CANADIAN WHO'S WH

CANADIAN WHO'S WHO

CANADIAN
WHO'S
WHO

1982

VOLUME XVII

Kieran Simpson
Editor

UNIVERSITY OF TORONTO PRESS

Toronto Buffalo London

© University of Toronto Press 1982
Toronto Buffalo London
Printed in Canada
ISBN 0-8020-4604-5
ISSN 0068-9963

CONTENTS

CANADIAN WHO'S WHO
1982

Canadian Who's Who is the largest and most authoritative publication of its kind in Canada, offering instant access to almost eight thousand prominent Canadians in all walks of life. Published annually to provide current and accurate information, the familiar bright-red volume is recognised as the standard reference source of contemporary Canadian biography.

Until University of Toronto Press acquired publication rights in 1978, the *Canadian Who's Who* was issued triennially, with five supplementary booklets (the *Canadian Biographical Service*) published at intervals between editions of the main volume. This publication policy was found on examination to have many drawbacks. Because purchase of the main volume was separate from subscription to the supplementary booklets, librarians and others were never quite sure if their holdings were complete. Also, with the three-year period between editions, the biographies in the main volume became too dated and the current information, scattered in the supplements, was not easily accessible. An annual edition obviated the need for such supplements by locating the most recent information conveniently in one place. Thus while the *Canadian Who's Who 1979* was cumulative for the years 1976–9, the 1980 edition was the first to cover a one-year period.

Canadian Who's Who 1982 includes close to eight thousand biographies of persons who are of current national interest for reference or inquiry. Over two thousand individuals were invited to complete questionnaires from which new biographies were compiled. Those already listed in earlier editions were given the opportunity to update their biographies.

The *Canadian Who's Who* was first published in 1910 by *The Times Publishing Company* of London, England, and contained some two thousand biographies of important living Canadians. The late A. L. Tunnell acquired copyright from *The Times* in 1932, and in 1936 published a substantially larger second edition which incorporated *Canadian Men and Women of the Time*, a parallel reference work edited by Henry J. Morgan. Beginning with the 1936 edition, the *Canadian Who's Who* was published under the continuous editorial direction of A. L. Tunnell for forty-two years, until his retirement in 1978 and the acquisition of the work by University of Toronto Press.

While the appearance and the publication cycle of the *Canadian Who's Who* have changed in recent years, the guiding principle governing selection for inclusion has not. There is no charge, nor is there any obligation whatsoever, for the inclusion of a biography in the *Canadian Who's Who*. Biographees are chosen on merit alone. This long-standing editorial policy has distinguished the *Canadian Who's Who* in its long history and will be rigorously maintained in the future.

The editor would like to acknowledge the invaluable assistance of biographer Nancy Passy; also Connie Foss, Leslie Jeanneret, and Harry Marquis who all helped with the compilation and editing of this volume.

Kieran Simpson
May, 1982

BIOGRAPHIES

A

AACH, Kurt; executive; b. Oldenburg, Germany 15 May 1921; s. Emil and Kaethe (Schwarting) A.; e. high sch. and coll. West Germany; Harvard Univ. AMP 70; m. Inge d. Paul Grasshoff 16 Dec. 1950; children: Manfred, Hannelore; CHRMN. OF BD. HOECHST CANADA INC. 1980- ; Pres. Hoechst Industries Ltd.; Dir. Trans American Chemicals Ltd.; joined American Hoechst; Hoechst Mexico 1963-67; Vice Pres. Hoechst Canada Inc. 1967, Extve. Vice Pres. 1973, Pres. and Chief Extve. Offr. 1975-80; Dir. and Vice Pres. German Sch. of Montreal, Alexander von Humboldt; mem. Soc. Chem. Industry; German/Candn. Chamber Industry & Comm.; Lutheran; recreations: gardening, sailing, ham operation; Club: Royal St. Lawrence; Home: 2 Ave. Laberge, Senneville, Que. H9X 3P9; Office: 4045 Côte Vertu, Montreal, Que. H4R 1R6.

ABBIS, Hon. Mr. Justice Joseph Chaiker, B.C.L.; retired judge; b. Beirut, Lebanon 11 Nov. 1911; s. Michael and Mary (Farah) A.; came to Can. 1911; e. Edmundston (N.B.) Pub. Sch.; Seminaire de Qué. 1931; St. Francis Xavier Univ. B.A. 1935; McGill Univ. B.C.L. 1948; JUDGE, COURT OF QUEEN'S BENCH, N.B.; Teacher, Edmundston High Sch. 1935-45; called to Bar of N.B. 1948; cr. Q.C. 1968; practised law Edmundston, N.B. 1948-73; Chrmn., N.B. Study Comte. on Nursing Educ. 1970; rec'd George Findlay Stephens Award, Candn. Hosp. Assn. 1971; Citation for Meritorious Services, Am. Hosp. Assn. 1976; "Judge Chaiker Abbis Award" estbd. by N.B. Hosp. Assn. 1977; recipient Queen's Silver Jubilee Medal 1977; served with Carleton & York Regt. (Reserve); Pres., N.B. Hosp. Assn. 1953-58, Candn. Hosp. Assn. 1966-68; Del.-at-Large, Am. Hosp. Assn. 1966-79; author various articles on trusteeship, health; Liberal; R. Catholic; recreations: travel, reading, golf, philately, numismatics, collecting first editions; Home: 89 - Nineteenth Ave., Edmundston, N.B. E3V 2A8

ABBOTT, Albert Clifford, B.A., M.D., C.M., LL.D.(Hon.), F.R.C.S.(C), F.R.C.S.(Edin.). F.A.C.S., F.I.C.S.; retired surgeon; b. Stockton, Man., 5 Aug. 1897; s. Albert Edward and Annie (Brown) A.; e. Univ. of Man., B.A. 1917, M.D., C.M. 1921; Travelling Scholarship (Univ. of Man.), 1922 and 1923; Banting Research Grants, 1932-62; Nat. Research Council Grant, 1937; Univ. of Winnipeg, LL.D. (Hon.) 1977; m. Mary Eileen d. late W.J. Bulman, Winnipeg, Man., 2 Jan. 1925; children: C. Edward B., Frances Eileen; Assoc. Prof. of Surgery, Univ. of Manitoba; Publications: over 40 papers on various surg. topics, mainly bone formation and thyroid disease; mem., Winnipeg Med. Soc.; Man. Med. Assn; Candn. Med. Assn.; Am. Urol. Assn.; N. Central Br.; Am. Urol. Assn.; Candn. Urol. Assn.; Western Surg. Assn.; Candn. Soc. of Clinical Surgs.; Treas. (1973-74 Internat. Coll. Surg. (Pres. 1968-69); City of Winnipeg Community Service Award 1972; Golden Boy Award (Good Citizenship Award, Prov. of Man. 1970); Hon. Life mem., Winnipeg Med. Assn.; Man. Med. Assn.; Can. Med. Assn.; Winnipeg Skating Club; Winnipeg Gyro Club (past Pres.) Protestant; recreations: skating, fishing, shooting, curling; Clubs: Winnipeg Winter (Pres. 1949); Manitoba Gyro: Home: 130 Handsart Blvd., Tuxedo, Winnipeg, Man. R3P 0C5.

ABBOTT, Hon. Anthony C., P.C., lawyer; b. Montreal, Que. 26 Nov. 1930; s. Douglas Charles and Mary Winifred (Chisholm) A.; m. Naomi Siddall d. E. Norman Smith 19 Feb. 1955; children: Douglas Chisholm, Hilary Smith, Timothy Alexander; Liberal; Anglican; recreation golf; Clubs: University (Toronto); Rideau; Home: 12 Lakeview Terrace, Ottawa, Ont. K1S 3H4.

ABBOTT, Hon. Douglas Charles, P.C. (Can.) 1945, B.C.L., D.C.L., LL.D., Q.C.; b. Lennoxville, P.Q., 29 May 1899; s. Lewis Duff and Mary Jane (Pearce) A.; e. Bishop's Coll., P.Q., Hon. D.C.L. 1950; McGill Univ. B.C.L., Hon. LL.D. 1951, Dijon Univ., France; m. (1) Mary Winifred, d. W. C. Chisholm, K.C., Montreal, 22 Sept. 1925; (2) Elizabeth, d. Charles Geddes Scarth, Edmonton, 11 July 1981; children: Elisabeth, Anthony, Lewis; 1st el. to H. of C., g.e. 1940; re-el. g.e. 1945, 1949 and 1953; apptd. Min. of Nat. Defence for Naval Services & Min. of Nat. Def. (Army) Aug. 1945; apptd. Minister of Finance 1946, resigning 1 July 1954; Justice, Supreme Court of Can. 1954 till resigned Dec. 1973; served in 1st World War 1916-18 with 7th (McGill) Siege Batty.; R.A.F. 1918; Chancellor, Bishop's Univ. 1958-68; Anglican; Clubs: University; Royal Montreal Curling (Montreal); Rideau (Ottawa); Home: 45 Lakeway Dr., Rockliffe Park, Ottawa, Ont. K1L 5A9

ABEL, Elie, B.A., M.Sc., LL.D.; journalist; educator; b. Montreal Que., 17 Oct. 1920; s. Jacob and Rose (Savetsky) A.; e. Baron Byng High Sch., Montreal, 1933-37; McGill Univ., B.A., 1941; Columbia Univ. M.Sc. 1942; LL.D. McGill, 1971; LL.D., West. Ont., 1976; m. Corinne, d. Clifford A. Prevost, 28 Jan. 1946; children: Mark, Suzanne; Harry and Norman Chandler Professor of Communication, Stanford University 1979-; mem., Intl. Cmsn. for the Study of Communication Problems at UNESCO, 1977-79; U.S. delegation to UNESCO's 21st Gen. Conf. at Belgrade, Yugoslavia, 1980; Dean, Sch. of Journ., Columbia Univ. 1970-1979; Reporter, "Windsor Daily Star", 1941; Asst. City Ed., "Montreal Gazette", 1945; Foreign Corr., North American Newspaper Alliance, 1946-47; U.N. Corr. Overseas News Agency, 1947-49; Reporter and Foreign Corr., "New York Times", 1949-59; Washington Bureau Chief, "The Detroit News", 1959-61; Reporter-Commentator, Nat. Broadcasting Co. Inc. 1961-70; served with RCAF 1942-45; co-author (with W. Averell Harriman) Special Envoy to Churchill and Stalin, 1941-46. (Random House, New York.) co-author, "Roots of Involvement: The U.S. in Asia 1784-1971" author, "The Missile Crisis", 1966; ed., "What's News: The Media in American Society", 1981; rec'd. George Foster Peabody Award for "outstanding radio news", 1967; Overseas Press Club Award for "best interpretation of foreign news", 1969; Sigma Delta Chi; Jewish; Clubs: The Century (New York); Office: Department of Communication, Redwood Hall, Stanford University, Stanford, California, 94305.

ABELL, John Norman, M.A.: investment dealer; b. Kent, Eng., 18 Sept. 1931; s. Sir George Edmund Brackenbury K.C.I.E. and Susan (Norman-Butler) A.; e. Marlborough Coll., Wiltshire, UK, 1950; Worcester Coll., Oxford Univ., M.A. 1954; m. Mora Delia; d. Anthony George Clifton-Brown, Rome 17 Nov. 1957; children: Sarah Elizabeth, Martin George, Antony Philip Norman; VICE CHRMN. AND DIR., WOOD GUNDY LTD. since 1977; Dir; W.H. Smith & Son Canada Ltd.; joined present Firm Vancouver 1955; Mgr. Money Market Dept., Toronto 1957; Mgr. Wood Gundy (International) 1962; served on staff of Royal Comn. on Atlantic Acceptance and became Head of Wood Gundy N.Y. Office 1966 then became Pres. Wood Gundy Inc., also Vice Pres. and Dir. Wood Gundy Ltd.; served with Brit. Army Rifle Bgde. 1950-51; rank 2nd Lt.; Dir., Candn. Arthritis Rheumatism Soc. Nat. Comte.; mem. Candn.-Am. Comte.; Anglican; recreations: shooting, fishing, tennis; Clubs: York; Toronto; The Queen's Caledon Mountain Trout; Tadanac; India House (N.Y.); Home: Foxcote Farm, R.R. 1, Hillsburgh, Ont.; Office: Box 274,Toronto Dominion Center, Toronto, M5K 1M7.

ABRAHAMS, Vivian Cecil, B.Sc., Ph.D., D.Sc.; educator; b. London, Eng. 19 Oct. 1927; s. Woolf Shusterman A.; e. City of London Sch. 1945; Edinburgh Univ. B.Sc. 1952, Ph. D. 1955, D.Sc. 1978; m. Pamela Phyllis Julia d. Ewart Dance, Swallowfield, Berks., Eng. 10 Sept. 1955; children: Graham, Mark, Carolyn, Jennifer; PROF. OF

PHYSIOL. AND HEAD OF DEPT. QUEEN'S UNIV. since 1976; Fulbright Fellow, Univ. of Pa. 1955-56; Beit Mem. Fellow, Med. Research Council, Nat. Inst. for Med. Research 1956-59, mem. scient. staff 1959-63; Assoc. Prof. present univ. 1963, Prof. 1967; M.R.C. Visiting Scient. Univ. Coll. London 1970-71; Chrmn. Ont. Grad. Scholarship Bd. 1977-78; served with RA 1945-48; author various articles in prof. journs.; mem. Scitec (Past-Pres.); Candn. Physiol. Soc.; Internat. Assn. for Study of Pain (Founder-mem.), Physiol. Soc.; Soc. Neuroscience; Can. Assn. for NeuroSci. (Pres. 1981-82); Am. Physiol. Soc.; Vice Pres., Cmte. of Parl., Sci. and Eng.; Br. Pharmacol. Soc.; recreations: skiing, sailing; Home: 259 Fairway Hills Cres., Kingston, Ont. K7M 2B5; Office: Kingston, Ont. K7L 3N6.

ABRAM, George Stanley, B. Arch., F.R.A.I.C.; architect; b. Regina, Sask., 6 Dec. 1923; s. William Gordon and Lyra Viola (Chalmers) A.; e. Central Coll. Inst., Regina, Sask.; Univ. of Toronto, B. Arch. 1949; m. Persis Ross, d. John A. Hughes, Toronto, Ont., 4 Oct. 1952; PARTNER, ABRAM/NOWSKI; served in 2nd World War as Pilot Offr. with R.C.A.F. 1943-45; mem. Ont. Assn. Arch.; Royal Architectural Inst. of Can., Address: 6 Lansing Square, Willowdale, Ont. M2J 1T5

ABRAMOV, Ayala Fleg Zacks, O.C., LL.D.; b. Jerusalem 31 Dec. 1912; d. Samuel and Rache (Berman) Bentovim; e. Jerusalem; Coll. Feminin de Bouffemont, Paris 1930; Sorbonne, Cours de Civilisation Française 1931-32; London Sch. of Econ. Social Science & Social Work 1933-34; Columbia and N.Y. Univs. Art Hist., Museum of Modern Art N.Y. Museum Adm. 1951-53; Univ. of Toronto LL.D. 1971; m. Maurice Fleg (d. 1940) 1938; m. Samuel J. Zacks, Toronto, Ont. 1947 (d. 1970); m. S. Zalman Abramov 1977; i/c French Pavilion, Levant Fair, Palestine 1936, Palestine Pavilion, Internat. Exposition Paris 1937; active in French Resistance 1940-45, Eng. 1942 with Free French, landed with Allied Forces Europe 1944, rank Capt., Liaison Offr. to Allied HQ G5 Displaced Persons SHAEF Frankfurt, assimilated rank Col., relief work concentration camps, active participation "Aliyah Beth" 1945-46; came to Can. 1947; Pres. Toronto Chapter Candn. Wizo-Hadassah 1949, Toronto Chapter Friends of Hebrew Univ. 1950; Chrmn. Women's Div. state of Israel Bonds 1970-71; rec'd Eleanor Roosevelt Humanities Award (1st Candn.) 1970; estbd. Hazor Archaeol. Museum (Ayelet-Haschachar, Israel (The Ayala and Sam Zacks Museum) 1955-57; donated some 100 Candn. paintings, sculpture and Eskimo art to Queen's Univ. (Agnes Etherington Art Centre) 1963; Sam and Ayala Zacks Collection to Art Gallery of Ont. and Royal Ont. Museum 1970; Chair of Art Hist. Hebrew Univ. Jerusalem 1970; Chair of Geophysics, Weizmann Inst. of Science, Rehovot, Israel 1970; exhns. of Ayala and Sam Zacks Collection incl. Art Gallery of Ont. and maj. museums Can., USA and Israel 1955-57; Tribute to Samuel J. Zacks, Art Gallery of Ont. 1971, Israel Museum Jerusalem 1976, Tel-Aviv Museum 1977; mem. of Bd.: Art. Gallery of Ont.; Internat. Council of Museums (Hon. mem. 1977, Gov. of Foundation); Can-Israel Cultural Foundation; Am.-Israel Cultural Foundation N.Y. and Israel; Bezalel Acad. of Art Jerusalem; Hon. Patron Royal Ont. Museum; mem. Internat. Council Museum of Modern Art N.Y.; co-founder and Past Pres. Nat. Youth Orchestra Can; former Chrmn. Henry Moore Sculpture Centre Comte. Toronto; mem. Internat. Bd. Israel Museum Jerusalem (Hon. Fellow 1978), Tel-Aviv Museum (extve. Bd.); Gov., Weizmann Inst. of Science, Rehovot; Hebrew Univ. Jerusalem; Tel-Aviv Univ.; Home: 13 Ben Gurion Blvd., Tel-Aviv, Israel.

ABT, Peter, Ph.B.; industrialist; b. Macklin, Sask., 1 Aug. 1931; s. Kilian and Ramona (Sieben) A.; e. St. Anthony's High Sch., Edmonton, Alta., Univs. of Denver, Notre Dame, Indiana, Ph.B. (Comm.); m. Jean, d. J.R. Robson, Vermilion, Alta., 30 Aug. 1958; children: Peter, Edward, Margaret, Barbara, Suzanne; PRESIDENT, ENERGAS

LTD., OIL AND MINING EXPLORATION, XEREX EXPLORATION LTD., ELKHORN PETROLEUMS LTD., A.U. MINES INC., CIMARRON COAL CO.; (formerly Pres. of Scurry-Rainbow Oil Ltd.); R. Catholic; recreations: hunting,water sports; Clubs: Calgary Petroleum; Canyon Meadows Golf & Country; Calgary Curling; The 400; Home: 1235 Bel-Aire Drive S.W., Calgary, Alta.T2V 2C1; Office: Suite 2415, 400 - 4 Avenue S.W., Shell Centre, Calgary, Alta. T2P 0J4

ACHESON, John S., B.Com., F.S.A., F.C.I.A.; insurance executive; b. Boissevain, Man., 12 Apr. 1922; s. Sidney Richards and Margaret Bell (Scott) A.; e. Laura Secord Pub. and Gordon Bell High Sch., Winnipeg, Man.; Univ. of Manitoba, B.Comm. 1951 (Gold Medalist) F.S.A. 1955; m. Frances Marjorie, d. Joseph Matkin, Victoria, B.C., 7 July 1945; children Kathleen, Robert, Scott, Gail; PRESIDENT, DOMINION LIFE ASSURANCE CO., since 1971; with Royal Bank of Canada 1939-41 and 1945-46; joined Actuarial Dept. of present Co., 1951-52; apptd. Asst. Actuary 1952; with Underwriting dept., 1952-60; became Underwriting Extve. 1959; Research Extve., Agency Dept., 1960; Supt. of Agencies 1962; Asst. Dir. of Agencies 1964; Vice-Pres. and Dir. of Agencies 1965; Extve. Vice-Pres. and Dir. 1970; Pres. (1974-75) Kitchener-Waterloo Fed. Appeal; Dir., Lincoln Nat. Life Ins. Co., Ft. Wayne, Ind.; Gray Coach Lines Ltd., Toronto, Ont.; Waterloo Ins. Co., Waterloo, Ont.; Island Life Ins. Co. Ltd., Jamaica; Kitchener Rotary Club served in 2nd World War as Navig. (aircrew) 1941-45; P.O.W. in Germany 1943-45; discharged with rank of Flt-Lt.; mem., P.O.W. Assn.; United Church; recreations: golf, curling, bridge; Club: Westmount Golf and Country (Dir.); Home: 33-54 Blue Springs Dr., Waterloo, Ont. N2J 4M4; Office: 111 Westmount Rd. S., Waterloo, Ont. N2J 4C6

A'COURT, James H., C.A.; company executive (retired); b. Toronto, Ont., 26 Nov. 1914; s. Henry James and Mary Anne (Baker) A'C.; e. North Toronto Coll. Inst.; Univ. of Toronto, B.A., 1937; m. Sarah Elizabeth d. late John Hunter, 29 Aug. 1942; four d.; joined Clarkson Gordon & Co., 1937; C.A., 1942; became Asst. Treas., Brascan Ltd., 1947-51; held various posts with subsidiaries in Brazil, 1951-61; apptd. Vice-Pres., Finance, 1961; el. a Dir., 1967-79; mem., Inst. Chart. Accts. of Ont.; Anglican; Clubs: Toronto; Toronto Cricket, Skating & Curling; Toronto Racquet; Home: R.R. No. 2, Maple, Ont. L0J 1E0

ACZÉL, János Dezsö, M.A., Ph.D., F.R.S.C.; mathematician, educator; b. Budapest, Hungary 26 Dec. 1924; s. late Dezsö and Irén (Adler) A.; e. Primary Sch. 1934, Eng. Sch. 1935 and Berzsenyi High Sch. 1943, Budapest; Univ. of Budapest B.A. 1946, M.A. 1947, Ph.D. 1947; m. Susan Kende d. late Lajos Kende 14 Dec. 1946; children: Catherine (Mrs. Schulze), Julie (Mrs. M. More); PROF. OF MATH. UNIV. OF WATERLOO; author "Funktionalgleichungen der Theorie der geometrischen Objekte" (with S. Golab) 1960; "Vorlesungen über Funktionalgleichungen und ihre Anwendungen" 1961; "Ein Blick auf Funktionalgleichungen und ihre Anwendungen" 1962; "Lectures on Functional Equations and their Applications" 1966; "On Applications and Theory of Functional Equations" 1969; "On Information Measures and their Characterizations" (with Z. Daróczy) 1975; over 200 articles; Editor-in-Chief Aequationes Mathematicae, editor Journal of Geometry, Utilitas Mathematica, Series Editor, Encyclopedia of Mathematics and Its Applications; rec'd M. Beke Award 1961; Hungarian Acad. Sciences Award 1962; Distinguished Prof. 1969; fellow, Royal Soc. Can. 1971; mem. Candn. Math. Soc. (Council 1971-73); Am. Math. Soc. (Organizer of Special Meeting); Royal Soc. Can. (Convenor Math. Div. 1974-75, Chrmn. Acad. Science Ed. Comte. 1977-78, Ed. Math. Reports since 1978); N.Y. Acad. Science; Oesterr. Math. Ges.; R. Catholic; recreations: swimming, literature; Home: Apt. 2 - 1908, 300 Regina St. N., Waterloo, Ont. N2J 4H2; Office: Univ. of Waterloo, Centre for Information Theory, Faculty of Mathematics, Waterloo, Ont. N2L 3G1.

ADAIR, Hon. James Allen; politician,; b. Edmonton, Alta. 13 May 1929; s. late James Wilfred and late Beatrice (Shewfelt) A.; e. Athabasca, Mayerthorpe, Edmonton (Westglen High Sch.); State Seed Lab. St. Paul, Minn.; m. Joyce Helen d. Rev. C. Alvin Johnson, Wetaskiwin, Alta. 31 Oct. 1960; children: Richard, Catherine, Robert; MINISTER OF TOURISM AND SMALL BUSINESS ALTA. since 1979; Feed Mill Operator and Grain Buyer, Searle Grain Co. 1948-49; Seed Buyer, Peace Milling Co., Peace River 1953-59; Catering Supvr., Fortier & Associates Catering, Peace River 1960-64; Salesman and Sports Dir. CKYL Radio, Active Partner and Secy. Treas. Peace River Broadcasting Corp. 1964-71; el. P. Cons. mem. for Peace River Alta. g.e. 1971, re-el. since; apptd. Min. without Portfolio for N. Devel. and Indian-Metis Liaison 1971, Min. of Recreation, Parks and Wildlife 1975-79; Past Sr. Councillor, Un. Comm. Travellers of Am. 1958-59; Dir. Alta. Wildlife Foundation 1970-71; Pres. Peace River & Dist. Assn. Mentally Retarded 1969-70; mem. Alta. Adv. Council Air Cadet League Can. 1972-73; Registrar, Alta. Amateur Hockey Assn. Peace Country 1967-70; Peace River Campaign Chrmn. Red Shield 1967; Secy.-Treas. and Stat., N. Peace Hockey League 1965-70; former Dir. Alta. Golf Assn.; P. Conservative; Anglican; recreations: golf, swimming, baseball, hockey, hunting, fishing; Clubs: Peace River Toastmaster (Charter Pres. 1966-67); Optimist (Peace River Past Pres. and Past Lt. Gov. 1955-57); Peace River Curling (Pres. 1959); Home: 9634-83 Ave., Peace River, Alta. T0H 2X0; Office: Legislature Bldg., Edmonton, Alta. T5K 2B6.

ADAM, François, F.I.I.C.; exécutif d'assurance; né Montréal, Qué., 22 oct. 1913; f. Louis (décédé) et Blanche (Ménard) (décédé) A.: e. l'Ecole la Mennais: Hautes Etudes Comm. de Montréal; études spécialisées à l'Inst. d'Assurance du Can.; ép. Lucille, f. Joseph Lamoureux, 14 sept. 1940; enfants: Marie-José, Louis-Pierre, Monique, Richard; PRESIDENT, SOCIETE D'ASSURANCE DES CAISSES POPULAIRES; Prés., Sécurité Co. d'Assurances Générales du Canada; Administrateur, La Féd. de Qué. des Caisses Populaires Desjardins et de La Corp. Immobilière Place Desjardins; Provincial Bank of Canada; Adm. et Vice-Prés., Bureau d'Expertises des Assureurs Ltée; Adm., Bureau des Assureurs du Can.; la Conf. des Cos. d'Assnce. Indépendantes; Fonds d'Indemnisation des Victimes d'Accidents d'Automobiles; au service des cos. d'Assnce. Générales et Phoenix de Paris, Montréal 1931; asst. gérant, succursale de Qué., Co. d'Assurance Halifax 1939; dir. gén. adjoint, Cos. d'Assurances Générales de Commerce, Canadienne Mercantile et Canadienne Nationale de St-Hyacinthe 1942; dir. gén., Soc. d'Assnce. des Caisses Populaires 1950 an Pres. 1971; mem., Comité Consultatif du Service des Assnces.; Comité de Placements, Soc. Financière pour le Comm. et l'Indust.; Comités de Finance et d'Expansion de l'Univ. Laval; catholique r.; recreations: golf, pêche, lecture, voyages; Club: Garnison; Residence: 16 Belleau, Lévis, Qué. G6V 4A9; Bureau: 100 est Trans-Canada, Lévis, Qué. G6V 4Y7

ADAMS, David; ballet master; teacher, choreographer, dancer; b. Winnipeg, Man. 16 Nov. 1928; s. Charles George and Stella Maude (Mozley), A.; e. Winnipeg, Man.; m. Lois Smith 13 May 1950 (divorced); one d. Janine; remarried 8 Nov. 1980 Edmonton, Alta. to Meredith Wood; HEAD OF DANCE AND THEATRE ARTS DEPT. GRANT MACEWAN COMMUNITY COLL., 1980- Founding mem. Royal Winnipeg Ballet 1938-46; Nat. Ballet of Can. 1951-61; Alta. Ballet 1977-79; mem. Sadlers Wells Ballet 1946, Metropolitan Ballet 1947-48, Festival Ballet 1961-69, Royal Ballet 1970-77 (all Eng.); Choreographer of Ballets, Winnipeg Ballet, Nat. Ballet, Festival Ballet, Alta. Ballet; lead roles in all accepted classical ballet repetoire in above companies; recreations: music, elec-

tronics, jewelry making; Address: #1151 Knottwood Rd. E., Edmonton, Alta. T6K 2K5.

ADAMS, Gordon Albert, B.A., M.Sc., Ph.D., F.R.S.C., F.C.I.C.; biochemist; b. Watford, Ont. 5 Aug. 1907; s. Richard and Laura Emily (Long) A.; e. Queen's Univ. B.A. 1928; Univ. of W. Ont. M.Sc. 1930; Univ. of Chicago Ph.D. 1938; m. Mary Ballantyne d. William Tanton, Strathroy, Ont. 27 Dec. 1938; Demonst. in Chem. Univ. of W. Ont. 1928-29, Instr. in Biochem. 1929-39; Princ. Biochem. Div. Biol. Sciences, Nat. Research Council, Ottawa 1939-72; Visiting Prof. in Biochem. Microbiol. Colo. State Univ. 1973-74; contrib. author "Methods in Carbohydrate Chemistry" Vol. V 1965, Vol. VI 1972; author 118 scient. publs. on original research mainly in field of carbohydrate chem.; mem. Candn. Biochem. Soc.; Protestant; Address: 99 Front St. W., Strathroy, Ont. N7G 1X9.

ADAMS, James Franklin, M.B., M.D. Tor., L.R.C.P. Lond. Eng., M.R.C.S. Eng., F.R.C.S.(C); b. Hanover, Ont., 21 May 1893; s. James Henry and Elizabeth (Boyd) A.; e. Owen Sound, Ont., Coll. Inst.; Univ. of Toronto; children: James, Mary; Capt. R.C.A.M.C. 1916-19; Major R.C.A.M.C. Med. Bd. 1939-43; Fellow Roy. Coll. of Surg. Can.; Essex Co. Med. Soc.; Ont. Med Assn.; Candn. Med. Assn.; Alpha Omega Alpha Fraternity; United Ch.; Club: Essex Golf and Country; Address: Home: 1929 Ontario St., Windsor, Ont., N8Y 1N1; Office: Medical Arts Bldg., 1011 Ouelette Ave., Windsor, Ont. N9A 4J9

ADAMS, John W., F.C.A.; executive; b. 17 June 1924; e. C.A. Ont. 1949; m. Kathleen, 18 April, 1953; children: Peter, Paul, Annemarie; PRESIDENT AND CHIEF EXTVE. OFFR., EMCO LTD. 1978- ; Dir. Canada Malting Co. Ltd.; F. W. Woolworth Co. Ltd.; Canada Trustco Mortg. Corp.; B. F. Goodrich Canada Inc.; F. W. Woolworth (USA); Sifton Properties Ltd.; D. H. Howden Co.; joined Emco as Comptroller 1950, Dir. 1956, Extve. Vice Pres. & Treas. 1970; rec'd Queen's Silver Jubilee Medal 1977; named Kt. Commdr. Order St. Sylvestre (Papal Honour) 1978; Dir. London Cancer Soc.; Chrmn. of Bd. St. Joseph's Hosp. London; mem. Adv. Bd. Sch. of Business Adm. Univ. of W. Ont.; Chrmn. Special Comte. to Examine Role of Auditor (Adams' Report 1978); mem. Acct.'s Internat. Study Group 1973-76, Chrmn. 1976; Pres. Candn. Inst. C.A.'s 1978-79; Clubs: London; London Hunt & Country; Toronto; Home: 1448 Corley Dr., London, Ont. N6G 2K4; Office: 1108 Dundas St. E., London, Ont. N6A 4N7.

ADAMS, Peter Frederick, M.Eng., Ph.D.; educator; b. Halifax, N.S. 4 Feb. 1936; s. Gordon Vincent and Freda (Fraser) A.; e. Dalhousie Univ. Dipl. in Engn. 1956; N.S. Tech. Coll. B.Eng. 1958, M.Eng. (Civil Engn.) 1961; Lehigh Univ. Ph.D. (Civil Engn.) 1966; m. Barbara Elaine Dickey; three s. 1976- ; DEAN OF ENGINEERING, UNIV. OF ALTA. 1976- and Prof. of Civil Engn. 1970- ; Design Engr. Gen. Engn. Dept. Internat. Nickel Co. of Canada, Copper Cliff, Ont. 1958-59; Asst. Prof. of Civil Engn. Univ. of Alta. 1960-63; Research Asst. Fritz Engineering Laboratory, Lehigh Univ. Bethlehem, Pa. 1963-66; Assoc. Prof. Univ. Alta. 1966-70; Design Engr., Project Planner, Dominion Bridge Co. Toronto (sabbatical leave) 1973-74; Dir. Petroleum Recovery Inst.; Computer Modelling Group; Coal Mining Research Centre (Extve. Comte.); Mang. Adv. Inst.; Hydrocarbon Research Centre (Chrmn.); Candn. Welding Bureau; mem. organ. comtes. various confs.; mem. Adv. Comte. Plastic Design Unbraced Multi-Storey Steel Frames, Am. Iron & Steel Inst. 1970- ; Civil Engn. Grant Selection Comte. Nat. Research Council 1973-76; Adv. Comte. Effects Beam Yielding Column Stability, Am. Iron & Steel Inst. 1973- ; Edmonton Br. Extve. Engn. Inst. Can. 1972-73; rec'd Cert. of Merit Candn. Soc. Civil Engn. 1978; co-author 3 maj. texts instr. structural steel design; contrib. various monographs aspects structural stability & steel design; author or co-author over 70 publs.; presented over 40 lectures, addresses; mem. Assn. Prof. Engrs., Geols. & Geophysicists Alta.; Candn. Council Prof. Engrs.; Internat. Assn. Bridge & Structural Engn. (Vice Pres. Internat.; Chrmn. Candn. Group; Nat. Comte. 1984 Cong.); Am. Soc. Civil Engrs.; Candn. Soc. Civil Engrs. (Assoc. Ed. "Canadian Journal of Civil Engineering"); mem.-at-Large Structural Stability Research Council; mem. Candn. Standards Assn.; Internat. Standards Organ.; Community League; Salvation Army (Red Shield Appeal Extve. 1979-); Club: Skyscraper Toastmasters; Office: 5-1 Mechanical Engineering Bldg., Edmonton, Alta. T6G 2G8.

ADAMS, Welburn John, F.S.A., F.C.I.A.; actuarial executive; b. Toronto, Ont., 9 June 1908; s. late James Henry A. and Nellie S. (Welburn) A.; e. Toronto Schs., m. Bessie (d. 1965), d. late James Campbell, 15 Sept. 1933; children: Nancy (Mrs. P.G. MacDonnell), Sally (Mrs. J.W.R. Medland) and Peter; 2ndly, Helen Beaton, (nee Walker), 1971; Dir., Arbitrators' Inst. of Canada; joined The Canada Life in 1925; Vice-Pres. Associated Senior Executives; President Life Office Mang. Assn., New York, 1949-50; Life Ins. Inst. of Can. 1950-51; Ont. Chamber of Comm. 1962-63; Vice-Chrmn., Extve. Council, Candn. Chamber of Comm. 1958-59; United Church; recreation: sailing; Clubs: Canadian (Pres. 1971); Toronto; Albany; R.C.Y.C.; Home: 55A Rowanwood, Toronto, Ont. M4W 1Y8

ADAMSON, Anthony, O.C. (1974), M.A., LL.D., F.R.A.I.C.; b. Toronto Ontario, 7 October. 1906; s. Col. Agar, D.S.O., and Mabel (Cawthra) A.; e. Elementary School, Port Credit, Ontario; Wellington College, England, Grenoble University, France; Cambridge Univ., M.A., London Univ., Eng. (Post-Grad.); Queen's, LL.D. 1975; m. Augusta, d. Judge Angus Bonnycastle, 11 Sept. 1931; children: Adrian C., Inigo H.T.C.(d.), Jeremy E.A.; Assoc. Prof. of Town Planning 1955-65, Univ. of Toronto; Vice-Chrmn., Nat. Capital Comn., Ottawa, 1959-67; served for ten yrs. as el. municipal offr. in Twp. of Toronto, Sch. Bd. and Councillor; Reeve 1953-54; Chrmn. of Public Utilities Comn., 1955-56; Pres., Children's Aid Soc., Peel Co., 1956; Pres. (1964), Ont. Welfare Council; Pres. (1951), Town Planning Inst. Can.; Dir., Nat. Theatre Sch. 1967-69; Nat. Ballet Sch. 1975; mem. Ontario Heritage Foundation; Ont. Council for Arts (Chrmn. 1969-74); co-author "The Ancestral Roof", co-auth. "The Gaiety of Gables" and "The Hallowed Walls" Gov. Gen.'s Award for non-fiction) 1975; awarded Coronation Medal; Jubilee Medal; Award of Merit, City of Toronto 1978; LL.D. Queen's 1975; Gabrielle Leger Medal, Heritage Can. 1981; Conservative; Anglican; Home: 23 Rosedale Road, Toronto, Ont. M4W 2P1

ADAMSON, Gordon Sinclair, B.Arch., F.R.A.I.C., R.C.A. architect; b. Orangeville, Ont., 19 May 1904; s. late John Birrell and Margaret Jane (Lamont) A.; e. Pub. and High Schs., Orangeville, Ont.; Univ. of Toronto, B.Arch. 1928; m. Bessie Arlene, d. late John J. Graham, 6 Jan. 1934; one d., Mrs. Paul Montgomery; in private practise of his prof. since 1934; expanded (1960) and (1964) with various partners; among his commissions have been industrial bldgs., community projects, univ. bldgs., schs., etc.; chosen one of prize winners in competition new Nat. Art Gallery, Ottawa, and several other important medals; Cert. of Merit for outstanding Service in beautification of Toronto; Pres., Ont. Assn. of Arch., 1953; mem. Assn. of Candn. Indust. Designers (Life); mem. (1956-60) Senate, Univ. of Toronto; United Church; recreations: gardening, photography, art appreciation; Clubs: Arts and Letters; Granite; Rosedale Golf; Kiwanis (W. Toronto); Home: 111 Park Rd., Toronto, Ont. M4W 2N8; Office: Adamson Associates, 2 Gloucester St., Toronto, Ont. M4Y 1L5

ADASKIN, Frances James (Mrs. Murray Adaskin); soprano; concert and radio artist; b. Saint John, N.B.; of U.E.L. descent from Anne Faucht, first girl born in Saint John after landing of Loyalists in 1783; d. Frederick W.

James (newspaperman); e. Montreal, P.Q., High Sch.; McGill Conservatorium of Music (four-years' Scholarship); specialized study with Emmy Heim of Vienna, authority on German Lieder, and with Madame Lisette Patterson, specialist in French; later studied with Enrico Rosati and Madame Maria Kurenko in New York, and Roland Hayes in Boston; moved to Montreal, P.Q., as a child; at 16 was soloist at St. James' United Ch., Montreal; thereafter appeared for a season at Chateau Frontenac, Que., where her interpretation of French songs was highly praised; concert artist at Banff Springs Hotel for a number of seasons and, when there, performed for H.M. King Geo. VI and Queen Elizabeth; met and married in Banff, Murray Adaskin, violinist and composer; sang leading role in first Candn. hour length opera produced in CBC, "Transit Through Fire", by Dr. Healey Willan, and was also chosen to sing the title role in CBC's first full-length opera, "Deirdre of the Sorrows" (Willan); sang leading soprano role, "Ellen Orford", in Benjamin Britten's opera "Peter Grimes"; this performance was such a success that, on public demand, it was repeated the following week, setting a precedent in Candn. music; sang the role of "Anne" in the CBC's first performance of Stravinsky's "Rake's Progress"; gave first performance in Can. and made first recording of Paul Hindemith's "Das Marienleben"; sang with Sir Ernest MacMillan conducting Toronto Symphony and Mendelssohn Choir many times; has appeared on numerous occasions with Little Symphony of Montreal, Calgary Symphony, Regina Symphony, Cathedral Singers of Montreal, Ottawa Choral Union; recital tours in Can. and U.S.; Address: 3020 Devon Rd., Victoria, B.C. V8R 6C9

ADASKIN, Gordon, R.C.A.; painter; educator; b. Toronto, Ont. 7 June 1931; s. Harry Adaskin; e. apprentice of Frank Lloyd Wright 1951; Vancouver Sch. of Art grad. 1952 (Drawing & Painting Hons.); Prov. Normal Sch. Vancouver grad. 1955; children: Jon, Susan; Docent and Asst. Curator Vancouver Art Gallery 1955-56; Art Teacher and Counsellor Vancouver Sch. System 1956-62; Instr. in Drawing, Painting, Anat. and Art Hist., Alta. Coll. of Art Calgary 1963-66; Painting Instr. Banff Sch. of Fine Art summers 1964, 1965, 1970, Instr. in Drawing summers 1975, 1976, Lectr. in Basic Design Banff Centre Theatre Crafts 1972-77, Educ. Program Consultant to Theatre Div. 1977; Instr. in Design Univ. of Alta. summers 1963, 1966; Asst. Prof. of Environmental Studies Univ. of Man. 1966, Assoc. Prof. 1971, Chrmn. of Basic Design (5 yrs.) 1975; Guest Lectr. Univ. of B.C. 1973; considerable radio and TV experience as commentator, interviewer, script writer and program consultant; solo exhns. incl.: London (Eng.) House 1953; Maison Canadienne Paris 1954; Tempus Gallery Vancouver 1963, Little Gallery 1966; Applied Arts Centre Calgary 1965; Banff Sch. of Fine Arts 1964, 1965; Univ. of Man. 1967, 1969, 1980; Griffiths Gallery Vancouver 1967, 1968, 1969; Studio Gallery West Vancouver 1973; Private Studio Shows Vancouver 1973, Banff 1975, Winnipeg 1976; Peter Whyte Gallery Banff 1976; Bau-Xi Gallery Vancouver 1981; Melnychenko Gallery Winnipeg 1981; rep. in numerous group shows Can. and USA, pub. and private colls.; mem. Council Royal Candn. Acad. Arts; Home: 375 Lilac St., Winnipeg, Man. R3M 2S8; Office: Faculty of Architecture, Univ. of Manitoba, Winnipeg, Man. R3T 2N2.

ADASKIN, Harry, O.C., LL.D. (Dalhousie), LL.D.(Simon Fraser), LL.D.(U.B.C); violinist; b. 1901; m. Frances Marr (C.M.); original of Hart House String Quartet 1923-38 and toured with them in Can., U.S., U.K., France, Italy, Holland, Denmark and Sweden; made N.Y. solo debut Feb. 1947; for some yrs. C.B.C. Intermission Commentator on the Sunday Afternoon N.Y. Philharmonic broadcasts; Prof. of Music, Univ. of B.C., Head of Dept. of Music, 1946-58 (retired 1972); autobiography: "A Fiddler's World," Vol. 1, 1977 (Vol. 2 expected 1981); Address: 4958 Angus, Vancouver, B.C. V6M 3M5

ADASKIN, Murray, Q.C., LL.D. (Lethbridge), D. Mus. (Hon.), O.C.; D. Mus. (Univ. of Brandon, Man.); D. Mus. (Univ. of Windsor, 1977); composer; b. Toronto, Ont., 28 Mar. 1906; s. Samuel and Nisha (Perstnov) A.; e. Royal Conserv. of Music, Toronto; Ecole Normale, Paris, France: Music Acad. of the West, Calif.; Aspen Sch. of Music, Colo., Univ. of Lethbridge, LL.D. 1970; Univ. of Windsor, D. Mus. (Hon.) 1977; m. Frances, d. Frederick William James. 16 July 1931; Composer-in-Residence, Univ. of Sask., since 1966 (Prof. and Head of Dept. of Music, 1952-66); mem. Canada Council 1966-69; for many years Violinist with Toronto Symphony Orchestra; composer of many publ. and recorded vocal, chamber music and orchestral works, Centennial opera "Grant Warden of the Plains," and many commissioned works, incl. "Of Man and the Universe" for Expo, "Coronation,Overture" and "Algonquin Symphony"; rec'd. Sr. Arts Fellowship, Canada Council, 1960-61, to work in Europe; chosen "Citizen of the Year". Saskatoon 1969; two hr. CBC broadcast, "Profile of Murray Adaskin at 65" 1971; Bd. mem. Saskatoon Art Centre, 1966-67; Hon. Life mem., Saskatoon and Toronto Musicians' Assns.; Dir., Candn. Music Centre; mem. Candn. League of Composers; Royal Soc. of Arts; Humanities Assn. of Can.; C.A.P.A.C.; Centennial Medal, 1967; D.Mus. Univ. of Brandon 1972; Clubs: Arts & Letters (Toronto); Joel (Saskatoon); Address: 3020 Devon Road, Victoria, B.C. V8R 6C9

ADASKIN, Mrs. Murray — see: Adaskin, Frances James.

ADDERLEY, John P.; company president; b. Liverpool, Eng., 5 March. 1913; s. John Leo and Agnes Glynne (Cousins) A.; e. St. Edwards Coll., Liverpool Eng.; m. Frances Marie, d. the late Laurence Smith, 6 Sept. 1939; children; Ann-Marie, John Damian, Magdalen Mary, Laurence Peter, Edmund Mark; PRES. AND CHIEF EXTVE. OFFR.. G.U.S. CANADA INC.; Legare (1978) Inc.; Woodhouse (1978) Inc.; dir. The Great Universal Stores Ltd., London, Eng.; Burberrys Ltd.; Chrmn., Patersons (Australia) Ltd.; served in 2nd World War for five and a half yrs.; Commissioned in Adm. and Special Duties Br., R.A.F.; Roman Catholic; Home: 32 Ballantyne Ave. N. Montreal, Que. H4X 2B8; Office: 5375 Côte de Liesse, Montreal, Que. H4P 1A2

ADDISON, J. Harry; executive; b. Toronto, Ont., 13 Apl. 1905; s. late Hardill and the late Rosabell A.; m. Eleanore Clarke Haney; children: John H., Harry J., Clarke A., Wayne H.; PRES., ADDISON CADILLAC LTD.; Addison Leasing of Can. Ltd.; Chrmn. of Bd., St. Alban's Boys' Club; mem. Toronto Harbour Comn., Dir., Metrop. Indust. Comn; Metrop. Safety Council; The Jockey Club Ltd.; recreation: thoroughbred horses, Addison Hall Farms, Aurora, Ont.; Clubs: Granite; Jockey Club Ltd.; Big Bay Point (Ont.) Golf & Country; Thoroughbred Club of America (Lexington, Ky); Home: Elhara, 228 Steeles Ave. E., Thornhill, Ont. L3T 1A6; Office: 832 Bay St., Toronto, Ont. M5S 1Z6

ADDY, The Hon. Mr. Justice George Arthur, B.A., E.D., C.D.; judge; b. Ottawa, Ont. 28 Sept. 1915; s. late Frederick William and Clorida Richer (de la Flèche) A.; e. Ecole St-Jean-Baptiste, Ottawa; Univ. Ottawa, B.A.; Osgoode Hall Law Sch., Toronto; m. Joyce Rose Sylvia, d. late John Head, April 1942; children: Paul, Clive, Nicole, Vincent, George; mem. Court Martial App. Bd. 1953-59; app. Sup. Court of Ont. 1967; Fed. Court of Canada, 1973; COURT MARTIAL APPEAL COURT, 1974; called to Bar of Ont. (in absentia) 1942; Q.C. 1960; Partner Vincent & Addy 1945-55, Partner Vincent, Addy & Charbonneau 1955-60, Sr. Ptner. 1960; served with Militia (Regt. de Hull) 1934-40, active service Eng. and Aleutian Islands 1940-45; Commdr. Univ. Ottawa C.O.T.C. 1945-56; C.O. Regt. de Hull (21st Armoured) 1956-58; retired rank Lt.-Col.; apptd. Hon. Col. Regt. de Hull 1973; Past Pres. and

Life mem. R.C.A.C. Assn.; mem., Roy. Candn. Mil. Inst., Toronto; Founding mem., (Hon. mem. and Past Pres.) Cercle Universitaire d'Ottawa; Hon. Gov. Ottawa Univ.; R. Catholic; recreation: yachting; Home: 737 Island Park Dr., Ottawa, Ont.K1Y 0B9; Office: Supreme Court Bldg., Wellington St., Ottawa, Ont. K1A 0H9

ADELMAN, Maurice, M.A.Sc., Ph.D., F.C.I.C.; retired university professor; b. Welland Ont., 1 July 1915; s. Paul and Rachel (Gonickman) A.; e. Welland (Ont.) High Sch.; Univ. of Toronto, B.A.Sc. (Chem. Engn.) 1937, M.A.Sc. 1940, Ph.D. 1946; m. Dorothy Myra, d. Shimson Koldofsky, London, Eng., 1 Sept. 1941; children: Abela S., Paul Wm.; ADJUNCT, UNIV. OF WINDSOR, Dir., Indust. Research Inst. (Univ. of Windsor); Chart. mem. Experiments Adv. Comte, Chalk River Nuclear Labs.; joined Assumption Univ. as Assoc. Prof., 1956; Prof. of Chem., 1957-64 and Head, Dept. of Chem. Engn., 1959-74; Asst. Chemist, Canada Cement Co. Ltd., July-Sept. 1937; Demonst. in Chem. Engn. and Organic Chem., Univ. of Toronto, 1937-40 and Instr. in Chem. Engn. there, 1940-45; Special Instr. (part time), Dept. of Chem. Engn., Univ. of Toronto, Sept. 1948-Apl. 1950; Prof., Chem. Engn. 1951-81; Assoc. Dean, Grad. Studies 1964-81; Fellow, Am. Assn. for Advanc. Science; mem., Am. Soc. Engn., Assn. Prof. Engrs. Ont.; Chem. Inst. Can. (Fellow; Chrmn. Bd. 1966); Adv. Council on Occupational and Environmental Health Hazards, Ont. (Chrmn. Standards and Guidelines sub-comm.); Dir., Temple Beth El.; Extve. Comte., Windsor Jewish Community Council; Beta Sigma Rho (Eta Chapter); recreations: golf, skiing, squash, bridge, music; Home: 3858 Mt. Royal Drive, Windsor, Ont. N9G 2B7

ADILMAN, Sid; newspaper columnist; b. Saskatoon, Sask. 27 Oct. 1937; s. Lawrence and Clarice (Goldstein) A.; e. Tecumseh Pub. Sch., South Coll. Inst., Central Coll Inst., London, Ont.; Univ. of W. Ont. B.A. work in Eng. and Sociol. plus degree course in Journalism; m. Toshiko Suzuki, Japan 1 May 1965; two s. Mio, Nobu; ENTERTAINMENT COLUMNIST, TORONTO STAR since 1971; Candn. Bureau Chief; Variety; joined Toronto Star 1960-63; Toronto Telegram 1963-71; co-author "Dining Out in Toronto"; contrib. to various books; author articles Candn. and U.S. mags. and newspapers; mem. Assn. Candn. TV & Radio Artists; Jewish; recreation: reading; Home: 74 Albany Ave., Toronto, Ont. M5R 3C3; Office: One Yonge St., Toronto, Ont. M5E 1E6.

ADRIAN, Donna Jean, M.L.S.: librarian; b. Morden, Man. 28 Aug. 1940; d. William Gordon and Dorothy Jean (Gregory) Frazer; e. Brandon (Man.) Coll. Inst.; Brandon Coll. B.A. 1962; McGill Univ. B.L.S. 1963, M.L.S. 1968; Que. Class I Teacher's Cert.-Lib. Science 1965; m. James Ross Adrian 17 July 1965; LIBRARIAN, ROSEMERE HIGH SCHOOL (part-time) 1980- ; Lib. Consultant (part-time) Laurenval Sch. Bd. 1980- ; Lectr. (part-time) Concordia Univ. Lib. Studies Program 1974- ; Lib., Rosemere High Sch. and Supvr. Laurenvale Elem. Sch. Libs. 1963-66; Lib.-Dept. Head, Rosemere High Sch. 1966-74; Lib. Consultant (part-time) North Island Regional Sch. Bd. and Lib. (part-time) Rosemere High Sch. 1974-79; Lib. Consultant, Laurenval Sch. Bd. 1979-80; mem. Mayor of Laval's Lib. Comte.; mem. ed. bds. "Canadian Materials"; "Emergency Librarian"; mem. Candn. Lib. Assn. (Pres. CSLA); Que. Assn. Sch. Libs. (Pres.); Corp. Prof. Libs. Que.; Am. Lib. Assn.; Internat. Assn. Sch. Librarianship (Conf. Co-Chrmn.); Protestant; recreations: scuba diving, bridge, bowling, swimming; Home: 194 Roi Du Nord, Ste-Rose, Laval, Que. H7L 1W5; Office: 530 Northcote Rd., Rosemere, Que. J7A 1Y2.

AFFLECK, W. Bruce, Q.C., B.A., LL.B.; lawyer; b. Oshawa, Ont. 3 May 1931; s. William Affleck; e. O'Neill Coll. & Vocational Inst. Oshawa 1950; Univ. of Toronto Victoria Coll. B.A. 1953; Osgoode Hall Law Sch. Toronto LL.B. 1957; m. Frances Myrtle Walker 14 Feb. 1981; two s. Robert Bruce, William John; step-children: Derek William,

Kelly April, Jason Michael; PARTNER, AFFLECK, SOSNA & SHAUGHNESSY; called to Bar of Ont. 1957; cr. Q.C. 1970; Asst. Crown Atty. Co. Ont. 1959-61; Crown Atty. Co. Ont. Region Durham 1961-77; Dir. Crown Attys. E. Central Ont. Region 1975-77; Chrmn. Bail Comte. Ont. Crown Attys. Assn. (brief 1967), Secy. of Assn. 1965-67; Dir. and former Secy.-Treas. Oshawa Gen. Hockey Club 1962- ; Vice Pres. Whitby Warriors Sr. "A" Hockey Club 1973-74; Dir. Oshawa Falcon TV Sr. "A" Football Club 1975-77; Pres. Cardiac Rehabilitation Assn. 1976-77; Dir. Oshawa Green Gaels 1977-79; Nat. Pres. Candn. Assn. Children Learning Disabilities 1969-71; Pres. Ont. Assn. Children Learning Disabilities 1964-68, 1968-69; Pres. Boy Scouts Can. Oshawa & Dist. 1974-75; Guest Lectr. Queen's Univ. Law Sch., Windsor Univ. Law Sch., Osgoode Hall Law Sch.; Lectr., RCMP Coll. Ottawa 1966-77; Ont. Prov. Police Coll. 1962-74; Candn. Fire Investigator's Sch. 1967; Coroners for Prov. Ont. on Inquest Evidence 1962-77; Prov. Judge's Assn. 1976- ; named Hon. Col. State of Miss. 1964; one of top 3 Crown Attys. in Can. (Candn. Mag.) 1977; recipient Outstanding Young Man Award Jr. Chamber Comm. 1968, named Hon. Life mem.; Queen's Medal for Outstanding Performance 1977; author various articles prof. journs.; el. Bencher Law Soc. Upper Can. 1979; Dir. Criminal Lawyers Assn. 1981; mem. Candn. Bar Assn.; P. Conservative; Protestant; recreations: public speaking, reading, hiking, swimming; Home: R.R.1, Hampton, Ont. LOB 1J0; Office: 57 Simcoe St. S., Oshawa, Ont. L1H 7V5.

AGNEW, Robert Gordon, B.A., D.D.S., L.D.S., M.Sc.D., Ph.D.; b. Toronto, Ont., 4 Sept. 1898; s. John Henry and Mary Eliza (Law) A.; e. elem. schs., Toronto, Ont.; Victoria Coll. Univ. of Toronto, B.A. 1920; Roy. Coll. of Dental Surg., L.D.S.; Univ. of Toronto, D.D.S., 1921, M.Sc. (Dent.) 1934, Ph.D 1941; post-grad. work, Univ. of Vienna; Research Fellow, Peking Union Med. Coll.; accredited specialist (Periodontist) Can. (Ont.) & U.S.A.; Diplomate, Am. Bd. of Oral Med., 1966; m. Mary Anna (divorced 1961), d. Rev. Henry Caldwell, 7 Aug. 1923; children: Marie (d.), Robert, Margaret, Ruth; 2ndly, Ella B., d. James J. Magee, 9 Sept. 1961; Research Fellow, 1921-22 and Staff Mem., Roy, Coll. of Dental Surgeons, Univ. of Toronto, 1922-23; proceeded to China under Un. Ch. of Can. 1923; joined staff of W. China Union Univ. 1925-48 (Acting Dean of Dentistry, 1945-46). Prof. of Biol. Sciences and Periodontology in Coll. of Med. & Dent. there, also teacher of Music (Voice) and teacher in Divn. of Religious Educ.; Prof. of Periodontology, and Dir., Clinic in Periodontia, conducting research in joint studies in Oral Pathology with Bernard Gottlieb, Baylor Univ., Dallas, Texas, 1948; Assoc. Prof., Univ. of Cal. S.F. Sch. of Dent., 1948-66, Prof. of Oral Biol. Emeritus Sch. of Dent., and Prof. of Pathology Emeritus Sch. of Medicine; has conducted seven research expeditions into W. China Border Tribes' Country and into E. Tibet in fields of Nutrition, Oral Pathol. and Folk-Music; has taken part in relief activities in China under Candn. Red Cross, Candn. Aid to China; Am. Bureau for Med. Aid to China; has lectured throughout Can. and U.S.A. on subjects dealing with relations between Am. and the East and on scient., religious and educ. problems in China, while on furlough; former mem., Nat. Dental Health Bd., Min. of Health, Govt. of China; West China Dent. Assoc.; West China Border Research Assn. (Past-Pres.); Master, Internat. Coll. of Dent. (Pres., Coll. at Large 1961); Am. Geog. Sec.; Am. Assn. for Advanc. of Science; mem., Cal. State Dental Assn.; Pierre Fauchard Acad.; Pan-Am. Odontol. Assn.; Internat. Assn. for Dental Research; (Regent.) Chengtu Section, Internat. Coll. of Dents.; Candn. Dental Assn.; Ont. Dental Assn.; Am. Dental Assn.; W. China Dental Assn.; Am. Acad. of Periodontology; W. China Border Research Assn. (Past Pres.); Am. Acad. of Oral Pathol.; Fed. Dentaire Internat.; Royal Soc. Health; Chrmn., Asilomar Conferences, Mental Health Assn. N. Cal. 1952-61; Chrmn., Bd. of Dirs., Pac. Foundation, 1957, permanent Hon. Chrmn. 1966; Editor ICD Scientific

and Educ. Journal 1965-78; Advisory Bd., Cal. Inst. of Integral Studies; Pres., Internat. Pioneer Acad. of Internat. Re-educ. Foundation 1971-72; has contrib. approx. 80 articles dealing with scient. subjects, internat. affairs, etc., pub. in Can., U.S.A. and China; Freemason; Phi Tau Phi; Unitarian Universalist (Unitarian Humanist); recreations: music (choral conducting), philosophic research, travel; Address: 7707 Tommy Dr., Apt. H-1, San Diego, Ca. 92119.

AGOSTINI, Lucio; composer; conductor; b. Fano, Italy, 30 Dec. 1913; s. Giuseppe A. (well known Montreal musician); m.; children: Lola, Elio; came to Montreal, P.Q., 1916 and began musical studies two yrs. later; at age of eight, showed great talent as a 'cellist, later studied all wind instruments and the piano; early prof. engagements on 'cello and saxophone in orchestras of Palace and Capital theatres at age of 15, under his father who directed the orchestras; entered radio shortly afterward and quickly gained reputation as orchestra leader and arranger; has thorough knowledge of Cuban and other Latin Am. rhythms, and music in the modern manner; prolific contributor to radio and TV music, including scores for CBC radio dramas; Chrysler Festival Shows (1956-57). "Pick The Stars" Toronto, (1956-57), "Front Page Challenge", (1957-59), "Appointment with Agostini" (1958); Musical Director of Assoc. Screen News in Montreal; speaks English, French, Italian and Spanish; composed and conducted music for almost every movie made by Nat. Film Bd. during 2nd World War; awarded Nice (France) Music Festival Award in 1957 for being "the most successful Candn. Arranger of Popular Music"; mem., Composers, Authors & Publ. Assn. Can.;

AHL, Erwin E., insurance executive; b. Brugg, Switzerland, 17 Apl. 1915; s. Edward and Frieda (Klarer) A.; e. primary and secondary schs. Brugg, Switzerland; Grad. Sch. for Business Adm. Zurich; m. Rita d. late A.A. Hunter, Ste. Anne de Bellevue, Que., 15 Feb. 1947; one s. David; PRES., FEDERATION INSURANCE CO. OF CANADA 1981; Vice-Chmn. and Dir. of Galaxy Reinsurance Comp.; H.O. Del. Candn. Br. Switzerland Gen. Insurance Co. and Helvetia Swiss Fire Insurance Co. 1939-46; Asst. Mgr. Baloise Insurance Co. Candn. Br. 1947-50; Mgr. for Can., Switzerland Gen. Ins. Co. Ltd. and Helvita Swiss Fire Ins. Co. Ltd. 1951-64; Vice Pres. and Mang. Dir., Federation Ins. Co. of Can. 1964-81; Dir. Swiss-Candn. Chamber Comm.; Protestant; Club: Cercle Place d'Armes; Home: 245 Revere Ave., Town of Mount Royal, Que. H3P 1B9; Office: 275 St. James St. W., Montreal, Que. H2Y 1M9

AIKEN, Gordon Harvey, Q.C.; b. Ripley, Ont., 26 Sept. 1918; s. late Albert Henry and Rhetta (Treleaven) A.; e. Pub. & Continuation Sch., Allenford, Ont.; Owen Sound Collegiate, Ont.; Osgoode Hall, Toronto, Ont. (Grad. Hons.) 1940; m. Marie Kathrine Miller, Prince George, B.C., 7 Dec. 1945; children: Carol Jane, Anne Shirley, George Arthur Miller, Clare Ruth; m. 2ndly, Ingrid Krall, 26 Aug. 1978; son, Roger Lee; PARTNER, AIKEN & CHRISTENSEN & HEATH; cr. K.C. (Q.C.) 1952; practised law Tara, Bracebridge & Gravenhurst, Ont. 1940 to date; Judge, Juvenile & Family Court, Muskoka 1951-56; served as officer in Canadian Army 1941-1946, Signals, Mil. Intelligence and Platoon Commander R.H.L.I. overseas; el. to H. of C. 1957, re-elected 1958, 1962, 1963, 1965 and 1968. Not a candidate subsequently; del. to U.N. Gen. Assembly 1961; Chairman Banking & Commerce Committee, H. of C. 1962; leader Cdn. Delegation to Rome, I.P.U. 1972; author "The Backbencher" 1974; mem. Royal Canadian Legion (past Pres., Tara Br.); Conservative; United Church; recreations: camping, outdoor life; Clubs: Rotary International since 1946 (Pres. Grav. club 1952-53); Home: Gravenhurst, Ont.; Office: 141 Muskoka Rd. N., Gravenhurst, Ont. P0C1G0.

AIRD, Alexander Ross, B.A.; management consultant; b. Toronto, Ont. 2 April 1936; s. William Hugh and Margaret Grace (Cameron) A.; e. Lower Canada Coll., Montreal; McGill Univ. B.A. 1958; m. Margot Knox. d. Herbert Knox McLean, 13 Dec. 1958; one s. William Cameron; three d. Wendy Birks, Linda McLean, Philippa Ross; MANAGEMENT CONSULTANT, TOUCHE ROSS & PARTNERS and TOUCHE ROSS & CO.; joined Payne Ross Ltd., Montreal, 1958; Partner-in-Charge, P.S. Ross & Partners, Winnipeg 1964-68, Toronto 1968-70; Managing Partner, 1972-79; Chrmn. since 1979; served as Reserve Officer, Black Watch (R.H.R.) of Canada, 1957-64; mem., Inst. Management Consultants of Ont.; Inst. Management Consultants of U.S.; Alpha Delta Phi; Presbyterian; recreations: golf, squash, tennis; Clubs: York; Toronto Golf; Mount Bruno Country (Montreal); Badminton and Racquet Club of Toronto; Home: 187 Douglas Drive, Toronto, Ont. M4W 2B6

AIRD, Hon. John B., O.C. (1976), Q.C., B.A., LL.D. (Wilfrid Laurier U.); b. Toronto, Ont., 5 May 1923; s. late Hugh Reston and May (Black) A.; e. Upper Can. Coll.; Trinity Coll. B.A. 1946; Osgoode Hall Law Sch.; Wilfrid Laurier, LL.D. (Hon.) 1975; m. Lucille Jane, d. Harry Housser 27 July 1944; one s. Hugh Housser, three d. Lucille Elizabeth (Mrs. W.J. Menear), Jane Victoria (Mrs. T.G. Blackmore), Katherine Black; LIEUTENANT GOVERNOR OF ONTARIO, 1980-; read law with Wilton & Edison, assoc. with same 1949-53; Partner, Edison, Aird & Berlis 1953-74; Aird Zimmerman & Berlis 1974-78; Partner, Aird and Berlis 1978-; cr. Q.C. 1960; mem. Senate of Can. 1964-74; Chrmn. Candn. Sec., Can.-U.S. Perm. Jt. Bd. on Defence Oct. 1971-Oct. 1979; mem. Comte. of Nine (of the North Atlantic Assembly) Mar. 9, 1973-Oct. 1973; Chrmn. Inst. for Research on Public Policy since Nov. 28, 1974; served as Lt. R.C.N.V.R. 1942-45; Hon. Pres. Naval Off. Assns. of Canada; rec'd hon.LL.D. Wilfred Laurier U. 1975, and from Royal Military College of Canada, 1980; apptd. Chancellor of Wilfrid Laurier U. 1977; mem. Bd. Govs. Lester B. Pearson Coll. of the Pacific; Honorary Counsel, St. Paul's Anglican Church Toronto; Clubs: York; Toronto; Toronto Golf; Granite; Office: Lieutenant Governor's Suite, Queen's Pk., Toronto M7A 1A1

AIROLA, Paavo, Ph.D., N.D., R.C.A.; author; artist; naturopathic physician; b. Karelia, Finland 14 June 1918; e. Prep. Coll. Viborg, Finland 1936; Univ. of Leningrad Ph.D. 1939; Isac Grünewald Art Sch. Stockholm 1945-47; Brantridge Forest Sch. Eng. N.D. (doctorate in Naturopathic Med.) 1962; came to Can. 1952, Candn. citizen 1957; children: Anni, Evi, Paul, Karen, Paula; author "There Is A Cure For Arthritis" 1968 (rec'd Award of Merit Am. Inst. Pub. Affairs); "Sex and Nutrition" 1970; "Health Secrets From Europe" 1970; "Are You Confused?" 1971; "How To Keep Slim, Healthy and Young With Juice Fasting" 1972; "Cancer: Causes, Prevention and Treatment-The Total Approach" 1972; "Rejuvenation Secrets From Around The World That Work" 1974; "Swedish Beauty Secrets" 1971; "Stop Hair Loss" 1965; "How To Get Well" 1974; "Hypoglycemia: A Better Approach" 1977; "The Miracle of Garlic" 1978; "Everywoman's Book" 1979; "The Airola Diet and Cookbook" 1981; author regularly featured columns in various mags.; solo painting exhns. Toronto, Montreal, N.Y., Boston, Phoenix, Stockholm, London, Paris; rep. in perm. colls. Sweden, Can. and USA; former Pres., Candn. Colour & Form Soc.; mem. Ont. Soc. Artists; Academician, Royal Candn. Acad. of Fine Arts; Internat. Acad. Biol. Med. (Pres. and Founder); Internat. Naturopathic Assn.; Internat. Soc. Research Civilization Diseases & Environment; Address: (P.O. Box 22001) Phoenix, Ariz. U.S. 85028.

AITKEN, Hugh T., C.A.; insurance executive; b. Montreal, P.Q., 2 July 1912; s. James Taylor and Annie Currie (Forgan) A.; e. Kensington Pub. Sch. and West Hill High Sch., Montreal (Matric. 1929); C.A. 1935; m. Margaret T. Marshall, 15 Nov. 1971; with P.S. Ross & Sons, C.A.'s, Montreal, 1929-37; A.T. Ross Ltd., Invest. Dealers, Montreal, 1937-38; P.S. Ross & Sons, C.A.'s, Montreal, 1938-40; Asst. Dir. of Finance British Purchasing Comn., New York, 1940-45; Past Pres. Export Devel. Corp. (Crown Co.) 1945-75; Chmn., Finance Comte., Boy Scouts of Can.; Past Pres., Chart. Accts. Club of Ottawa; Ottawa Boy Scouts; Union d'Assureurs ,des Credits Internationaux; mem., Parish Council, Christ Church Cathedral; awarded Coronation Medal, 1953; Centennial Medal, 1967; Protestant; recreations: golf, bridge, fishing; Clubs: Rideau; Royal Ottawa Golf; Commandine de Bordcaux Home: 32 Tennyson St., Ottawa, Ont. K2E 7G9. or Glocca Morra, Shawville, Qùebec J0X 2Y0

AITKEN, Sir (John William) Max, Bart., D.S.O. 1942, D.F.C. 1940; journalist; newspaper director; b. Montreal, P.Q., 15 Feb. 1910; e. Westminster; Pembroke Coll., Cambridge; m. 2ndly, Mrs. Jane Lindsay, d. R. O. R. Kenyon-Slaney 1946; (2 d.); 3rdly, Violet, d. Sir Humphrey de Trafford, Dec. 1950 (1s., 1d.), LIFE PRES., EXPRESS NEWSPAPER LTD., publishers of: Daily Express, Sunday Express, Scottish Daily Express, Scottish Sunday Express, Evening Standard, London), Dir.,; Associated Television Ltd.; Chancellor (el. 1966), Univ. of New Brunswick; Hon. Citizen of Moncton, N.B. (1966); Commissioned in No. 601 Sqdn., Royal Auxiliary Air Force, 1935; served in 2nd World War 1939-45 with R.A.F.; promoted Group Capt. 1944; awarded Czech War Cross; el. to H. of C. for Holborn, g.e. 1945; Cambridge Assn. Football Blue 1930-31; Conservative; Presby.; recreation: sailing, golf; Clubs: White's; Royal Yacht Squadron, New York Yacht; Home: 46 Chelsea Square, Landon S.W.3, England; Office: Daily Express, Fleet St., London, England.

AKENSON, Donald Harman, Ph.D., F.R.S.C., F.R.S.A.; historian; educator; b. Minneapolis, Minn. 22 May 1941; s. Donald Nels and Fern L. (Harman) A.; e. Yale Univ. B.A. 1962; Harvard Univ. Ed.M. 1963, Ph.D. 1967; PROF. OF HIST. QUEEN'S UNIV. since 1974; Publisher and Owner, Langdian Press ("Canadian Papers in Rural History"); Allston Burr Sr. Tutor, Dunster House, Harvard Coll. 1966-67; Asst. Prof. of Hist. and Asst. Dean, Yale Coll. 1967-70; Assoc. Prof. of Hist. Queen's Univ. 1970-74; Hon. Research Fellow, Inst. Irish Studies, Queen's Univ. of Belfast 1976-77; Hon. Prof. of Educ. Trinity Coll. Dublin 1976-77; comm. sheep farmer; rec'd Am. Council Learned Socs. Research Award 1976-77; author "The Irish Education Experiment: The National System of Education in the Nineteenth Century" 1970; "The Church of Ireland: Ecclesiastical Reform and Revolution 1800-1885" 1971; "Education and Enmity: The Control of Schooling in Northern Ireland 1920-50" 1973; "The United States and Ireland" 1973; "A Mirror to Kathleen's Face: Education in Independent Ireland 1922-60" 1975; "Local Poets and Social History: James Orr, Bard of Ballycarry" 1977; "Between Two Revolutions: Islandmagee, County Antrim, 1798-1920" 1979; "The Lazar House Notebooks" 1981; "A Protestant in Purgatory: Richard Whately, Archibishop of Dublin" 1981; Phi Beta Kappa; Clubs: Yale (N.Y.C.); Co. Antrim Yacht (N. Ireland); Office: Kingston, Ont. K7L 3N6.

AKHURST, Harold Weldon; company executive; b. Vancouver, B.C., 17 Aug. 1913; s. late William Adolphus and Winifred Eliza (Nunns) A.; e. Prince of Wales High Sch., Vancouver, B.C.; University Sch., Victoria, B.C.; Univ. of British Columbia; m. Jeanne Elizabeth, d. James Loghrin, White Rock, B.C., 14 Sept. 1940; two s. William Bruce, Brian James; PRESIDENT, AKHURST MACHINERY LTD., since 1950; began with Grinnell Cooper Co. Ltd., Vancouver, B.C., 1934; Hammond Cedar Products Ltd., Hammond, B.C., 1935-42, leaving in post of Assistant Sales Manager; served in 2nd World War for three years with R.C.N.V.R.; discharged with rank of Lieut.; Phi

Gamma Delta; United Church; recreations: boating, golf, fishing; Home: 1354 Balfour Ave., Vancouver, B.C. V6H 1X7; Office: 216 W. 2nd Vancouver, B.C. V5Y 1C6

AKRIGG, George Philip Vernon, M.A., Ph.D., F.R.H.S., F.R.S.C.; Shakespeare scholar and historian; b. Calgary, Alta. 13 Aug. 1913; s. George Straker and Rose Edith (Norton) A.; e. Central Sch. and Lethbridge (Alta.) Coll. Inst.; Calgary (Alta.) Normal Sch.; Univ. of B.C. B.A. 1937, M.A. 1940; Univ. of Cal. Berkeley Ph.D. 1944; m. Helen Brown d. late E. C. Manning 2 Sept. 1944; children: Marian, Daphne, George; Prof. of Eng. Univ. of B.C. 1958-79; Dir. Discovery Press; Research Fellow, Folger Shakespeare Lib. Washington, D.C. 1946-47; Lectr. Shakespeare Seminar, Stratford, Ont. 1966; Renaissance Inst. Ashland Shakespeare Festival, Ore. 1972; Can. Council Leave Fellowship 1970-71, 1975-76; mem. Can. Council On-Site Inspection Teams (Laval Univ. 1975, Univ. of Toronto 1976, 1980); frequent speaker; Pres. Vancouver Inst. 1963-64; author "Jacobean Pageant or the Court of King James I" 1962; "Shakespeare and the Earl of Southampton" 1968; "1001 British Columbia Place Names" 1969 (co-author); co-author "British Columbia Chronicle 1778-1846" 1975; "British Columbia Chronicle 1847-1871" 1977; numerous articles on Shakespeare, Eng. lit. and hist. of Renaissance; mem. Modern Lang. Assn.; Anglican; recreations: travel, gardening; Home: 4633 W. 8th Ave., Vancouver, B.C. V6R 2A6.

ALARIE, Pierrette. (Madame Simoneau); O.C. (1967); artiste lyrique; educateur; née Montréal, Que., 9 novembre, 1921; f. Sylva et Amanda (Plante)Alarie; é. écoles primaires et secondaires; études musicales au Curtis Institute de Philadelphia; ép. Léopold Simoneau, 1 juin, 1946; enfants: Isabelle, Chantal; Direction scénique San Francisco Conservatory of Music Banff Summer School of the Arts and Shawnigan-Victoria Festival. Antérieurement du Metropolitan Opera; Opera de Paris, de San Francisco; festivals d'Aix-en-Provence, Edinburgh, Vienne, Munich, Salzburg, etc.; Medaille du Centenaire; Catholique; recreations: théâtre, lecture, haute cuisine, marche, natation; Adress: aux soins de Conservatory of Music, San Francisco, Cal. 94122

ALBINO, George Robert, A.B., M.B.A.; mining executive; b. Boston, Mass., e. Harvard Business Sch.; Columbia Coll., Columbia Univ. (A.B. 1950; M.B.A. 1954); came to Can. 1965; m. Julianne E.; three s.: William, Robert, George Jr.; CHMN., PRES. AND C.E.O., RIO ALGOM LTD.; Lornex Mining Corp. Ltd.; Dir., Confederation Life; Barclays Can. Ltd.; Rio Tinto Zinc Corp. Ltd.; Rossing Uranium Ltd.; Served with U.S. Marine Corps, 2nd Marine Div., Capt.; Clubs: Toronto National, Mississauga; Home: 2242 Highriver Court, Port Credit, Ont. L5H 3K4; Office: 120 Adelaide St. W., Toronto, Ont. M5H 1T1

ALCOCK, Charles Benjamin, Ph.D., D.Sc., F.R.I.C.; educator; consultant; b. London, Eng 24 Oct. 1923; s. Arthur Charles and Margaret (Francis) A.; e. Imp. Coll., B.Sc. 1944; Univ. of London, Ph.D. 1955, D.Sc. 1969; m. Valerie Marie Daniel Robinson 20 Aug. 1949; children: Deborah Susan, Martin Charles, James Benjamin; PROF. METALL. AND MATERIALS SCIENCE, UNIV. OF TORONTO; Extractive Metall. Lectr., Am. Inst. Metall. Engrs. 1974; Author, "Principles of Pyrometallurgy"; coauthor, "Metallurgical Thermochemistry" (5th ed.); "Electromotive Force Measurements in High Temperature Systems" and author over 130 tech. papers; Le Beau Medallist, Soc. des Hautes Températures, 1976; Chrmn., chemical Eng. Div. Visiting Comte. and M.H.D. Interdivision Comte., Argonne Nat. Lab. U.S.A., Mem. Can. Nat. Comte. for IUPAC; Fellow, Inst. Mining & Metall., London; Amer. Inst. Met. Engrs.; Royal Soc. Arts; Anglican, recreations: sports, music; Home: 20 Dunbar Rd., Toronto, Ont. M4W 2X6; Office: 184 College St., Toronto, Ont. M5S 1A4

ALCOCK, Norman Zinkan, B.Sc., M.S., Ph.D.; physicist; b. Edmonton, Alta., 29 May 1918; s. late Joseph Benjamin and late Edith Alma (Zinkan) A.; e. Queens Univ., B.Sc. (Elect. Engn.) 1940; Cal. Tech., M.S. (Elect. Engn.) 1941; McGill Univ., Ph.D. (Physics) 1946; m. Patricia Christian Sinclair Hunter, 29 June 1948; children: Stephen, Christopher, David, Nancy; PRESIDENT AND DIR., CANADIAN PEACE RESEARCH INST., since 1962; Research Engr. (ground radar), Nat. Research Council Can., 1941; Telecommunications Research Estab., Great Malvern, Eng. (airborne radar) 1943; McGill Univ., Research Physicist (cyclotron design), 1945; Atomic Energy of Canada Ltd. (neutron diffraction research), 1946; Vice-Pres. and Dir., Isotope Products Ltd., Oakville, Ont., 1950; Gen. Mgr. of Isotopes Products Div., Canadian Curtiss-Wright, 1957, and Dir. of Engn. there 1958; self employed on peace research, 1959; Commissioned in R.C.A.F. 1942; mem., Sigma Xi; Address: Gryffin Lodge, Huntsville, Ont. P0A 1K0;

ALDERSON, Delos Earl, B.Sc.; association executive; b. Brantford, Ont.; s. Ernest Walton and Vera Isula (Earl) A.; e. Brantford Coll. Inst.; Queen's Univ. B.Sc.; m. Rhea Eleanor d. Robert Lucas 9 Oct. 1948; children: Philip, Catherine, Susan (Mrs. R. Mackenzie); PRES., CHIEF ADM. OFFR. AND DIR., CANDN. GAS ASSN. 1981- ; Pres. and Dir. Candn. Gas Research Inst. 1981- ; Staff Engr. Gatineau Power Co. Ottawa 1948; Div. Plant Engr. Canadian International Paper Co. Gatineau 1951; Mgr. Projects, M.W. Kellogg Co. New York 1961; Chief Engr. E. B. Eddy Co. Ottawa 1967; Asst. to Pres. (Pulp & Paper Group) Domtar Inc. Montreal 1973; Past Chrmn. Assn. Maj. Power Consumers Ont.; Past Dir. Industrial Gas Users Assn.; Reddy Mem. Hosp. Corp. Montreal; Past Chrmn. Candn. Pulp & Paper Industry's Energy Task Force; mem. Governmental Energy Conserv. Comte.; mem. Assn. Prof. Engrs. Prov. Ont.; Internat. Gas Union (Switzerland); World Energy Conf.; Candn. Chamber Comm.; Bd. Trade Metrop. Toronto; Candn. Nat. Exhn. Assn.; recreations: sailing, golf, cross-country skiing; Clubs: Beaconsfield Golf; Empire; Canadian; Lambton Golf & Country; Home: 2 Riverstone Dr., Toronto, Ont. M9P 2R6; Office: 55 Scarsdale Rd., Don Mills, Ont. M3B 2R3.

ALDOUS, John Gray, M.A., Ph.D.; university professor; b. Bristol, Eng., 16 Nov. 1916; s. Frederick Gray and Mary Ursula (Macfarlane) A.; came to Can. 1919; e. Univ. of Btsh. Columbia, B.A. 1939, M.A. 1941; Univ. of Toronto, Ph.D. 1944; m. the late Elsie Eileen Hooley, Vancouver, B.C., 22 July 1944; children: Joleen, Peter, Donald; PROF. OF PHARMACOLOGY, DALHOUSIE UNIV.; Asst. in Gen. Physiol. and Biol., Univ. of B.C. 1939-41; Demonst. in Gen. Physiol., Univ. of Toronto 1941-45; Asst. Prof. of Pharmacol., Dalhousie, 1945-48 and Assoc. Prof. 1948-50; Alpha Omega Alpha; mem., Candn. Physiol. Soc., Pharmacol. Soc. of Can. (Pres. 1970); N.S. Inst. of Science (Hon. Life mem.; Pres. 1956-58); Biol. Council Can. (Treas. 1973, Vice Pres. 1974); N.S. Comn. on Drug Dependency (Bd. mem. 1972-81); Hon. mem., N.S. Pharm. Soc. 1977; Professor Emeritus (1981); recreations: photography, music, sports; Home: R.R. 1, Newport, Hants Co., N.S. B0N 2A0

ALDRIDGE, Gordon James, M.A., M.S.W., Ph.D.; university professor, b. Toronto, Ont., 19 Oct. 1916; s. Eugene Froyard and Alicia Louisa (Jourdan) A.; e. N. Toronto (Ont.) Coll. Inst. 1934; Univ. of Toronto, B.A. (Sociol.) 1938, Dipl. in Social Science 1939, M.A. (Psychol.) 1948, M.S.W. 1949; Univ. of Mich., Ph.D. (Community Devel.) 1955; Univ. of London (Dipl. in Educ. 1963; m. Gladys Parker, d. late Rev. Joseph Fletcher Chapman, 21 June 1941; one s., Major Ronald Gordon; PROF. OF SOCIAL WORK, ARIZONA STATE UNIV.; Social Caseworker, Big Brother Movement, Toronto, 1939-41; Casework Supvr., 1946-50 (Asst. Extve. Dir. 1949-50); Lectr. in Psychol., Univ. of Toronto, 1946-50;

Dir., Ont. summer camp for emotionally disturbed boys, 1947-49; Assoc. Prof. of Social Welfare and Dir. of Human Relations Inst., Fla. State Univ., 1950-52; Assoc. Prof. to Prof., Michigan State Univ. 1952-78; Dir., Sch. of Social Work, 1959-66; Consultant on social work educ. incl. Inst. of Higher Educ., Columbia Univ., periodic consultant with state and nat. organs. concerning programs and services in aging and retirement; served with Candn. Army in Can. and Europe 1941-46; rank Maj. on discharge; author: "Social Issues and Psychiatric Social Work Practice", 1959; Co-author: "Social Welfare and the Aged", 1959; "Social Welfare of the Aging" (Vol. II of "Aging Around the World"), 1962; "Liberal Education and Social Work", 1965; "Undergraduate Social Work Education", 1972; many articles and book reviews; mem., Council Social Work Educ.; Nat. Assn. Social Workers; Gerontol. Soc.; Internat. Assn. Gerontol.; Can. Assoc. on Gerontol.: Protestant; recreations: music, theatre, swimming; Home: 7709 East Sheridan Street, Scottsdale, Ariz.; Office: Tempe, Ariz.

ALEXANDER, David Gerald; trust company executive; b. Belfast, N. Ireland 31 Oct. 1925; s. William Alexander; came to Can. 1926; e. Mimico (Ont.) High Schl. 1946; York Univ. Business 1972; m. Marion d. Edward Prince, Port Credit, Ont. 20 March 1952; two d. Donna Joy, Sandra Beth; VICE PRES. FIDELITY TRUST CO. since 1975; served Beneficial Finance Co. 25 yrs. becoming Vice Pres. (Can.) and Dir. Beneficial International Insurance Co.; Extve. Vice Pres. New Horizons Tower; Dir. Christian Nat. Evangelical Comn.; Christian Horizons; Yonge St. Mission; Baptist; recreations: golf, sailing, music (violinist); Club: Toronto Squash; Home: 18 Woodway Trail, Toronto, Ont. M8Y 2B8; Office: 350 Bay St., Toronto, Ont. M5H 2S6.

ALEXANDER, John Clark, B.Sc. (C.E.); manufacturer; b. Moose Jaw, Sask., 1 Aug. 1912; s. Robert M. and Katherine McNeil (Clark) A.; e. Univ. of Man. B.Sc. (C.E.) 1934; Harvard Business Sch. Advanced Mang. Program 1957; m. Noreen George; formerly President, Joy Manufacturing Co. (Canada) Ltd. (ret.); formerly Pres., The Craig Bit Co. Ltd. (ret.); mem. Candn. Inst. Mining & Metall.; recreations: golf, cross country skiing; Club: Galt Country (Dir.); Home: 95 Cambridge St. Apt. 1703, Cambridge, Ont. N1R 3S2;

ALEXANDER, Lincoln MacCauley, P.C., Q.C., B.A., M.P.; politician; b. Toronto, Ont. 21 Jan. 1922; s. Lincoln MacCauley and May Rose)Royale) A.; e. McMaster Univ. B.A. 1949; Osgoode Hall Law Sch. 1953; m. Yvonne d. late Robert Harrison 10 Sept. 1948; one s. Keith; CHRM., ONT. WORKMEN'S COMPENSATION BD., 1980-; Min. of Labour Can. 1979-80; called to Bar of Ont. 1953; cr. W.C. 1966; former Partner, Millar, Alexander, Tokiwa & Isaacs, Hamilton, Ont.; def. cand. fed. g.e. 1965; el. to H. of C. for Hamilton W. g.e. 1968, re-el. since; mem. Inter-Parlty. Union (Candn. Group); Commonwealth Parlty. Assn. (Candn. Br.); Candn. NATO Parlty. Assn.; U.N. Observer 1976, 1978; mem. Hamilton Goodwill Africa Foundation; Hamilton Chamber Comm.; Nat. Council Candn. Human Rights Foundation; Hon. Patron Hamilton Kiwanis Club Music Festival; rec'd St. Ursula Award 1969; Clk. and Legal Advisor Stewart Mem. Ch. Hamilton; served with RCAF 1942-45, rank Cpl.; mem. Hamilton Lawyers' Club; Wentworth Co. Law Assn.; Candn. Bar Assn.; Freemason; Shriner; P. Conservative; Baptist; recreations: music, gardening; Clubs: Optimist (Past Pres.); Hamilton Cricket (Hon. mem.); Home: 30 Proctor Blvd., Hamilton, Ont. L8M 2M3; Office: House of Commons, Ottawa, Ont. K1A 0A6.

ALEXANDER, Norman J.; investment consultant; b. Regina, Sask. 1909; Dir. Dome Petroleums Ltd.; Continental Illinois Bank (Canada) Ltd.; Marinav Corp.; Ampower Canada Ltd.; Former Vice-Pres. James Richardson

& Sons Ltd. and Former Mang. Partner Richardson Securities of Canada; Past Pres. B.C. Bond Dealers Assn.; Vancouver Stock Exchange; Investment Dealers Assn. of Can.; Clubs; Manitoba; St. Charles Country; Winnipeg Winter; Vancouver; Capilano Golf & Country; Home: 85 Yale Ave., Winnipeg, Man. R3M 0K9; Office: Suite 2410, One Lombard Place, Winnipeg, Man. R3B 0X4

ALEXANDER, William Edward, M.Sc., Ph.D.; educator; b. North Battleford, Sask. 19 Apl. 1934; s. William Henry Gordon and Eleanor (Arnold) A.; e. Univ. of Sask. B.Sc. (Pharm.) 1958, M.Sc. 1960; Univ. of Sydney Ph.D. 1965; m. Grace Marion Gorchynski; children: Bradley Dean, Megan Nicole, Jeffrey Todd; PROF. VICE-PRES., PERSONNEL & STUDENT AFFAIRS, UNIV. OF TORONTO; author articles various journs.; mem. Sask. Pharm. Assn.; Candn. Pharm. Assn.; Anglican; recreations: swimming, tennis, skiing, woodworking, gardening; Home: 18 Pipers Green Ave., Scarborough, Ont. M1S 3J8; Office: Simcoe Hall, Toronto, Ont. M5S 1A1

ALFORD, (William) Parker, B.Sc., Ph.D., F.A.P.S.; physicist; educator; b. London, Ont. 22 March 1927; s. William Alexander and Ruby (Parker) A.; e. Univ. of W. Ont. B.Sc. 1949; Princeton Univ. Ph.D. 1954; m. Jeannette d. Dr. W. H. Wadland, Stratford, Ont. 1949; two s. William David, Stephen Charles; PROF. AND CHRMN. OF PHYSICS, UNIV. OF W. ONT. 1973- ; Instr. Princeton Univ. 1953-55; Instr. Univ. of Rochester 1955, Asst. Prof. 1956, Assoc. Prof. 1960, Prof. 1966-73; Visiting Scient., Inst. for Nuclear Research, Amsterdam 1961-62; Visiting Prof., Univ. of Munich 1971-72; Univ. of Colo. 1978-79; author or co-author over 75 papers various aspects nuclear physics; mem. Candn. Assn. Physicists; Am. Assn. Physics Teachers; Sigma Xi; recreations: skiing, sailing, hiking; Home: 4 Grosvenor St., London, Ont. N6A 1Y4; Office: London, Ont. N6A 3K7.

ALIUS, John; journalist; b. Chemnitz, Germany, 24 Sept. 1925; s. Alfred W. and Elise (Vogel) A.; came to Canada 1930; e. Strathearn High Sch., Montreal, Que.; Montreal High Sch.; Sir George Williams Coll.; Univ. de San Marcos (Lima, Peru); m. Dorothy Jean, d. Gordon Reeves, 30 June 1951; children: Yara, Linda, John, Marc; GEN. MGR., INTERNAT. FEATURES DIVISION, UNITED PRESS INTERNATIONAL; joined British United Press in 1943 while still attending coll.; Mgr. Calgary Bureau 1950; mem. Parlty. Press Gallery 1951-53; joined present organ. as Mgr. for Peru-Ecuador-Bolivia 1954-55, Mgr. for Brazil 1956-58, Mgr. N. Div. Latin Am., Mexico City 1959-67; Mgr., UPI of Canada, Montreal 1968-70; Dir. Internat. Services 1970-72; Mormon; recreations: outdoor living, skiing, reading; Club: Overseas Press; Homes: Mt. View Estates, Washingtonville, N.Y. and 1850 Boucherville Blvd., St. Bruno, Que. J3V 4H4; Office: 220 E. 42nd St., New York, N.Y.

ALLAN, Douglas Henry Wilson, B.A.Sc., P.Eng., b. Toronto, Ont., 18 Nov. 1919; s. Thomas Henry and Edna Mae (Wilson) A.; e. Univ. of Toronto, B.A.Sc. (Metall.) 1942; m. Evelyn Anne Grace, d. late W.A. Wagner, Richmond Hill, Ont., 29 Sept. 1945; children: Marilyn Grace Giekes, Warren Douglas; Chief Eng. Export Dev. Corp., Ottawa, 1980-; held various metall. positions, Hamilton Works, The Steel Co. of Canada Ltd., 1945-55; Metall. Engr., American Iron and Steel Inst., N.Y., 1955-64; Chief, Iron and Steel Div., Materials Br., Dept. of Industry, Ottawa, 1964-68; Mgr. of Marketing, Peace River Mining and Smelting Ltd., Amherstburg, Ont., 1968-71; Vice-Pres. & Gen. Mgr. Industrial Research Inst., Univ. of Windsor 1971-75; Assistant to President of Co-Steel International Ltd. 1975-76; Fellow Am. Soc. for Quality Control; Mem. Assoc. of Professional Engrs. of Ont.; American Inst. of Mining Metall. and Petroleum Engrs.; Am. Soc. Metals; The Metals Soc. (U.K.); Freemason; United Church; recreations: gardening, boating, curling; Home: 6437 Sugar Creek Way, Orleans, Ont. K1C 1X9;

Office: Export Development Corp., 110 O'Connor St., Ottawa, Ont.

ALLAN, Hugh David, B.A.Sc.; industrial executive; b. Toronto, Ont., 25 Feb. 1925; s. Arthur Alexander and Gladys (Gurney) A.; e. Rosedale Pub. Sch., Toronto, 1930-34; Univ. of Toronto Schs., 1934-42; Univ. of Toronto, B.A.Sc. 1946; m. Susan, d. W. Christie Barclay, Toronto, Ont., 17 May 1947; children: H. Michael, Barbara S., David G.; PRES., EMERSON ELECTRIC CAN. LTD. 1980-; Group Vice-Pres., Worthington Pump Inc. 1979; Dir. and Mem. Extve. Comte. of Worthington Pump Inc. 1976-79; joined John Inglis Co. Ltd. as Prod. Engr., 1946-47; apptd. Application Engr. 1947-49; Sales Engr. 1949-55; joined present firm as Asst. to Gen. Mgr., 1956; apptd. Gen. Sales Mgr. 1957-60; Vice Pres. and Gen. Mgr. 1960-65; Chairman and Pres. 1965-76; mem., Assn. Prof. Engrs. Ont.; Am. Mang. Assn.; Delta Kappa Epsilon (Pres. 1945); United Church; recreations: tennis, squash, hunting, fishing, photography; Clubs: Rosedale Golf; Badminton & Racquet; Home: 418 Russell Hill Rd., Toronto, Ont. M5P 2S3; Office: Markham, Ont.

ALLAN, Vice-Adm. John, C.M.M., C.D., B.Sc.; Canadian Forces; b. Kirkland Lake, Ont. 31 March 1928; e. Queen's Univ. B.Sc. (Elect. Engn.) 1955; children: Sandra Kathryn, James, William; DEPUTY CHIEF OF DEFENCE STAFF 1980-; joined RCN 1946 as Ordinary Seaman; Cadet 1950 (Queen's Univ.); comnd. 1954; commanded HMCS Qu'Appelle 1968-70; prior to present appt. served as Proj. Mgr. DDH 280 Prog., Nat. Def. Hdqts. 1970-73: Apptd. Offr. in Order of Military Merit for serv. in DDH 280 prog.; Cmmdr. First Destroyer Sqdn. Halifax, N.S. 1973-74; Chief of Staff Mar. Cmmd. Hdqts., Halifax, N.S. 1974-75; Dir. Gen. Mar. Engin. and Maint., Nat. Def. Hdqts. in rank of Commodore 1975-77; Assoc. Asst. Dep. Min. Materiel, Nat. Def. Hdqts., 1977-79 in rank of Rear-Admiral; awarded Order of Military Merit in the grade of Cmmdr. June 1979; promoted Vice-Admiral July 1979 and in Aug. appt. Cmmdr. of Mar. Cmmd. in Halifax, N.S.; Office: Canadian Forces; National Defence Headquarters, Ottawa, Ont.

ALLAN, John Dykes, B.A.Sc.; industrialist; b. Vancouver, B.C., 31 July 1925; s. William A.; e. Lord Byng High Sch. Vancouver; Univ. of B.C. B.A.Sc. (Mech. Engn.) 1947; m. Marjorie Alice Pearson, 26 Nov. 1949; PRESIDENT,and CHIEF OPERATING OFFICER STELCO INC.; Dir. Stelco.; Dir.; Royal Trustco Ltd.; Dir. Royal TrustCorp of Canada; Dir. Rockwell International of Canada Ltd.; Dir. Gulf Canada Ltd.; Dir. C-I-L Inc.; mem. Am. Iron & Steel Inst.; Int. Iron and Steel Inst.; Candn. Mfrs.' Assn.; Delta Upsilon; Protestant; recreations: golf, cross-country skiing; Clubs: Canadian; Toronto Golf; Hamilton Golf & Country; St. James's (Montreal); Union Club of Cleveland; Home: 2238 Shardawn Mews, Mississauga, Ont. L5C 1W5; Office: (P.O. Box 205) Toronto-Dominion Centre, Toronto, Ont. M5K 1J4

ALLAN, Spence A., M.B.E., E.D., B.A. b. Hamilton, Ontario, 20 February 1906; s. George and Clara Mabel (Carey) A.; e. Hamilton College Inst.; Univ. of Toronto B.A. (Pol. Econ.) 1929; m. Dorothy Walker, d. Alexander F. Zimmerman, 20 June 1931; children: George A., Mrs. Charles E. Parker, Deborah M.; Past Pres. Chedoke Hospitals (retired); joined Reid Press Ltd. 1929 as Plant Superindt;. Asst. to Mang. Dir., 1945-51; Pres. 1954; served with Argyll & Sutherland Highlanders, N.P.A.M., 1930-40 (now Hon. Col.); 2nd World War with R.C.A.F. 1940-45, Adm. Br. trans. to Reserve with rank of Group Capt.; awarded M.B.E.; Past. President, Canadian Paper Box Manufacturers Association; Past Chrmn., Hamilton Br., Candn. Inst. Internat. Affairs; Past Chrmn. Bd. of Govs., Art Gallery of Hamilton; Senator Stratford Shakespearean Festival Foundation; mem. Extr. Comte., Royal Botanical Gardens; Hon. Col., 91st Argyll Sutherland High-

landers of Can.; Kappa Alpha; Conservative; Presbyterian; recreations: boating, horticulture; Clubs: The Hamilton; Royal Hamilton Military Institute; Tamahaac; Badminton & Racquet (Toronto); Home: 53 Markland St., Hamilton, Ont. L8P 2J5

ALLAN, Ted; playwright and author; b. Montreal, P.Q., 25 Jan. 1916; s. Harry and Anne (Elias) Herman; e. Elementary Schs., Montreal, and Baron Byng High Sch. there; m. Kate Schwartz, 25 Aug. 1939, (divorced 1966); children: Julia Iona, Norman Bethune; Member of Internat. Bgde., Spanish Civil War; stage plays: "The Money Makers", produced in Toronto, 1954; "The Ghost Writers", produced at Arts Theatre, London, 1955; "Legend of Pepito", at Theatre Workshop, London, 1956; "Double Image" (with Roger MacDougall), Savoy Theatre, London, produced by Sir Laurence Olivier, 1957, and in Paris, 1959-64, Michodière Theatre under title "Gog et Magog"; "Secret of the World", produced Theatre Royal, Stratford East, 1962; "Oh What a Lovely War", produced by Joan Littlewood, London and New York, 1965; 'Chu Chem-A Zen Buddhist-Hebrew Musical", produced by Albert Marre, N.Y., 1965; "I've Seen You Cut Lemons", produced by Fortune Theatre, London, 1970; "My Sister's keeper", produced at Lennoxville Festival, 1974; books: "This Time a Better Earth", 1940; "The Scalpel, The Sword — The Story of Dr. Norman Bethune" (in collab. with Sydney Gordon), 1955; "Willie the Squowse" (1977); radio drama, documentaries, medical documentaries, television drama, in Can., U.S.A. and Eng.; also short stories have appeared in "New Yorker", "Harpers", "Mademoiselle", "Colliers", etc.; Academy Award Nom. Best Orig. Screen Play, "Lies My Father Told Me" (1975); Socialist; recreations: reading; Address: c/o Mike Zimring, William Morris Agency, 151 El Camino, Beverly Hills, Calif. U.S.A. 90212.

ALLAN, William Norman, B.A., M.Com., F.R.Econ.S.; executive; b. Toronto, Ont., 30 May 1925; s. Leslie Brown and Anne Lillian (Morrison) A.; e. Allenby Public School, Lawrence Park Coll. Inst.; Univ. of Toronto (Victoria Coll. B.A. 1948), (Grad. Sch. of Business Adm., M.Com. 1951); m. Jean Mary, d. Lewis and Agnes Pryzdial, 22 May 1965; CHAIRMAN AND PRES., FISCAL INVESTMENTS LTD., since 1961; Economic Realty Corp. Ltd.; Great Lakes Commercial & Holdings Corp. Ltd.; Great North Uranium & Energy Resources Inc.; Chrmn., Transprovincial Financial Corp. Ltd.; Vice-Pres. and Dir., Reserve Acceptance Co., Ltd.; Dir. Miller Fluid Engineering Co. Ltd.; Founder, Anglo-Permanent Corporate Holdings Ltd.; Economist, Treas. Dept., Govt. of Ont., 1949-52; Consultant and Econ., 1952-57; Extve. Asst. to Fed. Minister of Finance, Ottawa, 1957-61; Former Pres., Audubon Soc.; Pres., Bus. Admin. Course, University of Toronto; Life Gov., Royal Humane Soc.; Chrmn. & Gov., Fidelity Charitable Foundation; mem., Nat. Trust for Scotland; Life Fellow, Acad. of Pol. Sci. (Columbia Univ.); Roy. Commonwealth Soc.; Roy. Econ. Soc., London, Eng. (el. 1965); mem., Ont, Hist. Soc.; Bd. of Trade for Metro Toronto; Life, Empire Club of Can.; St. Andrew's Soc; Tor; Candan. Econ. Assn.; Life mem., Kappa Sigma Fraternity (Internat.); Am. Internat. Acad.; Freemason (Shriner); Protestant; P. Conservative; recreations: fishing, ornithology, history, astronomy, mycology; Clubs: Albany; Kensington Fishing (Gatineau); Sommerville Recreation & Country; Board of Trade Club: University (Ottawa); Home: 157 Golfdale Road, Toronto, Ont. M4N 2C1; Office: 44 Eglinton Ave. W., Suite 410, Toronto, Ont. M4R 1A1

ALLANSON, Bruce D., C.D.; trust company executive; b. Sherbrooke, Que. 29 Jan. 1930; s. Joseph George and Lilian Grace (Hatch) A.; e. Sherbrooke Elem. and High Schs. 1947; m. Audrey Joan d. Clifford Coates 13 Oct. 1951; two s. Mark Douglas, Peter Bruce; EXTVE. VICE PRES., MANG. DIR. AND DIR., SHERBROOKE TRUST CO. 1980-; Dir. Trust General du Canada; CW Dunn Insurance; Brompton Construction Inc.; Sherbrooke Real Estate Co.; joined present Co. 1955, Acct. 1955, Comptroller 1962, Secy.-Treas. 1968, Asst. Gen. Mgr. 1972, Gen. Mgr. 1975, Vice Pres. 1977, Extve. Vice Pres. 1978; served with Sherbrooke Hussars Militia 15 yrs.; Dir. Bishop's Univ.; Sherbrooke Hosp.; Sherbrooke Hosp. Foundation; Wales Home; mem. Trust Co's Assn.; Indust., Comm. & Inst. Accts.; Liberal; Anglican; recreations; curling, golf, skiing; Clubs: Sherbrooke Country; Sherbrooke Curling; Home: 755 Buck St., Sherbrooke, Que. J1J 3L6; Office: 75 Wellington St. N., Sherbrooke, Que. J1H 5B5.

ALLARD, Hector J. M., M.A., LL.D.; diplomat; b. Notre Dame de Grace, Man., 11 May 1902; s. Alexander and Virginie (Beauchemin) A.; e. St. Boniface Coll., Man., (B.A., 1924); Univ. of Man., M.A. 1926, LL.D. 1971; Oxford Univ. (Rhodes Scholar.) B.A. 1928, M.A. 1949; m. Marie-Nicole, d. Jules Auffray, Paris, France, 6 July 1929; seven children; Inst. of Internat. Relations, Geneva, 1928; Lect. in French, Wesley Coll. and Univ. of Man., Winnipeg, Man., 1924-26; Lect., Asst. Prof. in French, Univ. of Alberta, 1930-32; joined Dept. of External Affairs as Third Secy. Dec. 1932; Third Secy., Washington, 1937-40; Second Secy., May 1940; First Secy., Jan. 1944; Mexico City 1944-46; Chargé d'Affaires A.I. 1944-45; Counsellor, Brussels, 1946-49; seconded to Internat. Refugee Organ., 1949-52; returned to Dept. of External Affairs, 1952; in Nov. 1953 apptd. Permanent Del., then Permanent Rep. of Can. to the European Office of U.N.; attended confs. either as Observer. Alternate Del. of ICEM, WHO, ILO and ECOSOC, Big Four in July 1955, and Big Four Foreign Mins. in 1955; Ambassador to Cuba, Dominican Republic and Haiti, 1957-59; Ambassador to Denmark, 1960-67; Secretary to Adhoc Comm. for erection of monument to Louis Riel, inaugerated in Winnipeg 1971; Roman Catholic; recreations: riding, hunting, farming; Home: "Baie St. Paul", R.R. 1, Box 77, Headingly, Man. R0H 0J0

ALLARD, Gen. Jean Victor, C.C., C.B.E., D.S.O., E.D., C.D.; army officer (retired); b. Nicolet, P.Q., 12 June 1913; s. Ernest and Victorine (Trudel) A.; e. Coll. St. Laurent, Montreal, 1921-29; Coll. St. Jérome. Kitchener, Ont., 1929-31; D.S.S. Laval 1958; LL.D. Ottawa 1959; St. Mary's; St. Thomas; D.M.Sc. Royal Mil. Coll.; m. Simone, d. Gustave Piché, 7 Jan. 1939; children: Michèle, Andrée; joined Three Rivers Regt., N.P.A.M., 1933, later promoted Capt.; trans. to Active Force 1939 and became Major; served in 2nd World War 1939-45; Co. of London Yeomanry 1940-41; attended Candn. Army Staff Coll., Kingston, 1941-42; returned overseas and posted to 5th Candn. Armoured Div.; Instr. Candn. Army Staff Coll., Kingston, July 1942; served as 2nd in Command Regt. de la Chaudière and assumed same appt. with Royal 22e Regt. in Italy in 1943; promoted Lt. Col. Jan. 1944 and apptd. C.O. Royal 22e Regt.; promoted Brig. March 1945 and apptd. Commdr. 6th Candn. Inf. Bgde. in Holland; Mil. Attaché to Moscow Nov. 1945-Feb. 1948; subsequently assumed command of Eastern Quebec Area; attended Imperial Defence Coll. in England 1950-51, at conclusion of which apptd. Vice-Q.M.G. in Ottawa: apptd. Commdr. 25th Candn. Inf. Bgde. Group in Korea Apl. 1953; Commdr., 3 Candn. Inf. Bgde. Group, Valcartier, Sept. 1954; Eastern Quebec area, Sept. 1956; promoted Maj. Gen. and apptd. Vice Chief of Gen. Staff, Ottawa, Apl. 1958; Commdr., 4th Div., Brit. Army of the Rhine in Germany, Nov. 1961 (first Canadian to command a Brit. Div.); Maj. Gen, Survival, Ottawa, Nov. 1963; on integration of Candn. Armed Forces Sept. 1964 promoted Lt. Gen. and apptd. Chief of Operational Readiness in Ottawa; Commdr., Mobile Command in St. Hubert, P.Q. 1965; promoted General and apptd. Chief of Defence Staff 1966-69; awarded C.B.E., D.S.O. and 2 bars, Bronze Lion (Netherlands). Croix de Guerre and Légion d'honneur (France), Legion of Merit (U.S.); Chrmn., Bd. of Govs., Ottawa Univ., 1966; Kt. of Magistral Grace, Sovereign and Military Order of Malta, 1967; recreations:

golf, music, fishing, hunting; Clubs: Quebec Garrison; Royal Candn. Mil. Inst.; Cercle Universitaire d'Ottawa; Royal 22e Regt. Assn.; La Regie du 22e; Roy. Soc. of Arts; R.C.A.F. Assn.; R.C.N. Service Assn.; Mount Royal (Montreal).

ALLARD, Jeanne Grisé; writer; b. Saint-Césaire, P.Q., 27 March 1902; d. Henri and Alice (Bergeron) Grisé; e. Couvent de Saint-Césaire; Univ. of Montreal (Econ., Pol. and Social Sciences, Hist. and Sociology); m. 1 Oct. 1938; three s. (twins) Pierre and Michel, Daniel; Women's Editor "Le Bulletin des Agriculteurs", Montreal, (under the pseud. Alice Ber) 1938-75; Women's Editor, "Le Canada-Francais", Saint-Jean, P.Q., 1928-31; "La Patrie", Montreal 1935-38; Radio CHLP 1936-1948, CKAC 1945-50, CBF 1971-73, Télémétropole 1971-74; Co-Founder Les Ecrivains pour la Jeunesse, 1948 (Pres. 1951); Publications: "Gouttes d'eau", 1929; "Médailles de cire", 1933; "Mystères" 1947; "Chagrins d'enfants", 1948; "Un billet pour lEpagne", 1960; "Mille Trucs Madame" 1971; Douze cents nouveaux Trucs 1972, Encore des Trucs 1973, Toujours des Trucs 1974, 222 recettes pour deux, 1973 1500 prénoms et leur signification 1973; Author, "Le Tissage" (1975), coll. with Germaine Galerneau; Ed. "J'apprends l'Anglais" (1976), coll. with Gino Silicani; "J'apprends l'anglais", Tome II (1978) Assoc. Editor, "Lady-in-Waiting" and "Je serai mère"; awarded Médaille de Vermeil de l'Académie francaise, 1937; mem., Candn. Women's Press Club; Le Club des Femmes Journalistes; AIJPF Ass. inter. des journalistes de la presse féminine et familiale; Vice-Pres., Service d'Educ. familiale de l'Amicale des Présentines de Montréal;Membre Honoraire de l'ACRA, 1980; Roman Catholic; recreations: travelling, cooking, reading, receptions; Home: 5493 ave Earnscliffe, Montreal, P.Q., H3X 2P8.

ALLARD, (Joseph) Claude, B.Com., C.A.; retired accountant and management consultant; b. St. Constant, P.Q., 22 May 1926; s. Joseph Normand and Marie Jeanne (Lefebvre) A.; e. McGill Univ., B.Com. (Hon. Econ.) 1949; Inst. Chart. Accts. Que., C.A. 1951; m. Kathleen Isabel, d. late Denis John McCarthy, 18 June 1951; children: Claudette, Richard, Nicole; started with Price Waterhouse & Co., Chartered Accountants, Montreal, 1949-60; joined Dom. Steel & Coal Corpn., Ltd. as Asst.-Comptroller 1960, Vice-Pres., Finance and Treas., Dosco Industries Ltd., and Dominion Coal Co. Ltd., 1964-68; Partner, Price Waterhouse and Co., Price Waterhouse and Co., and Mineau, Allard, Mantha et Associes, Montreal 1964-81 (ret.); served in 2nd World War with R.C.C.S. 1945-46; Alderman, Town of St. Bruno, 1962-68; Mayor 1968-69; mem., Order of Chart. Accts. Que. Financial Extves. Inst.; R. Catholic; recreations: golf, farming; Home: 117 De Touraine, St. Lambert, Que. J4S 1H3

ALLEN, (Alexander) Richard, M.A., Ph.D.; educator; author; b. Vancouver, B.C. 10 Feb. 1929; s. Harold Tuttle and Ruby Rhoda (Reilly) A.; e. Fernie (B.C.) High Sch. 1947; Univ. of B.C. 1947-50; Toronto Teachers Coll. 1954; Univ. of Toronto B.A. 1956; Univ. of Sask. M.A. 1961; Duke Univ. Ph.D. 1967; m. 1stly Margaret Jane Ritchie 1951; m. 2ndly Nettie d. Daniel Shewchuk, Hamilton, Ont. 24 Apl. 1965; children: Daniel Richard, Philip Andrew; PROF. OF CANDN. HISTORY, McMASTER UNIVERSITY 1976- ; Pub. Sch. Teacher, Ottawa 1954-55, Crystal Bay, Ont. 1956-57; Gen. Secy. Student Christian Movement Can., Univ. of Sask. 1957-61; mem. Dept. Hist. Univ. of Regina 1964-74, Dir. Candn. Plains Area Studies Program 1968-74; joined McMaster Univ. 1974, mem. Senate 1976-78; rec'd Can. Council Sr. Leave Fellowships 1971-72, 1978-79 (Fellow, Faculty Religious Studies McGill Univ.); Principal Founder Candn. Plains Research Center Univ. of Regina; Nat. Student Chrmn., Student Christian Movement Can. 1952-53; sometime rep. on Social Science Research Council Can.; mem. Archives Comte. Un. Ch. of Can., Consultant on Ch. and Labour; author "The Social Passion: Religion and Social

Reform in Canada 1914-1928" 1971; Ed. "A Region of the Mind: Interpreting the Western Canadian Plains" 1973; "The Social Gospel in Canada" 1975; "Man and Nature on the Prairies" 1976; various articles, biog. studies and colls. religion and soc. in post-confed. Can.; mem. Program Comte. and Council Candn. Hist. Assn. 1972-74; mem. Candn. Meth. Hist. Soc.; Institut d'histoire de l'Amerique Française; NDP (Prov. Council); United Church; recreations: skiing, log cottage restoration, music, French; Home: 85 Haddon Ave. N., Hamilton, Ont. L8S 4A4; Office: Hamilton, Ont. L8S 4L9.

ALLEN, Clive Victor, B.A., B.C.L.; executive; b. Montreal, Que., 11 June 1935; s. John Arthur and Nora (Barnett) A.; e. McGill Univ., B.A. 1956, B.C.L. 1959; m. Barbara Kantor, 22 Feb. 1964; two s. Drew Keith, Blair John; VICE-PRESIDENT & GENERAL COUNSEL, NORTHERN TELECOM LIMITED; read law with Hackett, Mulvena, Drummond & Fiske and an Assoc. there 1960-63; called to Bar of Que. 1960; Partner, Fiske, Emery, Allen & Lauzon 1964-66; Asst. Secy. Allied Chemical Canada Ltd. 1966-69, Secy. 1969; Vice-President & Secretary 1972-74; joined Northern Telecom Limited (then Northern Electric Company, Limited) May, 1974; Lect. in Mang. Sir George Williams Univ. 1961-74; mem., Candn. Bar Assn.; Bar of Quebec (Montreal Sec.); Am. Soc. of Corp. Secretaries; Candn. Tax Foundation; International Bar Assn; Protestant; Clubs: Montreal Badminton & Squash; St. James's (Montreal); Granite; Home: 18A Deer Park Cres., Toronto, Ont. M4V 2C2; Office: 33 City Centre Dr., Mississauga, Ont. L5B 2N5

ALLEN, Frank Bowie; advertising and publishing executive; b. Montreal, Que., 14 Jan. 1923; s. late Frank Barclay and Kathleen Ross (Bowie) A.; e. Montreal High Sch.; Feller coll., Que.; m. Barbara Jean, d. late Dr. Charles Albert Marlatt, 28 Sept. 1946; two s., Dr. Dana, Frank Jr.; PRESIDENT; TELE-DIRECT Ltée. since 1971; started with Bell Canada, Comm. Dept., Montreal 1940; rejoining Co. after War 1945 served in various line and staff mang. assignments; Dist. Account Mgr. (responsible for Airlines indust.) 1963; Mgr., new Business Communications Seminar Centre, Montreal 1966; Gen. Supv., Sales Methods and Training 1967; Gen. Supv., Personnel and Training 1967; Gen. Supv., Marketing 1969; Asst. Vice-Pres. (Directory) 1970; Chrmn. Bd. of TDL WWoodtreating Ltd.; Tele-Direct Inc. (U.S.A.); National Telephone Directory Corp. (New Jersey, U.S.A.); Tele-Direct Canada Ltd.; the Sanford Evans group of cos.; Tele-Direct International Ltd.; Y.P. Publishing Australia Pty. Ltd.; Dir., Tele-Direct Ltd.; Edward H. O'Brien Pty. Ltd. (Australia); Dir. Ronalds-Federated Ltd.; Intelterm Systems Ltd.; Bell Communication Systems Ltd.; Que. Soc. for Crippled Children; Gov., Montreal Gen. Hosp.; enlisted Candn. Army 1942, serving with distinction in Can., U.K. and France; rank at discharge Capt.; Liberal; Anglican; recreations: golf, hunting, tennis, fishing; Clubs: Rotary; Summerlea Golf; Cornwall Pointer; St-James; Forest & Stream; Home: 12233 Somerset Rd., Montreal, Que. H4K 1S1; Office: 1600 Dorchester Blvd. W., Montreal, Que. H3H 1P9

ALLEN, Fraser Hall, B.A.Sc., M.S., Ph.D.; petroleum executive; b. Toronto, Ont. 19 Oct. 1918; s. Russell James and Edna (Bryans) A.; e. Univ. of Toronto Schs. 1937; Univ. of Toronto B.A.Sc. 1941; Univ. of Texas M.S. 1943, Ph.D. 1947; m. Eloise d. late James H. McCabe 22 Dec. 1942; children: Joanne Victoria Walker, Douglas Fraser, Stephen James; PRESIDENT, AMOCO CANADA PETROLEUM CO. LTD. since 1975; held various engn. assignments 1941-51 Stanolind Oil & Gas and Pan American Petroleum Corp.; became Dist. Engr. latter Co. Corpus Christi, Texas 1951, Div. Engr. Oklahoma City 1955, Chief Engr. Tulsa 1960, Div. Production Supt. Fort Worth 1961-62; Co-ordinator Crude Oil Production Purchasing & Transport. Standard Oil Co. (Ind.) Chicago 1962-66; Mgr. Production Amoco International Oil Co. N.Y. 1966, Mgr. Operations Co-ordination Chicago 1968-69; Pres. and Gen. Mgr. Amoco Argentina Buenos Aires 1969-72; Vice Pres. Production Amoco International 1972-75; service Naval Research Lab. Washington; Dir. Calgary Philharmonic Society; Chrmn. Tulsa Boy Scout Circus; Dir. Jr. Achievement S. Alta.; mem. Adv. Comte. Internat. Oil & Gas Educ. Center; S.W. Legal Foundation Dallas; Petroleum Engn. Visiting Comte. Univ. of Texas; Dir., Univ. of Okla. Research Inst.; Candn. Petrol. Assn. (Gov.); Soc. Petrol. Engrs. (Dir. 1963-66); AAPG; AIChE; Sigma Xi; Presbyterian; recreations: golf, fishing, skiing, canoe tripping, scuba diving; Clubs: Calgary Petroleum; University (Chicago); Gormandizers (Buenos Aires); Ranchmen's; Calgary Golf & Country; Office: Amoco Canada Bldg., 444 Seventh Ave. S.W., Calgary, Alta. T2P 0Y2

ALLEN, The Hon. Gordon Hollis, Q.C., LL.B.; (retired) judge; b. Chestertown, N.Y., 28 May 1901; s. Fletcher William and Flora (Baker) A.; e. Public and High Schs., Chestertown, N.Y., and Calgary, Alta.; Univ. of Alberta, LL.B. 1922; m. Helen H. Coughlin, 4 Aug. 1943; children: Fred, Sally, Sue; formerly Justice of Appellate Div., Supreme Court of Alberta; read law with Taylor, Moffat & Co.; called to Bar of Alta., 1923, cr. K.C. 1945; Bencher, Law Society of Alta., 1951-62; Past Pres., Law Soc. of Alta.; Calgary Bar Assn.; Calgary Golf and Country Club; Freemason; Protestant; recreations: golf, hunting; Home: 222 Eagle Ridge Drive S.W., Calgary, Alta. T2V 2V7; c/o MacKimmie Matthews, 7th Fl., Gulf Canada Square, 401-9th Ave. S.W., P.O. Box 2010, Calgary, Alta. T2P 2M2

ALLEN, William R., Q.C.; b. Ottawa, Ont., 1919; e. St. Michael's Coll., Univ. of Toronto and Osgoode Hall, Toronto, Ont.; m. Marjorie A.; children: Frank, Rosemary, Jane; Dir., Norwich Union Insurance Soc. Ltd.; The Molson Companies Ltd.; for 12 consecutive years a member of Toronto City Council (Ward 1 Alderman, 1950-55, Controller 1956-61); member of Metro Council, 1953-55 and 1959-61; has served on all City Council and Metro Council Standing Committees; member of Metro Extve. from mid-1959; Chrmn. of Council of Metrop. Toronto 1962 till resigned Sept. 1969; served in 2nd World War; Capt. with Queen's York Rangers; with Candn. Army Hdqrs., five yrs. service in Eng., France, Belguim, Holland and Germany; acted as Extve. Offr. of Civil Service Assn. of Ont., 1940; mem. Bd. of Govs., St. Michael's Hosp.; Pres., Candn. Nat. Exhn. Assn.; Chrmn., Bd. of Mang., Exhibition Place Stadium; Pres. and Chrmn., Kinross Mortgage Corp. 1969-74; Pres., The Dominion Realty Co. Ltd. 1972-75; Asst. Treas. (rec'd. Human Relations Award (Can. Council of Christians & Jews); Office: 40 Ridge Drive. M4T 1B7., Toronto, Ont.

ALLIN, Eardley Samuel, M.D., F.R.C.S., Eng., F.R.C.S. (C); surgeon; b. Toronto, Ont., 26 Aug. 1907; s. Edgar William and Rose Mary (Kember) A.; e. Pub. Schs. and Strathcona High Sch., Edmonton, Alta.; Univ. of Alta., B.Sc. 1927; Univ. of Toronto, M.D. 1931; post grad. studies at Toronto Gen. Hosp., Prince of Wales Gen. Hosp., Princess Beatrice Hosp., London, Eng., Roy. Gwent Hosp., Newport, Eng. and surg. studies at St. Bartholomew's Univ. Coll. Middlesex, St. Thomas's, and Roy. National Hosps., all of London, Eng.; m. Florence Gertrude, d. Francis W. Crang, M.D., Edmonton, Alta., 30 Sept. 1933; children: Shirley Jane, John Edward, Edgar Francis, Grace Jill and Robert Eardley; Clin. Instr., Dept. of Surg., Univ. of Alta.; Chief Surgeon Allin Clinic, Edmonton (ret. 1976); Hon. Surgeon, Royal Alexandra Hosp.; Assoc. Staff, Mineral Springs Hosp., Banff; Hon. Life mem., Edmonton Acad. of Med.; Alta. Med. Assn.; Candn. Med. Assn.; Dir., Commercial Life Assuuance and Halifax Insurance Companies; ret. Feb. 1979 after 20 yrs.; Freemason (Scot. Rite; 32XXX); Clubs: Cascade Lodge (Banff); Banff Shrine; Banff Rotary; Liberal; United Church; Home: 517 Buffalo St., Box 1776, Banff, Alta. T0L 0C0

ALLMAN, Richard Thomas, B.S.A., Ph.D.; b. Toronto, Ont., 29 Mar. 1915; s. Richard and Martha Rachel (Wrigglesworth) A.; e. Univ. of Toronto, B.S.A. 1936; Cornell Univ., Ph.D. 1941; m. 1st, Nancy Beckwith Humphreys (d. 1952), 5th Nov. 1947; 2ndly, Audrey C. Gartrell, 6 Feb. 1960; children: Richard Thomas, Nancy, Catherine; PRESIDENT, BRADFORD FERTILIZER LIMITED, Livestock Specialist, Blatchford Feeds Co., Toronto, Ontario 1936-37; Animal Nutritionist, Ayerst, McKenna & Harrison Co. Ltd., Montreal, 1938-39; Agronomist, Canadian Malting Co., Toronto, 1940; Livestock Specialist, Quaker Oats Co., 1941-42; i/c Field Research in Man., N. Am. Cyanamid and Chemical Co., Toronto, Ont., 1945-46; Fertilizer Specialist with UNRRA in China, 1947, i/c of fifteen million dollar programme; served as Regional Agric. Rehabilitation Officer with UNRRA in Greece, 1946; Mgr., Fertilizers, Chem. Div., Shell Canada Ltd., 1965-74; mem. of Panel of Experts that devel. FAO/UNICEF Milk Conserv. Project in Finland, Poland, France, Italy, Czechoslovakia, Yugoslavia, Greece, Austria and Malta; Chief of UNICEF mission in Chile, 1951-52; awarded Legion of Merit (Chile); served in 2nd World War, 1942-45; Flight Lieut., Nutrition Specialist, Med. Br., R.C.A.F.; Hon. Lectr. in Biochemistry, Univ. of Alberta, 1943-45; mem., Am. Assn. for the Advanc. of Science; Agric. Inst. Can.; Plant Food Producers of E. Can.; Pres. (new) Candn. Fertilizer Assn., 1958-59; author of "Nutritional Deficiencies in Livestock", 1948; many other tech. articles and treatises on nutrition; United Church; recreation: colour photography, still and movie; Home: 50 Dawlish Ave., Toronto, Ont. M4N 1H1; Office: P.O. Box 1000, Bradford, Ontario. L0G 1C0

ALLMAND, Hon. Warren, P.C., M.P.; politician; b. Montreal, Que., 19 Sept. 1932; s. Harold W. and Rose Irene (McMorrow) A.; e. Loyola High Sch., Montreal; St. Francis Xavier Univ.; McGill Univ.; Univ. de Paris; children: Patrick, Julianne, Robin; called to Bar of Que. 1958; el. to H. of C. for Montreal-N.D.G. in g.e. 1965, 1968 1972, 1974, 1979, 1980; Min., Consumer & Corporate Affairs, 1977-79; sometime Min. of Indian and Northern Affairs; sometime Sol. Gen. of Canada; member: Civil Liberties Union; Candn. Consumers Assn.; Comte. for Independent Can.; Soc. to Overcome Pollution; U.N. Assn.; World Feds. Can.; mem.: Que. Bar Assn.; Candn. Bar Assn.; Liberal; recreations: skiing, hockey, tennis, football; Club: Mount Royal Tennis Home: 2525 Cavendish Blvd., Montreal, Que. H4B 2Y6; Office: House of Commons, Ottawa, Ont. K1A 0A6

ALLOWAY, Donald Miller, B.A.Sc., P.Eng.; company chairman and president; b. Oshawa, Ont., 9 June 1921; s. late Arthur Roy and Mary Kelly (Sickle) A.; e. N. Simcoe Pub. Sch. and O'Neil Coll. Vocational Inst., Oshawa, Ont.; Univ. of Toronto, B.A.Sc. 1945; Univ. of W. Ont., Mang. Training Course 1958; Reg'd Prof. Engr., Prov. of Ont.; m. Norma Marian, d. Frederick Raymer. Pike, Weston, Ont., 9 June 1945; children: Heather Elizabeth, Donald Miller II, Wendy Jane, Robert Raymer, Graham Frederick; CHAIRMAN AND CHIEF EXTV. OFFR., CONSOLIDATED GRAPHICS LTD., Chrmn., United Graphics Inc., (Seattle); Chrmn. J.T. Gilmore & Comp., Ltd.; Vice Chrmn., Dominion Corrugated Paper Co., Ltd.; Pres., Maplex Mang. & Holdings Ltd.; Pres., Trans-Canada Investment Corp. Ltd.; Dir., Abstainers' Insurance Co.; Dir., Maplex Gen. Ins. Comp; Midwest Litho Ltd. (Sask.); Ed. Council of Graphic Arts Ind. (U.S.A.); Island Press Ltd., Bermuda; Plant Engr., Times Gazette, Oshawa, 1946; held various extve. positions 1947-50; Vice Pres.-Mang. Dir., General Printers Ltd., 1950; Pres. 1956; joined present Co. as Mang. dir. 1957, Pres. 1959; Dir., Maplex Mang. & Holdings Ltd. 1972, Vice Pres. 1977, Pres. 1979; Past Pres., Graphic Arts Industries Assoc. (Ottawa); Spring Garden Baptist Church; rec'd Centennial Medal 1967; recreations: golf, boating; Clubs: Granite; National; Muskoka Lakes Golf & Country; Ocean Reef (Key Largo, Fla.); Home: 13 Sonata Cres., Don Mills,

Ont. M3B 2C3; Summer: Port Carling, Ont.; Office: 180 Duncan Mill Rd., Don Mills, Ont. M3B 1Z6

ALMOND, Paul, M.A., A.R.C.A.; cineaste; b. Montreal, Que. 26 Apl. 1931; s. Eric and Irene Clarice (Gray) A.; e. B.C.S.; McGill Univ.; Balliol Coll., Oxford B.A. 1952, M.A.; m. Geneviève Bujold, Sept., 1976; Producer Dir. with CBC 1953-66 and TV co's in New York, London and Hollywood; wrote produced and directed film "Isabel", 1968; "Act of the Heart", 1970; "Journey" 1972; Subject of book by Janet Edsforth "The Flame Within", Publ. Cdn. Film Inst.: Canadian Film Award Best Director 1970 (ETROG); Best TV Director, 1979 (Genie); Address: Quest Film Productions Ltd., 1272 Redpath Cres., Montreal, Que. H3G 2K1

ALTON, Thomas R., C.A.; financial executive; b. Walkerton, Ont., 29 July, 1939; e. C.A. 1962; m. Janet Ann, 21 April, 1962; children: Sharon, Linda, Carol Ann; PRESIDENT AND CHIEF EXTVE. OFFR., SCOTIA MORTGAGE CORP. 1971- ; Gen. Mgr. Mortgages & Invests. The Bank of Nova Scotia 1980- ; articled with Coopers & Lybrand, Toronto becoming Mgr. 1957-63, trans. to London, Eng. 1963-64; Gen. Mgr. Scotia Mortgage Corp. 1964-71; Clubs: Albany; Adelaide; Oakville; Oakville Curling; Tamarack Island Fishing & Shooting; Home: 349 Gloucester Ave., Oakville, Ont. L6J 3W8; Office: 44 King St. W., Toronto, Ont. M5H 1H1.

AMABILE, George, M.A., Ph.D.; writer; educator; b. Jersey City, N.J., 29 May 1936; s. Anthony Thomas and Josephine (Masi) A.; e. Princeton (N.J.) High Sch., 1953; Amherst Coll., A.B. 1957; Univ. of Minn., M.A. 1961; Univ. of Conn., Ph.D. 1969; ASSOC. PROF. OF ENGLISH, UNIV. OF MANITOBA since 1971; joined the Univ. as Lectr. 1963, Asst. Prof. 1966-68, 1969-71; Visiting Writer in Residence, Univ. of B.C. 1968-69; Dir. Can. Periodical Pub. Assn.; Dir., Reach Out today (ex-convict employment & re-entry organ.); mem. Comte. of Artists to advise Min. of Tourism & Culture; has given readings of own work at Man. Theatre Centre and on radio, TV and at the Montreal Olympics 1976; rec'd Hunter Prize; Anna Von Helmholz Phelan Prize, Univ. of Minn. 1961; Can. Council Grants 1968, 1969, 1981-82; author, "Blood Ties", 1972; "Open Country", 1976; "Flower and Song", 1977; "Ideas of Shelter," 1981; "The Presence of Fire" 1982; other writings published in numerous anthols., journs. and periodicals; co-founder and Ed., "The Far Point"; Ed. "Northern Light"; has ed. "The Ivory Tower"; "The Penny Paper"; mem., w. Candn. Publishers' Assn. (Founding & Constitutional Comte.); Modern Langs Assn.; League Candn. Poets; Candn. assn. Univ. Teachers; Assn. Candn. Univ. Teachers Eng.; Delta Phi Lambda; recreations: fishing, tennis, guitar, swimming; Home: 17-75 Young St., Winnipeg, Man. R3C 1Y7; Office: Dept. of English, Univ. of Man., Winnipeg, Man.

AMATO, Lanfranco; company executive; b. Rovereto, Italy, 19 Apl. 1922; s. Joseph and Adile Valdagni A.; e. Univ. of Bocconi, Milan, Italy, degree in Comm. and Finance; m. Dr. Liliana, d. Joseph Conte, 23 Oct. 1954; one s. Sergio; HON. CHAIRMAN BD. AND DIR., OLIVETTI CANADA LIMITED; Dir., Four Seasons Hotels Ltd.; began as Sales Rep for Olivetti in Italy, 1950; apptd. Special Rep. for the market devel. of overseas agents in 1952, during the course of which gained an intimate knowledge of many countries in the Far East, W. and N. Africa and in Europe; i/c Agent-Dealer Operations for the newly formed Candn. subsidiary of Olivetti, 1955; apptd. following merger of Underwood and Olivetti, apptd. Gen. Sales Mgr. and Dir., of Underwood Ltd. 1960; Vice-Pres., Marketing 1962; Extve. Vice-Pres. 1965; Pres. and Gen. Mgr. Olivetti Underwood Ltd., 1966; Chrmn. of the Board, 1973; served in 2nd World War with Italian Army; Lieut., 1st Regt. of Grenadiers; with U.S. Army from

Sept. 1943; Mentioned in Despatches by Gen. Sir Harold Alexander; Kt. of Obedience Sovereign Mil. Order of Malta; Grand Offr. Republic of San Marino; Kt. Commander Mil. Order St. Lazarus of Jerusalem; Knight of Corona D'Italia; Commdr. Order of Merit of Italian Republic; Chevalier de la Confrerie du Tastevin (Burgundy); Golden Mercury "Ad Honorem" (Italian Oscar for Comm. and Indust.); Former Gov., Toronto Arts Production; Dir., Italian Chamber of Comm. of Toronto (Past Pres.); Candn. Opera Co.; Canadian Club of Toronto; Candn. Assn. Kts. of Malta (mem. Extve. Comte.); Candn. Council of Christians and Jews (mem. Extve. Comte.); mem. Bd. Trade of Metrop. Toronto; Candn. Chamber of Comm.; Candn.-Italian Business & Prof. Men's Assn.; R. Catholic; recreations: tennis, swimming, reading; Clubs: Empire; Rotary International; Home: 108 Sandringham Drive, Downsview, Ont. M3H 1C9; Office: 50 Gervais Dr. Don Mills, Ont. M3C 1Z3

AMES, John Cuthbert; corporate executive; b. London, Eng. 12 Nov. 1919; s. late Walter Thomas and late Mary Kate (Kemp) A.; e. St. John's High Sch. Winnipeg, Man.; Univ. of W. Ont. Mang. Training Course 1964; m. Bettie Marguerite d. late William Owen Randolph, Winipeg, Man. 12 Jan. 1946; children: John Randolph, Jeffrey Kenneth; VICE PRES. AND SECY. CANADIAN PACIFIC LTD. since 1978; Asst. Secy. Canadian Pacific Air Lines Ltd.; held clerical and secretarial positions CP Steamships and CP Rail, Winnipeg, Man. 1937-41, secretarial and supervisory positions CP Rail, Winnipeg and Vancouver 1946-55, Office Mgr. Office of Vice Pres. present co. Montreal 1955-58, Asst. to Vice Pres. 1958-65, Asst. Corporate Secy. 1965-72, Secy. of Co. 1972-78; served with RCASC Can. UK N.W. Europe 1941-46, rank Capt.; Affiliate, Inst. Chart. Secys. and Adms.; mem. Am. Soc. Corporate Secys. Inc.; Anglican; Clubs: Canadian Railway; Ile Perrot Golf & Country; Home: 307 Penn Rd., Beaconsfield, Que. H9W 1B5; Office: Room 202, Windsor Stn., Montreal, Que. H3C 3E4.

AMIEL, Barbara, B.A.; writer; b. Herts., Eng.; d. Col. Harold Joffre and Vera Isserles (Barnett) A.; e. N. London Coll. Sch. Canons Park, Eng.; Univ. of Toronto B.A. 1963; m. George Jonas 11 Oct. 1974; Assoc. Ed., "Toronto Sun", 1981-; Columnist, "Maclean's" since 1976; rec'd Can. Council Grant 1974; Media Club of Can. Award 1976; Periodical Publishers Assn. Award 1977; co-author "By Persons Unknown" 1977; author of "Confessions" 1980; winner Mystery Writers of America Edgar Allan Poe Award for best fact crime book; contrib. to various journs. TV and radio documentaries; Jewish; Address: c/o Toronto Sun, 333 King St. E., Toronto, Ont.

AMYOT, Laurent, B.A., B.A.Sc., M.Sc., P.Eng.; b. Verdun, Que. 18 Jan. 1931; s. Olivier-René and Anita (Hébert) A.; e. Coll. de Montréal B.A. (honours) 1950; Ecole Polytechnique de Montréal B.A.Sc. (honours) 1955; Univ. of Birmingham M.Sc. 1957 (Athlone Fellow 1956-57); m. Siglinde d. Robert Drobek, Krefeld, W. Germany 8 June 1963; two s. Normand, Marc; CORP. VICE-PRES., QUEBEC OPERATIONS, ATOMIC ENERGY OF CANADA LTD.; 1982-; Chrmn. and Dir., Nuclear Engn. Inst. Ecole Polytechnique 1970-81, Prof. there since 1968 Dir., Nuclear Analysis mem. Atomic Energy Control Bd. 1971-1979; Nuclear Engr. Associated Electrical Industries & John Thomson, Manchester, UK 1955-56; C.D. Howe Engn. Consultants 1957-58 Montreal; Canadair Ltd. Montreal 1958-59; Research staff mem. General Atomic, San Diego 1959-62; Euratom, Ispra (Italy) 1962-68; mem. Reactor Safety Adv. Comte. (Ont. 1970-76, Chrmn. Que. 1972-76, Acting Chrmn. N.B. 1974-76); Home: 50 Aberdeen, Candiac, Que. J5R 2C3; Office: Atomic Energy of Canada Ltd.; Montreal, Que.

AMYOT, René, Q.C., B.A., LL.L., M.B.A.; barrister; b. Quebec City, Que., 1 Nov. 1926; s. Omer Amyot and Caroline (Barry) L'Espérance; e. Coll. Des Jesuites De

Que., B.A. 1946; Laval Univ. Law Sch., LL.L. 1949; Harvard Univ. Grad. Sch. of Business Adm., M.B.A. 1951; m. Monique, d. Fernand Boutin, 4 Dec. 1954; children: François, Eric, Dominique, Isabel-Sophie; PARTNER, AMYOT LESAGE BERNARD DROLET ET ASSOCIES; Vice-Pres. and Dir. The Imperial Life Assurance Company of Canada; Northern Life Assur. Co. of Can.; Dir. and Sec., Fiducia Ltd.; Cdn. Helicopters; Logistec Corp.; Chrmn. of Audit Comte., Rothmans of Pall Mall Can. Ltd.; Chmn. of Bd., Air Canada; Dome Mines Ltd.; Le Vieux Port de Que.; called to Bar of Que. 1949; cr. Q.C. 1965; joined Procter & Gamble, Montreal, 1951; Bouffard & Associates, Quebec, 1952; mem., Candn. Bar assn.; Gov., Candn. Tax Foundation; Internat. Chamber Comm.; Assn. des MBA du Québec; Liberal; R. Chatholic; recreations: skiing, swimming, tennis, farming; Clubs: Quebec Garrison; Toronto; Home: 1155, rue Turnbull, #201, Québec, Qué. G1R 5G3; Office: 1 Place Ville Marie, Montreal, Que. H3B 3P7

ANDERSON, Donald Sutherland; company executive; b. Winnipeg, Man., 21 Sept. 1913; s. James Wilson and Madeleine Caroline Mary (Chivers) A.; e. Earl Grey Jr. and Kelvin Tech. High Schs., Winnipeg, Man.; m. Margaret Richmond, d. late Dr. T. W. Stoddart 16 Aug. 1941; two s. Ian Sutherland, Robert James; one d. Jocelyn Mouat (Mrs. Roger A. Green); CHAIRMAN, CANADA REALTIES LIMITED since 1975; Dir. Royal Bank of Canada; Slough Estates (Canada) Ltd.; Denison Mines Ltd.; Crum & Forster of Canada Ltd.; Herald Insurance Co.; Continental Group of Canada Ltd.; National Life Assurance Co. Ltd. of Canada; Inglis Ltd.; Hardee Farms International; Algonquin Mercantile Corp.; Wheeling-Pittsburg Steel Corp.; joined Royal Bank of Canada, Winnipeg 1930 serving in numerous branches Man. and Supvrs. Dept. Winnipeg; trans. H.O. Montreal 1941, Candn. Credits H.O. 1945, Asst. Mgr. Winnipeg Br. 1947, Mgr. Calgary 3rd St. Br. 1949, Calgary Br. 1951, Toronto Br. 1952, Asst. Gen. Mgr. H.O. 1957, Toronto 1958, Ont. Gen. Mgr. 1961, Vice-Pres. and Dir. 1964, Sr. Vice-Pres. 1970; apptd. Chrmn. and Chief Extve. Offr. Metro Centre Developments Ltd. 1971-1975; served with R.C.O.C. 1942, discharged Capt. 1945; Trustee, Toronto Gen. Hosp.; Past Pres., Bd. Trade Metrop. Toronto; mem. Nat. Adv. Council, Boys' and Girls' Clubs of Can.; Bd. Hon. Govs. Candn. Assn. for Retarded Children; recreations: golf, shooting, fishing; Clubs: York; Toronto; Rosedale Golf; Goodwood (Toronto); Ranchmen's (Calgary); Manitoba (Winnipeg); Lost Tree (Florida); Royal and Ancient Golf Club of St. Andrews (Scotland); Ristigouche Salmon (Matapedia); Home: 42 Arjay Cres., Willowdale, Ont. M2L 1C7; Office: Ste. 916, 40 University Ave., Toronto, Ont. M5J 1T1

ANDERSON, Doris Hilda, O.C. (1974), B.A.; writer, editor; b. Calgary, Alta. 10 Nov. 1925; d. Thomas and Rebecca (Laycock) McCubbin; e. Crescent Heights (Alta.) High Sch.; Univ. of Alta., B.A. 1945, hon. LL.D. 1975; m.; children: Peter David, Stephen Robert, Mitchell Richard; Pres., Candn. Adv. Council on the Status of Women 1979-81; Editor, Chatelaine Magazine 1958-77; defeated Lib. cand. in Toronto's Eglinton riding in Oct. 1978 by-election; former Dir., Maclean-Hunter Publishing Co.; MacMillan Publishing Co. Can. Ltd.; Canadian Film Development Corp.; Dir., Board of Can. Civil Liberties; Trustee, Inst. of Research on Public Policy Planning; former mem. Bd., Metropolitan Children's Aid; mem., Tri-Lateral Comn. for North America; former Gov., York Univ.; mem., Ontario Press Council 1977-; author "Two Women" 1978; "Rough Layout", 1981; commenced as Edit. Asst., Star Weekly 1945; Claire Wallace radio programme script writer 1946; with T. Eaton Co., Advertising Dept. 1946-50; joined Chatelaine 1951 and held positions of Edit. Asst., Asst. Ed., Assoc. Ed. and Mang. Ed. prior to editor; awarded Centennial Medal 1967; City of Toronto Award 1981; Can. Press Club Hall of Fame 1981;

Anglican; recreations: reading, travel, gardening; Home: 174 Dufferin Court, Apt. 11, Ottawa, Ont. K1M 2A6

ANDERSON, G.S.L., D.F.C., B.A.; advertising executive; b. Sweden, 25 Feb. 1920; s. Gustav and Anna (Bengtson) A.; came to Canada 1923; e. Pub. and High Schs., Hanover and Mount Forest, Ont.; Univ. of W. Ont., B.A. (Hons.) Business Adm. 1949; m. Florence, d. William McIntyre, 20 Nov. 1945; children: Kenneth, Heather, Edith, Joan; Honorary Chrmn. Ronalds-Reynolds and Co. Ltd. since 1979; Media Supvr., Cockfield Brown & Co. Ltd. 1949, Acct. Extve. 1951; Advertising & Promotion Mgr., Milko Products Ltd. 1952; joined present Co. as Acct. Extve. 1953, Acct. Supv. 1954, Vice-Pres. and Dir. 1956, Sr. Vice-Pres. and Gen. Mgr. 1965, Extve. Vice-Pres. 1971; Pres. 1973, Chmn. 1977; served in 2nd World War, R.C.A.F. 1941-45, Flight Lt. and Pilot, awarded D.F.C.; Past Chrmn., Inst. Candn. Advertising; Member, Bd of Gov. ICA; Past Pres. Advertising Guild; Past chmn. U.W.O. London Conference; Past V.P. Am. Mktg. Assoc.; Member Bd. of Gov. Frontier College; Past Dir. and mbr. Exec. Com. of Junior Achievement of Can.; Un. Church; recreations: golf, curling, music, farming, antiquing, fishing; Clubs: Mississaugua Golf & Country; Oriskany Club; Stonecrop Fishing; Boulevard; Royal Canadian Military Inst.; R.C.A.F. Burma Squadrons Assoc.; Home: PH 7, 2185 Marine Dr., Oakville, Ont. L6L 5L6; Farm, RR2 Markdale, Ont.: Office: 154 University Ave., Toronto, Ont. M5H 3B1

ANDERSON, John Ansel, Ph.D., D.Sc., LL.D., F.R.S.C., F.C.I.C., F.A.I.C.; chemist; b. Sidcup, Kent, Eng., 16 Aug. 1903; s. Alfred William and Agnes (Hanna) A.; e. Univ. of Alta., B.Sc. 1926, M.Sc. 1928; Leeds Univ., Ph.D. 1930; Univ. of Graz, Austria; Univ. of Birmingham, Eng.; Univ. of Sask., D.Sc. 1964; Alta., LL.D. 1965; Man., LL.D. 1978; m. Isla Doune, d. T. J. Scott, Edmonton, Alta., 1931; children: Garet Sean, Jason Alfred; Biologist, Divn. of Applied Biol. and Agric., Nat. Research Council, Ottawa, Ont., 1930-39; Dir., Grain Res. Lab., Can. Grain Comn. 1939-62; Dir., Winnipeg Research Stn., Can. Dept. Agric., 1962-63; Dir.-Gen., Research Branch, Canada Dept. of Agric., 1963-68; Research Prof., Dept. of Plant Science, Univ. of Manitoba 1968-71; mem., Am. Assn. of Cereal Chem (Pres., 1952-53); Internat. Assn. Cereal Chem. (Pres., 1959-60); ed. of "Enzymes and Their Role in Wheat Technology", 1946; Editor, "Storage of Cereal Grains and Their Products", 1954; has written some 100 scient. papers publ. mainly in "Cereal Chem."; awarded Thomas Burr Osborne Medal by Am. Assn. of Cereal Chemists, 1957; Protestant; recreations: golf, chess; Home: 1505 - 620 Toronto St., Victoria, B.C. V8V 1P7

ANDERSON, John Harold Cameron, B.A.Sc.; manufacturer; b. Perth, Ont. 17 Apl. 1924; s. John McLaren and Irene F. (Cameron) A.; e. Perth (Ont.) Coll. Inst. 1946; Univ. of Toronto B.A.Sc. 1950; m. Willa Florence Ward 6 Sept. 1952; children: W. Darlene, John B.; PRESIDENT, JENKINS CANADA INC. since 1978; Pres. and Dir. Smith Valve Corp. of Canada Ltd.; Indust. Engr. Orange Crush Ltd. 1950-52, Advertising Mgr. 1953-55; Sales Rep. Toronto present Co. 1955, Vice Pres.-Mfg. and Dir. 1970; mem. Assn. Prof. Engrs. Prov. Ont.; Order Engrs. Que.; Anglican; recreations: golf, workshop hobbies; Club: Beaconsfield Golf; Home: 138 Flamingo Dr., Beaconsfield, Que. H9W 2T2; Office: 170 St. Joseph Blvd., Lachine, Que. H8S 2L6.

ANDERSON, John Murray, B.Sc.F., Ph.D., LL.D., D.Ped.; educator; b. Toronto, Ont., 3 Sept. 1926; s. Murray Alexander and Eleanor Montgomery (Valentine) A.; e. Jarvis Coll. Inst., Toronto; Univ. of Toronto, B.Sc.F. 1951, Ph.D. 1958; St. Thomas Univ., LL.D. 1974; Univ. of Maine, D.Ped. 1976; LL.D. Dalhousie Univ., 1979; m. Eileen Anne, d. Dr. A. M. McFaul, Collingwood, Ont., 3 Nov. 1951; children: Nancy, Susan, Peter, Katherine;

PRES., J.M. ANDERSON CONSULTANTS INC. 1980-; Asst. Prof. Biol., U.N.B. 1958; Assoc. Prof. Biol., Carleton Univ. 1963; Dir. Fisheries Research Bd. Can. Biol. Stn., Saint Andrews, N.B. 1967; Pres., Univ. of New Brunswick 1973-79; Dir.-Gen., Research and Devel. Fisheries & Marine Service, Dept. of Environment, Ottawa 1972; mem. Scient. Adv. Comte., World Wildlife Fund (Can.); Council Can. Steering Comte. Candn. Energy Problems; Chrmn. Scient. Adv. Group, Internat. Atlantic Salmon Foundation; Pres. & Chrmn. of Bd. Huntsman Marine Lab., St. Andrews, N.B.1973-77; Assn. of Univ. and Coll. of Canada; Fraser Companies, Ltd. and Fraser Paper Ltd.; Bd. of Govs.: Inst. Candn. Bankers; Rothesay Coll. School; Kenya Technical Teachers Coll., Nairobi, Kenya; Extve. Comte., N.B. Museum; Vice-Pres. Biolog. Council of Canada; Chrmn. Ass. of Atlantic Univ.1978-79; Mem., Bd. of Dir., Int. Atlantic Salmon Foundation, 1979-; Mem., Bd. of Dir., John R. Bradford Ed. Fund (Noranda), 1979-; Vice-Chrmn.; Sunbury Shores Arts and Nature Centre Inc. 1979-; served with RCNVR 1945; author over 40 scient. publs. in area animal physiol.; mem. Candn. Soc. Zools. (Past Pres.); Sigma Chi; Unitarian; recreations: skiing, boating, tennis; Home: P.O. Box 547, St. Andrews, N.B. E0G 2X0; Office: P.O. Box 547, St. Andrews N.B. E0G 2X0

ANDERSON, Myles Norman, B.Sc., (Geo Eng.); mining executive; b. Flin Flon, Man. 22 Jan. 1931; e. Flin Flon, Man.; Univ. of Man. B.Sc.; m. Tania Lorette Babienko; children: Kristopher, Paul, Kathryn; CHMN., AND CHIEF EXECUTIVE OFFICER., COMINCO LTD.; Vice Pres. and Dir. West Kootenay Power & Light Co. Ltd.; Dir. Toronto-Dominion Bank; Fording Coal Ltd.; Pine Point Mines Ltd.; Aberfoyle Ltd.; Cominco Australian Pty. Ltd.; Cominco Binani Zinc Ltd.; Cominco American Inc.; Vestgron Mines Ltd.; author various publs.; mem. Mining Assn. Can.; Candn. Inst. Mining & Metall.; Am. Inst. Metall. Engrs.; B.C. Prof. Engrs.; Missouri Prof. Engrs.; Alta. Prof. Engrs.; Coal Assn. Can.; recreations: hunting, fishing, curling, golf; Clubs: Vancouver Club; Shaughnessy Golf & Country; Home: 6825 Adera St., Vancouver, B.C. V6P 5C2.

ANDERSON, His Hon. N. Robert, LL.B.; judge; b. Sherbrooke, Guysborough Co., N.S., 30 Nov. 1930; s. Robert Clarence and Ida Lyll (Morris) A.; e. Elem. and High Sch., Sherbrooke, N.S.; Dalhousie Univ. Law Sch., LL.B.; m. Edith Louise, d. H. E. Pyle, Boylston, N.S., 14 Jan. 1961; children: Shirley L., Katherine I., Caroline M., John M.; JUDGE, CO. COURT DISTRICT NO. 1, N.S. since Dec. 1971; read law with A. W. Cameron, Q.C.; called to Bar of N.S. 1957; in law practice, Sherbrooke, N.S. 1957-65; apptd. Dir. (Criminal), Dept. Atty. Gen., N.S., Halifax 1965; def. Cand., Prov. Lib. Party 1960; mem. N.S. Barrister Soc.; Candn. Bar Assn.; Freemason; Presbyterian; recreations: fishing, hunting, camping, reading; Office: Court House, Halifax, N.S. B3J 1S7

ANDERSON, Philip Robley; construction executive; b. Newcastle, Eng., 4 May 1921; s. Joseph Walton and Vida Caroline (Robley) A.; e. Jordan Hill Coll. Sch., Glasgow, Scot.; Glasgow Univ.; m. Audrey Jewel, d. late William Broadbridge, 22 March 1947; children: Jane, Blair, Lois; VICE-PRESIDENT, R.G. KIRRY & SONS LTD., since 1981-; Field Engr., The Foundation Co. of Canada Ltd., Toronto, 1947-48; Project Mgr., Toronto, 1948-50; Gen. Supt., Toronto, 1950-53; Br. Mgr., Calgary, 1953-57; W. Div. Mgr. and Vice-Pres., Calgary, 1957-63; joined as Extve. Asst. to Pres., Montreal, 1963-64; V.P., Operations 1964-68; E.G.M. Cape and Co. Ltd., Pres. 1978-80; served with R.E. in Europe during 2nd World War; rank Maj.; P. Conservative; Anglican; recreations: golf, swimming, skiing; Clubs: National; Rosedale; Home: 173 Golfdale Road, Toronto, Ont. M4N 2C1; Office: 250 Consumers Rd., Willowdale, Ont. M2J 4V6

ANDERSON, Raymond Cecil, B.A., LL.B.; diplomat; b. Wetaskiwin, Alta., 6 June 1929; s. Rudolph Thure and Alice Woodrow (Shantz) A.; e. Univ. of Alta., B.A. 1952, LL.B. 1957; Harvard Univ. (Advanced Mang.) 1971; m. Joyce Ralphene, d. J. Russell Love, Edmonton, Alta., 21 Aug. 1954; children: Douglas Russell, Calvin Blair, Catharine Alice, Doris Dorothy; CDN. HIGH COMMR. TO AUSTRALIA, 1980-; joined Trade Commr. Service, Dept. Industry, Trade & Comm. 1957; Vice Consul, Sâo Paulo, Brazil 1955; Vice Consul and Trade Commr., Los Angeles 1961; Chargé d'Affair, Manila 1963; Consul and Sr. Trade Commr., Boston 1965; Dir. (Personnel) Trade Commr. Service, Dept. External Affairs 1968, Dir. Personnel Operations, 1971-74, Consul Gen., Seattle; Asst. Dep. Minister Industry, Trade and Commerce 1974-76; Consul General Los Angeles 1978; with R.C.A.F., Course Dir. Univ. Flying Trainees 1955-56; mem. Prof. Assn. Foreign Service Offrs.; Zeta Psi; United Church; recreations: boating, music, bridge; Clubs: Harvard Business; Rotary; Candn. Soc. of Los Angeles; Home: 32 Mugga Way, Red Hill, A.C.T. 2603; Office: Cdn. High Comm., Commonwealth Ave., Canberra A.C.T. 2600

ANDERSON, Hon. Richard Philip, B.A., LL.D.; b. Victoria, B.C., 1 Jan. 1921; s. Herbert Glass A.; e. Univ. of B.C., B.A., LL.D.; m. Margaret Chapman d. Foster Bingham, Seattle, Wash., 4 Feb. 1965; children: Kathryn, Marion, Christine, Graeme, Heather; step d. Pamela, Susan; JUSTICE, COURT OF APPEAL, B.C.; read law with law A. R. McDougall; called to Bar of B.C. 1949: cr. Q.C. 1969; former Justice, Supreme Court, B.C.; served with Candn. Army and RCAF during World War II, Flight Lt.; mem., Law Soc. B.C.; Candn. Bar Assn.; Phi Gamma Delta; recreation: golf; Clubs: Vancouver; Point Grey Golf & Country; Home: 1063 West 7th Ave., Vancouver B.C. V6P 1W4; Office: Court House, Vancouver, B.C.

ANDERSON, Robert Bernard, A.B., M.S., Ph.D., F.C.I.C.; educator; b. Moline, Ill. 31 Aug. 1915; s. Gustav Adel and Hilda (Benson) A.; came to Can. 1965; e. Augustana Coll., Ill. A.B. 1938; State Univ. of Iowa M.S. 1940, Ph.D. 1942; m. Jane Udden 3 July 1942; children: Robert Udden, Susan Jane (Shawki); PROFESSOR, DEPT. OF CHEM. ENG., MCMASTER UNIV. 1981- ; Research Assoc., Dept. of Chem. Eng., Johns Hopkins Univ. 1942; Supervising Chemist, Bureau of Mines, Bruceton, Pa. 1944; Visiting Prof., Queen's Univ. (Belfast) 1965; Professor Emeritus of Chem. Eng., McMaster Univ. 1965; Fellow, Chemical Inst. of Can. (1968); author "The Fischer-Tropsch and Related Syntheses" 1951; ed. and co-ed. "Experimental Methods in Catalytic Research" Vol. 1 1968, Vols. 2 and 3 1976; over 150 papers in technical journals; 5 patents; Chrmn., Div. of Catalysis, Chem. Inst. of Can.; mem. Ed. Bd., Journal of Catalysis; Amer. Chemical Soc.; Catalysis Soc.; Sigma Xi; rec'd Amer. Chem. Soc.'s Ipatieff Prize 1953; Pittsburgh Award 1960; U.S. Dept. of Interior Dist. Service Medal 1966; Chem. Inst. of Can. Catalysis Medal 1979; Spinks Lectr., Univ. of Sask. 1982; recreations: cross-country skiing, canoeing; Home: 149 Colleen Cres., Ancaster, Ont. L9G 1J2; Office: Hamilton, Ont. L8S 4L7.

ANDERSON, Robert Newton, B.A., B.Ed., M.A., Ph.D.; educator; b. Saskatoon, Sask. 14 March 1929; s. George W. and Bertha M. (Sloan) A.; e. Univ. of Sask. B.A. 1949, B.Ed. 1951; Univ. of Minn. M.A. 1959, Ph.D. 1963; m. Shirley Anne Bennett 24 March 1951; children: Janis, Ellen, Jeff, Paul, David; Dean of Educ. Univ. of Lethbridge 1974-79 and Prof. of Educ. there since 1969, mem. Bd. of Govs. 1970-74; Visiting Fellow, Univ. of Aberdeen, Scotland 1979-80; Hist. Teacher and Head of Dept. Regina Coll. System 1950-58; Assoc. Dir. of Curriculum Prov. Sask. Dept. Educ. 1958-59; Prof. of Educ. and Head of Dept. Univ. of Calgary 1959-65; Prof. of Secondary Educ. and Head of Dept. Univ. of Sask. Regina 1965-69; Candn. Rep. to World Conf. on Educ. Asilomar, Calif. 1970; Visiting Prof. Univ. of Lagos and Advisor to Govt. of Nigeria

1970-71; author "Institutional Analysis of Mount Royal College" 1964; "Two White Oxen: A Perspective on Early Saskatoon" 1972; co-author "Foundation Disciplines and the Study of Education" 1968; "Trends in Teacher Education" 1977; "Lifelong Education in a World Perspective" 1978; contrib. to educ. journs.; Fellow, Philos. Educ. Soc.; mem. Comparative & Internat. Educ. Soc.; World Council on Curriculum (Founder and mem. Bd. Dirs.); Candn. Soc. Studies Educ.; Candn. Assn. African Studies; Candn. Educ. Assn.; Candn. Coll. Teachers; Candn. Foundations Educ. Assn. (Founding Pres. 1962, 1970); N.W. Regional Philos. Educ. Soc. (Pres. 1965-66); rep. of N. Am. at World Conf. on Curriculum in Istanbul Aug. 1977; United Church; Home: 2615 Sixth Ave. S., Lethbridge, Alta. T1J 1C9

ANDERSON, Roy Clayton, B.Sc., M.A., Ph.D.; university professor; b. Camrose, Alta., 26 Apl. 1926; s. Leslie and Nina (Wager-Keller, U.E.L.) A.; e. Pub. and High Schs., Camrose, Alta.; Univ. of Alta., B.Sc. 1950; Univ. of Toronto, M.A. 1952, Ph.D. 1956; Univ. of London, 1956-57; Univ. of Paris, Dipl. Helminthology 1958"; m. Phylliss Cathleen, d. Addison Brox, 1948; children: Douglas Roy, Michel Brock; PROF. OF ZOOL., UNIV. OF GUELPH, since 1965; CHMN: DEPT. ZOOL. 1979-; Research Assoc. and Sr. Research Scientist, Ont. Research Foundation, 1958-65; served with R.C.N.V.R. 1943-45; Consultant Ed., "Journal of Parasitology"; Co-ed., "Systematic Parasitology"; Official Correspondent, Commonwealth Inst. of Helminthology (Commonwealth Agric. Bureaux), St. Albans, Eng.; rec'd Henry Baldwin Ward Medal, Am. Soc. Parasitologists, 1968; Rec'd Distinguished Service Award, Wildlife Disease Assoc. 1978; author of over 130 scient. papers and Ed. of two books in Parasitology and Commonwealth Inst. of Helminthology Keys to the Nematodes of Vertebrates; has contrib. to understanding of Helminth diseases of wild and domesticated animals; mem., Am. Soc. Parasitol. (Vice-Pres. 1977); Helminthol. Soc. Washington, D.C.; Candn. Soc. Zool. (Pres. 1975); Wildlife Society; Wildlife Disease Assn. (member Council and Ed. Board "Journal of Wildlife Diseases", Pres. 1981-83); Royal Soc. Tropical Med. & Hygiene; Sigma xi; Protestant; recreation: literature; Home: 40 Westminster Ave., Guelph, Ont. N1E 4C1

ANDERSON, Wilfred Duncan Essery, B.A.; telecommunications executive; b. London, Ont., 10 Apl. 1923; e. Univ. of Toronto, B.A. 1944; Nat. Defence Coll. Kingston 1955; VICE PRES., BELL CANADA since 1971, AND VICE-PRES (OPERATIONS), TRANSCANDA TELEPHONE SYSTEM, 1980-; joined present Co. Montreal 1944, held various positions E. Area Engn. Dept. becoming Area Equipment Engr. 1955, returned to Montreal as Area Equipment Engr., E.A. 1956 and apptd. Outside Plant Engr. Montreal Area 1959, Area Chief Engr. 1960, Asst. Comptroller Systems and Procedures 1962, Asst. Vice Pres. Organ. Studies 1964, Vice Pres. and Gen. Mgr. Toll Area 1964, resigned 1965; held various positions vice pres. level Northern Electric Co., Ltd.; returned Bell Canada 1971; mem. Ottawa Bd. Trade; Candn. Chamber Comm.; Order Engrs. Que.; Assn. Prof. Engrs. Ont.; Clubs: Royal Ottawa Golf; Rideau (Ottawa); Home: 17 Amberwood Cr., Nepean, Ont. K2E 7B7; Office: F11, 410 Laurier Ave. W., P.O. Box 2410. Stn. D., Ottawa, Ont. K1P 6H5

ANDERSON, Lt. Gen. William Alexander Beaumont, O.B.E. (1945), C.D., D. Mil. Sc. (1977); is descended of a family many yrs. active in Candn. Mil.; b. Montreal P.Q., 7 May 1915; s. Maj.-Gen. William Beaumont and Lois Winnifred (Taylor) A.; e. Rothesay Coll., N.B.; Queen's Univ., B.A. 1937; Roy. Mil. Coll., Grad. 1936; Staff College., Camberley, Eng., 1941; U.S. Army and Navy Staff Coll., 1945; Nat. Defence Coll., 1950; Imp. Defence Coll., Eng., 1956; m. late Caroline Jane, d. Col. R. H. Waddell, Kingston Ont., 4 Nov. 1939; two s. Robert (died 1954), Anthony; SPECIAL ADVISER TO FEDERAL GOVERN-

MENT ON LAMBERT AND D'AVIGNON REPORTS 1980-; joined Candn. Mil., Roy. Candn. Horse Arty. 1936; trans. from Kingston to Winnipeg 1938; served in World War 1939-45 with Canadian Army Overseas; staff appts. include Personal Asst. to Gen. Crerar 1942; Gen. Staff Offr., 1st Grade (Operations) in N.W. Europe 1944-45; Chief Instr., R.M.C., 1945; Dir. of Mil. Intelligence, Ottawa, 1946-49; Dir., Canadian Army Staff Coll., 1950-51; Comdr. W. Ont. Area, 1952-53; Commdr., 1st Candn. Inf. Bgde., Germany, 1954-55; Vice-Adj. Gen. 1957-59; Depy. Chief of Gen. Staff, Ottawa, 1959-60; Comdt. Royal Mil. Coll., 1960-61; Adj.-Gen., 1962-64; Deputy Chief Reserves 1965-66; Commdr., Mobile Command, 1966-69; apptd. Chrmn. Ont. Civil Service Comn. 1969 and Depy. Min. Ont. Dept. Civil Service 1971; Secy., Mang. Bd., Ont. Cabinet 1974; Depy. Prov. Secy., Resources Development 1979; Mentioned in Despatches (N.W. Europe) 1944; Offr., Belgian Order of Leopold (1948); Offr. Belgian Order of the Crown with Palm (1946); Belgian Croix-de-Guerre with Palm (1946); Anglican; recreations: golf, boating; Club: York; Home: 1 The Mews, Ottawa, Ont. K1M 2G3; Office: Treasury Board, Ottawa, Ont., K1A 0R5

ANDERSON, The Honourable William Joseph; b. Oakville, Man., 20 April 1918; s. William Victor and Adeline (Whitmore) A.; e. Gladstone Pub. Sch., Winnipeg and Teulon (Man.) High Sch.; Univ. of Man.; Osgoode Hall Law Sch.; m. Alison Rosamond, d. late Dr. Charles L. Morgan, 2 July 1951; two s., William Hugh, Charles Edward; JUDGE, HIGH COURT OF JUSTICE FOR ONTARIO since 1977; read law with H. Fred Parkinson, Q.C.; called to Bar of Ont. 1948; cr. Q.C. 1960; practised law with Gardiner, Roberts or predecessor firms from 1948; served with Candn. Army Reserve 1939-42; Active Service 1942-45; mem., Advocates' Soc.; Candn. Bar. Assn.; Foundation Legal Research Can.; York Co. Law Assn.; Phi Delta Phi; Anglican; recreations: reading, fishing; Clubs: Lawyers, National; Home: 43 Roxborough St. E., Toronto, Ont. M4W 1V5; Chambers: Osgoode Hall, Toronto, Ont. M5H 2N5

ANDRAS, Kenneth Bertram; stock broker; b. Toronto, Ont., 5 Apl. 1909; s. Edward Bertram Gay and Gwendolyn Osler (Francis) A.; e. Brown Pub. Sch., Toronto, Ont.; Univ. of Toronto Schs., 1920-27; m. Elizabeth Boyd, d. late Dr. Joseph Graham, 12 Sept. 1936; children: Kenneth, John, Jane, Elizabeth; CHAIRMAN, ANDRAS, HATCH & HETHERINGTON LTD., Dir. Fireman's Fund Insurance Co. of Canada; Founding Chrmn. and now Director, CARE of Can.; Dir., The Donwood Institute; CNIB Amateur Radio Club; Fort York Branch, Royal Candn. Legion; Vice Pres., Tippet Foundation; Hon. Secy., St. George's Soc.; commenced career as Jr., Mara & McCarthy, Toronto, Ont., 1927; became Partner, 1939 (firm name changed to Stanton, Hatch & McCarthy in 1941, to Andras, Hatch & McCarthy in 1952 and to present style, 1963); served in 2nd World War, 1941-45 with R.C.A.F.; Overseas, 1941-44; retired with rank of Sqdn. Ldr.; Mentioned in Despatches; Univ. Toronto Schs. Old Boys' Assn. (Past Pres.); Hon. Chrmn. 1967 Junior Board of Trade; Past Pres., Bureau Municipal Research; past chrmn., Metro Toronto Hospital Planning Council; Adv. Comte., Boy Scouts Assn.; Conservative; Anglican; recreations: fishing, golf, photography, amateur radio (Stn. VE3UU); Clubs: Rotary Club of Toronto (Past Pres.); Progressive Conservative Business Men's; Badminton & Racquet; Albany Club (Past Pres.); Toronto Hunt; National; Home: 2 Rose Park Cres., Toronto, Ont. M4T 1P9; Office: Suite 1400, 4 King St. W., Toronto, Ont. M5H 1B8

ANDRAS, Hon. Robert Knight, P.C., LL.D.; b. Lachine, Que., 20 Feb. 1921; s. late John Donald and Angela Eva (Knight) A.; e. Wesley Coll., Winnipeg, Man.; Northland Coll., Ashland, Wis., Hon. Doctorate of Pub. Service 1970; LL.D. (Hon. Causa) Lakehead Univ. 1978; m. Frances Hunt, d. Edgar Gilbert Hunt, 20 Oct. 1945; children:

Robert Hunt, Angela Knight; Sr. Vice-Pres., Dir. and Mem. Exec. Comte., Teck Corp.; Bd. Chrmn. and Dir., TDC Technology Development Corp.; Dir., Lornex Mining Corp.; Tech Research U.S. Inc.; Intermagnetics General Corp., U.S.A.; Mag-Sep Corp., U.S.A.; Seagold; CDC Development Corp.; served with Queen's Own Cameron Highlanders of Canada in France, Belgium, Holland and Germany 1942-46; Winnipeg Light Infantry 1947-48; retired as Major; in executive positions with Ford Motor Co. of Can. Ltd. and Moffats Ltd. in Winnipeg, Saint John, Windsor and Toronto, 1948-58; purchased Gibson Motors Ltd. becoming Pres. of four firms dealing in automotive sales and car rentals, Thunder Bay 1958; el. M.P. for Port Arthur in g.e. 1965; re-el. 1968, 1972, 1974, 1979; served on H. of C. Comtes. (incl. Transport and Communications, Finance, Trade and Econ. Affairs) and Jt. Comte. of House and Senate on Consumer Prices; Del. to Candn.-U.S. Interparlty. Conf. 1967; Del. to 51st Internat. Labour Organ., Geneva 1967; Nat. Campaign Chrmn. to manage Hon. Paul T. Hellyer's campaign for Leadership of Lib. Party; apptd. to Cabinet and sworn into the Queen's Privy Council for Canada as Min. Without Portfolio (with responsibility regarding Indian Affairs) 1968; Min. responsible for Housing 1969; Min. of State for Urban Affairs 1971, Min. of Corporate Affairs 1972; Min. of Manpower and Immigration 1972 (with responsibility for Unemployment Insurance Commission); Pres., Treasury Bd. 1976; Pres., Bd. of Economic Development Mins. 1978; Retired from politics before Feb. 1980 election; Patron 1981 Canada Games (Thunder Bay); Dir., Can. Chamber of Comm.; Dir. and Mem., Vancouver Board of Trade; Mem. Adv. Comm. Max Bell Bus.-Govt. Studies Program (York Univ.); rec'd Centennial Medal; Liberal; Clubs: Vancouver Club; Shaughnessy Golf & Country; Home: 1450 Angus Dr., Vancouver, B.C. V6G 1V3; Office: Teck Mining Group, 1199 West Hastings St. Vancouver, B.C. V6E 2K5

ANDRE, Valve; actress; lecturer; free lance journalist; b. Estonia 10 Sept. 1923; d. August and Ida Silm; e. Coll. of Comm. Tallinn, Estonia 1943; Nat. Theatre Sch. Tallinn 1944; m. Rein Andre, 25 March 1944; children: Anneli, Maiki-Margo, Rein Jr.; Secy. and Special Asst. to former Estonian Ambassador to Sweden 1946-48; Founding mem. and Mgr. Estonian Theatre Sweden 1945-48; came to Can. 1948; Mgr. and Founding mem. Estonian Theatres Can. and Cultural Assn. Estonian Youth 1951; Chrmn. New Candn. Theatre 1964- ; Del. Heritage Ont. Cong. and mem. Comte. to Assess Heritage Ont. 1972; Vice Pres. Toronto Multicultural Centre Assn. 1975- ; Del. and mem. Sponsoring Comte. Multicultural Conf. Candn. Unity, Toronto 1978; Del. Confed. '78 1978; mem. Council for Candn. Unity, Ont. Comte., 1978; Vice Chrmn. Multicultural Comte. Nat. Unity 1979; Pres. (1976-) Rabindranath Tagore Lectureship Foundation; mem. Candn. Consultative Council on Multiculturalism 1974-79; Vice Pres. Multi-Heritage Community Alliance of Toronto 1980-; Dir. Couchiching Inst. on Pub. Affairs 1980-; leading roles CBC Radio and TV Drama since 1952, Nat. Film Bd. Can., New Candn. Theatre, Estonian Theatres Can., and Sweden, Royal Swedish Broadcasting Co. and Estonian Nat. Broadcasting; guest appearances and poetry recitals Europe, Can. and USA; author various articles, travelogues, poetry in nat. and foreign newspapers and mags.; teacher N. Vocational Sch. Evening Classes, Personality Development; private tutoring in speech, drama; mem. Assn. Candn. TV & Radio Artists; Empire Club; Lutheran; Address: 45 Donino Ave., Toronto, Ont. M4N 2W8.

ANDREW, Arthur Julian, M.A., D.C.L.; retired Canadian public servant; b. Pictou, N.S., 20 Nov. 1915; s. late Rev. Canon Albert Edward and Ethel (Sinclair) A.; e. Kings Coll. Sch., Windsor, N.S.; Dalhousie Univ., B.A. 1937, M.A. 1947; Kings Coll., Halifax, D.C.L. 1971; m. Joyce Mowbray, d. Lieut-Col. G. C. Sircom, Halifax, N.S., 24 Oct. 1940; two d.: Stephanie Victoria; apptd.

Asst. Under-Sec. of State for Ext. Affairs in 1974 (formerly Dir.-Gen., Asia & Pacific Bur. 1971-74); joined Dept. of Exter. Affairs, Aug. 1947; 2nd and 1st Secy., Candn. Embassy, Bonn, 1950-52; 1st Secy and Chargé d'Affaires, Candn. Legation, Vienna, 1953-54; Head of Information Div., Ottawa, 1955-57; Counsellor and Chargé d'Affaires, Candn. Legation, Prague, 1957-60; Head of Inspection Service, Ottawa, 1961-62; Candn. Ambassador to Israel & High Commr. to Cyprus, 1962-65; Candn. Ambassador to Sweden, 1965-69; Foreign Service Visitor, Univ. of Toronto, 1969-70; Ambassador to the Hellenic Republic; Dir.-Gen., Asia and Pacific Bur. 1971-74; Asst. Under-Sec. of State for Ext. Affairs 1974-79 (ret.); Foreign Service Visitor, Univ. of Kings Coll., Halifax (1978); author of "Defence by Other Means — Diplomacy for the Underdog" 1970; from 1937 to 1939 sub-editor Canadian Press, Atlantic Bureau; served in 2nd World War; Princess Louise Fusiliers (MG); Lieut., Sept. 1939; retired as Capt., March 1946; Anglican; Address Visiting Prof., Univ. of Kings College, Halifax, N.S. B3H 2A1

ANDREW, Geoffrey Clement, M.A., D.C.L.LL.D.; b. Bayfield, Antigonish, N.S., 3 July 1906; s. Canon A.E., M.C., M.A., and Ethel (Sinclair) A.; e. King's Coll., Dalhousie Univ.; Balliol Coll., Oxford, B.A., M.A. 1935; D.C.L., Univ. of King's Coll., 1962, Bishop's 1970, Univ. of N.B. 1971; D. es. L. Laval 1968; m. Margaret Monro, d. late Dr. William Lawson Grant, 28 June 1937; children: Alison, Edward, Caroline, Joan, Katherine; Teacher, Rothesay (N.B.) Coll. Sch., 1929-30; Upper Can. Coll., Toronto, 1930-33 and 1935-42; Secy., Wartime Information Bd., Ottawa, 1943-45; Dir., Candn. Information Service, 1945-47; apptd. Chief, Information Divn., Dept. of External Affairs, 1947; Advisor to Candn. Del., U.N. Assembly, London and New York, 1946-47; Prof. Eng., Univ. of B.C., 1947-62; Dean and Depy. to the Pres., 1953-62; Extve. Dir. Assn. of Univs. & Colls. of Can., Ottawa, Ont., 1962-71; mem. Vancouver City Council's Comm. on the Arts (1975-78); Chrmn. Bd. of Govs. Leon and Thea Koerner Foundation 1975-81; Anglican; recreations: reading, fishing, golf; Clubs: University (Vancouver); Canadian; Address: 4633 W. 13th Ave., Vancouver, B.C. V6R 2V6

ANDREW, John D., B.Com.; company executive; b. Glasgow, Scotland, 16 April 1921; s. Hugh David and Mary Clare (Burns) A.; e. St. Aloysius' Coll., Glasgow, 1938; Univ. of London; McGill Univ., B.Com. (Hon. Econ.) 1949; m. Frances Joan, d. late William Henry Smith, 1 Aug. 1947; one s. John David; EXECUTIVE VICE-PRESIDENT, CORPORATE AFFAIRS, CONSOLI-DATED-BATHURST INC.; Candn. Pulp & Paper Assn., Market Analyst, Statistician and Mgr., Trade Sections, 1949-58; Consolidated Paper Corp. Ltd., Asst. to Vice-Pres., Wayagamack Sales, 1958-63; Pres., Consolidated Paper Sales Ltd., 1966; Vice-Pres., Corporate Sales, l966 Pres. Consolidated- Bathurst Newsprint Ltd. 1967; Vice-Pres. Consolidated-Bathurst Ltd. 1967; served during 2nd World War with R.N.V.R., 1940-46; discharged with rank of Lieut.; mem., Candn. Pulp & Paper Assn.; Roman Catholic; recreations: fishing, hunting, curling, golf, reading; Clubs: St. James's; Montreal Thistle Curling; Forest & Stream; Mt. Bruno Country; Home: 738 Upper Belmont Ave., Westmount, Que. H3Y 1K2; Office: 800 Dorchester Blvd. W., Montreal, Que. H3B 1X9

ANDREWS, Rev. Elias, M.A., Ph.D., B.D., Litt. D., D.D. (Un. Ch.); b. Winterton, Nfld., 29 Jan. 1906; s. Allan and Adelia (Downey) A.; e. Meth. Coll. and Normal Training Sch., St. John's, Nfld.; Dalhousie Univ., B.A. 1933; Pine Hill Divinity Hall, Halifax, N.S., B.D. 1935; D.D. 1962; Drew Univ., M.A., 1940, Ph.D. 1947; Mount Allison Univ., Hon. Litt.D.; m. the late Flora Shannon, d. Edgar J. Green, Winterton, Nfld., 17 June l941; one s. Paul; 2ndly Mildred Jean, d. Robt. Caughey, Kingston, Ont. 1969; PROF. OF RELIGION, QUEEN'S UNIV., and Prof. of New Testament Studies at Queen's Theol. Coll.

1955-74 (Principal there 1955-70); o. 1935; Minister, Deer Lake, Nfld., 1936-37; Lect. in Philos. and Psychol. of Religion, Pine Hill Divinity Hall, 1937-39; Lect. in Biblical Studies and Religion, Brothers' Coll., Drew Univ., Madison, N.J., 1939-41; Prof. of New Testament Lang. and Lit. Pine Hill Divinity Hall 1941-55; Lect. in Biblical Lit. at Dalhousie Univ., 1947-55; Pres., Bay of Quinte Conf., Un. Ch. of Can., 1962-63; Publications: "Modern Humanism and Christian Theism", 1939; "The Meaning of Christ for Paul", 1949; "Apostle of Grace", 1979; Contrib., "Encyclopaedia Britannica, 15th edn." ("St. Paul"); "The Interpreters Dictionary of the Bible"; Address: 237 Bath Road, Bowling Green II, Kingston, Ont. K7M 2X8

ANDREWS, John Hamilton, A.O. M.Arch., L.F.R.A.I.A., Hon. A.I.A., F.R.A.I.C., A.R.I.B.A.; architect; b. Sydney, N.S.W., 29 Oct. 1933; s. Kenneth Dalmore and Margaret (Hamilton) A.; came to Can. 1958; e. N. Sydney Boys High Sch., Australia 1950; Sydney Univ., B. Arch. 1956; Harvard Univ. M. Arch. 1958; m. Rosemary Randall, 6 Sept. 1958; children: John Dalmore, Lee Bowen, Craig Randall, James Hamilton; with Univ. of Toronto Sch. of Arch. as Lect. 1962, Asst. Prof. 1963, Assoc. Prof. 1965, Prof. and Chrmn. Dept. 1967-69, since when in private practice under name of John Andrews Architects; bldgs. completed incl. Scarborough Coll., Univ. of Toronto; Art Centre, Kent State Univ.; Weldon Lib., Univ. of W. Ont., Harvard Graduate School of Design, Cameron Offices (Canberra, Aust.), King George Tower (Sydney, Aust.); Royal Australian Inst. of Architects Gold Medal, 1980; Juror, Australian Parl. House Competition, 1980; Winner of Internat. Architectural Competition for the Intelsat HQ., Wash. D.C., 1980; rec'd Massey Medal for Arch. (Scarborough Coll.); Centennial Medal 1967; Arnold Brunner Award U.S. Acad. of Arts and Letters 1971; Amer. Inst. of Arch. Honour Award 1973; Life Fellow, Royal Australian Inst. of Archs.; recreation: fishing; Offices: 47 Colborne St., Toronto, Ont. M5E 1P8 and 1017 Barrenjoey Road, Sydney, N.S.W.

ANDREWS, John Hobart McLean, M.A., Ph.D.; educator; b. Kamloops, B.C. 15 May 1926; s. John Ernest and Cynthia Maria (Robinson) A.; e. Univ. of B.C. B.A. (Physics) 1947, M.A. (Educ.) 1954; Univ. of Chicago Ph.D. (Educ.) 1957; m. Doris Deborah d. late Wilfrid Reid Payne 28 Aug. 1948; children: William J., Donald W., Jeffrey P., Lorraine D.; PROF. OF EDUC., UNIV. OF BRIT. COLUMBIA since 1973, Dean, Faculty of Educ. 1973-79; Prof. of Educ. Univ. of Alta. 1957-65; Prof. of Educ. and Asst. Dir. Ont. Inst. for Studies in Educ. Toronto 1965-73; Unitarian; Home: 4923 College Highroad, Vancouver, B.C. V6T 1G7

ANDREWS, Stephen James, R.C.A.; painter; b. Saskatoon, Sask. 16 May 1922; s. Samuel James and Ida Gertrude (Atkinson) A.; e. Windsor Sch. and Glenlawn Coll. Inst. St. Vital, Winnipeg 1940; The Winnipeg Sch. of Art 1942; Chelsea Polytechnic Sch. of Art 1946; Camberwell Sch. of Art & Crafts 1948; Academie Julian Paris 1948-49; studied with Martin Bloch, London, Eng. 1950; Scuola del Mosaico Ravenna, Italy 1953; solo exhns. Waddington Galleries, Tor. 1982; Gallery Moos, Calgary, 1982; incl. Hanover Gallery London, Eng. 1957; Winnipeg Art Gallery 1958; Montreal Museum of Fine Arts 1959, 1963; Overseas Press Club of Am. New York 1964; Jacox Galleries Edmonton 1968; Walter Phillips Gallery Banff 1977; Thomas Gallery Winnipeg 1978; S. African Assn. Arts Cape Town, Pretoria, Durban 1979; Galeria Kreisler Dos Madrid 1981; group exhns. incl. John Moores Liverpool Exhn. I 1957-58; 2nd Candn. Biennale Prints & Drawings touring 1980-82; rep. in various pub., corporate and private colls. incl. Herbert Art Gallery & Museum Coventry; Montreal Museum of Fine Arts; Nat. Coll. Fine Arts Smithsonian Inst. Washington; Nat. Gallery Can.; S. African Nat. Gallery; Sask. House London, Eng.; Aluminum Co. of America; Winnipeg Art Gallery; Toured India in 1955 and 1961 and studied under Maharishi Mahesh Yogi; Visiting Lectr. St. Paul's Sch. London; Univ. of Alta.; Univ. of Cape Town; McMaster Univ.; York Univ.; Banff Sch. Fine Arts; Univ. Calgary; has designed for theatre and film; Artist-in-Residence and Head of Winter Studio Art Program, Banff Centre Sch. Fine Arts 1976-77; author various art and travel articles; served with RCNVR 1942-45; mem. Alta. Soc. Artists; recreations: swimming, skiing; playwriting; collecting (antiques, african sculpture); Address: Finca La Jordana, Casares, Malaga, Spain.

ANGEL, John Bartlett, CM, D.Eng., P.Eng., F.E.I.C.; b. St. John's, Nfld., 12 June 1913; s. Fredk. Wm., M.B.E., B.A.Sc., M.E.I.C. and Mary Elizabeth A.; e. Meth. Coll.; Memorial Univ. (D.Eng. 1974); McGill Univ. (B.Eng. 1935); m. Agnes Helen Templeton, 1943; children: Roger, Jane, Barbara, John, Margaret; PRESIDENT, UNITED NAIL AND FOUNDRY CO. LTD., since 1948; President, William Noseworthy Co. Ltd.; Angel Manufacturing and Supply Co. Ltd.; Chairman, Heap and Partners (Nfld.) Ltd.; member Norcross-Bartlett Expedition., N.E. Greenland 1931; member Peary Mem. Expedition to N.W. Greenland 1932; Norcross-Bartlett Expedition to Foxe Basin, Canadian Arctic, 1933; Bartlett Expedition to N.W. Greenland 1935; International Nickel Co., Copper Cliff, Ont., 1934; joined present Co. as Engr. 1935; Pres., Nfld. Bd. Trade. 1944; mem. Pub. Libs. Bd. 1956-64; Prov. Councillor, Nfld. Div., Candn. Cancer Soc., (Pres. 1962-63; Nat. Dir.); Dir., Coughlan Coll., Memorial Univ.; has served on bds. of various acad., business and community groups; Charter mem. Nfld. Br. and Vice Pres. Atlantic Region 1958-60, Engn. Inst. Can.; Fellow Eng. Inst. of Canada 1978; Charter mem. and Pres., Assn. Prof. Engrs. Nfld. 1965; Pres., Candn. Council Prof. Engrs. 1970-71; Nfld. Rep. Engrs. Confed. Comn. 1961-62; mem. McGill Grad. Soc.; Hon. Secy. Bd. of Govs., United Ch.. Coll. 1951-62; Vice Chrmn. Nfld. Cancer Treatment & Research Foundation; Pres., Mental Health, Nfld. 1973-76; Freemason; United Church; Clubs: Rotary (Pres. St. John's 1949); Murray's Pond Fishing; Bally Haly Golf & Country; Explorers'; Home: 146 Hamilton Ave., St. John's, Nfld. A1E 1J3; Office: (P.O. Box 1555) St. John's, Nfld. A1C 5P2

ANGERS, Hon. Joseph Alexandre Jean-Claude, B.C.L.; judge; b. Valleyfield, Que. 30 March 1942; s. Alexandre and Gabrielle (LePage) A.; e. Univ. St. Louis (Edmunston, N.B.) B.A. 1961; Univ. of N.B. B.C.L. 1965; m. Joan Marie d. Adolphus Gerard MacDonald 19 Aug. 1967; children: Joseph Alexandre Paul, Marielle Joan, Marie-Claude Nicole; JUDGE, COURT OF QUEEN'S BENCH, N.B. since 1979; called to Bar of N.B. 1965; cr. Q.C. 1977; Solr., Dept. Justice N.B. 1965; Crown Prosecutor, Edmunston, N.B. 1967; mem. Rice & Angers, Edmunston 1968; apptd. Judge, Co. Court N.B. 1979; part-time Lectr. in Law, Univ. of N.B. 1976-77; Lectr. Bar Admission Course; Bd. Govs. Univ. of Moncton 1977-80; mem. Extve. Bd. Dirs. Coll. St. Louis Edmundston 1976-77; def. Lib. Cand. for Edmunston prov. g.e. 1974; Vice Pres. Organ. Comte. N.B. First Summer Games; rep. N.B. Lawyers CBC TV "On the Evidence"; Offr. N.B. Barristers' Soc. 1971-72 1976-77; Prov. Offr. Candn. Bar Assn. 1973; mem. N.B. Legal Aid Comte. 1971-79; R. Catholic; recreation: sports; Club: Edmundston Golf; Home: 22 Patterson St., Campbellton, N.B. E3N 1E4; Office: (P.O. Box 5001) Campbellton, N.B. E3N 3H5.

ANGLIN, Douglas G., M.A., D.Phil.; university professor; b. Toronto, Ont., 16 Dec. 1923; s. George Chambers and Ruth Cecilia (Cale) A.; e. Forest Hill Village (Ont.) Schs., 1929-41; Univ. of Toronto, B.A. (Hons., Pol. Science & Econ.) 1948; Univ. of Oxford (Rhodes Scholar for Ont., 1948), Corpus Christi Coll. and Nuffield Coll., B.A. (Philos., Pol. Econ.) 1950, M.A. 1954, D.Phil. 1956; m. Mary Elizabeth, d. Orville Pierce Watson, Toronto, Ont., 26 June 1948; two d., Margaret Alice, Deirdre Ruth;

PROF., DEPT. POL. SCIENCE, CARLETON UNIV. since 1965; Asst. and Assoc. Prof. of Pol. Science and Internat. Relations, Univ. of Manitoba, 1951-58; Assoc. Prof. and Prof. of Pol. Science, Carleton Univ., 1958-65; Assoc. Research Fellow, Nigerian Inst. of Soc. & Econ. Research, Univ. of Ibadan, Nigeria, 1962-63; Vice-Chancellor, Univ. of Zambia, 1965-69; Research Ass. with Center of Internat. Studies, Princeton Univ. 1969-70; served with R.C.N.V.R. as Lt. 1943-45; co-editor of "Canada, Scandinavia and Southern Africa," 1979, "Conflict and Change in Southern Africa," 1979; Co-author, "Zambia's Foreign Policy: Studies in Diplomacy and Dependence," 1979, author of "The St. Pierre and Miquelon Affaire of 1941", 1966; Co-Ed., "Africa: The Political Pattern", 1961; has written numerous articles for various learned journs.; mem., African Studies Assn. (U.S.A.); Candn. Inst. Internat. Affairs; Candn. Pol. Science Assn.; Candn. Assn. of African Studies (Pres. 1973-74); United Church; Address: Ottawa, Ont.

ANGLIN, James P., Q.C., B.C.L.; company executive; b. Westmount, Que., 28 Jan. 1912; s. James Penrose and Florence E. (Christy) A.; e. Westmount High Sch. 1929; McGill Univ., B.A. 1933, B.C.L. 1936; Univ. of Paris, France, Faculty of Law; m. late Julia Elizabeth, d. H. M. Moore, Montreal, 14 Sept. 1938; children: Susan Elizabeth (Mrs. Eric W. Winn), Julia Christine, James Penrose; CHRMN. BRITISH COLUMBIA ADV. BD., CROWN TRUST CO. since 1970; read law with Gordon W. MacDougall, K.C.; called to Bar of Que. 1936; Partner, Smith, Anglin, Laing, Weldon & Courtois and predecessor firms, (Montreal) 1937-70; Lectr., Faculty of Law, McGill Univ. 1945-55; mem. Bd. of Bar Examiners of Que. 1947-55; mem. Council, Bar of Montreal 1955-58; Past Pres., Montreal Boy's Assn., Royal Candn. Golf Assn.; Past Pres., Candn. Cancer Soc. B.C. & Yukon Div.; mem., Candn. Bar Assn. (mem. Extve. 1966-70); recreations: golf, fishing, boating; Clubs: The Vancouver; Shaughnessy Golf and Country; Royal Montreal Golf; Royal & Ancient Golf (St. Andrews, Scot.); Home: 1855 Acadia Road, Vancouver, B.C. V6T 1R2; Office: 750 West Pender St., Vancouver, B.C. V6C 2B2

ANGUS, Donald Lloyd, B.SC., P.Eng.; consulting engineer; b. Toronto, Ont.; e. Univ. of Toronto, B.Sc. (Mech. Engn.) 1941; m. Edith Katherine Gordon, Orillia, Ont.; one s. and one d.; PRESIDENT H. H. ANGUS & ASSOCIATES LTD., Toronto; Pres., Queen Elizabeth Hospital, Toronto; Chrmn., Granite Club; Past Pres., Assn. of Prof. Engrs. of Ont.; served in 2nd World War in RCEME; recreations: sailing, golf, curling, colour-photography; Home: 25 Bayview Wood, Toronto, Ont. M4N 1R8; Office: 1127 Leslie St., Don Mills, Ont. M3C 2S6

ANGUS, M. G., B.Com., company president; b. Stratford, Ont., 19 Jan. 1911; s. late William D. and late Elizabeth (Graham) A.; e. Stratford Coll. Inst.; Univ. of Toronto, B.Com. 1932; m. Ada Madeline, d. late James Hutchison, Montreal, P.Q. 1936; children: William David, Elizabeth Anne (Mrs. G.H. Eberts), Gillian Margaret (Mrs. Michel Côté); PRESIDENT, MADEG HOLDINGS INC. 1980-; Pres., National Trust Co. Ltd.; Chrmn. Montreal Gen. Hosp. Foundation; Founding mem., Candn. Shipowners Assn. and Candn. Shipowners Mutual Assurance Assn.; joined Dom. Mortg. & Investments Assoc. 1932, becoming Asst. Secy.-Treas.; joined with brother in Angus & Company, 1936 (mems. Toronto & Montreal Stock Exchanges); during war went to Nova Scotia as Secy.-Treas. and later Pres. of Clark Ruse Aircraft Ltd., operating aircraft plants for Govt. at Dartmouth, N.S., and Moncton, N.B.; returned to Montreal in 1946 and entered the shipping business; Pres., Lonham & Moore Ltd. and associated companies 1948-80; Phi Kappa Sigma; Presbyterian; Clubs: Mount Royal; St. James's; Mount Bruno Country; University; National (Toronto); Home: Apt. 1602, Two Westmount Square, Westmount, Que. H3Z 2S4; and Hermitage Club Grounds,

Lake Memphremagog, P.Q.; Offices: Suite 1410, One Westmount Sq.,Montreal, Que. H3Z 2R5

ANGUS, Margaret, B.A., LL.D.; author; conservationist; b. Chinook, Mont. 23 May 1908; d. Ulysses S. Grant and Cora (Krauss) Sharp; e. Univ. of Mont. B.A. 1930; Queen's Univ. LL.D. 1973; m. William Angus 28 Aug. 1929; children: Barbara (Mrs. Owen Morgan), James; Dir. of Radio, Queen's Univ. 1957-1968, museum curator since 1968; Chrmn. Kingston Centennial Comte. 1966-67, Kingston Comte. Arch. Review 1970-72; Dir. Ont. Hist, Studies Series since 1972; Pres. Frontenac Hist. Foundation 1973-1976, 1979-81; Gov. Heritage Can. 1974-79; Dir. Ont. Heritage Foundation 1975-81; Gov. Kingston Gen. Hosp. since 1972; Consultant Candn. Hist. Sites Div.; named "Citizen of the year" by Kingston Jaycees 1968; Queen's Univ. Alumni Award 1968 and Medal 1975; Cruikshank Gold Medal 1974; Heritage Can. Travel Award 1975; Silver Jubilee Medal 1977; author "The Old Stones of Kingston" 1966; "The Story of Bellevue House" 1967; "History of Kingston General Hospital" 1972; contrib. "Oliver Mowat's Ontario" 1972; "Kingston 300" 1973; over 30 short stories on hist. subjects for CBC, 4 documentaries, radio plays and hist. studies; Editor of series: Buildings of Architectural and Historic Significance in Kingston; mem. Ont. Hist. Soc. (Pres. 1969-71); Arch. Conservancy Ont.; Kingston Hist. Soc. (Pres. 1972-74); Home: 191 King St. E., Kingston, Ont. K7L 3A3.

ANGUS, William, B.S., A.M., Ph.D., F.I.A.L.; professor emeritus; b. Dundee, Scotland, 22 March 1897; s. James and Eliza (Black) A.; e. Bowdoin Coll., B.S. 1919; Harvard Univ. 1921-22; Northwestern Univ., A.M. 1928; Cornell Univ., Ph.D. 1935; New York Univ. and Columbia Univ., 1945; m. Margaret, d. late U.S. Grant Sharp, 28 Aug. 1929; children: Mrs. (Barbara) Morgan, James Grant; taught at Northwestern Univ., 1922-25; Indiana Univ. Extension Dept., 1923-25; Grinnell Coll., Iowa, 1925-27; State Univ. of Montana, 1927-32; Cornell Univ., 1934-35; N. Illinois State Teachers Coll., 1935-37; joined staff of Queen's Univ., 1937; Visiting Prof., Univ. of Hawaii, 1956; taught at Mayville (N.D.) State Coll., 1965-66; St. Hilda's and St. Hugh's Sch. (N.Y.) 1966-67; mem., Theatre Arch. Comte. of A.E.T.A., 1950-53; three times Regional Chrmn. of Dom. Drama Festival for E. Ont.; Founder and Dir., Queen's Summer Radio Inst., 1945-49; Guest Dir., Community Theatre; Rockefeller Foundation Fellowship, 1945; rec'd. Candn. Drama Award, 1948; Nuffield Foundation Research Grant, 1958; Centennial Medal, 1967; served in U.S. Army, Depot Bgde., Camp Devens, Mass., 1918; mem. Heritage Canada; Frontenac Hist. Foundation; Ont. Hist. Soc.; Kingston Hist. Soc.; Publications: numerous contrib. to scholarly and prof. journs.; "Uncle Willie's Nonsense: Poems for Children"; Ed. of "Historic Kingston"; mem., Psi Upsilon; recreation: grandchildren, theatre; Home: 191 King St. E., Kingston, Ont. K7L 3A3

ANHALT, Istvan; composer; educator; b. Budapest, Hungary, 12 Apl. 1919; s. Arnold and Katalin (Harmat) A.; e. D. Berzsenyi, Realgymnasium, Budapest, 1937; Hungarian Acad. of Music 1936-41; Conservatoire Nat. De Musique, Paris, 1946-48; private study with N. Boulanger and S. Stravinsky; m. Beate, d. late Paul Frankenberg, Jan. 1952; two d., Helen, Carol; PROF. MUSIC DEPT., QUEEN'S UNIV.; Head Music Dept. Queen's Univ., 1971-81; Asst. Conductor, Hungarian Opera, 1945; Asst. Prof. (Lady Davis Fellow), Assoc. Prof. and Prof., McGill Univ., 1949-71; also served as Chrmn., Dept. of Theory, Faculty of Music, 1963-69; Dir. of Electronic Music Studio 1964-71; mem. Senate 1968-71; Visiting F. Slee Prof. of Composition, State Univ. of N.Y., Buffalo, 1969; rec'd Centennial Medal 1967; compositions incl. Symphony No. 1; Cento; Fantasia; Foci; Symphony of Modules; Trio; Sonata for Piano; Sonata for Violin and Piano; "La Tourangelle"; Four Electronic Compositions; numerous recordings; mem., Candn. League Composers;

Home 274 Johnson St., Kingston, Ont. K7L 1Y4; Office: Music Dept., Queen's University, Kingston, Ont. K7L 3N6

ANKA, Paul Albert; singer; composer; b. Ottawa, Ont., 30 July 1941; s. Andrew Emile and late Camelia (Tannis) A.; e. Connaught Sch. and Fisher Park High Sch., Ottawa, Ont.; m. Anne Alison, d. Charles De Zogheb, Paris, France, 16 Feb. 1963; 5 children; estbd. Paul Anka Productions; Mgr., John Prine & Steve Goodman; set up with father Spanka Music Corp. recipient of 15 Gold Records (rec'd when single record sells 1 million copies); has rec'd over 21 Citations for writing from BMI; Young Can. Award 1961; invited to White House 1967; Alsac Service Award (St. Jude Children's Research Hosp. for Leukemia Foundation) 1968; composer: "Diana", "Puppy Love", "My Way" (for Frank Sinatra), "She's A Lady" (Tom Jones), Tonight Show theme, "The Longest Day" for movie of same name; mem., Un. Cerebral Palsy Assns., Inc. (Nat. Hon. Co-Chrmn.); Syrian Orthodox; Club: Friars; Address: c/o Lazarow & Co., 9454 Wiltshire Blvd., Beverly Hills, Calif. 90212

ANNABLE, Robert Graham, B.A.; executive; b. Moose Jaw, Sask., 10 March 1927; s. George Reynolds and Muriel (McVicar) A.; e. Prince of Wales High Sch., 1945; Univ. of B.C., B.A. 1951; m. Janice Elizabeth, d. Douglas Rowley McColl, 24 Nov. 1951; children: Blake Malcolm, Tanyss Jane, Peter Douglas, Mark Graham; CHRMN. AND CHIEF EXTVE. OFFR., ANCORE INTERNATIONAL (CANADA) LTD. (founded Co. 1961; trading, shipping ins.); past mem. Econ. Council Can.; The East Asiatic Co. (export lumber marketing) 1951-61; has founded many cos' in Can. and abroad engaged in internat. comm.; Phi Delta Theta; Anglican; recreations: golf, tennis, squash; Clubs: Vancouver; Capilano Golf & Country; Hollyburn Country; Canadian Men's; Home: 735 King George's Way, W. Vancouver, B.C. V7S 1S2; Office: P.O. Box 91608, West Vancouver, B.C. V7V 3P3

ANNETT, John C., B.A.Sc., M.B.A. (York 1974); mfr.; b. Detroit, Mich., 30 Jan. 1937; s. Francis C. and Cecile M. (Dwyer) A.; e. St. Michael's Coll. Sch., Toronto, 1954; Univ. of Toronto, B.A.Sc. (Elect. Engn. 1958; m. Gail R., d. Alex Stewart, 20 June 1959; children: Matthew, Kirsten, Megan; MANAGER CORP. DEVELOPMENT, JAN-NUCK LTD. 81-; Applications Engr., Andrew Antenna Co. Ltd., 1958; Sales Mgr., Douglas Randall Canada Ltd., 1964; mem., Assn. Prof. Engrs. Ont.; recreations: golf, fitness programs; Clubs: Bayview Golf & Country; Canadian; Office: P.O. Box 43, Toronto Dominion Centre, Toronto, Ont. M5K 1B7

ANNETT, Kenneth Hugh, C.D., F.C.C.T.; b. Gaspé, Que., 18 Aug. 1914; e. High Sch. New Carlisle, Que.; Macdonald Coll. McGill Univ. teaching educ.; Bishop's Univ. B.A., post-grad. M.Ed. courses; Columbia and Harvard Univs. post-grad. M.Ed. courses; m. Velma Law; three s.; CONSULTANT, EDUC. AND GENEALOGY; Counsellor Superior Council of Educ. Que. 1974-79; Supvr. of Schs. R-D-A Central Sch. Bd. 1958-62; Dir. of Guidance Protestant Schs. Que. Dept. of Pub. Instr. 1962-65; Asst. Dir. Guidance Bureau Que. Dept. Educ. 1965; Asst. Dir. Gen. Elem. and Secondary Educ. Br. 1966; Counsellor Office Depy. Min. Educ. 1973-74; served with RCAF Active Service Radar 1942-45; Secy. and Pres. St. Francis Teachers' Assn.; mem. Sr. Adms. Group; Consultant Sherbrooke Hosp. Sch. of Nursing; Chief Instr. Cadet Services Can.; Author "Huguenot Influence in Quebec"; "The Annett Family of Gaspé"; "Saga I"; "Gaspé of Yesterday"; Ed. "Quebec Educational Record", "Guidance Bulletin"; Fellow Candn. Coll. Teachers; founding mem. Candn. Guidance & Counselling Assn. and Richmond Hist. Soc.; mem. Que. Assn. Sch. Adms.; Lit. & Hist. Soc. Que.; Huguenot Soc. Can. (Pres.); Que. Family Hist. Soc.; Richmond Trust; Anglican; recreations: travel, boating, hist. research, photography; Home: 1225 Lavigerie, Ste. Foy, Que. G1W 3W8; Office: 2046 Chemin St-Louis, Sillery, Que. G1T 1P4.

ANNIS, Charles Arthur, B. Com., M.A., Ph.D.; b. Pickering, Ont., 18 Feb 1909; s. late Charles Albert and Sarah M. (Taylor) A.; e. Univ. of Toronto, B.Com. 1930; Cornell Univ., M.A. (Econ.) 1932, Ph.D. (Econ. & Internat. Finance) 1936; m. Margaret E. Fenton, Ottawa, Ont., 15 Sept. 1946; children: Ruth, Robert, Mary; Instr. in Econ., 1930-32 and in Econ., Banking and Internat. Trade, 1934-36, Cornell Univ.; Research Fellow, Brookings Inst., Washington, D.C., 1933-34; served as Offr. of Dept. of Finance, Can., specializing in fields of tariffs, trade, foreign exchange and internat. econ. policy, 1936-68; Chrmn. Machinery & Equipment Adv. Board 1968-70; Chairman Textile & Clothing Board (1970-75); participated in numerous internat. confs. and negotiations, particularly on tariffs and trade; apptd. Dir. of Tariffs 1960; Sr. mem., Candn. Del., Kennedy Round Tariff Negotiations, Geneva, 1964-67; served at Candn. Embassy, Washington; United Church; recreations: sailing, skiing; Home: 121 Buell St., Ottawa, Ont.

ANTON, Frank Robert, C.D., B.Sc. (Econ.), M.A., Ph.D.; educator; b. Leix, Ireland 24 July 1920; s. Norman James and Teresa Beatrice (Baker) A.; e. London Sch. of Econ. B.Sc. 1950; Univ. of Calif. Los Angeles M.A. 1956; Univ. of London Ph.D. 1961; PROF. OF ECON., UNIV. OF CALGARY 1957- ; Head of Econ. 1967-73, mem. Senate 1966-68; Research Econ., Govt. Can. Ottawa 1950-51; Inst. Indust. Relations UCLA 1953-56; Visiting Prof. Middle E. Tech. Univ. Ankara (OECD Sponsorship) 1964; recipient various Can. Council and Killam Fellowships; Chrmn. numerous Arbitration, Adjudication & Conciliation Bds. Govts. Alta., Can.; Assessor, Can. Council Killam Fellowships; served with RAF Bomber Command Navig. 1940-43, P.O.W. Germany 1943-45; author "Government Supervised Strike Voting" 1961; "The Role of Government in the Settlement of Industrial Disputes in Canada" 1962; "Wages and Productivity: The New Equation" 1969; "Worker Participation: Prescription for Industrial Change" 1980; "The Canadian Coal Industry: Challenge in the Years Ahead" 1981; co-author "Economics in a Canadian Setting" 1964; articles various internat. journs.; Founding mem. and Dir. Econ. Soc. Alta. 1966-68; mem. Candn. Econ. Assn. (Extve. Council) 1971-74; Am. Econ. Assn.; Candn. and U.S. Insts. Indust. Relations; Internat. Wine & Food Soc.; Town & Gown Calgary; Liberal; Anglican; recreations: swimming, hiking, music, travel, theatre; Club: Commonwealth (London, Eng.); Home: P.O. Box 1, Site 9, S.S. 3, Calgary, Alta. T3C 3N9; Office: Calgary, Alta. T2N 1N4.

APPELT, David Clemens, M.A., A.B.L.S.; librarian; b. Upper Moutere, New Zealand, 3 Aug. 1915; s. Arthur and Margarethe (Darsow) A.; came to Canada, 1925; e. Univ. of Alberta, B.A. (Hons. Eng.) 1936, M.A. 1937; Univ. of Michigan, A.B.L.S. (Hons.) 1946; m. Natalie, d. Fred Schmidt, Duval, Sask., 22 July 1946; children: Jane Elizabeth, Timothy James; Librarian, Univ. of Sask. 1945-80; Instr. in Eng., Mount Royal Coll., Calgary, Alta., 1937-39; Head Cataloguer, Univ. of Alberta Lib., 1941-45; Pres., Candn. Assn. of Coll. and Univ. Libs., 1966-67; mem., Candn. Lib. Assn.; Sask. Lib. Assn.; Royal Candn. Coll. of Organists; Lutheran; recreation: music; Home: 18 Sunnyside Dr., St. Catharines, Ont. L2M 2A1.

APPLE, Barbabas William Nixon, Q.C., B.A. LL.D.; barrister and solicitor; b. Toronto, Ont. 29 Jan. 1924; s. Elmer Albert and Beatrice Muriel (Nixon) A.; e. sec. sch. Pickering Coll. 1936-40; Univ. of Toronto B.A. 1946; Osgoode Hall Law Sch. LL.D. 1949; m. Sonia Jane d. John Skinner 14 June 1947; children: Heather Elizabeth, William Nixon, Sara Jane, Derek Phin; SR. PARTNER, SALTER, APPLE, COUSLAND, AND KERBEL; Dir. Penant Resources Ltd., Delhi Pacific Resources Ltd., Wimberley Resources Ltd., Dasher Resources Ltd., Belle Aire Resources Ex-

plorations Ltd.; called to the Bar of Ont. 1949; cr. Q.C. 1963; served with RCNVR 1943-45; author of "Filing of Prospectuses by Mining Companies," 1964 (printed under the auspices of the Ont. Securities Comn.); other writing incl. "Shareholders' Agreement," 1968; "Financing Through the Toronto Stock Exchange," 1972; and Osgoode Hall Cont. Legal Ed. Series; Conservative; Church ofEngland; Clubs: National; York Downs Golf and Country; recreations: golf, gardening; Home: R.R. #3, Uxbridge, Ont. L0C 1K0; Office: 10 King St. E., St. 900, Toronto, Ont. M5C 1C3.

APPLEBAUM, Louis, O.C., LL.D; composer; conductor; Arts Administrator; b. Toronto, Ont., 3 Apl. 1918; s. Morris Abraham and Fanny (Freiberg) A.; e. Harbord Coll. Inst., Toronto, 1931-36; Univ. of Toronto, 1940; Toronto Conserv. of Music 1928-40; private study under scholar. in N.Y. with Bernard Wagenaar and Roy Harris, 1940-41; m. Janet, d. Lewis Hershoff, Toronto, 19 July 1940; one s. David Hersh; CHRMN. FED. CULTURE POLICY REVIEW COMTE. 1980-; Extve. Dir., Prov. of Ont. Council for the Arts, 1971; Pres., Group 4 Productions; Music Consultant, C.B.C.-TV; joined staff of National Film Board of Can. as Composer 1941; Music Dir., 1943, composing and cond. scores for about 200 theatrical and nonthreatical documentary films; invited to Hollywood 1945, to compose and conduct score for "Tomorrow the World", produced by Lester Cowan for Un. Artists; returned 1946 to score "The Story of G.I. Joe", same studio; later returned to Can. to continue work at Nat. Film Bd.; resigned in 1947 to engage in study and research in N.Y.; composed scores for many documentary producers, incl. UNO, U.S. Army, March of Time, Nat. Film Bd., etc.; also writing lect. and teaching film music; won two prizes in Candn. Performing Right Soc. competition 1938 and 1939; score for "Tomorrow the World" won special citation from Hollywood Writers Mobilization; score for "Story of G.I. Joe", nominated for an Acad. Award; has contributed to "Film Music Notes", "Journ. of Aesthetics and Art Criticism", "Music in Canada", "The Stratford Scene", "Film Music"; Music Director, Stratford Festival 1953-60; Candn. Film Award 1968; Wilderness Award 1973; Candn. Film Award, 1975; Anik Award, 1977; concert works have been performed by orchestras in many countries, over CBC, BBC (U.K.), by the League of Composers, New York, and in recital in Canada, the U.S.A. and England; Chrmn., Composers, Authors & Publishers Assn. of Can. Comte. for Promotion of Candn. Music, 1964-71; Music Consultant, Nat. Arts Centre, Ottawa, 1964-67; mem. Adv. Panel, Can. Council, 1965-69; Lecturer, York Univ. 1974-78; mem. Bd. of Directors, Candn. Music Centre; Candn. League of Composers; CAPAC; Planning Council of OECA; Nat. Ballet Sch.; Candn. Conf. for the Arts; Candn. Music Council; mbr. Royal Soc. of Arts; Clubs: Arts & Letters; Cercle Universitaire; awarded Centennial Medal 1967; Order of Canada 1977; Queens Jubilee Medal, 1977; LL.D.(Hon) York U. 1979; Hon. Fellow, Ont. Coll. of Art. 1981; Beta Sigma Rho; Hebrew; Address: 151 365 Laurier Ave. W., Ottawa, Ont. K1A 0C8

APPLETON, John Miles, B.S.A., M.Sc.; agricultural executive; b. Winnipeg, Man., 7 June 1912; s. John and Amy (Coleman) A.; e. Pub. and High Schs., Toronto, Ont.; Ont. Agric. Coll., B.S.A. 1935; Univ. of Wales, M.Sc. 1937; m. Mary Davison, d. late Gilbert Hill, Saskatoon, Sask., 10 Aug. 1941; children: David John, Timothy. Mary, Christopher; Dir. of operations, agric. div., Maple Leaf Mills Ltd., (retired); began business career with Fertilizer & Feed Div., Maple Leaf Mills Ltd., 1937; joined Quaker Oats Co. of Can. Ltd. as Div. Mgr. 1938, apptd. Vice-Pres. 1958; became assoc. with present Co. 1968; is concerned with the devel. of a better appreciation of the importance of sound agric. to the National Econ.; has spoken to numerous gatherings in Chicago, St. Petersburg, Montreal, Toronto, Guelph, Chatham, London, etc.; Chrmn., Wallaceburg (Ont.) Pub. Sch. Bd., 1946-47-

48; Pres., Ont. Elevators Assn., 1956-57; Pres., Ont. Agric. Coll. Alumni Assn.; mem., Agric. Inst. Can.; mem., Bd. of Govs., Agric. Econ. Research Council (Pres. 1967); awarded Ont. Agric. Coll. Centennial Medal Sept. 1974 (for distinguished service to agric.); Anglican; recreation: agriculture; Home: 63 Widdicombe Hill Blvd., Weston, Ont. M9R 4B2; Office: P.O. Box 710, Station K, Toronto, Ont. M4P 2X5

APPLEYARD, Edward Clair, M.Sc., Ph.D.; geologist; educator; b. Strathroy, Ont. 22 June 1934; s. Harold Frederick Gaviller and Muriel Chanter (Jarvis) A.; e. Meaford (Ont.) High Sch.; Brantford (Ont.) Coll. Inst. 1952; Univ. of W. Ont. B.Sc. 1956; Queen's Univ. M.Sc. 1960; Cambridge Univ. Ph.D. 1962; m. Elizabeth Ann d. Albert Edward Curtis 28 July 1962; children: Gregory David Jarvis, Mary Louise Desborough; PROF. OF GEOL., UNIV. OF WATERLOO; mem. Geol. Assn. Can.; Mineral. Assn. Can.; Geol. Soc. Norway; Anglican; Home: 61 Larkspur Cres., Kitchener, Ont. N2M 4W8; Office: Waterloo, Ont. N2L 3G1.

APPLEYARD, Rt. Rev. Harold F., M.C., C.D., B.A., D.D.; bishop (Ang.); b. Grey Co., Ont. 1905; e. Univ. of Western Ont. (grad. 1927); Huron Coll. (grad. 1929); m. Muriel Chanter Jarvis, London, Ont.; children: Dr. Edward Clair, David Charles, Nancy Evelyn; ordained 1929 by Archbishop of Huron; first served a parish at Bervie, Ontario, 1929-32; Kerrwood 1932-38; Meaford, Ont., 1938-49; (except for war service); joined Candn. Army, 1942 and attached as Chaplain to Candn. Fusiliers; later joined Prince of Wales Rangers and Queen's York Rangers before proceeding overseas; Chaplain, Candn. Ordnance Reinforcement Unit, July 1942-43; in Apl. 1943 joined Royal Regt. of Can. serving with that Regt. to end of war; took part in Normandy invasion, campaign in N.W. Europe; awarded M.C.; apptd. Rector of Grace Ch., Brantford, Ont., 1949; named Archdeacon of Brant, 1954; Bishop of Georgian Bay, Diocese of Huron 1961-74; since 1970 Bishop Ordinary to the Candn. Forces 1970-77; Address: 720 Springbank Dr., London, Ont. N6K 1A3

APPLEYARD, Peter; composer; vibraphonist; percussionist; b. Cleethorpes, Eng. 26 Aug. 1928; drummer Brit. dance and Central RCAF Bands prior to moving to Bermuda 1949 and to Toronto 1951 where he began playing vibraphone; performed with Billy O'Connor, Park Plaza Hotel 1954-56, CBC Radio & with Cal Jackson; formed own group 1957 travelling widely in N. Am.; co-host CBC Radio "Patti and Peter" 1961-62; CBC TV "Mallets and Brass" with Guido Basso 1969; served as Music Dir. various Toronto nightclubs and cocktail lounges incl. Park Plaza Hotel, Sutton Place Hotel, Toronto-Dominion Centre; performed as leading percussionist in theatre, radio and TV, recording orchestras; toured Middle E. through CBC and UN; joined Benny Goodman's sextet early 1970's touring Europe 1972, 1974, Australia 1973; joined an orchestra incl. Count Basie Band for special Broadway engagement accompanying Frank Sinatra 1975; appeared in concert annually 1976-79 Ont. Place; Host "Peter Appleyard Presents" (TV jazz and variety program) Toronto and syndicated in N.Am. 1977; composer incidental music radio shows and themes for his jazz groups; various recordings; mem. CAPAC;

ARBUCKLE, Franklin, R.C.A., O.S.A.; artist, illustrator, teacher; b. Toronto, Ont. 17 Feb. 1909; s. George Lyons and Isabelle Jane (Gier) A.; e. Ont. Coll. Art, grad. 1931; m. Frances-Anne, d. Franz H. Johnston, 15 June 1934; two d.: Robin, Candace; Dir., Advertising Dept., Ont. Coll. Art, since Sept. 1962; rep. in many pub. and private collections; many one-man shows and group Candn. and Internat. shows; murals painted for Candn. Pacific Rly. and City Hall, Hamilton; tapestry murals, Royal Bank of Canada, H.O. for Ont., Toronto; twice winner, Jessie Dow Prize, Montreal; winner, Internat. Business Machines' Medal; Past Pres., Royal Candn. Acad. Arts;

Address: 278 Lawrence Ave. East, Toronto, Ont. M4N 1T4

ARCHAMBAULT, André, B.A., B.Sc.Phm., D. Pharm.; educator; b. St. Antoine-sur-Richelieu, Que., 22 May 1928; s. Wilfrid and Aline (Jacques) A.; e. Univ. of Montreal, B.A. 1949, B.Sc. Phm. 1954; Univ. of Paris (Grad studies and research in Biochem.), D.Pharm. 1956; m. Fleur-Ange, d. late Rosario Chrétien, 2 Oct. 1954; two s.; VICE-PRÉS., ACADEMIC, UNIV. OF MONTREAL, since 1968; Dir., Poulenc Canada Lté; Asst. Prof. of Biochem., Faculty of Pharm., Univ. of Montreal, 1956-60; Vice-Dean and Dir. of Studies, 1960; Assoc. Prof. of Biochem. and Dir. of Research, Univ. of Montreal, 1960-65, Prof. June 1965; Dean and Dir. of Studies (Pharm.), 1965-68; Pres., Comn. of Grad. Studies there, since 1962; mem. of Bd., Med. Research Council, P.Q. 1964-69; Dir., Candn. Foundation for Advanc. of Pharm.; mem., Coll. of Pharmacists of Que. Prov.; Pharmacy Examining Bd. Can.; Internat. Pharm. Fed.; Brit. Pharm. Comn.; Soc. de Chimie biol. de France; Candn. Acad. of Hist. of Pharm.; Am. Acad. of Hist. of Pharm.; Am. Chem. Soc.; Candn. Soc. of Chemotherapy; mem. Conseil supérieur de l'éducation du Québec; Fellow, Am. Assn. Advanc. Science; Hon. mem., Am. Bd. of Diplomates in Pharm; del. to a no. of Internat. Congs. (Pharm.); has rec'd a no. of Hon. Mentions and Prizes incl. Ltd. Gov's Medal of P.Q.; Publications: over 23 research papers, over 15 prof. articles; Home: 650 Dollard, Outremont, P.Q. H2V 3G3; Office: Montreal, Que.

ARCHAMBAULT, Louis, B.A., LL.B., F.T.C.I.; executive; b. Montreal, Que. 18 Dec. 1928; s Auguste and Georgette A.; e. Loyola Sch. Montreal; Coll. Ste-Marie, Montreal B.A. 1949; Univ. of Montreal LL.B. 1953, postgrad. Law Sch. 1954; m. Monique LL.L.d. late Paul-Émile Gagnon, Q.C. Rimouski, Que. 27 Aug. 1955; children: Nicole, Louis Jr., Marie; PRESIDENT AND CHIEF EXTVE. OFFR. TRUST GÉNÉRAL DU CANADA since 1978; Member, Board of Dir. and Executive Comte. 1976-; Pres. and Chief Executive Officer Sherbrooke Trust 1980-; Member Board of Dir. and Executive Comte. 1978-; Dir. RoyNat; Prêt Ville-Marie Inc.; Canadian Equitable Corp.; Stérling Trust Corp.; called to Bar of Que. 1954; joined present co. as Legal Counsel 1955, Founding Mgr. Trois-Rivières Br. 1957, Mgr. Que. Br. 1966, Gen. Mgr. 1970, Extve. Vice Pres. and Gen. Mgr. 1976; mem. Law Faculty Council Univ. of Montreal; mem. Extve. Cloutier of Cap-de-la-Madeleine and Ste-Thérèse of Shawinigan Hosps.; Co-Founder Que. Heart Foundation (Quebec City 1967-68), Dir. 1970, Campaign Pres. Quebec City Sec. 1968-69; Fellow, Trust Co's Inst.; Pres. Young Bar Assn. Trois-Rivières 1964; mem. Counsel and Executive Comte. Trust Co's Assn. Can. Que. Sec. (Secy. 1971-73, Treas. 1973-75, Vice Pres. 1975-77, Pres. 1977-79); R. Catholic; recreations: swimming, tennis; Clubs: Chambre de Comm.; St-Denis; St. Jame's Club of Montreal; Home: 18 Thurlow Rd., Hampstead, Que. H3X 3G6; Office: 1100, rue Université, Montreal, Que. H3B 2G7.

ARCHAMBAULT, Louis, , OC., B.A., D.E.B.A.M., A.R.C.; sculpteur; né Montréal, Qué., 4 avril 1915; e. Coll. des Jésuites Jean-de-Brébeuf, B.A. 1936; Ecole des Beaux-Arts de Montréal, (dipl. en céramique) 1939; ép. Mariette Provost, 1941; enfants: Aubert, Eloi, Patrice; expositions"Essai De Renouvellement Formel De Quelques Symboles Mystiques," Centre Culturel Canadien, Paris, et etinérante en grande Bretagne 1980; "Les Sculptures Urbains de Louis Hrchambault" Musee D'Art Contemporain, Montréal 1972; Festivals de Gde-Bretagne, Londres, 1951; Xe et XIe Triennale de Milan 1954 et 1957; XXVIIIe Biennale de Venise, 1956; Internationale, Pittsburgh, 1958; 300 Ans d'Art Canadien, Galerie Nat. du Can., 1967; Exposition Internat. de Sculpture Contemporaine, Expo 67; Ve Expo Internat. de sculpture, Legnano, Milan, Italie, 1969; 11e Biennale de Middleheim, Anvers, 1971; Bourses: gouv. can., Séjour en France 1953-54; Conseil des Arts du Can., 1959, 1962 et 1969; Ministère de l'Education du Québec, recherche, 1969-70, 1970-71; Collaboration: Pavillon du Can., Bruxelles, 1958; aeroport d'Ottawa, 1960; Place des Arts, Montréal, 1963; aéroport de Toronto, 1964; Esplanade, Galerie d'Art, Expo 67, Montreal; Pavillon du Can., Expo 67, Montréal; Pavillon du Canada, San Antonio, Texas, 1968; The Macdonald Block, Queen's Park, Toronto, 1969; Médaille des Arts connexes, Inst. Royal d'Architecture du Can., 1958; Ordre du Canada, 1968; Académicien, Académie Royale des Arts du Canada, 1968; Artiste en rés., Univ. du Qué., Montréal, 1969-71; Professeur, Univ. du Québec Et Concordia, Montréal; Résidence: 278 avenue Sanford, St-Lambert, Qué. J4P 2X6

ARCHAMBAULT, Hon. Maurice, B.A.; judge; b. St. Hyacinthe, P.Q., 5 Apl. 1914; s. Sylvani and Emma (Beaudry) A.; e. Acad. du Sacre-Coeur, Granby, Que.; Semy. de St-Hyacinthe, B.A. 1935; Univ. of Montreal (Law) 1935-38; called to the Bar of Que., 1938; cr. Q.C. 1950; m. Rolande, d. Aimé De Laboursodiere, 8 June 1940; children: Nicole, Ghislaine, Andrée, Maryel, Louise; JUSTICE, SUPERIOR COURT OF QUE., since 1962; Crown Prosecutor Dist. of Bedford, Que., 1950-60; formerly Counsel for many Mun. and Sch. Corps.; Pres., Rural Bar Assn. of P.Q., 1961; awarded Merite universitaire, Univ. of Montréal; R. Catholic; recreations: golf, travel; Home: 86 Claude-Champagne Ave., Outremont, Que. H2V 2X1; Office: Court House, Montreal, P.Q.

ARCHER, David Bruce, C.M.; trade union executive; b. Edinburgh, Scotland, 12 Jan. 1912; s. John and Agnes (Sheills) A.; came to Canada, 1920; e. Toronto Public Schs., Night Schs., Univ. Extension courses; m. Doris Mary, d. William Smith, Toronto, Ont., 1938; children: Ian Bruce, James David, Mrs. (Sheila) Arnott; Past President, Ont. Fed. of Labour; mem., Bd. of Trustees, United Appeal for Metro. Toronto; mem. of Bd., Candn. Nat. Exhn., Bd. Govs. York Univ.; Bd. Dirs. St. John Ambulance; apptd. Staff Rep. of Textile Workers Union in 1943 on discharge from the army; in 1945 el. Secy., Toronto & Lakeshore Labour Council, becoming Pres. in 1950; apptd. to Ont. Labour Relations Bd., 1948; apptd. Extve. Secy., Ont. Fed. of Labour, 1948-58; became Vice-Pres. of the Toronto and Dist. Labour Council on the merger of AFL-CIO in 1956; Extve. mem. Ont. Econ. Council; Past Chrmn. Toronto Housing Authority; Dir., The Toronto Symphony Orchestra Assn.; served in 2nd World War with Candn. Signal Corps; Signal Sergt. with 1st Bn., Candn. Machine Gun Corps; N.D.P.; United Church; Home: 9 Crescent Place, Apt. 2011, Toronto, Ont.; M4C 5L8

ARCHER, John H., B.L.S., M.A., Ph.D.; educator; b. Broadview, Sask., 11 July 1914; s. Charles H. and Mary (Archer) A.; e. Broadview (Sask.) High Sch.; Scott Coll. Inst., Regina, Sask.; Univ. of Sask., B.A. (Hons) 1947 and M.A. 1948; McGill Univ. Library Sch., B.L.S. 1949; Queen's, Ph.D. 1969; LL.D. Univ. of Regina 1981; m. Alice Mary, d. late Leonard Widdup, Kipling, Sask., 24 Aug. 1939; children: John Widdup, Alice Mary-Lynn; Pres. Univ. of Regina 1974-76; Pres. Emeritus Univ. of Regina 1976; Saskatchewan Pres. Council for Can. Unity, 1979; Queen's Silver Jubilee Medal, 1978; Candn. ed., Project Offr. Comn. on Govt. Organ. (Can.) 1961-62; Past Dir., Univ. Libs., McGill Univ., Archivist and Assoc. Prof. of Hist., Queen's Univ. 1967-69; won Undergrad. Scholarship, Univ. of Sask., 1946 and Dafoe Scholarship 1947; served in 2nd World War, U.K. and Mediterranean Theatres 1940-45, 1st Candn. Survey Regt., R.C.A.; Comn. Overseas 1943; Hon. Col. 10th Fld. Reg't, R.C.A., Regina; author of "Historic Saskatoon", 1948; "Saskatchewan: A History", 1980; co-author "The Story of a Province" (jr. hist. of Sask.), 1955; "Footprints in Time: Saskatchewan", 1965; Ed., "West of Yesterday", 1965; "Land of Promise", 1969; author, "History of Saskatchewan" 1980; mem., Candn. Lib. Assn. (Pres.

1966-67); Chrmn., Comte. on Intellectual Freedom 1962-65; mem., Bd. of Dirs., Candn. Centenary Council; mem. Candn. Hist. Assn., Inst. Pub. Adm. of Can., Candn. Citizenship Fed.; Inst. Prof. Lib. Ont.; Quebec Lib. Assn., Royal Candn. Legion; Anglican; recreations: bridge, golf, football spectacles, curling, Clubs: Canadian; Men's University; Assiniboia; United Services Inst.; Home: 1530 MacPherson Ave., Regina, Sask. S4S 4C9

ARCHER, Brig.-Gen. Maurice, M.B.E., E.D., B.Sc., civil engineer; b. Quebec, Que., 4 Oct. 1910; s. Edouard and Juliette (Hudon) A.; e. Comm. Acad., Quebec City; Royal Mil. Coll., Kingston, Ont. (Grad. 1932); McGill Univ., B.Sc. (Civil Engn.), 1933; m. Cécile Giroux, d. Jean-Baptiste Giroux, 22 Oct. 1937; children: Georges, Joan, Edouard, André, Isabelle; Chrmn. Archer, Seaden & Assocs.; Sr. Vice-Pres. Candn. Nat. Railways, 1971-76 (Vice Pres. Research & Devel. 1963-71); Dir. Missisquoi-Rouville; Vice Chmn. Metric Commission of Canada; Dir. Labrador Mining and Exploration Co. Ltd.; Mount Royal Rice Mills Ltd.; Consulting Engr. with Archer & Dufresne, Quebec City (except for war yrs.) 1937-52; Vice-Chrmn., Nat. Harbours Bd., July 1952-58, Chrmn., 1958-61; Extve. Asst. to Pres., E. G.M. Cape & Co. Ltd., 1961-63; served in 2nd World War in 4 M.E.D. Regt., R.C.A. in N.W. Europe; awarded M.B.E.; Pres., Royal Candn. Arty. Assn., 1954; Fellow, Engn. Inst. Can., mem. Corp. Prof. Engrs., Que., Roman Catholic; recreations: golf, tennis; Home: R.R. 1, Brome, Que. J0E 1K0; Office: 1134 Ste. Catherine St. W., Montreal, Que. H3B 1H4

ARCHER, Violet B., D.Mus., composer, pianist; university professor adjudicator; b. Montreal, P.Q., 24 Apl. 1913; d. Balestreri Cesare Angelo and Beatrice (Azzi) A.; e. McGill Univ., Teacher's Licentiate in Piano, 1934, B.Mus. 1936; Assoc. Candn. Coll. Organists, 1939; Yale Univ., B.Mus. 1948. M.Mus. 1949; McGill Univ., D.Mus. 1971; Instr. in Music, McGill Univ. 1943-47; Resident Composer, N. Texas State Coll., Denton, Texas, 1950-53; visiting Prof. of Music, Cornall Univ. 1952; Asst. Prof. of Music, Univ. of Oklahoma 1953-61; Assoc. Prof. of Music, Univ. of Alberta, 1962, Prof. there 1970-78, Prof. Emeritus since 1978; Composer in residence, Banff School of Fine Arts 1978, 79; Chmn. Div. Theory and Composition 1962-1978-won several scholarships and awards from 1948-59; Can. Council Sr. Fellowship, 1958-59; works have been performed at Internat. Festival of Edinburgh, Brussels World Fair, Osaka Festival, Japan, Expo 67, Stratford Shakespearean Festival, Vancouver Festival, also throughout Can., U.S., France, Switzerland, Italy, Scotland, Czechoslovakia, Eng. and in several networks in these countries incl. many Composers' Symposia in U.S.; comnd. by Internat. House of New Orleans for 1st Inter-Am. Music Festival (1st Candn.) "Trio for Piano, Violin and Cello", in 1958; Montreal Brass Quintet for 100th concert of Sarah Fischer Series, "Divertimento for Brass Quintet", 1963; comnd. by C.B.C. (1964, 65, 72, 78, 80), by Can. Council (1965, 1978 and 1979), by Montreal Jr. Symphony Orchestra, Edmonton Symph. Orch. and Saskatoon Symph. Orch.; etc., has composed numerous works (chamber, orchestral, keyboard, organ, choral, songs a capella, electronic music and others); awarded Composition Trophy, Que. Music Festival Competition 1939, Woods-Chandler prize for composition, Yale Univ., 1949, Ladies' Morning Musical Club of Montreal, 1949 (for work abroad); Queen's Jubilee Silver Medal 1978; rec'd Fellowship, MacDowell Colony, Peterborough, N.H. 1956; nominated recipient of Alumni Award for distinguished service in field of music by extve. comte., Yale Sch. of Music Alumni Assn. 1968; rec'd Merit Award, Govt. Alta. for contrib. to music in Prov., 1971; award for Outstanding Music 1980-81; author of numerous articles on music in journs., Publications (over 50), incl. "Prelude and Allegro for Violin & Piano" 1954; "Fanfare and Passacaglia for Orchestra" 1956; "Three Sketches for Orchestra" 1966; "Sonata for Clarinet and Piano" 1973; "Sganarelle", opera 1973; "Psalmody"; for orchestra, chorus and baritone voice 1978; "Sonata for Alto Saxophone and Piano" 1972; "Sonata for Oboe and Piano" 1973; Four Duets for Violin and Cello, 1979; Serveral Song Cycles, 1979-80; Piano Sonato No. 2, 1979; Two film scores: "Someone Cares," 1977 "Whatsoever Things Are True," 1980; mem., Candn. League of Composers; Music Educators' Nat'l Conf. Assoc.(U.S.A.); Internat. Folk Music Council; Candn. Folk Music Soc., Am. Music Centre; Candn. Music Centre, Am. Women Composers Inc.; Edmonton Musician's Assn., Candn. Fed. Music Teachers; Alta. Reg'd Music Teachers' Assn., Assn. Acad. Staff of Univ. of Alta., Candn. Assn. Univ. Teachers; Edmonton Chamber Music Soc., Composer member, Frau und Musik, Internationaler Arbeitskneis; Cologne, Germany 1979; Amer. Soc. of Univ. Composers; Amer. Women Composers Inc.; Assoc. of Can. Women Composers Nominated Life Academy Member of Accademia Tiberina of Rome, Italy 1979; Candn. Music Educators' Soc.; rec'd. Creative & Performing Award from City of Edmonton 1972; Honour Certificate for contribution to Alta's Musical Heritage, 1980; Hon. Mem. Sigma Alpha Iota; Home: 10805-85th Avenue, Edmonton, Alta. T6E 2L2

ARCHIBALD, Adams Gordon, B. Com., public utility executive; b. Truro, N.S., 7 Jan. 1911; s. Harry Adams and Wilanna (Archibald) A.; e. Colchester Co. Acad., 1924-27; Dalhousie Univ., B.Com. 1933; m. Marion Dean, d. George D. Muggah, 14 Sept. 1938; children: Mrs. Murray Fraser, David Dean, George Gordon, William Harry; CHAIRMAN OF BD. I.C.G. SCOTIA GAS LTD., 1979-; Dir., Eastern Telephone & Telegraph Co. Ltd.; Stanfield's Ltd.; Halifax Insurance Co.; Commercial Life Insurance; joined Maritime Telegraph & Telephone Co. Ltd. 1934 as a Salesman; Chief Clrk. in Sydney, N.S., 1935-38, trans. to Amherst, N.S., as Local Mgr., Feb. 1939; trans. to H.O. as Comm. Supervisor, Feb. 1940; apptd. Gen. Comm. Mgr., 1943, Gen. Plant Mgr., 1956, Gen. Mgr., 1958, Vice-Pres. 1959, Pres. 1963; Chrmn. of Board and Pres. 1968; Chrmn. of Board and Ch. Exec. Off. 1975; Chrmn. of Board, 1976; Chmn. of Bd. of Govs., Dalhousie Univ.; Pres., Candn. Chamber of Comm., 1970-71; United Church; Hobbies: riding, fishing, skiing; Clubs: Halifax; Saraquay; Home: 6083 Belmont Rd., Halifax, N.S. B3H 1N3; Office: 1505 Barrington St., Halifax, N.S. B3J 2W3

ARCHIBALD, Charles Roger, M.B.E., Q.C.; b. Toronto, Ont., 23 July 1910; s. Dr. Thomas Dickson and Muriel (Dumble) A.; e. Upper Canada Coll., Toronto, Ont., 1925; Trinity Coll. Sch., Port Hope, Ont., 1927; Roy. Mil. Coll., Kingston, Ont., 1931; Trinity Hall, Cambridge (Eng.) 1932; Osgoode Hall, Toronto, Ont.; m. Margaret, d. Basil B. Carter of Toronto and Quebec City, 5 Sept. 1940; children: Janet Dobree, Gillian Mary, Susan Margaret, David Carter Roger; PARTNER, STRATHY, ARCHIBALD & SEAGRAM; Dir., Giant Yellowknife Mines Ltd.; called to the Bar of Ont., 1935; cr. Q.C. 1953; served in Candn. Arty. and staff appts. 1939-45; Kappa Alpha; Conservative; Anglican; recreations: golf, squash, skiing; Clubs: University; Toronto Golf; Home: 17 Ancroft Place, Toronto, Ont. M4W 1M4; Office: Commerce Court West, Toronto, Ont. M5C 1T4

ARCHIBALD, Percy Alexander Howard, B.Sc., transportation executive; b. Glenelg, N.S., 16 Apl. 1920; s. Elwyn Oresta and Catherine Annabelle A.; e. Glenelg, N.S.; N.S. Agric. Coll., 1939; McGill Univ., B.Sc. (Agric.) 1942; m. Doris May, d. G. Buckley Simpson, Boylston, N.S., 1947; children: Lynn (Mrs. Brian Knudsen), Dale, Jane (Mrs. Brian McMillan), Brent, Sandy, Shari; PRESIDENT, ARCHIBALD'S BUS CO. LTD.; Pres., Archibald Motors Ltd.; Tigo Development Group Ltd.; Antigonish Electrical Enterprises; Secy.-Treas. Braeside Bowling Ltd.; Pres., Antigonish Cable Vision Ltd.; with Dept. of Veterans' Affairs 1946-49; Mgr., Keltic Motors Ltd., 1949-57; self-employed since 1957; served with Candn. Army in Europe during World War II; Liberal;

United Church; recreations: bowling, golf, fishing; Club: Liberal Century; Home: 87 Hawthorne, Antigonish, N.S. B26 1AG; Office: Antigonish, N.S.

ARCHIBALD, Raymond Douglas, B.A., LL.B.; barrister and solicitor; b. Saskatoon, Sask., 10 Mar. 1921; s. Raymond and Jane (McPhee) A.; e. Univ. of Sask., B.A. 1940 and LL.B. 1942; m. Jocelyn Fallis, d. W.G. Yule, Regina, Sask., 24 Mar. 1945; children: Peter D., Edna Jane, Jocelyn Joan; Partner, Lang, Michener, Cranston, Farquarson & Wright; read law with Estey, Moxon & Schmidt, Saskatoon, Sask.; called to Bar of Sask. 1945 & Ont. 1972; Secy., Dom. Textile Co. Ltd., 1951-60; Vice-Pres. and Gen. Mgr., Caldwell Linen Mills Ltd. 1960-69; Dir., CBS Records Canada Ltd.; CBS Television Network Sales of Canada Ltd.; CBS Musical Instruments, Ltd.; Central States can of Canada Ltd.; Shorewood Packaging Corp. of Canada Ltd.; served in 2nd World War with Calgary Tank Regt. and Candn. Grenadier Guards as Lieut.; wounded in action at Falaise, 1944; mem., Law Soc. of Sask.; Law Soc. of Upper Can.; Inst. of Chart. Sec. & Admin.; The Royal Cdn. Legion, Univ. Club of Montreal; H.R.H. Duke of Edinburgh's Study Conf. Oxford 1956; United Church; recreation: golf; Home: Iroquois, Ont. K0E 1K0; Office: One First Canadian Place, Toronto, Ont. M5X 1A2

'ARDAL, Páll Steinthórsson, M.A., Ph.D.; educator; b. Akureyri, Iceland 27 June 1924; s. Steinthór Pálsson and Hallfridur (Hannespóttir) 'A.; e. Menntaskolinn 'A Akureyri 1944; Univ. of Edinburgh M.A. 1949, M.A. (Hons.) 1953, Ph.D. 1961; m. Harpa Asgrimsdottir d. late Asgrimur Pe tursson 7 Sept. 1946; children: Hallfridur, Maja, Steinthor, Grimur; JOHN AND ELLA G. CHARLTON PROF. OF PHILOS., QUEEN'S UNIV. 1981-; teacher Menntaskolinn 'A Akureyri 1944-45, 1949-51; Univ. of Edinburgh 1955-69; Visiting Prof. Dartmouth Coll. 1963, 1971; Prof. of Philos. Queen's Univ. 1969; author "Passion and Value in Hume's Treatise" 1966; various book chapters, papers, reviews, critical studies; book ed.; mem. Soc. Health & Human Values; Hume Soc.; Candn. Philos. Assn.; Am. Philos. Assn.; Parkinson Foundation Can. (Pres. Kingston Chapter); NDP; Lutheran; recreations: squash, tennis, bridge; Home: 277 Welborne Ave., Kingston, Ont. K7M 4G7; Office: Kingston, Ont.

ARDIEL, June Victoria M., M.A.; advertising executive; b. London, Ont., 24 May 1921; d. late John Joseph Lorne and Daisy Blanche (Robinson) A.; e.Bishop Strachan Sch., Toronto, Ont. (Grad. 1939); University Coll., Univ. of Toronto, B.A. (Fine Art) 1943; M.A. 1968; VICE-PRESIDENT, ARDIEL ADVERTISING AGENCY LTD.; Dir., Leidra Lands Ltd.; joined the present Co. in 1943 as a Junior; former Creative Dir., Delta Delta Delta; Anglican; recreations: painting, reading; Clubs: University Women's; Granite; Home: 10 Fifeshire Rd. S. Willowdale, Ont. M2L 2G5; Office: 4 Lawton Blvd., Toronto, Ont. M4V 1Z4

ARES, Rév. Richard, O.C., B.A., M.A., lic.sc.soc., lic. phil. lic.théol., Ph.D., D. de l'U. (Paris), F.R.S.C., (R.C.); n. Marieville, Comté Rouville, P.Q. 7 janv. 1910; f. Georges et Dorila (Théberge) A.; e. Sém. St-Hyacinthe, B.A. 1931; Univ. de Montréal, M.A. 1935, lic.sc.soc. 1939; Scholasticat Immaculée-Conception, lic.phil. 1937, lic.théol. 1945; Inst. Catholique, Paris, Ph.D. 1948, Doct.Sc.soc. 1948; Univ. de Paris, D.U.P. (Droit international) 1948; mem., Commission royale, Problémes constitutionnels, 1953-56 (Qué.); Académie Sciences morales & pol. du Can., Prés., Sciences sociales du Can. dir. revue "Relations" 1956-69; Société royale du Can., depuis 1963; Publications: "Notre question nationale", 1945; "L'Eglise et la société internationale", 1949; "La Conférération, Pacte ou Loi?", 1949; "Pour un Québec fort", 1963; "Le role de l'Etat dans un Québec fort", 1962; "Dossier sur le Pacte fédératif de 1867", 1967; "Les positions-ethniques, linguistiques et religieuses-des Canadiens français à la suite du recensement de 1971", 1975; L'Eglise dans le monde d'aujourd'hui, 1977; etc., Residence: 25 ouest, rue Jarry, Montréal, Qué. H2P 2L9; Bureau: 8100, Bd. St.-Laurent, Montréal, Qué. H2P 1S6

ARGUE, Hon. Hazen Robert, B.A.Sc., senator (Regina); b. Jan. 1921; s. Howard B. and Legia (Scharf) A.; e. Avonlee Pub. and High Sch., Sask.; Univ. of Sask., B.A.Sc., m. Jean, d. Arcarde Ignatescue, Kayville, Sask., 24 July 1945; 1st. el. to H. of C. for Wood Mountain, g.e. 1945; re-el. g.e. 1949; el. for Assiniboia, g.e. 1953, 1957, 1958; el. Nat. Leader, C.C.F. Party, Aug. 1960 resigned from N.D. Party, Feb. 1962; re-el., g.e., 1962 in Liberal interest; def. g.e. 1963 and 1965; summoned to Senate of Canada, Feb. 1966; Minister of State responsible for the Can. Wheat Board, 1980-; United Church; Address: Ormiston, Sask. S0H 3H0

ARISS, Herbert Joshua; painter, art teacher; b. Guelph, Ont., 29 Sept. 1918; s. William Minno and Wilhemina Helen (Zinger) A.; e. Toronto (Ont.) Public and High Schs., Ont. Coll. of Educ. (1947); Ont. Coll. of Art (1940); m. Margot Joan, d. Earl D. Phillips, London, Ont., 5 July 1950; two s. Joshua Herbert, Jr., Jeffrey Earl; began as Designer for Vibra-Lite Co. (outdoor adv.); Illustrator and book Designer, Copp Clark, Macmillans, Longmans, Green, etc., 1947-62; Head of Art Dept., H.B. Beal Secondary School, London, Ont., 1966; taught painting, Doon Sch. of Fine Arts, 1952-56; Lect. widely throughout Ont. to art socs., awarded Can. Council Sr. Fellowship for Painting, 1960-61; served in 2nd World War with Candn. Army (Engrs.), 1942-46; Trustee, London Lib. & Art Museum, 1956-59; rep. in colls. of Nat. Gallery, Ottawa, Art Gallery of Toronto, London Art Gallery, Winnipeg Art Gallery, ACA Gallery, Calgary, Alta., Vancouver Art Gallery, N.B. Museum, Saint John, N.B., etc., mem., Ont. Soc. Artists; Candn. Soc. Painters in Water Colour (2nd Vice-Pres.) Candn. Group of Painters; Past Pres., Western Art League; Candn. Graphic Arts; el. to Roy. Candn. Acad. of Arts 1978; Anglican; Address: 770 Leroy Crescent, London, Ont. N5Y 4G7

ARMSON, Kenneth Avery, B.Sc.F., R.P.F.; educator; consultant; b. Newton Brook, Ont., 19 Feb. 1927; s. Harold P. and Gladys D. (Wraight) A.; e. Royal Grammar Sch., Worcester, Eng., Univ. of Toronto, B.Sc.F. 1951; Oxford Univ., Dipl. Forestry 1955; m. Harriett E. C., d. late James T. Coltham, 12 Apl. 1952; one child, Erling J. T.; CHIEF FORESTER, ONT. MIN. NAT. RESOURCES since 1979; Prof. of Forestry, Univ. of Toronto, 1952-79; Consultant in Silviculture and Forest Soils to indust. and govt.; joined Research Div., Ont. Dept. of Lands and Forests, 1951-52; served with Candn. Army 1945-46; Can. Forestry Achievement Award, 1978; author, "A Manual of Forest Tree Nursery Soil Management", 1974; "Forest Soils—Properties and Processes", 1977; also over 35 papers in scient. journs; mem. Ont. Prof. Foresters Assn.; Candn. Inst. Forestry; Soc. Am. Foresters; Soil Science Soc. Am.; Ont. Forestry Assn.; United Church; Home: 446 Heath St. E., Toronto, Ont. M4G 1B5

ARMSTRONG, Charles F., B.Com.; transportation executive; b. Nelson, B.C. 1927; e. Univ. of B.C. B.Com.; m. Margaret Kyle; 3 children; PRES., CN HOLDINGS 1979- ; Chrmn. of Bd. and Dir. NorthwesTel; Terra Nova Tel; CN Marine; CN Tower and various companies which comprise CN Trucking; served Econ. Research and Control Div. Air Canada and Rly. Assn. Can. prior to joining Research and Devel. Dept. CN 1953 Montreal and Transport. Dept. W. Can.; Asst. Area Mgr. Toronto 1961; Operations Mgr. London, Ont. 1963 and subsequently Mgr. S.W. Ont. area; Asst. Chief of Transport. Planning, System HQ 1967, Chief of Transport. 1969; Asst. Vice Pres. Adm. 1972; Vice Pres. Mang. Services 1973; Vice Pres. Mountain Region 1974; recreations: skiing, racquet sports, sailing; Clubs: M.A.A.A.; Mount Royal; Home: 12

Rosemount Ave., Westmount, Que. H3Y 3G7; Office: (P.O. Box 8100) Montreal, Que. H3C 3N4.

ARMSTRONG, Charles N.; insurance executive; b. Truro, N.S., 5 August 1936; s. Charles D. and Annie M. (Hayman) A.; e. Acadia Univ., B.A. (economics) 1960; m. Patricia Anne, d. Lyman G.R. Baiden, 20 August 1960; three children, Kimberly, Michael, Deanna; PRESIDENT CANADIAN OPERATIONS, METROPOLITAN LIFE INS. CO. since Nov. 1978; joined Metropolitan as a clerk in Canadian Head Office 1960; progressed through Personal Ins., Electronics, Mgt. Services; Asst. Vice-Pres. Personal Ins. 1971; transferred to New York Office as Asst. Vice-Pres. Personal Life Ins. Admin. & Policyholder Services 1972; Gen. Mgr. New England Head Office 1973; Vice Pres. Personal Ins. Operations 1974; Vice-Pres. in charge Atlantic Head Office 1976; President Canadian Operations Nov. 1978; mem., Bd. Govs., Univ. of Ottawa; Co Vice-Chrmn., Ottawa Civic Hosp. Devel. Campaign Committee; Co-Chrmn. U. of Ottawa Achievement fund Campaign Committee; Bd. of Dirs., Candn. Life & Health Ins. Assn.; mem., Business Council on Nat. Issues; Chmn., External Relations Steering Comm.; mem., Gout. Relations Comm.; recreations: skiing, bridge; Club: Rideau; Home: 3543 Paul Anka Dr., Ottawa, Ont. K1V 9K7; Office: 99 Bank St., Ottawa, Ont. K1P 5A3

ARMSTRONG, Christopher Gillette Russell, B.A.Sc.; O.L.S.; consulting engineer; b. Merlin, Ont., 8 Oct. 1896; s. Christopher and Alice Avilla (Miffin) A.; e. Univ. of Toronto, B.A.Sc. 1920; Ont. Land Surveyor 1924; m. Edith Helen, d. Frederick S. Archer, Howey, Florida, 20 July 1921; children: Mrs. Harriett Frye, Maurice; PRESIDENT, C. G. RUSSELL ARMSTRONG LTD.; joined Internat. Nickel as Engr. 1917 was successively Engr. for Cities Service Oil & Gas Co., 1918; J. J. Newman (Consulting Engr.) 1919; Owen McKay, Consulting Eng., Windsor and Walkerville, Ont. 1920; Supt. of Construc., Brunner Mond. Canada Ltd., Amherstburg, Ont., 1921; mem. of staff, University of Toronto, 1922-23; formed partnership, Newman & Armstrong, Consulting Engrs. and Surveyors, 1923; firm taken over under the name of C. G. Russell Armstrong, Consulting Engrs. and Land Surveyors 1943 whereupon he became Pres. in the new firm; Past President, Ontario Land Surveyors' Assn., mem., Am. Pub. Works Assn.; Assn. Prof. Engrs. of Ont.; Life mem., Engn. Inst. of Can.; Past Dir. and Hon. mem., Am. Waterworks Assn. (Past Pres., Candn. Sec.); Past Pres., Candn. Inst. on Pollution Control; Past Dir., Water Pollution Control Fed.; Protestant; Freemason recreations: hunting, fishing; Club: Lions International; Home: 3905 Riverside Dr. E., Windsor, Ont. N8Y 1B3; Office: 76 University W., Windsor, Ont. N9A 5N7

ARMSTRONG, Donald Eugene, B.A., B.Com., Ph.D.; management consultant; educator; b. Nanton, Alta. 10 May 1925; s. Samuel Timothy and Laura (Bridges) A.; e. Univ. of Alta., B.A., B.Com. 1950; McGill Univ. Ph.D. 1954; m. Muriel Gladys d. Dr. Frank G. Buchanan 14 May 1947; children: Susan Deryl, Joanne Patricia, Terrence Bruce; PRINC., MANECON ASSOCIATES LTD.; Prof. of Econ. McGill Univ.; mang. consultant practice 1954- ; author "Competition Versus Monopoly: Combines Policy In Perspective" 1982; "Education and Achievement" 1970; various articles transport., econ. forecasting, energy; served with Candn. Inf. Corps 1943-45, rank Lt.; mem. Candn. Chamber Comm. (various nat. comms.); Candn. Econ. Assn.; recreations: swimming, dancing; Address: 3 Westland Dr., Montreal, Que. H4X 1M1.

ARMSTRONG, Doris Marie, B.S., M.Ed. R.N.; nursing administrator; b. Georgetown, Ont. 2 Apl. 1926; d. Frederick Nasau and Pearl (Boomer) A.; e. Elem. and High Schs., Georgetown, Ont.; Brantford (Ont.) Gen. Hosp. Sch. of Nursing, Dipl. 1947; Univ. of Toronto, Course in Clin. Supervision in Operating Room, 1948-49; Johns

Hopkins Univ., B.S. 1957, M.Ed. 1967; Harvard U. Exec. Prog. in Health Systems Management;ASST DIR., HARTFORD HOSP. AND DIR. DEPT: OF NURSING., HARTFORD CONN. Operating Room Nurse, Brantford (Ont.) Gen. Hosp. 1947-48, 1949-50; joined Johns Hopkins Hosp. as Staff Nurse/Head Nurse Operating Room 1950, Instr. Supvr. Operating Room 1953, Asst. Dir. of Nursing, Gen. Operating Room 1958, of Nursing Operative and Acute Care Services 1967-70; former Trustee, St. Paul's Sch. for Boys, Brooklandville, Md.; author of various articles prof. journs.; co-author film "Oral Endoscopy" 1968; mem. Am. Nurses' Assn. Extve Comte. Nursing Service Facilitators 1974; Md. Nurses' Assn. (mem. Bd. Dist. 2 1973); Assn. Operating Room Nurses; American Hosp. Assoc., Council on Professional Services: American Soc. Nursing Admins.; Conneticut Nursing Assoc.; Conneticut Hosp. Assoc.; Hon. mem. The Johns Hopkins Sch. the Nursing Alumni Assoc.; mem. Sigma theta tan; Anglican; recreations: tennis, skiing; Home: 515 Walker Ave., Baltimore, Md. 21212; Office: 601 N. Broadway, Baltimore, Md.

ARMSTRONG, Frederick Henry, M.A., Ph.D.; educator; b. Toronto, Ont. 27 March 1926; s. Silas Henry and Dorothy Lillian (Goode) A.; e. Parkdale Coll. Inst. 1946; Univ. of Toronto B.A. 1949, M.A. 1951, Ph.D. 1965; m. Josephine Joan. d. late Ladislas Biberovich 6 Aug. 1960; children: Dale Henry, Irene Eleanor; PROF. OF HISTORY, UNIV. OF W. ONT. 1975- : served gen. ins. business as underwriter and broker 1951-60; Asst. in Numismatics Royal Ont. Museum 1948-51 (part-time); Instr. in Hist. Univ. of Toronto 1960-62 (part-time), 1962-63 (full-time); Lectr. Univ. of W. Ont. 1963, Asst. Prof. 1965, Assoc. Prof. 1968; Chrmn. Local Arch. Conserv. Adv. Comte, London, Ont. 1979, Vice Chrmn. 1977-78, mem. 1973-79; rec'd Am. Numismatic Soc. Newell Scholarship 1947, 1948; Centennial Comn. Grant 1966; Can. Council Awards 1968, 1969, 1971, 1973, 1974; Am. Soc. for State & Local Hist. Award 1976; Univ. of W. Ont. Pres.'s Medal 1979; Consultant, "Historical Atlas of Canada" 1979- ; mem. Nat. Archival Appraisal Bd. 1974- ; author "Handbook of Upper Canadian Chronology and Territorial Legislation" 1967; "Organizing for Preservation" 1978; co-author "Reflections on London's Past" 1975; "Bibliography of Canadian Urban History" 1980; Ed. or Co-ed. "Toronto of Old" Henry Scadding 1966; "Pioneering in North York" A History of the Borough" 1968; "Approaches to Teaching Local History Using Upper Canadian and Ontario Examples" 1969; "Aspects of Nineteenth Century Ontario; Essays Presented to James J. Talman" 1974; author numerous articles, reviews nineteenth century Ont. and urbanization; over 30 papers and presentations as mem. of panels learned socs.; univs.; mem. Am. Numismatic Soc.; Candn. Hist. Assn.; Champlain Soc. (Council 1974- , Vice Pres, 1980-); Ont. Hist. Soc. (Dir. 1963-65, 1972-80, Vice Pres. 1976-77, Pres. 1977-79); Royal Hist. Soc.; Presbyterian; recreations: photography, gardening, music, travel; Home: 1 Franklin Ave., London, Ont. N6C 2G6; Office: London, Ont. N6A 5C2.

ARMSTRONG, Herbert Stoker, M.A., Ph.D., D.Sc., D.U.C., F.R.S.C.; retired university dean; b. Toronto, Ont., 23 Nov. 1915; s. George Readie and Ethel Frances (Stoker) A.; e. Univ. of Toronto, B.A. 1938; M.A. 1939; Univ. of Chicago, Ph.D. 1942; D.Sc. McMaster 1967; D.U.C. Calgary 1972; m. Helen Kathleen, d. E. J. Halbert, Toronto, 6 Sept. 1941; two d., Catherine Frances, Margaret Shera; PROF. OF GEOLOGY Head, Dept. of Geology, McMaster Univ., 1941-53; Assoc. Prof. Geol. there 1947-48 and Prof. 1948-62; Asst. Dean of Arts and Science, 1946-48; Assoc. Dean of Univ. Coll. 1948-49; Dean of Arts and Science 1950-62; Univ. of Alberta, Prof. of Geol. 1962; Dean of Science 1962-63; Vice-Pres. (Academic) 1963-64; Pres. Univ. of Calgary 1964-68; Univ. of Guelph, Prof. of Geol. 1968-82; Dean of Grad. Studies 1968-80; mem., Candn. Inst. of Mining & Metall.; Geol. Assn. Can.; Geo-

chem. Soc.; Roy. Candn. Geog. Soc.; Candn. Soc. of Petroleum Geols.; Candn. Geol. Foundation; Geol. Soc. Finland; Heraldry Soc. Can., Sigma Xi; Kappa Epsilon Pi (Treas. 1941); Freemason; United Church; Address: 75 Glasgow St. N., Guelph, Ont. N1H 4W1.

ARMSTRONG, Jack Irwin, M.A.; consultant; b. Hamilton, Ont., 21 June 1914; s. Frank Irwin and Edna Banks (Green) A.; e. Delta Coll. Inst., Hamilton, Ont.; McMaster Univ., B.A. 1935, M.A. 1936; Osgoode Hall Law Sch., Toronto, Ont.; m. Rowena Mary, d. late Rev. E. J. Etherington, 5 July 1942; one s. John Gibsone; President, Canadian Textiles Institute, 1970-80; Deputy Services Adm., W.P.T.B., 1943; Deputy Wool Adm., W.P.T.B., 1944-46; Gen. Mgr., Candn. Textiles Inst. 1946-70; read law with Roebuck & Bagwell, Toronto, Ont.; called to the Bar of Ont. 1939; Past Pres. and mem., Inst. of Assn. Extves.; Delta Chi; Conservative; Protestant; recreations: woodworking, music, sports; Home: 34 Laurier Court, Beaconsfield, Que. H9W 4S8

ARMSTRONG, John A. (Jack), B.Sc.; industrial executive; b. Dauphin, Man. 24 March 1917; s. Louisa I. (McDonald) and late Herbert H. H.; e. Univ of Manitoba, B.Sc. (Geol.) 1937; Queen's Univ., B.Sc. (Chem. Engn.) 1942; hon. LL.D., Univ. of Winnipeg, 1978; Univ. of Calgary, 1980; m. June; three s. David, Douglas, Drew; CHAIRMAN AND CHIEF EXTVE. OFFR., IMPERIAL OIL LTD.; Chmn., School of Bus. Admin. Adv. Comte., Univ. of West. Ont., 1980; Dir. Royal Bank of Canada; joined the Co. as Geol., Regina, Sask. 1940; Exploration Mgr. Edmonton Dist. 1951; Gen. Mgr. Producing Dept. Toronto 1960, Dir. 1961, i.c. marketing operations 1963-65, Extve. Vice-Pres. 1966, Pres. 1970, Chief Extve. Offr. 1973, Chrmn. of Bd. 1974; mem., Bd. of Trustees of Fraser Institute; mem. Extve. Bd., Internat. Chamber of Comm.; mem. of numerous associations incl. B.-North American Committee, the Conference Board, Inc., etc.; recreations: golf, hunting; Office: 111 St. Clair Ave. W., Toronto, Ont. M5W 1K3

ARMSTRONG, John B., M.D., F.R.C.P.(C), Dip. Int. Med. (McGill); b. Toronto, Ont., 19 Oct. 1918; s. Charles Henry and Olive May (Buchanan) A.; e. Univ. of Toronto Schs. (1930-37); Univ. of Toronto, M.D. 1943; m. Dorothy Mae Green, Boharm, Sask., 27 May 1944; children: Robert, Stanley, Sheila, Mary; Sr. Med. Consultant, Govt. of Ont.; Assoc. Prof. in Preventive Medicine and Biostatistics, Univ. of Toronto; Res. Training, Royal Victoria Hosp., Montreal, P.Q. 1946-48; Fellow in Med., Duke Univ., Durham, N.C., 1948-49; Registrar, Roy. Post-grad. Med. Sch. of London, Hammersmith Hosp., 1949-50; Asst. Prof., Physiol. and Med. Research, Univ. of Manitoba, 1950-56 (concurrently Asst. Phys., Winnipeg Gen. Hosp.); apptd. Exec. Dir., Canadian Heart Foundation, 1957; Gov. for Ont., Am. Coll. of Cardiol.; mem., Admissions Comte., Duke Univ. Med. Sch.; served in 2nd World War, Capt. R.C.A.M.C. serving in Can., Nfld., U.K., Italy and N.W. Europe; mem., No. 1 Research Lab., R.C.A.M.C.; Fellow, Candn. Life Ins. Offrs. Assn. (1950-52); Markle Scholar in Med. Sciences 1952-56; Lic., Med. Council of Can.; mem., Candn., Cardiovascular Soc. (Councillor 1956-59); Pharm. Soc. Can. (Pres. 1972-3); Candn. Med. Assn.; Candn. Soc. for Clinical Investig. (founder mem.); Am. Heart Assn.; Nu Sigma Nu; United Ch.; Home: 51 Windy Golfway, Don Mills, Ont. M3C 3A6; Office: 15 Overlea Blvd., Toronto, Ont. M4H 1A9

ARMSTRONG, John Edward, M.A.Sc., Ph.D., F.R.S.C. (1950), F.G.S.A. (1945); geologist; Canadian public servant (ret.); b. Cloverdale, B.C., 18 Feb. 1912; s. David Edward and Mary Ellwood (White) A.; e. Univ. of British Columbia, B.A.Sc. (Geol. Engn.) 1934, M.A.Sc. (Geol. Engn.) 1935 (Carnegie Scholarship, 1935; Nicholson Scholarship 1936); Univ. of Toronto, Ph.D. 1939; m. Constance Lilian, d. Harold Crump, Vancouver, B.C., 2nd Oct. 1937; one s. John B.; former Sec.-Gen., XXIV Int.

Geol. Congress; entered Geol. Survey of Can. in 1934; retired 1976; Publications: over 110 papers by Govt. of Can., and in various scient. journals; Roy. Soc. Can. (Past Convener); Hon. Life mem. Geol. Soc. of America; Hon. Life mem. and Past Pres., Vancouver Natural Hist. Soc.; mem. Geol. Assn. of Can.; Gold Medalist, 24th Internat. Geol. Congress 1972; Merit Award, Pub. Service of Can. 1973; Queen's Jubilee Medal 1978; Medaland Diploma, XXVI Int. Geol. Congress (France), 1980; recreations: golf, natural history; Home: 206-2298 McBain Ave., Vancouver, B.C. V6L 3B1; Office: 2298 McBain Ave., Vancouver, B.C. V6L 3B1

ARMSTRONG, Richard Gary, B.Com.; transportation executive; b. North Bay, Ont. 22 Aug. 1938; s. Richard William A.; e. North Bay Coll. (Scollard Hall); St. Patrick's Coll. Ottawa B.Com. 1963; m. Therese Stringer, R.N. 27 June 1964; children: Carolyn, Beth, Richard, Jennifer; CHRMN., PRES. AND CHIEF EXTVE. OFFR., GREAT LAKES PILOTAGE AUTHORITY LTD. 1978- ; Dir. Seaway International Bridge Corp. Ltd.; Dir. of Personnel & Indust. Relations, St. Lawrence Seaway Authority 1972, Dir. of Adm. 1977-79; Secy., Seaway International Bridge Corp. Ltd. 1977-78; Past Dir. Kiwanis Club; Past Chrmn. St. Francis de Sales Parish Council; Past Chrmn. and Dir. Cornwall Youth Residence Inc.; mem. Personnel Assn. Toronto; R. Catholic; recreations: tennis, skiing; Home: 504 Riverdale Ave., Cornwall, Ont. K6S 2K4; Office: 132 Second St. E. (P.O. Box 95), Cornwall, Ont. K6H 5R9.

ARMSTRONG, Robert Douglas, B.Com., F.C.A.; retired mining executive; b. Ottawa, Ont., 25 Apl. 1916; s. William Allan and Jennie (Barry) A.; e. Pub. and High Schs., Ottawa, Ont.; Queen's Univ., B.Com. 1937; m. Dorothea, d. R. E. W. Fairleigh, Seattle, Wash., 29 Dec. 1944; children: Michael, Brock, Robert, Barbara; Chrmn., Ch. Ex. Off. and Director, Lornex Mining Corp. Ltd.; Preston Mines Ltd.; Vice Pres. and Dir., Tinto Holdings Ltd.; Dir., Canada Perm. Trust; Canada Perm. Mortgage; Marathon Realty; Algoma Steel Corp.; joined Price Waterhouse as C.A. Student 1937; assoc. with Imperial Oil Co. Ltd. for 10 yrs. in W. Can. at Calgary devel.; Div. of Finance and Adm., A. V. Roe (Hawker Siddeley); Vice Pres. Accounting and Finance, Canadian National Railway; Vice Pres., Corporate Planning, Chrysler Canada Ltd., Windsor, Ont. then Extve. Vice Pres.; subsequently went to U.S. in charge of Dealer Dev., U.S. Continental, Miami, Dallas, Houston, San Francisco; Asst. Gen. Mgr., Div. of Chrysler, Plymouth for U.S.; Pres., Chrysler Leasing Corp.; Chrmn., C.E.O. and Dir., Rio Algom Ltd. 1975-81 (ret.); served as Gunner during World War II; rank Lt.; Pres., Candn. Foundation, 1964; Clubs: St. James's (Montreal); The Toronto; The Vancouver; Lambton Golf & Country; Rosedale; Granite; Home: 30 Glenorchy Dr., Don Mills, Ont. M3C 2P9

ARMSTRONG, Robert L., B.A., LL.B.; trust company executive; b. Fredericton, N.B., 10 July 1914; s. Franklyn Ludlam and Willamina (Henry) A.; e. Univ. of N.B., B.A.; Dalhousie Univ. Law Sch., LL.B.; m. Lilian Irene, d. late Alexander McLean, 29 June 1940; four d., Margaret Patricia, Barbara Ann, Elizabeth McLean, Mary Jane; Vice Pres. Guaranty Trust Co. of Canada since 1972-80; Pres. Hospital Special Needs Inc.; read law with Hanson, Dougherty & West; called to Bar of N.B. 1940; law practice 1940-80; joined Guaranty Trust Co. 1945, Corporate Trust Dept.; held various appts. incl. Gen. Mgr. 1970; served with RCAF 1941-45; Flying Instr.; Mentioned in Despatches; Bd. Trade Metrop. Toronto (Past Chrmn., Club); Vice Pres., Candn. Cancer Soc., Toronto Unit; Chrmn., John Graves Simcoe Mem. Foundation; P. Conservative; Anglican; recreations: tennis, bridge, gardening; Clubs: Queen's (Dir.); Empire (Pres. 1973-74); Lawrence Park Tennis (Pres. 1980-81); Home: 61 Dalewood Rd., Toronto, Ont. M4P 2N4

ARMSTRONG, Robin Louis, B.A., M.Sc., Ph.D., F.R.S.C.; physicist; educator; b. Galt, Ont. 14 May 1935; s. Robert Dockstader and Beatrice Jenny (Grill) A.; e. Hespeler (Ont.) Pub. Sch. 1949; Preston (Ont.) High Sch. 1954; Univ. of Toronto B.A. 1958, M.Sc. 1959, Ph.D. 1961; Oxford Univ. post-doctoral studies 1961-62 (Nat. Research Council Fellowship, Rutherford Mem. Fellowship Royal Soc. Can.); m. Karen Elisabeth d. Carl Frederick Feilberg Hansen 8 July 1960; children: Keir Grill, Christopher Drew; DEAN OF ARTS AND SCIENCE, UNIV. OF TORONTO 1982- ; Asst. Prof. of Physics 1962, Assoc. Prof. 1968 and of Engn. Science 1969, Prof. of Physics 1971- , Prof. of Engn. Science 1971-74, Assoc. Chrmn. of Physics 1969-74, Chrmn. 1974-82; Dir. Candn. Inst. Advanced Research 1981- ; rec'd Herzberg Medal Candn. Assn. Physicists 1973; co-author "Mechanics, Waves and Thermal Physics" 1970; "The Electromagnetic Interaction" 1973; over 100 research publs. condensed matter physics various tech. journs.; mem. Candn. Assn. Physicists; Am. Phys. Soc.; Soc. Magnetic Resonance; recreations: jogging, skiing, golf; Home: 540 Huron St., Toronto, Ont. M5R 2R7; Office: University of Toronto, Faculty of Arts and Science, Toronto, Ontario, M5S 1A1

ARMSTRONG, William McColl, B.A.Sc., F.R.S.C. (1969), D.Sc.; retired educator; b. Hamilton, Ont., 27 Oct. 1915; s. William John and Ruth Hetherington (Armstrong) A.; e. Univ. of Toronto, B.A.Sc. (Hons.) 1937; m. Elsje Larson, d. Allard de Ridder, 10 March 1970; commenced as Supv., Metall. Labs., Steel Co. of Canada, Hamilton, Ont. 1937; Research Metall. (Dofasco Research Fellow) Ont. Research Foundation, Toronto 1943; with B.C. Research Council 1946; joined present Univ., Assoc. Prof., Dept. Metall. 1946, Prof. 1954, Prof. and Head Dept. 1964-65, Dean, Faculty Applied Science 1966-69, Depy. Acting Pres. 1967; Prof. of Metall. and Depy. Pres., Univ. of B.C. 1968-80 (ret.) Chrmn., Univ. of B.C. Comte. on Patents and Patent Rights since 1964; Council of Continuing Educ. for Engrs., Univ. of B.C. since 1966; Secy., Bd. Govs. 1967-; mem. Science Council Can.; Adv. Council, B.C. Inst. Tech.; Can. Council of Prof. Engrs.; Candn. Inst. Mining & Metall.; Am. Inst. Mining, Metall. & Petroleum Engrs.; Am. Foundrymen's Soc. (Past Chrmn. B.C. Chapter); Am. Soc. for Metals (Past Chrmn. B.C. Chapter); Am. Ceramic Soc.; Electrochem. Soc.; Engn. Inst. Can.; Candn. Research Mang. Assn. (mem. Extve. Comte.); mem. Bd. Mang., B.C. Research Council: NRC Adv. Comte on Applied and Engn. Research; Chrmn. Univs. Council of B.C. (1974); Exec. Dir., Research Secretariat, Govt. of B.C. (1978); Publications: numerous articles in leading learned and prof. journs.; rec'd Distinguished Lectr. Award, Candn. Inst. Mining & Metall.; Centennial Medal 1967; Alcan Award C.I.M.M. 1974; Fellow, A.S.M. 1974; Gold Medal of Candn. Council of Prof. Engrs. 1974; recreations: skiing, sailing, mountaineering, orchids, chamber music; Home: 2194 W. 57th Ave., Vancouver 14, B.C. V6P 1V4

ARMSTRONG, William T., B.A.; broadcasting executive; b. Wakefield, Que., 8 Dec. 1929; s. Francis Kenneth and Lillian Amy Daisy (Orme) A.; e. Wakefield (P.Q.) Consol. Sch.; Glebe Coll. Inst., Ottawa, Ont., Sr. Matric. 1947; Carleton Univ., B.A. 1952; m. Margaret, d. George Pilmer, Victoria, B.C., 4 June 1955; children: Andrew, Jessica, Alison; GENERAL MANAGER, NEW MASSEY HALL (TORONTO) 1981-; member, Bd. of Govs. Massey Hall; Managing Dir. Radio. CBC 1975-1979; with E. B. Eddy. Co., Hull, P.Q., 1952-58 in Indust. Relations Div. and finally (1956-58) Public Relations Offr.; joined C.B.C., Apl. 1958 as Audience Relations Coordinator; Dir. of Information Services, 1959-62; Secy., Commonwealth Broadcasting Conf. 1962-63; Extve. Asst. to Pres. 1963-65; Dir., Centennial Program Planning 1965-67; Dir., Corporate Relations 1967-69; Dir. Ottawa Area 1967; Vice Pres. Public Relations 1973; Asst. Gen. Mgr., Eng. Serv. Div. 1973-81; has been active in Ottawa theatrical circles, former Dir. of Ottawa Little Theatre, Organist and Choirmaster, St. Mathias Ch., Ottawa, 1955-64; Founding mem., Candn. Public Relations Soc. (mem. Nat. Council, 1959-61, Nat. Secy., 1961-62); mem. Royal Candn. Coll. Organists; Anglican; recreations: music, theatre; Clubs: Cercle Universitaire; Celebrity Club; The Country; Home: 5 Inglewood Dr., Toronto M4T 1G7

ARNASON, Thomas Johann, B.Sc., M.A., Ph.D.; professor emeritus; b. Brown, Man. 25 Nov. 1905; s. Thordur and Sigurros (Thomasson) A.; e. Univ. of Saskatchewan B.Sc. 1931, M.A. 1932; Univ. of Wisconsin Ph.D. 1934; m. Gwendolyn Evert 11 Sept. 1935; children: Lynn Katherine, Stefanie Thordis, Averil Evert; PROF. EMERITUS, DEPT. OF BIOLOGY, UNIV. OF SASKATCHEWAN (Dept. head 1967-68); Rawson Chair of Biol. 1970-73; served with COTC 1944; author of forty-five research articles in plant genetics and cytology; location of genes on wheat chromosomes; sterility in potatoes; cytoplasmic inheritance; effects of radiations and chemicals on chromosomes and genes; contributions made to knowledge of the effects of various treatments on chromosome breakage rates and gene mutation rates; mem., Am. Assn. for the Advancement of Science; Genetics Soc. of Can. (Pres. 1957-58); Home: 1032 Aird St., Saskatoon, Sask. S7N 0T1;

ARNFIELD, Robert Frank; company president; b. Vienna, Austria, 3 Apl. 1924; e. Rossall Sch., Lancs., Eng., 1939-42; Manchester Univ., 1942-45 (Hons. Chem); m. Mary Maughan Barnes, 2 Oct. 1948; two s. Richhard Nigel, Mark Robert; PRESIDENT, TORONTO POTTERY SUPPLIES and SERVICES LTD.; Pres. Arnfield Industrial Projects Ltd.; Research, Calico Printers, Eng., 1945-46; Unilever, Eng., 1946-54; served as Mang. Trainee, Asst. Plant Mgr., Eng. and Plant Mgr., Bangkok, Thailand; Mang. Consultant, Anne Shaw Organ., Eng., 1954-57; Plant Mgr., Bate Chemical Corp., Toronto, 1957-58; Plant Mgr., Davenport Containers, 1958-60; joined Consumers Glass Co. Ltd., Toronto, 1960; served as Asst. Plant Mgr., Mgr.-Engn. and Tech. Services; Vice Pres. (Tech. Services and Research), 1969; mem., Chem. Inst. Can.; Candn. Ceramic Soc. (Pres. 1970-71); Am. Ceramic Soc.; Assoc. Royal Inst. Chem.; Liberal; Anglican; Home: 14 Colwood Rd., Islington, Ont. M9A 4E3; Office: UNIT 1 7385 Torbram Rd. Mississauga, Ont., L4T 349

ARNOLD, Armin Herbert, Dr. ès Lettres, F.R.S.C.; educator; author; b. Zug, Switzerland 1 Sept. 1931; s. Franz and Ida (Baumgartner) A.; e. Univ. of Fribourg 1951-53, 1955-56 Dr. ès Lettres 1956; Univ. of Zurich 1953-54; Univ. of London 1954-55; PROF. OF GERMAN, McGILL UNIV. since 1968; Asst. Prof. of German, Univ. of Alta. 1959-61; Asst. Prof. McGill Univ. 1961, Assoc. Prof. 1964, Chrmn. German Dept. 1965-70, 1971-74; author "D. H. Lawrence and America" 1958; "Heinrich Heine in England and America" 1959; "James Joyce" Berlin 1963, Eng. transl. 1969; "D. H. Lawrence and German Literature" 1963; "G. B. Shaw" Berlin 1965; "Die Literature des Expressionismus" 1966, 2nd ed. 1971; "Felix Stümpers Abenteuer und Streiche" 1967; "Friedrich Dürrenmatt" Berlin 1969, 2d ed. 1971, 3rd ed. 1974, 4th ed. 1979, Eng. transl. 1972; "D. H. Lawrence" Berlin 1972; "Prosa des Expressionismus" 1972; "D. H. Lawrence: The Symbolic Meaning" 1962; "Kriminalerzählungen aus drei Jahrhunderten" 1978; "Interpretationen zu Georg Kaiser" 1980; "Sherlock Holmes auf der Hintertreppe" 1981; "Western-geschihten aus zwei Darhumderten" 1981; co-author with J. Schmidt "Reclams Kriminalromanführer"; co-editor "Studien zur Germanistik, Anglistik und Komparatistik" 106 vols. 1969-82; "Canadian Studies in German Language and Literature" 28 vols. 1969-82; co-ed. "Kanadische Erzähler der Gegenwart" 1967; "Das Goethe-Haus Montreal 1962-70" 1970; Lit. Critic "Neue Zürcher Zeitung" 1955-70; "Die Welt" 1964-71; numerous prefaces, introductions and articles in books, Candn. and foreign prof. journs.; R. Catholic; Home: 9e rang, Ste-Anne de la Rochelle, Que.

J0E 2B0; Office: 1001 Sherbrooke St. W., Montreal, Que. H3A 1G5.

ARNOLD, Edward S., B.Sc.; winemaker; b. B.C. 8 June; e. Univ. of B.C. B.Sc.; children: Stephen, Carolyn, David, Joanne; PRES. T. G. BRIGHT & CO. LTD.; Dir. T.G. Bright (Quebec) Ltd.; Les Vins La Salle; mem. Outward Bound; Ont. Inst. Agrols.; Wine Council Ont. (Chrmn.); recreations: swimming, golf; Club: Niagara Falls; Home: R.R.2 Mountain View Rd. S., Beamsville, Ont. L0R 1B0; Office: P.O. Box 510, Niagara Falls, Ont. L2E 6V4.

ARNOLD, John Timothy, B.A., M.B.A.; building supplies executive; b. Winnipeg, Man. 12 Feb. 1936; s. John Stewart Homer Arnold; e. Mount Royal High Sch. 1952; McGill Univ. B.A. 1958; Simon Fraser Univ. M.B.A. 1970; m. Maureen Gail d. William A. Patrick, Christina Lake, B.C. 17 Dec. 1960; children: Karen Elizabeth, Stephanie Gail, Kevin Patrick; PRES., OCEAN CONSTRUCTION SUPPLIES LTD., 1979- ; Mang. Trainee Halgary 1958-59; Supvr. Econ. & Evaluations Mobil Oil of Canada Ltd. Calgary 1959-63; Financial & Market Analyst B.C. Hydro & Power Authority Vancouver 1963-65; joined present Co. 1965 serving as Mgr. Planning & Devel., Mgr. Marketing, Vice Pres. & Gen. Mgr. Concrete Products & Bldg. Materials, Vice Pres. and Gen. Mgr. Ready Mix, Aggregate & Marine; mem. Vancouver Bd. Trade; Phi Delta Theta; Protestant; recreations: racquetball, squash, tennis; Clubs: Hollyburn Country; Vancouver Lawn Tennis & Badminton; Men's Canadian; Home: 3795 Southridge Ave., West Vancouver, B.C. V7V 3H9; Office: (P.O. Box 2300) Vancouver, B.C. V6B 3W6.

ARNOTT, Gordon R., B.Arch., F.R.A.I.C., F.A.I.A. (Hon.); b. Winnipeg, Man., 1 Aug. 1926; e. Univ. of Man. B.Arch. (Khaki Mem. Bursaries, R.A.I.C. Gold Medal) 1948; PRES., ARNOTT MACPHAIL ASSOCS. LTD. since 1974; Princ., Gordon Ryan Arnott 1950-51; Community & Regional Planning Central Mortgage & Housing Fellowship Univ. of B.C. 1951-52; Townsite Planning & Liaison Arch., Aluminum Co. of Canada, Vancouver-Kitimat 1952-53; Partner, Izumi & Arnott, Regina 1954, Izumi, Arnott, Sugiyama 1954-68; Princ., Gordon R. Arnott & Assoc. 1968-74; recent awards and comns.; Massey Medal Hon. Mention 1958; Vincent Massey Award of Excellence in Urban Environment (Midtown Plaza, Saskatoon) 1971; T.C. Douglas Bldg., Wascana Centre, Regina; First place, Wascana Centre Restaurant & H.Q. competition 1975; Addition to Western College of Veterinary Medicine, Saskatoon; Queen's Jubilee Medal 1977; Pres. (1970-71) Royal Arch. Inst. Can., mem. Sask. Assn. Archs. (Past Pres.); Candn. Inst. Planners; Nat. Design Council Can. (1973-79); Pres. Assiniboia Club, Regina 1977-78; Hon. mem. Mexican Soc. Archs., Office: 2275 Albert St., Regina, Sask. S4P 2V5

ARNUP, Hon. John Douglas, LL.D., D.Litt.S., judge; b. Toronto, Ont., 24 May 1911; s. Jesse Henry and Ella Maud (Leeson) A.; e. Oakwood Coll. Inst., Toronto, Ont.; Victoria Coll., Univ. of Toronto, B.A. 1932; Osgoode Hall, Toronto, Ont.; LL.D. Queen's Univ. 1967; York University 1969; D.Litt.S., Victoria Univ. 1976; m. Caroline Dora, d. Jan Ulrichsen, Beaverton, Ont., 2 Aug. 1941; children: Judith Ann (Dickson), Carol Elizabeth, Mary Katherine, Caroline Jane (Leising); JUDGE, COURT OF APPEAL, ONT. since 1970; Bencher, Law Soc. of Upper Can., 1952-70; called to the Bar of Ont., Sept. 1935; cr. K.C. 1950; former partner, Arnup, Foulds, Weir, Boeckh & Morris; mem. of Senate, Univ. of Toronto, 1945-50; Bd. of Regents, Victoria Univ., 1960-70; Treas., Law Soc, of Upper Can. 1963-66; mem. Candn. Bar Assn.; United Church; recreations: curling, golf; Clubs: Toronto Cricket, Skating, Curling; Lawyers (Past Pres.); Home: 88 Stratford Cres., Toronto, Ont. M4N 1C6; Office: Osgoode Hall, Toronto, Ont. M5H 2N5

ARONOFF, Samuel, A.B., Ph.D.; educator; b. Brooklyn, N.Y., 27 Feb. 1915; s. Esa and Sonia (Berchatsky) A.; e. Univ. of Calif. (Los Angeles) A. B. 1936, (Berkeley) Ph.D. 1942; m. Edith Elizabeth, d. Everett R. Moyer, Syracuse, N.Y., 1936; three d., Zena Katherine, Elizabeth Anne, Margaret Ruth; PROF. OF BIOCHEM., SIMON FRASER UNIV.; mem. Am. Soc. Biol. Chems.; Candn. Soc. Biol. Chem.; Can. Soc. Plant Physiol.; Am. Chem Soc.; Am. Soc. Plant Physiols.; Am. Soc. Advanc. Science; Home: Burnaby., B.C. V5B 1P9; Office: Burnaby, B.C. V5A 1S6

ARONOVITCH, Edgar Judah; real estate and insurance broker; b. Winnipeg, Man., 5 Oct. 1908; s. Abraham Herman and Gertrude (Leipsic) A.; e. Pub. Sch. and Kelvin High Sch., Winnipeg, Man., m. Reva, d. E. Greenberg, 4 June 1933; children: Brian Thomas, Donald Neil; joined Aronovitch and Leipsic Ltd. 1926; Chrmn. of Board 1976; President of Boyd Bldg. Ltd., Grant Park Plaza Corp., Arle Realty Ltd., Mid-Canada Mortg. Corp.; McGillivray Inv. Ltd.; Mountbatten Dev. Ltd.; Director of Graham Inv. Ltd., Can. Counc. of Christians and Jews, Can. Friends of the Hebrew Univ.; Gov. B'nai B'rith Fndn.; Past Pres. Downtown Bus. Men's Ass.; mem. Winnipeg Ch. of Comm., United Jewish Appeal, Soc. of Industr. Realtors, Int. Real Estate Fed., Nat. Ass. of Real Estate Boards, Am. Soc. of Real Est. Counsellors, Fellow at the Real Estate Institute; recreation: golf; Clubs: Glendale Country; B'nai B'rith; Home: 801—200 Tuxedo Blvd., Winnipeg, Man. R3P 0R3; Office: —167 Lombard Ave., Winnipeg, Man. R3B 0V3

ARONOVITCH, Hon. Harry L.; B.A., LL.M.; judge; b. Montreal, Que., 12 Feb. 1912; s. Isaac and Minnie (Miller) A.; e. High Sch. of Montreal, (Que.); Mcgill Univ., B.A. 1933; Univ. of Montreal, LL.M. 1938; m. Jean. d. Shei Resin, 24 Sept. 1942; children: Charles, Hilliard; JUDGE OF SUPERIOR COURT OF QUE. since 1969; called to Bar of Que. 1938; cr. Q.C. 1964; served with R.C.A.F. during World War II; Hon. Pres., Tifereth Beth David Jerusalem Synagogue; Past Chrmn., Que. Command Royal Candn. Legion; Home: 6505 Cote St. Luc Rd., Apt. PH6, Cote St. Luc, Que. H4V 1G3; Office: 1 Notre Dame St. E., Room 15.39, Montreal H2Y 1B6

ARONOVITCH, Michael, B.Sc., M.D., C.M., F.R.C.P.(C); physician; b. Montreal, P.Q. 15 Apl. 1910; s. Isak and Minnie (Miller) T.; e. McGill University, B.Sc. (Arts) 1931; M.D., C.M., 1935; m. Katherine Louisa, d. S. Silver, Montreal, P.Q., 30 Dec. 1945; children: Jane Ellen, Stephen Arnold, Carol Ann, Isaac Lawrence; Phys. in Chief, Mt. Sinai Hosp. Montreal; Consultant, Montreal Chest Hospital Centre;; Honorary Phys., Royal Victoria Hosp.; Chest Consultant, Herbert Reddy Mem. Hosp.; Bellechasse Hosp., Montreal; Former Assoc.Prof. of Med. and Clinical Med., McGill Univ.; former Chrmn. of Bd., Fulcrum Investment Co. Ltd.; Pres. Armika Corp. Ltd.; former Dir. and Chrmn of Bd., Alphatext Ltd.; Past Consultant, Grace Dart Hospital, Montreal and Dept. Veterans Affairs; private practice specializing in Internal Medicine and Chest Diseases; Major, R.C.A.M.C., 1942-46; author of many articles mostly on internal medicine; mem., Candn. Med. Assn., Med.-Chirurg. Soc. of Montreal; Montreal Clinical Soc. (Pres., 1952-53); mem. of Council, Jewish Health Agencies of Montreal; Fellow Royal Coll. of Physicians; Fellow Am. Coll. of Phys.; Fellow, Am. Coll. of Chest Phys.; Assoc. mem., Roy. Coll. of Phys., London, Eng.; Home: 1530 Dumfries, Town of Mount Royal, Que. H3P 2R4; Office: 5858 Cote des Neiges, Ste. 318, Montreal, Que. H3S 1Z1

ARSENAULT, Raymond L., B.A.Sc.; Eng. executive; b. Verdun, Québec, 24 July, 1929; e. Ecole Polytechnique de Montréal, Univ. de Montréal B.A.Sc. (Civil Engn.) 1956; McGill Univ. post-grad. work Business Adm.; m. Thérèse Bélisle, Arthur Bélisle; children: Raymond Jr., Louise and HélènePRESIDENT AND DIR., GLOBE REALTY LTD. (subsidiary of The Royal Bank of Canada)

1980; Vice Pres. and Dir. Globe Realty Management Ltd.; joined Royal Bank as Supvr. Bank Premises 1968, Asst. Gen. Mgr. 1970. Depy. Gen. Mgr. 1973, Vice Pres. Real Estate Resources 1978; mem. Ordre des Ingénieurs du Québec; Engn. Inst. Can.; Assn. des Diplômés de l'Univ. de Montréal; Assn. des Diplômés de Polytechnique; Gov. St-Luc Hosp.; Clubs: St. Denis; Laval-sur-le-Lac Golf; Home: 2299 Graham Boulevard, Town of Mount Royal, Quebec H3R 1H8. Office: (P.O. Box 6001) 1 Place Ville Marie, Montréal, Québec H3C 3A9

ARSENEAU, Robert John, B.A., B.C.L.; b. Bathurst, N.B. 10 Dec. 1942; s. Gerard C. and Margaret (Christie) A.; e. Harkins Acad. High Sch. Newcastle, N.B. 1960; Univ. of N.B. B.A. 1964, B.C.L. 1968; m. (Mary) Colleen d. Sam Howe, Newcastle, N.B. 3 May 1969; ASSOC., LADNER, DOWNS since 1981; Mem. Canada Labour Relations Bd. since 1975-81; Solr. N.B. Dept. of Justice 1968-71; Sr. Partner Bryden & Arseneau, Fredericton, N.B. 1971-75; called to Bar of N.B. 1968; called to bar of B.C. 1981; mem. N.B. Barristers Soc.; B.C. Law Society; Candn. Bar Assn.; recreation: long distance running; Home: 2997 West Seventh Ave., Vancouver, B.C. V6K 1Z7 Office: 2100 Pacific Centre South, Box 10021, 700 West Georgia St., Vancouver, B.C. V7Y 1A8.

ARTHUR, Eric Ross, C.C., B.Arch., M.A., LL.D., F.R.A.I.C., F.R.I.B.A., R.C.A.; prof. emeritus, arch. Univ. of Toronto; b. Dunedin, New Zealand, 1 July 1898; s. Frederick and Jean A.; m. Doris Debert; children: Paul, Jean (Mrs. Derrick Leach); D. Litt., Univ. of Guelph (Hon. Causa) 1982; Holt Travelling Scholar; Lord Leverhulme Prizeman, Civic Design (Univ. of Liverpool); Chairman of the Jury, Int. Competition for City Hall and Square in Toronto; cons. to the Steel Co. of Canada Ltd.; Univ. of Liverpool, Eng., Lord Kitchener Nat. Memorial Scholar 1919; one of Founders of Arch. Conservancy of Ont.; Appointed University College Architect, 1964; Companion Order of Canada 1968; Can. Council Medal 'for outstanding cultural achievement' 1968; Corp. of City of Toronto Award of Merit for distinguished pubic service; Am. Assn. of State and Local Hist. award of merit 1965; Centennial Medal 1967; Univ. of Alberta Gold Medal 1956 for disting. service to arts and arch. in Canada; author of 'Toronto, No Mean City' (1964); 'Old Buildings in Ontario', ''St. Andrew's Niagara-on-the-Lake''; ''18th and 19th Century Buildings in Ontario''; ''From Front St. to Queen's Park: The Story of Ontario's Parliament Buildings''; co-author, ''Iron: Cast and Wrought Iron in Canada from the Seventeenth Century to the Present,'' 1982; co-author, ''Moose Factory'', ''Old Forts in Upper Canada'', ''Guide to Hospital Building in Ontario'', ''The Barn, a Vanishing Landmark in North America'' (with Dudley D. Witney); co-author with James Acland, ''Buildings by the Sea''; served as rifleman with N.Z. Rifle Bgde., in World War I; as Ordinary Seaman in World War II; recreations: fishing, gardening; Clubs: Arts and Letters; Faculty: York; Home: 41 Weybourne Cres., Toronto, Ont. M4N 2R4

ARTHURS, Harry William, B.A., LL.M.; educator; b. Toronto, Ont., 9 May 1935; s. Leon and Ellen (Dworkin) A.; e. Oakwood Coll. Inst., Toronto 1952; Univ. of Toronto, B.A. 1955, L.L.B. 1958; Harvard Law Sch., LL.M. 1959; PROF. OF LAW, OSGOODE HALL LAW SCHOOL since 1968; read law with S.L. Robins, Q.C., Toronto; called to the Bar of Ont. 1961; Assist. Prof., Osgoode Hall Law Sch. 1961; Assoc. Prof. 1964, Prof. 1968, Assoc. Dean 1968-70; Dean 1972-77; Visiting Lectr. Faculty of Law, Univ. of Toronto 1965-66; Faculty of Law, McGill Univ. 1967-68; Visiting Fellow, Clare Hall, Cambridge 1971; Visiting Fellow, Centre for Socio-Legal Studies, Oxford, 1977-78; Arbitrator and Conciliator in Labour disputes since 1962; Impartial Chrmn., Men's and Ladies' Garment Industry, Toronto since 1967; Pres. Candn. Civil Liberties Assn. 1976-77; Chief Adjudicator, Public Service of Can. 1967-69; mem. Candn. Bar Assn., Candn.

Assn. Law Teachers; Assn. Am. Law Schs.; Labour Arbitration Panel, Ont. Dept. Labour; York Co. Law Assn.; Labour Arbitration Panel, Am. Arbitration Assn.; Candn. mem. Un. Auto Workers Public Review Bd. 1967-77; Mem. Economic Council of Can. 1978-81; Ben-cher, Law Soc. of Upper Can. 1979-; Chmn. Consultative Group on Legal Research and Ed. S.S.H.R.C. 1980-; author of numerous articles and monographs on labour relations law, civil liberties, adm. law, legal history and educ. in learned and prof. journs.; Home: 11 Hillcrest Park, Toronto, Ont. M4X 1E8; Office: York Univ., 4700 Keele St., Downsview, Ont. M3J 2R5

ASH, Stuart Bradley, RCA, AGI, AIGA, GDC; graphic designer and instructor; b. Hamilton, Ont. 10 July 1942; s. Clifford and Margaret A.; e. Western Tech. Sch. (graphic design); Ont. Coll. of Art (graphic design) grad. 1962; PRINCIPAL, GOTTSCHALK & ASH INTERNAT DESIGN CONSULTANTS TORONTO, MONTREAL, NEW YORK, ZURICH since 1966; design work has been published, exhibited, and given awards internationally; Instructor at Ontario Coll. of Art (Advanced Typography) 1978-80; recreations: sailing, skiing; Home: 167 Madison Ave., Toronto, Ont. M5R 2S6; Office: 322 King St.W., Toronto, Ont. M5V 1J4

ASHBY, Roger Arthur, B.Sc.(Comm.), C.G.A., R.I.A.; executive; b. Marieville, Que. 2 Nov. 1940; s. Emmett and Aurore (Ledoux) A.; e. Univ. of Montreal B.Sc.(Comm.) 1963; Soc. of Mgmt. Accts. of Can. C.G.A., R.I.A. 1966; m. Marguerite d. Louis Kelly 12 Feb. 1966; children: Eric, Alexandre; PRES., DOMTAR PULP AND PAPER PRODUCTS; Pres. and Chief Exec. Offr., Spruce Falls Power and Paper Co. Ltd.; Exec. Vice Pres. and Chief Operating Offr., Rolland Inc. 1978-80; served one year Royal Military Coll. - Navy; mem., Candn. Pulp and Paper Assn. (Technical Section); Catholic; Club: St. James; recreations: skiing, racquet ball, tennis; Home: 65 Pagnuelo, Outremont, Que. H2V 3B8; Office: 395 deMaisonneuve St. W., Montreal, Que. H3A 1L6

ASHFORTH, Albert Clifford; b. Toronto, Ont., 6 March 1893; s. late William of Manchester, Eng., and of late Mary (Hall) A.; e. Palmerston Sch., and Harbord Collegiate, Toronto, Ont.; m. Annetta Lillian, d. Henry Ross, Mount Albert, Ont., 5 Sept. 1921; two s.; Hon. Pres., Health League of Canada; Pres., Candn. Chamber of Com., 1958-60; mem. Advisory Comte., Boys Scouts Assn.; Hon. Pres., St. John's Convalescent Hosp., Newtonbrook, Ont.; Hon. member, Board of Regents, Victoria Univ., Toronto; mem. of Adv. Bd., CARE of Can.; began as Jr. with the Bank of Hamilton, Toronto, Ont., 1909; Jr., The Dominion Bank, Toronto, Ont., 1910; Gen. Mgrs. Secy., 1921; Supervisor, 1929; Mgr. Main Office, 1934; Asst. Gen. Mgr., H.O., 1946; Gen. Mgr., 1948; Vice-Pres. and Dir., 1951-55; Pres., The Toronto-Dominion Bank, 1955-60; Hon. director, Canada Life Ass. Co.; former mem., of Council, Toronto Bd. Trade; Freemason (P.M., R.A.M.); United Church; recreation: golf; Clubs: National; Rotary; Canadian; Board of Trade (Past Chrmn.); Home: 18 Glenallan Road, Toronto, Ont. M4N 1G7; Office: 68 Yonge St., Toronto, Ont. M5E 1L1

ASPER, Israel Harold, B.A., LL.M., Q.C.; b. Minnedosa, Man., 11 Aug. 1932; s. Leon and Cecilia (Zwet) A.; e. Univ. of Man., B.A. 1953, LL.B. 1957, LL.M. 1964; m. Ruth Miriam, d. J.M. Bernstein, Winnipeg, Man., 27 May 1956; children: David, Gail, Leonard; founder Buchwald, Asper, Henteleff; former M.L.A. and Leader of Liberal Party in Man.; Chairman of the Board: Global Ventures Western Ltd.; Global Communications Limited; CanWest Broadcasting Ltd.; Crown Trust Company; The Monarch Life Assurance Company; Universal Subscription Television, Inc.; Vice-Chairman: Na-Churs Plant Food Company; President and Chief Executive Officer: CanWest Direction and Planning Inc. read law with L.S. Matlin, Q.C. and Harold Buchwald, Q.C.; called to Bar of Man. 1957;

formed Asper & Co. 1959 and subsequently merged with Buchwald, Henteleff & Co.; Dir. and Law Teacher, Comm. Law, Man. Inst. C.A.'s, 1967-70; Dir. and Teacher of Taxation Course, Man. Bar Administrations Law Graduating Class; Special Lectr., Estate Planning, Univ. of Man. Law Sch., 1970-71; Co-Founder, Legal Accounting Assn.; Isaac Pitblado Lecture Series on Continuing Legal Educ.; Ford Foundation Visiting Prof., Univ. of W. Ont. Sch. of Business Adm., 1969; mem. Adv. Bd., Candn. Scholarship Trust; Dir., Man. Theatre Centre; Winnipeg Summer Theatre Assn.; Chrmn., Policies for Devel. Committee, Man. Govt. Commission on Targets for Econ. Devel., 1968-69; author: "The Benson Iceberg: A Critical Analysis of the White Paper on Tax Reform in Canada", 1970; weekly column on taxation nationally syndicated; also articles, papers and lectures; mem. Candn. Bar Assn. (Council Man. Sec.); Candn. Tax Foundation; Man. Law Soc.; Man. Bar Assn.; Candn. Council of Christians & Jews (Dir.); Prof. Lit. Assn.; Liberal; Hebrew; recreations: tennis, boating, music; Home: 1063 Wellington Cres., Winnipeg, Man. R3N 0A1; Office: 1900 Lakeview Square, Winnipeg, Man.

ASSELIN, Hon. Martial, P.C.(Can.), Q.C.,; senator; b. La Malbaie, P.Q., 3 Feb 1924; s. Martial and Eugénie (Tremblay) A.; e. Semy. Chicoutimi, B.A.; Laval Univ., LL.L.; Univ. de Montréal; m. Pierette Bouchard, d. Albert Bouchard Beauport, 14 Feb. 1953; two s., Bernard, Louis; called to the Bar of Que., 1951; cr. Q.C., 1963; Mayor of La Malbaie, P.Q.; during 2nd World War with C.O.T.C., Laval Univ.; Pres., Laval Univ. Student Council, 1950; mem. of H. of C. for Charlevoix 1958-62; apptd. Min. of Forestry in Diefenbaker Cabinet March 1963; def. in g.e. Apl. 1963; re-el. g.e. Nov. 1965; Del. of Can. at U.N., New York, 1959 and 1960; to Nato -Conf. in London, 1958; Del. of U.N. to Africa (Ruanda, Urundi), 1961; summoned to Senate of Can. 1972; P. Conservative; Roman Catholic; Address: C.P. 578, 320 St.-Etienne, La Malbaie, Charlevoix County, Que. G0T 1J0

ATCHISON, Clarence Edward, B.A., LL.D.; financial executive; b. Winnipeg, Man., 1913; e. Pub. Schs., Winnipeg, Man.; Univ. of Manitoba, B.A. 1933; LL.D. Univ. Winnipeg 1973; m. Mary L. Macoomb, Winnipeg, Man., 1945; three d.; Dir., Investors Group; Investors Group Trust Co. Ltd.; Investors Mutual of Canada Ltd.; Investors Growth Fund of Canada Ltd.; Investors International Mutual Fund Ltd.; Investors Dividend Fund; Investors Japanese Growth Fund Ltd.; Provident Stock Fund Ltd.; Canadian Indemnity Co.; mem. Winnipeg Chamber Comm. (Past Pres.); Offr., RCAF Navig. Br., 1941-45, rank Flt. Lt.; Invest. Dept., The Great-West Life Assnce. Co., Winnipeg, Man., 1936-47; joined the Investors Group 1 Jan. 1948; former Pres. and Chief Extve. Offr. and Vice-Chrmn. of the Board; United Church; Clubs: Manitoba; St. Charles Cuntry; Home: 1506 - 200 Tuxedo Blvd., Winnipeg, Man.; Office: 280 Broadway, Winnipeg, Man. R3C 3B6

ATHANS, George S., Jr., C.M. (1974), B.A.; athletic champion; b. Kelowna, B.C. 6 July 1952: s. George D., M.D. and Irene (Hartzell) A.; e. Concordia Univ. Sir George Williams Campus B.A. 1975, Communications-Pub. Relations Cert. 1975; Nikon Sch. of Photography Montreal 1972, 1975; McGill Univ. post-grad. courses in marketing; m. Claire Suzanne d. late Andre Sicotte 1 Dec. 1975; one d. Shawn Sacha; Mgr. Athans Skiing Enterprises Ltd., Vancouver; Sports Commentator CBC-TV; Pres. A.W.A. Marketing Ltd. Montreal; mem. Can.'s Nat. Water Ski Team 1966-75; holder World Slalom Record 1969-72; World and Candn. Champion 1965-75; Candn. Champion 33 times; winner over 100 water ski titles; rec'd Nat. Health & Welfare Educ. Scholarship 1970-73; Loyola Univ. Award Modern Sculpture 1970; named to Can.'s Amateur Hall of Fame Ottawa 1971 and Can.'s Sports Hall of Fame Toronto 1974; B.C. Athlete of the year 1971; Candn. Amateur Athlete of the Yr. 1972, 1973;

Que. Athlete of the Yr. 1973; mem. First Gallery of Athletes Montreal 1975 and various other distinctions and awards; author "Water Skiing" 1975 (also published in French and Russian); Hon. Life mem. Candn. Water Ski Assn.; recreations: squash, swimming, running, snow skiing, 35mm still photography, rock music; Club: La Cité; Address: 3669 Jeanne Mance, Montreal, Que. H2X 2K4

ATKINS, Gordon Lee, B.Arch., R.C.A.; architect; b. Calgary, Alta. 5 March 1937; s. Grant Lee Kearl and Dorothy A.; e. Univ. of Wash. B.Arch. 1960 (Faculty Medal for Design Excellence; Am. Tile Inst. Award); m. C. Joan Lecoq 21 March 1956; children: Lisa, Laura, Drew, Ryan, Murray, Seth; PROP., GORDON ATKINS AND ASSOCIATES ARCHITECTS LTD. 1963- ; Partner with Alton McCaul Bowers (religious works) 1961-62; sessional instr. Mount Royal Coll., S. Alta. Inst. of Technol.; lectr. Univ. of Calgary 4 yrs.; solo exhn. Edmonton Art Gallery 1970; recipient many design awards incl. Massey Medal (Melchin Summer Homes); Hon. Mention Design for Candn. Flag; 2nd Place Calgary Centennial Planetarium Competition; award & nat. exhn. R.C.A. Drahanchuk Studios, A.G.T. Elbow Park; Mayland Hts. Sch. display Nat. Schs. Conf., Union Internationale Archs. Budapest; Eighth Ave. Mall Design Award Candn. Arch.; Urban Design Awards Leavitt Residence 1979, Varsity Estates Condominiums Calgary 1979, Calgary Indian Friendship Center 1980; Pinebrook Golf Club Exhn. Olympic Games Montreal; Stoney Adm. Bldg. Hon. Mention Candn. Arch. 1978; Shouldice Athletic Change Pavilion Calgary, Candn. ARch. Yearbook Award 1980; Practice Profile Award, Alta. Assn. of Arch., 75th Anniversary; subject various TV programs; Exhn. Nickle Arts Gallery Univ. of Calgary 1980; served as Bishop of Mormon Ch.; mem. Bd. Examiners Univ. Alta.; Dir. Calgary Centennial Comte.; Council Community Services; Gov. Calgary Allied Arts Centre; mem. Alta. Assn. Archs. (Pres. Calgary Br.); Royal Arch. Inst. Can.; Mid-Can. Corridor Foundation; Rural Devel. Assn. (Dir.); Mormon; recreations: books, music, skiing; Home: 1008 Durham Ave. S.W., Calgary, Alta. T2T 0P7; Office: 1909 - 17th Ave. S.W., Calgary, Alta. T2T 0E9.

ATWOOD, Margaret, A.M., D.Litt., LL.D.; poet and book author; b. Ottawa, Ont., 18 Nov. 1939; d. Dr. Carl Edmund and Margaret Dorothy (Killam) A.; e. Victoria Coll., Univ. of Toronto, B.A., 1961; Radcliffe Coll., A.M., 1962; Publications: "Double Persephone" (poetry) 1961; "The Circle Game" (poetry) 1966; "Animals in that Country" (poetry) 1968 "The Edible Woman" (novel) 1969; "Procedures For Underground" (poetry) 1970; "The Journals of Susanna Moodie"(poetry) 1970; "Power Politics" (poetry) 1971; "Surfacing" (novel) 1972; "Survival, A Thematic Guide to Canadian Literature" (prose) 1972; "You Are Happy" (poetry 1974); "Lady Oracle" (novel) 1976; "Dancing Girls" (short stories) 1977; "Selected Poems" 1976; "Two-Headed Poems" 1978; "Life Before Man" (novel) 1979; "True Stories" (poetry) 1981; "Bodily Harm" (novel) 1981; rec'd E. J. Pratt Medal, 1961; President's Medal, Univ. of Western Ontario, 1965; Gov. Gen. Award, 1966, all for poetry; 1st Prize, Centennial Comn. Lit. Competition, Poetry Div. 1967; Can. Booksellers' Assn. Award, 1977, etc.; recreation: canoeing; Address: Oxford University Press, 70 Wynford Drive, Don Mills, Ont. M3C 1J9

AUBRY, Claude B., C.M. (1974), O.I.B.P.(1975): B.A., B.L.S.; librarian (retired); author; b. Morin Heights, Que. 23 Oct. 1914; s. Ernest and Augustine (Lafleur) A.; e. Univ. of Montreal (Coll. Ste-Marie) B.A. 1936; McGill Univ. B.L.S. 1945; Director, Ottawa Public Library 1953-1979; Depy. Chief Librarian, Ottawa Public Lib. 1949-53; Chief of Personnel, Montreal Civic Library 1945; Publications: "La vengeance des hommes de bonne volonté" 1944; "Miroirs déformant" 1945; "Les îles du roi Maha Maha II" (Eng. transl. "The King of the Thousand

Islands") 1960; "Le loup de Noël" 1963 (Eng. transl. "The Christmas Wolf" 1965); "Le violon magique" 1968 (Eng. transl. "The Magic Fiddler" 1968); "Agouhanna" (Eng. 1973, Fr. 1974); Candn. Authors Assn.; Alliance Française Ottawa; Association France-Canada; mem. Montfort Hosp. Corp.; Lib. Consultants Bd. Encyclopedia Canadiana; Ed. Bd. Candn. Childrens Lit.; Soc. des écrivains candns.; Ont. Lib. Assn.; Candn. Lib. Assn.; mem. Bd. Children Book Centre, Quebec Prov. Govt. Award for "The Christmas Wolf" (1943); Can. Library Assn. Bronze Medal for same (1965); A.C.B.L.F. Award "Littérature de Jeunesse" for "The King of the Thousand Islands" (1959); Cdn. Lib. Assn. Bronze Med. for same 1962; appt'd. "Officier de l'Ordre International du Bien Public" (1975); membre, "Ordre du Canada" 1974; recreation: writing; Address: 14 Claver St., Ottawa, Ont. K1J 6W7

AUBRY, (Joseph Charles Noël) Yves; air traffic controller; union representative; b. Hull, Qué. 26 June 1952; s. (Joseph) Charles (Edouard Frédéric Georges) and (Madeleine Antoinette) Pauline (de Bellefeuille) A.; e. St-Rédempteur, Gauvin, Polyvalente and St-Jean Baptiste, Hull, Qué. 1970; Carleton Univ. Elect. Engn. 1970-71; Dept. of Transport Air Traffic Control Licence 1973; Hull Music Conserv. 1968-69; m. (Marie) Jocelyne (Ann) d. Jacques Emond, Lac Ste-Marie, Qué. 27 May 1972; two d. Julie Sonia, Annick Pauline; Nat. Vice Pres., Candn. Air Traffic Control Assn. Inc. 1979-80; mem. Bargaining Team 1979-80 Contract, Rep. on NJC Fed. Govt.; Secy. Treas. Côte-Nord Br., Sept-Iles, Que. 1975-76, CATCA, Chrmn. of Br. 1977, Qué. Regional Dir. 1978-79; mem. Ottawa Guitar Soc. 1969-71; Drum Corps: Amicalists de Hull 1965-66, Les Troubadours Hull 1966-68; R. Catholic; recreations: classical and flamenco guitar, woodworking, electronics; Home: BG 3533, 58 de l'Epane, Place Ferguson, Sept-Iles, Que. G4R 4K2

AUCLAIR, Jacques Lucien, B.Sc., M.Sc., Ph.D.; educator; b. Montreal, Que. 2 April 1923; s. Alfred and Clothilde (Boucher) A.; e. Univ. of Montreal B.Sc. 1942; McGill Univ. M.Sc. 1945; Cornell Univ. Ph.D. 1949; m. 1stly Suzanne d. Auguste Strub 28 Apr. 1951; children: Danielle, France-Eve; m. 2ndly Monique d. Tancrede Marsil; PROF., DEPT. OF BIOLOGY, UNIV. DE MONTREAL; author over 80 research papers on insect physiology and biochemistry; Fell.; Entomological Soc. of Can.; mem. Entom. Soc. Que. (past Pres.); Sigma Xi; Entom. Soc. Amer.; Amer. Inst. of Biol. Sciences; awarded Médaille du Centenaire Canada 1967; recreations: tennis, swimming, gardening, travel; Home: 405 Riverside Dr., St-Lambert, Qué. J4P 1B2; Office: Succ. A., C.P. 6128, Montreal, Qué. H3C 3J7

AUDET, Adrien; retired banker; b. Montreal, Que., 8 Dec. 1910; s. Jean Louis and Albertine (Lacoste) A.; e. Maisonneuve Superior Coll.; Post-grad. courses in Can. and U.S.; m. Hermine, d. Adolphe Simard; children: Jacques, Gilles; joined Montreal City and District Savings Bank as Jr. Clerk, 1927; Asst. Acct. 1938; Chief Acct. Dept., Head Office, 1943; Asst. Chief Acct., 1954; Asst. Gen. Mgr., 1958; Depy. Gen. Mgr. 1967 mem. Montreal Bd. of Trade; Chambre de Comm. du District de Montréal; Roman Catholic; Club: Cercle de la Place d'Armes; Home: 3445 Drummond St., Apt. 702, Montreal, Que. H3G 1X9

AUDET, Henri, B.A., B.A.Sc.A., M.Sc., D.Sc.; communications executive; b. Montréal, Que. 7 Aug. 1918; s. Victor F. and Alice (Turgeon) A.; e. Jean-de-Brébeuf Coll., B.A.; Ecole Polytech. B.A.Sc.; Mass. Inst. Technol., M.Sc.; Univ. de Qué., D.Sc. m. Marie, d. Henre-S. Labelle, 24 June 1950; children: Louis, François, Denise, Bernard, Geneviève; CHAIRMAN, COGECO, INC.; Dir., Télévision St-Maurice Inc.; Télévision St-François Inc.; La Belle Vision Inc.; Past Chrmn., Que. Univ. (Trois-Rivières); avec La Soc. Radio-Canada 1945-57; Can. Assn. Broadcasters ACRTF; TV Bureau of Advertising;

Caisse Populair de Normanville; Comité Trifluvien des Concerts Symphonique de Qué.; Symphonic Concerts of Que.; Cultural Centre; mem., Order of Engineers; Eng. Inst. of Can.; Chamber of Comm.; Festivals de Musique of Qué.; r. catholique; Recreations: sailing; Clubs: St. Denis, St.-Maurice Yacht; Laviolette; Radisson; Ki-8-Eb Golf; Home: 2355 De Normandville, Trois-Rivières, Qué. G8Z 3R3; Office: P.O. Box 277, Trois-Rivières, Qué. G9A 5G3

AUDET, (Joseph Philippe) Jean-Paul, Ph.D.; educator; b. Saint-Anselme, Qué. 7 Dec. 1918; s. Alphonse and Marie-Anne (Gagné) A.; e. Dominican Faculty of Philos. and Theol. Ottawa 1940-47; St. Thomas Univ. Rome Ph.D. 1949; Inst. Egyptology Oxford 1949-50; Ecole Biblique et Archéologique Francaise de Jerusalem 1950-52; m. Jeanne-Marie d. Napoleon Gingras, Augusta, Me. 16 July 1975; children: Isabelle, Paul-Emmanuel; PROF. OF PHILOS. UNIV. DE MONTREAL; Chrmn. of Philos. there 1974- 78; rec'd Molson Award, Can. Council 1970; author "La Didache: Instructions des Apôtres" 1958; over 250 other publs.; mem. Royal Soc. Can.; Academie des Sciences Morales et Politiques; Assn. Canadienne de Philosophie; Soc. de Philosophie du Qué.; Home: R.R. 2, Magog, Qué. J1X 3W3; Office: (C.P. 6128) 2910 Boul. Édouard-Montpetit, Montréal, Que.

AUDET, Louis-Philippe, B.A., M.Sc., D.Paed., F.R.S.C. (1956); b. Sainte-Marie, Beauce, P.Q., 16 Nov. 1903; s. of Louis and Eugénie (Turcotte) A.; e. Normal Sch., Limoilou and Montreal, P.Q.; Univ. of Montreal, B.A. 1932, B. Paed. 1932; Laval Univ., M.Sc. 1937, D.Paed. 1952; one d. Louise: taught Primary and Normal Sch., 1921-30, Secondary school 1930-34; Prefect of Studies, Acad. de Québec, 1935-38, Sch. of Fisheries and Agric., Ste-Anne de la Pocatière, 1939-40; Supt. of Popular Educ., Ministry of Social Welfare and of Youth, Que., 1942-57; Secy. of the Gen. Direction of Studies of Specialized Schs. 1957-59; Dir. of âStudies of all the Insts. of Dept. of Social Welfare, Que., 1959-61; Secy. of Roy. Comn. of Inquiry on Educ. in Prov. of Que., 1961-65; Prof. "titulaire" of Hist. of Educ. in Can., Fac. of Educ., Univ. de Montréal, 1965-70; retired 1970; in the meantime Prof. of Sch. System, Laval and Montreal Univs.; Zool. Soc., Orsainville, 1945-70; Life mem., Roy. Soc. of Can. (Secy., Sec. I, 1957-66; Pres., Sec. I, 1967-68); Bourse Geo. W. Brown de la Soc. royale du Canada 1969; Publications: (natural hist.) "Le Chant de la Forêt", 1949; "Ceux qui nous servent", 1953; "Les Fauves et leurs victimes", 1954; "La Cité des Animaux", 1956; (education) "Le Frère Marie-Victorin, ses idées pédagogiques", 1943; "La chanson du Bonheur", 1948; "Le Centenaire du Système scolaire de la province de Québec", 1947; "Où mène le cours primaire de la province de Québec", 1948; "La Paroisse et l'Education", 1949; "Le Système scolaire de la province de Québec (6 vols.) 1950-56; "La Cabane Enchantée", 1960; "Éducateurs, Parents, Maîtres", 1963; "Histoire du Conseil de l'Instruction publique", 1964; "Bilan de la Reforme scolaire au Québec", 1969; "Histoire de l'Enseignement au Québec", 2 vol. 1971; co-author, "Le Système scolaire du Québec", 1967, 1968; "Canadian Education: A History", 1970; has contributed to "Mémoires de la Société Royal du Canada", 1956-70; "Dictionnaire biographique du Canada"; mem., Soc. des Dix (one article per year) since 1959; awarded Prix David, 1955, Casgrain Prize, 1956; mem., Soc. Zool. Que. (Pres. 1949-52); Soc. Des Ecrivains Canadiens; Soc. Des Etudes Hist.; R. Catholic; Home: 1305 av. Leblanc, Sillery, Qué. G1T 2G8

AUDET, Paul-A.; newspaperman; b. Quebec. Que., 14 March 1923; s. Sylvio and Rose-Aimee (Cloutier) A.; e. Acad. de Québec (Que.); Laval Sch. of Comm.; m. Michèle Richard, 13 Sept. 1947; children: Francine, André, Marc; PRESIDENT AND GEN. MGR,. LE SOLEIL LTEE.; Pres. Edimedia Inc.; Dir., Perspectives Inc.; Better Business Bureau of Can.; Vice-Chrmn., Newspapers Marketing Bureau; Past Pres., Newspaper Advertising Extve.

Assn. Can.; mem. Internat. Newspaper Advertising Extve. Assn.; Chambre de Comm. de Qué.; Chambre de Comm. Francaise du Can.; R. Catholic; recreations: swimming, golf, fishing, skiing; Home: 9 Jardins Merici, Apt. 1803, Québec, Que. G1S 4N8; Office: 390 St. Vallier, Québec, Que. G1K 3P6

AUDETTE, Louis de la Chesnaye, O.C. (1974), Q.C. (1953), B.A., L.Ph., LL.B.; Canadian public service (retired); b. Ottawa, Ont. 7 April 1907; s. Hon. Justice Louis Arthur and Mary Grace (d. Hon. Justice Sir Andrew Stuart) A.; e. Univ. of Ottawa, B.A., L.Ph.; Univ. of Montreal LL.B.; called to Bar of Qué. 1931; practised law with Audette & OBrien 1931-39; R.C.N. 1939-45, commanding various ships in N. Atlantic and Mediterranean; retired as Commdr. R.C.N.(R); mentioned in Despatches; 1st Secy., Dept. of External Affairs 1945-1947; Commr. Candn. Maritime Comn. 1947-1953, Chrmn. 1954-59; mem. Comm. of Inquiry into R.C.N. 1949; Dir. Export Devel. Corp. 1946-71; Dir. Crown Assets Disposal Corp. 1953-60; Dir. 1948-1959 and Pres. 1954-59 Park Steamship Co. Ltd.; mem. N.W.T. Council 1947-59; Court Martial Appeal Bd. 1951-59; Chrmn. Prep. Comte. U.N. Intergovt. Maritime Consultative Organ.1954-59 and Pres. First Assembly (London, 1959); Chrmn. Tariff Bd. of Can. 1959-72; Administrator, Maritime Pollution Claims Fund 1973-78; Past Pres. Canadian Club (Ottawa) and of Ottawa Philharmonic Orchestra; mem. Que. Bar; R.C.; Club: Cercle Universitaire; Residence: 451 Besserer St., Ottawa, Ont. K1N 6C2

AUGER, Fred S., B.Sc.; b. Calgary, Alta., 7 June 1907; s. Albert Raymond and Mabel Christine (Saunders) A.; e. Calgary Pub. and High Schs.; Univ. of Idaho, B.Sc. (Business); m. Dorothy Kathleen, d. late Norman Colin Hill, Calgary, Alta., 18 June 1934; children: Barry Norman, Timothy Frank; Formerly Dir., Southam Press Ltd.; Publisher "Vancouver Province" and "Winnipeg Tribune"; Phi Gamma Delta; United Church; recreations: hunting, fishing; Clubs: Manitoba (Winnipeg); Shaughnessy Golf; Vancouver; Black Watch of Canada (Montreal); Home: 4266 Staulo Cres., Vancouver, B.C. V6N 3S2

AUGER, Paul Emile, O.C., B.A., D.Sc., F.R.S.C., F.G.S.A.; geologist; b. St. Croix, Lotbinière Co., P.Q., 30 Sept. 1908; s. Arthur and Valeda (Boisvert) A.; e. Laval Univ., B.A. 1929, B.Sc. 1933; Queen's Univ., B.Sc. 1936; Mass. Inst. of Tech., D.Sc. 1940; m. Gabrielle, d. Joseph Hébert, 3 Feb. 1940; childen: Jacques, Louise, Michèle; named to Que. Prov. Econ. Council, July 1961; Depy. Min. of Natural Resources, Que., 1961-71; former Prof. of Econ. Geol. and i/c of Structural and Engn. Geol. at the Sch. of Mines, Laval Univ.; Geol. for Que. Bur. of Mines, 1938-41; Lect. in Econ. Geol., Laval Univ. Sch. of Mines, 1941; Asst Prof. 1943; has written many reports and papers on minerals in Que.; Wing Commdr., C.O. Laval Univ. Sqdn., R.C.A.F.; mem., Candn. Inst. of Mining & Metall. (Pres. 1968-69); Corp. Prof. Engrs. Que.; Cong. of Candn. Engrs.; Geol. Assn. of Can. (Pres. 1962); Soc. of Econ. Geols.; R. Catholic; Address: 1400 Parc Champoux, Sillery, Quebec G1S 1L6 Que.

AUGUSTYN, FRANK JOSEPH, O.C., dancer; b. Hamilton, Ont., 27 Jan. 1953; s. Walter and Elizabeth (Schmider) A.; student Nat. Ballet Sch., 1965-70; LL.D. (hon.), York U., 1977, McMaster U., 1979. Mem. Corps de Ballet,, Nat. Ballet Co. of Can., Toronto, . 1970-71, soloist, 1971-72, prin., 1972-; co-founder Ballet Revue; has performed in Can., U.S., London Festival Ballet, Germany, France, Holland, Monaco, Belgium, USSR, Italy, Switzerland, Cuba; TV appearances include Giselle (CBC), 1975, La Fille Mal Gardé (CBC), 1979 Pleasure of Your Company, Magic Show. Winner best couple award 2d Internat. Ballet Competition, Moscow, 1973; decorated Order of Can. Author: Kain-Augustyn, 1977. Office: 157 King St E Toronto Ont. M5C 1C9

AULD, Frank, M.A., Ph.D.; psychologist; educator; b. Denver, Colo. 9 Aug. 1923; s. Benjamin Franklin and Marion Leland (Evans) A.; e. Drew Univ. A.B. 1946; Yale Univ. M.A. 1948, Ph.D. 1950; m. Elinor Florence d. Rev. Jacob Ellis James 29 June 1946; children: Mary Elinor, Robert Franklin, Margaret Elizabeth; PROF. OF PSYCHOL., UNIV. OF WINDSOR 1970- ; Instr. and Asst. Prof. of Psychol. Yale Univ. 1950-59; Assoc. Prof. and Prof. of Psychol. Wayne State Univ. 1959-67; Prof. of Psychol. Univ. of Detroit 1967-70; Chrmn. Dearborn (Mich.) Community Council 1963; Consultant Advertising Research Detroit Un. Fund 1965-68; mem. Adv. Comte. Coll. Work Epis. Diocese Mich. 1963-71; mem. Psychol. Licensing Bd. State of Mich. 1968-71; served with U.S. Army 1943-46; author "Steps in Psychotherapy" 1953; "Scoring Human Motives" 1959; over 40 papers psychotherapy and psychol. testing; Convenor Accreditation Council Ont. Psychol. Assn.; mem. Candn. Psychol. Assn.; Am. Psychol. Assn.; Brit. Psychol. Soc.; recreations: hiking, music; Club: Economic (Detroit); Home: 1340 Pierce St., Birmingham,, Mich. 48009; Office: 401 Sunset Ave., Windsor, Ont. N9B 3P4

AULD, Lt. Col. the Hon. James Alexander Charles, LL.D.; merchant; b. Toronto, Ont., 22 July 1921; s. James Cresswell and Dorothy (May) A.; e. Rosedale Public and Elm House Schs., Toronto, Ont.; St. Andrew's Coll., Aurora, Ont.; Univ. of Toronto Schools; Hon. LL.D. Dundee Univ.; m. Nancy Eleanor, d. Alan Gilmour, 3 May 1946; children: James Alan Gilmour, Alexandra Christine Gilmour; Chrmn., St. Lawrence Parks Comm. 1981-; Vice Chrmn., St. Lawrence Parks Comm., Apl. 1958-Oct. 1962, Acting Chrmn., 1962-63; joined Gilmour & Co. Ltd., Brockville, Ont. 1947 (becoming Dir. and Secy-Treas. 1953) after employment with Tip Top Tailors Ltd., Toronto, and Nisbet & Auld Ltd., Toronto, 1945-47; Alderman, Corp. of Brockville, 1951-54; first el. to Ont. Leg. in by-el. Sept. 1954; re-el. 1955, 1959, 1963, 1967, 1971, 1975, 1977; did not seek re-election in 1981; Min. of Transport, 1962-63; Tourism and Information, 1963-71; Pub. Works 1971-72; Environment 1972-74; Min. of Colls. & Univs. 1974-75; Chrmn. Man. Board of Cabinet 1975-78; Min. of Energy, 1978-79; Min. of Nat. Resources 1978-81; served in 2nd World War; Q.O.R. of Can. 1941-45; discharged with rank of Capt.; service in Can., U.K., N.W. Europe with 1st Bn.; Major, 60th L.A.A. Regt. Brockville 1952 (R); Hon. Lt. Col. Brockville Rifles since 1978; mem., Royal Can. Mil. Inst.; Canadian Legion; Freemason; P. Conservative; Anglican; recreations: woodworking, photography, boating; Clubs: Albany (Toronto); Roy. Candn. Mil. Inst. (Toronto); Brockville Yacht; Home: 173 Hartley St., Brockville, Ont. K6V 3N4;

AULD, (Walter) Murray, B. Eng.; company executive; b. Regina, Sask., 16 Aug. 1916; s. Francis Hedley and Lily Elizabeth (Smith) A.; e. Central Collegiate, Regina, Sask., Sr. Matric., 1935; Univ. of Sask., B. Eng. (Mech. Engn.) 1940; m. Isabel George, d. Charles George Hutcheson, 21 Sept. 1942; children: Nancy Elizabeth, Fraser Hedley, Catherine Margaret; DEPUTY CHRMN. AND DIR., BRISTOL AEROSPACE LTD.; Dir. Great West Life Assurance Co., Telesat Can., Rolls Royce Holdings North America Ltd.; with Dept. National Defence, 1940-42; Div. Mgr., MacDonald Bros. Aircraft, 1942-45, Sales Mgr., 1945-54; Asst. Gen. Mgr., Bristol Aircraft (Western) Ltd., 1955-57; Vice Pres. and Gen. Mgr., Bristol Aero-Industries Ltd., Winnipeg Div., Bristol Aero-Industries Ltd., 1959-65; Dir., Rolls-Royce Holdings Canada Ltd.; mem. Candn. Aero. & Space Inst.; Protestant; Clubs: Manitoba; St. Charles Country; Home: 293 Overdale St., St. James, Man.; Office: (P.O. Box 874) Winnipeg International Airport, Winnipeg, Man. R3C 2S4

AULT, Samuel Gordon Keyes, B.S.A.; dairy executive; b. Winchester, Ont. 2 Feb. 1916; s. Jack Wellesley and Eliza Jane (Keyes) A.; e. Winchester (Ont.) High Sch.; Univ. of Toronto B.S.A.; m. Betty Margaret d. Dr. Lewis

S. Beattie, Toronto, Ont. 20 June 1942; children: Jane Campbell, Patricia Olsen, Stephen; CHRMN. AULT FOODS LTD.; Pres. Dundas Cheese Co. Ltd.; Beurrerie Lafreniere Ltèe; Laiterie Dallaire Ltèe; Dominion Dry Milk Ltd.; Dir. Ogilvie Flour Mills; Chrmn., Stacey Bros. Ltd.; Dominion Dairies Ltd.; Dir. Nat. Dairy Council (Past Pres.); Past Pres. Ont. Dairy Council; mem. Adv. Bd. Candn. Dairy Comn.; Vice Pres. St. Lawrence Parks Comn.; Past Chrmn. N. Dundas Sch. Bd.; Pres. P. Cons. Assn. Grenville-Dundas, Stormont-Dundas; served with Candn. Army 1941-45, Overseas 1942-45, rank Capt.; Mentioned in Dispatches; P. Conservative; Protestant; recreations: boating, golf, hunting, fishing; Clubs: Laurentian (Ottawa); 100; Morrisburg Golf; Home: 65 Lakeshore Dr., Morrisburg, Ont.; Office: Winchester, Ont. K0C 2K0.

AUMENTO, Fabrizio, M.Sc., Ph.D.; marine geologist; educator; b. Rome, Italy 19 Jan. 1940; s. Romualdo and Alda (Veronesi) A.; e. Univ. of London B.Sc. 1961; Dalhousie Univ. M.Sc. 1962, Ph.D. 1965; children: Paul, Lara, Patrick; CHIEF GEOL.; ELC-ELECTRONCONSULT (Milano, Italy); joined Geol. Survey of Can. 1965-69; Dalhousie Univ. 1969-78, Chrm. of Geol. 1973-75; Visiting Prof. Univ. of Geneva 1977, Instituto de Geociencias Dos Acores 1978; rec'd Nat. Research Council Steacie Fellowship 1976; APICS Young Scient. Award 1975; author "Initial Reports of the Deep Sea Drilling Project" Vol. 37 1977; over 80 publs. on marine geol. and assoc. topics; Fellow Royal Soc. Can.; recreation: sailing; Club: R.N.S.Y.S.; Office: ELC-Electroconsult via Chiabrera 8 20151 Milano, Italy

AUSTIN, Jacob (Jack), P.C., Q.C., B.A., LL.B.; LL.M.; Senator; b. Calgary, Alta., 2 March 1932; s. Morris and Clara Edith A.; e. Crescent Hts. High Sch., Calgary; Univ. of B.C.; Harvard Law Sch.; Univ. of Cal. (Berkeley); B.A.; LL.B.; LL.M.; m. Natalie Veiner Freeman, d. Harry Veiner, 4 Feb. 1978; three d., Edith, Sharon, Barbara; apptd. to Fed. Cabinet as Min. of State 1981; President, Uranium Canada Limited; Director, Panarctic Oils Ltd.; read law with N. T. Nemetz, Q.C.; called to Bar of B.C. and Yukon; cr. Q.C. 1970; Asst. Prof. of Law, Univ. of B.C., 1955; Law Partner, Nemetz, Austin & Co., Vancouver, 1958; Extve. Asst. to Min. of N. Affairs & Nat. Resources, Ottawa, 1963; Law Partner, J. Austin, Vancouver, 1966; Andrews, Swinton, Margach, Austin & Williams, 1966; Pres., Giant Mascot Mines Ltd., Vancouver, 1968; Brameda Resources Ltd., 1970; Depy. Min., Energy, Mines and Resources 1970-74; summoned to Can. Senate 1975; Lib. Cand. for Vancouver-Kingsway g.e. 1965; author, "Canadian-United States Practice and Theory Respecting the International Law of International Rivers"; co-author, "Canadian View of Territorial Seas and Fisheries"; recreations: boating, reading; Clubs: University (Vancouver); Canadian (N.Y.); Rideau; Cercle Universitaire d'Ottawa: Home: 1461 Connaught Dr., Vancouver, B.C.; Office: Room 668-S, The Senate, Ottawa, Ont. K1A OA4

AVERY, Burton Albert, B.A.Sc.; professional engineer; b. Kincardine, Ont., 28 April 1922; s. Roy Wilbert and Margaret May (McLeod) A.; e. High Schs., Kirkland Lake and Weston, Ont.; Univ. of Toronto, B.A.Sc. (Mech. Engn.) 1946; m. Mildred Shirley, d. Clifford r. Marchant, Weston, Ont., 23 July 1949; children: Jane, James; DEPY. GEN. MANAGER, B&K MACHINERY DIV., HAWKER SIDDELEY CANADA INC.; Inspector National Steel Car Co. Ltd., Aircraft Div., Malton, Ont. 1940-42; joined A. V. Roe Canada Ltd. (predecessor Co.) in 1946 as Design Engr. in Compressor Sec.; Acting Chief Design Engr. March 1953; Chief Design Engr. 1954-57; Deputy Chief Engr., 1957-59; Gen. Mgr. Orenda Div. of Hawker Siddeley Canada Ltd., 1959-65; Dir. of Engn., Orenda Ltd. 1966-81; mem., Governing Council, Univ. of Toronto, 1978; Assn. Prof. Engrs. Ont.; Fellow, Candn. Aero. Inst.; mem. Soc. of Auto Engrs.; Toronto Bd. of Trade;

United Church; Club: Bd. of Trade Golf; Home: 11 Mountbatten Rd., Weston, Ont. M9P 1Y8; Office: 6855 Airport Rd., Mississauga, Ont. LAV 1E7

AXWORTHY, Hon. Lloyd, P.C., M.P., M.A., Ph.D.; politician; b. North Battleford, Sask. 21 Dec. 1939; s. Norman Joseph and Gwen Jane A.; e. Univ. of Winnipeg B.A.; Princeton Univ. M.A. Ph.D.; MIN. OF EMPLOY-MENT AND IMMIGRATION, CAN. 1980- and Min. of State for Status of Women 1980-81; Dir. Univ. Research Inst.; Assoc. Prof.; def. cand. fed. g.e. 1968; el. M.L.A. Man. g.e. 1973, re-el. 1977; el. to H. of C. for Winnipeg-Fort Garry g.e. 1979, re-el. 1980; Liberal; United Church; Office: House of Commons, Ottawa, Ont. K1A 0A6.

AXWORTHY, Thomas Sidney, B.A., M.A., Ph.D.; civil servant; b. Winnipeg, Man. 23 May 1947; s. Norman J. and Gwen J. (Thomas) A.; e. Univ. of Winnipeg B.A. 1968; Queen's Univ. M.A. 1970; PH.D. 1979; Visiting Student, Univ. of Oxford, England 1972-73; m. Roberta Dojack d. Charles E. Dojack 23 July 1971; PRINC. SECY. TO THE PRIME MINISTER OF CANADA, 1980- ; joined Fed. Govt. 1974 as Special Asst. on Urban Policy to Min. of State for Urban Affairs and Spec. Asst. (Cabinet Briefing) to Min. of Nat. Rev.; Consultant, The Canada Consulting Group, 1975; Spec. Asst., Office of the P.M., 1975-76; Policy Advisor, 1977-78; Asst. Princ. Secy. (Policy) 1978-79; Sen. Policy Adv., Office of the Leader of the Opposition, 1979-80; Acting Dir., Lib. Laucus Research Bur., 1979-80; Instr., Dept. of Pol. Studies, Queen's Univ. (part-time) 1979-80; author various artices; mem. Amer. Pol. Sci. Assn.; Candn. Pol. Sc. Assn.; Candn. Inst. of Internat. Affairs; Oxford Union Soc.; Vice-Pres., Candn. Univ. Students, Univ. of Winnipeg, 1966-67; Academic Affairs Director, Univ. of Winnipeg, 1967-68; Premier, Tuxis and Older Boys' Parl. Assn. of Man. and N.W. Ont., 1968; Man. Organizer, John Turner Leadership Campaign, 1968; Vice-Pres., Candn. Univ. Liberals, Lib. Federation of Can., 1968-69; mem. Grad. Studies Comte., Dept. of Pol. Studies, Queen's Univ., 1969-70; Queen's Chrmn. and Kingston Vice-Pres., Comte. for an Independent, Can. 1970-71; Liberal Party; United Church; Home: 22 Grove St., Ottawa, Ont. K1S 3A6; Office: Langevin Block, Room 218, Ottawa, Ont. K1A 0A2

AYEARST, Morley, Ph.D.; professor emeritus; b. Courtright, Ont., 15 Oct. 1899; s. Rev. John Alma and Maude (Crothers) A.; e. Univ. of Toronto (Ont.) Schs.; Univ. of Toronto, Victoria Coll. B.A. 1921, M.A. 1924; study and travel in France (Ont. Govt. War Mem. Scholarship), 1922-23; Princeton Univ., Ph.D. 1932; m. Marjorie Douglas, d. Rev. B. Canfield Jones, 15 June 1929; one d., Patricia Anne; Prof. Emeritus of Govt. (Pol. Science), New York Univ., since 1966; Dir., Weschester Center, N.Y. Univ. 1948-50; Dir. of Evening Studies, Washington Sq. Coll. of Univ., 1950-59; Prof. of Govt. and Chrmn., Dept. of Govt. and Internat. Affairs there, 1962-66; Fulbright Research Scholar in Brit. W. Indies, 1953; during World War II served as Senior Intelligence Officer Bd. of Econ., Warfare, Washington, D.C.; Chief Intelligence Offr., U.S. Embassy London and SHAEF France, Belgium and Germany, 1943-45; Consultant, War Hists. Div., Bureau of the Budget, Washington, D.C., 1946; Pres., Preservation Soc. of E. End (Long Is.); Vice Pres., Springs Improvement Soc.; author: "The British West Indies: The Search for Self-Government", 1960; "The Republic of Ireland, its Government and Politics", 1969; co-author: "The Governments of Europe", 4th ed. 1954; other writings incl. numerous reviews and articles in various periodicals; mem., Am. Pol. Science Assn.; Internat. Pol. Science Assn.; recreations: travel, gardening; NYU Faculty Club; Home: 53 Buell Lane Ext., East Hampton, N.Y. 11937.

AYLEN, John Alden, Q.C.; b. Aylmer, P.Q., 2 June 1894; s. Henry and Desiré Elise (Bourinot) A.; e. Ashbury Coll., Ottawa; Harvard Univ., B.A. 1915; Univ. of Montreal,

LL.M. 1918; m. Jean Oliver Anderson, 15 June 1922; children: John Gordon, Priscilla; PARTNER, SCOTT & AYLEN: Lect. on Comm. Law, Faculty of Law, Univ. of Ottawa, 1955-63; called to Que. Bar, Jan. 1919; Batonnier, Bar of Hull, Que., 1942-44; called to Bar of Ont., Mar. 1931; cr. K.C., Feb. 1931; Chrmn. of Bd. (1955-63) V.O.N. for Can.; Vice-Chrmn., Dominion Drama Festival, 1947-49; Pres., Ottawa Little Theatre Inc. 1952-54; recreations: theatre activities, golf; Clubs: Rideau (Pres. 1949-50); Country; Royal Ottawa Golf (Pres. 1955-57); Home: 10 Carlyle Ave., Ottawa, Ont. K1S 4Y3; Office: 170 Laurier Ave. West, Ottawa, Ont. K1P 5V5

AYLESWORTH, John; TV and film writer-producer; b. Toronto, Ont., 18 Aug. 1928; s. Dr. Fredrick Allen and Thelma Marie (Bansley) A.; e. Forest Hill Coll. Inst., Toronto; m. Ann, d. Joe Martin, Palm Springs, Cal., children: John, Cynthia, William, Thomas, Linda, Robert, Martin; performer-writer, CBC "After Hours"; "The Big Review"; "On Stage"; creater-writer, "Front Page Challenge", writer, "Cross Canada Hit Parade"; "The Andy Williams Show", "The Judy Garland Show", "Hullabaloo", "Kraft Music Hall"; "Frank Sinatra — A Man and His Music", producer-writer, "The Jonathan Winters Show"; "Hee Haw"; "Herb Alpert Special"; "Happy Days"; "Don Adams Special"; "Sonny and Cher" series; "Shields and Yarnell" series; "Dorothy Hammill Presents Winners" special; "Hee Haw Tenth Anniversary" special, "The Grady Nutt Show", "The Nashville Palace", NBC; rec'd Emmy and Peabody Awards for "Frank Sinatra — A Man and His Music"; author: "Fee Fi Fo Fum", 1961; "Service!", 1971; Anglican; recreations: travel, reading, writing novels; Club Riviera Country (Los Angeles); Home: 1836 Loma Vista Drive, Beverly Hills, Cal.; Office; 357 N. Canon Dr., Beverly Hills, Cal.

AYRE, Anthony Green, O.B.E.; consultant; b. St. John's Nfld. 20 Nov. 1916; s. late James Garfield Green and Carlotta P. (Glassey) Ayre; e. Holloway and Prince of Wales Schs. Nfld.; Caldecott Prep. Sch. Eng. 1929-31; Ley's Pub. Sch. Cambridge, Eng. 1931-33; Macdonald Coll. McGill Univ. Dipl. Agric. 1937; self-employed Anthony G. Ayre Associates; Company Director; Rep., Byrne's Real Estate Ltd.; Consul for Belgium and for the Netherlands since 1965; joined RCN and comnd. 1941, service various naval vessels Pacific Coast and Atlantic 1942-45, joined HMCS Cabot as Reserve Offr. and promoted Lt. Commdr. 1949, C.O. Memorial Univ. Naval Training Div. 1949, Chief of Staff to Commodore Nfld. rank Acting Commdr. 1950, Area Offr. Sea Cadets Nfld. 1952-55; Extve. Mgr. Nfld. Bd. Trade 1959-70; Pres., Chamber of Commerce Executives of Canada, and Dir., Am. Chamber of Commerce Executives, 1968-69; Gen. Mgr. St. John's Bd. Trade 1970-71; Secy. St. John's Shipping Assn. Ltd. 1959-78; Extve. Secy. Nfld. Real Estate Bd. 1973-75; mem. Bd. Referees Unemployment Ins. Comn. since 1961; Area Supply Offr. Emergency Measures Organ, 1962-75; mem. Nfld. Labour Relations Bd. 1959-74; Court of Revision City of St. John's 1976-79; Dir. St. John's Tourist Comn.; Chrmn., Bd. of Govs., Nfld. Div. Candn. Corps of Commissionaires; former Chrmn. Pub. Libs. Bd. Nfld.; Regional Drama Festival Soc. Nfld.; former Dir. John Howard Soc.; has farmed in Eng., Nfld., Que. and Ont.; free lance writer and broadcaster; mem. AC-TRA; Royal Candn. Legion; Naval Assns. Central and Eastern Nfld.; Anglican; recreations: agriculture, reading, broadcasting, walking; Clubs: Crow's Nest; Naval (London, Eng.); Home: Trail's End, Box 1506 Topsail Rd., St. John's Nfld. A1C 5N8; Office: Bldg. 2, Finger Pier, Harbour Dr., St. John's, Nfld.

AYRE, Fred W., B.A.; company director; b. St. John's Nfld., 25 Nov. 1915; s. Harold Cecil and Agnes Marion (Miller) A.; e. Methodist Coll., St. John's Nfld.; Mostyn House, Cheshire, and Shrewsbury Sch., Eng.; Cambridge Univ. (Peterhouse) B.A. 1937; m. Doris Ethel, d.

Albert Harvey, Hastings, Eng., 15 Dec. 1938; children: Harvey, Sally, Nicholas; MANAGING DIR., BOWRING BROTHERS LTD. (Gen. Merchants, Estd. 1811) since 1947; joined Coca Cola co. (England) July 1937; apptd. Mgr. of Oxford Br., July 1938; after war service, joined Bowring Brothers Ltd. in Apl. 1946 (specialty: retail distribution, all phases); served in 2nd World War; enlisted R.A.S.C., Sept, 1939; 2 yrs. Home Service (Eng.), three yrs. Middle E. Forces, two yrs. Central Mediterranean Forces; demob. March 1946 with rank of Major; twice Mentioned in Despatches; Past Pres., St. John's Jr. Chamber Comm.; Nfld. Div., Candn. Red Cross Soc.; GWVA Extve.; Candn. Legion, etc.; Past Pres., Retail Div. Nfld. Bd. Trade; mem. Nfld. Officers Club (Crows Nest); Methodist; recreations: reading, writing; Home: 50 Roserill Avenue; Toronto, Ont.; Office: Apt. 412, 100 Wellesley East, Toronto, Ont. M4Y 1S2

AYRE, Lewis H. M.; company executive; b. Newfoundland 1914; s. Harold and Agnes (Miller) A.; e. Wrekin Coll., Eng.; m. Olga Crosbie; children: Miller H., Penelope M. Rowe; Chrmn, Ayre & Sons, Ltd. (estbd. 1859) which he joined 1931; Chrmn., Ayre's Ltd.; The Newfoundland Telephone Co. Ltd.; Job Bros. & Co. Ltd.; Holiday Lanes Ltd.; Northatlantic Fisheries.; Blue Buoy Foods Ltd.; Holly's Ltd., J. Michaels Fashions Limited; Dir., Newfoundland and Labrador Hydro; The Bank of Nova Scotia; Dominion Stores Ltd.; Robinson Blackmore Holding Ltd.; Labrador Mining & Exploration Co., Ltd.; mem. Adv. Bd., Canada Permanent Trust Co.; Pres. Nfld. Bd. of Trade, 1948-49; Clubs: Bally Haly Golf; Toronto; Canadian (N.Y.); Home 26 King's Bridge Rd., St. John's, Nfld. A1C 3K5; Office: Ayre and Sons, Limited, P.O. Box 70, St. John's, Nfld. A1C 5H8

AYRE, Robert, LL.D. (Concordia); writer, editor, critic; b. Napinka, Man., 3 Apl. 1900; s. William John and Sadie (Millar) A., both natives of Ireland; m. Thelma Mary, d. Henry Everett. 18 Apl. 1925; one s. Nicholas; engaged on staff Winnipeg "Telegram" and Winnipeg "Free Press", 1917-27; Montreal "Gazette", 1934-37; with C.N. Rlys. Pub. Relations, Winnipeg, Toronto, Montreal, 1927-63; Aft Critic Montreal "Standard" 1938-42 and Montreal "Star" 1950-70; Jt. Ed., "Canadian Art" 1944-59; author, "Mr. Sycamore", 1937 (O'Brien's Best Short Stories, 1938; other anthologies and theatre, film, TV and radio versions); author, "Sketco, the Raven", based on West Coast Indian legends, 1961; has written a number of short stories; contrib. to various pubs.; received Candn. Drama Award 1942; recreations: reading, music, walking, looking at pictures: Address: 5745 Cote St. Luc Road, Hampstead, Montreal H3X 2E5 Que.

AZIZ, David, M.A.Sc., Ph.D.; chemical engineer; b. Toronto, Ont., 7 May 1924; e. Univ. of Toronto, B.A.Sc. 1945, M.A.Sc. 1946, Ph.D. 1949; m. Margaret Cousins, 10 May 1952; children: Timothy David, Douglas Cameron, Louise; PRES. AND MANAGING DIRECTOR, INTERNATIONAL WAXES LTD. 1982-; Instr., Univ. of Toronto, 1946-49; Dir. of Research, Defence Research Bd., Dept. of Nat. Defence, 1949-50; Dir. of Production, Internat. Waxes Ltd., 1950-54 when appt. Vice-Pres.; apptd. Pres. 1955-66 when apptd. Chrmn. after co-acquisitions of M. Nicol & Co. and Boler Petroleum Co., which brought about formation of The INTERNATIONAL Group; mem., Assn. of Prof. Engrs. of Ont.; Club: Scarborough Golf; Home: 3 Lichen Pl., Don Mills, Ont. M3A 1X3; Office: 50 Salome Drive, Agincourt, Ont. M1S 2A8

AZIZ, Philip John Andrew Ferris, B.F.A., M.F.A.; painter, sculptor, designer, architectural designer, graphic artist; b. St. Thomas, Ont. 15 Apl. 1923; s. late Charles and Cecelia (Fakhoury) A.; e. St. Martin's and Wortley Rd. Primary Schs., H. B. Beal Secondary Sch., London, Ont.; Yale Univ., B.F.A. 1947, M.F.A. 1949; Harvard Univ., post-grad. work 1949; Lectr. in Art, Univ. of W. Ont., 1950-55; One-Man Shows: Eaton Fine Art Gallery, 1950

and 1957; Montreal Museum of Fine Arts 1952; Univ. of Waterloo 1967; One-Man Show, New York Culture Centre, 1969; Minnesota Museum of Fine Arts 1972; London Arts Gallery, Detroit 1975; One-Man Show, David Findlay Gallery, New York, 1976; Gruenebaum Gallery, New York 1978; exhns.; Royal Soc. of Portrait Painters, London, Eng., 1966 and 1967; Candn. Pavilion, Expo '67; Nat. Gallery, Ottawa, 1966-67; rep. in perm. collections of: Detroit Art Inst.; Montreal Museum of Fine Arts; Metropolitan Opera, Lincoln Centre Plaza, N.Y.; Univ. of Toronto; portraits incl. Eugene Cardinal Tisserant (hangs in Monteal Museum of Fine Arts), Rise Stevens, Yousuf Karsh, Lady Eaton, Erik Bruhn and mems. of Ford and Du Pont families: cr. Lady Chapel, St. Peter's Basilica, London, Ont., 1958-59, also St. Joseph Chapel and Chapel of Christ The King; cr. West Chapel, Timothy Eaton Mem. Ch., 1960-61; non-religious art and portraiture in private colls. in Can., U.S.A., Gt. Brit., Europe (incl. Vatican Museum); cr. Panels of The Four Seasons for Mich. Consolidated Gas Co. Bldg., Detroit, 1962; Permanent Coll. Norto Simon Inc., New York etc., dealer, Gruenebaum Gallery; Artist-in-res. Aspen Inst. Of Humanistic Studies 1972 and 1976; pioneer in use of eggtempera medium and works exclusively in it; served with RCAF 1942-45; mem., Yale Alumni Assn. Can. (Vice-Pres.); Phi Alpha; Liberal; Clubs: Yaum;le Univ. (N.Y.); University (Toronto); Address: 1180 Western Rd., London, Ont. N6G 1G8

B

BABBITT, John D(avid), D.Phil., F.R.S.C.; physicist; b. Fredericton, N.B. 2 Fed. 1908; s. Harold Randolph and Ethel Mary (Hatt) B.; e. Fredericton (N.B.) High Sch. 1925; Univ. of N.B. B.A. 1929; Oxford Univ. B.A. 1932, D.Phil. 1935; m. Dorothy Elizabeth d. late Joseph Rooney 16 Oct. 1948; children: David Harold, John Robert, Susan Elizabeth, Cynthia Anne, James Edward; retired Nat. Research Council 1973; Ed. "Science in Canada, Selections from the Speeches of E. W. R. Steacie"; author over 40 articles on thermal conductivity, diffusion, science policy; Hon. Treas. Royal Soc. Can. 1959-62; mem. Candn. Assn. Physicists; recreations: skiing, angling, outdoor life; Home: 436 Meadow Dr., Ottawa, Ont. K1K 0M4.

BACARDI, Jose Alberto, B.A.; company executive; b. Santiago, Cuba, 15 Sept. 1938; s. Joaquin and Caridad (Bolivar) B.; e. Santiago and Havana, Cuba; Fessenden School, West Newton, Mass.; Tabor Academy, Marion, Mass.; Rutgers Univ. (Econ. and Pol. Science) B.A. 1962; Univ. Syracuse. Grad. Sch. Internat. Marketing; came to Canada 1969; m. Maria, d. Daniel Bacardi, 27 Feb. 1965; children: Victoria, Maria, Cristina, Juan Alberto; PRES & CHIEF EXEC OFFR., FBM DISTILLERY CO. LTD. since 1968; began in gen. adm. with Bacardi Co. of Spain, 1962-63; Marketing Research, Bacardi International Ltd. in France, Can., Eng. 1963-65; Brand Mgr. and Overseas Sales Mgr., Bacardi Imports Inc., Miami, Fla., 1965-68; mem. Assn. Candn. Distillers; Board of Trade of Metrop. Toronto; R. Catholic; recreations: golf, tennis, handball; Clubs: Toronto Cricket, Skating & Curling; Metro Board of Trade; Home: 18 Wilket Road, Willowdale, Ont. M2L 1N6; Office: 2100, 44 King St. W., Toronto Ont. M2L 1N6

BACHAND, André, C.M., B.A., LL.L., L.Sc.Com.,M.S., FRSA; university administrator; b. Sherbrooke, Que., 1 April 1917; s. Charles Emile and Emilie (Codère) B.; e. St-Charles Borromée, Sherbrooke, B.A.; Univ. de Montréal, LL.L. 1941, L.Sc.Com. 1942; Harvard Grad. Sch. of Business Adm. 1942-43; Columbia Univ., M.S. 1944; m. Madeleine, d. late Senator Vien, 1944; two s. Claude, Raymond; DIR. OF DEVELOPMENT FUND, UNIV. DE MONTREAL since 1967; Dir., Renault Automobiles (Canada) Ltd.; The Mercantile Bank of Canada; called to Bar of Que. 1941; trained with C.A. firm Montreal 1943-44;

managed, reorganized and subsequently acquired Robin Frères Ltée 1945-52; joined present Univ. as Lectr. in Accounting, Sch. of Comm., 1945-52 and Faculty of Law 1952-56; Dir. of Pub. Relations and Asst. to Secy. Gen. 1952-62; Asst. to Rector 1962-67; TV and Radio regular series, guest panelist and moderator; Founder, Town of Mount Royal Mun. Lib.; Community Concerts Assn.; Dir., Candn. Automobile Assn. (Extve. 1972-74); Touring Club Montreal (Pres. 1972-73); Atelier Libre de Recherches Graphiques Inc.; Co-chmn. du Maurier Council in Performing Arts; Musées Nationaux du Can. (Vice Prés. 1974-78); former Bd. mem. Soc. Canadienne de la Croix-Rouge (Montréal); La Comédie Canadienne; Montreal Museum of Fine Arts; Past Vice Pres., Festivals de Montréal; First Pres., Town of Mount Royal Chamber Comm.; Past mem. Bd., Chambre de Comm. Française au Can.; Chambre de Comm. du Dist. Montréal; mem. Soc. Canadienne des Relations Publiques; Am. Alumni Council; Am. Coll. Pub. Relations Assn. (Past Dir.-1st Candn.); Candn. Assn. Univ. Devel. Offrs.; Asst. to Gen. Secy., Assn. des Univs. entièrement ou partiellement de langue française; Mem. Order of Can. 1979; Clubs: St. Denis; St. James's (Comte. 1965-67); Canadian (Pres. 1961-62); Home: 246 Willowdale, Montréal, Qué. H3T 1G7

BACHYNSKI, Morrel Paul, B.E., M.Sc., Ph.D., F.A.P.S., F.C.A.S.I., F.R.S.C., F.I.E.E.E.; scientist; executive; b. Bienfait, Sask. 19 July 1930; s. Nickolas and Karoline B.; e. Univ. of Sask. B.E. 1952, M.Sc. 1953; McGill Univ. Ph.D. (Physics) 1955; m. Slava Krkovic, Arvida, Que. 30 May 1959; children: Caroline Dawn, Jane Diane; FOUNDER, PRES. AND DIR. MPB TECHNOLOGIES INC. since 1977; Dir. Bytek Electronics; Lab. Dir. Microwave & Plasma Physics RCA Ltd. 1958, Dir. Research & Devel. 1965, Vice Pres. Research & Devel. 1975-76; rec'd David Sarnoff Outstanding Achievement Award in Engn. 1963; Prix Scientifique Du Qué. 1973; Can. Enterprise Award 1977; Queen's Silver Jubilee Medal; author "The Particle Kinetics of Plasmas" 1968; over 80 scient. articles various journs.; Fellow, Inst. Elect. & Electronic Engrs.; Am. Phys. Soc.; Can. Aeronautics and Space Inst.; mem. Candn. Assn. Physicists (Pres. 1968-69); SCI-TEC (Pres. 1974-75); Royal Soc. Can. (Vice Pres. Acad III); Am. Inst. Aeronautics & Astronautics; Am. Geophys. Union; recreation: tennis; Home: 78 Thurlow Rd., Montreal, Que. H3X 3G9; Office: (P.O. Box 160) 21051 North Service Rd., Ste. Anne de Bellevue, Que. H9X 3L5.

BACK, Frédéric, R.C.A.; animated film producer; interior decorator; painter; b. Sarrebruick, Territoire de la Sarre 8 Apl. 1924; s. Jean and Guillemette (Siegel) B.; e. Ecole de l'Académie Strasbourg, France 1937; École Estienne Paris, France 1939; Fine Arts Rennes, France 1939-43; m. Ghylaine d. Lucien Paquin 2 July 1949; children: Christian, Süzel, Francis; Prof., École du Meuble Montreal 1948-53; Prof., Fine Art Sch. Montreal 1948-51; Freelance work Radio-Canada T.V. 1953-56; Illustrator, Film Animator, small scale sets for film 1959- ; Set Designer for Niagara Films 1956-59; interior decorator for restaurants; La Saulaie, Hélène de Champlain, Pescatore, Roma Antiqua; churches: Pierreville, Aylmer, Ste-Agathe, South-Colton, Chateauguay, Brushton (USA); stained glass mural Place des Arts Montreal; rec'd Can. Council Art Scholarship for study animation film in Europe 1963; various prizes internat. animation film festivals; mem. Soc. québécoise pour la défense des animaux (Adm.); Green Peace; Soc. pour vaincre la pollution; Nature Can.; Internat. Animated Film Assn.; Soc. des Décorateurs Ensembliers du Qué.; recreations: beekeeping, gardening, tree planting, caring for wild animals, drawing; Home: 3514 ave. Kent, Montréal, Qué. H3S 1N2; Office: Société Radio-Canada, 1400 est blvd. Dorchester, Montréal, Qué. H2L 4R9.

BACON, Hon. Roger Stuart, M.L.A.; politician; b. Upper Nappan, N.S. 29 June 1926; s. Robert Clinton and Lillian May (Smith) B.; e. Upper Nappan schs.; m. Clara Emily d. Albert Hawthorne, St. Stephen's, N.B. 30 Nov. 1944; children: Douglas, Diana, Deborah; MIN. OF AGRIC. & MARKETING, N.S.1979- ; dairy farmer; auctioneer; former Councillor, Depy. Warden Cumberland Co.; mem. and Chrmn. Amherst Mun., Vocational and Regional High Sch. Bds.; Cumberland Co. and Towns Jt. Expenditure Bds.; Past Pres. Cumberland Co. P. Cons. Assn.; el. M.H.A. for Cumberland East prov. g.e. 1970, re-el. since; Min. of Tourism, Min. of the Environment and Min. Responsible for Adm. Emergency Measures Organ. N.S. Act and Regulations 1978; P. Conservative; United Church; Clubs; Curling; Toastmaster; Office: (P.O. Box 190) Hollis Bldg., Halifax, N.S. B3J 2M4

BADGLEY, Robin Francis, M.A., Ph.D.; educator; sociologist; b. Montreal, Que., 6 May 1931; s. Clement Montagu and Joan Gordon (Coles) B.; e. McGill Univ., B.A. 1952, M.A. 1954; Yale Univ. M.A. 1955, Ph.D. 1957 (Sr. Sterling Fellow); m. Jean Winifred, d. George Duncan, Northumberland, UK, 18 June 1959; children: Anne Duncan, Mary Elizabeth, Peter Francis; PROF. AND CHRMN. (1968-75) OF BEHAVIOURAL SCIENCE, FACULTY OF MED. UNIV. OF TORONTO and Prof. of Sociol. since 1968; Lectc., Sch. of Pub. Health, Columbia Univ. since 1965; Russel Sage Foundation Post-Doctoral Fellow, Yale Univ. 1957-58; Assoc. Prof., Dept. of Social and Preventive Med., Univ. of Sask. 1959-63 (Acting Chrmn. 1962-63); Sr. mem. Milbank Mem. Fund, N.Y. 1963-68; Visiting Lectr., Dept. of Epidemiol., Yale Univ. 1963-68; Consultant, Expert Adv. Comte. on Health Manpower, World Health Organ. 1969-70); mem. Research & Demonstration Grants Program, Welfare Adm., Washington, 1966-69; Rev-Comm., Nat. Inst. Child Health & Human Devel., U.S. Pub. Health Service, Washington 1966-70; Comm. on Candn. Public Health Assn. 1967-69; Health Services Committee, Ontario Council of Health, 1974-81; Health Promotion Committee, Conference of Federal- Provincial Health Ministers, 1974-76; Chrmn. Committee on the Operation of the Abortion Law, Privy Council, Govt. of Canada 1975-77; mem. Adv. Comte. on Med. Research, World Health Organiz. (PAHO) 1976-; Chmn., Task Force on User Charges, Ont. Council of Health, 1978-79; Fellowship, World Health Organiz. 1978; Chmn., Comte. on Social Sci-Health Research 1979- ; Comte. on Sexual Offences Against Children, Dept. of Justice & Nat. Health & Wel., Gov. of Can. 1980-; Working Group in Collective Bargaining, Ont. Council of Health 1980-; Expert Consultant for World Health Organ. to Israel, Nicaragua and Dominican Republic 1981; co-author, "Doctors' Strike: Medical Care and Conflict in Saskatchewan" 1967, 2nd ed. 1971; "The Family Doctor" 1972 (US), 1973 (Can.); Ed. "Milbank Memorial Fund Quarterly" 1963-68; "Behavioural Science and Medical Education in Latin America" 1966, Spanish transl. 1967; "Social Science and Health Planning: Culture, Disease and Health Services in Columbia" 1968, Spanish transl. 1968; "Social Science and Health in Canada" 1971; co-author, Report of the Comte. on the Operation of the Abortion Law, 1977-; "User charges for Health Services", 1979; author of book chapters, articles and reviews in prof. journs.; mem. Am. Sociol. Assn. (Secy.-Treas. Med. Sociol. Sec. 1965-68); Internat. Sociol. Assn. (Secy'.-Treas. Comte. Med. Sociol. since 1970); Home: 1104 Balmoral Pl., Oakville, Ont. L6J 2C9; Office: Toronto, Ont.

BAETZ, Reuben C., M.A. B.S.W., LL.D.; politician; b. Chesley, Ont., 9 May 1923; s. Harry William and Alice F. (Henrich) B.; e. Univ. of W. Ont., B.A. (cum laude) 1947; Columbia Univ., M.A. 1948; Univ. of Toronto, B.S.W. 1957; Extv. Devel. Sch., Am. Red Cross, 1960; m. Jule Annette, d. Dr. George Anderson, Minneapolis, Minn., 5 Aug. 1950; children: Mark Conrad, Annette Alice, Carla Patricia; MIN. OF RECREATION AND TOURISM, 1982-; Min. of Culture & Recreation, 1978-82; mem., Bd. of Govs., Waterloo Lutheran Univ.; Pres., Internat. Council on Social Welfare; Caseworker, Lutheran World Fed.,

Lubeck, Germany, 1949, and apptd. Dir. of the German Operation of the Fed., 1951; Asst. Dir., Lutheran World Fed. worldwide Operation, Geneva, 1952, and Dir., 1953; appt. Asst. Nat. Commr., Candn. Red Cross, Toronto, Ont., 1956; Extve. Dir., Candn. Welfare Council, Ottawa, 1962; el. to Ont. Leg. June 1977; Parlty. Assist. to Attorney-General Sept. 1977; Min. of Energy Jan. 1978; served in 2nd World War, Candn. Active Service Force, Oct. 1939-Nov. 1942; mem., Candn. Assn. Social Workers; Bd. of Social Ministry, Lutheran Ch. in Am.; Ont. Econ. Council; Trustee for Candn. Inst. for Research on Policy; Lutheran; recreations: golf, fishing, gardening; Club: Rideau; Home: 2400 Georgina Dr., Ottawa, Ont., K2B 7M7; Office: 77 Bloor St. W., Toronot, Ont. M7A 2R9

BAGBY, Robert R.; accountant; b. Casper, Wyo. 9 Nov. 1921; s. Joel Yancy and Margaret Agnes (McDermott) B.; e. Elem. and High Schs. Casper, Wyo.; Creighton Univ. Comm. Coll. 1940-42; Univ. of Denver, Business Adm. 1946-48; Banff Sch. Mang. Course 1965; m. Phyllis Ellen Yarian 6 Feb. 1943; children: Theresa, Michael, Jon, Timothy, Thomas, Patricia; PRESIDENT, GUSTAVSON ARCTIC DRILLING CO.; Extve. Vice Pres., Gustavson Group since 1959; Dir. Kamik Oil Ventures Ltd.; Jasper Sky Tram Ltd.; Gustavson Drilling (1964) Ltd.; started as Shipping Clerk Great Lakes Carbon Corp. 1939-40; Pub. Acct. Chapin & McNamara CPA 1945-46; Drilling Contractor Acct., Fred M. Manning Inc. 1947; Treas. and Office Mgr. Lowell Drilling Inc. 1950 and Gustavson Drilling Co. Ltd. 1953-59; served with U.S. Army Air Corps 1942-45; rank Pilot Offr. A.T.C.; P.O.W. Burma 1944-45; U.S. Army Air Force, Reserve, 1945; rank Lt.; (Past Pres. Candn. Assn. Oilwell Drilling Contractors); R. Catholic; recreations: golf, ranching; Clubs: Calgary Petroleum; Earl Grey Golf & Country; Home: R.R. 2, Cochrane, Alta. T0L 0W0; Office: Algas Mineral Enterprises, P.O. Box 2870, Calgary, Alta. T2P 2M7

BAGNALL, Rt. Rev. Walter E., D.D., LL.D. (Ang.); retired bishop; b. County Tipperary, Ireland, 22 Sept. 1904; e. Primary and Secondary Schs., Dublin, Ireland; Huron Coll., Univ. of Western Ont., grad. 1927; D.D. 1948; McMaster Univ., LL.D. 1959; m. Freida E., d. A.C. Nobbs of London, Ont., 1928; Curate All Saints Ch., Windsor, Ont., 1927; St. Marks, London, 1928; St. John's, Preston, Ont.; Rector, All Saints', Hamilton, Ont., 1936; St. George's, St. Catharines, Ont., 1940; apptd. Canon 1945 and later apptd. Rector of Christ Ch. Cathedral and Dean of Niagara; apptd. Bishop of Niagara 1949, now retired; served in 2nd World War as Padre with R.C.A.F. for 2½ yrs.; Address: 252 James St. N., Hamilton, Ont. L8R 2L3

BAGNELL, Hon. Glen, M.L.A., Ph.C.; pharmacist; b. Truro, N.S. 15 Feb. 1936; s. Alonzo Vernon and Greta Estelle (Montrose) B.; e. Pub. Schs., Truro, N.S.; Acadia Univ., B.Sc. 1957; Dalhousie Univ., Ph.C. 1959; m. Shirley Joan, d. Frank Edward Smith 16 Sept. 1957; children: Paul, Peter, Kenneth, Stephen; Minister of Municipal Affairs, (until 1978) N.S.; 1st elected mem. House of Assembly, 1969; in pharm. practice with Shannon Pharmacy, Dartmouth, N.S.; Past Pres. Dartmouth Chamber Comm.; Un. Appeal Fund; mem. N.S. Pharm. Soc. (Past Examiner); Dartmouth (N.S.) Pharm. Assn. (Past Pres.); Halifax Co. Regional Pharm. Assn.; Freemason; Liberal; recreations: curling, skiing; Clubs: Kiwanis (Past Pres.); Dartmouth Curling; Home: 54 Raymoor Dr., Dartmouth, N.S.;

BAGULEY, Robert, M.A., Ph.D.; economist; b. Niagara Falls, Ont. 28 Jan. 1942; s. Donald and Jean Marian (Stringer) B.; e. Univ. of W. Ont. B.A. 1963; Harvard Univ. M.A. 1966, Ph.D. (Econ.) 1969; m. Nancy Louise, d. Wilfred Samuel Ratz, 12 Oct. 1968; two d. Karen Jane Louise, Jocelyn Suzanne; ASST. GENERAL MANAGER AND DEPUTY CHIEF ECON., THE ROYAL BANK OF CANADA; Asst. Prof of Econ. Univ. of W. Ont. 1967-71;

Chief Econ., Econ. Analysis and Fiscal Policy Div., Dept. of Finance Ottawa 1971-73; mem. Am. Econ. Assn.; Candn. Econ. Assn.; Am. Stat. Assn.; Am. Management Assoc.; Can. Inst. Internat Affairs; Nat. Assoc. Bus. Economists; Nat. Planning Assoc.; Can. Bankers Assoc.; mem. Bd. Dirs., Inst. of Applied Econ. Research, Concordia Univ. Montreal Econ. Assn.; Clubs: University; Canadian; Harvard (Montreal); Home: 403 Walpole Ave., Beaconsfield, Que. H9W 2G6; Office: (P.O. Box 6001) Montreal, Que.

BAILEY, Alfred Goldsworthy, OC, M.A., Ph.D., LL.D., D.Litt., F.R.S.C.; educator; author; b. Quebec, P.Q., 18 Mar. 1905; s. Loring Woart and Ernestine Valiant (Gale) B.; e. Univ. of New Brunswick, B.A. 1927, D.Litt.; Univ. of Toronto, M.A. 1929, Ph.D. 1934; awarded Roy. Soc. Can. Fellowship for Research, 1934; Sch. of Econ. and Pol. Science, Univ. of London, Eng., 1934-35; St. Thomas Univ., LL.D.; McGill U., D.Litt.; Mount Allison, LL.D.; Officer of the Order of Canada, 1978; m. Jean Craig, d. Samuel Alexander Hamilton, Moose Jaw, Sask., 8 Sept. 1934; Prof. Emeritus of Hist. and formerly Prof. of Hist. and Head of Dept., and Vice Pres. (Acad.) Univ. of New Brunswick; Asst. Dir. and Assoc. Curator, N.B. Museum, 1935-38; Univ. of N.B., Lecturer in Anthrop., 1941-50; Dean of Arts, 1946-64; Hon. Librarian, Bonar Law Bennett Lib., 1946-61; mem. Hist. Sites & Monuments Bd. of Canada, 1951-62; former mem., Nat. Lib. Adv. Council; Harold Innis Visiting Prof., Univ. of Toronto, 1955-56; former Pres. of the St. John Art Club, 1936 former Gov., Lord Beaverbrook Art Gallery; former Chrmn., Bd. of Govs., Beaverbrook Playhouse; former Chrmn., Prov. Tree Comn. for N.B.; former mem., Gov.-Gen's Lit. Awards Comte.; Humanities Research Council of Can.; Extve. Comte. of Social Science Research Council of Can.; former Pres., York-Sudbury Hist. Soc.; author of "Songs of the Saguenay and Other Poems", 1927, "Tao: A Ryerson Poetry Chap Book", 1930; "The Conflict of European and Eastern Algonkian Culture, 1504-1700, a study in Canadian Civilization", 1937 (2nd ed. 1969); "Border River", 1952; "Culture and Nationality: Essays", 1972; "Thanks for a Drowned Island", 1973; his poems have appeared in "Candn. Poetry Mag". Vol.1 "Dalhousie Review"; "Canadian Forum"; "Preview"; "Voices"; "Here and Now"; "Oxford Book of Canadian Verse"; "Book of Canadian Poetry"; "First Statement"; "Northern Review"; "Penquin Book of Canadian Verse"; "Ninety Seasons: Modern Poems of the Maritimes"; "Wascana Review"; "Canadian Literature"; "Contemporary Verse"; "Poems of a Snow-Eyed Country; "Anthology of Common Wealth Verse"; "Reflections on a Hill Behind a Town; "Antholgy Commemorating the 35th Anniversary of the founding of the Fiddlehead Anthology of Magazine Verse and Handbook of American Poetry"; etc.; Anglican; recreation: travel; Home: 2 Acacia Grove, Fredericton, N.B. E3B 1Y7

BAILEY, Brig. Gen. Anthony John Beswick, D.S.O., O.B.E., E.D., C.D.; b. Sandwick, B.C., 16 Apl. 1914; s. Maj. John Beswick, D.S.O. and Ida Gertrude Barrow (Mogg) B.; e. Pub. and High Schs., Vernon, Chemainus and Duncan, B.C.; Jr. War Staff Coll., 1941-42; Imp. Defence Coll., 1964; m. Rosemary Dorothy, d. late George Edward Botting, 28 Nov. 1938; children: Christopher John Beswick, Barbara Patricia (Mrs. Robert Longe); enlisted NPAM as Boy Signaller, 1930; comnd. 2nd Lt. RCA 1936; served in various regt'al and staff appts. in Can., U.K., Italy and N.W. Europe, 1939-45; and in sr. staff appts. in Can., 1945-50; commanded 2 RCHA in Korea, May-Nov. 1951; promoted Col. to Command Royal Candn. Sch. of Arty., Camp Shilo, Man., 1951; Dir. of Arty, Ottawa, 1954-57; Chief of Staff, W. Command, Edmonton, 1957-59; Dir. of Mil. Operations and Plans, Ottawa, 1959-60; promoted Brig. and Commdr., E. Ont. Area, Kingston, 1960; Commdr., 2 Candn. Inf. Bgde. Group, Camp Petawawa, 1962-63; Chief of Staff, Training Command, Winnipeg, 1965-66; Dir., Nat. Defence Coll., 1966-

68 when retired; Vice. Pres., Adm., Mt. Allison Univ., 1969-76; awarded M.B.E. 1944, D.S.O. 1945, O.B.E. 1951; Mentioned in Despatches 1944; Anglican; recreation: farming;

BAILEY, R. Bruce, B.Sc.; geologist; petroleum executive; b. Edmonton, Alta. 8 Aug. 1922; s. Robert Henry Manning and Ida Dawson (Hosford) B.; e. Univ. of Alta. B.Sc. 1949; m. Shirley Kathleen d. late E. Atkinson 20 Sept. 1948; children: Lyndsay Jean, Shirley Kim, Robert Bruce Jr., Colleen Joyce; PRES., R. BRUCE BAILEY & ASSOC. LTD., 1980-; Pres. and Dir. Can. Reserve Oil & Gas Ltd., 1975-80; Dir. Reserve Oil and Gas Co. (Los Angeles); Petroleum Geol. Stanolind Oil and Gas 1949-54; Chief Geol. Petrofina Canada 1954-62; Vice Pres. Exploration and Production Banff Oil 1962-63; Div. Mgr. Champlain Petroleum 1963-68; Pres. R.B. Bailey and Assoc. 1968-69; Vice Pres. Exploration Canadian Reserve Oil and Gas Ltd. 1959-75; served with Univ. Air Training Corps; Fellow, Geol. Assn. Can.; mem. Am. Assn. Petrol. Geols.; Candn. Soc. Petrol. Geols.; Assn. Prof. Engrs. Alta.; Past Pres. Royal Candn. Golf Assn.; Past Dir. and Pres., Alta. Golf Assn.; P. Conservative; Protestant; recreations: golf, curling, hunting, photography; Clubs: Calgary Golf & Country; Glencoe; Calgary Petroleum; Home: 911 Edinburgh Rd., Calgary, Alta. T2S 1L7;

BAILLARGEON, Paul Felix, LL.B.; b. Montreal, Que., 16 Feb. 1902; s. late Oliva Leon and Marie Caroline Alphonsine (Mercier) B.; e. St. Mary's Coll., Montreal, P.Q., 1914-18; Loyola Coll., Montreal, 1918-22, arts course; McGill Univ., 1922-24, legal studies; Univ. of Montreal, 1924-25, legal studies and 1927-29, econ. and pol. studies; B.A. 1922; LL.B. 1925, and Master in Econ. and Pol. Science, 1929; m. Marie Thérèse, d. late Napoleon D'Amour, 15 Apl. 1926; children: Guy, Claire, Adele, Andre, Jacques, François; Advocate, Bar of Que. 1925; in gen. practice of law 1925-29 at Montreal, P.Q.; Princ. Translator and Acting Asst. Secy., Bd. of Rly. Commrs. of Can., Ottawa, 1929-32; practised law in Montreal, 1932-35; Secy., Bd. of Rly. Commrs. and Bd. of Transport Commrs. Can. 1935-52; Legal Adv., Bd. of Transport Commrs. Can. 1952-57; in employ of Atty.-Gen. of Que. 1958-62; of Que. Labour Relations Bd. in a legal capacity 1966-70; returned to law practice 1970-75; retired 1975; Home: 10605 Lille St., Montreal, P.Q. H2B 2R4

BAILLIE, Aubrey Wilton; company director; b. Toronto, Ont., 6 July 1908, s. late (Lady) Edith Julia (White) and Sir Frank Wilton B.; e. Appleby Coll., Oakville, Ont. (1918-27); Royal Mil. Coll., Kingston, Ont. (1927-29); Univ. of Toronto, 1929-30; m. Mary Frances, d. late William Finlayson, 5 Jan. 1933; Children: Frank, Phyllis; CHAIRMAN OF BD., BOWES COMPANY LTD., since 1967; Dir., General Accident Assurance Co. Ltd.; served with 48th Highlanders of Can. (Reserve,) 1931-34; 2nd World War (Active), 1940-45; invasion of Sicily and Italy; Anglican; recreations: hunting, fishing; Clubs: Toronto Hunt; Toronto Golf; Home: 1124 Lakeshore Rd. W., Oakville, Ont. L6J 4I5; Office: 75 Vickers Rd., Islington, Ont. M9B 6B6

BAILLIE, Donald Chesley, M.A., F.C.I.A.; consulting actuary; b. Toronto, Ont., 3 April 1915; s. Alexander Hamilton and Mary Garfield (Chesley) B.; e. Univ. of Toronto Schs. (1924-31); Univ. of Toronto, B.A. (Math. and Physics; Gov. Gen. Medal, Trinity) 1935, M.A. 1936; Columbia Univ., 1936-38; m. Mary Jane, d. S.F. Holmes, Wellesley Hills, Mass., 3 Aug. 1957; two d. Christina Mary, Martha Hamilton; ECKLER, BROWN, SEGAL & CO. LTD.; former Assoc. Prof. Dept. of Statistics, Univ. of Toronto, 1958-80; Lect. 1938-41; Ass-Prof. 1945; served in the 2nd World War with R.C.N.V.R., 1941-45; on loan to R.N. for radar duties, at sea in E. Mediterranean, N. Atlantic; ashore in N. Africa and Ireland; mem.-at-large (1961-62), Founding Extve. Comte., Candn. Pension

Conf.; author of "Compound Interest" (with N.E. Sheppard), 1958; various journal articles; Pres., Candn. Assn. for Humane Trapping; Past Pres., Men of the Trees Soc.; Fellow, Can. Inst. of Actuaries; Assoc., Soc. of Actuaries; mem. Task Force on Employee Benefits under Part X of Ont. Employment Standards Act (1973-75); Delta Kappa Epsilon; Anglican; recreations: growing trees, hiking, reading; Home: 20 Wychwood Park, Toronto, Ontario. M6G 2V5

BAIN, George William, Ph.D.; geologist; b. Lachute, Que., 8 May 1901; s. James and Margaret (McFaul) B.; e. Lachute (Que.) Acad., 1916; McGill Univ., B.Sc. (Mining Engn.) 1921, M.Sc. 1923 (Brit. Assn. Medal 1921; Le Roy Fellow 1921); Columbia Univ., A.M. 1923, Ph.D. 1927 (Univ. Fellow 1924); Amherst Coll., A.M. (hon.) 1941; m. Anne Elizabeth, d. Herman H. Kahrs, New York, 18 Sept. 1926; children: Elizabeth Anne, Iris Louise, Bruce Kahrs; Prof. Emeritus of Geol., Amherst Coll., since 1966; Consultant, Vermont Marble Co.; Georgia Marble Co.; Volunteer Extve., Internat. Extve. Service Corps; Asst. Geol. Survey of Can., 1921-24; Asst. Vt. State Geol., 1925; Field Geol., McIntyre Porcupine Mines, 1926; Geol., Vermont Marble Co., 1927-36; Advisor, Nfld. Comte. of Govt. on Marble, 1936; Consultant, Phelps Dodge Copper Corp., 1949-51; U.S. Atomic Energ. Comn., 1950-54; mem. Baruch Comte. for control of Atomic Energy, 1946; Asst. Prof of Geol., Univ. of Vt., 1925-26; joined Amherst Coll. as Instr., 1926; during World War II served as Consultant to Bd. of Econ. Warfare, 1942-43; Manhattan Engr. Dist., U.S. War Dept., 1944-46; rec'd Citation for Exceptional Service from Dept.; awarded Pres.'s Gold Medal, Candn. Inst. Mining & Metall., 1926; Hon. mem., Vocational Assistance Comn. of Republic of China; Dir., Pratt Museum of Geol., 1937-66; author: "Flow of Time Through the Connecticut Valley", 1942, 2nd ed. 1963; "Principles of Geology", 1959; "A Laurasian Looks at Gondwanaland", 1966; contrib. to "Encyclopedia of Science and Techonology" and "Encyclopedia of Earth Science Series"; other writings incl. more than 100 articles on geol. and mineral resource subjects; discoveries incl. Lumar (translucent marble); recovery of uranium from very dilute solutions; recognized recoverable uranium in Witwatersrand gold ores; Hon. Pres., Adams Club, McGill Univ., 1960; mem., Candn. Inst. Mining & Metall.; Am. Inst. Mining Engrs.; Soc. Econ. Geol.; Geol. Soc. Am.; Mineral. Soc. Am.; Geol. Soc. S. Africa; Dir. Hampshire Chapter Red Cross; Geol. Soc. Australia; Chi Phi; Sigma Xi; Episcopal; recreation: travel; Home: 33 Dana Pl., Amherst, Mass. 01002

BAINES, William Douglas, B.Sc., M.S., Ph.D.; mechanical engineer; university professor; b. Edmonton, Alta., 11 Feb. 1926; s. Cyril John Douglas and Mary Winifred (Neale) B.; e. Univ. of Alta., B.Sc. (Engn. Physics) 1947; Univ. of Iowa, M.S. 1948, Ph.D. 1950; m. Alaine Mae, d. Arthur Holmes Barrett, Peekskill, N.Y., 10 Aug. 1950; children: Ian Douglas, Janice Linell, Ross Barrett, Marc Douglas: PROF. OF MECH. ENGN., UNIV. OF TORONTO, since 1966 and Chrmn. of that Dept. 1971-76; Fellow of Massey College; Asst. Prof. of Civil Engn., Mich. State Univ., 1950-51; Research Offr., Nat. Research Council, 1951-59; Head of Hydraulics Lab., 1954-59; joined present Univ. as Assoc. Prof. of Mech. Engn. 1959-66; Acting Dean of Grad. Studies 1970-71; Consultant to Pulp and Paper Inst. of Can. on Papriformer and Papridryer devel.; mem. Gloucester Twp. Sch. Bd. 1957-59; rec'd J.C. Stevens Award, Am. Soc. Civil Engs., 1953; author of over 35 papers in scient. and engn. journs.; mem. Assn. Prof. Engrs. Ont.; Soc. Sigma Xi; Internat. Assn. Hydraulic Research; Internat. Union Theoretical & Applied Mech.; Lambda Chi Alpha; Anglican; recreations: skiing, swimming, sketching, hiking; Home: 1675 Wedmore Way, Mississauga, Ont. L5J 2J7; Office: 5 King's College Rd., Toronto M5S 1A4, Ont.

BAIRD, Charles F., B.A.; executive; b. Southampton, N.Y., 4 Sept. 1922; s. George White B.; e. Middlebury (Vt.) Coll., B.A. 1944; New York Univ. Grad. Sch. of Business Adm.; Advanced Mang. Program, Harvard Univ. Grad. Sch. of Business Adm.; m. Norma Adele White; children: Susan F., Stephen W., Charles F. Jr., Nancy W.; CHMN. AND CHIEF EXECUTIVE OFFICER AND DIR., INCO LTD.; Director Bank of Montreal, ICI Americas Inc.; Aetna Life & Casualty Co.; Financial Extve., Standard Oil Co. of New Jersey 1948-65 (Depy. European Financial Rep., London, 1955-58; Asst. Treas. 1958-62; Dir. and mem. Extve. Comte. Esso Standard S.A. Française, Paris, 1962-65); Asst. Secy. (Financial Mang.) U.S. Navy 1966-67; Under Secy. of the Navy 31 July 1967-20 Jan. 1969; served U.S. Marine Corps 1943-46, 1951-52 (Capt.); Business Council on Nat. Issues; British North-American Comte.; mem. Canadian-American Committee; Council on Foreign Relations; Chairman, Bd. of Trustees, Bucknell Univ.; Candn. Inst. Mining & Metall.; Clubs: Toronto; Queens; Toronto Lawn Tennis Club; Economic; Links; India House (N.Y.); Short Hills; Chevy Chase, Metropolitan (Washington, D.C.); International Lawn Tennis (Washington, D.C.); Home: 35 Rosedale Rd., Toronto, Ont. M4W 2P5; Office: 1 First Canadian Place, Toronto, Ont. M5X 1C4.

BAIRD, David McCurdy, Ph.D., D.Sc., F.R.S.C. (1958); geologist; b. Fredericton, N.B., 28 July 1920; e. Univ. N.B., B.Sc. 1941; Univ. Rochester, M.Sc. 1943; McGill Univ., Ph.D. 1947; D.Sc., Memorial 1972; D.Sc., U.N.B. 1973; DIR., NAT. MUSEUM OF SCIENCE & TECH., since 1966; Teach. Asst., Univ. of Rochester, 1941-43; Demonst., McGill Univ., 1943-46 and Lectr., Dawson Coll. there, summer session 1947; Asst. Prof. of Geol., Mount Allison Univ., 1946-47 and Univ. of N.B., 1947-50; Assoc. Prof. 1950-52; Prov. Geol. for Nfld., 1952-58; Prof. of Geol., Memorial Univ. of Nfld., 1953-54; Head of Dept. and mem. of Univ. Senate, 1954-58; Prof. of Geol. and Chrmn. of Dept., Univ. of Ottawa, 1958-66; Secy., Faculty of Science and mem. of Senate, 1960-62; prof. and field experience incl. N.B. Dept. of Mines; Geol. Survey of Can.; Geol. Survey of Nfld. 1939-66; mem. and Chrmn., Pub. Sch. Bd., Township of Gloucester, 1960-66; has appeared on nat. radio and T.V. programs; rec'd Past Pres.' Medal of Candn. Inst. Mining and Metall., 1965; author of guidebooks to geol. and scenery of Nat. Parks of Can.; mem., Geol. Assn. Can. (Councillor 1956-58); Candn. Inst. Mining & Metall. (Chrmn., Nfld. Br., 1954-55; Councillor 1955-57); Am. Assn. Advance. Science.; Nat. Assn. Geol. Teachers; Candn. Museums Assn.; Nat. Adv. Comte. on Research in Geol. Sciences, 1953-58; Secy., Geol. Sec., Royal Soc. Can., 1960-63 (winner of Barlow Award 1970); Office 1867 St. Laurent Blvd., Ottawa, Ont.

BAIRD, Donald Alexander, B.A., M.S.; librarian/archivist; b. Edmonton, Alta., 29 Jan. 1926; s. Alexander and Elizabeth Morrison (Thompson) B.; e. Univ. of B.C., B.A. 1950; Columbia Univ., M.S. 1951; Pub. Arch. of Can. certificate, 1978; m. Josephine Irene, d. late Sydney Thompson Barlow, 18 May 1957; children: Alexis Rawlings, Brenan Thompson; UNIV. ARCHIVIST AND DIR. OF PUB. HIST., SIMON FRASER UNIV. since 1978; Cataloguer, Vancouver Pub. Lib., 1951-54; Head, Cataloguing Dept., Victoria Pub. Lib., 1954-57 and Univ. of Alta. 1957-60; Asst. Lib., Univ. of Alta. Libraries, 1960-64; Univ. Librarian, Simon Fraser Univ., 1964-77; Adjunct Prof. of Hist., Simon Fraser Univ., 1981-; rec'd Can. Medal; co-author, 'The English Novel, 1578-1956', 1958; other writings incl. articles in prof. journs.; mem. Assn. of B.C. Archivists; Assn. of Can. Archivists; Society of Archivists; Soc. of American Archivists; Am. Lib. Assn.; Candn. Museums Assn.; Candn. Assn. Univ. Teachers; NDP; recreations: gardening, golf; Home: 3052 Armada St., Port Coquitlam, B.C. V3C 3S3; Office: Burnaby, B.C. V5A 1S6

BAIRD, Keith Alexander, B.A.; publisher; b. Kitchener, Ont. 19 Aug. 1925; s. James Roy and Myrtle Adelaide (Waldron) B.; e. Univ. of W. Ont. B.A. 1949; m. Constance Mary d. Benjamin Franklin Hamel 5 Aug. 1949; one d. Judith Leigh Yormak; PUBLISHER, KITCHENER-WATERLOO RECORD LTD. 1975- ; joined present Co. 1949, Asst. Publisher 1969, Vice Pres. 1971; served with RCN 1942-45; contrib. "Historic Heights" 1967; recipient W. Ont. Press Awards 1967, 1969, 1972, 1974; mem. Extve. Comte. The Presbyterian Record; mem. Candn. Daily Newspaper Publishers Assn. (Past Dir.); Candn. Press (Past Dir.); Internat. Press Inst. (Candn. Dir.); Commonwealth Press Union; Ont. Press Council; Freemason; Presbyterian; recreation: power-boating; Clubs: Toronto Press; Westmount Golf & Country (Kitchener); Home: 429 St. Leger St., Kitchener, Ont. N2H 4M8; Office: 225 Fairway Rd. S., Kitchener, Ont. N2G 4E5.

BAIRSTOW, David Steele, B.A.; motion picture executive; producer; b. Toronto, Ont., 27 April 1921; s. William and Florence Ida (Steele) B.; e. Earl Grey Pub. Sch. and Univ. of Toronto Schs. (Toronto, Ont.) 1938; Univ. of Toronto, B.A. 1944; m. Frances Lillian, d. William Kanevsky, Seal Beach, Cal., 17 Dec. 1954; children: Dale Owen, David Anthony; Extve. Producer, Nat. Film Bd. and Prod. of Eng. lang. versions of French films 1971-74; Exchange Prod. with Australian Commonwealth Film Unit 1969-70; has prod. and directed numerous films inc. "Road of Iron" 1954; "Perspective" (a series of T.V. documentaries) 1957; "Frontiers" (Documentary series) 1958-60; "Morning on the Lievre"; "On Their Merit" 1961; "Arctic Circle" 1963; "The Lord of the North" 1964; "Autobiographical"; "Judoka"; "Max in the Morning"; "Instant French" 1965; "Long Ways To Go"; "Once Upon a Prime Time" 1966; "The Accessible Arctic"; "The North has Changed" 1967; "The Stories of Tuktu" 1968-69; Executive Producer of film "Grierson", 1972; awards and recognitions incl. U.S. Nat. Comte. on Films for Safety 1949; Brit. Acad. Award for Documentary; Sydney, Australia Film Award 1952; Edinburgh Festival 1952 and 1961; Am. Film Festival 1960; Montreal Internat. Film Festival; San Francisco Film Festival: Berlin — Silver Bear 1961; Columbus, Ohio 1962; Gold Medal, Australian Nat. Film Festival 1971; Candn. Film Awards 1951, 56, 59, 62; Cork Festival (Ireland), Award for Best Film Short ("Paddington Lace") 1971; Robert Flaherty Award for Documentary Great Britain 1973; served with Candn. Inf. Corps 1945-46; Dir. and Past Pres. Soc. Film Makers; recreations: skiing, theatre; Home: 593 Lakeshore Dr., Beaurepaire, Que. H9W 4K5

BAKER, Bruce Earle, D.Sc.; of U.E.L. descent; b. Stanbridge E., P.Q. 1 Aug. 1917; s. Harry Arnold and Blanche Vivian (Soule) B.; e. Bedford (P.Q.) High Sch., 1937; Fessenden Scholarship for Math. 1939; Bishop's Univ. B.Sc. (1st Hons.) 1940; Laval Univ. D.Sc. 1943; m. late Saxe Clare. d. Earl Currie Cornell, Stanbridge E., 22 May 1948; children: Peter Cornell, Susan Jane, Philip Bruce, Robert Saxe, Jeffrey Arnold; PROF. FACULTY OF AGRIC. MACDONALD COLL. OF McGILL UNIV., since 1964; Chrmn., Dept. Agric. Chem. 1972-76; began as Research Chemist, Mallinckrodt Chemicals, 1944-45; Monsanto Chemicals, 1945-46; Lectr. Agric. Chem., McGill Univ. 1946-48; Asst. Prof., 1948-57; Assoc. Prof. 1957-64; devel. methods of producing sulfanilythioureas; process for hydrolysis of proteins; author and co-author of numerous scient. articles on milk and seed proteins, protein hydrolysates, milk chemistry, pharmaceuticals, pollution of soil and water with pesticides and industrial chemicals, radioactive fallout in arctic and sub-arctic regions and constitution of milks from arctic animals' furage fermentation; mem., Nat. Dairy Council of Canada; mem., Candn. Inst. Food Technol.; Am. Dairy Sc. Assn.; Am. Chem. Soc.; Candn. Inst. Chem.; Sigma Xi; Anglican; recreations: travel, tree farming, reading; Address: P.O. Box 208, Macdonald College, Ste. Anne de Bellevue, Que. H9X 1C0

BAKER, Lt. Col. Charles; executive; b. Toronto, Ont. 10 June 1920; s. late Charles Robert and late Frances Gladys (Stipe) B.; e. Upper Can. Coll., Toronto; Univ. of Toronto; m. Susanne Elizabeth, d. late Frederick Arthur Gaby; children: Charles, (Mrs.) Susanne Young; CHRMN., BD. OF TRUSTEES, THE ONTARIO JOCKEY CLUB and Chrmn., Extve. Comte.; Founder and Pres., Airport Advertising VIP Ltd.; Dir., AGF Japan Fund Ltd.; AGF Spcial Fund Ltd.; American Growth Fund Ltd.; Canadian Security Growth Fund Ltd.; Canadian Gas and Energy Fund Ltd.; Corporate Investors, Ltd.; Corporate Investors Stock Fund Ltd.; Growth Equity Fund Ltd.; Holt, Renfrew & Co. Ltd.; The Quaker Oats Co.; Ritz Carlton, Montreal; Gov., AGF Money Market Fund; AGF Option Equity Fund; Canadian Trusteed Income Fund; Steward, Jockey Club of Canada; Dir. of Thoroughbred Racing Associations; member the Jockey Club, N.Y.; joined Candn. Armoured Corps, Gov. Gen.'s Horse Guards 1940; served overseas as Lt., Italy, France, Belgium and Holland; twice wounded; rank Lt. Col. on discharge; thrice Mentioned in Despatches; Trustee, Gov. Gen.'s Horse Guards; Past Pres. and mem. Extve. Comte. Royal Agric. Winter Fair; recreations: farming, thoroughbred horses; Clubs: Toronto; York; Toronto & North York Hunt; Home: Norcliffe Farms, R.R. 3, King, Ont; Winter Residence: 12 Heronsnest, Sewell's Point, Jensen Beach, Florida 33457; Office: P.O. Box 156, Rexdale, Ont. M9W 5L2

BAKER, Frank P.; paint company executive; b. London, Eng., 29 Jan. 1929; s. Frank P., M.B.E. and E.A. (McDermott) B.; came to Can. 1968; e. St. Peters Sch., York, Eng.; Royal Mil. Acad., Sandhurst, Eng., grad. 1948; m. Anne, d. A. Gilmour, C.M.G. June 1957; children: Francis, Catherine; PRESIDENT AND MANG. DIR., INTERNATIONAL PAINTS (CANADA) LTD., since 1971; Pres. ROC Manufacturing of Canada Ltd., commenced with Pinchin Johnson Paints, Eng., Far East Rep., 1955-58; Mang. Dir. Shalimar Paints Ltd., India, 1958-68; joined present Co. as Extve. Vice-Pres. and Dir., at amalg. with Roxalin of Canada Ltd. 1969; with Brit. Regular Army, 1946-55; retired 1955, rank of Capt.; Anglican; recreations: polo, fencing, hunting, Golf; Clubs: St. James's; Royal Montreal Golf; Marine (Toronto); United Services (London, Eng.); Oriental (London, Eng.); Home: 17 Willow Ave., Westmount, Que. H3Y 1Y3; Office: 6615 Park Ave., Montreal, Que. H2V 4P6

BAKER, Loran Ellis, M.C. Canadian public service (retired); b. Yarmouth, N.S. 21 Sept. 1905; s. George Prescott and Mabel T. (Ellis) B.; e. Bishop's Coll. School, Lennoxville, P.Q.; McGill Univ., 1923-24; O'Sullivan Business School, Montreal 1924-25; m. Elizabeth, d. Arthur S. Creighton, 11 Oct. 1937; one d. Margaret; elected to H. of C. for Shelburne-Yarmouth-Clare in g.e. 1945; Parlty. Asst. to Min. of Nat. Defence, 1949; did not stand for re-el. to H. of C. g.e. 1949; previous to World War 1939-45 was Office Mgr. of coal business, L.E. Baker & Co., Yarmouth; Pres., L.E. Baker & Co. Ltd. 1948-49; apptd. Dir. of Inspection & Consumer Service, Dept. of Fisheries, Ottawa, 1950; Area Dir. of Fisheries (Maritimes) apptd. 1953; served as Pres., Yarmouth 20th Century Club 1935; Yarmouth Bd. of Trade 1936; Vice-Pres., N.S. 20th Century Club 1936; mem., Yarmouth Town Council 1934-37; served in World War 1939-45 with Roy. Candn. Arty. in Mediterranean Theatre and N.W. Europe with rank of Maj.; awarded M.C.; Hon. Lt. Col. 84 Ind. Field Batty.; a member of British Empire Team which won the international Tuna Angling Match at Wedgeport, N.S., 1937; mem. of same team when it waS defeated by the Cuban Team at Liverpool, N.S., 1938; also participated in internat. matches in 1947, '48 and '49; Kappa Alpha; Liberal; Anglican; Clubs: Yarmouth Golf & Country; Address: 10 Grand St., Yarmouth, N.S. B5A 2Z6

BAKER, Ronald James, OC, M.A., LL.D.; president emeritus, university professor; b. London, Eng., 24 Aug. 1924; s. James Herbert Walter and Ethel Frances (Miller) B.; e. Chistlehurst and Sidcup Grammar Sch. Eng.; Univ. of B.C., B.A. 1951, M.A. 1953; Grad. work, Sch., of Oriental and African Studies, Univ. of London 1954-56; LL.D. Univ. of New Brunswick 1970; LL.D. Mount Allison Univ. 1977; came to Can. permanently 1947; m. Helen Gillespie, d. late Thomas Elder, East Lothian, Scot., 3 Sept. 1949; children: Sharon Ann, Lynn Frances, Ian James, Sarah Jane, Katherine Jean; 2ndly, Frances Marilyn Frazer; one s. Ralph Edward; UNIV. PROF,UNIV. OF P.E.I. since 1978; Dir., Inst. for Departmental Leadership (Assoc. Atlantic Universities); Lectr. in Eng., Univ. of B.C., 1953; Assoc. Prof. 1962; first faculty appt. as Head of Eng. Dept. and Dir. of Acad. Planning, Simon Fraser Univ., 1964; First Pres., Univ. of P.E.I., 1969-78; served with RAF in Eng. and Germany, 1943-47; rank Flight Lt., Navig.; Bd. of Examiners, B.C., 1964-66; Acad. Bd., B.C. 1964-69; mem. Bd. of Govs., N.S. Tech. Coll. 1969-78; Holland Coll., Charlottetown 1969-78; mem., Can. Council 1970-76; Bd. of Dirs., Assn. Univs. and Colls. of Can., 1972-78; Pres., Assn. Atlantic Univs., 1976-78; rec'd Centennial Medal 1967; Queen's Jubilee Medal 1977; Offr., Order of Can., 1978; author of a no. of articles in acad. and educ. journs.; mem. Assn. Candn. Univ. Teachers Eng. (Pres. 1967-68); Modern Lang. Assn.; Nat. Council Teachers Eng.; Candn. Council Teachers Eng. (Extve. 1969-77); Candn. Linguistic Assn.; Candn. Soc. for Study of Higher Educ. (Pres. 1975-76); Fellow Roy. Soc. of Arts; Roy. Commonwealth Soc.; recreations: fishing, photography, music, conversation; Clubs: 1864 (Charlottetown) Canadian (Pres. 1974-75); Office: Univ. of P.E.I., Charlottetown, P.E.I. C1A 4P3

BAKER, Hon. Walter David, P.C., Q.C., M.P.; politician; b. Ottawa, Ont. 22 Aug. 1930; s. David Edward and Olive Delphine (LaBerge) B.; e. Albert Coll. Belleville, Ont. 1950; Carleton Univ. B.A. 1953; Osgoode Hall Law Sch.; m. Lois Patricia d. Henry R. Welch 2 June 1956; children: David Richard, Jeffrey Andrew, Nancy Patricia; read law with Hon. A. Kelso Roberts, Q.C. 1956; called to Bar of Ont. 1957; cr. Q.C. 1969; Partner, Bell, Baker, Thompson, Oyen & Webber, 1957-79 Ottawa; Associate counsel, Bell, Baker, 1980-; 1st el. to H. of C. for Grenville-Carleton g.e. 1972, re-el. 1974, re-el. for Nepean-Carleton 1979, 1980; Depy. Opposition House Leader 1973, Opposition House Leader 1976; sworn Pres., Queen's Privy Council for Can. and Min. of Nat. Revenue 1979-80; Leader of Govt. in H. of C. 1979; mem. Community Planning Assn. Can.; Carleton Co. Law Assn.; Bd. Govs. Albert Coll.; Ottawa Bd. Trade; Ont. Mun. Assn. (Assoc. mem.); Ont. Fed. Agric.; Candn. Br. Commonwealth Parlty. Assn.; Candn. NATO-Parlty. Assn.; Can.-U.S. Interparlty. Group; Candn. Group-Interparlty. Union; P. Conservative; United Church; recreations: golf, fishing, cross-country skiing, reading; Clubs: Richmond Curling (Hon. mem.); Carleton Heights Curling (Hon. mem.); Prescott Fish & Game; City View Kiwanis (Past Dir.); Mem. Nepean-Kanata C. of C.; Home: 8 Commanche Dr., Nepean, Ont. K2E 6E9; Office: House of Commons, Ottawa, Ont. K1A 0A6.

BALCER, Hon. Leon, P.C. (Can.) 1957, Q.C., B.A., LL.L.; b. Trois-Rivières, P.Q., 13 Oct. 1917; s. Leon and Berthe (Harnois) B.; e. Semy. des Trois-Rivières, B.A. 1938; Laval Univ., LL.L. 1941; m. Geneviève, d. Hon. Elisée Thériault, C.L., Quebec City, 8 Sept. 1943; children: Pierre, Nicole; EXTVE. VICE-PRES., ELECTRICAL AND ELECTRONICS MFRS. ASSN.; Pres., Elinca Communications Ltd.; Past Pres., Electronics Industry; Past Pres., P. Conservative Assn. of Can.; Past Prov. Organizer, P. Conservative Party, Que. Prov.; called to the Bar of Que., 1941; cr. Q.C., 1952; el. to H. of C. for Trois-Rivières, g.e., 1949-65; Solr. Gen. of Can., 1957-60; Min. of Transport, 1960-63; served in World War, 1941-45 as Lieut.,

R.C.N.V.R.; Roman Catholic; Home: 85 Range Rd., Ottawa, Ont.;Office: 77 Metcalfe St., Ottawa, Ont. K1P 5L6

BALDWIN, Lt. Col. Frederick H., E.D., C.I.B.; insurance executive; b. Sherbrooke, Que., 22 June 1911; s. Frederick A. and Mabel E. (Blue) B.; e. Mitchell Sch. Sherbrooke High and Bishop's Coll. Schs.; Bishop's Univ.; m. Helen McManamy, 28 April 1941 children: Janet, Patricia, Brian; Dir., Baldwin, Fuller and Downey Inc.; Dir., Sherbrooke Trust Co.; President, Sherbrooke Hosp.; joined Orient Hosiery Ltd. 1933; Asst. Supt. 1952; entered Ins. business 1957, purchasing McManamy Insurance Agencies 1957; amalg. with Watson & Fuller Ltd. 1970; joined Sherbrooke Regt. as Pte. 1933; Capt., Sherbrooke Fusilier Regt. 1939; active service in Europe (first Sherbrooke Fusilier to land in Normandy on D. Day); Mentioned in Despatches; C.O., Sherbrooke Regt. 1948-50; Life mem. Royal Candn. Armoured Corps; Past Hon. Pres., Sherbrooke Br., Royal Candn. Legion; Candn. Red Cross (Past Pres.); Bishop's Univ. Alumni Assn. (E.T. Br.) (Past Pres.); Clubs: St. George's (Past Pres.); Compton Fish & Game; Longchamps Country; Sherbrooke Curling; Home: 175 Bryant St., Sherbrooke, Que. J1J 3E6; Office: Continental Bldg., Sherbrooke, Que.

BALDWIN, Gerald William, Q.C., LL.D.; b. Palmerston, N. New Zealand, 18 Jan. 1907; s. Vaudrey Richardson and Maud (Friend) b.; e. High Sch., Edmonton, Alta.; Univ. of Alta. (law); m. Beulah Grace, d. John W. Freeland, Peace River, Alta., 5 Dec. 1930; children: Pat Leatherdale, Barbara Ann Baldwin, Gwennyth Cameron, Gerald, Bruce, Gregory; called to Bar of Alta. 1927; cr. K.C. 1942; served with R.C.A. in Can., Brit. and Europe during 2nd World War; cand. in Prov. g.e. 1935 and Fed. g.e. 1957; el. to H. of C. in g.e. 1958; re-el. until 1979 when retired from politics; Longtime supporter of freedom of information; apptd. Parlty. Secy. to Prime Min., Aug. 1962; el. Chrmn., Pub. Accounts Comte., Oct. 1963; Chrmn. Caucus Comte. on Justice and Special Comte. on Constit.; 1st apptd. Official Opposition House Leader 1968-73; re-apptd. 1977; mem. Law Soc. of Alta.; Royal Candn. Legion; Peace River & Dist. Bar Assn. (Pres.); P. Conservative; Anglican; recreations: skiing, sailing; Home: 206 Kamloops Ave., Ottawa, Ont. K1V 7C9

BALDWIN, Matthew M., B.Sc.; executive; b. Blucher, Sask. 3 May 1926; s. Robert Norman and Lillian Sarah (Martyn) B.; e. Univ. of Alta. B.Sc.(Petroleum Engn.) 1951; m. Elizabeth Jean d. W. Scott Hamilton 9 June 1951; three d. Susan Jane, Sally Elizabeth, Leslie Ann; Pres., Embee Consulting Ltd.; Grizzly Well Servicing Ltd.; Pemball Rentals Ltd.; Dir., Northwell Rentals Ltd.; Eastern Acres Ltd.; Bo-Em Rentals Ltd.; Hi-West Servicing Ltd.; Wardin Well Servicing Ltd.; Dir. Alberta Energy Co.; estbd. Baldwin & Knoll Ltd. 1950; Pres., Edmonton Eskimo Football Club; winner Alta. Curling Championship 1954, 1956-58, 1971; Candn. Curling Championship 1954, 1957, 1958; mem. Can., Alta., Edmonton and Can. Curling Sports Halls of Fame; recreations: curling, golf; Clubs: Edmonton Petroleum; Derrick Golf & Winter; Home: 59 Westbrook Dr., Edmonton, T6J 2C8; Office: 6820-103 St., Edmonton, Alta. T6H 2J2

BALDWIN, R. George, M.A., Ph.D.; educator; b. Vancouver, B.C. 13 Jan. 1927; s. late Sidney George and Vera Berkeley (Bailey) B.; e. Vernon (B.C.) Public Sch. and Preparatory Sch. 1938; Point Grey Jr. and Prince of Wales High Schs. Vancouver, B.C. 1944; Univ. of Brit. Columbia B.A. (Hons. Eng.) 1948; Univ. of Toronto, M.A. 1949, Ph.D. 1957; m. Barbara Kathleen, d. late Joseph Vernor Chew 28 Aug. 1948; children: Christopher George, John Robert (deceased), Janet Kathleen, (Werner); VICE-PRES. (ACADEMIC); UNIV. OF ALBERTA since 1979, and Prof. of English since 1963; joined the Univ. as Lectr. 1951, Asst. Prof. 1954, Assoc. Prof. 1958, Chrmn. Dept. of Eng. 1967-71, Assoc. Dean Arts 1971, Dean of Arts 1972-79; mem. Senate Univ. of Alta.; mem. Assn. Candn.

Univ. Teachers of Eng. (Past Vice-Pres.); Internat. Assn. Univ. Profs. of Eng.; Candn. Assn. Univ. Teachers; Can. Council Sr. Fellow 1966-67; Past Gov. Univ. of Alta.; Alpha Delta Phi; Anglican; Home: 6504-124 St., Edmonton, Alta. T6H 3V3; Office: Edmonton, Alta. T6G 2E1

BALFOUR, James Grant; retailer; b. London, Ont. 1 Aug. 1917; s. Richard Colgan and Ethel Margaret (Grant) B.; e. Univ. of Western Ont., Hons. Business Adm. 1938; m. Margaret Adele, d. late Charles Schmalz, 9 Sept. 1945; children: Richard James, Ian Grant, Barbara McGill; CHRMN. OF BD.; ZELLER'S LTD. since 1979; joined the Co. 1938, apptd. Vice-Pres. and Dir. 1964; Pres. and C.E.D. 1974; recreations: golf, skiing; Club: Royal Montreal Golf; Home: 1009 Hunt Club Mews, London, Ont. N6H 4R7; Office: 5250 Decarie Blvd., Montreal, Que. H3X 3T9

BALFOUR, R. James, Q.C.,; b. Regina, Sask. 22 May 1928; s. Reginald McLeod and Martha (McElmoyle) B.; e. Luther Coll., Regina; Univ. of Sask., LL.B.; m. Beverly Jane, d. Charles Roberts Davidson, Q.C., Regina, Sask. 6 June 1951; children: John Alan, James Roberts, Reginald William, Beverly Ann; PARTNER, BALFOUR, MOSS, MILLIKEN, LASCHUK, KYLE, VANCISE; Dir., KCL Enterprises Ltd.; Royal Trustco Ltd.; The Royal Trust Comp., Royal Trust Corp. of Can.; Comaplex Resources International Ltd.; Ducks Unlimited (Canada); Colonial Oil & Gas Ltd.; read law with R.M. Balfour, Q.C.; called to Bar of Sask. 1952; cr. Q.C. 1969; el. M.P. for Regina East 1972-79; apptd. to Senate 1979; mem. Regina Bar Assn. (Pres. 1956); Sask. Law Soc.; Candn. Bar Assn.; United Services Inst.; Freemason; P. Conservative; Protestant; recreations: sailing, skiing, shooting; Clubs: Assiniboia; Regina Can. Club of New York; Home: 175 Lansdowne Rd. S. Ottawa, Ont. K1M 0N8; Office: 1850 Cornwall St., Regina, Sask. S4P 2K3 or The Senate of Can., Parl. Bldgs., Ottawa, K1A 0A4

BALFOUR, St. Clair, D.S.C., B.A., LL.D.; publisher; b. Hamilton, Ont., 30 April 1910; s. St. Clair and Ethel May (Southam) B.; e. Highfield Sch., Trinity Coll. Sch., Port Hope, Ont.; Trinity Coll., Univ. of Toronto, B.A., 1931; m. Helen Gifford, d. E.G. Staunton, Toronto, Ont., Jan. 1933; children: Elizabeth Staunton, St. Clair; CHAIRMAN, SOUTHAM INC. since 75; Hon. Life mem., Commonwealth Press Union; Canadian Press; Dir., Can. Extve. Service Overseas; Ont. Heart Foundation; Toronto Redevelopment Adv. Council; Gov., Toronto Stock Exchange; Univ. of Toronto; served in 2nd World War; Commander R.C.N.(R.); awarded D.S.C.; Zeta Psi; Anglican; Clubs: Tamahaac; Hamilton; Toronto; Toronto Golf; York; Badminton & Racquet; Home: 17 Ardwold Gate, Toronto, Ont. M5R 2W1; Office: 321 Bloor St. East, Toronto, Ont. M4W 1H3

BALIKCI, Asen, Ph.D.; anthropologist; educator; b. Istanbul, Turkey 30 Dec. 1929; s. Cosma and Nidela (Janeva) B.; e. Internat. Sch. of Geneva 1948; Univ. of Geneva licence ès sciences géographiques 1953; Columbia Univ. Ph.D. (Anthrop.) 1962; m. Verena Ossent (divorced); children: Nicolas, Anna; PROF. OF ANTHROP., UNIV. OF MONTREAL 19.-; anthropol. field work: Macedonian Ethnic Group Toronto 1955; Candn. Eskimos 1957-61; Vunta Kutchin Indians, Y.T. 1961; Peasants in S. Yugoslavia 1962; anthropol. films Netsilik Eskimos 1963-68; Danakil pastoralists in Ethiopia 1969-70; pastoral nomads Afghanistan 1973-76; films incl. "The Netsilik Eskimo Film Series", "Sons of Haji Omar", Nat. Film Bd.; "Man: A Course of Study"; recipient Can. Council, Harvard Univ., Smithsonian Inst., NEH, NSF, Nat. Geographic Soc. grants; author "Vunta Kutchin Social Change" 1962; "The Netsilik Eskimo" 1972; over 50 scholarly articles various anthropol. subjects; mem. Candn. Ethnol. Soc.; Am. Anthropol. Assn.; Greek Orthodox; Home: 476 Outremont Ave., Montreal, Que. H2V 3M3; Office: (P.O. Box 6128) Montreal, Que. H3C 3J7.

BALKE, Mary Noel, B.A.; retired librarian; b. Londonderry, N. Ireland, 25 Dec. 1918; d. Maj. William, M.M. and Jenny (Wilson) Schoales; e. Londonderry (N. Ireland) High Sch., Belvedere and Godolphin Schs., Eng.; Sheffield Univ., B.A. 1939; Reg'd. Prof. Lib. of Ont. 1960; m. Maj. Nicholas Balke, C.D., 2 Sept. 1944; children: William Greer, Jennifer Mary Eileen; trained in Sheffield (Eng.) Pub. Libs. 1939-40; Asst. Lib., Patents and Alloys, Brown-Firth Research Labs., Sheffield, 1940; Research Asst. X-Ray Crystallography, 1942; Lib. and Information Offr., Ministry of Supply, Signals Research & Devel. Estab., Christchurch, Hants., 1943-44; Cataloguer, UN Information Office, London 1945; freelance writing and broadcasting 1948-58; Reference Lib., Ottawa Pub. Lib., 1959-61; Asst. Head, Business & Technol. Dept., 1962-63; Chief Librarian, Nat. Gallery of Can. 1964-79 (ret.); author of various newspaper articles, scripts and interviews for CBC; rec'd. Mem. Award, Candn. Women's Press Club, 1956; mem., Lib. Assn. Gt. Brit. (el. Assoc. 1942); Candn. Lib. Assn. (founding mem. and chrmn., Art Libraries Comte. 1967-69; Special Libraries Assn. (Chrmn. Museums, Arts & Humanities Div. 1974-75); Int. Fed. of Library Assns. & Insts. (Secy., Art Librarians Round Table 1978-79); Anglican; recreations: walking, reading, writing, theatre, swimming; Home: Box 27, Sea Dog, Nanoose Bay, B.C. V0R 2R0

BALKIND, Alvin, B.A.; curator; b. Baltimore, Md., 28 March 1921; s. Benjamin and Nessie (Bers) B.; e. Johns Hopkins Univ., B.A. 1953; Univ. of Paris, Sorbonne, 1954-55; Curator of Contemp. Art, Art Gallery of Ont. 1973;75; Chief Curator Vancouver Art Gallery 1975-78 (lv. of absence, Italy 1978-79); Candn. Commissioner, Paris Biennale, 1980; mem. Arts Adv. Panel of Can. Council; Dir., New Design Gallery, Vancouver, 1955-62; Fine Arts Gallery, Univ. of B.C., Vancouver, 1962-73; served in USN 1943-46; former prof. Univ. of B.C.; past mem. Visiting Comte., Nat. Gallery; author of various catalogues and articles for art journs.; recreation: travel; Home: 4177 W. 14th Ave., Vancouver, B.C.; Office: c/o 4177 West 14th Ave., Vancouver, B.C. V6R 2X6

BALLACHEY, Frank George, B.A., banker; b. High River, Alta. 31 July 1920; s. Alec Addington, Q.C., and Florence Genevieve (Macdonnel) B.; e. High River (Alta.) High Sch. (1938); Univ. of California (Berkeley). B.A. 1947; Nat. Defence Coll., Kingston, Ont. (1957-58); m. Kathleen Beatrice, d. Charles Rivet, Dallas, Texas, 3 Oct. 1959; MANAGER, GOVT. AFFAIRS, THE ROYAL BANK OF CAN. Regional Mgr., Export Financing The Royal Bank of Canada, since Feb. 1970; began as Reporter, Calgary Albertan, 1945-46; with Dept. of External Affairs of Can., 1947-60; Consul, Shanghai, 1948-51; Acting Commr., Internat. Supervisory Comm. Laos, 1954; Pol. Advisor to Candn. Commrs. in Indo-China, 1955-56; Candn. Del. to Malayan Independence Celebrations, 1957; First Secy. and Consul, Stockholm, 1958-59 and Chargé d'Affairs there 1959; Extve. Asst., Canadian Imperial Bank of Commerce, 1960-70; Regional Mgr., Export Financing, The Royal Bank of Can. 1970-80; served in 2nd World War with R.C.A.F. 1942-45, Flying Offr. (Pilot); Montreal Br., Candn. Inst. Internat. Affairs; Candn.-Scandinavian Foundation; Kappa Alpha; R. Catholic; recreations: golf, fishing, bridge; Clubs: University; Montreal, Knowlton Golf; Sombrero Country Club, Marathon Florida; Rideau; Royal Ottawa Golf Club; Home: R.R. 1 Ashton, Ont.; Seaview Dr., Plantation Island, Duck Key Fla. 33050; Office: Royal Bank Centre, 90 Sparks St. Ottawa, Ont. K1P 5T6

BALLANTYNE, Harold Kerr; reinsurance executive; b. Toronto, Ont., 8 Oct. 1919; s. Robert and Ethel (Scriven) B.; e. Toronto (Ont.) Pub. and High Schs.; m. Dorothy Brookes; one d. Heather Lynn; Chmn., JOHN F. SULLIVAN CO. OF CANADA LTD. Underwriter, London and Lancashire Ins. Co. Ltd. 1936-43; Inspr., Central Mutual Ins. Co. Ltd., 1943-50; Supt. of Agencies, National of Hartford Ins. Co., 1950-53; Sr. Vice Pres., Canadian Reinsurance Co., 1954-78; joined present co. 1978; Past Pres., Ins. Inst. Ont. (Award of Merit 1974); Anglican; recreations: curling, golf; Clubs: Donalda; Ontario; R.C.Y.C.; Home: 35 Caravan Dr., Don Mills, Ont. M3B 1M9; Office: Ste. 2100, Commerce Court North, Toronto, Ont.

BALLEM, John Bishop, Q.C., M.A., LL.M.; b. New Glasgow, N.S., 2 Feb. 1925; s. John C., M.D. and Flora (Miller) B.; e. Dalhousie Univ., B.A., 1946, M.A. 1948, LL.B. 1949; Harvard Univ. Law Sch., LL.M. 1950; m. Grace Louise, d. Aird Flavelle, Vancouver, B.C., 31 Aug. 1951; children: Flavelle Bishop, Mary Mercedes, John Flavelle; PARTNER, BALLEM, McDILL & MacINNES: author of several novels incl. "The Moon Pool", "Alberta Alone" and "Sacrifice Play"; a legal textbook "The Oil and Gas Lease in Canada" and numerous articles in various legal journs. and nat. mags.; TV host and narrator; mem. Phi Delta Theta; Presbyterian; Clubs: Calgary Golf & Country; Petroleum; Address: 3600 Scotia Centre, 700 2nd Street SW, Calgary, Alta. T2P 2W2

BALLMANN, Franz; banker; b. Germany 11 November 1924; s. Wilhelm Karl and Elsa (Gruener) e. Dilthey School, Wiesbaden, Germany; Goethe University, Frankfurt/Main; First Legal State Examination 1950, Great Legal State Examination 1953; m. Kwee Fong How, Singapore; 2 sons 1 daughter; VICE PRES. AND ASSOC. CHIEF ECON. (INTER-NAT) BANK OF MONTREAL 1978- ; Pres., Alexander von Humboldt School, Montreal; Assoc. Atty. at Law, Wiesbaden 1953; Assoc. Counsellor, Hessian Ministry of Econ. & Transport 1954; Assoc. Counsellor, Fed. Ministry of Econ., Bonn 1955; Counsellor: Fed. Ministry of Econ., Bonn 1958; Legal Dep't. I.M.F. Washington 1960 to 1967; Sr. Counsellor: Fed. Ministry of Econ. Bonn (on leave of absence) 1965; Special Consultant on Currency, Banking & Foreign Exchange to Depy. Prime Min. and Min. for Finance, Singapore 1967-70; Temporary Alternate Gov. IBRD. for Singapore 1968; Dir.Fed. Min. Econ. Bonn (on leave of absence) 1969; Financial Adv. Bank of America NT and SA, London, Eng. 1970; Vice Pres. and Chief Financial Adv. 1971; resigned from German Civil Service 1971; Sr. Banking Adv. The Monetary Authority of Singapore 1974; Vice Pres. Internat. Banking Europe, Middle E. & Africa Div. Bank of Montreal, London, Eng. 1975; Served in Second World War 1943/45 as Company Commander; Mem: Can. Institute of Inter. Affairs (C.I.I.A.); Société Universitaire Européenne de Recherches Financiéres (S.U.E.R.F.); the British Sub Aqua Club; Recreations: Deep sea fishing; scuba diving; underwater photography; Home: 345 Leacross, Town of Mount Royal, Qué. H3P 1L9; Office: 129 rue St. Jacques, Montréal, Qué. H2Y 1L6

BALLOCH, Anthony Edward, O.B.E., B.A., D.C.L., LL.D.; retired paper manufacturing executive; b. Woking, England, 29 March 1916; s. Gideon and Muriel Sutcliffe Montagu (Mort) B.; e. Winchester Coll., 1929-34; Magdalen Coll., Oxford, B.A. (Hons.) 1937; D.C.L. Acadia 1967; LL.D., St. Francis Xavier 1968; m. Mary Chase, d. Admiral H. S. Howard, U.S.N., Washington, D.C., 1946; children: Patricia Ann (Tuff), Josephine Mary Chase (Ahrens), Howard Robert, Hugh McCauley; Dir., Bowater Corp. and Bowater Inc.; with Bowater Paper Corp. 1938-80 in various capacities in Britain, U.S.A. and Canada; Bowaters Nfld. Pulp & Paper Mills Ltd., 1952-61, and a Dir. of that Co., 1958-61; Commd. in Royal Arty. (T.A.) 1936; served in 2nd World War; London A.A. Defences, Brit. Army Staff in Washington, and 15th Army Group and 5th U.S. Army in Italy; retired as Lieut.-Col.; O.B.E.; Mentioned in Despatches; U.S. Legion of Merit; U.S. Bronze Star Medal; mem. of Tech. Sec., Candn. Pulp & Paper Assn.; Anglican; recreations: golf, tennis, photography; Clubs: St. James's (Montreal); Conanicut Yacht (Jamestown, R.I.); Montreal Badminton; Home: 7 Glen Hill Lane, Wilton, Conn., 06897;

BALLS, Herbert Ryan, B.A., D.M.Sc. (Ottawa 1973); b. Winnipeg, Man., 24 May 1910; s. George Herbert and Alma Myrtle (Ryan) B.; e. Kelvin High Sch., Winnipeg, Man.; Univ. of Manitoba, B.A. (Hons.) 1931; Post-grad. studies in Pol. Science and Econs. at Univ. of Manitoba and Univ. of Toronto; m. Evelyn Marjorie, d. James Alexander Clarke, Ottawa, Ont., 7 Sept 1937; Dir. Northern Ont. Pipeline, Crown Corp., 1956-68; Dir., Candn. Nat. (W.I.) Steamships Ltd., 1960-71; staff of Auditor-Gen. of Can.; 1931-50; mem. of Research Staff, Royal Comm. on Dom.-Prov. Relations, 1938; Special Asst. to Dir. of Public Accounts Enquiry for Dom.-Prov. Conf., 1941-42; Special Asst. to Deputy Min. of Finance, 1950-54; Dir. of Financial Adm. and Accounting Policy Div., Dept. of Finance, 1954-58; Pres., Civil Service Co-op. Credit Society Ltd., 1957-59; Comptroller of the Treasury, 1958-68; Deputy Min. of Services and Deputy Rec. Gen. for Can. 1968-75, Skelton Clark Fellow, Queens Univ. (1975-76); Research Fellow, Inst. of Public Admin. of Canada; mem. Bd. of Govs., Candn. Council on Social Devel.; mem. Bd. of Govs., Huntington Univ. 1968-71; Pres. Un. Appeal of Ottawa and Dist., 1963-65; Chrmn., Community Funds and Councils of Can., 1965-69; Chrmn. Nat. Agency Review Comte, 1971-74; Director, Ont. Share and Deposit Insur. Corp.; mem., Inst. of Public Adm. Can. (Nat. Pres. 1960-61); United Church; recreations: painting, writing, gardening; Club: Rideau; Home: 2026 Thistle Cres., Ottawa, Ont. K1H 5P5

BALTZAN, David M., M.D., C.M., LL.D., F.A.C.P., F.R.C.P.(C), F.R.S.M., F.R.S.A. b. Bessarabia, 1897; s. Moses Alter and Yetlac (Bondar) B.; e. McGill Univ., M.D., C.M.; Diplomate, Am. Bd. of Internal Med.; m. Rose, d. Abe Cristall, 1927; three s. Dr. M.A., Dr. Don M., Dr. R.B.; Emeritus Prof. of Clinical Med., Univ. of Sask., former Chief of Staff and Chief of Dept. of Med., St. Paul's Hosp., Saskatoon; Consultant in Med., Univ. Hosp., Univ. of Sask.; Canadian National Rlys; Tuberculosis Sanatorium, Saskatoon; Dir. Sask. Heart Foundation; mem., Candn. Heart Foundation; Candn. Med. Assn. (Sr. mem. 1966); Am. Med. Assn.; Brit. Med. Assn. Internat. Soc. Internal Medicine; Acad. of Internal Med. of Sask. (Past Pres. and Founder); John Howard Soc. (Past Pres.); Canda. Council of Christians & Jews (Nat. Dir.); Candn. Inst. Internat. Affairs; Trustee, Queen Elizabeth II Candn. Fund for Research; Commr., Royal Comn. on Health Services; first Clinical Dir., Sask. Cancer Clinic; Past Pres., Sask. Med. Assn.; Acad. of Med. of Sask.; Publications: "Text Book-Internal Medicine"; "A Hepata-Cerebral Syndrome", 1936: "Hereditary Cynanosis"; "Bronchomoniliasis", 1940; "Brucellosis", 1937, and more than 50 other scient., med. and nursing publs.; awarded Coronation Medal, King Geo. VI; rec'd. Human Relations Award, Candn. Council Christians & Jews; Life mem., St. John of Jerusalem, Order Grand Priory Eng.; world traveller all continents, health, medical interests; Endowments: Baltzan Med. Canadiana Library (Univ. of Sask.); Drs. Baltzan Scholarship (Nutana Coll.); Baltzan-Baltzan (Hebrew Univ. Scholarship); mem. Candn. Authors' Assn.; New York Acad. of Science; B'Nai Brith; Address: Baltzan Associate Medical Clinic, Saskatoon, Sask. S7K 0A6

BAMFORD, Ralph Leonard, B.Acc., F.C.A.; b. Moose Jaw, Sask., 16 June 1910; s. Harry Holden and Ida Jane (Marks) B.; e. Victoria Pub. Sch., Moose Jaw, 1923; Central Coll. Moose Jaw, 1928; Univ. of Sask., B.Acc. 1931; Inst. of C.A.'s, Sask., 1934; F.C.A. 1956; m. Katharine Miriam, d. late Dr. Angus A. Graham, London, Ont., 10 June 1939; children: Margaret Anne (Mrs. Geo. Serviss), Janet Elizabeth (Mrs. Don Martin), David Graham, Douglas Murray; with Hodge, Bamford & Wilder, Chart. Accts., 1930-36; joined Ernst & Ernst, Toronto, 1936-40; Asst. Comptroller, Candn. Pacific Air Lines, Winnipeg and Montreal, 1942-44; Auditor, Subsidiaries of C.P.R., Montreal, 1944; became Sr. Partner, Hodge, Bamford & Wilder, Moose Jaw, 1944-50; R. L. Bamford & Co., 1950-

65; Resident Partner (Regina) McDonald Currie & Co. 1965-70; served as Comptroller, No. 3 Air Observer Sch., Regina, 1940-42; Local Treas. and mem. Prov. Extve., Candn. Red Cross; Past Pres. and Past Dist. Gov., Lions Club; Past Pres., Candn. Inst. of C.A.'s; former member, Senate, University of Sask.; former Trustee, Moose Jaw General Hospital Building Fund; Finance Chairman, Diocese of Qu'Appelle; Past Local and Prov. Pres., Chamber Comm.; Past mem. Extve Comte., Candn. Chamber Comm.; Past Pres., Sask. Inst. C.A.'s; Founding Dir., Sask. Soc. Indust. & Cost Accts.; Freemason; Conservative; Anglican; recreations: golf, curling, gardening, carpentry, music; Club: Kiwanis; Home: 2355 Arbutus Rd., Victoria, B.C. V8N 1V6

BANASCHEWSKI, Bernhard, F.R.S.C.; university professor; b. Munich, Germany, 22 March 1926; s. Adalbert Schremmer and Anna Magdalena B.; e. Hamburg Univ.; Dr. rerum naturarum; came to Canada, 1955; Asst., Hamburg Univ., 1953-55; Asst. Prof., McMaster Univ., 1955-57; Assoc. Prof., 1957-59; Prof., 1959; Dept. Chrmn. 1961-67; McKay Prof. of Math. 1964; served in 2nd World War in German army (Wehrmacht) 1944-45; prisoner-of-war, 1945-47; Assoc. Ed., Candn. Journal of Math. 1968-79; Ed. Bd., Gen. Topology and Its Applications, 1970; author of over 75 papers on algebra, gen. topology and related fields; mem., Candn. Math. Cong.; Am. Math. Soc.; Home: 100 Bay St. S., Apt. 503, Hamilton, Ont. L8P 3H3

BANDEEN, Robert Angus, O,C., B.A., PH.D., LL.D. D.C.L. (Hon.); transportation executive; b. Rodney, Ont., 29 Oct. 1930; s. John Robert and Jessie Marie (Thomson) B.; e. Univ. of W. Ont., B.A. (Hons.) 1952; Duke Univ., (1952-55) Ph.D. 1959; U. of Western Ont. Hon. LL.D. 1975; Dalhousie U. Hon. LL.D. 1978 Bishop's U. Hon. D.C.L. 1978 m. Mona Helen, d. S.M. Blair, Bolton, Ont., 31 May 1958; children: Ian Blair, Mark Everett, Robert Derek, Adam Drummond; President and Chief Extve. Offr., Candn. National 1974-82; Chrmn. and Dir., Grand Trunk Corp.; Grand Trunk Western Railroad; Central Vermont Rly., Duluth Winnipeg & Pacific Rly.; Detroit, Toledo Ironton Railroad; CNCP TeleCommunications; CN (France); Dir., Crown Life Ins. Co.; Mortgage Ins. Co.; Extendicare Ltd. Intercast S.A.; Eurocanadian Shipholdings Ltd.; joined present Co. as Asst. Econ. 1955; Research Stat. 1957; Staff Offr., Planning 1959; Chief, Costs and Stat. 1960; Chief, Devel. Planning 1961; Dir., Corp. Planning 1966; Vice-Pres., Corp. Planning and Finance 1968; Vice Pres., Great Lakes Region 1971; Extve. Vice Pres., Finance and Adm. 1972; Senator, Stratford Shakespearean Festival; Chancellor, Bishop's Univ. (Dir. of foundation, mem. of Corp.); British-North American Comte.; Howe Inst. Policy Analysis Comte Quebec Prov. Council of Boy Scouts of Canada, Hon. Vice-Pres.; (hon. mom. of Nat'l Council); Candn. Railway Club; Candn. Transport. Research Forum; Nat. Freight Traffic Assn.; Toronto Railway Club; Dir., Concordia Centre for Management Studies; Festival Lennoxville; Gov., Sport Participation Can.; mem., Adv. Comm., Can. Sk, Council; recreations: tennis, squash, skiing; Knight, The Order of St. John; Clubs: M.A.A.A.; St. James's (Montreal); Mount Royal; Delta Upsilon Fraternity; Home: 3120 Daulac Road, Westmount, Que. H3Y 2A2

BANFIELD, Alexander William Francis, M.A., Ph.D., university professor; b. Toronto, Ont., 12 March 1918; s. Rev. Alexander Woods and Althea (Priest) B.; e. Univ. of Toronto, B.A. 1942, M.A. 1946; Univ. of Michigan, PhD 1952; research fellow, Univ. Edinburgh 1975-76; m. Martha Fern, d. Fraser Duncan Munro, Lancaster, Ont., 3 Oct. 1942; children: Brian Alexander, Candace Anne, Martha Kim; PRES., RANGIFER ASSOCIATES ENVIRONMENTAL CONSULTANTS since 1979; joined Canadian Civil Service as Mammalogist, Nat. Parks Bureau, 1946-47; Chief Mammalogist, Candn. Wildlife Service, 1947-57; joined Nat. Museum of Natural Sciences, Ottawa as Chief Zoologist 1957; Dir., 1964-69; Prof. of Biol. Sciences, Brock Univ. 1969, Dir. Inst. of Urban & Environmental Studies 1974-79; Prof. Emeritus, Brock Univ., 1980; served in 2nd World War; enlisted Apr. 1942; discharged Oct. 1945; Overseas service with rank of Capt., Signal Corps and later Arty.; Publications: "Mammals of Canada" 1974, 2 books and over 100 scientific articles dealing with mammalogy, ornith, and wildlife management; Fellow, Arctic Inst. N.Am.; Am. Assn. Advance. Science; mem., Am. Soc. of Mammal; Candn. Soc. of Zool.; Fauna Preservation Soc. of Britain; Centennial Medal 1967; Phi Sigma; Sigma Psi; United Church; Address: 37 Yates St., St. Catharines, Ont. L2R 5R3

BANISTER, Eric W., B.Sc., M.P.E., Ph.D.; educator; b. Kirby-in-Furness, Lancs. Eng., 18 May 1932; s. Eric and Alice Ann (Halshall) B.; e. Manchester Univ., B.Sc. 1953; Loughborough Coll., Dipl. (PE) 1954; Univ. of B.C., M.P.E. 1962; Univ. of Ill., Ph.D. 1964; m. Maureen d. Stanley Landless, N. Wales, 6 Aug. 1960; children: Simon John, Fiona Jane, Susan Pia; PROF. OF KINESIOLOGY, SIMON FRASER UNIV. and Chrmn. of Dept. since 1970; Dir., Inst. for Human Performance, 1980-; Pres., Western Fitness Consultants Ltd., Vancouver; mem. Med. Adv. Comte., Remedial Gymnast Association (B.C.) 1971-73 and Candn. Soccer Assn. 1972-79; joined Univ. of B.C. as Asst. Prof.; Dept. of Phys. Educ. 1964-67; joined present Univ. as Asst. Prof. Dept. of Phys. Devel. Studies, 1967-69, Assoc. Prof. of Kinesiology, 1970; Acting Chrmn. of Dept. 1970; served with Parachute Regt., Brit. Army, 1954-56; rank 2nd Lt.; Ed. Chrmn., Proceedings 5th Internat. Hyperberic Conf., 1973; author of book chapters, reviews and over 60 articles in scient. journs.; Fellow, Am. Coll. Sport Med.; mem., Undersea Med. Soc.; Candn. Ass. Sports Sciences (Pres. 1977-78); Am. Soc. Sports Med.; Human Factors Assn. Can.; Human Factors Soc. Am.; Vice Pres., Sport Med. Council Can.; Ed., Candn. Journal of Applied Sports Sciences 1980-; Anglican; Home: 2651 Haywood Ave., W. Vancouver, B.C. V7V 1Y7; Office: Burnaby B.C. V5A 1S6

BANISTER, Rodger Thorson, B.Com.; construction executive; b. Calgary, Alta. 23 Aug. 1945; s. Ronald Kitchener and Inez Adelaide (Thorson) B.; e. Strathcona Composite High Sch. Edmonton; Univ. of Alta. B.Com.; m. Joan Ilene d. Robert Lucy 9 May 1970; children: Rodger Ronald, Jody Lucy; PRES. AND CHRMN. OF BD., BANISTER CONTINENTAL LTD. 1975- ; Pres., K. R. Ranches (1970) Ltd.; Rodban Holdings Ltd.; L.R.H.M. Investments Ltd.; Secy.-Treas. The Banister Corp.; Dir.; Cambridge Developments Ltd.; Saxon Properties Ltd.; Extve. Asst. and Dir. Banister Construction (1963) Ltd. Edmonton 1968; Asst. Vice Pres. Continental Computer Associates Inc. Edmonton 1969; Pres. K. R. Ranches (1970) Ltd. Edmonton 1970; Dir. and Chrmn. Extve. Comte. Banister Continental Ltd. 1974-75; Dir. Edmonton Art Gallery; Dir. Edmonton Air Services Authority; Dir. Construction Industry Dev. Council; mem. Young Pres.' Organ.; Phi Delta Theta; recreations: flying, skiing, reading; Clubs: Mayfair Golf & Country; Petroleum; Home: 4807 - 138 St., Edmonton, Alta. T6H 3Y9; Office: (P.O. Box 2408) 9910 - 39 Ave., Edmonton, Alta. T5J 2R4.

BANKES, John Maxwell; banker (ret.); b. Victoria, B.C., 28 June 1915; s. Stanley Fownes and Frances Victoria (McArthur) B.; e. Monteray at Oak Bay, Victoria; Oak Bay High Sch.; Victoria Coll.; m. Betty Jean, d. George Ingraham, Calgary, Alberta, 2 Nov. 1950; one s.; two d.; Pres. and Dir., Laker Air Travel (Can.) Ltd.; Chrmn. and Dir., Monsanto Canada Ltd.; Majestic Wiley Contractors Ltd.; Ont. Director, Can. Schenley Distilleries Ltd.; Dir., Heuga Can. Ltd.; commenced with the Royal Bank in Canada in 1934 at Victoria, B.C.; served at various brs. in B.C. and at Supv. Dept., Vancouver till 1941 when attached to Asst. Gen. Mgrs. Dept., Toronto; Asst. Mgr., Hamilton, Ont. 1946; Mgr. Bus. Devel. Dept., Calgary, 1950; Mgr., Portage Ave. Winnipeg 1952; Ottawa 1953, at Toronto Main Br. 1957; apptd. Asst. Gen. Mgr. 1961; Depy. Gen. Mgr. 1964-71; Vice-Pres. 1971-75; served in Royal Candn. Navy, 2nd World War 1942-45; mem. R.C.N.V.R.; Protestant; recreations: golf, swimming, boating, Clubs: Toronto; Granite; Toronto Hunt; Rosedale Golf; Royal Poinciana Golf; Port Royal (Naples, Fla.); Home: 113 Mildenhall Road, Toronto, Ont. M4N 3H4; Office: Ste. 1015, Royal Bank Plaza, Toronto, Ont. M5J 2J5

BANKS, Peter, M.D., F.R.C.P.(C), D.Sc., F.R.C.P. (Lond.), F.R.C.P.I., F.A.C.P.; consultant physician; b. Eng., 12 June 1922; s. Joseph Charles Richard and Kathleen Grace (Harvey) B.; e. Epsom Coll., Eng.; St. Bartholomew's Hosp., Univ. of London; m. Mary Barbara, d. late F. R. Way, O.B.E. 1946; three children; Pres. B.C. Med. Assn. 1965, Candn. Med. Assn. 1973-74; British Med. Assn. 1973-74; Commr., B.C. Medical Service Commission 1968-71; served in R.A.F.; Pres., Community Chest, Victoria, B.C.; Gov., Shawinigan Lake Sch.; Fellow Royal College of Physicians (Eng.); recreations: fly fishing, bird hunting, library; Club: Union; Home: 2997 Seaview, Victoria, B.C. V8N 1L2; Office: 360-1105 Pandora Ave., Victoria, B.C. V8V 3P8

BANKS, Tommy (Thomas Benjamin); pianist; conductor; composer; b. Calgary, Alberta. 17 Dec. 1936; CHRMN., ALTA FOUNDATION FOR PERFORMING ARTS 1978- ; Prop. Tommy Banks Music Ltd., music production and publishing; affiliate PRO Canada; began career as pianist at 14 with Don Thompson's band; Mus. Dir. Orion Musical Theatre, Edmonton 1954-59 and also led own groups' performances W. Can. and USA; accompanied many pop performers as pianist or orchestra conductor 1960-68; led jazz quintet Expo '67; produced and directed "Klondike Follies" starring Paul Anka 1967; Host, pianist, arranger and conductor "The Tommy Banks Show" (CBC-TV Edmonton 1968-71, CBC Nationally 1971-74, ITV international syndication 1974-76, CBC Edmonton 1980-); "Celebrity Revue", independent int'l synd. 1977-78; Music co-ordinator and occasional conductor ITV "In Concert" series for int'l synd.; also "Palace" starring Jack Jones (US singer) with Hamilton Philharmonic Orch. 1979; frequent guest conductor Edmonton Symphony incl. premiere and recording Rod McKuen's "Ballad of Distances" 1973; performer and occasional host CBC "Jazz Radio Canada"; performed Montreux Jazz Festival Switzerland 1978 (double LP of concert rec'd Juno Award 1979); composer "The Lady That's Known as Kate", "The Gift of the Magi" and score for CBC production Pierre Berton's "Klondike"; producer of numerous jingles; Board of Governors, Alberta College 1977-79; Member Nat'l Adjudicators Comte. Cdn. Stage Band Festival; occasional adjudicator, Canada Council 1977- ; Achievement Awards Prov. of Alberta 1971 and 1978; Outstanding Achievement Awards City of Edmonton 1975 and 1979; Hon. member Cosmopolitan International 1979; Hon. Diploma of Music, Grant MacEwan College 1979; Grand Prix du Disque - Canada 1979; Address: 2, 12227 - 107th Avenue, Edmonton, Alberta T5M 1Y9

BANMAN, Hon. Robert David, M.L.A.; politician; b. Winnipeg, Man. 10 Jan. 1945; s. Jacob G. and Barbara (Enns) B.; e. Steinbach (Man.) High Sch.; m. Joanne d. Art Baerg, Steinbach, Man. 11 July 1968; one s. David Robert oned. Heidi;MIN. OF FITNESS, RECREATION & SPORT, MAN., Min. of Co-operative Devel. 1978- and Min. responsible for Man. Lotteries & Gaming Act 1979-; mem. Steinbach Town Council 1970-73; el. M.L.A. for La Verendrye prov. g.e. 1973, re-el. 1977; Min. of Industry & Comm., Min. of Tourism, Recreation & Cultural Affairs, Min. Responsible for Adm. Man. Devel. Corp. Act 1977; P. Conservative; Mennonite; Clubs: Steinbach Curling; Steinbach Flying; Office: 333 Legislative Bldg., Winnipeg, Man. R3C OV8.

BANTING, Peter Myles, B.A., M.B.A., Ph.D.; educator; marketing consultant; b. Hamilton, Ont., 17 March 1936; s. Joseph Maitland and Beatrice Aline (Myles) B.; e. McMaster Univ., B.A. 1958, M.B.A. 1965; Mich. State Univ., Ph.D. 1971; m. Wendy Sharon Papple 24 Apr. 1981; PROF. OF BUSINESS McMASTER UNIV. since 1967; Ed., "The Harvester", Internat. Harvester Co. of Canada Ltd., 1959-64; Instr., Mich State Univ., 1965-66; Consultant, Prov. Fed. and Foreign Govts. and Indust.; author, "Marketing in Canada", 1973, "Canadian Marketing: A Case Approach", 1977; co-author, "Canadian Cases in Marketing", 1968; other writings incl. monographs and articles in learned and prof. journs.; Gov., Acad. of Marketing Science; mem. Am. Fed. Musicians; Am. Marketing Assn.; Sales & Marketing Extves. Internat.; Beta Gamma Sigma; Anglican; Home: 2153 Paisley Ave., Burlington, Ont. L7R 1W1; Office: Hamilton, Ont. L8S 4M4

BANZ, George, M.S., R.C.A.; architect; b. Lucerne, Switzerland 21 Dec. 1928; s. Robert and Josephine (Simeon) B.; e. elem. and secondary schs. Lucerne 1947; Swiss Fed. Inst. of Technol. Zurich Dipl. Arch. 1951; Okla. State Univ. (U.S.-Swiss Exchange Fellowship) M.S. (Arch. Engn.) 1952; m. Josette d. late Paul Charmillot 3 Sept. 1958; children: Paul Eric, Caroline Louise; self-employed GEORGE BANZ ARCHITECT: Pres. Urbanprobe Associates Ltd.; mem. Univ. of Toronto Sch. of Arch. Faculty 1960-64, 1970-75; Sessional Lecturer 1978- ; Associate of Inst. for Environmental Studies 1971- ; Special Consultant to Min. of State for Urban Affairs, Ottawa 1972-74; Part-time mem. Faculties of Ont. Coll. of Art (Indust. Design) 1980-; Univ. of Waterloo (Sch. of Arch.) 1980-81; recipient numerous design awards and distinctions; author "Elements of Urban Form" 1970; numerous articles and papers on architecture, planning and computer-sided design; mem. Comte. of Adjustment City of Toronto 1980- ; mem. Ont. Assn. Archs.; Royal Arch. Inst. Can.; Royal Candn. Acad. of Arts; Home: 498 St. Clair Ave. E., Toronto, Ont. M4T 1P7; Office: (P.O. Box 12 Station Q) Toronto, Ont. M4T 2L7.

BARABAS, Silvio, D.Sc.; scientist; b. Sarajevo, Yugoslavia 10 June 1920; s. Samuel and Sarah (Kabiljo) B.; came to Can. Nov. 1951; e. Univ. of Padua, Italy D.Sc. 1950; m. Louise Sofonio 12 Sept. 1959; children: Allen, Bertrand; HEAD OF ANALYTICAL RESEARCH, CAN. CENTRE FOR INLAND WATERS, INLAND WATERS DIRECTORATE, ENVIRONMENT CANADA, 1971- ; Mgr., World Health Org. Internat. Collaborating Centre on Surface and Ground Water Quality; Editor, 'Water Quality Bulletin'; Chief Chemist, Noranda Research Centre, 1953-66; Managing Dir., Technicon Corp., Tarrytown, N.Y., Montreal 1966-71; author of over 120 articles and patents in Analytical Chemistry, Instrumentation and United Nations Global Water Quality Monitoring; Fellow, Chem. Inst. of Can.; Amer. Chem. Soc.; Nat. Geographic Soc.; Spectroscopy Soc. of Can.; rec'd Fisher Scientific Lecture Award, Chem. Inst. of Can., 1975; Home: 428 Breckonwood Rd., Burlington, Ont. L7L 2T7; Office: National Water Research Inst., Box 5050, Burlington, Ont. L7R 4A6

BARBEAU, André, O.C., B.A., M.D., Ph.D. (Hon. Causa,) F.R.C.P.(C), F.A.C.P., F.A.A.N., F.R.S.C.; physician; educator; b. Montréal, Qué. 27 May 1931; s. Antonio and Rachel (Jodoin) B.; e. Coll. Stanislas Montréal 1948; Royal Roads Naval Coll. 1950; Univ. de Paris B.A. 1948; Univ. de Montréal M.D. 1956; Univ. of Uruguay Ph.D. (Hon. Causa) 1979; m. Lise d. late Louis-Georges Trudeau 10 June 1956; children: Claire, Claude, Michel, Dany; PROF. TITULAIRE DE NEUROLOGIE, UNIV. DE MONTRÉAL since 1970, Chrmn. of Neurol. since 1976, Prof. (Assoc. mem.) of Exper. Med. McGill Univ. since 1970, Dir. Programme de Neurologie since 1976; Dir. Dépt. de Neuro-biologie, Inst. de Recherches Cliniques de Montréal since 1967; Dir. Lab. de Neurologie, Univ.

de Montréal 1961-67, Asst. Prof. de Neurologie 1961-66, Prof. agrégé 1966-70; Chef du Service de Neurologie, Hôtel-Dieu de Montréal 1976-77; Residency in Neurol. Univ. of Chicago 1957-59, McGill Univ. 1959-60; Consultant en Neurologie, Hôpital du Sacré-Coeur and Montreal Neurol. Inst.; mem. Conseil (Recherches) Clinique Médicale Henri-Bourassa and Clinique Neurologique Bois-de-Boulogne; First Annual Harry M. Dent Lectr. Univ. of Buffalo 1963; Third Annual Neurol. Lectr. Univ. of Pittsburg 1970; 6th Allan Bailey Mem. Lectr. and Visiting Prof. (Saskatoon) 1975; Centennial Neurol. Lectr. Johns Hopkins Univ. 1976; Visiting Prof. Dalhousie Univ. 1977, Brooks Army Med. Center San Antonio, Texas 1977, Univ. of Ariz. Coll. Med. 1978, Univ. of Miami 1978; Univ. of Vt. 1978, Univ. of Uruguay 1979; Visiting Annual Lectr. in Neurol. Loyola Univ. Chicago 1978; Guest Lectr. and Visiting Prof. Nagoya Univ. Japan 1978; Markle Scholar 1960-66; rec'd numerous awards incl. 1970 Gold Medal Candn. Parkinson's Disease Assn., I.C.N. Annual Award for Research in Med. Sciences 1970, Prix de Recherches Cliniques Assn. des Médecins de Langue Française du Can. 1974, Cert. of Merit Multiple Sclerosis Soc. Can., Cert. of Appreciation ALS Soc. Am.; Prix Marcel Piché, 1979; Prix Pariseau (ACFAS) 1980; Officer, Order of Canada 1980; served with R.C.N. (R) 1948-56; mem. various scient. and med. ed. comtes.; mem. numerous med. and scient. adv. bds., research groups; past extve. various med. and scient. assns. and organs. incl. Past Pres. Candn. Soc. Clin. Investigation, Candn. Neurol. Soc.; Councillor, Extve. Bd. Am. Acad. Neurol. 1975-79; Hon. mem. Soc. Française de Neurologie; Italian Neurological Soc.; Japanese Neurol. Soc.; Sociedad de Neurologia de Chile; Sociedad de Neurologia del Uruguay; Brit. Brain Research Assn.; European Brain & Behavior Soc.; mem. numerous nat. and internat. med. and scient. assns.; has edited and/or published 25 vols.; author or co-author numerous scient. and para-med. papers or abstracts; R. Catholic; recreations: tennis, archaeology, swimming; Home: 3769 Wilson Ave., Montréal, Qué. H4A 2T7; Office: 110 W. Pine Ave., Montréal, Qué. H2W 1R7.

BARBEAU, Jacques, B.A., LL.B., L.L.M., C.G.A.; b. Montreal, Que., 20 May 1931; s. Alphonse and Marguerite (Beaulieu) B.; e. Univ. of B.C. B.A. (Econ.), LL.B.; Harvard Law Sch. LL.M. 1960, Dipl. Internat. Program in Taxation 1960; m. Margaret Ann d. The Hon. Walter S. Owen, Q.C., LL.D., Victoria, B.C., 12 Apl. 1958; children: Jean, Paul, Monique, Jacqueline; PARTNER, BARBEAU, McKERCHER, COLLINGWOOD & HANNA; Dir., Atlantic Foundation: An Educational Trust (U.K.); Kwik Lok Ltd.; Beaumont Timber Co. Ltd.; The Shepard Bank; read law with Thomas E. Ladner, Q.C.; called to Bar of B.C. 1957; Solr. Taxation Div. Dept. Nat. Revenue Ottawa 1957-60; Finance Offr. Taxation Div. Dept. of Finance Ottawa 1960-61; Dir. of Research Candn. Tax Foundation 1961-62; Lectr. Banff Sch. of Advanced Mang. and Banff Tax Seminar; Dir. Endeavour Soc. for Benefit of Arts, Sciences & Health; Vice-Chrmn., Emily Carr College of Art; Trustee Vancouver Sch. Bd. of Vancouver 1973-74; mem. Candn. Bar Assn.; B.C. Law Soc.; Candn. Tax Foundation; Delta Kappa Epsilon; Liberal; R. Catholic; recreations: jogging, swimming, squash; Clubs: Vancouver; Arbutus; Home: 1998 Hosmer St., Vancouver, B.C. V6J 2S8 and 1499 Edwards Dr., Point Roberts, Wash.; Office: Suite 2400, Oceanic Plaza, P.O. Box 12534, 1066 W. Hastings St., Vancouver, B.C. V6E 3X1

BARBEAU, Marcel; artiste peintre; sculpteur; né à Montréal, Qué. 18 février 1925; f. Philippe et Elisabeth (St-Antoine) B.; é. Diplôme de l'école du meuble de Montréal (design) 1947; étudié avec des maîtres tels que le peintre Paul-Emile Borduas, l'architecte Marcel Parizeau et l'historien d'art Maurice Gagnon; ép. Ninon, fille de Gérard Gauthier et Fleurette Rose 26 avril 1975; enfants: Manon, François; co-signataire du "Refus Global", il participe à toutes les manifestations du groupe "Automatiste" 1946-54; séjour à Paris 1962-64, New York 1964-68; voyage en Californie 1969, séjour 1970 et Paris 1971-74; représénte par le Dominion Gallery à Montréal; également représenté par Art & Intégration, Galerie Pierre Bernard à Hull, Galerie Gille Corbeil à Montréal, la Galerie Dresdnere à Toronto et la Galerie Felix Vallée, à Que.; expositions individuelles: Foyer de l'Art et du Livre Ottawa 1951, 1953; Wittenborn and Shutz New York 1952; Exposition rue Jeanne Mance Montréal 1952; Galerie Agnès Lefort Montréal 1952, 1953, 1955, 1956; Palais Montcalm Qué. 1955; Galerie de l'Actuelle Montréal 1955; Centre d'Art de Ste-Adèle 1957; Musée des Beaux Arts Montréal 1962; Galerie Denise Delrue Montréal 1961, 1962, 1963; Galerie Iris Clert Paris 1964; Galerie Dorothy Cameron Toronto 1963, 1964; Galerie du Siècle Montréal 1964, 1965, 1967; East Hampton Gallery New York 1965, 1966; Jerold Morris Toronto 1965; Carmen Lamana Gallery Toronto 1967, 1968; Nouvelle Galerie Denise Delrue Montréal 1969; Retrospective: Winnipeg Art Gallery, Musée d'Art Contemporain Montréal et, Scarborough Coll. Toronto 1969; Centre Culturel Canadien Paris 1971; Relais Culturel Aix-en-Provence 1971; Galerie St-Georges Lyon 1971; Galerie "Le Point d'Or" Grenoble 1972; Hôtel de Ville de Poitiers 1972; Théâtre de Caen 1972; Galerie III Montréal 1972; Centre Culturel Français Luxembourg 1972; Centre Culturel Asselt, Namur, Liège 1972; Galerie Yala Tunis 1974; Galerie de l'Union des Arts Plastiques Alger 1974; Galerie de Marseille 1974; Musée de Québec 1975; Musée d'Art Contemporain Montréal 1975; Bau-Xi Gallery Toronto 1977; "Dessins de Marcel Barbeau 1957-62" Musée des Beaux Arts de Montréal 1977; Centre Culturel, Université de Sherbrooke, Sherbrooke 1978; Galerie Dresdnere, Toronto, 1980; Galerie Dresdnere, Toronto, 1980; Galerie Pierre Bernard, Hull, 1981; Galerie Gilles Corbeil, Montreal, 1981; collections permanentes: Galerie Nationale du Can.; Musée Stedelijk Amsterdam; Musée Chrysler Norfolk, Va.; Musée du Nouveau Brunswick; Musée des Beaux Arts de Montréal; Art Gallery of Ontario; Musée d'Art Contemporain Montréal; Musée du Québec; Musée de Vancouver; Agnes Etherington Art Centre, Queen's University; Univ. du Mass.; Amherst; Musée Rose Hart, Brandeis Univ., Waltham, Mass.; Winnipeg Art Gallery; Conseil des Arts du Canada; Ministère des Affaires extérieures du Canada; Banque d'œuvres d'art, C.A.C.; Hart House Univ. de Toronto; Maison des étudiants canadiens Cité Universitaire Paris; Musée des Grondines, Quebec; Confederation Centre Art Gallery and Museum P.E.I.; Centre Culturel de Poitiers, France; Musée des Beaux-Arts de Lyon; Edmonton Art Gallery; Musée de Joliette; Toronto City Corp.; Municipalité de St. Laurent; Municipalité de Joliette; Collection Lavalin; Esso Collection; INCO Collection; Northern Central Collection; Aird & Berlis Collection, Tor.; Shell Collection; Union-Vie; Richard Brown Baker Coll., N.Y.; nombreuses expositions collectives au Can. et à l'étranger; concepteur et producteur du film "Désirs mouvements" et concepteur du film "Instants privilégiés"; autres activités: nombreuses conférences et séminaires; participation à plusieurs émissions de radio et de télévision au Canada et en France; Prof. d'arts plastiques: expression plastique et initiation à l'histoire de l'art: enseignement privé et au Centre culturel canadien à Paris; artiste résident, Bishop Univ., 1977-78 et 1978-79; bourses et prix: ler prix de peinture de la Royal Candn. Acad. 1963; Séminaire Internat. des Arts de l'Université Fairleigh-Dickinson 1965; Bourse Lynch-Staounton, Conseil des Arts du Canada 1973; diverses bibliographies; mem. Ass. Artistes visuels Qué.; Candn. Conf. Arts; récréations: lecture, musique, opéra, spectacles de danse, ski de fond, marche, golfe; résidence: 1631 Amherst, Montréal, Québec. H2L 3L4Rng Terrebonne St-Irénée, Charlevoix, Que. G0T 1V0 (été)

BARBEAU, Victor, O.C. (1970); educateur, auteur; né Montréal, Qué., 18 août 1896; f. Zotique et Victoria (Beaudouin) B., é. Coll. Sainte-Marie, Montréal: Univ. Laval; Univ. de Paris; Ecole des Hautes Etudes urbaines; Docteur honoris causa de l'Univ. d'Aix-Marseille, de Laval et de Montréal; ép. Lucile Clément 1919; enfants: Michèle (Dr. Claude Monfette), Nicole (M. Fernand Picard), Pierre, Claudine (Me. James Williams), François; Prof. de langue et de littérature françaises, École des Hautes Études commerciales de Montréal, 1925-63; prof. de littérature française contemporaine, Univ. McGill, 1939-42; prof. de coopératisme, Univ. Laval, 1939-43; Prés.-fondateur, "La Familiale" 1937-60; l'Alliance des Coopératives de consommation; mem. du Conseil supérieur de la Coopération (Qué.); Prés., Soc. des Auteurs canadiens, section française, Montréal 1927-30; Prés. et cofondateur, Soc. des Écrivains canadiens, Montreal 1937-44; Prés.-Fondateur, l'Academiee Canadienne Française, 1944; l'Académie des Sciences morales et politiques, 1961; fondateur-dir., revue littéraire "Liaison", 1946-50; Prés., P.E.N. Club de Montréal, 1939-44; Prés. "ad honorem", Acad. berrichonne, France; Lt. de R.F.C. 1916; auteur de: "Mesure de notre taille" 1936; "Pour nous grandir" 1937; "Le Ramage de mon pays" 1939; "Ville, ô ma ville", en coll-1942; "L'avenir de notre bourgeoisie", en coll-1939; "Initiation à l'humain" 1944; "La Société des Écrivains canadiens" 1944; "Géraldine Bourbeau" en coll-1954; "L'Académie canadienne-française" 1954; "Libre examen de la démocratie" 1960; "Le Français du Canada" 1963; "Grammaire & linguistique" 1966; "La Face et l'Envers" 1966; "Dictionnaire bibliographique du Canada Français" 1974; "La Tentation du passé" 1977; "Le Choix de Victor Barbeau dans l'Oeuvre de Victor Barbeau" 1981; Lauréat de l'Acad. Française; prix Duvernay; LL.D.(Hon.), Univ. d'Aix-en-Provence, Univ. Laval, Univ. de Montréal; catholique r.; résidence: 4300 blvd. de Maisonneuve, apt. 1003, Montréal, Qué. H3Z 1K8

BARBER, Alexander Hamilton; executive; b. Montreal, Que. 8 Aug. 1930; s. Walter James and Ruth N. (Ellis) B.; e. McGill Univ., Engn.; m. Linda Blair, d. G. Blair Gordon, Montreal, 15 Jan. 1955; children: Philippa, Mark; EXTVE. VICE PRES., KRUGER PULP & PAPER CO. LTD.; Vice Pres., Trois Rivières Pulp & Paper Co.; Dir., Blair & Co.; joined Canadian Liquid Air Co., Montreal, 1953; Canadian Chemical & Cellulose Co. 1954; Columbia Cellulose, Pulp Sales, Vancouver 1956, trans. to Montreal 1959, Pres. 1965-68; mem. Candn. Pulp & Paper Assn.; Anglican; recreations: fishing, skiing, shooting, sailing; Clubs: Mount Royal; Knickerbocker (N.Y.); Orleans Fish & Game (Dir.); Home: 14 Rosemount, Westmount, Que. ; Office: 600 Dorchester Blvd. W., Montreal, Que. H3B 1N4

BARBER, Clarence Lyle, M.A., Ph.D.; economist; university professor; b. Wolseley, Sask., 5 May 1917; s. Richard Edward and Lulu Pearl (Lyons) B.; e. Wolseley High Sch., 1930-34; Univ. of Sask., 1937-40 (B.A.1939); Clark Univ., M.A. 1941; Univ. of Minnesota, 1941-43 (Ph.D. 1952); m. Barbara Anne, d. Ernest Luther Patchet, Toronto, Ont., 10 May 1947; children: Paul Edward, Richard Stephen, David Stuart, Alan Gordon; PROFESSOR OF ECONOMICS, UNIVERSITY OF MANITOBA, since 1956; mem., Nat. Comn. on Inflation 1979; Commr., Royal Comn. on Farm Machinery; served R.C.A.F. 1943-45; Economist, Dom. Bureau of Stat., 1945-48; Asst. Prof.; McMaster Univ., 1948-49; Assoc. Prof., Univ. of Manitoba, 1949, Head of Econ. 1963; visiting Prof., Queen's Univ., 1954-55, McGill Univ., 1964-65; Dir., Research, Royal Comn. on Flood, Cost Benefit, Manitoba, 1957-59; Special Adviser on Nat. Income to Govt. of Philippines, U.N. Tech. Asst. Adm., 1959-60; Publications incl. "Inventories & The Business Cycle"; The Canadian Electrical Manufacturing Industry (Royal Comn. on Can. Econ. Prospects), Canadian Tariff Policy; Pres., Candn. Assn. of Univ. Teachers, 1958-59; Pres.-elect (1971-72) Candn. Econ. Assn.; Fellow Roy. Soc. of Canada 1977; Protestant; recreations: curling, skiing; Home: 320 Kingsway, Winnipeg, Man. R3M 0H4

BARBER, James C., B.A.; financial executive; b. England 1927; e. Trinity Coll. Univ. of Toronto B.A. 1950; m. Ann Hamilton 15 Sept. 1951; children: Anthony J.H., Brian C.W., Jennifer A; PRESIDENT, COAST UNDER-WRITERS LTD. 1969- ; Vice Pres. present co. 1965-69; Vice Pres. present co. 1965-69; Pres. Assn. Marine Underwriters B.C. 1960-62, 1966-67, 1978-79, 1979-80; Chrmn. W. Coast Comte. Candn. Bd. Underwriters and mem. Extve. Comte. (1979-80); recreations: skiing, hiking; Clubs: Terminal City; Evergreen Squash; Home: 6272 St. George's Cres., West Vancouver, B.C. V7W 1Z4; Office: 407, 1199 West Pender St., Vancouver, B.C. V6E 2R6.

BARBER, John Barron, B.Com.; industrial executive (ret.); b. Sault Ste. Marie, Ont., 4 June 1912; s. Roland and Alice Helena (Moorehouse) B.; e. Queen's Univ., B.Com. 1935; m. Hilda Elaine, d. Richard Crawford, Sault Ste. Marie, Ont.; children: Susan, Leslie; Sr. Vice Pres., Vice Chrmn., Dir. and Mem. Extve. Comte., The Algoma Steel Corp. Ltd.; until retired 1977; Dir. and mem. Extve. Comte., Dominion Bridge Co. Ltd.; Dir. and Pres., Cannelton Iron Ore Co.; Dir. and Vice-Pres. Tilden Iron Ore Co.; Sault Marine Services Ltd.; Sault Windsor Hotel Ltd.; The Southern Algoma Railway Co.; Yankanuck Steamships Ltd.; Kremzar Gold Mines Ltd.; Dir. and Asst. Treas., Maple Meadow Mining Co.; Asst. Treas., Cannelton Industries, Inc.; mem. Bd. Govs., Ont. Research Foundation; joined present Co., as Clerk, Treasurer's Dept., 1937; apptd. Asst. Treas. 1939; Asst. Comptroller, 1944; Comptroller 1946; Vice-Pres., Finance, 1956; mem., Am. Iron & Steel Inst.; Internat. Iron and Steel Inst.; Protestant; recreation: golf; Clubs: Sault Ste. Marie Golf; National (Toronto); Hidden Valley Golf (Michigan); Home: 13 Summit Ave., Sault Ste. Marie, Ont. P6B 2S2

BARBER, Lloyd I., O.C., B.A., B.Comm., M.B.A., Ph.D.; university president; b. Regina, Sask., 8 Mar. 1932; s. Lewis Muir & Hildred (Ingram) B., e. Regina Beach Sch., 1948; Luther Coll., Regina, 1949; Univ. of Sask., B.A. (Econ.) 1953, B.Comm. 1954; Univ. of Cal., Berkeley, M.B.A. 1955; Univ. of Wash., Ph.D. 1964; m. Muriel Pauline, d. late F. MacBean, 12 May 1956; children: Muir, Brian, Kathy, David, Susan, Patti; PRESIDENT AND VICE CHANCELLOR, UNIV. OF REGINA, SASK. 1976; Dir., Sinco Dev.; Regina United Way; Muir Barber Ltd.; Burns Foods Ltd.; Bank of Nova Scotia; Can. Arctic Co-operative Federation Ltd. (1974-78); SED Systems Ltd.; OPCAN (Katimavik) 1977-78; Molson Companies; Husky Oil Ltd.; Indian Equity Foundation (1977-79); Sask. Computer Utility Corp. 1973-75; Past mem., N. W. Terr. Leg. Council (1967-70); Instr. in Comm., Univ. of Sask., 1955; Asst. Prof. 1959; Assoc. Prof., 1964, Dean of Comm. 1968, Vice-Pres. 1968-74; Commr., Sask. Royal Comn. on Govt. Adm., 1964; Chrmn., Sask. Prov. Youth Review Comte., 1965; Indian Claims Comr., (apptd. by Privy Council of Can.) 1969-77; Special Inquirer for Elder Indian Testimony (apptd. by Privy Council of Canada) 1977-81; author of Brief to Carter Comn. for Retail Merchants Assn. Can. and several articles for learned journs.; awarded Can. Council pre-doctorial Fellowship; Ford Foundation Dissertation Grant; Centennial Medal; Vanier Medal; Hon. Sask. Indian Chief; mem., Amer. Econ. Assn; Cdn. Econ. Assn.; Inst. of Pub. Admin. of Can.; Assn. Candn. Schs. of Business (Pres. 1967-68); Pres. Univ. & Coll. of Can. 1981; Hon. Lt.-Col., 16 Serv. Battalian (M), Regina; Freemason; Liberal; United Church; recreations: hunting, fishing, sailing, swimming, reading, travel; Clubs: Regina Beach Yacht; Assiniboia; Faculty; Roy. United Serv. Inst.; Regina Officers Mess; Home: 2500 Cross Place, Regina, Sask. S4S 4C7

BARBOUR, David A., B.A.; brewery executive; b. Montreal, Que. 24 May 1940; s. (late) Ronald Granville and Stella Victoria (Smallhorn) B.; e. Trinity Coll. Sch. Port Hope, Ont.; McGill Univ.; Sir George Williams Univ. B.A.; m. Mary Helen d. late Dr. Thomas Harper 23 Jan. 1965; children: David Gregory, Heidi Anne, Ronald Geoffrey, Peter Thomas; PRES., MOLSON'S BREWERY (ONTARIO) LTD. 1981- ; Dir. and mem. Extve. Comte. Brewers Warehousing Co. Ltd.; Molson Breweries of Canada Ltd.; Dir., Traffic Inquiry Research Foundation; Sales Rep., Asst. Advertising Mgr. Dominion Textile Co. Ltd. 1964-65; Advertising Mgr. Consumer Products, Cyanamid of Canada 1966-67; Advertising & Pub. Relations Mgr., Mgr. Marketing Communications Molson's Western Breweries Ltd. 1968-71, Vice Près. Marketing 1976-78; Dir. Market Communications, Molson Breweries of Canada Ltd. 1972-76; Vice Pres. Marketing, Molson's Brewery (Ontario) Ltd. 1979-81; Delta Upsilon; P. Conservative; Protestant; recreations: squash, golf, gardening; Home: 34 Chartwell Rd., Oakville, Ont. L6J 3Z4; Office: 640 Fleet St., Toronto, Ont. M5V 1B2.

BARCLAY, Ian Andrew, B.C.L., M.P.A.; forestry executive; b. Montreal, Que., 7 Mar. 1921; s. Hon. Gregor and Jean Gertrude (Fleck) B.; e. Ashbury Coll. Sch., Jr. Matric., 1939; McGill Univ. B.C.L. 1948; Harvard Univ. M.P.A. 1949; m. Ann Victoria, d. G. W. Hadrill of Montreal, 21 Sept. 1951; one d., Deborah Ann; CHAIRMAN, B.C. FOREST PRODUCTS LTD. since 1976; Dir., United Corporations Ltd.; Blandin Paper Co.; Donohue St-Félicien Inc.; Hudson's Bay Co.; Hudson's Bay Oil and Gas Co. Ltd.; Royal Bank of Canada; Simpsons, Ltd.; C. D. Howe Research Inst.; mem. Econ. Council of Can.; called to the Bar of Que., 1948; practised law with Scott, Huggesen, Macklaier, Chisholm & Hyde; entered commerce as Dir. of Industrial Relations, Sheraton Hotels (Can.) Ltd.; subsequently Asst. Secy., Canadian Chemical & Cellulose Co. Ltd.; Vice-Pres. and Secy., Columbia Cellulose Co. Ltd.; joined B.C. Forest Products Ltd. as Vice-Pres. and Secy., 1962; Extve. Vice-Pres. 1967-68; Dir. 1968; Chrmn. and C.E.O. 1972; served with R.C.N.V.R., 1940-45; Dir., Boys' and Girls' Club of Can.; Governor, B.C. Lions Football Club (played football for Montreal and McGill); rec'd Newton D. Baker II Award (Un. Community Funds and Councils of Am. Award); Kappa Alpha (McGill, Pres. 1946-47); recreation: golf; Clubs: Vancouver; Shaughnessy Golf & Country; Home: 5925 Chancellor Blvd., Vancouver, B.C. V6T 1E6; Office: 1050 W. Pender St., Vancouver, B.C. V6E 2X3

BARCZA, Peter Josef; barritone, classical opera; b. Stockholm, Sweden 23 June 1949; came to Can. 1952; s. Josef and Katherine Elizabeth (Tamasi) B.; e. Royal Conservatory of Music, Toronto 1966-68; Univ. of Toronto, Diploma, Faculty of Music, 1968-71; postgrad training, Villa Schifanoia, Florence, Italy, 1971; CLASSICAL OPERA SINGER; leading roles incl. Canada Opera Co., 1972-; Toronto Symphony, 1972-; CBC Radio and TV, 1972-; Guelph Spring Festival, 1975-; Manitoba Opera, 1975-; Opera-In-Concert (Toronto), 1976-83; S. Alta. Opera (Calgary), 1978-; Theatre Royal de Wallonie (Belgium), 1978; Rochester Opera, 1978; Tehran Symphony, 1978; Rainbow stage, 1979; Regina symphony, 1979; Algoma Festival, 1979; Paris Opera, 1980-81; Kentucky Opera, 1980; Memphis Opera, 1980; Westchester Lyric Festival, 1981; Vancouver Opera, 1982; Comus Music Theatre, 1982; has appeared on TV, Radio-France, 1981; co-author of "Trivia - Inconsequential but Irresistible Facts About Canada," 1980; mem., Actors Equity; ACTRA: AGMA (USA); Home: 17 Strathallan Blvd.; Toronto, Ont. M5J 1S8.

BARD, Hon. Samuel Schwarz, B.A., LL.L.; judge; b. Quebec City, Que. 13 Aug. 1913; s. Jacob Schwarz and Rose (Ortenberg) B.; e. High Sch. of Quebec 1929; McGill Univ. B.A. 1933, Dipl. in Romance Langs.; Laval Univ. LL.L. 1936; m. Brauna d. late Harry Lax 1 July 1942; children: Perry, Joel; JUDGE, SUPERIOR COURT OF QUE. 1969- ; called to Bar of Que. 1936; cr. Q.C. 1961; Sr. Partner, Bard, L'Heureux, Philippon & Tourigny until 1969; mem. Can. Pension Appeals Bd. since 1971; Sessional Lectr. in Comm. Law Laval Univ. 1956-69; Founding mem. and 1st Pres., Que. Lodge B'nai B'rith 1938; Hon.

Vice Pres. Jeffery Hale's Hosp. Bldg. Campaign Quebec 1954-55; mem. Adv. Bd. Que. YWCA 1962; Vice Pres. Que. Salvation Army financial campaigns 1961-65, Hon. Co-Chrmn. 1966-68; mem. Vanier Inst. of the Family 1965-67; Dir. St. John Ambulance 1962-66; Hon. mem. Royal 22nd Regt. 1966; mem. Bd. Quebec Symphony Orchestra 1966-67; Gov., Théâtre de l'Estoc 1966; mem. Institut Canadien 1966; Comité France-Amérique 1960-66; Founding mem. and Past Pres. Les Amitiés Judéo-Chrétiennes 1952-72; Dir. Kiwanis Club 1967; mem. privilégié de la Fondation Univ. Laval; served with RCA 1942-45, rank Lt.; mem. Ed. Bd. "Quebec Bar Review" 1967-69; Chrmn. Comm. Law Comte. 1957, Pub. Relations Comte. 1960 Que. Br. Candn. Bar Assn.; mem. Candn. Judges Conf.; Hebrew; recreations: golf, tennis, skiing, bridge; Clubs: Hillsdale Golf & Country; Côte de Liesse Racquet; Home: 1745 Cedar Ave., Montreal H3G 1A7; Office: Court House, 1 Notre Dame E., Montreal, Que. H2Y 1B6.

BARFORD, Ralph M., B.Com., M.B.A.; executive; b. Toronto, Ont., 1 Nov. 1929; s. Ralph Alexander and Geraldine Edna (MacKenzie) B.; e. Univ. of Toronto, B.Com. 1950; Harvard Univ.; m.; children: Ralph M., Jr., Anne E., John A., Patricia S., Elizabeth, Jane; PRESIDENT, VALLEYDENE CORP.LTD.; Chrmn. GSW Inc.; Chrmn. Canadian Appliance Mfg. Co. Ltd.; Vice-Pres. and Dir. National Trust Co. Ltd.; Dir.; Union Gas Ltd.; MasseyFerguson Ltd.; Canadian General Investments Ltd.; Harding Carpets Ltd.; Thiokol Corp.; Wosk's Ltd.; De Havilland; Tor. Gen. Hosp.; Tor. Symphony; Niagara Inst.; Empire Life Ins. Co.; The Dom. of Canada Gen. Ins. Col; E-L Financial Corp.; Pres. (1967-68) Candn. Elect. Mfrs. Assn.; mem. Young Pres. Organ.; Phi Gamma Delta; Home: 11 Valleyanna Dr., Toronto, Ont. M4N 1J7; Office 161 Eglinton Ave. E., Toronto, Ont. M4P 1J5

BARIBEAU, Lt.-Col. Herve, E.D.; industrialist and broadcasting executive; b. St. Stanislas de Champlain. P.Q., 1 Nov. 1900; s. J. Alfred and Josephine (Mailhot) B.; e. Levis College, Commercial Grad. 1918; m. Cécile, d. Alfred Couillard-Després, 3 July 1926; children: Simon, Michel, Richard, Lise; CHRMN. OF BD. BARIBEAU & SON, INC., (estbd. 1922); Unigesco Inc.; Inter-Quebec Publicité Ltée; C.K.R.S.; Radio Saguenay Ltée; Vice Pres., Union Canadienne Ins., Co., Past Pres., Levis School Board; Dir., La Fédération des Oeuvres du Dist de Qué. Chamber of Comm., Levis Dist.; Past Pres., Gen. Assn. Professionelle des Industriels; Dir., Hosp. St. Augustin; Gov., Ecole de Comm. de Lavel; Pres. for 2 years of local Candn. Red Cross Campaign; served in World War 1939-45; O.C. of B Co., 35th Inf. Bn. 1944-45 and Lt. Col. and O.C. Levis Regt. 1945-49; has been active in welfare and social work, both in city and dist. of Levis; P. Conservative; R. Catholic; recreations: fishing, golf; Clubs: Rotary (Pres.) 1943-44; Garrison; Home: 13 Place Baribeau, Levis, Qué., G6V 6L5; Office: 381 St. Laurent St., Levis, Que. G6V 3W6

BARIBEAU, Michel; executive; b. Lévis, Qué., 4 May 1931; s. Herve and Cecile (Despres) B.; e. St. Louis de Conzague, Qué.; Acad. de Qué.; Laval Univ., Business Adm., R.I.A. 1953; m. Marielle, d. Arthur Simoneau, StAgapit, Qué., 13 Oct. 1956; children: Louis, Jean, Alain, Bernard; VICE PRES., BARIBEAU & FILS INC.; Pres.; Charrier & Dugal Ltée; Imprimerie Laflamme Ltée; Terrac Inc.; Chrmn. L'Unique Cie d'Assurance Vie Inc.; Dir., Banque Canadienne Nationale; Inter Québec Publicité Inc.; Télé-Capitale Ltée; Radio Saguenay Ltée; Enterprises Télé-Capitale Ltée; Télé-Capitale Unicom Ltée; Soc. de la Croix Rouge; Québec Aviation Ltée; R. Couillard & Ass. Inc.; R. Catholic; Clubs: Garrison, Rotary; Home: 654 St. Augustin, Breakeyville, Lévis, Qué. G6V 6L5; Office: 381 St-Laurent, Lévis, Qué. G6V 3W6

BARKER, Arthur Edward, Ph.D., D. Litt., F.R.S.C.; professor; B. Toronto, Ont., 21 Jan. 1911; s. Frank Harold and Gertrude (Arthur) B. e. Trinity Coll., Univ. of Toronto, M.A. 1934; I.O.D.E. Overseas Memorial Schol. 1935-37; Univ. of London, Ph.D. 1937; m. Dorothy, d. Very Rev. Chas. Edward Riley, Toronto, 4 June 1938; has one s. and one d.; PROF. EMERITUS OF RENAISSANCE LIT., UNIV. OF W. ONT., since 1980; Teaching Fellow Trinity Coll. Univ. of Toronto, 1933-35; Lectr. 1937-39; Assoc. Prof. 1939-42; Prof. of Eng. 1942-61; Resident Prof., Adams House, Harvard Univ., Cambrige, Mass. 1944-45; John Simon Guggenheim Mem. Fellow (Can.); Prof. (summer session) Columbia Univ., N.Y. 1945-46, 1960, 1961; Univ. of Wisconsin, 1949; Univ. of Cal., Los Angeles, 1961; Prof. of Eng., Univ. of Ill., 1961-70; Assoc., Center for Advanced Studies, Univ. of Illinois, from 1965; Prof. of Renn. Lit., Univ. of W. Ont., 1970-80; F.R.S.C. 1974; author of "Milton and the Puritan Dilemma", 1942; "Milton: Modern Essays in Criticism"; "The Seventeenth Century: Baconthrough Marvell," 1979; 1965; Anglican; Home: 1109 Sunset Ave., London, Ont. N6A 2Y5

BARKER, Clifford Albert Victor, C.D., D.V.M., M.Sc., D.V.Sc.; university professor; veterinarian; b. Ingersoll, Ont; 5 Jan. 1919; s. Albert Pelerin and Martha (Hansler) B.; e. Ingersoll (Ont.) Pub. and High Schs.; Univ. of Toronto, D.V.M. 1941 (Gold Medal), D.V.Sc. 1948; McGill Univ., M.Sc. 1945; m. Lily Jean, d. late Lorne Healey, 19 Sept. 1942; children: Ian K., Eric J., Graham Edward; PROF. (THERIOGENOLOGY) DEPT. OF CLINICAL STUDIES, ONT. VETERINARY COLL., UNIV. OF GUELPH, since 1953; Lectr., Animal Husbandry, Macdonald Coll., McGill Univ., 1941-45; Asst. Prof. 1948-51; Assoc. Prof. 1951-53; served with Ont. Agric. Coll. C.O.T.C. and McGill Univ. C.O.T.C.; Personnel Offr., Central Command Personnel Selection Unit attached 11 Field Arty. Regiment with rank of Major, 1953-65; Past Chairman, Wellington-Waterloo Airport Commission; Trustee, Caprine Research Foundation (U.S.A.); Past Pres., Candn. Society for Study of Fertility; Univ. of Guelph Alumni Assoc.; author of over 60 pub. scientific papers; rec'd Mary A. Farley Award from Am. Dairy Goat Assn., 1962; Carlo Del Bo Award, Italy, 1964; Spallanzani Research Inst. Medal, Italy, 1964; Society Award of the Candn. Soc. Study Fertility, 1955, 1965, 1971; Distinguished Alumnus Award, Ont. Veterinary Coll., 1977; Hon. mem., Coll. of Veterinary Med. of Venezuela; mem., Foreign Soc. (Italy, Spain, Brazil); Pres., Candn. Veterinary Med. Assn., 1965-66; Past Pres., Ont. Veterinary Assn.; Ont. Vet. Coll. Alumni Assn.; mem. Roy. College of Veterinary Surgeons; Charter mem., Cryobiol. Soc.; Soc. for Study of Reproduction; Internat. Lectr. on Animal Reproduction; Hon. mem., Omega Tau Sigma; former Business Mgr., Candn. Veterinary Journ., 1963-65; former mem. Ed. Bd., Candn. Journ. Comp. Med.; Ed., Ont. Veterinary Coll. Alumni Bulletin; Chart. Diplomate, Am. Coll. of Theriogenologists (1971); Protestant; recreation: sailing; Home: 61 Dean Ave., Guelph, Ont. N1G 1L3

BARKER, James Rollins, C.D., B.A.; diplomat; b. Kingston, Ont., 17 Apl. 1921; s. Harry Christie, M.C. and Jessie Kathleen Polson (Rollins) Fortye; e. Queen's Univ., B.A. 1948; Univ. of Geneva; Inst. Univ. de Hautes Etudes Internat., Geneva; Nat. Defence Coll.; m. Barbara Jane, d. Col. C. J. Bermingham, Ancaster, Ont., 5 May 1951; two s. Jonathan Fortye Bermingham, Christopher James Rollins; joined Dept. of External Affairs, 1950; 2nd Secy., Moscow, 1953-55; Counsellor, London, Eng., 1959-63; Head Aid and Financing Sec., Ottawa, 1963-66; Depy. Head, USA Div., 1967-69; First Dir., Operations Centre, 1969-71; High Commr. to United Republic of Tanzania with concurrent accreditation to Mauritius and to Zambia, 1971 and Ambassador to Somali Rep. 1974; Chief of Protocol, Ottawa 1975; apptd. Ambassador to Greece 1978; Dir., Vice Pres., Tradex Mutual Fund for Civil Servants, 1964-71; served UK and N.W. Europe 1941-46; rank Capt; United Church; recreation: early New Brunswick hist.; Home: 631 Hemlock Rd., Rockliffe Park, Ottawa, Ont. K1M 2E9; Office: 4 Ionnou Ghennadiou St. Athens 140, Greece.

BARKHOUSE, Hon. Ronald Theodore, M.H.A.; politician; b. New Ross, Lunenburg Co., N.S. 22 Apl. 1926; s. Alfred Simpson Barkhouse; e. New Ross Pub. Sch.; Horton Acad. Wolfville, N.S.; m. Eleanor Plunkett d. late Ernst Grant 1 Nov. 1951; children: Dawn, Robert, Leslie, Jimmie; MIN. OFMINES AND ENERGY, N.S.1978- ; retired from wholesale lumber business and gen. store 1974; mem. Chester Mun. Council 1952-67; Chester Mun. Sch. Bd. 1952-61; el. M.H.A. for Lunenburg E. 1974, reel. since; Former Dir. Bonny Lea Farm for Physically & Mentally Handicapped; rec'd Centennial Medal 1967; Queen's Silver Jubilee Medal 1978; Hon. Patron Ross Farm Agric. Museum (Past Chrmn. New Ross Dist. Museum Soc.); Hon. Ky. Col.; Freemason (P.M.); P. Conservative; Baptist; recreations: collecting records & tapes pre-1955 jazz; Clubs: Chester Golf; Chester Curling; Halifax Press; Home: New Ross, R.R. 2, Lunenburg Co., N.S. BOJ2MO; Office: (P.O. Box 1087) Halifax, N.S. B3J 2X1.

BARLOW, Leonard Edgar, B.A., C.F.A.; investment dealer (ret.); b. Hamilton, Ont., 27 Aug. 1914; s. Edgar and Minerva (Laforce) B.; e. McMaster Univ., B.A., 1937; m. Margaret Olive, d. Col. H.C. Craig; Dir., Global Communications Ltd.; Realcap Holdings Ltd.; Pres., Toronto Soc. of Financial Analysts, 1962-63; Pres., Inst. of Chart. Financial Analysts, 1969-70; Dir., Financial Analysts' Fed., 1965-66 and 1969-70; Trustee, Research Foundation, Financial Analysts 1971-74; United Church; recreations: golf, gardening, sailing; Club: Royal Canadian Yacht; Ontario; York Downs Golf & Country; Home: 103 Cortleigh Blvd., Toronto, Ont. M4R 1K7; Office: Commercial Union Tower, P.O. Box 433, Toronto Dominion Centre, Toronto, Ont. M5K 1M2

BARNES, James A., B.Sc.; telecommunications executive; b. Calgary, Alta. 7 Dec. 1919; e. Univ. of Alta. B.Sc. (Elect. Engn.) 1951; m. Georgina Carnell; PRES., ALBERTA GOVERNMENT TELEPHONES;served with RCN 1941-45, N. Atlantic; mem. Royal Candn. Legion; Assn. Prof. Engrs., Geols. & Geophysicists Alta.; Past Dir. ACCESS; Clubs: Rotary; Edmonton Electric; Edmonton Club; Edmonton Office: (P.O. Box 2411) Edmonton, Alta. T5J 2S4.

BARNES, Leslie William Charles Seaman, M.A.; economist, author; b. London, Eng., 13 Feb. 1920; s. William and Ada Minnie Amy (Seaman) B.; m. Dorothy Mary Waters; two s. Charles, Michael; e. Shooters Hill Sch., London, Eng.; London Univ.; Cambridge Univ.; Univ. of Zurich; B.A. 1949, M.A. 1952; Exec. Dir., Prof. Inst. Public Service of Canada 1965-74; served with Brit. War Office and Ministry of Supply; Dir. of Proof & Ballistics, Dept. of Nat. Defence 1951-65; Gov., Ashbury Coll., Ottawa 1965-75; rec'd Centennial Medal 1967; lately visiting Sr. Research Fellow, Ind. Relations Centre, Queen's Univ.; Chrmn. Int. Affairs Committee, Assn. Profs. of Ottawa; author of "Consult and Advise"; "Canada's Guns"; etc.; mem., Royal Econ. Soc.; Candn. Indust. Relations Research Assn.; Internat. Indust. Relations Research Assn.; Public Service Arbitration Tribunal; Anglican; Clubs: Chelsea; Royal Overseas (London, Eng.); Address: 60 McLeod St. Apt. 801 Ottawa, Ont. K2P 2G1

BARNETT, Henry Joseph Macaulay, M.D., F.R.C.P.(C), F.A.C.P. F.R.C.P.; educator; b. Eng. 10 Feb. 1922; e. Univ. of Toronto M.D. 1944; CHRMN., DEPT OF CLIN. NEUROL. SCIENCES, UNIV. OF WESTERN ONT. 1974- ; Chief, Dept. Clin. Neurol. Sciences, Univ. Hosp. London, Ont. 1974- ; Residency and Grad. Training Toronto Gen. Hosp., Banting Inst. Univ. of Toronto, Sunnybrook Hosp. Toronto, Nat. Hosp. London, Eng., Oxford Univ. (Research Asst. Neurol.) 1944-52; Phys., Toronto Gen. Hosp. 1952-67; Consultant in Neurol. Sun-

nybrook Hosp. 1953-66, Chief Div. of Neurol. 1966-69; Consultant in Neurol. Clarke Inst. Psychiatry 1953-68 and Toronto Hosp. Weston, Ont. 1954-66; Chief Div. of Neurol. Victoria Hosp. London, Ont. 1969-72 and Univ. Hosp. London 1972-74; Clin. Teacher, Univ. of Toronto 1952, Assoc. (Med.) 1954, Asst. Prof. 1963, Assoc. Prof. 1966; Prof. of Neurol. Univ. of W. Ont. 1969; has held numerous guest lectr. and visiting prof. positions incl. 1978 Willis Lectr. Montreal Neurol. Inst., 1979 Wartenberg Lectr. Am. Acad. Neurol., Allison Mem. Lectr. Queens Univ. Belfast, G. Robinson Mem. Lectr. Mississauga Hosp., Mississauga, Ont.; co-author "Syringomyelia" 1973; author or co-author many book chapters, articles, papers, abstracts, conf. proceedings; mem. various ed. bds. med. journs.; Fellow, Am. Acad. Neurol. (Dir. 1970-74); Non-Resident Fellow, Royal Soc. Med.; mem. Candn. Neurol. Soc. (Secy. 1964-68, Vice Pres. 1974-75, Pres. 1975-76); Toronto Neurol. Soc. (Pres. 1968); Am. Assn. Neurol. Surgs.; Am. Neurol. Assn. (1st Vice-Pres.); Am. Heart Assn. (Extve. Comte.); London Neurosciences Assn. (Pres.); Candn. Stroke Soc. (Past Pres.); Candn. Heart Foundation (Dir. & mem. Med. Adv. Comte.); Ont. Heart Foundation (Dir.); Ont. Deafness Research Foundation (Scient. Adv. Comte.); Home: 1571 Gloucester Rd., London, Ont. N6G 2S5; Office: University Hosp., London, Ont. N6A 5A5.

BARNETT, William Eddison, B.Arch.; architect; b. Toronto, Ontario., 7 June 1914; s. Walter George and Muriel Gordon (Marchant) B.; e. Danforth and Central Tech. Schs., Toronto, Ont.; Univ. of Toronto, B.Arch. 1938 (Arch. Guild Silver Medal; Darling & Person Prize); m. Hazel Pearl, d. Wilfred Dynes, Toronto, Ont., 15 Mar. 1941; children: Robert Eddison, Janice Elizabeth; PARTNER, W. E. BARNETT ARCH.; Pres., Guardex Services Ltd.; formerly engaged with arch. firms of Catto & Catto, Charles Dolphin, S. B. Coon & Son, Page & Steele, all of Toronto, leaving the latter firm in 1946 to commence own practice; with Alexander Murray Co. 1939-42 as Tech Advisor; Wartime Housing Ltd., 1942-44 as Supervisor; has been engaged on Sch. (Elem. and Secondary), Indust. and Comm. work and some Church and Residential structures; fellow, Royal Arch. Inst. Can.; mem., Ont. Assn. of Arch.; Ont. Arch. Assn. (Toronto Chapter); Toronto Bd. Trade; Conservative; United Church; recreations: philately, art; Clubs: Rotary (Leaside); Engineers'; Albany; Granite; Home: 300 Bessborough Drive, Toronto 17, Ont.; M4G 3L1; Office: 121 Avenue Rd., Toronto, Ont. M5R 2G3

BARR, John Roderick, Q.C.; lawyer; b. Toronto, Ont. 9 Sept. 1921; s. Peter and Anne (Peardon) B.; e. Hillfield Sch. Hamilton to 1938; Westdale Coll. Inst. Hamilton 1939; Osgoode Hall Law Sch. Toronto 1945-48; m. Rhoda Henrietta d. Robert James Marshall, Stella, Ont. 9 Oct. 1948; children: Peter Marshall, Rhoda Elizabeth Anne; SENIOR PARTNER, HARRIS, BARR, HILDEBRAND, DANIEL & WILSON; called to Bar of Ont. 1948; cr. Q.C. 1961; practice civil litigation St. Catharines since 1948; el. Bencher, Law Soc. Upper Can. 1979; Student Pilot, RCAF 1940-41, Instr., Flying Instructors Sch. and Central Flying Sch. 1942-43; Pilot, RAF Bomber Command 1944-45; mem. Advocates' Soc. (Past Vice Pres.); Candn. Bar Assn.; P. Conservative; Presbyterian; recreations: rowing, running, aerobatic flying, skiing; Clubs: St. Catharines; St. Catharines Rowing; St. Catharines Flying; St. Catharines Golf; Royal Candn. Mil. Inst. (Toronto); Home: 33 Hillcrest Ave., St. Catharines, Ont. L2R 4Y2; Office; 39 Queen St., St. Catharines, Ont. L2R 6V7.

BARR, Maj. Gen. (ret.) John Wilmer Browning, C.M.M., C.D., M.D., C.M., K.St. J., Q.H.P.; b. Lanark, Ont., 7 Dec. 1916; s. late James and late Mary Allen (Browning) B.; e. Lanark (Ont.) Cont. Sch., 1933; Perth (Ont.) Coll. Inst., 1934; Queen's Univ., M.D., C.M. 1940; Candn. Army Staff Coll., psc 1947; Royal Army Med. Coll., London, Eng., 1952-53; Univ. of Toronto, Dipl. in

Hosp. Adm. (Robert Wood Johnson Award) 1959; Nat. Defence Coll., 1964-65; m. Marion Sarah, d. late James Crawford, Thedford, Ont., 10 May 1945; Internship: Nichols' Hosp., Peterborough, Ont., 1939, Ottawa Civic Hosp. 1940; Gen. Duty Med. Offr., various units of 3 Candn. Inf. Div. 1940-44; C.O. 23 Candn. Field Ambulance and 6 Candn. Field Dressing Stn. 1945-46; various med. staff appts. Candn. Army 1947-50; C.O., RCAMC Sch., 1950-52; C.O., 2 Field Ambulance and Sr. Candn. Med. Offr., Europe, 1953-54, Asst. Dir. Med. Services, Army HQ 1954-57; C.O., Candn. Forces Hosp. Kingston, 1959-61; Dir. of Med. Personnel, Candn. Forces HQ 1961-64; Depy. Surg. Gen. (Operations) 1966-70; Surg. Gen., Candn. Forces, 1970-73; Col. Com. Can. Forces Medical Services 1976; Chief Med. Off., Order of St. John, Priory of Canada 1977-81; Registrar, Med. Council Can. 1973-81; Queen's Hon. Physician, 1967-73 and since 1977; Kt. of Grace, Order of St. John of Jerusalem, 1978; Hon. Vice-Pres., Def. Med. Assn. of Can., 1978; mem. Royal Scot Country Dance Soc., Ottawa Br.; Freemason; United Church; receations: scot. country dancing, gardening; Home: 429 Huron Ave., Ottawa K1Y 0X3, Ont.

BARR, Murray Llewellyn, O.C. (1968), B.A., M.Sc., M.D., LL.D., D.Sc., F.R.C.P. (C), F.A.C.P., F.R.S.C., F.R.S. (London); b. Belmont, Ont., 20 June 1908; s. William Llewellyn and Margaret (McLellan) B.; e. Univ. of W. Ont., B.A. 1930, M.D. 1933, M.Sc. 1938; m. Ruth Vivian, d. Wallace King, Ashtabula, Ohio, 1934; Children: Hugh, Robert, Carolyn, David; Prof. Emeritus of Anatomy, U. of W.O.; served with Res. R.C.A.M.C., 1936-39; 2nd World War on active service with R.C.A.F. 1939-45; on Res. since 1951 with rank of Wing Commdr.; main interest is cytol. research as it applies to sex anomalies and mental retardation; author of numerous publs. in field of cytol., principally cytol. of the nervous system and human cytogenetics; mem., Candn. Neurol. Soc.; Anatomical Soc. of Gt. Brit. & Ireland; Am. Assn. of Anatomists; Assn. for Research in Nervous & Mental Diseases; Candn. Assn. Anat.; awarded Flavelle Medal by Royal Soc. Can., 1959; the Charles Mickle Fellowship, 1960; rec'd from Pres. Kennedy one of the first Joseph P. Kennedy Foundation Awards to assist work in overcoming mental retardation, 1962; the Ortho Medal of the Am. Soc. for the Study of Sterility (1962), the Medal of the Am. Coll. of Physicians (1962), the Award of Merit of the Gairdner Foundation (1963) the Papanicolaou Award of the Am. Soc. of Gynecol. (1964); and the Maurice Goldblatt Award, Internat. Acad. Cytology, 1968; Alpha Omega Alpha; Protestant; Clubs: Harvey; Cajal; Home: 452 Wonderland Road, S. London, Ont. N6K 1L4

BARRETT, Hon David, M.L.A., B.A., M.S.W. LL. D. (Hon.); politician; b. Vancouver, B.C. 2 Oct. 1930; s. Samuel and Rose (Hyatt) B.; e. Britannia High Sch., Vancouver 1948; Seattle Univ. B.A. 1953; St. Louis Univ., Mo. M.S.W. 1956; Home. LL.D., St. Louis Univ. 1974; m. Shirley Hackman, 16 Oct. 1953; children: Daniel Alexander, Joseph Samuel, Jane Rosanne; Leader of Opposition, B.C. 1976-; formerly engaged in: social work, Probation Office, St. Louis 1956; Supervisor, Social Training, Haney Correctional Inst. 1957-79; Supvr., Counselling Services, John Howard Soc. of B.C., Vancouver 1959-64; Extve. Dir., Jewish Family Service Agency, Vancouver 1965-70; first el. to B.C. Leg. g.e. 12 Sept. 1960; re-el. g.e. 1963, 66, 69, 72, 76, 79; Leader of the Opposition 1969; Premier of B.C., Pres., Extve. Council and Min. of Finance 1972-75; N.D.P.; Jewish; Address: Parliament Bldgs., Victoria, B.C.

BARRETT, H. O., C.D., B.A., D.Paed., K.St.J.; educator; b. Brantford, Ont., 26 Aug. 1908; s. Charles and Elizabeth (Cook) B., e. Univ. of Toronto (Ont.) Schs., 1926; Univ. of Toronto, B.A. 1931, B.Paed. 1938, D.Paed. 1948; m. Isabel Alford (d), d. late Alexander Weddell, 10 Aug. 1946; children: Charles Alexander, Judith Isabel, John William; Teacher, St. Pauls Sch. for Boys, Toronto, 1935;

Teacher and subsequently Head of Guidance, E. High Sch. of Comm., Toronto, 1939-42, 1946-59; N. Toronto Coll. Inst. 1959; Prof. of Educ. Psychol., Ont. Coll. of Educ., Univ. of Toronto, 1962, Asst. Dean 1966-73; Dean 1973-74; appt'd. Prof. Emeritus of Educ. 1976; served with Candn. Army 1942-46; Overseas 1944-46; Militia 1949-57; rank Maj.; author, "A Job for You" 1958; "English" 1972; "History" 1980; also numerous journ. and mag. articles; Past Pres., Toronto Dist. Business Educ. Assn.; Fellow, Ont. Teachers Fed. (Past Pres.); Life mem. Ont. Secondary Sch. Fed. (Past Pres. Toronto and Prov. Dists.); Candn. Psychol. Assn. (Life); Life mem. and Secy.-Treas. Ont. Educ. Research Council (Past Pres.); Phi Delta Kappa; Mason; P. Conservative; United Church; recreations: theatre, reading, summer cottage; Home: 90 Berkinshaw Cres., Don Mills, Ont. M3B 2T2

BARRETT, Matthew W.; b. Ireland 20 Sept. 1944; e. Harvard Business School Advanced Management Program; m. Sept. 1968; children: Tara, Kelly, Andrea, Jason; SR. VICE PRES. AND DEPY. GEN. MGR., INTERNAT. BANKING, BANK OF MONTREAL; Home: 3 Poplar Place, Baie D'Urfé, Que. H9X 3H5; Office: 129 St. James, Montreal, Que. H2Y 1L6

BARRETT, Col. Ormonde Herbert, O.B.E., E.D., C.D.; trust company exec.; b. Hamilton, Ont., 2 March 1904; s. Herbert and Ellen Frances B.; e. Hamilton (Ont.) Public Schools and Coll. Inst.; Osgoode Hall, Toronto, Ont., Grad. 1926; m. 1st late Gladys Mary Handrahan; 2ndly, Lillian Mary Stuart (1960); Chrmn. and Dir., Guardian Trustco Inc. and Guardian Trust Co.; Vice-Pres., Secy. and Dir. Hunt and Moscrop (Canada) Inc.; Dir. Kindermann (Canada) Inc. Dir. and secy. Quebec-Labrador Found. Inc.; Hemlu Placements Inc.; Napierville Junction Railway Comp.; Candn. Devices Ltd.; Victoria Square Corp.; called to the Bar of Ont., 1926; (Can.) Law Dept., Goodyear Tire & Rubber Co. of Can. Ltd. 1924; Secy. and Gen. Counsel 1932; Asst. to Pres. 1946-50; Personnel Mgr., Ford Motor Co. of Can. Ltd., ·1951-53; Pres., Candn. Vickers Ltd., 1953-58; Pres., Zinc Oxide Co. of Canada Ltd. and Durham Industries (Can.) Ltd., 1960-63; Chrmn., McGill Associates, 1959-61; Chrmn., Que. Div. Candn. Mfrs. Assn., 1961-62; served in 2nd World War 1939-45 Overseas with Candn. Army; Col. Commandant, R.C.A.S.C., 1949-1957; Vice Pres., Que. Prov. Council, Boy Scouts of Can.; Pres. United Church Montreal Homes for Elderly People 1975-78; Pres. 1974-75 Sir Arthur Currie Br., Roy. Can. Legion; Pres. (1972-74) Candn. Forces Logistics Assn.; Pres. (1971) Un. Services Inst., Montreal; Pres. (1967) Candn. Club, Montreal; Freemason; Phi Delta Phi; recreations: music; Office: 614 Rue St. Jacques, Montreal, Que. H3C 1E2

BARRETT, Richard E., B.Sc.; mining engineer; b. Cobden, Ont., 20 June 1905; s. Lawrence Atholstane and Etta June (McCrum) B.; e. McGill Univ., B.Sc. (Mining Eng.) 1926; m. Margaret Robertson, d. late William MacNairn Shaw, Walkerton, Ont., 16 June 1934; one s., Lawrence Shaw; Dir., Ore Procurement, Eldorado Mining & Refining Co. Ltd., 1955-63; with Cerro de Pasco Copper Corp., Peru, S.A., 1926-29; Indust. Engr., Preston Furniture Co., 1929-33; Mgr., Parkhill Gold Mines, Wawa, Ont., 1933-36; Central Patricia Gold Mines, N.W. Ont., 1936-47; Prof. of Mining and Head, Dept. of Mining Engn., Univ. of Toronto, 1947-53; Mgr., Beaverlodge Operation, Eldorado Mining & Refining Co. Ltd., Uranium City, Sask., 1953-55; Extve Dir., Candn. Inst. of Mining & Metall., 1963-65; mem., Candn. Inst. Of Mining and Metall.; Assn. Prof. Engrs. of Ont.; Freemason; Anglican; Club: Engineers; Home: 3 Silver Crescent, Port Hope, Ont. L1A 2C4

BARRETTE-JONCAS, Hon. Madam Justice Claire, Q.C., B.A., LL.L.; b. Montreal, Que., 18 May 1933; d. Hon. Jean and Cecile (Guindon) Barrette; e. Acad. St-Paul; Pensionnat d'Outremont; Coll. Jésus-Marie, B.A.

1953; Univ. de Montréal, LL.L. (cum laude) 1956; m. Judge Claude Joncas, s. late Louis E. Joncas, Westmount, Que., 21 Dec. 1963; children: Louis, Lucie; called to the Bar of Quebec 1957; cr. Q.C. (fed.) 24 Dec. 1971; was only woman ever to preside over Jr. Bar of Montreal (1961-62) and first to sit on Bar Council of Montreal (1962-63); first woman to sit on Bar Council of Que. 1962-63 and first woman to plead before the Criminal Assizes in Quebec (Montreal 1958); former Dir., John Howard Soc. of Montreal; Treas., Inst. Philippe Pinel de Montréal (until 1975); former Secy., Legal Aid Bureau, Bar of Montreal; former Pres., Comte. of Criminal Affairs of Former Bureau; Elder, St-Viateur Ch., Outremont, Que. (1971-74); French Secy., Jr. Assocs. Montreal Museum Fine Arts 1960-61; Past Pres., Assn. Women Lawyers, P.Q.; Jr. Bar Assoc. of Montreal; Past mem. Council, Bar of Montreal and Bar of P.Q.; Lectr. in Criminal Law, Univ. of Montreal 1962-64 and McGill Univ. 1967-70; part-time mem. Law Reform Comm. of Canada 1971-75; Justice of the Superior Court of Quebec; R. Catholic; recreations: geneology, reading, travel; Home: 261 Côte Ste-Catherine Rd., Outremont, Que. H2V 2B2; Office: Court House, 1 est. rue Notre Dame, Ch. 16.66, Montreal, Que. H2Y 1D6

BARRON, Alex Ethelred; financier; b. Paris, Ont. 4 August, 1918; s. Dr. Fred and Ethel (Rutherford) B.; e. Schs. of Paris, Ont.; m. Nina Marion Burrows, 1 June 1946 (deceased 16 July, 1976); two s.; Paul Douglas, James Frederick; m. 2ndly, Beverley Mollet, 5 May 1978; PRESIDENT AND DIR., CANADIAN GENERAL INVESTMENTS LTD. (INVESTMENT TRUST); Chrmn. and Dir., Canadian Tire Corp. Ltd.; Chrmn. and Dir. of Extve. Comte, Domtar Inc.; Vice-Pres. and Dir., Spinrite Yarns and Dyers Ltd.; Dir. and mem. Extve. Comte., Canada Trustco Mortg. Co., The Canada Trust Co.; Dir., Halliburton Co., (Dallas, Texas); Steel Co. of Canada Ltd.; Protestant; recreation: fishing, skiing, golf; Clubs: Briars Golf & Gountry; Rosedale Golf; Granite; Toronto; Home: 75 Bayview Ridge, Willowdale, Ont. M2L 1E3; Office: Suite 1702, 110 Yonge St., Toronto, Ont. M5C 1T4

BARROW, Hon. Augustus Irvine, F.C.A.; senator; b. Montreal, Que. 15 Feb. 1913; s. Hartley F. J. and Margaret Edith (Irvine) B.; e. Halifax Pub. Schs.; Maritime Business Coll., Halifax; m. Joyce Frances, d. Fred Barnstead, 7 June 1941; children: Fred Foster, Barbara Frances; PRESIDENT, HALIFAX CABLEVISION LTD; Past Pres., Halifax Jr. Bd. Trade; Halifax Bd. of Trade; Inst. of C.A.'s of N.S.; Halifax Comm. Club; Halifax Co. Lib. Assn.; N.S. Lib. Assn.; Past Chrmn., Halifax Civic Comte. re Obtaining City Mgr.; Halifax-Dartmouth Metrop. Comte. on Problems of Regional Devel.; former Vice-Pres. for N.S., Atlantic Prov. Econ. Council; Freemason; Liberal; Baptist; recreations: golf, fishing; Clubs: Halifax; R.N.S.Y.S.; Halifax Golf & Country; Home: 1040 Ridgewood Dr., Halifax, N.S. B3H 3Y4; Office: 301 Bank of Nova Scotia Bldg., Halifax, N.S.

BARROW, Jack C.; company director; b. Toronto, Ont., 9 July, 1914; s. John and Alice E. B.; e. Riverdale Coll., Toronto, Ont.; m. Margaret E. (Betty), d. George A. J. Cook, 19 Nov. 1941; children: Peter C., Mary E.; DIR., SIMPSONS-SEARS LIMITED, Simpsons-Sears Acceptance Company Limited; Allstate Insurance Co. of Canada, Allstate Life Insurance Co. of Canada; Jannock Limited; Canadian Imperial Bank of Commerce; General Foods, Limited; Chrmn., Pirelli Canada Inc.; Business Council on National Issues; Past Pres., Retail Council of Can.; Chrmn. Corporate Div., Un. Appeal Metrop. Toronto, 1965; Pres., Un. Community Fund of Greater Toronto, 1968, Chrmn. Bd. Trustees, 1969-70; Asst. Buyer, Women's Ready-to-wear. Mail Order Div., The Robert Simpson Co. Ltd., 1946-49; Buyer, Girls' Wear, 1950-52; Mail Order Sales Mgr., Simpsons-Sears Ltd., 1953-55; Merchandise Supvr., Men's Wear, 1955-58, Men's and Boys' Wear, 1958-60; Gen. Retail Merchandise Mgr., 1960-62; Extve. Asst. to Pres., 1962; Extve. Vice-Pres.,

1962-66; Chrmn. and C.E.O., 1966-79; served during 2nd World War with Candn. Army 1941-44; recreation: golf; Clubs: Canadian; Toronto; York; Lambton Golf & Country; Toronto Hunt; The Mt. Royal; The Country (Fla.); Home: Apt. 1001, 150 Heath St. W., Toronto, Ont. M4V 2Y4 and 400 South Ocean Blvd., Manalpan, Palm Beach, Florida; Office: 222 Jarvis St., Toronto, Ont. M5B 2B8

BARRY, Lieut.-Col. Eric Lawrence, C.D.; association executive; b. Montreal, P.Q., 15 April 1927; s. William Henry and Beatrice Dillon (Lawrence) B.; e. St. Leo's Acad., Westmount, P.Q., 1933-45; McGill Univ. Sch. of Comm. 1945-49; Sir Geo. Williams Univ., B.A. (Econ.) 1966; m. Mae Christine, d. John Joseph O'Brien, Montreal, P.Q., 11 Oct. 1952; children: Christopher John, Lisa Maureen, Mary Catherine, Erica Jane, David William; PRES., CANADIAN TEXTILES INSTITUTE, 1980-; employed in Advertising Dept. of Henry Morgan & Co. Ltd., Montreal, 1950-52; Exec. Vice-Pres., Can. Paint Manufacturers Assn., 1964-79; joined Can. Paint Manufacturers Assoc. as Asst. to Pres. and Gen. Mgr., Jan. 1952; apptd. Secy., Sept. 1957; Gen. Mgr. 1958; Lieut. 17th Hussars, 1949-52, Capt., 1952-55, Major 1955-58; Lieut. Col. and C.O., Royal Candn. Hussars, 1960-1964; mem., Am. Soc. Assn. Extves.; Inst. of Assn. Extves.; R. Catholic; Commander Order of St. John of Jerusalem (1976); Club: St. James's (Montreal); Home: 4549 Sherbrooke St. West, Westmount, Que. H3Z 1E8; Office: 1080 Beaver Hall Hill, Montreal, Que. H2Z 1T6

BARRY, Francis Leopold(Frank), M.A., R.C.A.; artist; educator; b. London, Eng. 16 Apl. 1913; s. Hubert Charles and Olive (Armstrong) B.; e. Ealing Sch. of Art London, Nat. Dipl. in Design 1950; Hornsey Sch. of Art London, Art Teachers Dipl. 1951; Sir George Williams Univ. M.A. (Art Educ.); m. Hilda Patricia d. Pat Rawlinson 1945; children: Christopher, Ailsa; INSTR. IN DESIGN, DEPT. OF ART EDUC. CONCORDIA UNIV.; rep. in Nat. Gallery, McGill, Carleton and Concordia Univs. and in private colls.; monograph publ. Yvan Boulerice "Frank Barry"; served with R.A.F. (Intelligence) 1943-46; mem. Soc. des Peintures du Qué.; Anglican; recreations: cross-country skiing, swimming; Home: 201 Bedbrook Ave., Montreal, West, Que. ; Office: Montreal, Que.

BARRY, Ivor, B.A.; actor and writer; b. Merthyr, Glamorganshire, S. Wales, 12 April 1919; s. William John and Lily Maude (Phillips) B.; e. Univ. Coll. of Wales, B.A. (Hons. in French Lang. and Lit.); 1947; m. Helen Joy, d. Geoffrey Brameld of Somerset, Eng. and Mysore, India, 23 June 1950; one d. Bronwen Anne; began as Secondary Sch. Teacher and Pte. Tutor in London, Eng., 1948-52; came to Canada, 1953 and has since been engaged as a TV, Film, Radio, and Stage Actor, and as a script writer for these media, specializing in translation adaptations from the French (most work in close assoc. with CBC); served in 2nd World War, Royal Arty., 1940-46; Commnd. 1941, Overseas service (1941-46) in Middle E. and Italy; demob. with rank of War Subst. Lieut.; Pres., Assn. of Candn. Radio & Television Artists, 1961-62 (Council mem. 1959-61 and 1962-63, Dir. 1965); Dir., Candn. Council of Authors and Artists, 1962; mem. Acad. Motion Picture Arts and Sciences; recreation: work; Address: 360 South Burnside Ave., Apt. 5J, Los Angeles, Calif. 90036.

BARRY, Hon. John Paul, B.C.L.; judge; b. Saint John, N.B. 11 Nov. 1915; s. John A. and Julia P. (Wilson) B.; e. St. Patrick's Sch., Saint John High Sch.; Univ of N.B. B.C.L. 1936; m. Rita Marie d. John L. and Marie T. (Ready) Feeney 29 Dec. 1941; children: John, David, Mary, Norah, Thomas, Martha, Moira, Michael; JUDGE, SUPREME COURT OF N.B. since 1966; called to Bar of N.B. 1936; cr. Q.C. 1953; mem. Common Council Saint John 1940-44; Candn. Bar Assn.; R. Catholic; recreation: golf; Club: Westfield Golf & Country; Home: 213 Lancaster St., Saint John, N.B. E2L 2J4; Office: Provincial Bldg., 110 Charlotte St., Saint John, N.B. E2L 2J4.

BARRY, Leo, B.A., B.Sc., LL.M., Q.C.; b. Red Island, Placentia Bay, Nfld. 7 Aug. 1943; s. Leo Maurice & Elizabeth (Ryan) B.; e. High Sch. Brigus, Conception Bay, Nfld. (Gov. Gen.'s Medallist, Imperial Oil and Electoral Scholar) 1958; Memorial Univ. B.Sc. 1962, B.A. 1963; Dalhousie Law Sch. LL.B. 1967; Yale Univ. LL.M. 1968; m. Mary Elizabeth, d. Gerald Maloney 19 Feb. 1963; children: Sheila, Diane; BARRISTER AND SOLICITOR, HALLEY, HUNT 1981-; called to Bar of Nfld. 1969; practised law with firm of Thoms, Fowler, Rowe & Barry 1969-72; el. M.H.A. March 1972, apptd. Depy. Speaker 1972; Min. of Mines and Energy, Nfld., 1972-75; assoc. Prof. of Law, Dalhousie Law Sch. 1977-79; re-el. M.H.A. June 1979-81; mem. Candn. Human Rights Foundation; Law Soc. of Nfld.; Candn. Bar Assn.; Am. Soc. Internat. Law; Fellow, Foundation for Legal Research in Can.; P. Conservative; R. Catholic; recreations: squash, golf, chess, reading, bridge; Home: 11 Parsons Pl., St. John's, Nfld.; Office: Confederation Bld., St. John's, Nfld.;

BARTHOLOMEW, Gilbert Alfred, Ph.D., F.A.P.S., F.R.S.C., F.A.A.A.S.; nuclear physicist; b. Nelson, B.C. 8 Apl. 1922; s. Alfred Bartholomew; e. Univ. of B.C. B.Sc. 1943; McGill Univ. Ph.D. 1948; m. Rosalie May d. late Edwin Hugh Dinzey 19 Apl. 1952; RESEARCH DIR. PHYSICS DIV. ATOMIC ENERGY OF CANADA RESEARCH CO. since 1971; Jr. Research Offr. Nat. Research Council, Ottawa 1943-44; joined Atomic Energy of Canada Ltd. Chalk River 1948, Head of Neutron Physics Br. 1962-71; author over 100 scient. publs. incl. 7 review articles neutron capture y-rays, neutron physics and low energy nuclear physics; mem. Candn. Assn. Physicists; Sigma Xi; recreations: underwater swimming, canoeing, tree farming; Home: (P.O. Box 1258) RR #1, Deep River, Ont. K0J 1P0; Office: Chalk River, Ont. K0J 1J0.

BARTKIW, Roman, R.C.A.; artist; b. Montreal, Que. 8 March 1935; s. Ivan (Jan) (John) B.; e. Beamsville (Ont.) High Sch. 1956; Ont. Coll. of Art A.O.C.A. 1960 (Henry Birks Medal; Gov. Gen. Medal; J. S. McClean Scholarship 1960); Sheridan Sch. of Design Mississauga glass blowing 1969; Alfred Univ. N.Y. glass blowing 1970, glass technol. and arch. glass concepts 1974-75; one d.; owned and operated pottery studio Toronto and Markdale, Ont. 1961-71; glass blowing studio Combermere, Ont. 1975-77; pottery teacher own studio Toronto 1961-62; Northern Coll. Inst. Toronto 1962; Head of Ceramics Ont. Coll. Art 1968-69; instr. in ceramics and glass blowing Georgian Coll. Applied Arts 1971-74; estbd. arts & crafts program Chesterfield Inlet, N.W.T. 1978; instr. various summer and night courses; res. mastercraftsman potter, St. Clair College, Chatham, Ont. Demonst. and Panel mem. Internat. Glass Symposium Denmark 1976; pottery workshop Cambrian Coll. 1977; solo ceramic exhns. incl. Candn. Guild of Crafts Gallery Toronto 1964; Candn. Guild of Potters 1967; solo glass exhns. incl. Wells Gallery Ottawa 1976; Thomas Gallery Winnipeg 1976; Alice Peck Gallery Hamilton 1976; recipient Candn. Guild Crafts Design Award Ceramics 1965; Carling Festival of Arts Award Toronto 1969; Can. Council Award 1969; Candn. Scandinavian Foundation Travelling Scholarship 1974; Candn. Guild Crafts Travel Grant to Sweden 1975; Marriott Award for hand blown glass "Man" 1977; Ont. Arts. Council Grant 1979; rep. glass exhn. Umea and Gothenburg Museums, Sweden, Denmark and Finland 1974-76; Masters Exhn. Toronto 1976; rep. in various perm. colls. incl. Royal Ont. Museum, Umea and Gothenburg Museums Sweden, Museum of Decorative Arts Copenhagen; mem. Visual Arts Ontario; N.S. Designer's Craftsman; Candn. Crafts Council; Crafts Council; Candn. Ceramic Soc.; Ont. Potters Assn.; Ont. Arts Council; Address: R.R. 2 Granville Ferry, (Port Wade) Annapolis Co., N.S. B0S 1K0.

BARTLETT, Donald Sinclair, M.Sc.; executive; b. Beamsville, Ont., 21 April 1929; s. Harry Alfred Benjamin and Anne Spence (Sinclair) B.; e. Mich. State Univ. B.Sc. 1949; Wash. State Univ., M.Sc., 1951; m. Lilly Malene, d. Omil Thorstvedt, 29 Sept. 1951; children: Inger Anne, Margaret Lynn, Donald Benjamin Sinclair, Brenda Louise; PRESIDENT, BAR-WELL FOODS LTD., since 1971; Past Dir., Candn. Food Processors. Assn.; Dir., F.A.V.P.E.P. (Fruit & Vegetable Products Export Promotion Counsel of Can.); Dist. Mgr., Continental Can Co. of Canada Ltd., 1951-56; Clark Foods from 1956 to 1966 retired as Vice President; mem., Advertising & Sales Executives Club; Inst. of Food Tech.; Montreal Bd. of Trade; Montreal Kiwanis Club; mem. Consultative Comte., Faculty of Concordia; Sigma Chi; Freemason; United Church; recreations: skiing, golf; Clubs: Beaconsfield Golf; Mississaugua Golf & Country (Port Credit, Ont.); M.A.A.A.; Royal Montreal Golf; Home: 1779 Laird Blvd., Town of Mount Royal, P.Q.; Office: 1320 Graham Blvd., Town of Mount Royal, Montreal, Que. H3P 3C8

BARTON, Thomas Herbert, Ph.D., D.Eng.; educator; b. Sheffield, Eng. 28 May 1926; s. Herbert Ambrose and Annie (Jackson) B.; e. Univ. of Sheffield B.Eng. 1947 (Mappin Medal), Ph.D. 1949, D.Eng. 1968; m. Patricia Stokes 24 March 1951; DEAN, FACULTY OF ENGINEERING, UNIV. OF CALGARY since 1975 and Prof. of Elect. Engn. there; Acting Dir. Academic Computer Services, 1979-80; Grad. Apprentice English Electric Co. Stafford, Eng. 1949-50, Research Engr. 1950-51; Lectr. in Elect. Engn. Univ. of Sheffield 1951-57; Asst. Prof. McGill Univ. 1957, Assoc. Prof. 1960, Prof. 1965-75, Acting Dir. Dept. Extension 1966-67, Assoc. Dean Acad. Faculty of Engn. 1972-75, Acting Dean of Engn. 1974; Brit. Council Visitorship 1968; Visiting Prof. Univ. of Grenoble 1971; Consultant to General Motors Research Lab. for Elect. Engn. 1971-74; mem. Grants Comte. Elect. Engn. Nat. Research Council Can. 1973-76; Bd. Petroleum Recovery Research Inst. Alta. since 1975; Alta. Inter-Univs. Council 1977-81; Nat. Comte. Deans Engn. & Applied Science (Secy. 1977-78; Chrmn. 1978-79); Engn. Accreditation Comte. Queen's Univ. Chrmn. 1977; Past mem. and mem. various McGill Univ. and Univ. Calgary Comtes.; Fellow, Inst. Elect. Engrs. (London, Eng.); Fellow, Inst. Elect. & Electronic Engrs. (N.Y.), Chrmn. and mem. various comtes.; mem. Assn. Prof. Engrs., Geols. & Geophysicists Alta. (Bd. Examiners, Bd. Ed., Bd. on Candn. Content); Sigma Xi; recreations: gardening, carpentry; Home: 1115 Varsity Estates Rise, Calgary, Alta. T3B 2X4

BARTON, William Hickson, B.A., L.L.D.; retired; b. Winnipeg, Man. 10 Dec. 1917; s. Ernest James and Norah (Hickson) B.; e. Univ. of Brit. Columbia, B.A. (Hons.) 1940, Mt. Allison U., L.L.D., 1978; m. Jeanie, d. late F. B. Robinson, 27 Dec. 1947; one s., Scott Donald; Ambassador and Permanent Rep. of Can. to U.N. 1976-80; joined Defence Research Bd., Secy. 1946; Secy., Nat. Aeronautical Research Comte. 1950 until seconded to Dept. External Affairs 1952; joined that Dept. 1954 serving abroad in Vienna and at U.N., New York; Alternate Gov. for Can., Internat. Atomic Agency 1957-59; External Affairs mem., Permanent Jt. Bd. Defence 1959; Head, U.N. Div., Dept. External Affairs, Ottawa 1964, Asst. Under-Secy. State for External Affairs 1970; served in World War, R.C.A. 1940-46; rank on retirement Maj.; mem. Candn. Inst. Internat. Affairs; Chmn., Int. Program Candn. Comprehensive Auditing Found.; mem. Bd. of Trustees, U.N. Inst. of Training and Research; recreations: reading, swimming; The United Nations, New York, N.Y.

BARTRAM, Edward John, M.A., R.C.A.; artist; educator; b. London, Ont. 21 March 1938; s. Edward Alexander and Olive (English) B.; e. Neuchatel, Switzerland 1958; Univ. of W. Ont. B.A. 1961; Univ. of Toronto M.A. (Fine Arts) 1964; m. Mary Elizabeth d. William E. Bromley and Helen (Doig) 8 June 1980; Printmaking Instr. Central

Tech. Sch. Toronto; solo exhns. incl. Univ. of Guelph 1966; York Univ. 1969; Univ. of Toronto 1972; Aggregation Gallery Toronto 1975; 1640 Gallery Montreal 1975; 2719 Gallery Dallas, Texas 1975; Mira Godard Gallery Toronto 1977 10 years; 1979-82; rep. in numerous group exhns. incl. Internat. Printmakers Annual Seattle 1969, 1971; 2719 Gallery Dallas 1970, 1971, 1978; Salon Internat. de La Gravure Montreal 1971; Pratt Invitational N.Y. 1971; Candn. Artists Invitational Art Gallery Hamilton 1972; Candn. Heritage Art Gallery Ont. 1973; Premio Internazionale Biella, Italy 1973; 5 Printmakers Can. House London, Eng. and Centre Culturel Paris 1974-75; Norwegian Print Biennale 1980; 10 Contemporary Print Artists Japan 1981; rep. in various pub., corporate and private colls. incl. Art Gallery Ont., Can. Council Art Bank, Dept. External Affairs Ottawa; recipient Graphex II Purchase Award 1974; Arts Council Publ. & Purchase Award; G.A. Reid Award C.P.E. Annual, Sir George Williams Univ.; Ont. Soc. Artists 103rd and 105th Annual Purchase Awards; ''Imprint'' Praga Industries Award, Print & Drawing Council Can. 1976; Graphex IV Ont. Arts Council Editions Award 1976; mem. Ont. Soc. Artists; Print & Drawing Council Can.; Roy. Can. Acad.; Address: P.O. Box 188, King City, Ont. L0G 1K0.

BASFORD, S. Ronald, Q.C, P.C., B.A., LL.B.; b. Winnipeg, Man., 22 Apl. 1932; s. Douglas and Elizabeth (Menagh) B.; e. Gen. Steele Elem. Sch., Fort Garry, Man.; Comox (B.C.) High Sch.; Univ. of B.C., B.A. 1955, LL.B. 1956; m. Madeleine Nelson Kirk, 3 June 1967; two children: Daniel, Megan; PARTNER, DAVIS & CO., BARRISTERS & SOLICITORS since 1979; appt. Dir., North East Coal Development Project, Feb. 1981; Dir., General Distributors of Can. Ltd.; I.T.T. Industries; Alltrans Group of Can. Ltd.; mem., Bd. of Management, B.C. Research Council; Vancouver Public Aquarium Assn.; Vancouver Gen. Hosp. Foundation; practised law as partner in a Vancouver firm prior to el. to H. of C., def. cand., for Vancouver-Burrard, g.e. 1962; el. 1963, re-el. 1965; el. 1968, 1972, 1974 for riding of Vancouver Centre; Parlty. observer 18th Session of U.N. Gen. Assembly, 1963; Special Adviser to Govt. Del., 49th Conf. of the Internat. Labour Organ., Geneva, 1965; Leader, Candn. Del., 11th Commonwealth Parlty. Assoc. Conf., Wellington, N.Z., 1965; Del., 12th Conf., Ottawa, 1966; Co-Chrmn. with Senator David Croll of Special Joint Comte. of Senate & H. of C. on Consumer Credit & Cost of Living, 1967; Min. Consumer & Corporate Affairs 1968, Urban Affairs 1972, Nat. Revenue 1974, Justice and Attorney-General 1975; resigned from Cabinet Aug. 1978 and from H. of C. Feb. 1979; mem., Vancouver Bar Assn.; Vancouver Bd. Trade; Law Soc. of B.C.: recreation: fishing; Club: Vancouver; Home: 1870 W. 43rd Ave., Vancouver, B.C. V6M 2C5; Office: 14th Fl., Burrard Building, 1030 W. Georgia St., Vancouver, B.C. V6E 3C2

BASINSKI, Zbigniew Stanislaw, D.Phil., D.Sc., F.R.S.C., F.R.S.; research scientist; b. Wolkowysk, Poland 28 Apl. 1928; s. Antoni Basinski and Maria Z.A. Hilferding Basinska; e. Lyceum of Krzemieniec, Poland; Univ. Oxford B.Sc. 1952, M.A. 1954, D.Phil. 1954, D.Sc. 1966; m. 1 Apl. 1952; children: Stefan Leon Hilferding, Antoni Stanislaw Hilferding; Research Scient. Div. Physics, Nat. Research Council; Ford Distinguished Visiting Prof. Carnegie Inst. Technol. 1964; Commonwealth Visiting Prof. Metall. & Materials Science, Univ. Oxford, Visiting Fellow, Wolfson Coll. 1969-70; Visiting Research Scientist, Cavendish Laboratory Cambridge, and Overseas Fellow, Churchill College Cambridge, 1980-81; First recipient (1977) Candn. Metal Physics Medal; Fellow of the Royal Soc. of London, 1980; author over 60 scient. research articles various internat. journs.; mem. Metall. Soc. AIME; Sigma Xi; service Polish Army Cadet Sch. Camp Barbara, Palestine 1943-47; Home: 108 Delong Dr., Ottawa, Ont. K1J 7E1.

BASMAJIAN, John V., M.D., F.A.C.A., F.R.C.P.(C); university professor and administrator; b. Constantinople (of Armenian parentage) 21 June 1921; s. Mihran and Mary (Evelian) B.; e. (came to Canada, 1923) Univ. of Toronto, M.D. (with Hons.) 1945; St. Thomas's Hosp., London, Eng., Post-grad. studies, 1953; Saddington Medal, Univ. of Toronto, 1943, and Cody Silver Medal, 1945; m. Dora, d. Samuel Lucas, Leamington, Ont., 4 Oct. 1947; children: Haig Lucas, Nancy, Sally Ann; PROF. OF MEDICINE AND DIR. OF REHABILITATION MEDICINE PROGRAMS, McMaster Univ. since 1977; Dir. Regional Rehab. Research & Training Centre & Prof. of Anat., Physical Med. & Psychiatry, Emory Univ. 1969-77; Dir. of Neurophysiol., Georgia Mental Health Inst. 1969-77; Research Assoc., Hosp. for Sick Children, Toronto, 1955-57; Hon. Secy.-Treas., Banting Research Foundation, Toronto, 1955-57; Demonst. of Anat., Univ. of Toronto, 1946-47; Post-grad. work at Sunnybrook Hosp., and Hosp. for Sick Children, Toronto, 1947-48; Lect. in Anat., Univ. of Toronto, 1949-51, Asst. Prof., 1951-54, Assoc. Prof., 1954-56; Prof., 1956-57; Prof. and Head of Anat., Queen's Univ. 1957-69; awarded Starr Medal for Research, Univ. of Toronto, 1956; served in R.C.A.M.C., 1943-45 with rank of Capt.; N.R.C. exchange scientist to Soviet Acad. of Sciences, 1963; Publications: ''Primary Anatomy'', 8th ed., 1982; ''Surface Anatomy,'' 1977; ''Muscles Alive: Their Functions Revealed By Electromyography'', 4th ed., 1979; ''Grant's Method of Anatomy'' 10th ed., 1980; ''Clinical Electroneurography'' (with M. Smorto) 2nd ed., 1980; ''Computers in Electromyography'' (with H. Clifford, W. McLeod and N. Nunnally); ''Electrodiagnosis'' (with M. Smorto) 1977; ''Therapeutic Exercise'', 3rd ed. 1977; ''Biofeedback'' 1979; ''Electrode Placement in EMG Biofeedback'' (with R. Blumenstein), 1980; Neuromotor Examination of the Limbs'' (with M. Smorto), 1980; ''Therapeutic Exercise D2 Student Edition,'' 1980; many scientific articles in various medical journals; mem., Am. Assn. of Anats. (Extve Comte. 1975-79); Anat. Soc. of Gt. Brit. & Ireland; Biofeedback Res. Soc. (Extve. Comte 1975-77); Candn. Neurol. Soc.; Acad. of Med., Toronto; Fellow, N.Y. Acad of Med., mem., Ont. Coll. of Phys. & Surg.; Candn. Assn. Anats. (mem. Extve. Council and Secy., 1965-68); Am. Acad. Neurol.; Cajal Club (Neurol.); Hon. mem., Mexican Assn. of Anats.; Am. Assn. Advance. Science; Neuroscience Soc.; Soc. for Psychophysiol.; Biomed. Engn. Soc.; Am. Cong. of Rehabilitation; Internat. Soc. of Electromyographic Kinesiol. (Pres. 1968-72); Internat. Soc. Biomechanics (Extve. Comte. 1974-76); Biofeedback Soc. of America (Pres. 1979); mem., Ed. Bd., Candn. Journal of Surgery (1957-68); the International Journal ''Electromyography''; the ''Queen's Quarterly'' (1961-68); Am. Journ. of Phys. Med.; Assoc., Ed., Am. Journ. of Anat.; Anatomical Record; mem. of Senate, Queen's Univ., (1965-68); Chrmn., subcomte. on Med. Electronics and Electrotherapy, Comte. on Electrical Definitions, Candn. Standards Assn. (1960-67); Dir., Ont. Div., Candn. Cancer Soc. (mem., Med. Adv., Publicity & Educ. Comtes.; Chrmn., sub-comte. on sch. ed. programmes) mem., Nat. Fitness Research Review Comte. (Chrmn., 1967-69) Dept. of Health and Welfare, Ottawa, Trustee, Kingston Bd. of Educ. (Chrmn. of Bd., 1964, 1965); mem. Fitness Council of Can. 1968-69; Study Sec. on Orthopedics and Applied Physiology, Dept. Health, Educ. Welfare, Washington; rec'd Kabakjian Award for Contributions to Science, New York, 1967; named to ''2000 Men of Achievement'', 1973, and 1974; Gold Key Award 1977, Am. Congress of Rehabilitation Medicine; Honorary Fellow, Roy. Coll. of Phys. and Surgeons 1978; visiting lecturer in many universities in Europe, Japan, Australia, New Zealand, etc; United Church; recreations: drawing, gardening; Home: 106 Forsyth Ave. N., Hamilton, Ont. L8S 4E4

BASSETT, Douglas Graeme, OStJ, KCLJ; executive; b. Toronto, Ont. 22 June 1940; s. John White Hughes and Eleanor (Moira) B.; e. Bishop's Coll. Sch., Lennoxville, Que.; Upper Can. Coll., Toronto; Univ. of N.B.; m. Susan Joan Temple, d. C. R. Douglas, 19 Oct. 1968; three d.: Deborah Elizabeth, Stephanie Alexandra, Jennifer Moira; PRES. AND CEO, CFTO-TV LTD.; Baton Broadcasting Inc.; Vice-Pres., Glen-Warren Productions Ltd.; CFGO Radio Ltd.; Chrmn., Telegram Corp. Ltd. Director: Telegram Corp. Ltd.; Baton Broadcasting Inc.; CFTO-TV Ltd.; Glen-Warren Prod. Ltd.; CFGO Radio Ltd.; CKLW Radio Broadcasting Ltd.; Eaton's of Canada Ltd.; CFQC Broadcasting Ltd.; Argus Corp. Ltd.; All-View Interphase Inc.; C.F. Haughton Ltd.; Canadian Imperial Bank of Commerce; Ravelston Corp. Ltd.; Hollinger Argus Ltd.; Nurcan Energy Resources Ltd.; Pres. Arthritis Soc. (Ont. Div.); Vice Pres. & Dir. St. John's Ambulance (Ont. Council); Trustee, Hosp. for Sick Children; Toronto Sch. of Theology; Gov., Havergal Coll., Toronto; Bishop's Coll. Sch., Lennoxville, Que.; Variety Village Sport Training and Fitness Club; Dir., The Council for Canadian Unity; Nat. Ballet of Can.; Ireland Fund of Can.; Olympic Trust of Can.; Hospital for Sick Children Foundation; mem., Young Pres. Organ.; Conservative; Anglican; recreations: squash, tennis, sailing, golf, skiing; Clubs: The Toronto; York; Toronto Golf; Granite; Badminton & Racquet; Primrose; Muskoka Lakes Golf & Country; Albany (Toronto); Canadian (Toronto); Lyford Cay (Nassau); North Hatley Sailing (Que.); Variety (Toronto); Empire (Toronto); Mount Royal (Montreal); Rideau; Caledon Ski; Officer of The Order of St. John; Kt. Commander of the Military and Hospitaller Order of St. Lazarus of Jerusalem; Home: 424 Lytton Blvd., Toronto, Ont. M5N 1S4; Office: 9 Channel Nine Court, Toronto, Ont. M4A 2M9

BASSETT, Maj. John White Hughes, B.A.; broadcasting executive; b. Ottawa, Ont., 25 Aug. 1915; s. John and Marion Wright (Avery) B.; e. Ashbury Coll., Ottawa, Ont.; Bishop's Coll. Sch., Lennoxville, P.Q.; Univ. of Bishop's Coll., B.A. 1936; m. Eleanor Moira; d. Dr. F. H. Bradley, Sherbrooke, Que., 26 Apl. 1938; children: John, Douglas, David; 2ndly Isabel Glenthorne, d. Dr. Ian Macdonald, July 1967; children: Avery, Sarah, Matthew; CHAIRMAN OF BD., BATON BROADCASTING INC.; Chrmn. CFTO-TV Ltd.; CFQC-TV and Radio (Saskatoon); CKLW-AM, FM (Windsor); Haughton Graphics Ltd.; Dir., CTV Television Network Ltd.; served in 2nd World War as Major, Seaforth Highlanders of Can.; saw action in Italy and N.W. Europe; def. cand to H. of C. for Sherbrooke, Que. 1945 and Toronto Spadina, g.e. June 1962; mem., Candn. Legion; P. Conservative; Anglican; recreations: riding, tennis; Clubs: York The Toronto; Empire; Badminton & Racquet; Mount Royal (Montreal); La Coquille (Fla.); Canadian; Primrose; Queens; International Lawn Tennis; Rideau (Ottawa); St. James's (Montreal); Home: 76 Binscarth Road, Toronto, Ont. M4W 1Y4; Office: Suite 1206-08, 101 Richmond St. W., Toronto, Ont. M5H 1T1

BASSNETT, Peter J., F.L.A.: librarian; b. Sutton Coldfield, Eng. 16 Nov. 1933; s. Lionel and Phyllis (Maw) B.; e. Steyning Grammar Sch. matric. 1951; Hammersmith Sch. of Arch. & Bldg. Intermediate A.I.Q.S. 1956; North-Western Poly-tech. Sch. of Librarianship 1961-63; m. Ann Gorham 12 Dec. 1959; two d. Madeline, Sarah; DIR., SCARBOROUGH PUBLIC LIBRARY BD. 1975- ; Quantity Surveyor Godfrey & Burgess, London, Eng. 1955-58; Librarian-in-Charge Haringey, London, Eng. 1964-66; Calgary Pub. Lib. Bd. 1966-72, Adm. Asst. to Dir.; Dir. Systems & Mang. Services N. York Pub. Lib. Bd. 1972-75; served with RAF 1952-54; author various articles pub. lib. adm. and research; Pres. Alta. Lib. Assn. 1968-69; mem. Lib. Assn. (Eng.); Candn. Lib. Assn.; Ont. Lib. Assn.; Private Libs. Assn.; recreations: bibliography, horticulture, musicophile, art appreciation; Home: 25 Brimwood Blvd., Unit 106, Scarborough, Ont. M1V 1E2; Office: Administration Centre, 1076 Ellesmere Rd., Scarborough, Ont. M1P 4P4.

BASSO, Guido; flugelhornist; trumpeter; arranger; composer; conductor; b. Montreal, Que. 1937; began playing trumpet at 9; played in dance and show bands and at 18 was heard by Vic Damone at club El Morocco and subsequently toured with him; toured throughout N. Am. with Pearl Bailey and her husband (Louis Belson's) orchestra 1957-60; settled in Toronto 1960 becoming a first-call studio musician and leader; Music Dir. CBLT "Nightcap" 1963-67 and CBC TV "Barris and Company" 1968-69; co-starred with Peter Appleyard in CBC TV "Mallets and Brass" 1969; Music Dir. CBC Radio "After Noon" 1969-71 and led orchestras for 2 CBC TV series on big band era "In the Mood" 1971-72 and "Bandwagon" 1972-73; organized CNE big band concerts with Dizzy Gillespie, Quincy Jones, Woody Herman and Benny Goodman 1975; also performed Toronto nightclubs and hotel lounges with own groups; soloist with Boss Brass, Nimmons 'N' Nine Plus Six and big bands of Ron Collier and others; recordings incl. several pop instrumental LPs; many Jazz LP's with the Boss Brass, Singers Unlimited, Hi Lo's and others; sought after studio musician whose distinctive flugelhorn sound can be recognized on numerous radio & TV jingles.

BATA, George Lewis, B.A.Sc., M.Sc.; chemist; b. Budapest, Hungary 18 Nov. 1924; e. Univ. of Budapest B.A.Sc. (Chem. Engn.) 1946, M.Sc. (Chem.) 1947; Univ. of Utah Tutorial Extr. Metall. 1972; Mass. Inst. of Technol. Turorial Polymer Rheology 1981; m. Judith Eve Belgrader 25 March 1950; one d. Catherine; DIR., INDUST. MATERIALS RESEARCH INST., NAT. RESEARCH COUNCIL OF CAN. 1978- ; Works Engr. Monoplast Ltd. Budapest 1947-49; Consultant New Product Devel. Société Gentia, Vincennes, France 1949-50; Devel. Group Leader, Arborite Ltd., LaSalle, Que. 1950-53; Dir. and Vice Pres. Resinous Products Inc., Dorval, Que. 1953-54; R & D Mgr. Varcum Chemicals Ltd. Lindsay, Ont. 1954-55; Staff Asst. Union Carbide Canada Ltd. 1955, Assoc. Dir. of Devel. 1956, Dir. of Devel. 1958, Dir. of Technol. 1968-78; Dir. Candn. Welding Bureau 1980- ; mem. Adv. Panel Strategic Grants, Nat. Sciences & Engn. Research Council Can. 1980- ; mem. Assoc. Comte. on Tribology present Council 1978-79, Task Force Study Que. Lab. on Engn. Materials 1977, Adv. Comte. Biomed. Engn. 1976-81; Gov., Sodalitas Danubiana Foundation & Lib. Inc. 1974- ; Candn. Del. to Internat. Organ. Standardization (Plastics) 1968- ; Dir. Physico-Med. Systems Corp. 1968-78; Chrmn. Consultative Comte. Coll. Educ. in Plastics, Ministry Educ. Que. 1966-73; Chrmn. Candn. Chem. Engn. Conf. (25th); Treas. II World Cong. Chem. Engn. Montreal 1981; holds 27 nat. and internat. patents; author numerous publs., book chapters; rec'd Candn. Research Mang. Assn. Award 1980; Médaille de Vermeil La Société d'encouragement de la recherche et de l'invention Paris, France 1979; mem. Chem. Inst. Can.; Am. Soc. Testing & Materials; Candn. Inst. Mining & Metall.; Assn. Scient., Engn. & Technol. Community Can. (Pres. 1981); Candn. Research Mang. Assn. (Chrmn. 1977-79); Soc. Plastic Engrs. (Chrmn. Internat. Relations Comte. 1967-68); Candn. Soc. Chem. Engn. (Vice Pres. 1970-71, Dir. 1967-68); l'Ordre des chimistes du Qué. (Past Dir.); Sigma Xi; R. Catholic; recreations: archaeology Central Asia, biomedical engineering, ocean sailing, Canadian science policy; Club: Mount Royal Tennis; Home: 43 Maplewood Ave., Outremont, Que. H2V 2L9; Office: 750 Bel-Air St., Montreal, Que. H4C 2K3.

BATA, Sonja Ingrid, LL.D.; director; b. Zurich, Switzerland, 8 Nov. 1926; d. Dr. George, C.B.E. and Pati (Suter) Wettstein; e. Swiss Fed. Inst. of Technol. Zurich; Wilson Coll. Pa. LL.D.; Loyalist Coll. Belleville Hon. Dipl. for Applied Arts & Technol.; m. Thomas J. Bata, 26 Oct. 1946; children: Thomas G., Christine, Monica, Rosemarie; Dir. Bata Ltd.; Candn. Commerical Corp.; Alcan Aluminum Ltd.; Urban Transportation Development Corp.; Candn. Council for Business and Arts; Gov., York Univ.; North York Gen. Hosp.; Extve. Comte., Jun. Achievement of Can.; World Wildlife Fund (Can.); Bd. Trustees, Pres., World Wildlife Fund (Internat.); Hon. Gov. Toronto French Sch.; mem. Candn. Adv. Council Shastri-Indo Candn. Inst.; mem. Nat. Bd. Candn. C. of C., 1976-80 (Extve. Council 1976-78); mem. Nat. Design Council Can. 1964-76 (Chrmn. 1973-75); Bd. Trustees Art Gallery Ont. 1968-74; active in Girl Guide World Assn. (mem. W. Hemisphere Comte. and World Finance Comte.) 1953-64; Hon. mem. Internat. Business & Prof. Women's Assn.; Home: 44 Park Lane Circle, Don Mills, Ont. M3C 2N2; Office: 59 Wynford Dr., Don Mills, Ont. M3C 1K3

BATA, Thomas J., C.C. (1971); manufacturer; b. Praha, Czechoslovakia, 17 Sept. 1914; s. Thomas and Marie B.; e. Elem. Schs., Zlin, Czechoslavakia; Private Schs., Eng. and Switzerland; Acad. of Comm., Uherske, Hradiste; m. Sonja Ingrid, d. Dr. George Wettstein, Zurich, Switzerland, 26 Oct. 1946; PRESIDENT BATA LTD.; Chrmn., Bata Industries Ltd.; Bata Financial Corp. of Can. Ltd.; Dir., IBM Canada Ltd; IBM World Trade Americas/Far East Corp.; CP Airlines; Dir., Candn. Council, Internat. Chamber Comm., French Chamber Comm. in Can.; Candn. Extve. Service Overseas; mem., Bd. Govs., Trent Univ.; past Chrmn. Bd. Govs. Candn. Assn. Latin Am.; mem. Bd. Govs. Candn. Export Assn.; Chrmn. Comte. on Development for Business & Industry Adv. Comte. to OECD; Fellow, Internat. Acad. Mang.; mem. Adv. Council Nat. Ballet of Can.; mem. Chief Extves. Forum; Candn. Inst. Internat. Affairs; Candn. Econ. Policy Comte.; Young Pres. Organ. (Founding mem. and Past Dir.); came to Can. 1939; under his leadership was built up a new plant at Batawa, Ont.; served in Candn. Reserve Army as Capt., Hastings & Prince Edward Regt.; R. Catholic; recreations: riding, swimming, skating, skiing, tennis, aviation; Clubs: Rotary (Trenton); Granite; Royal Can. Yacht.; Royal Automobile (London, Eng.); Rideau (Ottawa); Canadian (N.Y.); Home: 44 Park Lane Circle, Don Mills, Ont. M3C 2N2; Office: 59 Wynford Drive, Don Mills, Ont. M3C 1K3

BATEMAN, Leonard A., P.Eng.; consultant; b. Winnipeg, Man., 14 Jan. 1919; e. Lord Roberts, Riverview and Kelvin High Schs., Man.; United Coll.; Univ. of Man., B.Sc. (Elect. Engn.) 1942, M.Sc. 1948; Banff Sch. of Advanced Mang. (Business Adm.); Macro Eng. Seminar, M.I.T.; m.; three children, one s., two d.; PRES., BATEMAN & ASSOCIATES LTD.; design and operating responsibilities, City of Winnipeg 1942, Gen. Supt. i.c Power Production when resigned 1956; joined Manitoba Hydro Electric Bd. as Systems Planning Engr. 1956, Dir. of Production 1961, Dir. Systems Planning 1967, Asst. Chief Engr. 1970, Asst. Gen. Mgr. — Engn. and Chief Engr. 1971; Gen. Mgr. Engineering 1971; apptd. Chrmn. and Chief Extve. Offr. 1972; formed Bateman Consulting Services Jan. 1979, Bateman & Associates, 1980; Chrmn., CIGRE Study Comte. 14 (1st Candn. appted. chrmn.); Candn. Rep., World Power Conf., Moscow, Aug. 1968; Candn. Elect. Assn. Rep. on Tech. Adv. Comte., Hydro-Quebec Inst. Research 1971-74; Past Dir., Banff Sch. Advanced Mang.; Sr. mem. Inst. Elect. & Electronic Engrs.; mem. Candn. Elect. Assn. (Past Pres.); Fellow, Engn. Inst. Can. (Past Vice-Pres. Can. Nuclear Assoc.; mem., World Energy Conference; Conf. International des Grands Réseaux Electriques (CIGRE); Chmn. Can. National Comte of CIGRE, 1980-84; mem., Winnipeg Ch. of Commerce; Assn. Prof. Engrs. Man. (Past Pres., Past mem. council); author of numerous papers in prof. journs.; Address: 231 Brock St., Winnipeg, Man. R3N 0Y7;

BATEMAN, Robert McLellan, B.A.; artist; b. Toronto, Ont. 24 May 1930; s. Joseph Wilbur and Anne (McLellan) B.; e. Forest Hill High Sch. Toronto 1950; Univ. of Toronto B.A. 1954; Ont. Coll. of Educ. 1955; m. Birgit Ilse d. Ulrich Freybe, West Vancouver, B.C. 1 Aug. 1975; children: Alan, Sarah, John, Christopher, Robbie; Commr. Niagara Escarpment; Educ. Chrmn. Halton Region Con-

serv. Authority for Crawford Lake; high sch. art teacher 20 yrs.; guest lectr. art, photography, nature, conserv. various educ. and service groups; frequent tour leader and lectr. Lindblad Travel New York; films incl. "Robert Bateman" CBC TV "This Land" 1972; "Images of the Wild: A Portrait of Robert Bateman" Nat. Film Bd. Can. 1978; "The Nature Art of Robert Bateman" 1981; comns. incl. World Wildlife Fund co-designer limited ed. silver bowl 1976; 5 stamps Candn. Govt. Endangered Species Series 1976-81; Metrop. Toronto Bd. Trade painting "Window Into Ontario" 1977; Candn. Govt. wedding present to Prince Charles "Northern Reflections - Common Loon Family" 1981; named American Artist Magazine Artist of Yr. 1980; Master Artist Leigh Yawkey Woodson Art Museum 1982, Wausau, Wisc.; rec'd Excellence Award in Arts for Contrib. to Artistic Community Wentworth Co.; biog. "The Art of Robert Bateman" by Ramsay Derry 1981; maj. Candn. travel Exhn. Nat. Museum of Natural Sciences Ottawa "Images of the Wild" 1981; rec'd Queen's Silver Jubilee Medal 1977; Past Dir., Hamilton Naturalist Assn., and Fed. Ont. Naturalists; Hon. Life mem. Audubon Soc., and Nat. Wildlife Fed., and Sierra Club; Hon. Dir. Niska Wildlife Foundation, and Long Point Bird Observatory; Hon. Life mem. Burlington Cultural Centre 1980; mem.; Pollution Probe; World Wildlife Fund; Soc. Animal Artists N.Y.; Royal Candn. Acad. Arts; Brit. Soc. Wildlife Artists; United Church; Address: R.R. 2, Milton, Ont. L9T 2X6.

BATEMAN, William B., B.A., M.B.A.; banker; b. S. Kingstown, R.I. 1924; e. Brown Univ. B.A. 1945; Harvard Bus. Sch. M.B.A. 1947; m. Nancy Sherman 1948; children: 4; EXTVE. VICE-PRES. & GEN. MGR., WORLD CORPORATE BANKING, BANK OF MONTREAL, 1981- ; joined Chase Manhattan Bank N.A. Special Training Prog. 1947, Credit Dept. 1948, U.S. Dept. New Eng., Midwest 1949, Asst. Treas. 1940, Asst. Vice Pres. 1953, Petroleum Dept. 1956, Vice Pres. 1961, U.S. Dept. S.W., Ohio, Pa. 1962, Sr. Vice Pres. Metrop. Dept. W. Side Manhattan 1967, Extve. Vice Pres. Human Resources Dept. 1971, Real Estate & Mortgage Loan Dept. 1973; Sr. Vice Pres. and Chief Agt. U.S. Div. and N.Y. Agency, Bank of Montreal 1976; Extve. Vice-Pres. & Gen. Mgr. Internat. Banking, 1980; Home: 20 Avoca Ave., Toronto, Ont. M4T 2B8; Office: 1 First Canadian Place,Toronto, Ont. M5X 1A1

BATEMAN, William Maxwell, D.F.C., B.A.Sc., P.Eng.; company president; b. Winnipeg, Man., 7 May 1920; s. Norman Silver and Veda (Maxwell) B.; e. Bayside High Sch. (L.I., N.Y.); Univ. of Toronto, B.A.Sc. 1949; m. Gaye Marjorie, d. late Frederick George Lister, 22 Oct. 1949; children: Kathryn, Paul, Anne, Leslie; PRESIDENT, GENSTAR CONSTRUCTION LTD., 1979; Dir., Sales Engr., Construction Improvements Ltd. 1949; project Engr., C. A. Pitts General Contractors Ltd. 1951; Chief Engr. 1957; Vice Pres. and Chief Engr. 1963; Dir. 1967; Sr. Vice Pres. 1971; Pres. and Dir., Lake Ont. Cement 1972-79; Dir. G. & H. Steel Co.; Vice Chrmn., Mississauga Gen. Hosp.; served in 2nd World War, R.C.A.F.; rank at discharge Flight Lt.; mem. Assn. Prof. Engrs. Ont.; Engn. Inst. Can.; Concrete Comte. of Candn. Standards Assn.; author of various tech. articles and contrib. to "Heavy Construction"; Anglican; recreations: boating, golf; Clubs: Ontario; Mississaugua Golf and Country (Past Pres.); Home: 2415 Bayview Pl. S.W., Calgary, Alta. T2V 0C&; Office: Suite 300, 11012 Macleod Trail S.W.; Calgary, Alta. T2J 6A5

BATES, Albert E., B.Comm., F.C.I.B.; banker; b. Loon Lake, Sask., 30 June, 1937; s. Edward & Doris (Lockyer); e. Western Canada High School, Calgary, McGill Univ., Montreal; m. Constance Jo-Anna d. the late C.A. Wear, March 8, 1958; Children: Jo-Anne, Cathy, Kevin; SR. VICE PRES. MAN. & SASK. DIV., BANK OF MONTREAL since April, 1980; joined present bank June, 1955, held various positions in Alberta; attended McGill Univ.

Sep., 1965 to May, 1969 attaining B.of Comm. degree, winner of Gold Medal; returned to present bank, various exec. positions to October, 1973, VP Master Card to 1976, VP Retail Banking to March, 1978, VP Retail Operations to Sep., 1979, VP E. & N. Ont. to March 31, 1980; Director of Manitoba Theatre Centre, Manitoba Opera, Royal Winnipeg Ballet, Health Sciences Centre Research Foundation, Manitoba Sanitorium Board, Manitoba Forestry Assoc. Inc.; Home: 34 Newbury Cresc., Winnipeg, Man. R3P 0V5; Office: P.O. Box 518, Winnipeg, Man. R3C 2J7.

BATES, David Vincent, M.D., F.R.C.P., F.R.C.P. (C), F.A.C.P., F.R.S.(C); educator; b. West Malling, Kent, Eng., 20 May 1922; s. Dr. John Vincent and Alice Edith (Dickins) B.; e. Rugby Sch. 1935-39; Pembroke Coll., Cambridge 1939-41; St. Bartholomew's Hosp., Univ. of London 1941-44; M.B. Cambridge 1945, M.D. 1954; m. Gwendolyn Margaret, d. W. F. Sutton, 24 March 1948; children: Anne Elizabeth, Joanna Margaret, Andrew Vincent; Dean, Faculty of Med., Univ. of Brit. Columbia 1972-77; Prof. of Medicine and Physiology since 1972; sometime Sr. Phys., Roy. Victoria Hosp., Montreal, Prof. Exper. Med., McGill Univ., Chrmn. Dept. of Physiol. and Assoc. Dean, Grad. Studies there; Chrmn., Adv. Panel on Aviation, Defence Research Bd. Can.; Chrmn., Roy. Comn. on Uranium Mining, Prov. of B.C. 1979-80; Visiting Prof: Univ. N.C.; Univ. of Otago, N.Z.; Univ. of Cal.; Johns Hopkins Univ.; Harvard Med. Sch.; Univ.of Wisc.; Dalhousie; asst. Visiting Prof., Univ. of Melbourne, Australia; served in Royal Army Med. Corps. 1945-48; service in India, Japan and Malaya; mem. Roy. Coll. of Phys.; Physiol. Soc. of London; Med. Research Soc.; Am. Physiol. Soc.; Candn. Physiol. Soc.; N.Y. Acad. Science; Am. Soc. for Clin. Investig.; Candn. Soc. for Clin. Investig.; Roy. Soc. Med.; Candn. Thoracic Soc. (Pres. 1973); Candn. Assn. for Club of Rome; awarded Robert A. Cooke Medal, Am. Acad. of Allergy 1966; Queen's Jubliee Medal 1978; Certificate of Special Merit, Candn. Meteorol. Soc. 1973; author of "Respiratory Function in Disease" 1971; "A Citizen's Guide to Air Pollution" 1972; over 150 papers in scient. journs.; recreation: sailing; mem., Science Council Can.; Office: Univ. of Brit. Columbia, Vancouver, B.C. V6T 1W5

BATES, John Seaman, D.Sc., Ph.D.; consulting chemical engineer; b. Woodstock, Ont., 9 June 1888; s. Joseph Ivimey and Lavinia Cutler (Read) B.; e. High Sch., Amherst, N.S.; Acadia Univ., B.A. 1908, B.Sc. 1909, D.Sc. 1940; Columbia Univ., Chem. E. 1913, Ph.D. 1914; Univ. of Ottawa, D.Sc. 1957; Univ. of New Brunswick, D.Sc. 1971; m. 1st, Jeanette Ingraham, North Sydney, N.S., 22 Apl. 1916; 2nd, Ruby Windsor, Bathurst, N.B., 24 Apl. 1931; children: Mary Stuart (Mrs. Michael Lynch-Watson), David Windsor; began as Asst. Chem. Engr., Arthur D. Little, Inc., Boston, Mass., 1913-14; Supt., Forest Products Labs. of Can., Dept. of Interior, Montreal, 1914-19; Rep. in matters pertaining to acetone, Imp. Munitions Bd., 1916-18; Tech. Supt., Price Bros. & Co. Ltd., Kenogami, P.Q., 1919-21; Chem. Engr., Bathurst Co., Ltd., Bathurst, N.B., 1921-26; Chief Chem. and mem. Extve., Price Bros. & Co. Ltd., Quebec P.Q., 1926-32; Tech. Adviser, Price & Pierce Ltd., London, Eng., 1933-40; Candn. Mgr., Price & Pierce, Ltd., Montreal, P.Q., 1940-51; Consulting Engr., Montreal, 1952-59; Chrmn., N.B. Forest Devel. Comn., 1955-57; mem., N.B. Electric Power Comn., 1957-60; Chrmn., N.B. Water Authority 1958-67; Chrmn., N.S. Water Authority 1963-66; P.E.I. Water Authority 1966; Tech. Sec., Candn. Pulp and Paper Assn. (Chrmn., 1915-18, Hon. Life mem. 1956, Permanent Hon. Chrmn. 1974); Chem. Inst. Can. (Pres. 1922-23); Tech. Assn. Pulp & Paper Indust. (Life mem.); Engn. Inst. Can. (Life mem.); Candn. Forestry Assn. (Chrmn. 1949-53); Tech. Div. Brit. Paper & Board Makers' Assn.; (Hon. Life mem. 1956); Ont. Water Resources Comn., Distinguished Service Award 1965; Centennial Medal 1967; Protestant; Address: 72 Bridge St., Sackville, N.B. E0A 3C0

BATES, Peter John Henry, B.Sc.; information scientist; b. Maidenhead, Berks, Eng. 22 Dec. 1940; came to Can. 1967; s. Richard Henry and Eleanor (Milson) B.; e. Merchant Taylor's Sch., London 1959; London Univ. B.Sc. 1964; m. Janet Margaret Clothier 1 July 1967; children: Alexander Richard, Evan Daffyd; INFORMATION SPECIALIST, SYNCRUDE CANADA LTD. since 1972; Dir., Alta. Information Retrieval Assn.; Asst. Librarian, Associated Lead Manufactures, 1964-67; Library Asst., Univ. of Sask., 1967-68; Librarian, Alta. Research Council, 1968-72; Ed., Alta. Oil Sand Index, 1972; Clubs: Gateway Camera; recreations: photography, cross country skiing, reading, travelling; Office: Hwy. 16A and 17th St., P.O. Box 5790, Edmonton, Alta. T6C 4G3.

BATES, Ronald William, B.A., M.Com.; company executive; b. Toronto, Ont. 17 March 1925; s. Nelson Cedric and Esther Elizabeth (Bernardo) B.; e. N. Toronto Coll. Inst.; Univ. of Toronto, B.A. 1947, M.Com. 1949; m. Helen Myra, d. J. Harold Mabley, 27 Jan. 1951; children: John, Warren, Adam, Henry, Myra, Martha, Sarah; PRESIDENT AND CHIEF EXTVE. OFFR., LEVER BROTHERS LTD.; Dir. Thomas J. Lipton Ltd.; served in RCAF and Candn. Army 1944-45; mem. Grocery Products Mfrs. Can. (Past Chrmn. Marketing Council); Delta Upsilon; Protestant; recreations: art, travel, reading; Home: 27 Fifeshire Rd., Willowdale, Ont. M2L 2G4; Office: 1 First Canadian Place, Toronto, Ont. M5X 1A9

BATSHAW, Hon. Harry; Q.C.; judge; b. Dubrovna, Russia, 14 Oct. 1902; s. Thomas and Golda (Gillman) B.; came to Can. 1905; e. Pub. and High Schs., Montreal, P.Q.; McGill Univ., B.C.L. 1924; Univ. of Grenoble, France; The Sorbonne, Paris; m. Dr. Anne, d. late Lewis S. Tarshis, 18 Jan. 1928; children: Zipporah (Prof. Fredk. Wiseman); Lewis David; Justice, Superior Court of Quebec (ret. 1977); Depy. Judge Federal Court of Canada 1978; Arbitrator, Que. Labour Dept., 1979; Hon. Judge World Macabi Ass. 1980; read law with Maxwell Goldstein, K.C.; called to Bar of Que. 1925; cr. K.C. 1940; served in 2nd World War; Pilot Offr. with R.C.A.F. attached to Air Cadet Corps; now on Reserve; mem., Adm. Comte., United Nations Assn. of Montreal; Candn. Inst. of Internat. Affairs; Internat. Law Assn.; Hon. Vice-Pres., Zionist Organ. of Can., which he rep. at 22nd Internat. Cong. held in Bale, Switzerland, 1946, and 23rd Cong. at Jerusalem, 1951 (el. Judge of Cong. Court of Hon.); former Secy., Baron de Hirsch Inst.; Trustee, Shaar Hasho-Mayim Cong.; Hon. Fellow Hebrew Univ. 1976; Co-Chrmn. Amitie Culturelle Can. Française Israel; mem., Candn. Legion (Hon. Pres., Brig. Frederick Kisch Br.); on grad. from McGill Univ. was awarded Elizabeth Torrance Gold Medal for highest standing, the McDonald Travelling Scholar., and the Montreal Bar Prize for Comm. Law; Pres., Candn. Friends of the Alliance Israelite Universelle; Co-Chrmn., Candn. Council Christians & Jews (Human Relations Award, 1957); Medal of Merit of French Govt., 1962; Chrmn. Human Rights Comte., Interat. Law Assn.; Candn. Govt. Del., U.N. Conf. on Human Rights, Teheran, 1968; formerly Liberal; Hebrew; recreations: carpentry, photography, sailing; Clubs: Montefiore; Lord Reading Yacht (first Hon. Commodore); Canadien; Gatineau Fish and Game (Dir.); Home: 4557 Sherbrooke W., Apt. 101, Montreal, Que. H37 1E8

BATTEN, Alan Henry, D.Sc., Ph.D., F.R.S.C., F.R.A.S.; astronomer; b. Whitstable, Eng. 21 Jan. 1933; s. late George Cuthbert and Gladys (Greenwood) B.; e. Wolverhampton Grammar Sch. 1950; Univ. of St. Andrews B.Sc. (Astron.) 1955, D.Sc. 1974; Univ. of Manchester Ph.D. 1958; m. Lois Eleanor d. late Albert Ernest Dewis, Bedworth, Eng. 30 July 1960; children: Michael Henry John, Margaret Eleanor; SR. RESEARCH OFFR. DOMINION ASTROPHYSICAL OBSERVATORY since 1976; Research Asst. and Jr. Tutor, St. Anselm Hall of Residence, Univ. of Manchester 1958-59; Nat. Research Council Fellow, Dom. Astrophys. Observatory 1959-61, staff mem. since

1961; Part-time Lectr. in Astron. Univ. of Victoria 1961-63; Guest Investigator Vatican Observatory 1970 and Instituto de Astronomia/Fisica Del Espacio Buenos Aires 1972; rec'd Queen's Silver Jubilee Medal 1977; Pres. Parent-Teacher Assn. Willows Elem. Sch. 1971-73; mem. Synod Diocese of B.C. 1967-69, 1974; Gov. Ang. Theol. Coll. Vancouver 1967; author "Binary and Multiple Systems of Stars" 1973; Ed. "Extended Atmospheres and Circumstellar Matter in Spectroscopic Binary Systems" 1973; co-ed. "Determination of Radial Velocities and Their Applications" 1967; trans. "L'Observation des Etoiles Doubles Visuelles" par P. Couteau, 1980; 2 correspondence courses in Astron. for B.C. Dept. Educ., over 80 research papers and articles in prof. journs., 2 catalogues Orbital Elements of Spectroscopic Binary Systems; mem. Am. Astron. Soc.; Astron. Soc. Pacific (Vice Pres. 1965-68); Can. Council mem. Royal Soc. of Can. 1980-81; Royal Astron. Soc.; Pres. Victoria Centre 1970-72, Nat. Pres. 1976-78; Ed. Journal of Royal Astron. Soc. of Can. 1981-; Candn. Astron. Soc. (Charter mem. 1971, Pres. 1972-74); Internat. Astron. Union (Pres. Comn. 30 (Radial Velocities) 1976-79, Vice-Pres. Comn. 42 1979-, mem. Candn. Nat. Comte. 1964-70 and since 1976, Chrmn. Nat. Organ. Comte. XVII Gen. Assembly Montreal 1976-79); Fellow, Explorers Club 1979; Anglican; Home: 2987 Westdowne Rd., Victoria, B.C. V8R 5G1; Office: 5071 W. Saanich Rd., Victoria, B.C. V8X 4M6

BATTEN, Donald M., F.I.I.C., F.C.I. Arb., F.A.I.C.; insurance executive; b. London, Eng., 30 April 1930;, s. Archibald G. M. and Agnes M. (Spooner) B.; came to Canada 1953; e. Barrister at Law. Gray's Inn, U.K. 1953; m. Lois E., d. late Dr. Jim McClelland, 30 June 1955; children: Lynne E., D. Michael, David C.; PRESIDENT, GEN. MGR. AND DIR., THE MERCANTILE & GENERAL REINSURANCE CO. OF CANADA LTD. since 1972; joined the Co. in Claims Div. 1958, Asst. Gen. Mgr. 1971; Vice-Pres. Fed. Soc. of Fellows Ins. Inst. of Can.; Fellow, Inst. of Arbitrators (U.K.); past Chrmn., Arbitrators' Inst. of Can.; Pres., Ins. Inst. of Ont. 1981-82; Anglican; recreations: boating, theatre; Clubs: Ontario; National; Bayview Golf and Country; Home: 34 Harnish Cresc., Toronto, Ont.; Office: 141 Adelaide St. W., Toronto, Ont. M5H 3L5

BATTEN, Jack Hubert, B.A., LL.B.; author, journalist, radio broadcaster; b. Montreal, Que. 23 Jan. 1932; s. Jack Hubert Sr. and Mary Kathleen (Soward) B.; e. Univ. of Toronto Schools; Univ. of Toronto B.A. 1954, LL.B. 1957; Osgoode Hall Law Sch. 1959; m. 2ndly Marjorie Harris 20 April 1968; children (by 1st m.): Russell Bradshaw, Sarah Jane; FREELANCE JOURNALIST, AUTHOR, BROADCASTER since 1968; called to the Bar of Ontario 1959; lawyer, McLaughlin, Macaulay, May and Soward, 1959-63; writer, Maclean's Magazine, The Canadian, and managing ed., Saturday Night Magazine, 1963-68; author of twelve books incl. "The Honest Ed Story," 1972; "The Leafs in Autumn," 1975; "Lawyers," 1980; "In Court", 1982; several articles for Chatelaine, Toronto Life, Saturday Night, etc.; mem., Writers' Union of Can.; Kappa Alpha; Protestant; recreations: tennis, jazz; Home/Office: 41 Salisbury Ave., Toronto, Ont. M4X 1C5.

BATTEN, Reginald A.; film and broadcasting executive; b. Toronto, Ont., 19 April 1932; s. Alexander and Helen (Wallace) B.; e. Forest Hill Pub. Sch., Cantab Coll. and Upper Canada Coll., Toronto, Ont.; Appleby Coll., Oakville, Ont.; McMaster Univ.; children: Reginald Jr., Kim Alexandra, Deborah Louise; PRESIDENT, RABKO LTD. since 1958; Pres., Medallion Film Laboratory Ltd.; Filmpro. Ltd.; Arco Ltd.; Dir., Bomac Batten Ltd. since 1971; studied in Radio and T.V., N.Y. City, 1954; with Batten Films Ltd., 1955-57; founded present Co. 1958; instituted Filmpro Ltd., 1959, and ARCO Advertisers Revisions Ltd., 1963; became Extve. Vice-Pres., Rapid Grip & Batten Ltd. on amalg. of RABKP, Filmpro and ARCO with that Co. in 1964; Pres. and Mang. Dir., 1965-71; mem.,

Bd. Trade Metrop. Toronto; Soc. Motion Picture & T.V. Engrs.; Anglican; recreations: golf, skiing; Clubs: St. Georges; Craigleith Ski; Home: 19 Edgehill Rd., Islington, Ont. M9A 4N1; Office: 240 Richmond St. W., Toronto, Ont. M5V 1W1

BATTEN, W. Howard, B.A.; company executive; b. Toronto, Ont., 23 June 1929; s. W. Howard and Margaret Grace (Banfield) B.; e. Upper Canada Coll. (1939-46) and Cantab Coll. (1946-48), Toronto, Ont.; Univ. of Toronto, B.A. 1951; m. Sharon R., d. Gary Roggen, Melbourne, Fla.; children: W. Howard, Jr., Wendy Elizabeth, Geoffrey David; PRES., BATTEN GRAVURE LTD., Brampton, Ont.; Pres. Batten Graphics Ltd., Dir. A.V. House; mem. Adv. Bd., Fiscal Investments Ltd.; with Rapid Grip & Batten Ltd., 1951-71; Pres. Ottawa Bd. Trade, 1962-63; Past Pres., Ottawa Ad & Sales Club (1959); Ottawa Extves. Assn. (1961); Hon. Fellow, Inst. of Comm. & Indust. Mgrs., Birmingham, Eng.; Kappa Alpha; United Church; recreations: golf, skiing; Clubs: Granite; Royal Ottawa Golf; Toronto Golf; Craigleith Ski; Cambridge; Office: 553 Richmond St. W., Toronto, Ont. M5V 1Y6

BATTLE, Edward Gene, B.Sc.; company executive; b. Mont Belvieu, Texas, 19 June 1931; s. Paul E. and Annie-Mae B.; e. Texas A & M Univ. B.Sc. (Petrol. & Geol. Engn.); PRESIDENT AND DIR., NORCEN ENERGY RESOURCES LTD. since 1975; Dir. Northern and Central Gas Corp. Ltd.; Coleman Collieries Ltd.; Gaz Metropolitain, Inc.; Greater Winnipeg Gas Co.; joined Continental Oil Co., Texas 1954; Evaluation Engr. Medallion Petroleums Ltd. (subsequently Canadian Industrial Gas & Oil Ltd. 1965) 1957, Vice Pres. Production 1965, Extve. Vice Pres. 1966, Pres. 1973; Pres. and Chief Operating Offr. Northern and Central Gas Corp. Ltd. (subsequently present Co. 1975) 1974; mem. Assn. Prof. Engrs. Geols. & Geophysicists Alta.; Assn. Prof. Engrs. Ont.; Soc. Petrol. Engrs.; Am. Inst. Mining Metall. & Engn.; recreations: golf, skiing, tennis; Club: Calgary Golf & Country; Rosedale Golf (Toronto); Toronto; Home: 46 Chestnut Park, Toronto, Ont. M4W 1W8; Office: 4600 Toronto-Dominion Centre, Toronto, Ont. M5K 1E5

BATTLE, Helen Irene, M.A.,Ph.D., D.Sc., LL.D.; professor emeritus; b. London, Ont., 31 Aug. 1903; d. Edward Barrow and Elizabeth Ida (Hodgins) B.; e. Univ. of Western Ontario B.A. 1923, M.A. 1924, LL.D. 1971; Univ. of Toronto, Ph.D. 1928; D.Sc. Carleton 1971; joined Univ. of W. Ont. 1923 as Demonst. in Zool.; Instr. 1924; Asst. Prof., 1929; Assoc. Prof., 1933; Prof. 1949-72; Fellow, Am. Assn. for Advanc. of Science; Hon. Life mem. Nat. Assn. Biol. Teachers; awarded Centennial Medal 1967; Pres. (1962-63) Candn. Soc. Zool (Hon Life 1969); Fry Medallist, Can. Soc. Zool. 1977; J.C.B. Grant Award, Can. Soc. Anat. 1977; has written scient. papers with special reference to teleosts in the field of embryology, experimental. biol., spawning rhythms, embryological effects of carcinogens; Inheritance of Mackinder's brachydactyly; history of Zoology in Canada; Pi Beta Phi; Anglican; Clubs: University Women's; Soroptomist; Home: 132 Mamelon St., London, Ont. N5Z 1Y1

BATTLE, Robert Felix, O.C. (1974); retired public servant. b. Delia, Alta., 9 Apl. 1916, s. John and Fay (Friedley) B.; e. Mount Royal Coll. and Univ. of Alta., 1934-37, Cooper Inst., Higher Accountancy & Business Adm., 1950; Banff Sch. of Advanced Mang. 1954; Nat. Defence Coll., 1969-70; m. Lois Morrison, 4 Oct. 1942; children: Kenneth, Murray, Ellen; with Albertan Publishing Co. 1937-38; Delia Crown Lumber Co. Ltd. 1938-41; International Harvester Co. 1941-42; joined fed. civil service, Indian Affairs Br., Alta., 1945; served as Field Agt., Indian Supt., Regional Supvr. of Indian Agencies (Alta., N.W.T.); Chief, Econ. Devel., Ottawa 1960; apptd. Asst. Dir., Operations then Dir., Indian Affairs; subsequently Asst. Depy. Min., Indian & Eskimo Affairs (made Hon. Chief, "Mountain Chinook Wind", Stoney Tribe); Asst.

Depy. Min., Dept. Indian & N. Affairs (Finance & Adm.) 1970 until retirement; served in Brit. and N.W. Europe 1942-45; recreation: sailing; Home: 962 Saturna Pl., Victoria, B.C. V8Y 1H4

BATTS, Michael Stanley, B.A., D.Phil., M.L.S., D.Litt., F.R.S.C.; educator; b. Mitcham, Eng. 2 Aug. 1929; s. Stanley George and Alixe (Watson) B.; e. Sir Walter St. John Sch. London 1947; Univ. of London B.A. 1953, D.Litt. 1973; Univ. of Freiburg D.Phil. 1957; Univ. of Toronto M.L.S. 1974; m. Misao d. Ryuichi Yoshida, Victoria, B.C. 19 March 1959; one d. Anna Yuri; PROF. OF GERMAN, UNIV. OF B.C.; teaching positions Univs. Mainz, Basle, Wurzburg, Calif. (Berkeley); served with Brit. Army 1947-49; Vice Pres. Can Ass. of Univ. Teachers of Ger.; mem. Candn. Ethnic Studies Adv. Comte.; Trustee, Vancouver Museums & Planetarium Assn.; author "Die Form der Aventiuren im Nibelungenlied" 1961; "Bruder Hansens Marienlieder" 1963; "Studien zu Bruder Hansens Marienliedern" 1964; "Gottfried von Strassburg" 1971; "Das Nibelungenlied: Paralleldruck der Hss A, B und C nebst Lesarten der übrigen Handschriften" 1971; "A Checklist of German Literature 1945-75" 1977; "The Bibliography of German Literature: An Historical and Critical Survey" 1978; co-author "Scandinavian Literature in English Translation 1928-77" 1978; Ed. "Essays on German Literature in Honour of G. Joyce Hallamore" 1968; "A Short Account of a Northwest Voyage Performed in the Years 1796, 1797 and 1798" 1974; "Translation and Interpretation: the Multi-cultural Context" 1975; "The Canadian Settlers Guide" Part 2 1975; "In Praise of Scribes" 1977; various articles and reviews on medieval and modern lit., bibliog., book hist.; mem. Modern Lang. Assn. Am.; Candn. Lib. Assn.; Candn. Assn. Univ. Teachers German; Internationale Vereinigung für germanische Sprach- und Literaturwissenschaft; Humanities Assn. Can. (Ed. Bd.); Modern Humanities Research Assn.; Medieval Acad. Am.; Philol. Assn. Pacific Coast; recreations: badminton, squash, gardening; Home: 5587 Holland St., Vancouver, B.C. V6N 2A7; Office: Germanic Studies, Univ. of B.C., Vancouver, B.C. V6T 1W5:

BAUDOUX, Mt. Rev. Maurice, O.C., S.T.D. (R.C.); Archbishop of St. Boniface, 1955-74; retired 1974; Titular Archbishop of Preslavo, and Coadjutor Archbishop of St. Boniface (with right of succession) 1952-55; ordained priest, Prud'homme, Sask. 1929; formerly Curate and Pastor, Prudhomme, Sask. and Bishop of St. Paul, 1948-52; Hon. doctorates: D ès L, D. Phil., D.D., D.LL., D.C.L.; Address: 151 Cathedrale, St. Boniface, Man.

BAUM, Gregory G., M.A., Th.D. (R.C.); university professor; author; b. Berlin, Germany, 20 June 1923; s. Franz S. and Bettie (Meyer) B.; came to Canada (from Eng.) 1940; e. McMaster Univ., B.A. (Math and Phys.) 1946; Ohio State Univ., M.A. (Math) 1947; Univ. of Fribourg, Switzerland, Th.D. 1956; Hon. Doctorates: Huron Coll., St. Francis Xavier, Ohio Wesleyan, Lafayette, Waterloo Lutheran, McMaster & Dubuque; PROF. OF RELIGIOUS STUDIES, ST. MICHAEL'S COLL., UNIVERSITY OF TORONTO; Ed. The Ecumenist; Assoc. Ed., Journal of Ecumenical Studies; mem. Edit. Comte., Concilium; author of "That They May Be One" 1958; "The Jews and the Gospel" 1961 (rev. ed. paperback under title "Is the New Testament Anti-semitic"); "Progress and Perspective" 1962 (paperback ed. under title "Catholic Quest for Christian Unity" 1965); "Ecumenical Theology Today" 1965; "Ecumenical Theology No. 2" 1967; "The Credibility of the Church Today" 1968; "Faith and Doctrine" 1969; "Man Becoming" 1970; "New Horizon" 1972; "Religion and Alienation"1975; "the Social Imperative" 1978; "Catholics and Canadian Socialism" 1980; mem., Candn. Theol. Soc.; Candn. Soc. for Study of Religion; Am. Theol. Soc.; Address: St. Michael's College, Univ. of Toronto, Toronto, Ont. M5S 1J4

BAWTREE, Michael, M.A.; theatre and television director; producer; writer; b. Newcastle, Australia 25 Aug. 1937; s. Raymond Francis and Kathleen (McKeachran) B.; e. Radley Coll. U.K. 1956; Worcester Coll. Oxford Univ. B.A. 1961, M.A. 1963; ARTS PLANNER AND DIR. INTER-ARTS PROGRAMS, BANFF SCH. OF FINE ARTS, 1979- ; Head of Musical Theatre Div. 1978- ; actor, writer and TV host Toronto 1962-65; Instr. Victoria Coll. Univ. of Toronto 1963-64; Dramaturge, Stratford Festival 1964, Asst. to Artistic Dir., Literary Mgr. and Dir. of Third Stage 1971, Assoc. Dir. 1973-74; Book Critic "Toronto Telegram" 1965; Theatre Resident, Simon Fraser Univ. 1965-69, Founding mem. of Senate; Teatro Experimental de Cali, Colombia 1968-69 (Can. Council Bursary); Dir. of Eng. Theatre, Nat. Arts Centre 1970-71; Co-founder, Pres. and Artistic Dir. COMUS Music Theatre of Can. 1975- ; dir. various Candn. (incl. Shaw Festival, Stratford Festival & Guelph Spring Festival) and U.S. productions; Stage productions include "She Stoops to Conquer" (Stratford 1972, 1973, CBC-TV 1974); "The Medium" (Stratford 1974, Toronto 1977, produced for TV 1978, Emmy nomination 1979); author "The Last of the Tsars" (play) 1973 (Avon Theatre, Stratford Festival 1966); served with Brit. Army 1956-58, Cyprus, rank 2nd Lt.; mem. Candn. Actors' Equity Assn.; Candn. Conf. Arts; Soc. Stage Dirs. & Choreographers (U.S.); Assn. Candn. TV & Radio Artists; recreations: piano, photography, travel, reading, language study; Club: Vincents' (Oxford Eng.); Home: 286 Sherbourne St., Toronto, Ont. M5A 2S1; Office: (P.O. Box 1020) Banff, Alta. T0L 0C0.

BAXTER, James Douglas, M.D., C.M., M.Sc., F.R.C.S.(C); educator; otolaryngologist; b. Montreal, Que. 2 Oct. 1923; e. Mem. Univ. Coll. Nfld. 1940-42; McGill Univ. M.D., C.M. 1947, M.Sc. 1952; m. Dorothy Rowena Hardy 7 June 1947; two d. Carolyn Ann, Barbara Hardy; PROF. OF OTOLARYNGOLOGY, McGILL UNIV. since 1972, Chrmn. since 1970; apptd. Otolaryngol.-in-Chief, Royal Victoria Hosp. 1970; Montreal Gen. Hosp. 1977; Dir. Inst. of Otolaryngol. McGill Univ. and Royal Victoria Hosp. 1970, Consultant, Reddy Mem. Hosp., Queen Elizabeth Hosp., Montreal Chest Hosp., Jewish Gen. Hosp.; Internship Royal Victoria Hosp., Queen Mary Veterans' Hosp., Grad. Hosp. Univ. of Pa., Children's Hosp. of Philadelphia 1947-53; rec'd J.B. Collip Fellowship in Med. Research 1951-52; joined McGill Univ. 1954; apptd. to Dept. Otolaryngol. Royal Victoria Hosp. 1953, The Children's Mem. Hosp. (now Montreal Children's Hosp.) 1954; apptd. to Med. Staff Shriner's Hosp. for Crippled Children as Otolaryngol. 1969; Dir. of On-Going Survey and Project of Ear Disease and Hearing Loss Eskimo Population E. Candn. Arctic, Dept. Nat. Health & Welfare Can. under auspices McGill Univ. Baffin Zone Project since 1972; author or co-author numerous articles, papers, reports; Hon. Dir. Montreal Oral Sch. for the Deaf, Inc. since 1969; Visites Interprovincials 1978-; Fellow, Am. Acad. Ophthalmol. & Otolaryngol.; Am. Laryngol. Assn. (2nd Vice Pres. 1971-72); Am. Broncho-Oesophaol. Soc. (Vice Pres. 1978-79); mem. Candn. Med. Assn.; Candn. Otolaryngol. Soc. (Council 1968-76, Program Chrmn. 1970, Secy. 1970-72, Vice Pres. 1972-74, Pres. 1974-75); Montreal Medico-Chirurgical Soc. (Pres. Otolaryngol. Sec. 1965-67); Pan Am. Assn. Oto-Rhino-Laryngol. & Broncho-Esophagol. (Vice Pres. 1974-76, 1980-81); Internat. Assn. Bronchol. & Esophagol.; Assn. Otolaryngols. Prov. Que. (Vice Pres. 1971-72); Am. Laryngol., Rhinol. & Otol. Soc. Inc.; Collegium Oto-Rhino-Laryngologicum Amicitiae Sacrum; Am. Triol. Soc. (Secy. E. Sec. 1979-80); Protestant; Home: 74 Fernlea Cres., Town of Mount Royal, Que. H3P 1T6; Office: 687 Pine Ave. W., Montreal, Que. H3A 1A1.

BAXTER, (Joseph) Iain (Wilson), B.S., M.Ed., M.F.A.; artist; visual arts consultant; b. Middlesborough, Eng., 16 Nov. 1936; s. Andrew and Annie (Wilson) B.; e. Crescent Heights High Sch., Calgary, Alta. 1955; Univ. of Idaho, B.S. (Zool.) 1959, M.Ed. 1962; Washington State Univ.,

M.F.A. 1964; m. Elaine Ingrid, d. George Hieber, Spokane, Wash., 5 Sept. 1959; children: Tor Iain Gion, Erian; Assoc. Prof. and Univ. Res. in Visual Arts, Communications Centre, Simon Fraser Univ., 1966; Pres., N. E. Thing Co.; one-man exhns. incl.; Yamada Contemporary Gallery, Kyoto, Japan, 1961; Washington State Univ., 1964; Art Gallery of Greater Victoria (B.C.), 1966; Vancouver Art Gallery 1966; Albert White Gallery, Toronto, 1966; Rolf Nelson Gallery, Los Angeles, 1966; Norman McKenzie Art Gallery, Regina, 1966; McIntosh Art Gallery, Univ. of W. Ont., 1966; York Univ. Art Gallery 1966; Douglas Gallery, Vancouver, 1967; Simon Fraser Univ. 1969; rep. in numerous group exhns. in Can., U.S.A. and Europe since 1961; special exhns. incl. Sculptor and Dir. of "Beauty Through Destruction Creator", Univ. of B.C., 1965; Designer of Visual Sec. "Medium is the Message" Univ. of B.C., 1966, also "Bagged Place" and "Piles" at Univ. 1966 and 1968; rep. in perm. colls. of Washington State Univ., Calgary Art Centre, Montreal Museum of Fine Art, Norman McKenzie Art Gallery, Univ. of Victoria, Nat. Gallery of Can., Vancouver Art Gallery; 1st Candn. to do vacuum forming as an art form and to work with plastic and inflated sculpture and water in bagged landscapes; conceived "Total Length of Canada Film", 1968 to be shown at nat. expns.; Co-author and Illustrator, "Wildlife of the Northern Rocky Mountains", 1961; Producer "How" 1965 and "Portfolio of Piles" 1968; awards incl.: Japanese Govt. Foreign Painting Scholarship, 1961-62; Frances F. Reeve Foundation Travelling Grant 1962; Hon. Mention, Candn. Flag Design Competition 1963; Grad. Teaching Fellowship, Painting, Washington State Univ., 1962-64; Can., Council Short Term Grant and Travel Grant 1966, Sr. Grant 1969; Purchase Prize, Graphics, Victoria Art Gallery, 1966; Centennial Purchase Award Exhn. 1966; Purchase Prize, Painting, Vancouver Centennial Award Exhn. 1966; "Perspective 67" award for prints and drawing with vacuum-formed work, 1967; 1st Prize Printmaking, Centennial Arts Exhn. 1967; "Canadian Artists '68" Prize in Painting, Toronto, 1968 producing an Environment, Nat. Gallery of Can., 1969; rep. Can. at Sao Paulo Biennial Exhn., 1969; mem., Soc. Plastics Engrs.; recreations: skiing, ecology, hiking; Address: 1419 Riverside Dr. N. Vancouver, B.C. V7H 1V6

BAYDA, Hon. Edward Dmytro, B.A., LL.B.; judge; b. Alvena, Sask., 9 Sept. 1931; s. Dmytro Andrew and Mary (Bilinski) B.; e. Alvena (Sask.) High Sch.; City Park Coll. Inst., Saskatoon, Sask., 1948; Univ. of Sask, B.A. 1951, LL.B. 1953; m. Marie Thérèse Yvonne, d. Joseph Rosaire Gagnè, 28 May 1953; children: Paula, Christopher, Margot, Marie-Thérèse, Sheila, Kathryn; CHIEF JUSTICE OF SASKATCHEWAN, 1981–; called to Bar of Sask. 1954; cr. Q.C. 1966; practised law in Regina, Sask., 1953-72; Sr. Partner, Bayda, Halvorson, Scheibel & Thompson, 1966-72; Queen's Bench 1972; Justice of Appeal 1974; Past Nat. (Can.) Registrar, Assn. Kinsmen Clubs (Past Pres., Regina Kinsmen); mem., Regina Bar Assn. (Past Pres.); Law Soc. Sask. (former Bencher); Candn. Bar Assn. (former Sask. Chrmn. Civil Justice Sec.); K. of M.; R. Catholic; Club: Assiniboia (Past Dir.); Home: 9 Turnbull Pl., Regina, Sask. S4S 4H2; Office: Court House, Regina, Sask.

BAYEFSKY, Aba, C.M., R.C.A.; artist; b. Toronto, Ont., 7 Apl. 1923; s. Samuel and Hetty (Simon) B.; e. Central Tech. Sch., Art. Dept., Toronto, Ont.; Acad. Julian, Paris, France; m. Evelyn, d. of Paul Swartz, Oshawa, Ont.; Children: Anne, Edra, Eban; Staff mem., Ont. Coll. Art, Toronto; Dir., art classes, Hart House, Univ. of Toronto 1957-69; awarded French Govt. Scholar., 1947-48; Can. Council Fellowship for travel and study in India; mem., Internat. Jury for 2nd Internat. Exhn. prints, Tokyo; won first Purchase Prize of Candn. Soc. of Painters in Watercolour, 1953; J.W.L. Forster award of Ont. Soc. Artists, 1958; Work in war art coll. of Nat. Gallery Ottawa; Nat. Gallery of Victoria, Melbourne, Australia; Art Gallery of Ont.; Hamilton; London (Ont.); Sarnia; Metropolitan

Museum, N.Y.; Library of Congress, Wash.; Hebrew Univ., Jerusalem; École des Beaux Arts, Que.; Loyola Coll., Que.; Concordia Univ., Montreal; Hart House, Univ. of Toronto; Beaverbrook Gallery, Fredericton, N.B.; and various colls. in Can., U.S.A., India; 32 one-man exhns. since 1942 including "Bayefsky at the Market", Ont. Coll. of Art 1976; Exhibition of Portfolio "Legends" and "Forces of Earth and Sky", Candn. Consulate, N.Y. 1973; and Candn. Embassy, Washington, D.C. 1971; Retrospective Exbn. Art Gallery of Hamilton 1973; Albert White Gallery, Toronto 1966 awarded Order of Can. 1979; served in 2nd World War with R.C.A.F. as Official War Artist, 1942-46; mem. Candn. Soc. Graphic Art (Past Pres.); Candn. Soc. Painters in Watercolour; Candn. Group of Painters (Pres.); Fed. of Candn. Artists (Past Pres., Ont. Region); Home: 7 Paperbirch Dr., Don Mills, Ont. M3C 2E6

BAYLAUCQ, Jacques G., B.A., B.Com.; company executive; b. Pau, France, 5 Jan. 1931; s. Jean and Jeanne (Hourticq) B.; e. Coll. Stanislas, Montreal, B.A. (Univ. of Paris); Friley Inst., Ecole Supérieure de Commerce de Paris; Queen's Univ. B.Com. 1955; m. Sylvie, d. André Bieler, 1957; children: Philippe, Véronique, Nathalie; SR. VICE-PRES., ADM. AND PLANNING, ST. LAWRENCE CEMENT CO.; prior to joining present firm was partner I/C P.S. Ross & Partners, Que. Region; served with DuPont of Canada Ltd. (Kingston), Canadian National (Montreal), Canadian Industries Ltd. (Montreal and Toronto); mem. Montreal Chamber Comm.; Bd. of Dir., French Chamber Comm. Can.; Inst. Mang. Consultants Que.; Queen's Univ. Council (1972-75); Metrop. Montreal YMCA Bd. Dirs.; recreations: golf, cross-country skiing, swimming; Clubs: St. James's; Laval-sur-le-Lac; St. Denis; Home: 216 Portland Ave., Town of Mount Royal, Que. H3R 1V2; Office: 11,175 Métropolitain Blvd., Montreal East, Que. H1B 1A4

BAYLEY, C. C., M.A., Ph.D., F.R.S.C., (1961); university professor; b. Congleton, Eng., 5 March 1907; s. Harry and Hannah (Calvert) B.; e. Univ. of Manchester, B.A. 1928, M.A. 1929; Univ. of Marburg (1930); Univ. of Chicago, Ph.D. 1938; m. Ethel Mary, d. U. B. Woolliscroft, 11 Sept. 1936; two d. Ann Margaret, Susan Nancy; PROF. DEPT. OF HISTORY, McGILL UNIV. (Chrmn. of Dept. 1961-65); Lectr. in Hist., Univ. of Toronto, 1931; Asst. Prof. of Colorado Coll., 1932; Univ. Fellow, Univ. of Chicago, 1935; joined McGill Faculty, 1935; Guggenheim Fellowship 1948; Can. Council Sr. Fellowship 1966; Killam Fellowship 1970; Publications: "The Formation of the German College of Electors", 1949; "War and Society in Renaissance Florence", 1961; "Mercenaries for the Crimea: The German, Swiss, and Italian Legions in British Service, 1854-1856", 1977; Anglican; recreation: travel; Home: 3610 McTavish St., Apt. 34, Montreal, Que. H3A 1Y2

BAYLY, George Henry Uniacke, D.F.C., M.Sc.F.; forester; b. Toronto, Ont., 13 Feb. 1918; s. George William and Adeline Mary (Cartwright) B.; e. The Grove Sch., Lakefield, Ont., 1928-32; N. Toronto Coll. Inst., 1932-35; Univ. of Toronto, B.Sc.F. 1939, M.Sc.F. 1952; m. Fay Mavis, d. N. L. Anderson, Toronto, Ont. 30 May 1944; children: John, Ann, Richard; with Dom. Forest Service, Alberta, 1939; Price Brothers and Co., Que., 1939-40; Spruce Falls Power and Paper Co. Ltd., Kapuskasing, Ont., 1940; joined Ont. Dept. Lands and Forests, Reforestation Div., 1945; apptd. Chief of Div., 1954 and Asst. Depy. Min. of Dept. 1957 and Depy. Min. 1966-71; apptd. Secy. Treasury Bd. Ont. 1971; Depy. Prov. Secty. Resources Devel. Ont. 1974-75; now G.H.U. Bayly Consulting Ltd.; served with R.C.A.F. as Sqdn. Ldr. U.K., Africa, S.E. Asia, 1940-45; mem., Candn. Inst. Forestry; recreations: skiing, voyageur and whitewater canoeing, gliding; Address: Heathcote P.O., Ont. N0H 1N0

BAZOS, Frank A.; dairy executive; b. Greece, 6 Aug. 1901; s. Anthony D. and Helen (Viglas) B.; came to Can. 1920; e. St. Alban's Pub. Sch., Toronto, Ont.; Harbord Coll. Inst.; Shaw Business Coll.; m. Matilda, d. Wm. Edwards, June 1926; two d. Helen, Constance; two s. James F., Robert; FOUNDER, CHRMN. OF BD., CHIEF EXTVE. OFFR. AND DIR. THE BECKER MILK CO. LTD., since 1957; Chrmn. of Bd., Perrette Dairy Ltd., P.Q.; Puretest Dairy Ltd.; Pres., Euclid Securities Ltd.; Partner, Karrys Bros. Ltd., 1926-31; Founder and Pres., Devon Ice Cream Ltd., 1931; mem., Bd. of Trade of Metrop. Toronto; Candn. Chamber of Comm.; Gov., Central Hosp., Toronto; Freemason; Greek Orthodox; recreation: golf; Clubs: Summit Golf & Country; Progress (past mem. Nat. Bd.); Y.M.C.A. Business Men's (Past Pres. and Dir.); Home: 1 Benvenuto Place, Toronto, Ont. M4V 2L1; Office: 671 Warden Ave., Scarborough, Ont. M1L 3Z7

BEACH, Earl Francis, A.M., Ph.D., university professor; b. Chicago, Ill., 13 Mar. 1912; s. Albert and Florence (Kraft) B.; came to Can. 1916; e. Queen's Univ., B.A. 1934; Harvard Univ., A.M. 1936, Ph.D. 1938; m. Katharine, d. H. N. MacAdam, Ottawa, 3 Sept. 1938; children: Elizabeth, Charles; PROF. EMERITUS, McGILL UNIV.; Guggenheim Fellow, 1949-50; Chrmn., Social Sciences Research Council, 1958-60; Publications: "Economic Models", 1957; mem., Can. Econ. Assn.; Roy. Econ. Soc.; Am. Econ. Assn.; recreations: walking, reading; Home: 508 Victoria Ave., Westmount, Que. H3Y 2R5

BEACOCK, Ernest Stanley, M.L.S.; librarian; b. Ont. 21 Jan. 1921; s. Lambert Asel and Eva May (Tebbey) B.; e. Queen's Univ. B.A. 1942; Univ. of Toronto B.L.S. 1947, M.L.S. 1968; m. Nadine Mary Southwell 7 Sept. 1946; one s. Brian (d.); DIR. AND SECY.-TREAS., LONDON PUBLIC LIBRARY BD. 1974- ; Adjunct Prof. Sch. of Librarian & Information Science, Univ. of W. Ont. 1975- ; Librarian, Lambton Co. Lib., Ont. 1947-49; Kenton (Ohio) Pub. Lib. 1949-53; Troy-Miami (Ohio) Co. Pub. Lib. 1953-61; Asst. Dir., London Pub. Lib., 1961-66; Dir., Midwestern Regional Lib. System, Kitchener, Ont. 1966-74; served with Candn. Army 1942-46; rec'd Ont. Lib. Trustees Assn. Award 1972; mem. Ont. Lib. Assn.; Candn. Lib. Assn.; Candn. Assn. Lib. Schs.; Club: Rotary; Home: 668 Cranbrook Rd., London, Ont. N6K 1W6; Office: 305 Queens Ave., London, Ont. N6B 3L7.

BEAGRIE, George Simpson, D.D.S., F.D.S., F.R.C.D.(C), F.I.C.D.; educator; b. Peterhead, Scot. 14 Sept. 1925; s. late Eliza Lawson and George B.; came to Canada 1968; e. High Sch. Lasswade, Scot. 1943; Dental Sch. Edinburgh 1947; Royal Coll. Surgs., (Edinburgh), L.D.S. 1947, F.D.S. 1954; Univ. of Edinburgh, D.D.S. 1966; m. Marjorie Ena, d. late John McVie 30 Sept. 1950; children: Jennifer Hunter, Lesley Elizabeth, Ailsa Marjorie, Elspeth Simpson; DEAN, FAC. OF DENTISTRY, UNIV. OF BR. COL. 1978; formerly Prof. and Head (1st) Dept. Restorative Dent., Edinburgh Univ.; served in R.A.F. as Dental Offr. 1948-50, rank Flight Lt.; mem. Council, Royal Coll. Dent. of Can. (elected Pres. 1977-79); mem. Candn. Dental Assn.; Brit. Dental Assn.; Féd. Dentaire Internat. (Vice-Chrmn. Comn. on Dent. Educ. 1976-80, Chrmn. 1981-); Internat. Assn. Dent. Research, (Pres. 1977-78); Candn. Acad. Periodontists; Brit. Soc. Periodontol.; Ont. Soc. Periodontists; Med. Research Council Can. (mem. Dent. Sciences Comte.; Scient. Offr. Dent. Science 1971-76); Pierre Fauchaud Academy; Fellow, Amer. Coll. of Dentists; Past Council mem. Brit. Soc. Periodontol.; Past mem. Dent. Council Royal Coll. Surgs. Edinburgh; Dent. Ed. (Cont. Educ.) Candn. Dent. Assn.; Liberal; United Church (Elder); recreations: golf, riding, music, travel, gardening; Office: Faculty of Dentistry, Univ. of British Columbia, Vancouver, B.C. V6T 1W5

BEALL, H. W., B.Sc.F.; b. Ottawa, Ont., 29 Sept. 1908; s. Herbert Pelton and Gertrude Helen Evelyn (Wilson) B.; e. Pub. Sch. and Lisgar Coll. Inst., Ottawa, Ont.; Queen's Univ.; Univ. of Toronto, B.Sc.F. 1932; m. Mary Gertrude, d. late Hon. Robert Forke, 20 Oct. 1934; children: Elma Gertrude, James Herbert Forke; Forest Fire Research Offr., Candn. Public Service 1932-40; in charge of Forest Fire Research, 1946-50; Chief, Forestry Operations Divn., Dept. N. Affairs and Nat. Resources, 1951-60; Dir. Adm. Br., Dept. of Forestry, 1961-64; Special Advisor 1965-69, since when retired; served in R.C.A.F. 1941-45 (Radar duties in U.K.; Radar staff appts in Middle East); retired with rank of Sqdn. Leader; Mentioned in Despatches; mem. Candn. Inst. of Forestry; Ont. Prof. Foresters Assn.; author or jt.-author of some 30 publ. and articles on devel. of forest fire danger rating techniques and fire control planning methods; Freemason; Psi Upsilon; Anglican; recreations: photography, fishing; Home: 331 Mountbatten Ave., Ottawa, Ont. K1H 5W2.

BEAMENT, George Edwin, O.B.E. (1943), K. St. J. (1964); E.D., C.D., Q.C.,; b. Ottawa, Ont., 12 Apl. 1908; s. Thomas Arthur and Edith Louise (Belford) B.; e. Roy. Mil. Coll. of Can. 1929; Univ. of Toronto, B.A.Sc. (M.E.) 1931; Osgoode Hall, grad. 1934; m. Brenda Yvonne Mary, d. Henry James Macthomas Thoms, Scot., 22 Feb. 1941; children: Justin Geoffrey, Meriel Virginia Mary; COUNSEL, BEAMENT, GREEN, YORK since 1968; called to the Bar of Ont. 1934; cr. K.C. 1948; Assoc. Beament & Beament 1934; Offr. Commdg., 2 Field Batty., Roy. Candn. Arty. 1939; Offr. Commdg., 2/14 Field Batty., do., 1940; proceeded to U.K. 1940; Bdge. Maj., 1st Candn. Armoured Bgde. 1941; Lt.-Col., Commdg. Offr., 6th Candn. Field Regt., Roy. Candn. Arty. 1942; G.S.O. 1, 4th Canadian Armoured Divn. 1942; G.S.O. 1 (Ops.) 1st Candn. Army 1943; Col., Gen. Staff, First Candn. Army 1943; Brig., Gen. Staff, 1st Candn. Army 1945; Pres., Khaki Univ. of Can. in U.K. 1945-46; Mentioned in Despatches; Croix de Guerre (avec Palme); Order of the White Lion; Mil. Cross (Czechoslovakia); Hon. Pres., Ottawa YM-YWCA 1968-73; Gov., Corps of Commissionaires (Ottawa); Bencher, Law Soc. of Upper Can. 1964-75; Commr., Nat. Capital Comm., 1961-1966; Chancellor, Priory of Canada, Order of St. John of Jerusalem 1975-78; Hon. Col 30 Field Regt. R.C.A. 1968-78; Kappa Alpha; Conservative; Anglican; Club: Rideau; Home: Snowberry, Notch Rd., Old Chelsea, Que. J0X 2N0; Office: 10th Floor, 100 Sparks St., Ottawa, Ont. K1P 5B7

BEAMENT, Commander Thomas Harold, V.R.D., R.C.A.; artist b. Ottawa, Ont., 23 July 1898; s. Herman Joseph and Lillian (Perkins) B.; e. Model Sch., Ottawa; Ottawa Coll. Inst.; Osgoode Hall; Ont. Coll. of Art, Toronto; m. Ida Lawson McDougall, 14 Oct. 1939; S. Thomas Harold read law with George F. Henderson, K.C.; called to Bar of Ont. 1923; practised law for one year; Candn. fine arts rep. at the Brit. Empire Expn.; has practised his art exclusively since 1924; exhibited in all important Candn. exhns. since 1922, London, Paris, Buenos Aires, Southern Dominions, and the U.S.; designed Candn. ten cent Eskimo stamp, 1955; rep. in Nat. Gallery, Ottawa, Dom. Archives, Montreal Museum of Fine Arts; Prov. Art Gallery, Que., Art Gallery of Hamilton, Art Gallery of London, Ont., and many smaller collections; received Jessie Dow Prize, Montreal Spring Exhn., 1935; served in World War 1917-18 with R.C.N.V.R. as ordinary seaman and later warrant offr.; served as Offr. in R.C.N.V.R. since 1924; commanded Montreal Divn. 1930-35; served in World War 1939-45 with R.C.N.V.R.; Lieut. Commdr. 1939; spent two years afloat in command of minesweepers and escort vessels in the Atlantic; appt. Sr. Naval War Artist and promoted to Commdr. 1943; retired 1947; spent one and a half yrs. overseas during which time he painted mostly in the Channel and the Mediterranean, his subjects including the Normandy assault and the revolution in Greece; has painted in the Brit. Isles, West Indies, Italy, Greece, Panama, Southern

States, Baffin Island, Spain, Portugal, and many parts of Can.; Pres., Roy. Candn. Acad. of Arts 1964-67 (el. a full academician 1946); Address: 208—1160 St. Mathew St., Montreal, Que. H3H 2P4

BEAMENT, Tib.M.A., R.C.A.; artist; b. Montreal, Que. 17 Feb. 1941; s. Harold and Ida Lawson (McDougall) B ; e. Fettes Coll. Edinburgh, Scot. (Crerar Scholarship) 1959; Beaux-Arts Montreal Dipl. 1963, post grad. studies Print Making 1964-66; Specialist's Dipl. Art Ed 1969; Accademia Delle Belle Arti, Rome 1963-64; Sir George Williams Univ. M.A. (Art Ed.) 1972; Art Teacher, Miss Edgars Sch. 1966-79; Concordia Univ. (Design) 1975; McGill Univ. (Drawing) 1973; exhns. Can., USA, Europe during last 20 yrs.; solo exhns. Can. since 1965, Zurich 1981; rep. pub. and private colls. Can., USA, S. Am., Europe; rec'd Italian Govt. Grant 1963, 1964; Can. Council Grant 1966; Que. Govt. Grant 1966, 1973; Greenshields Foundation Grant 1971, 1975; Royal Can. Acad. (Chrmn. Centennial Comm., Que. 1978-80); mem. Extve. Comte. and Dir. Greenshields Foundation; mem. Print & Drawing Council Can.; Accademia Delle Arti Italia; Protestant; recreations: sailing, gardening (raising orchids), scuba diving; Address: 121 Lewis Ave., Montreal, Que. H3Z 2K7.

BEAMES, James W., Q.C., LL.B.; b. Calgary, Alta., 13 April 1931; s. Ivor Beames; e. Univ. of Alta., B.A. 1952, LL.B. 1953; m.; three children; PARTNER, MILNER AND STEER since 1975; read law with Hon. Justice W.J.C. Kirby; called to Bar of Alta. 1955; cr. Q.C. 1972; Past Pres. Red Deer Bar Assn.; Central Alta. Bar Assn.; Central Alta. Alumni Assn.; Univ. of Alta.; Past Vice Pres., Red Deer Chamber of Comm.; mem., Law Soc. Alta.; Candn Bar Assn. (Past Pres. Alta.); Bencher, Law Soc. Alta. 1971-79, Pres. 1978; Kappa Sigma (Treas.); P. Conservative; Unitarian; recreation: golf; Clubs: Kinsmen (Past Pres.); Red Deer Golf & Country (Past Vice Pres.); Office: 9th Floor, Milner Bldg., 10040—104 St., Edmonton, Alta. T5J 0Z7

BEAMISH, Robert E., B.A., B.Sc., M.D., F.R.C.P. (Can) (Edin) (London), F.A.C.P., F.A.C.C., F.C.C.P., F.I.C.A.; b. Shoal Lake, Man. 9 Sept. 1916; s. William Henry and Margaret May (McLeod) B.; e. Shoal Lake (Man.) Pub. Sch. 1930; McConnell High Sch. 1933; Brandon Coll. McMaster Univ. B.A. 1937; Univ. of Man. M.D. 1942, B.Sc.(Med.) 1944; m. Mary Kathleen, d. late Abel Seneca Weekes, 26 June 1943; three d., Catherine Margaret, Judith Millicent, Mary Anne; CONSULTANT THE GREAT-WEST LIFE ASSURANCE CO. since 1981; Assoc. Prof. of Med. Univ. of Manitoba since 1964-81; Prof. of Med. 1981-; Assoc. Phys. Health Sciences Centre, Winnipeg since 1957; Nuffield Dominion Travelling Fellow Gt. Brit. 1947-48 subsequently part-time Tutor in Med. Univ. of Man.; Phys. and Cardiologist, Man. Clinic 1948-70; apptd. Med. Dir. Great West Life Assurance Co. 1970; Vice Pres. Underwriting and Medical 1975-81; served with RCAMC 1944-46, rank Capt.; Distinguished Service Award, Brandon Univ., 1979; Candn. Heart Foundation, 1980; Gen. Chrmn. Winnipeg Centennial Symposium on Dilemmas of Modern Man; Dir. Candn. Heart Foundation; Man. Heart Foundation; Candn. Assn. for the Club of Rome; Trustee Am. Coll. Cardiology 1975-80; mem. Coll. Phys. & Surg.'s Man. (Pres. 1960-61); Man. Med. Assn. (Pres. 1970-71); Candn. Med. Assn. (Gen. Council 1966-72); Candn. Cardiovascular Soc. (Pres. 1968-70); Am. Coll. Phys. (Gov. Man.-Sask. 1972-76); Interam. Soc. Cardiol. (1st Vice Pres. 1972-76-80); Candn. Life Ins. Med. Offrs. Assn. (Pres. 1978-79); Vice Pres., U.N. Assn. in Can.; past Pres., Candn. Inst. of Internat. Affairs (Winnipeg Br.); mem. Bd. Gov., Univ. of Man.; Pres., Bd. Dirs., Brandon Univ. Foundation; United Church; recreations: medical history, philosophy; Club: Manitoba; Home: 176 Oxford St., Winnipeg, Man. R3M 3J6 Office: 60 Osborne St., Winnipeg, Man. R3C 3A5

BEAN, Roy M.; newspaperman; publisher; b. Waterloo, Ont., 19 Dec. 1911; s. Roy Sylvester and Margaret Jane (McDougall) B.; e. Schs. of Waterloo and Kitchener, Ont.; m. Kathleen Ethel, d. Geo. Herbert Wade, 23 May 1936; has one d., Donna G.; VICE-PRES., REEVE BEAN LTD., formerly Mang. Dir., Bean Printing & Publishing Co. Ltd.; former Publisher of Waterloo "Chronicle"; mem. Candn. Weekly Newspapers' Assn. (Dir. for many years and Pres. 1949-50); mem., Waterloo and Kitchener Chambers of Comm.; United Church; recreations: riding, yachting; Club: Rotary; Westmount Golf and Country; Address: 505 Dutton Dr., Waterloo, Ont. N2L 4C7

BEAN, Walter Alexander, C.B.E., E.D., C.D., B.Com; trust company extve.; b. Kitchener, Ont., 26 July 1908; s. late David Alexander and Rose Anna (Winter) B.; e. Kitchener-Waterloo Coll. Inst.; Univ. of Toronto, B.Comm. 1930; m. Eleanore Elizabeth, (died May 1971), d. late George D. Fearman, 30 May 1934; children: Douglas A., W. Donald; Chrmn Economical Mutual Insurance Co. of Canada, Perth Insurance Co., Missisquoi and Rouville Ins. Co.; Dir. & mem. Extve. Comte., CanaTrustco Mtge. Co., Can. Trustco; Mutual Life Ins. Co. of Canada; Waterloo Ins. Co.; with B. F. Goodrich Co. of Canada, 1925-26; joined Waterloo Trust now merged with Canada Trust as Statistician, 1930; apptd. Treas., 1935; Depy Gen. Mgr. 1951; el. a Dir. 1957; subsequently apptd. Vice-Pres. and Gen. Mgr. and Pres. Dir. and Gen. Mgr. 1964; Depy. Chrmn. and Vice Pres., Canada Trustco and Huron-Erie Mortgage Corp., 1968; retired 1978; Lieut. and Capt., Scots Fusiliers of Can., N.P.A.M., 1930-40; served in 2nd World War, 1940-45; Capt. Highland Light Inf. of Can.; Capt., Major, Lieut.-Col. and Brig. various hdqrs.; Commanded 2nd Candn. Inf. Bgde. (Reserve) 1949-52; Hon. Col. Highland Fusiliers of Can; 1966-72; Past Pres., K-W Gyro Club; Past Pres., Trust Co's Assn. of Can.; Kitchener Chamber of Comm.; Delta Kappa Epsilon; Conservative; Anglican; recreation: golf; Clubs: Westmount Golf & Country; Toronto; Muskoka Lakes Golf & Country; Rotary; Gyro; Home: 238 Stanley Drive, Waterloo, Ont. N2L 1H8 Office: 305 King St. W., Kitchener, Ont. N2E 4B9

BEARDMORE, Harvey, Ernest, B.Sc., M.D., C.M., F.R.C.S.(C), F.A.C.S.; surgeon; educator; b. Windsor, Ont. 4 Feb. 1921; s. Harold Beardmore; e. McGill Univ. B.Sc. 1946, M.D., C.M. 1948; m. Frances Seymour d. Kenneth Seymour Barnes 1 Sept. 1945; children: Richard Murdoch, Ann Elizabeth, Patricia Louise, Ian Harold, Carol Harvey, Diane Frances; PAEDIATRIC GEN. SURGEON, THE MONTREAL CHILDREN'S HOSP. 1954-; former Assoc. Prof. of Surgery McGill Univ. 1972-; served with P.P.C.L.I. 1943-45, Italy & N.W. Europe, rank Lt.; R.C.A.M.C. 1949-59 (Reserve Active Offrs.), rank Capt., Supplementary Reserve 1959; Fellow, Am. Acad. of Pediatrics; Protestant; Home: 4501 Sherbrooke St. W., Apt. 6E, Montreal, Que. H3Z 1E7; Office: 2300 Tupper, Montreal, Que. H3H 1P3.

BEARE, Rev. Francis Wright, Ph.D. (Ang.); emeritus professor; b. Toronto, Ont., 16 Aug. 1902; s. George and Ellen Orr (Doole) B.; e. Univ. Coll., Univ. of Toronto, B.A., with McCaul Gold Medal in Classics 1925; Prince of Wales Scholarship 1921; Ont. Govt. Scholar; Ecole des Hautes Etudes, Univ. of Paris 1926; Knox Coll.; Carnegie Fellow, Roy. Soc. of Can. 1932; Univ. of Chicago, Ph.D. 1945; D.D. (honoris causa), Univ. of Toronto with Trinity College (Joint convocation) 1980; m. 1stly late Marion Gurd 1932, 2ndly Marianne, d.August Pleus 20 August 1973; Professor Emeritus, New Testament Studies, Trinity Coll., Univ. of Toronto since 1968; Lectr. in Latin, Queen's Univ., 1925-26; Lectr. in Greek, McMaster Univ., 1928-30; Lectr., Church Hist., Presb. Coll., 1933-35; Prof. of Theol. & Registrar there 1935-46; Prof. of New Testament Studies Trinity Coll., Univ. of Toronto 1946-68; Visiting Lectr. in New Testament, Union Theol. Semy., N.Y., 1944-45; in Divinity, Univ. of Cambridge, 1950; Vis. Lect. in Divinity: Vanderbilt Univ. 1972-73,

Coll. of Emmanuel and St. Chad, Univ. of Sask., 1975; foreign mem., Inst. Français d'archéologie Orientale; Sr. Fellow, Can. Council, 1957-58; author of "The First Epistle of Peter" (the Greek Text with introduction and notes) 1947, 2nd ed. 1958, 3rd ed. (revised and enlarged) 1971; The Epistle to the Ephesians in "The Interpreter's Bible", Vol. X, 1953; "The Epistle to the Colossians in "The Interpreter's Bible", Vol. XI, 1955; "The Epistle to the Philippians", 1959, 3rd ed. 1962; "St Paul and his Letters", 1962; "The Earliest Records of Jesus", 1962; "The Gospel According to Matthew" 1981; Contrib. (20 articles) to "The Interpreter's Dictionary of the Bible", 1962; "Biblisch-historisches Handwörterbuch", 1964; Pres., Soc. of Biblical Lit. 1969; mem. Council on Study of Religion 1969-71; Conservative; Home: 21 Dale Ave. apt. 903, Toronto, Ont. M4W 1K3

BEATON, George H., M.A., Ph.D.; educator; b. Oshawa, Ont. 20 Dec. 1929; s. late John H. and Madeline I. (Rogerson) B.; e. elem. and high sch. Oshawa; Univ. of Toronto B.A. 1952, M.A. 1953, Ph.D. 1955; m. Mary P. d. late James C. Clarke 15 Aug. 1953; children: James H., Patricia M., Dorcas E.; PROF. OF NUTRITIONAL SCIENCES, FACULTY OF MEDICINE UNIV. OF TORONTO; Chmn. of Dept. 1975-81; joined Univ. of Toronto 1955, Head, Dept. Nutrition Sch. of Hygiene 1963-75, Acting Dir. Sch. of Hygiene 1973-75, Acting Dean Faculty of Food Sciences 1975-78; rec'd Borden Award of Nutrition Soc. of Can.; Co-ed. "Nutrition: A Comprehensive Treatise" 3 Vols. 1965; Co-ed. and author "Nutrition in Preventive Medicine" 1977; author over 75 scient. papers in field of nutrition; mem. Nutrition Soc. Can. (Secy., Pres.); Am. Inst. Nutrition (Council); Am. Soc. Clin. Nutrition; Candn. Physiol. Soc.; Office: FitzGerald Bldg., Univ. of Toronto, Toronto, Ont. M5S 1A8.

BEATON, Neil Stewart, M.Sc., Ph.D.; consulting geologist; b. Ouray, Colo., 10 Dec. 1904; s. William and Ana Christine (Stewart) B.; a naturalized Candn. came to Can. June 1913; e. Haileybury Sch. of Mines (Matric. 1922); Queen's Univ., B.Sc. 1927, M.Sc. 1931; Mass. Inst. of Tech., Ph.D.; Geol. Rhodesian Anglo American Corp., N. Rhodesia, 1927-30; North American Mines Inc., Boston, Mass., 1934-38; Geol. to Mang. Dir., Northern Canada Mines Ltd.; and Kirkland Lake Gold Mining Co. Ltd., Toronto, Ont., 1938-79; Consulting Geol. since 1956; currently Tech. Consultant, Ont. Securities Comn. and Toronto Stock Exchange; mem., Candn. Inst. Mining & Metall.; Soc. of Econ. Geols.; Candn. Geol. Assn.; Am. Inst. Mining & Metall. Engrs.; United Church; recreation: curling; Clubs: Engineers; Granite; Address: 37 Blyth Hill Rd, Toronto, Ont. M4N 3L6

BEATON, William Henry, B. Eng.; consulting engineer; b. Montreal, Que., 4 May 1921; s. William Alexander and Cécile (Décarie) B.; e. Loyola Coll. 1938; McGill Univ. B. Eng. (Civil Engn.) 1947; m. Annah Jean, d. Russell Meikle, 29 Sept. 1951; children: Karen, Marilyn, Gordon, Gregory; PARTNER & DIR., BEAUCHEMIN-BEATON-LAPOINTE INC.; Chrmn. Cansult Ltd.; Dir., International Airport Consultants of Montreal Ltd.; in 1951, Porject Engr. with Beauchemin & Hurter on projects for Dept. of Nat. Defence; in 1954 became an Associate of J.A. Beauchemin & Assocs. engaged on various defence and pub. works developments in E. and N. Can.; joined present partnership on formation 1956 since when has contrib. to management technical & devel. aspects of the firm inc..; feasibility studies and masterplans for three USAF air bases projected for Que.; the complete devel. of new resource towns in Que. and Labrador; also been engaged in internat. devel. projects which include: the conceptual planning and project management of a new internat. airport, a harbour development and currently extensive dredging and reclamation works for navigation channels and industrial sites in the United Arab Emirates; airport extensions in several Caribbean islands; environmental engn. projects for cities

of Riyadh and Medinah, Saudi Arabia; highway project in Saudi Arabia and in the Sultanate of Oman; also became engaged on project management for the new Montreal International Airport, Mirabel, Que.; served in RCAF (Pilot Offr.) 1942-44; mem. Engn. Inst. Can.; Am. Inst. Civil Engrs.; Assn. Prof. Engrs. Nfld.; Order of Engrs. Que.; Assn. of Consulting Engrs. Can.; Protestant; recreations: reading, music, sailing; Clubs: M.A.A.A.; University; Home: 604 Clarke Ave., Westmount, Que H3Y 3E4; Office: 1134 St. Catherine St. W., Montreal, Que. H3B 1H4

BEATTIE, Allan Leslie, Q.C., B.A.; b. Copper Cliff, Ont., 25 March 1926; s. Robert Leslie and Amelia Edna (Allen) B.; e. Copper Cliff Pub. and High Schs.; St Andrew's Coll. Aurora, Ont., 1944-45; Trinity Coll., Univ. of Toronto, B.A. 1948; Osgoode Hall Law Sch., 1948-51; m. Elizabeth Agnes Mary, d. late Maurice Ogilvie Tremayne, 20 July 1951; four d., Elizabeth Anne, Barbara Allen, Mary Louisa, Leslie Anne; PARTNER, OSLER, HOSKIN & HARCOURT; Dir. & Chrmn. Eaton Bay Financial Services Ltd., Life Assurance Co., Trust Co. and Group of Mutual Funds; Dir. and mem. of Extve. Comte. Eaton's of Canada Ltd.; Dir., Telegram Corn Ltd.; Baton Broadcasting Inc.; Sklar Manufacturing Ltd.; Canadian Mist Distillers Ltd.; C.F. Haughton Ltd.; read law with Osler, Hoskin & Harcourt; called to Bar of Ont 1951; cr. Q.C. 1962; Trustee: Hospital for Sick Children, Toronto; Eaton Retirement Annuity Plan; Toronto School of Theology; Timothy Eaton Mem. Ch.; mem., Candn. Bar Assn.; Candn. Tax Foundation; United Church; recreations: golf, skiing; Clubs: York; The Toronto; Toronto Golf; Craigleith Ski; Home: 80 Chestnut Park Rd., Toronto, Ont. M4W 1W9; Office: P.O. Box 50, First Canadian Pl., Toronto, Ont. M5X 1B8

BEATTIE, Jessie Louise; author; lecturer; b. Blair Ont., 2 Oct. 1896; d. late Francis Walker and Janet (Fleming) B.; e. Blair, Ont.; Tassie Hall, Galt, Ont.; Univ. of Buffalo (Ed. Writing); spent 6 years in library work in Ont., New York, Brit. Col., and New Jersey; former dir. Cultural Use of Leisure, Community Welfare Council of Ont.; librarian and tchr. of creative writing, Ont. Dept. Prisons and Reforms; case worker, Big Sister Assoc. Toronto; in charge of music and drama, School for the Retarded, Hamilton; free-lance writer and book author; "Blown Leaves" (verse), 1929; "Shifting Sails" (verse), 1931; "Hilltop" (novel), 1935; "Three Measures" (novel), 1938; "White Wings Around the World" (travel, as told to her by Donald M. Green), 1953; "Along the Road" (life sketches), 1954; "John Christie Holland" (biography), 1956; "Black Moses" (biog.), 1958; "Split in the Sky" (non-fiction), 1960, "Hasten the Day" (short stories), 1961; "Strength for the Bridge" (novel) 1966 and reproduced as univ. text book in Japan 1969; "A Season Past" (autobiog. sketches) 1968; "The Log-Line" (biog., Capt. C. Dixon) 1972; "A Rope in The Hand" (biog., Capt. Francis J Brown) 1973; "Winter Night" (collected poems) 1975; "A Walk Through Yesterday" (personal memoirs) 1976; "William Arthur Deacon" (biog.) 1978; "A Skylark's Empty Nest" (novel dedicated to year of the Child) 1979; "Black Sheep They Were Not" (stories of remittance men 1841-1914) 1981; contrib. verse, children's stories and articles to various Candn. and Am. mags.; conducted a column known as "Library Bookshelf" in the Galt "Reporter", 1928; mem., Candn. Authors Assn.; Candn. Women's Press Club, Hamilton Br.; Protestant; Address: 30 Roanoke Rd., Hamilton, Ont. L8S 3P7

BEATTY, David S.; financial consultant; b. Toronto, Ont., 11 May 1915; s. Harold Eastwood and Ann Lois (Duggan) B.; e. Upper Can. Coll., Toronto; m. Eugenie Isabel, 19 July 1979; children: David Ross. Barbara Elise; Pres., Beatinvest Ltd.; Chrmn., Old Canada Investment Corp. Ltd.; Dir., Campeau Corp. Ltd.; CSA Management Ltd.; Gerling Global Life Ins. Co.; Gold Trust Ltd.; Lexington Gold Fund Inc.; K-Vet Labs. Ltd.; Spar Aerospace

Ltd.; Versatile Corp.; Trustee, Canada permanent Income Investments; with Dominion Securities, 1932-39; Burns Bros. and Denton Ltd. 1939-67 (Pres. 1952-65, Depy. Chrmn. 1965-67); served Overseas with Royal Regt. Can. in 2nd World War; demob. with rank Maj.; awarded C. in C. Cert. of Gallantry; Past Pres., Invest. Dealers' Assn. Can.; Bd. Govs., Toronto Stock Exchange; Anglican; recreations: golf, fishing, music, nature study; Clubs: Empire; Toronto; Granite; Glenmajor Angling; Rosedale Golf; Canadian; Franklin; York; Home: Ste. 301, 616 Avenue Rd., Toronto, Ont. M4V 2K8; Office: Ste. 2510, Royal Bank Plaza, P.O. Box 174, Toronto, Ont. M5J 2J4

BEATTY, (Henry) Perrin, P.C.M.P. B.A.; politician; b. Toronto, Ont. 1 June 1950; s. George Ernest and Martha L. (Perrin) B.; e. James McQueen Pub. Sch. Fergus, Ont. 1962; Upper Can. Coll. Toronto 1968; Univ. of W. Ont. B.A. 1971; m. Julia Florence Carroll d. late Robert A. Kenny and Mrs. Roy Hall Hyndman, Ottawa, Ont. 23 Feb 1974; Min. of State (Treasury Bd.) June 1979-Feb. 1980; el. to H. of C. g.e. 1972, re-el. since; mem. Comte. on Univ. Affairs Govt. of Ont. 1971-72; Asst. to Min. of Health Ont. 1971-72; Hon. mem. Royal Candn. Legion; P. Conservative; United Church; recreations: photography, music; Home: P.O. Box 33, Fergus, Ont. N1M 1Z4; Office: House of Commons, Ottawa, Ont. K1A 0A6.

BEATTY, Robert Lawler, B.A.; consultant; b. Yellow Grass, Sask., 24 June 1916; s. William Alexander and Eva Mary (Small) B.; e. Swift Current, Sask., Univ. of Toronto, B.A. (Math. and Phys.) 1938; Ont. Coll. of Educ., High Sch. Specialist standing in Math. and Phys. 1939; m. Helen Elizabeth, d. late Kenneth McLeod Munro, 20 Dec. 1941; children: Jane Weir, David Munro, Kenneth William Robert, John Edward; SPECIAL ADVISER, UN-EMPLOYMENT INSURANCE COMN.; Dir. General Insurance Service 1970; Teacher, Toronto Coll., 1939-40; joined federal govt. 1947 holding various positions in Unempl. Insur. Comm., Dept. of Nat. Health and Welfare and Privy Council office; Asst. Dir. of Unemployment Ins., 1962; apptd. Dir. Gen. 1966; Special Adviser to Comm. 1972-77; Trustee Ottawa Bd. of Education since 1972, Chrmn. 1973, 1974; Pres., Large School Bds. of Ont., 1980; sessional Lectr. in Math, Carleton Univ. since 1950; served as an Officer with RCN in N. Atlantic and with RN, 1940-45; Chrmn., Group Comte. of Boy Scouts Assn.; Elder, Parkdale Un. Ch.; Dir., Inst. Gen. Mang.; recreations: travelling, golf, tennis, curling, skiing; Home: 2397 Georgina Dr., Ottawa, Ont K2B 7M9;

BEAUBIEN, Rév. Irénée, S.J., B.A., L.Ph., D.D. (R.C.); n. Shawinigan, 26 janv. 1916; é Sém. des Trois-Rivières, P.Q.; études en lettres, sciences, philosophie et théologie chez les Pères Jesuites, Montréal, P.Q.; ordonné prêtre en 1949; fit séjours d'études spéciales aux Etats-Unis et en Europe en vue de mieux comprendre le problème des relations entre catholiques et non-catholiques; fonda en 1952 à Montréal le Catholic Inquiry Forum (centre de renseignements sur le catholicisme); a collaboré à l'organisation de plusieurs centres d'information catholique au Canada et à l'étranger; a contribué des articles à plusieurs revues et journaux; en 1958 inaugure dialogue mensuel entre pasteurs protestants et prêtres catholiques; en 1962 nommé par S.E. le cardinal Léger président de la Commission d'oecuménisme de Montréal et, en 1963, directeur-fondateur du Centre d'oecuménisme; président du Pavillon Chrétien à l'Expo 67 de Montréal; en 1966, nommé par l'épiscopat canadien au poste de directeur du Centre national d'oecuménisme; en 1975, fusion du Centre et de l'Office national d'Oecuménisme qui deviennent, sous sa direction, le Centre Canadien d'Oecuménisme; Résidence: 25 ovest, rue Jarry, Montréal, Qué. H2P 1S6; Bureau: Centre Canadien D'Oecuménisme, 2065 ouest, rue Sherbrooke, Montreal, Que. H3H 1G6

BEAUBIEN, Hon. Louis P.; senator; b. Montreal, P.Q., 3 March 1903; e. Montreal; m. Frances, d. late J.R. Douglas; children: Charles Douglas, Margot Lucile; Dir.: Beaubran Corpn.; Holt Renfrew & Co. Ltd.; Marshall Steel; Inter City Papers Ltd.; summoned to Senate of Can., Nov. 1960; served in 2nd World War as a Major in R.C.A.P.C. and was Overseas for four yrs.; Clubs: Mount Royal; St. James's; Montreal Racket; Rideau (Ottawa); Office: The Senate, Ottawa, Ont. K1A 0A4

BEAUBIEN, Philippe de Gaspé, O.C. (1967), B.A., M.B.A., LL.D.; broadcasting executive; b. Montreal, Que., 12 Jan. 1928; s. Philippe de Gaspé and Lucille (Mercier) B.; e. Univ. of Montreal, B.A.; Harvard Sch. Business Adm., M.B.A.; York University, LL.D.; m. Nanbowles, d. Michael Frederick O'Connell, 28 Jan. 1956; children: de Gaspé, Nanon, François; CHRMN. OF BD. AND PUBLISHER, TV GUIDE INC. (TORONTO) AND TV HEBDO (MONTREAL) since 1977; Chrmn. of Bd., Beausud Inc. (Publishers of Canadian Living); Chrmn. of Bd. and. C.E.O., Télémédia communications Ltée, since 1967; Chrmn. of Bd. of Télémédia subsidiaries; Chrmn. of Bd. Télémedia Ont. Inc.; Dir. Bombardier Inc.; Canada Devel. Corp.; Reitman's (Canada) Ltd.; Banff Sch. of Fine Arts; York Univ.; commenced as Sales Mgr., Philippe Beaubien & Co. Ltd. 1954; Mang. Consultant, Leetham Simpson Ltd. 1956; Mgr. and Pres., Beaubien Distribution Co. Ltd. 1960; Dir. of Operations, Candn. Corp. for 1967 World Exhn. (Mayor of Expo '67) 1963-67; founder and Hon. Chrmn., ParticipAction; awarded Centennial Medal 1967; Czechoslovakia Gold Medal; R. Catholic; recreation: all sports; Clubs: Mount Royal; York; Home: 37 Surrey Gardens, Westmount, Que H3Y 1N5; Office: 1400 Metcalfe St., Montreal, Que. H3A 1X2

BEAUCHAMP, Jacques; retired executive; b. Montreal, Que. 28 July 1926; s. Rosario and Lucienne (Bourdeau) B.; e. Levis (Que.) Coll.; Lasalle Extension Univ. Montreal; Sir George Williams Univ.; m. Pierette Mainville 9 Sept. 1946; one d. Elise; President and Dir. Gaz Metropolitain, Inc 1976-81; Sr. Vice Pres. and Dir. Northern and Central Gas Corp.; Acct. Montreal Coke & Manufacturing Co. 1943-55, Chief Acct. 1955-57; Mgr. Gen. Accounting present Co. 1957, Controller 1962, Treas. 1964, Vice Pres. Finance and Treas. 1970, Group Vice Pres. Finance and Treas. 1973, Extve. Vice Pres. 1975; mem. Financial Extve. Inst.; Conf. Bd. Can.; Candn. Tax Foundation; Am. Gas Assn.; Candn. Gas Assn.; Montreal Bd. Trade; Dr., Montreal Symphony Orch.; Univ. de Qué. à Montréal; R. Catholic; recreations: music, reading, golf, bowling; Clubs: Canadian; St. James's; Mount Royal; St-Denis; Home: 150 Willowdale, Outremont, Que. H3T 1E9

BEAUCHEMIN, J. Jacques, Q.C., B.A.; company executive; b. Amos, Que., 12 Oct. 1923; s. Pierre and Germaine (Lafleur) B.; e. Académie Querbes, Outremont, Que.; Coll. of Montreal; Loyola Coll., B.A.; Univ. of Montreal, grad. in Social Sciences 1946, law grad. 1947; m. Louise M., d. J. Roméo Boucher, 8 Jan. 1949; children: Jean-Jacques, Suzanne, Robert, Hélène, Marie; Pres.; East Sullivan Mines Ltd.; Brompton Mines Ltd.; Brunswick Tin Mines Ltd.; Chester Mines Ltd.; Courvan Mining Corp. Ltd.; D'Estrie Mining Corp. Ltd.; Eastern Explorers Corp.; Federal Metals Corp. Ltd.; Nigadoo River Mines Ltd.; Peninsula Metals Corp.; Standard Gold Mines Ltd.; Weedon Mines Ltd.; Vice Pres. and Dir. L'Economie Mutuelle d'Assurance-Vie; Dir. Banque Canadienne Nationale; The Belmont Park Co. Ltd.; Clinton Copper Mines Ltd.; F. Pilon Inc.; Johns-Manville Corp.; mem. Adv. Bd.; Guaranty Trust Co. of Canada (Montreal Sec.); called to Bar of Que. 1947; cr. Q.C. 1968; active in law firm of Beauchemin, Valiquette & Gervais full time to 1968; mostly active in mining field since 1968; twice Ald. of City of Outremont; Dir., Notre Dame Hosp.; mem., Montreal Bar; Mining Assn. Can.; Que. Metal Mining Assn. Inc.; R. Catholic; recreations: golf, gardening;

Clubs: Cercle Place d'Armes; Canadian; Office: 500 Place d'Armes, Montreal, Que.

BEAUCHEMIN, Micheline, O.C. (1973), F.R.S.C., R.C.A.; tapestry weaver; b. Longueuil, Qué.; e. Ecole des Beaux Arts, Montreal, Qué.; studied with Ossip Zadkine in Paris 1953, working on stained glass windows, Chartres, France; took up embroidery and tapestry, Greece 1955; returned to Can. 1957 working as wardrobe keeper and designer C.B.C.; full-time tapestry and weaving 1958; specialized in tapestry weaving, Japan 1962; created Curtain, Nat. Arts Centre, Ottawa; exhns. incl. Montreal and Toronto (all one-woman); Mexico, Tokyo and Paris; rec'd. Can. Council Grants 1959, 1965, 1973; Centennial Medal 1967; mem. Candn. Council of Esquimaux Arts; has travelled widely in China and India; researched weaving with Andes and Jungle Indians, S.Am. 1973; Address: 22 Chemin du Roy, Les Grondines, Qué. G0A 1W0

BEAUCHEMIN, Paul T., B.A.Sc.; consulting engineer and urbanist; b. Montreal, Quebec, 26 March 1931; s. Jules Armand and Marie-Anne (Gervais) B.; e. Coll. de Montréal; Ecole Polytechnique, B.A., B.Sc., C.E., P.Eng.; m. Lise, d. Paul-Henri Roy, 8 Oct. 1955; children: Louis, Sophie, Patrick; SR. PARTNER, BEAUCHEMIN-BEATON-LAPOINTE INC; Chmn. of Bd., SOMER (multi-disciplinary planning & research group); Dir. CAIM (Consultants en Aéroports Internat. de Montréal Ltée); Cansilo Inc.; Chmn. Construction Ind. Dev. Council; mem. Assn. of Consulting Engrs. of Can. (Pres. 1976-77); Assn. Consulting Engrs. Que. (Pres. 1974-76); Order of Engrs. Que.; Prof. Corp. of Urbanists of Que.; Soc. francaise d'urbanisme; Candn. Inst. of Planners; Engn. Inst. Can.; R. Catholic; recreations: flying, fishing, swimming, boating, gardening; Club: Cercle Universitaire; Home: 3781 The Boulevard, Westmount, Que. H3Y 1T3; Office: 1134 St. Catherine St. W., Montreal, Que. H3B 1H4

BEAUCHEMIN, Roger Olivier; consulting engineer; executive; b. Donnacona, Que., 20 May 1923; s. Jules Armand and Marie-Anne (Gervais) B.; e. Coll. Mont Saint-Louis; Ecole Polytechnique, Univ. de Montréal, B.A.Sc. 1950; m. Andrée, d. Dr. Noël Décarie, 29 June 1950; children: François, Denys, Anne Marie; Roger; PARTNER, BEAUCHEMIN-BEATON-LAPOINTE INC. since 1956; Dir. Mont Tremblant Lodge (1965) Inc.; Martin Black Inc.; B.G. Checo Engr. Ltd.; Un. Provinces Ins. Co.; Candn. Marconi Co.; Chrmn. Montreal Port Authority (Chrmn. Montreal Port Council 1970-71); Engr., Tech. Sales Dept., Canada Cement Co. 1950; Partner, J.A. Beauchemin & Associates 1955 (became present firm 1956, inc. 1972); responsible for transp., structural and certain engn. projects such as: the Macdonald-Cartier Bridge and other bridges in Que. and Cameroons, several freeways and parkways Que., transport and parking facilities Expo '67; consultant to French Govt. on transport. planning for Grenoble Winter Olympic Games 1968; conducted study for Lebanese Govt. on devel. Mt. Hermon summer and winter resort complex; Councillor, Mun. of Mont Tremblant; Pres., Chambre de Comm. du Dist. de Montréal 1969-70; Montreal Heart Inst. 1977-78; mem. Order of Engrs. (Que.); Assn. Consulting Engrs. Can.; Inst. of Transport Engrs. (Pres. 1971); Engn. Inst. Can.; R. Catholic; recreations: golf, history, skiing, travel; Clubs: Mount Royal; St-Denis; Home: 4345 Westmount Ave., Westmount, Que. H3Y 1W4; Office: 1134 St. Catherine St. W., Montreal, Que. H3B 1H4

BEAUDET, Guy, E.D., C.D., B.A., B.A.Sc.; civil engineer; b. Thetford Mines, Que., 8 Oct. 1911; s. J. Eugène and Lucina (Langlois) B.; e. Laval Univ., B.A.; Univ. of Montreal, B.A.Sc.; Ecole Polytechnique de Montréal, Civil Engn. 1938; m. Andrée, d. late Robert LeBlond de Brumath, 11 Oct. 1940; children: Alain, Marie Christine; PRES., GUY BEAUDET & ASSOCIÉS INC. CONSUL-

TANTS (LAVALIN GROUP) since 1976; City Engr., Thetford Mines, Que., 1938-41; Mgr., E. Div., Central Mortgage and Housing Corp., 1946; Asst. Port Mgr., Port of Montreal 1947, Acting Port Mgr. 1954, Port Mgr. 1955; mem. Nat. Harbours Bd. since 1971, Vice Chrmn. 1973; served with R.C.E. in Can., U.K. and N.W. Europe during World War II; Mentioned in Despatches, Europe; Consultant to Port Comte., W. Indies Fed., 1958; comnd. to survey and report on adm. and operational problems of Ports of Lebanon, 1967; directed similar mission Jamaica 1968; mem., Corp. Engrs. Que.; Engn. Inst. Can.; Candn. Mil. Engn. Assn.; Internat. Assn. Ports & Harbors; Am. Assn. Port Authorities (Pres. 1967-68); Perm. Internat. Assn. Navig. Congresses; Mil. & Hospitaller Order St. Lazarus Jerusalem; R. Catholic; recreation: philately; Clubs: Grunt; Cercle Universitaire; Home: 635 Powell Ave., Town of Mount Royal, Montreal, Que. H3R 1L7; Office: 1130 Sherbrooke St. W., Montreal, Que. H3A 2R5

BEAUDOIN, Gérald-A., O.C., c.r., B.A., M.A., LL.L., D.E.S.D.; avocat et éducateur; né Montréal, Qué. 15 avril 1929; f. Armand et Aldéa B.; é. études primaires Montréal, secondaires chez les Jésuites, Montréal; Univ. de Montréal, B.A. 1950, LL.L. 1953, M.A. (droit) 1954; Univ. Toronto Law Sch. (boursier Carnegie) 1954-55; Univ. d'Ottawa, D.E.S.D. 1958; ép. Renée, f. E. Desmarais, Montréal, Qué. 11 sept. 1954; enfants: Viviane, Louise, Denise, Françoise; DOYEN UNIV. D'OTTAWA. Faculté de droit, Sec. de droit civil, 1969-79; Conseiller juridique au Min. de la Justice, Ottawa, 1956; Conseiller parlementaire adjoint de la Chambre des Communes 1965; nommé c.r. 1969; Vice-Prés. (Can.) de l'Inst. de droit d'expression française; mem. de l'exécutif du Sénat de l'Univ. d'Ottawa; mem. Barreau du Qué.; Assn. du Barreau candn. (Prés. nat., Sec. de droit constit. 1971-73); l'Inst. candn. des Affaires publiques; l'Inst. d'adm. publique du Can.; mem. de la Galerie Nat.; membre de la Comm. sur l'Unité can. (Comm. Pépin-Robarts) 1977-79; mem. de la Société Royale du Canada 1977; Officier de l'Ordre du Canada, 1980; Professeur de droit constitutionnel; a donné un grand nombre de conférences sur la Constitution au Canada et à l'étranger; auteur d'une cinquantaine d'articles en droit constitutionnel et de deux ouvrages intitulés "Essais sur la Constitution" 1979, Editions de l'Université d'Ottawa; "Le partage des pouvoirs" 1980, Edition de l'Universite d'Ottawa; co-auteur de "Mecanismes pour une nouvelle Constitution" 1981; catholique r.; loisirs: lectures, voyages, natation; Club: Cercle Universitaire; residence: 4 St-Thomas, Hull, Qué. J8Y 1L4

BEAUDOIN, Gérard, M.D.; psychiatrist; university professor; b. Montreal, Que., 4 Feb. 1922; s. Médéric and Blandine (Brûlé) B.; e. Coll. de St-Jean, 1935-40 and Coll. Ste-Marie, Montreal, B.A. 1942; Univ. de Montréal, P.C.B. 1943, M.D. 1948; m. Ruth, d. J. Théo Legault, Montreal, Que., 31 July 1950; one d., two s.; DIR. DEPT. OF PSYCHIATRY, UNIV. DE MONTREAL and mem., Council Faculty of Med., since 1965; Dir., Dept. of Psychiatry, Hôpital Général du Christ-Roi, Verdun, Que., since 1953; residency: Hôpital Général de Verdun, 1948-49; Montefiore Hosp., N.Y., 1950-51; N.Y. Hosp., White Plains, N.Y., 1951-53; C.S., P.Q., 1955; Asst. Prof., Dept. Psychiatry, Univ. de Montréal, 1956-64; Assoc. Prof. 1964; mem. "Comité Consultatif", since 1965; mem., Candiac Catholic Sch. Comn.; Candn. Psych. Assn. (Dir. since 1963); Que. Psych. Assn. (Dir. since 1962); Candn. Med. Assn.; Assn. des Médecins de Langue Française du Can.; Société Médicale de Montréal; R. Catholic; Home: 58 Place de Bretagne, Candiac, Que. J5R 3M9; Office: C.P. 6128 Montreal, Que.

BEAUDOIN, Laurent, O.C. (1973), M.Com.; industriel; né à Laurier Station, comté de Lotbinière, Québec, 13 mai 1938; f. P.A. et Yvonne (Rodrigue) B.; é. Coll. Ste. Anne, B.A. 1957; Univ. de Sherbrooke, maîtrise en commerce

1960; Institut des Comptables Agréés, Comptable agréé 1961; Docteur "hon. causa" en science de L'administration, Univ. de Sherbrooke 1971; ép. Claire, f. J.-Armand Bombardier 29 août 1959; enfants: Nicole, Elaine, Denise, Pierre; PRESIDENT ET DIR. GENERAL, BOMBARDIER LTEE depuis 1966; pratique privée, Beaudoin, Morin, Dufresne et Ass., Québec, 1961-63; contrôleur, Bombardier Ltée 1963, Dir. Général 1964; Président Bombardier Ltéé et Directeur Général Groupe Valcourt 1975; Prés. Bombardier Ltée et MLW-Worthington Limited 1975; Prés. et Chef de la Direction Bombardier Ltée et Bombardier Inc. 1977; Pres. du Conseil et Chef de la Direction, Bombadier Ltée. et Bombadier Inc. 1979; Membre du Conseil d'Administration de: Bombardier Corp. Inc.; Héroux Inc.; Banque Nationale du Canada; Corp. de Développement du Canada; Les Industries Ltée Maislin Industries Ltée; B.C. Forest Products Ltd.; CDC Ventures Inc.; Celanese of Can. Inc.; membre: Institut des Comptables Agréés; Conseil Canadien des Chrétiens et des Juifs; Young Presidents' Organization Inc.; Vice-Prés. Les Boy Scouts du Canada, Gen.-Prov. Council; Chevaliers de Colomb; Clubs: Saint-Denis; Mont-Royal; Loisirs: motoneige, golf, bâteau, lecture; Résidence: Casier postal 307, Knowlton, Que.; Bureau: Bombardier Inc., 800 Boul. Dorchester Quest, Ste 1520, Montréal, Que. H3B 1X9

BEAUDRY, Jean; labour executive; b. St-Julienne, Que., 14 Aug. 1929; e. Labour Coll. of Can.; Rep. for United Steelworkers of Am. since 1954 (formerly Extve. Vice Pres. Candn. Labour Cong. 1970-74); trade union career began Noranda Mines, N. Que.; Asst. Geol. for 7 yrs.; joined Internat. Union of Mine, Mill and Smelter Workers 1947; el. departmental steward; joined Canadian Congress of Labour Volunteers' Organ. Comte. 1948; el. Recording Secy., Local 4278, Un. Steelworkers of Am., 1949; served on various local comtes. during next 5 yrs.; also served as Secy., N.W. Que. Mining Council for several terms; apptd. Internat. rep., Un. Steelworkers of Am., 1954; has also worked on various comtes of Que. Fed. of Labour and travelled overseas on behalf of steelworkers and Candn. labour movement; Labour Rep. on Royal Comm. on Safety and Health of Miners in Ontario 1974-76; NDP; R. Catholic; Club: Canadian; Home: 117 Lotta Ave., Ottawa. Ont. K2G 2B8; Office: 141 Laurier St. W., ste. 903, Ottawa, Ont. K1P 5J3.

BEAULIEU, Hon. Lucien Arthur, B.A., M.S.W., LL.B.; judge; b. Mutrie, Sask. 10 Sept. 1933; s. Magloire and Elodie (Boudreau) B.; e. Philomath Sch. Mutrie, Sask. 1950; Maison St. Joseph, Otterburne, Man. 1951; Coll. Mathieu, Gravelbourg, Sask.; Univ. of Ottawa B.A. 1955, M.S.W. 1960; Osgoode Hall Law Sch. LL.B. 1966; m. Joan Patricia d. Edmond J. Andrecheck, Barry's Bay, Ont. 13 Aug. 1962; children: Andre J., Noel W.; SR. JUDGE, PROV. COURT (FAMILY DIV.) YORK AND PEEL 1977- ; Chrmn. Task Force on Vandalism 1979- ; called to Bar of Ont. 1968; Social Worker, Sask. Dept. Social Welfare 1956-58; Cath. Children's Aid, Toronto 1960-63, Caseworker and Dept. Supvr.; Group Home Supvr. 1961-69; Asst. Crown Atty. Toronto 1968-71; Asst. Prov. Dir. Legal Aid Ont. 1971-73, Prov. Dir.; Prov. Judge Family Div. 1973-77; Commr. Royal Comm. on Violence in Communications Industry 1975-77 (co-author 7 vol. Report 1977); author various articles on violence in the family; winner Jaycees Effective Speaking Contest, 1957 Nat. Winner - Impromptu Debates Osgoode Hall; served with Candn. Militia, rank 2nd Lt.; mem. Prov. Family Court Assn. (Pres.); Internat. Youth Magistrate Assn. (Vice Pres.); Candn. Bar Assn.; Candn. Assn. Corrections & Criminology; K. of C.; R. Catholic; recreations: hockey, music, reading, walking, theatre; Clubs: Celebrity; Grange Racquetball Acad.; Home: 51 Lawrence Ave. E., Toronto, Ont. M4N 1S2; Office: 311 Jarvis St., Toronto, Ont.

BEAULIEU, Mario, B.A. LL.L.; notaire et conseiller juridique; né Plantagenet, Ont., févr. 1930; f. Henri de Montpellier-Beaulieu et Berthe (Lalonde) B.; é Coll. St-Ignace

& Coll. Ste-Marie (Montréal) bachelier és-arts; faculté de droit, Univ. Montréal; licencié en droit 1955; ép. Louise, f. René Thomas Montréal, Qué., 8 sept. 1956; enfants: François, Martine, Louis, Stephane, Charles; NOTAIRE, SÉNIOR DE L'ÉTUDE LÉGALE; BEAULIEU; MANOLA-KOS et BISANTE; Pres., Conseil d'administration de constructions, Simard Beaudry Inc., 1981; Jeunesse musicale, 1981; admis. en tant que membre de la Chambre des Notaires du Québec, 1956; Prés. de Collet Frères Ltée; Candidat défait dans Laurier, U.N., élections gén. 1962; coordinateur assises gén. de l'Union Nationale, 1965; prés. de la compagne électorale du parti 1966; dir. Cabinet du premier ministre Johnson et sous-ministre de l'exécutif 1966; dir. gén. Union Nationale 1968; élu député Dorion, 1969; Min. Immigration (mars), Ministre Inst. fin. (avril), Min. finances (juillet); membre: Canadian Bar Assn.; catholique; Recreation: golf; Clubs: Chambre Commerce (Montréal); Laval-sur-le-Lac; Towers Club; Le Club International (Fort Lauderdale); Residence: 1139 Blvd Mont-Royal, Outremont Qué. H2V 2H6; Bureau: 3033 est, rue Jarry, Montreal, Que. H1Z 2C3

BEAULIEU, Paul André, Q.C., B.A., LL.L., F.R.S.C. (1957); diplomat; b. Outremont, P.Q., 1 April 1913; s. Louis Emery, Q.C., and Attala (Malette) B.; e. Coll. Ste-Marie, Montreal (1933); Univ. of Montreal, B.A., LL.L.; m. Simone Aubry, d. late Dr. Hector Aubrey, Montreal, P.Q., 16 May 1942; children: Marie, Louis; read law with Beaulieu, Gouin, Tellier & Bourbon, called to Bar of Que., 1937; cr. K.C. 1947; joined Dept. of External Affairs as Third Secy., 1940; Third Secy., Washington, Apl. 1944, Second Secy., Oct. 1944, Paris 1945; consul, Boston, Mass., 1949; Dept. of External Affairs, Ottawa, 1951; Counsellor, Office of the High Commr. for Can., London, 1954; Chargé d'Affaires a.i., Candn. Legation, Beirut, Apl. 1958; successively Ambassador to Lebanon and Iraq, then to Brazil; Assoc. Perm. Rep. and Ambassador of Can. to the Un. Nations, 1967; Ambassador to France, 1968; then to Portugal 1970; formerly held various extve. posts with La Féd. des Scouts Cath. de Qué.; mem., Candn. Gen. Council, Boy Scouts Assn. (awarded Silver Wolf); Publications: "Jacques Revière", 1955 rec'd 1er Prix Concours littéraires de la P.Q., 1953; contrib. articles to various journs. in Can. and France; R. catholic; recreations: tennis, swimming; Club: Cercle Universitaire d'Ottawa.5754 av. Deom, Montreal, Que. H35 2N4

BEAULIEU, Roger L., Q.C., B.A., B.C.L., M.B.A.; b. Montreal, Que., 26 Sept. 1924; s. Guillaume A. and Eulalie (Galibert) B.; e. Coll. Jean de Brébeuf, B.A. 1944; McGill Univ., B.C.L. 1947; Harvard Grad. Sch. of Business Adm., M.B.A. 1949; m. Andrée, d. late Jules Prieur, 5 March 1955; children: Marc, Nicole, Michèle; PARTNER, MARTINEAU WALKER (formerly Martineau, Walker, Allison, Beaulieu, MacKell & Clermont); Dir., Canada Permanent Mortgage Corp.; Brown Boveri Canada Inc.; Place Desjardins, Inc.; Netcom Inc.; Laurentian Mutual Insurance; World Wildlife Fund (Canada); Cara Operations Ltd.; Pirelli Canada; Canada Permanent Trust Co. (Chrmn. Montreal Adv. Bd.); Kesmark Ltd.; Canadian Provident Gen. Ins. Group; Dir., National Cablevision Ltd.; Télémedia Communications Ltd.; Omnimedic Inc.; Chateau MontLabert Inc., Chrmn., Montreal Hdgrs. Comte.; Arts Council, Montreal Urban Community; Gov., MBA's Assoc. of Que.; called to Bar of Que. 1947; cr. Q.C. 1958; mem. Candn. Bar Assn.; P. Conservative; R. Catholic; recreation: travel; Clubs: University; Mount Royal; St-Denis; Home: 3044 St. Sulpice Rd., Montreal, Que. H3H 1B5; Office: 800 Victoria Sq., Montreal Que. H4Z 1E9

BEAULIEU, Victor-Lévy; écrivain, journaliste, éditeur; n. St-Paul-de-la-Croix (Rimouski) 2 Sept. 1945; f. Edmond et Léonie (Bélanger) B.; é Ecole Pie IX; cours études secondaires, Univ. de Montréal; ép Francine, f. Pierre-Paul Cantin, 11 avril 1969; Dir. Littéraire des Editions du Jour et il donne également au niveau universitaire, des cours de création littéraire; a publié: "Mémoires d'outre-tonneau" et "Race de monde" 1968; "La Nuitte de Malcomm Hudd" 1969; "Quand les écrivains Quebecois jouent le jeu" (en collaboration) et "Jos Connaisant" 1970; "Pour saleur Victor Hugo" et "Les Grand-Péres" 1971; aussi articles de critique littéraire dans Le Devoir, Liberté, l'Illettré, La Presse et Maintenant; lauréat du Prix Littéraire, Hachette-Larousse 1967; récu Grand Prix Littéraire (pour "Les Grand Péres") 1972; mem. du Parti Québecois; récréations: jardinage, patinage, casse-tête;

BEAULNE, Joseph-Charles-Leonard Yvon, B.A., Ph.L.; diplomat; b. Ottawa, Ont., 22 Feb. 1919; s. Leonard and Yvonne (Daoust) B.; e. Univ. of Ottawa, B.A., Ph.L. 1941; m. Thérèse, d. Herve Pratte, 7 Feb. 1946; children: Pierre, François, Louise, Leonard, Gilles; served with Post Office Dept., 1939-40; Dept. of Secy. of State, 1940-42; Parlty. Translator, 1947-48; joined Dept. of External Affairs 1948; served in Rome, 1949; seconded to CBC (IS), Montreal, 1952; returned to External Affairs 1953; served in Buenos Aires 1956; Ottawa 1959 and 1960; Havana 1960; apptd. Ambassador to Venezuela 1961; concurrently accredited to Dominican Republic 1963; served in Washington 1964; Ambassador to Brazil 1967; Perm. Rep. and Ambassador to U.N., New York, 1969; seconded from External Affairs and named Asst. Secy. of State 1972; Dir., Bureau of African & Middle Eastern Affairs. Dept. External Affairs 1974;Can. Rep. to U.N. Human Rights Comm. 1976; Perm. Del. of Canada to UNESCO 1976; Ambassador to Holy See, 1979; served with Candn. Army 1942-46; rank Capt. on discharge; R. Catholic; Office: 125 Sussex Dr., Ottawa, Ont.

BEAUPRÉ, Bernard, B.A., M.A.Sc., M.Sc.; retired civil engineer; b. Montreal, Que. 11 March 1914; s. Léandre and Adrienne (Gibeau) B.; e. St. James Parochial Sch., Montreal 1919-27; Coll. de Montréal & Semy. de Philosophie, B.A. 1935; Conservatoire Nat. de Mus. (piano and organ) 1935-36; Ecole Polytech. de Montréal, B.Sc.A. and C.Eng. 1941; Univ. of Toronto, M.A.Sc. (Pub. Health Engn.) 1943; Harvard Univ., M.Sc. (Indust. Hygiene) 1946; m. Georgette, d. late J. E. de Serres, 29 Nov. 1941; children: Pierre, Louise, Françoise: Pres., Bernard Beaupré Traductions Ltée; with Dominion Bridge Co. Ltd., Estimator and Designer, Plate and Boiler Dept., Lachine, Que. 1941; Engr. i/c Surveys, Div. Indust. Hygiene, Que. Dept. Health 1942; Assoc. Prof., Sch. of Hygiene, Univ. of Montreal 1947-65; Extve. Secy. Engn. Div., Dept. Public Works, City of Montreal 1947, Supt. Smoke Control Div. 1950, Asst. Dir., Dept. of Parks 1954-57, Tech. Adviser to Dir. of Pub. Works 1958; Gen. Mgr., E. Can., Aero-Hydraulics Corp., Montreal 1965-71; Comr., Internat. Joint Comm. 1969-81; Research Co-ordinator, Ecole Polytech., Dept. Sanitary Engn. 1968-71; Chrmn., Richelieu Chapter, Candn. Red Cross Soc.; Chrmn., Town of Richelieu Sch. Bd. 1956-66, Chrmn. Club Richelieu-Chambly 1953; Vice-Pres., Que. Sch. Bd. Fed. 1960-63; mem. Corp. Engrs. Que.; Am. Water Works Assn.; Water Pollution Control Fed.; R. Catholic; recreations: music, book and stamp collecting, gardening, tapestry work; Home: 128, 6th Ave., Richelieu, Que. J3L 3M9

BEAUREGARD, Hon. Marc, B.A., B.C.L.; judge; b. Montreal, Que., 14 July 1937; s. François and Gertrude (Levesques) B.; e. Stanislas Coll. Montreal; B.A.(Paris) 1956; McGill Univ. B.C.L. 1959; m. Mireille d. Conrad Lefebvre, Montreal, Que., 17 Sept. 1960; children: Patrick, Charles, Emmanuelle; JUSTICE, COURT OF APPEAL OF QUE.; called to Bar of Que. 1960; Council mem. Jr. Bar of Montreal 1965-66; Bar of Montreal 1967-68; Bar Prov. of Que. 1967-68; Que. Sec. Candn. Bar Assn. 1974-75; R. Catholic; recreations: bridge, hunting, tennis, fishing; Home: 733, rue Hartland, Outremont, Montreal, Que. Office: Court House, 1 Notre Dame E., Montreal, Que. H2Y 1B6

BEAVERBROOK, Lady, LL.D.; b. Sutton, Surrey, Eng., 27 July 1910; d. John Christoforides and Mildred Nightingale-Boyes; came to Can. 1932; Dalhousie Univ., LL.D. (honoris causa) 1967; m. 1stly Sir James Dunn, Bt., Q.C., 7 June 1942; 2ndly The Rt. Hon. Lord Beaverbrook, 7 June 1963; Chancellor, Dalhousie Univ.; recreation: horse racing; Address: Dayspring, Saint Andrews, N.B. E0G 2X0

BÉCHARD, Albert, B.A., LL.L.; diplomat; b. St. Aléxis of Matapédia, Qué. 18 Nov. 1922; s. late Georges and late Ezéphise (Gendron) B.; e. St. Aléxis-de-Matapédia, Qué. 1937; Gaspé(Qué.) Coll. B.A. 1945; Laval Univ. LL.L. 1949; admitted to Bd. of Notaries 1950; m. Lucette Gabrielle Eva d. late Siméon Elisée Fortin and Anne-Marie Cazes, 1 Sept. 1952; children: Carl, Pierre, René; CONSUL GEN. OF CAN. IN NEW ORLEANS 1979- ; practised law (notarial) Carleton, Qué. 1950-79; Secy.-Treas. Mun. of Carleton, Qué. 1951-60; Lib. M.P. for Bonaventure 1962-79 (Magdalen Islands added 1968); served as Chrmn. Qué. Lib. M.P.'s 1963-65; Parlty. Secy. to Secy. of State 1965-68, to Min. of Justice 1970-72; Asst. Depy. Speaker 1968-70; Chrmn., Standing Comte. on Fisheries & Environment 1972-79; National Liberal Caucus, 1977-78; rec'd Candn. Centennial Medal 1967; Queen's Silver Jubilee Medal 1978; mem. L'assn. des notaires du Bas St-Laurent & Gaspésie; Prov. Qué. Fed. Assn. Notaries; Candn. Bar Ass. Pres., Carleton Bd. Trade 1959-61; K. of C.; Liberal; R. Catholic; recreations: fishing, golf; Club: Plimsoll (New Orleans); Home: 4725 Gary Mikel Ave., Metairie, La. 70002; Office: 2110 International Trade Mart, 2 Canal St., New Orleans, La. 70130

BECHTEL, Stephen Davison, Jr., B.Sc.E., M.B.A., D.Eng.; engineering-construction executive; b. Oakland, Cal. 10 May 1925; s. Stephen Davison and Laura (Peart) B.; e. Purdue Univ. B.Sc.E. 1946, D.Eng. 1972 (Hon.) Stanford Grad. Sch. of Business M.B.A. 1948; Univ. of Colo. 1943-44; m. Elizabeth Hogan; 5 children; CHRMN. OF BD. AND EXTVE. COMTE., BECHTEL GROUP INC.1973- ; Chrmn. Sequoia Ventures Inc.; Bechtel Canada Ltd.; Sequanda Ventures Inc. (formerly Canadian Bechtel Ltd.); Dir. International Business Machines Corp.; Southern Pacific Co.; mem. and former Vice Chrmn. The Business Council; Life Councillor and former Chrmn. The Conf. Bd. Inc.; Mang. Partner, Lakeside Co. 1946-47; Asst. Secy. Bechtel Corp. 1947-52, Supt. and Job. Supt. 1950-51, Mgr. Pipeline Div. 1952, Vice Pres. & Mgr. Pipeline Div. 1952-55, Treas. 1953-54, Sr. Vice Pres. 1955-57, Extve. Vice Pres. & Sr. Sponsor Pipeline & Internat. Divs. 1957-60, Pres. 1960-73; Field Engr. Bechtel-Price-Conyes 1948-59, Job Engr. 1949-50; Vice Pres. and Constr. Mgr. Canadian Bechtel Ltd. 1951-52, Chrmn. 1957-79; Mang. Partner, Bechtel Associates 1954-73; served various USA Presidential Comtes. 1967-74; Trustee, Cal. Inst. Technol.; mem. Pres.'s Council Purdue Univ. and Gov. Purdue Foundation; mem. Nat. Action Council on Minorities in Engn.; rec'd Purdue's Distinguished Alumnus Award 1964; Ernest C. Arbuckle Award Stanford's Grad. Sch. of Business 1974; Distinguished Service Award 1978 and Distinguished Engn. Alumnus Award 1979 Univ. of Colo.; Engn. News Record's Constr.'s Man of Yr. Award 1974; Moles' Award Outstanding Achievement in Constr. 1974; ASCE Civil Engn. Mang. Award 1979; Am. Soc. Mech. Engrs. Centennial Award 1980; author various publs.; served with U.S. Marine Corps Reserve 1943-48; U.S. Navy Reserve 1948-50; Offr., French Legion of Honour; Fellow, Am. Soc. Civil Engrs.; Hon. Fellow, Inst. Chem. Engrs. (UK); mem. Am. Inst. Mining, Metall. & Petroleum Engrs.; Nat. Acad. Engn.; Hon. Trustee, Cal. Nat. Acad. Sciences; Beta Theta Pi; Tau Beta Pi; Chi Epsilon; Protestant; recreations: golf, tennis, fishing, shooting, hiking, photography; Clubs: Mount Royal (Montreal); Vancouver (B.C.); York (Toronto) and many social and business clubs USA; Home: (P.O. Box 3809) San Francisco, Cal. 94119; Office: 50 Beale St., San Francisco, Cal. 94105.

BECK, Frederick Allan, Q.C.; b. Penetanguishene, Ont., 26 May 1902; s. of Walter John and Helen (McGibbon) B.; e. Upper Canada Coll., grad. 1920; Univ. College, Univ. of Toronto, B.A. 1925; Osgoode Hall, 1925-28; m. Marjory, d. Brigadier F. A. Lister, D.S.O., 15 March 1939; children: Nancy; Vice-Pres., Gates Rubber Co. of Can. Ltd.; Dir., Volkswagen (Can) Ltd., Crown Trust Co.; United Canada Insurance Co.; Gardner Denver (Can.) Ltd.; G. and H. Steel Industries Ltd.; and other Cos.; called to the Bar of Ont., 1928; cr. K.C. 1945; began practice with Bain, Bicknell, White & Bristol, 1928; served in Royal Navy and Royal Canadian Navy in 2nd World War, 1940-45, in N. Atlantic Escort Service; advanced to rank of Lieut. Commdr. (Captain of Corvette HMCS "Battleford" 1942-44 and of Frigate HMCS "Lasalle" 1944-45); Mentioned in Despatches; Hon. Counsel Eglinton & Caledon Hunt Club; Anglican; recreations: riding, sailing, curling; Clubs: University; Granite; Eglinton & Caledon Hunt; Home: 115 Strathallan Blvd., Toronto, Ont. M5N 1S8; Office: 330 University Ave., Toronto, Ont. M5B 1R7

BECK, George Hammersley; investment dealer; b. Toronto, Ont., 20 Nov. 1914; s. Harry Thatcher and Marian Frances (Asbury) B.; e. Crescent Sch. (Toronto); Upper Can. Coll.; m. Kathleen, d. James Davie, 14 Nov. 1942; children: Marian Ruth, Patricia Mary; SENIOR VICE-PRES. & DIR., ANDRAS, HATCH & HETHERINGTON LTD.; joined Bartlett Cayley Ltd., investment dealer, at inception, 1933, as Jr. mem.; following active war service held various positions in sales and mang.; Partner 1955; held positions of Asst. Treas.; Treas.; Vice-Pres., 1955-65; Pres. 1965-79; served in 2nd World War with Candn. Inf. 1942-44; on loan to Brit. Army as a "Canloan" Offr., 1944; wounded Aug. 1944; rank Lieut.; Vice Chrmn., Wycliffe Coll. (Univ. of Toronto); Past Nat. Pres., and mem. Nat. Council C.N.I.B.; Ed., "Canloan Review"; Past Pres., Canloan Army Offrs. Assn.; St. George's Soc.; Fort York Br., Roy. Candn. Legion; mem. and Past Pres., Imp. Offrs. Assn. Can.; Anglican; recreations: gardening, swimming; Clubs: Bd. of Trade; Rotary; Home: 47 Lascelles Blvd., Toronto, Ont. M5P 2C9; Office: Suite 1100, 4 King St. W., Toronto, Ont. M5H 1B8

BECK, Howard Leighton, Q.C., B.A., LL.B., LL.M.; b. Vancouver, B.C. 15 March 1933; s. late Ralph J. and Freda R. B.; e. Univ. of B.C. B.A., LL.B.; Columbia Univ. LL.M.; m. Delores Wright 9 Sept. 1971; PARTNER, DAVIES, WARD & BECK since 1963; Dir. Warrington Products Ltd.; Block Bros. Industries Ltd.; Canadian Manoir Industries Ltd.; read law with Lawson, Lundell, Lawson & McIntosh; called to Bar of B.C. 1957, Ont. 1963; cr. Q.C. 1971; Assoc. Lawson, Lundell, Lawson & McIntosh Vancouver 1957-61; Jt. Secy. Atty. Gen.'s Comte. on Securities Leg. (Kimber Comte.) 1963-65; Lectr. Mergers and Acquisitions Course, Univ. of Toronto Extension; Seminar on Corporate Finance, Osgoode Hall Law Sch., York Univ.; Candn. Inst. C.A.'s Mergers and Acquisitions; Going Public, Univ. of Toronto Extension 1969; co-author "McDonald's Current Taxation to 1966"; Assoc. Ed. "McDonald's Canadian Income Tax to 1966"; contrib. author to "Acquisitions and Mergers in "Canada" 1977; mem. Candn. Bar Assn.; Canadn. Tax Foundation; Home: 3 Ormsby Cres., Toronto, Ont. M5P 2V2; Office: 4700 Commerce Court West, Toronto, Ont.

BECK, James Murray, M.A., Ph.D., F.R.S.C.; professor emeritus, researcher, writer; b. Lunenburg, N.S. 2 Dec. 1914; s. Allan Clyde and Florence Louise (Silver) B.; e. Lunenburg (N.S.) Acad.; Acadia Univ. B.A. 1934, M.A. 1938; Univ. of Toronto M.A. 1946, Ph.D. 1954; hon. LL.D., Dalhousie Univ. 1981 PROF. EMERITUS OF POL. SCIENCE; DALHOUSIE UNIV. since 1963; teacher pub. and high schs. N.S. 1934-41; Instr. in Pol. Science Univ. of Toronto 1948-50; Asst. Prof. of Pol. Science and Hist. Acadia Univ. 1950-52; Asst., Assoc. and Full Prof. of Pol. Science, Royal Mil. Coll. of Can. 1952-63; Consultant to

N.S. Govt. on constitutional matters 1967-70; served with RCAF 1941-45, radar officer, rank Flight Lt.; author "Government of Nova Scotia" 1959; "Pendulum of Power: Canada's Federal Elections" 1968; "The History of Maritime Union: A Study in Frustration" 1969; Ed. "Joseph Howe: Voice of Nova Scotia" 1964; "The Shaping of Canadian Federalism: Central Authority or Provincial Right?" 1971; contrib. to "Dictionary of Canadian Biography"; over 50 booklets and articles on Candn. govt. and politics; mem. Candn. Pol. Science Assn.; Candn. Hist. Assn.; United Church; Office: Halifax, N.S.

BECK, John Christian, M.Sc., M.D., C.M., F.R.S.C. (1970), F.R.C.P.(C), F.A.C.P.; physician; educator; b. Audubon, Iowa, 4 Jan. 1924; s. Wilhelm and Marie (Brandt) B.; e. McGill Univ., B.Sc. 1944, M.D., C.M. (Holmes Gold Medal) 1947, M.Sc., 1951, Dipl. in Med. 1952; m. Mary Frances, d. Col. C. N. Mitchell, 28 May 1951; one s., Philip; Dir. Multicampus Div. of Geriatrics; UIC.L.A. School of Medicine; Chrmn., Exper. Med., McGill Univ., 1969-79 and Dir., Univ. Clinic, 1964-79; Phys.-in-Chief, Royal Victoria Hosp.; Sr. Consultant in Med., Queen Mary Veteran's Hosp.; Hon. Consultant, Lakeshore Gen. Hosp.; Consultant in Med., Royal Edward Chest Hosp.; postgrad. work Royal Victoria Hosp., Cleveland (Ohio) Clinic, New Eng. Med. Center, Rigshospitalet (Copenhagen) and Univ. Coll. Hosp. (London, Eng.), 1949-53; Lectr. in Med. and Clin. Med., McGill Univ., 1954-55; Asst. Prof. of Med. 1955-57; Asoc. Prof. 1957-64; Prof. 1964-69; Research Assoc., McGill Univ. Clinic, 1954-55; Research Fellow since 1955; Clin. Asst., Royal Victoria Hosp., 1952-54; Asst. Phys. 1955-59; Phys. 1960-64; Chief, Endocrine-Metabolic Unit, 1964; Markle Scholar in Med. Sciences 1954-59; mem. Ed. Bd., "Journal of Clinical Endocrinology and Metabolism"; "Current Topics in Experimental Endocrinology"; Dir., Que. Camp for Diabetic Children; Dir., Am. Bd. Internal Med.; Secy.-Gen., Internat. Soc. for Endocrinology, Inc.; Hon. Fellow, Royal Coll. Phys. (London), 1971; mem., Am. Soc. Clin. Investigation; Assn. Am. Phys.; Candn. Soc. Clin. Investigation (Pres.,) Endocrine Soc. (Vice Pres., Chrmn., Post-grad. Assembly); Am. Fed. Clin. Research (Council, E. Div.); Candn. Med. Assn. (post-grad. educ. comte.); Am. Diabetes Assn.; Candn. Diabetes Assn.; McGill Osler Reporting Soc. (Secy.); Montreal Physiol. Soc.; Montreal Med. Chirurg. Soc.; Candn. Physiol. Soc.; Hon. Fellow, Royal Soc. Med.; Laurentian Hormone Conf.; Candn. Assn. Profs. Med.; Hon. mem., Peruvian Endocrine Soc.; Sigma Xi; Alpha Omega Alpha; Lutheran; Office: Dir., Multicampus Div. of Geriatric Medicine, 10833 Le Corte Ave. (CHS), Los Angeles, Cal. 90024

BECK, Roger Lyne, M.A., Ph.D.; educator; b. London, Eng. 11 Jan. 1937; s. Henry Wolfestan and Mathilda Genevieve (Lyne) B.; e. Radley Coll. Eng. 1955; New Coll. Oxford Univ. B.A. 1961; Univ. of Ill. M.A. 1963, Ph.D. 1971; m. Janet d. Carl Coffin 20 Apl. 1968; one d. Winifred; ASSOC. PROF. OF CLASSICS, ERINDALE COLL. UNIV. OF TORONTO; Lectr. in Classics Univ. of Man. 1963-64; Univ. Coll. Univ. of Toronto 1964-65; Asst. Prof. of Classics present Coll. 1968 becoming Assoc. Prof.; mem. Gov. Council Univ. of Toronto 1979-81, Chrmn. Acad. Affairs Comte. 1980; Review Ed. "Phoenix" 1978-81; author various articles classical topics especially Petronius and the ancient novel, the cult of Mithras; served with R.A. 1955-57, rank 2nd Lt.; mem. Classical Assn. Can. (Secy. 1977-79); Am. Philol. Assn.; Anglican; recreations: astronomy, antique collecting (china); travel; Home: R.R. 4, Acton, Ont. L7J 2M1; Office: Mississauga, Ont. L5L 1C6.

BECKEL, William Edwin, B.A., M.S., Ph.D.; university president; b. Kingston, Ont., 11 Apl. 1926; s. Elmer Ernest and Beatrice Mary (Driver) B.; e. Kingston (Ont.) Coll. & Vocational Inst.; Queen's Univ., B.A.; State Univ. of Iowa, M.S.; Cornell Univ., Ph.D.; m. Dorothy Kathleen, d. E. W. Brown, Claresholm, Alta., 3 Sept. 1953;

children: John, Margaret, Julia, Millie; PRES. AND VICE CHANCELLOR, CARLETON UNIV., since 1979; Head, Entom. Sec., Defence Research N. Lab., 1948-54; Physiol. Ecol., Entom. Lab., Chatham, Ont., 1955; Asst. Prof. of Zool., Univ. of Toronto, 1956-60; Assoc. Prof. 1960-63; Prof. 1963; Dean of Science, Scarborough Coll., Univ. of Toronto, 1963-64 and of Coll. 1964-68; Vice-Pres., Acad. and Finance of Univ. of Lethbridge 1968-71; Pres. and Vice Chancellor 1972-79; pioneered educ. TV in Can. for higher educ.; rec'd Allied Dye and Chem. Fellowship, Cornell Univ.; author of over 50 publs. for prof. journs.; mem., Candn. Soc. Cell Biols.; Candn. Soc. Zool.; recreations: skiing, hunting; Home: 1 Linden Terrace, Ottawa, Ont. K1S 1Z1

BECKER, His Excellency John Joubert, B. Comm; diplomat; b. Klerksdorp, S. Africa, 29 June 1925; s. late Johannes Jacobus and Francina Jacoba (Joubert) B.; e. Klerksdorp High School; Univ. of Potchefstroom, B.Comm; m. Magdalena Maria d. late Gen. H.N. Botha, 12 Aug. 1950; children: Annalise and Francine; AMBASSADOR OF S. AFRICA TO CANADA since 1978; since 1947 served in Pretoria, London, Vienna, Geneva and Bonn; recreations: hiking, golf, reading; Home: 5 Rideau Gate, Ottawa, Ont.; Office: 15 Sussex Drive, Ottawa, Ont.

BECKET, Ralph Wilson, Q.C., B.A., B.C.L.; b. Montreal, P.Q., 3 June 1909; s. Ralph Alexander and Laura Eliza (Langhoff) B.; e. King's Sch.; Westmount (P.Q.) High Sch.; McGill Univ., B.A. 1931, B.C.L. 1934; m. Mary Evelyn, d. late Rev. J. W. MacKenzie, 30 Nov. 1938; children: Heather, Joanna, Wilson; retired Vice-Pres. and Gen. Counsel, Canadian International Paper Company; GEN COUNSEL THE IMPERIAL TRUST CO. ; DIR. ST. RAYMOND PAPER LTD.; called to the Bar of Que., 1935; cr. Q.C. 1955; Manager, Prince Edward Island Trust Co., 1936-39; mem., Montgomery, McMichael, Common, Howard, Forsyth & Ker, 1945-50; served in 2nd World War, 1939-45; Adjt., P.E.I. Highlanders (Black Watch); Lieut.-Col. and O.C., 3rd Regt. First Special Service Force (Parachute); awarded U.S. Silver Star; mem., The Candn. Legion; mem., Candn. Bar Assn.; Protestant; recreations: fishing, numismatics; Clubs: St. James's; Rideau (Ottawa); Home: 3497 Walkley Ave., Montreal, Que H3B 2K2

BECKMAN, Margaret Lilas Armstrong, B.A., M.L.S.; librarian; b. Hartford, Conn. 1926; d. Ewen Cameron and Anne Armstrong; e. Kitchener-Waterloo (Ont.) Coll. Inst.; Univ. of Western Ont., B.A. 1946; Univ. of Toronto, B.L.S. 1949, M.L.S. 1969; m. Arthur Kenneth B. 16 Sept. 1950; children: Christopher, Susan, David; CHIEF LIBRARIAN, UNIV. OF GUELPH since 1971; Lectr. in Lib. Planning Sch. of Lib. and Information Science, Univ. of W. Ont. since 1970; Lib. Bldg. Consultant to several acad., public and govt. libs.; Head Cataloguing Dept. Univ. of Waterloo 1960, Dir. Tech. Services 1964; joined present Univ. as Systems Lib. 1966, Depy. Lib. 1970; mem. Candn. Assn. Coll. and Univ. Libs. (Past Pres.); Ont. Lib. Assn.; Am. Inst. of Information Science; Am. Lib. Assn.; Candn. Assn. Univ. Teachers; Adv. Bd. on Scient. and Tech. Information Nat. Research Council (Pres. 1980–); Nat. Lib. Task Force on Nat. Union Catalogue; author numerous books, book chapters and articles in prof. journs.; Past Chrmn. Waterloo Public Lib. Bd.; Presbyterian; Conservative; recreations: hiking, skiing, swimming, canoeing; Home: 168 John Blvd., Waterloo, Ont. N2L 1C5

BEDARD, Hon. Jean-Jacques, B.A., LL.L.; juge; né Québec, 10 sep. 1916; fils J. Ephraim Bédard, C.R.; é Séminaire de Québec; Univ. St.-Dunstan, Charlottetown, P.E.I., B.A.; Univ. Laval, Qué., LL.L.; ép Bérengère Bélanger, 26 juin 1943; enfants: Jean-Pierre, Lise, Bérengère, Claire, Mireille; JUGE PUINE DE LA COUR SUPERIEURE, DIST. DE QUE., depuis 1 Nov. 1966; juge d'office à la Cour du Banc de la Reine de la prov. de Qué.; dirigea une étude légale avec Mes Francois Veil-

leux, C.R., Auguste Choquette, M.P., et Raymond Caron, LL.L.; élu une première fois á l'Assemblée Lég., 1952; réélu, 1960 et 1962; nommé Prés. du Comité des Bills Privés et adjoint parlementaire du Procureur Général, 1961; Vice-Prés., l'Assemblée Lég. de la Prov. de Qué. jusqu'au 1 nov. 1966; entré au service de l'armée Canadienne, 1942, fut attaché militaire au bureau du juge-avocat général du Ministère de la Défense Nationale jusqu'en déc. 1945, avec le grade de capitaine; mem., Conseil Laval des Chevaliers de Colomb et de l'Assemblée Gén. Archevêque Mathieu; mem. à vie, Club Optimiste St-Laurent-Québec, ancien Prés., Jeune Barreau de Qué.; Chambre de Comm. de Charlesbourg; Bureau: 6880 Boul. Bourassa, Charlesbourg, Qué. G1H 3C7

BÉDARD, Hon. Marc-André, M.N.A., B.A., LL.D.; b. Ste-Croix, Qué. 15 Aug. 1935; s. Lorenzo and Laurette (Bilodeau) B.; e. St-Honoré Primary Sch.; Chicoutimi Semy.; Univ. of Ottawa; m. Nicole d. Edgar Girard, Arvida, Qué, 19 June 1965; children: Eric, Stéphane, Louis, Maxime;MIN. OF JUSTICE AND MIN. OF STATE FOR ELECTORAL REFORM, QUE. 1979- ; el. M.N.A. for Chicoutimi prov. g.e. 1973, re-el. since; Min. of Justice and Atty. Gen. 1976; Parti Quebecois; R. Catholic; Office: 1200, route de l'Eglise, Ste-Foy, Qué. G1V 4M1.

BEDDOES, John Michael, B.Sc.; electrical engineer; b. Kidderminster, Eng. 2 Sept. 1929; s. John and Edith B.; e. Univ. of London B.Sc. 1954; Carleton Univ. course work M.Eng. 1966; Univ. of Mich. Solid State Physics 1963; McMaster Univ. Advanced Math., several short courses Mang., Finance & Business; m. Priscilla d. Albert Wacker, Eng. and Germany; children: Ursula, Rebecca, Jonathan, Matthew. EXECUTIVE VICE PRES. COMMERCIAL PRODUCTS, ATOMIC ENERGY OF CANADA LTD. since 1975; Circuit Design Engr. Decca Radar, Eng. 1954-57 and Racal Engineering Ltd. Eng. 1956-57; Part-time Lectr. in Electronics, Hamilton Inst. Technol. 1961-62; Sr. Engr. Canadian Westinghouse Co. Ltd. Hamilton 1957-63; mem. Scient. Staff Northern Electric Co. Ottawa 1963-65, Mgr. Applications Engn. & Design 1965-68, Mgr. Tech. Resources Advanced Devices Centre 1968-69; Tech. Dir. Microsystems International Ltd. Ottawa 1969-70, Acting Gen. Mgr. 1970-71, Operations Mgr. Data Products 1972-73, Vice Pres. Tech. Devel. 1972-73; Product Mgr. Memories/Microprocessors, General Instrument Microeletronics Div., Hicksville, Long Island, N.Y., Dir. of Technol. 1974-75; served with Brit. Army 1948-50; holds 3 patents, 8 disclosures accepted; author various papers, articles; Queen's Jubilee Medal 1977; mem. Assn. Prof. Engrs. Prov. Ont.; Royal Candn. Coll. Organists; Protestant; recreations: music, equestrian sports, gardening; Home: R.R.1, Kanata, Ont. K2K 1X7; Office: P.O. Box 6300 Stn. J, Ottawa, Ont. K2A 3W3.

BEECROFT, Eric Armour, M.A., Ph.D., F.R.S.A.; professor emeritus; b. Toronto, Ont. 7 Sept. 1903; s. Frank Lloyd and Eva (Armour) B.; e. Univ. of Toronto B.A. 1925, M.A. 1927 (Mackenzie Fellow in Pol. Econ.); Yale Univ. Ph.D. 1934; m. Ann Granger 1952; one s. Douglas Armour; PROF. EMERITUS OF POL. SCIENCE, UNIV. OF W. ONT. 1976- ; Asst. Prof. of Pol. Science Univ. of Calif. Los Angeles 1931-39, Berkeley 1939-41; Extve. Secy. Internat. Econ. Studies, Nat. Planning Assn. Washington, D.C. 1941-42; Chief Far E. Div. Bd. Econ. Warfare U.S. Govt. 1942-43; Special Rep. in India Foreign Econ. Adm. 1943-45; Special Asst. to Secy. of Interior U.S. 1945-47; Loan Offr. The World Bank 1947-54 serving in Washington, Philippines 1948-49, India 1949, Sri Lanka 1949-51, Pakistan 1951, Ethiopia 1950-51; Nat. Dir. Community Planning Assn. Can. 1954-60; Rep. in Ottawa Candn. Fed. Muns. 1960-65; Prof. of Pol. Science 1965-76 and Prof. of Urban Studies Faculty Engn. Science 1969-73 Univ. of W. Ont.; Founder, Candn. Council on Urban & Regional Research 1962, Chrmn. Bd. Dirs. 1966-69; Candn. mem. Gov. Bd. Internat. Fed. Housing & Planning 1958-68 and Extve. Internat. Union Local Authorities 1970-71; mem. Urban Devel. Comte. Science Council Can. 1969-71; Extve. Comte. Candn. Council on Educ. 1960-62; author numerous articles prof. journs.; Ed. "Community Planning Review" 1954-60; mem. Soc. Internat. Devel.; City of London (Ont.) Mang. Comte. 1974-76; Consultant to UN report on Credit Insts. for Local Authorities 1970-72; recreation: music; Clubs: Cosmos (Washington, D.C.); University (London, Ont.); Home: 727 Old Hunt Rd., London, Ont. N6H 4K7; Office: London, Ont. N6A 5C2.

BEECROFT, Norma Marian; composer, producer (music); b. Oshawa, Ont., 11 Apl. 1934; d. Julian Balfour and Eleanor Chambers (Norton) B.; e. Royal Conserv. of Music, Toronto (piano, flute & composition) 1950-58; Berkshire Music Centre, Tanglewood, composition with Aaron Copland and Lukas Foss, 1958; Acad. of Saint Cecilia, Rome, grad. in composition, 1961; private studies in Darmstadt, Germany and Dartington, Eng, 1960-61; major compositions incl.: "Tre Pezzi Brevi," 1960-61; "Improvvisazioni Concertanti," 1961; "Contrasts for Six Performers," 1962; "From Dreams of Brass," (Jane Beecroft) 1963-64; "Elegy and Two Went to Sleep" (Leonard Cohen), 1967; "Piece Concertante No. 1." 1966; "Undersea Fantasy" (electronic score), 1967; "The Living Flame of Love" (St. John of the Cross), 1967, "Rasas I", Commission 1968 — "Soc. de Musique contemp. du Qué."; "Improvvisazioni Concertanti No. 2", Nat. Arts Centre Commission, 1971; "Rasas II" CBC Commission, 1972-73, for contralto, chamber ensemble and tape; "Three Impressions from Sweetgrass" (Wayne Keon), Ontario Youth Choir Commission, 1973, for mixed choir and percussion; "Improvvisazioni Concertanti No. 3", Toronto Symphony Women's Committee commission, 1973, for flute, timpany and orch.; "Rasas III", New Music Concerts commission, 1974, for soprano, chamber ensemble and tape; "11 and 7 for 5+", 1975 CBC commission for Canadian Brass quintet and tape; "Piece for Bob", 1975, CBC commission for solo flute and tape; "Collage '76" for solo flute, chamber ensemble and tape, Ont. Arts Council Comm. 1976; "Consequences for Five", Candn. Electronic Ensemble commission, 1977, for piano, 3 brass, synthesizers and electronics; "Collage '78", Music Inter Alia Commission, 1978, for bassoon solo, ensemble and tape 1978; "Quaprice", 1979-80, commissioned by James MacDonald for solo horn, percussion and tape; "Cantorum Vitae", 1980-81, commissioned by Days, Months & Years to Come (Vancouver) for flute, cello, 2 pianos, percussion & tape; "Hedda" 1981, ballet score for orchestra and tape, Nat. Ballet of Can. comm.; Producer, Music Dept. (Radio), CBC; since 1969 freelance commentator on contemporary, music (host of CBC-FM series "Music of Today"] and documentarist on Canadian composers, music and technology); rec'd schols. in composition Royal Conserv. of Music, Berkshire Music Centre, Canada Council, Italian Ministry of Foreign Affairs; Armstrong Award for Excellence in FM Broadcasting; Victor M. Lynch-Staunton Award (Can. Council) for distinguished artists, 1978-79; producer of CAPAC/RCI record series "Music Canada" etc.; comns.; Charlottetown Festival, 1966; Ten Centuries Concerts (Pres.) 1967; Expo '67; Waterloo Lutheran Univ., 1967; Crest Theatre Hour Co., 1967; Pres., New Music Concerts, Toronto, 1971; Secy., Candn. League Composers, 1966-67; mem., ACTRA Composers, Authors & Publishers Assn. Can.; Address 10 Lyndhurst Court, Toronto, Ont. M5R 1X7

BEEKMAN, Philip E., A.B.; distiller; b. Glenridge, N.J. 3 Oct. 1931; s. Chester Carlyle and Madeline Frances (Davis) B.; e. Dartmouth Coll. A.B. 1953; m. Nancy d. late Clarence V. Bush 22 Sept. 1952; children: Elizabeth E. Robinowitz, Leslie Ann, Philip E. Jr., Nancy Leigh; PRESIDENT, SEAGRAM CO. LTD. since 1977; joined Colgate-Palmolive Co. as Indust. Engr. 1953, Plant Production Indust. Relations 1957, Marketing Man. 1961, Asst. to Pres. and Chrmn. of Bd. 1963, Extve. Vice Pres.

Argentina 1964, Area Mgr. Caribbean 1965, Pres. Candn. Co. 1968, Vice Pres. Latin Am. 1969 and Domestic Co. Household Div. 1970, Pres. Internat. 1974; active YMCA Can. 1968, USA since 1969; Beta Theta Pi; R. Catholic; recreations: golf, tennis, squash; Clubs: Cricket (Toronto); Racquet (New York); Home: 10 Wildwood Dr., North Caldwell, N.J.; Office: 1430 Peel St., Montreal, Que. H3A 1S9

BEER, Harry M., B.A.; educator (retired); b. Brandon, Man. 15 Apl. 1913; s. Dr. Edwin Charles and Eleanor Tweed (McWaters) B.; e. Pickering Coll. 1931; Univ. of Toronto B.A. 1937; m. Elizabeth Greenway d. late William Wendell Holmes 28 June 1939; three s. David H., Charles M., James M.; Headmaster, Pickering College, Newmarket, Ont. 1953-78; Headmaster Emeritus, mem. of the Yonge St. Meeting of the Religious Soc. of Friends (Quakers); Address: 602 Pearson Street, Newmarket, Ont. L3Y 1G3

BEETZ, Hon. Jean, M.A., LL.L., LL.D., D.C.L.; juge; né Montréal, Qué., 27 mars 1927; f. Jean et Jeanne (Cousineau) B.; é. Univ. de Montréal, B.A. 1947, LL.L. 1950; Oxford Univ. B.A. 1953, M.A. 1958; JUGE, COUR SU-PREME DU CANADA depuis 1974; reçu avocat (Qué.) 1950; C.R. 1965; boursier Rhodes 1951; Prof. adjoint, Univ. de Montréal 1953, Prof. agrégé 1959; Dir., Inst. de Recherche en Droit Public, Univ. de Montréal 1961-63; Doyen, Faculté de Droit 1968-70; Prof. titulaire 1966-73; nommé à la Cour d'Appel du Qué. 1973; Secrétaire adjoint du Cabinet et Greffier adjoint du Conseil Privé 1966-68; Conseil Spécial du P.M. du Can. pour les affaires constitutionelles 1968-71; mem. de la Société Royale du Can.; Fellow Hon. du Collège Pembroke, Oxford; catholique r.; Clubs: Cercle Universitaire (Ottawa); Résidence: 400 rue Stewart, Ottawa, Ont. K1N 6L2; Bureau: rue Wellington, Ottawa, Ont. K1A 0J1

BEGG, R. W., OC, E.D., C.D., M.Sc., M.D., D.Phil., F.R.C.P. (C) D.C.L., LL.D.; b. Florenceville, N.B., 27 Dec. 1914; s. Henry Todd and Annie Cullen (Keith) B.; e. Univ. of King's Coll., B.Sc., 1936; Dalhousie Univ., M.Sc. 1938, M.D. 1942; Oxford Univ., D. Phil. 1950; m. Elsie Eileen, d. C. H. Baker, Winnipeg, Man., 19 Nov. 1943; children: Robert, Catherine (Mrs. John Barron), Ronald, Beverley (Mrs. Ronald Bowman); 1975 (Principal of Saskatoon Campus and Vice Pres. Univ. of Sask. 1967-75); Asst. and Research Assoc. Professor of Biochem., Dalhousie University., 1946-50; Assoc. Professor and Prof. of Med. Research, Univ. of W. Ont. (Collip Lab.), 1950-57; Prof. of Cancer Research and Dir., Sask. Research Unit, Nat. Cancer Inst., Saskatoon, 1957-62; Dean of Med. and Prof., Chem. Path., Univ. of Sask., 1962-80; Pres. Emeritus & research ass. Pathology Dept., Univ. of Sask., 1975-80; mem. N.P.A.M. (P.E.I. Highlanders) 1929-42; served in R.C.A.M.C. with 1st Candn. Parachute Bn. in Can., U.K., N.W. Europe, 1942-45; Col., Militia Group Commdr. C.A. (M), 1950-65; Hon. Col., 20 Med. Co., RCAMC; author of research papers, publ. in Cancer Research, Candn. Journ. of Biochem., etc.; Address: University of Sask., Saskatoon, Sask. S7N 0W0

BÉGIN, Hon. Monique, P.C., M.P., M.A.; politician; b. Rome, Italy 1 March 1936; d. Lucien and Marie-Louise (Vanhavre) B.; e. Notre-dame-de-Grâce Elem. Sch. Montreal; Esther Blondin High Sch. Montreal; Teachers' Coll. Rigaud, Que.; M.A. in Soc., Univ. of Montreal; Univ. of Paris; McGill Univ.; MIN. OF HEALTH & WELFARE, CAN. 1980- ; Founding mem. Fed. de Femmes du Qué., 1965-67; Extve. Secy. Gen. Royal Comn. on Status of Women in Can. 1967-70; mem. Candn. Human Rights Foundation; el. to H. of C. for Montréal Saint-Léonard-Anjou g.e. 1972, re-el. since; apptd. Parlty. Secy. to Secy. of State for External Affairs 1975; Min. of Nat. Revenue and Sworn of Privy Council 1976; Min. of Nat. Health & Welfare 1977; hon. Ph.D. St. Thomas Univ. N.B., 1977; Distinguished Service Award, Candn. Soc. for Clinical

Investigation, 1979; Liberal; R. Catholic; Home: 4101 Jarry St. E., Montreal, Que.; Office: House of Commons, Ottawa, Ont. K1A 0A6.

BEGIN, Robert, F.S.A.; b. Giffard, Que., 20 Oct. 1925; s. Joseph and Germaine (Blais) B.; e. Primary Sch., Giffard, Que.; Academie de Québec; Laval Univ.; Univ. of Manitoba; m. Marie, d. Gaston Cancade, Findlay, Man., 8 Oct. 1949; children: Lorraine, André (deceased), Gisele, Danielle, Céline; PRESIDENT & CHIEF EXTVE OFFICER, INDUSTRIAL LIFE INSURANCE CO., 1977-81; Pres. and Dir., The Equitable General Insurance Co. and Industrial General Insurance Co., since 1972; Dir, Industrial Life-Technical serv. Inc.; MICR Systems Ltd., Industrial Life, Real Estate Serv. Inc.; Fiducic Prêt et Revenu; joined Co. in 1947, Asst. Actuary 1954, Actuary 1958, Vice-Pres. and Controller 1966; Extve. Vice Pres. 1967; mem., Candn. Inst. of Actuaries; Candn. Life Ins. & Health Assn.; Life Office Mang. Assn. (Atlanta, Ga.); Que. Chamber Comm.; R. Catholic; recreations: hockey, fishing, hunting, gardening; Home: 3445 Hawey Blvd., Quebec, Que. G1E 1P4; Office: 1080 St. Louis Rd., Quebec, Que. G1K 7M3

BEHRENS, Herman H.; manufacturer; b. Isle of Wight, England, 27 May 1910; s. Henry and Edith Hamilton (Lillis) B.; e. Liebig Gymnasium, Frankfort, Germany; m. Frances, d. John J. O'Brien, 23 Feb. 1952; children: Anne, Peter, Mary; joined Consolidated Dyestuff Corpn., Montreal, P.Q. in 1934; Sales Mgr. for Ont. for successor Co., Irwin Dyestuff Corpn., 1950-52 apptd. Mgr. of Dyestuff Div., Chemical Developments of Can. Ltd., 1952; Asst. Gen. Mgr., 1955-57; Vice-Pres. and Dir. 1957-76; mem. Candn. Assn. Textile Colourists & Chemists; Am. Assn. Textile Colourists & Chemists; Roman Catholic; Liberal; recreation: golf; Home: 4991 Grosvenor Ave., Montreal, P.Q. H3W 2M2

BEIGIE, Carl E., A.B., economist; b. Cleveland, Ohio 9 Apl. 1940; s. George C. and Carol Elizabeth (Chamberlin) B.; e. Cleveland Heights (Ohio) High Sch. 1958; Muskingum Coll. A.B. 1962; Mass. Inst. Technol. Grad. work in Econ. 1962-66 (Woodrow Wilson Fellow 1962; Presb. Fellow 1962, 1964); m. Mary Catherine d. Late William H. Hall 3 June 1961; children: David P., Darin E.; PRESIDENT, C. D. HOWE RESEARCH INST. since 1978; Dir. Fraser Companies Ltd.; Assoc. Prof. (Part-Time) Faculty of Mang. McGill Univ.; Asst. Vice Pres. and Internat. Econ. Irving Trust Co. New York City 1968-71; Extve. Dir. present Inst. 1971-77; Lectr. Dept. Econ. Univ. W. Ont. 1966-68; Dir. Candn. Foundation for Econ. Educ.; Zinor Holdings Ltd., 1979-; frequent speaker and media commentator on Econ.; business consultant; participant govt. adv. groups; mem., Dept. of Communications' Consultative Comte. on the Implications of Telecommunications for Candn. Sovereignty, 1979; author "The Canada-U.S. Automotive Agreement: An Avaluation" 1970; "Inflation Is a Social Malady" 1979; co-author "The Disappearance of the Status Quo"; author or co-author numerous articles in fields of telecommunications policy, energy issues, trade policy and gen. econ. conditions; mem. Time Canada's Bd. of Econs. 1973-75; mem. Montreal Econ. Assn.; Candn. Econ. Assn. (Extve. Concil 1972-75); Nat. Assn. Business Econs. (Adolph G. Abramson Award 1971); Candn. Assn. Business Econs.; Am. Econ. Assn.; United Church; recreations: reading, philately, athletics; Home: 85 Elgin Cres. #556, Beaconsfield, Que. H9W 2B3; Office: 2064 Sun Life Bldg., Montreal, Que. H3B 2X7.

BÉIQUE, Pierre, C.M., B.Com.; concert manager; b. Montreal, Que. 7 Sept. 1910; s. Paul Albert and Thérèse (Merrill) B.; e. Colls. Ste-Marie and Jean-de-Brébeuf; Chauncy Hall Sch. Boston; McGill Univ. B.Com. 1936; SPECIAL ASST. TO MUSICAL DIR., MONTREAL SYMPHONY ORCHESTRA; joined present Orchestra as Hon. Treas. 1936, Gen. Mgr. 1939-71; Bd. of Trustees, Nat.

Arts Centre 1981-84; Liberal; R. Catholic; recreations: golf, fishing; Club: Kanawaki Golf; Home: 3450 Drummond St., Montreal, Que. H3G 1Y3; Office: Place des Arts, 200 de Maisonneuve Blvd., Montreal, Que. H2X 1Y9.

BEIRNE, Bryan Patrick, M.A., M.Sc., Ph.D., M.R.I.A.; entomologist; educator; b. Rosslare, Co. Wexford, Ireland, 22 Jan. 1918; s. late Patrick James and late Margaret (Kelly) B.; e. Trinity Coll., Univ. of Dublin, B.Sc., M.Sc., M.A., Ph.D.; m. Elizabeth, d. late James Curry, 12 Apl. 1948; children: Patrick J., Anne M.; PROF. OF PEST MANG. AND DEAN OF GRAD. STUDIES, SIMON FRASER UNIV.; Dir. of Pestology Centre there 1967-79; Lectr. in Entomol., Univ. of Dublin, 1945; Research Scientist (Insect Systematics), Can. Dept. of Agric., Ottawa, 1949; Dir., Research Inst. (Biol. Control), Belleville, Ont., 1955; participant in various internat. confs. and symposia on biol. pest control and pest mang incl. FAO, WHO, IBP and IACBC (Chrmn.); Gold Med. Entomol. Soc. of Canada 1976; author, "The Origin and History of the British Fauna", 1952; "British Pyralid and Plume Moths", 1952; "Pest Management", 1968; "The Leafhoppers of Canada and Alaska", 1956; "Collecting, Preparing and Preserving Insects", 1955; also over 160 research papers on insect systematics and morphology, pest ecology, biol. and integrated controls, zoogeog.; mem., Entomol. Soc. Can.; Entomol. Soc. Am.; Office: Burnaby, B.C. V5A 1S6

BELANGER, Fernand, B.A., M.S.C.; professeur titulaire; né Daveluyville, Qué., 15 juil. 1930; f. J.-Henri et Blanche (Fournier) B.; é Séminaire de Nicolet; Univ. Laval; études doctorales en "Business Admn."; ép 1 juin 1961; enfants: Josée, Jean, Claude; DOYEN DE LA FACULTE DES SCIENCES DE L'ADMINISTRATION DE L'UNIV. LAVAL depuis 1970; Dir., L'Unique Compagnie d'assurances; Delivro Group; Daveluyville Furniture; Fire Ins. Co. of Canada; carrière entière à l'Univ. de Laval, prof. titulaire depuis 1961; Secrétaire du Dépt. de Gestion des entreprises de la Faculté des Sciences de l'Admn. 1964-66; Dir. du Dépt. de Gestion des entreprises 1966-69; Dir.-fondateur de la maîtrise en admn. 1970->; consultant pour les gouvernements du Québec et du Canada, ainsi que pour quelques grandes compagnies nat. et internat., telles que: ALCAN, Canadian International Paper, Dominion Textile, C.E.C.M., etc.; catholique; Bureau: Sainte Foy, Québec, Qué.

BELANGER, Jean-Robert, B.A., B.Ph., M.A., newspaper publisher; b. Hull, Que., 5 Aug. 1922; s. Henri and Agnès (Plouffe) B.; e. Elem. Sch., Hull Que.; High Sch., Chambly, Que.; Univ. of Ottawa, B.A., B.Ph. 1943, M.A. (Pol. & Écon.) 1947; LaSalle Extension Univ., Accounting & Business Admn.; Univ. of Toronto, R.I.A. 1956; m. Marguerite Léger, 1 Sept. 1947; children: Pierre, Paul, Jean, Claire, Lise, Céline; PUBLISHER AND GEN. MGR., LE DROIT LTEE since 1972; Chrmn., Imprimerie Leclerc Ltée; Dir., Perspectives Inc.; Dir., Foyer du Bonheur Inc. (Hull, Que.), Hebdo-Revue du Canada Français Ltée, Candn. Press; Candn. Daily Newspaper Publishers Ass.; with Provincial Bank of Canada 1943; joined Le Droit Ltée 1944, Chief Acct. 1948, Treas. and Dir. Labour Relations 1957-72; mem. Bd. Trustees, Health Centre, E. Bruyère; mem. Extve. Comte. Bd. of Govs., Univ. of Ottawa; Chrmn. of Bd., Hull C.E.G.E.P. 1969-72; R. Catholic; recreations: golf, fishing, reading; Home: 33 rue Gendron, Hull, Que. J9A 1B7; Office: 375 Rideau St., Ottawa, Ont. K1N 5Y7

BELANGER, Leonard-Francis, M.A., M.D., F.R.S.C., F.R.M.S., F.A.C.N.(E); professor emeritus; b. Montreal, P.Q., 11 Mar. 1911; s. Dr. Joseph Amedee Deus and Frances Ann Kathleen (Leonard) B.; e. Univ. of Montreal, B.A. 1931, M.D. 1937; Northwestern Univ.; Harvard Med. Sch., M.A. (Med. Sc.) 1940; Marine Biol. Lab., Woods Hole, Mass. (course in Exper. Embryol.); m. Marie Cecile, d. Joseph Lefebvre, Quebec, 11 June 1938; children: Nicole, Richard; professor emeritus, Dept. of Anatomy, School of Med., Univ. of Ottawa; Prof. and Head, Dept. of Histo. and Embryol., 1946-77 (first prof. and founder); began gen. practice of med., Lacolle, Que., 1937; Asst., Dept. of Histol., Univ. of Montreal, 1938; Fellow of Prov. Govt. of Que. and Rougier-Armandie Foundation of Paris 1939; Asst. Prof. of Histol. and Embryology, Univ. of Montreal, 1941; Research Assoc., Dept. of Anat., McGill Univ., 1945; Visiting Prof., Dept. of Phys. Biol., Cornell Univ., 1956-62; Anat., Univ. of Brit. Columbia, 1963-64; Local Chrmn. and Co-ed., 3rd Parathyroid Conf. (Mont. Gabriel) 1967; awarded Claude Bernard Medal, 1965; Dow Award and Medal 1968; Parizeau Medal (ACFAS) 1968; rec'd Steindler Award of U.S. Orthopedic Research Soc. 1972; Queen's Jubilee Medal 1977; served in World War 1941-45 as Med. Offr. with R.C.A.F.; mem., Am. Assn. of Anat.; Histochem. Soc.; Candn. Physiol. Soc.; Hon. Fellow, Candn. Orthopedic Research Soc.; has contrib. a variety of scient. writings to the field of med., incl. important papers on use of radioisotopes as biol. tracers, histochem.; bone and endocrine physiol.; R. Catholic; recreations: photography, history, travel; Address: 1618 Sir John's Lake, R.R. 7, Lachute, Que. J8H 3X1

BELANGER, Marcel, O.C. (1974), C.A.; b. Montreal P.Q., 2 June 1920; s. late Victorien and Alice (Beaudet) B.; e. Laval Univ., B.A. 1940, M.Comm. 1943; Harvard Univ., M.A. (Econ.) 1948; Hon. Ph.D. (Adm.) Sherbrooke and Laval; m. Simone, d. late J. E. Gagnon, Quebec City, P.Q., 17 July 1948; one d. Marie Veitch; PRES., GAGNON & BÉLANGER INC.; formerly mem., Royal Comn. on Coastal Trade (1955-58); Study Comte. on Public Assistance in Que. (1962-63); Ind. Review Comte. on Office of Auditor Gen. (1974-75); Chrmn. Que. Prov. Roy. Comn. on Taxation, 1963-65; mem. Que. Comn. on Trade of Alcoholic Beverages 1968-71; Dir., Great-West Life Assnce. Co.; Abitibi-Price Inc.; La Compagnie Price Co. Ltée.; Celanese Canada Inc.; John Labatt Ltd.; Commerce Group Insurance; The National Bank of Canada; Eldorado Nuclear Ltd.; La Fondation J. Armand Bombardier; Bell Canada; Provigo Inc.; Pratt and Whitney Aircraft of Canada Ltd.; Scan Marines Inc.; Hudson's Bay Co.; Past Pres., Candn. Inst. Chart. Accts. (1975-76) R. Catholic; recreations: swimming, fishing, skiing; Home: 839 Eymard Ave., Quebec, G1S 4A3 Office: 2050 Boul. St.-Cyrille W., Quebec, Qué. G1V 2K8

BELANGER, Michel Ferdinand, B.A., B.Sc.; b. Lévis, Que., 10 Sept. 1929; s. Ferdinand and Jeanne (Blouin) B.; e. Coll. de Lévis (Que.) B.A. 1949; Univ. Laval, B.Sc. Social Science (Econ.) 1952; McGill Univ. Post-Grad. Studies (Central Mortgage & Housing Corp. School) 1952-54; m. Hélène; 6 children; PRESIDENT, CHRMN. OF BOARD AND CHIEF EXTVE. OFFR., NATIONAL BANK OF CANADA; Dir. Bank of Canada; Simpson-Sears Ltd.; Bangue de l'Union Occidentale Française et Canadienne; CIP Inc.; Power Corp of Can.; MICC Investments Ltd.; joined Dept. Finance, Treasury Bd., Ottawa 1954, with Econ. and Internat. Affairs Div. 1957-60; on loan to research staff, Royal Comn. on Energy (Borden Comn.) 1958-59; Econ. Adv., Que. Dept. Hydraulic Resources 1960; Dir. Planning, Que. Dept. Nat. Resources 1961; Asst. Depy. Min. 1963; Depy. Min., Que. Dept. Indust. and Comm. 1966; Econ. Adv. to the Que. Extve. Council 1969; Secy. Treasury Bd. 1970; Pres. and Ch. Exec. Off. Montreal Stock Exchange 1973-76; mem. Régie de la Place des Arts; Dir., Institut de Recherches Cliniques de Montreal; C.D. Howe Research Inst.; R. Catholic; Clubs: St-Denis; St. James's; Mount Royal; Home: 615 Dunlop, Montreal, Que. H2V 2W1; Office: 500 Place d'Armes, Montreal, Que. H2Y 2W3

BELBECK, Kenneth George, B.A.; management consultant; b. London, Ont., 11 Feb. 1928; s. George Jerald and Lily May (Jolliffe) B.; e. London (Ont.) Central Coll. Inst., 1941-46; Univ. of W. Ont., Sch. of Business Adm., B.A.

1950; m. Patricia Ann, d. Murray Leslie McCulloch, London, Ont., 19 May 1951; children: Gregory, Jeffrey, David, Susan; PRESIDENT, THORNE, STEVENSON & KELLOGG, since 1967; dir.; L. E. Shaw Ltd.; Comptroller, Geo. Pattison & Co. Ltd., 1950-53; joined present Co. 1953; apptd. Consultant and subsequently Princ.; Founding mem., Inst. Mang. Consultants Ont.; Past Pres., Candn. Assn. Mang. Consultants; Zeta Psi; United Church; recreations: golf, skiing; Clubs: Granite; Rideau; Home: 27 Pettit Dr., Weston, Ont. M9R 2W6; Office: 2300 Yonge St., Toronto, Ont. M4P 1G2

BELFORD, John A., B.Com.; retired company executive; b. Ottawa, Ont., 16 Jan. 1918; s. John Alexander and Lillian Jane (Wingfield) B.; e. Glebe Coll. Inst., Ottawa, Ont.; McGill Univ, B.Com. 1941; m. Jeanne, d. Thomas Nelson Woods, 13 Sept. 1945; children: John Alexander Jr., Glenys Jane; Consultant in Personnel and Indust. Relations; Vice-Pres.-Personnel & Indust. Realtions, Massey-Ferguson Ltd. from 1957, retired as Corp. Vice-Pres. 1979; Personnel Mgr., Belding-Corticelli Ltd., Montreal, P.Q., 1946-50; Asst. to Vice Pres.-Personnel Brazilian Traction, Rio de Janeiro, 1951; Asst. Labour Relations Mgr., Canadian Nat. Rlys., Montreal, P.Q., 1952-56; Lect. in Indust. Relations and Dir. of field Work, Grad. Sch. of Indust. Relations, Univ. of Montreal, 1947-50; Pres., Montreal Personnel Assn., 1950; served in 2nd World War; enlisted as Cadet, R.C.A., Candn. Army, Apl. 1941; overseas service, U.K. and N.W. Europe, 1941-45; retired with rank of Maj., 1946; mem. Toronto University Club; Home: 1097 Lakeshore Road E., Oakville, Ont.L6J 1K9

BELHUMEUR, David, B.A., L.Sc.Com., D.B.A. (H.C.), C.A.; executive; b. St-Guillaume, Que., 21 April 1919; s. Omer and Annette (Bonin) B.; e. Laval Univ., B.A. 1940; Univ. of Montreal, L.Sc.Com. 1945, D.B.A. (H.C.) 1975; m. Andrée, d. Raoul Cavet, Quebec, P.Q., 10 Sept. 1951; children: Jean, Hélène, Pierre, Josée; PRESIDENT, AIR FOOD CATERERS LTD.; Kebec Restaurants & Management Inc.; Fonds D.B. Inc.; Vice-Pres. SOGERO Inc.; Dir., Trust Général du Canada; Inst. de Cardiologie de Montréal 1970-79; Advisor, Export Credit Insurance Corp. 1959-63; Gov., Faculty of Adm., Univ. of Sherbrooke; Marie-Enfant Hosp.; Dir., Symphonic Orchestra of Québec 1966-68; Prov. Chamber Comm. 1964-66; Pres., Trois-Rivières Chamber of Comm. 1963-64, Chevalier de l'Ordre Equestre du St-Sepulcre de Jerusalem (1974); R. Catholic; recreation: yachting, golf; Clubs: St.-Denis; Montreal Yacht; Laval-Sur-Le-Lac Golf; Home: 16 Fernlea Cres., Town of Mount Royal, Qué. H3P 1T6; Office: 1 Place Ville Marie, Montréal, Qué.

BELISLE, Louis-Alexandre; lexicographer; author; publisher; b. Saint-Eloi de Témiscouata, Qué. 7 March 1902; s. Georges and Hélène (Rioux) B.; e. Teachers' Schs., Marists Brothers, Lévis and Saint-Hyacinthe; Queen's Univ. A.C.B.A. (Practical Banking and Business Practice) 1923; m. Gabrielle d. Dr. Bernard Miville Deschênes, Saint-Pascal de Kamouraska, Qué. 2 Sept. 1929; children: Pierre, Helène (Mrs. Claude Pattey), Robert, Bernard; Financial Ed., "Le Soleil", Que 1929-36; Publisher-owner "La Semaine Commerciale" 1936-74 and Bélisle, Editeur, Inc. 1950-74 (Past Pres. and Ed.); taught Business French and Stock and Produce Exchanges Operations, Laval Sch. of Comm. 1940-49; author-publisher "La Bibliothèque de l'Homme d'Affaires" 13 vols. 1942-66; author "Le Français des Affaires"; "Tenue de Bureau"; "Petit Dictionnaire Canadien de la Langue Française"; "Dictionnaire Général de la langue Française au Canada" 1958, abridged version 1969, revised ed. 1979; "Organisation et Financement des Enterprises"; "Crédits et Recouvrements"; "Marchés Mobiliers et Placements"; supervised "Dictionnaire Technique Géneral Anglais-Français; co-author "Plomberie et Tuyauterie"; "Chauffage et Ventilation"; "Installations Electriques"; "Charpente et Menuiserie"; "Hygiène et Plomberie"; "Peinture-

Vitrerie"; "Maçonnerie-Matériaux"; adapted numerous European books dealing with Business Management Industrial Engineering and Marketing Trade; transl. "Techniques Modernes de Supervision" (Alfred Lateiner) and numerous books mecaniciens de machines fixes, travail des metaux, Publisher of "La collection des Grands Auteurs"; author "Références Biographiques" 5 vols. 1978; twice invited to act as Mayor of Sillery, Lib. cand. 1960, Union Nationale cand. 1960 (refused both); cofounder Citizen League of Sillery and Credit Union of Sillery; Past Dir. Printers' Employers Union; taught printing in Qué. 2 yrs.; rec'd Medal of L'Académie Française 1958; Medal of La Vie française en Amérique 1971; res., Soc. canadienne de Technologie (Founder 1945); Pres., Soc. des Editeurs canadiens du Livre français 1958-60; twice Pres. of Le Salon du Livre de Qué.; mem. Royal Soc. Can.; French Publishers' Assn. (Pres. 1959-60); Educ. Book Publishers' Assn.; Soc. des Ecrivains (sec. Qué.); Parti Québécois; recreations: music, gardening, collecting old Qué. words and expressions; Home: 1404 ave. des Pins, Sillery, Qué. G1S 4J5; Office: (C.P. 162 Station B) 105 Côte-de-la Montagne, Qué. G1K 7A6.

BELISLE, Hon. Rhéal, LL.D.; senator; b. Blezard Valley, Ont., 3 July 1919; s. J.-B. and Philomène (Nault) B.; e. Blezard Valley, Ont. and Chelmsford (Ont.) High Sch.; Univ. of Toronto; Laurentian Univ. LL.D. 1971; grad. in Theology, St. Paul's Univ. of Ottawa 1977; m. Edna Rainville, 21 Aug. 1941; four s., four d.; Dir. Fielding Lumber Co. Ltd.; Whitefish Pallet Co. Ltd.; Dir., Montfort Hospital; Dir., Banque Canadienne Nationale; Union du Canada; summoned to Senate 1963; Rep. NATO Conf. Paris 1963; Observer 19th Gen. Assembly UN 1964; Rep. UN visit Pope Paul VI 1965; mem. Senate Special Comtes. on Divorce, Science Policy, Poverty; Del. Commonwealth Parlty. Assn. Conf. Trinidad and Tobago 1969; Rep. Senate and C.P.A. fact-finding tour Malawi, Zambia, Tanzania, Uganda, Kenya and Ethiopia 1970, Israel (guest of Premier) 1970; Del. European Common Market Brussels and Strasbourg 1973; Rep. 28th Session UN 1973; Veterans and Senate Rep. 30th Anniversary Landing in Normandy — Beny-sur-Mer 1974; Rep. 20th Commonwealth Parlty. Conf. Sri Lanka, Ceylon 1974; mem. Candn. Del. to Poland and Denmark 1975, Union of Soviet Socialist Republics 1975; 22nd Session Western European Union in Paris 1976; South 1977; South African fact-finding tour 1977; Can. Del. to Mexico 1977; Can. Del. of Interparliamentary Canada-U.S.A. Conference in Victoria 1977; VIIIth Conf. of International Assoc. of French Parliamentarians, Paris 1977; Del. 64th Interparliamentary Conference in Switzerland, Hungary, and Bulgaria 1977; Rep. Candn. Sec., Internat. Assn. French Parliamentarians, Brussels 1978; visited Japan, China, Hong Kong as del. of Candn. Wildlife Fed. 1978; observer, 33rd U.N. Gen. Assembly 1978; observer to Namibia's first elections 1978; attended political seminar in Fed. Republic of Germany sponsored by Konrad-Adenaver Foundation 1979; Candn. del. to 20th meeting of Can.-U.S. Inter-parlty. Group in Alta., Yukon, Alas. 1979; Councillor of Rayside 1944, Mayor 1945-52, Clk. Treas. for 2 yrs.; Pres. and Dir. Sudbury and Dist. Mun. Assn.; Dir. Sudbury and Dist. Home for Aged; served with Candn. Army 1941-43; el. M.P.P. Ont. 1955, re-el. 1959; Chrmn. and mem. various comtes. Ont. Leg; Gov. Sudbury Univ. 1963 (Chrmn. 1964-74, Lifetime Hon. Pres.); Hon. Pres. l'Assn. d'éduc. d'Ont.; Life mem. l'Ordre de mérite de la culture française au Can. 1969; Pres. and Dir. Sudbury and Dist. Chamber Comm. 1950-55, Chelmsford & Valley Chamber Comm. 1952; Charter mem. Nat. Adv. Council, Candn. Cystic Fibrosis Found. (Chrmn. Finan. Comte. 1975); Dir., Ottawa Symphony Orchestra; Candn. Wildlife Federation; Trustee, Candn. Wildlife Found.; Club: Wellington, Ottawa (Hon. Pres.); P. Conservative; R. Catholic; Home: 403 Simpson Rd., Ottawa, Ont. K1H 5A8; Office: The Senate, Ottawa, Ont. K1A 0A4

BELIVEAU, Jean Arthur; executive; hockey player (retired); b. Trois-Rivieres, Que., 31 Aug. 1931; m. Elise (Couture); one d. Helene;SR. VICE PRES. AND DIR. REL. CLUB DE HOCKEY CANADIEN INC.; Dir., Alliance Mutual Life Insur. Co.; Dominion Textile Inc.; Investors Mutual of Canada Ltd.; The Molson Co.'s Ltd.; Royal Trust Co.; played with Montreal Canadiens 1953-71; Captain 1961-71; scored 507 regular season goals (all time record for centre), 79 more in playoffs; 712 regular seas. assists, and record 97 in 162 playoff hockey games; on 10 Stanley Cup winners; mem. Hockey Hall of Fame; Winner of Art Ross Trophy; twice Hart Trophy (MVP); Conn Smythe Trophy; Address: 155 Victoria St., Longueuil, Que. J4H 2J4

BELL, Alistair Macready, R.C.A.; artist-printmaker; b. Darlington, Eng. 21 Oct. 1913; s. Archibald and Gladys Mary (Vassie) B.; e. elem. schs. Darlington, Eng., Toronto, Ont. and Galt, Ont.; Galt Coll. Inst. & Vocational Sch. 1928; m. Lorna Beatrice d. Kenneth Rivers Streatfeild 5 July 1941; one s. Alan Streatfeild; full-time artist-printmaker since 1967; rep. in various internat. graphics exhns. particularly Xylography; many one-man exhns. Can.; rep. in pub., corporate and private colls. incl. Nat. Gallery Can., Museum of Modern Art New York, Victoria and Albert Museum, Museo Ugo da Carpi Italy; Co-Trustee Emily Carr Scholarship Trust 6 yrs.; rec'd Can. Council Sr. Artists' Fellowship 1959, 1967; Past Pres. B.C. Soc. Artists; Candn. Group of Painters; Address: 2566 Marine Dr., West Vancouver, B.C. V7V 1L4.

BELL, C. Randolph; executive; b. St. John's, Nfld., 30 May 1944; s. Charles Renfrew and Ruth (Hickman) B.; e. Bishop Field and Bishop's Coll., St. John's; Memorial Univ. of Nfld.; m. Mary Virginia, d. Col. H.E.C. Price, Ottawa, Ont., 15 Apl. 1966; children: Christopher, Timothy, Andrew, Ruth; PRESIDENT AND DIR., CHARLES R. BELL LTD., since 1972; Dir., Bell Holdings Ltd.; Nfld. Offshore Services Ltd.; Nfld. Steamships Ltd.; A.D.C. to Lieut. Gov. of Nfld.; joined present firm 1964; Dir., Internat. Grenfell Assn.; Grenfell Labrador med. Mission, Ottawa; Grenfell Assn. Nfld.; mem. Bd. Trustees, St. John's Heritage Found.; mem., CNIB (Past Chrmn. Nfld.); Dir. and mem. Nat. Council); Presbyterian; recreations: yachting, tennis, gardening; Clubs: Bally Haly Golf & Country; Royal Nfld. Yacht; Fort William Racquets Club of St. John's; York Club, Toronto; Home: 44A Circular Rd., St. John's, Nfld. A1C 2Z1; Office: 81 Kenmount Rd., St. John's, Nfld. A1B 3P8

BELL, Charles Renfrew; company executive; b. St. John's, Nfld., 2 Dec. 1901; s. Hon. S.K. and M.E. (Crosbie) B.; e. Meth. Coll., St. John's; King's Coll. Sch., Windsor, N.S.; Lower Can. Coll.; Roy. Mil. Coll.; McGill Univ.; m. late Ruth, d. Albert E. Hickman, St. John's, 3 June 1939; 2ndly Margaret D. Harvey, Victoria, B.C., 1963; CHAIRMAN, CHARLES R. BELL LTD.; Dir., Internat Grenfell Assn.; Lieut., Gen. Reserve of Offrs. (Cavalry); Delta Sigma Phi; Presbyterian; recreations: sailing, fishing, hunting, golf; Club: Royal Nfld. Yacht (Past Commodore); Home: 44 Circular Rd., St. John's, Nfld. A1C 2Z1; Office: 81 Kenmount Rd., St. John's, Nfld. A1B 3P8

BELL, Very Rev. Clifford Ritchie, D.C.L., D.D. (Pres.); b. Sherbrooke, P.Q., 11 Aug. 1905; s. late William and late Jane (Coupland) B.; e. Bishop's Univ., B.A. 1929; Presby. Coll., B.D. 1936; Univ. of New Brunswick, B.A. (ad eundem) 1931; Presb. Coll., Montreal, D.D. 1949; Bishop's D.C.L. 1969; Order of Westminster 1978; m. Margaret Farnie, d. late Capt. George William Watson Clark, Aberdeen, Scotland, 23 Aug. 1930; children: David Ritchie, Janet Farnie; retired 1980; Minister Emeritus of the Margaret Rodger Memorial, Presbyterian Church, Lachute, Qué.; Pastor Macvicar Mem. Ch., Montreal, 1936-50; Prof. of Pastoral Theol. and Homiletics, Presbyterian Coll., Montreal, 1950-65; Pastor, Margaret Rodger Mem.

Ch., Lachute, 1966-79; Acting Principal, Presbyterian Coll. 1968; Moderator, Gen. Assembly of Presb. Ch. in Can., 1948-49; Rep. of Presb. Ch. in Can. at first meeting, World Council of Churches, Amsterdam, 1948; Pres., Montreal Prot. Min. Assn., 1946-47; o. 1929; Pastor, St. James, Truro, N.S., 1929-35; mem. of Extve., Lord's Day Alliance for N.S.; mem. of Senate, Presb. Coll., Montreal, 1932-35; mem. of Gen. Assembly's Bd. of Sunday Schs. and Young People's Soc., 1932-35; mem., Extve., N.S. Bible Soc., 1932-33; Pres., Truro Min. Assn., 1933; Moderator, Presby. of Halifax and Lunenburg, 1933; Vice-Pres., Candn. Bible Soc., 1965; Dir. Christian Pavilion Expo '67; mem., Prot. Comte., Superior Council of Educ. for Prov. of Que., since 1965; Ed. of 'The Theol. Review', publ. by the Presby. Coll. 1928-29; inaugurated radio program (Sunday religious period), "Make Life Worth While", 1952; author of "Purple Vapours", 1st series, 1927, 2nd series, 1931; Reserve Chaplain, R.C.N.; Freemason; recreation: reading; Club: Lions; Address: 644 Main St. E., Lachute, Que. J8H 1Z1

BELL, Gordon Ross; journalist; b. Imperial, sask., 29 Sept. 1925; s. late George Melrose and Edna Mae (Parkin) B.; e. Pub. Schs., Regina, Sask.; Magee and King Edward High Sch., Vancouver, B.C.; Univ. of B.C. 1945-46; m. Shelagh Noreen, d. late C.J. O'Grady, Calgary, Alta., 2 June 1952; children: Kevin Alexander, Colin Ross, Cecilia Noreen; MANG. EDITOR, VICTORIA TIMES-COLONIST, since 1968; joined Circulation Department, Edmonton Bulletin, 1947; Cub Reporter, The Albertan, Calgary, 1949; became City Ed., Assoc. Ed. and Asst. Mang. Ed.; joined Victoria Times as Financial Ed., 1960; apptd. Asst. Ed. 1965; served on active duty with RCNVR 1944-45; Clubs: Racquet; Capital City Yacht Club; Home: Lancelot Pl., Saanichton, B.C. V0S 2M0; Office: 2621 Douglas St., Victoria, B.C. V8W 2N4

BELL, J.A. Gordon; banker; b. Rivers, Man., 16 Aug. 1929; s. John Edwin, D.D. and Mary MacDonald (McIlraith) B.; e. Pub. and High Schs. at Brandon, Man., St. John's, Nfld., St. Catharines and Toronto, Ont.; m. Charlene Elizabeth, d. John McCabe, Detroit, Mich., 10 Jan. 1959; PRES. AND CHIEF OPERATING OFFICER, THE BANK OF NOVA SCOTIA, since 1979; Chmn. & Dir., Scotia Mortgage Corp.; Vice-Chmn. and Dir., Scotia Factors Ltd.; Scotia Leasing Ltd.; Scotia-Toronto Dominion Leasing Ltd.; Vice-Pres., Scotia Realty Ltd.; Dir., The Bank of Nova Scotia; The Bank of Nova Scotia Jamaica Ltd.; The Bank of Nova Scotia Trust Co. of Jamaica Ltd.; Bank of Nova Scotia Trust Co. (Bahamas) Ltd.; Bank of Nova Scotia Trust Co. (Caribbean) Ltd.; Bank of Nova Scotia Trust Co. (Cayman) Ltd.; Bank of Nova Scotia Trinidad & Tobago Ltd.; Bank of Nova Scotia Trust Co. of the West Indies Ltd.; The West India Company of Merchant Bankers Ltd.; Nova Scotia Corporation; Scotiafund Financial Services Ltd.; BNS International (Hong Kong) Ltd.; R.L. Crain Inc.; Ont. Hydro; joined present Bank, Queen and Church Branch, Toronto 1948; Inspection Staff, General Office, 1953; transferred to London, Eng. as Special Rep., 1955; Mgr., W. End, London, 1957; Asst. Mgr., Toronto Br., 1959; Mgr., Halifax Br. 1962, Ottawa Br. 1964, Kingston, Jamaica 1965; Asst. Gen. Mgr., Kingston, Jamaica, 1966; Mang. Dir., The Bank of Nova Scotia Jamaica Ltd., 1967; Gen. Mgr., Metrop. Toronto Region, 1968, Deputy Chief Gen. Mgr. 1969; Exec. V.P. and Chief Gen. Mgr. 1972; Hon. Chmn., The Canadian Bankers' Association; Vice Pres., Boys and Girls Clubs of Can.; Clubs: National; Granite; The Toronto; Office: Executive Offices, 44 King St. W., Toronto, Ont. M5H 1H1

BELL, J. Milton, O.C. (1972), Ph.D., F.R.S.C. (1973), F.A.I.C.; b. Islay, Alta., 16 Jan. 1922; s. Milton Wilfred and Elsie Joyce (Larmour) B.; e. High Sch., Scott, Sask.; Sch. of Agric., Vermilion, Alta., 1940; Univ. of Alta., B.Sc.A. 1943; Macdonald Coll., McGill Univ., M.Sc. 1945; Cornell Univ., Ph.D. 1948; m. Edith Margaret Joan, d. Charles William Smith, 21 Sept. 1944; three s. two d;

Prof. Animal Science, Coll. of Agric.; Nat. Comte. for Internat. Union of Nutritional Sciences; Sask. Adv. Council on Animal Production; named Can.'s (first) Laureate of Agric., 1970; rec'd Borden Award, Nutrition Soc. Can., 1962; Fellow, Agric. Inst. Can., 1966; mem., Am. Inst. Nutrition; Candn. Soc. Animal Prod.; Am. Soc. Animal Prod.; United Church; recreation: photography; Home: 1530 Jackson Ave., Saskatoon, Sask. S7H 2N2

BELL, Joel, B.A., B.C.L., LL.M.; petroleum executive; e. McGill Univ. B.A. 1962, B.C.L. 1965; Harvard Univ. LL.M. 1967, doctoral studies Business Sch.; EXTVE. VICE PRES., PETRO-CANADA; Research Asst. Grad. Sch. of Business Adm. McGill Univ. 1962, Lectr. in Econ. 1965-66; Economic Research Corp. 1963; Research Asst. to Project Dir. Private Planning Assn. Candn. Trade Comte. 1964; Special Asst. to Dir. Combines Investigation & Research Dept. Justice 1965; mem. law firm Riel, LeDain, Bissonnette, Vermette & Ryan, Montreal 1965-66; Prime Ministerial Task Force on Labour Relations Ottawa and Consultant Econ. Council Can. 1967-68; Staff Consultant Can. Dept. Labour 1968-70; Counsel and Dir. Research Royal Comn. Labour Leg. Nfld. and Labrador and Special Advisor to Min. of Consumer & Corporate Affairs 1969-72; Consultant to Govt. of Indonesia on Employment Stimulation & Labour Policy 1972; Chrmn. Working Group on Foreign Invest. Govt. Can. 1970-73; Special Counsel CRTC 1973; Special Advisor Dept. Energy, Mines & Resources 1973-74; Econ. Advisor Office of Prime Min. 1974-76; Sr. Vice Pres. Petro-Canada 1976; author numerous writings leg. matters; Office: (P.O. Box 2844) Calgary, Alta. T2P 3E3.

BELL, John W., M.B.E., B.A.Sc., F.I.E.E.; retired company executive; b. Toronto, Ont. 2 Sept. 1911; s. Arthur Cecil and Bertha May (Laws) B.; e. Central Tech. Sch., Toronto, Ont.; Univ. of Toronto, B.A.Sc. 1933; Post-grad. course in Photography; Univ. of W. Ont. (summer) Business Adm. 1950, m. Evelyn Gertrude, d. Charles Snelgrove, Toronto, Ont., 2 July 1934; two d. (Mrs.) Marilyn Grace Myrvold, (Mrs.) Jocelyn Helen Tait; with Nat. Research Council, Radio Sec., Ottawa, Ont., 1937-45 becoming Chief Scient. Offr. of Radio Div., 1942-45; awarded M.B.E. for work in radar; joined Smith & Stone Ltd., Georgetown, Ont. as Dir. of Research, 1945; Plant Mgr. 1949-51, Gen. Mgr. 1952-57; estbd. and owned a profitable automatic vending machine operation, 1951-57; joined CAE Electronics Ltd. as Vice Pres.-Engn. 1957; Vice Pres., Development 1969; mem. of N. Halton High Sch. Bd., 1951-54 (Chrmn. for one yr.); mem., Corp. of Prof. Engrs. Que.; Assn. Prof. Engrs. Ont.; Anglican; recreation: golf; Club: Beaconsfield Golf; Home: 157 Stonehenge Drive, Beaconsfield, Que. H9W 3X6

BELL, Norman Brooke, B.A.; investment dealer; b. Toronto, Ont. 8 Nov. 1920; s. late Norman Brooke and late Helen Monro (Murray) B.; e. Upper Can. Coll., Toronto, 1929-39; Trinity Coll., Univ. of Toronto, B.A., 1942; m. Cicely Barlow d. Douglas White Ambridge, Toronto, 18 Sept. 1953; children: Patricia Brooke (Mrs. Gary L. Reid), Douglas Ambridge Brooke; VICE-PRES. AND DIR., BELL GOUINLOCK LIMITED, since 1967; Dir., Zurich Life Ins. Co.; Chrmn., Sunnybrook Med. Centre; joined present Co., 1946; apptd. Dir. and Treas., Jan. 1957; served with 48th Highlanders of Can., 1941-45; Zeta Psi; Anglican; Clubs: University; Badminton & Racquet; Home: 215 Lonsdale Rd., Toronto, Ont. M4V 1W7; Office: P.O. Box 110, First Canadian Place, Toronto, Ont. M5X 1B6

BELL, Norman Henry; corporate executive; b. Brantford, Ont., 21 Nov. 1911; s. Frederic Wallace and Mary (Tunnicliffe) B.; e. Brantford (Ont.) Pub. Sch. and Coll. Inst. and Vocational Sch.; Univ. of Toronto (Sch. of Applied Science) 1931-32; Mang. Training, Univ. of W. Ont. 1955; m. Winnifred, d. late Robert James Miller, St. Thomas, Ont., 26 July 1941; one d. Kathryn Joanne; Dir., Euclid Canada

Ltd.; commenced as Sales Rep. in Ont., Geo. Weston Ltd., 1932-38; Gen. Mgr. and Dir. (1955-58) in Brantford Coach and Body Ltd. 1938-58; Pres., White Motor Corp. of Can. Ltd. 1958-76; served in 2nd World War; enlisted in R.C.O.C. as Pte., 1942; remustered to R.C.A.F., Sept. 1943; Navigator's Wing and Pilot Offr., June 1944; posted Overseas Sept. 1944; returned to Can. Jan. 1946 and discharged with rank of Flying Offr.; Hon. Dir., Can. Safety Council; Lambda Chi Alpha; Freemason (Scot. Rite); Anglican; Clubs: Mississaugua Golf & Country; Home: 1560 Stavebank Road, Mississauga, Ont. L5G 2V7;

BELL, (Philip) Michael, M.A.; art administrator; historian; b. Toronto, Ont. 31 Dec. 1942; s. William Harvey and Alice W. (Stone) B.; e. Aurora (Ont.) & Dist. High Sch. 1961; Univ. of Toronto B.A. 1966, M.A. (Fine Arts) 1967; m. Natalie Maria d. Prof. George N. Luckyj 15 Aug. 1977; DIR. & CEO McMICHAEL CANADIAN COLLECTION 1981- ; Teacher, Dr. G. W. Williams Secondary Sch. Aurora, Ont. 1967-68; Hist. Research Offr. and Head, Paintings, Drawings & Prints Sec. Pub. Archives of Can. 1968-73; Dir. Agnes Etherington Art Centre, Kingston, Ont. 1973-78; Visual Arts Offr. Ont. Arts Council Toronto 1978-79; Asst. Dir. Pub. Programs Nat. Gallery Can. 1979-81, Acting Dir. 1981; author "Painters In A New Land" 1973 (Gov. Gen.'s Award Non-Fiction 1974); numerous articles, papers, reviews, exhn. catalogues; mem. Candn. Conf. of Arts; Vice Pres. and Secy.-Treas. Ont. Assn. Art Galleries 1976-78, 1979-80 (Past Chrmn. various comtes.); mem. Candn. Museums Assn.; United Church; Home: 59 Ritchie Ave., Toronto, Ont. M6R 2K1; Office: Kleinburg, Ont. L0J 1C0.

BELL, Hon. Richard Albert, P.C. (Can.), Q.C., B.A.; b. Britannia Heights, Ont. 4 Sept. 1913; s. Wm. Frederick and Mary Ellen (Graham) B.; e. Grant Consol. Sch., Britannia Heights, Ont.; Nepean High Sch., Westboro, Ont.; Univ. of Toronto, Hon. B.A. in Law 1934; Osgoode Hall, Toronto, Grad. 1938; m. late Winifred Osborne, d. R.V. Sinclair, K.C., Ottawa, 24 Dec. 1939; one d., Judith Miriam (Oyen) Q.C.; 2ndly, Ruth M. Rolph, widow of Prof. W.K. Rolph, 4 May 1963; Sr. Partner, Bell and Baker; mem. Ont. Law Reform Commission since 1964; mem. Bd. of Govs., Carleton Univ. since 1974; Bd. of Dirs., Queensway-Carleton Hosp. since 1972, Pres. and Chrmn. of Bd. 1979-81; mem. Adv. Comn. on Parlty. Accommodation 1974-75; Assistant Private Secretary to Minister of National Revenue 1934-35; Assistant Dom. Organizer of Conservative Party, g.e. 1935; Private Secy. to successive Leaders of the Opposition (Hon. R.J. Manion, Hon. R.B. Hanson, Gordon Graydon) 1938-43; Secy. of Nat. Cons. Conv. Comte. 1942, and took charge of Organ. of Conv.; el. Joint Secy., Nat. Cons. Conv. 1942; Secy., P. Cons. Assn. of Can., 1943-44; Nat. Dir., P. Cons. Party of Can., 1943-49; Organ. P. Cons. Nat. Conv., 1948; Chrmn. of Campaign Comte., P. Conservative Party, 1952-53; Jt. Chrmn., P. Cons. Nat. Convention, 1956; Nat. Campaign Chairman, Candn. Cancer Society 1970-72; Pres., Candn. Cancer Soc. Ont. Div. 1974-75, hon. Pres. 1981-; read law with F.B. Matthews, K.C., and C.M. Colquhoun, K.C.; called to the Bar of Ont. 1938; cr. K.C. 1950; Past Pres., Univ. of Toronto Alumni (Ottawa Valley Br.); Past Pres., Co. of Carleton Law Assn.; formerly Dir., Ont. Chamber of Comm.; Ottawa Bd. Trade; el. to H. of C. for Carleton, g.e. 1957, 1958; and apptd. Parlty. Asst. to Min. of Finance, 1957 and Parlty. Secy. to Min. of Finance 1959; re-el. in g.e. June 1962; apptd. Min. of Citizenship & Immigration, 9 Aug. 1962; def. in g.e. Apl. 1963; re-el. in g.e. Nov. 1965; def. in g.e. June 1968; Bencher, Law Soc. of Upper Can., 1956-61; P. Conservative; Anglican; Home: "Fairfields", 3080 Richmond Rd., Nepean K2B 7J5, Ont.; Office: Suite 500, 116 Lisgar St., Ottawa, Ont. K2P 0C2

BELL, Robert E., C.C. (1971), M.A., Ph.D., F.R.S.C., F.R.S., physicist, univ. prof.; b. New Malden, Surrey, Eng. (of Candn. Parents), 29 Nov. 1918; s. Edward Richardson and Edith Emily (Rich) B.; e. Univ. of Brit. Columbia, B.A. (Hons. Math and Physics) 1939, M.A. (Physics) 1941; McGill Univ., Ph.D. (Physics) 1948; D.Sc.: Univ. New Brunswick 1971, U. Laval 1973, U. de Montréal 1976, McMaster U. 1978, U. Brit. Col. 1978, Concordia 1979, McGill 1979, Carleton U. 1980; LL.D. U. of Toronto 1971; D.C.L. Bishop's U. 1976; m. (Lillian) Jeanne, d. G.R. Atkinson, Kemptville, Ont., 5 July 1947; one d. Alison Ann; RUTHERFORD PROF. OF PHYSICS, McGILL UNIV. since 1960; (formerly Principal and Vice Chancellor there, 1970-79; Vice Dean, Physical Sciences, Faculty of Arts & Sciences 1964-67; Dean, Faculty of Grad. Studies & Research 1969-70); Demon. in Physics, Univ. of B.C., 1939-41; Research Physicist on radar devel., Nat. Research Council, Ottawa, 1941-45; joined Atomic Energy Div. at Chalk River, 1946; with Candn. Army Active. 1941-45 (seconded to Nat. Research Council, Ottawa, without army rank or pay); Nat. Research Council Fellow, 1945-46; Pres. Royal Soc. Can. 1978-81; Visitng Scientist, Bohr's Inst. for Theoretical Physics, Copenhagen, 1958-59; Contrib. author, "Alpha, Beta, and Gamma Ray Spectroscopy", 1965; "Annual Review of Nuclear Science", 1954; has publ. over 50 scient. papers on various topics in nuclear physics; mem., Candn. Assn. of Physicists (Pres., 1965-66); Medal for Achievement in Physics, 1968; Fellow Am. Physical Soc.; Sigma Xi; recreations: gardening, reading; Home: 363 Olivier Ave., Montreal, Que. H3Z 2C8

BELL, Robert Gordon, O.C., M.D.; b. St. Mary's, Ont. 11 July 1911; s. Robert and Elizabeth (Oliver) B.; e. St. Mary's Coll. Inst.; Univ. of Toronto M.D.; m. Mary Irene d. Ernest P. Lamping, Ridgeway, Ont. 18 June 1938; children: Ronald Gordon, Janice Marie Hambley, Mary Linda, Mary Elizabeth Plouffe, Brian Joseph; PRES., THE DONWOOD INST. 1960- ; Pres., Glenmaple, Highland Creek 1946-47; Shadow Brook Health Foundation, Willowdale 1948-54; Willowdale Hosp. 1951-54; The Bell Clinic, Willowdale 1954-67; served with R.C.A.M.C. 1942-46, dir. psychol. retraining and rehabilitation centres; rec'd Honour Award, Students' Adm. Council Univ. of Toronto 1930; Citation of Merit, Malvern Inst., Pa. 1958; Centennial Medal 1967; Queen's Silver Jubilee Medal 1977; author "Escape from Addiction" 1970; Officer of Order of Can., 1979; over 20 educational films; over 100 articles for clin. and lay publs.; Hon. Consultant, Am. Assn. Against Addiction; sr. mem. Candn. Med. Assn.; mem. Candan. Psychiatric Assn.; Ont. Med. Assn. (life mem.); recreations: reading, gardening, bridge, travel; Club: Aesculapian; Home: 47 York Rd., Willowdale, Ont. M2L 1H7; Office: 175 Brentcliffe Rd., Toronto, Ont. M4G 3Z1.

BELL, Robert Murray, Q.C., B.A.; insurance executive; b. Aurora, Ont., 11 Sept. 1913; s. Robert Norman and Agnes R.T. (Alexander) B.; e. Univ. of Alta., B.A. 1934; Osgoode Hall Law Sch. 1938; m. Ann Elizabeth, d. Harold C. Walker, Q.C., Toronto, Ont., 5 Nov. 1955; one s., d.; read law with Messrs. Fraser and Beatty; called to the Bar of Ont. 1938; cr. Q.C. 1962; joined Fraser, Beatty, Palmer & Tucker 1938; entered Legal Dept. of Confederation Life Insurance Co. 1946, Extve. Asst. 1953, Gen. Counsel 1957, Vice-Pres. and Gen. Counsel 1961 retired as Vice-Pres., Gen. Counsel and Secy. 1978; Comnd. in Q.O.R. of Can. 1940 serving overseas; later with Candn. Intelligence Corps. in N. Africa, Italy and N.W. Europe; mem. Assn. Life Ins. Counsel; Bd. Trade Metrop. Toronto; Champlain Soc.; Phi Delta Phi; United Church; Clubs: University; Lawyers; Home: 134 Forest Hill Rd., Toronto, Ont. M4V 2L9

BELL, T. Patrick; executive; b. Lemsford, Sask. 1924; e. Univ. of Sask. Coll. of Comm. 1946-48; Banff Sch. Advanced Mang. 1967; m. Willa, June, 1948; 2 children; CHIEF EXTVE. OFFR., FEDERATED CO-OPERATIVES LTD.,CONSUMERS' CO-OPERATIVE REFINERIES LTD., INTERPROVINCIAL LTD. 1979- ; joined Fed.

Govt. 1948-50; Federated Co-operatives Ltd. 1950 holding various positions incl. Auditor, Retail Finance Dir. 1957-62, Finance Dir. 1962, Treas. 1970, Corporate Secy. 1977-79; mem. Bd. Western Co-op Fertilizers; Conf. Bd. Can.; instrumental setting up Canadian Co-operative Resources Co.; served with RCAF Overseas 1943-46; mem. Bd. Trade; Un. Ch. Bd.; recreations: golf, tennis; Office: (P.O. Box 1050) 401 - 22nd Street E., Saskatoon, Sask. S7K 3M9.

BELL, Thomas Johnston, B.Com., LL.D.; company executive; b. Southampton, Ont., 26 June 1914; s. Charles M. and Hazel (Hamilton) B.; e. Ridley Coll., St. Catharines, Ont. (Grad. 1932); Univ. of Toronto, B.Com. 1936, LL.D. 1979; m. Gertrude, d. late George Alexander Harshman, 2 Apl. 1948; two s. and four d.; CHAIRMAN AND DIR., ABITIBI-PRICE INC., since 1967; Dir., Royal Bank of Canada; Canada Cement Co. Ltd.; Simpsons Limited; Fiberglas Canada Limited; Chairman Board of Trustees, Toronto General Hospital, joined Federal Wire & Cable Co. Ltd., Guelph, Ont., 1936; Vice-Pres. 1951; Pres., Fiberglas Canada Inc., Toronto, Ont. 1956-67; served in 2nd World War; 12th Field Regt., R.C.A., 1942-46; awarded M.C.; Lieut.-Col., 11th Field Reg. (Reserve), 1946-52; Conservative; Anglican; recreations: golf, skiing; Clubs: Mount Royal (Montreal); The Toronto; Rosedale Golf; York; Augusta National Golf; Home: 175 Teddington Park, Toronto, Ont. M4N 2C7; Office: Toronto-Dominion Centre, Toronto, Ont.

BELL, Thomas Miller, B.C.L.; barrister; b. Saint John, New Brunswick, 11 Jan. 1923; s. Thomas M. and Edith Berry (Miller) B.; e. Univ. of New Brunswick, B.C.L.; married; four children; el. to H. of C. in g.e. 1953; Asst. to Minister of Trade & Comm., 1957-58; Parlty. Secy. to Minister of Justice, 1959-63; Pres., Young Conservative Party, 1968; apptd. Prov. Court Judge 1974; served in 2nd World War with Merchant Navy; P. Conservative; Anglican; Office: Provincial Building, Saint John, N.B.

BELL, Thomas Reid; textile executive; b. Montreal, Que. 13 June 1923; s. Finlay Turiff and Nora (O'Connor) B.; m. Anne-Marie d. Benjamin Hammond 5 June 1954; children: Stephen, Ian, Brian, Paula, Carole; PRESIDENT, CHIEF EXTVE. OFFR. AND DIR., DOMINION TEXTILE INC. 1977- ; Dir. Royal Trust Co.; Canada Starch Co. Inc.; Swift Textiles Inc. (Ga.); Columbian Chemicals Canada Ltd.; joined Analytical Dept. present Co. 1940, Asst. Gen. Sales Mgr. 1963, Dir. of Marketing 1967, Vice Pres. Marketing 1969, Group Vice Pres. Operations 1970, Extve. Vice Pres. 1973, Pres. and Chief Operating Offr. 1974; served with RCNVR N. Atlantic World War II; Clubs: Mount Royal; Montreal Badminton & Squash; Kanawaki Golf; recreations: golf, skiing; Home: 881 Isle de France Cres., St. Lambert, Que. J4S 1T8; Office: 1950 Sherbrooke St. W., Montreal, Que. H3H 1E7.

BELL, William H.; management consultant; b. Hamilton, Ont., 1 Apl. 1917; s. John Henry and Ellen (Gallagher) B.; e. Hamilton Pub. Schs.; Mimico High Sch.; Business Adm. Courses; m. Ella Tyler, 14 Sept. 1940; children: Margaret, Terry, Judith, William Jr.; PRESIDENT W.H. BELL & ASSOCIATES; commenced in Math. and Marketing Depts., Sun Life Assnce. Co., 1937-48; sales and marketing positions leading to Vice-Pres., Marketing, Royal Typewriter Co. Ltd., 1946-60; Pres. Victor Comptometer Limited 1960-72; Vice-Pres. Marketing Interroyal Corporation Ltd. 1972-74; Dir. Cello Products Inc.; Mem. and Dir. Cambridge Red Cross; Dir. South Waterloo Memorial Hospital (Vice-Chrmn. 1977-78); Mem. and Group Comm. Chrmn. Boy Scouts of Canada Waterloo Region; served with R.C.A.F., attached to R.A.F. Coastal Command, 1942-45; Candn. Business Equipment Mfrs.' Assn. (Pres. 1966-67); recreations: golf, curling, fishing, photography; Club: Galt Country; Home: 40 Lansdowne Road South, Cambridge, Ont. N1S 2T3

BELLEAU, Bernard R., M.Sc., Ph.D., D.Sc., LL.D., F.C.I.C., F.R.S.C., O.O.C.; educator; b. Montreal, Que. 15 March 1925; s. Roland and Marguerite (Croteau) B.; e. Univ. of Montreal B.Sc. 1947, M.Sc. 1948; McGill Univ. Ph.D. 1950; Dalhousie Univ. LL.D. 1978; m. Pierrette d. late Jean-Marie Lavoi 28 Nov. 1950; children: Marc, François, Francine; PROF. OF CHEMISTRY, McGILL UNIV. since 1971; Consulting Dir. of Research, Bristol Laboratories of Canada; Research Asst. Sloan Kettering Inst. for Cancer Research 1950-52; Postdoctoral Fellow, Case Inst. of Technol. 1953; Research Assoc. Reed and Carnick, Jersey City 1954-55; Asst. prof. of Biochem. Laval Univ. 1955-58; Assoc. Prof. Univ. of Ottawa 1958, Prof. of Biochem. 1961, Vice Dean for Research, Faculty of Science & Engn. 1969-70; mem. Comité de Direction du Centre d'Etudes et de Recherches de Chimie Organique Appliquée CNRS Paris; conceived and developed non-narcotic analgetics and synthetic antibiotics; Rennebohm Lectr. Univ. of Wis. 1975-76; Centennial Lectr. Am. Chem. Soc. N.Y. 1976; Léo Marion Lectr. Nat. Research Council 1978; rec'd Prix de la Prov. de Qué. 1956; Merck, Sharp and Dohme Award 1961; Centennial Medal 1967; Parizeau Medal Candn. Assn. Advanc. Science 1970; Am. Chem. Soc. Award in Medicinal Chem. 1976; Izaak Walton Killam Mem. Scholarship 1977-79; Prix Marie-Victorin 1978; McLaughlin Medal. Roy. Soc. Can. 1979; Chem. Inst. Can. Medal 1979; former Chrmn. Adv. Comte. for Chem. Research, Defence Research Bd. Can.; former Ed. "Life Sciences"; mem. or former mem. various ed. bds.; author over 125 refereed scient. publs. dealing with drug action, medicinal chem., molecular pharmacol.; mem. Am. Chem. Soc.; N.Y. Acad. Sciences; 541 Victoria Ave., Office: 801 Sherbrooke St. W., Montreal, Que. H3A 2K6.

BELLEMARE, Raymond, R.C.A.; graphic designer; b. Nicolet, Que. 25 Jan. 1942; s. Jean-Baptiste and Rita (Dubuc) B.; e. primary sch. Nicolet, Que. 1954; Coll. l'Assomption, Que. classical course 1958; Montreal Sch. of Fine Arts grad. Graphic Design 1962; PRES., RAYMOND BELLEMARE DESIGNERS INC.; Partner, Bellemare, De Passille & Associes Inc.; Dir. Graphic Design Dept. Olympic Comte. 1976; Design Consultant, CBC; awards: Packaging Assn. Can. 1962; Graphica Club of Montreal 1966, 1969; Soc. Graphic Designers Can. 1968, 1970; Communication Arts Mag. USA 1970, 1973, 1977; Deco Press Italy 1974; Design Canada 1975; Arts. Dirs.' Club N.Y. 1977; VII Miedzynarodowe Biennale Plakatu, Warsawa 1978; corporate image designs, Candn. postage stamps, posters, signalling, printed material; mem., Royal Cdn. Academy of Arts; Am. Inst. Graphic Arts; Soc. des Graphistes du Qué.; R. Catholic; recreations: farming, hunting, cycling, fishing, travel, sailing; Home: Office: 28 St. Paul St. East Montreal, Que. H2Y 1G3.

BELL-IRVING, Hon. Henry Pybus, D.S.O., O.B.E., D.Sc.M., E.D., C.D.; b. Vancouver, B.C. 21 Jan. 1913; s. Henry Beattie and Annie Hilda (Pybus) B-I; e. Shawnigan Lake Prep. Sch. Vancouver Is. 1927; Loretto Sch. Musselburgh, Scot. 1930; Univ. of B.C. 1931; m. Nancy Isobel d. Reginald Symes 8 Apl. 1937; three s. Henry Symes, Roderick, Donald Reginald; Lieut. Seaforth of C., N.P.A.M., 1933-39; C.A.S.F., 1939-45, U.K., Sicily, Italy, N.W. Europe. Commanded in turn, Canadian O.C.T.U., Battle School, in U.K., Loyal Edmonton Regt., Seaforth of C. in Italy, 10 Cdn. Inf. Bde. in N.W. Europe promoted Lt. to Brig., awarded D.S.O. and bar, O.B.E., m.i.d.x2; Post War: Honorary Colonel Seaforth Highlanders of Canada; Chrmn. and Pres. Bell-Irving Realty Ltd. 1948-72; Chrmn. and Pres. A. E. LePage Western Ltd.; Dir. A. E. LePage Toronto; Boy Scouts: Akela, Dist. Commr, Vice-Pres. B.C. and Yukon 1949-; Chrmn. B.C. Real Estate Agents Licencing Bd. 1954-58; Gov. rep. on Board of Vancouver Children's Hospital 1962-78; B.C. Corps Commissionaires C.O. 1967-71, Trustee 1971-78; Pres. Vancr. Real Estate Bd. 1958; Cdn. Real Estate Assn. 1972; a founding Fellow, Cdn. Inst. of Realtors (F.R.I.); accredited appraiser, Cdn. and U.S. Institutes, (A.A.C.I.,

M.A.I.); Vancouver Board of Trade Council 1965—President, 1974; Sworn in as Lt. Gov. of British Columbia 18 May 1978; K.St.J.; Anglican; recreations: boating, fishing, shooting; Clubs: Vancouver; Vancr. Lawn Tennis and Badminton; Address: Government House, Victoria, B.C. V8S 1V9

BELSHAW, Cyril Shirley, M.A., Ph.D., F.R.S.C.; anthropologist; educator; b. N.Z. 3 Dec. 1921; s. Prof. Horace Belshaw; e. Auckland Grammar Sch.; Auckland Univ. Coll., Univ. of N.Z. M.A. 1945; London Sch. of Econ. Ph.D. 1949; m. (late) Betty Joy Sweetman; children: Diana Marion, Adrian William; PROF. OF ANTHROP. UNIV. OF B.C., Head of Anthrop. 1968-74, mem. Senate 1963-72 and 1975-78, Secy. Faculty Assn. 1957-58, Extve. 1959-64, Pres. 1960-61; mem. Extve., Internat. Social Science Council 1973-77, Vice Pres, 1976-77; mem. Extve. Social Science Research Council of Can. 1968-71, Vice Pres. 1970-72; Del. to Assembly, Internat. Council Philos. & Humanistic Studies 1977 and 1979; Candn. Del. UNESCO Gen. Conf. 1972, 1974; Extve., Candn. Comn. UNESCO 1971-72, Mem.-at-Large since 1973; Consultant variously to UNESCO, UN Bureau of Social Affairs, UN ECOSOC, OECD; Dir. UN Training Centre Vancouver 1961-62; mem. UN ECOSOC Mission Thailand 1965; Colonial Service, Brit. Solomon Islands 1943-46; field work in Solomon Islands, New Caledonia, New Hebrides, New Guinea, Fiji, B.C., Thailand, Switzerland; mem. Acad. Bd. for Higher Educ. B.C. 1971-72; Emslie Horniman Scholar 1947-49; Sr. Scholar in Econ. Univ. N.Z. 1942; John Simon Guggenheim Fellow 1965-66; Hon. Life Fellow, Royal Anthropological Inst.; Lon. Life fellow, Assoc. of Soc. Anthropologists in Oceania; Lon. Life mem., Pacific Sci. Assoc.; author "Island Administration in the South West Pacific" 1950; "Changing Melanesia" 1954; "In Search of Wealth" 1955; "The Great Village" 1957; "Under the Ivi Tree" 1964; "Anatomy of a University" 1964; "Traditional Exchange and Modern Markets" 1965; "Comercio Tradicional y mercados modernos" 1973; "The Conditions of Social Performance" 1970; "Towers Besieged: The Dilemma of the Creative University" 1974; "The Sorcerer's Apprentice: An Anthropology of Public Policy" 1976; co-author "The Indians of British Columbia" 1958; various articles and reports; Ed. "Current Anthropology" since 1974; Pres., Internat. Union of Anthropological and Ethnological Sciences 1978-83; Pres., XIth Internat. Congress of Anthropological and Ethnological Sci. 1983; Pres., XLIII Internat. Congress. of Americanists, 1979; Extve. Am. Anthrop. Assn. 1969-71; Pres., Educational Foundation for Anthropology and the Public 1981-; Founding mem. Candn. Univ. Service Overseas. Internat. Assn. Scient. Eds' Assn. (Extve. 1978), Internat. Assn. Anthrop. Eds.; mem. Internat. Union Anthrop. & Ethnol. Sciences (Extve. Ch. Finance & Ch. Projects); Pacific Science Assn. (Candn. Nat. Comte., Chrmn. Social Sciences & Humanities 1968-77); Fellow, Explorers Club, N.Y.; Club: University; Home: 5749 Chancellor Blvd., Vancouver, B.C. V6T 1E4; Office: 6303 N.W. Marine Dr., UBC Campus, Vancouver, B.C. V6T 2B2.

BELTON, Edward F. "Ted"; association and insurance executive; b. Toronto, Ont. 4 March 1931; s. Francis S. and Margaret A. (Malone) B.; e. De La Salle Coll. "Oaklands" Toronto 1949; m. Joan Marie, d. Albert Drury 23 Oct. 1954; children: Kelly-Ann, Gregory Scott, Lisa Marie, Edward Patrick; PRES. AND CHIEF EXTVE. OFFR., INSURERS' ADVISORY ORGAN. OF CAN. since 1974; joined Halifax Insurance Co. Toronto 1949 serving in Fire, Casualty, Auto. and Claims Depts.; Toronto Field Rep. 1953; Field Rep. Federation Insurance Co. 1956, Service Office Supv. Windsor, Ont. 1956, Ont. Br. Casualty Supv. 1958; Casualty Mgr. for Can., Halifax Insurance Co. 1959, Chief Underwriter 1960, Supt. of Brs. 1962, Mgr. W. and E. Divs. 1964, Vice-Pres. Marketing 1972; Mgr. for Can. Safeco Insurance Cos. 1973; mem. Ins. Inst. of Ont.; Inst. Assn. Extves.; Planning Executive

Inst.; Adv. Bd., Brebeuf Coll.; The Presidents Assoc.; Clubs: National (Toronto); Bd. Trade Metrop. Toronto; recreations: sailing, reading, tennis; Home: 5 Creekside Rd., Willowdale, Ont. M2M 3R5; Office: 180 Dundas St. W., Toronto, Ont. M5G 1Z9

BELYEA, Helen R., O.C. (1976), Ph.D., F.R.S.C., LL.D., D.Sc.; geologist; b. Saint John, N.B., 11 Feb. 1913; d. Arthur Sefton and Eleanor Fraser (Reynolds) B.; e. Dalhousie Univ. B.A. 1934, M.A. 1936, LL.D. 1977; Northwestern Univ. Ph.D. 1939; Univ. of Windsor D.Sc. 1976; geol. lab. asst. and science teacher private schs. 1940-43; Technol. Geol. Survey of Can., 1945, Tech. Offr. 1946, Geol. 1947, Geol. (Calgary) 1950, Sr. Geol. (Calgary) 1960-74; served with WRCNS 1943-45, rank Lt. (SB); cochrmn. First Internat. Symposium on Devonian System, Calgary 1967; lectr. on Devonian of W. Can. univs. and geol. soc's France; rec'd Barlow Award Medal 1959; Alberta Achievement Award 1976; author over 30 publs.; mem. Calgary Philharmonic Women's League Comte. for Independent Can.; Hon. mem., Candn. Soc. Petroleum Geols. Geol. Assn. Can.; Internat. Assn. Sedimentols.; Soc. Econ. Paleontols. & Mineralogs.; Calgary Region Arts Foundation; Trustee, Calgary Zoolog. Soc.; mem., Glenbow Alta. Inst.; Alpha Gamma Delta; recreations: skiing, hiking, gardening, swimming; badminton, concerts, lectures; Clubs: Calgary Golf & Country (lady elect.); Glencoe; Home: 230 21st Ave. S.W. Apt. 14, Calgary, Alta. T2S 0G6

BELZBERG, Samuel, B.Com.; financial executive; b. Calgary, Alta., 26 June 1928; e. Cliff Bungalow Pub. Sch., Rideau Park Jr. High and Central High Sch., Calgary; Univ. of Alta., B.Com. 1948; m. Frances, d. late David Cooper, Los Angeles, Cal., 8 Oct. 1950; PRESIDENT, FIRST CITY FINANCIAL CORP. LTD.:Chmn., Yeshiva Univ. of Los Angeles; founder, Dystonia Medical Research Foundation and Simon Wiesenthal Center for Holocaust Studies; mem., Univ. Council of B.C.; recreations: golf, tennis; Clubs: Richmond Golf & Country; Vancouver Lawn Tennis and Badminton; Royal Vancouver Yacht; Office: 777 Hornby St., Vancouver, B.C.

BELZILE, Hervé, B.A., M.Com., C.A., Dr. Com.Sc.; insurance executive; e. Rimouski (Que.) Semy. B.A. 1943; Univ. of Montreal M.Com. 1955, Dr.Com.Sc. 1970; C.A. 1948; Harvard Business Sch. AMP 1959; CHRMN. AND CHIEF EXTVE. OFFR., ALLIANCE MUTUAL LIFE INSURANCE CO.; Dir. Alliance mutuelle-vie; National Bank of Canada; Québec-Téléphone; General Foods; Inglis Ltd.; Prof., Ecole des Hautes Etudes Commerciales 1945-52; joined present co. as Controller 1952, Secy. 1955, Mang. Dir. and mem. Bd. 1957, mem. Extve. Comte. 1962, Pres. 1963; Dir. Opéra de Montréal; Univ. de Moncton; Clubs: Saint-Denis; Cercle Universitaire de Qué.; Laval-sur-le-Lac; Home: 157 Dobie Ave., Town of Mount Royal, Qué. H3P 1S3; Office: 680 Sherbrooke St. W., Montréal, Qué. H3A 2S6.

BEMBRIDGE, William Edward, B.Sc.; executive; b. Montreal, Que. 2 Nov. 1928; s. Albert Edwin and Elizabeth (Nixon) B.; e. High Sch. of Montreal 1946; McGill Univ. B.Sc. 1950; children: Douglas Neil, Wendy Ellen; PRES., MERCK FROSST LABS. since 1978; Production Supvr. Merck & Co. Ltd. 1950; Extve. Vice Pres., Merck Frost Labs, 1973; Pres. Merck Sharp & Dohme 1975; past Chrmn. Pharm. Mfrs. Assn. Can.; Dir., Royal Victoria Hospital, M.H.; Protestant; recreation: sports; Clubs: Royal St. Lawrence Yacht; Office: P.O. Box 1005, Pointe-Claire-Dorval, Que. H9R 4P8

BENCOSME, Sergio Arturo, M.D., M.Sc., Ph.D.; educator; b. Monte Cristy, Dominican Republic, 27 Apl. 1920; s. Sergio and Rosalba (Ruiz) B.; e. Escuela Normal Superior, Santo Domingo, B.Sc. 1938; Univ. of Montreal, M.D. 1947; McGill Univ. M.Sc. 1948, Ph.D. 1950; m. Bertha Josephina, d. late José Rojas, 31 May 1947; children: Rosanna Margarita, Yolanda Ivonne, Violetta Josefina, Rolando Sergio, Humberto Cirilo; Prof. of Pathology, Queen's Univ. 1965; Pathol., Kingston (Ont.) Gen. Hosp. since 1959; Dir., Inst. Biomed. Studies, Santo Domingo; internship Santo Domingo and Montreal, Que. 1942-51; Research Fellow in Pathol., Douglas Fellow, Grad. Med. Research Fellow, McGill Univ. 1947-50; Asst. Pathol. Ottawa Gen. Hosp. 1951-53; Pathol. Kingston Gen. Hosp. 1953-57; Acting Dir. Hotel Dieu Hosp., Kingston, 1957; Asst. Prof. of Pathol. Univ. of Ottawa 1951-53; joined present Univ. as Assoc. Prof. 1953-57, 1959-65; Asst. Pathol. Univ. of Calif. Los Angeles 1957-59, Visiting Lectr. in Anat. there 1956; Consultant to Hitachi Corp. 1959-65; Prof. Faculty of Med. Universidad Nacional Pedro Henriquez Urena, Santo Domingo; Advisor, Dominican Republic Min. Pub. Health for Research & Med. Educ.; Faculty of Med. Universidad Catolica Madre y Maestra Santiago; Armed Forces Med. Corps for Research & Med. Educ.; estbd. modern technol. for identifying pancreatic islet cells 1949; rec'd. Medal of Duarte Sanchez y Mella 1974; author or co-author over 150 scient. publs. and 5 maj. monographs; Ed. Council Mexican Journal of Pathologia; Ed. Bd. Laboratory Investigation; Ed. Adv. Bd. Microstructures; mem. various scient. assns. incl.: Biol. Soc. Montreal; Ont. Assn. Pathols.; Candn. Assn. Pathols.; Am. Assn. Anats.; Candn. Physiol. Soc.; Internat. Acad. Pathol.; Am. Assn. Pathols. & Bacteriols.; Am. Assn. Exper. Pathol.; Electron Microscope Soc. Am.; Pathol. Soc. Gt. Brit. & Ireland; Soc. Exper. Biol. & Med. (Council, Champlain Chapter); Nat. Acad. Science Dominican Repub. (Dir.); R. Catholic; recreations: riding, bicycling, chess, photography, dancing, piano; Clubs: Royal Mil.; Rotary Internat. Santo Domingo (Hon. mem.); Rotary Moca (1st Hon. mem.); Home: 71 Avenida Juan Pablo Duarte, Santiago, Dominican Republic

BENETEAU, Basil A., B.Sc.; b. Windsor, Ont., 28 Aug. 1925; e. Holy Rosary Sch., Toronto, Ont., 1935; Univ. of Ottawa High Sch., 1941; Ottawa Tech. Sch., 1942; Queen's Univ. B.Sc. (Elect. Engn.) 1948; PRESIDENT AND DIR., NORTHERN TELECOM CANADA LIMITED; Dir. Bell-Northern Research Ltd.; Northern Telecom Inc.; ABN Bank Can. (Chrmn.); mem., Export Trade Development Bd.; Chrmn., Can. - Korea Bus. Council; recreations: fishing, winter sports, hunting; Office: Ste. 900, 304 The East Mall, Islington, Ont. M9B 6E4

BENHAM, Hugh Avery, LL.D.; executive; b. Winnipeg, Man., 18 May 1911 s. Alfred William and Grace Moreton (Harvey) B.; e. Winnipeg Pub. Schs. and Kelvin High Sch.; m. Mary Lile, d. William Donald Love, 16 Oct. 1935; chil.: Patricia Joan, Hugh John, William Drewry, Donald Bruce; Dir., Tees and Persse Ltd.; Investors Mutual of Can. Ltd.; Investors Growth Fund of Can.; Investors Internat. Mutual Fund; Provident Stock Fund; Trustee, Canada Permanent Income Investments; The Mercantile Bank of Canada; Bird Construction Ltd.; Citadel Life Ass. Co.; Citadel Gen. Assur. Co.; Winterthur Canada Financial Corp.; Chmn. McDonald Grain Co. Ltd.; with McCabe Grain Co. Ltd., 1931-40; Depy. Chrmn., Payroll Savings Div., Nat. War Finance Comte. (Manitoba) 1941-43; joined Staff of Royal Securities Corp. Ltd., 1945 and apptd. Mgr. at Winnipeg 1948; appt. Chief of the Securities Dept., Bank of Canada, 1953; formerly Chrmn., Man. Civil Service Superannuation Bd.; Vice-Pres. of Invest. Dealers Assn. of Can., 1952-53; Winnipeg Chamber Comm., 1963; formerly Trustee, City of Winnipeg Sinking Fund; Chrmn. Finance, Vanier Inst. of the Family, Anglican; Home: 249 Waverley St., Winnipeg, Man. R3M 3K4; Office: 600-360 Broadway, Winnipeg, Man.

BENHAM, Mary Lile, B.A.; writer; b. Winnipeg, Man. 8 Oct. 1914; d. Wm. Donald Love and Laura Augusta (Drewry); e. Univ. of Manitoba B.A. 1935; m. Hugh Avery Benham 16 Oct. 1935; children: Patricia Joan (Porth), Hugh John, Wm. Drewry, Donald Bruce; served with

P.R. Div., Natl. War Finance Cmte. 1943-45; performed freelance radio work; co-author of "Winnipeg", 1974; author of "Manitoba Club 1874-1974," 1974; "Nellie McClung," 1975, "Paul Kane," 1977, "La Verendrye," 1980; other writings incl. puppet plays, articles, book reviews, and poems publ. in several popular magazines; Bd. of Dir., Candn. Writers Foundation; mem., Writers' Union of Can.; Candn. Authors Assn.; Candn. Soc. of Children's Authors, Illustrators and Performers; Penhandlers; GammaPhi Beta; Club: Jr. League; recreations: swimming, painting, tennis; Home/Office: 249 Waverley St., Winnipeg, Man. R3M 3K4.

BENIDICKSON, Hon. William Moore, P.C. (Can); senator; barrister; of Icelandic descent; b. Dauphin, Man., 8 Apl. 1911; s. Christian and Gertrude May (Moore) B.; e. Dauphin. Man. Pub. Schs.; Humberside Coll. Inst., Toronto; Kelvin High Sch., Winnipeg; Univ. of Man.; m. Agnes McCausland, d. late James A. Richardson, Winnipeg, Man.; three children; called to the Bar of Man. 1936; Ont. 1937; served in 2nd World War with R.C.A.F., rank of Wing Commdr.; 1st el. to H. of C. for Kenora-Rainy River, g.e. 1945; Parlty. Asst. to the Min. of Transport, 1951-53, to the Min. of Finance, 1953-57; Min. of Mines & Tech. Surveys 1963; summoned to Senate of Can., 1965; Hon. Solr., Kenora Trades & Labour Council; Phi Delta Theta; Hon. Life mem. Kenora (Ont.) Royal Can. Leg.; Knight of the Order of the Falcon (Iceland); Freemason; Liberal-Labour; United Church; Club: Manitoba (Winnipeg); Home: Kenora, Ont.; Office: The Senate, Ottawa, Ont. K1A 0A4

BENNETT, Hon. Claude Frederick, M.P.P. politician; b. Ottawa, Ont. 19 Sept. 1936; e. Ottawa, Ont.; m. Deborah; children: Natalie, Claude Winston;MIN. OF MUN. AFFAIRS AND HOUSING, ONT.1981; el. Ald. Ottawa City Council 1961; re-el. 1963, 1965, 1967; mem. first Ottawa-Carleton Regional Govt. 1968-70; el. to Ottawa Bd. of Control 1970 serving as Sr. Controller and Acting Mayor; mem. Extve. of Ottawa-Carleton Regional Council 1970 and Chrmn. Ottawa Planning Bd.; el. M.P.P. for Ottawa S. 1971 and apptd. Parltv. Asst. to Min. of Treasury, Econ. & Intergovernmental Affairs; Min. Without Portfolio 1972; Min. of Industry & Tourism 1973; Min. of Housing 1978; as an independent ins. agt. rec'd Three Outstanding Young Men Award, Ont. Jr. Chamber of Comm. 1968; Dir. Central Can. Exhn. Assn.; Trustee, Grace Hosp. Ottawa; part-owner London Knights Hockey Club; voted Man of the Yr. by Ottawa Shrine Club 1980; Office: Parliament Bldgs., Queen's Park, Toronto, Ont. M7A 1A1.

BENNETT, Colin E., Q.C.; executive; b. Meaford, Ont., 5 March 1908; s. Thomas Emerson and Ellen Haggart (Stewart) B.; e. Univ. of Toronto (Pol. Econ.), 1931; Osgoode Hall, 1936; m. late Mary Dorothy, d. Franklyn H. Tindale, 16 April 1938; children: Cynthia, Laurence, Mary Ellen; 2ndly Fern Eleda Butchart, d. Jasper A. Stuart, 28 Aug. 1965; VICE-CHRMN. OF BOARD, VICTORIA & GREY TRUST CO.; Pres. and C.E.O. Victoria and Grey Trust Co. 1974-78; called to Bar of Ont., 1936; Dir.: Casualty Co. of Canada, Dom. of Can. General Insur. Co., Empire Life Insur. Co., E-L Financial Corp. Ltd.; Judge, Co. Court of Grey 1957, Chief Judge, Ont. Co. and Dist. Courts 1969-73; served in 2nd World War 1941-45 with R.C.A.F., retiring as Group Cap.; 1st el. to H. of C. for Grey N., g.e. 1949; re-el. g.e. 1953; Party Asst. to Minister of Veterans' Affairs, 1953-57; First Chrmn. Criminal Injuries Compensation Board 1968-71; Dir., John Howard Soc. of Ont.; Freemason; United Church; recreations: curling, golf; Address: Apt. 201, 2 Clarendon Ave., Toronto, Ont. M4V 1H9

BENNETT, Donald George; executive; b. Ottawa, Ont. 6 Jan. 1925; s. George C. and Margaret (Stewart) B.; e. Ottawa (Ont.) Tech. High Sch. 1943; Humber Coll. Mang. Studies; m. Mabel Iris d. late Walter Fitzpatrick 22 June

1948; children: Diane J. (Mrs. Michael Cook), Douglas D., David J.; PRES. AND DIR. HOUSEHOLD FINANCE CORP. OF CANADA; Dir. Household Realty Corp.; Merchant Retail Services Ltd.; Lend Lease Transportation Co. Ltd.; served with present co. 32 yrs.; served with RCAF 1943-45, pilot; mem. Assn. Candn. Financial Corps.; Bd. Trade Metrop. Toronto; United Church; recreations: golf, squash, sports; Clubs: R.C.Y.C.; Markland Wood Country; Home: 1927 Pagehurst Court, Mississauga, Ont. L4X 1Y8; Office: 85 Bloor St. E., Toronto, Ont. M4W 1B4.

BENNETT, Hon. Gordon Lockhart, M.Sc., D.C.L. L.L.D.; b. Charlottetown, P.E.I. 10 Oct. 1912; s. J. Garfield and Annie (Lockhart) B.; e. Elem. Schs. Charlottetown, P.E.I.; Prince of Wales Coll.; Acadia Univ. B.Sc. 1937, M.Sc. (Chem.) 1947, D.C.L. 1976; m. Doris L., d. H. Bruce Bernard 10 Aug. 1937; one d. F. Diane (Mrs. David Campbell); LIEUTENANT GOVERNOR, PROV. OF PRINCE EDWARD ISLAND 1974-80; Teacher (elem., secondary and univ.) 1939-66; el. to Prov. Leg. P.E.I. 1966, re-el. 1970, 1974; Pres. Extve. Council 1966-74, Min. of Educ. 1966-72, Min. of Justice and Attorney Gen. 1970-74; Prov. Secy. 1970-74; Candn. Del. to UNESCO, Paris 1972, to Commonwealth Parlty. Assn., Sri Lanka 1974; Hon. Recording Secretary, Can. Bible Soc.; Pres., P.E.I. Br., Council for Can. Unity; Mason (PGM); Liberal; United Church; recreations: gardening, golf, curling (Past Pres. Dom. Curling Assn.); Address: 14 Charlotte Dr., Box 1123, Charlottetown, P.E.I. C1A 2N5

BENNETT, Harry; insurance executive; b. Staten Isld., N.Y., 14 Jan. 1923; s. William and Annie (Thomson) B.; e. William Penn Charter Sch., 1940; Univ. of Penna., grad. 1947; m. Carol, 8 May 1954; PRESIDENT, OSBORN & LANGE, INC.; Pres. Osborn and Lange (U.S.A.) Inc.; with Fire Assn. of Philadelphia, 1947-49; Ocean Marine Ins. Co., London, Eng., 1949-50; L. Hammond & Co., 1950-51; F.B. Hall & Co., N.Y., 1951-52; Osborn & Lange (U.S.A.), Inc., 1952-54; mem. of Corp., Bishop's University; served during 2nd World War with U.S.N.R.; discharged with rank of Lieut.; Dir., Mariners House of Montreal; mem., Candn. Comte. of Lloyds Register of Shipping; Candn. Maritime Law Assn.; mem. Psi Upsilon; recreations: golf, travel; Clubs: St. James's; Royal and Ancient Golf Club of St. Andrews; Pine Valley Golf (New Jersey); Mt. Bruno Country; National (Toronto); Cercle De La Place D'Armes; Whitehall (N.Y.); Home: 30 Holton Ave., Westmount, Que. H3Y 2E8; Office: 759 Victoria Square, Montreal, Que. H2Y 2K5

BENNETT, Brig.-Gen. Robert Taylor, O.B.E. 1945, C.D., O.St.J. 1970, B.A.; Canadian Forces (retired), b. Ottawa, Ont., 15 July 1918; s. late Charles Herbert and Winnifred Gwendolyn Alice (Dawson) B.; e. Glebe Coll. Inst., Ottawa, 1935; Royal Mil. Coll., Hon. grad. 1939; Royal Mil. Coll. of Science, 1940 (I.O.O.); Candn. Army Staff Coll. 1943 (psc); U.S. Command & Gen. Staff Coll. 1945; NATO Defence Coll. 1952 (NADC); Nat. Defence Coll. 1962 (NDC); Univ. of Man., B.A. 1979; m. Evelyn Mary, d. late Harry Albert Underwood, 18 Dec. 1947; three s., Geoffrey Taylor, Robert George, Richard James; overseas, 2nd and 5th Divs., 1st & 2nd Candn. Corps, 1st Candn. Army, CMHQ and Pacific Force World War II; Lt. 1939; Capt. 1940; Maj. 1941; Lt. Col. 1943 (youngest in Candn. Army); Col. 1953; Brig. Gen. 1971; Mentioned in Despatches; Instr., Army Staff Coll., Kingston, 1946-50; Army HQ, QMG Br., Ottawa, 1950-51; SHAPE, Paris, 1952-53; Mil. Asst. to Secy. Gen., NATO HQ, 1953-56; Chief of Staff, Central Command, Oakville, 1956-58; Garrison Commdr., Longue Pointe, Montreal, 1958-61; Internat. Control Comn., Indo-China, 1961-62; Dir. Ordnance Services, AHQ/CFHQ, Ottawa, 1963-67; Dir. of Organ., CFHQ, 1967-71; Sr. Candn. Mil. Offr. Indo-China and Sr. Mil. Adviser and acting Commissioner, Internat. Control Comn., Viet-Nam, 1971-72; Dir.-Gen. Restructuring CFHQ 1973; retired 1974; man. cons., E.A.C. Amy and

Sons, Ltd. Ottawa since 1974; Commandant, Can. Army Bisbey Cadet Rifle Team 1966-69; mem. Que. and Federal Dists. Councils St. John of Jerusalem; Ottawa Diocesan Extve. Comte., 1975-7; Pres. Nat. Supply Comte., Boy Scouts of Can.; mem. Boy Scout Gen. Council, 1980; Pres., Can. Youth Publications 1981; Fisher Park Adv. Comte.; Secy.-Treas., Un. World Coll. (Candn. Comte.); Mil. Lay Del. Gen. Synod 1959, 1969; Delegate to Ottawa Anglican Synod 1965-70, 1972-77; Extve. Comte. Gen. Council Royal Mil. College Club Can., 1968-71; Pres. RMC Club of Can. (Ottawa branch) 1978; Hon. ADC to Gov. Gen. of Can. 1959-61; Assoc., Brit. Inst. Mang.; mem., Brit. Commonwealth Soc.; Anglican; recreations: curling, skiing, golf, gardening; Club: Pathfinders' (UK); Amberwood Golf and Country; Home: 20 Kittansett Court, Amberwood Village, Stittsville, Ont. K0A 3G0

BENNETT, Roy Frederick, F.C.A.; industrialist; b. Winnipeg, Manitoba, 18 March 1928; s. Charles William and Gladys Mabel (Matthews) B.; e. N. Toronto Coll. Inst.; Inst. Chart. Accts. Ont., F.C.A. 1953; children: Bruce Roy, Brenda Laurie, Lynne Susan; remarried Aug. 26, 1978 to Dr. Gail C.A. Cook; DIR. AND FORMER CHRMN., FORD MOTOR CO. OF CANADA LTD.; mem. Policy Comm., Business Council on National Issues; Premier's Advisory Comm. on Ontario's Econ. Future; Bd. of Govs., York Univ.; Canadian-American Committee; Niagara Institute; Protestant; recreations: golf, squash, tennis, skiing; Clubs: Mississauga Golf & Country; Toronto; Office: The Canadian Road, Oakville, Ont. L6J 5E4

BENNETT, Victor Robert, B.Com., LL.B.; transportation executive; b. St. John's Nfld., 13 Dec. 1928; s. Victor Sydney and Winefride Mary (Browne) B.; e. Bishop's Coll. Sch., Lennoxville, Que., 1946; McGill Univ. B.Com. 1951; Univ. of B.C. LL.B. 1955; m. Constance, d. Arthur Cyr, 4 June 1955; two s., four d.; PRESIDENT INNOTECH AVIATION LTD.; Secy., Timmins Aviation Ltd., 1956-59; Gen. Mgr. 1960-64; Vice Pres. 1965-66; served with RCAF (R) as Pilot 1947-59; rank Flight Lt.; R. Catholic; recreations: skiing, fishing; Clubs: Laurentian; Royal St. Lawrence Yacht; Home: 38 Watterson Rd., Baie D'Urfe, Que. H9X 3C6; Office: Montreal Int. Airport, Dorval, Que.

BENNETT, William John, O.B.E., LL.D.; consultant; b. Schreiber, Ont., 3 Nov. 1911; s. Carl Edward and Mary Agnes (Downey) B.; e. Schreiber (Ont.) Pub. Sch.; Fort William (Ont.) Coll. Inst.; Univ. of Toronto, B.A. (Hons.) 1934, LL.D. 1955; m. Elizabeth Josephine, d. John Palleck, Fort William, Ont., 12 Nov. 1936; children: Paul, Mary Sue, Ann, John, Barbara, Kristin & Hilary; consultant, the Iron Ore Co. of Canada; Chmn. of the Bd., Philips Canada Ltd.; Dir., Investors Group; Eldorado Nuclear Limited; Canadian Reynolds Metals Company Ltd.; Canadian Pacific Limited; Canron Limited; Cominco Limited; Peterson, Howell and Heather Can. Inc., Chmn. C.D. Howe Inst.; Private Secretary to Minister of Transport 1935-39; Chief Exec. Asst. Min. of Mun. & Supply 1939-46; Vice-Pres. and Gen. Mgr., Eldorado Mining & Refining Ltd. 1946, and Pres. and Mang. Dir., 1947 till 1958; Pres., Atomic Energy of Canada Ltd. 1953-58; Canadian British Aluminum Co. Ltd. 1958-60; Vice-Pres. and Dir., The Iron Ore Co. of Can. 1960-65; Pres. of that comp. 1965-77 (ret.); Roman Catholic; Club: Mount Royal; Home: Apt. F-41, Chateau Apts., 1321 Sherbrooke St. W., Montreal, Que. H3G 1J4; Office: Ste. 1650, 1245 Sherbrooke St. W., Montreal, Que. H3G 1G8

BENNETT, Hon. William Richards; politician; b. Kelowna, B.C., 14 Apr. 1932; s. Hon. William Andrew Cecil (former Premier of B.C.) and Annie Elizabeth May (Richards) B.; e. Kelowna (B.C.) Pub. Schs.; m. Audrey Lyne d. Percival George James, Vesuvius Bay, B.C., 16 Apl. 1955; children: Bradford, Kevin, Stephen, Gregory; PREMIER OF BRIT. COLUMBIA since 1975; joined B.C. Social Credit Party 1952; el. mem. Leg. Assembly B.C. for

S. Okanagan 1973; el. Leader B.C. Social Credit Party 1973; Past Pres. Kelowna Chamber Comm.; Kelowna Toastmasters Club; United Church; recreations: tennis, skiing; Clubs: Kelowna Gyro (Past Dir.); Kelowna Club; Kelowna Golf and Country; Home: R.R. 1, Pritchard Dr., Westbank, B.C. V1Y 7P9; Office: Parliament Bldgs., Victoria, B.C.V8V 4R3

BENNETT, Winslow Wood; executive; ranch owner; b. Minneapolis, Minn. 18 March 1925; s. Russell H. and Miriam von S. (Fletcher) B.; e. Phillips Acad. Andover, Mass. 1943; Univ. of Minn. Bachelor of Mech. Engn. 1949; m. Adele d. Lucien Wulsin, Cincinnati, Ohio 20 Oct. 1951; children: Winslow Wood Jr., Peter W., Frank B., Russell H.; Chrmn., Equity Silver Mines 1979- (founded former Equity Mining Corp. 1969); Gold Run Mining Inc.; Pres., Adanac Mining and Exploration Ltd. 1971- ; Owner Shoderee Ranch, Pincher Creek, Alta.; joined Armco Steel Corp., Middletown, Ohio 1949-51; Electro Manganese Corp. Knoxville, Tenn. (merged with Foote Mineral Co. Philadelphia) 1951-61; Laird & Co., invest.bankers., 1961-63; Molybdenum Corp. 1963; Placer Development, Vancouver 1964-69; Gov. Vancouver Pub. Aquarium; Dir. B.C. Cancer Foundation; served with U.S. Navy 1943-46, rank Lt. j.g.; mem. Candn. Inst. Mining; Am. Inst. Mining Engrs.; Anglican; recreations: horseback riding, ranching, fishing, tennis, skiing; Clubs: Vancouver; Vancouver Lawn Tennis; Pennask Fishing; Home: 1341 Matthews Ave., Vancouver, B.C. V6H 1W7; Office: (P.O. Box 49277) Four Bentall Centre, Vancouver, B.C. V7X 1L3.

BENOIT, Germain Edmour, B.A., transportation executive; b. Montreal, Que., 19 June 1919; s. Ovila Joseph and Louisa (Leduc) B.; e. Loyola Coll., B.A. 1940; m. Edith Diana Beasley, 4 Nov. 1951; VICE PRES., ATLANTIC REGION, CANADIAN PACIFIC LTD.; Pres. and Dir., Aroostook River Railroad Cc.; Brunterm Ltd.; Great Field Investment Corp.; Houlton Branch Railroad Co.; International Railway Co. of Maine; Newport and Richford Railroad Co.; Dir., Fredericton Railway Co.; mem., Assn. Rr. Supt's; Vt. State Rr's Assn. (Past Pres.); Montreal Bd. Trade; Montreal Chamber Comm.; Quebec Safety League (past Pres.); recreations: golf, curling; Clubs: Canadian Railway; Traffic; Sherbrooke (Que.) Golf & Country; Meadowbrook Golf; Home: P.O. Box 521, Snowdon Branch, Montreal, Que. H3X 3T7; Office: 1134 Ste. Catherine St. W., Montreal, Que. H3C 3E4

BENSLEY, Edward Horton, M.B.E. (1946), B.A., M.D., D.Sc., F.R.C.P. (C), F.C.I.C., F.A.C.P. educator; b. Toronto, Ont., 10 Dec. 1906; s. Benjamin Arthur and Ruth (Horton) B.; e. Univ. of Toronto, B.A. 1927, M.D. 1930 (1st Alex T. Fulton Scholar, in Natural & Phys. Sciences (1924), Jean Balmer Scholar. Science (1924), Edw. Blake Scholar. in Biol. and Med. Sciences (1925), Daniel Wilson Scholar. in Biol. and Med. Sciences (1926), Brit. Assn. for Advanc. of Science Bronze Medal (1927), Gold Medal for highest aggregate standing in med. course (1930); D.Sc. Acadia 1964; Emeritus Prof. of Med., Hon. Lectr. in Hist. of Med., and Hon. Under Librarian, McGill Univ.; Ed., Osler Library Newsletter; Consulting Phys., Montreal Gen. Hosp.; mem., Staff of Montreal Gen. Hosp. since 1932, and of McGill Univ. since 1941; formerly Vice Dean, Faculty of Med.; Publications: over 160 articles in med. and other journs.; Chrmn. Nutrition Panel, Def. Res. Bd. of Canada 1949-52; mem. Can. Council on Nutrition 1948-58; Chrmn. Comm. on Nutrition, C.M.A., 1951-54; Consult. in Nutrition, Can. Forces Med. Council 1957-60; Pres. Nutrition Soc. of Canada 1961-62; Pres. Can. Soc. of Clinical Chemists 1957-58; Hon. Sec. Can. Fed. of Biol. Societies 1957-61; Hon. Pres. Osler Soc. of McGill Univ. 1956-57, 1980; Pres. James McGill Scholar of McGill U. 1978-80; Hon. Consultant Royal Victoria Hospital 1962-67; Consultant in Metabolism and Toxicology, Reddy Memorial Hospital 1950-61; awarded Centennial Medal; served in 2nd World War, Major, R.C.A.M.C. (Advisor in Nutri-

tion); Alpha Omega Alpha; Unitarian; Home: 157 Morrison Ave., Montreal, Que. H3R 1K5; Office: McIntyre Medical Sciences Bldg., 3655 Drummond St., Montreal, Que. H3G 1Y6

BENSON, Hon. Edgar John, P.C., M.P., B.Com., LL.D., F.C.A.; b. Cobourg, Ont., 28 May 1923; s. Franklin M. and Julia A. (Minifie) B.; e. Pub. Sch., Cobourg, Ont.; Cobourg Coll. Inst.; Queen's Univ., B.Com. 1949; Inst. of C.A.'s of Ont., C.A. 1952; PRES., CANDN. TRANSPORT COMN. since 1972; Partner, England, Leonard, Macpherson & Co., Kingston, Ont. 1953; Asst. Prof. of Comm., Queen's Univ. 1952-62; served in 2nd World War in Can. 1941; overseas 1942-46; el. to H. of C. for Kingston in g.e. 1962; apptd. Parlty. Secy. to Min. of Finance, 1963; Min. of Nat. Revenue, July 1964; Pres., Treasury Bd. 1966; Min. i/c Housing, Jan.-Apr. 1968; Min. of Finance 1968-72 and Min. of National Defence 1972; member, American Accountant Association; Canadian Tax Foundation; Freemason; Liberal; Protestant; recreations: hunting, fishing; Clubs: Kiwanis; Cataraqui Golf & Country; Home: 44 Strathcona Cres., Kingston, Ont. K7M 1N8; Office: Ottawa, Ont. K1A 0N9

BENSON, Kenneth Peter, C.A.; forestry executive; b. Vancouver, B.C. 1 March 1927; s. Lawrence Benson; e. Univ. of B.C.; C.A. 1953; m. Joyce d. Charles Heino 5 Nov. 1949; children: David, Sally; PRES. AND CEO, DIR., BRITISH COLUMBIA FOREST PRODUCTS LTD. since 1979; Dir. Trans Mountain Pipe Line Co. Ltd.; Blandin Paper Co.; Donohue St.-Felician Inc.; Finlay Forest Ind. Ltd.; Muir Creek Logging Co. Ltd.; Pinette & Thorrion Mills Ltd.; Western Forest Products Ltd. (Chrmn.); joined Powell River Co. 1955, Asst. Controller 1958; present Co. 1962 Comptroller, Vice Pres. Finance 1967, Dir. 1970, Extve. Vice Pres. Operations 1972, Sr. Extve. Vice Pres. 1974, Pres. and Chief Operating Offr. 1976; mem. Inst. C.A.'s; Clubs: Vancouver; Vancouver Lawn Tennis & Badminton; University; Home: 6329 Angus Dr., Vancouver, B.C. V6M 3P4; Office: 1050 W. Pender St., Vancouver, B.C. V6E 2X3.

BENTALL, Rev. Charles Howard, B.A., B.D., D.D. (Bapt.); b. Vancouver, B.C., 19 Oct. 1913; s. Charles and Edna Olive (Gilmour) B.; e. Univ. of British Columbia, B.A. 1934; McMaster Univ., B.D. 1937, D.D. 1957; m. Shirley Franklyn, d. Frank May, 15 June 1946; children: Louise, Kathleen, Joan, Barnard; formerly Sr. Pastor First Ch., Calgary, Walmer Rd. Ch., Toronto, Ont., and First Church, Regina, Sask.; formerly Interim Principal Bapt. Leader Training Sch., now Adm. Dean, Div. of Christian Studies and Asst. Exec. Min., Bapt. Union of W. Can., Pres. Bapt. Fed. of Can. 1956-59; Home: R.R. 4, Calgary, Alta.

BENTALL, Harold Clark, B.A.Sc., P.Eng.; company executive; b. Vancouver, B.C., 4 May 1915; s. Charles and Edna Olive (Gilmour) B.; e. Univ. of British Columbia, B.A.Sc. 1938; m. Phyllis Emily Weedon, 16 June 1938; children: Mrs. Helen Wyder, Charles Ernest, Mrs. Mary George, David Clark; CHRMN., THE BENTALL GROUP LTD. Dominion Construction Co. Ltd.; Bentall Investments Ltd.; B.C. Millwork Products Ltd.; Canem Systems Ltd.; Dir., Scott Paper Ltd., Cominco Ltd., Toronto-Dominion Bank, Finning Tractor & Equipment Co. Ltd., B.C. Forest Products Ltd., Trustee, TD Realty; joined Dominion Construction in 1938, el. a Dir. 1943, Vice-Pres. 1950, Pres. 1955, Chmn. & CEO, 1975-80; Baptist; recreations: yachting; Clubs: Vancouver; Shaughnessy Golf & Country; Royal Vancouver Yacht; Home: 2194 S.W. Marine Drive, Vancouver, B.C. V6P 6B5; Office: 3100 Three Bentall Centre, Vancouver, B.C.

BENTALL, Robert G., B.A.Sc., P.Eng.; company executive; b. Vancouver, B.C., 6 Nov. 1922; s. Charles and Edna Olive (Gilmour) B.; e. Univ. of B.C., B.A.Sc. 1944; m. Thelma J., Turner, 20 May 1948; children: Robert,

Mrs. Laura Nelson, Mrs. Ruth Anderson; PRESIDENT AND CHIEF EXECUTIVE OFFICER, THE BENTALL GROUP LTD.; Bentall Investments Ltd.; B.C. Millwork Products Ltd.; Chief Exec. Offr., Dominion Construction Ltd.; Dir., Canem Systems Ltd., Royal Trustco Ltd.; joined Dominion Construction as Project Engr. 1945; Project Mgr. and Br. Mgr. 1945-1950; apptd. to extve. staff 1950; Extve. Vice Pres. 1955-75; Pres. 1975-80; Baptist; Clubs: Vancouver; Capilano Golf & Country; Home: Penthouse 11, 111-18th St., West Vancouver, B.C. V7V 3V3; Office: 3100, 3 Bentall Centre, Vancouver, B.C. V7X 1B1

BENTLEY, Charles Frederick, M.Sc., Ph.D.; university professor Emeritus; b. Cambridge, Mass., 14 March 1914; s. Charles Fred and Lavina Ann (Mackenzie) B.; e. Victoria High Sch. (1932), and Edmonton Normal Sch. (1933), Edmonton, Alta; Univ. of Alberta, B.Sc. 1939 M.Sc. 1942; Univ. of Minnesota, Ph.D. 1945; m. Helen Signe, d. Thorwald Petersen, 16 Sept. 1943; children: Ann Catherine, Theodore Carl; PROF. EMERITUS UNIV. OF ALBERTA, since 1979; Bd. Govs., Internat. Devel. Research Centre 1970-74; taught school, 1933-36; Research Asst., Can. Dept. of Agric., 1939-40, Univ. of Alta., 1940-41; Instr. in Soil Science, Univ. of Minn., 1942-43; Instr. and Asst. Prof., Soil Science, Univ. of Sask., 1943-46; Asst. Prof., Assoc. Prof., Prof. of Soil Science, Univ. of Alta., 1946-56; Can. Colombo Plan Specialist in Ceylon, 1952-53; Dean, Faculty of Agric., Univ. of Alta., 1959-68; Prof. of Soil Science there 1969-79; F.A.O. Consultant in Thailand, Oct.-Dec. 1962; recipient of Univ. of Minn. Outstanding Achievement Award; Centennial Lect., Agric. Inst. of Can., 1967; awarded Centennial Medal; Queen's Jubilee Medal; Leader, Can. Agric. Task Force to India, 1967; Agric. Advisor External Aid Office, Ottawa, 1968-69; Consultant in Uganda, Candn. Internat. Devel. Agency Aug. 1971; Leader, Can. Agric. Team to Sri Lanka, 1979 and 1980; Past Pres., Edmonton Br., Un. Nations; Edmonton Br., C.I.I.A.; mem. and Chrmn. Gov. Bd. ICRISAT, Hyderabad, India 1972-82; Fellow, Royal Society of Canada; Fellow, Am. Soc. of Agronomy; Fellow, Soil Science Soc. of America; Fellow, Am. Assn. Adv. Science; Agric. Inst. Can. (Pres. 1963-64); Candn. Soc. Soil Science (Past Pres.); mem. Alta. Inst. Agrols. (Past Pres.); Am. Soc. Soil Sciences; Am. Soc. Agron.; Past Pres. Int. Soc. Soil Sci. (Pres. 1974-78); Klink Lecturer, Agric. Inst. Can. 1981-82; author of some 80 scient. papers, usually jt. authorship; recipient, Alberta Premier's Award for Excellent; Gamma Alpha; recreations; golf, photography; Home: 13103 - 66 Ave., Edmonton, Alta. T6H 1Y6

BENTLEY, Gerald Eades Jr., B.A., B.Litt., D.Phil.; b. Chicago, Ill., 23 Aug. 1930; s. Gerald Eades and Esther (Felt) B.; e. Princeton Univ., B.A. 1952; Oxford Univ., B.Litt. 1954, D.Phil. 1956; m. Anne Elizabeth Kathryne Louise, d. Raymond Budd, 22 June 1952; two d., Sarah Elizabeth Esther, Julia Greenwood; PROF. OF ENGLISH, UNIVERSITY OF TORONTO; Teacher, Univ. of Chicago 1956-60, Univ. d'Alger 1967-68; Univ. of Poona 1975-76; joined present Univ. 1960; Visiting Lectr., Eng., Japan, Australia, New Zealand, Thailand, Sri Lanka, India, Can., U.S.A.; Guggenheim Fellow 1958-59; Can. Council Fellow 1963-64, 1970-71, 1977-78; research also in France, Germany, Switzerland, Italy, Taiwan, Hong Kong, Iran, Egypt, Tanzania; Ed., Wm. Blake's "Vala or the Four Zoas", 1963; "The Early Engravings of Flaxman's Classical Designs", 1964; Ed., Wm. Blake's "Tiriel", 1967; "Blake Records", 1969; "The Blake Collection of Mrs. Landon K. Thorne", 1971; Ed., Wm. Blake "America" 1974; "William Blake: The Critical Heritage", 1975; Ed., "Editing Eighteenth-Century Novels", 1975; "A Bibliography of George Cumberland", 1975; "Blake Books", 1977 (Jenkins Award for Bibliography 1979); Ed., Wm. Blake, "Europe", 1978; Ed., "William Blake's Writings", 2 vols. 1979; author of articles in various lit. journs.; mem., Modern Lang. Assn.; Bibliog. Soc.; Oxford Bibl-

iog. Soc.; Printing Hist. Soc.; Conf. Ed. Problems (occasional Chrmn.); recreations: travel, book collecting, bearcatching; Home: 246 MacPherson Ave., Toronto, Ont. M4V 1A2

BENTLEY, James M., O.C. (1967), B.Com.; farmer; b. Dawson City, Yukon, 23 June 1906; s. Samuel James and Mary Annie (McRae) B.; e. Univ. of Alta., B.Com. 1930; m. Marion, d. Michael J. Saunders, 11 Nov. 1936; children: Donald J., Linda (Mrs. John J. Chalmers), Merle E. (Mrs. Kenneth Kew), Ila (Mrs. David Scott); former Pres., Candn. Fed. of Agric. 1962-68; Dir., Edmonton Dist. Milk Producers, 1953; Dir., Alta. Milk Producers Assn. 1953-76; Un. Farmers of Alta. Co-op. Assn.; Alta. Fed. of Agric. (Pres. 1957-63); Dir. Un. Farmers of Alta., 1935-43; Candn Co-op. Implements Ltd., 1949-57; mem. of Senate, Univ. of Alta.; mem. Candn. Council on Rural Devel.; Alta. Adv. Council; Alta. Dairy Control Bd., 1969; Freemason; P. Conservative; United Church; recreations: golf, curling; Address: R.R. 6, Edmonton, Alta.

BENTLEY, Peter John Gerald; executive; b. Vienna, Austria, 17 March 1930; s. Leopold Lionel Garrick and Antoinette Ruth B.; e. St. George's Sch., Vancouver, B.C.; Univ. of Brit. Columbia Sch. of Forestry; Banff Sch. Advanced Mang.; m. Sheila Farrington McGiverin, 23 May 1953; four d. Barbara Ruth, Susan Patricia, Joan Katherine, Lisa Maria; one s. Michael Peter; PRES., CHIEF EXTVE. OFFR. AND DIR., CANADIAN FOREST PRODUCTS LTD.; Canfor Ltd.; Canfor Investments Ltd.; Dir., Bank of Montreal; Prince George Pulp & Paper Ltd.; Intercontinental Pulp Co. Ltd.; Takla Forest Products; Balco Industries Ltd.; Westcoast Cellufibre Industries Ltd.; Versatile Corp.; Burrard Yarrows Corp.; Shell Canada Limited; mem. International Advisory Bd., Chemical Bank, New York; Business Counsel on Nat. Issues, Toronto; Past Chrmn. and Mem. Exec. Comm. Seaboard Lumber Sales Co. Ltd.; Seaboard Shipping Co. Ltd.; Dir. Forest Industrial Relations Ltd.; Past Pres. and Dir. Canadian Forestry Assn. of B.C.; Past Chrmn., B.C. Sports Hall of Fame; Trustee, Olympic Trust of Can.; Hon. Dir., Candn. Prof. Golfers Assn.; Gov., St. George's School; Clubs: Capilano Golf & Country; Marine Drive Golf; Vancouver Lawn Tennis & Badminton; Vancouver Gun Club; Vancouver Club; Thunderbird Country (Palm Springs, Calif.); Royal and Ancient Golf Club, St. Andrews, Scotland; Office: 2800-1055 Dunamuir St., P.O. Box 49420, Bentall Postal Stn., Vancouver, B.C. V7X 1B5

BENY, Roloff (Wilfrid Roy), O.C. (1972), M.A., M.F.A., LL.D., R.C.A.; b. Medicine Hat, Alta., 7 Jan. 1924; s. Charles John Francis and Rosalie M. (Roloff) B.; e. Elem. and High Schs., Medicine Hat, Alta.; Banff Sch. of Fine Arts, 1939; Trinity Coll., Univ. of Toronto, 1941-45, B.A., B.F.A.; State Univ. of Iowa, 1946-47, M.A., M.F.A. (Graphic Arts); Columbia Univ. and Inst. of Fine Art, N.Y. Univ., 1947-48; travel and study in Greece, Italy and France, 1948-49 and in Spain, Eng., Italy and Germany, 1951-52; 1st pub. showing Man. Soc. of Artists at age 15; during World War II period work accepted by many exhns. in Can.; has had 25 one-man exhns. incl.: Hart House, Toronto, 1941, 1944 and 1951; Weyhe Gallery, N.Y., 1947; Art Gallery of Palazzo Strozzi, Florence, Italy, 1949; Fine Art Gallery, Eaton's Coll. St., Toronto, 1950 and 1953; Knoedler Gallery, N.Y., 1950, 1951 and 1954; Gallery 'del Corso', Merano, Italy, 1951; Gallery 'del Calibano', Vicenza, Italy, 1951; Paul Morihien Gallery, Palais Royal, Paris, 1952; Galleria Del Milione, Milano, Italy, 1952; Art Gallery of Ont., 1954; Robertson Gallery, Ottawa, 1954; Waldorf Galleries, Montreal, 1954; Tour, W. Can. Art Circuit, 1955; The Contemporaries Gallery, N.Y., 1956; Inst. of Contemporary Art, London, 1955; Sagittarius, Rome, 1956; Paolo Barozzi Galleries, Venice, 1967; San Francesco, Sorrento, 1980, One man exhibition in the Palazzo dell'Esposizione, Rome (then touring capitals of Europe); work has been represented in many nat. exhns. in U.S. and Can. incl.: San Francisco Museum; Art

Inst. of Chicago; Lib. of Congress, Washington, D.C.; Carnegie Inst.; Dallas Museum of Fine Art; Nat. Gallery of Can.; paintings and graphic art are in perm. colls. of: Nat. Gallery of Can.; Art Gallery of Ont.; Fogg Museum, Boston; Yale Univ. Museum; Knoedler Gallery, N.Y.; Brooklyn Museum; N.Y. Pub. Lib.; Museum of Modern Art, N.Y.; Wesleyan Univ.; Milione Gallery, Milan; Redfern Gallery, London, Eng.; Bezalel Museum, Jerusalem; work also represented in many private colls.; has prepared 9 maj. pub. photographic exhns. in Can. and Europe incl. "A Time of Gods" (1962), "Metaphysical Monuments", "Pleasure of Photography" (1966), "Sculpture of the Renaissance" (1967), "Image Canada" (comnd. for Expo 67), "The Renaissance" (1968), "A Visual Odyssey" (Gallery of Modern Art, N.Y. 1968, and Toronto 1971); books incl.: "The Churches of Rome" (text by peter Gunn (1981); "Odyssey: Mirror of the Mediteranean" (text and anthology by Anthony Thwaite) 1981); "The Thrones of Earth and Heaven" (text by late Bernard Berenson), 1958 (awarded Internat. Prize for Design at Leipzig Book Fair); "A Time of Gods," 1962; "Pleasure of Ruins" (text by Rose Macaulay), 1964, rev. edn. 1977; "To Every Thing There Is A Season" (presented by Candn. Govt. to visiting heads of state and govt. leaders during Centennial Yr.), 1967; "Japan In Colour" (text by Anthony Thwaite), 1967, "India", 1969; "Island: Ceylon", 1971; "In Italy" 1974; "Persia: Bridge of Turquoise" 1975; "Iran, Elements of Destiny" 1978; numerous photographs and articles have appeared in Candn., Am., Eng. and European publs.; rec'd John Simon Guggenheim Fellowship for printmaking and painting, 1953; Centennial Medal, 1967; Can. Council Visual Arts Award, 1968; el. Kt. of Mark Twain, 1967; his book "Japan in Colour" selected as "the world's finest book" and awarded a gold medal by Internat. Book Fair, Leipzeig, E. Germany, 1968; Life mem. R.C.A. 1973; LL.D. Univ. Lethbridge 1972; Address: Lungotevere Ripa 3-B, Rome, Italy 00153 and 432 - 13th St. S., Lethbridge, Alta. T1J 2V9

BERCUSON, David Jay, M.A., Ph.D.; educator; b. Montreal, Que. 31 Aug. 1945; s. Joseph Myer and Sylvia (Green) B.; e. Monklands High Sch. Montreal 1962; Sir George Williams Univ. B.A. 1966; Univ. of Toronto M.A. 1967, Ph.D. 1971; m. Cheryl Joy d. Bertram Baron, Calgary, Alta. 19 June 1966; children: Michael Solomon Baron, Sharon Rena Baron; PROF. OF HISTORY, UNIV. OF CALGARY1978- ; Visiting Asst. Prof. Univ. Calgary 1970, Asst. Prof. 1971, Assoc. Prof. 1975, Pres. Faculty Assn. 1974-75, mem. Gen. Faculties Council 1977-80; Dir. Calgary Hebrew Sch.; rec'd Lt. Gov.'s Silver Medal for Hist. 1966; Can. Council Doctoral Dissertation Fellowships 1966-70 and Leave Fellowship 1975; Social Science & Humanities Research Council Leave Fellowship 1979; Killam Resident Fellowship 1981; Ed. "Canadian Historical Review" 1977- ; author "Confrontation at Winnipeg" 1974; "Winnipeg Strike: 1919" 1974; "Canada and the Burden of Unity" 1977; "Fools and Wise Men" 1978; various articles w. Candn. labour & social hist., the middle e. and Candn. regionalism in numerous mags., newspapers; mem. Candn. Hist. Assn. (Council); Candn. Profs. for Peace in the Middle E. (Vice Pres.); Jewish; Clubs: Men's Canadian; B'nai Brith; Home: 36 Dalroy Cr. N.W., Calgary, Alta. T3A 1G3; Office: 2500 University Dr. N.W., Calgary, Alta. T2N 1N4.

BERCZI, Andrew, B.Sc., B.A., M.B.A., Ph.D.; educator; b. Budapest, Hungary 15 Aug. 1934; s. Stephan and Iren (Bartha) B.; e. Univ. of Tech. Sciences, Budapest Indust. Engn. 1951-56; Sir George Williams Univ. B.Sc. 1961, B.A. 1963; McGill Univ. M.B.A. 1965, Ph.D. 1972; m. Susan d. Zoltan Bartok, Budapest, Hungary 29 Aug. 1958; two s. Thomas Edgar, Peter Alexander; DEAN, FACULTY OF GRAD. STUDIES, WILFRID LAURIER UNIV. since 1978; served as Engr., Supvr. Engn., Supvr. Computer Systems in Engn., HQ and Business Information Systems Depts., Bell Telephone Co. of Canada 1956-65;

Prof. of Quantitative Methods and Chrmn. of Dept., Sir George Williams Univ. 1965-72; Dean, Fac. of Comm. and Adm., Concordia Univ. 1972-78; rec'd Can. Council and Prov. Que. Scholarships; McConnell Fellowship; NRC research grants; author several textbooks, monographs and over 50 articles and papers in mang. science area various journs. and confs.; mem. Data Processing Mang. Assn.; Assn. Computing Machinery; Systems & Procedures Assn.; Candn. Operations Research Soc.; Operations Research Soc. Am.; Inst. Mang. Science; Am. Mang. Assn.; Am. Assn. Advanc. Science; R. Catholic; recreations: tennis, skiing, sailing, swimming; Home: 76 McCarron Cresc., Waterloo, Ont. N2L 5N1; Office: 75 University Ave. W., Waterloo, Ont. N2L 3C5

BERESFORD-HOWE, Constance Elizabeth, Ph.D.; (Mrs. C.W. Pressnell); writer; b. Montreal, P.Q., 10 Nov. 1922; d. Russell and Marjory Mary (Moore) B.-H.; e. West Hill High Sch., Montreal, P.Q.; McGill Univ., B.A. 1945 (with Shakespeare Gold Medal for Eng. Lit. and Dorothy Peterson Prize for creative writing), M.A. 1946 (with $1200) scholar. from P.Q.); Brown Univ. Ph.D. 1950; m. Christopher W. Pressnell, M.A., 1960; one s., Jeremy Howe; author of "The Unreasoning Heart", 1946; "Of This Day's Journey"; "My Lady Greensleeves", 1955; "The Book of Eve", 1973; "A Population of One", 1977; "The Marriage Bed", 1981 awarded Dodd, Mead Intercoll. Lit. Fellow. 1945; Candn. Booksellers Award 1973; Can. Council Sr. Arts Award 1975; Ont. Arts Council Grant 1976; short stories have appeared in Toronto "Sat. Night", "Candn. Home Journal", "Chatelaine" and "Maclean's", articles in "The Writer" and "The Montrealer"; mem., The Writers' Union of Canada; Internat. P.E.N. Club (Past Pres. Montreal Centre); Phi Beta Kappa; Anglican.16 Cameron Cresc., Toronto, Ont. M4G 1Z8

BERGER, Carl, M.A., Ph.D.; Educator; b. The Pas, Man. 25 Feb. 1939; e. Univ. of Man. B.A. 1961; Univ. of Toronto M.A. 1962, Ph.D. 1967; two d. Rachel, Clare; PROF. OF HISTORY, UNIV. OF TORONTO; author "The Sense of Power: Studies in the Ideas of Canadian Imperialism 1867-1914;; 1970; "The Writing of Canadian History" 1976; rec'd Gov. Gen.'s Award for Non-Fiction 1977; mem. Royal Soc. Can.; Home: 30 Duggan Ave., Toronto, Ont. M4V 1Y2; Office: Toronto; Ont. M5S 1A1.

BERGER, Gerald A., B.A., M.B.A.; Canadian public service; b. Toronto, Ont., 31 Dec. 1937; s. Louis and Salome (Lubetsky) B.; e. Forest Hill Coll. Inst., Toronto, 1956; Univ. of Toronto, B.A. 1959; Columbia Univ., M.B.A. 1961; m. Ruth Bryna, d. late Phillip Cohen, 25 June 1967; children: Michael Robert, Lisa Miriam; ASST. DEPY. MIN. (COMM. SUPPLY), DEPT. OF SUPPLY & SERVICES since 1974; Vice Pres. and Dir., Crown Assets Disposal Corp.; joined Fed. Pub. Service as Project Offr., Small Business Br., Dept. of Trade & Comm. 1961; Project Offr., Mang. Control Group, Dept. of Defense Production 1963; Extve. Asst. to Asst. Depy. Min., Finance and Adm. of Dept. Defense Production and Dept. Industry 1964; Extve. Asst. to Asst. Depy. Min. of Operations, Dept. Industry 1965 and to Depy. Min. of Industry 1966; Extve. Asst. to Secy. of Treasury Bd. 1968; Sr. Program Offr., Treasury Bd. Secretariat 1969; Secy., Prices and Incomes Comn. 1969; Dir. Gen. (Supply Planning) Dept. of Supply and Services 1972; author, "Canada's Experience with Incomes Policy—1969-70"; Jewish; Home: 384 Hamilton Ave. S., Ottawa, Ont. K1Y 1C7; Office: 17A1 Place du Portage, 11 Laurier St., Hull, Que. K1A 0S5

BERGER, Monty (Montague), B.A., M.Sc.; business consultant; b. Quebec, Que., 26 July 1918; s. Julius and Rebecca (Fitch) B.; e. Elem. and High Schs., Montreal; McGill Univ., B.A. (Hons. Econ. and Pol. Science) 1939; Columbia Univ., Pulitzer Grad. Sch. of Journalism, M.Sc. 1940; m. late Sonia, d. Isaac Mindel, London, Eng., 4

Sept. 1947; children: Ann Rebecca, Joy Diane, Eric Jules; PRESIDENT, BERGER & ASSOCIATES INC.; Gen. Mgr., Saje Publications Ltd.; formerly City Ed., Quebec Chronicle-Telegraph; Rehab. Ed., Montreal Gazette; Public Relations Mgr., Canadian Industries Ltd.; estbd. course in Pub. Relations, Dept. Continuing Educ., McGill Univ.; served in C.O.T.C., McGill and Laval Univs.; qualified as 2nd Lt., Arty.; F/Lt. with R.C.A.F., Overseas 1941-45; Sr. Intelligence Offr., 126 (Spitfire) Wing; crossed channel, D-Day 1944 seeing action in France, Belgium, Holland and Germany; Past Pres., Canadian Club of Montreal; Allied Jewish Community Services; Dir., Grads. Soc. (McGill); Les Festivals de Montréal; Fed. Appeal of Gtr. Montreal; Royal Victoria Hosp.; St. Mary's Hosp.; YMCA (MH metropolitan); mem. Council, Montreal Bd. Trade; Candn. Indust. Eds. Assn. (Past Pres. Que. Chapter); Candn. Pub. Relations Soc. (Past Pres. Que. Br.; Pres. Toronto Soc.; Lamp of Service Award;); Pub. Relations Soc. of Am. (Candn. Rep.); Internat. Pub. Relations Assn. (Candn. Rep.); Dir., Lib. Assn., Fed. Co. of Mount Royal (a Cand. for Lib. Nomination, Mount Royal Riding 1965); recreations: swimming, tennis, chess, reading; Club: University (Montreal); Home: 590 Kindersley Ave., Town of Mount Royal, Que. H3R 1S4; Office: 615 Dorchester Blvd. W., Montreal, Que. H3B 1P5

BERGER, Hon. Thomas Rodney, B.A., LL.B.; b. Victoria, B.C., 23 March 1933; s. Maurice Theodore and Nettie Elsie Perle (McDonald) B.; e. Univ. of B.C., B.A. 1955, LL.B. 1956; m. Beverley Ann, d. Joseph O. Crosby, 5 Nov. 1955; children: Erin Frances, David Bruce; JUDGE, SUPREME COURT OF B.C. since 1971; called to Bar of B.C. 1957; practised law in Vancouver 1957-71; Chrmn., Royal Comn. on Family and Children's Law (B.C.) 1973-74; Commr., Mackenzie Valley Pipeline Inquiry (Can.) 1974-77; Comr., Indian and Inuit Health Consultation 1978-80; served as M.P. (NDP) for Vancouver-Burrard 1962-63; M.L.A. for Vancouver-Burrard 1966-69; Anglican; Clubs: Jericho Tennis; Office: 800 Smithe, Vancouver, B.C. V6Z 2E1

BERGERON, Hon. Anthime; juge; né Montréal, Qué., 22 Jan. 1925; fils Donat et Aline (Héneault); é. Coll. Ste-Marie B.A. 1945; Univ. de Montréal LL.B. 1948; ép. Thérèse, f. Damase Parizeau (décédé) 27 juin 1949; enfants: Yves, Luc; JUGE, COUR SUPÉRIEURE DU QUEBEC depuis 1973; admis au Barreau du Québec, 12 juillet 1948; nommé C.R. 1958; Associate, Lacoste & Lacoste 1948-54; Associé sr., Tansey, de Grandpré, Bergeron, Johnston, Lavery, O'Donnell, Clark & Carriere 1955-73; Catholique romain; Clubs: St. Laurent-Kiwanis (Prés. 1967); Club de Golf Laval-sur-le-Lac; Résidence: 4540 Promenade Paton, Laval, Qué. H7W 4W6; Bureau: Palais de Justice, Montréal, Qué.

BERGERON, Hon. Camille Léopold, B.A., Ph.B., Th.B., LL.L.; judge; b. LaReine, Qué. 7 Dec. 1928; s. Ernest and Alexina (Doyle) B.; e. Univ. of Ottawa B.A. 1950, Ph.B. 1950, Th.B. 1952; Laval Univ. LL.L. 1956; m. Huguette J. A. Oscar Bellemare 7 Sept. 1957; children: Louise, Claire, Denis, Diane; PUISNE JUDGE, SUPERIOR COURT OF QUE.; called to Bar of Que. 1957; Appointed to the Bench, 1969; mem. Candn. Judges Conf.; R. Catholic; recreations: oil painting, woodcarving; Home: 79 Trémoy Rd., Noranda, Que. J9X 1W2; Office: Court House, 2 Ave. du Palais, Rouyn, Que. J9X 2N9.

BERGERON, Marcel, B. ès A., L.Com.; employé civil; né St. Grégoire de Nicolet, Co. Nicolet, Qué., 5 Déc. 1922; fils Henri et Alice (Trudel) B.; é., école primaire, St. Grégoire, Co. Nicolet; Séminaire de Nicolet, B. és A.; Ecole Hautes Etudes Commerciales, B.Com., L. ès Com.; ép. Lina Lebebvre, 7 juin 1957; enfant: François; DÉLÉGUÉ DU GOUVERNMENT DU QUÉBEC Sousministre Adjoint, Ministere De L'Industrie, Commerce et Tourisme, Quebec; Vérificateur Interne Junior, The Texas Co. (S.A.) Ltd., Rio de Janeiro, Brésil, 1947-54; Associé, Comercial E

Importadora Lejes S.A., Rio de Janeiro, Brésil, 1954-57; Propriétaire, A. Canadense Auto Pecas Ltds., Rio de Janeiro, Brésil, 1957-60; Gérant Général des ventes, Laboratoires Dr. Leo Lorrain Ltée, 1960-63, et des Produits Familex Ltée, Montréal 1963-65; Dir. Gén. de l'Indust., Min. de L'Industrie de du Comm., Qué. 1965; Délégué général du Québec pour les Etats-Unis 1978; mem., Montreal Board of Trade; Chambre de Comm. de Montréal; Catholique; récréations; yachting, ski; Bureau: Sanno Grand Bldg., Ste. 501, 14-2 Nagata-Cho, 2 Chome Chiyoda-Ku, Tokyo 100, Japan

BERGSMA, John, M.A.Sc., M.B.A., P.Eng.; manufacturer; b. The Netherlands 11 Nov. 1945; s. Folkert and Antje (Brouwer) B.; came to Canada 1953; e. St. Catharines (Ont.) Coll. Inst. 1964; Univ. of Waterloo, B.A.Sc. (Mech. Engn.) 1969, M.A.Sc. (Civil Engn.) 1971; McMaster Univ. M.B.A. 1973; m. Barrie-Ann, d. E. Kennard 20 June 1968; children: Glynis Rachelle, Katharine June; PRESIDENT, GEN. MGR. AND DIR., COLUMBUS McKINNON LTD. since 1975; joined the Co. as Asst. to Gen. Mgr. 1971, Gen. Mgr. 1974; mem. Business Adv. Council, McMaster Univ.; mem. Engn. Inst. Can.; Assn. Prof. Engrs. Ont.; Candn. Soc. Mech. Engrs.; Am. Soc. Mech. Engrs.; Candn. Chamber Comm.; Clubs: Rotary; Burlington Lakeshore; Home: 1990 Kerns Rd., Burlington, Ont. L7P 3A5; Office: 760 Brant St., Burlington, Ont. L7R 3Y3

BERGSTROM, Lyle Herbert, B.A., B.Paed.; retired civil servant; b. Barron, Wis., 19 Apl. 1912; s. late Eric N. and Laura M. (Breen) B.; e. Melville (Sask.) High Sch., 1930; Univ. of Sask., B.A. 1940; Univ. of Toronto, B.Paed. (Hons.) 1944; m. Dorothy Alice, d. late Ernest Charles Dumbleton, 31 Aug. 1935; one s.: Wayne L.; Teacher and Sch. Princ., 1931-44; Supt. of Schs., Sask., 1944-56; mem. Faculty, Teachers Coll., Sask., 1956-58; Chief Supt. of Schs., Sask., 1958-63; Asst. Dep. Min. of Educ., Sask., 1963-65; Dep. Min. of Educ., Sask. 1965-73; Special Adv. to Min. of Educ. 1973-79 (ret.); part-time Lectr., Univ. of Sask., in Educ. Adm., 1953-62; mem., Pilot Short Course in Educ. Leadership, 1953; mem. Staff Short Course for Candn. Insprs. and Supts., 1954 and Consultant, 1959; Chrmn., Candn. Nat. Comn. for Sch. Broadcasting (Chrmn., Eng. Council); mem., Candn. Nat. Comn. for UNESCO; mem., Candn. Del. to Commonwealth Conf. on Educ., Ottawa, 1964, Lagos, Nigeria 1968, Canberra 1971, Accra 1977, and to 14th and 15th Conf. of UNESCO, Paris, 1966 and 1968; Head, Candn. Del. to Conf. of Internat. Bureau of Educ., Geneva, 1967; mem., Bd. Dirs., Candn. Educ. Assn., since 1958 (el. Pres. 1967); Freemason; United Church; recreations: golf, fishing; Home: 26 McNab Cres., Regina, Sask. S4S 4B1; Office: Parkview Place, 2220 College Ave., Regina Sask.

BERIAULT, Ronald Joseph, C.L.U.; insurance executive; b. Toronto, Ont., 28 March, 1930; s. Elie and Anne (Mazin) B.; e. Public and High Schs., Hamilton, Ont.; McMaster Univ.; m. Vera, d. John Gordon Benedict, 27 March 1954; two children: Mark, Laurel; VICE-PRES. AND DIR., SKYWAY LIFE INSURANCE AGENCIES INC.; commenced as Ins. Agent, Life & General Ins. Co., Hamilton, Ont., 1950-57; Dist. Mgr., The Monarch Life Assurance Co., Hamilton, 1957-59; Branch Mgr., Zurich Life Insurance Co. of Canada, 1959-62; Supt. of Agencies, 1962-68; apptd. Vice-Pres., The Western Life Assurance Co., Hamilton, 1968; mem. C.L.U., Soc. for Crippled Children, Can. Hearing Soc., HIABA, MDRT, Hamilton Sertoma Club (Pres.); Home: Burlington, Ont.; Office: 105 Main St. E., Hamilton, Ont. L8N 1G6

BERLAND, Alwyn, M.A., M.Litt.; academic administrator; b. Chicago, Ill., 31 July 1920; s. Jacob and Elizabeth (Berg) B.; e. Univ. of Chicago, M.A. 1948; Cambridge Univ., M.Litt. 1953; m. Jayne Epstein, 3 Aug. 1941; 4 children; DEAN OF HUMANITIES, MCMASTER UNIV. since 1973; Professor and Chairman, Department of English, Univ. of Sask., Regina, 1963-67; Dean of Arts and Science, 1967-68; Extve. Dir. Candn. Assn. Univ. Teachers 1968-72; served as Ensign with U.S.N. during 2nd World War; Fulbright Scholar 1951-52, 1952-53; rec'd Can. Council Grant 1968; Can. Council Fellowship 1978-79; "Culture and Conduct in the Novels of Henry James," 1981 Ed., "The Wascana Review"; author or numerous articles for journs. in Eng., U.S. and Can.; Pres., Humanities Assn. Can.; mem., Assn. Candn. Univ. Teachers Eng.; Humanities Research Council Can.; Soc. of Friends; Home: 210 Bay St. S., Hamilton, Ont. L8P 3J1; Office: Hamilton, Ont.

BERLINGUETTE, Vincent Raymond, B.Com.; retired public servant; statistician; b. Ottawa, Ont., 28 Jan. 1919; s. Edgar and Rosa (Sayer) B.; e. Univ. of Ottawa, B.Com. 1941; m. Marie (deceased), d. late Joseph Rubben, 25 May 1946; three children; m. Ellen, d. late Arthur P. Nugent; Acct. & Stat., Imperial Tobacco Co. Ltd., Montreal, 1941-42; joined Bur. Bureau as Stat. and subsequently Chief, Business Stat. Sec., Research & Devel. Div., 1945-59; Asst. to Dir., Indust. & Merchandising Div., 1959-63; Dir., Indust. Div., 1963-67; Dir.-Gen., Econ. Br. 1967-73; Asst. Chief Stat. (Bus. Stat.), Statistics Can. 1973-78 (ret.) served Overseas as Arty. Offr. with 1st Medium Regt., RCA, 1942-45; R. Catholic; Home: 1890 Louisiana Ave., Oshawa, Ont. K1H 6V1

BERLIS, Douglas Albert, Q.C., B.A.; barrister and solicitor; b. Toronto, Ont., 25 Dec. 1920; s. Henry Albert and Annie Jean (Henderson) B.; e. Trinity Coll., Univ. of Toronto, B.A. 1942; Osgoode Hall; PARTNER, AIRD & BERLIS (Established 1974); Vice Pres., Dir. and Gen. Counsel, Algoma Central Railway; Pres. and Dir., All Canadian-American Investments Ltd.; Chrmn. and Dir., Canadian Worcester Controls Ltd.; Dir., and Secy., Permali (Can.) Ltd.; Petersen Can. Ltd.; Hamilton Kent of Can. Ltd.; Dir., Bralorne Resources Ltd.; Bathurst Paper Ltd.; Consolidated-Bathurst Inc.; Can. Tungsten Mining Corp. Ltd.; Domglas Inc.; The Investors Group; Montreal Trust Co.; Old Canada Investments Corp. Ltd.; Philips Canada Ltd.; Rolland Inc.; Sogepet Ltd.; read law with Manning, Mortimer & Kennedy, Toronto, Ont.; called to the Bar of Ont., 1949; cr. Q.C. 1961; Partner, Edison, Aird & Berlis 1953-74; served in 2nd World War; Pilot in R.C.A.F., 1941-45, Can., Eng., N. Africa, Italy, Flight Lieut.; mem. Int. Advisory Board, Amax Inc.; Trustee, Bank of Nova Scotia Pension Fund; Chrmn. N. York Gen. Hosp.; mem., Extve. Comte., Trinity Coll.; Presbyterian; recreations: golf; boating; Clubs: Toronto; Badminton & Racquet; Toronto Golf; Granite; Home: 1 Suncrest Drive, Don Mills, Ont. M3C 2L1; Office: 145 King St. W., Toronto, Ont. M5H 2J3

BERLIS, Norman Frederick Henderson, B.A.; barrister-at-law; diplomat; b. Toronto, Ont., 8 Apl. 1914; s. Henry Albert and Annie Jean (Henderson) B.; e. Trinity Coll., Univ. of Toronto, B.A. 1937; Osgoode Hall Law Sch., Toronto, grad. 1940; m. Oriel Louise Pollock, 11 March 1949 (deceased 1975); children: Michael Ernle, Anna Louise; read law with Joy & Chitty and with Mason, Foulds, Davidson, Carter & Kellock, Toronto; called to Bar of Ont. 1946; joined Dept. of External Affairs, Can. 1947; Offr. i/c Perm. Mission of Can. to European Office of U.N., Geneva, 1948-52; Depy. Head of European Div., Ottawa, 1952-54; Head of Estabs. & Organ. Div., 1954-56; Counsellor, Candn. Embassy, Rome, 1956-59; Head of Information Div., Ottawa, 1960-62; High Commr. to Tanzania, 1962-65 and concurrently accredited as High Commr. to Uganda, 1962-65 and to Kenya, 1963-65; Ambassador to Poland, 1965-67; Chief of Protocol, Ottawa, Ont. 1967-69; Ambassador to Austria 1969-75 and concurrently Perm. Rep. of Can. to the U.N. Indust. Devel. Organ., and to Internat. Atomic Energy Agency, also Candn. Gov. on I.A.E.A. Bd. of Govs., Vienna, 1970-73; Ambassador and Rep. of Can. to U.N. Econ. & Social Council N.Y. and Geneva, and concurrently Dir. U.N.

Econ. & Social Affairs Div., Dept. External Affairs, Ottawa 1973-75; Ambassador to Denmark 1975-79; retired from diplomatic service 1979; served with RCNVR 1943-46; enlisted as Ordinary Seaman; discharged with rank of Lt.; awarded Centennial Medal, 1967; Club: Le Cercle Universitaire, Ottawa; Home: 6A Egerton Gardens, London SW3 2BP

BERNARDI, Mario, C.C. (1972); b. Kirkland Lake, Ont., 20 Aug. 1930; s. Leone and Rina (Onisto) B.; e. Coll. Piox, Treviso, Italy; Benedetto Marcello Conserv., Venice, Italy; Mozarteum, Salzburg, Austria; Royal Conserv., Toronto; m. Mona d. Philip T. Kelly 12 May 1962; MUSIC DIR. & CONDUCTOR NATIONAL ARTS CENTRE ORCHESTRA, 1979-; Former Musical Dir., Sadler's Wells Opera Co.; has guest conducted the Royal Philharmonic, the London Symphony, the Quebec City, Montreal, Toronto, Edmonton, Vancouver, Indianapolis, Chicago and Pittsburgh Orchestras, as well as L'Orchestre de la Suisse roman de, the Los Angeles Chamber, the BBC Welsh, the Slovak Philharmonic Orchestras; as NAC Music Dir. & Conductor has toured Canada, the USA, Mexico, Europe and USSR; began musical career as pianist, Italy; on return to Can. was Soloist in various orchestras; Asst. Conductor, Toronto Opera Festival (later Candn. Opera Co.); conducted for radio and television; first worked as coach at Sadler's Wells on schol., 1962; makes annual performances at Stratford, Ont. Music Festival; U.S. debut, San Francisco Opera, Nov. 1967; annual appearances Vancouver Opera Assn. and C.B.C.; Club: Savage; Home:

BERNER, Rev. Norman, B.A., D.D.; minister; b. Guelph, Ont. 8 Oct. 1910; s. Ulrich Rudolf and Clara (Nieghorn) B.; e. Waterloo Coll. Univ. of W. Ont. B.A. 1935; Waterloo Lutheran Semy. 1938; Waterloo Lutheran Univ. D.D. 1972; m. Ruth M. d. late Henry Ludwig 14 Apl. 1941; three d. Carole (Mrs. Norman McLeod), Suzanne (Mrs. Larrie Brown), Heather (Mrs. Dalton Pinkerton); DIR., LUTHERAN CH. IN AM. CANADA FOUNDATION 1980- ; Min., Brantford-Woodstock Parish 1938-45; St. Lawrence Parish 1945-46; Ed., Lutheran Publication House, Philadelphia 1946-50; Mgr. Lutheran Ch. Store, Kitchener 1950-54; Asst. to Pres. Lutheran Synod 1955-79; Vice Pastor Zion Lutheran Ch. Stratford, Ont. 1979-80; Del., World Council Chs. Nairobi 1975; mem. Lutheran Seminar Japan 1972; Lutheran Observer-Consultant, Gen. Comn. Ch. Union (Ang.-Un. Ch.) 1968-72; Consultant, Candn. Lutheran World Relief, India, Jordan, Israel 1975; attended Lutheran World Fed. Conf. on Social Responsibility, Vienna 1969; author daily devotions "Home Altar"; mem. Candn. Council Chs. (Pres. 1972-76); Lutheran Council in Can. (Pres. 1978-79); Secy. Candn. Sec. Lutheran Ch. in Am. 1969-75; Home: 120 Blueridge Ave., Kitchener, Ont. N2M 4E1

BERNIER, Hon. Leo, M.P.P.; politician; b. Sioux Lookout, Ont., 12 Aug. 1929; s. Joseph and Leah (Jubinville) B.; e. Sioux Lookout (Ont.) Cont. Sch.; m. Marjorie, d. Dallas Gastmeier, 22 Aug. 1949; children: Janice (Mrs. Brian Evans), Karen (Mrs. Ralph Cast Jr.), Donald, John; MIN. OF NORTHERN AFFAIRS ONT. since 1977; el. M.P.P. 1966, re-el. since; apptd. Min. of Mines & Northern Affairs 1971 and Min. of Lands & Forests 1972 holding both portfolios until two Depts. merged into present Ministry; apptd. Ontario's first Min. of Northern Affairs 1971; also mem. Management Board of Ont. cabinet; former mem. Hudson (Ont.) Pub. Sch. Bd.; mem. Jr. Chamber Comm. Internat.; Senator 610; K. of C.; P. Conservative; R. Catholic; recreations: hunting, fishing, curling; Home: Hudson, Ont. P0V 1X0; Office: 10 Wellesley St. East, Toronto, Ont. M4Y 1G2

BERNIER, Roger B., librarian; b. Drummondville, Que. 28 Sept. 1942; s. Armand W. and Jeanne (Ouellette) B.; e. Seminaire de Sherbrooke B.A. 1964; Univ. de Montréal B.Bibl. 1965; Univ. de Sherbrooke 1966; m. Denise d. Gerard Marquis 26 Sept. 1967; divorced; one d. Hélène;

HEAD, BIBLIOTHEQUE DES SCIENCES, UNIV. DE SHERBROOKE 1981- ; Head of Cataloging & Classification Seminaire de Sherbrooke Bibliotheque 1965-67; Supvr. of Classification Univ. de Sherbrooke Bibliotheque 1967-69; Head, Service du Catalogage Univ. du Qué. à Montréal Bibliotheque 1969-70; Head, Bibliotheque des Sciences Univ. de Sherbrooke 1970, Head, Centres de documentation de la Bibliotheque 1972, Head, Bibliotheque Générale 1976, Head, Documentation Centre Program de Recherche sur l'Amiante 1977-81; Teacher, Lib. Congress Classification, Stage en Bibliotheconomie de La Pocatiere summers 1966, 1967, 1969, 1970; CEGEP Maisonneuve 1969; author "Classification Library of Congress: Manuel Pratique d'Utilisation (traduction) 1969; "Abrege de la Classification Library of Congress" 1970; "La Classification Library of Congress: Cours et Exercices" 1973; Vice Pres. de la Comn. de Credit, Caisse Populaire Ste-Jeanne d'Arc, Sherbrooke; Mem. ASTED.; Corp. des Bibliothecaires Professionels du Qué.; R. Catholic; recreations: skiing, sailing; Club: Optimist; Home: (C.P. 54) Plage Southiere R.R. 2, Magog, Que. J1X 3W3; Office: Sherbrooke, Que. J1K 2R1.

BERNIER, Hon. Yves, C.D., B.A., LL.L., B.Sc.Soc.; judge; b. Lévis, Qué. 17 Feb. 1916; s. late Henri and Yvonne (Picard) B.; e. Coll. de Lauzon; Séminaire de Qué. B.A. 1937; Univ. Laval LL.L. 1940, B.Sc.Soc. 1941; m. Victoire d. late Joseph T. Bernier 8 June 1942; children: Josée, Simon, Pierre; JUDGE, COURT OF APPEAL, QUE. 1973- ; called to Bar of Que. 1940; cr. Q.C. 1956; law practice Bernier & Bernier 1940; Moraud, Alleyn, Labreque & Bernier 1951; mun. Judge, City of Lauzon 1956-61; Judge, Superior Court Que. 1961-73; Prof. of Law (Bankruptcy) Laval Univ. 1961-72, Qué. Bar Sch. 1972-73; Depy. Judge, Admiralty Court 1965-70; apptd. to Court Martial Appeal Court 1961; Chrmn. Royal Comn. on Pilotage 1962-70; active service Candn. Army 1940-46, rank Lt. Col.; Reserve Army 1946-57, rank Lt. Col. (35e A/tk Régt. R.C.A.); mem. Candn. Bar Assn.; R. Catholic; Home: 349 St-Joseph St., Lauzon, Qué. G6V 1G5; Office: Court House, 12 St-Louis St., Québec City, Qué. G1R 4P6.

BERNSTEIN, Harold Joseph, M.A., Ph.D., F.C.I.C., F.R.S.C.; research chemist retired; b. Toronto, Ont. 26 Aug. 1914; s. Benjamin and Molly (Cohen) B.; e. Univ. of Toronto B.A. 1935, M.A. 1936, Ph.D. 1938; Univ. of Copenhagen 1939-40 (1851 Exhn. Research Scholar); Univ. of Chicago 1946; m. Dorothy d. late A. Snipper 28 Nov. 1947; children: Lee Ruth, Mark Aaron, Susan Elizabeth; retired 1978; Research Chem. Nat. Research Council, Div. of Chem.; rec'd Chem. Inst. Can. Medal 1974; Herzberg Award Spectroscopy Sc. Can. 1977; Pittsburgh Spectroscopy Conference Award 1980; co-author "High Resolution Nuclear Magnetic Resonance" 1959; over 200 research papers various nat. and internat. scient. journs.; interned Germany 1940-45; NDP; Jewish; recreations: music, golf; Club: Rideau View Golf & Country; Home: 616 Fraser Ave., Ottawa, Ont. K2A 2R5;

BERRILL, Norman John, Ph.D., D.Sc., LL.D., F.R.S., F.R.S.C.; b. Bristol, Eng., 28 Apl. 1903; s. Percy and Kate Eliza (Stiles) B.; e. Univ. of Bristol, B.Sc. 1924; Univ. Coll., Univ. of London, Ph.D. 1929; D.Sc. 1931; Univ. of Windsor, LL.D. 1967; Univ. Br. Col. D.Sc. 1972; McGill Univ. D.Sc. 1973; Fellow A.A.A.S. 1978; Travelling Rockefeller Fellow. 1927; Lect. Physiol. Sch. of Med., Leeds, 1927-28; Asst. Prof. Zool., McGill Univ., 1928-31; Assoc. Prof. 1931-38; Chrmn., Zoology Dept., 1938-47; apptd. Strathcona Prof. of Zool. 1946; Guggenheim Fellowship, 1964; author of "Man's Emerging Mind", 1955 (Gov.-Gen. Award for Creative Non-Fiction, 1955 and 1956); "Developmental Biology", 1971; "Development" 1976; Address: 410 Swarthmore Ave., Swarthmore, Pa. 19081.

BERRY, Edmund Grindlay, M.A., Ph.D., F.R.S.C.; educator; b. Leslie, Aberdeenshire, Scot. 12 March 1915; s.

Rev. James Garrow and Agnes (Henderson) B.; e. Dumfries Acad. 1925-26; Fredericton, N.B. 1926-32; Univ. of N.B. 1932-33; Queen's Univ. B.A. 1936, M.A. 1937; Univ. of Chicago Ph.D. 1940; m. Virginia d. Fred J. Gingerick, North Manchester, Ind. 25 Aug. 1943; children: Julia, Margaret; EMERITUS PROF. OF CLASSICS, UNIV. OF MAN. Lectr. present univ. 1940, Asst. Prof. 1946; Assoc. Prof. 1949, prof. 1957-80 Head of Classics Dept. 1961-78, Dir. of Summer Sch. 1946-49, Asst. Dean of Arts & Science 1949-51; mem. Queen's Univ. Council 1963-75; Candn. Council Acad. Panel 1966-69; Chrmn. Humanities Research Council 1972-74; mem. St. John's Coll. Council 1972-76; rec'd Guggenheim Fellowship 1951-52; Nuffield Foundation Research Grant 1969; author "Emerson's Plutarch" 1961; articles on Plutarch, Anacreon, classical influences on Am. and Eng. lit.; Chrmn. Ed. Bd. "Mosaic" 1976-80; mem. Classical Assn. Can. (Pres. 1970-72); Humanities Assn. (Pres. 1961-63); Hellenic Soc.; Am. Philol. Assn.; Classical Assn. Middle W. and S.; Anglican; recreations: reading, travel; Home: 310 Dromore Ave., Winnipeg, Man. R3M 0J5; Office: 210 Dysart Rd., Winnipeg, Man. R3T 2N2.

BERRY, Gerald L., M.A., Ed.D.; educator; b. Provost, Alta., s. Herbert and Ruby May (Hudson) B.; e. Provost (Alta.) High Sch., 1932; Camrose (Alta.) Normal Sch., 1934; Univ. of Alta., B.A. 1942, M.A. 1950, B.Ed. 1952; Univ. of Colo., Ed.D. 1963; m. Ruth Isabelle, 7 July 1945; children: Gregory Richard, Anne Marie, Margaret Elaine; Prof. Emeritus, Univ. of Alberta since 1978; Teacher and Princ. 1934-52; Supt. of Schs., High Prairie, 1952; Inspr. of High Schs. Alta., 1957; joined present Univ. 1961, Prof. and Chrmn., Dept. of Secondary Educ. 1965-78; author, "Religions of the World", 1947; "The Whoop-up Trail", 1951; "Champlain", 1967; "Problems and Values", 1967; also numerous articles, briefs, monographs and reports; mem. Edmonton Educ. Soc.; Phi Delta Kappa Internat.; Freemason; Liberal; Protestant; recreations: golf, bridge; Home: 12607-51A Ave., Edmonton, Alta. T6H 0N6

BERRY, Howard Townsend, B.Sc.; mining executive; b. 30 Dec. 1917; e. Queen's Univ. B.Sc. (Metall. Engn.) 1940; m. Betty Isabel Colles, 14 Sept. 1942; children: Brian, Michael, Jane; Chairman, PRES., CHIEF EXTVE. OFFR. AND DIR.,FALCONBRIDGE NICKEL MINES LTD.; Dir. Indusmin Ltd.; Corp. Falconbridge Copper; Falconbridge Dominicana; joined Cominco, Trail, B.C. 1946; Falconbridge Nickel Mines Ltd., Falconbridge, Ont. 1953, Toronto 1969- ; recreations: golf, skiing; Office: (P.O. Box 40) Commerce Court West, Toronto, Ont. M5L 1B4.

BERRY, L. Michael, B.A.; diPlomat; b. Bolton, U.K. 28 Sept. 1937; s. Leonard and Margaret (Wynne) B.; e. McGill Univ. B.A. 1961, grad. studies internat. relations 1963-64; m. Linda Kathleen d. Alan M. Randal, Rockburn, Que. 17 Aug. 1963; children: Elizabeth, Mark, Kathryn; CANDN. HIGH COMMR. TO SINGAPORE 1979- ; Special Asst. to Min. of Justice 1961-63; joined Dept. External Affairs 1964, Second Secy. Berlin 1966-68, Counsellor (Econ.) London 1971-75, Dir. Comm. & Econ. Policy Div. Ottawa 1977-79; Protestant; recreations: squash, cricket; Clubs: Toronto Cricket Skating & Curling; Singapore Cricket; Home: la Bishopsgate, Singapore 1025; Office: 230 Orchard Rd., Singapore 0923.

BERRY, Leonard Gascoigne, M.A., Ph.D., F.R.S.C., F.G.S.A., F.M.S.A., university professor; b. Toronto, Ont., 17 Aug. 1914; s. Francis Richard and Amelia (Gascoigne) B.; e. Univ. of Toronto Schs. (1924-32); Univ. of Toronto, B.A. 1937, M.A. 1938, Ph.D. 1941; m. May Catherine, d. late James Milthorpe, 11 Apl. 1941; children: Paul Richard, Susan Elizabeth; Miller Memorial Res. Prof. Geol., Queen's Univ. 1956-79; Emeritus Prof. since 1979; Editor, "The Canadian Mineralogist" and "Powder Data File"; Teaching Asst., Univ. of Toronto, 1937-40; Geol. (summers), Ont. Dept. Mines, 1936-40;

Engr., Research Enterprises Ltd., Toronto, Ont., 1940-44; joined Queen's Univ. as Lectr. in Mineral. 1944; John Simon Guggenheim Fellow, 1953-54; Can. Silver Jubilee Medal, 1977 Publications: "Mineralogy" (with Brian Mason), 1959; "X-Ray Powder Data for Ore Minerals" (with R. M. Thompson) 1962; "Elements of Mineralogy" (with Brian Mason) 1968; "Mineral Powder Diffraction File, Data Book and Search Manual" with P. Bayliss, Mary E. Mrose, Deane K. Smith, 1980; numerous short papers in scient. journs.; Hon. Dir., Royal Ont. Museum; Geol. Soc. Amer.; Mineral. Soc. Japan; Am. Crystallographic Assn.; Internat. Mineral Assn. (Treas. since 1960, Acting Secy. 1976-78); Hon. mem. Clube de Mineralogia, Recife (Brazil); Walker Mineral. Club: Mineral. Soc. Gt. Brit.; Mineral. Assoc. Can. (Vice-Pres. (1974) Pres. (1976) Editor Emeritus since 1975); Fellow Geol. Assn. Can.; Mineral. Soc. Am.; Vice-Pres. (1963) and Pres. (1964), Home: 1693 Hillview Rd., Kingston, Ont. K7M 5E3

BERRY, Rt. Rev. Robert Edward Fraser, B.A., D.D. (Ang.); b. Ottawa, Ont., 21 Jan. 1926; s. Samuel and Clara (Hartley) B.; e. Connaught Sch., Montreal, Que. 1939; High Sch. of Montreal 1943; Sir George Williams Coll., B.A. 1950; Montreal Diocesan Theol. Coll., L.Th. 1953, D.D. (Hon.) 1972; McGill Univ., B.D.1953; m. Margaret Joan Trevorrow, d. Dr. W. H. T. Baillie, Toronto, Ont., 12 May 1951; children: Christopher Fraser, Elisabeth Joan; BISHOP of KOOTENAY; o. Deacon, 1953, Priest 1954, Rector, St. Margaret's, Hamilton, Ont. 1955, St. Mark's, Orangeville, Ont. 1961, St. Luke's, Winnipeg, Man. 1963; Rector, St. Michael and All Angels, Kelowna, B.C. and Supvy. Pastor, Central Okanagan Region 1967; el. Bishop 8 May and consecrated 24 June 1971; served in 2nd World War, R.C.A.F., Air Crew 1943-45; Chaplain, B.C. Dragoons 1970-72; recreations: boating, fishing; Home: 1857 Maple St., Kelowna, B.C. V1Y 1H4; Office: Box 549, Kelowna, B.C. V1Y 7P2

BERRY, Wallace Taft, B.Mus., Ph.D.; educator; composer; b. La Crosse, Wisc. 10 Jan. 1928; s. Edward Carl and Louise (George) B.; e. Univ. of S. Calif. Los Angeles B.Mus. 1949, Ph.D. 1953; Conservatoire Nat. de Musique Paris 1953-54; m. Maxine Cecile d. late Abraham Metzner 11 May 1954; PROF. AND HEAD OF MUSIC, UNIV. OF B. C. 1978- ; Lectr. Univ. of Calif. Los Angeles 1956-57; Instr. Univ. of Mich. 1957; Asst. Prof. 1960, Assoc. Prof. 1963, Prof. 1966-67; composer various published works; author "Form in Music" 1966; "Structural Functions in Music" 1975; articles prof. journs.; recipient Fulbright Award Paris, France 1953-54; Univ. of Mich. Distinguished Faculty Award 1963; ASCAP Composer Awards N.Y. 1966-81 (intermittent); Pittsburgh Flute Club Nat. Competition Compositions for Flute 1st Prize 1970; Univ. S. Calif. Outstanding Music Alumnus 1973; Composer Award Am. Acad.- Inst. Arts & Letters 1978; el. to Univ. of Mich. Soc. Fellows 1975; served with U.S. Army 1954-56; mem. Candn. Univ. Music Soc.; Coll. Music Soc.; Soc. Music Theory (Press.-Elect); Am. Soc. Composers, Authors & Publishers; recreations: swimming, cooking; Home: 1104 - 1835 Morton, Vancouver, B.C. V6G 1V3; Office: 6361 Memorial Rdd., Vancouver, B.C. V6T 1W5.

BERTALANFFY, Felix D., M.Sc., Ph.D., F.R.M.S.; educator; b. Vienna, Austria, 20 Feb. 1926; s. late Prof. Ludwig and late Maria (Bauer) von B.; e. Univ. of Vienna Med. Sch. 1945-48; McGill Univ. M.Sc. 1951, Ph.D. 1954; m. Gisele Lavimodière, 20 Jan. 1954; PROF. OF ANATOMY, UNIV. OF MANITOBA since 1965; joined present Univ. as Asst. Prof. 1955, Assoc. Prof. 1959; med. and biol. research incl. cell div. and kinetics, cancer and carcinogenesis, regeneration, exfoliative cancer cytol., fluorescence microscopy and histochem., histophysiol. and pathol. of respiratory system, cancer chemotherapeutic agts.; developed acridine orange fluorescence microscopy for exfoliative cancer diagnosis (clin. application); writings incl. over 120 contribs. to biol. and med. journs. publ. in 6 langs.; over 150 articles on Japanese

philately and postal hist. in various Eng. and German philatelic publs.; Hon. Fellow, Pan Am. Cancer Cytol. Soc.; Fellow, Roy. Microscopical Soc. (London); Amer. Philatelic Soc.; Writers; Hall of Fame; mem. Am. Assn. Anatomists; Candn. Assn. Anatomists; Am. Assn. Cancer Research; Candn. Soc. Cytol.; Internat. Soc. Stereol.; Sigma Xi; R. Catholic; recreation: Japanese philately; Home: 886 Lindsay St., Winnipeg, Man. R3N 1H8; Office: Dept. of Anatomy, Univ. of Manitoba, 730 William Ave., Winnipeg, Man. R3E 0W3

BERTON, Pierre, O.C. (1974), B.A., LL.D., D.Litt.; author; b. Whitehorse, Yukon, 12 July 1920; s. Francis George and Laura Beatrice (Thompson) B.; e. Victoria Coll., Victoria, B.C.; Univ. of B.C., B.A. 1941; m. Janet Constance, d. A. L. Walker, Haney, B.C., 22 Mar. 1946; children: Penny Margaret, Pamela Beatrice, Patricia Dorothy, Peter Andrew, Paul Francis, Peggy Ann, Perri Robin; Dir., McClelland & Stewart Ltd.; Natural Science of Can., Ltd.; Panelist, "Front Page Challenge" (CBC-TV); Host: "The Great Debate" and "My Country" and Commentator: Radio CKEY "Dialogue"; Pres., Pierre Berton Enterprises Ltd.; My Country Productions Ltd.; Chrmn., Bd. of Govs. Heritage Canada; City Editor, Vancouver "News Herald" 1942; Feature Writer, "Vancouver Sun", 1946-47; Assistant Editor, "Maclean's Mag.", 1947-51; Assoc. Ed. 1952, and Mang. Ed. 1953-59; Assoc. Editor & Columnist, Toronto "Star", 1958-62; rejoined "Maclean's Mag.", 1962-63; Editor-in-chief, Canadian Centennial Library, 1964-68; served in 2nd World War with Candn. Inf. Corps. as Pte., Cpl., 2nd Lt. and Lt.; Royal Mil. Coll. (Intelligence Staff as Acting Capt., G.S.O. III); author of "The Royal Family", 1954; "The Golden Trail", 1955; "The Mysterious North", 1956 (Gov. Gen. Award for Creative Non-Fiction 1956); "Klondike", 1958 (Gov. Gen. Award for Creative Non-Fiction, 1958); "Just Add Water and Stir", 1959 (Leacock Medal for Humour, 1960); "Adventures of a Columnist", 1960; "The New City", 1961; "The Secret World of Og", 1961 and 1974; "Fast, Fast, Fast Relief", 1962; "The Big Sell," 1963; "The Comfortable Pew", 1965; "The Smug Minority", 1968; "The National Dream", 1970; "The Great Railway" (Illustrated) 1972; "The Last Spike" (Gov. Gen. Award for Non-Fiction) 1971; "Drifting Home", 1973; "Hollywood's Canada", 1975; "My Country" 1976; "The Dionne Years: A Thirties Melodrama" 1977; "The Wild Frontier" 1978; "The Invasion of Canada, 1812-13", 1980; "Flames Across the Border, 1813-1814", 1981; Nat. Newspaper Awards for Feature Writing and Staff Corresponding, 1961; ACTRA award (best public affairs broadcaster in radio, 1978); ACTRA'S Gordon Sinclair Award—Integrity and outspokenness in broadcasting—1972; Stephen Leacock Medal for Humour 1960; recreations: painting, bird watching, gardening, sketching, conversation; Home: R.R. 1, Kleinburg, Ont. L0J 1C0; Office: 21 Sackville St., Toronto, Ont. M5A 3E1

BERTRAM, David; petroleum executive; b. Calgary, Alta. 7 Feb. 1937; e. R.I.A. 1963; m. Olga, 18 April, 1959; children: David, Janice, Karen; SR. VICE PRES. FINANCE & ADM., CANADIAN OCCIDENTAL PETROLEUM LTD. 1976- , Dir. 1978- ; Controller present co. 1971, Treas. & Controller 1972, Vice Pres. Finance & Adm. 1974; mem. Soc. Mang. Accts.; Financial Extves. Inst.; Clubs: Willow Park Golf; Calgary Petroleum; Home: 611 Willow Park Pl. S.E., Calgary, Alta. T2J 1P3; Office: 1600 McFarlane Tower, 700 - 4th Ave. S.W., Calgary, Alta. T2P 3J5.

BERTRAND, Claude, C.C. (1971), B.A., M.D., F.A.C.S., F.R.C.S.(C); neurosurgeon; b. Sherbrooke, Que., 28 March 1917; s. Stella (Gamache) B.; e. St. Charles Borromée Semy., Sherbrooke, B.A. 1934; Univ. de Montréal, M.D. 1940; Rhodes Scholar elect; grad. and post-grad. training in Can. and USA; Research Assoc., Dept. of Anat., Oxford Univ., 1946-47; m. Claire Paradis, 16 May 1942; children: Hélène (Mrs. George Cantlie), Denise

(Mrs. Luc Pelland), Lucie (Mrs. Charles Wheeler), Louis; Emeritus Chief, Dept. of Neurosurgery, Hôpital Notre-Dame; Pres. of Extve., Med. Bd. there since 1969; Prof. of Neurosurg., Univ. de Montréal, 1969; joined present hosp. as Acting Chief, Dept. of Neurosurg., 1947; mem. Med. Research Comte. in Surg. 1965-66; joined Univ. de Montréal as Asst. Prof. of Surg. (Neurosurg.), 1947; Assoc. Prof. 1952; consulting neurosurg.; Montreal Neurol. Inst.; Barrie (Ont.) Mem. Hosp.; Hôtel-Dieu (Montreal and Sherbrooke); Santa Cabrini Hosp., Montreal (Hon.); Visiting Prof., Nat. Inst. of Health, Bethesda, Md., 1962; Bowman-Gray Sch. of Med., Winston-Salem, N.C., 1962; Univ. of Vermont 1966; Univ. of Alta. 1968; Dartmouth Univ. 1971; Exchange Prof., Univs. of Strasbourg, Paris, Marseille, Lyon, 1961; Univ. of Mexico 1964; Max Planck Inst., Frankfurt, 1969; served with RCAMC 1943-45; rank Capt. (Acting Maj.); Traveler for James IVth Assn. 1969; mem. Med. Research Council Can. 1969-71; rec'd Lawrence Poole Prize, Univ. of Edinburgh, 1970-71; Bd. of Dir., Sun Life; Crédit Foncier; Digital Equipment; C.E.D.; mem., Am. Assn. Neurol. Surgs.; Soc. Neurol. Surgs.; Neurosurg. Soc. Am. (Founding mem.); Pres. 1963); Soc. de Neurochirurgie de Langue Française Paris (Pres. 1964); Assn. des Neurochirurg. de la Prov. de Qué.; Candn. Neurosurg. Soc. (Pres. 1961); Soc. Brit. Neurol. Surgs. (Hon. mem. 1970); Montreal Neurol. Soc. (Pres. 1952); Am. Acad. Neurol. (Assoc. mem. 1956): Soc. Neurol. de Paris (Hon. mem.); Candn. Med. Assn. and other med. assns.; R. Catholic; recreations: skiing, tennis, golf; Clubs: Mount Bruno Golf; Montreal Tennis; Mount Stephen; Home: 15 Springgrove Cres., Outremont, Qué. H2V 3H8; Office: 15 Springgrove Cres., Outremont, Que. H2V 3H8

BERTRAND, Gérard, Q.C., B.A., LL.L; b. Donnacona, Que. 13 Apl. 1927; s. Joseph Alfred and Yvonne (Gravel) B.; e. Ecole du Sacré coeur Donnacona, Que.; Coll. de Lévis; Séminaire de Qué.; Laval Univ. B.A., LL.L.; Royal Candn. Sch. Inf.; Univ. of Toronto and York Univ. M.B.A. course 1971 (Pub. Service Bicultural Devel. Fellow); children: Louis, Anne Pascale; CHIEF LEG. COUNSEL, LEG. SEC., DEPT. OF JUSTICE since 1980; called to Bar of Que. 1952; cr. Fed. Q.C. 1975; rec'd comn. (COTC) 1950, Staff Learner H.Q.E. Que. Area 1951-52; joined Dept. External Affairs 1952-63 serving in Ottawa, Tokyo (1953-56), Paris (Second and First Secy. 1958-62); Candn. Corp. for 1967 World Exhn. 1963-67 serving as Extve. Asst. to Pres. and Commr. Gen. and Project Offr. "Man in the Community" Pavilion; Gen. Mgr. Nat. Film Bd. Can. 1968-71; Asst. Secy. to Cabinet (Leg. and House Planning) Privy Council Office 1972-76; Registrar, Supreme Court of Can. 1976-78; Assoc. Chief Leg. Counsel, Leg. Sec., Dept. of Justice 1978-80; mem. Hull Bar; Bar Prov. Que.; R. Catholic; recreations: cycling, tennis, reading; Clubs: Cercle Universitaire d'Ottawa (Founding mem.); Ottawa Bicycle; W. Ottawa Tennis; Home: 10-333 Metcalfe St., Ottawa, Ont. K2P 1S5; Office: West Memorial Bldg., 344 Wellington St., Ottawa, Ont. K1A 0J1

BERTRAND, Gilles, B.A., M.Sc., M.D., F.R.S.C. (1956); neurosurgeon; b. Montreal, Que., 5 Aug. 1924; s. Albert and Françoise (Demers) B.; e. Univ. de Montréal, Coll. Jean-de-Brebeuf, B.A. 1943; Univ. de Montréal, M.D. 1949; McGill Univ., M.Sc. 1954; m. Louise, d. late Napoleon Lafleur, 20 June 1953; children: Marise, François, Martin; PROF. OF NEUROSURGERY, McGILL UNIV. since 1971; Lect. neurosurg. there 1955; Asst. Prof. 1960, Assoc. Prof. 1963; Neurosurgeon-in-Chief, Montreal Neurol. Hosp. (1973); Consultant Neurosurg. Physician's Hosp., Plattsburgh N.Y.; Hosp. Jean-Talon, Montreal; Brome Missisquoi Perkins Hosp.; Pres., Candn. Assn. Neurol. Surg.; mem. Am. Assn. of Neurosurgs.; Am. Acad. Neurol. Surg.; Society of Neurological Surgeons 1977; Soc. de neurochirurgie de langue française; Montreal Neurol. Soc. (Past Pres.); Assn. des neurochirurgiens Prov. Que. (Sec., Pres. 1965-69); R. Catholic; recreations:

sailing, skiing; Club: Royal St. Lawrence Yacht; Home: 1317 Redpath Cresc., Montreal, Que. H3G 1A1; Office: 3801 University, Montreal, Que. H3A 2B4

BERTRAND, Rev. Hector-L., S.J., Ph.D., D.Sc. (R.C.); priest; educator; b. Warren, Ont., 10 March 1907; s. William James and Eugénie (Gervais) B.; e. Sacred Heart Coll., Sudbury, Ont., B.A. 1928; S.J. 1928; Georgetown Univ., D.Sc.; VICE PRES.-ADM., UNIV. OF SUDBURY since 1965; Publisher and Ed., "Le Voyageur" (weekly French paper) since 1975; o. 1939; Prof. of Apologetics and Dean of Discipline (Prefectus Disciplinae), Sacred Heart Coll. of Sudbury (now present univ.) 1941; Founder, 1st Conv. and Exhn. for Hosps., Prov. Que. 1948; Founder and Dir., L'Ecole Supérieure d'Administration Hospitalière, 1948; "L'Hopital d'Aujourd'Hui" (journ.), 1955; Founder, Med. Dirs. course, 1957; Hosp. and Med. Adm. courses (evening), 1961; Regent, Coll. of Medicine, Bangalore, India, 1963-65; consultant in hosp. adm.; during World War II served as Chaplain, Parachutists Corps (Candn.) 1943; Maj. and Commdg. Chaplain, Mil. Dist. No. 10, Can., 1944; rec'd George Findlay Stephens Mem. Award for "Outstanding services to Hospitals of Canada", citations from various prof. assns.; Pres. and Extve. Dir., Cath. Hosp. Assn. Can. 1945-52; Founder, Pres. and 1st Extve. Dir., Comité des Hôpitaux du Qué. 1947; Gov., Candn. Hosp. Assn., 1947-63 (with 2 yrs. exception; Chrmn. Comte. on Educ.); Founder, Assn. Med. Dirs. Prov. Que., 1957; Assn. Hosp. Adms. Prov. Que., Assn. Practical Nurses Prov. Que. (Hon. mem.), Assn.: Baby-Nurses Prov. Que.; Assn. Med. Record Librarians Prov. Que., 1960; Co-founder, Candn. Council on Hosp. Accreditation; Hon. Fellow, Am. Coll. Hosp. Adms.; Hon. mem., Que. Assn. Hosp. Adms.; Candn. Med. Record Librarians; Life mem., Assn. Consultants in Indust. Relations; mem., Acad. Hosp. Counsellors; Address: Univ. of Sudbury, Sudbury, Ont.

BERUBE, Jean-Yves, C.M.; exécutif; né Cap Chat, Qué. 5 mars 1928; f. Ephrem et Marie Leda Isabelle Bérubé; é. Ecole Cap Chat cours primaire; St-Alexandre et Gaspé cours classique; Université du Quebec a Polyvalente Ste-Anne-des-Monts cours adm. 1972-75; ép. Blandine f. Edouard Coulombe 23 octobre 1967; enfant: Louise; EXTVE., THE NAVY LEAGUE OF CAN., QUE. DIV.; Adjoint (surveillant) sur les constructions de quai Payroll 1949-51; Gérant personnel et traffic, Ungava Transport Inc. (Ste-Anne-des-Monts et Sept-Iles) 1951-63; Gérant du personnel et traffic, Agence Maritime Inc., dirigeant le tout du bureau Ste-Anne-des-Monts 1963-68; dirigeant ses propres affaires (appartements à loyers, commerces, etc.) 1968-72; entre 1960-77 mem. de l'exécutif du Conseil de dével. du territoire de la Gaspésie (2 ans); Administrateur du Conseil régional de Développement de l'Est du Qué.; Prés., Chambre de Comm. de Cap Chat et de la Gaspésie; Dir., Chambre de Comm. prov. de Qué.; Prés., Ligue Navale du Can. (sec Cap-Chat); Prés. de l'Office d'Habitation municipal de Cap-Chat; Echevin de la ville de Cap-Chat (terminé 1974); Prés. du Comité du dével. de la ville de Cap-Chat; Administrateur au CEGEP de Matane; postes actuels: mem. actionnaire du syndicat minier Boisbuisson (Mines Madeleine); Propriétaire édifice à logements; mem. Chevaliers de Colomb Cap-Chat; Prés., Camp aventurier de la Gaspésie (cadets) incorporé sous le nom de Ligue Navale de Cap-Chat Inc. (Fondateur); Prés. fondateur, Festival Nat. de Folklore inter-ethnique à St-Octave de l'Avenir (1977); Dir. régional de la Ligue Navale du Can. (secteur Qué.- Gaspé et Iles-de-la-Madeleine) et mem. du conseil d'adm.; mem. consel adm. Soc. des Arts Traditionnels du St-Laurent; Vice-Prés. Finance (Provinciale) de la LIGUE NAVALE du Canada; Admin. de l'Ass. Touristique de la Gaspésie; Catholique; récreations: tennis, skiing, ping-pong, baseball, hockey; bureau: 4846 Sherbrooke St. W., Westmount, Qué. H2Z 1G8; adresse: (L.P. 10) Lap-Lhat Lte., Gaspe G0J 1E0.

BÉRUBÉ, Hon. Yves Gilles Alexandre, M.N.A., D.Sc.; politician; b. Montréal, Qué. 28 March 1940; s. Armand and Fleur-Ange (Ménard) B.; e. St-Laurent Coll. Montréal; Mass. Inst. Technol.; m. Francine d. Marc Leroux, Montréal 24 Aug. 1963; children: Sylvie, Dominique;MIN. OF ENERGY & RESOURCES,QUE. 1979- and Pres., Treasury Bd., 1981- ; engr.; Prof. of Mines & Metall. Laval Univ.; el. M.N.A. for Matane prov. g.e. 1976, re-el. since; Min. of Lands & Forests and Min. of Natural Resources 1976; recipient Gold Medal Soc. pour l'Encouragement de la Recherche et de l'Invention Paris 1978; mem. Order Engrs. Que.; Parti Quebecois; R. Catholic; Office: 1050, St.-Augustin, 3e étage, Québec, Qué. G1R 4Z5.

BESANT, Derek Michael, B.F.A., R.C.A.; artist; educator; b. Fort MacLeod, Alta. 15 July 1950; e. Univ. of Calgary B.F.A. 1973, grad. studies 1974; m. Alexandra Haeseker 1 Aug. 1974; INSTR., ALTA. COLL. OF ART 1977- , Drawing Chrmn. 1978-80; apptd. to Legislative Art Comm., Minister of Culture, Alta.; Exhn. Designer, Glenbow-Alta. Inst. Art Gallery & Museum 1973-77 (design and layout for new museum location Calgary opening 1976); recent exhns. incl. Winnipeg Art Gallery Print Project; Nat. Print and Drawing Exhibition, Ont.; 10 Candn. Print Artists, Nat. Museums Can. tour of Japan; R.C.A. Contemporary Work in Alta., Nickle Arts Museum Calgary; New Work from Can., World Print Council San Francisco; Candn. Prints, Assn. Print Workshops Gt. Brit., Edinburgh, Scot.; Nine from Can., Candn. Consulate Boston; Painting in Alta.-An Hist. Survey, Edmonton Art Gallery; 10th Annual Nat. Works on Paper, S.W. Texas State Univ.; 150 Yrs. of Watercolour Painting in Alta., Glenbow Museum, Calgary; "Derek Besant" Mira Godard Gallery Toronto; Eau Claire Peel, Mural Calgary Comm.; "Faltiron Mural" W. wall Godderham Flatiron Bldg. Toronto 1980; Candn. Rep. Brit. Internat. Biennale 1979; rec'd 2nd Prize Miami Internat. Biennale 1977; Alta. Ed. "Artmagazine" 1975- ; author various articles, reviews; mem. Candn. Artist Representation; Univ. Art Assns. Can.; Alta. Soc. Artists; Boston Printmaking Soc.; World Print Council; Print & Drawing Council Can.; (Vice Chrmn. 1976-78, Extve. mem. 1979-80); Home: P.O. Box 520, Midnapore, Alta. T0L 1J0; Office: 1301, 16 Ave. N.W., Calgary, Alta. T2M 0L4.

BESSE, Ronald D.; publisher; b. Stayner, Ont., 7 Dec. 1938; e. Stayner (Ont.) Pub. Sch.; Collingwood (Ont.) Dist. Coll. Inst.; Ryerson Inst. of Technol., Business Adm. 1960; m. 26 Jan. 1963; children: Christopher, Alison; PRESIDENT AND CHIEF EXECUTIVE OFFICER, GAGE PUBLISHING LIMITED 1977; began publishing career with McGraw-Hill, Inc.; served as Vice Pres., McGraw-Hill Can. 1968-70; Mang. Dir., McGraw-Hill Mexico 1970-73; Pres. McGraw-Hill Ryerson 1973-76; Pres. and C.E.O., Consolidated Graphics Ltd.; Protestant; Home: 8 Lawrence Cresc., Toronto, Ont. M4N 1N1; Office: 164 Commander Blvd., Agincourt, Ont. M1S 3C7

BESSETTE, Gérard, M.A., L.ès L., D.ès L., F.R.S.C., university professor; b. Sabrevois, Que., 25 Feb. 1920; s. Jean-Baptiste and Victoria (Bertrand) B.; e. Univ. de Montréal, B.A. 1941; M.A. 1946, L.ès L. 1946, D.ès L. 1950; m. Irene, d. Jan Bakowski, 3 Sept. 1971; PROF. OF FRENCH, QUEEN'S UNIV., since 1960; Univ. of Sask. 1946-49; Duquesne Univ., Pittsburgh, Pa., 1951-58; Royal Mil. Coll., Kingston, Ont. 1958-60; author of "Poèmes Temporels", 1954; "La Bagarre", novel, 1958; "Le Libraire", novel, 1960; "Les Images en poésie canadienne-francaise", 1960; "Les Pédagogues", novel, 1961; "Not For Every Eye" (trans. of "Le Libraire"), 1962; "L'Incubation", novel, 1965; Ed., "Anthologie d'Albert Laberge", 1962; rec'd Gov. Gen.'s Lit. Award for French Fiction, 1966 and 1972; "Une Littérature en ébullition" (criticism) 1968; "Trois romanciers québécois" (criticism) 1974; "Incubation (trans. of "l'Incubation"H6; "Le Cycle" (novel) 1971; "La Commensale" 1975; "Les

Anthropoïdes" 1977; "Mes romans et moi" (memoirs) 1979; "La Garden-party de Christophine" (short stories) 1980; (in collab.) "Histoire de la littérature canadienne-française", 1968; "Le Semestre" (novel) 1979; Ed., "De Québec à Saint-Boniface", (anthol. of French-Candn. short stories), 1968; Address; 270 Frontenac St., Kingston, Ont. K7L 3S8

BESSIN, Hyman company president; b. Ottawa, Ont., 7 March 1910; s. Moses and Rachel (Wolinsky) B.; m. Marion, d. Samuel Friedman, New York City, 31 May 1942; children: Leya, Moshe, Berl, Hershel; PRESIDENT AND DIR., ACKLANDS LTD. and its 57 subsidiaries, since 1961; President, Lanark Investments Limited; Rachel Investments Limited; Fort Garry Court Limited; B&V Management Services Ltd.; Winston Hall, Ltd.; Secy.-Treas., Community Video Ltd.; Dir., Mizrachi Bank of Israel; Pres., Hotel Winchester, 1939-60; Eastview Bus Lines, 1946-50; served 7 yrs. on Winchester, Ont. Mun. Council and Hydro Comn.; Pres., Candn. Friends Bar Ilan Univ. (mem. Global Bd. of Trustees); Candn. Foundation of Jewish Educ.; Candn. Friends of Yeshiva Univ. (Trustee of Univ.); Founder and Trustee, Bar Ilan Univ., Israel; Nat. Treas. Mizrachi Zionist Organ. of Can.; mem., World Zionist Organ., Jerusalem; Candn. Zionist Fed. (Past Pres.); Ottawa Jewish Community (Past Pres.); Freemason; Hebrew; recreations: photography; antique coin collecting; Home: 438 Daly Ave., Ottawa, Ont. K1N 6H4

BEST, Brian Desmond, M.D., F.R.C.S. (Edin.), F.R.C.S. (C); b. Chandlers Ford, Eng., 20 Aug. 1910; s. Robert Moore and Ann (McBride) B.; came to Canada 1911; e. Killarney Pub. and High Schs., Man.; Univ. of Manitoba, M.D. 1934; Lic., Med. Council of Can. 1934; F.R.C.S. (Edin.) 1937; F.R.C.S.(C.) 1949; m. Jean Margaret, d. Herman Prior, Portage la Prairie, Man., June 1940; one s. and one d.; Emeritus Prof. of Obstet. and Gynaecol., Univ. of Manitoba, until retired 1980; Hon. Obstet. and Gynaecol., Winnipeg Gen. Hosp.; mem., Candn. Med. Assn.; Winnipeg Med. Soc.; Coll. of Phys. & Surg. of Man. (Pres. 1946-47); Soc. of Obstet. & Gynaecols. of Can.; Candn. Gynaecol Past Pres., Soc.; has contrib. scient. papers to various med. publs.; Protestant; Home: 204-1 Evergreen Pl., Winnipeg, Man. R3L 0E9;

BEST, Douglas W.; company president; b. Toronto, Ont., 13 Jan. 1917; s. Thomas Wilbur and Lila (Wilson) B.; e. Univ. of Toronto Schs. 1934; m. Betty-Jane, d. Hon. Harold Kirby, June 1947; children: Thomas H., J. Kirby; PRESIDENT, T. H. BEST PRINTING CO. LIMITED since 1953; Pres., Ontario Publishing Company Limited; Director, Royal Canadian Mint; joined present Company, 1934; Vice-Pres. and Gen. Mgr., 1945; joined Ontario Publishing Co. as Sales Mgr., 1937; Vice-Pres. and Gen. Mgr., 1945, Pres. 1966; served in 2nd World War, Lieut., R.C.N.V.R. 1941-45; mem. Book Mfrs. Inst. Inc. (Extve. Comte.); Candn. Mfrs. Assn; Toronto Bd. Trade; Graphic Arts Indust. Assn.; Council of Printing Industries; Liberal; United Church; recreations: skiing, golf; Clubs: Empire; National; Granite; Home: 119 Strathallan Blvd., Toronto, Ont. M5N 1S9; Office: 33 Kern Rd., Don Mills, Ont. M3B 1S9

BEST, Edward Willson, B.Sc., Ph.D.; geologist; b. Windsor, Ont., 15 April 1927; s. William and Della Pearl (Willson) B.; e. Univ. of W. Ont., B.Sc. 1949; Univ. of Wis., PhD. 1953; m. Bette Ilene Rushlow, 1951; children: Wendy Elizabeth, Alan Randall, Carolyn Leslie; VICE-PRES. (NATURAL RESOURCES)BP CANADA INC.; Chief Geologist, Triad Oil Company, 1958; Exploration Manager 1963; Vice President 1969; Dir., BP Can. 1980-Home: 116 Roxboro Rd. SW, Calgary, Alta. T2S 0R1; Office: 333 5th Ave. S.W., Calgary, Alta. T2P 3B6

BEST, Henry Bruce Macleod, M.A., Ph.D.; educator; b. Toronto, Ont. 9 Oct. 1934; s. late Dr. Charles Herbert and

Margaret (Mahon) B.; e. Upper Can. Coll. Toronto; Univ. of Toronto B.A. 1956; Laval Univ. M.A. 1957, Ph.D. 1969; m. Janna Mairi de Grasse d. Iain Ramsay, Isle of Islay, Scot. 28 Dec. 1964; children: Mairi, Bruce; PRES. LAURENTIAN UNIV. OF SUDBURY and Prof. of Hist.; Extve. Asst. to Secy. of State and asst. to other cabinet mins. 1958-60; Extve. Asst. to Leader of Opposition Nfld. 1960; Extve. Secy. Internat. Diabetes Fed. 1963-64; Research Assoc. to Pres. York Univ. 1964-65, Asst. to Pres. 1965-66; Lectr. in Candn. Hist. 1964-66, Dir. of Student Services and Lectr. Candn. Hist. & Humanities 1966-69, Asst. Prof. of Hist. Atkinson Coll. and Fellow of McLaughlin Coll. 1969-71, Assoc. Prof. and Acting Coordinator of Candn. Studies 1971-74, Assoc. Dean of Atkinson 1971-73, Assoc. Prof. and Jt. Coordinator Candn. Studies 1975-77; mem. Sudbury 2001 Comte. 1977-; Chrmn. First Special Council Ont. Univs. Comte. on Support of Bilingualism (francophones) 1978, mem. Second Special Council (anglophones); Chrmn. Univs. Centennial Comte. Ont. 1965-67; Chrmn. Centennial Programme in Arts AUCC 1965-67; regular commentator in French and Eng. on pol. and cultural affairs radio and TV Toronto and Montreal 1965; mem. Governing Council Ont. Coll. Art 1972-74 (Chrmn. 1973-74); Course Dir. New Horizons Programme Fed. Govt. 1973-74; mem. Planning Bd. Twp. Nassagaweya 1970-73 (mem. and Chrmn. Comte. Adjustment 1971-74); Dir. Ont. Educ. Communications Authority 1978-; Sudbury & District Chamber of Commerce; Laurentian Hospital; Elliot Lake Centre; recipient Can. Council Grants for Candn. Studies; author various acticles, papers, book chapters, contrib. to "The Dictionary of Canadian Biography"Vol. 1 and V; mem. Candn. Assn. Scot. Studies; Candn. Profs Peace in Middle E.; Adv.Bd., "Language and Society"; P. Conservative; Presbyterian; recreations: farming, collection antiques; Clubs: University Toronto); Idylwylde Golf & Country (Sudbury); Home: 179 John St., Sudbury, Ont. P3E 1P5; Office: Sudbury, Ont. P3E 2C6.

BEST, James Calbert, B.A.; Canadian public servant; b. New Glasgow, N.S., 12 July 1926; s. Albert T. and Carrie Mae (Prevoe) B.; e. New Glasgow (N.S.) High Sch., 1943; King's Coll., Dalhousie Univ., B.A. 1948, Dipl. Journalism 1948, post-grad. work, Pol. Science-Pub. Adm. 1949; m. Barbara Doreen, d. Isaac Charles Phills and Mary Phills (Alda), Sydney, N.S., 17 Oct. 1957; children: Christene, Jamie, Stephen, Kevin; (Asst. Depy. Min. (Operations) 1970-73); Asst. Dep. Min. (Adm.), Dept. of Manpower and Immigration 1974-75; Dir. Applied Studies in Govt. Prog., Commonwealth Secretariat, London, Eng. 1975-77; Special Policy Advisor to Dep. Min./Chrmn. Can. Employment and Immigration Comm./Dept. 1978; Extve. Dir., Immigration and Demographic Policy 1978; Nat. Pres., Civil Service Assn., Can., 1957-66; Dir., Personnel & Adm., Office of Comptroller of Treasury, Can., 1966-69; Dir.-Gen., Adm., Dept. Supply & Services, Can., 1969-70; former mem. Bd. of Govs., King's Coll., Halifax; rec'd Centennial Medal 1967; mem., Inst. Pub. Adm. Can. Fed. Inst. Gen. Mang. (Dir.); Fed. Financial Offrs.' Inst.; Anglican; recreations: reading, photography, music; Home: 2067 Delmar Dr., Ottawa, Ont. K1H 5P6; Office: Place Du Portage, Phase 4, Hull, Quebec K1A 0J9

BETHUNE, Gordon Wallace, B.Sc., M.D., C.M., F.R.C.S.(C), F.A.C.S.; surgeon; educator; b. Toronto, Ont. 22 Oct. 1919; s. John Hamilton Gordon and Mabel (Hickey) B.; e. Baddeck (N.S.) High Sch.; Acadia Univ. B.Sc. 1939; Dalhousie Univ. M.D., C.M. 1943; m. Helen Lorraine d. late Gordon Daley 27 Oct. 1943; children: Graeme H.G., M.D., Drew C.G., M.D.; PROF. AND HEAD OF SURGERY, DALHOUSIE UNIV. 1967- ; Head of Surgery, Victoria Gen. Hosp.; Consultant in Surg., Camp Hill Hosp., Halifax Infirmary, Saint John Gen. Hosp., N.S. Govt.; Lectr. in Surg. Dalhousie Univ. 1951, Prof. and Head of Clin. Surgery 1964; conducted private practice of surgery; apptd. Asst. and Assoc. Surgeon,

Victoria Gen. Hosp.; Trustee, Dennis Med. Fund Dalhousie; served with R.C.A.M.C. Can. and Europe 1943-46, rank Capt.; initiated program of offshore yacht racing (Bluenose Offshore Racing Circuit); author various articles and papers related to breast carcinoma; mem. Ed. Bd. "Canadian Journal of Surgery"; mem. Council Royal Coll. and mem. Extve. Comte. Council; Founding mem. Candn. Assn. Gen. Surg.; mem. Candn. Med. Assn.; Assn. Gen. Surgs.; Candn. Assn. Clin. Surgs.; A.O. Whipple Surg. Soc.; Soc. Surg. Chrmn.; Soc. Candn. Surg. Chrmn.; A.O.A.; Phi Rho Sigma; recreations: sailing, golf, bridge; Clubs: R.N.S.Y.S.; Chester Yacht; Saraguay; Home: 1618 Oxford St., Halifax, N.S.; Office: Victoria General Hospital, Halifax, N.S. B3H 2Y9.

BETTERIDGE, Lois Etherington, M.F.A., R.C.A.; silversmith and goldsmith; b. Drummondville, Que. 6 Nov. 1928; d. Alfred George and Dorothy May (Young) Etherington; e. Ont. Coll. of Art 1948; Univ. of Kans. B.F.A. 1951; Cranbrook Acad. of Art Mich. M.F.A. 1957; m. Keith James Betteridge, Hants., Eng. 11 Sept. 1960; children: Eric Beasley, Lise Miranda, rep. 9 solo exhns. and over 75 group exhns.; rep. in various pub. colls. incl. Royal Scot. Museum; Massey Foundation Coll. of Contemporary Candn. Crafts; Nat. Museum of Natural Sciences Ottawa; Candn. and Ont. Crafts Council Perm. Works; lectr. USA, Gt. Brit., Scandinavia and Can.; Juror Workshops Can. and abroad; secular and ecclesiastical holloware; gold and silver jewelry; recipient Citation for Distinguished Prof. Achievement Univ. of Kans. 1975; Saidye Bronfman Award for Excellence in Crafts 1978; Can. Council Travel Grant to attend opening of her exhn. at Candn. Cultural Centre Paris 1979; Debeers Ring Competition Award; Craft Dimensions Award; cited various publs.; author various articles; mem. Adv. Bd. Algonquin Coll. Applied Art Technol. Ottawa; mem. Soc. N. Am. Goldsmithing; Ont. Crafts Council; Candn. Crafts Council; Visual Arts of Ottawa (Vice Pres.); Alpha Delta (Vice Pres. 1950-51); Protestant; recreations: skiing, swimming, canoeing; Address: 62 Parc Champlain, Mt-St-Hilaire, Que. J3H 3R6.

BETTS, Donald Drysdale, M.Sc., Ph.D.; university professor; b. Montreal, Que., 6 May 1929; s. Wallace Havelock and Mary (Drysdale) B.; e. Dalhousie Univ. B.Sc. (Physics) 1950, M.Sc. (Physics) 1952; McGill Univ., Ph.D. (Physics) 1955; m. Vilma Florence, d. late Horace Mapp, 5 June 1954; div. 1980; children: Malcolm R., Sylvia M., Eric K., Douglas R.; DEANOFARTS AND SCIENCE AND DALHOUSIE UNIV.; mem. of organizing comte. of internat. summer schs. in physics, 1957,1961,1965 and 1968; rec'd. Nat. Research Council of Can. Post-doctoral Fellowship, 1955-56 and Grants; NATO Science Fellow 1963-64; Nuffield Foundation Fellow, 1970-71; mem., Candn. Assn. Physicists (Vice Pres. 1968-69; Pres. 1969-70); SCI-TEC (Vice Pres. 1970); recreations: camping, badminton; Home: 908 6369 Coburg Rd., Halifax, N.S. B3H 4J7

BEVERIDGE, James MacDonald Richardson, OC, Ph.D., M.D., LL.D., D.Sc., F.R.S.C. (1960); university president; b. Dunfermline, Scotland, 17 Aug. 1912; s. James and Margaret (Spence) B.; e. Dunfermline High Sch.; came to Can., 1927; Horton Acad., Wolfville, N.S. (1933); Acadia Univ., B.Sc. 1937, and D.Sc. 1962; Univ. of Toronto, Ph.D. 1940; Univ. of W. Ont., M.D. 1950; LL.D. Mount Allison 1966; D.Sc., Queen; Univ. 1978; m. Jean Frances, d. Rev. Dr. F. H. Eaton, 26 Dec. 1940; children: Catherine, James, Alexander, Robert, Duncan, William, Elizabeth; Pres. Acadia Univ. 1964-78; Craine Prof. of Biochem., Queen's Univ. and Head of Dept., 1950-64; Chrmn., Bd. of Grad. Studies there 1960-63; Dean of School 1963-64; mem., Candn. Nat. Comte. of Internat. Union of Biochem., since 1955 (Chrmn. 1959-62); Chrmn., Defence Research Bd. Panel on Nutrition & Metabolism, 1961-65; Dir., C.B.C., 1965-68; mem., Fisheries Research Bd. Can., 1959-68; Research Asst., Univ. of Toronto, 1940-44; Scient. Asst. and later Assoc. Biochemist,

Pacific Fisheries Exper. Stn., Vancouver, 1944-46; Lectr., Univ. of W. Ont., 1946-50; Publications; about 100 scient. papers; mem., Am. Inst. Nutrition; Am. Soc. for Clinical Nutrition; Candn. Bio-chem. Soc.; Candn Physiol. Soc (Secy. 1953-56); Candn. Soc. for Clinical Chem; Chem. Inst. Can.; Council on Arteriosclerosis; Nutrition Soc. Can. (Pres., 1964-65); Science Council of Can. 1968-71; Alpha Omega Alpha; United Church; recreations: golf, fishing, bridge; Clubs: Ken-Wo Golf & Country; Home: R.R. 1, Canning, N.S. B0P 1H0

BEWICK, Howard Albany, M.A., Ph.D.; consultant; retired chemist; b. Toronto, Ont., 9 Sept. 1916; s. Albany and Maude (Coupland) B.; e. Univ. of Toronto, B.A. 1940, M.A. 1941, Ph.D. 1945; m. Lenore, d. Karl D. Knechtel, Hanover, Ont. 28 Apr. 1945; children: Brenda, Paul, David, Brian; Chemist, Imperial Oil, Sarnia, Ont., 1943-44; Research Chem., Nat. Research Council, Toronto and Ottawa, 1944-45; Research Supv., Solvay Process Div., Allied Chemical Corp., Syracuse, N.Y., 1946-52, Asst. Dir. Research 1952-58; Dir., Devel., Allied Chemical Canada Ltd., Montreal, 1959-67; Vice-Pres. Development and Planning (Pte. Claire) 1967-73; Technical Director (Amherstburg) 1973-75; Directr Environment Services (Amherstburg) 1975-76; Director Special Projects (Amherstburg) 1976; mem. Am. Chem. Soc.; Soc. of Chem. Indust.; Chem. Inst. Can.; Nat. Assn. of Accts.; Protestant; Home: 1030 Morand St., Windsor, Ont. N9G 1J6

BEZNAK, Margaret, M.D.; b. Budapest, 10 May 1914; d. Bela Hortobagyi, M.D. and Dr. Margaret (Winter) H.; e. Univ. of Budapest, M.D. 1939; m. A. B. L. Beznak, M.D., 1936; came to Canada 1953; retired 1979; Prof. of Physiol. 1976-79; Acting Dean, Faculty of Med. Univ. of Ottawa 1975-76, Vice-Dean 1969-75; Prof. and Chrmn. Dept. of Physiol. 1960-69; mem. Bd. of Govs. of Univ. 1968-74); mem. Bd. of Trustees, Children's Hospital Eastern Ont. until 19079; author of close to 80 scient. publ.; mem. Physiol. Soc. (Eng.); Candn. Physiol. Soc.; Home: 61 Reid, Ottawa, Ont. K1Y 1S8

BHATIA, Avadh Behari, M.Sc., D.Phil., Ph.D., F.R.S.C., educator; b. Barabanki, India 16 Aug. 1921; e. Univ. of Allahabad B.Sc. 1940, M.Sc. 1942, D.Phil. 1946; Univ. of Liverpool Ph.D. 1951; PROF. OF PHYSICS, UNIV. OF ALTA. since 1960; Lectr., Univ. of Allahabad 1944-47; 1851 Exhn. Scholar Univs. of Bristol and Liverpool 1947-49; Prof. of Theoretical Physics, Phys. Research Lab. Ahmedabad, India 1950-52; Imperial Chemical Industries Fellow, Univ. of Edinburgh 1952-53; Nat. Research Council Fellow Ottawa 1953-55; Asst. and Assoc. Prof. Univ. of Alta. 1955-60, Dir. Theoretical Physics Inst. 1964-69; Hon. Prof. Univ. of Liverpool 1963-64; Science Research Council (UK) Sr. Visiting Fellow, Univ. of Oxford 1978-79; author "Ultrasonic Absorption" 1967; over 70 research papers nat. and internat. journs.; Fellow of the American Physical Society; Fellow of former Phys. Soc. Eng.; mem. Candn. Assn. Physicists; Assoc. mem. Acoustical Soc. Am.; recreations: walking, music, reading; Home: 8734 - 117 St., Edmonton, Alta. T6G 1R5; Office: Edmonton, Alta. T6G 2J1.

BHERER, Wilbrod, C.M., Q.C.; radio and television executive; b. St-Fidèle, Qué. 11 Aug. 1905; s. Wilbrod and Laure (Lapointe) B.; e. Laval Univ. B.A., Faculty of Law studies; m. Françoise d. A. O. Pruneau 13 Oct. 1931; one d. Hélène (Mrs. Jean Pelletier); PRESIDENT AND CHIEF EXTVE. OFFR. TELE-CAPITAL LTD. 1978- ; Dir. Ritz Carlton Hotel, Montreal; called to Bar of Que. 1930; cr. K.C. 1945; law practice 1930-58; Pres., George T. Davie & Sons Ltd. 1958-64; Depy. Chrmn. Canadian Vickers Ltd. 1964-67, Chrmn. 1967-76; mem. Extve. Comte. present Co. 1976-78; Chrmn. R. Cath. Sch. Bd. City Quebec 1958-71; mem. Bd. Laval Univ. 1967-72, Chrmn. Med. Center 1968-79; Vice Pres. Centre Hospitalier; Kt. Commandor Ordre Equestre du St-Sépulcre de Jérusalem and Ordre Equestre de St-Lazarre; served with Que. Regt., rank Lt. Col.; mem. Candn. Bar Assn.; R. Catholic; recreation: gardening; Clubs: St. James's; Mount Royal; Cercle Universitaire; Home: 835 des Braves, Quebec City, Que. G1S 3C5; Office: 2136 Ste-Foy Rd., Ste-Foy, Que. G1K 7X2.

BIANCHINI, Lucian, M.A.L.S.; librarian; b. Ferrara, Italy, 15 March 1929; s. Amedeo and Jole (Bruni) B.; e. Cermenate, Como, Italy; Aquinas Coll. 1950-51 and Rosary Coll., M.A.L.S. 1954; Sacred Heart Semy., Melrose Park, Ill., 1951-54; Gregorian Univ., Rome, 1960-61; M.P.A., Dalhousie Univ. 1981; LIBRARIAN, MOUNT ST. VINCENT UNIV. since 1973; Cataloguer, Univ. of Calgary Lib., 1967, Head, Humanities Div., 1969; mem., Candn. Lib. Assn.; Atlantic Provs. Lib. Assn.; R. Catholic; Home: 9 School Ave., Halifax, N.S. B3N 2E1; Office: Halifax, N.S.

BICKFORD, James G.; banker; b. Huntingdon, Que., 22 July 1928; s. Harold Gordon and Jean Forbes (Stark) B.; e. Huntingdon (Que.) Acad. 1945; m. Jetta Florence Georgina, d. Merlin Aubrey Goodger-Hill, Toronto, Ont., 6 Aug. 1951; EXTVE. VICE PRES., ADMINISTRATION, CANADIAN IMPERIAL BANK OF COMMERCE Chrmn. and Pres., Dominion Realty Co. Ltd.; Imbank Realty Co. Ltd.; Dir., Great Lakes Re. Management Corp., N.Y.; Canlea Ltd.; Delta Hotels Ltd.; Commerce First Ltd.; Ont. Heart Foundation; joined present Bank 1945; served at various brs. Que. Region until 1959; Mgr., Lachine, Que. 1959, Regional Gen. Mgr.'s Dept., Montreal, special assignment 1961, Mgr., Kingston, Jamaica 1964-66, London, Eng. 1967, Vice Pres., Internat. 1970; Senior Vice-Pres., Internat 1973; Exec. Vice-Pres., Internat, 1978; Extve. Vice Pres., Admin., 1980; mem. St. Andrews Soc.; Toronto Black Watch Assn.; Freemason; Presbyterian; recreations: shooting, fishing, photography, chess; Clubs: National; (Toronto) City of London (Eng.); Overseas Bankers (London, Eng.); Metropolitan Club, New York; Can. Club of New York; Home: 55 Harbour Square, Ste. 1013, Toronto, Ont. M5J 2L1; Office: Commerce Court West, Toronto, Ont.

BIDWELL, Roger Grafton Shelford, B.Sc., M.A., Ph.D., F.R.S.C.; biologist; educator; b. Halifax, N.S., 8 June 1927; s. late Adm. Roger Edward Shelford and Mary Grafton (Bothamly) B.; e. Dalhousie Univ., B.Sc. 1947; Queen's Univ., B.A., M.A., Ph.D. 1954; m. Shirley Mae Rachel, d. late Ernest Mason, 1 July 1950; children: Barbara Mary Grafton, Alison Deborah, Roger John Shelford, Gillian Frances; Tech. Offr., Defence Research Bd. of Can., Kingston, Ont. 1951; Asst. Research Offr., Nat. Research Council, Halifax, 1956; Assoc. Prof. of Bot., Univ. of Toronto, 1959; Prof. of Biol., Case W. Reserve Univ., Cleveland, 1965-69 (Chrmn. of Dept. 1966-69); Prof. of Biology, Queen's Univ. 1969-79; I.W. Killam Research Prof. and Prof. of biology, Dalhousie Univ., 1981-; External Examiner in Botany, Nanyang Univ. Singapore 1974-77; Sc. Exch. Visitor, People's Republic of China, 1975 and 1977; Visiting Prof., Cornell Univ., summers 1961-63; Visiting Scientist, NRC, Halifax, 1966, 1976-77; mem. Adv. Bd., Atlantic Regional Lab. of NRC (1972-75); has participated in internat. confs. on plant science in USA, Brit., Poland and Can.; conducted research in photosynthesis, plant metabolism, seaweed metabolism, nitrogen and proteins in plants; author, "Plant Physiology", 1974, 1979; Assoc. Ed., "Canadian Journal of Botany", 1970-1980; Ed., "Biological Council of Canada Newsletter", 1972-76; other writings incl. over 90 scient. papers, book chapters; Convener, Plant Sciences Sec., Royal Soc. Can. 1975-77; Pres., Halifax Br., Civil Service Assn., 1959; mem., N.S. Inst. Science; Candn. Soc. Plant Physiols. (Founding Comte.; Secy.-Treas. 1963-65, Pres. 1972-73); Am. Assn. Advanc. Science; Biol. Council Can. (Secy, 1972-76); Fellow, Explorers Club 1978; Queen's Jubilee Medal 1977; Candn. Soc. of Plant Physiols. Gold Medal 1979; Anglican; recreations: sailing, skiing, walking, music; Office: Atlantic Research Associates, Box 202, Wallace, N.S. B0K 1Y0

BIELER, André, R.C.A. (1955), LL.D. (Queen's 1969); artist; b. Lausanne, Switzerland, 8 Oct. 1896; s. Prof. Charles and Blanche (Merle d'Aubigne) B.; e. Stanstead Coll.; Beaux-Arts, Paris; m. Jeannette, d. Theodore Meunier, Montreal, P.Q., 27 April 1931; has four children; studied painting in Paris, Switzerland and New York; Resident Artist and Prof. of Art, Queen's Univ., Head of Dept. and Dir., Agnes Etherington Art Centre, 1936-63; Emeritus Prof. since 1963; Banff Sch. of Fine Arts, 1940, 1947, 1949 and 1952; organ. Fed. Candn. Artists, 1941; rep. in Toronto, Vancouver, Edmonton, Windsor, Hamilton, Winnipeg, Oshawa, London, Ont. Art Galleries; National Gallery, Ottawa; Montreal Museum of Fine Art; Hart House, Toronto; Le Musée de la Prov. Qué.; Queen's Univ., Sir George Williams Univ., McMichael Candn. Collection, Kleinberg, and many private collections; won competitions for Mural at Shipshaw for Aluminum Co. of Can. (1946); in new D.V.A. Bldg. (E. Mem. Bldg.), Ottawa (1954); Mosaic in Chalmers Ch. Hall, Kingston, Ont.; Frontenac Tile Co., Kingston, Ont.; Internat. Exhns., Paris 1936; Coronation 1937; Tate 1938; Chicago Watercolor 1938: Chicago 1939; World Fair, New York and San Francisco 1939; Brooklyn Internat. Biennial 1941; Andover 1942; Yale 1944; Rio 1946; Boston Museum of Fine Arts 1946; U.N.E.S.C.O. 1946; Fifty Years of Canadian Painting 1949; Virginia Museum, Richmond, 1949; Painters of Can. 1949; Contemp. Candn. Art 1950; Brazil 1950; San Francisco 1956; one-man shows, Geneva, paintings and drawings, 1924; Montreal Art Assn. 1924; Ritz, Montreal, paintings and drawings 1926; Kingston, paintings, 1937; Toronto, Montreal, Winnipeg, Ottawa watercolours, 1940; Ecole des Beaux Arts, Que., paintings, 1941; Eaton;s Coll. St., Toronto, paintings, 1946; Garfield Gallery, Toronto, paintings and drawings 1950; Museum of Fine Arts, Montreal paintings and drawings, 1952; Robertson Art Gallery, Ottawa, paintings, 1954; Kingston, paintings, 1955; Retrospective Exhn. 1924-63, Agnes Etherington Art Centre, 1963; Mexico (San Miguel Allende) 1964; Irene McKim Gallery, Kingston, 1966; Walter Klinkhoff, Montreal 1969; Organizer and Chrmn., Conf. of Candn. Artists, Queen's Univ. 1941, publ. proc. jointly with Mrs. Elizabeth Harrison, 1941; Montreal Medal (Queen's) 1976; Retrospective (in 10 Canadian cities) 1970-71; Wallack's Gallery, Ottawa 1970; Kaspar Gallery, Toronto 1977; one-man show, Roberts Gallery, Toronto 1978, 1980; numerous articles in Maritime Art, Canadian Art and other periodicals; has been on extensive lecture tours throughout Can.; has had works reproduced in "Seven Painters of Quebec" (film by Nat. Film Bd.), "Bieler" 1973 (film by Quarry Films, Queen's Univ. and C.B.C.) and in "The Arts in Canada", 1958; served in World War with P.P.C.L.I., 1915; Candn. Corps Hdqrs., 1918; awarded Meritiorious Service Medal; mem. Ont. Soc. Artists (J.W.L. Foster Awards, 1957; Candn. Group Painters (Vice-Pres. 1943); Candn. Soc. of Painters in Water Colour; Fed. Candn. Artists (Pres. 1942-44); Candn. Soc. Graphic Art; Home: Apt. 304, 185 Ontario St., Kingston, Ont. K7L 2Y7

BIELER, Ted, B.A.; sculptor; b. Kingston, Ont., 23 July 1938; s. André and Jeannette A. (Meunier) B.; e. studied sculpture with Ossip Zadkine, Paris, 1953-54; painting, with Singier at Academie Ranson, Paris; tapestry design, under Jean Lurcat at St. Céré, France; graphic art, under John Buckland-Wright at the Slade Sch. of Art, Univ. of London, 1954; Summer Sch. of Fine Arts, Queen's Univ. (under Tondino and Alex Millar) 1956; Kingston Coll. and Vocational Inst. 1957; Cranbrook Acad. of Art, Bloomfield Hills, Mich., B.A. (Fine Arts) 1961; schol. Summer Sch. of Painting, Saugatuck, Mich., 1960; CO-ORD., GRAD STUDIES PROG. IN VISUAL ARTS AND ASSOC. PROF., FACULTY OF FINE ARTS, YORK UNIV., 1981-; 6 months tour Europe and Asia, Can. Council Award, 1967-68; Lecturer, Dept. of Fine Arts,

Univ. of Toronto, 1962-68; Instr. in Sculpture. Albright Sch. of Art, Univ. of Buffalo, 1961; Exhibitions: Spring Exhn. Montreal Museum of Fine Art, 1957, 1959, 1965; Ont. Soc. of Artists, Art Gallery of Toronto 1957 and 1960; Four Candns., (with Michael Snow, Gerald Gladstone, and Bain Ireland) at the Art Gallery of Toronto, Feb. 1959 with Chambers, Ingles, and Markle, at the Isaacs Gallery, Toronto, Jan. 1962 (one man show there 1964); Albright-Knox Art Gallery, Buffalo, 1964; outdoor, Sculpture Soc. of Can., Stratford, Ont., 1965; Nat. Gallery Centennial Sculpture Exhn., Toronto City Hall, 1967; Candn. Artists '68, The Art Gallery of Ont. 1968; One-Man Show; York Univ., 1977; commissions include freestanding concrete sculpture for Lakehead Terminal Airport, Fort William, Ont., 1964; Expo '67, relief walls for News & Adm. Bldg. and fountain for Ont. Pavilion; freestanding sculptures for Med. Science Bldg., Univ. of Toronto, 1967; courtyard sculpture, Civic Hall, London, Ont., 1967; rep. in coll. of Agnes Etherington Art Centre, Kingston, Ont., McMaster Univ., Montreal Museum of Fine Arts; York Univ.; The Canada Council; Univ. of Toronto; Allied Arts Medal, Royal Architect Assn., 1969; mem., Exec. Comte., The 10th Intl. Sculpture Conf., Toronto, 1978; Address: Glenstreams, R.R.1, Locust Hill, Ont. L0H 1J0

BIETENHOLZ, Peter Gerard, D.Phil.; university professor; b. Basel, Switzerland, 7 Jan. 1933; s. Alfred and Mary (Gerhard) B.; e. Univ. of Basel, D.Phil. 1958; m. Doris S., d. Franz Huber, Basel, Switzerland, 29 Aug. 1958; children: Michael F., I. Balthasar, Samuel A.; came to Can. 1963; Professor, Dept. of History, Univ. of Sask.; author: "Der italienische Humanismus und die Blütezeit des Buchdrucks in Basel", 1959; "Pietro Della Valle (1586-1642)", 1962; "History and Biography in the Work of Erasmus of Rotterdam", 1966; "Basle and France in the Sixteenth Century", 1971; Ed., "Collected Works of Erasmus"; mem. Ed. Bd., "Canadian Journal of History/Annales Canadiennes d'Histoire"; mem., Candn. Hist. Assn.; Rennaissance Soc. Am.; Am. Soc. Reformation Research; Swiss-Am. Hist. Assn. (Dir.); Home: 117 Albert Ave., Saskatoon, Sask. S7N 1E6

BIGELOW, Robert, Q.C.; b. London, Ont., 25 Sept. 1905; s. William John and Alice E. (Talbot) B.; e. Univ. of Western Ont., 1927; Osgoode Hall, Toronto, Ont.; m. Madelon, d. late Fred W. Coles, 22 Dec. 1934; one. d. Susan; PARTNER, BIGELOW, HENDY, SHIRER & UUKKI-VI; called to the Bar of Ont. 1930; cr. K.C. 1945; Conservative; Anglican; recreation: golf, fishing, hunting; Clubs: Granite; Rosedale Golf; Kiwanis (Past Pres.); Caledon Mountain Trout; The Goodwood; Home: 169 Teddington Pk. Ave., Toronto, Ont. M4N 2C7; Office: Suite 1525, Forester House, 789 Don Mills Rd., Don Mills, Ont. M3C 1T5

BIGELOW, Wilfred Gordon, O.C., B.A., M.D., M.S., LL.D., F.R.C.P.S.(C), F.A.C.S.; surgeon; educator; b. Brandon, Man., 18 June 1913; s. Wilfred Abram and Grace Ann Carnegie (Gordon) B.; a direct descendent of Isaac B., emigrated from New. Eng. to N.S. 1761; e. Brandon (Man.) Coll.; Brentwood Coll., Victoria, B.C.; Brandon College 1931; Univ. of Toronto, B.A. 1935, M.D. 1938, M.S. 1938; LL.D., Brandon Univ. 1967; m. Ruth d. William Arthur Jennings, 9 July 1941; children: Mary, John, Dan, William; SR. SURGEON AND HEAD, CARDIOVASC. SURG., TORONTO GEN. HOSP. and Prof. Emeritus, Dept. of Surg., Univ. of Toronto; started as Research Fellow, John Hopkins, Baltimore, Md. 1946-47; joined staff, Toronto Gen. Hosp. and apptd. Assoc., Dept. Surg., Univ. of Toronto 1948; served in R.C.A.M.C., Field Transfusion Unit 1941-42; Graded Surg., 6th Candn. C.C.S., Eng. and N.W. Europe 1942-45; mem. Defence Research Bd. 1967-72; mem. Bd. Dirs., Ont. Heart Foundation, Nature Conservancy of Canada; Hon. Fellow, Royal Coll. of Surgs. (Eng.); rec'd Lister Prize and Peters Prize, Univ. of Toronto 1949; Gairdner

Award, Toronto 1959; Centennial Medal 1967; Nat. Heart Foundation of Canada, Award of Merit and Queen's Medal 1977; Award of Merit, City of Toronto 1978; mem. Candn. Med. Assn.; Ont. Med. Assn.; Coll. of Physicians & Surgs. of Ont.; Central Surg. Assn.; Soc. of Univ. Surgs.; Am. Surg. Assn.; Cardiovasc. Surg. Council, Am. Heart Association; Am. Assn. Thoracic Surg. (Pres. 1975); James IV Assn. of Surgs.; Candn. Soc. Clin. Surgs.; Candn. Soc. Clin. Investigators; Internat. Cardiovasc. Soc. (Vice-Pres. 1971); Candn. Cardiovasc. Soc. (Pres. 1970-72); Soc. for Vascular Surg. (Pres. 1968-69); Nu Sigma Nu; recreations: fishing; hunting, skiing; Clubs: University; Osler Bluff; Home: 7 Castle Frank Rd., Toronto, Ont. M4W 2Z3;

BIGGAR, James H., O.C. (1968); M.A.; b. Toronto, Ont., 15 Dec. 1908; s. George Coltman and Ethel Boswell (Tate) B.; e. Upper Canada Coll., Toronto, Ont.; Univ. of Toronto, B.A.; Oxford Univ., M.A.; m. Elspeth Holland, d. late Russel Britton; children; J. Russel, George A., Elspeth M., Patricia B.; retired Teacher, Upper Canada Coll.; Founder (1936) and Dir. Visites Interprovinciales; Home: 98 Walmsley Blvd., Toronto, Ont. M4V 1X6

BIGGAR, Warren; manufacturer; b. Hamilton, Ont., 29 May 1931; s. Ralph and Frances (Kelly) B.; e. Pub. and High Schs., Hamilton, Ont.; McMaster Univ., grad. in Metall. 1949; m. Barbara Ann, d. James Hughes, Oct. 1955; children: Craig, James, Susan; PRESIDENT, FROST METAL PRODUCTS LTD.; Dir., David Porteous Ltd.; commenced career with U.S. Steel 1949; joined Canadian Drawn Steel Co., Hamilton, Ont. 1952, becoming Gen. Mgr. 1960; purchased present Co. 1961; mem. Hamilton Chamber Comm.; Conservative; United Church; recreations: skiing, golf, sculpting; Club: Limberlost; Home: 360 Aurora Cres., Burlington, Ont. L7N 2A9; Office: 170 Chatham St., Hamilton, Ont. L8P 2B6

BIGGS, Kenneth A., C.A., R.I.A., F.S.M.A.C.; executive; b. Edmonton, Alta., 9 Apl. 1929; s. Walter A. and Evelyn N. (Rudd) B.; e, Strathcona High Sch., Edmonton, 1947; Extve. Devel. Inst., Montreal, 1959-60; Univ. of W. Ont., Summer Mang. Sch., 1963; m. Leone R. Hoffman, 10 Sept. 1958; SR. VICE PRES., FINANCE, CANADIAN UTILITIES LTD., since 1973; Sr. Vice-Pres. Yukon Electric Co. Ltd.; Dir., Alberta Power Ltd.; Northwestern Utilities Ltd.; Canadian Western Natural Gas Co. Ltd.; Canadian Utilities Ltd.; Q.C.T.V., Edmonton; held various financial positions Celanese Canada Ltd. incl. Vice Pres., Finance, 1951-72; Dir., Bralorne Oil and Gas Co. Ltd., 1970; formerly Pres., Trans-Canada Computer Utility Ltd.; Sr. Vice Pres., Alberta Power Ltd. 1972; Dir.; Citadel Theatre mem. Bd. of Gov., Edmonton Club; mem. Soc. Mang. Accts. Can. (Pres. 1973-74), el. Fellow 1979; Inst. C.A.'s Alta.; Campaign Chmn., Salvation Army Edmonton; Protestant; recreations: golf, gardening, music; Clubs: Edmonton; Edmonton Petroleum; Glendale Club Home: 13708 - 84 Ave., Edmonton, Alta. T5R 3R4; Office: 10040 - 104 St., Edmonton, Alta. T5J 2V6

BILD, Fred, B.A.; diplomat; b. Leipzig, Saxony 7 Aug. 1935; s. late Joseph and Ida (Kleinmann) B.; e. Sir George Williams Univ. B.A. 1957; Univ. Coll. Univ. of London 1958-60; Ecole Nationale d'Adm. Dipl. 1968; m. Eva d. late W.A. Kornpointer 17 Dec. 1958; children: Eva Rebecca, Maia Lilith, Sarah Harumi; AMBASSADOR TO THAILAND, THE SOCIALIST REPUBLIC OF VIETNAM AND THE LAO DEMOCRATIC PEOPLES REPUBLIC 1979- ; Third Secy., Can. Embassy, Tokyo 1963, Second Secy. 1964, Sr. Pol. Advisor to Candn. Del. to Internat. Control Comn. in Laos 1966, Counsellor, Can. Embassy, Paris 1968, Extve. Asst. to Under-Secy. of State for External Affairs Ottawa 1970, Counsellor (Econ.) Paris 1972, Dir. Personnel Operations Ottawa 1977; Trustee, Asian Inst. of Technol. Bangkok; recreations: billiards, anthropology; Clubs: Martel Mem. Billiards; Address: P.O. Box 500 (BNGKK), Ottawa, Ont. K1N 8T7.

BILLINGSLEY, Robert William, B.Sc.; industrialist; b. Toronto, Ont., 26 April 1937; s. William Benson and Marjorie Eileen (Munro) B.; e. Univ. of Pa., B.Sc. (Econ.) 1960; m. Sandra Lynn, d. Nelson Kulz, 30 Sept. 1961; one d. Anne Elizabeth; Pres., Billvest Ltd.; Chrmn. and Dir., BCM Technologies Ltd.; Bramalea Ltd.; I.R.C. Professor, Colgate Darden Grad. School of Business, Univ. of Virginia; former President, Chief Extve. Offr., Reed Paper Ltd.; Chrmn. Canadian Wallpapers Manufacturers Ltd.; Pres. and Chief Extve., Offr., Anglo-Canadian Pulp and Paper Mills Ltd.; Dir. Canadian Glassine Co. Ltd.; Intercontinental Pulp Co.; Reed-Ingram Corp.; Reed International Ltd.; Takla Forest Products Ltd.; Takla Logging Co.; Prince George Pulp and Paper Ltd.; started as Sales Representative, Broad Base Retailing, Marketing Research, Information Systems, Shell Canada Ltd. 1960; Area Mgr.-E., Pulp & Paper Div., Div. Mgr. Pulp & Paper, Erco Chemicals (Electric Reduction Co. of Canada Ltd.) 1967; with Hooker Chemical Corp., Prod. and Sales Mang., Engn., Tech. Sales and Devel. 1970; mem. C.D. Howe Inst.; Home: R.R. 1, Orton, Ont. L0N 1N0

BILODEAU, Rodrigue, B.Eng., P.Eng.; company chairman and chief exec. off.; b. Levis, Que., 23 April, 1921; s. Theodore H. and May (Shink) B.; e. St. Patrick's High Sch., Quebec City; St. Francis Xavier Univ.; McGill Univ. B.Eng.; Harvard Business Sch. A.M.P.; m. Betty June Parker, 3 June 1950; children: Carol, Dale, Patricia, Anita; CHAIRMAN AND CH. EXEC. OFFICER, HONEYWELL LTD., since 1974; Pres. Honeywell Holdings Ltd.; Chrmn. Amplitrol Electronics Ltd.; Dir. Texaco Canada Ltd.; N.E.I. Canada Ltd.; Lever Brothers Ltd., Exechequer Financial Corp. Ltd.; joined present Co. as Salesman, Montreal 1950; E. Can. Sales Mgr., Comm. Div. 1953; Nat. Sales Mgr., Indust. Div., Toronto 1956; Mgr. Indust. Products Group (Europe), Honeywell Inc., Frankfurt, Germany 1959; Asst. Dir., European Operations 1961; Pres., Honeywell S.A., Paris, France 1964; Vice Pres., Market. and Dir., Honeywell Ltd., 1968; Pres. 1970; served in 2nd World War, R.C.A.F.; Pilot (Flying Offr., 407 Sqdn.); Past Pres. Can. Manuf. Assn.; Past Pres. & mem Extve Comte., Can. Council of the International Chambers of Commerce; mem. Policy Comm., Bus. Council on Nat. Issues; Canadian-American Committee; Assoc. of Prof. Engineers of the Prov. of Ont.; recreations: skiing, golf; Clubs: Canadian, Toronto; Toronto Board of Trade; Bayview Country; National C. Toronto; Delta Sigma Phi; Home: 22 Hi Mount Drive, Willowdale Ont. M2K 1X4; Office: 155 Gordon Baker Rd., Willowdale, Ont. M2H 3N7

BINGLEMAN, George Leo, C.A.; b. Simcoe, Ont. 4 Dec. 1933; e. Brantford (Ont.) Coll. Inst. 1952; Inst. C.A.'s Ont., C.A. Ont. 1959, Alta. 1977; m. Joan Loraine Miller 1 June 1957; two children; VICE PRES. FINANCE, FORDING COAL LTD. since 1978; joined Clarkson Gordon & Co. 1954-62; Controller, AMF Atomics 1962-64; Canadian Westinghouse 1964-65; Secy. and Asst. Treas., Greening Donald Ltd. 1965-73; Treas., Fording Coal Ltd. 1974-77; recreations: golf, fishing, skiing; Club: Willow Park Golf; Office: 205 Ninth Ave. S.E., Calgary; Alta. T2G 0R4.

BINNS, Hon. Patrick George, M.L.A., M.A.; politician; b. Weyburn, Sask. 8 Oct. 1948; s. Stanley Ernest B.; e. St. Dominic Savio, Weyburn, Sask.; Meridian Sch. Lloydminster, Sask.; Univ. of Alta. B.A., M.A.; m. Carol Isobel d. M. J. (Buster) MacMillan, Charlottetown, P.E.I. 8 May 1971; three s. Robbie, Mark, Bradley; MIN. OF COMMUNITY AFFAIRS, P.E.I. 1979- and Min. responsible for P.E.I. Housing Corp.; Devel. Offr. Govt. Alta 1971-72; Devel. Offr./Asst. Mgr. Rural Devel. Council P.E.I. 1972-75, Co-ordinator Kings Co. Regional Services Centres 1975-78; family farm operator Hopefield, P.E.I. since 1972; el. M.L.A. for Dist. of Kings 1978, re-el. 1979; rec'd Queen's Silver Jubilee Medal 1978; Phi Kappa Pi (Pres. 1970-71); P. Conservative; R. Catholic; recreations: hockey, skiing; Home: Murray River R.R.4, P.E.I. C0A 1W0; Office: (P.O. Box 2000) Charlottetown, P.E.I. C1A 7N8.

BIRCH, Daniel R., M.A., Ph.D.; educator; b. Ganges, B.C., 1 Sept 1937; s. George Alfred and Grace Lilian (Poland) B.; e. Delta High Sch., Ladner,B.C. 1954; Northwest Bapt. Theol. Coll., Dipl. in Theol. 1958, B.R.E. 1960; Univ. of B.C., B.A. 1963, M.A. 1968; Univ. of Cal. (Berkeley) Ph.D. 1969; m.Rose Arlene, d. late Donald McDonald, 1962; one d., Carol Leah; PROF. AND DEAN OF EDUCATION, UNIV. OF B.C., since 1981; Teacher of Hist. 1959-61 and High Sch. Counsellor 1961-63, Maple Ridge, B.C.; Social Studies Dept. Head and Vice Princ. 1964-65; Assoc. Sch. of Educ., Univ. of Cal. (Berkeley) 1968-69; joined Simon Fraser Univ. as Assoc., Educ. Foundations Centre, 1966-67, Asst. Prof. of Educ., 1969-71; Chrmn., Prof. Devel. Centre, 1970-71; Dean, Faculty of Education 1971-75; Prof. of Educ. and Assoc. Vice Pres. (Academic) 1975-80; co-dir. research training programs in U.S. and Can. on guided self-analysis and teacher educ.; author, "Gandhi"; "Life in Communist China"; "Asia" (all 1969); "Early Indian Cultures of North America"; "Voyages of Discovery"; "Life in Early North America"; "Growth of a Nation"; "Culture Realms of the World" (all 1974); also prof. articles in various educ. journs.; Am. Educ. Research Assn.; Nat. Council Social Studies; Candn. Soc. Study Educ.; Home: 945 Esquimalt Ave., West Vancouver, B.C. V7T 1J9; Office: 2125 Main Mall, Vancouver, B.C. V6T 1Z5

BIRCH, Lewis Bernard, B.Sc., M.A., F.B.Ps.S. (1967); university professor; b. Burton on Trent, Eng., 24 Feb. 1913; s. Lewis and Emily Dunkley (Hodgkinson) B.; e. Grammar Sch., Burton on Trent, 1924-30; Univ. of Birmingham, B.Sc. 1934, Dipl. in Psychol. of Childhood 1947, M.A. 1951; Fellow, Wolfson College, Cambridge 1976; m. Mary, d. Sidney Bristow, Whitchurch, Salop, Eng., 3 Sept. 1939; two d.: Katherine Mary, Patricia; MACDONALD PROF. OF EDUC., McGILL UNIV., since 1967; Schlmaster, 1934-40; Educ. Psychol., 1948-52; Lectr. in Educ. Psychol., Univ. of Sheffield and Depy. Dir. of Inst. of Educ., 1952; Sr. Lectr. 1959; Asst. Ed., "British Journal of Educational Psychology," 1952, Ed. 1961-67; author of numerous articles for prof. journs.; joined Brit. Army 1940; comnd. into Lincolnshire Regt. 1941; Capt. 1942, Maj. 1944 (D.A.A.G.); served in Burma from 1941; Mentioned in Dispatches; mem., Brit. Psychol. Soc. (Chrmn., Educ. Sec. and mem. Council); recreations: lawn tennis, squash, cabinet making; Clubs: National Liberal (London, Eng.); Home: 19 Cambridge Rd., Baie d'Urfe, Que. H9X 2V5; Office Faculty of Education, McGill University, Montreal, Que. H3A 1Y2

BIRCH, Hon. Margaret, M.P.P.; b. Leamington, Ont., 13 June 1921; d. Wallace Edward and Mary Jane (Ferguson) Stewart; e. Pub. and High Schs., Leamington, Ont.; m. Guy Cochran Birch, 27 Sept. 1941; children: Randolph Guy, Ellen Jane; PROV. SECY. FOR SOCIAL DEVEL. ONT.; since Feb. 1974 (Min. without Portfolio 28 Sept. 1972-Feb. 1974); mem. Scarborough Bd. Health 8 yrs. (Chrmn. 3 yrs.); mem. Bd. of Mental Health Council for Scarborough (Chrmn. 3 yrs.); mem. Scarborough Social Planning Council 10 yrs. (Vice Pres. 2 yrs.); Charter mem. Bd. of Govs., Scarborough Centenary; P. Conservative; Protestant; Clubs: Cedarbrae Golf & Country; Scarborough Golf & Country; Albany; Home: 53 Burnview Cres., Scarborough, Ont.M1H IB4; Office: Parliament Bldgs., Queen's Pk., Toronto, Ont.

BIRD, Hon. Florence Bayard CC. (1971); senator, journalist, broadcaster, and author (pseud. Anne Francis); b. Philadelphia, Pa. 15 Jan. 1908; d. Dr. John H.W. and Elizabeth (Kane) Rhein; e. Agnes Irwin Sch., Philadelphia; Bryn Mawr Coll.; LL.D. York (Hon.) 1972; D. Hum.L. Mt. (Hon.) St. Vincent 1974; Award of Merit, the Art Directors' Club of Toronto 1973-74; LL.D. (Hon.) Carleton Univ. 1975; LL.D. Queen's Univ. (Hon.) 1975; two

Women's National Press Club Awards; m. John Bird (d. 1978), 14 Nov. 1928; member Canadian Del. to UNESCO Conf., New Delhi, 1956; produced documentaries for C.B.C. in Germany Denmark, France, Switzerland, Belgium, Netherlands, U.S. and Hungary, 1958-66; news commentator on nat. and internat. service of CBC, 1946-66; Chrmn., Royal Comn. on Status of Women in Can., 1967-70, consultant to Task Force on Status of Women in C.B.C., 1974; summoned to Senate of Canada 1978; Special CIDA Consult. to the Govt. of Jamaica 1975-76; to Govt. of Barbados 1977; author "Anne Francis — An Autobiography" 1974; "Holiday in the Woods" 1976; mem. Candn. Inst. Internat. Affairs (Past Chrmn., Winnipeg and Ottawa Women's Br.); Can. Res. Inst. for the Adv. of Women; Can. Writers' Foundation Inc.; recreations: swimming, walking, reading; Address: 333 Chapel St., No. 201, Ottawa, Ont. K1N 8Y8

BIRD, Hon. John Williston(Bud), M.L.A.; politician; b. Fredericton, N.B. 22 March 1932; s. John Leo and Edith Margaret (Williston) B.; e. Fredericton High Sch. 1949; m. Margaret Roberta Huet d. Walter L. Lawson, Minto, N.B. 27 Dec. 1969; children: Catherine, Stephen G., Nancy E. (Stafford), J. William, Michael Huet, Karen, Margot;MIN. OF NATURAL RESOURCES, N.B.1978- ; founded J. W. Bird and Co. Ltd. 1959 becoming Pres. (now in trust); purchases Wm. Stairs, Son & Morrow Ltd. 1975, merged to form Bird-Stairs; founded Bird Holdings Ltd. 1965 (now in trust); Mayor, City of Fredericton 1969-74; Pres. Candn. Fed. of Mayors 1973-74; Vice Pres. N.B. P. Cons. Party of Can. 1977- ; el. M.L.A. for Fredericton S. 1978; introduced and piloted "Crown Lands and Forests Act" and "Fish and Wildlife Act" 1980; rec'd Internat. Atlantic Salmon Conserv. Award 1980; T.B. Happy Fraser Award 1981 for salmon conservation; served with R.C.M.P. 1949-51; Freemason; P. Conservative; United Church; recreations: salmon fishing, flying (pilot), hunting, golf, bridge, skiing; Clubs: Fredericton Garrison; Fredericton Country; Miramichi Salmon; Home: 7 Simcoe Court, Fredericton, N.B. E3B 5C6; Office: (P.O. Box.6000) Centennial Bldg., Fredericton, N.B. E3B 5H1.

BIRD, Richard Miller, M.A., Ph.D., F.R.S.C.; economist; educator; b. Fredericton, N.B. 22 Aug. 1938; s. Robert Bruce and Annie Margaret (Miller) B.; e. Sydney (N.S.) Acad. 1954; Univ. of King's Coll. B.A. 1958; Columbia Univ. M.A. 1959, Ph.D. 1961; London Sch. of Econ. 1960-61; m. Marcia Gladys d. Alfred Abbey, Littleover, Eng. 10 May 1958; children: Paul, Marta, Abbey; DIR, INST. FOR POLICY ANALYSIS AND PROF. OF ECON. UNIV. OF TORONTO since 1980; Instr. Harvard Univ. 1961-63; Sr. Research Assoc. Columbia Univ. 1963-64; Adv., Ministry of Finance, Govt. of Colombia 1964-66; Lectr. Harvard 1966-68; Assoc. Prof. present Univ. 1968-70, Prof., 1970-80; Chief, Tax Policy Div. Internat. Monetary Fund 1972-74; Killam Fellow 1969-70; Lincoln Inst. of Land Policy Fellow 1976-77; Consultant to numerous foreign countries and internat. organs.; Dir. Comission on Intergovernmental Finance, Colombia, 1980-81; author "Financing Urban Development in Mexico City" 1967; "Taxation and Development" 1970; "Growth of Government Spending in Canada" 1970; "Taxing Agricultural Land in Developing Countries" 1974; "Charging for Public Services" 1976; "Residential Property Tax Relief in Ontario" 1978; "Growth of Public Employment in Canada" 1979; over 100 papers on pub. finance and econ. devel.; mem. Internat. Inst. Pub. Finance; Nat. Tax Assn. - Tax Inst. Am. (Dir.); Am. Econ. Assn.; Candn. Econ. Assn.; Candn. Tax Foundation; Home: 1065 Stockwell Ave., Mississauga, Ont. L5H 1B5; Office: 150 St. George St., Toronto, Ont. M5S 1A1.

BIRD, William Richard, D.Litt.; author; b. East Mapleton, N.S., 11 May 1891; s. Stephen and Augusta Caroline B.; e. Cumberland Co. Acad. Amherst, N.S.; Mt. Allison Univ., D.Litt. 1949; m. Ethel May, d. late John Sutton, 18 June 1919; one d., Mrs. Dr. I.M. Murray, s. Stephen Stanley (killed in action in World War II); selected by "Maclean's Magazine" to tour the old battle front preparatory to furnishing a series of articles, 1931: contrib. for 15 yrs. to veterans' publications in Can., U.S.A., Great Britain, S. Africa, New Zealand and Australia; served in World War I with 42nd Royal Highlanders as Scout Cpl.; awarded M.M.; author "A Century at Chignecto", 1928; "And We Go On", 1930; "Private Timothy Fergus Clancy", 1930; "Thirteen Years After", 1932; "The Communication Trench", 1935; "Maid of the Marshes", 1936; "Here Stays Good Yorkshire", 1945, co-winner Ryerson Press All-Can. Fiction Award; "Sunrise for Peter", 1946; "Judgment Glen", 1947, co-winner Ryerson Press All-Can. Fiction Award; "The Passionate Pilgrim", 1949; "This is Nova Scotia", 1950; "So Much to Record" (novel), 1951; "To Love and To Cherish", 1952; "No Retreating Footsteps" (history of North N. S. Highlanders), 1953; "The Two Jacks", 1954; "Done at Grand Pre" and "The Shy Yorkshireman", 1955 "Off-Trail in Nova Scotia", 1956; "Tristram's Salvation", 1958; "These Are the Maritimes", 1959; "Atlantic Anthology", 1959; "Despite The Distance", 1961; "The North Shore Regiment", 1963; "Ghosts Have Warm Hands", 1968; numerous short stories and articles; his stories listed in O. Henry Mem. Award Collections and O'Brien Best Short Stories; Nat. Pres., Candn. Authors' Assn. 1949-50; Hon. Pres., Candn. Authors' Ass.; Chrmn., N.S. Hist. Sites Adv. Council; Fellow, Haliburton Soc. of King's Coll.; Writers' Council of Nova Scotia (hon. life mem.); Pres. (1958), St. George's Soc. of Halifax; Life mem., N.S. Hist. Soc. (1967); hon. chief North Dakota Indians; Yarmouth Historical Society (hon. life mem.); Liberal; United Church; Address: 963 Marlborough Ave., Halifax, N.S. B3H 3G9

BIRINGER, Paul Peter, M.A.Sc., Ph.D.; educator; consultant; b. Marosvasarhely, Hungary 1 Oct. 1924; s. Arpad Biringer; e. Tech. Univ. Budapest Dipl. Engn. 1947; Royal Inst. of Technol. Stockholm M.A.Sc. 1951; Univ. of Toronto Ph.D. 1956; m. Eva Barbro Gunnarsdotter, M.A. d. Axel Gunnar Rengman 15 Apl. 1952; two d. Anne Barbro, M.D., Monica Eva, B.A.; PROF. OF ELECT. ENGN., UNIV. OF TORONTO 1965- ; Head, Research & Devel., Hatch Associates Ltd., Toronto 1980- , Consulting Engr. 1970- ; Dir. Electrical Engineering Consociates Ltd.; Consulting Engr., Ajax Magnethermic Corp. Warren, Ohio 1958- ; General Engineering Co. Ltd. Toronto 1953-58; Asst. Prof. Univ. of Toronto 1957, Assoc. Prof. 1961; Gov., George Brown Coll. Applied Arts & Technol. 1972-78; recipient Pleyel Award for Research 1951; Candn. Dist. Prize AIEE 1958; Sons of Martha Medal Assn. Prof. Engrs. Prov. Ont. 1968; Prize Paper Award Indust. Appl. Soc. of IEEE 1979; author over 100 publs.; holds over 40 patents in fields of magnetic frequency changers, solid state frequency changers, indust. electroheat; participant several internat. projects designing and bldg. electrometallurgical plants and electric furnaces; Sr. Research Fellow, Japan Soc. Promotion Science; Fellow, Inst. Elect. & Electronics Engrs.; Chrmn. Awards Comte. Internat. Electric Comn.; mem. Assn. Prof. Engrs. Prov. Ont.; recreations: tennis, skiing; Clubs: Toronto Lawn Tennis; Empire; Kiwanis; Bennington Height Tennis; Home: 6 Lumley Ave., Toronto, Ont. M4G 2X4; Office: 35 St. George St., Toronto, Ont. M5S 1A4.

BIRKETT, E. Roy, B.Com., M.B.A., C.F.A.; private investor b. Eng.; s. Edward Thomas and Jessie Rose (Chapman) B.; e. Public and High Schs. Sask.; Univ. of Brit. Columbia B. Com. 1951; Harvard Univ. M.B.A. 1956; Chart. Financial Analyst 1971; m. J. Ruth, d. Edward J. Breithaupt 1959; children: Martha Jessie, Sally K., A. Leslie, Donna J.; Pres., Kayty Exploration Ltd. (and U.S. subsidiary); Dir., K. T. Resources (1981) Ltd. (listed Alta. Stock Exchange) & subsidiaries; Time Savers Quick Print Centres Ltd.; Investment Analyst, Corp. Finance, Mead & Co. Ltd. 1979-80; Pres., K.T. Mining Ltd. (O.T.C.), 1977-80; Pres. Dennisteel Corp. Ltd. 1962; Financial Ana-

lyst A.E. Ames & Co. 1964; Mgr. Research, Midland Osler Securities Ltd. 1966-68; Mgr. Research, T. A. Richardson & Co. Ltd. 1969; Pres., A.E. Osler, Gendron Ltd. 1970-75; former dir. Toronto Soc. Financial Analysts and Candn. Council of Financial Analysts; mem. Lytton Park Ratepayers Assn.; Protestant; recreations: sailing, reading, travel; Home: 137 Hillhurst Blvd., Toronto, Ont. M5N 1N7; Office: 80 Continental Pl., Toronto, Ont. M1R 2T4 and 2½ 2081 Yonge St., Toronto, Ont. M4S 2A4

BIRKS, George Drummond, B.Com.; executive; b. Montreal, P.Q., 18 Feb. 1919; s. Henry Gifford and Lilian Cockshutt (Drummond) B.; e. Selwyn House Sch., Montreal, P.Q.; St. Andrew's Coll., Aurora, Ont.; McGill Univ. B.Comm.; m. late Muriel Anne, d. late T. J. Scobie, M.D., 4 Apl. 1942; five children; PRES. AND CHIEF EX. OFFR., HENRY BIRKS & SONS LTD.; Dir., Central Investment Corp.; Rolland Inc.; Monarch Investments Ltd.; Fidmor Mortgage Investment Corp.; Bank of Montreal Mortgage Corp.; United Corporations Ltd.; Harvey Woods Ltd.; U.A.P. Inc.; Formula Growth Ltd.; Royal Trustco; C.A.E. Industries Ltd.; Vancouver Centre Development Ltd.; Adv. Comte., Mitsubishi (Canada) Ltd.; Trustee, Montreal Childrens Hospital Foundation; Gov., Montreal Children's Hospital; McGill Univ.; mem. Adv. Bd., Salvation Army; served with Black Watch (R.H.R.) of Canada; Mentioned in Despatches; United Church; Clubs: Mount Royal; St. James's; Mount Bruno Country; National (Toronto); Home: 1321 Sherbrooke W., Montreal, Que. H3Y 2C8; Office: 1240 Phillips Square, Montreal, Que. H3G 1J4

BIRNBAUM, Eleazar, B.A., Dipl. O.A.S.; educator; b. 23 Nov. 1929; s. Solomon Asher and Irene (Grunwald) B.; e. Holt Sch. Liverpool, Eng. 1946; City of London (Eng.) Sch. 1947; Univ. of London Sch. Oriental & African Studies Dipl. Hebrew Palaeography & Epigraphy 1949, B.A. (Arabic) 1950, B.A. (Turkish) 1953; m. Rebecca d. late Moszek Pardes, Brussels, Belgium 30 May 1962; children: Nathan J., Samuel M., Abraham U., Sarah M., Miriam D.; PROF. OF MIDDLE EAST & ISLAMIC STUDIES; UNIV. OF TORONTO 1970- ; Asst. Lib., Oriental Sec. Durham Univ. Lib. (Eng.) 1953-60; Near E. Bibliog. Dept. Near E. Langs. & Lits. Univ. of Mich. 1960-64, Head of Lib.'s Near E. and S. Asian Unit 1960-64; Assoc. Prof. present Univ. 1964-70; Consultant to research fund granting agencies Can. and U.S.A.; Consultant and book reviewer scholarly journs.; author "Books on Asia, from the Near East to the Far East" 1971; "The Islamic Middle East" 1975; 'The Book of Advice' by King Kay-Ka'us Ibn Iskandar: The Earliest Old Ottoman Turkish 'Kabusname' " 1981; co-author "Introduction to Islamic Civilisation" 1976; numerous articles Orientalist Turkish and Jewish studies scholarly journs.; Dir., Eitz Chaim Schs., Beth Jacob High Sch., Maimonides Coll. and Agudath Yisroel Cong., Toronto; mem. Am. Oriental Soc.; Middle E. Studies Assn. N. Am.; Turkish Studies Assn.; Middle E. Libs. Assn.; Am. Research Inst. Turkey; Assn. Orthodox Jewish Scients.; Jewish; recreations: research Middle E. langs., lits., hist. & bibliog., swimming; Clubs: Faculty; Oriental; Home: 132 Invermay Ave., Downsview, Ont. M3H 1Z8; Office: Toronto, Ont. M5S 1A1.

BIRNEY, Alfred Earle, O.C. (1970), Ph.D., D.Litt., LL.D., F.R.S.C. (1954); author; of a Western pioneer family, his father having arrived in Alta. on horseback, 1883, later prospecting in various parts of the Rockies; b. Calgary, Alta., 13 May 1904; s. William George and Martha Stout (Robertson) B.; e. Univ. of B.C., B.A. 1926; (scholar. to Univ. of Toronto 1926-27); Univ. of Toronto, M.A. 1927; Ph.D. 1936; Univ. of California (grad. sch.) 1927-30; Univ. of London (Roy. Soc. of Can. Fellowship) 1934-35; LL.D., Univ. of Alta. 1965; D.Litt., McGill 1979; m. Esther, d. Emmanuel Bull, Hampstead Garden Suburbs, London, 6 Mar. 1940, divorced 1977; one s., William; began career as Teaching Fellow, Univ. of California, 1927-30; Lectr. Summer Sch., Univ. of B.C., 1927 and eight other summers; Instr. Univ. of Utah 1930-32, 1933-34; Leonard Fellow, Univ. of Toronto 1932-33; Lect. in Eng., Univ. Coll., Univ. of Toronto, 1936-41; Asst. Prof. 1941-42; Supervisor of European Foreign Lang. Broadcasts, Internat. Shortwave Service, CBC 1945-46; Prof. of Eng. Univ. of B.C. 1946-63, and Head, Dept. of Creative Writing there 1963-65; Writer-in-Residence, Univ. of Toronto, 1965-67; Univ. of Waterloo 1967-68; Univ. of Western Ont. 1971-72; Lit. Ed., "Canadian Forum" 1936-40; Editor-in-Chief, "Canadian Poetry Magazine" 1946-48; Editor-in-Chief, "Prism International" 1964-65; Advisory Ed., "New Canadian & American Poetry" 1964-68; served with Reserve Army (C.O.T.C.) 1940-42, with rank of Lieut.; served in World War 1942-45 with Inf. Personnel Selection Service, Overseas 1943-45; Maj. in charge, Personnel Selection for Candn. Army Belgium and Holland; invalided home; winner of Gov.-Gen's Award in Poetry, 1942 and 1945; author of "David and Other Poems", 1942; "Now is Time", 1945; "Strait of Anian", 1948; "Turvey", a military picaresque (novel) 1949; "Trial of a City", 1952; "Twentieth Century Canadian Poetry", an anthology, 1953; "Down the Long Table", a novel, 1955; (ed.) U.B.C. "Record of Service in Second World War" 1955; "Ice Cod Bell or Stone", poems, 1962; (ed.) "Selected Poems of Malcolm Lowry", 1962; "Near False Creek Mouth", poems, 1964; "Selected Poems", 1966; "The Creative Writer", 1966; "Memory no Servant", poems, 1968; co-ed., "Lunar Caustic", Malcolm Lowry 1968; "pnomes, jukollages & other stunzas", 1969; "poems of earle birney", 1969; "rag & bone shop", poems, 1971; "The Cow Jumped Over the Moon/ the writing & reading of poetry", 1972; "The Bear on the Delhi Road", poems, 1973; "What's so Big about Green?" poems, 1973; "Collected Poems 1920-74", 1975; "Alphabeings", visual poems 1976; "The Rugging and the Moving Times", poems 1976; "The Damnation of Vancouver", stage play 1977; "Ghost in the Wheels", sel. poems 1977; "Fall by Fury", poems 1978; "Big Bird in the Bush", sel. stories and sketches 1978; "Spreading Time", essays and memories, Book I: 1904-49, 1980; "The Mammoth Corridors", poems, 1980;numerous poems, stories, essays, lit. articles, book reviews, etc. to Candn., Am. and Brit. publs.; awarded Borestone Poetry Award (U.S.A.) 1951; Lorne Pierce Gold Medal for Lit. (Royal Soc. Can.) 1952; Leacock Medal for Humour by Stephen Leacock Mem. Comte., 1949; Candn. Govt. Overseas Fellowship to France, 1953; Nuffield Scholar, England, 1958-59; Visiting Prof., Univ. of Oregon, 1961; Regents Prof., Univ. of California, 1968; Can. Council Sr. Arts Fellowship, 1962-63, 1968-69, 1975, 1978-81; mem., League of Candn. Poets; Writers Union of Canada; Assoc. of Can. Television and Radio Artists; awarded Can. Council Medal "for outstanding cultural achievement" 1968; recreations: swimming, gardening, cycling; Address: c/o McClelland & Stewart, 25 Hollinger Rd., Toronto, Ont. M4B 3G2

BIRTLES, Robert J.; advertising executive; b. Toronto, Ont. 19 July 1934; s. John J. and Jean E. (Parkinson) B.; e. Malvern Coll. Inst. Toronto; Univ. of Toronto Extension; m. M. Ann d. William S. Laidley 12 March 1960; children: James, Susan, Ian, Douglas; Sr. Vice Pres. Baker Lovick Ltd.; Dir. Sterling Trust Corp. Ltd.; United Church; recreations: squash, sailing, skiing; Clubs: RCYC; Craigleith Ski; Home: 34 Tarlton Rd., Toronto, Ont. M5P 2M4; Office: 60 Bloor St. W., Toronto, Ont. M4W 3B8

BISHOP, Charles Johnson, B.Sc., A.M., Ph.D., F.R.S.C., F.A.S.H.S., F.A.I.C.; horticulturist; b. Semans, Sask. 6 Jan. 1920; s. Lewis Leander and Nellie Erdine (Illsley) B.; e. elem. schs. Wolfville, Berwick and Somerset (N.S.); high schs. Berwick, Kentville (N.S.); Acadia Univ. B.Sc. 1941; Univ. of W. Ont. 1941-42; Harvard Univ. A.M., Ph.D. 1947; m. Katherine Adele d. late Frank L. Corey 19 June 1951; one s. John; Research Coordinator (Crop Production) Research Br. Agric. Can. since 1978; Weather Forecaster (RCAF) Dept. Transport 1942-45, Flying Offr. 1945; Research Scient. Tree Fruit Breeding Exper. Stn.

Can. Dept. Agric. Kentville, N.S. 1947-52, Supt. Exper. Stn. 1952-58; Acting Supt. Exper. Stn. Summerland, B.C. 1958-59; Assoc. Dir. Program (Crops) Research Br. Can. Dept. Agric. Ottawa 1959-63, Research Coordinator (Hortic.) 1963-78; rec'd Candn. Hortic. Council Merit Award; Queen's Silver Jubilee Medal; author over 25 papers scient. research genetics & fruit breeding; Past Pres. Broadview Home & Sch. Assn.; Fellow, Am. Soc. Hortic. Science; Fellow, Agric. Inst. Can. (Past Hon. Secy.); Hon. Pres. and Hon. Life mem. W. Candn. Soc. Hortic.; Past Pres. & Secy. Science Soc. Royal Soc. Can.; Past Pres. Candn. Soc. Hortic. Science; Genetics Soc. Can.; mem. Internat. Soc. Hortic. Science (Council); Genetics Soc. Am.; Baptist; recreations: curling, photography, gardening; Club: Granite Curling; Home: 548 Hillcrest Ave., Ottawa, Ont. K2A 2M9; Office: Central Experimental Farm, Ottawa, Ont. K1A 0C5.

BISHOP, Claude Titus, B.Sc., B.A., Ph.D., F.R.S.C.; scientist; Canadian public servant; b. Liverpool, N.S., 13 May 1925; s. Claude Wetmore and Elva (Titus) B.; e. Acadia Univ., B.Sc. 1945, B.A. 1946; McGill Univ., Ph.D. (Chem.) 1949; m. Pierrette Marie Therese (deceased 1975), d. late Eugene Picard, 8 July 1951; one s., Scot; EDITOR-IN-CHIEF, RESEARCH JOURNALS, NAT. RESEARCH COUNCIL, since 1970 and Dir., Div. of Biol. Sciences since 1978; joined NRC as Jr. Research Offr. 1949; served as Asst., Assoc., Sr. and Princ. Research Offr. 1949-65; Asst. Dir., Biochem. Lab., 1969-72; Assoc. Dir., Div. of Biol. Sciences 1972-78; Dir., Div. Biol. Sci. since 1978; Asst. Ed. and Ed., Canadian Journal of Chemistry, 1964-70; author of over 85 scient. papers; Chrm., USA Nat. Acad. Sciences Comte. on Specifications & Criteria for Biochem. Compounds, 1965-68; mem. Candn. Biochem. Soc.; recreations: golf, skiing; Club: Rideau View Golf; Home: 39 Fern Ave., Ottawa, Ont. K1Y 3S2; Office: 100 Sussex Dr., Ottawa, Ont. K1A 0R6

BISHOP, Olga Bernice, M.A., A.M.L.S., Ph.D., LL.D.; professor emeritus; b. Dover, N.B., 24 June 1911; d. Thomas Cochrane and Minnie Earle (Colpitts) B.; e. Mount Allison Univ., B.A. 1938, M.A. 1951, LL.D. 1971; Carleton Univ., B. Pub. Admin. 1946; Univ. of Michigan, A.M.L.S. 1952, Ph.D. 1962; prof. Univ. of Toronto Fac. of Library Science 1970-77; Secy., Mount Allison Mem. Lib., Sackville, N.B. 1932-40; Asst. Lib., 1946-53; apptd. Gen. Lib., Univ. of Western Ont., 1953-54; Med. Lib., 1954-65; Assoc. Prof., Univ. of Toronto Sch. of Lib. Science 1965-70; served during 2nd World War as Sr. Adm. Offr. R.C.A.F. Record of Service, Can. Civil Service, Ottawa, 1940-46; Dir., London Community Concert, 1963-66; author of "Publications of the Governments of Nova Scotia, Prince Edward Island, New Brunswick 1758-1952", 1957; "Publications of the Government of the Province of Canada 1841-1867", 1963; "Publications of the Government of Ontario 1867-1900", 1976; "Bibliography of Ont. Hist., 1867-1976: Cultural Economic, Political, Social" 1980; "Canadian Official Publications" 1981; has written articles and book reviews for various lib. journs.; mem., Candn. Lib. Assn.; Candn. Assn. Coll Univ. Libs. (Secy. 1965-66); Ont. Lib. Assn.; Ont. Assn. Coll. Univ. Libs. (Councillor 1963-65, Vice Chrmn. 1965-66, Chrmn. 1966-67); Inst. Prof. Libs. Ont. (Dir. 1964-68, Pres. 1966-67); Candn. Assn. Univ. Teachers (UTFA Toronto Councillor 1968-1973): Med. Lib. Assn.; Bibliog. Soc. Can. (Pres. 1976-78); rec'd Marie Tremaine Medal in Can. Bibliography 1981; CASLIS AWARD 1981; Beta Phi Mu; Progressive Conservative; United Church; recreation: handicrafts; Club: University Women's; Home: 62 Thornton Ave., London, Ont. N5Y 2Y3

BISHOP, Hon. Wilfred G., M.L.A.; lumber executive; politician; b. Chipman, N.B. 24 Sept. 1917; s. Amos and Annie E. (Dykeman) B.; m. Margaret M., d. Hugh Wilson, 28 Sept. 1937; children: Sandra Ann, Darrel Wilfred; MIN. OF TRANSPORTATION, N.B., since July 1972; Min. Natural Resources 1970-72; Pres., Bishop Lumber

Co. and Bishop Sawmills Ltd., Chipman, N.B.; M.L.A., N.B., since 1952; mem., Royal Candn. Legion; P. Conservative; Baptist; recreation: boating; Club: Chipman Curling Home: Chipman, N.B. E0E 1C0; Office: P.O. Box 6000, Fredericton, N.B. E3B 5H1

BISSELL, Claude Thomas, C.C. (1969), M.A., Ph.D., D.Litt., LL.D., F.R.S.C.; ex-univ. president and administrator; b. Meaford, Ont., 10 Feb. 1916; s. George Thomas and Maggie Editha (Bowen) B.; e. Runnymede Coll. Inst., Toronto, Ont.; Univ. Coll., Univ. of Toronto, B.A. 1936 and M.A. 1937; Cornell Univ., Ph.D. 1940; D. Litt. of Univ. of Manitoba, Univ. of Western Ont., Lethbridge, Leeds, Toronto, LL.D. of McGill Univ., Queen's, New Brunswick, Carleton, Montreal, St. Lawrence Univ. (Canton, N.Y), Brit. Columbia, Michigan, Columbia, York, Prince of Wales Coll., Windsor, St. Andrew's (Scotland); Docteur ès Lettres, Laval; m. Christina Flora, d. William Gray, Glasgow, Scot., 12 Sept. 1945; one d., (Mrs.) Deirdre Macdonald; Instr. in Eng., Cornell Univ. 1938-41; Lectr. in Eng., Univ. Coll. Univ. of Toronto 1941; Dean of Residence, University Coll., 1946-56; Asst. Prof. 1947; Assoc. Prof. 1951; Prof. 1962 and since July 1971; Asst. to the Pres., Univ. of Toronto 1948-52; Vice-Pres., 1952-56; President, Carleton Univ., 1956-58; Pres., Univ. of Toronto 1 July 1958-30 June 1971; Univ. Professor (Toronto) since 1971; Dir., Confed. Life Ins. Co.; Gen. Accident Assnce. Co. of Can.; served in 2nd W.W. with Candn. Inf. Corps 1942-46; with Argyll and Sutherland Highlanders of Can. in N.W. Europe campaign; discharged with rank of Capt.; Award of Merit, City of Toronto 1962; Hon. Mem. Am. Acad. of Arts and Science 1968; Editor of "University College: A Portrait", 1953; "Canada's Crisis in Higher Education" and "Our Living Tradition", 1957; "Great Canadian Writing", 1966: author of "The Strength of the University", 1968; "Halfway Up Parnassus: A Personal Account of the University of Toronto 1932-71" 1974; "The Humanities in the University" 1977; "THE YOUNG VINCENT MASSEY", 1981 (Co-winner of City of Toronto annual book award, 1982); named Chairman of The Canada Council, 1960-62; Pres., World University Service of Can. (2 yr. term) Nov. 1962; Pres., Nat. Conf. of Candn. Univs. and Colls., 1962-63; Chrmn., Candn. Universities Foundation, 1962-63; Chrmn. Carnegie Foundation for the Advancement of Teaching 1966; Pres. World University Service of Canada 1962-63; Chrmn. Comm. of Presidents of Universities of Ontario 1962-66; Visiting Prof. of Candn. Studies, Harvard Univ., 1967-68; Commonwealth Fellow, Sch. of English, Leeds Univ. 1973; Aggrey-Fraser-Guggisberg Memorial Lecturer, Univ. of Ghana 1976; mem. Council of the Arts (Ont.) 1972-75; author of various articles in Candn. and Eng. lit. in Candn. and Am. journals; United Church; Clubs: Arts and Letters; York; Home: 229 Erskine Ave., Toronto, Ont. M4P 1Z5; Office: University of Toronto, Toronto, Ont.

BISSON, Hon. Claude, B.A., LL.L.; juge; né Trois-Rivières, Qué., 9 mai 1931; f. Roger Bisson, C.R., (Maintenant Juge à la Retraite) et Marcelle (Morin) B.; é. Univ. Laval, Québec, B.A., 1950; Univ. Laval, LL.L., 1953; ép. Louisette, f. Gaston Lanneville, 12 Oct. 1957; enfants: Alain, Marie, Louis; JUGE DELA COUR D'APPEL DU QUEBEC depuis le 1 Mai, 1980 Juge Puine de la Cour Superieure du District de Montreal, Du 27 fév. 1969Au 1 Mai 1980; admis au Barreau du Québec, 1954; Catholique; Bureau: Palais de Justice, Montreal, Qué.

BITTORF, Donald George, M.Arch., R.C.A., F.R.A.I.C.; architect; b. Edmonton, Alta. 13 Aug. 1926; s. George Nicholas and Edna Elizabeth (Seibel) B.; e. Eastwood High Sch. Edmonton; 1945; Univ. of Wash. B.Arch. 1954; Harvard Univ. Grad. Sch. Design M.Arch. 1955; m. Loa Rae Mackenzie 9 June 1956; children: Donald Blair, Graeme Reed, Elizabeth Ann, Marin Rae; PRES., BITTORF HOLLAND AND COMPANY ARCHITECTS LTD.1975-; Pres., Paer-Maric Investments Ltd.; Assoc.

Partner, K. C. Stanley and Co. Edmonton 1956-59; Green Blakstein Russel & Associates Winnipeg 1959-70; Annett and Bittorf Architects Edmonton 1959-64; Bittord Wensley Architects Edmonton; D.G. Bittorf Architect Ltd. 1970-75; exhns. incl. Nickle Gallery Calgary 1980; City of Edmonton Design Awards, 1979, 1980, 1981; rec'd Am. Inst. Archs. Scholarship 1951; Grad. Award 1954; Univ. of Wash. Arch. Alumni Travel Scholarship 1953; Structural Clay Products Inst. Award 1954; Winnipeg City Hall Competition co-recipient 1st Prize 1960; Alta. Assn. Archs. Design Award 1965 (Edmonton Art Gallery); Dir., Fort Edmonton Hist. Foundation; Northern Lights Theatre; Trustee Govt. House Foundation; mem. Alta. Assn. Archs. (Council 1963-65, Bd. Examiners 1971-75, 1979); Urban Design Inst.; Heritage Can. Foundation; Phi Beta Kappa; Tau Sigma Delta; Bd. mem. Edmonton Art Gallery 1960-74; P. Conservative; Unitarian; recreations: skiing, wilderness hiking, canoeing; Clubs: Faculty; Calgary Professional; Home: (P.O. Box 14.3) R.R. 5, Edmonton, Alta T5P 4B7; Office: #420 Boardwalk Bldg., 10310 - 102 Ave., Edmonton, Alta. T5J 2X6.

BLACHFORD, Henry Lloyd, B.Sc., F.C.I.C.; chemical engineer; manufacturer; b. Montreal, P.Q., 31 May 1896; s. Henry and Agnes Louis (Williams) B.; e. Montreal High Sch.; McGill Univ., B.Sc. 1918; m. Grace I., d. Prof. N.M. Trenholme, 19 Dec. 1928; children: Ann, Norman, Nancy, John; CHAIRMAN AND OWNER, H. L. BLACHFORD LTD. (estbd. 1921; Chem. Mfrs. and Distributors) and of H. L. Blachford, Inc., Detroit, (Chem. Mfrs.); Alderman, City of Westmount, 1951-54; served in 1st World War with Air Force; mem. Am. Chem. Soc.; Soc. of Chem. Industry (England); Conservative; Protestant; recreation: golf; Clubs: St. James's; York; Lyford Cay (Nassau); Mississaugua Golf: Home: 39 Old Mill Road, Toronto, Ont. M8K 1G6; Office: c/o H. L. Blachford Ltd., 2323 Royal Windsor Drive, Mississauga, Ont. L5J 1KS

BLACHUT, Teodor Joseph, M.Sc., Dr.Sc.Techn., F.R.S.C.; scientist; b. Czestochowa, Poland 10 Feb. 1915; s. Aleksander Blachut; e. Tech. Univ. of Lwow, Poland M.Sc. (Geodesy) 1938; Tech. Univ. of Zurich Dr.Sc.Techn. 1971; Tech. Univ. of Mining & Metall. Krakow, Hon. Dr. Degree 1974; m. Schawalder 28 Dec. 1948; children: Jan. Daniel, Piotr; HEAD OF PHOTOGRAMMETRY RESEARCH SEC., NAT. RESEARCH COUNCIL since 1951; joined Wild Co., Switzerland 1946; came to Can. 1951; invented and was responsible for devel. no. photogrammetric concepts and instruments; holds several patents; mem. various Candn. and internat. comtes.; invited lectr. various acads. of science, univs. and learned socs. Europe, N. and S. Am.; Visiting Scient., Univ. of Brasilia 1970; Pres., Comte. on Large Scale and Urban Surveying & Mapping, Pan Am. Inst. Geog. & Hist. 1969-77; initiated and promoted devel. photogrammetric instrument mfg. in Can.; organizer numerous scient. and prof. internat. confs. Can. and abroad; rec'd Hon. Medal Tech. Univ. of Milan 1960; Photogrammetric Award and Luis Struck Award, Am. Soc. Photogrammetry 1973; served with Polish Armed Forces in France during World War II; Editor and main author "Urban Surveying and Mapping" 1979; author over 100 publs. geodetic, photogrammetric and cartographic subjects in Eng., Polish, French, Spanish and German; "History of Photogrammetry"in progress; Past Ed. "The Candian Surveyor"; mem. Candn. Inst. Surveying (Past Pres.); Am. Soc. Photogrammetry, MOLDS (Dir.); Pan Am. Inst. Geog. & Hist.; Internat. Soc. Photogrammetry; Corr. mem. Polish Geodetic Soc.; Hon. mem. Corp. des Arpenteurs-Géomètres Prov. Qué.; Brazilian Cartographic Soc.; R. Catholic; Home: 29 Cedar Rd., Ottawa, Ont. K1A 0R6; Office: Ottawa, Ont. K1A 0R6.

BLACK, Conrad M., B.A., M.A., LL.L., Litt.D., LL.D., K.L.J.; businessman; publisher; b. Montreal, Que. 25 Aug. 1944; s. late George Montegu and late Jean Elizabeth (Riley) B.; e. Carleton Univ. B.A. 1965; Laval Univ.

LL.L. 1970; McGill Univ. M.A. 1973; LL.D., St. Francis Xavier Univ. 1979, McMaster Univ. 1979; Litt.D., Univ. of Windsor 1979;CHRMN. OF BD. AND CHRMN. EXEC. COMTE. ARGUS CORP. LTD. Chmn. of Bd. and Chmn. of the Extve. Comte., Norcen Energy Resources Ltd.; Vice-Chrmn. and Chrmn. Exitve. Comte., Hollinger Argus Ltd.; Chrmn., Ravelston Corp. Ltd.; Pres., Western Dominion Investment Co. Ltd.; mem. Extve. Comte. and Dir., Cdn. Imp. Bank of Comm.; Dominion Stores Ltd.; Standard Broadcasting Corp. Ltd.; Dir., CFRB Ltd.; Carling O'Keefe Ltd.; Confederation Life Ins. Co.; Eaton's of Can. Ltd.; T. Eaton Acceptance Co. Ltd.; Iron Ore Co. of Can.; Labrador Mining and Exploration Co. Ltd.; author "Duplessis" 1977; Clubs: Toronto; York; Toronto Golf; University (Montreal); Mount Royal Club (Montreal); Office: 10 Toronto St., Toronto, Ont.M5C 2B7

BLACK, Rev. J. Bernard, B.A., M.L.S., S.T.B.; librarian; b. Toronto, Ont., 31 May 1926; s. Frederick Gerald and Alma Helen (Sampson) B., e. St. Michael's Coll. Sch. (1939-44); St. Michael's Coll. Univ. of Toronto, B.A. 1949, B.L.S. 1952, M.L.S. 1956, S.T.B. 1955; Univ. of Mich., 1959-61; LIBRARIAN, ST. MICHAEL'S COLL. UNIV. OF TORONTO, since 1961; mem., Tor. Public Library Board since 1979, chmn. since, 1981; Instr., Univ. of Toronto Lib. Sch. 1963-65; Univ. of Western Ont. Sch. Lib. and Info. Science 1971; Asst. Lib., St. Basil's Semy., 1953-56; Lib. and Asst. Prof of Eng., St. Thomas More Coll. in Univ. of Sask. 1956-59; mem. of Adv. Council. Sask. Lib. Assn., 1958-59; served in Royal Candn. Inf., 1944-45; mem., Candn. and Am. Lib. Assns.; Candn. Coll. of Teachers; Roman Catholic; joined Basilian Fathers, 1946; Address: 50 St. Joseph St., Toronto, Ont. M5S 1J4

BLACK, James Thompson, C.A.; b. Montreal, P.Q., 16 July 1925; s. James and Agnes Lang (McCartney) B.; e. High Sch. of Montreal (Matric. 1941); C.A. 1949; PRES., DIR. & CHIEF EXTVE. OFFR., THE MOLSON COMPANIES LTD. since 1973; Dir.: Canron Inc., Mutual Life Assurance Co. of Canada; Rio Algum Ltd.; Petro-Can.; with McDonald Currie & Co., Chart. Accts., Montreal, P.Q., 1941-49 (except war service); joined Molsons Brewery Ltd., 1949 as Asst. to the Treas.; Asst. Treas., 1953-55; Comptroller, 1955-61; Molsons Western Breweries Ltd., Vice-Pres. and Gen Mgr., 1961, Pres. 1966; Molson's Breweries Ltd., Vice-Pres., Operations, 1966; Dir., 1967; Sr. Vice Pres., Brewing Group Molson Industries Ltd., and Pres., Molson Breweries of Can. Ltd. 1968; Extve. Vide Pres., Operations, Molson Industries Ltd. 1970; Extve. Vice Pres., Molson Ind. Ltd. 1972; served in 2nd World War with RCAF; Flying Offr.-Navigator, 1943-45; Gov., Junior Achievement of Can.; Chmn. Niagara Inst.; Treas., Candn. Mfrs. Assn.; Dir., Business Council on Nat. Issues; Council for Candn. Unity; Trustee, Fraser Inst.; Regular mem., Conference Bd.; mem., Candn. Council; Conference Bd. in Can.; The Toronto; Office: 2 International Blvd., Rexdale, Ont. M9W 1A2

BLACK, Joseph Laurence, E.D., LL.D.; company president; b. Middle Sackville, N.B., 28 May 1900; s. Frank B. and Eleanor L. (Wood) B.; e. Sackville, N.B. Public Schs.; Upper Canada Coll., Toronto, Ont. (1917-18); Royal Mil. Coll., Kingston, Ont. (Grad. 1921); m. Gwendolyn, d. Nathaniel McDonald, Thedford, Ont., 1935; children: Joseph, Laurence, jr., Janet McDonald, John Donald; PRESIDENT, J.L. BLACK & SONS LTD. (Rentals, Investments, Estbd. 1847); Dir., Atlantic Industries (N.B.) Ltd.; mem. Bd. of Regents, Mt. Allison University; served in N.P.-A.M., 1921-39; 2nd World War with Candn. Active Army, 1940-45; Conservative; Protestant; recreations: golf, curling, hunting, fishing; Clubs: Sackville Country; Sackville Curling; Aesculapius Fishing; Albert Fishing Club; R.M.C. of Canada; Home: Middle Sackville, N.B.; Office: (P.O. Box 68), Sackville, N.B. E0A 3C0

BLACK, Sam; R.C.A.; R.S.W.; artist; educator; b. Ardrossan, Scot. 5 June 1913; s. James Black; e. Ardrossan

Acad.; Glasgow Sch. of Art; Jordanhill Coll. of Educ. Glasgow grad. D.A. (Glas), A.T.D. (Lon) 1936; m. Elizabeth Morton d. William Howie June 1941; four d.; PROF. EMERITUS EDUC., UNIV. OF B.C. 1978- ; teacher elem. and secondarysch. Scot.; after war service His Majesty's Inspr. of Schs. Eng.; Prince. Lectr. in Art, Jordanhill Training Coll. Glasgow 1949-58; Prof. of Fine Arts and Art Educ. Univ. of B.C. 1958-78; Commonwealth Visiting Fellow to Australia 1963; has held many solo exhns.; rep. in various pub., corporate and private colls. incl. Imp. War Museum (London), Can. Council Art Bank, Nat. Gallery Can. and other colls. Can., Europe, Australia, Japan; author and illustrator "China Sketchbook" 1976; several illustrated travel articles and numerous articles in prof. journs.; contrib. to various publs. incl. UNESCO's "Art and Education"; "Thought" 1961; served with Royal Scots Fusiliers 1939-45, Camouflage Offr. 1st Brit. Corps Normandy, rank Maj.; Mentioned-in-Despatches, Oak Leaf; rec'd Belgian Medal Civile 2 Class for bravery; Candn. Centennial Medal 1967; Univ. of B.C. Master Teacher Award 1970; Hon. Life mem. Univ. of B.C. Alumni 1980; Candn. Soc. for Educ. Art (Past Pres.); B.C. Art Teachers Assn.; Founding mem. Internat. Soc. for Educ. Art (Past Vice Pres.); mem. Roy. Can. Acad. Arts.; Royal Scot Soc. Painters in Watercolour; Candn. Soc. Painters in Watercolour; Print & Drawing Council Can.; Presbyterian; recreations: art, travel, AddressThe Shieling, Cardena Rd., Bowen Island, B.C. V0N 1G0.

BLACKBURN, Robert Harold, M.A., B.L.S., M.S., LL.D.; librarian; editor; b. Vegreville, Alta., 3 Feb. 1919; s. John H. and Palma G. (Olson) B.; e. Univ. of Alberta, M.A. 1941; Univ. of Toronto, B.L.S. 1942; Columbia Univ., M.S. 1948; Univ. of Waterloo, LL.D. 1965; m. F. Patricia, d. H.A. Gibson, M.D., Calgary, Alta., 31 Dec. 1942; children: Robert G., Karen M., John H.; LIBRARIAN, UNIVERSITY OF TORONTO, 1981-; Gen. Asst., Calgary Pub. Library, 1945-46; Asst. Librarian, Univ. of Toronto, 1947-54; Chief Librarian, Univ. Of Toronto 1954-81 Editor of Nfld. 'Supplement to "Encyclopedia of Canada", 1949; "Joint Catalogue of Serials in Toronto Libraries", 1953, author of various poet. articles, poems and short stories; mem., Candn. Library Assn. (Pres. 1958-59); Ont. Library Assn.; Am. Library Assn.; Pres. (1963-64) Candn. Assn. of Coll. & Univ. Libs.; Bd. mem. (1965-67), Assn. of Research Libs.; Bd. Chrmn. (1967), Centre for Research Libs.; Dir., Am. Lib. Assn. and Council, Assn. of Coll. & Research Libs.; Bd. mem. Mass. Inst. of Tech. Bd. of Lib. Visitors 1970-73; Bd. mem. Assn. of Research Libs. 1971-73; mem. Can. Assn. of Research Libs; Consultant for Can. to "Colliers Encyclopedia"; Protestant; Home: 5324 Durie Rd., Streetsville, Ont. L5M 2C7; Office: University of Toronto, Toronto, Ont.

BLACKBURN, Walter Juxon, B.A.; publisher; broadcaster; b. London, Ont., 18 March 1914; s. late Arthur Stephen and late Etta Irene (Henderson) B.; e. London Central Coll. Inst.; Univ. of Western Ont., B.A. (Hons. Business Adm.), 1936; m. Marjorie Ludwell, d. late Lawrence Dampier, 9 Nov. 1938; children: Susan Marjorie, Martha Grace; CHAIRMAN, DIR. AND PUBLISHER, LONDON FREE PRESS PRINTING CO. LTD.; Chrmn. of Bd., CFPL Broadcasting Ltd.; Dir., The Canada Trust Co.; mem., Candn. Assn. of Broadcasters; The Canadian Press; Newspaper Advertising Bureau, Am. Newspaper Publishers Assn. (Secy. of the Assn. 1954-59); apptd. Pres. and Mang. Dir., London Free Press Printing Co. Ltd., Jan. 1936; Chrmn. CKNX Broadcasting Ltd.; Pres. Wingham Investments Ltd.; Secy., American Newspaper Publishers Assn., 1954-59; mem. of Adv. Bd., Y.M.C.A.-Y.W.C.A.; Adv. Bd., Orchestra London; served as Second Lieut., First Hussars, 1938-39; Hon. Col., 9 Signal Regt. (1959-64); Delta Upsilon; Freemason; Independent; Anglican; recreations: fishing, boating; Clubs: The London; London Hunt & Country; Home: 11 Kingspark

Cresc., London, Ont. N6H 4C3; Office: (Box 2280, Terminal A), 369 York St., London, Ont. N6A 4G1

BLACKER, Rowland John; publisher; b. Somerset, Eng., 4 Apl. 1904; s. John and Annie (Short) B.; m. Edith Maude Mills, 15 Oct. 1930; children: Maureen Elizabeth, John Stratton; came to Can. 1928; e. Shepton Mallet Sch., 1916; Queens Coll. (Business) 1920; Dir., Sir Isaac Pitman & Sons (Canada) Ltd.; Chrmn., Copp Clark Ltd. until 1974; with Pitman Press, Bath Eng., 1920; London publ. office of Pitman Publishing, 1927; Asst. Mgr., Sir Isaac Pitman & Sons, Toronto, Ont., 1928; subsequently Pres., Sir Isaac Pitman & Sons (Canada) Ltd. till 1970 (chrmn. until 1974); Founder and Jt. Sponsor of Squadron 61, Toronto Air Cadets, 1940; mem., Bd. Trade Metrop. Toronto; awarded Distinguished Prof. Services Award of Chart. Inst. of Secys. 1967; Anglican; recreations: golf, gardening; Home: 52 Pine Crescent, Toronto, Ont. M4E 1L4;

BLACKWELL, John Henry, E.D., M.Sc., Ph.D.; educator; b. Melbourne, Australis 9 July 1921; s. Mathew Drummond and Vera Isabel Marion (Lillies) B.; e. Univ. of Melbourne B.Sc. 1941; Univ. of W. Ont. M.Sc. 1947, Ph.D. 1952; m. Betty Stanmore d. late Thomas Herbert Smith 19 Apl. 1947; children: Stephen D., J. Gerald, Patricia F. M. (Morden), Thomas M.; PROF. OF APPLIED MATH., UNIV. OF W. ONT. 1981- ; Instr., Asst. Prof. Assoc. Prof., Prof., Dept. of Physics 1947-1960; Prof. Dept. of Math. 1960-67; Prof. and Chrmn. of Applied Math. 1967-76, Prof. of Applied Math. and Extve. Asst. to Pres. (Planning) 1976-80; Visiting Fellow, Australian Nat. Univ. Canberra 1955-56; UK Commonwealth Fellow, Oxford Univ. 1964-65; served with Citizen Mil. Forces (Inf.) Australia 1939-42, Australian Imp. Force (RAEME) 1942-46 (Australia, UK and N.W. Europe), rank Capt.; Candn. Offrs. Training Corps 1958-66, rank Lt. Col.; author various articles heat transfer, magnetohydrodynamics, microwave spectroscopy in Candn. and foreign scient. & engn. journs.; Fellow, Inst. Math. & its Applications; mem. Candn. Soc. Mech. Engrs. (Past Vice Pres.); Candn. Applied Math. Soc.; Engn. Inst. Can.; Royal Candn. Legion; P. Conservative; Anglican; recreations: golf, photography, model railways; Clubs: University; London Hunt & Country; Home: 2 Runnymede Cres., London, Ont. N6G 1Z8; Office: London, Ont. N6A 5B9.

BLACKWOOD, Allister Clark, M.Sc., Ph.D., F.R.S.C.; microbiologist; educator; b. Calgary, Alta. 22 Nov. 1915; s. Allister Chester and Bessie Emerson (Saunders) B.; e. Univ. of Alta. B.Sc. 1942, M.Sc. 1944; Univ. of Wis. Ph.D. 1949; m. Mildred d. Jack Marsh, Drumheller, Alta. 1 May 1943; children: Alan Clark, Marsha Ellen, Susan Mildred; Prof. Emeritus, Dept. Microbiol. Faculty of Agric. Macdonald Coll. McGill Univ. 1981-, Prof. of Microbiology 1957-81, Chrmn. of Dept. 1957-68, Dean of Faculty and Vice Princ. of Coll. 1972-77; joined Div. of Applied Biol. Nat. Research Council, Ottawa 1944-46, Prairie Regional Lab. Saskatoon 1948-57; holds US Patent Production of Glycerol by Fermentation; rec'd Centennial Medal 1967; Silver Jubilee Medal, 1977; author or co-author numerous articles, reviews, book chapters; Hon. mem. Que. Soc. de Microbiologie (Pres. 1962-63); mem. Candn. Soc. Microbiol. (Pres. 1964-65); Am. Soc. Microbiol.; Soc. Gen. Microbiol.; Soc. Applied Bacteriol.; Soc. Indust. Microbiol.; Assn. Faculties Agric. Can. (Pres. 1975-76); Kappa Sigma; Anglican; recreations: curling, swimming; Home: 2131 Wenman Dr. Victoria, B.C. V8N 2S3

BLACKWOOD, David Lloyd, R.C.A.; artist; b. Wesleyville, Nfld. 7 Nov. 1941; s. Capt. Edward and Molly (Glover) B.; e. Wesleyville Mem. High Sch. 1959; Ont. Coll. of Art Toronto (Govt. Nfld. Centennial Scholarship) Hon. Grad. Drawing & Painting 1963, rec'd Travelling Scholarship to visit maj. Am. Colls. Washington and N.Y., grad. work Painter-Printmaker 1963-64; m. Anita Elizabeth d. Adrian Bonar, Toronto, Ont. Sept. 1970; one s. David Bonar; Assoc., Ont. College of Art, 1963; Artist-in-Residence Erindale Coll. Univ. of Toronto 1969-75; Art Master, Trinity Coll. Sch. Port Hope, Ont. 1963- ; rep. in pub. and private colls. incl. Nat. Gallery Can., Nat. Gallery Australia, Montreal Museum Fine Arts, Art Gallery Ont., Uffizi, Florence, various Candn. and USA univs. and business firms, private coll. Queen Elizabeth; maj. exhns. incl. Univ. of Me. 1980, Blackwood Prints 1967-80 Milan, Italy 1980 also Bologna, Venice and Rome; Dir., Sault Coll. Applied Arts; Candn. Prison Arts Foundation; co-author "Wake of the Great Sealers" 1974; subject of NFB film Blackwood 1974; rec'd 10 internat. film awards incl. Oscar nomination; maj. awards incl. Purchase Award Biennial Exhn. Nat. Gallery Can. 1964; Purchase Award Nat. Gallery Australia 1967; Ingres Medal Govt. France 1963; Internat. Graphics '71 Award Montreal Museum Fine Arts; First Internat. Norweigian Biennial Prints Award 1972; Biennale Internat. de L'estampe Paris 1973; 8th Burnaby Internat. Biennial 1975; Hon. Academician with Gold Medal, Italian Acad. Fine Arts 1980; el. mem. Royal Candn. Acad. 1975 (Vice Pres.); mem. Ont. Soc. Artists; Print & Drawing Council Can.; Candn. Soc. Painters Water Colour; recreations: hist. research related to Nfld., collecting Candn. art & antiques, reading, writing, photography, music; Address: 22 King St., Port Hope, Ont. L1A 2R5.

BLAIR, Hon. D. Gordon, LL.B., B.C.L.; judge; b. Regina, Sask. 23 Dec. 1919; S. Duncan and Eliza Martha (Elliott) B.; e. Regina Pub. and High Schs.; Univ. of Sask. B.A. 1939, LL.B. 1941; Oxford Univ. (Rhodes Scholar 1941) B.C.L. 1947; m. Sarah Margaret d. Charles William Milton 24 June 1946; two s. David Allen, Stephen Gordon; JUDGE, COURT OF APPEAL ONT. since 1976; called to Bar of Sask. 1942, Ont. 1952; cr. Q.C. 1975; Foreign Service Offr. Dept. External Affairs 1945-47; Partner, Francis, Woods, Gauley & Blair, Saskatoon 1948-50; Extve. Asst. to Min. of Justice 1951-52; Partner, Herridge, Tolmie, Gray, Coyne & Blair, Ottawa 1953-75; el. to H. of C. for Grenville-Carleton 1968-72; Chrmn. H. of C. Comte. on Procedure & Organ. 1968-72; Del. 25th Gen. Assembly U.N. 1970; Vice Chrmn. Ont. Comn. of El. Contributions & Expenses 1975; served as Lieut. with Irish Regt. of Can., gravely wounded Italy 1944, Capt. A.G. Br., N.D.H.Q. 1944-45; mem. Internat. Comn. Jurists (Candn. Sec.), Pres. 1973-76; Candn. Bar Assn.; Royal Candn. Legion; United Church; recreations: golf, reading; Clubs: Rideau; Royal Ottawa Golf; Links O'Tay Golf & Country (Perth, Ont.); Royal Candn. Mil. Inst. (Toronto, Ont.); Home: Apt. 1608, 65 Harbour Sq., Toronto, Ont. M5J 2L4; Office: Osgoode Hall, Toronto, Ont. M5H 2N5.

BLAIS, Hon. Jean-Jacques, Q.C., P.C., M.P., B.A., LL.B.; b. Sturgeon Falls, Ont., 27 June 1940; s. Rodolphe Gaston and Claire (Rochon) B.; e. Ecole Sacré-Coeur and Sturgeon Falls (Ont.) High Sch. 1958; Univ. of Ottawa B.A. 1961, LL.B. 1964; Osgoode Hall 1966; m. Maureen Ann d. late Edward Michael Ahearn, Ottawa, Ont., 20 May 1968; children: Stéphane, Alexandre, Marie-José; MIN. OF SUPPLY AND SERVICES, CAN. 1980-; Solicitor General for Canada 1978; apptd. Postmaster Gen. of Can. and Depy-House Leader Sept. 1976; read law with Joseph Sedgwick, Q.C.; called to Bar of Ont. 1966; assoc. law practice with George Campbell Miller, Toronto and retained for firm Miller and Blais by various labour groups 1966-70; practised at Criminal Bar appearing before criminal tribunals incl. Supreme Court of Can.; became Partner Blais, McLachlan & Duchesneau-McLachlan, N. Bay 1970; mem. Adv. Comte. on French Educ. Metrop. Toronto 1969; Cand. Toronto Bd. of Educ. 1969(def.); el. to H. of C. 1972, re-el. 1974, 1979 and 1980; apptd. Parlty. Secy. to the Pres. of the Privy Council 1975; Hon. mem. Offrs.' Mess CFB and Algonquin Regt.; mem. Chamber Comm.; Nipissing Bar Assn.; Law Soc. Upper Can.; Candn. Bar Assn.; Amnesty Internat.; Liberal; R. Catholic; recreations: skiing; swimming; Clubs: Richelieu Internat.; Liberal Internat.; Davedi; Home: 200 Parsons Ave., North Bay, Ont. P1A 1S7; Office: House of Commons, Ottawa, Ont. K1A 0A7

BLAIS, Marie-Claire, C.C. (1972); author; b. Quebec, Que. 1939; studied lit. and philos. Laval Univ.; awarded Guggenheim Fellowship 1963 and 1964; author of "La belle Bête" 1959, (trans. into Eng. as "Mad Shadows" 1960); "Tête blanche" 1960, (Eng. trans. 1961); "Le jour est noir" 1962 (trans. into Eng. as "The Day is Dark"); "Pay voilés (poems) 1963; "Existences" (poems) 1964; "Une saison dans la vie d'Emmanuel" 1965, (Eng. trans. "A Season in the Life of Emmanuel" 1966); "Les Voyageurs Sacrés"; "L'insoumise" 1971, (trans. into Eng. as "The Fugitive" 1978); "L'exécution; pièce en deux actes" (play) 1968, (trans. into Eng. as "The Execution" 1976); "Manuscrits de Pauline Archange" 1968 and "Vivre, Vivre" 1969 (both trans. into Eng. as "The Manuscripts of Pauline Archange" 1970); "Vivre, Vivre" 1969; "Les Apparences" 1970 (trans. into Eng. as "Durer's Angel" 1972); "Le Loup" (novel) 1972 (trans. into Eng. as "The Wolf" 1974); "Un Joualonais sa Joualonie" 1973 (trans. into Eng. as "St. Lawrence Blues" 1974); "Une liaison parisienne" 1976 (trans. into Eng. as "A Literary Affair" 1978); "L'Ocean" 1977 (trans. into Eng. as "The Ocean" 1978); "Les nuits de l'underground" 1978 (trans. into Eng. as "Nights in the Underground" 1979); "Le Sourd Dans La Ville," 1980 (trans. into English as "Death to the City" 1981) ; Address: c/o Louise Myette, 3507, Aylmer St., Montreal, Que. H2X 2B9

BLAIS, Pierre G., M.B.A.; food processing executive; b. Montreal, Que. 5 Aug. 1931; s. Lucien and Claire (Delorme) B.; e. Mont-Saint-Louis Coll. Montreal 1950; McGill Univ. Faculty of Comm. 1953, M.B.A. 1971; m. Claudette d. Lionell Ethier, Montreal, Que. 3 Sept. 1956; children: A. Pierre, Patrice; TREAS. KELLOGG SALADA CANADA INC. since 1977; Adm. Mgr. present co. Montreal 1970, Cost Controller Toronto 1971, Mgr. Auditing 1975; on loan to Anti-Inflation Bd. Ottawa 1976; mem. Candn. Mang. Assn.; Candn. Tax Foundation; R. Catholic; recreations: tennis, reading; Club: Richelieu (Internat. Pres. 1981-82); Home.56 Allangrove Cres., Agincourt, Ont. M1W 1S5; Office: 6700 Finch Ave. W., Rexdale, Ont. M9W 5P2.

BLAKELY, W. Thomas; association executive; b. Hamilton, Ont., 2 Oct. 1913; s. William Robert and Lydia Lucretia (Deynarde) B.; e. High Schs., Hamilton, Ont.; m. Patricia Norma, d. late Robert John Leader, 19 Oct 1956; children: Thomas Patrick; DEPUTY CHRMN., ASSN. OF CANDN. ADVERTISERS since 1970; admitted to printing apprenticeship, Hamilton "Herald" (now defunct), Sept. 1932; successively attached to Ed. and Advertising Depts. till suspension of paper in 1936; Freelance fiction writer, 1936-38; Advertising Mgr. and Asst. Ed of Temiskaming "Speaker", New Liskeard, Ont., 1939; Asst. Advertising Mgr., Fort William "Times-Journal", 1940-42, and after war services became Indust. Promotion Mgr.; Copywriter and Creative Dir., McKim Advertising Ltd., 1946-49; Dir. of Advertising & Pub. Relations, Yardley of London (Canada) Ltd., 1949-53; named Mgr. of Montreal Office of McConnell, Eastman & Co. Ltd., Sept. 1953, Vice-Pres. 1954, Dir. 1958; Dir., Pub. Relations, Domtar Ltd. 1967; apptd. Mang. Dir. of present Assn. 1970; Dir., Candn. Advertising Research Research Foundation (Press. 1971); Candn. Advertising Adv. Bd.; Better Business Bur. of Can.; Children's Broadcast Inst.; served in 2nd World War with R.C.N. as Ordinary Seaman in 1942; service in mid-Atlantic convoy duty; discharged with rank of Lieut. 1945; mem. Pub. Relations Soc.; Protestant; Clubs: Naval Officers; Toronto and Montreal Press; Advertising & Sales Executives; Home: 265 Chaplin Cresc., Toronto, Ont. M5P 1B1; Office: 180 Bloor St. W. St., Toronto, Ont. M5S 2V6

BLAKENEY, Hon. Allan Emrys, Q.C., M.L.A., M.A., LL.B.; b. Bridgewater, N.S., 7 Sept. 1925; s. John Cline and Bertha May (Davies) B.; e. Bridgewater (N.S.) High Sch.; Dalhousie Univ., B.A. 1945, LL.B. 1947; Nova Scotia Rhodes Scholar 1947; Oxford Univ., B.A. 1949, M.A. 1955; m. Mary Elizabeth (Molly) Schwartz d. Dr. Hugh W. Schwartz, Halifax, N.S. (d. 1957) Sept. 1950; m. Anne Louise, d. Cyril H. Gorham, Halifax, N.S.; May 1959; children: Barbara, Hugh, David, Margaret; PREMIER OF SASKATCHEWAN, since 1971; formerly a Dir. of several Co-op. Assns.; read law with W. P. Potter, Q.C., Lunenburg, N.S.; called to the Bar of N.S. 1950, and Sask. 1951; cr. Q.C. 1961; Secy. and Solr. for Crown Corps. Prov. of Sask., 1950-55; Chairman, Sask. Securities Comm., 1955-58; in private practice, Davidson, Davidson & Blakeney, 1958-60; Griffin, Blakeney, Beke, Koskie & Lueck, 1964-70; Min. of Educ., Sask., 1960-61; Prov. Treas. 1961-62, Min. Pub. Health, 1962-64; el. to Sask. Leg. for Regina City, 1960; re-el. for Regina W. 1964, and for Regina Centre 1967, 1971, for Regina Elphinstone 1975 and 1978; Leader of the Opposition 1970-71; Hon. Doctor of Civil Law, Mt. Allison Univ.; Hon. Doctor of Laws, Dalhousie Univ.; mem., Law Soc. Sask.; Cdn. Bar Assoc.; N.D.P.; Baptist; Office: Legislative Bldg., Regina, Sask. S4S 0B3

BLAKLEY, Harold W., B.A.Sc.; executive; b. Grimshaw, Alta. 1 Feb. 1923; s. Everett Thomas and Mabel (Archibald) B.; e. Grimshaw (Alta.) High Sch. 1939; Univ. of Toronto B.A.Sc. 1950; m. Bertha Florence d. Sam Brett, Toronto, Ont. 11 Sept. 1948; CHRMN., PRES. AND C.E.O., VICKERS CAN. INC. 1978-; Sales Engr. Ashland Oil & Refining Co. Inc. Cleveland, Ohio 1950-52; Babcock & Wilcox Ltd. Galt, Ont. 1952-56; Gen. Mgr.-Can. Illinois Tools Ltd. Don Mills, Ont. 1956-59; Pres. Crane Canada Ltd. Montreal 1959-63; Consolidated Bakeries Ltd. Toronto 1963-64; Carling Breweries Ltd. Toronto 1964-67; Formosa Spring Brewery Ltd. Toronto 1967-71; Columbia Brewing Co. Ltd. Vancouver 1971-77; Extve. Vice Pres. and Dir., Vickers Can. Inc. 1977-78; served with RCAF 1942-45 Can. UK and Europe; Anglican; recreation: tennis, golf, hiking; Club: Vancouver; St. James's; Capilano Golf & Country (Vancouver); Royal Montreal Golf; Office: 5000 Notre Dame St. E., Montreal Que. H1V 2B4

BLAKNEY, John Frederick; executive; b. Glendale, Cal., 12 Nov. 1921; s. John Albert and Ethel (Hartley) B.; e. Brantford (Ont.) Coll. Inst., 1937; m. Mary G., d. Frederick W. Holt, 1 Feb. 1944; two s. John F., Robert M.; VICE-PRES., INDUST. FOODS DIV., OGILVIE MILLS LTD.; Pres., Flour Division; with Slingsby Manufacturing, Brantford, Ont. 1937-41; joined present Co. as Asst. Mgr., Brantford, Head-1953; Mgr. 1954-55; Plant Mgr., Keewatin, Ont., 1955-57; Winnipeg, 1957-61; Montreal, 1961-63; Gen. Mgr., Winnipeg, 1963-66; Vice Pres., Flour Div., Montreal, 1966-68, Pres., Indust. Div., 1969; served with RCAF as Flying Offr.-Navig., 1941-45; Parks Commr., Brantford, 1952-54; Ald., Brantford City Council, 1955; mem., Assn. Operative Millers; Candn. Nat. Millers Assn. (Chrmn. 1974-76, 1980-82); Can. Grains Council (Dir. 1978-84); Protestant; recreations: golf, fishing, gardening; Clubs: Mount Stephen; Beaconsfield Golf; Home: 169 Regatta Ave., Pointe Claire, Que. H9S 3Z5; Office: Ste. 2100, 1 Place Ville Marie, Montreal, Que. H3B 2X2

BLANCHARD, J. Ewart, B.Sc., M.A., Ph.D.; geophysicist; b. Truro, N.S. 22 March 1921; s. Aubrey B. and Agnes George (Blair) B.; e. Dalhousie Univ., B.Sc. 1940; Univ. of Toronto, M.A. 1947, Ph.D. 1952; m. Mary Helena, 5 July 1958; children: Jonathan Sandilands, Megan Blair; PRESIDENT NOVA SCOTIA RESEARCH FOUNDATION CORPORATION, Geol. Survey of Can., summer 1940; Asst. Forecaster, Meterol. Service, Dept. of Transport, 1940-42; Party Chief Geophys. Surveys, Conwest Exploration Ltd., summers 1946 and 1947; Geophysicist, Newmont Mining Corp., 1948-49; Lectr. in Physics, Dalhousie Univ., 1949-52; Asst. Prof. 1952-57; Assoc. Prof. 1957-64; Prof. 1964-66; Dir. Geophysics Div., N.S.

Research Foundation, 1949-66, Vice Pres. 1966-68; Acting Dir., Dalhousie Inst. of Oceanography, 1964-65; served with RCN 1942-45; rank Lieut.; author of numerous papers for learned journs.; Fellow Roy. Soc. of Can.; mem. Soc. Exploration Geophysicists; Am. Geophys. Union; European Assn. Geophysicists; Candn. Assn. Physicists; Seismol. Soc. Am.; Can. Inst. Mining and Metall.; N.S. Inst. Science; Presbyterian; recreations: golf, skiing, tennis; Home: 6470 Coburg Rd., Halifax, N.S. B3H 2A7; Office: (Box 790) Dartmouth, N.S. B2Y 3Z7

BLAND, Alan Goldworth, B.Sc., P.Eng.; b. Ottawa, Ont., 19 Jan. 1926; s. Charles H. and Ethel (Farrow) B.; e. Queen's Univ., B.Sc. (C.E.) 1949; m. Sylvia Alice, d. Rowley Frith, Ottawa, Ont., 6 Aug. 1955; children: Margaret Susan, Rowley Peter; PRESIDENT AND GENERAL MANAGER, DEFENCE CONSTRUCTION (1951) LTD., since 1963; began with L.P. Stidwell, Consulting Engr., and Ont. Land Surveyor; joined Central Mortgage and Housing Corp., 1951; trans. to present Co., Engr. in Charge, Navy Projects, 1954; R.C.A.F. Projects, 1955; N. Ont. Sec., Trans-Can. Pipeline 1956; Adm. Engr., 1959; Asst. Chief Engr. (Constr. Planning), 1962; Course XVI, Nat. Defence Coll., Kingston, Ont., 1962; Protestant; recreations: Golf, curling, boating, swimming; Home: 22 Riverside Dr., (P.O. Box 227) Manotick, Ont. K0A 2N0; Office: SBI Building, Billings Bridge Plaza, 2323 Riverside Dr., Ottawa, Ont. K1A 0K3

BLAND, John, B.Arch., A.A.Dipl., D.Sc., F.R.A.I.C., R.C.A.; university professor; b. Lachine, P.Q., 3 Nov. 1911; s. Widmer Clarence and Clara (Ford) B.; e. Loyola Coll.; McGill Univ., B. Arch., 1933; Arch. Assn. Sch., London, Eng., 1937; m. Fay, d. A.C.M. Thomson, Dec. 1942; children: Clara Katherine, Andrew Widmer, John Christie, Alfred Henry; EMERITUS PROF. OF ARCH., McGILL UNIV., 1979-; Former Partner, Bland, Le Moyne, & Shine, Archs. and Planning Consultants, Montreal, P.Q.; Extve. Secy., Sch. of Arch., McGill Univ., 1939-41, and apptd. Dir. in 1941; Macdonald Prof. 1950-79 mem. of Council, Royal Arch. Inst. of Can.; mem., P.Q. Assn. of Arch. (Past Pres.); Clubs: Faculty; University; Home: 21094 Lakeshore Road, Ste. Anne de Bellevue, Que. H9X 1S2

BLANK, Harry, Q.C., M.N.A., B.C.L., B.Sc., advocate; b. Montreal, P.Q., 24 May 1925; s. Udel and Molly (Zinman) B.; e. Baron Byng High Sch., Montreal, (Grad. 1941); McGill Univ., B.Sc. 1947, B.C.L. 1950; m. 2ndly, Elaine Sloane, d. late Jacob Sloane, Boston, Mass., 18 Nov. 1967; children: David, Joyce, Gale, Caren, Andrew, Michael; called to the Bar of Que., 1950; served in 2nd World War; No. 2 Candn. Army Univ. Corp., 1943; Candn. Inf. Corps, 1944; overseas with North Shore Regt. (N.B.), 1945; wounded in action, 1945; Royal Montreal Regt., 1945; McGill C.O.T.C., 1946-50; el. to Nat. Assembly of Que. for Montreal-St. Louis, g.e. June 1960; re-el. since; Depy. Speaker, National Assembly 1971-76, Joint Chrmn. of Committees since 1976; el. Extve. mem. Commonwealth Parl. Assn. representing Canadian region 1975, del. to Assn. conferences Australia 1970, Mauritius 1976, Ottawa 1977, Jamaica 1978, also exec. meetings St. Lucia 1976, Sierra Leone 1977, Penang 1978; mem., Cercle de Juif Langue Française; Canadian Legion; B'Nai Brith; K. of P.; Liberal; Hebrew; recreations: flying (pte. pilots lic.), golf, fishing; Club: Montefiore; Garrison; Home: 9 Redpath Row, Montreal, Que. H3G 1E6; Office: 1255 University St., Montreal, P.Q.

BLANKSTEIN, Cecil Nat, B.Arch., F.R.A.I.C.; b. Winnipeg, Man., 15 Aug. 1908; s. Max Zoel and Lena (Goldin) B.; e. Univ. of Manitoba, B.Arch. 1929; m. Claire Sara, d. late Harry Lyon Diamond, 24 Aug 1936; children: Arthur Martin, Max Zoel; PRESIDENT. GBR ASSOCIATES, Architects & Engineers; Dir., TransAir Ltd.; started arch. practice with Mr. L. J. Green, 1931; formed arch. firm 1934; formed present firm 1944; mem. Urban Land Inst.;

Manitoba Assn. Archs.; Que. Assn. Archs.; recreations: golf, stamp collecting; Home: 1201-200 Tuxedo Blvd., Winnipeg, Man. R3P 0R3; Office: 303-323 Wellington Cres., Winnipeg, Man. R3M 0A4

BLASER, Lorenz Paul, B.Sc.; company executive (ret.); b. Markinch, Sask., 12 Feb. 1916; s. Paul and Barbara (Appenheimer) B.; e. Univ. of Sask., B.Sc. (Chem. Engn.); m. Marjorie Jean, d. late Herbert Orr, 4 July 1942; children: Barbara Lynn, Paula Jean, David Lorenz Paul; Pres., Gulf Canada Products Co., 1976-81 and Pres., Gulf Canada Products Co.; joined British American Oil Co.'s Calgary Refinery, 1939 and transf. to Moose Jaw Refinery as Asst. Chemist, 1941; subsequently apptd. Refinery Chemist in Moose Jaw; Resident Process Engr. at Moose Jaw, 1945; Head, Process Engn. Div., Toronto, 1949-52; Asst. Mgr., Moose Jaw Refinery, 1952-54; Chief Engr., Toronto, 1954-58; Gen. Mgr. of Mfg., 1958-63; Vice-Pres. (Mfg.) 1963-65; Vice Pres., Personnel, Trans., Crude Products Supply 1965; World Wide Coordinator of Refining, Gulf Oil Corp. 1966-67; returned to Canada as Senior Vice-Pres. 1967; Extve. Vice Pres. and Dir. 1976; Dir., Canadian Opera Company, Toronto; mem., Ont. Assn. Prof. Engrs.; Am. Petrol. Inst.; United Church; recreations: curling, golf, gardening; Clubs: Engineers; Donalda; Granite; National; Engineers' (Toronto); Home: 37 Daneswood Rd., Toronto, Ont. M4N 3J7;

BLATCHFORD, Mrs. Douglas H. (Ellen H.C.), M.B., M.D., F.R.C.P.(C).; physician-anaesthetist (retired); b. Maple Valley, Wis., 17 July 1900; d. late Charles Joseph Comisky and Sarah Agnes (Clements) B.; e. High Sch., Aurora, Ont.; Univ. of Toronto, M.B. 1923; served internship in Philadelphia and in St. John's Hosp., Toronto; specialized in anaesthesia under late Dr. McKesson, Toledo, Ohio, and Dr. S. Johnston, Toronto Gen. Hosp.; m. Douglas H., s. late T. W. Blatchford, 4 July 1925; with Women's College Hosp., Toronto, mem. Anaesthesia Staff 1926-30, Chief of Anaesthetic Staff 1930-56, active consultant 1956-66; mem., Am. Anaesthetists Soc.; Candn. Anaesthetists Assn.; Acad. of Med., Toronto; Internat. Anaesthesia Research Soc.; Candn. Med. Assn.; Coll. of Phys. & Surg.; United Church; recreations: music, travel; Address: 4000 Yonge St., Apt. 612, Toronto, Ont. M4N 2N9

BLATT, Jack, F.B.S.C., F.I.C.; industrialist; b. Warsaw, Poland, 1909; s. Eva (Kasimereska) and late Isaac B.; e. Polytech. Schs., Warsaw, Poland, and Regina, Sask.; m. Devida, d. Richard Williams, Cornwall, Ont., 1941; children: Howard Edward, Margaret, Elsa, Cora, Joyce; CHMN. OF THE BD., ELECTRICITÉ STANDARD INC.; Pres., Standard Enterprises Corp.; Standard Holdings Ltd.; Blaman Investments Inc.; Henja Investments Corp.; Bonaventure of Florida, Prime Corporation; Pres., Madabar Ltd.; Secy. Treas., Building Enterprises Inc.; Life Gov., Y.M.H.A., Montreal; Gov., United Parochial Schs. of Montreal; Camp B'nai Brith; Jewish Gen. Hosp.; Jewish Hosp. of Hope; Dir., Hillel Foundation; McGill Univ.; B'Nai B'Rith; Hewbrew; recreations: golf, curling; Clubs: Elmridge Country; Mt. Stephen, St. Denis (Montreal); Montefiore; Bonaventure Golf & Country; Florida; Office: 4480 Cote de Liesse Road, Montreal, Que. H4N 2R3

BLEY, Paul; pianist; composer; b. Montreal, Que., 10 Nov. 1932; s. Joseph and Betty (Marcovitch) B.; e. Que. Conserv.; McGill Sch. of Music (rec'd jr. dipl. at age 11); Juilliard Sch. of Music; began study of violin at 5 yrs., piano at 8 yrs.; played N.Y. City clubs, midwestern and Cal. coll. concerts and nightclubs in Los Angeles (incl. a group with Ornette Coleman and Don Cherry), 1954-60; toured Germany with Jimmy Guiffre "Three", 1960 and Japan with S. Rollins, 1963; re-formed own trio for Bard Coll. Concert, 1964; mem. Jazz Composers Guild 1964-65; Trio concerts at Museum of Modern Art and Newport Jazz Festival, 1965; 1st European tour with own trio, 1965, 2nd tour 1966; won 2nd place in Jazz & Pop Mag.

Internat. Critics Poll, 1965 and 1969 (Pianists category); has recorded over 30 L.P.s 1953-72; 1st Moog Synthesizer Soloist Concert, Philharmonic Hall, N.Y. 1969; 4 European tours with Synthesizer Show, 1970-71; 6 European solo piano tours 1972-74; formed IAI Records & Videotapes 1975; toured Europe, solo piano concerts 1978, 1979; Home: 4930 St. Kevins Ave. Apt. 11, Montreal, Que. H3W 1P4; Office: IAI, P.O. Box 225, Village Station, New York, N.Y. 10014

BLICQ, Anthony Norman; publisher; b. Guernsey, C.I. 15 Nov. 1926; s. A. Sandford and Marjorie E. (Steele) B.; m. Laura P. Engelbach; children: Sarah Louise, Justine Emma; EXTVE. DIR. THE UNIV. OF B.C. PRESS since 1970; came to Can. 1940; former mem. Candn. Civil Service and Oxford (England) University Press; author "Rise and Fall of Married Charlie" (novel) 1970; photographs and short stories under pseudonym; Office: 2075 Wesbrook Mall, Vancouver, B.C. V6T 1W5.

BLISHEN, Bernard Russell, M.A.; university professor; b. Harlesdon, Eng., 21 Sept. 1919; s. Henry Charles Adolphus and Lilly Anne (Shipp) B.; came to Can. 1935; e. McGill Univ., B.A. 1949, M.A. 1950; Columbia Univ. 1955-56; m. Ruth Edith, d. Ernest Popkin, 14 May 1947; children; Jennifer, Joan, Susan, Peter; Chief Institutions Sec., Dom. Bureau of Stat. 1950-56; Lect., Univ. of Brit. Columbia, 1956-60; Asst. Prof. 1961; Research Dir., Royal Comn. on Health Services, 1961-64; Assoc. Prof., Trent Univ. 1964-66; Prof. and Chrmn., Dept. of Sociology, 1966-67; Dean of Grad. Studies 1967-73; professor York Univ. since 1973; served in 2nd World War, R.C.N. 1939-45; received Columbia University Fellowship; Laidlaw Fellowship; Nuffield Travelling Fellowship; Soc. Sci. and Humanities Research Council Leave Fellowship; member, Canadian Sociol. & Anthrop. Assn. (Pres. 1977-78); author "Canadian Society" (1964); "Doctors & Doctrines" (1969); "Does Money Matter" (1973) and articles in learned journals; Anglican; recreation: sailing; Home: 531 Hunter St. W., Peterborough, Ont. K9H 2M9; Office: York University, Downsview, Ont. M3J 1P3

BLISS, Harvey John, LL.B., Q.C.; lawyer; b. Toronto, Ont. 6 Oct. 1933; s. Henry and Ida (Hoffman) B.; e. Jarvis Coll. Inst. Toronto; Univ. of Toronto B.Com. 1955; LL.B. 1958; m. Eileen May d. Joseph Sullivan 4 Feb 1966; two d. Kimberley Anne, Deborah Leigh; SR. PARTNER, BLISS, KIRSH: called to Bar of Ont. 1960; cr. Q.C. 1978; Partner, Levinter, Whitelaw, Dryden, Bliss & Hart 1965-73; mem. Nat. Council on Adm. of Justice in Can., Chrmn. 1975-78, Vice Chrmn. 1978- ; Dir. Candn. Inst. for Adm. Justice 1977-, Vice-Pres., 1980-; mem. Gov. Council Candn. Sec., Internat. Comn. Jurists 1974-, Vice-Pres. 1980-81; Instr. in Trial Practice, Osgood Hall Law Sch. York Univ. 1970-76; Instr. in Civil Procedure, Bar Admission Court 1962-71; Ont. Legal Adv. to Fed. campaign comte. since 1972; Chrmn. Constitution Comte. Lib. Part in Ont. 1971-74, mem. Policy Comte. 1964-65; Chrmn. Constitution Comte. Toronto & Dist. Lib. Assn. 1966-71, mem. Extve. Bd. 1965-71; Chrmn. Task Force on Justice Ont. Lib. Party Conf. 1971; Chrmn. Justice Sec. Policy Research Centre 1971; Policy Chrmn. Ont. Young Lib. Assn. 1964-65; author or co-author various party briefs, speeches, papers; mem. Candn. Bar Assn. (Nat. Council 1968-); Co. York Law Assn.; Medico-Legal Soc. Toronto; Advocates' Soc. Toronto; Internat. Bar Assn.; Law Soc. Upper Can.; Sigma Alpha Mu (Pres. 1954-55); Liberal, recreations: growing bonsai, collecting wine, travel, languages; Home: 19 Chelford Rd., Don Mills, Ont. M3B 2E4; Office: 133 Richmond St. W., Suite 402, Toronto, Ont. M5H 2L3.

BLISS, John William Michael, Ph.D.; educator; author; b. Leamington, Ont. 18 Jan. 1941; s. Quartus and Anne Lavelle (Crowe) B.; e. Kingsville Pub. Sch. and Dist. High Sch.; Univ. of Toronto B.A. 1962, M.A. 1966, Ph.D. 1972; m. Elizabeth Jane d. Robert Haslam, Harrow, Ont. 29 June 1963; children: James, Laura, Sara; PROF. OF HIS-

TORY, UNIV. OF TORONTO; secondary sch. teacher Hamilton and Toronto 1962-65; Teaching Asst. Harvard Univ. 1967-68; mem. Gov. Council Univ. of Toronto 1975-78; mem. Council Royal Candn. Inst. 1980- ; author "Canadian History in Documents 1763-1966" 1966; "A Living Profit: Studies in the Social History of Canadian Business 1883-1911" 1974; "A Canadian Millionaire: The Life and Business Times of Sir Joseph Flavelle, Bart." 1978 (Sir John A. Macdonald Prize Candn. Hist.; Univ. of B.C. Medal Candn. Biog.; City of Toronto Book Award; Toronto Hist. Bd. Award of Merit); co-author "The Wretched of Canada: Letters to R. B. Bennett 1930-35" 1971; numerous scholarly and popular articles maj. Candn. journs. and newspapers; Gen. Ed. "Social History of Canada Series" 1971-77; currently writing hist. discovery insulin and biog. of Sir Frederick Banting; mem. Candn. Hist. Assn.; Ont. Hist. Soc.; Business Hist. Conf. (USA); Methodist; recreations: skiing, baseball, children; Home: 314 Bessborough Dr., Toronto, Ont. M4G 3L1; Office: History Dept, Univ. of Toronto, Toronto, Ont. M5S 1A1.

BLISSETT, William Frank, M.A., Ph. D., F.R.S.C.; educator; b. East End, Sask. 11 Oct. 1921; s. Ralph Richardson and Gladys Anne (Jones) B.; e. Victoria High Sch. 1939; Victoria (B.C.) Coll. 1941; Univ. of B.C., B.A. 1943; Univ. of Toronto M.A. 1946, Ph.D. 1950; PROF. OF ENGLISH, UNIV. COLL., UNIV. OF TORONTO 1965- ; Teaching Asst., Lectr. and Instr. in Eng. Univ. of Toronto 1946-50; Assoc. Prof. of Eng. Univ. of Sask. 1950-57; Prof. 1957-60; Prof. and Head of English, Huron Coll. London, Ont. 1960-65; Ed. "University of Toronto Quarterly" 1965-76; "Imitation and Design" 1953; "Editing Illustrated Books" 1980; co-ed. "A Celebration of Ben Jonson" 1972; author "The Long Conversation with David Jones" 1981; various articles Shakespeare, Ben Jonson, Spenser, David Jones, lit. Wagnerism; Hon. Fellow Huron Coll. 1966; mem. Assn. Candn. Univ. Teachers Eng.; Candn. Fed. for Humanities; Toronto Wagner Soc. (Vice Pres.); Anglican; Home: 36 Castle Frank Rd., Apt. 212, Toronto, Ont. M4W 2Z7; Office: University College, University of Toronto; Toronto, Ont. M5S 1A1.

BLOEDEL, Prentice; lumber company executive; b. Bellingham, Wash., 13 Aug. 1900; s. Julius H. and Mina (Prentice) B.; e. Yale Univ., A.B. 1921; m. Virginia L. Merrill, 16 Aug. 1927; children; Virginia P.(Mrs. Charles B. Wright, Jr.), Eulalie M. (Mrs. Ernst Schneider); Instr. Thatcher Sch. Ojai, Cal., 1921-22; engaged in lumber business, Bellingham, 1923-28; with Bloedel, Stewart & Welch Ltd., Vancouver, B.C., 1929-35, Pres. 1942-51; Vice Chrmn., MacMillan & Bloedel Ltd., Vancouver, 1951-56, Dir., 1951-59; Dir., MacMillan, Bloedel & Powell River Ltd., 1956-65; Dir., MacMillan Bloedel Ltd., 1966-72, National Bank of Commerce (Seattle) 1956-73; The Bank of Montreal, 1951-53; Marine Bancorporation, 1963-73; mem., Adv. Comte., Toronto General Trusts Corp., 1947-63; B.C. Council of Boy Scouts (mem. 1942-47, Pres. 1947-48); made Freeman of City of Vancouver March 1971; Episcopalian; Clubs: Vancouver; University and Rainier (Seattle, Wash.); Address: 7701 N.E. Dolphin Drive, Bainbridge Island, Washington 98110.

BLONDEAU, Gilles, B.A., B.Com., F.S.A., F.I.C.A.; actuary and insurance executive; b. Quebec City,Que. 5 Oct. 1940; s. Cylien and Rose (Drolet) B.; e. Coll. des Jésuites [Garnier] 1958; Univ. Laval B.A. 1960, B.Com. 1963; m. Claudette d. René Houde, Greenfield Park, Que. 15 June 1963; children: Nathalie, Anabelle; PRES. AND GEO, GROUPE OPTIMUM INC. 1979-; Pres., Gestion Optimum Inc.; Chmn., St. Laurent, Compagnie de Réassurance; Société Nationale d'Assurances; Blondeau and Co.; Vice Chmn., Domtar Inc.; Pres., Blondeau and Co. 1969-79; Dir. La Solidarité (Paris); joined Swiss Reinsurance Co. Zurich 1963-65; Vice Pres. Canadian Reassurance Co. Toronto 1965-69; Pres., Blondeau and Co. 1969-79; Fellow, Soc. of Actuaries 1967; R. Catholic; Home: 5

Lansdowne Ridge, Westmount, Que.; Office: 740 ouest, rue Notre Dame, Montreal, Que. H3C 3X6

BLOOM, Myer, M.Sc., Ph.D., F.R.S.C., F.A.P.S.; physicist; educator; b. Montreal, Que. 7 Dec. 1928; s. Israel and Leah (Ram) B.; e. Baron Byng High Sch. Montreal 1949; McGill Univ. B.Sc. 1949, M.Sc. 1950; Univ. of Ill. Ph.D. 1954; m. Margaret Patricia d. late Roy Franklin Holmes 29 May 1954; children: David, Margot; PROF. OF PHYSICS, UNIV. OF B.C. since 1963; Nat. Research Council Postdoctorate Fellow, Univ. of Leiden 1954-56; Asst. Prof. Univ. of B.C. 1957-60, Assoc. Prof. 1960-63; Visiting Prof. Harvard Univ. 1964-65; Univ. de Paris-Sud 1971-72; rec'd Alfred P. Sloan Fellowship ù1961-65; Steacie Prize 1967; Biely Prize 1969; Candn. Assn. Phys. Gold Medal 1973; Izaak Walton Killam Mem. Scholarship 1978; author numerous research and review articles; mem. Candn. Assn. Physicists; recreations: skiing, hiking, squash; Home: 5669 Kings Rd., Vancouver, B.C. V6T 1K9; Office: Vancouver, B.C. V6T 1W5.

BLOOMFIELD, Arthur Irving, M.A., Ph.D.; university professor; economist; b. Montreal, Que., 2 Oct. 1914 (U.S. citizen since 1945); s. Samuel and Hanna Mai (Brown) B.; e. McGill Univ., B.A. 1935, M.A. 1936; Univ. of Chicago, Ph.D. 1942; PROF. OF ECON., UNIV. OF PENNSYLVANIA, since 1958; Econ., Fed. Reserve Bank of N.Y., 1942-58 (Sr. Econ. and Offr. 1953-58); Consultant to Foreign Econ. Adm. of U.S. Govt., 1944-45; Adviser to Bank of Korea and Korean Ministry of Finance, 1949-50; Adviser to U.N. Korean Reconstr. Agency in Korea, 1951-52; Econ. Consultant to U.S. Govt. agencies in Vietnam, Cambodia and Laos, 1953, 1954, Korea 1956, 1960 and Congo 1966, 1967, 1968; Consultant to Ford Foundation in Malaysia, 1964; Sr. Econ. on prof. staff of Comn. on Foreign Econ. Policy of U.S. Govt., 1954; Head, U.S. Del. to Working Party of Experts on Financial Aspects of Econ. Devel. Programs in Asia and Far E., Bangkok, 1954; mem. adv. Comte. to Philippine Central Bank Comn., 1955-56; Visiting Prof. of Econ., The Johns Hopkins Univ., 1961, Princeton Univ. 1963, The City Univ. of N.Y. 1965; rec'd Allen Oliver Gold Medal and Grad. Fellowship (Econ.), McGill Univ., 1935; Pre-Doctoral Fellowship, Social Science Research Council, 1939-40; Guggenheim Fellowship 1956 (not availed of); Rockefeller Foundation Fellowship, 1957-58; Ford Foundation Faculty Research Fellowship, 1962-63; Consultant to U.S. Dept. of State since 1970; Visiting Prof. of Economics, Univ. of Melbourne 1972; Observer, Annual Meeting, African Devel. Bank, Abidjan, 1979; Editorial Board, Journal of Post-Keynesian Economics; author: "Capital Imports and the American Balance of Payments, 1934-1939", 1950; "Banking Reform in South Korea", 1961; "Monetary Policy under the International Gold Standard, 1880-1914", 1959; "Speculative and Flight Movements of Capital in Postwar International Finance", 1954; "Short-term Capital Movements under the Pre-1914 Gold Standard", 1963; "Patterns of Fluctuation in International Investment before 1914", 1968; other writings incl. articles in prof. journs. and in symposia; mem., Am. Econ. Assn.; Royal Econ. Soc.; Am. Assn. Univ. Profs.; Jewish; Home: Rittenhouse Claridge Apts., Philadelphia, Pa. 19103

BLOOMFIELD, Bernard Manfred, K.St.J., Ph.D., LL.D.; petroleum executive; b. Montreal, P.Q., 16 Oct. 1904; s. Harry and Sadie (Davis) B.; e. Westmount (P.Q.) High Sch.; McGill Univ.; m. Nery Judith, d. Frederick Loewy, Germany, 8 June 1943; children: Henry Joseph Frederick, Evelyn Ruth; PRESIDENT, CANADIAN MANUFACTURERS SALES CO. (Exporters and Distributors); Pres., Israel Continental Oil Co. Ltd.; Eldee Foundation; Nat. Pres., Candn. Histadrut Campaign; Vice-Pres. and Dir.; Am. Comte. for Labour Israel, U.S.A.; Nat. Treas., Candn. Friends of Hebrew Univ., Nat. Chrmn. Bd. 1978; Past Pres., Jewish Immigrant Aid Services, Nat. V.P.; E. Can. Region; Nat. Treas., Israel Maritime League; mem.

Nat. Extve. Fed. Zionist Organs. Can.; a Founder and Chrmn., Jewish Nat. Fund, Candn. Centennial Forest (Israel); Founder and past. Nat. Treas., Candn.-Israel Chamber of Comn. in Israel; Hon. Dir., Baron de Hirsch Inst. and Child Welfare Bur.; Hon. Vice-Pres. (1976) and Life Gov., Jewish Peretz Sch., Jewish People's Sch., Montreal and Bialik Sch., Toronto; Leader of Candn. trade mission to Israel, 1962; mem., Bd. Govs., Technion Israel Inst. of Technology 1970, Nat. Pres. 1975; Internat. Bd. of Govs., Hebrew Univ. of Jerusalem, 1964, Extve. Comte. Bd. of Govs. 1977; Internat. Bd. of Govs., Tel Aviv Museum; Bd. of Dirs., Solomon Schechter Academy Inc. 1977; Bd. of Dirs., Hebrew Free Loan Assn. 1977; rec'd. Histadrut Humanitarian Award, 1965; Vice-Pres., Que. Prov. Council, St. John Ambulance; Kt. of Justice (Assoc.) Ven. Order of St. John of Jerusalem; Grand Commdr., Order of Star of Africa (accorded by Pres. of Liberia), 1970; rec'd D. Phil., Hebrew Univ.; D. Sc. and Technol. (Hon.), Technion-Israel Inst. Technol. 1978; apptd., mem., Bd. of Govs., St. Francis Xavier Univ.; Chrmn., Internat. Adv. Compet., Coady Inst., 1966; Gov., Inst. de Cardiologie de Montreal; Pres., Lady Davis Med. Research Inst.; Jewish Gen. Hosp. of Montreal; Pres., Antigonish Human Resources Foundation; Hon. Consul Gen. of Korea in Montreal; mem., Hon. Adv. Council, Congregation Shaar Hashomayim 1977; Cand. Heraldry Soc. Can. 1974; Pi Lambda Phi; Hebrew; Clubs: Montefiore; Elm Ridge Country; Home: 3180 St. Sulpice Rd., Montreal, P.Q.; Office: 1080 Beaver Hall Hill, Montreal, Que. H2Z 1S8

BLOOMFIELD, Louis Mortimer, Q.C., LL.M., Ph.D., D.C.L., LL.D., K.St.J.; L.M.B.; b. Montreal, Que., 8 Aug. 1906; s. Harry and Sadie (Davis) B.; e. McGill Univ., B.A. 1927; Univ. of Montreal, LL.M. (Hons.) 1930; LL.D., St. Francis Xavier 1964; m. Justine Stern; Sen. Partner, Bloomfield & Bloomfield; Vice-Pres., Reddy Mem. Hosp.; mem., Bd. Govs., Weizmann Inst. of Science, Rehovoth, Israel; Consul-General (Hon.) of Liberia; Hon. President and Director, Quebec Council, and Knight of Justice (A) 1965. Most Venerable Order of the Hospital of St. John of Jerusalem; Life Governor, Jeanne d'Arc Hospital; L.G. Children's Memorial Hospital; Y.M.H.A.; Charter Patron, International Bar Assn.; Co-Founder and Dir., Can. Human Rights Foundation; Publications: "The British Honduras-Guatemala Dispute", 1953; "Egypt, Israel and the Gulf of Aquaba in International Law", 1957; "Grunding und Aufbau Kanadischer Aktiengesellschaften", 1960; co-author "Boundary Waters Problems of Canada and the United States", 1958; "Crimes Against Internationally Protected Persons" 1975; Guest Lectr., McGill Univ. Inst. of Air & Space Law, Hebrew Univ., The Ford Foundation, etc.; Vice Pres., World Wildlife Fund (Can.); Hon. Pres., Internat. Law Assn.; Ph.D. Hebrew Univ. 1971; D.C.L. St. Thomas Univ. 1973; Home: 3 Westmount Square, Apt. 1211, Westmount, Que. H3Z 2S5; Office: 1080 Beaver Hall Hill, Room 2020, Montreal, Que. H2Z 1S8

BLOOMFIELD, Morton Wilfred, M.A., Ph.D.; university professor; b. Montreal, Que., 19 May 1913; s. Samuel and Hanna Mai (Brown) B.; e. McGill Univ. B.A. 1934, M.A. 1935; Univ. Coll., Univ. of London grad. study 1935-36; Univ. of Wisc., Ph.D. 1938; Harvard Univ., A.M. (Hon.) 1961; m. Caroline, d. Col. Chester Lichtenberg, Ft. Wayne, Ind., 16 March 1952; children; Micah Warren, Hanna, Samuel; PROF. OF ENGLISH, HARVARD UNIV., since 1961 and Chrmn. of Dept. 1968-72; Asst. Lectr. of Eng. McGill Univ., 1934-35; Asst. Instr. of Eng., Univ. of Wisc., 1936-38; Instr. 1938-39; Instr. of Eng., Univ. of Akron, 1939-41; Asst. Prof. 1941-46; Asst. Prof. of Eng., Ohio State Univ., 1946-51; Assoc. Prof. 1951-54; Prof. 1954-61; served as Master Sgt. AUS 1942-45; attached to Am. Embassy, London 1943-45; Special Civilian Consultant to Secy. of War 1945-46; awarded Bronze Star 1946; author: "Seven Deadly Sins: An Introduction to the History of a Religious Concept", 1952; "Piers Plowman as a 14th Century Apocalypse", 1962; "Essays and Explorations: Studies in Ideas, Language and Literature", 1970; co-author: "Ten Plays", 1951; "Great Plays", 1963; "Form and Idea", 1953 and 1961; "A Linguistic Introduction to the History of English" (with L. Newmark), 1963; Editor, "In Search of Literary Theory", 1972; "Language as a Human Problem" (with E. Haugen) 1973; Consulting Ed., "American Speech", 1955-57; Adv. Ed., "Manuscripta", "Chaucer Review", "Annuale Mediaevale", Journal of the History of Ideas, 1976-79; "Language and Style", "New Literary History", "Poetica" & "Viator"; member Editorial Staff Board Funk & Wagnalls "New College Standard Dictionary" and Adv. Ed., "American Heritage Dictionary"; Fellow & recipient of Haskins medal (1964), Medieval Acad. (Vice Pres. 1975-76); Pres. Medieval Acad. 1976-77; Corresponding mem., British Academy; Corresponding Fellow, Medieval Society of Southern Africa; Adv. Editor, Journal of the History of Ideas 1977-80; mem., Modern Lang. Assn. Am. (Extve. Council 1966-69); Am. Renaissance Soc.; Am. Dialect Soc.; Candn. Linguistic Soc.; Linguistic Soc. Am., Am. Dante Soc. (Council 1971-74 and since 1979); International Assn. University Profs. Eng. (Adv. Extve. Bd. Council since 1962); Modern Humanities Research Assn.; Société internat. pour L'étude de la philosophie médievale; Bd. Trustees, Nat. Humanities Center, Research Triangle, N. Carolina (Chrmn. 1976-79); Fellow Am. Acad. Arts & Sciences (Vice Pres. 1972-76); Amer. Philosophical Soc.; mem. Center for Advanced Study in Behavioral Sciences, Palo Alto, Cal. 1967-68; Inst. for Advanced Study, Princeton, N.J., 1972; Phi. Beta Kappa (Hon.); Home: 13 Kirkland Pl., Cambridge, Mass. 02138

BLOUIN, Georges Henri, B.A., LL.B.; diplomat; b. Montreal, Que., 4 June 1921; s. Charles Henri and Hermine (Panneton) B.; e. Collège Sainte-Marie, Montreal, B.A. 1944; Université de Montréal, LL.B. 1948; m. Denise, d. Auguste Angers, St. Lambert, Que., 12 Feb. 1948; children: Pierre A., Micheline; AMBASSADOR TO THE NETHERLANDS since 1979; 2nd Secy., Candn. Embassy, New Delhi, 1951-53; Consul in San Francisco, 1955-58; Counsellor, Candn. Embassy, Athens, 1961-63 and Brussels, 1963-65; Ambassador to Federal Republic of Cameroun (Yaoundé) and also accredited to Republic of Gabon, of Chad and Central African Republic, 1965-67; Min. Candn. Embassy, Washington, 1967-70; Dir. Gen. Personnel, Dept. of External Affairs, Ottawa, 1970-73; Ambassador to Spain and Morocco 1973-77; Assist. Under-Secy. of State for External Affairs 1977-79; R. Catholic; recreation: golf; Home: 215 MacKay St., Ottawa, Ont.; Office: Dept. of External Affairs, Ottawa, Ont. K1A 0G2

BLUME, Helmut; musician; broadcaster; professor; b. Berlin, Germany, 12 April 1914; s. Dr. Gustav and Romana (Sachs) B.; M. Ljerka Putić; e. Univ. of Berlin (1932-33); Acad. of Music, Berlin, Grad. (1933-38); Toronto Conservatory of Music, (1942-43); Dean, Faculty of Music, McGill Univ. 1963-76; Prof. Emeritus; Fellow, Roy. Soc. of Arts 1976; joined Staff of the Univ. in 1946; regular contrib. to CBC programs as writer, commentator and pianist; Music Consultant, CBC Internat. Service; Pres. of Ger. Benevolent Soc. of Montreal 1980-; co-author of "Canada's Story in Song", 1960; author of "Form in Music" (record-album) 1960; various short stories and numerous Candn. newspaper reviews of recitals, radio and television programs; Piano Recitalist, 1942-43; Head of German Sec., CBC Internat. Service, Montreal, 1944-46; awarded (first) for "Music to See", produced by Ted Pope (22nd Am. Exhn. of Educ. Radio-TV Programs, Ohio State Univ. 1958); Lutheran; recreations: boating, swimming; Home: 20 Windsor Ave., Westmount, Que. H3Y 2L6

BLUMENAUER, George Henry, B.A.Sc.; executive b. Nelson, B.C., 13 Oct. 1921; s. Alice May (Swanell) and late John Richard B.; e. Cranbrook (B.C.) High Sch.; Univ. of B.C., B.A.Sc. (Mech. Engn.); m. Margaret

Emma, d. late Christian M. Nielsen, 18 Oct. 1947; three s. Richard, William, Christian; CHRMN., OF THE BOARD AND CEO, OTIS ELEVATOR CO. LTD., 1981; Dir., Alpin-Otis Elevator Co. Ltd.; DOFASCO Inc. Mutual Life Assurance Co. of Canada; The Royal Bank of Canada; Hudson's Bay Oil & Gas Co. Ltd.; Franki Canada Ltd.; Union Gas Ltd.; Works Engn., 1947; Service Sales, Toronto (Ontario) District, 1948; New Sales Rep., 1949; Asst. District Manager, Toronto (Ont.) Dist., 1950, Dist. Mgr., 1953; Gen. Mgr., Operations, Hamilton, Ont., Oct. 1959; Vice-Pres., 1961; Chrmn. of Bd. and Pres., 1969; served during 2nd World War with R.C.E.M.E.; mem., Bd. Govs., McMaster Univ.; mem., Assn. Prof. Engrs. Ont.; Engn. Inst. Can.; Candn. Mfrs. Assn.; NEEA; Un. Church; recreations: golf, fishing, Clubs: Mississauga Golf & Country; Hamilton Golf & Country; Hamilton; Caledon Mountain Trout; St. James's (Montreal); York (Toronto); Tamahaac (Ancaster); Home: 142 Claxton Dr., Oakville, Ont. L6J 4N9; Office: 414 Victoria Ave. N. (P.O. Box 650), Hamilton, Ont. L8N 3M1

BLUMENFELD, Hans; O.C.; town planner and consultant; b. Osnabrueck, Germany, 18 Oct. 1892; s. Martin Jacob and Anna (Warburg) B.; e. studied Arch., Polytech. Insts., Munich, Karlsruhe, Darmstadt, Germany 1911-14, 1919-21; Dr., hon. caus., Univ. de Montreal, 1968; Univ. of Waterloo, 1974; Tech. Univ. of N.S., 1981; came to Canada 1955; Prof. of Urban & Regional Planning (part-time) Univ. of Toronto; in Arch. practice, Germany, U.S. and Austria 1921; Arch. and City Planner, U.S.S.R. 1930; Site Planner, N.Y. and Jersey City 1938-40; Research Dir., Philadelphia Housing Assn. 1941-44; Head, Div. of Planning Analysis, Philadelphia City Planning Comm. 1945-62; Asst. Commr., Metrop. Toronto Planning Bd., 1955-61; has lect. widely in Can., U.S., U.K., France, Italy, Germany, Austria, Denmark, Puerto Rico, Israel, Turkey; served in German Army 1914-18, Pte. 1st Class; mem. Nat. Extve., Candn. Peace Congress; Fellow, Town Planning Inst. Can.; Am. Inst. of Planners; Corp. des Urbanistes du Que. (Hon.); German Acad. for Urban and Regional Planning (Corr.); rec'd Award for Merit, Am. Inst. Planners; Royal Can. Academy of Arts; Officer, O.C., 1978; author of "The Modern Metropolis" 1967; "Metropolis and Beyond" 1980; and numerous articles in prof. journs.; portrait painted by O. H. Hagemann 1919; Lambda Alpha; Marxist; Address: 66 Isabella St., Apt. 2602, Toronto, Ont. M4Y 1N3

BLUMSOM, Henry Thomas; motion picture executive (retired); b. Toronto, Ont. 5 Sept. 1921; s. Henry James and Adelaide Mae (Inwood) B.; e. Scarborough (Ont.) Coll. Inst.; m. Grace Mary (d. 1978), d. late Ernest Jones, 15 Nov. 1974; m Mary Bowers, 24 Oct. 1981; PRESIDENT, ODEON THEATRES (CANADA) LTD. since 1974; Accounting Dept. York Trading Ltd. 1936-40, 1945-46; Acct., Eagle Lion Films, 1946; joined present Co. Chief Acct. 1954, Asst. Treas. 1955, Treas. 1957, Secy. Treas. 1959, Dir. 1963, Vice Pres. 1972; served with RCAF as Flying Instr. 1940-45; rank Flying Offr.; Secy. Treas., Entheos Lodge Found., 1980-; Freemason (P.D.D.G.M.); Anglican; recreations: photography, golf; Home: Apt. 215, 325 5th Ave. N., Saskatoon, Sask. S7K 2P7

BLUNDELL, William Richard Charles, B.A.Sc.; company executive; b. Montreal, Que., 13 Apr. 1927; s. Richard Charles and Did Aileen (Payne) B.; e. Univ. of Toronto, B.A.Sc. 1949; m. Monique, d. Paul Audet, Quebec, Que., 20 March 1959; children: Richard Paul, Emily Claire, Michelle Ann, Louise Chantale; PRES. & CHIEF EXTVE. OFFR., CAMCO INC. since 1979; joined Canadian General Electric Co. Ltd. 1949; apptd. Vice Pres., Finance 1968, Consumer Products, 1970, Apparatus & Heavy Machinery 1972; Anglican; recreation: sports; Club: Granite; Mount Royal; Home: 45 Stratheden Rd., Toronto, Ont. M4N 1E5; Office: 185 Wright Ave., Weston Ont. M9N 1E7

BLYTH, Colin Ross, M.A., Ph.D.; educator; b. Guelph, Ont. 24 Oct. 1922; s. Colin McDonald and Gladys Irene (Martin) B.; e. Guelph Coll. Inst. 1940; Queen's Univ. B.A. 1944; Univ. of Toronto M.A. 1946; Univ. of N.C. 1946-48; Univ. of Calif. Berkeley Ph.D. 1950; m. Margaret Valerie d. Edward Vivian Thompson, Guelph, Ont. 27 Aug. 1955; children: Mary Alice, Georgina, Colin M., Heather, Alexander, Donald; PROF. OF MATH. STAT., QUEEN'S UNIV. 1974- ; Asst. Prof. to Prof. Univ. of Ill. 1950-74; Stat. Consultant Ill. State Geol. Survey 1952-54; Assoc. Ed. "Journal of American Statistical Association" 1968-71; author various research papers math. stat.; Fellow, Am. Stat. Assn.; Inst. Math. Soc.; mem. Candn. Math. Soc.; Stat. Soc. Can.; Math. Assn. Am.; Kingston Gaelic Soc. (1st Pres.); Loyal Orange Assn.; Freemason; P. Conservative; Presbyterian; recreations: bagpipes, Scottish poetry and music, Gaelic language & music; Home: 138 Albert St., Kingston, Ont. K7L 3V2; Office: Kingston, Ont. K7L 3N6.

BOAG, T.J., M.B.Ch.B.F.R.C.P.(c); F.R.C. Psych.; Liverpool, Eng. 11 Apl. 1922; s. John Harvey and Elizabeth (Johnson) B.; e. Merchant Taylor's Sch. Crosby, Eng. 1939; Univ. of Liverpool M.B.Ch.B. 1944; McGill Univ. Dipl. in Psychiatry 1953; Candn. Inst. of Psychoanalysis 1954-58; m. Lorna Christian d. late Herbert Stewart Milne 1 July 1950; children: Peter Thomas, Graham Stewart, Patricia Janet, Alexander Harvey; DEAN, FACULTY OF MEDICINE, QUEEN'S UNIV. and Prof. Dept. Psychiatry there since 1975; Consultant, Kingston Gen. Hosp., Hotel Dieu Hosp., St. Mary's of the Lake Hosp., Kingston Psychiatric Hosp.; Asst. Dir. Allan Mem. Inst. 1959-61; Asst. Prof. of Psychiatry McGill Univ. and mem. Attending Staff Royal Victoria Hosp. Montreal 1953-61; Prof. of Psychiatry and Chrmn. of Dept. Univ. of Vt. 1961-67; Attending Psychiatrist and Chief of Servic, Mary Fletcher Hosp., DeGoesbriand Mem. Hosp. and Med. Centre of Vt. 1961-67 also Consultant Vt. State Hosp. Health and Vt. State Hosp.; joined present Univ. as Prof. and Head Dept. Psychiatry and Psychiatrist in Chief Kingston Gen. Hosp. 1967-75; served with RAMC 1944-47, rank Capt.; author 32 prof. publs.; Fellow, Am. Psychiatric Assn.Royal College of Phsycians and Surgeons of Can.; Royal College of Psychiatrists; Assn. Am. Med. Colls.; Candn. Psychiatric Assn.; Assn. Candn. Med. Colls.; Candn. Med. Assn.; Candn. Psychoanalystic Soc.; Internat. Psychoanalytic Assn.; Ont. Psychiatric Assn.; Ont. Med. Assn.; Alpha Omega Alpha; Assoc. mem. Sigma Xi; Anglican; recreations: sailing, cross-country skiing, antique collecting; Home: 82 Centre St., Kingston, Ont. K7L 4E6

BOBYN; Edward Joseph, B.Sc., M.E.E., F.C.A.S.I.; Canadian Public servant; b. Krydor, Sask. 11 Dec. 1921; s. James D. and Katherine (Borytzki) B.; e. Univ. of Sask. B.Sc., 1944; Johns Hopkins Univ. M.E.E. 1948; m. Helen Lydia d. late Jacob Bubniuk 11 Oct. 1945; children: James Edward, Patricia Joan, John Dennis, Diane Christine, Stephen Michael, Michèle Lynne; CHIEF OF RESEARCH AND DEVEL. DEPT. OF NAT. DEFENCE since 1974; Head, Instrumentation Sec. Candn. Armament Research & Devel. Estab. 1948, Depy. Supt. Guided Missile Wing 1950 and Supt. 1955, Supt. Systems Wing 1958-60; Chief of Systems Research, SHAPE Air Defence Tech. Centre, Holland 1960-63; Dir. Systems Evaluation RCAF HQ 1963-64; Chief Supt. Suffield Exper. Stn. Ralston, Alta. 1964-68; Dir.-Gen. Defence Research Estab. Valcartier, Que. 1968-72; Depy. Chrmn. (Scient.) Defence Research Bd. 1972-74, served with Royal Candn. Corps of Signals 1943-45, rank Lt.; mem. Scient. Comte. Nat. Reps. SHAPE Tech. Centre Holland (Candn. Nat. Rep.); NATO Adv. Group for Aerospace Research & Devel. (Nat. Del.); NATO Defence Research Group (Nat. Del.); Non-Atomic Mil. Research & Devel. Sub-comte. (Candn. Princ.); mem. Armed Forces Communications and Electronics Assn., Engn. Inst. Can.; Candn. Research Mang. Assn.; Assn. Scient. Engn. & Technol. Community Can.;

Ukrainian Prof. & Businessmen's Assn.; Fellow, Cdn. Aero. and Space Int.; Rotary Club Can.; Sigma Xi; Awarded Queen's Silver Jubilee Medal, 1977, Centennial Medal, 1967; Recreations: Woodworking, Fishing, Photography, Music; Home: 2218 Aster St., Ottawa, Ont. K1H 6R6; Office: 101 Colonel By Dr., Ottawa, Ont. K1A 0K2.

BOCK, Jacques, B.S.; industrialist, lumberman; b. Montreal, P.Q., 10 Dec. 1932; s. Roland and Jeanette (Francoeur) B.; e. Universidad de Las Americas; Univ. of S. Cal., B.S. (Pub. Adm.) 1957; Pres. and Gen. Mgr. Bock & Tétreau Inc.; Chrmn. of Bd., The Eagle Lumber Co. Ltd.; Dir., Bock & Frère Ltée; Shearer Lumber Co. Ltd.; Thibault & Desjardins Ltée; J. S. Gosselin Ltée; Daigle & Paul (1980) Inc. Air Canada; Texaco Canada Inc.; Past Pres. Candn. Lumbermen's Assn.; Nat. Assn. of Independent Bldg. Materials' Distributors; Past Dir. N. Am. Wholesale Lumber Assn.; Que. Forestry Assn.; mem., Am. Assn. Pub. Adm.; Am. Acad. Pol. & Social Science; Newcomen Soc.; Office: 300 Stinson, Montreal, Que. H4N 2N2

BOCK, Roland;, lumberman; b. Papineauville, Que., 29 Sept. 1900; s. J. S. and Elisa (Lauzon) B.; two s. Jacques, Michel; CHRMN. OF THE BOARD, BOCK & TETREAU LTD. (Estbd. 1919, lumber dealers); Pres., Shearer Lumber Co. Ltd.; Dir.; Hôpital Saint-Luc; Past Pres., Candn. Lumbermen's Assn.; Roman Catholic; Club: St. Denis; Home: 3940 Cote des Neiges Rd., Montreal, Que. H3H 1W2

BODEL, Donald H., B.Com., C.A., F.R.I., C.R.E.; real estate consultant; b. Kingston, Ont., 25 Jan. 1938; s. James Howard and Mary Olive (Bodel) Fairbanks; e. Univ. of B.C., B.Com. 1961; C.A. 1964; Real Estate Dipl. Course 1964-67; m. Muriel Joan, d. Ronald Gourlay, Vancouver,B.C., 22 Aug. 1964; s. Kenneth H., David R., John M.; PRES. RICHARD ELLIS Inc. since 1976; Dir. R.E. Holdings Ltd., Richard Ellis Inc., joined Peat Marwick Mitchell & Co., Vancouver, B.C. 1961; Gen. Mgr., Dominion Management Co., Vancouver, 1964; Exec. Vice-Pres., Fidelity Trust 1974; mem. Bd. of Govs., Regent Coll., 1969-74; (Chrmn. 1973-74); mem. Inst. C.A.'s Ont.; Real Estate Inst. of Canada; Real Estate Bd. Chicago; Am. Soc. of Real Estate Counselors; Protestant; Home: 840 Sheridan Rd., Winnetka, Ill. 60093; Office: Ste. 6545, 200 E. Randolph Dr., Chicago, Ill. 60601

BODILEY, Arthur Phineas, M.B.E., F.C.I.I.; insurance executive (retired); b. Northampton, Eng., Sept. 1913; s. late Phineas Walgrave and Mary (Beeby) B.; e. Prince Henry's Grammar Sch., Otley, Eng.; m. Dod, d. late Charles Leazell 1945; two d., one s.; formerly Pres. for Can., Prudential Assurance Co. Ltd.; joined the Co., 1930, successive appts. in U.K. and Can. since that time and now mem. Cdn. Bd.; 1938-45, 2nd Middlesex Yeomanry (T.A.); Royal Signals, N. Africa, Syria, India, Burma, rank Major; awarded M.B.E. (mil.); past Pres. Can. Save the Children Fund; Dir.; Montreal Family Service Foundation; Montreal Children's Hospital Corp. and Foundation; recreations: music, books, nature; Home: 20746 Gay Cedars Drive, Baie d'Urfe, Que. H9X 2T4

BODSWORTH, Frederick; writer; b. Port Burwell, Ont., 11 Oct. 1918; s. Arthur John and Viola (Williams) B.; e. Port Burwell Cont. Sch.; m. Margaret Neville, d. late Joseph Banner, 8 July 1944; children: Barbara, Nancy, Neville; Reporter, St. Thomas "Times-Journal", 1940-43; Reporter and Editor, Toronto "Daily Star" and "Star Weekly", 1943-46; Asst. Editor, "Maclean's Magazine", 1947-55; author: "Last of the Curlews", 1955; "The Strange One", 1960; "The Atonement of Ashley Morden", 1964; "The Sparrow's Fall", 1966; "The Pacific Coast" (Illustrated Natural History of Canada series); co-author "Wilderness Canada" 1970; approx. 100 articles in "Maclean's Mag.", and many articles in other Candn.

and Am. mags.; Past Pres., Fed. Ont. Naturalists; recreations: bird watching, nature study; Clubs: Toronto Ornithological; Toronto Field Naturalists'; Brodie; Address: 294 Beech Ave., Toronto, Ont. M4E 3J2

BOESCHENSTEIN, Hermann, Ph.D., LL.D., F.R.S.C. (1957); emeritus professor; b. Switzerland; e. Univ. of Zurich, Munich, Berlin and Rostock; post-grad. work in Naples, Paris and Toronto, LL.D. Queen's 1968; came to Can. 1926 and joined staff of Univ. of Toronto, 1931; Prof. of German and Head of Dept. Univ. Coll. there, 1956-68; during 2nd World War was Dir. of War Prisoners' Aid of Y.M.C.A.; Visiting Prof., Univ. Coll., London, Eng., 1955; Univ. of Chicago 1964; McGill Univ. 1970-74; Home: 103 Bedford Rd., Toronto, Ont. M5R 2K4

BOGERT, Maj.-Gen. Mortimer Patrick, C.B.E. (1953), D.S.O. (1943); officer; b. Toronto, Ont., 17 Mar. 1908; s. Mortimer Selwyn and Georgina Maud (Crombie) B.; e. Selwyn House Sch., Montreal; Ashbury Coll., Ottawa; Roy. Mil. Coll. 1926-30; McGill Univ. 1930-31; Commissioned in Black Watch (Royal Highlanders of Canada) 1930; Royal Canadian Regiment (Permanent Force), Canada, 1932; proceeded overseas on staff of 1st Candn. Div. 1939; attended Staff Coll., Camberley, Eng., 1940; attached to Brit. Army in Middle East 1942; Commanded W. Nova Scotia Regt., Sicily and Italy 1943; wounded 1943; served as G.S.O.1, 1st Candn. Div. (Italy) 1944; awarded O.B.E. 1944; commanded (temp.) 3rd Candn. Inf. Brig. 1944; Brig.; Commndg. 2nd Candn. Inf. Bgde. in Italy and Holland 1944-45; commanded 8th Candn. Inf. Bgde., Candn. Occupation Force in Germany 1945-46; awarded Croix de Guerre (France) 1944; awarded Aristian Andreas (Greece) 1944; Commanded Eastern Ont. Area 1946; subsequently B.C. Area; Commdr., 25th Candn Inf. Brigade, Korea, Apl. 1952-Apl. 1953; awarded Legion of Merit (officer, U.S.A.) 1953; Depy. Adj.-Gen. Army Hdqrs., Ottawa, 1953-54; Commandant, Candn. Army Staff Coll., Kingston, Ont., 1954-58; promoted to rank of Maj.-Gen., G.O.C. Eastern Command, Halifax, N.S., 1958; retired from Candn. Army, 1962; named by Brit. Colonial Office as one of two-man Comn. to investigate the future of Kenya's northern prov., Oct. 62; Anglican; recreation: shooting; Address: Grove Cottage, Donnington, Newbury, Berkshire, England

BOGGS, Jean Sutherland, O.C. (1973), Ph.D., LL.D., F.R.S.C., b. Negritos, Peru, 11 June 1922; d. Oliver Desmond and Humia Marguerite (Sutherland) B.; e. Alma Coll., St. Thomas, Ont.; Trinity Coll., Univ. of Toronto, B.A. 1942; Radcliffe Coll. A.M. 1946, PhD. 1953; unm.; Appointed by Prime Minister Trudeau in 1982 to head a Commission to plan a new NATIONAL GALLERY and Museum of Man; Dir., Philadelphia Museum of Art, 1979-81; Educ. Secy., Art Assn. of Montreal, 1942-44; Asst. Prof. Skidmore Coll., N.Y., 1948-49; Asst. Prof. Mount Holyoke Coll., Mass., 1949-52; Asst. and Assoc. Prof. Univ. of Calif. 1954-62; Curator, The Art Gallery of Toronto, 1962-64; apptd. Steinberg Prof. of Art Hist., Washington Univ., St. Louis, 1964-66; Dir., The National Art Gallery of Canada, 1966-76; Prof. of Fine Arts, Harvard Univ., 1976-79; arranged Picasso and Man. Exhn., The Art Gallery of Toronto; Dir. Coll. Art Assn. of Am.; Publications: "Portraits by Degas", 1962 and various articles on Degas; "The National Gallery of Canada" 1971; Anglican; Address: Ottawa, Ont.

BOGGS, William Brenton, O.B.E., B.Eng., F.C.A.S.I., company executive; b. Douglas, Arizona, 18 Dec. 1918; s. William B. Boggs; (naturalized Canadian); e. McGill Univ., B.Eng. (Mech.) 1940; m. Hughene, d. A. T. Parkes, 7 Feb. 1948; children: William B., Talbot H., Mary Catherine; PRES. AND CHIEF EXTVE. OFFR., CANADA SYSTEMS GROUP LTD. since 1971; Chrmn. and Dir.: MFS Ltd.; Dir.: Guardian Insurance Co.; Montreal Life Ins.; Can. Man. Assn.; Dir. Canadian Nat. Exhibition; Toronto Symphony; Nat. Ballet; Pres. Canadian

Assn. of Data Processing Organizations 1976-77; with Trans-Canada Air Lines, 1945-50; Canadair Ltd. 1950-57; joined Hawker Siddeley Canada Ltd., 1957, and subsequently Vice-Pres., Transp. Equipment; Pres., and C.E.O. de Havilland Aircraft of Can. Ltd. 1965-70; served in 2nd World War with R.C.A.F., 1940-45 as Sqdn. Ldr.; awarded O.B.E.; Baptist; recreations: golf, tennis; Clubs: Canadian; Rosedale Golf; Granite; Queen's; Rideau (Ottawa); Home: 190 Roxborough Dr., Toronto, Ont. M4W 1X8; Office: 2599 Speakman Dr., Sheridan Park, Ont. L5K 1B1

BOGLE, Hon. Robert John, B.A.; politician; b. Calgary, Alta. 29 Aug. 1943; s. Robert and Phoebe Alberta (Orford) B.; e. Masinasin Sch. City of Warner; Erle Rivers High Sch. Milk River, Alta.; Mount Royal Coll. Calgary; Univ. of Lethbridge; Sir George Williams Univ.; m. Dr. Elizabeth Christine d. Dr. Hans Lewke, Calgary, Alta. 30 July 1977;MIN. OF SOCIAL SERVICES & COMMUNITY HEALTH, ALTA.1979- ; former high sch. teacher and businessman; mem. Milk River Town Council 1969-75; el. M.L.A. for Taber-Warner prov. g.e. 1975, re-el. 1979; Min. without Portfolio responsible for Native Affairs 1975; Charter mem. Kinsmen Club; mem. Chamber Comm.; Businessmen's Assn.; P. Conservative; Anglican; Office: 424 Legislative Bldg., Edmonton, Alta. T5K 2B6.

BOHME, John David Sumner, Q.C., B.A., LL.B.; b. Toronto, Ont. 9 Nov. 1921; s. William F.R. and Edith Mary (Drinkwater) B.; e. Univ. of Toronto Schs.; Univ. of Toronto; Osgoode Hall Law Sch.; m. Willy Cornelie d. Hendrik Willem van Brakel 8 July 1957; children: Christopher Hendrik, Elizabeth Mary; PARTNER, AIRD & BERLIS since 1974; Dir. and Secy. Place Gas & Oil Co. Ltd.; Dir. Thompson-Lundmark Gold Mines Ltd.; Consolidated Marbenor Mines Ltd.; Pango Gold Mines Ltd.; Prado Explorations Ltd.; United Reef Petroleums Ltd.; read law with Slaght, McMurtry, Ganong, Keith & Slaght; called to the Bar of Ont. 1953; cr. Q.C. 1966; Lawyer, Wright & McTaggart, Toronto, 1954-56; Edison, Aird & Berlis, Toronto 1956-58; Partner 1958-73; served with RCNVR 1941-46; N. Atlantic, rank Lt. Commdr.; mem. Candn. Bar Assn.; Psi Upsilon; P. Conservative; Anglican; recreations: sailing, golf; Clubs: Albany; Lawyers; Granite; Home: 120 Glencairn Ave., Toronto, Ont. M4R 1M9; Office: 145 King St. W., Toronto, Ont. M5H 1J8

BOHNE, Harald; publisher; b. Darmstadt, Germany 15 March 1929; s. Fritz and Anna Louisa (Landmann) B.; e. Bunsen Real Gymnasium, Heidelberg, Germany 1950; came to Can. 1954, naturalized 1960; m. Jean Marcelle Shaver 1 July 1955; DIR., UNIV. OF TORONTO PRESS since 1977; Mgr. Univ. of Toronto Bookstore 1958, Business Mgr. Univ. of Toronto Press 1960; Asst. Dir. 1970, Assoc. Dir. 1975; co-author "Publishing: The Creative Business" 1973; Ed. "Canadian Books in Print" 1970, 1971, 1972, 1973; mem. Candn. Booksellers Assn. (Pres. 1962-64); Assn. Candn. Publishers (Pres. 1977-78); Assn. Candn. Univ. Presses; Assn. Am. Univ. Presses; Soc. for Scholarly Publishing; Winner of Eve Orpen Award for Publishing Excellence, 1980; United Church; Office: Front Campus, Toronto, Ont. M5S 1A6.

BOILARD, Hon. Jean-Guy, B.A., LL.L.; judge; b. Lyster, Co. Megantic, Que. 15 Aug. 1937; s. Donat and Juliette (Fillion) B.; e. St. John's Coll. Co. Iberville, Que. B.A. 1957; Univ. of Montreal Law Sch. LL.L. 1960; m. Lise d. Horace Leroux, Montreal, Que. 9 Sept. 1959; children: François, Stéphane; JUSTICE, SUPERIOR COURT OF QUE.; called to Bar of Que. 1961; R. Catholic; recreation: vintage automobiles; Club: Vintage Automobile Club of Montreal Inc.; Home: 10510 Verville St., Montreal, Que. H3L 3E8; Office: Court House, Montreal Que.

BOISCLAIR, Marc-André; company president; b. Montreal, Que., 1 Dec. 1922; s. Thérèse (Lalumière) B.; e.

Montreal, Que.; PRESIDENT, INVESTER INC.; served in 2nd World War with R.C.N.V.R. as Lieut.; R. Catholic; recreations: skiing, fishing, sailing, flying; Home: 756 McEachran, Outremont, Que. H2V 3C7; Office: 5540 Cote des Meiges, Montreal, Que.

BOIVIN, Bernard, L.Sc., Ph.D.; botanist; b. Montréal, Qué. 7 June 1916; s. Alexis and Marie (Tremblay) B.; e. Univ. de Montréal B.A. 1937, L.Sc. 1941; Harvard Univ. Ph.D. 1944; m. Cosette d. late Charles-Eugène Marcoux 1946; children: Lilian (Mme Pierre Lavigne), Hélène (Mme Yvon Saint-Onge), Jacques; LECTURER, UNIV. LAVAL since 1980; Botanist, Nat. Museum 1946-47; Research Assoc. Harvard Univ. 1947-48; Research Scient. Agric. Can. 1948-65, 1967-69, 1970-81; Professeur-visiteur, Univ. Laval 1965-66; Visiting Prof. Univ. of Toronto 1969-70; served with Candn. Army 1943-46; rec'd Guggenheim Fellowship 1946; Médaille Marie-Victorin 1973; Médaille du Centenaire de la Soc. de Géog. de Qué. 1978; author "American Thalictra and Their Old World Allies" 1944; Enumération des plantes du Canada" 1966; "Flora of the Prairie Provinces" 5 vols. "Provancheria" 1967-81; "Survey of Canadian Herbaria," 1980; over 140 papers bot., linguistics, biog., bibliog.; mem. Royal Soc. Can.; New Eng. Bot. Club; Soc. botanique du Quebec; R. Catholic; Home: 380 Ch. Saint-Louis, apt. 1107, Quebec, Que. G1S 4M1; Office: Herbier Louis-Marie, Pavilion Comtois, Cité Universitaire, Quebec G1K 7P4.

BOLAND, Hon. Janet Lang, B.A.; judge; b. Kitchener, Ont. 6 Dec. 1928; d. George W. and Miriam (Geraghty) Lang; e. Kitchener, Ont.; Convent of Sacred Heart (Kenwood) Albany, N.Y.; Waterloo Coll.; Univ. of W. Ont. B.A.; Osgoode Hall Law Sch.; m. 1 Oct. 1949; children: Michael Frederic, Christopher John, Nicholas James; JUDGE, TRIAL DIV. SUPREME COURT OF ONT. since 1976; called to Bar of Ont. 1950; cr. Q.C. 1966; began private law practice 1950; reported in Court of Appeal for Ont. Weekly Notes and Ont. Reports; mem. Panel Reform for Women Jt. Comte.; joined White, Bristol, Beck & Phipps, Toronto 1958; Partner, Lang, Mitchener, Farquharson, Cranston & Wright, Toronto 1968; apptd. Judge Co. of York 1972; R. Catholic; recreations: skiing, tennis, travel; Home: 164 Inglewood Dr., Toronto, Ont.; Office: Osgoode Hall, Toronto, Ont.

BOLIN, Allan Patrick; company executive; b. Winnipeg, Man. 20 Nov. 1926; e. St. Edward's Sch., Winnipeg 1940; St. Paul's Coll. 1945; m. Mary Frances Proctor 16 Sept. 1952; children: Mary Kiloren, Louise Ann (Mrs. David Sage), Patrick Arthur, Nancy Jane; EXECUTIVE VICE-PRES, CORPORATE DEVELOPMENT, CONTINENTAL BANK OF CAN. since 1981; Sr. Vice-Pres. and Gen. Mgr.; IAC Ltd.; Pres. Niagra Finance Co. Ltd. Dir., IAC Ltd.; Capital Funds (IAC) Ltd.; Capital Funds (IAC Ont.) Ltd.; Niagara Finance Co. Ltd.; Niagara Realty of Canada Ltd.; Niagara Realty Ltd.; Premier Property Ltd.; began with CN Rlwys. Passenger Dept. Winnipeg 1945-46; joined IAC Ltd. Winnipeg, serving successively as Trainee, Accts. Rep., Sales Rep. and Asst. Mgr. 1947-51; Asst. Mgr. Calgary 1951, Br. Mgr. Red Deer 1953, Saskatoon 1954, Winnipeg 1956, Regional Mgr. Business Devel. Winnipeg 1960, Toronto 1965, Asst. Vice-Pres. Ont. Div. Toronto 1966, Vice-Pres. W. Div. Montreal 1969, Vice-Pres. and Div. Gen. Mgr. W. Div. Vancouver 1970, Sr. Vice-Pres. and Gen. Mgr., Business Devel., Toronto 1974, Sr. Vice-Pres., Corporate Devel., Toronto 1976; Sr. Vice-Pres. and Sr. Gen. Mgr., Toronto 1978, Sr. Vice-Pres. and Sr. Gen. Mgr.-Domestic Operations, Toronto 1979; Clubs: Vancouver; Capilano Golf & Country; Lambton Golf and Country; Office: Continental Place, 130 Adelaide St. W., Toronto, Ont. M5H 3R2

BOLTON, James Linden, M.Sc., Ph.D.; agrologist; b. Plumas, Manitoba, 4 Oct. 1906; s. James Moir and Agnes Moore (Connolly) B.; e. Bellhampton (Man.) Public Sch., Grad. 1919; Sch. of Agric., Vermilion, Alta., Dipl. 1927;

Olds, Alta., Matric.1930; Univ. of Alberta, B.Sc. 1933; M.Sc. 1936; Univ. of Minnesota, Ph.D. 1947; m. Mary Margaret, d. A. R. McFadden, Bluffton, Alta., 6 Sept. 1935; children: James Robert, Agnes Louise, John Linden; began as Student Asst. at Exper. Farm, Lacombe, Alta., 1927-34; and in charge of field crop experiments, 1929-34; Grad. Asst. in forage crop breeding, Univ. of Alta., 1935-36 financed by Carnegie Research Fund with special research project on seed setting in alfalfa; Agric. Supervisor, Exper. Farm, Swift Current, Sask., 1936-41 in charge of regrassing, irrigation, plant taxonomy, and plant breeding projects; on loan to Univ. of B.C., 1939-40 to lecture in range management and weed control; Research Asst., Dom. Forage Crops Lab., Saskatoon, 1942-56 in charge of research and crop improvement of alfalfa; did basic work which led to production of "Rambler" and "Beaver" alfalfas, important varieties especially adapted in W. Can.; Head, Crops Sec. Research Station, Saskatoon, 1956-64; Research Coordinator (Forage Crops) Research Br., Can. Dept. of Agric. 1964-71; Professional Assoc., Dept. of Plant Science, Univ. of Alta. since 1971; Publications: "Alfalfa"; numerous scient. and popular papers and bulls. dealing principally with the breeding and management of alfalfa; Fellow, Agric. Inst. Can.; Am. Assn. Advanc. Science; mem., Agric. Inst. Can. (Pres. 1958-59); Candn. Soc. Agron.; Am. Soc. Agron.; Sask. Inst. Angrols. (Registrar 1946-52); Prof. Inst. Public Service Can. (Pres., Sask. Br. 1957-58); Alta. Inst. Agrols; United Church; recreations: curling, plant collecting; Address: Apt. 1703, 9835 - 113 St., Edmonton, Alta. T5K 1N4

BOLTON, Richard Ernest, B.Sc., F.R.A.I.C., R.C.A.; b. Montreal, Que., 18 March 1907; s. William Ernest and Catharine Hamilton (McClure) B.; both of Montreal, Que.; e. Westmount (Que.) High Sch.; McGill Univ.; Mass. Inst. Tech.; m. Elizabeth Armour, d. late A. Armour Robertson, M.D. of Montreal, P.Q.; one d. and one s.; in private practice as a principal 1933-70; Chancellor, Coll. of Fellows, Roy. Arch. Inst. Can. 1970-73; Pres., P.Q. Assn. of Architects, 1961; served in 2nd World War; Lieut.-Commdr., R.C.N.V.R.; mem. Acad., Royal Candn. Acad. Arts; Fellow Royal Architectural Inst. of Canada; Director Heraldry Society of Canada; Anglican; Clubs: St. James's; Royal St. Lawrence Yacht; Home: 4325 Montrose Ave., Westmount, Que. H3Y 2A8

BOLTON, Thomas Gilbert; b. Toronto, Ont., 5 April 1914; s. late Thomas Edward and late Ruth Louise B.; e. Riverdale Coll. Inst., Toronto; Cert. Gen. Accts. Assn.; m. Vera Isabel Thompson, 28 Sept. 1940; two s. Thomas Christopher, Kimberley James; DEPY. CHRMN. AND DIR., DOMINION STORES LTD.; Dir.: Argus Corp. Ltd.; Hollinger Argus Ltd.; Roy. Agric. Winter Fair; joined the Co. 1936, Toronto, Hamilton, Montreal, Halifax 1936-42, Vice-Pres. Corp. Planning 1967, Vice-Pres. Corp. Devel. 1969, Pres. and Dir. 1973; Dir. Hollinger Argus Ltd.; served in 2nd World War R.C.A.F. 1942-46, rank F.Lt.; Past Pres. Cert. Gen. Accts. Assn.; Anglican; Clubs: Granite; Toronto; National; Lambton Golf & Country; Home: 12 Kingsford Court, Islington, Ont. M9A 1X4; Office: 605 Rogers Rd., Toronto, Ont. M6M 1B9

BOMBARDIER, André J. R., B.A.; company executive; b. Valcourt, Que. 31 Dec. 1942; s. J. Armand and Yvonne (Labrecque) B.; e. Primary Sch., Valcourt, Que.; Semy. of Sherbrooke, B.A.; Univ. of Sherbrooke 1966-69; Adm. Faculty (B.Com. option Finance); div; children: Jean-François, Isabelle, Charles, and Louis; PRÉSIDENT LES ENTREPRISES DE J.-ARMAND BOMBARDIER LTÉE Vice-Pres., Bombardier Inc.; Bd. of Dir., Cdn. Safety Council; R. Catholic; recreations: snowmobiling, hockey, golf, hunting, fishing; Home: 761 St. Joseph St., Valcourt, Que. J0J 1E0; Office: 800 West Dorchester Blvd., Montreal, Que. H3B 1X9

BONE, Allan Turner, B.Sc.; construction engineer; b. Glasgow, Scotland, 2 Feb. 1895; s. late Peter Turner and Elizabeth Lusk (Allan) B.; e. Western Canada Coll., Calgary, Alta. (1903-11); McGill Univ., B.Sc. 1916; m. Enid Margaret, d. late Alfred Price, 8 March 1922; children: Margaret, Elizabeth, John; Alderman, City of Westmount, P.Q., 1953-57; Dir., Metropolitan Y.M.C.A., Montreal, P.Q.; Jr. Engr. with Candn. Govt. Rlys., Halifax Ocean Terminals, 1916-19; with George A. Fuller Co. of Canada as Engr. in Moncton, Temiskaming and Montreal, 1919-22; Engr., Shawinigan Engineering Co. (on La Gabelle Power Devel.), 1922-24; joined George A. Fuller Co. of Canada again in 1924 (Asst. Supt. and Supt. Metropolitan Bldg., Toronto; Metropolitan Life Bldg., Ottawa; Royal Bank Bldg., Montreal), 1924-29; Constr. Mgr., Montreal Office, 1929-31; Vice-Pres. and Chief Engr., J. L. E., Price Co. Ltd., 1932-49 Pres. & Gen. Mgr., 1949-62, Chairman 1962-64; mem., Corp. of Prof. Engrs. Que.; Life mem., Engn. Inst. of Can.; mem., Canadian Construction Assn. (Pres. 1956-57); Conservative; United Church (Elder); recreations: golf, skiing, gardening; Clubs: Royal Montreal Golf; Laurentian Lodge; Home: Apt. 1803, 4000 Maisonneuve W., Westmount, Que. H3Z 1J9

BONE, Peter W.; executive; b. London, Eng., 28 May 1926; s. Andrew Walton and Mary (Piggott) B.; e. Balham Grammar Sch., Eng. 1935-43; Jr. Cambridge (Hons); m. Patricia Nellie, d. Alan Maryson Cockrell, Wellingore, Lincs., Eng., 7 April 1956; one d. Vanessa Walton; EXECUTIVE DIRECTOR CORPORATE AFFAIRS, ROTHMANS OF PALL MALL CANADA LTD.; Dir., Craven Foundation; joined J. Arthur Rank Organ., Gt. Brit., 1947; Brit. Film Inst., 1951; Gen. Mgr., Calgary, (Alta.) Jubilee Auditorium 1957; joined present Co. 1959; served with RN (Fleet Air Arm) 1943-46; rank Sub-Lt.; Past Dir., Ont. Chamber Comm.; Past Pres., Italian-Candn. Chamber Comm.; mem. Roy. Can. Military Inst.; Rotary Internat.; Candn. Pub. Relations Soc.; P. Conservative; Anglican; recreations: reading, shooting, antique cars; Clubs: Royal Candn. Mil. Inst. Toronto Press; Home: 1 Benvuto Pl., Toronto, Ont. M4V 2L1; Office: 1500 Don Mills Rd., Don Mills, Ont. M3B 3L1

BONGARD, Gordon R. P., B.A.Sc., M.B.A.; stock broker and investment dealer; b. Toronto, Ont., 15 June 1925; s. Gordon R. and Dorothy (Pearson) B.; e. Univ. of Toronto Schs. (Grad. 1944); Univ. of Toronto, M.A.Sc. (Mech. Engn.) 1949; Harvard Business Sch., M.B.A. 1951; m. Eve. d. Graham Cassels, Toronto, Ont., 2 May 1953; three d., Deborah Anne, Susan Jane, Catherine Joan; SR. VICE PRES., AND DIR., NESBITT THOMSON BONGARD INC. 1980-; Pres., Bongard, Leslie & Co. Ltd. since 1970; mem. Toronto Stock Exchange; apptd. General Mgr. of Bongard & Co. in 1953; Extve. Vice Pres. 1964-70; Partner 1957-64; served in 2nd World War with Royal Candn. Navy, 1944-45; Anglican; Clubs: Badminton & Racquet; Toronto; Toronto Golf; Home: 209 Forest Hill Rd., Toronto, Ont. M5P 2N3; Office: 17th Fl., Royal Trust Tower, Toronto-Dominion Centre, Toronto, Ont. M5K 1C4

BONGARD, Gordon Ross, B.Sc.; (ret.) stock broker; b. Toronto, Ont., 13 Jan. 1899; s. Robert Ross and Elsie (Johnston) B.; e. Univ. of Toronto Schs. Royal Mil. Col., Univ. of Toronto. B.Sc. (Applied Science) 1922; m. Dorothy Isabel, d. W. H. Pearson, 1 Sept. 1923; children: Gordon R. P., Ian A., Blair C.; Ret. Hon. Chrmn., Nesbitt Thomson Bongard Inc.; Pres., Toronto Stock Exchange 1940-41; served in World War 1916-18 as Lieut., Royal Arty.; Conservative; Anglican; recreations: golf, fishing; Clubs: Toronto; Ristigouche Salmon; University; Home: 28 Hawarden Crescent Toronto, Ont. M5P 1M7;

BONGARD, William Lester, B.A.Sc., P.Eng.; executive; b. Norwood,Ont., 29 Sept. 1921; s. George Claude and Grace Lavina (Brown) B.; e. Norwood Pub. and High Schs.; Univ. of Toronto, B.A.Sc. (Mech. Engn.) 1949; m Norah Louise, d. Leonard B. Robertson, 9 June 1944; children: Robert, Reid, David, Norah; MGR., ENVIRONMENTAL AFFAIRS, ESSO CHEM. CAN., 1980- ; Dir. Environmental Services, Allied Chemical Canada Limited joined Cyanamid of Canada Ltd. as Project Engr., Niagara Plant, 1949; Prod. Supv., 1951; Mgr. 1960; Mgr., Welland Plant, 1961; Mgr., Mfg. Services, H.O., Montreal, 1965; served with R.C.A.F. 1941-45; discharged with rank of Flying Offr.; mem. Assn. Prof. Engrs. Ont.; Protestant; recreations: golf; Office: Esso Chemical Canada, 2300 Yonge St., Toronto, Ont. M5W 1K3

BONGIE, Laurence L., Ph.D.; educator; b. Turtleford, Sask. 15 Dec. 1929; s. Louis Basil and Madalena (Pellizzari) B.; e. Univ. of B.C., B.A. 1950; Univ. of Paris Ph.D. 1952; m. Elizabeth A. E. d. William G. Bryson 14 July 1958; one s. Christopher L.; PROF. AND HEAD OF FRENCH, UNIV. OF B.C. 1966- ; Lectr. present Univ. 1953, Instr. 1954, Asst. Prof. 1956, Assoc. Prof. 1961; recipient Humanities Research Council Fellowship 1955-56; Can. Council Sr. Fellowship 1963-64, 1975-76; Social Sciences & Humanities Fellowship 1982-83; Killam Sr. Fellowship 1982-83; author "David Hume, Prophet of the Counter-Revolution" 1965; "Diderot's Femme Savante" 1977; "Condillac, Les Monades" 1980; various articles; mem. French, Internat., Am. and Candn. Soc's 18th Century Studies; Founding mem. and Dir. B.C. Soc. Translators & Interpreters; R. Catholic; recreations: cycling, hobby farming; Home: 3746 West 13th Ave., Vancouver, B.C. V6R 2S6; Office: Vancouver, B.C. V6T 1W5.

BONNEAU, Louis P., O.C., B.A.Sc.; university official; b. St. Francois, Co. Montmagny, P.Q., 21 Aug. 1916; s. Adelard and Rose-Delima (Goupil) B.; e. Ecole Polytechnique, 1937-38; Laval Univ., B.A.Sc. (Hons.) 1942; m. Agathe, d. Nérée Tremblay, Quebec, P.Q., 16 Sept. 1939; children: Micheline, Jacques, Rachéle, Louise Hélène, Pierre, Michel; VICE-RECTOR, LAVAL UNIV. since 1961; mem., Nat. Research Council; Assoc. Comte. for Science & Med. of Expo. '67; Bd. of Govs., l'Hôtel-Dieu de Qué.; Inst. of Candn. Bankers; Engr. with Canadian Johns-Manville Co. Ltd., 1942-47; Lect. Laval Univ., 1947-50; Assoc. Prof. and Asst. Secy. to Faculty of Science, 1951-54; Prof. of Thermodynamics and Founder and Head of Mech. Engn. Dept., 1954-59; Vice Dean, Faculty of Science, 1956-60 and Dean., 1960-61; mem., Engn. Inst. Can. (Pres. Que. Br. 1956); Am. Soc. of Metals; Corp. of Prof. Engrs. Que.; Am. Soc. Mech. Engrs.; Am. Soc. Heating & Refrigeration Engrs.; La Chambre de Comm. de Que; Candn. Inst. Mining & Metall. (Vice-Pres., Que. Br. 1957); O.C. 1979; R. Catholic; Home: St-François, Co. Montmagny, Que. G0R 3A0; Office: ST. Francois Co., Montagny Quebec, Que. G0R 1A0

BONNELL, Rev. John Sutherland, D.D., LL.D. (Presb.); b. Prince Edward Island, 1893; e. Prince of Wales Coll., Charlottetown, P.E.I.; Dalhousie Univ. B.A.; Pine Hill Divinity Hall B.D. 1927, D.D. 1934; Washington & Jefferson Coll., LL.D. 1943; Lafayette Coll., D.D. 1950, Univ. of New Brunswick 1958; Acadia Univ., N.S., LL.D.; m. Bessie Louise Carruthers, 26 June 1923; children: George Carruthers, Catherine Cameron, Elizabeth Louise, Jessie Margaret; Pastor, St. Andrew's Presb. Church, Saint John, N.B., 1923-29; post grad. work, London, Eng., and the continent 1927-28; Pastor, Westminster United Ch., Winnipeg, Man., 1929-35; Min., Fifth Ave. Presb. Ch., New York 1935, Min. Emeritus since 1962; Pres., New York Theol. Semy. 1967-69; declined call to Metropolitan Un. Ch., Toronto, 1934; his pastorate in Winnipeg was marked by success in all depts., organized several city-wide mass meetings, overflow congregations weekly; the first Candn. to hold the charge of Fifth Ave. Ch., NY.; Sprunt Lectr., Union Theol. Semy., Richmond, Va., 1943; Chancellor's Lectr., Queen's Univ. 1944; Norton Lectr., The Southern Baptist Theol. Semy., Louisville, Ky., 1944; Ashlin Bible Lectr., First Presb. Ch., Mooresville, N.C.,

1949; Chas. C. Beam Lect., First Presby. Ch., Charlotte, N.C., 1953; Weber Mem. Lect., Moravian Theol. Semy., Bethlehem, Pa., 1956; Radio Broadcaster since 1946 on WJZ Nat. Vespers, Oct. to May; Perkins Lect., First Meth. Ch., Wichita Falls, Texas, 1950; served in World War as Sgt., 5th Candn. Siege Batty., Candn Arty. 1916-18; twice wounded; invalided to Can. 1918; at various times preached at summer camp meetings at Regina, Sask., and Berwick, N.S., special summer preacher in such British pulpits as St. Martin-in-the-Fields, (Trafalgar Square, London), The City Temple (London), American Cathedral (Paris), American Cathedral (Wash.); preaching mission in Presbyterian churches in Sydney, Aust., 1963; author: "Fifth Avenue Sermons", 1936; "Pastoral Psychiatry", 1938; "Britons Under Fire", 1941; "Psychology for Pastor and People", 1948; "What Are You Living For?", 1950; "The Practice and Power of Prayer", 1954; "Heaven and Hell", 1955; "No Escape From Life", 1958; "I Believe in Immortality", 1959; "Certainties for Uncertain Times", 1962; "Do You Want to be Healed", 1968; "Presidential Profiles", 1970; contrib. to religious pubs. and other mags.; specializes in spiritual counselling; awarded by King Geo. VI in 1949 "The King's Medal for Service in the Cause of Freedom"; The Edward Lectureship, Shadyside Presby. Ch., Pittsburgh, Pa., 1958; el. Pres., Candn. Soc. of New York, 1959; Co-Chrmn., Relig. Comn., Nat. Conf. of Christians & Jews; played prominent role in discrediting Sen. McCarthy; visited Soviet Union on three occasions; met with Govt. Comm. on Churches in Russia; Clubs: University (N.Y.); Canadian (Hon.); Home: 468 Riverside Drive, New York, N.Y. 10027; Summer Home: Home by the Sea, Georgetown, P.E.I. C0A 1L0

BONNELL, Hon. M. Lorne, C.M., M.D.; senator; physician; b. Hopefield, P.E.I., 4 Jan. 1923; s. Henry George Horace and Charlotte Matilda (MacEachern) B.; e. Hopefield Sch., P.E.I. 1929; West Kent Sch., Charlottetown, P.E.I. 1934; Prince of Wales Coll., Charlottetown, P.E.I. 1939-43; Dalhousie Univ., M.D. (Master Surg.) 1949; Lic, Med. Council of Can.; m. late Ruby, d. John Jardine, Freetown, P.E.I., 6 July 1949; children: Mark Lorne, Linda Florence; Phys. and Surg., Murray River and Montague, P.E.I.; mem., Med. Staff King's Co. Mem. Hosp., Montague; entered prov. politics in Fourth Dist. Kings Co. P.E.I. April 1951; el. as Private mem. until 1955, re-el. 1955 and apptd. Min. of Health; re-el. as a mem. of Opposition 1959 and 1962; re-el. 1966 and apptd. Min. Welfare and Min. Tourist Devel.; Min. Responsible for Housing 1970; resigned from Prov. politics Nov. 1971 and summoned to Senate of Can., 15 Nov. 1971; mem. P.E.I. Centennial Comn.; Chrmn., Murray River P.E.I. Centennial Comn.; mem. P.E.I. Med. Assn.; Candn. Med. Assn.; Freemason (P.M.); Liberal; Presby.; recreation: golf; Home: Murray River, P.E.I. C0A 1W0; Office: The Senate, Ottawa, Ont. K1A 0A4

BONNER, Robert William, Q.C., B.A., LL.B.; barrister and solicitor; b. Vancouver, B.C., 10 Sept. 1920; s. Benjamin York and Emma Louise (Weir) B.; e. Pub. and High Schs., Vancouver, B.C.; Univ. of British Columbia, B.A. (Econ. and Pol. Science) 1942; Univ. of B.C. (Faculty of Law) Grad. 1948; m. Barbara, d. Rodney Robinson Newman, Vancouver, B.C., 16 June 1942; children: Barbara Carolyn, Robert York, Elizabeth Louise; CHRMN. AND DIR., BRITISH COLUMBIA HYDRO AND POWER AUTHORITY, 1976-; Dir., SCOR Reinsurance Co. International Nickel Co. of Canada Ltd.; Montreal Trust Co.; Energy Supplies Allocation Board; read law with firm Clark, Wilson, White, Clark and Maguire Vancouver, British Columbia; called to the Bar of B.C., 31 July 1948; cr. Q.C. 1 Aug. 1952; before entering B.C. Govt. practised law with the firm of Clark, Wilson, White, Clarke & Maguire, Vancouver, B.C.; following grad. joined Candn. Army in 1942; served with Seaforth Highlanders of Can. in Can., U.K., N.Africa, Sicily and Italy; wounded in action in Italy; retired from active service with rank of Ma-

jor in 1945; apptd. Lieut.-Col. in Reserve Force, commanding Univ. of B.C. Contingent, C.O.T.C., 1946 till retiring in Dec. 1953; entered B.C. Govt. as Atty.-Gen. in Aug. 1952, and el. mem. for Columbia, 24 Nov. 1952; re-el. mem. for Vancouver-Point Grey, 9 June 1953, cont. as Atty.-Gen.; apptd. Min. of Educ., 19 Oct. 1953, relinquishing this portfolio 14 April 1954; re-el. in g.e. 1956 cont. as Atty.-Gen.; in addition to post of Atty.-Gen. apptd. Min. of Indust. Devel. Trade & Comm. 1957-64; re-el. in g.e. 1960 and 1963; re-el. mem. for Cariboo in by-el. Nov. 1966; retired as Atty.-Gen. May 1968; joined MacMillan Bloedel Ltd. as Sr. Vice-Pres., Adm. 1968; Extve. Vice-Pres., Adm. 1970; Vice-Chrmn. 1971, Pres. and Chief Extve. Offr. 1972, Chrmn. 1973-74; mem., Candn. Bar Assn.; Law Soc. of B.C.; Vancouver Bar Assn.; Delta Upsilon; Freemason; Social Credit; Anglican; recreations: boating, photography; Clubs: Union; Vancouver; Capilano Golf & Country; Home: 5679 Newton Wynd, Vancouver, B.C. V6T 1H6; Office: 970 Bouvrard St., Vancouver, B.C. V6Z 1Y3

BONNYCASTLE, Charles Humphrey, B.A., L.L.D.; b. Winnipeg, Man., 26 Dec. 1904; s. Angus Lorne (descendant of Sir Richard Bonnycastle) and Ellen Mary (Boulton) B. (d. of Maj. Boulton, organizer of Boulton's Scouts in N.W. Rebellion, later a Senator of Russell, Man.); e. St. John's Coll. Sch., Winnipeg; Trinity Coll. Sch., Port Hope; Trinity Coll., Univ. of Toronto, B.A. 1925; St. John's Coll., Oxford, 1925-26; Univ. of N.B., LL.D. 1953; m. Millicent Veronica Allen, d. C. E. Clarke, Toronto, 29 June 1938; children: Hilary, Angus; joined Hudson's Bay Co. (Can.) at H.O., Winnipeg; served in Accounting Dept., 1929; Secy's Office, 1932; Retail Store 1934; joined staff of Upper Can. Coll. as Jr. Housemaster 1934; Sr. Housemaster 1936; Headmaster, Rothesay Coll., N.B. 1938-70; Capt., R.C.N.(R); served in 2nd World War, 1939-45; Zeta Psi; Anglican; recreations: golf, tennis; Address: 27 Grove Ave., Rothesay, N.B. E0G 2W0

BONNYCASTLE, Lawrence Christopher, B.A., F.A.S., D.S.L.; company executive; b. Russell, Man., 19 Nov. 1907; s. Angus L. (Judge) and Ellen M. (Boulton) B.; e. Univ. of Man., B.A. 1929; Wadham Coll., Oxford, Eng., B.A. (Juris.); m. Mary F. Andrews; has three s.; DIR., CANADIAN CORPORATE MANAGEMENT CO. LTD. (Pres. 1963-72, Vice Chrmn. 1972-79); Dir.: Harlequin Enterprises Ltd.; Eldorado Nuclear Ltd.; mem. Addiction Research Foundation; with Northern Life Assnce. Co. of Canada, London, Ont., 1932-40; joined John Labatt Ltd. as Treas. 1940; apptd. Vice-Pres. and Asst. Gen. Mgr., 1948; Gen. Mgr., Nat. Life Assnce. Co. of Can. 1949-52; Office: P.O. Box 131, Commerce Court West, Toronto, Ont. M5L 1E6

BONUS, John L.; association executive; b. Mons, Belgium, 27 Jan. 1913; s. Henry Pem Kingsford and Margaret Elisa (Tournay) B.; e. Royal Athenaeum (Humanities-Classics), Mons, Belgium; Kings Coll., Univ. of London; m. Brigitte Paule, d. Gustave van Assche, 7 June 1934; children: Beatrice Mary (Mrs. R. A. Short), Harold Paul, John Arnold (dec.); MANG. DIR., MINING ASSN. OF CANADA, since 1968; Partner in family business (footwear mfg.), Brussels, 1935-40; engaged in import-export business (leather and hides), Brussels, 1937-40; Secy. Gen., Brit. Chamber of Comm. in Belgium and Rep. of Fed. of Brit. Industries, 1945-50; Gen. Mgr., Brit. Candn. Trade Assn., Toronto (HQ), Montreal and Vancouver, 1951-67; served with R.A. 1940-45; comnd. 1941; Maj. 1943-45; prewar internat. ranked tennis player; Past Pres., Candn. Lawn Tennis, Assn.; R. Catholic; recreation: tennis; Clubs: National (Toronto); Rideau; International of Can.; HomeL 619 Manor, Rockcliffe Park, Ottawa, Ont. K1M 0J1; Office: Suite 705, 350 Sparks St., Ottawa, Ont. K1R 7S8

BOONE, James Edward, M.D., F.R.C.P.(C); physician; educator; b. Hamilton, Ont. 31 July 1927; s. Frank H. and

Helen G. Boone; e. Earl Kitchener and Westdale Secondary Sch. Hamilton; Univ. of Toronto M.D. 1951; m. Joan G. d. Enna E. Dauphinee, Sarnia, Ont. 24 May 1958; children: Thomas J., Charles M., Peter D.; PROF. AND CHRMN. OF PEDIATRICS, UNIV. OF W. ONT. since 1973; Asst. Prof. of Pediatrics, Univ. of Toronto 1964, Assoc. Prof. 1967; Chrmn. Postgrad. Manpower Comte., Council Ont. Faculties of Med. 1972-79; mem. Med. Manpower Adv. Comte. Ont. 1977-79; author various publs. juvenile rheumatoid arthritis, med. manpower; mem. Candn. Pediatric Soc. (Dir.); Anglican; recreations: wilderness canoeing, fishing; Home: 1 Harrison Cres., London, Ont. N5Y 2V3; Office: War Mem. Children's Hosp., 392 South St., London, Ont. N6B 1B8.

BOONE, Maurice Perry, M.A., B.L.S.; librarian (retired); b. Houlton, Maine, 25 July 1907; s. Charles Edward and Annie Margaret (Kirkpatrick) B.; came to Canada, 1913; e. Fredericton (N.B.) High Sch.; Univ. of New Brunswick, B.A. (Hons. in Classics) 1929; Univ. of Toronto, M.A. (Classics) 1931, B.L.S. 1941; Lectr., Univ. of Toronto Lib. Sch., 1941-42; Asst. Lib. and Lectr. in Lib. Science, Ont. Coll. of Educ., 1942-43; Chief Cataloguer, Univ. of Sask. Lib., 1943-44; Chief Lib. and Asst. Prof. of Lib. Science, Acadia Univ., 1944-50; Lecturer in Lib. Science, Bowling Green State Univ., Bowling Green, Ohio (summer 1963); Librarian, N.B. Leg. Lib. 1950-70; Editor; Union List of Scientific and Technical Periodicals in Libraries of the Maritime Provinces and Newfoundland, 1951; mem., Candn. Lib. Assn.; Baptist; Home: 338 Saunders St., Fredericton, N.B. E3B 1N8

BOOTH, Andrew Donald, D.Sc., Ph.D.; university president; b. East Molesey, Surrey, Eng., 11 Feb. 1918; s. Sidney Joseph, O.B.E., and Katherine Jane (Pugh) B.; e. Univ. of London, B.Sc. (1st Class hons.) 1940; Univ. of Birmingham, Ph.D. 1944; Inst. for Advanced Study, Princeton, 1947; Univ. of London, D.Sc. 1951; m. Kathleen Hylda Valerie, Ph.D., d. F. Britten, Warwickshire, Eng., 30 Aug. 1950; children: Ian Jeremy Macdonald, Amanda Jane; Chrmn. of Bd., Autonetics Research Associates since 1978; Pres., Lakehead Univ. 1972-78; Interdisciplinary Prof. of Autonetics, Case-Western Reserve Univ., Cleveland 1963-72; Scient. Adv., Internat. Computers & Tabulators Ltd. (Eng.); Dir., Wharf Engn. Labs (Eng.); Asst. Chief Engr., Morris Engines, Coventry, 1939-40; Sr. Research Scholar Brit. Rubber Producers' Assn., 1940-44; Research Phys., 1945, Nuffield Fellow, Birbeck Coll., Univ. of London 1946-49; Visiting (full) Prof. of Theoretical Physics, Univ. of Pittsburgh, 1949; Dir., Computer Project, Birkbeck Coll., Univ. of London, 1950-55; Univ. Reader in Computational Methods, London, 1955-62; Head, Dept. of Numerical Automation, Birkbeck Coll., 1957-62; Head, Dept. of Elect. Engn., Univ. of Sask. 1962-63; Dean, Coll. of Engn. mem., Research Comte., Marie Curie Mem. Foundation, 1957-62; mem. Council of Nat. Res. Council of Canada since 1975; awarded Hon. Fellowship, Inst. of Linguists, 1961; Hon. Dir. of Research, Birbeck Coll., 1962; author of "Fourier Technique in X-Ray Organic Structure Analysis", 1948; "Automatic Digital Calculators", 1st ed. 1953, 2nd ed. 1956; "Numerical Methods", 1st ed. 1955, 2nd ed. 1956; and others; over 300 scient. papers in journs; inventor of Magnetic Storage Drum for computers; basic patents on Magneto-strictive store, multi-core magnetic storage; awarded Centennial Medal 1967; Gov., Ladbroke Sch., London, 1956-59, Eastbourne Training Coll. (Eng.); 1960-62; Fellow, Inst. Electronic and Radio Engrs.; mem., Brit. Inst. Radio Engrs. (mem. Council 1955-62; Chrmn., Papers Comte., 1955-62; Chrmn., Computer Group, 1957-62; Vice Pres., 1965-67; Chrmn., Canadian Div., 1965); Fellow, Brit. Inst. Physics; Church of England; recreations: motoring, mountaineering, music; Clubs: Athenaeum (London); Royal Canadian Military Inst. (Toronto); Hon. mem. Univ. Club of Toronto; Home: Timberlane, 5317 Sooke Rd., R.R. 1, Sooke, B.C. V0S 1N0

BOOTH, Ronald Findlay, B.A., LL.B.; b. Brandon, Man. 29 July 1935; s. Wilfrid Gatley and Eleanor Jean (Findlay) B.; e. Pub. Schs. Brandon and Dauphin, Man.; Univ. of Man. B.A. 1957, LL.B. 1960; m. Ruth Caroline d. Walter T. Murray 16 May 1958; children: Pamela Lynn, Jennifer Caroline, Jillian Tracy; VICE PRES., CORPORATE DEVELOPMENT, REDPATH INDUSTRIES LTD. since 1981; read law with Thompson, Shepard, Dilts, Jones & Hall, Winnipeg; called to Bar of Man. 1960, Bar of Ont. 1964; practised law with Kerr, Meighen, Haddad & Booth, Brandon, Man. 1960-64; Asst. Solr. The Steel Co. of Canada Ltd., Hamilton, Ont. 1964, Asst. Secy. and Sr. Solr. 1967-72; Secy. and Legal Counsel, RCA Ltd. Ste. Anne-de-Bellevue, Que. 1972, Vice Pres., Secy. and Gen. Counsel 1974-76; Vice Pres. and Gen. Counsel 1976-80; Extve. Vice Pres., Redpath Ind. Ltd. 1980-81; mem. Bd. Trade Metrop. Toronto; Law Soc. Upper Can.; Law Soc. Man.; Candn. Bar Assn.; Zeta Psi; Anglican; recreations: tennis, sailing, skiing; Club: Toronto Cricket Skating & Curling, Cambridge Club; Home: 8 Doncliffe Dr., Toronto, Ont. M4N 2E6; Office: (P.O. Box 66) Suite 2100, S. Tower, The Royal Bank Plaza, Toronto, Ont. M5J 2J2.

BOOTHROYD, (Eric) Roger, M.Sc., Ph.D.; univerity professor; b. Lennoxville, P.Q., 2 April 1918; s. Eric Edward and Lois Muriel (Rimmer) B.; e. Bishop's Coll. Sch., Lennoxville, P.Q. (Grad. 1935); Bishop's Univ., B.Sc. 1938; McGill Univ., M.Sc. 1940, PhD. 1943; m. Etta, D. Karl Kaïfer, Zurich, Switzerland, 8 June 1957; children: Arnold I., Karin J., Derek B.; PROF. OF BIOLOGY, McGILL UNIV., since 1971; Lectr. in Biol. and Chem., Bishop's Univ., Lennoxville, P.Q., 1945-46; joined McGill as Lectr., in Genetics, 1946; Asst. Prof. 1949; Assoc. Prof. 1959, Prof. 1967; served in Candn. Army 1944-45 (Chem. Warfare); enlisted as Pte., retired as Lieut.; Publications: research papers in cytol. in Candn. and foreign journs.; mem., Genetics Soc. Can.; Genetics Soc. Am.; Am. Soc. Cell. Biol.; Candn. Soc. Cell. Biol.; Fellow, Am. Assn. Advance. Science; Sigma Xi; Home: 5522 Borden Ave., Côte St. Luc, Que. H4V 2T3

BORDEN,Henry, O.C. (1969), C.M.G. (1943), Q.C., D.C.L., LL.D.; b. Halifax, N.S., 25 Sept. 1901; s. Henry Clifford and Mabel (Ashmere) Barnstead B.; e. King's Coll. Sch., Windsor, N.S.; McGill Univ. B.A. 1921; Dalhousie Law Sch., 1922-24; Rhodes Schol. N.S. 1924; Exeter Coll., Oxford 1924-27, B.A. 1926; St. Francis Xavier, LL.D. 1960, Dalhousie 1963, Toronto 1972; Acadia, D.C.L. 1960; m. Jean Creelman, d. late Dr. Donald Alexander MacRae, 1 June 1929; children: Robert L., Ann Creelman, John Perry, Mary Jean, Henry MacRae; Chrmn., Canada Security Assurance Co.; Candn. Board, Norwich Union Life Ins. Soc.; Norwich Union Fire Ins. Soc., Ltd., 1939-76; Hon. Dir., Massey-Ferguson Ltd.; Dir. and mem. Extve. Comte. and Past Pres., Royal Agric. Winter Fair, Toronto; Chrmn., Royal Comn. on Energy, 1957-59; Hon. Dir. Canada Trustco Mortgage Co.; Hon. Trustee, Roy. Ont. Museum; with Roy. Bank of Can., 1921-22; called to Bar, Lincoln's Inn, London, 1927; called to Bar of N.S. 1927, Ont. 1927; cr. K.C. 1938; Sr. Member, Borden, Elliot, Kelley & Palmer, 1936-46; Gen. Counsel, Dept. of Munitions & Supply, Ottawa, 1939-42; apptd. Chrmn., Wartime Indust. Control Bd., Ottawa & Co-ordinator of Controls, Dept. of Munitions & Supply, 1942-43; formerly Pres., Brazilian Light & Power Co. Ltd. (now Brascan Ltd.) 1946-63, Chrmn. 1963-65; Dir. Emeritus, Canadian Imperial Bank of Commerce; Vice-Chrmn. (1945-64), Chrmn. (1964-68), Hon. Chrmn. (1968-71), Bd. of Govs., Univ. of Toronto, formerly Lectr. on Corpn. Law, Osgoode Hall Law Sch., Toronto; joint author (Fraser & Borden) "Handbook of Canadian Company Law", 1931; Ed. "Robert Laird Borden: His Memoirs" 1938; "Letters to Limbo" by Sir Robert L. Borden, 1971; Past Pres., Canadian Club of Toronto; Past Pres., Lawyers Club of Toronto; cr. Grand Offr. of Nat. Order of the Southern Cross (Brazil) 1962; Phi Kappa Pi; Conservative; Anglican; recreations: farming, fishing;

Clubs: York; Home: Vinegar Hill, R.R. 2, King, Ont. L0G 1K0; Office: Suite 2096, Commerce Court W., (P.O. Box 125, Commerce Court Postal Station), Toronto, Ont. M5L 1E2

BORINS, Hon. Stephen, B.A., LL.B.; judge; b. Toronto, Ont. 3 Oct. 1934; s. Norman, Q.C. and Adeline (Fine) B.; e. Forest Hill Coll. Inst. 1952; Univ. of Toronto B.A. 1956, LL.B. 1959; Law Soc. Upper Can. Bar Admission Course 1961; m. Elaine F., M.D., F.R.C.P.(C) d. Dr. Bernard Manace 10 July 1960; two d. Jennifer, Gwen; JUDGE, CO. AND DIST. COURTS OF ONT. since 1975; called to Bar of Ont. 1961, Bar of Yukon 1975; Law Clk. to Chief Justice High Court of Ont. 1961-62 private law practice 1962-69; co-counsel to Royal Comn. Inquiry into Civil Rights 1966-71; Prof. of Law, Osgoode Hall Law Sch. 1969-75, Assoc. Dean 1972-75; Dir., Candn. Judicial Seminar 1970-74; mem. Senate York Univ. 1970-74; Bencher, Law Soc. Upper Can. 1971-75; rec'd Treas.'s Medal, Law Soc. First Prize, Lawyers Club First Prize 1961; co-author "Canadian Civil Procedure" 1973, 2nd ed. 1977; author various book chapters, articles and addresses on legal topics; Jewish; recreations: tennis, golf; Clubs: Oakdale Golf & Country; Home: 31 Dunbar Rd., Toronto, Ont. M4W 2X5; Office: 361 University Ave., Toronto Ont. M5G 1T3

BORN, Allen, B.Sc.; executive; b. Durango, Colo. 4 July 1933; e. Univ. of Texas B.Sc. (Geol. & Metall.) 1958; m. Patricia A. Beaubien 1953; three s. Michael, Scott, Brett; PRES. AND CHIEF EXTVE. OFFR., PLACER DEVELOPMENT LTD. 1981- ; Exploration Geol. Oil & Gas, El Paso Natural Gas 1958-60; Metall., Vanadium Corp. of America 1960-62; Gen. Foreman, Pima Mining Co. 1962-64; Asst. Supt. Molycorp 1964-67; Chief Metall., Supt., Mgr., Amax Inc. 1967-76; Pres. and Chief Extve. Offr. Canada Tungsten Mining Corp. Ltd. 1976-81; Pres., Amax of Canada Ltd. 1977-81; Vice Pres. Amax Northwest 1976, Pres. 1980-81; served with U.S. Army Far E. Command 1952-55; mem. Am. Inst. Mining Engrs.; Candn. Inst. Mining & Metall.; Clubs: Engineers'; Vancouver; Arbutus; Home: 2009 West 28th Ave., Vancouver, B.C. V6J 2Y8; Office: 1600-1055 Dunsmuir Street, Vancouver, B.C. V7X 1P1

BORRIE, Wilfrid John; investment dealer; b. New Westminster, B.C., 3 Apl. 1895; s. Robert Gibb and Sarah Ann (Masterman) B.; e. King Edward High Sch., Vancouver, B.C.; m. late Elizabeth, d. Harry Taylor, N. Vancouver, B.C., 10 Mar. 1923; children: Harry Robert, Betty Doreen; Pres., Boreen Holdings Ltd.; Dir., Pacific Western Airlines Ltd.; Dillingham Corp. Canada Ltd.; The Presbyterian Extension Fund (B.C.) Ltd.; Hon. Gov., The Leon and Thea Koerner Foundation; mem. of Council, Vancouver Bd. of Trade (Pres. 1946-47); Pres., Investment Dealers Assn. of Can. 1951-52; B.C. Internat. Trade Fair 1964; Past Pres., Candn. Chamber of Comm.; Vice Pres. and Dir., B.C. Internat. Trade Fair, 1967; served in 1st World War with Candn. Engineers as C.S.M.; awarded M.M. and Order of St. George; mem., Extve. Assn. of Vancouver; Freemason; Protestant; recreations: gardening; Clubs: Terminal City; Canadian; The Vancouver; Home: 902 Park Gilford, 1025 Gilford St., Vancouver, B.C. V6G 2P2; Office: (Box 49160) Bentall Three, Vancouver, B.C. V7X 1K6

BORWEIN, David, Ph.D., D.Sc., F.R.S.E.; educator; b. Kaunas, Lithuania 24 March 1924; e. Univ. of Witwatersrand, S. Africa B.Sc. 1945, B.Sc. (Hons.) 1948; Univ. Coll. London, Eng. Ph.D. 1950, D.Sc. 1960; m. Bessie Flax 30 June 1948; children: Jonathan Michael, Peter Benjamin, Sarah Tanya; PROF. AND HEAD OF MATH., UNIV. OF W. ONT. 1967- ; Lectr. in Math. St. Salvators Coll. St. Andrews Univ. Scot. 1950-63; Visiting Prof. present Univ. 1963-64, Prof. 1964- ; served with S. African forces 1945; author over 70 research articles math. journs.; co-ed.: Analysis, Internat. Journ. of Analysis & its Applica-

tion; mem. Candn. Math. Soc.; Math. Assn. Am. (Assoc. Ed. Am. Math. Monthly); Am. Math. Soc.; London Math. Soc.; recreations: jogging, tennis, bridge, reading, theatre; Home: 1032 Brough St., London, Ont. N6A 3N4; Office: Middlesex Coll., London, Ont. N6A 5B7.

BOSA, Hon. Peter, C.L.U.; senator; insurance executive; b. Bertiolo - Udine - Italy 2 May 1927; s. late Antonio and late Angela (Moro) B.; e. Elem. Sch. Bertiolo - Udine - Italy; Hamilton (Ont.) Mt. High Sch. 1951; C.L.U. 1968; m. Teresa d. late Alessandro and Concetta Patullo, Boiano, Italy 20 July 1968; children: Angela, Mark; PRESIDENT, P. BOSA INSURANCE AGENCY LTD. since 1965; Foreman Cutting Dept. Sainthill Levine Co. Ltd. Toronto 1948-57; Life Underwriter Northern Life Assurance Co. 1957-63; Ald. Ward 3 Borough of York 1969, re-el. 1972, 1974; Special and Extve. Asst. to Min. of Citizenship & Immigration, Govt. House Leader and Postmaster Gen. 1963-65; summoned to Senate 1977; Dir. Northwestern Gen. Hosp. since 1970; Chrmn. Candn. Consultative Council on Multiculturalism 1976-79; mem. Candn. Italian Business & Prof. Men's Assn. Toronto; Toronto Life Underwriters' Assn.; Toronto Ins. Agts. Assn.; Liberal; R. Catholic; recreations: chess, golf; Clubs: Famee Furlane; York Lions; Home: 22 Neilor Cres., Etobicoke, Ont. M9C 1K4; Office: 1055 Wilson Ave., Downsview, Ont. M3K 1Y9

BOSANQUET, L.C.; company executive (retired); formerly Vice-Pres. Marketing and Dir., Pilkington Brothers (Canada) Ltd.; started with parent Co. in Bristol, Eng., 1927; came to Can. 1949; served with Eighth & First Armies in North Africa and Italy, 1940-46; Mentioned in Despatches; retired 1978; Past Pres., Candn. Importers Assn.; mem., Toronto Bd. of Trade; Granite; Home: 12 Aldenham Cres., Don Mills, Ont. M3A 1S2

BOSHER, John Francis, B.A., Ph.D., F.R.S.C.; educator; b. Sidney, B.C. 28 May 1929; s. John Ernest and Grace (Simister) B.; e. North Saanich High Sch. 1946; Victoria Coll. B.C. 1946-48; Univ. of B.C. B.A. 1950; Univ. of Paris D.E.S. d'Histoire 1954; Univ. of London Ph.D. 1957; m. Kathryn Cecil d. Henry Deryck Berry, Mexico 28 May 1968; children: Kathryn Grace, George Henry Francis; PROF. OF HIST. YORK UNIV. since 1969; Administrative Offr. Civil Service Comn. Ottawa 1951-53; Asst. Lectr. King's Coll. Univ. London 1956-59; Prof. Univ. of B.C. 1959-67, Cornell Univ. 1967-69; author "The Single Duty Project" 1964; "French Finances 1770-1795" 1970; ed. and contrib. "French Government and Society 1500-1850" 1973; many articles on 18th century France and Can.; guest lectr. various insts. France, U.S. and Can.; mem. Econ. Hist. Soc. (Eng.); Hist. Soc. (Eng.); Soc. French Hist. Studies (U.S.); Anglican; recreations: plumbing, wiring, gardening; Office: 4700 Keele St., Downsview, Ont.

BOSLEY, Murray Arthur William, B.Com., F.R.I., C.R.E.; real estate broker; b. Toronto, Ont. 7 March 1915; s. William Henry, O.B.E. and Elsie M. (Crokam) B.; e. University of Toronto Schs. (1932); Trinity Coll., Univ. of Toronto, B.Com. 1936; CHRMN., W. H. BOSLEY & COMPANY LTD. General Real Estate Estbd. 1928; Past Pres., Candn. Assn. of Real Estate Bds. (1958); Past Pres., Candn. Inst. of Realtors (1960); Past Pres., Toronto Real Estate Bd., (1951 and 1952); Past Pres., Ont. Assn. of Real Estate Bds., (1954); Real Estate Advisor to Dept. of Nat. Defence, Ottawa, 1939-41; Asst. to Gen. Mgr., Wartime Housing Ltd., 1941-42; Trustee Sunnybrook Health Centre; Past Pres. Can. Chapter Int. Real Estate Federation; served in 2nd World War with 12th Candn. Field Regt. Delta Upsilon; Anglican; recreations: Golf, photography; Clubs: National (Past Pres.); Badminton & Racquet; Toronto Hunt; Rosedale Golf (Past Pres.); Rotary (Past Pres.); Home: 24 Maple, Toronto, Ont. M4W 2T6; Office: 188 Eglinton Ave. E., Toronto, Ont. M4P 2E4

BOSLEY, Raymond Sedgemore Lock, F.R.I., C.P.M.; real estate broker; b. Toronto, Ont., 22 Aug. 1921; s. William Henry, founder of the firm of W. H. Bosley & Co., and Elsie M. (Crokam) B.; e. Univ. of Toronto Schs.; Northern Vocational Sch., Toronto, Ont. (special courses in Real Estate Appraisal and Property Mang.); m. Dorothy Claire, d. T. H. Dickinson, 2 June 1943; three s. Michael, Thomas, William; PRESIDENT, W. H. BOSLEY & COMPANY LTD., Real Estate Brokers, Estabd. 1928; Pres., Toronto Real Estate Bd. 1958; Hon. Life Mem. Toronto Real Estate Bd.; Sr. Vice Pres. and mem. of Gov. Council, Inst. of Real Estate Management of the Nat. Assn. of Real Estate Bds., Chicago; Charter Pres., Ont. Chapter, Inst. of Real Estate Mang.; Past Secy., Bldg. Owners & Managers Assn.; Past Pres. Toronto Central Branch, Can. Red Cross Soc.; Past Pres., Rotary Clubs of Toronto (1970); served in 2nd World War with R.C.N.V.R. and R.C.A., rank Lieut.; Anglican; recreations: golf, photography, boating; Clubs: National; Granite; Rosedale Golf; Rotary (Past Pres.); Past Pres. Rotary Laughlen Centre; Home: 10 Arjay Cresc., Willowdale, Ont. M2L 1C7; Office: 188 Eglinton Ave. E. Toronto, Ont. M4P 2E4

BOSS, Bill (Gerard William Ramaut), B.A.; university administrator; writer; broadcaster; b. Kingston, Ont., 3 May 1917; s. Lt.-Col. William and Marcelle-Blanche (Ramaut) B.; e. McDonald Pub. Sch., Kingston, Ont.; Lisgar Coll. Inst., Ottawa, Ont. (Grad. 1935); Univ. of Ottawa, B.A. 1941; unm.; Dir. of Public Relations and Publications, Univ. of Ottawa, and Lectr. in Pol. Science there; Freelance writer and broadcaster; Sports Reporter, "The Citizen", Ottawa, 1932-36; varied assignments, "The Times", London, Eng., 1936-38; Reporter, "The Citizen", Ottawa, 1938-42; joined The Candn. Press, 1944; as War Corr. reported campaigns of 1st Candn. Corps. in Italy and N.W. Europe; Germany, Holland, Austria, Italy, 1945-46; C.P. Bureau in Toronto, New York, Winnipeg, Edmonton, and Vancouver 1947-48; C.P., London, Eng. (reported from Sweden, Norway, Denmark, Holland, Germany, France, Italy) 1948-50; War Corr. with Candn. Forces in Korea (reported from Indo-China Thailand, Formosa, Hong Kong, Japan, Korea) 1950-53; Candn. Army & R.C.A.F. in Germany, France, 1953; C.P. Resident Corr. in Moscow, 1953-54; Editor, C.P. Head Office 1954-55; Ont. Ed. 1955-56; Parlty. Press Gallery, 1957-58; won Nat. Newspaper Awards 1951 (feature writing), 1954 (staff corresponding); served in 2nd World War; Comnd. in 2nd Lanark & Renfrew Scottish Regt., 1940; Lieut., Pub. Relations Offr., HQ 4th Candn. Armoured Div. in Can. and U.K. 1942-43; with Candn. Army N. Africa, Sicily, Italy 1943-44; discharged in Italy June 1944; mem., Ont. Older Boys Parlt. (E. Ottawa) 1933; Asst. Dir. of Music, Ottawa Collegiates, 1934-35; Founder and Conductor, Ottawa Concert Orchestra; speaks French, Italian, German, Dutch, Russian; mem., Candn. War Correspondents' Assn.; Candn. Pub. Relations Soc., Vice-Chrmn., Pub. Relations, Candn. Conf. on Educ., 1962; Publications incl. "Canadian Army Official Handbook on Korea", 1951; Roman Catholic; recreation: music; Clubs: Press (London, Tokyo, Ottawa); Royal Overseas League; Office: University of Ottawa, Ottawa, Ont.

BOSTOCK, Hugh Samuel, M.Sc., PhD., F.R.S.C., F.G.S.A.; geologist (retired); b. Vancouver, B.C., 6 Jan. 1901; s. Hon. Hewitt and Lizzie Jean (Cowie) B.; e. Pub. Sch., Monte Creek, B.C.; Ashbury Coll., Ottawa, Ont.; Hillside Sch., and Charterhouse Sch., Godalming, Surrey, Eng.; Roy. Mil. Coll. Can., Dipl. 1922; McGill Univ., B.Sc., 1924, M.Sc. 1925; Univ. of Wis., Ph.D. (Geol.) 1929; m. Violet Craigie, d. Charles R. Hamilton, K.C., Nelson, B.C.; two s., two d.; long with Geol. Survey of Can. retiring as Sr. Geologist; awarded Royal Candn. Geog. Soc. Massey Medal, 1965; Fellow, Arctic Inst. of N. America; mem., Candn. Inst. Mining & Metall.; Geol. Assn. Can.; Home: 2150 Westbourne Ave., Ottawa, Ont. K2A 1N5

BOSWORTH, Norman Lang; manufacturer; b. Toronto, Ont., 26 Aug. 1912; s. John Edward and Hanna (Hicks) B.; e. Public and High Schs., Aurora, Ont.; m. Laura B. Prince, 17 Oct. 1936; children: Robert P., Margaret-Ann; CHAIRMAN OF THE BOARD AND DIR., CANADA DRY LTD. (Founded 1890), since 1968; began career with O'Keefe Beverages, Toronto, Ont., 1935; moved to Canada Dry Ltd., Toronto, Ont., 1936; Sales Staff, 1936-41; Supv., 1941-45; Br. Mgr., 1945-47; Div. Mgr., 1947-53; Vice-Pres. and Gen. Sales Mgr., 1953-57; Vice-Pres. and Gen. Mgr., 1957-68; el. a Dir., 1953; Pres. 1968-79; CEO and Chrmn. of Bd. Can. Dry Ltd. 1976-77; Adanac Beverages Ltd. 1977-79; mem., Bd. Trade Metrop. Toronto; Candn. Tourist Assn.; Anglican; recreation: curling, boating, hunting; Clubs: R.C.Y.C.; Canadian; Granite; Home: 48 Hawkesbury Drive, Willowdale, Ont.; Office: 2 Champagne Drive, Downsview, Ont. M3J 2C5

BOTHWELL, Rt. Rev. John G., D.D. (Ang.); bishop; b. Toronto, Ont., 29 June 1926; s. William Alexander and Anne (Campbell) B.; e. Runnymede Pub. Sch. 1939 and Humberside Coll. Inst. 1944 Toronto; Trinity Coll. Univ. of Toronto B.A. 1948, B.D. 1951; D.D. 1972; m. Joan d. Hector Cowan, 29 Dec. 1951; Children: Michael, Timothy, Nancy, Douglas, Ann; BISHOP OF NIAGARA since 1973; Asst. Priest St. James Cath. Toronto 1951-53 and Christ Ch. Cath. Vancouver 1953-56; Rector St. Aidan's Oakville 1956-60 and St. James Dundas, Ont. 1960-65; Canon of Christ Ch. Cath., Hamilton, Ont. 1963; and Programme Dir. Niagara Diocese 1965-69; Extve. Dir. of Program Nat. HQ Ang. Ch. Toronto 1969-71; el. Bishop Coadjutor Niagara Diocese 1971; Exec. Mem. Hamilton Soc. Planning Council 1972-76 (Pres. 1976-78); Bd. mem., Hamilton United Way and Ontario Council for Social Development; Official Visitor Ridley Coll. St. Catharines, St. John's Boys Sch. and St. Margaret's Girls' Sch. Elora, Ont. and Candn. Ch. of the Sisters of the Church; mem. Gen. Synod and Ont. Prov. Synod Ang. Ch. of Can.; mem. various ecumenical and inter ch. comtes. and bds.; Club: Dundas Valley Golf & Country; Home: 838 Glenwood Ave., Burlington, Ont. L7T 2J9; Office: 67 Victoria Ave. S., Hamilton, Ont. L8N 2S8

BOTHWELL, Mary; artist; singer; b. Toronto, Ont.; e. Toronto Conserv.; Toronto Sch. of Art; Salzberg, Austria; her flower paintings, in which she specializes, have been only paintings exhibited in Swiss Pavillions of world fairs and at Swiss Center, N.Y.; works in numerous collections incl. Hunt. Bot. Lib., Carnegie-Mellon Univ., and of Eisenhower Univ.; regular one-man shows at Chase Gallery (N.Y.) and N.Y. Hortic. Soc. Carlyle Gallery, N.Y. 1979; as a leading soprano has sung throughout U.S., in Holland, Switzerland, Austria, France and Eng., only internat. recognized Liedersinger born and educ. in Can. and U.S.; frequent radio appearances in U.S., Paris, Switzerland, Holland and on B.B.C., London, Eng.; starred in own radio program "The Mary Bothwell Show", N.Y.; special Bicentennial Exhns. U.S. State Flowers, N.Y. Parks Dept. 1975; Past Pres., Candn. Women's Club, N.Y. and actively engaged in promoting their Schol. Fund for young Candn. artists; Summer Home: St. Moritz, Switzerland; Office: c/o Betty Smith Associates, 322 E. 55th St., New York, N.Y. 10022.

BOTTERELL, E. Harry, O.C., O.B.E., M.D., M.S., F.R.S.C.(C), D.Sc., LL.D.; neurosurgeon; b. Vancouver, B.C. 28 Feb. 1906; s. John Esterbrook and Louise Ethel (Armstrong) B.; e. Ridley Coll., St. Catharines, Ont.; Univ. of Manitoba M.D. 1930; Univ. of Toronto M.S. 1936; D.Sc. McGill 1972; LL.D. Queen's 1973; winner Lister Prize 1937, George Armstrong Peters Prize 1939; m. Margaret Talbot, d. Mt. Rev. Archbishop Samuel Pritchard Matheson; children: Daphne, Jocelyn; Prof. Emeritus of Surgical Neurol. and Clinical Anatomy, Queen's Univ. since 1974; House Surg. Winnipeg Gen. Hosp. 1929, Resident in Gen. Surg. 1930; Resident Physician, Montreal Gen. Hosp. 1931; Resident Surg. Toronto Gen. Hosp.

1933; Intern and Extern neurol. and neurosurg. Nat. Hosp. London U.K. 1934; Research Fellow Neurophysiol. Yale Univ. 1935; Lect. in neurophysiol. and Resident Neurosurg. Lect. and Jr. Neurosurg., and Consulting Neurosurg. Toronto 1936-40; Sr. Neurosurg. 1945-62 and Assoc. Prof. Neurosurg. Univ. of Toronto 1952-62, Prof. of Surg. (Neurosurg.) 1962; Dean of Med. Queen's Univ. 1962-70, Vice-Princ. Health Scs. 1968-71, Special Advisor to Princ. Health Scs. 1971-74; served in 2nd World War RCAMC 1940-45, rank Lt.-Col.; Sr. Neurosurg., Christie St. Hosp. Jt. Services Neurosurg. Unit and Sunnybrook Hosp. Neurosurg. Unit D.V.A., 1945-55; Neurolog. Consultant and mem. Med. Adv. Bd. Lyndhurst Hosp.; One-man Comte. Enquiry into Health Care System in Min. Correctional Services in Ont. 1971; One-man Comte. enquiring into animal health care services Ont. Min. Agric. and Food 1974; Chrmn. Nat. Health Services Adv. Comte. for Candn. Penitentiary Service; Hon. Fellow, Roy. Coll. of Surgeons (Edinburgh); Hon. mem. Soc. Brit. Neurol. Surgs.; Hon. mem. Australasian Neurosurg. Assn.; Sr. mem. American Neurosurg. Assn.; Hon. mem. Can. Assn. Phys. Med. and Rehabilitation; Soc. de Neurochirurgie de langue Francais; Soc. Neurol. Surgs.; Am. Neurol. Assn.; Candn. Assn. Physical Med. and Rehabilitation; Sr. mem. Acad. Neurol. Surg.; Sr. mem. Am. Assn. Neurol. Surgs.; Sr. mem. Candn. Med. Assn.; F.N.G. Starr Award of Can. Med. Assn. 1977; 1980 Comm. Citation, Correctionals Services of Can. Zeta Psi; Anglican; recreation: sailing; Home: 2 Lakeshore Blvd., Kingston, Ont. K7M 4J6; Office: Kingston, Ont.

BOUCHARD, Jacques; advertising executive; b. Montreal, Que.; 29 Aug. 1930; s. Bernard and Lucienne (Leduc) B.; e. St. Laurent Coll., B.A. 1948; Univ. of Montreal, L.S.P. 1952; Head Univ., Fla., M.A. (Educ.); m. Caroline, d. Antoine Maranda, 13 June 1969; one d. Veronique; PRESIDENT, BCP ADVERTISING LTD.; commenced as Translator, Vickers & Benson Ltd., Montreal 1949; Mgr., French Advertising, James Lovick Ltd. 1955; Acct. Supv., J. Walter Thompson Co. Ltd. 1956; Advertising Mgr., La Brasserie Ltd. 1957; recreations: horseriding, billiards; Clubs: Le Publicité de Montreal; Advertising & Sales Executive; Young Presidents' Organization Inc.; Political Consultants; Canadien; Home: 630 Dunlop Ave., Outremont, Que. H2V 2V9; Office: Room 444, 1010 St. Catherine St. W., Montreal, Que. H3B 1G3

BOUCHARD, Son Honn. Louis-Philippe, B.A., L.èsD.; né Amos, Qué., 28 juil. 1918, f. Dalmas et Laurette (Fortin) B.; é. Séminaire de Qué., B.A. (cum laude, médaille du lt.-gov.) 1939; Univ. Laval, L. ès D. (cum laude, médaille du lt.-gov.) 1946; Ecole des Hautes Etudes Comm., Univ. de Montréal; études en comptabilité et cours de perfectionnement en adm., en collab. avec l'Univ. d'Harvard 1961; ép. Gilberte Savoie, 26 juin 1945; enfants: Marie, Jacqueline, Guy; JUGE DE LA COUR PROVINCIALE, QUE.; Vice-prés. Comm. des transports du Qué.; Prés.-dir. gén., Régie de l'assurance-depôts du Qué.; Prés., Comité d'étude sur l'industrie des valeurs mobilières au Qué.; Vice-prés. honoraire, Conseil Saint-Jean de Qué.; Dir., Assn. canadienne pour santé mentale; avec le Trust Général du Canada, Dir.-gérant, succursale de Qué. 1955, Dir. Gén. adjoint de la Cie 1965; Conseiller spécial auprès de l'Executif, P.Q. 1968; admis au Barreau 1946; nommé C.R. 1968; catholique romaine; récréation: golf; Clubs: Cercle universitaire; Club de golf Royal Québec; résidence: 3 Jardins de Mérici, app. 707, Québec, Qué. G1S 4M4; bureau: 585 est boul. Charest, Québec, Qué. G1K 7W5

BOUDREAU, Jacques J., B.A., B.Sc.A.; consulting engineer; b. St-Jerome, Que. 13 Feb. 1936; s. Dr. Yvan C. and late Corine (Teasdale) B.; e. Coll. Jean de Brébeuf, B.A. 1955; Ecole Polytech., Montreal B.Sc.A 1959; post-grad. studies in business adm., water pollution, solid wastes and air pollution control; m. Carmen, d. late Ernest Dupras, 3 Oct. 1959; children: Jacques, Louis, Danièle;

PROJ. DIR., JR. PARTNER, VEZINA, FORTIER & ASSOC. Pres. and Gen. Mgr. Boudreau Dubeau, Lemieux Inc., 1975; with Steel Co. of Canada Ltd., Utilities Engr. Hamilton, Ont. 1959; Production Supvr., DuPont of Canada Ltd., Shawinigan, Que. 1962; Production Supt., St-Lawrence Fertilizers Ltd., Valleyfield, Que. 1966; Production and Tech. Supvr., Gulf Oil Canada Ltd., Varennes, Que. 1967; joined present Co. as Project Mgr. 1980; mem. Ord. Engrs. Que.; Air Pollution Control Assn.; Association Qué. des Techniques de l'eau; recreations: golf, swimming; Home: 277 Mgr. de Belmon, Boucherville, Que. J4B 2L3. Office: 3300 Cavendish Blvd., Suite 385, Montreal, Que. H4B 2M8

BOUEY, Gerald Keith, O.C., B.A., LL.D.; banker; b. Axford, Sask., 2 Apl. 1920; s. John Alexander and Inez Amanda (Hathaway) B.; e. Trossachs (Sask.) High Sch.; Queen's Univ., B.A. (Hons.) 1948; Queen's Univ., LL.D.; m. Anne Margaret, d. William Acheson Ferguson and late argaret Martin (Nicol), 8 Aug. 1945; children: Kathryn Anne, Robert Gerald; GOV. AND DIR., BANK OF CANADA, since 1 Feb. 1973; Dir., Federal Business Development Bank; Export Development Bank; Canada Deposit Ins. Corp.; joined Royal Bank of Canada 1936-41; joined present bank 1948; Chief Research Dept., 1962; Adviser 1965; Depy. Gov. 1969, Sr. Depy. Gov. 1972; served with RCAF 1941-45; mem., Bd. Trustees, Queen's Univ.; Candn. Econ. Assn.; United Church; recreations: golf, cross country skiing; Clubs: Royal Ottawa Golf; Country; Canadian; Home: 79 Kamloops Ave., Ottawa, Ont. K1V 7C8; 234 Wellington St., Ottawa, Ont.

BOUGHNER, Clarence Clarkson, M.A.; climatologist (retired); Canadian public service; b. Simcoe, Ont., 6 Sept. 1910; s. John Stewart and Minnie May (Smith) B.; e. Simcoe (Ont.) High Sch.; Univ. of Toronto (Victoria), B.A. (Hon. Math. and Physics) 1933 and M.A. (Meteorol.) 1934; m. Jessie Eleanor, d. late Dr. John King, 4 Mar. 1939; joined staff of the Head Office of the Meteorol. Service of Can., 1934, as Asst. Climatologist; apptd. Supt. of the Climatol. Sec. 1950, Chief of Climatol Div. 1957-70; Dir.-Gen. Central Services Br., Atmospheric Environment Service 1970-73; mem. of World Meteorol. Organ. Tech. Comn. on Climatol. 1950-73 (Pres. 1960-69); World Meteorol. Organ. Tech. Comn. on Agric. Meteorol. 1947-73; mem., Royal Meteorol. Soc.; awarded Patterson Medal for distinguished service in meteorol., 1967; United Church; recreation: golf; Home: 28 Boxbury Rd., Etobicoke, Ont. M9C 2W2

BOULANGER, Maurice, B.A., C.A.; b. Quebec, Que. 16 Mar. 1900; s. Frederick and Corinne (Poulin) B.; e. Levis Coll., P.Q.; Laval Univ., B.A. 1921; C.A. 1927; m. Germaine, d. A. E. Couet, 11 May 1929; four s. and three d.; CONSULTANT: MALLETTE, BENOIT, BOULANGER, RONDEAU & ASSOC., (estbd. 1940); Formerly Titular Prof. in Dept. of Accountancy at the Faculty of Law; mem., Que. City Comte. of Chart. Accts. (Past Pres.); life mem., Order of Chart. Accts. of Que.; Knight of Columbus, 4th degree; Roman Catholic; Clubs: Kiwanis; University (Que.); Home: 7, Jardins Mérici, App. 302, Québec, Que. G1S 4N8; Office: 990, de Bourgogne, C.P. 10350, Ste-Foy, Que. G1V 4H5

BOULET, Albert, B.A., M.Com., C.A.; insurance executive; b. Quebec City, P.Q., 15 Aug. 1916; s. late J. Wilfrid, C.A., and Bernadette (Camiré) B.; e. Sémy. de Québec, P.Q.; Laval Univ., B.A. 1936, M.Com. 1945; C.A. 1946; m. Marguerite, d. J. Herménégilde Boulet, Québec City, P.Q., 17 May 1941; three d.: Louise, Hélène, Denyse; PRESIDENT, LA SOLIDARITE, COMPAGNIE D'ASSURANCE SUR LA VIE (Estbd. 1942) since 1954; Hamel Transport Ltée.; Expeditex Inc.; J. Lucien Allard Ltée; Les Immeubles Allard Ltée.; Accountancy with Boulet & Boulet, C.A., 1936-41; Albert Boulet & Partners, 1941-50; Boulet, Morin, Lachance, Motard & Robitaille, 1950-54; Founder and Secy.-Treas. of present firm, 1942;

Vice-Pres. & Treas., 1952-54; Gov., Faculty of Comm., Laval Univ.; R. Catholic; K. of C. (Past Grand Kt.); recreations: fishing, golf; Clubs: Cap Rouge Golf; Chasse et Pêche des Neuf Lacs; Home: 600 Ave. Laurier, Québec City, Que. G1R 2L4; Office: 925 Chemin St. Louis, Québec City, P.Q. G1S 1C1

BOULET, Lionel, OC, B.A., M.Sc., D.Sc., D.Gén.; utilities executive; research engineer; b. Québec City, Qué., 29 July 1919; e. Univ. Laval, B.A. 1938, B.Sc. (elect. engn.) 1944, D.Sc. 1972; Illinois, M.Sc. 1947; doctoral courses 1948; Sir George Williams Univ., D.Sc. 1968; Univ. Ottawa, D.Gén. 1971; Fellow Eng. Inst. of Canada 1973; D.Sc. (hon. causa) Laval 1972, McGill 1977; m. Ruth Millette; children: Christiane, Geneviève, Jean-François, Isabelle; DIRECTOR, RESEARCH INST., HYDRO-QUEBEC since 1967; with Boulet & Boulet, C.As. 1938-40; Student Engr., Saguenay Power Co., Ile Maligne, 1941; Jr. Acct., Boulet & Boulet 1942; Student Engr., R.C.A. Victor Co. 1943; Jr. Engr. 1944; Lab. Asst., Univ. Laval 1945; Champaign Research Asst., Univ. Illinois 1946, Assoc. 1947; Lectr., Elect. Engn., Univ. Laval 1948; helped estb. Research Lab., R.C.A. Victor Co. 1948-50; Asst. Prof., Elect. Engn., Univ. Laval 1950, Prof. 1953; Research Consultant, C.A.R.D.E. 1950-53; Head of Dept. and Research Lab. 1954; taught Operations-Research math. to econ. and business adm. profs.; joined present Co. as Consultant 1964; Tech. Adv. to Gen. Mgr. 1965; awards incl., Prince of Wales Decoration; Corp. Prof. Engrs. Qué. Prize and Engn. Inst. Can. Prize 1943; Inst. Elect. & Electronic Engrs. Prize 1944 (Montreal Sec. Award 1943); Canada Medal 1967; Archambault Medal 1970; Pres., Ext. Adv. Bd., Faculty of Science, Laval Univ.; Pres., "Conseil de la Politique scientifique du Québec"; Past Chrmn., Qué. Sec., Am. Inst. Elect. Engn.; Chrmn., Univ. Prof. Sec., Candn. Elect. Assn.; Comte. on Research, Corp. Prof. Engrs. Qué.; Pres. Int. Electric Res. Exch. 1976; Sigma Xi; R. Catholic; Home: 11285 Pasteur, Montreal 356, Qué.; Office: Monté3 Ste-Julie, Varennes, Qué. J0L 2P0

BOULT, Reynald, Q.C., B.A., B.Ph., LL.L.; lawyer; b. Hull, Que. 20 Nov. 1916; s. Richard and Alice (Larose) B.; e. Univ. of Ottawa B.A., B.Ph. 1938, LL.L. 1958; Dominican Coll. Ottawa 1939-40; m. Lyône Migneron 5 Oct. 1940; children: Francine, Marcel, Lucile; Librarian, Supreme Court Of Canada 1962-79; called to Bar of Que. 1959 with Gold Medal of Paris Bar; cr. Fed. Q.C. 1976; Offr. Inspection Bd. UK and Can. 1940-45; Adm. UNRRA sponsored European relief campaigns 1945-46; Reviser Bureau for Transl's Debates Div. 1947-60; Solr. Secy. of State Dept. 1960-62; author "A Bibliography of Canadian Law" New ed. 1977; contrib. to various legal journs.; Club: Cercle Universitaire; Home: 330 Metcalfe St., Ottawa, Ont. K2P 1S4;

BOULTER, Cedric Gordon, Ph.D.; university professor; archaeologist; b. Tryon, P.E.I., 9 May 1912; s. James Wilfred and Charlotte Wright (Muirhead) B.; e. Prince of Wales Coll., Charlottetown, P.E.I., 1927-30; Acadia Univ., B.A. 1933; Johns Hopkins Univ., 1933-34; Am. Sch. of Classical Studies, Athens, 1934-35; Univ. of Cincinnati, Ph.D. 1939; m. Elizabeth Patricia, d. Henry J. Neils, Minneapolis, Minn., 28 May 1953; two s., John Neils, Edward Gordon; PROF. OF CLASSICS, UNIV. OF CINCINNATI, since 1954 and Fellow of Grad. Sch. since 1965; joined present Univ. as Instr. 1939-45; Asst. Prof. 1945-52; Assoc. Prof. 1952-54; Annual Prof. 1965-66 and mem. Mang. Comte., since 1950, Am. Sch. of Classical Studies, Athens; served with RCNVR (Special Br.) 1942-45; discharged with rank Lt. Commdr.; mem., Archaeol. Inst. Am. (Gen. Secy. 1955-57; Pres., Cincinnati Soc. 1958-70); mem. Am. Philol. Assn.; Classical Assn. Can.; Soc. Promotion Hellenic Studies; Club: University; Home: 1 Rawson Woods Circle, Cincinnati, Ohio 45220

BOULVA, Charles, B.Sc.A.; executive; b. Cannes, France, 9 Feb. 1918; s. Dr. René and Yvonne (Quigneaux) B.; e. Coll. Stanislas, Cannes, France; Coll. Mont St-Louis, Montreal, Que.; Ecole Polytechnique, Montreal, B.Sc.A. (Civil Engn.); m. Betty Van der Poorten; children: Jacques, Yves (deceased), Louise (Mrs. P. Grignon), Francine; PRES. & CHRMN. OF BD., SOCIÉTÉ DE DÉVELOPPEMENT DE LA BAIE JAMES; Chrmn. of Bd., Sotel inc.; Société de tourisme de la Baie James; apptd. Study and Site Engr., Provincial Electricity Bd., Montreal, 1939; served with Rural Electrification Bureau, Que. Govt. as Dist. Engr. 1946, Chief Engr. 1953; Chief Engr. and Partner, Cartier, Côté, Piette, Boulva, Wermenlinger et Associés, 1961; Asst. Extve. Dir., Asselin, Benoît, Boucher, Ducharme, Lapointe, 1967; Chief Engr. and Dir., Dept. of Pub. Works, City of Quebec, 1970; mem. Corp. Engrs. Que.; Am. Soc. Civil Engrs.; Candn. Nat. Comte. on Large Dams; R. Catholic; Club: St-Denis; Home: 205, chemin de la côte Ste-Catherine, apt. 601, Outremont, Qué. H2V 2A9; Office: 800 de Maisonneuve Blvd. E., Montreal, Que. H2L 4M6

BOURASSA, Hon. Robert, M.N.A., M.A., lawyer; economist; b. 14 July 1933; e. Jean-de-Brébeuf Coll. (Arts) 1953; Univ. de Montréal (Law; Gov. Gen. Medal); Oxford Univ. (Rhodes Scholar), M.A. (Econ.) 1959; Harvard Univ., M.A. (Internat. Tax and Corp. Law); m. Andrée, d. late Joseph Simard, Sorel, Que.; one s. Françoise; one d. Michelle; Prime Minister of Quebec 1970-76; first el. to Que. Nat. Assembly for Mercier, g.e. 1966; former Financial (Opposition) Critic in Assembly; chosen Leader of Que. Liberal Party 17 Jan. 1970; sworn in as Prime Min. of Que. and Min. of Finance 12 May 1970; assumed the Portfolios of Finance till Nov. 1970, and of Intergovernmental Affairs, Feb. 1971-Feb. 1972; joined Fed. Civil Service 1960 as a Fiscal Advisor in Nat. Revenue Dept.; Lectr. on Econ. and Public Finance, Univ. of Ottawa; apptd. Secy. and Research Dir. for Bélanger Comn. on Taxation, Que. 1963-65

BOURASSA, Yves Gustave, M.B.E., C.D., B.A.; educator; b. Montreal, Que. 21 March 1910; s. Eugene and Adrienne (Labelle) B.; e. Univ. de Montréal B.A. 1930; m. Marcelle Landreau 1937; div. 1977; m. 2ndly Hélène Lanctôt 1978; two d. Liette Ferron, Danielle; VISITING PROF. AND DIR. MANG. DEVEL. PROGRAMS, ECOLE DES HAUTES ETUDES COMMERCIALES, UNIV. DE MONTREAL: Announcer, Program Dir. Radio Stn. CKAC 1932-40; joined Spitzer & Mills Advertising 1945-46; Founding Pres. French Advertising Services 1946-49; Dir., Vice Pres., Partner, Walsh Advertising Co. 1949-60; Sr. Vice Pres., Mgr., French Services, McCann-Erickson (Canada) Ltd. 1960-63; Commissaire Gén. des Fêtes du Can. Français 1963-64; Pres., Bourassa, Gagnon et Associés Ltd. 1964-67; Sr. Vice Pres., BCP Advertising Ltd. 1967-72; Pres., The BCP Group Ltd. 1973-76, Chrmn. 1976-79; served with Candn. Army 1940-45, rank Lt. Col.; Kt. Commdr. Mil. & Hospitaller Order St. Lazarus; Offr. Order St. John Jerusalem; Club: St-Denis; Home: 95 McNider, Apt. 501, Outremont, Qué. H2V 3X5; Office: 5255 ave. Decelles, Montréal, Qué. H3T 1V6.

BOURGAULT, Jean-Julien, O.C. (1970); artiste et sculpteur; né St Jean Port Joli, Qué. le 24 juin 1910; f. Magloire et Emélie (Legros) B.; é. à l'école du village; Coll. Montréal; Ecole Anglaise; ép. Antoinette, f. Leonce Caron, 8 Oct. 1934; enfants: Gils, Claudette, Nicole, Pierre, Micheline; il vient d'une famille des sculpteurs depuis des générations du côté maternel; un des premiers à promouvoir le renouveau de l'art en sculpture en 1930 à Québec et à St Jean Port Joli où il fonda une école de sculpture en 1939 et il a fourni au moins 100 sculpteurs à travers les Etats-Unis et Can. depuis cette date; reçu Merite Nat. Français 1964; Prés. Chambre de Comm., St. Jean Port Joli; Catholique Roman; récréations: chasse, pêche, le bateau, peinture; Adresse: St. Jean Port Joli, Qué. G0R 3G0

BOURGAULT, Pierre L., B.A., B.Sc., Ph.D., F.C.I.C.; P.Eng.; electrochemist; Vice-Rector (Admin.) U. of Ottawa; b. St. Brieux, Sask. 5 July 1928; s. Georges and Louise (Boissière); e. Coll. Mathieu (Lib. Arts) B.A. 1950; Univ. of Sask., Engn. 1951; Univ. of Ottawa B.Sc. 1953, Ph.D. (summa cum laude) 1961; m. Denise, d. Elzéar Tremblay, Ottawa, Ont., Aug. 1957; children: Bernard, Robert, Adèle, Jérôme, Louise; with Johnson, Matthey and Mallory, Toronto in various positions leading to Div. Mgr. 1960-69; Science Advisor, Science Council of Can., Ottawa 1969; apptd. Dean of Engn., Univ. of Sherbrooke 1971-72; Asst. Secy. (Policy) Min. State for Science and Technol. 1972-75, Asst. Deputy Min., Energy, Mines and Resources 1975-80; former Mem. Board of Governor, Univ. of Ottawa; Nat. Design Council of Canada; Standards Council of Canada; Assn. Prof. Engrs. Ont.; Candn. Research Mang. Assn.; author of "Innovation and the Structure of Canadian Industry"; also numerous articles in prof. and learned journals; holds various patents for batteries, capacitors and other electrochemical devices; R. Catholic; Home: 23 Parkwood Cres., Blackburn Hamlet, Ottawa, Ont. K1B 3J5; Office: 550 Cumberland St., Ottawa, Ont. K1N 6N5

BOURGEAU, Pierre G., B.A. Pol. Sc., LL.B., barrister and solicitor; executive; b' Ont. 21 Jan. 1939; s. Gerard Roger and Colombe (Handy) B.; e. Guigues., Bréboeuf and Académie de la Salle, Ottawa; Univ. of Ottawa B.A. Pol. Sc. 1961, LL.B. 1965; Post Graduate Studies-Doctorate Course-Civil Law, Univ. of Ottawa 1965-66; Osgoode Hall — Bar Admission Course 1967-68; m. Nicole d. Jacques de Terwangne, Hudson, Que., 21 July 1973; one s. Pierre-Daniel; GEN. COUNSEL AND SECRETARY, CELANESE CANADA LTD. and Gen. Counsel & Secy. 1979-; Dir. and Vice-Pres. and Sec., Milhaven Fibres Ltd.; Dir. & Pres. Celcan Properties Ltd.; called to Bar of Ont. 1968; mem. Candn. Dipl. Corps, Dept. External Affairs 1968-70, Legal Advisor UN Session 1969, to Dept. Secy. of State on behalf of Fed. Dept. of Justice 1970-72; Legal Advisor Canadair Ltd. Montreal 1972-74; joined Churchill Falls (Labrador) Corp. Ltd. as Gen. Counsel and Secy. 1974; Vice Pres., Legal, and Gen. Counsel and Sec. 1975-79; Dir. & Vice-Pres., Constance Lethbridge Rehabilitation Centre; mem. Law Soc. Upper Can. (Bar of Ontario); Bar of Que.; Candn. Bar Assn.; Cdn. Council on Internat. Law; Aff., Inst. Chartered Secretaries and Administrators; R. Catholic; recreation: travel; Club: St. James's; St. Denis; Home: 615 Lazard Ave., Town of Mount Royal, Que. H3R 1P6; Office: 800 Dorchester W, 29th Floor, Montreal, Que. H3C 3K8

BOURKE, Douglas T., B.Eng.; executive; b. Montreal, Que. 9 Aug. 1925; s. George Wesley and Beatric Minerva (Mitchell) B.; e. Westmount (Que.) High Sch.; McGill Univ., B.Eng. 1949; Mang. Training Course, Univ. of Western Ont. 1966; Advanced Mang. Program, Harvard Univ. 1971; m. Sheila Ross, d. late William Adams Ramsay, 1 March 1950; children: Andrew Thomas, Jane Cynthia, Diana Ramsay; PRESIDENT AND DIR., DRUMMOND McCALL INC. since 1972; Pres., DMC Metals Inc.; Drummond McCall Metals Corp.; Dir., GBC Capital Ltd.; Dominion-Scottish Investments Ltd.; SKF Can. Ltd.; joined present Co. 1951; Steel Products Mgr. Montreal 1959, Asst. Mgr. 1963, Operations Mgr. 1967, Vice-Pres. 1971; served in 2nd World War, R.C.A.F., Pilot Offr. — Flight Engr. 1943-45; Past Pres., McGill Grad. Soc.; Candn. Steel Service Centre Inst.; Past Chrmn., Study Corp.; Gov., Conseil du Patronat du Québec; mem. Bd. Mang., Montreal Gen. Hosp. Corp.; Gov., McGill Univ.; Delta Upsilon; United Church; recreations: squash, tennis, golf, skiing; Clubs: University; Mount Royal; Montreal Indoor Tennis; Royal Montreal Golf; Badminton & Squash; Home: 5 Rosemount Ave., Westmount, Que. H3Y 3G6; Office: 5205 Fairway, Lachine, Que. H8T 1C1

BOURKE, George Mitchell; investment consultant; b. Montreal, Que., 8 Feb. 1923; s. George Wesley and Beatrice Minerva (Mitchell) B.; e. Westmount High Sch., 1940; Roy. Mil. Coll., grad. 1942; McGill Univ., B.Eng., 1948; m. Barbara Ann, d. Adolphus William Brown, 11 Dec. 1948; children: Steven Mitchell, Michael George, Julia Elizabeth; CHAIRMAN AND DIR., BOLTON, INC. TREMBLAY; joined Investment Dept., Sun Life Assnce. Co. of Can., 1948; promoted Asst. Treas., 1957; Assoc. Treas., 1960; Secy.-Treas., Cornwall Street Rly., Light & Power Co. Ltd., 1951-61; Dir., 1961; joined present Co., Oct. 1961; mem., Montreal Inst. Invest. Analysts; Alderman, City of Dorval, 1958-60; served overseas during second World War with Roy. Candn. Arty. in Eng., France, Belgium and Holland, 1942-45; discharged with rank of Capt.; Dir., Montreal Boys Club; Unitarian; recreation: photography; Club: University; M.A.A.A.; Home: 3460 Redpath St., apt 106, Montreal, Que. H3G 2G3; Office: 1100 University St., Montreal, Que. H3G 1H1

BOURKE, Richard David, M. Arch., R.C.A., F.R.A.I.C.; architect, university administrator; b. Montreal, Que. 22 Oct. 1931; s George Wesley and Beatrice (Mitchell) B.; e. Westmount (Que.) High Sch. 1948; McGill Univ. B.Arch. 1954; Harvard Univ. M.Arch. 1959; m. Judith Margaret (d.) d. Veith (deceased) daughter of late George Selwyn Veith 19 March 1955; children: Meredith Margaret, Thomas David; DIR. OF UNIV. RELATIONS, McGILL UNIV. 1981- ; joined J. B. Parkin Architects Toronto 1955-58; Dobush, Stewart, Bourke, Montreal 1960-65; Dobush, Stewart, Bourke, Longpre, Marchand, Goudreau 1965-72; Extve. Asst. to Princ. McGill Univ. 1972, Dir. Devel. & Communications 1975; Dir. Miss Edgar's and Miss Cramp's Sch. Montreal 1972-75; Council mem. Order Archs. Que. 1964-66; Liberal; United Church; recreations: sailing, skiing, tennis; Club: University; Home: 3470 Redpath St. Montreal, Que. H3G 2G3; Office: 845 Sherbrooke St. W., Montreal, Que. H3A 2T5.

BOURKE, Thomas John, B.Sc.; publisher; b. Chesterville, Ont. 21 Feb. 1937; s. Thomas John B.; e. Mich. Technol. Univ. B.Sc. 1961; m. Melodie Ann d. late Arthur J. Booth 24 Aug. 1963; three d. Gillian, Jacqueline, Jennifer; PRESIDENT, TELE-DIRECT (PUBLICATIONS) INC. 1981- ; Dir. Tele-Direct Ltd.; Edward H. O'Brien Pty. Ltd., Australia; Sanford Evans, Winnipeg; National Telephone Directory, N.J.; Marketing Rep. Bell Canada 1961, Directory Dept. 1968, Div. Directory Production Mgr. 1970; Vice Pres. Production, Tele-Direct Ltd. 1971, Vice Pres. Marketing 1972, Vice Pres. Directory Operations 1973, Operating Vice Pres. 1978; mem. YMCA fund-raising campaigns; R. Catholic; recreations: golf, tennis, squash; Clubs: Royal Montreal Golf; Weston Golf & Country (Ont.); Montreal Board of Trade; Toronto Board of Trade; Canadian; Home: 17 Fredmir Blvd., Dollard des Ormeaux, Que. H9A 2R1; Office: 1600 Dorchester Blvd. W., Montreal, Que. H3H 1P9.

BOURNE, John G.; company chairman; b. Montreal, P.Q., 1918; s. late Dr. Wesley and Sara Beatrice (McGillis) B.; e. Selwyn House Sch., Montreal; Westmount High Sch.; McGill Univ. (one year science); m. Joan Elspeth, d. late A. Sidney Dawes, 10 Oct. 1942; children: Thomas, Elspeth; CHAIRMAN, ATCONCORP.; Dir., Atlas Maritimes Ltd.; G. M. Gest (1977) Inc.; G. M. gest Contractors (1977) Inc.; Past-Pres., Que. Road Builders Assn., 1957-58; Past-Pres., Montreal Constr. Assn., 1960-61; with Royal Bank of Can., 1935-39; joined present Co. in 1940; served in 2nd World War with the Black Watch (R.H.R.) of Can., 1939-42 in Can. and U.K.; First Special Service Force, 1942-44 as Lieut.-Col. Commanding a Bn.; served in Aleutian Islands, Italy and S. France; having joined N.P.A.M. in 1934, rejoined in 1946 and took Command of the Black Watch (R.H.R.) Can. in 1952; retired, 1955; Colonel of the Regt., the Black Watch (R.H.R.) of Can. 1968, Hon. Col. 1973; Clubs: St. James's; Murray Bay Golf; Forest & Stream; Mt. Bruno Country; Home: 3

Westmount Square, Apt. PH. H, Montreal, Que. H3Z 2S5; Office: 255 Norman St., Montreal, Que.H8R 1A3

BOURNE, Larry Stuart, M.A., Ph.D.; educator; b. London, Ont. 24 Dec. 1939; s. Stuart Howard and Florence Evaline (Adams) B.; e. Univ. of W. Ont. B.A. 1961; Univ. of Alta. M.A. 1963; Univ. of Chicago Ph.D. 1966; m. Paula T. d. J.A. O'Neill, Liverpool, Eng. 14 Aug. 1967; children: David S. A., Alexandra L. E.; PROF. OF GEOGRAPHY, UNIV. OF TORONTO since 1973 and Dir. Centre for Urban and Community Studies there since 1972; Research Assoc. Centre for Urban Studies, Univ. of Chicago 1965-66; Asst. Prof. of Geog. present Univ. 1966, Assoc. Prof. 1969, Assoc. Dir. Centre for Urban and Community Studies 1969; Visiting Prof. London Sch. of Econ. 1972-73; Centre for Environmental Studies, London 1978-79; Consultant and Advisor to various levels govt.; mem. numerous internat. research and policy groups incl. Internat. Inst. for Applied Systems Analysis (Austria), Internat. Comn. on Urbanization (Poland), Urban Affairs Assn. (USA); author "Private Redevelopment of the Central City" 1967; "Urban Systems: Strategies for Regulation" 1975; "The Geography of Housing," 1981; Ed. "Internal Structure of City" 1971, 2nd ed. 1982; coed. "Urban Systems Development in Central Canada" 1972; "The Form of Cities in Central Canada" 1973; "Urban Futures for Central Canada" 1974; Co-ed., "Systems of Cities" 1978; "Urban Housing Markets" 1979; author numerous journ. articles, reports and papers; rec'd Can. Council Research Fellowship 1972-73; second Can. Council Leave Fellowship 1978-79; mem. Regional Science Assn.; Candn. Assn. Geographers; Assn. Am. Geographers; Urban Studies; Candn. Assn. Univ. Teachers; Delta Upsilon; Lambda Alpha; recreations: tennis, basketball, hockey; Home: 26 Anderson Ave., Toronto, Ont. M5P 1H4 Office: 150 St. George St., Toronto, Ont. M5S 1A1

BOURNE, Robert Porter (Robin), C.D., B.A.; Canadian public servant; b. Tunbridge Wells, Kent, U.K. 5 Aug. 1930; s. Kenneth Morrison Bourne; e. Ridley Coll. St. Catharines, Ont. 1948; Royal Mil. Coll. of Can. 1952; Univ. of W. Ont. B.A. 1954; Sch. of Arty., Larkhill, U.K. Long Gunnery Staff Course 1958; Staff Coll. Camberley, U.K. 1962-63; m. Patricia d. late Donald Robert Agnew; children: Mark Kenneth, Anne Susan Blossom, John Frederick, Peter David Anthony; Asst. Depy. Min.-Police and Security Planning and Analysis, Dept. Solr. Gen. Can. 1972-79; comnd. Lt., R.C.A. 1952; served Korean War 1952-53, Germany 1955-57, Cyprus (U.N.) 1967-68, Can. 1953-55, 1958-62, 1964-67, 1968-72, retired as Col. 1972; seconded as Lt. Col. to Privy Council Office, Cabinet Secretariat for Foreign Policy and Defence 1968-71; seconded as Col. to Dept. Solr. Gen., Head Security Planning 1971; joined Candn. Pub. Service 1972; granted extve. devel. leave at Carleton U., 1979-80; Dunning Trust Lect'r. Queen's Univ. 1976; Commr., Comn. Inquiry into RCMP Pub. Complaints, Discipline and Grievance Procedures (Marin Comn.) 1974-76; extve. dir. Comm. Inquiry into Post Office security, and investigation function, 1980; Asst. Depy. Min., Police Serv., B.C. Min. of Att. Gen. 1981; rec'd Centennial Medal 1967; Anglican; recreations: squash, canoeing; Home: 301-2333 Beach Dr., Victoria, B.C. V8R 6K2; Office: 609 Broughton St., Victoria, B.C. V8V 1X4

BOURNS, Arthur Newcombe, B.Sc., Ph.D., D.Sc., L.L.D., F.R.S.C., F.C.I.C.; chemist; b. Petitcodiac, N.B., 8 Dec. 1919; s. Evans Clement and Kathleen (Jones) B.; e. Acadia Univ., B.Sc. 1941, D.Sc. 1968; McGill Univ., Ph.D. 1944; McGill Univ. D.Sc. 1977; Brock U. L.L.D. 1980; Univ. of M.B., D.Sc. 1981; McMaster Univ., D.Sc. 1981; m. Marion Harriet, d. William S. Blakney, Petitcodiac, N.B., 23 June 1943; children: Mrs. Douglas Brown, Mrs. William Milne, Robert Evans, Brian Hugh; PRES., McMASTER UNIV., 1972-80; Research Chem., Research Labs., Dominion Rubber Co. Ltd., 1944-45; Lectr., Acadia

Univ., 1945-46; Asst. Prof. of Chem., Univ. of Sask., 1946-47 and McMaster Univ. 1947-49; Assoc. Prof. 1949-53; Prof. since 1953; Dean, Faculty of Grad. Studies, 1957-61; Chrmn., Dept. of Chem., 1965-67; Vice-Pres., Science and Engn. Div. 1967-72; Acting Pres. 1970; Nuffield Travelling Fellowship in Sciences, Univ. Coll., of London, Eng., 1955-56; memberships: Ancaster Pub. Sch. Bd. 1963-64; Comte. on Univ. Affairs, Prov. of Ont. 1964-69; Nat. Research Council of Can. (mem.: Council, Extve. Comte., Sub-comte. on Negotiated Grants, Allocations, Adv. Bd. to Div. of Chem. 1969-75; Standing Comte. on Scient. Publications 1969-71; Striking Comte. 1971-72; Comte. on Regional Devel. Program 1971-75; Grant Selection comte. in Chem. 1966-69, Adv. Comte. on Ind. Research and Devel. 1979-; Gp. Chrmn., Chem. and Chem. Engn./Metall. Grant Selection Comtes. 1969-72; Co-Chrmn. 1971 and Chrmn. 1972-75, Comte. on Grants and Scholarships) Weizmann Inst. Science (Sc. Adv. Council of Can. Bd. 1974-); Royal Botanical Gdns. (mem. Bd. and Vice-Chrmn. 1972-80); Assn. Univs. and Colls. Can. (mem. Bd. Dirs. 1974-77); Natural Sciences and Engineering Research Council (mem.: Council, Extve. Comte., Allocations Comte., Comte. on Strategic Grants 1978-; Univ.-Ind. Interface Adv. Comm 1979-; Chrmn. Comte. on Grants and Scholarships 1978-); Candn. Comte. for Financing of Univ. Research 1978-80; Council of Ont. Univs. (mem. Council 1972-80 and Vice-Chrmn. 1976-78 Extve. Comte.); Candn. Bureau Internat. Educ. (Pres. and Chrmn. Extve. Comte. 1973-76); McMaster Univ. Medical Centre (mem., Bd. Trustees, Extve. Comte. 1972-79; Chedoke-McMaster Hosp. (mem. Bd. Trustees, Extve. Comm. 1979-80); Bd. of Gov., Mohawk Coll. of Applied Arts & Technol. 1975-; Ed. Bd. "Science Forum" 1967-73; Dir. Slater Steel Co., 1975-80; Vice-Chrmn. 1959-60 and Chrmn. 1961-62 Gordon ResearchConf. on Chem and Physics of Isotopes; Brit. Council Lect. 1963; writings incl. numerous research pubis. in field of phys. organic chem. for various prof. journs.; recreations: travel, gardening; Address: RR #7, Brantford, Ont. N3T 5L9

BOUSFIELD, Edward Lloyd, M.A., Ph.D., F.R.S.C.; biologist; b. Penticton, B.C. 19 June 1926; s. late Reginald Harker and Marjorie Frances (Armstrong) B.; e. Riverdale Coll. Inst., Toronto, 1944; Univ. of Toronto, B.A. 1948, M.A. 1949; Harvard Univ., Ph.D. 1954; m. Barbara Joyce, d. late Hugh William Schwartz, 20 June 1953; children: Marjorie Anne, Jessie Katherine, Mary Elizabeth, Kenneth Lloyd; SENIOR SCIENTIST, NAT. MUSEUM OF NATURAL SCIENCES, since 1974; Adjunct Prof. of Biol., Carleton Univ., since 1969; Invertebrate Zool., present Museum, 1950-64; Chief Zool. 1964-74; Sr. Visiting Investigator, Systematics — Ecol. Program, Marine Biol. Lab., Woods Hole, Mass., 1963-70; Prof. visiteur, Univ. de Laval 1971; has participated in numerous scient. expeditions in N. Am.; rec'd "Hudson 70" Medal for participation in Hudson 70 expedition in Cape Horn region, S. Am.; prof. fields incl. taxonomy and distribution of amphipod crustaceans, intertidal ecol., evolution and phylogeny of crustaceans, post-glacial dispersal of marine animals in Can.; author of over 80 scient. and popular publs. and books on marine biol. and crustaceans since 1947; mem., Ottawa Field-Naturalists' Club (Pres. 1959-60); Arctic Inst. N. Am.; Ecol. Soc. Am.; Am. Soc. Limnology & Oceanography; Candn. Soc. Zoologists.; (Pres. 1979-80;) Biol. Council Can.; Sigma Xi; Salvation Army; recreations: curling, golf, lawnbowling, music; Clubs: RA Curling (Pres. 1972-73); Highland Park Lawn Bowling (Pres. 1977-78); SPEBSQSA: Home: 48 Farlane Blvd., Ottawa, Ont. K2E 5H5; Office: 2378 Holly Lane, Ottawa, Ont. K1A 0M8

BOUSQUET, Jean P., B.A.; stockbroker; b. Montreal, Que., 29 Sept. 1918; s. Josephine (Wiallard) and late Dr. J. P. E. Bousquet; e. Univ. de Montréal, B.A.; m. Helen, d. John Popovitch, 9 Aug. 1945; children: Paul, Marie-Elaine (Mrs. Afilalo), Suzanne (Mrs. Francisci); VICE-PRESIDENT, GREENSHIELDS INCORPORATED;

Dir., Greenshields Inc.; Cassidy's Ltd.; Rep., Jones-Heward & Co., Montreal, 1945-57; Exec. Vice-Pres. Crang & Ostiguy Inc. 1957-77; served as Offr., R.C.N., 1939-45; Gov., Hôpital Marie-Enfant; Past Pres. and Dir., Montreal Inst. of Cardiology; Cammdr. Mil. and Hospitaller Order of St. Lazarus of Jerusalem; mem. Montreal Soc. of Financial Analysts; Liberal; R. Catholic; recreations: fishing, golf, swimming; Home: 249 Stanstead Ave., Town of Mount Royal, Que. H3R 1X4; Office: 4 Place Ville Marie, Monteal, Que. H3B 2E8

BOUTON, Charles Pierre, D.E.S., D. ès L.; educator; b. Paris, France, 17 Feb. 1926; s. Pierre Alexandre and Madeleine Augustine (Guillot) B.; e. Baccalauréat (1st and 2nd) Paris, France 1943-44; Univ. de Paris (Sorbonne) Lic. ès Lettres 1947, Dipl. d'Etudes supérieures 1949, D. ès L. 1969; m. Eliane Pierrette, d. late Pierre Ernest Poulet, 3 Aug. 1946; children: Jean-Francois Pierre, Denys Pierre Gérard; PROF. OF FRENCH & LINGUISTICS, SIMON FRASER UNIV. and Chrmn. Modern Langs. Dept. since Sept. 1973; Prof. French Lit. and Lang., Educ. Nat., France 1947; Asst. Lectr. in French, Dundee Univ. Coll., Scot. 1951; Alliance Française, Ecole pratique de Paris 1952-67 (Prof. 1952, Asst. Dir. de l'Ecole and Séminaire de pédagogie, ling. et psycholing. 1958); Prof. French and Ling., Converse Coll., Spartanburg, S.C. 1967; Prof., present Univ. 1971; author of "Le dévelopment du langage", 1976; "La signification", 1979; "La linguistique appliquée", 1979; "Les Mécanismes d'Acquisition du français langue étrangère". 1969; "Les Grammaires françaises de Claude Mauger" 1972; "L'Acquisition d'une langue étrangère 1974; Edit. "Le Misanthrope" 1962; "Madame Bovary" 1969; "La Démocratie en Amérique" 1973; Co-author "Des Machines et des Hommes" 1964; "La Langue de l'Automobile" 1966; "Regardons, Ecoutons, Parlons" 1968; "Glosssaire de français scientifique" 1970; also articles in various prof. mags. and journs.; el Chevalier, La Conférie des Chevaliers du Tastevin (1974); mem. Assn. française de ling. appliquée; Candn. Assn. Univ. Teachers; Ling. Assn. B.C.; R. Catholic; Home: 1843 Rufus Dr., North Vancouver, B.C. V7J 3L8; Office: Burnaby, B.C.

BOUVIER, Rev. Emile, S.J., Ph.D.; labour economist; educationalist; b. Montreal, P.Q., 29 Mar. 1906; s. Joseph Ephrem and Charlotte Marion B.; e. St. Mary's Coll., Montreal; Boston Coll., A.B. 1928; A.M. 1929; Georgetown Univ., PhD. 1932; Harvard Univ., post-grad. work in Econ. 1939-41; PROF., DEPT. OF ECON., UNIV. OF SHERBROOKE, since 1963, and Pres. Emeritus 1980; (Pres., Univ. of Sudbury 1959-60, Laurentian Univ. of Sudbury 1960-63); former Chairman and Prof. (1955-59) of Labour Econ. and Industrial Relations, Dept. of Econ., Georgetown Univ., Washington, D.C., apptd. 1955; Dir., Industrial Research Centre, Institut Social Populaire, since 1951; Acting Director, Sch. of Industrial Relations and Sch. of Business and Admin., Universidad Iberoamericana, Mexico City, since 1953; Vice-Pres. (1954) and Pres. (1955) of the Catholic Economic Assn.; mem., Candn. Social Science Research Council (Comte. on Indust. Relations); Econ. Advisor, Candn. Indust. Assn.; Ed. Bulletin "Social des Industriels", 1943-48; mem., Ecole Sociale Populaire (Ed. of Relations); Montreal Personnel Assn.; Am. Econ. Assn.; Indust. Relations Research Assn.; Am. Assn. for Pub. Adm.; Candn. Pol. Science Assn.; Am. Management Assn.; author of "Economique Industrielle", 1943; "Votre Tache, Jeunesse"; "Le Travail Feminin"; "La Cogestions des Entreprises"; "Les Méfaits du Socialisme"; "La Profession en Relations Industrielles"; "Health Insurance in Canada"; "Les Pensions de Vieillesse"; "l'Assurancechômage au Canada", "Unemployment Insurance in Canada", "Industrial Relations as a Profession", "A Discussion on Pension Plans", "Patrons et Ouvriers", "Neither Right nor Left in Labor Relations"; "Fautil un Contrôle des Prix", "Le Revenu national du Canada", "Le Droit du Travail au Québec", "Le Salaire annuel

garanti", "The Guaranteed Annual Wage", "L'Organisation corporative est elle réalisable au Québec"; "Les Rouages de l'Economie", 1970; "L'Economique et la coexistence du secteur public et du secteur privé"; "Les Relations du Travail au Québec", 1980; R. Catholic; Address: University of Sherbrooke, 2625 Portland, Sherbrooke, Que.

BOVEY, Edmund Charles; C.M. (1978), company executive; b. Calgary, Alta., 29 Jan. 1916; s. Charles A. and Dorothy Bovey; e. Univ. Sch., Victoria, B.C.; m. Margaret Snowdon, d. Gordon and Mary S.; two children; DIRECTOR AND MEMBER OF THE EXECUTIVE COMMITTEE, NORCEN ENERGY RESOURCES LTD.; Dir., Abitibi-Price Inc.; Canada Packers Inc.; Can. Imperial Bank of Commerce; Coleman Collieries Ltd.; Duplate Can. Ltd.; Hollinger Argus Ltd.; Labrador Mining and Exploration Co. Ltd.; MONYLife Ins. Co. of Can.; PPG Ind. Inc.; PPG Ind. Can. Ltd.; Northern and Central Gas Corp. Ltd.; Past Pres., Can. Gas Assoc.; Bd. of Govs. Univ. of Guelph; mem., Canadian Econ. Policy Comm.; Trustee and Past Pres. of Art Gallery of Ontario and Art Gallery of Ont. Foundation; Vice-Pres. and mem. Bd. of Govs. Massey Hall; Chmn. of Bd., Wellesley Hosp.; Vice Chmn., Int. Council of Museum of Modern Art, N.Y.; Chrmn. Council for Business and the Arts in Canada; hon. mem. of Nat. Council of the Boy Scouts of Canada; recreations: golf, swimming, shooting; Clubs: Duquesne (Pittsburgh, Penn.); Rosedale Golf; Granite; Manitoba; The Toronto; Empire (Life mem.); York; The Links (New York); Duquesne (Pittsburgh, Penn.); recreations: golf, swimming, shooting; Home: 33 York Ridge Rd., Willowdale, Ont. M2P 1R8; Office: 4600 Toronto-Dominion Centre, Toronto, Ont. M5K 1E5

BOW, Malcolm Norman; diplomat (retired); b. Regina, Sask., 30 Sept. 1918; s. Dr. Malcolm Ross and Norma (Wallace) B.; e. Garneau Public and High Schs., Edmonton, Alta.; Univ. of Alta. (1938-40); Univ. of Brit. Columbia (1947-48); Acad. of Internat. Law, The Hague, Netherlands, 1948; m. Betty Rundle, d. Bertram R. Roberts, Shoreham-by-Sea, Sussex, Eng., 6 March 1945; children: Paul (deceased), Jane, Michael, Neil; Vancouver "Daily Province", 1946-49; joined Dept. of External Affairs, Ottawa, 1949; Vice Consul, New York, 1950-53; Ottawa 1953-56; First Secy., Candn. Embassy, Madrid, 1956-58 and Chargé d'Affaires a.i. there 1958-59; Ottawa, 1959-60; Counsellor and Chargé d'Affaires, Candn. Embassy, Havana, Cuba, 1961; Special Asst. to Secy. of State for External Affairs, Ottawa, 1962-64; Ambassador to Czechoslovakia (1964-68) (concurrently to Hungary 1965-68); apptd. Dir. Arms Control and Disarmament Div., Dept. External Affairs, Dec. 1968, Dir. of Latin Am. Div. March 1971; apptd. Ambassador to Cuba, 1973-75 (and concurrently to Haiti 1975); Dir.-Gen. of Security and Intelligence 1975-76; served in 2nd World War; Candn. Army, 1940, Calgary Highlanders, Eng., Lieut.; British Army, Burma, Capt.; Candn. Army Pacific Force, Major, 1946; recreations: golf, jogging, travel, research, writing; Home: 655 Richmond Rd., Unit #27, Ottawa, Ont. K2A 3Y3

BOWDEN, William Norman, B.Com.; insurance executive; b. Dunnville, Ont., 6 March 1912; s. Norman and Mary Jane (Gregory) B.; e. Univ. of Toronto, B.Com. 1933; m. Georgina Beryl, d. late Lt. Col. George W. Nelson, 30 Sept. 1939; children: Richard, Timothy, William, Margaret; retired as Sr. Vice-Pres. Crown Life Insurance Co.; mem., Saugeen Memorial Hospital Bd.; South Hampton Parks Bd.; Festival Theatre Bd.; Fellow, Life Office Mang. Inst.; Freemason; Anglican (Rector's Warden); Recreations: golf, fishing; Home: (Rector's Warden) Southampton, Ont. N0H 2L0

BOWELL, Gordon Stephen Johnson, M.B.E., M.B.A.; pulp and lumber executive; b. Vancouver, B.C., 27 Dec. 1918; s. Stephen Robert and Charlotte (Johnson) B.; e. Queen's Univ., B.A. 1941; (Rhodes Scholar 1941); Harvard Univ., M.B.A. 1947; m. Frances, d. C. E. Webb, Vancouver, B.C.; children: Shelley, Christopher; PRES., BOWELL CONSULTANTS LTD. since 1975; joined Bloedel Stewart & Welch Ltd., 1947; apptd. Vice Pres., MacMillan and Bloedel Ltd., 1957 and Vice Pres. and Gen. Mgr., Pulp and Paper Group, 1962; Pres., Rayonier Canada (B.C.) Ltd. 1964-70; Pres., Weldwood of Can. Ltd. 1971-75; Dir., Seaboard Lumber Sales 1964-75; served with R.C.A. Overseas as Maj., 1941-45; Anglican; recreations: fishing, skiing, tennis; Clubs: Vancouver; Shaughnessy Golf; Vancouver Lawn Tennis; Home: No. 15, 4350 Valley Dr., Vancouver, B.C. V6L 2K9; Office: Ste. 1070, 1055 W. Hastings St., Vancouver, B.C. V6E 2E9

BOWERING, George Harry, M.A.; poet and fiction writer; b. Okanagan Falls, B.C., 1 Dec. 1936; s. Ewart Harry and Pearl Patricia (Brinson) B.; e. S. Okanagan High Sch., Oliver, B.C.; Victoria (B.C.) Coll.; Univ. of Brit. Columbia, B.A. 1960, M.A. 1963; Univ. of Western Ontario; m. Angela Maya, d. E. H. Luoma, Courtenay, B.C., 14 Dec. 1963; Editor of "Imago" (internat. mag. of longer poems); Vice-Pres., The Nihilist Party of Can. (London); former L.A.C. in R.C.A.F. (photographer); author: "Sticks & Stones", 1963; "Points on the Grid", 1964; "The Man in Yellow Boots", 1965; "The Silver Wire", 1966; "Mirror on the Floor", 1967; "Baseball", 1967; "Rocky Mountain Foot", 1969; "Two Police Poems", 1969; "The Gangs of Kosmos", 1969; "Sitting in Mexico", 1970; "Al Purdy", 1970; "George, Vancouver", 1970; "Genève", 1971; "The Story So Far", 1970; "Touch: Selected Poems", 1971; "Autobiology", 1972; "In the Flesh", 1974; "Curious", 1974; "Flycatcher and Other Stories", 1974; "At War with the U.S.", 1975; "Allophanes", 1976; "The Concrete Island", 1977; "A Short Sad Book", 1977; "Poem & Other Baseballs", 1977; "Protective Footwear", 1978; "Concentric Circles", 1978; "Another Mouth", 1979; "Three Vancouver Writers", 1979; "Burning Water" (Novel) 1980; ed., "Fiction of Contemporary Canada", (Stories) 1980; "Particular Accidents" (poetry) 1980; ed.,; "Great Canadian Sports Stories", 1979; Gov. Gen. Award for Poetry, 1969; Can. Council Sr. Arts Award 1971; second Canada Council Sr. Arts Award 1977; Gov. Gen. Award for Fiction 1980; Romantic Anarchic Left; Religion: Protestant Agnostic; recreation: softball; Address: 2499 W. 37 Ave., Vancouver, B.C. V6M 1P4

BOWERING, Marilyn Ruthe, M.A.; author; b. Winnipeg, Man. 13 Apl. 1949; d. Herbert James and Elnora May (Grist) B.; e. Claremont Sr. Secondary Sch. Victoria 1966; Univ. of Victoria B.A. 1971, M.A. 1973; Univ. of B.C. 1968-69; mem. Ed. Bd. Press Porcepic; author "Sleeping with Lambs" poetry 1980; "The Visitors Have All Returned" fiction 1979; "The Killing Room" poetry 1977; "One Who Became Lost" poetry 1976; "The Liberation of Newfoundland" poetry 1973; "Organ's Eye" fiction and "Grandfather Was A Soldier" poetry, to be published; poetry pamphlets: "Third Child/Zian" 1978; "The Book of Glass" 1979; co-ed. "Many Voices" 1977; rec'd Nat. Mag. Award Poetry 1978; Lectr. in Creative Writing, Univ. of Victoria 1978-80; Ed. and Writer gregson/graham 1978-80; freelance Ed. Noel Collins (Edinburgh), Blackwoods (Edinburgh) 1981; freelance book reviewer various periodicals; rep. in journs. and anthols.; mem. Writers' Union Can.; League Candn. Poets; recreations: travel, hill-walking, sailing, watercolour painting, piano; Home: Manzer Rd., Sooke, B.C. V0S 1N0; Office: 3777 Jennifer Rd., Victoria, B.C. V8P 3X1

BOWERMAN, Hon. G. R., M.L.A.; b. Shellbrook, Sask., 3 Nov. 1930; s. E. L. and Laura Rosalee (Anderson) B.; e. Shellbrook (Sask.) Pub. Sch.; Candn. Vocational Training Sch., Prince Albert, Sask., Agric.-Resources Mang. & Adm. Course; m. Dagmar Alma Louise Christiansen, d. late Christian Ludwig, 14 Feb. 1959; two s., Curtis Christian, Mark Aaron; MIN. OF ENVIRONMENT; formerly Min. for Nothern Sask.; served Dept. of Natural Resources, Sask. for 17 yrs.; superv. prov. comm. fishing

indust. 1955-65; estbd. and operated private co., Reindeer Fisheries Ltd. 1965-67 when co. sold; subsequently pursued vocation of farming; cand. for mayor Prince Albert, Sask., 1964; el. M.L.A. for Shellbrook Constit. 1967; apptd. Min. of Mineral Resources and Min. responsible for Sask. Indian & Metis Dept., Sask. Water Resources Comn. and Sask. Water Supply Bd. 1971; Min. of Natural Resources 1972; served on local Saskatchewan Wheat Pool Committee, co-op. and credit union bds.; o. Elder of Reorganized Ch. of Jesus Christ of Latter Day Saints; served in Sask. as Dist. Pres. and as Pres. of various congs. in Prince Albert and other points; NDP; recreations: canoeing, fishing, hunting; Club: Kinsmen; Home: 3431 Queen St., Regina, Sask. S4S 4B7; Office: Legislative Bldg., Regina, Sask.

BOWIE, George Leslie; insurance executive; PRES. AND DIR., THE NORTHERN LIFE ASSURANCE CO. OF CANADA: Dir. and Vice Chrmn. of Bd., The Personal Insurance Co.; Dir. Sterling Trust Co.; Dale-Ross Holdings Ltd.; Dir. & Vice-Chmn of the Bd., St. Joseph's Hosp.; Office: 380 Wellington St., London, Ont. N6A 4G3.

BOWKER, Her Hon. Marjorie Hope Montgomery, B.A., LL.B., LL.D.; judge; b. P.E.I., 4 Jan. 1916; d. William Frank Hale and Mary (Carr) Montgomery; e. Garbutt Business Coll., 1934; Univ. of Alta., B.A. 1938, LL.B. 1939; Ewha Women's Univ. (Korea), LL.D. 1968; m. Wilbur Fee Bowker, Q.C. 12 Oct. 1940; children: Blair Montgomery, Lorna Ethel, Keith Wilbur; JUDGE, JUVENILE & FAMILY COURT, ALTA., since 1966; Judicial Supervisor, Family Court Conciliation Service since 1972; read law with George Hobson Steer, K.C.; called to Bar of Alta. 1940; practised law with firm of Milner, Steer & Co., Edmonton; served as Parliamentarian at Nat. Convention, YWCA of Can., 1965; only woman mem. of comte. set up by Govt. of Alta. to study adoption in that prov., 1966; presented brief on mental retardation to Alta. Leg. Comte. on Preventive Health Services, 1967; guest speaker at Nat. Convention, Jr. Leagues of Am. in Montreal, 1967; guest speaker at Ewha Women's Univ., Seoul, Korea, 1968; only Candn. speaker at Am. Conf. of Conciliation Courts, Los Angeles, 1969; speaker at 14 Candn Clubs in Can. & W. Germany during 1978-79 on subject "Can the Family Survive?"; recipient Queen's Silver Jubilee Medal, 1978; Alta. Achievement Award 1981; mem. International Federation of Women Lawyers; Candian Comm. of Jurists; Vanier Inst. of the Family; Trustee, Univ. of Alta. Hosp. 1965-77; Bd. of Dir. of Association of Family Conciliation Courts (1969-79); writings incl. "Supplementary Report on Adoption in Alberta", 1965; mem., Jr. League of Am.; Pi Beta Phi; United Church; Home: 10925-85 Ave., Edmonton, Alta. T6G 0W3; Office: 500 Century Place, 9803—102A Ave., Edmonton, Alta. T5J 3A6

BOWKER, Wilbur Fee., Q.C., B.A., LL.M., LL.D.; b. Ponoka, Alta., 18 Feb. 1910; s. George Elwyn and Ida Ethel (Pritchard) B.; e. Univ. of Alberta, B.A. 1930, LL.B. 1932; Univ. of Minnesota, LL.M.; m. Marjorie Hope, d. late W. F. H. Montgomery, 12 Oct. 1940; two s., Blair, Keith; one • d. Lorna; read law with George Hobson Steer, K.C.; called to Bar of Alta., 1933; mem., legal firm of Milner, Steer, Edmonton, Alta., 1933-45; Dean Faculty of Law, Univ. of Alberta 1945-68; Dir., Inst. Law Research & Reform, Prov. of Alta. 1968-75; served in 2nd World War, 1942-45; with Candn. Army in Can.; discharged with rank of Capt.; mem., Candn. Bar Assn.; Law Soc. of Alta.; Assn. of Can. Law Teachers 1955-56; Delta Kappa Epsilon; Freemason; United Church; Club: Rotary; Home: 10925-85th Ave., Edmonton, Alta. T6G 0W3

BOWLAND, John P., M.Sc., Ph.D.; educator; b. Portage la Prairie, Man. 10 Feb. 1924; s. Herbert John and Gertrude Evelyn (Patterson) B.; e. Univ. of Man. B.S.G. (Agric.) 1945; Wash. State Univ. M.Sc. 1947; Univ. of Wis. Ph.D. 1949; m. Helen May; d. Alan Campbell, Brandon,

Man. 28 May 1946; two d. Margaret Anne Lytviak, Dorothy Lynne; DEAN OF AGRIC. AND FORESTRY, UNIV. OF ALBERTA since 1975; joined present Univ. 1949, Asst. Prof. of Animal Husbandry 1949, Assoc. Prof. of Animal Nutrition 1954, Prof. since 1962; sabbatical leave Nat. Inst. for Research in Dairying, Reading, Eng. 1959-60, Swiss Fed. Tech. Inst. Zürich 1968-69 and Australasia 1981; participant several missions Latin Am., S.E. Asia and Peoples' Repub. of China; rec'd Borden Award Nutrition Soc. Can. 1966; Fellow, Am. Assn. Advanc. Science; Agric. Inst. Can.; Distinguished Service Award, West. Sec., American Soc. of Animal Services, 1977; United Church of Can.; recreations: skiing, swimming, philately; Home: 11243-79 Ave., Edmonton, Alta. T6G 0P2

BOWLBY, Bradford Hugh Blaikie, Q.C., M.A.; b. Toronto, Ont., 20 June 1916; s. Allington Tupper, Q.C. and Mary (Blaikie) B.; e. Univ. Toronto Schs.; Trinity Coll., Univ. Toronto, B.A. 1938, M.A. 1939; m. Anne Elizabeth, d. William Otter Morris, 18 Sept. 1948; children: David Bradford Tupper, Margaret Jane, Sarah Elizabeth; PARTNER, BOWLBY & BOWLBY; Chrmn., Assessment Review Court 1976-; Fed. Organizer, P.Cons. Party 1965; Chrmn., Inter Church Comte. on Legal Affairs; read law with Bowlby, Macdonald & Co., Toronto, Ont.; called to Bar of Ont., 1942; cr. Q.C., 1954; mem., Candn. Bar Assn.; Co. York Law Assn.; Toronto Central P.C. Assn. (Pres. 1955); Pres. St. Paul's P.C. Assn. 1963; P. Cons.; Anglican; recreations: curling, boating; Clubs: R.C.Y.C.; Toronto Cricket, Skating & Curling; Albany; Lawyer's; Home: 115 Glenforest Rd., Toronto, Ont. M4N 2A1; Office: 330 Bay St., Toronto, Ont. M5H 2S8

BOWLBY, John Douglas, Q.C.; b. Hamilton, Ont., 12 Sept. 1926; s. late Mr. Justice Charles William Reid and Elsie (Dixon) B.; e. Westdale Coll., Hamilton, Ont.; Pickering Coll., Newmarket, Ont.; McMaster Univ.; Osgoode Hall Law Sch., Toronto, Ont.; m. Louise Elizabeth, d. late Ferdinand Haas; children: Jennifer Christine, Carolyn, John Dixon; SR. PARTNER, BOWLBY, LUCHAK, MARTINO, THOMAN, LOFCHIK; read law with Mason Foulds Arnup Walter Weir & Boeckh and with John J. Robinette, Q.C.; called to Bar of Ont. 1951; cr. Q.C. 1964; el. Bencher, Law Soc. of Upper Can., 1966, 1971, 1975, 1979; apptd. Treas. of the Law Soc. of Up. Can., 1980; upon grad. joined father's firm; engaged exclusively in trial work both criminal and civil; Pres., Hamilton E. Lib. Assn.; Past Pres., Hamilton Lawyers Club; Delta Upsilon; Liberal; United Church; recreation: golf; Clubs: Hamilton; Hamilton Golf & Country; Home: 4114 Lakeshore, Burlington, Ont. L7L 1A1; Office: 46 Jackson St. E., Hamilton, Ont. L8N 1L1

BOWLBY, Kathleen E., B.A.; b. Aylesford, N.S., 5 Apl. 1904; d. Norman I. and Eunice R. (Sanford) B.; e. Pub. and High Schs., Aylesford, N.S.; Acadia Univ., B.A., 1923; Librarian, Dept. Indian Affairs & Northern Development, 1959-69; Nat. Secy., U.N. Assn. in Can., 1948-59; Teacher of Math. and Science, Alma Coll., St. Thomas, Ont., 1923-26; Branksome Hall, Toronto, 1926-37; Principal, Ottawa Ladies' Coll., 1937-42; Wartime Tech. Asst., Bureau of Mines, 1942-46; Registrar, Carleton Coll., Ottawa, 1946-48; Home: 16 Sandridge Rd., Ottawa, Ont. K1K 0A8

BOWLEN, Patrick Dennis, B.B.A., J.D.; lawyer; executive; b. Prairie du Chien, Wisconsin, 18 Feb. 1944; s. Paul Dennis and Arvella (Woods) B.; e. Campion Jesuit High Sch., Prairie du Chien; Univ. of Oklahoma Sch. of Business, B.B.A. 1966; Univ. of Okla. Sch. of Law grad. J.D. 1968; PRESIDENT, BOWLEN HOLDINGS LTD. 1979-; read law with Saucier, Jones, Calgary, Alta.; called to the Bar of Alta. 1969, practising law with Saucier, Jones 1969-70; Asst. to the Pres. of Regent Drilling Ltd. 1970-71; Pres., Batoni-Bowlen Enterprises Ltd. 1971-79; mem. Law Soc. Alta.; Candn. Bar Assn.; Young Presidents Organ.;

R. Catholic; recreations: golf, skiing, surfing; Clubs: Mayfair Golf & Country; Edmonton Petroleum; Outrigger Canoe (Honolulu); Home: 28A, 11135-83 Ave., Edmonton, Alta. T6G 2C6; Office: 21st Floor, 10201 Jasper Ave., Edmonton, Alta. T5J 3N7

BOYCE, Harry MacKenzie, B. Com.; company director; b. Phoenix, B.C., 28 Sept. 1907; s. John S. and Annie M. (Mackenzie) B.; e. McGill Univ., B.Com. 1930; m. Dorothy Jane, d. Gordon Farrell, Vancouver, B.C., 15 May 1937; children: Farrell M., K. Jane; Dir. Yorkshire Trust Company; Dir. (former Vice-Pres. and Treas.), B.C. Telephone Co.; Okanagan Telephone Co.; Past Chrmn., Vancouver Pub. Library Bd.; Past Pres., Community Chest & Council, Vancouver; Clubs: Canadian (Past Pres.); Vancouver; Home: 1830 S.W. Marine Dr., Vancouver, B.C. V6P 6B2; Office: 900 West Pender St., Vancouver, B.C. V6C 1L1

BOYD, Dawson C.; executive (retired); b. Moose Jaw, Sask., 4 Oct. 1911; s. James Allen and Edith Evelyn B.; e. Belleville (Ont.) Vocational Sch.; m. Margaret Irene, d. Richard Thomas Graham, 31 Oct. 1936; children: David Richard, Paul Dawson; PRESIDENT, INTERNATIONAL HARDWARE OF CANADA LTD. since 1972; Dir., Moira Investments Ltd.; joined the Corbin Lock Co. (predecessor firm), Time Study and Prod. Control 1933, Supt., Belleville, Ont. 1935, Sales Rep. 1937, Procurement Offr., War Material 1939, Sales Rep. 1945, W. Can. Sales Mang. 1952; Gen. Sales Mgr., Russwin Lock Div. of International Hardware Co. 1956, Gen Sales Mgr., Corbin Lock Div. 1958; apptd. Vice-Pres. and Gen Mgr. present Co. (on change of name from Corbin Lock Co. of Canada Ltd.) 1962; served as Flight Lt., R.C.A.F. (Air Cadet); mem. (Toronto Chapter) Am. Hardware Consultants; Freemason; P. Conservative; Protestant; recreations: golf, fishing, hunting; Club: The Belleville; Home: R.R. 1, Carrying Place, Ont. K0K 1L0

BOYD, James Henderson, R.C.A., F.I.A.L.; artist; b. Ottawa, Ont. 16 Dec. 1928; s. William Abercrombie and Mary (Henderson) B.; e. Ottawa Tech. High Sch.; Art Students League N.Y.; Nat. Acad. N.Y.; Contemporaries Workshop N.Y.; Vignette Engraver Canadian Bank Note 1946-52; free-lance CBC; Resident Artist Univ. of W. Ont. 1967-69, mem. Senate Hon. Degree Comte. 1968-69, Chrmn. Art Acquisitions Comte. and Curator Art Coll.; Head of Printmaking Ont. Coll. of Art 1970-71, Faculty mem. 1971-73; part-time lectr. Univ. of Ottawa 1973-81; Condordia Univ. 1976-77; rec'd First Prize 1st Nat. Print Show Vancouver; Best Foreign Artists Venezuela, Chile; executed mural Univ. of Ottawa Macdonald Bldg.; carved doors Campbellton Lib.; Maritime Museum, Summerside, P.E.I.; PSAC Bldg. Ottawa; rep. in various perm. colls. incl. Nat. Gallery Can.; Museum of Modern Art N.Y.; Victoria & Albert Museum; Lugano Art Gallery; Art Gallery Ont.; Nat. Art Gallery S. Africa; mem. Accademia Italia delle Arti & del Lavoro (with Gold Medal); Candn. Artists Representation (Spokesperson, Local Rep. Ottawa 1978; Vice Spokesperson Ont. 1974-75); Home: 481 Sunnyside Ave., Ottawa, Ont. K1P 0S8; Office: (P.O. Box 2400 Stn. D.) Ottawa, Ont. K1P 5W5.

BOYD, Liona, B.Mus.; musician; classical guitarist; b. London, Eng.; d. John Haig and Eileen (Hancock) B.; came to Can. 1957; e. Kipling Coll. Inst. 1967; Univ. of Toronto B.Mus. 1972; Eli Kassner Guitar Acad.; studied with Alexandre Lagoya, internat. concert artist and T.V. personality; 5 long playing records "The Guitar", "Liona", "Miniatures for Guitar", "The First Lady of the Guitar", (CBS) "Liona Boyd with Andrew Davis conducting Eng. Chamber Orchestra" (CBS) sound tract to "I am a Guitar"; record with Chet Atkins "The First Nashville Guitar Quartet" 1979; TV performances incl. CBC Superspecial "Liona" 1978; opening act for Gordon Lightfoot; compositions and arrangements sound tract to CBC TV Drama 1979 rec'd Juno Award 1978; Vanier Award

1979; mem. Am. Fed. Musicians; Candn. Assn. Publishers & Authors; Am. Assn. Publishers & Authors.

BOYD, Robert A. Eng., B.A., B.Sc.; retired public utility executive; b. Sherbrooke, Que., 21 June 1918; e. Ecole Polytechnique de Montréal, B.Sc. (Mech. & Elect. Engn.) 1943; m. Claire Letendre, 1943; children: Robert, André, Louise, Suzanne, Daniel, Muriel; President & Chief Extve. Offr., Hydro-Québec to 1981; Chmn, bd. of dir., Nouveler; mem. bd. of dir. Hydro-Quebec, Société d'énergie de la Baie James; Hydro-Qué. Internat.; Sidbec; Sidbec-Dosco; Candn. Electrical Ass.; Churchill Falls (Labrador) Corp.; mem. Inst. of Electrical and Electronics Engineers; The Conference Bd., Inc.; The Conference Bd. in Can.; Ordre des Ingénieurs du Québec; Holder of hon. doctorates from Univ. de Montréal, Concordia Univ., Univ. de Sherbrooke; recreations: hunting, golf, winter sports; Clubs: Mount Royal; St. Denis; Office: 75 Dorchester Blvd. W., Montreal, Que. H2Z 1A4

BOYD, Winnett, B.A.Sc., P.Eng.; b. Prestatyn, N. Wales, 17 Oct. 1916; s. Winnett Wornibe (Candn.) and Marjorie Sterne (St. George) B. (Am.); came to Can. 1917; e. Trinity Coll. Sch., Port Hope, Ont.; Somers Coll., Bermuda; Jarvis Coll. Inst., Toronto, Ont.; Univ. of Toronto, B.A.Sc., 1939; Mass. Inst. Tech. post grad. studies; m. Jean Winnifred Ransom, d. Mrs. N. C. Sutherland, Town of Mount Royal, Que., 30 May 1942; two d., Wendy Susan Lee Lloyd, Pamela Ann Boyd; PRESIDENT, WINNETT BOYD LTD. 1981-; Teaching asst., Mass. Inst. Tech., 1939-40; Jr. Engr., Demerara Bauxite Co., Brit. Guiana, 1940-41; Engr., Aluminum Co. of Canada Ltd., Montreal, 1941-42; Shawinigan Falls, P.Q., 1942-43; with Nat. Research Council, 1943-44, studying jet engines in England; with Turbo Research Ltd., 1944-46 (i/c Engine Design Sec., 1945-46); joined A. V. Roe Can. Ltd., Gas Turbine Engn. Divn., 1946-50; Chief Designer, 1946-48; Asst. Chief Engr. and Chief Designer, 1948-50; Sr. Partner, Winnett Boyd Associates, Pres., Winnett Boyd Ltd., 1951-59; Pres., Arthur D. Little of Can. Ltd. 1959-81; 1951-57, Chief Mech. Engr., in charge NRU reactor design for the C. D. Howe Co. Ltd.; during period of employment with Turbo Research Ltd., and A. V. Roe Can. Ltd., undertook and completed design of Canada's first jet engine the "Chinook", and later the "Orenda"; since April 1956 conceived, designed and promoted the Daniels-Boyd Nuclear Steam Generator (world rights acquired by Arthur D. Little Inc.); mem., Assn. of Prof. Engrs. Ont.; joined R.C.N.V.R., Sept. 1943 as Sub. Lieut. (E), and seconded to Nat. Research Council, Nov. 1943 to engage in jet engine work in Eng.; def. cand. for York-Scarborough, g.e. Oct. 1972; founded BMG Publishing Limited 1974; currently promoting patented back-pedalling brake for multi-speed bicycles; Anglican; recreations: riding, skiing, swimming, cycling; Clubs: Toronto; Toronto and North York Hunt; Lambton Golf & Country; Montreal Badminton & Squash; Home: 38 Restwell Crescent, Willowdale, Ont. M2K 2A3; Office: Flexmaster Bldg., 36 Shelley Rd., Richmond Hill, Ont. L4C 5G3

BOYLE, Vice-Admiral Douglas Seaman, C.M.M., C.D.; b. Revelstoke, B.C. 29 Nov. 1923; s. Allan Douglas and Suzanne Dorothy B.; e. Schs. Revelstoke, B.C.; Royal Naval Coll. Dartmouth and Conway, Eng.; Imp. Defence Coll.; m. Janet Black Thompson 30 April 1943; children: Beth, Isobel, Heather, Margaret, Patricia; entered RCN as Cadet 1941 subsequently serving on destroyer HMCS "Chaudiere"; joined staff RCN Coll., Royal Roads, B.C. 1945 and subsequently Navig. Direction Specialist U.K., Naval HQ Can. and Pacific Coast with service on HMCS "Ontario"; promoted Lt.-Commdr. 1951 and apptd. Navig. Offr. HMCS "Magnificent" 1952; joined staff of Naval Member Candn. Jt. Staff, London, Eng. 1953, promoted Commander and later returning to Can. as Depy. Dir. Naval Training; following two commands at sea (HMCS "Athabaskan" and "Saguenay") served as Asst. Chief Staff (Training and Adm.) Staff Flag Offr. Pacific Coast; promoted Capt. and apptd. Commdr. Fourth Candn. Escort Sqdn. 1962; Dir. Naval Training Naval HQ Sept. 1964; Dir. Sr. Appts. (Navy) Dec. 1964; promoted Commodore and apptd. Dir. Gen. Postings and Careers 1966; Commdr. Standing Naval Force Atlantic 1970; Dir. Gen. Personnel and Production 1971; promoted Rear-Admiral May 1972 and apptd. Chief of Personnel; Commander, Maritime Command 1973; promoted Vice-Admiral 1975; retired 1977; presently Requirements Manager, Scan Marine Inc.; mem. Bd., World Press Digest; Anglican; recreation: boating; Home: 28 Queensline Dr., Nepean, Ont. K2H 7H9

BOYLE, Harry J., O.C. (1977); D.Litt.; executive and writer; b. St. Augustine, Ont., 7 Oct. 1915; s. William A. and Mary Madeleine (Leddy) B.; e. Wingham (Ont.) High Sch.; St. Jerome's Coll., Kitchener, Ont.; m. Marion, d. Michael McCaffrey, 3 Jan. 1937; children: Patricia, Michael; publisher of small mag. 1934; subsequently freelance writer and newspaper stringer in W. Ont., especially for "The London Free Press" and "The Toronto Globe and Mail"; Radio Stn. CKNX, Wingham, Ont., 1936-41; "The Stratford Beacon-Herald", 1941-42; joined CBC as Farm Commentator, 1942; became Supvr., Farm Broadcasts, Program Dir., Trans-Can. Network and Radio Network Supvr. of Features; Dir., Nat. Farm Radio Forum, 1942-46; Visiting Fellow, Inst. of Candn. Studies, Carleton Univ. 1968-69; mem. Faculty, Banff Sch. of Fine Arts; radio credits incl.: "CBC Wednesday Night", "Assignment" and "Project" series; weekly columnist "The Toronto Telegram", 1957-68; Vice-chrmn. 1968-76, Chrmn., C.R.T.C. Comm. 1976-77; Columnist, Montreal Star 1978; mem. Ont. Arts. Council, 1979-; wrote no. of radio plays incl. "Strike" and "The Macdonalds of Oak Valley"; also stage play "The Inheritance" produced by Museum Theatre, Toronto, 1950; author of "Mostly in Clover" (essays), 1961; "Homebrew and Patches" (essays), 1963 (winner of Leacock Medal for Humour); "A Summer Burning" (novel), 1964; "With a Pinch of Sin" (novel), 1966; "Straws in the Wind" (essays) 1969; "The Great Canadian Novel" 1972; "Memories of a Catholic Boyhood" (novel) 1973; "The Luck of the Irish" (novel) 1975; John Drainie Award by Assn. Candn. Television and Radio Artists for his contrib. to broadcasting, 1970; winner, Leacock Medal for Humour 1975; Hon. D.Litt. Trent Univ. 1974 and Hon. Fellow of Lady Eaton Coll. there; Hon. L.L.D. (Concordia Univ.) 1978; named to Candn. Newspaper Hall of Fame 1979; Jack Chisholm Award, Candn. Film & TV Dir. Ass., 1980; Dir., The Vanier Inst.; Donwoods Inst.; mem., Ont. Arts Council 1980; Assoc., Executive Consultants Ltd., Ottawa.; R. Catholic; Club: Arts & Letters; Home: 12 Georgian Crt., Toronto, Ont. M4P 2J8

BOYLE, J. Allan; banker; b. Orillia, Ont., 10 May 1916; s. Mr. and Mrs. W. J. Boyle; e. Orillia (Ont.) Coll. Inst.; Univ. of W. Ont., Mang. Training Course; DIRECTOR, TORONTO-DOMINION BANK Dir.; Excelsior Life Insurance Co.; Costain Ltd.; Aetna Casualty Co. of Canada; Jannock Limited; Dir., Echo Bay Mines Ltd. joined the Bank, Orillia, Ont. 1934, serving subsequently at Toronto and N.Y., Special Rep. N.Y. 1956, Agent N.Y. 1964, Asst. Gen. Mgr. H.O. Internat. Div. 1966; Gen. Mgr. Adm. 1968, Depy. Chief Gen. Mgr. 1968; Exec. Vice-Pres. Chief Gen. Mgr. 1972; Pres. 1978; served with R.C.A.F. 1940-45; Candn. Bankers' Assn. (Pres. 1974-75); Past Pres. Can. Club of Toronto; Regtor Investments Ltd.; Exec. Vice-Pres. & Dir., Toronto-Dominion Centre Ltd.; Toronto-Dominion Centre West Ltd.; Dir. & mem. Exec. Comte., The C.K. Clarke Psychiatric Research Foundation; mem., Bd of Governors, York University; mem., Advisory Committee, Sch. of Bus. Admin., Univ. of W. Ontario; Toronto Redevelopment Adv. Council; recreations: golf, curling, bridge; Clubs: Bd. Trade Metrop. Toronto; Thornhill Country; Granite; York; Toronto Club; Sara Bay Country Club, Sarasota, Fla.; Office: Toronto-Dominion Centre, Toronto, Ont. M5K 1A2

BOYLE, R. W., M.A.Sc., Ph.D., F.R.S.C., F.R.G.S.(C); geochemist; b. Chatham Twp., Kent Co., Ont. 3 June 1920; s. Robert and Jane (Murray) B.; e. Univ. of Toronto, B.A.Sc. (Mining Geol.) 1949, M.A.Sc. 1950, Ph.D. (Geochem.) 1952; m. Marguerite Lois, d. Elgin Brown, Wallaceburg, Ont., 3 Nov. 1945; children: Heather Ann, Daniel Robert; PRINCIPAL RESEARCH SCIENTIST, SPECIAL PROJECTS, GEOL. SURVEY CAN. (formerly Sr. Geologist); joined the Geol. Survey of Canada, 1952; served overseas during 2nd World War with R.C.A. in U.K., France, Belgium, Holland, Germany, 1939-45; mem., Prof. Inst. Public Service; Mineral. Assn. Can.; Geochem. Soc.; Soc. Econ. Geol. (Councillor, 1980-83); Candn. Inst. Mining & Metall.; Internat. Assn. Genesis of Ore Deposits (Vice-Pres.); Geol. Assn. Can.; Assn. of Exploration Geochem., Pres. 1975-76; Internat. Assn. Geochem. and Cosmochem.; rec'd. Barlow Mem. Medal, Candn. Inst. Mining and Metall. 1967; Willet G. Miller Medal, Roy. Soc. Can. 1971; Pub. Service Comn. of Can. Merit Award 1971; Distinguished Lecturer, Can. Institute of Mining and Metall., 1980-81; author of "The Geology, Geochemistry and Origin of the Gold Deposits of the Yellowknife District, N.W.T."; "Geology, Geochemistry and Origin of the Lead-Zinc-Silver Deposits of the Keno Hill-Galena Hill area, Yukon Territory"; "Geochemistry of Silver and its Deposits"; "Geochemistry of Gold and its Deposits"; "The Geology, geochemistry, and origin of the barite, manganese, and lead-zinc-copper-silver deposits of the Walton-Cheverie area, N.S."; over 100 papers in prof. journs.; Anglican; recreation: photography; Home: 2024 Neepawa Ave., Ottawa, Ont. K2A 3L6; Office: 601 Booth St., Ottawa, Ont. K1A 0E8

BOYLE, Willard Sterling, M.Sc., Ph.D., F.A.P.S.; physicist; association executive; b. Amherst, N.S. 9 Aug. 1924; s. Ernest Sterling and Bernice Teresa (Dewar) B.; e. Lower Can. Coll. 1942; McGill Univ. B.Sc. 1947, M.Sc. 1948, Ph.D. (Physics) 1950; m. Aileen Elizabeth d. Alfred Leslie Joyce 15 June 1946; children: Robert, Cynthia, David, Pamela; PRESIDENT AND DIR., ATLANTIC RESEARCH ASSOCIATES; Asst. Prof. Royal Mil. Coll. Kingston 1951-53; mem. Tech. Staff Bell Labs 1953-62; Dir. Space Science Centre Bell Communications 1962-64; Dir. and Extve. Dir. Semicontor & Integrated Circuit Devel. Bell Labs 1964-74, Extve. Dir. Research on Lightwave Communication, Quantum Electronics, Digital Electronics 1974-79; Consultant to govt. and industry on mang. science and technol. in affiliation with Atlantic Research Associates 1979; served with RCNVR 1942-46, Fleet Air Arm, Pilot Operations with RN, rank Lt.; author over 40 tech. papers electronics, solid state physics, plasma physics; holds 16 patents incl. Fundamental Patents on Charge Coupled Devices and Semi Conductor Junction Laser; recipient Ballantine Medal Franklin Inst.; Morris Liebman Award Inst. Elect. & Electronic Engrs.; el. to Nat. Acad. Engn. 1973; Fellow, Inst. Elect. & Electronic Engrs.; mem. Am. Assn. Advanc. Science; Royal Candn. Legion; recreation: sailing; Club: Corinthian; Home: (P.O. Box 179) Wallace, N.S. B0K 1Y0; Office: (P.O. Box 202) Wallace, N.S. B0K 1Y0.

BOYNTON, Herbert Welch Beames; company president; b. Toronto, Ont., 30 Oct. 1902; s. late John Herbert and Maude Elizabeth (Fellowes) B.; e. Toronto Pub. Schs.; Oakwood Coll. Inst., Toronto; m. Eileen Ruth, d. late William Lutton, Toronto, Ont., 1931; one s. John William; CHRMN. BD., TORONTO MUTUAL LIFE INSURANCE CO. (Estbd. 1935) since 1972; Vice-Pres., United Stationery Co. Ltd.; on Sales Staff, Underwood Ltd., Toronto, Ont., 1920-53; Dir. of present Co. since 1935, Vice-Pres. 1942-62; Pres. 1962; Dir., St. Bernard's Convalescent Hosp.; Mgr., Argonaut Jr. and Sr. Football Teams, 1927-41; Anglican; recreations: boating, sports; Clubs: Granite; Argonaut Football; Argonaut Rowing (Life mem.); Home: 95 Thorncliffe Pk. Dr., apt. 4102, Toronto, Ont. M4H 1L7; Office: c/o United Stationery Co. Ltd., 30 Production Dr., Toronto, Ont.

BRACE, John H., B.A.Sc., P.Eng.; industrialist; b. Toronto, Ont., 21 May 1926; s. George Arnold and Gwendolyn Julia (Welham) B.; e. John Ross Robertson Pub. Sch., Toronto: 1931-37; Univ. of Toronto Schs., 1937-44; Univ. of Toronto, B.A.Sc. (Mech. Engn.) 1949; Harvard Bus. Sch. (AMP); m. Alma Josephine, d. William Alexander Piitz, 8 July 1950; children: Paul, Janette, James; PRESIDENT, HONEYWELL LIMITED since 1974 (Dir., Operations Honeywell Europe 1971-74); Honeywell Controls Ltd.; joined Hinde and Dauch Paper Company as Indust. Engr., 1949-50; joined Honeywell Controls Ltd. as Indust. Engr., 1950-51; apptd. Foreman, 1951-52; Asst. to Factory Mgr., 1953-54; Plant Supt., 1954-57; Factory Mgr., 1957-64; Operations Mgr., 1964-66; Vice Pres., Adm. 1966-71; served with R.C.N.V.R., 1944-45; Dir., Boys Clubs of Can.; Candn. Standards Assn.; Trustee, Hospital Council of Metro Toronto; mem., Assn. Prof. Engrs. Ont.; R. Catholic; Office: The Honeywell Centre, 155 Gordon Baker Rd., Willowdale, Ont. M2H 3N7

BRACKEN, Alexander McKnight, A.B., J.D., LL.D.; manufacturer; b. Toronto, Ont., 7 May 1908; s. Thomas Edward and Margaret Acheson (McKnight) B.; e. Muncie (Ind.) High Sch., 1925; Ball State Teachers Coll.; Univ. of Mich., A.B. 1929, J.D. 1931; LL.D., Ball State Univ., Ind. State Univ., Anderson Coll.; m. Rosemary Wright, d. Frank Clayton Ball 14 July 1932; children: Frank Alexander, Thomas Ball, Elizabeth Ann, William McKnight, Alexander Elliott; CHRMN. EMERITUS OF BD., DIR. AND MEM. OF EXTVE. COMTE., BALL CORP.; Chrmn. Bd. of Dirs. and mem. Extve. Comte., Merchants National Bank of Muncie; Pres. and Dir., Muncie and Western Railroad Co.; Dir. and Offr., Ball Brothers Research Corp.; called to Bar of Ind. 1931; mem. Bar U.S. Supreme Court 1945; assoc. with Bracken, Gray & DeFur, Muncie, Ind., 1931-33; joined present Co. as Legal Counsel 1933; Pres. Emeritus Bd. of Trustees, Ball State Univ.; Trustee, Carleton Coll.; Vice Pres. and Dir., Ball Bros. Foundation; Pres. and Dir., George and Frances Ball Foundation; Dir. Emeritus, Ball Mem. Hosp. Assn.; Past Pres. and mem., Muncie Chamber Comm.; Hon. mem., Muncie Jr. Chamber Comm.; Pres., Bd. of Trustees, YMCA; Past Dir., Un. Fund Muncie; Past mem. Extve. Council, Boy Scouts; served on various comtes. Epis. Diocese Indiapolis and as mem. Bd. of Proctors of Cathedral; former mem. Vestry and Sr. Warden, Grace Epis. Ch.; mem., Am. Bar Assn.; Ind. State Bar Assn.; Del. Co. Bar Assn.; Beta Theta Pi; Clubs: Rotary (Past Pres.); Delaware Country; Leland Golf; Columbia (Indianapolis); Indiana Soc. Chicago; University (Chicago); Lawyers' & Presidents' Univ. of Mich.; Home: 2200 W. Berwyn Rd., Muncie, Ind. 47304; Office: Suite 520, Merchants National Bank Bldg., 100 S. Mulberry St., Muncie, Ind. 47305.

BRACKEN, Harry McFarland, M.A., Ph.D.; university professor; b. Yonkers, N.Y. 12 March 1926; came to Can. 1966; s. Harry S. and Grace (McFarland) B.; e. Trinity Coll., Hartford B.A. 1949; Johns Hopkins Univ. M.A. 1954; Univ. of Iowa Ph.D. 1956; div. Eva Maria Laufkotter 24 Dec. 1949; children: Christopher, Timothy; PROF. OF PHILOSOPHY, MCGILL UNIV. since 1966; Instr., Univ. of Iowa 1955-57, Asst. Prof. 1957-61; Assoc. Prof. Univ. of Minnesota (Mpls.) 1961-63; Prof. Arizona State Univ. 1963-66; Prof. Phil. Univ. of Calif. (San Diego) 1970; Visiting prof. of Phil., Trinity Coll., Dublin; Univ. of Metaphysics, Univ. Coll., Dublin; Natl. Univ. of Ireland 1972-73; 1979-80; served with U.S. Navy, Pacific theatre, 1943-46; author of "The Early Reception of Berkeley's Immaterialism: 1710-1733", 1959 (rev. 1965); other writings incl. articles on seventeenth and eighteenth century philosophers (Descartes, Melebranche, Bayle, Locke, Hume, Reid), and on the philosophical aspects of the work of Noam Chomsky; rec'd. Acad. Freedom Award, Arizona Civil Liberties Union, 1966; J.K. Segal Found. for Jewish Culture, Educ. Award, 1972; mem., Am., Candn. and Irish Philosophical Assn.; Am. and Candn. Societes for eighteenth century studies; Candn. Assn. for Irish Studies;

Office: 1001 Sherbrooke St. W., Montreal, Que. H3A 1G5.

BRADBURY, Louis Stanley; business executive; b. Bay Roberts, Nfld. 12 June 1913; s. late Emily (Parsons) and late William Stanley B.; m. Margaret Paula, d. late William Brophy, 10 Oct. 1938; children: William, Robert, Jean (Mrs. K. W. Crawford); CHRMN., CANADIAN SALTFISH CORP. 1974-79; joined Nfld. Fisheries Bd. 1936, for several years its W. Indies Rep. and later Extve. Secy.; Dir. Nfld. Fisheries, Can. Dept. Fisheries 1949; Chief Supvr. (Nfld.) and Chrmn. Nfld. Fisheries Bd. 1952; trans. to Ottawa 1955 to organize Indust. Devel. Br., Fisheries & Marine Service; has served as mem. Nfld. Fisheries Loan Bd.; Candn. Commr. Internat. Comn. for N.W. Atlantic Fisheries; Can. del. to United Nations (FAO, Fisheries); Office: 320 Queen St., Ste. 2100, Ottawa, Ontario K1R 5A3

BRADEN, Bernard; actor; b. Vancouver, B.C., 16 May 1916; s. Dr. Edwin B.; e. Magee High Sch., Vancouver, B.C.; m. Barbara Kelly, Vancouver, B.C., 1942; children: Christopher, Kelly, Karma; auditioned for radio as a singer, stn. CJOR, Vancouver, B.C., 1935; serious illness ended this career so he turned to writing, acting and producing; worked in Vancouver, B.C., with Andrew Allan of the C.B.C., and the comedian Alan Young; went to Toronto, Ont., with Young in 1943 as part of Buckingham Show; contrib. to and acted in C.B.C.'s Stage Annuals; wrote and produced the popular radio serial, "John and Judy", and broadcast a regular week-day program called "Bernie Braden Tells a Story"; was also heard as "Gabby", the old timer on the "Wayne and Shuster Show"; now engaged in similar work in Eng.; recreations: golf, dialects; Address: c/o B.B.C., London, Eng.

BRADEN, Mrs. Bernard — see: Kelly, Barbara.

BRADFIELD, John R., CC., LL.D.; industrialist; HON. CHAIRMAN, NORANDA MINES LTD.; Home: 151 Dunvegan Road, Toronto, Ont. M5P 2N8; Office: Commerce Court W., Box 45, Toronto, Ont. M5L 1B6

BRADFORD, William Elwood, B.Com., F.C.G.A.; banker; b. Montreal, Que. 14 Oct. 1933; s. Elwood J. and Jessie (Murray) B.; e. Concordia Univ. Montreal B.Com. 1960; Cert. Gen. Acct. 1960; m. Dolores d. late J. A. MacDonnell 6 Nov. 1954; children: Michael, Gary, Sandra, Maureen, Laurie, Joseph, Janet; PRES., BANK OF MONTREAL 1981-; Dir., Bank of Montreal; joined Northern Electric Co. Ltd. 1950-59; Canada Iron Foundries Ltd. 1959-62; Asst. Controller, Reynolds Extrusion Co. Ltd. 1962-66; Vice Pres. and Controller, Churchill Falls (Labrador) Corp. Ltd. 1967-70; Vice Pres. and Sr. Financial Offr. for Brinco Group of Co's 1970-74; Extve. Vice Pres. Finance present Bank 1975, Extve. Vice Pres. Finance and Adm. 1976; Extve. Vice Pres. and Depy. Gen. Mgr. Domestic Banking 1978; Exec. Vice Pres. and Gen. Mgr. Domestic Banking 1979; Extve. Vice Pres. and Chief Gen. Mgr. 1980; Dir., Sunnybrook Medical Centre; Chrmn., Extve. Council, Can. Bankers' Assn.; mem. Cert. Gen. Accts. Assn. Ont.; Financial Extves. Inst.; Bd. Trade Metrop. Toronto; mem., Adv. Council, Vanier College; Adv. Comm. to Rector on Public Affairs, Concordia Univ.; R. Catholic; recreations: tennis, squash, golf, skiing, hunting, fishing; Clubs: Mount Royal (Montreal); M.A.A.A.; Cambridge Club, Adelaide, National, Lambton Golf (Toronto), Ontario Racquet; Home: 1333 Watersedge Rd., Mississauga, Ont. L5J 1A3; Office: (P.O. Box 4) First Bank Tower, First Canadian Pl., Toronto, Ont. M5X 1C6.

BRADLEY, Richard Alan, M.A.; educator; b. Portland, Dorset, Eng., 6 Oct. 1925; s. Reginald Livingstone and Phyllis Mary (Richardson) B.; e. Milner Court, Kent, Eng.; Marlborough Coll. (Wiltshire, Eng.); Trinity Coll., Univ. of Oxford, M.A.; m. Mary Anne Vicary, 23 Nov. 1971; one s., two ds. (of former marriage); Asst. Master,

Dulwich Coll., London, Eng. 1949; Asst. Master and Head Hist. Dept., Tonbridge Sch., Kent, Eng. 1950-66; Head Master, St. Edward's Sch., Oxford, Eng. 1966-71; Head Master, Ridley Coll., St. Catharines, Ont. 1971-81; Head Master, The Rivers School, Weston, Mass.; served in 2nd World War with Royal Marines 1943-46; Comnd. and served in India and Java with 34th Amphibian Support Regt.; Anglican; recreations: sports, drama, mountaineering; Clubs: Vincent's (Oxford, Eng.); University (Toronto); Public Schools (London, Eng.); Oxford and Bermondsey (U.K.); Address: The Rivers School, 333 Winter St., Weston, Mass. 02193.

BRADLOW, John, M.B.A.; banker; b. Johannesburg, South Africa 10 Aug. 1943; e. Univ. of Witwatersrand, B. Comm.; Harvard, M.B.A.; m. Brenda Merle 14 June 1969; children: Richard and Michael; SR. VICE PRES. PROJECT FINANCING, BANK OF MONTREAL; mem. Inst. of Chartered Accountants of Ont.; Home: 481 St. Clements Ave., Toronto, Ontario M5N 1M3; Office: 1 First Canadian Place, Toronto, Ont. M5X 1A1

BRADY, Alexander, O.C. (1970), Ph.D., D.Litt., LL.D., F.R.S.C.; university professor; b. Kilkenny, Ireland, 26 Jan. 1895; s. Samuel and Anne (Moore) B.; e. Univ. Coll., Univ. of Toronto, B.A. 1919; M.A., Ph.D. 1926; Balliol Coll., Oxford, 1919-21; EMERITUS PROF. OF POLITICAL ECON., UNIV. OF TORONTO; Prof. of History, Wesley Coll., Winnipeg, Man., 1921-24; author of "Life of Thomas d'Arcy McGee", 1925; "William Huskisson and Liberal Reform", 1928, 2nd. ed., 1967; "Canada", in "Modern World Series", 1932; "Democracy in the Dominion's", 3rd ed., 1958; Introd. to "Essays on Politics and Society" by John Stuart Mill, 1977; has contrib. to the "Encyc. Brit."; "Cambridge Hist. of the Brit. Empire"; "Encyc. of the Soc. Sciences"; has also written articles appearing in "Round Table", "Can. Journ. of Econ. and Pol. Science", "American Political Science Review"; etc.; rec'd Innis-Gerin Medal of Royal Soc. Can. 1969; Hon. mem. of the Candn. Inst. Internat. Affairs; Anglican; Home: 147 Boulton Drive, Toronto, Ont. M4V 2V5

BRADY, Frank Patrick, Q.C., B.C.L.; textile manufacturer; b. Montreal, Que. 8 Feb. 1923; s. Hugh F. and Catherine (O'Connor) B.; e. McGill Univ. pre-Engn., Arts, B.C.L. 1949; m. Grace Adeline d. late Thomas Bamford 2 Dec. 1944; children: Thomas Erskine Frank, Timothy Wesley John; SR. VICE PRES. CORPORATE SERVICES, DOMINION TEXTILE INC. since 1979; called to Bar of Que. 1949; cr. Q.C. 1968; law practice Quinlan, Colas, Carignan & Brady 1949-57; Legal Counsel present Co. 1951, Asst. Corporate Secy. 1955, Asst. Vice Pres. Mfg. 1960, Mgr. indust. Relations 1964, Gen. Counsel 1969, Vice Pres. and Gen. Counsel 1974; Past Chrmn. Business Linguistic Centre Montreal; Dir. and Chrmn. of Bd., Candn. Textiles Inst.; mem. Task Force Textiles & Clothing Fed. Govt.; Co-chrmn., Perm. Adv. Comte. Min. of Indust. Trade & Comm.; Past Chrmn. Que. Div. Candn. Mfrs. Assn.; mem. Bar Prov. Que.; served with RCN 1942-45; R. Catholic; recreations: golf, sailing, skiing; Clubs: Mount Stephen; Royal Montreal Golf; Pointe Claire Yacht; Home: 114 Bathurst Ave., Pointe Claire, Que.; Office: 1950 Sherbrooke St. W., Montreal, Que.

BRADY, George Robert; transportation executive; b. Baskatong, Que., 22 June 1911; s. Robert Malcolm and Mary Elizabeth (Wolfendale) B.; e. Ottawa (Ont.) Public and Tech. Sch.; Urwick-Orr (England) Management Inst.; m. Helen, d. late Adam McGregor, 6 Jan. 1939; children: Mrs. Patrick McCue (Nancy), Michael Charles, Sheila Elizabeth; former Gen. Mgr., Ottawa Transportation Commission, retired 1976; joined staff of Ottawa Electric Rly. Co. (predecessor Co.) as Office Boy, 1939; apptd. Dir. of Claims & Safety, 1947 and reorgan. that Dept.; Dir., Assoc. Bd., Ottawa YM-YWCA; Dir., John Howard Soc.; Bd. of Manag., St. Giles Presb. Ch.; mem., Ottawa Bd. Trade; Canadian Transit Assn. (Pres. 1964-65;

Chrmn. of Claims and Safety Comte., 1951-54); Anglican; recreations: skiing, fishing, art; Club: Kiwanis (Dir.); Home: 290 Holmwood Ave., Ottawa, Ont. K1S 2R3

BRADY, Patrick E.H., B.A.; management consultant; b. Montreal, Que., 9 Jan. 1917; s. William Charles and Rose (Hearty) B.; e. Pub. Sch., Montreal; High Sch., N. Que.; Queen's Univ.; m. Jean, d. H.H.J. Nesbitt, 16 May 1942; five children; PRES. AND CHIEF EXTVE. OFFR., P.E.H. BRADY CONSULTANTS LIMITED, Housing and Mang. Consultants, since 1968; Pres., J.B.T. Properties Ltd.; Chrmn. Torgroup; Pres. Brady Fin. Group; Assoc., J. B. Sparling Co. Montreal; former Extve. Dir., Ontario Assn. of Housing Authorities; Sr. Offr., Central Mortgage & Housing Corp., 1945-56; Asst. Dir. Housing, Ontario Housing Corp., 1956-59; Extve. Dir., Metrop. Toronto Housing Authority, 1959-64; Depy. Mang. Dir., Ont. Housing Corp. and Dir., Ontario Student Housing Corp., 1964-68; served in 2nd World War with 2nd Candn. Field Regt. in Italy, Germany, France; discharged with rank of Lieut., 1945; mem. Queen's Univ. Alumni Assn. (Past Vice-Pres.); Am. Nat. Assn. Housing and Redevel. Officials (Extve. Comte.); awarded Centennial Medal, 1967; National Housing Award, 1964; United Church; Clubs: Celebrity Club; Bd. of Trade of Metro Toronto; Boulevard; Home: 55 The Kingsway, Toronto, Ontario M8X 2T3; Office: 181 University Ave., Toronto, Ont. M5H 3M7

BRAIT, A.A., B.A.Sc., P.Eng.; telecommunications executive; b. Cooksville, Ont., 12 Dec. 1924; s. Otto and Adele Bassi) B.; e. Port Credit (Ont.) High Sch.; Univ. of Toronto, B.A.Sc. 1946; m. Margaret Rebecca, d. Samuel Norris, 2 Sept. 1950; one s., Richard; PRES. & CHIEF EXTVE. OFFR., NEWFOUNDLAND TEL. CO. LTD., since 1970; mem., Bd. of Mang., Trans Canada Tel. System, since 1970; joined Bell Canada in Toronto, 1946; held a variety of engn. positions with Bell until apptd. Chief Engr., Avalon Tel. Co., St. John's, Nfld., 1964; returned to Bell in 1966 and held several extve. positions in Montreal and Ottawa before returning to Nfld. in 1970; Dir., Candn. Cancer Soc.; mem., Assn. Prof. Engrs. Nfld.; St. John's Bd. Trade; Candn. Chamber Comm.; Past Pres., Candn. Telecommunications Carriers Assn. (Dir.); Past Pres., Atlantic Provs. Econ. Council; Anglican; recreation: golf; Clubs: Bally Haly Golf; Murray's Pond; Rotary; Home: 21 Rennie's Mill Rd., St. John's, Nfld. A1C 3P9; Office: Ft. William Bldg., 6th Floor, Duckworth St., St. John's, Nfld. A1C 5H6

BRAITHWAITE, John Victor Maxwell; writer; b. Nokomis, Sask. 7 Dec. 1911; s. George Albert Warner and Mary (Copeland) B.; e. Nutana Coll. Inst. Saskatoon, Sask. 1930; Saskatoon Normal Sch. 1931; Univ. of Sask.; m. Ida Marguerite Aileen d. Robert Alexander Treleaven 12 Oct. 1935; children: Beryl Marie, Sharon Maxine, Christopher Maxwell, Sylvia Aileen, Colin Scott; became full-time freelance writer 1945; author radio plays CBC Stage Series "Ford Theatre", "Buckingham Theatre" and CBC Sch. Broadcast Dept.; author various articles popular mags., textbooks, 6 juvenile novels; humorous books incl. "Never Sleep Three in a Bed", "The Night We Stole the Mountie's Car", (Winner Leacock Memorial Medal, 1972); "The Commodore's Barge is Alongside"; adult novels incl. "Why Shoot the Teacher", "A Privilege and a Pleasure", "Lusty Winter", "McGruber's Folly"; numerous scripts for radio, TV and movies incl. "Voices of the Wild" nat. network 17 yrs.; mem. Streetsville Sch. Bd. 5 yrs.; Town Council Orangeville, Ont. 2 yrs.; served with RCNVR 1941-45, rank Lt. Commdr.; Life mem. ACTRA; mem. Writers Union Can.; Acad. Candn. Writers; Liberal; Protestant; recreations: walking, canoeing, movies, baseball, ornithology; Home: (P.O. Box 163) Port Carling, Ont. P0B 1J0.

BRAITHWAITE, Leonard, Q.C., B.Com., M.B.A.; b. Toronto, Ont., 23 Oct. 1923; s. Reginald and Wilhelmina

(Cox) B.; e. Harbord Coll. Inst., Toronto; Univ. of Toronto, B.Com. 1950; Harvard Univ., M.B.A. 1952; Osgoode Hall Law Sch., 1958; two s., Roger John Austin, David Leonard; read law with the late H.L. Rowntree, Q.C. and H.G. Chappell, Q.C.; called to Bar of Ont. 1958; cr. Q.C. 1971; served in Can. and Overseas with RCAF during World War II; el. to Bd. of Educ. for Twp. of Etobicoke 1960 and served on various comtes, incl. Adv. Vocational Comte.; served on Etobicoke Planning Bd. for 2 yrs.; el. to Council of Twp. of Etobicoke for Ward 4 in 1962; el. M.P.P. in prov. g.e. 1963 (first Negro el. to Parl. in Can.); mem. Bd. of Govs., Etobicoke Gen. Hosp.; Past Pres., Royal York Garden's Community Assn.; Lectr., Inst. of Business Adm., Univ. of Toronto, 1953-54; sponsor of boys' and girls' sports teams; mem., Candn. Bar Assn.; Co. York Law Assn.; Advocates' Soc.; Criminal Lawyers' Ass.; Metro. Toronto Bd. of Trade; Phi Delta Phi; Liberal; Anglican; recreations: outdoor sports, reading; Clubs: Harvard Business; Kiwanis; Office: Suite "E", 1500 Royal York Rd., Etobicoke, Ont. M9P 3B6

BRAITSTEIN, Marcel, R.C.A.; sculptor; educator; b. Belgium 11 July 1935; s. Arthur and Paula (Eckstein) B.; e. École des Beaux-Arts de Montréal 1953-59; Instituto Allende, San Miguel de Allende, Mexico 1959-60; m. Dianne Carol d. William Farrar 2 Oct. 1965; two d. Paula, Lara;PROF. OF FINE ARTS, UNIV. DU QUE.1969- ; Visiting Prof. Mt. Allison Univ. Sackville, N.B. 1973-75; one-man exhns.: Galerie Ptah Brussels 1960; Galeria Agnés Lefort Montreal 1961, 1963, 1965; Galeria Jacobo Glantz Mexico 1961; Montreal Museum of Fine Arts 1963; Whitney Gallery Montreal 1970; Galerie Entremonde Paris 1970; Romi Goldmuntz Centrum Antwerp 1971; Gallery 93 Ottawa 1972; Owens Art Gallery Sackville, N.B. 1973; Confederation Centre Art Gallery P.E.I. 1974; Univ. de Moncton 1975; Univ. du Qué. 1979; rep. in group exhns. Can., USA, Mexico and Europe since 1957; rep. pub. colls. Montreal Museum of Fine Arts, Art Gallery Ont., Winnipeg Art Gallery, Confederation Centre P.É.I.; recreations: sailing, cross-country skiing, reading; Club: Hudson Yacht; Home: 61 Macaulay Lane, Hudson Heights, Que. J0P 1J0; Office: (P.O. Box 8888 Stn. A) Montreal, Que. H3C 3P8.

BRAKELEY, George A., Jr., B.A.; public relations and fund raising counsel; b. Washington, D.C., 18 Apl. 1916; e. Chestnut Hill Acad., Philadelphia, Pa., 1934; Univ. of Penna., B.A. 1938; m. Roxana Byerly, Sept. 1946; children: George A. III, Deborah, Joan, Linda; CHAIRMAN OF BOARD AND CH. EXEC. OFFR., BRAKELEY, JOHN PRICE JONES INC. NEW YORK; Founding Chrmn. G.A. Brakeley Co. Inc. Los Angeles, Cal.; Dir., Am. Assn. of Fund-raising Counsel; with John Price Jones Co. Inc., New York City, fund raising counsellors, 1937-50; organ. John Price Jones Co. (Canada) Ltd. in 1950 (control in Can. taken over in 1953 and name changed in Jan. 1953 to G.A. Brakeley & Co. Ltd.); as fund raising counsellor, served Harvard Univ., McGill Univ., the (Montreal) Jt. Hosp Fund, the Toronto Gen. Hosp., the (Winnipeg) Jt. Hosp. Bldg. Fund, U.B.C., Univ. of Toronto, Queens, U. of Cal. and others, in all fields of philanthropy; served in 2nd World War; hon. discharged 1946 with rank of Capt.; Anglican; recreations: tennis, fishing; Clubs: Montreal Racket; Wee Burn Golf, (Darien); Racquet & Tennis (Phila.); University (N.Y. & Chicago); Mill Reef, (Antigua); Anglers Club (New York); Fly Fishers Club (London); Home: 1 Pilgrim Road, Darien Conn.; Office: 6 E. 43rd St., New York, N.Y.

BRAND, John Charles Drury, Ph.D., D.Sc.; chemist; educator; b. Durban, S. Africa 21 May 1921; s. Andrew Nevill and Helen Mabel (Drury) B.; e. Michaelhouse, Balgowan, Natal, S.Africa; Univ. of London B.Sc. 1941, M.Sc. 1943, Ph.D. 1946, D.Sc. 1956; m. Evelyn Grace d. late Bertram Leonard Meek 25 Sept. 1943; one s. David Andrew; PROF. OF CHEM. UNIV. OF W. ONT. since 1969; Sr. Lectr. Univ. of Glasgow 1947-64; Prof. Vanderbilt Univ. 1964-69; co-author "Molecular Structure" 1959, 2nd ed. 1974; "Applications of Spectroscopy" 1965; scient. papers various journs.; mem. Chem. Soc. (London); Candn. Assn. Physicists; Candn. Inst. Chem.; Royal Soc. Can.; Home: 1518 Western Rd., London, Ont. N6G 1H7; Office: London, Ont. N6A 5B7.

BRAND, Oscar, B.A.; writer; composer; entertainer; b. Winnipeg, Man., 7 Feb. 1920; s. I.Z. and Beatrice (Shulman) B.; e. Brooklyn Coll. of Coll. of City of N.Y., B.A. (Psychol.); m. Karen Grossman; children: Jeannie, Eric, Anthony, Jordan; Pres., Gypsy Hill Music; mem. Creative Bd. Sesame Street; Curator, Songwriters Hall of Fame; Critic, CBC "Playdate"; Host, "Let's Sing Out" CBC, CTV; mem. Faculty, Hofstra Univ., N.Y. and New Sch., N.Y.; author of 10 published books incl.: "Singing Holidays", "The Ballad Mongers", "Bawdy Song Book"; has recorded 65 L.P.s and written 76 documentary and indust. films (rec'd Venice, Edinburgh and Cannes Festival awards, Golden Reel, Scholastic, Freedoms Foundation, Peabody, Ohio State and Emmy Awards); creator of score for "In White America", "How To Steal An Election", "The Joyful Noise", "The Education of Hyman Kaplan"; presently composing score and writing lyrics for musical "Thunder Bay"; served with US Army as Psychol., 1942-45; rec'd Unit Award; Legion of Merit; Co-ordinator of Folk Music for N.Y. Mun. Stn.; Trustee, Newport Festival Foundation; mem., N.Y. State Folklore Assn.; Dramatists Guild; ACTRA; SAG; Address: 141 Baker Hill, Great Neck, New York, 11023, N.Y.

BRANDER, F. Gerald; b. Brantford, Ont., 30 Dec. 1920; s. Gordon Wheeler and Ella F. (Chalcraft) B.; e. North Toronto (Ont.) Coll. Inst. (1939); m. Frances Fisk White, Toronto, Ont., 3 Sept. 1946; children: Judith, Robert, Stephanie; remarried Sylvia, 21 June, 1969; joined Maclean-Hunter Ltd., 1939; PRES. & CHIEF EXEC. OFFR. TOURISM INDUSTRY ASSOCIATION OF CANADA; successively in Accounting, Circulation, Advertising, Editorial and Mang. functions, Group Publisher, Business Publs.; former Publisher, "Maclean's m Magazine", and "Le Magazine Maclean"; Dir. of Co. 1964-71; Vice-Chmn. & Dir., Ontario Motor League, Toronto Club; Dir., Ont. Motorist Insurance Company; Dir., OML World Wide Travel Agency (Toronto) Ltd.; United Church Observer; Past Pres., Sales Research Club; Magazine Publs. Assn. Can.; Periodical Press Assn. Can.; United Church; Clubs: Canadian; Home: 129 Mildenhall Rd., Toronto, Ont. M4N 3H4; Office: 130 Albert St., Ottawa, Ont. K1P 5G4

BRANDT, Don R., D.F.C., B.Com.; executive; b. Minneapolis, Minn., 22 Apr. 1920; s. Emil A. and Edith W. (Larson) B.; e. High Sch., Minneapolis Minn.; Univ. of Minn., B.Com. (Business Adm.) 1947; m. Mary Elizabeth, d. C.O. Brown, Rochester, Minn., 23 Apr. 1948; VICE PRES., CORP. DEVEL., CANADIAN UTILITIES LTD. since 1973; Dir., Regent Drilling Ltd.; Northern Development Ltd.; served in 2nd World War with U.S. Army Air Force (1st Lieut.); D.F.C. and Air Medal; Psi Upsilon; Lutheran; recreation: golf; Clubs: Edmonton Petroleum; Mayfair Golf & Country; Home: 9911 136th St., Edmonton; Office: 10040-104 St., Edmonton, Alta. T5J 2V6

BRANDY, Stuart Cameron; broadcast management consultant; b. Windsor, Ont. 5 Oct. 1932; s. Thomas Stuart and Bessie Ellen (Cameron) B.; e. Beck Coll. Inst. London, Ont.; m. Sheila Patricia McLaren 30 Apl. 1955; children: David, Kimberley, Tracey; FOUNDER AND OWNER, CAMERON McLAREN INC. 1981- ; served radio broadcasting 32 yrs. incl. 18 yrs. with Maclean Hunter Ltd. as Sr. Broadcast Exte. and Pres. 3 broadcasting subsidiaries; Chrmn., Radio Bureau Can. 1971-73; recreation: woodworking; Club: Rideau; Address: 118 Lisgar Rd., Rockcliffe Park, Ont. K1M 0E6.

BRASSARD, Paul G., B.Arch., F.R.A.I.C.; architect; b. Montreal, P.Q., 20 Dec. 1912; s. Raoul Adolphe (an architect) and Marie-Rose (LeSage) B.; e. Mont St. Louis Coll., 1927-33 (Grad. in Scient. course); Ecole des Beaux-Arts Sch. of Arch., B.Arch. 1939; m. Réjane, d. Ernest Carrière, Outremont, Que. 7, March 1942; one d. Denyse; PARTNER, BRASSARD & WARREN, Estbd. 1946, Montreal; 1939-44 employed by Foundation Co. of Canada Ltd. on the design of the St. Paul l'Ermite Munition Plant, and then as Asst. to the Vice-Pres. as H.O. Rep. on the Aluminium Co. contracts at Shipsaw, Arvida and Ile Maligne; 1944-46 worked with Ross & McDonald, architects, estbd. present partnership in 1946; arch. for a no. of office bldgs., schools, etc.; Counsellor, City of Outremont since 1967; mem., P.Q. Arch. Assn.; Roman Catholic; recreations: golf, curling, hunting; Club: Laval-sur-le-Lac; Home: 165 Cote Ste. Catherine Rd., Apt. 909, Outremont, Que. H2V 2A7; Office: 934 St. Catherine St. E., Montreal, Que. H2L 2E9

BRAULT, Lucien, M.A., Ph.D., D.Lett. (St. Francis Xavier, Antigonish, N.S., 1973); b. Ottawa, Ontario., 10 July, 1904; s. Aimé and Délisca (Proulx) B.; e. Ottawa Schs. 1911-19; La Salle Acad. 1919-22; Queen's Univ. 1930-32; Univ. of Ottawa, B.A. 1936; M.A. 1938; Ph.D. 1940; m. Florence, d. Albert Harwood, 10 Oct. 1936; children: Jean-Harwood, Louise, Paul; Prof. of Can. Hist., Univ. of Ottawa 1937-62; retired; Prof. of Mil. Hist., Royal Military College of Canada, Kingston, Ont.; Emeritus Prof. of Univ. of Ottawa and Hon. Historian cities of Ottawa and of Hull; Pres., Ottawa Hist. Information Inst.; Past Pres., Soc. d'Hist. d'Ottawa; Vice-President, soc. généalogique can.-française; Corr. mem., Inst. d'Hist. d'Amérique française; mem., Soc. des Ecrivains; Canadn. Hist. Assn.; awarded Que. Prov. Lit. and Science Prize 1943; author: "Gaspé depuis Cartier" 1934; "Historical Gaspé" 1935; "Francis-J. Audet et son Oeuvre, Bibliographie" 1940; "Ottawa, Capitale du Canada, de son Origine à nos Jours" 1942; "Mémoires de la Société royale du Canada, Index 1882-1943"; "Le Canada, Guide du Lecteur 1945"; "Ottawa, Old and New", 1946; "Histoire de Saint-François-de-Sales de la Pointe-Gatineau" 1948; "Hull, 1800-1950" 1950; "Index, Soc. d'Histoire de l'Eglise, 1933-1958"; "Le Canada au XXe Siècle" 1965; "Histoire des comtés unis de Prescott et de Russell", 1965; "Un Siècle d'Administration scolaire", 1960; "Bref Exposé de l'Enseignement bilingue au XXe Siècle", 1966; "A Century of Reporting", 1967; "Sainte-Anne d'Ottawa, Cent Ans d'Histoire, 1873-1973", 1973; "Académie De-La Salle, un édifice patrimonial reprend vie" 1975; "Parliament Hill—La Colline parlementaire" 1976; "The Grand Hotel, a Heritage Hostelry" 1979; "A Mile of History in Ottawa" 1980; "Aylmer d'Hier/of Yesteryear" 1981; Roman Catholic; Recreations: skiing, sailing, horticulture; Home: 36 Aylmer Road, Aylmer, Que. J9H 1A5

BRAUN, H.S., B.A., LL.D., C.D., D.Sc.; educator; b. Hanover, Ont., 13 Nov. 1913; s. Samuel L. and Elizabeth (Voelzing) B.; e. McMaster Univ., B.A. 1936, LL.D. 1964, D.Sc. 1977; m. Margaret, d. Dr. C.R. McComb, 6 July 1940; four ds.; Principal Emeritus, Lakehead University since 1974; Dean of University Schools (retired 1977); Head, Science Dept., Port Arthur Coll. 1937-41; Port Arthur Coll. Inst. 1946-48; Principal, Lakehead Tech. Inst. 1948-59; Principal, Lakehead Coll. of Arts, Science & Tech. 1958-65; served in 2nd World War, R.C.N. 1942-46; rank Commdr.; mem. Bd. Govs., Port Arthur Gen. Hosp.; Port Arthur Public Lib. Bd.; Dir., Scholarships (Trust Fund); mem. Candn. Assn. Physicists; Freemason: United Church; recreations: sailing, curling, duck hunting; Clubs: Country; Gyro; T.R. Sailing: Home: 1104 Waverley Park Towers, 405 Waverley St., Thunder Bay "P", Ont. P7B 1B8; Office: Thunder Bay, Ont.

BRAWN, Robert Gerald, B.Sc.; petroleum executive; b. Calgary, Alta. 24 Sept. 1936; s. Gerald and Daisy (Mamini) B.; e. Pub. and High Schs. Calgary; Univ. of Alta.

B.Sc. (Chem. Engn.) 1958; m. Carole d. Oliver Stevens, Calgary, Alta. 19 July 1958; children: Sheryl, Dean, Kelly, Patti; PRES., CEO AND DIR., TURBO RESOURCES LTD.; Challenger Int. Services, Turbo & Challenger subsidiary companies; Dir., Panarctic Oils Ltd.; Queenston Gold Mines Ltd.; Lariat Oil & Gas Ltd.; Candn. Foremost Ind.; Bankeno Mines Ltd.; Chem./Drilling Engr., Mobil Oil of Canada 1958-60; Engr. and Mgr. International Drilling Fluids 1960-65; estbd. S & L Oil Refineries Ltd. 1965 (now Turbo Refineries Ltd.); sold Turbo Oils Ltd. to Leduc Calmar Oils Ltd. 1970 (became present Co. 1971); mem. Dean's Adv. Comte. Faculty of Business Adm. & Comm., Univ. of Alta.; Can. West Found.; Vice Pres. and Dir., Calgary Chamber Comm.; Dir., Can. Chamber Comm.; Past Pres. Springbank Community Assn.; Pres. and Dir., Independent Petroleum Assn. Can.; mem. Assn. Prof. Engrs. Alta.; Young Pres.'s Organ. Inc.; Fraternity Phi Delta Theta; P. Conservative; Anglican; recreations: hockey, skiing; Clubs: Calgary Petroleum; Rotary S. Calgary; Home: P.O. Box 4, Site 8, S.S. 3, Calgary, Alta. T3N 3N9; Office: 1035 - 7th Ave. S.W., Calgary, Alta. T2P 3E9.

BRAY, Harry S., Q.C., B.A.; provincial civil servant; e. Univ. Coll. Univ. of Toronto B.A. 1948; Osgoode Hall Law Sch. Toronto; VICE CHRMN.,ONT. SECURITIES COMN. 1968- called to Bar of Ont. 1951; Sr. Counsel Ont. Securities Comn. 1958; Asst. Dir. Pub. Prosecutions, Ministry of Atty. Gen. 1963; Dir. Ont. Securities Comn. 1964; Pres. N. Am. Securities Adm. Assn. Inc. 1977-78; Chrmn. OSC Study on Problems of Disclosure Raised to Investors by Business Combinations & Private Placements 1970; Chrmn. Interministerial Comte. on Commodity Futures Trading 1975; Study Dir. and mem. OSC Comte. on Securities Industry Ownership 1972; Shriner; Freemason; mem. Bd. Trade Metro. Toronto (Chrmn. 1974-75); Goodwill Services (Bd. Govs. 1976-79); Candn. Bar Assn.; recreations: boating, fishing, photography; United Church; Clubs: Lawyer's; Empire; Home: 73 Willamere Dr., Scarborough, Ont. M1M 1W5: Office: Ministry of Consumer & Commercial Relations, 10 Wellesley St. E., Toronto, Ont. M7A 2H7.

BRAYBROOKE, David, M.A., Ph.D., F.R.S.C.; educator; b. Hackettstown, N.J. 18 Oct. 1924; s. Walter Leonard and Netta Rose (Foyle) B.; e. Hobart Coll. 1941-43; New Sch. for Social Research 1942; Downing Coll. Cambridge 1945; Columbia Univ. 1946; Harvard Univ. B.A. 1948; Cornell Univ. M.A. 1951, Ph.D. 1953; Am. Council Learned Soc's Fellow, New Coll. Oxford 1952-53, Rockefeller Foundation Grantee 1959-60; m. Alice Boyd Noble 31 Dec. 1948; div. 1982; children: Nicholas, Geoffrey, Elizabeth Page; PROF. OF PHILOS. AND POLITICS, DALHOUSIE UNIV. 1965- ; Instr. in Hist. and Lit. Hobart and William Smith Colls. Geneva, N.Y. 1948-50; Teaching Fellow in Econ. Cornell Univ. 1950-52; Instr. in Philos. Univ. of Mich. 1953-54; Bowdoin Coll. Brunswick, Me. 1954-56; Asst. Prof. of Philos. Yale Univ. 1956-63; Assoc. Prof. of Philos. and Politics present Univ. 1963-65; Dean of Liberal Arts, Bridgeport (Conn.) Engn. Inst. (part-time) 1961-63; Visiting Prof. of Philos. Univ. of Pittsburgh 1965, 1966; Univ. of Toronto 1966-67; Visiting Prof. of Pol. Science Univ. of Minn. 1971; Univ. of Calif. 1980; recipient Guggenheim Fellowship 1962-63; Leave Fellowship Social Sciences & Humanities Research Council Can. 1978-79; mem. Acad. Adv. Panel Can. Council Ottawa 1968-71; Council for Philos. Studies 1974-79; Ed. "Philosophy in Canada" 1973-78; mem. various journ. ed. bds.; Chrmn. Guilford (Conn.) Town Democratic Comte. 1961-62; Cand. for All. Halifax 1974; mem. Bd. Educ. Guilford (Conn.) 1957-59; Dir. N.S. Civil Liberties Assn. 1976- ; author "Three Tests for Democracy: Personal Rights; Human Welfare; Collective Preference" 1968; "Traffic Congestion Goes Through the Issue-Machine" 1974; co-author "A Strategy of Decision: Policy Evaluation as a Social Process" 1963; numerous articles prof. journs. and colls.; served with U.S. Army 1943-46,

Corps of Engrs., Signal Corps, Code Clk. European Theatre; mem. Am. Philos. Assn. (Extve. Comte. E. Div. 1976-79); Am. Pol. Science Assn. (Vice Pres. 1981-82); Am. Soc. Pol. & Legal Philos.; Candn. Assn. Univ. Teachers (Vice Pres. 1974-75, Pres. 1975-76); Candn. Peace Research & Educ. Assn.; Candn. Philos. Assn. (Pres. 1971-72); Candn. Pol. Science Assn.; Royal Inst. Pub. Adm.; recreations: reading, music, walking, swimming; Club: Waegwoltic; Home: 6045 Fraser St., Halifax, N.S. B3H 1R7; Office: Halifax, N.S. B3H 3J5.

BRAYLEY, Jack; LL.D. (Dalhousie), journalist; b. Saint John, N.B., 17 Feb. 1912; s. late John and Emma (Walker) B.; e. Saint John, N.B. High Sch.; m. Zeversa Lorraine, d. M.T. Gibbon, Saint John, N.B., 9 Dec. 1936; children: Sally, John Fenwick; retired as Chief of Bureau (Atlantic), The Canadian Press 1946-77; Reporter, Saint John "Times-Globe", 1931-33 and Sports Ed., 1933-35; served with A.P. in London, Eng. in 1935, then trans. to London Bureau of Candn. Press; returned to Can. 1941; Montreal Bureau, 1941-43; Ottawa, 1943-46; apptd. Atlantic Supt. at Halifax, N.S., 1946; reported activities of Candn. Armed Forces and repatriation of Mackenzie-Papineau Battalion from Spanish Civil War; as a mem. of London Bureau and later was Mil. Writer attached to Parlty. Press Gallery staff, Ottawa; also visited Korean War, Suez Theatres; Nat. Newspaper Award for coverage of 1958 Springhill Mine disaster and N.N.A. citations for Korean and Suez coverage; other awards for writing and conservation effort; Queen's Jubilee Medal; C.B.C. Atlantic Neighborly News-Caster, 1953-76; ex-mem. Senate, Acadia Univ.; Candn. War Correspondents Association; N.S. Bird Soc.; mem. Adv. Council of Nat. & Prov. Parks Assn. Can.; a founding Dir., N.S. Opera, Symphony and Ballet Assns.; Anglican; Recreations: riding, natural history; Home: "Elderslie," Kerr's Mill Road, Wallace, Cumberland Co., N.S. B0K 1Y0

BRECHER, Michael, M.A., Ph.D.; F.R.S.C. university professor; b. Montreal, Que., 14 March 1925; s. Nathan and Gisella (Hopmeyer) B.; e. Strathcona Acad., Outremont, Que.; McGill Univ., B.A. (1st Class Hons. Econ. and Pol. Science) 1946; Yale Univ., M.A. (Internat. Relations) 1948, Ph.D. (Internat. Relations) 1953; m. Eva, d. His Eminence, Chief Rabbi Nissim Danon of Palestine, 7 Dec. 1950; children: Leora, Diana Rose, Seegla; PROF. OF POL. SCIENCE, McGILL UNIV.; Publications: "The Struggle for Kashmir", 1953; "Nehru, A political biography", 1959 (abridged ed. 1961; transl. into Hindi, German, Italian, Japanese); "The New States of Asia", 1963; "Succession in India: A Study in Decision — Making", 1966; India and World Politics", 1968; "Political Leadership in India: An Analysis of Elite Attitudes", 1969; "The Foreign Policy System of Israel: Setting, Images, Process", 1972; "Decisions in Israel's Foreign Policy", 1974; "Studies in Crisis Behavior", 1979; "Decisions in Crisis", 1980; many articles in international journals; Visiting Prof. of Pol. Sci., Univ. of Chicago 1963, Univ. of California, Berkeley 1979, Stanford Univ. 1980; Visiting Prof. of Internat. Relations, the Hebrew Univ., Jerusalem 1970-75; awarded the Watumull Prize by Am. Hist. Assn. for Nehru biography, 1960; Woodrow Wilson Foundation Award of Am. Pol. Science Assn. for "Foreign Policy System of Israel" 1973; Nuffield Fellowship 1955-56; Rockefeller Fellowship 1964-65; Guggenheim Fellowship 1965-66; Killam Awards (of Canada Council) 1970-74 and 1976-79; mem. Internat., Am. Candn., Israeli Pol. Science Assns.; Jewish; Address: c/o McGill University, Montreal, Que.

BRECKON, Sydney Wilson, B.Sc., Ph.D.; university professor; b. R.R., Georgetown, Ont., 26 Sept. 1918; s. Sydney Smith and Annie Leona (Wilson) B.; e. Queen's Univ., B.Sc. (Hons. in Physics) 1941; McGill Univ., Ph.D. 1951; m. Gwyneth, d. Hon. Justice H.A. Winter, 10 Feb. 1945; children: Sydney Lawrence Winter, Harry Ross, Margaret Anne, Peter Douglas, Robert Paul; VISITING

PROF., DEPT OF PHYSICS, UNIVERSITY OF WATER-
LOO 1976-77, Prof., Dept. of Physics, Mem. Univ. of
Nfld., since 1953 (Dept. Head 1953-76); Jr. Research
Physicist (Nuclear Physics Sec.) N.R.C., Chalk River,
Ont., 1946; Demonstrator, Physics Dept., McGill Univ.,
1946-47; Research Asst. (part-time), Radiation Lab.,
McGill Univ., 1947-50 (awarded N.R.C. Studentship,
1947 and 1948); Research Asst., Radiation Lab., McGill
Univ., 1950-51 and Research Assoc., there 1951-53;
served in 2nd World War, 1941-46 with R.C.N.V.R. (on
loan to Royal Navy, 1941-43); principal appts.: H.M.S.
"Dorsetshire"; staff of Commdr.-in-Chief, South Atlan-
tic; Staff of Capt. "D", Nfld.; co-author of several papers
on short half-life radio-activities induced by proton bom-
bardment; mem. Candn. Mil. Colls. Adv. Bd. 1970-73;
Senate, Memorial Univ. of Nfld., 1954-69; mem. Candn.
Assn. of Physicists (Councillor 1954-55, 1963-64); Am.
Physical Soc.; Assn. of Prof. Engrs., Nfld.; Am. Assn. for
Advan. of Science; Candn. Assn. of Univ. Teachers;
Sigma Xi; Protestant; recreations: fishing, gardening;
Home: 5 Winter Place, St. John's, Nfld. A1B 1J5

BREEN, J.M.; executive; b. Detroit, Mich., 8 Aug. 1927;
s. Joseph Lawrence and Mary Margaret (Phipps) B.; came
to Can. 1938; e. Renfrew (Ont.) Coll., Sr. Matric. 1945; m.
Janet Teresa, d. late Charles Watters, 23 Sept. 1950; chil-
dren: Michael, Mary Jane, Wendy, Douglas, Maurice:
VICE PRES., MARKETING, NORTHERN LIFE ASSUR-
ANCE CO. OF CAN. since 1979; with H.J. Heinz Co.
Ltd. as Salesman 1947; joined Crown Life as Agent 1952,
Asst. Agency Supv., H.O. 1954, Agency Supv. 1957,
Supt. of Agencies 1961, Agency Vice-Pres. 1966, Agency
Vice-Pres. (U.K.) 1968, Mang. Vice-Pres. (U.K.) 1970,
Vice Pres. and Gen. Mgr. (U.K.) 1972; R. Catholic; recrea-
tions: golf, reading; Club: London; London Hunt and
County; London Chamber of Commerce; Home: 389
Dundas St., Apt. N-15-1, London Towers, London, Ont.
N6B 3L5; Office: Northern Life Assurance Co. of Canada,
380 Wellington St., London, Ont. N6A 4G3

BREGMAN, Sidney, B.Arch.; architect; b. Warsaw, Po-
land s. Frieda (Granadier) and the late Max B.; e. Central
Tech. Sch., Toronto, Ont.; Univ. of Toronto, Sch. of
Arch., Honour Grad., 1951; children: Charles Ross,
Lloyd Elliot, Nina Diane, Susanne Mae; PARTNER,
BRÉGMAN & HAMANN, since 1953; Dir.: Vanguard
Trust of Canada Ltd.; Seel Mortgage Investment Corp.
(Vice Pres.); Mount Sinai Hospital, Toronto; mem., Royal
Arch. Inst. Can.; Ont. Assn. Arch.; Que. Assn. Arch.;
Beth Tzedec Cong.; Recreations: squash, sailing, Home:
98 Elm Ave., Toronto, Ont. M4W 1P2; Office: 50 Gervais
Drive, Don Mills, Ont. M3C 1W2

BREITHAUPT, John Duncan, B.A.Sc.; steel company ex-
ecutive; b. Peterborough, Ont. 31 July 1927; s. John Ed-
ward and Elspeth G. (Mavor) B.; e. Brown Sch. and
Univ. of Toronto Schs. 1945; Univ. of Toronto B.A.Sc.
1949; Univ. of W. Ont. Mang. Training Course 1968; m.
Margaret Isabel d. late George Dealtry Woodcock 31 Dec.
1949; children: Mary, Catharine, George, Barbara, James,
Jill; GEN. MGR. CORPORATE PLANNING, STEEL CO.
OF CANADA LTD. since 1978; Dist. Sales Mgr. Page
Hersey Tubes Ltd. Calgary 1960; Plate Sales Mgr. Steel
Co. of Canada Ltd. 1965, Asst. Gen. Sales Mgr. 1972,
Gen. Sales Mgr. 1975; Dir. Hamilton Chamber Comm.;
Extve. Comte. Hamilton & Dist. Candn. Mfgrs. Assn.;
mem. Assn. Prof. Engrs. Prov. Ont.; Phi Delta Theta; P.
Conservative; Anglican; Clubs: Hamilton; Engineers (To-
ronto); Burlington Golf & Country; Home: 115 Edgecliffe
Pl., Burlington, Ont. L7L 3Z2; Office: Stelco Tower 22,
100 King St. W., Hamilton, Ont. L8N 3T1.

BRENT, John Elford, B.A., LL.D.; industrialist (ret.); b.
Brantford, Ont., 26 Sept. 1908; s. late John Elford and late
Rosa Mae (Walker) B.; e. Univ. of Western Ont., B.A.
(Business Adm.) 1931; Waterloo Lutheran Univ., LL.D.
1966; Western 1972; m. Paula Mary Tillmann, 24 Sept.

1938; children: William, Susan, Peter, Paul; Dir., Ellis-
Don Ltd.; Hon. Mem., Adv. Council, The Toronto Sym-
phony; Hon. mem. Bd. Trustees, Toronto Western
Hosp.; Hon. Mem., Advisory Committee of School of
Business Administration, University of Western Ontario;
Hon. Governor, Massey Hall.; Dir., Can. Geriatrics Re-
search Soc.; Clubs: Canadian (Toronto); Rosedale Golf;
York; Toronto; Empire; Naples Bath & Tennis (Fla.);
Home: 61 St. Clair Ave. W. Apt. 502, Toronto, Ont. MR4
2Y8; Office: (P.O. Box 156, Station Q, Toronto, Ont. M4T
2M1

BRESVER, Abraham, C.A.; transportation executive; b.
Hirsh, Sask. 13 May 1917; s. Hyman and Fanny (Redman) B.; e. Regina Coll. 1936; Univ. of Toronto 1946;
Chartered Acct.; MANG. DIR. METRO CAB CO. LTD.;
Pres. Active Taxi Ltd. and seven other taxi co's; Founder
and Treas., Coachman Insurance Co. 1979; resigned
1979, mem. Candn. Radio Tech. Planning Bd.; began to
practise accountancy 1946; entered taxi business 1955;
control of present Co. 1956; served with Candn. Inf.
Corps 1945-46; Candn. Vice Pres. Internat. Taxicab
Assn.; Pres. Ont. Assn. Taxicab Operators; P. Conservative; Hebrew; recreation: reading; Home: 330 Spadina
Rd., Apt. 605, Toronto, Ont. M5R 2V9; Office: 811 King
St. W., Toronto, Ont. M5V 1N4

BRETON, Albert, B.A., Ph.D.; economist; b. Montmartre, Sask., 12 June 1929; s. Albéric T. and Jeanne (Nadeau) B.; e. Coll. de S. Boniface, Univ. of Man. B.A. 1951;
Columbia Univ. Ph.D. (Econ.) 1965; m. Margot, d. Gilbert Fournier, Montreal, Que.; children: Catherine, Natalie, Françoise, Robert; PROF. OF ECONOMICS, UNIV.
OF TORONTO since 1970; Asst. Prof. of Econ. Univ. de
Montréal 1957-65; Dir. of Research The Social Research
Group, Montreal 1956-65; Visiting Assoc. Prof. Carleton
Univ. 1964-65; Professeur invité, Université Catholique
de Louvain (Belgique) 1968-69; Lectr. in Econ. 1966-67
and Reader in Econ. 1967-69 London Sch. of Econ.; Visit-
ing Prof. of Candn. Studies Harvard Univ. 1969-70;
awarded Candn. Social Science Research Council Grant
1955-56; Can. Council Grant 1959-60; Guest of the Inst.,
Mass. Inst. of Technol. 1959-60; Post-Doctoral Fellow,
Univ. of Chicago 1965-66; co-recipient Can. Council Killam Sr. Research Scholarship 1972, 1977; mem. Candn.
Econ. Policy Comte. C.D. Howe Research Inst.; Vice-
Chmn., Fed. Cultural Policy Review Comm.; author "A
Conceptual Basis for an Industrial Strategy", 1974; "The
Economic Theory of Representative Government", 1974;
co-author with A.D. Scott, "The Economic Constitution
of Federal States" 1978, "The Design of Federation" 1980;
Co-author with R. Breton, "Why Disunity" 1980; author
or co-author numerous articles in various journs.; Home:
160 Rosedale Hts. Dr., Toronto, Ont. M4T 1C8

BRETON, Raymond Jules, M.A., Ph.D.; educator; b.
Montmartre, Sask. 19 Aug. 1931; s. Albéric T. and Jeanne
(Nadeau) B.; e. St. Boniface Coll.; Univ. of Man. B.A.
1952; Univ. of Chicago M.A. 1958; Johns Hopkins Univ.
Ph.D. 1961; m. Lily Thérèse d. Alexandre Laliberté, Cap-
de-la-Madeleine, Qué. 20 Aug. 1955; children: Marc, Michèle, Suzanne, Lorraine, Daniel; PROF. OF SOCIOL.
UNIV. OF TORONTO; Dir., Grad. Studies in Sociology;
Program Dir. Inst. for Research on Pub. Policy 1976-81;
Research Dir. The Social Research Group, Montreal 1957-
64; mem. Comte. on Aid to Publs. Social Science Re-
search Council 1969-72; Can. Council Acad. Panel 1970-
72, Chrmn. Consultative Group on Social Surveys 1973-
75, mem. Univ. of Toronto Task Force on Council's
Comn. on Grad. Studies in Humanities and Social Sci-
ences 1974; mem. ad hoc Comte. on Research, Ont. Econ.
Council 1976-77; rec'd Samuel S. Fels Fellowship 1960-61;
Can. Council Leave Fellowship 1972-73 and 1981-82; au-
thor "Academic and Social Factors in Career Decision-
Making: A Study of Canadian Secondary School
Students" 1972; "The Candian Condition: A Guide for
Research Development" 1977; co-author "The Social Im-

pact of Changes in Population Size and Composition: An Analysis of Reactions to Patterns of Immigration" 1974; "Cultural Boundaries and the Cohesion of Canada," 1980; "Why Disunity: An Analysis of Linguistic and Regional Cleavages in Canada," 1980; Ed., "La Langue de Travail au Québec"; "Aspects of Canadian Society" 1974; "Canadian Review of Sociology and. Anthropology" 1973-76, mem. or past mem. various ed. bds.; author various articles immigrant integration, inter-ethnic relations, language policies, etc.; mem. Royal Soc. Can.; Candn. Social. & Anthrop. Assn. (Extve. Comte. 1970-72); Internat. Sociol. Assn.; Candn. Ethnic Studies Assn. (Extve. Comte. 1973-77); Am. Sociol. Assn.; R. Catholic; recreations: cinema, theatre, music, travel, cross-country skiing, swimming; Home: 48 Alexandra Blvd., Toronto, Ont. M4R 1L7; Office: 563 Spadina Ave., Toronto, Ont. M5S 1A1.

BRETT, John Roland, M.A., Ph.D., F.R.S.C.; research biologist; b. Toronto, Ont. 25 June 1918; s. George Sidney and Marion Grace (Kernick) B.; e. Brown Sch. Toronto 1929; Univ. of Toronto Schs. 1938; Univ. of Toronto B.A. 1941, M.A. 1944, Ph.D. 1951; m. Phyllis d. late Ruben Walls 23 Dec. 1948; children: Stephen Sidney, Eric Ian; Research Scient. Pacific Biol. Stn. Dept. Fisheries since 1948; Hon. Lectr. Univ. of Wash. since 1968; Research Asst. Ont. Fisheries Research Lab. 1939-41; Med. Assoc. RCAF 1941-43, rank Flying Offr.; co-author and ed. "Fish Physiology" Vol. VIII; "Bioenerjetics and Growth" 1978; author or co-author over 90 scient. papers environmental physiol. fishes; mem. Candn. Soc. Zools. (Assoc. Ed. 1968-71, Secy.-Treas. 1970-72); Am. Fisheries Soc. (Assoc. Ed. 1959-63); Prof. Inst. Can.; Panel Experts Fisheries Div. FAO; Candn. Power Sqdns.; recreations: boating, fishing, hiking, building, reading; Club: Nanaimo Yacht; Home: 3586 Oakridge Dr., Nanaimo, B.C. V9T 1M4; Office: Pacific Biological Station, Nanaimo, B.C. V9R 5K6.

BRETT, Katharine Beatrice (Mrs. Gerard Brett); museum curator (ret.); b. Hull, Eng., 26 June 1910; d. Samuel Herbert and Katharine Elizabeth (Monk) Maw; came to Canada, 1912; e. Ont. Coll. Art., grad. 1931; m. Gerard Brett, 8 Oct. 1948; Assoc. Curator (former Curator 1950-68) Textile Dept., CURATOR, 1973, Royal Ont. Museum of Toronto; now CURATOR, EMERITUS; Assoc. Prof. Dept. of Fine Art, Univ. of Toronto; has exhibited with Royal Candn. Acad., Ont. Soc. Artists, Candn. Soc. Graphic Art; joined staff of Royal Ont. Museum, as Draughtsman, 1938, Textile Dept., 1945; Centre Internat. d'Etude des Textiles Ancien, Lyon, France; Costume Soc. (London); INTERNAT. COUNCIL of Museums, COSTUME Comte.; Anglican; recreation: painting; Clubs: Heliconian; Needle & Bobbin (N.Y.); Home: 567 Avenue Rd., Toronto, Ont. M4V 2K1.

BRETT, Hon. Roy Charles, M.H.A.; politician; b. Barr'd Island, Nfld. 18 Aug. 1936; s. William Richard and Phoebe Elizabeth (Keats) B.; e. Barr'd Island High Sch.; Mem. Univ. of Nfld.; m. Norma d. Baxter Rice, Botwood, Nfld. 15 Dec 1956; children: Debra Ann, Charles Todd;MIN. OF TRANSPORTATION & COMMUNICATIONS, NFLD.1979- ; el. M.H.A. prov. g.e. 1972, re-el. since; Parlty. Asst. to Premier 1972; Min. of Social Services 1975; Min. of Consumer Affairs & Environment 1979; P. Conservative; United Church; Club: Clarenville Lions; Office: 6th Floor, Water St., St. John's, Nfld. AIC 5T7.

BREWIN, Francis Andrew, Q.C.; b. Hove, Sussex, Eng., 3 Sept. 1907; s. Rev. Francis Henry and Amea Fenerty (Blair) B.; e. Radley Coll., Berks, Eng.; Osgoode Hall, Toronto, grad. 1930; m. Margaret Isabel, d. Geo. C. Biggar, June 1935; children: John, Margaret, Martha, Mary, Jane; Counsel, Cameron, Brewin & Scott; read law with Blake, Lash, Anglin & Cassels; called to Bar of Ont. 1930; cr. K.C. 1948; practised with J.C. McRuer, K.C., 1930-43; Rep., Co-op. Comte. on Japanese Candns. in constitutional reference to P.C. 1946; acted in Supreme Court of

Can. for Atty. Gen. of Sask. and in P.C.; Lieut. 2nd Bn., Roy. Regt. of Can. (R); def. cand. to H. of C. for St. Pauls, 1949; to Ont. Leg. for St. Georges, 1943; 1st el. to H. of C. for Toronto Greenwood, g.e. June 1962 (retired from Parliament 1977); Pres., Ont. C.C.F. 1946-49 (Nat. Extve. Council); mem., Founding Comte. and Federal Extve., N.D.P., 1961; mem., Extve., Synod of Diocese of Toronto; del., (Ang. Church of Can.), 3rd Assembly, World Council of Chs., New Delhi, 1961; del., Brit. Commonwealth Relations Conf., London, Eng., 1945, and Bigwin Inn, 1949; author: "Stand on Guard: The Search for a Canadian Defence Policy", 1965; co-author (with David MacDonald, M.P.), "Canada and the Biafra Tragedy"; mem., Candn. Inst. of Internat. Affairs; Delta Chi; N.D.P.; Anglican; Home: 686 Echo Dr., Ottawa, Ont. K1J 1P3

BREWSTER, Donald Burgess, Ph.D.; pulp and paper executive; b. Leeds, Eng. 17 Nov. 1931; s. John Duncan and Jessie Mathieson (Ross) B.; e. Ripon (Eng.) Grammar Sch. 1950; Leeds Univ. B.Sc. 1954, Ph.D. 1958; Harvard Grad. Sch. of Business 1968; Oxford Centre for Mang. Studies 1978; one d. Claire; PRES., PROFIGARD INC. since 1981; Plant Supvr. Texaco Trinidad Inc. 1958-60; Sr. Devel. Engr. Dupont of Canada 1960-61; Adv. Systems Engr. IBM Canada 1961-64; Research Dir. Westvaco Corp. 1964-69; Vice Pres., SDK & H Ltd. (consultants) 1969-71; Task Force Mgr., Marketing Mgr., Mang. Dir. S. Pacific, Marketing Dir. Europe, Measurex Corp. 1971-77; Corp. Tech. Dir., Kruger Inc., 1978-81; contributor "Paper Making Systems and Their Control" 1970; over 20 publs. and patents; mem. Candn. Pulp & Paper Assn.; Tech. Assn. Pulp & Paper Indust.; recreations: classical music, tennis, squash, skiing, travel; Clubs: Montreal Amateur Athletic Assn.; Mt. Royal Tennis; Home: 73 Chesterfield Ave., Westmoung, Que. H3Y 2M6; Office: 75 boul. Hymns, Pointe Claire, Que. H93 1E2.

BREWSTER, Elizabeth Winifred, A.M., B.L.S., Ph.D., D.Lit.; poet; novelist; educator; b. Chipman, N.B. 26 Aug. 1922; d. Frederick John and Ethel May (Day) Brewster; e. Sussex (N.B.) High Sch. 1942; Univ. of N.B., B.A. 1946, D.Lit. 1982; Radcliffe Coll. A.M. 1947; Kings Coll. Univ. of London 1949-50; Univ. of Toronto B.L.S. 1953; Ind. Univ. Ph.D. 1962; PROF. OF ENGLISH, UNIV. OF SASK. 1980- ; served various libs. incl. Queen's Univ., Carleton Univ., Ind. Univ., Mount Allison, N.B. Leg., Univ. of Alta.; teacher Victoria Univ. B.C. 1960-61; joined present Univ. 1972; author "East Coast" poems 1951; "Lillooet" poem 1954; "Roads" poems 1957; "Passage of Summer" poems 1969; "Sunrise North" poems 1972; "In Search of Eros" poems 1974; "The Sisters" novel 1974; "Sometimes I Think of Moving" poems 1977; "It's Easy to Fall on the Ice" 10 stories 1977; to be published "The Way Home" poems, 1982; "Digging In" poems, "Junction" novel, 1982; recipient E. J. Pratt Gold Medal and Prize Univ. of Toronto 1953; Univ. of W. Ont. Pres.'s Medal and Award for Poetry 1979; Can. Council Sr. Artists Awards Poetry 1971-72, 1976, 1978-79; mem. League Candn. Poets; Writers Union Can.; Sask. Writers Guild; Assn. Candn. Univ. Teachers Eng.; Assn. Candn. & Que. Lit.; Candn. Assn. Commonwealth Lit. & Lang. Studies; Home: 1226 College Dr., 10, Saskatoon, Sask. S7N 0W4; Office: Saskatoon, Sask. S7N 0W0.

BREYFOGLE, Peter Nicholas, B.Eng., M.B.A.; executive; b. Barcelona, Spain, 24 Sept. 1935; s. Robert Joshua and Elsia (McLaughlin) B.; e. Winchester Coll., Eng., 1949-54; Cambridge Univ., B.Eng. 1957; Harvard Univ., M.B.A. 1959; came to Can. 1936; m. Josephine Mary, d. B.A. King, Dorset, Eng., 11 Dec. 1965; one s. Nicholas Brenton; SENIOR VICE-PRES., FINANCE DOME PETROLEUM LTD. 1978- since 1975; joined Massey-Ferguson as Financial Analyst, Toronto, Ontario, 1959; Plans and Controls Coordinator, Massey-Ferguson Export, Coventry, Eng. 1961; Gen. Financial Analysts Mgr., Massey-Ferguson Ltd., Toronto 1964; Comptroller, MF

Inc./MF Industries, Toronto and Des Moines 1965; Comptroller, Massey-Ferguson Ltd., Toronto 1969; Vice Pres., Corp. Operations 1972; Extve. Vice-Pres., Europe, 1975-78; Dir., Credit Suisse (Can.) Ltd.; member Financial Executives Institute; Anglican; recreations: golf, squash, tennis, bridge; Clubs: Royal Canadian Yacht; Badminton & Racquet; Ranchmen's; Home: 4216 Britannia Dr., S.W., Calgary, Alta. T25 1J3; Office: Calgary Atla.

BRIDGES, Harold, B.Sc., F.Inst.Pet.; b. Dronfield, Eng. 14 March 1916; s. George H. and Alice M. (Allen) B.; e. Durham Univ. B.Sc. 1937; m. Shirley May d. Percy T. J. Cresswell, Nhill, Australia 26 June 1943; children: Margaret E., Jennifer S., John H. C.; Dir., International Nickel Co. Ltd. Toronto; Alaska Interstate Co., Houston; Geosource Inc., Houston; held various positions Royal Dutch-/Shell Group 1937-66 (internat. service); Dir. Shell Petroleum, London 1966-68; Pres. and CEO, Shell Canada Ltd. Toronto 1968-71, Shell Oil Co., Houston 1972-76, retired 1976; served with Royal Australian Air Force 1942-44, Flight Lt.; Protestant; recreation: golf; club: Montreux Golf (Switzerland); Address: Residences de la Côte, 70-1110 Morges, Vaud, Switzerland.

BRIEN, Francis Staples, M.B., F.R.S.M. (Lond.), F.R.C.P.(C.), F.A.C.P.; university professor; b. Windsor, Ont., 9 Apl. 1908; s. James Wilbert Brien, M.B., and Josephine Elizabeth (Staples) B.; e. Coll. Inst., Windsor, Ont.; Univ. of Toronto, B.A. 1930, M.B. 1933; post-grad. studies in London, Eng., M.R.C.P., 1937; F.R.C.P. (London) 1958; LL.D., Univ. W. Ont. 1979; m. Mildred Isabel, d. John Herman Appel, 12 June 1937; one d., Mary; Hon. Prof., Univ. of Western Ont. since 1972; Prof. of Medicine there 1945-72; Emeritus Staff, Victoria Hosp., London, Ont.; Medical Consultant, Northern Life Assurance Co. of Can.; former mem., Med. Adv. Bd., Ont. Cancer Treatment & Research Foundation; served as House Phys., Toronto Gen. Hosp., 1933-36; in gen. practice with father in Windsor, Ont., 1937-42; served in World War 1942-45 with No. 10 Candn. Gen. Hosp.; rank at discharge Lieut.-Col.; twice Mentioned in Dispatches; author of scient. papers in medical lit.; former mem. of Council and vice. pres. (med.), Royal Coll. of Phys. & Surg. of Can., and Coll. of Phys. & Surg. of Ont. (Chrmn. of various comtes. of both organ.); life mem., London Acad. of Med.; Ont. Med. Assn.; Candn. Med. Assn.; Candn. Heart Assn.; Candn. Rheumatism Assn.; Candn. Arthritis & Rheumatism Soc.; Emeritus mem., N.Y. Acad. of Sciences; Am. Geriatrics Soc.; Phi Chi; Alpha Omega Alpha; Liberal; Baptist; recreations: photography, fishing, hunting; Home: 144 Iroquois Ave., London, Ont. N6C 2K8

BRIGGS, Geoffrey Hugh, M.A.; librarian; b. Leeds, Eng. 14 Apl. 1926; s. Harry and Charlotte Irene (Black) B.; e. King's Sch. Rochester, Eng. (King's Scholar); St. John's Coll. Cambridge Univ. M.A. 1947, Choral Scholar; Univ. Coll. London Dipl. Archives and Dipl. Librarianship 1949; m. Judith Mary d. Frederick A. de la Mare, Hamilton, N.Z. 6 Dec. 1950; two s. Nicholas, Peter; UNIV. LIBRARIAN, CARLETON UNIV. 1969- ; Asst. Librarian, London Univ. 1949-54; Depy. Librarian, Victoria Univ. of Wellington, N.Z. 1954-67; Univ. of Calgary 1967-69; mem. Candn. Assn. Research Libs. (Pres. 1979-80); Candn. Lib. Assn.; recreations: music, fishing; Home: 2125 Fillmore Cres., Ottawa, Ont. K1J 6A1; Office: Colonel By Dr., Ottawa, Ont. K1S 5B6.

BRINDLE, John Arthur; insurance executive; b. Manchester, Eng. 22 Dec. 1922; s. Arthur George and Gertrude Ellen (Campbell) B.; e. St. Margaret's Sch. Manchester; Northern Univ. Sch. Cert. and Matric.; m. 1stly Muriel Jones (d.) 30 Oct. 1948; m. 2ndly Kathleen (Billyard) Hawkins 9 July 1977; children: Michael John, Richard David Henry, Helen, Grace Penelope; EXTVE. VICE PRES., SUN LIFE ASSURANCE CO. OF

CANADA 1980- ; Dir. Sun Life Assurance Co. of Canada (U.K.) Ltd.; joined present Co. as Rep. Manchester Br. 1947, Asst. Mgr. Southampton Br. 1953, Mgr. Manchester Central Br. 1953, Asst. Mgr. of Agencies 1955, Mgr. of Agencies 1959, Asst. Gen. Mgr. and Mgr. of Agencies 1971, Depy. Gen. Mgr. for Gt. Brit. and Ireland 1972, Gen. Mgr. 1973, Sr. Vice Pres. and Gen. Mgr. 1975, Sr. Vice Pres. 1979-80; served in Middle E. and European Theatres, Royal Tank Regt 1942-47; mem. Inst. of Dirs.; E. India Sports & Pub. Schs.; Ends of the Earth; P. Conservative; Anglican; recreations: golf, swimming, reading; Clubs: Granite; Canada; Chislehurst Golf; Home: 61 St. Clair Ave. W., Apt. 408, Toronto, Ont.; Office: (P.O. Box 4150, Stn. A) Toronto, Ont. M5W 2C9.

BRISBIN, Rev. Frank G., B.A., B.D., D.D. (Un. Ch.); b. Holden, Alberta, 9 May 1919; s. late Charles Nelson and Mary Elizabeth (Kennedy) B.; e. Pub. and High Schs., Edmonton, Alta.; Univ. of Alta., B.A. 1939 and B.D. 1944; St. Stephen's Coll., Edmonton, Alta. (Theol.) 1942; m. Charlotte Louise, d. late H. V. Clendenning, 18 July 1944; children: M. Lorraine, Virginia L., Helen J., Eleanor R., Allen G.; SECY. DIV. OF COMMUNICATION, UN. CHURCH CAN. since 1968 (former Min. St. Giles Ch., Hamilton, Ont. 1959-67); Secy., World Assoc. for Christian Communication 1975-78; mem. World Council of Churches Communication Comte. 1976-; o. 1942, and thereafter spent two yrs. on the pastoral charge of Cadomin, Alta.; Stavely, Alta. for four yrs.; Asst. Min., Metropolitan Un. Ch., Toronto 1948-50 and Acting Min. 1951 and Min., 1952-59; Pres., Toronto Council of Chs. (1956); Chrmn., Toronto East Presbytery, Un. Ch. (1956); mem., Un. Ch. Bd. of Publ. Extve., 1952-69; mem. of Extve., Un. Ch. Gen. Council, 1964-68; Chrmn., Hamilton Presbytery, 1965-66; D.D. St. Stephen's Coll. 1969; Home: 143 Bessborough Drive, Toronto, Ont. M4G 3J7; Office: 85 St. Clair Ave. East, Toronto, Ont. M4T 1M8

BRISCOE, Robert, B.Sc., M.B.A.; manufacturer; b. Montreal, Que. 20 Dec. 1941; s. John Richard and Anna Pearl (Pitcher) B.; e. Chambly Co. High Sch. St. Lambert, Que. 1960; Sir George Williams Univ. B.Sc. 1967, M.B.A. 1973; m. Marielle Raymonde, d. Jacques Rousseau, 28 Oct. 1961; children: Lorraine, Tracey, Susan, Robert Glen; PRESIDENT, LES FROMAGES GEMME INC. since 1981; Chrmn. of Bd., Lallemand Inc.; Young Presidents Organ.; recreations: golf, skiing, fishing; clubs: St.-Denis; Brome Lake Boating; Knowlton Golf; Home: 694 Victoria Ave., Westmount, Que.; Office: 616 Russeau Barré, Marieville, Que. Que. J0L 1J0

BRISSENDEN, William Guy, P.Eng.; consulting engineer; b. Halifax, N.S., 28 March 1915; s. William Ernest and Esther Susanna (Olson) B.; e. Lachine (Que.) High Sch., 1932; McGill Univ., B. Eng. (Mining) 1937, M.Eng. (Ore Dressing) 1938; m. Jean Winnifred Mary, d. late Watson S. Hammond, 15 May 1943; children: Richard William, Janet Mary, Jane Elizabeth, Robert Charles; PRES., WILLIAM G. BRISSENDEN INC.; Chrmn. Can. National Committee, World Mining Congress; Dir., Brascan Ltd.; joined Paymaster Consolidated Mines Ltd. 1945-1948 as Mine Superintendent; Mine Superintendent, Hallnor Mines Ltd., 1948-51; Gaspé Copper Mines Ltd. 1951-62; served as Supt., Asst. Mgr. and as Mgr. from 1957; Mgr. Noranda Mines Ltd., Noranda, Que., 1962-65; Gen. Mgr. 1965-68; Vice Pres. Mines 1969-75; Brunswick Mining & Smelting Corp., Ltd. (Pres. 1971-75); Gaspe Copper Mines Ltd. (Pres. 1971-75); served with RCNVR 1940-45; rank Lieut. Commdr. (Elect.) on discharge; mem., Corp. Engrs. Que.; Am. Inst. Mining & Metall.; Candn. Inst. Mining & Metall.; Can. Inst. of Int. Affairs; Prof. Eng. of Ontario; United Church; recreations: golf, photography; Clubs: York Downs Golf; Bd. of Trade of Metro Toronto; National; Granite; Home: 25 Glenallan Road, Toronto, Ont. M4N 1G6; Office: P.O. Box 299, Ste. 3903, Royal Trust Tower, Toronto-Dominion Centre, Toronto, Ont. M5K 1K2

BRISSON, Germain J., M.Sc., Ph.D.; educator; b. St-Jacques, Que. 12 Apl. 1920; s. Antonio and Clara (Gaudet) B.; e. Univ. of Montreal B.A. 1942; Laval Univ. B.Sc. (Agric.) 1946; McGill Univ. M.Sc. (Animal Nutrition) 1948; Ohio State Univ. Ph.D. 1950; m. Yvette d. Laurent Dalpé, Ste-Marie Salomée, Qué. 7 July 1948; 5 children; PROF. OF NUTRITION DEPT. ANIMAL SCIENCES UNIV. LAVAL, Dir. Program de doctorat en nutrition 1977- , Dir. Centre de recherche en nutrition 1968-78; author "Lipids in Human Nutrition" 1982; over 70 articles various aspects nutrition; recipient Golden Award Candn. Feed Industry Assn. 1979; mem. Agric. Inst. Can.; ACFAS; Am. Inst. Nutrition; R. Catholic; Home: 1084 de Nouë, Ste-Foy, Qué. G1W 4L3; Office: Pavillon Comtois, Québec City, Qué. G1K 7P4.

BRISSON, Jean-Roch, B.A., B.Sc.A.; b. Ottawa, Ont. 20 Apl. 1927; s. J.T. and B. (Delorme) B.; e. Laval Univ. B.A. 1947, B.Sc.A. (Chem. Engn.) 1951; 1951-53 Brit. Ministry of Educ. Athlone Scholarship for studying and training with leading mfg. corps. in Brit.; m. Eliane d. late P.O. Dubé 5 Sept. 1951; children: Claude, Pierre, Francine, Ginette; PRESIDENT AND CHIEF OPERATING OFFR. AND DIR. MARINE INDUSTRIE LTÉE since 1977; Dir. Quebec Hospital Service Assn; Quebec Mutual Life Assurance Co.; Quebec Industrial Relations Inst.; Foresteel Industrie Ltee; Marine Industrie (Montage) Ltée; Société Milthom; Canadian Export Assn; Plant Engr. Canadian Arsenals Ltd. Quebec 1953-56, Dir. of Engn. Services 1956, Div. Mgr. 1959, Gen. Mgr. Canadian Arsenals Ltd., Ottawa 1962 Pres. and Gen. Mgr. 1963, also Dir. of Machinery and Armament Br. Dept. Defence Production Ottawa 1963; Mgr. Munitions Div. Canadian Industries Ltd. Montreal 1969, Dir. of Engn. 1972-77; (Bd. Gov.): Candn. Shipbuilding & Ship Repairing Assn; Candn. Assn-Latin America; mem. Order Engrs. Que.; Engn. Inst. Can.; Candn. Mfrs. Assn. (Extve. Comte., Que. Div.); Montreal Chamber Comm.; Lloyd's Register of Shipping (Can. Comm.); Can. Electrical Assn.; Presidents Assn. R. Catholic; recreations: golf, skiing; Club: St. Denis; Home: 128 Strathcona Dr., Town of Mount Royal, Que. H3R 1E6; Office: P.O. Box 550 Sorel, Que. J3P 5P5

BRITTAIN, Donald Code, RCA, motion picture director; b. Ottawa, Ont., 10 June 1928; s. Abram Code and Elise Adrienne (Duclos) B.; e. Glebe Coll. Inst., Ottawa; Queen's Univ.; m. 1stly Barbara Ellen Tuer (d. 1953), 8 Apl. 1950; 2ndly Brigitte Irmgard Halbig, 6 July 1963; children: Christopher Duclos, Jennifer Birgit; Journalist, "Ottawa Journal", 1951-54 (Nat. Press Award 1952); film maker, Nat. Film Bd. of Can., 1954-68; Fuji Group, Japan 1968; independent since 1970; films incl.: "Volcano" (Academy Award Nomination); "Henry Ford's America" (Internat. Emmy Award); "Memorandum" (Grand Prize Venice Film Festival, N.Y. Festival); "Bethune" (Grand Prize, Leipzig); "Never a Backward Step" (Grand Prize, San Francisco); "The Champions" (four Cdn. Film Awards); "Paperland (four Cdn. film Awards) "The Dionne Quintuplets; "Fields of Sacrifice"; 6 times chosen Best Candn. Dir.; Major Retrospectives Boston, Montreal and New York Museum of Modern Art; past pres., Can. Soc. of Film Makers; Guest Lectr. on Film, Univ. South. Cal.; Standford Univ. N.Y. Univ., Univ. British Columbia; rec'd Centennial Medal 1967; mem. Soc. Film Makers (Pres. 1964, 1971); Anglican; Home: 471 Clarke Ave., Westmount, Que. H3Y 3C5

BRITTAIN, William Bruce, D.F.C., B.Sc.; Canadian public service; b. Truro, N.S., 10 Feb. 1922; s. William Harold and Mary Macdonald (Cruickshank) B.; e. Macdonald Coll., McGill Univ., Teaching Cert. 1941. B.Sc. and High Sch. Teaching Dipl. 1949; m. Catherine Ewing, d. late John W. Wood, 17 June 1947; children: Elizabeth Ewing, Catherine Bonney, William Harold Bruce; DEPY. MIN., DEPT. VETERANS AFFAIRS, since 1975; joined Dept. of Agric., Ottawa, as Asst. Dir. of Personnel, 1949-

50; apptd. Chief, Adm. Div., Science Service, 1950-54; joined as Asst. Dir., Indian Health Service, 1954-62; apptd. Assoc. Dir., Medical Services, 1962-65; Dir.-Gen., Adm. 1965; with Treasury Bd., Management Improvement Br. 1969-70; Asst. Dep.-Min. Dept. Veterans Affairs 1970; served with R.C.A.F. 1941-45; AC2 to Squadron Leader; Flying Instr., Training Command; Bomber Command — 6 (Candn.) Group, U.K.; P.O.W. Denmark, Germany; awarded D.F.C.; mem., Fed. Inst. Mang.; Am. Mang. Assn.; past Pres. Can. Inst. Pub. Adm. 1980-81; United Church; recreations: Canadiana, skiing, boating; Home: 10 Chinook Cr., Nepean, K2H 7E1, Office: Veterans Memorial Bldg., Ottawa, Ontario.

BRITTON, William Leonard, B.A. LL.B.; b. Kirkland Lake, Ont., 15 Dec. 1935; s. Leonard William and Jeanne (LaFleche) B.; e. Univ. of W. Ont. B.A. 1958; Univ. of B.C. LL.B. 1962; m. Linda Susan d. Don Menzies, Kamloops, B.C., 26 Dec. 1960; children: Christopher, Angela, Daniel, Jane; mem. law firm Bennett, Jones; Dir. ATCO Ltd.; Candn. Utilities Ltd.; Easton United Securities Ltd.; read law with Chambers, Might & Co.; called to Bar of Alta. 1963; Dir. Calgary & Dist. Foundation; Stampeder Football Club Ltd.; mem. Candn. Bar Assn.; Delta Upsilon; P. Conservative; R. Catholic; recreations: squash, skiing, golf; Clubs: Calgary Petroleum; Willow Park Golf; Glenmore Racquet; Home: 408 Wilderness Pl. S.E., Calgary, Alta. T2J 2G5; Office: 3200, Shell Centre, 400-4th Ave. S.W., Calgary, Alta. T2P 0X9

BROADBENT, J. Edward, M.P., M.A., Ph.D.; b. Oshawa, Ont., 21 March 1936; s. Percy Edward and Mary Anastasia (Welsh) B., Tweed, Ont.; e. Univ. of Toronto, B.A. (Philos.) grad. 1st, M.A. (Philos. of Law), Ph.D. (Pol. Science); London Sch. of Econ., post-grad. work; m. Lucille Allen, 29 Oct. 1971; children: Paul Charles, Christine Elizabeth; LEADER, NEW DEMOCRATIC PARTY since 1975; Prof. of Pol. Science, York Univ. 1965-68; el. to H. of C. for Oshawa-Whitby g.e. 1968; re-el. since; el. Chrmn., Fed. Caucus 1972; elected Leader of N.D.P. 1975; elected Vice-Pres. of Socialist International 1976; re-elected Leader of N.D.P. 1977, 1979 and 1981; served with RCAF; rank Pilot Offr.; two Univ. of Toronto Open Fellowships and two Canada Council Scholarships for post-graduate study in Canada and England; mem. Branch 43, Royal Can. Legion; author, "The Liberal Rip-Off" 1970; mem. Candn. Pol. Science Assn.; Candn. Civil Liberties Ass.; recreations: cross-country skiing; reading; music; Home: 450 Laurier Ave. E., Ottawa, Ont.; Office: House of Commons, Ottawa, Ont. K1A 0A6

BROADBENT, R. Alan, B.A.; b. Toronto, Ont. 20 July 1945; s. Joseph Alan Scace and Marjorie Jean (McEacheran) B.; e. Univ. of B.C. B.A. 1968; Queen's Univ.; BUSINESS CONSULTANT 1981; Dir. of Information Rubber Assn. of Can. 1973-77; Pres. 1977-81 Rector, Queen's Univ. 1969-72; Pres., Maytree Foundation; mem. Bd. Trustees Queen's Univ.; mem. Cort Soc.; recreations: tennis, canoeing; Club: Queen's; Home: 155 Westminster Ave., Toronto, Ont. M6R 1N8; Office: 100 University Ave., Toronto, Ont. M5J 1V6

BROADFOOT, Barry Samuel, B.A.; writer; b. Winnipeg, Man. 21 Jan. 1926; s. Samuel James and Sylvia Marie (Scoular) B.; e. Univ. of Man. B.A. 1949; children: Susan Elaine, Ross Archer; served newspaper and wire services 29 yrs. as photo ed., sports ed., night city ed., city ed., news ed., travel ed., book ed., mag. ed., roving corr., columnist; commentator 13 part TV series Alta.'s Pioneers; author "Ten Lost Years" 1973; "Six War Years" 1975; "The Pioneer Years" 1976; "Years of Sorrow, Years of Shame" 1977; 5 books travel in Can.; popular mag. articles, special assignments Candn. newspapers, Am. and Eng. mags.; rep. in anthologies; served with Candn. Inf. Corps 1943-45; recreations: fishing, boating, hiking, antique hunting, backroads travel, reading and correspondence; Address: 3996 Morningside Rd., Nanaimo, B.C. V9T 1N5.

BROCK, Rear Admiral Jeffry Vanstone, D.S.O., D.S.C., C.D.; R.C.N. (retired); b. Vancouver, B.C., 29 Aug. 1913; s. late Capt. Eustace Alexander B. and Margaret Phoebe (Jukes) B.; e. St. John's Coll. Sch., Winnipeg, Man.; Univ. of Manitoba; m. Patricia Elizabeth, d. late John Henry Folkes, 11 March 1950; children: Jeffrey Patrick Alexander, Constance Alexandra (Mrs. P.R. McCurdy), Wm. Ranulf Augustus D'Aguilar; began career with business associations with Great West Life Assnce. Co. and Cockfield, Brown & Co. of which he was W. Mgr.; 1st Lieut., Winnipeg Div., R.C.N.V.R. 1934; in Command Vancouver Div. 1936; Staff Signals Offr. to Flag Offr. Pac. Coast, 1939; on loan service with Royal Navy, Mar. 1940; and until Nov. 1944 served afloat in N. Atlantic, W. Africa, N. Africa, Italy and E. Mediterranean, and during this period held appts. in Command of HMS "Kirkella," HMS "Rununculus", HMS "Stonecrop", HMS "Bazely", and as spare Escort Commander W. Approaches; Mentioned in Despatches; D.S.C.; promoted Commdr.; Nov. 1944-July 1945, Sr. Offr., 6th Candn. Escort Group; 1945-47, Sr. Offr., W. Naval Reserve Divns., in Command HMCS "Ontario", R.C.A.F. Staff Coll.; Dir. of Naval Plans, Ottawa, 1948-50; May 1950, apptd. Capt. (D) West Coast Candn. Destroyer Flotilla; departed for Far East and Korean War as Commdr., Candn. Destroyers Far East; Mentioned in Despatches; D.S.O.; U.S. Legion of Merit (Offr.); returned to Can. July 1951 on appt. as Naval mem. of Dir. Staff, Nat. Defence Coll. of Can.; Naval Member, Candn. Jt. Staff, London, Eng., and Naval Adviser to the High Commr. for Can., 1953-57; apptd. Sr. Candn. Offr. Afloat (Atlantic), June 1957; Asst. Chief of the Naval Staff (Air & Warfare) and mem. of the Naval Bd., 1958; promoted Rear Adm. and apptd. Vice Chief of Naval Staff July 1961 and mem. of Can. U.S. Permanent Jt. Bd. on Defence; apptd. Flag Offr. Atlantic Coast and Maritime Commdr. Atlantic, July 1963; retired June 1965; P. Conservative cand. for Nanaimo, Cowichan and The Islands, g.e. 1968; author, "The Dark Broad Seas" 1981; Anglican; recreations: fishing, sailing, travel; Homes: Westport, Ont. K0G 1X0, and 2225 Queen Anne Drive S.E., Fort Myers, Fla. 33905

BROCK, Stanley E., C.M., F.S.A.; actuary; b. Winnipeg, Man., 9 Sept. 1912; s. William R. and Anne (Williams) B.; e. Univ. of Manitoba, Hon. B.A. 1933; m. Gertrude, d. Col. E. Blondeau of Chateau d'Eau, Que., 26 Sept. 1942; children: Donald, Alan, Joyann; VICE-CHRMN. BOARD OF DIR., INDUSTRIAL LIFE INSURANCE CO.; Dir., Levesque, Beaubien Inc.; Canadian Financial Corp.; Industrial Life Technical Services Inc.; The Equitable General Insurance Co.; Industrial General Insurance Co.; mem., Royal Trust Adv. Bd., Quebec; Vice Pres., Jeffery Hale's Hosp. Centre; Pres., Jeffery Hale's Hosp. Corp.; Protestant; Clubs: Rotary; Royal Quebec Golf; Garrison; Atlantis; Home: Thornhill Park, Quebec, Que.; Office: 1080 St. Louis Rd., Quebec, Que. G1S 1C7

BRODEUR, Alphonse Toner; industrialist; b. Montreal, Que., 20 Feb. 1902; s. late Alphonse and Nellie (Toner) B.; e. Montreal High Sch.; Loyola Coll.; Ottawa Univ.; m. Nora, d. W.W. Hope, Ottawa, Ont., 14 June 1928; children: Dr. Michael T. H., Alphonse William H., James H., Christopher John; CHAIRMAN, CASSIDY'S LTD.; Lorlea Steels Ltd.; Continental Olivier Ltd.; Gaylord Régéthermique Canada Ltée; Modern Kitchen Equipment Ltd.; Cody Food Equipment Ltd.; Chrmn. G.H. Kitchen Equipment Inc.; Continental Manufacturers Ltd.; Chrmn., Deurcol Inc.; A.B.C.-Cassidy Inc.; Imbrex-Cassidy Ltd.; Packer Floor Coverings Ltd.; Terminal Sheet Metalworkers Ltd.; Gov., Montreal Children's Hosp.; Past Pres., Canadian Importers Assn.; Past Pres.; Hotel & Restaurant Suppliers Assn.; Past Pres. and Dir., Quebec Assn. for Retarded Children; Bd. of Hon. Govs., Candn. Assn. for Mentally Retarded; Dir., Candn. Council, Inter-

nat. Chamber of Commerce; served as offr. of Royal Montreal Regiment from 1925 to end of 2nd World War; Gov., Notre Dame Hosp.; Douglas Hops.; Hôpital Marie-Enfant; Liberal; Roman Catholic; recreations: golf, curling, gardening; Clubs: Royal Montreal Golf; Royal Montreal Curling; Royal St. Lawrence Yacht; Mount Royal; Montreal Badminton & Squash; Home: 60 Summit Crescent, Westmount, Que. H3Y 1L6; Offices: 2555 Matte Blvd., Brossard, Que. J4Z 3M1; and Ste. 965, Sun Life Bldg., Montreal, Que. H3B 2W6

BRODEUR, Alphonse William; company president; b. Montreal, Que. 15 April 1931; s. Alphonse T. and Nora (Hope) B.; e. High Sch., Montreal; Trinity College Sch., Port Hope, Ont.; McGill Univ., B.Com. 1953; m. Heather Ruth, d. late Grand Gordon, 3 March 1962; three s.; PRESDIENT, CASSIDY'S LTD., since 1968; Dir., Round Agencies Ltd.; Equipment Finance Corp. Ltd.; Standard Cottons Ltd.; joined Co. 1953; apptd. Office Mgr., 1956; Sales Mgr., Toronto, 1957; Asst. Gen. Mgr., 1962; Gen. Mgr., 1964; awarded Centennial Medal, 1967; mem. Montreal Bd. Trade; Candn. Restaurant Assn.; Quebec Hotel & Suppliers Assn.; Anglican; recreations: squash, golf, curling, gardening; Clubs: Royal Montreal Golf; Badminton & Squash; Home: 33 Whitney Ave., Toronto, Ont. M4W 2A7; Office: 95 Eastside Dr., Toronto, Ont.

BRODIE, Jessie Bruce, Ph.D.; home economist (retired); b. Bethesda, Ont., 10 Nov. 1897; d. George Alexander and Luella Kate (Terry) B.; e. Pub. Sch., Bethesda; Pickering Coll. and High Sch., Newmarket, Ont.; Univ. of Toronto, B.A. 1920; Ont. Coll. of Educ.; Columbia Univ., M.A. 1925, Ph.D. 1931; Teacher, Coll. Inst., Virden, Man., 1920-21; Coll. Inst., Fort William Ont., 1922-23; High Sch., New Liskeard, Ont., 1923-24; Asst. in Research, Columbia Univ., 1925-30; Prof. of Home Econ., George Peabody Coll. for Teachers, Nashville, Tenn. 1930-36; Univ. of Toronto, 1936-52; Nutrition Specialist, Queen Aliya Coll., Baghdad, Iraq. under F.A.O. of U.N., 1952-54; Home Econ. Adv., F.A.O. of U.N. 1954; mem., Am. Dietetic Assn.; Am. Home Econ. Assn.; Candn. Dietetic Assn; Candn. Home Econ. Assn.; Sigma Xi; Kappa Delta Pi; Home: 10 William Morgan Dr., Toronto, Ont. M4H 1E7

BROEN, John E., B.Sc., M.B.A.; manufacturer; b. Edmonton, Alta. 10 Dec. 1938; s. late Asa T. Broen; e. Univ. of Alta. B.Sc. (Civil Engn.); Univ. of W. Ont. M.B.A.; m. Della Gail d. Charles Rayburn 6 Oct. 1962; children: John Eric, Thomas Asa, Carey Lynn; VICE PRES., MARKETING OPERATIONS, ROTHMANS OF PALL MALL CAN. LTD. since 1978; Special Risks Inspr. Candn. Underwriters Assn. Calgary 1961-63; Fire Protection Engr. Reed, Shaw, McNaught, Toronto 1963-65; Group Product Mgr. Benson & Hedges Tobacco Co. Montreal 1969, Vice Pres.-Dir. Marketing 1971, Extve. Vice Pres. 1974-75; Vice Pres. Asia/Pacific Philip Morris International, Melbourne and Hong Kong 1975-76; Pres., Benson and Hedges (Can.) Ltd. 1977-78; Delta Kappa Epsilon; recreations: squash, cross country skiing; Home: 137 Rochester Ave., Toronto, Ont. M4N 1N9; Office: 1500 Don Mills Rd., Don Mills, Ont.

BROMBERG, Maurycy-Moshe Bar-Am. B.A.; artist; b. Piotrcov-Tryb, Poland 20 Dec. 1920; s. Yeshayu and Regina (Bresler) B.; e. Koenigshutte, Silesia, Poland 1933; Sch. of Applied Art, Sosnovitz, Poland grad. dipl. in Graphics 1935; Acad. Fine Arts, Cracov, Poland B.A. Art Teacher 1939; Govt. Inst. Plastic Arts, Lvov, Poland Tech. Drawing Teacher 1941; m. Berta d. Baruch Aaron 1939; children: Edward, Miriam; Art Counsellor and Art Dir. Ramat-Gan (Israel) Municipal Museum; exhns. incl. various galleries Lodz 1946-50; Mun. Fine Art Gallery Cracov 1949; Art Centre Tel-Aviv 1951; Cata Gallery Jérusalem 1953; Museum Bnei-Brit 1963; Ramat-Gan 1964, 1967, 1972, 1977; Jewish Art Centre Buenos-Aires 1973; Internat. Fine Art Graphic Berlin 1973; Fine Art Centre Cambridge 1974; Gallery Zavier Toronto 1976; Koffler Art Gallery Toronto 1978; paintings, sculpture and monuments in collections of Martyrology Museum Warshaw; Mun. Fine Art Museum Lodz; Jewish Art Centre Lodz; Yad Ben-Zvi Museum Jerusalem, Yad Vashem Museum; Mun. Fine Art Museum Ramat-Gan, Yad Lebanim House; Martyrology Museum Chulon; rec'd Lodz Mun. Fine Art Museum Award 1946, Jewish Cultural Centre Award 1947; Annual Grant Polish Artists Assn. Warshaw 1949; Berlin Medal for Graphics 1973; author various articles in Israeli newspapers; mem. Israel Teacher Assn.; Israel Artists & Sculptors Assn.; Address: 20 Waggoners Wells Lane, Thornhill, Ont. L3T 4K3.

BROMKE, Adam, M.A., Ph.D.; university professor; b. Warsaw, Poland 11 July 1928; came to Can. 1950; s. Waclaw and Romualda (Beckmann) B.; e. St. Andrew's Univ. M.A. 1950; Univ. of Montreal Ph.D. 1953; McGill Univ. Ph.D. 1964; m. Alina B. d. Boleslaw Kosmider 7 June 1958; children: Adam Robert, Aleksander Richard; PROF. OF POLITICAL SCIENCE, MCMASTER UNIV. since 1973; Chrmn. of Dept., 1973-79; Lectr. Univ of Ottawa, 1952-53; Lectr. Univ. of Montreal, 1952-54; Ed.-in-Chief, Polish Overseas Proj., Free Europe Cmte., N.Y., 1955-57; Conference leader and lectr. McGill Univ., 1957-60; Research fellow, Russain Res. Centre. Harvard Univ., 1960-62; at Carleton Univ. as Asst. Prof., 1962; Chrmn. Soviet and European Studies, 1963-66; Assoc. Prof., 1964; Prof., 1967; Chrmn. of Dept., 1968-71; Man. Ed., "Candn. Slavonic Papers", 1963-66; served with Polish Underground Army 1944-45; Polish Forces under Britain's Comm., 1945-47 (Germany, Italy, U.K.); discharged as Offr.-in-Comn.; twice awarded Polish Army Medal; author of "The Labour Relations Board in Ontario", 1961; "Poland's Politics, Idealism vs. Realism", 1967; "Poland: The Last Decade", 1981; Ed., "The Communist States at the Crossroads", 1967; Ed., "The Communist States and the West", 1967; Ed., "The Communist States in Disarray, 1965-1971", 1972 (Polish Trans., 1973); Ed., "Gierek's Poland", 1973; Ed., "The Communist States in the Era of Detente, 1971-1977", 1978; papers on intl. politics and Eastern Europe in several professional jnls. and N.A. newspapers; mem., Candn. Assn. of Slavists (Vice Pres. 1966-68, Pres. 1968-69); Candn. Political Assn.; Am. Assn. for the Advancement of Slavic Studies; Intl. Political Science Assn.; Intl. Cmte. for Soviet and European Studies (Pres. 1974-80); R. Catholic; recreations: serious reading, light music; Home: 165 Little John Rd., Dundas, Ont. L4H 4H2; Office: Hamilton, Ont. L8S 4M4.

BROMLEY, David Allan, B.Sc., M.Sc., M.A., M.S., Ph.D., F.A.P.S., F.A.A.A.S., F.R.S.A. (London), Dr. Nat. Phil. (Frankfurt); Dr. d'Etat, Science (Strasbourg); Dr. Sc.(Queen's); LiH. D. (U. of Bridgeport); physicist, university professor; b. Westmeath, Ont., 4 May 1926; s. Milton Escort and Susan Anne (Anderson) B.; e. Queen's Univ., B.Sc. (Engn. Physics) 1948, M.Sc. (Physics) 1949; Univ. of Rochester, M.S. 1950 Ph.D. (Nuclear Physics) 1952; Yale Univ., M.A. 1961; m. Patricia Jane, d. Thomas Patrick Brassor, Kingston, Ont., 30 Aug. 1949; children: David John, Karen Lynn; HENRY FORD II PROF. OF PHYSICS, YALE UNIV., since 1961 and Chrmn. of Dept. 1970-77; Dir., A.W. Wright Nuclear Structure Lab. since 1962; Operating Engr., Ont. Hydro Elect., 1946; Demonst., Queen's Univ., 1947; Jr. Research Offr., NRC (Can.) 1948; Univ. of Rochester, Instr. 1952-54, Asst. Prof. 1954-55; Atomic Energy of Canada Ltd. 1955-60 (Assoc. Research Offr., 1955-56; Sr. Research Offr., 1957-60; Sec. Head, Accelerators, 1958-60); Assoc. Prof. of Physics, Yale Univ., 1960-61 and Assoc. Dir. Heavy Ion Accelerator Lab.; with J.M. McKenzie devel. first room temp. semiconductor nuclear detectors and first used these in nuclear research; with E. Almqvist first used light helium istopes as projectiles in nuclear research; discovered first nuclear molecules; with H.W. Fulbright designed and built first variable energy cyclotron; with Chalk River and High Voltage Engn. staff devel. first tandem accelerator and first Emperor tandem accelerator respectively; with J. Birnbaum (IBM) devel. first completely integrated computer based nuclear data acquisition system; pioneered in use of heavy ion beams in precision study of nuclear phenomena; Dir., United Nuclear Corp.; Extrion Corp.; United Illuminating Co.; Union Trust Co.; Northeast Bancorp Inc.; General Ionex Co. Oak Ridge Assoc. Univs.; Univ. of Bridgeport; Consulting Ed., McGraw Hill Book Co.; Consulting Ed. Nuclear Instruments and Methods; American Scientist; Annals of Physics; Il Nuovo Cimento; Nuclear Science Applications; Science, Technology and the Humanities; Journal of Physics; Technology in Society; Consultant, Brookhaven, Los Alamos, Argonne, Oak Ridge Nat. Labs., Bell Telephone Labs., IBM Corp., High Voltage Engn., Gen. Telephone and Electronics Co.; awarded Gov. Gen. of Canada Medal 1948, Queen's Univ. Medal 1948, Shell Fellowship 1949, NRC (USA) Fellowship 1952, Guggenheim Memorial Fellowship 1977; Humboldt Prize 1978; Chrmn. U.S. Nat. Comte., Internat. Union of Pure and Applied Physics; Pres. International Union of Pure and Allied Physics; Chrmn., Nat. Physics Survey Comte., Nat. Acad. Sciences; Chrmn., Office of Physical Scs., N.R.C.; mem. Candn. Assn. of Physicists; Conn. Acad. Science & Engn.; Fellow, Brantford Coll., Yale Univ.; Am. Acad. Arts & Sciences; Am. Assn. Advanc. Science (Chrmn. Physics Sect. 1977); Pres., Am. Assn. Advanced Sci. 1979, Chmn. of Bd. 1982; Benjamin Franklin Fellow, Royal Soc. of Arts (London) 1979; mem. at Large, Nat. Research Council (Chrmn. Comte. on Nuclear Science NAS-NRC); mem., Naval Sc. Bd. NAS-NRC; High Energy Physics Adv. Panel, ERDA; Nuclear Sci. Adv. Comm. USDOE/NSF Jt. U.S.-U.S.S.R. Working Group on Science Policy and on Research on Fundamental Properties of Matter; Chrmn., CSCPRC formal U.S. nuclear science delegation to Peoples Republic of China 1979; co-author of "Proceedings of the Kingston Conference" 1960, and "Perspectives in Physics" 1969; "Physics in Perspective" 1972-73; author of over 350 publ. in scient. and tech. lit.; "Large Electrostatic Accelerators" 1976; "Detectors in Nuclear Science" 1978; "Heavy Ion Science" 4 vols., 1981; Sigma Xi; Presbyterian; recreations: archeology, music, photography; golf; Clubs: New Haven Lawn; Mory's; Cosmos (Washington, D.C.); Office: 260 Whitney, New Haven, Conn.; Home: 35 Tokeneke Dr., Hamden, Conn. 06518.

BRONFMAN, Charles Rosner; industrialist; b. Montreal, Que. 27 June 1931; s. Saidye (Rosner) and late Samuel B.; e. Selwyn House Sch. Montreal; Trinity Coll. Port Hope, Ont.; McGill Univ. 1948-51; two children: Stephen Rosner, Ellen Jane; DEPUTY CHRMN., CHRMN. EXTVE. COMTE., THE SEAGRAM COMPANY LTD. 1979; Chrmn., Joseph E. Seagram & Sons since 1975; Chrmn. Cemp Investments Ltd.; Montreal Baseball Club Ltd.; Hon. Chrmn. and Dir. Supersol Ltd., Israel; Dir. Bank of Montreal; Canadian Pacific Air Lines Ltd.; joined Joseph E. Seagram & Sons Ltd. 1951; Nat. Sales Mgr. 1954; Vice-Pres. Marketing 1955; Vice-Pres. and Dir. The Seagram Co. 1958; Pres. 1958; Extve. Vice-Pres. 1971; Chrmn. 1975 Past Pres. Allied Jewish Community Services Montreal; Life Gov. Jewish Gen. Hosp.; Gov. the Jewish Agency for Israel, Montreal YM-YWHA; La Jeune Chambre de Montréal Inc.; Dir. Jerusalem Found. Inc., Candn. Council Christians and Jews; Chairman of the Board, Can.-Israel Securities Ltd. (State of Israel Bonds, Can.); mem. Montreal Bd. Trade; Shaar Hashomayim Cong., Westmount; Clubs: Montefiore; Mount Royal; Saint-Denis; Hillside Tennis; Elm Ridge Golf & Country; Hollywood Golf (Deal, N.J.); Office: 1430 Peel Street, Montreal, Que. H3A 1S9

BRONFMAN, Edgar M., B.A.; industrialist; b. Montreal, Que. 20 June 1929; s. Saidye (Rosner) and Samuel B.; e. Trinity Coll. Sch. Port Hope, Ont.; McGill Univ., B.A. 1951; Williams Coll., Mass.; M. Georgina (Webb), 1975; CHAIRMAN BD. AND CHIEF EXTVE. OFFR., THE

SEAGRAM COMPANY LTD. 1977-; Chmn. & CEO, Joseph E. Seagram & Sons; CHMN., GULFSTREAM LAND & DEVELOPMENT CORP.; Dir., E.I. duPont de Nemours & Co.; Trustee, Mount Sinai Hosp.; Park East Synagogue; Salk Inst. for Biol. Studies; Hon. Trustee Bank of New York; Trustee and Pres. Samuel Bronfman Foundation; Dir. Am. Cancer Society (N.Y. City Div. Inc.); Clevepak Corp. (Chrmn.); International Executive Service Corps; Am Technion Soc.; Interracial Council for Business Opportunity; Weizmann Inst. of Science; mem. Am. Jewish Committee (exec. comte.); Am. Jewish Congress; Anti-Defamation League of B'Nai B'rith (National Comm.); Business Comte. for the Arts, Inc.; Center for Inter-Am. Relations, Inc.; Comte for Economic Development; Council of Foreign Relations; Foreign Policy Association; Hundred Year Assn. of N.Y.; Nat. Urban League (Finance Comte); United Jewish Appeal/Federation of Jewish Philanthropies; Pres., World Jewish Congress Extve. Bd. Govs. N.Y. Council Boy Scouts of Am.; Founding mem. Rockefeller Univ. Council; Office: 375 Park Ave., New York, N.Y. 10152

BRONFMAN, Edward M., B.Sc.; executive; b. Montreal, Que., 1 Nov. 1927; s. Allan and Lucy (Bilsky) B.; e. Bishop's Coll. Sch.; Babson Coll. (Mass.), B.Sc. (Business Adm.) 1950; children: Paul Arthur, David Eric, Brian Anthony; DEP. CHAIRMAN BD. AND DIR. EDPER INVESTMENTS LTD.; Chrmn., Nat. Hees Enterprises Ltd.; Ranger Oil (Canada) Ltd.; National Hees Enterprises Ltd.; Trizec Corp. Ltd.; Brascan Ltd. mem. Bd. Govs., Jewish Gen. Hosp.; Y.M.H.A.; Que. Student Intra-Exchange Program; E. Regional Chrmn., Candn. Friends of the Hebrew Univ.; Jewish; recreations: skiing, tennis, jogging; Office: Royal Bank Plaza, P.O. Box 93, Toronto, Ont. M5J 2J2

BRONFMAN, Gerald, B.Com.; industrialist; b. Yorkton, Sask., 2 Dec. 1911; s. Harry and Ann (Gallaman) B.; e. Public Schs. in the West; Montreal High Sch.; McGill Univ., B.Com.; m. Marjorie Meta, d. late Jacob Schechter of New York, 9 Feb. 1941; children: Joan Eileen, Judith Lynn, Corinne Marcia, Jeffrey Mark; PRESIDENT, GERBRO INC.; Pres., Gerin Inc.; Roslyn Developments Ltd.; Dir., Hasboro Industries (Can.) Ltd.; Chmn., Gerboro Properties Ltd.; Dominion Dairies Ltd.; began with Distillers Corporation-Seagrams Limited.; Montreal, Quebec, and Seagrams-Distillers Corporation, New York, New York; served in 2nd World War with R.C.A.F., Sqdn. Leader; awarded United States Legion of Merit (Officer); Life Gov., Verdun Prot. Hosp.; Hon. mem. of Council of Montreal Museum of Fine Arts; Trustee, Candn. Red Cross Soc. (Que. Dir.); Trustee, YM-YWHA and HHS; Gov. Montreal Children's Hosp.; Jewish Gen. Hosp.; Jewish Hosp. of Hope; Pres., Mt. Sinai Hosp. Corp.; Pres., Marjorie and Gerald Bronfman Foundation; Harry Bronfman Family Foundation; mem. Senate, Stratford Shakespearean Festival Foundation; mem. McGill Grads. Soc.; Phi Lambda Phi; Mu Sigma; B'nai B'rith Orthodox Jewish; recreations: golf, photography, skiing; Clubs: Montefiore; St. Denis; Elmridge Country; Home: 475 Roslyn Ave., Westmount, Que. H3Y 2T6; Office: Suite 1700, 1245 Sherbrooke St. W., Montreal, Que. H3G 1H4

BRONFMAN, Peter F., B.A.; business executive; b. Montreal, Que., 2 Oct. 1929; s. Allan and Lucy (Bilsky) B.; e. Lawrenceville Sch., N.J.; Yale Univ., B.A. 1952; m. Diane Feldman, 8 Dec. 1953, divorced; m. 2ndly, Theodora Reitsma, 4 Feb. 1976; children: Linda, Bruce, Brenda; CHAIRMAN, EDPER INVESTMENTS LTD.; Chrmn. Bd., Carena-Bancorp Inc.; Dir. and Chrmn. of Board, Trizec Corp. Ltd.; Dir. and Chrmn. of Bd.; Brascan Ltd.; Continental Bank; Dir., John Labatt Ltd.; London Life; Scott Paper; Hebrew; recreations: tennis, swimming; Clubs: Montefiore; Office: Royal Bank Plaza, P.O. Box 93, Toronto, Ont. M5J 2J2

BROOK, Adrian Gibbs, Ph.D., F.C.I.C., F.R.S.C.; university professor; b. Toronto, Ont., 21 May 1924; s. Frank Adrian and Beatrice Maud (Wellington) B.; e. Lawrence Park Coll. Inst., Toronto, Ont.; Univ. of Toronto, B.A. 1947, Ph.D. 1950; m. Margaret Ellen, d. Samuel E. Dunn, Ottawa, Ont., 18 Dec. 1954; children: Michael Adrian, Katherine Mary, David Lindsay; PROF. OF CHEMISTRY, UNIV. OF TORONTO, since 1962 and Chrmn. of Dept. 1971-74; Lectr. in Chem., Univ. of Sask., 1950-51; Nuffield Foundation Fellow in Chem., Imp. Coll. of Science & Tech., London, Eng., 1951-52; Post-doctoral Fellow, Iowa State Univ., 1952-53; Lectr., Univ. of Toronto, 1953-56, Asst. Prof., 1956-59, Assoc. Prof., 1959-62, Assoc. Chrmn. of Dept. 1968-69, Acting Chrmn. 1969-71; awarded Regents Gold Medal in Physics and Chem., 1947; Kipping Award in Organsilicon Chem. (Am. Chem. Soc.) 1973; author of 105 articles in scient. and prof. journs.; mem. Am. Chem. Soc.; Chem. Inst. of Canada; served in 2nd World War with R.C.N.V.R., 1943-45; United Church; recreations: sailing, water skiing; Home: 79 Glenview Ave., Toronto, Ont. M4R 1P7

BROOK, Philip R., D.F.C., B.Arch.; architect; b. Salmon Arm, B.C., 7 Feb. 1918; s. John Smith and Dorothy Margaret Maxwell (Gibbons) B.; e. Niagara Pub. Sch. Niagara-on-the-Lake, Ont., 1934; St. Catharines (Ont.) Coll. Inst., 1939; Univ. of Toronto, B.Arch. 1950; m. Sonia, d. John Dixon, 9 Dec. 1950; children: Michael, Gregory, Debora, Dinah, Matthew; PARTNER, BROOK-CARRUTHERS-SHAW; associated with Allward and Gouinlock Arthur Eadie and Earl C. Morgan, '1950-56; entered private practice 1957 and formed firm Brook & Banz, 1959; received Massey Medal, Royal Candn. Acad. Arts; Royal Arch. Inst. Can., 1961 and 1967; served as Night Fighter Pilot with RCAF in Britain, North Africa, Sicily and Europe (Sqdns. 410, 255 & 418), 1940-45; awarded D.F.C.; mem., Royal Arch. Inst. Can.; Ont. Assn. Archs.; Royal Academy of Arts; recreations: sports, painting; Home: 18 Munro Park Ave., Toronto, Ont. M4E 3M3; Office: 200 Adelaide St. West, Toronto, Ont. M5A 1W7

BROOK, Richard L., textile manufacturer; wool merchant; b. Simcoe, Ont., 3 Feb. 1909; s. Harry J. and Martha I. (Lea) B.; e. Appleby Coll., Oakville, Ont.; Lowell Textile Inst., Lowell, Mass.; m.; two d., Judith, Betty; PRESIDENT, SIMCOE WOOL STOCK CO. LTD. (estd. 1890); Partner, Norfolk Wool Co.; Dir., Brook Woolen Co. Ltd.; Conservative; Anglican; recreations: fishing, hunting, golf; Office: 449 Norfolk St. S., Simcoe, Ont. N3Y 2W8

BROOKE, Hon. John W.; Justice, Court of Appeal Ontario, since 1969; previous to elevation to the High Court of Justice of Ont. in 1964 was mostly engaged in Counsel work; as specialist in labour law was Counsel in that field for Candn. Broadcasting Corp. and Cand. Coll. of Nurses; as a Lectr. at Osgoode Hall Law Sch. was a Dir. of the school's Bar Administration Comte. on Criminal Procedure; Home: 186 Glencairn, Toronto, Ont. M4N 1N2; Office: Osgoode Hall, Toronto, Ont. M5H 2N6

BROOKER, Douglas Jack; company president; b. Brantford, Ont. 12 Jan. 1919; s. F. W. and Elva (McGuire) B.; e. Pub. and High Schs., War Staff Coll., Brantford, Ont.; m. Jane, d. Marcel T. Morgan, 17 June 1944; 2 s. and 2 d.; PRESIDENT, AERO ENVIRONMENTAL LTD. since 1964; Pres., D. J. Brooker Industries Ltd.; Liberty Building Ltd.; Asst. to Pres., present Co. (then Aero Tool Works Ltd.), 1947; Vice-Pres. and Gen. Mgr.; 1949; served in 2nd World War with R.C.A.F., rank Wing Commdr. A.F.C., 1939-47; mem., Oil Heating Assn. of Can. (Past Pres.); Bd. of Trade Metrop. Toronto; Candn. Mfrs. Assn.; Royal Candn. Mil. Inst.; Freemason; Anglican; recreations: flying, fishing; Home: 42 Saintfield Ave., Don Mills, Ont. M3C 2M6; Office: 37 Hanna Ave., Toronto, Ont. M6K 1W9

BROOKES, John E.; economic adviser; b. Montreal, Que. 3 Dec. 1916; s. Charles and Mary Ann (Carter) B.; e. Comm. High Sch., Montreal 1930-34; night courses in Econ. and Corp. Finance, McGill Univ. and Sir George Williams Univ.; m. Monique. d. Joseph Chevalier, Lachine, Que. 29 May 1956; one step-d., Claudette Viau; Chrmn., C.B.R.S. Ltd.; Dir., Normick Perron Inc.; Dustbane Enterprises Ltd.; with Barclays Bank (Canada) as Banker and Investment Officer, Montreal 1934-42; joined Greenshields Inc., Security Deliveries 1944-45, Underwriting 1946-47, Manager Bond Trading 1948-57, Vice-President 1957-64, Managing Dir. 1965-66, Sr. Vice-Pres. 1967, Vice-Chrmn. 1972-76; served in World War, R.C.A. 1942-44; Anglican; recreation: golf; Clubs: Kanawaki Golf & Country; Home: 1990 Louisbourg, Montreal, Que. H3M 1M3; Office: 1600 Dorchester Blvd. W., Ste. 610, Montreal, Que.

BROOKING, Ruth Patricia, B.A., B.L.S.; librarian; b. West Whitby Twp., Ont. 17 March 1928; d. Ernest Covini and Hazel Olive (Hutchings) B.; e. Brooklin Continuation Sch. 1945; Oshawa Coll. & Vocational Inst. 1946; Queen's Univ. B.A. 1958; Univ. of Toronto B.L.S. 1962; CHIEF LIBRARIAN, OSHAWA PUBLIC LIBRARY 1974- ; Head of Tech. Services present Lib. 1962, Head of Adult Services 1964, Asst. Chief Librarian 1967, Acting Chief Librarian 1973; mem. Candn. Lib. Assn.; Ont. Lib. Assn.; United Church; recreations: farming, skiing, curling, swimming, reading; Clubs: Canadian; University Women's; Home: R.R. 1, Whitby, Ont. L1N 5R5; Office: 65 Bagot St., Oshawa, Ont. L1H 1N2.

BROOKS, Frank Leonard; artist; b. London, Eng., 7 Nov. 1911; s. Herbert Henry and Ellen (Barnard) B; came to Can. 1912; e. Pub. and High Schs., North Bay, Ont.; Central Tech. Sch. and Ont. Coll. of Art, Toronto, Ont.; travelled and studied in Eng., France and Spain 1932-34; Ont. Teachers' Training Coll., Hamilton, Ont.; Escuela Universitaria de Bellas Artes, San Miguel de Allende, Mexico, lithography and fresco, 1947; m. Reva, d. M. Silverman, Toronto, Ont., 18 Oct. 1935; has exhibited throughout Can., also in Eng. and N.Y.; paintings in collection of Nat. Gallery, Ottawa, Art Gallery of Ontario, Museum of Modern Art, Mexico, Palacio de Bellas Artes, Mexico, D.F. (Exhibition of Paintings and Tapestries 1976), S. J. Zacks Coll., Toronto and Art Gallery, London, Ont.; Worcester Art Museum (US); Carpenter Gallery, Dartmouth Coll., N.H., Ohio Univ., as well as in many private collections; Exhibitions at Ohio Univ., Athens, Ohio; Dartmouth Coll.; Santa Barbara Museum of Art; Lucien Labaudt Art Gallery, San Francisco; Witte Museum, San Antonio; appointed Teacher of Art, N. Vocational School, Toronto, Ont. 1937; served in World War 1943-45 with R.C.N.V.R. as Lieut.; Official War Artist 1944; mem. Roy. Candn. Acad. of Arts; author: (books) "Watercolor ... A Challenge", 1957; "Oil Painting Traditional and New", 1959; "Wash Drawing" and "Casein" 1961; "Painting and Understanding Abstract Art", 1964; "Painter's Workshop", 1969; Home: Calle de la Quinta S/N (Guadiana) Box 84, San Miquel de Allende, Gto., Mexico.

BROOKS, James M., B.A.; banker; b. Walkerton, Ont. 1 May 1926; e. Univ. of Toronto B.A. 1961; m. Ethel Ivison Oct. 1949; children: David J., Barbara J.; VICE-PRES. MORTGAGE DIVISION, CANADIAN IMPERIAL BANK OF COMMERCE; joined Kinross Mortgage Corp. as Asst. Sec. 1964, becoming Mgr. Ont., Asst. Gen. Mgr., Gen. Mgr., Pres. 1973 and Deputy Chairman and C.E.O. 1981; Kinross name changed to CIBC Mortgage Corporation Feb. 1982; Home: 73 Elvaston Drive, Toronto, Ont. M4A 1N5; Office: 750 Lawrence Avenue West, North York, Ont.

BROOKS, Reva; photographer; b. Toronto, Ont. 10 May 1913; s. Morris and Jennie (Klein) Silverman; e. Dovercourt Pub. Sch., Central High Sch. of Comm., Central Tech. Sch., Toronto; Univ. of Toronto night courses; m. Frank Leonard Brooks 18 Oct. 1935; Exhns.: Toronto, London, Montreal, Vancouver galleries; Santa Barbara Museum of Art; Anglo-Mexican Inst. Mexico; Witte Museum, San Antonio, Texas; Museum of Modern Art N.Y.; Dartmouth Coll.; Group Show Creative Photography 1956; Salon Internat. du Portrait Photographique, Bibliothèque Nationale, Paris 1961; Grands Photographes de Notre Temps, Versailles 1962; Expo Montreal 1967; Palacio de Bellas Artes Mexico 1970; Centro Cultural Instituto Nacional de Bellas Artes, San Miguel de Allende, Mexico; Casa de Cultura Aguascalientes, Mexico; Universidad de Guanajuato; Travelling Exhn. USA 1971; Royal Ont. Museum 1972; rep. in coll.: Bibliothèque Nationale Paris; Museum of Modern Art N.Y.; Instituto Nacional de Bellas Artes Mexico; David Alfaro Siqueiros Mexico; Rufino Tamayo Mexico; Rico Lebrun Los Angeles; John Huston Ireland; MacKinley Helm Coll. Santa Barbara; Ansel Adams Carmel; Ayala & Samuel J. Zacks Toronto; Helen Hayes N.Y.; Kate Simon N.Y.; Henry Miller Calif.; Freeman Tovell Ottawa and other Candn. Mexican Am. and European artists and collectors; various publs. of works; contrib. "Enciclopedia del Sapere" Milan; Nat. Univ. of Mexico 1974; San Francisco Museum of Modern Art 1975 and Travelling Exhn. 1976; Nat. Film Bd. Can. 1975; Catalogue "Photography 75"; Home: Calle de la Quinta s/n (Guadiana), San Miguel de Allende, Gto., P.O. Box 84, San Miguel de Allende, Gto., Mexico.

BROOKS, Robert Leslie, B.Sc., M.B.A.; banker; b. Kelvington, Sask., 2 June 1944; e. Univ. of Man. B.Sc. 1965; Univ. of W. Ont. M.B.A. 1968; m. Brenda Mary 28 Dec. 1968; children: Derek, Keith and Ian; GEN. MGR. FINANCE & ADM., THE BANK OF NOVA SCOTIA; Systems Comptroller present Bank 1971, Supvr. Systems Planning 1972, Chief Acct. 1973, Comptroller & Chief Acct. 1978; mem. Financial Extves. Inst.; Home: 220 Donessle Dr., Oakville, Ontario; Office: 44 King St. W., Toronto, Ont. M4H 1E2.

BROOKS, Vernon Bernard, M.Sc., Ph.D.; neuroscientist; educator; b. Berlin, Germany 10 May 1923; s. Martin and Margarete (Hahlo) B.; e. Univ. of Toronto B.A. 1946, Ph.D. 1952; Univ. of Chicago M.Sc. 1948; m. Nancy Fraser 29 June 1950; children: Martin Fraser, Janet Mary, Nora Vivian; PROF. OF PHYSIOL. UNIV. OF W. ONT. 1971- , Chrmn. of Physiol. 1971-76; Lectr. in Physiol. McGill Univ. 1950-52, Asst. Prof. 1952-56; Visiting Fellow in Physiol. Australian Nat. Univ. 1954-55; Asst. Prof. Rockefeller Univ. 1956-60, Assoc. Prof. 1960-64; Prof. of Physiol. New York Med. Coll. 1964-71, Chrmn. of Physiol. 1964-69; author over 100 publs.; ed. "Motor Control" 1981; mem. ed. bds. various scient. journs.; mem. Am. Physiol. Soc.; Candn. Physiol. Soc.; Internat. Brain Research Organ.; Soc. Neuroscience; Unitarian; recreations: reading, cottage; Home: 99 Euclid Ave., London, Ont. N6C 1C3; Office: London, Ont. N6A 5C1.

BROOMFIELD, Adolphus George, R.C.A. (1973); artist; b. Toronto, Ont., 26 Aug. 1906; s. George Thomas and Esther May (Hathaway) B.; e. Queen Victoria Sch. and Parkdale Coll Inst., Toronto, Ont.; Ont. Coll. of Art; summer schs. of art, N.Y. and Vt.; m. Isadora Bettina Hellmuth, 3 July 1948; children: Ann Hellmuth, John Gay; Lect. on Color Hist. and Application to Service Clubs and Industrial Training Schools, 1954-56; served in 2nd World War with R.C.A.F. as Squadron Leader in Newfoundland, England, Normandy, Belgium, Holland, Germany and Denmark; with Bomber Command and Tactical Airforce 1942-46; mem. Candn. Painter-Etchers (1941); mem., Ont. Soc. of Artists (1942); Candn. Graphic Arts Soc. (1939); Ont Inst. Painters; Royal Candn. Acad. Art: Painting (1973); has written occasional reviews of art books and an article on Tom Thomson; a charcoal portrait of him sketched by Olive Snell, official "Tatler" artist while he was in Eng., and publ. in "Tatler"; included in "terrible Beauty" by H. Robertson, 1977; "The Many Ways of Waters and Color, 1979; "Canada Crafts" by G. Schaming, 1978; Coll. of 143 T.A.F. Drawings (Normandy to Germany) recorded in check-list of war colls., Nat. Gallery, Ottawa "Memories, 1913" a painting included in Nat. Gallery diploma collection, R.C.A.; Conservative; Protestant; recreation: skiing; Studio-Home: 232 Isabella Ave., Mississauga, Ontario L5B 1A9.

BROSSARD, Nicole, B.A., L.ès L.; writer; b. Montreal, Qué., 27 Nov. 1943; d. Guillaume and Marguerite (Matte) B.; e. Univ. Montreal, B.A. 1965, L.ès L. 1968; Univ. Québec (Montreal), Bt. d'Enseignement specialise 1971; m. 22 Jan. 1966; co-Dir., "La Barre du Jour" (Literary Review); "Beau" 1968; "Suite Logique" 1970; Le Centre author: "Mordre en sa Chair" 1966; "L'Echo Bouge Blanc" 1970; "Un Livre" 1970; "Sold Out" 1972; co-author, "Trois (Aube à la Saison)" 1965; Anarchist; Home: 665, Crevier, Montreal, Qué. H4L 2V6

BROSSEAU, Bernard Louis Persillier, O.B.E., M.C., C.D., M.D.; association executive; b. Beloeil, Que., 21 Aug. 1912; s. Bernard Louis and Angéline (Benoit) B.; e. Mount St. Louis Coll., Montreal, 1922-33; Univ. of Montreal, M.D. 1941; Royal Army Med. Coll., London, Eng.; Royal Coll. of Physicians and Surgeons, Dipl. in Tropical Med. and Hygiene 1947; Univ. of Toronto, Dipl. in Hosp. Adm. 1958; m. Margaret Jean, d. late Horace Stuart, 18 March 1958; one s., Julien; ASST. EXTVE. DIRECTOR, CAN. COUNCIL ON HOSPITAL ACCREDITATION; Vice Pres., Council of Can.; served with R.C.A.M.C. 1940-45; Regtl. Med. Offr., Repatriation, U.K., 1946-47; C.O. Fort Churchill Mil. Hosp., 1948-50; Sr. Med. Offr., Candn. Army Far East, 1950-52; C.O. 25 Field Ambulance, Korea; Area Med. Offr., Eastern Que., 1952-54; Med. Liaison Offr., Candn. Army Liaison Estab., London, Eng. and SHAPE, Paris, France, 1954-56; Area Med. Offr., Eastern Ont., Kingston, 1958-60; Med. Liaison Off., Candn Joint Staff, Washington, D.C., 1960-62; retired Candn. Army 1962; with Ont. Hosp. Services Comn. as Dir., Hosp. Services, 1962-63; Commr. of Hosp. 1963-65; Dir. Hosp. Services, Coll. of Physicians and Surgeons, Que. 1965-66; mem., Soc. Grads. Hosp. Adm.; Defence Med. Assn.; Assn. des Médecins de Langue Française du Can.; R. Catholic; recreation: hiking; Club: Royal Candn. Mil. Inst.; Address: 1815 Alta Vista Rd., Ottawa, Ont. K1G 3Y6

BROTT, Alexander, Mus.D., F.R.S.A., LL.D.; conductor, composer, violinist; professor; b. Montreal, Que., 14 March 1915; s. Samuel and Annie (Fuchsman) B.; e. McGill Univ.; Julliard Sch. of Music, New York; Univ. of Chicago, D.Mus.; D. Mus (honoris causa) McGill Univ., 1980; m. Charlotte, d. Walter Goetsel, Montreal, P.Q., 11 March 1943; two s. Boris, Denis: PROF. OF MUSIC, McGILL UNIV., and Conductor in Residence there; Musical Dir., McGill Chamber Orchestra; Montreal "Pops" Concerts Inc.; Kingston "Pops" Concerts; has composed a number of works involving various instruments and several solo pieces; most recent compositions incl. "Martlet's Muse" commissioned by McGill Grad. Soc. (symphonic work based on McGill tunes); "Centennial Celebration", "La Corriveau" (ballet), "Pristine Prims in Polychrome", "Paraphrase in Polyphony" 1967; "Spasms for Six", "Accent" 1971; Symphonic works: "From Sea to Sea", "Concordia", "Oracle", "Fancy & Folly", "Royal Tribute", "Analogy in Anagram", "Spheres in Orbit", "War & Peace", "Prelude to Oblivion", "Violin Concerto", "Arabesque for Cello and Orchestra"; String Orchestra: "Lullaby & Procession of the Toys", "Ritual", "Dirge", "Three Astral Visions"; A Capella Choir: "Canada Case History", "Israel", "The Emperor's New Clothes" 1971, "The Young Prometheus", 1971; and a number of chamber works; Compositions incl. over 50 symphonic works, chamber works and works for solo instruments; toured U.S.S.R. (1966), Switzerland, Mexico, France, Poland, Hungary, Czechoslovakia, U.S., Can.

with McGill Chamber Orchestra; commissioned by C.B.C. to research and orchestrate unpub. works of Beethoven, two of which ("The Young Prometheus" and "7 Minuets 6 Canons") rec'd world premiers in Can.; Conductor and Mus. Dir. Kingston Symphony Orch. 1965-80; apptd. Musical Div. Emeritus 1981; Hon. mem. Zoltan Kodaly Acad. and Inst.; Awards: two Olympic Medals for compositions (London and Helsinki); Sir Arnold Bax Gold Medal; Lord Strathcona Scholarship; Elizabeth Sprague Cooledge Award (twice); Loeb Mem. Award (twice); CPAC Award (thrice); Hon. LL.D., Queen's Univ. 1973; Candn. Music Council Medal for contribution to music in Can. 1976; Queen's Jubilee Medal 1978; Medal of Order of Can. 1979; mem., Composers Authors & Publishers Assn.; Musicians Guild of Montreal; Home: 5459 Earnscliffe, Montreal, Que. H3X 2P8

BROTT, Boris; music director and conductor; b. Montreal, Que., 14 March 1944; s. Alexander and Lotte (Goetzel) B.; e. Conservatoire de Musique, Montreal; McGill Univ.; studied conducting with Pierre Monteux, Igor Markevitch, Leonard Bernstein and Alexander Brott; MUSIC DIRECTOR AND CONDUCTOR, THE HAMILTON PHILHARMONIC since 1969; Principal Guest Conductor, BBC Welsh Symphony Orchestra and Princ. Conductor, CBC Winnipeg Orchestra; made debut as violinist with Montreal Symphony 1949; founded Philharmonic Youth Orchestra of Montreal 1959; Asst. Conductor, Toronto Symphony 1963-65; Principal Conductor, Northern Sinfonia, Eng. 1964-68; Asst. Conductor, N.Y. Phillharmonic 1968-69; Music Dir. and Conductor, Lakehead Symphony 1968-72, Regina Symphony 1971-72; has guest conducted all major orchestras in Can.; BBC Symphony Orchestras in Glasgow, Manchester, London and Cardiff; The Philharmonia; Royal Philharmonic; Liverpool Philharmonic; L'Orchestre des concer's Colonne, Paris; RIA, Rome and Milan; RIAS Berlin; Berlin Philharmonic; Los Angeles Philharmonic; Chautaugua Symphony; Orquesta Sinfonica de El Salvador, del Estado de Mexico; Jerusalem Symphony; has recorded for Mace Studios and Canadian Talent Library; awarded + an American Conductor's Prize 1958; Gold Medal, Dimitri Mitropoulos Internat. Conductors Competition 1968; writer-host-conductor of numerous TV and Radio shows incl. "Music from Bach to Rock" (Ohio State Award Winner), "Music — Why Bother?", "Hear Out" (Ohio State Award Winner), "Brott to You", "Brott Backstage", also featured on numerous CBC-TV specials incl. Musicamera, Glenn Gould Series "Music in our Time" and "Boris and those Magnificent Music Machines"; Music div., series of syndicated TV programmes, "The Palace"; music dir. and conductor of "Great Artists in Concert" TV series; rec'd Can. Jaycee Award "One of Five Outstanding Young Canadians" 1973; Hon. Chmn.mas Seal Campaign 1980-81; Home: 301 Bay St. South, Hamilton, Ont.; Office: Hamilton Place, 50 Main St. W., Hamilton, Ont. L8P 1H3

BROWER, Robert L., Q.C., B.A., LL.B.; b. Edmonton Alta., 2 Feb. 1925; s. Lorin B. and Elizabeth Christina (Miller) B.; e. Victoria and Westglen High Schs., Edmonton, 1943; Univ. of Alta., B.A. (Pol. Econ.) 1950, LL.B. 1953; children: Robert Lorin Taylor, Kimberley Anne, Catherine Christine; PARTNER, BROWER & CO. President and Director, Battleford Mortgage Co. Limited; Great Alberta Capital Corp.; read law with Dubensky, Belzil & Clark; called to Bar of Alberta 1954; cr. Q.C. 1969; served as Flight Sgt., Coastal Command. RCAF 1943-45; Progressive Conservative candidate province g.e. 1955; cand., City of Edmonton civic el. 1964; Pres. P. Conservative, Fed. Constit. of Edmonton Strathcona 1963-65; mem., Edmonton and Alta. Bar Assns.; Phi Delta Theta (Pres. 1952; alumni Pres. 1955; Pres. Alta. 1954-60); P. Conservative; Protestant; recreations: golf, jogging; Clubs: Oilfield Tech. Soc.; Edmonton; Home: 1002, 9940-112 st., Edmonton, Alta. T5K 1L8; Office: 814 Imperial Oil Building 10025 Jasper Ave., Edmonton, Alta.

BROWN, Hon. A. Garnet, M.L.A.; politician; food broker; b. Halifax, N.S., 22 May 1930; s. Alexander Garnet and Margaret B.; e. Halifax, N.S. m. Elizabeth Anne, d. Earl Lowe, Sheet Harbour, N.S., 22 Aug. 1953; children: Karen, Robert, James, Jacqueline; MIN. OF RECREATION; Pres. A. G. Brown & Son Ltd.; Brown Brokerage Ltd.; D & G Leasing; Vice Pres. Halifax Cable Vision; Dartmouth Cable; Digby Cable, Past Pres. Candn. Food Brokers; served as campaign mgr. for former Premier of N.S. fed. g.e. 1965, prov. el. 1967 and prov. leadership Lib. Party 1966; Pres. N.S. Lib. Assn. 1968-71; el. M.L.A. for Halifax-E. Shore 1969; re-el. since; apptd. Min. of Highways and of Pub. Works 1970; Min. of Tourism 1971; Prov. Secy. & Min. of Recreation 1975; has rec'd numerous awards during govt. service; led N.S. del. to Munich in successful bid to bring first World Canoe Championships to Dartmouth, N.S. 1978; has served as Exte. mem. Dir. and participant in many prof. and community organs. incl. Nat. Dir. Duke of Edinburgh Awards; Past Pres. N.S. Food Brokers' Assn., Halifax Ad & Sales Club; Former Nat. Dir. Candn. Roads & Transport. Assn.; el. Pres. 1975-76, Candn. Food Brokers' Assn.; mem. N.S. Hall of Fame; mem. Halifax Bd. Trade; Young Pres' Internat.; Liberal; R. Catholic; recreations: golf, bridge, swimming; Clubs: Halifax; Ashburn Golf & Country; Waegwoltic; Home: 7061 Fielding Ave., Halifax, N.S. B3L 2H1; Office: Brown Building, 3500 Kempt Rd., Halifax, N.S.

BROWN, Anthony William Aldridge, M.B.E., B.Sc.F., M.A., Ph.D. F.R.S.C.; b. Horley, Surrey, Eng. 18 Nov. 1911; s. William and May (English) B.; e. Winchester Coll. Eng., 1925-29; Univ. of Toronto, B.Sc.F. 1933; M.A. 1934; Ph.D. (Bio-chem.) 1936; London Sch. of Hygiene and Tropical Med., 1936-37; m. Jocelyn, d. Norman Evill, Hampstead, London, Eng. 11 June 1938; children: Hilary, Virginia, Kathryn; formerly Prof. and Head, Dept. of Zool., Univ. W. Ont. (apptd. 1947); formerly Assoc. Comte. mem., Defence Research Bd., U.S. Nat. Research Council, World Health Organ.; Special Consultant, U.S. Pub. Health Service; Biologist, World Health Organ. 1956-58 (special leave of absence); mem., Edit. Bd., "Annual Review of Entomology"; in 1937 became Sessional Lectr. in Entom., Macdonald Coll., McGill Univ.; 1938-42 served as Asst. Entom., Dom. Dept. of Agric., i/c Candn. Forest Insect Survey; 1940-42, Ed. "The Canadian Field-Naturalist"; served in 2nd World War 1942-45; Maj., Directorate of Chemical Warfare; awarded M.B.E.; appt. Head, Entom. Sect., Experimental Station, Suffield, of Defence Research Bd., 1945-47; Research Fellowship of Royal Soc. of Can. in the Biol. Sciences, 1936-37; awarded Entomol. Soc. Can. Gold Medal for Achievement, 1963; Pres., Entomol. Soc. Can. 1962; Am. Mosquito Control Assn., 1965; Entomol. Soc. Am., 1967; Candn Soc. Zool. 1968; Am. Assn. of Econ. Entom.; Hon. mem. Entom. Soc. Ont.; Entom. Soc. Am.; author; "Insect Control by Chemicals", 1951; "Insecticide Resistance in Arthropods", 1958; "Ecology of Pesticides" 1978; co-author: "Entomology Medical & Veterinary", 1954; many scient. papers for tech. journs.; currently John A. Hannah Distinguished Prof. Emeritus, Mich. State Univ.; Kappa Alpha; Anglican; Address: Sous-la-ville, 1261 Genolier, Switzerland

BROWN, Arnold, D.D., L.H.D., O.C. (1981); Salvation Army officer; b. London, Eng. 13 Dec. 1913; s. Arnold Rees and Annie (Horrocks) B.; came to Canada 1923; e. Belleville (Ont.) Coll. Inst.; Trinity Coll. of Music; L.H.D. Asbury Coll. 1972; DD. Olivet Coll., 1981; m. Jean Catherine, d. late James Barclay, 15 Sept. 1939; children: Heather Jean, Beverley Ann; Comnd. Salvation Army Offr. 1935, i.c. Salvation Army work, Bowmanville, Ont. 1935, Asst. Ed. "The War Cry" (Can.) 1936, Nat. Information Offr. (inaugurating Salvation Army Radio & TV work) 1946, Nat. Youth Offr. 1962, Dir. Internat. Public Relations, Salvation Army London, Eng. 1964, Chief of Staff. Internat. Salvation Army, London, Eng. 1969-1974;

Territorial Commdr. — Can. and Bermuda, Toronto, Ont. 1974-77; General 1977-81; mem. Inst. Public Relations (U.K.); author of "What Hath God Wrought?" 1952; also numerous articles in mags. and journs.; made Freeman of City of London (Eng.) 1978; Protestant; recreations: reading, writing, music; Clubs: Rotary (Past Pres. and hon. mem., London, Eng. Br. 1970-71); hon. mem., Downtown Toronto; Home: 117 Bannatyne Dr., Willowdale, Ont. M2L 2P5

BROWN, Cassie, author; b. Rose Blanche, Nfld. 1 Oct. 1919; d. Wilson Gordon and Caroline (Hillier) Horwood; e. Rose Blanche Ang. Sch. 1927; St. Michael's Convent, St. George's Nfld. 1930; Mercy Convent, St. John's, Nfld. 1937; m. Donald Frank Brown 10 Sept. 1945; children: Derek L., Christine L.; PRESIDENT, KARWOOD LTD.; author "Death on the Ice" 1976; "A Winter's Tale" 1976; "Standing Into Danger" 1979; radio plays, articles, fiction; Journalist, "The Daily News" St. John's, 7 yrs.; published "Newfoundland Woman" mag. 1961-64; participated amateur dramatics 1956-66, also radio and TV; Protestant; Address: (P.O. Box 5806) St. John's, Nfld. A1C 5X3.

BROWN, Donald I., CIB; insurance broker; b. Montreal, Que., 19 Dec. 1931; s. late Charles Arrol and Estelle (Lynch) B.; e. Loyola of Montreal; Sir George Williams Univ. comm.; children: Karen Norma, Deborah Susan, Stephen Scott; PRESIDENT AND CHIEF EXTVE. OFFR. AND DIR., JOHNSON & HIGGINS WILLIS FABER LTD. since 1975; Dir. Johnson & Higgins Willis Faber Inc.; Dupuis Parizeau Tremblay Inc.; J. & H.W.F. Inc.; Les Conseilliers D.P.T. Inc.; Pres. & Dir., Devitt-McClure Limited; Pres. and Dir., Johnson & Higgins Willis Faber (Alberta) Ltd.; Chrmn. of Bd. and Dir., Johnson & Higgins Willis Faber (Aviation) Ltd.; joined Johnson & Higgins (Canada)Ltd. 1950, Mgr. Production Dept. 1963; joined E. A. Whitehead as Partner 1965, Vice Pres. and Dir. 1966. Vice Pres. and Dir.-Ont. 1970; Vice Pres. and Dir. Tomenson Saunders Whitehead Ltd. 1973, Extve. Vice Pres. and Dir. 1975 and Dir. Tomenson Alexander Ltd. 1975; Past Pres. Montreal Central Lions Club; Inter Service Club Council; mem. Bd. Trade Metrop. Toronto; Ins. Brokers Assn. Que.; Toronto Ins. Conf.; R. Catholic; recreations: golf, curling, skiing, reading; Clubs: Mount Royal (Montreal); Royal Canadian Military Institute (Toronto); Royal Montreal Golf; St. George's Golf & Country (past Dir.); Toronto Golf; Cambridge; Home: 19 Roxborough St. W., Toronto, Ont.; Office: P.O. Box 70, 36th Floor, First Canadian Place, Toronto, Ont. M5X 1C2

BROWN, Downie; manufacturer; b. Glasgow, Scot. 17 June 1943; s. Robert and Helen Margaret (Marshall) B.; e. Hutcheson's Boys Grammar Sch. Glasgow 1960; Inst. C.A.'s Scot. Apprentice 1960-65, mem. 1965; Glasgow Univ. 1962-64; m. Moya d. George McAuley, N. Ireland, 3 Oct. 1975; VICE PRES. CORPORATE DEVELOPMENT, INDAL LTD.; held various accounting positions R.T.Z. Industries (formerly Pillar Holdings) 1968-72; Extve. International Financial Management, London, mang. sports personalities and entertainment celebrities 1972; joined present Co. 1973 holding various positions incl. mang. two subsidiaries; served as Capt. Scot. and Brit. Internat. Swim Teams, competed in Commonwealth Games 1966 and 1970; mem. Inst. C.A.'s Scot.; Protestant; recreations: swimming, squash, golf, photography, reading, music; Home: 102 St. Leonards Ave., Toronto, Ont. M4N 1K5; Office: 4000 Weston Rd., Weston, Ont. M9L 2W8.

BROWN, Eldon Leslie, B.A.Sc., M.E.; mining engineer (retired); b. Toronto, Ont., 19 Aug. 1900; s. Samuel and Fanny Leach (Cole) B.; e. Public Schs. and Parkdale Coll. Inst., Toronto; Univ. of Toronto, B.A.Sc. 1922 and M.E. 1933; m. Margaret Louise, d. David Drybrough, 4 March 1930; children: Margaret Carol, Sheila Leslie and Eldon Leslie; engineer with Mond. Nickel Co. and Victoria Syndicate (Mond subsidiary) 1923-27; Supt. and later Gen. Supt. Sherritt Gordon Mines Ltd., 1927-32; Mgr., God's Lake Gold Mines Ltd., 1933-37; Consulting Engineer, Madsen Red Lake Gold Mines, 1937-39 and Sachigo River Exploration Co. Ltd. 1937-42; General Manager, Sherritt Gordon Mines Ltd., 1936-46 becoming Pres. and Mang. Dir. till retired from that post Apl. 1968; Vice-Pres. and Gen. Mgr., Michipicoten Iron Mines Ltd., 1942-46; Pres., Candn. Metal Mining Assn., 1950-51; Dir., Eldurado Mining and Refining Ltd. 1951-61; mem., Candn. Inst. Mining & Metall.; Assn. Prof. Engrs. Ont.; Univ. of Toronto Engn. Alumni Medal 1954; Candn. Inst. Mining & Metall. Blaylock Medal 1968; Conservative; Presbyterian; Clubs: Engineers'; Home: Mardon Farm, Brechin, Ont.

BROWN, Eric Joseph, Q.C., B.A., C.T.C.I.; trust company executive; b. Staffs., Eng. 6 Oct. 1921; s. Harry and Eva (Betteley) B.; e. Elem. Sch. Staffs., Eng.; High Sch. Walkerville, Ont.; Carleton Univ. B.A. 1949; Osgoode Hall Law Sch. 1953; m. Norrine, d. James Garvin 25 May 1956; children: Stephen, Eric, Victoria; CHAIRMAN, CANADA PERMANENT TRUST CO.; since 1981 Chrmn. Canada Permanent Mortgage Corp.; called to Bar of Ont. 1953; cr. Q.C. 1968; Trust Offr. Chartered Trust Co. 1953, Estate Mgr. 1958, Mgr. Toronto Br. 1962, Asst. Gen. Mgr. 1963; Asst. Vice-Pres. Canada Permanent Cos. (as consequence of merger) 1968; Vice-Pres. Planning 1971, Sr. Vice-Pres. Planning and Services Div. 1972, Extve. Vice-Pres. 1974; Pres. 1975; served in 2nd World War R.C.A.F. 1940-45, service in U.K. and N. Am,; rank on discharge W.O.l; mem Candn. Chamber Comm.; Candn. Bar Assn.; Trust Cos. Assn. of Can.; Bd. Trade Metrop. Toronto; Anglican; Clubs: National; Granite; recreations: boating, swimming; Home: 42 Aldenham Cres., Don Mills, Ont. M3A 1S2; Office: 320 Bay St., Toronto, Ont. M5H 2P6

BROWN, Maj. Gen. George Grenville, C.D.; retired army officer; b. Saskatoon, Sask., 17 June 1922; s. late Arthur Richardson, B.Sc., LL.D. and Marie Pauline (Grambo) B.; e. Pub. and High Schs., Lloydminster and Regina, Sask., 1940; Royal Mil. Coll., 1940-42 mq; Staff Coll. Camberley Eng., 1956 psc; Assoc. Inf. Offrs. Advanced Course USA, 1952; Nat. Defence Coll., 1968-69 NDC; m. Constance Helen Bridgman (d. 1971) 27 Oct. 1946; children: Shaun Richardson Grenville, Shelley Jean Marie, Patrick Arthur Raymond; 2ndly, Pauline Hazel Boismenu, April 1972; one. s. Steven John; comnd. and posted overseas 1942; joined Loyal Edmonton Regiment, Italy, 1943; wounded in Battle of Naviglio Canal 1944; served as operations officer Holland 1945; returned to Canada to join Pacific Force 1945; joined PPCLI Regular Army 1946; served in Shilo, Manitoba, Calgary and as Staff Learner, HQ W. Command Edmonton 1947; Area Cadet Offr. for B.C., Vancouver, 1947-50; Sqdn. Commdr. Royal Roads Services Coll., 1950-52; promoted Maj. 1952 and co. commdr. 2 PPCLI Calgary and Germany 1953-55; Bgde. Maj. 1st Candn. Inf. Bgde. Group, 1957-60; GSO 2 1st Brit. Div., Army on Rhine, 1960-62; promoted Lt. Col. 1962 and C.O. 1st PPCLI Victoria (named Hon. Citizen 1963); Germany 1963-65, returned to Can. to help formation of HQ Mobile Command; Col. 1966 and apptd. Chief of Inf., Candn. Forces HQ Mobile Command; Dir. of Equipment requirements (Land Forces), CFHQ, 1969; Brig. Gen. and Chief of Staff Operations, HQ Mobile Command, 1970-72; Commdr. 1 Combat Group & Can. Forces Base, Calgary 1972-74; promoted Maj. Gen. Aug. 1974 and apptd. Chief Land Operation NDHQ Ottawa; Depy-Commdr. Mobile Command 1975; conducted Jubilee Celebration of PPCLI in Germany reviewed by Col.-in-Chief (Lady Patricia Ramsay), 1964; made Honorary Indian Chief "Defender", 1964; awarded Centennial Medal 1967; Serving Brother, Order of St. John 1976; apptd. Col. of the Regt. PPCLI 1977; joined Alberta Energy Co. 1978; mem. Bd., Calgary Chamber of Comm.; Hon. Pres., Prov. Que. Rifle Assn. and 1st Bn. PPCLI Rod & Gun Club; mem., Royal Mil.

Coll. Club of Can.; Loyal Edmonton Regt. Assn.; PPCLI Regt'al Assn.; Camberley Staff Coll. Grad. Assn.; Royal Alberta United Services Inst.; Dev. Bd.; Centre for Conflict Studies U. of N.B.; hon. life mem., Earl Mountbatten Mem. Soc.; recreations: skiing, gardening; Home: 844 Oakside Circle S.W. Calgary, Alta. T2V 4P7; Office: Alberta Energy Co. Ltd., 639 Fifth St. S.W., Calgary, Alta. T2P 0M9

BROWN, Gerald Daniel; executive; b. Windsor, Ont., 3 Apl. 1929; s. Wiltrude (Dunwoody) and late Gerald M. B.; e. Pub. and High Schs., Toronto, Ont.; m. Valerie, d. late William McKay, May 1949; children: Drew, Victoria, Deborah, Michael; CHRMN. AND C.E.O., PUBLIC & INDUSTRIAL RELATIONS LTD., since 1979; Pres. B.L. Associates Ltd.; Chairman, PIR Advertising Ltd.; Chrmn. Hill and Knowlton Canada Ltd.; Director, Canada Newswire Ltd.; T.E.C. Printing Ltd.; served as Editor of Canadian daily, weekly and business pubs. and as Pub. Relations Consultant till joining present Co. in 1952 as Acct. Extve.; el. a Dir., 1955; apptd. Vice-Pres. and Mang. Dir., 1958; Pres., Public and Ind. Relations Ltd.; mem., Candn. Public Relations Soc.; Inst. of Public Relations; Public Relations Soc. of Am.; Candn. Chamber Comm.; Anglican; recreations: charitable activities, outdoor sports; Clubs: Ontario; Granite; Empire; Devil's Glen Country Home: 98 Cortleigh Blvd., Toronto, Ont. M4R 1K6; Office: One Yonge St., Toronto, Ont. M5E 1N4

BROWN, Harcourt, M.A., Ph.D.; professor emeritus; b. Toronto, Ont., 30 May 1900 s. Newton Harcourt and Grace Amanda (Young) B.; e. Univ. of Toronto, B.A. 1925; M.A. 1926; Columbia Univ., Ph.D. 1934; m. Dorothy Elizabeth, d. Dr. Charles Edward Stacey, 27 Apl. 1927; has one d., Jennifer; in Dom. Bank, Toronto and Ottawa, 1917-20; Queen's Univ. 1926-29; Brooklyn Coll., N.Y., 1930-31; Univ. of Rochester, 1931-32; Travelling Fellow, Am. Council Learned Socs., 1934-35; Washington Univ., St. Louis, Mo., 1935-37; Prof. of French Lang. and Lit., Brown Univ. 1937-69; Co-Founder and Assoc. Ed., "Annals of Science", 1935-74; mem. Bd. Eds., "Journal of the History of Ideas", 1944-76; Past Pres., Hist. of Science Soc.; mem., Modern Lang. Assn. Am.; Modern Humanities Research Assn.; Can. Historical Assn.; Soc. for French Studies; corr. mem. Acad. des Sciences, Arts et Belles-Lettres, Caen, France; author of "Scientific Organizations in Seventeenth Century France", 1934, 1967; editor and contributor to "Science and the Creative Spirit", 1958, 1971; author of "Science and the Human Comedy" 1976; articles in "University of Toronto Quarterly", Studies in the Renaissance, Studies on Voltaire and the 18th Century, "Diogenes"; "Isis"; Journal of Higher Education, Journal of the History of Ideas, Dictionary of Scientific Biography, Revue d'Histoire de la Littérature française, Bulletin de la Société d'Histoire du Protestantisme français, Daedalus, "Rendiconti" of Accademia Nazionale dei Lincei, Rome, Annals of Science; etc.; mem. Bd. of Festival of the Sound; Address: 14 Avenue Rd., Parry Sound, Ont. P2A 2A7;

BROWN, Jack Ernest, B.A., B.L.S., M.A., LL.D.; librarian; b. Edmonton Alta., 1 March, 1914; s. Ernest William and Maud Alice (Jarman) B.; e. Univ. of Alta., B.A. 1938; McGill Univ. B.L.S. 1939; Univ. of Chicago M.A. 1940; L.L.D. Univ. Waterloo 1965, McMaster Univ. 1978; m. Estelle A., d. late Frank Coles, 26 Dec. 1944; children: Frances, Keith; Prof., Grad Sch. Library Sci., McGill Univ. since 1978; Dir. Can. Inst. Scientific and Tech. Information, NRC 1974-77; (Nat. Science Librarian 1957-74); Reference Librarian, Edmonton Public Library 1942; Library Assistant, New York Public Library, Science and Tech. Div., 1947; Asst. Librarian, Brown Univ., Providence, R.I. 1946-47; sometime Visiting Lectr., McGill Univ. Lib. Sch., Toronto Univ. Lib., Sch., Ottawa Univ. Lib Sch.; mem., Candn. Lib. Assn. (Councillor 1961-64); Assn. of Coll. & Research Libs. (Dir. 1961-64); Nat. Research Council Assoc. Comte. on Scient. Information

(Secy.); Candn. Nat. Comte. for Internat. Fed. for Documentation (Secy.); Internat. Fed. for Documentation (Vice Pres., 1965-67); mem. OECD Information Policy Group; NRC Adv. Bd. on Scient. & Tech. Information; Can. Assoc. Information Science; Can. Library Assn.; Special Libs. Assn.; Candn. Library Assn. Outstanding Service to Librarianship Award, 1979; Libraries & Inf. Services, Award for Special Librarianship in Can., 1979; Anglican; recreations: music, gardening; Home: 417 Meadow Dr., Ottawa, Ont. K1K 0M3; Office: McGill Univ., Graduate Sch. of Library Science, 3459 McTavish St. Montreal, Que. H3A 1Y1

BROWN, Kenneth Charles, B.A.; diplomat; b. Ann Arbor, Mich., 13 Feb. 1925 (came to Can. 1925); s. late Prof. George Williams and Vera Beatrice (Kenny) B.; e. Univ. of Toronto, B.A. 1945; Oxford Univ. (Rhodes Scholar), B.A. 1948; m. Ruth Louise, d. Earl Johnston, Sarnia, Ont., 3 July 1948; children: David, Deborah, Christopher, Andrew; joined Dept. of External Affairs in London, Eng., July 1948; Ottawa Dec. 1948; Second Secy., Havana 1951; Ottawa 1954; Second Secy., Berne 1957; First Secy. 1959; Ottawa 1960; Counsellor, Washington 1963; Ottawa 1967; Ambassador to Cuba and Haiti 1970; Ottawa 1973; Ambassador to Sweden 1976; Chmn., Refugee Status Advisory Comte., Can. Employment and Immigration Commission; served with Candn. Army in N.W. Europe 1944-46; rank Sgt. on discharge; Un. Church; recreations: skiing, camping, bridge, tennis; Home: 285 Mariposa Ave., Ottawa, Ont. K1M 0T4; Office: Refugee Status Advisory Comte., Employment and Immigration Commission, Ottawa, Ont. K1A 0J9

BROWN, Logan Rae, B.A.; industrialist; b. Guelph, Ont., 6 Aug. 1927; s. C. H. Sherman and Vera Irene (Rae) B.; e. Pub. Sch. and London (ont.) Central Coll. Inst.; Univ. of W. Ont., Sch. of Business, Hon. B.A. 1950; m. Betty Catherine, d. Sam McMahon, Toronto, Ont., 3 July 1951; children: Jordan, Christopher, Sandra; PRES., ROBIN HOOD MULTIFOODS INC. since 1969 and Chief Extve. Offr. since 1970; Vice-Pres., International Multifoods, Minneapolis, Minn. since 1971; began career as Sales Rep., Lever Brothers Ltd. 1950; Marketing Research Dept. 1950; Brand Mgr. 1952; New Products Mgr. 1955; Marketing Mgr. 1957; joined Libby, McNeill & Libby of Canada Ltd. as Dir.-Marketing, 1960; Pres. and Mang. Dir. 1964; Vice-Pres., International, Libby, McNeill & Libby, Chicago 1966-69; with C.O.T.C., sch. of Inf., Camp Borden, 1946-50; qualified as Lt.; Past Offr., Elgin Regt., St. Thomas, Ont.; Candn. Intelligence Corps, Toronto, qualified as Capt.; Nat. Dir., Am. Marketing Assn. 1958-60, (Past Pres. Toronto Chapter 1955-56); mem. Ed. Review Bd., "Marketing in Canada" (1958); Chmn. (1974) Grocery Products Mfrs. of Can.; mem. Adv. Council Banff Sch. Fine Arts 1971; Dir. The Council for Canadian Unity; Chmn. (1973) Food & Beverage Industry Comte., Outlook Conf.; mem. Candn. Mil. Intelligence Assn.; 2nd Vice-Pres. and Chrmn. 1976 Building Fund Campaign, Montreal YMCA; mem., Bd. Gov., North York Gen. Hosp.; mem., Advisory Council, Fred C. Manning Schl. of Business, Acadia Univ.; Dir. Epilepsy Ont., 1980; Advisory Bd., Liberty Mutual, 1978; Zeta Psi; Protestant; recreation: golf; Clubs: Granite; St. James's; Royal Montreal Golf; Toronto Badminton & Racquet; Toronto Hunt; Home: 15 Glenallan Rd. Toronto, Ont. M4N 1G6; Office: 243 Consumers Rd., Toronto, Ont. M2J 4R4

BROWN, Col. Milton H., O.B.E.(1942), M.D., D.P.H., F.C.C.P., F.R.C.P.(C), F.R.S.M.; prof. emeritus; university professor; b. Havelock, Ont., 6 Sept. 1898; e. Trenton, (Ont.) High Sch.; Univ. of Toronto. M.B. 1924, B.Sc., M.D. 1928 D.P.H.; m. 26 June 1950; began med. career as Clin. Assoc., Connaught Labs., 1928-34; Research and Clin. Assoc. there 1934; went to Univ. of Toronto. Dept. Hygiene and Preventive Med., as Demonst., 1931-32; Lectr. 1932-35; Asst. Prof. 1935-40; Assoc. Prof. 1940-45; Prof. and Head of Dept. of Public Health, 1955-67; Assoc.

Dir. of Sch. of Hygiene, 1955-67; Asst. Dir. Connaught Laboratories 1955-67; served with Candn. Mil. 1932-39; served in World War 1939-45 in Eng., Italy and N.W. Europe as Dir. of Hygiene with the rank of Col.; Fellow Acad. of Med.; Fellow Emeritus Am. Coll. of Chest Phys.; Chrmn., Panel on Infection and Immunity, Defence Research Bd., 1951-65; mem., Public Health Research Adv. Comte., Dept. of Nat. Health and Welfare, 1960-67; Chrmn., Editorial Bd. of "Modern Medicine", 1964-80; staff (Chest Clinic) Toronto Western Hospital 1930-77; Chest Consultant, Geriatric Centre 1966-76; mem., Candn. Pub. Health Assn.; Am. Pub. Health Assn.; Candn. Med. Assn.; Ont. Med. Assn.; has contrib. numerous scient. article of med. journs.; Freemason; Nu Sigma Nu; Anglican; Home: 42 McRae Dr., Toronto, Ont. M4G 1R9

BROWN, Murray Thompson; broadcasting executive; b. Kitchener, Ont., 2 June 1917; s. Ira Sylvester and Isabel Ada (Thompson) B.; e. Amherstburg, (Ont.) High Sch. (1930-35); Parkdale Coll. Inst., Toronto, Ont., 1935-36; Univ. of Western Ont. (Management Training), Aug. — Sept. 1948; m. Clarice Victoria, d. Russell Gibson, Montreal, P.Q., 10 Apl. 1948; children: Judith Belle, Murray Craig; PRESIDENT, CFPL BROADCASTING LTD., operating Stns. CFPL AM-FM-TV; Pres., CKNX Broadcasting Ltd.; Wingham, Ont.; Dir., London Free Press Holdings Ltd.; Pres., Central Can. Broadcasters Assn., 1952; began as Clerk, Confed. Life Assn., Toronto. Ont., 1936-37; joined Burt Business Forms Ltd. (now Moore Business Forms Ltd.), 1937; held various stat. and sales positions, 1937-45; apptd. Announcer and Writer for CFPL, 1945; Commercial Mgr., 1946-49; apptd. Stn. Mgr. 1949, Gen. Mgr. 1955; Pres., Candn. Assn. of Broadcasters, 1960; Chrmn. (1974-75) Candn Advertising Adv. Bd.; Campaign Chrmn. London Un. Way (1973); United Church; recreations: golf, tennis; Clubs: London; London Hunt & Country (Pres. 1976); Home: 139 Wychwood Place, London, Ont. N6G 1S7; Office: CFPL-TV, Communications Rd., London, Ont. N6A 4H9

BROWN, Robert Craig, M.A., Ph.D.; educator; b. Rochester, N.Y. 14 Oct. 1935; s. Ralph Nelson Jennings and Marion F. (Black) B.; e. Livonia (N.Y.) Central Sch. 1953; Univ. of Rochester B.A. 1957; Univ. of Toronto M.A. 1958. Ph.D. 1962; m. Gail d. John Detgen, Haworth, N.J. 21 May 1960; children: Bradley Bower, Brenda Bekeley, Brian Blair; PROF. OF HISTORY, UNIV. OF TORONTO since 1970; Asst. Prof. of Hist. Univ. of Calgary 1961-64; present Univ. 1964, Assoc. Prof. 1966, Dir. of Grad. Studies 1972-73, Assoc. Chrmn. Dept. Hist. 1974-77; Assoc. Dean, Sch. of Grad. Studies 1981-; red'd various Can. Council Fellowships; Izaak Walton Killam Sr. Research Scholarship; S.S. H.R.C. leave grant; author "Canada's National Policy 1883-1900" 1964; "Robert Laird Borden, A Biography" Vol. 1 1975, Vol. 2 1980; co-author "Canada Views the United States" 1966; "Confederation to 1949" 1966; "The Canadians 1867-1967" 1967; "Canada 1896-1921" 1974; author various articles, essays and reviews; mem. Candn. Hist Assn. (Council 1964-67, Vice-Pres. 1978-79, Pres. 1979-80); Am. Hist. Assn.; United Church; Home: 175 Glenview Ave., Toronto, Ont. M4R 1R4

BROWN, Robert Douglas, B.Com., M.A., F.C.A.; b. Stratford, Ont., 3 Aug. 1934; s. late Ernest William and Mary Ellen (Keil) B.; e. Pub. and Secondary Schs., Stratford, Ottawa and Toronto, Ont.; Parkdale Coll. Inst., Toronto 1952; Univ. Coll., Univ. of Toronto, B.Com. 1956; Univ. of Chicago, Div. of Social Sciences, M.A. (Econ.) 1957; C.A.(Gold Medal, Ont. Inst. and Silver Medal Award, Candn. Inst. Chart. Accts.) 1960; m. Wendy Frances, d. late Frank Day, 23 Dec. 1961; children: Michelle Mary Lorraine, Robert Carleton; SR. TAX PARTNER, PRICE WATERHOUSE & CO. since 1968; admitted to the Partnership 1966; Member of Firm's Exec. Committee 1976-; Executive Partner—Tax, Price Waterhouse International, 1974-79; Chrmn., Toronto French Sch. 1980-

82; Lecturer, then Asst. Prof. (part-time) Dept. of Pol. Economy, Univ. of Toronto 1962-72; Special Lect., Advanced Tax, Osgoode Hall Law Sch. 1972-77; served as tax consultant to various govts.; Inst. Chart. Accts. Ont.; Candn. Inst. Chart. Accts. (Chrmn. Tax Course Study Group 1973-75; Chrmn. Taxation Comte. 1971-73); Candn. Br., Internat. Fiscal Assn.; (Candn. Reporter at the World Congress 1971); Mem. Taxation Adv. Comm. of Revenue Canada 1975-78; Chrmn. Task Force on Resources of Canada West Found., 1975-77; Bd. Trade Metrop. Toronto; Publications: numerous articles on taxation and other subjects in leading newspapers, mags. and professional journals; speaker at prof. and indust. conferences; recreations: swimming, reading; Clubs: National; Granite; Cambridge; Home: 164 St. Leonard's Ave., Toronto, Ont. M4N 1K7; Office: (P.O. Box 51) Toronto-Dominion Centre, Toronto. Ont. M5K 1G1

BROWN, Robert Stewart, M.A., Ph.D.; college professor (retired); b. Campbellford, Ont., 9 Sept. 1911; s. George Alexander and Elizabeth Douglas (Stewart) B.; e. Queen's Univ., Hon. B.A. 1933; M.A. 1934; McGill Univ., Ph.D. 1936; m. Ernest Patterson Rolph, June 1955; children: Margaret Elizabeth, Mary Roberta; formerly Prof., Dept. of Chemistry, Univ. of Guelph; Chem., Hendry Cornell Research Foundation, Kingston, Ont., 1936-37; Instr. & Lectr., Roy. Mil. Coll., 1937-42; Research Chem. there 1942-43; Head, Dept. of Chem., Ont. Agric. Coll., 1946-65; Prof. and Head, Dept. of Chem., Univ. of Guelph 1965-68; served in World War 1943-46 with Candn. Army (overseas), 1st Candn. Chem. Warfare Lab., Hdqrs. 1st Candn. Army, Khaki Univ. of Can.; promoted Capt. and Major; United Church; recreations: curling, music, fishing; Club: Curling; Home: 4 University Ave. W., Guelph, Ont. N1G 1N1

BROWN, Robert Taylor, B.B.A.; petroleum executive; b. Brantford, Ont. 1 Apl. 1921; s. George Franklin and Grace Jean (Taylor) B.; e. Univ. of W. Ont. B.B.A. 1948; m. Evelyn Rae d. late John Jenkins Vizzard 5 June 1943; children: Beverley Joan, Robert Jon, Martha Marie, John Jay; PRES., GULF CANADA PRODUCTS CO. 1981- ; Dir. Trans Mountain Pipe Line Co. Ltd.; held various financial and advertising positions Candn. automotive and advertising industries 1940-42, 1948-66; Co-ordinator of Advertising & Merchandising, Gulf Canada 1966, Dir. Corporate Advertising 1967, Vice Pres. Marketing 1971, Vice Pres. Planning & Control 1975; Vice Pres. Strategy Center Business Plan Analysis, Gulf Oil Corp. 1977, Vice Pres. Corporate Planning 1979; served with RCAF 1942-45; Protestant; Clubs: Granite; National; Office: (P.O. Box 460, Stn. A) Toronto, Ont. M5W 1E5.

BROWN, Ronald C., B.A.; barrister and solicitor; b. Sarnia, Ont. 12 June 1929; s. Jacob Laverne and Hilda (Spittlehouse) B.; e. Public Schs.,Stratford, Windsor and Hamilton, Ont., High Sch., Hamilton, Ont.; McMaster Univ., B.A. 1952; Osgoode Hall Law Sch.; m. Mary, d. Charles W. Bowyer, 28 Aug. 1954; children: Christine, Robert, Ian; PARTNER, BLAKE CASSELS & GRAYDON; Dir. Windsor Raceway Holdings Ltd.; Industrial Life Insurance Co.; MICC Investments Ltd.; Mortgage Insurance Co. of Canada; Delta Benco Ltd.; read law with present Firm; called to Bar of Ont. 1956; mem. Candn. Bar Assn.; Candn. Tax Foundation; Bd. Trade Metrop. Toronto; Un. Church; recreations: golf, curling; Clubs: Donalda; National; Home: 62 Airdrie Rd., Leaside, Ont. M4G 1M2; Office: (Box 25) Commerce Court W., Toronto, Ont. M5L 1A9

BROWN, Rosemary, M.L.A., B.A., M.S.W.; b. Jamaica, B.W.I., 17 June 1930; d. Ralph and Enid (James) Wedderburn; e. Wolmer's Sch. for Girls, Jamaica; Mcgill Univ., B.A. 1955; Univ. of B.C., M.S.W. 1964; St. Vincent Univ., Halifax, D.H.L. 1981; m. William T.; s. William B., 12 Aug. 1955; children: Cleta Denise, William Garrison, Jonathan Llewelyn; Founding mem.-trainer, Volunteers for

Vancouver Crises Intervention and Suicide Prevention Centre; Social Worker, Children's Aid Soc. of B.C.; Montreal Children's Hosp.; Vancouver Neurol. Soc.; Counsellor, Simon Fraser Univ. since 1969; Ombudswoman, Status of Women Council B.C. 1970-72; el. to B.C. Leg. 1972 (becoming 1st ever Black woman to hold elected office in any Candn. Parlt.); re-el. 1975, 1979; Adv. Council, Sch. of Social Work, Univ. of B.C. 1974; U.N. Human Rights Fellowship 1973; Black Award, Nat. Black Coalition of Can. 1974; mem. Status of Women Council of B.C.; Council of Continuing Educ., Univ. of B.C.; N.D.P.; recreations: reading, weaving; Clubs: University Women's; National Black Coalition of Canada; Home: 5551 Elwyn Dr., Burnaby, B.C. V5E 4A3.

BROWN, Rt. Rev. Russel F., B.A., D.C.L., D.D., (Ang.); assistant Bishop, Montreal; b. Newcastle-on-Tyne, England, 7 Jan. 1900; s. Henry John George and Lucy Jane (Ferguson) B.; came to Canada, 1909; e. Bishop's Univ., B.A. 1933, D.C.L. 1961; Montreal Diocesan Theol. Coll., D.D. 1968; m. late Priscilla Marian, d. Frederick Oldacres, 20 June 1940; children: Nicholas, Francis, Richard; Asst. Bishop of Montreal; former Bishop of Quebec; Address: 3473 University St., Montreal, Que. H3A 2A8

BROWN, Thomas Campion, M.D, F.C.A.P., F.R.C.P.(C); physician; b. Winnipeg, Man., 27 March 1920; s. Frank Herbert, C.B.E. and Elizabeth (McIlroy) B.; e. Univ. of Toronto Schs.; Univ. of Toronto, M.D. 1943; m. Joye Louise, d. Vorwerk Ernst, Waterloo, Ont., 23 Aug. 1943; children: Sheila Joye (Mrs. R. K. Munro), Lynda C. E., Thomas C.; PATHOL.-IN-CHIEF, PRINCESS MARGARET HOSP.; Dir. of Clin. Pathol., The Wellesley Hosp., Toronto; served with R.C.A.M.C. during 2nd World War, rank Maj.; mem., Toronto Acad. of Med. (Past Pres.); Ont. Med. Assn.; Candn. Med. Assn.; Ont. Assn. Pathols.; Candn. Assn Pathols.; Medico-Legal Soc. Toronto; Am. Assn. for Advance. of Science; Am. Soc. Clin. Pathols.; Coll. Am. Pathols.; Electron Microscope Soc. Am.; Internat. Acad. Pathol.; Nu Sigma Nu; Presbyterian; Clubs: York Downs Golf & Country; University; Aesculapian; Arts and Letters; Home: 38 Glengrove Ave. W., Toronto. Ont. M4R 1N6; Office: 500 Sherbourne St., Toronto, Ont. M4X 1K9

BROWN, William Thomas, M.B.E., E.D., M.A., investment dealer; b. Vancouver, B.C. 10 May 1912; s. Albert Malcolm and Edith Elizabeth (Wootton) B.; e. Univ. of Brit. Columbia B.A. 1932; Oxford Univ., B.A. 1934, M.A. 1937; m. late Daphne Georgina, d. Philip H. Jackson, Fordingbridge, Hants., Eng., 29 Dec. 1937; children: Michael Jack, Peter Thomas, Jane Daphne (Mrs. Gordon S. Ball); CHAIRMAN, ODLUM BROWN & T. B. READ LTD., Dir., Wardair International Ltd.; B.C. Telephone Co.; Bank of Brit. Col.; Century Insurance Co. of Canada; Fidelity Life Assur. Co.; Vancouver Foundation; National Second Century Fund of B.C.; Chris Spencer Foundation; Chairman, Public Library Bd., City of Vancouver (1960-61); Pres. Men's Candn. Club of Vancouver, 1950-51; Pres. (1966-67) Investment Dealers Assn. of Can.; apptd. a mem., Royal Comm. on Banking & Finance (Fed.) Oct. 1961; with Odlum Prown Co., 1935-39; served in 2nd World War; with Irish Fusiliers (Vancouver Regt.) 1939-44; Staff Hdqrs., Candn. Army and then Essex Scottish Regt.; wounded in Normandy, Aug. 1944 awarded M.B.E.; retired from Army with rank of Lieut.-Col.; Psi Upsilon; Freemason; P. Conservative; Anglican; Club: Vancouver; Home: 311 Shaughnessy Pl., 4900 Cartier St., Vancouver, B.C. V6M 4H2; Office: 1800-609 Granville St., Vancouver B.C. V7Y 1A3

BROWNE, J. S. L., M.D., Ph.D., LL.D, F.R.S.C., F.R.C.P., F.A.P.C.; physician; emeritus professor; b. London, Eng., 13 Apl. 1904; s. William Lyon and Ellen Winifred (Nealor) B.; e. McGill Univ., B.A. 1925; M.D., C.M. 1929, B.Sc. (Med.), (Holmes Gold Medal and

William's Prize), Ph.D. (with Gov. Gen.'s Silver Medal) 1932; Univ. of Gottingen; Univ. of Graz, and Univ. Coll., London, Eng. (Roy. Soc. of Can., Travelling Fellow) 1932-33; Queen's Univ., LL.D. 1953; W. F. Mickle Fellowship, Univ. of Toronto 1963; Emeritus Prof. of Med., McGill Univ. since 1971; Research Fellow, Lectr., Asst. and Assoc. Prof. of Med., McGill Univ., 1933-45; Asst. Phys., Asst. and Acting Dir., Roy. Victoria Hosp., Montreal, P.Q., 1937-44; Asst. and Acting Dir., McGill Univ. Clinic, 1940-44; Phys., Royal Victoria Hosp., 1944-66; Hon. Consultant there 1966; Prof. of Med. and Chrmn., Dept., McGill Univ. 1947-55; Prof. of Investigative Med. and Chrmn. Dept. 1955-69; Prof., Dept. Experimental Med. 1969-71; Consultant, Scient. Inst. de Recherches Cliniques de Montreal 1967; Dir., McGill Univ. Clinic, Royal Victoria Hosp., 1947-55; Secy., Sub-Comte. on Blood Substitutes, Assoc. Comte. on Med. Research, Nat. Research Council (Can.) 1942-46 (mem. Advisory Comte. 1946-49); mem., Am. Soc. for Clin. Investigation (Pres. 1947-48); Candn. Soc. Clin, Investig.; Endocrine Soc. (Pres. 1948); Montreal Medico-Chirurg. Soc. (Pres. 1949); Candn. Med. Assn.; Assn. Am. Phys.; Am. Clinical & Climatol. Assn.; Candn. Physiol. Soc.; Brit. and Am. Physiol. Socs.; has contrib. over sixty articles dealing mainly with endocrinology to various med. journs.; Nu Sigma Nu; Anglican; Residence: 900 Sherbrooke St. W., Apt. 100, Montreal. Que. H3A 1G3

BROWNE, Hon. William Joseph, P.C. (Can.), Q.C., B.A., B.A.Sc., LL.D.; b. St. John's Nfld., 3 May 1897; s. Liberius and Bridget (O'Reilly) B.; e. Holy Cross Sch. and St. Bonaventure's Coll., St. John's Nfld. (Winner of Jubilee Scholar, 1915); Univ. of Toronto, B.A.Sc. (Hons. Civil Engn.), 1919; Rhodes Scholar, Nfld., 1918; Merton Coll., Oxford, 1919-22 (B.A.,Oxon 1921); LL.D. (Hon.) Memorial Univ. of Nfld. 1975; m. 1st, Mary Grace (died 14 Feb. 1930), d. Hon. John Harris, 7 July 1924; children: Marjorie, Madeleine, William, Peter; 2ndly, Mary (died 16 Feb. 1944), d.Richard Roche, 4 July 1933; children: Edward, Mary Antonia (died April 5, 1939); 3rdly, Margaret Fleming (d. 1970), widow of Alan C. Fleming, K.C., Ottawa, Ont., and d. H Buckley, Bathurst, N.B.; 4thly, (Dr.) Norah C. Renouf, widow G.Rex Renouf of St. John's and d. Canon Maurice Elphinstone of England, 12 Sept. 1973; called to the Bar of England, June 1922; Nfld., Oct. 1922; cr. K.C. 1934; practiced law, 1922-34, and since 1949; Asst. Clerk, Nfld. House of Assembly, 1923-24; def. cand. for Dist. of Placentia-St. Mary's; el. to H. of A. for St. John's W., 1924; def. 1928; el. for Harbour Main Bell Island, 1932; Minister without Portfolio, Alderdice Govt., 1932-34; Acting Min. of Finance, 1932; Acting Min. of Justice, 1933; apptd. Judge, Central Dist. Court, July 1935; resigned in 1949 and contested St. John's W. in Fed. g.e. and elected; def. in g.e. 1953; el. to Nfld. H. of A. by acclamation, 1954, and re-el. 1956; el. to H. of C. for St. John's W., g.e. 1957 and 1958; apptd. Min. without Portfolio, Can., 1957; Solr.-Gen., 11 Oct. 1960; el. Nfld. H. of A. Nov. 1962 in g.e.; rep. Canada at Colombo Plan Conf., Saigon, Oct. 1957; Vice-Chrmn., Candn. del. to U.N. Gen. Assembly, Sept.-Dec. 1958; K. of C. (P.G.K. of Terra Nova Council); P. Conservative; Roman Catholic; Address: 97 Rennie's Mill Road., St. John's, Nfld. A1B 2P1

BROWNING, Gordon E., B. Com., F.C.A.; b. Cobalt, Ont., 31 July 1916; s. Harry Strand and Mary Beatrice (McCrea) B.; e. Toronto Public Schs.; Sudbury (Ont.) Public and High Schs.; Univ. of Toronto, B. Com. 1938; m. Sally Christine, d. late John A. McPhail, Q.C., Sault Ste. Marie, Ont., 22 Feb. 1941; children: John H. Foster (stepson); J. G. Desbrisay, Beverly, Gordon, Jr.; SR. PARTNER, BRUNTON BROWNING DAY AND PARTNERS (Chart. Acct., Estbd. 1938); Acct. with Canada Packers Ltd., 1938-42 (sometime Salesmen); articled with S. R. Brunton, C.A., 1942-45 (C.A. 1946) and formed partnership with him in 1946 (F.C.A. 1959); Capt., Soo-Sudbury Regt. (reserve); Pres., Ont. Chamber of Comm.

1959-60; Past Chrmn. Sudbury Gen. Hosp. Adv. Bd.; Sudbury and Dist. Hosp. Council; Chmn., Extve. Comte. Bd. of Govs., Laurentian Univ.; Extve. Comte. Bd. of Regents, Univ. of Sudbury; Past Pres., N. Ont. Golf Assn.; Sudbury & Dist. Chamber of Comm.; Past Dir., Candn. Chamber of Comm., Ont. Div., P. Conservative; Roman Catholic; recreations: golf, bridge; Club: Idylwylde Golf & Country (Past Pres.): Home: Apt. 913, 250 St. Anne's Rd., Sudbury, Ont. P3C 5M8; Office: 469 Bouchard, Sudbury, Ont. P3E 2K8

BROWNRIDGE, Hon. Russell Lawrence; judge; b. Saskatoon, Sask., 23 Nov. 1914; s. Alvin Arthur and Ethel Anna (Bates) B.; e. Univ. of Sask. (Arts 1937); Law, 1939; m. Mary Esther, d. Robert Roycroft, 4 July 1942; two s. Robert Alvin, James Russell; JUSTICE, COURT OF APPEAL, SASK., since Oct. 1961; read law with J. G. Diefenbaker, Q.C.; called to the Bar of Sask. 1940; cr. Q.C. 1951; entered the firm of Ross, Gilmour & Brownridge 1941 and successor firm Gilmour & Brownridge, 1943-47 practising alone 1947-58 when organ. firm of Brownridge & Schollie (1958-59); Justice, Court of Queen's Bench, Sask., 1959-61; served five years as Alderman, City of Moose Jaw; Past Pres. of Canadian Club, Family Services Assn.; Past Lt.-Gov., Kiwanis Club and many other civic organs.; National Pres., Candn. Red Cross Soc.; Chrmn. Regina Chapter, Candn. Council of Christians & Jews; mem. Bd. of Govs., Regina Orchestral Soc.; Chrmn., Sask. Electoral Boundaries Comn.; mem., Candn. Bar Assn.; Elder St. Andrew's United Church; Moose Jaw & Lakeview United Church, Regina; Freemason; recreations: golf, swimming, curling; Home: 90 Academy Park Rd., Regina, Sask. S4S 4T7; Office: Court House, Regina, Sask.

BROWNRIGG, Garrett M., C.B.E. (1949), M.D., D.Sc., F.A.C.S.; F.R.C.S.(C); b. St.John's, Nfld., 13 Aug. 1907; s. Garrett and Agnes (Murphy) B.; e. St. Bonaventure's Coll., St. John's, Nfld.; St. Mary's Coll. Sch. Halifax, N.S.; McGill Univ., M.D., C.M. 1932; D.Sc. Mem. Univ. 1968; m. Ena Marjorie, d. W. C. Winsor, M.B.E., 22 Sept. 1930; children: Garrett, Ann, Lynn; Clinical Prof. of Surg., Memorial Univ. of Nfld.; mem., Resident Staff; Montreal Gen. Hosp. 1932-34, and Grace Dart Hosp., Montreal, 1934-35; Asst. Surg., St. John's Gen Hosp 1935-43 and Surg. there since 1943; Chrmn., Dept. Surg. 1959-67; mem. Avd. Council, St. John's Gen Hosp. 1943-67; Consulting Surg., Grace Gen. and Janeway Children's Hosps.; Surg., Sanatorium for Tuberculosis, St. John's, Nfld., since 1935; mem. Bd. Govs., St. Clare's Mercy Hosp.; Nfld. Med. Bd.; Chief Surg., St. Clare's Mercy Hosp. 1957-77 and Chief of Staff 1957-78; Hon. Ch. of Staff 1978; Chief of Service (Surgery) D.V.A., Nfld.; has contrib. articles on surg. subjects to "Am. Journ. of Surg." and "Journ. of Candn. Med. Assn."; Newfoundland Medical Assoc. (Pres. 1946-47); Fellow, Amer. Assoc. Surgery of Trauma; St. John's Clinical Soc. (Pres. 1942-43); mem. Bd. of Govs. Amer. College of Surgeons 1958-70; Pres. Federation Medical Licensing Authorities of Canada 1977-78; Am. Assoc. for Thoracic Surgery; Phi Chi; Independent; R.C.; recreation: fishing; Clubs: Royal Nfld. Yacht; Bally Haly Golf & Country; Address: 47 Queen's Road, St. John's Nfld. A1C 2A7

BRUCE, Allan Wallace; retired association executive; b. Hamilton, Ont., 26 Oct. 1907; s. William Wallace and Florence Amelia (Lamport) B.; e. Upper Canada Coll., Toronto, Ont. (1925); m. Doreen Olive, d. Caldwell Henderson, Windsor, Ont., 22 Feb. 1936; one d. Beverly Ann; United Church; Clubs: Board of Trade. Toronto Hunt; Home: 21 Dale Ave., Toronto, Ont. M4W 1K3

BRUCE, Fraser W., B.A.Sc.; b. Newmarket, Ont., 1 Dec. 1903; e. Beaverton (Ont.) Public Sch.; Upper Canada Coll., Univ. of Toronto, B.A.Sc. (Mech. Engn.) 1927; former Pres. & CEO of the Aluminum Co. of Can.; Director, C.D. Howe Foundation; Director of Canadian Executive

Service Overseas; joined Aluminum Company of Canada Ltd., Toronto Sales Office, following grad.; Mgr., Aluminium Ltd.'s sales in Japan, 1930-34; Asst. to the Pres., Aluminium Co. of Can. Ltd., 1934; Mgr., Alcan (U.K.) Ltd., London, Eng., 1936-39; Mgr., Aluminum Co. of Canada Ltd., Ottawa Office 1939-44; Gen Sales Mgr., Aluminum Co. of Canada Ltd., 1944-46; Vice-Pres. and Gen. Sales Mgr., 1946-52; Mang. Dir., Alcan Industries Ltd., London, Eng., 1952-57; Director, Alcan Aluminium Ltd. 1959-73; Clubs: Mount Royal; Rideau (Ottawa); University (Montreal); Home: 1321 Sherbrooke St. W., Montreal, Que. H3G 1J4

BRUCE, Geoffrey F., M.A.; diplomat; b. Kingston, Ont., 30 June 1925; s. Dr. Everend Lester and Mary B.; e. Queen's Univ. B.A. 1947, grad. work 1948 Columbia Univ., M.A. 1952; New Sch. for Social Research 1948-49; Nat. Defence Coll. 1970-71; Goethe Inst. Germany 1963; m. Dr. Erika von Conta, 19 Sept. 1972; children: David Ian, Karen; HIGH COMMISSIONER OF CANADA TO KENYA AND CONCURRENTLY TO UGANDA 1978; Candn. Embassy Tel Aviv 1955-57; Candn. High Comn. Colombo, Sri Lanka 1960-63; Candn. Embassy Vienna, Austria and Candn. Mission to Internat. Atomic Energy. Agency, Vienna, 1963-67; Dir., Science and Environmental Relations, Dept. External Affairs, Ottawa 1971-73; Min. and Depy. Perm. Rep to United Nations, and Candn. Rep. to Econ. and Social Council UN, New York 1973-77; Commnd. 2nd Lt. Candn. Army Reserve; Trustee Am. Internat. Sch. Vienna 1965-67; Fellow, Harvard Univ. Center for Intern. Affairs 1977-78; Chrmn. U.N. Commission on Transnational Corporations 1978; High Commr. for Can. to Kenya and concurrently to Uganda 1978; Permanent Rep. of Canada to U.N. Environment Program and to U.N. Centre for Human Settlements 1978; Adjunct Prof. Pol. Sci., Winthrop College, Rock Hill, South Carolina since 1976; mem. Prof. Assn. Foreign Service Offrs.; Candn. Pol. Science Assn.; recreations: theatre, music, visual arts, travel, swimming, tennis; Canadian High Commission, P.O. Box 30481, Nairobi, Kenya

BRUCE, W. Robert, M.Sc., Ph.D., M.D., F.R.S.C., F.R.C.P.S.; physicist; b. Hamheung, Korea, 26 May 1929; s. George Finalay and Ellen (Tate) B.; e. Univ. of Alta., B.Sc. (Chem.) 1950; Univ. of Sask., M.Sc. (Physics) 1956; Univ. of Chicago, M.D. 1958; Lic., Med. Council of Can.; m. Willa Margaret, d. William Graham MacFarlane, June 1957; children: Graham D., Kevin R., Lynda J.; DIR., LUDWIG INST. FOR CANCER RESEARCH, TORONTO BRANCH.; Prof., Dept. of Med. Biophysics, Univ. of Toronto, since 1966; joined present Univ. Dept. as Lectr., 1959-60; Asst. Prof. 1960-64; Assoc. Prof. 1964-66; joined Physics Div. of present Inst., 1959; awarded Medal for Med., Royal Coll. Phys. and Surgs. Can., 1968; McLaughlin Gold Medal 1980; Dir., Am. Assn. Cancer Research; United Church; Home: 4 Marshfield Court, Don Mills, Ont.

BRUCE, (William) Harry, B.A.; editor; author; freelance journalist; b. Toronto, Ont. 8 July 1934; s. Charles Tory and Agnes (King) B.; e. Brown Pub. Sch. and Oakwood Coll. Inst. Toronto; Mount Allison Univ. B.A. 1955; London Sch. of Econ. 1956-57; Massey Coll. Univ. of Toronto 1969-70; m. Penny d. Clifford A. Meadows 10 Sept. 1955; children: Alexander, Annabel, Max; Pres., EAST COAST EDITORIAL LTD.; Contrib. Ed., "Atlantic Insight"; Reporter, "The Ottawa Journal" 1955-59; mem. Parlty. Press Gallery 1958-59; Reporter, "The Globe and Mail" 1959-61; Asst. Ed., "Maclean's" mag. 1961-64; Mang. Ed. "Saturday Night" mag. 1964-65; Mang. Ed. (Founding), "The Canadian Magazine" 1965-66; Assoc. Ed. and Featured Columnist, "The Star Weekly" 1967-68; Columnist, "The Toronto DailY Star" 1968-69; Reports and Reviews Ed., Columnist, Maclean's" 1970-71; Extve. Ed., Nova Scotia Light and Power Co. Ltd. 1971; TV Talk-Show Host "Gazette" CBC Halifax 1972; freelance writer 1973-

79; Editor, "Atlantic Insight" 1979-80; Extve. editor, 1981; mem. Founding Bd., Writers' Fed. of N.S.; rec'd ACTRA "Nellie" for "Word From An Ambassador of Dreams", best radio drama 1977; winner first annual Evelyn Richardson Mem. Lit. Award for "Lifeline", best non-fiction book by a Nova Scotian 1978; author "The Short Happy Walks of Max MacPherson" 1968; "Nova Scotia" 1975; "Lifeline" 1977; "R.A. - The Story of R.A. Jodrey, Entrepreneur" 1979; commentary, short articles in several anthols., numerous essays, reviews and columns in maj. Candn. newspapers and mags.; mem. Periodical Writers Assn. Can. (Past Dir.); Assn. Candn. TV & Radio Artists; Protestant; recreations: sailing, jogging, swimming; Clubs: Halifax Press; Dalhousie Faculty; Home: 1381 Le Marchant St., Halifax, N.S. B3H 3P8

BRUCHESI, Jean, B.A., LL.M., D.Litt., D.Pol. Science, LL.D., F.R.C.S. Canadian diplomat; of French and Italian descent; b. Montreal, P.Q., 9 Apl. 1901; s. Charles, K.C., and Elmire (Desnoyers) B.; e. Coll. de Montreal (Sulpicians), 1912-19; Coll. Ste Marie (Jesuits), B.A. with Hons. 1921; Univ. of Montreal, LL.L. with Hons. 1924 (Schol. of P.Q.); Ecole Libre des Sciences Politiques de Paris, France, 1924-26; Lic. in "Sciences Politiques", 1926; Faculty of Letters, the Sorbonne, Paris, and Ecole des Chartes, Paris, 1926-27; Univ. of Montreal, D. Pol. Science; D. Litt. Univ. of Caen; Manitoba; Laval; LL.D. Univ. Cian Inst. 1968; m. Berthe, d. Wilfrid Denis, notary, Nicolet, P.Q., 20 June 1930; two d., Anne (Mrs. Otto Nowotery), and Nicole (Mrs. Richard McKinnon); Advocate 1924; Prof., Internat. Politics, Univ. de Montreal, 1929-52; Prof., Hist. of Can., Coll. Marguerite Bourgeoys, 1932-59; Candn. Ambassador to Spain 1959-64 and to Morocco 1962-69; Candn. Ambassador to Argentina, Uruguay and Paraguay 1964-67; Prof. Econ. Hist. of Can., Laval Univ., 1943-52; Lectr., Sorbonne (Paris), 1948; Former Ed., "La Revue Moderne", Montreal. 1930-36; and of "L'Action Universitaire", a monthly pub. of the Montreal Univ. Alumni, 1935-37; official Lect. of Royal Soc. Can 1951; mem., Candn. del. with the Candn. Exhn. Train in France 1923; Rep., Univ. of Montreal at the 50th anniversary of the Inst. Cath. of Paris (France) and of the Cath. Univ. of Angers (France) in 1925; official del. of the Univ. of Montreal at the 400th centenary of Joan of Arc, 1929 and 1931, in Paris, Tours and Rouen; and at the 400th centenary of the Coll. de France, Paris, 1931; Corr., Montreal newspaper "Le Canada", and del. of the Univ. of Montreal in Poland, Rumania, Turkey, Bulgaria, Yugoslavia, Hungary and Austria, delivering lects. on Can. 1929; Secy. of Candn. Postmaster Gen. and Candn. del. to Cong. of l'Union Postale Universelle held in Cairo, Egypt, 1934; attached to the ed. staff of "Le Canada", 1928-31; Past Pres.-Gen., Candn. Cath. Hist. Assn. and Candn. Hist. Assn.; La Société des Ecrivains Canadiens (Pres.); Candn. Arts Council (Pres.); Les Visites Interprovinciales (Pres.); Offr. at Nat. Order of "Honneur et Mérite" (Haiti); Chevalier Legion Hon. (France); Commr. Cultural Order St. Charles (Monaco); Knight Grand Cross, St. Gregory the Great (Vatican); Knight Grand Cross, Isabel (Spain); Pres., Institut Canadien de Qué., 1946-59; Royal Soc. of Can. 1953-54 (awarded Tyrrell Medal for Hist. Research 1951); former Pres. and Founder of L'Assoc. des Anciens Etudiants d'Europe and founder of La Société des Ecrivains Canadiens; mem., La Soc. Hist., Montreal; La Soc. des Poètes, P.Q.; Internat. PEN Club; Polish Inst. Arts and Sciences; Under-Secy. of State and Deputy Registrar for P.Q., 1937-59; Mem., Candn. del. to Unesco Conf. on Adult Educ. (Elsinore, Denmark), 1949; author of "Coups d'Ailes", poems, 1922; "Jour Eteints", 1929 (Pris d'Action Intellectuelle); "Aux Marches de l'Europe", hist., pol., econ. of Central & Oriental Europe 1932; (Prix d'Action Intellectuelle); "Histoire du Canada", 1934-35 and 1951, (Prize of the French Acad.); "L'Epopée Canadienne" (illustrated album for young readers) 1934; "Rappels", 1941; "de Ville-Marie à Montréal", 1942; "Le Chemin des Ecoliers", 1943; "Evocations", 1947; "Canada, Realités d'hier et d'aujourd'hui" 1948 (Prize of French Acad. and Prix Du-vernay) translated in Eng. under title "A History of Canada"; "Le Canada" (Illustrated); "L'Université", 1953; "Voyages — — — Mirages — — — ", 1957; "Témoignages d'hier" 1961; "Souvenirs à Vaincre" (1901-1959) 1974; "Souvenirs d'Ambassade" (1959-1972) 1975; Research Fellow (Hist.) Univ. Ottawa 1969-71; awarded the Médaille de l'Acfas for his contribution to the advancement of science, 1949; is a contributor to "Book of Knowledge" (French); Roman Catholic; recreations: swimming, fishing.

BRUCK, Robert J.; company executive; b. N.Y. 1919; Grad. from Hun School, 1936; attended Univ. of Virginia, 1936-39; EXECUTIVE VICE-PRESIDENT, & DIR. BRUCK MILLS LTD., since 1948; joined Co. 1939; el. Dir. 1947; served in World War 1942-45 with U.S. Navy; Past Pres., Candn. Fabrics Foundation; Montreal Symphony Orchestra; Home: 517 Clarke Ave., Montreal, Que. H3Y 3E1;

BRUEMMER, Fred, R.C.A.; author; photographer; b. Riga, Latvia 26 June 1929; came to Can. 1950; m. Maud van den Berg 31 March 1962; two s.; author "The Long Hunt" 1969; "Seasons of the Eskimo" 1971; "EnCounters with Arctic Animals" 1972; "The Arctic" 1974; "The Life of the Harp Seal" 1977; "Children of the North" 1979; "Bear River" 1980; various articles Am., Candn. and European mags. in Eng., French and German; rec'd Queen's Silver Jubilee Medal 1977; Protestant; Address: 5170 Cumberland Ave., Montreal, Que. H4V 2N8.

BRUK, John, B.Com., LL.B.; mining executive; b. Blato, Yugoslavia 5 March 1930; s. Kuzma Bosnic and Jelica (Kalogjera) B.; e. Univ. of B.C. B.Com. 1957, LL.B. 1958; m. Carol d. George Sparling, Sidney, B.C. 20 Dec. 1954; children: Mark, Ian, Bruce, Steven; PRES. AND CHIEF EXTVE. OFFR., CYPRUS ANVIL MINING CORP. 1975- ; Dir. Canadian Commercial Corp.; Western Can. Resources Fund Ltd. Lectr. Univ. of Wash. 1957-58; articling student Lawrence & Shaw, Vancouver 1959-60; called to Bar of B.C. 1960; Partner, Nemetz, Austin, Christie & Bruk, Vancouver 1960-63; Lawrence & Shaw 1963-74; Chrmn. of Bd. Dynasty Explorations Ltd. Vancouver 1974-75; Gov. B.C. Inst. Technol.; mem. Candn. Bar Assn.; Law Soc. B.C.; Nat. Adv. Comte. Mining Industry; Can. Japan Business Coop. Comte.; Mining Assn. Can. (Dir.); R. Catholic; recreations: reading, music; Clubs: Vancouver; Capilano Golf & Country; Home: 5662 Cypress St., Vancouver, B.C. V6M 3R6; Office: 300, 355 Burrard St., Vancouver, B.C. V6C 2G8.

BRUNEAU, Marc Y., B.Com., L.Sc.Com., C.A.; b. St. Damase, Que. 28 May 1935; s. J. Roméo and Fabiola (Beauregard) B.; e. St. Charles Garnier Sch.; St. Stanislas High Sch. 1957; Hautes Etudes Commerciales Univ. of Montreal B.Com. 1956, L.Sc.Com. 1957; C.A. 1958; m. Claire L. d. Roméo Lussier 10 June 1967; one s. Marc G.; MANAGING PARTNER,MacGILLIVRAY & BRUNEAU 1962- ; Partner, MacGillivray & Co. 1969- ; Dir. and mem. Audit Comte. Trust General du Canada; Dir. and mem. Extve. Comte. Trust General Inc.; Sr. to Mgr. McDonald, Currie & Co. 1958-62; Dir. and Asst. Secy. Candn. Heart Foundation; Chrmn. and mem. Extve. Comte. Que. Heart Foundation; mem. Chart. Inst. C.A.'s; Chambre de Comm. de Montréal; R. Catholic; Clubs: Laval-sur-le-Lac (Past Pres.); St-Denis; Home: 1274 Mont-Royal Blvd., Outremont, Que. H2V 2H8; Office: 3610, 1155 Blvd. Dorchester W., Montreal, Que. H3B 3T9.

BRUNEL, Louis, B.A., L.Sc.Com.; executive; b. Montreal, Que. 21 June 1941; s. Donat and Maria (Perron) B.; e. Coll. des Eudistes Montréal B.A. 1962; Ecole des Hautes Etudes Commerciales L.Sc.Com. 1965; m. Carole d. Henri Pérusse, Ste-Foy, Que. 10 May 1975; children: Marie-Hélène, Jean-Lou, Ludovic, Rosalie; VICE PRES., GEN. DIR. AND DIR., CABLEVISION NATIONALE

LTÉE. 1981- (Dir. 79-); Chrmn. Informatech) Quebec 1980-81; Vice-Pres. Communications and Dir. Univ. of Québec 1971-80; Dir., Télécâble Vidéotron (1979) Ltée; Data Processing Machine Operator, Les Pharmacies Universelles Montreal 1958, Analyst Programmer 1962, Chief Acct. 1964-66; Asst. to Dir. Adm. Computer Center Univ. of Montreal 1966, Dir. of Center 1967-69; Dir. of Computer Center, Quebecair 1969; Dir. Computer Systems Devel. Univ. of Que. 1969, Asst. Vice Pres. Communications 1970; Vice-Pres. Communications and Dir., 1971-79; Chmn. and Gen. Dir., Ecole Nat. D'Administration Publique 1979-81; Dir. Télé-Université 1973-76; Assn. des diplômés de l'Ecole des Hautes Etudes Comm. 1971-74; mem. Assoc. Comte. Instructional Technol. Nat. Research Council Can. 1976-79; Chrmn. Le Presses de l'Université du Québec 1975-79; rec'd "Prix du Journalisme Scientifique du Canada" 1975; author "Telecommunications: Des Machines et Des Hommes" 1978; co-author "University at Home" 1977; numerous articles and lectures on computers, satellites, information, telecommunications, cable and innovation; mem. Corp. des Administrateurs Agréés; R. Catholic; recreations: tennis, reading, painting, camping; Home: 196 Pierre Foretier, Ile Bizard, Que. H9C 2B1; Office: 90 Beaubien Ouest, Montreal, Que. H2S 1V7.

BRUNELLE, Hon. Rene, b. Penetanguishene, Ont., 22 Jan. 1920; s. Pierre and Ida (Beaupre) B.; e. High Sch., Timmins, Ont.; Ottawa (Ont.) Normal Sch.; Khaki Univ., London Eng.; Univ. of Toronto; Laurentian Univ. LL.D. 1978; m. Andree Hebert, Nov. 1956; children: Louis, Suzanne, Pierre, Kelly; Prov. Sec. for Resources Development 1977-81; Minister of Social and Family Services, Ont. 1972; 1st el. to Ont. Leg., by-el. May 1958; re-el. since; apptd. Min. Lands and Forests, Nov. 1966, Min. Mines, Nov. 1967; apptd. Chrmn., Ont. Parks Integration Bd., March 1968; formerly Chrmn., Select Comte. of Leg. on Mining; enlisted in R.C.A. 1942; Comnd. 2/Lt. 1943; Overseas 1944, serving as Canloan Offr. with Monmouthshire Regt. till discharge 1946; Tourist Operator, Remi Lake, Moonbean. Ont.; P. Conservative; R. Catholic; K. of C.; recreations: hunting, fishing, canoeing, skiing; Club: Albany; Home: Moonbean, Ont. P0L 1V0

BRUNET, Michel, B.A., M.A., Ph.D.; professeur titulaire; né à Montréal, Qué., 24 juillet 1917; fils de Léo et Rose (DeGuise) B.; e. B.A., Univ. de Montréal, 1939; Diplôme supérieur d'enseignement, Dép. de l'Instruction publique du Québec, 1941; Lic. en sciences sociales, écon. et pol., Univ. de Montréal, 1946; M.A. (Histoire), Univ. de Montréal, 1947; Ph.D. (Histoire), Clark Univ., 1949; Boursier de la Fondation Rockefeller, 1947-49; ép. Berthe Boyer, 7 mai 1945 (d. 1974); ép. Léone Dussault, 5 déc. 1975; PROF. TITULAIRE DÉPT. D'HISTOIRE, UNIV. DE MONTREAL depuis 1959; Prof. asst., 1949, agrégé 1950-59; dir. du dépt. d'histoire 1959-67, Secrétaire (1962-1966) et Vice-Doyen (1966-1967) de la Faculté des lettres, et mem. du conseil (1959-1967); mem. de l'Académie canadienne-française depuis 1961 (secrétaire 1962 à 1972); Prés. de l'Association des professeurs de l'Université de Montréal 1965-66; mem., comme associé étranger, de l'Académie des Sciences d'Outre-Mer de France, 1969; Soc. historique de Montréal; Soc. historique du Canada; Institut d'histoire de l'Amérique française; auteur: "Canadians et Canadiens" 1954; "La Présence anglaise et les Canadiens" 1958; "Histoire du Canada par les textes" 1963; "Québec — Canada anglais: deux itinéraires, un affrontement" 1968; "Québec 1800: paysages et témoignages" 1968; "Les Canadiens après la Conquête 1759-1775" mem. "Notre Passé, le présent et nous" 1976; Prix littéraire du Gouverneur Général et Prix France-Québec, 1970; Médaille de la Soc. hist. de Montréal 1978; auteur de nombreux articles, brochures et comptes rendus critiques. Adresse: Department d'Histoire, Université de Montréal, Case Postal 6128, Succursale A, Montreal, Que. H3C 3J7

BRUNET, Pierre, C.A.; investment dealer; b. Verdun, Que., 3 March 1939; s. Paul E. and Liliane (Brisson) B.; e. Coll. Olier, classical studies, 1951-59; Univ. of Montreal (HEC). C.A. degree 1964; m. Louise, d. Adolphe Simard, 17 June 1961; children: Lucie, Isabelle, Philippe, Bernard; MANAGING DIR. AND EXECUTIVE VICE-PRESIDENT, LEVESQUE, BEAUBIEN INC.; Chrmn. Montreal Stock Exchange (1974-75); commenced as Auditor, Samson, Bélair, Côté, Lacroix & Associés, Chart. Accts. 1959-64; Treas. and Dir., Morgan, Ostiguy & Hudon Inc. 1964-70; Dir., Montreal Symphony Orchestra; Montreal Chamber of Comm.; Chairman, Financial Administrators section of Invest. Dealers Assn. of Can. 1968-69; Chrmn., National Contingency Fund 1972; Chairman (1974-75); Dir. of the Order of Chartered Accountants of Quebec 1978-79; Dir., Order of Char. Accts. of Qué. 1978-79; R. Catholic; recreations: swimming, skiing, tennis; Clubs: Club Saint-Denis; St. James's; Home: 31 Pagnuelo Ave., Outremont, Que. H2V 2B8; Office: 360 St. Jacques St., Montreal, Que. H2Y 1P7

BRYANS, Alexander McKelvey, M.D. M.Ed., F.R.C.P. (C); physician; b. Toronto, Ont., 16 Sept. 1921; s. Dr. Fred Thomas and Barbara (McKelvey) B.; e. Univ. of Toronto Schs. (1932-39); Univ. of Toronto, M.D. 1944; Mich. State Univ. M.Ed. 1971; m. Elaine, d. S. G. Fildes, Town of Mount Royal, P.Q., 30 May 1954; children: John Alexander, Susan Gail, Mary Catherine; Prof. of Paediatrics, Queen's Univ., since 1959; served in R.C.A.M.C., 1942-46; Fellow, Royal College of Physicians and Surgeons of Canada; Fellow, Am. Acad. Pediatrics; mem., Candn. Med. Assn.; Ont. Med. Assn., Candn. Paediatric Soc.; Dir. Health Sciences Office of Educ., Queen's Univ. since 1972; United Ch.; recreations: skiing, camping; Address: Health Sciences Office of Education, Queen's University, Kingston, Ont. K7L 3N6

BRYANS, Frederick Edward, M.D., F.R.S.C.(C), F.R.C.O.G.; educator; b. Toronto, Ont. 2 March 1924; s. Frederick Thomas Bryans; e. Univ. of Toronto Schs. 1941; Univ. of Toronto M.D. 1946, B.Sc. 1949; m. Jane Folwell d. Dr. Neil McKinnon 25 June 1975; step-children: Elizabeth Calvin, Margot Calvin, Brian Calvin; PROF. OF OBSTETRICS & GYNAECOLOGY, UNIV. OF B.C. since 1960; served with RCAMC 1944-46; rec'd Queen's Silver Jubilee Medal; United Church; Home: 1750 W. 36th Ave., Vancouver, B.C. V6M 1K2; Office: Vancouver General Hospital, Vancouver, B.C. V5Z 1M9

BRYCE, Robert B., C.C. (1968), B.A.Sc., M.A., LL.D. F.R.S.C. (1961); Canadian public servant; financier; b. Toronto, Ont., 27 Feb. 1910; s. Robert Alexander and Edna Gertrude (Baxter) B., e. Univ. Toronto, B.A.Sc. 1932; Cambridge Univ., B.A. 1934; Harvard Univ. 1935-37; m. Frances Robinson, Spokane, Wash., 1937; two s. and one d.; first position with Sun Life Assurance Co., Montreal, Que., as an Economist; joined Dept. of Finance, Ottawa, 1938; during 2nd World War was Secy. to the Govt. Econ. Advisory Comte.; appt. (first) Candn. Dir. Internat. Bank in Wash., 1946; apptd. Asst. Depy. Min. of Finance and Secy. of the Treasury Bd., 1947; Clerk of the Privy Council and Secy. to the Cabinet, 1954; Depy. Min. Finance 1963; Econ. Adv. to Prime Min. on Constitution 1970; apptd. Extve. Dir., Internat. Monetary Fund 1971; Royal Comn. on the Concentration of Corporate Power 1975-77; Address: 14 Monkland Ave., Ottawa, Ont. K1S 1Y9

BRYNELSEN, Bernard Orlando, B.A.Sc.; mining engineer; b. Vancouver, B.C., 22 Aug. 1911; s. John and Anna (Knutsen) B.; e. Pub. and High Schs., Vancouver; Univ. of British Columbia, B.A.Sc. 1935; one yr. Geol. postgrad. work 1936; m. Eileen Manning, d. William R. Simon, Portland, Ore., 15 May 1937; one d., Karen Lorene; Chmn., Alaska Apollo Gold Mines Ltd.; Brenda Mines Ltd.; Pres. B & B Mining Co.; Norancon Exploration Ltd.; Dir., Wenatchee Silica Sand Company and several mining companies; began as Field Engineer, Inca Mining

Corporation, 1932; joined Polaris Taku Mining Co., as Mine Supt., 1936-42; Mgr., Consolidated Nicola Goldfields, 1942-43; Constr. Supt., Keyes Constr. Co., 1943-45; Mgr. for B.C. with Que. Gold Mining Corp., 1945-74; West. Mgr., Noranda Exploration Co. 1974-; mem. Prof. Engrs. of B.C.; Candn. Inst. of Mining & Metall.; Assoc. Inst. of Mining Engrs.; Sigma Phi Delta; United Ch.; recreations: Yachting, fishing; Clubs: Royal Vancouver Yacht; Capilano Golf & Country; Terminal City; Vancouver; Home: 1962 Knox Road, University Hill, Vancouver, B.C. V6T 1S6;

BRYSON, G.S., B.Com.; provincial civil servant; e. Univ. of B.C., B.Com. 1942; DEPY. MIN. OF FINANCE, B.C. 1957- ; Secy. Treasury Bd.; mem. & Secy. B.C. Sch. Dists. Capital Financing Authority; B.C. Regional Hosp. Dists. Financing Authority; B.C. Educ. Insts. Capital Financing Authority; Asst. Commr. Social Services Tax 1948, Commr. 1950; Asst. Depy. Min. of Finance 1954; Clubs: Union; Gyro Internat.; Home: 1420 Beach Dr., Victoria, B.C. V8S 2N3; Office: Parliament Bldgs., Victoria, B.C. V8V 1X4.

BRZESKI, Oleg W., D.Sc.; executive; b. Poznan, Poland 19 Feb. 1921; s. Leon and Anna (Braunek) B.; came to Canada 1950; e. Lyceum High Sch., Wetzikon, Switz.; Fed. Polytech. Sch. Zurich; Chem. Engr. 1946, D.Sc. 1948, McGill Univ.; m. Maria, d. late Bronislaw Lasocki 1957; children: Ada Maria, Anna Barbara, Veronika Julia, Marina Kateri; PRES., CHIEF EXTVE. OFFR. AND DIR., SANDOZ (CANADA) LTD. since 1975; Chrmn. of Bd., Anca Inc.; Dir. Wander Ltd.; Hospal Canada Ltd.; Sandoz Holdings Ltd.; Rockefeller Research Fellow, ETH Organic Lab., Zurich 1945; Scient. Office, Sandoz Ltd., Basle 1948, Asst. Promotion Mgr. Can. 1950, Marketing Mgr. 1961; Vice-Pres. i.c. Pharmaceutical Div., Sandoz (Canada) Ltd. 1965; served in 2nd World War with French Army; mem. Chem. Inst. Can.; Montreal Physiological Soc.; Polish Inst. Arts and Sciences; R. Catholic; Clubs: MAAA; Forest and Stream; Home: 4135 Grand Blvd., Montreal, Que. H4B 2X4; Office: P.O. Box 385, Dorval, Que. H9R 4P5

BRZUSTOWSKI, Thomas Anthony, B.A.Sc., A.M., Ph.D., P.Eng.; educator; b. Warsaw, Poland 4 Apl. 1937; s. Jerzy Michal and Helena (Bielicka) B.; e. N. Toronto Coll. Inst. 1954; Univ. of Toronto B.A.Sc. (Engn. Physics) 1958; Princeton Univ. A.M. 1960, Ph.D. (Aeronautical Engn.) 1963; m. Louise Marguerite d. John A. Burke, Montreal, Que. 4 Apl 1964; three s. John Michael, Marc-André, Paul Thomas; VICE PRES. ACAD., UNIV. OF WATERLOO since 1975 and Prof. of Mech. Engn. there since 1966; Engr. in Training Combustion Sec. Orenda Engines, Malton 1958; mem. Research Staff General Electric Research Lab. Schenectady, N.Y. 1960; Asst. Prof. of Mech, Engn. present Univ. 1962, Assoc. Prof. 1964 and Chrmn. of Dept. 1967-70, Assoc. Dean of Engn. for Grad. Studies 1971-74; Engn. Assoc. Environmental Control and Safety Div. Esso Research and Engineering Co. Florham Park, N.J. 1970-71; Consultant on environmental control and safety to various comp. in the energy ind-; rec'd various scholarships 1954-58 (Wallberg, APEO, McKee-Gilchrist, Avro Aircraft); Air Reduction Fellowship 1958-60; Ford Foundation Residency in Engn. Practice 1970-71; Angus Medal, Eng. Inst. of Can. 1976, 1978; mem. Bd. of Govs. Univ. of Waterloo 1973-77; Bd. Dirs., Stratford Shakespearean Festival; Kitchener-Waterloo Philharmonic Choir; developed widely-used design methods for flares in oil refineries and chem. plants; author "Introduction to the Principles of Engineering Thermodynamics" 1969; author or co-author over 50 research papers in combustion, flame aerodynamics, fire safety; also contrib. to "McGraw-Hill Encyclopedia of Energy" 1976; Fellow, Eng. Inst. of Can.; Fellow, Inst. of Energy (UK); mem. Assn. Prof. Engrs. Prov. Ont.; Candn. Soc. Mech. Engrs. (mem Ed. Bd.); Am. Soc. Mech. Engrs.; AIAA; ASEE; Combustion Inst.; R. Catholic; recreations: tennis, squash, hiking, skiing, photography; Clubs: Waterloo Tennis; Chicopee Ski; Home: 23 Sunbridge Cres., Kitchener, Ont. N2K 1T4

BUCHANAN, Hon. J. Judd, P.C., B.A., M.B.A.; politician; b. Edmonton, Alta. 25 July 1929; s. Nelles Victor and Helen (DeSilva) B.; e. Univ. of Alta. B.A. 1953; Univ. of W. Ont. M.B.A. 1955; m. Kay Eleena d. late Harry Ezra Balfour 3 May 1952; children: Duncan Grant, Gregg Balfour, James Harry; Pres. of Treasury Bd., 1978-79; Min. of Public Works 1976-78 and Min. of State for Science and Technol. 1977-78; el. to H. of C. 1968, re-el. 72, 74, 79, 80 (resigned from H. of C. 1980); Parlty. Secy. to Min. of Indian and N. Affairs 1970 and to Min. of Finance 1972, apptd. Min. of Indian & N. Affairs 1974; Liberal; United Church; recreations: skiing, canoeing;

BUCHANAN, Hon. John MacLennan, Q.C., M.L.A., B.Sc., LL.B., D.Eng.; politician; b. Sydney, N.S. 22 Apl. 1931; s. Murdoch William and Flora Isabel (Campbell) B.; e. Sydney Acad.; Mount Allison Univ. B.Sc.; Dalhousie Univ. LL.B.; m. Mavis Olive Charlotte d. Daniel Forsyth, Bear River, N.S. 1 Sept 1954; children: Murdoch William, Travis Campbell, Nichola Ann, Natalie Flora, Natasha Heather; PREMIER OF N.S.,Pres. of Extve. Council and Chrmn. of Policy Bd. 1978- ; cr. Q.C. 1972; el. M.L.A. for Halifax Atlantic prov. g.e. 1967, re-el. since; Min. of Pub. Works and Min. of Fisheries 1969; Leader of P. Cons. Party N.S. 1971; Min. of Finance 1978-79; Freemason; P. Conservative; United Church; Clubs: City; Lions; Office: Province House, Halifax, N.S. B3J 2T3.

BUCHANAN, Mervin Arthur, D.F.C., B.A.Sc.; executive; b. Leamington, Ont. 29 June 1923; s. Russell and Annie (Coulter) B.; e. Leamington High Sch.; Univ. of Toronto B.A.Sc. (Engn. & Business) 1951; m. Elspeth Alston d. Daniel Fraser 15 Sept. 1948; three s. Douglas, Alan, Grant; PRES., GEN. MGR. AND DIR., SQUARE D CANADA ELECTRICAL EQUIPMENT INC.; held various positions Square D incl. Field Engr., Hdqrs. Sales Supvr., Regional Sales Mgr., Sales Mgr., Vice Pres. Marketing, Extve. Vice Pres.; served with RCAF 1941-45, rank Flight Lt.; Dir., Elect. & Electronic Mfrs. Assn. Can.; Jr. Achievement Metrop. Toronto; mem. Thorncrest Homes Assn.; Bd. Trade Metrop. Toronto; Candn. Nat. Exhn.; Protestant; recreations: reading, golf, fishing; Club: Weston Golf & Country; Home: 1277 Kipling Ave., Islington, Ont. M9B 3N4; Office: 6303 Airport Rd., Mississauga, Ont. L4V 1S2.

BUCHANAN, William Gavin; transportation consultant; b. London, Ont. 8 June 1921; s. Edward Victor and Faith Chisholm (Turnbull) B.; e. St. George's Pub. Sch., London, Ont.; St. Andrew's Coll., Aurora, Ont.; Oxford Univ.; m. 1st Diana, d. Sir Hugo Cunliffe-Owen, 1947; 2ndly, Elizabeth F., d. D. H. Currer Briggs, Leeds, Yorkshire, 17 Oct. 1955; children: Gray, James, Victoria, Elizabeth; CONSULTANT CORPORATE AFFAIRS, EUR.-CAN. NAT. AND SPECIAL ADVISOR ON DISABLED BR. RAILWAYS BD. 1981-; Dir., CN France; Trade Advisor, Dept. of Trade & Indust. Ont.; Maclean-Hunter Publishing Co., Toronto, 1948-57; Mgr. for E. Can., The Financial Post, Montreal, 1957-67; joined present Co. as Asst. to the Pres. 1967; Gen. Mgr. 1968-71; Vice Pres., Europe 1978-81 served in WW II with RCA 1940-45; 1st Candn. Div. Sicily, Italy; A.D.C. to Lt.-Gov. of Ont. 1947-52; Vice Chrmn., Candn. Univ. Service Overseas; 1966-67; Nat. Chrmn. for Can., Royal Commonwealth Soc., 1966-67 (Depy. Chrmn., Central Council London Eng. 1973) Vice-Pres. Central Council, 1977; mem. Candn. Del. to NATO Planning Bd. for Ocean Shipping 1970-71; Pres., Can.-UK Chamber Comm., London, Eng. 1971-72; mem. Exec. Council Canada Club, London England, 1975-78; Chrmn., N. Amer. Comm., Lon. Cham. of Comm. and Ind. 1978-81; Chrmn. Maple Leaf Luncheon Club, London England, 1979-80; Sch. Commr., City of Westmount, Que. 1961-63; Bd. of Govs.,

Selwyn House Sch., Montreal, 1963-68; mem., Internat. Cargo Handling Co-ordination Assn. (Extve. Comte. 1970); Freeman, City of London 1974; Patron, Lester B. Pearson Coll. of the Pacific, and mem. Academic Comte. United World Colleges, 1978; recreations: fly fishing, Clubs: St. James's (Montreal); Turf (London, Eng.); Inst. of Directors (London, Eng.); Home: Black Wen Farm, Nutley, Sussex, Eng.; TN223EH; Office: British Railway, Board, 222 Marylebone, London, Eng.

BUCHANAN, William W., M.A.; farmer; poultry breeder; b. Winnipeg, Man., 11 Dec. 1911; s. David Wylie and Lily Grace (Power) B.; e. Univ. of Manitoba, B.A. (Hons.); Univ. of Toronto, M.A. 1937; m. Marguerite A., d. J. R. Oastler of East Selkirk, Man., 20 Sept. 1940; four children; former Vice Chrmn. Tariff Bd. Can., now an Econ. Consultant; Dir., R. O. P. Hatchery, Winnipeg, Man.; Man. Fed. of Agric.; Man. R. O. P. Breeders Assn.; Pres., Man. Poultry Council; V.-Pres., Nat. Poultry Council; mem., Tariff Bd. of Can., 1949-59; Chrmn. Anti-Dumping Tribunal 1969-72; has been a large-scale farmer & poultry breeder for a number of years; Protestant; Office: 83 Placel Rd., Ottawa, Ont. K1L 5B9

BUCHWALD, Harold, Q.C., B.A., LL.M.; b. Winnipeg, Man., 22 Feb. 1928; s. Frank and Bessie (Portigal) B.; e. Queenston Pub. Sch., Robert H. Smith Jr. High Sch. and Kelvin High Sch., Winnipeg, 1944; Univ. of Man., B.A. 1948, LL.B. 1952, LL.M. 1957; m. Darlene Joy, d. Joseph Besbeck, Los Angeles, Cal., 5 June 1960; children: Jeffrey Joshua, Richard Dan; PARTNER, BUCHWALD, ASPER, HENTELEFF, since 1970; Dir., Metropolitan Properties Corp.; CHUM (Man.) Ltd.; mem. Winnipeg Adv. Bd.; Montreal Trust Co.; called to Bar of Man. 1952; cr. Q.C. 1966; Lectr. on Co. Law, Man. Law Sch., 1957-61; Sessional Lectr. on Consumer Protection, Faculty of Law, Univ. of Man. since 1969; Chrmn., Isaac Pitblado Lectures on Continuing Legal Educ.; First James L. Lewtas Visiting Professor, Osgoode Hall Law School, York Univ., Toronto 1977; Visiting Research Fellow, Inst. for Legisl. Research and Comparative Law, Hebrew Univ. of Jerusalem 1978; Hon. Fellow of the Hebrew Univ.; Special Counsel to Man. Govt. on Consumer Protection Matters, 1965-70; Chrmn., Candn. Consumer Council (1971-73); Hon. Solicitor Jewish Foundation of Manitoba; Nat. Chrmn., Can.-Israel Comte.; Nat. Vice-Pres., United Israel Appeal of Can., Inc.; Dir. and Co-Chrmn., Deficit Retirement Comm.; Winnipeg Symphony Orchestra; Gen. Campaign Chrmn., Combined Jewish Appeal of Winnipeg 1980; Pres. Law Society of Manitoba 1975-76; Gov. Canadian Tax Foundation 1973-76; mem. Bd. of Govs., Hebrew Univ. of Jerusalem; Pres., Winnipeg Chapter, Candn. Friends of Hebrew Univ. (1969-77); Chrmn., Adv. Bd., B'nai Brith Hillel Foundation, Univ. of Man., 1953-56; Chrmn., B'nai Brith Camp Bd., 1960-63; Pres. (1974-76) and Dir., YMHA Community Centre, Winnipeg; Dir., Winnipeg Football Club 1966-70; Dir., Winnipeg Symphony Orchestra, 1966-68 (Hon. Solr. 1967-68); Dir., Rainbow Stage, Inc., 1966-68; author, "Administration & the Carter Report", 1967; co-author, "Farmers & the White Paper on Tax Reform", 1970; author of weekly column "The Tax Corner", Toronto "Globe & Mail Report on Business", 1966-68; Contrib. Ed., Can. Business Law Journ.; other writings incl. articles and papers for various publs.; mem. Law Soc. Man. (Life Bencher); Man. Bar. Assn. (Pres. 1970-71); Candn. Bar Assn. (Nat. Chrmn., Taxation Sec. 1970-71 and Pub. Relations Comte. 1965-67); Nat. Jt. Comte. of Candn. Bar Assn. & Candn. Inst. C.A.'s on Tax Matters (Co-Chrmn. 1970-71); Dir., Can. Scholarship Trust Foundation since 1974; Chrmn., Wpg. Adv. Bd., Can. Scholarship Trust Foundation; Vice Chrmn. Un. Way of Winnipeg Campaign 1974; Sigma Alpha Mu (Pres. Sigma Xi 1947-48; Regional Gov. 1956-58); Freemason; Jewish; recreations: water skiing, tennis, skating, cross-country skiing, spectator sports; Club: Glendale Country; Home: 411 Park

Blvd., N., Winnipeg, Man.; Office: 1 Lakeview Square, Winnipeg, Man.

BUCK, Carol, M.D., PH.D., D.P.H.; university professor; b. London, Ont., 2 Apl. 1925; d. Albert Henry and Evelyn Florence (Parsons) Whitlow; e. Univ. of W. Ont., M.D. 1947, Ph.D. 1950; London Sch. of Hygiene & Tropical Med., D.P.H. 1951; m. Robert Crawforth Buck, 1946; two d., Lucy Anne, Effie Louise; Prof. & Chmn., Dept. of Community Medicine, UWO 1967-72; Prof. and Chrmn., Dept. of Epidemiol. & Prev. Medicine, Univ. of Western Ont. 1972-77; Prof., Dept. of Epidemiology and Biostatistics 1978-; Rockefeller Fellow, Dept. of Epidemiol. and Med. Stat., London Sch. of Hygiene and Tropical Med., 1951-52; Asst. Prof., Dept. of Psychiatry and Preventive Med., Univ. of W. Ont., 1952-56; Assoc. Prof. 1956-62; Prof. of Preventive Med. 1962-66; Ass. Ed., American Jour. of Epidemiology, 1980; mem. Science Council of Can., 1970-73; mem., Candn. Pub. Health Assn.; Canadian Assn. Teachers of Soc. and Preventive Med.; Society for Epidemiologic Research; Pres.; Internat. Epidemiol. Assn. 1981-84; Club: University; Home: 181 Elmwood Ave., London, Ont. N6C 1K1

BUCK, Harold Derek Rogers, M.C., F.R.A.I.C., A.R.I.B.A.; architect; b. Beckenham, Kent, Eng. 21 May 1920; s. Harold Samuel and Dorothy Jessie (Rogers) B.; e. Clair House Sch.; Dover Coll.; children: Robin, Jeremy, Laura; SR. PARTNER, PAGE & STEELE since 1965; joined Gerald Lacoste, Arch. London, Eng. 1938; T. Laurie Price, London, Eng. 1946; Partner, T. Laurie Price & Derek Buck, Dublin 1952; Arch. present firm 1955, Partner 1962; joined Brit. Army 1940, comnd. RA 1942, served in N. Africa, Italy, Syria, Lebanon; Territorial Army Comn. Surrey Yeomanry 1946; K. St. J.; mem. St. John Ambulance Ontario (Past Pres.); Ont. Assn. Archs.; Anglican; Home: 19 Maureen Dr. Willowdale, Ont. M2K 137; Office: 1623 Yonge St., Toronto, Ont. M4T 2A1

BUCK, Robert John, B.A., M.A., Ph.D.; university professor; b. Vermilion, Alta. 5 July 1926; s. Frank Jackson and Katherine Elizabeth (MacKinnon) B.; e. Univ. of Alberta B.A. 1949; Univ. of Kentucky M.A. 1950; Univ. of Cincinnati Ph.D. 1956; m. Helen d. Sideris Vasiliou 31 July 1955; children: George H., Zoe E.; PROF. OF CLASSICS, UNIVERSITY OF ALBERTA since 1966; Asst. Prof. Univ. of Kentucky, 1955-60; Assoc. Prof. Univ. of Alberta, 1960-66; Head of Dept. of Classics, 1964-72; served with RCAF, 1944-45; author of "History of Bocotia", 1979; 20 articles and monographs on topics in Greek Hist., Greek and Roman archaeology; Fellow of the Candn. Inst. in Rome, 1976; mem., Managing Comte. Am. Sch. of Classical Studies, Athens, 1961; Bd. of Dir. Candn. Mediterranean Inst., 1979- ; Past Vice Pres. Candn. Archaeological Inst. at Athens, 1973-79; of Classical Assn. of Can., 1970-73; Kappa Sigma; N.D.P.; Anglican; Clubs: Faculty, Univ. of Alta.; recreations: skiing, model railroading; Home: 11752 University Ave., Edmonton, Alta. T6G 1Z5; Office: University of Alberta, Edmonton, Alta. T6G 2E6.

BUCKLAND, Ross; executive; b. Sydney, Australia 19 Dec. 1942; s. William Arthur Haverfield Buckland; e. Sydney Boys' High Sch. 1958; Australian Soc. Accts.; Inst. Chart. Secys. & Administrators; m. Patricia Ann d. William Bubb, Warriewood, Australia 22 Jan. 1966; two s. Sean, Mark; VICE PRES., KELLOGG COMPANY, since 1981. Vice Pres., Kellogg Intl.; Dir of European Operations and Mang. Dir., Kellogg Co. of Great Britain; 1979-80; joined English, Scottish & Australian Bank Ltd. 1958; subsequently held various financial and adm. positions with firms engaged in engn., office equipment and food industry; joined Elizabeth Arden Pty. Ltd. 1966; Kellogg (Australia) Pty. Ltd. 1973, held various positions incl. Asst. Mang. Dir. and Mang. Dir.; Fellow, Australian Soc. Accts.; Inst. Chart. Secys. & Administrators; mem. Australian Computer Soc.; Anglican; recreation: squash;

Home: 1 Bowdon Rise, Bowdon, Cheshire WA 142RP, England; Office: Kellogg Company of Great Britain, Ltd. (Stretford), Manchester, M32 8RA, England.

BUCKLER, E. J., M.A., Ph.D., F.C.I.C., LL.D.; chemist b. Birmingham, England; e. Univ. of Cambridge, M.A., Ph.D.; CONSULTANT, POLYSAR LTD. since 1979; began as Research Chem., Trinidad Leaseholds Ltd. and Imperial Oil Ltd.; loaned to St. Clair Processing Corp. Ltd. (subsidiary) during war years; remained with Polymer Corp. Ltd. now Polysar Ltd. (sythetic rubber plant) when Imperial Oil withdrew 1945; apptd. Mgr. of Research & Devel. Div. 1947; Vice-Pres. Research & Devel. 1958-79; Past Chrmn., Candn. Research Mang. Assn. and Research & Devel. Comte.; Candn. Mfrs. Assn.; mem., Am. Chem. Soc.; Soc. of Chem. Industry; 1980 Technical Award, Internat. Inst. of Synthetic Rubber Producers; Office: Sarnia, Ont.

BUCKLER, Ernest, O.C. (1974), B.A., M.A., Litt. D., LL.D.; author; b. Dalhousie West, N.S., 19 July 1908; s. Appleton and Mary Elizabeth (Swift) B.; e. Dalhousie West Common Sch.; Bridgetown High Sch.; Dalhousie Univ., B.A. 1929; Univ. of Toronto, M.A. 1930; LL.D. Dalhousie 1971; Litt.D. New Brunswick 1969; unm.; prize winning article appeared in "Coronet", 1938; short stories and articles in "Esquire", 1939-42; "Saturday Night", 1940-47; "Maclean's", 1948-51; radio plays, C.B.C., 1940-45; author of Maritimes Letter, "Saturday Night", 1947-48; "The Mountain and the Valley" (novel), 1952; "The Cruelest Month" (novel), 1963; "Whirligig" 1977 (winner Leacock Award, 1977); also contributed to "Colliers", "Ladies Home Journal", "Chatelaine", "Country Gentleman", "Atlantic Monthly", and other journs.; Radio Talks (CBC), 1954-1959; President's Medal, 1957 and 1958, for best short story published by a Canadian during the preceding year, awarded Can. Council Scholar. 1960; Book reviewer "New York Times", 1962; awarded Can. Council Fellowship, 1964 and 1968; author (memoir) "Ox Bells and Fireflies", 1968; "Nova Scotia: Window on the Sea" (text for pictorial study of N.S.) 1973; Address: R.R. 3, Bridgetown, N.S. B0S 1C0

BUCKLEY, Jerome Hamilton, A.M., Ph.D. university professor; literary historian; b. Toronto, Ont., 30 Aug. 1917; s. James Ora and Madeline Isabelle (Morgan) B.; e. Victoria Coll., Univ. of Toronto, B.A. 1939; Harvard Univ., A.M. 1940, Ph.D. 1942; m. Elizabeth Jane, d. late John Alexander Adams, 19 June 1943; children: Nicholas, Victoria, Eleanor; GURNEY PROF. OF ENG. LIT., HARVARD UNIV., 1975-; Instr. to Prof. of Eng., Univ. of Wisc., 1942-54; Prof. of Eng., Columbia Univ., 1954-61; Prof. of English, Harvard Univ. 1961-75; Guggenheim Fellow 1946-47 and 1964; rec'd Christian Gaus Award 1952; Am. Philos. Soc. Grant 1956; author: "William Ernest Henley", 1945; "The Victorian Temper", 1st publ. 1951; "Tennyson: The Growth of A Poet", 1st publ. 1960; "The Triumph of Time", 1966; Ed.: "Poetry of the Victorian Period", 1965; "Poems of Tennyson", 1959; "Masters of British Literature", 1962; "The Pre-Raphaelites", 1968; "Victorian Poets and Prose Writers" (bibliog.), 1977; author, "Season of Youth: From Dickens to Golding" 1974; Editor, "The Worlds of Victorian Fiction" 1975; mem., Modern Lang. Assn. (Ed. Bd. 1963-68); American Academy of Arts and Sciences; Tennyson Soc. (Vice Pres.); Internat. Assn. Univ. Profs. Eng.; Acad. of Lit. Studies; Fellow, Huntington Library 1978; Democratic; Anglican; recreations: travel, skating; Home: 191 Common St., Belmont, Mass. 02178; Office: Widener Library 245, Cambridge, Mass.

BUCKWOLD, Hon. Sidney, B.Com.; senator; wholesaler; b. Winnipeg, Man., 3 Nov. 1916; s. Harry and Dorothy (Freedman) B.; e. McGill Univ., B.Com. 1936; m. Clarice, d. Samuel Rabinovitch, 17 Sept. 1939; children: Jay Murray, Judith Miriam, Linda Ruth; Pres. and Gen. Mgr., Buckwold's Ltd. (joined Co. in 1936); Dir., Bank of

Montreal; Consolidated Pipelines Co.; Mutual Life Assurance Co. of Can.; Sed Systems Ltd.; served in 2nd World War, R.C.A.S.C. 1942-45; Mayor of Saskatoon, Sask. 1958-63 and 1967-71; summoned to Senate of Can., Nov. 1971; Freemason; Jewish; Liberal; recreations: golf, curling; Clubs: Saskatoon; Riverside Golf & Country; Home: 824 Saskatchewan Cres. E., Saskatoon, Sask. S7N 0L3; Offices: 75-24th St., Saskatoon, Sask. S7K 0K3, and The Senate, Ottawa, Ont. K1A 0A4

BUGG, William John Franklin, M.D., C.R.C.S.(C).; b. Wingham, Ont. 25 Jan. 1912; s. James Herbert and Margaret Nielen (Galbraith) B.; e. Central Coll. Inst. London, Ont. 1932; Univ. of W. Ont. M.D. 1938; Candn. Hosp. Assn. Mang. Course 1954; Inter Agency Inst. for Hosp. Adms. Washington 1964; m. Blanche Mary d. Donat Godin 16 June 1942; children: Judith, William, James, Stephen; former Asst. to Asst. Depy. Min. Veterans Affairs Ottawa; mem. Senate, Univ. of W. Ont. 1968-71; served with R.C.A.M.C. Can. and Overseas World War II, rank Capt.; rec'd Centennial Medal 1967; Candn. Red Cross Citation; Chrmn. and Founding mem. London & Dist. Health Assn.; mem. Royal Candn. Legion (Extve.); recreations: hunting, fishing, amateur radio; Address: R.R. 1, Morpeth, Ont. N0P 1X0.

BUGOLD, His Hon. John N., B.A., B.C.L., L.L.D.; judge; b. Maria, Que., 8 Sept. 1906; s. late James and Philomene (Bernard) B.; e. Campbellton (N.B.) High Sch., Saint Joseph Univ., B.A. 1933; Univ. of New Brunswick Law Sch., B.C.L. 1936; St. Thomas Univ., L.L.D. 1977; m. Veronica M. Murray, 14 July 1940; JUDGE, SUPREME COURT OF N.B., APPEAL DIV. since 1970; called to the Bar of N.B. Sept. 1936; cr. Q.C. 1958; practised his prof. in Campbellton, N.B., 1936-41 and 1946-68; Judge, County Court, Cos. of Northumberland, Gloucester and Restigouche, 1968-70; formerly Magistrate, City of Campbellton, Judge of Probate, Co. of Restigouche, Clerk of the Peace, Co. of Restigouche, City Solr., City of Campbellton; Chrmn. N.B. Motor Carrier Bd.; N.B. Bd. of Commrs. of Pub. Utilities; Adm. Bd., Hotel Dieu Hosp., Campbellton, N.B.; served in Can. and overseas with R.C.A.F. 1941-46; def. Liberal Cand. Fed. by-el. 1955; former Ald. and Mayor, City of Campbellton; Past Pres. various community organs.; mem.; Can. Pension Appeal Bd.; Candn. Bar Assn.; N.B. Barristers' Soc., Fed. of Ins. Counsel; Royal Candn. Legion; Royal Candn. Air Force Assn.; K. of C. (past State Depy. for N.B.); Roman Catholic; recreations: motoring, gardening; Club: Campbellton Curling.

BUIK, William A., M.A.; investment executive; b. Toronto, Ont., 1 Jan. 1930; e. Univ. of Toronto B.A. 1950, M.A. 1958; Chart. Financial Analyst 1968; m. Elizabeth Ann (Creighton) 10 June 1961; children: Catharine Ann, Sandra Helen; PRESIDENT, BURNS FRY INVESTMENT MANAGEMENT; Dir. Burns Fry Ltd.; Monument Well Services Inc.; Colo.; joined present co. 1964; Trustee, Havergal Coll. Foundation; St. James-Bond Ch.; Clubs: Cambridge; Osler Bluffs Ski; Home: 28 Mason Blvd., Toronto, Ont. M5M 3C7; Office: (P.O. Box 150) 5000, First Canadian Place, Toronto, Ont. M5X 1H3.

BUISSON, Gabriel; industrialist; b. Shawinigan, Que., 29 June 1927; s. Rosario and Rose (Martin) B.; e. Immaculée Conception and Shawinigan (Que.) Tech. Sch.; Internat. Correspondence Schs. Inc., Dipl. in Chem. Engn.; m. Pauline, d. Patrick Arseneault, 19 Nov. 1949; children: Claude, Serge, Josette, André; PRESIDENT AND GENERAL MGR. LAURENTIDE CHEMICALS INC.; Pres., 81735 Canada Ltée; Soc. de Gestion Cascade Ltée; Sidgens Ltée; Laurentide Chemicals, Atlantic Div. Ltd.; Peinture Nationale Ltée; Past Vice Pres., Shawinigan Sr. Chamber Comm.; mem., Candn. Mfrs. Assn.; Past Dir., Centre des Dirigeants D'Entre prise; R. Catholic; recreations: golf, curling, hunting, fishing, reading; Club: Shawinigan Golf & Curling (Founder & Pres.; Dir.);

Home: 90 Terrasse Cascade, Shawinigan-Sud, Que. G9P 2V3; Office: 4650 12th Ave., Shawinigan-Sud, Que. G9N 6V2

BUITENHUIS, Peter Martinus, B.A. Ph.D.; university professor, writer; b. London, Eng. 8 Dec. 1925; came to Can. 1959; s. John A. and Irene (Cotton) B.; e. elem sch. Essex, Eng.; Jesus Coll. Oxford, Eng., B.A. 1949, M.A. 1954; Yale Univ. Ph.D. 1955; m. Marguerite Ann d. Ross Stephenson 11 Dec. 1977; children: Juliana Polley, Adrian Peter Ross, (and by previous marriages) Paul Jason, Penelope Ann, Pym Susan, Beatrix Cameron, Hugo Donald; PROF. OF ENGLISH, SIMON FRASER UNIV. since 1975 (Chrmn. of Dept. 1975-81); Instr. Univ. of Oklahoma, 1949-51; Instr. Am. Studies Yale Univ. 1954-59; Asst. and Assoc. Prof. Vict. Coll. Univ. of Toronto, 1959-66; Visiting Prof. Univ. of Calif., Berkeley, 1966-67; Prof. McGill Univ., 1967-75; Visiting Prof. and Lectr. Macalester College, Minn., 1961-62; Wesleyan Univ. Middletown, Conn., 1958; State Univ. of Buffalo, N.Y., 1964; Berlin, Wurzburg, Kiel, Hamburg, Manchester; served with Royal Navy, 1943-46, rank Sub. Lt.; France and Germany Star, 1939-45, author of "Hugh Maclennan", 1968; "Viewpoints on Henry James's Portrait of a Lady", 1968; Ed. "Selected Poems of E.J. Pratt," 1969; "The Grasping Imagination:" the American Writing of Henry James", 1970; "The Canadian Imagination", (contrib. to) 1978; "The Restless Analyst: Essays by Henry James", 1980; essays on Saul Bellow, Stephen Crane, Arnold Bennett, H.L. Mencken, Mary McCarthy, J.D. Salinger, Propaganda of the Great War; regular reviewer for the "Globe and Mail"; mem., Am. Studies Assn.; Br. Assn. for Am. Studies; Candn. Assn. for Am. Studies (Pres. 1968-70); Candn. Assn. for University Teachers; Candn. Assn. for Chrmn. of English (Pres. 1978-79); Candn. Council Fellow, 1963-64; Am. Council of Learned Societies Fellow, 1972-73; SSHRC Leave Fellowship, 1982-83; recreations: skiing, sailing, squash, jogging; Home: 7019 Marine Dr., W. Van., B.C. V7W 2T4; Office: Burnaby, B.C. V5A 1S6.

BUJOLD, Geneviève actress; b. Montreal, Que., 1 July 1942; d. Firmin and Laurette (Cavanaugh) B.; e. Hochelga Convent for 12 years; Conserv. of Dramatic Arts. Montreal, 3 yrs; m. Paul Almond (div.), 18 March 1967; one s. Matthew James; rec'd Susanne Bianchetti Award, Paris, for "La Guerre est Fini", 1966; Emmy nomination for "Saint Joan", 1967; Best Actress Award, Carthagenia Film Festival; winner of ETROG for best actress "Isabel", 1968; Hollywood Golden Globe Award and Acad. Award nomination for "Anne of the Thousand Days", 1969; winner of ETROG for best actress, 1970; Earle Grey Award (ACTRA) "for most outstanding performer in Canada" 1972; Films include: "King of Hearts", "THE THEIF," "Alex and the Gypsy," "KAMOURASKA," "OBSESSION," "Murder by Decree", "COMA"; Chrmn. of the Bd., Gendon Distribution Co.; mem., ACTRA; Union des Artistes; Parti Quebecois; R. Catholic;

BULL, Hon. Ernest Bolton; judge; b. Vancouver, B.C., 23 Aug. 1907; s. Alfred Edwin and Margaret Elizabeth (McKenney) B.; e. Public Schs., Vancouver, B.C.; University Sch., Victoria, B.C., Univ. of British Columbia, B.A.; m. Margaret Jean, d. late Dr. Edwin Dixon Carder, Vancouver, B.C., 15 Dec. 1934; JUSTICE, COURT OF APPEAL, B.C., since Nov. 1964; read law with Hon. J.W. deB. Farris; called to the Bar of B.C. 1931; cr. Q.C. 1956; Assoc., Farris & Co. 1931-33; Partner, Farris, Stultz, Bull & Farris 1933-64; served with Candn. Army as Major, June 1941 to Jan. 1946, Seaforth Highlanders of Can. (Reinforcement Offr.); Legal Offr., Judge Advocate-Gen. Br. Nat. Defence Hdqrs., Dec. 1941-43; Asst. Judge Advocate-Gen. C.A., Mil. Dist. No. 7, N.B., June 1943; G.S.O. 2 (Instr. Mil Law) Candn. War Staff Course, Royal Mil. Coll., 1944; Asst. Depy. Judge Advocate, G.H.Q. (21 Army Group), H.Q. 1 Candn. Army, 1945; Depy. Judge Advocate, 3 Candn. Inf. Div. till discharge, Jan. 1946; mem. of Council, Candn. Bar Assn., 1949-52; Pres., Vancouver Bar Assn., 1952 and 1953; Pres. and Dir., Children's Aid Soc. of Vancouver 1958-1961; contrib. to Drynan & Sangster "Words and Phrases - Legal Maxims"; Zeta Psi; Anglican; recreations: golf, fishing; Clubs: The Vancouver; Union (Victoria); Capilano Golf & Country; Pennask Lake Fishing and Game; Home: 1264 West 39th Ave., Vancouver, B.C. V6M 1T1; Office: Court House, Vancouver, B.C.

BULLER, Herman, B.A., B.Ed., B.C.L.; author; teacher; b. Montreal, Que., 30 April 1923; s. Joseph and Lily (Fruchter) B.; e. Strathcona Acad., Montreal, 1939; Sir George Williams Univ., B.A. 1943; Univ. of Toronto, B.Ed. 1970; McGill Univ., B.C.L. 1946; Univ. of Toronto, Ont. Coll. Educ., Perm. High Sch. Cert. 1957; m. Adele Eve, d. Adolph Gottlieb, Toronto, Ontario, 11 June 1946; presently teaching econ. hist. and theory for N. York Bd. of Educ.; previously taught Eng. lit. and creative writing; served with C.O.T.C., Sir George Williams Univ. and McGill Univ.; author of "One Man Alone", 1963; "Quebec in Revolt", 1965 (paperback ed. 1966); "The Revolt of the French Canadian Youth", 1966; "This My Land" (novel) 1968; critical reviews have appeared in "The Telegram", Toronto, "The Montreal Star", "La Presse", Montreal, "Toronto Daily Star", etc.; has written several short stories; rec'd Canadiana Award for "One Man Alone", 1963; "Days of Rage" (novel) 1974; "Tania: The Liberation of Patty Hearst" (play) 1975; mem., Ont. Secondary Sch. Teachers Fed.; Candn. Authors Assn.; Hebrew; Address: 9 Kingsbridge Court, Willowdale, Ont. M2R 1L6

BULLOCH, John F. D., M.B.A.; association executive; b. Toronto, Ont. 24 Aug. 1933; s. John A, and Belle (Halter) B.; e. Univ. of Toronto, grad. (Engn. and Business) 1956, M.B.A. 1964; m. Mary Helen, d. Gerald D. McCleneghan, 22 Aug. 1955; children: Peter, Martha; PRES., CANADIAN FED. OF INDEPENDENT BUSINESS since 1971; mem. Advisory groups reporting to Prime Minister of Canada and Ontario Premier; Vice-Pres. & Dir., John Bulloch Ltd. (Mfrs. & Retailers, Men's Clothing); with Imperial Oil Ltd., Indust. Sales, 1956-57; Mgr., Heavy Oil Sales, Cities Service Oil Ltd. 1957-59; Mgr., Baier Fuels Ltd.; Kitchener, Ont. 1959-63; Lectr., Ryerson Polytechnical Inst. 1964-70; Pres. and Founder, Candn. Council for Fair Taxation, organ. challenging White Paper on Tax Reform 1970-71; Chrmn. (1972-73) and Dir., Candn. Centre for Entrepreneurial Studies, Ryerson, Polytech. Inst.; mem. Assn. Prof. Engrs. Ont.; Protestant; recreations: tennis, boating, summer cottage; Club: Tennis; Office: 4141 Yonge St., Willowdale, Ont. M2P 2A6

BUMSTEAD, R. Glenn, B.A., LL.B.; b. Meaford, Ont. 20 Oct. 1938; s. David L. and Margaret S. (Miller) B.; e. Meaford (Ont.) High Sch.; Univ. of Alta. B.A. 1965; Osgoode Hall Law Sch. LL.B. 1968; m. P. Joan d. Frederick Angell 13 Sept. 1965; children: John G., Andrea M.; SR. VICE PRES., GEN. COUNSEL AND SECY. THE TORONTO-DONINION BANK since 1976 and Vice Pres. & Dir. Pension Fund Soc. there; Pres. and Dir. Leamor Holdings Ltd.; Dir. Tordom Corp.; Pacific Centre Limited; Toronto-Dominion Centre Limited; Toronto-Dominion Centre West Limited; Regtor Investments Ltd.; Toronto Dominion Realty Co. Ltd.; Edmonton Centre Ltd.; Terbett Investment Properties Ltd.; Edmonton Centre West Ltd.; ECW Leaseholds Ltd.; 82195 Can. Ltd.; Dir. and Sec., 94027 Can. Inc.; read law with Thomson, Rogers; called to Bar of Ont. 1970; law practice Thomson, Rogers 1968-72; Gen. Counsel and Asst. Secy. General Motors of Canada Ltd. 1972-76; served with RCAF 1957-63; mem. Candn. Bar Assn.; York Co. Law Assn.; P. Conservative; Anglican; recreations: wood-working, skiing, reading; Club: University; Home: 2254 Bethnal Green Rd., Oakville, Ont. L6J 5J9; Office: Toronto-Dominion Centre, Toronto, Ont.M5K 1A2

BUNGE, Mario Augusto, Ph.D., LL.D.; educator; author; b. Buenos Aires, Argentina 21 Sept. 1919; s. Augusto and Maria (Müser) B.; e. Universidad Nacional de La Plata Ph.D. 1952; Simon Fraser Univ. LL.D. 1981; m. Marta Irene d. Ricardo Cavallo, Buenos Aires 5 Feb. 1959; children: Carlos F., Mario A.J. (by first marriage); Eric R., Silvia A.; FROTHINGHAM PROF. OF LOGIC & METAPHYSICS, McGILL UNIV. 1981- ; Teaching Asst. in Exper. Physics Universidad Nacional de La Plata 1943, Prof. of Theoretical Physics 1956-59; Teaching Asst. in Math. Physics Universidad Nacional de Buenos Aires 1946-52, Prof. of Theoretical Physics 1956-58, Prof. of Philos. 1957-62; Visiting Prof. Univ. of Pa. 1960-61, Univ. of Texas 1963, Temple Univ. 1963-64, Univ. of Del. 1964-65, Universität Freiburg 1965-66, Aarhus Univ.; 1972, ETH Zurich 1973, Universidad Nacional Autónoma de México 1975-76; Prof. of Philos, present Univ. 1966-81; Fellow, Alexander von Humboldt Stiftung 1965-66, John Simon Guggenheim Foundation 1972-73; author "Temas de educación popular" 1943; "Causality" 1959; "Metascientific Queries" 1959; "Etica y ciencia" 1960; "Cinemática del electrón relativista" 1960; "Intuition and Science" 1962; "The Myth of Simplicity" 1963; "Scientific Research" 2 vols. 1967; "Foundations of Physics" 1967; Teoría y realidad" 1972; "Philosophy of Physics" 1973; "Method, Model and Matter" 1973; "Sense and Reference" 1974; "Interpretation and Truth" 1974; "The Furniture of the World" 1977; "A World of Systems" 1979; "Epistemología" 1980; "The Mind-Body Problem" 1980; "Ciencia y desarrollo" 1980; "Scientific Materialism" 1981; over 260 scient. articles; Founder and later Headmaster, Universidad Obrera Argentina, Buenos Aires 1938-43; mem. Asociación Física Argentina; Agrupación, Rióplatense de Lógica y Filo-sofía Científica (Past Pres.); Asociación Mexicana de Epistemología (Past Pres.); Inst. Internat. de Philosophie; Académie Internationale de Philosophie des Sciences; Philos. of Science Assn.; Soc. Exact Philos.; Candn. Philos. Assn.; Candn. Soc. Hist. & Philos. Science; Brit. Soc. Philos. Science; Ed. 7 collective works; gen. ed. book series "Studies in the Foundations and Philosophy of Science"; "Library of Exact Philosophy"; Episteme"; "Foundations and Philosophy of Science and Technology"; biog. "Scientific Philosophy Today: Essays in Honor of Mario Bunge" 1982; Liberal; recreations: reading, music, walking, swimming, cross-country skiing; Home: 29 Bellevue Ave., Westmount, Que. H3Y 1C4; Office: 3479 Peel St., Montreal, Que. H3A 1W7.

BUNTING John Pearce, B.Comm.; stockbroker; b. Toronto, Ont., 6 Sept. 1929; s. Alfred and Harriet (Lee) B.; e. Appleby Coll., Oakville; McGill Univ., B.Comm., 1952; m. Stephanie Keeley, 26 Sept. 1977; children: Mark Alfred, Elsa Brenda, Harriet Elizabeth, Alexandra Keeley, Charles Pearce; PRESIDENT AND CHIEF EXEC. OFFICER, TORONTO STOCK EXCHANGE; Dir., Canadian General-Tower Ltd.; Gov. Appleby Coll.; Dir. St. John's Convalescent Hosp.; Pres. Ticker Club 1976-77; Vice Pres., Fed. Internat. des Bourses de Valeurs 1981-82; with McLeod, Young & Weir, 1952-55; joined Alfred Bunting & Co. Ltd. 1955 (apptd. Pres. 1967); mem. Bd. of Council Bd. of Trade of Metrop. Toronto; Lakeland Conserv. Ltd.; Anglican; Kappa Alpha; recreations: golf, squash, skiing; Clubs: University (Pres. 1979-80); Toronto Golf; Granite; Osler Bluff Ski; Home: 21 Shorncliffe Ave., Toronto, Ont. M4V 1S9; Office: 234 Bay St., Toronto, Ont. M5J 1R1

BURBIDGE, Frederick Stewart, B.A., LL.B.; transportation executive; b. Winnipeg, Man. 30 Sept. 1918; s. Frederick Maxwell and Susan Mary (Stewart) B.; e. Ravenscourt Sch. Winnipeg; Univ. of Manitoba, B.A. 1939; Man. Law Sch., LL.B. 1946; m. Cynthia Adams Bennest, 27 April 1942; children: John Bennest, George Frederick; CHMN. AND CEO, CANADIAN PACIFIC LTD. since 1981; Dir., Can. Pacific Ltd.; CP Steamships Ltd.; Cominco Ltd.; Can. Pacific Enterprises Ltd.; C.I.L. Inc.; Canadian Pacific (Bermuda) Ltd.; Marathon Realty Co. Ltd.; Soo Line Railroad Co.; Bank of Montreal (mem. Exec. Comm.); CP Air; CNCP Telecommunications; Royal Victoria Hospital Foundation; called to Bar of Man. 1946; entered Candn. Pacific Law Dept., Winnipeg 1947 as Asst. Solr.; Asst. Solr. Montreal, 1950; Solr. 1957; Asst. Gen. Counsel 1960; Asst. Vice-Pres., Traffic 1962; Vice-Pres., Rail Admn. 1966; Vice-Pres. and Extve. Asst. 1967; Vice-Pres., Admn. 1969; Vice-Pres., Marketing and Sales, CP Rail, 1969; Sr. Extve. Offr., CP Rail 1971; Vice-Pres., Canadian Pacific 1971; Pres., 1972; Mem. Adv. Council to Min. of Ind. Trade & Comm.; Mem. Gen. Council of Industry (Quebec); Hon. Vice-Pres., Boy Scouts of Canada (Quebec); Citizens Adv. Board, The Salvation Army; R.C.N. 1941-45, rank Lt.; Clubs: Saint James's; Candn. Railway; Mount Royal; Montreal Bd. of Trade; La Chambre de Commerce; Traffic Club of Montreal; Office: Windsor Station, Montreal, Que. H3C 3E4

BURBRIDGE, Kenneth Joseph, M.A., B.C.L., Ph.D.; b. Bathurst, N.B., 2 July 1911; s. Harry Joseph and Elizabeth (Foley) B.; e. St. Thomas Univ.; St. Francis Xavier Univ., B.A. (1935) and M.A. (1936); Univ. of New Brunswick, B.C.L. (1939); Univ. of Ottawa, Ph.D. (1942) m. Marion Catherine Smith, 20 Nov. 1943; children; John Kenneth, Sheila Marie; engaged in private practice of law at Saint John, N.B., 1939-41; ADMINISTRATOR, MARITIME POLLUTION CLAIMS FUND, OTTAWA; various positions in pub. service of Can. incl. Legal Counsel, Dept. of Munitions & Supply. Ottawa, 1941-43; Chief Legal Adv. to Nat. Selective Service, (Mobilization), Dept. of Labour, Ottawa, 1943-44; Legal Adv. to Unemployment Ins. Comn., Ottawa, 1945; Counsellor to Secy. of State and Dir., War Claims Branch, Dept. Secy. of State, Ottawa, 1945-47; Legal Adviser, Dept. of External Affairs, Ottawa and Counsel for Can. before Internat. Joint Comn. 1948-54; del. to Inter-Allied Reparations Agency, Brussels, 1947; Candn. Adv. to Allied Conf. on Enemy Property, London, 1947; Candn. del. to Allied Conf. on German Indust. Property Rights, Neuchatel; Candn. Observer at Council of Europe, Strasbourg; Legal Adv. to Candn. dels. to UNS., 1952-53; Candn. Depy. Permanent Rep. to N. Atlantic Council (NATO) and Organ. for European Economic Cooperation (O.E.E.C.) Paris, 1954-57; Candn. del. to Columbo Plan Conf., Seattle, 1958; Candn. Del., Inter-govtl. Maritime Consultative Organ. and Econ. Comn. for Europe Conf. on Internat. Combined Transport, London, Eng. and on Internat. Shipping Leg., Geneva, 1970; Candn. Del to Internat. Conf. on Unlawful Interference with Civil Aviation 1971; Consul Gen. of Can., Seattle 1957-62; High Commr. to N.Z. 1963-67; Dir., U.S.A. Div., Dept. External Affairs 1968-70; Exec. Dir., Intern. Transport Policy, Can. Transport Commission, Ottawa 1971-78; Can. del. to Gen. Assemblies of Intern. Civil Aviation Organization (ICAO) 1974, 1977; Can. del. to UNCTAD Conferences on international multi-modal transport, Geneva, 1972-77; recreations: oil painting, golf; Club: Royal Ottawa Golf; Home: 930 Sadler Cresc., Ottawa , Ont. K2B 5H7. Office: Tower "A", Place de Ville, Ottawa, Ont. K1A 0N5

BURCHELL, David G., B.Sc.; mining executive; b. Joggins Mines, N.S.; e. Mount Allison Univ., B.Sc.; PRESIDENT, BRAS D'OR COAL CO. since 1956; Vice-Pres. Fundy Industries Ltd.; Vice-Pres. Cape Breton Crane Ltd.; joined present Co. as Asst. Engr.; Pres., Mining Soc. of N.S. 1950; Secy. of Independent Coal Operations Assn. of N.S.; mem., Prov. Labour Relations Bd.; rep. Candn. Coal mining industry, I.L.O., Turkey 1956, Geneva 1970; Pres., Candn. Inst. Mining & Metall. 1958-59; mem. Vol. Econ. Planning Comte. for Prov. N.S.; Director, Atlantic Provs. Transportation Comn.; Office: P.O. Box 7, North Sydney, N.S. B2A 3M1

BURCHELL, Howard B., M.D., Ph.D.; cardiologist; b. Athens, Ont., 28 Nov. 1907; s. James Edward and Edith (Milligan) B.; e. Univ. of Toronto, M.D. 1932; Univ. of Minn., Ph.D., 1939; m. Margaret, d. Dr. Henry Helmolz, 14 Aug. 1942; children: Susan (Mrs. F. Profeta), Judith (Mrs. J. E. Bush), Cynthia, (Mrs. R. Patterson), Rebecca; Prof. of Med., Mayo Sch. of Med., Rochester, Minn., 1946-67; Prof. of Med., Univ. of Minn. 1968-75 Sr. Cardiol., Univ. Unit Northwestern Hosp. 1975-78; frequent visiting Prof., Stanford U., C.A.; various guest lectureships including New York, Boston, Tel Aviv, London (Eng.), Edinburgh, Dundee, Leyden, London (Ont.), Dayton and Houston; served with U.S. Air Force 1942-46; co-author: "Congenital Heart Disease"; Ed., "Circulation" (1965-70) (Am. Heart Assn. Journ.); other writings incl. various articles pertaining to pathol. and physiol. of circulation; mem., Assn. Am. Phys.; Am. Physiol. Soc.; Am. Heart Assn. (Past Chrmn., Research Comte.); Alpha Omega Alpha; Sigma Xi; Independent; Universalist; recreations: history of medicine, libraries; Home: 260 Woodlawn Ave., St. Paul, Minn.

BURGESS, Bernard Whittaker, M.Sc.; pulp and paper executive; b. Ottawa, Ont. 7 Jan. 1921; s. Cecil and Violet (Hervey) B.; e. Hopewell Ave. Sch., Ottawa; Glebe Coll. Inst., Ottawa; Ottawa Tech. High Sch.; Queen's Univ., B.Sc. 1944, M.Sc. 1946; m. Evelyn Pearl, d. Richard Stethem, 25 May 1946; children: Brian Stethem, John Bernard Scott, Kathryn Ann (Mrs. Douglas Lamb), Mary Elizabeth (Mrs. John Roy); PRES., CHIEF EXTVE. OFFR. & DIR., PULP AND PAPER RESEARCH INST. OF CAN. since 1979; Commenced as Sr. Chemist, The E.B. Eddy Co., Hull, Que. 1945; Tech. Asst., Tech. Sec., Candn. Pulp and Paper Assn., Montreal 1946; joined present Inst. as Asst. to Pres., 1952, Secy. and Business Mgr. 1955, Vice-Pres. Adm. 1967; Exec. Vice-Pres. 1971; Director 1977; Ch. Oper. Off. 1978; Alderman, Village of Senneville, Que. 1961-67 and Mayor 1967-75; Councillor, Montreal Urban Community 1970-75; mem. Tech. Sec., Candn. Pulp and Paper Assn.; Tech. Assn. Pulp and Paper Industry; Chem. Inst. Can.; Assn. Prof. Engrs. Ont.; mem. Adv. Council on Engn., Queen's Univ. 1968-75; Chrmn. 1973-74; Past Chrmn. 1974-75; mem. Queen's Univ. Council 1975-; mem., Bd. Trustees, Queen's Univ. 1980; mem., Exec. Comm., Bd. of Trustees, Queen's Univ. 1981; Candn. Research Mang. Assn.; mem. la Chambre de Commerce du District de Montréal; Montreal Bd. Trade; Church of England; recreations: skiing, golf, woodworking; Clubs: Beaconsfield Golf; Forest and Stream; Mount Royal; Home: 31 Pacific Ave., Senneville, Que. H9X 1A6; Office: 570 St. John's Blvd., Pointe Claire, Que. H9R 3J9

BURGESS, Horace Telfer; investment dealer; b. Toronto, Ont., 3 Aug. 1909; s. Charles Horace and Ella Hughene (Telfer) B.; m. Marion H., d. J. M. Gray, Port Credit, Ont., 14 Feb. 1935; CHRMN., BURGESS GRAHAM SECURITIES LTD.; Dir. and Secy., Silknit Ltd.; mem., Toronto Stock Exchange; Conservative; Anglican; Clubs: Kiwanis; Albany; Mississauga Golf; Home: 1301 Minaki Road, Mississauga, Ont.; Office: Royal Bank Plaza, P.O. Box 175, Toronto, Ont. M5J 2J4

BURGESS, James Allan; B.A.Sc.; manufacturer; b. Chatham, Ont., 29 June 1915; s. Herbert Wesley and Helen Rose (Fraser) B.; e. Univ. of Toronto, B.A.Sc. (Mech. Engn.) 1937; m. Nova May, d. late J.W. Christian, 29 June 1940; four children; Chrmn., Extve. Comm., Waltec Enterprises Ltd.; joined present Co. in May 1937, a Co. founded by his father in 1905; past Pres., Candn. Standards Assn.; mem., Candn. Inst. Plumbing & Heating; Plumbing Mfrs. Inst.; Presbyterian; Home: 542 Sandra Cresc., Wallaceburg, Ont. N8A 2C6; Office: 1355 Wallace, Wallaceburg, Ont. N8A 4L9

BURGESS, John Herbert, B.Sc., M.D., C.M.; physician; educator; b. Montreal, Que. 24 May 1933; s. John Frederick Burgess; e. Lower Can. Coll. Montreal 1951; McGill Univ. B.Sc. 1954, M.D., C.M. 1958; Univ. of Birmingham Research Fellow 1960-62; Univ. of Calif. San Francisco

Research Fellow 1964-66; m. Andrea Clouston d. Andrew Scott Rutherford, Westmount, Que. 30 May 1958; children: Willa, Cynthia, Lynn, John; DIR., DIV. OF CARDIOLOGY, MONTREAL GEN. HOSP. 1973- ; Prof. of Med. McGill Univ. 1975- and Chrmn. Cardiol. Training 1974- ; Consulting Cardiol. Douglas Hosp., Barrie Mem. Hosp., Centre Hospitalier Cote des Neiges, Huntingdon Gen. Hosp., Frobisher Bay Gen. Hosp.; Dir. Cardiorespiratory Lab. present Hosp. 1968-73, Med. Resident 1959-60, 1962-64, Intern. 1958-59; Asst. Prof. of Med. McGill Univ. 1966, Assoc. Prof. 1969-75; Examiner, Royal Coll. Phys. & Surgs. Can. 1970- (Mem. Council); Chrmn., McLaughlin Test Comte. Internal Med. 1978-81; Test Comte. in Med., Med. Council Can. 1978-81; recipient Wood Gold Medal 1958; Nuffield Travelling Fellowship in Med. 1960-62; R. Samuel McLaughlin Fellowship 1964-66; Med. Research Council Can. Scholarship 1966-71; Charles O. Monat Associateship 1971-74; author various research articles; mem. Candn. Heart Foundation (Vice Chrmn. Scient. Review Comte.); Am. Coll. Phys. (Gov. for Que.); Montreal Cardiac Soc. (Pres. 1978-80); Lafleur Reporting Soc. (Pres. 1977-78); Candn. Cardiovascular Soc.; Candn. Soc. Clin. Investigation; Med. Research Soc. Gt. Brit.; Am. Physiol. Soc.; Am. Assn. Advanc. Science; Am. Heart Assn.; Am. Coll. Cardiol.; N.Y. Acad. Sciences; Alpha Omega Alpha; recreations: swimming, cross-country skiing; Home: 639 Murray Hill, Westmount, Que. H3Y 2W8; Office: 1650 Cedar Ave., Montreal, Que. H3G 1A4.

BURGESS, Rachel Lillian, C.M., B.S., PH.D.; psychologist; teacher; counselor; b. Grand Falls, N.B. 9 Nov. 1935; d. Joseph I. and Aurolie (Leclerc) Cormier; e. Grand Falls, N.B. Pub. Sch.; Nursing Sch. Montreal 1951-52; Univ. of Me. Bachelor in Psychol. 1971, Master in Emotionally Disturbed 1974, B.S. 1975, Teacher's Licence 1976, Advance Degree in Counselling 1979; Hon. degree: Doctor of Laws (PH.D.) U. of St. Thomas 1980; m. Lee A. Burgess, Grand Falls, N.B. 4 Sept. 1956; children: Jimmy, Leah, Donna, Carl, Alison; PRINC. AND DIR., BURGESS CENTER FOR HANDICAPPED, founder of sch. and sheltered workshop, teacher and counselor; rec'd Record Achievement, Univ. of Me. 1971; Vanier Award 1971; Order of Canada, 1978; mem. Literacy Assn.; Mental Assn.; Psychol. Assn.; Mentally Retarded Assn.; Teachers' Assn. (Dir.); Counselors' Assn.; R. Catholic; recreations: skiing, guitar, reading, thinking; Address: (P.O. Box 597) Burgess Center, Grand Falls, N.B. E0J 1M0.

BURGOYNE, Gerald Wilfrid, B.Sc.; manufacturer; b. London, Eng. 5 Oct. 1919; s. late Wilfrid Omerod and late Anna Freda Clara (Grossman) B.; e. Erith Co. Sch. Eng.; Univ. of London B.Sc. (Chem.) 1944; Assoc., Royal Inst. Chem. 1944; m. Dorothy (Dee) Mary Worsley 28 June 1941; one s. Simon Richard; PRES. AND DIR., NACAN PRODUCTS LTD. 1979- ; came to Can. 1947; joined present Co. as Tech. Service Chem.; Asst. Sales Mgr. 1954, Sales Mgr. 1956, Vice Pres. 1960; Sales Dir., National Adhesives Ltd., Slough, Eng. 1962 (on loan to affiliated co.), Mang. Dir. 1966; rtn'd to Can. as Vice Pres., Gen. Mgr. and Dir. 1968; mem. Chem. Inst. Can.; Bd. Trade Metrop. Toronto; Club: Boulevard; Home: Suite 310, 1300 Bloor St., Mississauga, Ont. L4Y 3Z2; Office: 50 West Dr., Bramalea, Ont. L6T 2J4.

BURKA, Petra; figure skater; b. Amsterdam, Holland, 17 Nov. 1946; d. Ellen Ruth (Danby) and Jan B; came to Can. 1951; e. Kipling Coll. Inst., Vincent Massey Coll. Inst. and Lawrence Park Coll. Inst., Toronto, Ont.; Jr. Candn. Skating Champion 1961; Sr. Candn. Champion 1964-66; N. Am. Champion 1965; Third, Olympics, 1964; World Championships, Third 1964, First 1965, Third 1966; entered Prof. ranks 1966; Candn. Woman Athlete of the Year 1964, 1965; Lou Marsh Trophy Winner, 1965; subsequently worked in public relations capacity, Fitness & Amateur Sport Directorate, Dept. Nat. Health and Welfare, Ottawa, Ont.; researcher and production assistant

on television and feature film projects; commentator for CBC and CBS (U.S.) television coverage of figure skating events; mem., Sports Hall of Fame; Anglican; Hon. Life mem., Toronto Cricket, Skating & Curling Club;

BURNET, Jean Robertson, Ph.D.; educator; b. Toronto, Ont. 10 June 1920; d. Johnn and Jemima (Sheals) Burnet; e. Strathcona Pub. Sch. and Owen Sound (Ont.) Coll. & Vocational Inst.; Univ. of Toronto Victoria Coll. B.A. 1942, M.A. 1943; Univ. of Chicago Ph.D. 1948; PROF. OF SOCIOL. GLENDON COLL. YORK UNIV. 1967- ; Instr. to Assoc. Prof. Univ. of Toronto 1945-67; Visiting Lectr. Univ. of N.B. 1948-49; Chrmn. of Sociol. Glendon Coll. 1967-72, 1974-76, Co-ordinator of Candn. Studies 1973-74; Research Assoc. Royal Comn. of Bilingualism & Biculturalism 1966-69; Chrmn. Candn. Ethnic Studies Adv. Comte. Dept. Secy. of State 1973- , mem. Ethnic Hist. Adv. Panel 1975- ; rec'd Guggenheim Fellowship 1955-56; Can. Council Fellowship 1972-73; named Learned Assoc. Univ. of Windsor 1976; author "Next-Year Country" 1951; "Ethnic Groups in Upper Canada" 1972; various book chapters, articles on ethnic relations and multiculturalism; Ed.-in-Chief "Canadian Review of Sociology and Anthropology/La Revue Canadienne de Sociologie et d'Anthropologie 1963-68; mem. Multicultural Hist. Soc. Ont. (Dir.); Candn. Sociol. & Anthrop. Assn.; Candn. Ethnic Studies Assn.; Am. Sociol. Assn.; Home: 494 St. Clements Ave., Toronto, Ont. M5N 1M4; Office: 2275 Bayview Ave., Toronto, Ont. M4N 3M6.

BURNETT, David Grant, B.A., M.A., Ph.D., F.R.S.A.; curator; b. Lincoln, Eng. 1 Oct. 1940; s. Wilfred Burnett; e. Univ. of London, Birbeck Coll. B.A. 1965, Courtauld Inst. of Art M.A. 1967, Ph.D. 1973; children: Charles, Wenham, Emma;CURATOR OF CONTEMPORARY CANDN. ART, ART GALLERY OF ONT.1980- ; Lectr. in Hist. of Art Univ. of Bristol 1967-70, Assoc. Prof. of Art Hist. Carleton Univ. 1970-80, Chrmn. of Dept. 1974-77, 1978-79; exhns. and catalogues incl. "A Tribute to Paul Klee 1879-1940" Nat. Gallery Can. 1979; "Guido Molinari Drawings" Agnes Etherington Art Centre Kingston 1981; Robert Bourdeau and Phillip Pocock, A.G.O. 1981; 3 exhns. Candn. Printmakers Showcase Carleton Univ.; catalogues: "Guido Molinari: Quantificateur" Musée d'art contemporain Montreal 1979; numerous articles, reviews, papers field of art; series 5 programs on Modern Art CTV 1976-77 and on Landscape Painting 1979; various radio and TV interviews; recipient Catherine Jane Booth Mem. Prize 1965; Merit Increment 1979; Can. Council Grants 1974, 1980; served numerous comtes. Can. Council Awards to Artists; Univ. Art Assn. Can. (Secy.-Treas.); Assn. Univs. & Colls. Scholarship Bd.; A.C.A.P. Discipline Force (Chrmn. 1979-80); mem. Internat. Assn. Art Critics; recreations: music, reading, photography; Office: 317 Dundas St. W., Toronto, Ont.

BURNS, Charles Fowler Williams; investment dealer; stockbroker; b. Vancouver, B.C., 27 Sept. 1907; s. Herbert Deschamps and Marguerite (Williams) B.; e. Upper Can. Coll.; Trinity Coll. Sch., Port Hope, Ont.; Univ. of Toronto; m. Janet Mary, d. Norman F. Wilson, Ottawa, 23 Feb. 1934; children: Joan Harrison, Herbert Michael, Janet Mary Cairine; HON. CHRMN., BURNS FRY LTD.; Hon. Chrmn., Crown Life Ins. Co.; Dir., Baton Broadcasting Inc.; Denison Mines Ltd.; Trustee, Extendicare Ltd.; Trustee, The Ontario Jockey Club; steward and mem. The Jockey Club of Can.; Life Gov., Trinity Coll. Sch., Port Hope, Ont.; Past Pres. and now Dir. and mem. Extve. Comte., Royal Agric. Winter Fair, Toronto, Ont.; floor mem., Campbell, Stratton & Co. (stockbrokers), 1929-31; R. A. Daly & Co. (investment dealers), 1931-32; formed Chas. Burns & Co. 1932; enlarged this Co. by inclusion of Latham Burns and changed name to Burns Bros & Co., 1932, the firm becoming mem. of Toronto Stock Exchange; now operates through merger with Fry Mills Spence as Burns Fry Ltd.; Zeta Psi; Liberal; Anglican; recreations: swimming, tennis, riding; Clubs: Toron-

to; York; Toronto Hunt; University; Halifax (N.S.);
Home: Kingfield Farms, King City, Ont. L0G 1K0; Office:
1 First Canadian Pl., Suite 5000, P.O. Box 150, Toronto,
Ont. M5X 1H3

BURNS, Lieut.-Gen. Eedson Louis Millard, C.C. (1967),
D.S.O., O.B.E. (1935), M.C., LL.D.; b. Westmount, P.Q.,
17 June 1897; s. George Eedson and Louise (Wills) B.; e.
Lower Can. Coll., Montreal; Roy. Mil. Coll., Kingston;
LL.D., Univ. of British Columbia and Alberta; m. Eleanor, d. Daniel Phelan, M.D., 3 Dec. 1927; has one d.,
Mary Eleanor; comnd. in Roy. Candn. Engrs. 1915;
served in World War 1914-19; with 4th Div. Signal Co.
1916-18; Staff Capt., 12th Candn. Inf. Bgde. 1919;
awarded M.C. 1916; subsequently held various appointments, incl. Instr., Roy. Mil. Coll., and charge of Survey
Br., Dept. of Nat. Defence; Dir. of experimental work of
Br. in air photo survey and devel. methods largely used
in World War 1939-45; grad. from Staff Coll., Quetta, India 1929; apptd. Offr. in Charge, Geog. Sec., Gen. Staff,
Ottawa, 1929; served as Pres., Candn. Inst. of Surveying,
1936-37; served in World War 1939-45, attending Imperial
Defence Coll. at outbreak of war; Chief Gen. Staff Offr.
under Gen. Crerar, Candn. Mil. Hqrs., London, until
1940; then under him as Asst. Depy. Chief of Gen Staff,
Dept. of Nat. Defence, 1940-41; held various staff appts.
and commands, incl. 4th Candn. Armoured Bgde. and
2nd Candn. Divn., until Jan. 1944, when he took com-
mand of 5th Candn. Armoured Divn.; assumed com-
mand of 1st Cand. Corps, Mar. 1944, during operations
in Liri Valley and capture of Rimini; appt. in charge of
Candn. Sec. Hdqrs., 21st Army Group, 1944; Dir. Gen. of
Rehabilitation, Dept. of Veterans' Affairs, 1945-46; Depy.
Min., Dept. of Veterans' Affairs, 1950-54; 1955, trans to
Dept. External Affairs as Special Adviser and lent to
United Nations; Chief of Staff, U.N. Truce Supervision
Organ., Palestine, 1954-56; Commdr., U.N. Emergency
Force, Nov. 1956-Dec. 1959; promoted to Lt.-Gen.; Jan.
1958; Adviser to Govt. of Canada on Disarmament; Jan.
1960; rep. Can. at 10 Nation Disarmament Conf., Mar.-
June 1960, and at 18 Nation Disarmament Conf. Mar.
1962-68; Prof. of Strategic Studies, Carleton Univ. 1972-
75; author of "Between Arab and Israeli", 1962;
"Megamurder" 1966; "General Mud,", 1970; "A Seat at
the Table" 1972; "Defence in the Nuclear Age" 1976; has
contrib. various essays in Candn., Brit. and Am. periodicals; mem., Survey Inst. of Can.; Anglican; recreations:
gardening; Home: 5570 McLean Cres., Manotick, Ont.
K0A 2N0

BURNS, H. Michael, executive; b. Toronto, Ont., 19
June 1937; s. Charles F. W. and Janet M. (Wilson) B.; e.
Trinity Coll. Sch., Port Hope; Cornell Univ., Fthaca N.Y.;
m. Susan P., d. C.A. Cathers, Toronto; children: Charles
F. M., Janet Michelle; CHMN. AND DIR. CROWN LIFE
INSURANCE CO.; Chrmn., Dir. and CEO, Extendicare
Ltd.; Chrmn. and Dir., Datacrown Inc.; Dir., Algoma
Central Railway; Ivy Fund (Boston); Fiducary Investment
Co. (N.J.); Pres. and Treas., Kingsfield Investments Ltd.;
Chrmn. and Dir. Datacrown Ltd.; Dir., Ivy Fund; Fiduci-
ary Co. of New Jersey; Gov. Trinity Coll. Sch. Port Hope;
Dir. Candn. Council Christians and Jews; Kappa Alpha;
Anglican; Club: Toronto; York; recreation: farming;
Home: Kingswood, R.R. 3, King, Ont. L0G 1K0; Office:
120 Bloor St. E., Toronto, Ont. M4W 1B8

BURNS, James Edward, B.A.; insurance executive; b.
Toronto, Ont., 13 June 1916; s. Albert Edward and Elizabeth (Murphy) B.; e. St. Michaels Coll. Sch.; Univ. of Toronto, B.A. 1936; m. Beatrice Marie, d. Frank A. Cartan,
13 July 1940; children: Francis Edward, Lawrence John,
Mary Catherine, Joanne Marie; CHRMN., GENERAL
ACCIDENT ASSURANCE CO. of CAN.; Past Chrmn.
Underwriters' Adjustment Bureau; Past Chrmn. Ins. Bureau of Can.; Past Chrmn. Insurers Advisory Organization; served RCAF 1941-45; Liberal; Catholic; recreations:
golf, curling; Clubs: National; Oakville Golf; Home: 116

Caulder Dr., Oakville, Ont. L6J 4T3; Office: 357 Bay St.,
Toronto, Ont. M5H 2T7

BURNS, James William, (Jim) B. Com., M.B.A.; busi-
ness executive; b. Winnipeg, Man., 27 Dec. 1929; s. late
Charles William and Helen Gladys (Mackay) b.; e. Gor-
don Bell High Sch., Winnipeg; Univ. of Man., B. Com;
Harvard Univ., M.B.A.; m. Barbara Mary, d. G. F. Cope-
land, 12 Aug. 1953; children: James F. C., Martha J., Alan
W.; PRESIDENT, POWER CORP. OF CANADA Chmn.,
& Dir. The Great-West Life Assurance Co.; Pres. and
Dir., Trans-Can. Corp. Fund; Shawnigan Ind. Ltd.; Dir.,
The Investors Group; Genstar Ltd.; IBM Canada Ltd.; Ba-
thurst Paper Ltd.; Consolidated Bathurst Inc.; Montreal
Trust Co.; Domglas Inc. Honorary Lt. Col. Queen's Own
Cameron Highlanders of Canada; mem. Candn. Council
Christians & Jews; mem. Council for Business & Arts in
Can.; Trustee, N. Am. Wildlife Foundation; Trustee, The
Conference Board (New York)); mem. of Bd., The Con-
ference Bd. in Canada (Ottawa); mem. Bd. of Directors,
Council for Business and the Arts in Canada; Bd. of Di-
rectors, Can. Council of Christians & Jews; Ducks Unlim-
ited; The Arthritic Soc.; recreations: hunting, fishing, ten-
nis, golf; Clubs: St. Charles Country; Manitoba
(Winnipeg); Albany (Toronto); Mount Royal; Mount Bru-
no; Montreal Home: 51 Belvedere Circle, Westmount,
Que. H3Y 1G7 Office: 759 Victoria Sq., Montreal, Que.
H2Y 2K4

BURNS, Latham Cawthra, B.A.; investment dealer; b.
Toronto, Ont., 26 June 1930; s. Herbert Latham and Iso-
bel (Cawthra) B.; e. Trinity Coll. Sch., Port Hope, Ont.;
Collegiate Sch. (N.Y.); Cornell Univ., B.A.; m. Patricia-
Annette, d. Paul Higgins, 1 May 1971; children: Reed
Cawthra, Holton Latham, Farish Victoria, Cawthra Caro-
line, Ainsley Isobel; CHAIRMAN, BURNS FRY
LIMITED; Standard Products (Canada) Ltd.; United Keno
Hill Mines Ltd.; Dir., St. Michael's Hosp.; Dir., Gottas-
Larsen Shipping Corp.; Echo Bay Mines Ltd.; joined
present Co. 1952; Delta Kappa Epsilon; Liberal; Anglican;
recreations: golf, tennis; Clubs: York; The Toronto; To-
ronto Badminton & Racquet; Toronto Hunt; Home: 215a
Lonsdale Rd., Toronto, Ont. M4V 1W7; Office: (Box 39)
First Canadian Place, suite 5000, P.O. Box 150, Toronto,
Ont. M5X 1H3

BURNS, Patrick Dennis, insurance executive; b. Toronto, Ont., 9 Aug. 1928; s. Albert Edward and Elizabeth
(Murphy) B.; e. St. Michael's Coll. Sch., Toronto, 1942-
46; m. June Lorainne, d. Stanley Allcock, Toronto, 10
Nov. 1951; children: Patricia Anne, Barbara Lynn;
EXTVE. VICE-PRES. AND DIR., CONFEDERATION
LIFE INS. CO. since 1980; joined present Co. 1946;
apptd. Mgr., Planning, 1956; Data Processing Extve.
1961; Dir., Systems and Computors, 1965; Asst. Vice
Pres. 1967; Adm. Vice Pres., Corporate 1968; Vice Pres.
and Controller 1970; Vice Pres., Group Ins. 1971; Vice
Pres., Cdn. Oper. 1974; Fellow (1950), Life Office Mang.
Assn.; Liberal; R. Catholic; recreations: golf, curling;
Home: 156 Underhill Dr., Don Mills, Ont. M3A 2K5; Offi-
ce: 321 Bloor St. E., Toronto, Ont. M4W 1H1

BURR, Arthur Albert, M.A., Ph.D.; engineering educator; b. Manor, Sask., 23 Aug. 1913; s. Charles Albert and
Mary (Hay) B.; e. Univ. of Sask., B.A. 1938; M.A. 1940;
Pa. State Univ., Ph.D. 1943; m. Leslie Mae Dickin, 1 July
1941; children: Janet Leslie, Leonard Charles; RENSSE-
LAER PROF. EMERITUS AND DEAN EMERITUS,
RENSSELAER POLYTECHNIC INST. since 1978; Teacher, Sask. Pub. Schs., 1932-36; Teaching Asst., Univ. of
Sask. 1938-40 and Pa. State Univ. 1940-43; Research Physicist, Armstrong Cork Co., 1943-46; joined present Inst.
1946; Prof. and Assoc. Head. Dept. of Metall. Engn.,
1953-55; Head of Dept. 1955-61; Acting Dean, Sch. of
Engn., 1961-62; Dean 1962-74; Rensselaer Prof. 1974-78;
rec'd award for "Outstanding Teacher of Metallurgy",
Am. Soc. for metals; mem. Am. Inst. Mining Metall. &

Petrol. Engrs.; mem., Am. Soc. Engn. Educ.; Am. Soc. Metals; pub. in various tech. journals; Presbyterian; recreations: boating, fishing, photography; Home: 983 Spring Ave., Troy, N.Y. 12180.

BURR, Ronald C., M.D., C.M., F.R.C.S. (Edin.), F.R.C.S. (C.), F.A.C.R., K St.J.; radiologist; professor emeritus; b. Bloomfield, Ont., 1 Aug. 1904; s. Clayton W. and Ethelwyn Christina (Thom) B.; e. Coll. Inst., Picton, Ont., 1917-21; Prov. Normal Sch., Peterborough, Ont., 2nd class teacher's cert. 1922; Queen's Univ., M.D., C.M. 1932; Fellow, Royal Coll. of Surgeons, Edinburgh, 1935; Cert. Specialist in Diagnostic and Therapeutic Radiol., Roy. Coll. Physicians & Surg. of Can., 1943; Royal Coll. of Surgeons, Can. (ad eundem), 1947; Fellow Emeritus, Amer. Coll. of Radiology m. Theo., d. late Lt.-Col. David S. Tamblyn, 20 Sept. 1934; one d., Catherine; former Director, Ontario Cancer Foundation (Kingston Clinic); and Prof. of Radiotherapy, Queen's Univ., Kingston, Ont.; did post-graduate work as interne at Kingston (Ont.) Gen. Hosp. 1931-32; Jr. Interne at Hamilton (Ont.) Gen. Hosp. 1933; Resident Interne at Kingston Gen. Hosp. 1933-34; promoted to Asst. Radiologist, 1935; became Acting Head, Dept. of Radiology, Queen's Univ., and Kingston Gen. Hosp., 1939; apptd. Dir., Ont. Inst. of Radiotherapy, which in 1947 became the Ont. Cancer Foundation (Kingston Clinic); retired 1971; mem., Advisory Med. Bd., Ont. Cancer Treatment and Research Foundation; served in 2nd World War 1940-45; Lieut.-Col. commanding No. 1 Field Ambulance (Reserve); mem., Mun. Bd. of Educ., 1945-48; Pres., Kingston Acad. of Med.; Fellow Emeritus, Am. Coll. of Radiology; Life mem., Candn. Assn. of Radiologists (Pres. 1955); mem., Cont. Med. Assn. (Dir. 1953-55); Candn. Med. Assn.; Radiol. Soc. of N. Am.; Brit. Inst. of Radiol.; had pub. many tech. articles in med. Journs.; Kt. of Grace, St. John Ambulance 1979; Honoured by K.G.H. who named new Ronald C. Burr wing in 1977; United Church; Home: 67 Kensington Ave., Kingston, Ont. K7L 4B4

BURRIDGE, Kenelm Oswald Lancelot, M.A., B.Litt., Ph.D.; educator; b. St. Julian's, Malta 31 Oct. 1922; s. William and Jane Cassar Torregiani B.; e. Dragon Sch. Oxford, Eng. 1936; Blundell's Sch. Tiverton, Devon 1939; Exeter Coll. Oxford Univ. B.A. (Jurisprudence) 1948, Dipl. in Social Anthrop. 1949, B.Litt. 1950, M.A. 1952; Australian Nat. Univ. Ph.D. 1953; m. Rosabelle Elizabeth Griffiths (d. 1971), Sept. 1950; one s. Julian Langford; PROF. AND HEAD OF ANTHROP. UNIV. OF B.C. since 1974; Pres. S. Pacific Peoples Foundation of Can.; Govt. Scholar Oxford Univ. 1946-50; Scholar Australian Nat. Univ. 1953 (fieldwork New Guinea); Research Fellow Univ. of Malaya 1956; Prof. and Head of Anthrop. Univ. of Baghdad 1958; Univ. Lectr. in Ethnol. Pitt Rivers Museum, Univ. of Oxford 1968, Foundation Fellow St. Cross Coll.; Visiting Lectr. Univ. of W. Australian 1967; Visiting Prof. Univ. of B.C., Prof. 1968; served with RN 1939-46 Atlantic, Mediterranean, Indian Ocean, E. Indies, specialized submaries, POW 6 months (escaped), Twice Mentioned in Despatches, rank Lt.; rec'd Can. Council Award 1970, 1971; Guggenheim Fellowship 1972-73; Visiting Fellow and Lectr. Princeton Univ. 1977; Killam Fellow, S.S.H.R.C.C. Leave Fellowship 1979-80; author "Mambu: A Melanesian Millennium" 1961; "Tangu Traditions" 1969; "New Heaven, New Earth" 1969 (Spanish transl. 1970); "Encountering Aborigines" 1973; "Someone, No one" 1979; numerous reviews, essays incl. articles for "Encyclopaedia Britannica" and "Encyclopaedie de la Pleiade" on religious theoretical and ethnographic matters; Hon. Fellow, Royal Anthrop. Inst, Gt. Brit. & Ireland; Assn. Social Anthrops.; Am. Anthrop. Assn.; Candn. Sociol. & Anthrop. Assn.; Candn. Ethnol. Soc.; Royal Soc. Can.; R. Catholic; recreations: hiking, sailing, motoring; Home: Apt. 4, 2265 Acadia Rd., Vancouver, B.C. V6T 1R7; Office: 2075 Wesbrook Pl., Vancouver, B.C. V6T 1W5.

BURRIDGE, Robert Eric, M.S., Ph.D.; educator; university administrator; b. Plaster Rock, N.B. 29 Aug. 1931; s. Albert Charles and Bessie Anne (MacInnes) B.; e. Univ. of N.B. B.Sc.E. (Elect. Engn.) 1953; Univ. of Wisc. M.S. 1962; McGill Univ. Ph.D. 1968; m. Ardeth Elma d. late Edgar Ball 16 May 1953; children: Stephen Robert, Colin Andrew, Lori Anne; VICE PRES. (ACADEMIC) UNIV. OF N.B. and Prof. of Elect. Engn. 1980- ; Grad. Apprentice, British Thomson Houston Co. Rugby, Eng. 1953-55; Asst. Prof. of Elect. Engn. present Univ. 1955-63, Assoc. Prof. 1963-70, Chrmn. and Prof. of Elect. Engn. 1970-75, Dean of Engn. and Prof. 1976-80; Acad. Visitor, Imp. Coll. of Science & Technol. London, Eng. 1975-76; mem. Council, N.B. Research & Productivity Council; recipient Beaverbrook Scholarship 1948-53; Athlone Fellowship 1953-55; Sir George Nelson Award Engn. Inst. Can. 1966; mem. Bd. Govs. Univ. N.B.; author over 20 tech. articles electric power engn.; mem. Assn. Prof. Engrs. Prov. N.B. (mem. Council 1980-82, 2nd Vice Pres. 1982-83); Engn. Inst. Can.; Am. Soc. Engn. Educ.; Sr. mem. Inst. Elect. & Electronic Engrs.; Baptist; recreations: reading, skiing, local history; Home: 790 Windsor St., Fredericton, N.B. E3B 4G5; Office: (P.O. Box 4100) Fredericton, N.B. E3B 5A3.

BURT, George Graham, LL.D.; labour leader (retired); b. Toronto, Ont. 17 Aug. 1903; s. William Henry and Barbara Anne B.; e. Shaw's Business Coll. and Central Tech. Sch., Toronto, Ont.; Univ. of Windsor, LL.D. 1968; children: Barbara Hazel, William; was one of first mems. of Local 222, U.A.W.-C.I.O., in Oshawa; el. Treas. of 1st Extve. Bd. of Local 222 and subsequently el. by accl. on two succeeding yrs.; Candn. Dir. & Internat. Bd. mem. of U.A.W.-C.I.O., defeating C. H. Millard at the convention in Cleveland, 1939-68; led Ford Strike, 1945; negotiated contract which included the Rand formula; had long been Dir., U.A.W.-C.I.O., Vice-Pres. (at large) Candn. Labour Cong. (1958), mem. of Adv. Bd., Unemployment Ins. Comte., and Bd. mem., Candn. Assn. for Adult Educ.; served in Gov.-Gen's Body Guard; formerly mem. Bd. of Govs. Univ. of Windsor; Dir., Windsor Community Fund; mem., Nat. Youth Comm; Y.M.C.A.; Presbyterian; recreations: fishing, swimming, hockey, wrestling; Home: 197 Pineway Park, Kingsville, Ont. N9Y 2J1

BURTON, Clifford Chickering, B.S.; engineer; b. Chicago, Ill. 13 Dec. 1917; s. Clifford Eugene and Margaret Theresa (Murrell) B.; e. Calif. Inst. of Technol. B.S. 1940; m. Marcella Rogers d. Thomas S. Cole 29 Aug. 1946; one s. Dr. Thomas E.; Advisor to Mang. PCL-Braun-Simons Ltd. 1982- ; Dir. C F Braun & Co. of Canada Ltd.; Engr. Texaco Inc. New York 1940-48; Vice Pres. C F Braun & Co. Alhambra, Calif. 1971, Pres. and Dir. 1971-79, joined Co. 1948; Pres., Chief Extve. Offr., Dir. PCL-Braun-Simons Ltd. Calgary 1979-81; recipient Distinguished Alumni Award Calif. Inst. Technol. 1974; Clifford C. Burton Scholarship in Chem. Engn. estbd. Univ. of Calgary 1981; Fellow, Am. Inst. Chem. Engrs.; mem. APEGGA; recreations: hiking, skiing, photography; Clubs: Ranchmen's; California (Los Angeles); Alpine of Canada; Home: 4, 1754 - 8th Ave. N.W., Calgary, Alta. T2N 1C2; Office: 777 Gulf Canada Square, Calgary, Alta. T2P 3C5.

BURTON, Denis Eugene Norman; artist; teacher; illustrator; printmaker; b. Lethbridge, Alta., 6 Dec. 1933; s. Clarence Edward Frederick and Bertha Jean (Tiller) B.; e. Lethbridge Coll. Inst., 1950; Pickering Coll., Newmarket, Ont. 1952; Ont. Coll. of Art, Toronto (where rec'd R. S. McLaughlin, J.F.M. Stewart and R.C.A. scholarships) 1956; m. Diane Fern, d. Louis J. Pugen, 9 Sept. 1970; children: Varyn Erica Clare (by previous m.); Maihyet Etanya; Dir. "New School of Art," Toronto, 1971-77; founded (with R. Hedrick & J. Sime, Toronto, 1965) and was Pres. Arts' Sake Inc. "The Institute for Visual Arts," until Nov. 1978; One Man Retrospective Exhibition of Drawings, Lynnwood Art Centre, Simcoe, 1980; One Man Retrospective Cardigan-Milne Gallery, Wpg. 1980; apptd. Artist in Residence, Emily Carr Coll. of Art, Vancouver, 1979-80; full-time instructor, 1980-81; Retro exhibition travelled to ten major Can. galleries and universities 1977-79; Chrmn., Drawing & Painting Dept., Ont. Coll. of Art, 1970-71; employed as Graphic Designer, CBC, Toronto, 1957-60; T.V., Film Promotion & Advertising Designer, TDF Advertising-Artists Ltd., Toronto, 1963-64; has exhibited widely in leading galleries and museums throughout Can. and U.S.A.; awards incl. Walker Art Centre Biennial (3) 1958; Granby International 1959; Can. Council 1961, 1967, Sen. Awards 1969, 72, 73, 75, 76; purchase prize at Winnipeg Biennial Show 1968; works rep. in several Can. and Am. pub. and pte. Colls. incl: Walker Art Centre, Minneapolis, Metropolitan Museum of Art, N.Y., Pasadena Art Museum, Nat. Gallery, Ottawa; Montreal Museum of Fine Arts; Art Gallery of Ont. Can. Council Art Bank, etc.; commissioned murals for Mr. and Mrs. J. D. Eaton, 1962; and Edmonton Internat. Airport, 1963; designed Henry Kelsey Mem. postage stamp, 1970; has contrib. illustrations for several Can. mags. and articles to art and archaeol. journs in Can. and U.S.A.; Recreation: Jazz playing (saxophone, drums); Address: 454 East 8th Ave., Vancouver, B.C. V5T 1S7

BURTON, Edgar Gordon; merchant; b. Toronto, Ont., 14 Jan. 1935; s. Edgar Gordon and Clayton (Callaway) B.; e. Upper Can. Coll., Toronto; Trinity Coll., Univ. of Toronto; Advanced Management Plan of Grad. Sch. of Business, Harvard; m. Jane Sutherland Cody, Toronto, 3 Sept. 1957 d. Mr. and Mrs. Donald Cody; two s., Gregory James, David Edgar; two d., Jeanne Louise, Nancy Anne; joined Simpsons 1955; Asst. Gen. Man. Montreal Area 1965; Toronto Area 1968; Vice President and Director 1969; Vice President, Corp. Affairs 1975; President 1976; Pres. and Dir. 1977-81; Director: Can. Imp. Bank of Commerce; Dir. and Mem. Exec. Comm., Retail Council of Canada; Dir. Toronto General Hospital Foundation; Mem., Exec. Comm. Toronto Redevelopment Advisory Council; Bd. of Directors, Stratford Shakespearean Festival; Gov., Upper Canada College, Toronto; Hon. Director, Can Professional Golfers' Assoc. of Ontario; Gov., College of Churches of Christ (Disciples); past Pres., Bd. of Trade, Metro. Toronto; Canadian Club Inc.; Church of Christ (Disciples); Clubs: Granite; Rosedale Golf; St. James's (Montreal); Home: Greenbrook Farm, RR #2, King, Ont. L0G 1K0

BURTON, G. Allan, D.S.O., E.D., LL.D.; retired company chairman; b. Toronto, Ont., 20 Jan. 1915; s. late Charles Luther, C.B.E., D.C.Sc., LL.D. and Ella Maud. (Leary) B.; e. Lycee Jaccard, Lauzanne, Switzerland, 1929-30; Univ. of Toronto Schs., 1926-34; Univ. of Toronto (Arch.), 1934-35; m. Audrey Caro (deceased), d. late John Roy Syer, Toronto, Ont., 12 May 1938; one s., three d.; m. Mrs. Betty Kennedy, 15 Oct., 1976; Dir., The Royal Bank of Canada; Bell Canada; Standard Broadcasting Corp. Ltd.; CFRB Ltd.; Electrolyser Corp.; Hudson's Bay Co.; joined The Robert Simpson Co. ltd., Toronto, 1935; appointed General Manager, Toronto store, 1951; Director, 1953; Vice-President 1957; promoted as Vice-Pres. and Mang. Dir., 1958; Pres., 1964; Chmn. and Ceo 1968-79 comnd. 2nd Lt. in the Governor-General Body Guard, January 1933; Active Militia G.G.H.G., 1933-40; Active Service with G.G.H.G. in England, Italy, Holland and Germany, 1940-45; Lt. Col. Commanding G.G.H.G., 1948-50; Hon. Lt. Col. G.G.H.G. 1965-70; awarded D.S.O. Italy 1943 and E.D. 1949; Chrmn., United Appeal Metrop. Toronto, 1961; Pres., Bd. Trade Metrop. Toronto, 1962-63; Pres., Metrop. Toronto Indust. Comn., 1967-69, and Chrmn. Bd. 1969-71; Kt. of St. Lazarus of Jerusalem; Bro. Offr., St. John of Jerusalem, 1962; mem., Extve. Comte., Redevel. Adv. Council Metrop. Toronto Founding (Chrmn. 1960-62); Bd. Trustees, Hosp. for Sick Children, 1963-77; mem., Royal Candn. Inst.; Business Advisory Council, School of Business, U. of W. Ont. 1970-; G.G.H.G. Assn.; Psi. Upsilon; Freemason; United Church; recreations: riding, painting, fishing, shooting;

Clubs: Arts & Letters; York; Toronto; R.C.Y.C.; Mount Royal (Montreal); Royal Canadian Military Institute; Canadian; Empire; Eglinton Hunt (jt. M.F.H. 1953-70); Rolling Rock (Ligonier, Pa.); London (Ont.); Caledon Mountain Trout; Ristigouche Salmon (Dir.); Home: Limestone Hall Farm, R.R. 2, Milton, Ont. L9T 2X6; and 68 Old Mill Rd., Toronto, Ont. M8X 1G8

BUSH, John Nash Douglas, Ph.D., Litt.D., L.H.D.; b. Morrisburg, Ont. 21 Mar. 1896; s. Dexter Calvin and Mary Evelina (Nash) B.; e. Univ. of Toronto (Victoria Coll.), B.A. 1920, M.A. 1921; Harvard Univ. Ph.D. 1923; Litt.D. Tufts 1952, Princeton 1958, Toronto 1958, Oberlin 1959, Harvard 1959, Swarthmore 1960, Boston Coll. 1965, Michigan State 1968, Merrimack Coll. 1969; L.H.D. Southern Illinois 1962, Marlboro Coll., 1966; mem. Am. Philos. Soc.; Fellow, Brit. Acad.; m. Hazel d. E.H. Cleaver, K.C., Burlington, Ont., 3 Sept. 1927; one s., Geoffrey Douglas; Sheldon Travelling Fellow (Harvard) in Eng., 1923-24; Inst. and Tutor in Eng., Harvard, 1924-27; Asst. Assoc., and Prof., Univ. of Minnesota, 1927-36; Guggenheim Fellow in Eng. 1934-35; Assoc. Prof. of Eng., Harvard Univ., 1936-37, and Prof. 1937-57; Gurney Prof. of Eng. 1957-66; Pres., Modern Humanities Research Assn., 1955; author of "Mythology and the Renaissance Tradition in English Poetry", 1932, rev. ed. 1963; "Mythology and the Romantic Tradition in English Poetry", 1937; "The Renaissance and English Humanism", 1939; "Paradise Lost in Our Time", 1945; "English Literature in the Earlier Seventeenth Century, 1600-1660" (Oxford Hist. of Eng. Lit.), 1945, rev. ed. 1962; "Science and English Poetry", 1950; "Classical Influences in Renaissance Literature", 1952; "English Poetry: The Main Currents from Chaucer to the Present", 1952; "John Milton", 1964; "Prefaces to Renaissance Literature", 1965; "John Keats", 1966; "Engaged & Disengaged", 1966; "Pagan Myth and Christian Tradition in English Poetry" 1968; "Matthew Arnold", 1971; "Jane Austen", 1975; Editor: "The Portable Milton", 1949; "Tennyson: Selected Poetry", 1951; "John Keats: Selected Poems and Letters", 1959; "Shakespeare's Sonnets" (with A. Harbage), 1961; "Complete Poetical Works of John Milton", 1965; "Variorum Commentary on the Poems of John Milton", Vol. I, "The Latin and Greek Poems", 1970; Vol. II, (with A. S. P. Woodhouse), "The Minor English Poems", 1972; Home: 3 Clement Circle, Cambridge, Mass. 02138

BUSH, Robin Beaufort, R.C.A., A.C.I.D.; industrial design consultant; b. Vancouver, B.C. 18 May 1921; s. Herbert Joseph and Muriel Helen (Matheson) B.; e. Oak Bay High Sch. Victoria 1936; Lord Byng High Sch. Vancouver 1937; King Edward High Sch. Special Program; Vancouver Sch. of Art 1938-39; Jr. and Sr. Matric. 1940; Royal Roads Coll. 1941; Kings Coll. Halifax 1941-42 RCNVR Offr. Training Sch.; m. Joan Ogilvie d. late James MacMurray, Saint John, N.B. 10 Nov. 1945; children: Susan Muriel Haberman, Janice Anne, Matthew Robin, Sara Joan Alderson; PRES. ROBIN BUSH DESIGN INC. 1952- ; Pres. Mosaic Communications Inc.; Interdesign Marketing Consultants Ltd.; designed and devel. large resort and fishing lodge Genoa Bay, Vancouver Is. 1946-50; indust. design practice Vancouver and Toronto 1950-81 (3 pavilions Expo '67), Montreal 1968-72 (maj. client Nat. Museums of Man & Natural Science Ottawa); Dir. Sheridan Coll. Sch. of Design 1972-75; mem. Adv. Bd. Ont. Craft Foundation 1966-71; Nat. Design Council Ottawa 1954-58; Thirteen Nat. Design Awards; Diplomas Milan Triennale 1954 and 1957; active regional civic comtes. urban planning; served with RCNVR 1941-46 N. Atlantic, N. Africa, Europe, Pacific Volunteer, rank Lt. Commdr.; mem. Assn. Candn. Indust. Designers (Past Pres.); Academician, Royal Candn. Academy of the Arts; P. Conservative; United Church; recreations: sailing, photography, travel; Home: Apt. 1203, 66 High St. E., Mississauga, Ont. L5G 1K2; Office: 22 Bay St., Mississauga, Ont. L5H 1C1 and Suite 202A, 1102 Homer St., Vancouver, B.C. V6B 2X6.

BUSHNELL, Ernest L.; radio executive; b. near Lindsay, Ont., 19 Nov. 1900; s. James and Adeline (Stinson) B.; e. Victoria Univ., Toronto; Toronto Conservatory of Music (vocal training) for five years.; m. Edna A., d. Edward Wood, Toronto, 19 Aug. 1926; one d., Marilyn Elaine; HONORARY CHAIRMAN - BUSHNELL CÓMMUNI-CATIONS LTD. since 1975; sang on prof. concert platform for five yrs.; started first radio advertising agency in Can.; Mgr. of Radio Stns. CFRB and CKNC, Toronto, 1929-33; Dir. Gen. of Programs, CBC 1945-53; Asst. Gen. Mgr., 1953-58, Vice-Pres., 1958-59 when resigned; Freemason; Protestant; recreations: golf, fishing; Home: 1602, 211 Wurtemburg St., Ottawa, Ont. K1N 8R4; Office: 1500 Merivale Rd., Ottawa, Ont. K2E 6Z5

BUSSIÈRES, Hon. Pierre, M.P.; politician; b. Normandin, Que. 8 July 1939; s. Jean-Baptiste and Thérèse (Poison) B.; e. Normandin Elem. Sch.; Desbiens High Sch. Lévis, Que.; m. Gertrude d. Georges Cloutier, Normandin, Que. 18 July 1964; children: Denis, Marie-Pierre; MIN. OF STATE FOR FINANCE, CAN. 1980- ; el. to H. of C. for Charlesbourg g.e. 1974, re-el. since; Parlty. Secy. to Min. of Energy, Mines & Resources and to Min. of State for Science & Technol. 1978; Liberal; R. Catholic; Home: Charlesbourg, Que.; Office: House of Commons, Ottawa, Ont. K1A 0A6.

BUTLER, Esmond Unwin, C.V.O., B.A., C.St.J.; Canadian public servant; b. Wawanesa, Man., 13 July 1922; s. Rev. Thomas B. and Alice Lorna (Thompson) B.; e. Weston (Ont.) Coll.; Univ. of Toronto, B.A.; Univ. of Geneva; Inst. of Internat Studies, Geneva, Licencié ès Sciences politiques; m. Georgiana Mary, d. Hon. John North, 19 March 1960; children: Mark William, Clare Martine; SECRETARY TO GOVERNOR GENERAL OF CAN., since 1959 and Secy. Gen. of the Order of Can. and of the Order of Military Merit; Journalist, United Press, Geneva, Switzerland, 1950-51; Asst. Secy. Gen., Internat. Union of Official Travel Organs., Geneva, 1951-52; Information Offr., Dept. of Trade and Comm. 1952-53, Dept. of Nat Health and Welfare, 1953-54; Asst. to Secy. to Gov. Gen. 1955-58; Asst. Press Secy. to The Queen, London, 1958-59; Acting Press Secy. to The Queen, Royal Tour of Can., 1959; served with RCNVR 1942-46; Overseas service in HMCS Stormont and HMCS Algonquin; following War served with Naval Reserve; rank Lt. Commdr.; Zeta Psi; Anglican; recreations: fishing, shooting, Canadiana, skiing; Home: Rideau Cottage, Government House, Ottawa, Ont.; Office: Government House, Ottawa, Ont. K1A 0A1

BUTLER, Gordon Cecil, B.A., Ph.D., F.R.S.C.; biochemist; b. Ingersoll, Ont. 4, Sept. 1913; s. Irvin and Edna M. (Harris) B.; e. Ingersoll Coll. Inst. (1926-31); Univ. of Toronto, B.A. 1935, Ph.D. 1938; Univ. of London, 1938-40; m. Jean S., d. G. D. Meeke, Hamilton, Ont., 3 July 1937; children: Judith, Stephen, Gregory, Susan; DIR. OF BIOL. SCIENCE DIV., NAT. RESEARCH COUNCIL OF CAN., 1968-78; mem. U.N. Scient. Comte. on Effects of Atomic Radiation (past chrmn.) 1956-80; Internat. Comn. on Radiological Protection Comte. 4 and 2, 1963-77; Research Chemist, Chas. E. Frosst & Co., 1940-42; N. R. C. Atomic Energy Project 1945-47; Prof. of Biochem., Univ. of Toronto, 1947-57; Research Dir. of Biol. & Health Physics Div., Atomic Energy of Can. Ltd., 1957-65; Sci. Comm. on Problems of Environment (chrmn., Cdn. Nat. Comm. (1978-81); Cdn. Physiol. Soc.; Cdn. Biochem Soc. (past pres.); Am. Soc. Biol. Chemists; Health Physics Soc.; Am. Assn. Advanc. Sci.; Cdn. Soc. for Cell Biol.; Assn. Sci., Engn. & Tech. Community of Can.; Cdn. Fed. Biol. Socs. (past Bd. Chrmn.); Roy. Soc. of Can. (pres. Acad. of Sci. 1974-75); Internat. Foundation for Sci. (vice pres. 1975-81); Scientists and Engineers for Energy and Environmental Security Inc. (mem. Bd. Dirs. 1981-82); joined present Council as Dir., Radiation Biol. Div. 1965; served in 2nd World War in Chem. Warfare, 1942-45; retired with rank of Major; United Church; recreations:

golf, carpentry; Home: 260 Sandridge Rd., Ottawa, K1L 5A2; Office: N.R.C., Ottawa, Ont. K1A 0R6

BUTLER, Sir Michael, Bart., Q.C.; b. Devonport, England, 22 April 1928; s. Marjorie Brown (Woods) and late Sir Reginald Thomas Butler, Bart.; e. (came to Canada 1940) Brentwood Coll., Victoria, B.C.; Univ. of Brit. Columbia, B.A.; Osgoode Hall, Toronto, Ont., divorced; children: Richard Michael, Geoffrey MacLean, Patrick Colman, Thomas David; PARTNER, BUTLER, ANGUS; Officer and/or Director of: Teck Corp.; Place Gas & Oil Co. Ltd.; Elco Mining Ltd.; Highland-Crow Resources Ltd.; MacDonald Dettwiler Assoc. Ltd.; and other public and private companies; Chrmn. Bd. of Gov., Brentwood College Association; read law with John G. Edison, Q.C., Toronto, Ont.; called to the Bar of Ont. 1954, and to Bar of B.C. 1967; Home: 634 Avalon Rd., Victoria, B.C.; Office: 736 Broughton St., Victoria, B.C.

BUTT, Gene Willard, B.A.; b. Toronto, Ont., 15 June 1918; s. George Willard and Lillian May (Stewart) B.; e. Oxford House Grammar Sch. and private tuition; Royal Conserv. of Music Toronto; York Univ. B.A. (Hons.) (Sociol.) 1972 (Pol. Science) 1974; m. Margaret L. d. Harold Baker, Lindsay, Ont., 25 Nov. 1950; farmer Vaughan Twp. Ont. 1938-40; Head of Exhns. Fine Art Dept. Robert Simpson Co. Ltd. 1940, adm. positions various depts. 1945, Design Consultant 1950-56; Lectr. various acad. subjects Ont. Coll. of Art 1957, Chrmn. Dept. Extension & Evening Classes 1965, Depy. Princ. 1966, Acting Pres. 1969-71; Co-ordinator of Educ. Services, Art Gallery of Ont. 1974-76; retired 1978 to do research and writing; mem. Curriculum Comte. Ont. Coll. of Art and Wellington Coll. Univ. of Guelph 1965-66; undertaken several restorations of pub. bldgs. in Ont. incl. Victoria Hall (Cobourg); mem. Arnold Arboretum Harvard Univ.; Essex Inst. Salem, Mass.; Life mem. Art Gallery of Ont.; Ed. "Colour Comments" 1962-65; author various articles; Fellow Royal Hortic. Soc. (Eng.); member-at-large, Am. Herb. Society; mem. Candn. Pol. Science Assn.; Candn. Hist. Assn.; Candn. Sociol. & Anthrop. Assn.; Am. Sociol. Assn.; Teilhard Centre for Future of Man. (Eng.); P. Conservative; Anglican; recreations: music, books, gardening, dogs; Clubs: University; St. George's Soc.; Home: "Glendyer", R.R. 4, Mabou, Cape Breton, n.S. B0E 1X0

BUTTRICK, John Arthur, B.S., M.A., Ph.D.; economist; university professor; b. Rutland, Vermont 12 Sept. 1919; came to Can. 1970; s. late George Arthur and Agnes (Gardner) B.; e. elem. and sec. sch. N.Y. City; Haverford Coll., Haverford, Pa., B.S. 1941; Yale Univ. M.A. 1947, Ph.D. 1950; m. 2ndly Ann Garnet d. late Kenneth Tatlow 24 July 1958; children (by 1st m.): Peter Miller, Hilary Jacob, Michael Samuel; PROF. OF ECONOMICS, YORK UNIV. since 1970; Dir. of Grad. Prog. 1979-; Instr. Yale Univ., 1948-49; Asst. Prof. Northwestern Univ., 1949-53; Assoc. and Full Prof. Univ. of Minn. 1953-73, Chrmn. 1961-63, Dir., Grad Studies 1967-69; Chief, Minn.-los Andes Project (Colombia), 1965-66; Visiting Prof. at Stanford, Harvard, Vanderbilt, Berkely, Los Andes, Tokyo, Singapore; a C.P.S.;U.S.A., 1941-45, assigned to Forest Services performing surveys, econ. research, etc., in various locations; author of "Economic Development", 1954 (also Indian, Japanese and Spanish eds.); "Theories of Economic Growth" 1960 (also Spanish ed.); "Consumer, Producer and Social Choice", 1968; "Who Goes to University from Toronto", 1977; "Educational Problems and Some Policy Options", 1977; "Aid and Development", 1979; other writings incl. bk. reviews and articles relating to econ. dev. or economics of educ. in several publs. and professional jnls.; Pres. O.E.O., Minneapolis 1967-68; Offr. DFL Ward, Minn. 1968-69; Chrmn., Task Force on Child Care, Ont. Govt. 1972; Natl. Task Force of Anglican Ch. on the Econ. 1975-77; ACAP and COU Cmte. on Index Nos. 1975-78; Bd. Mem. Hiroshima, Nagasaki relived; past bd. mem. Reform Metro; competed for N.Y.

Sch. Bd., Ont., 1979 (defeated); mem., Am. Econ. Assn; Candn. Econ. Assn. (Ed. Bd. 1978-81); CLU, AGO, Canada-Argentina Cmte; awarded Univ. Scholarship and Jr. Sterling Fellowship, Yale 1946-49; Faculty Fellowship, Fund for Advance. of Educ. 1952-53; Faculty Fellow., Ford Found., 1960-61; Fulbright Fellow. (Japan and Singapore) 1963-64; Research Fellow, Ont. Econ. Council, 1976-77; Mayflower Medal; listed in Who's Who in America, American Men of Science; Club: 39ers; recreation: woodworking; Home: 31 Henry St., Toronto, Ont. M5T 1W9; Office: 4700 Keele St., Downsview, Ont. M3J 1P3.

BYERS, Donald N., Q.C., LL.D.; Partner law firm of Byers & Casgrain; Chrmn., Renold Canada Ltd.; RHP Canada Inc.; Tioxide Can. Inc.; Dir. and mem. Extve. Comte. Royal Trustco Ltd.; Zellers Ltd.; Dir. Excelsior Life Insurance Co.; Tioxide Can. Inc.; Major Box Ltd.; Batonnier Bar of Montreal 1972-73; Past Pres. Montreal Bd. of Trade; Chambre de Comm. de la Prov. de Qué.; Past Chrmn. Extve. Council, Candn. Chamber of Comm.; Home: 562 Grosvenor Ave., Westmount, Que. H3Y 2S7; Office: Suite 2401, 800 Place Victoria, Montreal, Que.

BYERS, Neil E., M.L.A., B.Ed.; teacher; politician; b. Fertile, Sask., 7 Dec. 1928; s. Erland Newton and Kathleen Mary (McDonald) B.; e. Pub. and High Schs., Fertile and Frobisher, Sas.; Moose Jaw (Sask.) Normal Sch.; Univ. of Sask., B.Ed. 1961; m. Margaret, d. Walter Engelke, Frobisher, Sask., 8 Nov. 1952; children: Douglas Wayne, Valerie Maureen, Eleanor Elaine, Sandra Ruth, Roland Newton, Candyce Jean; sch. teacher for 21 yrs. in Saskatchewan; el. M.L.A. in prov. g.e. June 1969; re-el. 1971, 1975 and 1978; mem. Elks and Masonic Lodges; recreations: music; Home: 225 Durham Dr., Regina, Sask. S4S 4Z4; Office: Room 214, Legislative Bldgs., Regina, Sask.S4S 0B3

BYLEVELD, Herbert C., M.A.; economist; b. The Hague, Netherlands; 21 March 1922; s. Willem F. B. and Gretchen (Koehler) B.; e. Erasmus Univ., Rotterdam, B.A., M.A. (1946) (Econ.); m. Mona, d. late Michael Fragasso, Quebec City, 22 June 1957; two d., Lucy Anita, Lisa Maria; SENIOR POLICY ANALYST, DEPT. OF INDUSTRY, TRADE & COMMERCE, with Rubber Study Group, London, Eng., 1946-48; became Mgr. of an assn. of rubber, tea and coffee estates, Indonesia, 1948-50; came to Can. 1951; joined Bathurst Paper Ltd. as Economist, 1957; Research Dir., Conf. Bd., 1961-67; Econ. Adv., Candn. Imperial Bank of Commerce, 1967-68; Dir. Corp. Devel., Provincial Bank of Can. 1968-75; Chief, Industrial Analysis Div., Foreign Investment Review Agency 1975; lectured at McGill and Université de Montréal (H.E.C.); mem. Montreal Econ. Assn. (Past Pres.); Nat. Assn. Business Econs.; Protestant; recreations: gardening, tennis, skiing; Office: 235 Queen St., Ottawa, Ont. K1A 0H5

BYNOE, Brian Clive, B.A., Q.C.; barrister and solicitor; b. Toronto, Ont. 16 Sept. 1928; s. Clive Vickers Bynoe; e. McMaster Univ. B.A. 1953; Osgoode Hall Law Sch. LL.B. 1957; m. d. A. N. S. Jackson, Jamaica 15 Sept. 1953; m. Audrey May d. A.N.S. Jackson, Jamaica 15 Sept. 1953; children: Roberta Ann, Nora Elizabeth, Brian Clive Vickers; sole practitioner B. CLIVE BYNOE, Q.C.; Offr. and Dir. various private co's incl. Vice Pres. and Dir. Canadian Protection Services Ltd.; Dir. Shandon Associates Ltd.; called to Bar of Ont. 1957, N.W.T. 1962; cr. Q.C. 1971; Lectr. in Criminal Law & Procedure Ont. Bar Admission Course 1960-80; Lectr. Continuing Educ. Series Law Soc. Upper Can.; sometime Lectr. in Criminal Law & Procedure Fed. Law Soc's; Counsel to several Royal Comns. incl. Royal Comn. Toronto Jail & Custodial Service; former mem. Ed. Bd. Criminal Reports (Can.); author numerous articles various aspects criminal law; Bencher, Law Soc. Upper Can.; mem. Advocate Soc.; Criminal Lawyers' Assn. (Past Pres.); Candn. Bar Assn.; Co. York Law Assn.; Lawyers' Club; P. Conservative;

Anglican; recreations: racquet sports, boating, swimming, hunting, fishing, shooting; Clubs: Scarborough Rod & Gun; Toronto Lawn Tennis; Home: 12 Gordon Rd., Willowdale, Ont. M2P 1E1; Office: 111 Elizabeth St., 6th Floor, Toronto, Ont. M5G 1R9.

BYRD, Kenneth Frederic, B.A., B.Sc. (Econ.) M.A., LL.D., F.C.A.; professor emeritus; b. Durban, Natal, S.A., 31 Oct. 1903; s. Frederic and Elise Mary (Dymond) B.; e. Howard Gardens Sch., Cardiff, S. Wales 1915-19; Univ. of London, B.A. (1st Class Hons. in Eng. with subsidiary French) 1929; M.A. (Eng.) 1932; B.Sc. Econ. (with 2nd Class Hons. in Internat. Law & Relations) 1940; LL.D.(Hon.) Mount Allison 1968; LL.D.(Hon.) Dalhousie 1974; m. Iris Madeline, d. late Benjamin Sparks, Durban, S.A., 28 June 1930; children: David Kenneth, Christopher John; qualified A.C.A. 1927; admitted C.A. (S.A.) 1944, and Que., 1955; articled to L.D. Williams of Deloitte, Plender, Griffiths & Co., Chart. Accts., Cardiff, Wales 1921-26; Sr. Lectr. in Accounting & Auditing, Natal Univ. Coll., 1929-43; apptd. to first chair of Accounting & Auditing, Natal Univ. Coll. 1944; mem. of Senate, Univ. of S.A., 1929-47 and Natal Univ. Coll. 1940-47; Dean, Faculty of Commerce and Dir. of Comm. Bldg., Natal Univ. Coll., 1946-48; Prof. of Accountancy, Faculty of Management, McGill Univ. 1948-72; mem. of External Studies Comte., Univ. of S.A., 1945-47; Chrmn. of League of Nations Union (Durban Br.) during 2nd World War and later of U.N. Assn.; mem. of Indo-European Council, Durban till 1947; served in S.A. Coastal Defence Corps 1941-43; Hon. Life mem. Candn. Assn. Univ. Teachers 1967; Liberal; United Church; recreations: walking, reading; Home: 565 Huron St., Woodstock, Ont. N4S 7B1

BYRNE, Edward G., Q.C., B.Sc., LL.D., D.Sc.Soc., D.C.L.; b. Chatham, N.B., 23 July 1912; s. Thomas Ives, M.D., and Rita Blair (Ross) B.; e. Dalhousie Univ., B.Sc. 1934, LL.B. 1936, D.Sc.Soc. 1950; LL.D. 1964; D.C.L. 1975; m. Lt. N/S Ruth Anne Corr, R.N., 27 June 1946; children: Anne Mary, Joseph Ross; COUNSEL G. BYRNE, RIORDON, LENIHAN, WILLIAMSON & THERIAULT; Pres., Overseas Insurance Ltd.; Dir., Benmore Ltd.; Alnes Ltd.; Read Stenhouse Int. Ltd.; Gotras Larsen Shipping & Corp.; Chmn. audit comte., Gotas Larsen Shipping Corp.; called to the Bar of N.S. and N.B., 1936; cr. K.C. 1952; Mayor of Bathurst, N.B., 1948-50; Pres., Bathurst Bd. Trade; County Chairman of Nat. War Finance Comte., 1940-46; mem. of Bathurst Sch. Bd. 1941-49; mem., Canadian Bar Assn.; New Brunswick Bar Assn.; Nova Scotia Bar Assn.; Nat. Dir. and former mem., Internat. Comm.; Can. Chamber of Comm.; served in R.C.A.F., 1939-40; Phi Delta Phi; Roman Catholic; recreations: sailing, fishing, swimming, golf, hunting; Clubs: Union (Saint John); Halifax (N.S.); St. James's (Montreal); R.N.S.Y.S.; Ashburn; Saraguay; Mid-Ocean (Bermuda); Rotary; Gowan Brae Golf & Country; Home: "Greensleeves", Tuckers Town, Bermuda; Office: Dorchester Bldg., Suite 2, Church St., Hamilton, Bermuda

BYRNE, Jerome Cotter, B.A.; mining executive; b. Sault Ste. Marie, Ont., 11 April 1910; s. John Jerome (Mine Mgr. and Mining Extve.) and Mabel Gertrude (Spafford) B.; 4th generation of mining developers in Can.; e. Public and High Schs.; Haileybury, Ont.; St. Michaels Coll., Toronto, Ont.; Queen's Univ., B.A. 1934 (Econs. Geol. and Mineral.); m. Mabel Kathleen, d. R. H. McHoull, Cornwall, Ont. 17 Aug. 1935; children: John Jerome, Patricia Ann (Mrs. D.R. Crombie), Mary Teresa (Mrs. G.E. Kaiser); CHMN. & CEO, RAYROCK RESOURCES LTD.; Discovery Mines Ltd.; Chmn. & CEO, Pyx Explorations Ltd.; Camlaren Mines Ltd.; Johnsby Mines Ltd.; Dir., Northgate Exploration Ltd.; Pominex Ltd.; Cullaton Lake Gold Mines Ltd.; miner and field scout, 1930-35; Mine Mgr. Lake Athabasca Dist., Sask. and Yellowknife area of N.W.T., 1935-42; apptd. Pres. and Mang. Dir., Rayrock Mines Ltd. and Discovery Mines Ltd. 1946; during 2nd World War, served as Civilian Engr. with U.S. Army

Corp of Engrs. in N.W.T. constr. oil pipe lines, pumping stns., roads, airfields, townsites and communications, 1942-45; Life mem., Candn. Inst. of Mining and Metallurgy Dir., Treas. and mem. Extve. Comte., Mining Assn. of Can.; Dir. and mem., Extve. Comte., The Gold Inst.; Prospectors & Developers Assn.; R. Catholic; recreation: golf; Clubs: Engineers; Granite; York Downs Golf & Country; Wigwam Golf & Country, Arizona; Home: 616 Avenue Road, Toronto, Ont. M4V 2K8; Office: Ste. 1011, 2200 Yonge St., Toronto, Ont. M4S 2C6

BYRNES;James J., banker; b. Schenectady, New York 23 July 1941; e. Cornell Univ., B.Sc. 1963, M.B.A. 1964; m. Terry Reimers 24 June 1972; SR. VICE PRES. AND DEPY. GEN. MGR. CORPORATE BANKING, BANK OF MONTREAL; Home: R.R. 2, King City, Ont. L0G 1K0; Office: 1 First Canadian Place, Toronto, Ont. M5X 1A1.

C

CABANA, Aldée, M.Sc., Ph.D.; chemist; educator; b. Beloeil, Qué. 20 July 1935; s. Germain and Marie-Ange (Laquerre) C.; e. Univ. de Montréal B.Sc. 1958, M.Sc. 1959, Ph.D. 1962; Princeton Univ. 1961-63; m. Lise d. Lionel Couillard, St-Marc-Sur-Richelieu, Qué. 28 June 1958; children: Bruno, Marianne, Louise, Yves; DEAN OF SCIENCES, UNIV. DE SHERBROOKE 1978- , Prof. of Chem. 1971- ; Lectr. present Univ. 1963, Asst. Prof. 1964, Assoc. Prof. 1967; recipient Gerhard Herzberg Award Spectroscopy Soc. Can. 1976; mem. Nat. Research Council Can.; author over 40 scient. papers vibrational spectroscopy; mem. Order of Chems.; C.I.C. CAP; Spectroscopy Soc. Can.; ACFAS; Sigma Xi; R. Catholic; recreations: sailing, skiing; Home: 264 Heneker, Sherbrooke, Qué. J1J 3G4; Office: Sherbrooke, Que. J1K 2R1.

CABANA, Most Rev. Georges, B.A., B.C.L., LL.D., (R.C.); retired archbishop; b. Granby, Qué., 23 Oct. 1894; s. Joseph and Angélina Desgré C.; e. Elem. Sch., Granby, Qué.; Seminaire de Sherbrooke (Qué.); Seminaire de St. Hyacinthe, Qué.; Univ. Laval, B.A., B.C.L., LL.D., Sherbrooke, Bishop's; Prof., St. Hyacinthe Semy., St. Augustine's Semy., St. Hyacinthe Grand Semy.; Asst. at St. Pierre de Sorel; Chaplain at St. Charles Hospital, St. Hyacinthe; Archbishop, St. Boniface, Man. 1941-52; Archbishop of Sherbrooke, Qué. 1952-68; K. of C.; Address: Pavillon Mgr Racine, 1415 Godbout, Sherbrooke, Qué. J1K 2C7

CABANA, Maurice L.; insurance executive; b. Granby, Que. 1922; e. Sacred Heart Coll. Granby; m.; 4 children; VICE PRES. PERSONAL INS. MARKÉTING, METROPOLITAN LIFE INSURANCE CO. 1974- ; joined present co. 1948, Sales Mgr. 1953, Field Training Instr. 1957, Field Training Supvr. 1961, Dist. Sales Mgr. 1962, Regional Sales Mgr. 1963; served with Candn. Army 1941-44, rank Sgt. Maj.; mem. Ottawa Bd. Trade; Candn. Life Ins. Assn. (Chrmn. Individual Ins. Comte.); Chart. Life Underwriters Assn.; recreations: skiing, skating, golf, reading; Club: Richelieu; Home: 350 Queen Elizabeth Dr., Suite 1003, Ottawa, Ont. K1S 3N1; Office: 99 Bank St., Ottawa, Ont. K1P 5A3.

CADIEUX, Jean, B.A. Laval 1943, L.Comm. Montreal 1946, D.Sc.Eco., Aix en Provence 1970; recteur; né L'Original, Ontario, 25 août 1923; f. Fortunat et Elvina (LaBelle) C.; ép. Françoise, f. Esdras Chamard, St. Jean Port Joli, Qué., 5 juillet 1947; enfants: Louise, Bernard, Marie, Pierre, Hélène, Chantal, Jean P.; RECTEUR, UNIV. de MONCTON: Dir., La cie de Gestion Atlantique; mem. Conseil d'adm., Beaverbrook Art Gallery; Musée du Nouveau-Brunswick; Institut de Memramcook; Hôpital Dr. Georges-L. Dumont; Campagne Ensemble; Prés., Entraide Univ. Modiale de Can.; Prof. invité; Faculté des sciences écon. Aix en Provence 1970-71; auteur:

"Le bilinguisme au Nouveau Brunswick" 1967; "L'Hôpital de Maria" 1970; "Les coûts sociaux au Nouveau Brunswick" 1972; Dir., "Revue Economique" 1963-67; "Revue de l'Université de Moncton" 1968-69; rec'd Ordre du Mérite du Canada; mem. Assn. des Comptables Agréés; catholique; récréations: natation; golf, bridge; Club: Richelieu; Résidence: 1119 rue Main, Shediac N.B. EA0 3G0; Bureau: Moncton, N.B. E1A 3E9

CADIEUX, Brig. Gen. John Paul Anthony, ret'd, C.D., B.Eng., M.Sc., M.B.A., P.Eng.; Candn. Armed Forces, Transport Canada; Office of Comptroller Gen. of Can.; b. North Bay, Ont. 27 Oct. 1934; s. Joseph Anthony and Clare Margaret (O'Grady) C.; e. Royal Mil. Coll., Grad. Dipl. 1957; McGill Univ., B.Eng. 1958; Queen's Univ., M.Sc. 1966; Harvard Business Sch., M.B.A. 1969; rec'd RCAF Pilot Wings 1957; served with 423 All-Weather (Fighter) Sqdn., 2 (Fighter) Wing. Grostenquin, France, 1958-62; Lectr., Royal Mil. Coll. 1962-65; Depy. Sqdn. Commdr., RCAF Gimli, Man., 1965-67; Commandant, 433 e. Escadrille Tactique de Combat, CFB Bagotville, Que. 1969-71; Commandant, Coll. militaire royal de Saint-Jean, 1971-73; Treasury Bd. 1973-74; Dir. Gen. Recruiting, Educ. Trg., Hdqrs. Ottawa 1974-75; Aide-de-Camp to Gov. Gen. 1971-75; Commdr., 1 Candn. Air Group (NATO), Lahr, W. Germany 1975-77; Dir. Gen. Airports & Const. Services, Ottawa, 1977-80; Ass't Comptroller Gen. 1980-; mem. Assn. Prof. Engrs. Ont.; Dir., Air Cadet League; United Way; etc.; R. Catholic; Home: 1108-530 Laurier Ave., Ottawa, Ont. K1R 7T1.

CADIEUX, (Joseph David Romeo) Marcel, C.C. (1969), Q.C., LL.D., F.R.S.C. (1967); retired diplomat; b. Montreal, P.Q., 17 June 1915; s. Roméo and Berthe (Patenaude) C.; e. Grasset Coll., Montreal, P.Q. B.A. 1936; Univ. of Montreal, LL.L. 1939, LL.D. 1964; McGill Univ. (Post Grad. studies) 1939-40; m. Anita, d. Jean Comtois, Quebec, P.Q., 21 Jan. 1956; two s.; Head, Candn. Mission To European Communities 1975-78; chief negotiator for Can./U.S.A. fisheries and boundaries disputes 1977-79; retired 1979; joined Dept. of External Affairs as Third Secy., 1941; Third Secy., London, 1944; Second Secy., Brussels, 1945; Ottawa, 1947; Personnel Offr., 1949-51; First Secy., Paris 1951; attended courses at NATO Defence Coll., Paris, Nov. 1951; Counsellor, Permanent Del. to NAC and OEEC, Paris, June 1952; Sr. Advisor to the Candn. Commrs., Internat. Supervisory Comns., Indochina, Sept. 1954; Head U.N. Div., 1955-56; subsequently apptd. Legal Advisor and Asst. Under Secy. of State for External Affairs; Depy. Under Secy. of State, 1960, Under Secy. of State for External Affairs 1964-70; Prof. of Public Internat. Law. Faculty of Law, Univ. of Ottawa, 1956-63; Head, Can. Mission to European Communities, Brussels 1975; el. to Internat. Law Comn. by U.N. Gen. Assembly 1961; called to the Bar 1939; invested with Vanier Medal; outstanding achievement award 1969; author: "Le Ministère des Affaires Extérieures"; "Premières Armes"; "Embruns"; "Le Diplomate Canadien"; R. Catholic; Home: 2047 Chalmers Rd., Ottawa, Ont.

CADIEUX, Hon. Léo, P.C., O.C. (1974); diplomat; b. St.-Jerome, Que., 28 May 1908; s. Joseph E. and Rosa (Paquette) C.; e. Commercial Coll., St-Jerome; Semy. of St-Therese de Blainville; m. Monique, d. Placide Plante, Mont Laurier, Quebec, 1 Aug. 1962; after grad. entered field of journalism with LA PRESSE (1930); Dir. of L'Avenir du Nord and La Revue Moderne; War Corr. for La Presse of Montreal, 1944; sometime Prothonotary of Superior Court, Terrebonne District; Mayor, St-Antoine des Laurentides (1948); engaged with Candn. Army in Public Relations, 1940-44; 1st el. to H. of C. for Terrebonne, g.e. 1962; re-el. 1963, 1965, 1968; Min. of National Defence, Sept. 1967-17 Sept. 1970; Ambassador to France 1970-75; Liberal; Catholic; Home: 20 The Driveway, Ottawa, Ont.

CADWELL, Roy, M.A.; retired lawyer; b. Wilcox, Sask., 8 July 1907; s. Howard and Martha (Fletcher) C.; e. Riverdale Coll., Toronto, Ont.; Univ. of Toronto, B.A., 1930, M.A. 1932; Osgoode Hall Law Sch. 1933; m. Priscilla Ward, d. the late Walter Jones, Clearwater, Florida; CHAIRMAN, LESTER B. PEARSON PEACE PARK INC.; Dir., Cadwell Properties Ltd., Madoc-Tweed Art & Writing Centre; read law with Ludwig, Ludwig and Schuyler; called to the Bar of Ont., formed firm and practised law with Cadwell & Piper, Toronto, 1933; Asst. Registrar, Osgoode Hall 1937; Inspr. Legal Offices 1939-40; organized Cadwell Properties Ltd. as a private holding co. 1949; Legal Advisor, Candn. Truce Commrs., Vietnam, Laos and Cambodia, Dept. External Affairs 1955-56; returned to private practise 1957; retired 1958; Offrs. Training Course, Niagara-On-The-Lake, R.C.A.S.C. 2nd. Lieut. 1939; enlisted R.C.A.M.C. Lieut. 1940, Capt. 1942; organized mil. hosps. Canada and England; part time in Personnel Selection Br.; now Reserve Offr., Capt.; Service & Overseas Medals; author of "Communism in the Modern World"; (M.A. thesis), "The Incidence of Automobile Accidents"; "Clearwater, A Sparkling City"; Lecturer, Dept. Univ. Extension, Univ. of Toronto 1949-52; Liberal cand., Riverdale, Toronto, 1935; Fed. Liberal cand., Hastings-Frontenac 1965; first Pres., Don Valley Conservation Assn. 1946 and helped organize Authority 1948; Chairman, Jr. Bar Sec.; Prov. of Ont.; mem., Toronto Lawyers Club (to retirement); Life mem., Candn. Bar Assn.; former mem., Candn. Authors' Assn., National Writers' Club, Kiwanis Club; Past-Pres., Royal Candn. Legion, Forest Hill, Toronto; Freemason; United Church; recreations: writing, art, music, people; Royal Candn. Legion (Madoc, Ont.); Homes: (spring, summer, fall) R.R.3, Tweed, Ont.; (winter) 1109 N. Betty Lane, Clearwater, Florida; Office: Trans-Canada Hwy. No. 7, Tweed, Ont. K0K 3J0

CAHOON, Margaret Cecilia, M.Ed., Ph.D.; educator, nurse and researcher; b. Hallowell Twp., Prince Edward Co., Ont. 5 May 1916; d. Gordon Milton and Mary Maude (Black) C.; e. Women's Coll. Hosp. Sch. for Nurses Toronto 1943; Univ. of Toronto Cert. in Pub. Health Nursing 1946, B.Ed. 1953, M.Ed. 1960; Queen's Univ. B.A. 1950; Univ. of Mich. Ph.D. 1967; Univ. of Edinburgh Post-doctoral Fellowship (Research) 1976; PROF. OF NURSING, UNIV. OF TORONTO with cross-appt. to Health Adm. Faculty of Med. 1970- , mem. Gov. Council of Univ. and mem. from Gov. Council to Counsils of Faculties of Dentistry and Pharm.; 1980-82 Rosenstadt Prof. of Health Research, Sunnybrook-Univ. of Toronto Nursing Project; Staff to Supvr. Prince Edward Co. Hospt. 1943-44; Pub. Health Nurse, Town of Picton 1944-45; Pub. Health Nurse, Ont. Cancer Treatment and Research Foundation, Kingston Clinic and Instr. in Community Health Nursing Kingston Gen. Hosp. Sch.-of Nursing 1946-49; Fellow in Pub. Health Sch. of Hygiene Univ. of Toronto 1950-52, Assoc. in Pub. Health 1952-64, Asst. Prof. 1964-68, Assoc. Prof. of Nursing with cross-appt. to Sch. of Hygiene 1968-70; Community Health Service E. York-Leaside Health Unit 1950-68; Visiting Prof. of Nursing Univ. of Man. 1980; mem. Bd. Health Borough of E. York 1971-75, Vice Chrmn. 1973-75; rec'd Yaffe Award Candn. Cancer Soc. 1947; Centennial Award Ont. Educ. Assn. 1960; Fellowship in Gerontology Nat. Council Jewish Women 1961; World Health Organ. Award 1963; Hon. Clin. Fellowship Ont. Cancer Treatment & Research Foundation 1971-72; Ont. Ministry of Health Fellowship 1975; Sesqui-centennial Award Univ. of Toronto 1977; Educ. Devel. Award 1978; author-consultant (Candn. ed.) Health Science Books 4-8 1968-71; author and co-author various articles, papers, book chapters; mem. Reg'd Nurses" Assn. Ont.; Candn. Nurses" Assn.; Candn. Nurses" Foundation (Chrmn. Comte on Research in Nursing 1971-72); Ont. Pub. Health Assn. (Pres. 1963-64); Can. Pub. Health Assn. (Gov. Council 1961-64); Am. Pub. Health Assn. (Gov. Council 1979-81); Candn. Assn. Univ. Teachers; Ont. Regional Council

Assn. Univ. Schs. Nursing (Chrmn. Comte. on Studies 1970-75, mem. Council 1976-80); Pi Lambda Theta; P. Conservative; Presbyterian; recreations: spinning, weaving, fishing, cross-country skiing, travel, painting; Home: 45 Elswick Rd., Toronto, Ont. M4B 2Z7; Office: 50 St. George St., Toronto, Ont. M5S 1A1.

CAIN, Michael Haney, B.A., B.C.L.; ex-judge; b. Chicoutimi, Que., 26 March 1929; s. Murray Vincent and Anna Marie (Feeney) C.; e. St. Patricks High Sch., Arvida, Que., 1946; McGill Univ., B.A. 1950, B.C.L. 1953; m. Huguette, d. Joseph Potvin, Chicoutimi, Que., 20 Sept. 1954; children: Murray, Evelyn; PARTNER, BERGERON, CAIN & ASSOCIATES (former 1971-72, Justice of Superior Court of Que.); called to Bar of Que. 1954; cr. Q.C. 1971; Pres., Foundation of Univ. of Que. at Chicoutimi Inc.; Bâtonnier of Bar of Saguenay 1970-72; mem., Bar of Que. (Gen. Council 1970-71; Extve. Comte. 1970-71 and Vice Pres. of Comte. 1971); Prov. Que. Bar Assn. (Vice Pres. 1969-70; Pres. 1971); Candn. Bar Assn. (Dir., Que. Sec. 1969-72); Vice Pres., Que. Br., Candn. Bar Assn. 1973-74; Que. Br., Candn. Bar Assn. Pres. 1974-75; Candn. Inst. for Admin. of Justice; Que. Human Rights Comm.; Phi Gamma Delta; R. Catholic; recreations: tennis, golf; Home: 315 Chabanel, Chicoutimi, Que. G7H 3S1; Office: 110 Racine, Chicoutimi, Que. G7H 5E8

CAIRD, John Fenwick, F.I.I.C., F.C.I.I.; insurance executive; b. Leeds, England, 30 Sept. 1921; s. John and Madge (Fenwick) C.; e. Froebelian, Leeds, Eng.; Woodhouse Grove Sch., Apperley Bridge, Eng.; m. Barbara, d. Wilfred Hubbard; children: Martin, Melanie, Andrew; PRESIDENT AND C.E.O., HALTON-CAIRD INSURANCE AGENCY LTD.; Pres., John Caird Investments Ltd.; Pres., Insurance Brokers Ass'n. of Ont.; Eagle Star Group, 1956-73; Supt. of Agencies for Can. 1961-63; Pres. and Mang. Dir. for Can., 1963-73; served in 2nd World War with R.A.F. as Pilot in Can., India and Burma, 1941-46; discharged with rank of Flight Lieut.; Freemason; Rotarian; Anglican; recreations: tennis, squash, golf; Clubs: Bd. of Trade Oakville; Royal Military Institute; Oakville Golf; Home: 400 Randall St., Oakville, Ont. L6J 1X4; Office: 257 Randall St., Oakville, Ont. L6J 5A2

CAIRNS, Albert MacNaughton; broadcasting consultant; b. Edmonton, Alta., 9 Apl. 1911; s. Albert William and Theodore Isabella (MacNaughton) C.; e. Univ. of Alta. 1929-33; m. Mary Grace, d. T. F. Cadzow, 1115 Colbourne Cres., Calgary, 15 May 1937; children: Michael, Penelope; Vice Pres. and Gen. Mgr. Calgary Television Limited, 1960-66; Mgr. Radio Station CFAC 1942-60; with Radio Stn., CJCA, Edmonton, 1934-37; All-Canada Radio Facilities Ltd., Toronto, 1937-40; A. McKim Ltd. (Advertising), Toronto, 1940-41; Pres., Calgary Allied Arts Council, 1963-65; Conservative; Protestant; Recipient, Canadian Drama Award 1960; Special Award from John Howard Soc. 1968; Hon. mem. Candn. Red Cross Soc.; recreations: golf, shooting; Clubs: Calgary Golf & Country; Calgary Arts and Letters; Home: 3029-2nd St. S.W., Calgary, Alta. T2S 1T4

CAIRNS, John Campbell, M.A., Ph.D.; university professor; b. Windsor, Ont., 27 Apl. 1924; s. William Garroway and Mabel Elizabeth (Campbell) C.; e. Tower House and Emanuel Schs., London, Eng.; Lawrence Park Coll. Inst., Toronto, Ont.; Ridley Coll., St. Catharines, Ont.; Univ. of Toronto, B.A. 1945, M.A. 1947; Cornell Univ., Ph.D. 1951; PROF. OF HIST., UNIV. OF TORONTO, since 1964; Instr., Univ. of N. Carolina, 1951-52; Lectr., Univ. of Toronto, 1952, Asst. Prof. 1956, Assoc. Prof. 1962-64; Visiting Prof., Cornell Univ., 1962, Stanford Univ. 1968; served with R.C.A.F. 1943-45; author of "France", 1965; Co-Author, "The Foundations of the West", 1963; Ed.; "The Nineteenth Century", 1965; "Contemporary France", 1978; has written various articles on modern French hist. and aspects of historiography for learned journs.; mem., Am. Hist. Assn.; Soc.

d'Hist. Mod.; Soc. for French Hist. Studies; recreations: music, travel, sailing; Home: 165 Roxborough St. E., Toronto, Ont. M4W 1V9

CAIRNS, Richard Blakely, C.A.; greeting card executive; b. Los Angeles, Cal. 9 Apl. 1934; s. late Robert and Evelyn (Harris) C.; came to Can. 1936; e. Rolph Rd. Pub. Sch., Leaside High Sch. Toronto; Univ. of Toronto 1954; Queen's Univ. 1956-61; C.A. degree; m. Hazel d. Albert Campbell 15 Nov. 1957; children: Michael, Diane; PRES., COUTTS HALLMARK CARDS, WILLIAM E. COUTTS CO. LTD. since 1976; Pres. and Dir. Hallmark Cards of Canada Ltd.; Ambassador Cards of Canada Ltd.; CHI Gifts Ltd.; Auditor and student, Glendinning, Jarrett & Gould, Toronto 1956-60; Audit Asst. through Sr. Audit Mang., Arthur Andersen & Co. Toronto 1960-71; Controller, Coutts Hallmark Cards, Toronto 1971, Secy. Treas. 1972, Vice Pres. Finance 1973-75; Chrmn., Gift Packaging & Greeting Card Assn. (Dir. 1975, Treas. since 1975); Past Pres. Candn. Waterski Assn. Ont. Region; mem. Bd. Trade Metrop. Toronto; P. Conservative; United Church; recreations: water skiing, squash, skiing, golf; Club: Granite; Home: R.R. 1, Uxbridge, Ont. L0C 1K0 Office: 2 Hallcrown pl., Willowdale, Ont. M2J 1P6.

CAISERMAN-ROTH, Ghitta, B.A., R.C.A.; artist; b. Montreal, Que. 2 March 1923; d. Hanane and Sarah (Wittal) Caiserman; e. Parsons Sch. of Design New York City B.A.; Ecole des Beaux-Arts Montreal 1961; m. Max Roth 1962; one d. Kathe; has been assoc. with Concordia Univ., Saidye Bronfman Centre, Univ. de Que.; paintings incl. in various pub., corporate and private colls. such as McMichael Conserv. Gallery Kleinberg, Montreal Museum of Fine Arts, Nat. Gallery of Can., Vancouver and Winnipeg Art Galleries, London (Ont.) Pub. Lib. & Art Museum, Beaverbrook Art Gallery, Dept. External Affairs Ottawa; rec'd Canada Council Fellowship; numerous purchase prizes; Centennial Medal 1967; author "Creativism" 1980; Pres. Atelier Graphia; mem. Council Royal Candn. Acad. Arts; Print & Drawing Council Can.; Candn. Soc. Artists; recreations: tennis, cross-country skiing; Club: Mount Royal Tennis; Home: 4266 de Maissonneuve W., Westmount, Que. H3Z 1K6.

CALDER, Brendan Robert, B.Math.; trust company executive; b. 20 Sept. 1946; e. Univ. of Waterloo B.Math. 1969; m. Mary Ellen, 25 June 1971; children: one d. Kate; PRESIDENT, CHIEF EXTVE. OFFR. AND DIR.,THE FIDELITY TRUST CO.; Dir. Fidelity Trustco Ltd.; Patrician Land Corp. Ltd.; Kraftkell Canada Ltd.; joined Canavest House Ltd. 1969-78 becoming Gen. Mgr. and Dir.; Consultant, The Metropolitan Trust Co. 1978-80; Fellow, The Candn. Securities Inst.; mem. N. Am. Soc. Corporate Planning; Toronto Soc. Financial Analysts; World Future Soc.; Club: National; Home: 95 Alcorn Ave., Toronto, Ont.; Office: 350 Bay St., Toronto, Ont. M5H 2S6.

CALDER, Frank Arthur, L.Th.; b. Nass Harbour, Nass River, B.C., 3 Aug. 1915; s. Job Henry Clark and Emily (Leask) C.; e. Ang. Theol. Coll., Univ. of B.C., L.Th. 1946; married; served as Member Legislative Assembly (M.L.A.) in B.C. for 26 yrs, first with C.C.F.-N.D.P., then with Social Credit. First Canadian Native Indian to be elected to any Candn. Parl't., 1949, and first Canadian Native Indian appointed Minister of the Crown in Canada: Minister without Portfolio, 1972-73. Known for famous "Calder Case", a landmark decision of the Supreme Court of Canada, 1973, on the Nishga Land Claims, a decision upon which current Indian land settlements are being considered in Can. Founder, Nishga Tribal Council, Pres. 1955-74, Research Dir. since 1974, "Chief Lissims" of Nishga tribe; Director, Domain Consultants; Social Credit Party; Anglican; Home: 906 Parklands Dr., Victoria, B.C. V9A 4L7

CALDER, Col. (James) Allan, E.D., C.D.; b. Westmount, Que., 4 June 1908; s. Robert Ernest and Florence

Emmeline (Osborne) C.; e. Lower Can. Coll.; McGill Univ. 1926-29; m. Eva Jessie Doris (Monica), d. H. B. Bishop, London, Eng., 10 July 1943; one d., Susan Monica; joined Imperial Tobacco Co. of Can. Ltd. 1929; Asst. Comptroller, 1935; Comptroller, 1946; Treas. 1950; el. a Dir., 1950; Vice-Pres. and Treas., 1953; retired as Dir. Extve. Vice-Pres., March 1967; served with Canadian Mil. 1930-39; served in World War 1939-45, overseas; Lt.-Col. commanding Roy. Montreal Regt. (M.G.) 1941-43, (Hon. Lieut.-Col. 1958; Hon. Col. 1965-70); Acting Col. commandg. "A" Group, Candn. Reinforcement Units, 1943-44; Lieut.-Col. Commandg. Sask. Light Inf., Feb. to July 1944, and Acting Brig. commandg. 1st Candn. Inf. Bgde., July to Dec. 1944, in Italy; Mentioned in Despatches; Nat. Pres., Canadian Mfrs. Assn., 1954-55; Past Chairman, Inst. of Administration; Past Chrmn., Bd. of Govs., Lower Can. Coll.; Delta Upsilon; Protestant; recreations: golf, fishing; Clubs: United Services; Kanawaki Golf; Home: Apt. 1212, The Regency, 3555 Cote des Neiges Rd., Montreal, Que. H3H 1V2 Winter address: Apt. M305, Longboat Harbour, 4430 Exeter Dr., Longboat Key, FLA 33548

CALDWELL, Jessie (Mrs. Alexander Lorne Caldwell), B.Sc.; b. Manchester, Eng., 17 Oct. 1901; d. Thomas and Gertrude Mary (Williamson) Rowles; came to Canada 1910; e. St. Luke's Sch., Manchester, Eng.; Pub. Sch.; Crandall, Man.; High Sch., Empress, Alta.; Normal Sch., Saskatoon, Sask.; Univ. of Sask., B.Sc. 1924; m. 10 Nov. 1924; one s., Thomas David Roberts, Q.C.; Pres., Nat. Fed. of Liberal Women of Can., 1956-59 (hon. life mem.); Vice-Pres., Saskatchewan Liberal Assn., 1957-59; mem., Nat. Film Bd. of Can., 1950-56; Senate, Univ. of Sask. 1929-50; Bd. of Evangelism & Social Service, Un. Ch. of Can., 1961-66; Bd. of Govs., St. Andrew's Coll. (Un. Ch. of Can.) 1964-70; Vice-Pres., Nat. Council of Women of Can., 1950-53 (hon. life mem.); Chrmn., Cabri (Sask.) Consol. Sch. Bd., 1929-41; mem., Dependents Regional Advisory Comte. of N. Sask., 1942-46; Cand. (def.) for Prov. Leg. for City of Saskatoon, g.e. 1952; Alternate Del., Candn. del. to 8th Gen. Assembly of U.N., 1953; def. cand. for Saskatoon, Fed. g.e. 1958; mem., Candn. Inst. Internat. Affairs for 20 yrs.; Candn. Fed. of Univ. Women; Nat. Extve. Comte. and Vice-Pres., U.N. Assn. in Can. 1958-62; Joint Chrmn. Sask. World Refugee Year Committee, 1958-62; Chrmn. Sask. Nansen Centenary Appeal Committee, 1961; Hon. life mem., Sask. and Saskatoon Councils of Women of Can.; Past Pres. and Hon. Pres. Saskatoon Archaeol. Soc.; Hon. Life Mem. Sask. Achaeol. Soc.; Liberal; United Church; recreations: amateur archaeology, gardening; Address: 807 University Dr., Saskatoon, Sask. S7N 0J5

CALLAGHAN, Hon. Frank Woods, B.A., LL.B.; judge; b. Toronto, Ont. 7 Jan. 1930; s. Frank Walker, Q.C. and Elizabeth (Woods) C.; e. Univ. of Toronto Schs. 1948; Univ. of Toronto B.A. 1952, LL.B. 1955; Osgoode Hall Law Sch. 1957; m. Mary Florence (Mollie) d. S. H. O'Brien, M.D., Hamilton, Ont. 8 Oct. 1955; children: Frank Stephen, Brian Patrick, Mark Joseph, John Edward; JUDGE, SUPREME COURT OF ONT. since 1978; called to Bar of Ont. 1957; cr. Q.C. 1966; private law practice 1957-63; Dept. of Atty. Gen. Ont. 1963-70, Sr. Crown Counsel 1967, Asst. Depy. Atty. Gen. for Ont. 1968; private practice, Toronto, Counsel to Tory, Tory, DesLauriers & Binnington 1970-72; Depy. Atty. Gen. and Depy. Min. of Justice for Ont. 1972-77; Sr. Co. Court Judge Dist. of York 1977; mem. Law Soc. Upper Can.; Candn. Bar Assn.; Club: Toronto Hunt; R. Catholic; recreations: golf, sailing; Home: 50 Glengowan Rd., Toronto, Ont. M4N 1G2; Office: Osgoode Hall, Toronto, Ont. M5H 2N5.

CALLAGHAN, J. Clair, B.A., B.Eng., M.S.; educator; b. Ebbsfleet, P.E.I. 21 Feb. 1933; s. Harris William Patrick and Cora (Shea) C.; e. St. Dunstan's Univ. B.A. 1953; St. Francis Xavier Univ. Dipl. Engn. 1954; N.S. Tech. Coll. B.Eng. 1956; Mass. Inst. Technol. M.S. 1963; m. Ellen

Catherine (d) d. George Mullally, Souris W. P.E.I. 14 June 1958; children: Kevin, Mary Jane, Jeffrey; PRESIDENT, TECHNICAL UNIV. OF NOVA SCOTIA (formerly N.S. Technical Coll.) since 1977; Prof. of Engn. St. Dunstan's Univ. 1956-58; Research Asst. Mass. Inst. Technol. 1958-60; Prof. of Engn. N.S. Tech. Coll. 1960-66; Prof. of Engn. and Chrmn. Elect. Engn. Dept. Sir George Williams Univ. 1968-70, Dean Faculty of Engn. and Prof. 1969-77; Consultant, Warnock Hersey, Computing Devices of Canada, Fairey Canada Ltd., Chemcell, Consultant to Canadian Internat. Devel. Agency 1975; mem. Nat. Research Council Comte. on Scholarship 1975-78 Selection (Chmn. 1976-78); Nat. Res. Council-Adv. Bd. on Scientific & Technological Info. 1980-83; Candn. Engn. Manpower Council 1975-77; mem. Extve. Comte., Assn. Atlantic Univs.; Chmn. Council Univ. Pres. of N.S.; Chmn. N.S. Educational Computer Network Bd.; Dir., N.S. Research Found. 1978-80, 80-82; N.S. Tidal Power Corp. 1979-81; Assn. Univs. & Colls. Can.; Dir., Extve. Council, Adv. Comm. Int. Dev. Office, Liaison Comm. Int. Relations, Council of Univ. Pres.; mem. Council of Maritime Premiers Comte on Research & Development; N.S. Task Force on Research and Technology; City of Halifax Task Force on Offshore Activities (1981); Candn. Coll. Advanced Engn. Practice; served with RCAC 1953-58, rank Lt.; holds Patent on Cable Tension Control; author over 20 tech. articles in prof. journs.; mem., Assn. Prof. Engrs. N.S.; Order Engrs. Que.; Am. Soc. Elect. Engrs.; Inst. Elect. & Electronic Engrs.; Fellow Engn. Inst. Can.; R. Catholic; recreations: sailing, swimming; Club: Halifax; Home: 1334 Barrington St., Halifax, N.S. B3J 2X4

CALLAGHAN, Morley Edward; novelist; b. Toronto, Ont.; s. Thomas and Mary (Dewan) C.; e. St. Michaels Coll., Univ. of Toronto, B.A. 1925; Osgoode Hall Law Sch.; m. Lorette Florence, d. late Joseph Dee, 16 Apl. 1929; two s., Michael, and Barry; has been writing seriously since 1923; author of "Strange Fugitive", 1928; "Native Argosy", 1929; "It's Never Over", 1930; "Broken Journey", 1932; "Such Is My Beloved", 1934; "They Shall Inherit the Earth", 1935; and "More Joy in Heaven", 1937; sold "Turn Again Home" to the New York Theatre Guild, 1940; "Just Ask for George" (play), 1940; "The Loved and the Lost" (novel), 1951 (Gov. General's award 1952); "The Many-Colored Coat" (novel), 1960; "A Fine and Private Place", 1975 (Novel); "Close to the Sun Again", 1975 (novel); "No Man's Meat and The Enchanted Pimp", 1978; awarded $15,000 Can. Council Prize, and $50,000 Royal Bank of Canada Award 1970; has written more than 100 published short stories; engaged in radio work 1944; became well known as Chrmn. for the Forum Series "Of Things to Come"; rec'd. L.L.D., Univ. of Toronto, 1966; L.L.D., Univ. of Western Ont., 1965; Hon. Litt.D., Windsor 1973; R. Catholic; Address: 20 Dale Ave., Toronto, Ont. M4W 1K4

CALLEN, John Manfred, C.D.; transportation executive; b. Toronto, Ont., 27 March 1921; s. late Charles A. and Agnes Mary (Kilkeary) C.; e. De La Salle Coll. (Oaklands), Toronto, Ont. 1939; m. Marjorie Bernice, d. late Lawrence Moore, 7 Sept. 1946; children: Sean Charles, Mary Margaret; SR. VICE-PRES. ONT. (TOR.) AIR CANADA since Feb. 1979; Reg. Vice Pres., Tor., 1970-79; joined Trans-Canada Airlines (predecessor Co.) as Reservations Agent, Toronto 1946, Passenger Agent i/c Toronto 1948, Sales Rep. 1950, Reservations Mgr. 1953, Sales Mgr. 1956, Sales Mgr.-U.K. 1959, Internat. Sales Mgr., Montreal 1961, Dist. Mgr. N.Y. 1966; Dir. CN Tower; Bd. Trustees, Ont. Travel Industry Fund; served with Toronto Scottish Regt. (Active Service) 1939-45, (Militia Service) 1945-59; enlisted as Pte.; discharged active service Staff Sgt.; Comnd. 2nd Lt. 1946; rank on discharge Maj. 1959; R. Catholic; recreations: golf, water sports; Clubs: Granite; Lambton Golf & Country; Toronto; Home: 1469 Halyard Court, Mississauga, Ont. L5J 1B2; Office: 130 Bloor St. W., Toronto, Ont. M5S 1P5

CALLWOOD, June (Mrs. Trent Frayne), O.C. (1978); writer; b. Chatham, Ont., 2 June 1924; d. Harold and Gladys (LaVoie) Callwood; m. Trent Gardiner Frayne, 13 May, 1944; children: Jill Callwood, Brant Homer, Jennifer Ann, Casey Robert; Vice Pres., Candn. Civil Liberties Assn. 1965-; Founder, Yorkville Digger House 1967; Chairman, Writers' Union of Canada 1979-80; President Justice for Children 1979-80; Exec. Comte. Writers' Development Trust 1977-81; President Learnxs Foundation 1972-79; executive Canadian Council of Christians and Jews 1978-82; President and Founder Nellie's 1974-77; member Council of Amnesty International (Canada) 1979-82; Dir., Cdn. Soc. for Abolition of Death Penalty 1981; Chmn. Ian Adams Defence Comte 1980; Pres. Jessie's Centre for Teenagers 1980-82; Member Order of Canada 1978; Humanities Award Canadian Council of Christians and Jews 1978; co-chairman with Gordon Fairweather 1st annual conference of federal Human Rights Commission 1978; named B'nai B'rith Woman of the Year 1969; City of Toronto Award of Merit 1974; host, CBC television "In Touch" 1975-78; author, "Love, Hate, Fear and Anger", 1964; co author "A Woman Doctor Looks at Life and Love" (Dr. Marion Hillard), 1957; "Mayo, The Story of My Family and Career" (Dr. Charles W. Mayo) 1968; "Canadian Women and the Law" (with Marvin Zuker)1971; "How to Talk to Practically Anybody about Practically Anything" (Barbara Walters) 1973; "We Mainline Dreams" (Dr. Judianna Densen-Gerber) 1974; "Otto Preminger Remembers" 1975; "The Law is Not for Women" (Pitman, 1976) with Marvin Zuker; "Naughty Nineties, Canada's Illustrated Heritage" 1978; "Portrait of Canada" 1981; "A Full Life" with Helen Gahagan Douglas, 1982; other writings incl. mag. articles, TV and radio scripts; Home: 21 Hillcroft Dr., Islington, Ont. M9B 4X4

CAMERON, Alastair Duncan, M.B.E., B.Sc.; consulting engineer; b. Fredericton, N.B. 28 Oct. 1920; s. Adam and Dora Isabel (Davidson) C.; e. Univ. of N.B. B.Sc. (Civil Engn.) 1942; McGill Univ. Dipl. in Mang. 1970; m. Audrey d. late H. O. Charlton 17 may 1951; children: Duncan, Harry, Sheila, Janet; VICE PRES. UTILITY MANG. MONTREAL ENGINEERING CO. LTD. since 1976; Chrmn. of Bd. and Dir. Maritime Electric Co. Ltd.; Chrmn. and Mang. Dir. Monenco Jamaica Ltd.; Pres. and Dir. Newfoundland Light & Power Co. Ltd.; Vice Pres. and Dir. Ottawa Valley Power Co.; Vice Pres. and Dir. Canelco Services Ltd; Dir., Monenco Ltd.; Monenco Holdings Ltd.; Draftsman and Design Engr. Dominion Bridge Co. Ltd. 1946-47; various assignments Montreal Engineering Co. Ltd. as Design Engr., Resident Engr. and Supervising Engr. in Civil and Constr. Depts. 1947-56; Gen. Mgr. Maritime Electric Co. Ltd. Charlottetown 1957-63, Asst. Mgr. Econ. and Valuation Div. Montreal Engineering Co. Ltd.; 1963 becoming Mgr. 1969, Vice Pres. and Mgr. Mang. Consulting Div. 1972, Vice Pres. Mang. Consulting 1975-76; served with RCA Can. UK N.W. Europe 1942-45; Past Pres. Charlottetown Bd. Trade; former Dir. Atlantic Provs. Econ. Council; mem. Order Engrs. Que.; Candn. Soc. Civil Engn.; Engn. Inst. Can.; Candn. Elect. Assn.; Can. Nat. Committee, World Energy Conference; Anglican; recreations: sailing, skiing; Clubs: Mount Stephen; M.A.A.A.; Home: 70 Union Blvd., St. Lambert, Que. J4R 2M5; Office: P.O. Box 6088 Stn. A, Montreal, Que. H3C 3Z8.

CAMERON, Hon. A.M. (Sandy), B.Sc.; politician; businessman; b. Sherbrooke, N.S. 16 Dec. 1938; s. Alex Whitcomb, Q.C. and Mary Kathryn (MacLean) C.; e. Sherbrooke (N.S.) Elem. and St. Mary's Rural High Schs.; N.S. Agric. Coll.; McGill Univ. B.Sc., (Agric.); m. Shirley Elaine; d. late Milton Vatcher, N. Sydney, N.S. 12 Aug. 1961; children; Moira K., Alex Whitcomb; GENERAL MGR., BICKERTON INDUSTRIES; Min. of Development for N.S. 1976-1978; el to N.S. House of Assembly by-el. 1973, Min. of Fisheries 1973, Min. of Lands and Forests 1975; mem. N. Brit. Soc.; Fish & Games Assn.; Liberal;

United Church; Home: (P.O. Box 70) Sherbrooke, N.S. B0J 3L0; Office: Bickerton Industries, Bickerton West, Guys Co., N.S. B0J 3C0

CAMERON, Rev. Angus de Mille, B.D. (Unitarian); b. Sussex Corner, N.B., 9 June 1913; s. James Logan and Harriett Bernice (de Mille) C.; e. Univ. of N.B.; Acadia Univ., B.A. 1934; Univ. of Chicago 1935-37; Meadville Theol. Sch., Chicago, B.D. 1937; m. Esther Cary, d. Frank W. Horner, Montreal, 9 Nov. 1942; children: Jean, Sheila, James, Bruce; o. 1937; Min., Adams Memorial Ch., Dunkirk, N.Y., 1937-41; Ch. of the Messiah, Montreal, Que. 1941-59; First Unitarian Ch. of Philadelphia, 1963-67; served on Bd. of Govs. of Montreal Council of Social Agencies, 1942-46; Vice-Pres., Am. Unitarian Assn. (rep. Can. on Bd. of Dirs.) 1948-51; contrib. Editor of "The Christian Register"; author of chapter in "Voices of Liberalism 1", 1947; recreations: tennis, music, hunting, fishing; Clubs: Montreal Indoor Tennis; Riverside Country; Home: "Lochiel" Clifton Royal, N.B. E0G 1N0

CAMERON, Hon. Donald, B.Sc., M.Sc., LL.D.; senator; educator; b. Devonport, Eng., 6 March 1901; s. Donald and Marion (MacFadyen) C.; came to Canada 1906; e. Univ. of Alta, B.Sc. 1930, M.Sc. 1934; Univ. of B.C. LL.D. 1959; Univ. of Calgary, LL.D. 1978; m. Stella Mary, d. Samuel Joseph Ewing, 6 July 1932; one d., Mary Jean (Mrs. T. J. Elliott); Prof., Dir. Dept. of Extension, Univ. of Alberta, 1936-56; Dir., Baff Sch. of Fine Arts, 1936-69; Dir. Banff Sch. Advanced Mang. 1952-69, Chrmn. 1969-75; Dir., Nat. Film Soc. of Can. 1936-50; Pres., Alta. Br. Candn. Handicrafts Guild 1946-49; mem., Nat. Film Bd. of Can., 1943-50; Chrmn. Candn. Legion Educ. Services, Alta. Command 1939-46; mem., Nat. Adv. Comte. on Candn. Citizenship 1939-45; mem., Candn. Inst. of Agric.; Am. Acad. of Pol. Science; Council, Candn. Assn. for Adult Educ.; West. Can. Consultant, Encyclopedia Britannica; Candn. Govt. del. to Ninth Gen. Conf. UNESCO, New Delhi, 1956; Leader, Candn. Del. to UNESCO 1960; Leader, Candn. Del., 9th Commonwealth Parlty. Assn., Kuala Lumpur, Malaysia, 1963; Chrmn., Roy. Comm. on Educ., Alta. 1958-59; Dir., CDP Computer Data Processors Ltd. since 1968; Vice chrmn., Senate Comm. on Sci. Policy 1968-76; chrmn, duMaurier Council for Performing Arts 1972-78; first chrmn., Cdn. Comm., United World Colleges 1962-72; summoned to Senate of Can., July 28, 1955; has contrib. articles and features to various mags. and periodicals on educ. and sociol.; author, "Campus in The Clouds"; "China Revisited"; "The Impossible Dream"; Zeta Psi; United Church; Home: Banff, Alta. T0L 0C0 and 394 Third Ave., Ottawa, Ont.

CAMERON, Donald Charles, B.Com.; security analyst; b. Chesterville, Ont., 22 May 1923; s. Norman Scott and Essie Mary (Dwyer) C.; e. Primary Sch., N.Y., Montreal, Chesterville; Chesterville High Sch., 1938-42; Queen's Univ., B.Com. 1946; Univ. of Virginia, Chart. Financial Analyst, 1965; m. Lyla Anne, d. Frederick William Paynter, 10 July 1948; children: Donald Alexander, Bruce William, Jean Anne; CHRMN., C.E.O. AND DIR., JONES HEWARD & CO. LTD., since Jul. 1981; Dep. Chmn. 1975-; Past Gov., Montreal Stock Exchge.; Vice Pres. and Dir., Jones Heward Securities Ltd.; Dir., Jones Heward Adv. Services Ltd.; Jones Heward Fund Ltd.; De Vegh Mutual Fund Inc.; MPG Investment Corp.; joined present Co. 1946; held various positions in Invest. Mang. Dept. for 2 yrs.; trans. to Research Dept.; apptd. Dir. of Research, 1958; admitted to Partnership 1959; became Dir. of Invest. Policy, 1963 and in addition Vice Pres. 1965; Pres. 1966; mem., Montreal Society Financial Analysts (Pres. 1960); R. Catholic; recreations: golf, swimming, tennis, bridge; Home: 23 Castle Frank Cres., Toronto, Ont.; Office: Suite 909, 141 Adelaide St. W., Toronto, Ont. M5H 3L5

CAMERON, Donald F., M.B.E., C.D., B.A., M.D., F.A.C.A., F.R.C.P.(C); educator; b. Edmonton, Alta., 19 Aug. 1920; s. Donald Ewing and Winnie Fletcher (Macphee) C.; e. Univ. of Alta., B.A. 1947, M.D. 1949; m. Patricia, d. Cecil Harrison, Lewis, Sussex, 20 May 1944; children: Jane Elizabeth, Michael Donald, Judith Anne, Peter Forbes; PROF., DEPT. OF ANAESTHESIA, UNIV. OF ALBERTA and Dean, Faculty of Medicine there; served with Royal Candn. Armoured Corps, during World War II; rank Lt. Col.; Mentioned in Despatches; Vice-Pres., Alta. Motor Assn.; Past Pres., Med. Council Can.; Pres. Assn. of Candn. Med. Colleges; mem. Candn. Anaesthetists Soc.; Candn. Med. Assn.; Am. Soc. Anesthesiol s. Zeta Psi; Anglican; recreations: fishing, gardening, skiing; Home: 9015 — Sask. Dr. W., Edmonton, Alta. T6G 2B2; Office: Edmonton, Alta.

CAMERON, Douglas George, O.C., M.C., M.D., C.M., F.R.C.P.&S. (C), F.R.C.P., F.A.C.P.; e. McGill Univ., M.D., C.M. 1940; post grad. at Montreal General Hosp. and Nuffield Dept. of Clinical Med., Oxford (resident physician 1946-48 and Research Asst. 1948-49); CHRMN. DEPT. OF MED., McGILL UNIV.; Physician-in-Chief, Montreal Gen. Hosp. and Dir. of McGill Univ. Med. Clinic there; Rhodes Scholar 1940; Sr. Med. Research Fellow, Nat. Research Council, 1949-52 when joined staffs of Montreal Gen. Hosp. and McGill Univ.; a Specialist in hematology and internal med.; served in 2nd World War with R.C.A.M.C. 1940-46 in U.K., Africa, Sicily, Italy and N.W. Europe; awarded M.C. while a Regt. Offr. with Royal Canadian Regt.; discharged with rank of Lieut.- Col.; Past Pres., Royal College of Physicians and Surgeons (Can.); Past Pres., Candn. Soc. for Clinical Investigation; Montreal Physiol Soc.; Osler Reporting Sec. of McGill Univ.; Past Gov. for Que., Am. Coll. Physicians; Master, Am. College of Physicians, 1979; Past Pres., Que. Med. Assn.; mem., Am. Clin. & Climatol. Assn.; Centennial Lectr. in Med., Royal Coll. of Phys. & Surg., Can., 1967 (Vice Pres. for Med., 1970-71); Officer of the Order of Canada, 1979; awarded Centennial Medal; Queen'S Jubilee Medal; author of over 60 med. publications; Address: The Montreal General Hospital, Montreal, Que.

CAMERON, George Donald West, O.C. (1968), LL.D., M.D., C.M., D.H.P., F.R.C.P. (Lond.), F.A.P.H.A.; K.G.St.J.; b. Omemee, Ont., 10 Sept. 1899; s. George Stewart and Norah (West) C.; e. Public Schs., Peterborough, Ont.; Lakefield Prep. Sch., Ont. 1911-16; Royal Mil. Coll., Kingston, Ont., 1916-18; Queen's Univ. Med. Sch., M.D., C.M. 1927; Sch. of Hygiene, Univ. of Toronto, D.P.H. 1928; LL.D. Queen's 1951, Manitoba 1956, Alta. 1962, Dalhousie 1964; mem. of Founders Group, Am. Bd. of Preventive Med.; Specialist Cert. in Pub. Health, R.C.P. & S. Can.; m. Margaret Vansittart, d. late L. B. C. Livingstone, 3 Nov. 1928; one s. Donald John Vansittart; one d. Norah Isobel; mem. of Council, Queen's Univ.; on Staff of Sch. of Hygiene and Connaught Labs., Univ. of Toronto, 1929-38; joined Dept. of Pensions & Nat. Health, Ottawa as Chief of Lab. of Hygiene, 1939; apptd. Dir. of Health Services, Dept. of Nat. Health & Welfare, 1945; Depy. Min. of Nat. Health & Welfare, 1946; Depy. Min. of Nat. Health, 1946-65; Chrmn. of Jt. Comte. of the St. John Ambulance & Candn. Red Cross Soc.; Nat. Pres., V.O.N.; Past Pres., Candn. Public Health Assn.; Sr. mem., Candn. Med. Assn.; Brit. Med. Assn.; Toronto Acad. Med.; Ottawa Acad. Med.; served in 1st World War, 1918-19 2nd Lieut., R.G.A. Eng., France and Belgium; 4th Btty., R.C.A., Peterborough, 1920-27; Anglican; recreations: canoeing, reading, carpentry; Home: 221 Engleburn Ave., Peterborough, Ont. K9H 1S5

CAMERON, Keith G., C.A.; financial executive; b. Woodford, England 21 May 1947; e. England; m. Luz Maria 28 Dec. 1974; VICE PRES. ADM., TREAS. & CONTROLLER, ASAMERA INC.; Fellow, Inst. C.A.'s Eng. & Wales; mem. Inst. C.A.'s Alta.; Home: 339 Point McKay

Gardens, Calgary, Alta. T3B 5C1; Office: Suite 2100, 144 4th Ave. S.W., Calgary, Alta. T2P 3N4

CAMERON, Peter Alfred Gordon, B.Com.; company executive; b. Toronto, Ont. 1930; e. Appleby Coll., Oakville, Ont.; McGill Univ. B.Com.; m. Suzanne M. S. Noble 1955; children: Ian, Janet, Patricia; Pres. and Dir., Canadian Corporate Management Co. Ltd. since 1978; Dir. The Halifax Insurance Co.; The Commercial Life Assurance Co. of Canada; Chromalox Canada Inc.; Cashway Building Centres Ltd.; RBW Inc.; Regal Greetings & Gifts; Dominion Forge Co.; Direct Film; Mang. Trainee, Ford Motor Co. of Can. Ltd., Windsor, Ont. 1953; Asst. to Advertising Mgr., Brading's Breweries Ltd., Toronto, Ont. 1954; Sales Rep., Wm. B. Stewart & Sons Limited 1955; Assistant Advertising Manager then Product Manager, Proprietaries Division, Warner Lambert (Canada) Limited 1956; Acct. Executive, MacLaren Advertising Co. Limited 1958; Sr. Acct. Extve., Foster Advertising Ltd. 1960, Group Supv. 1962, Vice-Pres. 1965, Group Vice-Pres. 1969; Vice Pres., Candn. Industries ltd. 1970-78; continuous service in Candn. Army Mil. 1948-70; retired as Lt. Col., C.O. 48th Highlanders of Can.; re-activated 1975 as Col. Commander, Montreal Military District until 1978; awarded Order of Military Merit 1977; Commander of the Order of St. John; Chrmn. of the Bd., Appleby Coll.; Dir., Sunnybrook Medical Centre Inst.; Candn. Liver Foundation; mem. Advertising and Sales Executives Club; American Marketing Assn.; recreations: music, squash, skiing, golf; Clubs: University (Toronto); Badminton and Racquet (Toronto); Toronto Golf; St. James's (Montreal); Raquets (Montreal); Hermitage (Magog, Que.); Office: P.O. Box 131, Commerce Court West, Toronto, Ont.

CAMERON, Robert Burns, O.C. (1970), D.S.O., LL.D., D.Eng.; industrialist; b. New Glasgow, N.S., 28 July 1919; s. Hugh Scott and Christine (Fraser) C.; e. New Glasgow (N.S.) High Sch.; Royal Mil. Coll. 1939; N.S. Tech. Coll.; LL.D., St. Mary's Univ. 1968, St. Francis Xavier 1969; D.Eng., N.S. Tech. Coll. 1969; m. Florence Anna, d. Donald Colin Campbell, 15 Jan. 1943; children: Peggy(deceased), Christine, Hugh, Elizabeth, Robert, James, Donald, Harry; Pres., Cape Breton Heavy Water Ltd.; Deuterium of Canada Ltd.; Chrmn. and CEO, Maritime Steel and Foundries Ltd.; Dir., Royal Bank of Canada; Dover Mills Ltd.; R.B. Cameron Ltd.; Carmichael Construction Ltd.; Candn. Geriatrics Research Soc.; served with R.C.E. in Eng., Italy and W. Europe, rank Maj.; Presbyterian; Office: 379 Glasgow St., New Glasgow, N.S. B2H 5C3

CAMERON, Robert Ian Page, B.A.; tobacco executive; b. England, 5 Feb. 1919; s. Donald and Nancy (Page) C.; e. Univ. of Toronto Schs.; Univ. of Toronto, B.A. (Modern Hist.); m. Jane Elizabeth; d. W. J. Beaton, Q.C., Toronto, Ont., 16 March 1946; children: William James, John Dugald, Nancy Jane; PRESIDENT AND DIR., CLARENDON IMPORTS INC.; Gen. Mgr., Alfred Dunhill of London, Ltd.; served with Candn. Army Overseas, 1942-46; Capt. R.C. Signals 3rd Div.; Anglican; recreations: tennis, squash, sailing, skiing; Clubs: Badminton & Racquet; Thornhill Country; Home: 7456 Bayview Ave., Thornhill, Ont. L3T 2R7; Office: 1500 Don Mills Rd., Toronto, Ont. M3B 3L1

CAMERON, Robert Parke, B.A.; diplomat; b. Montreal, Que. 15 Oct. 1920; s. late Edward Parke and late Isabel MacFarlane (Fraser) C.; e. Perth (Ont.) Coll. Inst. 1938; Univ. of Toronto Univ. Coll. B.A. 1943; m. Katharine Isobel d. late Arnold Whiteley 17 July 1948; children: Bruce Allison Fraser, Alexander Brian, Lesley Isabella; Instr. Dept. Pol. Econ. Univ. of Toronto 1946-47; joined Dept. External Affairs 1947, Third Secy. Havana 1948-50, Econ. and European Divs. Ottawa 1951, First Secy. Stockholm 1955, Defence Liaison Div. Ottawa 1958, Counsellor (Pol. Affairs) Washington 1962, Min. Counsellor Bonn 1966,

Head NATO and N. Am. Div. Ottawa 1969, Dir.-Gen. Bureau of Defence and Arm Control Ottawa 1970, External Affairs Rep. Can.-USA Perm. Jt. Bd. Defence 1970, Ambassador to Yugoslavia, Roumania and Bulgaria 1974 and to Yugoslavia and Bulgaria 1976-77; Diplomat in Residence U. of British Columbia 1977-78; Ambassador to Poland and to the German Democratic Republic, 1978-80; Dir.-Gen. Bureau of Int. Security Policy and Arms Control Affairs; served with Candn. Army 1943-45, UK and N.W. Europe, rank Lt.; Protestant; recreations: tennis, skiing, fishing; Office: Dept. External Affairs, Pearson Bldg., Ottawa; Home: 72 Kilbarry Cres., Ottawa, Ont. K1K 0H3

CAMERON, Rev. Ross Ketchen, C.D., M.A., D.D. (Presb); retired; b. Stratford, Ont., 20 March 1904; s. Rev. Robert Fleming and Margaret Anderson (Ketchen) C.; e. Georgetown (Ont.) Pub. and High Schs.; Univ. of Toronto, Knox Coll., B.A., 1929, M.A., 1932, D.D., 1959; m. Audrey Maude, d. Harry Bradley, 17 July 1931; one s.; Donald Ross; served in St. Andrews, Streetsville, Ont., 1932-33, Rogers Mem., Toronto, 1933-36, First Ch., Edmonton, Alta., 1936-40; Min., Dovercourt Rd., Toronto, 1940, and of York Mem., Toronto, 1965-75; Moderator of 88th Gen. Assembly of the Presby. Church in Can., 1962-63; served during 2nd World War with R.C.A.F. as Chaplain, 1942-45; Chaplain, 48th Highlanders, 1947-59, Hon. Major; Freemason; mem., St. Andrews Soc.; Home: 8 Wilberton Rd., Toronto, Ont. M4V 1Z3

CAMERON, Silver Donald, M.A., Ph.D.; author; b. Toronto, Ont. 21 June 1937; s. Maxwell A. and Hazel B. (Robertson) C.; e. Univ. of B.C., B.A. 1959; Univ. of Calif. M.A. 1962; Univ. of London Ph.D. 1967; m. 1stly Catherine Ann d. late Sam Cahoon 21 Aug. 1959; children: Maxwell, Ian, Leslie, Steven; m. 2ndly Marie Louise d. Arthur Terrio, D'Escousse, N.S. 17 May 1980; one s. Mark Patrick Terrio-Cameron; author "The Education of Everett Richardson" 1977; "Faces of Leacock" 1967; "Conversations with Canadian Novelists" 1973; "Seasons in the Rain" essays 1978; "Dragon Lady" novel 1980, paperback 1981; "The Baitchopper" children's novel to be published; numerous articles, radio drama, reviews, short stories, TV scripts; teacher B.C., N.S. and N.B. before becoming freelance writer and broadcaster 1971; Writer-in-Residence Coll. of Cape Breton 1978-80; rec'd several ACTRA Award nominations radio drama; 2 Nat. Mag. Awards; nominated Internat. Prix Italia Radio Drama 1980; Pres. Richmond Co. NDP Assn.; mem. Prov. Council N.S. NDP; mem. Writers' Union Can.; Periodical Writers' Assn. Can.; ACTRA; Writers' Fed. N.S.; recreations: sailing, canoeing, scuba diving, woodwork; Club: Lennox Passage Yacht; Address: D'Escousse, N.S. B0E 1K0.

CAMP, Dalton Kingsley, B.A., M.Sc.; publicist; columnist; b. Woodstock, N.B., 11 Sept. 1920; s. Harold and Aurilla (Sanborn) C.; e. Pub. Sch., Piedmont, Cal., U.S.A.; Horton Acad., Wolfville, N.S.; Univ. of N.B., B.A.; Columbia Univ., M.Sc.; London Sch. of Econ. (Beaverbrook Overseas Scholar); m. Linda, d. George S. Atkins, 28 Aug. 1943; children: David Kingsley, Michael George Harold, Linda Gail, Constance Marilyn, Cheryl Ann; Pres. and Dir., Travel Directions (Public Relations) Ltd.; Chrmn. of Bd., Candn. Civil Liberties Assn.; mem. Ont. Royal Comn. on Book Publishing 1971-72; Chrmn. Ont. Comn. on Legislature 1973-75; def. cand. to H. of C. in g.e. 1965 and 1968; Pres., Nat. P. Conservative Party Can. 1964-69; mem. Bd. Govs. Acadia Univ.; Candn. Inst. International Affairs; Skelton-Clark Fellow, Queen's Univ., 1968-69; author "Gentlemen, Players and Politicians" 1970; "Points of Departure," 1979; P. Conservative; recreation: tennis; Clubs: Albany; Bayview Country; Badminton & Racquet; Home: Northwood, Cambridge, Queens Co., N.B. E0E 1B0; Office: 43 Eglinton Ave. E., Toronto, Ont. M4P 1A2

CAMPANARO, John Anthony; retired company executive; b. Brooklyn, N.Y., 2 May 1913; s. Anthony and Marie (Pecorella) C.; e. Bushwick and Brooklyn (N.Y.) Evening High Schs.; Brooklyn Polytechnic. Inst., 1934-35; Pratt Inst., Brooklyn, 1936-39 (Indust. Elect. Engn.); Vice Pres., Comm. Devel., Westinghouse Canada Ltd., 1970-1976; held various Sales and Sales Adm. positions, Westinghouse Electric International Co., 1933-51; apptd. Gen. Mgr., Comm. Devel. of present Co., 1951-54; Gen. Mgr., Project Devel., 1954-57; Vice-Pres., Project Devel., 1957; Vice-Pres., Apparatus Sales, 1959; Vice Pres. Central Region 1961-70; served with U.S. Army Air Force, 1942-44; mem., Candn. Elect. Assn.; recreations: golf, music, art; Clubs: Toronto Electric (Dir.); Canadian; Bayview Golf & Country; Home: 44 Stubbs Dr., Apt. 703, Willowdale, Ont. M2L 2R3

CAMPBELL, Alan Newton, Ph.D., D.Sc., F.R.S.C., F.R.I.C., F.C.I.C.; professor emeritus; b. Halifax, England; s. Henry and Elizabeth Ann (Newton) C.; e. higher grade sch., Burntisland, Fife, Scotland; Birkzeck Coll., London, B.Sc., 1920; King's Coll., London, M.Sc., Ph.D. 1924; Univ. of Aberdeen, D.Sc. 1929; m. Alexandra Jean Robson, d. John Kerr, Aberdeen, 28 Aug. 1931; one d. Morag Dorothea; mem. of Nat. Research Council of Can., 1951-57; began teaching career as Asst. Lectr., Univ. of Aberdeen, 1925-30; Asst. Prof. of Chem., Univ. of Man., 1930-33; Asst. Prof. 1936-45; Prof. 1945-69 (retired); created Emeritus Prof., 1969; part author of "The Phase Rule", 9th ed. 1952, German ed. 1958; has contrib. about 200 original research papers to chem. journs.; Liberal; Anglican; recreations: music, travel; Home: 1254 Corydon Ave., Winnipeg, Man. R3M 0Z2

CAMPBELL, His Hon. Alan Royal; judge; b. Toronto, Ont., 15 April 1917; s. William Elmo and Frances Amelia (Flint) C.; e. Fern Ave. Pub. Sch., Toronto, 1929; Parkdale Coll. Inst., Toronto, 1934; Univ. of Toronto, B.A. (Hon. Law) 1938; Osgoode Hall Law Sch., Toronto, 1941; m. Marian Christine, d. John Caspar Dressel, St. Catharines, Ont., 4 Aug. 1945; children: Susan Frances, Stuart John, Mary Ann, Thomas Secord; JUDGE, FRONTENAC COUNTY, since 1966; practiced law in Toronto 1941-66; part-time Lectr., Univ. of Toronto, 1945-47; read law with John B. Allen, Q.C.; called to the Bar of Ont. 1941; cr. Q.C. 1957; Trustee, Toronto Bd. Educ., 1954-56; mem. Metrop. School Bd., 1954-56; mem., Toronto Pub. Lib. Bd. 1962-66; mem., City of Kingston Police Comn.; Kingston Pub. Library Bd. 1966-76; Bd. of Govs., Kingston Gen. Hosp.; United Church; recreations: bridge, reading, water sports; Address: Court House, Kingston, Ont.

CAMPBELL, Alexander; executive; b. Perth, Ont. 6 Aug. 1918; s. Neil and Helen (Keir) C.; e. Kensington and West Hill Schs. Montreal, Que.; m. Mary Elizabeth d. late George S. Herringer Dec. 1947; children: Ian David, Hugh Alexander, Christine; VICE PRES. OPERATIONS, SIMPSONS-SEARS since 1972; Vice Pres. Simpsons-Sears Acceptance Co. Ltd.; Dir. Photo Engravers & Electrotypers Ltd.; Dir. Toronto Symphony; Trustee Simpsons-Sears Profit Sharing Retirement Fund; joined Inspection Dept. Toronto-Dominion Bank 1947, Gen. Mgr.'s Secy. 1949, Br. Mgr. Toronto 1952-53; joined present Co. Toronto 1953, Regional Credit Mgr. Vancouver 1955, Supt. Vancouver 1959, Asst. to Vice Pres. Retail Adm. Toronto 1960, Gen. Mgr. Retail Operations Toronto 1963, Vice Pres. Retail 1969; served with Candn. Army Eng. and N.W. Europe 1942-45, rank Capt., HQ 4th Inf. Bgde. (Reserve) BRASCO 1950-52; Depy. Campaign Chrmn. Un. Appeal Vancouver, Campaign Chrmn. Burnaby; mem. Retail Council Can.; Bd. Trade Metrop. Toronto; The Conf. Bd.; Royal Candn. Inst.; Army Officers Assoc.; Presbyterian; recreations: golf, skiing, tennis, fishing; Clubs: Caledon Ski; Lambton Golf & Country; Home: 33 Baby Point Cres., Toronto, Ont. M6S 2B7; Office: 222 Jarvis St., Toronto, Ont. M5B 2B8

CAMPBELL, Hon. Alexander Bradshaw, P.C. (1967), Q.C., M.L.A., B.A., LL.B., LL.D.; b. Summerside, P.E.I., 1 Dec. 1933; s. late Hon. Thane A. and Cecilia (Bradshaw) C.; e. Dalhousie Univ., B.A. and LL.B. (1959); McGill Univ., LL.D., 1967; University of P.E.I., L.L.D., 1979; m. Marilyn, d. Melville Gilmore, Guelph, Ont., 19 Aug. 1961; children: Blair Alexander, Heather Kathryn, Graham Melville; Appt. JUSTICE, SUPREME COURT OF P.E.I., Nov. 1978; called to Bar of P.E.I., 1959; cr. Q.C., 1966; el. M.L.A. in by-el. for 5th Prince, Feb. 1965 and Leader of P.E.I. Liberal Party, Dec. 1965; Min. of Justice and Attorney Gen. 1966-69, Min. of Development 1969-72, Min. of Agric. 1972-74; Premier of P.E.I., July 1966-Sept. 1978, re-el. to fourth term Apr. 1978, resigned Sept. 1978; former Secy. Summerside Bd. of Trade and Vice Pres. Young Liberal Assn.; Liberal; Director, Institute of Man and Resources; United Church; recreations: curling, skiing, golf; Home: 330 Beaver St., Summerside, P.E.I. C1N 2A3; Office: Sir Louis Davies Law Courts Bldg., Charlottetown, P.E.I.

CAMPBELL, Alexander John, Q.C., LL.B., LL.M., B.A.; advocate; b. Truro, N.S., 4 Apl. 1904; s. Alexander John and Blanche (Tremaine) C.; e. Truro, N.S. (Primary); Ashbury Coll., Ottawa, Ont.; Dalhousie Univ., B.A. 1925, LL.B. 1927; Harvard Law Sch., LL.M. 1929; m. the late Frances Vivian, d. late Philip Weatherbe, Halifax, N.S., 11 July 1940; two d., Susan Frances, Elizabeth Jane; m. 2ndly Mary Claire Gordon, widow of late Grant Gordon, Q.C., Oct. 1963; COUNSEL, CAMPBELL, PEPPER AND LAFFOLEY; Dir. Cdn. Ultramar Ltd.; Dir. Ultramar Can. Inc.; Chrmn. and Dir., Delta-Benco Ltd.; Chrmn. and Dir., Redifusion Inc.; Pres. and Dir., Les Cinemas Odéon Ltée.; Chrmn. and Dir., Redifusion (Canada) Inc.; read with A. J. Campbell, Q.C., 1925-27; called to the Bar of N.S. 1927 and of Quebec 1930; cr. K.C. 1946; began practice with father A. J. Campbell, Q.C., in Truro, N.S.; moved to Montreal, Que., in 1929; practising with Brown, Montgomery & McMichael; with Audette & O'Brien till 1932 when assoc. with Hon. F. Philippe Brais, Q.C., in 1931 till apptd. as a Puisne Judge of the Superior Court of Que., Nov. 1946; in July 1949 resigned from the Bench and resumed practice in partnership with Hon. F. P. Brais, Q.C. till 1970; Bâtonnier, Bar of Montreal 1966-67, and of Que. Prov. 1966-67; mem., Bar of Montreal; Bar, Prov. of Que.; Cdn. Bar Assn.; Amer. Bar Assn.; Internat. Law Assn.; Fellow Am. Coll. of Trial Lawyers; Liberal; Protestant; recreation: golf; Clubs: St. James's; University; Kanawaki Golf; Home: 3980 Cote des Neiges Road, Apt. A31, Montreal, Que.; Office: Suite 1414, 1 Place Ville Marie, Montreal, Que. H3B 2B3

CAMPBELL, Alistair Matheson, M.A., F.I.A., F.S.A., b. Strachur, Argyllshire, Scot., 3 July 1905; s. Peter and Catherine (MacRae) C.; e. Inverness Roy. Acad., Scot.; Univ. of Aberdeen, M.A. 1927; Research Scholar in Math. 1928; m. Barbara Isabel Alexander, d. late E. Greville Hampson, 2 April 1948; has one s. Michael Alexander and three ds. Catherine, Barbara, Jill; CHRMN. EMERITUS, SUN LIFE ASSURANCE CO. OF CANADA; Hon. Dir. Canadian Enterprise Development Corp. Ltd.; and Royal Trustco Ltd.; Royal Trust Corp. of Can.; Dir., Digital Equipment of Canada Ltd.; The Royal Trust Mortgage Corp.; Royal Trust Co. Ltd.; joined present Co. in Actuarial Dept. 1928, Asst. Actuary 1934, Assoc. Actuary 1940, Actuary 1946, Assist. Gen. Mgr. & Actuary 1947; Vice-Pres. and Actuary 1950, Vice-Pres. and Chief Actuary 1954, Extve. Vice-Pres. and Dir. 1956, Pres. and Chief Extve. Offr. 1962, Chrmn. and Chief Extve. Offr. 1970, Chrmn. 1973; Chrmn. of Extve. Comte. 1978; on loan to Foreign Exchange Control Bd., Ottawa 1939-40; served with Royal Candn. Arty. 1940-45; Past Gov. (1953-55 and 1957-59) Soc. of Actuaries; Pres. (1957-58) Candn. Life Ins. Assn.; Candn. Assn. Actuaries (Pres. 1947-48); mem. Bd. Div. Trustees, Past Vice-Pres., Hon. mem. (1956) and Hon. Gov. (1975), Candn. Red Cross Soc. (Que. Div.); Past Prov. Vice-Pres. (Que.) (1962-63) and mem. Extve.

Comte. (1965), Am. Life Convention; Past Dir., Life Ins. Assn. of Am. (1968-71); Clubs: University (Montreal); Mount Royal; The Country (Ottawa); the Rideau; Home: 4 Coltrin Place, Rockcliffe, Ottawa, Ont. K1M 0A5

CAMPBELL, Arthur Grant, B.A.; retired diplomat; b. Montreal, Que., 18 Sept. 1916; s. Donald Grant and Sophy Edith (Field) C.; e. Upper Canada Coll., Toronto, 1934; McGill Univ., B.A. 1938; Columbia Univ., Postgrad. Studies 1951; m. Carol, d. Albert Michael Wright, 6 April 1940; one s. Ian Andrew Grant; Ambassador to Norway and Iceland 1977-81; commenced as Asst. to Secy., Candn. Chamber of Comm. and Assoc. Ed. "Canadian Business" 1938-41; UN Secretariat, Dept. Pol. and Security Council Affairs 1946-56 (UNAEC 1946, Disarmament Comn. 1952-56); Asst. Secy., UN Comn. for India and Pakistan 1948; Political Adviser, UN Rep. for India and Pakistan 1950; joined Dept. Ex. Affairs, UN Div. 1956; Counsellor, Ten Nation Conf. on Disarmament, Geneva 1960; Counsellor, New Delhi 1960; Head, Commonwealth Div., Ottawa 1963; Min.-Counsellor, Eighteen Nation Disarmament Conf., Geneva 1967; Minister, Bonn 1969; Ambassador to South Africa, and High Commissioner to Botswana, Lesotho and Swaziland; 1972; served in R.C.A. 1941-46, U.K., Central Mediterranean, N.W. Europe; Mentioned in Despatches; Psi Upsilon; United Church; recreations: golf, skiing, music; Home: 7 Rothwell Dr., Ottawa, Ont.

CAMPBELL, Hon. Bennett; teacher; politician; b. Montague, P.E.I. 27 Aug. 1943; s. Wilfred Laurier and Edith Florence (Rice) C.; e. Poplar Point Sch.; St. Dunstan's High Sch. grad. 1960; St. Dunstan's Univ. 2 yr. Teacher Educ. Program; m. Margaret Shirley, d. Joseph Chaisson, Souris, P.E.I. 1 Aug. 1970; children: Kelly Dawn, Colin, Grant, Sherry Lee, Grace; Leader of Opposition, P.E.I. 1979-81; Chrmn. of Treasury Bd. 1976-79; el. mem. Prov. Leg. 1970, re-el. 1974, 1978, 1979; Min. of Educ. 1972-78, Prov. Secy. and Min. of Educ. 1974-76; Premier of P.E.I. 1978-79; Chrmn. Council of Mins. of Educ. Can. 1976; Liberal; R. Catholic; recreations: golf, boating, camping; Club: Lions; Home: (Box 28) Cardigan, P.E.I. C0A 1G0;

CAMPBELL, Bruce Dewar, B.Com.; executive (ret.); b. St. Thomas, Ont. 11 July 1923; s. John D.; e. Pub. and High Schs., St. Thomas, Ont; Queen's Univ., B.Com. 1950; m. Barbara I., d. William Gordon Fraser, Oct. 1959; with International Business Machines Co. Ltd., Sales Div. 1950-61; Mgr., IBM Canada Ltd. Montreal 1962; Gen. Mgr., IBM Project Expo '67, 1967 Regional Mgr. Br. Adm. 1968; joined SDI Associates Ltd. as Vice-Pres. and Dir. 1969; Pres., 1970-79; Dir. Computel Systems Ltd.; mem. Candn. Assn. for Corp. Growth; Institute of Dir. in Can.; Baptist; Club: Lambton Golf & Country recreations: golf, travel, bridge; Home: 32 Kingsway Cres., Islington, Ont. M8X 2R3;

CAMPBELL, Clarence Sutherland, M.B.E. (1945), Q.C., LL.B., M.A.; sport executive; b. Fleming, Sask., 9 July 1905; s. George Alexander and Annie May (Haw) C.; e. Strathcona High Sch., Sask.; Univ. of Alta., B.A. 1924; LL.B. 1926 (Rhodes Schol. for Alta. 1926); Oxford Univ., M.A. in Jurisprudence, 1928; m. Phyllis Loraine King, 11 Nov. 1955; Pres., National Hockey League 1946-77; read law with Wood, Buchanan, Macdonald & Campbell; called to the Bar of Alta., 1931; cr. Q.C. 1947; served in World War 1941-46 with Candn. Army; overseas with 5th Candn. Anti-Tank Regt., Roy Candn. Arty. 1942; commanded Hdqrs., 4th Candn. Armoured Div. Sqn., 1944-45; Prosecutor, Candn. War Crimes Unit 1945-46; Mentioned in Despatches; Pres., Lakeshore Gen. Hosp. Foundation; mem., Alta. Law Soc.; rec'd Centennial Medal 1967; has written Candn. War Crimes Reports; Liberal; United Church; recreation: golf; Clubs: Royal Montreal Curling; Beaconsfield Golf; Home: St. Georges Apts., 3465 Redpath St., Montreal, Que. H3G 2G8; Office: 960 Sun Life Bldg., Montreal, Que.

CAMPBELL, Colin Alexander, O.B.E. (1943), M.I.D. (1944), D.S.O. (1945), P.Eng.; b. Shedden, Ont., 17 Jan. 1901; s. Archibald C. and Flora (McCallum) C.; e. Lawrence Station Public Sch.; Dutton High Sch.; Queen's Univ.; m. Vera M., d. M. S. Smith, Dutton, Ont., 25 May, 1923; four children; Pres. and Dir., Amos Mines Ltd.; Vice Pres. and Dir. International Mariner Resources Ltd.; Silver Shield Mines Inc.; Bardyke Mines Ltd.; Associated Senior Extves. of Canada Ltd.; engaged in mining and special field work with Hollinger and McIntyre mines, 1921-28; Mgr. Dunkin Golf Mines, Narrow Lake, 1928-30; Bey Mines Ltd., Northbrook, Ont., 1930-33; Barry Hollinger Golf Mines, Boston, Creek, 1933-34; engaged in consulting practice, 1934-37 and since 1946; el. to H. of C. for Frontenac-Addington, 1934 and re-el. 1935; resigned and contested Addington, (def.) Prov. g.e. 1937; el. to Prov. Leg. for Sault Ste. Marie by acclamation by-el. Nov. 1937; apptd. Mininster of Public Works in Hepburn Cabinet, 1937; served in 2nd World War; enlisted as 2nd Lieut. with Royal Candn. Engrs., 1939; promoted 1st Lieut. and later in Eng. promoted to Capt., and subsequently Major, Lieut.-Col. and Brig.; O.B.E., M.I.D., D.S.O. and Legion of Merit, U.S.A.; Hon. Col. 2nd Field Engr. Regt. (Militia) 1967, Brig. Gen. Feb. 1968; mem., Assn. of Prof. Engrs. Ont.; Candn. Inst. Mining & Metall; Royal Candn. Inst.; Past Pres., Toronto Liberal Business Men's Club; Past Pres., Candn. Curling Assn.; Pres., Internat. Curling Fed.; Freemason (Royal Arch); Liberal; Presbyterian; Clubs: Granite; Hamilton Thistle; Home: Apt. 1615, 25 Maybelle Ave., Islington, Ont.;

CAMPBELL, D. Ralph, D.F.C. and Bar, M.A., LL.D.; b. Foxboro, Ont. 14 Nov. 1918; s. Fred H. and Florence Pearl (Hollinger) C.; e. Univ. of Toronto, B.A. 1949; Oxford Univ., B.A. 1951, M.A. 1958; Rhodes Scholar 1949-51; m. late Muriel Joy, d. L. S. Winch, 18 June 1949; children: Hugh Frederick, Catherine Anne, Elizabeth Mary; 2ndly, Ruth Marion, d. W. Heron, 11 Feb. 1977; Pres., Univ. of Manitoba, 1976-81; commenced as Lect., Dept. Agric. Econ., Ont. Agric. Coll. 1951 and Head of Dept. 1952-62; mem., Ont. Marketing Enquiry 1958-59; Econ. Advisor and Acting Dir. of Planning, Govt. of Jordan 1962-64; Assoc. Dean, Faculty of Arts and Science, Univ. of Toronto 1964-68; Chrmn., Discipline Comte. 1968-70; mem. Task Force on Agric., Govt. of Can. 1968-70; Econ. Advisor, Ministry Finance and Planning, Govt. of Kenya 1970-72; Prof. of Econ., Univ. of Toronto and Principal, Scarborough Coll., 1972-76; Hon. L.L.D. Univ. of Guelph, Univ. of Winnipeg; served in 2nd World War, R.C.A.F., rank Pilot, Flight-Lt.; awarded D.F.C. and Bar; co-author of "Canadian Agriculture in the Seventies" 1970 and many articles in econ. and agric. econ. journs.; Agric. Inst. Can. (Pres. 1960); Candn. Agric. Econ. Soc. (Pres. 1959); Office: c/o The Rockefeller Foundation, P.O. Box 47543, Nairobi, Kenya

CAMPBELL, Donald G., F.C.A. (1973); communications executive; b. Toronto, Ont., 14 Aug. 1925; s. late James Lindsay and Margaret (Graham) C.; e. C.A. 1950; m. Audrey Irene d. late Garnet Percy Reid, 12 Aug. 1944; children: David, Reid, Marc, Craig, Scott; CHRMN. AND CHIEF EXTVE. OFFR. MACLEAN HUNTER LTD. since 1977; Chrmn. Design-Craft Ltd.; Key Radio Ltd.; Maclean-Hunter Publishing Corp. (Chicago); Pres. and Chrmn., Greatlakes Broadcasting System Ltd.; Dir. National Market Reports Inc.; Maclean Hunter Cable TV Ltd.; Transkit Corp.; CFCN Comm. Ltd.; Data Business Forms Ltd.; Toronto-Dominion Bank; Texasgulf Inc., Steinberg Inc.; joined Price Waterhouse 1945-50; Treas. Noma Lites Ltd. 1950-51; Secy.-Treas. Atomic Energy Can. Ltd. Chalk River 1952-57; joined present Co. 1957, Controller and Dir. 1958, Vice Pres. Finance 1960, Extve. Vice Pres. Broadcasting and Finance 1969, Pres. and Chief Extve. Offr. 1970, Chrmn. and Pres. 1976; served with RCAF 1942-45, rank Flying Offr.; Trustee Hosp. for Sick Children Toronto; mem., Toronto Redevelopment Adv. Council; Protestant; recreations: golf, squash, skiing; Clubs: Georgian Peaks Ski; Toronto Golf; University; York; Home: 53 Widdicombe Hill Blvd., P.H. 2, Weston, Ont. M9R 1Y3; Office: 481 University Ave., Toronto, Ont. M5W 1A7

CAMPBELL, Edward Christopher; hotel executive; b. Straford, Ont. 26 Dec. 1916; s. Christopher Nicholas Campell; e. Lord Roberts Pub. Shc. 1930 and Central Coll. Inst. 1963, London, Ont.; Univ. of W. Ont. 3 yrs. Business Adm.; m. Henriette Mary d. late Thomas Duffy 3 June 1954; children: Christopher, Duff, Jennifer, Carolyn; SR. VICE PRES.-OPERATIONS ADMINISTRATOR, COMMOMWEALTH HOLIDAY INNS OF CANADA LTD. since 1974; family reasurant business 1940-42, 1946-64; Dir. Food & Beverage presnt hotel chain 1964, Vice Pres. Food & Beverage 1968, Vice Pres. Operations 1971; served with RCA 1942-45, Can. Eng. Italy N.W. Europe; mem. Candn. Restaurant Assn.; Ont. Restaurant Assn.; Ont. Hotel Assn.; P. Conservative; Protestant; receation: Golf; Clubs: London Hunt & Country; London; Home: 481 Regent St., London, Ont. N5Y 4H5; Office: (P.O Box 5707) 304 York St., London, Ont. N6A 4S6.

CAMPBELL, Finley Alexander, B.Sc., M.A., Ph.D., F.R.S.C.; geologist; educator; b. Kenora, Ont. 5 Jan. 1927; s. Finley McLeod and Vivian (Delve) C.; e. Kenora High Sch. 1944; Brandon Coll. Univ. of Man. B.Sc. 1950; Queen's Univ. M.A. 1956; Princeton Univ. Ph.D. 1958; m. Barbara Elizabeth d. late Dr. R. P. Cromarty, Brandon, Man. 17 Oct. 1953; children: Robert Finley, Glen David, Cheryl Ann; PROF. OF GEOL. UNIV. OF CALGARY since 1976; Dir. and Vice Chrmn. of Bd. Candn. Energy Research Inst.; Exploration and Mining Geol. 1950-58; Asst. Prof. of Geol. Univ. of Alta. 1958, Assoc. Prof. 1963-65; Prof. and Head of Geol. Univ. Calgary 1965, Vice Pres. Capital Resources 1969, Acad. Vice Pres. 1971-76; rec'd Queen's Silver Jubilee Medal; author over 30 articles topics relating to econ. geol. and mineral deposits; mem. Geol. Assn. Can. (Councillor); Mineralol. Assn. Can.; Soc. Econ. Geol.; Mineralol. Soc. Am.; P. Conservative; Presbyterian, recreations; sailing, skiing, music, photography; Clubs: Glenmore Yacht; Zig Zag Yacht; Clearwater Bay Yacht; Home: 3408 Benton Dr. N.W., Calgary, Alta. T2L 1W8; Office: Calgary, Alta. T2N 1N4.

CAMPBELL, Henry Cummings, B.L.S., M.A.; librarian; b. Vancouver, B.C., 22 Apl. 1919; s. Henry and Margaret Kennedy (Cummings) C.; e. Univ. of British Columbia, B.A. 1940; Univ. of Toronto, B.L.S. 1941; Columbia Univ., M.A. (Adult Educ.) 1948; m. Sylvia Frances, d. Harold F. Woodsworth; children: Shiela Margaret, Bonnie Kathleen, Robin Woodsworth; GENERAL MGR. ESPIAL PRODUCTIONS LTD. TORONTO; Librarian, National Film Bd. of Can., 1941-43; Head, Foreign Productions there, 1943-46; Research Assoc., Inst. of Adult Educ., Teachers Coll., N.Y., 1946-48; Librarian and Archivist, United Nations, N.Y., 1948-49; Head, Bibliographical and Research Library Development, UNESCO, Paris, France, 1949-51; Head, UNESCO Clearing House for Libraries, Paris, France, 1951-56; Chief Librarian, Toronto Public Libraries, 1956-78; United Church; Home: 373 Glengrove Ave. W., Toronto, Ont. M5N 1W4

CAMPBELL, Air Marshal Hugh, C.B.E., K.St.J., C.D., B.Sc., LL.D., D.Sc.; Salisbury, N.B., 13 July 1908; e. Pub. and High Schs., Salisbury and Moncton, N.B.; Univ. of New Brunswick, B.Sc. (E.E.) 1939, LL.D. 1952; m. Helen Elizabeth Mary Sutherland, Vancouver, B.C., 15 Dec. 1936; Dir. Inglis Co. Ltd.; Canada Trust Co.; Vice Chancellor, St. John Ambulance; granted R.C.A.F. Pilots Wings Camp Borden, 1930; Engr., Canadian General Electric, 1930-31; commissioned R.C.A.F. 1931; subsequently served as Pilot, Flying Instr., Adjt., Staff Offr. and C.O. at R.C.A.F. Stations; Dir. of Training Plans, British Commonwealth Air Training, Air Force Hdqrs., during early part of Second World War; mem. Chief of

Air Staff Mission U.K., 1940; Dir. of Air Staff R.C.A.F. Hdqrs., Gt. Brit., 1941; served in U.K. and Middle East; apptd. Asst. Chief of Air Staff with rank Air Commodore, 1944; apptd. to the Air Council as mem. for Personnel with rank Air Vice Marshal, 1945; Imp. Defence Coll., London, Eng., 1948; A.O.C., N.W. Air Command Hdqrs., Edmonton, Alta., 1949; Chrmn., Candn. Jt. Staff, Washington, 1949-52; Candn. mem., NATO Mil. Comte., 1950-52; A.O.C., Candn. Air Div. Europe, 1952-55; Vice Air Depy., SHAPE, Europe 1955-57; Chief of Air Staff, R.C.A.F., 1957-62; awarded U.S. Legion of Merit; Order of the White Lion (Czec.); War Cross; Clubs: Royal Ottawa Golf; Rideau; Address: S-802-20 Queen Elizabeth Dr., Ottawa, Ont. K2P 1C8

CAMPBELL, Ian Lachlan, B.A., M.Sc. (Econ.); college principal; b. Ottawa, Ont., 3 Nov. 1927; s. Dr. George. A. and Hazel (Jeffrey) C.; e. Trinity Coll. Sch., Port Hope, Ont., 1941-42; Lisgar Coll. Inst., Ottawa, 1942-46; Carleton Coll., B.A. 1951; London Sch. of Econ. and Pol. Science, M.Sc. (Econ.) 1953; m. Marion d. William Wellwood, 14 July 1950; children: Heather, Diarmid, Colin, Mora; PRINCIPAL AND VICE-CHANCELLOR, RENISON COLL., UNIV. OF WATERLOO, since 1977; Bd. of Govs., Univ. of Waterloo, since 1978; Asst. Prof. of Pol. Science and Sociol., Mount Allison Univ., 1954-56; Asst. Prof. of Sociol. 1956-65; Dir. of Extension, Dir. of Pub. Relations, 1963-65; Dean, Faculty of Arts and Prof. of Pol. Science and Sociol., Bishop's Univ., 1965-69; Acting Head, Dept. of Sociol., 1967-69; Dean, Faculty of Arts, Sir George Williams Univ., 1969-73; Sir George Williams Faculty of Arts, Concordia Univ., 1973-77; Pres., Candn, Assn. of Deans of Arts & Science, 1975-76; held various civic and educ. positions incl. Ald. 1958-59 and Mayor 1962, Sackville, N.B.; Pres., Bd. Trade Sackville, 1961; First Pres., Atlantic Provs. Corrections Assn., 1963; mem. Acad. Council, Maritime Sch. of Social Work, 1961-65; Gov., Dom. Drama Festival, 1964-65; mem. ad hoc Comte. on Govt. Grants to Que. Univs., 1965-68; Chrmn., Sherbrooke Regional C.E.G.E.P. Planning Comte., 1968-69; mem. Panel of Consultants to Candn. Comte. on Corrections, 1966-69; Commr., Govt. of Can. Comn. of Inquiry into Non-Med. Use of Drugs, 1969; rec'd Henry Marshall Tory Award, Carleton Coll., 1951; Can. Council Grants, 1951, 1969; Marjorie Young Bell Fellowship 1963; talks given for CBC on various programmes; author of publs. in sociol. field; Anglican; Home: 86-A McDougall Rd., Waterloo, Ont. N2L 5C5

CAMPBELL, J. Brian, B.Sc., P.Eng. executive; b. Winnipeg, Man. 2 June 1937; s. Hugh A. and Marion B. (Levins) C.; e. Univ. of Man. 1954-58; Letourneau Coll. Texas B.Sc. (Indust. Engn.) 1960; Banff Sch. Advanced Mang. 1966; Internat. Corr. Schs. Metall. and Hydraulics; m. Carole Marion; d. late Harry H. Pielou 24 June 1961; children: Grant I., Lynne E.; PRESIDENT, & CHAIRMAN, J.B.C. MANAGEMENT RESOURCES LTD. 1980-; Analyst and Mgr. Indust. Engn. Manitoba Rolling Mills (Div. Dominion Bridge Co.) 1960, Mang. Mfg. Services 1968-74; Extve. Vice Pres. and Gen. Mgr., Candn. Bronze Co. Ltd. 1974-76, Pres. and Dir. 1976-78; Pres., Dir. & Gen. Mgr., Cae-Montupet Diecast Ltd. 1978-80; served with RCAF Reserve 1954; Chrmn. Jt. Use Parks Comte. Transcona, Man.; Sr. mem. Am. Inst. Indust. Engn.; Chrmn., Candn. C.W.S. Group; Vice Chrmn. Materials Comte. and Adv. mem. Man. Research Council; mem. Bd. Examiners Assn. Prof. Engrs. Prov. Man.; P. Conservative; Protestant; recreations: golf; tennis, squash, camping; Home: 4 Camelot Court, St. Catharines, Ont. L2T 3R3; Office: 4 Camelot Court, St. Catharines, Ont., L2T 3R3

CAMPBELL, James, M.A., Ph.D.; university professor; research scientist; b. Glasgow, Scotland, 18 July 1907; s. late Robina Stirling (Wylie) and late James C.; came to Can. 1922; e. Ayr Acad., Ayr, Scotland, 1920-22; Harbord Coll. Inst., Toronto and N. Toronto Coll. Inst., 1922-26; Univ. of Toronto, B.A. 1930, M.A. 1933; Ph.D. 1938; m.

Mary Louise, d. late Arthur Elliott Allen, 17 Apl. 1954; children: James, Elizabeth Mary, Christine Louise, Sheila Wylie; PROF. EMERITUS OF PHYSIOLOGY, UNIV. OF TORONTO, 1979; research at Univ. of Toronto, Dept. of Biochem., 1930-32; Dept. of Physiol. Hygiene, 1934-36, Dept. of Physiol. 1933-34 and 1936-39; McGill Univ., Dept. of Physiol., under Fisheries Research Bd., 1932-33; assisted in initiating prod. of adrenaline and posterior pituitary extract for clin. use and growth hormone for experimental use by Connaught Med. Research Labs., Toronto; discovered fat-mobilising actions of anterior pituitary extracts and effects of growth hormone in prod. of diabetes through destruction of insulin-producing cells of pancreatic islets; proved that growth hormone elicits increased secretion of insulin prior to appearance of diabetes; discovered new process for prod. of canned potable water and emergency foods; apptd. Asst. Prof., Univ. of Toronto, 1940; Assoc. Prof. 1955; Prof. 1959; mem. of Panel on Nutrition and Metabolism, Defence Research Bd., 1948-62 (Chrmn. 1958-61); served with R.C.N.V.R. 1941-45; Lt. (SB) 1941; Lieut.-Commdr. (SB) 1943; played role in advances in nutrition for Service personnel and prod. of emergency rations; has contrib. to no. of med. books and written papers for scientific journs.; mem., Candn. Biochem. Soc.; Candn. Physiol. Soc.; Nutrition Soc. Can.; Biochem. Soc (U.K.); Am. Chem. Soc.; Am. Diabetes Assn.; Am. Physiol Soc.; Freemason; Liberal; Protestant; recreations: sailing, canoeing, sketching; Clubs: Arts and Letters (Toronto); Faculty; Home: 54 Summerhill Gdns., Toronto, Ont. M4T 1B4; Office: Medical Sciences Bldg., Univ. of Toronto, Toronto, Ont. M5S 1A8

CAMPBELL, John Colin Armour, E.D., C.D., Q.C., B.A.; Formerly Canadian public service 1956-75; b. St. Catharines, Ont., 24 July 1905; s. Col. (His Hon.) John Samuel, V.D., K.C., and Elizabeth (Oille) C.; e. Bishop Ridley Coll.; St. Catharines Coll.; Univ. Coll. of Toronto, B.A. 1927; Osgoode Hall Law Sch., Toronto, 1927-30; m. Margaret Kathryn, d. G. A. Welstead, St. Catharines, Ont. 14 Oct. 1939; served in 2nd World War proceeding overseas in Dec. 1939 with 10th (St. Catharines) Field Bty., 2nd Field Regt., R.C.A.; posted to 1 A/T Regt., R.C.A. 1940; trans. to Office of Judge Advocate Gen., Oct. 1942; served in 1 Cdn. Inf. Div. in Sicily and Italy and at C.M.H.Q. London, Eng.; returned to Can., 1945; apptd. Pres. of Standing Courts-Martial, Camp Borden, subsequently held appt. as Asst. Judge Advocate Gen. at Camp Borden, Ottawa, Central and Western Commands and Cdn. Jt. Staff, London, Eng.; Dept. of Nat. Defence Rep. at Internat. Red Cross meeting, Toronto, Ont. 1952 and at Status of Forces Conf., Bonn, W. Germany 1955-56; retired from Army with rank of Lt.-Col. March 1957; mem., Royal Candn. Legion; Royal Candn. Mil. Inst., Toronto; Psi Upsilon Fraternity; Anglican; recreation: travel; Home: Apt. 1001-20 Driveway, Ottawa, Ont., K2P 1C8

CAMPBELL, John James Ramsay, Ph.D., F.R.S.C. (1961); professor; b. Vancouver, B.C., 29 Mar. 1918; s. Murdoch and Margaret J.; e. Univ. of B.C., B.S.A. 1939; Cornell Univ., Ph.D. 1944; m. Emily Ann Fraser, 4 Sept. 1942; four children; PROF. AND HEAD OF MICROBIOLOGY, UNIV. OF BRITISH COLUMBIA; with Science Service, Central Exper. Farm (Grad. Asst. in Bacteriol.) 1939-40; Dept. of Nat. Defence, Research Worker, 1944-46; Prof. of Dairying UBC, 1946-65; Head, Dept. Micro biology, UBC, 1965——; Fellow, Am. Assn. for the Advance of Science; mem., Soc. of Am. Bacteriol.; Soc. for Gen. Microbiol.; Candn. Soc. Microbiol.; rec'd Harrison Prize of Royal Soc. Can. 1969; Sigma Tau Upsilon; Gamma Alpha; Sigma Xi; Phi Kappa Phi; Protestant; Home: 3949 West 37th Ave., Vancouver, B.C. V6N 2W4

CAMPBELL, Marjorie Wilkins (Mrs. Angus); author; b. London, Eng.; e. Swift Current, Sask., and Toronto, Ont.; lived seven years on farm near Fort Qu'Appelle,

Sask.; m. late Prof. Angus A. Campbell, M.D., 1931; First Editor, Magazine Digest; author of ''The Soil Is Not Enough'', 1938; ''The Saskatchewan'', published in ''The Rivers of America Series'', 1950, revised 1965; ''Ontario'', 1953; ''The Nor'westers'', ''Great Stories of Canada'' series; ''The North West Company'', 1957; ''The Face of Canada'', with four other writers, 1959; rec'd Guggenheim Fellowship for research and biog., re William McGillivray (1764-1825), 1959-60; ''McGillivray, Lord of the Northwest'' (biog. of Wm. McGillivray) 1962; ''No Compromise'' (biog. of Col. E. A. Baker), 1965; ''The Savage River'' (biog. of Simon Fraser), 1968; ''Two Jack Daws'', ''The Fur Trade'' and ''Push to the Pacific'' 1968; ''Northwest to the Sea'', 1975; received Arts Award, The Canadian Council, 1967; awarded Gov. Gen. Award for Creative Non-Fiction (''The Saskatchewan'') 1950; Gov. General's Award for Juveniles (The Nor'westers) 1954; Consultant to National Heritage Ltd. re Restoration of Fort William, by Govt. of Ont. 1971-76; mem. Order of Canada, 1978; sometime mem. Candn. Authors' Assn.; Candn. Women's Press Club (Past Pres., Toronto Br.); mem. Writers' Union of Canada; Anglican; Club: Toronto Heliconian. Address: 50 Rosehill Ave., Apt. 1106, Toronto, Ont. M4T 1G6

CAMPBELL, Richard H., B.A.; manufacturer; b. Greenfield, Mass. 4 Jan. 1936; s. Richard William and Elizabeth Rose (Welcome) C.; e. Deerfield Acad. 1954; Colby Coll. B.A. 1958; Univ. of Mass. grad. courses; m. Carolyne Jean d. Chester J. Zywna, Greenfield, Mass. 20 Apl. 1963; children: Carolyn, Shannon, Sean, Reagan; PRES., GEN. MGR. AND DIR., BLACK & DECKER CANADA INC. 1979- ; Advertising/Sales Promotion Mgr. Millers Falls Co. 1962-67; Marketing Mgr. 1967-70; Dir. of Marketing Black & Decker Manufacturing Co. 1970, Gen. Sales Mgr. 1974-75; Vice Pres. Marketing present Co. 1975, Vice Pres. Operations 1978; served with U.S. Marine Corps active duty 1958-61, ready reserve 1961-66, rank Capt.; Dir. and Chrmn. Finance Comte. St. Vincent's Hosp. Brockville; mem. Ont. Adv. Comte. on Global Product Marketing within Secondary Industry; Past Dir. and Sr. Vice Pres. Candn. Hardware & Housewares Mfrs.' Assn.; Treas. Alpha Tao Omega; R. Catholic; recreations: boating, reading, competitive sports; Club: Brockville Country; Home: 371 Pearl St. W., Brockville, Ont.; Office: 100 Central Ave., Brockville, Ont. K6V 4N8.

CAMPBELL, Robert W.; oil company executive; b. Valentine, Nebraska, 22 Oct. 1922; s. Harry Lee and Margaret (Haley) C.; CHAIRMAN AND CHIEF EXTVE. OFFR., PANCANADIAN PETROLEUM LTD.; Dir., Bank of Canada; Canadian Pacific Enterprises Ltd.; Celanese Canada Inc.; Fording Coal Ltd.; Cominco Ltd.; AMCA International Limited; Maple Leaf Mills Ltd.; Westinghouse Canada Ltd.; served in 2nd World War; Capt., 101st Airborne Div., U.S. Army; served in Europe; Roman Catholic; Home: 3819-10th St., S.W., Calgary, Alta. T2T 3J2; Office: 125 9th Ave. S.E., Calgary, Alta. T2G 0P6

CAMPBELL, Ross, D.S.C., B.A.; former diplomat; b. Toronto, Ont., Nov. 4 1918; s. Helen Isabel (Harris) and late William Marshall C.; e. Univ. of Toronto Schs.; Univ. of Toronto (Trinity Coll.), Faculty of Law, B.A., 1940; m. Penelope d. late Dr. Clermont Grantham Hill, M.B.E., 6 June 1945; two children; PARTNER, CANUS TECHNICAL SERVICES CORPORATION since 1981; began career Legal Div., Dept. of External Affairs 1945; as Third Secy.; Candn. Legation, Oslo, 1946-47; Second Secy., Copenhagen, 1947-50; European Div. Dept. of Ex. Affairs, Ottawa, 1950-52; First Secy., Candn. Embassy, Ankara, 1952-56; Head, Middle East Div., 1957-59; Special Asst. to Secy. of State for External Affairs 1959-62; Asst. Under Secy. of State for External Affairs, 1962-64; Adv., Candn. Dels. to U.N. Gen. Assemblies and Candn. Ministerial Dels. to N. Atlantic Council, 1958-64; Candn. Ambassador to Yugoslavia, 1964-67 (concurrently), Algeria 1965-67; Ambassador and Perm. Rep. to NATO 1967-72, Paris

May 1967, Brussels Oct. 1967; Ambassador to Japan, 1972-75; Rep. of Korea 1973-74; Chairman, Atomic Energy of Canada Ltd., Jan. 1976-May, 1979; Pres., Atomic Energy of Can. Internat'l, 1979; Nuclear Consultant 1980-81; served with R.C.N. 1940-45; awarded D.S.C. 1944; promoted to Lt. Commdr., R.C.N.(R.) (retired), 1949; mem. Naval Offrs. Assn. Can.; Delta Kappa Epsilon; Anglican Church; recreations: gardening, hunting; Address: Home: Rivermead House, 179 Aylmer Rd., Aylmer, Que. J9H 5T8; Office: Ste 2200, Tower A, Place de Ville, Ottawa, Ont. K1R 5A3

CAMPBELL, Virginia A., M.Sc., Ph.D.; educator; b. Saint John N.B., 12 Aug. 1930; d. J. Packard and Mary Gertrude (Kierstead) C.; e. Fairville (N.B.) Superior Sch., 1944; Saint John (N.B.) High Sch., 1947; Acadia Univ., B.Sc. 1951; Pa. State Univ., M.Sc. 1959, Ph.D. 1963; PROF. AND DEAN, SCH. OF HOME ECON., ACADIA UNIV. since 1971; Internship Harper Hosp., Detroit 1951; Dietitian, Hartford (Conn.) Hosp. 1952-56; Research Asst., Univ. of Pittsburgh, 1959; Instr., Pa. State Univ., 1962; Sch. of Medicine, Univ. of Wash., 1963, Chief Nutrition Div., Child Devel. Mental Retardation Centre 1963-71; author of various articles in prof. journs.; dir., Acadia Inst.; Extve. of Board, mem. Bd. of Gov. Acadia U. 1979-82; mem., Candn. Dietetic Assn.; Candn. Home Econ. Assn.; N.S. Dietetic Assn.; N.S. Home Econ. Assn.; Nutrition Soc. of Can.; Nutrition Today Soc.; Omicron Nu; Sigma Delta Epsilon; recreations: fishing, golf, curling, cycling, carpentry, painting; Home: West Wood Dr., Wolfville, N.S. B0P 1X0; Office: Wolfville, N.S. B0P 1X0

CAMPBELL, William; insurance executive; b. Glasgow, Scot. 20 May 1932; d. late Duncan and Jane (McNicol) C.; e. Port Ellen Sch. Isle of Islay; Hillhead High Sch. Glasgow; Royal Tech. Coll. Glasgow; m. Doris d. late James Robertson Linkison 18 Oct. 1958; children: Mairi Linkison, Alasdair Linkison; EXTVE. VICEPRES., ROYAL INSURANCE CO. OF CANADA; Extve. Vice Pres. Western Assurance Co.; Quebec Assurance Co.; Dir. Underwriters Adjustment Bureau; Presbyterian; recreations: horticulture, golf, curling, philately; Clubs: Ontario; Donalda; Royal Montreal Curling; Home: 299 Roehampton Ave., Apt. 930, Toronto, Ont. M4P 1S2; Office: 10 Wellington St. E., Toronto, Ont. M5E 1L5.

CAMPBELL, Maj. William Allan, Q.C., B.A.; b. Peterborough, Ont., 6 June 1913; s. William Stanley and Elizabeth Isabelle (Westlake) C.; e. Univ. of Toronto, B.A. 1935; Osgoode Hall, Toronto, Ont.; m. Gladys Aird, d. Dr. George Munroe, 17 Aug. 1940; one d. Laird, one s., Duart; PARTNER, HAMILTON, TORRANCE, STINSON, CAMPBELL, NOBBS & WOODS; read law with F. G. McBrien and J. C. Macfarlane, K.C., Toronto, Ont.; called to the Bar of Ont., 1938; engaged in Corp. and Labour Law, 1938-42; joined Canadian Westinghouse Co. Ltd., as Solr. in 1946; apptd. Secy. and Gen. Counsel, 1947, Vice-Pres. & Secy., 1953; served in 2nd World War in Candn. Army; Overseas, 1943-45; discharged 1946 with rank of Major; apptd. Chrmn., Indust. Develop. Comte. of Econ. Council, Ont., 1962; mem., Law Soc. of Upper Can.; Candn. Bar Assn.; Hon. Gov., Hamilton-Burlington YMCA and Metro YMCA; Phi Kappa Sigma; United Church; recreations: skiing, golf, sailing; Clubs: University (Toronto); Oakville; P.C.Y.C. (Port Credit); Home: 391 Galt Ave., Oakville, Ont. L6J 1Z7; Office: 196 Adelaide St. W., Toronto, Ont. M5H 1W7

CAMPBELL, William Clarke, B.A.; lawyer; b. Haileybury, Ont., 3 Dec. 1918; e. Haileybury, (Ont.) High Sch.; Victoria Coll., Univ. of Toronto, B.A.; m. Kathleen Joan Jenkins, 3 July 1943; children: William Clarke, Bryan James, Kathleen Joan; PARTNER, DAY, WILSON, CAMPBELL; Ch. and Dir., Consolidated Candn. Faraday Ltd. and other Candn. co.'s; read law with Thomas J. Day; served with R.C.N.V.R. 1943-45; Bailli Delegue;

Confrer'e de la Chaine des Rotisseurs; Clubs: Engineers; Eglinton Hunt; Royal Candn. Mil. Inst. Metropolitan, (N.Y.); Homes: Apt. 502, 330 Spadina Rd., Toronto, M5R 2V9 and Coventry Farm, R.R. 1, Bolton, Ont. L0P 1A0; Office: 250 University Ave., Toronto, Ont. M5H 3E7

CAMPBELL, William James; newspaper officer; b. Orangeville, Ont., 15 Feb. 1900; s. John Henry and Sophia (Dobbin) C.; e. Pub. and High Schs.; m. Ruth Marie, d. late George E. Sutton, Toronto, Ont., June 1928; children: Mrs. Crofton Harvey, William James, Jr.; Dir., Toronto Star Ltd.; Trustee Atkinson Charitable Foundation, 1957; joined the Toronto Star. Feb. 1919; served in 1st World War, Pte., 75th Bn., Toronto Scottish, 1915-18; Freemason; Liberal; Protestant; recreation: golf; Clubs: Granite; Weston Golf; Mayacoo Golf & Country (W. Palm Beach); Sunningdale Golf (Eng.); Home: 15 Cobble Hills, Islington, Ont. M9A 3H6

CAMPEAU, Lucien, M.ès A.; prêtre jésuite; éducateur; né Waterville, Maine 15 juillet 1914; f. Aimé et Marie-Anne (Bureau) C.; é. Courcelles, Qué. et Séminaire du Sacré-Coeur, St-Victor, Beauce, Qué.; Univ. Laval B.ès A. 1936; Univ. de Montréal M.ès A. 1940; Immaculée-Conception, Montréal licence en philosophie 1942, licence en théologie 1949; Univ. Grégorienne licence en Histoire ecclésiastique 1956, doctorat en Histoire ecclésiastique 1967; PROFESSEUR EMERITE D'HISTOIRE, UNIV. DE MONTREAL 1968-1980; entré chez les Jésuites 1936; prof. de Théologie de l'Immaculée-Conception, Montréal 1951; Professeur d'Hist., Univ. de Montreal 1968-80; membre de l'Institutum Historicum Societatis Iesu, Rome; l'Institut d'Histoire de L'Amérique française; la Société Royale du Can.; Comité des Fondateurs de l'Eglise du Can.; Société des Dix; Académie des Sciences morales et politiques; éditeur des "Monumenta Novae Franciae 'I' La première mission d'Acadie (1602-1616)" 1967, II "Etablissement à Québec (1616-1634)" 1979; auteur "La première mission des Jésuites en Nouvelle-France (1611-1613) et Les commencements du Collège de Québec (1626-1670)" 1972; "Les Cent-Associés et le peuplement de la Nouvelle-France" 1974; "L'Evêché de Québec (1674): Aux origines du premier diocèse érigé en Amérique française" 1974; "Les Finances publiques de la Nouvelle-France sous les Cent-Associés 1632-1665" 1975; contrib. "Sacrae Congregationis de Propaganda Fide Memoria Rerum: 350 ans au service des missions 1622-1972" Vol. 1/2 1972; "L'Hôtel-Dieu de Montréal 1642-1973" 1973; plusieurs articles sur l'histoire de l'Eglise et l'histoire de la Nouvelle-France; catholique; Adresse: Maison des Jésuites, 175 boul. des Hauteurs, St-Jérôme, Qué. J7Z 5T8; Bureau: (C.P. 6128) Montréal, Qué. H3C 3J7.

CAMPEAU, Robert; real estate development executive; b. Sudbury, Ont. 3 Aug. 1923; m. Ilse Luebbert; CHRMN. AND CHIEF EXTVE. OFFR., DIR., CAMPEAU CORP.; mem. Adv. Bd. Guaranty Trust Co. of Canada; Gov., Ashbury Coll. Ottawa; Clubs: Lambton Golf and Country, Rideau, Ottawa Hunt and Golf, Mount Royal, Rivermead Gold, Country (Aylmer), Laval sur-le-lac, Jupiter Hills, Met; Home: 64 The Bridle Path, Don Mills, Ont. M3B 2B1; Office: 320 Bay St., Toronto, Ont. M5H 2P6.

CAMPO, Alfredo Felice Michele, O.C.; industrialist; b. Castel di Lucio, Italy, 22 Jan. 1905; s. Cavalier Uff. Placido and Matilde Lo (Forti) C.; e. Royal Univs. of Palermo and Catania (LL.D.); m. Priscille, d. A. Dubé, Montreal, Que, 9 Dec. 1977; one d. Giovanna; Life Gov., Montreal Gen. Hosp. and Queen Elizabeth Hosp. (Montreal), Gov., Douglas Hosp, Hôpital Ste-Justine; Montreal Children's Hosp.; Joined McColl-Frontenac Oil Co. Ltd. (now Texaco) in 1926, leaving in 1953 when sales mgr. founded Petrofina Can. Ltd. in 1953. Retired as Chief Executive Officer in 1973 and Chairman in 1977; attended Sch. for Officers, Palermo, Italy (Field Arty.); awarded

Grande Ufficiale al Merito della Rep. Italiana; Commandeur de l'Ordre de la Couronne Belge., Mem. Order of Canada. recreation: bridge; Clubs: St. James's; Forest & Stream; Home and Office: R.R. 1, Ste.-Marguerite Station, Que. J0T 2K0

CAMU, Pierre, O.C. (1976), Ph.D., L.Litt., F.R.S.C. (1966); transport executive; b. Montreal, Que., 19 March 1923; s. Pierre and Jeanne (Duval) C.; e. Montreal, Univ., M.A. 1947, Ph.D. 1951, L.Litt, 1947; Post-grad. studies at St. Johns Hopkins Univ., 1947-49; Dr. of Geog., Ottawa Univ. 1968; m. Marie-M., d. T. R. Trudeau, 4 Nov. 1950; children: Suzanne, Marie-Hélène, Pierre; PRESIDENT, MARCH SHIPPING LTD. since 1979; with Geog. Branch, Department of Mines & Tech. Surveys, Ottawa, 1949-56; Prof. of Econ. Geog., Laval Univ., Quebec, 1956-60; Vice-Pres., St. Lawrence Seaway Authority, 1960-65, Pres. 1965-73; Adm., Candn. Marine Transport., Min. of Transport 1970-73; Pres. (1973-77) Candn. Assn. of Broadcasters; Chrmn., CRTC 1977-79; author of several articles dealing with trans. and econs. of transport; co-author, "Economic Geography of Canada", 1964; R. Catholic; recreations: skiing, boating; Club: Rideau; Office: 360 St. Jacques, Ste.1400, Montreal Que. H2Y 1K1

CANDLISH, Stanley M., B.Sc.; company executive; b. Montreal, Que., 23 Nov. 1925; s. Dr. H. M. and Lillian (Holtby) C.; e. Alfred Joyce (Outremont) Pub. Sch., 1930-37; High Sch. of Montreal, 1938-42; McGill Univ., B.Sc., 1946, Postgrad. study in Bacter., 1946-47; m. Bridget Suzanna (Naomi) d. late David J. Coady, Glace Bay, N.S., 17 July 1948; one s., Ross Maiben; MANAGER, RESEARCH AND DEVELOPMENT, IMPERIAL TOBACCO LTD. 1980-; joined present Co. as Chem., 1947; Asst. Mgr. Tech. Service Lab., 1957; Asst. Mgr. Devel. & Tech. Service Lab., 1964; Mgr. Devel. & Tech. Service 1966-69; Div. Head. Mgr., Product Devel. & Tech. Services Dept., 1978-80; McGill C.O.T.C., 1942-47; mem., Packaging Assn. Can. (Pres., 1967-68); Liberal; Protestant; recreations: boating, boat building, skiing; Club: Iroquois Yacht; Home: 815-48th Ave., Lachine, Que. H8T 2S4; Office: 3810 St. Antoine, Montreal, Que. H3C 3L6

CANDLISH, Violet Elizabeth, B.Sc.A., M.Sc., Ph.D.; research consultant; b. Regina, Sask. 9 July 1931; d. James Garfield and Christy Violet (Macewen) Gardiner; e. elem. sch. Ottawa, Ont.; Luther Coll. Regina, Sask. 1948; Macdonald Coll. McGill Univ. B.Sc.A. 1952; Univ. of Man. M.Sc. 1968, Ph.D. 1970, post-doctorate 1971-72; m. John Henry Candlish 25 July 1953 (separated); children: Lucy Ellen, Patricia Jane, Jill Elizabeth, William Edwin, Christy Alice; estbd. Beth Candlish Ph.D., Research Consultant 1978; Lecturer Candn. Internat. Grains Inst.; Research Officer and mem. Winnipeg Chamber Comm.; Science Council Can.; Research Assoc. Plant Science, Univ. Man. 1972; Research Scient. Feed Grain, Grain Research Lab. Winnipeg 1973; Research Specialist, Can. Grains Council 1976; Lib. Cand. for Ft. Garry, Man. g.e. 1977; Vice Pres. (2nd) Lib. Party of Man. 1978; Field Underwriter, N.Y. Life Ins. Co.; mem. Bd. of Regents, U. of Winnipeg; Man. Inst. of Agrologists; Assn. Am. Cereal Chems.; Candn. Soc. Animal Scients.; Nutrition Today Soc.; Man. Action Comte. Status Women; Liberal; Anglican; recreations: flying, music, theatre; Club: Winnipeg Flying; Home: 62-One Snow St. Winnipeg Man. R3T 2M4; Office: 62 One Snow St., Winnipeg, Man. R3T 2M4.

CANN, Christopher John; executive; b. Eng. 22 Feb. 1941; s. Harold John and Ada Mary (Trueman) C.; came to Canada 1964; e. Grammar Sch. Lewes, Eng.; Reading Univ. 1961; C.G.A. 1973; M.T.C.I. 1977; m. Jean, d. George Speaight, 21 Nov. 1964; children: Deborah Jane, Michael John; SR. VICE PRESIDENT TRUST DIVISION, EATON BAY FINANCIAL SERVICES LTD. since 1979; Pres., Eaton Bay Trust Co. (Alberta); Trainee, Westminster Bank, Sussex, Eng. 1961; British Bank of Middle East 1964; Import and Export Dept., Candn. Imperial Bank of

Commerce, H.O. 1964; Acct. Triarch Corp. 1966, Controller 1971, Treas. 1972, Vice-Pres. and Treas. 1973, Extve. Vice-Pres. and Treas. 1974, Pres. 1974; Pres., Commerce Capital Mortgage Corp., 1976; Senior Vice President, Commerce Capital Corporation Ltd. and Subsidiaries, 1978; mem. Ont. Mortgage Brokers Assn.; CGA Association of Canada; Trust Companies Association of Canada; Anglican; Clubs: Domn. Rabbit and Cavy Breeders Assn.; Pres., Ont. Commercial Rabbit Growers Association; Home: R.R.2, Whitby, Ont. L1N 5R5; Office: Eaton Bay Financial Services, 595 Bay St., Toronto, Ont., M5G 2C6

CANNING, Robert H., B. Com., Investment Dealer; b. 1926, March 21, Montreal, P.Q.; e. Univ. of Toronto, B. Com. 1948; m. 1950, Irma Elizabeth Perry, deceased; children: Barbara Jane and Peter Robert; CHAIRMAN, PRES. AND DIR.,BELL GOUINLOCK LTD. Gov., Toronto Stock Exchange; Dir. present firm 1959; Vice Pres. 1967; Pres. 1972; Chrmn 1981; Club: Ontario; Home: 75 Ardwold Gate, Toronto, Ontario, M5R 2W1; Office: (P.O. Box 110), 1 First Canadian Place, Toronto, Ontario, M5X 1B6

CANNON, Edward Patrick, B.Com., C.A.; executive; b. Quebec City, Que., 26 March 1940; s. Edward Lawrence and Mary Margaret (McKeown) C.; e. Univ. of Ottawa, B.Com. 1962; Laval Univ. Maitrise en Sciences Commerciales 1963; m. Jacqueline Mary d. Cecil Vivian Parker, Ottawa, Ont., 10 Aug. 1962; three s. Lawrence Parker, Bruce Patrick, Charles Jeffrey; PRESIDENT AND CHIEF EXECUTIVE OFFICER, COMPUTEL SYSTEMS, LTD.; Dir., Computel Systems Ltd.; served with Peat, Marwick, Mitchell & Co. Montreal 1963-65; joined The Royal Trust Co. 1965; Asst. Vice Pres. and Comptroller 1972-75; mem. Inst. C.A.'s Que.; Financial Extves. Inst.; R. Catholic; recreations: golf, tennis, youth activities; Clubs: Laurentian; Cambridge; Larrimac & Donalda Golf; Office: 45 St. Clair Ave. W., Toronto, Ont. M4V 1K9

CANVIN, D.T., B.S.A., M.Sc., Ph.D., F.R.S.C. (1977); university professor; b. Winnipeg, Man., 8 Nov. 1931; s. Victor T. and Maria (Clouston) C.; e. Univ. of Man., B.S.A. 1956, M.Sc. 1957; Purdue Univ., Ph.D. 1960; m. Lois Marie, d. J. E. Endersby, Winnipeg, Man., 13 July 1957; children: Steven, Paul, Sarah, Robert; PROF. OF BIOLOGY, QUEEN'S UNIV.; writings incl. various scient. papers in fields of plant physiol.-biochem.; mem., Candn. Soc. Plant Physiols.; Am. Soc. Plant Physiols.; Candn. Biochem. Soc.; Biol. Council Can.; Am. Assn. Advanc. Science; Am. Soc. Agron; Anglican; recreations: curling, bridge, fishing; Home: 17 Queen Mary Rd., Kingston, Ont. K7M 2A3

CAPE, John Christopher, B.A.; Eng.; M.E.I.C.; General contractor; b. Montreal, Que. 2 July 1937; s. John Meredith and Mary Elizabeth C.; e. Trinity Coll. Sch. Port Hope, Ont. 1955; Bishop's Univ. B.A. 1958; Univ. of Scranton, Engn. 1966; Alexander Hamilton Inst., Business Adm. 1970; m. Beverley Joyce d. Geoff Rogers; children: Jim, Geoff, Pam; VICE PRES., E. G. M. CAPE & CO. LTD. since 1978; joined present Co. 1961; Anglican; Clubs: Badminton & Racquet; Granite; Office: 180 Duncan Mill Rd., Don Mills, Ont. M3B 3K2.

CAPLAN, Herbert, B.A., D.D.S., F.A.C.D., F.I.C.D.; b. Montreal, Que., 3 June 1921; s. Morris and Ethel (Gerkin) C.; e. Aberdeen Sch., Montreal, Que.; Strathcona Acad., Outremont, Que.; Loyola Coll., Montreal, Que., B.A.; McGill Univ., D.D.S.; post-grad. training, Temple Univ., 1958; m. children: Melissa Alfreda; Chief, Dept. Dentistry, Reddy Memorial Hosp., Montreal, Que.; Courtesy Staff mem., Queen Elizabeth Hosp., Montreal, Que.; Gov., Coll. Dental Surgeons of Que., 1968-72; Candn. Dental Assn., 1971-72; Judge on War Mem. Comte.; Candn. Dental Assn., 1964-65; Pres., Am. Acad. Dental Med., Montreal Sec., 1963-64 and alternate del. to Nat.

Body, 1964; served as Lt. during 2nd World War with Candn. Inf. Corps, 1943-45; Publications: Clinical and Prof.; mem., Candn. Dental Assn.; Am. Inst. Oral Biol.; Am. Assn. Hosp. Dental Chiefs; Chicago Dental Soc.; Fed. Dentaire Internat.; served on Extve. Bd., Mt. Royal Dental Soc.; Alpha Omega (Pres., Montreal Alumni Chapter, 1955-56; Regent, Que. and Ont., 1957-58; Nat. Comte. Chrmnships 1958-61; Internat. Treas. and Internat. Convention Rep., 1961-64; Internat. Pres.-Elect. 1964-65; Internat. Pres., 1966); mem., McGill Grads Soc. and Past Faculty Chrmn. (Dentistry) of the Alma Mater Fund, 1960-61; apptd. Consultant in Dent., Reddy Mem. Hosp. 1967; official Del. to Fed. Dentaire Internat. by Candn. Dent. Assn. 1966; apptd. Chrmn. of Scient. Program for Candn. Dental Assn. in Montreal, 1969; Fellow, Am. Coll. of Dents.; Fellow, Internal Coll. of Dentists; mem. Loyola Alumni Assn.; Founder mem., Dental Sch., Hebrew Univ. and mem. Supporting Alumni; Hebrew; recreations: golf, photography; Club: Hillsdale Golf & Country; Home: 5160 MacDonald Ave., Montreal, Que. H3X 2V8; Office: Suite 315, 3535 Queen Mary Rd., Montreal, Que. H3V 1H8

CAPON, Frank Samuel, executive (retired); b. Romford, Eng., 15 Dec. 1915; s. Frank C. and Lillian M. (Apps) C.; e. Royal Liberty Sch., Romford, Eng.; C.A. (Que.); came to Canada, 1 Aug. 1930; m. Marjorie, d. H. E. O'Connell, 27 Apl. 1940; two d. Gail, Susan; Dir., Genstar Ltd.; Consumers Glass Co. Ltd.(Bd. Chmn.); Dennison Mfg. Co. of Can. Ltd. (Bd. chrmn.); Union Minière Can. (Bd. Chrmn.); Past Pres. Montreal General Hospital; joined Candn. Industries Ltd., 1938; Asst. Treas. 1946, Treas. 1949; apptd. Secy. and Treas., DuPont of Canada Ltd. 1954, Dir. 1957, Vice-Pres. 1960-70; Pres., Candn. Inst. Chart. Accts. 1971-73, mem., Financial Extves. Inst. (Past Pres. and Dir.); Inst. Chart. Accts. Que.; Clubs: Mount Bruno Golf & Country; Mount Royal; Ashburn Golf (Halifax, N.S.); Home: P.O. Box 520, Chester, N.S. B0J 1J0

CARBONNEAU, Côme, O.C., M.A.Sc., Ph.D.; mining executive; b. Saint-Jean-des-Piles, Qué. 24 Nov. 1923; s. Omer and Edith (Bordeleau) C.; e. Laval Univ. B.A. 1943, B.A.Sc. 1948; Univ. of B.C., M.A.Sc. 1949; McGill Univ. Ph.D. (Geol.) 1953; m. Françoise d. Lucien Pettigrew 15 Sept. 1951; children: Hélène, Marie, Jean, Pierre, Lise, Alain; PRES. AND CHIEF EXTVE. OFFR., CORPORATION FALCONBRIDGE COPPER 1981- ; Chrmn. of Bd. and Dir. Bachelor Lake Gold Mines Inc.; Dir. Les Relevés Géophysiques Inc.; Assoc. Prof. of Geol. Ecole Polytechnique and Univ. of Montreal 1951-63; Consulting Geol., St-Lawrence Columbium, Oka area 1953-59; Extve. Vice Pres. 1963-65; Founding Pres. and Chief Extve. Offr. SOQUEM, Quebec 1965-77; Prof. of Geol. and Mineral Econ. Laval Univ. 1977-81, Chrmn. of Geol. Faculty of Sciences & Engn. 1979-81; Nomination: Officer Order of Canada, 1978; recipient A. O. Dufresne Award Candn. Inst. Mining & Metall. 1978; mem. Nat. Adv. Comte. on Mining Policies 1971-75; Nat. Adv. Comte. on Mining & Metall. 1980; Pres. Assn. Canadienne-Française pour l'Avancement des Sciences 1975-76; Dir., Univ. Laval 1970-71, Pres. Assn. des Anciens 1970-71; Gov. McGill Univ. 1973-77; author various articles scient. and prof. journs.; mem. Order Engrs. Que.; Candn. Inst. Mining & Metall.; Geol. Assn. Can.; Assn. des Géologues du Qué.; Sigma Xi; recreations: reading, skiing, cycling; Clubs: Cercle Universitaire Qué.; Engineers' (Toronto); Home: Apt. 105, 80 Quebec Ave., Toronto, Ont. M6P 1B4; Office: (P.O. Box 40) Commer. Court West, Toronto, Ont. M5L 1B4.

CARBOTTE, Mrs. Marcel; — see: Roy, Gabrielle.

CARDIN, Hon. Louis-Joseph-Lucien, P.C. (1963), Q.C., B.A., LL.B.; b. Providence, R.I., 1 March 1919; s. Octave and Eldora (Pagé) C.; e. Loyola Coll.; Montreal, B.A.; Univ. de Montréal, LL.B.; m. Marcelle, d. late Armand Petitclerc, Sorel, Qué., 3 June 1950; children: Jean-Fran-

cois, Celine, Louis, Michel; first el. H. of C. for Richelieu-Verchères, by-el., 6 Oct. 1952; apptd. Assoc. Min. o Nat. Defence 22 Apl. 1963; Min. of Public Works, 12 Feb 1965; Min. of Justice and Atty.-Gen. 7 July 1965-68; mem Immigration Appeal Bd. 1970-72; Asst. Chrmn., Tax Review Bd. 1973-75; Chrmn., Tax Review Bd. since 1975 served overseas in 2nd World War with R.C.N., 1941-45 discharged with rank of Lieut.-Commdr.; called to the Bar of Que., June 1950; Liberal; Catholic; Home: 88 Isabelle, Hull, Que. J8Y 5G7; Office: Kent Professiona Bldg., 381 Kent St., Ottawa, Ont. K1A 0M1

CARDY, A. Gordon, M.C., B.Com., K.L.J.; hotelier; b Brockville, Ont., 14 June 1919; s. Roland Hastings and Jean (Gordon) C.; e. Trinity Coll., Univ. of Toronto B.Com. (Hons.) 1941; m. Alice Elizabeth, d. Wilber C. Cochrane, 18 Sept. 1948; children: Barbara, Roland, Gordon, Rosemary; CHAIRMAN PRESIDENT AND CHIEF EXECUTIVE OFFICER, CP HOTELS LTD. Aug. 1978 and Gen. Mgr., Royal York Hotel, Toronto since 1968, Dir., Cochrane Dunlop Hardware Ltd. 1972; Gen. Mgr., Prince Edward Hotel, Windsor, Ont. 1951, Sheraton Connaught Hotel, Hamilton, Ont. 1952, Sheraton Brock Hotel, Niagara Falls, Ont. 1954, Sheraton Hotel, Rochester, N.Y. 1955, King Edward Sheraton Hotel, Toronto, Ont. 1956; served in 2nd World War, Lt., R.C.A. 1942-45; served in Europe; awarded M.C.; Past Pres., Ont. Hotel & Motel Assn. of Can.; Past Pres. Hotel Assn. of Can. 1975; Convention & Tourist Bureau Metrop. Toronto; Pres., Ont. Heart Foundation 1969; United Church; recreations: golf, horseback riding; Clubs: Kiwanis (Dir.), Goodfellowship; Lambton Golf & Country; Home: 53 Dunvegan Rd., Toronto, Ont. M4V 2P5; Office: 100 Front St. W., Toronto, Ont. M5J 1E3

CARELESS, James Maurice Stockford, B.A., A.M.,Ph.D., F.R.S.C. (1962); university professor; b. Toronto, Ont. 17 Feb. 1919; s. late William Roy Stockford and Ada Josephine (de Rees) C.; e. Univ. of Toronto Schs.; Univ. of Toronto, B.A. 1940; Harvard Univ., A.M. 1941 and Ph.D. 1950; m. Elizabeth Isobel, d. late Gordon Robinson, 31 Dec. 1941; five children; PROF. OF HISTORY, UNIV. OF TORONTO, since 1959; (former Chrmn. of History there); Sheldon Trav. Fellowship, Harvd., 1942-43; joined Hist. Dept., Univ. of Toronto as a Lectr. 1945; Co-Chrmn. of Archeol. & Hist. Sites Bd. of Ont.; Asst. to the Naval Historian, Naval Service Hdqrs., Ottawa 1943; Special Wartime Asst., Dept. of External Affairs, Ottawa, 1943-45; engaged in latter stages of War as Candn. Diplomatic Offr. on Exchange Ship "Gripsholm"; has served as Hist. Consultant on C.B.C. radio and television programs; author of "Canada, A Story of Challenge", 1953; (awarded Gov. Gen. Medal, 1954); "The Union of the Canadas", 1967; Jt. author, "Canada and the Commonwealth", 1953; "Canada and the Americas", 1953; "Canada and the World", 1954; "Brown of the Globe" (biog.) Vol. 1 (1959) and Vo. 2 (1963); "Colonists and Canadiens", 1971; "The Pioneers", 1969; also numerous articles on hist. subjects in reviews and journs.; awarded Tyrrell Medal for Candn. Hist. 1962; rec'd Gov. Gen's Award for non-fiction ("Brown of the Globe") 1964; Cruickshank Medal of Ont. Hist. Soc. 1968; Trustee, Ont. Science Centre 1963-73; Dir., Ont. Heritage Foundation since 1975; Trustee, Ont. Hist. Studies Series since 1973; mem. Comn. on Post-Secondary Educ. in Ont. 1968-72; Hist. Sites & Monuments Bd. of Can. since 1972; mem., Candn. Hist. Assn. (Pres. 1967-68); Ont. Hist. Soc. (Pres. 1959); Address: Toronto, Ont.

CAREY, Lewis Stafford, M.D., C.M., M.Sc., M.S., F.R.C.P. F.A.C.R. radiologist; educator; b. Yorkton, Sask. 9 July 1925; s. Edward H. and Gladys C.; e. Edward High Sch. Vancouver; Univ. of B.C.; Queen's Univ. M.D., C.M. 1950, M.Sc. (Med.) 1956 (John Franklin Kidd Essay Prize in Surg. 1949); Univ. of Minn. M.S. 1959; m. Beverly Jane d. Dr. Wallace Baxter, Burlington, Ont. Sept. 1950; children: Richard, Mark, Susan, John,

David; patient care (clin. work), teaching and research, Univ. Hosp., Univ. of W. Ont.; residency in Surg., Mayo Clinic 1953-55, in Diagnostic Radiol. 1955-58; Diplomate Am. Bd. Radiol. 1958; holds patent Devel. Mobile X-Ray Unit for Bedside Pacemaker Insertion - Visa Cart (1972); Exper. Leader, Telemed. Exper. U-6 Using CTS Satellite Hermes 1976-77; Chrmn. Northern Health Services 1973-79; co-author "Congenital Heart Disease: Correlation Pathological Anatomy and Angio-cardiography" 2 vols. (French and Eng.) 1965; author or co-author numerous med. publs.; Fellow, Am. Coll. Radiol.; mem. Alumnae Assn. Mayo Foundation for Med. Ed. & Research; Am. Roentgen Ray Soc.; Assn. Univ. Radiols.; Candn. Assn. Radiols.; Candn. Med. Protective Assn.; Candn. Profs. Radiol.; Council on Cardio-vascular Radiol.; Minn. Radiol. Soc.; N. Am. Soc. Cardiac Radiols.; Radiol. Soc. N. Am.; Solar Energy Soc. Can.; Home: 45 Blackburn Cres., R.R. 3, Komoka, Ont. N0L 1R0; Office: University Hospital, P.O. Box 5339, Terminal A, London, Ont. N6A 5A5.

CARIGNAN, Pierre, Q.C., M.A., LL.L.; b. Lachine, Que., 21 Apl. 1922; s. Anatole and Marie-Rose (Parker) C.; e. Coll. de Montreal, 1934-40; Semy. de Philos., B.A. 1942; Univ. of Montreal, LL.L. 1946; Harvard Univ., M.A. (Econ.) 1947; m. Rita, d. Donat Heroux, Verdun, Que., 26 Feb. 1949; two d.; Isabelle, Genevieve; PROFESSOR OF LAW, UNIV. OF MONTREAL, (formerly Dean of Faculty there); former mem. Consultative Comte. on Bankruptcy Leg.; Dir. Public Law Research Inst. Univ. of Montreal; former mem. Restrictive Trade Practices Comn.; called to Bar of Que. 1945; cr. Q.C., 1959; Home: 4845 West Broadway, Montreal, P.Q. H4V 1R5

CARLEY, Robert H. e. Univ. of Toronto, B.Com. (Comm. and Finance; co-winner of Edw. Blake Scholarship) 1943; m.; four children; JUDGE OF COUNTY COURT, COUNTY NORTHUMBERLAND; Practised law in Peterborough, 1951-79; Appt'd Q.C. 1967; former Dir., The Consumers' Gas Co.; Raybestos — Manhattan (Can.) Ltd.; Past Chrmn., Presb. Church Bldg. Corp.; Peterborough Industrial Devel. Organization; Bencher, Law Soc. of Upper Can. 1971-75; served in 2nd World War with RCNVR (HMCS "Sarnia"); Past Pres., Peterborough Law Assn.; Peterborough Auto. and Rotary Clubs; Presbyterian; Home: 262 Walton St., Cobourg, Ont. K9A 3W8; Office: Judges' Chambers, P.O. Box 38 Cobourg, Ont. K9A 4K2

CARLILE, Jack C., B.A.Sc., B.Com.; telecommunications executive; b. Vancouver, B.C., 28 Nov. 1921; s. John Edward and Agnes Jamieson (Maclachlan) C.; e. Univ. of B.C., B.A.Sc. 1944, B.Com 1946; m. Leone Carey, d. Joseph A. Legree, 19 Oct. 1946; PRES. & CHIEF OPERATING OFFICER, BRITISH COLUMBIA TELEPHONE CO. 1980-; held various engn. and staff sales assignments, Canadian Industries Ltd., 1946-50; various staff administrative positions, Brazilian Traction Light and Power Co. subsidiaries in Brazil, 1951-54; various engn. and operational positions and subsequently Vice Pres.-Finance 1966-71, British Columbia Telephone Co., 1954-71, Vice Pres. — Adm. 1974-75; Pres., TransCanada Telephone System 1971-74; Vice Pres-. Operations, B.C. Telephone 1976-80; served with Candn. Inf. Corps. 1944-45; rank Lt.; Anglican; recreations: golf; Clubs: Vancouver; Capilano Golf & Country; Home: 3591 Capilano Rd., N., Vancouver, B.C. V7R 4H9; Office: 3777 Kingsway, Burnaby, B.C. V5H 3Z7

CARLSON, Donald Arthur, P.Eng., B. Sc., M.E.I.C. construction executive; b. Edmonton, Alta. 27 Oct. 1931; s. Arthur Victor and Belle Pearl (Snider) C.; e. Oliver Sch. and Westglen High Sch. Edmonton 1950; Univ. of Alta. B.A.Sc. (Civil Engn.) 1954; Mass. Inst. Technol. postgrad. work in constr. mang.; m. Elizabeth d. Mike Manasterski 27 Dec. 1958; children: Dennis Arthur, Susan Leslie, Douglas Scott, John David; CHMN. OF BD., A. V. CARLSON CONSTRUCTION CORP. LTD 1979-;. (Edmonton and Calgary); Pres., Edmonton Eskimo Football Club, 1979-80; Pres., Carlson Development Corp. Ltd. since 1964; Pres. Tradewinds Travel; Pres., Carlson Resources, Inc.; Mem. Bd. of Directors, National Trust Co.; Melcor Developments Ltd.; Princeton Developments Ltd.; Nu-Alta Developments Ltd.; Alta. Motor Assn; AMA Insurance; Brentwood College; Project Mgr. A. V. Carlson Construction Ltd. 1950-64; Chmn. Bd. of Governors, Edmonton Eskimo Football Club; mem. Prof. Engrs. Prov. Alta.; Engn. Inst. Can.; Candn. Constr. Assn.; Young Pres. Organ; Chief Executives Forum, Inc. World Business Council; Edmonton Chamber of Commerce; Society Delta Upsilon; recreations: travel, skiing, jogging, scuba; Clubs: Skal; Edmonton Petroleum; Center; Royal Glenora; Home: 2 Laurier Pl., Edmonton, Alta. T5R 5P4; Office: 14904 - 123rd Ave., Edmonton, Alta. T5V 1B4

CARLSON, Donald H. E.; publisher; b. Edmonton, Alta., 25 Aug. 1918; s. Theo Gustav and Grace Helen (Ockenden) C.; e. Elem. and High Schs., Wetaskiwin and Edmonton, Alta.; Univ. of Alta. 1940 B.A. (Gold Medallist); m. Madeline Frances, d. E. M. Beetlestone, Surrey, B.C. 5 March 1941; children: (Mrs.) Madeline Ellis, (Mrs.) Elizabeth Davis, (Ms.) Susannah Wyndham, Anthony, Gustav; PUBLISHER, FINANCIAL TIMES OF CANADA, since 1974; Journalist, Ed., Toronto Star, Vancouver Sun, Vancouver Province, 1942; Dir., Pub. Relations, James Lovick & Co. Ltd., 1953; Crown Zellerbach Canada Ltd. 1955; Ford Motor Co. of Canada, Ltd., Div. Pub. Rel. 1959-63; Secy., 1964-67, Vice Pres. and Secy. 1968-74; Anglican; recreations: handball, sailing, skiing; Clubs: National; Royal Canadian Yacht Club, Toronto; Oakville Club; Home: 32 Colonial Crescent, Oakville, Ont. L6J 4K9; Office: 920 Yonge St. Toronto, Ont. M4W 3L5

CARLSON, Roy L., M.A., Ph.D.; archaeologist; educator; b. Bremerton, Wash., 25 June 1930; s. Peter Lincoln and Margaret Mary (Clark) C.; e. Univ. of Wash., B.A. 1952, M.A. 1955; Univ. of Ariz., Ph.D. 1961; m. Maureen Joyce, d. James Kelly, Vancouver, B.C. 13 June 1953; children: Catherine Carroll, Daniel James, Arne Kelly, Christopher Clark; PROF. DEPT. OF ARCHAEOL., SIMON FRASER UNIV. since 1971; Curator, Klamath Co. Museum, Klamath Falls, Ore. 1957-58; Teaching and Research Asst., Univ. of Ariz., 1959; Asst. Prof., Univ. of Colo. Boulder, 1961; Field Dir., Univ. of Colo. 4th Nubian Expdn., Africa, 1965; joined present Univ. as Asst. Prof. 1966, Assoc. Prof. 1967-71; author, "Teachers Manual for Early Indian Cultures of North America", 1973; "White Mountain Red Ware", 1970; "Eighteenth Century Navajo Fortresses of the Gobernador District", 1965; "Basket Maker III Sites Near Durango, Colorado", 1963; Ed., "Current Research Reports", Dept. of Archaeol., Simon Fraser Univ., Publ. No. 3, 1976; "Salvage '71: Reports on Salvage Archaeology in British Columbia", 1973; "Archaeology in British Columbia New Discoveries", 1970; mem. Candn. Archaeol. Assn.; Soc. Am. Archaeol.; Home: 888 Seymour Dr., Coquitlam, B.C. V3J 6V7; Office: Burnaby, B.C. V5A 1S6

CARLYLE, Grant Morton, B.Com.; company director; b. Calgary, Alta., 12 July 1913; s. late Thomas Morton and Stella Winnifred Alice (Young) C.; e. University Sch., Victoria, B.C., 1930-32; McGill Univ., B.Com., 1934; m. firstly Joyce Kathleen, d. late Richard Stanley Law, 15 May 1940 died Feb. 18, 1978; one d. Barbara Joan; m. secondly Mabel Pearl (Kennedy) Webb, W. John B. Webb of calgary; Pres., The Quest for Handicrafts Can. Ltd. (Calgary-Banff-Victoria); president until retirement of Alminex Petroleum Ltd.; Dir. Silverwood Industries Ltd.; Pres., National Dairy Council of Canada 1954-55; Pres., Calgary Chamber Comm., 1963-64; Chrmn., Banff Sch. of Fine Arts Bd. of Govs. 1970-81; Club: Kiwanis; Address: 2905 Carlton St. West, Calgary, Alta. T2T 3L1

CARMICHAEL, Donald W.; financial executive; b. St. Catharines, Ont., 29 Jan. 1923; s. Harry John and Marie (Moran) C.; e. Pub. and High Schs., St. Catharines, Ont.; Assumption Coll.; McGill Univ.; m. Maryon, d. Isaac Edward Misener, 26 June 1948; one s. Harry John Jr., one d. Lee Anne; PARTNER, CHAIRMAN OF THE BOARD and CHIEF EXTVE. OFFICER, WATT CARMICHAEL SECURITIES LTD. since 1976 and 1981; estab. Carmichael Power Co. Ltd. 1947; joined Baker Weeks, New York, N.Y. as trainee 1957; trans. to Toronto office, Securities Sales 1958; Partner, Donald R. Watt Securities 1971; apptd. Partner, Vice. Pres. and Dir., Watt Carmichael Securities Ltd. 1972, Pres. 1976; Chmn. of the Bd. 1981; mem., Toronto Stock Exchange; Metrop. Toronto Bd. Trade; Past mem. Bd. Govs., Lady of Mercy Hosp.; Scarborough Gen. Hosp.; Delta Kappa Epsilon; R. Catholic; recreations: golf, yachting, race horses; Clubs: Rosedale Golf; Granite; Canadian; Toronto Hunt; Metrop. New York City; Home: 15 Lauderdale Drive, Willowdale, Ont. M2L 2A8; Office: Suite 3470, First Canadian Place, Box88, Toronto, Ont. M5X 1B1

CARMICHAEL, Hugh, B.Sc., M.A., Ph.D., F.R.S.C.; physicist; b. Farr, Sutherland, Scotland, 10 Nov. 1906; s. Rev. Dugald and Agnes Macmillan (Macaulay) C.; e. Univ. of Edinburgh, B.Sc. (1st Class Hons. in Physics) 1929; Univ. of Cambridge, Ph.D. 1937, M.A. 1939; Fellow, St. John's Coll., Cambridge, 1937-40; m. Margaret Elizabeth May, d. Thomas Forbes Maclennan, 23 Oct. 1937; children: Dugald Macaulay, Margaret Lind (Mrs. Wilson Stuart), Elizabeth Agnes (Mrs. Gary Cooper), Hugh Alexander Lorne; Carnegie Research Fellow, University of Edinburgh, 1929-33; Clark Maxwell Research Scholar, Univ. of Cambridge, 1933-37; Demonst., University of Cambridge, 1937-44; Senior Principal Scient. Offr., Min. of Supply, Atomic Energy Mission to Can., 1944-50; Principal Research Offr., Head of Gen. Physics Br., Atomic Energy of Can. Ltd. 1950-71; during 2nd World War, Meteorol. Office, 1939-40 Hankey Scheme, 1941-44; member of Wordie Expdn. to N.W. Greenland 1937, conducting first free balloon exper. to measure cosmic radiation near the geomagnetic pole up to an altitude of 18 miles; mem., Inter-Union Comm. on Solar-Terrestrial Physics, 1966-72; has written scient. and tech. reports and papers on cosmic radiation, space physics, solar flares, nuclear reactor control and instrumentation, fused silica micro-balance, nuclear physics, radio-active contamination control; mem. Candn. Assn. Physicists; American Geophys. Union; Protestant; recreations: sailing, golf, curling, hunting; Home: 9 Beach Ave., Deep River, Ont. K0J 1P0

CARMICHAEL, John B.W., Jr.; B.A.; executive; b. Toronto, Ont. 14 Feb. 1952; e. Upper Can. Coll. Toronto; Univ. of W. Ont. B.A. 1974; m. Kerry MacBeth 9 Oct. 1976; children: Christin, Michael; PRESIDENT AND CHIEF EXTVE. OFFR., BRODIE BRUSH CO. LTD., CARWOODS INDUSTRIES INC. 1981- ; Dir. City National Leasing Ltd.; City Buick Pontiac Cadillac Ltd.; Domestic Tank & Equipment Ltd.; joined City National Leasing Ltd. 1974 becoming Pres. prior to present appt.; recreations: golf, tennis, skiing; Home: 825 Highland Dr., West Vancouver, B.C. V7S 2G6; Office: 58 W. Sixth Ave., Vancouver, B.C. V5Y 1K1.

CARMICHAEL, John Bernard Woods, B.A.; company president; b. St. Catharines, Ont., 18 June 1926; e. Assumption Coll., Windsor, Ont.; McGill Univ., B.A. 1949; m. Collen Fitzpatrick, d. J.G. Fitzpatrick, Montreal, P.Q., 20 May 1950; children: John Jr., Colleen (deceased), Patricia, Julie, Jill; PRESIDENT, CITY BUICK PONTIAC CADILLAC LTD.; Chrmn., City National Leasing Ltd.; Chrmn., Domestic Tank & Equipment Ltd.; Dir., Warner-Lambert Canada Ltd.; Imperial Life Assurance Co. of Can.; The Northern Life Assurance Co. of Can.; Wellesley Hosp.; began career in Buffalo, N.Y. as Pres., Turb-O-Tube Furnace Inc., 1949-56; apptd. Pres., Domestic Tank

& Equipment Ltd., Scarborough, Ont., 1951; entered auto field as Pres. of City Buick Ltd. (predecessor Co.), 1955; mem., World Business Council; Jockey Club of Canada; Delta Kappa Epsilon; R. Catholic; recreations: golf, tennis; Clubs: Granite; National; Queens (Toronto); Rosedale Golf; Lyford Cay, Nassau; Home: 155 Warren Road, Toronto, Ont. M4V 2S4; Office: 1900 Victoria Park Ave., Scarborough, Ont. M1R 1T6

CARON, H. Marcel, C.A.; docteur hon. causa (Univ. de Montréal); O.C.; comptable agréé; né Montréal, Qué., 16 sept. 1919; f. Henri et Eva (Mercure) C.; é. Coll. Mt. St-Louis et Ecole des H.E.C., Montréal; ép. Madeleine, f. Henri Dussault, 26 nov. 1949; enfants: Pierre, Michèle, Marie, François, Robert; ASSOCIE EXE., CLARKSON GORDON depuis 1949 et Assoc. Woods, Gordon depuis 1957 et H. Marcel Caron et Associés depuis 1975; ancien président, Ordre des Comptables Agréés de Qué., Chambre de Commerce du District de Montréal, Club Laval-sur-le-Lac, Assoc. Can. d'Etudes Fiscales, Revue Commerce, Opéra du Quebec; Comité Canada Comté consultatif du Min. du Revenu du Qué.; Inst. Can. des Comptables Agréés; Aviseur, Corp. de l'Ecole des H.E.C. et Verificateur General du Canada; administrateur croix Blue, chaire sciences comptables; Eglise Notre Dame de Montréal; Loisirs: golf, voile, ski; Clubs: Laval-sur-le-Lac; St-Denis; Nekabong; St. James's; Résidence: 8 Courcelette, Outremont, Qué. H2V 3A6; Bureau: 2000-630 ouest, blvd. Dorchester, Montréal,Qué. H3B 1T9

CARON, Raymond, Q.C.; b. Montreal, Que., 27 Sept. 1906; s. late Adolphe Louis and late Agnes (Dulude) C.; e. High Sch. of Montreal, 1924; McGill Univ., B.A. 1928, B.C.L. 1931; m. Brenda Beryl, d. late Charles Spurr Harding, Montreal, 21 May 1932; children: Trevor Harding, Daphne Lorraine (Mrs. L.W. Shick), Derek Raymond, Melodie Molson (Mrs. H.B. Yates); COUNSEL, COURTOIS, CLARKSON, PARSONS & TETRAULT since 1965; read law with Mitchell, Ralston, Kearney & Duquet; called to Bar of Que. 1931; cr. Q.C. 1959; in practice with Mitchell, Ralston, Kearney & Duquet 1931-33; private practice 1933-36; Caron & Gillean 1936-41; Defence Industries Ltd. 1941-46; Caron & McKay and later Caron, McKay & Trépanier, 1946-65; specialist in labour law; internat. lectr., exhibitor and judge for photographic salons in Can. and U.S.; Past Pres., Royal Automobile Club of Can.; Montreal Parks & Playgrounds Assn.; Westmount Mun. Assn.; Montreal Track & Field Club; Montreal Camera Club; Montreal Clean-up Campaign; mem., Bar of Montreal; Candn. Bar Assn.; Montreal Bd. Trade; Montreal Museum of Fine Arts; Fellow, Photographic Soc. Am.; Assoc., Royal Photographic Soc. Gt. Brit.; recreations: photography, music, golf; Clubs: St. James's; Canadian; The Hermitage; Home: 4300 Blvd. DeMaisonneuve W., Westmount, Que. H3Z 1K8; Office: 22nd Floor, 630 Dorchester Blvd. W., Montreal, Que. H3B 1S6

CARPENTER, Major General Frederick S., A.F.C., C.D. (ret.); b. Toronto, Ont., 19 Sept. 1914; e. Upper Can. Coll., Toronto; Royal Mil. Coll., Kingston; RCAF War Staff Coll., 1944; Imp. Defence Coll., 1952; joined RCAF after grad. in 1937 and trained as a pilot; served with bomber reconnaissance sqdns. during Battle of Atlantic and later commanded 117 (BR) Sqdn. at North Sydney, N.S., and 9 (BR) and 160 (BR) Sqdns., both on the Pacific coast; also commanded wartime stns. at Bella Bella and Coal Harbour, B.C. before being selected for air staff duties at W. Air Command HQ, Vancouver; apptd. Dir. of Plans, AFHQ, 1943 and later became mem. Candn. Air Liaison Mission to S.E. Asia; named Dir. of Organ. and Estab., AFHQ, 1944; trans. to N.W. Air Command HQ as Sr. Personnel Staff Offr., 1947; apptd. Sr. Air Staff Offr., Training Command HQ, 1949; Chief of Training AFHQ, 1951; Chief of Operations, AFHQ, 1953; named Air Offr. Commanding Air Transport Command, 1956; returned to Ottawa as Chief of Special Studies Group, AFHQ, 1961; became Air Offr. Commanding, Maritime Air Command,

1963; apptd. Depy. Commdr., Mobile Command, 1965; Commandant, Nat. Defence Coll. 1966; Home: R.R. 1, Seeleys Bay, Ont. K0H 2N0

CARPENTER, George W., B.S.M.E.; retired utilities executive; b. Okla., 27 Aug. 1915; s. G.E. Carpenter; e. Univ. of Okla., B.S.M.E. 1936; came to Can. 1963; m. Erdine C.; children: Joe, James, Judith; Dir., Tecumseh Gas Storage Ltd.; Underwater Gas Developers Ltd.; Niagara Gas Transmission Ltd.; Home Oil Co. Ltd.; mem. Assn. Prof. Engrs. Prov. Ont.; Home: 407, 170 Roehampton Ave., Toronto, Ont. M4P 1R2

CARPENTER, Helen M., B.S., M.P.H., Ed.D.; educationalist; b. Montreal, P.Q., 29 March 1912; d. Robert George and Janet Maude (Brown) C.; ed. Univ. of Toronto (Nursing Dipl.) 1933; Teachers Coll., Columbia Univ., B.S. 1943, Ed.D. 1965; Johns Hopkins Sch. of Hygiene and Pub. Health, M.P.H. 1945; Outpost Service, Ont. Red Cross Hosps., 1933-34; Staff Supv., Asst. Dir., V.O.N., Hamilton and Toronto, 1934-42; Consultant in Pub. Health Nursing, Prov. Dept. of Health (B.C.), 1943-44; Dir., Public Health Nursing East York-Leaside Health Unit, 1945-48; Asst. Prof., Univ. of Toronto Sch. of Nursing, 1948-62, Dean, Faculty of Nursing, 1962-72, Chrmn., Grad. Dept., 1970-76, Prof. 1962-77; retired June 1977; Prof. Emeritus, 1977——; Rockefeller Foundation Fellowship (Grad. study), 1944; Candn. Red Cross Scholarship, 1959; mem., Metro Toronto District Health Counsil, 1980-; Candn. Nurses' Assn. (Pres. 1960-62); Reg'd. Nurses Assn. Ont.; Internat. Council of Nurses (Educ. Comte.); Vice-Pres., Can. Red Cross Society; Protestant; recreation: photography; Home: Apt. 1208, 77 St. Clair Ave. E., Toronto, Ont. M4T 1M5;

CARR, David William, B.A., B.S.A., M.Sc., Ph.D.; publisher; consulting economist; b. Leney, Sask., 9 Dec. 1911; s. Samuel Henry and Lillian (Moore) C.; e. Univ. of Saskatchewan, B.A., B.S.A. 1948; Univ. of Wisconsin, M.Sc. 1949; Harvard Univ., Ph.D. 1953; m. Frances Eleanor, d. Chauncey Wayne Close, Cut Knife, Sask., 10 Nov. 1939; children: Glenna Lea, Candace Gail, Gertrude Lillian (d.), Frances Lynn; PUBLISHER, "Carr's Report For Executives" 1975-76; Head, D.W. Carr & Assoc. since 1959; has served as Econ. Adviser to Dept. of Northern Affairs; St. Lawrence Seaway Authority; several Fed. Royal Comms. (Price Spreads, Transp., Banking, Finance) Nfld. Agric; Comte. on Manitoba's Econ. Future, Resources of Tomorrow, Farm Credit Corp., Emergency Measures, Atlantic Devel. Bd., Fed. Dept. of N. Devel. (Y. Terr.), etc. Director of numerous research projects in agricultural and other resource development; served in 2nd World War with R.C.A.F., 1940-45, rank on discharge Flying Offr.; author of "Recovering Canada's Nationhood" 1971; mem., Am. Econ. Assn.; Am. Men of Science; Candn. Pol. Science Assn.; United Church; Home and Office: 211 Fourth Ave., Ottawa, Ont. K1S 2L7

CARR, Ernest Patterson Cameron; company chairman; b. Ottawa, Ont., 11 Aug. 1913; s. late Albert Ernest and Florence Beatrice Cameron (Wood) C.; e. Dewson St. Pub. Sch. and Central Tech. Sch. (Scholarship 1st and 2nd yrs.), Toronto, Ont.; m. Annie Phyllis, d. late Robert Harvey Nixon. Clarkson, Ont., 19 May 1939; children: John Cameron, Elizabeth Margaret Cameron (Keddie), Joanne Cameron (Losos); CHAIRMAN, HOWELL WAREHOUSES CO. LTD. (Estbd. 1913); began business career in 1929 with T. Eaton Co. Ltd., Toronto, and held various posts with them till 1935 when he joined the present Co. as Asst. to the Vice-Pres.; Past Pres., Candn. Warehousemen's Assn.; Candn. Industrial Traffic League; Past Pres., Candn. Importers & Traders Assn.; United Church; Clubs: Granite; Empire; Board of Trade; Rotary; Home: 37 York Ridge Road, Willowdale, Ont. M2P 1R8; Office: 514 Carlingview Dr., Rexdale, Ont. M9W 5R3

CARRADINE, William J., B.A., M.B.A.; communications company executive; b. Smooth Rock Falls, Ont., 21 Jan. 1929; s. Dennis Charles and Elsie (Darby) C.; e. Univ. of W. Ont., B.A. 1951, M.B.A. 1954; m. Jacqueline Ann, d. E. Allen Millsap, London, Ont., 22 Jan. 1955; children: Susan, Catherine, Christopher; SENIOR VICE PRES. SOUTHAM INC. Chrmn., Newspaper Marketing Bureau; Dir., Today Magazine Inc.; Kitchener-Waterloo Record Ltd.; Pacific Press Ltd.; Sun Publishing Co. Ltd. (Brandon); National Ballet of Can.; Clubs: Royal Candn. Yacht; Badminton and Racq; Board of Trade; Home: 68 Warren Rd., Toronto, Ont. M4V 2R5; Office: Suite 801, 321 Bloor St. E., Toronto, Ont. M4W 1G9

CARR-HARRIS, Ian Redford, B.L.S.; artist; b. Victoria, B.C. 12 Aug. 1941; S. Gordon Grant McDonald and Rosamond (Green) C-H; e. Osgoode St. Pub. Sch. Ottawa 1952; Ashbury Coll. Ottawa 1959; Queen's Univ. B.A. 1963; Univ. of Toronto Sch. of Lib. Science B.L.S. 1964; Ont. Coll. of Art A.O.C.A. 1971; m. 1966; one d. Lise Renée; Dir. of Lib Services Ont. Coll. of Art and Faculty mem. Exper. Arts Dept.; solo exhns. incl. A Space Gallery Toronto 1971; Mezzanine Gallery N.S. Coll. Art & Design 1972; Yajama/Galerie, Montreal, 1981; Dalhousie Art Gallery, Halifax, N.S., 1982; Carmen Lamanna Gallery Toronto 1973, 1975, 1977, 1979 (2), 1981; rep. in maj. group exhns. Can., USA, Europe since 1973; rec'd several Can. Council Project Cost Grants, Jr. Arts Grant 1976, 1980 , Travel Grant 1978; Home: 68 Broadview Ave., 4th Floor, Toronto, Ont. M4M 2E6; Office: c/o Carmen Lamanna Gallery, 840 Yonge St., Toronto, Ont. M4W 2H1.

CARRICK, Donald, O.B.E., Q.C., B.A., LL.B.; b. Port Arthur, Ont., 18 Sept. 1906; s. John James and Mary Jane (Day) C.; e. N. Ward Pub. Sch., Port Arthur, Ont.; St. Andrews Coll., Toronto, Ont., 1918-24; Univ. of Toronto, B.A. 1928; Harvard Law Sch., LL.B. 1931; Osgoode Hall, Toronto, Ont.; m. Elizabeth Frazee, d. late Gerald Bunker, 1 June 1934; children: George Manton, Ellen Grover; Counsel, Carrick, O'Connor, Coutts & Crane until retired 1967; read law with the late James Bain and late Peter White, Toronto, Ont.; called to the Bar of Ont., Sept. 1934; mem. of firm of Slaght, Ferguson & Carrick, 1934-41; practised alone, 1945-49; appt. Queen's Counsel, 22 Dec. 1955; with N.P.A.M. 1940-41; served in 2nd World War, 1941-45; on active service with 12th Field Regt., R.C.A., 1941; trans. to Office of Judge Advocate Gen. in Feb. 1942 till Sept. 1945 and stationed in U.K. and Italy; Mentioned in Despatches; el. to H. of C. for Trinity (Toronto), Nov. 1954-June 1957; mem., Law Soc. of Upper Can.; Psi Upsilon; Liberal; United Church; recreation: golf; Clubs: Rotary; Rosedale Golf (Life Mem.); Scarboro Golf (Life mem.); Home: 329 Lytton Blvd., Toronto, Ont. M5N 1R9

CARRIER, Denis, M.Comm., D. de l'Un. (Paris); éducateur; né Windsor, Qué. 6 avril 1938; f. Arthur et Germaine (Desloges) C.; é. Univ. de Sherbrooke, M. Comm. 1959; Inst. d'Etudes politiques (Univ. de Paris) Dipl. Sc. pol. 1961, D. de l'Un. (Paris) 1966; ép. Lise Thibault; enfants: Luc, Julie, Marc; PROF. DES SCIENCES SOCIALES, UNIV. D'OTTAWA depuis 1962 et Vice-Recteur, Adjoint (Enseignement et Recherche) depuis 1980; Chargé de cours 1962, Prof. adjoint 1966, Prof. agrégé 1969; Dir. des études (Faculté des Sciences sociales) 1965, Secrétaire 1967, Administrateur 1969; Prés. de Comm. de révision des structures d'enseignement et de recherche de l'Univ. d'Ottawa 1972-74; Doyen de la Faculté des sciences sociales, 1970-81; auteur de "La stratégie des négociations collectives" 1967; Egalement auteur de "Une stratégie pour le changement — A Strategy for Change", 1974; résidence: 45 rue Brady, Hull, Qué. J8Y 5L5

CARRIGAN, David Owen, B.A., M.A., Ph.D.; university professor b. New Glasgow, N.S., 30 Nov. 1933; s. Ronald and Marion Constance (Hoare) C.; e. New Glasgow (N.S.) High Sch., 1951; St. Francis Xavier Univ.,

B.A. 1954; Boston Univ., M.A. 1955; Univ. of Maine, Ph.D. 1966; m. Florence Catherine, d. Ronald L. Nicholson, Sydney, N.S., 1958; children: Nancy, Janet, David. Glen. Sharon, Douglas; PROFESSOR OF HISTORY, ST. MARY'S UNIV. since 1979; Asst. Prof. of Hist., Xavier Coll., St. Francis Xavier Univ., 1957-61; Assoc. Prof. and Chrmn of the Dept. 1961-67; Assoc. Prof. of Hist., Wilfrid Laurier University, 1967-68; Principal and Dean of Arts, King's Coll., Univ. of W. Ont., 1968-71; Pres., St. Mary's Univ. 1971-79; mem., Can. Council; Council of Trustees, Inst. for Research on Public Policy; author, "Canadian Party Platforms 1867-1968", 1968; also articles for various journs.; mem., Am. Hist. Assn.; Am. Cath. Hist. Assn.; Phi Kappa Phi; Address: St. Mary's Univ.; Halifax, N.S. B3H 3C3

CARRINGTON, John W., B.A.Sc.; mining consultant; b. Fort William, Ont., 6 May 1913; s. Charles Kemp and Mary Dorothea (Shackleton) C.; e. Univ. of Toronto, B.A.Sc. (Mining Engn.) 1934; m. Clara Malcolm, d. late Alex Gray, 30 April 1938; children: Mary Catherine, Molly Malcolm, John Kemp; Retired editor, The Northern Miner; Dir., Gray Forgings and Stampings Ltd.; served in 2nd World War, Lieut., R.C.N.V.R. 1942-45; mem. Candn. Inst. Mining & Metall.; Am. Inst. Mining, Metall. & Petroleum Engrs.; Assn. Prof. Engrs. Ont.; Anglican; Clubs: Engrs. (Past Pres.); R.C.Y.C.; Beaver Fishing; Home: 85 Plymbridge Rd., Willowdale, Ont. M2P 1A2

CARROLL, Joy; journalist; author; b. Melfort, Sask. 8 July 1924; d. John Robert and Elsie (Lee) Holroyd; e. Melfort (Sask.) High Sch. Sr. Matric. 1943; Business Course 1944; Royal Conserv. of Music; m. John Alexander Carroll 17 May 1952; children: Anne Elizabeth, Barbara Evelyn, Scott Alexander, Angus John Gregory; sometime Women's Ed. Prince Albert Daily Herald; News writer C.B.C.; Script writer, Claire Wallace; Feature Ed. New World Mag.; Extve. Ed. National Home Monthly; Candn. Ed. Better Living (N.Y.); Ed. Harlequin Books; Travel Ed. Chatelaine Mag.; author of "Canadian Etiquette" (with Claire Wallace); "Night of Terror"; "Murdered Mistress"; "God & Mrs. Sullivan"; "Weekend"; "The Restless Lovers"; "The Moth"; "Soul's End"; "Five over Eden"; "Pioneer days 1840-1860"; "Proud Blood"; "Pride's Court"; also numerous articles and short stories in various Candn. and Am. newspapers, mags. and journs.; portrait painted by Harold Town 1948; Anglican; recreations: music, swimming; Home: 71 Brown St., Port Hope, Ont. L1A 3E2

CARROTHERS, Hon. (Alexander) Brian (Beatty), B.A., LL.B.; judge; b. Saskatoon, Sask. 18 Jan. 1923; s. late William Alexander and late Agnes Elizabeth (Godber) C.; e. Univ. Hill Sch.; Univ. of B.C. B.A., LL.B.; m. late Jean Elizabeth d. late Clifford O. Foss 4 March 1950; children: Douglas Alexander, Robert Brian, Linda Jean; JUSTICE OF APPEAL, COURT OF APPEAL FOR B.C. AND JUDGE, COURT OF APPEAL FOR YUKON TERRITORY since 1973; called to Bar of B.C. 1949; cr. Q.C. 1967; law practice Davis & Co. 1949-56; Douglas, Symes and Brissenden 1956-73; served with Candn. Army UK N.W. Europe (wounded Normandy beachhead), rank Capt.; Life Bencher and Treas. (1972-73) Law Soc. B.C.; former Chrmn. Nat. Sec. and Prov. Br. Pres. (1966-67) Candn. Bar Assn.; Founding Dir. and sometime Pres. B.C. Med. Services Foundation; Life Fellow and sometime Pres. Foundation for Legal Research; Trustee W. Vancouver Un. Ch.; Zeta Psi; United Church, recreation: gardening; Club: Vancouver; Home: "Stonehaven" 4648 S. Piccadilly Rd., W. Vancouver, B.C. V7W 1J7; Office: The Law Courts, 800 Smithe St., Vancouver, B.C. V6Z 2E1.

CARROTHERS, Alfred William Rooke, S.J.D., LL.D. (Sask. McMaster, Calgary); research executive; b. Saskatoon, Sask., 1 June 1924; s. William Alexander and Agnes Elizabeth (Godber) C.; e. Univ. of Brit. Columbia, B.A.

1947, LL.B. 1948; Harvard Law Sch., LL.M. 1951; S.J.D. 1966; LL.D., Univ. of Sask. 1974, McMaster 1975, Calgary 1976; Order St. Lazarus of Jerusalem; m. Margaret Jane, d. Col. Macgregor Macintosh, 1 July 1961; two s. Matthew, Jonathan; one d. Alexandra; DEAN, COMMON LAW SECTION, FACULTY OF LAW, UNIV. OF OTTAWA since 1981; President, Inst. for Research on Public Policy, since 1974; Pres., Univ. of Calgary, 1969-74; called to the Bar of B.C. 1948, Ont. 1965, Alberta 1969; Lectr., Univ. of Brit. Columbia, 1948-50; Asst. Prof. 1952-55; Assoc. Prof. 1955-60; Dir., Inst. Indus. Relations, 1960-62; Prof. 1960-64; Asst. Prof., Dalhousie Univ., 1951-52; Dean and Prof. of Law, Univ. of W. Ont. 1964-68; author of "The Labour Injunction in British Columbia", 1956; "Labour Arbitration in Canada", 1961; "Collective Bargaining Law in Canada", 1965; mem., Candn. Assn. Univ. Teachers (Past Pres.); Candn. Assn. Law Teachers; Protestant; Club: University (Vancouver, B.C.); Address: Faculty Hall, 57 Copernicus, Univ. of Ottawa, Ottawa, Ont. K1N 6N5

CARROTHERS, Gerald A.P., M.Arch., M.C.P., Ph.D.; Educator; b. Saskatoon, Sask. 1 July 1925; s. late William Alexander and late Agnes Elizabeth (Godber) C.; e. Univ. Hill Sch. Vancouver, B.C. 1943; Univ. of Man. B.Arch. 1948, M.Arch. 1951; Harvard Univ. M.C.P. 1953; Mass. Inst. of Technol. Ph.D. 1959; PROF. IN ENVIRONMENTAL STUDIES, YORK UNIV. since 1968; Lectr. and Research Planner, Univ. of Man. 1948-53; Research Asst. Mass. Inst. of Technol. 1953-56; Asst. Prof. Univ. of Toronto 1956-60; Assoc. Prof. and Prof. Univ. of Pa. 1960-67, Chrmn. Dept. City & Regional Planning 1961-65, Founding Dir. Inst. Environmental Studies 1965-67; Educ. Advisor, Central Mortgage and Housing Corp. Ottawa 1966-77; Founding Dean Faculty of Environmental Studies York Univ. 1968-76; Interim Dir., U. Of Toronto/York U. Joint Program in Trans. 1976-78; Visiting Professor, University of Nairobi, Kenya, 1978-80; Consultant advisor to various educ. prof. govt. and other pub. bodies in Can., U.S. and overseas; co-author "Methods of Regional Analysis" 1960; Founding Ed. "Plan" 1959; "Papers and Proceedings of the Regional Science Association" 1955-62; Fellow, World Acad. of Art & Science; Fellow Royal Arch. Inst. Can.; mem., Ont. Assn. Archs.; Candn. Inst. Planners; Am. Inst. Of Certified Planners; Ont. Soc. Environmental Mang.; Regional Science Assn. (Pres. 1970-71); Home: (P.O. Box 121) Concord, Ont. L4K 1B2; Office: 4700 Keele St., Downsview, Ont. M3J 2R2

CARRY, Charles William, M.Sc.; manufacturer; b. Winnipeg, Man., 19 March 1905; s. Henry Dulmage and Ida Anna (Bowler) C.; e. Pub. Schs., Winnipeg, Man.; Univ. of Manitoba, B.Sc. (Civil Engn.) 1926, M.Sc. 1929; m. Muriel Gladys, d. Thos. H. Gilmore, Kelwood, Man., 13 June 1931; one s. Roger Gilmore; with Dominion Bridge Co. Ltd., Winnipeg. Man. as Jr. Draftsman, Designer, Contract Engr., Asst. Plant Engr. of W. Plants, 1927-32; Manitoba Bridge & Engineering Works, Winnipeg, Plant Appraisal and Sales, 1932-35; Engn. and Sales Work, Riverside Iron & Engineering Works, Dom. Bridge Co., Calgary, Alta., 1936-38; Chief Engr., Standard Iron & Engineering Works, Edmonton, Alta. 1938-45; Founded C.W. Carry Ltd. and Calgary Structural Steel Ltd., in 1945 (sold both to Canada Iron Foundries Ltd. in 1958); retired from Canron 1967 as Dir. and Regional Vice Pres. and re-purchased C.W. Carry (1967) Ltd.; mem., Edmonton Chamber of Comm. (Council 1955-57; Pres., 1958-59); Engn. Inst. Can. (Life Member); Canadian Inst. of Steel Constr.; Freemason; Conservative; United Ch.; recreations: golf, travel; Clubs: Edmonton; Petroleum; Mayfair-Edmonton; Home: 701-11920 100 Ave., Edmonton, Alta. T5K 0K5; Office: 5815, 75 St., Edmonton, Alta. T6E 0T3

CARSCALLEN, Air Vice-Marshal H.M., D.F.C., C.D., B.Sc.; R.C.A.F. (retired); b. Hamilton, Ont., 9 Nov. 1908; s. Henry Gurney and Marion Susan (Myles) C.; e. Royal

Mil. Coll., Kingston, Ont., 1930; Queen's Univ., B.Sc. (Civil) 1932; m. Nancy Isabelle Frances, d. Lieut.-Col. W.B. Almon, Halifax, N.S., 14 Aug. 1940; children: Henry A., Mary M., William E., Laleah A.; Comnd. Flying Officer, R.C.A.F., June 1933; Air Survey, W. Coast and E. Can., 1934-37; promoted Flt. Lieut., 1937; Seaplane Operations, Dartmouth, N.S., 1938-39; promoted Sqdn. Leader, Nov. 1939; No. 5 (FB) Sqdn., Anti-submarine patrols from Dartmouth, N.S., from outbreak of war to June 1940; land based No. 10 Sqdn. A-S patrols, Gander, Nfld., June 1940 to end of year; promoted Wing Commdr., 1941; engaged in various patrols on E. coast, 1941-42; Bomber Command No. 6 Group, R.C.A.F. in U.K. and formed No. 424 (Bomber Sqdn.) and Commanded Squadron, 1942-43; promoted Group Captain June 1943; Stn. Commdr., 6 Group, U.K., 1943-44; Stn. Commander, R.C.A.F. Stn., Dartmouth N.S. for 9 mths. of 1944; Army-Navy Staff Coll. U.S.A. in fall of 1944 to spring of 1945; attached to XXI Bomber Command USAF, Guam. at time of Japanese surrender; Air Attaché, Washington, D.C., 1945-47; Dir. of Personnel Adm., Air Force Hdqrs., Ottawa, 1947-48; promoted Air Commodore 1948; Chief Staff Offr., N.W. Air Command, Edmonton, Alta., 1948-50; Chief of Air Operations Air Force Hdqrs., Ottawa, 1950-53; attended Nat. Defence Coll., Kingston, Ont., 1953-54; A.O.C. Air Transport Command, 1954-56; Chief of Staff Fourth Allied Tactical Air Force, Germany, 1956-60; promoted to Air Vice Marshal 1960; A.O.C., Training Command, 1960-63; retired July 1963; Zeta Psi; Anglican; recreations: fishing, hunting; Clubs: Rideau; Five Lakes Fishing; Address: 771 Acacia Lane, Ottawa, Ontario K1M 0M9

CARSON, John Jarvis, O.C. (1976), M.A. LL.D., D.U.: educator; b. Vancouver, B.C. 11 Oct. 1919; e. Univ. of B.C. B.A. 1943; Univ. of Toronto M.A. (Psychol.) 1948; York Univ. LL.D. 1972; Univ. of Ottawa D.U. 1975; widower; children: Elizabeth, John, Faith, Deborah, Daniel, Katharine; DEAN, FACULTY OF ADM., UNIV. OF OTTAWA since 1976; Prof., Fac. of Admin. 1981-; Sr. Personnel Consultant J.D. Woods & Gordon Ltd. Toronto 1946-52; Mgr. of Manpower Planning & Devel. Ont. Hydro 1952-54, Dir. Employee Relations 1954-56; Dir. Indust. Relations B.C. Electric, Vancouver 1956, Vice Pres. Indust. Relations 1958, Vice Pres. and Asst. to Pres. 1960-61; Dir. of Manpower Project Royal Comm. on Govt. Organ. Ottawa 1961-62; Mgr. Staff Services B.C. Hydro & Power Authority, Vancouver 1962-64; Special Advisor on Personnel to Secy. of Treasury Bd. Can. Ottawa 1964-65; Chrmn. Pub. Service Comn. of Can. 1965-76; Past Pres. Children's Foundation of B.C.; Narcotic Addiction Foundation B.C.; Nat. Council YMCA's Can.; Prov. Commr. St. John Ambulance Bgde. B.C.; Dir. CUSO; Community Fdn. of Ottawa and District; Cercle Universitaire; named Commdr. Order St. John Jerusalem; rec'd Alumni Merit Award Univ. of B.C. 1968; Order of Can. 1976; frequent guest speaker; author numerous publs.; Hon. Life mem. Nat. Council YMCA's Can.; mem., B.C. Psychol. Assn.; Candn. Psychol. Assn.; Indust. Relations & Personnel Mang. Assn. B.C.; Internat. Civil Service Adv. Bd.; Internat. Personnel Mang. Assn.; Spec. Adv. Bd., Min. of Employment and Immig.; Office: 115 Wilbrod St., Ottawa, Ont.

CARTER, Most Rev. Alexander, B.A., L.Th., J.C.L., LL.B. (R.C.); bishop; b. Montreal, Que., 16 April 1909; s. Thomas J. and Mary (Kelty) C.; e. St. Patrick's Sch. (Grad. 1924); College de Montréal (Grad. 1930); Semy. of Philosophy, B.A. 1932; Grand Semy. of Theol., L.Th. 1936; Appolinaris Law Sch., Rome, J.C.L. 1939; Laurentian Univ., LL.B. (honoris causa), 1962; BISHOP OF SAULT STE. MARIE, since 1958; Chancellor, Univ. of Sudbury; Vice-Chancellor, Montreal, 1940-46; Chancellor, Winnipeg, 1946-47; Vice-officials Matrimonial Tribunal, Montreal, 1948-53; Parish Priest, Holy Family, Montreal, 1953-57; apptd. Bishop of Sault Ste. Marie, 1958;

Publication: "Answers"; recreations: fishing, hunting; Address: 480 McIntyre, North Bay, Ont. P1B 2Z4

CARTER, (Mrs.) Alixe; novelist; journalist; b. Ottawa, Ont., d. late Percy Alexander and late Pearl Bennett Carson; e. St. Hilda's Sch. for Girls, Calgary, Alta.; m. Rudolph Leon, Pauls Valley, Okla., 1937 (divorced 1965); children: Nancy, Carson, Rudolph; a Dir., CBC, 1958-64; Candn. Comm. of UNESCO, 1960-64; Vice-Chrmn., Salmon Arm B.C. Sch. Bd., 1948-54; Candn. Women's Press Club mem. award, for news 1956; Media Club of Can. award for columns (Ottawa "Journal") 1976; Clubs: Media; National Press; Zonta; Mystery Writers of America; Home: 150 Queen Elizabeth Dr. Ottawa, Ont. K2P 1E7

CARTER, David Giles, M.A., F.S.A.; art consultant in fine arts and museology; b. Nashua, N.H., 2 Nov. 1921; s. Eliot Avery and Edith Berdan Gardner C.; e. Fessenden Sch., W. Newton, Mass. (Dipl. 1936); Phillips Acad., Andover, Mass. (Dipl. 1941); Princeton Univ., A.B. 1944; Harvard Univ., M.A. 1949; New York Univ., 1949-51; m. Louise, d. Chauncey Belknap; children: Mrs. Charles J. (Deborah Lamont) Carter Conroy, Howard Giles, Margaret Belknap, Pamela Hobart; DIR., MONTREAL MUSEUM OF FINE ARTS, 1964-76; Volunteer, Metrop. Museum of Art, N.Y., 1950 and Student Fellow M.M.A., 1951; Fellow, Brussels Art Seminar Belgium, 1951; Curatorial Asst., Dept. of Paintings, Metrop. Museum of Art, N.Y., 1952-54; Curator of Paintings & Prints, The John Herron Museum of Art, Indianapolis, 1955-59; Dir. Museum of Art, Rhode Island Sch. of Design, Providence, 1959-64; U.S. Diplomatic Courier, 1944-47; awarded by Italian Govt. Gold Medal of Culture, 1963; Juror at various exhns.; author of articles, reviews in various art journs., catalogues and bulls.; mem. Am. Assn. (Museums); Armour & Arms Soc. (Corr.); Armour & Arms Club of Am.; Coll. Art Assn. Am.; Deutscher Verein für Kunstwissenschaft; The Mediaeval Acad. of Am.; AAM-ICOM; former mem., Assn. of Art Museum Dir.; Candn. Assn. Museum Dirs. Organ. (past pres.); CAN-ICOM; mem., Comte. des biens culturels du Qué. 1974-76; Trustee, Eli Whitney Museum, Hamden, C.T.; Bd. mem., Preservation Trust of New Haven, C.T.; Hon. mem., United Services Club Ltd.; Protestant; recreations: hiking, sailing, photography, collecting art; Clubs: The Terrace; The Grolier; New Haven Lawn; Home: 100 Edgehill Road, New Haven, Conn.

CARTER, Edward Robert Erskine, B.C.L.; Q.C.; b. Saint John, N.B., 20 Feb. 1923; s. Arthur Norwood, Q.C. and Edith Isobel (Ireland) C.; e. Univ. of New Brunswick, 1940-42; Osgoode Hall, Toronto, Ont., 1945-47; Rhodes Scholar for N.B., 1947; Univ. of New Brunswick Law Sch., B.C.L. 1947; Oxford Univ., B.C.L. 1949; m. Verna Leman, d. Rev. H. Andrews, Pointe Claire, Que., 31 May 1947; children: Edward Robert Erskine, Jr., Ian Christopher, Jennifer Ann, Sandra; COUNSEL, BORDEN AND ELLIOT; former President and Chief Extve. Offr., Hambro Canada Ltd. 1973-75; Chrmn. and Pres., Advocate Mines Ltd.; Dir., Bank of Montreal; Westrox Industries Ltd.; Sun Alliance Insurance Co.; Global Nat. Resources Ltd; British Candn. Resources Ltd., read law with McMillan, Binch, Wilkinson, Berry & Wright, Toronto, Ont.; called to Bar of New Brunswick 1947 and Ontario 1951; associated with A.N. Carter, Q.C., in practice of law, Saint John, N.B. 1949-53; Legal Officer, Abitibi Power & Paper Co. Ltd., Toronto, Ont., 1953-54; joined Fennell, McLean, Seed & Carter, 1954; became a Partner, 1955-58; former President, Patino Mining Corporation. 1957-72; served in 2nd World War with Royal Candn. Arty., 1942-44; on loan to 7th K.O.S.B., 1st Brit. Airborne Div., 1944; P.O.W. Sept. 1944-Apl. 1945; mem., Mining Assn. of Can. (Dir.); Zeta Psi; Anglican; recreations: swimming, tennis; Clubs: University; Toronto; Office: 250 University Ave., Toronto, Ont.

CARTER, His Eminence G. Emmett, L.Th., M.A., LL.D., D.D., D.H.L., Ph.D.; Cardinal (R.C.); b. Montreal, Que., 1 March 1912; s. Thomas Joseph and Mary (Kelty) C.; e. St. Patrick's Boy's Sch., Montreal; Montreal Coll.: Univ. of Montreal, B.A. 1933, B.Th. 1936, M.A. 1940, Ph.D. 1947; LL.D., Univ. of W. Ont., LL.D. (hon.) Concordia Univ. 1976, Univ. 1976, Univ. of Windsor 1977; D.D. (hon.) Huron Coll., Univ. of W. Ont. 1978; D. Litt., St. Mary's University, Halifax, 1980; LL.D. McGill Univ., Montreal, 1980; LL.D. Notre Dame Univ., 1981; Elevated to Sacred College of Cardinals, June 1979; app'ted Mem. Secretariate for Non-Christians and Secretariate for Christian unity 1979; D.H.L. Duquesne; ARCHBISHOP OF TORONTO, since June 1978; Titular Bishop of Altiburo, 1961 (consecrated 2 Feb. 1962); o. Priest 1937; Supv., Montreal Cath. Sch. Comn., 1937-39; Founder and Principal, The St. Joseph Teachers Coll.; Charter mem. and first Pres., Thomas More Inst. for Adult Educ., 1945; Eng. Commr. of the Montreal Cath. Sch. Comn., 1948-61; Rector, St. Lawrence Coll., Quebec, 1961; Chaplain, Newman Club of McGill Univ., 1941-56; three terms as Nat. Chaplain, Candn. Fed. of Newman Clubs; elevated Hon. Canon of the Basilica of Our Lady Queen of the World, Montreal, 1953; Commdr. of Order of Scholastic Merit of Que., 1958; Conventual Chaplain, Kts. of Malta, 1960; Auxiliary Bishop of London, 1961-64; Bishop of London, 1964-68; apptd. Chancellor. Assumption Univ., 1964; apptd. by Pope Paul VI Candn. Rep. at Consilium for Liturgy, Rome, 1966; Chrmn., Candn., Liturg. Comm. (Eng. Sector) and Pres., Office of Liturgy (Eng. Sector) C.C.C.B., 1966; Vice-Pres., Doctrine and Faith Dept. C.C.C.B., 1969; C.C.O. 1971-73; C.C.C.B. 1973-75; Pres., C.C.C.B. 1975-77; mem., Sacred Cong. for Divine Worship 1970; Perm. Council of the Synod, 1978; Chrmn., Internat. Comte. for Eng. in the Liturgy 1971; Publications: "Catholic Public Schools of Quebec", 1957: "Psychology and the Cross", 1959; "The Modern Challenge to Religious Education", 1961; recreations: skiing, tennis, swimming; Address: 355 Church St., Toronto, Ont. M5B 1Z8

CARTER, Harriet Estelle, R.C.A.; artist (prof. name Harriet Manore Carter); b. Grand Bend, Ont. 22 March 1929; d. late Lloyd Avery and late Clarissa (Hamilton) Manore; e. H. B. Beal Tech. & Comm. High Sch. London, Ont. 1948; Dundas Valley Sch. of Fine Art 1967-68; m. John G. Carter 20 Jan. 1951; children: Mrs. Lynn Anne Powell, Brian John, Scott Lloyd; prof. painter since 1969; comm. designer for glass co. 1948-51; exhns. incl. Nat. Acad. Gallery N.Y. City 1972; Harbour Front Toronto 1975; Art Gallery of Ont. 1975-76; Tokyo, Hiroshima, Nagoya 1976, also Montreal, Toronto and Calgary; Equinox, B.C. 1977; exhn. and seminar Sarnia Pub. Gallery 1977; solo exhns. Nancy Poole's Studio 1972, 1974, 1976, 1977, 1980; Group show W. End Gallery Edmonton 1980; 1981 Group Exhibition, "Cloud Flowers, Rhododendrons East and West", on tour until 1983; rep. in various private and pub. colls. incl. Lt. Gov.'s Coll., Can. Council Art Bank, Hart House Toronto; mem. Candn. Soc. Painters in Water Colour; Ont. Soc. Artists; Royal Candn. Acad.; Liberal; Anglican; recreations: wild-flowers, exploring small towns and villages, auctions; Home: 78 MacLennan Ave., Hamilton, Ont. L8V 1X6; Office: Nancy Pooles Studio, 16 Hazelton Ave., Toronto, Ont.

CARTER, Harry Havilland, M.A.; diplomat; b. Toronto, Ont., 4 Jan. 1918: s. Basil Brooke and Mary Isobel (Casey) C.; e. Lakefield Prep. Sch. (1929-32); Upper Canada Coll. (1932-34); Univ. of Toronto, B.A. (Pol. Science and Econs.) 1938, M.A. 1940; m. Pamela Christine, d. Stephen W. Price, 4 Dec. 1948: two d. Vivien P., Valerie I.; joined Dept. of External Affairs after war service: has served in Wash., The Hague, New York and New Delhi; apptd. Head of U.S.A. Div., Jan. 1961: subsequently Ambassador to Finland then to S. Africa: currently Dir. Historical Division; served in 2nd World War; enlisted as Gunner. 1940, Commnd. Aug. 1940; served with 1st Field

Regt., R.C.H.A. 3rd Medium Regt., R.C.A.; discharged with rank of Capt., 1944; Kappa Alpha; Anglican; recreations: photography, reading, music; Home: 155 Blenheim Drive, Rockcliffe Park, Ottawa, Ont.; Office: Dept. of External Affairs, 125 Sussex Drive, Ottawa, Ont. K1A 0G2

CARTER, Madame Justice Mary Yvonne, B.A., LL.B.; judge; b. Cromer, Man. 11 Oct. 1923; d. William George and Jean May (Marshall) Munn; e. Nutana High Sch. Saskatoon 1941; Univ. of Sask. B.A. 1944, LL.B. 1947; m. Roger Colenso Carter 14 June 1947; children: Stephen, Sarah, Martha, Michael, Mark, Adam; COURT OF QUEEN'S BENCH since July, 1981; Local Judge, Court of Queen's Bench and Judge of Unified Family Court since 1978; called to Bar of Sask. 1948; practiced law in partnership with spouse 1948-53; Part-time Magistrate and Judge of Magistrate's Court 1960-72; Judge of Magistrate's Court 1972-78; Anglican; recreations: gardening, cooking, bird watcher; Home: 420 Cumberland Ave. S., Saskatoon, Sask. S7H 2L4; Office: Unified Family Court, 9th Floor, Canterbury Place, 224 4th Ave. S., Saskatoon, Sask. S7K 5M5

CARTER, Thomas Le Mesurier, M.C., B.A., M.Sc.; diplomat; b. Toronto, Ont., 10 June 1915; s. Basil Brooke and Mary Isabel (Casey) C.; e. Bishop's Univ., B.A. 1934; Univ. of London M.Sc. (Econ.) 1939; m. 1stly, Marie-Louise (d. 1973), d. Charles Pattin, 11 Sept. 1954; one d. Monique; m. 2ndly, Alice, d. Jean Cléjan, 6 June 1974; joined Candn. Foreign Service, 1945; served in Dept. of External Affairs, Ottawa, and in Missions in Brussels, Berne and Rome; Chargé d'Affaires, Candn. Legation, Warsaw, 1952-54; Candn. Commr., Internat. Supv. Comn., Vietnam, 1957-59; attended Imp. Defence Coll., London, 1959; High Commr. to Nigeria, 1960-64; Ambassador to Arab Republic of Egypt 1967; Ambassador to the Netherlands 1972-76; currently Ambassador to Austria; served in 2nd World War; enlisted in R.C.A.; 2nd Lieut. 1940; U.K., Italy and France; discharged with rank of Capt. 1945; Anglican; recreation: golf; Address: 10 Karl Luegerring, Vienna 1, Austria

CARTER, Tullis Ninion, E.M.; construction executive; b. Winnipeg, Man., 6 Jan. 1906; s. William Henry and Julia (Tullis) C.; e. St. John's Coll. Sch., Winnipeg; Univ. of Minnesota, E.M., 1931; m. Margaret Wilmot, d. George W. Swaisland, Vancouver, June 1934; children: William Swaisland, Julia Anne, Patricia Jane; PRESIDENT & DIR., THE CARTER CONSTRUCTION CO. (1973) LTD.; organ. The Carter Constr. Co. Ltd., Toronto, 1943; Nat. Pres. Candn. Construction Assn. 1957-58; Chrmn., Constr. Safety Assn., 1940-42; Pres., Ont. Gen. Contractors' Assn., 1943-44; Dir., Ont. Road Builders' Assn.; mem., Prof. Engrs. Ont.; Delta Kappa Epsilon; Sigma Gamma Epsilon; United Church; recreation: golf; Clubs: Engineers'; Rosedale Golf; Home: 3 Valleyana Dr., Toronto, Ont. M4N 1J7; Office: 66 Sixteenth E., Thornhill, Ont. L3T 3P4

CARTER, Hon. Walter C., M.H.A.; b. Greenspond, Bonavista Bay, Nfld. 8 March 1929; s. Ethelred and Beatrice (Pond) C.; m. Muriel d. late Allan Baker; children: Roger, David, Donna, Gregory, Bonnie, Susan, Glen, Paul; Min. of Fisheries, Nfld. 1975-79; el. St. John's Mun. Council 1961, re-el. 1965, Depy. Mayor 1966; el. M.H.A. for White Bay North 1962; el. to H. of C. for St. John's West 1968, re-el. 1972, 1974, resigned 1975 to re-enter prov. politics; el. M.H.A. for St. Mary's-The Capes 1975; Anglican; Home: 27 Cambridge Ave., St. John's, Nfld. A1A 3N5; Office: Viking Bldg., Wishingwell Rd., St. John's, Nfld. A1C 5T7.

CARTIER, Céline; bibliothécaire; né Lacolle, Qué. 10 mai 1930; f. Henri et Marie-Reine (Boudreau) Robitaille; é. Univ. de Montréal, Diplôme supérieur pédagogie 1948, Certificats en litt. et ling. 1952; Ecole de bibliothécaires-docum. Paris, Diplôme 1962; Ecole nationale d'adm. publique, Qué. Maîtrise en adm. publique 1976; ép. Georges Cartier 29 novembre 1952; enfants: Nathalie, Guillaume; DIRECTEUR GENERAL DES BIBLIOTHEQUES, UNIV. LAVAL 1979- ; Dir. de la Bibliothèque centrale, Commission des écoles catholiques de Montréal 1964-73; Dir. des collections spéciales Univ. du Qué., Montréal 1973-76, Dir. des bibliothèques de secteurs 1976-77; Chef de la Bibliothèque générale, Univ. Laval 1977-78; auteur "Cours de français" 1958; "Recontre sur la bibliothéconomie québécoise" 1975; textes radiophoniques á Radio-Can., confs., articles, contrib. aux revues professionnelles dans les sciences de l'information; mem. Candn. Lib. Assn.; Am. Lib. Assn.; récreations: musique, lire, skiing, natation; Adresse: 1130, Chemin Ste-Foy, #106, Québec, Qué. G1S 4P7; Bureau: Québec, Qué. G1K 7P4.

CARTIER, Georges, B. ès A., L. ès L.; bibliothécaire; écrivain; n. L'Assomption, Qué., 4 avr. 1929; f Rosaire-D. et Marguerite (Mathieu) C.; e Externat classique Sainte-Croix; Univ. de l'Assomption; Univ. de Montréal, B. ès A . 1948, L. ès L., 1951, Bacc. en bibliothéconomie, 1952, D. ès L. (scolarité), 1955; Coll. de France, Paris, Cours d'esthétique, 1956-57; ép Céline, f d'Henri Robitaille, Rosemont, Qué., 29 nov. 1952; enfants: Nathalie, Guillaume; Directeur général des Arts et des Lettres au ministère des Affaires culturelles depuis 1977; Bibliothèque Saint-Sulpice, Montréal (Ministère des Affaires culturelles du Qué.), conservateur, 1964-67; conservateur en chef, Bibliothèque Nationale du Qué. 1967-73; Directeur de l'Ecole de Bibliotheconomie de l'Université de Montreal 1973-77; UNESCO, Paris, chargé du Service de distribution de la Div. de la presse, Dépt de l'information, 1961-64; Collège Sainte Marie, directeur de la bibliothèque, 1958-61; Commission des Ecoles catholiques de Montréal, asst-dir. des bibliothèques scolaires, 1955-57, et coordonnateur du Service technique (classification et catalogage), 1952-55; Publications: "Hymnes-Isabelle", 1954; "La Mort à Vivre", paru en Belgique, (Prix Inter-France, 1955); "Laves et Neiges", 1954; "Obscure navigation du temps", 1956; "Le Poisson pêché", (Prix du Cercle du Livre de France), 1964; 'Chanteaux" (poemes) 1976; et collaboré: revues, journaux, Radio-Canada; mem. Corp. des bibliothécaires professionels du Qué.; Bureau: 225, av. Grande-Allée E., Quebec, Qué. G1R 5G5

CARTIER, Max K., executive; b. Thun, Switzerland, 13 Nov. 1926; e. Dipl. Business Adm. Switzerland; Univ. of Syracuse studies in Finance; m. children: Robert, Kenneth, Carine, Alissa; PRESIDENT ANDCHIEF EXTVE. OFFR., CREDIT SUISSE CANADA; Asst. Treas. The Singer Co. New York 1960-67; Vice Pres. Morgan Guaranty Trust Co. of New York 1967-77; Sr. Vice Pres. Credit Suisse, Zurich 1977; Office: (P.O. Box 179) Commerce Court W., Toronto, Ont. M5L 1K2.

CARTON, Gordon Robert, Q.C., B.A.; company executive; b. Toronto, Ont., 14 July 1921; s. Arthur and Isabella Lucinda (Bain) C.; e. Victoria Coll., Univ. of Toronto, B.A. 1946; Osgoode Hall Law Sch., 1949; m. Marjorie Helen, d. Lt. Col. Frank Davis, 13 Sept. 1941; two d., Heather Diane, Janice Anne; VICE-PRES., LEGAL & CORP. AFFAIRS, SILVERWOOD INDUSTRIES LTD.; Bd. of Dirs., Direct Transportation Ltd.; Bd. of Govs., York Univ.; called to the Bar of Ontario 1949; cr. Q.C. 1961; el. M.P.P. 1963; re-el. 1967, 1971; apptd. Min. of Labour, Ont., March 1971; Min. of Transport & Communications Feb. 1972; served with RCAF 1941-45; rank Flying Offr., Navig.-Bombardier; Past Nat. Pres., Candn. Progress Club; Past Pres., YMCA; mem., Candn. Bar Assn.; Co. York Law Assn.; P. Conservative; United Church; Home: 4000 Yonge St., Toronto, Ont. M4N 2N9; Office: 6205 Airport Rd., Mississauga, Ont. L4V 1E1

CARTWRIGHT, Alton S., B.Sc.; manufacturer; b. Casper, Wyo., 7 Oct. 1922; s. Blanche (Harper) and late Stuart C.; e. Univ. of Denver (Econ.) 1942; Oregon State Univ., B.Sc. (Elect. Engn.) 1944; Harvard Univ. Grad.

Sch. of Business Adm. 1968-69 (Advanced Mang. Program); m. Adelaide, d. late Frank Igoe, 22 Dec. 1951; children: Stuart Andrew, Matthew Alton, David Francis, Patrick Harper; CHRMN., CHIEF EXTVE. OFFR. AND DIR., CANADIAN GENERAL ELECTRIC CO. LTD. since 1977; Dir., Dominion Engineering Works Ltd.; commenced with General Electric Co., Engn. — Consumer Products, Bridgeport, Conn. 1946, Engn. — Meters and Instruments, Lynn, Mass. 1947, Research and Devel. Center — Devel. Engn., Motors and Generators — Engn., Apparatus Sales Engr., Schenectady, N.Y. 1948; Product Planner — Motors, Lynn. Mass. 1952. Advertising Mgr., Erie, Pa. 1953, Production Control Supv. 1956, Mgr. — Sales, Adjustable Speed Drives 1957, Mgr. — Marketing, Direct Current Motors 1960, Mgr. — Product Sec., Adjustable Speed Drives 1963, Gen. Mgr. — Direct Current Motor & Generator Dept. 1965; joined present Co. as Vice-Pres., Apparatus & Heavy Machinery Div., Montreal 1970, Extve. Vice-Pres., Toronto 1972, Pres. and Dir. 1972; Special assignment General Electric Co. in Europe and Asia (incl. estab. Drive Systems Co. Ltd., Tokyo, Japan) 1965-70; served in U.S. Army Signal Corps 1942-46; enlisted Pte., Hon. Discharge with rank of First Lt.; Past Dir., Red Cross (United Fund Campaign Vice-Chrmn., Erie, Pa.); Mercyhurst Coll., Pa.; Hamot Hosp.; St. Vincent Hosp., Erie, Pa.; Reg'd P.Eng., Commonwealth of Mass.; mem. Conference Bd. of Can.; Conference Bd. Inc. (N.Y.); Policy Comte, Business Council on Nat. Issues; Wellesly Hosp. Research Advisory Bd.; Sigma Alpha Epsilon; recreations: tennis, skiing; Clubs: Toronto Lawn Tennis; Toronto; Home: 259 Dunvegan Rd., Toronto, Ont.; Office: P.O. Box 417, Commerce Court Postal Stn., Toronto, Ont. M5L 1J2

CARVER, David H., A.B., M.D.; physician, educator; b. Boston, Mass. 18 Apl. 1930; s. Elias and Charlotte (Jaffe) C.; e. Harvard Univ. A.B.; Duke Univ. M.D.; m. Patricia Jo d. late Israel Nair 2 Aug. 1963; children: Randolph Nair, Rebecca Lynn, Leslie Allison; PROF. AND CHRMN. OF PEDIATRICS, UNIV. OF TORONTO since 1976; Phys.-in-Chief, Hosp. for Sick Children since 1976; Intern (Med.) Johns Hopkins 1955-56; Research Fellow (Pediatrics), Western Reserve 1956-58; Jr. Resident, Children's Hosp. Boston 1958-59, Sr. Resident 1959-60, Chief Resident 1960-61; Research Fellow (Pediatrics) Harvard 1961-63; Asst. Prof. of Pediatrics and Microbiol. Albert Einstein 1963-66; Assoc. Prof. of Pediatrics, Johns Hopkins 1966-73, Assoc. Prof. of Microbiol. 1966-76, Prof. of Pediatrics 1973-76; served with USPHS Epidemic Intelligence Service 1956-58; rec'd Schaffer Award for Teaching, Johns Hopkins 1973; Bain Award for Teaching, Hosp. Sick Children 1978; mem. Ed. Bd. Pediatrics 1972-78; Comte. on Infectious Diseases Am. Acad. Pediatrics 1973-79; Study Sec. USPHS Center for Disease Control 1971-73; Prov. Research Grants Review Comte. Ont. Ministry of Health since 1977 (Chmn. since 1981); author various articles research virology and infectious diseases; mem. Soc. Pediatric Research; Am. Pediatric Soc.; Am. Acad. Pediatrics; Infectious Disease Soc. Am.; Candn. Pediatric Soc.; Candn. Infectious Disease Soc.; Am. Soc. Microbiol.; Am. Soc. of Virology; Am. Assn. Advanc. Science; Jewish; Home: 17 Lynwood Ave., Toronto, Ont. M4V 1K3; Office: 555 University Ave., Toronto, Ont. M5G 1X8.

CARVER, Hon. Horace Boswell, Q.C., M.L.A., LL.B.; politician; b. Charlottetown, P.E.I. 29 Dec. 1948; s. Gordon Russell and Celia Mae (White) C.; e. Prince of Wales Coll. Charlottetown; Dalhousie Univ. B.A., LL.B.; m. Lucile Barbara d. Laurie Burton Conrod, Dartmouth, N.S. 19 May 1973; children: Jonathan Boswell (d.), Julie Lucile; ATTY. GEN. AND MIN. OF JUSTICE P.E.I. and Govt. House Leader 1979- ; called to Bar of P.E.I. 1973; cr. Q.C. 1979; Partner, Foster, Carruthers, Carver & O'Keefe 1975-79; Carver, Matheson & Matheson, 1981-; P. Cons. cand. Third Queens prov. g.e. 1974 (def.); el. M.L.A. for Third Queens prov. g.e. 1978, re-el. 1979; apptd. Atty. Gen.

and Min. of Pub. Works 1979; del. from P.E.I. to 1980 Constitutional Confs.; Past Pres. Protestant Family Service Bureau; Hon. mem. Un. Services Offrs. Club; mem. Candn. Bar Assn.; P.E.I. Law Soc.; P. Conservative; Church of Christ; recreations: reading, gardening, travel; Home: 55 Goodwill Ave., Charlottetown, P.E.I. C1A 3E4; Office: (P.O. Box 2000) Charlottetown, P.E.I. C1A 7N8.

CARVER, Humphrey Stephen Mumford, LL.D.; b. Birmingham, Eng. 29 Nov. 1902; s. Frank and Annie J. H. (Creswell) C.; e. Rugby Sch. Eng. 1921; Corpus Christi Coll. Oxford Univ. 1924; Sch. of Arch. London, Eng. A.R.I.B.A.; Queen's Univ. LL.D. 1979; came to Can. 1930; m. 1stly Mary Robertson d. Rev. Dr. Charles W. Gordon Sept. 1933; one s. Peter Gordon King; m. 2ndly Anne Harley d. Mr. Justice George Sedgewick Nov. 1951; two d. Deborah Anne, Jane Mary Creswell; Partner, Borgstrom & Carver, Landscape Archs. & Town Planners 1931-37; Lectr. Sch. of Arch. Univ. of Toronto 1938-41, Research Assoc. Sch. of Social Work 1946-48; Chrmn. Research Comte. Central Mortgage & Housing Corp. 1948-55, Chrmn. Adv. Group 1955-67; served with Candn. Army NDHQ Ottawa 1942-45, rank Maj.; author "Cities in the Suburbs" 1962; "Compassionate Landscape" 1975; numerous articles on city and community planning, urbanization, housing; Fellow and former Pres. Candn. Inst. Planners; Hon. mem. Candn. Soc. Landscape Archs.; NDP; recreation: watercolour painting; Club: Arts & Letters (Toronto); Home: 421 Lansdowne Rd. N., Ottawa, Ont. K1M 0X8.

CASAVANT, Marcel J.M., banker; b. Granby, Qué. 19 Sept. 1932; m. Thérèse Lacroix 14 May 1955; children: two sons, two daughters; SR. VICE-PRÉS., PROVINCE OF QUÉBEC, CANADIAN IMPERIAL BANK OF COMMERCE 1981- ; joined Bank, Granby, Qué. 1950; Mgr., Pie IX & Jean Talon, Montréal 1959; Asst. Mgr., Main Branch, Montréal 1968; Mgr., Main Branch, Montréal 1971; Asst. Gen. Mgr., Québec 1975; Vice-Pres. and Regional Gen. Mgr., Montréal Region 1977; Sr. Vice-Pres. and Regional Gen. Mgr., Montréal Region 1981; mem. Bd. Fondation de l'UQAM; Hôtel-Dieu de Montreal; Orchestre Symphonique de Montréal; Montreal Assoc. for the Blind; Past Chairman of the Candn. Council of Christians and Jews (Montréal); Mem. Adv. Bd. Salvation Army; Gov. Spera Foundation Inc.; Clubs: Saint-Denis; Mount Royal; Forest & Stream; Royal Montréal Golf; Home: 64 Franklin, Town of Mount Royal, Qué. H3P 1B7; Office: 1155 Dorchester Blvd. W., Montréal, Qué. H3B 3Z4

CASE, Frank Elliott; retired trust company officer; b. Montreal, Que., 11 Feb. 1910; s. Thomas Robert Francis and Grace Edith (Elliott) C.; e. Public School and Collegiate, Toronto, Ont.; m. Jessie Olga, d. Rudolph Dunbar, Barrie, Ont., 10 April 1939; children: Thomas Robert, Isabel Julia, Peter Elliott; Dir., Imperial Life Assurance Co. of Canada; Shawinigan Group Inc.; Quebec Iron and Titanium Corp.; Arlen Realty Inc., New York; Pres., Kennecott Canada Ltd.; entered the Royal Bank of Canada in Toronto, Ontario, 1928; served in various branches throughout Ontario and in Ontario Supervisor's Dept.; trans. to Credit Dept. H.O., 1939; appt. Asst. Mgr., Montreal Br., 1941; served in R.C.N., 1942-45, retiring with rank of Lieut.; after war returned to Invest. Dept. at H.O. 1945; Supv. of Investments 1953, Asst. Gen. Mgr. 1960, Depy. Gen. Mgr. 1963-64, Gen. Mgr. 1964-67; Pres. and Chief Extve. Offr., Montreal Trust Co. 1967-71, Chrmn. and Chief Executive Officer 1971-75; retired 1975; Anglican; Clubs: Brockville Country; The Toronto; Canadian (N.Y.); Mount Royal; Forest & Stream; Home: (P.O. Box 711) Brockville, Ont. K6V 5V8

CASEY, Daniel William; retired banker; b. Amherst, Nova Scotia, 6 Dec. 1910; s. William Weldon and Mina Lucinda (Almy) C.; e. Public and High Schs., Amherst, N.S.; Fellow, Candn. Bankers' Assn., Queen's Univ.;

Univ. of W. Ont. (Business Mang. summer course); m. Dorothy Bertha Pinkney, 8 May 1948; children: John William, Deborah Jane, Janet Elizabeth; Dir., Lloyds Bank International. Can.; Acklands Ltd.; Dylex Ltd.; served in 2nd World War, Capt. R.C.A.P.C.; Anglican; Club: Rosedale Golf; Home: Apt. 803, 62 Wellesley St. W., Toronto, Ont. M5S 1C3

CASGRAIN, (C.) Perrault, O.C. (1973), Q.C.; LL.D. b. Que., Que., 18 Jan. 1898; s. Charles Perrault and Germaine (Mousseau) C.; e. Que. Semy.; Coll. of Ste-Anne de la Pocatière, Que.; St. Procopius Coll. nr. Chicago, Ill.; Laval Univ., B.A. LL.L.; m. Lydie, d. J.E. Prince, K.C., LL.D., Quebec, Que., 25 May 1921; children: Suzanne (Mrs. Douglas Hart), Andre Perrault, Pierre, Phillippe, Michelle (Mrs. Michel Bérard), Louise (Mrs. Jacques Brillant); SR. COUNSEL, LAVERY, O'BRIEN; cr. K.C. 1930; served in 1st World War with 1st Canadian Tank Bn., April 1918; M.L.A., Quebec, 1939-44; Minister without Portfolio, Que., 1942-44; mem., Candn. Bar Assn. (Pres. 1966-67); Pres., Que. Rural Bar Assn., 1943-44; Vice Pres. for Can., Union Internationale des Avocats, 1968-73; LL.D. HONORIS CAUSA, Dalhousie University, 1967; Liberal; R. Catholic; recreation: golf; Clubs: Hermitage, University (Montreal); Home: 33 Azgyle Ave., St. Lambert, P.Q. J4P 3P5; Office: 2 Complexe Desjardins, 31st Fl., Montreal, Que. H5B 1G4

CASGRAIN, Hon. Therese (Mrs. Pierre F.), C.C. (1974), O.B.E., LL.D.; senator; b. Montreal, Que.; d. Sir Rodolphe and Lady Forget; e. Sacred-Heart Convent at Sault-aux-Récollets, Montreal, Que.; Hon. LL.D., Montreal 1968, McGill, Trent, Queens 1974, Waterloo, Bishop, Notre-Dame (B.C.), Mt. St. Vincent, York, Ottawa 1979, Concordia, 1980, Windsor, 1981; m. Pierre Casgrain (d. 1950); founder of French Jr. League 1926 and co-founder, French Fed. Charities; Past Pres., League of Women's Rts. and is credited with having won, almost single handed, the right for women to vote in that Prov.; has been Vice-Pres., Nat. Fed. of Liberal Women's Clubs of Can; French Sec., Candn. Assn. Adult Education; helped found Soc. des Concerts Symphoniques de Montréal; rec'd O.B.E. for organ. of Wartime Prices Bd.; Vice Pres., Nat. Council of N.D.P. (C.C.F.), 1948-61; served three times as Prov. Leader, C.C.F. Party of Que.; former Vice-Chrmn., Nat. Council of that party; def. (N.D.P.) Montreal, Outremont, St. Jean, g.e. June 1962; C.C.F. observer at Asian Socialist Conf., Bombay, India; attended meetings of Internat. Socialist Council in Haifa and Rome; joined "Voice of Women" group 1960, Nat. Pres. 1962; founded La Fédération des Femmes du Qué. 1966; mem. Expo 67 Nat. Council of Women; Past Pres., League of Civil Liberties; Pres., Que. Med. Aid Comte. to Vietnam; mem. Adv. Council on Adm. of Justice in Que.; author of "Une Femme chez les Hommes" 1971 (transl. as "A Woman in a Man's World"); awarded Medal for Criminology, Univ. of Montreal 1967; "Woman of the Century" Medal (Que.), Nat. Council Jewish Women; apptd. O.C. 1967, el. to C.C. 1974; summoned to the Senate of Can. Oct. 1970; medal "Persons Case" 1979; retired July 1971; Home: 250 Clarke, Montreal, Que. H3Z 2E5

CASHMAN, John P. (Jack); executive; b. Gt. Brit. 19 Nov. 1940; s. John A. and Nora (Keogh) C.; e. Univ. of London (Chem.); PRES., GEN. MGR. AND DIR., JOHNS-MANVILLE CANADA INC. 1981- ; Dir. Johns-Manville Sales Corp.; Johns-Manville H. F. Iceland; Polymer Corp.; joined Johns-Manville Great Britain 1964, Sales Mgr. 1967; trans. to Johns-Manville Europe Corp., France 1969 becoming Group Marketing Mgr. Europe for Fiber Glass and Bldg. Products; mem. Inst. Marketing; Inst. Dirs., London; recreations: skiing, golf, tennis; Clubs: Boulevard; Lambton Golf & Country; National; Toronto; Home: 100 Quebec Ave., Apt. 1606, Toronto, Ont. M6P 4B8; Office: 295 The West Mall, Toronto, Ont. M9C 4Z7.

CASHMAN, Hon. Leslie Frederick, LL.B.; judge; b. Toronto, Ont. 18 Oct. 1920; s. late Frederick George and Elizabeth Ellen (Cooper) C.; e. Northwestern Univ. 1940-41; Univ. of B.C. LL.B. 1949; m. Edna May d. late Frederick Newman 7 Oct. 1944; children: Frederick George, Leslie Ellen Scherileese; JUDGE, CO. COURT OF VANCOUVER ISLAND since 1971; called to Bar of B.C. 1949; law practice Cashman & Currie, Quesnel, B.C. 1949-58; G. Roy Long & Co. Vancouver 1958-63; Cashman, Hope & Heinrich, Prince George, B.C. 1963-71; served with Candn. Intelligence Corps Can., UK and N.W. Europe 1942-46; rec'd Medal of Merit Boy Scouts Can.; Delta Upsilon; Anglican; recreations: yachting, golf; Home: 404 - 375 Newcastle Ave., Nanaimo, B.C. V9S 4H9; Office: Court House, 35 Front St., Nanaimo, B.C. V9R 5J1.

CASS, Frederick McIntosh, Q.C.; b. Chesterville, Ont., 5 Aug. 1913; s. William Joseph, Q.C., and Agnes I. (McIntosh) C.; e. Victoria Univ., Toronto, B.A. 1933; Univ. of Toronto, M.A. 1935; Osgoode Hall, Toronto, Ont.; m. C. Olive, d. William H. Casselman, 15 July 1950; Regent of Victoria Univ., Toronto 1960-1977; Past Pres., Candn. Good Rds. Assn.; Hon. Chief of Six Nations Indian Confed., and of Ojibway Tribe; read law with Rogers & Rowland, Toronto, Ont., and W.J. Cass, Q.C., Winchester, Ont.; called to the Bar of Ont., June 1936; cr. Q.C. 1955; Partner in the law firm of Cass & Cass; el. to Ont. Leg. for Grenville-Dundas, g.e. 1955; (Min. of Highways 1958-61, and of Mun. Affairs 1961-62, Atty. Gen. 1962-64, Speaker of the Leg. 1968-71); with Stormont-Dundas & Glengarry Highlanders, 1937-46 (now Hon. Col.); Overseas with this Regt. (C.M. H.Q., London); retired with rank of Major; Magistrate of Cos. of Grenville and Dundas, Ont., 1950-55; mem., Law Soc. of Upper Can.; Roy. Candn. Mil. Inst.; Candn. Bar Ass'n.; Ont. Good Roads Assn. (Past Pres.); Freemason; United Church; P. Conservative; Clubs: Rotary (Chesterville); Winchester 100; Albany; Home: Chesterville, Ont. K0C 1H0; Office: (Box 390), Winchester, Ont. K0C 2K0

CASS-BEGGS, David Norman, M.Sc.Tech., F.I.E.E.; retired public utility executive; b. Manchester, Eng., 2 Oct. 1908; s. late Laura (Coulter) and Alfred Beggs; e. Hulme Grammar Sch., Manchester; Manchester Univ., M.Sc. Tech.; m. Barbara, d. late the Rev. Bingley Cass, London, Eng., 17 Dec. 1932; children: Michael, Rosemary, Ruth; Chrmn., B.C. Hydro & Power Authority 1973-76 (ret.) (formerly Chrmn., Manitoba Hydro-Electric Bd. 1970-73); Tech. Apprentice, Lancaster Dynamo and Crypto Co., Manchester, Eng., 1929-31; Lectr., Wolverhampton and Staffordshire Tech. Coll., 1931-35; Schs. of Tech., Oxford, 1935-39; Lectr., Asst. Prof., Assoc. Prof. of Elect. Engn., Univ. of Toronto, 1939-52; Prof. of Elect. Engn., Univ. Coll., Swansea, U.K., 1952-55; Gen. Mgr., Sask. Power Corp., 1955-64; Head, Man the Producer Exhibit, EXPO 67, Montreal, 1965-66; Science Adviser, Science Secretariat and Science Council of Can., 1966-70; Past Pres., Candn. Gas Assn. (1964); mem., Engn. Inst. Can.; Candn. Elect. Assn. (Dir. and Pres. 1960-61); Homes: Apt. 901, 60 MacLaren St., Ottawa, Ont. K2P 0K7; Great Studio, Limnerslease, Compton, Surrey, Eng. GU3 7JD.

CASSELMAN, Mrs. A.C. — see: Wadds, Jean

CASSELL, William F.; insurance executive; b. Toronto, Ont. 1920; e. N. Toronto Coll. Inst.; VICE PRES. GROUP INS. & PENSIONS, METROPOLITAN LIFE INSURANCE CO. 1967- ; joined City of Toronto Dept. Health 1936; Underwriter, U.S. Fidelity & Guaranty Co. 1945; mgt. trainee Procter & Gamble 1948; Service Supvr. president Co. 1949; Mgr., 561 Avenue Rd. Ltd. 1956; National Life Assurance Co. of Canada, Group Secy., Group Supvr., Mgr. Group Adm., Asst. Supt. Agencies, Mgr. Special Accounts, Group Sales Mgr., Dir. Group Div. - 1958; served with RCAF 1942-45, rank Flying Offr. (pilot); Life mem. Children's Aid Soc. Metrop. Toronto; mem. Bd. Trade Metrop. Toronto; Candn. Life Ins. Assn.;

Candn. Life and Health Assn.; recreations: classical music, Canadian art, photography; Home: 85 Range Rd., Apt. 1004, Ottawa, Ont. K1N 8J6; Office: 99 Bank St., Ottawa, Ont. K1P 5A3.

CASSELS, Gordon Thomson, M.B.E., M.C.; retired stockbroker; b. Toronto, Ont., 5 Oct. 1894; s. Walter Gibson and Esther Eugenie (Lownsbrough) C.; e. St. Andrews Coll., Toronto; Royal Mil. Coll., Kingston, Ont.; formerly with Cassels, Blaikie & Company; served in 1st World War, gaz. Lieut. (1914) Candn. Field Arty.; Capt., R.C. Horse Arty., France and Belgium; awarded M.C. (Somme) 1916; 2nd World War, gaz. (1941) Major 2i/c 14 Field Regt. R.C.A.; D.A.A. & Q.M.G. (1942) "C" Group C.R.U.; Lieut.-Col. C.A.R.U. Eng. 1944; M.B.E. 1943; Past Pres., Ont. Golf Assn.; Clubs: Toronto Golf (Past Pres.); University (Past Pres.); Home: 19 Poplar Plains Crescent, Toronto. M4V 1E9; Office: 110 Yonge St., Toronto, Ont. M5C 1V9

CASSIDY, Michael Morris, M.P.P., B.A.; politician; b. Victoria, B.C. 10 May 1937; s. Harry Morris and Beatrice (Pearce) C.; e. Univ. of Toronto Schs.; Petit Seminaire de Québec; Univ. of Toronto Trinity Coll. B.A. 1958; London Sch. of Econ. 1959-61; m. Maureen Kathleen d. Rev. Wilfred Waddington, London, Eng. 30 March 1961; children: Benedict, Adam, Matthew; Leader, Ont. New Democratic Party 1978-81; Ed. The Varsity Univ. of Toronto 1957-58; reporter Vancouver Sun, Candn. Press, Birmingham Post (Eng.); Reporter, Financial Times of Canada 1964-70; Ottawa Bureau Chief 1966-70; Prof. Sch. of Journalism Carleton Univ. Ottawa 1970-71; Ald. City of Ottawa 1970-72; first el. to Ont. Leg. g.e. 1971, re-el 1975, 1977; elected Leader Ontario N.D.P., February 1978; Unitarian; recreations: cross-country skiing, tennis, piano; Home: 160 Waverley St., Ottawa, Ont. K2P 0V6; Office: Ontario Legislature, Queen's Park, Toronto, Ont. M7A 1A2.

CASSON, Alfred Joseph, LL.D., R.C.A.; artist; b. 1898 Toronto, Ont.; e. local schs.; LL.D., Univ. of W. Ont. 1970; worked for a period in an engraving house, Hamilton, Ont.; joined staff of Rous & Mann Ltd., Toronto; rec'd. his art educ. attending night classes and studying under Harry Britton, A.R.C.A.; became known for his blockprints, which were much sought after; later devel. a distinct mastery of oil and water colour media; mem. of Council, Art Gallery of Toronto; Chrmn. of Council, Ont. Coll. of Art; el. to Roy. Candn. Acad. 1939 (Vice-Pres. 1945-47, Pres. 1948); mem., Group of Seven, 1926; Ont. Soc. Artists (Pres. 1941-43, 1945-46); Candn. Soc. of Painters in Water Colour; Candn. Group of Painters; Nat. Acad. of Design (U.S.); LL.D. Univ. of Saskatchewan, 1971; LL.D. Univ. of Toronto, 1975; Officer of the Order of Canada, 1978; Home: 43 Rochester Ave., Toronto, Ont. M4N 1N7

CASTEL, Jean Gabriel, Q.C., B.Sc., LL.B., J.D., S.J.D.; Fellow, Royal Soc. of Canada; professor of Law, Osgoode Hall Law Sch., York Univ.; Barrister and Solicitor; e. LL.B. Univ. of Mich.; Harvard Univ., S.J.D.; Lic. en droit (Paris); Dipl., Inst. de Droit Comparé (Paris); Fullbright Scholar, 1950; Commonwealth Scholar (1962); Legal Research Asst., Un. Nations, Dept. of Econ. Affairs, 1952; sometime with Dewey, Ballantine, Busby, Palmer & Wood, New York City, 1953; Asst. Prof. of Law, McGill Univ., 1954-55, Assoc. Prof. 1955-59; Secy. of the Faculty 1957-59; Visiting Prof. of Comparative Law, Laval Univ., 1959-65; Univs. Montreal (1965, 1977), Mexico (1963), Lisbon (1964), Nice (1968), Toronto (1974), Puerto Rico (1973), McGill (1978-80), Ottawa (1979-80), Paris (Sorbonne) (1981); mem. Bd. of Eds., Candn. Yearbook of Internat. Law; Editor, "Canadian Bar Review", since 1957, and Faculty Advisor to McGill Law Journ., 1954-59; Publications: "Foreign Judgments: A Comparative Study", 1957; "Canadian-American Private International Law", 1960; "Cases, Notes and Materials on Conflict of Laws",

1961, and eds. 1968-1978; "The Civil Law System of the Province of Quebec", 1962; "International Law as Interpreted and Applied in Canada" (1965); "Droit international privé québecois" 1980, "Canadian Conflict of Laws" 2 Vols. (1975-78); Can. Criminal Law, Internat'l and Transnat'l Aspects (1981); Secy-Gen., Candn. Assn. of Comparative Law, 1960-1965, Pres., 1971-74; mem. Council, Candn. Bar Assn. (ex-officio); Candn. Inst. Internat. Affairs; Internat. Law Assn.; Office Revision Civil Code (Québec), 1965-1975; Academic in residence, Dept. of External Affairs (1980); French Resistance 1943-1945; Address: Osgoode Hall, York University, Downsview, Ont.

CASTONGUAY, Claude, C.C. (1974), D.C.L., F.S.A., F.C.I.A.; actuary; b. Quebec, Que. 8 May 1929; s. Emile and Jeanne (Gauvin) C.; e. Académie de Qué. 1948; Laval Univ. 1948-50; Univ. of Man. 1950-51; D.C.L. Bishop's 1972; LL.D. McGill 1974, Toronto 1975; D. de l'U. Sherbrooke 1975; LL.D. U. Manitoba 1980; m. Mimi d. Hon. Gaspard Fauteux 22 Sept. 1956; children: Monique, Joanne, Philippe; Chrmn. of Bd., Imperial Life Insurance Co.; Pres. Fonds Laurentien Inc.; Chmn. of Bd. Loyal American Life Ins. Co.; Vice-Chmn. of Bd., Laurentienne Mutuelle d'Assurance; Chrmn. of Bd., Northern Life Assur. Co.; Vice Chmn. of Bd., Canadian Provident; General Ins.; Personal Ins. Co.; Paragon Ins.; Professional Reinsurance Consultants Ltd.; Credit Foncier; Imbrook Properties Ltd.; Dir. F.I.C. Fund Inc.; Dir., Impco Properties Ltd.; Dir. La Prévoyance, Cie d'Assurances; La Laurentienne Cie d'Assurances Générales; Le Bouclier Laurentien, Compagnie d'Assurance; Montreal City and District Savings Bank; Trustees of the Montreal City and District; Cdn. Industrial Renewal Bd.; Assoc. Actuary Industrial Life Insurance 1951-55; Actuary La Laurentienne Cie Mutuelle d'Assurance, Mutual Life Assurance Co. 1955-58; Administrator and Actuary La Prévoyance, Cie d'Assurances 1958-62; Founded Castonguay, Lemay & Associates Inc. 1962, Consulting Actuary and Partner Castonguay, Pouliot, Guérard & Associates Inc. 1962-70, 1973-77; Chargé de cours Actuarial Dept. Laval Univ. 1951-55, Prof. agrégé 1955-57; Chrmn. Royal Comn. Inquiry Health & Social Welfare 1966-70; Pres. Task Force on Minimum Wages and Work Conditions 1974; mem. Steering Comte. Fed.-Prov. Jt. Review Candn. Social Security System 1973-75; Pres. Govt. Que. Task Force Urbanization 1974-76; mem. Fed. Anti-inflation Bd. 1975-76; el. mem. Que. Nat. Assembly for Louis Hébert 1970-73, Min. of Health and Min. of Family & Social Welfare 1970-71, Min. of Social Affairs 1971-73; served with RCNVR 1947-50, rank Sub-Lt.; Pres., La Fondation Bherer; mem., Trilateral Commission; Fellow, Candn. Inst. Actuaries; mem. Candn. Inst. Pub. Adm.; Candn. Assn. Club de Rome; Dir., Inst. for Research on Public Policy; Fellow, Soc. of Actuaries; Candn. Inst. Internat. Affairs; Liberal; R. Catholic; recreations: skiing, reading, painting, fishing; Club: Cercle Universitaire; Cercle de la Place d'Armes and St. James's Club of Montreal; Home: 1155 rue Turnbull, App 811, Quebec, P.Q. G1R 5G3; Office: 500 Grande-Allée, Est, Québec, Qué. G1R 2J7; 95 St. Clair Avenue W., Toronto, Ont., M4V 1N7

CASTONGUAY, Nelson Jules Valois, LL.D.; Canadian public servant; b. Ottawa, Ont., 31 Dec. 1913; s. Jules (former Chief Electoral Offr. Can.) and Florence (Valois) C.; e. Loyola High Sch., Montreal, Que. (1931-34); LL.D. (1968), St. Mary's Univ., N.S.; m. Jean Embyl, d. Alexander Workman, Ottawa, Ont., 23 Feb. 1939; children: Lynne, Gillian, Peter, Sandy: Representation Commissioner, Canada, until retirement Dec. 31, 1978. (Office of Representation Commissioner officially abolished Aug. 1, 1979); joined the Chief Electoral Office in 1934 as a Messenger; Chief Electoral Offr., 1949-66; served in 2nd World War on various H.M.C. ships, 1941-45 with R.C.N. in N. Atlantic; now Lieut.-Commdr., R.C.N. (R); Roman Catholic; recreation: fishing; Home: 202 Cloverdale, Rockcliffe Park Village, Ottawa, Ont. K1M 0X2

CATTANACH, Hon. A(ngus) Alexander; judge; b. Winnipeg, Manitoba, 26 July 1909; s. Angus Archibald and Jennie Elizabeth (Young) C.; e. Public and High Schs., Winnipeg, Man.; Univ. of Manitoba, B.A., 1929; Univ. of Sask., LL.B., 1932; m. Verena Margaret, d. James W. Miller, Carleton Place, Ont., 29 Oct. 1944; one d. Heather Edmonde; PUISNE JUDGE, FEDERAL COURT OF CAN., since March 1962 (formerly Asst. Under Secy. of State, Dept. of Secy. of State and Acting Under Secy. of State, Sept. 1961-Mar. 1962); called to the Bar of Sask.; 1934; cr. Q.C. (Dom.) 1952; served in 2nd World War with R.C.A.F., 1940-45, rank Wing Commdr.; Life mem., Clan Macpherson Assn.; United Church; Home: 753 Island Park Drive, Ottawa, Ont. K1Y 0B9; Office: Federal Court, of Canada, Ottawa, Ont.

CATTO, Rev. Charles, C.M., B.A., B.D.; b. Toronto, Ont. 7 June 1929; s. Charles Edward and Marion (Haddow) C.; e. Ryerson Pub. Sch. London, Ont. 1938; Blythwood Pub. Sch. Toronto 1940; Univ. of Toronto Schs. 1946; Univ. of Toronto B.A. 1951, B.D. 1955 (Emmanuel Coll.); m. Barbara Jean d. late Albert F. Loveys 25 Sept. 1954; children: Charles Daniel, Linda Jean, Wanda Marie, Roderick; EXTVE. DIR., FRONTIERS FOUNDATION since 1968; Dir., Keekandahsowin; Missy. with Cree Indians, God's Lake, Man. 1954-57; Missy. Bd. of World Mission, Un. Ch. Can. under Un. Ch. of Zambia 1957-62; Min. of Hampton Charge 1963-68; founded Operation Beaver under Candn. Council Chs. 1963; Operation Causepeace 1968; produced two LP albums "Zambezi Valley Songs", "The Third World Sings"; Order of Can. 1979; Guest of Honour, Native Council of Can. Banquet, 1981; mem. Un. Ch. Can. Comte. on Internat. Affairs since 1963; NDP; United Church; recreations: skating, model shipbuilding, banjo playing, table tennis; Home: 712 Kingfisher Dr., Pickering, Ont. L1W 1X5; Office: 2328 Danforth Ave., Toronto, Ont. M4C 1K7.

CATZMAN, Marvin Adrian, judge; b. Toronto, Ont. 1 Sept. 1938; s. Fred M., Q.C. and Irene (Meyers) C.; e. Univ. of Toronto B.A. (Gold Medal Sociol.) 1959, LL.B. (Dean's Key) 1962; Law Soc. Upper Can. (Treas.'s Medal for Highest Standing) 1964; m. Ruth Lynn d. Sidney Kaplan, M.D., Vancouver, B.C. 20 Aug. 1972; children: Penny Gayle, Julie Beth, David Aaron; JUDGE, SUPREME CRT. OF ONTARIO, July 1981; called to Bar of Ont. 1964; cr. Q.C. 1976; Law Clk. to Chief Justice High Court, Supreme Court of Ont. 1964-65; Lectr. in Bankruptcy and Insolvency Osgoode Hall Law Sch. 1974-75; Course Adm. and Lectr. Principles of Business Law Course York Univ. 1967- ; Lectr. Civil Procedure Sec. Bar Admission Course Law Soc. Upper Can. 1966-76; mem. Supreme Court of Ont. Rules Comte. 1975- ; Secy. Adv. Comte. Ont. Personal Property Security Act 1976- ; el. Bencher, Law Soc. Upper Can. 1979 (Vice Chrmn. Legal Educ. Comte. 1979-); Law Soc. Upper Can. Special Lectures Series Lectr. and Panel Chrmn. Torts 1973, Contracts 1975, Employment Law 1976, Professions 1977; Chrmn. Series on Estate Planning & Adm. 1980, Remedies 1981; mem. Senate Univ. of Toronto 1968-72; mem. Candn. Bar Assn. (Ont. Council 1978-80); Co. of York Law Assn.; Advocates' Soc.; Jewish; Club: Northwood Country; Home: 23 Pinnacle Rd., Willowdale, Ont. M2L 2V6; Office: Judges' Chambers, Osgoode Hall, Toronto, Ont. M5H 2N5.

CAVANAGH, Hon. James Creighton, B.A., LL.B.; judge; b. Ernfold, Sask. 15 June 1916; s. late James Thomas and late Elizabeth Somerville (Creighton) C.; e. Univ. of Sask. LL.B. 1949, B.A. 1950; m. Margaret Anne d. late Angus Norman MacDonald 3 Sept. 1951; children: Elizabeth (Pegoraro), Norman, Paul, Peter, Jane, Ruth, Mark; JUDGE, COURT OF QUEEN'S BENCH, ALTA. 1979- , Depy. Judge Supreme Court of N.W.T. 1975- , Judge Court Martial Appeal Court 1981- ; called to Bar of Alta. 1951; cr. Q.C. 1964; Judge, Trial Div. Supreme Court of Alta. and Ex officio Judge Appellate Div. 1973;

Dir. St. Joseph's Hosp. Edmonton; Dir. and Treas. Candn. Judges Conf.; served with RCAF 1941-45, Navig. Eng. and Tunisia, rank Flying Offr.; Bencher, Law Soc. Alta. 1969-73; K. of C.; R. Catholic; recreations: curling, travel; Club: Royal Glenora; Home: 9307 - 147 St., Edmonton, Alta. T5R 0Y8; Office: Law Courts, Edmonton, Alta.

CAVANAGH, Patrick E., B.A.Sc.; metallurgist; b. Winnipeg, Man., 30 Mar. 1915; s. Edgar Lawrence and Margaret (Gillies) C.; e. Univ. of Manitoba, 1930-32; Univ. of Toronto, B.A.Sc. 1937; m. Doris Aileen, d. Dr. A.E. Proctor, Winnipeg, Man., 14 Sept. 1940; children: Nancy, Clare, Patrick, Kelly; PRES., LONE STAR MINING AND EXPLORATION CO. LTD., 1972-; Internat. Iron Ores Ltd., 1962-; with Ont. Research Foundation, 1937-39; Metallurgist, Steel Co. of Can. Ltd., 1939-42; Chief Metall., Dumont Labs. 1942-45; apptd. Dir., Dept. of Engn. and Metall., Ont. Research Foundation, 1946-57; Vice-Pres., Premium Iron Ores Ltd. 1958 and Pres. 1960; Lambda Chi Alpha; Anglican; Clubs: Seigniory; Engineers: Mount Royal; Home: 606 Avenue Rd., Toronto, Ont. M4V 2K9; Office: 2222 S. Sheridan Way, Mississauga, Ont. L5J 2M4

CAVERS, His Hon. Harry Peter; judge; b. St. Catharines, Ont., 27 Dec. 1909; s. Harry A. and Laura Mabel (Lyons) C.; e. Univ. of Toronto; Osgoode Hall, 1935; m. Dorothy Alma, d. Hon. Frank L. Bastedo, Q.C., Regina, Sask., 18 Mar. 1944; one d. Dorothy Anne (Mrs. John L. Carruthers); JUDGE, CO. COURT OF ONTARIO, read law with late J.J. Bench, K.C.; called to the Bar of Ont. 1935; cr. Q.C. 1961; in partnership with late Hon. J.J. Bench, K.C. (Bench & Cavers) 1935-42; Partner, Cavers, Chown, Cairns & Hicks, St. Catharines, Ont. 1950-64; served in 2nd World War 1942-45; Lt. R.C.N.V.R.; 1st el. to H. of C. for Lincoln, g.e. 1949; re-el. g.e. 1953; def. g.e. 1957 and 1958; mem., Lincoln Co. Law Assn. (Past Pres. 1961) 1935-64; Candn. Bar Assn. (mem. Council 1961, 62, 63); Secy.-Treas., Co. & Dist. Judges' Assn. of Ont. 1970-74; Royal Candn. Legion; Delegate, Commonwealth Party. Conf., Nairobi 1954, Jamaica 1956; Freemason; United Church; Clubs: St. Catharines Kiwanis (Past Pres. 1961); University Club of Toronto; St Catharines Club; Home: 207-16 Towering Heigts Blvd., St. Catharines, Ont. L2T 3G9; Office: Court House, King St., St. Catharines, Ont.

CAVERS, James Ross, B.S.A., M.S.; retired university professor; agricultural journalist; b. Millgrove, Ont., 24 July 1906 s. late Rev. Charles A. and Ada Annetta (Leask) C.; e. St. Catharines Coll. Inst., 1921-25; Ont. Agric. Coll., B.S.A. 1929; Univ. of Minnesota, M.S. 1932; m. Jane Ewing, d. late Archibald A. Parks, Owen Sound, Ont., 3 Aug. 1935; with Ont. Agric. Coll., 1933-37; in charge of Poultry Husbandry, Univ. of Manitoba, 1937-46; Prof. of Poultry Sci., Univ. of Guelph 1946; Chrmn. Dept., 1948-68; Assoc. Ed. of Canadian Poultry Review 1968-72; ret. 1972; mem. Agric. Inst. Can. (Pres., Winnipeg Br. 1944); Poultry Science Assn. (Can. and U.S., Pres. 1954); World's Poultry Science Assn.; United Church; recreations: gardening, curling; Home: 26 Maple, Guelph, Ont. N1G 2G2

CEDRASCHI, Tullio, M.B.A.; investment executive; b. Zurich, Switzerland 4 Oct. 1938; e. Coll. of Technol. Zurich Civil Engn. degree 1960; McGill Univ. M.B.A. 1968; PRES. AND CHIEF EXTVE. OFFR., CN INVESTMENT DIV. 1977- ; Dir., Markborough Properties Ltd.; Canadian Commercial and Industrial Bank; Morguard Investment Securities Ltd.; Helix Investments Ltd.; Toronto College Street Centre Ltd.; Conventures Ltd.; Civil Engr., Conrad Zschokke, S.A. Zurich 1960-61; Bureau d'Etudes Quoniam Paris 1961-63; BBR Switzerland and Can. 1963-65; R.R. Nicolet & Associates Montreal 1965-66; CN Invest. Research Offr. 1968, Gen. Mgr. 1973; mem. Montreal Soc. Financial Analysts; Swiss-Candn. Chamber Comm.; recreations: tennis, squash, skiing; Clubs: M.A.A.A.; Mount Royal Tennis; Outremont Ten-

nis; Home: 517 Habitat '67, Cité du Havre, Montreal, Que. H3C 3R6; Office: (P.O. Box 155) Place Bonaventure, Montreal, Que. H5A 1A8.

CHABOT, Hon. James Roland, M.L.A.; politician; b. Farnham, Que. 8 May 1927; s. J. Gustave and Blanche (Bernier) C.; e. pub. and private schs. Que. and Vt.; m. Grace Carr, Chilliwack, B.C. 1950; children: James, Robert, Linda, Dawn, Mark, Allan Bruce; MIN. OF LANDS, PARKS & HOUSING, B.C.1978- ; former Supvr. C.P.R.; Ald. Village of Invermere 4 yrs.; Trustee Windermere Dist. Hosp. Bd. one yr.; Past Pres. Kinsmen Club Invermere; el. M.L.A. for Columbia River prov. g.e. 1963, re-el. since; Min. of Labour 1971-72; Min. of Mines & Petroleum Resources 1976; Social Credit; R. Catholic; Office: Parliament Bldgs., Victoria, B.C. V8V 1X4.

CHADWICK, James Barton, Q.C., LL.B.; barrister; b. Toronto, Ont. 28 Oct. 1936; s. James Kent and Helen T. (O'Connor) C.; e. St. Francis Xavier Univ. B.A. 1959; Univ. of Ottawa LL.B. 1962; m. Julie V. Hayes 25 Aug. 1962; children: Thomas K., Robert J., Kevin, Laura; PARTNER, BURKE-ROBERTSON, CHADWICK & RITCHIE; called to Bar of Ont. 1964; cr. Q.C. 1977; Chrmn. Ont. Legal Aid Plan; Bencher, Law Soc. Upper Can.; mem. Advocates Soc.; Internat. Bar Assn.; Candn. Bar Assn.; R. Catholic; Clubs: Seigniory; Laurentian; Home: 91 Beaver Ridge, Nepean, Ont. K2E 6E5; Office: Suite 1800, 130 Albert St., Ottawa, Ont. K1P 5G4.

CHADWICK, William Franklin, B.A., B.Com., M.Sc.; banker; b. Regina, Sask., 25 May 1929; s. Alvin William and Edna (Andrews) C.; e. Univ. of Sask., B.A. 1952, B.Com. 1953; Columbia Univ., M.Sc. 1956; m. Sheila Barron, 15 Sept. 1962; 2 children; VICE PRES., HUMAN RESOURCES, BANK OF MONTREAL: Home: 270 Connemara Cres., Beaconsfield, Que. H9W 2N7; Office: 129 St. James St. W., Montreal, Que. H2Y 1L6

CHAFE, James Warren, B.A., B.Ed.; writer, teacher; b. Springfield, Man., 13 Dec. 1900; s. James Warren and Adelaide (Roberts) C.; e. Winnipeg Pub. Schs.; Univ. of Man., B.A. 1934; B.Ed. 1938; m. Georgina Maude, d. George Swanton Norwood, Man., 30 June 1934; children: Beverley Elizabeth, Warren James; Asst. Dir., R.C.A.F. Dependents' Sch., Zweibrüken, Germany, 1958-60; Past Pres., Winnipeg Br., Assn. Candn. Radio & Television Artists; Man. Teachers' Soc.; author of "We Live Together", 1942; "Early Life in Canada", 1943; "Canada, a Nation" (with Dr. A.R.M. Lower), 1948; "Canada, Your Country", 1950; "An Apple for the Teacher", 1967; "A History of the Manitoba Teachers' Society", 1969; also "When We were Young . . . Winnipeg and I" (to be pub.), "Extraordinary Tales from Manitoba History", 1974; "Adventure in Riel Country" (to be pub.); radio scripts and articles in mags. and prof. journs.; has travelled over 50,000 miles as an actor with prof. dramatic co.'s in U.S. and Can. 1924-29; Protestant; recreation: golf; Clubs: Southwood Country; Fellowship; Home: 197 Oak St., Winnipeg, Man. R3M 3P7

CHAGNON, Roland, C.A.; company exec.; b. Montreal, Que., 4 Jan. 1910; s. Pierre and Antoinette (Dubé) C.; e. St-Henri Sch., Montreal; Ecole des Hautes Etudes Commerciales, Montreal, Lic. in Comm. 1930; Lic. in Accountancy 1932; m. Mariette, d. Hector Gagné, 19 Oct. 1940 (d. 19 March 1962); m. 2ndly, Doris Kimber, Oct. 1963; one s. Jean, two d. Nina, Louise; PRES., EXEC. COMM., LALLEMAND INC. 1981-; Pres. 1952-75; Chrmn. 1952-75, Chmn. 1975-81; Pres.; Falco Inc.; Alibon Ltée; Dir.; Sovereign General Assurance Co.; Sovereign Life Assnce. Co.; Family Life Assnce. Co.; Jano Inc.; Topsy Inc.; mem., Inst. of C.A.'s, Que. (1932); practising C.A. 1932-38; Compt., Le Syndicat de Québec, 1938-41; Dir., Treas., Stores Mgr., Dupuis-Freres, 1947-52; Dir., Candn. Retail Fed., 1945-46; Pres., Que. City Credit Bureau, 1946-47; Montreal Chamber of Comm. (Pres. 1956-57); Institut des Recherches Cliniques de Montreal; mem., Montreal Bd. of Trade (Dir. 1962-64); Candn. Mfrs. Assn.; Candn. Chamber of Comm.; Fed. Appeal of Greater Montreal (Pres. 1968); prepared "Study of Taxation of Co-Operatives" for Que. Chamber of Comm. 1945; R. Catholic; recreation: golf; Club: St. Denis; Mount Royal; Montreal Badmington & Squash; Home: 1414 Redpath Cres., Montreal, Que. H3G 1A2; Office: 1620 Prefontaine St., Montreal, Que. H1W 2N8

CHALMERS, David Bay, B.A.; petroleum executive; b. Denver, Colo. 17 Nov. 1924; s. late David Twiggs and Dorrit (Bay) C.; e. Public and High Schs., Denver, Colo.; Dartmouth Coll., Hanover, N.H., B.A. 1947; one s. David B. Chalmers Jr.; PRES., CORAL PETROLEUM, INC. since 1973; Chrmn. of Bd. Coral Petroleum Ltd., Coral Petroleum (Canada) Inc., Coral Petroleum Development, Inc., Leeward Petroleum Ltd.; United Refining Co., Warren Pa.; joined Bay Petroleum Corp., Denver 1947, Landman Oklahoma City 1951, Mgr. Crude Oil Purchases 1954; Mgr. Crude Oil Purchases and Sales, Tennessee Gas Transmission (now Tenneco) 1955, Vice-Pres. 1961; Vice-Pres., Occidental Petroleum Corp. 1967 then Pres. and Mang. Dir., Jefferson Lake Petrochemicals of Canada Ltd.; Pres. of Canadian Occidental Petroleum, Ltd. and Offr. and Dir. of various affiliates and subsidiaries 1971-73; served in 2nd World War, Lieut. U.S. Marine Corps 1943-45, in Korean War 1949-50 as First Lieut.; former mem. Board of Governors, Canadian Petroleum Association; Indep. Petroleum Assn. of Am.; National Petroleum Refiners Association; American Petroleum Institute; Texas Indep. Petroleum & Royalty Owners Assn.; Epis.; recreation: golf, tennis; Clubs: Calgary Petroleum; Denver Petroleum; Denver Country; Calgary Golf and Country Club;; Lakeside Country (Houston); Metropolitan (New York); The Houstonian (Houston); Houston Petroleum; The Houstonian; Woodlands Country (Houston); Home: 5600 San Felipe, No. 4, Houston, Texas; Office: 908 Town and Country Boulevard, Suite 600, Houston, Texas, 77024.

CHALMERS, Floyd Sherman, O.C., LL.D., Litt.D., B.F.A.; b. (of Candn parentage) Chicago, Ill., 14 Sept. 1898; s. James Keeler and Anna (Dusing) C.; e. Pub. and High Schs., Orillia and Toronto, Ont.; Khaki Coll., Ripon, England; Univ. of W. Ont., LL.D. 1962, Waterloo Lutheran 1963; Trent Univ., Litt.D. 1968; York Univ., B.F.A. 1973; m. Jean Alberta, d. Walter G. Boxall, Toronto, Ont., 28 Apl. 1921; Children: Wallace G., Joan; Dir., American Growth Fund Ltd.; AGF Special Fund Ltd.; AGF Japan Fund Ltd.; AGF Money Market Fund; Canadian Gas and Energy Fund Ltd.; Canadian Security Growth Fund Ltd.; Corporate Investors Ltd.; Corporate Investors Stock Fund Ltd.; Canadian Trusteed Income Fund Ltd.; Growth Equity Fund Ltd.; Option Equity Fund; Trustee, Ont. Historical Studies; Encyclopedia of Music in Can.; Junior with Bank of Nova Scotia, 1914; Reporter on Toronto "World" and Toronto "News"; joined "Financial Post" 1919; Ed., 1925-42; Extve. Vice-Pres., Maclean-Hunter Ltd. 1942-52; Pres., 1952-64, Chairman 1964-69, Hon. Chmn. since 1978; overseas with 1st Candn. Tank Bn. in World War I; attended Commonwealth Press Conferences U.K. 1946, Can. 1950, Australia-N.Z. 1955, Pakistan-India 1961; author of "A Gentleman of the Press", Doubleday 1969; Pres., Canadian Club of Toronto 1932-33; Periodical Press Assn. of Can. 1947-49; Candn. Opera Co. 1957-61; Stratford Shakespearean Festival Fndn. 1965-67; Chancellor, York Univ. 1968-73; founder of the Floyd S. Chalmers Foundation, chrmn. 1963-79, now admin. by Ont. Arts Counc. as The Floyd S. Chalmers Fund; Liveryman, Worshipful Co. of Stationers & Newspapermakers, London, Eng. 1957; Freeman, City of London 1957; Fellow, Internat. Inst. Arts & Letters 1957; O.C. 1967; Centennial Medal 1967; Civic Medal of Merit, Toronto, 1974; Diplôme d'Honneur, Candn. Conf. of the Arts, 1974; Candn. News Hall of Fame 1975; Queen's Jubilee Medal 1977; Candn. Music

Council Special Award 1977; Independent; recreation: golf; Clubs: Canadian; York; Toronto Hunt; Arts and Letters (hon. life mem.); Ticker Hon. Chmn., Founder and First Pres., 1929-30); Home: Apt. 4611, 44 Charles St. W., Toronto, Ont. M4Y 1R8; Office: 481 University Ave., Suite 805, Toronto, Ont. M5W 1A7

CHAMBERS, Frederic William, B.A.Sc.; mechanical engineer; b. Brandon, Man., 15 July 1899; s. William and Jean (Marshall) C.; e. Brandon Coll., Man.; Univ. of Toronto, B.A.Sc. 1923; Ont. Coll. of Educ., Toronto 1923-24; m. Margaret Florence, d. Col. James Robertson Gordon, Sudbury, Ont., 18 May 1929; children: Helen Jean, Margo Leslie; m. Phillis Dorothy, d. Lieut. Col. Frederick William Vallat O.B.E, 28 Jan. 1979; PRESIDENT, F.W. CHAMBERS & CO. LTD.; with Bell Telephone Co., Toronto, 1924-25; Asst. Schedule Engr., do., Montreal 1925-26; Townsite Engr., Aluminum Co. of Can. Ltd., Arvida, Que. 1926; Chambers & Carley (Distrib. of Engn. Equip.), Toronto 1927, and their successors F.W. Chambers & Co., Toronto 1931; incrp. as F.W. Chambers & Co. Ltd. 1937; served in World War 1917-19 as Flight Sub-Lieut., R.N.A.S.; mem., Assn. of Prof. Engrs. of Ont.; Corpn. of Prof. Engrs. of Que.; Am. Soc. of Heating, Refrigerating & Air Conditioning Engrs.; author of numerous articles on radiant heating, air conditioning and allied subjects publ. in Candn. and Am. mags. and trade journs.; Freemason; Independent Liberal; United Church; recreations: golf, bowling; Clubs: Optimist (Pres., 1955-56); Lawrence Park Lawn Bowling (Pres. 1969); Home: 55 Glengowan Rd., Toronto, Ont. M4N 1G3; Office: 1821 Avenue Road, Toronto, Ont. M5M 3Z4

CHAMBERS, Hon. Thomas William, M.L.A., B.A.Sc., P.Eng.; politician; b. Port Arthur, Ont. 7 July 1928; s. William Edward and Mary Jane C.; e. Port Arthur Coll. Inst.; Univ. of Toronto B.A.Sc.; m. Margaret Lenore d. Norris Green, Lindsay, Ont. 22 Dec. 1952; children: Steven William, Robert Norris, Joan Maureen, Susan Lenore; MIN. OF HOUSING & PUBLIC WORKS, ALTA.1979- ; petroleum engr.-consultant; el. M.L.A. for Edmonton Calder prov. g.e. 1971, re-el. since; mem. Alta. Assn. Prof. Engrs.; Candn. Inst. Mining & Metall.; Edmonton Chamber Comm.; RCAF Assn.; P. Conservative; Protestant; Office: 207 Legislative Bldg., Edmonton, Alta. T5K 2B6.

CHANASYK, Victor, B.Sc. (Ag.), B.S. (L.A.), M.L.A.; professor; b. Vegreville, Alta., 15 Oct. 1926; s. Nicholas and Xenia (Tymchuk) C.; e. Olds Sch. of Agriculture and Univ. of Alta., B.Sc. (Ag.) 1949; Univ. of Cal. (Berkeley) B.S.(L.A.) 1957; Harvard Univ. M.L.A. 1958; m. Lillian Iris d. William Nicholas Pidruchney, 14 July 1955; PROF., SCH. OF LANDSCAPE ARCH., UNIV. OF GUELPH since 1975 (Dir. of Sch. 1964-75); horticulturist, Can. Exper. Stn., Beaverlodge, Alta. 1949-55; Commr., Mun. Art Comm., Seattle, Wash., 1959-61; landscape arch. and urban planner, Puget Planners, Inc., Seattle, 1958-61; landscape arch. and site planner, Skidmore, Owings & Merrill, San Francisco, 1961; Prof. of Landscape Arch., Dept. of Horticulture, Univ. of Guelph, 1962-64; mem. adv. comte., Ryerson Inst. of Tech. (1968) and Humber Coll. of Applied Arts (1967); princ., Victor Chanasyk Assoc. 1969; mem. ed. bd. Bd. of Gov., Can. Soc. of lanscape Architects; "Water, Air and Soil Pollution: An International Journal of Environmental Pollution," 1970; developed first B.L.A. program in landscape arch. in Can.; planned Forillon Nat. Park, Que., co-recipient, Nat. Mfg. Design Award of Can. 1965; Centennial Medal 1967; Can. Council Research Grant, 1970; Life Fellow, Roy. Soc. of Arts 1972; Fellow, Candn. Soc. of Landscape Arch., 1973; Extve. Council (1965) Candn. Soc. of Landscape Arch.; Pres. (1965) Ont. Assn. of Landscape Arch.; Press., Wash. Soc. of Landscape Arch. 1959-61; mem. Candn. Soc. of Landscape Arch. Nat. Accreditation Council (1980-) (Chrmn. Comte. on Educ. 1975); Ont. Assn. of Landscape Arch. Exec. Council (1980-81), Pres., Ont. Assn. of Landscape Arch., 1981-Ed. Comte. 1980; author of articles in govt. and learned publs.; Ukrainian Orthodox; recreation: horticulture, conservation, bonsai; Home: 64 Woodside Rd., Guelph, Ont. N1G 2H2

CHANDLER, David L., B.A.; executive; b. Greensboro, N.C., 28 Aug. 1926; s. Virgil and Beatrice (Dillon) C.; e. Pub. Sch., Greensboro, N.C.; Riverside Acad.; Univ. of Virginia, B.A. 1949; m. Ann, d. Henry L. Phillips; children: Allyn, David, Jr.; CHRMN. OF BD., & C.E.O., GALT-BRANTFORD MALLEABLE IRON LTD.; Grand Rapids Metalcraft, Grand Rapids, Mich.; Founders of American Investment Corp., Springfield, Missouri; Chrmn. and Pres., Redlaw Ind. Inc., Toronto; Chmn., G.I. Export Copr., Waterbury, N.Y.; Acct. Extve., Merrill Lynch Pierce Fenner & Smith, 1950-56; Resident Manager, Baker-Weeks & Co., Toronto, Ont., 1956-61; Vice-Pres. and Dir. Bache & Co. 1961-66; served with U.S. Army during 2nd World War, 1942-45; Sigma Alpha Epsilon; Anglican; recreations: fishing; golf; Clubs: Rosedale Golf; Badminton & Racquet; Jupiter Island (Hobe Sound, Florida); Home 126 Warren Rd., Toronto, Ont. M4V 2S1; Office: 60 Kerr St., Cambridge, Ont. N1R 5V8

CHANT, Dixon S., F.C.A., company executive; b. Toronto, Ont., 25 Apl. 1913; s. Christopher William and Minnie Jane (Butler) C.; e. Pickering Coll., Newmarket, Ont.; Inst. of Chart. Accts. Ont.; C.A. m. Marion K., d. Roderick K. MacNaughton, Gananoque, 13 June 1942; two s. Brian William, Murray James; EXTVE. VICE PRES. & MEM. OF EXTVE. COMTE., ARGUS CORP. LTD.; Extve. Vice Pres. & mem. Extve. Comte. Hollinger Argus Ltd.; Dir. & Chrmn. of Extve. Comte., Standard Broadcasting Corp. Ltd.; Dir. & Extve. Vice Pres., Hollinger North Shore Exploration Co. Ltd.; Labrador Mining & Exploration Co. Ltd.; The Ravelston Corp. Ltd.; Vice-Pres., Men. Exec. Comte. and Dir., Dominion Stores Ltd.; Crown Trust Co.; Dir. & mem. Extve. Comte. Norcen Energy Resources Ltd.; Chrmn. of Bd. & Chrmn. of Extve. Comte., VS Services Ltd.; Dir. & mem. of Investment Comte., Fireman's Fund Ins. Co. of Can.; Dir., Bushnell Communications Ltd.; CFRB Ltd.; Grew Corp.; St. Lawrence Cement Co.; United Church; recreations: curling, golf, photography; Clubs: Granite (Past Pres.); Rosedale Golf; Toronto Board of Trade; Canadian; Toronto; Empire; Muskoka Lakes Golf & Country; (Past Pres.); Residences: 167 Coldstream Ave., Toronto, Ont. M5N 1X7; P.O. Box 212, Port Carling, Ont. P0B 1J0 (summer); Office: 10 Toronto St., Toronto, Ont. M5C 2B7

CHANT, Donald, M.A., Ph.D., LL.D. (Hon.), F.R.E.S., F.R.S.C., F.E.S.C.; educator; b. Toronto, Ont., 30 Sept. 1928; s. Sperrin Noah Fulton and Nellie Irene (Cooper) C.; e. Univ. of Brit. Columbia, B.A. (Hons.) 1950, M.A. 1952; Univ. of London, Ph.D. 1956; Dalhousie Univ., LL.D.; divorced; children: Patrick, Jeffrey, Timothy; m. K.M. Hanes, 1975; DIR., JOINT STUDY CENTRE FOR TOXICOLOGY, UNIV. OF TORONTO 1980-; Chrmn. of Bd., Ont. Waste Management Corp., 1980-; Chrmn., Pollution Probe Foundation 1964-1980; Chmn., Canadian Environmental Advisory Council; Scientific Advisory Comte., World Wildlife Fund (Can.); Dir., Inst. of Ecology, Washington, D.C.; Chrmn., Candn. Comte. of Univ. Biol. Research Offr.; Can. Dept. Agric. 1950; Dir., Research Lab., Can. Dept. Agric., Vineland, Ont. 1960; Chrmn., Dept. of Biol. Control, Univ. of Cal., Riverside, Cal. 1964; Chrmn., Dept. of Zool., University of Toronto 1967-75; mem., Candn. Soc. of Zools. (Pres.); Canadian Entomol. Soc.; Ont. Environmental Assessment Bd.; Chrmn. Premier Davis Steering Comte. on Environmental Assessment Regulations, 1976-1980; author of "Pollution Probe" 1970; "This Good Good Earth" 1971; co-author of several other prof. books and author of over 60 prof. research publs.; rec'd. Univ. Brit. Columbia Alumni Award 1970; White Owl Conservation Award 1972; Vice-Pres. and Provost, U. of T. 1975-80; Awarded Honorary LL.D. Dalhousie Univ., 1976; Univ. of Toronto Alumni Faculty Award 1980; recreations: fishing, camp-

ing; Home: 9 Beaumont Rd., Toronto, Ont. M4W 1V4; Office: Room 103, 121 St. Joseph St., Univ. of Toronto, Toronto, Ont. M5S 1A1

CHAPDELAINE, Jean, M.A.; diplomat; b. Montreal, Que., 1914; e. Ste. Marie Coll., Montreal, Que., B.A.; Oxford Univ. (Rhodes Scholar) M.A.; m. Rita Laframboise; children: Claude, Annick, Antoine; Diplomatic Adv. to Que. Govt. since 1976; joined Dept. of External Affairs in 1937; Third Secy., Candn. Legation, Wash., D.C., 1940-43; on loan to Privy Council, Ottawa, for a time; First Secy., Candn. Embassy, Paris, 1946-49; Charge d'Affairs, Dublin 1950; Counsellor, Candn. Diplomatic Mission to Bonn, 1950-53; Head of European Div. of the Dept. at Ottawa, 1953; Asst. Under Secy. of State, 1954-55; Ambassador to Sweden and Min. to Finland, 1956-59; to Brazil 1959-63; to United Arab Republic 1964; mem. of a number of Candn. del. to internat. confs., incl. Peace Conf., Paris, 1946, and Assemblies of the U.N.O., Sept.-Dec. 1948 and 1963; Agent Gen. for Que. in France 1965-76; Home: 165 Grande Allée E., Quebec, Que.; Office: 1225 Place Georges V., Quebec, Que. GIR 427

CHAPIN, Vincent L., B.A.; company executive; b. Fort William, Ont. 16 April 1916; s. LeRoy and Elizabeth (Rowley) C.; e. Public and High Schs. Weyburn, Sask.; Univ. of Ottawa, B.A. 1938; m. Olivia, d. John Henry 16 Nov. 1940; children: Vincent John, Paul Henry, Theresia Mary, Peter Joseph; PRESIDENT AND DIR., ROMAN CORPORATION LTD. since 1975; Vice-Pres. Denison Mines Ltd.; with American Can of Canada Ltd. as Extve. Understudy 1939-41; joined Foreign Service 1946 and apptd. Asst. Comm. Secy. Candn. Embassy The Hague 1947-1950 Brussels 1950-54; Comm. Councillor The Hague 1954-56, Rio De Janeiro 1956-59; Dir. Internat. Trade Policy, Dept. Trade and Comm. Ottawa 1959-64; Min. (E-cons.) Canada House London, Eng. 1964-68; Vice-Pres. (Fed.) Export Devel. Corp. 1968-75; Past Vice-Chrmn. Foreign Invest. Ins. Comn. Berne Union; Vice Chrmn., Deputy Chrmn., Sharelife Appeal; mem., Candn. Inst. of Internat. Affairs; served with Queen's Own Cameron Highlanders (Winnipeg), European Theatre 1941-46; rank on discharge Maj.; recreation: golf, swimming, outdoor sports; Clubs: Bd. of Trade; Canadian; Empire; Royal Ottawa; Reform (London, Eng.); Home: 704-4005 Bayview Ave., Willowdale, Ont. M2M 3Z9; Office: Suite 3900, South Tower, Royal Bank Plaza, P.O. Box 40, Toronto, Ont. M5J 2K2

CHAPLIN, James Dhu; manufacturer; b. St. Catharines, Ont., 26 Dec. 1932; s. James Elliot Gordon and Helen Elizabeth (Goring) C.; e.Ridley Coll., St. Catharines, Ont.; m. Janet Catherine d. Robert Hamilton Rough; Newmarket, 11 May 1956; divorced; children: Helen Elizabeth Anne, Richard Robert Gordon, Janet Suzanne, Julia Dianna; CHRMN. OF BD. & CHIEF EXTVE. OFFR., CANADIAN GENERAL-TOWER LTD.; Dir., PCL Industries Ltd.; Woodbridge Foam Corp.; Ald., City of Galt 1963, re-el. 1965; apptd. Depy. Mayor 1967; def. cand. (Fed.) in Waterloo S. 1964 and 1965; P. Conservative; Anglican; Club: Toronto; Home: R.R. 4, Inglewood Farms, Cambridge, Ont. N1R 5S5; Office: 52 Middleton St., Cambridge, Ont. N1R 5T6

CHAPMAN, C. Norman; company executive; CHMN. OF THE BD., EMCO LTD.; Dir., Crown Trust Co.; Past Pres., Candn. Inst. of Plumbing & Heating; Founding Dir., LP Gas Ass'n of Can.; joined present Co. as a Salesman in Vancouver in 1939 after four yrs. educ. at Univ. of British Columbia; in 1945 appointed Gen. Sales Mgr. and transf. to Head Office, London, Ont.; elected a Director in 1950 and subsequently has held posts of Vice President-Sales, Vice President-Marketing, Extve. Vice-Pres., Pres., and C.E.O.; Home: 51 Westchester Drive, London, Ont. N6G 2K6; Office: (P.O. Box 5300, Terminal "A") 1108 Dundas St., London, Ont. N6A 4N7

CHAPMAN, Christopher Martin, R.C.A.; film maker; b. Toronto, Ont. 25 Jan. 1927; s. Alfred Hirschfelder and Doris Helen (Dennison) C.; e. Northern Vocational Sch. Toronto; m. 1stly Aljean Pert (d.); m. 2ndly Barbara Glen d. Gerhard Kennedy; one s. Julian Christopher; PROP., CHRISTOPHER CHAPMAN LTD. 1951- ; served 6 yrs. in advertising agency prior to 1951; films incl. "The Seasons" (Candn. Film of Yr. Award 1954, medal from Salerno); "A Place to Stand" (Etrog Candn. Film of Yr., 2 Hollywood nominations, Acad. Award Oscar); "Loring and Wyle"; "Quetico"; "The Persistent Seed"; "Canada"; "Festival" (Expo 70 Osaka); "Impressions 1670-1970" (tercentenary Hudson's Bay Co.); "Volcano" (70 mm Imax); "The Happy Time" (created film component); "Toronto the Good" (multi-media 35 mm film and slide presentation); "A Sense of Humus" (rec'd recognition from Techfilm, Czechoslovakia); "Rome With Anthony Burgess" (dir., filmed, ed. for Nielsen Ferns Internat.); "Saskatchewan Land Alive" (Sask.'s Diamond Jubilee 1980); "Kelly" (feature film) (Famous Players Film Corp., dir.); recipient over 35 recognitions internationally; rec'd R.C.A. Medal for distinguished contrib. to art of film; Centennial Medal 1967; Queen's Silver Jubilee Medal 1977; Pres., Royal Candn. Acad. Arts; Past Pres., Dirs. Guild Can.; mem. Candn. Soc. Cinematographers; Candn. Soc. Eds.; Club: Arts & Letters; Home: R.R. 4, Sunderland, Ont. L0C 1H0; Office: 93 Roxborough Dr., Toronto, Ont. M4W 1X2.

CHAPMAN, Ross Alexander, B.S.A., M.Sc., Ph.D., D.Sc., F.C.I.C.; government administrator; b. Oak Lake, Man., 10 Dec. 1913; s. Frank Richards and Helen Elizabeth (Ross) C.; e. Galt Coll. Inst. (Ont.), 1933; Ont. Agric. Coll., B.S.A. 1940; Macdonald Coll., McGill Univ., M.Sc. 1941, Ph.D. 1944; Univ. of Guelph, D.Sc. 1971; m. Jean McBain Currie, 7 July 1942; children: Karen Bickell, Grierson Currie PRIVATE CONSULTANT TO INTERNATIONAL AND GOVERNMENT AGENCIES on food and drug control since 1974; Asst. Prof. of Chem., Macdonald Coll., McGill Univ., 1944-48; Chief, Food Chem. Div., Food & Drug Directorate, 1948-55 and 1957-58; Dir., Research Labs., 1958-63; Asst. Dir.-Gen. (Foods), 1963-65; Asst. Depy. Min. (Food and Drugs), 1965-71; Special Adviser to Depy. Min. (Health) 1971-72; Dir.-Gen., Internat. Health Services 1972-73; Scientist, Food additives, WHO, Geneva, 1955-57; apptd. mem. Panel of Experts on Food Additives, WHO, 1958; mem. Expert Comte. on Food Additives, Rome, 1959; mem. Candn. Del. to Conf. on Food Standards, Geneva, 1962; Codex Alimentarius Comn., Head Candn. Del., Rome, 1963 and mem. Candn. Del., Geneva, 1964; Chrmn., Codex Comn. on Food Labelling, Ottawa, 1965 and 1966; mem. Panel on Food Safety, White House Conf. on Food, Nutrition & Health, 1969; Head, Candn. Del., U.N. Comn. on Narcotic Drugs Special Sessions, 1970 and to 24th regular session, 1971; Alternate rep. and Acting Head, Candn. Del. to U.N. Conf. to Adopt Protocol on Psychotropic Substances, Vienna, 1971; consultant, to World Health Organization, Geneva 1974-75; to South Pacific Comn. Noumea, New Caledonia 1975-76; to Pan Amer. Health Organization, Washington, D.C. 1977-78; to Drug Abuse Policy, White House, Washington, D.C. 1978; to Saudi Arabia, 1979; to Trinidad and Tobago and to Brazil, 1980; rec'd. Internat. Award, Inst. Food Technols., U.S.A., 1959; William J. Eva Award, Candn. Inst. Food Technol., 1969; hon. D.Sc., Guelph Univ., 1971; Underwood-Prescott Mem. Lectureship 1972; mem., Internat. Narcotic Control Bd. 1973-76; author of over 30 scient. publs.; Fellow, Assn. Official Analytical Chems.; mem., Candn. Inst. Food Technol. Inst. Food Technols.; recreations: golf, skiing; Home: 655 Richmond Rd., Unit 48, Ottawa, Ont. K2A 0G6

CHAPPELL, Hon. Prowse Corrill, M.L.A.; politician; farmer; b. Kitchener, Ont. 30 Sept. 1928; s. Alexander Chappell; e. Summerside (P.E.I.) High Schs. farm short courses; m. Ethelbert d. Rex Dawson, Albany, P.E.I. 25

Apl. 1951; children: Ronald, Wayne, Deborah, Cindy; MIN. OF AGRIC. AND FORESTRY, P.E.I. 1979- ; Past Pres. P.E.I. Fed. of Agric.; Past Prov. Dir. Candn. Fed. Agric.; el. M.L.A. 1978; P. Conservative; Baptist; recreations: golf, reading; Home: R.R. 2, Summerside, P.E.I. C1N 4J8; Office: (P.O. Box 2000) Charlottetown, P.E.I. C1A 7N8.

CHAPUT-ROLLAND, Mme Solange, O.C. (1975); écrivaine; née Montréal, Qué. 14 mai 1919; f. Emile et Rosalie (Loranger) Chaput; é. Couvent d'Outremont (Qué.); Univ. Sorbonne 1939-40; ép. André Rolland 12 mars 1941; enfants: Suzanne Monange, Claude D.; élue deputé libéral du comté de Prévostà làssemblie Nationale, Novembre 1979; auteure "Dear Enemies" (avec Gwethalyn Graham); "Mon pays Québec ou le Canada"; Québec année Zéro; "Une ou deux Sociétés Juste "; "la Seconde conquête"; "Les Heures Sauvages"; "Watergate "; "Les Maudits Journalistes"; "Lettres ouvertes à treize personnalités politiques"; "Une cuisine toute simple" (avec Suzanne Monange); "Face-to-Face" (avec Gertrude Laing); editorialiste; journaliste; écrivain politique; modérateur des radio et télévision; mem. de la Commission Pepin-Robarts sur l'unité Canadienne; Conseil des Arts du Can.; Conseil de l'Université de Montréal; Cercle des Femmes journalistes; l'Union des Artistes; Comn. sur la capitale nationale 1975; reçu Prix Mem. Award 1971-73 pour ses éditoriaux; Don MacArthur Award 1975 pour ses reportages radiophoniques sur la guerre en Israel; résidence: Poste du Lac Guindon, Qué. J0R 1B0

CHARBONNEAU, Hon Guy, B.A.; C.I.B.; C.L.J.; insurance executive; b. Trois-Rivières, Que. 21 June 1922; s. Charles F. and Marie-Rose (Lajoie) C.; e. Primary Schs., Trois Rivières, Que.; Coll. Jean-de-Brebeuf; Univ. of Montreal, B.A. 1941; McGill Univ., Economics, 1941-42; m. Jeanne, d. late Dr. André Bielle, Paris, France, 4 Aug. 1945; m. 2ndly, Yolande Bourguignon, 29 Sept. 1972; App. Mem. Senate of Can., Sept. 1979; CHAIRMAN OF THE BOARD, AND C.E.D., CHARBONNEAU, DULUDE & ASSOC. LTD.; Appointed Men. of Senate of Can. 1979; Dir., Charbonneau, Ledgerwood, Leipsic, Ryan, Simpson & Assocs. Ltd.; Maynard Energy Inc., VS Services Ltd.; Chmn. of Board La Société VS Ltée; mem. Advisory Board, Guaranty Trust Co. of Can.; Montreal Bd. of Trades; served during 2nd W.W.; Commnd. in 1942, Les Fusilliers Mont-Royal; Army Intelligence Course Staff Coll., Kingston, Ont., 1943; Capt. Overseas in 1944 and Air Liaison Offr. with French Wing of TAF in N.W. Europe; Commndr., men., Military and Hospitalier, Order of St. Lazarus of Jerusalem; Chambre de Commerce Francaise au Canada; Can. and Que. Feds. of Ins. Agents and Brokers Assn.; Chambre de Comm. de Mtl.; recreations: bridge, golf, theatre, the arts; Clubs: Laval-sur-le-Lac; Mt. Royal; Home: 3620 Ridgewood Ave., Montreal, Que. H3V 1C3; Office: 4150 St. Catherine St. W., Suite 460, Westmount, Que. H3Z 2W0

CHARBONNEAU, Roger, B.A., L.Sc.Com., M.B.A., LL.D. (Hon.), C.A., O.C.; educator; b. Montreal, Québec 26 Nov. 1914; s. Edouard and Bernadette (Larivière) C.; e. Collège Jean de Brébeuf (Montreal) B.A. 1936; Ecole des Hautes Etudes Comm., L. ès Sc. Com. 1939; Harvard Sch. of Business Adm. M.B.A. 1942; Inst. of C.A. of Qué., C.A. 1945; LL.D. (Hon.), McGill; m. Yvette, d. late Georges Plourde, 1940; children: Francine, Michelle, Gilles, Alain, François; President, Lab. Anglo-French Cie Ltée; Chrmn., BNP Can. Inc.; Dir. Anglo Canadian Telephone Co.; Canadian Surety Co.; Donohue Co. Ltd.; Donohue St-Félicien Inc.; Ecole des Hautes Etudes Commerciales; Fondation Lionel Groulx; Fondation Crudem Canada-Haiti Inc., Gaz Metropolitain; Le Groupe Sobeco; Québec Téléphone; Rolland Inc.; Trust Gén. du Can.; Prof. Ecole des Hautes Etudes Commerciales 1940-60; Asst. Dean, 1959-62; Dean 1962; currently Chrmn. Advisory Comte.; Partner, Charbonneau & Murray, C.A. 1945-54; Co-owner Radio-Nord Inc. 1948-56; mem., Econ.

Council of Can. 1964-65; Pres., Chambre de Comm. de Montréal, 1964-65; R. Catholic; recreation: travelling; Club: St-Denis: Home: 31 Thornton Ave., Town of Mount-Royal, Qué. H3P 1H3; Office: 5255 Decelles Ave., Montréal, Que. H3T 1V6

CHARLAND, Claude Talbot, B.A., B.C.L.; diplomat; b. Quebec City, Que 29 Oct. 1933; s. late Maurice and Lucienne (Talbot) C.; e. Loyola Coll. Montreal B.A. 1954; McGill Univ. B.C.L. 1957; m. Marguerite d. Dr. Jean Panet-Raymond, Frelighsburg, Que. 31 Aug. 1957; children: Louis Christian, Bernard Robert, Anne-Elizabeth; AMBASSADOR TO MEXICO with accreditation to Guatemala, 1979- ; apptd. Foreign Service Offr. 1957, Vice Consul and Asst. Trade Commr. New Orleans 1958, Asst. Comm. Secy. Paris 1958-61, Lagos 1961-62, Extve. Asst. to Depy. Min. of Industry, Trade & Comm. 1962-65, Consul and Trade Commr. Sao Paulo 1965-67, Comm. Counsellor Brussels 1967-69, Min.-Counsellor (Comm.) Paris 1970-73, Asst. Depy. Min. Trade Commr. Service and Internat. Marketing, Industry, Trade & Comm. Ottawa 1973-79; R. Catholic; Club: Bankers (Mexico City); University (Mexico City); Home: Montes Carpatos 825, Mexico 10, D.F.; Office: P.O. Box 500 (MEX), Ottawa, Ont. K1N 8T7 or Schiller 529, Mexico 5, D.F.

CHARLES, William Bruce, M.D., F.R.C.P.(C) (1946); F.A.C.P. (1967); physician; b. Toronto, Ont., 23 Nov. 1913; e. Univ. of Toronto, M.D. 1938; Diplomate, Am. Bd. of Internal Med., 1948; Consultant Staff, Toronto East Gen. Hosp.; Active Consulting Staff, Dept. of Medicine, Sunnybrook Medical Centre; Emeritus, Prof., Dept. of Med., Univ. of Toronto; served in 2nd World War, 1941-46; Major, No. 2 Candn. Gen. Hosp., Eng. and N.W. Europe; United Church; Home: 115 Rochester Ave., Toronto, Ont. M4N 1N9

CHARPENTIER, Fulgence, M.B.E. (1944), C.M. (1978); b. Ste. Anne de Prescott, Ont., 29 June 1897; e. Classical Coll., Joliette, P.Q.; Laval Univ., B.A. 1917; Osgoode Hall, Toronto, 1919; m. Louise Dionne, 1934; joined Department of External Affairs, 1947; Adviser, UNO Conference, Paris, 1948; Candn. Delegate, UNESCO Fourth Session, Paris, 1949; Information Officer, Canadian Embassy, Paris, 1948-53; Adviser, UNO Conf., Paris, 1951; Del., 8th UNESCO Conf., Montevideo, 1954; Chargé d'Affaires, Candn. Embassy, Uruguay, 1953-56; Brazil, 1956-57 and at Haiti, 1957-60; Ambassador to Cameroun, Gabon, Chad, Congo (Brazzaville) and Central African Republic 1962-1965; apptd. Asst. to the Commr.-Gen. Candn. World Exhn., Montreal 1967; apptd. Asst. Editor-in-Chief "Le Droit" 1968; Pres., L'Alliance Française; formerly Parlty. Corr., "Le Droit", Ottawa; later with "La Presse", Montreal; mem., Parlty. Press Gallery (Pres. 1926); Private Secy., Hon. Fernand Rinfret, 1926-30; Chief French Journals, H. of C., 1936-47; apptd. Chief Press Censor, 1940; Asst. Dir. of Censorship, 1943, and Dir., 1944-45; Alderman, Ottawa, 1929-30; Controller, there, 1931-35; defeated cand. for Mayor, 1935; served in World War with C.E.F. 1918; author "Le Mirage Américain", 1934; "Les Patriotes" (drama), 1938; editorialist, "Le Droit", Ottawa; Bailli national Confrérie Chaîne des Rôtisseurs; Confederation Medal, and several foreign orders; King's Coronation Medal; R. Catholic; Home: 42 Southern Drive, Ottawa, Ont. K1S 0P6; Office: 375 Rideau St., Ottawa, Ont. K1N 5Y7

CHARRON, André, C.R., B.A., LL.L.; administrateur; né Montréal, Qué., 10 décembre 1923; f. Ernest, D.D.S., D.S.C., et Antoinette (Champagne) C.; é. Collège de Montréal, 1936-42; Collège Ste-Marie, B.A. 1944; Université de Montréal, LL.L. 1947; C.R. 1964; ép. Louise, fille de Berthold Mongeau, 14 juin 1956; enfants: André, Caroline, Guy-Philippe, Fannie; PRES., LEVESQUE, BEAUBIEN INC.; Pres. du Conseil et Admin. L'Industrielle Cie d'Assurance sur la Vie; Mt.-Tremblant Lodge (1965) Inc.; Admin., Fonds F-I-C Inc.; Admin., Steinberg Ltée; Eagle Lumber Co. Ltd.; Lallemand Inc.; Librairie Beauchemin Ltée; Admin., Atlific Inns Inc.; Atpro Inc.; Beaubran Corp.; Campeau Corp. Ltd.; Domlim Inc.; Pres., Inst. Armand-Frappier; Admin., Hôpital Marie Enfant; Sandvick Canada S.C.C.; N.G. Valiquette Ltée; La Prévoyance Cie d'Assurances; La Laurentienne Cie d'Assurances générales; La Paix, Cie d'Assurances générales du Canada; Dir. Cie du Trust National Ltée; Ancien prés., Assn. candnne. des Courtiers en Valeurs mobilières; Prés. du Comité des Gouv., Bourse de Montréal; études légales avec Brais Campbell & Assoc., 1947-48; André Charron, 1948-58; Charron & Mercier, 1958-63; Catholique R.; Clubs: Mount Royal; St.-Denis; Résidence: App. 1260, 1250 avenue des Pins, Montréal, Qué. H3G 2P5; Bureau: 360 Rue St.-Jacques, Montréal, Qué. H2Y 1P7

CHARRON, Hon. Claude, N.N.A.; politician; b. Ile Bizard, Qué. 22 Oct. 1946; s. Lucien and Béatrice (Théoret) C.; e. St-Raphael des Missions Sch St-Laurent Coll. Montréal; Univ. of Montréal;Parlty. House Leader And Min. For Parlty. Affairs, Que. 1979-82; el. M.N.A. for St-Jacques prov. g.e. 1970, re-el. since; Min. Responsible for High Comn. on Youth, Recreation & Sports 1976; Prof. of Pol. Science; Vice Pres. Internat. Affairs Students' Union Qué. 1968; co-author "Les Etudiants Québécois" 1969; mem. Mouvement Souveraineté-Assn. since foundation; Parti Quebecois;

CHARTERS, Robert Burns, D.F.M.; construction executive; b. Brampton, Ont., 9 May 1923; late s. Clarence Victor and Ida Mary (Harcourt) C.; e. Brampton (Ont.) High Sch.; m. Kathleen, d. late T. H. McKillop, 13 March 1947; children: Thomas Victor, Lorie Louise; CHAIRMAN OF THE BOARD AND DIR., ARMBRO HOLDINGS, since 1972; Dir. and Extve. Vice Pres., Armstrong Holdings (Brampton) Ltd.; Dir. and Chmn. of the Bd., Montcalm Construction Inc.; Armbro Materials & Construction Ltd.; Armbro Transport Ltd.; Dir., Ont. Golf Assn.; Dir., Candn. Construction Assn.; joined Armstrong Bros. Construction 1946; served in many fields and H.O. particularly heavy constr. and highway constr. operations 1946-66; named a Dir. and Extve. Vice Pres. of all operating co's, 1966; served with RCAF 1941-46; attached to RAF Bomber Command 1942-45; rank Flight Lt. on retirement; awarded Croix-de-Guerre; mem., Candn. Br., RAF Escaping Soc.; P. Conservative; Anglican; recreation: golf; Clubs: Chinguacousy and the Toronto Golf Club; Home: 1400 Dixie Road, Mississauga, Ont. L5E 3E1; Office: (Box 1000) Brampton, Ont. L6V 2L9

CHARYK, Joseph Vincent, Ph.D., LL.D.; company president; b. Canmore, Alta., 9 Sept. 1920; s. late John and Anna (Dorosh) C.; e. St. Patrick's High Sch., Lethbridge, Alta., 1938; Univ. of Alta., B.Sc. in Engineering Physics 1942, LL.D. 1964; Cal. Inst. of Technol., M.S. 1943, Ph.D. 1946; D.Engineering (Hon.) U. Bologna, 1974; m. Edwina Elizabeth, d. late William Rhodes, Aug. 1945; children: William R.; J. John, Christopher E., Diane E,; PRESIDENT AND DIR., COMMUNICATIONS SATELLITE CORP., 1963-1979; PRESIDENT, C.E.O., and DIR., 1979 —, Jet Propulsion Lab., Cal. Inst. of Technol., 1943-46; Instr. in Aeronautics at Inst., 1945-46; Asst. Prof. of Aeronautics, Princeton Univ., 1946-49; Assoc. Prof. (assisting in estb. of Guggenheim Jet Propulsion Center, Forrestal Research Center of Univ.) 1949-55; Dir. Aerophysics & Chem. Lab., Missile Systems Div., Lockheed Aircraft Corp., 1955-56; Dir. of Missile Technol. Lab. and later Gen. Mgr. of Space Technol. Div., Aeronutronic Systems (subsidiary Ford Motor Co.), 1958-59; Chief Scientist, U.S. Air Force and later Asst. Secy. for Research & Devel., 1959-60; Under Secy. of Air Force 1960-63; Dir., Abbott Laboratories; American Security Corp.; mem. of Corporation, C.S. Draper Laboratory, Inc.; Fellow, Am. Inst. Aeronautics & Astronautics; mem., Nat'l Acad. Engring; Internat. Acad. Astronautics; National Inst. Social Sciences; National Space Club; Fellow, Inst. Elect. & Electronic Engrs.; Sigma Xi (Past Pres. Princeton Chapter); recreations: golf, tennis, photography; Clubs: Burning Tree; 1925 F. Street; Chevy Chase; Metropolitan Club; Home: 5126 Tilden St., N.W. Washington, D.C. 20016; Office: 950 L'Enfant Plaza, S.W. Washington, D.C. 20024

CHASTON, John G.; investment dealer; b. Calgary, Alta., 5 March 1915; s. Leon Christopher and Mrs. (Greer) C.; e. W. Can. High Sch., Calgary; children: John Lionel, Margaret Elizabeth, Christina Leone, Martha Jane; CHAIRMAN OF THE BOARD, PEMBERTON SECURITIES LTD., since 1975; Dir., Balco Forest Products; Block Bros. Industries; Secy.-Treas., Pemberton & Son Vancouver Ltd., 1946, Dir. 1952, Vice Pres. 1966; served with R.C.A. and Royal Candn. Ordnance Corps during World War II; rank Lt. on discharge; mem. Inst. C.A.'s B.C.; Anglican; recreation: golf; Clubs: Capilano Golf & Country, The Vancouver, Royal and Ancient Golf (St. Andrews); Valley C. (Montecito Calif.); Home: 2866 Bellevue, W. Vancouver, B.C. V7J 1E8; Office: The Bentall Centre, Vancouver, B.C. V7X 1K6

CHATILLON, Claude, B.A., L.P.H.; diplomate; né à Ottawa, 29 déc. 1917; fils William et Eugénie (Poulin) C.; é. Univ. d'Ottawa, B.A., BPH (1940), LPH (1941); m. Simone Boutin, 24 jan. 1948; enfants; Pierre-Yves, Elisabeth, Annick; Vice Counsul, New York 1946; Deuxième Secrétaire, Ambassade du Canada, New Delhi, fév. 1950; Ottawa ministère mars 1950; Deux. Secrétaire Paris, nov. 1953 et Premier juillet 1955; Coll. de la Défence nat., Kingston, Ont. sept. 1956; Ottawa, août 1957 (Dir. de l'Information — Min. des Affaires Extérieures); Consul, Seattle, mars 1959, Boston 1962; Conseiller, Ambassade du Can., Madrid et Rabat, 1965; Ottawa sept. 1970 (Dir. des affaires consulaires); Dir. de la Politique consulaire nov. 1972; Ambassadeur au Cameroun, Gabon, R.C.A. et Tchad, oct. 1975 à juillet 1978; rep. du Ministère au Comité consultatif de Statut de Réfugié depuis 1978; vol. armée canadienne 1942 (soldat), service Royaume-Uni, Afrique du Nord, Sicile, Italie; démob. en 1945 (lieut.); mem. Assn. des anciens de l'Univ. d'Ottawa; Assn. du Royal 22e Régt.; Catholique R.; intérêts particuliers: peinture, tennis, natation, pêche, golf; Address d'affaires: Ministère des Affaires Extérieures, Ottawa, Ont.

CHATTERTON, George L., B.Sc.; b. Boshof, Union of S. Africa, 16 Jan. 1916; s. Harry Butler & Charlotte Elizabeth (Van Zyl) C.; e. Boys' High Sch., Kimberley, S.A., Sr. Matric. 1933; Univ. of Pretoria, B.Sc. (Agric.) 1937; Cornell Univ. 1939-40; came to Canada 1940; m. Katherine M., d. late James Cavanagh; children: Drewie W., Sharlie E., Peter G., Valerie J.; served in 2nd World War in R.C.A.F. as Flying Offr.; Regional Supervisor, Veterans' Land Act, Dept. of Veterans' Affairs, 1946-61; el. to H. of C. for Esquimalt-Saanich (B.C.) in by-el. 1961; re-el. 1962 and 1963 and 1965; mem., Saanich Sch. Bd., 1957-61, Reeve, Mun. of Saanich; Dir., Gr. Victoria Water Bd.; 1958-61, Dir., Victoria & Vancouver Island Publ. Bur.; Victoria Chamber of Comm.; Gr. Victoria Art Gallery; 1959-61, Trustee, Gr. Victoria Centennial Fund; 1960, Pres., Vancouver Island Mun.; Extve. mem., Union of B.C. Mun.; 1960-61, Chrmn., Capital Region Planning Bd. of B.C.; mem., Capital Improvement Dist. Comn. of B.C.; Prov. Adm., Home Owner Assistance, 1968-73; Chrmn. B.C. Housing Management Comn., 1970-73; Assoc. Depy. Min., first of Dept. of Housing, then Min. of Mun. Affairs and Housing, 1973-78; Exec. Dir., Urban Development Inst. (Pacific Region); since 1 April 1978; mem., Agric. Inst. of Can.; Inst. of B.C. Agrol.; Appraisal Inst. of Can.; Comm. Planning Assn. of Can.; Centennial and Jubilee Awards; P. Conservative (fed.); Social Credit (prov.); Protestant; recreations: gardening, swimming; Home: 2180 Beach, Victoria, B.C. V8R 6J8

CHATWIN, Leonard William, B.A.; Canadian public service; retired; b. Vancouver, B.C., 22 Apl. 1913; s. late Henry William and Annie Louise (Murgatroyd) C.; e. Pub. and High Sch., Vancouver, B.C.; Univ. of British Columbia (1930-31; 1938-43) B.A.; m. Norma Isobel Young, 29 Dec. 1956; Extve. Producer, Challenge for Change Program, Nat. Film Bd., 1971-75; employed in business in Vancouver, B.C., 1932-38; in charge of visual educ. in the Extension Dept., Univ. of B.C. 1938-43; joined Nat. Film Bd. as Organizer of Indust. and Trade Union Circuits for B.C.; apptd. Regional Supervisor for B.C., 1943 and for Alta. also, 1945; trans. to Ottawa, 1947 as Co-ordinator of Candn. Distribution; apptd. Dir. of Distribution 1949; Gen. U.S.A. Rep. 1962-66, Asian Rep. 1967-69; Chief, Media Studies & Production Liaison 1969-71; Protestant; recreations: mountain climbing, photography; Clubs: B.C. Mountaineering; Alpine of Canada; Address: Mayne Island, B.C. V0N 2J0

CHEESEMAN, Roy L.; company president; b. Port au Bras, Newfoundland, 1921; s. Hon. John T. Cheeseman; e. Bishop Feild Coll., St. John's Nfld.; King's Coll. Sch., Windsor, N.S.; Shaw's Business Sch., Toronto, Ont.; m. Vicki Butler, Bishop's Falls, Nfld.; four children; PRESIDENT, WEST ATLANTIC PRODUCTS LTD.; Dir., Conception Bay Sea Products Ltd.; Past Pres., Nfld. Board of Trade; served in 2nd World War with R.A.F. 1940-45; after war became a Partner in General Traders Ltd., in 1949 joined Bowring Bros. Ltd., St. John's Nfld. as Wholesale Mgr.; joined present firm as Mang. Dir., 1955, el. Pres. 1958; el. M.H.A. (P.C.) 1972; Past Vice-Pres., St. John's Jr. Chamber Comm.; Past Pres., St. John's Rotary Club; Address: St. John's, Newfoundland.

CHEESMAN, Ralph Leslie, M.Sc., D.I.C., Ph.D., F.G.S.; consulting geologist; b. Southborough, Tunbridge Wells, Eng., 19 Jan. 1924; s. Leslie H. S. and Ethel (Miller) C.; e. Eltham Coll., Eng., 1935-41; Imperial Coll., London Univ., B.Sc. (Hons. Geol.) 1950 (A.R.C.S.), M.Sc. (Geol.) D.I.C. 1951; Univ. of London, Ph.D. (Geol.) 1955; m. Hilda, d. Henry Hughes, St. Lucia, B.W.I., 2 Sept. 1950; two s., Christopher Ralph, Timothy Andrew; mem. of Teaching Staff, Dept. of Geol., Imp. Coll., Univ. of London, 1951-55 (also served as Librarian for Watt's Lib. of Geol., 1952-55); joined Dept. of Mineral Resources, Sask. as Sr. Geol. (Precambrian) 1955, Chief Geol. 1956-69, since when Consulting Geol.; Mgr.-Consultant, Sask. Mining Assn. since 1973; Hon. Aide to Gov. Gen. 1971-74; served with R.N.V.R. (active 1942-46; Lieut., Reserve, since 1946; L.Cdr. R.C.N.R., 1962, Cdr. 1971; in command H.M.C.S. "Unicorn" N.R. Div., Saskatoon 1971-74; H.M.C.S. Queen, N.R. Div. Regina 1975-76; Fellow Geol. Soc. London; Mineral. Assn. Can.; Geol. Assn. Can.; mem. Senate, Coll. of Emmanuel and St. Chad; mem., Geol. Assn. (London); Geol. Soc. Am.; Candn. Inst. Mining & Metall.; Assn. Prof. Engrs. Sask. and Man. Eng. Advis. Council, Sask.; Anglican; recreations: private flying, philately, travel; Address: 730-2002 Victoria, Regina, Sask. S4P 0R7

CHERCOVER, Murray; television executive; b. Montreal, Que., 18 Aug. 1929; s. Max M. and Betty (Pomerance) C.; e. Port Arthur, Ont., Matric.; Acad. Radio & Television Arts, Toronto, Ont.; Neighbourhood Playhouse, Sch. of Theatre, New York, N.Y.; m. Barbara Ann d. C. J. Holleran, Atlanta, Ga.; children: Hollis Denny, Sean Peter; PRESIDENT, MANG. DIR. AND DIR. CTV TELEVISION NETWORK LTD., since 1969: Pres. and Dir., Avanti Management Ltd.; Lancer Teleproductions Ltd.; Dir., Toronto Arts Productions; International Council, National Academy of Television Arts and Sciences; Futures Secretariat; began career with CFPA Radio Stn., Port Arthur, Ont., 1944; in radio and theatre, with New Play Soc., Toronto 1946-48; in U.S., 1948-52; Extve. Dir., Stock Co. in Kennebunkport. Me., Long Island Tent Theatre, Atlantic City Circle Theatre; Producer-Dir., of Network Television Drama for Louis G. Cowan Agency, "Cosmopolitan Theatre"; Film Dir., independently to Canada, 1952; until 1960 Drama Producer-Dir., C.B.C.; "General Motors Presents", Proctor & Gamble "On Camera"; Ford Motor "Playbill", "Space Command" etc.; also Comm.

Producer on all maj. nat. accounts; joined CFTO-TV, Baton Broadcasting Ltd., as Extve. Producer of all Prod., 1960; Dir., Programming, 1961; Vice-Pres., Programming, 1962; joined present interest as Extve. Vice Pres. and Gen. Mgr. 1966, Chief Operating Offr. and Dir. 1966; mem. Adv. Comte. for Theatre Arts; The George Brown Coll. of Applied Arts & Technol.; Radio & Television Arts Advisory Comm. Ryerson Polytechnical Inst.; Advisory Committee for Film/TV Production Program, Humber College; Advisory Council of Canadian Friends of Tel Aviv University; Canadian Association of Broadcasters; Broadcast Executives Society; Central Canada Broadcasters' Association (former Director); International Platform Association; International Press Institute; National Academy of Television Arts & Sciences (Internat'l Council); Royal Canadian Yacht Club; Bloor Park Club; Radio Control Club; Model Aeronautics Association of Canada; Antique & Classic Car Club; Morgan Owners Club, MGT Registry; Ferrari Car Club.; recreations: theatre, antiques, collection of fine art, aviation, antique and classic cars; Club: R.C.Y.C.; Home: 34 Dunbar Road, Toronto, Ont. M4W 2X6; Office: 42 Charles St. East, Toronto, Ont. M4Y 1T5

CHERNEY, Brian, M.Mus., Ph.D.; composer; educator; b. Peterborough, Ont. 4 Sept. 1942; e. ARCT 1961; Univ. of Toronto B.Mus. 1964, M.Mus. 1967, Ph.D. 1974; Royal Conserv. Music Toronto piano and composition; taught theory and composition Univ. of Victoria 1971-72 and McGill Univ. 1972- ; compositions incl. "Variations for Orchestra", "Quintet", "Mobiles" (1968-69), "String Trio" 1976 (tied for top position Internat. Rostrum of Composers 1979); author "Harry Somers" 1975; numerous other writings; affiliate PRO Canada; Assoc., CM Centre.

CHERNIACK, Saul, Q.C., LL.B.; b. Winnipeg, Manitoba, 10 January 1917; s. Joseph Arthur, Q.C. and Fannie (Golden) C.; e. Peretz Folk, Machray and St. John's High Schs., Winnipeg; Univ. of Man.; LL.B. 1939 m. Sybil Claire, d. late Joseph Zeal, 10 July 1938; children: Lawrie, Howard D.; read law with Joseph A. Cherniack, Q.C.; called to Bar of Man. 1940; cr. Q.C. 1963; private law practice since 1940; served with Intelligence Cor., Candn. Army, during World War II; rank Capt.; mem. Winnipeg Sch. Bd. 1950-54; Councillor, Twp. of Winnipeg Beach, 1958-59; Ald., City of Winnipeg, 1959-60; Councillor, Metro Corp. Greater Winnipeg, 1960-62; M.L.A. 1962-81; re-el. since; Min. of Finance and Min. of Urban Affairs 1969 resigning 3 Jan. 1975; Past Nat. Vice Pres., Candn. Jewish Congress; mem., NDP; Jewish; Home: 333 St. John's Ave., Winnipeg, Man. R2W 1H2; Office: Legislative Bldg., Winnipeg, Man.

CHERNICK, Victor, M.D., F.A.A.P., F.R.C.P.(C); pediatrician; educator; b. Winnipeg, Man. 31 Dec. 1935; s. Jack J. and Mina (Tapper) C.; e. Univ. of Man. M.D. 1959; Johns Hopkins Hosp. 1960-64; m. Norma d. Saul Fordman, Winnipeg, Man. 19 May 1957; children: Mark, Sharon, Richard, Lisa; PROF. & HEAD OF DEPT. OF PEDIATRICS, UNIV. OF MAN. 1971-79; Pediatrician-in-Chief, Health Sciences Centre 1971-79; Prof. of Pediatrics, Univ. of Man. 1979-; Head, Section of Pediatric Respirology, Childrens Hosp. of Winnipeg 1979-; Scient. Offr. Med. Research Council Can.; Lectr. in Pediatrics, Johns Hopkins Univ. 1964, Asst. Prof. 1965-66; Asst. Prof. of Pediatrics Univ. Man 1966, Assoc. Prof. 1967-71; Visiting Prof. of Pediatrics, Harvard Univ. 1976-77; mem. Med. Adv. Comte. Richardson Foundation; Queen Elizabeth II Scientist 1967-73; Am. Men of Science 1968; Candn. Pediatric Soc. Medal for Research 1970; Hon. Citizen City of New Orleans 1976; Trustee, Queen Elizabeth II Scient. Fund; External Examiner, Med. Research Council of N.Z.; Assoc. Ed. "Disorders of the Respiratory Tract in Children" 3rd ed. 1977; Guest Ed. "Onset and Control of Fetal and Neonatal Respiration" Vol. 1 1977; co-author, "Respiratory Therapy of Newborn Infants and Children" 1982; author or co-author numerous reviews, papers, abstracts and presentations; Fellow, Am. Thoracic Soc. 1962-64, Chrmn. Scient. Assembly Pediatrics 1970; mem. Soc. Pediatric Research (Council 1973-76); Candn. Soc. Clin. Investigation; Midwest Soc. Pediatric Research (Pres. 1976-77); Am. Physiol. Soc.; Candn. Pediatric Soc.; N.Y. Acad. Science; Candn. Physiol. Soc.; Am. Acad. Pediatrics (Extve. Comte. Sec. Diseases of chest 1973-77); Dir. Candn. Thoracic Soc. 1971-72; Secy. Internat. Cystic Fibrosis Assn. 1973-76; mem. Council Royal Coll. Phys. & Surgs.; mem. Cystic Fibrosis Panel, Internat. Pediatric Assn.; mem. Ed. Bd. several prof. journs.; Home; 14 Montcalm Cres., Winnipeg, Man. R2V 2N4; Office: Children's Hospital, 685 Bannatyne Ave., Winnipeg, Man. R3E 0W1.

CHERRY, Zena Mary; newspaper columnist; b. Prince Albert, Sask. d. Dr. Stanley Butler and Belle (Thomas-Brown) MacMillan; e. Sacred Heart Convent, Prince Albert; Bishop Strachan Sch. Toronto; m. late Westcott Warren Christopher Cherry; COLUMNIST, THE GLOBE AND MAIL; mem. volunteer comtes. Candn. Opera Co., Nat. Ballet, Multiple Sclerosis Soc., Toronto Symphony, Jr. League of Toronto; former Bd. mem. Candn. Red Cross Soc.; Past Regent, Lady Tweedsmuir Chapter IODE; Founding Chrmn. Children's Theatre; mem. Founding Extve. Comte. for Theatre, York Univ.; Dir., Toronto Outdoor Art Exhn.; four-time winner Candn. Women's Press Club Mem. Award; mem. Internat. Press Inst. Switzerland; Media Club Can.; Heraldry Soc. Can.; Anglican; recreations: reading, travel, hagiography; Clubs: Badminton & Racquet; Canadian; Empire; Garden; Heliconian; Royal Candn. Mil. Inst.; Royal Canadian Yacht; Home: "Cherrywood", 200 Heath St. W., Toronto, Ont. M4V 1V4; Office: 444 Front St. W., Toronto, Ont. M5V 2S9.

CHETWYND, Sir Arthur Ralph Talbot, Bt.; communications consultant; b. Walhacin, B.C., 28 Oct. 1913; s. Frances M. (Jupe) and the late Hon. William Ralph Talbot C., M.L.A.; e. Pub. and High Sch., B.C.; Vernon Prep. Sch. B.C.; m. Marjory M. M., d. late Robert Bruce Lang; children: Robin John Talbot, William Richard Talbot; CHRMN., CHETWYND FILMS LTD.; Pres., Brocton Hall Communication Ltd.; Dir., N.Z. Lamb Co. Ltd.; prior to 2nd World War, engaged in ranching and teaching in B.C.; on staff of Univ. of Toronto, 1945-51 (Assoc., Sch. of Physical and Health Educ.; Publicity Offr., Univ. of Toronto Athletic Assn.); Field Supervisor Candn. Red Cross Water Safety Programme, 1946-49; formed Chetwynd Films Ltd., 1950, specialising in sponsored films for bus., indust., govt. and T.V.; production work of Co. includes educ. films on med.; advertising, instructional, travel, safety, sports and other related subjects; has produced over 3,000 films since 1950; over 100 nat. and internat. awards; served in 2nd World War with R.C.A.F., 1943-45; Chief Instr. of Med. Reconditioning at end of war; mem., Candn. Film and T.V. Assn. (Past Pres.); Soc. of Motion Picture and T.V. Engrs.; Information Film Producers of Am. Inc.; Travel Industry Assn. Can.; Ist. of Assn. Extves.; Metrop. Toronto Bd. of Trade; Candn. Chamber of Comm.; Monarchist League Can.; Vice-chrmn., Roy. Commonwealth Soc.; past pres., Empire Club of Can.; Anglican; recreations: swimming, golf, volunteer work; Clubs: Toronto Hunt; Albany (Toronto); Hart House; Naval & Military (England); Home: 95 Thorncliffe Park Dr., Apt. 402, Toronto, Ont. M4H 1L7; Office: #402, 95 Thorncliffe Park Dr., Toronto, Ont. M4H 1L7

CHEVALIER, Leo Charles, C.M.; fashion designer; b. Montreal, Que. 8 Oct. 1934; s. Leo John and Mary Ellen (Whitten) C.; e. Loyola Coll. 1948-52; Sch. Art.Design, Montreal Museum of Fine Arts 1951-53; Ecole des Beaux Arts de Montréal 1955; m. Monica Solange d. Michael A.V. Perdriel 21 June 1980; OWNER, LEO CHEVALIER

INTL. LTD.; Asst. Mgr., Henry Morgan Co., 1955-59; Designer/costumer, Montreal Theatre Ballet, 1958; Asst. Mgr./Display, R. Simpson Co., 1959-60; Freelance Fashion designer and Interior designer, 1960-61; Mgr./Buyer Fraid's Co., 1961-63; Mgr./Buyer De St. Victor. 1963-65; Prop. Cheval Boutique, 1966-68; Fashion Designer numerous cos. Ladieswear, Brodkin Ind., 1973-; Designed/Executed costumes Mtl. Ballet Theatre, 1958; Murals Bell Can. Head Off., 1965; Costumes, Théathre de Repentigny, 1967; Designer of Year, Intl. Ladies' Garment Assn., 1967; Order of Can. 1979; Founding mem. and past pres. Fashion Designers' Assn. of Can.; mem., Fashion Can.; Designer Development Cmte. (Past Dir.); Bd. mem. Can. Colour Council; Office: 416 de Maisonneuve Blvd. W., Ste. 7, Montreal, Que. H3A 1N9.

CHEVRIER, Jean-Marc, B.A., B.Péd., Doctorat en psychologie; psychologist; publisher; b. Cheneville, St-Félixdeé Valois, Qué. 2 March 1916; s. Joseph Honoré and Olévina (Malette) C.; e. Univ. de Montréal B.A., B.Péd. 1940, Licence en Sciences pédagogiques 1942, Baccalauréat en psychologie 1943, Licence en psychologie 1945, Doctorat en psychologie 1949; Ecole normale Jacques-Cartier High Sch. Teacher Dipl. 1939; Diplomate Am. Bd. Examiners Prof. Psychol. Counseling Psychol. 1956; m. Madeleine d. Télesphore Bourassa 4 Jan. 1941; children: Marie-Paule, Marcel, Claudette, Madeleine, Robert; PRESIDENT AND EXTVE. DIR., INST. OF PSYCHOLOGICAL RESEARCH INC. 1964- ; Extve. Dir. JMC Press Ltd. 1968- ; Founder & Chief Psychol. Guidance Bureau Ministry of Youth Que. Govt. 1947-53; Consultant, Comte. of Apprenticeship Printing Trades 1947-73; Laval & Chambly Coll. 1949-58, Hôpital Pasteur de Montréal 1953-60; Prof. (chargé de cours) Inst. Psychol. Univ. de Montréal 1951-57, Sch. of Rehabilitation Faculty of Med. 1953-57, Sch. of Educ. 1959-61; Founder and Dir. Psychol. Dept. Rehabilitation Inst. Montreal 1953-62; Dir. of Guidance Montreal Cath. Sch. Comn. 1962-64; Prof. (chargé de cours) Ecole Normale Secondaire 1962-63; Adm. and Pres. Edi-Quebec 1973-75; Dir., Treas., Vice Pres. Le Centre de Psychologie et de Pédagogie 1945-57; recipient Silver Medal Ecole Normale Jacques Cartier 1939; Bronze Medal Graphic Arts Industries Prov. Que. 1958; Graphic Arts Industries (USA) Award; Stothers Exceptional Child Foundation Scholarship; Ministry Health & Social Welfare Can. Grant 19..; author numerous textbooks and psychol. tests; mem. Assn. Psychols. Prov. Que. (Past Pres.); Candn. Psychol. Assn.; Am. Psychol. Assn.; Candn. Guidance & Counselling Assn.; Ont. Psychols. Assn. and other prof. assns.; R. Catholic; recreations: skiing, photography; Home: 524 de Marigny, Laval-Des-Rapides, Ville de Laval, Qué. H7N 5A3; Office: 34 Fleury St. W., Montreal, Que. H3L 1S9.

CHEVRIER, Hon. Lionel, P.C. (Can.) 1945 C.C. (1967); Q.C., D.C.L., LL.D.; b. Cornwall, Ont., s. late Joseph Elphège and late Malvina (De Repentigny) C.; e. Primary and Secondary Schs., Cornwall, Ont.; Ottawa Univ., B.A. and Ph.B. 1924; LL.D. Ottawa Univ. 1946, Laval 1952, Queen's 1956; D.C.L. Bishop's 1964; Osgoode Hall, Toronto, Ont.; m. Lucienne, d. Thomas J. Brûlé, Ottawa, Ont., 22 Oct. 1932; children: Lucie (Mrs. Pierre Thomas), Robert, Jean, Bernard, Adèle (Mrs. Jean Besner), Marie (Mrs. Richard Gervais); active with law firm of Geoffrion & Prud'homme; called to the Bar of Ontario, 1928 and Bar of Quebec 1957; cr. K.C. 1938; Secretary, Bd. of Trade, Cornwall, Ont., 1928-34; Hon. Col., S.D. & G. Highlanders; el. to H. of C. for Stormont, g.e. 1935; re-el. g.e. 1940, 1945, 1949 and 1953; Depy. Chief Govt. Whip 1940; Chrmn., Special Parlty. Sub-comt. on War Expenditures, 1942; Del., Empire Parlty. Assn., Washington, 1943; apptd. Parlty. Asst. to Min. of Mun. & Supply, 1943; Del., Bretton Woods Conf., 1945; Minister of Transport, 1945-54; Chrmn. Candn. Del. to U.N. Gen. Assembly, Paris, 1948; Chrmn., Special Mission to francophone Africa 1968; Mission to Candn. Consular posts in U.S. 1968; Pres., St. Lawrence Seaway Authority, 1954-57;

apptd. Pres. of the P.C. Apl. 1957; re-el. to H. of C. for Montreal-Laurier, g.e. 1957, 1958, 1962, '63; Min. of Justice, Canada, 1963-64; Candn. High Commr. to the U.K. 1964-67; apptd. Commr.-Gen. for visits of State, Candn. Centennial Exhn. Montreal 1967; retired from the pub. service 31 Dec. 1968; Author "The St. Lawrence Seaway"; President, Montreal Rehabilitation Institute; President, Windsor Hotel; Director, Québecair, Imperial Trust Company, Canadian Fur Investments Ltd., Newsco Investments Ltd.; Clubs: Rideau (Ottawa); St. James's; Mount Stephen, (Montreal); Address: 500, Place d'Armes, Suite 1200, Montreal, Que. H2Y 2W4

CHICOINE, F. Luc, B.A., M.D.; paediatrician; b. Montreal, Que. 19 Apl. 1929; s. Henri and Lucienne (Danis) C.; e. Univ. of Montreal B.A. 1948, M.D. 1953; m. Pierrette d. late Charlemagne Legault 27 June 1957; one s. Jean-François; PROF. AND CHRMN. OF PEDIATRICS, UNIV. OF MONTREAL since 1974; Dir. Dept. of Pediatrics and Poison Control Center, Ste-Justine Hosp.; Residency Univ. of Montreal 1953-55; Babies and Children Hosp. Western Reserve Univ. Cleveland 1955-57; Assoc. Prof. present univ. 1964, Prof. 1971; co-author "Precis de Pediatric" 2nd ed. 1977; "Poisons, Emergency Treatment"; mem. Royal Coll. Phys.; Am. Acad. Pediatrics; Candn. Med. Assn.; Candn. Pediatric Soc.; Am. Assn. Poison Control Centres; R. Catholic; recreation: golf; Club: Oka Golf; Home: 115 Duchastel, Outremont, Que. H2V 3E9; Office: 3175 Chemin Ste-Catherine, Montreal, Que. H3J 1C5.

CHILCOTT, W. Dan, Q.C., LL.B.; barrister and solicitor; b. Ottawa, Ont. 15 May 1929; s. James Chilcott; e. Dalhousie Univ.; Dalhousie Law Sch. LL.B.; m. Jean Davidson Pyper 21 July 1962; children: Alison, Jenifer; PARTNER, BINKS, CHILCOTT & SIMPSON: called to Bar of N.S. 1954, Ont. 1956; cr. Q.C. 1966; Trustee, Salvation Army Grace Hosp. Ottawa; Vice. Pres. Central Can. Exhn. Assn.; mem. Police Comn. Ottawa; Bencher, Law Soc. Upper Can.; Protestant; Clubs: Ottawa Hunt & Country; Cercle Universitarie; Home: 3194 Riverside Dr., Ottawa, Ont. K1V 8N7; Office: 19 Daly Ave., Ottawa, Ont. K1N 6E1.

CHILD, Arthur James Edward, B.Com., M.A., F.C.I.S. (1952); company executive; b. Guildford, Surrey, Eng., 19 May 1910; s. William Arthur and Helena Mary (Wilson) C.; e. Gananoque (Ont.) Pub. and High Schs.; Queen's Univ., B.Com. 1931; Harvard Business Sch. AMP, 1956; Univ. of Toronto M.A. 1960; PRES. AND CHIEF EXTVE. OFFR., BURNS FOODS LTD., since 1966; Chmn., Palm Dairies Ltd.; Scott National Co. Ltd.; Stafford Foods Ltd.; Food Svces. Ltd.; Canbra Foods Ltd.; Pres., Ajex Invests. Ltd.; Candn. Dressed Meats Ltd.; Jamar, Inc.; A.R. Clarke and Co. Ltd.; Dir., La Verendrye Mang. Corp.; Allendale Mutual Insurance Co.; Nova, an Alta. Corp.; The Canada Life Assurance Co.; Dir., Newsco Investments Ltd.; Canoe Cove Mfg. Ltd.; Detroit Marine Terminals Inc.; Energy Equipment Systems Inc.; Grove Valve & Regulator Co.; Imperial Trust Co.; WAGI Internat. Corp.; Hydroblaster Inc.; Imperial Trust Co.; Chmn., Canada West Foundation; Ronalds-Federated Ltd.; author: "Economics and Politics in U.S. Banking"; co-author: "Internal Control" with Bradford Cadmus; International President, Inst. of Internal Auditors, 1948-49; mem., Royal Candn. Mil. Inst.; International Inst. for Strategic Studies; Clubs: University (Toronto) R.C.Y.C. (Toronto); R.C.M.I. (Toronto); Mt. Royal (Montreal); St. James's (Montreal); Vancouver; Harvard (Boston); Ranchmen's; Calgary Golf & Country; Home: 1320 Baldwin Ave. S.W., Calgary, Alta.; Office: (P.O. Box 2520) Calgary, Alta. T2P 2M7

CHIPMAN, Robert A., M.Eng., Ph.D.; university professor; b. Winnipeg, Man., 28 April 1912; s. George F. and Emily R. (Christie) C.; e. Univ. of Manitoba, B.Sc. (E. Eng.) 1932; McGill Univ., M.Eng. 1933; Cambridge

Univ., Ph.D. 1939; Harvard Univ., 1937-38; m. Lois M., d. Garnet S. L. Retallack, 29 June 1938; children: Eric George, Ralph Oliver, Julie Anne; PROF OF ELECT. ENGN., UNIV. OF TOLEDO, 1957-78; emeritus 1978; Assoc. Prof. of Elect. Engn., McGill Univ., 1947-57; Fellow, Inst. of Elect. and Electronic Engrs.; mem., Soc. for Hist. of Tech.; Sigma Xi; Protestant; Home: 3547 Rushland, Toledo, Ohio 43606.

CHISHOLM, Donald Alexander, B.A.Sc., M.A., Ph.D.; physicist; b. Toronto, Ont., 7 May 1927; s. Douglas Alexander and Daisy (Smith) C.; e. Adam Beck Sch. and Malvern Coll. Inst., Toronto, 1945; Univ. of Toronto, B.A.Sc. 1949, M.A. 1950, Ph.D. 1952; m. Marilyn, d. Frederick G. Bayliss, 15 May 1953; children: Leslie Megan, Christopher Andrew; CHRMN. AND PRES., BELL-NORTHERN RESEARCH LTD., since 1977; Pres., Innovation & Development, Northern Telecom Ltd. since 1981; Dir., BNR Inc. (U.S.A); Northern Telecom Inc. (U.S.A.); Northern Telecom Can. Ltd.; Northern Telecom Internat. Ltd.; Vice Chrmn., Ont. Research Foundation; Bell Telephone Laboratories, New Jersey, 1953-68; Dir. from 1964; Mang. Dir., System Studies, Bellcomm Inc., Washington, 1968-69; Vice Pres. Research and Devel., Northern Electric Co. Ltd., 1969-70; Pres., Bell-Northern Research Ltd., 1971-76, Extve. Vice Pres., Technology, Northern Telecom Ltd. 1976-81; Fellow, I.E.E.E.; mem. Sci. Council Can.; Hon. Dr. Engineering Univ. of Waterloo 1979; Hon. Dr. Science Univ. of Toronto 1980; Clubs: Country; Mt. Royal; Mississauga Golf & Country; Home: 1523 Knareswood Dr., Mississauga, Ont. L5H 2L9; Office: P.O. Box 458 Station A, Mississauga, Ont. L5A 3A2

CHISHOLM, John Foster, D.S.C., D.F.C., Q.C., b. Toronto, Ont., 3 Aug. 1896; s. late William Craig and Gertrude (Foster) C.; e. Toronto Model Sch.; Univ. of Toronto Schs.; McGill Univ., B.C.L. 1921; m. Kathleen (died 1934), d. late Arthur J. Darling, 1924; 2ndly, Frederica, d. Kenneth MacLaggan, Fredericton, N.B. 1 June 1940; two d.; COUNSEL, COURTOIS, CLARKSON, PARSONS, & TETRAULT; called to the Bar of Que. 1922; cr. K.C. 1937; served in 1st World War, enlisting with R.N.A.S., 1915, serving Overseas as Flight Lieut.; later Capt. with R.A.F.; awarded D.S.C. 1917, and D.F.C., 1918; Zeta Psi; Presbyterian; recreations: golf, curling; Clubs: Royal Montreal Golf; Royal Montreal Curling; St. James's; Home: 15 Willow Ave., Westmount, Que. H3Y 1Y3; Office: 22nd Floor, 630 Dorchester Blvd., Montreal, Que. H3B 1V7

CHISHOLM, Robert Ferguson, O.B.E. (1945), B.Com.; company exeuctive; b. Battleford, Sask., 16 Oct. 1904; s. Robert Ferguson and Eva (Kitson) C.; e. Univ. of Toronto, B.Com. 1926; m. Dorothy Alice, (d. 1960); d. Robert Pinchin, Toronto, Ont. 7 Apl. 1934; children: Judie, Janet; m. 2ndly Rosemary, d. Robert Fennell, Q.C., 3 Jan. 1963; DIRECTOR, WILLIAM MARA CO.; Dir., R. L. Crain Ltd.; Confed. Life Assn.; Thompson Paper Box Co. Ltd.; Capital Growth Fund Ltd.; Formosa Brewery Ltd.; mem. Bd. of Govs., Univ. of Toronto, 1960-70; mem., Bd. of Regents, Victoria Univ., Toronto; Asst. to Mang. Dir., De-Forest Crosley Radio Ltd., Toronto, 1926-33; Indust. Engr., J. D. Woods & Co. Ltd., 1933-38; Vice-Pres. and Gen. Mgr., Gordon Mackay & Co. Ltd., 1938; Extve. Vice-Pres., Dominion Stores Ltd. 1958; mem. Bd. of Stewards, Rosedale Un. Ch.; awarded O.B.E. for wartime work for Candn. Govt. in charge of distribution; Pres., Toronto Symphony 1968-69; author of: "The Darlings" 1971; United Church; Clubs: University; Rosedale Golf; Toronto; St. James's (Montreal); Canadian (Pres. 1950-51); Home: 79 Highland Crescent, Willowdale, Ont. M2L 1G7; Office: Suite 800, 234 Eglinton Ave. E., Toronto, Ont. M4P 1K5

CHITTY, Dennis Hubert, M.A., D.Phil.; professor emeritus; b. Bristol, U.K. 18 Sept. 1912; s. Hubert Chitty; came to Can. 1930; e. Univ. of Toronto B.A. 1935; Oxford Univ. M.A. 1947, D.Phil. 1949; m. Helen Marie d. late Robert

O. Stevens, St. Catharines, Ont. 4 July 1936; children: Jane Carol, Kathleen Joanna, Stephen Gwilym; Prof. Emeritus of Zool. since 1978; Ont. Fisheries Research Lab. summers 1932-35; Small Mammal Research, Bureau of Animal Population, Oxford Univ. 1935-61; taught Hist. and Principles of Biol. Univ. of B.C. 1961-78 (Master Teacher Award 1973); author various scient. papers regulation numbers in natural populations animals especially small mammals; mem. Royal Soc. Can.; Candn. Soc. Zool.; Liberal; Home: 1750 Knox Rd., Vancouver, B.C. V6T 1S3; Office: Univ. of B.C., Vancouver, B.C. V6T 1W5.

CHMIELENSKI, Andrew; civil engineer; b. Warsaw, Poland, 16 April 1909; s. Jan Brug-Chmielenski and Maria (Kossowski) C.; e. Tech. Univ. of Warsaw, Dipl. (Civil Engn.) 1934; m. Eileen Ann. d. Joseph Duffield, 25 July 1949; Design Engineer in Poland, 1934-39; Messrs. Braithwaite and Co., Engrs. Limited, London, Eng., 1946-48, Branch Manager in charge of Co.'s office in Warsaw 1951; came to Canada Dec. 1951; Design Engr., The Foundation Co. of Canada Ltd., 1952-53; joined subsidiary Found. of Can. Engineering Corp. Ltd. (Fenco), 1953 as Design and Project Engr.; apptd. Div. Engr.-Marine Structures, 1957, Vice-Pres. 1960 (co-ordinated the work of the FENCO Reg. Offices), Pres. 1962, Chrmn. Bd. 1973, retired 1975; consultant since 1976; Publications: "Modernization of a Harbour, St. John's, Nfld."; served in 2nd World War, Polish, Middle East and Italian Campaigns, 1939-45 with Polish Army; awarded Polish Crosses (Krzyz Waleczvch and Krzyz Zaslugi); mem., Corp. Prof. Engrs., Que.; Assn. Prof. Engrs., Ont.; Inst. Civil Engrs. Gt. Britain; Roman Catholic; recreations: tennis, gardening; Home: 139 Burbank Dr., Willowdale, Ont. M2K 1N9

CHOLETTE, Jean; marketing executive; b. Montreal, Que. 7 May 1930; s. Edouard Cholette; m. Laurence Legault; children: Claudine, Sylvie, Manon; Pres. Thor Industries Canada Ltée.; sales and marketing consultant Jean Cholette & Associés; Club: Garrison (Quebec); Lambton Golf; Home: 1333 Bloor St. W., Apt. 2503, Mississauga, Ont. L4Y 3T6; Office: 59 Westmore, Rexdale, Ont. M9V 3Y6

CHOQUETTE, Hon. Jerome, Q.C., B.A., LL.L., Doctorate in economics; lawyer; b. Montreal, Que., 25 Jan. 1928; s. Claude and Pauline (Geoffrion) C.; e. Stanislas Coll., B.A.; McGill Univ., B.A., LL.L. 1949; Univ. of Paris, Doctorate in econ. (Jean Bertrand Nogaro Prize); Columbia Univ., Sch. of Business Adm.; m. Françoise Bédard; children: Danielle, Claude, Anita, Céline, Frédéric; Min. of Justice, Que., 1970-75; called to Bar of Que. 1949; cr. Q.C. 1964; Assoc. of: Guy Favreau; Jean Martineau, Battonier of Que. Bar Assn.; Desjardins & Ducharme; Vice-Pres., Que. Lib. Fed.; Head Fed's Pol. Comm.; el. M.N.A. for Outremont in prov. g.e. 1966; re-el. 1970; Min. of Justice, Que. 1970-75; Min. of Educ. 1975; resigned from govt. 1975; founded Popular Nat. Party; Pres., Jr. Bar Assn.; Liberal; R. Catholic; recreations: golf, travel; Home: 7 Ave. Nelson, Outremont, Que. H2V 3Z5

CHOQUETTE, Son. Honn.,Marc, B.A., LL.L.; juge; né Québec 18 fév. 1929; f. l'Hon Fernand, Juge de la Cour d'Appel de la Prov. de Qué. (à sa retraite depuis 1970) et de Dame Marguerite (Vallerand) C.; é. Séminaire de Québec; Coll. St-Charles Garnier; Univ. Laval; ép. Marie, f. M. et Mme Jean-Paul Galipeault; enfants: Claude, Marie, Bernard, Danièle, Philippe, Marc, Anick: JUGE DES SESSIONS DE LA PROVINCE DE QUEBEC, depuis 1971; étude légale: Des Rivières, Choquette, Rioux, Paquet, Goodwin & Vermette, Qué. (Assoc. Sen.); admis au Barreau 1954; créé c.r. 1970; Dir., Trés., 2ième Vice-Prés., 1er Vice-Prés., et Prés. du Jeune Barreau de Qué.; Dir., Jeune Chambre de Comm. de Qué.; mem., Conseil Légis. et substitut au Conseil Gén. et conseiller du Barreau de Qué.; du bureau de l'Assistance judiciaire et du Comité du Service de Référence du Barreau de Qué.; de l'Assn. du Barreau Candn.; de la Chambre de Comm. de Qué.; substitut de la Couronne pour le dist. judiciare de Qué. 1960-66: Procureur, de la Couronne dans les causes de Douanes et Accise, de l'Impôt sur le revenu et autres; de la Comn. de Police du Qué.; de la Cour Municipale de Sillery, 1977-80 représentant du Québec, membre du comité Exécutif et secrétaire général de l'Association Canadienne des juges de Cours Provinciales; nommé juge coordonnateur de la Cour des Sessions de la Paix pour le district du Quebec, 1980; Clubs: Kinsmen; Garnison (Québec): Golf de Cap-Rouge Inc.; Résidence: 1340 rue Leblanc, Sillery, Qué. G1T 2G7; Bureau: Cour des Sessions de la Province de Québec, Local B-16, Québec, P.Q.

CHOQUETTE, Robert, C.C. (1968), LL.D.; poet; novelist; playwright; b. Manchester, N.H., 22 April 1905; s. J. Alfred, M.D., and Ariane (Payette) C.; e. Notre Dame-Coll. and St-Laurent Coll., Montreal, P.Q.; Loyola Coll., B.A. 1926; m. Marguerite, d. Wilfred Canac-Marquis, 1 Apl. 1937; children: Michel, Danielle; Assoc. Cmmr. of Centennial Comn., Can., 1963-64; Candn. Consul-Gen. to Bordeaux, France, 1964-68; Ambassador to Argentina, Uruguay and Paraguay 1968-70; Special Adviser, Information Can., 1971-72; awarded David Prize for Poetry, 1926, and ex aéquo with Alfred DesRochers for Poetry, 1931; awarded Lord Willingdon Prize for Lit. Essay, 1930; has contrib. reg. to the French Candn. press of both Que. and New Eng. States for number of yrs.; was, for a period of three yrs., Secy. to the "Ecole des Beaux-Arts de Montreal": has written regularly for radio and television (Montreal) from 1933 to 1961; spent 1942 at Smith College, Northampton Mass.; was "resident author"; author of "A Travers les vents", poems, 1925 and 1926; "La Pension Leblanc", a novel, 1927, 2nd ed. 1976; "Metropolitan Museum", poem, 1931; "Poésies nouvelles", 1933; "Le Fabuliste La Fontaine à Montreal", 1935; "Suite Marine", poem, 1953 (Special Prize by French Acad., 1954; Prix Duvernay, 1954; David Prize, 1956; Prix Edgar Poe (Paris), 1956; Prix international des Amitiés françaises (Paris), 1962); "Le Curé de Village", 1936; "Les Velder", a novel with preface by André Maurois, 1941; "Oeuvres poétiques", 1956; "Elise Velder", novel, 1958; "Robert Choquette", collection "Classiques canadiens" 1959; "Metropolitan Museum" and other poems, published in Paris, 1962; "Oeuvres Poétiques", revised ed. 1968; "Poèmes choisis" 1970; "Sous le règne d'Augusta", comedy, 1974; " 'Le Sorcier d'Anticosti' and Other Canadian Legends" 1975; "Moi, Pétrouchka," fable, 1980; wrote scenario and dialog. for film, "Le Curé de Village", made by Quebec Productions Corpn.; Past Pres., Acad. canadienne-française; Acad. Ronsard (Paris); P.E.N. Club; Société des Poètes français (Paris); Past President, La Soc. des Ecrivains canadiens; Roman Catholic; recreations: theatre, travel, piano; Address: Apt. B-80, Château Apts., 1321 Sherbrooke St. W., Montreal, Que. H3G 1J4

CHORLTON, Ronald William, B.Sc.F.; business executive; b. Birmingham, Eng., 13 Apl. 1925; s. William and Minerva (Cummings) C.; came to Can. 1928; e. Britannia Pub. and High Schs.; Univ. of B.C., B.Sc.F.; m. Mary, d. Harold Housden, 12 Sept. 1946; children: Michael William, Bruce Whitham, Lesley Bronwen, Jennifer Mary; CHAIRMAN & C.E.O., WAJAX LTD. AND SUBSIDIARIES; Dir., Innocan Investments; Credit Suisse (Canada) Ltd.; Innotech Aviation Ltd.; served as Able Seaman, RCNVR, 1944-45; Past Pres., Candn. Assn. Equipment Distributors; mem., Ont. Prof. Foresters Assn.; Candn. Inst. Forestry; Anglican; recreations: sailing, skiing, tennis; Clubs: Rideau; The Country; Royal St. Lawrence Yacht (Montreal); University (Toronto); Home: 41 Lyttleton Gardens, Rockcliffe Park, Ottawa, Ont. K1L 5A4; Office: 350 Sparks St., Ottawa, Ont. K1R 7S8

CHOTE, Canon Arthur Abel, B.A., L.Th., D.D.; b. Toronto, Ont. 7 Oct. 1914; s. late Samuel and late Flora (Spary) C.; e. Riverdale High Sch. Toronto 1932; Univ.

Coll. Univ. of Toronto B.A. 1947; Wycliffe Coll. L.Th., D.D. 1948; children: Paul S., Ruth A.; Chaplain, North York Gen. Hosp.; Industrial Chaplain, Consolidated Graphics Ltd.; mem. Bd. Govs. Humber Mem. Hosp.; Fort York Officers Legion; served with Toronto Scot. Regt. (Non-Perm.) 1937-39, RCAF 1939-45; rec'd King's Commendation for valuable services in the air; mem. Bd. Trade Metrop. Toronto; Hon. Doctor of Divinity, Univ. of Toronto; Royal Candn. Legion; Comm. Travellers' Assn.; P. Conservative; Anglican; Club: Empire; Address: 40 High Park Ave., Apt. 2105, Toronto, Ont. M6P 251.

CHOUINARD, Hon. Julien, O.C., C.D., M.A., LL.L.; judge; b. Quebec City, 4 February 1929; s. Joseph Julien and Berthe C.; e. Coll. St. Charles Garnier, Que., B.A. 1948; Faculty of Law, Laval Univ., Que., LL.L. 1951; Univ. of Oxford, M.A. 1953; m. Jeannine, d. Lucien Pettigrew, Que. City, 6 Sept. 1956; children: Julien, Lucie, Nicole; SUPREME COURT OF CANADA 1979-; called to the Bar of Quebec, 1953; cr. Q.C. 1965; member of Council, Faculty of Law, University Laval, Que.; Lect. of Corp. Law, Laval University, 1959-66; formerly Gen. Secy. of the Cabinet, Que. and sometime Depy. Min. of Justice; served in Canadian Mil. since 1948; Lieut.-Col., C.O., 6 Field Regt. R.C.A.(M) 1965-68; mem., Que. and Candn. Bars (Pres. Jr; Bar of Que. 1961-62); mem. of Council Que. Br. Nat. Council of Candn. Bar Assn. 1965; Roman Catholic; recreations: skiing; sailing; Clubs: Cercle Universitaire; Home: 200 Clearview, Ottawa, Ont. K1Z 8M2; Office: Supreme Court of Canada, Ottawa, Ont. K1A 0J1

CHOWN, Bruce, O.C. (1967), B.A., M.C., M.D., D.Sc., LL.D., D.U.C., F.A.C.O.G.(Hon.), F.R.C.O.G.(Hon.), F.R.S.C., F.R.C.P. (Can.) (Hon.); retired physician; b. Winnipeg, Man., 10 Nov 1893; s. Henry Havelock and Katherine (Farrell) C.; e. McGill Univ., B.A. 1914; Univ. of Man., M.D. 1922, D.Sc.; Univs. of W. Ont., Winnipeg and Sask., LL.D.; Univ. of Calgary, D.U.C.; m. Gladys, d. Taylor Webb, 29 March 1922; 4 children; 2ndly Allison, d. William Grant, Winnipeg, Man., 27 May 1949; one child; Professor of Paediatrics, Univ. of Man., 1950; Dir. RH Lab. of Winnipeg (Founder, 1943); served on staff of Children's Hosp. of Winnipeg, 1925-75; joined Univ. of Man. 1925; Head, Dept. of Paediatrics, 1950-53; served with Candn. Field Arty. 1914-19; rec'd. F.N.G. Starr Medal, Candn. Med. Assn.; writings incl. many articles in scient. journs; mem., Candn. Med. Assn.; Candn. Paediatric Soc.; Genetics Soc. Can. (Past Pres.); Am. Pediatric Soc. (Past Vice Pres.); Delta Upsilon; recreation: gardening; Home: 1284 Transit Rd., Victoria, B.C. V8S 5A3

CHRETIEN, Hon. Joseph-Jacques Jean, P.C., M.P., B.A., LL.L.; lawyer, politician; b. Shawinigan, Que., 11 Jan 1934; s. Wellie and Marie (Boisvert) C.; e. St. Joseph Semy., Three Rivers, Que.; Laval Univ.; m. Aline Chainé, Shawinigan, Que., 10 Sept. 1957; children: France, Hubert, Michel; JUSTICE MINISTER, ATTORNEY-GEN., AND MIN. OF STATE FOR SOCIAL DEVELOPMENT 1980-; first el. to H. of C. in g.e. 1963; apptd. Parlty. Secy. to Prime Minister July 1965 and to Min. of Finance Jan. 1966; apptd. Min. of State attached to the Min. of Finance, 1967; Min. of Nat. Revenue Jan. 1968; Min. of Indian Affairs & Northern Development, July 1968; Pres. Treasury Bd. 1974-76; Min. of Industry, Trade & Commerce, 1976-77; Min. of Finance 1977-79; Dir., Bar of Trois-Rivières, 1962-63; Liberal; R. Catholic; Home: 1171 Rhodes Cres., Ottawa, Ont.; Office: Justice Bldg., 3rd Floor, 239 Wellington St., Ottawa, Ont. K1A 0H8

CHRISTENSEN, Ione Jean; commissioner; b. Dawson Creek, B.C. 10 Oct. 1933; d. Gordon Irwin Cameron; e. Duncan, B.C. and Whitehorse, Yukon 1953; San Mateo (Cal.) Coll. Business Adm., Assoc. Arts Degree 1955; m. Arthur Karsten Christensen 1 Feb. 1958; two s. Paul Cameron, Philip Karsten; PRES., HOSPITALITY NORTH

LTD. 1981-; Dir., Petro Canada; Commr. of Yukon Territory 1978-79; held clerical positions with Taylor & Drury, Yukon Electrical Co. and Govt. of Yukon 1955-62; Pay and Personnel Supvr. Govt. of Yukon 1962-65, Princ. Clk. Estimates 1965-66, Personnel Supvr. and Acting Dir. 1966-67; apptd. Justice of the Peace and Juvenile Court 1971; Small Debt Official 1974; el. Mayor of Whitehorse 1975, re-el. 1977 but resigned 1978 upon appt. as Commr.; Dir., Boy Scouts of Can. Provincial Yukon B.C.-Council; The Yukon Fdn.; Council for Can. Unity; Yukon Nurses Soc.; Mem. Whitehorse Chamber Comm.; Vice-Pres., N. Lights Toastmistress Club; Dir. and Vice-Pres., MacBride Museum; Anglican; recreations: camping, fishing, hunting, gardening, dressmaking and design, arts and crafts; Home: 26 Takhini Ave., Whitehorse, Yukon Y1A 3N4;

CHRISTENSEN, Jorgen Vibe, LL.D.; executive; b. Vejle, Denmark, 9 Nov. 1917; e. High Sch. Univ. Entrance Vejle, Denmark, various business courses; LL.D, h.c. Simon Fraser Univ. 1978; came to Can. 1946; m. Alice 1956; PRESIDENT AND DIR. TAHSIS CO. LTD.: Pres. and Dir. Ucona Holdings Ltd.; Nootka Transportation Co. Ltd.; Dir., Eacom Timber Sales Ltd.; Dir. The East Asiatic Co. (Canada) Ltd.; Hon. Consul for Denmark in B.C. and Yukon 1960-70; served with R.A. Hong Kong 1940-46; P.O.W.; Chrmn. Vancouver Gen. Hosp. 1973; B.C. Med. Centre 1973-76; Dir. Vancouver Civic Museum and Planetarium. Chrmn. Maritime Museum Sec. 1970-73; Past Chrmn. Council Forest Industs.; Employers Council; Extve. Comte. Forest Indust. Relations Ltd. and mem. Pulp & Paper Indust. Relations Bureau; recreation: yachting; Clubs: Vancouver; Royal Vancouver Yacht; W. Vancouver Yacht; Home: 4246 Staulo Cres., Vancouver, B.C. V6N 3S2; Office: 1201 West Pender St., Vancouver, B.C. V6E 2V4

CHRISTENSEN, Lauritz Royal, B.Sc., Ph.D.; educator; b. Everson, Wash. 2 Aug. 1914; s. Carl and Garnet (Remley) C.; e. Univ. of Wash. B.Sc. 1939; St. Louis Univ. Ph.D. 1941; m. Ann d. late Edwin Berliner 27 Aug. 1960; children: Laurie, David and Jeff Bloom (stepsons); PROF. Emeritus OF MED. BIOPHYSICS AND DIR. DIV. LAB. ANIMAL SCIENCES, UNIV. OF TORONTO 1980-; Grad. Fellow Univ. of Wash. 1938; Teaching Fellow St. Louis Univ. Med. Sch. 1938-41; Med. Fellow; NYU-Bellevue Med. Sch. 1941-42; Instr. in Bacteriol. NYU Med. Sch. 1942-46, Asst. Prof. 1946, Assoc. Prof. 1955-59, Assoc. Prof. of Pathol. 1959-67; Visiting Fellow in Chem. Univ. of Wis. summer 1964; Dir. Berg inst. Scient. Services 1953-67; Prof. of Med. Biophysics and Dir. Div. Lab Animal Sciences, Univ. of Toronto 1967-80; Chrmn. Adv. Comte. Sheridan Community Coll.; Assoc. Ed Lab. Animal Science; rec'd Nat. Research Council Med. Fellowship 1941-43; Lasker Award 1949; Charles A. Griffin Award 1973; author numerous articles prof. journs.; Fellow, N.Y. Acad. Science; mem. Candn. Assn. Lab. Animal Science; Am. Assn. Advanc. Science; Sigma Xi; recreations: machine shop work, gunsmithing, varmint hunting; Home: 49 Wildwood Ave. Madison, Wisc. 06443 U.S.A.; Office: 1 Taddle Creek Rd., Toronto, Ont. M5S 1A8.

CHRISTENSEN, Rosemary Lorraine, B.A., B.C.L.; b. Walton-on-Thames, Eng.; e. The Sorbonne, Paris, Cour de Civilisation Française 1959-60; McGill Univ. B.A. 1964, B.C.L. 1967; PRESIDENT AND DIR., THE SOMERVILLE HOUSE CORP.; Pres. & Dir. Somerville House Management Ltd.; Somerville House Productions; Somerville House Securities; Somerville House Commodities Inc.; called to Bar of Que. 1968; mem. Candn. Assn. Motion Picture Producers; Que. Assn. Motion Picture Producers; Acad. Candn. Cinema; Home: 608, Two Westmount Sq., Montreal, Que. H3Z 2S4; Office: 750, 1310 Greene Ave., Montreal, Que. H3Z 2B2.

CHRISTENSON; Elvin Arnold, F.C.A.; b. Jarrow, Alta. 18 Nov. 1918; s. Arnold and Edith (McCune) C.; m. Halina Wyka, children: Dwight, Eric, Karyn, Lynne, Marnie; SR. PARTNER, THORNE RIDDELL & CO.; Regional Extve. Partner-Prairie Region, Internat. Liaison Partner 1969-74 present firm; founded predecessor firm Christenson. Morrison & Co. 1944; Chrmn. Comte. of Alta. Inst. Report on Role of Prov. Auditor 1974; inst. Rep. Adv. Council to Faculty of Business Adm. and Comm. Univ. of Alta. 1968-69, mem. Senate; Chrmn. Bd. Trustees Univ. Hosp. Foundation; mem. Inst. C.A.'s Alta. (Pres. 1962-63); Pres. Candn. Inst. C.A.'s 1976-77 (Council 1962-63); rec'd Centennial Medal 1967; P. Conservative; United Church; recreations: golf, photography, cottage; Clubs: Kiwanis; Edmonton; Mayfair Golf & Country; Edmonton C.A.'s; Pacioli Dining; Edmonton Petroleum; Home: 12903 - 66 Ave., Edmonton, Alta. T6H 1Y6; Office: 1200 Royal Trust Tower, Edmonton Centre, Edmonton, Alta. T5J 1V4.

CHRISTIE, James Hamilton, F.R.A.I.C., A.R.I.B.A., F.R.S.A.; Architect; b. Glasgow, Scot., 13 July 1929; s. late John Alexander and Ruby Kirk (Hamilton) C.; e. High Sch. of Glasgow, 1947; Glasgow Sch. of Arch., 1954; m. Jean Stuart Campbell, d. James Wallace, Bath, Eng., 24 June 1960; children: Sarah Hamilton, James Andrew, David Francis; Senior Partner, Stevenson Raines Barrett Christie Hutton Seton and Partners, Calgary. Associated with Gillespie, Kidd & Coia, Scot., 1952-57; joined Moody & Moore, Winnipeg, 1957; founding Partner MMP Vancouver, 1974; associated with design of Manitoba Cultural Centre and growth and development of several western Universities; has served as President of Social Planning Council of Winnipeg and Chairman of its Housing and Urban Renewal Committee; Chairman, Manitoba Provincial Housing Committee and Delegate 1968 Canadian Conference on Housing; Vice President Manitoba Theatre Centre; Member Alberta Association of Architects; Architectural Institute of British Columbia; Manitoba Association of Architects (Council 1964-69, President 1968); Freeman of City of Glasgow, Scot., Presbyterian; recreations: golf, swimming, rugger; Clubs: Manitoba; The Canadian (Pres.); Hollyburn Country; Earl Grey Golf & Country Club; Home: 2375 Longridge Dr., S.W., Calgary, Alta. T3E 5N7; Office: 1106-4th St., S.W., Calgary, Alta. T2R 0X6

CHRISTIE, Robert (Wallace), B.A.; actor, director, b. Toronto, Ont., 20 Sept. 1913; s. David Wallace, D.D., and Barbara Wilson (Alexander) C.; e. Public Schs.; Woodstock, Ont.; Public and Riverdale Coll. Inst., Toronto, Ont.; Victoria Coll., Univ. of Toronto, B.A. 1934; m. 1st Margot Syme, 14 Apl. 1937; 2ndly Grania Mortimer, 12 July 1958; children: Dinah Barbara, Cedar Townsend, Geraldine Fiona, Matthew Alexander, David MacIvor; with The John Holden Players, Toronto, Bala and Winnipeg, 1934-36; went to England, 1936 engaging in Prov. Repertory, then a London Production and tour; with Old Vic Co., 1938-39 (Buxton Festival and Mediterranean Tour); after war service returned to Toronto as Freelance; Stratford Shakespearean Festival during its first 4 yrs., incl. Edin. Festival; "Ti-Coq" in English at Montreal; Musical and Revue: "Sunshine Town", "Mother Goose"; "Fine Frenzy", "Beggars' Opera"; Broadway Openings: "Tambourlaine", "Love and Libel"; Vancouver Internat. Festival: "Mary Stuart"; starred as Noah Hatch in CBC series "Hatch's Mill", 1967; on numerous occasions "Sir John A. Macdonald", etc., etc.; 1971-79 Teacher of Acting, Theatre Dept., Ryerson Polytech. Inst.; served in 2nd World War, 1940-45, enlisting in London, Eng.; with R.C.A.M.C. and R.C.A.S.C., Eng., France, Belgium, Holland, Germany; mem., Actors' Equity Assn.; Assn. Radio & TV Artists; N.D.P.; Club: Arts & Letters; Home: 42 Dale Ave., Toronto, Ont. M4W 1K6

CHRISTIE, Ven. William Douglas McLaren, B.A. (Ang.); b. St. Johnsbury, Vermont, 12 Nov. 1910; s. William Edward and Mabel (Mathewson) C.; e. Lennoxville (P.Q.) High Sch.; Bishop's Univ., B.A. (Theol.) 1935; Washington Coll. of Preachers; m. Pamela Kerrigan, d. Andrew Louis Henderson, England, 7 Sept. 1948; children: Peter Andrew, Mary Pamela; o. Deacon 1935 and Priest 1936; Curate at Bury, Que., 1935-36; Incumbent of Montage and Franktown (Diocese of Ottawa), 1936-39; Vankleek Hill, Ont., 1939-43; Rector of Renfrew, 1943-46; All Saints, Westboro, Ottawa, 1946-58; Rector of Trinity Ch., and Archdeacon of Cornwall, 1958; Diocesan Archdeacon & Dir. of Programme for Diocese of Ottawa, 1967-72; Diocesan Archdeacon & Rector of St. Bartholomew's Church, Ottawa, 1972; Chaplain to the Governor General, 1967; Rural Dean of Ottawa, 1951-57; Part-time Chaplain, R.C.A.F., 1941-43; Chaplain, Gov.-Gen. Foot Guards (5th Canadian Guards), 1947-58; Retired, June 30, 1979; Order of St. Lazarus of Jerusalem; Efficiency Decoration; recreation: curling. Home: 22 MacKay St., Apt. 2, Ottawa, Ont.

CHRISTNER, William C., B.S.A.; company executive; b. Kitchener, Ont., 16 Oct. 1926; s. Charles A. and Violet (Otto) C.; e. Univ. of Guelph, B.S.A. 1949; Univ. of W. Ont., Mang. Training Course 1967; Advanc. Mang. Harvard Business Sch. 1969; m. Shirley E., d. Robert J. Cousineau, Elmira, Ont., 6 March 1949; children: Barbara, Robert; SR. VICE-PRES. AND DIR., THOMAS J. LIPTON, INC., since 1963; Chief Chemist, Burns & Co. Ltd., 1949-53; Tech. Asst., Vice-Pres. Mfg., Kraft Foods Ltd., 1953-58; Prod. Mgr., Salada Foods Ltd., 1958-63; mem., Chem. Inst. Can.; Packaging Assn. Can. (Past Chrmn.); Bd. Trade Metrop. Toronto; Pres., C.F.P.A.; Campaign Chrmn., Metrop. Toronto United Way, 1977; Liberal; Protestant; recreations: skiing, fishing; Clubs: Thornhill Country; University; Home: 59 Forest Grove Dr., Willowdale, Ont. M2K 1Z4; Office: 2180 Yonge St., Toronto, Ont. M4S 2C4

CHRONES, James, M.Sc., S.M., F.C.I.C.; b. Weyburn, Sask., 6 Sept. 1925; s. late James Peter and late Helen (Dennis) C.; e. Univ. of Sask., B.Sc. (Chem. Engn.) 1946, M.Sc. (Chem.) 1948; Mass. Inst. of Tech., S.M. (Chem. Engn.) 1950; m. Matina Prassas, Swift Current, Sask. 6 June 1951; children: Eleni, Tom, James; Pres., Dynawest Projects Ltd., Calgary 1979-80; Research Engr., Atomic Energy of Canada Ltd., Chalk River, 1950-53; Research & Devel. Engr., M. W. Kellogg, Jersey City, N.J., 1953-55; Process Engr., New York, 1955-58; Sr. Process Engr., Kellogg International Corp., London, Eng., 1958-60; Process Mgr., M. W. Kellogg, New York, 1960-64; Consulting Engr., Saskatoon, Sask., 1965-66; Pres., Cambrian Engineering Ltd., Saskatoon, 1966-71; Assoc., Hatch Associates Ltd., Toronto, Ont., 1971-73; Vice Pres. and Gen. Mgr., Pullman Kellogg Canada Ltd., 1973-79; from Sept. 1980, Consultant for the petroleum, petrochem. & energy ind.; holds patents on ethylene production, heavy water production, vegetable oil processing; mem., Registered Prof. Engr. Ont. and Alta.; Am. Inst. Chem. Engrs.; Candn. Soc. Chem. Engn.; recreations: swimming, tennis; Home: 330—25 Ave., S.W. Calgary, T2S 0L4

CHUNG, Hung, R.C.A.; artist; b. Canton, China 8 Feb. 1946; s. Chung Fook-kuan and Chiu Yee-wah; e. Nung Lin 1st Primary Sch. CAnton 1957; Tak Ming Middle Sch. Hong Kong 1963; Chu Hai Coll. Civil Engn. 1965; Vancouver Sch. of Art (Sculpture) grad. 1973; award-winning sculptures incl.: 1st Internat. Sculpture Competition Autopista Del Mediterraneo Barcelona 1974; Competition of monument for s.s. "Beaver" 1975; Wood Sculpture Symposium of the Americas 1977; Competition for a commemorative sculpture Capt. George Vancouver 1980; project sculptures for B.C. Provincial Bldgs., Vancouver, and National Capital Commission, Ottawa, 1981; rec'd Can. Council Arts Grant 1976; Address: 4012 Maple Cres., Vancouver, B.C. V6J 4B2.

CHURCH, Douglas Hamilton, B.Sc.; petroleum executive; b. Calgary, Alta. 5 Nov. 1932; s. William Kenneth and Eleanor (Hamilton) C.; e. Univ. of Alta. B.Sc. 1954; m. Linda Gail d. late Thomas George Potts 16 Jan. 1965; two s. Dean Allan, Craig Stuart; EXTVE. VICE PRES., CAN DEL OIL LTD. 1980- ; joined Canadian Gulf Oil Co. and British American Oil Co. 1954-61; Texas Gulf Sulphur 1961-72; present Co. 1972; mem. Assn. Prof. Engrs. Alta.; Phi Delta Theta; recreation: golf; Clubs: Calgary Petroleum; 400; Gyro; Earl Grey Golf; Home: 2905 Lindstrom Dr. S.W., Calgary, Alta. T3E 6E5; Office: 28 Floor 330, 5 Ave. S.W., Calgary, Alta. T2P 0L4.

CHURCH, Kenneth Robert, B.Com., C.A.; comptroller; b. Ottawa, Ont. 20 Mar. 1921; s. George Alexander and Ethel (Turley) C.; e. Queen's Univ. B.Com. 1942; Inst. of C.A.'s of Ont. C.A. 1948; m. Elsie May d. Late Edwin Chambers 9 Dec. 1944; children: Kenneth Edward, Thomas Robert; COMPTROLLER, HAWKER SIDDELEY CAN. INC. 1981- ; Auditor, Price Waterhouse 1942-50; Treas., Orenda Internat. Ltd. 1963-81; Vice-Pres. Finance, Orenda Ltd. 1966-73; Dir. of Finance, Orenda Div., Hawker Siddeley 1974-80; mem. and past Dir. of Toronto Branch, Financial Extves Inst. of Can.; extve. mem. and past Chrmn. of Contracts and Finance Cmte., Air Industries Assn. of Canada; Anglican; Clubs: Weston Golf & Country; Toronto Bd. of Trade; recreations: sailing, curling; Home: 30 Cedarland Dr., Islington, Ont. M9A 2K3; Office: 7 King St. E., Toronto, Ont. M5C 1A3

CHURCH, Robert Bertram, M.Sc., Ph.D.; geneticist; educator; b. Calgary, Alta. 7 May 1937; s. Bertram Cecil and Alexa Winnifred (Black) C.; e. Crescent Hts. High Sch. Calgary 1955; Olds (Alta.) Coll. Dipl. 1956; Univ. of Alta. B.Sc. 1962, M.Sc. 1963; Univ. of Uppsula Dipl. 1961; Univ. of Edinburgh Ph.D. 1965; m. Joyce Maryanne d. Harry Brown, Calgary, Alta. 2 May 1958; children: Jeffrey Robert, Eileen Alexa; PROF. AND HEAD OF MED. BIO-CHEM. & BIOL. FACULTY OF MED. UNIV. OF CALGARY since 1969; Dir. Highfield Stock Farms; Dir., Connaut Laboratories Ltd., Toronto, 1979—; Exec., Natural Sciences and Engineering Research Council of Canada, Ottawa, 1978—; Pres. Church Livestock Consultants; Lochend Luing Ranches; Dir. Calgary Exhn. & Stampede; Chmn. Research and Technology Comte, Calgary Chamber of Cmmerce 1979-; Research Assoc. Univ. of Wash. 1965-67; Asst. Prof. Univ. Calgary 1967-69; Visiting Scient. Soviet Acad. Sciences 1972, Murdoch (W. Australia) Univ. 1977, Animal Reproduction Lab. Colo. State Univ. Fort Collins 1978; author over 50 scient. papers molecular genetics, manipulation of reproduction in domestic animals and genetics of higher organisms; numerous articles on applied animal livestock mang.; United Church; recreations: livestock, ranching; Home: R.R.1, Airdrie, Alta. T0M 0B0; Office: 2920 - 24 Ave. N.W., Calgary, Alta. T2N 1N4.

CHURCHILL, Hon. Gordon, P.C. (Can.) 1957, D.S.O., Q.C., M.A., LL.B.; retired; b. Coldwater, Ont., 8 Nov. 1898; s. Rev. J. W. and Mary E. (Shier) C.; e. Public and High Schs., Port Arthur, Ont., and Winnipeg, Man.; United Coll.; Univ. of Manitoba; m. Mona Mary, d. C.W. McLachlin, Dauphin, Man., 9 Aug. 1922; one d. Winona; sometime a Teacher and High Sch. Principal; Past Pres., Manitoba Teachers Soc.; subsequently studied law and on grad. joined the law firm of Haig & Haig, Winnipeg, Man.; el. to Manitoba Leg. as Army Rep. (Independent), 1946; resigned in 1949; def. cand. to H. of C., g.e. 1949; 1st el. to H. of C. for Winnipeg South-Centre, by-el. 25 June 1951; apptd. Min. of Trade & Comm. 22 June 1957; Min. of Veterans Affairs, 11 Oct. 1960; Min. of Nat. Defence, Feb.-Apl. 1963; retired from politics 1968 (did not contest el.) and resumed practice of law Jan. 1969 with D'Arcy and Deacon, Winnipeg; served in 1st World War Overseas as a Vickers Machine Gunner, 1916-19; 2nd World War, 1939-45 with Fort Garry Horse; C.O., 1st Candn. Armoured Carrier Regt., in N.W. Europe; Dean of Faculty, Khaki Univ., England, 1945; mem., Royal Candn. Legion; P. Conservative; United Church; Home: 2469 Mill Bay Rd., Mill Bay, B.C. V0R 2P0

CHUTE, Andrew Lawrence, O.B.E., M.A., M.D., Ph.D., F.R.C.P.(C); emeritus professor; b. Kodai Kanal, India, 31 May 1909; s. Jesse Edmund and Pearl (Smith), M.D. (decorated by King Geo. V with the "Kaiser-i-Hind" for Distinguished Service to India) C.; e. Univ. of Toronto, B.A., M.A., M.D., 1935; Univ. of London, Ph.D., 1939; m. Helen Evans (M.D.), d. Robert Mills Reid, Vegreville, Alta., 6 Oct. 1939; children: Judith, Douglas; Dean of Medicine, Univ. of Toronto, since 1966 and Prof. of Pediatrics there since 1951, now Dean Emeritus; served in World War 1940-45 as Lieut. with 2nd Light Field Ambulance 1940; Lieut.-Col. and O.C. No. 1 Candn. Research Lab.; served in Eng., N. Africa, Italy and N.W. Europe; invested O.B.E., Military Division, for research work on tank warfare in N. Africa; Sir Arthur Sims Commonwealth Travelling Prof. 1966; mem., Candn. Diabetes Assn., Candn. Med. Assn.; Acad. of Med. (Toronto); Toronto Diabetes Assn.; Alpha Kappa Kappa; Alpha Omega Alpha; Address: R.R. #1, Loretto, Ont. L0G 1L0

CHUTTER, Sturley Donald Charles, M. Com., C.A.E.; management consultant and association executive; b. Vancouver, B.C. 9 Aug. 1924; s. Thomas Sturley, M.C., and Clover May, R.N., (Walker) C.; m. Johanna Margaretha Helling, 1959; d. Jessica Caroline; s. Brian Andrew; e. Univ. of British Columbia, B.Com. (1st Class Hons.) 1944; Univ. of Toronto, M.Com. (1st Class Hons.) 1946; Northwestern Univ., Diploma in Trade Assn. Management (1st Class Hons.) 1954; Ottawa Bureau Chief, Revay & Ass. Ltd. Extve. Dir., Construction Ind. Dev. Council; Cert. Assn. Extve. (C.A.E.); Chrmn., Metric Comn. Sector Comte. for Construction; formerly Gen. Mgr., Candn. Construction Assn., 1954-75; Past Mem., Extve. Comm., Nat. Bldg. Code; Past Dir., Nat. Construction Industry Devel. Foundation; Past Vice Chrmn., Accreditation Brd., Inst. Assn. Extves.; Past Vice-Chrmn., Nat. Capital Region Br., Community Planning Assn. of Canada; Comnd. in Candn. Inf. Corps, Jan. 1945; demobilized with rank of Lieut., Nov. 1945; Past Pres. Univ. of B.C. Alumni Assn., Ottawa Br.; Past Dir., Inst. Assn. Extves.; a Candn. Del. to N.A. Apprenticeship Conf., San Diego, 1953, to ILO, Geneva, 1957, 1964 and 1971; Phi Kappa Sigma; Anglican; Clubs: Rideau; Ottawa Athletic; Rotary; Home: 18 Wren Road, Ottawa, Ont. K1J 7H7

CINADER, Bernhard, Ph.D., D.Sc., F.R.I.C., F.R.S.C.; scientist; educator; b. Vienna, Austria 30 March 1919; s. Leon and Adele (Schwarz) C.; e. Univ. of London B.Sc. 1945, Ph.D. (Biochem.) 1948, D.Sc. (Immunology) 1958; one d. Agatha; PROF. OF MED. BIOPHYSICS, MED. GENETICS AND CLINICAL BIOCHEMISTRY (1969-), FELLOW OF NEW COLLEGE, UNIV. OF TORONTO (1970-), since 1999, Prof. of Clin. Biochem. since 1970, Dir. Inst. of Immunology 1971-80; Mem. of the Governing Council, Univ. of Toronto (1980-83); Pres., Internat. Union of Immunological Societies (1969-1974); Pres., Canadian Society for Immunology, (1966-1969 and 1979-81); Beit Mem. Fellow 1949-53; Grantee Agric. Research Council, Lister Inst. Preventive Med. London 1953-56; Fellow of Immunochem. Inst. Pathol. Western Reserve Univ. Cleveland 1948-49, Enrique E. Ecker Lectr. in Exper. Pathol. 1964; Princ. Scient. Offr. Dept. Exper. Pathol. Inst. Animal Physiol. Babraham Hall, Cambridge 1956-58; Head, Subdiv. Immunochem. Div. Biol. Research Ont. Cancer Inst. 1958-69; Assoc. Prof. Depts. Med. Biophysics & Pathol. Chem. Univ. Toronto 1958-69; Lectr.: Société de Chimie Biologique Paris 1954; Institut Pasteur Paris 1960; Univ. Coll. London 1963; State Univ. of N.Y. Buffalo (A. Harrington Lectr.) 1974; Acads. of Science Czechoslovakia and Hungary, Acad. of Med. Rumania 1974; Advance Sch. of Immunology, Zinkovy, Czechoslovakia 1978; Visiting Prof. Univ. of Man. 1967, Univ. of Alta. 1968; W.H.O. Consultant, Bombay, India,

1981; Prof. Bankok, Thailand, 1982; Jt. Chrmn. Sec. Immunochem. Internat. Cong. Biochem. Belgium 1955; Dir. Sec. Immunochem. 4th World Cong. Biochem. 1958; Past Chrmn./mem. various comtes. Med. Research Council, Biol. Council Can., Nat'l Cancer Inst.; mem. World Health Organ. Expert Adv. Panel on Immunology and various Task Forces; Session Chrmn. Cong. on Immunology of Reproduction, Varna, Bulgaria 1975; mem. Candn. Scient. Del. U.S.S.R. 1975; Session Chrmn. Internat. Cong. Allergy. Buenos Aires 1976; Chmn. Workshop on Ageing of the Immune System, 4th Int. Congress of Immunology, Paris 1980; mem. Adv. Comtes. Center for Immunology, State Univ. of N.Y. Buffalo and Dept. Basic & Clin. Immunology Med. Univ. S.C.; Chrmn. Adv. Bd. WHO-IUIS Inst. for Training & Research in Immunology Amsterdam; Dir. Candn. Fed. Biol. Sciences; Chmn., I.U.I.S.-W.H.O. Nomenclature Comte. 1980-; I.U.I.S. rep. at I.C.S.U. (1980-1; Pres. of the Comte. for the 6th Int. Cong. of Immunology to be held in Toronto 1986; mem. of Editorial Bds: Can Journ. of Biochemistry (1967-71), Immunochemistry (1965-69), Journ. of Immunological Methods (1970-74), Excerpta Medica Foundation — Immunology, Serology and Transplantation Section (1966 —), Immunological Communications (1974—), Bolletino Dell' Istituto Sieroterapico Milanese (1973—), Immunology Letters (1979—), Journ. of Immunogenetics (1976), Receptors (1980—), Chrmn Ed. Bd. Journ. Immunogenetics (1977—). rec'd Old Student Prize Queen Mary Coll. Univ. London 1944; Jenner Mem. Studentship 1946; Société de Chimie Biologique Medal 1954; Ignac Semmelweis Medal Budapest 1978; Queen's Silver Jubilee Medal; Ed. "Antibody to Enzymes - A Three-Component System" 1963; "Antibodies to Biologically Active Molecules" 1967; "Regulation of the Antibody Response" 1968, 2nd. ed. 1971; co-ed. "Immunological Response of the Female Reproductive Tract" 1976; ed. "Immunology of Receptors" 1977; Series ed. Books on Receptors, 1980 —; author over 210 scient. articles, also articles and catalogues Candn. Indian art; Home: 73 Langley Ave.,, Toronto, Ont. M4K 1B4; Office: M.S.B. Univ. of Toronto, Toronto, Ont. A8O 1A8.

CLAIR, Hon. Michel, M.N.A., LL.L.; politician; b. St-Germain de Grantham, Qué. 16 June 1950; s. Lucien and Thérèse (Grandmont) C.; e. St-Germain de Grantham Primary Sch.; Seminaire de Nicolet; Coll. Jean-de-Brébeuf; Univ. de Sherbrooke; Univ. of Montréal; MIN. OF TRANSPORT,QUE. 1981- ; called to Bar of Qué. 1974; mem. Drummondville Office Legal Aid 1974-76; el. M.N.A. for Drummond electoral circ. g.e. 1976, re-el. since; Min. of Revenue, 1979-81; Parti Québécois; R. Catholic; Office: 700 est, boul. St. Cyrille, Québec, Qué. G1R 5H1.

CLARK, Alden Richardson, B.A., D.C.L. (Hon.); merchant; b. Fredericton, N.B., 23 Sept. 1903; s. Hon. William George and Harriet (Richardson) C.; e. Acadia Univ., B.A. 1924; D.C.L. (Hon.) Acadia 1978; m. Helen, d. David Crowe, 5 Sept. 1928; children: John, Nancy, Richard; CHAIRMAN, J. CLARK & SON LTD.; Pres., Rainsford Realty Ltd.; Gen. Mgr. Helark Investment Ltd.; Western Realty Ltd.; Dir. Provincial Artisans Inc.; Oromocto Development Corp.; Fredericton Foundation Inc.; Capital Winter Club Ltd., joined present Co. 1924; Mgr., St.John Br. 1927-40; Gen. Mgr., 1940; served in Reserve Army, 1942-44 as Offr. Commdg., 28th L.A.D.(R) Roy. Candn. Ordnance Corps; Hon. Col., Roy. N.B. Regt.; First Chrmn., Military Compound Bd.; Fredericton Garrison Club; N.B. Sports Hall of Fame; Past Pres., N.B. Automobile Dealers Assn.; Fed. of Auto Dealers Assns. of Can.; mem., St. Andrew's Soc.; United Empire Loyalist Assn.; Liberal; Baptist; recreations: curling, fishing, gardening; Clubs: Fredericton Golf; Curling; Country Club of Fredericton; Maritime Srs. Golf Assn.; Gov. General's Curling; City; Union (Saint John); Home: 1 Forest Acres, Fredericton, N.B. E3B 4L2; Office: 117 York St., Fredericton, N.B. E3B 4Z2

CLARK, Hon. Barry Roy, M.L.A., B.A., B.Th., M.Th.; politician; b. Charlottetown, P.E.I. 5 July 1948; s. Roy Leard and Irene Blanche (MacPherson) C.; e. Prince of Wales Coll., Univ.; m. Judith Ann d. Merritt Kerrick, Elizabethtown, Ky. 20 Aug. 1973; children: Amie Charissa, Jeremy Roy; MIN. DEPT. OF TOURISM, INDUSTRY & ENERGY, P.E.I.1980- ; facilitator/instr. Leadership Inst. Holland Coll.; el. M.L.A. for 6th Queens prov. g.e. 1978, re-el. 1979; Min. without Portfolio and Min. Responsible for Housing Corp. 1979-80; P. Conservative; Church of Christ; Office: (P.O. Box 2000) Shaw Bldg., Charlottetown, P.E.I. C1A 7N8.

CLARK, Charles David, M.B.A.; food executive; b. Hamilton, Ont. 22 Feb. 1939; s. Charles Henry and Marguerite Sandel (Waller) C.; e. McMaster Univ. B.A. 1963; Univ. of W. Ont. M.B.A. 1966; m. Mary Edna d. Late Ward Aubrey Kelly, Hamilton, Ont. 27 Aug. 1965; children: Alexandra Sandel, Sarah Frances, Hazel Ann; PRES. AND DIR., THOMAS J. LIPTON INC. since 1978; Dir., mem. of Exec. Comte., Chmn., Government Policy Task Force; Grocery Products Manufacturers Assoc. of Can.; Sr. Group Product Mgr. Colgate-Palmolive Ltd. 1966-72; Dir. of Marketing Seven-Up (Canada) Ltd. 1972-74; Vice Pres. Marketing and Dir. present Co. 1974-77, Extve. Vice Pres. 1977-78; Vice Pres. Ont. Council Boy Scouts Can.; Dir. Central Ont. and Lakeshore YMCA: mem. Ontario Chapter, Young Presidents' Organization, Inc.; recreations: skiing, jogging, tennis, squash, sailing; Club: Donalda; Home: 25 Farmington Cres., Agincourt, Ont. M1S 1E9; Office: 2180 Yonge St., Toronto, Ont. M4S 2C4.

CLARK, Rt. Hon. Charles Joseph (Joe), P.C. M.P., M.A., LL.B. (Hon); politician; b. High River; Alta. 5 June 1939; s. Charles A. and Grace R. (Welch) C.; e. Univ. of Alta. B.A. 1960, M.A. 1973; Univ. of N.B. LL.B. (Hon) 1976; m. Maureen Anne d. late John J. McTeer 30 June 1973, one d. Catherine Jane; LEADER OF THE OPPOSITION 1980-Nat. Leader, Preg. Cons. Party of Canada and Leader of Official Opposition H. of C. 1976-79and 1980-; Prime Minister of Can. 1979-80 el. to H. of C. for Rocky Mountain, Alta. 1972, re-el. 1974; el. Yellowhead, Alta. 1979 and 1980; Prog. Cons. Caucus Chrmn. on Youth 1972-74 and on Environment 1974-76; Advisor to Hon. R. L. Stanfield 1967-70; Special Asst. to Hon. Davie Fulton 1966-67; careers in teaching, journalism and broadcasting; R. Catholic; recreations: cross-country skiing, tennis travel, reading; Clubs: Ottawa Athletic, Cercle Universitaire (Hon. mem.); Home "Stornoway", 541 Acacia Ave. Ottawa, Ont.Office: House of Commons, Ottawa, Ont.

CLARK, Colin Whitcomb, Ph.D.; educator; b. Vancouver, B.C. 18 June 1931; s. George Savage and Irene (Stewart) C.; e. Magee High Sch. Vancouver 1949; Univ. of B.C., B.A. 1953; Univ. of Wash. Ph.D. (Math.) 1958; m. Janet Arlene d. James A. Davidson, Georgeville, Que. 17 Sept. 1955; children: Jennifer Kathleen, Karen Elizabeth, Graeme David; PROF. OF MATH., UNIV. OF B.C. 1970- ; Instr. in Math. Univ. of Calif. (Berkeley) 1958-60; Asst. Prof. present Univ. 1960, Assoc. Prof. 1966; Visiting Scholar, Univ. of Calif. Berkeley 1965-66; Visiting Scient., New Mexico State Univ. 1970-71 and C.S.I.R.O. Div. of Fisheries & Oceanography, Sydney, Australia 1975-76; mem. Fisheries & Oceans (Can.) Research Adv. Council 1981-84; mem. Program Adv. Comte. Internat. Center Living Aquatic Resources Mang. (Manila) 1982-85; author "Elementary Mathematical Analysis" 1981; "Mathematical Bioeconomics; the Optimal Management of Renewable Resources" 1976; "Bioeconomic Modelling and Fishery Management" (in preparation); numerous articles prof. journs. on pure & applied math., resource econ., biol.; mem. Candn. Applied Math. Soc. (Pres. 1981-83); Assn. Environmental & Resource Econs. (Council 1982-84); Soc. Indust. & Applied Math.; recipient Killam Sr. Research Fellow 1975-76, 1981-82; Prof. Jacob Biely Faculty Research Prize 1978; recreations: hiking,

cross-country skiing, gardening; Club: North Shore Hikers; Home: 9531 Finn Rd., Richmond, B.C. V7A 2L3; Office: Vancouver, B.C. V6T 1W5.

CLARK, Brig. Donald M., E.D., Q.C.; b. Vancouver, B.C., 12 Apl. 1915; s. late Brig-Gen. John Arthur, C.M.G., D.S.O., V.D., C.D., Q.C., LL.D., and Jean Abercrombie (McGillivray) C.; e. Univ. of British Columbia (1931); Royal Mil. Coll., Kingston, Ont., Dipl. of Grad. 1936; Vancouver Law Sch., 1936-39; m. Joan Napier, d. late Herbert McKenzie Ross, 25 Apl. 1941; children: Donald Ross, Campbell McGillivray, Sally Joan; SR. PARTNER, CLARK, WILSON; Dir. and Secy., Bank of British Columbia; Trustee, BBC Realty Investors; Governor, Canadian Tax Foundation; 1954-56, 1972-75; read law with John A. Clark, Q.C.; called to the Bar of British Columbia, 1939; cr. Q.C. 1960; served in 2nd World War ; Overseas, 1939-45 in Eng., Italy. Holland, Belgium and Germany with Seaforth Highlanders of Can. (latterly as C.O.); Mentioned in Despatches; Commdr. of 15th Inf. Bgde. Reserve Army, 1950; of 24th Militia Group, Vancouver, B.C., 1955-57; Dir., Children's Hosp.; B.C. Prov. Council Boy Scouts; Vancouver Foundation; mem., Candn. Bar Assn.; B.C. Law Soc.; Vancouver Bar Assn. (Past Pres.); Delta Upsilon; Conservative; Presbyterian; Club: Vancouver; Home: 5087 Connaught Drive, Vancouver, B.C. V6M 3G2 Office: 1700-750 W. Pender St., Vancouver, B.C. V6C 2B8

CLARK, (Edward) Ritchie, B.Com.; retired banker; b. Toronto, Ont., 3 Feb. 1912; s. Herbert Abraham, K.C., B.A., and Mary Laura Adeline (MacNicol) C.; e. N. Toronto and Oakwood Coll. Insts., Toronto, Ont.; Univ. of Toronto, B.Com. 1933; Fellow, Candn. Bankers' Assn.; m. Eileen, d. Rev. T. J. Campbell Crawford, M.A., W. Kilbride, Ayrshire, Scotland, 11 Oct. 1945; children: Alison, Ritchie, Rosemary, Lorna; joined Bank of Nova Scotia in Economics Dept., 1933; employed in various brs. and depts of the Bank in Toronto and New York, 1934-42; after war service entered Credit Dept. at the Gen. Mgr.'s Office, 1946; joined Industrial Devel. Bank (Crown Corp.) as a Credit Offr., Toronto Br., 1947; trans. to Vancouver as Credit Offr. in Vancouver Br. and subsequently apptd. Asst. Supv. at that office; apptd. Supv., Winnipeg Br., 1956, Montreal, 1959; Asst. Gen. Mgr. 1962; Depy. Gen. Mgr. 1966; Gen. Mgr. 1969; Chief Gen. Mgr. 1973; Vice Pres. and Chief Gen. Mgr. of Federal Business Development Bank 1975; Extve. Vice Pres. and Chief Gen. Mgr. 1976; retired 1977; mem. Admin., Council & Finance Comte. of Presbyterian Church in Can.; served in 2nd World War with R.C.A.F., 1942-46; attached to R.A.F. Overseas, 1944-46; attained rank of Flying Offr.; commanded R.A.F. units as Radar Offr.; Presbyterian; recreations: music, photography, reading; Clubs: St. James's; Home: 65 Franklin Ave., Town of Mount Royal, Que. H3P 1B8

CLARK, Eileen, B.Sc.; association executive; b. Twechar, Scot. 8 Jan. 1924; d. Thomas James Campbell and Isabel Sharpe (Hastings) Crawford; e. Ardrossan (Scot.) Acad.; Univ. of St. Andrew's B.Sc. 1943; m. E. Ritchie Clark 11 Oct. 1945; children: Alison (Mrs. W. D. Vannah), H. C. Ritchie, Rosemary (Mrs. Clark-Beattie), Lorna; PRES., CANDN. FED. OF UNIV. WOMEN 1979- ; held several positions Nat. Extve. Comte. of present Fed. incl. Vice Pres. (Que.) and Chrmn. Internat. Relations, 1968-79; mem. Council Internat. Fed. Univ. Women 1977-79; 2nd. Vice-Pres., Virginia Gildersleeve Internat'l Fund for Univ. Women, 1981-; served as Radar Tech. Offr. WAAF 1943-46, rank Sec. Offr.; Chrmn. Comte. on Arts & Letters, Montreal Council of Women 1972-73; mem. St. Andrew's Soc. Montreal (2nd Vice Pres. 1979-, Welfare Chrmn. 1973-); L'Assn. des femmes diplômées des univs. (Montréal); P. Conservative; Presbyterian; recreations: skiing, curling, golf, English smocking, antique porcelain; Clubs: University Women's Club of Montreal Inc; Town of Mount Royal Curling; Home: 65 Franklin

Ave., Town of Mount Royal, Qué. H3P 1B8; Office: Univ. de Montréal, Case postale 6128, succursale A, Montréal, Qué. H3C 3J7.

CLARK, George Denton, B.Sc., M.Eng.; executive; b. Summerside, P.E.I., 29 Jan. 1924; s. William Andrew Heath and Mary Lillian (Murray) C.; e. Prince of Wales Col., Charlottetown, P.E.I. 1945-46; Univ. of N.B., B.Sc. (Elect. Engn.) 1950; McGill Univ., M.Eng. 1952; m. Janet Eileen, d. Norman MacMurdo, North Bedeque, P.E.I., 7 Aug. 1946; children: Bryan Denton, Dr. Elizabeth Mary Heather, Barbara Ann; CHAIRMAN & PRESIDENT, RCA INC.; Dir., Coronet Carpets Ltd., Farmham Que.; Past-Chmn., Can. Chamber of Commerce; mem. Can.-U.K. Comte. and Can.-U.S. Comte. Candn. Mfrs. Assn., Toronto; joined Nat. Research Council, Ottawa, as Research Offr. 1956; joined present Co., Montreal, as Mgr., Field Operations, 1956; Mgr., Montreal Engn. Liaison Office, Camden, N.J., 1957; RCA Service Co., Mgr. Site Operations, Greenland and Alaska, 1959; Mgr., Missile Test Project, Cape Canaveral, Fla., 1960; Mgr. Range Projects, Cocoa Beach, Fla., 1968; Vice Pres., Range Projects, Cocoa Beach 1969, Vice Pres. Operations, Cherry Hill, N.J., 1972; apptd. Pres., RCA Ltd., 1973, Chrmn. of Bd. and Pres. 1976; Dir. and Past Bd. Chrmn., Fla. Inst. of Technol.; served as Pilot, RCAF, 1942-45; Offr. RCEME, 1949-55; mem. Inst. Elect. & Electronic Engrs.; recreations: golf, boating; Clubs: Royal Montreal Golf, Forest and Stream; Mount Royal; Rideau; Lambton Golf and Country Toronto; Office: P.O. Box 161, Royal Bank Plaza, Toronto, Ont., M5J 2J4

CLARK, Hart Duncan, B.A.; Canadian public servant; b. Winnipeg, Man., 30 July 1914; s. Frederick W. and Edith A. (Sutherland) C.; e. Univ. of Man., B.A. 1935 (Gold Medal Arts Hons. Course), grad. studies and teaching fellowship in Math., 1935-37; Rhodes Scholar, Merton Coll., Oxford Univ., 1937-40 (Math.); m. Lenore Morgan, Winnipeg, Man. 12 June 1943; four s: Terence, Alan, David, John, one d: Barbar; Part-time Adviser, Internat. Claims for Dep. Min. of Finance; Consultant, Pension & Insur. Benefits for Human Rights Commission; Spec. Pensions Adv., Treasury Bd., 1976-80; special asst. to Depy. Min. of Finance particularly in internat. claims; Lectr., Univ. of Man. 1945-46; Carleton Univ. (evening classes) 1949-51; joined present Service 1947; held various positions Dept. of Finance and Treasury Bd. incl. Dir., Pensions and Ins. Div. 1953-76; served in 2nd World War, Exper. Offr. in Admiralty; posted E. coast Scot. 1940-43; various bases in U.S. 1943-45; United Church; recreations: curling, golf, camping; Club: Ottawa Curling; Home: 94 Avenue Rd., Ottawa, Ont. K1S 0P2; Office: Place Bell Canada, Ottawa, Ont. K1A 0R5

CLARK, Howard Charles, M.Sc., Ph.D., Sc.D., F.R.S.C., F.C.I.C.; educator; b. Auckland, N.Z. 4 Sept. 1929; s. Eric Crago Clark, e. Takapuna Grammar Sch. Auckland 1947; Univ. of Auckland B.Sc. 1951, M.Sc. 1952, Ph.D. 1954; Cambridge Univ. Ph.D. 1958, Sc.D. 1972; m. Isabel Joy d. late Leslie Dickson 10 Apl. 1954; children: Carolynn Joy, Kristin Elizabeth; VICE PRES. ACAD. UNIV. OF GUELPH since 1976 and Prof. of Chem.; Dir. Varian Associates of Canada Ltd.; Lectr. Univ. of Auckland 1954-55; Fellow, Cambridge Univ. 1955-57; Asst. prof. to Full Prof. Univ. of B.C. 1957-65; Prof. and Head of Chem. Univ. of W. Ont. 1965-76; mem. various comtes. Nat. Research Council Can. and Council Ont. Univs.; Ed. "Canadian Journal of Chemistry" 1974-78; mem. various ed. bds.; author or co-author over 200 articles and chapters in prof. journs.; mem. Am. Chem. Soc.; Chem. Soc. (London); United Church; recreations: tennis, swimming, gardening; Home: R.R.1, Moffat, Ont. L0P 1J0; Office: Guelph, Ont. N1G 2W1.

CLARK, Mt. Rev. Howard Hewlett, C.C. (1970), D.D., D.C.L., LL.D. (Ang.); b. McLeod, Alta, 23 Apl. 1903; s. Douglass and Florence Lilian (Hewlett) C.; e. Trinity Coll., Univ. of Toronto , B.A. 1932; Hon. D.D., Trinity Coll., Toronto, 1945, and from eleven other colls. and univs. 1955-66; D.C.L. Bishop's 1960, St. John's Coll. 1964; LL.D., Manitoba 1966; m. Anna Evelyn, d. W. Foster Wilson, 2 June 1935; children: Howard, Mary, Esther, Elizabeth; Archbishop and Metrop. of Rupert's Land 1961-69; Primate of Anglican Ch. of Canada 1959-70; Asst. Curate, Christ Ch. Cath. Ottawa, Ont. 1932; Priest in Charge of Christ Ch. Cathedral, Ottawa 1938; Rector 1939-53; Dean of Ottawa, Anglican Ch. of Canada 1945-53; Bishop of Edmonton, 1954-59 and Archbishop 1959, Hon. Chaplain. Gov.-Gen's Foot Guards, Ottawa, 1934-38; el. Chrmn. of (New) Ang. Council of N. America, Feb. 1969-70; Special Lect., Trinity Coll., Toronto 1970, Tutor and Fellow 1971-, also Chancellor since 1972; Home: 252 Glenrose Ave., Toronto, Ont. M4T 1K9

CLARK, Ian Christie, M.A.; museum executive; b. Toronto, Ont. 17 April 1930; s. Christie Thomas and Gwyneth (Shannon) C.; e. Upper Can. Coll. Toronto 1948; McGill Univ. B.A. 1953, M.A. 1958; m. Nancy Cynthia d. Henry Lloyd Blachford, Montreal, Que. Aug. 1958; children: Graeme Christie, Brenda Trenholme; SECY.-GEN., NAT. MUSEUMS OF CAN. since 1978; Instr. in Eng. McGill Univ. 1955; Ed. and Publs. & Reports Secy., Pulp and Paper Research Inst. Can. 1956; joined Dept. External Affairs Ottawa 1958; Third Secy. and Vice Consul Brussels 1961, Second Secy. 1962, Secy. Candn. Del. to 12th Gen. Conf. UNESCO Paris 1962, Cultural Affairs Div. Ottawa 1964-67, First Secy. (Information) Paris 1967, Counsellor (Information & Cultural Affairs) 1968, Cultural Counsellor London 1970-72; Dir. of Museums and Visual Arts, Dept. Secy. of State 1972, Special Advisor to Secy. of State, Cultural Property Export and Import Act 1974; Chrmn. Candn. Cultural Property Export Review Bd. 1977; author "Indian and Eskimo Art of Canada — Art Indien et Esquimau du Canada" 1970; poetry various mags.; critical reviews arts France 1967-70, U.K. 1971-72; Founding mem. Que. Archaeol. Assn. (Secy.) and Seminar on Aboriginal Populations Que. and Labrador 1954; Zeta Psi; Presbyterian; recreations: tennis, skiing, swimming, gardening, arts, Canadiana; Clubs: Badminton & Racquet (Toronto); Royal Automobile (London); Five Lakes; Rockcliffe Lawn Tennis; Country (Ottawa); Home: 393 Maple Lane, Rockcliffe Park, Ottawa, Ont. K1M 1H7; Office: 300 Laurier Ave. W., 21st Floor West Tower, Ottawa, Ont. K1A 0M8.

CLARK, Joseph Adair Porter; executive; b. Toronto, Ont., 2 Nov. 1921; s. Joseph W. G., C.B.E., D.F.C. and Hazel (Porter) C.; e. Univ. of Toronto; m. Patricia, d. W. G. Fraser Grant, Q.C., 28 Sept. 1946; children: Joseph, Thomas, Carolyn; Pres. AND CEO, CANADA NEWS-WIRE LTD.; Mills, Spence & Co., Toronto, 1945; Asst. to Dir. of Pub. Relations, Massey-Harris Co. Ltd., 1947; with partners formed Tisdall, Clark and Co. in 1952: now Tisdall, Clark and Partners, from which he retired in 1979; served with RCNVR in Atlantic Area and Europe 1940-45; awarded Centennial Medal 1967; mem., Toronto Rehab. Centre (Past Pres.); Candn. Rehab. Council (Past Pres.); former Chrmn., Adv. Comte. on Rehab. to Ont. Min. of Community and Social Services; accredited mem., Candn. Pub. Relations Soc., Pub. Relations Soc. of Amrica; mem. Advisory Comte., Branksome Hall School; Freemason; Anglican; recreations: fishing, reading; Club: Granite; Home: Highwoods, R.R. 2, King City, Ont. L0G 1K0; Office: 500-211 Yonge St., Toronto, Ont. M5B 1N3

CLARK, Robert Fisher; insurance executive; b. Kingston, Ont., 3 March 1919; s. Robert W., M.D., and Evva Harriet (Fisher) C.; e. Pub. and High Sch., Bowmanville, Ont.; m. Kathleen Eleanor, d. late Franklin F. Appleton; children: Peter, Stephen, David, Michael, Anne, Sarah; DEPY. CHRMN., CANADIAN REINSURANCE CO. since 1978 and chief agent in Canada, Swiss Reinsurance Co. since 1958; with Ocean Accident & Guarantee Corp. & Commercial Union Assnce. Co. Ltd., 1938-41; Extve.

Vice-Pres., Sterling Offices of Can. Ltd., 1941-52; Mgr. and Secy., Candn. Reins. Co., 1953; Pres. 1968; Hon. Chairman, Reinsurance Research Council; Dir., Can. Arthritis Soc.; Anglican; Clubs: Cutten (Guelph); Ontario; York Downs Golf & Country; Home: George St., Rockwood, Ont. N0B 2K0; Office: 95 St. Clair Ave. W., Toronto, Ont. M4V 1N9

CLARK, Samuel Delbert, M.A., Ph.D., LL.D., D.Litt., F.R.S.C. (1952), O.C.; educator; b. Lloydminster, Alta., 24 Feb. 1910; s. Samuel David and Mary Alice (Curry) C.; e. Univ. of Sask., B.A. 1930, M.A. 1931; London Sch. of Econ. & Pol. Science 1932-33; McGill Univ. M.A. 1935; Univ. of Toronto, Ph.D. 1938; m. Rosemary Josephine, d. late W. E. Landry, 26 Dec. 1939; children: Ellen Margaret, Samuel David, William Edmund; Prof. of Sociology, Univ. of Toronto, 1953-76, Prof. Emeritus since 1976; Lecturer Sociology, University of Manitoba, 1937; joined Univ. of Toronto as Lect. 1938; Visiting Prof. of Sociol., Univ. of Cal. (Berkeley) 1960-61; McCulloch Prof. of Soc., Dalhousie Univ., 1972-74; Visiting Prof. of Soc., Univ. of Guelph, 1976-78; Visiting Prof. of Soc., Lakehead Univ., 1978-80; Distinguished Visiting Prof., Univ. of Tsukuba, Japan, Spring 1980; Visiting Prof. of Candn. Studies, Univ. of Edinburgh, 1980-81; author of "The Canadian Manufacturers Assn." 1939; "The Social Development of Canada" 1942; "Church and Sect in Canada" 1959; "The Developing Canadian Community" 1963 (new ed. with additional chapters 1968); "The Suburban Society" 1966; "The Canadian Society in Historical Perspective" 1976; "The New Urban Poor" 1978; also numerous articles in learned and prof. journs.; rec'd. Guggenheim Fellowship 1944-45; Tyrrell Medal, Royal Soc. of Can. 1960; Officer Order of Can. 1978; LL.D. Univ. Calgary, 1978; D.Litt. St. Mary's Univ., 1979; LL.D. Dalhousie Univ., 1979; mem., Candn. Pol. Science Assn. (Pres. 1958-59); Candn. Assn. of Anthropol. & Sociol. (Hon. Pres.); Am. Sociol. Assn.; Pres. (1975-76) Royal Soc. Can.; Foreign Hon. mem., Am. Acad. Arts and Sciences (1976); Liberal; Address: 9 Lamont Ave., Agincourt, Ont. M1S 1A8

CLARK, Lieut.-Gen. Samuel Findlay, C.B.E., C.D.; b. Winnipeg, Man., 17 March 1909; s. James and Anne Elizabeth (Findlay) C.; e. Univ. of Manitoba, (B.Sc.) (Elect. Engn.) 1932; Univ. of Sask., B.Sc. (Mech. Engn.) 1933; Staff Coll., Camberley, 1942; Imp. Defence Coll., London, 1947; m. Blanche Leona, d. Joseph Hamilton Seagram, Barrie, Ont., 18 Sept. 1937; Lieut., Royal Candn. Corps of Signals, 1933; Assoc. Prof. Elect. and Mech. Engn., R.M.C., Kingston, Ont.; C.O., Lieut.-Col., 5th Canadian Armoured Divn. Signals, 1941; G.S.O. 1, Candn. Mil. Hdqrs., London, Eng., 1942; Chief Signal Offr., 2nd Candn. Corps, 1942-45; Depy. Chief, Gen. Staff, Army Hdqrs., Ottawa 1945-47; Candn. Observer, W. Union Defence Organ., 1948-49; promoted Maj. Gen. 1949, Lieut.-Gen. 1958; after 1948 prior to present appt. was successively Chrmn., Candn. Jt. Staff, London, and Candn. mem. N.A.T.O. Military Cmte. and Q.M.G., Ottawa (1951), then G.O.C. Central Command, Oakville, Ont.; Chief of the Gen. Staff, Ottawa 31 Aug. 1958-1 Oct. 1961; Chrmn. of Nat. Capital Comn., Ottawa, 1961-67; Commdr. Order of Orange-Nassau with Crossed Swords; Offr., Legion of Merit (U.S.A.); Offr., St John; mem., Royal Candn. Geog. Soc.; Engn. Inst. Can.; Assn. Prof. Engrs. Ont.; Anglican; Club: Union; Address: 301-1375 Newport Ave.,Victoria, B.C. V8S 5E8

CLARK, Thomas Henry, Ph.D., F.R.S.C., F.G.S.; paleontologist; b. London, Eng., 3 Dec. 1893; e. Harvard Univ., A.B. 1917, A.M. 1921, Ph.D. 1923; Logan Prof. of Paleontol., McGill Univ., 1929-62; Chrmn., Dept. of Geol. Sciences there 1952-59; Geol.; Geol. Survey of Can., 1927-31; Geol. Dept. of Mines, Que., 1938-60, Dept. Natural Resources 1960-63, Consultant 1963-69; Advisor in Geol. to Redpath Museum 1969; Dir., McGill Museums 1943-52; Asst. Geol., Harvard Univ., 1915-20; Instr. there 1920-24; Asst. Prof., McGill Univ., 1924-27; Assoc. Prof.,

1927-29, Prof. Emeritus, 1964; mem., Paleontol. Soc.; Geol. Soc. Am.; Candn. Inst. Mining & Metall.; Geol. Assn. Can. (Logan Gold Medal winner 1970); Sigma Xi; Phi Beta Kappa; Address: Dept. of Geol. Sciences, McGill University, 3450 University St., Montreal, Que. H3A 2A7

CLARKE, Austin Ardinel Chesterfield; author; b. Barbados, W.I. 26 July 1934; s. late Kenneth Trotman and Gladys Irene C.; e. St. Matthias' Boys' Sch., Combermere Sch. and Harrison Coll., Barbados; Trinity Coll. Univ. of Toronto; m. Betty Joyce d. late David Reynolds, Kingston, Jamaica, W.I. 14 Sept. 1957; two d. Janice Elizabeth, Loretta Anne; WRITER-IN-RESIDENCE, UNIVERSITY OF WESTERN ONTARIO, 1982-83; Visiting Prof. of Eng. and Am. Studies, Yale Univ. 1968-71; Jacob Visiting Prof. of Lit. Brandeis Univ. 1970-71; Margaret Bundy Scott Visiting Prof. of Lit. Williams Coll. 1971; Visiting Prof. of Black Studies, Duke Univ. 1972-73; Visiting Prof. of Ethnic Studies, Univ. of Texas, Austin 1973-74; Adviser to Prime Min. of Barbados 1974-76; Cultural Attaché Embassy of Barbados, Washington 1974-75; Gen. Mgr. Caribbean Broadcasting Corp. Barbados 1975-76; Writer-in-Residence, Concordia Univ. Montreal 1975-76; mem. Metrop. Toronto Lib. Bd. 1968; Yale Aurelis Club, Yale Univ., 1969-70; Yale Club of New Haven, 1970- ; P. Cons. cand. York S. Prov. Riding 1977; Trustee, Rhode Island Sch. of Design, Providence 1969-74; Fellow, Calhoun Coll. Yale Univ. 1968-70, Morse Fellow 1968; Fellow Sch. of Letters, Ind. Univ. 1969- ; rec'd Pres.'s Medal Univ. of W. Ont. 1965 Fiction; Saturday Night-Belmont Short Story Award 1965; Can. Council Lit. Award 1967, 1972, 1974-Fiction; Casa de las Americas Lit. Prize 1980 Fiction; author "The Survivors of the Crossing" 1964; "Amongst Thistles and Thorns" 1965; "The Meeting Point" 1967; "Storm of Fortune" 1973; "When He Was Free and Young", "He Used to Wear Silks" 1972; "The Bigger Light" 1975; "The Prime Minister" 1977; "Growing Up Stupid Under the Union Jack" 1980; "Under the Sandbox Tree," 1981; co-author "From the Green Antilles" 1966; "Voices, 2" 1965; "34 X Schwarze Liebe" 1968; "Stories From Ontario" 1974; "The Toronto Book" 1976; "Canada In Us Now" 1976; "Canada Writes!, 1977; "Stories Plus" 1979; "Toronto Short Stories" 1977; "Social Problems" 1964; Columnist, "The Nation Newspaper" Barbados 1979- ; P. Conservative; Anglican; Club: Bathurst Lions (Toronto); Address: 432 Brunswick Ave., Toronto, Ont. M5R 2Z4.

CLARKE, Brock Francis, Q.C., B.A., B.C.L.; b. Quebec City, P.Q., 30 Aug. 1919; s. Desmond Arthur, O.B.E. and Aline (Paradis) C.; e. Quebec City; Loyola High Sch., Montreal, Que.; Loyola Coll., B.A. (magna cum laude) 1939; McGill Univ., B.C.L. (Elizabeth Torrance Gold Medal) 1942; m. Simonne de Fonville Ethier, 14 June 1951; four s., Brian, David, Kevin, Gregory, one d. Brenda; PARTNER, OGILVY, RENAULT,; Vice-Pres. and Dir., Clarke Transport Canada Inc.; Dir., Liberian Iron Ore Ltd.; United Provinces Insurance Co.; Donohue Inc., Donohue St. Felicien Inc.; Donohue Charlevoix Inc.; Donohue Malbaie Inc.; Clarke Steamship Ltd.; read law with present firm; called to the Bar of Que., 1943; on active service with R.C.N.V.R. 1943-45; discharged with rank of Lieut.; mem., Candn. Bar Assn.; Candn. Tax Foundation; Roman Catholic; Clubs: Mount Royal; St. Jame's; Mt. Bruno Country; Murray Bay Golf; Home: 4 Hudson, Westmount, Que. H3Y 1Y7;Office: Place Ville Marie, Montreal, Que. H3B 1Z7

CLARKE, Donald Walter, M.Sc., Ph.D.; university professor; b. Vermilion, Alta., 12 April 1920; s. Harold James and Helena Leonora (Opfergelt) C.; e. Univ. of Alberta, B.Sc. 1941, M.Sc. 1943; Cal. Inst. Tech., Ph.D. 1951; m. Patricia Jean, d. H. L. Clary , San Marino, Cal., 28 Apl. 1951; children: Hugh James, Donald Clary, Catherine Emily; PROF. OF PHYSIOL., UNIV. OF TORONTO; Hon. Prof., Banting & Best Dept. Med. Research; Sr. Fellow, Trinity Coll.; joined present Univ. as Asst. Prof. in

Dept. of Physiol. 1951; served in 2nd World War with R.C.N.V.R. 1943-46 (Electrical), Lieut.; Mentioned in Despatches; Medal of Service, City of Toronto, 1977; author of several articles in scient. journs. and semi-tech. articles in soaring publs.; mem., Candn. Physiol. Soc.; Sigma Xi; Lambda Chi Alpha; United Church; Soaring Assn. of Can.; recreations: amateur radio (VE3 CHB), skating, volunteer agency work, soaring; Home: 108 Inglewood Dr., Toronto, Ont. M4T 1H5; Office: Medical Science Bldg., Univ. of Toronto, Toronto, Ont.

CLARKE, Ernest George, B.D., M.A., Ph.D.; educator; b. Varna, Ont. 16 June 1927; s. Melvin E. McK. and Eva M. (Epps) C.; e. Univ. of Toronto, Victoria Coll. B.A. 1949, Emmanuel Coll. B.D. 1952, M.A. 1953; Univ. of Chicago 1949-50; Leiden Univ. Holland Ph.D. 1962; m. Ruth G. d. Standish L. Hunt, Grand Valley, Ont. 8 Sept. 1951; children: Ernest Paul, Margaret Jean, Patricia Helen, David William; PROF. OF NEAR EASTERN STUDIES, VICTORIA COLL., UNIV. OF TORONTO, mem. Gov. Council of Univ.; Ed. "Newsletter for Targumic and Cognate Studies"; author "The Selected Questions of Ishó Bar Nun" 1962; "Wisdom of Solomon" 1972; mem. Soc. Mediterranean Studies (Dir.); Candn. Soc. Biblical Studies; Soc. Biblical Lit. (USA); Assn. Targumic Studies; Internat. Soc. Study Old Testament; P. Conservative; United Church; recreations: bookbinding, gourmet cooking; Clubs: Oriental; Arts & Letters; Home: 171 Collier St., Toronto, Ont. M4W 1M2; Office: Toronto, Ont. M5S 1A1.

CLARKE, Frank R., F.I.A., F.C.I.I., A.S.A., F.C.I.A; insurance executive; b. Manchester, Eng. 3 March 1920; s. Malcolm and Daisy (Burton) C.; e. Grammar Sch. Manchester, Eng.; m. Jean, d. Sydney Middleton 13 Oct. 1945; children: Hilary, Heather; SR. VICE PRES., CHIEF ACTUARY AND DIR., CONSTELLATION ASSURANCE CO. since 1975; Pres., Divien Mang. Ltd.; with Phoenix Assurance Co., Sales Mang. 1936, Asst. Actuary 1963; Actuary, Commercial Life Assurance Co., Toronto 1964; Actuary, Eaton Financial Services 1969; Vice Pres. and Actuary, Unionmutual Life Assurance Co. of Canada 1973; served in 2nd World War R.A.F. 1939-45, rank on discharge Flight Lt.; Assoc. Soc. of Actuaries; mem. Bd. Trade Metrop. Toronto; Anglican; recreations: golf, swimming, music, bridge; Home: 633 Shenandoah Drive, Mississauga, Ont. L5H 1W1; Office: 26 Wellington St. E., Toronto, Ont. M5E 1J6

CLARKE, George F.S., F.S.A., F.C.I.A.; b. Govan, Sask., 1 Feb. 1921; s. late E. Francene (Wallbridge) and late J. Orville C.; e. High Sch., Govan, Sask., 1939; University of Manitoba, B.Com. (Hons.) 1950; F.S.A. 1953; m. Sheila J.M. Stewart, 18 Sept. 1945 (d. 1975): one d. Georgia; m. 2ndly, Elsa Maryan McLeod, 7 May 1977; PRES. AND DIR., SUN LIFE ASSURANCE COMPANY OF CANADA, since 1978; Chrmn. and Dir., Sun Life of Can. Invest. Mgmt. Ltd.; Sun Life of Can. Benefit Mgmt. Ltd.; Suncan Equity Services Co.; Deputy chrmn. and Dir., Sun Life Assurance Co. of Can. (U.K.) Ltd.; Pres. and Dir., Sun Life Assurance Co. of Can. (U.S); Suncan Benefit Services Co.; Sun Growth Fund Inc.; Dir., Royal Trustco Ltd.; Candn. Cancer Soc.; Life Office Management Assn.; Mem., Bd. of Gov., Univ. of Waterloo; Manufacturers Life Insurance Co. 1950-67 (Group Vice-Pres. 1964-67); joined present Co. as Actuary 1967, Vice-Pres. and Chief Actuary 1968, Sr. Vice-Pres. 1970, Extve. Vice Pres. 1972; served with R.C.A.F. 1942-46, in U.K., Middle E., India, Ceylon, rank Flight Lt.; Fellow, Society of Actuaries; Fellow, Candn. Inst. of Actuaries; mem.; Internat. Cong. of Actuaries; Clubs: Masonic Lodge; Royal Montreal Golf; Royal Montreal Curling; Mt. Royal; Granite; Toronto; Home: 45 Dunvegan Rd., Toronto, Ont. M4V 2P5; Office: P.O. Box 4150, Station A, Toronto, Ont. M5W 2C9

CLARKE, Irene Fortune Irwin (Mrs. W.H.), C.M., M.A.; b. Toronto, Ont., 21 March 1903; d. John Irwin, Co. Leitrim, Ireland and Martha (Fortune) I. of Toronto; e. Parkdale Coll. Inst., Toronto; Victoria Univ., B.A. (Classics and Hons. English); Univ. of Toronto, M.A. (Greek Lit. and Philos); m. late William Henry Clarke, B.A.; 21 June 1927; children: Garrick Irwin, M.A. (Oxon.), B.D.., William Henry, Ph.D., Martha Cecily (Mrs. George Leibbrandt) B.A.; assoc. in business with her husband, founder and former Pres. of Clarke, Irwin & Co. Ltd., until his death; Pres. 1955-81, and Chrmn. of Bd. 1981-; Chrmn., Comn. on Legal and Econ. Status of Women, Candn. Fed. of Univ. Women, 1949-52; founding mem., Candn. Women's Voluntary Services, 1940; Hon. mem., Candn. Council Girl Guides Assn., 1954-57; Hon. Pres., Ont., Classical Assn., 1954-56; Regent, Victoria Univ., 1946-54; apptd. 1st woman mem., Bd. of Govs., Univ. of Toronto, 1958-72; Chrmn., Women's Div., Nat. Fund, Univ. of Toronto, 1959-60; Centennial Medal of Can, 1967; Mem., Order of Can., 1976; Hon. Trustee, Royal Ont. Museum; mem., Dom. Bd. of Finance, United Ch. of Canada 1960-65; Clubs: Toronto Ladies'; Heliconian; Address: 39 Old Mill Rd., Apt. 2004, Toronto, Ont. M8X 1G6

CLARKE, Kenneth Harry John, B.A.Sc., P.Eng.; industrialist; b. Toronto, Ont., 12 Oct. 1911; s. Harry John and Alice (Harkell) C.; e. Univ. of Toronto, B.A.Sc. (Metall. Engn.) 1936: Nat. Defence Coll., Kingston, Ont. 1953-54; m. Margaret Elizabeth, d. Harry Roland Winter, Toronto, 19 April 1940; one s. Kenneth; CHAIRMAN, SIMON-CARUES OF CANADA, Ltd. Consult., Corp. Affairs, Inco Ltd.; Chrmn. and Pres., Kaysea Consultants Ltd.; formerly Pres. Marketing Div. and Pres. Internat. Sales Ltd., Inco Ltd.; Chrmn., Candn. Industry and Business Internat. Adv. Comte. to Can.; Fed. Govt., Chrmn. Bus. and Indust. Adv. Comte. to D.E.C.D., Paris;Dir. Simon-Carves of Canada Ltd.; former mem. Adv. Comte. to Fed. Min. of Energy Mines & Resources; joined present Co. as Chemist, Port Colborne, Ont. 1934; Asst. Smelter, Consolidated Mining & Smelting Co. Ltd., Trail, B.C. 1935; Metall. Engr. Copper Refining Div., International Nickel Co. 1936, Asst. Mgr. Candn. Sales 1938, Mgr. Candn. Sales and Market Devel. 1957, Asst. Vice-Pres. 1967; served during 2nd World War Chief Allocations and Conserv. Div. also Extve. Asst. to Metals Controller Dept. Munitions and Supply, and Depy. Adm. Non-Ferrous Metals (Primary) Wartime Prices and Trade Bd. 1940; Special Asst. to Depy. mem. for Can., Combined Production & Resources Bd., Washington, D.C. 1944-45; Chrmn. Comte. on Utilization Nickel, Manganese, Cobalt, Tungsten & Molybdenum, Internat. Materials Conf., Washington, D.C. and Chrmn. Metall. Adv. Comte. Dept. Defence Production 1951-52; Candn. Del. U.N. Meeting on copper & zinc, London, U.K. 1957; Unido Copper Technol. Symposium, Moscow 1970; UNDP Multinat. Negotiations Symposium, Caracas 1974; Delegate, Law of the Sea Conf., Geneva and New York 1976-79; Chrmn. Internat. Standards Organ. Tech. Comte. TC-155 Nickel & Nickel Alloys; Past Internat. Pres. Pacific Basin Econ. Council; former Chancellor Senate and former Pres. Bd. Govs., Stratford Shakespearean Festival Foundation; former Pres. Silversmiths Guild of Can.; Candn. Copper & Brass Devel. Assn.; former Vice-Pres. & Dir. Candn. Export Assn.; former Chrmn. Comm. Intelligence Comte., Candn. Mfrs. Assn.; Can.-U.S. Comte.; Dir. Candn. Extve. Council Internat. Chamber of Comm.; mem. Extve. Comte. Can.-U.K. Comte., Candn. Chamber of Comm.; mem. Assn. Prof. Engrs. Ont.; Candn. Inst. Mining & Metall.; Bd. Trade Metrop. Toronto; Candn. Inst. Internat. Affairs; rec'd Centennial Medal 1967; Clubs: National; National; Rideau (Ottawa); Canadian, East India Devonshire Sports and Public Schools (London); Metropolitan (N.Y.); Home: "Post Manor", 1970 Brock Rd., Pickering, Ont. L1V 1Y3; Office: Box 44, 1 First Canadian Place, Toronto, Ont. M5X 1C4

CLARKE, Percy Raymond, B.Sc., P.Eng.; mining executive; b. Portage La Prairie, Man., 1 Sept. 1918; s. Victor Thomas and Alice Irene (Sexsmith) C.; e. Birch Hills (Sask.) Public Sch.; Portage Coll. Inst., Portage La Prairie, Man.; Univ. of Manitoba (2nd year Arts and Science) 1938; Univ. of Alta., B.Sc. (Mining Engn.) 1948; m. Pauline Mary, d. George Jennings, 9 June 1945; children: Angela, Jean, Irene, Michael; CHMN. AND C.E.O., KIDD CREEK MINES LTD. 1981-; Pres., Texasgulf Metals Co. Sr. Vice-Pres. Texasgulf Inc.; Pres. and Dir. Texasgulf Can. Ltd.; app'ted Sr. Vice Pres. Texasgulf Inc., 1976; — Vice Pres., Texagulf Inc., Kidd Creek Operation 1973; Extve. Vice Pres. and Dir., Texasgulf Can. Ltd. since 1976; joined Cominco, Trail Smelter as Jr. Engr. 1948; Mill Supt., Highland-Bell Ltd. 1950; Research Metallurgist, Noranda Mines Ltd. 1954; Mill Supt., Heath Steele Mines 1955; concurrently Base Metal Consultant (private practice) and Sr. Engr., Atomic Energy Control Bd., Univ. of Alta. 1958; Mill Supt. Kamkotia Mines Ltd. 1961; joined present Co. as Mill Supt., Timmins, Ont. 1964; served in 2nd World War, Queen's Own Cameron Highlanders of Can. 1939-45; comnd. Overseas 1941, on Dieppe Raid 1942; P.O.W. 1942-45; mem. Assn. Prof. Engrs. of Ont.; Candn. Inst. Mining & Metall.; Am. Inst. Mining & Metall. Engrs.; Dir., Zinc Institute; Mining Assn. of Can. (Dir.); Nat'l Advisory Comte on Mining Industry; Anglican; recreations: skiing, golf, camping; Home: 2095 Gatestone Ave., Oakville Ont L6J 2G2; Office: P.O. Box 175, Commerce Court, Toronto, Ont. M5L 1E7

CLARKE, Richard Morel, B.A.Sc., M.Eng.; b. Toronto, Ont. 17 July 1931; s. Roy Percy and Jean (Morel) C.; e. Allenby Pub. Sch. and Lawrence Park Coll. Inst. Toronto 1949; Univ. of Toronto B.A.Sc. 1954 (Chem. Eng.); Yale Univ. M.Eng. 1956; Rensaeller Polytechnic, Hartford, Conn. Business Mang. 1958; m. Jacqueline June d. Jack W. Eaton, Orillia, Ont. 23 Jan. 1960; two d. Stephanie S., Wendy E.; PRES. AND CHIEF EXTVE. OFFR., CELANESE CANADA INC. 1978- ; Pres., Celanese Canada Millhaven/Fibres Inc.; Dir., and Chmn. Cleyn & Tinker Inc.; Dir., Adv. Bd., Allendale Ins. Co.; Research & Devel. Engr. American Cyanamid 1954; Devel. Engr. Shell Oil Co. 1955; Vice Pres. & Gen.Mgr. Joclin Manufacturing Co. 1956-68; Devel. Mgr. Cabot, Celanese Chemical Co. 1968; Marketing Mgr. Resins, Celanese Plastics 1971, Vice Pres. & Gen. Mgr. Resins 1973; Sr. Vice Pres. Marketing Indust. & Smoking Products, Celanese Fibers Marketing Co. 1975; Extve. Vice Pres. & Gen. Mgr. Celanese Canada Ltd. 1978; Vice Chrmn. and mem. Extve. Comte. Candn. Textiles Inst.; mem. Extve. Comte. Soc. Chem. Industry; Dir. Candn. Export Assn.; mem. Candn. Chem. Producers' Assn.; Business Council on Nat. Issues; Am. Inst. Chem. Engrs.; Chem. Mfrs. Assn., Chrmn., Communications Comte.; Psi Upsilon; recreations: tennis, golf, skiing, photography; Clubs: Mount Royal; Montreal Badminton & Squash; Hillside Tennis; Home: 64 St. Sulpice Rd., Westmount, Que. H3Y 3B7; Office: 800 Dorchester Blvd. W., Montreal, Que. H3C 3K8.

CLARKE, Hon. Roderick Dunfield, B.A., B.C.L.; judge; b. Smiths Falls, Ont. 17 Apl. 1933; s. Vincent George and Helen Hogg (Dunfield) C.; e. St. George's Pub. Sch. and Quebec High Sch. Quebec City 1953; Univ. of N.B. B.A. 1958, B.C.L. 1961; Osgoode Hall Bar Admission Course 1966; m. Diane Dawne d. late Vernon Cooper, Rothesay, N.B. 14 Oct. 1961; children: Keltie Dawne, Fraser Aubrey Briar, Wilson Braymer; ONT. PROV. COURT JUDGE (CRIMINAL DIV.) since 1974; joined The National Trust Co. Toronto 1961-64; articled law student 1964-66; called to Bar of Ont. 1966; law practice Young & Clarke 1966-74; Dir. YM-YWCA; served on numerous bds. and comtes. prior to appt.; only civilian el. to Service Bn. Senate; contrib. to various legal publs.; former Secy.-Treas. and Vice Pres. Thunder Bay Law Assn.; Chrmn. Educ. & Sentencing Comte., Prov. Judges Assn. Ont. (Criminal Div.); Anglican; recreations: running, tennis, golf, boating; Home:

R.R. 13 Silver Harbour, Thunder Bay, Ont. P7B 5E4; Office: 1805 East Arthur St., Thunder Bay, Ont. P7E 5N7.

CLARKE, Stanley Desmond, B.Sc., P.Eng.; b. Quebec, Que., 18 Dec. 1917; s. Desmond and Aline (Paradis) C.; e. Quebec (Que.) High Sch.; Loyola Coll., Montreal, Que.; Royal Mil. Coll. Kingston, Ont.; Queen's Univ., B.Sc. (Mech. Engn.); m. Josefina Delgado Y Angulo, Havana, Cuba, 27 Feb. 1949; children: Desmond S., Donald I., Rosemary Josefina; PRESIDENT, CLARKE TRANSPORT CANADA INC., associated and subsidiary companies in marine and surface transport, pool car operations and internat. services; Dir., Texaco Can. Inc.; IAC Ltd.; Continental Bank of Canada; Quebecair; Halterm Ltd.; Marine Industrie Ltée.; began with Swan Hunter & Wigham Richardson Ltd., Eng., July-Dec. 1939; apptd. Asst. to Supt., Clarke Steamship Co. Ltd., 1945; Operating Mgr. 1945-50; Gen. Mgr. 1950; el. Vice-Pres. and Gen. Mgr., Clarke Transport Can. Inc. and assoc. cos., 1956; Pres. and Gen. Mgr., 1958; served with Candn. Army in Can., Europe and N. Africa, 1940-45; demobilized with rank of Lt.-Col.; Gen. Chrmn., 1963 Campaign Fed. Catholic Charities Inc.; Pres., St. Mary's Hosp., 1964-67; Gen. Vice Chrmn., 1970 Campaign of Federation Appeal of Greater Montreal; mem., Inst. Marine Engrs. (London); Order of Engrs. Que.; Soc. Naval Architects & Marine Engrs. (New York); recreations: golf, skiing; Clubs: St. James's; Mount Bruno; Mount Royal; Home: 2090 Cambridge Rd., Town of Mount Royal, Montreal, Que. H3R 2Y1; Office: 1155 Dorchester Blvd. W., Montreal, Que.

CLARKSON, Adrienne, M.A.; writer; TV interviewer; b. Hong Kong, 10 Feb. 1939; d. William George and Ethel May (Lam) Poy; e. Lisgar Coll. Inst., Ottawa, Ont., 1956; Univ. of Toronto, B.A. (Trinity Coll.) 1960, M.A. (Eng.) 1962; Sorbonne, 1962-63; 2 children; ONT. COMMISSIONER TO FRANCE, 1982-; Interviewer-host, CBC TV "Take 30", 1965-75; Host, "Adrienne At Large", 1974; "Fifth Estate", 1975-82; rec'd Centennial Medal 1967; Gen. Editor, "The New Woman" series, since 1970; author, "A Lover More Condoling", 1968; "Hunger Trace", 1970; "True To You In My Fashion", 1971; ACTRA Awards: best TV Journalist 1974; for outspokenness and integrity in broadcasting 1975; best documentary writing 1976; Internat. Emmy Award, Best Foreign Documentary, "Four Women", 1978; Address: c/o Candn. Speakers and Writers Service Ltd., 44 Douglas Cres., Toronto, Ont.

CLARKSON, Max Boydell Elliott, M.A.; educator, b. Lenzie, Scot. 14 Oct. 1922; s. George Elliott and Helene (Mannaberg) C.; e. Stowe Sch. Buckingham, Eng. 1939; St. Andrew's Coll. Aurora, Ont. 1940; Univ. of Toronto B.A. 1943, M.A. 1946; m. Madeleine d. Michael Earls 5 June 1948; children: Max Adam, Helene Edith; DEAN, FACULTY OF MANG. STUDIES, UNIV. OF TORONTO and Prof. of Mang. 1975-80; Dir. Value Line Development Capital Corp.; Graphic Arts Mutual Insurance; Tymshare; Eastern Utilities Ltd.; TransCanada Freezers Ltd.; Suncor; Vice Pres. Technical Charts, Inc. 1947-50; Pres. Clarkson Press Inc. 1950-57; Pres. Graphic Controls Corp. 1957-70, Chrmn. of Bd. 1970-75; served as Operations Offr. RCNVR 1943-45, rank Lt.; Chrmn. Mayor's Citizens' Adv. Comte. on Community Improvement Buffalo 1964-75; Allentown Community Centre 1970-75; Trustee D'Youville Coll. Buffalo 1975-77; Dir. The Niagara Inst. since 1972; The Shaw Festival 1969-79; mem. Council, Bd. Trade Metrop. Toronto; mem., Internat. Council for Quality of Working Life; Anglican; recreation: tennis; Clubs: Buffalo; Metropolitan (N.Y.); Bath (London, Eng.); York; Queens; Toronto Lawn Tennis; Home: 71 Old Forest Hill Rd., Toronto, Ont. M5P 2R3; Office: 246 Bloor St. W., Toronto, Ont. M5S 1V4

CLARKSON, Ross T., Q.C.; b. Montreal, P.Q., 29 March 1922; S. Ross and Elsie Florence (Trenholme) C.; e.

Selwyn House Sch. (Montreal), 1928-36; Lower Can. Coll. (Montreal) 1936-39; Univ. of Grenoble, 1947; McGill Univ.,B.A., 1942, B.C.L. (1st Class Hons.), 1948; Elizabeth Torrence Gold Medal, Civil Law; Montreal Bar Assn. Prize, Civil Law; I.M.E. Prize, Comm. Law; Univ. of Paris, 1948-49; m. Susan Jeanette d. late Ward C. Pitfield, 7 Sept. 1955; children: Linda Jane, Peter Ross; PARTNER, COURTOIS, CLARKSON, PARSONS & TETRAULT; Dir., National Trust Co. Ltd.; Menasco Can. Ltee.; Great Lakes Reinsurance Co.; Munich Reinsurance Co. of Canada; Munich Holdings Ltd.; S.K.W. Canada Inc.; Hoechst Canada, Inc.; Trans-American Chemicals Ltd.; Michelin Tires (Can.) Ltd.; mem., Montreal Children's Hosp.; Life Gov., Douglas Hosp. (Montreal); Dir. and Secy. Montreal Children's Hosp. Foundation; mem. Zeller Family Foundation; Gov., Foundation and mem., Reddy Mem. Hosp.; read law with W.B. Scott, Q.C.; called to the Bar of Quebec, 1948; cr. Q.C., 1963; joined present law firm, 1949; a Partner, 1958; Lectr. in Law, McGill Univ. 1959-71, and McGill Centre for Continuing Educ. 1968-70; mem., Canadn. Bar Assn.; Candn. Tax Foundation; Internat. Comn. of Jurists; Fellow, Internat. Acad. Law and Science; mem., Selwyn Old Boys Ass., (Dir. 1954-58, Pres. 1956-57); Alpha Delta Phi; United Ch.; recreations: reading, photography, swimming, music, cross-country skiing, hiking; Clubs: St. James's; University; M.A.A.A.; Hillside Tennis; Home: 220 Chester Ave., Montreal, Que. H3R 1W3; Office: 630 Dorchester Blvd. W., Montreal, Que. H3B 1V7

CLARKSON, Stephen, M.A., D.P.Sc.; educator; b. London, Eng., 21 Oct. 1937; s. George Elliott and Alice Helene (Mannaberg) C.; came to Can. 1939; e. Upper Can. Coll., Toronto, Ont. 1955; Univ. of Toronto, B.A. 1959; New Coll., Oxford, M.A. 1961 (Rhodes Scholar, Ont. 1958); Fondation Nat. de Science Pol., D.P.Sc. 1964 (Woodrow Wilson Fellow 1961); m. 1. Adrienne Louise Poy, div.; 2. Christina McCall Newman, 1 Sept. 1978; two d., Kyra Antoinette and Blaise Damaris PROF. OF POL. SCIENCE, UNIV. OF TORONTO; Policy Chrmn., Liberal Party in Ont. 1969-73; Dir., Social Planning Council Metrop. Toronto; mem. Edit. Bd., The Canadian Forum, 1965-79; joined the Univ. as Lect., Dept. Pol. Economy 1964, Asst. Prof. 1965, Assoc. Prof. 1967; Prof., 1980; Sr. Fellow, Research Inst. on Communist Affairs, Columbia Univ. 1967-68; Sub-Lt., R.C.N.V.R.; Cand. for Mayor, City of Toronto, 1969; Dir., Maison Française de Toronto 1972; author of "L'Analyse Soviétique des problèmes indiens du sous-développement" 1970; "City Lib: Parties and Reform in Toronto" 1972; "The Soviet Theory of Development: India and the Third World in Marxist-Leninist Scholarship" 1978; Ed., "An Independent Foreign Policy for Canada?" 1968; "Visions 2020: Fifty Canadians in Search of a Future" 1970; has contrib. Chapters to "Nationalism in Canada" 1966; "Peace, Power and Protest" 1967; "Living in the Seventies" 1970; "Canadian Independence" 1972; "The Egalitarian Option: Perspectives on Canadian Education" 1975; "Canada at the Polls: The General Election of 1974" 1975; "Nationalism, Technology and the Future of Canada" 1976; "party Politics in Canada" 1979; other writings incl. over 100 articles, chapters and reviews in leading journs., mags. and newspapers; has created new simulation technique for teaching univ. politics; Pres., Univ. League for Social Reform; Survival Found. 1973-77; mem., Candn. Pol. Science Assn. (Secy.-Treas. 1966-67); Candn. Assn. Slavists; Internat. Pol. Science Assn.; Am. Pol. Science Assn.; Candn. Assn. Asian Studies; Candn. Inst. Internat. Affairs; recreations: gardening, carpentry; Home: 44 Rosedale Rd., Toronto, Ont. M4W 2P6

CLARKSON, Stuart Winston, M.A.; Ontario civil servant; b. Stanley, N.B., 16 Sept. 1920; s. Elmer H. and Jane (Stewart) C.; e. N.B. Teachers Coll., Lic. 1938; Mount Allison Univ., B.A. 1949; Univ. of Toronto, M.A. 1951; m. L. Jean, d. late Carl Pardo Blenheim, Ont., 26 June 1944; children: Sherri, Wayne, James; Chrmn., Civil Service

Comn. (Ont.) 1974-79; Economist, Defence Research Board, Ottawa 1951; Department Trade and Commerce, Ottawa 1955, Atomic Energy of Can. Ltd. 1957; Depy. Min., Energy & Resources Ont. 1959; Trade & Devel. Ont. 1962; Revenue 1971; Chrmn., Ont. Eergy Bd. 1973; author of Report on Uranium and Atomic Energy; Extve. Dir. of Study "Energy in Ontario" 1973; Chmn. Residential Tenancy Comm. 1979; served in 2nd World War with R.C.A.F. 1940-45; United Church; Home: 100 Quebec Ave., Apt 1612, Toronto, Ont. M6P 4B8; Office: 77 Bloor St. W., Toronto Ont.

CLARRY, John Hamilton Cameron, Q.C., M.B.E., C.D., E.D., B.A.; b. Calgary, Alta., 21 Sept. 1919; s. Ernest Simpson and Jean Milne (Cameron) C.; e. Forest Hill Village (Toronto) Pub. Sch.; Univ. of Toronto Schs. 1938: Univ. Coll. Univ. of Toronto B.A. 1947; Osgoode Hall Law Sch. 1950 (Silver Medal); m. Elizabeth Joy d. Gordon Kennedy, Toronto, Ont., 17 Sept. 1955; children: Susan, David, Michael; PARTNER McCARTHY & McCARTHY; Dir. TransCanada PipeLines Ltd.; Canada Permanent Mortgage Corp.; Canada Permanent Trust Co.; The Canada Life Assurance Co.; called to Bar of Ont. 1950; cr. Q.C. 1963; joined Irish Regt. Can. 1937-38, COTC 1938-40, commnd. Royal Candn. Army Service Corps 1940, served overseas 1940-43, 1944-46; attBnded and instructed Candn. War Staff Course 1943-44, D.A.Q.M.G. First Candn. Army 1944; Royal Candn. Army Service Corps (Militia) 1946-58, C.O. 5 Column 1952-55, apptd. Hon. Lt. Col. 25 Toronto Service Bn. (Militia) 1971; mem. Bd. Govs. Candn. Tax Foundation 1967-70 and 1974-78 (Chrmn. 1976-77); mem. Council Bd. Trade Metrop. Toronto since 1975, Vice-Pres. 1980-; mem. Law Soc. Upper Can.; Candn. Bar Assn.; Offr. Order Orange Nassau with Crossed Swords; Liberal; Presbyterian; Clubs: Toronto; York; University; Royal Candn. Mil. Inst.; Home: 45 Glen Elm Ave., Toronto, Ont. M4T 1V1; Office: (P.O. Box 48) Toronto-Dominion Centre, Toronto, Ont. M5K 1E6

CLAS, André, B.A., M.A., D.Ph.; educator; b. Laning, France 1 June 1933; s. Eugène and Erna (Ditgen) C.; e. Univ. of Strasbourg B.A. 1953; Univ. of Montreal M.A. 1960; Univ. of Tübingen D.Ph. 1967; m. Sylviane d. Florimond Canepeel 18 July 1955; children: Sophie-Dorothée, David; PROF., DEPT. OF LINGUISTICS, UNIV. OF MONTREAL, 1976- ; Ed., META (Translators' Journal) 1968- ; joined present Univ. as Lectr. 1966, appointed Asst. Prof. 1967, Assoc. Prof. 1970, Chrmn. of Dept. 1972-81; author "Phonétique appliquée" 1967; "Le français, langue des affaires" 1969;"Guide de la correspondance" 1980; mem., Soc. de languistique romane; Ling. Soc. of Amer.; Candn. Ling. Soc.; Hon. Mem., Translator Soc. of Que.; Presbyterian; Home: 7405 Maynard, Montreal, Que. H3R 3B3; Office: (P.O. Box 6128, Succ. A) Montreal, Que. H3C 3J7

CLAXTON, John B., QC, B.C.L.; b. Montreal, Que., 13 Jan. 1927; s. Brooke and Helen G. (Savage) C.; e. Roslyn Sch., Lower Can. Coll. and Westmount (Que.) High Sch., 1944; McGill Univ., B.C.L. 1950; two s. David Frederick, Edward Brooke; called to Bar of Que. 1950; cr. Q.C. 1968; practised law in Montreal with Dixon, Claxton, Senecal, Turnbull & Mitchell and its successor firms from 1950-63; partner firm Lafleur Brown, Mtl. 1963-; served with Candn. Army 1945; Counsel to Royal Comn. on Can.'s Econ. Prospects (Gordon Comn.), 1955-56; Lectr., Faculty of Law, McGill Univ., 1956-68; Pres., McGill Law Grads.' Soc., 1970; Dir. Jr. Bar Assn. Montreal, 1951-54 (Secy. 1953-54); Chrmn., Group Ins. Comte., Bar of Montreal, 1970; mem., Candn. Bar Assn.; Liberal; Anglican; Clubs: University; Montreal Racket; Hillside Tennis; Canadian; Home: 1550 Dr. Penfield, Apt. 1507, Montreal, Que., H3G 1C2; Office: Lafleur, Brown, de Grandpré, 800 Victoria Sq., Suite 720, Montreal, Que. H4Z 1E4

CLEGHORN, John Edward, B.Com., C.A.; banker; b. Montreal, Que. 7 July 1941; s. H. W. Edward and Hazel M. (Dunham) C.; e. Westmount (Que.) High Sch. 1958; McGill Univ. B.Com. 1962; C.A. 1964; m. Pattie E. d. late Harry L. Hart 29 June 1963; children: Charles, Ian, Andrea; SR. VICE PRES. AND GEN. MGR. BRITISH CO-LUMBIA THE ROYAL BANK OF CANADA 1980- ; Dir. Pacific Forest Products Ltd.; joined Clarkson, Gordon & Co. 1962; St. Lawrence Sugar Ltd. 1964-66; Mercantile Bank of Canada, Montreal 1966, Mgr. Winnipeg Br. 1969, Vice Pres. W. Div. Vancouver 1970; Royal Bank H.O. Montreal 1974, Asst. Gen. Mgr. Project Financing Group 1975, Depy. Gen. Mgr. Corporate Lending 1976, Vice Pres. Nat. Accounts Div. 1978, Sr. Vice Pres. Planning & Marketing Internat. Div. 1979; Dir. Vancouver Gen. Hosp. Foundation; Vancouver Symphony Soc.; Vice Pres. and Gov., Greater Vancouver YMCA; Gov., Vancouver Pub. Aquarium; Trustee, Fraser Inst.; B.C. Sports Hall of Fame & Museum; mem. Que., Man. and B.C. Insts. C.A.'s; Clubs: Arbutus; Vancouver Lawn Tennis & Badminton; Vancouver; Home: 1491 West 26th Ave., Vancouver, B.C. V6H 2B3; Office: (P.O. Box 11141) 1055 W. Georgia St., Vancouver, B.C. V6E 3S5.

CLEGHORN, Robert Allen, M.D., D.Sc., F.R.C.P.(C); F.R.C. Psych.; b. Cambridge, Mass., 6 Oct. 1904; s. Allen Mackenzie and Edna Theresa (Gartshore) C.; e. Pub. and High Schs., London, Ont.; Univ. of Toronto Schs., 1921-22; Univ. of Toronto Med. Sch., M.D., 1928; Aberdeen Univ., D.Sc. 1932; m. Sheena (died 1976), d. late Sir John Marnoch, 1932; children: John Marnoch, Mhairi Jane (Santiago), Ailie Moir (Zimmermann); 2ndly Elizabeth, d. late Prof. H.H. Newman, 1977; Jr. Interne, Toronto Gen. Hosp., 1928-29; Asst. in Physiology, Marischal Coll., Aberdeen, 1929-32; Asst. Attending Phys., Toronto Gen. Hosp., 1933-46; Dir., Therapeutics Lab., Allan Mem. Inst., Montreal 1946-64; Asst. Prof. of Psychiatry, McGill Univ., 1946-49, Assoc. Prof. 1949-60, Prof. and Chrmn. of Dept. 1964-70, now Emeritus Prof.; Special lecturer, Psychiat., U. of T. 1978; Consultant Psychiatrist, SBMC, 1978-; served in 2nd World War as Major, with R.C.A.M.C.; service in Italy and N.W. Europe with No. 1 Research Lab.; mem., Candn. Med. Assn.; Physiol. Soc.; The Endocrine Soc. (Ed. Bd. 1953); Candn. Physiol. Soc.; Am. Soc. for Clinical Investigation; Am. Physiol. Soc.; Am. Psychosomatic Soc. (Past Pres.); N.Y. Acad. of Science; Am. Assn. Advanc. Science; Am. Psychiatric Assn. (Fellow 1954); Candn. Psychiatric Assn.; Am. Heart Assn.; Montreal Medico-Chirurg. Soc.; Acad. of Med., Toronto; Research Associate, Harvard Univ. 1953-54; Publications: 170; Office: Dept. of Psychiatry, Sunnybrook Med. Centre., 2075 Bayview Ave., Toronto, Ont. M4N 3M5

CLEMENT, Hon. Carlton William: judge; b. Waterloo, Ont., 1907; s. Charles B. and Gertrude (Unger) C.; m. Mary G. Lynch, June 1929; children: Charles M., Naomi G.; JUSTICE SUPREME COURT, ALTA.; mem., Edmonton Chamber Comm. (1959); Pres., Alta. & N.W. Chamber Mines (1960); Dir. for Alta., Candn. Chamber Comm.; Past Hon. Secy., Heart Fund of Alta.; mem. of Alta. Council, Candn. Bar Assn.; recreation: sailing; Clubs: Royal Glenora; Edmonton; Mayfair Golf & Country; Home: 14104-98 Ave., Edmonton, Alta. T5N 0G1; Office: Court House, Edmonton, Alta.

CLEMENTS;John Banks, Q.C.; barrister and solicitor; b. Winnipeg, Man. 23 Oct. 1925; s. late Garfield Leroy and late Florrie Ada (McKinnon) C.; e. Univ. Sch. Pasadena, Calif.; Univ. of Man. B.A. 1948; Osgoode Hall Law Sch. LL.B. 1952; m. Mary Louise d. late George E. Edmonds, Q.C. 31 Jan. 1959; children: Anne Elizabeth, John Edmonds; PARTNER, LASH, JOHNSTON 1959- ; Dir. Federal Pioneer Ltd.; Chesebrough-Pond's (Canada) Ltd.; Chesebrough-Pond's International Ltd.; John B. Clements Ltd.; Cornell-Dubilier Electronics (Canada) Ltd.; Fluidic Systems Ltd.; Sentinel Securities of Canada Ltd.;

Telnor Holdings Ltd.; Wynn's Canada Ltd.; called to Bar of Ont. 1952; cr. Q.C. 1964; joined law firm Lash & Lash (predecessor firm) Toronto 1952; served with RCNVR 1945; mem. Bd. Mang. Ont. Div. Candn. Nat. Inst. for Blind 1970-81; mem. Candn. Bar Assn.; Co. York Bar Assn.; Law Soc. Upper Can.; Zeta Psi; United Church; recreations: tennis, music, gardening; Clubs: R.C.Y.C.; National; Granite; Lawyers; Canadian; Empire; Home: 265 Inglewood Dr., Toronto, Ont. M4T 1J2; Office: (P.O. Box 11) Royal Bank Plaza, Toronto, Ont. M5J 2J1.

CLERMONT, Georges C., B.A., LL.B.; b. Montréal Qué., 27 Sept. 1936; s. Georges O. and Gabrielle (Grothé) C.; e. Coll. Jean de Brébeuf 1955; Univ. of Paris B.A. 1957; Univ. de Montréal LL.B. 1961; m. Marie d. late Hon. Jean Raymond, 9 Sept. 1961; children: Georges R., Anne-Marie, Jean-François; VICE PRES. DIVERSIFIED BUSINESS-ES, CIP INC. since 1975; Dir. CIP Daxion Inc.; Facelle Co. Ltd.; CIREM (Centre International de Recherches et d'Etudes en Management); read law with Duranleau, Dupré & Duranleau; called to Bar of Que. 1962; law practice Stewart, Crépeault & McKenna until 1968; joined Legal Dept. Bell Canada Montreal as Solr. becoming Asst. Gen. Counsel 1974; mem. Québec Bar; Candn. Bar Assn.; Montreal Chamber Comm.; R. Catholic; recreations: tennis, swimming, boating; Clubs: St-Denis; Canadian; Home: 366 Portland Ave., Town of Mt-Royal, Qué. H3R 1V5; Office: Sun Life Bldg., Montréal, Qué.I3

CLERMONT, Yves W., B.Sc., Ph.D.; educator; b. Montreal, Que. 14 Aug. 1926; s. Rodolphe and Fernande (Primeau) C.; e. Mont-Saint-Louis (Montreal) 1945; Univ. of Montreal B.Sc. 1949; McGill Univ. Ph.D. 1953; m. Madeleine d. Albert Bonneau 30 June 1950; children: Suzanne, Martin, Stéphane; PROF. AND CHRMN. OF ANAT. McGILL UNIV. since 1975; Lectr. McGill 1953, Asst Prof. 1956, Assoc. Prof. 1960, Prof. 1963; app'ted mem. Nat'l Bd Medical Examiners Anatomy Test Comte. (U.S.) 1979- ; mem. Grant Comtes. Med. Research Council Can. 1973-77, since 1978; mem. Review Group (1972-76) and Adv. Group, 1976-78; Expanded Program of Research in Human Reproduction, World Health Organ. Geneva; Secy. of the Arthur Lucian Award Comte. 1980-; mem. Ford Foundation Adv. Comte. in Reproductive Sciences 1976-79; rec'd Prix Scientifique de la Prov. de Qué. 1963; S. L. Siegler Award Am. Fertility Soc. 1966; Fellow, Anna Fuller Foundation USA 1954-55, Lalor Foundation USA 1962; author over 85 articles cytology, histology male reproductive organs; mem. Royal Soc. Can; Am. Assn. Anatomists (Vice Pres. 1970-73); Candn. Assn. Anatomists; Soc. Study Reproduction; Am. Soc. Andrology; Candn. mem., Microscopical Soc. of Can. 1981; R. Catholic; Home: 567 Townshend, St-Lambert, Que. J4R 1M4; Office; 3640 University St., Montreal, Que. H3A 2B2.

CLIFF, Denis Antony, B.Ed., R.C.A.; artists educator; b. Victoria, B.C. 8 Aug. 1942; s. Claire Henry and Ruth (Gregson) C.; e. Lampson Str. Sch., Esquimalt Jr. and Sr. High Schs. Victoria, B.C. 1960; Univ. of Victoria B.Ed. 1965; New Sch. of Art Victoria 1966-67; m. Margaret Joan d. John Watson Akins, Victoria, B.C. 23 Apl. 1965; children: Jason Alexander, Andrew Warren, Samantha Alison; PROF. OF VISUAL ART, YORK UNIV. 1979- ; cross appt. to Faculty of Educ., resp. for training art teachers; solo exhns. incl. Pollock Gallery Toronto 1968-72 annually, 1974, 1975, 1977, 1978, 1981; Artists Co-operative Toronto, Artist in Community Project Temagami, Smooth Rock Falls, Kirland Lake, Ont. 1976; Drawings 1977; York Univ. 1978; rep. in over 55 group exhns. since 1964; rep. in various pub., corporate and private colls. incl. Nat. Gallery Can., Can. Council Art Bank; comns. incl. Ostler Sch. of Nursing Mural 1969-70; Simcoe Bd. Educ. Mural 1971; Eaton Centre Toronto Mural 1978; recipient Best Painting Award City Hall Exhn. 1970, Best in Show Award 1971; 2nd Prize Aviva Art Exhn. 1971; Ont. Arts Council Awards 1976, 1978; Artist-in-Residence Canadore Coll. North Bay 1972-74; Dir. Artists Co-operative

Toronto 1975-; joined Art Gallery Ont. Artist in Community Program 1976; served jury Ont. Arts Council Artist in Schs. Program 1977-; Founding mem. and Dir. Arts" Sake Inc. 1977; Vice Pres. 1978, Pres. 1979; art teacher disabled people, Ont. Coll. of Art, Arts" Sake Inc. and New Sch. of Art; pioneered Art Trek sponsored by Ont. Govt. to bring prof. artists to remote Ont. communities; author "Colour" 1977; currently writing humorous book on art hist.; academic monitor for Bd. of Ed., Visual Art Prog.; Home: 207A Cowan Ave., Toronto, Ont. M6K 2N7; Office: 4700 Keele St., Downsview, Ont. M3J 1P3.

CLIFF, Ronald Laird, B.Com., C.A. (1954); company executive; b. Vancouver, B.C., 13 March 1929; s. Ronald Lorraine and Anna Georgina (Laird) C.; e. St. George's Sch., Vancouver, B.C. (Sr. Matric. 1946); Univ. of British Columbia, B.Com. 1949; m. June Dorrance, d. Fred B. Brown, Vancouver, B.C., 7 July 1951; children: Mrs. Diana Maughan, Leslie Georgina, Sheila Lorraine, Ronald Laird; CHRMN., INLAND NATURAL GAS CO. LTD.; Chmn., Candn. Aircraft Products Ltd.; Vice Chrmn., Pacific Press Ltd.; Dir., Balco Industries Ltd.; Bralorne Resources Ltd.; Burrard Yarrows Corp.; Canada Wire and Cable Co. Ltd.; Canfor Investments. Ltd.; Noranda Metal Industries Ltd.; Okanagan Helicopters Ltd.; Q Broadcasting Ltd.; Continental Bank of Can.; Versatile Corp.; mem; Adv. Bd., National Trust Co. Ltd.; Trustee, Olympic Trust of Can.; Trustee, Hockey Canada; Dir., Vancouver Symphony Society; mem., Institute of Chartered Accountants of B.C.; Lloyd's of London; Anglican; recreations: golf, yachting; Clubs: Shaughnessy Golf; Capilano Golf & Country; Vancouver; Royal Vancouver Yacht; Office: Ste. 3134, 1055 Dunsmuir St., Box 49273, Bentall Centre, Vancouver, B.C. V7X 1L3

CLIFFORD, Betsy; ski champion; b. Ottawa, Ont., 15 Oct. 1953; d. John F. and Margaret Isabel (Phillips) C.; e. Chelsea (Que.) Prot. Sch.; Notre-Dame de Lourdes, Ottawa; Hull (Que.) High Sch.; Philemon Wright High Sch., Hull, Que.; won Gold Medal in Giant Slalom, Val Gardena, Italy in World Championships 1969-70; nominated to Can.'s Sports Hall of Fame; on Candn. Nat. Ski Team for 8 yrs. (selected when 14 yrs. old); placed 5th in Downhill, Grindelwald, Switzerland, 1968-69; placed 2nd. in Slalom event at Badgastein, Austria and at Grindlewald, 1969-70, placed 5th in Giant Slalom, Val d'Isère, France; won world cup slaloms at Val d'Isère, France and Schruns, Austria 1970-71; tied for first place overall world cup slalom 1971; then injured; rejoined Can. World Cup team 1973 after winning 1973 CAN-AM circuit (1st Candn.) and winning all events for Candn. Championships, Thunder Bay, Ont. Feb. 1973; Catholic; Address: Link Road, Old Chelsea, Que. J0X 2N0

CLIFTON, John Terrence, R.C.A.; industrial designer; b. Peterborough, Ont. 26 July 1933; s. Harry Kelsey and Edna Menzie (Allin) C.; e. Ont. Coll. of Art Toronto grad. 1957 AOCA; m. Elizabeth Jane Leeson d. late Henry N. Blakeney 22 Oct. 1960; children: Scott Andrew, Leeson Alexandra, Christopher Kelsey; VICE-PRES., DIR. OF DESIGN, RADUN DESIGN PLANNING LTD.; rec'd Nat. Design Council Awards; Prof. Assn. Design Awards; Design Award Man. Design Inst.; mem. Assn. Candn. Indust. Designers (Ont. Chapter, Past Pres.); Phi Kappa Pi; P. Conservative; Protestant; recreations: flying, fishing, hunting; Club: Oshawa Flying; Home: R.R. 1, Bowmanville, Ont. L1C 3K2; Office: 204, 1992 Yonge St., Toronto, Ont. M4S 1Z7.

CLOSS, Maurice Joseph; manufacturer; b. Toronto, Ont. 14 Dec. 1927; s. late Wilfred Clinton and late Kathleen Rose (Skelly) C.; e. elem. and high schs. Oshawa, Ont.; Mang. Studies Univ. of W. Ont., Queen's Univ., Wayne State Univ.; children: Paul Maurice; Patricia Lynn; PRES., CHIEF EXTVE. OFFR. AND DIR., CHRYSLER CANADA LTD. 1980- ; Vice-Pres., Chrysler Corp.; Dir. Ontario Mortgage Corp.; Chrysler Credit Canada Ltd.; Chrysler

Insurance Canada Ltd.; joined General Motors 1943-55; Ford Motor Co. 1955-59; Chrysler Canada Ltd. 1959-79 serving as Mgr. Parts Inventory Control, Parts Marketing Mgr., Dir. Parts Marketing, Dir. of Merchandising, E. Area Sales Mgr., Gen. Sales Mgr., Gen. Vehicle Marketing Mgr., Vice-Pres.-Marketing; Sales Mgr.-West, U.S. Automotive Sales Group, Chrysler Corp. Detroit 1979; Extve. Vice Pres. present Co. 1980; R. Catholic; recreations: golf, tennis, swimming; Clubs: Beach Grove Golf & Country; Windsor; Renaissance; Home: 1063 Bell Isle View, Windsor, Ont. N8S 3G6; Office: 2450 Chrysler Centre, Windsor, Ont. N9A 4H6.

CLOUSTON, Ross N., B.Sc., M.B.A.; executive; b. Montreal, P.Q., 13 Sept. 1922; s. A. Roy and Maud (Neal) C.; e. McGill Univ., B.Sc. (Hons. Chem.) 1949; Harvard Univ., M.B.A. (with Distinction) 1951; m. Brenda Elizabeth, d. M.W. Kerson, Montreal, P.Q., 12 Feb. 1944; children: Robert, Brendan; PRESIDENT, GORTON GROUP; Chrmn. Trans World Seafood Inc.; Vice-Pres. General Mills Canada Ltd.; General Mills Inc.; Dir., Cape Ann Bank and Trust Co.; Founder, La Salle Foods Ltd. 1953; Blue Water Sea Foods Ltd. 1959; Past Pres. and Dir. National Fisheries Institute, Washington, D.C.; Dir. Gloucester Fisherman's Museum; employed by Royal Commission on Newfoundland Fisheries under Sir Albert Walsh, 1951-52; Salesman, A. Roy Clouston & Sons Ltd., 1952-53; Candn. Sales Mgr. for Fishery Products Ltd., 1955-59; served in 2nd World War with R.C.A.F., 1941-45; Past Pres. Fisheries Council of Can.; Dir. The New England Merchants Nat. Bank of Boston; Phi Kappa Pi; Club: Salem Country Club; Home: Normandy, off Hesperus Ave., Magnolia, Mass., 01930; Office: The Gorton Group, Gloucester, Mass.

CLOUTIER, Hon. François, B.A., M.D., F.R.C.P.(C), F.A.P.A.; psychiatrist, psychoanylist; b. Quebec, Que., 4 Apl. 1922; s. Jean Baptiste and Anna Marie (Tousignant) C.; e. Laval Univ., B.A., M.D. (with high hons.); Dipl. in Ethnology, Musée de l'Homme, Paris; m. late Solange Hollinger, M.A., M.D., 1953; two d. Sophie, Nathalie; m. secondly Hélène Daigneault; CHIEF OF DEPT. OF PSYCHOSOMATIC MEDICINE OF THE INSTITUTE PSYCHIATRIQUE LAROCHEFOUCAULD (PARIS) Min. of Education, Que. 1972-76; after grad. went to Europe (France) to specialize in psychiatry and was made Asst. in Neurol. and Psychiatry of Faculty of Med. of Paris; returned to Can. and began practice, becoming Chief of the Psychiatric Dept. at Notre-Dame Hosp. and a Sr. Consultant at Queen Mary Veterans' Hosp., Montreal; Dir. Gen., World Fed. for Mental Health (1962-66) (London and Geneva); el. to Que. Nat. Assembly for Ahunsic in g.e. April 1970; apptd. Min. of Cultural Affairs, 1970; Min. of Educ. 1972; Min. Intergovt. Affairs 1976; Delegate gen. of Que. Govt. in France 1976; resigned on advent of P.Q. to power; Publications incl. "Un psychiatre vous parle", 1954; "L'homme et son milieu", 1958, "La Santé Mentale", 1966; "Le Mariage Réussi" 1967; about 25 scient. papers; and a book of political memoirs: "L'Enjeu"; Liberal; R. Catholic; recreation: horseback riding; Address: 9 Rue Perronet 75007 Paris, France

CLOUTIER, Gilles G., B.A., B.Sc.A., M.Sc., Ph.D, F.R.S.C.; physicist; b. Quebec City, Que., 27 June 1928; e. Univ. Laval, B.A. 1949, B.Sc.A (Physics) 1953; McGill Univ., M.Sc. (Physics) 1956, Ph.D. (Physics) 1959; m. Colette Michaud; children: Hélène, Suzane, Pierre, Benoît, Nathalie; PRESIDENT, ALBERTA RESEARCH COUNCIL; Asst. Dir. of Research, Hydro-Quebec Institute of Research 1974-78, Dir. of Research 1971-74; member, National Research Council, 1973-76; Research Offr.; CARDE, Defence Research Bd., 1953-54; Sr. mem. Scient. Personnel, RCA Victor Co. Research Labs., 1959-63; Assoc. Prof., Univ. de Montréal 1963-67, Prof. 1967-68, Visiting Prof. 1968-69; joined Hydro-Quebec Inst. of Research as Scient. Dir., Basic Sciences Lab., 1968-71; Fellow, Royal Soc. of Can. (1976); Officer, Order of Can.

(1981); mem., Candn. Assn. Physicists (Pres. 1971-72); Am. Phys. Soc.; Inst. Elect. & Electronics Engrs.; Assn. of Engnrs., Geologists and Geophysicist, of Alta.; mem. du Conseil de l'universite de Montreal 1976-80; R. Catholic; Home: 926 Rice Rd., Edmonton, Alta. T6R 1A1; Office: 9th Floor, 9925-109 St., Edmonton, Alta. T5K 2J8

CLOUTIER, Rév. Raoul, O.C. (1971), B.A.; prêtre, éducateur; né St. Charles de Bellechasse, Qué., 14 août 1908, f. Docteur Norbert et Leonora (Terreau) C.; descendant de Zacharie Cloutier, immigrant en 1634; é. Collège Ste.-Anne de la Pocatière; Univ. Laval, B.A., 1927, études théologiques, 1927-31; Vicaire coadjuteur, St. Francois d'assise, 1931-40; dir. de l'Oeuvre des Terrains de Jeux de Qué., et dir. diocésain des Oeuvres de Jeunesse du diocèse de Qué., 1934-40; prof. de sociol., l'Ecole tech. du Qué., 1935-39: fonde Camp-Ecole Trois Saumons: Centre-lac Trois Saumons, Centre-lac Minogami, et dir. 1947-71; enseigne à l'Ecole Prov. de natation et de securité aquatique, 1949; Camp Marie-Victoire (sciences naturelles) 1955; Ecole de Cadres (cours de perfectionnement pour personnel qualifié des camps de vacances) 1960; École de Moniteurs (cours de formation de base) 1962; Aumônier militaire, 1940-47, en Angleterre, l'Afrique du Nord, l'invasion de Sicile et d'Italie, où blessé en 1944; démobilisé, 1947; reçu l'Etoile de Guerre (1939-45), l'Etoile d'Italie, Defense Medal, C.V.S.M., Médaille de Guerre (1939-45), (tout du Canada); recu Etat Pontifical du Vatican; Bene Merenti; Mérite diocésain, Ste.-Anne de la Pocatière; Insigne de Service de la Soc. canadienne de la Croix Rouge, 1952; Médaille du centennaire, 1967; 1ᵉ Decoration Prov. pour services eminents dans le domaine du loisir, 1973; Médaille du 25 Ann. du Couronnement de la reine Elizabeth; Officier de l'Ordre du Canada 1971; Catholique R.; récréations: chasse, pêche, voyages, lectures; adresse: 11 est, rue Crémazie, Québec, Qué. G1R 1Y1

CLOUTIER, Sylvain, O.C., M.A., M.Com., M.B.A.; executive; b. Trois Rivières, Qué. 1929; e. Univ. of Ottawa B.A. 1949; Univ. of Montreal M.Com., M.A. 1952; Harvard Business Sch. M.B.A. 1955; m. Denyse Sauvé 1953; children: Guy, Sylvie; CHRMN. OF THE BD. AND PRES., EXPORT DEVELOPMENT CORP.; mem. Pub. Service Comn. Can. 1965; Depy. Secy. Treasury Bd. 1967; Depy. Min. for Taxation Dept. Nat. Revenue 1970; Depy. Min. of Nat. Defence 1971; Depy. Min. of Transport 1975; present position 1979- ; rec'd Outstanding Achievement Award Pub. Service of Can. 1977; mem. Adv. Council Fed. Inst. of Mang. 1966-68; Gov., Algonquin Community Coll. Ottawa 1969-71; Montfort Hosp. Ottawa 1973-79; Univ. of Ottawa 1975- ; Hon. Gov. Inst. Internal Auditors 1972- ; Trustee, Ottawa Health Sciences Centre Gen. Hosp. 1978- ; Dir. Fed. Business Devel. Bank 1978- ; mem. Extve. Council Inter-Am. Centre Tax Adms. 1971; Adv. Bd. Candn. Mil. Colls. 1977-75; Defence Research Bd. 1971-75; mem. Order C.A.'s Qué.; Inst. Pub. Adms. Can. (Past mem. Extve. Comte.); mem. Extve. Comte. Nat. Jt. Council Pub. Service Can. 1966-67; Office: 110 O'Connor St., Ottawa, Ont. K1P 5T9.

CLUTE, Kenneth Fleury, B.A., M.D., F.R.C.P.(C); paediatrician; b. Toronto, Ont., 19 Dec. 1918; s. Arthur Roger, Q.C. and Laurine Adele (Fleury) C.; e. Univ. of Toronto Schs., grad. 1936; Univ. of Toronto, B.A. in Classics (with 1st Class Hons. and gold medal) 1940; Univ. of Toronto, M.D. (with Hons. and gold medal) 1945; m. Roberta Jessie, d. late George Brodie, Quebec, P.Q., 24 Sept. 1955; children: Alistair Kenneth, Thomas Brodie, Geoffrey Arthur; PROF. OF COMMUNITY HEALTH LAW, DEPT. OF HEALTH ADM., FACULTY OF MEDICINE, UNIV. OF TORONTO, since 1975, Sch. of Hygiene 1966-75; Jr. Interne, Toronto Gen. Hosp., 1945-46; Fellow in Surg., Hosp. for Sick Children, Toronto, 1946-47; Grey Nuns' Hosp., Regina and Regina Gen. Hosp., Res. in Path., 1947-48; Sr. Interne in Paediatrics, Children's Mem. Hosp., Montreal, 1948-49; Asst. Res. in

Paed., 1949-50; Asst. Psychiatrist in Children's Psych. Clinic, Johns Hopkins Hosp., Baltimore, 1950-51; Physician in Med. Care Clinic there and Fellow in Pediatrics, Johns Hopkins Univ.; 1951-52; Research Assoc. in Legal Med. and Paed., Univ. of Maryland, 1952-53; in private practice of paediatrics, Toronto and mem. of Staff, Hosp. for Sick Children, 1953-55; Dir. of Survey of Gen. Practice of Can., Dir. of Field Studies, Dept. of Pub. Health, Sch. of Hygiene, Univ. of Toronto, 1956-61; Research Secy., Candn. Assn. for Retarded Children, 1962-64; Assoc. Prof. of Med. Care 1962-66 and Albert G. Milbank Fellow in Law and Pub. Health 1964-68, Dept. of Pub. Health, Sch. of Hygiene, Univ. of Toronto, author of: "The General Practitioner: A Study of Medical Education and Practice in Ontario and Nova Scotia", 1963; served during 2nd World War with R.C.A.M.C, 1943-46; mem., Ont. Med. Assn.; Candn. Med. Assn.; Candn. Pub. Health Assn.; Roy. Coll. Phys. & Surg. Can.; Acad. of Med., Toronto; Nu Sigma Nu; Alpha Omega Alpha; Anglican; recreations: reading, music, gardening, astronomy, boating; Home: 48 Castle Frank Rd., Toronto, Ont. M4W 2Z6; Office: Dept. of Health Admin., Community Health Div., McMurrich Bldg., Faculty of Medicine, University of Toronto, Toronto, Ont. M5S 1A8

CLYNE, Hon. John Valentine, C.C. (1972) b. Vancouver, B.C., 14 Feb. 1902; s. Henry Notman and Martha Alice (Dillon) C.; e. Univ. of Brit. Columbia; King's Coll., Univ. of London (specialized in Marine Law);m. Betty Somerset, 10 Dec. 1927; children: Valentine Dorothy, John Stuart Somerset; Chancellor, Univ of B.C.; former Pres., Candn. Inst. for Advanced Legal Studies; Chrmn., B.C. Heritage Trust; former Chrmn. & Chief Extve. Offr., MacMillan Bloedel Ltd. 1957-73 and now Hon. Dir.; former Dir., Canada Trust; Candn. Pacific Ltd.; Philips Electronics Industries Ltd.; Dir. Emeritus, Candn. Imperial Bank of Comm.; Chrmn., Adv. Group on Extve. Compensation in Pub. Service 1968-71; Chrmn. Consultative Comte on the Implications of Telecommunications for Can. Sovreignty, (1979); Chrmn. Selection Comte, Royal Bank Award, (1967-); Governor, Consortium for Atlantic Pacific Affairs (1978-); former Chrmn., Inter-Gov. Maritime Consultative Organ. of U.N.; began practice, Vancouver, B.C., 1927, specializing in Admiralty Law; Chrmn., Maritime Comn. of Can.; 1947-50; Justice, Supreme Court of British Columbia, 1950-57; Past Pres., Vancouver Bar Assn.; served as Royal Commr. on Whatshan Power House Disaster 1954, Milk Indust. of B.C. 1955, Land Expropriation Methods in B.C. 1961; K.G.St.J. (1959); Home: 3738 Angus Dr., Vancouver, B.C. V6J 4H5

COATES, Robert C., M.P., Q.C., B.A., LL.B.; b. Amherst, N.S., 10 March 1928; s. Frederick Carman and Rita Bridget (O'Brien) C.; e. Amherst Sr. High Sch. (1949); Mount Allison Univ., B.A. 1951; Dalhousie Law Sch., LL.B. 1954; m. Mary Blanche, d. Dr. Arthur K. Wade, Perth Junction, N.B., 27 Dec. 1954; children: David Wade, Amy Marijo; Chrmn., Standing Comte on Mg'r and Members' Services; called to the Bar of N.S., June 1956; 1st el. to H. of C. for Cumberland, g.e. 1957; re-el. since; mem. Commonwealth Parlty. Assoc.; Inter-Parlty. Union; NATO Parlty Assoc.; Can.-U.S. Parlty Group; Chrmn., Can.-Korea Parlty Group; Pres., John G. Diefenbaker Memoril Foundation; Past Pres., P. Conservative Assn. of Can.; mem., N.S. Barristers Soc.: P. Conservative; Anglican; Address: 46 Regent St., Amherst, N.S. B4H 3T1

COBBOLD, Richard Southwell Chevallier, M.Sc., Ph.D., F.R.S.C.; educator; b. Worcester, Eng. 10 Dec. 1931; s. late Reynold Chevallier and Betty Joyce (Lindner) C.; e. Imp. Coll. of Science & Technol. Univ. of London A.R.C.S., B.Sc. 1956; Univ. of Sask. M.Sc. 1961, Ph.D. 1965; m. Margaret Mary d. late Henry St. Aubyn, Redditch, Eng. Aug. 1963; children: Adrian C., David C., Christopher M.; PROF. AND DIR. INST. OF BIOMED.

ENGN. UNIV. OF TORONTO since 1974; Asst. Exper. Offr. Ministry of Supply U.K. 1949-53; Scient. Offr. Defence Research Bd. Can. Ottawa 1956-59; Lectr. to Assoc. Prof. of Elect. Engn. Univ. of Sask. 1960-66; Assoc. Prof. Inst. Biomed. Engn. present Univ. 1966, Prof. 1970; co-recipient Premium Award Pub. Papers Inst. Elect. Engrs. 1965; author "Theory and Application of Field-Effect Transistors" 1970, Russian ed. 1975, Polish ed. 1975; "Transducers for Biomedical Measurements: Principles and Applications" 1974; book chapters, research papers semiconductor devices and biomed. engn. measurements; mem. Inst. Elect. & Electronic Engrs.; Candn. Med. & Biol. Engn. Soc. (Vice Pres. 1970-74); R. Catholic; recreations: tennis, skiing; Club: North Toronto Tennis; Home: 116 Ridley Blvd., Toronto, Ont. M5M 3L9; Office: Toronto, Ont. M5S 1A4.

COBURN, Kathleen, O.C. (1974), M.A., B.Litt., F.R.S.C. (1958); writer; b. Stayner, Ont., 7 Sept. 1905; d. John and Susannah Wesley (Emerson) C.; e. Harbord Coll. Inst., Toronto, Ont.; Univ. of Toronto, B.A. and M.A. 1930; (I.O.D.E.) War Mem. Scholarship) 1930; St. Hugh's Coll., Oxford, B.Litt. 1932; LL.D. Queen's 1964; Instructor English Dept., Victoria College, Univ. of Toronto, 1932; Asst. to Dean of Women there, 1932-35; Prof. of English, Victoria College, 1953; Prof. Emeritus, Victoria Coll. 1971; awarded Sr. Fellowship, Internat. Fed. of Univ. Women (for advanced research), 1947; Hon. Fellow, St. Hugh's Coll., Oxford, Eng., 1970; D.H.L. Haverford Coll. Pa. 1972; Hon. Fellow, Champlain Coll., Trent Univ., 1972; D.Litt. Trent Univ., 1973; D.Litt. (Cantab) 1975; D.Litt., Univ. of B.C. 1976; D.Litt., Univ. of Toronto 1978; Ed. of "The Philosophical Lectures of S.T. Coleridge" (hitherto unpubl.), 1949, author of "The Grandmothers", 1949; "Inquiring Spirit" (a new presentation of Coleridge), 1951, revised ed., Toronto, 1979; edited: "The Letters of Sara Hutchison", 1954: "The Notebooks of Samuel Taylor Coleridge", Vol. 1 1957, Vol. II 1961, Vol. III 1973; "In Pursuit of Coleridge", 1978; Gen. Ed., "The Collected Works of S.T. Coleridge", 1968-; edited "Twentieth Century Views", 1967; "Discourse", Royal Institution 1972; "Riddell Memorial Lectures 1972"; "Alexander Lectures" 1978; has written many articles for "Review of English Studies", "Gazette des Beaux Arts", "Canadian Forum", "The Listener", etc.; mem., Charles Lamb Soc., London; awarded John Simon Guggenheim Fellowship to study unpub. writings of Samuel Taylor Coleridge, 1953 and 1957-58; rec'd. Leverhulme Award 1948; Rosemary Crawshay Prize (Brit. Acad.) 1958; Commonwealth Visiting Fellowship, 1962-63; Chaveau Medal (1979) RS; recreations: canoeing in north country, skating; Office: University of Toronto, Toronto, Ont. M5S 1K7

COCHRAN, Hon. Bruce, C.D., M.L.A., B.Com.; politician; b. Mahone Bay, N.S. 1 Dec. 1919; s. Wilfred N., M.D. and Nora Louise (Nicol) C.; e. Mahone Bay Pub. and High Schs.; Lunenburg (N.S.) Acad.; Univ. of King's Coll. and Dalhousie Univ. B.Com.; m. Maxine Elizabeth d. F. Max Bishop, Lawrencetown, N.S. 3 May 1951; one s. Andrew Bruce Bishop; MIN. OF TOURISM, N.S. 1979- , mem. Extve. Council (Cabinet); Chief Adm. Offr. Naval Research Estab. Defence Research Bd. Halifax 1948-50; Publisher and Ed. "Dartmouth Patriot" 1950-51; Personnel Mgr. Simpsons-Sears Halifax and Toronto; Pres. and Publisher "Dartmouth Free Press" 1972-74; Pres., Bruce Cochran Associates Ltd. Halifax 1960- ; el. M.L.A. for Lunenburg Center prov. g.e. 1974, re-el. 1978-81; held portfolios Consumer Affairs, Housing, Communications & Information, Culture Recreation & Fitness; Gov., Univ. of King's Coll.; served with West N.S. Regt. UK, N.Africa, Sicily, Italy 1939-45, rank Capt.; rec'd Centennial Medal 1967; Queen's Silver Jubilee Medal; mem. Candn. Pub. Relations Soc.; Royal Commonwealth Soc.; Phi Kappa Pi (Past Pres.); P. Conservative; Anglican; Office: Province House, Halifax, N.S.

COCHRAN, J.F., M.A.Sc., Ph.D.; educator; b. Saskatoon, Sask. 29 Jan. 1930; s. John Alexander and Frances Edith (Latham) C.; e. University of British Columbia, B.A.Sc. (Engn. Physics) 1950; M.A.Sc. (Engn. Physics) 1951; University of Illinois, Ph.D. (Physics & Math.) 1955; m. Pieternella, d. Nicholas Neuteboom, 15 Jan. 1957; children: Stephanie Anne, Alexander John; PROF. OF PHYSICS, & DEAN OF SCIENCES, SIMON FRASER UNIV. 1981-; Chrmn. of Dept. 1971-74; started as Research Assoc. Physics Dept., Univ. Ill. 1955-56; Asst. Prof., Mass. Inst. Technol. 1957; Prof., Simon Fraser Univ., 1965; Acting Head Dept. Physics present Univ. 1968-69; Chrmn. of Dept. 1971-74; mem. Candn. Assn. Physicists (Chrmn. Comte. on Physics & Society, Past Chrmn. and Past Vice-Chrmn. Solid State Div., Past Councillor for B.C. and Yukon); Am. Physical Soc.; Nat. Research Council Physics Grants Selection Comte. 1971-74; awarded NRC Postdoctoral Fellowships 1956-57; Sloan Fellowships 1957-59; Assoc. Ed., Candn. Journ. Physics; Co-ed. (with R.R. Haering) "Solid State Physics": Vol. 1, "Electrons in Metals" 1968; recreation: squash; Club: University; Home: 4174 Rose Cres., West Vancouver, B.C. V7V 2N8; Office: Burnaby, B.C. V5A 1S6

COCHRAN, Jack, B.A.Sc.; retired consultant; b. Winnipeg, Man., 12 Oct. 1920; s. Hugh Taylor and Catherine (Harper) C.; e. Univ. of Brit. Columbia, B.A.Sc.; m. Elizabeth Katherine Specken, 29 Dec. 1943; children: Thomas Richard, Elizabeth June, Pamella Diane, Margaret Carol; Past President, Domtar Construction Materials, May 1968-Dec. '79; Chrmn. Bd., MacKay Specialities Inc.; early business experience included ten years at Domtar's salt plants at Unity, Sask., and Sarnia, Ont., then as Production Mgr., Sifto Salt, Montreal; joined Brantford Roofing, 1954, and served in various capacities; apptd. Vice-Pres., Marketing, Domtar Construction Materials Ltd., July 1961; Vice-Pres. and Mang. Dir., 1964-68; mem. Nat. House Builders Assn. (mem. Extve., 1966 and 1967; Chrmn., Mfrs. Council, 1967; mem., Econ. Research Comte., 1967-1980; Past Presidents' Adv. Comte, 1968-1981); Reciprocal Dir., Candn. Constr. Assn. and Housing & Urban Devel. Assn. of Can. 1969-71; mem. (First Chrmn.) Constr. Industry Devel. Council, Industry Trade & Comm.; Vice-Pres., MacKay Center For Deaf & Crippled Children; Chrmn., Candn. Comte. on Bldg. Research 1974-78; recreations: gardening, reading; Home: 65 York Rd., Beaconsfield, Que. H9W 4L1

COCHRANE, Rev. Arthur C., B.A., Ph.D., D.D. (Presb.); L.H.D.; professor; b. Belleville, Ont., 23 Sept. 1909; s. William and Margaret (McConaghy) C.; e. Univ. of Toronto, B.A. 1932; Knox Coll., Toronto, grad. 1935; D.D. 1963; Edinburgh Univ., Ph.D. 1937; Iowa Wesleyan Coll., L.H.D. 1967; m. Ilsa, d. Gustav Ehlentrup, Bielefeld, Germany, 27 Feb. 1937: children: Eduard, Gordon; VISITING PROF., WARTBURG THEOL. SEMY., since 1976; Min., St. Andrew's Presb. Ch., Tillsonburg, Ont., 1937-42; St. Andrew's, Port Credit, 1942-48; Prof. of Systematic Theology, Theol. Semy. of Univ. of Dubuque, 1948-71; emeritus 1977; Pittsburgh Theol. Semy. 1971-75; Visiting Prof. of Theol., Yale Univ. Divinity Sch., 1963-64; Publications: "The Church and the War", 1939; "The Existentialists and God", 1956; "The Church's Confession Under Hitler", 1962; translated Otto Weber's, "Karl Barth's Church Dogmatics", 1953; Ed. "Reformed Confessions of the 16th Century", 1966; "Eating and Drinking with Jesus", 1974; Past Pres., Am. Theol. Soc.; Presbyterian; Home: 2421 University Ave., Dubuque, Iowa. 52001

COCHRANE, Rev. Charles Clarke, B.A., D.D. (Presb.); b. Belleville, Ont., 30 Nov. 1910; s. William and Margaret (McConaghy) C.; e. Orillia (Ont.) Public Sch. and Coll. Inst.; Queen's Univ., B.A. 1938; Knox Coll., Toronto (Divinity), Dipl. 1939, D.D. 1969; Emmanuel Coll., Toronto, B.D. 1944; m. Isobel Jean, d. late Rev. A.E. Cameron, 25

April 1939; children: Donald Bryden, William Alexander, Douglas Charles; Minister, Presbyterian Tri-Congregations, Toronto, Ont., 1976-79, (ret'd); Min., St. Andrew's, Geraldton, Ont., 1939-41; Knox., Georgetown, Ont., 1941-48; Melville, Westmount, Que., 1948-76; mem. of Senate, Presb. Coll., Montreal, 1949-52; mem. of Bd., 1952-58; Lectr., 1964-66; mem. Bd. Westmount Y.M.C.A., 1950-58; Montreal Council for Social Order, 1952-53, Prot. Hungarian Service Assn., 1957-59, Greater Montreal Council of Chs., 1953-60 (Pres. 1957-60); Moderator, Presbytery of Montreal, 1955 and 1965, and Clerk 1957-58; Pres., Westmount Min. Assn., 1959-60; Advisor, Montreal Christian Youth Council, 1957-60; Sr. Teacher, Relig. Instr., Westmount High Sch., 1952-66; Vice-Pres., North Am. Area Council of World Alliance of Reformed Chs., 1960, Pres. 1965; mem. Bd., Children's Service Centre; Soc. for Protection of Women and Children; Elizabeth House; a trustee of the Fund to Contest the "Padlock Law"; author of "Jesus of Nazareth in Word and Deed", Eerdmans 1979; occasional contrib. to relig. journs.; Que. Corr., "The Christian Century", Chicago, 1958-66; Address: 300 Regina St. N., Richmond One, Apt. 212, Waterloo, Ont., N2J 3B8.

COCHRANE, Michael H., B.A., M.B.A.; mining executive; b. 7 Feb. 1937; e. Trinity Coll. Sch. Port Hope, Ont.; Univ. of W. Ont. B.A.; Northwestern Univ. M.B.A.; EXTVE. VICE PRES. FINANCE & ADM., DENISON MINES LTD. 1981- ; Chrmn. and Chief Extve. Offr. Sydney Steel Corp.; Pres. Can. China Trade Council; joined Ford Motor Co. 1961-69; Great West Life Assurance Co. 1969-70, Extve. Asst. to Pres.; Air Canada 1970-76, Controller, Vice Pres. Finance; Reed Ltd. 1976-78, Chrmn. of Bd. and Extve. Comte.; Massey-Ferguson 1978-80, Vice Pres. Planning & Business Devel. and Asst. to Pres.; Northern Telecom 1980-81, Extve. Vice Pres. Adm.; Dir. Adv. Council Faculty Adm. Studies York Univ.; Dir. Candn. Council Christians & Jews, Chrmn Adv. Comte. and Nat. Program Comte.; mem. Financial Extves. Inst.; Protestant; recreations: sailing, racquet sports; Clubs: Albany; Mount Royal; M.A.A.A.; Cambridge; Canadian (N.Y.); Empire; Manitoba; Granite; Oriental; Halifax; Home: 50 Buckingham Ave., Toronto, Ont. M4N 1R2; Office: (P.O. Box 40) Royal Bank Plaza, Toronto, Ont. M5J 2K2.

COCKBURN, Bruce; singer; songwriter; guitarist; b. Ottawa, Ont. 27 May 1945; e. Berklee Coll. of Music, Boston 1964-66, theory, composition and arranging; played in several rock bands incl. the Esquires and the Children, Ottawa; soloist various coffee houses and made first appearance Mariposa Folk Festival 1967; mem. folk-rock band Three's A Crowd CBC TV series 1968-69; made first cross-country tour 1972; appearances Philadelphia Folk Festival 1974, Alice Tully Hall New York 1977; toured Japan with Murray McLauchlan 1977 and as soloist 1979; writer numerous songs incl. "Goin' Down the Road"; "Goin' to the Country", "Musical Friends", "Laughter", "Mama Just Wants to Barrel-house All Night Long", "Burn"; recordings LP's incl. "Bruce Cockburn" 1970, "High Winds White Sky" 1971, Sunwheel Dance" 1972, "Night Vision" 1973, "Salt, Sun and Time" 1974, "Joy Will Find a Way" 1975, "In the Falling Dark" 1977, "Circles in the Stream" 1977, "Further Adventures of Bruce Cockburn" 1978, "Dancing in the Dragon's Jaws" 1979; rec'd Juno Awards as folksinger of yr. 1970, 1971, 1972, 1979; Numerous other awards; affiliate PRO Canada.

COCKBURN, Hon. G. William N., Q.C., M.L.A., B.A., B.C.L.; politician; b. St. Stephen, N.B., 14 Feb. 1931; s. late George H.I. and Bessie L. (Dinsmore) C.; e. Univ. of N.B., B.A. 1953; B.C.L. 1955; m. Marjorie M.T., d. late M. Allan Ryan, 14 Aug. 1954; children: G. William A., Beth Susanne, Richard Blair; CHRMN., N.B. ELECTRIC POWER COMN., since 1976; called to Bar of N.B. 1955; Q.C. 1978; el. M.L.A. 1967; re-el. 1970, 1974, 1978; Min.

of Fisheries and Environment, 1970-74; Min. of Health 1974-76; Past Vice Pres., N.B. Young P. Cons. Assn.; Past Lt. Gov., O.Q.M. District Kiwanis Internat.; Past Pres., Charlotte Co. Young P. Cons. Assn.; Past. Secy., Charlotte Co. Cons. Assn.; Past Chrmn., Bd. Trustees, Charlotte Co. Hosp.; Past Dir. St. Stephen-Milltown Assn. for Retarded Children; mem., Candn. Bar Assn.; N.B. Barristers Soc.; Freemason; (Shriner); P. Conservative; Presbyterian; recreations: golf, curling; Club: Kiwanis; Home: 40 Hawthorne St., St. Stephen, N.B. E3L 1W6; Office: Room 201, 527 King St., Fredericton, N.B. E3B 4X1

COCKER, Herbert; retired general contractor; b. Toronto, Ont., 15 Sept. 1908; s. Thomas and Alice (Stafford) C.; e. Pub. Schs., Saskatoon and Prince Albert, Sask., Detroit, Mich., Kingston and Hamilton, Ont.; Central Secondary Sch., Hamilton, Ont.; H.B. Beal High Sch., London, Ont.; m. A. Grace, d. Herbert Smith, 6 May 1939; children: Gail Elizabeth, Paul Herbert; Pres., McKay-Cocker Construction Ltd., 1961-76 (ret.); presently Hon. Chrmn. of Bd.; joined Bank of Montreal as Clerk for 2 yrs; with Pigott Construction Ltd. for 20 yrs. as Tradesman, Foreman and Supt.; joined present firm as Vice-Pres. and Gen. Mgr., 1946-61; mem., Vocational Training Adv. Council, Dept. of Labour, Ottawa; Dep. Chmn., Bd. of Trustees, First St. Andrew's United Church; Chmn., United Church Council, Middlesex presbytery; Past Chrmn., Bd. Stewards, First St. Andrews Ch., London, Ont.; Past Pres., London Builders Exchange; Past Pres., London Chamber Comm.; United Church; recreation: golf; Clubs: London Hunt; Rotary (Past Pres.); Home: 1174 St. Anthony Rd., London, Ont. N6H 2R1

CODE, Charles Frederick, B.S., M.D., Ph.D.; medical researcher and educator; b. Winnipeg, Man., 1 Feb. 1910; s. Abraham and Gertrude Casilda (Drewry) C.; e. Univ. of Man., B.S. and M.D. 1934; Univ. of Minn., Ph.D. 1940; m. Gwendolyn Irene, d. A.S. Bond, 30 Dec. 1935; three children: PROF. MEDICINE AND SURGERY UC SAN DIEGO; Assoc. Dir., Center for Ulcer Research & Educ., U.C.L.A. & V.A. Wadsworth Hosp. Center, Los Angeles 1975-80; (formerly Dir. for Med. Educ. & Research, Mayo Foundation 1966-72); Lecturer in Physiol., Univ. Coll., London and National Institute for Med. Research, London, 1936-37; joined Mayo Foundation as Fellow in Physiol. and Med., 1934-35; Asst. in Exper. Surg., 1938; Instr. in Physiol. then Asst. Prof., Med. Sch., Univ. of Minn., 1939-40; joined staff of Mayo Clinic as Consultant in Physiol. and Asst. Prof. in Physiol., Mayo Foundation, 1940; Prof. of Physiol., Mayo Foundation and Chrmn., Sec. of Physiol., Mayo Clinic and Mayo Foundation, 1942-65; during World War II conducted aviation research 1940-46; Visiting Prof. of Physiol., St. Thomas Med. Sch., London, Eng., 1966; Botazzi Lectr., Cong. of Italian Socs., of Exper. Biol., Physiol., Biochem. and Human Nutrition, Pavia, Italy 1970; Hon. Consultant, The London Hosp., London, Eng. 1971; rec'd Physiol. Research Prize and Gold Medal, Univ. of Man., 1930; Bayliss-Starling Mem. Scholarship, Univ. Coll., London, 1936; Theobald Smith Award and Medal for Research, 1938; D.Sc. (Hon.) Medical Coll., Wisconsin, 1978; D.Sc. (Hon.) Univ. of Man., 1981; co-author, "An Atlas of Esophageal Motility in Health and Disease", 1958; Ed., Handbooks of Physiology of Alimentary Canal, 1964-68; mem. Ed. Bd., "Gastroenterology"; other writings incl. over 400 original scient. publs.; discoveries incl. role of histamine in allergic reactions and gastric acid secretion; definition of Esophageal Motor Disorders; role of acid in Peptic Ulcer Disease Motor and Elect. Activity of Bowel; Am. Physiol. Soc. (mem. Ed. Bd. and Ed.-in-Chief of Physiol. Reviews, 1957-63; Past Chrmn., G.I. Sec.); mem., Candn. Physiol. Soc.; Physiol Soc., England; Assn. Am. Physicists; Am. Gastroenterol. Assn. (Past Pres. and mem. Gov. Bd.; Past Chrmn. G.I. Research Group and Research Comte.); Episcopalian; recreations: gardening, photography, sailing, fishing; Clubs: Balboa (Mazatlan, Mexico); Royal Lake of the Woods Yacht (Kenora, Ont.); Office: Section Gastroenterology, San Diego Va Medical Center, 3350 La Jolla Village Dr., San Diego C.A. 92161.

CODERRE, Guy; broadcasting executive; b. Ottawa, Ont., 13 Aug. 1928; s. Oscar and Cécile (Godbout) C.; e. Ottawa, Ont.; various prof. courses incl. Harvard Univ. PMD; m. Jovette, d. Rolland Forget, 2 Apl. 1956; children: Guy, Yves, Marc, Nicole, Eric; VICE PRES.,HUMAN RESOURCES, CANDN. BROADCASTING CORP.; Vice-Chrmn. CBC Pension Bd. Trustees; Ancien Prés., Le Cercle Universitaire d'Ottawa; Gouverneur, Hôpital St.-Louis-Marie-de Montfort; recreations: reading, music, golf; Clubs: Harvard Alumni; Cercle Univ. d'Ottawa; Home: 180 Lees, Apt. 1713, Ottawa, Ont. K1S 5J6; Office: (Box 8478) Ottawa, Ont. K1G 3J5

CODY, Hon. Donald William, M.L.A.; politician; b. Pilger, Sask. 28 March 1936; s. Edward and Rosella (Wirtz) C.; m. Joan Eileen Germsheid 3 July 1961; two s. Scott Gordon, Garnet Douglas;MIN. OF CO-OPERATION & CO-OPERATIVE DEVEL., SASK.1979- ; ins. claims extve.; el. M.L.A. for Watrous prov. g.e. 1971, Cand. 1975 (def.), re-el. M.L.A. for Kinistino, 1978; Min. of Co-operation & Co-operative Devel. 1974-75; Min. of Telephones 1978; NDP; R. Catholic; Office: 307 Legislative Bldg., Regina, Sask. S4S 0B1.

COFFIN, Hon. Thomas H., B.A., LL.B.; judge; b. East Jordan, Shelburne Co., N.S., 13 Feb. 1907; s. late Thomas Roy and Margaret Lyle (Martin) C.; e. Halifax Acad., Dalhousie Univ., B.A. 1927, LL.B. 1929; m. Madeline Hilda, d. Dr. Archibald Covert Canning, King's Co., N.S., 24 June 1944; children: Thomas A., Daphne E.; JUDGE, APPEAL DIV., SUPREME COURT OF N.S. since 1968; read law McInnes, Lovett and Macdonald; called to the Bar of N.S. 1929; cr. K.C. 1950; practised law with McInnes, Lovett and Macdonald 1929, John Y. Payzant and son 1930, Payzant and Coffin 1936, Payzant, Coffin and Blois 1946, Coffin, Blois and Hicks 1956; apptd. to Supreme Court of N.S. 1961; former Depy. Mayor, City of Halifax; former Pres. N.S. Barristers' Soc., Vice Pres. for N.S., Nat. Council Y.M.C.A.s of Can.; United Church; Freemason (Scot. Rite); recreations: golf, gardening; Clubs: Halifax; Saraguay; Ashburn Golf; Home: 1421 Thornvale Ave., Halifax, N.S. B3H 4C3; Office: Law Courts, Halifax, N.S.

COGSWELL, Fred(erick William) M.A., Ph.D.; poet, publisher; educator; b. East Centreville, N.B. 8 Nov. 1917; s. late Florence (White) and late Walter Scott C.; e. Prov. Normal Sch. 1936; Carleton Vocational Sch. 1939; Univ. of N.B., B.A. (hons.) 1949, M.A. 1950; Edinburgh Univ. (I.O.D.E. Scholar.) Ph.D. 1952; m. Margaret, d. late John Hynes 3 July 1944; children: Carmen Patricia, Kathleen Mary; Prof. Dept. of Eng., Univ. of N.B. since 1952; author of ''The Stunted Strong'' 1954; ''The Haloed Tree'' 1957; ''The Testament of Cresscid'' (trans.) 1958; ''Descent from Eden'' 1959; ''Lost Dimension'' 1960; ''Star-People'' 1968; ''Immortal Plowman'' 1969; ''One Hundred Poems of Modern Quebec'' (trans.) 1970 (2nd ed. 1971); ''A Second Hundred Poems of Modern Quebec'' (trans.) 1971; ''In Praise of Chastity'' 1971; ''Chains of Lilliput'' 1971; ''The House Without a Door'' 1973; ''Confrontation'' (trans.) 1973; ''Light Bird of Life'' 1974; ''The Poetry of Modern Quebec'' (trans.) 1976; ''Against Perspective'' 1977; ''A Long Apprenticeship: Collected Poems'' 1980; co-author ''The Arts of New Brunswick'' (with S. MacNutt and R. Tweedie) 1967; ''The Enchanted Land'' (with T.R. Lower) 1968; Ed. ''Five New Brunswick Poets'' 1961; contrib. ''Literary History of Canada'' 1966; ''Dictionary of Canadian Biography'' Vols. IX and X; ''On Canada'' 1971; Ed. (1952-66) ''The Fiddlehead'' lit. mag. and currently Ed. and Publisher, Fiddlehead Poetry Books; has contrib. poems, articles, reviews to numerous leading lit. and prof. journs.; awarded Nuffield Fellowship 1959; Can. Council Sr. Fellowship 1967; mem. League Candn. Poets (Regional Rep.); Candn. Authors Assn.; Assn. of Candn. Publish-

ers (Hon. Life mem.); Assn. Candn. Univ. Teachers of Eng.; Humanities Assn. Can. (Ed. Assn. Bulletin 1967-72); Cand. Assn. Univ. Teachers; Modern Lang. Assn.; Assn. of Que. and Candn. Literatures; (Pres. 1978-80) Comp. Lit. Assn.; Assn. of Candn. Translators; Protestant; N.D.P.; recreation: athletics; Club: PEN; Home: 769 Reid St., Fredericton, N.B. E3B 3V8; Office: University of New Brunswick, Fredericton, N.B. E3B 5A3

COHEN, Albert D.; merchant; b. Winnipeg, Man., 22 Jan. 1916; s. late Alexander and Rose (Diamond) C.; e. Winnipeg Pub. and High Schs.; m. Irena, d. late Ing. Eduard Kanka, Nov. 1953; children: Anthony Jan, James Edward, Anna Lisa; PRESIDENT AND CHIEF EXTVE. OFFR., GENERAL DISTRIBUTORS OF CANADA LTD.; Chmn. & CEO,, Sony of Can. Ltd.; Chrmn. Extve. Comte., Metropolitan Stores of Canada Ltd.; Cam-Gard Supply Ltd.; Dir. Pan-Canadian Petroleum Ltd.; served with RCNVR 1942-45; Pres., Man. Theatre Centre, 1968-69, 1970-71; Past Pres., Winnipeg Clinic Research Inst.; Past Pres. The Paul H.T. Thorlakson Research Found.; mem. Bd., Metric Comn., 1972-77; Du Maurier Council of the Performing Arts; recreations: golf, skating; Clubs: Glendale Country; Winnipeg Winter; Home: 305 Park Blvd., Tuxedo, Winnipeg, Man. R3P 0G8; Office: 1370 Sony Pl., Fort Garry, Winnipeg, Man. R3C 3C3

COHEN, Leonard, LL.D.; writer; b. Montreal, que., 1934; e. McGill Univ.; Columbia Univ. (postgrad. work); LL.D., Dalhousie Univ.; author of ''Let Us Compare Mythologies'' (poems) 1956; ''The Spice Box of Earth'' (poems) 1961; ''The Favourite Game'' (novel) 1963; ''Flowers for Hitler'' (poems) 1964; ''Beautiful Losers'' (novel) 1966; ''Parasites of Heaven'' (poems) 1966; ''Selected Poems: 1956-68'' 1968; ''The Energy of Slaves'' (poems) 1972; ''Death of a Ladies Man'' (novel) 1978; rec'd Gov. Gen.'s Award 1968; Address: c/o McClelland & Stewart Ltd., 25 Hollinger Rd., Toronto, Ont. M4B 3G2

COHEN, Matt(hew), M.A.; author; b. Kingston, Ont. 30 Dec. 1942; s. Morris and Beatrice (Sohn) C.; e. Fisher Park and Nepean High Schs. Ottawa 1960; Univ. of Toronto B.A. 1964, M.A. 1965, grad. studies 1966; WRITER-IN-RESIDENCE, UNIV. OF WESTERN ONTARIO 1981; Lectr. in Religion, McMaster Univ. 1967-68; Writer-in-Residence, Univ. of Alta. 1975-76; Visiting Prof. of Creative Writing, Univ of Victoria 1979-80; rec'd Sr. Can. Council Arts Award 1977; author ''Korsoniloff'' 1969; ''Johnny Crackle Sings'' 1971; ''Columbus and the Fat Lady'' 1972; ''The Disinherited'' 1974; ''Wooden Hunters'' 1975; ''The Colours of War'' 1977; ''Night Flights, And Other Stories, New and Selected'' 1978; ''The Sweet Second Summer of Kitty Malone'' 1979; ''Flowers of Darkness'', 1981; ''The Expatriate: Collected Short Stories'', 1982; Address: ''(P.O. Box 401) Verona, Ont. K0H 2W0.

COHEN Maxwell, O.C. (1976), Q.C., LL.D., F.R.S.A.; university professor; b. Winnipeg, Man., 17 Mar. 1910; s. Moses and Sarah (Wasserman) C.; e. Univ. of Manitoba, B.A. 1930, LL.B. 1934; Northwestern Univ., LL.M. 1936; Research Fellow, Harvard Law Sch., 1937-38; LL.D. Univ. of N.B.; Univ. of Man.; m. Isle Alexandra, d. Adolph Sternberg, Vancouver B.C.; one d., Joanne Sternberg (Mrs. Andrei Sulzenicio); PROF. EMERITUS OF LAW, McGILL UNIV. since 1978; formerly Macdonald Prof. of Law; called to the Bar of Man. 1939; Special Asst. and Jr. Counsel, Combines Investigation Comn., 1938-40; with Econ. Br., Dept. of Mun. & Supply 1940-41; Special Corr., ''Christian Science Monitor'', 1941-42; Lectr. in Law, McGill Univ. 1946-47; Assoc. Prof. 1947-52; Secy. of the Faculty 1947-53; Prof. 1952-78; Dean of Law 1964-69; Prof. Emeritus 1978; Scholar-in-Residence, Univ. of Ottawa 1980-82; Adjunct Prof., Inst. of Law & Internat. Relations, Carleton Univ., 1980-83; Impartial Chrmn., Men's Clothing Industry 1948-51; Special Asst. to Dir. Gen., Tech. Assistance Adm. of U.N. 1951; Dir., Inst. of Air &

Space Law, 1962-65; served with Candn. Army, 1942-46 with final rank of Major; attached to Nat. Defence Hdqrs., Ottawa 1942-45; Head, Dept. of Econ. and Pol. Science, Khaki Univ. of Can. in Eng. 1945-56; Hon. Fellow, Consular Law Soc. (N.Y.); Past Pres. and Hon. Vice-Pres., Candn. Br., The Internat. Law Assn.; mem., Candn. Bar Assn. (former Chrmn., Constitutional and Internat. Law Section); Montreal Bar Assn.; Law Soc. of Man.; Former Chmn. Intenat'l Branch, Candn. Inst. Internat. Affairs; Candn. Pol. Science Assn.; Hon. mem., Engn. Inst. of Can. 1977; Hon. Life mem., Can. Council Internat'l Law; Hon. Vice Pres., Am. Soc. of Internat'l Law, 1980-82; Ed. Bd., Can. yearbook of Internat'l Law; Foreign Affairs Ed., "Saturday Night" 1957-61; mem., Candn. del. to 14th Gen. Assembly of Un. Nations, 1959-60; Chrmn., Special Comte. on Hate Propaganda 1965-66; Impartial Chrmn., Que. Fur Mfg. Industry (1962); Special Counsel on Constitutional Law, Govt. of N.B., 1967-70; Chrmn. Roy. Comn. on Labour Leg., Nfld. 1969-72; Roy. Comn. on Collège Militaire, St. Jean 1968; Special Comte. of Inquiry into Unloading of Grain Vessels Montreal Harbour 1967-68; Pres., Que. Adv. Council on Adm. of Justice 1972-74; Chrmn. Adv. Comte. on Marine & Environmental Confs., (Law of the Sea) Depts. of Environment and of External Affairs 1971-74; Chrmn. Candn. Sec., Internat. Jt. Comn. (Can.-U.S.) 1974-79; articles in Canadian, U.S., U.K. and International Journals recreation: golf; Clubs: Faculty; University; Rideau; Montefiore; Elm Ridge Country; Home: 1302 - 200 Rideau Terrace, Ottawa, Ont. K1M 0Z3

COHEN, Morris, M.A., Ph.D., F.C.I.C.; research chemist (retired); b. Regina, Sask., 10 July 1915; s. Israel and Esther Liba (Brownstein) C.; e. Brandon (Man.) Coll., B.A. 1934; Univ. of Toronto, M.A. 1935, Ph.D. 1939; m. Beatrice, d. late J.M. Sohn, 15 July 1940; two s. Matthew, Andrew; Head of Corrosion Lab, N.R.C. (retired 1979); with Monarch Battery Mfg. Co., Kingston, Ont., 1940-43; joined Div. of Applied Chem., N.R.C., 1943; rec'd Willis Rodney Whitney Award of Nat. Assn. of Corrosion Engrs., 1959; author of over 90 papers on fundamental aspects of corrosion; rec'd. Outstanding Achievement Award, Corrosion Div., Electrochem. Soc. 1973; Hebrew; recreations: golf, fishing, music; Home: 391 Princeton Ave., Ottawa, Ont. K2A 0M6

COHEN, Dr. (Mrs.) Nina Fried, O.C., (1967), LL.D.; b. Glace Bay, N.S., 17 March 1907; d. Max and Rose (Hausner) Fried; e. Mount Allison Ladies Coll., Sackville, N.B., 1924; Mount Allison Univ. LL.D. 1967; m. 28 March 1928 to Harry Cohen; one s. Justin Stuart; blueprinted and founded Miners' Museum 1960; (Cape Breton's Centennial Project, 1967); Chrmn. Miners' Museum 1962-68; founded Miners Folk Soc., 1964; originated coal miners choral group known as "Men of the Deeps"; Trustee and exec., Nat. Museums of Can.; Hon. Chrmn., Cape Breton Miners Foundation 1962-68; Miners' Museum, Glace Bay, N.S. 1962-68; Citizenship and Migration, Nat. Council of Women; Gov., Hebrew Univ., Jerusalem and Candn. Chrmn., Jewish Nat. and Univ. Lib. Centre for Candn. Nat. Pres., Hadassah — W120 Organ. of Can., 1960-64 (Hon. Pres. 1964); Hon. Life Mem. and mem. World Extve., Women's Internat. Zionist Organ. 1971; Nina Cohen Baby Day Care Centre, Jerusalem, Israel, 1980; rec'd Centennial Medal 1967; Order of Canada, 1967; Lloyd MacInnis Humanitarian Award, 1968; Medal of Service, Hebrew Univ., 1969 and Candn. Red Cross Soc. Medal of Merit 1939-45; Queen's Jubilee Medal 1977; Tenth Anniv. Medallion of the Nat. Museums of Can. 1977; 60th Anniv. Jubilee Medal of the Hadassah-WIZO Organ. of Can. 1917-77; Bd. of Dir., Intl. Educ. Centre, Saint Mary's University, Halifax, 1978; named "Woman of the Century 1867-1967" for N.S.; "Nina Cohen Village" named after her, Shibolim, Israel 1955; Hon. Pres., Women's Business and Prof. Assn. 1967 privilege of using Can. Centennial Standard for personal use; 1960-69 pub. and wrote for "Orah" magazine; Hadassim

Children's Village, Israel, named in her honour: Nina F. Cohen dormitory; was active in War Orphan Placem't Serv. Can. Jewish Cong.; Adopted two war orphans, brothers; involved in many aspects devel't new State of Israel; Instituted & launched the "Lieut.-Col. Yonathan Netanyahu Memorial Scholarships" at the Hebrew Univ. of Jerusalem to honor the fallen ldr. of the Entebee raid 1976; mem. World Zionist Cong.; Rec. Certif. Pub. Distinction, City of Saskatoon, Sask.; Arr, first all-Can. exhib. contemp. art from Nat. Gall. Ottawa to Tel Aviv Mus., Israel, 1971. Apptd. Consultant to Annapolis Royal Dev. Comm. in its Historic Restoration 1605-1980; Gov., Annapolis Royal Heritage Foundation, 1981; Recognized in "International Who's Who of Intellectuals", and "World's Who's Who of Women"; Liberal; Hebrew; recreations: painting, writing, golf, travel; Address: 24 York Ridge Rd., Willowdale, Ont. M2P 1R7

COHON, George A., B.Sc.; company president; b. Chicago, Ill., 19 Apl. 1937; s. Jack A. and Carolyn (Ellis) C.; came to Can. 1968; e. Pub. and High Schs., Chicago; Drake Univ., B.Sc. 1958; Northwestern Sch. Law, Juris Doctorate in Law 1961; m. Susan, d. Abe and Ann (Liberman) Silver, 4 Sept. 1960; two s. Craig, Mark; PRESIDENT AND DIR., McDONALD'S RESTAURANTS OF CANADA LTD since 1971; Director of Canadian Jewish News; Canadian Council of Christians and Jews; Muscular Dystrophy Association of Canada; National Campaign Chairman for State of Israel Bonds, Canada; Governor of Participation House; Trustee of Ontario Crippled Children's Centre; Member of National Advisory Council of the Canadian Cystic Fibrosis Foundation; Advisory Board of Adelaide Court; Member of the Funding Committee of the Canadian Hearing Society; Member of the Crew-Variety Club of Ontario; Trustee of United Community Fund (United Way); Co-Chairman, North York Y.M.C.A. Building Fund; Board of Governors-Canadian Opera Company; Board of Governors-Mount Sinai Hospital; YMCA of Metro Toronto & Central Ont. Lake Shore 'Y'; Board of Dir., Young People's Theatre Centre; Patron, Toronto French Schools; Advocate, Ont. College of Art; practiced law with Cohon, Raizes and Regal 1961-67; Licensee, McDonald's Restaurants of Ont. 1967-71; served with U.S. Army and Air Force Reserve, 1962-68; Founder and Dir., Better Boys Foundation, Chicago; mem. Am., Ill. and Chicago Bar Assns.; Young Pres. Organ.; Candn. Restaurant Assn. (Past Dir.); recreations: tennis, skiing; swimming; Club: York Racquets; Home: 112 Forest Hill Rd., Toronto, Ont. M4V 2L7; Office: 20 Eglinton Ave., West, Toronto, Ont. M4R 2E6

COKE, Brig. William Lawrence, O.B.E., M.D.; b. Watford, Ont., 5 Apl. 1905; s. James Richard (reclaimed land from Brooke Swamp and devel. one of the finest small farms in Lambton Co.) and Margaret Mary (Kingston) C.; e. Univ. of W. Ont., M.D., 1928; m. Greta Estelle Minhinnick, 2 May 1936; children: James William Edward, Greta Mary; Lieut., R.C.A. M.C. 1929; Med. Offr., M.D. 3 (Ont.) 1929; M.D. 4 (Que.) 1929; M.D. 10 (Man.) 1930; promoted Capt., Oct. 1930; Dist. Med. Offr., M.D. 12 (Sask.) 1934; promoted Major 1935; a Lieut.-Col. 1940; posted to No. 10 Field Ambulance 1940; proceeded overseas Dec. 1940; apptd. to command, 24th Light Field Ambulance (U.K.) with rank Lieut.-Col., 1942; Candn. Army (Mediterranean) Oct. 1943; apptd. to command, 4th Candn. Field Ambulance (Italy) Mar. 1944; posted to Hdqrs., 1st Candn. Divn., as A.D.M.S. (Italy) Aug. 1944; promoted Col. Aug. 1944; trans. to Candn. Army (France) 1945; returned to Can. 1946; Mentioned in Despatches; apptd. Dist. Med. Offr., M.D. 4 (Que.) 1946; command Med. Offr. (Que.) Oct. 1946; Dir.-General of Med. Services, Ottawa, 1947-52; mem., Candn. Pension Comn. 1952-63; Supt., Veterans' Hosp't., Victoria, B.C., 1963, retired Oct. 1971; awarded Geo. VI Coronation Medal; Lic., Coll. of Phys. & Surgs. of Ont.; Theta Kappa

Psi; Anglican; recreations: walking, hunting, fishing; Home: 2834 Murray Dr., Victoria, B.C. V9A 2S5

COKER, John Martin; reinsurance executive; b. Bognor Regis, Eng., 29 Mar. 1920; s. late Maj. John Nelson, M.C., T.D., and late Hilda Muriel (Martin) C.; e. Felsted Sch.; m. Edith, d. Henry Williams, 12 June 1947; PRESIDENT AND DIR., MUNICH REINSURANCE CO. OF CANADA (Estbd. 1960), since May 1969; Pres. and Dir., Munich Holdings Ltd.; Munich-Canada Management Corp. Ltd.; Dir., Munich-London Management Corp. Ltd.; Extve. Vice Pres. and Dir., The Great Lakes Reinsurance Co. Caledonian Insurance Group, 1937-58; Resident Inspector for W. Indies, 1950-54; Asst. Mgr. New York, 1954-56; Group's Asst. Mgr. for Can. and Secy., Caledonian-Canadian Insurance Co., 1956-58; Asst. Secy., Western-British America Assurance Group, 1958-61; Gen. Mgr., Global General Insurance Co., 1961-63; joined present Group Jan. 1964; served in Munich 1964-66 and London (attached to C.E. Golding & Co. Ltd. and to Arbuthnot Insurance Services Ltd.) 1966-69; A.C.I.I. 1948; Dir., IBC, 1981; Pres. R.R.C. 1978; Major, R.E. in 14th Army, 1945; Anglican; Clubs: Cercle de la Place d'Armes (Montreal); Canadian; National; Empire; Home: Apt. 412, 1 Benvenuto Place, Toronto, Ontario M4V 2L1; Office: Suite 1103, 55 Yonge St., Toronto, Ont. M5E 1J4

COLAS, Emile Jules, Q.C., B.A., B.Eng., LL.B., LL.M., LL.D.; lawyer; b. Montreal, Que. 3 Oct. 1923; s. Emile and Elise (Pila) C.; e. McGill Univ. B.Engn. 1946; Univ. of Ottawa B.A. 1947; McGill Univ. LL.B. 1949, LL.M. 1950; Univ. of Ottawa, LL.D. 1980; m. Rejane Laberge 25 Oct. 1958; children: Bernard, Hubert, François; SR. PARTNER, de GRANDPRE, COLAS, DESCHENES, GODIN, PAQUETTE, LASNIER AND ALARY; called to the Bar of Quebec 1950; cr. Q.C. 1965; Dir., Secy., Legal Advisor, Quebec Trust Co. 1966-; Dir., Secy., Rototech-Smith Co. Ltd., 1966-; Jr. Bar of Mtl. Secy. 1953-54, Vice Pres. 1954-55, Pres. 1955-56; Commonwealth Bar Assn. Delegate to the Conf. in London, 1955; Bar of Mtl. Mem. of Council 1956-57, 1967-69; Belgium Inst. of Intl. and Comparative Law, corresponding mem. for Can., 1957-; Legal Aid Bureau of the Bar of Mtl., Founder 1956, Vice Pres. 1956-66, Pres. 1966-72; as repres. Natl. Conf. on Poverty (Ottawa) 1971, Honorary Pres. 1972-73; Conf. of Commiss. on Uniformity of Legislation in Can., delegate of the Bar of P.Q.: mem., 1956-63, 1965-; Vice Pres. 1968-69, Pres., 1969-70, Honorary Pres. 1970-71; Intl. Union of Young Lawyers, Vice Pres. as rep. of Can., 1962-68; Bar of P.Q.: mem. of Council 1967-69; Candn. Bar Assn.: mem. of Council for Que. 1961-, Vice Pres. for Que. 1971-72, Chrmn. sub-cmte. on civil justice, Chrmn. natl. cmte. on legal educ. and training; Intl. Union of Lawyers, Mem. of Council for Can., 1969-; Chrmn., Family Law Section, Natl. Conf. on Poverty (Ott.) 1972; Apptd. to Advisory Council on Justice of P.Q., 1973; Pres., Intl. Law Assn. 1976-; Dir., Council on Candn. Unity 1978; Intl. Law Assn. mem. of Natl. Council, Pres. of Intl. Convention 1982 (1st time in Can.); Extve. Cmte. St-John Ambulance; Trustee, Found. for Legal Research; author of several papers incl. "Le contrôle juridictionnel du pouvoir discrétionnaire", 1949; "Les Tribunaux du travail", 1952; "Le Procès de divorce", 1975; "La Troisième Voie. Une nouvelle constitution", 1978; and numerous articles in professional publs. on legal aid, civil law, arbitration and labour law; extensive mem. incl. Corp. of Engn. of Que.; Engn. Inst. of Can.; Bar of P.Q.; Candn. Bar Assn.; Chambre de Commerce Française au Canada; Welfare Assn. of the Bar of Mtl; rec'd Edwin Botsford Busteed Scholarship, 1950; Knight of Grace and Devotion, Order of Malta; Medaille de la France libérée; Chevalier de l'Ordre des Palmes académiques; Officier de l'Ordre du Bien Public; Chevalier de la Légion d'Honneur (France); R. Catholic; Home: 1 Summerhill Terrace, Montreal, Que. H3H 1B8; Office: 2501 Stock Exchange Tower Bldg., 800 Place Victoria, Montreal, Que. H4Z 1C2.

COLE, Clarence William; banker; b. Picton, Ont. 26 Jan. 1937; EXTVE. VICE PRES., CANADIAN IMPERIAL BANK OF COMMERCE 1981- ; served as Sr. Vice Pres. Cochran Murray & Wisener Ltd.; joined Bank 1975 as Vice Pres. Invest. Div., Vice Pres. Corporate Banking Div. 1978, Sr. Vice Pres. Finance 1980; Dir. Kinross Mortgage Corp.; Gov. Trent Univ. and mem. Extve. Comte.; Clubs: Lambton Golf & Country; Cambridge; Montreal Badminton & Squash; Office: Commerce Court W., Toronto, Ont. M5L 1A2.

COLE, Gordon Arthur, B.A.Sc., M.B.A.; petroleum executive; b. Ont. 11 May 1929; e. Univ. of Toronto B.A. Sc. 1951; Univ. of W. Ont. M.B.A. 1957; m. Betty Stanhope 1958; children: Jacqueline, Robert; V.P. & GEN. MAR., INTERPROVINCIAL PIPE LINE LTD.; mem. Assoc. of Prof. Eng. of Alta.; Clubs: Royal Glenora; Edmonton Petroleum; Centre, Mayfield Indoor Tennis; recreations: tennis, squash; Home: 3624-117A St., Edmonton, Alta. T6J 1V5; Office: P.O. Box 398, Edmonton, Alta. T5J 2J9.

COLE, John N.; financial consultant; b. Montreal, Que., 9 May 1910; m. late May Thomas, 1936; former Vice Chrmn., Wood Gundy Ltd.; Pres. The Cole Found.; Dir., Belding-Corticelli Ltd.; Donohue Company Ltd.; Peterson, Howell & Heather (Canada) Ltd.; Charlevoix Paper Co.; Atlantic Shopping Centres Ltd.; British American Bank Note Co. Ltd.; Domco Industries Ltd.; Gerin Ltd.; Gerbro Inc.; Malbaie Paper Co. Ltd.; North Am. Car Can. Ltd.; Chmn. Candn. Advisory Bd.; Prudential Assnce. Co. Ltd.; Vice Chrmn., Montreal Adv. Bd., Salvation Army; Chrmn., Montreal Children's Hosp. Found.; Protestant; Clubs: Mount Royal; Guards; Mount Bruno Golf & Country; Montreal Badminton & Squash; Brook's (London, Eng.); Murray Bay Golf; Garrison (Quebec); Toronto; St. James's; Home: 21 Ramezay Road, Westmount, Que. H3Y 3J7; Office: Suite 3625, 1 Place Ville Marie, Montreal, Que. H3B 3P2

COLEMAN, Albert John, M.A., Ph.D.; university professor; b. York Co., Ont., 1918; s. Frank and Phoebe (Gerrard) C.; e. Runnymede Coll. Inst., Toronto, Ont.; Univ. Coll. of Toronto, B.A. 1939; Princeton Univ., M.A. 1942; Univ. of Toronto, Ph.D. 1943; m. Marie-Jeanne Michele, d. Rodolphe de Haller, 23 July 1953; two s. William Frank, Michael Haller; PROF. DEPT. OF MATH. AND STATISTICS,QUEEN'S UNIV., since 1960; Head of Dept. 1960-80; Dir., Internat. Student Centre there 1965-80; Lectr., Math. Dept. there, 1943-45; Travelling Secy., World's Student Christian Fed., Geneva, 1945-49; Lectr., Asst. Prof., Assoc. Prof., Univ. of Toronto, 1949-60; Visiting Prof., Dublin Inst. for Advanced Study, 1952; author of "The Task of the Christian in the University", 1947, and 40 mathematical articles; Pres. Internat. Math. Comn.; Pres., Cdn. Math. Soc., 1972-74; mem., Lambeth Conference 1978; Consultant to Min. of Energy Mines and Resources, 1980; Chmn., Citizen's Advisory Comte., Millhaven Penitentiary, 1977-79; Chmn., Devel. Comm., Internat'l Mathematical Union, 1974-78; Anglican; recreations: music (piano, choir), Home: 185 Ontario St., Kingston, Ont. K7L 2Y7

COLEMAN, John Hewson, L.H.D. (Hon.), LL.D.; extve.; b. Joggins, N.S., 22 March 1912; s. William Bartholomew and Rosalie (Comeau) C.; e. Joggins Public Sch. (Jr. Matric. 1928); LL.D. St. Francis Xavier and Saint Mary's Univs.; m. Kathryn Marguerite, d. late F. Stanley Mitchell, Dartmouth, N.S., 12 Sept. 1939; children: Gerald Francis, Kathryn Claire (Mrs. J.H. Green); PRESIDENT, J.H.C. ASSOCIATES LTD.; Chrmn., Pres. and Dir., United Group of Mutual Funds; Chrmn. Northwest Nitro-Chemicals Ltd.; Chrmn. Bd. and Dir., Maritime Steel and Foundries Ltd.; Thomson Newspapers Ltd.; Internat. Minerals & Chemical Corp.; Gt. Lakes Reins. Co.; Hawker Siddeley Canada Ltd.; Imasco Ltd.; Munich Reinsurance Co. of Canada; Royal Bank of Canada; Chrysler Canada Ltd.; Exco Corp. Ltd.; Roman Corp.

Ltd.; Great-West Life Assurance Co.; Standard Products (Canada) Ltd.; TransCanada Pipelines Ltd ; Westburne International Industries Ltd.; Hunter Douglas Ltd.; Colgate-Palmolive Ltd.; Dir. (1st Candn.) Chrysler Corp.; Chrmn. Lehndorff Corp.; joined Royal Bank of Canada in Amherst, N.S., Nov. 1928; served at various brs. in N.S.; trans. to Montreal, Candn. Credit Dept., 1946; apptd. Mgr., Cornwall, Ont. 1949; Winnipeg 1954; Supvr., Sask. Brs., 1957; Gen. Inspr. 1960; Asst. Gen. Mgr., 1961; Depy. Gen. Mgr. 1964; Chief Gen. Mgr., 1964; Vice-Pres., Dir. and Chief Gen. Mgr., 1966; Extve. Vice Pres. 1968; Depy. Chrmn. and Extve. Vice Pres. 1970; Dir., St. Michael's Coll. Foundation; Bd. Regents, Mt. Allison Univ.; Kt. of Malta; Roman Catholic; recreations: golf, bridge; Club: Lambton Golf & Country; Toronto; Home: 561 Avenue Rd., Suite 603-4, Toronto, Ont. M4V 2J8; Office: Suite 2935, P.O. Box 14, Royal Bank Plaza, Toronto, Ont. M5J 2J1

COLEMAN, John Royston M.A., Ph.D., LL.D.; b. Copper Cliff, Ont., 24 June 1921; s. Richard Mowbray and Mary Irene (Lawson) C.; e. Univ. of Toronto, B.A. 1943; Univ. of Chicago, M.A. 1949, Ph.D. (Econ.) 1950; Beaver Coll., LL.D. 1963; Univ. of Pa., LL.D. 1968; Manhattanville Coll., L.H.D., 1975; Gannon Coll., LL.D. 1975; Emery & Henry Coll.; LL.D. 1977; Haverford Coll., 1980; m. Mary Norrington, d. William Andrew Irwin, Toronto, 1 Oct. 1943 (divorced 1967); children: John Michael, Nancy Jane, Patty Ann, Paul Richard, Stephen William; Pres., Edna McConnell Clark Found., N.Y.C.; former Pres., Haverford Coll.; Instr. and Asst. Prof., Mass. Inst. of Technol., 1949-55; Assoc. Prof., Prof., Head Dept. of Econ. and Dean, Humanities and Social Sciences, Carnegie-Mellon Univ., Pittsburgh, 1955-65; Program Offr. in Charge, Social Devel., The Ford Foundation, N.Y., 1965-67; Chrmn. Bd. Dirs., Fed. Reserve Bank of Philadelphia 1973-77; Dir., Provident Mutual Life Ins. Co.; Trustee, Philadelphia Savings Fund Soc.; Pres. N.Y. Reg. Assn. of Grantmakers, 1979-; author: "Readings in Economics", 1952, 1955, 1958, 1964, 1967; "Labor Problems", 1953, 1959; "Comparative Economic Systems", 1968; "The Changing American Economy", 1967; "Blue Collar Journal", 1974; also numerous articles; served with RCNVR 1943-45; rank Lt.; mem., Am. Econ. Assn.; Quaker; Address: 300 Central Park W., New York, N.Y. 10024

COLEMAN, Ronald Borden, B.Com., LL.B.; executive; barrister; solicitor; b. Middleton, N.S. 27 Dec. 1932; s. LeBaron Ernest and Jessie May (Banks) C.; e. King's Co. Acad., N.S. 1951; Dalhousie Univ., B.Com. 1955, LL.B. 1957; m. Margaret Alice; two s. Ronald Gary, Paul LeBaron; d. Tova Patricia; SR. VICE PRES. AND GEN. COUNSEL, HOME OIL CO. LTD.; Pres. and Dir., Cygnus Corp. Ltd.; Offr. and Dir. of various subsidiaries of above co; Pres., Independent Petroleum Assn. of Can.; read law with N.D. McDermid, Q.C.; called to Bar of Alta. 1958; joined Macleod, McDermid, Dixon, Burns, Love & Leitch, Calgary, 1957; joined present Co. as Solr. 1958; Gov., Shawnigan Lake Sch., B.C.; mem. Candn. Bar Assn.; Law Soc. Alta.; Calgary Bar Assn.; Chart. Inst. Secy's; recreations: golf, riding; Clubs: Calgary Petroleum; Ranchmen's; Glencoe; Earl Grey Golf; Home: 2902 Montcalm Cres. S.W., Calgary, Alta. T2T 3M6; Office: 2300 Home Oil Tower, 324-8th Ave., S.W., Calgary, Alta. T2P 2Z5

COLES, Gordon Ronald; construction & development executive; b. Calgary, Alta., 14 June 1919; s. Charles Henry and Henley May (Pearson) C.; e. Northern Vocational Sch., Toronto, Ont., Arch. (Hons.) 1936; m. Olga, d. John Chaban, 23 April 1942; one s., Ronald Charles; PRESIDENT, ALGORE DEVELOPMENTS LTD.; Treas., Bridgeview Invests. Ltd.; Secy. Treas., O & R Holdings Ltd.; all of Sarnia, with Forsey Page & Steel, Archs., Toronto, 1938; James, Proctor & Redfern, Const. Engrs., Toronto, 1938-41; Candn. Dredge & Dock, St. John, N.B.,

1941-42; Supt. of Constr., Polymer Corp. Ltd., Sarnia, 1942-45; formed Coles-Jeffrey Engn. Co., 1945; Coles-Jeffrey Construction Co. Ltd., 1946 (Pres. 1946-58) (dissolved and formed present firm, 1959); former mem. Sarnia Adv. Bd., Canada Trust-Huron & Erie; mem. Candn. Construction Assn.; Sarnia Builders Exchange; Sarnia Chamber Comm. (Dir. and Past Vice-Pres.); United Church; recreations: curling, boating; Clubs: Sarnia Riding (Past Dir.); Rotary (Past Dir.); Home: 504 Woodrowe Shores, Sarnia, Ont. N7V 2W2 Office: Algore Developments Ltd., Suite 703, Polysar Bldg., 201 North Front St., Sarnia, Ont.

COLHOUN, James Leslie Alexander, M.A., LL.B.; trust company executive; b. Toronto, Ont. 24 Sept. 1920; e. Royal Sch. Dungannon, N. Ireland; Trinity Coll., Dublin B.A., King's Inns, Dublin, LL.B.; Univ. of Toronto post-grad. work (Flavelle Scholarship); m. Heather Elizabeth Colhoun, B.A., M.A., LL.B., d. Arthur Frederick Colhoun 4 July 1970; children: Frederick Leslie; CHRMN. AND CHIEF EXTVE. OFFR., NATIONAL TRUST CO. 1977- ; Dir. Hoechst Canada Inc.; Victory Reinsurance Management Canada Ltd. (V.R.M. Canada); Roussel Canada Inc.; Personal Trust Dept. present co. 1951, Trust Offr. Corporate Trust 1952, Mgr. Corporate Trust 1961, Asst. Vice Pres. and Mgr. Corporate Trust 1964, Vice Pres. Corporate Trust 1966, Vice Pres. Toronto 1968, Extve. Vice Pres. 1969, Pres. 1972, Pres. and Chief Extve. Offr. 1974; Past Pres. and Dir. Ont. Heart Fndtn.; mem. Gov. Council Univ. of Toronto; Pres., Trust Co's Assn. of Can.; Freemason; Clubs: York; Toronto; National; Granite; Mount Royal; R.C.Y.C.; Toronto Golf; Home: 7 Peebles Ave., Don Mills, Ont. M3C 2N9; Office: 21 King St. E., Toronto, Ont. M5C 1B3

COLLARD, Edgar Andrew, C.M., M.A., D.Litt., D.Lit., F.R.S.A.; newspaper editor (emeritus); b. Montreal, Que., 6 Sept. 1911; s. Gilchrist and Florence May (Luttrell) C.; e. McGill Univ., B.A. 1935, M.A. 1937; Hon. D.Litt. 1962; Hon. D.Lit., Carleton Univ., 1981; m. Henrietta Elizabeth, d. late Rev. George H. Forde, Cookshire, Que., 23 Aug. 1947; awarded the Certificate of Merit by Candn. Hist. Assn. for outstanding contrib. to local history, 1967; apptd. Assoc. Editor of "The Gazette" Montreal 1944, Editor 1953-70; received National Newspaper Award for Editorial Writing, 1949, 1950, 1959, 1969; author of: "Oldest McGill" (a hist. of McGill Univ.) 1946; "A Tradition Lives" (a hist. of "The Gazette") 1953; "Canadian Yesterdays" (a collection of researches in Candn. hist.) 1955; wrote chapters on Principal Dawson and Principal Peterson in "The McGill Story", 1960; author of: "Montreal Yesterdays" (a hist. of 19th century Montreal) 1962; "Call Back Yesterday" (descriptions of old Montreal) 1965; "The Story of Dominion Square", 1970; "The Art of Contentment" (anthology) 1974; "The McGill You Knew 1920-60" 1975; "Montreal: The Days That Are No More" 1976; also histories of ten institutions; has written a column on the history of Montreal in the "Gazette", weekly, 1944-; apptd. Mem. of Order of Can. 1976; Donated the Collard Collection of Canadiana to the Public Archives of Can., and the Collard Library of History and Literature to Carleton Univ., Ottawa, 1979; Independent Conservative; United Church; Club: University, Montreal; Home: 400 Stewart St., Apt. 1609, Ottawa, Ont. K1N 6L2

COLLARD, (Henrietta) Elizabeth, M.A., LL.D., F.R.S.A.; writer; b. Sawyerville, Que., 20 Oct. 1917; d. late Rev. George Henry and late Anna Sophia (Kingston) Forde; e. St. Helen's Sch., Dunham, Que.; Cookshire (Que.) High Sch.; Mount Allison Univ., B.A. 1939, LL.D. 1971; Univ. of Maine, M.A. 1940 (Maritime Provs. Fellow); Univ. of Toronto, Exchange Student 1937-38; m. Edgar Andrew Collard, Montreal, Que., 23 Aug. 1947; Sr. Latin and Eng. Mistress, St. Helen's Sch., Dunham, Que., 1940-42; Educ. Ed. "The Gazette", Montreal, also frequent contrib. to "Toronto Saturday Night", 1942-47;

Consult. on ceramics to Nat. Museum of Man, Ottawa; has served on many bds. and comtes. incl. Ladies', Lib. and Acquisition Comtes., Montreal Museum of Fine Arts; Bd. Dirs., Montreal Children's Lib. and Greater Montreal Br. of Victorian Order Nurses (Publicity Chrmn. 10 yrs.); author, "Nineteenth-Century Pottery and Porcelain in Canada", 1967; contrib. author "Book of Canadian Antiques", 1974; contrib. author: "English Pottery & Porcelain" 1980; also many articles and reviews for various mags. in Gt. Brit., Australia, USA and Can.; mem., Eng. Ceramic Circle; United Church; recreation: amateur herpetologist; Home: Apt. 1609, 400 Stewart St., Ottawa, Ont. K1N 6L2

COLLIE, Michael John, M.A., F.R.S.A.; poet; educator; b. Eastbourne, Eng., 8 Aug. 1929; s. Leslie Grant and Elizabeth (Robertson) C.; e. St. Catharine's Coll , Cambridge Univ., M.A. 1956; m. Joanne Aline, d. Dr. Paul L'Heureux, St. Boniface, Man., 20 Dec. 1960; children: Peter, Jeremy, Nicholas, Katharine, Ursula; PROF. OF ENGLISH, YORK UNIV. since 1965 (Dean of Grad. Studies 1969-73); Asst. Prof., Univ. of Manitoba., 1957; Lectr. Univ. of Exeter, 1961; Assoc. Prof., Mount Allison Univ., 1962; joined present Univ. 1965; Chrmn., Dept. of Eng., 1967-69; served with Brit. Army Intelligence Corps, 1947-49; author, "Poems", 1959; "Skirmish with Fact", 1960; "Laforgue", 1964; "Jules Laforgue Derniers Vers", 1965; "The House", 1967; "Kerdruc Notebook", 1972; "New Brunswick", 1974; "George Meredith A Bibliography", 1974; "George Gissing: A Bibliography", 1975; "Jules Laforgue", 1977; "Jules Laforgue Les Complaintes", 1977; "George Gissing: A Biography", 1977; "The Alien Art", 1977; "George Borrow", 1982; mem., Modern Lang. Assn.; Internat. Assn. Univ. Profs. Eng.; Modern Humanities Research Assn.; Assn. Candn. Univ. Teachers Eng. (Pres. 1968-69); recreations: squash, fell-walking, chess: Home: 150 Farnham Ave., Apt. 210, Toronto, Ont. M4V 1H5; Office: Winters College, York University, Downsview, Ont., M3J 1P3

COLLIE, Wallace Homan; financial consultant; retired Vice Pres., Bank of Montreal, Head Office; b. London, Ont.; s. late Wallace and Georgina Peoples (Burns) C.; e. Ontario Pub. and High Schs.; Queen's Univ. Bankers' Course; m. Margery Black, d. late Albert R. Gibson, Toronto, Ont., 25 Sept. 1948; Consultant Common Ceuts Int. Group; Dir., Old Brewery Mission; Director, Canadian Corporation, Mtl.; Consultant, Femco Financial Corp., Edmonton Ltd.; entered Bank of Montreal at Welland, Ont. subsequently serving at London, Eng.; Paris, France, Montreal, Quebec City, Toronto, Ont.; Mgr. Main Office at Edmonton, Alta., 1952-55; Supt. Corporate Devel., H.O., 1955-59; Asst. Gen. Mgr., 1959-67; Vice Pres., 1967-68, Spec. Consultant 1968-75; served in 2nd World War, R.C.A.F., Adjt. and sr. adm. posts var. stns; transf. overseas to Base Stn., No. 6 Bomber Group, Yorkshire, in same capacity; discharged with rank of Flight Lieut., Aug. 1945; Trustee and Hon. Vice-Pres. Candn. Red. Cross Soc. (Pres., P.Q. 1957-58); Pres. (1970), Air Cadet League of Canada and Past Prov. Pres. for Alta., presently Hon. Pres. (Nat.); Past Prov. Treas. Candn. Cancer Soc. (Que.); Past Treas. Chamber of Comm., Edmonton, Alta.; Past Treas. Alta. & Northwest Chamber of Mines; Chrmn. of Trustees, Greater Montreal Poppy Day Relief Fund; Hon. Gov., Candn. Seniors' Golf Assn.; Anglican; recreation: golf; Clubs: Mount Royal; Mount Bruno Country; Royal Montreal Curling; Canadian; Toronto Golf; Royal & Ancient Golf Club of St. Andrews; Mid Ocean (Bermuda); Home: The Gleneagles, 3940 Cote des Neiges Rd., Montreal, Que. H3H 1W2; Office: The Gleneagles, 3940 Cote des Neiges Rd., Montreal H3H 1W2

COLLIER, Alan C., R.C.A.; artist; b. Toronto, Ont., 19 March 1911; s. Robert Victor and Eliza Frances (Caswell) C.; e. Harbord Coll. Inst., Toronto, Ont.; Ont. Coll. of Art, A.O.C.A. 1933; Art Students' League, New York City; m. Ruth Isabella, d. G.P. Brown, Brantford, Ont., 7 April 1941; one s. Ian Munro; Advertising Artist, New York, 1937-42; has maintained his studio in Toronto since 1946; Art Teacher, Ont. Coll. of Art, 1955-66; his paintings have been exhibited since 1934 with Ont. Soc. Artists, Royal Candn. Acad.; Montreal Spring Show, Hamilton Winter, First and Third Candn. Biennial, Nat. Gallery, Hart House, Candn. Portraits; rep. in Nat. Gallery, Ottawa, London (Ont.) Museum & Art Gallery, Art Gallery of Ont., Kitchener-Waterloo Art Gallery, Art Gallery of Hamilton, Sarnia Public Library and Art Gallery, McLaughlin Gallery, Oshawa, Arts and Culture Centre, St. John's, Nfld.; Tom Thomson Art Gallery, Owen Sound; Art Gallery of Algoma, Sault Ste. Marie; Can. Council Art Bank; Frye Art Museum, Seattle Wash.; Seagram Cities of Canada series and many private and business collections; One-Man Shows; 1951 and 1957 at Art & Letters Club, Toronto; Chas & Emma Frye Art Museum, Seattle, 1964; Retrospective Exhibition in ten Ont. Public Galleries, 1971; 1956 and 1957, 1958, 1961, and bi-annually to present at Roberts Gallery, Toronto; Rep. by Kensington Gallery, Calgary; Mural paintings in Bank of Can. bldg., Ryerson Polytech. Inst., and Parl. Bldg. Toronto; Pres., Ont. Soc. of Artists (1958-61); served in 2nd World War with Candn. Army, Arty. Survey, 1943-46; Protestant; Club: Arts & Letters; Address: 115 Brooke Ave.; Toronto Ont. M5M 2K3

COLLIER, Vice-Adm. Andrew Laurence, C.M.M., D.S.C., C.D.; b. Kamloops, B.C. 3 June 1924; s. Andrew and Kathleen (Cochenour) C.; e. Salmon Arm (B.C.) High Sch.; Royal Candn. Naval Coll. 1943; Royal Naval Staff Coll. Greenwich, UK 1962; Nat. Defence Coll. Can. 1970; m. Elizabeth Paton d. William Gilchrist, Dumfries, Scot. 16 May 1970; one s., one d. by previous marriage; joined RCN 1942; served Overseas 1943-45 followed by sea duty incl. Korea 1950-51; promoted Commdr. 1957, Commodore 1972, Vice-Adm. 1977; commanded Destroyer, Destroyer Sqdn. and Candn. Atlantic Flotilla; Naval Attache USA 1973-74; Chief of Maritime Operations 1974-75; commanded Pacific Coast 1975-77; named Commdr. Order of Mil. Merit 1977; Commdr. Maritime Command 1977-79 (ret.); Dir. N.S.Heart Foundation; mem. Salvation Army Adv. Council Halifax; Anglican; recreations: boating, walking; Home: 5004 Georgia Park Terrace, Victoria, B.C.

COLLIER, (Herbert) Bruce, M.A., Ph.D., F.R.S.C., b. Toronto, Ont., 10 Oct. 1905; s. Robert Victor and Eliza Frances (Caswell) C.; e. Harbord Coll. Inst., Toronto, Ont.; Univ. of Toronto, B.A. (Hons. Chem.) 1927; M.A. (Biochem.) 1929, Ph.D. (Biochem.) 1930; m. Mary Augusta, d. late R.J. Rodger, 24 July 1930; children: Carol Frances, Rodger Bruce; Fellow in Biochem., Univ. of Toronto, 1927-30; Head, Dept. of Biochem., West China Union Univ., Chengtu, China, 1932-39; Biochemist, Inst. of Parsitology, McGill Univ., 1939-42; Asst. and Assoc. Prof. Dept. of Biochem., Dalhousie Univ., 1942-46; Prof. and Head of Dept. of Biochem., Univ. of Sask. 1946-49; Prof. of Biochem., Univ. of Alta. 1949-64; Prof. of Pathol. Univ. of Alta. 1964-71 since when Prof. Emeritus; mem., Soc. of Biological Chemists; Sigma Xi; Home: 11808-100th Ave., Apt 704, Edmonton, Alta. T5K 0K4

COLLIN, Arthur Edwin, M.Sc., Ph.D.; Canadian public servant; marine scientist; b. Collingwood, Ont., 16 July 1929 s. Prof. William Edwin, F.R.S.C. and Louie Viola (Leggott) C.; e. Univ. of W. Ont., B.Sc. 1953, M.Sc. 1955; McGill Univ., Ph.D. 1962; Nat. Defence Coll., 1969-70; m. Christa, d. Herbert Dedering, Germany, June 1963: children: David, Andrew, Christiane; ASSOCIATE DEPUTY MINISTER, DEPT. OF ENERGY, MINES & RESOURCES, 1980-; Scientist, Fisheries Research Bd. of Canada, 1955; Oceanographer U.S. IGY Program Ice Island T-3 1958 and Polar Cont. Shelf Project, 1959-62; Visiting Research Instr., Univ. of Wash., 1962-63; Oceanographer in Charge of Arctic Research, Bedford Inst. of

Oceanography, Dartmouth, N.S., 1963-65; Sr. Oceanographer, Dept. of Nat. Defence Candn. Forces HQ, Ottawa, 1965-68; Dom. Hydrographer, Candn. Hydrog. Service 1968-71; Dir.-Gen. Marine Sc. Directorate 1971-73 and Dir. Gen. Fisheries Research 1972-73; Asst. Depy. Min., Ocean and Aquatic Sciences, 1974-77; Asst. Depy. Minister, Atmospheric Environment Service, Dept. of the Environment, 1977-80; Permanent Rep. for Canada, U.N. World Meteorological Organization; Lieut., RCN(R); author of a no. of scient. papers and articles; Fellow, Arctic Inst. N. Am.; mem. Candn. Meteorological & Oceanographic Soc.; U.S. Naval Inst.; Candn. Inst. Surveying; recreations: skiing, carpentry; Home: 17 Madawaska Dr., Ottawa, Ont. K1S 3G5; Office: 580 Booth St., Ottawa, Ont. K1A 0E4

COLLINGWOOD, Henry; general merchant; b. St. John's Nfld., 6 May 1918; s. Thomas W. and Mary A.W. (Petley) C.; e. Prince of Wales Coll., St. John's, Nfld.; m. Maureen Victoria O'Reilly, 15 Oct. 1953; three s. and one d.; PRESIDENT, BAINE, JOHNSTON & CO. LTD. (estbd. 1780); Chrmn. Cooper's Discount Foods (1973) Ltd.; Nfld. Marine Ins. Co.; Beothic Gen. Ins. Co., Ltd.; Nfld. Containers Co.; Nfld. Transportation Co., Ltd.; Dir., Royal Trustco; The Royal Trust Corp.; Newfoundland Offshore Services Ltd.; Donovans Wholesale Ltd.; Newfoundland Light and Power Co. Ltd.; Newfoundland Telephone Co. Ltd.; began with present Co., 1934; apptd. Pres. 1959; Anglican; recreations: golf, fishing; Clubs: Mount Royal (Montreal); Bally Haly Golf; City; Rotary; Murray's Pond Fishing; Home: 1 Kings Bridge Court, St. John's, Nfld. A1C 2R1; Office: 58 Kenmount Rd., St. John's, Nfld. A1B 1W2

COLLINS, A.F. (Chip); provincial civil servant; DEPY. PROV. TREAS., ALTA.; Dir. Alta. Home Mortgage Corp.; Alta. Housing Corp.; Alta. Mun. Financing Corp.; Alta. Resources Railway Corp.; Commr., Alta. Govt. Telephones; Secy., Treasury Bd. and Heritage Savings Trust Fund Invest. Comte.; mem. various cabinet and govt. comtes.; Office: 434 Terrace Bldg., Edmonton, Alta. T5K 2C3.

COLLINS, Arthur Stewart, D.F.C.; advertising executive; b. Peterborough, Ont., 4 Aug. 1920; s. Frederick and Henrietta (Stewart) C.; e. Renfrew (Ont.) Coll. Inst., 1938; Queen's Univ., 1938-40; m. Patricia Mary, d. Arnold L. Holden, Toronto, Ont., 11 Sept. 1948; children: Katherine E., Michael S., Terence A., Kevin J., Brian H.; CHRMN. AND CHIEF EXTVE. OFFR., FOSTER ADVERTISING LTD.; Extve. Vice Pres. and Creative Dir., Tandy Advertising Ltd., Toronto, 1946-59; Vice Pres. and Dir. of Account Services, Stanfield, Johnson & Hill Ltd., Montreal, 1959-62; Vice Pres. and Mgr., Montreal Office, James Lovick Ltd., 1962-63; joined present firm as Vice Pres., Automotive Div., 1963-69; Vice Pres., Central Div., 1969-73; Pres. 1973; served with RCAF 1940-46, Pilot; 400 Sqdn. Overseas; Anglican; recreations: golf, curling, skiing; Clubs: Albany; Granite; Peterborough Golf; Home: 3205 Palace Pier, 2045 Lakeshore Blvd. W., Toronto, Ont.; Office: 40 St. Clair Ave. W., Toronto, Ont. M4V 1M2

COLLINS, Darrall Stanley, C.D., Q.C., LL.B.; b. Bredenbury, Sask., 6 May 1925; s. John Stanley and Emma Edith Patience (Einboden) C.; e. Alameda (Sask.) High Sch.; Univ. of Sask., LL.B. 1949; m. Patricia Doreen Mae, d. of Cyril W. Joiner, Victoria, B.C., 15 Apl. 1950; children: Kelly Stanley, Darrall William, Vicki Patricia, Robin Cyril; read law with Arthur Parsons Dawe, Victoria, B.C., 1949-50; called to Bar of B.C. 1950, Y.T. 1958, N.W.T. 1966; cr. Q.C. (Fed.) Dec. 1968; practised his prof. at Terrace, B.C., 1950-53; mem. Office of Judge Advocate Gen., Dept. of Nat. Defence, 1953-58, during which time served in Europe as mem. of defending prosecuting team from Jan. 1954 to Aug. 1957; apptd. Legal Advisor for Y.T. Apl. 1958; in private practice in White-

horse from 1960; now Crown Prosecutor, Yukon Territory; served in 2nd World War in Can. and overseas 1943-45; C.O.T.C. and Militia 1945-53; regular force 1953-58; Militia 1959-66; commanded local militia unit, Whitehorse, Y.T., first C.O. Yukon Regt., 1963; former Ald., City of Whitehorse; Vice-Pres. Yukon Lib. Assn.; mem. Student's Financial Aid Comte., Y.T., 1960-68; mem. Candn. Bar Assn.; B.C. Law Soc.; Liberal; Anglican; recreations: golf, curling; Club: Associates

COLLINS, John; cartoonist; e. Sir George Williams Coll. (Art); joined the "Gazette", Montreal 1939; has had more than 10,000 editorial cartoons published while with the paper; Nat. Newspaper Award for cartooning 1954, 1973; only Candn. to have had two of his works chosen for a book of cartoons published by the Internat. Cartoon Show, London, Eng. 1958; Pres., Assn. of Am. Ed. Cartoonists, 1968-69; Office: 250 St. Antoine, Montreal, Que. H2Y 3R7

COLLINS, John Alfred, M.D.; obstetrician and gynecologist; educator; b. Kitchener, Ont. 2 Oct. 1936; s. John Bandel and Vera (Hannahson) C.; e. Univ. of W. Ont. M.D. 1960; m. Carole Joanne Sedwick d. Bruce West, Toronto, Ont. 22 July 1956; children: John Bruce, Blayne Linda, Anne Catherine; PROF. AND HEAD OF OBSTETRICS & GYNECOLOGY, DALHOUSIE UNIV. since 1977; Clin. Asst. Prof. of Obstetrics & Gynecology; Univ. of W. Ont. 1967, Clin. Assoc. Prof. 1971, Assoc. Prof. 1975 (Univ. Hosp.), Asst. Dean Undergrad. Educ. Faculty of Med. 1975; Clin. Research Fellow, Ont. Cancer Foundation London Clinic 1967-76; co-ed. "A Practical Manual on Reproduction" 1973; author or co-author various med. papers and publs.; mem. Candn. Med. Assn.; N.S. Med. Soc.; Soc. Obstets. & Gynecols. Can.; Candn. Fertility Soc.; Am. Coll. Obstets. & Gynecols.; Am. Fertility Soc.; Royal Coll. Phys. & Surgs. Can.; recreations: tennis, sailing; Home: 1124 Robie St., Halifax, N.S. B3H 3C7; Office: 5821 University Ave., Halifax, N.S. B3H 1W3.

COLLINS, Hon. Dr. John F., M.H.A.; politician;MIN. OF FINANCE, NFLD.1979- ; apptd. Pres., Treasury Bd., 1980; el. M.H.A. for St. John's South prov. g.e. 1975, re-el. 1979; Depy. Speaker 1975; P. Conservative; Office: Confederation Bldg., St. John's, Nfld. A1C 5T7.

COLLINS, Malcolm Frank, Ph.D.; educator; b. Crewe, Eng. 15 Dec. 1935; s. Bernard and Ethel (Smith) C.; e. Cambridge Univ. B.A. 1957, Ph.D. 1962; m. Eileen d. late Stanley Ray 1961; children: Adrian B., Andrew M., Gillian O.; PROF. OF PHYSICS, McMASTER UNIV. 1973- ; Chrmn. of Physics 1976-82; Staff Scient. Atomic Energy Estab. Harwell, Eng. 1961-69; Assoc. Prof. of Physics present Univ. 1969-73; author over 50 acad. publs. condensed matter physics, slow neutron scattering; mem. Bd. Eds. Solid State Communications 1970- ; Pres. Chess Fed. Can. 1976-77, Bd. Govs. 1972- ; mem. Candn. Assn. Physicists (Chrmn. Condensed Matter Div. 1979-80); recreation: chess; Home: 6 Penge Court, Dundas, Ont. L9H 4R4; Office: Hamilton, Ont. L8S 4M1.

COLLINS-WILLIAMS, Cecil, B.A., M.D., F.R.C.P.(C) (1950); physician; b. Toronto, Ont. 31 Dec. 1918; s. Ernest and Nellie (Hewitt) C-W.; e. Univ. of Toronto, B.A. (Victoria Coll.) 1941, M.D. 1944; m. Jean, d. late William Hamilton, 30 June 1944; children: Donald James, Joan; SR. STAFF PHYSICIAN, HOSP. FOR SICK CHILDREN and Head, Allergy Div. there; Professor of Paediatrics, Univ. of Toronto; Consultant, Ont. Crippled Children's Centre; post-grad. work in paediatrics and paediatric allergy in Toronto, Boston and New York, 1944-50; private practice in Toronto since 1950; joined staff of present Hosp. 1950; on full-time staff of Hosp. and Univ. of Toronto since 1968; served with RCN 1946-47; author, "Paediatric Allergy and Clinical Immunology (as applied to Atopic Disease)", Notes and Suggested Reading for Medical Students", also over 100 articles and papers for various med. journs. and book chapters; mem. various Ed. Bds.; Fellow, Candn. Soc. Allergy & Clin. Immunology (Past Pres.); Am. Acad. Paediatrics; Am. Acad. Allergy; Am. Coll. Allergists; Fellow, Acad. of Med., Toronto; Ont. Antibody Club; Ont. Allergy Soc. (Past Pres.); Candn. Paed Soc.; Candn. Soc. for Immunology; Ont. Thoracic Soc.; Candn. Thoracic Soc.; Am. Thoracic Soc.; Dir. Asthma Soc. of Can., Dir. and Past. Pres. Ass'n for the Care of Asthma; Dir. Asthma Care Ass'n of America Inc., Trustee, Asthmatic Children's Foundation; Roy. Soc. of Med.; Br. Soc'y for Allergy and Clinical Immunology, Roy. Coll. of Physicians and Surgeons of Can.; Sigma Xi; Alpha Omega Alpha; Protestant; recreation: photography; Cross-country skiing; Clubs: Granite; Toronto; Home: 39 Bennington Heights Dr., Toronto, Ont. M4G 1A8; Office: 555 University Ave., Toronto, Ont. M5G 1X8

COLOMBO, John Robert, editor; writer; poet; b. Kitchener, Ont. 24 March 1936; s. John and Irene (Nicholson) C.; e. Kitchener-Waterloo (Ont.) Coll. 1955; Univ. Coll., Univ. of Toronto, B.A. (hons.) 1959; Univ. of Toronto Sch. Grad. Studies 1960; m. Ruth F., d. Joseph Brown, Toronto, Ont. 11 May 1959; children: Jonathan, Catherine, Theodore; Ed. Bd., "The Tamarack Review"; book publications since 1974: "Colombo's Canadian Quotations" 1974; "The Sad Truths" 1974; "Translations from the English" 1974; "Colombo's Little Book of Canadian proverbs, Graffiti, Limericks & Other Vital Matters" 1975; "Colombo's Canadian References" 1976; "Colombo's Concise Canadian Quotations" 1976; "Mostly Monsters" 1977; "Variable Cloudiness" 1977; "Private Parts" 1978; "The Poets of Canada" 1978; "Colombo's Book of Canada" 1978; "Colombo's Names and Nicknames", 1978; "The Great Cities of Antiquity", 1979; "Other Canadas", 1979; "Colombo's Book of Marvels", 1979; "Colombo's Hollywood", 1979; "The Canada Colouring Book", 1980; "222 Canadian Jokes", 1981; "Blackwood's Books", 1981; "Not to be Taken at Night" (with Michael Richardson), 1981; "Friendly Aliens", 1981; "Poems of the Inuit", 1981; and, with Nikola Roussanoff: "Under the Eaves of a Forgotten Village" 1975; "The Balkan Range" 1976; "The Left-Handed One" 1977; "Depths" 1978; "Remember Me Well" 1978; Host, "Colombo's Quotes", wkly. nat.-network CBC-TV series; etc.; Rep., Commonwealth Arts Festival, U.K., 1965; Guest, Writers Union, Bulgaria, 1975-80; Writer-in-residence, Mohawk Coll., Hamilton, Ont. 1977; Centennial Medal 1967; adviser to Ont. Arts Council 1968-69; Can Council 1968-70; Award of Merit, Ont. Library Assn., 1977; Best Non-Fiction Paperback Book Award, Periodical Distributors, 1977; Esteemed Knight of Mark Twain, 1979; Laureate, Order of Cyril and Methodius; mems: ACTRA; PEN; Club: Celebrity; Address: 42 Dell Park Ave., Toronto, Ont. M6B 2T6

COLONNIER, Marc, M.D., M.Sc., Ph.D.; educator; b. Québec, Qué. 12 May 1930; s. Jean and Enilda (Bourguignon) C.; e. Univ. of Ottawa B.A., B.Ph. 1951, M.D. 1959, M.Sc. (Anat.) 1960; Univ. Coll. London Ph.D. (Neurobiol.) 1963; m. Lise d. Arthur DeGagné, Ottawa, Ont. 14 Nov. 1959; one child, Jean; PROF. OF ANAT. UNIV. LAVAL since 1976; Asst. Prof. of Anat. Univ. of Ottawa 1963-65, Prof. and Dir. of Anat. 1969-76; Asst. Prof. Physiol. Univ. de Montréal 1965-67, Assoc. Prof. 1967-69; rec'd Lederle Med. Award 1966-69; Charles Judson Herrick Award 1967; author various articles anat. studies parts of brain concerned with vision; mem. Royal Soc. Can.; Am. Assn. Anats; Candn. Assn. Anats; Soc. Neuroscience; Cajal Club; Home: 736 Pére Marquette, Apt. 301, Québec, Qué. G1S 2A2; Office: Laboratoires de Neurobiologie, Hôpital de l'Enfant-Jésus, 2075 ave. de Vitré, Québec, Qué. G1J 5B3.

COLTER, His Hon. William Edgar Charles; judge; b. Cayuga, Ont., 14 Sept. 1916; s. Richard S., Q.C., and Aletha M. (Birdsall) C.; e. Cayuga (Ont.) Pub. and High Schs.; Ridley Coll., St. Catharines, Ont.; Univ. of Toronto, B.A. 1937, LL.B. 1941; Osgoode Hall Law Sch., Toronto, 1940; m. Elizabeth M., d. late Reginald S. Duncan, 27 Sept. 1941; two d., Ann E., Patricia J.; CHIEF JUDGE, CO. & DISTRICT COURTS, ONT. since Feb. 1974; read law with City Solr., Toronto; called to Bar of Ont. 1940; cr. Q.C. 1957; practised law with Colter & Colter, Cayuga, Ont., 1940-42 and 1946-48; Macoomb, Colter & Sullivan, Welland, Ont., 1948-63; Colter & Sullivan, Welland, 1963-64; apptd. Jr. Judge, Co. Court of Middlesex, 1964, Sr. Judge 1967; Hon. LLD. Univ. Western Ont. 1976; served with Candn. Army 1942-46; discharged with rank of Capt., Royal Regt. of Can., 2nd Div.; mem., Candn. Bar Assn.; York Law Assn.; Sigma Chi; Anglican; Clubs: University; Lawyers; London Hunt & Country; Home: 9 Thornwood Road, Toronto, Ont. M4W 2R8; Office: Travellers Tower, 400 University Ave., Suite 1803, Toronto, Ont. M5G 155

COLVILLE, David Alexander, O.C., B.F.A.; artist; b. Toronto, Ont. 24 Aug. 1920; s. late David Harrower and late Florence (Gault) C.; e. Amherst, N.S. schs.; Mount Allison Univ. B.F.A. 1942; Hon. Degrees: Trent Univ.; Mount Allison Univ.; Dalhousie Univ.; Simon Fraser Univ.; Univ. of Windsor; Acadia Univ.; Memorial Univ. Nfld.; m. Rhoda d. late Charles H. Wright 5 Aug. 1942; children: Graham Alexander, John Harrower, Charles Wright, Ann Christian; teacher Mount Allison Univ. 1946-63; Visiting Artist Univ. of Calif. Santa Cruz 1967; Berliner Kunstlerprogramm 1971; solo exhns. incl.: Kestner Gesellschaft Hannover 1969; Marlborough London, Eng. 1970; Gemeent Museum, Arnhem, Kunsthalle, Dusseldorf, Fischer Fine Art London, 1977; Mira Godard Galleries Toronto, Montreal 1978; rep. in various pub., corporate and private colls. incl.: Nat. Gallery Can.; Art Gallery Ont.; Musée de Beaux Arts Montreal; N.B. Museum; Museum of Modern Art N.Y.; Sammlung Ludwig Aachen; Wallraf-Rickartz Museum Cologne; Kestner Gesellschaft Hannover; Musée Nat. d'Art Moderne Paris; Museum Boymans-van Beuningen Rotterdam; served with Candn. Army 1942-46, War Artist 1944-46; Trustee Nat. Museums Can.; Chancellor Acadia Univ.; P. Conservative; Home: 408 Main St., Wolfville, N.S. B0P 1XO; Office: (P.O. Box 550) Wolfville, N.S. B0P 1XO.

COMEAU, Hon. Benoit, M.L.A., b. Comeauville, N.S., 16 July 1916; s. late Hon. Senator Joseph Willie and Zoé (Doucet) C.; m. Marie Antoinette, d. Willis Doucet; three s., three d., M.L.A. For Clare 1979-81; Min. of Public Works, N.S., 1973-78 (formerly Min. Lands, Forests & Fisheries); apptd. Min. i/c Adm. of Liquor Control Act 1976; has served as Pres., B & M Construction Co.; Vice Pres., C & M & B Realty Co. Ltd.; partner Benoit & Medard Mink Ranch; Past Vice Pres., St. Mary's Bay Industries; served overseas with RCAF 1941-44; mem., Royal Candn. Legion; Liberal; R. Catholic; Club: Richelieu; Home: Little Brook, Digby Co., N.S. B0V 1A0

COMEAU, Louis Roland, B.Sc., B.Ed.; educator; ex-politician; b. Meteghan, N.S., 7 Jan. 1941; s. Désiré Joseph and Antoinette Marie (Saulnier) C.; C. Clare (N.S.) District High Sch.; St. Anne's Coll.; St. Mary's Univ., Dipl. Engn. and B.Sc. 1958-62; Dalhousie Univ., B.Ed., 1963, grad. requirements for M.Sc. 1967; m. Clarisse Marie, d. Émile Theriault, Belliveau Cove, N.S. 20 June 1964; children: Louise Anne, Jacques, Martine; PRES., KINGSTON LUMBER AND BUILDING SUPPLIES, Pres., College Ste-Anne 1971-77; Prof. of Physics and Math. there 1963-65 and 1967-68; 1st el. to H. of C. for S.W. Nova 1968; Owner and Pres., E. M. Comeau & Sons (1977) Ltd., since 1977; mem. Candn. Assn. of Phys.; Am. Assn. of Phys.; Dir., N.S. Power Corp.; Atlantic Trust Co. Ltd; Atlantic Management Institute (Past Chmn.); P. Conservative; Catholic; Clubs: Richelieu (Dir.); Clare Social; Clare Golf & Country; Address: Church Point, N.S. B0W 1M0

COMFORT, Charles Fraser, O.C. (1972), C.D., LL.D., R.C.A.; b. Edinburgh, Scotland, 1900; came to Can. in 1912, settling in Winnipeg; e. Winnipeg School of Art; Art Students League, New York; Kunsthistorich Instituut te Utrecht; Mt. Allison Univ., LL.D. 1958; LL.D. R.M.C. of Can., 1980; served in 2nd World War as Sr. Combat War Artist in U.K., Italy and N.W. Europe, 1943-46 (discharged with rank of Major); Dir., Dept. of Mural Painting, Ont. Coll. of Art, 1935-38; Assoc. Prof., Dept. of Art & Archaeol., Univ. of Toronto, 1938-60; Dir., Nat. Gallery of Canada, 1960-65; Pres., Roy. Candn. Acad., 1957-60; Past Pres., Can. Soc. of Painters in Water Colour; Past Pres. Candn. Group of Painters; mem., Ont. Soc. of Artists; Arts & Letters Club, Toronto; Hon. mem., Candn. Art Museum Dirs. Organ.; Art Dirs. of Can.; Candn. Soc. of Educ. through Art; Arts Club, Montreal; Hart House, Univ. of Toronto; awarded Italy's "Medaglia al Merito Culturale", 1963; Gold Medal for Painting and Allied Arts, Univ. of Alta., 1963; Roy. Soc. Fellowship for study in the Netherlands, 1955-56; work embraces landscapes, portraits and non-objectives in oil and water colour, murals and stone carvings; has exhibited in Can. and abroad since 1924; rep. in major Candn. Colls.; murals include Toronto Stock Exchange, 1938; Toronto-Dominion Bank, Vancouver, 1951; Neurol. Div., Toronto General Hosp., 1958; Nat. Lib. and Archives Bldg., Ottawa; 1967; Acad. of Medicine, Toronto, 1968; Publs. include "Canadian Painting", Massey Report, Roy. Comn. Studies, 1951; "Artist at War", 1956; "The Moro River and Other Observations", 1970; Address: 1201-100 Bronson Ave., Ottawa, Ont. K1R 6G8

COMMON, Frank Breadon, Q.C., B.C.L.; b. Montreal, Que., 16 April 1920; s. late Frank Breadon and late Ruth Louise (Lang) C.; e. Westmount High Sch.; Royal Mil. Coll., Kingston, Ont. (1938-40), Grad.; McGill Univ., Law Faculty, B.C.L. 1948 (Pres., Student Veterans Soc. 1946-47; Law Undergrad. Soc. 1948); cr. Q.C. 1959; Hon. Doctor of Laws, St. Francis-Xavier Univ., 1980; m. Katharine Ruth, d. Rev. Harold Stewart Laws, 7 Sept. 1946; children: Katharine Ruth, Anne Elizabeth, Diana Melanie, Ruth Elizabeth, Jane Laws, James Lang; MEMBER, OGILVY, RENAULT; Chrmn. of Bd. and Dir., Covent Canada Corp. Ltd.; Peterson, Howell & Heather Canada Inc.; Peterson, Howell & Heather (U.K.) Ltd.; Canadian Corporations Ltd.; Secy. and Dir., Ralston Purina of Canada Ltd.; Cadbury Schweppes Powell Ltd.; Dir., International Paper Sales Co. Inc.; Anglo American Chemicals Ltd.; Royal Bank of Canada; Beneficial Finance Co. of Canada Ltd.; Covent N. American Properties Ltd.; N. American Car (Canada) Ltd.; Place Ville Marie Corp.; Trizec Corp. Ltd.; Triton Shopping Centres Ltd.; Selco Mining Corp. Limited; Triton Shopping Centres of Canada Ltd.; CIBA-GEIGY Canada Ltd.; mem. Candn. Adv. Bd., Sun Alliance Insurance Company; mem. Corp. Bishop's Univ.; 1st Gen. Chrmn., Combined Health Appeal of Metro Montreal (1963); Life Gov. (Past Chrmn.) Douglas Hosp.; mem. Extve. Comte. and Bd. Mang., Canadian Red Cross Soc. (Que. Div.); Founder and First Chrmn., Murray Bay Festivals Inc.; Founder and First Pres., Candn. Foundation for Educ. Devel.; former Ald. City of Westmount, Que. and Commr. of Finance 1959-62; served in 2nd World War, R.C.E., 1940-45; in Canada till Sept. 1941 and Overseas in Eng. and N.W. Europe to Sept. 1945; Mentioned in Despatches; called to Bar of Que., June 1948; Lectr., Law Faculty, McGill Univ. (in Income Tax and Successions Duty Law) 1953-61; mem. Candn. Tax Foundation; Candn. Bar Assn. (Hon. Treas., Que. Sec. 1955-57, Chrmn., Que. Income Tax sub-sec. 1955-56, mem. Council 1956-59); United Church Clubs; Mount Royal; Forest & Stream; Murray Bay Golf; Mount Bruno Country; The Brook (NYC); Bayou (La.); Home: Apt. B-101, 3940 Cote des Neiges Rd., Montreal, Que. H3H 1W2; Office: 700 Place Ville Marie, Montreal, Que.

COMMON, Robert Haddon; B.Sc., B.A.S., M.A.S., Ph.D., D.Sc., LL.D., F.R.S.C., F.A.I.C., F.R.S.C.; b. Larne, Co. Antrim, N. Ireland, 25 Feb. 1907; s. Robert Hall and Alice Whiteside (Magill) C.; e. Campbell Coll., Belfast; The Queen's Univ. of Belfast, B.Sc. 1928, B.A.S. 1929, M.A.S. 1931, D.Sc. 1957, LL.D. 1974; Univ. of London (external), Ph.D. 1935 and D.Sc. 1944; m. Renate Liselotte, d. late Prof. F. H. Gueterbock, 16 Oct. 1935; six children; Prof. of Agric. Chemistry, McGill Univ., 1947-75, now Emeritus Prof.; Asst. in the Dept. of Agric. Chem., The Queen's Univ. of Belfast, and Research Asst. in Chem. Research Div., Min. of Agric. for N. Ireland, 1929-41; Lectr. in Agric. Chem., The Queen's Univ. of Belfast, 1945; Principal Scient. Offr., Min. of Agric. for N. Ireland, 1946; Special Supervisor for the Dir. of Canning Control. Min. of Food (U.K.), 1943-47; Depy. Sr. Gas Adviser for N. Ireland, 1939-45; author of papers in various scient. journs., mainly on agric. chem. and biochem.; Fellow, Chem. Inst. Can.; Roy. Chem.; Agric. Inst. Can.; Royal Soc. of Can; emeritus mem., Candn. Inst. Food Tech.; Nutrition Soc. of Canada; Sigma Xi; Anglican; Address: 12A Maple Ave., Ste. Anne-de-Bellevue, Que. H9X 2E4

COMMON, William B., Q.C., LL.D.; b. London, Eng., 1899; called to Bar of Ont. 1923; cr. K.C. 1933; entered Atty. Gen's. Dept. 1927; former Depy. Atty. Gen. for Ont.; retired 1971; Life Bencher, Law Soc. of Upper Can.; served in World War 1914-18 with R.A.F.; Address: 2635 Lakeshore Blvd. W., Toronto, Ont. M8V 1G5

COMTOIS, Roger, LL.L., LL.D.; 'educateur; né St-Eustache, Qué. 9 février 1921; f. Isidore et Malvina (Houde) C.; é. Coll. Bourget, Rigaud B.A. 1941; St.-Michael's Coll. Toronto 1941-42; Ecole Normale Jacques Cartier, Montréal Cert. 1943; Univ. de Montréal LL.L. 1946; Univ. d'Ottawa LL.D. 1964; (divorcé); enfants: Lorraine (Berthold), Denys, Marie-Andrée; PROFESSEUR DE DROIT, UNIV. DE MONTREAL; Notaire, Lachute, Qué. 1946-48, Montréal, Qué. depuis 1948; auteur "Loi du notariat annotée" 1959; "Traité de la communauté de biens" 1965; Essai sur les donations par contrat de mariage; Les libéralites, 1979; mem. Soc. Royale du Can.; Assn. du Barreau canadien; Dir. de la Revue du Notariat; Prés. de la Chambre des notaires 1966-69; catholique; récreations: skiing, golf; Adresse: 4938 Iona, Montréal, Qué. H3W 2A2; Bureau: 3101 Marie Guyard, Montréal, Qué. H3C 3T1.

COMTOIS, Roland, M.P., B.Sc.A., P.Eng.; b. Sainte-Julie, Verchères Co., Que., 3 March 1929; s. Arthur and Aurore (Charlebois) C.; e. Acad. St-Georges, Longueuil, Que. 1938; Coll. de Longueuil 1947; Mont. Saint Louis, Montreal 1950; Ecole Polytech., Univ de Montréal, B.Sc.A. 1954; m. Huguette, d. Alphée Desrosiers, 16 Sept. 1950; children: Ninon, Richard, Louise, Robert; with Que. Dept. of Roads 1952-53; Engr., Dept. N. Affairs and Nat. Resources 1954; Engr., Iberville Construction Inc., Repentigny, Que. 1955-60; Dir., Caisse Populaire of Repentigny, 1956-70; Joliette Asphalt Ltd. and North West Que. Enterprises Ltd., 1960-70; Que. Road Builders Assn., 1965-66; Gov., Le Gardeur Hosp. Corp., 1st el. to H. of C. for Joliette-l'Assomption-Montcalm, g.e. 1965, for Terrebonne 1968, re-el. 1972, 1974; resigned to run in Que. g.e. 1976, def.; re-el. to H. of C. in by-el. 1977 for Terrebonne; re-el. 1979 and 1980 g.e. Parlty. Secy., Min. of Communications, 1971-72; min. of Nat. Defence, 1972; Min. of Finance, 1972-74; Vice-Chrmn., Standing Comte. on Finance, Trade and Econ. Affairs, May 1975, Chrmn. Oct. 1975; Vice Chrmn., Stdg. Comte. on Mang. and Member's Services, July 1975; mem. of a no. of Parlty. and Govt. Delegations; Pres. of Can.-Fr. Interparliamentary, Appreciation, 1980; Vice-Pres., NATO Assn., Candn. Branch 1980; mem. of C.O.T.C. 1949-51; Lt. Candn. Army (supplementary Reserve) 1951-71; mem., Que. Order of Engrs.; Candn. Inst. Engrs.; Knights of Columbus (Terrebonne); Candn. Legion, Ste. Therese; Hon. Pres., Terrebonne Hts.; Hon. Ddir., Candn. Assn. of Exhns., 1975-76; Liberal; R. Catholic; Clubs: Optimist, Repentigny; Richelieu, Repentigny (hon.); Home: 201 boul. Iberville, Repentigny, Que. J6A 1Z3; Office: Pièce 108 East Block, Chambre des communes, Ottawa, Ont. K1A 0A6

CONACHER, Desmond John, M.A., Ph.D., F.R.S.C.; educator; b. Kingston, Ont. 27 Dec. 1918; s. late William Morison and late Madeline (Cashel) C.; e. Queen's Univ. B.A. 1941, M.A. (Classics) 1942; Univ. of Chicago Ph.D. (Greek Lang, & Lit.) 1950; m. Mary Kathleen d. late Bernard Smith 2 Aug. 1952; children: Hugh Anthony, Susan Mary; PROF. OF CLASSICS, TRINITY COLL. UNIV. OF TORONTO since 1965; Special Lectr. in Classics, Dalhousie Univ. 1946-47; Asst. Prof. of Classics, Univ. of Sask. 1947, Assoc. Prof. 1952-58; Assoc. Prof. of Classics present Coll. 1958-65, Head of Classics, Trinity College, 1966-72; Chrm., Intercollegiate Dep't of Classics, Univ. of Toronto, 1972-76; author "Euripidean Drama" 1967; "Aeschylus' Prometheus Bound: A Literary Study", U. of T. Press, 1980; author various articles and reviews mainly Greek Tragedy prof. journs.; Fellow, Royal Soc. of Canada (el. 1976); mem. Ed. Bd. "Phoenix" 1968-73; Hon. Adv. Bd. "University of Toronto Quarterly" since 1975; mem., Bd. of Dir., Can., Fed. for the Humanities (1981-); mem. Classical Assn. Can. (Council 1975-78); Am. Philol. Assn. (Dir. 1974-77); recreations: tennis, badminton; Home: 126 Manor Rd. E., Toronto, Ont. M4S 1P8; Office: Toronto, Ont. M5S 1H8.

CONACHER, James Blennerhasset, M.A., Ph.D.; educator; b. Kingston, Ont. 31 Oct. 1916; s. William Morison and Madeline (Cashel) C.; e. Regiopolis Coll. High Sch. Kingston; Queen's Univ. B.A. 1938, M.A. 1939; Harvard Univ. Ph.D. 1949; m. Muriel B. Foley 6 Nov. 1943; children: Desmond William, Patricia Madeline; PROF. OF HISTORY, UNIV. OF TORONTO 1963- ; Cabinet Secretariat, Privy Council Office 1940-41; served with Candn. Army 1941-46, rank Capt.; joined Dept. Hist. Univ. of Toronto 1946, Chrmn. Dept. 1972-77, former mem. Senate, Pres's Council, mem. Gov. Council 1978-81; Visiting Prof. Univ. of Notre Dame 1965-66; author "The Aberdeen Coalition 1852-1855" 1968; "The Peelites and the Party System 1846-52" 1972; "From Waterloo to the Common Market - Borzoi History of England" Vol. V 1975; Ed. "The Emergence of British Parliamentary Democracy in the Nineteenth Century" 1970; "History of Canada or New France" (Francois Du Creux) 2 vols. 1951, 1952; Jt. Ed. "Canadian Historical Review" 1949-56; various articles nineteenth century Brit. hist.; Hon. Vice Pres. Champlain Soc. 1980, Ed. 1952-56; mem. St. Vincent de Paul Soc. (Toronto Pres. 1959-62, 1963-65); Candn. Hist. Assn. (Pres. 1974-75); Royal Hist. Soc.; Conf. on Brit. Studies; Univ. of Toronto Faculty Assn. (Pres. 1971-72); Founding mem. Candn. Assn. Univ. Teachers; R. Catholic; Home: 151 Welland Ave., Toronto, Ont. M4T 2J6; Office: Dept. Hist, Univ. of Toronto, Toronto, Ont. M5S 1A1.

CONDON, Thomas Joseph, M.A., Ph.D.; university professor; b. New Haven, Conn. 27 July 1930; s. Edmond Francis and Helen (Heffernan) C.; e. Yale Coll. B.A. 1952; Boston Coll. M.A. 1953; Harvard Univ. Ph.D. 1962; m. Ann Kathleen d. late Joseph Gregory Gorman 30 May 1962; children: Katherine, Carine, Gregory; VICE PRES. (SAINT JOHN) UNIV. OF NEW BRUNSWICK since 1977 and Prof. of Hist. there; Teaching Fellow in Hist. and Tutor, Harvard Univ. 1959-1962 Research Asst. on Hist. Preservation and Urban Renewal Boston 1962; Asst. Prof. of Hist. Univ. of N.B. Fredericton 1962-66, Prof. of Hist. and Dean of Arts 1970-77; Acting Pres., Univ. of N.B. (Fredericton & St. John Campuses) 1979-80; Extve. Assoc. Am. Council Learned Socs. N.Y. 1966-70; visiting Assoc. Prof. of Hist. Ind. Univ. Bloomington 1967-68; Visiting Prof. of Hist. Grad. Centre City Univ. of N.Y. 1968-69; Hon. Research Fellow Inst. of U.S. Studies Univ. of London 1975-76; served with U.S. Naval Reserve 1953-57, rank Lt.; rec'd Holland Soc. N.Y. Grant 1962, Can. Council Research Grants 1964, 1965, Henry E. Huntington Lib. Summer Fellowship 1964; mem. Humanities Research

Council Can. 1972-73; Chrmn. Adv. Comte. on Arts in N.B. 1973-75; Gov. Rothesay Coll. Shc. 1977 and Univ. of N.B. 1977; Chrmn. Engn. Task Force Maritime Provs. Higher educ. Comn. 1977-78; has served on various other educ. bds. and comtes.; mem. Candn. conf. of Arts; N.B. Museum; Beaverbrook Art Gallery; author "New York Beginnings: The Commercial Origins of New Netherland" 1968; various articles and reviews, papers, lectures and addresses; Ed. "ACLS Newsletter" 1968-70; mem. Ed. Bd. "Computers and the Humanities" 1969-70 and "Acadiensis" 1970; mem. Am. Hist. Assn; Brit. Assn. Am. Studies; Candn. Assn. Am. Studies; Candn. Hist. Assn.; Candn. Univs. Soc. Gt. Brit.; N.B. Hist. Soc.; York-Sunbury Hist. Soc.; The Mory's Assn.; Saint John Bd. Trade; R. Catholic; recreations: tennis, squash; Club: Union; Home: 1 Jersey Lane, Rothesay, N.B. E0G 2W0; Office: (P.O. Box 5050) Saint John, N.B. E2L 4L5.

CONNAGHAN, Charles Joseph, M.A.; Industrial relations consultant;; b. Arranmore, Co. Donegal, Republic of Ireland 14 Feb. 1932; s. John and Sarah (O'Donnell) C.; e. St. Dominic's Sch. and Morrisons Acad. for Boys, Crieff, Pertshire, Scot. 1951; Univ. of B.C. B.A. 1959, M.A. 1960; m. Erma Grace d. late Walter Edwin McGuirk 27 Dec. 1958; children; Michael John, Susan Gail, Kathryn Patricia; PRES. C.J. CONNAGHAN & ASS. LTD. 1980-; Trainee MacMillan Bloedel Co. 1960-61; Mgr. Indust. Relations, Atlas Steels Ltd. Welland, Ont. 1961-66 and Anglo-Canadian Pulp & Paper Mills Ltd., Quebec City 1966-70; Pres. Construction Labour Relations Assn. of B.C. Vancouver 1970-75; served with Royal Army Service Corps 1951-53, rank Sgt.; mem. Univ. of B.C. Senate 1970-75, Bd. of Govs. 1972-75; Econ. Council of Can. 1976-79; Bd. of Dirs., Council for Candn. Unity since 1977; Bd. of Dirs., Contact Canada since 1977; Bd. of Trustees, St. Vincent Hosp., Vancouver, 1980-; Bd. of Trustees St. Paul's Hosp. Vancouver 1976-78; Memb. of Council, Candn. Council Christians & Jews (Pacific Region) 1974-77 Vice-Pres., Niagara Inst.; Mem. Caada-West Found'n; Chrmn., Citizes' Comte on Taxation, Munic. of West Vancouver, 1978-79; mem. Bd. Dirs., Candn. Club of Vancouver; Contact Canada since 1978; Mem. Nat. Council & B.C. & Yukon Council - The Duke of Edinburgh's Award in Canada; Vancouver Bd. of Trade; former mem. Constr. Indust. Adv. Council B.C.; Hon. mem. Boys & Girls Clubs Vancouver; prepared report on German Indust. Relations for Fed. Dept. of Labour 1976; Vice-Pres., Admin. Services, Univ. of B.C. 1975-80; prepared report on Japanese Industrial Relations for Fed. Dept. of Labour, 1981; author number articles indust. and labour relations fields; Past Extve. mem. Indust. Relations Sec. Candn. Pulp & Paper Assn.; recipient of Queen's Jubilee Medal; Beta Theta Pi; Liberal; R. Catholic; recreations: squash, tennis, fishing; Clubs: Tent 47; Clubs-(dir.) Candn. Club, Vancouver; Variety Clubs Internat.; Variety (W. Canada); Canadian Club; Faculty Club, Univ. of B.C.; Hollyburn Country; Home: 4626 Woodgreen Dr., West Vancouver, B.C. V7S 2V2

CONNELL, George E., Ph.D., F.C.I.C., F.R.S.C.; biochemist; b. Saskatoon, Sask., 20 June 1930; s. James Lorne and Mabel Gertrude (Killins) C.; e. Upper Can. Coll., Toronto; Univ. of Toronto, B.A. 1951, Ph.D. 1955; m. Sheila Harriet Horan, 27 Dec. 1955; children: James, Thomas, Caroline, Margaret; PRES., UNIV. OF WESTERN ONT., since 1977; Prof., Dept. of Biochem., Univ. of Toronto (Chrmn. 1965-70); Assoc. Dean Faculty of Med. 1972-74; Vice Pres. (Research & Planning) 1974-77; mem., Med. Research Council 1966-70; Ont. Council of Health, 1978; Chmn., Council of Ont. Univ., 1981-83; writings incl. over 50 scient. articles for various journs.; mem., Candn. Biochem. Soc. (Pres. 1973-74); Am. Soc. Biol. Chem.; Anglican; recreations: squash, sailing, Home: 1836 Richmond St., London, Ont. N6A 4B6; Office: University of Western Ontario, London, Ont.

CONNELL, J(ames) Peter; federal public servant; b. Halifax, N.S., 23 Sept. 1926; s. James Walter and late Kathryn Whitman (Sanders) C.; e. N.S. High Schs.; Acadia Univ.; m. Ella Catherine, d. late Murdoch Gordon MacLeod children: James, David, Bruce, Douglas, Jeffrey, Elizabeth, Barbara, Kathryn; DEPY. MIN. OF NATIONAL REVENUE FOR CUSTOMS AND EXCISE since 1975; Chrmn., Customs Co-operation Council (1980-82); Employment Supvr. Frigidaire Products of Canada Ltd. Toronto 1950-52; Asst. Personnel Mgr. Lucas-Rotax Ltd. 1952-55; Indust. Relations Mgr. Union Carbide Canada Ltd. Belleville and Montreal 1955-60; Dir. Employee Relations Allied Chemical Canada Ltd. Montreal 1961-66; Dir. Personnel, Dept. of Nat. Revenue Customs and Excise 1966-67; Dir. Gen. Personnel, Dept. of Transport 1967-68; Depy. Secy. Treasury Bd. 1969-75; United Church; recreations: fishing, farming; Home: Oxford Station, Ont. K0G 1T0; Office: Connaught Bldg., Mackenzie Ave., Ottawa, Ont. K1A 0L5

CONNELL, Philip F., B-A., F.C.A.; financial executive; b. Hamilton, Ont. 20 Jan. 1924; s. Maurice Williams and Kathleen C.; e. Delta Coll. Inst. Hamilton 1942; McMaster Univ. B.A. 1946; C.A. 1950; SR. VICE PRES. FINANCE, OSHAWA GROUP LTD. since 1976; joined Clarkson Gordon & Co. 1946-57; Comptroller, Canadian Westinghouse Co. Ltd. 1957-67; Controller, Domtar Ltd. 1967-68; Vice Pres. Finance, George Weston Ltd. 1968-75; mem. Financial Extves. Inst. (Past Pres. Hamilton Chapter); Candn. Inst. C.A.'s (Gov. & Treas.); FCA (1968); United Church; Clubs: National; Hamilton; Home: 400 Walmer Rd. Apt. 2510 W. Toronto, Ont.; M5P 2X7; Office: 302 The East Mall, Toronto, Ont. M9B 6B8

CONNELL, W. Ford, M.D., C.M., F.R.C.P. (Lond.), F.R.C.P.(C), F.A.C.P., LL.D.(1973); educator; b. Kingston, Ont., 24 Aug. 1906; s. Dr. Walter Thomas and Florence (Ford) C.; e. Queen's Univ. Med. Sch., Grad. 1929; Post Grad. training at Toronto Gen. Hosp. (1929-31) and at Freiburg-in-Breisgau, Manchester and London (1931-33); m. Merle Beatrice, d. the late James Bruce, Grand Valley, Ont., 16 Dec. 1933; children: James Douglas, Walter Bruce, Patricia Anne; Fellow in Med., Queen's Univ., 1933-34, Prof. and Chrmn., Dept. of Medicine, 1942-68, Emeritus Prof.; Dir., Heart Dept., Kingston Gen. Hosp. 1933-76, Sr. Consultant since 1976; Asst. Prof. of Med. 1934-37, Assoc. Prof. 1937-43, Capt. R.C.A.M.C. (Reserve); Fellow, Am. Coll. of Cardiology (1961) and Gov. for Ont., 1962; Gov. for Ont., Am. Coll. Phys., 1958-63; mem., Am. Bd. of Internal Med.; Conservative; Freemason (Scot. Rite); recreations: fishing, reading, philately; Home: 11 Arch St., Kingston, Ont. K7L 3L4

CONNELLY, Brig. Gen. Alan Burton, C.B.E. (1945), C.D., B.Eng., Army (retired); b. Amble, Northumberland, Eng., 25 March 1908; s. Thos. and Janet (Burton) C.; e. Pub. Schs. and Crescent Heights High Sch., Calgary, Alta.; Calgary Normal Sch.; Roy. Mil Coll. Can., grad. with Hons. and Gov. General's Silver Medal 1931; Nova Scotia Techn. Coll. (3rd year Elect. Engn.) 1932; McGill Univ., B.Eng. (Civil) 1933; m. Margaret Woodbury, d. G. R. Forbes of Halifax, N.S., 10 Sept. 1937; children: Margaret M., Alan B. F.; m. 2ndly Mary Evelyn Sharpe, d. James Brock, Meadville, Pa.; Lieut., R.C.E. 1931-36; empl. on surveys, training, engn. services, Ottawa, Halifax, Winnipeg and Eng.; Capt. R.C.E.1936-39; Camp Engr., Petawawa; Dist. Engr. Offr., Montreal and Kingston; served in World War 1939-46; Maj., R.C.E., 1939-41, and Adj., R.C.E. 1st Candn. Divn., Eng., attached R.E. 4 Br. Div., France, Apl.-May 1940; Instr. in staff course and staff offr. R.E., Corps Hdqrs.; Lieut.-Col. 1941-43 and C.O., R.C.E., 1st Candn. Divn., 4th Candn. Armoured Divn.; promoted Brig. 1943 and Chief Engr., 1st Candn. Corps, Italy; later Commanded B Group, Candn. Reinforcement Units and Candn. Repatriation Units; Commdr., Candn. Troops, N.W. Europe, July 1946; Depy. Chief of Gen. Staff and Depy. Adj. Gen., Candn.

Mil. Hdqrs., Lond., Eng., 1946; Mentioned in Despatches, Italy 1944; created C.B.E. Depy. Adj. Gen., Army Hdqrs., Ottawa, 1946-48; Commdr. and Chief Engr., N.W. Highway System, 1948-50; Commdr., Sask. Area 1950-51 and G.O.C., Prairie Command, 1951; Commdr. Candn. Mil. Mission, Far East, 1951-52; Korean Medal; U.N. Medal; Coronation Medal; retired 1952; Dufresne Engn., 1953-55; Vice-Pres. (Overseas Operations), Manix Ltd., 1955-56; Vice Pres. and Gen. Mgr., Empire Devel. Co. Ltd., 1956-57; Chief. Engn. Div., Dept. N. Affairs & Nat. Resources 1958-62, Dir., Capital Assistance, External Aid Office, 1963-69, and of Colombo Plan Bureau 1969-73; Adv. Min. Plannning and Finance, Burma 1974-75; Hon. Lt. Col. 3FD. Eng. Regt. (M); life mem. Engn. Inst. of Can.; Caan. Soc'y of Civil Engrs.; Assn. of Prof. Engrs. of Ont.; Mil. Engrs. Assn.; United Church; recreations: golf, diving; Club: University (Montreal); Home: 360 Lake St. Louis Rd., Ville de Lery, Que. J6N 1A3

CONNELLY, Eric, F.C.A.; company executive; b. Amble, Northumberland, Eng., 2 June 1910; s. Thomas and Janet (Burton) C.; e. Calgary Public and Crescent Heights High Sch.; admitted C.A., Alta., 1933; F.C.A. 1957; m. Barbara Violet Ella, d. William Toole, Calgary, Alta., 31 Mar. 1948; one s. Brian William; CHAIRMAN and DIR., Barber Engineering & Supply Co. Ltd.; Barber Engn. and Controls Ltd.; Besco Industrial Products Ltd., Canex Trading Ltd.; Canex Edible Oils, Ltd.; Dir., Turbo Resources Ltd.; Bankeno Mines Ltd.; Queenstown Gold Mines Ltd.; L.K. Resources, Ltd.; Eau Claire Estates, Ltd.; Merland Exploration Ltd.; Can. Exec. Overseas; Calgary Chamber of Commerce; Formerly: Chairman, Pembina Pipeline Ltd.; Pres. Panarctic Oils, Ltd.; Vice-Pres. and Dir. Loram Ltd.; Pres., Calgary Chamber of Comm.; Alta. Tuberculosis Assn. (Dir. 1943-48): Dir., Inst. of Chartered Accts. of Alta. (Council 1948-55; Pres. 1954); Hon. Treas., Calgary Exib. and Stampede, (1975-77); Newcomen Soc.; Freemason (32° Scot Rite), Shriner; Anglican; Clubs: Ranchmen's (Pres.); Calgary Petroleum; Calgary Golf & Country; Glencoe; Rotary; Mill Reef (Antigua); Wailea Golf (Hawaii); Home: Apt. 4 S., Covenant House, 222 Eagle Ridge Drive, S.W., Calgary, Alta. T2V 2V7; Office: 6th Floor, 1035-7th Ave. S.W., Calgary, Alta. T2P 1A8

CONNOLLY, Hon. John Joseph, P.C., O.B.E., Q.C., Ph.D., LL.D.; senator; b. Ottawa, Ont., 1 Oct. 1906; s. Patrick T. and Josephine (Macdonald) C.; e. Univ. of Ottawa; Queen's Univ.; Univ. of Notre Dame; Univ. of Montreal, LL.B.; m. Ida B., d. J. E. Jones, Ottawa, Ont., 1938; children: Peter Charles, John Macdonald; mem. Bars of Ont. and Que.; cr. Q.C. 1947; Extve. Asst. to Min. of Nat. Defence for Naval Services, 1941-45; Counsel to Honeywell Wotherspoon; former mem., Council of Candn. Bar. Assn.; mem. Parlty. Del. to Atlantic Cong. (NATO) 1959 and to NATO Parlty. meeting, Washington, 1959; Pres., Nat. Liberal Fed., 1961-64; summoned to the Senate of Can., June 1953; Min. Without Portfolio and Govt. Leader in the Senate, 1964-68; C.P.A., Chrmn. Gen. Council 1965-66, mem. Extve. Comte. 1967-70; Past Pres. Gen., Candn. Catholic Hist. Assn.; Past Pres., English Catholic Educ. Assn. Ont.; Co. Carleton Law Assn.; Liberal; R. Catholic; Clubs: Rideau; Royal Ottawa; Home: 281 Roger Road, Ottawa, Ont. K1H 5C5;

CONNOR, Harold P., B.A., LL.B.; executive; b. Montreal, Que., 9 Aug. 1913; s. Harold George and Theresa Eleanor (Palmatary) C.; e. Horton Acad. Wolfville, N.S.; Dalhousie Univ. B.A., LL.B.; m. Elisabeth Campbell d. Arnold Saunderson, Halifax, N.S., 21 Sept. 1938; children: Ann, Susan, Sara; Denis; Depy. Chrmn., Central & Eastern Trust Co.; Chrmn., Halifax Parking Co.; Dir. Halifax Developments: Phoenix Insurance Co. of Canada; Nat. Sea Products Ltd. (ret'd.); Acadia Life Ins. Co. Ltd.; mem. Lloyd's of London; read law with L. A. Lovett; called to Bar of N.S. 1937; served with RCNVR 1939-45, rank Lt.; mem. Bar of N.S.; P. Conservative; Anglican; recreations: golf, sailing, skiing; Clubs: Halifax; Ashburn

Golf; Royal Poinciana Golf; Royal & Ancient Golf (St. Andrews, Scot.); Royal Nova Scotia Yacht Squadron; Home: 1054 Ridgewood Dr., Halifax, N.S. B3H 3Y4

CONNOR, Robert Dickson, B.Sc., Ph.D.; educator; b. Edinburgh, Scot. 15 May 1922; s. Robert and Jane Black (Dickson) C.; e. George Heriot's Sch. Edinburgh; Univ. of Edinburgh B.Sc., 1942, Ph.D. 1949; m. Sheila Carmichael d. William Telfer, Edinburgh, Scot. 27 Dec. 1948; two s. David, Graham; PROFESSOR, FACULTY OF EDUCATION UNIV. OF MANITOBA 1979-; Asst. Lectr. Univ. Edinburgh 1947, Lectr. 1949-57; Assoc. Prof. of Physics Univ. Man. 1957-60, Prof. of Physics, Univ. of Man. 1960-79; Dean of Science Univ. of Man. 1970-79; Assoc. Dean Arts & Science 1963-68, Acting Dean Grad. Studies 1968, Vice Dean Arts & Science and Dean of Science 1968-70; mem., Univs. Grants Comn., Man. 1968-79; served with RAF Tech. Br. 1942-46; rec'd Centennial Award 1967; author over 40 papers in scient. journs. mainly field Nuclear Spectroscopy; mem. Candn. Assn. Physics; Soc. Sigma Xi; United Church; recreations: rare books, swimming; Home: 638 Elm St., Winnipeg, Man. R3M 3P4

CONRAD, Walter Grenville, D.F.C., B.A.; transportation executive; b. Melrose, Ont.; s. Rev. William Walter and Ena Eloise (Trethewey) C.; e. Bedford (Que.) High Sch.; McGill Univ., B.A. 1940; m. Kathleen Onita, d. J. S. Horton, Bergenfield, N.J., 22 Sept. 1945; children: Allan, Brian, Joanne; joined McLeod, Young, Weir & Co., Invest. Dealers, in Montreal, 1945; resigned and joined American Airlines in Montreal, Feb. 1946; seconded to Internat. Air Transport Assn. in Montreal, Jan. 1948-Feb. 1949; District Sales Mgr. for American Airlines in Montreal, Toronto and Baltimore, 1949-51; European Sales Mgr., 1951-54; Dir. of Sales, American Airlines de Mexico 1956-57; Vice Pres., Gen. Mgr. and Dir., 1957-60; Vice Pres., N. Region, 1960-64; Vice Pres. Field Sales, Eastern Air Lines Inc. N.Y. 1964; now a Sr. Extve. of Braniff Airlines, Texas; served in 2nd World War, 1940-45 with R.C.A.F. as Pilot with rank of Wing Commdr.; Grad. of War Staff Coll.; awarded D.F.C. and Bar; United Church; recreations: golf, hunting, fishing; Address: Braniff Airlines, Dallas, Texas.

CONVERY, Frank W., B.A.; advertising executive; b. Peterborough, Ont., 2 Aug. 1925; s. Frank Ernest and Iris (Wray) C.; e. Ridley Coll., St. Catharines, Ont., 1943; Univ. of W. Ont., B.A. 1948; m. Marilyn Joyce, d. MacIntosh Hebb, 11 Sept. 1954; children: Mark A., Steven M., R. Michael; B. Lynn; CHAIRMAN AND PRESIDENT AND DIR., F. H. HAYHURST CO. LTD., since 1970; joined St. Catharines Standard 1948-50; joined present Co. 1950; apptd. Vice Pres. 1960; Dir. of Account Services 1965; Dir. 1967; served with RCAF 1943-45; rank Pilot Offr.; R.N.V.R. (Air Arm) 1945; rank Sub Lt.; mem. Bd. Govs., North York Gen. Hosp.; Bd. of Dir., Inst. of Can. Advertising; mem., Business Council on Nat'l Issues; Kappa Alpha; Protestant; recreations: reading, music, gardening; Club: Donalda; Home: 16 Donmac Dr., Don Mills, Ont. M3B 1N5; Office: 55 Eglinton Ave. E., Toronto, Ont. M4P 1G9

CONVEY, John, Ph.D., D.Sc., F.A.P.S.; b. Craghead, Durham, Eng., 29 Mar. 1910; s. John and Mary (Catterson) C.; e. Alderman Wood Secondary Sch., Durham, Eng.; came to Can. 1929; Univ. of Alta., B.Sc. 1933; M.Sc. 1936; Dipl. of Educ. 1936; Univ. of Toronto, Ph.D. 1940; McMaster Univ., D.Sc. 1959, Univ. Windsor 1965; m. Annette Therese, d. Octave Lemieux, 9543 — 108 Ave., Edmonton, Alta., 30 Dec. 1939; children: Annette, Jaqueline, John, Nicole; Research Phys. on loan to Brit. Admiralty, 1940-46; Rep. of Brit. Admiralty Del. to U.S.A. and Can. 1945; with Brit. Intelligence 1946; served in World War, 1940-46, with R.C.N.V.R.; Assoc. Prof. of Physics, Univ. of Toronto, 1946-48; Chief, Physical Metall. Div., Mines Br., Dept. of Mines & Tech. Surveys, 1948-51; Dir., Mines Dr., Dept. of Energy Mines & Resources 1951-73, since when Sr. Advisor in Mining & Metall. Sc. and Technol. Div.; retired from public service 1975; Fellow Inst. of Phys. of Gt. Brit.; Am. Soc. for Metals; mem., Electro-chem. Soc. of Am.; Am. Inst. Mining & Metall. Engrs.; Candn. Inst. Mining & Metall.; Hon. mem. Inst. of Mining & Metall. of Gt. Britain; winner of Sorby Prize for Research Work in Metals, Sheffield, Eng., 1942; awarded The Blaylock Medal by Canadian Institute of Mining & Metall. for contrib. to devel. of controlled atomic energy in Can., 1956; Special Centennial Plaque by Candn. Inst. of Mining & Metall., 1967, for outstanding contrib. to mining and metall.; has contrib. many scient. articles to current journs.; R. Catholic; recreations: athletics, art; Club: Newman; Address: Box 265 Shore Lane, P.O. Box 70, Wasaga Beach, Ont. L0L 2P0

CONWAY, Brian Evans, Ph.D., D.I.C., D.Sc., F.R.S.C., F.R.I.C., F.C.I.C.; educator; b. London, Eng. 26 Jan. 1927; s. Arthur George and Ethel (Evans) C.; e. Imp. Coll. of Science & Technol. London B.Sc. 1946, Ph.D. 1949, D.I.C.; Univ. of London, D.Sc. 1961; m. Nina Protopopos; one child Adrian; PROF. AND CHRMN. OF CHEM., UNIV. OF OTTAWA since 1975; Consultant, Hooker Chemical Co.; Brookhaven National Lab.; Continental Group (N.Y.); Chrmn. of Chem. Univ. Ottawa 1966-69; mem. Nat. Research Council Chem. Grant Comte. 1975-78; rec'd Chem. Inst. Noranda Award 1964, Medal 1976; author "Electrochemical Data" 1952; "Theory and Principles of Electrode Processes" 1964; co-ed. "Chemical Physics of Ionic Solutions" 1966; "Modern Aspects of Electrochemistry" 13 vols. 1954-present; over 250 research papers scient. journs.; Home: 757 Acacia Lane, Ottawa, Ont.; Office: 365 Nicholas St., Ottawa, Ont. K1N 9B4.

CONWAY, Geoffrey, B.Com., D.B.A., C.A.; broadcasting executive; b. Toronto, Ont. 2 Nov. 1933; s. Dr. Clifford B. and Clara B. (Lisk) C.; e. High Sch., Victoria, B.C.; Victoria (B.C.) Coll., Gold Medallist 1952; Univ. of B.C., B.Com. (Gold Medallist) 1956; C.A. 1958 (B.C. Gold and Can. Silver Medallist); Harvard Univ. (Ford Foundation Fellowship) D.B.A. 1973; m. Sylvane, d. Henry G. Barnes, Pontypridd, Wales; children: Michael John, Alison Jane Ilitta, Amanda Roseann Elizabeth; PRESIDENT AND DIR., CUC LTD. since 1968; Pres. and Dir., Northern Cable Services Ltd.; Northern Microwave Ltd.; Sudbury Cable Services Ltd.; Timmins Cable Services Ltd.; Cable Communications Ltd. and Trillium Cable Communications Ltd.; Vice-Pres. & Dir. Bay Ridges Cable TV Ltd.; with Clarkson Gordon & Co. Vancouver and Toronto, Acct. and Income Tax Specialist 1956-61; Special Asst. to Min. of Finance, Ottawa 1963; Research Supv., Royal Comn. on Taxation 1963-67; Special Lectr., York Univ. Business Sch. 1967-73; Consultant, Finance and Broadcasting since 1967; mem. Candn. Inst. C.A.; Candn. Cable TV Assn. (Past Chrmn. Long Range Planning and Policy Comte.); author of "Supply of, and Demand for, Canadian Equities" (Toronto Stock Exchange and Fed. Govt. Task Force on Foreign Invest. co-sponsors) 1970; also two studies for Royal Comn. on Taxation and Capital Gains 1968; Pentacostal; Home: R.R. #3, Newmarket, Ont. L3Y 4W1; Office: Unit 33, 705 Progress Ave., Scarborough, Ont. M1H 2X2

COO, (Norman) Douglas, LL.B.; judge; b. Montreal, Que. 15 Feb. 1931; s. Hugh Douglas Coo; e. Upper Can. Coll. Toronto 1948; Univ. of Toronto Law Sch. LL.B. 1952; m. Anne Butchart Gibson 24 May 1974; one s. Christopher; SR. JUDGE, DIST. OF YORK since 1979; called to Bars of B.C. and Ont. 1953; cr. Q.C. 1964; practiced law with Shearer and Coo 1953-73; apptd. Co. Court Judge 1973; Past Gen. Counsel and Dir., Candn. Diabetic Assn.; Past mem. Operating Comte. Centre for Adult Educ. Toronto; Faculty of Law Capt. Varsity Fund 1962-63; mem. Faculty of Law Alumni Assn. (Past Pres.); Co. York Law Assn.; Advocates Soc. (Past Dir. and Program Chrmn.); Lawyers' Club Toronto; Candn. Bar Assn.;

Lectr. in Comm. Law, Univ. of Toronto 1956-57, Lectr. in Law (Extension) 1957-60; Anglican; recreation: travel; Clubs: Albany; Toronto Lawn Tennis; Home: Apt. 813, 44 Jackes Ave., Toronto, Ont. M4T 1E5; Office: 361 University Ave., Toronto, Ont. M5G 1T3.

COOK, (Charles) Reginald, C.A.; brewery executive; b. Montreal, Que. 21 Jan. 1919; s. Charles and Edith Mabel (Ironman) C.; e. St. Lambert (Que.) High Sch. 1936; Westhill High Sch. Montreal 1937; McGill Univ. C.A. 1947; m. Anne Margaret Milton 22 June 1946; three d. Dorothy Louise, Barbara Isabel, Carol Elaine; VICE PRES. AND SECY., THE MOLSON COMPANIES LTD.; articled with McDonald Currie & Co. 1937-49; held various positions incl. Vice Pres. Finance and Dir. Johnson & Johnson Ltd. 1949-65; Controller present Co. Montreal 1965, Vice Pres., Finance; Dir. Can. Safety Council; Dir. and Past Pres. Extve. Devel. Inst. Montreal; served with RCAF 1941-45, Africa & India; mem. & Comte. Chrmn. Toronto Chapter Financial Extves. Inst. (Past Pres. Montreal Chapter); Presbyterian; recreations: swimming, gardening, home repair and improvement; Club: National; Home: 17 Tettenhall Rd., Islington, Ont. M9A 2C2; Office: 2 International Blvd., Rexdale, Ont. M9W 1A2.

COOK, Hon. Eric, Q.C.; senator; b. St. John's Nfld., 26 July 1909; s. Hon. Sir Tasker and Henriettea L. (Pennock) C.; e. Bishop Feild Coll., St. John's, Nfld.; m. Mary A., d. Frederick W. Angel, St. John's, Nfld., 17 July 1935; children: Peter Pennock, David Angel, Jonathan Bartlett, Elizabeth Sheridan; summoned to Senate of Can., 14 Feb. 1964; called to Bar of Nfld. 1932; cr. K.C. 1946; Anglican; Address: The Senate, Ottawa, Ont. K1A 0A4

COOK, Gail C.A., M.A., Ph.D.; b. Ottawa, Ont.; d. William Harrison and Ina (Stephens) C. m. Roy F. Bennett; e. Rockcliffe Park Pub. Sch. 1953 and Lisgar Coll. inst. 1958 Ottawa; Carleton Univ. B.A. 1962; Univ. of Mich. M.A. 1965, Ph.D. (Econ.) 1968; EXTVE. VICE PRES. C. D. HOWE RESEARCH INST. 1977-78; Econ. consultant 1979-; Sr. Adviser to Chrmn. of Econ. Council of Can. 1979-80; Dir. The Manufacturers Life Insurance Co. and Hiram Walker-Consumer Home Ltd.; mem., Bd. of Dir., Inst. for Research on Pub. Policy 1979-80; mem. of Council & Extve. Comte., Soc. Sci. & Humanities Research Council 1978-81; mem. of Council & Research Policy Comte., Ont. Econ. Council, 1979-; mem. of Premier of Ont. Adv. Comte. on Confederation, 1979-; mem. of Bd., Candn. Opera Co., 1980-; Research Asst. Royal Comn. on Health Services 1962-63, Royal Comn. on Taxation 1964, Econ. Council of Can 1965, Doctoral Fellow in Urban & Regional Econ. Wayne State Univ. 1967-68; Asst. Prof. of Econ. Univ. of Toronto 1968-74; Dir of Research Candn. Econ. Policy Comte. and Project Dir. Stat. Can. Study on Econ. Role of Women in Can. present Inst. 1974-76; Expert Witness to Hamilton-Burlington-Wentworth Local Govt. Review 1969; Advisor to Govt. of Man. Local Govt. Boundaries Comn. Report 1970; Conrib. to Adv. Task Force on Housing Policy Prov. Ont.; mem. Ont. Econ. Council Task Force & Local Regional Govt. Data 1975; Ed. Bd. Candn. Pub. Policy-Analyse de Politiques; author various reports, articles book chapters reviews on pub. finance and urban econ.; Ed. "Opportunity for Choice: A Goal for Women in Canada" 1976; former mem. Extve. Council Candn. Econ. Assn.; Presbyterian; recreations: skating, skiing, tennis; Home: 844 Ingersoll Court Mississauga, Ontario L5J 2S1

COOK, Harry D.; company executive; Formerly Pres. and Gen. Mgr., Abbott Laboratories Ltd.; Pres., Pharm. Mfrs. Assn. of Can., 1950-51, 1963-65; Village Commissioner; mem. of Bd., Water Utility; Home: 1255 Commercial St., Kentville, N.S. B4N 3G3

COOK, Rt. Rev. Henry George, D.D. (Ang.); b. London, Eng., 12 Oct. 1906; s. Henry George and Ada Mary (Ovens) C.; came to Can. 1912; e. Huron Coll., London,

Ont., L.Th. 1935; Univ. of W. Ont., B.A. 1935, Hon. D.D. 1948; m. Opal May (B.A.), d. Wesley Thompson, London, Ont., 4 June 1935; children: David, Peter, Barbara; mem. Anglican Gen. Synod 1944-74; served as Missy. at Fort Simpson, N.W. Terr. 1935-43; Canon, Diocese of Athabasca 1940; Sr. Curate, St. Paul's Bloor St. Ch., Toronto, Ont., 1943-44; Rector of S. Porcupine 1944-45; Archdeacon of James Bay, 1945-47; Princ., Bishop Horden Sch., Moose Factory, 1945-47; Hon. Canon, Diocese of Moosonee, 1948; Supt., Indian Sch. Adm., Can., 1948-63; Suffragan Bishop of the Arctic; 1963-66, Bishop of MacKenzie 1966-74; Co-ordinator of Hist. Programs, Govt. of N.W.T. 1974-79; served some time apprenticeship of five yrs. to the trade of toolmaking and received papers from John Morrow Co., Ingersoll, Ont.; served four years with C.O.T.C.; Hon. Canon, Cath. of Athabasca (1940); Conservative; recreations: mechanical models, boating; Address: 15 Plainfield Court, Stittsville, Ont., K0E 3G0

COOK, Leslie Gladstone, M.B.E. F.C.I.C.; research chemist; b. Paris, Ont., 12 July 1914; s. late Rev. William Andrew and Maude Marion C.; e. Brantford (Ont.) Coll. Inst.; Univ. of Toronto, 1932-36 (1st Class Hons. Physics and Chem. and Gertrude Davis Exchange Fellowship); Univ. of Berlin (Kaiser Wilhelm Inst. für Chemie); Dr. of Nat. Sciences 1938; Cambridge Univ. 1938-40; m. Alfreda Mary, d. late Alfred Thomas Crutcher, 26 Dec. 1940; children: Patricia Joan, Leslie Pamela, Andrew George; PRES., L. G. COOK ASSOCS. INC. (consulting on energy sci. and technol.) since 1977; Research Chemist and Physicist, Aluminum Laboratories Ltd., Arvida, Que., Toronto and Kingston, Ont. 1939-45; National Research Council, Chalk River, Ont., 1945-52; Chemist, Atomic Energy of Can. Ltd., 1952-56; General Electric Research Lab., 1956-68 (Project Analyst, 1956-59, Mgr. Project Analysis and Program Planning Secs., 1959-68); Mgr., Program Planning and Analysis Group, Corp. Research Staff, Esso Research and Engn., 1969; Delegue Gen. for Policy and Planning, National Research Council 1968-69; United Church; recreations: music; piano; Office: 98 Hobart Ave., Summit, N.J. 07901

COOK, Melville, Mus.D., F.R.C.O.; musician; b. Gloucester, Eng., 18 June 1912; s. Harry Melville and Vera Louis (Samuel) C.; e. King's Sch., Gloucester, Eng.; m. Marion Weir Moncrieff, 1944; Organist and Choirmaster, All Saints Ch., Cheltenham, Eng. 1935, Leeds (Eng.) Parish Ch. 1937, Hereford (Eng.) Cath. 1956, All Saints' Ch. Winnipeg, Man. 1966, Metrop. Un. Ch., Toronto, since 1967; Conductor, Halifax Choral Soc., Eng., 1948-56; Leeds Guild of Singers 1948-51; Three Choirs Festivals 1958, 1961, 1964; Winnipeg Philharmonic Choir 1966-67; Metrop. Festival Choir, Toronto, since 1968; has examined for organ and piano in Eng. and Can.; adjudicated at music festivals in Gt. Brit., Can., Hong Kong and Europe; has recorded for EMI and RCA; appeared as concert pianist, lectr. and organist in Europe and Can.; served with RA in UK, E. Africa, Ceylon and India 1941-46; mem. Toronto Musicians Assn.; Inc. Soc. Musicians (Eng.); Royal Candn. Coll. Organists; recreation: hiking; Home: 6 Glen Gannon Dr., Toronto, Ont. M4B 2W4; Office: 51 Bond St., Toronto, Ont. M5B 1X1

COOK, Ramsay, M.A., Ph.D., F.R.S.C. (1968); university professor; b. Alameda, Sask., 28 Nov. 1931; s. George Russell and Lillie Ellen (Young) C.; e. Pub. and High Schs., Sask. and Man.; Univ. of Man., B.A. 1954; Queen's Univ., M.A. 1955; Univ. of Toronto, Ph.D. 1960; m. Margaret Eleanor, d. Dr. J. S. Glen, Thornhill, Ont.; children: Margaret Michele, Markham Glen; PROF. OF HISTORY YORK UNIV.; previously Prof. of History, Univ. of Toronto; Ed., Canadian Historical Review, 1963-68; Chmn. of Bd., Can. Inst. for Historical Microreproduction; Visiting Prof. of Candn. Studies, Harvard Univ., 1968-69; Bicentennial Prof. of Cdn. History, Yale Univ. 1978-79; awarded Pres.'s Medal (Univ. of W. (Ont.),

Scholarly Article Category 1966, 1968; author of "The Politics of John W. Dafoe and the Free Press", 1963; "Canada: A Modern Study", 1964; "Canada and the French Canadian Question", 1966; "Canada 1896-1921; A Nation Transformed" (with R. C. Brown) 1975; Ed. "The Dafoe-Sifton Correspondence", 1967; "Provincial Autonomy, Minority Rights and the Compact Theory", 1969; "The Maple Leaf Forever" 1971; Ed. "French Canadian Nationalism: An Anthology", 1969; "The Proper Sphere" (with W. Mitchinson) 1977; awarded Tyrrell Medal of Roy. Soc. Can. (for contrib. to hist. scholarship, 1975; mem., Candn. Hist. Assn.; Univ. League for Soc. Reform (Past Pres.); recreations: theatre, music, movies, bird watching; Home: 65 Woodlawn Ave. W., Toronto, Ont. M4V 1G6

COOK, Sidney Jabez, M.A., F.C.I.C.; economic chemist; b. Owen Sound, Ont., 22 Mar. 1889; s. late William and Louisa (Morgan) C.; e. Univ. of Toronto, B.A. 1914, with Hons. in Chem. and Minerol.; Fellow in Chem., 1914-15; Dipl. as Pub. Analyst, 1915; Univ. of Ottawa, M.A. (in French) 1936; m. 1st, Amy Rose (died 1946), d. late Captain Daniel Rooney; 2ndly, Gertrude Mary, d. Lieutenant-Colonel J. A. McKenna, Ottawa, Ont., 23 June 1951; Dom. Analyst, Food and Drug Labs., Trade and Commerce Dept., 1915-18; Chief of the Mining, Metall. and Chem. Br., Dom. Bur. of Stat. 1919-30; Research Investigator in the Divn. of Research Information, National Research Council, Ottawa, Ont., 1930-37; seconded for duty as Gen. Secy. and Ed., "Proc." (5 vols.), Fifth Pac. Science Cong. (Vancouver, 1933), 1932-34; Offr. i/c Research Plans and Publ. 1938-46; Offr. i/c Public Relations Br., Nat. Research Council, 1947-54, when retired; Lectr. in Chem., St. Patrick's Coll., 1955-61; Secy. Candn. Del., Brit. Commonwealth Scient. Conf., London, Eng., 1936; Secy., War Inventions Bd. 1939-43; Extve. Secy., Med. Research Comtes. 1942-46; made reports in govt. bulls. on food and drug analyses between 1915 and 1918; and stat. reports, 1919-30; author of "First Directory of the Chemical Industries in Canada", 1919; initiated the following reports "Chemicals and Allied Products", 1919; "Iron and Steel", 1920; "Non-Ferrous and Non-Metallic Manufactures.", 1919-23; and "Coal Statistics", made contrib. to scient. and trade journals on above subjects up to 1930 and later on scient. research and ed. practice; Assoc., Roy. Inst. Chem., 1918-54; mem. (1918) and Candn. Corr. (1918-64); Am. Chem. Soc.; one of the Founders and for 5 yrs Hon. Secy., Prof. Inst. Civil Service Can.; Fellow, Charter mem., and mem. of first Council, Chem. Inst. Can. (Chrmn., Ottawa Section, 1926); el. Hon. Fellow, Chem. Inst. of Can. 1980; mem. and 1958-64 a Dir., Ottawa Neighbourhood Services; United Church; Club: Canadian; Home: 140 Broadway Ave., Ottawa, Ont. K1S 2V8

COOK, William Harrison, O.C. (1969), O.B.E., M.Sc., Ph.D., LL.D., D.Sc., F.A.I.C., F.R.S.C., F.C.I.C.; retired; b. Alnwick, Northumberland, Eng., 2 Sept. 1903; s. Peter and Jean (Maitland) C.; came to Can. 1912; e. Claresholm, Alta., Sch. of Agric. diploma; Univ. of Alta., B.Sc. 1926 M.Sc. 1928; Leland Stanford Univ., Ph.D. 1931; Univ. of Sask., LL.D. 1948; Laval Univ., D.Sc. 1963; m. Ina Helen, d. Chas. Alex Stephens, 21 Aug. 1932; children: Glenn, Gail, Nancy; Hon. Secy., Royal Soc. of Can. 1950-53, Pres. of Sec. V, 1956-57, Vice-Pres. of the Soc. 1961-62 and Pres. 1962-63; Ed.-in-Chief "Canadian Journal of Research", 1943-47; served as Research Asst., Univ. of Alta. 1924-30; Jr. Research Biol., Nat. Research Labs., Ottawa, 1930-35; Assoc. Research Biol. 1935-41; Dir., Div. of Biosciences, Nat. Research Council, 1941-68; Extve. Dir., Nat. Research Council 1968-69; Dir. Gen., Candn. Comn. for I.B.P. 1969-74; has contrib. over 150 scient. and tech. papers in plant biochem., food chem., refrigerated storage and transport of food, structure of lipoproteins and macromolecules; Fellow, Agric. Inst. of Can.; Charter mem., Inst. of Food Tech.; Vice-Pres., Candn. Biochem. Soc., 1964-65; Pres. 1965-66; Pres., Biol.

Council of Can., 1968-69; Trustee, Biol. Abstracts 1955-60; mem., Bd. of Govs., Univ. of Guelph, 1965-71; Fellow, Am. Assn. Advanc. Science; Coronation Medal, 1952; Centennial Medal, 1967; Elizabeth II 25th Anniv. Medal, 1977; Phi Lambda Upsilon; Sigma Xi; United Church; Home: 201 Maple Lane, Rockcliffe, Ont. K1M 1G9

COOKE, Jack Kent; company executive; publisher; b. Hamilton, Ont., 25 Oct. 1912; s. Ralph Ercil and Nancy (Jacobs) C.; e. Malvern Coll. Inst., Toronto, Ont.; m. Barbara Jean, d. William Carnegie, Port Perry, Ont., 5 May 1934; children: Ralph, John; PRESIDENT AND TREAS., JACK KENT COOKE INC. (Cooke Publishing Co. and American Cablevision Co.); Owner, Los Angeles Kings Hockey Club; joined Northern Broadcasting and Publishing Ltd., 1935; Partner, Thomson Cooke Newspapers, 1937-52; Pres., radio stn. CKEY, Toronto; 1944-61; Pres. and Publisher, Liberty of Canada, Ltd. & Consolidated Press Ltd. 1947-61; Pres., Consolidated Frybrook Industries Ltd., 1952-61; Micro Plastics Ltd., 1955-61; Comn. of Bd., Transam Microwave Inc. 1965-69; 1st Vice-Pres. Pro Football Inc.; Pres., The Forum of Inglewood Inc., 1966-; Dir., Chmn Exec Comte H&B Am. Corp. 1969-70; Chmn. CEO Teleprompter Corp, 1974-; The Ercil Corp., The JKC Corp. jt. owner, Donald Cooke Inc., radio stn. and newspaper reps. N.Y.C., Chicago, San Francisco and Hollywood; Pres., Guild Radio Features, Toronto; Robinson Industrial Crafts Ltd., London, Ont., Aubyn Investments Ltd.; Vice Pres. and Dir., Pro-Football Inc. (Washington Redskins, Nat. Football League), Washington; purchased Los Angeles Lakers of Nat. Basketball Assn., 1965; Trustee, Little League Found., City of Hope; Bd. Govs., Arthritis Found. Clubs: National (Toronto); R.C.Y.C. (Toronto); Bel Air Country (Los Angeles); Eldorado Country (Palm Desert). Address: Fallingbrooke, Route 1, Box 72, Upperville VA. 22176

COOKSON, Hon. John William(Jack), M.L.A., B.Sc.; politician; b. Lougheed, Alta. 29 Oct. 1928; s. Herbert and Catherine C.; e. Banff (Alta.) High Sch.; Univ. of Alta. B.Sc. (Agric.), Prof. Cert. Educ. 1956; m. Winnifred Ann d. late Norman Doupe, Wetaskiwin, Alta. 23 June 1956; children: Bruce, John, Robert, Sally; farm operator; el. M.L.A. 1971, re-el. since; Party Whip 1971-75; MIN. OF ENVIRONMENT, ALTA. 1979- ; Co. Councillor Lacombe 1964-71; P. Conservative; Protestant; Home: R.R. 3, Lacombe, Alta. T0C 1S0; Office: Legislative Bldgs., Edmonton, Alta. T5K 2B6

COON, Burwell Ranscier, B.A.Sc. (Arch.), F.R.I.B.A., F.R.A.I.C.; b. London, Ont., 5 May 1892; s. Stephen Burwell and Elizabeth Ann (McLeod) C., e. Univ. of Toronto, B.A.Sc. in Arch. 1913; studied arch. in New York and Paris; m. Beatrice Hilda (d. 1963), d. F. A. Turner, Toronto, Ont., June 1923; children: Isabel Blanche, Eleanor Elizabeth; m. 2ndly, Mrs. Kathleen Squires Jackson, d. H. F. Squires, Toronto, 1966; has practised for many years with S. B. Coon & Son, Archs., Toronto, estbd. 1912; mem., Ont. Assn. of Archs. (Past Vice-Pres.); Past Pres., Roy. Arch. Inst. Can.; Past Chancellor Coll. of Fellows, R.A.I.C.; Freemason (P.M.); Protestant; recreation: golf; Clubs: Rosedale Golf; Weston Golf & Country; Arts & Letters; University; Home: 235 St. Clair Ave. W., Toronto, Ont. M4V 1R4

COOPER, Hon. Arthur Gordon, B.Comm., B.C.L., LL.D., D.C.L.; judge; b. Saint John, N.B., 11 Dec. 1908; s. George Thomas and Mary Jane Underhill (Peters) C.; e. Kings Coll. Sch., Windsor, N.S.; Dalhousie Univ., B.Com. 1931, LL.D. 1968; Oxford Univ., (Rhodes Scholar, N.S. 1932), B.A. 1934, B.C.L. 1935; m. Helen Olive Hendery, 27 Sept. 1939; three s., George Thomas Hendery, John Geoffrey, Stephen Hugh; JUSTICE, SUPREME COURT OF N.S. (APPEAL); read law with Russell McInnes, Q.C.; called to Bar of N.S. 1938; cr. Q.C. 1955; served with RCAF, Personnel (Legal) Br., during 2nd World War; Past Pres., Candn. Bar Assn.; LL.D.,

Dalhousie Univ.; D.C.L. Univ. of King's Coll., N.S.; Phi Kappa Pi; Anglican; recreation: reading; Clubs: Halifax, Saraguay; Home: 1036 Ridgewood Dr., Halifax, N.S. B3H 3Y4; Office: Law Courts, Halifax, N.S.

COOPER, Austin Morley, Q.C., B.Com.; barrister; b. Toronto, Ont. 10 Feb. 1929; s. Bert and Esther (Michaelson) C.; e. Univ. of Toronto Schs. 1945; Univ. of Toronto B.Com. 1949; Osgoode Hall Law Sch. 1953; children: Peter Meredith, Douglas Anthony, Paul Warren; called to Bar of Ont. 1953; cr. Q.C. 1964; law practice Toronto since 1953; Bencher, Law. Soc. Upper Can.; Fellow, Foundation for Legal Research in Can.; mem. Advocates' Soc.; Candn. Bar Assn. (mem. Special Comte. on Judiciary); Pi Lambda Phi; Jewish; recreations: sailing, skiing, walking; Home: Apt. 2014, 44 Jackes Ave., Toronto, Ont. M4T 1E5; Office: Suite 600, 111 Richmond St. W., Toronto, Ont. M5H 2H5.

COOPER, Hon. Donald E.; judge; b. Hamilton, Ont. 1 Jan. 1928; s. Edward James and Alice (Boardman) C.; e. Central Coll. Inst. 1946; McMaster Univ. B.A. 1950; Osgoode Hall Law Sch. 1954; m. Helen Louise; children: Edward Ralph Jay, Donald Bradley, Michael Randall, Pamela Jayne; JUDGE, UNIFIED FAMILY COURT 1979- ; called to Bar of Ont. 1954; cr. Q.C. 1964; law practice Agro, Cooper, Zaffiro, Parente, Orzel & Hubar 1954-76; private law practice 1976-79; apptd. Co. & Dist. Court Judge 1979; mem. Bd. Govs. McMaster Univ. 1976-79; Pres., Hamilton Lawyers' Club 1972-73; mem. Advocate Soc.; Candn. Bar Assn.; Hamilton Law Assn. (Trustee and Secy. 1966-67); Ont. Family Court Judges Assn.; County Court Judges Assn.; Candn. Inst. for the Admin. of Justice; Anglican; recreations: skiing, tennis; Club: Niagara Falls; Sertoma (Past Internat. Dir.); Home: 9317 Niagara Parkway, Niagara Falls, Ont. L2E 6S6; Office: 100 James St. S., Hamilton, Ont. L8P 2Z3.

COOPER, Keith E., M.B., B.S., M.Sc., M.A., D.Sc.; educator; b. Frome, Somerset, Eng. 7 Aug. 1922; s. Allen Cooper; e. Watford (Eng.) Grammar Sch. 1940; St. Mary's Hosp. Med. Sch. London M.B., B.S. 1945; Univ. of London B.Sc. 1948, M.Sc. 1950; Oxford Univ. M.A. 1960, D.Sc. 1971; m. Eileen Mary d. late George A. Cox, Watford, Eng. 22 Aug. 1946; children: John A., Peter Charles; VICE PRES. RESEARCH UNIV. OF CALGARY since 1979 and Prof. of Med. Physiol. since 1969; Lectr. in Physiol. St. Mary's Hosp. Med. Sch. London 1946-48; mem. M.R.C. Unit for Research on Body Temperature Regulation, Radcliffe Infirmary, Oxford, Eng. 1950-69 (Dir. 1960-69); Fellow, St. Peter's Coll. Oxford Univ. 1961-69; mem. Defence Research Bd. Cold Climatic Panel 1970-74, Biosciences Adv. Comte. since 1975; Prof. and Head of Med. Physiol. Univ. Calgary 1969-78; Assoc. Vice Pres., 1978-79; mem. Internat. Union of Physiol. Sciences Comn. on Thermal Physiol. and Teaching of Med. Physiol. since 1976; served with RAF 1948-50, Aviation Med. Inst. Farnborough, rank Flight Lt.; former Dir. and mem. Extve. Calgary Philharmonic Soc.; Dir. Calgary Div. Candn. Cancer Soc.; mem. Extve. Candn. Paraplegic Assn.; coauthor 'Hypothermia for Surgical Practice' 1960; book chapters and numerous articles in scient. journs. on temperature regulation, hypothermia and fever; mem. Am. Physiol. Soc.; Brit. Physiol. Soc.; Candn. Physiol. Soc. (Vice pres. 1974-75, Pres. 1975-76); Brit. med. Research Soc.; Candn. Soc. Clin. Research; Can. fed. Biol. Socs. (Chairman and Pres. 1979-80); Am. Assn. Advanc. Science; N.Y. Acad. Sciences; Undersea Med. Soc.; Sigma Xi; recreations: hiking, skiing, sailing, music, reading old scientific books; Home: 624 Sifton Blvd. S.W., Calgary, Alta. T2T 2K7; Office: 2500 University Drive, Univ. of Calgary, N.W., Calgary, Alta. T2N 1N4.

COOPER, Marsh A., M.A.Sc., D.Sc.; executive; b. Toronto, Ont., 8 Oct. 1912; s. Frederick Webster and Gertrude (Marsh) C.; e. Univ. of Toronto, B.A.Sc., M.A.Sc.; Harvard Univ., post-grad. work; m. Doris Elsie Roos,

1942; PRESIDENT, M.A. COOPER CONSULTANTS INC., Dir., Falconbridge Nickel Mines Ltd.; Corp. Falconbridge Copper; McIntyre Mines Ltd.; Burns Foods Ltd.; The Superior Oil Co.; Abitibi Price Inc.; Canadian Imperial Bank of Commerce; Crown Life Insurance Co.; Extendicare Ltd.; Falconbridge Dominica L. por A.; Kiena Gold Mines Ltd.; W.M. Keck Foundation; Indusmin Ltd.; mem., Assn. Prof. Engrs. of Provs. of Ont., B.C.; Am. Inst. of Mining, Metall. & Petroleum Engrs.; Candn. Inst. of Mining & Metall.; Engineering Inst. of Can.; Soc. Econ. Geologists; Pres. & CED Falconbridge Nickel Mines Ltd. 1969-80; United Ch.; Clubs: Boisclair Fish & Game; The Toronto; Engineers; National; York; Office: P.O. Box 40, Commerce Court West, Toronto, Ont. M5L 1B4

COPE, Raymond Robin, B.A.Sc.; administrator; b. New Westminster, B.C., 21 Aug. 1930; s. late Alice Louise (Hogberg) and Robin Cecil C.; e. Univ. of B.C., B.A.Sc., (Mech. Engn.) 1953; Carleton Univ. 1957-58; Sir George Williams Univ. 1961-63; McGill Univ., grad. work in Econ. 1962-64; m. Mae Margaret Anne, d. late Walter Hawn, 10 Dec. 1955; children: Roy Douglas, Margaret Elaine, Robert Walter; ASSIST. DIR. GEN. (TRAFFIC & INDUSTRY FINANCE) INTERNAT. AIR TRANSPORT ASSN.; Trainee Engr., Candn. Nat. Rlys., 1953-54; Asst. Supvry. Engr. & Supvry. Engr., C.N. Hotels, 1954-59; Planning Co-ordinator and Research Engr., 1960-64; Dir., Rly. and Highway Br. and Dir., Transport, Policy and Research, Dept. of Transport, 1964-68; Vice Pres. (Research) Candn. Transport Comn., 1969-75; joined Comn. 1968; mem., Assn. Prof. Engrs. Ont.; Candn. Transport. Research Forum (Founding Pres.); Protestant; recreations: golf, chess, reading; Home: 32 chemin de la Pralay, 1294 Genthod, Geneva, Switzerland; Office: 26 chemin de Joinville, 1216 Cointrin, Geneva, Switzerland

COPELAND, Clare Robert; b. Toronto, Ont., 1 Feb. 1936; s. Charles Ernest C.; e. Runnymede Coll. Inst., Toronto; Univ. of W. Ont.; m. d. of Edmund Kyes, 3 March 1962; children: Robert Gregory Bruce, Heather Anne; PRESIDENT, OFFICE OVERLOAD LTD.; previously with General Motors before joining present firm; Founding Pres., Candn. Inst. Temp. Services; mem., Bd. Trade Metrop. Toronto; Anglican; recreations: squash, skiing; Clubs: Canadian; R.C.Y.C. Home: 1 Colwood Rd., Islington, Ont. M9A 4E2; Office: 55 Bloor St. W., Toronto, Ont. M4W 1A5

COPES, Parzival, C.D., M.A., PH.D.; university professor; b. Nakusp, B.C., 22 Jan. 1924; s. Jan Coops and Elisabeth Catharina (van Olst) C.; e. Vierde Vijfjarige H.B.S., Amsterdam, 1936-41; Overtoom Business Coll., Amsterdam, 1941-42; Univ. of B.C., B.A. 1949, M.A. 1950; London Sch. of Econ. and Pol. Science, Ph.D., 1956; m. Dina, d. W. P. Gussekloo, Leersum, Netherlands, 1 May 1946; children: Raymond Alden, Michael Ian, Terence Franklin; PROF. DEPT. OF ECON. SIMON FRASER UNIV., since 1964 (Head Dept. 1964-69), Chrmn. 72-75) Director, Centre for Can. Studies Simon Fraser, since 1978; Dir., Inst. of Fisheries Analysis, 1980-; Econ. & Stat., Dom. Bureau of Stat., Ottawa, 1953-57; apptd. Assoc. Prof., Memorial Univ. and successively Head, Dept. of Econ. and Prof., 1957-64; instrumental in founding Inst. of Soc. and Econ. Research there and was 1st Director of Econ. Research; served as Chairman or member of numerous arbitration and conciliation boards; served with Netherlands Resistance Army, 1944; Candn. Army and Brit. Mil. Govt. in Germany, 1945-46; C.O.T.C. 1947-50; Canadian Army (Militia) 1950-63; author of "St. John's and Newfoundland — An Economic Survey", 1961; "The Resettlement of Fishing Communities in Newfoundland" 1972; Econ. Consultant specializing in fisheries resource management; Chrmn. Extve Comte., Pacific Regional Science Conf. Organ., since 1977; mem., Candn. Econ. Assn. (V.Pres. 1971-73); Am. Econ. Assn.; Candn. Assn. Uiv. Teachers; Regional Science Assn.; W. Regional Science

Assn. (Pres. 1977-78); Director, Social Science Fed'n of Can. since 1979 (Vice Pres., 1981-); Can. Regional Science Ass'n.; Law of the Sea Inst.; recreations: photography, travel; Home: 502 St. Andrews Rd., W. Vancouver, B.C. V7S 1V2

COPITHORNE, Maurice Danby, Q.C., B.A., LL.B.; diplomat; b. Vancouver, B.C. 3 July 1931; s. Cecil James and Margery (Hill) C.; e. Univ. of B.C., B.A. 1954, LL.B. 1955; m. Tamako Yagai Aug. 1963; two s. Dan, Asa; AMBASSADOR TO AUSTRIA, Gov. for Can., Internat. Atomic Energy Agency and Candn. Perm. Rep. to UN Indust. Devel. Organ. 1979-; Chmn. IAEA Bd. of Governors, 1980-81; called to Bar of B.C. 1956; joined Dept. of External Affairs as Foreign Service Offr. 1956 serving in various capacities Ottawa and abroad; Fellow, Centre for Internat. Affairs, Harvard Univ. 1974; Dir. Gen. Legal Bureau, Dept. External Affairs Ottawa 1975, Legal Adviser 1977; Candn. Rep. Sixth Comte., UN Gen. Assembly 1975, 1976, 1978; author various articles internat. law; mem. Law Soc. B.C.; Candn. Council Internat. Law; Candn. Bar Assn.; Candn. Human Rights Foundation; Am. Soc. Internat. Law; mem., Sigma Tau Chi Hon. Soc.; Address: Lannerstrasse 27, 1190, Vienna, Austria;

COPLAND, Robert Philip, B. Com., C.A.; b. Kitchener, Ont., 24 March 1922; s. Robert Y. and Eleanor (Gies) C.; e. Pub. and High Schs., Kitchener, Ont.; Univ. of Toronto, B. Com. 1944; Queens Univ., C.A., 1949; m. Doris A., d. Burton R. Lederman, 3 March 1945; two s., Robert Michael, Peter David; CONSULTANT, EXECUTIVE COMPENSATION CONSULTANTS LTD., served in 2nd World War with R.C.A.F., 1943-45; discharged with rank of Pilot Offr.; mem., Ont. Inst. of Chart. Accts.; Kitchener Chamber of Comm.; recreations: golf, skiing, gardening, music; Club: Westmount Golf & Country; Home: 373 Warrington Dr., Waterloo, Ont. N2L 2P7; Office: 678 Belmont Ave. W., Kitchener, Ont. N2M 1N6

COPP, Douglas Harold, O.C. (1971), C.C. (1980), M.D., Ph.D., LL.D., F.R.S.C. (1959), F.R.C.P.(C) (1974), F.R.S. (1971); physiologist; b. Toronto, Ont., 16 Jan. 1915; s. Charles Joseph and Edith M. (O'Hara) C.; e. Univ. of Toronto, B.A. 1936 and M.D. 1939; Ellen Mickle Fellow, 1939-40; Univ. of Calif., Ph.D. (Biochem.) 1943; Queens LL.D. 1970, Toronto 1970; D.Sc., Ottawa 1973, Acadia 1975, British Columbia 1980; m. Winnifred A. Thompson, 15 July 1939; children: Mary, Carolyn, Patricia; PROF. PHYSIOL., UNIV. OF B.C. and Head of the Dept. 1950-80; mem. of Advisory Comn., Medical and Dental Research, National Research Council; Lectr. in Biochem., University of California, 1942-43; Instr. in Physiol. there 1943-45, Asst. Prof. 1945-50; Research Associate, Radiation Lab., 1943-50; Consultant, Nat. Research Council; mem. of Advisory Comm. on Isotope Distribution, U.S.A.E.C. research; biol. studies with radioactive isotopes, iron metabolism, bone metabolism, heavy metals, phosphate depletion, calcium regulation in mammals and fishes, parathyroid and ultimobranchial function, discovered calcitonin and teleocalcin; mem., Am. Physiol. Soc.; Candn. Physiol. Soc. (Past Pres.); Soc. for Exper. Biol. & Med.; Scient. Secy., 2nd Internat. Conf. on Peaceful Uses of Atomic Energy, 1958; Pres., Nat. Cancer Inst. of Can., 1968-70; Faculty Assoc., Univ. of B.C., 1965-66; Acad. of Sci. and Vice Pres., Roy. Soc. of Can. 1978-81; rec'd. Gairdner Foundation Annual Award 1967; Nicolas Andry Award, Assoc. Bone and Joint Surg. 1968; Jacobaeus Mem. Lecture, Gothenbourg, Sweden, 1971; Helsinki Finland, 1980; Faculty of Med. Medal, Univ. of Lund, Sweden, 1971; Jacob Biely Research Prize, Univ. of B.C. 1971, Flavelle Medal, Royal Soc. of Can. 1972; B.C. Science and Eng. Gold Medal, 1980; Steindler Award, Orthopedic Research Soc., 1974; Address: 4755 Belmont Ave., Vancouver, B.C., V6T 1A8

CORBIN, J. Eymard Georges, M.P.; politician; b. Grand Falls, N.B., 2 Aug. 1934; s. late Georges J. and Mariane (Bard) C.; e. Coll. of Bathurst, Bathurst, N.B.; St. Louis Coll., Edmundston, N.B.; Séminaire des Eudistes, Charlesbourg, Que.; m. Yvette Michaud, Drummond, N.B.; three d. Sylvie, Louise, Isabelle; Sch. Teacher, Grand Falls, 1957-59; Journalist, "The Cataract", Grand Falls, 1959-60; Information Offr., Dept. of Youth, N.B., 1961-62; Asst. Dir. 1963-64; Journalist, "L'Evangéline", Moncton, 1962-63; Broadcaster, (NABET) CBC, CBZ Fredericton and CBD Saint John, 1964-66; Dir. of Information, Prov. Comte. for Centennial of Confederation (N.B.), 1966-67; Ed., "Le Madawaska", Edmundston, 1967-68; el. to H. of C. in g.e. 1968; re-el. 1972, 1974, 1979, 1980 for the riding of Madawask-Victoria; Parlty. Secy. to Min. of Fisheries and Forestry, 1970, Min. of Environment 1971-72; Chrmn., Nat. Lib. Caucus 1974-75; Atlantic Provs. Lib. Caucus 1975-76; Del. to Internat. Parlty. Conf. on the Environment, Bonn, June 1971, and the U.N. Conf. on the World Environment, Stockholm 1972; Co-Chmn., Joint Senate and House of Commons Special Comte. on Official Languages, 1980; President, Canadian Section and International Vice-President of the International French speaking parliamentarians association (A-IPLF); Liberal; Office: House of Commons, Ottawa, Ont. K1A 0A6

CORCORAN, Francis L., Q.C., B.A., LL.B.; b. Moncton, N.B., 25 Jan. 1917; s. John Henry and Regina (Gautreau) C.; e. Sacred Heart Acad., Moncton, N.B., and Aberdeen High Sch. there; St. Mary's Coll., Halifax, N.S., B.A. 1938; Dalhousie Law Sch., LL.B. 1941; m. Marie Emily, d. Tom Nowlan, St. Francis, N.B., 28 Dec. 1942; children: Marie, Maureen, Carolyn, Frank, Catherine; read law with W. E. McMonagle; called to the Bar of N.B. 1941; engaged in private practice, 1941-52; Clerk of the Peace (Crown Prosecutor), Westmorland County, 1952-58; apptd. a mem., Tariff Board of Can., 1958, Vice Chrmn. 1959-69; now Chrmn. Expropriations Adv. Bd., Prov. of N.B.; mem., N.B. Barristers Soc.; Candn. Bar Assn.; mem. Ont. Council of Regents, Colleges and Universities; K. of C. (Past Faithful Navigator); B.P.O.E. (Past Exalted Ruler); C.O.F.; United Services Institute; Navy League of Can.; Candn. Cancer Soc. (Vice-Pres., Westmorland Unit); P. Conservative; Roman Catholic; Home: 105 Upton St., Moncton, N.B. E1E 2Z9; Office: 774 Main, Moncton, N.B. E1C 1E8

CORCORAN, Richard S., B.A., C.A.; executive; b. Brantford, Ont. 6 Sept. 1933; e. Waterloo Coll. B.A. 1956; C.A. 1967; m. Joan Margaret, 6 July 1957; children: Stephen Richard, William John; VICE PRES. FINANCE & ADM., LUMMUS CANADA INC.; articled with Glendinning Campbell Jarrett 1956-62; Mgr. Accounting, Foster Wheeler Ltd. 1963-68; Chief Acct. Acres Canadian Bechtel of Churchill Falls 1968-70; Project Controller, Churchill Falls (Labrador) Corp. 1970-74; Brinco Ltd. 1974-75; joined present co. 1975; Home: R.R. 2, 18th Ave., Gormley, Ont. L0H 1G0; Office: 251 Consumers Rd., Willowdale, Ont. M2J 4H4.

CORCORAN, William John, B.A., LL.B.; investment dealer;. b. Toronto, Ont. 2 Apl. 1933; s. John Andrew and Aphra-Mary (Clark) C.; e. Univ. of Toronto Schs. 1951; Univ. of Toronto, Trinity Coll. B.A. 1954, LL.B. 1957; m. Mary Gertrude, d. Dr. Ray Lawson, Montreal, Que. 11 Sept. 1964; children: Heather Mary, William Terence, Michael Andrew, Martha Evans; VICE-PRESIDENT AND DIR., McLEOD YOUNG WEIR LTD. 1978; Dir. The National Life Assurance Co. of Canada; Daon Development Corp.; Debenture & Securities Corp. of Can.; Dominion & Anglo Investment Corp. Ltd.; Candn. & Foreign Securities Co. Ltd.; Victoria & Grey Trust Co.; joined Underwriting Dept. Dominion Securities Corp. 1957; Partner, Jackman Relyea Associates 1959; Asst. to Mr. E. P. Taylor, Argus Corp. 1961; joined Algonquin Building Credits 1963, Pres. 1965; Mem., Governing Council, U. of T.; Exec. Vice-Pres. and Dir. McLeod, Young, Weir, Ltd., Toronto, 1978; Liberal; United Church; recreations: golf, tennis; Clubs: Badminton & Racquet; National Club; Home: (P.O. Box 241) Kleinburg, Ont. L0J 1C0; Office: 4 King St. W., Ste. 1920, Tor. Ont. M5H 1B6

CORISTINE, Edward Stanley, M.B.E.; retired public servant; b. Montreal, Que., 12 March 1912; s. Stanley Budden and Nina (Maclean) C.; e. Bishop's Coll. Sch.; Lennoxville, Que.; Bishop's Univ.; Sir George Williams Univ., Montreal, Que.; m. Elizabeth Roberts; one d., Cynthia Elizabeth; served in 2nd World War, 1941-45 with R.C.A.F. retiring with rank of Sqdn. Leader; (M.B.E.); Anglican; recreation: golf; Clubs: Royal Montreal Golf; Hylands Golf, Ottawa; Home: 32 Marco Lane, Ottawa, Ont. K1S 5A2

CORK, Edwin Kendall, B.Com.; mining executive; b. Toronto, Ont.; s. Stuart Fraser and Ella (Kendall) C.; e. Univ. of Toronto Schs.; Univ. of Toronto Victoria Coll. B.Com. 1954; m. Eve d. late Sir William Slater 31 Dec. 1960; children: Sarah Jane, John Fraser Kendall, Peter Steven Kendall, Mary Elisabeth; SR. VICE-PRES. & TREAS. NORANDA MINES LTD; joined NORANDA MINES LTD. 1959- ; Dir. The Bank of Nova Scotia; E-L Financial Corp. Ltd.; Vice Chrmn. Gov. Council Univ. of Toronto; joined Gilbert Jackson & Associates 1954-59; Phi Gamma Delta; Christian Scientist; Club: National; Home: 94 Keewatin Ave., Toronto, Ont. M4P 1Z8; Office: (P.O. Box 45) Commerce Court West, Toronto, Ont. M5L 1B6.

CORMACK, Barbara Villy, B.A. (Mrs. Eric Wyld Cormack); writer; b. Manchester, Eng., 25 Jan. 1903; d. Ernest and Edith Anna (Lloyd) Villy; e. Manchester High Sch. for Girls, Eng.; Hillhurst Sch., Connaught Sch. and Crescent Hts. High Sch., Calgary, Alta.; Univ. of Alberta, B.A. 1924; m. Eric Wyld, s. John Ford Cormack, 20 Aug. 1925; children: Douglas Villy, David, Ernest Eric; Edmonton, Alta., Sch. Trustee, 1929-40; author of "Seed Time and Harvest", 1942; "Local Rag", 1951; "The House" (novel), 1955; "Red Cross Lady" (biog. of Mary H. Conquest), 1960; "Happy Music to You", 1963; "Westward Ho! 1903", 1967; "Landmarks", 1968; "Perennials and Politics" (biog. of Hon. Irene Parlby 1969); "History of 4H Clubs in Canada", 1971; "George", the biography of her retarded son, 1978; and plays, mag. stories and verse; mem., Candn. Authors Assn., Edmonton Br.; Teacher in Edmonton Sch. for Retarded Children; Home: R.R.3 Sherwood Park, Alberta. T8A 3K3

CORMACK, Robert George Hall, M.A., Ph.D., F.R.S.C.; botanist; b. Cedar Rapids, Iowa 2 Feb. 1904; s. Robert Muir and Jane Leith (Beveridge) C.; e. Peterborough (Ont.) Coll. Inst. 1925; Univ. of Toronto B.A. (Univ. Coll.) 1929, M.A. 1931, Ph.D. 1934; m. Margaret Evelyn d. late Samuel Archibald Dickson, Edmonton, Alta. 5 Sept. 1939; two s. Robert Douglas Dickson, David Stewart Sifton; Prof. Emeritus of Bot. Univ. of Alta. since 1969; Class Asst. Univ. of Toronto 1929-36; Lectr. to Prof. of Bot. Univ. Alta. 1936-69; Consultant to Alta. Forestry Dept. (Ecol. & Conserv. Studies E. Slopes Rockies) 1944-69; Consultant, MacKenzie River Gas Pipe Line Project (Ecol. Studies) 1970-71; served with Edmonton Fusiliers (R) 1940-45; author "Wild Flowers of Alberta" 1967; 2nd printing 1977; "Wild Flowers-Banff, Jasper, Kootenay, Yoho National Parks" 1972; numerous scient. papers and popular articles plant anat. and plant ecol.; internat. authority on devel. root hairs; Life mem. Candn. Inst. Forestry; Sigma Chi; P. Conservative; Protestant; recreation: lawn bowling; Club: Garneau Lawn Bowling; Home: #1106, 9835-113 St., Edmonton, Alta. T5K 1N4.

CORMIE, Donald Mercer, Q.C., B.A., LL.M.; b. Edmonton, Alta., 24 July 1922; s. George Mills and late Mildred (Mercer) C.; e. Pub. and High Schs., Edmonton, Alta.; Univ. of Alta., B.A. 1944, LL.B. 1945; Harvard Univ., LL.M. 1946; m. Eivor Elisabeth, d. Einar Ekstrom, 8 June 1946; children: John Mills, Donald Robert, James Mercer, Neil Brian, Bruce George, Robert Ekstrom, Alli-

son Barbara, Eivor Emilie; SR. PARTNER, CORMIE, KENNEDY, FITCH, PATRICK, COOK & CAMPBELL; Pres. and Dir., Principal Group Ltd., Collective Securities Ltd.; Chrmn., Principal Savings & Trust Co.; Pres. and Dir., Principal Life Insurance Co.; Principal Investors Corp. (U.S.A.); Principal Certificate Series Inc. (U.S.A.); Principal Venture Fund Ltd.; Collective Mutual Fund Ltd.; Cormie Ranch Ltd.; Secy. and Dir., George M. Cormie Enterprises Ltd.; studied law with S. Bruce Smith; former Chief Justice of Alta.; called to Bar of Alta. 1947; cr. Q.C. 1964; Partner, Smith, Clement, Parlee & Whitaker, Edmonton, Alta. 1947-53; estbd. present Firm 1954; Sessional Instr., Faculty of Law and Instr., Real Estate Law, Dept. of Extension, Univ. of Alta. 1949-53; served in Merchant Marine 1943-44; mem. Alta. Law Soc.; Candn. Bar Assn. (mem. Council 1961-81; Chrmn., Adm. Law Sec. 1963-65; Vice-Pres., Alta. 1968-69); Chrmn., Research Comm., Foundation for Legal Research; Young Presidents' Organ. Inc. (Alta. Chrmn. 1966-67; N. Pacific Area Vice-Pres. 1969-71); Dir., Banff Sch. Advanced Mang. 1968-71; Citadel Theatre 1968-70; author of "The Power of the Courts to Review Administrative Decisions" 1945; "Treaty Making by Canada" 1946; "The Nature and Necessity of Administrative Law" 1960; "Administrative Problems of Government — Alberta" 1964; "The Administrative Agency in 1965" 1965; United Church; recreations: hunting, sailing; Clubs: The Edmonton; Royal Glenora; Edmonton Petroleum; Derrick Golf & Country; Home: 12436 Grandview Drive, Edmonton, Alta. T6H 4K4; Office: 300 Principal Plaza, Edmonton, Alta. T5J 3N6

CORMIER, Clément, C.C., c.s.c.; priest; educator; b. Moncton, N.B. 15 Jan. 1910; s. Clément and Léontine (Breau) C.; e. St. Bernard's Sch. Moncton; St. Joseph's Univ. B.A. 1931; Univ. of Montreal L.Th. 1936; Laval Univ. Bachelor Degree in Social, Econ. & Pol. Sciences 1940; Hon. doctorates; Univ. of N.B. 1950, Univ. Montreal 1952, Laval Univ. 1957, Mt. Allison Univ. 1958, Univ. Sacred Heart Bathurst 1959, Laurentian Univ. 1967, Univ. de Moncton 1968, Univ. St. Thomas Fredericton 1975; Univ. of P.E.I. 1980; CHANCELLOR UNIV. DE MONCTON 1973-78; Dean of Studies, St. Joseph's Univ. 1940-47, Pres. 1948-53, Pres. Univ.'s Moncton Br. 1953-54, 1956-63; Dean of Studies, Coll. de l'Assomption, Moncton 1947-48; First Pres., Univ. de Moncton 1963-67, Dir. Centre of Acadian Studies 1968-74; mem. Royal Comn. on Bilingualism & Biculturalism 1963-70; mem. N.B. Human Rights Comn. 1967-74; Candn. Human Rights Foundation; Hon. Curator, Moncton Civic Museum 1973; mem. N.B. Rural Renewal League 1975; o. 1936; Mérite scolaire acadien, Assn. acadienne d'Educ. 1948; O.C. 1967, C.C. 1972; décoration de l'Assn. des Hautes Etudes commerciales (Montréal) 1966, Conseil de la Vie française 1974; author various publs.; Pres. N.B. Prov. Museum (Saint John) 1953-54; Pres. Assn. canadienne d'Educ. de langue française 1955-57; Founding Pres. Société française acadienne 1960-62; Vice pres. Assn. Univ. & Colls. Can. 1966-67; Found. Pres., Compagnie des Cent associés francophones, 1979-80; mem. Royal Soc. Can.; Life mem. N.B. Assn. Museums; Certificate of Merit, Cdn. Museums' Assoc.; Chevalier, Ordre de la Pléiade, 1979; The Military & Hospitalier Order of St. Lazarus of Jerusalem, 1978; Prix. au mérite de la Fondation J.-Louis Levesque, 1980; R. Catholic; recreations: travel, bridge; Address: 2 Kendra St., Moncton, N.B. E1C 4J8.

CORNELL, Paul Grant, E.D., M.A., Ph.D., F.R.H.S.; educator; b. Toronto, Ont., 13 Sept. 1918; s. Beaumont Sandfield and Margaret Grant (Wilson) C.; e. Lower Can. Coll., Montreal; Brampton (Ont.) High Sch.; Univ. of Toronto, B.A., M.A., Ph.D. (Hist.); m. Christina Mary, d. late James Jerome Suckling, Margate, Eng., 6 Dec. 1941; children: John Grant, Virginia Susan, Benjamin William, Jennifer Margaret; PROF. OF HIST., UNIV. OF WATERLOO, since 1960 Chrmn. History, 1960-68; (Dean, Faculty of Arts 1970-73; Acting Vice Pres. (Acad.) 1972), Hon. Archivist since 1977; Lectr.-Prof., Dept. of Hist. Acadia Univ., 1949-60; served with N.P.A.M. Peel & Dufferin Regt. 1932-36, Lorne Scots 1936-40; Candn. Army (Active) 1940-46; C.O.T.C. Univ. of Toronto 1947-50 and Acadia Univ. 1953-56; author, "The Alignment of Political Groups in the Province of Canada", 1962; "The Great Coalition", 1967 (reprinted 1971); co-author, "Canada, Unity in Diversity", 1967 (French transl. 1969); other writings incl. various articles in hist. journs.; Fellow of the Royal Hist. Soc.; mem., Candn. Hist. Assn. (Ed. "Report" 1953-56); Ont. Hist. Soc. (Pres. 1973-74), co-ed., "Ontario History", 1963-78); Inst. Pub. Adm. Can.; Anglican Lay Reader, Lay Asst.; Home: 202 Laurier Place, Waterloo, Ont. N2L 1K8

CORNELL, Ward MacLaurin; b. 1924; e. Pickering Coll. Ont.; Univ. of W. Ont.; m. Georgina Saxon; 5 children; DEPUTY MINISTER, ONTARIO MINISTRY OF CULTURE & RECREATION; commenced as Lect. in Eng. and Hist., Pickering Coll. 1949; Gen. Mgr. Broadcast Div. (Radio), Free Press Printing Co. 1954; Pres., Ward Cornell Ltd., Creative Projects in Communication 1967-72; a Free Lance Broadcaster of numerous T.V. and Radio programmes 1946-72; Visiting Lect. Conestoga Coll. 1968-72; Agent Gen. for Prov. Ont. in U.K. 1972-78; Gen. Mgr.-European Operations, Lenroc Internat. Ltd. since Sept. 1978-80; Ont. Dep. Provincial Secy. for Social Dev., 1980; Clubs: The London (Ont.); Lambs; Albany, Marks (UK); Home: R.R. 1, Uxbridge, Ont. L0C 1K0

CORRIGAN, Dorothy, C.M. (1978), R.N., LL.D.; b. Charlottetown; P.E.I., 26 July 1913; d. Andrew and Elizabeth (MacQuaid) Hennessy; e. Rochford Square Sch. and Prince of Wales Coll. Charlottetown; Charlottetown Hosp. Sch. of Nursing 1937; St. Dunstan's Univ. LL.D. 1969; m. 21 June 1944; children: Andrew Ernest, D.D.S., Mary Kathryn, R.N.; practiced nursing Montreal; served 11 yrs in mun. govt. as Ald., Depy. Mayor and Mayor of Charlottetown 1960-71; Head P.E.I. Symphony Assn. 1972-74; Pres. Chamber Comm.; mem. Adv' Council Atlantic Police Acad.; Holland Coll., Charlottetown; Can. Council; R. Catholic; recreations: skating, swimming, tennis; Clubs: Zonta; Women's Service; Address: 228 Graftan St., Charlottetown, P.E.I. C1A 1L4

CORRIGAN, Harold, B.Comm., C.A.; executive; b. Montreal, Que., 3 March 1927; s. Harold Willard and Dorothy M. (Cauldwell) C.; e. Westmount (Que.) High Sch.; McGill Univ., B.Com., C.A. 1950; Lic. im Acct. 1953; Centre D'Etudes Industrielles, Dipl. 1959; m. Eve, d. William James Howard Ellwood, 14 June 1952; two d., Susan, Ann; VICE PRESIDENT, CORPORATE RELATIONS, ALCAN ALUMINUM LTD. since 1980; Dir., Simpsons Sears, Ltd.; MICC Investments Ltd.; IAC Ltd.; Continental Bank of Can.; joined Alcan 1950; sales, financial & mang., Montreal and N.Y.; Pres., Alcan Can. Products Ltd. 1971-80; served with RCNVR 1945; Pres., Candn. Mfrs. Assn. 1975-76; mem. Inst. C.A.'s Que.; Anglican; Clubs: Mount Royal; Toronto, University (N.Y. City; Montreal; Toronto); Royal St. Lawrence Yacht; RCYC; Office: Box 6090, Montreal, Que., H3C 3H2

CORRIGAN, John Sinclair, B. Com.; association executive; b. Toronto, Ont., 13 Dec. 1911; s. Martha (Wickens) and late Frederick Sinclair C.; e. Univ. of Toronto Schs., 1921-30; Univ. Coll. Univ. of Toronto 1934; m. Margaret Isabel, d. late Robert Henderson, Toronto, Ont., 1 May 1937; children: John, Fred, Martha, Norah, Sheila; Pres., Candn. Nat. Exhibition Assn., 1971-72; Dir., Toronto Area Indust. Devel. Bd. (Pres. 1974-75); with Acct. Dept., General Steel Wares Ltd., 1934-56; Vice-Pres. and Gen. Sales Mgr., John Wood Co. Ltd., 1956-63 (Co. acquired by Anthes Imperial Ltd. 1963) and subsequently Vice Pres., Trade Relations, Anthes Eastern Ltd.; Reserve Commission, Univ. of Toronto C.O.T.C., 1940-45; mem., Bd. of Govs., Toronto Y.M.C.A., since 1940 (Pres., Broadview Y.M.C.A. 1953-54, Pres., Metrop.

Y.M.C.A., 1962-63); Pres., U.T.S. Old Boys Assn., 1960; mem., Nat. Indust. Design Council (Chrmn. 1957-58); Candn. Inst. Plumbing & Heating (Pres., 1960-61); Chrmn. Toronto Br., Candn. Mfrs. Assn., 1968-69; Dir., Candn. Nat. Exhibition; Toronto East Gen. Hosp.; Branksome hall School; Trustee, Toronto Gen. Burying Grounds; Alpha Delta Phi; Freemason (P.M.); Conservative; United Church; recreations: golf, sailing; Clubs: University, Lambton Golf (Dir.); Rotary; Home: 170 Roxborough Drive, Toronto, Ont. M4W 1X8

CORRY, James Alexander, C.C. (1968), LL.M., LL.D., D.C.L., F.R.S.C.; university principal; b. Millbank, Ont., 29 Nov. 1899; s. Andrew and Jean (Neilson) C.; e. Univ. of Sask., LL.B. 1923 and Hon. LL.D. 1951; Oxford Univ. B.C.L. 1927; Columbia Univ., LL.M. 1935; m. Alice Madeline, d. Rev. R. J. and Mrs. Russell, Swift Current, Sask., 29 Dec. 1934; read law with Bence, Stevenson & McLorg, Saskatoon, Sask.; called to the Bar of Sask. 1930, Ont. 1968; Prof. of Law, Univ. of Sask., 1927-36; Hardy Prof. of Pol. Science, Queen's Univ., 1936-61, Vice Principal there 1951-61; Principal, 1961-68; received Rhodes Scholarship for Sask., 1924; special Fellowship in Law, Columbia Univ., 1934-35; author of "Democratic Government and Politics" and "Elements of Democratic Government"; "Law and Policy", 1958; "The Changing Conditions of Politics", 1963; "Universities and Government", 1969; "Farewell The Ivory Tower" 1970; with Dr. L.-P. Bonneau, "Quest for the Optimum: Research Policy in the Universities of Canada", 1972; "My Life and Work-A Happy Partnership" (memoirs of J.A. Corry) 1981; mem. Canada Council 1966-72; mem., Bd. of Govs., Candn. Broadcasting Corp., 1949-58; Candn. Pol. Science Assn. (Pres. 1954-55); Pres., Nat. Conf. of Candn. Univs. and Colls., 1964-65; Chrmn., Candn. Univ. Chrmn., Candn. Univ. Foundation, 1964-65; Chrmn., Comte. of Presidents of Ont. Univs. 1966-68; LL.D., Univ. of Toronto, 1962; Univ. of St. Andrews, Scotland, 1963; Dalhousie Univ., 1964; Univ. of Montreal, 1965; Western Ont., 1965; Laval 1966; Calgary, 1967; Manitoba, 1967; Roy. Mil. Coll., 1968; St. Francis Xavier 1968; McGill 1968; Windsor, 1968; New Brunswick, 1969; Trent 1970; Queen's 1970, D.C.L. Bishop's 1970; Memorial of Nfld. 1975, York Univ. 1980; made Companion of Order of Canada, 1968; rec'd. Royal Bank of Canada Award 1973; Address: 44 Kensington Ave., Kingston, Ont.

CORY, Hon. Peter de C., B.A.; judge; b. Windsor, Ont. 25 Oct. 1925; s. Andrew and Mildred (Beresford Howe) C.; e. Univ. of W. Ont. B.A. 1947; Osgoode Hall grad. 1950; m. Edith, d. Claude Nash 14 September 1949; children: Christopher, Andrew, Robert; SUPREME COURT OF ONT., TRIAL DIV., since Dec. 1974; called to the Bar of Ont. 1950; cr. Q.C. 1963; served as Pilot, R.C.A.F. 419 Sqdn. 1943-45; Bencher, Law Soc. of Upper Canada 1971-74; Past Pres. Advocates Soc., York Co. Law Assn.; Past mem. Council, Candn. Bar Assn.; recreations: squash, fly fishing, skeet shooting; Club: University; Office: Osgoode Hall, Toronto, Ont. M5H 2N6

COSENS, Hon. Keith Alan, M.Ed.; politician; b. Teulon, Man. 7 July 1932; s. George Henry and Inez (Deacon) c.; e. Stonewall Coll. Inst. 1950; Univ. of Man. B.A. 1963, B.Ed. 1964, M.Ed. 1974; m. Marie Isabel d. James Smith, Shoal lake, Man. 27 Dec. 1952; children: Brant, Kevin, Lisa; MIN. OF EDUC. MAN. since 1977; teacher and sch. adm. Man. schs. 25 yrs.; el. to Prov. Leg. 1977; P. Conservative; Protestant; recreations: tennis, curling, hunting, fishing; Home: (P.O. Box 604) Stonewall, Man. R0C 2Z0; Office: Legislative Bldg., Winnipeg, Man.

COSGROVE, Hon. Paul, M.P., LL.B.; politician; b. Thunder Bay, Ont. 30 Dec. 1934; e. Agincourt Coll. Inst. Toronto; St. Michael's Coll. Univ. of Toronto B.A.; Queen's Univ. LL.B.; m. Frances; children: Conal, Mark, Darin, Cara; MIN. OF PUBLIC WORKS, CAN. 1980- and

Min. Responsible for Central Mortgage & Housing Corp. and Nat. Capital Comn.; Mayor of Scarborough 1973-78; el. M.P. for York-Scarborough g.e. 1980; Past. Dir. Assn. Muns. Ont.; Fed. Candn. Muns.; former Dir. Metro Zoo Soc.; Scarborough Centenary; Scarborough Gen. Hosps.; mem. Candn. Bar Assn.; Law Soc. Upper Can.; Lawyers Club; Thomas More Lawyers Guild; Liberal; R. Catholic; Home: 33 Elkwood Dr., Scarborough, Ont. M1C 2C2; Office: 356 Confederation Bldg., Ottawa, Ont. K1A 0A6.

COSSETTE, J.-Claude, M.Ed., Ph.D.; advertising executive; educator; b. Québec City, Qué. 1 Dec. 1937; s. Armand and Simonne (Labrecque) C.; e. Petit Séminaire de Qué. classical studies 1958; L'Ecole des Beaux-Arts de Qué. Dipl. in Advertising Art 1962, M.Ed. 1963; Laval Univ. Cert. in Marketing 1962, Cert in Business Adm. 1970, Ph.D. 1975; Ecole du Livre Estienne, Paris Cert. 1964; m. 1stly Claire Tremblay; children: François, Joëlle; m. 2ndly Suzanne d. Antonio Nadeau; one s. Guillaume; PARTNER, COSSETTE ASSOCIÉS COMMUNICATION MARKETING 1970- ; Pres., Graphème Inc.; Nadeau-Cossette Inc.; Habitex Inc.; Prof. Agrégé 1975- and Dir. Programmes de Communication Graphique, Laval Univ.; founded Cossette & Dupuis, Graphiste Associés 1964; Cossette Associés, Graphistes Conseils Ltée 1966; Bureau d'Esthétique Appliquée de Qué. Inc. 1966; service Royal Candn.Ordnance Corps, rank Lt.; Lectr. on Semiological Approach of Picture Communication ten Calif. univs. and research centres 1978; Pedagogical Dir. series 26 TV programs on Advertising in Que. 1977; lectr. on advertising, communication through pictures many internat. confs., univs. and colls.; author "Communication de Masse Consommation de Masse" 1974; "La Comportementalité et la Segmentation des marchés" 1980; 3 books of poetry; various papers, articles; mem. Assn. des dirigeants d'agences de publicité francophones du Qué. (Founding Dir.); Inst. Internat. de la Communication (Founding Dir.); Assn. Internat. de Sémiotique; Internat. Communication Assn.; Candn. Assn. Applied Social Research; Candn. Communication Assn.; Assn. des Compagnons de Lure; recreations: travel, walking, reading, swimming, tennis; Office: Ecole des Arts visuels, Pavillon cassault #4413, Univ. Laval, Qué. G1K 7P4.

COSSINS, Edwin Albert, B.Sc., Ph.D., D.Sc., F.R.S.C.; educator; b. Romford, Essex, Eng. 28 Feb. 1937; s. Albert Joseph and Elizabeth H. (Brown) C.; e. Clark's Coll. Romford, Eng. 1953; S.E. Essex Tech. Coll. Eng. 1955; Chelsea Coll. Univ. of London B.Sc. 1958, Ph.D. (Plant Biochem.) 1961, D.Sc. 1981; m. Lucille Jeanette d. Dr. Reginald Wilson Salt, Lethbridge, Alta. 1 Sept. 1962; children: Diane Elizabeth, Carolyn Jane; PROF. OF BOTANY, UNIV. OF ALTA. since 1969; Research Assoc. Purdue Univ. 1961-62; Asst. Prof. of Botany present Univ. 1962, Assoc. Prof. 1965, Acting Head of Botany 1965-66, Dir. Introductory Biol. Program 1974-77; Chrmn. Grant Selection Comte. Cellular Biol. & Genetics, Nat. Research Council Can. 1976-77; mem. Adv. Panel Strategic Grants, Natural Sciences and Engn. Research Council Can. 1978-81; rec'd Centennial Medal 1967; co-author "Plant Life in Anaerobic Environments" 1978; "The Biochemistry of Plants, A Comprehensive Treatise" Vol. II 1979; over 75 scient. publs. in nat. and internat. journs.; Assoc. Ed. "Canadian Journal of Botany" since 1969; Corr. Ed. "Plant Biochemical Journal" since 1974; Life mem. Royal Soc. Can. (Rapporteur, Plant Biol. Div. 1975-77); mem. Candn. Soc. Plant Physiols. (W. Dir. 1968-70, Secy. 1973-75, Vice Pres. 1975-76, Pres. 1976-77); Biochem. Soc. Gt. Brit.; Candn. Biochem. Soc.; Am. Soc. Plant Physiols.; Japanese Soc. Plant Physiols.; Plant Biochem. Soc.; Anglican; recreations: golf, curling, cross-country skiing; Club: Royal Glenora; Home: 99 Fairway Dr., Edmonton, Alta. T6J 2C2; Office: Edmonton, Alta. T6E 2E9.

COSTAIN, Cecil Clifford, D.S.C., Ph.D., F.R.S.C., F.I.E.E.E.; b. Ponoka, Alta. 16 June 1922; s. Henry Hud-

son and Elida Mary (Eakin) C.; e. Univ. of Sask. B.A. 1941, B.A. (Hons.), M.A. 1947; Cambridge Univ. Ph.D. 1951; Univ. of Mich. 1950-51; m. Cynthia Hazell d. late J. M. G. Ewing, M.D. 26 July 1949; children: Linda Carol, Charles Gordon; PRINC. RESEARCH OFFR. AND HEAD OF TIME & FREQUENCY SEC., DIV. OF PHYSICS, NAT. RESEARCH COUNCIL; joined Spectroscopy Sec. of present Div. NRC 1951-71, Time & Frequency Sec. 1971; Exhn. of 1851 Scholar 1947; served with RCN 1942-45, Radar Offr. HMS Indomitable 1942-45, retired Lt. Commdr. 1945; co-author "Advanced Treatese on Physical Chemistry" Vol. 4 1975; author over 40 papers on Microwave Spectroscopy and on Candn. Time & Frequency Standards; mem. Candn. Assn. Physicists (Vice Pres. 1979, Pres. 1980); Protestant; recreation: gardening; Home: 49 Cedar Rd., Ottawa, Ont. K1J 6L5; Office: Div. of Physics M-36, Nat. Research Council, Ottawa, Ont. K1A 0S1.

CÔTÉ, Bernard G., B.Com., M.B.A.; company executive; b. Montreal, Que. 16 Aug. 1931; e. Loyola Coll. B.Com. 1954; Univ. Western Ont. M.B.A. 1956; m. Isabelle McCubbin; has two s., one d.; PRES., B.G. CÔTÉ CONSULTING LTD.; Chrmn., Ducros, Meilleur, Roy & Associés Ltée; Dir., G. M. Plastic Corp.; Indust. Plastic Extrusions Ltd.; Korlin Plastics Ltd.; York Lambton Corp. Ltd.; CompAir Can. Inc.; Cie d'Assnce. du Qué.; Kruger Inc.; with IBM as Marketing Rep., Data Processing Div. 1956, Marketing Mgr. 1964, Br. Mgr. 1966, Dist. Mgr. Eastern Region 1967, Vice Pres. 1969; joined Omega Investments Ltd. as Pres. 1972; joined Celanese Can. Inc., 1974, Pres., C.E.O. & Chrmn. to June 1979; served as Lieut.; R.C.N.; Chrmn., l'Ecole de Technol. Supérieure l'Univ. Qué.; Pres., Candn. Council, Internat. Ch. of Comm.; Chrmn., Centraide Montreal (United Way); Vice Pres., Concordia Univ. Centre for Mgmt. Studies; Vice Pres., Canada World Youth; Dir., Juvenile Diabetes Research Fund; Hôpital Marie Enfant pour les Jeunes; mem., Sci. Council Can.; Candn. Econ. Policy Comte.; Conf. Bd. Can.; Chambre de Comm. Montreal (Pres. 1973); Montreal Bd. Trade; recreations: skiing, golf, tennis; Clubs: St. James's; Mt. Royal; Laval-sur-le-Lac; Forest and Stream; Hermitage Golf & Country; Canadian (Montreal); Address: P.O. Box 769 Station "A", Montreal, Que. H3C 2V2

CÔTÉ, Ernest Adolphe, M.B.E., B.Sc., LL.B.; retired diplomat; b. Edmonton, Alta., 12 June 1913; s. Cécile (Gagnon) and late Jean Léon C.; e. Jesuit Coll., Edmonton; Laval Univ., B.Sc.; Univ. of Alta., LL.B.; Imp. Defence Coll., 1949; m. Madeleine, d. late Charles Frémont, Quebec, Que., 16 June 1945; children: Michel, Benoît, Denyse, Lucie; Ambassador to Finland 1972-75; read law with Simpson and Macleod, Edmonton, Alberta; called to Bar of Alta., 1939; with Dept. of External Affairs, 1945-55; Asst. Depy. Min. N. Affairs and Nat. Resources, 1955-63; Depy. Min. (became Dept. of Indian Affairs & N. Devel., Oct. 1966), 1963-68; Depy. Min., Dept. of Veterans' Affairs 1968; Depy. Solicitor-Gen. 1966-72; served as Lieut., Royal 22nd Regt., and on staff, 1939-45; discharged rank Col.; M.B.E.; Mentioned in Despatches; Dir., Royal Candn. Geographical Society; Ottawa Public Library; Hôpital de Montfort, Ottawa; Roman Catholic; recreations: golf, swimming, skiing; Home: 2 Allan Pl., Ottawa, Ont. K1S 3T1

CÔTÉ, Hon. Jean-Pierre, P.C. (1965); LIEUT. GOV. of QUÉBEC; b. Montreal, Que., 9 Jan. 1926; s. Joseph Emile and Cedia (Roy) C.; e. Longueuil Coll. and Sch. of Dental Technol. Longueuil, Que.; m. Germaine, d. Charles Tremblay, Gaspé, Que., 31 July 1948; has eight children; prior to entering politics in 1963 owned and operated a dental laboratory; Pres., Longueuil Sch. Bd., 1961-63; 1st el. to H. of C. for Longueuil, g.e. 1963 and re-el. 1965 1968; apptd. Postmaster Gen. 18 Dec. 1965, Min. of Nat. Revenue 1968-70, returned as Post master Gen. 24 Sept. 1970; summoned to the Senate 1 Sept. 1972; Pres. 1974-78, Liberal Party of Can. (Que. Sec.); Candn. Rep. to

I.L.O., Geneva, 1964; Home: 1010 St. Louis Rd., Sillery, Que. G1S 1C7; Office: 1 Edifice Andre Laurendeau, 1050 St. Augustin St., Que. G1A 1A1

CÔTÉ, Pierre; exécutif; né Québec, 2 fév. 1926; f. feu Jules H. et d'Andrée (Fortier) C.; é. Académie de Québec; Ont. Agric. Coll.; ép. Marié à Hélène, fille du Juge André Taschereau, Québec 1950; enfants: Pierre, André; PRÉS. DU CONSEIL D'ADMINNISTRATION, CELANESE CAN. INC.; Administrateur, CAE Industries Ltée.; Canada Development Corp.; AES Data; Datacrown Ltée.; Drummond McCall; Ralston Purina du Canada Ltée.; Mutual Life Co. Assnce. du Canada; La Garantie Co. l'Amerique du Nord; Banque de Montréal; Canron Inc.; Domtar Inc.; Bombardier Inc.; Wordplex; Canreit; mem. Conseil consultatif de la succursale de Québec, du Trust Royal du Canada; Prés., le Conseil du Patronat du Qué.; ex-Gouv., Bourse de Montréal; Ex-Prés., Chambre de Comm. de Qué.; La Soc. Candn. de la Croix-Rouge; Conseil Nat. de l'Industrie Laitière du Can.; Conseil de Planification et de Dével. du Qué.; L'Orchestre Symphonique de Qué.; récréations: golf, pêche, chasse; Clubs: Garnison; Golf du Lac Saint-Joseph; Mount Royal; Royal Quebec Golf; Golf Mont Bruno; Résidence: 1271 Place de Mérici, Québec, Qué. G1S 3H8; Bureau: 2 Place Quebec, Suite 828, Quebec, Qué. G1R 2B5

COTTERILL, Benedict Gordon Ross; executive; Wareham, Dorset, Eng. March 26, 1918; s. late Gordon Edward Ross and Mary Angela (Herbert) C.; e. Beamsville (Ont.) High Sch.; m. Violet Lorraine d. late William H. Clark, 12 Jan. 1946; children: Stanley B., Paul C.; VICE PRES. BAG DIV. CONSOLIDATED-BATHURST INC. since 1977; Dir. Senior Vic-Pres. and Gen'l Mgr. Consolidated-Bathurst packaging Ltd.; Asst. to Export Mgr. Page-Hersey Tubes Ltd. 1938-43, Asst. Export Mgr. 1945-6; Export Mgr. and Secy. Sino-Canadian Development Co. 1946, Offr. Sinocan Forwarders Ltd.; Mgr. and Secy-Treas. Roy Peers Co. Ltd. 1946-52; Salesman, St. Regis Paper Co. (Canada) Ltd. 1952, W. Sales Mgr. 1953, Ont. Dist. Sales Mgr. 1957, Gen. Sales Mgr. 1962; Dir. of Marketing, Consolidated-Bathurst Packaging Ltd. Bag Division 1967; Vice-Pres. and Gen. Mgr. 1968; served with RCAF during World War II, Pilot; Anglican; recreations: golf, fishing, gardening, travel; Clubs: Saint James's Montreal; Empire (Toronto); Capilano Golf & Country (Vancouver) Lambton Golf & Country (Toronto); Mississauga Golf and Country Club; Royal Montreal Golf; Home: 140 Wilder Dr., Oakville, Ont. L6L 5G3; Office: 2070 Hadwen Rd., Mississauga, Ont. L5K 2C9.

COTTRELLE, James Elliot; company president; b. Toronto, Ont., 15 March 1911; s. George Richardson and Bessie (Elliot) C.; m. Dorothy, d. Samuel Gallaugher, Alliston, Ont., 19 May 1951; children: Janet, George, Stuart; PRESIDENT, DALE SECURITIES LTD.; Dir., Roy. Agric. Winter Fair; Candn. Nat. Exhn.; Protestant; Clubs: Toronto; Granite; Eglinton Hunt; Toronto & N. York; Home: 241 Warren Rd., Toronto; Ont. M4V 2S6; Office: Victoria Towers, 44 Victoria St., Toronto, Ont. M5C 1Y2

COUCILL, Irma Sophia; portrait artist; b. London, Ont. 8 Aug. 1918; d. Percival Harold and Mary (Krowa) Young; e. Holy Name Separate Sch. Toronto 1929; St. Angela's Coll. London, Ont. 1929-30; St. Joseph's High Sch. and St. Joseph's Convent Coll. Toronto 1934; Eastern High Sch. Comm. Toronto; m. Walter Jackson Coucill 17 June 1939; two s. John Thomas, Thomas Dean; Ed. Artist, Globe & Mail 1958-60; Toronto Star 1960-; Maclean's Magazine 1970-72; Canadian Forum; Syndicated Artist, Toronto Star Syndicate 1960-70; portrait colls.: Candn Hockey Hall of Fame (234) Toronto 1958-; Candn. Aviation Hall of Fame (105) Edmonton 1974-; Candn. Business Hall of Fame (25) Toronto 1980-; Candn. Indian Hall of Fame (30) Brantford; Candn. Press Coll. Toronto (Past Presidents, Gen. Mgrs., Broadcast News Mgrs.) and other colls.; portrait presented to Un.

Way Chairmen past 15 yrs.; portraits of prime mins. used for comm. coins/trade dollars; 20 exhns. Fathers of Confed. portraits centennial yrs. Toronto, Montreal, Ottawa, Kitchener; exhn. 55 portraits Prime Min. Trudeau Arts & Letters Club Toronto; book illustrations: "Founders and Guardians" 1968; "The Nation Makers" 1967; "The Journal Men" 1974; recreations: photography, music, etymology, gardening, painting; Address: 393 Broadway Ave., Toronto, Ont. M4P 1X5.

COUCILL, Walter Jackson, R.C.A. artist; b. Camden, N.J. 22 June 1915; s. Albert and Emilie (Jackson) C.; came to Can. 1923; e. pub. schs. Eng. and Toronto; Scarborough Coll. Inst. and Danforth Tech. Sch. Toronto; Ont. Coll. of Art; m. Irma Sophia d. late Percival Harold Young 17 June 1939; two. s. John Thomas, Thomas Dean; self-employed; art dir. Robert Simpson Co., Display Service Co.; art consultant; arch. delineator for arch. firms; free-lance designer and artist in exhn. and display design; rep. in various pub., business and private colls. incl. Nat. Gallery (War Records), Art Gallery of Ont., Nat. Archives Gallery, Metrop. Lib. Toronto, Ont. Govt. offices; served with RCAF, pilot training, Art Dir. official RCAF mag. "Wings", 1942-45; mem. Royal Candn. Acad. Arts; recreations: gardening, photography, flyfishing; Club: Arts & Letters (Past Vice Pres. and mem. Extve.); Address: 393 Broadway Ave., Toronto, Ont. M4P 1X5.

COUGHLAN, Dermot G. J.; executive; e. Banbury, Eng.; PRESIDENT & CHIEF EXTVE. OFFR., INDAL LTD. 1973-; Pres. and Dir. Indal Inc., Va.; Dir. R.T.Z. Industries Ltd., London, Eng.; Chubb Holdings (North America) Ltd.; joined Alcan Industries, U.K. 1957-62; Financial Dir. Hollands Distributors Ltd. 1962-68; Chief Financial Offr. R.T.Z. Pillar Ltd. Engineering Group 1968; Vice Pres. Finance, Indal Ltd., Can. 1970, Extve. Vice Pres. 1972; served with RAF 1954-56; Fellow, Assn. Cert. Accts. (UK); mem. Young Pres.' Organ.; Am. Mang. Assn.; Bd. Trade; Newcomen Soc. N. Am.; recreations: tennis, boating, fishing, reading; Home: Kleinburg, Ont.; Office: 4000 Weston Rd., Weston, Ont. M9L 2W8.

COUGHLIN, Violet L., M.A., D.L.S.; librarian; educator; e. McGill Univ. B.Sc. 1928, High Sch. Teacher's Dipl. 1928, B.L.S. 1938; Columbia Univ. M.A. 1958, D.L.S. 1966; PROF. EMERITUS, McGILL UNIV. LIBRARY SCHOOL 1975-; Tech., Med. Lab. Royal Victoria Hosp. 1928-29; Teacher Montreal High Sch. 1929-34; Cataloguer, Redpath Lib. McGill Univ. 1941, Lib. of Royal Victoria Hosp. 1941-51, Lectr. Lib. Sch. 1951, Asst. Prof. 1957, Assoc. Prof. 1965, Prof. 1969-75, Acting Dir. 1970, Dir. 1971-73; Visiting Prof. Emeritus Univ. of Toronto Faculty Lib. Science 1975-79; Visiting Lectr. Univ. of Pittsburgh Grad. Sch. of Lib. & Information Science 1966-67; Univ. of Hawaii Grad. Lib. Sch. summers 1968, 1970; recipient Can. Council Fellowship 1958-59; Miriam Tompkins Scholarship Columbia Univ. 1958-59; mem. Bd. Beta Phi Mu 1965-68; served various comtes. Candn. Lib. Assn.; Am. Lib. Assn.; Am. Assn. Lib. Schs.; Que. Lib. Assn. (Pres. 1954-55); Corp. Prof. Libs. Que. (Bd. 1972-75); author "Larger Units of Public Library Service in Canada" 1968; various papers, articles; Office: Montreal, Que.

COUILLARD, Pierre, B.A., B.Sc., PhD.; né Montmagny, Qué., 19 mars 1928; f. Dr. Jean-Marie et Germaine Daigneau C.; e. Petit Seminaire de Québec; Univ. Laval, B. ès A., 1947, B. ès Sc., 1951; Univ. de Pennsylvanie, Ph.D. (Zool.), 1955; boursier du Conseil Can. des Recherches, études poursuivies à l'Univ. Libre de Bruxelles, 1955-56; ép. Hélène, f. Prof. M. Pardé, Grenoble, France, 26 déc. 1955; enfants: Philippe, Catherine, Denis; Prof Titulaire, Dept. des Sciences Biol., Univ. de Montréal (Dir. du Dept. 1963-67); mem.; Soc. de Biol. de Montréal; Am. Assn. Advanc. Science; Soc. of Protozoologists; Assoc. des Physiols. (Paris); Soc. Biol. Cell. du Canada; Sigma

Xi; Catholique; recreation: camping; résidence: 631 rue Davaar, Outremont, Québec H2V 3B1

COULTER, Michael Arthur, B.Sc., P.Eng.; industrialist; b. Toronto, Ont. 22 May 1943; s. Warren Raymond Helen Patricia (Aldington) C.; e. Queen's Univ. B.Sc. 1966; m. Judith Constance d. Frank P. Labey, Georgetown, Ont. 28 Aug. 1965; one s. Marcus James; PRODUCT MGR., TRI CANADA INC. Vice Pres. Gasohol Inc.; Past Pres., Coulter Anodizing Ltd.; Booth-Coulter Inc.; Coulter Copper and Brass Ltd.; joined Coulter Copper and Brass Ltd. as Project Engr. 1969, Vice Pres. and Chief Engr. 1972; mem. Tech. Adv. Council Humber Coll. Toronto; Assc. mem. Master Brewers Am's; mem. Candn. Heat Exchanger and Pressure Vessel Mgrs. Assn. (Past Pres.); mem. Am. Soc. Mech. Engrs.; Engn. Inst. Can.; P. Conservative; Anglican; recreations: swimming, camping, skiing, chess, music, bridge; Club: Lambton Golf & Country; Home: 2158 Fowler Dr., Mississauga, Ont. L5K 1B8; Office: 6500 Northwest Dr., Mississauga, Ont. L4V 1K4

COULTER, Thomas Henry, B.S., M.A.; association executive (retired); b. Winnipeg, Man., 21 Apl. 1911; s. David and Sarah Anne (Allen) C.; e. St. Johns Coll. Sch. Winnipeg, 1925-27; Peabody High Sch., Pittsburgh, 1927-29; Carnegie Inst. of Technol., B.S. 1933; Univ. of Chicago, M.A. 1935; m. Mary Alice, d. Robert L. Leach, 24 Nov. 1937; children: Sara Anne, Anne, Jane Allen, Thomas H. II; CHIEF EXTVE. OFFR., CHICAGO ASSN. OF COMMERCE AND INDUSTRY, 1954-1980; Invest. Analyst, Shaw & Co., Chicago, 1935-36; Mgr.. Business and Product Devel. Div. and Mgr., Business Planning, The Zonolite Co., Chicago, U.P. 1936-45; Booz Allen & Hamilton, Hamilton Mgt. Consultants, 1945-50; el. to Partnership 1948; Pres., American Bildrok Co., Chicago, 1950-53; Hon. Trustee, Skokie Valley Community Hosp. (Pres. 1955-58 and 1966-69); Dir.: Chicago Crime Comn.; U.S. Olympians, Midwest Chapter; Citizenship Council Metrop. Chicago; Chicago Council on Foreign Relations; Better Business Bureau Metrop. Chicago; mem. various civic and philanthropic organs.; rec'd Alumni Citation for Pub. Service, Univ. of Chicago, 1954; Alumni Merit Award for Outstanding Prof. Achievement, Carnegie-Mellon Univ., 1956; Sports Illustrated Silver Anniversary All-Am. Award, 1957; "Honorary Citizenship" Scroll, Winnipeg, 1959; Commdr.'s Cross of Order of Merit, Fed. Repub. of Germany, 1961; U.S. Army's Outstanding Civilian Service Medal, 1961; Kt., Order of Merit of Italian Repub., 1961; Gold Badge of Honor for Merits to Repub. of Austria, 1962; Immigrants' Service League Distinguished Achievement Award, 1963; Kt. of 1st Class, Order of Lion of Finland, 1964; Offr., Royal Order of VASA of Sweden, 1965 and Commdr. 1972; Golden Badge of Hon. for Merits to Prov. of Vienna 1971; Citizen Fellowship Award, Inst. of Medicine of Chicago, 1976; Indust. Statesman Award, U.S.-Japan Trade Council, 1976; Chevalier of the Nat. Order of Merit of The Republic of France, 1978; Third Class of the Order of the Sacred Treasure of Japan, 1979; mem. State Dept.'s Top Mang. Seminar Team, Israel 1956 and Japan 1958; Dir. Japan Am. Soc. of Chicago, Inc.; mem., Amer. Mgt. Assn.; Chicago Council on Foreign Relations, Cook County Econ. Devel. Comte.; Nat. Planning Assn.; Nat. Sales Extves. Internat. Newcomen Soc. in N. Am.; Nat. Adv. Bd., Am. Security Council Extve. Comte.; Ill. Council on Econ. Educ.; U.S. Chamber of Comm.; Dist. Export Council, U.S. Dept. Comm.; Chicago Hist. Soc., Field Museum of Natural hist., Art Inst. of Chicago; Adv. Council on Aging, City of Chicago; Governor's Council on Health and Fitness; Nat. Adv. Council. Nat. legal Centre for the Public Interest and other business and prof. organs.; Protestant; Clubs: Commercial; Canadian; University; Glen View; Mid-America; Economic; Executives (Pres. 1950-51); Home: 58 Overlook Dr., Golf, Ill. 60029;

COULTER, Warren R., B.A.Sc., P. Eng.; retired manufacturer; b. Toronto, Ont., 3 Aug. 1911; s. William

Charles and Lydia Georgina (Woolidge) C.; e. Riverdale Coll. Inst., and Jarvis Coll. Inst., Toronto, Ont.; Univ. of Toronto, B.A.Sc. 1933; m. Helen Patricia, d. late Harold Aldington, 30 Sept. 1937; two s. Michael Arthur, Terence Douglas; Chrmn., Coulter Copper & Brass Ltd. 1976, resigned 1980, former Chrmn., Booth-Coulter Coppersmithing Ltd.; Aluminum Swimming Pools Canada Ltd.; mem., Assn. Prof. Engrs. Ont.; Conservative; Anglican; recreations: swimming, boating, golf; Clubs: Lambton Golf & Country; Rotary (Islington); Home: Apt. 1103-2010 Islington Ave., Weston, Ont. M9P 3S8

COUPLAND, Robert Thomas, Ph.D.; university professor; b. Winnipeg, Man., 24 Jan. 1920; s. Thomas John Winfred and Gertrude (Macleod) C.; e. Univ. of Manitoba, Cert. in Agric. 1938, B.S.A. 1946; Univ. of Nebraska, Ph.D. 1949; m. Marjory Ileen, d. Atley Roddick, 28 Feb. 1975; one d. Lorraine Dawn; PROF. AND HEAD OF PLANT ECOLOGY, UNIV. OF SASKATCHEWAN since 1948; and Dir. of the Matador Project (Internat. Biol. Programme); served as Asst. in Range Studies, Dom. Exper. Station, Swift Current, Sask., 1941-46; i/c Dom. Forest Exper. Station, Wasagaming, Man., 1946; Grad Asst. in Botany, Univ. of Nebraska, 1946-47; Johnson Fellow in Botany, Univ. of Nebraska, 1947-48 Ecol. Soc. of Am.; Sask. Inst. of Agrol.; Brit. Ecol. Soc.; Brit. Grassland Soc.; Agric. Inst. of Can.; Am. Inst. Biol. Science; Candn. Bot. Soc.; Soc. of Range Management; awarded Univ. of Man. Gold Medal, !946; Centennial Medal; Fellow Am. Soc. Advance. Science; author of several papers on native vegetation and the ecology of weedy plants; Sigma Xi; Home: 515 Copland Cres., Saskatoon, Sask. S7H 2Z4

COURTOIS, E. Jacques; Q.C.; B.A., LL.B.; b. Montreal, P.Q., 4 July 1920; s. Edmond and Cléophée (Lefebvre) C.; e. Univ. of Montreal, B.A., LL.B.; m. Joan, d. L. L. Miller, Hudson Heights, P.Q., 23 Oct. 1943; children: Nicole, Jacques, Marc; PARTNER COURTOIS, CLARKSON, PARSONS & TETRAULT; Chrmn. of Bd. Gaz Métropolitain inc.; United North American Holdings Ltd.; Pres. and Dir., La Compagnie Foncière du Manitoba (1967), Ltée.; Pres. & Dir., CIIT Inc.; Pres. & Dir., Elican Development Co. Ltd.; Dir., Club de Hockey Canadien Inc.; Vice Pres. and Dir., Bank of Nova Scotia; Chrmn. and Dir., Abitibi Asbestos Mining Co. Ltd.; Dir. Brinco Ltd.; CAE Industries Ltd.; Vice Pres. & Dir., Canada Life Assurance Co.; Dir., various Eaton/Bay Funds; McGraw-Hill Ryerson Ltd.; Norcen Energy Resources Ltd,; Phoenix Steel Corp; Ritz-Carlton Hotel Co. of Montreal, Ltd.; Rolland inc.; Trizec Corp. Ltd.; called to the Bar of Que.; 1946; cr. Q.C. 1963; mem., Candn. Bar Assn.; Bar of Montreal; mem. Bd., Montreal Children's Hosp. and Reddy Mem. Hosp.; served in 2nd World War with R.C.N.V.R.; R. Catholic; Clubs: Forest & Stream; St. Denis; York (Toronto); St. James's; Mount Royal; Mount Bruno Country; Office: 22nd Floor, 630 Dorchester Blvd. W., Montreal, Que. H3B 1V7

COURTRIGHT, James Milton, B.A., B.Sc., P.Eng.; retired university vice-principal; b. North Bay, Ont., 16 Dec. 1914; s. Milton and Sophia (Varin) C.; e. Glebe Coll. Inst., Ottawa; Univ. of Ottawa, B.A. 1937; Queen's Univ., B.Sc. (Hons.) 1941 Pres. of the Student Body (Alma Mater Soc.) 1940-41; (rec'd Jenkins Trophy 1941; John Henry Newman Honour Soc.); Columbia Univ., mang. course 1957; m. Mary Nora, d. Patrick Joseph Roche and Nora O'Rourke, 16 Oct. 1943; children: Joseph W., James H., Patricia N., Stephen M., John T., Mary Ellen, Anthony S., Francis G.; DIR, BEQUEST AND ESTATE PLANNING, QUEEN'S UNIV. part time; joined Shell Canada Ltd. as Refinery Engr., Montreal, 1941, Lubrication Engr., Toronto, 1943, Mgr. Lubricants Dept., 1945, Dist. Mgr., Niagara Peninsula, 1947, Asst. to Vice Pres. and Gen. Mgr., Vancouver, 1948; Retail Sales Mgr. 1949, Sales Mgr. 1949, Gen. Mgr., Purchasing, Toronto, 1951, E. Region Marketing Mgr., Montreal, 1958, Coordinator Pub. Relations, Toronto, 1966, Coordinator Environmental Control, 1968; Vice Principal, Devel. and Infor., Queen's Univ. 1970-79 (ret.) rep. Can. in javelin throw Olympic Games, Berlin, 1936; Commonwealth Games, Australia, 1938 (gold medal); Pan-Am. Games, Dallas, 1937 (gold medal); mem., Queen's Univ. Council (former Trustee of univ.); Past Pres., Newman Assn. Montreal; Ancien Secrétaire de la Fondation Saint-Thomas d'Aquin du Can.; author numerous papers and speeches on mang., purchasing, marketing, pub. relations and environmental control; mem. Ed. Adv. Bd., "Chemosphere" (internat. tech. publ.) 1970-75; Gouverneur de la Chambre de Comm. Prov. de Qué. 1962-65; Council mem., Montreal Bd. Trade 1965-66; Dir., Ont. Chamber Comm. 1967-72; Vice Pres., Cath. Sch. Bd., Vancouver, 1950; Gov., Council for Canadian Unity; Kingston District Chamber Comm., 1972-76; Dir. Kingston Rowing Club; Olympic Club of Can.; Past Dir., Air Pollution Control Assn.; Ont. Chapter; Past Chrmn., Oil Buyers Group, Nat. Assn. Purchasing Agts. (U.S.A.); mem. Bd., St. Mary's of the lake Hosp., Kingston; mem., Assn. Prof. Engrs. Prov. Ont.; Distinguished Service Award, Queen's Univ. 1980; Sports Hall of Fame, Univ. of Ottawa 1980; R. Catholic; recreations: swimming, skiing, walking, reading; Club: University (Montreal); National (Toronto); Home; 431 King St. W., Kingston, Ont. K7L 2X5

COUSE, Mervyn Austin, D.F.C., B.A.Sc.; consulting engineer; b. Toronto, Ont. 22 Jan. 1923; e. Univ. of Toronto B.A.Sc. 1950 (Civil Engn.); m. Agnes Anderson Mitchell; four d.; SR. VICE PRES. AND DIR., PROCTOR & REDFERN LTD.: Chrmn. and Dir. Housel & Associates, Fla.; Dir. Proctor & Redfern International Ltd.; joined present Co. 1950, presently Mgr. Urban Devel. Div.; Dir., S. Muskoka Mem. Hosp. Bracebridge, Ont.; served with RCAF 1942-45, rank Flying Offr.; mem. Assn. Prof. Engrs. Prov. Ont.; Engn. Inst. Can.; Am. Soc. Civil Engrs.; recreations: curling, golf; Club: Granite; Home: 100 Ruscica Dr., Toronto, Ont. M4A 1R4; Office: 75 Eglinton Ave. E., Toronto, Ont. M4P 1H3.

COUSLAND, Rev. Kenneth Harrington, M.C., M.A., B.D., D.D. (Un. Ch.); principal emeritus; b. Swatow, China, 18 Sept. 1894; s. Philip B., a med. missy. in China, and Susan (Harrington) C.; e. George Watson's Coll., Edinburgh, Scotland; Edinburgh Univ.; New Coll., Oxford, B.A. with Hons. 1921, M.A. 1925; Knox Coll., Toronto, B.D. 1927, D.D. 1958; Victoria Univ., Toronto, D.D. (Hon.), 1977; United Theol. Coll., Montreal, D.D. 1942; m. Mary Elizabeth, d. R. F. Rowlands, Toronto, Ont., 24 April 1925; children: Sheila Elizabeth, Richard Philip Kenneth, Mary Suzanne; Master, St. Andrew's Coll., Toronto, 1922-24; Min., Warden Pk. Un. Ch., Toronto, 1926-27; Lect., Union Theol. Coll., 1927-29; Assoc. Prof. of Ch. Hist., Emmanuel Coll., 1929-32; and Prof. 1932; Principal, Emmanuel Coll., 1956-63; served in World War 1914-18 with R.F.A., France and Flanders, gaz. 2nd Lieut., Aug. 1914; Capt., Oct. 1915, Maj. 1918; thrice wounded; Observer, R.F.C., 1917; Mentioned in Despatches 3 times; awarded M.C. and Croix de Guerre (France); mem., Am. Soc. of Ch. Hist.; Past Pres., Watsonian Club (Toronto); Past Pres., Emmanuel Coll. Alumni Assn.; Dir., Toronto Inst. of Church Music; Chrmn., Toronto Inst. of Pastoral Training; Pres., Toronto Conf. of United Church of Can. (1963-64); co-author with late Dr. T. B. Kilpatrick of "Our Common Faith", 1928; contrib. to "The Heritage of Western Culture" (Ed. R. C. Chalmers), 1952, and "The Ministers' Handbook of the United Church of Can.", 1952; author: "The Founding of Emmanuel College", 1978; "The Great War, 1914-18: A 'Gunner' of the First World War Looks Back"; Visiting Prof., McMaster Divinity Coll. 1964; Union Coll. of B.C., 1965-68; recreations: horticulture, music; Home: 30 Colin Ave., Toronto, Ont. M5P 2B9

COUTTS, Herbert Thomas, C.M. (1974), M.A., Ph.D., LL.D.; b. Hamilton, Ontario, 9 Feb. 1907; s. late Charles Alexander and late Harriet I. (Hartwell) C.; e. Georgetown, Ont.; Calgary and Claresholm, Alta.; Calgary Normal Sch.; Univ. of Toronto, B.A. 1935; Univ. of Alta., M.A. 1942; Univ. of Minn., Ph.D. 1950; LL.D., Mem. Univ. of Nfld. 1968; Univ. of Alta. 1979; m. late Clara Alberta, d. late George Simpson, 26 Dec. 1938; four s., one d.; m. Alice Polley, d. Martin Garrett, Sept. 23, 1978; Teacher, Cereal, Claresholm View, Starline, 1925-30; Princ., Stavely (Alta.) S.D., 1930-33; High Sch. Asst. and Princ., Claresholm (Alta.) S.D., 1935-43; Supt. and Inspr. of Schs., Wainwright (Alta.) Sch. Div., 1943-46; Assoc. Prof. of Educ., Univ. of Alta., 1946-50, Chrmn., Div. of Secondary Educ. there 1950-55, Prof. 1951, Dean, Faculty of Educ., 1955; presently Prof. Emeritus, v. of Alberta; has rec'd numerous honours for prof. contributions; co-author, numerous literary publications; Fellow, Canadian Coll. Teachers; Hon. Life mem., Canadian Educ. Assn. (Pres. 1965-66); Candn. College Teachers (Council 1969-75); Candn. Soc. Study Educ. (Pres. 1972-74); Phi Delta Kappa (Emeritus mem.);.I.O.O.F.; United Church; recreations: walking, skating, bridge; Club: Rotary; Home: 12345 - 66 A Ave., Edmonton, Alta. T6H 1Z2

COUTTS James A., LL.B., M.B.A.; b. High River, Alta., 16 May 1938; s. Ewart E. and Alberta (Allan) C.; e. Univ. of Alta. LL.B. 1961; Harvard Sch. of Business M.B.A. 1968; defeated liberal cand. Spadina by-election 1981; Princ. Secy. to Prime Minister of Canada, 1980-81; Princ. Sec'y to Prime Minister from 1975-79; Princ. Secy. to Leader of Opposition 1979-80; called to Bar of Alta. 1962; practised law with McLaws & Co. Calgary, Alta. 1961-63; Secy. to Prime Min. of Can. 1963-66; Consultant McKinsey & Co. Cleveland, Zurich and Toronto 1968-70; Partner, Canada Consulting Group 1970-75; Fed. Lib. Can. for McLeod, Alta. 1962; Sr. Pol. Advisor Prime Min.'s campaign 1974; Gov. Lester B. Pearson Coll. of the Pacific; Dir., Niagara Inst.; Liberal; United Church of Canada; recreation: tennis; Clubs: Rideau Tennis; Rideau; Harvard (Toronto).

COUTURE, Hon. Jacques, M.N.A.; politician; b. Québec, Qué. 23 Nov. 1929; s. Joseph and Irène (Marcoux) C.; e. Laval Univ.; Univ. of Montréal;MIN. OF IMMIGRATION,QUE. 1976- ; el. M.N.A. for St-Henri prov. g.e. 1976, re-el. since; Min. of Labour & Manpower 1976-77; Parti Quebecois; R. Catholic; Office: Edifice G. Quebec, Qué. G1R 5E6.

COUTURE, Jean-Claude, Q.C., B.A., LL.B., B.Comm.; b. Hull, Que., Jan. 1, 1924; s. Dr. Aimé and Lorette (Châtillon) C.; e. High Sch., Ottawa Univ., Ottawa, Ont.; Ottawa Univ., B.A. 1945, B. Comm. 1952; Laval Univ., LL.B. 1949; PARTNER, OGILVY, RENAULT; Dir., J. & P. Coates (Canada) Inc.; P. Bonhomme Ent. Ltd.; S.F. Iszard and Co., Elmira, N.Y.; Phoenix Assur. Co. of Can.; Acadia Life Ins. Co.; called to Bar of Que. 1949; cr. Q.C. 1965; with Dept. Nat. Revenue, Legal Br., Taxation 1950-62, joined present Firm 1963; mem. Estate Planning Council of Montreal; Candn. Bar Assn.; Candn. Tax Foundation; Internat'l Fiscal Assoc.; R. Catholic; recreations: golf, fishing; Clubs: Seigniory; Club de Golf Beaconsfield Inc.; Cercle Universitaire (Ottawa); Mount Royal; Home: 27 Laurier Court, Beaconsfield, Que. H9W 4S7; Office: 1981 McGill College, Montreal, Que. H3A 3C1

COUTURE, Jean-Marie, M.S.C.; administrateur professionel; né Lévis, Qué., 25 sept. 1925; f. F.-Xavier et Alice (Pelletier) C.; é. Ecole Secondaire St-Fidèle (Qué.); Univ. Laval, Faculté de Comm., M.S.C. 1948; ép. Paule, f. P. Albert Dion (Décédé), 25 mai 1953; enfants: André, Lucie, François, Simon; PRESIDENT, SOCIETIE DE FIDUCIE DU QUEBEC depuis 1973; Adm. Fédération de Québec des Caisses Populaires Desjardins; Fiducie du Québec; avec B. Houde & Grothé Ltée, Dir. adjoint de personnel de l'usine 1948-51; Dir. des services, Terrains de jeux de Québec 1952-54; Secrétaire-adjoint, Chambre de Comm. de Qué. 1955; Dir. des services adm., Féd. de

Qué. des Caisses Populaires Desjardins 1955-63; Directeur géneral Fiducie du Québec 1963, Dir. Gén. et adm. 1965; Prés. et Dir. Gén. 1972; Président 1973-77. Président, Société d'habitation du Québec depuis Juin 1977; mem. Corp. des Adm. Agréés; catholique; recreations: lecture, natation, camping; Clubs: St-Denis, Chambre de Commerce de Montréal; résidence: 2000 Arvida, St-Bruno de Montarville, Qué. J3V 3R8; Bureau: Bureau 3 Place Desjardins, Mtl. H5B 1E3; 1054 Rue Conroy, Que., G1R 5E5

COUTURE, Luc-André, Q.C., M.A., L.Ph. LL.L.. Canadian public service; b. Ottawa, Ont., 10 Nov. 1920; s. Florence (Patrice) and the late Dr. Ernest C.; e. Univ. of Ottawa, B.A., B.Ph. 1940, L.Ph. 1941, M.A. 1942; Laval Univ., LL.L. 1949; m. late Louise Duchaine; children: André, Raïssa, Stéphane; 2ndly, Paulette Juneau; VICE CHAIRMAN, RESTRICTIVE TRADE PRACTICES COMISSION, since 1963; Professor of Law, University of Ottawa, since 1954; called to Bar of Que. 1949; cr. Q.C. 1964; Prof. of Philos. and Social Sciences, Univ. of Ottawa for 2 yrs.; Sr. Adv. Counsel, Dept. of Justice 1949-56 and also Legal Adviser, Dept. of Citizenship and Immigration; Gen. Counsel, St. Lawrence Seaway Authority, 1957-63 and also Vice Pres. and Legal Counsel, Cornwall Internat. Bridge Co. Ltd.; Counsel, Indust. Inquiry Comn. on Disruption of Shipping (Norris Inquiry); mem. Bd. of Review under P.O. Act; research project on Royal Comns., Inquiries and Adm. Law; served as an offr. 1944-46; Gov., Univ. of Ottawa (Past Gen. Pres., Alumni Assn.); Founder-Dir., La Caisse Populaire du Sacré-Coeur d'Ottawa Ltée; former Chrmn., Extve. Bd., U.N. Assn. in Can. (Past Pres., Ottawa Br.; Chrmn., Candn. Comte. for 25th Anniversary of U.N.); Legal Counsel, Fed. of French-Speaking Parent-Teachers Assn.; Centennial Medal, 1967; contrib. to "La Revue du Notariat", 1949-54; to La Société juridique Henri Capitan (1952); various writings for Candn. Bar and other periodicals; mem., Candn. Inst. Internat. Affairs; Candn. Bar Assn.; R. Catholic; recreations: painting, swimming; Clubs: Cercle Universitaire; Federal Lawyers'; Home: 211 Wurtemburg St., Ottawa, Ont. K1N 8R4; Office: Dept. of Consumer and Corporate Affairs, Legion house, 359 Kent St., Ottawa, Ont.

COUVRETTE, Joseph-Gilles-André, B.A.; diplomate; né. Montréal, Qué., 15 jan. 1934; f. Bernard et Myrielle (Chartrand) C.; e. Coll. Jean-de-Brébeuf Montréal B.A.; Univ. de Montréal licencié en droit; Univ. de Georgetown cours de maîtrise en relations internationales; ép. Micheline fille de Aimé Godon, 24 mai 1958; enfants: Louis, Michel, Anne-Marie, Philippe; AMBASSADEUR DU CANADA EN SUÈDE 1981-; entré au Ministère des Affaires extérieures 1957, nommé aux Directions des Affaires juridiques, des Affaires d'Extrême-Orient, du Protocole et des Nations Unies avant d'être affecté à l'Ambassade à Rome en 1959; Direction des Affaires d'Europe et au Cabinet du Ministre 1962; Lagos 1965; l'Ecole Nationale d'Adm. à Paris 1967 et puis à l'Ambassade à Paris 1967-68; Directeur adjoint des Affaires culturelles 1968; Directeur des Affaires d'Afrique francophone 1971; Directeur des Affaires du Moyen-Orient 1973; Ambassadeur du Canada au Sénégal, en Mauritanie, en Guinée, au Mali et Haut-Commissaire en Gambie, 1974-77; Ambassadeur en Guinée-Bissao et au Cap-Vert 1975; Ambassadeur au Liban, en Syrie et en Jordanie 1977; Chef de Protocole 1978; Sous-secrétaire d'Etat adjoint aux Affaires extérieures 1979- ; Catholique R.; Récréation: lecture, tennis, ski, golf; Bureau: Ambassade du Canada, Boite postale 16 129, 103 23 Stockholm 16, Suède

COVERT, Frank Manning, O.B.E., D.F.C., Q.C.; b. Canning, Kings Co., N.S., 13 Jan. 1908; s. Archibald Menzies and Minnie Alma (Clarke) C.; e. Canning High Sch.; Kings Co. Acad., Kentville, N.S.; Dalhousie Univ., B.A. 1927, LL.B. 1929; Tech. Univ. of Nova Scotia, P. Eng. (Honourary) 1981; m. Mary Louise Stuart, d. Hon.

W. H. Covert, 25 Aug. 1934; children: Michael, Susan, Peter, Sally; PARTNER, STEWART, MacKEEN & COVERT; Pres., Maritime Paper Products Ltd.; Ben's Holdings Ltd.; Dir., Royal Bank of Canada; Candn. Keyes Fibre Co. Ltd.; Nat. Sea Products Ltd.; Phoenix Assurance Co. of Canada; Great Eastern Corpn.; Eastern Telephone & Telegraph Co.; Home Care Properties Ltd.; Maritime Steel & Foundries Ltd.; Minas Basin Pulp & Power Co. Ltd.; Sydney Engineering & Dry Docks Co. Ltd.; Bowater Mersey Paper Co. Ltd.; Sun Life Assurance Co. of Canada; Standard Brands Ltd. Lindwood Holdings Ltd.; Counsel, Royal Comn. on Transportation 1949; read law with James McG. Stewart, K.C., Halifax, N.S.; called to Bar of N.S. 1930; cr. K.C. 1944; practised in Halifax 1929-40; Asst. Gen Counsel, Dept. of Munitions & Supply, 1940-42; served in World War 1942-45; with R.C.A.F. as Navigator; awarded D.F.C.; mem., N.S. and Candn. Bar Assns.; Liberal; Anglican; recreation: golf; Homes: Spring Garden Terrace Apts., Spring Garden R., Halifax, N.S.; Hunts Point, Queens Co, N.S. B0T 1G0 Office: 1583 Hollis St., Halifax, N.S. B3J 1V4

COVERT, George David Napier, Q.C.; B.A., B.C.L., LL.M., M.B.A.; b. Halifax, N.S., 27 Sept. 1938; s. George Leslie and Mary Kathleen Kilgour (Napier) C.; e. Univ. New Brunswick, B.A. 1960, B.C.L. 1963; Harvard Univ., LL.M. 1965; York Univ., M.B.A. 1969; m. Eleanor Patricia, d. late Frank T. Stanfield, 14 June 1969; children: Meghan Patricia, Ian David, Brian Frank; PARTNER, STEWART, MacKEEN & COVERT; Dir., Stanfield's Ltd. Pres. Halifax Infirmary; Dir. Northlake Shipping Ltd.; read law with Donald A. Kerr, Q.C.; called to Bar of N.S. 1966; P. Cons.; Anglican; Home: 893 Marlborough Ave., Halifax, N.S. B3H 3G7; Office: 1583 Hollis St., P.O. Box 997, Halifax, N.S. B3J 2X2

COWAN, Charles Gibbs, C.D., Q.C.; lawyer; b. Cannington, Ont. 13 Nov. 1928; s. Charles Gibbs and Jean (MacFarlane) C.; e. Upper Can. Coll. Toronto 1946; Univ. of Toronto, Trinity Coll. B.A. 1950; Osgoode Hall Law Sch. 1954; Militia Staff Course msc 1959; m. Susan Mary d. late Philip Charles Tidy 24 Sept. 1954; children: Julia Mary, James Charles Strathy, Stuart Philip Gibbs; PARTNER, HOLDEN, MURDOCH & FINLAY; Dir. and Secy. Hollinger Argus Ltd.; Labrador Mining and Exploration Co. Ltd.; called to Bar of Ont. 1954; cr. Q.C. 1967; served with Queen's Own Rifles of Can. (Militia) 1947-63, rank Maj.; mem. Candn. Bar Assn.; Co. York Law Assn.; Heraldry Soc. Can.; Anglican; Club: University; Home: 8 Powell Ave., Toronto, Ont. M4W 2Y7; Office: (P.O. Box 80) First Canadian Place, Toronto, Ont. M5X 1B1.

COWAN, Edgar A.; publisher; b. Toronto, Ont. 29 May 1937; s. Maurice Charles and Ann (Finsten) C.; e. Oriole Park Pub. Sch. Toronto; N. Toronto High Sch. Sr. Matric.; Ryerson Inst. of Technol. Grad. in Business Adm.; Univ. Extension courses in Business Adm. and Journalism; m. Nuala Mary Cassidy 2 Jan. 1966; one s. Noah; PRESIDENT, LIVELY ARTS MARKET BUILDERS INC; Pres. and C.E.O., (publisher of "Saturday Night"); Readers Club of Canada (Book Club) 1975; Dir. and Founding Partner Channel CITY-TV SeventyNine Ltd.; Dir. New Leaf Publishing Co. Ltd.; Raventures Holdings Ltd.; Galanty Ltd.; Ed. Asst. "Toronto Telegram" 1961, Asst. Promotion Mgr. 1962; Acct. Extve. Pub. Relations MacLaren Advertising Co. Ltd. 1963, Pub. Relations Dept. Mgr. Vice Pres. 1968-70; Pres. Carleton, Cowan Public Relations Ltd. 1970-74; Serving Bro. Order St. John; mem. Lib. Party Can. St. Paul's Lib. Assn.; Dir. Writers Development Trust, Niagara Institute; Metrop. Toronto Zool. Soc.; Celtic Arts; Ireland Fund of Can.; mem. Candn. Periodical Publishers Assn.; Candn. Conf. Arts; Festival of Festivals; Candn. Pub. Relations Soc.; Liberal; Hebrew; Clubs: Variety; Toronto Press; Home: 144 Walmer Rd., Toronto, Ont. M5R 2X9; Office: 69 Front St. E., Toronto, Ont. M5E 1R9

COWAN, Hon. Gordon Stewart, M.A., LL.B., B.C.L., LL.D.; retired; b. St. John's, Nfld., 19 May 1911; s. Peter Haviland and Hattie (Gushue) C.; e. Methodist Coll. (now Un. Ch. Coll.), St. John's; Memorial Coll. (now Univ.); Dalhousie Univ. Law Sch.,; LL.B., 1932; LL.D., 1976; Rhodes Scholar, Nfld., 1933; Exeter Coll., Oxford, B.A. (lst Class Hon. in Juris.) 1935, B.C.L. (1st Class), 1936, M.A., 1937; m. 1st late Jean Elizabeth Rettie, 6 May 1937; children: James Stewart, Hugh Robert, Joan Elizabeth; 2ndly Jean C. Mann; Chief Justice, Trial Div., Supreme Court of N.S. 1967-81; read law with Raymond Gushue, St. John's and J. E. Rutledge, Halifax; called to Bar of N.S. 1932; cr. Q.C., 1950; Lectr. in Law, Dalhousie Law Sch., 1936-37; Asst. Prof., 1937-39; Asst. Prof. Manitoba Law Sch., 1939-41; practised law with Stewart, Smith, MacKeen & Rogers, Halifax, N.S., 1941-43; Partner, Stewart, MacKeen & Covert, 1943-66; apptd. Judge, Supreme Court of N.S., 1966; served as Capt., 2nd Reserve Bn., Princess Louise Fusiliers, Halifax, 1942-45; mem., Halifax Sch. Bd., 1951-54; House of Assembly, Halifax Centre, 1956-60; Candn. Red Cross (Pres., N.S. Div., 1947-49, Hon. Secy. 1950; Vice-Pres., 1958-76); Y.M.C.A. (Dir., Halifax, 1948-55, Trustee 1960-76); Dalhousie Univ., Alumni Gov., 1949-54; Chrmn., Victoria Gen. Hosp. Comn., 1956-57; Gov., Candn. Tax Foundn. 1960-62; Treas., Atlantic Provs. Econ. Council, 1960-61; Chrmn., N.S. Human Rights Comte. 1966-68; Chrmn., N.S. Human Rights Comte. 1966-70; United Church; recreation: gardening; Clubs: Saraguay; Halifax; R.N.S.Y.S.; Office: #1001-6095 Coburg Rd., Halifax, N.S. B3H 4K1

COWAN, Ian McTaggart, O.C. (1970), Ph.D., LL.D., D.Env.Sc., D.Sc., F.R.S.C.; university professor; b. Edinburgh, Scot., 25 June 1910; s. Garry McTaggart and Laura Alice (Mackenzie) C.; came to Can. 1913; e. Univ. of B.C., B.A. 1932; Univ. of Cal., PhD. 1935; LL.D. Alberta 1971; D. Env. St., Univ. of Waterloo 1975; D. Sc., Univ. B.C. 1977; LL.D.; Simon Fraser Univ. 1980; m. Joyce Stewart, d. Kenneth Racey, Vancouver, B.C., 21 Apl. 1936; children: Garry, Barbara Ann; PROF. OF ZOOLOGY, UNIV. OF B.C.; 1945-75; Head of the Dept. 1943-64; Asst. Dean of Arts & Sciences 1957-63; Dean of Grad. Studies 1964-75; Dean Emeritus since 1975; mem., Fisheries Research Bd. of Can.; Nat. Research Council of Canada; Wildlife Adv. Comte. to U.S. Secy. of Interior; IUCN Survival Service (V. Pres. 1970-76); Arctic Institute (Past Chrmn.); Pres., Biol. Council of Can. 1967-68; Asst. Biol., B.C. Prov. Museum, 1936-38; Asst. Dir. 1938-40; Consulting Biol., Nat. Parks of Can., 1943-46; mem. and Chrmn., Canadian Environmental Adv. Council 1972-79; Chrmn., B.C. Academic Bd. 1977-79; Academic Council (B.C.) sine 1978; Candn. Comte. on Whales and Whaling; Chmn., Habitat Conserv. Fund (Adv. Bd., B.C.) 1981-; Chancellor, U. of Victoria, 1979-85; Can. Centennial Medal, 1967; Fred Fry Medal, Can. Soc. Zoologists, 1977; Queen Elizabeth Jubilee Medal, 1978; mem., Am. Ornithologists Union; Am. Soc. of Mammologists; Am. Wildlife Soc. (Past Pres.; Leopold Medal 1970); Soc. Systematic Zool.; has contrib. many books and papers on mammals, birds, parasites and diseases of mammals to various tech. jours.; Sigma Xi; Anglican; Home: 3919 Woodhaven Terrace, Victoria, B.C. V8N 1S7

COWARD, Laurence, E., F.I.A., F.C.I.A., A.S.A., F.C.A.; company executive; b. London, Eng., 20 July 1914; s. Charles E. and Eleanor (Betts) C.; e. Royal Liberty Sch., Essex, Eng.; Jesus Coll., Cambridge Univ.; Inst. of Actuaries, 1939; m. Mollie Yeulett, 1 Jan. 1949; children: Michael, Jane, Anthony, Peter; DIR., WILLIAM M. MERCER LTD.; joined Brit. Civil Service, London, Eng. as Extve. Offr., Nat. Debt Office, 1935; Actuary 1937-41; apptd. Actuary of present Co. 1949; Vice Pres. 1953; Chrmn. Pension Comn. of Ont., 1963-65; Pres., Candn. Inst. of Actuaries, 1969-70; Candn. Pension Conf., 1963-65; author of "Canadian Handbook of Pension and Welfare Plans" (CCH); Anglican; recreations: skiing; music; Clubs: National; Granite; Alpine Ski;

Home: 100 Millwood Rd., Tor. Ont. M4S 1J7; Office: 1 First Canadian Place, Tor. Ont. M5X 1G3

COWASJEE, Saros, M.A., Ph.D.; author; educator; b. Secundrabad, India 12 July 1931; s. Dara Cowasjee; e. St. John's Coll. Agra, India B.A. 1951; Agra Coll. M.A. 1955; Univ. of Leeds Ph.D. 1960; PROF. OF ENGLISH, UNIV. OF REGINA 1971- ; Asst. Ed. Times of India Press, Bombay 1961-63; Instr. in Eng. present Univ. 1963; guest lectr. numerous univs. Europe, Australia, N. Am., India; author "Sean O'Casey: the Man Behind the Plays" 1963 (criticism); "O'Casey" 1966 (criticism); "Stories and Sketches" 1970; "Goodbye to Elsa" 1974 (novel); "'Coolie': An Assessment" 1976 (criticism); "So Many Freedoms: A Study of the Major Fiction of Mulk Raj Anand" 1977 (criticism); "Nude Therapy" 1978 (short stories); "The Last of the Maharajas" 1980 (screenplay); "Suffer Little Children" 1982 (novel); ed. with introductions "Private Life of an Indian Prince" 1970 (novel); "Untouchable" 1970 (novel); "Seven Summers" 1970 (novel); "Coolie" 1972 (novel); "Author to Critic: The Letters of Mulk Raj Anand" 1973 (letters); "Hindoo Holiday" 1979 (novel, introd. only); "Mulk Raj Anand: A Check-list" 1979 (bibliog., introd. only); "The Big Heart" 1980 (novel); "Modern Indian Fiction" 1981 (anthol.); "Modern Indian Short Stories" 1982 (anthol.); "Stories from the Raj" 1982 (anthol.); "Four Months of 'Forty-seven" 1983 (fict. anthol.); contrib. to various publs., numerous articles; recipient 3 Can. Council Leave Fellowships; mem. Assn. Candn. Univ. Teachers Eng.; Candn. Assn. Commonwealth Lit. & Lang. Studies; S. Pacific Assn. Commonwealth Lit. & Lang. Studies; Authors Guild India; Writers Union Can.; Cambridge Soc.; Zorastrian; recreations: driving, reading, travel; Address: Regina, Sask. S4S 0A2.

COWIE, Bruce Edgar; broadcaster; b. Prince Albert, Sask. 6 Mar. 1938; s. Louis Leroy and Janet (Anderson) C.; e. Prince Albert Coll. Inst.; m. Marlene Ann d. late-Michael Lehman 28 July 1958; children: Cameron Bruce, Brent Brent, Caron Dawn; VICE PRES. AND GEN. MGR., HARVARD COMMUNICATIONS (CKCK-TV, CKRM-AM, CFMQ-FM HARVARD CREATIVE SERVICES) 1981- ; Pres., Braeloch Consulting Ltd.; Vice-Pres., Harvard Developments Ltd.; Vice-Pres. Harvard Oil & Gas; Dir., Westernn Surety Co. Ltd.; CTV Television Network; Announcer, CKOM radio, Saskatoon 1956-59; Announcer, CKCK-TV, Regina 1959-68; Gen. Mgr., Armadale Productions 1968-72; Gen. Mgr., CKCK-TV, 1972-78; V.P. and Gen. Mgr., CKCK-TV, 1978-81; Alderman, City of Regina 1974-77; named Broadcaster of the Year 1981 by Western Assn. of Broadcasters; founding Chrmn. Can Pro (TV Program Festival); past Pres. Western Football Conference; life mem. and past Pres. Saskatchewan Roughriders Football Club; mem. Quarter Century Club, Candn. Assn. of Broadcasters; Liberal; Roman Catholic; Clubs: Assiniboia; Lakeshore Estates; recreations: skiing, swimming, horse show announcing; Home: 113 Tibbits Rd., Regina, Sask. S4S 2Y9; Office: P.O. Box 2000, Regina, Sask. S4P 3E5

COWIE, James F., B.Comm.; petroleum executive; b. Montreal, Que. 22 July 1934; s. Andrew James and Hilda Margaret (Thomson) C.; e. Various schs. Toronto Winnipeg Vancouver Victoria; Univ. of B.C., B.Comm. 1956; Advance Mgmt. Prog., Harvard Business School, 1977; m. Helen Betty Ann d. Berne C. Pickering 26 July 1957; children: James McRae, Donald Stuart, Kathryn Ann, Heather Lynn; PRESIDENT AND DIR. RYERSON OIL AND GAS LTD. joined: Landman, Amoco Canada Ltd. Calgary 1959, Pure Oil Co. 1964; Contracts Mgr. Central-Del Rio Oils, 1965-68; Land Mgr. and Asst. Secy. Canadian Homestead Oils 1968-72; Land Mgr. Pan Ocean Oil Ltd. 1972, Vice Pres. 1974, Pres. 1975-81; Zeta Psi; recreations: golf, squash; Clubs: Calgary Petroleum; Silver Springs Golf & Country; Home: 1045 Varsity Estates Pl.

N.W., Calgary, Alta. T3B 3X5; Office: 204, 6715-8 St. N.E., Calgary, Alta. T2E 7H7

COWING, Walter Lishman; publisher; b. London, Eng. 14 Feb. 1926; s. Walter and Clara Emma (Kelly) C.; e. Toronto pub. schs. and East York Coll. Inst.; m. Beverley Doreen d. Arthur James Hay, D.C.M., Toronto, Ont. 24 Aug. 1946; children: Paula Doris, Richard Walter, Glen Arthur; PRES. CANADA LAW BOOK LTD. since 1968; Pres. and Dir. Walbev Holdings Ltd.; Vice. Pres. and Dir. Garden City Press Ltd.; Jobborn Manufacturing (1975) Ltd.; Dir. Aurland Holdings Ltd.; joined present firm 1941, Asst. Gen. Mgr. 1959, Vice pres. 1967; served with Candn. Inf. Regt. 1944, Argylle & Sutherland Highlanders 1945; mem. Council Printing Industries; Candn. Aquanats; Anglican; recreations: golf, curling, scuba, boating, snowmobiling; Clubs: Bayview Country (Pres. 1977); National; Home: 24 Vintage Lane, Thornhill, Ont. L3T 1X6; Office: 240 Edward St., Aurora, Ont. L4G 3S9.

COWLEY, Hon. Elwood Lorrie, M.L.A., B.Ed., B.A.; politician; teacher; b. Saskatoon, Sask., 2 Aug. 1944; s. William Andrew and Edwina (Call) C.; e. Univ. of Sask., B.Ed. 1965, B.A. (distinction) 1967; m. Delores Gail, d. Stirling O. Major, Kinley, Sask., 26 June 1965; children: Sherry Loy, Carla Rae, Scott Joseph; PROVINCIAL SEC., MINISTER OF ECONOMIC DEVELOPMENT; GOV. OF SASKATCHEWAN Min. of Mineral Resources Saskatchewan; Chairman, Crown Investments Corp.; Sask. Mining and Devel't Corp. (S.M.D.C.); Chmn., Sask. Oil and Gas Corp.; Teacher, Assiniboia (Sask.) Composite High Sch. 1965, Thom Coll., Regina, Sask. 1967-72; el. M.L.A. for Biggar, Sask. 1971; mem., Sask. Teachers' Fed.; N.D.P.; United Church; recreations: curling, bridge; Home: 197 Hanley Cresc., Regina, Sask. S4R 5A9; Office: Rm. 38, Legislative Bldgs., Regina, Sask.

COWTAN, Stanley Alfred, B.Sc.; petroleum executive; b. Ottawa, Ont. 29 Oct. 1927; s. Albert Charles and Alice Harriet (Griffith) C.; e. Nepean High Sch. Ottawa; Queen's Univ. B.Sc. (Chem. Engn.) 1950; m. Patricia Ann d. Cecil Frederick Cross 4 Jan. 1957; children: Catherine, Stanley Jr., Linda, Cynthia; SENIOR EXECUTIVE VICE PRESIDENT SUNCOR INC.; reg'd Candn. patent agt.; mem. Assn. Prof. Engrs. Ont.; Clubs: Granite, National; Home: 11 Butterfield Dr., Don Mills, Ont. M3A 2L9; Office: 56 Wellesley St. W., Toronto, Ont. M5S 2S4

COX, Albert Reginald, B.A., M.D., F.R.C.P.(C), F.A.C.P., F.A.C.C.; educator; b. Victoria, B.C. 18 Apl. 1928; s. Reginald Herbert Cox; e. Victoria High Sch. 1946; Victoria Coll. 1948; Univ. of B.C. B.A. 1950, M.D. 1954; m. Margaret d. L. Douglas Dobson, St. John's, Nfld. May 1954; children: Susan M., David J., Steven F.; DEAN OF MEDICINE, MEMORIAL UNIV. OF NFLD. since 1974; consulting staff Gen. Hosp. St. John's Nfld.; Consultant, Grace Gen. Hosp., St. Clare's Mercy Hosp., Janeway Child Health Centre, St. John's, Nfld.; Asst. Prof. of Med. Univ. of B.C. 1961, Assoc. prof. 1964-69; Prof. and Chrmn. of Med. present Univ. 1969-74, Aoc. Dean Clin. Affairs 1972-74; author various scient. publs. cardiol. and cardiovascular physiol.; Dir. Internat. Grenfell Assn.; Bd. mem., Gen. Hosp. Corp.; Past Pres., Assn. Candn. Med. Colls.; mem. Candn. Cardiovascular Soc.; Candn. Soc. Clin. Investigation; Nfld. Med. Assn.; Candn. med. Assn.; Presbyterian; recreations: greenhouse gardening, photography; Home: 144 Waterford Bridge Rd., St. John's, Nfld. A1E 1C9; Office: Faculty Medicine, Health Sciences Centre, Memorial University, St. John's, Nfld.

COX, Kenneth Victor, B.Sc., D.Adm., D. Sc.; utilities executive; b. Allison, N.B., 14 May 1922; s. Charles Hilton and Hattie Mae (Mollins) C.; e. Moncton (N.B.) High Sch. 1938; Univ. of N.B., B.Sc. (Elect. Engn.); m. Mary MacNeill, d. late John Franklin Dow, June 1944; children: David R., Rodney A., Kenneth H., Marilyn L.; N.B. TELEPHONE CO. LTD.CHRMN. BD. & PRES. N.B. TEL

CO. LTD.; Dir., Bank of Nova Scotia; Pres. and Chief Extve. Offr., Bruntel Holdings Ltd.; Dir., Maritime Elect. Co. Ltd.; Eastern Telephone & Telegraph Co.; North American Life Assurance Co.; Fraser Inc.; Datacrown Inc.; SDL/Datacrown Inc.; Dir., Telesat Can.; Chrmn., N.B. Research & Productivity Council; Sr. mem., Conference Board Inc.; Bd. Hon. Governors, Candn. Assn. Mentally Retarded; mem., Assn. Prof. Engrs. Prov. N.B. (Past Pres.); Fellow, Engn. Inst. Can.; Hon. Dr. of Science, U. of New Brunswick; Hon. Dr. of Bus. Administration, Univ. of Moncton; recreation: flying, photography, fishing; Clubs: Westfield Golf & Country; Riverside Golf & Country; Union; Rotary; Home: 216 Roderick Row, Saint John, N.B. E2M 4J8; Office: One Brunswick Square Saint John, N.B. E2L 4K2

COX, Lionel Audley, M.A., Ph.D., P.Eng, F.C.S., F.C.I.C., F.A.A.A.S., F.T.A.P.P.I.; research chemist; b. Winnipeg, Man., 18 Sept. 1916; s. late Harry Audley and late May Julia (Racine) C.; e. Univ. of B.C., B.A. 1941, M.A. 1943; McGill Univ., Ph.D. 1946; m. Evelyn Juliet, d. Walter Emerson Bavis, M.D., 1 Sept. 1941; children: Victoria M. R.; C. Bruce R., David A. R.; Pres., Lionel A. Cox Inc. (Research Devel. and Innovative Consultants); (formerly Dir. of Research); Teacher, Math. and Science, Univ. Sch., Victoria, B.C., 1935-40; Lectr. in Chem., Univ. of B.C., 1943-44; Chief Chem. and Consultant, Sidney Roofing and Paper Co., Victoria, 1941-44; Research Chem., American Viscose Corp., Marcus Hook, Pa., 1946-51; Sr. Research Chem. 1951-53; Vice Pres. and Dir. of Research, Johnson & Johnson Ltd., Montreal, 1953-61; Vice Pres. and Dir. of Research and Engineering, Personal Products Ltd. (Div. of Johnson & Johnson), Milltown, N.J., 1961-65; Dir. of Research & Technology Assessment, MacMillan Bloedel Ltd. 1965-77; served with C.O.T.C. 1939-43; mem., Board of Mang., B.C. Research; Nat. Adv. Bd., Forest Products Research; Fed. Govt. and Pulp & Paper Indust. Coordinating Comte. on Water Pollution Abatement; Bd. of Editors, "Research Mngmt."; Journal of Ind. Research Inst. Inc; Bd. of Dirs., Educ. Inst. of B.C.; Fellow, Am. Assn. Advanc. Science; Tech. Assn. Pulp & Paper Industry; Chem. Inst. of Can.; Emeritus Rep., Indust. Research Inst. Inc.; mem., Am. Chem Soc.; Candn. Soc. Chemical Engrs.; Candn. Pulp & Paper Assn.; Candn. Research Mang. Assn.; Assn. of Prof. Engrs. of B.C. Engn. Inst. Can.; Fiber Soc., Inc.; Forest Products Research Soc.; Soc. Chem. Indust.; mem., Nat. Research Council 1971-74 and Sci. Council Can. 1974-77; Sigma Xi; mem. Bd. of Trustees, Shaughnessy Hosp., Vancouver, B.C.; recreations: golf, swimming, tennis; Clubs: University; Shaughnessy Golf & Country; Home: 4185 Yuculta Crescent, Vancouver, B.C. V6N 4A9

COX, Wallace, D., Q.C.; b. Toronto, Ont., 31 Jan. 1916; s. Frank W. and Ethel (Dunning) C.; e. Boxgrove Sch., Guildford, Surrey, Eng.; Canford Sch., Bournemouth, Hants, Eng.; Upper Can. Coll.; Univ. of Toronto; Osgoode Hall Law Sch.; m. Mary., d. Owen Ellis, Feb. 1946; one d. Susan Merridy; PARTNER, COX, ARMSTRONG & SMITH, since 1961; Dir., Sterling Offices of Canada Ltd.; Anglo Canada General Insurance Co.; Gibraltar General Insurance Co.; Chief Agent in Can., General American Life Assurance Co.; Chief Agent in Ont., Grain Insurance and Guarantee Co.; read law with Wilfrid M. Cox; called to Bar of Ont., 1941; cr. Q.C.; served during 2nd World War with Candn. Army in Normandy; discharged with rank of Capt.; mem., Candn. Bar Assn.; Co. York Law Assn.; Bd. Trade Metrop. Toronto; Beta Theta Pi; Un. Church; recreations: cricket, skiing, Office: 19 Richmond St. W., Toronto, Ont. M5H 1Y9

COXETER, Harold Scott Macdonald, Ph.D., LL.D., D.Math., D.Sc., F.R.S., F.R.S.C.; research mathematician; b. London, Eng., 9 Feb. 1907; s. Harold Samuel (mem. of London firm of Coxeter & Son) and Lucy (Gee) C.; e. St. George's Sch. Harpenden, Eng.; Trinity Coll., Cambridge, B.A. 1929; Ph.D. 1931 (winner of Smith's prize); Fellow there 1931-35; Rockefeller Fndn. Fell. at Princeton 1932-33; Procter Fellow at Princeton 1934-35, Alta., LL.D. 1957; Trent 1973; Toronto, 1979; Waterloo, D.Math. 1969; Acadia, D.Sc. 1971; m. Hendrina Johanna, d. Leonardus Brouwer, Vlaardingen, Holland, 20 Aug. 1936; children: Edgar, Susan; came to Can. 1936; PROF. EMERITUS OF MATHEMATICS, UNIV. OF TORONTO, 1980-; Asst. Prof. there 1936-44; Assoc. Prof. 1944-48; Prof. 1948-80; Visiting Prof. at Univ. of Notre Dame 1947; Columbia Univ. 1949; Dartmouth Coll., 1964; Florida Atlantic Univ. 1965; Univ. of Amsterdam, 1966, Edinburgh, 1967, East Anglia, 1968, Australian National, 1970, Sussex, 1972; Utrecht, 1976; Cal Tech, 1977; Bologna, 1978; awarded H. M. Tory Medal for outstanding contrib. to Math. Science, by Roy. Soc. of Can., 1950; author of "Non-Euclidean Geometry", 1942; "Regular Polytopes", 1948; "The Real Projective Plane", 1949; "Introduction to Geometry", 1961; "Projective Geometry", 1964; "Twelve Geometric Essays", 1968; "Regular Complex Polytopes", 1974; co-author of "The 59 Icosahedra", 1938; "Generators and Relations", 1957; "Geometry Revisited", 1966; "Zero-symmetric Graphs", 1981; revised Rouse Ball "Mathematical Recreations and Essays" (12th ed.) 1974; has contributed numerous papers to various scientific journals; discovered a new regular polyhedron having six hexagonal faces at each vertex, 1926; enumerated the n-dimensional kaleidoscopes, 1933; Editor-in-Chief Candn. Journal of Math., 1949-58; Pres. Can. Math. Cong. 1965-67; Int'l Cong. Mathematicians, 1974; Hon. mem., Edin. Math. Soc.; Mathematische Gesellschaft, Hamburg; Wiskundig Genootschap; London Math. Soc.; mem. Am. Math. Soc.; Math. Assn. Am.; Candn. Math. Soc.; Liberal; Protestant; recreation: music; Home: 67 Roxborough Dr., Toronto, Ont. M4W 1X2

COYLE, David Marshall, B.Com.; company executive; b. Aylmer, Ont. 1919; e. Vaughan Coll., Toronto, Ont.; Univ. of Toronto, B.Com.; m. Isabel Emmerson 1946; children: Elizabeth, Dudleigh, Jennifer, Margaret; VICE-PRES., C-I-L INC. since 1969 and Dir. since 1975; Chrmn. Bd., Douglas Estates Ltd.; Dir., J.P. Morgan of Can. Ltd.; joined the Co. as Acct., Montreal 1946, Asst. Credit Mgr. 1950, Finance Mgr. 1954, Mgr. Special Studies 1960, Mgr. Staff Devel. 1964; seconded to Imperial Chemical Industries Ltd. (India) as Finance Dr., 1966; returned to present position 1969; served in Merchant Navy 1941-46; Past Pres., Montreal Y.M.C.A.; mem. Montreal Soc. Fin. Analysts; Fin. Extves. Inst.; recreations: golf, skiing; Clubs: Oriental (London, Eng.); Tollygunge (Calcutta, India); St. James's; Royal Montreal Golf; Knowlton Golf; Home: 1398 Ave. Dr. Penfield, Montreal, Que. H3G 1B7; Office: 630 Dorchester Blvd. W., Montreal, Que. H3B 1S6

COYLE, Donald Walton, B.A.; television executive; b. London, Ont., 17 June 1922; s. Lorne Stanley and Pearle A. (Walton) C.; e. Amherst Coll., B.A.; m. Patricia Robinson, 6 June 1946; children: Donald Lorne, Deborah Ann, Sharon Robinson; Pres., Can West Communications Corp., Chm., Intercontinental Communications, Inc.; Dir., served with RCAF during World War II; Chi Psi, Episcopalian; Club: University (N.Y.); recreations: skiing; flying: Home: 86 Plymbridge Rd., Willowdale, Ont. M2P 1A3; Office: Suite 3800, First Canadian Place, Toronto, Ont. M5X 1A4

COYNE, James Elliott, B.A., B.C.L., LL.D.; financial consultant; b. Winnipeg, Man., 17 July 1910; s. Hon. James Bowes and Edna Margaret (Elliott) C.; e. Univ. of Manitoba, B.A. 1931, LL.D. 1961; Oxford Univ. B.A. 1933, B.C.L. 1934; m. Meribeth (Stobie) Riley, 26 June 1957; called to Bar of Man. 1934; practised law in Winnipeg, 1934-38; entered Bank of Canada Research Dept. 1938; Securities Advisor, Bank of Canada, 1944-49; Depy. Gov. 1950-54; Gov. 1955-61; resigned July 1961; Clubs: Toronto; Manitoba (Winnipeg); Home: 29 Ruskin Row, Winnipeg, Man. R3M 2R9

COYNE, John McCreary, D.F.C., Q.C., M.A.; lawyer; b. Winnipeg, Manitoba, 20 June 1919; s. Hon. James Bowes, Q.C., and Edna Margaret (Elliott) C.; e. Ravenscourt Sch.; Winnipeg, Man.; Univ. of Manitoba, B.A. (Hons.) 1940; Oxford Univ., B.A. 1947, M.A. 1951; m. Margery Joan, d. late Frank G. Daniels, Montreal, Que., 19 Sept. 1952; children: Jennifer, Deborah, Barbara, John, Ryland; PARTNER, HERRIDGE, TOLMIE; mem., Ottawa Adv. Bd., Canada Permanent Trust Co.; mem. Bd. of Gov., Can. Tax Found'n.; called to the Bar at Lincoln's Inn, London, 1947; to the Bar of Manitoba, 1948, and of Ont. 1948; cr. Q.C. 1964; served in 2nd World War with R.C.A.F. 1942-45; awarded D.F.C.; Gov., Trinity Coll. Sch., Port Hope, Ont.; mem., Candn. Bar Assn.; Zeta Psi; Anglican; Clubs: Rideau; Royal Ottawa Golf; Home: 235 Mariposa Ave., Rockcliffe Park, Ottawa, Ont. K1M 0T4; Office: 116 Albert St., Ottawa, Ont. K1P 5G3

COZENS, John; musician; heraldic artist; editor; adviser on protocol; b. Tottenham, Eng., 27 April 1906; s. Rev. Reginald and Mrs. C.; m. Winifred Pitman; children: Joyce Marian, John Francis; HON. SECRETARY, CANADIAN MUSIC COUNCIL; Conductor, Civil Service Choral Society and other choral groups; mem., Canadian Heraldry Society; Ont. Reg. Music Teachers Assn.; English-Speaking Union; Editor, Arranger and Composer of music publ. by U.S., Candn. and Eng. Co's; Centennial Medal, 1967; Candn. Music Council medal, 1976; Queen's Jubilee Medal, 1977; Club: Arts & Letters; Address: 188 Elmwood Ave., Willowdale, Ont. M2N 3M6

CRABTREE, Harold Roy, C.D., B.Sc., LL.D.; manufacturer; b. Montreal, P.Q., 2 March 1918; s. Harold and Louisa Alberta (Stafford) C.; e. Lower Canada Coll., Montreal, P.Q.; McGill Univ., B.Sc.; LL.D. Mount Allison, 1963; m. Caroline Ruth, d. A.A. Hanna, Montreal, P.Q., 17 Nov. 1945; children: Sandra, Harold, Stafford; CHRMN. AND PRES., WABASSO INC. and subsidiaries; Dir. and mem., Extve. Comte., Domtar Inc.; Vice Chrmn., Fraser Co's. Ltd.; Dir. & mem. extve. comte., Bank of Montreal; Sun Life Assurance Co. of Canada; RHP Canada; Renold Canada Ltd.; Velcro Corp.; Ptutt & Whitney of Can.; Douglas Inc.; Sherbrooke & Standard Insurance Cos.; Pres., Treeford Ltd.; mem., Canadian Advisory Board, Commercial Union Group of Ins. Co's.; Gov., Royal Edward Chest Hosp.; Laurentian Chest Hosp.; Royal Victoria Hosp. Fndn.; Alexandra Hosp., all Montreal; mem. of Corp. of Bishop's Univ., Lennoxville, P.Q.; Lower Can Coll.; Chancellor Emeritus, Mount Allison Univ.; served as Lieut., Canadian Army in 2nd World War; Hon. Col., Royal Canadian Hussars (Montreal); mem. Candn. Textiles Inst. (Pres. 1955-59); Cotton Inst. of Can. (Pres. 1954-59); Chrmn. of Extve. Council, Candn. Chamber of Comm., 1957-58; Past Pres., Candn. Mfrs. Assn., 1963-64; Pres., Montreal Bd. of Trade, 1960 Delta Kappa Epsilon; Conservative; Presbyterian; recreations: shooting; fishing; Clubs: St. James's, Mount Royal; University; Royal Montreal Curling; Canadian (N.Y.); Stadacona Fish & Game; Home: 58 Forden Cres., Westmount, Que. H3Y 2Y4; Office: 1825 Graham Blvd., Montreal, Que. H3R 1H2

CRABTREE, W. H. Aubrey, LL.D.; industrialist; 3rd generation engaged in papermaking indust. in Can.; b. Joliette, P.Q., 1 Apl. 1898; s. David and Alice (Woods) C.; e. Stanstead Coll., P.Q.; Berthier (P.Q.) Grammar Sch.; Burdett Coll., Boston, Mass.; Univ. of N.B., LL.D.; m. Dorothy, d. J. W. Hall, Edmundston, N.B., 12 June 1931; children: Mary Diana, J. Alan; Hon. Dir., Fraser Companies, Ltd.; Fraser Paper Ltd.; Dir., Wabasso Ltd.; with Edwin Crabtree & Sons, Sunapee, N.H., Adams Paper Co., Wells River, Vt., Howard Smith Paper Mills Ltd., at Crabtree Mills and Beauharnois, P.Q., 1920-28; Gen. Supt., Can. Paper Co., Windsor Mills, Que., 1928; later becoming Resident Mgr.; joined Fraser Co.'s as Mill Mgr., Fraser Paper Ltd., 1930; Gen. Mgr. 1935; Vice-Pres. and Gen. Mgr., Fraser Co.'s Ltd. and subsidiary Co.'s

1940; Pres. and Gen. Mgr., 1941-62, Chairman, 1956-66; served in World War 1916-19 with C.E.F.; sr. mem., Tech. Sec., Candn. Pulp & Paper Assn. (Past Chrmn. Extve. Bd.); mem., Am. Pulp & Paper Mills Supt. Assn.; life mem., Maritime Seniors' Golf Assn.; sometime mem., U.S.A. War Production Bd., Groundwood Paper Indust. Advisory Comte.; Anglican; recreations: golf, fishing; Clubs: The Edmundston Golf; Delray Dunes Golf and Country (Florida); Home: 1140 S.W., 22nd Ave., Delray Beach, Florida 33445

CRAGG, John Gordon, Ph.D.; educator; b. Toronto, Ont. 3 May 1937; s. Gerald Robertson and Evelyn Alice C.; e. Westmount (Que.) Jr. and Sr. High Schs. 1954; McGill Univ. B.A. 1958; Cambridge Univ. B.A. 1960; Princeton Univ. Ph.D. 1965; m. Olga d. Borris Browsin, Washington, D.C. 8 Sept. 1962; two s. Michael Ian, Philip Andrew; PROF. AND HEAD OF ECON., UNIV. OF B.C. 1976- ; Asst. Prof. 1967, Assoc. Prof. 1968, Prof. 1971; Asst. Prof. Univ. of Chicago 1964-67; Dir. of Research, Prices & Incomes Comn. Ottawa 1969-71; Dir. St. George's Sch. Vancouver; author "Wage Changes and Labour Flows in Canada" 1973; co-author "Expectations and the Structure of Share Prices" 1982; various articles econometrics & corp. finance prof. journs. recreations: skiing, boating, music; Home: 6 Semana Cres., Vancouver, B.C. V6N 2E2; Office: 997 - 1873 East Mall, Vancouver; B.C. V6T 1Y2.

CRAIG, Burton MacKay, B.Sc.A., M.Sc., Ph.D.; biochemist; b. Vermilion, Alta. 29 May 1918; s. Walter Alexander and Mary Jessie (Baillie) C.; e. Univ. of Sask. B.Sc.A. 1944, M.Sc. 1946; Univ. of Minn. Ph.D. 1950; m. Inez Gladys d. late John Kalmer Guttormson 5 July 1945; children: Wayne Keith, Cheryl Lynne; DIR., PRAIRIE REGIONAL LAB. 1970- ; Asst. Research Offr. 1950, Assoc. Research Offr. 1954, Sr. Research Offr. 1960, Princ. Research Offr. 1968, Assoc. Dir. 1969-70; mem. Council and Extve. Comte. Sask. Research Council 1974-83; Group Dir. Nat. Research Council 1979-83, mem. Council 1980-81; mem. Can. Agric. Research Council 1974; Can. Agric. Services Co-ordinating Comte. 1978- ; author over 60 scient. papers, 2 book chapters; holds 2 patents; Hon. Life mem. Agric. Inst. Can.; mem. Chem. Inst. Can.; Am. Oil Chem. Soc.; Candn. Inst. Food Technol.; Am. Assn. Advanc. Science; Candn. Research Mang. Assn.; Phi Lambda Upsilon; Sigma Xi; United Church; recreations: golf, curling; Home: 423 Lake Cres., Saskatoon, Sask. S7H 3A3; Office: 110 Gymnasium Rd., Saskatoon, Sask. S7N 0W9.

CRAIG, Gerald Marquis, Ph.D.; educator; b. Brighton, Ont. 2 Oct. 1916; s. Clarence Marquis and Florence (Cryderman) C.; e. Church St. Schs., N. Toronto Coll. Inst.; Univ. of Toronto grad. 1939; Univ. of Minn. Ph.D. 1947; m. Janet Stier 9 March 1943; children: Alan, Constance; PROF. OF HISTORY, UNIV. OF TORONTO; served with RCAF 1943-45; author "Upper Canada, The Formative Years" 1963; "The United States and Canada" 1968; various articles Candn. and Am. hist.; mem. Candn. Hist. Assn.; Am. Hist. Assn.; Organ. Am. Historians; Home: 137 Roxborough St. E., Toronto, Ont. M4W 1V9.

CRAIG, James Basil, B.Arch.; architect; b. Toronto, Ont., 10 April 1926; s. James Henry, B.A.Sc., F.R.A.I.C. and Grace MacFarlane (Morris) C.; e. St. Pauls Public Sch. for Boys, Toronto, Ont.; Univ. of Toronto Schs.; Univ. of Toronto, B.Arch. 1950; m. Charlotte Jane, d. W. Baldwin Clipsham, Regina, Sask., 2 May 1964; one d., Sheila Jane, one s., D'Arcy William; children (by former marriage) James Bruce, Tara Patricia; PARTNER, CRAIG, KOHLER AND EDMUNDSON, Archs. since 1963; former Partner, Craig, Madill, Abram & Ingleson, Toronto, 1954-63; has designed many schools and pub. bldgs., especially in Ont.; served with R.C.N.V.R., 1945; on active Reserve, R.C.N., 1949-55, retiring with rank of Acting Lt.; mem., Ont. Assn. Arch. (Chrmn., Toronto Chapter

1961-62, Ottawa Chapter 1965-67) First Vice-Pres. 1979; Royal Arch. Inst., Can.; Phi Delta Theta; recreations: sailing, photography, model-building; Club: Britannia Yacht; Office: 200 Tremblay Road, Ottawa, Ont. K1G 3H5

CRAIG, Rev. Canon James Hannington, M.A., D.D. (Ang.); b. Montreal, P.Q.; s. Rev. Dr. W. W. Craig, former Dean of Ont.; e. Univ. of British Columbia, B.A.; Trinity Coll., Univ. of Toronto, B.D., M.A., D.D.; m.; children: Myrna, John, David; taught school for a time in Vernon, B.C.; Dean of Residence and Lect. in Practical Theol., Huron Coll., London, Ont., and at the same time Rector of St. Luke's Ch. there, 1930-35; Incumbent, St. Mary's Ch., Vancouver, B.C., and Lect. at Ang. Theol. Coll. there, 1935-44, when apptd. Dean of Algoma; Dean of Calgary and Rector of Cath. Ch. of the Redeemer there 1951-53; Rector, Grace Church On-the-Hill, Toronto, 1953-72; Retired; Address: R.R. #1, Naramata, B.C., V0H 1N0

CRAIG, James S., M.Arch.; b. Moose Jaw, Sask., 17 Dec. 1912; s. Netson Ross and Carrie E. Shand (Fraser) C.; e. univ. of Toronto, 1929-31; Univ. of Man., B.Arch. (Gold Medal) 1934; Mass. Inst. of Tech., M.Arch. 1935; m. Marion Mollie, d. late Walter Stuart Moore, 30 Nov. 1940; Pres., 385 Madison Avenue Ltd.; Sherbrooke Farms Ltd.; Moorecraig Co. Limited; Dir., Deer Run Ridge Investments Ltd.; with W. L. Somerville, 1935-39 and W. R. L. Blackwell, 1939; Architect, Ford Motor Company of Canada, 1940-45; formed partnership Blackwell & Craig, 1945, becoming Blackwell, Craig and Zeidler, 1954; changed to Craig & Zeidler, 1956 and Craig, Zeidler and Strong, 1963; retired 1973; firm received Massey Medal awards, 1955, 1959, 1967; Nat. Design Awards, 1962, 1964, 1967; Ont. Masons Relations Council Awards, 1964, 1965, 1966, 1968, 1970, 1971; Canadian Architect Year Book Design Awards, 1967, 1969, 1970, 1971; Trustee, Art Gallery of Ont. and Chrmn. of Exhn. Comte. for AGO, 1970-74; Dir., Art Gallery of Peterborough 1974-79; author of several articles on hosp. design in "Candn. Hospital"; Chrmn. Peterborough Planning Bd., 1958, 1959; Peterborough United Way Campaign 1977-78, 1978-79; mem., Roy. Inst. Br. Arch.; Royal Arch. Inst. Can.; Freemason; Delta Kappa Epsilon; Protestant; recreations: skiing, sailing; Clubs: Peterborough; Peterborough Golf & Country; Granite (Toronto); Address: 21 Merino Rd., Peterborough, Ont. K9J 6M8

CRAIG, John A. D., O.B.E., E.D., B.Com., F.C.A.; chartered accountant; b. Montreal, P.Q., 30 Nov. 1907; s. John and Jeanne (Eluau) C.; e. Upper Canada Coll., Toronto, Ont.; Univ. of Toronto; m. Elizabeth Hunter, d. C. W. Rous, 7 Dec., 1937; two d., Sheila (Mrs. David Ward), Jane; formed the firm of Snyder, Craig & Co., Chart. Accts. in 1946; served with The Royal Regt. of Can. and The 3rd Candn. Inf. Div., in 2nd World War; awarded M.B.E., and O.B.E.; Order of Orange Nassau (Netherlands) and Mentioned in Despatches; mem., Inst. Chart. Accts. Ont.; Candn. Tax Foundation; Art Gallery of Toronto (Life); Royal Candn. Inst. (Life mem. and former mem. of Council); St. Andrew's Soc. (Past Pres.); Fort York Br., Candn. Legion (Past Pres.); Kappa Alpha; Presbyterian; Clubs: National; Toronto Cricket, Skating & Curling; Royal Candn. Mil. Inst.; Home: 204 Heath St. W., Toronto, Ont. M4V 1V5; Office: 372 Bay St., Suite 1902, Toronto, Ont. M5H 2W9

CRAIG, R. Ross; industrial executive; b. Hamilton, Ont., 18 Nov. 1915; s. Norman H. and Ethel (Maguire) C.; e. Burlington (Ont.) High Sch.; children: Dr. R., Mrs. Gaye Donat, R.N.; DIR. AND EXTVE. VICE-PRES.-COMMERCIAL, DOFASCO INC., since 1964; Pres. and Dir., Baycoat Ltd.; Dir., National Steel Car Corp., Ltd.; Maritime Life Assurance Co.; Guelph DoLime Ltd.; Beachvilime Ltd.; Prudential Steel Ltd.; Zeller's Ltd.; joined present firm in Time Office and Cost Distribution, 1935; trans. to Sales and Order Dept. 1939; apptd.

Vice-Pres., Tin Plate and Sheet Sales, 1951; Vice-Pres., Marketing, 1961; mem., Canadian Manufacturers Association; Hamilton Chamber Comm.; Am. Iron & Steel Inst.; Toronto Railway Club; Candn. Inst. Steel Constr.; Steel Indus. Adv. Council; Anglican; recreations: philately, gardening, golf, fishing, hunting, trap & skeet shooting; Clubs: Hamilton Golf & Country; Tamahaac Club; Hamilton; Home: Craiglea Farm, R.R. #1, Campbellville, Ont., L0P 1B0; Office: P.O. Box 460, Hamilton, Ont. L8N 3J5

CRAIGIE, E(dward) Horne, Ph.D., F.R.S.C.; professor emeritus; b. Edinburgh, Scot., 24 June 1894; s. Alfred Horne and Margaret Wilson (Deuchars) C.; e. Roy. High Sch., Edinburgh; Parkdale Coll. Inst., Toronto; Univ. of Toronto; post-grad. studies, Univ. of Chicago The Wistar Inst., Instituto Cajal, Madrid, Central Inst. for Brain Research, Amsterdam; m. Marguerite Cecile, d. William T. J. Homuth, 1919; children: Margaret Florilla, Louise Cecile; PROF. OF COMPARATIVE ANATOMY & NEUROLOGY, UNIV. OF TORONTO, 1945-62; Demonst. in Biol, Univ. of Toronto, 1916-19; Lect., 1919-25; Asst. Prof. of Comparative Anat. and Neurol., 1925-33; Assoc. Prof., 1933-45, Prof. 1945-62, since when Prof. emeritus of Zool.; Fellow of Roy. Soc. of Can.; Ed., "Transactions" of Sec. V., Roy. Soc. Can. 1941-61; mem., Royal Canadian Inst. (Hon. Librarian 1935-45; Hon. Ed., 1945-49); mem., Am. Assoc. of Anats.; Am. Assn. for Advanc. of Science; Toronto Medical Historical Club; Neurological Assn.; Toronto Guild for Colour Photography (Pres. 1953-54); author of "An Introduction to the Finer Anatomy of the Central Nervous System, Based Upon the Albino Rat", 1925; revised as "Craigie's Neuroanatomy of the Rat", 1963; "A History of the Department of Zoology of the University of Toronto", 1965; "A Laboratory Guide to the Anatomy of the Rabbit", 1951; The World of Ramon y Cajal" (with W.C. Gibson) 1968; trans. autobiography of S. Ramon y Cajal, "Recollections of My Life", 1937; 6th ed. Bensley's "Practical Anatomy of the Rabbit", 1938, 7th ed. 1944, 8th ed. 1948; Ed., Sec. D., "Canadian Journ. of Zoology", 1948-1955; has contrib. numerous papers to the Am. and European scient. journs.; club: Cajal; recreation: colour photography; Home: 52 Strathgowan Ave., Toronto, Ont. M4N 1B9

CRAIGIE, John Hubert, O.C. (1967); M.Sc., Ph.D., LL.D., D.Sc., F.R.S. (1952), F.R.S.C.; b. Merigomish (Piedmont Valley), Pictou Co., N.S., 8 Dec. 1887; s. John Yorston and Elizabeth (Pollock) C.; e. Dalhousie Univ., Oct. and Nov. 1914; Harvard Univ., A.B. 1924; Univ. of Minnesota, M.S. 1925; Univ. of Manitoba, Ph.D. 1930, D.Sc. 1959; Univ. of Brit. Columbia, D.Sc. 1946; Univ. of Sask., LL.D. 1948; Dalhousie LL.D. 1951; m. Miriam Louise, d. Allan R. Morash, Lunenburg, N.S., 4 Oct. 1926, Plant Path., Dept. of Agric., 1925-27; Sr. Plant Path., 1927-28; Sr. Plant Path. in Winnipeg, 1928-45, when also served as Offr. in Charge of Dom. Lab. of Plant Pathology; Assoc. Dir. of Science Service and Chief, Div. of Botany and Plant Path., 1945-52; retired as Princ. Plant Pathol., Science Service, Dept. of Agric., 8 Dec. 1958; Official Del. for Can., Internat. Hortic. Cong., London, 1930; 5th Pac. Science Cong., Victoria and Vancouver, 1933; 6th Pac. Science Cong., Berkeley & Los Angeles, Cal., 1939, and Imp. Agric. Bureaux Conf., London, Eng., 1946; has discovered the function of Pycnia and Pycniospores in rust fungi, and a method by which different physiol. form and races of a rust organism may be hybridized; served with Candn. Cycle Corps, Halifax, N.S., Nov. 1914-Feb. 1915; served in World War with C.M.R., 1915-18; with Indian Army, June 1918-Feb. 1920; Fellow Emeritus, Am. Phytopathol. Soc. (Pres. 1945-46); Hon. mem., Candn. Phytopathol. Soc. (Pres. 1934-35); Fellow, Agric. Inst. of Can. (Pres. Man. br., 1935-36); mem., Winnipeg Scient. Club; Hon. mem., Candn. Soc. of Microbiol.; rec'd Outstanding Achievement Award, Univ. of Minn., 1951; Roy. Soc. Can. (Flavelle Medal, 1942); Elvin Charles Stakman Award, Univ. of Minn., 1964; Centennial Medal, 1967; O.C. 1967; Queen's Jubilee

Medal, 1977; (First) Award & Merit (Medal) of Can. Phytopathological Society, 1979; Emeritus mem., Prof. Inst. of the Civil Service of Can. (1st award of Medal); Home: 950 Bank St., Ottawa, Ont. K1S 5G6

CRAIK, Donald W., M.L.A., M.Sc., P.Eng.; consulting engineer; b. Baldur, Man., 16 Aug. 1931; s. Ira Donald and Cordelia Bella Mae (Young) C.; e. Greenway (Man.) Rural Sch.; Baldur (Man.) Coll. 1947-49; United Coll. 1950; Univ. of Manitoba, B.Sc. (M.E.) 1956; Univ. of Minnesota, M.Sc. (M.E.) 1961; m. Shirley Yvonne, d. late J. Arthur Hill, Hilton, Man., 19 Sept. 1953; children: Judith, Polly, Donna; MINISTER OF ENERGY AND MINES, AND DEPUTY PREMIER OF MANITOBA; also i/c Man. Hydro, Man. Forestry Resources Ltd., & Man. Dev. Corp.; President, D. W. Craik Engineering; Pres. Donley Estates Ltd.; 1st el. M.L.A., Man. for St. Vital Constit. 1966-69 and for Riel since 1969, re-el. g.e. 11 Oct. 1977; Min. of Finance Oct. 1977- Jan. 1981; Min. of Energy & Mines 1979-; Deputy Premier, Jan. 1981-; Trainee Engr., Canadian Westinghouse Co. 1956; Prof. of Engn., Univ. of Man. 1957-64; Dir., Man. Research Council 1964-66; Min. of Mines & Natural Resources, Man. 1967, Min. of Educ., 1968-69; mem., Assn. Prof. Engrs. Man.; Dir., St. Vital Sch. Div. Bd. 1962-64 (Chrmn. 1964); Freemason; P. Conservative; Protestant; recreations: jogging, golf, cross country skiing; Home: 3 River Lane, Winnipeg, Man. R2M 3Y8; Office: Legislative Bldg., Winnipeg, Man. R3C 0V8

CRANG, James Harold; stock broker; b. Toronto, Ont., 11 Jan. 1902; s. James, Jr., and Lillian (McKay) C.; e. Upper Can. Coll.; m. Dorothy K. (died), d. late Harold F. Ritchie, 16 Sept. 1933; one s., James Harold Junior; 2ndly, Margaret A. Dunlap; InvestmentBroker, Mem. Emeritus Toronto Stock Ex.; Pres., J. H. Crang & Co.; Glenville Farms Dairy Ltd.; Dir. and Past Pres., Royal Agric. Winter Fair, Toronto; Adv., Royal Ont. Museum of Toronto; Dir., Candn. Equestrian Team and Candn. Equestrian Fed.; began his career in brokerage business, Sept. 1920; after purchasing seat, el. to Standard Stock & Mining Exchange, Toronto, 1924; later became mem., Calgary Stock Exchange; subsequently purchased seats on Winnipeg Grain, Vancouver Stock, Candn. Stock and Candn. Commodity Exchanges; mem., Montreal Stock Exchange, since 1951; Major, 7th Regt. Arty., 1942; Asst. Dir. of Arty., 1943-44; Depy. Dir.-Gen., Army Tech. Devel. Bd.; Conservative; Anglican; recreations: riding, shooting, fishing; Clubs: Toronto Hunt; Eglinton Hunt; Toronto; Toronto & N. York Hunt; York; Mount Royal (Montreal); Rolling Rock (Ligonier, Pa.); White's (London, Eng.); Address: 40 Burton Rd., Toronto, Ont., M5P 1V2, and Glenville Farms, R.R. 2, Newmarket, Ont. L3Y 4V9

CRANSTON, Robert Alexander, Q.C., LL.D.; b. Collingwood, Ont., 1 July 1912; s. William Thomas and Edith (Copeland) C.; e. Alliston (Ont.) High; m. Gladys Catherine, d. Dr. A. P. Rutherford, Hawkesbury, Ont., 28 Sept. 1940; children: Robert, Diane; PARTNER, LANG, MICHENER, CRANSTON, FARQUHARSON & WRIGHT; Dir., Broulan Reef Mines Ltd.; Iso Mines Ltd.; Ames Crosta Mills (Canada) Ltd.; Jacuzzi Canada Ltd.; Shafer Valve Co. of Canada Ltd.; Copperfields Mining Corp. Ltd.; Commercial Union Assnce. Co. of Can.; Orchan Mines Ltd.; called to the Bar of Ont., 1936; created K.C. 1954; mem., Candn. Bar Assn.; Theta Delta Chi; Presbyterian; Clubs: Lawyers; National; Home: 220 Cortleigh Blvd., Toronto, Ont. M5N 1P5; Office: Box 10, First Canadian Place, Toronto, Ont. M5X 1A2

CRANSTON, Toller; skater, artist; b. Hamilton, Ont. 20 Apr. 1949; e. Kirkland Lake, Ont.; École des Beaux Arts, Montreal; began skating at age of 8; won Candn. Jr. Skating Championship at age of 14 (1964); won Quebec Winter Games 1967; 1968-69 won 3rd Candn. Sr. Men's Championship; 1969 3rd Grand Prix Internat., St. Gervais France; 6th North Am.; 1970 2nd in Candn. Sr., 13th

World; 1971 won 1st Candn. Sr., 2nd North Am., 11th World; 1972 won 1st Candn. Sr., 9th Olympics, 5th World (1st in free-style singles div.); 1973 won 1st Candn. Sr., 5th World, won 1st Skate Canada; 1974 won 1st Candn. Sr., Bronze Medallist, World Championships (1st in free-style singles); 1975 won 1st Candn. Sr., 4th World (1st in free-style singles); 1976 won 1st Candn. Sr., Bronze Medal in Olympics; mem. ISU winter & summer tour 1971-74; turned prof. & launched own pro ice show 1976; mem. Candn. Sports Hall of Fame; Lis kaleidoscopic paintings have been exhibited worldwide; author & illustrator "A ram on the Rampage" 1977.

CRATE, Harold E., F.C.A.; b. Toronto, Ont., 20 Apl. 1902; s. Arthur E. and Susan (Reid) C.; e. Pub. and High Schs., Toronto, Ont.; Inst. of Chart. Accts. 1919-25; F.C.A. 1947; m. Leila Wilmot, d. David Plewes, 5 Sept. 1927; children: Marilyn, Ross, Graham, David; retired Partner of Thorne, Riddell, etc. Dec. 1969; consulting practice 1970-77; mem., Inst. Chart. Accts. Ont. (Pres. 1950-51); Past Pres., Public Accts. Council for Prov. of Ont.; former Gov., Candn. Tax Foundation; Conservative; Anglican; recreations: golf, curling, sailing; Clubs: Rosedale Golf; National; R.C.Y.C.; Rotary; Home: 33 Harbour Sq., Apt. 808, Toronto, Ont. M5J 2G2; Office: Box 262, Toronto-Dominion Centre, Toronto, Ont.

CRAWFORD, Edward Hamon, B.A.; insurance executive; b. Truro, N.S., 14 Aug. 1925; s. late Edward Smith and Marie Eva (Hamon) C.; e. Ruston Acad., Havana, Cuba; St. Andrew's Coll., Aurora, Ont.; Trinity Coll., Univ. of Toronto, B.A. (Pol. Science & Econ.); m. Barbara Mary, d. late W. H. Smith, 25 June 1955; children: Douglas Edward Smith, Robert Gordon Smith; PRESIDENT AND DIR., CANADA LIFE ASSURANCE CO. since 1973; Dir., Canadian Imperial Bank of Commerce; Gulf Canada Ltd.; Moore Corp. Ltd.; Chrmn., Candn. Enterprise Devel. Corp. Ltd.; Interprovincial Pipe Line Ltd.; Candn. Life Ins. Assn. 1980-81; joined Investment Department of present Company, 1948; Investment Rep., London, Eng., 1952-57; Asst. Treas., Home Office, 1957-63, Assoc. Treas., 1963-64, Treas., 1964-67; Vice Pres. and Treas. 1967-70; Extve. Vice Pres. 1970-73; el. a Dir. 1971; served with R.C.A.F., 1943-45; Dir., Am. Council of Life Ins.; mem. Bd. Govs., St. Andrew's Coll.; Bd. Trustees: Hosp. for Sick Children; The Banting Research Foundation; Anglican; Clubs: Granite; York; Toronto; Toronto Golf; Home: 47 Daneswood Rd., Toronto, Ont. M4N 3J7; Office: 330 University Ave., Toronto, Ont. M5G 1R8

CRAWFORD, George L., Q.C., LL.B.; b. Edmonton, Alta., 17 July 1915; s. late Georgie Kay (Biggs) and late John Lyndon C.; e. Univ. of Alberta, LL.B., 1938; m. Sheila, d. late J. A. Stewart, 24 Aug. 1940; children: Anne, Sally, Eve, Erica; ASSOCIATE, McLAWS AND CO.; Dir., Selkirk Communications Ltd.; Canada Security Assurance Co. Ltd.; Southam Inc.; Canadian Western Natural Gas Co. Ltd.; Norwich Union Insurance Societies; IAC Ltd.; Continental Bank of Canada; Candn. Utilities Ltd.; Past Pres., Calgary Exhibition & Stampede; called to the Bar of Alta. 1940; cr. Q.C. 1960; served with R.C.N.V.R. 1940-45; Delta Kappa Epsilon; Conservative; Anglican; recreations: riding, golf, curling; Clubs: Ranchmen's; Calgary Golf & Country; Glencoe; Home: Bedlam Ridge, Priddis, Alta. T0L 1W0; Office: 407-8th Ave. S.W., Calgary, Alta, T2P 1E6

CRAWFORD, John Richard Leathes, B.A.; retired publisher; b. Toronto, Ont., 2 April 1914; s. late Helen Mar (Silver) and John Thomas C.; e. Univ. of Toronto Schs., 1924-33; Univ. of Toronto, B.A. 1937; m. Pretha Rae, d. late Peter Keiller, 2 Nov. 1942; children: Allan Thomas, Joan Rae; Pres. & Treas., The Canadian Analyst Ltd., Financial Publrs., 1955-77; began as Stat., Acct., Office Mgr., Hutson & Dinnick, mems. of Toronto Stock Ex., 1945-48; Asst. Secy., Office Mgr., Burlington Steel Co. Ltd., Hamilton, Ont., 1948-55; Securities Adviser (Reg'd.

Ont. Securities Comn.) 1955-59; Dir., A. E. Osler Co. Ltd. mems. Toronto Stock Ex. 1959-72; served in 2nd World War, 1940-45; enlisted Toronto Scottish Regt.; final rank of Capt. and Adjt.; Cert. Gen. Acct., 1955; Delta Tau Delta; United Ch.; recreations: travel, bridge; Home: 3020 Glencrest Rd. Apt. 409, Burlington, Ont. L7N 2H2

CRAWFORD, John Sinclair, M.D., F.R.C.P.(C); educator; b. Toronto, Ont. 12 May 1921; s. James Sinclair and late Irene (Vokes) C.; e. Univ. of Toronto 1939; Univ. of Toronto M.D. 1944; m. Olive Margaret d. late Thomas Albert McAulay 16 Sept. 1944; three s.; PROF. AND CHRMN. OF REHABILITATION MED. FACULTY OF MED. UNIV. OF TORONTO since 1972; Dir. Dept. Rehabilitation Med. Toronto Western Hosp., mem. Attending Staff Phys. Dept. Med. and Past Chrmn. Med. Adv. Comte.; Med. Dir. Hillcrest Hosp. 1962-73; Chrmn. Med. Adv. Comte. Toronto Rehabilitation Centre 1960-70; Chrmn. Specialty Comte. Phys. Med. & Rehabilitation, Royal Coll. Phys. & Surgs.; served with RCAMC 1943-46; author various articles prof. journs.; mem. Ont. Med. Assn.; Candn. Med. Assn.; Candn. Assn. Phys. Med. & Rehabilitation (Pres. 1959); Protestant; recreations: boating, skiing; Clubs: Boulevard; Big Bay Point Yacht; Home: 70 Sir William's Lane, Islington, Ont. M9A 1V3; Office: 399 Bathurst St., Toronto, Ont. M5T 2S8.

CRAWFORD, Hon. Neil Stanley, Q.C., M.L.A., B.A., LL.B.; politician; b. Prince Albert, Sask. 26 May 1931; s. William Francis and Hannah (Hoehn) C.; e. Humboldt elem. and high schs.; Univ. of Sask, B.A., LL.B.; m. Catherine May d. J. Percy Hughes, Netherhill, Sask. 3 Sept. 1951; children: Scot, Teresa, Ian, Elaine, Sandra, Robert;ATTY. GEN. & GOVT. HOUSE LEADER, ALTA.1979- ; Extve. Asst. to Prime Min. 1961-63; Ald. City of Edmonton 1966-71; el. M.L.A. for Edmonton Parkallen prov. g.e. 1971, re-el. since; Min. of Health & Social Devel. 1971-75; Min. of Labour 1975-79; mem. Candn. Bar Assn.; P. Conservative; Protestant; Office: 227 Legislative Bldg., Edmonton, Alta. T5K 2B6.

CRAWFORD, Purdy, Q.C., B.A., LL.M.; b. Five Islands, N.S. 7 Nov. 1931; s. Frank and Agnes (Doyle) C.; e. Mt. Allison Univ. B.A. 1952; Dalhousie Univ. LL.B. 1955; Harvard Law Sch. LL.M. 1956; m. Beatrice, d. Wilfred Corbett 19 May 1950; children: David, Suzanne, Heather, Mary, Barbara, Sarah; SR. PARTNER, OSLER HOSKIN & HARCOURT since 1970; Dir. Imasco Ltd.; Hudson Bay Mining and Smelting Co. Ltd.; Keep Rite Inc.; UMEX Inc.; mem. Adv. Council, Industrial Estates Ltd.; called to Bar of N.S. 1956, of Ont. 1958; student with Osler Hoskin & Harcourt 1956, Assoc. Lawyer 1958, Partner 1962; cr. Q.C. 1968; Special Lectr. Osgoode Hall Law Sch. 1964-68, Univ. of Toronto Law Sch. 1969-71, Bar Admission Course 1969-72; Co.-Secy. Atty. Gen.'s Comte. on Securities Leg. 1964-65; Chrmn. Ont. Taxation Sub-sec., Candn. Bar Assn. 1966-68; Treas. Nat. Taxation Sec. 1968-70; Past mem. various comtes. on taxation and of Bd. Govs. Candn. Tax Foundation 1970-72; Cdn. Inst. of Ch. Accts. Special Comm. to Examine Role of Auditor 1977-78; Accounting Research Adv. Bd. 1977-79; United Church; recreations: golf, skiing, badminton; Clubs: Parrsboro Golf (N.S.); Granite; Toronto; York Downs Golf & Country; Caledon Ski; Homes: Five Islands, N.S. (summer) and 9 Ansley St., Toronto, Ont. M4R 1X5; Office: P.O. Box 50, First Canadian Place, Toronto, Ont. M5X 1B8

CRAWFORD, William Stanley Hayes, M.A., Ph.D., D.Sc.; educator; b. Saint John, N.B., 17 April 1918; s. Roy Elmer and Jane Isabel (Shaw) C.; e. Mount Allison Univ., B.A. 1939 (Rhodes Schol. for N.B.); Univ. of Minn., M.A. 1942, Ph.D. 1950; m. Marjorie Jane, d. F. H. Paulsen, Minneapolis, Minn., 11 Sept. 1943; has two s., William Stanley Hayes, Jr., Frederick Hunter Paulsen; Pres., Mount Allison Univ. 1975; Prof. of Math. Mt. Allison Univ. 1980-; Prof. of Math. Inst. of Math., Univ. of

Minn., 1942-43; Asst. Prof. of Math., Mt. Allison Univ., 1943-46, Prof. since 1946, Head of the Dept., 1946-72; Dean of Science 1956-62; Vice Pres. 1962-69; Dean of Arts and Sci. 1962-65; Acting Pres. 1962-63; Hon. D.Sc. awarded by U.N.B., 1979; Hon. Research Asst., Univ. College, London, 1954-55; Lieut., Reserve Army; Dist. Commr., Boy Scouts, 1945-47; mem., N.B. Higher Educ. Comn. 1967-74; Am. Math. Soc.; Math. Assn. of Am.; Candn. Math. Soc.; Am. Assoc. Advanc. Science; Sigma Xi; Freemason; recreation: golf; Home: Box 1050, Sackville, N.B. E0A 3C0

CRAWLEY, Frank Radford, O.C., C.A.; film producer; b. Ottawa, Ont., 14 Nov. 1911; s. Arthur Alfred and Ruth (Orme) C.; PRESIDENT AND DIRECTOR, CRAWLEY FILMS, Past Pres., Ottawa, Y.M.C.A.; mem., Inst. of Chart. Accts. of Ont.; United Church; Office: 19 Fairmont Ave., Ottawa, Ont. K1Y 3B5;

CREAGHAN, Hon. Paul, M.L.A., B.Comm., LL.M.; b. Moncton, N.B., 27 March 1937; s. William Vincent and Gretchen Catherine (Smith) C.; e. St. Francis Xavier Univ., B.Com. 1958; Dalhousie Univ., LL.B. 1961; Harvard Univ., LL.M. 1962; m. Sandra Ann, d. A. J. Fenwick Bathurst, N.B., 10 June 1963; children: Jason David, Amber Fenwick; SR. SOLICITOR, N.B. ELECTRIC POWER COMM.; Min. of Justice, N.B. 1974; Partner, Leger; Yeoman, Creaghan & Savoie, since 1969; called to Bar of N.B. 1962; Assoc., Edward G. Byrne, Q.C., 1962; Partner: Creaghan & Creaghan, 1963-67; Leger, Creaghan & Savoie, 1967-69; Lectr., Univ. of N.B., 1964-65; served as Pilot Offr., RCAF, R.O.T.P., 1954-58; Ald., City of Moncton, 1965-67; Councillor, Westmorland Co. Council, 1965-67; el. M.L.A. for City of Moncton, 1970; Min. of Health 1970, of Econ. Growth 1972; mem., N.B. Bar Assn.; Candn. Bar Assn.; Moncton Bd. Trade; Sigma Chi; Progressive Conservative; R. Catholic; recreations: curling, fishing, reading; Clubs: Rotary; Elks; Moncton City; Home: 12 Lakewood Dr., Moncton, N.B. E1E 3L7; Office: 527 King St., Fredericton, N.B E3B 4X1

CREAGHAN, Mr. Justice William Lawrence Marven; C.D., Court of Queen's Bench; b. Newcastle, N.B., 30 May 1922; s. John Adams and Alice D. (Marven) C.; e. Moncton High Sch., 1939; St. Francis Xavier Univ.; Dalhousie Univ., LL.B. 1948; m. Therese A., d. late Ben LeBlanc, 2 Sept. 1950; children: Lawrence, Andrew, Valerie; read law with J. A. Creaghan, Q.C.; called to the Bar of N.B. 1948; Registrar of Probate 1952-58; former Partner, Creaghan & Creaghan; served in 2nd World War; Capt. in R.C.A. in Europe and the Mediterranean; Ald., Moncton, N.B., 1952-58; el. to H. of C. for Westmorland 1958; app'ted to County Court, 1962; R. Catholic; Clubs: Fredericton Garrison; Office: Justice Bldg., Queen St., Fredericton, N.B.

CREAL, K. H. M., M.A., S.T.B.; b. Grenfell, Sask., 4 Oct. 1927; s. Howard Hubert and Colina (Macdonald) C.; e. Univ. British Columbia, B.A. 1948; Univ. of Toronto, M.A. 1949; Trinity Coll., Toronto, Ont., S.T.B. 1953; m. Dorothy Knowles, d. John H. Wright, Richmond, Va., 30 Aug. 1952; children: Margaret Colina, Mary Dorothy, Elizabeth Martha; MASTER OF VANIER COLLEGE, YORK UNIVERSITY, since 1974; Instr. in Hist., Univ. of S. Sewanee, Tenn., 1950; Rector, St. John's Ch., Winona, Ont., 1953-55; Diocesan Missioner, Diocese of Niagara, 1955-58; Gen. Secy., Gen. Bd. of Religious Educ., Ang. Ch. of Can., 1958-65; Dir., Humanities Programs, Atkinson Coll., York Univ., 1965-66; Prof. of Humanities since 1966; Div. of Humanities, Faculty of Arts, 1969-74; recreations: swimming, tennis, reading; Office: Vanier College, York University, Downsview, Ont. M3J 1P3

CREAN, John Gale, B.Com.; manufacturer; b. Toronto; Ont., 4 Nov. 1910; s. Gordon Campbell and Louisa Annie Evelyn C.; e. Upper Can. Coll., 1919-28; Univ. of Toronto (Comm. and Finance), B.Com. 1932; m. Margaret Eliza-

beth, d. late George A. Dobbie, 2 Dec. 1939; children: John F. M., Jennie E., Susan M., Patricia L.; PRESIDENT, ROBERT CREAN & CO. LTD.; Dir., Kelsey-Hayes Can. Ltd.; Scythes & Co.; Pres., Internat. Chamber of Comm., 1974-75; Chrmn. of Bd., Cdn. Org. for the Simplification of Trade Procedures, 1978-80; Candn. Council, Internat. Chamber of Comm., 1970-72, 1974-75; Ont. Science Centre 1964-69; Chrmn., Candn. Business & Industry Adv. Comte. to OECD, 1972-74; Candn. Cmte. on Multinat. Enterprises, 1974-80; Candn. Business Group for Multilateral Trade Negotiations, 1973-79; mem. Adv. Bd., Internat. Mang. and Devel. Inst., Washington, D.C.; Candn. Employer del. to Internat. Lab. Organ., Geneva, 1964; Chrmn. of Council, Bishop Strachan Sch., 1953-63; mem. Extve. Comte., Trinity Coll., Univ. of Toronto 1968-74; Pres., Candn. Inst. Internat. Affairs 1981; Duke of Edinborough's 80th Study Conference 1978-80; Chmn. of Bd., Ont. Science Centre, 1964-69; Pres., Wilton Park Assn. of Can.; Dir., Hillcrest Hosp., Toronto; Past Chrmn., Ont. Divn., Candn. Credit Men's Assn. (1948); mem., Candn. Chamber of Commerce (Pres. 1955-56); mem. of Can.-U.S. Comte. of combined Chambers of Comm., 1950-53; Chrmn., Can.-U.S. Comte., Candn. Chamber Comm., 1962; has travelled extensively throughout the world; served in Queen's Own Rifles, N.P.A.M.; 1928-36; C.O.T.C., Univ. of Toronto, 1942-45; Kappa Sigma (G.M.); P. Conservative; Presbyterian; recreations: tennis, badminton, sailing; Clubs: University; Badminton & Racquet; R.C.Y.C.; Queen's; St. James's (Montreal); Address: 161 Forest Hill Rd., Toronto, Ont. M5P 2N3

CREBER, George Edgar, Q.C.; b. Toronto, Ont., 12 Sept. 1927; s. Thomas Edgar and Clara Bernice (Humphries) C.; e. Univ. of Toronto (Econs. and Pol. Science) 1949; Osgoode Hall Law Sch., Toronto, Ont.; m. Edythe Elizabeth, d. Frederick A. Thorne, 21 June 1952; children: Kathryn Anne, Michael George; Dir. and Chmn., Blue Mountain Pottery Ltd.; Vice-Chmn. and Dir., Viceroy Manufacturing Co. Ltd.; called to the Bar of Ontario, 1953; Club: Scarborough Golf; Home: 273 Glen Manor Drive E., Toronto, Ont. M4E 2Y4

CREECH, Donald Havelock, B.B.A.; manufacturer; b. Victoria, B.C., 3 May 1924; s. William Havelock and Alice Maude (Briggs) C.; e. Univ. of Washington (Seattle), B.B.A. 1947; Univ. of Western Ont., Marketing Mang., 1959; m. Cynthia Mae, d. Edgar Horley Cowan, N. Vancouver, B.C., 1 March 1947; two s.: Miles Timothy, Christopher Havelock; MANAGING DIR., ARMSTRONG CORK CO. LTD.; Dir., Armstrong Cork Espana, Madrid; Armstrong Europe Services Ltd., London; Inarco Ltd., Bombay; joined Armstrong Cork Canada Ltd. as Sales Trainee in June 1947; Salesman, Toronto Dist., 1948; Montreal Dist. 1949; Dist. Mgr., Montreal, 1950; Mgr., Building & Floor Products Div., 1951; Vice-Pres. Oct. 1961; Vice-Pres. and Gen. Sales Mgr., Apl. 1962; el. Dir., June 1962; Pres., Gen Mgr. and Dir. 1970; Delta Kappa Epsilon; Protestant; recreation: golf; Office: Armstrong House, 3 Chequers Sq., Uxbridge, Middlesex, England.

CREED, Frank Cyprian, B.Sc., Ph.D.; electrical engineer; b. Windsor, Ont. 3 Apl. 1921; s. Ernest Alfred and Marjorie Cora (Shepherd) C.; e. Queen's Univ. B.Sc. 1945; Univ. of London Ph.D. (Elect. Engn.) 1952; m. Elizabeth Richmond d. Norman Stanley Case 26 March 1960; mem. (Past Chrmn.) Candn. Tech. Comte., Internat. Electro-Technical Comn. on High Voltage Testing Techniques 1958- ; High Voltage Engn. Research, Nat. Research Council Can. 1945-79; Candn. mem. CIGRE Study Comte. on High Voltage Testing 1961-79; Guest Lectr. Univ. of Toronto, Univ. of Denmark; recipient Morris E. Leeds Award Inst. Elect. & Electronic Engrs. 1981; author numerous papers impulse voltage measurement (rec'd Prize Paper Award IEEE); mem. Assn. Prof. Engrs. Prov. Ont.; Inst. Elect. & Electronic Engrs. (Past Dir.); Anglican; recreations: golf, sailing; Address: (P.O. Box 190) Hubbards, N.S. B0J 1T0.

CREEGGAN; Rt. Rev. Jack Burnett, L.S.T., D.C.L. (Ang.); ret. bishop; b. Bancroft, Ont., 10 Nov. 1902; b. Alfred Henry and Mary Laura (Sheffield) C.; e. Deseronto (Ont.) Pub. and High Schs.; Queen's Univ., B.A. 1925; Bishop's Univ., L.S.T. 1927; D.C.L. 1971; m. Dorothy Jarman, d. late Alexander Thomas Embury and Hester Mary (Jarman), 30 June 1931; children: (Mrs.) Mary-Isabel Wright, A. A. Burnett; retired Bishop of The Diocese of Ontario (1974); Freemason; recreations: golf, curling; Address: 67 Sydenham St., Apt. 304, Kingston, Ont. K7L 3H2

CREELMAN, Lyle, O.C. (1971), M.A., LL.D.; retired nursing executive; b. N.S., 14 Aug. 1908; d. late Samuel Prescott and late Laura C.; e. Vancouver Normal Sch. 1926; Univ. of B.C., B.A.Sc. (Nursing) 1936; Columbia Univ. Teachers' Coll., M.A. 1939; Univ. of N.B., LL.D. 1963; Elem. Sch. Teacher, Richmond, B.C., 1928-32; Dir. of Pub. Health Nursing, Metrop. Health Comte., Vancouver, B.C., 1940-44; Chief Nurse, Brit. Occupied Zone of Germany, UNRRA, 1945-46; Study of Pub. Health Nursing in Can., Candn. Pub. Health Assn., 1948-49; Nursing Consultant, World Health Organ., Geneva, 1949-54 and Chief Nursing Offr., 1954-68; rec'd Centennial Medal 1967; Queen's Jubilee Medal, 1977; Protestant; Club: University Women's; Home: Arbutus Point Rd., R.R. 1, Bowen Island, B.C. V0N 1G0

CREERY, Kenneth Andrew; company director; b. Vancouver, B.C., 11 Feb. 1894; s. Andrew McCreight and Anna (Hulbert) C.; e. Univ. Sch., Victoria, B.C.; McGill Coll., Vancouver, B.C.; McGill Univ.; m. Emma S., d. W. R. MacInnes, Montreal, Que., 5 June 1936; 2nd m. Marion Plaunt de Walleville, 30 Sept. 1960; Purchasing Agent, The British Metal Corporation (Canada) Limited, 1925-26; Secretary-Treasurer, 1926-34; Pres., 1934-59; Chrmn. 1959-64; served in World War, 1914-18, 16th Bn.; Dispatch Rider, 3rd Bgde., C.E.F. till Aug. 1915; Commissioned in R.F.C.; Zeta Psi; Conservative; Anglican; recreations: golf, tennis, fishing; Clubs: Montreal; University; Royal Montreal Golf; Home: Apt. 1103, 1460 Dr. Penfield Ave., Montreal, Que. H3G 1B8

CREGAN, James D.J., Q.C., B.A., LL.B.; b. Montmartre, Sask. 19 Apr. 1918; s. James and Noemie (Ecarnot) C.; e. Public Schs., Montmartre; Univ. of Ottawa, B.A.; Dalhousie Univ. LL.B.; m. 15 Feb. 1975; children: James E. Cregan, Colleen H. Currie; PARTNER, MILNER & STEER; called to the Bar of N.S. 1948, Alberta 1949, N.W.T. 1951; cr. Q.C. 18 Jan. 1960; began practice with present firm 1948 and admitted to partnership 1955; served in 2nd World War as a Pilot with R.C.A.F. overseas; mem. Edmonton Executive Assn.; K. of C.; R. Catholic; P. Conservative; recreations: fishing, golfing, boating; Club: Edmonton Golf & Country; Home: 323 Westridge, Edmonton, Alta. T5T 1C4; Office: 901-10040-104th St., Edmonton, Alta. T5J 0Z7

CREIGHTON, Kenneth David, B.A., B.Com., C.P.A.; university administrator; b. Vancouver, B.C., 27 Apl. 1922; s. Moses Dundas and Mary Euphemia May (Miller) C.; e. Univ. of B.C., B.A. 1946, B.Com.; Univ. of Cal., Berkeley, grad. work in Accounting, 1947-48; m. Christiana Maria, d. Dr. Sigfried Knauer, Los Angeles, 22 May 1950; children: Karyn Stephanie, David Dundas, Geoffrey Michael; ASSOC. VICE PRES. FOR BUSINESS & FINANCE AND CONTROLLER, STANFORD UNIV. since 1971 and 1960 respectively; pub. accounting practice with Lester Herrick and Herrick (now Arthur Young & Co.), San Francisco, 1947-54; Asst. Controller and Coordinator of Corporate Reports, Food Machinery and Chemical Corp. (now FMC Corp.), 1954-58; joined present Univ. as Asst. Controller, 1958; participated in seminar on "Higher Education and National Development in Asia",

Seoul, Korea, 1968; served with Candn. Navy during World War II; Consultant. Nat. Inst. of Health; Past President, National Assn. Coll. & Univ. Business Offrs.; mem., Am. Inst. C.P.A.'s; Sigma Tau Chi; Beta Alpha Psi; Psi Upsilon; Zeta Zeta; Christian Scientist; recreations: skiing, sailing, tennis; Home: 823 Pine Hill Rd., Stanford; Cal.

CREIGHTON, Mary Helen, C.M. (1976), LL.D., D.èsL., D.C.L., D. Litt.; folklorist; b. Dartmouth, N.S., 5 Sept. 1899; d. Charles Edward and Alice Julia C.; e. Halifax (N.S.) Ladies' Coll., Grad. 1916; Univ. of Toronto and Indiana Univ.; Mt. Allison, LL.D., 1957; D.èsL.; Laval 1961; D.C.L., King's Coll., 1967; D.Litt. St. Francis Xavier 1975, St. Mary's 1976; served in World War I as civilian subordinate, R.F.C., 1918; has contributed articles and stories to chief Candn. Journals; conducted broadcasts for children over C.H.N.S. and was first station "aunt" 1926-27; since 1931 has broadcast frequently for CBC on folksongs and folklore, and many songs from her collection have been transcribed prof. for the CBC's Internat. Service; has lectured extensively to organisations in Canada and the U.S.; Dean of Women, Univ. of King's Coll., 1939-41; awarded three Fellowships from Rockefeller Foundation for Folklore Research 1942, 1943 and 1946; since 1943 has recorded over 4000 folk songs, also folk tales, games, dances, instrumental music, and samples of dialect for Lib. of Cong., Washington (1943, 1944, and 1948); and Nat. Museum, Ottawa, 1947-67; has been on staff of Nat. Museum since 1947 to collect and record folklore in Maritime Provs., published "Songs and Ballads From Nova Scotia", 1932 and 1966; Folk Music from N.S. 1956 and Maritime Folk Songs (records by Folkways), 1962; "Twelve Folk Songs From Nova Scotia" in collab. with Doreen H. Senior, 1940; "Folklore of Lunenburg County" 1950; "Traditional Songs From Nova Scotia", with Doreen H. Senior, 1950; "Bluenose Ghosts", 1957; "Gaelic Songs in Nova Scotia", in collab. with Calum MacLeod, 1964; "Eight Folktales From Miramichi" in collab. with Edward D. Ives, 1962; "Bluenose Magic", 1968; "Folk Songs from Southern New Brunswick" 1971; "A Life In Folklore", 1975; "Eight Ethnic Folk Songs For Young Children" and "Nine Ethnic Folk Songs For Older Children" with Eunice Sircom, 1977; "Maritime Folk Songs" 1962 and 1979; subject of Nat. Film Bd. documentary, "Songs of Nova Scotia" 1958; "Land of the Old Songs", CBC 1960; "Lady of the Legends", CBC 1966, organized & performed with N.S. Folk Singers, a group of seven, 1967-73; compositions for the opera "The Broken Ring" (1953), the ballet "Sea Gallows" (1959), the symphonies "Two Maritime Aquarelles" (1970) and "Atlantic Suite" (1979), "A medley for strings" (1976) etc. were based on music from her books which also inspired music for the stage play, "Johnny Belinda"; arrangements of many of her songs in Can. and abroad, the best known being "Farewell to Nova Scotia" which has almost become the province's anthem; rec'd Can. Council grants, 1957, 1959; Maritimes Vice-Pres., Candn. Authors' Assn., 1958, Nat. Pres., 1962-64; Nat. Vice-Pres., Candn. Folk Song Soc., 1957-70; mem. EXtve., N.S. Hist. Soc., 1958-62; has been the subject of articles in Can. and abroad; Corr., Internat. Folk Music Council; Regent, Mayflower Chapter, I.O.D.E. 1932-33; Pres., Alexandra Soc. of King's Coll., 1940-45; Pres., Women's Canadian Club, Halifax, 1945-46; Council, Am. Folklore Soc., 1952; Charter Pres., Zonta Club, Halifax, 1951; Hon. mem., Dartmouth Univ. Women's Club; Hon. mem., N.S. Folk Arts Council, 1967; Fellow, Am. Anthropol. Assn., 1947-60; Fellow of Haliburton, Univ. of King's Coll., 1967; Fellow, Am. Folklore Soc. 1968; fellow, Royal N.S. Hist. Soc., 1979; Kiwanis Club "Citizen of the Year", Dartmouth 1966; Pres., Dartmouth Museum Soc. 1970-71; rec'd. Centennial Medal 1967; Candn. Music Council Medal 1974; Hon. Pres., Cdn. Folk Music Soc. 1974: rec'd Order of Canada, 1976; Queen's Jubilee Medal 1978; Hon. mem. Kodaly Inst. 1977 and Music for Children, Carl Orff Canada, 1979; Hon. mem. Candn. Assn. Music Libs. 1973;

mem. Bd. "Encyclopedia of Music in Canada" 1973-81; a musical biography by John Fred. Brown was produced in 1980; Anglican; Address: 26 Brookdale Cres., Apt. 207, Dartmouth, N.S. B3A 2R5

CREIGHTON, Wilson Lyall, B.S.E.E., B.S.M.E., P.Eng.; manufacturer; b. Ottawa, Ont. 3 Aug. 1926; s. Wilson Robert and Laura Pearl (Spratt) C.; e. Ottawa Tech. High Sch. 1945; Carleton Univ., Dipl. 1948; Indiana Inst. Technol., B.S.E.E. 1950, B.S.M.E. 1951; m. Sigrid Esther, d. Richard Winteler, 19 Dec. 1953; three d. Heidi, Ellen, Lori; PRESIDENT, ATOMIC ENERGY OF CANADA LTD.-INT. 1980-; President chief extve. offr. and dir., Brown Boveri Canada Ltd. 1973-1980; joined Brown Boveri, Engr.-in-Training, Baden, Switz. 1951; Sales Engr., Brown Boveri Canada Ltd. 1954; Asst. Sales Mgr. 1956, Dist. Sales Mgr. 1962, Gen. Mgr. Ont. Sales 1969; mem. Assn. Prof. Engrs. Ont.; Corp. Engrs. of Que.; Engn. Inst. of Can.; Inst. Electronics and Elec. Engrs.; Protestant; Clubs: Donalda; Mount Royal; recreations: tennis, golf; Home: 171 Minto Pl., Rockcliffe Pk., Ottawa, Ont. K1M 0B6; Office: 275 Slater St. Ottawa, Ont. K1A 0S4

CREPEAU, Paul-André, O.C., C.R. B.A., L.Ph., LL.L., B.C.L., Docteur en droit (Paris); mem. de la Soc. royale du Can. (1979); né, Gravelbourg, Sask., 20 mai 1926; fils Jean-Baptiste and Blanche (Provencher) C.; é Coll. de Gravelbourg; Univ. Ottawa, B.A., 1946; L.Ph., 1947; Univ. Montréal, LL.L., 1950 (Prix du Doyen, 1949; Prix du Lieut.-Gouv. et Prix Arthur Vallée, 1950); Univ. Oxford, B.C.L., 1952 (Bourse Rhodes); Univ. de Paris, Docteur en droit, 1955 (Prix R. Dennery); LL.D. Ottawa, 1971; ép. Nicole, f. Fernand Thomas, 26 juin 1959; enfants: François, Marie-Geneviève, Philippe; PROF. TITULAIRE DE DROIT, UNIV. McGILL Wainwright Prof. of Civil Law; et Dir. de l'Inst. de droit comparé; appelé au Barreau de Montreal, 1950; Conseil de la reine, 1969; Prés. de l'Office de revision du Code civil de Québec 1965-1977; Association. can. des Prof. de Droit (prés., 1964-65); Assn. qué des professeurs de droit (1965-66); Inst. International de Droit d'Expression Française (vice-prés.); Ass'n qué. pour l'étude compar. du droit, (prés 1974-) Assn. de Droit Internat., section de Montréal, (mem. du Conseil1970-75); Fac. Internat, pour l'enseignement du droit comparé (Strasbourg, mem. du Conseil); Reçu prix du Barreau de la Prov. de Qué., 1962; publ. "La responsabilité civile du médecin et de l'eétablissement hospitalier", 1956; "La dissertation juridique" avec Me Jean Roy, 1958; "Recueil de documents et arrêts en droit international privé québécois/Cases and Materials in Quebec Private International Law", 1968; "Recueil de documents et arrêts sur la théorie générale des obligations juridiques", 1974; "Eléments d'une introduction au droit international privé comparé", 1962; "L'Avenir du Fédéralisme canadien — The Future of Canadian Federalism" avec le Prof. C. B. MacPherson, 1965; "La responsabilité médicale et hospitalière: évolution récente du droit québécois", 1968; Rapport sur le Code civil du Québec (en collab.) 1978; "Code civil-Civil Code, 1866-1980" avec J.E.C. Brierley, 1981; nombreux articles and comptes-rendus dans plusieurs périodiques; prof. invité à maintes reprises aux. univ. de Québec, Montréal, Baton Rouge (La), Edimbourg, Ecosse, et Vienne, Autriche, Catholique; récréation: natation, golf; Résidence: 5 Place du Vésinet, Montréal, Québec H2V 2L6

CRESSWELL, Peter Ross, B.Sc., B.A.Sc.; transportation executive; b. Montreal, Que. 14 March 1935; s. Herbert Arthur and P. Ethelwynne (Carpenter) C.; e. Bishops Coll. Sch. Lennoxville, Que. 1953; Bishops Univ. B.Sc. 1955; Univ. of Toronto B.A.Sc. 1959; m. Nancy Elizabeth d. Trevor Moore, Toronto, Ont. 14 Nov. 1959; children: Robert, Tracy, Susan; VICE PRES. AND GEN. MGR.-MARINE DIV., DIR., ALGOMA CENTRAL RAILWAY; Pres., Algoma Steamships Ltd.; Herb Fraser and Associates Ltd.; Chmn. Dom. Marine Assn.; Dir. Candn. Lake Carriers Assn.; Jensens Montreal Ltd.; Assn. Prof. Engrs.

Prov. Ont.; Kappa Alpha (Past Pres.); Anglican; recreations: golf, tennis, skiing; Clubs: Sault Ste. Marie Golf; Toronto Golf; Home: 1993 Queen St. E., Sault Ste Marie, Ont. P6A 2G8; Office: (P.O. Box 7000) Sault Ste. Marie, Ont. P6A 5P6.

CRETE, Hon. Joseph Arthur Marcel; judge; b. La Tuque, Que.; 31 May, 1915; s. Alphida and Jeanne (Paquin) C.; e. Primary and Secondary Schs. in Grand'Mere and Trois-Rivière, Qué.; Laval Univ. (Law) 1937; Osgoode Hall, Toronto, Ont.; m. Berthe, d. H. L. Godin, Toronto, Ont., 14 June 1941; children: Louis, Marie, Lucille, Raymonde; CHIEF JUSTICE OF QUEBEC 1980-; engaged in private practice 1938; former Director of a number of Companies; called to the Bar of Que., 1937; cr. Q.C. 1961; practiced law with Leo Pinsonneault, Q.C., 1938-50, and with Auguste Desilets, Q.C., Denis Lévesque, Marcel Beaumier, and Yues Duhaime 1957-61; Justice, Superior Court of Que. 1962-72; Justice Québec Court of Appeal; President, Shawinigan-Grand'Mere Canadian Club; Catholic; recreations: hunting, fishing, Laurentide (Grand'Mere); Home: 100-6th St., Grand'Mere, Que. G9T 4P5; Office: Court House, Montreal, Que.

CRIGHTON, Arthur Bligh, D.M.A.; musician; educator; b. Calgary, Alta., 6 June 1917; s. Reginald James and Grace Carman (Armstrong) C.; Univ. of Toronto, L.R.C.T., Mus. Bac. 1948; Univ. of S. Cal., M.M. 1962, D.M.A. 1965; PROF. OF MUSIC, UNIV. OF ALBERTA; Chrmn., Div. of Music Hist. and Lit. 1967-80; has taught in fields of music theory, hist. and applied music at present univ.; Conductor, Univ. Symphony Orchestra, 1950-67; Examiner and Theory Consultant, W. Bd. of Music; "A Workbook for Music Analysis" 1980; served with RCAF during World War II; Bomber Pilot; P.O.W. Germany 1942-45; Active Reserve, Univ. of Alta. Sqdn., 1950-68; rank Lt. Col.; Assoc., Royal Candn. Coll. Organists (Past Chrmn., Edmonton Centre); mem., Candn. Assn. Univ. Schs. Music; Home: 8903-180 St., Edmonton, Alta. T5T 0Y3

CRIPTON, Michael John, D.D.S., F.R.C.D.(C.); orthodontist; b. Montreal, Que, 29 Sept. 1934; s. John and Veronica (Tchachuk) C.; e. Westmount (Que.) Jr. and Sr. High Schs.; McGill Univ. D.D.S. 1957; Univ. of Montreal Dipl. in Orthodontics 1961; m. Nancy Carroll, d. Carvell G. Green, Florenceville, N.B. 27 Sept. 1958; children: Michael, Mary, Peter, David; orthodontic practice Moncton since 1961; Partner MacRealty Ltd.; dental practice Fredericton 1957-59; el. Councillor-at-Large Moncton 1971; re-el. 1973; unsuccessful cand. for Mayor 1974; Chrmn. Easter Seal Campaign Moncton 1964; Pres. Moncton Boys' Club 1964-66 (Bd. mem. 1962-70); mem. Nat. Dent. Examining Bd. Can. 1970-75; Dent. Adv. Comte. Dept. of Health N.B. 1969-71; Atlantic Prov's Rep. Candn. Fund for Dent. Educ. 1971-78; Pres. Can. Dental Ass'n. 1976-77; Fellowship, Int'l College of Dentists, 1978; President, Can. Ass'n. of Orthodontists, 1979-80; mem. Adv. Comte. Moncton Minor Hockey Assn.; Dir. Moncton Figure Skating Club; Extve. Comte. 1974 Candn. Figure Skating Championships; Vice Chrmn., Skate Canada 77, Moncton; Assoc. mem. Offrs.' Mess CFB Moncton; mem. Greater Moncton Chamber Comm.; Candn. Dent. Assn. (Pres. Sept. 1976-77); Am. Assn. Orthodontics; European Assn. Orthodontics; Fed. Dentaire Internationale (Nat. Treas.-Can.); N.B. Dent. Soc. (Secy.-Treas.-Registrar 1964-67; Chrmn. Liaison Comte. N.B. Govt. 1969-71); Northeastern (US) Soc. Orthodontists; Anglican; recreation: curling; Clubs: Beaver Curling; Moncton City; Rotary (Pres. 1969-70); Home: 21 Alexander Ave., Moncton, N.B. E1E 1T3; Office: 567 St. George St., Moncton, N.B. E1E 2B8

CRISPO, John, B. Com., Ph.D.; university professor; b. Toronto, Ont., 5 May 1933; s. Francis Herbert and Elizabeth Brock (Gillespie) C.; e. Upper Can. Coll. Toronto, 1952; Trinity Coll., Univ. of Toronto, B. Com. 1956; Mass.

Inst. of Technol., Ph.D. (Indust. Econ.) two d., Carol Anne, Sharon Elizabeth; CHEVRON VISITING PROF. FACULTY OF MANG. STUDIES AND DEPT OF POL. EC., SIMON FRASER UNIV.; Assoc. of Centre for Industrial Relations; Teaching Assistant, Mass. Institute of Technol., 1959-60; Assistant Prof., Huron Coll., Univ. of W. Ont., 1960-61; joined present Univ. as Asst. Prof., 1961-64; Assoc. Prof. 1964-65; mem., Prime Min.'s Task Force on Labour Relations, 1967-69; Chrmn., Ont. Union-Mang. Council, 1967-74; frequent public speaker & media commentator author, "International Unionism — A Study in Canadian-American Relations", 1967; "The Public Right to Know — Accountability in the Secretive Society", 1975; "The Canadian Industrial Relations System", 1978; "Industrial Democracy in Western Europe", 1978; "A Mandate for Canada", 1979; ed. and co-ed. of several books; other writings include articles for learned journs.; recreations: farming; riding; skiing; Home: 425 Richview Ave., Toronto, Ont. M5P 3G7

CRITCHLEY, William Archibald, C.A.; company executive; b. Cochrane, Ont., 12 Aug. 1926; s. late John Archibald and Louise Matilda (Humble) C.; e. St. Catharines (Ont.) Coll. Inst., 1944; C.A. 1952; m. Jane MacDonald, d. John Johnston, St. Catharins, Ont., 22 Oct. 1947; children: Bruce, Leigh; m. Mary Allison, d. Dr. Donald News, Senneville, Que., 29 Aug. 1981; GROUP VICE PRES., FINANCE & ADM., POLYSAR LTD. since 1977; Secy.-Treas., Spinrite Yarns & Dyers Ltd., 1953-54; Internal Auditor and subsequently Mgr. Accounting. Chem. Div., Union Carbide Canada Ltd., 1955-57; Mgr. Internal Audit, Massey-Ferguson Ltd., 1958; subsequently served in several financial positions incl. Asst. Corporate Comptroller; served in Australia as Dir., Comptroller and Secy., 1963-66; Chief Financial Offr., Canada Wire and Cable Co. Ltd., 1966; Vice Pres. Finance 1967; Vice Pres. and Controller, The Molson Companies Ltd., 1971-73; Dir. Marketing Asia/Africa/Australasia, Massey-Ferguson Ltd. 1973-76; apptd. Vice Pres.-Finance, Polysar Ltd. 1976; served with RCNVR (Air Br.) 1944-46; Anglican; recreations: golf, music; Home: 2191 Lakeshore Rd., R.R. #3, Sarnia, Ont. N7T 7H4; Office: 201 Front St. N., Sarnia, Ont. N7T 7V1

CROCKER, Howard Graham; b. Newcastle, N.B., 4 Oct. 1912; retired; s. Rowland Waldo and Rita (Elliott) C.; e. Harkins Acad.; Mount Allison Univ. (two yrs. Finance and Comm.); m. Muriel, d. Archibald Cross, 28 Oct. 1936; children: Donald Graham, Muriel Anne; Pres., T. W. Crocker Co. Ltd. (Estbd. 1866; fresh and frozen fish exporters); elected to N.B. Legislature 1960-63-67-70; Minister of Lands & Mines, N.B. 1960-65; apptd. (1965), Chrmn., N.B. Electric Power Comn; Chrmn., N.B. Army Benevolent Fund; apptd. to Army Benevolent Fund Bd. (Can.) 1977; Dist. Gov., Canadian Corps of Commissioners; Dir., Newcastle Rink Assn.; Past Pres., Newcastle Br., Royal Candn. Legion; Past Dist. Commdr., B.E.S.L.; twice a mem., Newcastle Town Council; served in N.P.A.M., then in 2nd World War with R.C.A. in Sicily, Italy, France, Germany; Past Pres., Miramichi Shrine Club; Freemason (P.M.); Scot. Rite; 32°); Liberal; Anglican; recreations: curling, boating, fishing, hunting; Home: 503 King George Highway, Newcastle, N.B. E1V 1M6

CROCKETT, Arthur Holmes, LL.D.; banker; b. Westville, N.S., 12 Jan. 1917; s. late Frederick N. G. and Annabelle (Holmes) C.; m. Margaret Louise, D. Wentworth N. Macdonald, Sydney, N.S., 25 Aug. 1951; children: Margot Gwynneth, Pamela Jane, Arthur Ross; DEPUTY CHAIRMAN AND DIR., THE BANK OF NOVA SCOTIA, since 1972; Chrmn. & Dir., Scotia Centre Ltd.; Bank of Nova Scotia Jamaica Ltd.; The West India Co. of Merchant Bankers Ltd.; Vancouver Centre Development Ltd.; Siemens Electric Ltd.; Siemens Overseas Investments Ltd.; Vice-Pres. and Dir., Brunswick Square Ltd.; Scotia Realty Ltd.; Dir., Bank of Nova Scotia Trust Co. of

Jamaica Ltd.; Bank of Nova Scotia Trust Company of Jamaica Limited; Bank of Nova Scotia Trinidad and Tobago Ltd.; Bank of Nova Scotia Trust Co. of The West Indies Ltd.; Fintra Corp.; Can. Colors & Chemicals Ltd.; Carr Investments Ltd.; Eastbourne N.V.; Hawker Siddeley Can. Inc.; Mannesmann Demag Ltd.; Nova Scotia Corp.; GSW Inc.; Gerling Global Gen. Ins. Co.; Gerling Global Reins. Co.; Gerling Global Life Ins. Co.; Supreme Aluminum Industries Ltd.; Pres., Can. German Ch. of Ind. & Comm. Inc.; joined the Bank at Westville, N.S., 1934; Special Rep., New York Agency, 1946; Supervisor's Dept., Winnipeg, 1949; Mgr., Oshawa, Ont., 1950, London, Eng., 1953, Montreal, 1957, Toronto, 1958; Asst. Gen. Mgr. of Bank and Mgr. Toronto Br., 1962; Depy. Gen. Mgr., 1964; Gen. Mge., Montreal, 1966; Chief Gen. Mgr., 1968; Pres. and Dir., 1970; served as Offr., R.C.N., 1941-45; discharged with rank of Lieut.-Commander; Hon. President, Canadian Bankers Association, (Pres. 1969-70); mem., Bd. Govs. Dalhousie Univ.; Hon. LL.D., Mount Allison University 1971; Protestant; recreation: golf; Clubs: National; Toronto; Toronto Hunt; The York (Toronto); Rosedale Golf; Granite; Office: 44 King St. W., Toronto, Ont. M5H 1H1

CROLL, Hon. David Arnold, Q.C.; senator; b. Moscow, Russia, 1900; s. Hillel and Minnie (Cherniak) C.; e. Pub. and High Schs., Windsor, Ont.; Univ. of Toronto; Osgoode Hall Law Sch., Toronto, Ont.; m. Sarah Levin, 1925; children: Eunice, Constance Sandra Ruth; practising with Croll & Croll, Windsor, Ont., and Croll & Godfrey, Toronto, Ont.; read law with F. D. Davis, Q.C., Windsor, Ont., and Hughes & Agar of Toronto, Ont., called to Bar of Ont., 1925; cr. K.C. 1934; mem., Candn. Bar Assn.; Essex County Law Soc.; Yorks Law Soc.; el. Mayor of Windsor, 1930-34 and 1938-40; 1st el. to Ont. Leg. for Windsor-Walkerville, at g.e. 1934; sworn of the Extve. Council and apptd. Min. of Pub. Welfare, Mun. Affairs, and Min. of Labour, 19 July 1934; resigned apr. 1937; mem., Ont. Leg. 1937 to 1945; enlisted Pte. Candn. Army (Essex Scots) Sept., 1939; served overseas and promoted to Lt.-Col.: discharged 1945; el. to H. of C., 1945, for Toronto-Spadina; re-el. g.e. 1949 and 1953; apptd. to the Senate of Canada, 28 July 1955; Freemason (Shrine); Liberal; Hebrew; Home: 1603 Bathurst St., Toronto, Ont. M5P 3J2; Office: 99 Avenue Rd., 9th floor, Toronto, Ont. M5R 2G6

CROMARTY, Hon. John David Stuart; judge; b. Calgary, Alta., 1 Feb. 1912; s. William David and Beatrice (Prosser) C.; e. Lisgar Collegiate, Ottawa, Ont.; Trinity Coll., Univ. of Toronto, B.A. 1934; Osgoode Hall, Toronto, Ont.; m. Nancy Macleod, 26 June 1948; children: Brooke, (Mrs. D. W. Sharp), Barry; Justice, Supreme Court of Ont., Nov. 1971 (formerly a partner, Cromarty, Brooks & Macfarlane, Welland, Ont.); read law with R. M. Fowler; called to the Bar of Ont., June 1937 cr. Q.C., 1 Jan. 1955; served with R.C.N.V.R. 1940-5 as Commander; Anglican; Clubs: R.C.Y.C.; University (Toronto); Home: 500 Avenue Rd., Toronto, Ont. M4V 2J6; Office: Osgoode Hall, Toronto, Ont. M5H 2N5

CROMIE, Peter Esmond, B.Com.; industrialist; b. Vancouver, B.C., 10 Dec. 1920; s. Robert James and Bernadette Grace (McFeely) C.; e. Pub. and High Schs. Vancouver; Univ. of Brit. Columbia 1939-41 and B. Com. 1946; Univ. of Toronto 1941; m. Inez Patricia, d. Henry Ferdinand Knight, 10 Dec. 1948; children: Gail Patricia, Ronald Peter, Dana James, Edward Allan, Lin Inez, Jane Bernadette, PRES. AND DIRECTOR PLATO INDUSTRIES LTD.; Dir., Paisley Corp.; Tunstall Estates Ltd.; White Islets Corp.; D. C. Projects Ltd.; served in R.C.A. 1943-45; rank Sgt. Intelligence Corps; Convocation Founder, Simon Fraser University; Zeta Psi; Unitarian; recreations: tennis, golf, boating; Clubs: The Vancouver; Vancouver Lawn Tennis; Shaughnessy Golf and Country; Home: Suite 900, 1685 W. 14th Ave., Vancouver,

B.C. V6J 2J3 Office: Suite 300, 595 Howe St., Vancouver, B.C. V6C 2T5.

CRONE, John Porter, C.A.; financial consultant & company director; b. Belfast, N. Ireland 17 May 1930; s. Robert and Anna Frances (Porter) C.; e. Royal Belfast Acad. Inst. 1942-47; Belfast Coll. of Technol. A.C.A. 1952; m. Christine Evans 3 Apl. 1954; children: Judith, Michael, Jacqueline, Jennifer, Wendy; PRES. & DIR., QUINTET RESOURCES LTD.; Dir., Canada Northwest Land Ltd.; B.M.C. Oil and Gas Inc., San Antonio Group Vice Pres. Corporate, & Dir., Home Oil Co. Ltd. 1977-80; Extve. Vice Pres. and Dir., Scurry-Rainbow Oil Ltd. 1977-80; Dir. Home Petroleum Corp. Houston, Texas; Treas. Home Petroleum corp. 1968-69; Comptroller Home Oil co. Ltd. 1969-72; Mang. Dir. Home Oil (UK) Ltd. 1972-75; Vice Pres. Internat. Operations Home Oil co. Ltd. 1975-77; mem. Inst. C.A.'s Alta., Ireland; Anglican; recreations: golf, tennis, swimming, reading, bridge, Clubs: Calgary Petroleum; Ranchmen's; Uplands Golf; Royal Automobile (London, Eng.); Home: 5025 Lockhaven Dr., Victoria, B.C. V8N 4J6; Office:

CRONE, Robert Carl; film producer; b. Toronto, Ont., 7 Aug. 1932; s. The Rev. Walter S. and Dorothy Kathleen (Fitzsimmons) C.; e. Pub. ad High Schs., Peterborough, Ont.; Peterborough Business Coll.; Bob Jones Univ., Greenville, S.C.; m. Violet May, d. Roy Sanderson, 4 Sept. 1952; one s. David Carl; Operations Mgr. of a T.V. Stn., U.S.A., 1955; C.B.C., 1956; Freelance Motion Picture Producer, 1957; Vice-Pres., Robert Crone Pictures Ltd., 1958; Pres. and Dir., Crone Holdings Ltd., 1961; Crone Films Inc., U.S.A., 1961; Pres., Chief Extve. Offr. and Dir. Film House Ltd. 1968; Awards: T.V. Workshop, N.Y.; Gold Camera Award, 1955; Ohio State Univ. Film Award, 1959; 1981 joint recipient with wife of the special Air Canada Award, and jointly received Genie from the Acad. of Candn. Cinema for their outstanding contributions to the growth of the Canadian film industry; responsible for dir. and prod. of Motion Picture and T.V. for Nat. Lib. Fed.; rec'd Centennial Medal 1967; Civilian Citation, Board Commissioners, Metropolitan Toronto Police 1969; mem., Soc. of Motion Picture & T.V. Engrs.; Candn. Prof. Photographers Assn.; Am. Cinema Labs.; Soc. of Film Makers; Life mem. Directors Guild of Can.; Can. Soc. of Cinematographers; Can. Film Editors Guild; founding mem. Can. Acad. Film and Television Arts and Sciences; mem. Can. Film and Television Assn.; Dir., N. Rosedale Ratepayers Assn.; Liberal; United Church; recreations: travel, reading, music, skiing, gourmet, multi engine instrument rated pilot; Clubs: Granite; Canadian; Rotary; Ontario; Home: 400 Walmer Rd., Toronto, Ont. M5P 2X7

CRONIN, John J.; advertising executive; b. Charleville, Ireland, 10 Oct. 1931; s. Col. Edmund J. and Bridget (MacMahon) C.; e. Oxford Cambridge Higher Leaving Cert., 1950; Univ. of London, Dipl. in Eng. Lit. 1950; Univ. of London, Dipl. in Eng. Lit. 1950; m. Patricia, d. Maurice J. O'Connor, 29 Oct. 1955; children: Mark, Jonathan, Shane, Paul, Connor, Jacqueline; PRESIDENT AND CHIEF EXTVE. OFFR., J. WALTER THOMPSON CO. LTD.; Reporter, Limerick Chronicle, Ireland, 1951-53; The Candn. Press, Montreal. 1953-55; Pub. Relations and Advertising Supvr., The Great West Life Assurance Co., Winnipeg, 1954-60; Copy Chief and Creative Dir., Cockfield-Brown Advertising Agency, Winnipeg, 1960-63; joined present co. as Sr. Copywriter 1964; Creative Dir. 1966-72, Vice Pres. 1967-72, Dir. Montreal Office 1971, Extve. Vice Pres. and Dir., Candn. Operations 1972, Vice Pres. 1974, Pres. and Chief Operating Offr. 1976, Chief Extve. Offr. 1977, Sr. Vice Pres. 1977; mem., Inst. of Candn. Agencies; Broadcast Extves. Soc., Toronto; R. Catholic; recreations: reading; music; Club: Club; Home: 280 Riverside Dr., Toronto, Ont. M6S 4B2; Office: 102 Bloor St. W., Toronto, Ont. M5S 1M9

CRONIN, Robert Francis Patrick, C.D., M.D., C.M., M.Sc., F.R.C.P. (Lond.), F.R.C.P.(C); physician; educator, b. London, Eng., 1 Sept. 1926; s. Archibald Joseph and Agnes Mary (Gibson) C.; e. Princeton Univ. 1943-44 and 1947-49; McGill Univ., M.D., C.M. 1953, M.Sc. 1960; m. Shirley-Gian, d. Randal Killaly Robertson, 19 June 1954; children: David Robert, Diana Christine, Daphne-Gian: CONSULTANT TO THE AGA KHAN FOUNDATION, PROF., FACULTY OF MED., McGILL UNIV.; a mem. of the Faculty since 1959, Assoc. Dean 1969-72, Dean 1972-77; Sr. Phys., Montreal Gen. Hosp.; Consultant (cardiology), Queen Mary Veterans' and St. Anne's Hosp., 1961; Gov., Coll. of Phys. and Surg., Que., 1968; Vice Pres., Medical Research Council, Que., 1971; M.G.H. Research Inst., 1977; Dir., Can. Heart Foundation, 1978; Found. Armand Frappier, 1980; Consultant, World Bank Bank and C.I.D.A., 1980; Pres., Grad. Soc. of McGill Univ., 1978; served in 2nd World War, R.C.A.F. 1944-45; Brit. Army 1945-47, rank Lt.; R.C.A.F. Auxiliary 1956-64, rank Sqdn.-Ldr.; author of numerous articles in scient. journs. primarily in field of cardiovascular physiol., Fellow; Roy. Coll. Phys., London; Club: University; Home: Champ- Riond, 1815 Baugy, Montreux, Switzerland.

CRONYN, Hugh Verschoyle, G.M., F.R.S.A.; artist; painter; b. Vancouver, B.C., 30 April 1905; s. Verschoyle Francis and Mable Margaret (Philpot) C.; e. Ridley Coll., St. Catharines, Ont.; Franz Johnson Studio, Toronto; Art Students League, N.Y.; Acad. Lhote, Paris; American Sch. of Fine Arts, Fontainbleau; m. Jean Harris, M.A. (Oxon), d. Percy Harris, 1942; two d. Anna Catharine, Janet Margaret; before the 2nd World War worked in Paris Studios, and as Freelance artist, London, Eng; subsequent to the war, Dir. of Art at the Architectural Assn. Sch. of Arch., London, Eng.; full-time Lectr. in Painting at North East Essex Sch. of Art, Colchester, Eng., also Instr. in Lithography; exhibits at the Royal Acad., The London Group, Artists Internat. Assn., various U.K. Galleries; paintings and portrait colls. in Eng., Sweden, Canada, U.S.A., France; mural paintings C.P.S. Empress of Canada; one-man exhns.: Toronto, Montreal, Victoria, B.C., Canada House, London, Minories, Colchester, Edng., and other prov. galleries; currently painting in Can., Eng., Fr., served in 2nd World War: 1939, Royal Navy Auxiliary Patrol; 1940-46; Royal Navy, Lieut.-Commdr.; George Medal; Fellow of Roy. Soc. of Arts; Addresses: 47, Forsythe St., Marmora, Ont.; Studio 3, St. Peters Wharf, Hammersmith Terrace, London, England and Caufour 46800, Montcuq, France.

CRONYN, Hume; actor; writer; director; b. London, Ont., 18 July 1911; s. Hume Blake, distinguished financier and publicist, and Frances A. (Labatt) C.; e. Ridley Coll., St. Catharines, Ont.; McGill Univ.; N.Y. Sch. of Theatre; Mozarteum, Salzburg, Austria; Am. Acad. Dramatic Art, New York; Hon. LL.D., Univ. of W. Ont. 1974; m. Jessica Tandy (actress) 27 Sept. 1942; children: Christopher Hume, Tandy, Susan Tettemer; intended for the law, but after some amateur experience with a group of players in Montreal, Que., joined Cochran's Stock Co., Washington, D.C., and made prof. debut in "Up Pops the Devil", 1931; later estbd. a growing reputation when appearing in "Three Men on a Horse" (1935-36), followed by "High Tor", "Room Service", "Boy Meets Girl"; took first leading role "The Weak Link", 1940 entered motion pictures in "Shadow of a Doubt", 1943; directed an Actor's Lab. Theatre prod. of "Portrait of a Madonna", 1946, followed by "Now I Lay Me Down To Sleep", 1949, "Hilda Crane", 1950, "The Egghead", 1957; with Norman Lloyd staged the initial Phoenix Theatre prod. "Madam Will You Walk", 1953, in which he also co-starred with his wife; scored a great hit with prod. of "The Fourposter" 1952 (won Am. Theatre Wings' Antoinette Perry Play Award, 1952); on tour with "The Fourposter" 1951, '52, '53; inaugurated radio series "The Marriage" for NBC (with wife), 1953; has since appeared in "The

Honeys", 1955; "A Day by the Sea", 1955; "The Man In The Dog Suit", 1958; "Sunrise at Campobello" (film), 1960; "Cleopatra" (film), 1963; port. Polonius in Sir John Geilgud's prod. of "Hamlet", 1964; appd. in title role of "Richard III", 1965; played Yepihodov "The Cherry Orchard" and the title role "The Miser", 1965 at Tyrone Guthrie Thea., Minneapolis; "A Delicate Balance" at Martin Beck, N.Y., 1966 and in U.S. tour 1967; Revival "The Miser" 1968 at Mark Taper Forum, L.A.; title role of "Hadrian VII", Stratford 1969 and National Tour 1969-70; "The Caine Mutiny Court-Martial", Ahmanson Thea., Los Angeles 1971-72; appeared on stage in "Promenade All" at Alvin Theatre, N.Y.C. 1972; Samuel Beckett Festival at the Forum, Lincoln Centre, N.Y.C. ("Krapp's Last Tape", "Happy -days", and "Act without words I") 1972; tour "Promenade All" 1973; "Krapp's Last Tape" tour 1973; performed in "Krapp's Last Tape" and "Not I" (with Jessica Tandy) Toronto 1973; "Noel Coward in Two Keys" 1974 and tour 1975; 'Concert-recital' tour of "Many Faces of Love"(Oct.-Nov. 1974 and 1975); "Merchant of Venice" and "A Midsummer Night's Dream", Stratford Fest. (Ont.) 1976; "Many Faces of Love", London, Ont. and tour 1976; co-produced with Mike Nichols, and appeared in "The Gin Game" (Pulitzer Prize 1978) with Jessica Tandy, Long Wharf Thea., New Haven, Conn. and The Golden Thea., N.Y.C. 1977-78; "Gin Game" national tour U.S. 1978-79, and in Toronto, Canada, London, England, and U.S.S.R. 1979; co-authored (with Susan Cooper), "Foxfire" performed Stratford Festival, Ont. 1980 and Guthrie Theatre, Minneapolis, 1981; "Rollover", 1981; "Honky Tonk Freeway" 1980; additional films: "Gaily, Gaily", 1968; "The Arrangement", 1968; "There Was A Crooked Man", 1969; "Conrack", 1973; "Parallax View", 1973; made 1st appr. in TV in "Her Master's Voice", 1939; has acted in all major dramatic television series and appeared seven times on "Omnibus" and three times on the Ed Sullivan Show"; sometime lectr. on drama; has written a number of short stories and has collab. with Hitchcock on the screen treatment of "Rope" and "Under Capricorn" at request of the President and Mrs. Johnson, appeared with his wife at the White House in "Hear America Speaking", 1965; was nominated for an Academy Award for performance in "The Seventh Cross", 1944; rec'd (with his wife) Comoedia Matinee Club's Award for "The Fourposter", 1952; rec'd the Barter Theatre Award "for outstanding contribution to the theatre", 1961; nominated for Antoinette Perry (Tony) Award, 1961; awarded Delia Austria Medal from the N.Y. Drama League for performance in "Big Fish, Little Fish", 1961; rec'd Antoinette Perry (Tony) Award and won the "Variety" N.Y. Drama Critics Poll for portrayal of Polonius in "Hamlet", 1964; rec'd Am. Acad. of Dramatic Arts Ninth Annual Award for Achievement for Alumni, 1964; rec'd. Herald Theater Award for Tobias in "A Delicate Balance"; L.A. Drama Critics Circle Award for best actor in "Caine Mutiny Court Martial" 1972; 4th Annual Straw Hat Award for Best Dir. ("Promenade All") 1972; 1972-73 Obie Award ("Krapp's Last Tape"); Brandeis Univ. Creative Arts Awards for distinguished achievement 1978; nominated by Drama Desk for outstanding actor and for Antoinette Perry (Tony) Award for best actor in "The Gin Game", 1977-78; also rec. L.A. Critics' Award for performance in "Gin Game", 1979; el. to Amer. Theatre Hall of Fame, 1979; nominated for Candn. Olympic Boxing Team, 1932; named to Bd. Dirs., Stratford Fest. (1st actor) 1978; Address: 63-23 Carlton St., Rego Park, N.Y. 11374

CRONYN, John B., B.Sc., company director; b. London, Ont., 3 Dec. 1920; s. late Verschoyle Philip and Dorothy (Bruce) C.; e. St. George's Public Sch., London, Ont.; Ridley Coll., St. Catharines, Ont.; Univ. of Toronto, B.Sc. 1947; m. Barbara Jean, d. late Noble Duff, 22 June 1946, children: Hume Duff, Marilyn Ruth, Martha Ann; Dir., John Labatt Ltd.; Stambax Inc., Americaire Corp.; Can. Trustco Mortgage Co.; Econ. Investment Trust Ltd.; D. H. Howden & Co. Ltd.; Major Holdings and Develop-

ment Ltd.; Burnlea Holdings Ltd.; R.C.O. Investments Ltd.; Union Gas Ltd.; Talisman Resort Hotel; St. Joseph's Hospital; London Life Insurance Co.; Past Pres. London Chamber Comm., V.O.N., Boy Scouts Assn., London, Ont.; Assn. Prof Engrs. Ont.; apprentice brewer, John Labatt Ltd., Oct. 1947; completed brewmaster's course with Nat. Brewers Acad. 1949; apptd. Production Mgr., John Labatt Ltd., 1950, Dir. of Production, 1952, Vice-Pres. in charge of Production, 1956; el. a Dir., 1959, Extve. V.P. 1962; apptd. Chrmn., Ont. Gov. Productivity Improvement Project 1969; Vice Chrmn. of Bd., John Labatt Ltd. 1973; took early retirement, retaining directorship of John Labatt Ltd. 1976; served in 2nd World War; Lieut., R.C.E.; England and N. W. Europe, 1942-46; Kappa Alpha; Anglican; Clubs: London Hunt & Country; The London; Toronto; Great Lakes Cruising; Home: 21 Doncaster Ave., London, Ont. N6G 2A1

CROOKER, Arthur Mervyn, M.A., Ph.D.; retired university professor; b. Cayuga, Ont., 19 Sept. 1909; s. Mervyn Arthur and Evelyn Agnes (Crull) C.; e. McMaster Univ., B.A. 1930; Univ. of Toronto, M.A. 1931; Ph.D. 1935; post-grad. studies, Univ. of London, 1935-37; m. Helen Mae, d. John MacVicar, 3 June 1939; children: Mervyn; Prof. of Physics, Univ. of B. Columbia, 1945-75; N.R.C. Research Assoc., Goddard Space Flight Center, N.A.S.A., 1970-71, 1976-77; with Dunlop Tire and Rubber Co. as Chem., 1929; Research Asst. to Dr. J. C. McLennan 1931; 1851 Exhibition Research Student 1935-37; Lectr. and Asst. Prof., Univ. of B.C., 1937-38; with Research Enterprises Ltd. as Chief Physicist in charge of Optical Design, 1941-45; mem., Am. Phys. Soc.; Am. Assn. for Advanc. of Science; Liberal; United Church; Home: 1670 Wesbrook Cres., Vancouver, B.C. V6T 1W1

CROOKSTON, J. Ian; financial consultant; b. Ayr, Scotland, 19 July 1910; s. James and Agnes N. (Sovereign) C.; e. Boxgrove Sch., England, 1919-24; Stowe Sch., Eng., 1924-28; m. Cynthia D., d. Norman Copping, June 1937; children: Andrea (deceased), Dana, James; 2ndly, Anne D. Dumstrey, Nov. 1976; Retired Chairman and Dir., Nesbitt, Thomson and Company Limited, Dir., Trustee, Candn. Realty Investors; Governor, Investment Bankers Assn. of Am., 1966; Conservative; Anglican; recreation: golf; Clubs: Toronto; York; Toronto Hunt; Home: 187 Cottingham St., Toronto, Ont. M4V 1C4; Office: (Box 35) Toronto-Dominion Centre, Toronto, Ont. M5K 1C4

CROSBIE, Alexander Harris, D.S.O., B.A.; merchant; b. St. John's Nfld., 27 Feb. 1919; s. John Chalker and Mitchie Ann (Manuel) C.; e. Prince of Wales Coll., St. John's, Nfld.; Appleby Coll., Oakville, Ont.; Trinity Coll., Univ. of Toronto, B.A. (Philos. and Hist.); m. Gertrude, d. Andrew Murray, St. John's, Nfld., 25 Sept. 1947; three s. and two d.; PRESIDENT, A. H. MURRAY & CO. LTD. (Gen. Merchants, Steamship Agts., etc.); Pres., Colonial Cordage Co. Ltd.; Pres., Bold Lumber Co. of Ont.; Dir., Boys Club of Canada; Pres. (1956), Nfld. Bd. of Trade; served in 2nd World War; joined Gov.-Gen.'s Horse Guards, March 1941; discharged with rank of Major, Nov. 1945; awarded D.S.O.; fought for econ. union with U.S.A. during confed. issue; Zeta Psi (Pres. at Toronto, 1940); United Ch.; recreations: reading, raising family; Clubs: City; Murray's Pond; Zeta Psi (New York); Home: 25 Pine Bud Ave., St. John's, Nfld.; Office: Beck's Cove, St. John's, Nfld.

CROSBIE, Andrew C.; industrialist; b. St. John's, Nfld., 23 May 1933; S. Jessie E. and (late) Chesley A. married; three s. Alex, Robert, Timothy; one d. Cynthia, Chrmn., Crosbie Offshore Services Ltd.; Crosbie Services Ltd.; Crosbie Reed Stenhouse Ltd.; Eastminister Assur. Agency Ltd.; Mercury Internat. Travlsurance Agency Ltd.; Pres., Avalon Lounge Ltd.; Chimo Shipping Ltd.; Crosbie-Bowring Bases Ltd.; Crosbie Enterprises Ltd.; Crosbie Investments Ltd.; Crosbie O.S.A. Ltd.; Crosbie Realty Ltd.; Nfld. Engineering & Construction Co. Ltd.;

Robinson-Blackmore Printing & Publishing Ltd.; St. John's Development Corp. Ltd.; Trinity Brick Products Ltd.; Dir., Advocate Mines Ltd.; Avalon Lounge Ltd.; Chimo Shipping Ltd.; Colonial Cordage Company Ltd.; Crosbie-Bowring Bases Ltd.; Crosbie Investments Ltd.; Crosbie Offshore Services Ltd.; Crosbie O.S.A. Ltd.; Crosbie Realty Ltd.; Crosbie Reed Stenhouse Ltd.; Crosbie Services Ltd.; Eastern Provincial Airways Ltd.; Eastern Provincial Airways (1963) Ltd.; Eastminister Assurance Agency Ltd.; Hansa Canada Inc.; Mercury Interna. Travlsurance Agency Ltd.; Nfld. Engineering & Construction Co. Ltd.; Robinson-Blackmore Printing & Publishing Ltd.; St. John's Development Corp. Ltd.; Trinity Brick Products Ltd.; Central & Eastern Trust Adv. Bd.; Dir. Candn. Council Christians & Jews; Conference Bd. of Can.; Chrmn. and Pres., Jeux du Canada Games 1977; Past Pres., Nfld. Bd. Trade; United Church; recreations: hunting, fishing; Club: Bally Haly Golf & Country; Address: (P.O. Box 398) Virginia Waters, Logy Bay Road, St. John's, Nfld. A1C 5K3

CROSBIE, John Carnell, P.C., Q.C., B.A, M.P.; lawyer; politician; b. St. John's Nfld., 30 Jan. 1931; s. Chesley Arthur and Jessie Elizabeth (Carnell) C.; e. Bishop Feild Coll., St. John's, Nfld.; St. Andrew's Coll., Aurora, Ont.; Queen's Univ., B.A. 1953 (Univ. Medal in Pol. Science); Dalhousie Univ., LL.B. 1956 (Univ. Medal in Law); Univ. of London, post-grad. work in Law (Candn. Bar Assn. Viscount Bennett Fellowship for 1957); m. Jane Ellen Audrey, d. late Dr. John H. Furneaux, 8 Sept. 1952; children: Chesley Furneaux, Michael John, Beth; read law with P. J. Lewis, Q.C.; called to Bar of Newfoundland 1957; el. to St. John's City Council as Councillor, 1965, apptd. Depy. Mayor, 1966; resigned to accept appt. in Smallwood Lib. Adm. as Min. of Mun. Affairs & Housing, Nfld., July 1966; trans. to Health Portfolio, Sept. 1967; el. M.H.A. for Dist. of St. John's W. in prov. el. Sept. 1966; resigned from Cabinet due to policy disagreements, 14 May 1968; joined P. Conservative Party, June 1971; re-el. for St. John's W., Oct. 1971 and March 1972; apptd. Min. of Finance and Pres. of Treasury Bd. Jan. 1972-Oct. 1974; then apptd. Min. of Fisheries, Min. of Intergovernmental Affairs and Govt. House Leader until Oct. 1975, when apptd. Min. of Mines and Energy and Intergovt. Affairs; resigned Sept. 1976 to run for Parlt. and el. M.P., St. John's W. in by-el. 18 Oct. 1976; became Opposition Energy Critic and then Indust., Trade and Comm. Critic Oct. 1977; re-el. for St. John's W. May 1979, sworn into Privy Council June 4, 1979, and app'ted Min. of Finance; re-el. for St. John's W., Feb 1980 and appt. Opposition Finance Critic; subsequently named External Affairs Critic; el. to Univ. Council, Queen's University, 1967; mem. Newfoundland Law Society; Canadian Bar Association; Canadian Tax Foundation; P. Conservative; United Church; recreations: reading, swimming, hunting; Home: 16 Circular Rd., St. Johns, Nfld. A1C 2Z1; Offices: 220 Lemarchant Rd., St. John's, Nfld. House of Commons, Ottawa K1A 0A6

CROSBIE, John Shaver; association executive; author; b. Montreal, Que., 1 May 1920; s. Thomas Champion and Margaret Ruth (Shaver) C.; e. Univs. of N.B. and Toronto; m. Catherine Patricia James, 19 Nov. 1971; four s. Peter, Stephen, Andrew, Charles; one d. Kathryn; PRESIDENT, MAGAZINE ASSOCIATION OF CANADA since 1967; and Pres., John S. Crosbie Ltd., (1979); with Canadian Broadcasting Corp. until 1944 when apptd. Mang. Dir., Purdy Productions; Asst. Gen. Mgr., Dancer-Fitzgerald-Sample (Canada) Ltd., 1946; Gen. Mgr., Canadian Advertising Agency Ltd. Montreal, 1949; subsequently with J. Walter Thompson Co., Toronto and later as a Vice-Pres., Chicago and San Francisco; served in 2nd W.W. as Offr., Can. Army; Founding-Dir., Candn.-Am. Soc. of N. Calif.; Past Vice-Chrmn., Un. Appeal, Toronto; ex-Chrmn. and Dir. Can. Advertising Adv. Bd.; Gov., Candn. Club of New York; Founding Dir. Nat'l Mag. Awards Found'n.; Nat. Parks Assn.; au-

thor of "The Incredible Mrs. Chadwick"; "Crosbie's Dictionary of Puns", "Crosbie's Dicr'y of Riddles", etc.; Clubs: Granite; Canadian (N.Y.); Home: 107 Ridge Dr., Toronto, Ont. M4T 1B6; Office: 1240 Bay St., Toronto, Ont. M5R 2A7

CROSS, George E.; advertising and public relations counsel; b. New Glasgow, N.S., 25 April 1918; s. George Benjamin and Henrietta (McAulay) C.; e. Public Sch., Saint John, N.B.; Jarvis Coll. Inst., Toronto, Ont.; Ont. Coll. of Art; Univ. of Toronto (Extension); m. Marjorie Eleanor, d. William Salter, 16 Nov. 1940; three s. Douglas George, Robert William, Timothy Charles; MAN. DIR. GEO. CROSS AND CO. PUBLIC RELATIONS CONSULTANTS; Hon. Life Gov., Toronto East Gen. Hosp. 1953-80, 81-; onetime Advertising & Sales Promotions Mgr., Canada Dry Ltd., and later Moffats Ltd., Weston, Ont; recognized as a Specialist in Marketing Research and one of the Canadian pioneers in application of modern scient. research techniques to solution of marketing and distribution problems; Chart. mem. and first Pres. of Toronto Chapter, Am. Marketing Assn.; planned and conducted first forum on Marketing Research ever held in Can. in connection with 1946 annual convention of Assn. of Candn. Advertisers; planned and dir. first organ. course in Marketing Research in Canada (1946) under Extension Dept., Univ. of Toronto; joined Walsh Adv. Co. in 1948; apptd. Dir. and Br. Mgr., 1949, Vice-Pres., 1950; purchased partnership interest in Co. and its subsidiary, Editorial Services, in 1954; apptd. Ont. Div. Mgr. of both Co.'s in 1957 Sr. Vice-Pres. and Gen. Mgr. in 1958; joined Spitzer, Mills and Bates Ltd. as Sr. Vice-Pres; Pres. 1964-69; Chairman, 1969-79; Past Dir., Broadcast Executives Society; Advertising & Sales Club of Toronto (1946); Multiple Sclerosis Soc. of Can.; Speech Fdn. of Ont.; Offr. in Training, 21st Batty., 7th Toronto Regt., R.C.A.; Queen's Silver Jubilee Medal; Protestant; recreations: boating, gardening; Clubs: Granite; Ontario (Past Pres. and Dir.); A.G.O.; Home: 21 Dunkeld Way, Thornhill, Ont.

CROSSLEY, Desmond Ivan, B.Sc.F., M.Sc.; forester; b. Lloydminster, Sask., 7 Oct. 1910; s. Frederick Ivan and Bessie Holtby C.; e. Lloydminster Pub. and High Schs.; Univ. of Toronto, B.Sc.F., 1935; Univ. of Minnesota, M.Sc., 1940; m. Isobel Willis, d. late Joseph Boyd, 9 Oct. 1937; children: (Mrs.) Lynne Elizabeth Bowen, Robert Ivan; PRESIDENT, MASKUTA PROPERTIES LTD., Inventor, log building Constr: two patents; Forest Consulting, specializing in Mang. and Silviculture; Dir., Fab-a-Log Cabins Ltd., Edmonton; Supv. of Tree Planting, Forest Nursery Stn., Indian Head, Sask., 1935-40; Sr. Research Offr., Fed. Forestry Br., Calgary, 1945-55; Chief Forester, Northwestern Pulp & Power Ltd., 1955-75; special lecturer (Forestry) Universities of Alberta, Toronto, and British Columbia; served as Navig., R.C.A.F., 1941-45, rank of Sqdn. Ldr.; mem., Arctic Land Use Research Comte. 1973-78; Alta. Environment Council 1978; Univ. of Alberta Senate 1966-71; author of over 50 scient. publs.; Candn. Forestry Achievement Award 1970; Alta. Achievement Award 1975; mem., Candn. Inst. of Forestry (Pres. 1966-67) (Fellow 1979); 1978-79, mem. Forestry Panel, Envir. Council of Alberta; "The Environmental Effects of Forestry Operations in Alberta"; Sr. mem., Soc. of Am. Foresters; mem., Nat'l Bd. of Dir., Jr. Forest Wardens Assoc. of Can.; Sigma Xi; Agnostic; recreation: raising and training Arab horses; growing miniature (bonsai) trees; Club: Kiwanis (Past Pres.); Home: Hinton, Alta. T0E 1B0; Office: Hinton, Alta. T0E 1B0

CROSTHWAIT, Ven. Terence, M.A., L.Th. (Ang.); b. Winnipeg, Man., 24 March 1905; s. Samuel C.; e. Trinity Coll. Sch., Port Hope, Ont.; Trinity Coll., Toronto, M.A., L.Th.; m. Sylvia, d. Rev. E.C. Cayley; children: Eve, John; Asst., St. John's, Norway, Toronto, Ont., 1932; Grace Church on-the-Hill, Toronto, 1933; Rector, St. Mark's Ch., Port Hope, Ont., 1940; St. Alban's, Toronto,

1946, and Canon of St. James Cath.; Rector, St. Clement's Church 1956-70; Archdeacon of York 1957-70 when retired; Home: 44 Jackes Ave., Toronto, Ont. M4T 1E5

CROUSE, Lloyd Roseville, M.P.; b. Lunenburg, N.S., 19 Nov. 1918; s. Kenneth Eleazer and Mary Bertha (Lantz) C.; e. Lunenberg Co. Acad.; m. Marion Cavell, d. Lawson E. Fraser, Bridgewater, N.S., 7 Oct. 1942; children: Marilyn Diane (Mrs. Ken Williams), Stephen Lloyd; before entering politics estbd. Crouse Fisheries Ltd., Viking Fisheries Limited and Atlas Fisheries Ltd.; served with R.C.A.F. as Pilot 1941-45; mem., Lunenburg Town Council, 1950-52; mem., Lunenburg Sch. Commrs., 1950-52; Chrmn., Lutheran Youth Bd., 1950-54; Past Pres., Lunenburg Br. 23, Royal Candn. Legion; Chrmn. and Master of Ceremonies, N.S. Fisheries Exhn., 1946-56; mem. Council, Lunenburg Bd. Trade, 1946-56; 1st el. to H. of C. for Queens-Lunenburg g.e. 1957, re-el. in 1958, '62, '63, '65, el. in 1968 as first rep. for new "South Shore" constit., re-el. 1972, 1974, 1979 and 1980; Chrmn., Candn. Del., Commonwealth Parly. Conf. in U.K., 1962; Del. to NATO Parlty. Conf., Paris, 1963, 1964, 1966, to Brussels 1967; del. to Inter Parlty. Union Conf., Paris 1971; Del. Commonwealth Parlty. Conf. 1973; Del. C.P.A. Conf., Jamaica, 1978; Del. C.P.A. Conf. New Zealand 1979; Del. to 26th Commonwealth Parly. Conference 1980 at Lusaka, Zambia; Chairman Standing Comte. on Public Accounts 1974 and 1975; Delegate to 1981 U.N. Conference at Columbo, Sri Lanka; presently serving on House Standing Comtes. of External Affairs and Nat'l Defence, Fisheries, and Regional Economic Expansion; mem. Candn. Legion; N.S. Salmon Assn.; Candn. Group Interparlty. Union; Candn. NATO Parlty. Assn.; Candn. Commonwealth Parlty. Assn.; Fellow, N.S. Royal Commonwealth Society; P. Conservative; Lutheran; Clubs: Rod & Gun; Lunenburg Curling and Yacht; Address: 4 Linden Ave., Lunenburg, N.S. B0J 2C0

CROWE, Cameron Macmillan, B.E., Ph.D., F.C.I.C.; educator; b. Montreal, Que. 6 Oct. 1931; s. Ernest Watson and Marianne Verity (Macmillan) C.; e. Montreal West (Que.) High Sch. 1948; Royal Mil. Coll. grad. dipl. 1952; McGill Univ. B.E. 1953; Cambridge Univ. Ph.D 1957; m. Jean Margaret Gilbertson 15 Feb. 1969; PROF. OF CHEM. ENGN., McMASTER UNIV. 1970- ; Sr. Devel. Engr. Du Pont of Canada Ltd. 1957-59; Asst. Prof. present Univ. 1959, Assoc. Prof. 1964, Chrm. of Chem. Engn. 1971-74; Athlone Fellow 1953-55; C. D. Howe Mem. Fellow 1967-68; co-author "Chemical Plant Simulation" 1971; Assoc. Ed. "Canadian Journal of Chemical Engineering" 1971-74; mem. Am. Inst. Chem. Engrs.; Assn. Prof. Engrs. Prov. Ont.; recreations: tennis, skiing; Home: 821 Glenwood Ave., Burlington, Ont. L7T 2J8; Office: Hamilton, Ont. L8S 4L7.

CROWE, Rev. Frederick Ernest, S.J., B.Sc., B.A., S.T.D., Lic. Phil., (R.C.); theologian; educator; b. Jeffries Corner, N.B., 5 July 1915; s. Jeremiah Chesley and Margaret Lucinda (Mahoney) C.; e. Sussex (N.B.) High Sch. 1930; Univ. of N.B., B.Sc. 1934; Loyola Coll., Univ. of Montreal, B.A. 1943; Gregorian Univ., Rome, S.T.D. 1953; Coll. de l'Immaculée-Conception, Lic. Phil. 1962; D.Litt. (Hon.), St. Mary's 1971; D.D. (Hon.), Trinity College, Toronto, 1977; Teacher of Theol., Regis Coll., Toronto since 1953; Research Prof. there since 1975, Prof. Emeritus, 1980-; Founder The Lonergan Research Center 1972; o. Priest, Toronto 1949, S.J. 1936; Teacher, St. Mary's Coll., Halifax, N.S. 1943-46; Pres., Regis Coll. 1969-72; Visiting Prof., Gregorian Univ., Rome 1964; Consultant (to two Candn. bishops) First Synod of Bishops, Rome 1967; served in C.O.T.C. 1930-32; author of "A Time of Change" 1968; "Escatologia e missione terrena in Gesù di Nazareth" 1976; "Theology of the Christian Word: A Study in History" 1978; "The Lonergan Enterprise", 1980; Ed., "Spirit as Inquiry" 1964; contrib. "New Catholic Encyclopedia" 1967; Ed., "Collection: Papers by Bernard Lonergan" 1967; mem. Candn. Theol. Soc.; Catholic

Theol. Soc. Am.; Jesuit Philos. Assn.; Am. Catholic Philos. Assn.; John Courtney Murray Award 1977; Honoured with volume of essays by colleagues, Trinification of the World: A Festschrift in Honour of Frederick E. Crowe in Celebration of His 60th Birthday (Regis College Press, 1978); recreations: bridge, walking, reading; Address: Regis College, 15 St. Mary St., Toronto, Ont. M4Y 2R5

CROWE, Marshall Alexander, B.A.; b. Rossburn, Manitoba, 14 April 1921; s. William Johnston and Georgina (Gammon) C.; e. Daniel McIntyre Coll. Inst., Winnipeg, Man.; Univ. of Manitoba, B.A. 1946; m. Doris Mary, d. late Richard C. Scanes, 5 Dec. 1942; children: Thomas, Alison, Helen, Sheila, Abigail; PRESIDENT, M.A. CROWE CONSULTANTS, INC. since Jan. 1978; Dir., Assoc. Pullman Kellogg Ltd.; Dome Petroleum Ltd.; Energy Ventures Inc.; Gulf Interstate Co.; Hudson's Bay Oil and Gas Ltd.; Sulpetro Ltd.; Dept. of External Affairs, 1947-61; Econ. Adviser, Candn. Imperial Bank of Commerce, 1961-67; apptd. Asst. Secy. of the Cabinet and Asst. Clerk of the P.C. Canada 1967; Depy. Secy. of the Cabinet 1969; Pres. Can. Devel. Corp. 1971, Chrmn. 1971-73; Chrmn., Nat. Energy Bd., 1973-77; served in 2nd World War with Candn. Army (Inf.); discharged with rank of Capt.; Home: Portland, Ont. K0G 1V0; Office: 350 Sparks St., Suite 408, Ottawa, Ont. K1R 7S8

CROWLEY, Robert Wilfred, B.A.; public utilities executive; b. London, Ont., 1 Aug. 1923; e. Univ. of W. Ont., B.A. 1947; VICE PRES., CUSTOMER SERVICES, BELL CANADA, since 1979; joined present Co., London, 1947; held various mang. positions in Owen Sound, Windsor, Kitchener, London, Toronto and Montreal, 1947-62; apptd. Gen. Supvr.-Comm. Methods & Results, HQ Montreal, 1962; Comm. Dept. Mgr., S. Div., W. Area, Toronto, 1964; Area Comm. Mgr., Montreal, 1965; Gen. Mgr.-S. Div., W. Area, Toronto, 1968; Vice Pres. (W. Area), Toronto, 1970; Vice Pres. (Toronto Area) 1976; Vice-Pres. (Customer Services) Toronto 1979; served with Candn. Army 1943-45; Clubs: Ontario; Credit Valley Golf and Country; Home: 1363 Gatehouse Dr., Mississauga, Ont. L5H 1A6; Office: 393 University Ave., Toronto, Ont. M5G 1W9

CROZIER, Douglas Noel, M.D.; paediatrician; b. Toronto, Ont. 23 June 1926; s. George Crozier; e. Univ. of Toronto M.D. 1952; two d. Susan Jane, Stephanie Louise; SR. PAEDIATRICIAN AND CHEST PHYSICIAN, HOSP. FOR SICK CHILDREN; Asst. Prof. of Paediatrics Univ. of Toronto; Chest Consultant and mem. Med. Adv. Ont. Soc. Crippled Children; Chrmn. Ont. Cystic Fibrosis Clinicians Comte. and mem. Young Adult Cystic Fibrosis Comte. of Cystic Fibrosis Foundation; internship: Toronto E. Gen. Hosp. 1952-53, Hosp. for Sick Children 1953-55, 1956; Baby's Hosp.-Presbyterian Med. Hosp. N.Y. Fellow in Paediatric Pathol. 1955-56; Sunnybrook Hosp. 1957; Med. Dir. Bloorview Children's Hosp. 1960-70; mem. Med. Adv. Candn. Cystic Fibrosis Foundation 1960-67, Chrmn. 1960-63; Dir. Cystic Fibrosis Clinic Hosp. for Sick Children 1958-78; Med. Ed. "Candid Facts"; author or co-author numerous med. articles; United Church; recreations: skiing, tennis; Clubs: Devils Glen Country; Downtown Tennis; Rosedale Tennis; Home: 215 Seaton St., Toronto, Ont. M5A 2T5; Office: 555 University Ave., Toronto, Ont. M5G 1X8.

CRUICKSHANK, Donald James, M.Sc., P.Eng.; telecommunications executive; b. Edinburgh, Scot. 5 Nov. 1931; s. John Cecil and Mabel Elizabeth (Harvey) C.; e. Fessenden Sch. Boston, USA 1944; Highgate Sch. London, Eng. 1948; Royal Naval Engn. Coll. Plymouth B.Sc. 1953; Coll. of Aeronautics, Cranfield Inst. of Technol. Bedfordshire, Eng. M.Sc. 1958; m. Lesley-Joan d. Stanley Rowell, Hudson, Que.; children: Colin, Wendy, Sally, Paula, Jeffrey; VICE PRES., PUBLIC & ENVIRONMENTAL AFFAIRS, BELL CANADA; Mgr. Govt. Programs,

Bristol Aerospace Ltd. Winnipeg 1965-71; Vice Pres. and Gen. Mgr. Rolls-Royce Canada 1971-72, Pres. 1972-77; Pres., Candn. Telecommunications Carriers Assn. 1978-80; served with RN 1948-58, RCN 1958-65; mem. Assn. Prof. Engrs. Prov. Ont.; Anglican; recreations: sailing, skiing, tennis; Home: 5 Ryeburn Dr., Ottawa, Ont. K1G 3N3; Office: 800-160 Elgin Ave., Ottawa, Ont.

CRUICKSHANK, William Harvey, M.D.; company director; b. Bognor, Ont., 1 November 1912; s. Edgar Burnet and Effie Pearl (Elyea) C.; e. Malvern Coll. Inst., Toronto, Ont.; Univ. of Toronto, M.D. 1936; post-grad. diplomas in Psychiatry (1940) and Public Health (1941); children: Michael Burnet, Jeffrey Leigh, Andrea Elizabeth; Dir., Crown Life Insurance Co; Procor Ltd.; P.L. Robertson Mfg. Co. Ltd.; joined Bell Canada as Med. Dir., 1945-55; Asst. Vice-Pres., Personnel, 1955-56; Dir. of Pub. Relations, 1956-57; Vice-Pres. and Gen. Mgr., Toronto Area, 1957-63; Vice-Pres. and Gen. Mgr., Toronto Area, 1967-63; Vice-Pres., Public Relations 1963-70; Vice-Pres., Environmental Studies 1970; served in 2nd World W. Overseas with R.C.A.M.C., 1943-45; Mayor of Baie d'Urfe, 1955-57; Chrmn., City of Toronto Redevelop. Adv. Council, 1962-63; Campaign Chrmn., Un. Fund of Metrop. Toronto, 1960; Pres., Candn. Club of Toronto, 1962-63; Home: 4402, 95 Thorncliffe Park Dr., Toronto, Ont. M4H 1L7

CRUISE, James Edwin, B.A., M.S., Ph.D.; museum director; b. Port Dover, Ont. 26 June 1925; s. William Edward and Annie Gertrude (Walker) C.; e. Marburg Sch. Woodhouse 1937; Port Dover (Ont.) High Sch. 1941; Simcoe (Ont.) High Sch. 1943; Univ. of Toronto B.A. 1950; Cornell Univ. M.S. 1951, Ph.D. 1954; DIR. ROYAL ONTARIO MUSEUM since 1975; Teaching Asst. in Gen. Bot. & Taxonomy, Cornell Univ. 1951-54; Post-doctoral Fellow and Instr. in Bot. Philadelphia Acad. of Science (Ford Foundation Fellowship) 1954-56; Asst. Prof. State Univ. of N.J. 1956, Assoc. Prof. 1958, Prof. 1960-63; Adjunct Prof. of Bot. Princeton Univ. 1959-63; Assoc. Prof. Univ. of Toronto 1963, Prof. since 1969, Curator of Phanerogamic Herbarium 1969-75, Assoc. Chrmn. 1971-72, Assoc. Dean of Arts 1973-75; Consultant to Nat. Science Foundation, Washington, D.C. 1959-63; Participant NSF Summer Inst. for Coll. & Univ. Instrs. Vanderbilt Univ. Nashville 1962; Dir. Plant Systematice, NSF Summer Inst. Rutgers Univ. 1963; Ed. Consultant in Systematics and Exper. Taxonomy Am. Journ. of Bot., Castanea, The Am. Nat. and Am. Midland Nat. since 1963; served with RCAF 1943-46, Air Navig. and Navig. Instr., rank Flying Offr.; rec'd Queen's Silver Jubilee Medal 1977; mem. Canadian Art Museum Directors Organization, Association of Art Museum Directors, International Council of Museums; Ont. Soc. Biols. (Pres. 1967-68, 1970-71); Candn. Bot. Assn. (Secy. 1970-72); Am. Inst. Biol. Science; Bot. Soc. Am.; Am. Soc. Plant Taxonomists; Internat. Soc. Plant Taxonomists; Phi Kappa Phi; Sigma Xi; United Church; Home: 55 Maitland St. Apt. 1704, Toronto, Ont. M4Y 1C9; Office 100 Queen's Park, Toronto, Ont. M5S 2C6.

CRUMP, Norris Roy, C.C., M.E., D.Eng., LL.D., D.Sc., D.C.L.; transport executive (retd.); b. Revelstoke, B.C., 30 July 1904; s. Thomas Huntley and Eleanor Jan (Edwards) C.; e. Pub. Sch., Vancouver, B.C.; High Sch., Revelstoke, B.C.; Purdue Univ., B.Sc., 1929, ME., 1936 and D.Eng. 1951; Queen's LL.D. 1950, Montreal 1958, W. Ont. 1967, Manitoba 1974; D.Sc. Laval 1956, Clarkson Coll. of Tech. 1956; D.C.L. Bishop's Univ. 1957; Kt. of Grace, St. John Ambulance Assn., 1956; Companion Order of Can.; m. Stella Josephine, d. Edward Elmore Elvin, Uhrichsville, Ohio, 23 Aug. 1930; two d., Ann Louise, Janice; Hon. mem. Adv. Comte., Sch. of Business Adm., Univ. of W. Ont.; began with Canadian Pacific Railway as labourer at Revelstoke, Brit. Columbia, 1920; Machinist Apprentice, Field, B.C. 1920; Night Foreman, Roundhouse, Sutherland, Sask., 1930-31; Shop Foreman, Leth-

bridge, Alta., 1931-32 and Alyth, Alta., 1932-34; Locomotive Foreman, Wilkie, Sask., 1934-35; Night Foreman, Moose Jaw, Sask., 1935-36; Div. Master Mechanic, Regina, 1936-40; Chief Draftsman, Supt. Motive Power & Car Dept., Winnipeg, Man., 1940-41; Asst. Supt. Car Dept. there 1941-42; Asst. to Vice-Pres., Montreal 1942-43; Gen. Supt., Toronto 1943-44; Asst. Gen. Mgr., Eastern Lines 1944, Gen. Mgr. 1946; Vice-Pres. and Gen. Mgr., Jan.-Aug. 1947; Vice-Pres., E. Region 1947-48; Vice-Pres. (all lines), Montreal 1948; Dir. since 1949; Vice-Pres. of Co. and mem. of Extve. Comte., May 1949; Pres. 1955-61; Chrmn. and Pres. 1961, Chrmn. of the Co. and Chief Extve. Offr. 1964; Chrmn., C.P.L. 1969, retired chrmn. 1972, retired dir. 1974; Hon. Dir. Soo Line RR.; Mutual Life of Can.; Council, Calgary Chamber of Comm.; Life mem., Engineering Institute Canada; Hon. mem., Am. Soc. of Mech. Engrs.; recreations: handicrafts, archaeol.; Clubs: Mount Stephen (Hon. 1959); Ranchmen's; Address: 1209 Prospect Ave. S.W., Calgary, Alta. T2T 0X4

CRUTCHLOW, Lewis George, B.Sc.; Canadian public service; b. Saskatoon, Sask., 14 June 1921; s. James and Mary Anne (Jacobs) C.; e. Saskatoon Tech. Coll., Sr. Matric. and Indust. Cert. 1938; Univ. of Sask., B.Sc. (Elect. Engn.) 1950; Royal Military Coll., Hon. D. Eng., 1981; m. Edith Mae, d. late William James Dickson, 18 May 1943; children: Wayne Gordon, Richard James, Garry Lewis, Mary Anne; Asst. Depy. Min. (Materiel), Dept. of Nat. Defence 1972; Dir., Defence Construction (1951) Ltd.; Crown Assets Disposal Corp.; joined Nat. Defence HQ, naval engn. field, 1950; served as Chief Engr., Radar Engn. Div.; trans. to staff Asst. Depy. Min. (Requirements) 1956; subsequently Dir. Gen. of Requirements (Electronic & Communications); trans. to Treasury Bd. 1968 becoming Dir., Transport. & Communication Div., Programs Br.; returned to present Dept. as Asst. Depy. Min. (Logistics) 1971; served with R.C.A.F. 1942-45 as Radar Offr.; rank Flying Offr.; mem., Engn. Inst. Can.; Inst. Elect. & Electronic Engrs.; Inst. Gen. Mang. (Dir.); United Church; recreations: boating, fishing, hunting, photography; Club: North Lake Fish & Game; Home: 20 Avenue Rd., Ottawa, Ont. K1S 0N9.; Office: N.D.H.Q., Ottawa, Ont. K1A 0K2

CUDDY, Robert MacWilliam, B.Sc.; company vice president; b. Toronto, Ont., 18 Aug. 1920; s. Frank Roland and Katheline (Porte) C.; e. Pub. and Central Tech. Schs.; Toronto; Queen's Univ., B.Sc. (Mech. Engn.) 1949; m. Jean R., d. late Ottomar Wirges, 25 March 1950; children: David, Michael; VICE PRES., NORTHERN TELECOM CAN. LTD., since 1976; commenced as Regional Engr., Coca-Cola Ltd., Ottawa, 1949-51; Production Control Mgr., Reliance Electric Ltd. 1951-52, Production Mgr. 1952-54, Mgr., Motor Mfg., Reliance Electric Ltd., Welland, Ont. 1954-56; joined Beatty Bros. Ltd., Fergus, Ont., as Chief Engr. 1956-57, Chief Engr. and Mgr., Quality Control 1957-59, Mgr., Engn. and Engn. Sales 1959-61, Mgr., Operations and Indust. Sales, 1961-63; Gen. Mgr., Indust. Products Div., General Steelwares Ltd. 1963-64; Gen. Mgr., Beatty Bros. Div., General Steelwares Ltd. 1964-65; Pres. and Gen. Mgr., Varta Batteries Ltd. 1965-75; served in 2nd World War with R.C.A.F., overseas, (401 Sqdn.) as a Pilot, 1942-45; discharged rank Flying Offr.; mem., C.M.A.; A.P.E.O.; Anglican; recreations: reading, photography, travel; Clubs: Granite; Manitoba; Home: 49 Burnhamthorpe Pk. Blvd, Islington, Ont. M9A 1H8; Office: 304 The East Mall, Islington, Ont. M9B 6E4

CUERRIER, Jean-Paul, M.Sc.; biologist; retired Canadian public service (1979); b. St. Polycarpe, Soulanges Co., P.Q., 8 Apl. 1916; s. Adelard and Antoinette (Lalonde) C.; e. Coll. Ste-Marie, Montreal, P.Q.; Coll. Bourget, Rigaud, P.Q., B.A. 1938; Univ. of Montreal, L.Sc. 1942, M.Sc. 1949; m. late Georgette Bouchard, 4 June 1942; five children; m. Marthe, d. late B. DuSault, 12 Feb. 1972; formerly Sr. Scientific Adv., Canadian Wildlife Service (apptd. 1949 as Chief Specialist, Limnol.); Prof. of Zoology, Univ. of Montreal, 1942-49; mem., Am. Fisheries Soc.; Am. Inst. Fishery Research Biols.; Prof. Inst. of Civil Service of Can.; R. Catholic; Home: 241 Jeanne-Mance St., Ottawa (Vanier), Ont. K1L 6L8;

CULINER, John William; sculptor, advertising executive; b. Hearst, Ont., 6 Jan. 1913; s. Harry and Mary (Milder) C.; e. Humberside Coll. Inst., Toronto, Ont.; Univ. of Toronto (Grad. 1935); m. late Lillian, d. late Nathan Seper, 20 June 1943; children: Ross Allan, Jill Arlene, Cathy Ann; m. 2ndly Elaine James, 2 July 1962; CHRMN., PIR ADVERTISING LTD.; Hebrew; recreations: golf, collecting fine art, tennis; Clubs: Oakdale Golf & Country, York Racquets; Home: Apt. 5011, 44 Charles St. W., Toronto, Ont. M4Y 1R8; Office: One Yonge St., Toronto, Ont. M5E 1E5

CULLEN, Hon. Jack Sydney George Bud, P.C., Q.C., M.P., B.A.; politician; b. Creighton Mine, Ont. 20 April 1927; s. Chaffey Roi and Margaret Evelyn (Leck) C.; e. Creighton Mine (Ont.) Public Sch.; Lansdowne Public Sch.; Sudbury (Ont.) High Sch; Univ. of Toronto; Osgoode Hall Law Sch.; former Minister of Employment & Immigration, CAN; 1976-79; former Minister of National Revenue, Can. 1975-76; commenced as Barrister; 1st el. to H. of C. for Sarnia-Lambton, g.e. 1968, re-el. 1972, 1974, defeated 1979, re-el. 1980; Chmn., Standing Comte. on Finance, Trade and Econ. Affairs; formerly Parlty. Secy. to Min. of Nat. Defence, of Energy, Mines & Resources and of Finance; 1st Pres. Sarnia Educ. Authority; mem. Sarnia Sch. Bd.; Life mem. Sarnia Kinsmen Club; mem. Sarnia and Dist. Assn. for Mentally Retarded; United Church; Liberal; Home: 206 N. MacKenzie St. Sarnia, Ont.; Office: 151 Bay St., Ottawa, Ont.;

CULLENS, Williams S., B.Sc., P. Eng.; manufacturer; b. Stirling, Scot. 10 Jan. 1930; s. James and Elizabeth Laura (Scott) C.; e. Stirling (Scot.) High Sch.; Univ. of Glasgow B.Sc. (Engn.) 1951; m. Elizabeth S. Stewart d. Alexander Brewster, Stirling, Scot. 18 March 1953; four d. Kim, Gail, Laura, Jane; PRES., AND CHIEF OPERATING OFFR. AND DIR. CANRON INC. since 1981; Project Supt. Robert McAlpine Ltd., Montreal 1954-60; Sales Eng., Structural Steel Ltd., 1960-61; Sales and Gen. Mgr., present Co. 1961-70, Group Vice Pres. 1970-76; Exec. Vice-Pres. and C.E.O., 1976-81; Dir., 1980-; Hon. Dir. and former Chrmn. Candn. Inst. Steel Constr.; former Chrmn. Candn. Welding Bureau; Councillor, Welding Inst. of Can.; Dir., Russell Burdsall & Ward Corp., Presbyterian; recreations: golf, tennis, squash; Clubs: Adelaide, Toronto Golf; Home: 78 The Kingsway, Toronto, Ont.M8X 2T5; Office: — Suite 6300 First Canadian Place, P.O. Box 134, Toronto, Ont. M5X 1A4.

CULLITON, Hon. Edward Milton, B.A., LL.B., D.C.L.; judge; b. Grand Forks, Minn. 9 Apl. 1906; s. John Joseph and Katherine Mary (Kelly) C.; came to Can. 1906; e. Pub. and High Schs. Elbow, Sask.; Univ. of Sask. B.A. 1926, LL.B. 1928, D.C.L. 1962; m. Katherine Mary d. late Frank Hector, Dysart, Sask. 9 Sept. 1939; CHIEF JUSTICE OF SASK. to April 1981 called to Bar of Sask. 1930; cr. Q.C. 1947; practiced law Gravelbourg, Sask. 1930-51; el. to Leg. Assembly Sask. by-el. 1935, re-el. 1938, def. 1944, re-el. 1948; Prov. Secy. and Min. in Charge of Tax Comn. 1938-41, Min. without Portfolio 1941-44, resigned on appt. to Court of Appeal Sask. 1951; mem. Bd. Govs., Univ. of Sask. 12 yrs., Chrmn. 2 yrs., Chancellor 1962-68, apptd. Chief Justice, 1962; served with Candn. Army 1941-46, R.C.A. and Judge Advocate's Br. Can. and Overseas, rank Maj.; Companion of Order of Can.; Kt. Commdr. St. Gregory; mem. Un. Services Inst.; R. Catholic; recreations: golf, curling, travel; Clubs: Assiniboia, Wascana Country; Home: Apt. 1303; 1830 College Ave., Regina, Sask. S4P 1C2; Office: 2425 Victoria Ave., Regina, Sask. S4P 3V7.

CULVER, David Michael, B.Sc., M.B.A.; executive; b. Winnipeg, Man., 5 December 1924; s. Albert Ferguson and Fern Elizabeth (Smith) C.; e. Selwyn House Sch., Montreal, P.Q., 1931-39; Lower Canada Coll., 1939-40; Trinity Coll. Sch., Port Hope, Ont., 1940-41; McGill Univ., 1941-43 and 1945-47, B.Sc.; Harvard Bus. Sch., M.B.A., 1949; Centre d'Etudes Industrielles, Geneva, Switzerland, 1949-50; m. Mary Cecile Powell, d. Ray Edwin Powell, 20 Sept. 1949; three s., Michael, Andrew, Mark; one d., Diane; PRES.AND C.E.O., ALCAN ALUMINIUM LTD.; Chrmn., Can. Japan Business Cooperation Comte.; Dir., Canadair Ltd.; MacMillan Bloedel Ltd.; American Express Co.; joined Alcan in 1949; served on the Staff, Centre d'Etudes Industrielles, Geneva, Switzerland, 1950-52; joined Sales Staff, New York Sales Office 1952; apptd. Mgr. 1954; Vice-Pres. and Dir., Alcan International Ltd., 1956; Chief Sales Offr., Alcan Aluminium Ltd., and Pres., Alcan International Ltd., April 1962; Extve. Vice Pres., Fabricating and Sales, and Dir., Alcan Aluminum Ltd. Jan. 1968; Pres. Alcan Aluminium Ltd. 1977; Chmn. Aluminium Co. of Can. Ltd. 1978; pres. & Ce. Alcan Aluminium Ltd. 1979; served in 2nd World War with Candn. Inf. Corps, 1942-45; Alpha Delta Phi.; Anglican; recreations: golf, skiing, racquets, music; Clubs: St. James's; Mt. Royal; Mt. Bruno Country; Montreal Racket; Montreal Indoor Tennis; Home: 627 Clarke Ave., Montreal, Que. H3Y 3E5; Office: 1 Place Ville Marie, Montreal, Que. H3C 3H2

CUMMING, George Stewart, Q.C., B.A., LL.B.; b. Vancouver, B.C.; 1 May 1928; s. George and Jessie Robertson (Stewart) C.; e. Oak Bay High Sch., Victoria, B.C. 1945; Victoria Coll., Univ. of Brit. Columbia, B.A. 1950, LL.B. 1951; m. Margaret Isabella, d. Ernest Theodore Rogers, 10 Nov. 1956; children: Catherine Irene, Brian George, Hamish Arthur; PARTNER, CUMMING, RICHARDS, UNDERHILL, FRASER, SKILLINGS; read law with T. G. Norris; called to the Bar of B.C. 1951; cr. Q.C. Sept. 1969; mem. Candn. Bar Assn.; Vancouver Bar Assn.; Beta Theta Pi; Conservative; Anglican; recreations: skiing, riding; Clubs: The Vancouver; Home: 7226 Blenheim St., Vancouver, B.C. Office: 900 W. Hastings St., Vancouver, B.C. V6C 1G1

CUMMING, Glen E.; art gallery director; b. Calgary, Alta. 2 July 1936; s. Alexander Edward Brown and Johanna Maria Christina (Van Der Doorn) C.; e. Alta. Coll. of Art grad. 1963 (Queen Elizabeth Prize 1960; Alta. Govt. Visual Arts Bd. Scholarships 1961-62); DIR., ART GALLERY OF HAMILTON 1973- ; Supvr. Art Educ. Edmonton Art Gallery and Assn. to Dir. 1964; Dir. of Expressive Arts City of Edmonton Parks & Recreation 1965; Curator, Regina Pub. Lib. Art Gallery 1967-69; Dir. Kitchener-Waterloo Art Gallery 1969-72; Dir. Robert McLaughlin Gallery Oshawa 1972-73; author various publs.; Pres., Candn. Art Museums Dirs. Organ. 1981; Ont. Assn. Art Galleries 1974; Chrmn., Art Adv. Comte. Mohawk Coll. Applied Arts & Technol. 1979-82; mem. Organizing Comte. Art Toronto 1980; Internat. Council Museums; Assn. Art Museums Dirs.; Candn. Museums Assn.; Hamilton & Dist. Chamber Comm.; Club: Hamilton; Home: 1502 - 222 Jackson St. W., Hamilton, Ont. L8P 4S5; Office: 123 King St. W., Hamilton, Ont. L8P 4S8.

CUMMING, Thomas Alexander, B.A.Sc.; banker; b. Toronto, Ont. 14 Oct. 1937; e. Univ. of Toronto B.A.Sc. 1960; m. E. Mary 12 Mar. 1965; children: Jennifer, Alison, Katy; VICE PRES. AND GEN. MGR., THE BANK OF NOVA SCOTIA; Dir. Scotia Centre Ltd.; Gov., Strathcona Tweedsmuir Sch.; Dir. Calgary Philharmonic; Dir. Calgary Chamber of Commerce; mem. Candn. Wildlife Fed.; Clubs: Calgary Golf & Country; Calgary Petroleum; Home: 10412 Willow Crest Rd. S.E., Calgary, Alta. T2J 1P1; Office: 700 - 2nd St. S.W., Calgary, Alta. T2P 2W2.

CUNNINGHAM, J. Stewart M., F.S.A., F.C.I.A.; PRESIDENT AND CHIEF EXTVE. OFFR., FIDELITY

LIFE ASSURANCE CO. 1973- ; joined Friends' Provident Life Office (parent co. of Fidelity Life) London, Eng. 1952; trans. to Fidelity Life Assurance Co., Regina 1958, H.O. moved to Vancouver 1961, Actuary 1968, Vice Pres. and Actuary 1971, Pres. 1973, Dir.; Chrmn. B.C. Life Insurance Pub. Relations Comte.; Trustee, Simon Fraser Univ. Acad. Staff Pension Plan; Gov., Employers' Council B.C.; mem. Adv. Council, Faculty of Comm. & Business Adm. Univ. of B.C.; Past Chrmn. Ins. Council B.C.; Clubs: Vancouver; University; Home: 5947 Highbury St., Vancouver, B.C., V6N 1Y9; Office: 1600, 1130 West Pender St., Vancouver, B.C. V6E 2S2.

CUNNINGHAM, James William, B. Com; business consultant; b. Montreal, Que., 22 July 1922; s. James Thomas and Margery Annie (Green) C.; e. High Sch., Montreal Que. 1939; Sir George Williams Coll., B. Com. 1952; C.A. courses, McGill Univ. 1943-47; m. Sheila Dorothy, d. late Gordon Dickson Flett, 16 Oct. 1954; children: Joanne Wendy (Mrs D. Thomas), Geraldine Gail (Mrs J. Pfeiffer), Heather May, James Gordon; articled with P. S. Ross & Sons (C.A.) 1943; Acct., Power Corp. of Canada 1947, Assistant Secretary 1950; Assistant Treasurer, Shawinigan Water & Power Co. and Southern Canada Power Co. 1958; Schering Corp. Ltd., Comptroller 1963; Secretary-Treas. 1966; Vice Pres. 1969-75; entered independent business consulting since 1975; served in 2nd World War, R.C.A.F. 1941-42; Past Cndn. Chrmn., Chart. Inst. of Secys. and mem., Extve. Council, National Body, Quebec Chapter; founding President, Chateauguay Homeowners' Association; mem. Institute Chart. Accts.; former mem. Bd., Central Y.M.C.A.; Liberal; Baptist; recreations: golf, jogging; Home: 19 Lang Ave., Chateauguay, Que. J6J 2A7

CUNNINGTON, Brig. Gen. Douglas Wightman, G.M. (1940), C.D., B.Sc., P.Eng., army officer (retired), b. Calgary, Alta., 24 Aug. 1916; s. Douglas George Leopold, O.B.E., M.C. and Elsie May (Wightman) C; e. Central Coll. Inst., Calgary, 1933; Royal Mil. Coll., 1937; Queen's Univ., B.Sc. (Civil) 1938; Cndn. Army Staff Coll.; U.S. Command and Gen. Staff Coll.; NATO Defence Coll.; m. Ivy Louise d. Herbert Austin Brown, Victoria, B.C., 6 Oct. 1939; children: Desmond Charles, Claudia; comnd. R.C.E. 1937; served in Eng. and France 1940-44 and with U.S. Forces in Leyte and Okinawa 1945; Command Engr. Offr., Que. Command, 1947-49; Instr., Cndn. Army Staff Coll., 1949-52; Commandant, Royal Cndn. Sch. of Mil. Engn., Chilliwack, B.C., 1953-56; Instr., NATO Defence Coll., Paris, 1956-58; Chief Engr., Cndn. Army, 1958-62; Commdr., Cndn. Army Contingent, U.N. Emergency Force, Gaza Strip, 1964-65; Dir. Gen. Sr. Appts., Cndn. Forces HQ, 1965-67; Commdr., Cndn. Defence Liason Staff (London), 1967-71; Priory Secy., Priory of Canada, Order of St. John of Jerusalem since 1972; Brig. Gen. 1967; mem. Assn. Prof. Engrs. Ont.; Mil. Engrs. Assn. Can.; Anglican; recreations: skiing, travel; Home: 36 Linden Lea, Ottawa, Ont. K1M 1A8

CURLEY, Paul Roger, B.Com.; executive; b. Ottawa, Ont. 28 Aug. 1942; s. Matthew and Winnifred (Smith) C.; e. Univ. of Ottawa B.Com. 1967; Univ. of Oslo grad. dipl. in Econ. 1970; m. Sharon Jane Hlywka 28 Dec. 1977; Nat. Dir., P. Cons. Party Of Can. 1979-81; business extve. Imperial Oil Ltd. 1967-72, 1974-79; Special Asst. to Hon. Robert L. Stanfield 1972-74; Nat. Treas. P. Cons. Party Can. 1977-79; mem., Bd. Gov., Univ. of Ottawa; P. Conservative; R. Catholic; Clubs: Albany (Toronto); Calgary Petroleum; Home: 307 Glen Rd., Toronto, Ont. M4V 2X4; Office: 178 Queen St., Ottawa, Ont. K1P 5E1.

CURLOOK, Walter, M.A.Sc., Ph.D.; metallurgist; mining executive; b. Coniston, Ont. 14 March 1929; s. William and Stephanie (Acker) C.; e. Sudbury (Ont.) High Sch. 1946; Univ. of Toronto B.A.Sc. 1950, M.A.Sc. 1951, Ph.D. 1953; Nuffield Research Lab. Imp. Coll. Science & Technol., Post-doctorate Fellowship 1954; m. Marie

Jeanne Burak 28 May 1955; children: Christine, Paul, Michael, Andrea; PRES. AND CHIEF EXTVE. OFFR., INCO METALS CO. 1980- ; Research Metall., Inco. Copper Cliff. Ont. 1954, Supvr. Research Stn. Port Colborne, Ont. 1959, Supt. of Research Copper Cliff 1960, Asst. to Gen. Mgr. 1964; Dir. Technique COFIMPAC, Paris, France 1969, Gen. Mgr. Inco Oceanie 1972; Vice Pres. Adm. and Engn. Inco, Copper Cliff 1972, Vice Pres. Corporate Planning New York 1974, Sr. Vice Pres. Production Toronto 1977; first Chrmn. of Bd. Cambrian Coll. Applied Arts & Technol. Sudbury; Task Force mem. Geol.-Mining-Mineral Engn. Univ. of Toronto; rec'd Airey Award 1979; holds patents on process metall.; author various tech. papers; Pres., Ont. Mining Assn.; Dir., Great-West Life Assur. Co.; mem. Candn. Inst. Mining & Metall.; Am. Inst. Mining Engrs.; Nat'l Adv. Comte on the Mining Ind.; Catholic; recreations: hockey, walking, skiing; Clubs: Duquesne (Pittsburgh, Pa.); Adelaide; Home: 25 Cluny Dr., Toronto, Ont. M4W 2P9; Office: (P.O. Box 44) 1 First Canadian Place, Toronto, Ont. M5X 1C4.

CURRAN, Howard Wesley, B.S., M.A., Ph.D.; b. Schenectady, N.Y., 12 Feb. 1908; (naturalized Canadian, 1947); s. Howard Daniel and Harriet Maud (Ferguson) C.; e. Syracuse Univ.; Hobart Coll., B.S. 1931; Univ. of Mich., M.A. 1932 and Ph.D. 1942; m. Alice Dorletta, d. George Harrison Arnold, Syracuse, N.Y., 19 Sept. 1933; children: David Arnold, Dorletta Jane, Frances Elizabeth; mem. of Syracuse-Andean Expdn. to Venezuela, 1930; with Brazilian Govt. 1935-36 with Fishculture Comn. of N.E. Brazil; engaged in Biol. Surveys for N.Y. State Conservation Dept. 1936; apptd. to the Dept. of Biology, Queen's Univ., 1936; Dir. of Queen's Univ. Biol. Stn. on Lake Opinicon 1944-52; Dir., Dept. of Extension 1952-71; Ret. 1971 as Prof. Em. in Biology; twice selected as "Man of the Year in Kingston", 1948, 1964; Honorary Life mem., Kingston Dist. Ch. of Comm.; Ont. Fed. of Anglers & Hunters; Candn. Assn. of Dirs. of Extension & Summer Schools; active in Kingston Field Naturalists, Kingston Hist. Soc., Frontenac Hist. Foundation; author of "A Biological Survey of Lake Opinicon", 1947; United Church: recreations: stamps & coins; fishing, camping; Clubs: Kinsmen (Past Pres.); Home: 90 Bagot St., Kingston, Ont. K7L 3E5

CURRAN, Lawrence Donald; manufacturer; consultant; b. Toronto, Ont., 10 Aug. 1924; s. late James Howard and Mary Irene (Gouett) C.; e. St. Helen's Pub. Sch.; De La Salle Coll. 1946; various adm. courses sponsored by YMCA (Rochester, N.Y.) 1948; m. Laurette Margaret, d. late George Marchand, 30 June 1949; children: Mary Louise, James Donald, Michael Joseph; PRESIDENT AND MANAGING DIR., BAUSCH & LOMB OPTICAL CANADA INC. since 1967; joined Co. under Dept. Veteran Affairs "Training on the Job" Plan, 1947; initially hired for supervisory material and later made Group Ldr., Pilot Plant, Midland, Ont.; at Rochester Univ., N.Y. for additional training in management, personnel relations and adm. courses, 1948; Foreman in Charge Mfg., (Midland, Ont. plant), 1949; Mgr. 1951; el. a Dir. 1954; served in 2nd World War with Elgin Regt., 25th C.A.D.R., 1942-45; Mang. Chrmn., Midland Separate Sch. Bd., 1960-67; Past Pres., Rotary Club; Past Chrmn., C.N.I.B.; former Vice-Pres., Georgian Bay Boy Scouts Assn.; Conservative; R. Catholic; K. of C.; recreations: golf, boating, hunting; Home: 23 Bridlewood Blvd., Agincourt, Ont. M1T 1P3; Office: 16 Coldwater Rd., Don Mills, Ont. M3B 1Y7

CURRAN, Robert Linton; retired newspaper publisher; b. Sault Ste. Marie, Ont., 19 Oct. 1911; s. James Watson and Edith Mary (Pratt) C.; e. Sault Coll. Inst.; Empire State Sch. of Printing, Ithaca, N.Y. (Grad. 1930); m. Camilla Anna, d. late Joseph O'Connor, 11 May 1936; children: (Mrs.) Suzanne Pihlaja, (Mrs.) Constance Nadeau, Paul, Robert Jr.; Pres. and Publisher, The Sault Star Ltd.,

1952-75 (ret.); Dir., Royal Trust Co. Adv. Bd.; entered business as Printer on return from sch.; subsquently served briefly in Advertising, Circulation and Business Depts., trans. to Edit. Dept. serving as Reporter, Dist. Editor, Telegraph Edit., Sports Edit. and City Edit.; became Mang.-Director, Oct. 1941 (as well as Edit. of Editorial page); with Reserve Army, 2nd Bn. Sault Ste. Marie & Sudbury Regt. (Lieut.), 1940-45; Pres., Sault Ste. Marie Chamber of Commerce, 1948-50 (Dir. 1946-70); Pres., Candn. Daily Newspaper Publ. Assn., 1963-64; Independent; United Church; recreations: fishing, camping, carpentry, hunting, sailing; Clubs: Algoma Steel Men's; Rotary; Home: 1168 Queen St. E., Sault Ste. Marie, Ont. P6A 2E4

CURRAN, William Victor, C.A.; b. McLean Twp., Ont. 23 May 1918; s. late William John and Mary Lea C.; e. Bracebridge (Ont.) High Sch.; C.A. 1950: m. Marion Thelma d. late Peter Williamson 16 July 1946; 6 s. Michael, James, Andrew, Robert, Joseph, Geoffrey and 4 d. Kathryn, Jane, Jennifer, Victoria; PARTNER, DUNWOODY & CO. since 1954; Pres. Dunwoody Ltd. since 1958; joined present Co. 1945, Nat. Mang. Partner 1972; served with 48th Highlanders of Can. 1940-44 Can. UK Sicily Africa Italy; served King Sch. Bd. 3 yrs., King Twp. Council 4 yrs.; Pres. York N.P. Cons. Assn. 5 yrs.; Chrmn. Bldg. Comte. King City Community Centre; Past Chrmn. King City Community Centre Bd.; mem. Business Club Metrop. Toronto (Past Pres.); Freemason; Lions Internat.; P. Conservative; United Church; recreations: golf, gardening; Clubs: National; Carrying Place Golf & Country; Home: R.R.4, King City, Ont. L0G 1K0; Office: Royal Bank Plaza, Bay and Front Streets, Toronto, Ont.

CURRIE, David Vivian, V.C.; b. Sutherland, Sask. 8 July 1912; s. David Henry and Mabel (Brimble) C.; e. High Sch. and Tech. Sch. (Mech. & Welding) Moose Jaw, Sask.; m. Isabel Goodall d. late Foster Civil, Owen Sound, Ont. 24 Aug. 1934; one s. David; Motor Mech. and Welder Moose Jaw 1930-39; Equipment supt. Quebec North Shore Paper Co. Baie Comeau 1945-52; Vice Pres. Bonnard Manufacturing, Lachine, Que. 1952-56, Logging Rep. Chas. Cussons, Montreal 1956-60; Sgt.-at-Arms, House of Commons, Ottawa 1960-78; served with pub. sch. cadets 1925-27, militia Moose Jaw 1928-39; 1939-1942, Saskatoon Light Infantry (M.G.) Machine Gun Training Centre, Engineer Training Centre Dundurn Camp, 1942-45 Armoured Corp Training Centre, Camp Borden and South Alberta Regt. (R.C.A.C.); Awarded the Victoria Cross 21 Aug. 1944; rec'd Coronation Medal 1953, Centennial Medal 1967, Silver Jubilee Medal 1977; Life mem. Royal Candn. Legion; Army Navy & Air Force Veterans; Royal Candn. Armoured Corps Assn.; Hon. Lt. Col. Sask. Dragoons Moose Jaw (ret.); Elks (Life mem.); United Church; recreations painting, gardening; Clubs Moose Jaw Mil. Garrison Sgts Mess, Moose Jaw (Life mem.); Inst. (Life mem.); Royal candn. Mil. Inst. Toronto (Life mem.); Address: 1582 Drake Ave., Ottawa, Ont. K1G 0L8.

CURRIE, George Napier McDonald, B.Eng., M.Sc.; b. Montreal, Que., 13 Dec. 1927; s. George Selkirk and Louisa Hope (Napier) C; e. Selwyn House Sch., Montreal, 1933-42; Trinity Coll. Sch., Port Hope, Ont., 1942-45; Royal Candn. Naval Coll., 1st Class Cert. 1947; McGill Univ., B.Eng. 1951; Univ. of Toronto, M.Sc. 1953; m. Daphne Louise, d. William Grant Fisher, London, Ont., 16 Apl. 1955; children: Stephanie Louise, Gordon Andrew McDonald, Janet Hope, George Timothy Grant; EXTVE. VICE-PRES. & DIR., A.E. AMES & CO. LTD. 1980-; president & chief extve. offr., F.P. Publications Ltd., 1978-80; Chrmn., Currie, Coopers & Lybrand Ltd., 1973-78; Pres. Urwick, Currie and Ptnrs Ltd. 1960-73; Director, Graham Fibre Glass Ltd.; Charles E. Napier Co., 1951-56; Consultant, Urwick, Currie & Partners 1956; Gov., McGill Univ.; Gov., Mackay Center for Deaf &

Crippled Children; Pres. (1968-69) Candn. Assn. Mang. Consultants; mem., Que. Inst. Mang. Consultants; Engn. Inst. Can.; Assn. Prof. Engrs. Ont.; Kappa Alpha; Protestant; recreations: skiing, fishing; tennis; Clubs: Toronto Golf; University; Osler Bluff Ski (Collingwood, Ont.); Toronto Badminton & Racquet; Maganissippi Fish & Game; Home: 69 Bayview Ridge, Toronto, Ont. M2L 1E3; Office: 320 Bay St. Toronto, Ont. M5H 2P7

CURRIE, Neill Edward, D.F.C., B.A., B.Sc., B.Phil., M.A., economist; b. Port Arthur, Ont., 24 June 1921; s. Anna Bryant (Snook) and late Alexander Clapperton Currie; e. Gordon Bell High Sch. and United Coll. Winnipeg; Univ. of Man., B.Sc. 1942; Queen's Univ., B.A. 1945; Univ. of Toronto, M.A. 1947; Oxford Univ. (Rhodes Scholar), B.Phil. 1951; ECON. ADVISER, Can. Chamber of Commerce, since May 1979; with Candn. Pacific Telegraphs, Winnipeg and Port Arthur, 1937-41; High Sch. teacher, United coll., Winnipeg, 1945-46 and Asst. Prof. of Econ. there, 1947-48; Econ. & Statistics Br., Dept. of Defence Prod., 1951-52; Foreign Service offr., Dept. of External Affairs, 1952-61 (Candn. Consul. Colombia and 2nd Secy., Candn. Embassy, Bogota, Col., 1954-56; Econ. and U.N. Divs., 1956-58; 1st Secy., Canadian Permanent Mission to U.N., 1958-61); Asst. Econ. Adviser, Bank of Montreal, 1961; Econ. Adviser, 1966; Vice-Pres. and Econ. Adviser 1967; served with R.C.A.F. 1942-45 as Flying Offr. Pilot of heavy bombers in European Theatre; former Chrmn., Economists Comte., Candn. Bankers' Assn.; Gov., Fraser-Hickson Inst.; Dir., McGill Chamber Orchestra; Chrm. Westmount Senior Citizens' Centre; mem., Candn. Assn. of Business Economist's; Candn. Inst. Internat. Affairs; Montreal Econ. Assn.; Moneco Forum; Nat. Assn. Business Econ.; Candn. Econ. Assn.; former Dir., Candn. Council Internat. Chamber of Comm.; United Church; recreations: music, gardening; Clubs: Mtl. Bd. of Trade; Oxford (Eng.) Union Soc.; Home: 307 Roslyn Ave., Westmount Que. H3Z 2L7

CURRY, Andrew Gibson, B.A.; retired investment dealer; b. Windsor, N.S., 6 Apl. 1901; s. Rufus and Cornelia Augusta (Faulkner) C.; e. Kings Coll. Sch., Windsor, N.S., 1916; St. Andrew's Coll. Sch., Toronto, Ont., 1918; Univ. Coll., Univ. of Toronto, B.A. 1922; m. Dorothy Dawson, d. late Dr. John Randolph Page, New York, 14 January 1938; children: John Page, Mrs. Cornelia Curry Thornber; joined A. E. Ames & Co. after grad.; after service in Toronto, London, Eng., and Montreal, moved to N.Y. in 1930; apptd. Pres., A. E. Ames & Co., Inc., 1951-65; Chrmn., Bd. of Dirs., 1965-68; Dir. A. E. Ames & Co. Ltd. and Partner, A. E. Ames & Co., 1951-65; Phi Gamma Delta; Republican; Episcopalian; recreations: yachting; Clubs: Canadian (N.Y.); Scarsdale (N.Y.) Golf; Metropolitan (N.Y.); Chester (N.S.) Yacht; Home: Brook Lane, Hartsdale, N.Y. 10530; (Summer) Strawberry Hill, Chester, N.S. B0J 1J0

CURRY, Duncan Steele, B.A., M.B.A.; retailing, concrete, manufacturing; b. Winnipeg, Man. 4 Aug. 1940; s. Peter Duncan and Noreen (Murphy) Curry; e. Ridley Coll., St. Catharines, Ont. 1957; Stanford Univ., B.A. 1962; Harvard Business Sch., M.B.A. 1964; m. Judith Ann, Ph.D. (Psychology) d. Benjamin J. Kaganov, Montreal, Quebec, 15 May 1980 PRESIDENT AND CHIEF EXTVE. OFFR., REVELSTOKE COMPANIES LTD.; Pres. and Dir., Venture Funding Corp. Ltd.; Dir., R. Angus Alberta Ltd; Can. Gen. Electric Co. Ltd.; Domtar Inc; Val Royal Lasalle Ltée.; Vice-Chrmn. Business Council on Nat'l Issues and Mem. of Policy Comte.; Chrmn., Salvation Army Advisory Bd.; recreations: reading, skiing, tennis; Clubs: The Toronto; Ranchmen's; Glenmore Racquet; Office: 508 - 24 Ave. S. W., Calgary, Alta. T2S 0K4

CURRY, Peter Duncan, LL.D.; company executive; b. Copenhagen, Denmark, 12 July 1912; s. Duncan Steele and Bertha (Laxdal) C.; e. Ridley Coll., St. Catherines, Ont., 1928-31; Bishop's Univ., 1931-34; Univ. of Man.,

Hon. LL.D., 1963; children: Duncan Steele, Gerald Mark, Patrick Murphy, Constance Kathleen; DEPUTY CHAIRMAN POWER CORP. OF CANADA LTD. Chrmn., of the Extve. Comte and Dir. Great West Life Assnce. Co.; Chmn. and Dir. Cablecasting Ltd.; Pres., Dromore Invest. Co. Ltd.; Greater Winnipeg Cablevision Ltd.; Dep. Chmn. Trans-Canada Corp. Fund; Shawinigan Industries Ltd.; Dir., Bathurst Paper; Inco Ltd.; Domglas Ltd.; Ford Motor Company of Canada Limited; CAE Industries Ltd.; C.S.L. Group Inc. Montreal Trust Co.; Consolidated Bathurst Ltd.; The Investors Group; mem., Bd. Trustees, North American Wildlife Foundation; Anglican; recreations: fishing, skiing; Clubs: Manitoba; Mt. Royal; Toronto; Home: 7 Braeside Place, Westmount, Que. H3Y 3E8; Office: 759 Victoria Sq., Montreal, Que. H2Y 2K4

CURTIS, Charles Edward, F.C.A.; b. Winnipeg, Man. 28 July 1931; s. Samuel and May (Goodison) C.; e. Prince Edward Sch.; E. Kildonan Coll. Inst.; Univ. of Man. C.A. 1955; m. Hilda Marion d. late Jack F. Simpson 30 Oct. 1954; one d. Nancy Maude; DEPY. MIN. DEPT. OF FINANCE MAN. since 1976; Vice-Chrmn Man. Hydro Bd.; mem. Superannuation Bd.; Teachers Retirement Invest. Fund; Univ. of Winnipeg Invest. Fund; Workers Compensation Bd. Invest. Fund; Acting Clk. Extve. Council; joined Dunwoody & Co. 1949-54; Dept. of Nat. Revenue Income Tax Div. 1954-67, Chief Assessor N.B. Div.; Dept. of Finance Man. since 1967, Asst. Depy. Min. Budget, Accounting, Finance & Adm.; Past Chrmn. Group Comte. Cubs & Scouts Fort Garry; Past mem. and Chrmn. Bd. of Stewards Fort Garry Un. Ch.; Pres. Inst. C.A.'s Man. 1975-76; United Church; recreations: badminton, tennis, swimming; Clubs: Winnipeg Rotary (Hon. Treas.); Winnipeg Winter Past Gov.; Manitoba; Home: 812 Kebir Pl., Winnipeg, Man. R3T 1W9; Office: Room 109, Legislative Bldg., Winnipeg, Man. R3C 0V8.

CURTIS, Donald William; hotel executive; b. Dover Ohio, 11 March 1923; s. Michael O'Connor and Gertrude (Schneider) C.; e. Miami (of Ohio) Univ.; Texas A & M Coll.; Univ. of Md. (Foreign Lang. Inst.); Salzburg, Austria; m. Jill Evolin, d. Col. Kennard S. Vandergrift, 6 Apl. 1957; children: Donald William Jr., David Bruce, Jill Evolin; PRESIDENT, C.E.O. AND DIR. OF BOARD OF SKYLINE HOTELS LTD. Gen. Mgr., U.S. Govt. Recreational Centres, Germany, 1948-58; Foreign Dir. and Asst. to Pres., Steigenberger Hotel Corp., Germany, 1958-61; Gen. Mgr. & Shareholder, Hotel Corp., Switzerland, 1961-64; Vice Pres.-Internat. Div., Hotel Corp. of America, London, Eng., 1964-67; Pres. and Extve. Dir., Johannesburg Hotel President and Development Co., S. Africa, 1967-69; Dir. Arwa South Africa (Pty) Hosiery Manufacturers Johannesburg, 1967-69; Sr. Extve. Vice Pres., Club Mediterranée, France, 1969-71; Advisor to Baron Edmond de Rothschild (Hotel Invests.), Paris, 1969-71; Chrmn., Pres. and Chief Extve. Offr. present co. 1972-1978; served with U.S. Army in Europe 1944-48; Consultant: Hotel Sch., Bad Reichenhall, Bavaria; USAF, Wiesbaden (Club Mang.); US Embassy Bonn (Labor Mang.); Honoured by Oberbergurmeister of Bad Reichenhall and Landrat of Landkreis; rec'd Gold Medal for Outstanding Hotel Mgr. of Yr., Germany, 1953; 4 Gold Medals Hunting. All-round Trophy Competition, Germany 1957; awarded title Hon. Chef by Can. Fed. of Chefs de Cuisine, 1976; Recipient, Bold Medal Award of the Comte of European Excellence, 1976; mem., Confrerie des Chevaliers du Tastevin, Dijon and Toronto; Commanderie de Bordeaux, Toronto; Internat. Hotel Assn.; Am. Soc. Travel Agents; Bd. of Trade, Metro Toronto; Dir.,; Travel Indust. Assn.; Can./Israel Chamber of Comm.; Delta Tau Delta; recreations: hunting, fishing; Clubs: Metropolitan (N.Y.); Rotary; Address: 37 Edenbridge Dr., Islington, Ont. M9A 3E8

CURTIS, Francis William; contractor; b. Winnipeg, Man., 22 April 1908; s. Charles and Mary Agnes (Ritchie) C.; e. Pub. Sch., Winnipeg, Man.; Pub. and High Schs.,

Toronto, Ont.; m. Ruth Roberta, d. late John M. Rattenbury, Charlottetown, P.E.I., 5 Oct. 1940; children: John, Catherine, Ritchie, Nora; Pres. and Chrmn., Georgetown Shipyards, Inc.; Gen. Mgr., Roadbuilders Assn.; Past Pres. and Dir., Charlottetown Y.M.C.A.; Past Pres., Charlottetown Bd. Trade; P.E.I. United Appeal; Past Gov. APEC (Atlantic Provinces Economic Council); Past Pres. Maritime Bd. of Trade; mem. Labor. Mang. Relations Bd. of P.E.I.; Presbyterian; recreations: golf, curling, gardening, tennis; Clubs; Rotary (Past Pres.); Belvedere Golf; Home: 24 Ambrose St., Charlottetown, P.E.I. C1A 3P2

CURTIS, George Frederick, B.A., LL.B., B.C.L., D.C.L., LL.D.; retired; b. Stogumber, Somerset, Eng., Sept. 1906; s. William George and Florence Giles (Thorne) C.; came to Can. 1913; e. Univ. of Sask., LL.B. 1927; Oxford Univ., B.A. 1930; B.C.L. 1931; m. Doris Gwendolyn, d. Judge J. Willis Margeson, Bridgewater, N.S., 15 May 1940; children: John, Joan, Robert, Peter; Prof. of Law and Dean of the Faculty, Univ. of Brit. Columbia, 1945-71; read law with N.R. Craig, K.C., Moose Jaw, Sask.; P.H. Gordon, K.C., Regina, Sask.; called to Bar of Sask., 1931; N.S. 1944; B.C. 1948; practised his prof. with Gordon & Gordon, Regina, 1931-34; Assoc. Prof. of Law, Dalhousie Law Sch., 1934-38; Russell Prof. of Law there 1938-44; Viscount Bennett Prof. of Law there 1944-45; mem., MacQuarrie Comn. on Combines Leg., 1950-52; Visiting Prof., Harvard Law Sch., 1955-56; A.N.U. 1965; London 1971-72; Calgary 1978; Prof. of Law, 1971-77; Pres., Assn. of Candn. Law Teachers, 1951-52; Chrmn., Halifax Br.; Candn. Inst. of Internat. Affairs, 1937-39 and Vancouver Men's Br., 1950-52; Pres., Halifax Candn. Club, 1939-40.; Dir., Halifax Y.M.C.A., 1937-43, Regina 1932-34, Vancouver 1948; Halifax Sch. for the Deaf 1943-45; Chrmn., Candn. Commonwealth Scholarship Comte., 1959-71; Del., U.N. Conf. Law of the Sea, Geneva, 1958, 1960; Commonwealth Educ. Conf., London, Oxford, 1959, New Delhi 1962, Ottawa, 1964; Dir. Candn. Foundation for Legal Research, 1960-71; Gov., Crofton House Sch. 1960-71; Koerner Foundation 1957-71; mem., Candn. Bar Assn.; Anglican; recreation: camping; Clubs: Faculty; University; Home: 1808 Allison Rd., University Hill, Vancouver, B.C. V6T 1S9

CURTIS, Glenn H, B.A.Sc., M.B.A.; consulting engineer; b. Toronto, Ont., 1926; s. Air Marshal Wilfred A., and the late Pearl Elizabeth (Burford) C.; e. Univ. of Toronto, B.A.Sc. 1948; Harvard Univ. M.B.A. 1950; m. Margaret Harrington, 1956; PRESIDENT, GLENN H CURTIS & ASSOCIATES LIMITED since 1972; Anglin-Norcross Corp. Ltd., Montreal, 1950-55; joined Stone & Webster Canada Ltd. in 1955, Pres. 1962-68; Vice Pres. and Chief Engr., The International Nickel Co. of Can., Ltd. 1968-72; served in Royal Naval Fleet Air Arm, 1945; The Black Watch (Royal Highland Regt.) of Can. (Reserve), 1952-55; Dir., Interprov. Pipe Line Ltd.; mem. Candn. Inst. Mining & Metall.; Assn. of Prof. Engrs., Alberta; Assn. of Prof. Engrs. Ont.; Engn. Inst. of Can.; Order of Engrs. of Que.; Office: (P.O. Box 17) Toronto-Dominion Centre, Toronto, Ont. M5K 1A1and Suite 810, Selkirk House, 555 4tth Ave. S.W., Calgary, Alta T2P 3E7

CURTIS, Hon. Hugh Austin; politician; b. Victoria, B.C. 3 Oct. 1932; s. Austin Ivor and Mary Helen (Shepherd) C.; e. high sch. grad. 1950; m. Sheila Diane d. Charles Whitmore Halford, Vancouver, B.C. 16 March 1957; children: Gary Hugh Austin, David Charles, Susan Diane Helen; MINISTER OF FINANCE, B.C.; career in private broadcasting B.C. 1950-72; Ald. Mun. of Saanich 1962-64; Mayor Dist. of Saanich 1964-73; Chrmn. Capital Regional Dist. 1966-72; Pres. Union of B.C. Muns. 1969-70; Chrmn.Mun. Finance Authority B.C. 1970-72; former Extve. mem. Fed. Candn. Muns.; first el. to B.C. Leg. 1972; former Prov. Sec'y and Min. Gov't Services; Social Credit; Anglican; recreations: gardening, swimming, music; Club: Union; Home: 4585 Leyns Rd., Victoria, B.C.

V8N 3A1; Office: Parliament Bldgs., Victoria, B.C. V8V 1X4.

CURTIS, Norman; insurance executive; b. Hull, Eng. 15 Nov. 1927; s. Harry C.; e. Hull (Eng.) Grammar Sch. 1946; Univ. Coll. Hull 1946-47; London Business Sch. 1974; m. Patricia Mary d. late Harold Jessop Nall 22 Oct. 1951; children: Simon Rolf, Alison Judith; PRES. AND DIR. GUARDIAN INSURANCE CO. OF CANADA since 1980; Dir. Montreal Life Ins. Co.; Insurers' Adv. Organ.; Underwriters' Adjustment Bureau; Insurance Bureau of Can. Vice Pres., Underwriters' Laboratories of Canada; joined Royal Exchange Assurance, London, Eng. 1950-56, Vancouver 1957-65, Br. Mgr. Toronto 1966-69; Marketing & Planning Mgr. Guardian Royal Exchange Group (subsequently present co.) 1969-74, Vice Pres. 1974, Sr. Vice Pres. 1976; Extve. Vice Pres. 1977; UK Nat. Service (Army) 1948-50; Fellow, Ins. Inst. Can.; P. Conservative; Anglican; recreations: travel, music, reading (European hist.); Club: Albany; Home: 55 Harbour Square, suite 3313, Toronto, Ont. M5J 2L1; Office: Guardian of Canada Tower, 181 University Ave., Toronto, Ont. M5H 3M7.

CURTIS, Ross R.; banker; b. Peterborough, Ont. 23 Nov. 1919; e. Univ. of Western Ont. AMP 1968; Univ. of Indiana AMP 1970; m. Margaret Anne Lennox Wilson 12 May 1942; children: Dr David R., Bryan R.; SR VICE PRES. PETROLEUM DIVISION, WORLD CORPORATE BANKING, BANK OF MONTREAL 1981- ; served present bank various positions and locations incl. Sen. Vice Pres Alberta Div. 1971-76; Sen. Vice Pres. Corp. Banking, Nat. Resources 1976-79; Sen. Vice Pres. & Dep. Gen. Mgr. Corporate Banking, Western Operations 1979-81; Former Pres. Alberta Heart Foundation; Clubs: Calgary Golf & Country; The Ranchmen's Club; Lampton Golf & Country Club, Toronto; Union Club of B.C.; Office: Suite 3000, 300 - 5th Ave. S.W., Calgary, Alta.

CUTTS, Kenneth L.; trust company executive; b. Saskatoon, Sask., 25 June 1924; s. Leonard George and Jean Russell (McGowan) C.; e. Alexander High Sch., Medicine Hat, Alta.; m. Patricia Marie, d. late James Hansen, 15 Feb. 1946; children: Robin Leonard (Finland), Terry Jean, Patricia Joan, Kenneth James, Pamela Jill, Christopher John; former Vice-Chrmn, Fort Garry Trust Co.; Pres., Bestlands Development Ltd.; K. L. Cutts & Assoc.; Acct., Canadian Imperial Bank of Commerce, Dawson Creek, B.C. becoming Br. Mgr., Drumheller and Calgary, Alta.; Regional Mgr., Business Devel. (Alta.), Calgary; Supt., Business Devel., H.O. Toronto; formerly Gen. Mgr., Bank of Western Canada; R.C.N.V.R. 1942-45; Latter Day Saints; Home: 103 Fulham Crescent, Winnipeg, Man. R3N 0G5;

CVETANOVIC, Ratimir J., B.Sc., B.A.Sc., M.A., Ph.D., F.R.S.C., F.C.I.C.; research scientist; b. Belgrade, Yugoslavia, 19 May 1913; s. Josif and Natalija (Urosevic) C.; e. Univ. of Edinburgh, B.Sc. 1936; Univ. of Belgrade, B.A.Sc. 1941; Univ. of Toronto, M.A. 1950, Ph.D. 1951; m. Jean Elizabeth, d. H.M. Macdonald, Antigonish, N.S., 15 Aug. 1955; children: Michael Ratimir, Angela Natalia, Nadine Elizabeth; Visiting Prof., Dept. of Chemistry, University of California, SENIOR RESEARCH SCIENTIST, OFFICE OF ENVIRONMENTAL MEASURES, NAT. BUREAU OF STANDARDS, WASHINGTON, D.C. 1980-; Special Lect., Univ. of Toronto, 1955; Visiting Prof., Cornell Univ., 1963; Distinguished Visiting Prof., Univ. of Calif. (Davis), 1966; Overseas Fellow, Churchill Coll., Cambridge, 1967; Head, Kinetics, Photochem. and Catalysis Sec., Div Chem., Nat. Research Council 1952-78; -80; author of numerous scient. papers and articles in field of chem.; served in 2nd World War as Reserve Lieut. in Yugoslav army; Home: 18 Wick Cres., Ottawa, Ont. K1J 7H2; Office: National Bureau of Standards, Washington, D.C.

CYBULSKI, John M., B.Sc., M.B.A.; executive; b. Poland 2 Aug. 1936; s. Henry and Czeslawa (Florianowicz) C.; e. Mech. Trade Sch. Warsaw, Dipl. 1951; Mech. Tech. Coll. Warsaw, Dipl. Technol. 1955; Sir George Williams Univ. B.Sc. 1966; McGill Univ. Grad. Dipl. in Mang. 1974, M.B.A. 1978; m. Susan d. Aladar Marton, Montreal, Que. 7 May 1966; VICE PRES. AND GEN. MGR.-RAIL & DIESEL PRODUCTS DIV., BOMBARDIER LTÉE 1978- ; joined RCA Victor Co. Montreal 1960-65 holding various positions Special Products Div. incl. Production Engr.; Sr. Indust. Engr., Canadian Marconi Co. Ltd., Town of Mount Royal 1965, Div. Mfg. Analyst 1968, Procurement Mgr. 1969-74; Mgr. Purchasing & Traffic, Dominion Engineering Works Ltd. Lachine, Que. 1974, Mgr. Quality Assurance 1976, Mgr. Production Planning & Control 1978; mem. Candn. Soc. Mech. Engrs.; Chambre de Comm. Montréal; McGill Grad. Soc.; Liberal; R. Catholic; recreations: sailing, skiing, travel, classical music; Club: Ile Perrot Sailing; Home: 4078 Cote des Neige Rd., Montreal, Que. H3H 1W6; Office: 1505 Dickson St., Montreal, Que. H1N 2H7.

CYR, J.V. Raymond, B.A.Sc.; executive; b. Montreal, Que. 11 Feb. 1934; s. Armand and Yvonne (Lagacé) C.; e. Ecole Polytech. Univ. of Montreal B.A.Sc. 1958; Bell Labs., N.J. post-grad. studies in engn.; Nat. Defence Coll. 1972-73; m. Marie, d. Alphonse Bourdon, Montreal, Que. 1 Sept. 1956; children: Hélène, Paul-André; EXTVE. VICE PRES. ADMINISTRATION, BELL CANADA Dir. Steinbergs, Inc.; Dir. Banque Nationale du Canada; Dir. Télébec Ltée; Telesat Canada; Eaton/Bay Mutual Funds; joined Bell Canada as Engr. 1958, Staff Engr. Montreal 1965, Chief Engr. Québec City 1970, Vice Pres. Operations Staff E. Region Montreal 1973, Vice Pres. Montreal Area 1975; Chmn., Cdn. Telecommunications Carriers Assoc.; Dir., Centre de développement technologique de l'Ecole Polytechnique; Ecole national d'administration publique; Revue Commerce; Quebec Arthritis Soc.; mem., Ordre des Ingénieurs du Qué.; Engn. Inst. Can.; R. Catholic; recreations: golf, squash; Clubs: St-Denis; Islesmere Golf; St. James Club; Home: 3201 Hélène Boullé, Montreal, Qué. H3M 1Z4; Office: Extve Vice-Pres., Bell Canada, 1050 Beaver Hall Hill, Suite 1900 Mtl. Que. H2Z 1S3

D

DACEY, John Robert, M.B.E., M.Sc., Ph.D., F.C.I.C., C.M.; educator; chemist; b. Eng. 28 Apl. 1914; s. Harry and Arabella (Wilson) D.; e. Dalhousie Univ. B.Sc. 1936, M.Sc. 1938; McGill Univ. Ph.D. 1940; m. Jane Dean d. Hugh Campbell 1940; children: John W. H., Joan E. (Mrs. D. M. Bowie), Diane (Mrs. W. G. Sprules); PROFESSOR EMERITUS, ROYAL MILITARY COLL. OF CANADA; former Principal, R.M.C.; Scientific Consultant; served with Candn. Army 1940-47, rank Maj.; author over 50 scient. papers; mem. Am. Chem. Soc.; mem. Order of Canada; Sigma Xi; Anglican; Address: Bateau Chauel Estates, R.R. #1, Kingston, Ont. 2 Hewett House, RMC, Kingston, Ont.

DADSON, Douglas French, B.A., B.Ed.; educator; b. Toronto, Ont., 1 May 1913; s. Alexander Turnbull and Eva Stewart (Grafftey) D.; e. Univ. of Toronto Schs., 1931; Univ. of Toronto, B.A. 1935; Ont. Coll. of Educ., B.Ed. 1955; m. Patricia Grace, d. Charles Adamson, 22 Aug. 1942; children: Elizabeth Ann, Douglas Alexander; PROF. OF EDUCATION, UNIV. OF TORONTO since 1973; Dean, Fac. of Educ., Univ. of Toronto, 1963-73; Teacher, Secondary Schs., 1936-42; Instr., Univ. of Toronto Schs. 1945; Inspr., Ont. Secondary Schs. 1950; Prof., Ont. Coll. of Educ. 1954, Dean of Coll. 1963; Dean., Faculty of Educ., Univ. of Toronto 1970; served with R.C.A. 1942-44; rank Lt.; Capt., Educ. Services, 1944-45; Club: Reswick; Home: 97 St. Leonards Ave., Toronto, Ont. M4N 1K4

DAGENAIS, Camille A., O.C.(1973), D.A.Sc., D.Sc., LL.D., F.E.I.C.; engineering consultant and contractor; b. Montréal, Qué., 12 Nov. 1920; s. Gilbert and Charlotte (Mitchell) D.; e. Ecole Polytech. Univ. of Montreal, B.A.Sc. 1946; Alexander Hamilton Inst., Business Adm.; École des Hautes Études Comm., Business Adm.; D.Sc. Royal Mil. Coll. of Can. 1975, Laval 1977; D.A.Sc. Sherbrooke 1975; LL.D. Toronto 1973; m. Pauline; d. Emile Falardeau, 23 Aug. 1947; children: Guy, Alain, Claude; CHRMN. AND CHIEF EXTVE. OFFR., SNC GROUP OF COMPANIES; Chrmn. and Chief Extve. Offr. SNC Enterprises Ltd. and Surveyer, Nenniger & Chênevert Inc. since 1975; Dir., Société d'investissement Desjardins; Royal Bank of Canada; Canadian Liquid Air Ltd.; Spar Aerospace Ltd.; began as Engr. radar stns. Pine Tree Line, H. J. Doran, Consultants, Montreal and subsequently Constr. Overseer Canadian Industries Ltd.; joined Surveyer, Nenniger & Chênevert as Liaison Engr. 1953, Engr. 1954, Partner 1959, Chrmn. Bd. and Gen. Mgr. 1965; Pres. 1966; apptd. Pres. SNC Enterprises Ltd. 1967; mem., Order of Engrs. Que. (Vice Pres. Consulting Engrs. Sec. 1966); Assn. Consulting Engrs. Can. (Pres. 1967-68; Dir., 1966-70); Candn. Soc. for Civil Engn. (Pres. 1973); Internat. Comn. on Large Dams (Vice Pres. Zone Am. 1974-77); Pres. Candn. Comte. 1967-70) Candn. Nuclear Assn. (Past Pres. and Dir.); Candn. Good Roads Assn. (Past Dir.); Warden and Dir., Corp. of Seven Wardens; Candn. Council, The Conference Bd.; Corresp. mem. Acad. Mexicana de Ingenieria; Adv. Comtre., Centre for Internat. Business Studies, École des Hautes Études Commerciales; Gov., Conseil du Patronat; Am. Mang. Assn.; The Pres.'s Assn.; Chambre de Comm. du Dist de Montréal; Chambre de Comm. française au Can.; R. Catholic; recreations: hunting, fishing; Clubs: St. Denis; Mt. Stephen; Mt. Royal; Home: 3495 Avenue du Musée, Apt. 401, Montreal, Que. H3G 2C8; Office: 1 Complexe Desjardins, P.O. Box 10, Montreal, Que. H5B 1C8

DAGENAIS, Pierre, M.A., L.ès L., Ph.D., F.R.S.C. (1961); geographer; b. Montreal, P.Q., 3 Oct. 1909; s. J. Alcidas and Berthe (Claude) D.; e. Coll. Sainte-Marie, Montreal, B.A. 1932; Ecole des Hautes Etudes, M.A. (Comm.) 1935; Sorbonne, Paris, L.ès L. 1938; Univ. of Grenoble, Ph.D. (Geog.) 1939; m. Yvette Jamieson, 4 July 1936; children: Nicole (Mrs. Robert Boily), Bernard; DIR. AND FOUNDER; INST. OF GEOG., UNIV. OF MONTREAL; Dean, Faculty of Letters there 1962-67; Teacher, Jacques Cartier Normal Sch., Montreal, and Prof. Faculty of Educ. since 1968; author of several books and numerous articles related to his special field; Fellow, Artic Inst. of N. Am. (Pres., Montreal Sec. 1952); mem., la Soc. de Geog. de Montréal; l'Assn. Canadienne des Géog. (Pres. 1951); since 1935 has taken part in more than three geog. expeditions; Major in Reserve Army in 2nd World War; Roman Catholic; recreations: riding, farming; Home: 1605 Bernard Ave., Outremont, Que. H2V 1X2; Office: C.P. 6203, Station "A", Montreal, Que. H3C 3T3

DAIGLE, Roland, B. ès A., B.Com., L.Sc.C. M.B.A.; banker; b. St-Romuald, Que., 11 June 1939; s. Maurice and Hélène (Filteau) D; e. Coll. de Lévis, B.ès A. 1961; Laval Univ., B.Com. 1963, L.Sc.C. 1964, M.B.A. 1969; MGR., CAISSE POPULAIRE LES ETCHEMINS; Pres., Domaine Taniata Inc.; Secrétaire, Chambre de Comm. de St-Romuald, 1965-66; mem., Administrateurs Agréés; Chambre des Directeurs de Crédit; R. Catholic; recreation: golf; Club: Lions (Secy. 1966); Home: 1166 Dion Bernières, St. Nicolas, Que.; Office: 82 Principale, St-Romuald, Que.

DAKIN, John Kenneth, M.Com.; transportation executive; b. Nanaimo, B.C., 20 Apl. 1920; s. John Charles and Hilda May (Shaw) D.; e. Univ. of B.C., B.Com. 1948; Queen's Univ., M.Com. 1952; m. Gustine Alice, d. late

Carl L. A. Lietze, 2 Dec. 1954; children: Michael, Christie; EXECUTIVE VICE PRES. C.P. AIR; Dir. Canadian Pacific Transport Co. Ltd.; joined CP Air, Vancouver, as Spec. Asst. to General Manager. Operations 1950, Supervisor Labour Relations 1951, Direct or Industrial Relations 1952, Organization Planning and Executive Development 1959, Assistant Vice President Marketing and Sales 1962; appointed Dir. Personnel Planning of CP Ltd. 1971, Personnel & Organ. Planning 1972, Vice Pres. Personnel & Pensions 1973; returned to CP Air 1976 in present position; served with Royal Candn. Ordnance Corps 1941-46; United Church; recreations: sailing, skiing; Clubs: Vancouver; One Grant McConachie Way, Vancouver Int'l Airport, B.C. V7B 1V1

DAKSHINAMURTI, Krishnamurti, M.Sc., Ph.D., F.R.S.C. (U.K.); educator; b. Vellore, India, 20 May 1928; s. Sattanamcheri Venkataswami Krishnamurti and Kamakshi (Sundaradekshadar); e. Univ. of Madras, B.Sc. 1946; Univ. of Rajputana, M.Sc. 1952, Ph.D. 1957; m. Ganga Bhavani, d. S. Venkataraman, Madras, India, 28 Aug. 1961; children: Shyamala Lalitha, Sowmitri Sowmya; PROF. OF BIOCHEM., UNIV. OF MANITOBA since 1973; Visiting Prof. Rockefeller Univ., N.Y., 1974-75; Sr. Lectr. in Biochem. Christian Med. Coll., Vellore, India, 1952; Research Assoc. in Nutritional Biochem., Univ. of Ill. 1957; Research Assoc., Mass. Inst. of Technol. 1962; Assoc. Dir. of Research, St. Joseph Hosp., Lancaster, Pa., 1963; joined present Univ. as Assoc. Prof. of Biochem. 1965; rec'd Borden Award, Nutrition Soc. Can. 1973; author of over 130 research publs.; Assoc. Ed. "Canadian Journal of Biochemistry"; mem. Am. Soc. Biol. Chems.; Soc. for Neuroscience; Am. Soc. Neurochem.; Am. Inst. Nutrition; Am. Diabetes Assn.; Candn. Biochem. Soc.; Biochem. Soc. (UK); Nutrition Soc.; Hindu; Home: 934 Crestview Park Dr., Winnipeg, Man. R2Y 0V7; Office: Faculty of Medicine, Univ. of Manitoba, Winnipeg, Man. R3E 0W3

DALE, Robert Gordon, D.S.O., D.F.C., C.D.; industrialist; b. Toronto, Ont., 1 Nov. 1920; s. Dr. Gordon McIntyre and Helen Marjorie (Cartwright) D.; e. Univ. of Toronto Schs., 1930-39; Univ. of Toronto, Trinity Coll. 1939-40, Business Adm. Cert. Course 1946; m. Mary Austin, d. H. A. Babcock, Toronto, Ont., 3 Apl. 1948; two s.; Robert Austin, John Gordon; CHMN. AND CHIEF EXTVE. OFFR., MAPLE LEAF MILLS LTD., 1981; Dir., National Life Assur. Co. of Can.; McGavin Toastmaster Ltd.; Eastern Bakeries Ltd.; Manpower Serv. (Ont.) Ltd.; Corporate Foods Ltd.; Koppers International Canada Ltd.; Leitch Transport Ltd.; Candn. Extve. Services Overseas; joined pres. in 1947; appointed Plant Mgr., Toronto, 1957; Gen. Prod. Mgr. 1961; Asst. to Pres. 1965; Extve. V. Pres. & Dir., 1967; Pres. and C.E.O. 1969-81; joined RCAF 1940; served with RAF Bomber Command and Pathfinder Force 1941-45; retired with rank Sqdn. Leader 1945; Pres. (1972) Air Cadet League of Can.; Hon. Lt. Col., 400 Squadr. (Reserves) Candn. Armed Forces; mem., Adv. Bd., Bloorview Childrens Hosp.; mem. Bd. Trustees, Un. Community Fund of Greater Toronto; Chrmn. Extve Comte., Trinity College; mem., Bd. Trade Metrop. Toronto: Phi Kappa Pi; P. Conservative; Anglican; recreations: tennis, squash, golf, fishing; Clubs: Empire; Rosedale Golf; Badminton & Racquet; National; Home: 103 Dawlish Ave., Toronto, Ont. M4N 1H4; Office: P.O. Box 710, Stn. K, Toronto, Ont. M4P 2X5

DALE, William Scott Abell, M.A., Ph.D., F.R.S.A.; b. Toronto, Ont., 18 Sept. 1921; s. late Ernest Abell and late Mary (Bulloch) D.; e. Univ. of Toronto Schs.; Univ. of Toronto (Trinity), B.A. 1944, M.A. 1946; Harvard Univ. (1946-48), Ph.D. 1955; Courtauld Inst., London Univ., 1948-50; m. Jane Gordon, d. late Albert T. Laidlaw, Toronto, Ont. 19 Apl. 1952; children: Michael William, John Randall, Thomas Ernest Abell; PROF., VISUAL ARTS DEPT., UNIV. OF W. ONT., since 1967; with National Gallery of Canada, 1950-57; Curator, Art Gallery of Toronto, 1957-59; Director, Vancouver Art Gallery, 1959-61; Asst. Dir., Nat. Gallery of Canada 1961-66, Acting Dir., 1965-66, Depy. Dir., 1966-67; Chairman, Fine Art (now Visual Arts) Dept. Univ. of W. Ont., 1967-75; Res. Fellow, Dumbarton Oaks Research Library & Collection, Washington, 1956-57; served in 2nd World War with Royal Navy, Fleet Air Arm., 1944-45; author of articles and book reviews in "Art Bulletin", "British Museum Yearbook", "Burlington Magazine", "Canadian Art" and "Speculum"; mem., Coll. Art. Assn. of Am.; Mediaeval Acad. of Am.; Royal Soc. of Arts; Conservative; Anglican; Address: Univ. of Western Ontario, London, Ont. N6A 5B7

DALE-HARRIS, Robert Baldwin, D.S.O., F.C.A.; farmer, b. Montreal, P.Q., 20 July 1913; s. Spencer Lewin and Margaret (Cassels) D.-H.; e. Univ. of Toronto Schs.; Ridley Coll., St. Catherines, Ont.; Trinity Coll., Toronto, Ont.; m. Leslie Ruth, d. Leslie Howard, 2 May 1942; children: Carolyn, Lindsay, Victoria; CHRM. OF THE BD., BRINCO LTD. Dir., Gerling Group Co.; Chrmn., Candn. Equestrian Team; Past Chrmn. Clarke Institute of Psychiatry; Canadian Tax Foundation; partner, Coopers and Lybrand (formerly McDonald Currie and Co.) 1945-79; served in 2nd World War with Royal Canadian Artillery; on active service 1939-45 (Militia 1937-39); awarded D.S.O.; Kappa Alpha; Anglican, Clubs: Toronto; York; Toronto & North York Hunt; Home: Wotton House, Uxbridge, Ont. L0C 1K0; Office: 20 King St. W., Toronto, Ont. M5H 1C4

DALES, John Harkness, M.A., Ph.D.; university professor; b. Toronto, Ont., 20 Aug. 1920; s. John Franklin and Grace (Cochrane) D.; e. Univ. of Toronto Schs.; Univ. of Toronto, B.A. 1943, M.A. 1945; Harvard Univ., Ph.D. 1953; m. Elizabeth Eleanor, d. D. H. Bell, Elora, Ont., 5 June 1943; two s. John Robert, Gregory Franklin; PROF. OF POLITICAL ECONOMY, UNIV. OF TORONTO, since 1963; Mang. Editor, "The Canadian Journal of Economics and Political Science" 1957-67; taught at McGill Univ., Montreal, Que. 1949-54; Publications: "Hydroelectricity and Industrial Development: Quebec 1898-1940", 1957; "The Protective Tariff in Canada's Development" 1966; "Pollution, Property and Prices" 1968; articles in various journs.; trained as Pilot in R.C.A.F. 1943-45; Pres. (1974-75) Candn. Economics Assn.; Home: 232 Rose Park Dr., Toronto, Ont. M4T 1R5

DALES, Samuel, M.A., Ph.D.; educator; b. Warsaw, Poland 31 Aug. 1927; s. James and Helen (Ochs) D.; e. Tadcaster Grammar Sch. Yorks. Eng. 1943; Univ. of B.C. B.A. 1951, M.A. 1953; Univ. of Toronto Ph.D. 1957; m. Laura Lilli Ruth d. late Emil Fischer 1952; children: Adam Charles, Pamela Ann; PROF. OF MICROBIOL. & IMMUNOLOGY, UNIV. OF W. ONT. since 1976; Post-Doctoral Fellow, Nat. Cancer Inst. Can. 1957-60; Asst. Prof. The Rockefeller Univ. New York 1961-65, Assoc. Prof. OSC N.Y. Univ. 1966-69, Research Prof. 1969-76; author book chapters and over 100 scient. papers, reviews on cell-virus interactions and virus diseases; mem. Ed. Bd. 'Virology', 'Intervirology', 'Journal Cell Biology'; mem. Fed. Socs. Exper. Biol.; Harvey Soc.; Am. Soc. Cell Biol.; The Josiah Macy Jr. Foundation Faculty Scholarship 1981-82; Home: 1588 Hillside Dr., London, Ont. N6G 2P8; Office: London, Ont. N6A 5C1.

DALEY, LeRoy MacKenzie; executive; b. St. Catharines, Ont., 6 Nov. 1923; s. Ollie LeRoy and Elsie Blanche MacKenzie (Morrison) D.; e. St. Catharines Pub. Sch. and Coll. Inst.; m. Doris Elsie, d. Percy Richard Gretton, 15 June 1946; children: Richard J., Robert M., Deas M.; PRESIDENT AND CHIEF EXTVE. OFFR., VARIAN CANADA INC., served R.C.A.F. as AC2, LAC, Sgt. Pilot, Pilot Offr., Flying Offr., 1941-44; recreation: boating; Home: RR# 5, Georgetown, Ont. L7G 4S8; Office: 45 River Dr., Halton Hills (Georgetown), Ont. L7G 2J4

DALGLEISH, Harold David, B.Sc., M.D., F.R.C.S. (C); surg.; b. Gull Lake, Sask., 25 Apl. 1907; s. Robert William and Mary Elizabeth (Kearney) D.; e. Melfort (Sask.) High Sch.; Univ. of Sask., B.Sc. 1932; Univ. of Man., M.D. 1936; Cert. Gen. Surg., Royal Coll. of Can., 1952; Honorary LL.D., Univ. of Manitoba, 1969; m. Mildred Ida, d. W.R. Thackeray Palmerston, Ont., 30 Sept. 1934; children: Mrs. Elizabeth Zemmels, Patricia, Mrs. Julia Kurylo; in gen. practice, Saskatoon, 1936-60; limited gen. surg. since 1960; Teacher, Surg., Univ. of Sask. Med. Sch.; Chief of Staff, City Hosp., Univ. of Sask. since 1964; Bd. of Dir. Saskatoon Medical Arts, 1969-70; mem. Surg. Staff Univ., St. Pauls and City Hosps., Saskatoon; Hon. mem. College of Family Practice of Canada, 1979; College of Physicans and Surg. of Sask, 1976; Life mem. Sask. Med. Assoc.; Saskatoon & Dist. Med. Soc.; Senior Life mem. Can. Med. Assoc.; Past Pres., City Hosp., Staff, 1949; a Founder, Med. Services, 1965-7; mem. Sask. Coll. Phys. & Surgs., Pres., 1961-63, Registrar 1970-75; Pres., Candn. Medical Assn., 1968-69 (President, Saskatchewan Division, 1961-63); President, Family Welfare Association, Saskatoon, 1947-48; Trustee, Nixon Benevolent Fund; mem. Sask. Cancer Comn., 1945-49 (Pres., Saskatoon Dist. Soc., 1944); Pres., Univ. of Sask. Alumni, 1955-56; Can. Med. Assn., Medal of Service, 1979; Silver Jubilee Medal, 1978; Award of Merit, Sask. Med. Assoc., 1972; Canada Confederation Medal, 1967; Protestant; recreations: golf, curling, bridge; Clubs: Saskatoon (Past Dir.); Riverside Golf; Lions (Past Pres.); Home: 112-325-5th Ave. N., Saskatoon, Sask. S7K 2P7

DALGLIESH, (Wilbert) Harold, Ph.D.; professor emeritus; b. London, Ont., 13 March 1902; s. William James and Margaret Louise (McCallum) D.; e. Univ. of W. Ont., B.A. 1922, M.A. 1923; Univ. of Pa., Ph.D. 1931; studied at Univs. Paris, Dijon, Toulouse, Mich. and Cornell; m. Elizabeth Jessie, d. William Newton Rhodes, Philadelphia, Pa., 10 June 1929; children: Mrs. Margaret Elizabeth Broun, William John; Asst. Instr. in Hist., Univ. of Pa., 1925-26; Instr. in Hist., Lafayette Coll., 1927-33; Lectr., Asst. Prof., Assoc. Prof. and Prof. of Hist. and Pol. Science, Univ. of Utah, 1933-47; Prof. of History 1947-70; Head, Hist. Dept. 1960-63; visiting Staff mem., Univ. of W. Ont., summer 1929 and San Diego State Coll., summer 1964; Research Assoc., Council on Foreign Relations (N.Y.) 1945-46; Past Chrmn., Salt Lake City Comte. on Foreign Relations; Sr. Warden, St. Paul's Epis. Ch., 1959-60; Registrar, Archivist, Historiographer, Epis. Dioc. of Utah 1973-80; historiographer emeritus 1980-; author: "Company of the Indies" 1933; "Community Education in Foreign Affairs", 1946; "World War II and Ensuing East West Controversy", 1969; other writings incl. book chapters, articles and reviews for prof. journs.; mem., Am. Assn. Univ. Profs.; Utah Historical Society; Utah Acad. Science, Letters and Arts; Phi Alpha Theta; Episcopalian; recreations: gardening, travel; Home: 1108 E. South Temple, Salt Lake City, Utah.

DALGLISH, Keith Gordon, B.A., F.C.A.; executive; b. Toronto, Ont. 20 Feb. 1930; s. late T. Gordon and late Kate I. (Pearson) D.; e. Univ. of Toronto Schs. 1948; Trinity Coll. Univ. of Toronto B.A. 1952; Univ. of W. Ont. Mang. Training Course 1979; m. Gail E. d. George B. Bagwell, Q.C., Toronto, Ont. Sept. 1958; children: Tracy, Todd, Ian, Alison; TORONTO REGION EXTVE. PARTNER, THORNE RIDDELL 1977- ; joined Price Waterhouse, Toronto 1953-60; Secy.-Treas. ICT (Canada) Ltd. Toronto 1960-62; Partner, Thorne Gunn Helliwell & Christenson, Toronto 1963-67; Pres. George Weston Ltd. Toronto 1968-69; Partner, Thorne Riddell, Toronto 1969-77; mem. Inst. C.A.'s Ont. (Pres. 1981-82); Candn. Tax Foundation; Candn. Comprehensive Auditing Foundation; recreations: golf, curling; Clubs: University; Toronto Golf; Granite; Home: 65 Douglas Dr., Toronto, Ont. M4W 2B2; Office: (P.O. Box 262) Commercial Union Tower, Toronto-Dominion Centre, Toronto, Ont. M5K 1J9.

DALLAIRE, Raymond; industrialist; b. St-Hénédine. Qué. 16 Feb. 1932; s. late Albert and Régine (Lacasse) D.; e. St-Hénédine, (Que.) and Coll. des Marianistes, St-Anselme, Qué.; m. Rolande, d. late Clément Fortier, 12 Feb. 1966; two d. Andrée, Caroline; PRESIDENT AN DIR., P.H.-TECH INC. (formerly P. H. Plastics Inc.); Pres., Celtech Plastics Inc.; Vice Pres., Les Industries Dallaire Ltée; Dir., Candn. Windows & Doors Mfrs. Assn.; has served in various capacities constr. field Que., Ont. and B.C.; co-founded Dallaire Enterprises Inc. 1958, Quincaillerie Panoramique Inc. 1962, Plastique Futurama Inc. 1964; above firms merged under present name in 1971; named "Man of the Year" by Soc. Plastic Indust. Can. 1974; holds Candn. and foreign patents window and constr. industs.; co-founder Nordiques Hockey Club; mem. Soc. Plastic Indust. Can.; Soc. Plastics Engrs. Inc.; Centre des Dirigeants d'Enterprise; Comité Can.; Invention Qué. Inc.; Un. Inventors Scientists; Chambre de Comm. de Prov. Qué.; Candn. Standards Assn.; mem. Insul. Glass Mfrs. Assn.; Nat. Woodworkers Mfrs. Assn.; Nat. Sash & Door Jobbers Assn.; Candn. Bldg. Officials Assn.; Nat. Assn. of Home Builders; R. Catholic; recreations: golf, skiing, ski-dooing, physical fitness; Home: 587 de la Falaise, St-David, Lévis, Qué. G6W 1A4; Office: 790 Jean-M. Morin, Lauzon, Qué.

DALTON, William Henderson; association executive; b. Toronto, Ont., 20 Nov. 1916; s. Charles Skiffington and Gertrude Margaret (Hobbs) D.; e. Toronto, Ont.; m. Joyce Lucille, d. John Sweatman, 7 May 1940; children: David, Jonathan, Diana (Mrs. R. Cruickshank); PRES. AND DIR., THE CANADIAN GAS ASSOCIATION, since 1955; Pres. and Dir., Candn. Gas Research Inst. since 1974; Clk. in family business Dalton Brothers 1935; Estates Clk., Accounts Office, Supreme Court of Ont., 1936; served in securities business with Toronto brokerage firm for 3 yrs. after World War II; Pub. Relations staff, Ont. Hydro, 1948; Special Asst. to Chrmn. 1950; served with Candn. Army 1940-45; rank Maj.; Perm. Rep., Internat. Gas Union Council (Switzerland); Companion, Inst. Gas Engrs. (Eng.); Charter mem., Standards Council Can.; (Extve. Comte. 1971-72); mem., Candn. Chamber Comm.; Bd. Trade Metrop. Toronto; Queen's Jubilee Medal 1977; recreation: boating; Clubs: Empire, Canadian; Granite; Home: 19 Governor's Rd., Toronto, Ont. M4W 2E9

DALY, Norman A.; insurance executive; b. Vancouver, B.C.; s. James Arthur Claude and Johnann (Apperson) D.; e. Chart. Life Underwriter 1959; m. Catherine Joan Macdonald 15 Apl. 1948; children: Scott, Christie, Margot; VICE PRES. AND DIR. CANDN. DIV. THE CANADA LIFE ASSURANCE CO. 1980- ; joined present Co. as Sales Rep. Vancouver Br. 1945, Br. Supvr. 1948, Asst. Mgr. 1955, Br. Mgr. 1963, Agency Vice Pres. Can. and mem. Extve. Comte. H.O. Toronto 1968, Vice Pres. and Assoc. Dir. of Agencies, Individual Ins. 1977, Vice Pres. and Dir. Candn. Agencies, mem. Mang. Comte. 1978; served with RCAF, RAF Overseas World War II; Pres. Life Underwriters Assn. Vancouver 1966; mem. Candn. Life Ins. Assn. (Extve. and mem. various comtes.); Director, Life Ins. Marketing & Research Assn. recreations: golf, swimming, skiing; Clubs: Granite; Bd. Trade Golf & Country; Home: 41 Daneswood Rd., Toronto, Ont. M4N 3J7; Office: 330 University Ave., Toronto, Ont. M5G 1R8.

DALY, Richard Arthur, Jr.; investment dealer; b. Toronto, Ont., 28 May 1914; s. Richard Arthur and Katherine Evelyn (Cullen) D.; e. Brown Pub. Sch., Toronto, 1921-24; Upper Canada Coll., 1924-32; Univ. of Toronto, 1932-36; m. Genevieve, d. Rene Hubert, Paris, France, 1 June 1946; children: Patrick Arthur Hubert, Michelle Mary; CHAIRMAN AND DIR., R. A. DALY & CO. LTD.; since 1968; (mems., all principal Canadian Stock Exchanges, and Invest. Dealers' Assn. of Can.); with Bank of Toronto, 1936-42; joined present Co., 1946; apptd. a Dir., 1949 and Vice-Pres., 1953, Pres. 1961-68; Past Pres., Toronto

Soc. of Financial Analysts; Past Chmn., Ont. District, Exec. Comm., Investment Dealers' of Can.; served in 2nd World War as Lieut. with Candn. Armoured Carrier Regt. (Overseas), 1943-45; Clubs: National; Toronto Golf; Granite; Arts and Letters; Home: 99 Bayview Ridge, Willowdale, Ont. M2L 1E3; Office: Suite 800, Continental Place, 130 Adelaide St. West, Toronto, Ont. M5H 3R9 P.O. Box 42, Toronto-Dominion Centre, Toronto, Ont. M5K 1E1

DAMANT, Laurence Vasile; company executive; b. Nove-Mesto, Czechoslovakia, 25 Apl. 1913; s. Ivan and Anna (Valda) D.; e. Univ. of Karlsruhe, Dipl. Engn.; m. Franciska, d. Prof. Emil Probst, Ph.D., London, Eng.; one d.; VICE PRES., INDUST. CONTAINERS DIV. AND DIR., SONOCO PRODUCTS OF CANADA LTD.; Fact Engr., Chief Engr. and Asst. Prod. Mgr., Indus. Sarmei, S.A., Cluj, Roumania, 1934; came to Can. 1940 and estbd. present Co.; Production Mgr. for two years and subsequently Gen. Mgr., dur. World War 1939-45 instrumental in devel. new types of shell containers; mem., Inst. of Internat. Affairs; Greek Orthodox; recreations: tennis, skiing; Club: Mt. Royal Tennis; Home: 704, 65 Brittany Ave., Montreal, Que. J6W 3L4; Office: (P.O. Box 480) Terrebonne, Que. H3P 1A4

DAMPIER, John Lawrence, O.B.E., B.A.; executive; b. Strathroy, Ont., 29 Dec. 1914; s. Lawrence Henry and Edith Isabel (English) D.; e. Ridley Coll., St. Catherines, Ont., 1932; Univ. of W. Ont. B.A. 1936; m. Hilda Margaret Ingram, 17 June 1939; children: Mrs. Raymond Gamlin, Lawrence Paul, Marjorie Anne (Mrs. Frank Denhoed), Helen Louise (Mrs. R.A. Wilson); CHMN. OF THE BD., NABOB FOODS LTD., Dir., Nabob Foods Limited; B.C. Bearing Engineers Ltd.; Pope & Talbot Inc. (Portland, Ore.); Northwest Sports Enterprises Ltd. (Vancouver Canucks); Vancouver Foundation; Pres., Lawrence Dampier & Assoc. Ltd., joined Lever Bros. Ltd., Toronto, 1936-39; Sales Mgr., 1945-47; el. a Dir. 1947-50; trans. as Vice Pres., Lever Bros. Co. New York City, 1950; Vice-Pres., McCann-Erickson (Can.) Ltd., 1953-57; served with N.P.A.M., Q.O.R. of Can., 1936-39; Q.O.R. of Can., C.A. Overseas, 1939-42; HQ 3 Candn. Inf. Div., 1942-45; O.B.E.; Order of Oranje-Nassau; Past Pres., Council mem., Vancouver Board Trade; Past Pres., Boy Scouts of Can.; recreations: boating, curling, fishing; Clubs: Vancouver; Arbutus; Home: Apt. 305, 5475 Vine St., Vancouver, B.C. V6M 3Z7; Office: 116-525 Seymour St., Vancouver, B.C., (P.O. Box 35609 Vancouver) V6M 4G9

DANBY, Kenneth Edison; artist; printmaker; b. Sault Ste. Marie, Ont. 6 March 1940; s. M. G. Edison and Gertrude (Buckley) D.; e. Sault Tech. & Comm. High Sch.; Sault Coll. Inst.; Ont. Coll. of Art Toronto 1958-60; children: Sean, Ryan, Noah; one-man exhns. incl.: Gallery Moos Toronto 1964, 1965, 1967-72, 1974-79; Galerie Godard Lefort Montreal 1966; Cologne (Germany) Kunsmarkt 1969; William Zierler Gallery New York 1972, 1973; Images Gallery Toledo, Ohio 1972; Nancy Poole Gallery London, Ont. 1972; Galerie Allen Vancouver 1975; Continental Art Agencies Vancouver 1973; Fleet Gallery Winnipeg 1973; Galerie Moos Montreal 1974; Algoma Arts Festival Sault Ste. Marie 1975; Retrospective Exhn. S. Ont. circulated by Kitchener Waterloo Art Gallery 1974-75; Candn. Consulate New York 1977; de-Vooght Galleries Vancouver 1977, 1980; Arras Gallery New York 1977; Wallack Galleries Ottawa 1974; rep. numerous group shows Can., USA, Europe, rep. perm. colls. Museum of Modern Art, Montreal Museum of Fine Art, Art Inst. Chicago, Nat. Gallery Can.; comns. incl. designs for Series III Olympic Coins 1976; rec'd Jessie Dow Award for best painting Montreal Exhn. Drawings & Waterclolours, Nat. Gallery Can. 1964; Queen's Silver Jubilee Medal; R. Tait McKenzie Chair for Sport, Nat. Sport & Recreation Centre Ottawa 1975; incl. in various bibliogs.; Address: R.R. 4, Guelph, Ont. N1H 6J1.

DANCEY, Travis Eugene, B.A., M.D., C.M.; psychiatrist; b. Alymer (West), Ont., 22 Dec. 1905; s. Leon Eugene and Phoebe Alberta (Travis) D.; e. Aylmer Public and High Schs.; McGill Univ. (combined course), B.A. 1930, M.D., C.M. 1934, L.M.C.C. 1934; Cert. Specialist in Psychiatry, R.C.P. & S.(C) 1946, Que. C. of P. & S. 1950; m. Marjorie Janet, d. Dr. John Robertson McEwen, Huntington, Que., 17 Aug. 1935; one s. John Travis, M.D.; Sr. Psychiatrist, Dept. of Psychiatry, Montreal Gen. Hosp.; Consultant in Psychiatry, Verdun Prot. Hosp.; Assoc. Prof. of Psychiatry, McGill Univ.; Rotating Interne, Montreal Gen. Hosp., 1934-35; Post-grad. training and Res. Psychiatric, Verdun Prot. Hosp., 1935-42; Dist. Psychiatrist, Montreal Area, 1942-44; Specialist in Psychiatry, No. 1 Neurol. Hosp., England, 1944; C.O., No. 1 Candn. Exhaustion Unit, N.W. Europe, 1944 to end of war; discharged with rank of Major; Dir., Dept. of Psychiatry, Queen Mary Veterans Hosp., and Adviser in Psychiatry to Dir. Gen. of Treatment Services, Dept. of Veterans Affairs, 1945-69; private practice in psychiatry 1945 to present; Presbyterian (mem. of Session Knox Crescent and Kensington Chs., Montreal); Address: 6550 Sherbrooke St. W., Montreal, Que. H4B 1N6

DANCY, Keith Jules; broadcasting executive; b. Toronto, Ont., 30 June 1929; s. Frank and Daisy (Smith) D.; e. Toronto Pub. and High Schs.; m. Jeannine Margaret (Walker); children: Michelle (Mrs. Stone), Robert, David, Melissa; PRES. ADAM/DANY INC., CJRN 710 INC. TI-CAT FOOTBALL NETWORK; Dir., Grant Broadcasting Ltd.; Radio Bureau of Can.; began as High Sch. Reporter with CFRB, Toronto 1945-47; Announcer CHVC Niagara Falls, Ont. and CKDO, Oshawa, Ont. 1947; Announcer/writer with Northern Broadcasting, Kirkland Lake and Peterborough, 1948, CFNB Fredericton 1949; Announcer, Sports Dir. and Sales Mgr. at CFCF Montreal 1950-58; Mgr. CKSL London, Ont. 1959; co-founded CFOX Montreal and was Extve. Vice Pres. and Gen. Mgr. 1960-67; founded CKJD Sarnia 1968; merged his interests with Rogers Broadcasting and named Pres. and Dir. 1971; Past-Pres., Broadcast Extve. Soc.; former Rotary Club mem., London, Sarnia and Port Credit, Ont.; Past Pres., Lakeshore Rotary, Montreal, Que.; mem., Thousand Island Assn.; CAB Quarter Century Club; Anglican; recreations: tennis, swimming, boating, golf; Clubs: Hamilton Thistle; Toronto Downtown Tennis; Cedar Springs Racquet (Burlinton); Long Boat Key Golf Tennis (Florida); Hamilton Chamber of Comm.; Home: 104 Colonial Crt., Burlington, Ont.; Office: Suite 1408, 2 Carlton St. Toronto, Ont. M4P 2C9

DANCY, Terence E., B.Sc., A.R.C.S., Ph.D., D.I.C.; process metallurgist; b. Coulsdon, Surrey, Eng., 5 March 1925; s. Ernest William and Phyllis Nancy (Sharpe) D.; e. Highgate Sch., London, 1936-42; Imp. Coll. of Science Technol., B.Sc., (Chem.) and A.R.C.S. 1945, Ph.D. (Fuel Technol.) and D.I.C. 1948; Howe Mem. Lectr. (AIME) 1977; m. Edna Annis, d. Albert Ernest Abnett 12 Feb. 1947; two d. Marion Julia, Helena Mary; VICE PRES. TECHNOLOGY, SIDBEC AND SIDBEC-DOSCO LTD. since 1971; Dir., Sidbec-Normines Inc.; Sr. Scient. Offr. Brit. Iron & Steel Research Assn., Iron Making Div., London, 1947-53; Comm. Devel. Offr. 1954-56; U.K. Rep., Comité Internat. du Bas Fourneau, Liège, 1950-53; Scient. Liaison Offr., Brit. Commonwealth Scientific Office, Washington, D.C., 1953-54; with Jones & Laughlin Steel Corp., Pittsburgh, Pa., 1956-71; served as Research Supvr., Asst. Dir. Research, Asst. to Vice Pres. Engn. & Planning and Mgr., Process Engineering; Bethel Park, Pa. Planning & Zoning Comn., 1970-71; rec'd Hunt Medal (A.I.M.E.) 1960; Kelley Award (A.I.S.E.) 1963; Institute Medal (A.I.S.I.) 1965 & 1981; 1977 Howe Memorial Lecturer (AIME); author numerous tech. papers and ed. several books incl. co-ed., "Blast Furnace Theory and Practice", 1970; mem., Am. Inst. Mining Metall. & Petroleum Engrs.; Am. Soc. Metals (Fellow 1974); Metall. Soc. (Dir. 1969-71); Assn. Iron & Steel Engrs.; Can. Inst. of

Min. & Metall.; Office: 507 Place d'Armes, Montreal, Que. H2Y 2W8

D'ANDREA, Antonio, Dottorato in Filosofia, F.R.S.C.; b. Messina, Italy 22 Nov. 1916; s. Nunzio and Italia (Bassi) D'A.; e. High Sch. Messina 1931, Liceo Classico Messina 1934; gained first place Concorso competition admission Scuola Normale Superiore, Pisa 1934; Univ. of Pisa, Dottorato in Filosofia 1939; PROF. OF ITALIAN, McGILL UNIV. since 1964; chargé de cours Univ. of Pisa 1944-45; Visiting Prof. McGill Univ. 1949, Assoc. Prof. 1956, Chrmn. of Italian 1964-76; Dir. Italian Cultural Inst. Montreal 1962-64; Pres. F.C.A.C. Que. Dept. Educ. 1971-73; Pres. Sous-comité d'évaluation Conf. des Recteurs 1976-78; Visiting Prof. of Italian Univ. of Cal. 1978; rec'd Stella della Solidarietà italiana; Commendatore, Ordine al Merito della Repubblica (Italiana); Queen's Silver Jubilee Medal; Vice Provveditore agli Studi, Prov. of Pisa 1944-45; co-ed. "Discours contre Machiavel" 1974; "Yearbook of Italian Studies" 1971-75; author various articles; mem. Candn. Soc. Italian Studies (Past Pres.); Assn. des Profs. d'Italien du Qué. (Past Pres.); Candn. Soc. for Renaissance Studies; Royal Soc. of Canada; Club: University; Home: 66 Sunnyside Ave., Westmount, Que. H3Y 1C2; Office: Samuel Bronfman Bldg., 1001 Sherbrooke St. W., Montreal, Que. H3A 1G5.

DANE, Nazla L.; public relations consultant; b. Indian Head, Sask., 6 June 1906; d. John James and Nazla (Atolla) D.; e. Heward (Sask.) Cont. Sch.; Regina (Sask.) Coll. Inst.; Regina (Sask.) Normal Sch.; taught pub. and secondary sch. in Sask. 1925-33, during last 2 yrs. was Princ. of sch. in Cadillac; held positions in business organs. in Regina, Vancouver and then in Depts. of Munitions and Supply and Transport, Ottawa, during World War II; apptd. Dir., Educ. and Women's Divs., Candn. Life Ins. Assn. 1945-71; has been active in Candn. Pub. Relations Soc. (Toronto Branch), Women's Candn. Club, Toronto, Local Council of Women Toronto, Inter-Club Council for Women in Pub. Affairs Toronto, Soroptimist Club Toronto, YWCA of Can.; mem. Bd., VON Toronto; Metro Toronto Legal Services Clinic; has been Club, Prov. and Nat. Pres., Candn. Fed. of Business & Prof. Women's Clubs (Life mem. 1966); Vice Pres. and mem. Extve., Internat. Fed. of Business & Prof. Women, 1968, Pres. 1971 (Immediate Past Pres. and U.N. Chrmn. 1974-77); recreations: reading, writing, volunteer work, Canadiana; Address: 117 Old Forest Hill Rd., Toronto, Ont. M5P 2R8

DANIEL, C. William, B.A.Sc., P.Eng.; industrialist; b. Toronto, Ont., 17 Feb. 1925; s. Thomas Edward and Emily Anna (Hicks) D.; e. John Ross Robertson Pub. Sch. and Lawrence Park Coll. Inst., Toronto; Univ. of Toronto, B.A.Sc. (Mining Engn.) 1947; m. Ruth Elizabeth, d. late Dr. Harry Roberts Conway, 27 Dec. 1947; children: David William, Colleen Elizabeth (Mrs. Greg Sumner), Karen Louise (Mrs. H. Terrence Kelly), Robert Conway; PRESIDENT, CHIEF EXTVE. OFFR. AND DIR., SHELL CANADA LTD. since 1974; Pres. and Dir. Shell Investments Ltd.; Dir., Shell Can. Resources Ltd.; Bank of Montreal; Mutual Life Assurance Co. of Can.; joined Royal/Dutch Shell group 1947; served in petroleum engn. assignments USA, The Netherlands, Venezuela and Can.; mang. assignments Production Dept., Shell Canada Ltd., Calgary, Alta. 1959-62; Gen. Mgr., Shell Trinidad Ltd., Port Fortin, 1963; Production Dept. Mgr., Shell Canada Ltd. Calgary 1965, Gen. Mgr. Information and Computer Services, Toronto 1968, Vice Pres. Transport. and Supplies 1969; Dir., The Conc. for Candn. Unity; Vice-Chmn. and Dir. of Conference Bd. of Can.; Wellesley Hospital; Trustee, Ont. Sci. Centre; Chmn., Dir. and mem., Nat. Bd. of Governors, Junior Achievement of Can.; mem., Policy Comm., Bus. Council on Nat. Issues; mem., Assn. Prof. Engrs. Ont.; Univ. of Toronto Engn. Alumni Assn. United Church; recreations: golf, fishing, skiing; Clubs: Toronto; Rideau (Ottawa); Rosedale Golf

Club; The Goodwood Club; Office: 505 University Ave., Toronto, Ont. M5G 1X4

DANIELS, James Maurice, M.A., D.Phil. F.R.S.C., F. Inst. P., F.R.S.A.; b. Leeds, Eng., 26 Aug. 1924; s. Bernard and Mary Mahala (Proctor) D.; e. Cross Flatts Sch., Leeds, 1930-35; Leeds (Eng.) Grammar Sch., 1935-42; Jesus Coll., Oxford Univ., B.A. 1945; M.A. 1949, D.Phil. 1952; children: Ian Nicolas James, Maurice Edward Bruce; PROF. OF PHYSICS, UNIV. OF TORONTO, since 1961 and Chrmn. of Dept. 1969-73; Exper. Asst., Radar Research and Devel. Estab., Malvern, 1944-46; Tech. Offr., I.C.I. Explosives, 1946-47; Nuffield Fellow, Oxford Univ., 1951-52 and I.C.I. Fellow 1952-53; Asst. Prof., Univ. of B.C., 1953-56, Assoc. Prof. 1956-60, Prof. 1960-61; UNESCO "Expert", Univ. of Buenos Aires, Dec. 1958-Jan. 1959; Visiting Prof., Instituto de Fisica Bariloche, Argentina, 1960-61; Visiting Prof., Low Temp. Lab., Helsinki Univ. of Technology 1974; Visiting Prof., Columbia Univ., 1978-79; has served on various govt. comtes.; author, "Oriented Nuclei - Polarized Targets and Beams", 1965; other writings incl. over 60 publs. in various journs.; Guggenheim Fellow; socio activo de la Asociacion Fisica Argentina; mem. Amer. Physical Soc.; Candn. Assn. of Physicist's; N.Y. Acad. of Sciences; recreation: skiing, mountaineering; Home: 44 Charles St. W., Apt. 4003, Toronto, Ont. M4Y 1R8

DANIHER, Ernest Clayton, B.A., M.B.A.; advertising executive; b. Toronto, Ont., 1 June 1923; s. Ernest Leroy and Ethel May (Noble) D.; e. Univ. of Toronto Schs.; Univ. of W. Ont., B.A. (Hons. Bus. Adm.) 1949; Harvard Grad Sch. of Bus. Admn., M.B.A. 1951; m. Marion Elizabeth, d. Howard C. Norris, 18 Aug. 1951; children: Michael Shaun, Katharine Anne; PRES., COMCORE HOLDINGS INC.; Dir., Canadian National Sportsmen's Shows; Assoc. Br., Promotion Manager, Procter & Gamble Company (Canada) Limited, 1951; F. H. Hayhurst Company Limited, 1957; Vice-President, 1959; Executive Vice-President, 1961; Pres., 1965; Pres., James Lovick Ltd., 1970; served in R.C.A.F., rank Flying Offr. (Pilot); mem. Inst. Candn. Advertising; Delta Upsilon; Conservative; United Church; recreations: golf, fishing, farming; Clubs: Rosedale Golf; Granite; Caledon Trout; Home: 61 St. Clair Ave. W., Ste. 208, Toronto, Ont. M4V 2Y8; Office: 60 Bloor St. W., Toronto, Ont. M4W 3B8

DANN, Ven. Robert Philip, B.D., M.A. (Ang.); e. Univ. of Toronto, B.A., M.A.; Wycliffe Coll., Toronto; RECTOR, ST. PAUL'S CH.; o. 1941 and served in the Diocese of Fredericton, N.B., till 1944; Incumbent of the Parish of N. Essa, Ont., 1944-47; apptd. Archdeacon of Etobicoke, 1953 and prior present post was Rector of St. George's-on-the-Hill, Islington, Ont.; Home: 114 Roxborough Drive, Toronto, Ont. M4W 1X4; Office: St. Paul's Church, 227 Bloor St. E., Toronto, Ont. M4W 1C8

DANNER, William Edward; pharmaceutical manufacturer; b. Perth, Ont., 16 Sept. 1928; s. late Helen (McNeely) and E. L. Danner; e. Public School and Coll. Inst., Perth, Ont.; Univ. of B. Columbia, 1952; separated; is Chmn. of the Bd., Wampole Inc. (Estbd. 1905); mem. Proprietary Assoc. of Canada; Clubs: Granite; Laurentian (Ottawa); York Downs Golf; Links O'tay Golf (Perth); Sigma Chi; Anglican; recreations: golf, fishing, hunting, boating, curling; Home: R.R. #2, Portland, Ont. K0G 1V0; Office: Dufferin St., Perth, Ont. K7H 3E6

DANSEREAU, Bernard, Q.C., B.A., LL.B.; lawyer (retired); b. Outremont, Que., 29 July 1914; s. Alfred and Georgianna (Payette) D.; e. Querbes Academy, Outremont; Jean-de Brébeuf Coll. B.A. 1934; Univ. of Montreal, LL.B. 1937; m. Viola, d. James Prevost, Port Daniel W., P.Q. 20 July, 1940; read law with Brown, Montgomery & McMichael, Montreal, 1934-37; called to Bar of Montreal, 1938; cr. Q.C. 1953; practised law originally with the Hon. John Hall Kelly, Q.C., M.L.C., New Carli-

sle, P.Q. 1938-40; joined Imasco Ltd. as Solicitor, 1946; Gen. Solr., 1953; Gen. Counsel, 1963; Vice-Pres. & Dir., 1969; served in 2nd World War as Lieut. R.C.N.V.R. 1939-45; Gov., Univ. of Sherbrooke; Child Mary Hospital, Montreal, Que.; Montreal General Hospital; mem., Candn. Bar Assn.; Quebec Bar Assn; Assn. Candn. Gen. Counsel; Clubs: Chapleau, La Minerve, Que.; Saint James's; Montreal Badminton & Squash; R. Catholic; Home: 4855 Côte St. Luc Road, Montreal, Que. H3W 2H5

DANSEREAU, Dollard, Q.C.; b. Montreal, Que., 21 Nov. 1909; s. J.-Emile and Eveline (Guertin) D.; e. Collège Ste.-Marie, Montreal, Que.; Faculty of Law, Univ. of Montreal; m. Mariette, d. Wilfrid Fleury, 3 March 1935; children: Hélène, Colette, Lucien, Gilles, Anne-Marie; Judge, Court of the Sessions of the Peace, Montreal, since 1971; Dir., Campagnie d'Assurance vie La Solidarite de Québec; began his career in journalism as Ed. with "L'Ordre", 1933-35; became Ed.-in-Chief, "L'Illustration" (now "Montreal Matin"), 1936; read law with Pager, Cloutier and Archambault, Montreal, Que.; with Prov. Secy's Dept. and Advocate of Dept. of Insurance, a post which he occupied until 1941; named Crown Prosecutor, 1944; Asst. Atty.-Gen. for Dist. of Montreal, 1950-53; called to Bar of Que., 1936; cr. Q.C., 1953; mem., Soc. Amicales des Aveugles (Pres.); Conservative; R. Catholic; Home: 3250 Forest Hill, Montreal, Que. H3V 1C8

DANSEREAU, Jean-Claude; Petroleum executive; political party executive; b. Montreal, Que. 11 July 1930; s. late Gaston and late Flore (Guimond) D.; e. Externat Ste-Croix, Classical Studies; Univ. of Chicago, Adm. Course; m. Jeannine d. late Ls.-Theophile Ayotte 24 Apl. 1954; one d. Danielle; Services Coordinator, Imperial Oil Ltd.; joined Co. 1949; Pres., Les Entreprises J.P.C. Inc.; Vice Pres. Erenaure Inc.; mem. Organ. Comte. Jean Lesage Team 1960; Regional Dir., Lib. Party of Can. (Que.) 1966, Co-Chrmn. Prov. Convention 1968, Secy. 1968-70 and 1972-79, Acting Pres. 1979, Pres. 1979, 1982-83; Organ. Secy. and Jt. Dir. Trudeau Leadership Team 1968; Pres., Lib. Assn. Mercier Riding 1971- ; Vice Pres. Bd. Dirs. Louis-Hyppolite Lafontaine Hosp.; K. of C.; Liberal; R. Catholic; recreations: golf, tennis, swimming; Club: Kiwanis Metropolitan (Past Pres.); Home: 2735 Mercier St., Montreal, Que. H1L 5H8; Office: 10515 Notre-Dame St. E., Montreal East, Que.

DANSEREAU, Pierre, C.C. (1969), B.Sc., D.Sc., F.R.S.C.; university professor (emeritus); b. Montreal, Que., 5 Oct. 1911; s. Jean Lucien and Marie (Archambault) D.; e. Coll. Ste. Marie, B.A. 1931; Inst. Agricole d'Oka, B.Sc. (Agric.) 1936; D.Sc. Univ. de Genève 1939, Univ. of N.B. 1959, Sir George Williams 1971; Univ. of Sask., LL.D. 1959; Univ. de Strasbourg 1970; Sherbrooke 1971; Memorial 1974; Guelph 1973; Western Ont. 1973; McGill 1976; Ottawa 1978; Dr. Environmental Studies Waterloo 1972; m. Francoise, d. Henri Alexandre Masson, 29 Aug. 1935; Prof. of Ecol., Centre de Recherche Ecol., Univ. du Quebec 1972-76; Prof. Emeritus Univ. du Que., à Montréal since 1976; member Science Council of Can.; Vice Pres. Candn. Comte for the Internat. Biol. Program; Bot., Montreal Bot. Gdn., 1939-42; Dir., Service de Biogéographie, Montreal, 1943-50; Asst. and Assoc. Prof. Dept. of Bot., Univ. of Mich., 1950-55; Dir., Inst. Botanique, Univ. de Montréal, and Dean, Faculty of Science, 1955-61; Asst. Dir., N.Y. Bot. Gdn., Prof. of Bot. and of Geog., Columbia Univ., 1961-68; Trustee, Cranbrook Inst. of Science, Mich., 1953-62; received Médaille Fermat, Toulouse, 1960; Consejero de Honor - Consejo Superior de Investigaciones Cientificas, Madrid, 1960; Massey Medal, Royal Canadian Geog. Soc. 1973; NATO Sen. Scientist Fellowship, 1977; author: "Biogeography, An Ecological Perspective", 1957; "Contradictions & Biculture", 1964; "Inscape and Landscape", 1973; "La terre des hommes et le paysage intérieur", 1973; "Harmony and Disorder in the Canadian Environment,"

1975; "Harmonie et désordre dans l'environment canadien" 1980; ed. "Challenge for survival: Land, Air, and Water for Man in Megalopolis", 1970; contrib. to many Candn. and foreign journs.; also chapters in several books; Pres. Candn. Mental Health Assn. (Que. Div.); Vice-Chrmn. Candn. Env. Adv. Council; co-winner of Molson Prize 1974; member, Ecological Society America (Vice President 1969); Royal Society N.Z. (hon.); Candn. and Am. Geog. Socs.; R. Catholic; recreations: swimming, skiing; Home: 76 Maplewood, Outremont, Montreal, Que. H2V 2M1

DANSON, Hon. Barnett J., P.C. (1974); b. Toronto, Ontario, 8 Feb. 1921; s. late Joseph B. and late Sadie W. D.; e. Pub. and High Schs., Toronto; m. Isobel, d. J. Robert Bull, London, Eng., 6 Feb. 1943; four s., Kenneth B., John A. H., Timothy S. B., Peter T. J.; VICE CHMN. AND DIRECTOR, THE DEHAVILLAND AIRCRAFT OF CAN. LTD.; Dir., Victoria and Grey Trust Co., Methon Energy Corp. Inc.; el. to H. of C. for York N. in g.e. 1968; re-el. 1972 and 1974; Parlty. Secy. to Prime Min. 1970-72; Min. of State for Urban Affairs 1974-76; Min. of Nat. Defense 1976-79; Danson Corporation Limited established 1953; served with Q.O.R. of Canada 1939-45; rank Lt. on discharge; Dir., North Atlantic Council; Bd. Trade Metrop. Toronto; Organization for Rehabilitation through Training; Liberal; Jewish; recreation: fishing; Clubs: Royal Candn. Mil. Inst.; Donalda Club; Craighleigh Ski; Home: 133 Seaton St., Toronto, Ont. M5A 2T2; Office: 15b Front St. W., Toronto. Ont. M5J 2L6

DANZKER, Mark Harold, O.C.; executive; sportsman; philanthropist; b. 27 Feb. 1902; s. Harry and Rose (Buchwald) D.; e. Winkler, Man. Pub. Sch.; m. Dorothy Miriam d. late John N. Sternberg, Winnipeg, Man. 11 Oct. 1931; Pres., Dort-Mark Ltd.; has served as Chief Extve. Comet Investments Ltd., Danzker Press Ltd., Dormark Oils Ltd., Prairie Drum & Reconditioning Ltd., Rex Billiards Ltd., Twin River-Venus-Sioux Petroleum Exploration Syndicate, Rex Oil & Development Co. Ltd., Winnipeg Baseball Club Ltd.; holds various directorships Cand. co's; consultant on adm. various enterprises and invest. interests; past mem. Winnipeg Grain Exchange; el. to Winnipeg City Council as Ald. 1959, re-el. 5 succeeding 2 yr. terms, served as Acting Depy. Mayor and held numerous positions in addition to regular Council duties; former Chrmn. Winnipeg Finance Comn. and Winter Works Comte.; proponent urban unification; apptd. to Bd. Candn. Freshwater Fish Marketing Corp. 1969; chrmn. many fund raising events and functions; served as Pres. or Chrmn. of Jewish Foundation Man. 1972-76, Chmn. Bd. of Gov. 1980-, Winnipeg Enterprises Corp., Y.M.H.A. Community Centre Winnipeg, Fargo Disaster Fund, Un. Israel Appeal Winnipeg, Winnipeg Goldeyes Baseball Club and other organs.; served as Dir. or Extve. mem. Misericordia Hosp., Community Chest (Div. Chrmn.), Assn. Retarded Children & Adults, Red River Exhn., Candn. Good Roads Assn., Winnipeg and Man. Chambers Comm., Winnipeg Art Gallery, Candn. Centennial Comte. Greater Winnipeg (Treas.), Candn. Olympic Comte., Candn. Jewish Cong.; mem. Citizens' Comte. to acquire Pan-Am. Games for Can., Chrmn. Winnipeg's successful negotiating comte. Brazil 1963; rec'd Centennial Medal 1967; Man. Good Citizenship Award 1974; Fifth Annual Y.M.H.A. Sportsmen's Dinner Award 1977; granted Order of Canada, 1978; Liberal; Hebrew; Club: Glendale Golf & Country (Past Pres.); Address: 1003 - 323 Wellington Cres., Winnipeg, Man. R3M 0A4.

DAOUST, Sylvia, O.C.; R.C.A. (1951); sculptor; b. Montreal, P.Q., 24 May 1902; e. Beaux-Arts, Montreal; winner of 1st Prize, Willingdon Arts Compet. 1929; P.Q. Schol. to Europe, 1929; assoc., Roy. Candn. Acad.; 1943; has executed portraits busts for Candn. Bar Assn. and Que. Govt.; has exhibited in Can. and U.S., and at Rio 1946; awarded Scholar., Soc. Royale du Can. 1955-56;

Royal Arch. Inst. Can. Medal and Allied Arts Award, Sculpture 1961; executed "Edouard Montpetit" Monument, Univ. de Montréal 1967; "Marie-Victorin E.C." Monument, Jardin Botanique de Montréal 1954; one-man Exhns. incl. Musée du Qué. 1974. Dorval Cultural Centre 1975; Exhn.; "Trois Sculpteurs", Museum of the St. Joseph Oratory of Mt. Royal, 1979-80; mem., Sculptors' Soc. Can.; Address: 2525 Havre Des Iles, C #802, Chomeday, Laval, Que. H7W 4C6

DARBELNET, Jean L., F.R.S.C.; professor emeritus; b. Paris, France 14 Nov. 1904; s. Louis and Augusta (Lailavoix) D.; e. Lycée Carnot and Sorbonne; Agrégé de l'Université de France 1929; m. Elizabeth d. late William P. Matheson, Billings, Mont. 20 Aug. 1938; children: Anne, Robert; Prof. Emeritus Laval Univ. since 1975; Instr. in French, Harvard Univ. 1938-39; Prof. and Chrmn. of French, Dir. French Summer Sch., McGill Univ. 1940-46; Prof. of French Lang. and Lit. Bowdoin Coll. 1946-62; Prof. of Linguistics, Laval Univ. 1962-75; Consultant to Office de la langue française (Quebec); Visiting prof. at Universities of Ottawa, Montreal, Toronto, Alta., and B.C.; served with French Army 1930-31, 1939-40; Palmes académiques (France) 1949; Chevalier de l'Ordre national du Mérite (France) 1967; author "Regards sur le français actuel" 1963; "Pensée et Structure" 1969; co-author "Words in Context" 1973; "Stylistique comparée du français et de l'anglais" 1958; author various articles (in Meta, Babel etc.); mem. du Conseil internat. de la langue française (Paris); Candn. Linguistic Assn. (Pres. 1966-68); Modern Lang. Assn. Am. (Life Emeritus mem.); Translators' Soc. Que. (Hon. mem.); Assoc. of Translators and Interpreters of Ont. (Hon. mem.); recreations: walking, reading; Home: 3034 Louvigny, Quebec City, Quebec G1W 1B1; Office: Laval University, Quebec City, Que. G1K 7P4.

DARE, Lt. Gen. Michael R., C.M.M., D.S.O., C.D.; b. Montreal, Que., 7 Aug. 1917; e. Brantford, Ont.; Imperial Defence Coll., 1965; m. five children; DIR. GEN., R.C.M.P. SECURITY SERV.; joined Dufferin and Haldimand Rifles of Can., 1937; served with Royal Candn. Regt., 1940-42; served in N.W. Europe 1940-43 and 1944-45; apptd. Second-in-Command, Lincoln and Welland Regt., 1945 after serving as Bgde. Maj. with 4th Armoured Bgde.; later became Asst. Adjt. and Q.M. Gen., 4th Candn. Armoured Div.; held several staff offr. appts. in Vancouver, Edmonton and Camp Borden; apptd. G.S.O., HQ. 1st Commonwealth Div. in Korea, 1953; Commdr., Royal Candn. Armoured Corps Sch., Camp Borden, 1954; Candn. base units, Middle East, 1956; returned to Armoured Corps Sch. 1957 and became Dir. of Armour for Candn. Army, 1958; apptd. Dir. of Mil. Training, 1959 and Commdr., 3rd Candn. Inf. Bgde. Group, 1962; became Commdr., 4th Candn. Inf. Bgde. Group, W. Germany, 1962; apptd. Chief of Staff Operations and Training, Mobile Command, 1966; Depy. Chief, Reserves, Candn. Forces Hdqrs., 1966-68; promoted Maj. Gen. 1966, Lt. Gen. 1969; Vice-Chief of Defence Staff 1969-72; seconded to Privy Council, May 1972; Address: RCMP, Ottawa, Ont. K1A 0R2

DARLING, F. Peter; banker; b. Birmingham, Eng., 21 Oct. 1923; s. Frank George and Dora (Humphries) D.; e. Edgbaston Prep. Sch., Birmingham, Eng., 1937; St. Paul's Sch., London, Eng., Sr. Matric. 1940; Queen's Univ. (External); m. Dora Andresen, 6 Dec. 1944; two s., Mark William, Antony Peter; EXTVE. VICE PRES., BANK OF BRITISH COLUMBIA since 1973; Mang. Trainee, Ottoman Bank, London, Eng., 1946-47; Mgr. Foreign Dept., Bank of Toronto, Toronto and Vancouver, 1947-52; Mercantile Bank of Canada, Vancouver, 1954-64; private ins. and real estate business 1965-68; joined Bank of B.C., H.O., as Mgr. Internat. Banking, 1968, Supt. Internat. Banking 1968-69, Asst. Gen. Mgr. 1969, Vice Pres. 1972; served with R.A.F. Active Duty 1941-46; Pilot, Training and Fighter Commands; Fellow. Inst. Candn. Bankers;

recreations: golf, riding, music; Club: The Vancouver; Home: R.R. 1 Galiano Island, B.C. V0N 1P0; Office: 555 Burrard, Vancouver, B.C. V7X 1K1

DARNLEY, Arthur George, M.A., Ph.D.; geoscientist; b. West Hartlepool, Co. Durham, Eng., 28 Feb. 1930; s. Arthur and Dora Lilian (Archer) D.; e. Workshop Coll., Notts., Eng., 1948; Christ's Coll., Cambridge Univ., B.A. 1952, M.A. 1956, Ph.D. 1958; m. Joan, d. Frederick Allen, Cheltenham, Eng., 28 Aug. 1954; children: Robert Arthur, Elizabeth Ann, Ian Gordon; CHIEF, RESOURCE GEOPHYSICS & GEOCHEM. DIV., GEOL. SURVEY OF CAN., since 1972; Geol., Rhodesian Selection Trust (Services) Ltd., N. Rhodesia, 1952-54; Geol., Geol. Survey of Gt. Brit., Atomic Energy Div., London, Eng., 1957; Sr. Geol. 1960; Princ. Geol. 1963; Head, Remote Sensing Methods, Exploration Geophysics Div., Geol. Survey of Can. 1966-71; Chief of Div. 1971; served as tech. adviser and consultant to Internat. Atomic Energy Agency since 1965; Leader Candn. Mineral Exploration del., Brazil, 1972; served with R.A.F. 1948-49; author of numerous publications; mem., Canadian Institute of Mining & Metall.; Geol. Society London; Society Exploration Geophysicists; recreations: flying, travel, silviculture, carpentry; Home: 39 Trimble Cres., Ottawa, Ont. K2H 7M9; Office: 601 Booth St., Ottawa, Ont. K1A 0E8.

da ROZA, Gustavo Uriel, B.Arch., F.R.A.I.C., R.C.A.; university professor; architect; b. Hong Kong, 24 Feb. 1933; s. late Gustavo Uriel and Cecilia Maria (Alves) de R.; e. Liceu Nacional, Macau, 1945-57; La Salle Coll., Kowloon, Hong Kong, 1947-50; Univ. of Hong Kong, B.Arch. (Hons.) 1955; m. Gloria, d. late Stephen Go, 17 June 1961; children: Guia Maria, Gabriella Maria, Gina Maria, Gustavo Uriel III; Gil Vasco; Prof. of Arch., Univ. of Man.; in private arch. practice since 1961; Asst. Arch to late R. Gordon Brown, Hong Kong, 1955; joined teaching staff, Univ. of Hong Kong and began private practice, 1956; taught at Coll. of Environmental Design, Univ. of Cal., Berkeley, 1958-60; joined teaching staff, Univ. of Man., 1960; Finalist in Limited Arch. Comp. for Nat. Gallery of Canda., 1977; rec'd Award, Winnipeg Art Gallery Design Competition, 1967; winner (with assoc. Archs.), nat. competition for design of 1968 Winter Olympic Games Project in Banff; rec'd 1st Prize and 2 Hon. Mentions in nat. House Design Competition, 1965; winning design built as "Man and His Home" Pavilion, Expo 67; rec'd Centennial Hon. Mention for House Design for Sale, Tuxedo, Man.; arch. work shown on nation-wide TV program "This Land is People", 1967; rec'd Can. Council Special Arts Award to study residential arch. in Scandinavia, 1967; drawings exhibited at Royal Acad., London, 1956; Chmn., Can. Housing Design Council, 1775-77; Apptd. Hon. Consul of Portugal in Winnipeg, 1970; el Academician of the Royal Can. Acad. of Arts, 1973; mem., Man. Assn. Archs.; Royal Arch. Inst. Can.; Assn. of Coll. Schools of Arch.; Consular Corps of Winnipeg; Portuguese Assn. of Man.; Can. Equest. Fed.; Visiting Lectr. and design critic numerous Univ. in. N. Am.; R. Catholic; recreations: travel, equestrianship, music; Home: 515 Shaftesbury Blvd., Winnipeg, Man. R3P 0M3

DARRACH, Neil Campbell, B.Sc.A., M.Sc.; company executive; b. Sarnia, Ont. 20 Sept. 1917; s. late Roy Angus and the late Sadie (Campbell) D.; e. Univ. of Guelph, B.Sc.A. 1942; Univ. of Toronto, M.Sc. 1946; Univ. of Western Ont., Business Mang. 1949; PRES. & C.E.O., THE CONTINENTAL GROUP OF CANADA, LTD., Vice-Pres., The Continental Group Inc.; Dir., S.K.D. Mfg. Co. Ltd.; Mill Paper Fibres Ltd.; entire career with present company: Mgr. Research Dept. 1947; Quality Control Supv. 1950; Asst. Plant Mgr. 1951, Plant Mgr. 1952, Gen. Mgr. Mfg.-Metal 1956, Vice-Pres. & Gen. Mgr. 1964; Extve. Vice Pres. 1970-76; served with Candn. Army in European theatre as Lieut. 1942-45; various service decorations; mem., Adv. Council, York Univ.; Business Council on Nat'l Issues; Bd. of Trade of Metro Toronto; Cdn. Chamber of Commerce; Can. Food Processors, Grocery Products Manufacturing Assn.; Adv. Bd. Liberty Mutual Ins. Co.'s; Ont. Business Adv. Council; Atlantic Salmon Assn.; recreations: water painting, antiques; fishing; Clubs: Rosedale Golf; University; Home: 55 Harbour Square, Suite 1112, Toronto, Ont. M5J 2L1; Office: 3080 Yonge St., Toronto, Ont. M4N 3N1

DAS, Jagannath Prasad, M.A., Ph.D.; educator; b. Puri, India, 20 Jan. 1931; s. Sri Biswanath and Nilomoni (Mohanty) D.; came to Canada 1967; e. Utkal Univ. B.A. 1951; Patna Univ. M.A. (Gold Medallist) 1953; Univ. of London, Inst. of Psychiatry, Ph.D. 1957; m. Gita, d. R.C. Dasmohapatra, Jamirapalgarh, India 1955; children: Satya, Sheela; PROF. OF EDUCATIONAL PSYCHOL., UNIV. OF ALBERTA and Dir. Centre for Study of Mental Retardation there; began teaching in India; subsequently at George Peabody Coll. and Univ. of Calif. at Los Angeles before present position; rec'd Kennedy Foundation Fellowship 1963-64; Nuffield Fellowship 1972; Harris Award of International Reading Assoc.; Fellow, Am. Psychol. Assn.; Candn. Psychol. Assn.; mem., Am. Assn. Advanc. Science; Assn. Cross-cultural Psychol.; author of "Intelligence and Learning" 1981; "Simultaneous & Successive Cognitive Processes" 1979. "Mental Retardation for Special Educators" 1978; "Verbal Conditioning and Behaviour" 1969; "Manasika Byadhi" (Mental Illness) 1962; "Samaja" (Society) 1956; also numerous scient. articles in learned and prof. journs.; Home: 11724-38a Ave., Edmonton, Alta. T6J 0L9; Office: Edmonton, Alta.

DATTELS, David Roland; investment dealer; b. Basle, Switzerland, 9 Dec. 1909; s. Christian Henry and Helen Margaret (Allard) D.; e. Toronto Schs.; m. Norma Elliott, d. Norman J. Emlem, Montreal, Que., 19 June 1943; four s. Michael, Stephen Roland, Peter Grant, Timothy David; one d.; Janet Mary (Mrs. Ortrved); President, Dattels & Co. Ltd.; served in 2nd World War 1940-45 with R.C.N.; enlisted as Lt. 1940; trained at H.M.S. "King Alfred" and H.M.S. "Excellent"; served with R.N. destroyers and battleship in Eng., Africa and Mediterranean; survivor of H.M.S. "Airedale" during convoy trip to Malta 1942; returned to Can. 1943 as Extve. Offr., H.M.C.S. "Montreal" and later C.O., H.M.C.S. "Tecumseh" Calgary as Commdr.; retired 1945; Dir., Ont. Soc. for Crippled Children, Toronto; Clubs: Toronto Security Analysts; National (Toronto); Caledon Mountain Trout; Westmount Golf & Country; Home: "Glencaledon", R.R. 2, Caledon, Ont. L0N 1C0; Office: 305 King St. E., Kitchener, Ont. N2G 1B9

DAUDELIN, Charles, R.C.A.; sculptor; b. Granby, Que. 1 Oct. 1920; s. Aimé and Berthe (Lamothe) D.; e. Ecole du Meuble Montreal 1943; studied painting with Fernand Léger N.Y. 1943, 1944 and Paris 1946, 1947-48, also with Henri Laurens (sculptor) Paris; m. Louise d. Marc Bissonnette 1 Oct. 1946; children: Eric, Nanouk, Rémy, Katia, Valérie; concepts for churches and sculpture pieces from tabernacles to baptismal fonts; rep. in various pub. colls.; recipient French Govt. Scholarships Paris 1946-48; Can. Council Arts Award 1968-69, 1972-73 (Lynch-Staunton); sculpture prizes Nat. Arts Centre Ottawa 1966, Place des Arts Montreal 1967, Nouveau Palais de Justice Montreal 1972; Royal Arch. Inst. Can. Allied Arts Award 1973; Address: 17166 chemin Ste-Marie, Kirkland, Que. H9J 2K9.

DAUGHNEY, V. Edward, M.B.A., C.A.; oil company executive; b. Fredericton, N.B., 27 Oct. 1940; s. late Ralph Herman D. and Catherine Cecilia Jones Kinnaird; e. Univ. of N.B., B.B.A. 1961; C.A. 1964; Univ. of W. Ont. M.B.A. 1966; m. Judith, d. Wilfred Boucher, Ravens Head, Eng. 4 Jan. 1969; children: Trevor, Charlotte, Bridget; PRESIDENT, ROXY PETROLEUM LTD. 1981-; Dir., Export Development Corp.; joined Chemcell Ltd. 1966-67; Controller, Dir., Seabrook Farms Frozen Foods Ltd. 1967-69; Analyst, International Capital Corp. 1969-70; Vice Pres. Security Capital Corp. 1970-73; Vice Pres.

and Dir. Slater Walker of Canada, Pres. United Trust Co. 1975-76; Pres., Great Northern Financial Corp. 1976-80; served with R.C.N. (R), rank Sub-Lt.; mem. Candn. Inst. C.A.'s; Office: 480, 708-11th Ave. S.W., Calgary, Alta T2R 0E4

DAUPHINEE, James Arnold, O.B.E., M.D., F.R.C.P.(C), F.R.S.C.; retired; b. New Westminster, B.C., 9 Jan. 1903; s. Lindsay Arnold and Isabella St. Clair Paul (Muirhead) D.; e. Univ. of Brit. Columbia, B.A. 1922; Univ. of Toronto, Ph.D. 1929, M.D. 1930; m. late Doris Anita, d. Rev. Dr. Charles E. Manning, 18 May 1929; children: Catherine; 2ndly Luella Muriel, d. Rev. Charles E. Manning, 7 Oct. 1960; engaged in Hosp. and private practice, 1938-41; returned to private practice after Mil. Service 1945; Hon. Consultant, Dept. of Med., Toronto Gen. Hosp.; Special Lectr., Dept. of Med., Univ. of Toronto; Prof. and Head Dept. of Pathol. Chem., Univ. of Toronto 1947-66, Prof. Emeritus 1968; served in World War 1941-45 with Royal Canadian Army Medical Corps.; with No. 7 Light Field Ambulance, overseas, Medical Specialist, No. 8 Canadian General Hospital, 1942-43; Officer in charge of Medical, No. 11 Candn. Gen. Hosp. and No. 8 Candn. Gen. Hosp., Eng. and N.W. Europe; promoted Capt. 1941, Maj. 1942, Lieut.-Col. 1943; Pres., The Coll. of Phys. & Surg. of Ont., 1954-55; Pres., Med. Council of Can., 1957-58; mem., Candn. Med. Assn.; Ont. Med. Assn.; Am. Soc. of Clin. Investigation; Biochem. Soc.; Toronto Biochem. and Biophys. Soc.; Candn. Physiol. Soc.; Toronto Acad. of Med.; has contrib. various articles to med. journs.; Alpha Omega Alpha; Phi Gamma Delta; Conservative; Anglican; recreations: golf, photography; Clubs: Sydenham; Rosedale Golf; York; Home: 214 Inglewood Drive, Toronto, Ont. M4T 1H9

DAUPHINEE, John; journalist (retired); b. Vancouver, B.C., 6 Aug. 1913; s. Thomas Thore and Eva Bell (McCaul) D.; e. Univ. of Brit. Columbia (two yrs.); m. Isabel Alison, d. Rev. A. W. McIntosh, Vancouver, B.C., 1 Jan. 1938; one s., William Alexander Drew; General Mgr. of The Canadian Press, 1969-78; Reporter, Vancouver "Daily Province", 1935-36; with CP, Vancouver, B.C., 1936-40; Toronto, 1940; News Ed., Ottawa, 1940-44; Gen. Night Ed., Toronto, 1944; News Ed. and Chief of Bureau, London, Eng., 1944-48; Chief of Bureau, New York, 1948-49; Chief of Bureau, Winnipeg, 1950-51; Edmonton, 1951-52; author of "Opportunity in Canada", 1948 and 1958; Gen. News Editor, H.O. 1952-63; Gen. Supt., H.O. 1963-65; Asst. Gen. Mgr. 1965-69; United Church; recreation: photography; Home: Box 384, Deseronto, Ont. K0K 1X0

DAVENPORT, Alan Garnett, M.A.Sc., M.A., Ph.D., F.R.S.C.; engineer; b. Madras, India 19 Sept. 1932; s. late Thomas and May (Hope) D.; e. Cambridge Univ. B.A. 1954, M.A. 1958; Univ. of Toronto M.A.Sc. 1957; Univ. of Bristol Ph.D. (Civil Engn.) 1961; m. Sheila Rand d. late Sidney Earle Smith 13 Apl. 1958; children: Thomas Sidney, Anna Margaret, Andrew Hope, Clare Rand; PROF. AND DIRECTOR, BOUNDARY LAYER WIND TUNNEL LAB., FACULTY OF ENGINEERING SCIENCE, UNIV. OF W. ONT.; recipient Noble Prize 1963; Gzowski Medal, Engn. Inst. Can. 1963, 1978, Duggan Medal 1965; Golden Plate Award, Am. Acad. of Achievement 1965; Prize in Applied Meteorol., Candn. Meteorol. Soc. 1967; Can-Am Civil Eng. Amity Award, Am. Soc. Civil Engrs. 1977; Silver Medal, Assn. Prof. Engrs. Prov. Ont. 1977; co-recipient State-of-Art Civil Engn. Award for report "Structural Safety", Am. Soc. Civil Engn. 1973; Dr. of App. Sc., (honoris causa) Univ. of Louvain 1979; cited in 1981 by Engineering News Record for service to the construction industry; served with RCN (Air Br.) VC 920 Sqdn. 1957-58; mem. Assn. Prof. Engrs. Prov. Ont.; Am. Meteorol. Soc.; Candn. Meteorol. & Oceanographic Soc.; Royal Meteorol. Soc.; Candn. Soc. Civil Engn.; Engn. Inst. Can.; Internat. Assn. Bridge & Structural Engn.; Internat. Assn. Shell Structures; Am. Acad. Mechanics;

Seismol. Soc. Am.; Am. Soc. Civil Engrs.; Am. Concrete Inst.; recreations: tennis, squash; sailing; Home: 412 Lawson Rd., London, Ont. N5G 1X2; Office: London, Ont. N6A 5B9.

DAVEY, E. L., M.D., D.P.H., F.R.C.P.(C).; physician; Canadian public service; b. Toronto, Ont., 1 Nov. 1911; s. Allen George and Rosabel (Scott) D.; e. Univ. of Toronto, M.D. 1935; Sch. of Hygiene, Univ. of Toronto (Rockefeller Foundation Fellowship), D.P.H., 1938; m. Jean May, d. late W. B. Meiners, 16 Jan. 1943; three s. and one d.; Intern, Toronto Western Hosp., 1935-36; Post-Grad. trng. in Eng., 1936-37; in general practice, Toronto, Ont., 1938-40; temporary M.O.H., St. Catherines, Ont., 1940-41; served in 2nd World War; with N.P.A.M., R.C.A.M.C., 1939-40; enlisted in Candn. Army, May 1941 and promoted Capt. and Major in same year; Maj and apptd. to mobilize and command No. 1 Candn. Field Hygiene Sec., R.C.A.M.C., May 1942; proceeded Overseas and apptd. to command No. 7 Candn. Field Hygiene Sec., 3rd Candn. Inf. Div., May 1943 engaged in U.K. and N.W. European operations; apptd. A.D.M.S. (A.M.D.5), Dir. of Hygiene, D.M.S. Directorate, Candn. Mil. Hdqrs., London, Eng., and promoted Lieut.-Col., July 1945; returned to Can. and apptd. A.D.M.S. (A.M.D.5), Dir. of Hygiene, Candn. Army (Active Force), Army Hdqrs., Dept. of Nat. Defence, June 1946; discharged from the Army, Jan 1947; apptd. Asst. Chief, Civil Service Health Divn., Dept. of Nat. Health & Welfare, Feb. 1947 and Chief 1953; Dir. Ottawa Bureau 1962; Comm., Can. Pension Comm. until retirement 1981; cert. as Specialist in Public Health by Royal College of Physicians and Surgeons, 1951; Home: 100 Acacia Ave., Rockcliffe Park, Ont. K1M 0P7

DAVEY, Frank W., M.A., Ph.D.; poet; educator; b. Vancouver, B.C., 19 Apl. 1940; s. Wilmot Elmer and Doris (Brown) D.; e. Univ. of B.C., B.A. 1961, M.A. 1963; Univ. of S. Cal., Ph.D. 1968; m. Linda Jane, d. W. E. McCartney, Vancouver, B.C., 20 Nov. 1969; children: Michael Gareth, Sara Genève; Teaching Asst., Univ. of B.C., 1961-63; Lectr., Royal Roads Mil. Coll., Victoria, 1963-66, Asst. Prof. 1967-69; Writer-in-Residence, Sir George Williams Univ., Montreal, 1969-70; Asst. Prof., York Univ., Downsview, Ont. 1970, Assoc. Prof. 1972, Prof. since 1980; rec'd Can. Council Grants or Fellowships 1966, 1971-73, 1974-75; Dept. of Nat. Defence Arts Research Grant 1965, 1966, 1968; author, "D-Day and After", 1962; "City of the Gulls and Sea", 1964; "Bridge Force", 1965; "The Scarred Hull", 1966; "Five Readings of Olson's Maximus", 1970; "Four Myths for Sam Perry", 1970; "Weeds", 1970; "Earle Birney" (Studies in Candn. Lit. No. 11), 1971; "Griffon", 1972; "King of Swords", 1972; "L'an Trentiesme", 1972; "Arcana", 1973; "The Clallam", 1973; "From There to Here: a Guide to English-Canadian Literature since 1960", 1976; "War Poems", 1979; "The Arches", 1980; "Louis Dudek and Raymond Souster", 1980; 1974 Founding ed. two lit. mags., "Tish", 1961-63. "Open Letter", since 1965; Humanities Research Council Subvention, 1974, 1979; mem. of editorial board of The Coach House Press, 1974-; mem., Candn. Assn. Univ. Teachers; Assn. Candn. Univ. Teachers Eng.; Assn. Can. Que. Lit.; Home: 104 Lyndhurst Ave., Toronto, Ont. M5R 2Z7; Office: York University, Downsview, Ont.

DAVEY, Hon. Keith, senator; b. Toronto, Ont., 21 Apr. 1926; s. Charles Minto and Grace Viola (Curtis) D.; e. North Toronto Coll. Inst.; Victoria Coll., Univ. of Toronto, B.A. 1949; children: Douglas, Ian, Catherine; estbd. own communications consultancy, Continuing Communications Ltd. 1969; Dir., AHED Music Corp. Ltd.; Cantol Ltd.; after graduation became Sales Mgr., Radio Stn. CKFH, Toronto, for 11 yrs.; Pres., Toronto and York Young Lib. Assn., 1950; Past Pres., Eglinton Lib. Assn.; Chrmn., Publicity Comte., Ont. Prov. election, 1959; apptd. Nat. Campaign Dir., Liberal Party Can. 1961; subsequently Nat. Organizer of the Party and Extve. Dir.,

Lib. Fed. of Can. till summoned to the Senate, Feb. 1966; Co-Chrmn. Nat. Campaign 1973, 79, 80; Commr. of Candn. Football League, 1966-67; past mem. Bd. Govs., Toronto General Hosp.; Pres., Sportsmen's Mutual Funds; Dir., Shaw Festival; Advisory Bd. of World Press Digest; Candn. Sports Hall of Fame; Candn. Oldtimers Hockey Assoc.; Candn. Opera Co.; Patron of Ronald McDonald House, Toronto; Liberal; United Church; recreations: reading, hockey; Clubs: Rideau; Empire; Hyperion; Home: 33 Warren Rd., Toronto, Ont.; Office: 1867 Yonge St. Ste. 600, Toronto, Ont. M4S 1Y5 and The Senate, Ottawa, Ont. K1A 0A4

DAVEY, Kenneth George, M.Sc., Ph.D., F.R.S.C., F.E.S.C.; b. Chatham, Ont. 20 Apl. 1932; s. William and Marguerite (Clark) D.; e. McKeough Pub. Sch. and Chatham (Ont.) Coll. Inst. 1950; Univ. of W. Ont. B.Sc. 1954, M.Sc. 1955; Cambridge Univ. Ph.D. (Insect Physiol.) 1958; m. Jeannette Isabel d. late Dr. Charles S. Evans 28 Nov. 1959; children: Christopher Graham, Megan Jeannette, Katherine Alison; DEAN OF FACULTY OF SCIENCE, YORK UNIV. 1981-; Prof. of Biol., 1974-; Nat. Research Council Post-doctoral Fellow, Dept. Zoo. Univ. of Toronto 1958-59; Drosier Fellow, Gonville and Caius Coll. Cambridge Univ. 1959-63; Assoc. Prof. Inst. Parasitol. McGill Univ. 1963-66, Dir. of Inst. 1964-74, Prof. of Parasitol. and Biol. 1966-74; Chmn. of Biol., York Univ. 1974-81; Pres. and Chrmn. Bd. Dirs. Huntsman Marine Lab. St. Andrews, N.B. 1977-80; mem. Tropical Med. & Parasitol. Panel, US Nat. Insts. Health; Candn. Nat. Comte. Internat. Union Biol. Sciences; author "Reproduction in the Insects" 1965, Spanish ed. 1966; over 100 scholarly articles in various scient. journs. dealing with endocrinology of invertebrate animals; Assoc. Ed. "Canadian Journal of Zoology"; "International Journal of Invertebrate Reproduction"; Ed. Bd. "International Journal for Parasitology"; rec'd Queen's Silver Jubilee Medal; mem. Candn. Soc. Zools. (Extve., Nominating Comtes. V.P. 1979, 1980, Pres. 1981); Mem., Animal Biology Comte., Nat. Sciences and Engineering Research Council Canada; European Soc. Nematol.; Soc. Exper. Biol.; Entomol. Soc. Can.; Candn. Comte. Univ. Biol. Chrmn. (Chrmn. 1975-77); Biol. Council Can. (Pres., 1979-81); recreation: wine and food; Home: 194 Banbury Rd., Don Mills, Ont. M3B 3C5; Office: 4700 Keele St., Downsview, Ont. M3J 1P3:

DAVID, Jacques Lefaivre,B.Arch., R.C.A.; architect; b. Montreal, Que. 11 Nov. 1921; s. Charles, D.Sc. and Pauline (Lefaivre) D.; e. Coll. Mont-St-Louis Montreal Dipl. Science 1941; McGill Univ. B.Arch. 1946; SR. PARTNER, DAVID, BOULVA, CLEVE-ARCHITECTS; maj. projects incl. Palais de Justice de Montréal; Dow Planetarium Montreal; Place des Arts Master Plan; Théâtres Port-Royal & Maisonneuve; Hdqrs.: Banque Canadienne Nationale; Banque Nationale du Can.; Bell Canada Que. Region; Mercantile Bank of Can.; Alliance-Mutuelle-Vie Montreal; Royal Bank Centre Ottawa; Fed. Govt. Accommodation Program Hull, Que. (Phase III); Le Régence Hyatt Hotel Montreal; mem. Ordre des Architectes du Qué.; Ont. Assn. Archs.; Royal Arch. Inst. Can.; Zeta Psi (Pres.); R. Catholic; recreations: golf, tennis, reading, writing; Club: Mount Bruno Country; Home: 1455 Sherbrooke St. W., Apt. 2606, Montreal, Que. H3G 1L2; Office: 1253 McGill College Ave., Suite 800, Montreal, Que. H3B 2Z9.

DAVIDSON, Albert, C.A.; manufacturing executive; b. Toronto, Ont. 28 Jan. 1917; s. Hedley and Maggie Ann (Fordyce) D.; e. Public Sch. and Central High Sch. of Commerce, Toronto, Ont. (Gen. Business Cert. 1934); Inst. of C.A.'s of Ont.; C.A. 1942; m. Elizabeth Donald, d. late Wm. Ferguson, Toronto, Ont., 5 Sept. 1942; children: Wm. Donald, Catharine M., Elizabeth Ann; Pres. and Dir., Harding Carpets Ltd., 1967-78; Dir., Western Foundry, Wingham, Ont.; Harvey Woods Ltd.; Assoc. Dir., C.N. Exhibition; mem. Candn. Advisory Bd. of Ark-

wright Boston Insurance; engaged in auditing with C.P.A., Toronto, 1934-36, and Jenkins & Hardy, C.A.'s 1936-42; Jr. Partner, Lever & Hospin, C.A.'s Toronto, Ont. 1945-46; Secy.-Treas., Lily Cups Ltd., 1946-50; Comptroller, Carpet Div., Harding Carpets Ltd., 1950-54, Asst. Gen. Mgr., 1954-57, Gen. Mgr., 1957; apptd. Gen. Mgr. of the Co., Dec. 1959; el. a Dir., 1960; Extve. Vice Pres. 1962; served in 2nd World War; Capt., Candn. Army, R.C.O.C., 1942-45; Past Pres., Candn. Carpet Inst.; Past Chrmn., Brantford United Appeal; Past Chmn., Ont. Div., Candn. Mfrs. Assn.; Presbyterian; recreations: yachting, skiing, tennis; Club: Brantford (Past Pres.); Home: Woodend Place, R.R. 2, Woodbridge, Ont. L4L 1A6

DAVIDSON, Alexander Thomas, M.A.; public servant; b. Fort William, Ont., 11 Jan. 1926; s. Oliver Mowat and Charlotte Emma (Potter) D.; e. Queen's Univ., B.A. 1948; Univ. of Toronto, M.A. 1951; m. Joan Adeline, d. Frederick Alexander, 6 Aug. 1955; four s.: Chuck, Ronald, James, John; ASST. DEPY. MIN. PARKS CANADA, Dept. of Indian & Northern Affairs since 1973; Adm. Asst. to Depy. Min. of Nat. Resources, Sask., 1950; Sr. Planning Offr., 1951; Asst. Depy. Min., 1953; Chief, Resources Div., Dept. N. Affairs & Nat. Resources, 1958; Dir., Agric. Rehab. & Devel., Dept. of Agric., 1961-65; Asst. Depy. Min., Rural Devel., Dept. of Forestry, 1965-66; Asst. Depy. Min. (Water), Dept. Energy, Mines and Resources, 1966-71, Policy, Planning and Research, Dept. of the Environment 1971-73; served in 2nd World War in R.C.N.V.R., 1944-45; Dir., Candn. Assn. of Geographers; Mem. of Bd. of Royal Canadian Geographical Society; Mem. of Bd. of Governors of Heritage Canada; Mem. of Can. Inst. of Forestry; Inst. of Public Administration; United Church; recreations: fishing, skiing, curling; Home: 5 Okanagan Dr., Ottawa, Ont. K2H 7E7; Office: Rm. 2106, 400 Laurier Ave. W., Ottawa, Ont. K1R 5C6

DAVIDSON, George Forrester, C.C. (1973), M.A., Ph.D., LL.D., L.H.D., D.Litt.; b. Bass River, N.S., 18 Apl. 1909; s. Oliver Wendell and Emma Jane (Sullivan) D.; e. Elem. Sch., Bass River; Duke of Connaught High Sch., New Westminster, B.C.; Univ. of Brit. Columbia, B.A. 1928, LL.D. 1955; Harvard Univ., M.A. 1930, Ph.D. 1932; L.H.D. Brandeis Univ. 1961; LL.D., Univ. of Victoria, 1968; D.Litt. Acadia 1973; LL.D. McMaster 1973; D. Adm., Univ. of Ottawa, 1977; m. Elizabeth Ruth, d. Frank Henderson, Vancouver, 9 July 1935; children: Roger Reynolds, Craig Sullivan, Barbara Louise; m. (2nd) Anneke Irene, d. Johannes Kuiper Kent, Connecticut, 15 June 1975; SPECIAL ADVISER TO EXCTVE. DIR., UNITED NATIONS FUND FOR POPULATION ACTIVITIES 1980-; Prov. Supt. of Welfare and Neglected Children, Prov. of B.C., 1934-35; Extve. Dir., Vancouver Welfare Fed. and Council of Social Agencies, 1935-39; Dir. of Social Welf., Prov. of B.C., 1939-42; Extve. Dir., Candn. Welf. Council, 1942-44; Depy. Min. Dept. Nat'l Health & Welfare 1944-60; Depy. Min. Dept. Citizen & Immig. 1960-62; Dir., Bureau of Govt. Organ., Privy Council Office 1963-64; Secy. of Treas. Bd., Dept. of Finance, 1964-68; Pres. CBC 1968-72; Under Sec'y. Gen. for Admin. & Management, U.N. 1972-79; Candn. Rep. to U.N. Social Comn., 1947-50; mem. of Candn. del. to U.N. Econ. and Social Council on numerous occasions, 1946-52; Chairman, Social, Humanitarian and Cultural Committee United Nations General Assembly, 1953; Pres., U.N. Econ. & Social Council, 1958; President, Can. Conf. on Social Work, 1952-54; Internat. Conf. of Social Work, 1956-60; Chrmn., Nat. Jt. Council of the Pub. Service of Can., 1954-60; has written numerous reports and articles on social welfare and U.N. problems; United Church; Home: 400 E. 54th St., Apt. 24C, New York, N.Y.; Office: U.N. Headquarters, United Nations Plaza, New York, N.Y. 10017

DAVIDSON, Very Rev. Hugh Fleming, M.A., D.D. (Presb., retired); b. Newton, Ont., 14 Jan. 1909; s. late Alexander M. and May (Fleming) D.; e. Listowel (Ont.) High Sch.; Univ. Coll., Univ. of Toronto, B.A. 1930, M.A. 1933; Knox Coll., Dipl. 1933, D.D. 1960; D. D. (Hon.) Emmanuel College, Victoria Univ., 1975; m. Margaret Elizabeth, d. late William A. MacKay, 1936; children: Janet E. (Mrs. J. L. Sturgis), Alexander M., John R., Mary C.; Apptd. Asst. to the Minister, Knox Church, Listowel, Sept. 1978-; Assoc. Secy., Stewardship Resources, Bd. of Cong. Life 1974-77; Asst. Min., Knox Ch., Toronto, 1933-37; Min., Knox & St. Andrews Ch., Fort Erie, 1938-41; Knox Ch., Oshawa, 1945-50; First Ch., Chatham, Ont., 1951-60; Secy., Bd. of Stewardship & Budget, 1960-73; mem. Comn. on Stewardship, Nat. Council of Ch's. USA, 1960-74; Chrmn., Candn. Interch., Stewardship Comte., 1972-74; Moderator, Presb. Church in Can. 1974-75; served as Chaplain, RCAF, in Can., Eng., N. Africa and Italy, 1941-45; mem. Sch. Bd., Fort Erie, Ont., 1939-41; Bd. of Referees, Unemployment Ins. Comn., Oshawa, 1949-50; Lib. Bd., Chatham, Ont., 1952-60; Victoria Order Nurses Bd., Chatham, 1952-60; Chaplain, Royal Candn. Legion, Oshawa 1945-50 and Chatham 1951-60; recreations: golf, theatre; Home: 520 Argyle Ave. N., Listowel, Ont. N4W 1N6

DAVIDSON, John Roberts, Q.C.; b. Regina, Sask. 28 May 1925; s. Charles Roberts and Alice Isabel (McAra) D.; m. Elsie Ruth Wudrick 2 Sept. 1948; children: John Roberts, Barbara, Margaret; Pres., Alwest Leasing Ltd.; Dir., Orion Petroleums; Almark Resources; Frontier Mudlogging Inc.; called to Bar of Sask. 1952; cr. Q.C. 1972; served with RCNVR 1943-46; mem. Adv. Bd. YWCA; Past Pres. Regina Chamber Comm.; Sask. Chamber Comm.; Past Dir. Candn. Chamber Comm.; mem. Regina Bar Assn.; Sask. Law Soc.; Candn. Bar Assn.; Home: 2721 McCallum Ave., Regina, Sask. S4S 0P8; Office: 2230 Lorne St., Regina, Sask. S4P 2M7

DAVIDSON, Melville Whitelaw, M.A.; association executive; b. Calgary, Alta., 12 June 1912; s. David D. and Jean (Whitelaw) D.; e. McGill Univ., B.A. 1936; Geneva Sch. of Internat. Studies, Switzerland 1936; Columbia Univ., M.A. 1939; War Staff Coll. 1944; Harvard Univ., Advanced Mang. 1967; m. Frances Audrey, d. Herbert A. Locke, 18 Nov. 1944; children: Mrs. Douglas Scott, Ian David, Derek Locke, Leigh Anthes; PRESIDENT, CANADIAN SUGAR INSTITUTE; Vice Pres., Redpath Industries Ltd., 1958-75; joined Redpath at Chatham, Ont. 1945; moved to Montreal H.O. 1960; resident Vice Pres., Ont. 1968-75; served in 2nd World War, R.C.A.F. 1939-45; Air Navigator; Wing Commdr. ret.; awarded Air Force Cross; Polish Air Force Navigator's Award; Dir., Toronto Extve. Comte.; Candn. Mfrs. Assn.; Anglican; recreations: swimming, fishing; Clubs: National; Montreal Univ. Club; Home: 72 Highbourne Rd., Toronto, Ont M5P 2J4; Office: Suite 1904, 7 King St. E., Toronto, Ont. M5C 1A2

DAVIDSON, Neil Anderson, Q.C., LL.B.; b. Stettler, Alta., 23 Feb. 1916; s. Robert Anderson and Jane Simpson (Ogg) D.; e. Univ. of Alta., LL.B. 1940; m. Isabel Muriel, d. Russell Stanley, Edmonton Alts., 29 Apl. 1942; children: Diane Isabel Beaumont, Barbara Jean Reich, Margaret Muriel Newell, Gordon Neil Stanley; MAYOR, CITY OF VERNON, B.C. June 1979-; read law with Hon. R. L. Maitland, Q.C.; called to Bar of B.C. 1941; cr. Q.C. 1969; com. practice of law in Vernon, B.C. as Partner in firm of Morrow and Davidson, 1946; firm became Morrow, Davidson & Seaton 1951; Sr. Partner, Davidson & Co. 1966-77; Chrmn. of B.C. Liquor Board 1973-77; served with RCAF for 4 yrs. during World War II; served on Silver Star Parks Board (Chrmn. 15 yrs.) and with Coll. and Prof. Groups; mem., Candn. Bar Assn.; B.C., Vernon and Yale Bar Assn. (Past Pres.); Liberal; Un. Ch.; recreation: outdoor sports; Home: 1801-27th Ave., Vernon, B.C. V1T 1R3; Office: 4th Floor, 3205-32nd St., Vernon, B.C. V1T 5M7

DAVIDSON, Robert Lyndon, B.A.; banker; b. Willits, Cal. 29 Dec. 1929; s. late Henry B. and late Madge R. (Rupe) D.; e. Univ. of S. Cal. B.A.; Am. Inst. Foreign Trade; m. Corinne d. Reginald Longman, Eng. 21 May 1955; children: Mark, Craig, Brian; CHMN., PRES. AND CEO, MERCANTILE BANK OF CANADA since 1977; served with U.S. Navy 1951-54; recreation: golf; Office: 625 Dorchester Blvd. W., Montreal, Que. H3B 1R3.

DAVIDSON, Roy Mitchell, M.A.; Canadian public servant; b. Los Angeles, Cal., 5 July 1923; s. William and Margaret Lawson (Mitchell) D.; e. Pub. and High Schs., Calgary, Alta.; Univ. of Alta., B.A. 1944; Univ. of Toronto, M.A. 1947; Depy. Head, Bureau of Competition Policy, Dept. of Consumer & Corp. Affairs, since 1974 (formerly Sr. Econ. Adv.); joined govt. service as Jr. Adm. Asst., Dept. of Justice, 1947; apptd. Combines Offr. 1948; Dir. of Merger & Monopoly Br., Combines Investigation Office, 1960; served with RCAF 1944-45; rank Pilot Offr., mem., Candn. Econ. Assn.; Am. Econ. Assn.; YMCA; United Church; recreations: tennis, handball; Clubs: Cercle Universitaire; Pinecrest Tennis Club; Home: 173 Cooper St., Apt. 1101, Ottawa, Ont. K2P 0E9; Office: Place du Portage, Ottawa-Hull K1A 0C9

DAVIDSON, William Donald, B.A.Sc., M.Comm., P.Eng.; executive; b. Toronto, Ont. 20 Mar. 1924; s. Frank Perry and Florence Irene (Salter) D.; e. Central Tech. Sch., Tech. Dipl. 1941; Parkdale Coll. Inst., Sr. Matric. 1942; Univ. of Toronto, B.A.Sc. (Engn. and Business) 1950, M.Comm. 1951; Soc. of Indust. Accts., R.I.A. 1962; m. Alice Sylvia Weiss 4 June 1949; children: Andrea Dawn, Blair Foster; PRES., DOMTAR CHEMICALS GROUP, DOMTAR INC. since 1976; Extve. Vice-Pres., Domtar Chemicals Ltd., 1975; Vice-Pres., Corp. Devel., Domtar Ltd., 1974; Vice-Pres. and Gen. Mgr., Domtar Newsprint Ltd. 1970; Partner, P.S. Ross & Partners, Nat. Dir. Consulting Services 1957; Partner/Princ. Nat. Dir., Operations Mang. Services, Touche Ross & Co. (U.S.) 1969; served in 2nd World War, R.C.A.F. Heavy Bomber Navig. 1942-46; Past Trustee, Candn. Hunger Foundation; Past Dir., Assn. Prof. Engrs. Ont.; Presbyterian; recreations: golf, swimming, tennis, cycling, cross country skiing; Clubs: Donalda (Toronto); St. James's; Beaconsfield Golf Club; Home: 25 Parfield Dr., Willowdale, Ont. M2J 1C1; Office: 20 Queen St. W., Box 5, Toronto, Ont. M5H 3R3

DAVIES, Arthur Llewellyn; publisher; b. Brantford, Ont., 18 Aug. 1903; s. late Senator William Rupert, (President, The "Kingston Whig-Standard") and Florence (MacKay) D.; e. Renfrew (Ont.) Coll. Inst.; Central Tech. Sch., Toronto; m. Dorothy Eleanor, d. Dr. S. E. Porter, 5 May 1934; two s., Michael, Christopher; m. 2ndly Jean Rowe, 8 July 1969; VICE PRES., THE KINGSTON "WHIG-STANDARD" CO. LTD.; Officer Order of St. John, Honorary; Doctor of Laws, (Queen's); Past Pres., The Kingston Whig-Standard Co. Ltd.; The Peterborough Examiner Co. Ltd.; Frontenac Broadcasting Co. Ltd.; Past Chrmn. of Extve. Comte., Queen's Univ.; Past Chrmn., Kingston Gen. Hosp.; Past Pres., Kingston and District United Fund; Kingston Chamber of Comm.; Ont. Prov. Dailies Assn.; Candn. Daily Newspaper Publishers Assn.; Kingston Community Chest; Freemason; Presbyterian; Clubs: National (Toronto); Kingston Yacht; Home: 245 Alwington Place, Kingston, Ont. K7L 4P9; Office: 306 King St., Kingston, Ont. K7L 4Z7

DAVIES, Frank Thomas, M.Sc., F.R.S.C.; research scientist (retired); b. Merthyr Tydfil, Glam., Wales, 12 Aug. 1904; s. Richard and Jessie (Starr) D.; e. Univ. Coll., Aberystwyth, B.Sc., 1925; came to Canada, 1925; Univ. of Sask., 1925-26; McGill Univ., M.Sc. 1928; Hon. D. Sc. 1978; York Univ. Hon. D.Sc. 1977; m. Ada Eleanor, d. Isaac Edward Bennett, 29 July 1931; two d.: Marian (Mrs. S. N. Nash), June Margaret; Lectr. in Math. and Demonstr. in Physics, Univ. of Sask., 1925-26; Demonstr.,

Physics, McGill Univ., 1926-28; Physicist, First Byrd Antarctic Expdn., 1928-30; Scient., Carnegie Inst., Washington, 1930-32, 1934-39; Leader, Candn. 2nd Polar Expdn. (N.W.T.), 1932-34; Dir., Carnegie Geophysical Observatory, Huancayo, Peru, 1936-39; joined Defence Research Bd. as Scientist; successively Supt. Radio Physics Lab., Dir., Physical Research, Asst. Chief Scientist; Dir.-Gen. Telecommunications 1949-69; author of numerous papers in scient. journs; served in 2nd World War as a civilian working with R.C.N. in scient. and intelligence positions; awarded Antarctic Medal by U.S. Cong., 1930; Gov. and Fellow, Arctic Inst. N. Am.; mem.; Candn. Assn. Physicists; Anglican; recreations: gardening, swimming, reading; Club: Artic Circle; Home: 22 Clegg St., Ottawa, Ont. K1S 0H8

DAVIES, Haydn Llewellyn,R.C.A.; sculptor; b. Rhymney, Wales 11 Nov. 1921; s. Emrys and Rosina (Gallop) D.; e. Central Tech. Sch. (Art) Toronto grad 1939; Ont. Coll. of Art (Fine Art) grad. A.O.C.A. 1947; Univ. of W. Ont. Marketing Management 1964; Univ. of Toronto Fine Art 1972-74; m. Eva d. John Koller 26 June 1948; two s. Haydn Bryan, Trevor Koller; following grad. O.C.A. entered film, TV and advertising business becoming Sr. Vice Pres. and Dir. McCann-Erickson Advertising of Canada Ltd. and Pres. Trevan Properties; resigned 1976 to become full-time sculptor; rep. in pub., corporate and private colls. incl. Lambton Coll. of Arts and Technology, Sarnia, Ont., City Hall West Vancouver, Ont. Govt. Offices Windsor, Burlington Cultural Centre, Galleria Nazionale d'Arte Moderna e Contemporanea Rome, Museo d'Arte Moderna Venice, Musée Royaux des Beaux-Arts de Belgique Brussels, Nat. Museum of Wales; rep. various exhns. incl. Wood Scuplture of the Americas 1977, Monumental Sculpture-7 Sculptors Toronto 1978, Steel-the Engineer and the Sculptor Univ. of W. Ont. 1980; served with RCAF 1941-45; recreation: collecting antiques, art; Club: R.C.Y.C.; Home: 10 Rose Park Cres., Toronto, Ont. M4T 1P9;

DAVIES, John Arthur, M.A., Ph.D., F.C.I.C., F.R.S.C.; research scientist; b. Prestatyn, N. Wales, U.K. 28 March 1927; s. late Francis James and Doris (Edkins) D.; e. Univ. of Toronto B.A. (St. Michael's Coll.) 1947, M.A. 1948, Ph.D. 1950; Univ. of Leeds Post-doctoral Fellow 1954-56; m. Florence Mary d. late Alfred Smithson 29 July 1950; children: Susan Mary, J. Christopher, Catherine M., Paul M., James N., Anne E.; PRINC. RESEARCH OFFR. CHALK RIVER NUCLEAR LABS. ATOMIC ENERGY OF CANADA LTD.; Prof. in Physics and in Engn. Physics (Part-time) McMaster Univ.; joined present Labs. 1950; Visiting Prof. Inst. of Physics, Aarhus Univ. Denmark 1964-65, 1969-70; Cal. Tech. Pasadena 1969; Noranda Award Chem. Inst. Can. 1965; T.D. Callinan Award (first) Am. Electrochem. Soc. 1968; mem. Deep River & Dist. High Sch. Bd. 1959-68, Chrmn. 1 term; Renfrew Co. Bd. Educ. 1969; Deep River & Dist. Hosp. Bd. 1977-83; author "New Uses for Low-Energy Accelerators" 1968; "Ion Implantation of Semiconductors" 1970; "Channeling — Theory, Observation and Applications" 1972; over 120 research papers; Fellow, Danish Royal Akademy of Arts & Sciences; mem. Assn. Chem. Prof. Ont. (Past Chrmn.); R. Catholic; recreations: canoeing, cross-country skiing; Home: 7 Wolfe Ave., Deep River, Ont. K0J 1P0; Office: Chalk River, Ont. K0J 1J0.

DAVIES, John Lovatt, B.Arch.; architect b. Shropshire, Eng., 1914; Grad of Liverpool Univ. Sch. of Arch.; widowed; has two s. and one d.; came to Canada settling in Vancouver in 1947 establ. his own practice two yrs. later; Past Pres. of Royal Arch. Inst. of Canada and of Arch. Inst. of B.C.; Home: Roberts Creek, B.C. V0N 2W0; Office; 923 Denman St., Vancouver, B.C. V6G 2L9

DAVIES, Malcolm Norman, B.A.; retired association executive; b. Liverpool, England, 14 Jan. 1920; came to Can. 1923; e. McGill Univ., B.A., 1940; joined Bell Canada as Traffic Student, Montreal, 1945; held various mang. positions in Traffic, Stat. Rev. Requirements & Acct. 1946-59; Area Traffic Manager, Montreal, 1960; Regional Marketing Mgr. 1961; Asst. Vice Pres. (Revenue Requirements) 1964; Asst. Vice Pres. (Labour Relations) 1965; Vice Pres. (Operations Staff) 1967; Vice Pres. (Planning) 1968, (Business Devel.) 1970; Pres., Candn. Telecommunications Carriers Assn. 1972-78; served with RCAF 1940-45; rank Flight Lt.; Finance Commr., Montreal W., 1965-69; mem., Grad. Soc. McGill Univ.; Clubs: Ottawa Rotary; Montreal Rotary (Past Pres.); Home: 495 Buchanan Cres., Ottawa, Ont. K1J 7V2

DAVIES, Michael Bruce Cook, B. Com., LL.B.; investment banker; b. Berwyn, Alta, 8 Aug. 1939; s. Robert Eric Cook and Nancy Louisa (French) D.; e. Univ. of B.C. B.Com. 1961, LL.B. 1964; m.Susan London, M.A. d. Robert Phillip Kirchheimer, Chicago, Ill. Dec. 1972; one s. Robin Wendel Cook, one d. London Erica; VICE-PRES. CAN. ENERGY GROUP, MORGAN & STANLEY & CO. INC. 1980-; Vice-Pres. Finance, Polar Gas Project 1976-80; Dir. American Hoist of Canada Ltd.; Machinery Investment Co. of Canada Ltd.; joined First National City Bank, New York and The Mercantile Bank of Canada, Toronto serving as Trainee and bank offr. 1966-71; Vice Pres. and Dir. McLeod, Young, Weir & Co. Ltd. Toronto and Montreal 1971-76; read law with Davis & Co. Vancouver; called to Bar of B.C. 1965; mem. Law Soc. B.C.; Candn. Bar Assn.; Anglican; Clubs: Toronto Racquet; RCYC; National; Home: 1148 Fifth Avenue, New York, NY 10028; Office: 1251 Ave. of the Americas, New York, NY 10020

DAVIES, Michael Rupert Llewellyn, B.A., F.R.S.A.; publisher; b. Kingston, Ont., 22 July 1936; s. Arthur Llewellyn and Dorothy Eleanor (Porter) D.; e. Kingston (Ont.) Pub. Sch.; Trinity Coll. Sch., Port Hope (Ont.); Queen's Univ., B.A. 1959; m. Elaine, d. Earl Stephens, 8 Oct. 1960; children: Gregory, Eric, Andrew, Timothy, Jennifer; OWNER & PUBLISHER, THE KINGSTON WHIG-STANDARD CO. LTD., pub. of "The Kingston Whig-Standard" daily newspaper; Gen. Mgr. 1962; Publisher 1968; Sole Prop. 1976; Past mem., Ontario Council for the Arts, 1968-76; Mayor's representative to obtain and install large outdoor sculptures to commemorate Kingston's Tercentenary, 1973; Past Chrmn., Grand Theatre Bd.; Past Pres., Kingston Symphony Orchestra; Past Pres., Ont. Fed. of Symphony Orchestras; Hon. Chrmn., Commonwealth Press Union, Candn. Sec.; Past Pres., Candn. Daily Newspaper Publishers' Assn.; Ont. Prov. Dailies Assn.; Dir., Canadian Press; Past mem., Extve. Comte. and Campaign Chrmn., Stratford Shakespearean Festival; Founding Pres., Kingston Rowing Club; mem. Olympic Organizing Comte. 1976; mem. Mang. Comte. (1965-76) and Pres. (1975), Kingston General Hosp.; mem. Bd. Trustees, Queen's Univ.; Dir., Marine Museum of the Great Lakes, Kingston; Queen's Jubilee Medal 1977; recreations: sailing, music; Clubs: Kingston Yacht; Cataraqui Golf & Country; Toronto; Roy. Dart Yacht; Home: 226 Alwington Place, Kingston, Ont. K7L 4P8; Office: 306-310 King St. E., Kingston, Ont. K7L 4Z7

DAVIES, Robert Henry; C.A.E.; executive; b. Liverpool, Eng., 13 Jan. 1929; s. Joseph and Delia (Dignum) D.; e. De La Salle Grammar Sch. 1946 and Liverpool Tech. Coll. 1949; Univ. of B.C. Extve. Mang. Dipl. 1958; m. Helen, 27 July 1957; four d. Carolyn, Diana, Rita, Linda; EXTVE. DIR. B.C. HEART FOUNDATION since 1968; Lectr., Vancouver Jr. Chamber and Fac. of Comm. and Bus. Adm., Univ. B.C.; Candn. Cancer Soc. 1961-68; served several engn. consulting firms for 13 yrs.; served with Royal Naval Air Service 1949; Certified Assn. Extve. of Inst. of Assn. Extves. and Examiners; Past Pres. Inst. Assn. Extves. (Past Pres. Vancouver Chapter); Cunsultant, Amer. Heart Assoc.; Int. Soc. & Fed. of Cardiology; mem., Amer. Soc. Assoc. Executives; mem. Welsh Soc.; R. Catholic; Clubs: Marine Drive Golf; West Point Golf;

Home: 3295 West 23rd Ave., Vancouver, B.C. V6L 1P9; Office: 1212 West Broadway, Vancouver, B.C. V6H 3V2

DAVIES, Robertson, C.C. (1972), B. Litt., D.Litt., D.C.L., LL.D., F.R.S.C. (1967); author; educator; b. Thamesville, Ont., 28 Aug. 1913; s. Senator William Rupert and Florence (Mackay) D.; e. Upper Can. Coll.; Queen's Univ.; Balliol Coll., Oxford, B.Litt.; Univ. of Alta., LL.D. 1957; McMaster Univ., D.Litt. 1959, York 1973; Mt. Allison, 1973; Memorial, Western, McGill, Trent 1974; Windsor, 1971; Queen's Univ., LL.D. 1962, Manitoba 1972; Bishop's D.C.L. 1967; Calgary, D. Univ., 1975; D.Litt., Univ. of Lethbridge, Waterloo and Toronto 1981; m. Brenda Mathews, 2 February 1940; children: Miranda, Jennifer, Rosamond; Master, Massey College, Toronto, 1963-; Professor of Eng., Univ. of Toronto until retirement 1981; Professor Emeritus and Master Emeritus, Univ. of Toronto; Senator, Stratford Shakespearean Festival 1953; sometime actor and mem. Old Vic Repertory Co. and teacher in Old Vic Theatre Sch., Eng.; returned to Can. as Lit. Ed., "Saturday Night", 1940; became Ed., "Examiner", 1942; author of "Shakespeare's Boy Actors", 1939; "Shakespeare for Young Players", 1942; "Diary of Samuel Marchbanks" 1947; "Eros at Breakfast and Other Plays", 1949; "Fortune My Foe", 1949; "The Table Talk of Samuel Marchbanks", 1949; "At My Heart's Core", 1950; "Tempest Tost", 1951; "A Masque of Aesop", 1952; "Leaven of Malice" 1954; "A Jig for the Gypsy", 1954; "A Mixture of Frailties", 1958; "A Voice from the Attic", 1960; "A Masque of Mr. Punch", 1963; "Marchbanks' Almanack", 1967; "Stephen Leacock", "Feast of Stephen", "Fifth Business", 1970; "The Manticore" 1972; "Hunting Stuart and Other Plays" 1972; "World of Wonders", 1975; "The Revels History of Drama in English", Vol. 6, 1750-1880, (with others), 1975; "One Half of Robertson Davies", 1977; "Question Time", 1975; "The Enthusiasms of Robertson Davies", ed. by Judith Skelton Grant, 1979; "Robertson Davies: The Well-Tempered Critic", ed. by Judith Skelton Grant 1981; "The Rebel Angels" 1981; author with Sir Tyrone Guthrie of "Renown at Stratford", 1953; "Twice Have the Trumpets Sounded", 1954; "Thrice the Brinded Cat Hath Mew'd", 1955; 3-act plays produced: "Fortune My Foe", 1948; "King Phoenix", 1950; "At My Heart's Core", 1950; "A Jig for the Gypsy", 1954; "Hunting Stuart", 1955; "Love and Libel", 1960; "Brothers in the Black Art" (TV) 1974; "Question Time", 1975; "Pontiac and the Green Man", 1977; awarded Louis Jouvet Prize for direction "Taming of the Shrew", Dom. Drama Festival, 1949; Stephen Leacock Medal; 1955; Lorne Pierce Medal for Lit. from R.S.C., 1961; Gov.-Gen.'s Award for Fiction, 1973; Hon. mem., American Acad. & Inst. of Arts & Letters, 1980; Anglican; recreation: music; Clubs: Long Christmas Dinner; York (Toronto); Athenaeum (London); Address: Massey College, 4 Devonshire Pl., Toronto, Ont. M5S 2E1

DAVIES, Hon. William Hugh, LL.B.; judge; b. Chilliwack, B.C. 2 June 1931; s. John Lorimer D. and Mabel Helen (Currie) D.; e. Chilliwack High Sch.; Univ. of B.C. LL.B. 1955; m. Judith Ann d. Harry Jack Stevens, Chilliwack, B.C. 16 June 1962; children: Steven John, Jacklyn Ann; CO. COURT JUDGE, LOCAL JUDGE SUPREME COURT B.C.; Dir., Conf. of Can. Judges; Past Chrmn. Cultus Lake Park Bd.; rec'd Silver Jubilee Medal; served with RCAF, rank Flying Offr.; Delta Upsilon (Past Pres.); Baptist; recreations: golf, tennis; Home: 48489 Camp Road, R.R. 2, Chilliwack, B.C. V2P 6H4; Office: The Law Courts, Begbie Square, New Westminster, B.C. V3M 1C9.

D'AVIGNON, Guy; Canadian public servant; b. Montreal, Que., 6 Feb. 1923; s. Albert and Aggie (Reed) D.; e. McGill Univ.; m. Denise, d. Dr. Hector Dansereau, 18 Oct. 1952; children: Nicole, Pierre, Marie; DEPUTY MIN. OF SUPPLY, SUPPLY AND SERVICES CANADA, 1979-; Chmn. of Bd., Roy. Can. Mint; Dir., Crown Assets Disposal Corp.; Chmn., Dir. Gen., Information Con. 1972-

76; Chmn., Anti-Dumping Trib., 1976-78; Chmn., Spec. Comm. on Review of Personnel Management and the Direct Principle 1978-79; with Belding-Corticelli Ltd., Montreal, Que. 1947; Canadian Westinghouse Ltd., Hamilton, Ont. 1955; joined Civil Service Comn., Ottawa 1957; Unemployment Ins. Comn., Ottawa 1963; with City of Montreal 1964; Dir. of Planning and Asst. Dir. Gen., Public Service Comn., Can. 1966; Asst. Depy. Min., Dept. Industry, Trade & Comm., Ottawa 1971; served in 2nd World War overseas 1940-45; Fellow of the Royal Can. Geograph. Soc.; Clubs: The Country (Ottawa); National Press: Home: 16 Elgin, Lucerne, Que. J9H 1E1; Office: Ottawa, Ont.

DAVIS, Rev. Canon Alfred Henry, B.A., L.Th., D.D. (Ang.); b. Edgbaston, Birmingham, Eng. 17 Feb. 1902; s. late James William and late Elsie Gertrude (Sheldon) D.; came to Canada, 1912; e. Jarvis St. Coll. Inst., Toronto, Ont.; University Coll., Univ. of Toronto, B.A. 1930; Wycliffe Coll., Toronto, L.Th. 1931, D.D. 1955; m. late Ethel Maude Louise, d. late Robert King, 15 Aug. 1931; o. Priest 1931; successively Rector of St. Mary Magdalene, Winnipeg; Diocese of Rupert's Land; Rector of Hagersville, Ont., 1936-40; Holy Trinity, Welland, Ont., 1940-53; apptd. Field Secy., Missy. Soc. Ang. Ch. Can., 1953, Asst. Secy., 1957-59, Gen. Secy. 1959-67; Dir., Nat. and World Program Div. 1967-69; onetime Archdeacon of Lincoln and Welland Co.'s., and Canon of Christ Ch. Cath., Hamilton, Ont.; Pres. for two terms, Welland Co. Children's Aid Soc.; Editor: "Who dares stand idle", 1955; Home: 55 Belmont St., Toronto, Ont. M5R 1R1

DAVIS, Andrew, Mus.B.; conductor; b. Herts., Eng. 2 Feb. 1944; s. Robert James and Florence (Joyce) D.; e. King's Coll. Cambridge Organ Scholar Mus.B. 1967; studied conducting with Franco Ferrara, Rome 1967-68; MUSIC DIR., THE TORONTO SYMPHONY 1975- ; first maj. conducting Janacek's "Glagolitic Mass" with BBC Symphony Orchestra 1970 followed by 2 yrs. with BBC Scottish Symphony Orchestra, Glasgow; apptd. Assoc. Conductor New Philharmonia Orchestra 1973; and toured Far E. with Eng. Chamber Orchestra 1973 and began first of many visits to Israel Philharmonic Orchestra; served 3 seasons as Princ. Guest Conductor Royal Liverpool Philharmonic Orchestra; has appeared at many maj. internat. festivals incl. Edinburgh, Flanders, Berlin and for past 5 summers has conducted at Glyndebourne Opera Festival; has guest conducted in London, Los Angeles, Boston, Cleveland, Rome's Santa Caecilia Orchestra, Berlin Philharmonic Orchestra, Stockholm Philharmonic, N.Y., Chicago, Israel, Detroit, Radio Symphony of Berlin, Vienna Symphony; Metro Opera debut conducting Richard Strauss' "Salome", 1981; Paris Opera 1982 and Covent Garden, 1983 conducting Richard Strauss' "Der Rosenkavalier"; return Metro Opera to conduct Rossini's "Barber of Seville", 1982; rec'd 2 Grand Prix du Disque awards (Orchestral & Lyric) for recording of Maurice Duruflés "Requiem" with London Philharmonic 1978; Office: 215 Victoria St., Toronto, Ont. M5B 1V1.

DAVIS, Charles Carroll, M.A., Ph.D.; biologist; educator; b. Calif. 24 Nov. 1911; s. William Allen and Maude (Snyder) D.; e. Pasadena Jr. Coll. 1929; Oberlin Coll. B.A. 1933; Univ. of Wash. M.A. 1935, Ph.D. 1940; m. Sally May d. John P. Jacobsen June 1936; children: Peter T., Betsy A. Gimbel; Prof. of Biol. (retired) Mem. Univ. of Nfld. 1977- ; Instr. Jacksonville Jr. Coll. 1945-46; Asst. Prof. Univ. of Miami 1946-48; Case Western Reserve Univ. Asst. Prof., Assoc. Prof., Prof. of Biol. 1948-68; Prof. of Biol. Mem. Univ. of Nfld. 1968-77; Gjeste-professor, Universitetet i Tromso 1975-76; author "The Pelagic Copepoda of the Northeastern Pacific Ocean" 1949; "The Marine and Freshwater Plankton" 1955; over 113 papers prof. journs.; Fellow, Am. Assn. Advanc. Science; Ohio Acad. Science; mem. Am. Soc. Limnology & Oceanography; Ecol. Soc. Am.; Candn. Soc. Zool.; Plankton Soc. Japan; Marine Biol. Assn. UK; Freshwater Biol. Assn. UK;

Internat. Soc. Limnology; Am. Microscopical Soc.; Soc. Candn. Limnols.; Crustacean Soc.; Assoc. Ed. Internationale Revue der Gesamten Hydrobiologie; NDP; recreations: gardening, cooking, hiking, reading; Home: (P.O. Box 15) Site 3, R.R.1, Paradise, Nfld. A0A 2E0; Office: St. John's, Nfld. A1B 3X9.

DAVIS, Harry Floyd, S.M., Ph.D.; mathematician; educator; b. Colby, Kans. 2 Oct. 1925; s. Leo Lloyd and Edna Miars D.; e. Mass. Inst. Technol. S.B. (Physics) 1948, S.M. (Math.) 1953, Ph.D. (Math.) 1954; m. Myrna Joan d. late Harold Hugh MacPhie 9 Sept. 1961; two s. Harry Floyd, Kenneth Hugh; PROF. OF MATH., UNIV. OF WATERLOO 1961- , mem. Senate; Instr., Armed Forces Inst. 1945-46; Lowell Inst. Sch. Cambridge 1948-54; Mass. Inst. of Technol. 1948-54; Asst. Prof., Miami Univ. of Ohio 1954-55; Univ. of B.C. 1955-58; Assoc. Prof. Royal Mil. Coll. Can. 1958-61; served with U.S. Navy 1944-46; author "Fourier Series and Orthogonal Functions" 1963; co-author "Introduction to Vector Analysis" 4th Revised Ed. 1979; mem. Candn. Math. Soc.; Soc. Indust. & Applied Math.; Am. Math. Assn.; Sigma Xi; Beta Theta Pi; Anglican; Home: 355 Pommel Gate Cres., Waterloo, Ont. N2L 5X7; Office: Univ. of Waterloo, Waterloo, Ont. N2L 3G4.

DAVIS, Henry Francis, C.V.O., B.A., B.C.L.; retired Canadian public service; b. Ottawa, Ont., 30 Jan. 1914; s. Michael Patrick and Gertrude Ann (McGrady) D.; e. Lisgar Collegiate, Ottawa; Bishop's Univ., B.A. 1932; McGill Univ., B.C.L. 1935; Nat. Defence Coll. 1951; m. Isobel Margaret, d. James O'Reilly, 9 Jan. 1946; children: Ann, Martha, Thomas H.P., Jane; CANDN. SECY. TO HER MAJESTY THE QUEEN, FORMER SECY., CANDN. INTERGOVERNMENTAL CONFERENCES since 1973; Co-ord. for 1978 Royal Visit; Executive Assistant General Mgr., Royal Trust Co., Montreal, Que., 1936-40; with Dept. of External Affairs, Ottawa, 1946-47; Secy., Candn. Embassy, Buenos Aires, 1947-50; Ottawa, 1951-54; Min. Counsellor, Candn. Embassy, Paris 1954-58; Head of European Div., Ottawa, 1958-61; (periods as Acting Asst. Under Secy. of State for External Affairs); Chief of Protocol and Chrmn. of Govt. Hospitality Comte., 1961-64; Special Adv. Privy Council 1964-69; Secy. Constitutional Conf. 1969-72; read law with Col. J. L. Ralston, Q.C.; called to the Bar of Que. 1936; served in 2nd World War with R.C.A.F. 1940-46, Overseas, Bomber Pilot; Past Pres. Nat. Council of YMCA of Can.; mem., Extve. Comte. World Alliance of YMCA; Past Pres. Ottawa YM/-YWCA; Past Pres., Ottawa Red Cross; Past Pres. Nat. Gallery Assn.; Past Dir. Ottawa Social Planning Council; apptd. Commdr. Roy. Victorian Order 1978; Roman Catholic; Clubs: Rideau; Canadian (Past Pres.); Home: 80 MacKinnon Rd., Rockcliffe Park, Ont. K1M 0G3; Office: 100 Argyle Ave, Ottawa, Ont. K1Y 4J3

DAVIS, Hon. Jack, M.A., Ph.D., D.Sc.; politician; engineer; economist; b. Kamloops, B.C. 31 July 1916; s. Fred and Eveline Margaret (Blunsdon) D.; e. Univ. of B.C., B.A.Sc.; Oxford Univ. B.A., B.Sc., M.A. (Rhodes Scholar B.C. 1939); McGill Univ. Ph.D.; Univ. of Ottawa D.Sc.; m. Anna Georgina Margaret d. late Fred Worthing and Flora C., 4 Sept. 1942; children: Mrs. Merilyn McKelvey, John Brock, Steven Victor; MIN. OF ENERGY, TRANSPORT & COMMUNICATIONS, B.C.; Pres., Apex Consultants Ltd.; former Min. of Environment Can. and of Fisheries Can.; served with RCAF during World War II; named Engr. of Yr. Can. 1975; author "Canada's Energy Prospects"; "Mining and Mineral Processing in Canada"; "Outlook for Canada's Forest Industries"; "Canada's Chemical Industry"; numerous articles, columns and pamphlets; mem. Assn. Prof. Engrs. B.C.; Sigma Phi Delta; Protestant; recreations: tennis, badminton, skiing; Clubs: Mens Canadian; University; Hollyburn; Home: 855 Farmleigh Rd., West Vancouver, B.C. V7S 1Z8; Office: Legislative Bldgs., Victoria, B.C. V8V 1X4.

DAVIS, J(ames) R(obert) Leighton, B.F.A.; curator; artist; b. Winnipeg, Man. 14 May 1941; s. Robert Leighton Davis; City Mgrs.' Assn. Planning Adm. Dipl. Washington, D.C. 1969; Capilano Coll. Vancouver 1969-76; Dalhousie Univ. grad. studies Personnel & Financial Adm. 1978-79; N.S. Coll. of Art & Design B.F.A. 1979; m. Arlene I. d. J. E. Graham, Winnipeg, Man. 14 Sept. 1963; DIR./CURATOR, ST. MARY'S UNIV. ART GALLERY; Artist in Residence, St. Mary's Univ. 1980-; printmaker, watercolourist; 9 one-man exhns. organized nationally by Burnaby Art Gallery 1978-79; rec'd Vancouver Foundation Scholarship, Helen Pitt Fund for Fine Arts 1977; Address: St. Mary's University Art Gallery, Halifax, N.S. B3H 3C3

DAVIS, Kent John; transportation executive; b. Toronto, Ont., 29 Oct. 1917; s. Thomas Irving and Lillian Elizabeth D.; e. Univ. of Toronto 1939-40 and 1946; Oxford Univ., Royal Aero. Soc. 14th Air Transport Course 1969; m. Vivian J. McLaughlin, 12 July 1974; children: Laura, Julia, Virginia, Nancy, John; Vice Pres.-Flight Operations, Air Canada, 1971-77; joined Trans Canada Air Lines upon release from R.C.A.F.; First Offr. 1941; Capt. 1944; based in Winnipeg, Toronto, Montreal and Moncton has flown all of Co.'s routes; Flight Instr. 1951; Supvry Pilot, Toronto, 1952; converted to DC-8's in 1960 in charge of DC-8 flying at Toronto Base; Chief Pilot 1961; Flight Operations Mgr., Toronto, 1966; Flight Operations Dir. 1968; served with RCAF as Pilot during World War II; Secy.-Treas., Boy Scouts N.W. Br. for 2 yrs.; Protestant; Clubs: Toronto Cricket Skating & Curling; Toast Masters'; Home: 33 Blair Athol Crescent, Islington, Ont. M9A 1X6;

DAVIS, Murray Earl; manufacturer; b. Glenside, Sask. 22 Oct. 1919; s. William John and Matilda (New) D.; m. Carmen Parent 7 June 1943; children: Christine Michelle, Timothy Colin, Richard Brian; PRES. AND GEN. MGR. — HARVESTING & IMPLEMENTS, MASSEY-FERGUSON INDUSTRIES LTD.; Dir. Wilco-Canada Inc.; Candn. Farm & Indust. Equipment Inst.; mem. Adv. Comte. Indust. Accident Prevention Assn.; mem. Bd. Trade Metrop. Toronto; Protestant; recreation: golf; Club: Mississauga Golf & Country; Home: 54 Colonial Cres., Oakville, Ont. L6J 4K9; Office: 915 King St. W., Toronto, Ont. M6K 1E3.

DAVIS, Nathanael V.; executive; b. Pittsburgh, Penn., 26 June 1915; s. late Rhea (Reineman) and late Edward Kirk D.; e. Harvard Coll., A.B. 1938; post-grad. at London Sch. of Econ.; m. Lois H. Thompson of Jamaica, B.W.1., 15 Apl. 1941; children: James Howard Dow, Katharine Vining; CHAIRMAN BD., ALCAN ALUMINIUM LIMITED, since 1972; Dir., Bank of Montreal; Canada Life Assnce. Co.; except for wartime services, has been continuously assoc. with Alcan group since joining in 1939; Pres., Alcan Aluminium Limited 1947-72; Chrmn. Bd. and C.E.O. 1972-79; Clubs: Mount Royal (Montreal); Somerset (Boston); University (N.Y.C.); St. James's (Montreal); Office: (Box 6090), Place Ville Marie, Montreal, Quebec. H3C 3H2

DAVIS, Reginald C., M.A., Mus.M., M.Ed., Ph.D.; educator; b. Toronto, Ont. 10 Oct. 1916; s. John Ratcliffe and Dora Jean (Macklam) D.; e. Bloor St. Coll. Inst.Toronto 1935; Toronto Teachers Coll. 1936; Univ. of Ottawa B.A. 1941, M.A. 1943, Ph.D. 1944; Univ. of Rochester (Eastman Sch. Music) Mus.M. 1950; Univ. of Toronto M.Ed 1960; A.T.C.M. (piano) 1938; m. Eleanor Ethel d. Albert Michel, Petawawa, Ont. 29 June 1956; one d. Kathryn Eileen; PRINCIPAL, TRAFALGAR CASTLE SCHOOL; retired and mem. Bd. of Dirs. since 1968; Head Music Dept. Danforth Tech. Sch. 1949-54; Princ. Corvette Pub. Sch. Scarborough 1954-57; Inspr. Pub. Schs. Brantford, Ont. 1957-60; Princ. Cobourg Coll. W. 1960-63 and Cobourg Coll. E. 1963-65; Educ. Supvr. Instructional Programs W. Vancouver 1965-68;; mem. Brantford and Suburban Planning Bd.; former Conductor Port Hope and Community

Male Chorus; Conductor Whitby Rotary Male Choir; former mem. Bd. Dirs. Cobourg YMCA; Past Pres. Community Concert Assn. Cobourg; Past Vice Pres. Brantford Symphony Orchestra Assn.; Lectr. Sch. Princ. Course Queen's Univ.; mem. comte. Ministry of Educ. preparing course study Man in Soc. (Grade 11 & 12 Ont.); Past Pres. Bay of Quinte Secondary Sch. Headmasters' Assn.; Hon. Life mem. Sch. Insprs. Assn. Ont.; Pres. Oshawa Music Teachers' Assn.; Vice Chrmn. Candn. Assn. Princ's Independent Schs. for Girls; Freemason (organist); Phi Delta Kappa; P. Conservative; United Church; recreations: piano and organ duos; Club: Rotary; Address: 112 Glenwood Ave., Oshawa, Ont. L1G 3A9

DAVIS, Richard Edward Gillmor, O.C. (1974), D.Sc. Soc., LL.D.; Social scient.; b. Toronto, Ont., 6 Oct. 1894; s. Thomas Edward and Minnie (Gillmor) D.; e. U. of Toronto, B.A. 1920; McGill U. (Econ., Sociol.), M.A. 1927; Columbia Univ.; London School of Econ., 1936; Laval Univ., D.Sc. Soc. 1953; Univ. of B.C., LL.D. 1955; m. Margaret, d. Gunnar Svendsen, 8 Mar. 1941; one s., Eric Gillmor; Boys' Work Secy., Y.M.C.A., London, Ont., 1915-17; Gen. Secy., 1918-19; Indust. Secy. Boys' Work Secy. and Assoc. Gen. Secy., Y.M.C.A., Montreal, P.Q., 1920-28; joined staff of Nat. Council of Y.M.C.A.'s Toronto, Ont., 1928; organ. Candn. Inst. of Pub. Affairs (Couchiching Conf.) which has met annually since 1931; on leave of absence from Y.M.C.A. to serve as Extve. Dir., Candn. Youth Comn., 1942-46; Extve. Dir., Candn. Welfare Council, 1946-63; Consultant to the Special Comte. of the Senate on Aging, 1963-65; Visiting Prof. 1965, and subsequently Special Lectr. (1966-69) Sch. of Social Work, Univ. of Toronto; 1st Pres., Community Planning Assn. of Can.; mem., Ont. Govt. Comte. on Portable Pensions, 1960-61; Fed. Govt.'s Nat. Council on Welfare 1965-68; Bd. of Trustees, Ontario Hist. Studies Series since 1971; Candn. Inst. of Internat. Affairs; Clubs: Rideau; Faculty; Arts & Letters; Home: 18 Brookfield Rd., Willowdale, Ont. M2P 1A9

DAVIS, Hon. William Grenville, M.P.P., Q.C., B.A.,; b. Brampton, Ont., 30 July 1929; s. late Albert Grenville and Vera (Hewetson); e. Brampton (Ont.) High Sch.; Univ. of Toronto, B.A. 1951 Osgoode Hall Law Sch.; LL.D. (Hon.), Waterloo Lutheran 1963, W. Ont. 1965, Toronto 1967, McMaster 1968, Queen's, Windsor; D.U.C. (Hon.) Ottawa 1980; m. Helen (died 1962) d. Neil MacPhee, Windsor, Ont; m. Kathleen Louise, d. Dr. R. P. Mackay, Illinois; children; Neil, Nancy, Cathy, Ian, Meg; PREMIER OF ONT. and Pres. of the Council, Ont. since Mar. 1971; called to Bar of Ont. 1955; first el. to Ont. Leg. 1959; mem., Select Comte of Ont. Leg. to study Adm. and Extve. Problems of Govt. of Ont., 1960-63; 2nd Vice-Chrmn., Ont. Hydro-Electric Power Comn., 1961-62; Min. of Educ. 1962-71 and Min. of Univ. Affairs 1964-71; attached to Candn. Del. to UNESCO Conf., Paris, Nov. 1966; el. first Chrmn., Council of Mins. of Educ., Can., Sept. 1967; rec'd Greer Mem. Award, Ont. Educ. Assn., 1966; Award of Merit, Phi Delta Kappa Univ. of Toronto Chapter 1967; Publications: "The Government of Ontario and the Universities of the Province" (Frank Gerstein Lectures, York Univ.), 1966; "Education in Ontario", 1965; "Building an Educated Society 1816-1966", 1966; "Education for New Times", 1967; Cert. of Merit, Edinboro Univ., Pa.; Am. Transit Assn. Man of the Year 1973; mem., Candn. Bar Assn.; Ont. Bar Assn.; Freemason; United Church; P. Conservative; Clubs: Kiwanis; Albany; Address: Parliament Bldgs., Toronto, Ont. M7A 1A1

DAVIS, Most Rev. William Wallace, D.D., D.C.L., B.A., B.D. (Ang.); retired archbishop; b. Woodlawn, Ont., 10 Dec. 1908; s. Isaac and Margaret Celina (Dixon) D.; e. Univ. of Bishop's Coll., B.A. 1931, B.D. 1934; King's Coll., Halifax, D.D. 1953; Bishop's Univ., D.C.L. 1958; St. Francis Xavier Univ. Antigonish, N.S., LL.D. 1973; m. late Kathleen Aubrey, d. late Geo. B. Acheson, 20 July 1933; children: Robert, Mary, Arthur, Margaret;

m. 2ndly, Helen Mary Lynton of Ottawa, Ont. 1968; Reserve Army Chaplain, 1937; R.C.A.F. Chaplain, 1940-44; Army Chaplain (R) 1952-57; Bishop Co-adjutor of N.S., 1958-63; Bishop of N.S. 1963; Archbishop of N.S. and Metropolitan of the Eccl. Prov. of Can. 1972-75; Hon. asst. to Bishop of Ottawa; Publications: "This Canada"; Conservative; recreations: golf, tennis, handball, colour-photography; Home: Apt. 712, 1465 Baseline Rd., Ottawa, Ont. K2C 3L8; Office: 71 Bronson Ave., Ottawa, Ont. K1R 6G6

DAVISON, Edward Joseph, B.A.Sc., M.A., Ph.D., Sc.D., F.I.E.E.E., F.R.S.C.; educator; b. Toronto, Ont. 12 Sept. 1938; s. Maurice John and Agnes (Quinlan) D.; e. Royal Conserv. of Music Toronto A.R.C.T. Piano 1957; Univ. of Toronto B.A.Sc. 1960, M.A. (Applied Math.) 1961; Cambridge Univ. Ph.D. (Control. Engn.) 1964, Sc.D. 1977; m. Zofia d. M. C. Perz; 4 children; PROF. OF ELECT. ENGN. UNIV. OF TORONTO since 1974; Vice-Pres., (Technical Affairs), IEEE Control Systems Soc., 1979-80; mem of Edit. Adv. Bd. "Proceedings of the IEEE" 1980-; Dir. of IEEE Control Systems Soc. Magazine, 1980-; Dir., Elect. Engineering Consociates Ltd., Tor., 1977-; Asst. Prof. Univ. of Toronto 1964-66, 1967-68, Assoc. Prof. 1968-74; Asst. Prof. Univ. Calif. Berkeley 1966-67; Athlone Fellow 1961-63; E. W. R. Steacie Mem. Fellow 1974-77; Killam Research Fellowship 1979-80, 1981-82; author over 200 scient. articles math. system theory, multivariable control systems, large scale system theory, computational methods, application system theory to biol.; Fellow, Inst. Elect. & Electronic Engrs.; Fellow, Royal Society of Canada (1977); Designated Consulting Engr. Prof. Engrs. Prov. Ont.; Office: Toronto, Ont. M5S 1A4.

DAVISON, Stanley M.; banker; b. Enderby, B.C., Sept. 12, 1928; s. Ronald and Janet Grace (Livingstone) D.; e. Harvard AMP, 1980; m. Bette Irene, d. Aldo Rusconi, 12 June 1957; children: Loreen Joyce, Diane Janine, Ronald James; VICE-CHRMN. AND DIRECTOR, BANK OF MONTREAL, since 1980; joined present Bank 1947; held various positions in B.C., Que. and Alta.; Mgr., 10th & Granville, Vancouver, 1966-68; Vice Pres., Man. & Sask. Div., March 1968; Sr. Vice Pres. of Div., Nov. 1968; Extve. Vice Pres., Domestic Banking, Montreal 1971; Extve. Vice-Pres. and Chief Gen. Mgr., 1976-80; Protestant; recreations: curling, tennis, golf; Clubs: Petroleum (Calgary); Mount Royal; Toronto Club; Home: 3125 Linden Dr., Calgary, Alta. T3E 6C9; Office: 300 5th Ave. S.W., Calgary, Alta. T2P 3C4

DAWE, Chester; manufacturer; b. Bay Roberts, Conception Bay, Nfld., 17 May 1904; s. William and Mary E. (Russell) D.; e. Bay Roberts, Nfld.; m. Phyllis May, d. late William J. Carson, Montreal, Que., 30 Sept. 1930; two d. Janet, Sonia; PRESIDENT, CHESTER DAWE LIMITED; Dir., Canada Bay Lumber Co. Ltd.; Chester Dawe Inc.; Better Homes Ltd.; Freemason; Anglican; Club: Bally Haly Golf; Home: 50 Circular Rd., St. John's Nfld. A1C 2Z1; Office: (P.O. Box 8280) St. John's, Nfld. A1B 3N4

DAWE, Hon. Ronald Gilbert, M.H.A., B.P.E., B.Ed.; politician; b. Topsail, Conception Bay, Nfld. 21 June 1944; e. Prince of Wales Coll. Inst. St. John's, Nfld. 1961; Mem. Univ. of Nfld. B.P.E., B.Ed. 1970; m. Linda Hope Tricco; children: Michele, Craig, Todd; MIN. OF TRANSPORTATION, NFLD. 1981- ; former teacher Baie Verte Integrated High Sch., St. John's Un. Jr. High and Belanger Mem. High, Codroy Valley; Past Dir. Parks & Recreation, Stephenville and Recreation Consultant Dept. of Rehabilitation & Recreation; el. M.H.A. for St. Georges prov. g.e. 1979; apptd. Min. of Tourism, Recreation & Culture 1980; Min. of the Environment and Min. of Culture, Recreation & Youth 1980; Home: Millville, Codroy Valley, Nfld. Office: Atlantic Place, Water St., St. John's, Nfld.

DAWSON, David Collins, B.A.; company president (ret.); b. Vancouver, B.C., 9 Nov. 1902; s. George Warren and Malvina Rebecca (Buttimer) D.; e. Lord Roberts Sch. and King George High Sch., Vancouver, B.C.; Univ. of Brit. Columbia, B.A. 1924; Sprott Shaw Sch., Vancouver, B.C.; m. Laura Call, d. Thomas N. Dickie, Campbellton, N.B., 19 Apl. 1934; Pres., the Owl Drug Co. Ltd., 1939-1978; Pres., Pac. Coast Wholesale Drugs Ltd., since 1945; with Warehouse and Purchasing Dept., Kelly, Douglas & Co., Vancouver, B.C., for several yrs.; Asst. to Acct., The Owl Drug Co. Ltd., 1928; Dir. and Secy.-Treas., 1929; A.R.P. Warden, Civilian Defence Corps., Vancouver, B.C., during 2nd World War; mem., Vancouver Bd. of Trade; United Church; recreation: photography; Clubs: Rotary; Vancouver; Home: Suite 701 - 2155 W. 38th Ave., Vancouver, B.C. V6M 1R8;

DAWSON, Graham Russell, B.A.Sc., P.Eng.; contractor; b. Vancouver, B.C., 18 Nov. 1925; s. Frederick James and Marion Patterson (Russell) D.; e. Prince of Wales High Sch., Vancouver, 1943; Royal Canadian Naval Coll., grad. 1945; Univ. of B.C., B.A.Sc. 1949; Lieut. (Ret'd.), R.C.N.; m. Dorothy Eva Drape, d. late Col. R. D. Williams, 19 May 1949; children: Rebecca, Bruce, Ian, Murray, Marion; Chmn. and Dir., Dawson Construction Ltd.; mem. Adv. Bd., Nat. Trust Co. Ltd.; Trustee, Can. Realty Investors; Dir., Bank of Montreal; Canada Life Assurance Co.; Canadian Natural Resources Ltd.; The Hamilton Group Ltd.; Paccar of Canada Ltd.; Q Broadcasting Ltd.; Zeller's Ltd.; Dir., Andres Wines Ltd.; Sceptre Dredging Ltd.; Can. Mine Services Ltd.; Interprovincial Construction Co. Ltd.; Pres. and Dir., Interior Contracting Co. Ltd.; Dawson & Hall Ltd.; Shotcrete Inter. Ltd.; Imperial Paddock Pools Ltd.; LeDuc Paving Ltd.; Chmn., Daon Development Corp.; mem. Vancouver Board Trade (Past President); Bd. of Govs., Vancouver Public Aquarium; mem. Convocation, Univ. of B.C. and Simon Fraser Univ.; Past Pres., B.C. Div.; Candn. Arthritis Soc.; mem., Candn. Tech. Asphalt Assn.; Phi Delta Theta; United Church; recreations: golf, fishing, skiing; Clubs: Vancouver; Shaughnessy Golf & Country; Home: 1459 McRae Avenue, Vancouver, B.C. V6H 1V1; Office: 735 Clark Dr., Vancouver, B.C. V5L 3J4

DAWSON, John A., B.Sc., M.S., Ph.D.; economist; b. Montreal, Que., 14 Sept. 1923; s. Carl Addington and Mary Alice (Dixon) D.; e. McGill Univ., B.Sc. (Agric.) 1947; Univ. of Ill., M.S. (Agric. Econ.) 1949; Univ. of Chicago, Ph.D. (Econ.) 1957; m. Eunice Irene, d. Joseph William Hutchison, 20 Sept. 1947; children: Robert John, Kathleen Eunice; CONSULTANT, 1980-; Dir., Economic Council of Canada 1973-76; Econ., Can. Dept. of Agric. 1947; Sr. Econ. Advisor, Bd. of Broadcast Govs. 1960; joined Economic Council as Staff Econ. 1964; Extve. Dir., Candn. Energy Research Institute, 1976-80; served with RCNVR 1942-45; United Church; recreations: fishing, skiing; Address: 1837 Beattie Ave., Ottawa, Ont. K1H 5R7

DAY, Geoffrey Walter Gordon; banker; b. London, Eng. 21 Dec. 1929; s. Francis William and Ada Beatrice (Norris) D.; e. Ilford Co. High Sch. 1945; Banff (Alta.) Sch. Advanced Mang. 1968; m. Karen Audrey d. late Arthur Kemp 4 Nov. 1960; children: Anne Louise, Hilary Lee, Kevin Geoffrey Kemp; SR. VICE PRES., WORLD CORPORATE BANKING, BANK OF NONTREAL 1979; Law Student, Thomas Cooper & Co., London, Eng. 1950-53; joined Bank of Montreal 1953 holding various positions Kelowna and Vancouver, B.C., Sr. Asst. Mgr. Main Office, Victoria, B.C. 1965 and Calgary 1967, Dist. Mgr. E. Ont. 1969, Mgr. Main Office Hamilton, Ont. 1971, Comm. Marketing Mgr. H.O. Montreal 1974, Vice Pres., Corporate Banking, Toronto 1976-79; Vice Pres., Internat. Banking 1979-81; served with R.A.F. 1948-50, Radio Operator, rank Cpl.; P. Conservative; United Church; recreations: tennis, curling, golf; Dir., Candn. Coll. Bowl; Clubs: Ontario; Mississauga Golf & Country; Home: 1500 Larchview Trail, Mississauga, Ont. L5E 2S1; Office: First

Canadian Pl. 18th Floor, 100 King St. W., Toronto, Ont. M5X 1A1.

DAY, Grant Hall, Q.C., B.A., B.C.L., b. Montreal, P.Q., 2 Sept. 1923; s. Henry Stockwell and Madeleine (Hall) D.; e. Selwyn House Sch., Montreal, P.Q.; Bishop's Coll. Sch., Lennoxville, P.Q.; Bishop's Univ., B.A. 1946; McGill Univ., B.C.L., 1949; children: (of former marriage); Penelope, Audrey, Sarah; former Senior Partner DOHENY, DAY, MACKENZIE, GRIVAKES, GERVAIS & LeMOYNE; Former Dir., Allergan Canada Ltd.; Pilkington's Tiles (Canada 1961) Ltd.; National Drug & Chemical Co. of Can. Ltd.; read law with late George H. Montgomery, Q.C.; called to the Bar of P.Q. 1949; served in 2nd World War, chiefly at sea with R.C.N.V.R., 1941-45; Hon. mem. Can. Red Cross Soc. and Trustee Que. Div.; former Dir., Westmount Lib. Assn.; Treas. Montreal Bar, Hon. Solr., Montreal Farmers' Club; Class Agent, Bishop's Univ.; Dir., St. Andrew's Youth Centre; Hon. Solr., Nat. Ballet (Que.); mem., Naval Offrs. Assn.; Anglican; recreations: golf, farming; Clubs: Mount Bruno Golf & Country; Hillside Tennis; St. James's; Home: Ararat Farm, Glen Sutton, Que. J0E 2K0; Office: Suite 1203, 5 Place Ville Marie, Montreal, Que. H3B 2H1

DAYMOND, John Henry; company president; sales representative; b. Hamilton, Ont., 30 July 1928; s. John Herbert and Irene (Ferguson) D.; e. Public Sch. and Westdale Coll. Inst. Hamilton, Ont.; Univ. of Toronto Extension; m. Mary Margaret, d. Thomas, Pherigo, Lambeth, Ont. 20 May 1950; children: John Thomas, Deborah Lee, David Michael, Catherine Elizabeth, Patricia Lyn, Douglas Henry; DIR. AND PRES., HENRY DAYMOND SALES LTD. (Mfrs. Reps.); Dir., L. H. Frost & Co. Inc.; Lux Time Canada Ltd.; Tutco Inc.; with "Hamilton Spectator", 1945-46; Steel Co. of Can. Ltd., Hamilton, Ont., 1947-48; joined General Steel Wares Ltd., Toronto, Ont., 1948; trans. to McClary Div., London, Ont., 1950; Purchasing Agent, John Inglis Co. Ltd., Toronto, Ont., 1952-55; apptd. Vice-Pres. and Gen. Mgr. L. H. Frost (Canada) Ltd. 1955; former Vice-Pres., Young Conservatives, Broadview-Riverdale Toronto; Dir., Toronto Jr. Bd. Trade; Freemason (Rameses Shriner); Conservative; United Church; recreations: sports, boating, reading, standard bred horses; Clubs: "Jesters"; "Le Club"; Argonaut Rowing; Oakville; Conservative Men's; Home: R.R. #1, Alton, Ont. L0N 1A0; Office: 262 Kerr St. N., Oakville, Ont. L6K 3B2

DEACHMAN, Grant; b. Calgary, Alta., 4 May 1913; s. late Robert John and Elizabeth (Grant) D.; e. Pub. and High Schs., Calgary and Ottawa; Bishop's Univ., m. Helen, d. John Anderson, Ottawa, Ont., 24 May 1938; one s., Robert John; FIRST VICE-CHRM., TARIFF BD., 1979-; mem., Tariff Bd., since 1973; following war joined Montreal pub. relations firm as writer; Gen. Mgr., Retail Merchants' Assn. of B.C., Vancouver, 1951; estbd. own pub. relations firm; el. to H. of C. for Vancouver-Quadra in g.e. 1963; re-el. 1965, 1968; served as Chrmn. of Standing Comtes. on Fisheries and on Nat. Defence; Chief Govt. Whip; Chrmn., Candn. Group, Interparlty. Union, 1968-70; led dels. to world confs. of Union in Dakar, Lima, Vienna and New Delhi; served Overseas with RCA during World War II; Served on Extve. Comte. of UNICEF in Can., 1973-76; Liberal; Protestant; Club: Union (Victoria, B.C.); Home: 200 Rideau Terrace, Ottawa, Ont. K1M 0Z3; Office: 365 Laurier Ave. W., Ottawa, Ont. K1A 0G7

DEACON, Donald MacKay, M.C., B.A.; b. Toronto, Ont., 24 Apl. 1920; s. late Frederick Herbert and Ethel Read (Emmerson) D.; e. Univ. of Toronto Schs. (1937); Univ. of Toronto, B.A. 1940; m. Florence, d. Gordon D. Campbell, C.A., Toronto, Ont., 17 May 1947; children: Campbell, David, Martha, Douglas, Richard, Colin Paul; Chmn., Candev Financial Services Ltd.; Dir., F. H. Deacon Hodgson Inc.; Marks & Spencer Canada Inc.; Riverside Yarns Ltd.; Pres., Canadian Club of Toronto, 1968-

69; Deputy-Reeve, Twp. of Markham, Ont., 1957; served in 2nd World War, 1940-46 with Royal Candn. Arty., awarded M.C.; Liberal; United Church; recreations: gardening, Scouts; Home: 27½ Water St., Charlottetown, P.E.I. C1A 1A2; Office: 105 Adelaide St. W., Toronto, Ont. M5A 1R4

DEACON, F(rederick) Coulter; investment dealer; b. Toronto, Ont., 5 Aug. 1910; s. Col. F. H. and Ethel (Emmerson) D.; e. Univ. of Toronto Schs.; m. Margaret F., d. the Rev. J. Bruce Hunter of Toronto, Ont., 13 July 1946; children: Bruce Hunter, Thomas Wilson, Kathleen Mary, Margaret Elizabeth; Retired Chmn. of Bd., F. H. Deacon & Co. Ltd.; Dir., F. H. Deacon Hodgson Inc. (estbd. 1897, members principal Canadian exchanges; Invest. Dealers Assn. of Can.); Liberal; United Church; Clubs: The Toronto Hunt; York Downs Golf & Country Club; Home: 21 Dale Ave., Ste. 801, Toronto, Ont. M4W 1K3; Office: 105 Adelaide St. W., Toronto, Ont. M5H 1R4

DEACON, John Scott; stock broker; b. Toronto, Ont., 9 June, 1912; s. Col. Frederick Herbert and Ethel (Emmerson) D.; e. Univ. of Toronto Schs., grad. 1929, Victoria Coll. Univ. of Toronto B.A. 1934; m. Marian, d. Robt. Davidson Hume, K.C., of Toronto, 8 Sept. 1939; children: Peter Robert, John Scott, Barbara Cooper (Mrs. E. G.), Susan Porter (Mrs. D. Q.); DIR. F. H. DEACON, HODGSON INC. (estbd. 1897); Chairman, Toronto Stock Exchange 1966-68; entered F. H. Deacon & Company as Junior, 1934; served in 2nd World War 1939-45, enlisting as a Signalman 1939; commission May 1941; promoted Capt., 2nd Corps Signals, June 1942; Major, Canadian Army Hdqrs. in Europe, 1945; Lieut.-Col. commanding 2 Armoured Divn. Signals (RF), Nov. 1949; Mentioned in Despatches; Kappa Sigma; Clubs: National; Rosedale Golf; Beaumaris Yacht; Home: Terrace E, 21 Dale Ave., Toronto, Ont. M4W 1K3; Office: 105 Adelaide St. W., Toronto, Ont. M5H 1R4

DEACON, Paul Septimus, B.A., M.Com.; b. Toronto, Ont., 9 June 1922; s. Frederick Herbert and Ethel Record (Emmerson) D.; e. Univ. of Toronto Schs.; Univ. of Toronto, B.A. 1943, M.Com. 1947; m. Charlotte Adelle, d. Kenneth M. Smith, 25 Feb. 1950; children: (Charlotte) Anne, Wendy (Elizabeth), James (Kenneth), Andrew (Paul Donald), Jennifer (Emmerson); VICE-PRES., MACLEAN-HUNTER BUSINESS PUBLISHING CO., Feb. 1979-; Dir., Maclean-Hunter Ltd.; Key Radio Ltd.; joined The Financial Post, July 1947; Montreal Office, 1948-52; Investment Editor, 1952-64; Editor 1964-77; Publisher 1968-79; served in 2nd World War, with R.C.A.F., July 1942-Nov. 1945 as Pilot; served Overseas with No. 620 R.A.F. Sqdn.; Commissioned Apl. 1943; discharged with rank of Flight Lieut.; Mentioned in Despatches; Pres., Toronto Soc. of Financial Analysts 1961-62; Nat. Ballet of Canada 1975-78; Kappa Sigma; United Church; recreations: golf, squash, tennis, flying; Clubs: Rideau; Royal Ottawa Golf; University; Rosedale Golf; Canadian; Office: 309,151 Sparks St., Ottawa Ont. K1P 5E3

DEALY, John Michael, Ph.D.; educator; consulting engineer; b. Waterloo, Iowa 23 March 1937; s. Milton David and Ruth Marion (Dorton) D.; e. Univ. of Kansas B.S.Ch.E. 1958; Univ. of Mich. M.S.E. 1959, Ph.D. 1963, postdoctoral Fellow 1963-64; m. Jacqueline Mary Barbara d. Leo Déry, Town of Mount Royal, Que. Aug. 1964; one d. Pamela Ruth; PROF. OF CHEM. ENGN., McGILL UNIV. 1973- ; Asst. Prof. Chem. Engn. McGill Univ. 1964, Assoc. Prof. 1967; Visiting Prof. Univ. of Cambridge 1970; Univ. of Del. 1978-79; author "Rheometers for Molten Plastics" 1982; over 29 research publs. chem. engn., polymer rheol., plastics processing; Candn. Rep. Internat. Rheol. Comte.; mem. Candn. Soc. Chem. Engn.; Order Engrs. Que.; Am. Inst. Chem. Engrs.; Soc. Plastics Engrs.; Soc. Rheol. (Extve. Comte.); Brit. Soc. Rheol.; Am. Soc. Engn. Educ.; McGill Assn. Univ. Teachers (Pres. 1968-69); Scient. Research Soc. (Pres. McGill

Chapter 1972-73); Sigma Xi; Pres. McGill Faculty Club 1972-73; recreations: music, reading; Home: 305 Grosvenor Ave., Westmount, Qué. H3Z 2M1; Office: 3480 University, Montréal, Qué. H3A 2A7.

DEAN, Geoffrey, B.A.; publisher; b. Newcastle-on-Tyne, Eng. 18 Sept. 1940; s. Thomas Craig D.; e. Heaton Grammar Sch. Newcastle-on-Tyne; N. Toronto Coll. Inst. 1957; Victoria Coll. Univ. of Toronto B.A. 1961; m. Philma Marina Patterson 10 Aug. 1963; children: Andrea Samantha, Christopher Michael; PRES. AND DIR. JOHN WILEY & SONS CANADA LTD. since 1977; Pres. and Dir. Wiley Publishers of Canada Ltd. 1977-1981; Coll. Rep. and subsequently Coll. Ed. McGraw-Hill Co. of Canada Ltd. 1961-65; Sales Mgr. Methuen Publications (Div. of Carswell Co.) 1966-69; Van Nostrand Reinhold Ltd. 1970-76, Marketing Mgr., Vice Pres. Marketing 1972, Vice Pres. and Gen. Mgr. present co. 1976; Offr., Candn. Book Publisher's Council, 1st Vice Pres. 1982; Protestant; recreation: music; Club: Granite; Office: 22 Worcester Rd., Rexdale, Ont. M9W 1L1.

DEAN, Rt. Rev. Ralph Stanley, B.D., M.Th., A.L.C.D., D.D. (Ang.); b. London, England, 22 Aug. 1913; s. Frederick Mark and Emma (Middleton) D.; e. Roan Sch., Greenwich, Eng., 1924-28; Wembley County Sch., Eng. (1928-30 Matric.); London Coll. of Divinity, Univ. of London, B.D. 1938 and A.L.C.D. (Hons.); M.Th. 1944; Wycliffe Coll., Toronto, D.D. 1953; Emmanuel Coll., D.D. Saskatoon, 1957; Anglican Theological Coll., Vancouver, D.D. 1965; Huron Coll., London, D.D.; Trinity Coll., Hartford, Conn., S.T.D., 1966; Rector, Church of the Redeemer since 1979; m. Irene Florence, d. Alfred Bezzant Wakefield, London, Eng. 4 Nov. 1939; Archbishop of Cariboo and Metropolitan of the Eccl. Province of British Columbia, 1971-73 (Bishop of Cariboo 1957-71); Curate of St. Mary Islington, London, 1938-41; Curate-in-Charge, St. Luke, Watford, England, 1944-45; Chaplain and Tutor, London Coll. of Divinity, 1947-51; Principal, Emmanuel Coll., Saskatoon, Sask., 1951-56; apptd. Extve. Offr. of World-wide Ang. Communion, July 1964; recreations: sports, fishing; Address: 293 Riverbend Apts., Greenville, S.C. 29601

DEAN, William George, M.A., Ph.D.; university professor; b. Toronto, Ont., 29 Nov. 1921; s. William Ashton and Alice Mary (Firstbrook) D.; e. Brown Pub. Sch. and Upper Can. Coll., Toronto; St. Andrew's Coll., Aurora, 1940; Univ. of Toronto, B.A. (Trinity Coll.) 1949, M.A. (Geophysics and Geog.) 1950; McGill Univ., Ph.D. 1959; m. Elfreda Elizabeth, d. R. B. Johnston, Q.C., St. Catharines, Ont., 18 Sept. 1948; children: Peter Hugh, Robin Elizabeth; PROF. OF GEOG., UNIV. OF TORONTO, since 1969; Lab. Asst., Dept. of Geog. at present Univ. 1947; Lab. Demonst. 1948-49; Teaching Fellow 1949-50; Lectr. 1956-58; Asst. Prof. 1958-63; Assoc. Prof. 1963-69; Dir. of Field Camps 1958-67; Research Asst., Meteorol. Br., Dept. of Transport, 1947; Geog., B.C. Dept. of Lands, Victoria, 1951-53; Asst. Prof. and Chrmn. of Geog., Un. Coll., Winnipeg, 1953-56; Research Consultant on Arctic for Rand Corp., Santa Monica, Cal., 1954-56; Research Geog., Dept. of Mines and Tech. Survey, Ottawa, 1956-57; Visiting Fellow, Univ. Coll., Cambridge Univ., 1969-70; Project Supvr., Ont. Jt. Hwys. Research Programme on N. Ont. Roads Survey, 1961-64; Research Consultant, Bd. of Govs., Georgian Coll. of Applied Arts and Technol., 1967-68; has also served as consultant for various firms and govt. depts.; summer research and field work incl. N.W.T., N. Ont. and Ottawa; served with RCA (Militia), Toronto, 1940-42 and with RCA in Can., UK and N.W. Europe 1942-46; rank Lt.; Capt., C.O.T.C., Univ. of Man., 1954-56; awarded D.V.A. Schols. 1947-52; Archibald Lampman Schol. 1947; Trinity Coll. Prize for Proficiency 1949; Carnegie Arctic Research Fellow 1950-52; U.S. Nat. Science Foundation Fellowship 1963; Can. Council Fellowship 1969 and 1977; Ed., "The Canadian Geographer", 1960-67; Research Dir. and Ed.,

"Economic Atlas of Ontario" (Gold Medal, Leipzig, 1970); W. W. Atwood Gold Medal, Pan. Am. Inst. of Geography and History, 1973; Sr. Fellow, Trinity Coll., mem. Adv. Comte., Nat. Atlas of Canada; Dir., Hist. Atlas of Can. project; mem., Candn. Assn. Geogs.; Candn. Cartographic Assoc.; Kappa Alpha; mem. Toronto Brigantine Inc.; Dir., N.Y.C. Sailing School; Unitarian; recreations: curling, sailing, reading, music; Clubs: Faculty Club; Royal Canadian Curling; National Yacht; Home: 62 St. Andrews Gdns., Toronto, Ont. M4W 2E1

DEANS, Matthew Bruce; investment dealer; b. Toronto, Ont., 9 Aug. 1931; s. late Matthew Clifford and Dorothy Ann (Sutherland) D.; e. Univ. of Western Ont., B.A. (Honours Business Adm.) 1955; m. Donna Elizabeth d. of late Gordon C. Pautz, 28 Jun. 1955; two s. Gordon M., Mark A. and one d., Karen E.; SEN. VICE-PRES. AND DIR., GREENSHIELDS INC.; Pres., Bankers Securities Ltd.; Tamaraks Estates Ltd.; Delta Upsilon; Conservative; Protestant; recreations: golf, hunting; Clubs: Toronto; Boulevard; Empire; Home: 15 Country Club Dr., Islington, Ont. M9A 3J3; Office: Suite 3000, 1 First Canadian Pl., Toronto, Ont. M5X 1E6

DE BANE, Hon. Pierre, M.P., B.A.; politician; e. Brébeuf Elem. Sch.; St-Alexandre Coll.; Séminaire Trois-Rivières; Laval Univ.; m. Elizabeth Nadeau, Dec. 1980; one s. Jean-Manuel; MIN. OF REGIONAL ECON. EXPANSION, CAN. 1980– ; called to Bar of Que. 1964; el. to H. of C. for Matapédia-Matane g.e. 1968, re-el. since; Parlty. Secy. to Min. of External Affairs 1972, Min. of State for Urban Affairs 1974; Sworn of the Privy Council; apptd. Min. of Supply & Services 1978; Liberal; Office: 485 Confederation Bldg.; House of Commons, Ottawa, Ont. K1A 0A6.

de BELLEFEUILLE, Pierre, O.C. (1967), B. Phil.; b. Ottawa, Ont., 12 May 1923; s. Lionel Lefébure and Annette (Senécal) de B.; e. Univ. of Ottawa, B.Phil. 1944; children: Louis, Anne; with Le Droit, Ottawa, as Reporter, Music Critic, Foreign Ed. and Parlty. writer, 1945-51; joined Nat. Film Bd. of Can. as Chief of Ed. and Cataloguing Services and Co-ordinator of French Distribution, 1951-60; Founding Ed., "Le Magazine Maclean" 1960-64; apptd. Dir. of Exhibits, Candn. Corp. for the 1967 World Exhn., 1964-68; Free-lance journalist, writer, broadcaster and information consultant 1968-76; el. M.N.A. (Parti Québécois) for Deux-Montagnes, 15 Nov. 1976; apptd. Parlty. Asst. to Min. Cultural Affairs 1976, to Min. Intergovt. Affairs 1978; Past Pres., l'Institut Canadien des Affaires publiques; Ottawa Press Club; Le Syndicat des Journalistes d'Ottawa; la Société d'Histoire de Deux-Montagnes; Past Vice-Pres., Candn. Citizenship Council; l'Union Canadienne des Journalistes de langue française; mem. Québec Press Council (1974-76); awarded Gold Medal, Czechoslovak Soc. of Internat. Relations; Address: 83 Rue Chénier, Saint-Eustache, Qué. J7R 1W9

DECARIE, Guy, P.Eng.; b. Montreal, Que., 10 Nov. 1925; s. Wilbrod and Mercedes (Ouimet) D.; e. Ecole Notre-Da-e de Grâce; D'Arcy McGee High Sch. 1944; McGill Univ., B.Eng. 1948; m. Solange, d. Ernest Lapointe, 24 June 1952; children: Guy Philippe, Jacques, François; PRESIDENT AND GEN. MGR., CANAMONT CONSTRUCTION INC. Chrm. of the Bd. of Directors, La Société d'Ingénierie Cartier Ltée; with Harney Construction Co. Ltd., Quebec, Que. as Dir. and Secy. 1948-50; Project Mgr., North Shore Construction Co. Ltd., Montreal 1950; Marine Div. Engr., E. Area Engr., Mannix Ltd., Calgary and Chief Engr. and Dir., Mannibec Ltd. (Mannix subsidiary Calgary and Montreal) 1952; Vice-Pres and Operations Mgr., J. D. Stirling Ltd. 1957-59; mem. Corp. Engrs. Que.; Engn. Inst. Can.; R. Catholic; recreations: golf, tennis, skiing, swimming; Clubs: Mount-Royal; M.A.A.A.; Rosemere Golf; Home: 1321 Sherbrooke W., Apt. E60, Montreal, Que. H3G 1J4; Office: Suite 1500, 2045 Stanley St., Montreal, Que. H3A 2V4

DECARIE, Thérèse Gouin, O.C. (1977), B.A., Ph.D.; professeur; née Montréal, Qué., 30 sept. 1923; f. Léon et Yvette (Ollivier) Gouin; é. Univ. de Montréal, B.A. 1945, L.Ph. 1947, Ph.D. 1960; ép. Vianney D. 1948; doctorat honorifique, Univ. d'Ottawa 1981; enfants: Pascale, Dominique, Jean-Claude, Emmanuel; PROF., DEPT. DE PSYCHOLOGIE, UNIV DE MONTREAL; auteur de "Le développement psychologique de l'enfant" 1953 (5e éd. 1971); "De l'adolescence à la Maturité" 1955 (3e éd. 1971); "La Fasi della Crescita" (éd. italienne abrégée des deux livres précédents) 1960; "L'intelligence et l'affectivité chez le jeune enfant" 1961 (traduction anglaise 1965, espagnole 1970 et italienne 1980); éditeur, "La réaction du jeune enfant à la personne étrangère" (1972) (traduction anglaise 1974); aussi divers articles en français et en anglais sur les mêmes sujets; mem. Soc. Candnne. de Psychol.; Corp. des Psychol. de la P.Q.; Soc. for Research in Child Devel.; Soc. de Psychanalyse; Soc. Royale; Conseil Nat. de Recherches du Canada 1970-76; Ordre du Canada; catholique; r.; résidence: 79 McNider, Outremont, Qué. H2V 3X5; bureau: B.P. 6128, Montréal, Qué. H3C 3J7

DECARY, Hon. Raymond Gervais, B.A., LL.B.; judge; b. Montreal, Que., 16 Oct. 1921; s. Louis-Amédée and Germaine (Marchand) D.; e. Brebeuf Coll. (Jesuits) B.A. 1942; Univ. of Montreal LL.B. 1945; N.Y. Univ. 1946; divorced; children: Raymond Jean, Claude Champagne, Matthieu; JUSTICE, FEDERAL COURT OF CANADA since 1973; read law with C. G. Heward, Q.C.; called to Bar of Que. 1945; cr. Q.C. 1961; practised law Satterlee, Warfield & Stephens, New York 1945-46; Counsel Taxation Div. Dept. Nat. Revenue 1947-55; Geoffrion & Prud'homme 1955-69; Decary, Guy, Vaillancourt, Bertrand & Bourgeois 1970-73; Gov. Business Adm. Faculty Sherbrooke Univ.; mem. Candn. Bar Assn. (Pres. Tax Sub-Sec.); Candn. Tax Foundation (Extve.); R. Catholic; recreations: skiing, tennis, hiking; Clubs: Cercle Universitaire; Cercle Place d'Armes (Montreal); Office: Supreme Court Building, Wellington St., Ottawa, Ont. K1A 0H9.

DeCEW, William Howard; lumber merchant (retired); fifth generation of lumbermen; gggrandf., Capt. John DeCew, started in lumber business at DeCew Falls, Ont., 1810; b. Sand Point, Ont., 28 Dec. 1904; s. William Mark and Sarah Helena (Church) D.; e. Univ. of Brit. Columbia, 1927; m. Frances Clark, d. C.C. Browne, Vancouver, 31 Aug. 1935; has two d. and one s., Former President and Managing Director, DeCew Lumber Co. Ltd.; Advertising and Sales Bureau (Chrmn. 1944); Vancouver Bd. of Trade; Assn. of Kinsmen Clubs (Nat. Pres. 1942); B.C. Wholesale Lumber & Shingle Assn. (Past Pres.); past Dir., Nat.-Am. Wholesale Lumber Assn.; Freemason (32°); hon. life mem., Kinsmen; Hoo-Hoo Internat.; Protestant; Clubs: Terminal City (Past Pres., hon. life mem.); Southlands Riding & Driving (Past Pres.); Home: 228-14990 North Bluff Rd., White Rock, B.C. V4B 3E4

de CHANTAL, René, B.A., L. ès L., Dr. de L'U. (Paris), Dr. de l'Université Ottawa (honoris causa); F.R.S.C.; university professor; b. Moose Creek, Ont., 27 June 1923; s. William Joseph and Antoinette (Ladouceur) de C.; e. McGill Univ., B.A. 1948; Univ. de Paris, L. ès L. 1951, Dr. de l'U. 1960; Sorbonne, Diplôme de professeur de français à l'étranger 1951; m. Geneviève Marguerite Andrée. d. late Raoul Penot, 1951; children: Marie-Laure, François; MINISTER, CULTURAL AFFAIRS AND INFORMATION; CANDN. EMBASSY IN PARIS, since 1979; Vice Rector Academic Affairs, Univ. of Montreal 1975-79; Prof. of Modern French Lit. and French-Candn. Linguistics since 1964 and Dean, Faculty of Letters 1967-71; Dean, Faculty of Arts and Sciences, 1971-75; Lectr., Faculty of Arts, Univ. of Ottawa, 1951; Asst. Prof. 1955; Assoc. Prof. 1961; Asst. to Dean of Faculty, 1962; joined Univ. of Montreal as Assoc. Prof., Faculty of Letters and Head, Dept. of French Lit., 1962; participant in Weekly CBC program 'La langue bien pendue" from 1964 and of "La

Parole est d'or" until 1968; Head of Cultural Affairs, Dept. of External Affairs, 1966-67; Mem. and Pres., National Library Adv. Bd. 1975-79; served with RCAF 1942-45; author: "Chroniques de français", 1956, revised ed. 1961; "Marcel Proust, critique littéraire", 2 vols., 1967; other writings incl. articles for various newspapers and journs. and a weekly column on linguistics problems from "Le Droit" from 1953-63; Dir. and Founder, "Etudes françaises", 1965; mem., Académie Canadienne-française, Sec. perpétuel 1974-79; Royal Society of Canada, since 1966; Pres., Académie des lettres et des sciences humaines, 1977-78; Conseil internat. de la langue française, Vice-Pres., since 1976; Soc. des Gens. de lettres de France; R. Catholic; recreations: skiing, swimming; Address: 35, Ave. Montaigne, 75008 Paris, VIII, France

de CHASTELAIN, Brig. Gen. Alfred John Gardyne Drummond, C.D., B.A.; Canadian armed forces; b. Bucharest, Rumania 30 July 1937; s. Alfred George Cardyne and Marion Elizabeth (Walsh) de C.; e. Fettes Coll. Edinburgh 1955; Mount Royal Coll. Calgary 1956; Royal Mil. Coll. Can. Kingston B.A. 1960; Brit. Army Staff Coll. Camberley grad. 1966; m. Maryann d. Rev. Dr. A. M. Laverty, Kingston, Ont. 9 Sept. 1961; children: Duncan John Drummond, Amanda Jane; comnd. 2nd Lt. 2 Bn. PPCLI Edmonton 1960; promoted Capt. and named aide-de-camp to Chief of Gen. Staff Army HQ Ottawa 1962-64; Co. Commdr. 1 PPCLI Hemer, W. Germany 1964-65; promoted Maj. and Co. Commdr. 1 PPCLI Edmonton and later served with 1 Bn. UN Force Cyprus 1967-68; promoted Bgde. Maj. 1 Combat Group Calgary 1968-70; C.OO 2 PPCLI Winnipeg 1970-72 and promoted Lt. Col.; Sr. Staff Offr. Quartier Général Dist. 3 Qué. (Milice) Québec City 1973; promoted Col. and Commdr. Candn. Forces Base Montreal 1974; Depy. Chief of Staff HQ UN Forces Cyprus and Commdr. Candn. Contingent 1976; promoted to present rank 1977 and apptd. Commandant Royal Mil. Coll. Can. Kingston; assumed command 4 Candn. Mechanized Bgde. Group Lahr, W. Germany 1980-82; Presbyterian; recreations: fishing, painting, jogging, langlauf, skiing; Club: Royal Kingston Un. Services Inst.; Office: HQ 4 CMBG, CFPO 5000, Belleville, Ont. K0K 3R0.

DECHENE, Hon. André Miville, LL.B.; b. Edmonton, Alta., 25 Mar. 1912; s. Jos. Miville and Maria (Gariepy) D.; e. Edmonton Jesuit Coll., Laval Univ. (affiliate) 1925-32; Univ. of Alberta, LL.B. 1939; m. Therese, d. B. J. Dessureau, Bonnyville, Alta., 6 Aug. 1938; children: Charles, Claire; JUSTICE, COURT OF QUEEN'S BENCH OF ALBERTA, since Feb. 1965; read law with Chief Justice G. B. O'Connor; called to Bar of Alta. 1940; formerly practiced law in firm Duncan, Miskew, Dechene, Bowen, Craig & Broseau, Edmonton. Alta.; appt. Dist. Judge N. Alta., Aug. 1963; served as Agent for Imperial Oil Ltd., Marketing Divn., Bonnyville, and also sold fire and life ins., 1932-36; served in 2nd World War 1941-45, with Candn. Armoured Corps, Gen. Staff; discharged with rank of Capt.; def. cand. for Grouard in g.e. 1948 and for Edmonton, g.e. 1952; mem., Bonnyville (Alta.) Sch. Bd., 1940; Edmonton Archives & Land Marks Comte.; Pres., Alta. Young Liberal Assn., 1934; Pres., Edmonton Bar Assn. 1949; mem., Candn. Bar Assn.; K. of C. (Grand Kt. 1947; Dist. Depy. 1949; State Depy. 1954-55); Chairman, Canada Pension Appeals Bd.; mem., Edmonton Separate School Board (Chairman, 1953, 1955, 1956); mem. Extve. Assn. Canadienne des Educ. de Langue Française (1957); Pres., Assn. Canadienne Française de l'Alberta, 1950-56; mem.; Conseil de vie Française en Amerique (Pres. 1965-69); Chrmn. (1968) Friends of Univ. of Alberta; R. Catholic; recreations: curling; Clubs: Canadian; Mayfair Golf & Country; Home: 13845 Summit Dr., Edmonton, Alta. T5N 3S8; Office: Law Courts, Edmonton, Alta. T5J 0R2

DECKER, Franz-Paul; music director; b. Cologne, Germany, 1923; s. Kaspar and Elisabeth (Scholz) D.; e. Cologne Univ. and State Conserv.; Conductor and Music

Dir., Montreal Symphony Orchestra, 1966-76; Choir Dir. and Music Dir., Municipal Theatre, Giessen and Music Dir., Cologne Opera 1945; Perm. Conductor, Krefeld Opera and Orchestra, 1946; Conductor, Wiesbaden State Opera 1950-53; Wiesbaden Mun. Orchestra 1953-56; Gen. Dir., Bochum Orchestra, 1956-64; and Rotterdam Orchestra, 1962-68; has conducted all maj. orchestras in Athens, Brussels, Vienna, Salzburg, Paris, Zurich, Geneva, London, Edinburgh, Berlin, Munich, Lisbon, Madrid, Buenos Aires, Rio de Janeiro, Australia and New Zealand; rec'd German "Bundesverdienst Kreuz" 1st Class; Edgard Roquette Pinto-Medaille, Brazil and "Herscheppend schepik" Medal, Holland; mem., Soc. Contemporary Music; Address: Place des Arts, 200 Maissoneuve, Montreal, Que.

DECORE, The Hon. Mr. Justice John N., Q.C., B.A., LL.B., LL.D.; judge; b. Andrew, Alberta, 9 Apl. 1909; s. Nykola and Hafia (Kostiuk) D.; e. Pub. and High Schs., Alta.; Edmonton (Alta.) Normal Sch. (Grad. 1930); Univ. of Alta., B.A. (Arts) 1937, LL.B. 1938; m. Myrosia, d. Victor Kupchenko, Edmonton, Alta., 22 Sept. 1935; three s., John Victor, Lawrence George, Lionel Leighton; SUPERNUMERARY JUDGE OF THE COURT OF QUEEN'S BENCH OF ALBERTA since 1979; Chief Judge of the District Ct. of Alta. to June 30, 1979; formerly practised with law firm of Decore and Co., which he estbd. having offices in Vegreville and Edmonton, Alta.; called to Bar of Alta. 1939; cr. Q.C. 1963; Prov. Pres. Alta. Liberal Assn., 1958; mem. for Vegreville to H. of C., 1949-57; Parlty. Adviser to Candn. Del., U.N. Gen. Assembly, 1950; moved the nomination of Lester Pearson for the leadership of the Liberal Party succeeding Louis St. Lawrent; Ukrainian Greek Orthodox; Home: 8339 Saskatchewan Dr., Edmonton, Alta. T6G 2A7; Office: The Law Courts, Edmonton; Alta. T5J 0R2

DE COSTER, Robert, O.C., M.Sc., C.A.; né à Montréal, P.Q. 20 aout 1918; f. Albert et Aurore (Chateauvert) DeC.; é Académie de Québec; Univ. de Laval (Sc. de L'Administration); èp. Rita, f. J.-Ed. Verreault (décédé) 5 Juin 1943; enfants: Jean, Elise, Louis, Claude; PRESIDENT DU CONSEIL ET CHEF DE LA DIRECTION, SIDBEC ET SIDBEC-DOSCO, 1979: Hôpital Universitaire Laval; Prés., Camp Ecole Trois-Saumons; Institut Canadien des Affaires Internationales; Verificateur public, McDonald, Currie 1946-56; Contrôleur, Rock City Tobacco 1956-57, Irving Oil Inc. et Les Pétroles Inc. 1957-59; Gérant, Royal Trust 1959-65; Pres.-Fondateur, Régie de Rentes du Québec 1965-70; Sous-ministre, Ministère de l'Industrie et du Comm. 1970-75; Prés., Conseil général de l'Industrie du Qué. 1975-76; Prés.-fondateur, Régié des mesures anti-inflationistes (1975-76); Pres. Foundateur, Regie de l'assurance Automatobile du Québec (1976-79); Admin., Chambre de Comm. de Québec 1963-65, de la Province de Québec 1962-65; Trésorier, Carnaval d'hiver de Québec 1959; Vice-Pres., Campagne de Souscription, Univ. Laval 1967 et Conseil des Oeuvres; servit avec l'Armée Canadienne 1942-46, Officier; mem. Chambre de Comm. française du Canada; Chambre de Comm. Qué.; Am. Iron & Steel Inst.; Internat. Iron & Steel Inst.; Catholique romain; récréations: golf, pêche; Clubs: Cercle universitaire (Québec); Club de Golf Cap-Rouge (Québec); St. Denis (Montreal); Cercle de la Place d'Armes (Montreal); Résidence: 2172 Parc Bourbonière, Sillery; Québec. G1T 1B4; Bureau: 1134 Chemin Saint-Louis, Sillery, Qué. G1S 1E5

DEDEKAM, Hans J., B.L.; transportation executive; b. Oslo, Norway, 31 July 1917; s. Andre and Louise (Sparre) D.; e. Univ. of Oslo, Bachelor of Law; Business Adm., Paris, France; m. Phyllis, d. Ole Jesperson, Taber, Alberta, 20 Oct. 1952; one s. Eric; MANAGER FOR CANADA, SCANDINAVIAN AIRLINES SYSTEM; Trustee, Candn. Scandinavian Foundation; Chief Exec. Officer (secondment) British West Indian Airways, Trinidad, 1972, served in 2nd World War; wartime commission in Brit.

Army. Lieut., R.A.; Capt. Norwegian Army; mem., Montreal Bd. Trade; United Church; Clubs: Ad & Sales Executives; The Wings (New York); M.A.A.A.; Home: 121 Vivian Ave., Montreal, Que. H3P 1N8; Office: 1200 McGill College Ave., Suite 1420, Montreal, Que. H3B 4G7

de GOUMOIS, Michel, B.A. LL.L.; diplomat; b. Quebec City, Que. 21 March 1935; s. late Maurice and Marguerite (Picard) de G.; e. Laval Univ. B.A. 1954, LL.L 1957; called to Bar of Que. 1958; joined Dept. of External Affairs 1958, Third Secy. Karachi 1960, Adviser Laos and Vietnam Internat. Control Comns. 1961, Second Secy. London 1963, Legal and Fed. Prov. Divs. Ottawa 1966, Counsellor Dakar 1968, Dir. Francophone Insts. Div. Ottawa 1971, Ambassador to Ivory Coast, Mali, Upper Volta, Niger 1975; Depy. Under-Secy. of State for External Affairs 1978; Ambassador to Switzerland 1981-; Naval Cadet UNTD 1952-56, Lt. RCN(R), retired 1958; R. Catholic; recreations: golf, tennis, skiing; Club: Cercle Universitaire; Office: Dept. External Affairs, c/o Pearson Bldg., Sussex Dr., Ottawa, Ont. K1A 0G2

de GRANDPRE, A. J., Q.C.; b. Montreal, Que., 14 Sept. 1921; s. Roland and Aline (Magnan) de G.; e. Coll. Jean-de-Brebeuf, Montreal, Que., B.A. 1940; McGill Univ., B.C.L. 1943; Ph.D. (Hon. causa), Univ. of Que., 1979; m. Hélène, d. Azarie Choquet, Montreal, Que., 27 Sept. 1947; children: Jean-François, Lilianne, Suzanne, Louise: CHMN. AND CHIEF EXTVE. OFFR., BELL CANADA 1976-; Chrm. of the Bd. and Chrm. of Exec. Comm., Northern Telecom Ltd.; Dir., Toronto-Dominion Bank; Northern Telecom Ltd.; Northern Telecom Inc.; Chrysler Corp. (Detroit); Stelco Inc.; Dupont Canada Inc.; Trans-Canada Pipe Lines Ltd.; The Seagram Co. Ltd.; former partner, Tansey, de Grandpré, de Grandpré, Bergeron & Monet; Gov. McGill Univ.; read law with Hon. F. Philippe Brais, Q.C.; called to the Bar of Que., 1943; Legal Counsel, Roy. Comn. on Broadcasting 1956-57; cr. Q.C. 1961; Life mem., Candn. Bar Assn.; mem. Montreal Chamber Comm. (Dir. 1969-70); Assn. Candn. Gen. Counsel (emeritus); Bar of Que. Liberal; R. Catholic; Clubs: St. Denis; St. James's; Mount Bruno Country, Canadian; Home: Apt. 92, 445 St. Joseph Blvd. W., Montreal, Que. H2V 2P8; Office: 1050 Beaver Hall Hill, Montreal, Qué. H2Z 1S3

de GRANDPRE, Louis-Philippe, C.C., Q.C., B.A., B.C.L., L.L.D.; b. Montreal, Que., 6 Feb. 1917; s. Roland and Aline (Magnan) de G.; e. Coll. Sainte-Marie, Montreal; Univ. of Montreal, B.A. 1935; B.C.L., McGill Univ. 1938; LL.D. McGill Univ. 1972; LL.D. Ottawa Univ. 1973; Hon. D.C.L. (McGill Univ.) Hon. D. Phil. (Univ. of Quebec); m. Marthe Gendron d. late Hon. Lucien H. Gendron, P.C. Q.C., Montreal, 25 October 1941; children: Michel, Ivan, Sylvie, Francine; SR. PARTNER, LAFLEUR, BROWN, de GRANDPRE 1977; called to Bar of Que. 1938; K.C. 1949; Bâtonnier, Montreal Bar 1968-69; Prov. Que. 1968-69; Pres. Canadian Bar Assn. 1972-73; practised law in Montreal 1938-73; Justice, Supreme Court of Can. 1974-77; admitted to the Law Soc. of Upper Can. 1978, and the Law Soc. of Sask. 1981; Dir., Guardian Insurance Co. of Can.; Montreal Life Ins. Co.; Montreal Trust Co.; Soc. de Gestion Katerina Inc.; R. Catholic; Club: Mount Royal; home: 310 Trenton Ave., Town of Mount Royal, Que. H3P 1Z9; Office: Suite 720, Stock Exchange Tower, Place Victoria, Montreal, Que. H4Z 1E4

De GUISE, Yvon, B.A. Sc.; utilities executive; b. Montreal, Que. 10 March 1914; e. Ecole Polytech. de Montréal, B.A.Sc.(Engn.) 1937; m. Georgette Garneau; children: Claire, Lorraine; ENERGY CONSULTANT, LAVALIN INC. 1976-; vice president, hydro-Quebec 1974-76 and Commissioner there since 1965; Dir. Churchill Falls (Labrador) Corp. Ltd.; Place Desjardins Inc.; Atomic Energy of Canada Ltd.; with Canadian General Electric Co., test

courses and training Peterborough and Toronto 1937; Prof. of Hydrology and Power Projects, Ecole Polytech. 1943-55; joined Prov. Que. Hydraulic Dept. 1939; Chief Engr's Office Hydraulic and Power Stns. Dept., Hydro-Québec 1945, subsequently Operations Engr. Beauharnois Power Stn. 1947, Supt. Engr. Power Stns. 1951, Asst. Chief Engr. Regional Operating Div. 1954, Gen. Mgr. Operations and Sales 1962, Production and Transmission 1962, apptd. Acting Commr. 1964; Chrmn. Canadn. Comte. World Energy Conf. 1976-79; Extve. mem. Bd. Dirs. Canadn. Buclear Assn.; mem. Science Council of Can. 1976-79; Order of Engrs. Qué.; Engn. Inst. Can.; Am. Inst. Elect. Engrs. American Nuclear Soc.; Chambre de Comm. Montréal; Past mem. Candn.-Am. subcomte. i.c. planning regulation of St. Lawrence River Lake Ont. exit flow; R. Catholic; Office: 1130 Sherbrooke St. W., Montreal, Que. H3A 2R5

dekERGOMMEAUX, Duncan Chassin, R.C.A.; artist; educator; b. Premier, B.C. 15 July 1927; s. Robert Chassin and Cecilia Roberts (Halliwell) deK.; e. Banff Sch. of Fine Arts 1951; Hans Hoffman Sch. of Fine Arts, Provincetown, Mass. 1955-57; Instituto Allende, Mexico 1958; full-time student of Jan Zach, Victoria, B.C. 1951-54; children: Davin Jay, Byron Drew, Laurie Gillian; CHRMN. OF VISUAL ARTS, UNIV. OF WESTERN ONT. 1981- and Prof. 1980-; Project Designer Expo 67, Dir. Candn. Pavilion Art Gallery Expo 67; Project Designer Dept. of Secy. of State and Man. Govt., Man. Centennial Caravan 1970; Instr. Univ. of W. Ont. 1970, Asst. Prof. 1972, Assoc. Prof. 1974-80; over 30 solo exhns. since 1956; rep. many maj. group exhns. Can. and abroad; paintings toured Can. by Nat. Gallery 1967-68; several comns. Fed. Govt. and private architects; rep. maj. pub. colls. Can. and several abroad incl. Nat. Gallery Can., Art Gallery of Ont.; mem. Candn. Univ. Teachers Assn.; Univ. Art Assn.; Home: 437 Everglade Cres., London, Ont. N6H 4M8; Office: London, Ont. N6A 5B7.

De KORT, Joseph A., B.A.; trust company executive; e. Univ. of W. Ont. B.A. 1965; Ryerson Polytech. Inst.; M.T.C.I. 1976; SR. VICE PRES., THE METROPOLITAN TRUST CO. 1978- ; Dir. Canada First Mortgage Co.; InternationalSavings & Mortgage Co.; Systems Analyst, Woods Gordon 1965-69; Mang. Consultant 1970-72; Mgr. Mortgage Dept. present co. 1972, Vice Pres. Corporate Systems 1974-78; Ald. Ward 12 Scarborough 1975-80; mem. Works & Transport. Comte. 1975, 1978; Recreation & Parks Comte. 1976, 1977, 1979; Gov. Scarborough Gen. Hosp. 1976-79; mem. Alliance of Gas Operators; Bd. Trade Metrop. Toronto; Scarborough N. Prov. Lib. Assn.; York Scarborough Fed. Lib. Assn.; Home: 64 Blueberry Dr., Agincourt, Ont. M1S 3M3; Office: 353 Bay St., Toronto, Ont. M5H 2T8.

de LALANNE, Brig. James Arthur, C.B.E., M.C., O.St.J., E.D., LL.D (McGill, 1980), B.A., C.A.; b. Westmount, Que., 1897; e. McGill Univ., B.A.; m. Mildred Pollock Eakin, (died 1962) 1924; has one s.; Consultant, McDonald, Currie & Co. (now Coopers & Lybrand), Chart. Accts.; Dir., Longtin Conduits Inc.; former Dir., Pirelli Can. Ltd.; Lunham & Moore Ltd.; Spencer Supports (Canada) Ltd.; Aldger Ltd.; Pres., Candn. Inst. Chart. Accts. (1957-58); former Gov., McGill Univ., Ald. and Mayor of Westmount, Que.; mem. Prot. Comte. Council of Educ.; Montreal Adv. Bd., Canada Permanent Trust Co.; Pres., Inst. Chart. Accts. Que. (1952-53); McGill Grad. Soc. (1950-52); Rotary Club of Westmount (1939-40), Chrmn., Westmount Bd. of Sch. Commrs.; Pres., Candn. Rugby Union (1939-40); Past Pres. and Life mem. Que. Amateur Hockey Assn., Vice-Pres., M.A.A.A.; served in 1st World War; enlisted as a Pte. with P.P.C.L.I. and commissioned in the field; M.C. and Bar; thrice wounded; joined McDonald, Currie & Co. on full-time basis in 1920; served in 2nd World War joining Active Army with rank of Major, 1940; held various staff appts. travelling between Can. and Europe, and promoted to rank of Brig.; apptd. Vice Adj.-Gen. 1945; Awarded Commander of the Order of the British Empire; Order of the White Lion (Czechoslovak Republic); Hon. Lt. Col., McGill Univ. Contingent, C.O.T.C.; Vice Patron and former Pres., P.P.C.L.I. Assn.; Chrmn., and Gov., Candn. Corps of Commissionaires, Montreal Div.; Pres., Montreal United Services Inst. 1970-71; Hon. Chrmn. (former chrmn.), Paraplegique Assn. Que. Div.; Offr. Brother, Order of St. John; Grand Pres. and former Dom. Hon. Treas., Royal Candn. Legion, and Trustee, Centennial Foundation; Hon. Vice-Pres., Commonwealth Games Assn. of Can.; former Pres., Last Post Fund; Home: 633 Lansdowne Ave.; Westmount, Que. H3Y 2V7

DELANEY, Austin B.; manufacturer; b. London, Eng., 28 Oct. 1933; s. Francis George and Marie (Cockx) D.; e. Finchley Grammar Sch., London, Eng.; m. Maria Leontine, d. E. Neefs, Veltem, Belgium, 5 Aug. 1957; children: Danielle, Austin Paul; PRESIDENT, BELL & HOWELL LTD. Pres. since 1971, Mgr., Marks and Spencer Ltd., London, Eng., 1956-58; Mgr., Sawyer's Photographic Products (U.K.) Ltd., London, 1958-68; Sales and Marketing Mgr., Bell and Howell Ltd., London, 1968-69; came to Can. 1970 and apptd. Extve. Vice Pres. of present Co.; mem., Bd. Trade Metrop. Toronto; R. Catholic; recreations: skiing, photography, reading; Home: 10 Meadow Height Court, Thornhill, Ont. L4J 1V6; Office: 230 Barmac Dr., Weston, Ont. M9L 2X5

DE LERY, Alexandre C., B.A., B.A.Sc.; executive; b. Quebec, Que., 25 Aug. 1921; s. Suzanne (Gourdeau) and late C. de L.; e. Séminaire de Québec 1933-39; Univ. Laval, B.A. 1942, B.A.Sc. (Elect. Engn.) 1948; m. Paule, d. late Eugène Loignon, 14 Oct. 1950; children: Claude, André, Renée; PRESIDENT AND MANG. DIR., ASEA LTD. since 1964; Dir., ASEA Industries Ltd.; Sidbec-Dosco Ltée; with Northern Electric Ltd. in various engn. positions 1948 and subsequently with John Inglis Ltd.; Mgr., Que., English Electric Canada Ltd. 1957; Asst. Co-ordinator, Candn. Council of Resources Mins. 1963; Chrmn., Illuminating Engn. Soc., Que. Chapter 1952-53; mem. Order of Engrs. of Que.; Engn. Inst. of Can. (mem. Publ. Comte. 1967-70); Inst. Elect. and Electronic Engrs.; R. Catholic; recreations: golf, tennis, skiing; Club: Beaconsfield Golf; Home: 2 Fifth Ave., Pointe Claire, Que. H9S 5C7; Office: 10300 Henri-Bourassa Blvd. W., Saint Laurent, Que. H4S 1N6

DELISLE, Jacques, Q.C., B.A., LL.L; lawyer; b. Montréal, Que. 4 May 1935; S. Roch and Cecile (Miller) D.; e. Collège de Jésuites, Québec B.A. 1954; Univ. Laval, Québec, LL.L. 1957; Univ. de Paris 1958-59; Univ. de Toronto 1959-60; m. Nicole Rainville 17 Sept. 1960; children: Elène, Jean; LAWYER, LETOURNEAU AND STEIN; called to the Bar of Québec, 1958; cr. Q.C. 17 Sept. 1973; Home: 1240 de Samos Sillery, Que. G1T 2K4; Office: 65 Ste-Anne St., Ste. 400, Que. G1R 3X5.

DELISLE, Jean-Louis, B.A., M.A., LL.L.; diplomat (retired); b. Quebec City, P.Q., 14 Jan. 1912; s. François and Antoinette (Côté) D.; e. Petit Seminaire de Québec, B.A. 1933; Laval Univ., LL.L. 1936; Rhodes Scholar, Oxford Univ., B.A. (Hons.) 1939; M.A. 1968; m. Constance, d. Ovila Charette, Ottawa, Ont., 28 Oct. 1946; children: Martin, Sylvie; called to the Bar of Quebec, 1936; Secy., Prime Minister's Office, Ottawa, Ont., 1942-46; 2nd Secy., Canadian Embassy, Rio de Janeiro, 1946-49; Consul of Canada, Boston, Mass., 1951-54; Chargé d'Affaires and Head of Post Canadian Legation, Warsaw, 1954-56; mem., United Nations Comn. on French Togoland, 1957; Head of Legal Div., Dept. of External Affairs, Ottawa, Ont., 1958-59; Counsellor, Press and Cultural Affairs, Candn. Embassy, Paris, 1959-61; Ambassador to Costa Rica, El Salvador, Honduras, Nicaragua and Panama, 1961-64; Ambassador to Turkey 1964-67; Ambassador and Permanent Rep. to the U.N. and other internat. organs. in Geneva 1967-70; Dir., Academic Relations, Dept. Ex-

ternal Affairs 1970-73; Consul Gen. of Can., Boston, Mass. 1973-76; Lectr., Laval Univ. 1977; Pres., Int. Assoc. of Francophone Elders 1981; Catholic; recreations: swimming, skiing; Address: 1155, rue Turnbull (app 602), Quebec, Que. G1R 5G3

DELISLE, Jules, L.Ph., B.Sc.A., M.Sc.A.; engineer; university professor; b. Quebec City, Que. 9 April 1929; s. Gérard and Anna (Girard) D.; e. Univ. Laval, Que., B.Sc.A. 1959; Ecole Nat. Sup. de l'Aréronautique, Paris, M.Sc.A. 1960; Faculté des Sciences, Paris, 1966; m. Mariette d. Emile Cantin 1 Aug. 1959; children: Sylvie, Pierre, Alain; ENGINEER and PROFESSOR, UNIVERSITE DE SHERBROOKE; Head of Elec. Engn. Dept. 1967-71; Dean of Engn. Faculty, 1973-81; Vice Chrmn. Candn. Accreditation Bd., 1981-; co-author of "Introduction aux circuits logiques;" "Travaux pratiques en CCTS logiques"; publ. articles on switching circuit designs and automatic audiometric measurement; 6 patents in the fields of electrical load controllers and automatic audiometry; mem., Ordre des Ingénieurs du Québec; Inst. of Electronics and Electrical Engn.; R. Catholic; recreations: jogging, swimming, skiing; reading, movies; Home: 275 Rioux, Sherbrooke, Que. J1J 2W9; Office: 2500 Blvd. Université, Sherbrooke, Que. J1K 2R1.

DELORME, J. Noé, M.T.C.I.; banker; b. Montreal, Que., 13 Nov. 1933; s. Ulric and Alice (Giguere) D.; e. St-Stanislas High Sch. Montreal 1951; Queen's Univ. grad. in Trust Business 1966; m. Claudette d. Joseph Valade, Montreal, Que., 5 May 1956; children: Carole, Fabienne, Christian, Stephane; GEN. MGR. AND CHIEF OPERATING OFFR. DIR. MONTREAL CITY AND DISTRICT TRUSTEES LTD. since 1976; joined Montreal City and District Savings Bank 1951-53; joined present Co. (subsidiary) 1954, Income Tax Offr. 1957, Acct. 1959, Office Mgr. 1963, Secy. 1969, Asst. Gen Mgr. and Extve. Secy. 1975; served with RCAF 1953-54, rank Flight Offr.; mem. Trust Co.'s Assn. & Inst.; R. Catholic; recreations: tennis, skating, skiing; Home: 1561 O'Brien, Chambly, Que. J3L 3C7; Office: 1253 McGill College, Montreal. Que. H3B 2Z6

DELORME, Jean-Claude, O.C. (1967), B.A., L.LL.; b. Berthierville, Que.; 22 May 1934; s. Adrien and Marie-Anne (Rodrigue) D.; e. Coll. Sainte-Marie, Montreal, B.A. 1955; Univ. of Montreal, LL.L. 1959; m. Paule, d. Gérard Tardif, 2 Sept. 1961; two d. Catherine, Marie-Eve; PRES. AND CHIEF EXTVE. OFFR., TELEGLOBE CANADA (1971), formerly known as Candn. Overseas Telecommunication Corp.; Dir., C.B.C. 1968-76; Pres. La Régie de la Place des Arts; admitted Bar of Que. 1960; with law firm of Martineau, Walker, Allison, Beaulieu, Tetley & Phelan until apptd. Secy. and Gen. Counsel Expo '67 1963; Gen. Counsel and Asst. to Chrmn. and Chief Extve. Offr. Standard Brands Ltd. 1968; Vice-Pres. Adm. and Secy. and Gen. Counsel Telesat Canada 1969; apptd. Chrmn. Council of Commonwealth Telecommunications Organ. 1973; Dir., The Arthritis Soc. of Montreal; The Internat. Inst. of Music; L'Opera du Québec; mem. Que. Bar Assn.; Chambre de Comm. de Montreal; Confraternia Gastronom.; Accad. Italiana Della Cucina; Club Gastronom. Prosper Montagné; Confrérie des Vignerons de St-Vincent; La Confrérie des Vinophiles; Past Pres. les Grands Ballets Candns.; Coll. Ste-Marie; Assn. des Diplômes de l'Univ. de Montréal (1965-68): awarded Centennial Medal and Gold Medal. Czechoslovakian Sol. Internat. Relations; recreations: sailing, skiing; Clubs: St. James's; Cercle Universitaire; St. Denis; Home: 3 Glendale Ave., Beaconsfield, Que.; Office: 680 Sherbrooke St. W., Montreal, Que. H3A 2S4

DE LUCCA, John, B.B.A., M.A., Ph.D.; educator; b. Brooklyn, N.Y. 8 Oct. 1920; s. late Carlo and late Adela (Ianniello) De L.; e. City Coll. of New York B.B.A. 1941; New Sch. for Social Research M.A. 1950; Harvard Univ. grad. studies in philos. 1952-53; Ohio State Univ. Ph.D. 1955; m. Margaret Louise d. late Luther Williams 10 June

1956; children: Danielle Sue, David Jonathan; PROF. OF PHILOS., QUEEN'S UNIV. 1968- ; Pres. and Gen. Mgr. Johart International Corp. New York 1946-51; Lectr. in Philos. Pace Coll. N.Y. 1950-52; Acting Instr. in Eng. Ohio State Univ. 1955-56; Asst. Prof. of Philos. Wash. State Univ. 1956-62; Founding Chrmn. and Assoc. Prof. of Philos. Univ. of Victoria, B.C. 1962-68; served with U.S. Army 1942-45, W. Pacific Theatre; rec'd Unit Merit Citation; Ed. "Reason and Experience: Dialogues in Modern Philosophy" 1973; Ed. and Transl. "Descartes' Meditations on First Philosophy" 1975; author various articles, book reviews prof. journs.; Univ. Fellow, Ohio State Univ. 1954-55; mem. Beta Gamma Sigma; Candn. Philos. Assn.; Humanities Assn. Can.; Am. Philos. Assn. (Extve. Comte. Pacific Div. 1965-67; Chrmn. Program Comte. 1967); Philos. of Science Assn.; Northwest Conf. on Philos. (Pres. 1959-60); recreations: reading, photography, classical music and opera; Home: 10 Copperfield Dr., Kingston, Ont. K7M 1M4; Office: Kingston, Ont. K7L 3N6.

DeLURY, Daniel Bertrand, M.A., Ph.D.; professor; b. Walker, Minnesota, 19 Sept. 1907; s. Robert E. and Allie Marie (Bertrand) D.; e. Ottawa (Ont.) Coll. Inst.; Univ. of Toronto, B.A. 1929, M.A. 1930, Ph.D. 1936; m. Lila Eveline, d. John Thompson, Carduff, Sask., 1941; children: Lila Catherine, Robert Thompson; PROF. OF MATH., UNIV. OF TORONTO, since 1958; Instr. in Math., Univ. of Sask., 1931-34; Lectr. and Asst. Prof., Univ. of Toronto, 1937-45; Assoc. Prof. of Stat., Virginia Polytech. Inst., 1945-47; Dir., Dept. of Math. Statistics, Ont. Research Foundation, 1947-58; Publications: "Values and Integrals of the Orthogonal Polynomials up to n 26", 1950; "Confidence Limits for the Hypergeometric Distribution" (with J. H. Chung), 1950; mem., Candn. Statistical Soc.; Am. Math. Soc.; Am. Stat. Assn.; Inst. of Math. Stat.; Biometric Soc.; Internat. Stat. Inst.; Sigma Xi; Home: 35 Owen Blvd., Willowdale, Ont. M2P 1G2

DELWORTH, W(illiam) Thomas, M.A.; diplomat; b. Toronto, Ont., 24 Feb. 1929; s. Cecil Ivor and Jessie Strang (Corry) D.;e. Humber Heights Consol. Sch., Weston, Ont.; Weston (Ont.) Coll. Inst., 1947; Univ. of Toronto, B.A. 1951, M.A. 1956; m. Pamela Greene, d. B. B. Osler, Q.C., 27 Sept. 1969; apptd. Director General, Bureau of Asia/Pacific Affairs, Dept. of External Affairs, Ottawa, June 1978, Asst. Under-Sec'y, Oct. 1980; joined Dept. of External Affairs 1956; Extve. Asst. to Min. 1957-59; Candn. Embassy, Stockholm, 1959-63; Sr. Pol. Advisor to Candn. Commr., Internat. Comn. for Supervision and Control in Vietnam, Saigon and Hanoi, 1963-64; Far E. Div., Ottawa, 1964-70; Ambassador to Indonesia 1970-74; Ambassador and Head Candn. Del., Conf. on Security and Co-op. in Europe 1974; apptd. (first resident) Can. Ambassador to Hungary, 1975; concurrently Ambassador and Head Can. Del., Belgrade Conf. on Security and Co-op. in Europe, 1977-78; Address: 220 Lakeway Drive, Ottawa, Ont.

DeMARCO, Frank Anthony, M.A.Sc., Ph.D., F.C.I.C.; university administrator; b. Podargoni, Reggio Calabria, Italy, 14 Feb. 1921; s. Frank and Carmela (Scappatura) DeM.; e. North Bay (Ont.) Coll. Inst. 1938 (Robert Simpson Scholar.); Univ. of Toronto, B.A.Sc. 1942, M.A.Sc. 1943 (International Nickel Co. Scholar.), Ph.D. (Chem. Engn.) 1951 (Sch. of Engn. Fellowship); Inst. of Coll. Adm. & Coll. Prof.'s Workshop, Univ. of Mich., 1956; Computer Systems for Univ. Pres. course, 1969; Systems Analysis & Research course, 1970; m. Mary, d. late Tony Valenti, Toronto, Ont., 1 May 1948; children: Maria, Anna (Mrs. John Moore), Jean, Paula, Christine, John, Dante, Thomas, James, Teresa, Robert, Jerry; SR. VICE PRES., UNIV. OF WINDSOR since 1973; Instr., Univ. of Toronto 1943-46; Asst. Prof. and subsequently Prof. and Head, Chem. Dept., Assumption Coll. (became Assumption Univ. 1953), 1946-57, Dir. of Athletics 1949-55, Chrmn. Staff Comte., Essex Coll. of Univ. 1956-59, Act-

ing Head, Engn. Dept. 1957-59, Princ., Essex Coll. 1959-63, Assoc. Dean of Arts & Science 1958, Dean, Faculty of Applied Science 1959-64; Vice Pres., Univ. of Windsor 1963-73, Acting Dean of Engn. 1972-73, Acting Dean of Extension and Continuing Educ. 1975-76; Chrmn., Univ. Div. Devel Fund 1963-68; has served industry in various fields incl. research and as consultant in polyester resins, fiberglass laminates, fire-resistant cardboard; has held various offices Council Ont. Univs.; mem. 1st Council, Ont. Educ. Communications Authority Regional Council; mem. Organ. Comte. and Adv. Council, W. Ont. Inst. Technol.; Founding Chrmn. St. Clair Coll. of Applied Arts & Technol.; mem. Windsor (Ont.) Suburban Dist. High Sch. Bd.; Essex Co. Bd. of Educ. (mem. various comtes.); former Dir., Willistead Art Gallery; mem. Mang. Comte. and Chrmn. Inst. Div., Un. Fund Windsor; rec'd Coronation Medal 1953; Centennial Medal 1967; CKWW Citizen of Week Award for educ. and community work; Univ. of Windsor Alumni Award 1971; St. Clair Coll. Alumni Award; has conducted research in co-ordination compounds, brittle copper (electro-deposition), synthesis of cyanine dyes, solubilization properties of non-ionics; author of various articles in prof. journs.; Councillor and Chrmn. Chem. Educ. Div., Chem. Inst. Can.; mem. Am. Soc. Engn. Educ.; Assn. Prof. Engrs. Ont.; Candn. Soc. Study Higher Educ.; Windsor Art Gallery; mem. Ont. Min. of Health Comte. on the effects on Human Health of lead from the Environment; R. Catholic; recreations: curling, golf, squash, canoeing, art, travel; Clubs: Essex Golf; Windsor Curling; Home: 7750 Matchette Rd., Windsor, Ont. N9J 2J4

de MAYO, Paul, Ph.D., D.és Sc., F.R.S.C., F.R.S.; educator; b. London, Eng., 8 Aug. 1924; e. Univ. of London, B.A. 1944, M.A. 1952, Ph.D. 1954; Univ. of Paris, D.és Sc. 1969; m. Mary Turnbull, 19 May 1949; children: Ann Gabrielle, Philip Nicholas; PROF. OF CHEM., UNIV. OF WEST. ONT.; Dir.,Photochem. Unit there 1969-73; rec'd Merck, Sharp and Dohme Lecture Award 1966; Centennial Medal 1967; author, "The Higher Terpenoids", 1959; "Mono- and Sesquiterpenoids", 1959; Ed. "Molecular Rearrangements" 1963; Ed. "Rearrangments in Ground and Excited States", 1980; also numerous publs. in scient. lit.; mem. Am. Chem. Soc.; Chem. Inst. Can.; Chem. Soc. (London); Home: 436 St. George St., London, Ont. N6A 3B4; Office: London, Ont. N6A 5B7

DEMERS, Georges L., Q.C., LL.L., B.C.S.; b. Quebec, P.Q., 1 March 1920; s. Albert, K.C. and Yvonne C. (de Léry) D.; e. Quebec Little Semy.; Ottawa Univ. (Philos.), B.A. 1940; Laval Univ., LL.L. 1943; Laval Sch. of Comm., B.C.S. 1945; Pres. Sterling Securities Corp.; Dir., Northern Telecom Co. Ltd.; Grissol Foods Ltd.; Gounr. Laval Univ.; Hon. Swedish Consul in Que.; read law with Albert Demers and W. Desjardins and Jean Lesage; called to the Bar of Que. 1944; cr. Q.C. 1963; Part., Demers, Gosselin & Robitailles Attorneys; Past Pres., Que. Young Liberal Assn.; Pres., Que. Jr. Bar Assn. 1955; mem., Candn. Bar Assn.; Nat. 1st Vice Pres., Candn. Chamber Comm. 1971-72; Pres., Prov. Que. Chambre de Comm. 1968-69; Liberal; Roman Catholic; recreations: golf, fishing, hunting; Clubs: Reform; Garrison; University; Triton Fish and Game; Home: Town of St. Nicolas, Que.; Office: 425 est, Boul. Charest, Suite 502, Quebec, Que.

DEMERS, Pierre, B.E.; executive; b. Montreal, Que. 20 April 1929; s. Joseph Henri and Juliette (Lymburner) D.; e. Primary Sch., Noranda and Montreal, Que. 1942; Catholic High Sch., Montreal 1948; McGill Univ., B.A. (Elect. with Comm. option) 1952; m. Madeleine, d. Jean Jacques Charbonneau, 3 May 1952; children: Christiane, Yves, Jocelyne, Guy; PRESIDENT, AND GENERAL MANAGER, DGB CONSULTANTS INC., Systems Consultants since 1968; with Candn. Armament Research and Devel. Estab., Defence Research Bd. 1952-55; Sperry Gyroscope of Canada 1956; RCA Victor Co. Ltd. 1957-59; Partner, Demers, Homa, Baby, Consulting Engrs. 1960-

68; Commr., Preparatory Comn. for Conversion to Metric System; mem. Corp. Engrs. Que. (Pres. 1963); Assn. Consulting Engrs. Can. (Pres. 1971); Engn. Inst. of Can.; R. Catholic; Club: Cercle Universitaire; Home: 11 - 515 Laforest, Montréal, Que. H3M 2W5; Office: 1 Complexe Desjardins, P.O. Box 40, Desjardins Postal Stn., Montréal, Que. H5B 1B2

DEMERS, Pierre, B.A., L.Sc., M.Sc., D.Sc., F.R.S.C., nuclear physicist; university professor; b. Deal, Kent, Eng., 8 Nov. 1914; s. Alfred and Blanche (Legris) D.; e. Primary Schs. in Paris, Cannes, and Grasse, 1922-25; Coll. Sainte Marie, Montreal, P.Q., 1925-27; Coll. Jean de Brébeuf, Montreal, 1927-33; Univ. of Montreal, B.A. 1933, L.Sc. 1935, M.Sc. 1936; Ecole Normale Supérieure, Paris 1938-40; Agrégé de L'Univ. de France 1939; Coll. de France, 1939-40; Univ. of Paris, D.Sc. 1950; PROF. PHYSICS DEPT., FACULTY OF SCIENCE, UNIV. OF MONTREAL, since 1947; Physicist, Research & Devel. Lab., Canadian Industries Ltd., 1940-43; Atomic Energy Lab. and Chalk River Lab., Nat. Research Council of Can., 1943-46; Assoc. Prof. of Physics, Univ. of Montreal, 1947-52; Professeur Titulaire, 1952; winner of a number of prizes in acad. work and awarded a number of scholarships; mem., Candn. Assn. of Physicists (Past Treas.); Soc. de Physique et de Math. de Montréal (Pres. 1950-52); Ass. Can. Fr. Avanc. des Sciences; Am. Phys. Soc.; Italiana di Fisica, Italy; Assn. cath. des Intellectuels francais; Amicale des prof. francais au Can.; mem. du Conseil des Arts du Qué.; mem. Fondateur et Trés., Centre d'Etudes Prospective du Qué.; has contrib. scient. papers to "Canadian Journ. of Physics", "Physical Review" and others; Roman Catholic; recreations: reading, painting, swimming; Home: 1200 rue Latour, Montréal, Que. H4L 4S4; Office: C.P. 6128, Montreal, Que. H3C 3J7

DEMERS, Robert, B.A., B.C.L.; company president; b. Montreal, Que., 10 Oct. 1937; s. André and Berthe (Bélanger) D.; e. Coll. Stanislas, Montreal, B.A. (Univ. of Paris) 1957; McGill Univ., B.C.L. 1961; m. Liliane, d. Paul Densky, 15 May 1960; children: François, Catherine; PRES., MONTREAL STOCK EXCHANGE 1976-; called to the Bar of Que. 1961; Chrm., Quebec Securities Comm. 1972, Dir., Listings Dept., Montreal and Candn. Stock Exchanges 1962; Financial Advisor, Que. Dept. Educ. 1964; mem. of law firm, Desjardins, Ducharme, 1966; recreations: fishing, hunting, swimming; Home: 372 Deguire, Montreal, Que. H4N 1P6; Office: Stock Exchange Tower, Montreal, Que.

DEMIRJIAN, Arto, D.D.S., M.Sc.D.; educator; b. Istanbul, Turkey 11 Feb. 1931; s. Karekin and Teshkoyan D.; e. Coll. St-Michel, Istanbul, B.A. 1949; Univ. of Istanbul Dipl. Dental Surg. 1953; Univ. de Montréal D.D.S. 1959; Univ. of Toronto M.Sc.D. Anat. 1961; m. Giragosyan Garabet, Vancouver, B.C. Sept. 1959; 2 children; PROF. OF ANAT., FACULTY OF DENTAL MED., UNIV. DE MONTREAL 1971- ; Dir. Growth Research Center 1970- ; Asst. Prof. of Anat. Dept. Oral Biol. Faculty of Dentistry present Univ. 1961-65, Assoc. Prof. 1965-71; recipient Candn. Dental Assn.'s War Mem. Award; served with Turkish Army 1955, rank Capt.; author or co-author numerous publs.; mem. Armenian Gen. Benevolent Union; Soc. Armenians from Istanbul; Med. Research Council Dental Sciences Comte. 1971-74 (Chrmn. 1973-74); Candn. Dental Assn.; Coll. Dental Surgs. Prov. Que.; Internat. Assn. Dental Research; Am. Assn. Phys. Anthrop.; Internat. Assn. Anthropobiols.; Candn. Assn. Anats.; Am. Assn. Anats.; Internat. Soc. Cranio-Facial Biol. and other prof. assns.; Armenian Apostolic; recreations: camping, photography; Home: 1545 Lucerne Rd., Town of Mount Royal, Que. H3R 2J1; Office: 2801 Edouard-Montpetit, Montreal, Que. H3T 1J6.

DeMONE, Robert Stephen, B.Com., C.A.; executive; b. Dartmouth, N.S. 13 June 1932; s. Urban Roy and Effie Elfreda (Meisner) DeM.; e. Dartmouth pub. and high

schs. 1949; Dalhousie Univ. B.Com. 1952; C.A. 1954; Univ. of W. Ont. Dipl. Business Mang. 1970; m. Jean Valerie Ann d. Charles William Snedden 26 June 1954; two d. Susan Liane, Jill Carol; PRES., CHIEF OPERATING OFFR. AND DIR., MAPLE LEAF MILLS LTD. 1981- ; Dir. Eastern Bakeries Ltd.; Corporate Foods Ltd.; McGavin Foods Ltd.; Steep Rock Iron Mines Ltd.; Canadian Pacific Securities Ltd.; Great Lakes Forest Products Ltd.; Corporate Tax Assessor, Revenue Can. Halifax 1955-56; Works Acct. Canadian Rock Salt Co. Ltd. Pugwash, N.S. 1956-62; Comptroller, Ben's Ltd. Halifax 1962-67; various sr. finance and accounting positions Canadian Pacific Ltd. Montreal and Toronto 1967-79; Chrmn. and Chief Extve. Offr. Canadian Pacific Securities Ltd. Toronto 1977-81; Vice Pres. Finance & Accounting Canadian Pacific Enterprises Ltd. Toronto 1979-81; mem. Financial Extves. Inst. Can. (Dir. Toronto Chapter); author various articles; Anglican; recreations: tennis, skiing, bridge, gardening; Clubs: Canadian (Dir. Toronto Chapter); National; Ontario Raquet; Candn. Power Sqdn.; Freemason; Home: 274 Dalewood Dr., Oakville, Ont. L6J 4P5; Office: (P.O. Box 710 Stn. K) Toronto, Ont. M4P 2X5.

DEMPSEY, Lotta (Mrs. Arthur W. Ham); columnist; "Toronto Star" 1958-81; Feature Ed., "Chatelaine" for 10 yrs. and Editor, Jan.-Aug. 1952; Co-host CBC television program, "From Now On", 1978-9; sometime with Edmonton "Journal" and Edmonton "Bulletin"; apptd. to Ed. Staff, Toronto "Globe and Mail", 1949; won Candn. Women's Press Club Mem. Award, 1948, 1967 and 1976; named to Can. News Hall of Fame 1975; author of "No Life for a Lady", 1976; Home: R.R. 2, Markham, Ont. L3P 3J3

DENHAM, Frederick Ronald, B.Sc., Ph.D., M.B.A., F.E.I.C., C.M.C.; management consultant; b. Middlesbrough, Eng. 21 Oct. 1929; s. Frederick and Gladys (Tattersall) D.; e. Univ. of Durham B.Sc. 1950, Ph.D. (Mech. Engn.) 1953; Univ. of Buffalo M.B.A. 1960; m. Enid Lynn Hughes 19 Sept. 1953; children: John Frederick Hughes, Gillian Helen, Michael Edmond Graham; VICE PRES. AND DIR., THORNE STEVENSON & KELLOGG 1973- ; Scient. Offr. Defence Research Bd. 1953-54; Ford Motor Co. of Canada 1954-56; Union Carbide Canada 1956-61; joined present firm 1961, Partner 1967, Dir. 1966; Prof. of Adm. Studies York Univ. 1967-71; Trustee, N. York Bd. Educ. 1976-80; author "Distribution Management Handbook" 1981; various articles; mem. Inst. Mang. Consultants Ont. (Pres. 1982-83); Assn. Prof. Engrs. Prov. Ont.; Beta Gamma Sigma; Freemason; Liberal; Anglican; recreations: skiing, squash; Club: Rotary (Pres.- Eglinton 1972-73); Home: 15 Danville Dr., Willowdale, Ont. M2P 1H7; Office: 2300 Yonge St., Toronto, Ont. M4P 1G2.

DENHOLM, Douglas Andrew, B.S.P.; pharmacist; b. Comox, B.C., 25 Dec. 1921; s. late George Campbell and Blossom (Keye) D.; e. Pub. and High Schs., Courtenay, B.C.; Univ. of Brit. Columbia, B.S.P. 1951; m. Gladys Margaret, d. Roy Moulton, W. Vanvouver, B.C., 5 June 1958; one s., Neil Campbell and six d., Heather Anne, Carol Linda, Deborah Elizabeth, Donna Ricky, Sheilah Diane, Darlene Louise; former Extve. Dir., Vancouver-Richmond Assn. for the Mentally Retarded; Dir., and W. Vancouver Hosp. Soc.; Capilano Community Assn.; Councillor, B.C. Pharm. Assn. 1954-57, Pres. 1956-57, Registrar and Secy.-Treas. 1957-70; Councillor, Candn. Pharm. Assn. 1954-67, Pres. 1966-67, Hon. Life mem. since 1970; Dir., Candn. Foundation for Advanc. Pharm. 1955-58 and 1966-70; Dir., Narcotic Addiction Foundation of B.C. 1962-70, Pres. 1969-70, Extve. Dir. 1970-75; mem. Pharm. Examing Bd. of Can. 1964-70; Lectr., Pharm. Law, Univ. of B.C. 1964-71; Past Chrmn., Health Comte. Vancouver Bd. Trade; Pres., Univ. of B.C. Pharm. Alumni Assn. 1951-52; rec'd Dr. E. R. Squibb Pan-Am. Fed. Award 1968; served in 2nd World War, R.C.A.(Inf.) 1939-45; rank on discharge Lieut.; mem. Royal Soc.

Health; Presbyterian; recreations: golf, curling, swimming; Clubs: Canadian; Faculty (Univ. of B.C.); Home: 873 Hendecourt Rd., N. Vancouver, B.C. V7K 2X5; Office: 2979 West 41st Ave., Vancouver, B.C. V6N 3C8

DENIS, Hon. Azellus, P.C. (1963), Q.C., B.A., LL.B.; senator b. St. Norbert, Co. Berthier, P.Q., 26 Mar. 1907; s. Arsene Denis and Georgiana Laporte D.; e. St. Norbert and Joliette, P.Q.; Univ. of Montreal, B.A., LL.B.; 1st el. to H. of C. for Montreal-St. Denis at g.e. 1935; re-el. in g.e. 1940, '45, '49, '53, '57, '58, '62, '63; apptd. Postmaster Gen. Can., Apl. 1963; resigned from Cabinet, Dec. 1963; summoned to Senate of Can. Jan. 1964; mem. N. Montreal Bus. Men's Assn.; Cercle Paroissial Villeray; Assn. Libérale St.-Denis-Dorion; Liberal; Roman Catholic; Club: Montreal Reform; Home: 7319 Boyer St., Montreal, Que. H2R 2R6; Office: The Senate, Ottawa, Ont. K1A 0A4

DENIS, Camille A., B.Sc.A., P.Eng.; executive; b. Quebec City, Que. 19 Apr. 1930; s. Emile and Rose (Careau) D.; e. St.-Fidele High Sch.; Laval Univ. B.Sc.A.; m. Denise d. late J. Leon Godbout 20 Sept. 1954; VICE PRES. CORPORATE AFFAIRS. ROTHMANS OF PALL MALL CANADA LTD.; joined Canadian Resins and Chemicals Ltd. Shawinigan, Que. 1953-57 serving as Project Engr., Maintenance Engr., Head Film & Sheeting Dept.; joined present Co. 1958 serving as Maintenance Engr., Asst. Plant Mgr. and Plant Mgr. Quebec City and since 1968 Production Mgr., Vice Pres. Production and Vice Pres. Adm. Toronto; rec'd Silver Jubilee Medal 1977; Pres., Inst. for Political Involvement; Past Pres. Ont. Chamber Comm.; Dir. Candn. Chamber Comm.; Dir., Assoc. of Can. Advertisers; B.B.B. of Can.; Trustee & Vice-Pres. Communications, United Way of Greater Toronto; mem. Corp. Prof. Engrs. Que.; Can. Public Relations Soc.; Metro Toronto Bd. Trade; Candn. Mfrs. Assn.; Chambre de Comm. Francaise au Can.; R. Catholic; recreation: fishing; Club: Bayview Country; Home: 153 Underhill Dr., Don Mills, Ont. M3A 2K6; Office: 1500 Don Mills Rd. Don Mills, Ont. M3B 3L1

DENISET, Hon. Louis, B.A., LL.B.; b. St. Boniface, Man., 29 June 1919; s. François and Rachel (Bernier) D.; e. Provencher Sch.; St. Boniface Coll. B.A. 1939; Man. Law Sch. LL.B. 1949; m. Jeanne (d. 1977) d. of Jules Remillard, St. Boniface, Man., 21 Apl. 1951; children: Helene Clement, Pierre, Rachel, Jacques, Jean-Paul, Louise; 2ndly Helene Gaden d. of François Gaden, St. Boniface, Man. 27 Jan. 1979; JUSTICE, COURT OF QUEEN'S BENCH MAN. since 1965; read law with Bernier & Bernier; called to Bar of Man. 1949; lawyer for credit unions, caisses populaires and Banque Canadienne Nationale also Administrator for La Sauvegarde Insurance Co. prior to present appt.; el. to H. of C. for St. Boniface 1957-58; served with Royal 22ième Regt. of Que. 1940-46, then with Winnipeg Grenadiers, rank Lt. Col., service in Africa, Italy and Europe; R. Catholic; recreations: athletic activities, writing; Home: 301-227 Wellington Cres. Winnipeg, Man. R3M 3V7; Office: Law Courts Bldg., Winnipeg, Man.

DENNIS, Lloyd A., O.C. (1971), B.A., B.Ed., D.F.A.; educator; b. Aspdin, Ont., 9 Nov. 1923; s. Alfred James and Elizabeth (Grimes) D.; e. Pub. and High Schs., Muskoka Dist. and Huntsville, Ont.; Univ. of Toronto, B.A., B.Ed.; N.S. Coll. Art and Design, Hon. D.F.A.; m. 3 Dec. 1942; two d., Gale Sandra, Susan Elizabeth; former Dir. of Educ. and Secy., Leeds and Grenville Co. Bd. of Educ.; served as teacher, princ. and consultant in Toronto following World War II; served with Ont. Dept. of Educ. as Secy. and Research Dir., Prov. Comte. on Aims and Objectives of Educ. in Schs. of Ont. (Living and Learning) subsequently became Co-chrmn.; author, writer and commentator in field of educ.; lectures widely to sch. and service groups in N.Am.; served with Candn. Army, Active Service, 1942-46; Officer of Order of Canada, 1971; rec'd Greer Award for "outstanding service in educ.";

Ont. Pub. Sch. Men Teachers' Fed. Meritorious Award; Col. Watson Award for "outstanding contrib. to curriculum devel."; mem. Ont. Assn. Educ. Adm. Officials; Fellow, Ont. Inst. Studies in Educ.; Home: R.R. 1, Orillia, Ont. L3B 6H1

DENTON, His Hon. Francis William (Frank); retired judge, County of York; b. Toronto, Ont.; s. late Frank D., K.C.; e. Model Sch. and St. Andrews Coll., Toronto; U.T.S., Univ. of Toronto; Osgoode Hall Law Sch.; m. Kathleen Margaret, d. Rev. Trevor Hugh Davies, Toronto, 2 Nov. 1929; one d., two S.; former Judge, County of York; called to the Bar of Ont., 1919; Ald., City of Toronto, 1923-24; apptd. Commr., Bd. of Police Commrs., Toronto, 1934; sometime mem., Toronto Bd. of Educ.; formerly mem., Bd. of Trustees, Toronto Gen. Hosp.; Home: 16 Killarney Rd., Toronto, Ont. M5P 1L8;

DENVER, Robert Church; company executive; b. Montreal, Que., 27 Dec. 1910; s. Richard Church and Mary Morrison (MacKie) D.; e. Govan Sch., Scotland; Royal Arthur Sch., Montreal, Que.; Sir George Williams Univ., Montreal, Que.; m. Mary Georgina d. Francis Wallace, Montreal, Que., 17 June 1939; one s. Robert Wallace; VICE CHRMN. AND CHIEF EXTVE. OFFR., McFARLANE, SON & HODGSON LIMITED; joined the Co. 1925; Asst. Sales Mgr., 1945; Sales Mgr., March 1947; Vice-Pres. July 1947; Pres. and Mang. Dir. 1957; Gov., Montreal General Hospital; mem., Canadian Paper Trade Assn. (Past Chrmn.); Candn. Stationers Guild Association (Past Vice-Pres.); American Wholesalers Association (Past V-Pres.); Anglican; recreations: fishing, hunting, curling, golf; Home: 50 Hudson Ave., Apt. 401, Mount Royal, Que. H3R 1S6; Office: 200 DesLauriers, Montreal, Que.

DEOM, André, M.èsA.; né Rigaud, Qué., 25 juillet 1929; é. Collège Bourget, Rigaud; Univ. de Montréal, B. ès A., 1948, M. ès A. (Relations Industriel) 1951; PRES: ANDRÉ DÉOM & ASSOC: INC., et LE GROUPE INTERGESTION depuis 1977; Adm. Casavant Frères Ltée; Asst. Dir. du Pers., Que. Iron & Titanium Corp., Sorel, 1951-57; Dir. du Pers., Entreprises Brillant, Rimouski, 1957-63; Vice-prés. du Pers. et Rel. Publ., Qué.-Téléphone, Rimouski, 1963-65; Dir. du Pers., SIDBEC, 1965-66; Vice-prés., Personnel, Cie. de Papier Rolland Ltee, 1966-69; Consultant, Ducharme Déom & Associés Inc. 1969-72; Pres., La Société Internat. d'Equipment et de Conseil Inc. 1972-73; mem., Que. Nat. Assembly 1973-77; prés. du Comité d'enquête sur le chômage saisonnier, Conseil d'Orientation Econ. du Québec, 1965-67; vice-prés.(1956-57), Ass. des Diplômés en Rel. Ind.; mem. du Comité Exec., Ass'n. Prof. des Industriels; prof. invité, Dept. des Rel. Ind., Univ. Laval; Prés., Centre des Dirigeants d'Enterprise; membre, Comité de planification de l'éduc. des adultes, Min. de l'Educ, du Qué.; Conseil de Planification et de Dével. Econ.; Adm., Centre d'Etudes Univ. de Rimouski; Dir., Soc. des Conseillers en Relations Industrielles du Qué.; Président et Adm., CEGEP Edouard-Montpetit; co-fondateur de la première troupe de scouts du Collège Bourget et du Cercle des Jeunes de Rigaud; participa à la revue "Bleu et Or" en 1948; Résidence: 214 Place le Baron, Boucherville, Qué. J4B 2E1; Bureau: 1117 Ste-Catherine ouest, Bureau 906, Montréal, Qué. H3B 1H9.

dePAIVA, Henry Albert Rawdon, M.Sc., Ph.D., P.Eng.; educator; b. Edmonton, Alta. 29 Feb. 1932; s. Henry Albert and Louise Anna (Rowell) deP.; e. Univ. of Alta. B.Sc. (Civil Engn.) 1955; Univ. of Ill. M.Sc. 1960, Ph.D. (Engn.) 1961; m. Dorothy Anne Magee 19 Dec. 1964; three s. Allan, Stewart, Jeffrey; VICE PRES. (SERVICES) UNIV. OF CALGARY since 1972, Prof. of Civil Engn. since 1968; Dir. Fortress Mountain Resorts Ltd.; Asst. Dean of Engn. Univ. Calgary 1964-67, Acting Dean 1967-68, Prof. and Head of Civil Engn. 1969-72, Prof. and Acting Vice Pres. (Capital Resources) 1971-72; Nat. Research

Council Sr. Research Fellow 1968-69; Engn. Inst. Can. Gzowski Medal 1971; Am. Soc. Civil Engn. State of Art Award 1974; author various papers reinforced and prestressed concrete structures; mem. City of Calgary Bldg. Appeal Bd. 1969-72: Cub Leader Scouts Can. 1975-77; Rotary Club of Calgary; APEGGA Council mem. Calgary Zool. Soc.; Social Orientation Services; Engn. Inst. Can.; Candn. Soc. Civil Engn.; Am. Soc. Civil Engn.; Fellow, The Institution of Structural Engrs., Liberal; R. Catholic; recreations: skiing, hiking, camping, sailing; Home: 6 Varbow Pl. N.W., Calgary, Alta. T3A OB6; Office: 2500 University Drive N.W., Calgary, Alta.

de PEDERY-HUNT, (Mrs.) Dora, O.C. (1974), R.C.A.; sculptor; designer; b. Budapest, Hungary, 16 Nov. 1913; d. Attila and Emilia (Festl) de Pédery; e. State Lyceum, Budapest, 1932; Royal Sch. of Applied Art, Dipl. in Sculpture and M.A. 1943; came to Canada 1948; apptd.to Can. Council 1970-73; one-man shows and exhns.: Laing Galleries, Toronto; Internat. Exhn. of Contemp. Medals, The Hague 1963, Athens, Paris, Prague; Biennial of Christian Art, Salzburg; Dorothy Cameron Gallery; Douglas Gallery, Vancouver; Wells Gallery, Ottawa, 1967; Candn. Govt. Pavillion, Expo 67; Cologne 1971; Helsinki 1973; Cracow 1975; Budapest 1977; Lisbon 1979; Intern. Sculpture Symposium, Toronto 1978; Prince Arthur Gallerie, 1978; Hamilton Art Gallery, 1979; Gallery Stratford, 1979; rep. in pub. colls. of The Nat. Gallery of Canada, Ottawa; Art Gallery of Ontario, Toronto; Dept. of External Affairs, Ottawa; Museum of Contemp. Crafts, Charlottetown; Royal Cabinet of Medals, The Hague and Brussels; Pub. Archives, Ottawa; Smithsonian Inst., Wash., D.C.; The Massey College of Crafts; maj. comns. incl.: Can. Council Medal; Candn. Centennial Medal (rec'd. 1st Prize for design); Candn. Govt. Expo 70; rec'd Centennial Medal 1967; The Olympic Gold 100 Dollar Coin, 1976; The Ont. Arts Council Medal; Can. Natl. Arts Centre Medal; The Queen's Jubilee Medal 1977; The Can. Medal of Service; mem., Sculptors Soc. Can. (Past Pres.); Ont. Soc. Artists; Fed. Internat. de la Médaille, Paris (Candn. Rep.); R. Catholic; Address: 65 Glen Road, Toronto, Ont. M4W 2V3

de PENCIER, John D.; F.I.I.C.; insurance executive; b. Toronto, Ont. 5 May 1930; s. Evelyn Margaret (Richardson) and the late Joseph Christian de P.; e. Toronto and Ottawa pub. schs. Trinity Coll. Sch. Port Hope, Ont. 1949; Ins. Insts. Ont. and Can. grad.; Univ. of W. Ont. Mang. Training Course 1974; m. Marianne Frazer d. late James Hector Lithgow 29 June 1954; children: Joseph C., Jan S.; Adam R., Michèle L.; SR. VICE PRES. REED STENHOUSE LTD. since 1975; Dir. Stenhouse Reed Shaw Ltd. (London, Eng.); Seguridad S.A. (Panama); Clk. Trainee General Accident Assurance Co. 1949-50; joined Richardson Brothers 1950, el. Partner 1955; Vice Pres. and later Pres. Richardson, de Pencier Ltd.; formed Richardson, Garratt, de Pencier 1966; merger with Reed Shaw Osler 1970; Head Sales and Service Operation Toronto Br.; 1973 trans. to Head New Business Development Group; el. Underwriting mem. Lloyd's of London 1973; Chrmn. and Life Gov. Trinity Coll. Sch. Port Hope; Dir. and Extve. Comte. Toronto Symphony; Council for Candn. Unity; Adv. Bd. Family Day Care Centre; Can. Paraplegic Assoc.; former Dir. Nat. Ballet of Can.; Past Pres. Soc. Fellows Ins. Inst. Can.; served with 48th Highlanders of Can. 1951-55, rank Lt. (Reserve); Anglican; recreations: skiing, golf, squash, flying; Clubs: Toronto; Toronto Golf; Georgian Peaks Ski; Badminton & Racquet; Cambridge; University; Royal and Ancient (Scotland); Home: 219 Lonsdale Rd., Toronto, Ont. M4V 1W7; Office: (P.O. Box 250) Toronto-Dominion Centre, Toronto, Ont. M5K 1J6

de PENCIER, Michael, M.A.; publisher; b. Toronto, Ont., 19 Jan. 1935; s. Joseph Christian and Evelyn Margaret (Richardson) de P.; e. Trinity Coll. Sch., Port Hope, Ont., 1953; Trinity Coll., Univ. of Toronto, B.A. 1958;

Univ. of Mich., M.A. 1960; m. Honor Barbara, d. Richard H. G. Bonnycastle, 14 Apl. 1961; children: Nicholas John, Miranda Augusta, Mark Dumaresq; Pres., Key Publishers Co. Ltd.; Greey de Pencier Publications Ltd.; Dir., Romanco Systems Ltd.; Key West; Ottawa Magazine Inc.; Publisher, Toronto Life Magazine; Past Chrmn., Magazine Assoc. of Can.; Can. Periodical Publishers Assoc.; Nat. Magazine Awards Foundation; Dir., Toronto Arts Council; CB Media Ltd.; Tarragon Theatre; Perfect Mix Ltd.; Young Naturalist Foundation; Clubs: Toronto Golf; Badminton & Racquet; Osler Bluffs Ski Club; Home: 11 Highland Ave., Toronto, Ont. M4W 2A2; Office: 59 Front St. E., Toronto, Ont. M5E 1B3

DERBY, A. C., B.Sc., M.D., C.M., F.R.C.S.(C), F.A.C.S.; surgeon; Chief of Med.-Surg. Unit, St. Lawrence Psychiatric Centre (formerly to 1975, Surg.-in-Chief, Queen Elizabeth Hosp., Montreal, Quebec and Assoc. Prof. of Surgery, McGill Univ.; Consultant Surgeon to the Montreal Gen. Hosp.; a grad. of McGill Univ., completed postgrad, training at Montreal Gen. Hosp., Ottawa Civic Hosp., and the Brooke Army Med. Hosp., San Antonio, Texas; served with RCAMC in Europe during 2nd World War, then re-enlisting with R.C.A.M.C. and serving in Mil. Hosps. throughout Can. and Korea and Japan; prior to present appt. was Head of Dept. of Surg. and Chief of Med. Staff at Candn. Forces Hosp., Kingston, Ont. with rank of Col.; also for ten yrs. Asst. Prof., Med. Faculty of Queens Univ.; the posts held while in Montreal; Trustee, Montreal Med. Chi Soc.; mem. Comte. on Trauma, Am. Coll. Surg.; mem. Assn. for the Surgery of Trauma; numerous articles publ. in med. journs.; Home: R.R. 1, Iroquois, Ont. K0E 1K0; Office: Ogdensburg, N.Y.

de REPENTIGNY, Guy, M.Com.; insurance broker; b. Ste. Anne de Bellevue, Que., 23 May 1918; s. Aldéric and Louise (Deslauriers) de R.; e. Mont Saint Louis, Montreal, Que.; Univ. de Montréal, M.Com. 1941; m. Jeanne, d. Albert Lemay, 22 May 1948; children: Muriel, Marc, Nicole, André; MANG. DIR., MARSH & McLENNAN LTD. since 1976; Dir., Pratte-Morrissette Inc.; with Lukis, Stewart, Price, Forbes, 1942-62 (held position of Vice Pres. at time of departure); joined Marsh & McLennan Ltd. 1962; memj., Chambre de Comm. du District de Montréal; Candn. Council of Christians and Jews; Acquisition Comte., Montreal Museum of Fine Arts; Soc. des Amis de Marcel Proust; R. Catholic; recreations: art, literature, swimming, golf; Clubs: Mount Royal; Braeside Golf; Home: 23 Senneville Rd., Senneville, Que. H9X 1B7; Office: Les Terrasses, 1801 ave McGill College, Montreal, Que. H3A 2N4

DeROO, Mt. Rev. Remi Joseph, S.T.D. (R.C.); bishop; b. Swan Lake, Manitoba, 24 Feb. 1924; s. Raymond Peter and Josephine (DePape) DeR.; e. St. Boniface (Man.) Coll. and Semy.; Dominican "Angelicum" Pontifical Univ., Rome, S.T.D. 1952; BISHOP, DIOCESE OF VICTORIA, B.C. since Dec. 1962; o. priest, 8 June 1950; formerly Pastor, Holy Cross Parish, St. Boniface, Man.; Chrmn., Human Rights Comm. of Prov. of B.C. (1974-77); mem., Am. Cath. Theol. Assn.; Cndn. Bishops' Bd. of Admin. 1973-77; Chrmn. C.C.C.B. Social Action Comm.; Former Co-Chmn. Comte on Human Rights; Candn. Cath. Mariol. Assn.; Address: 740 View St., Victoria, B.C. V8W 1J8

DERRETH, Reinhard R.,R.C.A.; graphic designer; b. Berlin, Germany 20 Feb. 1928; s. Otto and Elfriede (Gosling) D.; e. High Sch. Germany; Vancouver Sch. of Art Comm. Design grad. 1958; Werkkunstschule Offenbach, Germany Stone Lithography 1961; m. Doreen Nancy Smetanuk 13 Nov. 1966; one s. Eugene; PROP., REINHARD DERRETH GRAPHICS LTD. 1970- ; display and poster designer, typesetter and printer Vancouver Pub. Lib. 3 yrs; formed partnership with Chris Bergthorson, Vancouver operating as typographic designers and printers 7 yrs.; design work incls. art exhn. catalogues, co.

symbols, postage stamps; designed Louis Riel commemorative stamp 1970, definitive series of 8 stamps issued 1972, 1977, 16 stamps ongoing Inuit series 1977 completed 1980, first day covers, aerograms; mem. Candn. Eskimo Arts Council 1974- ; Liberal; recreations: skiing, swimming, hiking; Home: 4820 Keith Rd., West Vancouver, B.C. Office: 1147 Homer St., Vancouver, B.C. V6B 2Y1.

DERRY, Duncan Ramsay, M.A., Ph.D., F.R.S.C.; consulting geologist; b. Eng., 27 June 1906; s. late Dr. Douglas E. and Margaret (Ramsay) D.; e. Rugby Sch., Eng.; Corpus Christi Coll., Cambridge, B.A. 1927; Univ. of Toronto, M.A. 1928; Ph.D. 1931; m. E. Alice, d. late Albert Langstaff, 29 Aug. 1935; two s., Ramsay, Douglas; Pres., Dejour Mines Ltd.; Duncan R. Derry Ltd.; Partner, Derry, Michener & Booth; Dir., Northgate Explorations Ltd.; United Keno-Hill Mines Ltd.; OBrien Resources Ltd.; Cullation Gold Mines Ltd. came to Canada 1927; Lectr. in Geol., Univ. of Toronto, 1931-35; joined Ventures Ltd. as Geol., 1935; Chief Geol., 1947; joined Rio Tinto Group, as Extve. Vice-Pres., Rio Tinto Canadian Exploration, 1954; apptd. 1956; served during 2nd World War with R.C.A.F., overseas, 1940-45; disch. with rank of Sqn. Ldr.; mem., Geol. Assn. Can. (Past Pres.); Geol. Soc. Am.; Candn. Inst. Mining & Metall.; Soc. Econ. Geols. (Past Pres.); Anglican; recreations: golf, hunting, riding; Clubs: University; Toronto Golf; Empire; Home: Adamson's Lane, Mississauga, Ont.; Office: Suite 2302, The Simpson Tower, Toronto, Ont. M5H 2Y4

DESBARATS, Peter; journalist; b. Montreal, Que., 2 July 1933; s. Hullett John and Margaret Ogston (Rettie) D.; e. Loyola High Sch., Montreal; Loyola Coll.; Feature Writer, The Gazette, Montreal, 1953-55; Local Reporter, Reuters, London, Eng., 1956; Pol. Reporter, The Winnipeg Tribune, Winnipeg, 1956-60; Pol. Reporter and Feature Writer, The Montreal Star, Montreal, 1960-65; Ed., Parallel Magazine, Montreal, 1966; Assoc. Ed., Saturday Night, Toronto, 1966-71; host of nightly CBC TV "Hourglass" pub. affairs show, 1966-71; Ottawa Ed., Toronto Star, 1971-73; Ottawa Bureau Chief, Global Television 1974-80; Political Commentator, CBC-TV, Ottawa; Senior Consultant, Royal Commission on Newspapers, 1980-81; Dean, Sch. of Journalism, Univ. of West. Ont. 1981-; author: "The State of Quebec", 1965; "Halibut York and More", 1966 and "Gabriel and Selena", both children's books and latter subject of an animated film; "Canada" (official publication Candn. Pavilion Expo 70 Osaka); "The Canadian Illustrated News", 1970; freelance contrib. to various mags.; former Candn. corr., The National Observer, Washington, D.C.; author play on Sir George Williams Univ. student sit-in and produced by Centaur Theatre, Montreal, 1970; author of "René—A Canadian in Search of a Country", 1976; "The Hecklers", 1979, a history of political cartooning in Canada; "Canada lost/Canada found — The Search for a New Nation" 1981; Actra award, "Best News Broadcaster", 1977; recreations: literature, skating, cycling; Club: National Press; Home: 209 Fourth Ave., Ottawa, Ont. K1S 2L7

DESBIENS, Br. Jean-Paul; journaliste; auteur; né à Metabetchouan, Qué., 7 Mar. 1927; fils Adélard et Alberta (Bouchard) D.; é. Ecole Paroissiale de St-Jérôme; Maison de Formation des Fréres Maristes; Ecole Normale Val-Cartier; Univ. Laval; Univ. du Latran; Univ. de Fribourg; REDACTEUR EN CHEF "LA PRESSE", MONTREAL 1970-72; en 1944 il prenait la soutane chez les Fréres Maristes; Dir., Service des Programmes de l'enseignement collegial et Examens Ministère de l'Educ. 1964; auteur, "Les Insolences du Frère Untel", 1960; "Sous le Soleil de la Pitié", 1965; "Introduction à un examen philosophique de la psychologie de l'intelligence chez Jean Piaget", 1968; R. Catholique; récréations: march, conversation, musique.

DESBRISAY, Lestock Graham, B.Sc.; executive; b. Campbellton, N.B.; e. Pub. Sch., Petit Rocher, N.B.; Mt. Allison Univ., B.Sc. 1942; retired President, Blakeny & Son Ltd.; Pres., BCP Holdings Ltd.; Secy.-Treas., Fundy Industs. Ltd.; Springhill Coal Mines Ltd.; Pres., Mt. Allison Fed. Alumni 1959; Maritime Prov.'s Bd. of Trade 1958; Moncton Bd. of Trade 1959-60; Vice-Chrmn., N.B. Br., Candn. Mfrs. Assn. 1958; Jr. Chamber Comm. of Can. (Nat. Vice-Pres. 1951); 1st el. to N.B. Leg. for Moncton City 1960; apptd. Prov. Secy.-Treas. 1960, Min. of Finance 1961, of Finance & Industry 1963, of Finance (N.B.) 1963-70 when retired; United Church; recreations: golf, boating; Clubs: Moncton Golf & Country; City; Beaver Society; Rotary; Elks; Home: 195 Bromley Ave., Moncton, N.B. E1C 5V5; Office: 42 Highfield St., P.O. Box 1265, Moncton, N.B. E1C 8P9

DESCHATELETS, Hon. Jean Paul, P.C. (1963), Q.C.; senator; b. Montreal, P.Q., 9 Oct. 1912; s. Sigefroy and Fabiola (Dequoy) D.; e. St. Mary's Coll., Montreal, P.Q.; Valleyfield Semy.; Univ. of Montreal; m. Fernande, d. Mrs. Candide Dufresne, 11 Nov. 1939; children: Helen, Bernard, Andrée; called to Bar of Quebec, July 1937; Enforcement Counsel for P.Q. W.P.T.B., 1942-51; Permanent Secy. of P.Q. Assn. of Architects. 1952-53; later Liaison Officer with R.C.M.P. for Black Market Investigations for Montreal and W. part of P.Q.; 1st el. to H. of C. for Maisonneuve Rosemount, g.e. 1953; Min. of Public Works from Apl. 1963 till resignation from the Cabinet, Feb. 1965; not a candidate in g.e. Nov. 1965; summoned to Senate of Can., Feb. 1966; named Depy. Govt. Leader in the Senate, 1966; Speaker of the Senate, 1968; mem. of Candn. PParlty. Del. to Commonwealth Parly. Conf. in Nov. and Dec. 1957 to New Delhi, Pakistan and Ceylon; K. of C.; Liberal; Roman Catholic; recreation: fishing. Club: Reform; Address: The Senate, Ottawa, Ont. K1A 0A4

DESCHÊNES, Hon. Jules, B.A., LL.M., LL.D., F.R.S.C.; judge; b. Montréal, Qué. 7 June 1923; s. Wilfrid and Berthe (Bérard) D.; e. Ecole St-Jean Baptiste Montréal; Coll. André-Grasset, Coll. de Montréal et Séminaire de Philosophie B.A. 1943; Univ. of Montreal LL.M. 1946 (Gov. Gen. & Lt. Gov. Medals); Concordia Univ. LL.D. 1981; m. Jacqueline d. Joseph-Edouard Lachapelle, Montréal, Qué. 26 June 1948; children: Louise, Mireille, Pierre, Yves, Jean-François; CHIEF JUSTICE, SUPERIOR COURT OF QUE. 1973- ; called to Bar of Qué. 1946; cr. Q.C. 1961; Barrister and Solr. 1946-72; Sr. Partner Deschênes, de Grandpré, Colas, Godin & Lapointe 1966-72; Justice, Court of Appeal Qué. 1972-73; Lectr. in Private Internat. Law Univ. of Montréal 1962-69; rec'd Order of Malta 1978; Pres., Montréal Port Council 1969-70; Qué. Adv. Council on Justice 1972; Qué. Br. Defence Research Inst. 1965-67; Warden, Paroisse St-Germain d'Outremont 1970-73; Trustee, Foundation for Law Research in Can. 1967-78; mem. Bd. Govs. 1967-73, Extve. Comte. 1970-73 and Hon. Gov. 1977, Univ. of Montréal; mem. Council Bar of Montréal 1962-64; Gen. Council Bar of Prov. Qué. 1963-64; First Pres. Qué. Interprof. Council 1965-67; mem. Extve. Comte. Candn. Judicial Council 1977- ; Pres., World Assn. Judges' Comte. on Expanding Jurisdiction of Internat. Court of Justice 1977- ; mem. Council World Peace Through Law Center 1980- ; Bd. Govs. and Extve. Comte. Candn. Inst. Advanced Legal Studies 1978- ; First Vice Pres. Candn. Inst. Adm. Justice 1980- ; author "The Sword and the Scales" 1979; "Les plateaux de la balance" 1979; "L'école publique confessionnelle au Québec" 1980; "Ainsi parlèrent les Tribunaux . . . Conflits linguistiques au Canada 1968-1980" 1981; co-author "L'Université: Son rôle, le rôle de ses composantes, les relations entre ses composantes" 1969; "Maîtres chez eux - Masters in their own House" 1981; numerous articles; Life mem. Montréal Lawyers' Benevolent Assn.; mem. Internat. Law Assn.; Internat. Comn. Jurists; Candn. Council on Internat. Law; Assn. québecoise pour l'étude comparative du droit; Hon. mem. Phi Delta Phi;

R. Catholic; recreation: music; Club: Cercle de la Place d'Armes; Home: 1702 Le Cartier, 1115 Sherbrooke St. W., Montréal, Qué. H3A 1H3; Office: Court House, 10 St. Antoine E., Montréal, Qué. H2Y 1A2.

DESCOTEAUX, Claude, B.A., L.Ph., LL.L.; provincial civil servant; b. Baie de la Trinité, Qué. 27 Feb. 1938; s. Jacques and Claire (Rouleau) D.; e. Univ. of Ottawa B.A. 1958, L.Ph. 1959; Univ. of Montreal LL.L. 1962; McGill Univ. 1963; Univ. de Paris, Inst. d'Etudes Politiques Dipl. Internat. Relations 1965, Faculté de Droit et de Sciences Economiques 3rd Cycle dipl. in Econ. 1966, Ecole Nationale d'Adm. de France Dipl. 1967; m. Micheline d. Jean Paul Crête, Quebec City, Que. 15 July 1961; children: Paule, Jacques, Annie; DEPY. MIN. ENERGY & RE-SOURCES, 1982- ; Depy. Min. of Industry, Trade & Tourism, Que. 1977-82; Dir. Sidbec-Dosco; Société Générale de Financement; called to Bar of Que. 1963; joined Dept. Industry & Comm. Que. 1967, Asst. Depy. Min. 1969, Depy. Min. 1977; Asst. Gen. Secy. Que. Extve. Council and Secy. of Perm. Ministerial Comte. on Econ. Matters 1973; Pres. and Chief Extve. Offr. Que. Indust. Research Center 1974; served with Candn. Army 1961-63 Ottawa and Montreal, rank Capt.; mem. Que. Bar Assn.; R. Catholic; Club: Officers' Mess La Citadelle Que.; Home: 879 Ave. Dessane, Quebec City, Que. G1S 3J7; Office: 710 Place d'Youville, Quebec City, Que.

DeSERRES, Roger, B.en Com.; exécutif; né Montréal, Qué. le 5 sept. 1914; fils Omer et Eugénie (Saucier) D.; é. Coll. Mont St-Louis, gradué Cours scient. 1934; Univ. McGill, B.en Com. 1937; ép. Monique, fille Rolland Préfontaine 1943; cinq enfants; PRESIDENT ET GERANT GEN., OMER DeSERRES LTEE depuis 1949; Prés. du Conseil, Produits Cellulaires Waterville Ltée; Adm. Banque Nationale du Canada; Adm. CIL Inc.; S.P.B. Canada Inc.; Formula Growth Ltd.; Québec Téléphone Ltée; Farinés Phenix; Guardian Insurance Co. of Canada; Montreal Life Insurance Co.; Prés. Nat., Chambre de Comm. du Can. 1966-67; Prés. Chambre de Comm. du Dist. de Montréal 1959-60; Prés. Inst. Candn. de Plomberie & Chauffage 1954-55; Prés., Fondation Hôpital Nôtre-Dame 1976-79; Comm. Undeur Grand Offr. de l'Ordre Equestre du St-Sépulcre de Jérusalem; Clubs: Mont Bruno Golf; Montreal Indoor Tennis; Saint-Denis; Laval-sur-le-Lac; loisirs; ski, golf, voyages; résidence: 566 ave. Grosvenor, Montréal, Qué. H3Y 2S7; bureau: 1200 rue Sanguinet, Montréal, Qué. H2X 3E7

DESJARDINS, Edouard, M.D., F.R.C.S.(C.), F.A.C.S.; surgeon; grands. of Dr Louis-Edouard D., Prof. of Opthalmology at Montreal Univ.; b. Montreal, P.Q., 17 July 1897; s. Edouard and Sara (Mathieu) D.; e. Maisonneuve Sch.; Coll. Ste.-Marie, 1917; Univ. of Montreal, M.D. 1922; Univ. of Paris, M.D. 1926; m. Anita (died 1972); d. A. Lambert, Granby, P.Q., 1 Sept. 1933; children: Nicole (Mrs. Wm. Thomas), Monique, M.D. Mrs. Yvon Benoit, M.D.), Micheline, D.E.S.; Emeritus Prof. of Surg., Univ. of Montreal; Consultant Surg., Hôtel-Dieu Hosp.; Pres., Med. Bd. of Hôtel-Dieu Hosp., Montreal, 1958; La Soc. Méd. de Montréal (Past Prés.); La Soc. de Chirurgie de Montréal (Past Prés.); Emeritus Ed. in Chief, L'Union Médicale du Can.; mem., Internat. Surg. Soc.; Montreal Medico-Chirurgical Soc.; Candn. Med. Assn.; Assn. des Médecins de Langue Française du Can. (Past Pres.); Chart. mem., Assn. of Surgs., P.Q.; Corr. mem., Soc. Chirurg. Lyon (France); Acad. de chirurg. de Paris; author of five books and numerous articles in various med. journs.; Editor: "La Médecine au Foyer", 1970; Roman Catholic; Residence: 279 ave. de l'Epée, Outremont, Montréal, Qué.

DESJARDINS, Hon. Gaston, L.ès D.; juge; né Baker Brook, N.B. 2 oct. 1932; f. J. Antoine et Marie (Bouchard) D.; é. Baker Brook, N.B. ecole primaire; Univ. Saint-Louis d'Edmundston gradué 1955; Univ. Laval L.ès D. 1958; ép. Louise f. Alphonse Cyr, Edmundston, N.B. 27

août 1957; enfants: Mireille, Yves; JUGE DE LA COUR SUPERIEURE DE LA PROV. DE QUE.; admis au Barreau de Qué. 1959; cr. Q.C. 1974; elu député libéral de Louis Hébert è l'Assemblée nationale du Qué. à l'élection du 1973; renouvellement de mandat non sollicité; catholique; récreations: tennis, skiing, pêche; Adresse: 3631, chemin St-Louis, Sainte-Foy, Qué. G1W 1T2; Bureau: 39, rue St-Louis, Québec, Qué. G1R 3Z2.

DESJARDINS, Marcel, B.A., B.Sc.A., M.B.A.; management consultant; b. Ste-Thérèse, Qué., 28 May 1939; s. Laurent and Fernande (Leroux) D.; e. Séminaire de Ste-Thérèse (Qué.) B.A. 1960; Ecole Polytechnique de Montréal B.Sc.A. 1964; Harvard Grad. Sch. of Business Adm. M.B.A. 1967; m. Madeleine d. Dr. Larose, Ste-Thérèse, Qué, 4 May 1963; children: Annie, Natalie, Eric; President CEGIR INC. (estbd. 1970); Treas. and Bd. mem., Mont-Trmblant Lodge; Bd. mem., Cdn. Export Assoc.; mem. Ordre des Ingénieurs du Qué.; Chambre de Comm. Montréal; R. Catholic; recreations: skiing, golf, reading, music; Club: St-Denis; Home: 706 Presseault, Ste-Thérèse-en-Haut, Qué.; Office: 2301 — 2 Complexe Desjardins, Montréal, Qué.

DESJARDINS, Régent; b. Montreal, Que., 30 Sept. 1926; s. Donat and Elisa (Paquin) D.; e. Salaberry, Tech. and Beaux Arts Schs., Montreal; m. Jacqueline, d. Hector Dubuc, Apl. 1955; children: Régent-Yves, Benoit, Michel, Johane, Line, Chantal; Pres., Simard & Denis Inc.; Pres., Regesco Inc.; T. L. Simard Inc.; Dir., Mediacom Industries Ltd.; Commr., Office Autoroute Montreal-Laurentides, 1958; Newspaper Publisher and Pres., Montreal-Matin 1962-74; Mun. Counsellor, City of Montreal, 1954; mem. Centre Sir Georges Etienne Cartier Corporation (Place des Arts), 1956; Hon. Treasurer, Junior Chamber Commerce Can. (Gov.); Founder & Hon. mem., Alouette Kinsmen Montreal; mem., Internat. Press Inst.; Jr. Chamber Comm. Internat. (Senator); Chambers Comm. Que. and Montreal; Kt. of Columbus; Assn. du 22e Inc.; Union National; R. Catholic; recreations: fishing, travel; Clubs: St-Denis; Canadien; Laval-sur-le-Lac; Home: 90 Fernlea, Ville Mont-Royal, Que. H3P 1T6; Office: 450 Sherbrooke E., Montreal, Que. H2L 1J8

DESLONGCHAMPS, Pierre, B.Sc., Ph.D.; educator; b. Laurentides, Que. 8 May 1938; s. Rodolphe and Madeleine (Magnan) D.; e. Univ. de Montréal B.Sc. 1959; Univ. of N.B. Ph.D. 1964; m. Shirley Elizabeth d. Walter Thomas, Jamaica 22 July 1976; children: Ghislain, Patrice; PROF. DE CHIMIE, UNIV. DE SHERBROOKE; rec'd Shell Canada Co. Fellowship 1963; Research Fellowship Harvard Univ. 1964; A. P. Sloan Fellowship 1970-72; Scient. Prize Que. 1971; E.W.R. Steacie Fellowship 1971-74 and Prize 1974; Médaille Vincent de l'ACFAS 1975; Izaak Walton Killam Mem. Scholarships in Science 1976-77; Merck, Sharp and Dohme Lectures Award Chem. Inst. Can. 1976; Fellowship "John Simon Guggenheim Memorial Foundation" (New York), 1979; Prize winner "Médaille Pariseau de l'ACFAS", 1979; Fellow of the Chem. Inst. of Can. 1980; author over 50 scient. publs. organic chem.; mem. Swiss Chem. Soc.; Royal Soc. Can.; Am. Chem. Soc.; Chem. Inst. Can.; Assn. Harvard Chems.; Corp. Prof. Chems. Que.; Am. Assn. Advanc. Science; Assn. Canadienne-Française pour l'Avancement des Sciences; Assn. Scient. Engn. & Technol. Community Can.; R. Catholic; Home: R.R.1, North Hatley, Que. J0B 2C0; Office: Sherbrooke, Qué. J1K 2R1.

DESMARAIS, Guy J., B.A., B.Com., C.Adm.; investment dealer; b. Sherbrooke, Qué., 13 Jan. 1939; s. Gaston and Adrienne (Végiard) D.; e. Univ. of Ottawa, B.A. 1960; Univ. of Sherbrooke, B.Com. 1962; Chart. Adm. 1967; m. Andrée, d. O. Ulric Léger, Sherbrooke, Qué., 2 May 1964; children: Guylaine, Sylvie; PRESIDENT AND CHIEF EXTVE. OFFR., GEOFFRION LECLERC INC. (mems. Montreal, Toronto and Vancouver Stock Exchanges and Invest. Dealers' Assn. Can.) since 1971;

Chmn. of Bd. and Extve. Comm., Canadair Ltd.; Dir. and mem. Extve. Comm., Fed. Bus. Devel. Bank; Dir., Inter City Papers Ltd.; entered, Nesbitt, Thomson & Co., Limited, 1962; Registered Representative 1963; Mgr., Sherbrooke Office, 1963 and Quebéc City Office, 1965; Asst. Mgr., Prov. of Qué., Jan. 1968 and Mgr. Oct. 1968; Dir. 1969; Vice Pres. 1970; Extve. Asst. to Pres. and mem. Extve. Comte., Morgan, Ostiguy & Hudon Inc., (now Greenshields) April 1970; Gen. Mgr. May 1970; Sr. Vice Pres. 1971; Allied mem. (Gen. Partner) N.Y. Stock Exchange 1968; served as Lt. (R), RCN (S); Extve. Offr., Univ. Naval Training Div., Sherbrooke Area, 1960-65 and of Sea-Cadets Div. 1964-65; Past Pres., Candn. Arthritis & Rheum. Soc. (Qué.); Vice Pres., Montreal Heart Inst.; Past Pres., Montreal Chamber of Comm.; Club: St. James's; Home: 1680 Place de Gros Bois, St. Bruno, Qué., J3V 4M9; Office: 800 Dorchester Blvd. W., Montreal, Qué. H3B 1X9

DESMARAIS, Jean Noel, Q.C., LL.D.; b. Buckingham, Que., 3 May 1897; s. Noel and Rose Anne (Cousineau) D.; e. Univ. of Ottawa B.A. 1919; Osgoode Hall Law Sch. 1922; LL.D. Laurentian 1976; m. Lébea d. late Louis Laforest 10 May 1922; children: Louis R. C.A.M.P., Jean Noel, Jr., M.D., Yolande Ducharme, Paul G., Jeannine Proulx, Francoise Le Poitevin, Pierre J., Robert C. Q.C.; read law with J.A. Mulligan, Sudbury; called to Bar of Ont. 1922; cr. K.C. 1947; Pres. Sudbury Copper Cliff Street Railway 1940-45 and Sudbury Bus Lines Ltd. 1945-50; Dir. Provincial Transport Enterprises Ltd.; Pres. Sudbury Investments Ltd.; Counsel, Desmarais, Keenan, Beaudry, Cull, Mahaffy & Young; Planner and co-Founder and original director Laurentian Univ. 1957-68; — Trustee Sudbury High Sch. 1928-34; Dir. V.O.N. 5 yrs.; Chrmn. of Bd. St. Joseph's Hosp. Sudbury 6 yrs.; Pres. Sudbury Law Assn. twice; Life mem. Law Soc. Upper Can.; mem. Candn. Bar Assn.; recreation: travel; Clubs: Idylwylde Golf & Country; The Copper Cliff; Home: 1170 Ramsey View Court, Sudbury, Ont. P3E 2E4; Office: 4 Durham N., Sudbury, Ont. P3C 5E5

DESMARAIS, Louis R., B.Com., C.A.; transportation executive; b. Sudbury, Ont., 16 Feb. 1923; s. Jean Noel and Lebea (Laforest) D.; e. Univ. of Ottawa; McGill Univ., B.Com., C.A.; m. Lucille, d. M. Normand, Ottawa, Ont., 19 Feb. 1949; children: Louis P., Luc, Bernard, Nicole, Monique, Natalie; MEM. OF PARLIAMENT Federal Riding of Dollard; First el. to House of Commons in gen. el. 1979; re-el. 1980; Vice Chrmn. Public Accounts Comte., Apr. 1980; appt. Parl'y Secy. to Min. of Labour, to Fitness & Sports, 1980; with Courtois, Fredette & Co., C.A.s, 1945-51; Desmarais & Parisien (now Desmarais, Arsenault & Co.) Sudbury, Ont. 1951-65; Pres., Dupuis Frères Ltée, Montreal 1965-66; Dir., Trans-Canada Corporation Fund 1966-67; Extve. Vice-Pres., Provincial Transport Enterprises Ltd. 1967, Pres. 1968; apptd. Pres. of Canada Steamship Lines 1970, Chief Extve. Offr. 1971 Chrmn. of the Bd. & C. & O. 1973, Chrmn. 1976; Deputy Chrmn. of Bd., Power Corp. of Can. Ltd. 1976; Dir., Candn. Home Assur. Co., Montreal; Montreal Baseball Club Ltd.; ; Chrm., Council for Canadian Unity, 1977-79; First Hon. Citizen, City of Sudbury, Depy. Mayor and Controller Sudbury 1963-65; Commr., Ontario Water Resources Comn. 1964-65; recreations: golf, cabinet making; Clubs: Mt. Royal; Mount Bruno Country; Royal Ottawa Golf; Home: 283 Acacia Ave., Rockcliffe Park, Ottawa, Ont. K1M 0L8

DESMARAIS, Paul, O.C. B.Com.; industrial extve.; b. Sudbury, Ont. 4 Jan. 1927; s. Jean Noel, Q.C., and Lebea (Laforest) D.; e. Univ. of Ottawa, B.Com.; Honorary degrees: LL.D., Univ. of Moncton; D., Wifred Laurier Univ.; D. Adm., Univ. of Ottawa; m. Jacqueline, d. Ernest Maranger, Ottawa, Ont., 8 Sept. 1953; two s., two d.; CHRMN. AND CHIEF EXTVE. OFFR., POWER CORPORATION OF CANADA; Chrm. of Extve. Comm., Consolidated-Bathurst Inc.; Dir., Compagnie financière

de Paris et des Pays-Bas; Consolidated Bathurst Inc.; Domglas Inc.; Gelco Enterprises Ltd.; Gesca Ltée; Great-West Life Assurance Co.; Hilton Canada Ltd.; The Investors Group; Montreal Trust Co.; Power Corp of Canada; La Presse Ltée; The Seagram Co. Ltd.; Steego Corp.; Sulpetro Ltd.; Clubs: Mt. Royal (Montreal); The "21" Club (N.Y.); Rideau (Ottawa); Toronto; Eldorado Country (Palm Desert); Bath and Tennis (Palm Beach); St. Andrews (Delray Beach); Office: 759 Square Victoria, Montreal, Que. H2Y 2K4

DES MARAIS, Pierre II, B.A., H.E.C.; company president; b. Montreal, Que., 2 June 1934; s. Pierre and Rolande (Varin) Des Marais ; e. Coll. Jean-de-Brébeuf, 1946-50; Coll. Sainte Marie, B.A. 1954; Graphic Arts Course, Toronto, 1954; Univ. of Montreal, Business Adm., H.E.C. 1958; m. Lise Blanchard, Jan. 21, 1956; children: Suzanne, Lison, Pierre III, Jean, Danielle, Sophie, Stéphane, Philippe, Anik; PRESIDENT AND GENERAL MANAGER, PIERRE DES MARAIS INC., since 1954; Pres., BTM Internat.; Dir., Canadian National; Imperial Oil Limited; Continental Bank of Canada; Telemedia Communications Limited; Schering Corporation Limited; Plough (Canada) Limited; Named "French Canadian Businessman of the Year" by Mutual Radio Network, 1968; Young Presidents' Organization Inc.; Advertising & Sales Executives Club Montreal; Le Publicité-Club de Montréal; Technical Association Graphic Arts; Centre des dirigeants d'Enterprise; Mayor City of Outremont, 1969-; Chairman of the Executive Committee of the Montreal Urban Community, 1978-; recreations: water skiing, skiing, yachting, golf, reading, rare books and binderies; Clubs: Club Saint-Denis; St. James's; Mt. Royal; Forest & Stream; Home: 10 McCulloch Ave., Outremont, Que. H2V 3L4; Office: 6125 Côte de Liesse Road, St. Laurent, Que. H4T 1C8

DESNOYERS, Sarto, Phm.B.; b. Kingsey, Que., 22 Jan. 1904; s. Dontagne, M.D. and Euphemie (Lefebvre) D.; e. Longueuil (P.Q.) Coll.; St. Hyacinthe (P.Q.) Semy.; Montreal Univ., Phm.B. 1927; Lic. in Pharm., 1927; MAYOR, CITY OF DORVAL; Dir., Blue Bonnets Raceway Inc.; Pres., Sogena Inc.; Vice Pres., Montreal Urban Community; Dir., Mount Royal Jockey Club; Hon. Vice-Pres., Boy Scouts of Can.; Fed. of Mayors of Can.; Gov., Canada's Sports Hall of Fame; Roman Catholic; recreations: skiing, golf, riding; Home: 1020 Bord du Lac, Dorval, Que. H9S 2C5; Office: City Hall, Dorval, Que. H9S 2C5

DESPRES, Robert, O.C.; M.Com.; C.G.A.; R.I.A.; F.S.M.A.C.; F.C.G.A.A.; executive; b. Quebec, Que. 27 September 1924; e. Laval Univ.; m. Marguerite Cantin, 1949; 4 children; CHRMN. OF THE BD. OF ATOMIC ENERGY OF CAN. LTD. 1980-; Dir., Campeau Corp.; Can. Malting Co. Ltd.; The Cn. Union Ins. Co. Ltd.; Le Centre Inter. de Recherches et d'Etudes en Management (CIREM); Domtar Inc.; Corp. Falconbridge Copper; La Fondation québécoise d'éducaton économique; Drummond McCall Inc.; I.A.F. Production Inc.; Nat. Trust Co. Ltd.; Netcom Inc.; Norcen Energy Resources Ltd.; Sidbec and Sidbec-Dosco Ltd.; Manufacturers Life Ins.; Public Gov., Montreal Stock Exchange; former mem. Roy. Comm. on Finan. Mang. & Accountability in Govt. of Can.; Que. Comm. of Inquiry on Finan. Institutions; Comptroller, Quebec Power Company, 1959-1963 and mem. Extve. Comte.; Mgr., Que. Regional Br., Administration and Trust Co., 1963-65; Depy. Min. of Revenue, Que., 1965-69; Pres. and General Manager, Quebec Health Insurance Board, 1969-73; Pres., Univ. of Quebec, 1973-78; Pres. & CEO, Netcom Inc., 1973-; Nat. Cablevision 1978-80; mem., Soc. of Indust. Accountants; Certified Gen. Accountants; Can. Tax Foundation; La Chambre de Commerce française du Canada; Pres.'s Assn. Am.; Officer of the Order of Canada, Dec. 1978-; Fellow Soc. of Management Accountants of Canada, Jul 1979-; Fellow, Can. Certified Gen. Accts. Assoc. 1981; mem., Que. Heart

Inst.; R. Catholic; recreations: golf, tennis, reading; Clubs: Le Cercle Univ. de Qué.; Mount Royal; Rideau; Lorette Golf; Home: 890 Dessane Ave., Quebec, Que. G1S 3J8

DESROCHERS, Louis A., Q.C., B.A., LL.D., D.Sc.Ed.; b. Montreal, Que. 21 March 1928; s. R. Armand and Lillian (Davignon) D.; e. Ecole Normale Jacques Cartier, Montreal; Coll. des Jesuites and Coll. St. Jean, Edmonton, Alta.; Univ. of Ottawa, B.A. 1949, LL.D.; Univ. of Alta., LL.B. 1952; Laval Univ., D.Sc.Ed.; m. Marcelle, d. Joseph Boutin, 30 Sept. 1953; children: Pierre, Marie, Claire, Isabelle, Dominique; PARTNER, McCUAIG DESROCHERS; Dir. L'Assurance-Vie Desjardins; Bank of Montreal; read law with S. H. McCuaig, Q.C., LL.D.; called to Bar of Alta. 1953; cr. Q.C. 1970; joined present Firm 1953; mem. Law Soc. Alta.; Candn. Bar Assn.; Liberal; R. Catholic; Home: 13722 Summit Point, Edmonton, Alta. T5N 3S7; Office: 1824 Royal Trust Tower, Edmonton, Alta.

DesROCHES, Antoine; publishing executive; b. Quebec City, Que. 9 Jan. 1924; s. Francis and Antoinette (Dubois) D.; e. St. Sacrement Superior Sch. 1939; Columbia Univ. Sch. of Journalism; Les Hautes Etudes Commerciales, Business Adm. 1967; Micrographics & Computer Output Microfilm Advanced Mang. Studies, Toronto 1974; m. Monique d. Fernand Nuytemans 24 Jan. 1969; children: Claude, Alain, José-Anne, France, Gisèle; ASST. TO THE PRES. AND DIR. OF PUB. RELATIONS, LA PRESSE LTEE; Pres. Les Editions La Presse Ltée; Information Expert UNESCO 1962-63; Treas. Que. Press Council 1974-79; mem. Candn. Consultative Videotex Comte. 1980-81; Vice Pres. Assn. des Editeurs Canadiens; mem. Internat. Press Inst.; Candn. Daily Newspaper Publishers Assn.; R. Catholic; recreations: skiing, tennis, travel; Home: 24 Buttonwood, Dollard-des-Ormeaux, Que. H9A 2N2; Office: 7 St-Jacques, Montreal, Que. H2Y 1K9.

DesROCHES, Jacques Marcel, B.Com.; association executive; b. Ottawa, Ont., 9 Apl. 1924; e. Carleton Univ., B.Com. 1950; m. Paulette Meunier, Sept. 1949; children: Pierre, Nicole, Hélène; PRES. AIR INDUST. ASSOC. OF CAN. 1979-; formerly Depy. Min. of Supply, 1973-79; Pres., Canadian Commercial Corp. 1975-78; Chrmn. of Bd., Royal Candn. Mint 1973-79; Chrmn., Candn. Govt. Specifications Bd. 1973-78; mem., Nat. Design Council 1974-78; Bd. of Dir., Crown Assets Disposal Corp. 1975-79; Pres. Candn. Arsenals Ltd. 1975-78; Chrmn., Unemployment Ins. Comn., 1967-72; Depy. Min. Dept. of Manpower & Immigration, 1972-73; Vice Pres. Bd. of Dirs., Algonquin Coll. 1973-79; mem. Bd. of Governors, Univ. of Ottawa 1980-; served with R.C.A. in Can. and N.W. Europe 1943-46; Clubs: Cercle Univ. d'Ottawa; Country; Home: 2152 Beaumont Rd., Ottawa, Ont. K1H 5V3; Office: Suite 601, 116 Albert St., Ottawa, Ont. K1P 5G3

DESTOUNIS, George P.; b. Montreal, Que., 7 May 1923; s. Peter and Mary (Poulmankos) D.; e. Westhill High Sch., Montreal; Sir George Williams Coll. (Business Adm.); PRES. AND MANG. DIR., FAMOUS PLAYERS CANDN. CORP. LTD., since Jan. 1969; Chrmn. and Pres., Consolidated Theatres Ltd.; President and Mang. Dir., United Theatres Ltd.; United Amusement Corp. Ltd., 1940; appt. Gen. Mgr. 1954; Extve. Vice-Pres., 1959; Extve. Vice-Pres., present Co., Sept. 1966; Liberal; Greek Orthodox; recreations: handball, golf; Home: 17 Ridgewood Rd., Toronto, Ont. M5P 1T4; Office: 130 Bloor St. W., Toronto, Ont. M5S 1N5

DEVER, Donald A., B.S.A., M.Sc., Ph.D.; agricultural scientist; b. Sudbury, Ont., 18 Sept. 1926; s. late John Andrew and Vona Mae (Chisholm) D.; e. Ont. Agric. Coll. (now Univ. of Guelph), B.S.A. 1949; Univ. of Wis., M.Sc. 1950, Ph.D. 1953; m. Elva May, d. late Charles Evan Carter, Guelph, Ont., 27 lia; SECY.-GEN., CAN. GRAINS COUNCIL; Past Dir., Western Transportation Adv. Coun-

cil; past Chrmn., Biomass Energy Inst., Winnipeg; Villa Rosa, Wpg.; Hon. Secy., Manitoba Club Wpg.; Project Leader, Fruit Insect Project, Biol. Control Laboratory, Canada Dept. of Agric., Belleville, Ont., 1946-49; Asst. Prof., Dept. of Entom., Univ. of Wis., 1953-56; Co-ordinator Fungicide Devel., Ortho Div., Chevron Chemical Co. (Div. of Standard Oil of Cal.), 1956-62; Tech. Dir., Niagara Chemicals (Div. of FMC Machinery & Chemicals Ltd.) 1962; Mgr. Internat. Devel., New York 1968-69; served with RCAF as Wireless Air Gunner, 1943-45; author or co-author of over 50 scient. and popular articles; el. Pres., Candn. Agric. Chemicals Assn., 1967; mem., Agric. Inst. Can. (Vice-Pres., Agric. Pesticide Tech. Soc., 1966-67); Entom. Soc. Am.; Entom. Soc. Can.; N.Y. Acad. Arts & Sciences; Past Dir., GIFAP, Brussels, Belgium; Anglican; recreations: golf, painting, woodworking; Home: 18 Holdsworth Ave., Winnipeg, Man. R3P 0P2; Office: 760, 360 Main St., Winnipeg, Man. R3C 3Z3

DEVERELL, William Herbert, B.A., LL.B.; lawyer; author; b. Regina, Sask. 4 March 1937; s. Robert J. and Grace Amy (Barber) D.; e. Univ. of Sask. B.A., LL.B.; m. Teka d. Joseph Melnyk, Canora, Sask. 17 Apl. 1960; children: Daniel Mark, Tamara Lise; PARTNER, DEVERELL, HARRUP, WOOD & POWELL 19..-; called to Bar of Sask. 1964; Past Pres. B.C. Civil Liberties Assn.; Past Chrmn. Criminal Justice Sec. Candn. Bar Assn.; mem. B.C. Bar Assn.; Writers Union Can.; author "Needles" 1979; "High Crimes" 1981; NDP; Home: North Pender Island, B.C. V0N 2M0; Office: 2 Gaolers Mews, Vancouver, B.C.

de VILALLONGA, Jesus Carlos; artist; b. Santa Colona, Spain, 10 Nov. 1927; e. Univ. of Madrid and Barcelona, Arch., 1944-49; Beaux Arts Sch. of San Jorge, Barcelona, 1947-52; Ecole des Beaux Arts, Paris (under Arnold and Gromaire), has exhibited in England, Canada and U.S. since 1957; 1970-80, Exhibitions in Montreal, Chicago, New York, Los Angeles, Rome, Kiev, Köln, London, Barcelona, Bilbao, Madrid; rep. in colls. of Art Gallery of London, Eng.; Collector's Gallery, Washington, D.C.; Dominion Gallery, Montreal; Univ. de Montréal; Univ. of Toronto; Musée de la Prov. de Québec; Palacio Episcopal de Gerona, Spain; Galeria Argos, Barcelona; Alexander Gallery, Los Angeles; Sagittarius Gallery, New York; etc.; Address: c/o Dominion Gallery, 1438 Sherbrooke St. W., Montreal, Que. H3G 1K4

de VISSER, John, R.C.A.; photographer; b. Veghel, North-Brabant, The Netherlands 8 Feb. 1930; s. Sebastian and Christine (van Hout) de V.; e. High Sch. Holland; children: Carole, Joanne, John; freelance photographer John de Visser Photographer Ltd.; 4 one-man exhns., several group exhns.; author "Portrait of Canada" New York Times 1970; "The North/East Coast" 1973; "Labrador" 1977; "Toronto" 1977; "Pioneer Churches" 1976; "Newfoundland and Labrador" 1979; "Quebec and the St. Lawrence" 1980; "Treasures of Canada" 1980; co-author "This Rock Within the Sea, A Heritage Lost" (with Farley Mowat) 1968; "Heritage, A Romantic Look at Early Canadian Furniture" (with Scott Symons) 1971; "Rivers of Canada" (with Hugh McLennan) 1974; "Winter" (with Morley Callaghan) 1974; maj. contrib. "Canada, A Year of the Land", "Call Them Canadians", "Between Friends/Entre Amis", "This was Expo", "Windows", "Doors", "The Yellowhead Route"; maj. mag. credits incl. "Life", "Time", "Macleans", "National Geographic", "Paris Match"; clients incl. Govts. of Can., Ont., India and maj. business firms; Past Council mem. R.C.A.; rec'd Nat. Film Bd. Gold Medal; Awards of Merit Art Dirs. Clubs Toronto, Montreal and N.Y.; Address: 2 Hagerman St., Port Hope, Ont. L1A 3G9.

DEVLIN, John H.; executive; b. Toronto, Ont. 23 March 1920; s. Charles D. and Florence Devlin; e. Upper Can. Coll. Toronto; m. Rosemary (Jukes) Woodward 8 Jan. 1973; three d. Julie, Jane, Lesley; CHRMN., ROTHMANS

OF PALL MALL CANADA LTD. 1969- ; Chrmn. Alfred Dunhill of London Ltd.; Dir. Rothmans International p.l.c. (London, Eng.); Bank of Montreal; Crown Life Insurance Co.; Carling O'Keefe Ltd.; B. F. Goodrich Canada Inc.; Advertising Mgr. Duplate Canada Ltd. and assoc. co's Toronto 1946-53; Gen. Sales Mgr. Smith & Stone Ltd. Toronto 1953-59; Pres. present Co. 1959-69; Chrmn. Carling O'Keefe Ltd. 1968; Trustee, Royal Ont. Museum; Dir. Council Business & Arts Can.; World Wildlife Fund (Can.); served as Pilot with RCAF World War II, rank Flight Lt.; recreations: tennis, fishing, swimming; Anglican; Clubs: Toronto; Turf; York; Home: "Foxgloves", St. John's Sideroad, R.R.2, Aurora, Ont. L4G 3G8; Office: 1500 Don Mills Rd., Don Mills, Ont. M3B 3L1.

DeVOE, Irving Woodrow, Ph.D.; scientist; educator; b. Brewer, Me. 4 Oct. 1936; s. Woodrow Donnison DeVoe; e. Aurora Coll. Ill. B.Sc. 1964; Univ. of Ore. Med. Sch. Ph.D. (Microbiol.) 1968; McGill Univ. post-doctoral fellow 1968-69; m. Lynne Rae d. Arthur Brookfield Parker 21 June 1960; children: Scott Irving, David Brookfield, Steven Patrick, Christopher James, Samantha Rae; PROF. AND CHRMN. OF MICROBIOL. & IMMUNOL, FACULTY OF MEDICINE, McGILL UNIV. 1978- ; Pres. and Owner Ferritech Laboratories Inc.; Research Assoc. Argonne Nat. Lab. U.S. Atomic Energy Comn. 1969-70; Asst. Prof. Aurora Coll. Ill. 1969-70; Asst. Prof. present Univ. 1970, Assoc. Prof. 1975, Prof. 1978- ; Nat. Inst. Predoctoral Fellow; served with U.S. Army (Arty.) 1954-58, U.S. Navy (Aviation) 1958-61, Vietnam; author "Microbiology" 1977; numerous scient. papers and reviews; mem. Candn. Soc. Microbiols.; Am. Soc. Microbiol.: Sigma Xi; Protestant; Home: 115 Chestnut Dr., Baie d'Urfé, Qué.; Office: 3775 University St., Montréal, Qué. H3A 2B4.

DEWAN, Patrick Michael, B.A., B.S.A., LL.D., K.S.G.; b. Osgoode, Ont., 23 Dec. 1890; s. John and Margaret (Shields) D., both Candn. of Irish descent; e. Univ. of Ottawa; St. Francis Xavier Univ., B.A. 1917, Hon. LL.D.; Ont. Agric. Col., B.S.A. 1922; m. Margaret Olive (died 29 Nov. 1970), d. Timothy Tierney, City View, Ont., 26 Sept. 1921; children: Rita Marie, John Tierney, Katherine Patricia, Wilfrid Francis, Margaret Teresa, Helen Josephine, David Michael; Hon. mem., Toronto Adv. Bd., Guaranty Trust Co. of Can.; Secy-Treas., Woodstock Agric. Soc., 1932-37; on teaching staff, Kemptville Agric. Sch., 1922-25; Trustee, St. Mary's Sch. Bd., Woodstock, Ont., 1927-30 (Chairman, 1929-30); Ald., Woodstock, 1931-34; mem., Woodstock Lib. Bd., 1930-37; 1st el. to Ont. Leg. for Oxford at g.e. 1934; re-el. at g.e. 1937; Min. of Agric. 1937-43; Dir., Ont. Chamber of Comm. (Chrmn. of Agric. Comte. 1955-56); Lt.-Gov., Internat. Kiwanis, Div. 3, 1956; Trustee, Alexandra Hosp. Trust, Ingersoll, Ont. for 25 yrs.; Dir., Ont. Hosp. Assn. 1961-70; Kt. of St. Gregory (1956); rec'd. Award of Candn. Council of Christians & Jews, 1956; K. of C.; Liberal; Roman Catholic; recreation: gardening; Club: Kiwanis (Pres. 1955); Address: Dawendine, Ingersoll, Ont.

DEWAR, Daniel Bevis, B.A.; Canadian public servant; b. Kenmore, Ont. 24 Aug. 1932; s. Daniel Peter and Greta Mae (Loney) D.; e. Kenmore, Ont.; Queen's Univ. B.A. 1953; m. Barbara Ann d. late William J. Sweeney 24 Apl. 1965; children: Peter, Sarah; DEPY. SECY. (OPERATIONS), PRIVY COUNCIL OFFICE since 1979; Cabinet Secretariat, Privy Council Office 1954-63; Treasury Bd. Secretariat 1963-73; Asst. Depy. Min. Med. Services, Dept. Nat. Health & Welfare 1973-75; Asst. Secy. Govt. Br., Ministry of State for Science and Technol. 1975-79; Protestant; Home: 9 Pellan Cres., Kanata, Ont. K2K 1J6; Office: Langevin Bldg., Wellington St., Ottawa, Ont. K1A 0A3.

DEWAR, John Stuart, B.Sc.; industrialist; b. Guelph, Ont., 24 June 1918; s. John George and Effie (Marshall) D.; e. Brown Pub. Sch. and Upper Can. Coll., Toronto,

Ont.; Queen's Univ., B.Sc. (Chem. Engn.) 1941; children: Helen, John, Peter, Kenneth; m. 2ndly, (Mrs.) Marian E. Prowse, 1968 who has three children; CHAIRMAN AND C.E.O., UNION CARBIDE CANADA LIMITED since 1981; Dir., Thomson Newspapers Ltd.; The Toronto-Dominion Bank; Manufacturers Life Ins. Co.; Ralston Purina Can. Inc.; Bd. of Trustees, Queen's Univ.; Bd. of Governors, Ont. Research Foundation; joined Nat. Carbon Co., Div. of Union Carbide Can. Ltd. in 1943 as Chem. Engr.; apptd. Pres. in 1955; apptd. Vice-Pres. of Union Carbide Can. Ltd. in 1956; Dir. 1959; Pres. 1965; Dir., Can. Manufacturers Assn.; Can. Chemical Producers' Assn. (Chmn. 1970); Can. Council of the Conference Bd.; Anglican; Clubs: Rosedale Golf; York (Toronto); Glen Abbey Golf; Toronto Club; Rideau (Ottawa); Mt. Royal (Montreal); Office: 123 Eglinton Ave. E., Toronto, Ont. M4P 1J2

DEWARE, Hon. Mabel Margaret, M.L.A.; politician; b. Moncton, N.B. 9 Aug. 1926; d. Hugh Fraser and Mary Elizabeth Ann (Adams) Keiver; m. Ralph Baxter Deware, Moncton, N.B. 1 Aug. 1945; children: Kimberly Jon, Peter Thomas, Michael Hugh, Joanne Christine; MIN. OF LABOUR & MANPOWER, N.B. 1978- ; Mgr. Keeware Management Ltd.; el. M.L.A. for Moncton West prov. g.e. 1978; P. Conservative; First United Baptist; Office: (P.O. Box 6000) Chestnut Complex, 470 York St., Fredericton, N.B. E3B 5H1.

DEWART, Leslie, M.A., Ph.D., LL.B.; educator; b. Madrid, Spain 12 Dec. 1922; s. Gerardo Gonzales and Adamina (Duarte) D.; e. Univ. of Toronto B.A. 1951, M.A. 1952, Ph.D. 1954, LL.B. 1979; Osgoode Hall Law Sch. 1981; m. Doreen Brennan 20 Aug. 1976; children (by first marriage): Leslie (Mrs. Philip Giroday), Elizabeth (Mrs. David McEwen), Sean, Colin; PROF. OF PHILOSOPHY OF RELIGION, ST. MICHAEL'S COLL., UNIV. OF TORONTO 1956- ; called to Bar of Ont. 1981; served with RCAF 1942-47; Home: 14 Prospect St., Toronto, Ont. M4X 1C6. Office: Toronto, Ont. M5S 1J4.

de WEERDT, Mark Murray, Q.C., M.A., LL.B.; b. Cologne, W. Germany, 6 May 1928; s. Hendrik Eugen and Ina Dunbar (Murray) de W.; e. various schs., Scot., 1935-46; Univ. of Glasgow, M.A. (Math. & Econ.) 1949; Univ. of B.C., LL.B. (Norgan Law Scholar 1953) 1955; m. Linda Anne, d. I. S. A. Hadwen, D.V.Sc., F.R.S.M., Toronto, 31 March 1956; children: Simon André, Murray Hadwen, David Lockhart, Charles Dunbar; GENERAL COUNSEL, VANCOUVER; senior counsel, Dept. of Justice at Vancouver since 1976; read law with T. P. O'Grady, Q.C., City Solr., Victoria, B.C.; called to Bar of B.C. 1956 and to Bar of N.W.T. 1958; cr. Q.C. (Fed.) 1968; Cross & O'Grady, Victoria, Assoc. Solr. 1956-57; Adv. Counsel, Dept. of Justice, Ottawa, 1957-58; Crown Atty., N.W.T., Yellowknife, 1958-63; Agt. of Atty. Gen. of Can., Yellowknife, 1958-66; Pub. Adm. for N.W.T., 1965-67; formed de Weerdt & Searle, 1963-64 and successor firms to 1971; Magistrate, Northwest Territories, 1971-73; General Solicitor, Insurance Corp. of B.C., 1974-76; held various extve. positions with Nat., N.W.T. and Mackenzie River P.Cons. Assns., 1959-68; Extve. mem., Yellowknife Bd. Trade, 1960-62; mem., Nat. Comte., N. & Arctic Scouting, Boy Scouts of Can., 1966-70; Trustee and Bd. Vice-Chrmn., Yellowknife Pub. Sch., 1964-68; Pres., N.W.T. Bar Assn., 1964-66 and 1969-70; mem., Candn. Bar Assn.; Home: 4005 West 39th Ave., Vancouver, B.C. V6N 3B1; Office: 19th Floor, 1055 West Georgia St., Vancouver, B.C.

DEWEY, John M., B.Sc., Ph.D., F.Inst.P.; educator; b. Portsmouth, Eng. 23 March 1930; s. Stanley George and Ilva (Hollingsworth) D.; came to Canada 1956; e. St. John's Coll., Portsmouth, Eng. 1947; Portsmouth Coll. of Technol. 1947-50; B.Sc. (London) 1950, Ph.D. (London) 1964; m. Jean Evelyn, d. Arthur Frederick Moon, 16 Aug. 1951; children: Elizabeth Sarah (Hall), Richard Kelvin; DEAN OF GRADUATE STUDIES, UNIV. OF VICTORIA and Prof. of Physics there since 1965;.Sr. Science and Math. Master, De La Salle Coll., Jersey, Channel Islands 1950; Head Aerophysics & Shock Tubes Sec., Suffield Exper. Station, Ralston, Alta. 1956; Fellow, Inst. Physics (U.K.); mem., Candn. Assn. Physicists; Am. Inst. Physics; has published numerous research reports and papers in learned and prof. mags. and journs.; recreations: sailing, badminton, tennis; Clubs: Victoria (B.C.) Racquet; Royal Victoria Yacht; Home: 1741 Feltham Rd., Victoria, B.C. V8N 2A4

DEWHURST, William George, B.M., B.Ch., F.R.S.M., F.R.C.P.(C), F.A.C.P. F.A.P.A.; educator, b. Frosterley, Eng.▵21 Nov. 1926; s. William and Elspeth Leslie (Begg) D.; e. Oxford Univ. B.A. 1947, B.M., B.Ch. 1950, M.A. 1962; M.R.C.P. 1955; London Univ. Acad. Postgrad. Dipl. in Psychol. Med. with Distinction 1961; Cert. Specialist Alta. 1970; Foundation mem. Royal Coll. Psychiatry 1971; m. Margaret d. Frank Dransfield, Southwater, Sussex, Eng. 17 Sept. 1960; children: Timothy Andrew, Susan Jane; CHRMN. OF PSYCHIATRY, UNIV. OF ALTA. 1975- and Prof. 1972-; Co. Dir., Neurochem. Research Unit 1979-; Hon. Prof., Pharmacy and Pharmaceutical Sci. 1979-; Consultant Psychiatrist, Royal Alexandra Hosp. and Edmonton Gen. Hosp.; Lectr. Inst. Psychiatry, London Univ. 1962-64; Sr. Lectr. and Consultant Physician, Inst. Psychiatry, Maudsley Hosp. London 1965-69; Assoc. Prof. Univ. of Alta. 1969-72; served as Offr. in charge of med. wards 33rd Gen. Hosp. Hong Kong 1952-54, rank Capt.; mem. Edmonton Local Bd. Health 1974-76; Past Univ. Alta. Rep. on Prov. Mental Health Adv. Council and mem. Research Comte.; mem. various ed. bds.; author or co-author numerous med. publs.; Past Pres. Alta. Psychiatric Assn.; Founding Vice Pres. Candn. Coll. Neuropsychopharmacol.; Past Chrmn. Candn. Assn. Prof. Psychiatry; Councillor, W. Candn. Dist. Br. Am. Psychiatric Assn.; Rep. on Scient. Council, Candn. Psychiatric Assn.; mem. various other internat. and nat. socs.; Anglican; recreations: books, football, athletics, hockey, music, chess; Home: 92 Fairway Dr., Edmonton, Alta. T6J 2C5; Office: 1-122 Clinical Sciences Bldg., Univ. of Alta., Edmonton, Alta. T6G 2G3.

DEWLING, Eric Garrett; financial executive (retired); b. St. John's, Nfld., 22 Sept. 1915; s. late Joseph W. and Emily R. D.; e. Bishop Feild Coll. and Prince of Wales Coll., St. John's, Nfld.; m. Doris Irene, d. A. D. MacCormack, New Glasgow, N.S., 21 Oct. 1946; children: Kathryn, Eric J., Alan, Peter; Vice Pres. and Secy., Canada Permanent Mortgage Corp. 1972-80 (Asst. V.P. and Secy. 1970-72); joined Eastern Trust Co. as Cashier, St. John's, Nfld. 1934; apptd. Acct., Montreal, 1941; Mgr. Charlottetown, P.E.I., 1949; Secy. and Chief Acct., Halifax, N.S., 1951; Asst. Gen. Mgr., Halifax, 1958; Gen. Mgr., Atlantic Region of Eastern & Chartered Trust Co. 1963; Depy. Gen. Mgr., Toronto, Ont. 1965; served with Royal Candn. Ordnance Corps. 1941-46; discharged with rank Warrant Offr. 1; Pres. (1966-67) Soc. Indust. Accts. of Can.; Fellow Soc. of Management Accts. of Can.; Fellow Chartered Inst. Secys.; Freemason; Anglican; recreations: music, curling, woodwork; Clubs: Donalda; National; Rotary; Home: Apt. 3101, 85 Thorncliffe Park Dr., Toronto, Ont. M4H 1L6; Office: 320 Bay St., Toronto, Ont. M5H 2P6

DeWOLF, Vice-Admiral Harry George, C.B.E. (1946), D.S.O. (1944), D.S.C.; R.C.N. retired; b. Bedford, N.S., 26 June 1903; s. Harry George and Kate A. (Fitzmaurice) D.; e. Roy. Naval Coll. of Can., Grad. 1921; Roy. Naval Staff Coll., Greenwich, Eng., Grad. 1937; m. Gwendolen Fowle, d. Thomas St. George Gilbert, Bermuda, 5 May 1931; children: Suzette, James; joined R.C.N.; 1918; Commdr. H.M.C.S. ''St. Laurent'', 1939-40, ''Haida'', 1943-44, ''Warrior'', 1947, ''Magnificent'', 1948; Rear Adm., Flag Offr. Pacific Coast, 1948-50; Vice Chief of Naval Staff 1950-52; Chrmn., Candn. Jt. Staff, Wash., D.C., 1952-55; promoted Vice-Adm., 1956; Chief of Naval Staff, 1956-60, retired 1961; Offr., Legion of Merit (U.S.A.)

1946; Legion of Hon. (France) 1947; King Haakon Cross of Liberation, 1948; D. M.Sc. h. RMC 1966, RRMC 1980; Presbyterian; recreations: fishing, golf; Homes: 200 Rideau Terrace, Apt. 1006, Ottawa, Ont. and Somerset, Bermuda.

DEXTRAZE, Gen. Jacques Alfred, C.C. C.B.E., C.M.M., D.S.O., C.D., LL.D.; transportation executive; b. Montreal, Que., 15 Aug. 1919; s. Alfred and Amanda (Bond) D.; e. St. Joseph de Berthier Coll., Montreal, 1930-37; MacDonald Business Coll., 1938-40; Columbia Univ., Business Adm., 1947; m. Frances Helena, d. Raymond E. Paré, 2 Sept. 1942; three s.; Jacques, Capt. Robert, John; CHMN. OF BD., CANADIAN NATIONAL 1977-; joined Fusiliers Mt. Royal (Res.), 1939; enlisted in Act. Serv., 1940; Overseas in various regimental & command appts. in U.K., Dir. of Canada Safety Council; Atlantic Council of Can.; Consortium For Atlantic-Pacific Affairs; apptd. C.O., Hastings and Prince Edward Regt. for service with Pacific Force in Far East, 1945; apptd. Mgr., Singer Mfg. Co., 1945-50; resumed army service at request of Min. of Nat. Defence, 1950 and apptd. C.O., Royal 22nd Regt. (Korea), 1950-52; served in various staff appts. in Can., 1953-57; Commandant, Royal Candn. Sch. of Inf., Camp Borden, 1957-60; Camp Valcartier, Que., 1960; promoted Brig. and apptd. Commdr., E. Que. Region, 1962; Chief of Staff, HQ U.N. Operations in Congo, 1963; returned to Can. to command 2 Candn. Inf. Bgde. Group, Camp Petawawa,1964-66; Chief of Staff Operations & Training, Mobile Command HQ, 1966-67; promoted Maj. Gen. and apptd. Deputy Commander, September 1967; Maj. Gen. and Deputy Chief of Personnel 1969; Lt. General and Chief of Personnel 1970-72; Promoted Four Star Gen. 1972; Chief of the Defence Staff of Candn. Armed Forces 1972-77; awarded D.S.O. (1944) and Bar (1945), O.B.E. 1952, C.B.E. 1964; awarded Commdr. of Order of Mil. Merit (1972); mem. of Chamber of Commerce (Mtl. District); Vice Patron of the Royal Candn. Military Inst.; Hon. Candn. Amateur Boxing Assn.; Candn. Infantry Assn.; Dominion Honorary Vice-Pres., Royal Candn. Legion; Knight of the Most Venerable Order of the Hospital of St. John of Jerusalem; Knight of the Military and Hospitaller Order of St. Lazarus of Jerusalem; R. Catholic; recreations: golf, skiing; Clubs: Saint Denis; St. James's (Montreal); Mount Royal, Candn. Railway Rideau Club of Ottawa; Quebec Garrison; Home: 467 Crestview Rd., Ottawa, Ont. K1H 5G7; Office: P.O. Box 8100, Montreal, Que. H3C 3N4

De YOUNG, H. George, B.Sc.; business consultant; b. Grand Haven, Mich., 13 July 1907; s. George and Gertrude (Sprick) De Y.; e. Mich. State Univ.; U.S. Naval Acad., B.Sc. (Engn.) 1931; m. Inez Adele, d. late Grant Stiff, Owosso, Mich., 15 Jan. 1933; children: George Gage, David John; Dir., Confederation Life Assn.; commissioned an Ensign in the U.S.N. which he resigned and joined Midvale Co., 1931; positions incl. Supervisor of Hammers, Supv. of Rolling Mills, and Chief Engr. (rec'd U.S. Govt. Award for research and develop. of armour-piercing projectiles at Midvale); Asst. to the Pres.; Treadwell Engn. Co., Easton, Pa., 1949-51; Works Mgr., Atlas Steels Ltd., Welland, Ont., 1951-52; Vice-Pres. (Operations), 1952-55; el. a Dir. 1954; Extve. Vice-Pres., 1955-56; Pres., 1956-63; Pres., Rio Algom Mines Ltd., 1963-65 when resigned; was a mem. of Candn. Govt. Mission to European Econ. Community, visiting Govts. of each mem. country and the Comn. of E.E.C.; on 28 Feb. 1961 named Chrmn., Nat. Productivity Council, Canada; Gen. Mgr. and Consultant, New Zealand Steel Ltd. 1966-69; mem., Am. Iron & Steel Inst.; Candn. Mfrs. Assn. (Extve. Council); Anglican; recreations: music, reading, fishing, retriever competition; Clubs: Niagara Falls; Maganassippi Fish & Game; York (Toronto); National (Toronto); Home: (P.O. Box 239) Fonthill, Ont. L0S 1E0

DEZIEL, Le Rev. Pere Roland Julien, B.A., L.Th; priest, Franciscan Fathers; b. St-Norbert, Berthier, Que. 7 March 1907; s. Achille and Malvina (Houde)D.; e. Laval Univ. Que., B.A. 1932; Sch. of Fine Arts, Montreal, 1940; Univ. of Montreal L.Th. 1944; Roman Catholic Priest; Pres., Société Généalogique Canadienne française since 1961, membre émérite 1975; Teacher, French Lit., Univ. of Montreal, 1944; Prof., Sch. of Fine Arts, 1945-64; Visiting lectr. at various coll. in the hist. of art; organized and accompanied 33 groups on cultural trips to Europe and USA; has given more than 400 educational broadcasts (Radio-Canada) on the subject of French Canadian families, from France to Can.; author of "Médaillons d'Ancêtres, I série", 1970; "Médaillons d'Ancêtres, II série", 1973; "Histoire de la ville de Verdun", 1976; "History of Verdun", 1978; "La famille Déziel-Labrèche, Histoire et généalogie", 1978; other writings include articles of history or genealogy publ. in various magazines; Chief Ed., "Memoires de la Soc. Généal. C.F."; rec'd. certificat de mérite "pour son importante contribution à l'histoire régionale" from Soc. Historique du Can., 1973; membre de l'Ordre du Canada, 1978; membre de Soc. Historique de Montréal; Soc. Généalogie de Québec; Home: 2010 Dorchester Blvd. W., Montreal, Que. H3H 1R6.

DIACHUK, Hon. Bill W.,M.L.A.; politician; b. Vegreville, Alta. 8 Oct. 1929; s. Nick and Helen (Drabit) D.; e. Two Hills High Sch.; Univ. of Alta. Cert. in Social Work; m. Olga Cymbaluk 31 May 1952; children: Glenn, Kenneth, Teresa, Brenda, Lynda; MIN. RESPONSIBLE FOR WORKERS' HEALTH, SAFETY & COMPENSATION, ALTA.1979- ; Pres., Diachuk Management and Consulting Services Ltd.; el. M.L.A. for Edmonton Beverly 1971, re-el. since; Depy. Speaker 1971-75; Caucus Secy. 1975- ; Past Pres., Star of North Retreat House; St. Basil's Parish Council; Alta. Cath. Sch. Trustee Assn.; former Trustee, Edmonton Cath. Sch. Bd.; served as mem. Alta. Sch. Trustee Assn.; Past Pres. and Hon. Life mem. Edmonton Ukrainian Prof. & Business Assn.; Hon. Pres. Ukrainian Cheremosh Soc.; K. of C.; Lions Internat.; Hon. Vice Pres. Norwood Br. Royal Candn. Legion; served various Leg. comtes.; apptd. to Adv. Comte. on Corrections and on Wildlife Resources; mem. Prov. Mun. Finance Council; Standing Comte. on Alta. Heritage Savings Trust Fund Act; P. Conservative; Ukrainian Greek Catholic; Office: 203 Legislative Bldg., Edmonton, Alta. T5K 2B6.

DIAMOND, Abel, J.,M.A., M.Arch., R.C.A., F.R.A.I.C.; architect; b. S. Africa 8 Nov. 1932; s. Jacob and Rachel (Werner) D.; e. Durban High Sch. 1950; Univ. of Capetown B.Arch (with Distinction) 1956; Oxford Univ. M.A. 1958; (Rugby Blue 1957); Univ. of Pa. M.Arch. 1962; m. Gillian Mary d. Kenneth Huggins 11 Aug. 1959; children: Andrew Michael, Alison Suzanne Katherine; PRINC., A. J. DIAMOND ASSOCIATES 1975- ; Pres. A.J. Diamond Planners Ltd.; Arch., Durban, S. Africa 1956; Partner, Cameron, Phillips & Diamond, Durban 1959-61; Sr. Asst. Arch., Louis I. Kahn, Philadelphia 1963-64; Arch., Toronto 1965-68; Princ., Diamond & Myers, Toronto 1969-75; Instr. in Arch. Univ. of Pa. and Drexel Inst. of Technol. Philadelphia 1962-63; Asst. Prof. Univ. Pa. 1963-64; Asst. Prof. Univ. of Toronto 1964, Assoc. Prof. (inaugurated postgrad. Urban Design) 1967-70; Assoc. Prof. (part-time) of Environmental Studies York Univ. 1970-72, Prof. (part-time) 1970-72; Tutor in Arch. Univ. Toronto 1980-81; keynote speaker various meetings incl. 150th Anniversary Royal Inst. Australian Archs. Perth 1979; juror various award programs; recipient Thornton White Prize in Arch. Univ. Capetown 1951; Graham Foundation Scholarship (USA) 1962; Marley Scholarship (S.Africa) 1962; Eedee Award Candn. Fed. Govt. 1967; Can. Council Grant 1967; Cert. of Excellence Soc. Graphic Designers Can. & Nat. Design Council 1966-68; Recipient various awards for architectural design; Fellow, Calumet Coll. York Univ. 1972; visiting critic and guest lectr. Univs. Alta., B.C., Calgary, Carleton, Laval, Man., McGill, N.S. Tech. Coll., Toronto, Harvard, Ill., Pa., Princeton, Wisc., Royal Melbourne Inst., W. Australia Inst.; author various publs. arch. and planning; Assoc. Ed. "Architecture Canada" 1965; mem. ed. bd. "Canadian Forum"; Tarragon Theatre Adv. Bd.; Dir., Chamber Players of Toronto Bd., mem. Royal Arch. Inst. Can.; Ont. Assn. Archs.; Ontario Assn. Archs. Registration Board 1976-79; member, National Capital Commission Design Advisory Committee 1981- ; Ordre des Architectes du Qué.; Royal Inst. Brit. Archs.; Royal Arch. Inst. Australia; Candn. Inst. Planners; Am. Inst. Planners; Heritage Can.; recreations: squash, music; Clubs: Vincents (Oxford); University; Home: 37 Glenrose Ave., Toronto, Ont. M4T 1K3; Office: 322 King St. W., Toronto, Ont. M5V 1J4.

DIAMOND, Allen Ephraim, B.Sc.; real estate developer; b. Montreal, Que., 1 March 1921; s. Meyer D.; e. Pub. Sch., Montreal, Que.; Brockville, (Ont.) High Sch.; Queen's Univ., B.Sc.; m. Shirley d. Charles Greenberg, 15 Sept. 1946; 4 s.; CHRMN. OF THE EXEC. COMM., CADILLAC FAIRVIEW CORPORATION LIMITED; Dir.; Cadillac Fairview Corp.; Ont. Hydro; formerly Chrm. of Bd. and Chief Exec. Officer of Cadillac Fairview Cor.; joined Principal Investments Ltd. as Project Manager (Constr.) 1946; founded Cadillac Contracting & Developments Ltd. (predecessor firm) 1953; served in 2nd World War with R.C.N.V.R. as Lieut.; Dir., Mt. Sinai Hosp.; YMHA; mem., Assn. Prof. Engrs. Ont.; Past Pres., Candn. Inst. Pub. Real Estate Co.'s; Vice Pres., Candn. Opera Co.; Alternate Gov., Hebrew Univ. of Jerusalem; recreations: golf, swimming; Home: 11 Dempsey Crescent, Willowdale, Ont. M2L 1Y4; Office: 1200 Sheppard Ave. E., Willowdale, Ont. M2K 2R8

DIAMOND, Air Commodore Gerald Gordon, A.F.C., C.D.;b. Gladstone, Man., May 1915; e. Pub. and High Schs., Vancouver, B.C.; RCAF Staff Coll., Toronto, 1947; Imperial Defence Coll., 1964-65; joined RCAF auxiliary 1937 and RCAF regular 1939; served with army co-operation and communications sqdns. on W. Coast; commanded wartime RCAF Stn., Annette Isl., Alaska, 1942-43 when named Offr. Commdg. 12 Communications Sqdn., Rockcliffe; joined Operations staff, 9 Transport Group, Rockcliffe (later became Air Transport Command), 1945; returned to command 12 Sqdn., 1946; was chosen for exchange duties with USAF, 1948; returned to Can. in 1951 to become Sr. Personnel Staff Offr., Air Material Command HQ, Ottawa; apptd. Dir. of Postings and Careers, AFHQ, Nov. 1951; named Commdg. Offr., RCAF Stn., Trenton, 1954; trans. to 4th Allied Tactical Air Force HQ, Ramstein, Germany, 1957; apptd. Chief of Personnel Service, AFHQ, 1960; Air Offr. Commdg., Air Transport Command, Dec. 1965; retired from Canadian Forces Mar. 1967; joined DeHavilland Aircraft of Canada Ltd. May 1967, now Ottawa rep.; Address: Apt. 603, 1405 Prince of Wales Dr., Ottawa, Ont.

diCENZO, Colin Domenic, C.M., C.D., M.Sc., D.I.C., F.E.I.C., F.I.E.E.E.; educator; engineer; b. Hamilton, Ont. 26 July 1923; s. Ferdanado and Kathleen (Quickenden) diC.; e. Hamilton Tech. Inst. Elect. Tech. Dipl. 1940; Univ. of N.B. B.Sc. 1952 (Brydon-Jack Scholar); M.Sc. 1957; Imp. Coll. of Science & Technol. D.I.C. 1953 (Athlone Fellow); m. Patricia Evelyn d. late Dr. H. Stanley Wright 12 Sept. 1950; children: Colin Stanley, Eileen Rose, Brian Wright, Frederic Mark, Peter David, Pamela Kathleen; DEAN OF ENGINEERING & APPLIED SCIENCE, MEMORIAL UNIV. OF NFLD. 1980- , mem. Senate, Council Faculty Grad. Studies, Chrmn. Council Faculty Engn. & Applied Science, mem. Nat. Comte. Deans of Engn. & Applied Science 1980- ; Lectr. in Elect. Engn. Royal Mil. Coll. Kingston 1954-57; Project Engr. and Depy. Head, Sonar Group, Naval HQ Ottawa 1957-60, Head, Underwater Fire Control Systems Design Group 1960-62; Sqdn Staff Offr. Second Candn. Destroyer Sqdn. Pacific 1962-64; Systems Engr. Candn. Forces HQ Ottawa

(Hydrofoil Ship Devel. Group) 1964-65; Assoc. Prof. of Elect. Engn. McMaster Univ. 1965-72, Prof. 1972-79 and Prof. of Elect. & Computer Engn. 1979-80, Prof. Emeritus 1980- , Dir. of Undergrad. Studies Engn. 1968-75, Assoc. Dean of Engn. 1975-79, Vice Chrmn. Faculty Engn. 1968-75; Visiting mem. Inst. Engrs. Australia 1979; Distinguished Visitor Inst. Engrs. India 1980; State Guest Govt. W. Bengal India 1980; Advisor, Jadavpur Univ. India 1981- ; Advisor, Petroleum Directorate Govt. Nfld. & Labrador 1981- ; Candn. mem. Engn. Comte. Oceanic Resources 1981- ; Advisor, Nfld. Inst. Cold Ocean Science; Dir. Bd. Govs. and mem. Research Program Adv. Comte. Centre for Cold Ocean Resources Engn. Nfld. 1980- ; Dir. Bd. Govs. Labrador Inst. N. Studies 1980- ; Pres., EIC Publishing Inc. 1979- ; served with RCN 1941-65, Reserve 1965-74, rank Commdr., C.O. HMCS Star 1969-71; decorated Order of Canada 1972; recipient Centennial Medal 1967; Pub. Servants Invention Act Award 1973; Assn. Prof. Engrs. Prov. Ont. Engn. Medal 1976; Queen's Silver Jubilee Medal 1977; Julian C. Smith Medal Engn. Inst. Can. 1977; Gov.-Gen.'s Commemorative Medal 1978; Candn. Soc. Elect. Engn. Commendation 1978; author over 46 publs. and patents; Fellow, Inst. Elect. & Electronics Engrs.; mem. Candn. Soc. Elect. Engn. (Pres. and Chrmn. Bd. Dirs. 1976-78); Candn. Dir. Pan-Am. Fed. Engn. Soc's 1981- , Candn. Del. 1980; mem. Commonwealth Engrs. Council; World Fed. Engn. Organs.; Pres., Engn. Inst. Can. 1979-80; Clubs: Hamilton Officers'; Crow's Nest Officers (St. John's, Nfld.); Home: 28 Millen Ave., Hamilton, Ont. L9A 2T4; Office: St. John's, Nfld. A1B 3X5.

DICK, Ronald Albert, M.Arch., R.I.B.A., F.R.A.I.C.; b. Paris, France, 3 June 1920; s. Leonard Albert and Elfrieda Annie (Gindle) D.; e. Sutton Valence Sch., Kent Eng.; Ecole Nationale Superieure des Beaux Arts, Paris, France; Bartlett Sch. of Arch., London Univ.; Cornell Univ.; m. Louise Spencer, d. Spencer Ervin, 24 June 1950; children: David Leonard, Andrew Ronald, Edwina Louise; SR. PARTNER, MARANI, ROUNTHWAITE & DICK, since 1964; joined Marani & Morris, Archs., Toronto, Ont., 1949; Assoc. Partner, Marani, Morris & Allan, 1953; Sr. Partner, 1962; served in 2nd World War with Royal Engrs., 1939-46, in U.K., S.E. Asia Command and N.W. Europe; attained rank of Major; with Candn. Militia, 1951-56; fellow, Royal Arch. Inst. Can.; Anglican; Clubs: Badminton & Racquet; University; Home: 319 Inglewood Drive, Toronto, Ont. M4T 1J4; Office: 112 Merton St., Toronto, Ont. M4S 2Z9

DICKEY, John Horace, Q.C.; lawyer; b. Edmonton, Alta., 4 Sept. 1914; s. Horace Arthur and Mary Catharine (Macdonald) D.; e. Morrison Sch., Antigonish, N.S.; Coll. St. Sch. and St. Mary's Coll., Halifax, N.S. 1936; Dalhousie Univ., LL.B. 1940; LL.D. St. Marys Univ., LL.D. 1980; Mount St. Vincent Univ., D.Hum.L. 1981; m. Eleanor Joyce, d. late Dr. M. J. Carney, Halifax, N.S., 18 Apl. 1959; PARTNER, McINNES, COOPER & ROBERTSON; Pres., Nova Scotia Pulp Ltd.; Dir., Atlantic Trust Co.; Candn. Commercial Corp.; Dover Mills Ltd.; Fraser-Brace Maritimes Ltd.; read law with W. C. MacDonald, K.C., M.P.; called to Bar of N.S. 1940; cr. Q.C. 1957; 1st el. to H. of C. for Halifax in by-el. 1947; re-el. g.e. 1949 and 1953; apptd. Parlty. Asst. to Min. of Def. Production 1952; def. in g.e. 1957, 1958; mem., Candn. del. to U.N. 1950; Candn. Rep. on Econ. and Social Council of U.N., 1950; Assoc. Prosecutor with Candn. War Crimes Liaison Detachment Far East; served in World War 1942-47 as Maj. with Candn. Army; Pres., N.S. Barristers Soc. 1966-67; Vice Pres., Candn. Bar Assn 1967-69; Liberal Fed. of Can.; Phi Delta Theta; Knight Comm.; Order of St. Lazarus; Liberal; R. Catholic; recreations: swimming, tennis, boating, skiing; Home: 1532 Larch St., Halifax, N.S. B3H 3W8; Office: 1673 Bedford Row, P.O. Box 730, Halifax, N.S. B3J 2V1

DICKINS, Clennell H., O.C. (1968), O.B.E., D.F.C., LL.D.; aviation consultant; b. Portage la Prairie, Man., 12 Jan. 1899; s. Ambrose and Jessie (Gouin) D.; e. Univ. of Alberta; m. Constance Gerrie, 1 Sept. 1927; children: John, Mary, William; Supt., McKenzie Dist., Candn. Airways Ltd. at Edmonton, 1929-34; promoted to Gen. Supt. at Winnipeg, 1935-40; Vice-Chrmn. and Chief Operations Offr., Air Services, C.P.R., 1941-42; Gen. Mgr., Atlantic Ferry Organization (ATFERO), Montreal, Vice-Pres. and Gen. Mgr., C.P. Airlines, Montreal, 1942-46; apptd. Sales Dir. of The de Haviland Aircraft of Canada 1947, Extve. Vice Pres., Apl. 1964; retired 1966; served in 1st World War 1917-19 with R.F.C. and R.A.F.; awarded D.F.C. 1918; mem., R.C.A.F., 1924-27; Pres., Air Industries & Transport Assn. of Can. 1952-53; mem. Canada's Aviation Hall of Fame, 1973-; Protestant; recreations: fishing, golf, flying; Home: Apt. 702, 1120 Beach Drive, Victoria, B.C. V8S 2N1

DICKSON, Arthur David, M.D.; university professor; b. Londonderry, N. Ireland, 2 March 1925; s. Arthur Edwin and Edith Elizabeth (McCandless) D.; e. Foyle Coll., Londonderry, 1932-43; Queen's Univ., Belfast, M.B., B.Ch., B.A.O. 1949, M.D. 1954; m. Dorothy, d. Edmund Crowe, Surrey, U.K., 30 Dec. 1952; two d. Kathleen, Susan; PROF. OF ANATOMY, UNIVERSITY OF CALGARY, since 1968; Assistant Lecturer, Queen's Univ., Belfast, 1951-54; Univ. Demonst., Cambridge Univ., 1954-56; Lectr., Aberdeen Univ., 1956-63; Assoc. Prof., Dalhousie Univ., 1963-66 and Univ. of W. Ont., 1966-67; Prof. 1967-68; writings incl. scient. papers on mammalian reproduction; mem., Candn. Assn. Anatomists; Am. Assn. Anatomists; Soc. Study Reprod.; recreations: ornithology, nature photography; Address: Univ. of Calgary, Calgary, Alta.

DICKSON, Hon. Frank Gordon William, B.A., LL.B.; judge; b. Regina, Sask. 22 Aug. 1931; s. Frank James and Edna Marion (Lewis) D.; e. Albert and Victoria Schs. Regina; Swift Current (Sask.) Coll. Inst. 1949; Univ. of Sask. B.A. 1962, LL.B. 1963; m. Jennie Ruth d. Andrew Anderson, Chaplin, Sask. 10 Aug. 1957; children: Gail Marion, Donna Helen, Joseph Andrew, David Frank; called to Bar of Sask. 1964; practiced law with MacDermid & Co. Saskatoon 1963-78; mem. Saskatoon Bar Assn. (Past Pres.); Law Soc. Sask.; Candn. Bar Assn.; Protestant; recreations: golf, badminton, swimming, camping, fishing; Clubs: Riverside Golf; Saskatoon Badminton; Home: 99 Leddy Cres., Saskatoon, Sask. S7H 3Y9; Office: 224, 5th Ave. South, Saskatoon, Sask. 57K 5M5

DICKSON, George H., B.S.A.; retired company executive; b. Westbourne, Manitoba, 4 July 1915; s. Rev. G. A., B.D., D.D., and Lillian (McLachlan) D.; e. Western Canada High Sch., Calgary, Alta. (1934); Ont. Agric. Coll., Guelph, Ont., B.S.A. 1938; m. Margaret Eleanor, d. late Matt Leggat, 18 May 1938; children: Beverley Ann, George Kent; Extve. Vice Pres. and Dir., Canada Packers Ltd., 1962-78; Dir., Canada Packers Ltd.; Haverhill Meat Products Ltd.; joined Canada Packers Ltd. in 1937 as Mail Clerk; Office and Plant Training, 1937-39; Hog Buying Operations, 1940; Pork Trading Operations, 1941; Mgr., Pork Operations at Toronto Plant, 1951, and Gen. Mgr. of Co's. Pork Operations, 1954; Dir. and Dir. of Marketing, 1956; Dir. and Gen. Mgr., 1960; Extve. Vice Pres. and Dir., 1962-77; Past Pres., Ontario Agricultural Coll. Alumni Assn.; mem. of Senate, Univ. of Toronto, 1953-56; mem. Bd. Govs., Univ. of Guelph; mem., Toronto Bd. Trade; Agric. Inst. of Can. (Past Pres., Central Ont. Local); United Church; recreations: golf, bowling, gardening; Clubs: St. George's Golf & Country; Toronto Badminton and Racquet; Home: 5 Edenbridge Drive, Islington, Ont. M9A 3E8

DICKSON, (Horatio Henry) Lovat, O.C. (1978), M.A., LL.D., Litt.D.; publisher; author; b. Victoria, Australia, 30 June 1902; s. Gordon Fraser and Josephine Mary (Cunningham) D.; e. Berkhamsted Sch., 1913-17; Univ. of Alta., B.A. 1927, M.A. 1929, LL.D. 1970; Univ. W. Ont., Litt.D. 1976; York Univ., Litt.D. 1981; m. Marguerite Isabella, d. late Alexander B. Brodie, 26 Dec. 1934; one s.; formed Lovat Dickson Ltd. (publishers of gen. lit.) in Can., 1968; Lectr. in Eng., Univ. of Alta., 1927-29; Assoc.-Ed., "The Fortnightly Review", London, 1929; Ed. 1930-32; Ed., "Review of Reviews", 1931-32; founded Lovat Dickson Ltd., London, 1932; served as Mang. Dir. to 1938; Asst. Gen. Ed. of Books, Macmillan & Co., London, 1938; Dir. and Gen. Ed. of Books, 1941-64; estbd. St. Martin's Press, New York on behalf of Macmillan's and served as Vice Pres. to 1964; Founding Dir., Reprint Soc., London and Pan Books Ltd.; served on Candn. Comte., Brit. Publishers Assn.; Past Pres., Publishers Circle; returned to Can. 1967; served with R.A.F. Toronto, 1918; Past Chrmn., Can. Scholarships, Cambridge Univ.; Pres., Candn. Univ. Soc. (U.K.), 1960-65; author: "The Green Leaf", 1938; "Half-Breed, The Story of Grey Owl" 1939; "Out of the West Land" (novel), 1944; "Richard Hillary" (biog.), 1950; "The Ante-Room" (autobiog.), 1950; "The House of Words" (autobiog.), 1963; "H. G. Wells: His Turbulent Life and Times", 1969; "Wilderness Man: The Strange Story of Grey Owl" 1973; "Radclyffe Hall at the Well of Loneliness" 1975; Liberal; Club: Arts & Letters, Toronto; Address: Apt. 808, 21 Dale Ave., Toronto, Ont. M4W 1K3

DICKSON, Jennifer, R.A.,R.C.A.; artist; b. Piet Rietief, S. Africa 17 Sept. 1936; d. late John Liston and Margaret Joan (Turner) Dickson; e. Goldsmiths Coll., Sch. of Art, Univ. of London 1954-59; Atelier 17, Paris 1960-65; m. Ronald Andrew Sweetman 13 Apl. 1961; one s. William David; Teacher, Eastbourne Sch. of Art 1959-62; directed and developed Printmaking Dept. Brighton Coll. of Art 1962-68; Graphics Atelier, Saidye Bronfman Centre Montreal 1970-72; Visiting Artist, Ball State Univ. 1967, Univ. of W. Indies 1968, Univ. of Wis. 1972, Ohio State Univ. 1973, W. Ill. Univ. 1973, Haystack Mountain Sch. of Crafts Me. 1973; Part-time Instr. of Drawing 1980-81; Visiting Artist Queen's Univ. 1977; rec'd Prix des Jeunes Artistes (Gravure) Biennale de Paris 1963; Maj. Prize World Print Competition San Francisco 1974; Biennale Prize 5th Norwegian Internat. Print Biennale 1980; author works incl "Genesis" 1965; "Alchemic Images" 1966; "Aids to Meditation" 1967; "Eclipse" 1968; "Song of Songs" 1969; "Out of Time" 1970; "Fragments" 1971; "Sweet Death and Other Pleasures" 1972; "Homage to Don Juan" 1975; "Body Perceptions" 1975; "The Secret Garden" 1976; "Openings" 1977; "Three Mirrors to Narcissus" 1980; "Il Paradiso Terrestre" 1980; "Il Tempo Classico", 1981; subject of CBC Special TV program 1980; rep. in maj. internat. museums incl. Metropolitan Museum New York, Victoria and Albert Museum, Hermitage Museum Leningrad; Can. Council Art Bank; National Gallery of Canada; Founding mem. Brit. Printmakers' Council; Print & Drawing Council Can.; Fellow, Royal Soc. Painter-Etchers & Engravers; Anglican; recreation: collecting antique clothes; Address: 508 Gilmour St., Ottawa, Ont. K1R 5L4.

DICKSON, Robert Clark, O.C. (1978), O.B.E., C.D., Q.H.P., M.D., LL.D., F.R.C.P., (C), F.R.C.P. (Lond), M.A.C.P.; physician; professor emeritus; b. St. Marys, Ont., 24 Sept. 1908; s. William Murray and Mable Earl (Clark) D.; e. Public School and Glebe Coll. Inst., Ottawa, Ontario; University of Toronto, M.D. 1934; LL.D. (Hon. c.) Dalhousie Univ., 1980; m. Constance Fraser, d. L. F. Grant, Kingston, Ont., 16 September 1939; children: William Fraser, Shelagh Margaret, Jane Alice Constance; mem. of Staff, Dept. of Med., Univ. of Toronto, reaching rank of Assoc. Prof., 1945-56; apptd. Prof. of Med., Dalhousie Univ. and Phy.-in-Chief, Victoria Gen. Hosp., Halifax 1956 retiring when Chrmn. of Dept. 1974; mem. of Staff, Toronto Gen. Hosp., 1945-52; Phys.-in-Charge of Wellesley Div., Toronto Gen. Hosp., 1952-55; served in 2nd World War with R.C.A.M.C. Active, 1939-45;

O.B.E., C.D.; then to Reserve with rank of Lieut.-Col.; Regimental Medical Officer, 48th Highlanders of Can. 1945-52; mem., Am. Gastroenterol Assn.; mem. of Council, Royal Coll. Phys. & Surg. Can. 1958-66 (Extve. Comte. 1964-66, President 1970-72); Gov., Am. Coll. of Physicians for Atlantic Provs. 1962-68 and Regent of the Coll. 1968-74; Dir., Internat. Grenfell Assn. 1974-81; Chrmn., Candn. Forces Med. Council since 1974; United Ch.; recreation: sailing; Clubs: R.N.S.Y.S.; Home: 1674 Oxford St., Halifax, N.S. B3H 3Z4

DICKSON, Hon. Robert George Brian, LL.B.; LL.D.; D.Cn.L.; b. Yorkton, Sask., 25 May 1916; s. Thomas and Sarah Elizabeth (Gibson) D.; e. Regina (Sask.) Coll. Inst.; Univ. of Man.; Man. Law Sch., LL.B. 1938; D.Cn.L., St. Johns Coll. 1965; LL.D. Univ. of Man., 1973; LL.D. Univ. of Sask., 1978; LL.D. Univ. of Ottawa, 1979; LL.D. Queen's Univ. 1980; called to Bar of Man., 1940; m. Barbara Melville, d. Henry E. Sellers, Winnipeg, Man., 18 June 1943; children: Brian H., Deborah I. (Mrs. Christopher B. Shields), Peter G., Barry R.; JUSTICE, SUPREME COURT OF CANADA since 1973; Chrmn. Bd. of Govs., Univ. of Man. 1980; practised law with Aikins, MacAulay & Co. 1945-63; Lectr., Manitoba Law Sch. 1948-54; apptd. to Court of Queen's Bench, Manitoba 1963, Court of Appeal 1967; Life Bencher, Law Soc. Man.; mem., Bd. of Trustees, The Sellers Foundation; called to the Bar of Man., 1940; cr. Q.C. 1953; served with Royal Candn. Arty., 1940-45; Anglican Church of Can. (Chancellor, Diocese of Rupert's Land 1960-71); recreation: riding; Clubs: Rideau; Maganassippi Fish & Game; Home: "Marchmont", Dunrobin, Ont. K0A 1T0; Office: Supreme Court Bldg., Ottawa, Ont.

DICKSTEIN, Joseph, B.Com., M.B.A., C.L.U.; insurance executive; b. Montreal, Que., 26 Jan. 1930; s. Moses and Lena (Feinberg) D.; e. McGill Univ., B.Com. 1951; Wharton Sch. of Finance and Economics; Univ. of Penna., M.B.A. 1952; C.L.U. 1953; m. Sibylle, d. Kurt Otto, 1 Oct.1974; children: Michael, Melanie, Oliver, Stephanie; PRES., DICKSTEIN INSURANCE AGENCIES LTD. (Estbd. 1977); with Crown Life Ins. Co., 1952-62; Pres., Westmount Life Ins. Co. 1962-76; Home: 31 Medalist Rd., Willowdale, Ont. M2P 1Y3; Office: 22 St. Clair Ave. W., Suite 1603, Toronto, Ont. M4Y 2S5

DIENES, Zoltan, Ph.D., LL.D.; mathematician; educator; b. Budapest, Hungary, 11 Sept. 1916; s. Paul Alexander and Valérie (Geiger) D.; e. Hungary, Paris and Eng.; Dartington Hall Sch., Devon, Eng., Matric. 1934; Univ. of London, B.A. 1937, Ph.D. PROF. OF MATH. EDUC., GOETHE UNIV. Frankfurt, Germany 1979; Prof. of Educ., Brandon Univ., Manitoba, 1975-78; Dir., of Research in Math. Learning, Univ. of Sherbrooke 1966-75; President International Study Group for Math. Learning; Dir., Assn. for Interdisciplinary Studies, Florence, Italy; Teacher, Highgate and Dartington Hall Schs., Eng., 1940-41; taught math. at Southampton Univ. 1941-43, Sheffield Univ. 1943-45, Manchester Univ. 1945-47, Leicester Univ. 1947-59; Dir. of Research Unit for investigation of generation insights, Brit. Assn. for Advanc. of Science, 1959-61; Research Fellow, Center for Cognitive Studies, Harvard Univ., 1960-61; Assoc. Prof. in Psychol., Adelaide Univ., Australia; Prof. of Educ. 1961-65; Math. Consultant: Leicestershire Educ. Authority, 1957-60; Organ. for European Econ. Co-op., 1960; Peace Corps, Hilo Campus, Univ. of Hawaii, 1964-70; Educ. Dept., State of S. Australia, 1962-65; Territory of Papua New Guinea, 1964-65; Minnemath Program, Univ. of Minn., 1965; Teachers Coll., Columbia Univ., 1966; Ministry of Educ., Paris, 1965; UNESCO, Paris, Budapest and Hamburg, 1962-68; Consultant for Tahiti 1976, State of Victoria, Aust. 1976, Univ. of Qué. 1978; Fellow of Howe Green Trust for developing interdisciplinary education in South Devon, 1978-81; author: "Concept Formation and Personality", 1959; "Building Up Mathematics", 1960, 2nd ed. 1964; "An Experimental Study of Mathematics Learning",

1964; "The Power of Mathematics", 1964; "Mathematics in the Primary School", 1964; "Modern Mathematics for Young Children", 1965; "Geometry Through Transformations" Parts I, II and III, 1967; "Fractions", 1968; "Power Roots and Logarithms", 1968; Co-author: "Thinking in Structures", 1965; "First Years in Mathematics" Parts I, II and III, 1966; "The Arithmetic and Algebra of Natural Number", 1966; "The Effects of Structural Relations on Transfer", 1968; "Approach to Modern Mathematics", 1968; "Les six étapes de l'apprentissage de la mathématique" 1970; "Elements of Mathematics" 1971; "Mathematique Vivante" 1979; "Giochi e Idee" I & II, 1979; "Parole e Idée 1980; "Ambiente, Uomini, Idee," 1980 3 vols.; other writings incl. articles and papers in field of math. for journs. and confs.; patent Multibase blocks; Phi Delta Kappa; Quaker; Home: "Golden October", Jubilee Rd., Totnes, Devon, England Office: Via Gioberti 34, 50121 Florence Italy

DIETRICH, Sister Dominica, M.A., LL.D.; b. Dashwood, Ont., 3 March 1916; d. Noah and Christine (Foster) D.; e. The Pines, Chatham, Ont.; Univ. of Toronto, B.A. 1943, M.A. 1945; St. Michael's Hosp., Toronto, Dipl. Dietitian 1944; Cornell Univ., pre-doctoral courses; Univ. of W. Ont., LL.D.; Superior Gen., Ursuline Religious of Chatham, 1969-77; Prof. and Head of Home Econ. Dept., Brescia Coll., London, Ont., 1945-69; Superior of Coll. 1954-60; Dean 1963-69; mem. Senate of Univ. of W. Ont. during same period; mem., Candn. Dietetic Assn. (Pres. 1968-69); Nat. Assembly of Women Religious; Women's Ordination Conf.; R. Catholic; recreation: bridge; Address: The Pines, Chatham, Ont.

DiGIACOMO, Thomas A., B.Com., M.B.A.; insurance executive; b. Toronto, Ont. 22 Dec. 1941; s. John R. and Alice M. (Caruso) DiG.; e. De La Salle Oaklands, Toronto 1960; Univ. of Toronto B.Com. 1964; Univ. of Chicago M.B.A. 1966; Vice Pres. Invests. Manulife; recreations: squash, flying; Clubs: Empire; Bloor Park; Home: 50 Groomsport Cres., Toronto, Ont. M1T 2K9; Office: 200 Bloor St. E., Toronto, Ont. M4W 1E4

DILLON, Richard Maurice, M.C., E.D., B.A., S.M., LL.D., F.E.I.C., P.Eng.; Ont. civil servant; b. Simcoe, Ont., 4 Aug. 1920; s. late Brig. Murray M., M.C., E.D. and Muriel Talbot (Hicks) D.; e. Pub. and High Schs., London, Ont.; Univ. of W. Ont., B.A. 1948, LL.D. Hon. 1979; Mass. Inst. of Technol., S.M. 1950; m. Elizabeth, d. late Henry Herbert Dempsey 1945; children: Kelly, Ann, Katherine; DEPY. MIN. OF MUNICIPAL AFFAIRS AND HOUSING 1980-, Depy. Prov. Sec. for Resources Development, Prov. of Ont., 1976-79; Depy. Min. of Energy, Ont. 1973-76; former Prof. of Engn., Univ. of W. Ont. and sometime Dean Faculty of Engn. Science there; Design Engr., M. M. Dillon & Co., 1948-49 and Project Engr., Sr. Structural Designer, Partner and Dir., 1951-60; Design Engr., Dominion Bridge Co. Ltd., Toronto, 1950-51; Dean of Engn. Science at Univ. of W. Ont., 1960-71; Project Offr., Scient. Research & Devel. Comn. on Govt. Organ. (Glassco Comn.) 1961-62; Colombo Plan Consultant on Eng. Educ. to Govt. of Thailand, 1963; mem. Prov.of Ont. Adv. Comte. on Confed., 1965-67; seconded to Extve. Dir., Task Force Hydro Comte. on Govt. Productivity, Toronto, 1971; served with Candn. Army 1933-56; served in Can., U.K., Italy 1939-45; retired as O.C. 3rd Bn. RCR; rec'd. M.C. 1942, E.D. 1953, Elizabeth II Coronation Medal 1953; Jubilee Medal, 1977; Assn. Prof. Engrs.-Sons of Martha Medal 1972; Pres., London P. Cons. Assn. 1967-69; mem. Ont. P. Cons. Extve. Comte. 1964-68; Past Pres., London and Ont. Brs. V.O.N.; Dir. London Contingent Candn. Corps of Commissionaires 1950-76; mem. Tor. Bd. of Governors, 1977; Warden, Bishop Cronyn Mem. Ch., 1961-65; Extv. Bd., Huron Coll., 1954-55; Vice Chrmn. and mem. Bd. of Govs., Fanshawe Coll. of Applied Arts & Technol., 1967-71; Gov., Ont. Research Foundation; Fellow Am. Soc. Civil Engn.; Fellow Engr. Inst. of Can.; mem. Assn. Prof. Engrs. Ont.

(Vice-Pres. 1978; Pres. 1979-80); Ont. Engn. Adv. Council 1968-71; Sigma Xi; P. Conservative; Anglican; reading, skiing, travel; Clubs: Toronto Hunt; Home: 11 Meredith Cres., Toronto, Ont. M4W 3B7; Office: 4th Floor, Hearst Block, Queen's Park, Toronto, Ont. M7A 2K5

DILTZ, Bert Case, M.A., LL.D. (Queens) 1960; b. Port Credit, Ont., 10 Feb. 1894; s. Charles Elisha and Martha Jane (Case) D.; e. Trinity Coll., Toronto; Queen's Univ., B.A. 1921 (Hons.) and M.A. 1922; Ont. Coll. of Educ., Special Cert. 1923; Columbia Univ. (summers) 1924-25; m. Agnes Marcella, d. Charles Peter Brown, 7 Aug. 1926; children: Charles Herbert, David Alexander, Douglas Graden; Lay Del. from Presby. Ch. Can. to First Assembly of World Coun. of Chs., Amsterdam, 1948; Head of Dept. of Eng., Lindsay Coll. Inst., Ont., 1923-28; Vice-Princ. there 1926-28; Instr. in Eng., Univ. of Toronto Schs. and Part-time Instr., Ont. Coll. of Educ., 1928-31; Prof. of Methods in Eng. and Hist., Ont. Coll. of Educ. 1931-58, and Dean of the Coll. 1958 till retired 1963; served in World War 1916-19 with Signal Sec., 10th Inf. Bgde., C.E.F., in France and Belgium; with Reserve Army, C.O.T.C., Univ. of Toronto, 1940-45; publications: "Models and Projects For English Composition", 1932; "Poetic Pilgrimage", 1943; "Pierian Spring", 1946; "New Models and Projects for Creative Writing", 1949; "The Sense of Wonder", 1953; "New Horizons", 1954; "Poetic Experience", 1955; "Word Magic", 1957; "Patterns of Surmise", 1962; "Frontiers of Wonder", 1967; "Stranger than Fiction", 1969, (a collection of original stories, sketches and poems); "A Flurry of Verses", (a collection of original poems), 1978; "Fleeting Fantasies for Fellow Travellers" (poetry) 1981; co-author of "Sense and Structure in English Composition", 1936; "Aim and Order in English Composition", 1937; "Living English", 1938; "Many Minds", Books I and II 1965; "Sense or Nonsense: Contemporary Education at the Crossroads", 1972; Presbyterian; recreations: reading, writing, gardening; Home: 92 Colin Ave., Toronto, Ont. M5P 2C2

DIMAKOPOULOS, Dimitri, B.Arch., F.R.A.I.C., R.C.A.; architect; b. Athens, Greece 14 Sept. 1929; came to Can. 1948; e. Experimental Sch., Univ. of Athens 1947; McGill Univ. B.Arch. 1955; m. Lydia d. Dimitri Chabaline 15 June 1960; children: Irene, Marina; PRINCIPAL, DIMITRI, DIMAKOPOULOS & PARTNERS: Dir., Hellenic-Canada Trust; Professor, Univ. of Montreal 1965; Visiting Prof. and Critic, McGill Univ.; Trustee, Hellenic College U.S.A. 1975; past Dir., St. George's Sch. of Montreal; Fellow, Royal Arch. Inst. of Can.; mem., Order of Archts. of Que.; Ont. Assn. of Archts.; Candn. Academy of the Arts; Bd. of Dirs., Candn. Archaeol. Inst., Athens 1980; Design Comte., Nat. Capital Commission, Ottawa 1981, 1982; recipient of numerous prizes & awards in nat. and internat. arch. competitions; participated in design of Salle Wilfrid Pelletier, Place des Arts, Place Ville Marie (in assn. with I.M. Pei of N.Y.), Place Bonaventure, Université du Qué., Greek Orthodox Cathedral (all in Montreal); Centre Scientifique Qué. (Ste-Foy, Qué.); Place d'Accueil (Hull, Qué.); "Palais de Justice" (Qué.); Cultural Centre (Ottawa); Cultural Center, Government Buildings (P.E.I.); Concert Hall and Theatre (Vancouver); and in planning of cities of Calgary, Quebec, Ottawa and Winnipeg; designed projects in Greece, Italy, Saudi Arabia, U.S.A., Algeria, Hong Kong; Greek Orthodox; Home: 461 Clarke Ave., Westmount, Que. H3Y 3C5; Office: 1253 McGill College Ave., Montreal, Que. H3B 2Y5

DIMITROV, Olga, R.C.A.; costume designer; b. Czechoslovakia 5 Jan. 1933; d. Svetoslav and Miskovska (Antonie) Dimitrov; e. Sch. of Ceramics Karls-Bad Czechoslovakia 1947-49; Acad. of Applied Arts Prague 1949-52; m. 7 Feb. 1957; one child; Prop., Dimitrov Design Services Ltd.; affiliation Errant Productions Ltd.; served as Resident Designer Civic Theatre Kladno and later at the Civic Theatre Presov; guest designer through-out Czechoslovakia for 4 yrs. creating designs for over

250 stage productions encompassing drama, opera, ballet and musical comedy; designed costumes for 18 feature films between 1964-68 incl. Acad. Award winning "Closely Watched Trains" and "The End of August in Hotel Ozone" (Vatican Peace Prize); came to Can. 1968; became Resident Costume Designer Neptune Theatre Halifax; Costume Designer Ind. Univ. Sch. of Music's Opera Dept. 1971-73; Resident Costume Designer Theatre London Co. and during this period also designed costumes for Toronto Arts Productions and Nat. Arts Centre Ottawa; Costume Designer "Fantastica" 42 short films for children; costume design for "In Praise of Older Women," 1977; "Agency," 1978; "Silence of the North," 1979; "Death Hunt," 1980; "Harry Tracy," 1980; mem. Assoc. Designers Can.-TV Film Theatre; Address: 132 Indian Rd., Toronto, Ont.

DIMMA, William Andrew, B.A.Sc., P.Eng., M.B.A., D.B.A.; diversified national real estate company executive; b. Aug. 13 1928; s. William Roy and Lillian Noreen (Miller) D.; e. Univ. of Toronto B.A.Sc. 1948; Harvard Univ. M.M.P. 1956, D.B.A. 1973; York Univ. M.B.A. 1969; m. Katherine Louise, d. W. M. Vacy Ash, 13 May 1961; children: Katherine, Suzy; PRES., AND DIR., A. E. LEPAGE LTD.; Chrmn., Polysar Ltd.; Dir., Capstone Investment Trust; Gen. Accident Assur. Co. of Canada; Simpsons-Sears Ltd.; The Continental Bank; Niagara Finance Ltd.; Niagara Inst.; Toronto Symphony; Vice Pres., Union Carbide Canada Ltd. 1966, Extve. Vice Pres. 1967, Dir., 1968 until leaving 1970 to pursue advanced studies; Dean Fac. of Adm. Studies, York Univ. 1974-75; Pres. & Dir., Torstar Corp. and Toronto Star Newspapers Ltd., 1976-78; Premier's Business Adv. Comte, (Ont.); Premier's Committee on the Economic Future (Ont.); Dir., Canadian Club of Toronto; Trustee, Hosp. for Sick Children; Bd. of Gov., York Univ.; author: "The Canada Development Corporation: Diffident Experiment on a Large Scale"; Beta Theta Pi; Anglican; recreations: golf, skiing; Clubs: Toronto; Toronto Golf; Granite; York; Mark's (London, Eng.); Home: 17 Dunloe Road, Toronto, Ont. M4V 2W4; Office: 33rd Floor, P.O. Box 100, Tor. Dom. Centre, Toronto, Ont. M5K 1G8

DIMSON, Theo Aeneas, R.C.A., F.G.D.C., A.O.C.A., A.G.I.; creative designer; b. London, Ont. 8 April 1930; s. Nicholas and Helen (Papadopoulos) D.; e. Pub. Sch. London, Ont.; Tech. Sch., Toronto; Ont. Coll. Art (scholar.), grad. 1950; Children: Lisa, Benjamin, Nicole, Emily Victoria; PRESIDENT AND CREATIVE DIR., DIMSON AND SMITH LTD. since 1965; began with Art Associates Ltd. as Graphic Designer 1950; Freelance 1953-60; rejoined Art Associates Ltd. as Vice-Pres., Creative Design, 1960; gold & silver awards of Excellence: Art Directors and Graphica Clubs of Toronto and of Montreal; Communication Arts Exhn., Los Angeles; Sr. Arts Fellowship by Can. Council 1961, 1971; Award of Excellence, 10th Candn. TV Commercials Festival; Best Show Award Gold and (triple) Silver Medallist, Art Dirs. Club of Toronto; 1st Prize Nat. Retail Merchants Assn. TV Conf. N.Y. and 21st Annual Retail Advertising Conf., Chicago 1973; exhibited in "100 Years of the Poster in Can., A.G.O. 1979; 2 gold, 5 silver awards, Art Dirs. Club, Toronto, 1980; exhibited 8th Internat. Poster Biennale, Warsaw, Poland; work exhibited internationally and rep. in internat. journals; one man articles in Idea Magazine (Japan), C.A. Magazine (U.S.A.), Creativity Magazine & Toronto Star (Canada); one man show, Toronto, 1978; Author, "Great Canadian Posters" 1979; mem. A.G.I.; Graphica Club, Toronto; Am. Inst. Graphic Arts, New York; Assoc., Ont. Coll. of Art; Greek Orthodox; Home: Greenwood, Ont. L0H 1H0; Office: 172 Davenport Rd., Toronto, Ont. M5R 1J2

DINGLE, D. Terence, B.A., B.C.L.; lawyer; b. Winnipeg, Man., 21 May 1935; s. Stanley Frederick and Katherine (Walsh) D.; e. Loyola High Sch., Montreal, Que.

1953; Loyola Coll., B.A. 1957; McGill Univ., B.C.L. 1960; m. Judith Elizabeth, d. H. W. Hingston, Montreal, Que., 16 Feb. 1963; children: Martha, Jill, Michael; PRES., SHAWINIGAN GROUP INC.; Dir., Shawinigan Consultants Internat. Ltd.; Kinney Shoes of Can. Ltd.; Nat. Hees Ent. Ltd.; called to Bar Que. 1961; mem. Montreal, Que. and Candn. Bar Assns.; recreations: golf, tennis, skiing, squash; Clubs: St. James's; Mt. Bruno Country; Montreal Badminton & Squash; University (Toronto); Office: 10th Floor, 620 University Ave., Toronto Ont.

DINN, Hon. Jerome William,M.H.A.; politician; b. St. John's, Nfld. 30 Jan. 1940; s. William and Alice (Power) D.; e. St. Patrick's Hall Sch. St. John's; m. Anna Lorraine d. Francis K. Lavigne, St. John's, Nfld. 9 June 1960; children: Brian, Suzanne;MIN. OF LABOUR & MANPOWER, NFLD.1979- ; el. M.H.A. for Pleasantville prov. g.e. 1975, re-el. 1979; Min. of Mun. Affairs & Housing 1976; RCAF Assn.; Sponsoring Comte. Air Cadets; P. Conservative; R. Catholic; Office: Confederation Bldg., St. John's, Nfld. A1C 5T7.

DINNICK, John S.; investment dealer; b. Toronto, Ont., 29 Oct. 1911; s. Wilfrid Servington and Alice Louise (Conlin) D.; e. St. Andrew's Coll., 1925-30; Upper Can. Coll., 1930; Trinity Coll., Univ. of Toronto, 1931-33; three d.; CONSULTANT McLEOD YOUNG WEIR LIMITED; (former Chrmn. of Bd.); Consultant, IFC World Bank; Dir., Canron Limited; Photo Engravers & Electrotypers Ltd.; mem. Bd. Govs. Central Hosp., Toronto; Pres. (1969-70), Invest. Dealers' Assn. Can.; joined present Co. in 1933, Dir., 1950; served in 2nd World War, 1940-45, with Candn. Army Overseas, Capt. in R.C.A.; on discharge, 2nd in Command, 665 Air Observation Post Sqdn., R.C.A.F.; Dir. and Past Pres., Woodgreen Community Centre; Dir., Ont. Heart Foundation; Kappa Alpha; Anglican; recreations: golf, skiing; Clubs: Strollers; Toronto Golf; Home: 31 Maple Ave., Toronto, Ont. M4W 2T8; Office: (P.O. Box 433), Toronto-Dominion Centre, Toronto, Ont. M5K 1M2

DINSDALE, Henry Begg, M.D., C.M., F.R.C.P.(C); physician; educator; b. Kingston, Ont. 22 Sept. 1931; s. Harry Hamlin and Doris Eileen (Donnelly) D.; e. Queen's Univ. M.D., C.M. 1955; m. Lyla June d. Bert T. Yates 11 June 1955; children: Janyce Hall, John Scott, Henry Yates, Martha Jane; PROF. AND CHRMN. DIV. OF NEUROL. QUEEN'S UNIV. 1971- , joined Dept. Med. 1963; mem. attending staff Kingston Gen. Hosp. 1963- ; Resident in Med. 1955-57; Registrar, Maudsley Hosp. London, Eng. 1957-59; Nuffield Fellow, Nat. Hosp. Queen's Sq. London, Eng. 1959-60; Resident and Research Fellow, Harvard Neurol. Unit Boston City Hosp. 1960-63; Past Chrmn. Ont. Heart Foundation; Ont. Mental Health Foundation and Ministry of Health Ont. Med. Research Comtes.; mem. various fed. and prov. task forces on Cerebrovascular Disease, Med. Manpower, High Technol. and Hypertension; mem. Med. Research Council Can. (Council 1977- , Extve. 1979-); recipient Brown Prize 1950; Morris Prize 1958; MacLachlan Fellow 1961-62; Bullard Fellow 1962-63; Weil Award Am. Assn. Neuropathol. 1976; author "The Nervous System, Structure and Function in Disease" 1972; numerous research articles and book chapters; mem. Candn. Neurol. Soc. (Past Councillor, Pres. 1981-); Am. Acad. Neurol. mem. Extve. 1979-); Colls. Phys. & Surgs. Ont. and Que.; Am. Neurol. Assn.; Candn. Soc. Clin. Investig.; Soc. Neurosciences; Candn. Assn. Neuroscientists; Internat. Soc. Cerebral Circulation & Metabolism; Candn. Stroke Soc.; Am. Heart Assn. (Council Cerebrovascular Div.); PanAm. Soc. Neurol.; Protestant; recreations: tennis, reading; Home: 95 Hill St., Kingston, Ont. K7L 2M8; Office: 78 Barrie St., Kingston, Ont. K7L 3J7.

DINSDALE, Hon. Walter Gilbert, P.C. (Can.) D.F.C., M.P., M.A., LL.D.; college lecturer; b. Brandon, Man., 3 Apl. 1916; s. George and Minnie (Lang) D.; e. Pub. Sch.

and Coll. Inst., Brandon, Man.; McMaster Univ. (Brandon Coll.), B.A. 1937; Salvation Army Training Coll., Toronto, Ont. 1940; Univ. of Toronto, M.A. 1951; Univ. of Chicago; LL.D. Brandon Univ., 1977; D.Hum. Richmond College (Tor.) 1977; m. Lenore Gunhild, d. Ludwig Gusdal, Erickson, Man., 17 Sept. 1947; children: Gunnar, Gregory, Beth, Eric, Rolf; with Canadian Pacific Express Co., 1936-39; engaged in Social work with the Salvation Army 1939-41 in Montreal and Toronto; Dir. of Adult Educ. and Asst. Prof. of Social Sciences, Brandon Coll. 1945-51; served in 2nd World War with R.C.A.F. 1941-45; awarded D.F.C.; 1st el. to H. of C. for Brandon. by-el. June 1951; re-el. since for Brandon-Souris; apptd. Parlty. Secy. to Min. of Veterans Affairs June 1957; Minister of N. Affairs & Nat. Resources in Diefenbaker Cabinet, 1960-63; mem., Central Region, Candn. Council of Christian & Jews; Royal Candn. Legion; Dir., Candn. Rehab. Council for the Disabled; Conservative; Salvation Army; recreations: photography, music, swimming; Clubs: Kiwanis; Canadian; Home: 3205 Rosser Ave., Brandon, Man.

DION, Rev. Gerard, O.C., L.Phil., M.Soc.Sc., LL.D., F.R.S.C. (1961); professor; b. Ste. Cécile de Frontenac, Que., 5 Dec. 1912; s. P-Albert and Georgianna (LeBlanc) D.; e. Collège de Lévis, B.A. 1935; Laval Univ., L.Th. 1939, L.Phil. 1943, M.Soc.Sc. 1943; o. Priest 1939; Prof. at Lévis Coll., Que., 1939-40; Curate, Sillery, Que., 1940-41; Prof., Faculty Soc. Sc., Laval Univ., 1944-80; Prof. Emeritus, Laval Univ. 1981; Prof. of Sociology, Sch. of Commerce, Laval Univ., 1944-52; LL.D. McGill, 1975, B.C., 1976, Tor., 1978; Concordia 1980; D.Litt. St. Francis Xavier, 1977; Killam Schol., 1974-76; Moral Advisor to Employers' Assns. of Que. 1944-56; Assoc. Dir., Dept. Indust. Relations, Laval Univ. 1946; Dir., 1957-63; mem., Prime Min's. Task Force on Labour Relations 1966-68; Chrmn., Candn. Textile Labour-Mang. Comte. 1967; mem. Constr. Indust. Devel. Council 1970-73; Past Pres. (1965-66). Candn. Indust. Relations Research Assoc.; mem. of the Sacerdotal Comn. of Social Studies 1947-60; Editor of (quarterly) bilingual "Relations Industrielles-Industrial Relations"; Author: "Dictionnaire canadien des relations de travail" ("Glossary of Terms used in Industrial Relations"); Co-author: "The Christians and Democracy", "The Christians and Elections", "Glossary of Terms used in Industrial Relations" (French-Eng.); author of many books, publications, articles publ. in French, Eng. and Spanish; has travelled widely in Can., U.S., Mexico, and S.Am.; Major in Reserve Army 1962; mem., Ec. Council of Can. 1976-80; Adv. Comm. on Univ. Affairs, Can. Council 1975-78; Soc. Sciences and Hum. Res. Council since 1978; Candn. Assn. Univ. Teachers; Candn. Pol. Science Assn.; Indust. Relations Research Assn.; Am. Management Assn.; Soc. des Ecrivains canadiens; Assn. internat. de relations professionnelles; Inst. canadien d'éduc. des adultes; Assn. Candn. des Sociol. et Anthropol. de langue française; mem. Bd. Dirs., Presses de l'univ. Laval, since 1975; R. Catholic; Address: 909 Msgr. Grandin, Quebec, Que. G1V 3X8

DION, Henry George, B.S.A., Ph.D.; agricultural scientist; b. Saskatoon, Sask., 18 Oct. 1915; s. Didie and Betty (Anderson) D.; e. Univ. of Sask. B.S.A. 1939; Univ. of Wisconsin, Ph.D. 1942; m. Wendy Marguerite, d. Ronald J. H. Ritchie, Middlesborough, Eng., 6 Nov. 1943; children: Paul, Vivian, Jeremy; Lectr., Soils Dept., Univ. of Sask., 1942-43; Agric. Research Council, Unit of Soil Enzyme Chem., Rothamsted Exper. Stn., Harpenden, Eng., 1943-45; Soil Survey Dept., Macaulay Inst. of Soil Research, Craigiebuckler, Aberdeen, Scot., 1945-46; Univ. of Sask., Assoc. Prof. of Soils, 1946-51; Soils Specialist, Land & Water Use Br., FAO, Rome, Italy, 1951-54; apptd. Prof. of Soil Chem., Macdonald Coll., McGill Univ. 1954 (sometime Dean, Faculty of Agric. and Vice Princ.); now Agricultural Consultant; Fellow, Agric. Inst. Can.; mem., Candn. Soc. of Soil Science; Anglican; Address: R.R. 2 Luskville, Que. J0X 2G0

DION, Leon, M.A., Ph.D., LL.D., F.R.S.C.; university professor; b. Saint-Arsène, Que., 9 Oct. 1922; s. Thomas and Alice (Dancause) D.; e. Laval Univ. (Rimouski Coll.) B.A. 1945, M.A. (Sociol. 1948, Ph.D. (Pol. Sc.) 1954; Univs. of Zurich, Cologne, Paris; London Sch. of Econ.; Harvard Univ.; LL.D. Queen's Univ.; m. Denyse, d. late Emile Kormann, Paris, France, 2 June 1951; children: Patrice, Stephane, Georges, Francis, France; PROF. OF POL. SCIENCE, LAVAL UNIV.; Special Adv., Comn. of Inquiry on Bilingualism & Biculturalism (1963-71); author of "Opinions publique et systèms idéologiques", 1962; "Les groupes et le pouvoir politique", 1965; "Le bill 60 et les publies", 1965; "Le bill 60 et la société québécoise", 1966, "Societé et politique", Tome I: "Fondements de la société libérale" 1971, Tome II; "Dynamique de la société libérale" 1972; has written many articles for learned journs., newspapers and mags.; mem., Candn. Pol. Science Assn.; Société Canadien de Science Pol. (former Prés.); Candn. Pub. Adm. Assn.; Inst. Canadien des Affaires Publiques; Ligue des Droits de l'Homme: Inst. Canadien de l'Educ. des Adultes; Home: 2555 Blvd. Liegeois, Sillery, Que. G1T 1W1

DIONNE, George Burton; F.R.G.S.; company executive; b. Montreal, Que., 17 Jan. 1922; s. Telesphore Octave and Louise Helen (Drolet) D.; m. Beryl Emily, d. Cyril Des-Côtes and Lillian (Haney), 26 Sept. 1942; children: Carolyn Lois, Bruce Charles, Arlene Beryl; VICE-PRES. ADMIN., THE DECLAN GROUP OF COMPANIES INC. Dir., Nova Drug Ltd./Ltée.; Frank W. Horner Ltd., 1939-54; served as Sales Rep., Sales Supvr., Asst. to Vice Pres.-Marketing and Export Mgr.; Arbuthnot Ewart (Canada) Ltd. (subsidiary of The Anglo-Thai Corp. of Great Britain), 1954-57; served as Mgr. for Can.; Mead Johnson of Canada Ltd., 1957-61; Dir. of Merchandising and subsequently Pres. of Mead Johnson of Quebec Ltd.; Schering Corp. Ltd., 1961-69; Dir. of Marketing and subsequently Vice Pres. of Corp. also Dir. and Vice Pres. of Pharmaco Canada Ltd. and White Laboratories; USV of Can. Ltd., 1969-73; Managing Dir. & Chief Exec. Officer of this Revlon Inc. Subsidiary; subsequently worked with Organizing Comm. 1976 Olympic games (Revenue Division) and as Exec. Vice-Pres. of Better Bus. Bureau of Canada; served with Candn. Active Army in Can. and Overseas during World War II; served with Victoria Rifles of Can. before and after War, rank Major; Past Dir. & Chrm., Membership Comm., Pharmaceutical Manufacturers Assoc. of Can.; Past Dir. & Hon. Treas., Candn. Foundation for the Advancement of Pharmacy; Past Dir., St. Lawrence Yacht Co.; Past Consul, ad honorem, Republic of Paraguay; Past Pres. and Treas., Archdiocesan Union of Montreal; Parents' Assoc. of Mt. Royal and St. Laurent, Que.; Past Dir. and Past Treas., Fed. of Home & Sch. Assns. Prov. of Que.; Past Dist. Treas., St. Lawrence Dist. of Candn. Power Squadrons and Past Commander, Montreal Squadron; Nat. Treas., Candn. Power Squadron 1970 conf.; Fellow, Royal Geographical Soc., 1979; mem., Royal Candn. Military Inst.; Bd. of Trade of Toronto; recreations: yachting, curling, duplicate bridge; Home: 11 Wincott Drive, Etobicoke, Ont. M9R 2R9; Office: Suite 1500, 55 University Avenue, Toronto, Ont. M5J 2H7

D'IORIO, Antonio, M.S., Ph.D.; educator; b. Montreal, Que., 22 April 1925; s. Giuseppe and Assunta (Torino) D'I.; e. Univ. of Montreal, B.S. 1946, M.S. 1947, Ph.D. (Biochem.) 1949; Heart Fellow, Univ. of Wisconsin, 1951; Post-doctoral Fellowship, Oxford Univ. 1955; m. late Ghislaine, d. Oscar Chatel, Montreal, Que., Sept. 1950; seven children; Vice-Rector (Academic) Univ. of Ottawa; Dean, Faculty of Science & Engn., Univ. of Ottawa, 1969-76 (Prof. of Biochem. and Chrmn. of Dept. 1961-69); Asst. Prof. of Physiol., Univ. of Montreal, 1949-56, Assoc. Prof. 1956-60; Publications: about 90 research papers in field of biol. sciences; Ed. Candn. Journl. of Biochemistry; acted as Editor of "Revue Canadienne de Biologie", 1956-60; mem., Am. Chem. Soc.; Biochem. Soc. (Eng.); Candn.

Biochem. Soc.; Am. Assn. Biol. Chem.; Roman Catholic; Home: 955 Plante Dr., Ottawa, Ont. K1V 9E3

DIRKS, John Herbert, M.D., F.R.C.P.(C), F.A.C.P.; educator; b. Winnipeg, Man. 20 Aug. 1933; s. Alexander P. and Agnes (Warkentin) D.; e. Mennonite Brethren Coll. Inst. Winnipeg 1950; Univ. of Man. B.Sc. and M.D. 1957; m. Fay Ruth d. Mark K. Inman, Ph.D., London, Ont. 3 July 1961; children: John Mark, Peter Benjamin, Martha, Carol; ERIC W. HAMBER PROF. AND HEAD OF MED. UNIV. OF B.C. since 1976; Dir. G. F. Strong Labs UBC, Prof. of Physiol. 1978; Phys.-in-Chief, Vancouver Gen. Hosp.; Rotating Intern and Jr. Asst. Resident Winnipeg Gen. Hosp. 1957-59; Renal Fellow, Deer Lodge Veterans Hosp. Winnipeg 1959-60; Med. Resident Montreal Gen. Hosp. and M.R.C. Fellow McGill Univ. 1960-62; M.R.C. Fellow and Visiting Scient. Lab. of Kidney & Electrolyte Metabolism, Nat. Heart Inst. Bethesda, Md. 1963-65; Dir. Renal Lab. Royal Victoria Hosp. 1965-76, Sr. Phys. 1971-76, Dir. Renal & Electrolyte Div. 1965-76; Med. Research Council Scholar, McGill Univ. 1965-70, Prof. of Med. 1971, Prof. of Physiol. 1974, John Fraser Research Assoc. 1971-76, mem. Endocrinol. & Nephrol. Grants Comte. Med. Research Council Can. 1972-77, Program Grants & Core Comte. 1977; Visiting Prof. Univ. Coll. Hosp. London 1973; mem. Scient. Adv. Bd. Nat. Kidney Foundation 1972; Vice Pres. C.O.S.C.I.N. Scient. Cong. Nephrol. 1974-78; Assoc. Ed. 'Canadian Journal of Physiology & Pharmacology' 1968-73; mem. Ed. Bd. several prof. journs.; author or co-author numerous publs. Candn. and foreign prof. journs.; mem. Candn. Soc. Clin. Investigation (Secy.-Treas. 1972-75, Pres. 1976-77); Candn. Soc. Nephrol. (Councillor); Am. Fed. Clin. Research (Councillor E. Sec. 1966-74); Coll. Phys. & Surgs. Prov. Que.; Fed. Med. Specialists Que.; Candn. Physiol. Soc.; Internat. Soc. Nephrol.; MRC Council; Am. Assn. Phys. and other Candn. and Am. prof. assns.; Protestant; Club: Arbutus; Home: 1250 Wolfe Ave., Vancouver, B.C. V6H 1W1; Office: 700 W. 10th Ave., Vancouver, B.C. V5Z 1M9.

DITHMER, Torben Gottschalck, LL.M.; diplomat; b. Copenhagen, Denmark 10 July 1929; s. Bernth Gottschalck and Thyra (Degn) D.; e. Univ. of Copenhagen LL.M. 1955; m. Margrethe Arenfeldt d. late Poul G. Mathiesen 31 May 1952; children: Ole Gottschalck, Charlotte; CONSUL GEN. OF DENMARK TO CAN. since 1979; joined Ministry of Foreign Affairs Copenhagen 1955; Secy. of Embassy, Danish Del. to NATO Paris 1959; Head of Sec. Copenhagen 1962; Alt. Rep. Denmark to 21st Gen. Assembly UN, N.Y. 1966; Counsellor of Embassy, Danish Mission to UN 1967; Alt. Rep. Denmark to Security Council UN 1967; Head of Dept. Copenhagen 1971; Danish nat. mil. service 1956-57; rec'd Kt.'s Cross First Class Order of Dannebrog; Offr.'s Cross Italian Order of Merit; Home: 44 Crescent Rd., Toronto, Ont. M4W 1S9; Office: Suite 310, 151 Bloor St. W., Toronto, Ont. M5S 1S4.

DIXON, Brian, M.Com., Ph.D.; sculptor, professor, consultant; b. Winnipeg, Man., 13 Jan. 1930; s. William Armstrong and May Alice (O'Brien) D.; e. Univ. of Man., B.A. 1950; Univ. of Toronto, M.Com. 1953; Univ. of Michigan, Ph.D. 1959; m. Anne Eleanore, d. late Richard M. Howard, 26 Aug. 1952 (div. 1978); children: Robert Brent, Allen Michael; PROF. BUS. ADM., YORK UNIV. since 1968; taught at Universities of Assumption, Michigan, McMaster, Queen's and McGill 1953-67; Founding Dir., Program in Arts Adm., York Univ., 1969-70; Associate Dean, 1972 & Acting Dean 1973-74, Faculty of Administrative Studies, York Univ.; mem., Candn. Assn. of Admin. Sci.; Candn. Conference of Arts; Can. Museums Assoc.; Internat. Council of Museums; exhns. of sculpture; Galerie Moos, Montreal, 1967; Ahda Artz Gallery, N.Y. 1969; Univ. of Toronto, 1970; Bau-xi Gallery, Toronto 1978; St. Lawrence Centre, 1979; Co-ordinator, Project for Restoration of the Egyptian Antiquities Muse-

um, Cairo 1981; author of some 3 books numerous articles in popular and learned journs.; recreation: running, poetry, travel; Home: P.O. Box 423, Gananoque, Ont. K7G 2T9; Office: 4700 Keele, Downsview, Ont. M3J 1P3

DIXON, Gordon H., B.A., Ph.D., F.R.S.C. (1970), F.R.S. (1978); university professor; b. Durban, S. Africa, 25 Mar. 1930; s. Walter James and Ruth (Nightingale) D.; e. High Sch., Cambridge, Eng.; Trinity Coll., Cambridge Univ., B.A.; Univ. of Toronto, Ph.D. 1956; came to Canada Nov. 1951; m. Sylvia Weir (Gillen) 20 Nov. 1954; children: Frances Anne, Walter Timothy, Christopher James, Robin Jonathan; served RCAF Reserve, Air Intelligence, 1952-54; Research Assoc., Univ. of Washington, 1954-55 (Asst. Prof. 1956-58); Staff mem., Med. Research Council Unit for research in cell metabolism, Univ. of Oxford, 1958-59; Asst. Prof., Biochem., Univ. of Toronto, 1960-62, Assoc. Prof., 1962-63; Assoc. Prof., Univ. of B.C., 1963-66 subsequently full Prof.; now Prof. of Med. Biochem. Univ. of Calgary; author of more than 180 articles in scient. journs.; winner of Ayerst Award, Candn. Biochem. Soc., 1966 and Steacie Prize for 1966; Josiah Macy Jr. Faculty Scholar Award, 1979; Flavelle Medal, Royal Society of Can. 1980; Candn. Biochem. Soc.; Am. Soc. Biol. Chem.; Conservative; recreations: hiking, gardening, skiing; Address: Fac. of Med., Div. Med. Biochemy Health Sciences Centre, University of Calgary, Calgary, Alta. T2N 4N1

DIXON, Harold Collier, B.Comm., F.C.A.; b. Toronto, Ont., 22 July 1910; s. George Ernest and Elinor Gertrude (Dadson) D.; e. Univ. of Toronto, B. Comm. 1932; LL.D., Honoris Causa, mcMaster Univ., 1979; m. Norma Irene, d. Howard Fife, Sharon, Ont., 11 June 1938; children: Joan Elaine, Barbara Jean, Robert Harold; Partner, Clarkson, Gordon & Co., 1947-75; Dir., Greening Donald Ltd.; mem. Bd. Govs., McMaster Univ.; joined firm 1932; C.A. 1936; F.C.A. 1956; Pres., Hamilton Assn. for Advanc. of Lit., Science and Art (1978-80); Baptist; recreations: gardening, swimming, fishing; Club: Hamilton; Home: 119 Dalewood Crescent, Hamilton, Ont. L8S 4B8

DIXON, Langford; poet and recitalist; b. Toronto, Ont., 2 June 1915; s. Henry and Margaret Diana (Rennie) D.; e. Balmy Beach public Sch.; Malvern Coll., Toronto; Private Tuition before attending London Sch. Engn. Tech. (U.K.); Oxford Univ. 1945; Hons. Grad., Lorne Greene's Acad of Radio Arts; m. Grace Marion, d. late George Morris Watson, 23 Aug. 1947; for some time Music Critic, CKEY, Toronto and later with Globe and Mail; Social Worker on Pilot Project sponsored by Bickell Foundation at core of Toronto's Gang Problems; Co-ordinator, Poetry Exchange Programme between B.W.I. and Ont. Schs.; Ont. Dept. Educ.; Pres., Wilson MacDonald Poetry Soc.; Candn Chrmn.; World Poetry Day Comte.; author of "The Ballad of Willy" 1964; "Comment" 1965; "The Devil You Say" 1965; "The Birds and Bees" 1965; "Seven" 1967; "When Laughter Put to Sea" 1968; "Once Upon a Time" 1970; "Though the World Cry", 1979; "On Reading Poetry in the Schools", 1981; has read his work widely throughout Ont. and U.S. in schs., colls., univs., theatres and on radio and TV; World Poetry Day Citation "for his contribution to International Understanding through Poetry" by World Poetry Day Comte., N.Y. 1971; Protestant; recreations: photography, furniture making and refinishing; Home: 57A Lytton Blvd., Toronto, Ont. M4R 1L2

DIXON, Michael E., M.D., C.M., M.Sc., F.R.C.P.(C); medical executive; b. Toronto, Ont. 16 June 1936; s. John Harkness and Edith Millicent (Bailey) D.; e. Lower Can. Coll. Montreal 1953; McGill Univ. B.Sc. 1958, M.D., C.M. 1960, M.Sc. 1963; m. Gail Susan d. F. Thurston Gunning 21 June 1958; children: Susan, Julia, Leanne, Andrew; REGISTRAR, THE COLL. OF PHYSICIANS & SURGEONS OF ONT. 1980- ; postgrad. training Royal Victoria Hosp., Montreal Gen. Hosp. and Queen Mary Veter-

ans Hosp., Montreal 1960-65; hosp. appts. Montreal Gen.
Hosp. 1967-69, Queen Mary Veterans Hosp. 1966-69,
Oshawa (Ont.) Gen. Hosp. 1970-72, Toronto Gen. Hosp.
1972-79; Lectr. in Med. McGill Univ. 1968-70, Univ. of To-
ronto 1972-75, Asst. Prof. 1975-79; Dir. of Med. Services,
Ont. Med. Assn. 1972-74; Vice Pres. Med. Affairs, To-
ronto Gen. Hosp. 1974-79; recreation: sailing; Clubs:
Queen City Yacht; R.C.Y.C.; Home: 106 Cortleigh Blvd.,
Toronto, Ont. M4R 1K6; Office: 64 Prince Arthur Ave.,
Toronto, Ont. M5R 1B4.

DIXON, Robert Kenneth, B.Sc.; petroleum executive; b.
Calgary, Alta. 20 July 1928; s. William John and Eebel
(Fisher) D.; e. Western Can. High Sch. Calgary 1946;
Mount Royal Coll. Calgary 1947; Univ. of Okla. B.Sc. (Pe-
trol. Engn.) 1950; m. Kathleen Marion d. late William
Wheat Myers 20 Sept. 1953; children: Suzanne Jane
(Rassmusen), Sydney Kathleen, Bradley James; PRESI-
DENT AND CHIEF EXTVE. OFFR., MERLAND EX-
PLORATIONS LTD. 1976- ; Dir., IPAC; Westroc Indus-
tries; Dist. Engr. New Superior Oils of Canada Ltd.,
Calgary 1950-53; Staff Engr. Tidewater Association Oil
Co., Regina 1953-54; Dist. Engr. Canadian Fina Oil Ltd.
Calgary 1954-63; Production Mgr. Uno Tex Petroleum
Corp. 1963-68; Dir. of Production, Petrangal, Luanda,
Angola 1968-71; Petroleum Engn. Consultant Calgary
1971-76; served with Candn. Reserve Army 1943-45;
mem. Assn. Prof. Engrs. Prov. Alta.; Calgary Chamber
Comm.; Royal Alta. Un. Services (Assoc. mem.); Protes-
tant; recreations: sailing, golf, basketball, curling, skiing;
Clubs: Calgary Petroleum; Earl Grey Golf & Country;
Home: 2817 Linden Dr. S.W., Calgary, Alta. T3E 6C8; Of-
fice: 300, 630 - 4th Ave. S.W., Calgary, Alta. T2P 0K2.

DJWA, Sandra Ann, B.Ed., Ph.D.; educator; b. St.
John's, Nfld. 16 Apl. 1939; d. Walter William and Dora
Beatrice (Hancock) Drodge; e. Mem. Univ. of Nfld.
Teacher Training 1955-56; Univ. of B.C., B.Ed. 1964,
Ph.D. 1968; m. Peter Djing Kioe Djwa 6 Sept. 1958; one s.
Phillip John; PROF. OF ENG. LIT., SIMON FRASER
UNIV. 19..- ; rec'd Killam Family Fellowship 1981-82,
1982-83; author "E. J. Pratt: The Evolutionary Vision"
1974; "Saul and Selected Poetry of Charles Heavysege"
1976; "F.R. Scott: Canadian" (in press), co-author; vari-
ous articles, book chapters; Dir. Candn. Fed. Humani-
ties; mem. Assn. Candn. Univ. Teachers Eng.; Assn.
Candn. & Que. Lits.; United Church; recreations: gardening, skiing; Home: 4677 Belmont Ave., Vancouver,
B.C. V6R 1C6; Office: Burnaby, B.C. V5A 1S6.

DLAB, Vlastimil, RNDr., C.Sc., Ph.D., D.Sc., F.R.S.C.;
educator; b. Bzi, Czechoslovakia 5 Aug. 1932; s. Vlastimil
and Anna (Stuchlikova) D.; e. elem. Sch. Bzi 1943; Real
Gymnasium, Turnov 1951; Charles Univ. R.N.Dr. 1956,
C.Sc. 1959; Habilitation 1962, D.Sc. 1966; Khartoum
Univ. Ph.D. 1962; m. Zdenka d. Josef Dvoràk 27 Apl.
1959; children: Dagmar, Daniel Jan; PROF. OF MATH.
CARLETON UNIV. since 1968; Fellow, Czech. Acad. Sci-
ence 1956; Lectr. and Sr. Lectr. Charles Univ. 1957-59,
Reader 1964-65; Lectr. and Sr. Lectr. Univ. of Khartoum
1959-64; Research Fellow and Sr. Research Fellow, Inst.
Advanced Studies, Australian Nat. Univ. 1965-68;
Chrmn. of Math. Carleton Univ. 1971-74; Visiting Prof.
Univ. de Paris VI, Brandeis Univ. and Universität Bonn
1974-75, Univ. of Tsukuba 1976, Univ. de São Paulo 1976,
Univ. Stuttgart 1977, Univ. de Poitiers 1978, Univ. Nat.
Auton. Mexico 1979, Universität Essen 1979; Univ. Biele-
feld 1980; rec'd Can. Council Leave Fellowship 1974; Nat.
Research Council Can. Scient. Exchange 1978; Japan Soc.
for the Promotion of Sci., Sr. Research Fellowship 1981;
Dipl. of Hons. Union of Czechoslovakia Mathematicians
1962; author over 60 research papers group theory, theory of rings and modules, gen. algebra, representation
theory; mem. Royal Soc. Can. (Convenor & mem. of
Council, 1980-81); Candn. Math. Soc. (Council 1973-77,
Chrmn. Research Comte. 1973-77); Am. Math. Soc.; London Math. Soc.; Math. Assn. Am.; recreations: sports,

music; Home: 277 Sherwood Dr., Ottawa, Ont. K1Y 3W3;
Office: Ottawa, Ont. K1S 5B6.

DOANE, Harvey Roy, F.C.A.; b. Halifax, N.S., 24 Mar.
1910; s. Stephen Angus and Sadie (DeMone) D.; e. Halifax (N.S.) County Acad.; Maritime Business Coll., C.A.;
m. Anne Margaret, d. late Ralph R. Hayden, 8 May 1933;
children: Lawrence, Alan, Beverly; FOUNDER, H. R.
DOANE & COMPANY; Pres., Atlantic Trust Company
until March 1979; Dir., Electrical Distributors Ltd.; Atlantic Electric Stores Ltd.; former mem. Bd. of Govs., Acadia
Univ.; Pres., Dom. Assn. of Chart. Accts.; Audit
Clk. with F. A. Nightingale, Halifax, N.S., 1927, Partner,
F. A. Nightingale & Co., 1933; Founded own firm 1937;
mem., Halifax Executives' Assn. (Past Pres.): Inst. of
Chart. Accts. of N.S. (Pres. 1942-43); Pres., N.S. Div.,
Candn. Red Cross Soc., 1958-60; Pres., N.S. Div. Cana-
dian Bible Society (1959-61); Freemason; (Scot. Rite 33%;
Sovereign Grand Commander for Canada) 1973-76; Liber-
al; Baptist; Clubs: Saraguay; Kiwanis (Pres. 1943; Lieut.-
Governor Ont.-Que.-Maritime Dist. 1945; Gov., 1946; Internat. Trustee 1950-52); Home: 967 Ritchie Drive, Halifax, N.S. B3H 3P4;

DOBB, Victor; banker; b. Letchworth, Eng., 8 May 1925;
s. Herbert Samuel and Gladys Victoria (Bacon) D.; e.
Bishop Winnington Ingram Sch., Ruislip, Eng., 1930-36;
Harrow Co. Sch., Middlesex, Eng., 1936-41; m. Sylvia
Olive, d. late Walter Neave, 7 Aug. 1947; children: Ken-
neth Stewart, Helen Linda; EXTVE. VICE PRES., BANK
OF BRITISH COLUMBIA; Dir., Johnston Terminals &
Storage Ltd.; Johnston Terminals Ltd.; Transtec Can.
Ltd.; Westbank Leasing Ltd.; joined Westminster Bank
Limited, London, Eng., 1941-56; joined Bank of Mont-
real, Montreal, 1956; Asst. Acct., Sun Life Bldg. Br.,
Montreal, 1958; Acct., Westmount Br., Montreal, 1961;
Credit Offr. H.O. 1963; Asst. Mgr., King & Yonge Sts.,
Toronto, 1967; Asst. Credit Mgr., Vancouver, 1968;
joined present Bank as Mgr. Vancouver Main Office
1970, Gen. Mgr. H.O. 1970; served with RAF in Middle
E. 1943-47; rank Flight Sgt./Air Gunner; Fellow, Inst.
Candn. Bankers; Inst. Bankers, Eng.; Anglican; recrea-
tion: golf; Clubs: Vancouver; Point Grey Golf & Country;
Home: 5988 Wiltshire St., Vancouver, B.C. V6M 3L9; Offi-
ce: 555 Burrard St., Vancouver, B.C. V7X 1K1

DOBBIE, George Herbert; textile manufacturer; b. Galt,
Ont., 15 Nov. 1918; s. late George Alexander and Jean
Edith (Scott) D.; e. Lakefield Prep. Sch.; Bishop Ridley
Coll.; McGill Univ. (Comm. & Finance); m. Marie Louise,
d. C. A. Reiser, Montreal, Que., 15 Mar. 1941; four s.
George, Murray, Brian, Alexander; CHMN., GLENELG
TEXTILES LTD.; Chmn., Agatex Devels. Ltd.; Dir., Do-
minion Life Assnce. Co.; Can. Trust Co.; Past Pres.,
Candn. Woolen & Knit Goods Mfrs. Assn.; Past Chrmn.,
Can. Textiles Inst., Galt Bd. of Trade; Galt Bd. of Ed.;
Past Pres., Dobbie Industries Ltd.; Newlands & Co. Ltd.;
Past Vice-Pres., Can. Manufacturing Assn.; Can. Comte.
of the Pacific Basin Economic Council; Past Governor,
Univ. of Waterloo; Lakefield College School; mem., Galt
Bd. Educ., 1948-54 (2 yrs. Chrmn.); served in 2nd World
War with Candn. Army, 1941-45; discharged with rank of
Capt.; Anglican; recreations: hunting, fishing; Clubs: To-
ronto; Home: 45 Blair Road, Galt, Ont. N1S 2H8; Office:
1201 Franklin Blvd., Galt, Ont.

DOBBS, Kildare Robert Eric, M.A.; writer and broadcaster; b. Meerut, United Provs., India, 10 Oct. 1923; s.
late William Evelyn Joseph, I.C.S., and Maud Clifford
(Bernard) D.; e. St. Columbia's Coll., Rathfarnham, Ireland, 1927-41; Jesus Coll., Cambridge, (Exhibitioner),
B.A. 1947, M.A. 1952; Inst. of Educ. London Univ.,
Teacher's Dipl., 1948; m. 1st Patricia Marjorie Agnes Parsons, 1944 (Div.); children: Kildare John Evelyn, Christian Tracey Allan; 2nd Mary, d. late C. L. McAlpine,
K.C., 1 March 1958; children: Lucinda McAlpine, Sarah
McAlpine; formerly Staff Writer, The Toronto "Star

Weekly", 1962-65 and Columnist, Toronto Star; studied privately with late G. D. Allt, ed. of "The Variorum Yeats"; employed in Brit. Colonial Service (now H. M. Overseas Civil Service), 1948-52; Educ. Offr., Moshi, Tanganyika, 1948-50; Dist. Offr., Iringa, 1950-52; came to Canada 1952; worked in Heinz' warehouse, Toronto; Teacher, High Sch., Lambton-Kent Co., 1953; Ed., Trade Books, Macmillan Co. of Canada Ltd., Toronto, 1953-61; Assoc. Ed., "Saturday Night", Dec. 1961-June 1962 and 1965-71; Ed. Bd., "The Canadian Forum"; Co-Founder, "The Tamarack Review"; rep. in "Oxford Book of Canadian Verse"; served in 2nd World War with Royal Navy, 1942-46; discharged with rank of Sub-Lt.; author of "Running to Paradise" (winner of Gov.-Gen's. Award, 1963), 1962; "Canada" (with Peter Varley), 1964; "Pride and Fall" (short stories) 1981; awarded Canada Council Sr. Arts Fellowship, 1964; Liberal; recreations: music, walking, photography; Club: Bookmen's; Address: 601-50 Prince Arthur Ave., Toronto, Ont M5R 1B5

DOBELL, Col. Sidney Hope, D.S.O., LL.D. (1959), C.A.; b. Quebec, Que., 1900; e. Sch. in Eng.; Roy. Mil. Coll., Kingston; McGill Sch. of Commerce, C.A. 1924; m.; two s.; Partner, firm of McDonald, Currie (Chart. Accts.) 1924-47; Comptroller and Extve. Asst. to the Principal, McGill Univ. 1947-55; Extve. Vice-Pres. and Dir., B. J. Coghlin Co. Ltd., 1955-56, Pres., 1956-61; served Overseas in 1st World War with British Army 1918-19; 2nd World War, Major in Command A/A Battery, 1939; trans. to Field Arty. Overseas with rank of Lieut.-Col., 1940 (a-warded D.S.O.); promoted Col. 1945; recreations: golf, bridge, reading; Clubs: Canadian (Pres. 1949); Mount Royal (Chrm. 1953); St. James's; Royal Montreal Golf (Pres. 1956); Home: 1227 Sherbrooke St. W., Montreal, Que. H3G 1G1

DOBRIN, Melvyn A.; executive; b. Montreal, Que. 26 March 1923; e. McGill Univ. Accounting; m. Mitzi 26 June 1949; children: Mrs. Terry Dobrin-Minzberg, Lewis, Ronald; CHMN. OF THE BD. AND CHIEF EXTVE. OFFR., STEINBERG INC. 1978- ; Dir. Montreal Trust Co.; joined Steinberg 1950 serving in various store depts. prior to becoming Store Mgr.; apptd. Produce Buyer and later Asst. to Sales Mgr.; Dir. of Store Operations; Vice Pres. 1960, Vice Pres. and Gen. Mgr. 1961, Miracle Mart Div., Dir. 1962, Extve. Vice Pres.- Retailing 1967, Pres. 1969; Dir. Montreal Heart Inst. Research Fund; Y.M./Y.W.H.A. Foundation (Chrmn. Trust Fund Comte.); Gov. Weizman Inst. of Science (Vice Pres. Candn. Soc.); Gov., Montreal Gen. Hosp.; Inst. Med. Research Jewish Gen. Hosp.; Spera Foundation; Miriam Home Foundation; Jewish Pub. Lib.; Co-Chrmn. Que. Region Candn. Council Christians & Jews; mem., Campaign Comte., Maisonneuve-Rosemount Hosp. Foundation; Life Gov. Douglas Hosp.; Heritage Gov. Un. Talmud Torahs; Life mem. Montreal Museum of Fine Arts; Hon. mem., Univ. du Qué. à Montréal Foundation; Hon. Vice Pres., Boy Scouts of Can.; served with RCAF World War II completing 32 missions European Theatre as Navig. Bomber Command Group, rank Flying Offr.; recreations: golf, tennis, skiing, art; Clubs: Montefiore; Elmridge Golf & Country; Office: 1500 Atwater Ave., Montreal, Que. H3Z 1Y3.

DOBSON, Thomas Smith; banker; b. Glasgow, Scot. 5 Aug. 1917; s. James Frederick Gordon and Ellen (McTole) D.; came to Canada 1919; e. Dundas (Ont.) High Sch., Sr. Matric.; m. Wilma Flora, d. William John McKee 7 July 1943; children: Richard, Virginia, Nancy; CHRM., EASTON UNITED SECURITIES LTD.; Calgary, Alta; Pres., T.S. Dobson Consultant Ltd.; Pres. & Dir., Commercial Trust Co. Ltd.; Threadneedle Management Ltd.; Lothian Holdings Ltd.; Dir., Zeller's Ltd.; TIW Industries Ltd.; Shawinigan Consultants Ltd.; Dynamar Energy Ltd.; Martin-Black Inc.; Barbecon Inc.; Robt. Mitchell Inc.; TransAlta Utilities Corp.; Pembina Pipe Line Ltd.; Can. Marconi Co., Steag Coal Power Ltd.; Clarion Petroleums

Ltd.; Bow Valley Resource Services Ltd.; South Alberta Pipe Lines Ltd.; former Exec. Vice-Pres., Royal Bank of Canada; served in 2nd World War with R.C.N. 1941-45, Lt. Commdr., Mentioned in Despatches; Fellow, Inst. Candn. Bankers; Presb.; recreations: golf, curling, fishing, hunting; Clubs: Calgary Petroleum; Ranchmen's (Calgary); Pinebrook Golf & Country; Canadian; Calgary Golf and Country; Home: 1200 6th St. S.W., Calgary, Alta. T2R 1H3; Office: 2nd Floor, 409 8th Ave. S.W., Calgary, Alta

DOBSON, William Arthur Charles Harvey, O.C. (1975), M.A., D.Litt., F.R.S.C. (1961); professor (ret.); b. 1913; children: Guy St. Clair, Iain St. Clair; Prof. Emeritus, Univ. of Toronto, 1979; Prof., Univ. Toronto, 1952-79 prior to this was Prof. and Head Dept. of E. Asian Studies, Univ. of Toronto, and before that Lectr. in Chinese, Oxford Univ.; elected to Ashley Fellowship, Trent Univ., 1980; Hon. Prof., Trent Univ. 1981; served in 2nd World War; Commnd. in Argyll and Sutherland Highlanders at Singapore, 1941; escaped the city after investment by the Japanese, and served under Field Marshal Wavell and Field Marshal Auchinleck; promoted Lieut.-Col. and became Personal Staff Offr. to Lord Mountbatten and Gen. Carton de Wiart; engaged in the same period in several diplomatic missions; loaned to Rt. Hon. Winston Churchill for the Cairo Conf.; concurrent with mil. duties in Far East was Adviser on Far Eastern matters to Dept. of External Affairs in India; awarded Order of the Cloud and Banner (China); on return to Eng., apptd. Asst. Adj. Gen. to Brit. Land Forces in Norway, and was responsible for drafting the Govt. Report on War Crimes there; later sent to Wash., D.C., as War Office Rep. for War Crimes; Publications: "The Civilization of the Orient", 1955; "Late Archaic Chinese", 1959; "Early Archaic Chinese", 1962; "Mencius" 1963, reprinted Paperbacks, 1966, 1969, 1974; "Late Han Chinese" (1964); ed. "The Contribution of Canadian Universities to an Understanding of Asia and Africa" (1964) revised and enlarged (1967); The Language of the Book of Songs" (1968); "A Dictionary of the Chinese Particles" 1974; awarded Can. Council Molson Prize 1973; Address: 279 Sherbrooke St., Peterborough, Ont. K9J 2N5

DOBSON, William Henry, F.R.I.; real estate and insurance agent; b. Toronto, Ont., 1 Nov. 1907; s. William C. T. and Harriet M. (Reeder) D.; e. Univ. of Toronto Sch. (Grad. 1928); m. Rita M. Cronin, 15 June 1931; one s., Douglas D'Arcy; PRESIDENT, W. H. DOBSON CO. LTD., since 1953 (City Agents for Hartford Ins. Co.); Head of W. H. Dobson, Real Estate, Estbld. 1890; Pres., Toronto Real Estate Bd., 1955 (Dir. 1949-56), Dir. (1953-54) Ont. Assn. Real Estate Bds.; Hon. Life mem. Toronto Real Estate Bd.; Pres., Orangeville Investment Club; mem. Nat. Assn. Real Estate Bds.; Chart mem., Candn. Inst. of Realtors; Conservative; Anglican; recreations: golf, photography, curling, farming; Clubs: Orangeville Curling; Orangeville Investment; Bd. of Trade; Home: Ridor Acres, R.R. 1, Orangeville, Ont. L9W 2Y8; Office: 1454 Yonge St., Toronto, Ont. M4T 1Y5

DOCKERTY, Malcolm Birt, M.D., C.M., Ph.D.; physician; pathologist; b. Cardigan, P.E.I., 19 Sept. 1909; s. late Robert Alexander and Addie Mae (Birt) D.; e. Prince of Wales Coll., Charlottetown, Hon. Dipl. and Anderson Gold Medal 1928; Ph.D. (Hon.) 1967; Dalhousie Univ., Gold Medal 1934; Ph.D. (Hon.) 1973; Mayo Grad. Sch.; Univ. of Minn., M.S. 1937; m. Marjorie Olive, d. John Stoddart, Jamestown, N. Dak. 29 Dec. 1937; one s., John Malcolm; Prof. of Pathol., Mayo Grad. Sch., Univ. of Minn., 1952; author; "Tumors of Mouth and Pharynx", 1968; "Rhymed Reminiscences of a Pathologist", 1979; "Streamside Reminiscences" 1980; other writings incl. several book chapters, outdoor mag. articles and over 450 prof. articles; Minn. Conservation volunteer; Hon. mem., N.S. Med. Soc.; St. Paul Surg. Soc.; mem., Am. Med. Assn.; Am. Soc. Clin. Pathols.; Minn. Soc. Clin. Pathols.

(Past Pres.); Central Assn. Obstetrics & Gynecol. (mem. Tumor Comte.); Civilian Consultant, Armed Forces Inst. Pathol., 1950-69; Republican; Presbyterian; recreations: trout fishing, hunting, archery, ornithology, carving; Club: Izaak Walton League; Home: 1344 2nd St. N.W., Rochester, Minn.

DODGE, David A., B.A., Ph.D.; b. Toronto, Ont. 8 June 1943; s. Andrew A. and C. Louise (Beatty) D.; e. Queen's Univ. B.A. 1965 (Medal in Econ.); Princeton Univ. Ph.D. 1972 (Woodrow Wilson Fellowship 1965-66, Princeton Nat. Fellowship 1966-67, Can. Council Fellowship 1968); m.; two children; EXEC. COORD., LABOUR MARKET DEVELOPMENT TASK FORCE, EMPLOYMENT AND IMMIGRATION, OTTAWA; 1980-; Prof. of Canadian studies, Johns Hopkins Univ., Wash. D.C., 1978-80; Asst. Prof. of Econ. Queen's Univ. 1968-72; Sr. Research Offr. Dept. Finance Ottawa 1972-73, Chief Quantitative Tax Analysis 1973-75; Extve. Dir. Indust. and Market Analysis Central Mortgage and Housing Corp. 1975-76; Dir. Gen., Econ. Research Br., Anti-Inflation Bd., 1976-77; Dir., Inter. Economics Program, Inst. for Research on Public Policy, Ottawa, 1979-80; author "Returns to Investment in University Training: The Case of Canadian Accountants Engineers and Scientists" 1973; "Structure of Earnings of Professional Engineers in Ontario" 1972; author or co-author various articles, papers and book chapters; Home: 3 Monkland Ave., Ottawa, Ont. K1S 1Y7; Office: Place du Portage, Phase IV, 140 Promenade du Portage; 4th Floor, Ottawa, Ont. K1A 0J9

DODGE, William, O.C. (1974), B.A.; ombudsman Canadian-Labour Congress; retired trade unionist; b. Verdun, Que.; 15 May 1911; s. William and Pauline (Ranieri) D.; e. Pub. and High Schs., Verdun, Que., Sir George Williams Univ., B.A. 1949; m. Lily Sidonie Headmanak, 21 Feb. 1941; one d. Valerie Anne; retired Secy.-Treas., Canadian Labour Congress; Hon. Dir., C.D. Howe Research Inst.; Howe Inst. Policy Analysis Comte.; mem., Brit.-N. American Comte.; served in 2nd World War; Lieut., 7th Candn. Medium Regt. R.C.A.; N.W. Europe campaign; four times Cand. (C.C.F.) Verdun Constit., Prov. and Fed. (def.); N.D.P.; United Church; Home: 706 Portage Ave., Ottawa, Ont. K1G 1T4;

DODWELL, Roland Bodington,M.A.; financial consultant; b. Williams Lake, B.C. 23 Feb. 1921; s. Claude Henry Dodwell; e. Oak Bay High Sch. Victoria, B.C. 1939; Univ. of B.C. B.A. 1944; Univ. of Toronto M.A. 1947; m. Audrey Joyce d. Harry Roy Day 5 June 1946; children: Lesley Joyce, Philip Henry; PRES. AND DIR., R. B. DODWELL LTD. 1977- ; Vice Chrmn. Spar Aerospace Ltd.; Dir. and Treas. Crowborough Investments Ltd.; Lectr. Univ. of B.C. 1947-49; Invest. Dealer (Dir.) Mills Spense & Co. 1949-68; Walwyn Stodgell & Co. 1968-74; served with RCNVR during World War II, rank Lt.; mem. Financial Analysts' Assn.; United Church; recreations: curling, golf, fishing, hunting; Clubs: Oakville Curling; Oakville Golf; Canard Gun; Home: 1112 Linbrook Rd., Oakville, Ont. L6J 2L1; Office: (P.O. Box 174) 2510 South Tower, Royal Bank Plaza, Toronto, Ont. M5J 2J4.

DOE, Roger Graham, B.A. b. Bermuda 25 June 1933; s. William Lestock and Helen M. O. (Franklin) D.; e. Saltus Grammar Sch. Bermuda 1945; Glebe Coll. Inst. Ottawa 1949; Univ. of W. Ont. B.A. 1953; Osgoode Hall Law Sch. 1958 (Silver Medal); children: Linda, Peggy, Gail, Douglas; m. Margaret Parker 1981; law practice Campbell, Godfrey & Lewtas since 1958; Dir. Dofasco Inc.; mem. Candn. Bar Assn.; Co. York Law Assn.; recreations: golf, skiing, squash; Clubs: Toronto; Toronto Golf; Granite; Home: 159 Glen Rd., Toronto Ont. M4W 2W7; Office: (P.O. Box 36) Toronto-Dominion Centre, Toronto, Ont. M5K 1C5.

DOEHRING, Donald Gene, M.A., Ph.D.; psychologist; educator; b. Pittsburgh, Pa. 7 Apl. 1927; s. Walter Alan

and Frances Elizabeth (Mehnert) D.; e. Montgomery Blair High Sch. Silver Spring, Md. 1944; Univ. of Buffalo B.A. 1949; Univ. of New Mexico M.A. 1951; Ind. Univ. Ph.D. 1954; m. Jean Margaret d. late William Kick 5 Aug. 1950; children: Nancy, Carrie, Carl, Laura, Peter; PROF. OF HUMAN COMMUNICATION DISORDERS & PSYCHOL. McGILL UNIV.; Research Dir. Sch. of Human Communication Disorders; Research Assoc. Central Inst. for Deaf, St. Louis, Mo. 1954-59; Asst. to Assoc. Prof. Ind. Univ. Med. Center 1959-63; joined McGill Univ. as Assoc. Prof. 1963; First Dir. Sch. Human Communication Disorder 1963-68; Visiting Scient. of Med. Research Council, Cambridge Univ. 1971-72; presently conducting research on devel. computer assisted instr. programs for children with reading disability; founded first Ph.D. program in speech & hearing in Can.; served with US Army 1944-47; author 'Patterns of Impairment in Specific Reading Disability' 1968; various book chapters, papers in scient. journs.; mem. Am. Psychol. Assn.; Candn. Psychol. Assn.; Internation Reading Assn.; Internat. Neuropsychol. Soc.; Liberal; recreations: music, reading, squash, canoeing, camping; Home: 4643 Sherbrooke St. W., Apt. 12A, Montreal, Que. H3Z 1G2; Office: 1266 Pine Ave. W., Montreal, Que. H3G 1A8.

DOERN, Hon. Russell, M.L.A., B.A. (Hons.); politician; b. Winnipeg, Man., 20 Oct. 1935; s. Karl John and Ruby (Henne) D.; e. Isaac Newton High School, Winnipeg, 1953; Un. Coll., B.A. 1959; Univ. of Man., B.A. 1965 (Hons.); m. 10 Apl. 1971; one d., Rachel Ruby; min. of public works, man., 1972-77; el. MLA for Elmwood since 1966; apptd. Min.-without-Portfolio 1970; Acting Min. of Pub. Works 1971; assoc. with Man. Theatre Centre, Winnipeg Art Gallery, Hist. & Scient. Soc. Man.; YMCA; Chrmn., Isaac Newton Alumni; Hon. mem., Candn. Assn. Occupational Therapists; Candn. UNICEF Comte.; taught 1960 and 1962-66; writings incl. numerous newspaper articles, TV programs for sch. broadcasts, freelance radio and TV; NDP; Unitarian; recreations: tennis, and skating; Address: Legislative Bldg., Winnipeg. Man.

DOERN, William; radiographer; b. Overstone, Man., 14 April 1902; s. Philip and Katherine (Zorn) D.; e. Pub. and High Schs., Morden, Man.; Sanitorium Bd. of Man. (affiliated with Univ. of Man.), 1926-29 (Radiography); Med. Technol. (R.T.), American Registry, April 1929; m. Louise Margaret, d. late Harry D. and Ada Kyle, 31 July 1935; children: William Robert, David Kyle, Catherine Margaret, Elsa Elizabeth; apptd. Chief Technician and Tech. Instr., Dept. of Radiology, Winnipeg Gen. Hosp. 1932; Tech. Dir., Sch. of Radiography, Dept. of Radiology there, 1956-65; and Dir. of Planning Dept. of Radiology there 1967-69; apptd. Chief Tech. to Sanitorium Bd. of Man. 1929; mem. Candn. Soc. of Radiological Techs. (Charter mem. since 1943; Pres. 1950-51, 1957-58; Chrmn., Comte. on Tech. Training, 1961; mem. Ed. Bd., 1963-65; Bd. of Examiners for Can. 1952-56); Am. Soc. of X-Ray Tech. (mem. Comte. on Educ. 1937; Counsellor for Can. 1949-50, 1954-65); Man. Soc. of X-Ray Tech. (instrumental in its organ. 1929; Past Pres., Hon. Life mem.); Hon. mem., Soc. of Radiographers, London (1951); Life mem., Am. Registry of Radiological Techs., 1957; mem. Adv. Comte. Man. Inst. of Tech., 1963. Life mem. (1967); Candn. Soc. Radiol. Tech.; awarded Centennial Medal 1967; honoured at 50th Anniversary of Man. Soc. of Radiol. Techs., Nov. 1979, by establishment and dedication of Wm. Doern Service Award, in recognition of his numerous contributions to radiology. K. of P.; Liberal; United Church; recreations: amateur cellist; do-it-yourself power tools; house trailering, hi-fi; Clubs: Winnipeg Cine; St. Andrews A.O.T.S.; Home: 366 Brock St., Winnipeg, Man. R3N 0Y9

DOHENY, Daniel O'C., Q.C., B.A., B.C.L.; advocate; b. Montreal, Que., 27 July 1915; s. Hugh and Mary Roycroft (O'Connell) D.; e. Selwyn House Sch., Montreal; Bishop's Coll. Sch., Lennoxville, Que.; McGill Univ.,

B.A. 1939, B.C.L. 1947; m. late Norah Deane, d. A. F. Baillie, 20 June 1946; children: Patrick, Norah Deane, Mary Lucille, Lisa Margot; PARTNER, DOHENY, MACKENZIE, GRIVAKES, GERVAIS & LEMOYNE; Dir., RCA Ltd.; Armstrong Beverley Engineering Ltd.; Burndy Ltd.; Trust Général du Can. Fonds Ltée; The Guarantee Co. of N.A.; Ritz-Carlton Hotel Co. of Montreal, Ltd.; read law with Errol MacDougall, Q.C.; called to the Bar of Que., 1947; cr. Q.C. 1958; served in 2nd World War with Fifth Field Regt., R.C.A.; Alpha Delta Phi; Roman Catholic; recreations: golf, tennis, skiing, fishing; Clubs: Montreal Racket; Mt. Royal; Mt. Bruno Country; Hillside Tennis; Knowlton Golf; Home: 41 Barat Rd., Westmount, Que.; Office: 1203, 5 Place Ville Marie, Montreal, Que. H3B 2H1

DOIRON, Hon. Joseph Aubin, D.D.S., D.Hum.Litt., LL.D.; lieutenant-governor; b. North Rustico, P.E.I. 10 June 1922; s. Adolphe Omer and Mary Emma (Pineau) D.; e. St. Anne's Coll. Church Point, N.S. B.A. 1946; Univ. of Montreal D.D.S. 1951; St. Anne's Univ. D.Hum.Litt. 1980; Dalhousie Univ. LL.D. 1981; Univ. of Moncton, Hon. Ph.D. 1982; m. Bernice Rose Gallant 17 June 1950; children: Paul, Robert, Pierre, Simonne, Colette, Omer, Marc; LT.-GOV. OF P.E.I. 1980- ; dentistry practice Summerside, P.E.I. since 1951; Founding Pres. and Chrmn. Acadian Mardi Gras Assn.; Charter mem. and Pres. Acadian Museum Assn.; mem. La Société St-Thomas d'Aquin; K. of C.; mem. Greater Summerside & Area Chamber Comm.; Past Dir. Summerside Cooperative Assn., St. Paul's Credit Union Ltd., P.E.I. Heritage Foundation; mem. 1973 P.E.I. Centennial Comn.; Past Island Rep. Candn. Folk Arts Council; Past mem. Summerside Bd. Sch. Trustees; Past Pres. Dental Assn. P.E.I.; Past Rep. Bd. Govs. Candn. Dental Assn.; Past Pres. St. Paul's Parish Council; P. Conservative; R. Catholic; recreations: choir singing, curling, golf, woodworking, painting, deep sea fishing, angling; Clubs: Kinsmen (Past Pres. Summerside); K-40 (Past Pres.); Address: "Fanningbank" Government House (P.O. Box 846), Charlottetown, P.E.I. C1A 7L9.

DOLEZEL, Lubomir, Ph.D.; educator; b. Lesnice, Czechoslovakia 3 Oct. 1922; s. Oskar Dolezel; e. Gymnasium Zabreh and Litovel, Czechoslovakia 1941; Charles Univ. Prague grad. 1949; Czechoslovak Acad. of Sciences Ph.D. 1958; m. Milena d. late Josef Velinger 27 Nov. 1961; children: Marketa, Milena, Pavla Kollert, Lubomir; PROF. AND CHRMN. OF SLAVIC LANGS. & LITS. UNIV. OF TORONTO 1980- ; High Sch. Teacher Czechoslovakia 1949-54; Research Fellow, Inst. for Czech Lang.; Czechoslovak Acad. of Sciences 1958-68; Assoc. Prof. (Docent) of Czech Lang. Charles Univ. Prague 1961-68; Visiting Prof. of Slavic Langs. & Lits., Univ. of Mich. 1965-68; Univ. of Toronto 1968-71, Prof. 1971- ; Visiting Prof. Univ. of Amsterdam 1976; Can. Council Research Leave Fellow 1977-78; author "O Stylu Moderní Ceské Prózy" (On the Style of Modern Czech Prose Fiction) 1960; "Slovník Spisovneho Jazyka Ceskeho" (Dictionary of Standard Czech) Vol. 1 1960 (co-author); "Narrative Modes in Czech Literature" 1973; Ed. "Teorie Informace a Jazykoveda" (Information Theory and Linguistics) 1964; co-ed. "Statistics and Style" 1969; various studies in stat. linguistics, stylistics, hist. of poetics, theory of fiction, Czech and Russian lit.; served with Anti-Nazi Resistance 1943-45; rec'd Mem. Medal of Resistance; mem. Soc. Linguistique de Paris; Toronto Semiotic Circle; Candn. Comparative Lit. Assn.; recreations: swimming, skiing; Home: 308 Carlton St., Toronto, Ont. M5A 2L7; Office: 21 Sussex Ave., Toronto, Ont. M5S 1A1.

DOLIN, Samuel Joseph, Mus.D.; composer; educator; b. Montreal, Que. 22 Aug. 1917; s. Joseph and Freda (Levin) D.; e. Baron Byng High Sch. Montreal 1933; Univ. of Toronto Mus.B. 1942, Mus.D. 1958; Toronto Conserv. of Music ATCM 1945; m. Inthia Leslie d. A. L. Pidgeon, Burlington, Ont. 7 March 1953; children: Elizabeth L.,

John J.; TEACHER COMPOSITION THEORY & PIANO, ROYAL CONSERVATORY OF MUSIC TORONTO, Founder Electronic Music Studio 1966; joined present Conserv. 1945; served 3 yrs. as Music Supvr. of Schs. Durham and Northumberland, Ont. prior to 1945; compositions incl.: (opera) "Casino" 1966-67; (orchestra) "Scherzo" 1950; "Serenade for Strings" 1951 (premiered by Finnish Nat. Radio during 1952 Olympiad); "Sinfonietta" 1950; "Sonata for String Orchestra" 1962; "Symphony No. 1 (Elk Falls)" 1956; "Symphony No. 2" 1957; "Symphony No. 3" 1976; (soloist(s) with orchestra) "Concerto for Piano and Orchestra" 1974; "Drakkar" 1972; "Fantasy for Piano and Chamber Orchestra" 1967; "Isometric Variables" 1957; (instrumental ensemble) "Adikia" 1975; "Barcarolle" 1962; "Concerto Grosso (Georgian Bay) 1970 (premiered CBC Summer Festival Toronto 1971); "Duo Concertante" 1977; "Little Sombrero" 1964; "Portrait" 1961; "Sonata" 1960; "Sonata" 1978; "Sonatina" 1954; (instrumental solo) "Little Toccata" 1959; "Prelude, Interlude and Fantasy" 1976; "Ricercar and Fantasy" 1975; "Sonata" 1970; "Stelcel" 1978; "Three Sonatas" 1973; (voice) "Chloris" 1951; "Deuteronomy XXXII" 1977; "Julia" 1951; "Ozymandias" 1951; (chorus) "The Hills of Hebron" 1954; "Marchbankantata" 1971; "Mass" 1972; (piano) "If" 1972; "Little Suite" 1964; "Little Toccata" 1959; "Prelude for John Weinzweig" 1973; "Queekhoven and A.J." 1975; "Slightly Square Round Dance" 1966; "Sonata" 1950; "Sonatina" 1959; "Three Piano Preludes" 1949; (2 pianos) "Concerto for Four" 1977; "Variation for Two Pianos" 1967; (incidental music) "Machina" 1970; "Missionaries" 1971; "Music from 'The Meeting Point'" 1971; (discography) "Ricercar"; "Sonata for Accordion"; "Sonata for Violin and Piano"; comns. many organs. and individuals incl. Stratford Festival, Toronto Repertory Ensemble, Royal Conserv. Music Toronto, Etobicoke Philharmonic Orchestra, CBC; mem. Adjudication Comte. Guitar Soc. Toronto's Internat. Guitar Festival 1978; mem. Candn. League Composers (Founding mem., Vice Pres. 1967-68, Pres. 1969-73); Internat. Soc. Contemporary Music (Vice Pres. 1972-76, Chrmn. Candn. Sec. 1972-74); Assoc. Composer, Candn. Music Centre (past Bd. mem.); Owner, Drakkar Music Publishing; mem. PRO Canada; Gov., Etobicoke Philharmonic; recipient Can. Council, Ont. Arts Council, Laidlaw Foundation and CBC grants; Home: 12 Reigate Rd., Islington, Ont. M9A 2Y2; Office: 273 Bloor St. W., Toronto, Ont.

DOLMAN, C. E., F.R.C.P., D.P.H., F.R.S.C; medical scientist; emeritus professor; e. London Univ., Eng., M.B., B.S., Ph.D.; Research mem., Connaught Medical Research Labs., Toronto, Ont., 1935-73; developed a new antitoxin to treat severe staphylococcus infection, 1933, and also a toxoid for active immunization against such infections; worked for many years on bacterial food poisoning incl. especially botulism; formerly Prof. and Head Dept. of Bacteriol. and Preventive Med. (1936-51) and Dept. of Bacteriology & Immunol. Univ. of B.C. (1951-65); Dir., Prov. Dept. of Health Labs. of B.C. (1935-56); Pres. (1969-70) Royal Soc. Can.; Pres. (1964-66) Candn. Assn. of Med. Bacteriols.; Silver Jubilee Medal, 1978; Coronation Medal 1953; results of his exper. publ. in several med. & scient. journs.; Hon. Life Mem., Candn. Public Health Assn., Candn. Assn. of Med. Microbiologists, Am. Soc. of Microbiology, Internat. Northwest Conference on Diseases in Nature Communicable to Man; author: "Medical Education in Canada and the United States", 1946; Editor, "Water Resources of Canada" 1967; Author of several articles in Dict. of Scientific Biog.; Home: 1611 Cedar Crescent, Vancouver, B.C. V6J 2P8

DOMBOWSKY, David S., B.Com.; executive; b. Avonlea, Sask. 1 Aug. 1938; e. Univ. of Sask. B. Com.; Carleton Univ. Dipl. in Pub. Adm. 1961; PRES. AND CHIEF EXTVE OFFR., POTASH CORP. OF SASK. 1975- ; Chrmn. of Bd., Potash & Phosphate Inst. and Foundation for Agronomic Research, 1975- ; joined Sask. Treasury Dept., Budget Bureau, 1958; Adm. Asst. to Depy. Prov. Treas. 1962; Secy., Johnson Royal Comn. 1964; Dir. Budget Bureau 1966; Depy. Prov. Treas. 1970; Depy. Min. Industry & Comm. 1972; Mang. Dir. Sask. Econ. Devel. Corp. 1973; Chrmn. of Bd. Potash Corp. of Sask. Feb.-Dec. 1975; mem. Nat. Council Inst. Pub. Adm. Can.; Office: 410 - 22nd Street E., Saskatoon, Sask. S7K 5T7

DOMVILLE, James de Beaujeu,B.A., B.C.L.; film commissioner; b. Cannes, France 1933; s. Henri de Gaspé and Elsie Welsh (Saltus) D.; e. Selwyn House Sch. Montreal; Trinity Coll. Sch. Port Hope, Ont.; Univ. de Fribourg Diplôme d'aptitude à l'enseignement du français à l'étranger 1951; McGill Univ. B.A. 1954, B.C.L. 1957; GOVT. FILM COMMR. AND CHRMN. NAT. FILM BD. OF CAN. 1979- ; Dir. CBC 1979- ; Ex-officio mem. Bd. Dirs. Candn. Film Devel. Corp. and Bd. Trustees Nat. Arts Centre since 1979; Dir. Institut de la musique du Can. since 1973; Gov. Le Théâtre du Nouveau Monde since 1972; mem. Bd. Govs., Extve. Comte. and Consultant Nat. Theatre Sch. 1968, Life Gov. 1968- (Co-founder and 1st Adm. Dir. 1960-64, Dir. Gen. 1964-68, Teacher 1960-70); Asst. Dir. of Eng. Production Nat. Film Bd. 1972, Extve. Producer Studio B. 1974-75, Depy. Govt. Film Commr. 1975-79; Producer, co-author, composer Candn. musical "My Fur Lady" 1956-58; Founder, Pres. Quince Productions Montreal 1958- ; co-producer theatrical productions incl. "Jubilee!" 1959, "Spring Thaw" 1960; Extve. Dir. Le Théâtre du Nouveau Monde 1968-72; Adviser and Consultant Entertainment Br. Candn. Fed. Pavilion Expo '67 1963-66; Rep. Internat. Theatre Symposia Rumania, Germany, Italy (Chrmn.), Sweden (Chrmn.) and Czechoslovakia 1964-68; guest lectr. various univ. theatre depts. 1964-68; Theatre Consultant to archs. Nat. Arts Centre Ottawa 1964-68; Theatre Rep. Internat. Colloquium on Can. Centre Culturel Internat. Cérisy la Salle, France 1968; mem. Selection Comte. First World Jewish Film Festival Jerusalem 1977; Gov. and mem. Extve. Dom. Drama Festival 1961; Chrmn. Festivals & Cultural Activities sub-comte. Candn. Centenary Council 1963; Treas. and Dir. Candn. Theatre Centre 1962, Secy. 1964-68; mem. Am. Educ. Theatre Assn.; Dir. U.S. Inst. Theatre Technol. 1966; mem. Comte. Prof. Training Internat. Theatre Inst. 1966-69; Co-chrmn. Theatre of Tomorrow Panel N.Y. 1967; mem. Adv. Arts Panel Can. Council 1968-69, Chrmn. 1969-72; Gov., Senator McGill Univ. 1969-74; Gov. Candn. Conf. of Arts 1975-77; recipient Candn. Centennial Medal 1967; Queen's Silver Jubilee Medal 1977; Home: 437 Mount Pleasant, Westmount, Que. H3Y 3G9; Office: 3155 Côte de Liesse, Ville St-Laurent, Qué. H4N 2N4 and (P.O. Box 6100 Stn. A) Montréal, Qué. H3C 3H5.

DON, Conway Joseph, M.B., B.S., F.R.C.R., F.R.C.P.(C), F.R.C.P.; radiologist; educator; b. Newcastle-on-Tyne, Eng. 1 Dec. 1922; s. Frank Austin and Rosanna (McHatton) D.; e. Univ. Coll. London 1941-43; Univ. Coll. Hosp. London 1943-46 (Liston Gold Medal in Clin. Surg. 1945), M.B., B.S. 1946; children: Felicity, Rosemary, Caroline, Paul, Penelope; PROF. AND CHRMN. OF RADIOLOGY, UNIV. OF OTTAWA; Dir. of Radiol. Ottawa Gen. Hosp., Chrmn. Med. Adv. Comte. and Chief of Med. Staff 1966-71, 1977-80; Hon. Consultant in Radiol. Riverside Hosp.; Royal Ottawa Hosp.; Consultant in Radiol. Ottawa Civic Hosp., Ont. Cancer Foundation (Ottawa Clinic), St. Vincent Hosp.; Med. Registrar, Univ. Coll. Hosp. London 1950-51, Registrar and Sr. Registrar 1951-56; Clin. Fellow, Mass. Gen. Hosp. and Teaching Fellow, Harvard Univ. 1956-57 (Richman Godlee Fellowship); Visiting Fellow, Mass. Gen. Hosp. 1968; Visiting Prof. Vanderbilt Univ. 1976-77; Visiting Prof. Univ. of Jedda, Saudi Arabia 1980; Research Grant Referee, Research Programs Br. Nat. Health & Welfare; author or co-author numerous scient. publs.; mem. Ont. Med. Assn.; Faculty of Radiols.; Candn. Assn. Radiols. (Councillor for E. Ont. 1965-67, Past Chrmn./mem. various

comtes.); Candn. Med. Assn.; E. Ont. Assn. Radiols.; Soc. Chrmn. Acad. Radiol. Depts. USA; Assn. Candn. Profs. Radiol.; Assn. Univ. Radiols. USA; Radiol. Soc. N. Am.; P. Conservative; recreations: squash, skiing, swimming, reading; Clubs: Rideau Lawn Tennis & Squash; Cercle Universitaire d'Ottawa; Ottawa Athletic; Home: 20 Rideau Terrace, Ottawa, Ont. K1M 1Z9; Office: Ottawa General Hospital, Ottawa, Ont. K1H 8L6.

DONAHOE, Richard Alphonsus, Q.C., B.A., LL.B., K.S.G.; senator; b. Halifax, N.S., 27 Sept. 1909; s. late James Edward and Rebecca Margaret (Duggan) D.; e. St. Mary's Coll., Halifax, N.S.; Dalhousie Univ., B.A. 1930, LL.B. 1932; Hon. LL.D., St. Mary's Univ. 1981; m. Mary Eileen, d. late Donald B. Boyd, 22 Sept. 1936; children: Arthur, Cathleen, Terence, Sheila, Nora, Ellen; read law with Burchell, Smith, Parker & Fogo, Halifax, N.S.; called to the Bar of N.S. 1932; cr. Q.C. 1950; contested N.S. Prov. el., 1937, in Halifax S.; Fed. el. 1940; contested Halifax N. (Prov.) 1949; el. Alderman for Ward 4, Halifax City, 1951, Mayor, 1952, re-el. by acclamation, 1953 and 1954; el. to Prov. Leg. for Halifax S., by-el. 1954; apptd. Atty. Gen., Min. Public Health, 1956; (both portfolios held until 1970); appointed Knight of St. Gregory the Great, 1969; appointed to Senate of Canada, 1979; mem., Charitable Irish Soc.; Royal Caledonian Curling Assn. of Scotland; K. of C.; P. Conservative; Roman Catholic; recreations: curling, fishing; Clubs: Halifax Curling; Canadian; Home: 456 Francklyn St., Halifax, N.S. B3H 1A9

DONAHOE, Hon. Terence Richard Boyd,M.L.A., B.Com., LL.B.; politician; b. Halifax, N.S. 30 Oct. 1944; s. Senator Richard Alphonsus and Mary Eileen (Boyd) D.; e. St. Mary's Univ. High Sch. 1960; St. Mary's Univ. B.Com. 1964; Dalhousie Univ. Law Sch. LL.B. 1967; m. Lynne Marie d. Bernard Harrison Sheehan 30 Dec. 1967; one d. Moira Eileen; MIN. OF EDUC. N.S. and Min. Responsible for Status of Women 1978- ; called to Bar of N.S. 1967; former Partner, Blois, Nickerson, Palmeter & Bryson; el. M.L.A. for Halifax Cornwallis prov. g.e. 1978; re-el. 1981; Gov. St. Mary's Univ. 1975-78; Head Candn. Del. Third Unesco Conf. Mins. of Educ Europe Region, Sofia 1980; Head Educ. Sector 21st Unesco Cen. Conf. Belgrade 1980; served Min. of Social Services' Comte. to review Family Court rules N.S.; former mem. Children & Youth Action Comte. on Child Welfare; former State Advocate K. of C.; former Hon. Counsel N.S. Div. Candn. Red Cross Soc.; mem. Prov. Extve. and Hon. Treas.; mem. Prov. Extve. John Howard Soc.; Past Pres. Halifax-Cornwallis P. Cons. Assn.; mem. Council of Mins. Educ. Can.; Candn. Comn. for Unesco; P. Conservative; R. Catholic; recreations: golf, skating; Club: Ashburn Golf & Country; Home: 1641 Walnut St., Halifax, N.S. B3H 3S3; Office: (P.O. Box 578) Halifax, N.S. B3J 2S9.

DONALD, Graham Edward Bruce, B.A., F.C.A.; chartered accountant; b. Warren, Ohio 23 Nov. 1926; s. Bruce and Joan (Clowes) D.; e. Brantford (Ont.) Coll. Inst.; Univ. of Toronto B.A. 1948; C.A. 1954; m. Joyce d. Roy P. Findlay 4 June 1955; children: Stephen, Graham, Elizabeth, Sarah, Anne; PARTNER, ERNST & WHINNEY; joined present firm 1953, Montreal 1958; Partner-in-Charge Hamilton Office 1962, Toronto 1970, Vice Chmn. 1981; Hon. Treas. Red Cross Hamilton Br. 1965-70; Ont. Div. Candn. Red Cross Soc. 1972-77; Campaign Extve. Un. Way Metrop. Toronto 1974-76; Gov. Hillfield-Strathallan Colls. 1966-71; Comte. Chrmn. Hamilton Chamber Comm. 1964-69; served with RCA, rank Capt.; mem. Insts. C.A.'s Ont. Man. Que. and B.C.; Accounting Research Comte., Candn. Inbst. C.A.'s 1973-77; Chrmn. Jt. Task Force on Ins. Candn. Inst. C.A.'s 1975-82; Delta Tau Delta (Treas. 1946); Anglican; recreations: golf, tennis, skiing, fishing; Clubs: Toronto Badminton & Racquet; Hamilton; Rosedale Golf; Albany; Caledon Ski; Home: 120 Roxborough St., E., Toronto, Ont. M4W 1W1; Office: Commerce Court W., Toronto, Ont. M5L 1C6

DONALD, James Richardson, O.B.E., B.Sc., B.A., D.Sc.; retired chemical engineer; b. Montreal, Que., 7 Oct. 1890's; s. James Thomas (a distinguished Chem. and Educ.) and Evelyn (Bellis) D.; e. Montreal High Sch.; McGill Univ., B.A., B.Sc.; m. Pensey S., d. David P. Irving, Vernon, P.E.I., 14 June 1916; one s. and one d; former Chrmn. of Bd., J. T. Donald & Co. Ltd., Chem. Engrs. & Economists, Consulting & Research Chemists, Inspecting & Testing Engineers, Dir.-Gen., Chem. & Explosives, Dept. of Munitions & Supply, 1939-45; Dir., Chem & Explosives Divn., Dept. of Defence Production, Mar. 1951-Oct. 1952; awarded Soc. of Chem. Industry (Candn. Sec.) Medal & Montreal Medal, C.I.C., for outstanding Services to Candn. Chem. Industry 1952 and 1962 respectively; special consultant to Fed. Govt. and author of "The Cape Breton Coal Problem", 1965-66; Fellow, Chem. Inst. Can.; mem. Engn. Inst. Can.; Am. Inst. Chem. Engrs.; Candn. Inst. Mining & Metall.; Soc. Chem. Indust. Gt. Brit. (Chrmn. Montreal Sec. 1929-30, 1955-56); author of various tech. papers; Psi Upsilon; United Church; Clubs: University; Royal Montreal Golf; Royal Montreal Curling; Chemists (New York); Address: 29 Crawford St., Brockville, Ont. K6V 1S2

DONGIER, Maurice Henri Jacques, M.D., F.R.C.P.(C); educator; b. Sorgues (Vaucluess), France 27 Nov. 1925; s. Raphael and Yvonne (Jouanen) D.; e. Univ. de Marseille, Cert. d'études physiques, chimiques et biologiques 1943, Thèse de doctorat en médecine 1951; McGill Univ. Dipl. in Psychiatry 1953; m. Suzanne d. Louis Montagnac, Cannes; France 1952; children: Pierre, François, Isabelle, Philippe; PROF. AND CHRMN. OF PSYCHIATRY, McGILL UNIV. 1974- ; Boursier du Ministère d'Affaires culturelles de France 1951-52; Chef de Clinique adjoint, Clinique des maladies nerveuses Univ. de Marseille 1954-57; Chef de Clinique titulaire 1957-60; Psychiatre chargé de recherches, Laboratoire de neurophysiologie clinique, Hôpital de la Timone, Marseille 1960-63; Professeur et Directeur, Département de Psychologie médicale et médecine psychosomatique, Univ. de Liège, Belgique 1963-71; Prof. of Psychiatry and Dir. Allan Mem. Inst., McGill Univ. 1971-80; named Officier de l'ordre de Léopold (Belg.); Chevalier de la Légion d'Honneur (Fr.); author "Névroses et troubles psychosomatiques" 1966-1967-1969, édit néerlandaise 1967; co-author "Contingent Negative Variations" 1969; "Divergent Views in Psychiatry" 1981; numerous book chapters, 250 articles, mem. Soc. Médico-Psychologique de Paris; Groupe de l'Evolution psychiatrique Paris; Soc. d'Electroencéphalographie de Langue Française; Soc. de Psychiatrie de Marseille; Internat. Coll. Psychosomatic Med. (Founding mem.); Candn. Psychoanalytic Soc. (Secy. Que. Eng. Sec. 1975-77); Candn. Psychiatric Assn.; Que. Psychiatric Assn.; Candn. Psychoanalytic Inst. (Secy.-Treas. 1977-79); Am. Psychiatric Assn.; Am. Psychopathol. Assn.; Am. Psychosomatic Soc.; R. Catholic; recreations: sailing, flying; Home: 3036 St. Sulpice Rd., Montreal, Que. H3H 1B5; Office: 1033 Pinee Ave. W., Montreal, Que. H3A 1A1.

DONNAY, J(oseph), D(ésiré) H(ubert), Ph.D., F.M.S.A., F.G.S.A.; educator; b. Granville-Oreye, Belgium 6 June 1902; s. Désiré Mathieu Joseph and Madeleine (Doyen) D.; e. Athenaeum Liège, Belgium 1920; Univ. Liège Candidat Ingénieur 1922, Ing. civil des Mines 1925; Stanford Univ. Ph.D. (Geol.) 1929; m. 1stly Marie-Madeleine Hennin 23 Dec. 1931; children: Robert V. J., Nicole; m. 2ndly Gabrielle Hamburger 25 July 1949; children: Albert H., Victor J.; RESEARCH ASSOC. IN CRYSTALLOGRAPHY, McGILL UNIV. 1975- ; Research Assoc. in Geol. and Teaching Fellow in Mineral. Stanford Univ. 1930-31; Assoc. in Mineral & Petrography The Johns Hopkins Univ. 1931-39, Visiting Prof. of Chem. Crystallography & Mineral. 1945 and Prof. 1946-71, Prof. Emeritus 1971- , Chrmn. Phys. Sciences Group 1951-53, Visiting Prof. 1972; Prof. ordinaire à la Faculté des Sciences 1946-47, Prof. honoraire 1948- , rec'd médaille de l'Université 1959 Univ. de Liège; Prof. agrégé Univ. Laval 1939-40, prof. ti-

tulaire 1940-45; Research Chem. Hercules Powder Co. Exper. Stn. Wilmington, Del. 1942-45; Fulbright Lectr. Univ. de Paris (Sorbonne) 1958-59; Guest Investigator, Carnegie Inst. of Washington, Geophys. Lab. 1959-70; Chargé de cours Univ. de Montréal 1970-72, Prof. invité 1972-76; Visiting Lectr. Univ. of Utah 1950, Ballistic Research Lab. Aberdeen Proving Ground, Md. 1961, Emory Univ., Ga. Inst. Technol., Univ. of Ga. 1963; Visiting Scient. U.S. Naval Postgrad. Sch. Monterey, Calif. 1955; Gastprof. Universität Marburg, Mineralogisches Inst. 1966, 1968; Guest Worker U.S. Nat. Bureau of Standards 1967-73; rec'd Queen's Silver Jubilee Medal 1977; ed. "Crystal Data" 1st ed. 1954, 2nd ed. 1963, 3rd. ed. vol. 1 1972, vol. 2 1973, vols. 3 and 4 1978; author "Spherical Trigonometry" 1945; "Space Groups and Lattice Complexes" 1973; over 150 papers scient. journs.; Fellow, Mineral. Soc. Am. (Pres. 1953; Roebling Medal 1971); Geol. Soc. Am. (Vice Pres. 1954; membre honoraire, Soc. géologique de Belgique (Vice Pres. 1946-47); Soc. française de Minéralogie et de Cristallographie (Vice Pres. 1949, mem. d'honneur 1978); Charter mem., Am. Soc. X-Ray & Electron Diffraction (Secy.-Treas. 1944, Secy. 1945-46); Crystallographic Soc. Am. (Pres. 1949); Am. Crystallographic Assn. (Pres. 1956); Geochem. Soc.; Vice Pres. Assn. française de Cristallographie 1959-60; mem. Assn. des Ingénieurs (médaille Trasenster 1977) Liège; Sigma Xi; Mineral. Soc. (UK) Phi Beta Kappa; del. various gen. assemblies and congs. Internat. Union Crystallography; Società Italiana di Mineralogia e Petrologia; Mineral. Assn. Can.; Académie royale des Sciences, des Lettres et des Beaux-Arts de Belgique; recreations philology; Home: 516 rue d'Iberville, Mont-St-Hilaire, Que. J3H 2V7; Office: 3450 University St., Montreal, Que. H3A 2A7.

DONNELLY, James; executive; b. Wishaw, Scot. 22 March 1931; s. Peter and Mary (Morris) D.; e. Royal Tech. Coll. Glasgow 1949-53; m. Brenda d. Ernest John Marks 29 March 1956; one d., three s.; PRES. AND CEO, ATOMIC ENERGY OF CANADA LTD. since 1978; held extve. positions General Electric of Eng. and English Electric Co. 1954-74; Vice Pres. Forestry Products, International Systems & Controls Corp. Inc., Montreal 1974; Assoc., Royal Tech. Coll. Glasgow; mem. UK Inst. Elect. Engrs.; recreations: tennis, skiing, theatre; Clubs: Cercle Universitaire; Ottawa Athletic; Ottawa Hunt; Home: 136 Dorothea Dr., Ottawa, Ont. K1V 7C6; Office: 275 Slater St., Ottawa, Ont. K1A 0S4.

DONNELLY, Hon. James Francis; retired judge; b. Greenock Twp., Bruce Co., Ont., 31 July 1901; s. Sen. James and Julia (McNab) D.; e. Pinkerton (Ont.) Pub. Sch.; St. Michael's Coll., Toronto; Univ. of Toronto, 1921; Osgoode Hall Law Sch.; m. Ina, d. John Kehoe, Pembroke, Ont., 27 Nov. 1926; children: Richard, James, Moyra C.; former justice, Supreme Court of Ont., since 1959; read law with Kilmer, Irving & Davis; called to Bar of Ont. 1924; cr. K.C. 1945; R. Catholic; recreations: golf, bridge; Clubs: University; London (Ont.) Hunt; Maitland Country; Home: University Club, University Ave., Toronto, Ont.;

DONNELLY, Murray Samuel, M.A., Ph.D. F.R.S.C.; educator; b. N.S. 23 July 1919; s. Melbourne Donnelly; e. Mt. Allison Univ. B.A. 1940; Univ. of Toronto M.A. 1946, Ph.D. 1954; m. Nancy Margaret d. late Malcolm H. Magee, Toronto, Ont. 17 Aug. 1946; children: Margaret Ann. Michael James; PROF. OF POL. SCIENCE, UNIV. OF MAN. and men. Bd. of Govs.; mem. 2 Royal Comns. of Inquiry (Prov.); Constitutional Adv. to Prov. Govt.; author 'The Government of Manitoba' 1963; 'Dafoe and the Free Press' 1968; numerous articles and book reviews; Fellow, St. Antony's Coll. Oxford; mem. Candn. Pol. Science Assn.; Clubs: Southwood Golf & Country; Winnipeg Winter; recreations: golf, curling; Home: 282 Ashland Ave., Winnipeg, Man. R3L 1L4; Office: 500 Dysart Rd., Winnipeg, Man. R3T 2M8.

DONOAHUE, James Thomas,R.C.A.; graphic designer; b. Walkerton, Ont. 15 Oct. 1934; s. Frank and Helene (Montpetit) D.; e. Central Tech. High Sch. Hamilton 1952; Ont. Coll. of Art 1956; children: Zoe, Noah, Colin; PROP., JIM DONOAHUE & ASSOCIATES LTD.; recipient numerous nat. and internat. awards from design organs. Toronto, Montreal, New York, Chicago; work featured in design publs. USA, Europe and Japan; mem. Art Dirs. Club Toronto (Past Pres.); Alliance Graphique Internationale; Home: 1148 Logan Ave., Toronto, Ont. M4K 3H1; Office: 20 Scollard St., Toronto, Ont. M5R 1E9.

DONOHUE, Mark, B.A., LL.L.; retired executive; b. Quebec City, 8 Sept. 1909; s. J. Timothy and Emilie (Normandin) D.; e. Private Sch., Laval Univ., B.A. 1931; Laval Univ. Law Sch., LL.L. 1934; Sch. of Business Adm., Harvard Univ., 1934-35; m. Lucile d. Joachim des Rivieres Tessier, Quebec City, 30 Sept. 1939; children: J. Thomas, Charles, Louise, Patricia; read law with Dupré, Gagnon, de Billy & Meighen; called to the bar of Que. 1934; mem., Can. Bar Assoc.; served as Mayor, Clermont, Charlevoix, Que., 1940-43; Hon. Mem. of Bd., Donohue Inc.; R. Catholic; recreations: fishing, golf, tennis; Clubs: Quebec Garrison; Cercle Universitaire; Mount Royal; The Everglades, Palm Beach (Florida); The Links (N.Y.); Home: 907-63 St. Clair Av. W., Toronto, Ont. M4V 2Y9; Office: 500 est, Grande Allée, Québec, Qué. G1R 2J7

DOODY, Hon. William, politician; b. St. John's, Nfld., 26 Feb. 1931; s. Matthew and Florence (O'Neil) D.; m. Doreen Jessop, 30 July 1961; children: Christine, Liam, Steven; SENATOR Since 1979; el. H. R. Main Dist. 1971; Min. of Mines and Resources 1972, of Indust. Devel. 1973, of Finance 1975-78; of Trans. and Comm., for Intergov. Affairs, of Pub. Works and Serv., 1978-79; P. Conservative; R. Catholic; Home: 32 Bennett St., Ottawa, Ont.; Office: The Senate, Ottawa, Ont. K1A 0A4

DORAIS, Léo A., B.A., M.B.A., Ph.D.; educateur; né Montréal, 21 sept. 1929; f. J. Armand et Lucienne (Cormier) D.; é. Univ. Montréal, B.A. 1952, B.Ph. 1953, L.Ph. 1955; Univ. Chicago, M.B.A. 1962; Univ. Chicago, Ph.D. 1964; ép. Suzanne, f. J. Roland Dansereau, 3 sept. 1955; enfants: André-R., Anne-Marie, Catherine, Jean-A.; SOUS-MINISTERE ADJOINT AUX ARTS ET À LA CULTURE 1980- ; mem. du Comité d'étude de la politique culturelle Fédérale (Comité Applebaum-Hébert); sous-secrétaire d'Etat adjoint aux Arts et à la culture 1979-80; vice président principal, Agence Canadienne de Développement International 1976-79; Recteur, Univ. du Quebec (Montreal) 1969-74; Vice-prés., Faroun Films (Canada) Ltée; Dir., Service d'éducation perm. Univ. Montréal, 1er février 1967-avril 1969; Dir. associé Service audiences Comm. Royale d'enquête sur le bilinguisme et le biculturalisme, 1964-65; membre; Comité planification de la recherche pédagogique 1967-68; Coordonnateur Comité élab. système informatique gestion universités 1968; membre: Canadian Indust. Trainers' Assn.; Candn. Assn. Adult Educ.; Musée Beaux-Arts, Montréal; Corporation des psychologues de la P.Q.; Soc. can. de psychologie; Soc. can. anthropologie et sociologie; Vice-Prés., Soc. de Math. appliquées; auteur du: "Manuel de méthodologie de la recherche", 1956; "l'Autogestion Universitaire: autopsie d'un mythe" 1977; de nombreux articles, Revue de Livres dans des périodiques; Catholique; Récréations: photographie, musique; sports aquatiques; Résidence: 261 River Rd., Vanier, Ont. K1L 8B8; Bureau: Ministère des Communications, Ottawa, Ont. K1A OM5

DORAIS, Marcel, B.A.Sc.; mining executive; b. Montreal, Que., 25 June 1924; s. Hororé and Albertine (Ladouceur) D.; e. Ecole Supérieure St-Stanislas and Mont St-Louis, Montreal 1944; École Polytech., Univ. de Montréal, B.A.Sc. (Civil Engn.); m. Marcelle, d. Marcel Rigaud, 4 Jan. 1947; children: Michel, Daniel, Anne; PRESIDENT, CHIEF EXTVE. OFFR. AND DIR., BELL ASBESTOS MINES LTD. since 1971; Dir., Candn. Oxy-

gen Ltd.; SNA (Société nationale de l'amiante) Forano Ltée; Mgr. (Constr.) C. Jobin Ltée, Québec City, 1950; Chief Engr. (Constr.) Michaud & Simard, 1959; Vice Pres. (Constr. Div.) Compagnie Miron Ltée, Montreal 1961-71; Dir., Thetford Indust. Clinic; mem. Que. Asbestos Mining Assn. (Dir.); Inst. Occupational & Educ. Health (Dir.); Corp. des Ingénieure du Qué.; Engn. Inst. Can.; Candn. Inst. Mining & Metall.; Can. Inst. of Mining and Metallurgy Foundation; R. Catholic; recreations: photography, swimming, travel, art; Club: St. Denis, Montreal; Home: 401 Lapierre St., Thetford Mines, Que. G6G 5T6; Office: (P.O. Box 99) Thetford Mines, Que. G6G 5S4

DORAN, Anthony Burke,Q.C., LL.B.; barrister; b. Ottawa, Ont. 17 May 1937; s. Anthony Burke and Margaret Felicite (Heney) D.; e. Univ. of Ottawa High Sch. 1954; Univ. of Ottawa 1955-56; McGill Univ. B.A. 1958; Osgoode Hall Law Sch. LL.B. 1961; m. Geralda Ruth d. late Rufus Savage 1 Apl. 1967; one s. Patrick John Wentworth; PARTNER, LANG, MICHENER, CRANSTON, FARQUHARSON & WRIGHT; called to Bar of Ont. 1963; cr. Q.C. 1978; author various articles legal topics; el. Bencher Law Soc. Upper Can. 1979; mem. Candn. Bar Assn. (Past Chrmn. Family Law Sec. Ont. Br.; mem. Nat. & Ont. Councils); Medico-Legal Soc.; Advocates' Soc. (Dir.); Thomas More Guild (Dir.); Kappa Alpha; Phi Delta Phi; Liberal; R. Catholic; Clubs: Rideau (Ottawa); Royal Ottawa Golf; Univ. Club of Toronto; Home: 44 Duncannon Dr., Toronto, Ont. M5P 2M2; Office: (P.O. Box 10) First Canadian Pl., Toronto, Ont. M5X 1A2.

DORE, Raymond, C.A.; banker; b. Sudbury, Ont. 25 March 1939; s. Albert and Anna (Leschishin) D.; e. Public and High Schs. Sudbury, Ont.; children: Steven, Glenn; CHAIRMAN OF THE BOARD, THE INTERIOR TRUST CO. 1981- ; Dir., Exeltor Inc.; Marshall Steel Ltd.; Williams Trading Inc.; C.A. with Arthur Crawley and Co., Montreal 1965; Treas. Commercial Trust Co., Montreal 1966-74; Vice Pres., Mercantile Bank of Can., Toronto 1975-77; C.E.O. Rolfe Reeve Group Ltd. 1977-78; Chrmn. of the Bd., Merchant Trust Co. 1978-79; Chrmn. of the Bd., Doré, Sutherland & Stuebing Inc. 1980; recreations: golf, squash; Clubs: Montreal Badminton & Squash; Royal Montreal Golf; Home: 33 Harbour Square, Toronto, Ont.; Office: P.O. Box 325, Toronto-Dominion Centre, Toronto, Ont. M5K 1K7

DORFMAN, Irwin, Q.C., B.A., LL.D.; b. Winnipeg, Man., 27 March 1908; s. Moses and Dora (Fidelman) D.; e. Univ. of Man., B.A. 1927, LL.B. (Gold Medallist) 1931; LL.D. 1977; m. Dorothy Evelyne, d. late William Plumm, 6 Sept. 1936; two d. Marcia, Louise; Partner, Thompson, Dorfman, Sweatman; called to Bar of Man. 1931; cr. K.C. 1950; Chrmn., Special Govt. Comte. to revise Man. Co.'s Act; Gov., Candn. Tax Fndn. 1967-70; Past Pres., S. Winnipeg Lib. Assn.; Past Dir., Royal Winnipeg Ballet; Past Pres., Shaarey Zedek Cong.; Pres., Man. Bar Assn., 1966-67; Past Pres., Law Soc. of Man.; Pres., Candn. Bar Assn. 1975-76; Liberal; Hebrew; recreations: fishing, golf; Clubs: Carleton; Glendale Golf & Country; Home: 1002 Hampton Green, Wellington Cres., Winnipeg, Man.; Office: 3 Lombard Place, Winnipeg, Man. R3B 1N4

DORION, Robert Bernard Joseph, B.Sc., D.D.S.; b. Montreal, Que. 16 Oct. 1944; s. Eugene Squires and Marcelle Fernande Sarah (Rochon) D.; e. St. Francis Xavier Univ. B.Sc. 1968; McGill Univ. D.D.S. 1972; Dipl. Am. Bd. Forensic Odontology 1976; m. Patricia Ann d. Alexander James Boyd, Morristown, Antigonish, N.S. 19 Aug. 1972; s. Robert Peter James; d. Melissa Sarah Jane; Demonst. Operative Dent. Univ. of Montreal since 1972, Lectr. in Forensic Dent. since 1975; Guest Lectr. Forensic Dent. McGill Univ. 1972-1974, Sessional Lectr. since 1974; Lectr. in Forensic Dent. Univ. Laval since 1977; Lectr. Can. Police College, 1978-; Consultant in Forensic Dent. Laboratoire de Medecine Légale, Ministry of Justice Que. (Dir. Odontological Identification) since 1973; author various articles prof. journs.; numerous lecture presentations in Can. and U.S.; Fellow, Am. Acad. Forensic Sciences; Can. Soc. Forensic Science (Dir. 1975-79, Pres. 1978-79, Chrm. of Bd. 1978-79, Ed. Bd. 1976-84); Am. Bd. Forensic Odontology (Dir. 1976-83); Mont. Dent. Club (Secretary 1979-80); mem. Candn. Dent. Assn.; Order Dents. Que.; recreations: photography, painting, skiing, swimming, writing, research; Office: 710-D, Sun Life Bldg., 1155 Metcalfe, Montreal, Que. H3B 2V6

DORN, Peter Klaus,R.C.A.; F.G.D.C. graphic designer; educator; b. Berlin, Germany 30 June 1932; s. Robert and Charlotte (Lemme) D.; e. Berufsschule für Grafisches Gewerbe Berlin 1949-51; Ont. Coll. of Art (evenings) 1962-63; Akademie für Grafik und Buchkunst Leipzig 1968; m. Charlotte d. Hans Graffunder, Berlin, Germany 25 Dec. 1954; children: Gregory, Jennifer, Jeffrey; DIR., GRAPHIC DESIGN UNIT, QUEEN'S UNIV. 1971-; Dir., Graphic Services, North Hatley Group of Companies and King Abulaziz Univ. Review Office, North Hatley, Que.; part-time Teaching Master, St. Lawrence Coll. Kingston 1979- ; Prop., Heinrich Heine Press; came to Can. 1953; Howarth & Smith, Typographers, Toronto 1954-59; Cornish & Wimpenny, Toronto 1960-63; Univ. of Toronto Press 1964-70; Guest Lectr. N.S. Coll. Art & Design 1980; Dir. Candn. Book Design Comte. 1975-78; Guild of Hand Printers 1963-70; rec'd Can. Council Grant 1968; over 50 nat. and internat. design awards; el. mem. Royal Canadian Academy, 1974; Fellow, Graphic Designers Can. (Nat. Pres. 1978-79); mem. Soc. Graphic Designers Can. (Pres. Kingston Br. 1977-79); Lutheran; recreations: private printing, sports; Home: 44 William St., Kingston, Ont. K7L 2C4; Office: 207 Stuart St., Kingston, Ont. K7L 3N6 or, P.O. Box 576, North Hatley, Que. J0B 2C0

DORRINGTON, Keith John, Ph.D., D. Sc.; educator; B. Tredegar, UK 26 Oct. 1939; s. Bruce D.; e. Univ. of Sheffield B.Sc. 1961, Ph.D. 1964, D.Sc. 1976; m. Jennifer d. Reginald Hampshire, Huddersfield, UK 24 Sept. 1960; children: Mark Julian, Jonathan Peter, Emma Justine; PROF. AND CHRMN. OF BIOCHEM. UNIV. OF TORONTO since 1977, Assoc. Dean of Medicine since 1978; Lectr. in Pharmacol. Univ. of Sheffield 1967-68; Sr. Scient. Med. Research Council, Molecular Pharmacol. Unit, Univ. of Cambridge 1968-70; Assoc. Prof. of Biochem. Univ. of Toronto 1970, Prof. 1975, Vice Provost (Health Sciences) 1976-77; rec'd Sir Henry Wellcome Travelling Fellowship 1966-67; Ayerst Award Candn. Biochem. Soc. 1977; Vice Chrmn. Univ. Teaching Hosps. Assn. 1976-77; mem. Am. Assn. Immunologists; Am. Soc. Biol. Chems.; Biochem. Soc.; Candn. Biochem. Soc.; Candn. Soc. Immunology; Chmn., Ed. Bd., "Molecular Immunology", 1980; Section Ed., "Journal of Immunology", 1977-; author or co-author over 120 scient. articles in areas of biochem. and immunology; recreations: music, literature; Home: 43 Gloucester St., Toronto, Ont. M4Y 1L8 Office: Toronto, Ont. M5S 1A8.

DORTON, Roger Anthony,B.Sc., Ph.D., P.Eng.; civil engineer; b. London, Eng. 23 March 1929; s. Harold William D.; e. Lexington (Mass.) High Sch. 1944; Hitchin Grammar Sch. Herts. Eng. 1947; Univ. of Nottingham B.Sc. (Engn.) 1951, Ph.D. 1954; m. Patricia Mary d. Horace George Upshall 4 Oct. 1958; children: Peter, Mary, Anne, Catherine; MGR. STRUCTURAL OFFICE HIGHWAY ENGN. DIV. MINISTRY OF TRANSPORT. & COMMU-NICATIONS, ONT.; came to Can. 1954; joined Dept. of Highways Ont. 1954-56; P.L. Pratley, Consulting Engrs. Montreal 1956-58; Chief Engr. H.H.L. Pratley Montreal 1958-65 (Champlain Bridge Montreal, Cornwall Bridge, Ogdensburg-Prescott Bridge); Partner, Pratley & Dorton Montreal (19 canal bridges Expo '67; A. Murray Mackay Suspension Bridge Halifax) 1965-72; joined present Ministry 1972 serving as Sr. Research Offr., Princ. Research Offr. R & D Div.; recipient 1st Prize Nat. Bridge Design Competition Expo '67 1965; Award of Merit A. Murray Mackay Bridge Assn. Consulting Engrs. 1970; Gzowski

Medal Engn. Inst. Can. for Best Paper of Yr. 1976; Candn. Soc. Civil Engn. 1977 Nat. Tour Lectr.; Assn. Prof. Engrs. Prov. Ont. Engn. Medal for Distinguished Engn. Achievement 1980; Queen's Silver Jubilee Medal 1977; Chrmn. Ont. Highway Bridge Design Code Comte.; author "The Champlain Bridge" 1962; "The Ontario Highway Bridge Design Code" 1979; various articles bridge design, research and testing, transit guideways; Assoc. Ed. "Canadian Journal of Civil Engineering"; mem. Assn. Prof. Engrs. Prov. Ont.; Candn. Standards Assn.; Internat. Assn. Bridge & Structural Engn.; Am. Concrete Inst.; Candn. Soc. Civil Engn. (Chrmn. Structural Div., Bd. Dirs.); Engn. Inst. Can.; R. Catholic; recreations: golf, music, reading, photography, history of bridges, antique prints; Home: 34 Kingland Cres., Willowdale, Ont. M2J 2B7; Office: 1201 Wilson Ave., Downsview, Ont. M3M 1J8.

DOUCET, Jean-Louis, Q.C.; Quebec; public service; b. St-Jacques-des-Piles, Co. Laviolette, Que., 23 Nov. 1909; s. Arthur and Aurore (Massé) D.; e. Séminaire Saint-Joseph, Trois-Rivières, Que., B.A. 1935; Laval Univ., LL.L. 1938; m. Claire, d. E. Alexandre Frenette, Quebec, 23 Sept. 1941; children: Danièle, Luc; Pres., Greater Québec Water Purification Bd., Jan. 1969-79 (Depy. Min. of Mun. Affairs 1950-69); Prof., Faculty of Law, Laval Univ.; called to the Bar of Quebec 1938; created K.C. 1951; was associated with his father's industry (J. Arthur Doucet, St-Jacques-des-Piles, Que.), 1932-35; apptd. Law Offr., Atty. Gen. Dept., Que., 1938; Assoc. Depy. Min. of Mun. Affairs, Dec. 1947; mem. of Prov., Nat. and Internat. Municipal Assns.; K. of C.; R. Catholic; recreation: reading, golf; Home: 2144 rue Boisjoli, Sillery, Que. G1T 1E5;

DOUGLAS, A. Vibert, O.C. (1967), M.B.E. 1918, Ph.D., LL.D., D.Sc., F.R.A.S.; b. Montreal, Que. 1894; e. McGill Univ., B.A. 1920, M.Sc. 1921, Ph.D. 1926, LL.D. 1960; D.Sc. (Queensland) 1965; LL.D. Queen's 1975; Cavendish Lab. and Cambridge Observatory, 1921-23; with War Office and Min. of Nat. Serv., London, 1916-18; Lect. in Physics & Astrophysics, McGill Univ., Montreal, 1923-39; Dean of Women, Queen's Univ., 1939-59; Prof. of Astronomy 1943-63; has contrib. numerous scient. articles to journs. of Gt. Brit., Can. and U.S.A.; general articles to Atlantic Monthly, Hibbert Journal and Univ. Quarterlies; Biographer of Sir Arthur Eddington, O.M., F.R.S.; mem. Roy. Astron. Soc. Can. (Pres. 1943-45); Am. Astron. Soc.; Am. Assn. Var Star Observers; Candn. Inst. Internat. Affairs; International Fed. of Univ. Women (Pres. 1947-50); Royal Astron. Soc. (G.B.); Internat. Astron. Union; Candn. Assn. for Hist. & Philos. of Science; Sigma Xi; Address: 402-67 Sydenham St., Kingston, Ont. K7L 3H2

DOUGLAS, Ian, C.M., O. St. J., C.D., Q.C., B.A.; barrister-at-law; b. Toronto, Ont., 12 June 1920; s. Clara S. (Simpson) and late Howard Riordon D.; e. Brown Sch. and Upper Canada Coll., Toronto, Ont.; Trinity Coll., Univ. of Toronto B.A. 1942; Osgoode Hall, Toronto, Ont.; m. Phyllis Mary Marguerite, d. late Lieut.-Col. Lionel H. Millen, D.S.O. and Bar, V.D., 6 June 1942; one s. and two d.; PARTNER, McCARTHY & McCARTHY; Dir., British American Bank Note. Inc.; C & M Products Ltd.; Plough (Can.) Candn. Acceptance Corp. Ltd.;Ltd.; Schering Inc.; W. H. Smith Canada Ltd.; called to the Bar of Ontario, June 1948; cr. Q.C. Jan. 1960; served with 48th Highlanders of Can., 1940 to 1954 with service overseas 1942-45; retired as Lieut.-Col.; Hon. Gov. and Hon. Solicitor, Canadian Corps of Commissionaires; Vice-Chmn. of the Bd., Sunnybrook Medical Centre; Zeta Psi; Conservative; Anglican; recreations: golfing, skiing, Clubs: Toronto; Toronto Hunt; Badminton & Racquet; Muskoka Lakes Golf & Country; Home: 156 Forest Hill Road, Toronto, Ont. M5P 2M9; Office: Toronto-Dominion Centre, Toronto, Ont. M5K 1E6

DOUGLAS, John Macdonald, B.E., M.Sc., P.Eng.; retired industrial executive; b. Zealandia, Sask., 10 Aug.

1917; s. John Macdonald and Marjorie May (Sweney) D.; e. Univ. of Sask., B.E. (Geol. Engn.) 1940; McGill Univ. M.Sc. (Geol.) 1941; m. Jessie Lucille, d. Col. J. G. Robertson, New Glasgow, N.S., 28 Nov. 1942; one d. Mrs. Jill Robertson Blok; DIR. OF REUTER-STOKES, INC. AND REUTER-STOKES CAN., LTD. 1977-; with Consolidated Mining & Smelting Co. of Canada, 1946-55, Property Supt., Pine Point Mines, N.W.T., for last 2 yrs.; with Eldorado Mining and Refining Ltd. 1955-63, Mine Mgr., Beaverlodge Mine, Uranium City, Sask., for last 4 yrs.; joined Babcock & Wilcox Canada Ltd. as Extve. Asst. to the Pres., 1963-65; apptd. Gen. Mgr. 1965; Vice Pres. and Gen. Mgr. 1966; Pres. and Chief Extve. Offr. 1968-76; Chrmn. Bd. 1976-78; Consultant, Gen. Mgr. and Secy., for Organ. of CANDU Industries 1979-; served with R.C.A.F. 1942-46, in Aero Engn. Br.; rose from Pilot Offr. to Squadron Leader; mem., Educ. Services Comte. 4 yrs., Hosp. Bd. 2 yrs., Councillor 4 yrs., Uranium City, Sask.; mem., Adv. Vocational Comte., Galt Bd. Educ., 1966; mem., Assn. Prof. Engrs. Ont.; Prof. Engrs. Assn. B.C.; Candn. Inst. Mining & Metall.; Pres. (1974-75), mem. Bd. of dir. 1980-81 Candn. Nuclear Assn.; Chrmn. Ont. Div., Candn. Mfrs. Assn. 1973-74; mem. Bd. of Governors, Univ. of Waterloo 1977-81; Freemason; Protestant; recreations: golf, curling, reading; Home: 24 Ridgewood Pl., Cambridge, Ont. N1S 4B4

DOUGLAS, Lloyd Robert, C.D., B.Sc.; company executive; b. Silverton, Man., 4 Aug. 1916; s. John Faircleugh and C. Mabel (Todd) D.; e. Strathclair (Man.) High Sch.; Univ. of Man., B.Sc. (Elect. Engn.) 1938; m. Frances Mary, d. T. L. Edwards, 12 Oct. 1940; children: Caroline, Elizabeth, William; Vice-Pres., Canadian General Electric Co. Ltd.; Test Engr., Canadian General Electric Co. Ltd., Peterborough, Ont., 1938, Sales Engr., Toronto, 1946, Mgr. Apparatus Marketing, Peterborough, 1955, Gen. Mgr., Apparatus Dept., 1964; Mgr. Bus. Dev. Apparatus & Heavy Machinery Division 1979; served in 2nd World War, 1940-45, Lt.-Col., Royal Candn. Signals; served overseas in Eng., N. Africa, Sicily, Italy, France, Germany and Holland; Mentioned in Despatches, 1944; Candn. Army Reserve, 1945-52; mem. Candn. Elect. Assn.; Assn. Prof. Engrs. Ont.; Corp. Prof. Engrs. Que.; Engn. Inst. Can.; recreations: curling, golf; Clubs: St. James's; Thornhill Golf & Country; Home: 79 Cachet Parkway, R.R. #2, Gormley, Ontario, L0H 1G0; Office: 1900 Eglinton Ave. East, Scarborough, Ont. M1L 2M1

DOUGLAS, Lieut.-Col. Malcolm Lyall, D.C.L.; b. Woodstock, Ont., 5 Feb. 1896; s. Malcolm and Christina (Hay) D.; e. Coll. Inst., Woodstock, Ont.; Univ. of Toronto, Ont.; D.C.L. King's Coll., Halifax; m. Aveleigh Margaret, d. Judge James Gamble Wallace 12 July 1922; one d., Mrs. Joan Avelleigh of Sault Ste Marie; mem. Bd. of Govs., Brockville Gen. Hosp.; joined Dom. Rubber Co. Ltd., Toronto, 1919, and went to Eng. for the Co., 1920, remaining as a Dir. of the Brit. subsidiary, in charge of Sales till 1929; apptd. Gen. Sales Mgr., Tires, for Can., 1929 and cont. till formation of the Candn. subsidiary of John B. Stetson Co., hat mfrs. of Philadelphia in 1935; Pres., John B. Stetson Co. (Can.) Ltd., 1935-59, Chrmn. of Bd., 1959-61; served in 1st World War 1914-18 with R.F.C., C.E.F. and R.A.F. and with Br. Royal Service under Gen. Hoare; Opened airport north Toronto, at Armour Hts; trained the first U.S. fliers; flew in France Belgium and Holland; during 2nd World War acted as Chairman of Nat. War Finance Comte. for Counties of Leeds and Grenville and also O.C. 2nd (R) Bn., Brockville Rifles; served overseas in air observation of the enemy in England, France & Belgium; has been active in Boy Scouts Assn. work since 1909; chosen in 1911 as one of contingent of Canadian Scouts at the coronation of King George V, mem. of Ontario Prov. Council and Extve. Comte., and Candn. Gen. Council (awarded Silver Wolf); mem., Anglican Church of Canada (in September 1952 el. Deputy Prolocutor of General Synod and a mem. of Extve. Council and el. Prolocutor of the Lower House

Sept. 1959 and re-el. 1962); former Pres., Rotary Club; mem. (62 yrs.) Royal Candn. Legion; Psi Upsilon; Freemason; Anglican; recreations: fishing, swimming, photography; Clubs: Brockville; Home: Apt. 708, Four Winds Apts., 109 King St. E., Brockville, Ont. K6B 1V8

DOUGLAS, Susan (Mrs. Jan Rubes); O.C.; actress; producer; b. Vienna, Austria, 13 March 1928; m. Jan Rubes, 22 Sept. 1950; children: Christopher, Jonathan, Anthony; came to Can. 1959; HEAD OF RADIO DRAMA FOR CBC DRAMA CANADA since 1979; as an actress has played on Broadway in "He Who Gets Slapped" (won Donaldson Award for best supporting performance 1946); "Druid Circle"; "Heart Song"; "Taming of The Shrew"; in Hollywood "Private Affairs of Bel'Ami" with George Sanders; "Lost Boundaries" with Mel Ferrer; "Five"; "Forbidden Journey" with husband; has acted in various TV shows incl.; "Studio One," "Kraft Playhouse", "Montgomery Presents"; played Kathy for 10 yrs. in "Guiding Light"; radio performances incl.: "Theatre Guild on the Air", "March of Time", "Inner Sanctum Mystery", "Helen Trent", "Backstage Wife", "Big Sister"; producer and founder of Young People's Theatre (estbd. 1965) and responsible for production of such plays as "Dandy Lion", "Popcorn Man", "The Diary of Anne Frank" with the Wallach family, and Laterna Magika's "The Lost Fairy Tale" (from Czechoslovakia); Bd. mem. of St. Lawrence Centre; Young People's Theatre; Int. Theatre Festival; awarded Order of Canada in 1977; voted "Woman of the Year" by B'nai Brith, Toronto, 1979; Home: 55 Sumner Heights Dr., Willowdale, Ont. M2K 1Y5; Office: Canadian Broadcasting Corp., P.O. Box 500, Station A, M5W 1E6

DOUVILLE, Raymond, B.Sc.; newspaper man; historian; b. La Pérade, Qué. 17 Sept. 1905; s. Alphonse and Alice Chavigny de La Chevrotière D.; e. Nicolet, Qué. Semy.; Univ. de Montréal B.Sc. (Journalism); m. Bella d. late Dr. Henri Beaulac 25 Sept. 1937; children: Renée (Mrs. Rejean Bouchard), Louise (Mrs. Cyrille Bernard), Charlotte (Mrs. Hubert Gaudry); Former Depy. Min. and Registrar Qué. Prov. Secy.; author "La vie quotidienne en Nouvelle-France" 1964; "La vie quotidienne des Indiens du Canada" 1967; "Daily Life in Early Canada" transl. 1967; "Na Nova França O Canada" transl. 1970; Ed. Françaises "La Vie d'Arthur Buies" 1933; Ed. du Bien Public "Aaron Hart" 1938; "Premiers Seigneurs et Colons de La Pérade" 1948; "Visages du Vieux Trois-Rivières" 1956; various hist. studies, booklets Candn. hist.; collab. "Biographical Dictionary of Canada"; mem. Royal Soc. Can.; Société des Dix; Académie de Clermont-Ferrand (France); recreation: genealogical research, travel; Address: 3309 rue L'Heureux, Apt. 6, Ste-Foy, Qué. G1X 1Y7.

DOW, A. Ray, B.Sc.; company executive; b. Toronto, Ont., 13 Dec. 1923; s. James Ray and Madelaine Helen (Gardiner) D.; e. Univ. of Toronto Schs.; University of Toronto, B.Sc. (Engn.) 1949; PRESIDENT, CANADIAN OXYGEN LTD. since 1973; Pres. and Dir., Arcweld Products Ltd.; Dir., Edwards High Vacuum (Can.) Ltd.; Medishield Products Ltd.; Can. Welding Bureau; joined Union Carbide Canada Limited, Gas Division as Service Engineer 1949, Sales Engineer 1951 Assistant District Manager 1956, Manager Distributor Sales 1956-58; Asst. Sales Mgr., Air Reduction (Canada) Ltd. 1960; joined present Co. as Gen. Sales Mgr. 1960; Vice-Pres. Sales, 1963; Exec. Vice-Pres. 1969; served in R.C.A.C. 1942-45; rank Lt.; mem. Engn. Inst. Can.; Assn. Prof. Engrs. Ont.; Compressed Gas Assn.; Am. Mang. Assn.; Bd. Trade Metrop. Toronto; Conservative; Catholic; recreations: golf, tennis; Clubs: Mississauga Golf & Country; Ontario Racquet; Home: 1498 Bunsden Ave., Mississauga, Ont. L5H 2B4; Office: 355 Horner Ave., Toronto, Ont. M8W 1Z7

DOW, Jack M., C.M., B.A. Mus.M.; b. Dutton, Ont. 17 July 1912; s. David Henry Dow, D.D.S.; e. Dutton, Ont.; Univ. of W. Ont. B.A. 1936; m. Maudie Loverne d. Frederick G. Taylor, London, Ont. 19 Nov. 1938; children: Judith Anne, Byron Douglas, John Robert, Laura Loverne; Secondary Sch. Teacher, Ottawa Tech. High Sch. 1937-39; N. Vocational Sch. Toronto 1939-46; N. Toronto Coll. Inst. 1946-58; Asst. Dir. of Music, Toronto Bd. Educ. 1958-71, Dir. of Music 1971-76; Vocal and Instrumental Specialist, Ont. Dept. Educ.; Hon. Life mem. Toronto Secondary Music Teachers' Assn.; Protestant; recreations: walking, golf; Home: 238 Belsize Dr., Toronto, Ont. M4S 1M4.

DOWIE, Ian R., M.A.; industrialist (retired); b. London, Eng., 4 Oct. 1907; s. George and Annie (Gollan) D.; e. George Heriot's Sch., Edinburgh, Scot.; Edinburgh Univ., M.A. 1929; m. Frances Margaret, d. J. A. Campbell, Toronto, Ont., 12 May 1937; children: Mark Ian George Campbell, Frances Elizabeth Anne Campbell, John Rodney Campbell; formerly with Canadian Breweries Ltd., (Pres., Oct. 1958-65); Chrmn., Ont. Comte. on the Healing Arts 1967-70; Campaign Chrmn., Ont. Red Cross, 1942-46; Red Cross, Cleveland, Ohio, 1950-51; Trustee, Cleveland Orchestra, Cleveland Community Fund; Presbyterian; recreation: golf; Clubs: Toronto Golf; Toronto; Oakville Golf; Caledonian (London, Eng.); Home: 5 Chartwell Rd., Oakville, Ont. L6J 3Z3

DOWNES, Peter Marsden; executive; b. Malvern, Eng., 23 May 1917; s. Donald Litt and Eldwyth (Marsden) D.; e. Sedbergh, Yorkshire, Eng.; St. Bees Sch., Cumberland, Eng.; came to Canada, 1936; m. Frances Patricia Secord, d. Ernest W. Lamprey, Sept. 1939; two d.: Susan, Judith; PRES., PETER DOWNES ASSOC. LTD. since 1977; joined Cockfield, Brown & Co. Ltd. in Vancouver, 1938; apptd. Mgr. of Vancouver Office, 1940, Vice-Pres. 1953, el. a Dir. 1954; Vice Pres., Corp. Communications, MacMillan, Bloedel Ltd., 1965-77; Pres., Vancouver Art Gallery, 1959-61; Dir., Vancouver Festival Soc., 1955-60; Anglican; recreation: gardening; Clubs: Vancouver; Shaughnessy Golf; Home: 2430 S.W. Marine Dr., Vancouver, B.C. V6P 6C2; Office: 1490 W. 72 Ave., Vancouver, B.C. V6P 3C9

DOWNEY, James, B.A., B.Ed., M.A., Ph.D.; educator; b. Winterton, Nfld. 20 Apl. 1939; s. Ernest Fletcher and Mimy Ann (Andrews) D.; e. Winterton (Nfld.) Un. Ch. Sch. 1955; Mem. Univ. of Nfld. B.A. 1962, B.Ed. 1963, M.A. 1964; Univ. of London Ph.D. 1966; m. Laura Ann d. late William Parsons 25 July 1964; children: Sarah Elizabeth, Geoffrey James; PRES. UNIV. OF NEW BRUNSWICK 1980-; Vice-Pres., (Academic), Carleton Univ. 1978-80; Dean, Faculty of Arts, Carleton Univ. 1975-78; Pres., pro-tempore, Jan. to May 1979; Chrmn. Dept. Eng., Carleton Univ. 1972-75, author "The Eighteenth Century Pulpit" 1969; co-editor "Fearful Joy" 1974; articles and reviews various learned journs.; Extve. Assn. of Universities; United Church; recreations: tennis, theatre; Home: 58 Waterloo Row, Fredericton, N.B. E3B 1Y9

DOWNEY, Hon. James Erwin,M.L.A.; politician;MIN. OF AGRICULTURE, MAN.1977- ; el. M.L.A. for Arthur prov. g.e. 1977; P. Conservative; Office: 165 Legislative Bldg., Winnipeg, Man. R3C OV8.

DOWNIE, Mary Alice Dawe, B.A.; writer; b. Alton, Ill. 12 Feb. 1934; d. Robert Grant and Doris Mary (Rogers) Hunter; came to Canada 1940; e. Univ. of Toronto B.A. 1955; m. John Downie 27 June 1959; children: Christine Avery, Jocelyn Grant, Alexandra Duncan; Stenographer, Maclean-Hunter, 1955; Reporter, Marketing Magazine, 1956; Editorial Assistant, Candn Medical Assn. Journal, 1956-57; Librarian and Publicity Manager, Oxford Univ. Press. 1958-59; Freelance Reviewer, 1959-78; Book Review Editor, Kingston Whig Standard, 1973-78; author 'The

Wind Has Wings' 1968; 'Scared Sarah' 1974; 'The Magical Adventures of Pierre' 1974; 'Dragon on Parade' 1974; 'The Witch of the North' 1975; 'The King's Loon' 1979; 'The Last Ship' 1980; 'And Some Brought Flowers' 1980; 'Jenny Greenteeth' 1981; 'Acadien pour de bon' 1982; 'Un huart pour le Roi' 1982; co-author (with John Downie) 'Honor Bound' 1971; (with George Rawlyk) 'A Proper Acadian' 1981; (with Jillian H. Gilliland) 'Seeds and Weeds' 1981; author various articles, stories and profiles in anthologies, The Hornbook Magazine, Candn. Children's Annual, Something About the Author (1978), Twentieth Century Children's Writers (1978), In Review (1978), Canada Writers (1977), Writers' Union of Can. Directory of Members, The Children's Book Centre Author Kit; creator and initial editor 'The Northern Lights Series' and 'Kids Canada Series'; rec'd Canada Council Arts Awards 1971-72, 1981-82; various Ontario Arts Council Awards; recreations: reading, travel, plants, music; Address: 190 Union St., Kingston, Ont. K7L 2P6

DOWNING, Alfred Eric, B.A.Sc.; company executive; b. Mount Elgin, Ont., 28 Feb. 1923; s. Alfred Henry and Florence (Davis) D.; e. Woodstock (Ont.) Coll.; Univ. of Toronto, B.A.Sc. 1947; m. Elizabeth Anna, d. Robert H. Pick, 26 June 1948; children: Janet, Eric; PRESIDENT & DIR., HIRAM WALKER-GOODERHAM & WORTS LTD. 1978-; Dir., Corby Distilleries Ltd.; Hiram Walker Resources Ltd.; Liquid Carbonic (Canada); Westinghouse Canada; served with R.C.N. 2nd World War; Chief Chemist and Distiller, H. Corby Distillery Limited, 1947-50; present Co. 1950-62; Plant Manager, Destilerias Hiram Walker & Sons, Argentina, 1962-64; Asst. to Vice-Pres., Hiram Walker-Gooderham & Worts Ltd. 1964-67; mem., Chem. Inst. of Can.; Assn. of Prof. Engrs. Ont.; Anglican; recreations: sailing, curling; Clubs: Windsor Yacht; Windsor Curling; Windsor Chamber of Comm.; Home: 1464 Victoria Avenue, Windsor, Ont. N8X 1P3; Office: 2072 Riverside Drive East, Walkerville, Ont.

DOWNING, John Arthur, B.Sc.; company president; b. Vernon, B.C., 14 Feb. 1916; s. Arthur George and Elizabeth (Hodder) D.; e. Univ. of Br. Columbia; Montana Sch. of Mines B.Sc. (Geol. Engn.) 1948; m. Mary Elaine, d. V.F. Barclay, Vancouver, B.C., 21 Dec. 1949; children: David, Laura, Lisa; Vice-President and Director, Houston Oils Limited; Consulting Geol., Nauss & Downing; began as Geol. with Bear Oil Co. and Pacific Petroleums Ltd., 1948-50; Link & Nauss Ltd., 1950-53; Link, Downing & Cooke Ltd., 1953-56; Vice-Pres., Gen. Mgr. and Dir., Cree Oil of Canada (1958) Ltd., and V. Pres., North Star Oil Ltd., 1956-61; Vice-Pres., Petroleum Operations and Dir., Teck Corp. Ltd., 1961-65; President, Ensign Oils Ltd. 1965; served in 2nd World War with R.C.A.F., 1941; Canadian Army, 1941-45, in England, Mediterranean and North West Europe areas; mem., Alta. Soc. Petroleum Geols.; Am. Soc. Petroleum Geols.; Candn. Inst. Mining & Metall.; Assn. Prof. Engrs. B.C., and Alta.; Geol. Assn. Can.; recreations: skiing, fishing; Clubs: Calgary Petroleum; Calgary Golf & Country; Home: 925 Royal Ave., Calgary, Alta. T2T 0L6; Office: 1050 Elveden House, Calgary, Alta.

DOWNING, Robert James,R.C.A.; sculptor; b. Hamilton, Oct. 1 Aug. 1935; s. Albert James and Dora Florence (Figgins) D.; e. grade sch. (self taught); m. Miriana d. Ratko Kaludjerovic, Toronto, Ont. 27 Sept. 1960; children: Sara Lynn, Michael John (by previous marriage); served with RCN as Photographer 1952-57 (awarded hon. mention for photog.); Police Constable City of Hamilton, co-founder Can.'s first police choir 1957-60; began sculpting 1960; apprenticeship with Ted Bieler, Prof. of Sculpture, Univ. of Toronto 1965 and completed largest precast concrete sculpture project ever attempted; Lectr. in Sculpture Univ. of Toronto 1967-69, completed series of 108 sculptures derived from the Cube; Part-time Lectr. in Art & Arch. Fanshawe Coll. of Art & Technol. London, Ont. 1969-71 and in Sculpture Processes & Systems

Ont. Coll. of Art 1971-72; Dir. of Art, Appleby Coll. Oakville, Ont. 1972; Visiting Lectr. in Sculpture, Banff Sch. of Fine Art and cert. as TIG Welder Can. Welding Sch. 1973-74; Part-time Lectr. on 3-D form, Cal. State Univ. Long Beach and completed series of sculptures exploring relationships between Platonic Solids and Fibonacci Ratio 1974-77; currently teaching Industrial Design, O.C.A.; solo exhns. incl. Dunkelman Gallery Toronto 1968; Galerie Agnes Lefort Montreal 1968; Whitechapel Art Gallery London, Eng. 1969; York Univ. Art Gallery Toronto 1970; Gallery House Sol Georgetown, Ont. 1971; Robert McLaughlin Gallery Oshawa 1972; Rodman Hall St. Catharines, Pub. Lib. & Art Museum London, Ont., Rothmans Art Gallery Stratford, Ont. Univ. of Guelph, Centennial Gallery & Lib. Oakville, 1972; Univ. of Alta. 1973; Lib. & Cultural Resources centre Huntington Beach, Cal. 1978; College Park, Toronto 1981; rep. in numerous group exhns.; rep. in various pub. and corporate colls.; rec'd Ont. Arts Council Awards 1967, 1977; Can. Council Awards 1967-71; Arts Council of Gt. Brit. Edinburgh Festival Award 1976, founded Ar Collection Policy Texaco Canada Inc. 1980; specialist in geometric sculpture; Founding mem. (1967) Candn. Artists Reps.; mem. Ont. Soc. Artists (Extve. Council); Sculpture Soc. Can.; Anglican; Address: 30 Gloucester St., Suite 1202, Toronto, Ont. M4Y 1L5.

DOWNS, Allan Rae, M.D., F.R.C.S.(C), F.A.C.S.; surgeon; educator; b. Preeceville, Sask. 14 Oct. 1930; s. Walter Harold and Violet Ellen (White) D.; e. Preeceville (Sask.) High Sch.; Univ. of Man. 1947-49; Man. Med. Coll. M.D. 1954; m. Janet P. Curran; children: Allan Craig, Allyson Merren; PROF. FACULTY OF MED. UNIV. OF MAN.; Prof. and Head, Dept. of Surg., Faculty of Med., Univ. of Man.; Surg.-in-Chief, Health Sciences Centre; mem., Society of Vascular Surg.; author or co-author various publs. and presentations; Past Pres. Candn. Soc. Vascular Surg.; mem. Candn. and Man. Med. Assns.; Candn. Cardiovascular Soc.; Candn. Assn. Clin. Surgs.; Internat. Cardiovascular Soc.; Soc. of Vascular Surgery; Central Surg. Assoc.; Candn. Univ. Surg. Chrmn. and other med. assns.; P. Conservative; Protestant; recreations: golf, tennis, hockey; Club: Niakwa Country Club; Home: 312 Hosmer Blvd., Winnipeg, Man. R3P OH6; Office: 700 William Ave., Winnipeg, Man. R3E OZ3.

DOWNS, Barry Vance,B.Arch., R.C.A., F.R.A.I.C.; architect; b. Vancouver, B.C. 19 June 1930; s. William Arthur and Milada Marie (Ruziska) D.; e. Queen Mary Primary Sch.; Lord Byng High Sch. 1947; Univ. of B.C. 1948-49; Univ. of Wash. B.Arch. 1954; m. Mary Hunter d. late Allan Stewart 24 Feb. 1955; children: William Stewart, Elizabeth Mary; PARTNER, DOWNS/ARCHAMBAULT ARCHITECTS 1969- ; Design Arch. Thompson, Berwick, Pratt Archs. 1956-63; private arch. practice 1963; Visiting Lectr. Univ. of B.C. 1960-63; recipient Massey Medal and numerous awards incl. Nat. Housing Design Awards, Candn. Arch. Yearbook Awards, RAIC Awards of Merit, Heritage Can. Regional Award; author "Sacred Places, British Columbia's Early Churches" 1980; various journ. articles; work cited numerous publs.; mem. Vancouver Civic Design Panel 1967-68; Hist. Adv. Bd. 1971-73; Heritage Adv. Comte. 1974-76; Candn. Housing Design Council Can. W. Region 1969-73; mem. Arch. Inst. B.C.; Phi Delta Theta; United Church; recreations: tennis, boating; Clubs: Vancouver Central Lions; Vancouver Lawn Tennis; Home: 6664 Marine Dr., West Vancouver, B.C. V7W 2S9; Office: 1272 Richards St., Vancouver, B.C. V6B 3G2.

DOWSETT, Robert Chipman, O St J, B.A., F.S.A., F.C.I.A.; insurance executive; b. Toronto, Ont. 27 June 1929; s. Reginald Ernest and Jean Shillington (Rose) D.; e. Univ. of Toronto Schs.; Univ. of Toronto, B.A. (Hon. Math. & Physics) 1950; m. Lois Eileen, d. Robert A. McHardy 28 June 1950; children: David Robert, Mary Isa-

bel, Carol Elizabeth; PRESIDENT AND DIRECTOR, CROWN LIFE INSURANCE CO. since 1971; Dir., Canada Permanent Companies; Datacrown Inc.; Dofasco Inc.; The Donwood Inst.; Extendicare Ltd.; Trustee, The McMichael Candn. Collection; joined Crown Life 1950; promoted successively to Asst. Actuary 1955, Assoc. Actuary 1959, Actuary 1964, Vice-Pres. and Actuary 1969, Extve. Vice-Pres. 1970; Fellow, Soc. of Actuaries 1954 (Secy. 1969-71]; mem. Bd. of Govs. [1971-74; 1975-78; mem. Canadian Association of Actuaries since 1953 (Secy. 1960) and its successor (1964) Candn. Inst. of Actuaries (Pres. 1973-74); el. Pres., The Candn. Life Ins. Assn. 1974-75; Chrm. Bd. of Dir., Council for Can. Unity, 1979-81; United Church; recreations: boating, water sports; Home: 15 Caravan Dr., Don Mills, Ont. M3B 1M9; Office: 120 Bloor St. E., Toronto, Ont. M4W 1B8

DOYLE, Donald, B.A.; Canadian public servant; b. Montreal, Que. 7 Oct. 1943; e. Univ. Ste-Anne, Church Point, N.S.; Univ. Laval B.A.; ASST. CHIEF OF STAFF, OFFICE OF THE LEADER OF THE OPPOSITION 1981; Journalist, La Presse Canadienne, Qué. 1965-66; Parlty. Corr., Tribune de La Presse, Qué. 1966-68; Ed. Nat. and Pol. News, Le Soleil, Qué. 1968; Parlty. Corr. for Le Soleil, Ottawa 1968-75, Dir. of Travel Sec., Qué. 1975-76; Press Secy. Office of Leader of Opposition 1976-79; Press Secy., Assistant Chief of Staff Prime Min.'s Office 1979-80; mem. Nat. Press Club; Office: House of Commons, South Block, Ottawa, Ont. K1A 0A6.

DOYLE, Frank Joseph; industrialist; b. Ottawa, Ont., 10 Mar. 1915; s. late Michael Joseph and late Helen (Sagadore) D.; m. Catherine Margaret, d. late Reuben I. and late Agnes (Convey) Cox, Toronto, Ont., 21 June 1941; children: Catherine Elizabeth, James Joseph; past Pres. and Dir., PPG Industries Can. Ltd.; Dir. Crouse Hinds Co. of Can.; Key Banks Inc. (Albany N.Y.); St. Joseph's Health Center, Toronto; Jr. Achievement Can.; Past Pres., Bd. Trade Metrop. Toronto; mem., Mfrs.' Council, Housing and Urban Devel. Assn. Can. (Past Chrmn.); Assn. Comte.-Order of St. John; Kts. of Columbus; Kts. of Malta; Clubs: Granite, Lambton Golf & Country; Home: 30 Kingsway Cres., Toronto, Ont. M8X 2R3;

DOYLE, Richard J.; newspaper editor; b. Toronto, Ont., 10 March 1923; s. James A. and Lillian (Hilts) D.; hon. LL.D., St. Francis Xavier Univ. 1981; m. Florence, d. late Francis Chanda, Jan. 1953; children: Kathleen Judith, Sean Gibson; Editor-in-Chief, "Globe & Mail", served in 2nd World War with R.C.A.F.; retired 1945 with rank of Flying Offr.; Publications: "The Royal Story", 1952; United Church; Home: 36 Long Crescent, Toronto, Ont. M4E 1N6; Office: 444 Front St. West, Toronto, Ont. M5V 2S9

DOYLE, Mt. Rev. Wilfred Emmett, B.A., J.C.D. (R.C.); bishop; b. Calgary, Alberta, 18 Feb. 1913; s. John J. and Mary Anne (O'Neill) D.; e. Sacred Heart Sch., St. Joseph's High Sch., and St. Joseph's Semy., Edmonton, Alta.; Univ. of Alberta, B.A. 1935; Univ. of Ottawa, J.C.D. 1949; BISHOP OF NELSON, since 1958; Asst. at St. Joseph's Cath., Edmonton, Alta., 1938-43, Asst. Chancellor, Archdiocese of Edmonton, 1938-43, and Chancellor, 1943-46 and 1949-58; Chancellor, Notre Dame Univ., Nelson, B.C. 1963-68 and Chrmn. of Bd. of Govs. 1963-74; Address: 813 Ward St., Nelson, B.C. V1L 1T4

DOZOIS, Paul, LL.D. (Sherbrooke); né 23 mai 1908; m. Pauline Crevier, 1942; enfants: Monique, Pierre, Martine; CONSEILLER, GÉRARD PARIZEAU LTÉ. 1978-; élu dép. Union Nat., comté St-Jacques 1956, 1960, 1962, 1966; appelé en 1956 au Conseil Exéc. de la P. de Q. comme tit. des Affaires Mun.; conserva les mêmes fonctions dans les cabinets des Hon. P. Sauvé et A. Barrette; Min. des Finances (1965-66), Min. des Affaires Mun. (1966-67), Min. des Inst. Financières, Compagnies et Coopératives (1968-69) dans le cabinet D. Johnson; Commre., Hydro-Que.

1969-78; adm., Soc. d'énergie de la baie James, 1971-78; Churchill Falls Corp. Ltd.; Prés. de la campagne, Féd. des Oeuvres de Charité Can.-Fr. 1950, prés. du Conseil d'Admin., 1955-57; prés. Chambre de Commerce des Jeunes, Montréal, 1940, gouv. hon. à vie; délégué au Conseil Mun. de Montréal: 1942-44 pour la C. de C.des Jeunes, 1946-56 pour la C. de C. de Montréal; membre du Comité Exéc. de Montréal 1947-56; mem. Chambre de Commerce de Montréal, Montreal Board of Trade, Club St-Denis; gouv. à vie, Hôp. Notre-Dame, Montréal. Bureau: 410, rue St. Nicholas, Montréal, Que. H2Y 2R1

DRABBLE, Bernard J., B.A.; Canadian civil servant; b. Eng. 1925; e. schs. Eng.; McGill Univ. B.A. ASSOC. DEPY. MIN. OF FINANCE, CAN. 1981- ; joined Bank of Canada 1947-81 holding various positions incl. Depy. Gov. 1974; Extve. Dir. for Can., Ireland and others International Monetary Fund, Washington, D.C. 1974-81 on leave of absence from Bank of Canada); Home: 2404 - 400 Stewart St., Ottawa, Ont. K1N 6L2; Office: 160 Elgin St., Ottawa, Ont. K1A 0G5.

DRABINSKY, Garth Howard,LL.B.; motion picture producer; lawyer; b. Toronto, Ont. 27 Oct. 1948; s. Philip D.; e. N. Toronto Coll. Inst.; Univ. of Toronto LL.B. 1973; m. Pearl, d. Harry Kaplan 22 June 1971; children: Alica Monica, Marc Lorne; PARTNER, ROBERTS & DRABINSKY 1978- ; Pres. and Dir. Tiberius Film; Cineplex Corp.; Pan-Canadian Film Distributors Inc.; Dir. CFMT-TV Toronto; Chrmn. On Stage '81: Toronto Theatre Festival; Vice Chrmn. Bd. Dirs. Acad. Candn. Cinema; called to Bar of Ont. 1975; Publisher "Canadian Film Digest" 1972-74 and Founding Pres. and Publisher "Impact", The Canadian Cinema Magazine"; Producer "Flick Flack" TV Series Global 1973-74; law practice Thomson, Rogers 1975-78; Producer motion picture "The Disappearance" 1977, "The Silent Partner" (Candn. Film Award Best Picture 1978) 1977, "The Changeling" (Candn. Film Award Best Picture 1980) 1979, "Tribute" (11 nominations incl. Best Picture 1981 Candn. Film Awards, Jack Lemmon Acad. Award nomination Best Actor) 1980, "The Amateur" 1981; Producer "Travesties" St. Lawrence Centre Toronto 1977; "By Strouse" musical Theatre-in-the-Dell Toronto 1978; guest speaker; author "Motion Pictures and the Arts in Canada-The Business and the Law" 1976; mem. Candn. Bar Assn.; Co. York Law Assn.; Jewish; recreations: sailing, squash, motion pictures, theatre, music, collector Candn. art; Club: Cambridge; Office: (P.O. Box 82) Suite 6965, First Canadian Pl., Toronto, Ont. M5X 1B1.

DRAESEKE, Gordon Cecil Ladner, B.A., F.C.I.S.; forestry executive; b. Vancouver, B.C., 24 June 1913; s. Gordon Cecil and Alice Parr (Ladner) D.; e. Shawnigan Lake (B.C.) Sch.; Univ. of B.C., B.A. 1936; Dalhousie Law Sch., 1939; m. 1stly Mildred Jeffrey Gow; 2ndly Dorothy Johnson, d. John Roy, Greenock, Scot., 18 Dec. 1957; children: Douglas, Kathie, Janice; stepsons: Bruce Allan, John Allan; retired as Pres. and Chief Extve. Offr., Council of Forest Industries of B.C. 1976; read law with Ladner Carmichael & Downs; called to Bar of B.C. 1939; Corporate Secy. and Legal Offr., Alaska Pine Co. (subsequently Alaska Pine & Cellulose Ltd. (1951) and Rayonier Canada Ltd. (1958), 1945; assumed same positions with Western Forest Industries Ltd., 1947; apptd. Vice Pres. Adm. and Secy., Rayonier Canada Ltd., 1958; Dir. 1960; Extve. Comte. 1967; Vice Pres., Dir. and mem. of Extve. Comte., Seaboard Lumber Sales Co. and Seaboard Shipping Co., 1963-68; Secy. and Dir., Canadian Puget Sound Lumber & Timber Co., 1946-68; served with RCN 1941-45; discharged as Lieut.-Commdr.; Dir., Candn. Forestry Assn.; Commr., Metric Comn.; Past mem., Vancouver Port Authority; Past Chrmn. Bd. of Trustees, Vancouver Gen. Hosp.; Past Pres., Med. Services Assn. B.C. (mem. Adv. Comte.); mem., Law Soc. B.C.; Candn. Bar Assn.; Fellows Foundation Legal Research in Can.; B.C. Research Council; Internat. Platform Assn.; Chrmn., Vancouver

Pub. Library 1966-70; Freeman, Dist. of Port Alice; Anglican; recreations: yachting, gardening, travel; Clubs: Vancouver; Union; Vancouver Lawn & Tennis; Home: Ste. 342, 658 Leg in Boot Square, Vancouver, B.C. V5Z 4B3

DRAINIE, Bronwyn Deborah Ann, M.A.; radio broadcaster; b. Toronto, Ont. 8 June 1945; d. John Robert Roy and Claire Paula (Wodlinger) D.; e. Whitney and Rosedale Pub. Schs., Jarvis Coll. Inst. Toronto; Univ. of Toronto B.A. 1967, M.A. 1969; Researcher and Story Ed., CJOH TV Ottawa 1969-70; Story Producer "Weekday" CBLT Toronto 1970-71; Student Counsellor, Scarborough Coll. Univ. of Toronto 1971-73; Crete, Greece writing and studying Greek 1973-74; B.B.C. and C.B.C. Radio London, Eng. 1974-75; C.B.C. Announcer Toronto "World at 6", "World at 8", "Identities", "Offstage Voices" 1975-76; Host of C.B.C. Radio "Sunday Morning" 1976-79; Host of C.B.C. Stereo "Celebration"; several film narrations Nat. Film Bd. 1978-79; recreations: reading, piano, travel, tennis; Home: 97 Pears Ave., Toronto, Ont. M5R 1S9; Office: (P.O. Box 500 Stn. A) Toronto, Ont. M5W 1E6.

DRAKE, Bryant Stillman Jr., A.B., LL.D.; educator; b. Berkeley, Ca. 24 Dec. 1910; s. Bryant Stillman and Flora (Frickstad) D.; came to Can. 1967; e. Univ. of Ca. Berkeley A.B. 1932; M. Florence Selvin d. late Sol Selvin 1 Apr. 1967; children: Mark Ernest, Daniel Lee; PROFESSOR EMERITUS, UNIV. OF TORONTO, 1979- ; Municipal Finance 1934; U.S. Govt. 1941; Municip. Bond Consultant 1958; Prof. 1967; author: "Discoveries & Opinions of Galileo" 1957; "Galileo Studies" 1970; "Galileo at Work" 1978; "Galileo" 1980; "Cause, Experiment & Science" 1981; translations of Galileo's books; articles on scientific revolution; mem., Internat. Acad. of History of Science (Paris); Amer. Acad. of Arts & Sci.; Fellowships, John Simm Gugenheim Mem. Foundation 1971-72, 1976-77; Protestant; recreation: music; Home: 219 Glen Rd., Toronto, Ont. M4W 2X2; Office: Toronto, Ont. M5S 1A6

DRAKE, Sir Eric (Arthur Eric Courtney), C.B.E., M.A., D.Sc., F.C.A.; company director; b. Rochester, Kent, Eng. 29 Nov. 1910; s. Dr. Arthur William Courtney and Ethel (Davidson) D.; e. Shrewsbury (Eng.) Sch. 1927; Pembroke Coll. Cambridge Univ. B.A. 1931, M.A. 1945; Hon. D.Sc. Cranfield Inst. 1972; m. Margaret Elizabeth d. Ralph Goodbarne Wilson 14 Sept. 1950; children: John Arthur Courtney, William Eric, Anna Freer, Felicity Low; Dir. Kleinwort Benson & Lonsdale Ltd.; Hon. Petroleum Adv. to Brit. Army 1971-; one of H.M. Lieuts. for the City of London; British Businessman of the Year Award 1971; Cadman Memorial Medal of Inst. of Petroleum, 1976; Gen. Mgr. British Petroleum Co. Ltd. Iran and Iraq 1950-51, Mang. Dir. 1958-75, Depy. Chrmn. 1962-69, Chrmn. 1969-75; awarded Legion of Honour France; Order of Homayun (Iran); Commdr. Order of Leopold (Belgium); Commdr. Order of the Crown (Belgium); Kt. Grand Cross Order of Merit (Italy); Hon. Fellow Pembroke Coll. Cambridge Univ.; Gov. Shrewsbury Sch.; Hon. Fellow Univ. Manchester Inst. of Science & Technol. 1974; Life Gov. City of London Univ.; Pres. Chamber Shipping UK 1964 (Vice Pres. 1963); Hon. Elder Brother Trinity House; Hon. mem. Hon. Co. of Master Mariners; recreations: sailing, shooting; Clubs: Royal Yacht Squadron (Cowes); Leander (Henley on Thames); Home: The Old Rectory, Cheriton, Alresford, Hampshire, Eng. SO24 OPZ; Office: Britannic House, Moor Lane, London EC2Y 9BU, Eng.

DRANCE, Stephen Michael, M.C., F.R.C.S.; ophthalmic surgeon; b. Bielsko, Poland, 22 May 1925; s. George Henry and Ida (Berger) C.; e. Univ. of Edinburgh, M.B. Ch.B. 1948, M.D. (Clin. Med.) 1949; Coll. of Surgs. of Eng., Dipl. of Ophthal. 1953; m. Betty Joan, d. Fred Palmer, Stamford, Eng., Jan. 1952; children: Jonathan Stephen, Michael George, Elisabeth Joan; PROF. & HEAD OF OPHTHAL., UNIV. OF BRIT. COLUMBIA and Co-ordinator of Research Ophthal.; mem., Med. Research Council; Research Asst. Ophthal., Oxford Univ., 1955-57; Asst. Prof. and Assoc. Prof., Univ. of Sask., 1957-63; joined present Univ. as Assoc. Prof., 1963; served with RAF Med. Service, rank Sqdn. Leader; former Ed., "Canadian Journal of Ophthalmology"; past Council mem., Candn. Ophthal. Soc. (past Pres.); rec'd McKenzie Medal, Glasgow Univ. 1972; Doyne Medal, Oxford Ophthal. Cong. 1975; Spaeth Medal, Philadelphia 1976; Richardson Cross Medal, S.W. England Soc. Opthalmology 1980; Liberal; recreations: swimming, skating, tennis, philately, music, cartography; Home: 1561 Wesbrook Cr., Vancouver, B.C. V6T 1V9

DRAPEAU, Jean, C.C., (1967), C.R., B.A., L.Sc.Soc. Econ. Pol., LL.D.; né Montréal, Qué., 18 fév. 1916; é. Coll. Jean-de-Brébeuf; Le Plateau; Univ. de Montréal, L. Sc. Soc. Econ. Po., 1937; B.A., 1938; LL.B. 1941; D.Hon., Univ. de Moncton, 1956; Univ. de Montréal, 1964; Univ McGill, 1965; Univ Loyola, Nouvelle-Orléans, 1966; Univ. Sir G. Williams et Laval, 1967; marié, 3 enfants; MAIRE DE MONTRÉAL depuis 1960; appelé au Barreau de Montréal, 1943; nommé C.R., 1961; maire de Montréal 1954-57; fondateur du Parti civique de Montréal, 1960; réélu maire de Montréal, 1960, 1962, 1966, 1970, 1974, 1978; oeuvres: Place des Arts, le Métro, Expo '67; C'est également grâce à son esprit de persévérance et de travail que la Ville de Montréal a été choisie comme lieu des Jeux Olympiques d'été de 1976; mem.: Am. Bar Assn. (hon.); autres assoc. nat. et internat.; trophée des Min. du Comm. et Indust. des dix prov. du Can. au can. ayant le plus contribué au dévelop. indust. du Can., 1965; Médaille d'Or, Inst. Royal d'Architect. du Can., 1967; Compagnon de l'Ordre du Can., 1967; représ. du Can. au Bur. Internat. des Expos. à Paris, 1967; Adresse: Hôtel de Ville, Montréal, Que.

DRAY, William Herbert, M.A., D. Phil., F.R.S.C.; educator; b. Montréal, Qué. 23 June 1921; s. William John and Florence Edith (Jones) D.; e. Rosedale Pub. Sch. and West Hill High Sch. Montréal 1938; Univ. of Toronto B.A. 1949; Oxford Univ. B.A. 1951, M.A. 1955, D. Phil. 1956; m. Doris Kathleen d. Col. Gilbert Best, Toronto, Ont. 23 Sept. 1943; children: Christopher Reid, Jane Elizabeth; PROF. OF PHILOS. UNIV. OF OTTAWA; Lect., Univ. of Toronto 1953-55; Asst. Prof. 1956-61; Assoc. Prof. 1961-63; Prof. 1963-68; Prof., Trent Univ. 1968-76 and Chmn. of Dept., 1968-73; served with RCAF 1941-46, Air Navig. Can. W. Indies UK S.E. Asia, RCAF (R) 1956-66, Wing Commdr.; author "Laws and Explanation in History" 1957; "Philosophy of History" 1964; "Perspectives on History" 1980; Ed. "Philosophical Analysis and History" 1966; "Substance and Form in History" 1981; numerous articles philos. hist., action and social sciences; mem. Aristotelian Soc.; Candn. Philos. Assn.; Candn. Hist. Assn.; Soc. de philosophie du Que.; Am. Philos. Assn.; ACLS Fellow (1960-61); Killam Fellow (1980-81); Home: 166 Rodney Cres., Ottawa, Ont. K1H 5J9; Office: Ottawa, Ont. K1N 6N5.

DREA, Hon. James Francis, M.P.P., B.A., L.H.D.; politician; b. St. Catharines, Ont. 7 July 1933; s. John Thompson and Joan Lavene (McCarthy) D.; e. Canisius Coll. Buffalo; m. Jeanne Elizabeth d. William Campbell, New Toronto, Ont. 22 Oct. 1955; children: Catherine Elizabeth, Denise Margaret, Kevin John; MIN. OF COMMUNITY & SOCIAL SERVICES, ONT.1981- ; journalist; rec'd Heywood Broun Award for Crusading Journalism 1961; mem. Nat. Comte. Cath. Social Life Conf. 1963-65; Internat. Rep. Un. Steelworkers Am. 1963-65; Vice Pres. and Dir. Candn. Register 1967-69; Vice Chrmn. Bd. of Review Ont. Dept. Social & Family Services 1969-72; Pres. Candn. Soc. Profl. Journalists 1970-72; Founding Dir. Credit Counselling Service Toronto; Dir. Candn. Scene; el. M.P.P. for Scarborough Centre prov. g.e. 1971, re-el. since; Parlty. Asst. to Min. of Consumer & Comm. Relations 1974; Min. of Correctional Services 1977; Min. of

Consumer & Comm. Relations 1978; P. Conservative; R. Catholic; Office: Queen's Park, Toronto, Ont. M7A 1A1

DREIMANIS, Aleksis, D.Sc., F.R.S.C.; university professor; geologist consultant; b. Valmiera, Latvia, 13 Aug. 1914; s. Peteris and Marta Eleonora (Leitis) D.; e. Latvian Univ., Mag. rer nat. 1938, habilitation 1942; Univ. of Waterloo, D.Sc. 1969; Univ. of W. Ont., D.Sc. 1980; m. Anita, d. late Rudolfs Kana, 18 Apl. 1942; children: Mara Love, M.D., Aija Downing, M.A.; Assist.-Lectr.-Privatdocent, Inst. of Geol., Univ. of Latvia, Riga, 1937-44; Consultant, Inst. of Mineral Resources of Latvia, 1942-44; Mil. Geol., Latvian Legion, 1944-45; Assoc. Prof. Baltic Univ., Hamburg and Pinneberg, 1946-48; Lectr. to Prof., Dept. of Geol., Univ. of W. Ont., 1948-80; Prof. Emeritus 1980-; Consultant on Pleistocene Geol. and Ground Water for various Candn. and U.S. Govt. agencies and private co.'s; Chrmn., Council of Latvian Nat. Fed. in Can., 1953-71; mem. Candn. Nat. Adv. Comte. on Research in Geol. Sciences and Chrmn. of its sub-comte. on Quaternary Geol., 1967-72; Candn. Del. to Internat. Geol. Cong. 1960 and to Internat. Assn. Quaternary Research 1965 and 1969, 73, 77; Assoc. Ed., Geosciences Canada 1976-78; served with Latvian Army 1939-40 and Latvian Legion 1944-45; rank 2nd Lt.; rec'd Kr. Barons' Prize 1935; Latvian Univ. Gold Medal 1936; Centennial Medal 1967; Silver Jubilee Medal, 1977; Hon. Award, Latvian Cultural Foundation 1977; Logan Medal 1978; Teaching Award of Ont. Confed. of Univ. Fac. Assoc. 1978; co-author, "Latvijas minerali un iezi" 1942; other writings incl. more than 150 scient. publs. mainly in Pleistocene and glacial geol.; mem. London Latvian Soc. (Pres. since 1948); fraternity "Lidums" (Pres. 1935-36); Royal Soc. of Can.; Geol. Assn. Can.; Geol. Soc. Am.; Soc. Econ. Paleontol. & Mineralog.; Internat. Assn. Gt. Lakes Research; Swed. Geol. Soc.; Germ. Quaternary Union; Baltic Research Inst.; Assn. for Advanc. of Baltic Studies; Latvian Am. Assn. of Univ. Profs.; Ont. Assn. of Geomorphs.; Internat. Glaciological Soc.; Quaternary Res. Assn.; Geol. Soc. in Stockholm; Candn. Quaternary Assn.; Swiss Geomorph. Soc.; Pres. of INQUA (Internat. Union for Quaternary Research) Comm. on Genesis and Lithology of Quaternary Deposits, 1973 to present; Councilor of AMQUA (Am. Quatenary Assn.) 1974-78, Pres.-elect 1978-80, Pres. 1980-82; leader, Can. Work Group, IGCP Project 24, 1975-82; recreation: photography; travel; Home: 287 Neville Dr., London, Ont. N6G 1C2

DREMAN, I.J.; investment broker; b. Winnipeg, Manitoba, 3 June 1910; s. Israel Jacob and Lea Yetta (Stark) D.; e. St. John's Tech. Sch.: m. Rae, d. Michael Trojan, 17 Feb. 1935; children: David Nasaniel, Solomon Bernard, Sherrill Elaine; PRESIDENT, DREMAN & CO. LTD. (Estbd. 1919); Pres., Hartford Investments Ltd. since 1963; Gov., Winnipeg Grain Exchange; joined Campbell Grain Co. Ltd., Winnipeg, Man. in July 1928 becoming Mgr. in 1929; joined North West Commission Co. Ltd. in 1932; became a member of Winnipeg Grain Exchange in 1937 and apptd. Pres. of North West Commission Co. Ltd. in 1951 (engaged entirely in grain business); el. an Assoc. mem. of Winnipeg Stock Exchange in 1957 and a full mem. in 1960; mem. of Winnipeg Clearing House Assn. (1951); former Pres. of Winnipeg Commodity Futures Brokers Assn. (for 18 yrs.); formerly a mem. Candn. Home Guard; Chairman of B'Nai B'rith Fresh Air Camp ($150,000) Campaign, Winnipeg; assisted in campaigns of Winnipeg Crippled Children's Soc. and Univ. of Manitoba Bldg. Fund; Dir., Winnipeg Talmud Torah; Chess Fed. of Can.; Mammonides Coll.; Shaarey Zedek Sch.; Candn. Foundation; mem., Winnipeg Grain & Produce Clearing Assn. Ltd.; Hebrew; recreations: chess, golf, travelling; Club: Glendale Country; Home: 600 Queenston St., Winnipeg, Man. R3N 0X5; Office: 6th Floor, 238 Portage Ave., Winnipeg, Man. R3C 0B1

DRENTERS, Josef Gertrudis, R.C.A.; artist; historian; b. Poppel, Prov. Antwerpen, Belgium 25 Nov. 1929; s. Joseph Antonius and Hendrika Maria (Swinkels) D.; e. schs. Belgium. Holland and Can.; classical studies Flanders monastary; came to Can. 1951; numerous sculptures diverse media, drawings and paintings in many colls. and Art Galleries Can., USA and Europe; maj. works Expo 67 incl. "Homage to the Pioneers of Canada" Ont. Pavilion and "Giant Toy" La Ronde; compiled large coll. hist. documents incl. data of Rockwood Acad. Ont. (early Candn. sch. founded by Yorks. Quaker William Wetheral 1850), engaged in extensive restoration Acad.'s structure; assoc. with Gustafsson Art Gallery Toronto; Address: Old Academy, Main St. S., Rockwood, Ont. N0B 2K0.

DRESEL, Peter E., B.Sc., Ph.D.; educator; b. Ulm, Germany 27 Feb. 1925; s. late Kurt M. and late Mathilde (Siegel) D.; e. Antioch Coll. Yellow Springs, Ohio B. Sc. 1948; Univ. of Rochester Ph.D. 1952; m. Anita d. late James T. Pitts 24 June 1947; D. children: K. Michael, Patricia Sparks, P. Evan; CARNEGIE AND ROCKEFELLER PROF. AND HEAD OF PHARMACOL. DALHOUSIE UNIV. since 1976; Instr. in Pharmacol. Univ. of Cincinnati 1952; Emory Univ. 1953-54; Sr. Research Pharmacol. Wm. S. Merrell Co. Cincinnati 1954-56; Asst. Prof. to Full Prof. Univ. of Man. 1956-76; Visiting Scient. in Physiol. Univ. Goteborg, Sweden 1963-64 and Univ. Coll. London 1970-71; served with U.S. Army 1943-45, rec'd Bronze Star with Oak Leaf Cluster, Purple Heart with Oak Leaf Cluster, Presidential Unit Citation; author over 55 scient. papers on pharmacol. of cardiac drugs; mem. Pharmacol. Soc. Can. (Secy. 1969-72, Vice Pres. 1974-75, Pres. 1975-77); Am. Soc. Pharmacol. & Exper. Therapeutics; Am. Assn. Advanc. Science; Cardiac Muscle Soc.; Sigma Xi; Unitarian; recreations: fishing, camping, travel; Home: 803 - 1074 Wellington St., Halifax, N.S. B3H 2Z8; Office: Halifax, N.S. B3H 4H7.

DRINKWATER, William Stanley, B.J.; retired Canadian civil servant; b. Toronto, Ont., 23 May 1921; s. William and Ellen (Duckworth) D.; e. Scarborough Coll. Inst., Ont.; Carleton Univ., B.J. 1949; m. June Mary, d. late Kenneth Goudie, 22 May 1948; children: David, Dulce; Editor, "Labour Gazette", Dept. of Labour, 1958-64; Chief, "Publications Div.", Dept. of Labour, 1964-78; with Ottawa "Citizen", 1940-41 and 1946-49; Editor, "Teamwork in Industry" (Dept. of Labour), 1950-51; Asst. Editor, "Labour Gazette", 1951-58; served in R.C.A.S.C., 1941-46 and 1949-50; mem., Prof. Inst. of Public Service of Can. (Editor of "Professional Public Service" 1958-61); Chrmn., Publicity Comte. Ottawa and Ottawa Valley Br., Candn. Red Cross Soc., 1955-59; mem., Corporate Communicators Can.; Information Services Inst.; Lectr., Carleton Univ.; Anglican; Home: 1517 Caverley St., Ottawa, Ont. K1G 0X9

DRISCOLL, Hon. Frederick Leo, M.L.A., M.A.; b. Mt. Herbert, P.E.I. 18 Aug. 1932; s. Joseph J. and Isabelle Suzanna (Coady) D.; e. St. Dunstan's Univ.; Univ. of N.B.; Univ. of Ottawa; m. Bernadette Mary d. William McManus, Charlottetown, P.E.I. 26 Oct. 1957; children: James William, Jennifer Elizabeth; MIN. OF EDUCATION, P.E.I.1979- ; Min. of Health 1979-80; Prof. of Candn. Hist.; served with Candn. Army Militia 1955-65, rank Lt.; el. M.L.A. for 3rd Queens prov. g.e. 1978, re-el. 1979; P. Conservative; R. Catholic; Clubs: United Services Officers"; Beleveedere Golf & Winter; Office: (P.O. Box 2000) Shaw Bldg., Charlottetown, P.E.I. C1A 7N8.

DRISCOLL, John F., B.Sc.; executive; b. Boston, Mass. 1 April 1942; e. Boston Coll. B.Sc. 1964; New York Inst. of Finance 1967; Candn. Inst. of Mang. P.Mgr. 1976; m. Merrilyn MacDonald 4 June 1968; children: Sean and Blair; VICE PRES. CORPORATE AFFAIRS & EXTVE. ASST. TO PRES., ACKLANDS LTD.; joined Technical Tape Corp. (U.S. Corp.) 1964-67; assoc. with invest. banking firms Paine Webber Jackson & Curtis, Thomson McKinnon & Auchincloss, Dominick Corp. 1967-73; joined Acklands Ltd. 1973; served with U.S. Marine

Corps Reserve 1961-66; mem. Candn. Mang. Assn.; Automotive Warehouse Distributors Assn. (Future Pres.); Bd. Trade; Automotive Industry Assn. (Pub. Relations Comte.); Candn. Assn. Corporate Growth; Home: 120 Heath St. W., Toronto, Ont. M4V 2Y6; Office: 100 Norfinch Dr., Downsview, Ont. M3N 1X2

DROLET, Jean-Paul, B.A., B.Sc.A., M.S., D.Sc.; mining engineer; civil servant; b. Québec City, Qué., 15 July 1918; s. Samuel and Florida (Bouré) D.; e. Laval Univ., B.A., B.Sc.A. (Engn.); Columbia Univ., M.S. (Mineral Econ.); (McGill Univ., D. Sc. (honoris causa), 1978; Laurentian Univ., D. Sc., (honoris causa), 1979; m. Françoise, d. Edouard Desrochers, 1949; SR. ASST. DEPY. MIN., (INTER. MIN.) DEPT. OF ENERGY, MINES AND RESOURCES, since 1963, Dir., Royal Can. Mint; Uranium Canada Ltd.; Royal Candn. Geograph. Soc.; Past Pres., Can. Inst. of Mining & Metallurgy; Chrmn., Candn. Permanent Comte. on Geog. Names; Specialist Lectr. in Mineral Econs., McGill Univ.; with Qué. Dept. of Mines as Engr.-Geologist, 1943-56; joined Qué. Cartier Mining Co. as Prospector-Engr., 1956-63; became Dir. and mem. of Bd. of Co., Hart Jaune Power Co., Cartier Railway Co.; mem., Am. Inst. Mining Engrs.; Prospectors & Developers Assn. Can.; Corp. Prof. Engrs. Qué.; R. Catholic; recreations: golf, Clubs: University; Home: 1294 Park Hill Circle, Ottawa, Ont. K1H 6K3; Office: 580 Booth Ave., Ottawa, Ont. K1A 0E4

DROUIN, Ross, Q.C., B.A., LL.L.; advocate; b. Quebec, Que., 18 Jan. 1904; s. U.F. and Anita (Côte) D.; e. Que. Semy., B.A. 1926; Laval Univ., LL.L. 1930; m. Theresa, d. Jos. E. Lemieux, 3 June 1931; children: Richard, Monique, Ross L., Jr.; SR. PARTNER, LANGLOIS, DROUIN & ASSOCIATES; Pres., Commercial Finance Corp. Ltd.; read law with Hon. Mark Drouin, Q.C.; called to the Bar of Que., 1930; cr. K.C. 1944; Bâtonnier of the Que. Bar, 1957-58; Roman Catholic; recreations: hunting, fishing, golf; Clubs: Garrison; Stadacona Fish & Game; Royal Quebec Golf; Home: 115 Turnbull, Québec, Qué. G1R 5G3; Office: 126 St. Pierre, P.O. Box 185, Stn. "B", Quebec, G1K 7A6

DRUMM, Alan L., C.I.B.; insurance executive; b. Montreal, Que, 3 Apl. 1929; s. Frederick Thomas and Marie Josephine (Beaubien) D.; e. elem. and high schs. Outremont, Westmount and Montreal W.; McGill Univ.; m. Robyn Audrey d. Donald Morton, Victoria, Australia 6 June 1959; children: Tracey Marie, Marc Christopher , Annemarie; SR. VICE PRES. AND DIR. MORRIS & MACKENZIE LTD.; Pres. O. Leblanc & Fils Ltée; Vice Pres., Dir. and mem. Extve. Comte. Macmor Ltd.; joined Federation Insurance Co. 1949-53, Clk. to Mgr. Casualty Dept. for Can.; joined present firm 1953, Casualty Expert; Dir. Ins. Brokers Assn. Prov. Que., Pres. & Founder Montreal Dist., Vice Pres.; Liberal; R. Catholic; recreations: golf, skiing, sailing; Clubs: Royal Montreal Golf; Petit Lac Nominique (Pres. and Dir.); Home: 4998 de Maisonneuve W., Apt. 822, Westmount, Que. H3Z 1N2; Office: 4141 Sherbrooke St. W. Suite 400, Westmount, Que. H3Z 1C1.

DRUMMOND, Brian Paul, M.B.A.; investment dealer; b. Montreal, Que., 17 Feb. 1931; s. Paul Cratherin and Elizabeth Pettingill (Sise) D.; e. Westmount (Que.) High Sch.; Dalhousie Univ.; Univ. of W. Ont., M.B.A.; m. Althea Margaret, d. Archibald D. McQueen, Town of Mount Royal, Que. 28 Oct. 1960; children: Kim Ann, Jeffrey Sise, Willa McQueen; PRESIDENT AND DIR. GREENSHIELDS INC.; Dir., Greenshields & Co. Inc., New York; Atco Industries Ltd.; Atco Gas & Oil Ltd.; Trizec Corp. Ltd.; B.P. Tanker Finance Ltd; Shieldings Ltd.; Greenshields Ltd.; Old Exchange Arts Foundation; Mount Bruno Association Ltd.; Lower Canada College (Gov.); mem., Adv. Council, Sch. of Bus. Admin., Univ. of Western Ont.; joined present Co., Corporate Finance, 1958; Mgr., Calgary Office, 1964-67; Mgr. Corporate Finance, Montreal, 1967; Dir. 1968; Extve. Vice-Pres. 1969; Vice Chrmn., Montreal Stock Exchange; Chrmn. (1975-76) Investment Dealers Association Canada; Dir., Cdn. Council of Christians and Jews; Zeta Psi; Anglican; recreations: skiing, squash, tennis; Clubs: Mount Royal; Mount Bruno Golf & Country; Montreal Badminton & Squash; Hillside Tennis; St. James's; Home: 371 Metcalfe Avenue, Westmount, Que. H3Z 2J2; Office: 4 Place Ville Marie, Montreal Que. H3B 2E7

DRURY, Brig. the Hon. Charles Mills, P.C. 1963, C.B.E., D.S.O., E.D., Q.C., civil servant; b. Montreal, Que., 17 May 1912; s. Victor Montague and Pansy Jessie (Mills) D.; e. Bishop's Coll. Sch., Lennoxville, P.Q.; Royal Mil. Coll. of Can.; McGill Univ., B.C.L.; Univ. of Paris, France; m. late Jane Ferrier Counsell, 1939; children: Diana, Leith, Victor M., Charles Gibbons; CHRMN., NATIONAL CAPITAL COMMISSION since 1978; practised law, 1936-39; served in 2nd World War, 1939-45 (final rank of Brig.); Chief of UNRRA Mission to Poland, 1945-46; with Department of External Affairs, Canada, 1947-48; Deputy Minister of National Defence, 1948-55; was President and Mang. Dir., Provincial Transport Ltd., 1955-60; el. to H. of C. for Montreal St. Antoine-Westmount, g.e. June 1962 and re-el. g.e. Apl. 1963; apptd. Min. of Defence Production, Apl. 1963 and Min. of Industry (new Portfolio), July 1963; re-el. g.e. Nov. 1965 and June 1968; Min. of Defence Production, Apl. 1963-July 1968; Pres. of the Treasury Bd. July 1968-Aug. 1974; Min. of Pub. Works and Min. of State for Sci. and Technol. 1974-77 (responsible for Nat. Research Council of Can. 1963-77); apptd. Special Rep. for Constitutional Devel. in N.W. Territories; resigned from H. of C. 1978; former mem. of Executive Committee, Montreal Chamber Comm.; Pres., Montreal Bd. Trade, 1961; Past Pres., Un. Nations Assn. of Can.; Dir., Royal Victoria Hosp.; mem. Extve. Comte. Montreal Chamber Comm.; Liberal; Clubs: St. James's; Home: 71 Somerset W. Apt. 1002, Ottawa, Ont. K2P 2G2; Office: 161 Laurier St. W., Ottawa, Ont.

DRURY, Chipman Hazen, O.B.E., B. Chem. Eng., M.B.A.; industrialist; b. Montreal, P.Q., 15 July 1917; s. Victor Montague and Pansy (Mills) D.; e. Selwyn House Sch., Montreal, 1924-29; Lower Can. Coll., 1929-34; Royal Mil. Coll. Can., 1934-38; McGill Univ., B.Sc. (Chem. Engn.) 1939; Harvard Univ. (Sch. of Business), M.B.A. 1947; m. Dorothy Janet, d. the late R. Reid Dobell, 27 Dec. 1945; children: Sally Katherine, Chipman M., Penny J., Pansy A., Reid Mills; PRESIDENT, QUEBEC INDUSTRIES LIMITED; Chrmn. of Bd., The Guardian Ins. Co. of Canada; Montreal Life Insurance Company; el. Mayor, City of Westmount, Que., Jan. 1963; Chief Engr. and Gen. Mgr., Quebec Industries Ltd. 1937; Research Asst., E.B. Eddy Co., Hull, Que., 1938; Adm. Asst., Canadian Car & Foundry Co. Ltd., Mexico City, 1939; Sales Engineer, Candn. Car & Foundry Co. Ltd., Montreal, Que., 1948-49, Asst. Gen. Mgr. 1949-50; Vice-Pres. i/c Purchasing, 1952-54; Vice-Pres., Dir. and Mgr., Canadian Gen. Transit Co. Ltd., 1954-56; Pres. and Mang. Dir., 1956-63; Extve. Vice Pres., Dom. Steel and Coal Corp., Ltd. 1963-64; Pres., Dosco Steel Ltd. 1964-68; Pres., Chrmn., Avis Transport of Can. Ltd. 1968-73; served in 2nd World War 1939-45; with Royal Candn. Arty., Can. 1939-40; U.K. 1940-43; served overseas in Italy, France, Belgium, N.E. Holland, 1943-45; Pacific Force, Oct.-Dec. 1945; awarded O.B.E.; trans. to Reserve 1945 with rank of Lieut.-Col. and Acting Col.; mem., Engn. Inst. of Can.; Corpn. of Prof. Engrs. of Quebec; Zeta Psi; Protestant; recreations: skiing, swimming, wood working; Clubs: University; Mount Bruno; Home: 422 Lansdowne Ave., Westmount, Que. H3Y 2V2; Office: Suite 446 - 1253 McGill College Ave., Montreal, Que. H3B 2Y5

DRYER, Douglas Poole, Ph.D., F.R.S.C.; educator; b. Toronto, Ont. 27 Nov. 1915; s. William Poole and Mabel (McLeod) D.; e. Harvard Coll. A.B. 1936, A.M. 1939;

Ph.D. 1980 m. 1stly Pegeen (d. 1963) d. J. L. Synge, Dublin, Ireland 22 March 1946; children: Dagny, Matthew, Moira; m. 2ndly Ellice d. late James Baird 29 May 1965; one step-d. Eleanor; PROF. OF PHILOS. UNIV. OF TORONTO; Instr. in Philos. Union Coll. Schenectady, N.Y. 1939-41, Harvard Coll. 1943-45; Lectr. in Philos. Tufts Coll. 1944-45; joined Univ. of Toronto 1945; author "Kant's Solution for Verification in Metaphysics" 1966; "Introduction to J.S. Mill" in "Collected Works" Vol. X 1969; articles on Kant and on pol. and social philos.; mem. ed. staff "Kant-Studien"; "Dialogue"; mem. Royal Scot. Country Dancing Soc.; Bruce Trail Assn.; Am. Philos. Assn.; Aristotelian Soc.; Candn. Philos. Assn.; Liberal; United Church; Club: Alpine; Home: 61 Lonsdale Rd., Toronto, Ont. M4V 1W4; Office: 215 Huron St., Toronto, Ont.

DRYER, Hon. Victor L., B.A.; judge; b. London, Eng., 23 Nov. 1910; s. Ernest Alfred and Maud (Smith) D.; e. Univ. of British Columbia, B.A. (with Hons, in Econ. and Pol. Science) 1933; Vancouver Law Sch.; m. late Isobel Marjory, d. George Wales, Strathmore, Alta.; 12 May 1938; children: Linda Meridel, David Victor; JUSTICE, SUPREME COURT, B.C.; Dep. Judge, Supreme Court of the Yukon Territory; read law with F.G.T. Lucas & E.A. Lucas; called to Bar of B.C., 1936; cr. Q.C. 1956; practised law, Ellis & Dryer, later Ellis, Dryer & McTaggart; Freemason (P.M., A. & A.S.R., A.Á.O.N.M.S.); Anglican; Clubs: Vancouver; Union (Victoria); Home: 1773 Knox Rd., Vancouver, B.C. V6T 1S4; Office: Court House, Vancouver, B.C.

DUBÉ, Hon. André, L.Ph., L.Sc.S., M.A., LL.L.; juge; né Matapédia, Qué. 12 mars 1918; f. J. Albert et Flore (Poirier) D.; é. Seminaire de Rimouski B.A. 1934; Univ. d'Ottawa L.Ph., L.Sc.S., M.A. 1937; Univ. Laval LL.L. 1947; ép. Lucile f. Jos. A. DesRosiers, Mont Joli, Qué. 5 mai 1941; enfants: Nyreille, Michelle, Marc, Jean, Nicole, Suzanne; JUGE, COURT D'APPEL DU QUE. depuis 1973; Bar de Qué. 1947; Q.C. 1963; ouverture bureau legal New Carlisle 1947; fonde bureau legal Dube & Arsenault, New Carlisle 1957; substitut Min. de la Justice 1963; Juge, Cour Superieure 1966; Cand. Lib. prov. 1948, 1952, fed. 1958; Vice Pres. Fed. Liberale Provinciale 1965; Pres.-Fondateur Fed. Liberale Federale (Prov. Qué.) 1966; enrolement volontaire 1940, licencié en 1945 au rang de Maj.; servit successivement dans Fusiliers du St-Laurent, le Regt. de Hull et le Royal 22e Regt.; prit part à la campagne d'Italie, de France, de Hollande et d'Allemagne; Croix d'or du mérite de la Pologne; Chevalier de l'ordre militaire et hospitalier de St. Lazare de Jerusalem; Queen's Silver Jubilee Medal; mem. Legion Canadienne (ancien Pres. New Carlisle); Chev. de Colomb (ancien député de dist.); Assn. R22e Regt. (ancien Pres.); récreations: golf, skiing, natation, chasse, pèche; catholique; Club: Garrison; Adresse: 7 Jardins Merici, Apt. 1205, Québec City, Qué. G1S 4N8; Bureau: Palais de Justice, 12 rue St. Louis, Québec City, Qué. G1A 1M8.

DUBÉ, Hon. Fernand Georges, Q.C., M.L.A., B.A., B.C.L.; politician; b. Edmundston, N.B. 29 Dec. 1928; e. elem. and high schs. Edmundston; Univ. of Ottawa B.A.; Univ of N.B. B.C.L.; m. Monique; 4 children: MIN. OF FINANCE, N.B. and Min. Responsible for Energy Policy 1978- ; called to Bar of N.B. 1957; Q.C. 1972; law practice Edmundston and Campbellton; el. M.L.A. for Campbellton prov. by-el. 1974, re-el. since; apptd. Min. of Tourism 1974 and Min. of Environment; Solr. for City of Campbellton 1969-74; Pres., Campbellton Centennial Comte. 1967; Cambellton Salmon Festival Comm. 1968-70; Cambellton Tigers Hockey Club 1971-75; Past mem. Council Barristers' Soc. N.B.; Past Pres., Restigouche Bar Assn.; Cambellton P. Cons. Assn.; mem. Campbellton Chamber Comm.; Office: (P.O. Box 6000) Fredericton, N.B. E3B 5H1.

DUBE, Hon. Jean-Eudes, P.C. (1968), Q.C., B.A., B.Ph., L.Ph., B.S.F.S., B.C.L., LL.D.(N.B.) 1971, D.C.L. Moncton 1973; barrister; b. Matapédia, Que., 6 November 1926; s. J. Albert and Flore (Poirier) D.; e. College of Gaspé, Que.; St. Joseph University, N.B.; Ottawa University, B.A., B.Ph., L.Ph.; Georgetown Univ., Sch. of Foreign Service, B.S.F.S.; Univ. of New Brunswick, Law Sch., B.C.L.; m. Noella, d. J. Edgar Babin, 25 June 1956; children: Marie Flore Rachelle, Jean-François; JUDGE, FEDERAL COURT OF CAN. AND COURT MARTIAL APPEAL COURT OF CAN. since 17 July 1975; Ald., Campbellton (N.B.) City Council, 1959-63; Crown Prosecutor 1960-61; 1st el. to House of Commons for Restigouche-Madawaska, 1962, re-el. 1963, 65, 68, 72, 74; President, Canadian NATO Parlty. Association, 1963 and re-el. 1964, 1965; Pres. (1st Candn.), N. Atlantic Assembly 1967; Chrmn., H. of C. External Affairs Comte., 1966 and 1967; sworn of Privy Council 1968; Min. Veterans' Affairs 1968-72; Min. of Public Works 1972 till resignation as M.P. 9 Apl. 1975 when apptd. to Fed. Court of Can.; cr. Q.C. 1969, and Q.C. (Fed.) 1974; Roman Catholic; Club: Rivermead Golf; Home: 1694 Playfair Dr., Ottawa, Ont. K1H 5S6

DUBIN, Anne R., Q.C.; b. Toronto, Ont., 19 Nov. 1926; e. Univ. of Toronto, B.A., LL.B., 1948; Osgoode Hall Law Sch., Toronto, Ont. (with Hons., Matthew Wilson Mem. Scholarship; Bronze Medal); m. The Hon. Mr. Justice Charles L. Dubin; PARTNER, TORY, TORY, DESLAURIERS & BINNINGTON; Trustee, Tor. Gen. Hosp.; Governor, York Univ.; Public Governor, Tor. Stock Exch.; read law with McMaster, Montgomery & Co., Toronto, Ont.; called to the Bar of Ont., 1951; cr. Q.C. 1961; Clubs: Canadian (Dir.) (Toronto); Queen's; Toronto Lawn Tennis; Home: 619 Avenue Road, Toronto, Ont. M4V 2K6 Office: Box 20, Royal Bank Plaza, Toronto, Ont. M5J 2K1

DUBIN, Hon. Charles L., b. Hamilton, Ont., 4 Apl. 1921; s. Harry and Ethel Dubin; e. Central Coll. Inst., Hamilton, Ont.; Univ. of Toronto, B.A. 1941; Osgoode Hall Schol. (with Hons.; Gold Medal; Chancellor Van Koughnet Schol.; Clara Brett Martin Mem. Schol. and Gurston Allen Prize); m. Anne Ruth Levine, 1951; JUSTICE, COURT OF APPEAL, SUPREME COURT, ONT.; 1973-; read law with Mason, Foulds, Davidson & Kellock; called to the Bar of Ont., June 1944; cr. K.C., Dec. 1950; formerly Sr. Partner, Kimber, Dubin, Brunner & Armstrong; Bencher, Law Society o Upper Canada, 1966-73; apptd. Royal Comm. to enquire into air safety in Canada, 1979; Clubs: Toronto Lawn Tennis; Queens; Home: 619 Avenue Road, Toronto, Ont. M4V 2K6; Office: Osgoode Hall, Toronto, Ont. M5H 2N6

DUBUC, Col. Jean-Claude, KSTJ., C.D. and Bar, ADC, B.Com., C.L.U., F.R.S.A., insurance executive; b. Montreal, Que., 10 Jan. 1924; s. Eugène, B.A. and Juliette (Martel) D.; e. completed science at Mont St. Louis Coll. and Faculty of Sciences, Univ. of Montreal; Univ. of London, Eng.; McGill Univ., B.Com.; m. Louise Flynn née McGovern; four children; Vice Pres., Johnson & Higgins Willis Faber Ltd.; Exec. Vice-Pres., Dupuis Parizeau, Tremblay, Inc.; Pres., J.C. Dubuc & Associates Ltd.; Vice Pres. and Dir., J. & H.W.F. Inc.; Les Conseillers D.P.T. Inc.; Dir. & Vice Pres., P.P. Lalonde Ltd.; Dir., Hicks Design Ltd.; Knowlton Golf Club; Dir. & Vice Pres., La Maison Bieler Inc.; Chancellor, Priory of Canada, Order of St. John; Governor, Institut de Cardiol. de Montréal and Hôpital Marie-Enfant; served during 2nd World War; landed in France and joined Les Fusiliers Mont-Royal in Belgium, Holland and Germany; discharged from active Force in 1946; commanded Le Régiment de Maisonneuve 1962-66; Commandant, Craig Street Armory, Montreal 1962-64; promoted to Col. and apptd. Commdr. of Dist. No. 2 (M) of Que. 1972-74; Hon. A.D.C. to Lt. Govs. of Que. since 1964; Awarded Knight of Justice of the Venerable Order of St. John; Knight of Magistral Grace, Sovereign & Military Order of Malta; Knight of Justice, Military & Hospitaler Order of St. Lazarus; Polonia Restituta (Poland); Military Cross (Poland); Order of Merit S.R. (France); Mil. Cross (Malta); Silver Medal (Paris); Bronze Medal (Versailles); Past Pres., Life Underwriters of Canada 1966; mem., Inst. Chart. Life Underwriters; Life mem. Million Dollar Round Table; mem. McGill Grad. Soc.; Royal Candn. Legion Past Pres., Jean Brillant VC Branch; Past Vice-Pres., Quebec Command; R. Catholic; Liberal; recreations: fishing, skiing, tennis; Clubs: St. Denis (Past Pres.); Royal Canadian Military Institute; Knowlton Golf; Home 2265 Kildare Rd., Town of Mount Royal, Que. H3R 3J6; Office: Suite 2300, Stock Exchange Tower, Place Victoria, Montreal, Que. H4Z 1E2

DUCHARME, Claude, Q.C.; SR. PARTNER, DESJARDINS, DUCHARME, DESJARDINS & BOURQUE; Chrmn. of Bd., La Sauvegarde Life Ins. Co.; Dir., UAP Inc.; Rogers Cablesystems Ltd.; Sodarcan Ltd.; National Reinsurance Co. of Can.; Nat. Bank of Canada; Christian Dior Can. Ltd.; Leisure Books Ltd.; Chrmn. of Bd. (1970-71) Chambre de Comm. de Montréal; Dir., Inst. de Diagnostic et de Recherches Cliniques de Montréal; Past Pres., Coll. Marie de France; Théâtre du Nouveau Monde; Past Vice Pres. Conseil Consultatif de la Justice; Home: 1250 Pine Ave. W., Apt. 860, Outremont, Montreal, Que. H3G 2P5; Office: Suite 1200, 635 Dorchester Blvd. W., Montreal, Que. H3B 1R9

DUCHARME, Jacques R., B.A., M.Sc., M.D.; b. Montreal, Que., 1 Jan. 1928; s. J. Oscar and Antonia (Gagnon) D.; e. Brebeuf Coll., Univ. of Montreal, B.A. 1948, M.D. 1954; Univ. of Pennsylvania, M.Sc. (Med.) 1961; Dipl. Am. Bd. of Pediatrics; Cert. Pediatrician and Endocrinologist, Que.; m. Monique, d. late Charles G. Smith, M.D., 6 June 1955; children: Andrée, Marie, Jean, Raymond, Anique; Chrmn., Dept. of Pediatrics, Univ. of Montreal 1968-75; Dir., Pediatric Research Center, L'Hôpital Ste-Justine, Montreal 1975-78; Dir., Pediatric Endocrine Lab. 1960-; Chrmn. Bd. Trustees Queen Elizabeth II Research Fund to aid research in diseases of children; has engaged in full-time acad. career since 1959 and research particularly in field of hormonal steroids in newborn, infants, childhood and adolescence; Pres., Candn. Soc. for Clin. Inves., 1966; Secy. Que. Med. Research Council 1964-69; mem., Candn. Med. Assn.; Soc. for Pediatric Research; Endocrine Soc.; Candn. Soc. Endocrinology & Metabolism; Club de Recherche Clinique du Que.; Candn. Pediatric Soc.; European Soc. for Pediatric Endocrinology; Lawson Wilkins Pediatric Endocrine Soc.; Assn. des Médecins des Langue Française du Can.; R. Catholic; recreations: skiing, swimming; Home: 505 Stuart Ave., Outremont, Que. H2V 3H1; Office: 3175 Ste. Catherine Rd., Montreal, Que. H3T 1C5

DUCKWORTH, Henry Edmison, O.C. (1976), B.A., B.Sc., Ph.D., D.Sc., LL.D., F.R.S.C.; educator; b. Brandon, Manitoba, Univ. Nov. 1915; s. Rev. Dr. Henry Bruce and Ann Hutton (Edmison) D.; e. Univ. of Manitoba, B.A. 1935, B.Sc. 1936; Univ. of Chicago, Ph.D. 1942; D.Sc. Ottawa 1966, McMaster 1969; Laval 1971; Mount Allison 1971; New Brunswick 1972; Queen's 1978; Western Ont. 1979; LL.D., Manitoba 1978; m. Katherine Jane, d. W.J. McPherson, Winnipeg, Man., 21 Nov. 1942; children: Henry William, Jane Edmison Maksymiuk; Pres. & Vice Chancellor, Univ. of Winnipeg 1971-81; Instr. in Math., Stonewall, Man., 1937-38; Lectr. in Physics, United Coll., Winnipeg, Man., 1938-40; Jr. Scientist N.R.C., Ottawa, 1942-44 and Asst. Research Physicist, Hamilton, Ont., 1944-45; Asst. Prof. of Physics, Univ. of Manitoba, 1945-46; Assoc. Prof. of Physics, Wesleyan Univ., Middletown, Conn., 1946-51; Prof. of Physics. Hamilton Coll., McMaster Univ., 1951-65; Dean of Graduate Studies, 1961-65; Vice Pres. (Devel.) Univ. of Manitoba 1965-66, Vice Pres. (Acad.) 1966-71; Prof. Visiteur, Univ. Laval 1970-71; Nuffield Foundation Travelling Fellowship, 1955; Dir., Wawanesa Mutual Ins. Co.; Chrmn., Advisory Commision on Nuclear Safety of Atomic Energy Control

Bd.; mem., Candn. Assn. of Physicists; Past Chrmn., Council of Assn. of Commonwealth Univs.; Past Pres., Roy. Soc. of Can.; Assoc. of Univ. and Coll. of Can.; Dir., Inst. for Research on Pub. Policy; United Church; recreation: philately; Club: Manitoba; Home: 76 Witton St., Winnipeg, Man. R3M 3C1

DUCKWORTH, John Walter Adam, M.B., Ch.B., M.D.; university professor; e. Harrow; Edin. Univ.; EMERITUS PROF. OF ANATOMY, FACULTY OF MED., UNIV. OF TORONTO, since 1979; before coming to Canada was House Surg. in Royal Simpson Maternity Hosp., and in Royal Infirmary, Edinburgh, and later Lect. at Edin. Univ.; served in 2nd World War (Comn. Surg.-Lieut. in R.N.V.R. 1938) with Royal Navy and promoted to Surg. Capt. R.C.N.R. in 1958; Assoc. Prof. of Anatomy, Univ. of Toronto, 1952-56; Prof. and Chmn., Dept. of Anatomy, 1956-64; research interests are the human heart and congenital heart disease; mem., Candn. Assn. of Anatomists; Anat. Assn. of Gt. Brit. & Ireland; awarded V.R.D. 1962, C.D. 1965; Hon. Physician to Queen 1975; Address: University of Toronto, Toronto, Ont.

DUCLOS, Gerard George, B.Com., M.B.A., R.C.D.S.; Canadian public service; b. Prince George, B.C., 15 June 1931; s. Noël Gerard and Blanche (Caus) D.; e. Secondary Sch., Kamloops, B.C., 1949; Univ. of Brit. Columbia, B.Com. (Hons.) 1954, M.B.A. 1960; m. Judith Patterson-Duclos, 1977; has three s. and two d.; ASSISTANT COMPTROLLER-GENERAL OF CANADA Apr. 1981-; joined Peace R. Glass Co. Ltd. as Comptroller and Asst. Treas. 1956-59; Asst. Prof. of Bus. Adm., Univ. of New Brunswick, 1960-63; Depy. Min. of Labour, Prov. of N.B., 1962-65; Chrmn., Bd. Dirs., Community Improvement Corp. of N.B., 1965-66; apptd. Asst. Depy. Min. and Dir. Gen. of Manpower Servs., Dept. Manpower, Can. 1966; Dir.-Gen. BSDT, PSC Can. 1968; Commr., Comn. of Inquiry into Indust. Safety, Province of New Brunswick, 1961; Dir. Gen., Staff Devel. Br., Pub. Serv. Comn. of Can., 1973; Royal College of Defense Studies, London UK, 1977; Sr. Policy Advisor, Treasury Bd. of Can., 1978; Candn. Internat. Devel. Agency (CIDA) 1979; mem., Candn. Assn. University Teachers; Candn. Mfrs. Assn.; Candn. Assn. Adms. Labour Leg.; Candn. Pol. Science Assn.; Candn. Educ. Assn.; recreations: skiing, reading, art. Address: Office of the Comptroller-General of Canada, 20th floor, Place Bell Canada, Elgin St., Ottawa, Ont. K1A 1E4.

DUCROS, Hon. Jacques F., B.A., B.C.L.; judge; b. Toulon, France, 18 May 1934; s. François and Françoise (Minville) D.; came to Can. 1934; e. Stanislas Coll., Outremont, Que., B.A. 1952; McGill Univ., B.C.L. 1956; m. Patricia, d. late Cleveland McCoshen, 10 Sept. 1960; children: Françoise, SusanMarie, Geneviève, Kateri, Caroline; JUSTICE, SUPERIOR COURT QUE. since 1971; Vice-Chmn., Law Reform Commission of Canada 1980-81; called to Bar of Que. 1957; Atty., Monette, Filion & Labelle 1957; Beique & Ducros 1959; Ducros, Tellier & Demers 1960-62; Crown Atty. (Part time) 1960-62; Permanent Crown Atty. 1962-64; Assoc. Depy. Min. Justice, Que. 1964-67; Partner, Geoffrion & Prud'homme 1967-71; Chrmn., Que. Criminal Justice Sub-sec., Candn. Bar Assn. 1968-69; Nat. Chrmn. Criminal Justice Sec., Candn. Bar Assn. 1970-71; appt. Commissioner of the Law Reform Comm. of Can., 1979, Vice-Chmn., 1980; R. Catholic; recreations: golf, bridge; Home: 4458 de Maisonneuve Blvd., Westmount, Quebec. H3Z 1L7; Office: Court House, Room 1624, 1 Notre Dame St. East; Montreal, Que. H2Z 16

DUDEK, Louis, M.A., Ph.D.; poet; teacher and editor; b. Montreal, Que., 6 Feb. 1918; s. Vincent and Rozynski (Stasia) D.; e. Montreal High Sch. (Sr. Matric 1936); McGill Univ., B.A. 1939; Columbia Univ., M.A. (History) 1947; Ph.D. (English and Comparative Lit.) 1955; m. Stephanie Zuperko, 1943 (div. 1965) m. Aileen Collins, 1970;

GREENSHIELDS PROF. OF ENGLISH, McGILL UNIV., since 1969; joined McGill 1951 as Lectr. in Eng.; Asst. Prof. 1953; Founder with Raymond Souster and Irving Layton of Contact Press, poetry publishing; Editor and Publisher of "Delta", literary mag., 1957-66 (ceased publ.); helped to edit and produce "First Statement" with John Sutherland and Irving Layton, 1941-43; assoc. with CIV/n magazine in Montreal, 1955-56; Ed. of Delta Canada, (later DC Books) book publishers; Instr. in English, City Coll. of New York, 1946-51; Publications; (poetry) "East of the City", 1946; "The Searching Image", 1952; "Twenty Four Poems", 1952; "Europe", 1955; "The Transparent Sea", 1956; "Laughing Stalks", 1958; "En Mexico", 1958; a prose work, "Literature and the Press", 1956; poems published in books: "Unit of Five", 1944; "Other Canadians", 1947; "Cerberus", 1952; co-ed. with M. Gnarowski "The Making of Modern Poetry in Canada", 1967; ed. "Poetry of Our Time", anthology of modern poetry, 1965; publ. long poem "Atlantis", 1967, "The First Person in Literature", 1967; "Collected Poetry", 1971; "Selected Essays and Criticism", 1978; "Technology and Culture", 1979; articles in "Dalhousie Review", "Queen's Quarterly", "Culture", "Canadian Forum", "Tamarack Review", "Delta", etc.; bibliography, Karol W.J. Wenek, "Louis Dudek: A Check-list," 1975; Address: 5 Ingleside Ave., Montreal, Que. H3Z 1N4

DUFF, Ann MacIntosh, R.C.A.; artist; b. Toronto, Ont., 14 July 1925; d. John MacIntosh Duff, Q.C., and Constance Hamilton (Townsend) D.; e. Branksome Hall Sch., Toronto, Ont.; Central Tech. Sch., Toronto, Ont.; Queen's Univ. Sch. of Fine Arts (summer); has exhibited with major group shows in Toronto, Montreal, Winnipeg, etc., since 1946; one-man shows at Picture Loan Soc., 1959, 1961, 1963, 1964, Gallery Ustel 1968, Merton Gall. 1970, 74, Sisler Gall. 1975, Prince Arthur Galleries 1980-82; also with four Toronto painters at Montreal Museum of Fine Arts and group show at Art Gallery, London, Ont.; exhibited at Candn. Nat. Exhn. (1951, 1954, 1956); incl. in 8th Burnaby Biennial 1975; Graphex 1, 2 and 3, 1973, 74, 75; "Fifty Years of Watercolour Painting", Art Gall. Ont. 1975; "Watercolours Japan-Canada", Tokyo, Montreal 1976-78; work in coll. of Art Gallery of Ont., Huron Coll., Dept. of External Affairs permanent coll. in N.Y.C., Agnes Etherington Gall., Sarnia Art Gall., Art Gall.ù of Brant, Nat. Gall. Can., London Art Gall., Toronto Dominion Bank, Dominion Foundries and Steel, Princess Margaret Hosp., Nat. Paper Goods, Esso Resources; Kitchener-Waterloo Art Gallery, Ont. Inst. for Studies in Education, John Labatt Ltd., Oregon State Univ., Corvallis, U.S.A., and many private colls. in Toronto, Montreal, Edmonton, Winnipeg and Vancouver and abroad; mem., Roy. Can. Acad. of Arts; Print and Drawing Council Can.; Candn. Soc. of Painters in Water Colour; Queen's Jubilee Medal 1977; Anglican; Address: 133 Imperial St., Toronto, Ont. M5P 1C7

DUFF, C. Alexander, B.Sc.; company executive; b. Renfrew, Ont., 22 Jan. 1914; s. Charles Alexander and Lena McIntyre (MacAdam) D.; e. Pub. and High Schs., Montreal W., Que.; McGill Univ., B.Sc. 1937; m. Pamela Catherine, d. Neil Thomas O'Connor, Kirkland Lake, Ont., 28 Sept. 1940; children: Judith, Marilyn, Sandra, Charles, Scott; VICE-PRES., HENRY BIRKS AND SONS LTD.; Pres. and C.E.O., Shreve Crump and Low Inc. Boston, Mass.; Pres. & CEO, Thomas Long Inc., Boston, Mass.; Dir., Henry Birks & Sons Ltd.; Birmanco Ltd.; Nat. Trust Co.; Chrmn. Bd. of Govs., Concordia Univ.; on grad. spent 4 yrs. as an Engr. in Toburn Gold Mines; joined present firm in 1966 after 21 yrs. with Henry Morgan & Co. Ltd.; a well known hockey player (amateur) 1934-40 and a mem. of Lake Shore Blue Devils, Allan Cup winners 1939-40; served in 2nd W.W. with R.C.A.F. in training, instructing and as Navigator for 4 yrs., retiring with rank of Flight Lieut.; mem. Royal Candn. Legion; Freemason; Presbyterian; recreations: tennis, hockey; Home:

79 Wolseley Ave., Montreal West, Que. H4X 1V6; Office: Phillips Square, Montreal, Que.

DUFF, Donald James, B.Ed., M.Sc., F.R.S.A.; development and community relations counsel; b. Calgary, Alta., 18 Sept. 1926; s. James and Julia Isobel (Middleton) D.; e. Central Coll. Inst., Calgary, Alta.; Calgary (Alta.) Business Coll., 1946; Univ. of Alta., B.Ed. 1949; Columbia Univ., M.Sc. (Grad. Sch. of Journalism), 1950; m. Beth Elinor, d. Connor W. Edwards, 19 Feb. 1948; children: James Connor, Julie Anita, Donald Jonathan; CHRMN., THE DUFF CONSULTING GROUP; Pres., Donald J. Duff & Associates Ltd., formed 1961; Oceanways Ltd.; journalist with Southam newspapers (Calgary "Herald", Edmonton "Journal", Vancouver "Province"), 1945-50; Dir., Pub. Relations, Vancouver Gen. Hosp. and B.C. Med. Centre, 1951-54; Vice-Pres., G.A. Brakeley & Co. Ltd. 1954-61; served with Candn. Army (Calgary Tank Regt.) 1943-45; author of articles on Candn. art and sculpture; consultant to Hudson Gallery; mem., St. Andrews Soc. of Montreal; Hudson Hist. Soc.; V.O.N. (Dir.); Anglican; recreations: golf, writing, photography; Clubs: Halifax; M.A.A.A.; Arts & Letters (Toronto); Whitlock Golf & Country; Ashburn Golf; Home: "Point of View", Hudson Heights, Que. J0P 1J0; Office: Village Centre, Hudson, Que. J0P 1H0

DUFF, George Francis Denton, M.A., Ph.D., F.R.S.C.; university professor; b. Toronto, Ont., 28 July 1926; s. George Henry and Laura (Denton) D.; e. Univ. of Toronto Schs.; Univ. of Toronto, B.A. 1948, M.A. 1949; Princeton Univ., Ph.D. 1951; m. Mary Elaine, d. George H. Wood, Ottawa, Ont., 16 June 1951; children: Valerie, John, Catherine, Janet, George; PROF. OF MATH., UNIV. OF TORONTO, since 1961; Chrmn., Dept. of Math., 1968-75; Editor, "Canadian Journal of Mathematics", 1958-61 and 1978-81; Moore Instr., Mass. Inst. Tech., 1951; Asst. Prof. Math., Univ. of Toronto, 1952-57; Assoc. Prof., 1957-61; Visiting Prof. of Math., Univ. of Sask., 1957; Publications: "Partial Differential Equations", 1956; "Differential Equations of Applied Mathematics", 1966; various math. papers in tech. journs.; mem., Am. Math. Soc.; Candn. Math. Soc. (Pres. 1971); Home: 20 Buckingham Ave., Toronto, Ont. M4N 1R2

DUFF, Grant Lawrence, B.A.Sc., P.Eng.; b. Cochrane, Ont. 13 March 1927; s. late Henry Donovan and Eva Gertrude D.; e. Jarvis Coll. Inst. Toronto; Univ. of Toronto, B.A.Sc., P.Eng.; m. Jean Elizabeth; d. late William Henderson 1955; children: Virginia, David; PRESIDENT, AND CHIEF EXECUTIVE OFFICER, COSTAIN LTD. 1981-; Dir. (Pres. 1978-80) Candn. Inst. of Public Real Estate Co's. Pres. Urban Devel. Inst. (Ont.) 1967; Devel. Mgr. present Co. 1963, Extve. Vice Pres. 196777; Pres. 1977-81; Dir. (Vice Pres. 1977-80) Nat. Retinitis Pigmentosa Foundation; mem. Assn. Prof. Engrs. Prov. Ont.; Clubs: Granite; Alpine Ski; Home: 92 Glengowan Rd., Toronto, Ont. M4N 1G4; Office: Ste. 2200, P.O. Box 428, 2 First Canadian Place, Toronto, Ont. M5X 1H9

DUFFELL, Stanley, B.Sc., MA.Sc., Ph.D., F.R.S.C.; geologist (retired); b. Port Moody, B.C. 3 Aug. 1908; s. George and Alice (Wilks) D.; e. Univ. of B.C. B.Sc. 1930, M.Sc. 1932; Univ. of Toronto Ph.D. 1935; m. Edith d. late Henry L. Rogers 1 Oct. 1941; children: Diane Patricia, Rodney Alexander; Geologist with private companies in Ont., B.C. and Que. 1935-40; R.C.A.F. Navigation Instructor 1941-45; Geologist, Geological Survey Canada 1945-67, Research Manager, 1967-73 (retirement); author "G.S.C. Memoirs on Geology of Ashcroft Map Area" 1952, "Whitesail Lake Map Area" 1959, "Terrace Map Area" 1964; over 20 publication on various aspects of geological research; Fellow, Royal Soc. of Can. (1967); Geological Assn. of Can.; Life Mem., Candn. Inst. of Mining and Mettalurgy; Presbyterian; recreations: curling,

sports, community affairs; Home: 894 Duberry St., Ottawa, Ont. K2A 3T3.

DUFFETT, Walter Elliott, B.Com., M.Sc.; statistician; b. Toronto, Ont., 19 Jan. 1910; s. late Herbert and late Margaret (Elliott) D.; e. Public and High Schs., Toronto and Galt, Ont.; Univ. of Toronto, B.Com. 1933; London Sch. of Econ., M.Sc. (Econ.) 1935; m. Agnes Isabel, d. late W.O. Rothney, 4 July 1940; two d., Margaret I., Barbara E.; with Invest. Dept., Sun Life Assnce. Co. of Canada, Montreal, P.Q., 1935-42; Economics Br., W.P.T.B., Ottawa, 1942-44; Asst. Chief, Research Dept., Bank of Canada, Ottawa, 1944-54; Dir. of Economics & Research Br., Dept. of Labour, Ottawa, 1954-56; Chief, Statistics Canada 1957-72; Vice-Pres., Conf. Bd. in Canda, 1972-78; mem., Candn. Economics Assn.; Internat. Stat. Inst.; Am. Stat. Assn. (Fellow); Inter-Am. Stat. Inst. (Pres.); Candn. Inst. Internat. Affairs; Home: 506 Driveway, Ottawa, Ont. K1S 3N4

DUFFIE, Msgr. Donald C., B.C.L., B.Th., D.C.L., LL.D., D.Sc.Adm.; b. Oromocto, N.B., 5 July 1915; s. Francis Carlston and Frances (Rutledge) D.; e. Fredericton (N.B.) High Sch., 1930; St. Joseph's Univ., B.A. 1934; Univ. of N.B., B.C.L. 1937, LL.D. 1967; Oxford Univ. (Rhodes Scholar), B.C.L. 1939; Holy Heart Semy., B.Th. 1944; Laval Univ. D.C.L. 1948; D.Sc.Adm. Moncton 1974; LL.D. St. Thomas Univ. 1979; Pres., St. Thomas Univ. 1961-75; Chrmn., Central Adv. Comte. on Educ., Atlantic Provs. 1970-73; read law with Winslow and MacNair; called to Bar of N.B. 1937; Prof. of Com.-Law-Canon Law Relation., Laval Univ., 1947-49; Prof. of Canon Law, Holy Heart Semy., Halifax, 1954-56; Prof. of Pol. Science, St. Mary's Univ., Halifax, 1957-61; Counsel (1951-61) and Assoc. Presiding Judge, 1976-, Regional Matrimonial Trubunal; R.C. Bishops of Atlantic Provs. and Chief Judicial Officer, Diocese of St. John 1979-; Vice-Pres., Assn. Atlantic Univs., 1968-71, Pres. 1971-73; Chrmn. Comte. of Pres.'s, N.B. Univs. 1969-75; mem., Rhodes Scholarship Selection Comte. for N.B., since 1965 and Sec. since 1974; and for N.S. 1956-61; mem. Senate, Univ. of N.B. 1963-75; Founding mem. and mem. Bd. of Dirs., N.B. Educ. Computer Network 1973-75; Bd. Dirs., Can. (N.B.) Studies since 1973; mem., N.B. Comte. on Health and Social Leg., 1935; Co-author, N.B.'s first Leg. on Co-ops, 1935; mem. N.B. Govt. Comte. on Mining Work Condns., 1937; Halifax City Comte. on Welf. and Soc. Studies, 1951; Dir., N.Am. Comm. of Pax Romana, 1951-53; Msgr., Pius XII, 1958; rec'd Sir Douglas Hazen Award for leadership in law, 1937; author, "Duffie Report — Teacher Education and Training", 1969; also articles for various newspapers and journs.; first and only hon. life mem. N.B. Safety Council; mem., N.B. Barristers' Soc.; Candn. Bar Assn.; Canon Law Soc. Am.; Candn. Canon Law Soc.; Candn. Educ. Assn.; Candn. Assn. of Rhodes Scholars; R. Catholic; recreations: N.B. Rugby Football League (Pres.); Oxford blue (hockey); Club: Canadian (Pres.-Fredericton); Home: 672 Fenety St., Fredericton, N.B. E3B 4H2

DUFFY, (John) Dennis, M.A., Ph.D.; educator; b. Louisville, Ky. 8 Oct. 1938; s. John Raymond and Agnes (Shouse) D.; e. St. Xavier High Sch. Louisville 1956; Georgetown Univ. Washington 1956-60; Univ. of Toronto M.A. 1962, Ph.D. 1964; m. Mary Ann d. Emory J. Gary, Louisville, Ky. 11 June 1960; children: Maura, Elaine, John Raymond; PRINCIPAL, INNIS COLL., UNIV. OF TORONTO and Prof. of Eng. there; Shastri Indo-Candn. Inst. Lectr. on Candn. Lit. in India 1982; author "Marshall McLuhan" 1968; "Gardens, Covenants, Exiles: Loyalism in the Literature of Upper Canada" 1982; broadcasting, numerous reviews, articles on Candn. lit.; NDP; R. Catholic; Home: 110 Cottingham St., Toronto, Ont. M4V 1C1; Office: Toronto, Ont. M5S 1J5.

DUFFY, Michael Dennis (Mike); broadcast journalist; b. Charlottetown, P.E.I. 27 May 1946; s. Wilfred Francis and

Lillian (McCarron) D.; e. Charlottetown Pub. Schs.; St. Dunstan, s Univ.; m. Nancy E. d. Robert K. Mann, Halifax, N.S. 9 May 1970; children: Miranda S., R. Gavin; PARLTY. REPORTER, CBC NAT. TV NEWS 1977- ; former newspaper reporter Charlottetown and broadcast journalist private radio stns. Amherst and Halifax; joined CFCF-TV Montreal 1969; Reporter CHUM group radio stns. Ottawa 1971; Parlty. Reporter CBC Radio 1974; Host of Duffy's Notebook CBC "Sunday Evening News"; frequent speaker symposiums and confs. Candn. politics and workings of Parlt.; cited in H. of C. for efforts to assist Vietnamese refugees 1975; Chrmn. Adv. Comte. Algonquin Coll. Sch. of Journalism Ottawa; author numerous mag. articles politics and journalism; mem. Center Investigative Journalism; R. Catholic; Club: National Press; Home: 1202, 100 Bronson Ave., Ottawa, Ont. K1R 6G8; Office: 800, 150 Wellington St., Ottawa, Ont. K1P 5A4.

DUFRESNE, Cyrille, B.A., B.Ap.Sc., M.Sc., Ph.D., P.Eng.; industrial executive; geologist; b. Quebec, Que., 28 Aug. 1919; s. Alphonse-Olivier and Louise (L'Espérance) D.; e. Primary Sch., Que.; St. Charles Garnier Classical Coll., Que., 1930-39; Laval Univ., B.A. 1939, B.Ap.Sc. (Mining) 1943; McGill Univ., M.Sc. (Geol.) 1948, Ph.D. (Geol.) 1952; m. Mabel, d. Solyme Tremblay, Pointe Claire, Que. 30 April 1949; children: Marc, Anne, Monique, Therese, Paul, Jean Louis, Marie Edith, François; PRES., SIDBEC NORMINES INC.; with various mining cos. during summers 1937-48; joined Labrador Mining & Exploration Co. Ltd. Geol. 1949-50; with Iron Ore Co. of Can. as Geol., 1950-51; apptd. Supvr. (Geol.), 1952-55; Exploration Supervising Engr., 1956-58; Chief Engr., Carol Project, 1958-63; Govt. Prov. of Que. Comité de Sidérugie, 1963; joined Sidbec as Tech. Adv. to Bd. of Dirs., 1964; apptd. Asst. to the Pres. 1965; Vice-Pres., Supply, Sidbec Dosco Ltee. 1970-76; served with R.C.E. as Lt., 1943-45; Founder and 1st Chrmn., Schefferville R.C. Sch. Bd., 1956-58; Labrador R.C. Sch. Bd., 1961-63; mem., Corp. Prof. Engrs. Que.; Assn. Prof. Engrs. Nfld.; Am. Inst. Mining, Metall. & Petroleum Engrs.; Geol. Assn. Can.; Candn. Inst. Mining Metall.; Am. Iron & Steel Inst.; Chambre de Comm. de Montréal; Assn. des Anciens de Laval; McGill Grad. Soc.; R. Catholic; recreations: fishing, swimming; Clubs: Cercle Universitaire (Quebec); Cercle de la Place d'Armes; Home: 244 Bloomfield, Outremont, Que. H2V 3R4; Office: Suite 1401, 440 Dorchester Blvd. W., Montreal, Que. H2Z 1V7

DUFRESNE, Col. F. Gérard, C.M. (1976), E.D., C.D.; insurance executive; b. East Angus, Que., 22 July 1918; s. Dr. Albert and Laetitia (Milette) D.; e. Shawinigan (Que.) Tech. Inst., 1939; m. Madeleine, d. Louis A. Cyr. Shawinigan, Que., June 1949; children: Monique, Luc, Suzanne; PRESIDENT, GERARD DUFRESNE INC.; Pres., Moreco Elektric Inc.; Vice Pres., Trois-Rivieres Chevrolet Ltd.; Dir., Canadian Universal Insurance Co.; Cascade Charcoal Ltd.; Plastishaw Co. Ltd.; Pelston Co.; Pres., Industrial and Economical Devel. Comn. of Shawinigan and Grand-Mere Que.; served with Candn. Militia, 1937-40, 1947-63; Candn. Army Overseas with Fusiliers Mont-Royal and 3rd Div. H.Q., 1940-46; C.O. 62 Regt. R.C.A. and G.S.O. 1 Mil. Gp.; former Mayor of Shawinigan; Gov., Candn. Commissioners Corps; Past Pres., local Junior Chamber of Comm.; Chamber Comm.; Corp. Prof. Techs.; Past Vice-President, Insurance Brokers Association Province Quebec; R.C.A. Assn.; mem., Inst. Prof. and Cert. Technols. Can.; Dir., Que. Council, St-John Ambulance; Liberal; Roman Catholic; recreations: hunting, fishing; Club: Shawinigan Golf; Home: 1363 Maple Ave., Shawinigan, Que.; Office: 769 5th St., Shawinigan, Que. G9N 1G2

DUGAL, Louis-Paul, O.B.E. (Civil 1946), M.Sc., Ph.D., LL.D., F.R.S.C.; LL.D. (Hon.) Toronto, 1965; Corcordia Univ., 1975; Ottawa Univ., 1978; b. Quebec, Que., 1 Oct. 1911; s. Arthur J. and Jeanne (Bolduc) D.; e. Laval Univ.,

B.A. 1931, M.Sc. 1933; Univ. of Penna., Ph.D. 1939; m. Marie, d. Marius H. and Blanche Necker, 24 May 1937; children: Monique, Lyse, Michel; Prof. Emeritus, Univ. of Sherbrooke, 1976, still acting as consultant; sometime Pres., Comte. Conjoint of Univ. Programs., Council of Univs.; sometime Depy. Dir., Science Secretariat, Privy Council Can.; Prof. of Biology, Univ. of Montreal, 1935-45; Prof. of Physiology, Medical Sch., Laval Univ., 1945-56; Prof. of Biology, Ottawa Univ. 1956-62; Dean, Pure & Applied Scs., Univ. of Ottawa, 1962-65; Vice Dean, Med. Faculty, Univ. of Sherbrooke, 1966-67; Vice Rector (Research and Administration) 1967; mem. (1964) of Comn. by Candn. Univs. Foundation to study univ. financing in next decade; Laureate of the French Acad. of Science (Physiology), 1952; Guggenheim Fellow, 1954-55; Publications: about 100 scient. papers (original) in scient. journs.; mem., Am. and Candn. Physiol. Soc.; Roman Catholic; recreation: golf, skiing, reading; Home: 340 de la Corniche, St. Nicolas, Levis, Que. G0S 2Z0

DUGGAN, Eric Milwyn; investment dealer; b. Solsgirth, Manitoba, 8 Oct. 1905; s. David Milwyn and Hannah Marion (Price) D.; e. Edmonton (Alta.) Pub. and High Schs.; Univ. of Alberta (Sch. of Comm.); m. Elise, d. Cecil A. Davidson, Edmonton, Alta., 24 June 1939; children: David Meyrick, James Winston, Barbara Elyse; RESIDENT DIR., EQUITABLE SECURITIES LTD.; Dir., Edmonton Stock Exchange; Pres., Edmonton Flying Club Holdings Ltd.; Adv. Bd., Air Cadet League of Can.; Adv. Bd., Edmonton Eskimo Football Club; Trustee, univ. of Alta. Found.; with Northwestern Utilities Ltd., 1923-28; served in 2nd World War with R.C.A.F.; served in Can. and U.K. in Adm. Br.; retired Nov. 1945 with rank of Wing Commdr.; Conservative; Baptist; recreation: golf; Clubs: Edmonton; Mayfair Golf; Royal Glenora; Home: 11712-Edinboro Road, Edmonton, Alta. T6G 1Z8; Home: Box 27, Site 17, R.R. 2, Winterburn, Alta.; Office: 300 Empire Bldg., Edmonton, Alta.

DUGRE, Roland A., B.A.Sc.; educator; b. Wotton, Que. 30 March 1924; s. Joseph and Alma (Lavigne) D.; e. Laval Univ. B.A.Sc. 1949; Bishops Univ. Business Adm. 1962-64; Sherbrooke Univ. Computer Course 1969; m. Jacqueline d. Raoul Gourdeau, Quebec City, 12, Nov. 1952; children: Bernard, Hélène, François; DIRECTEUR GENERAL, ECOLE DE TECHNOLOGIE SUPERIEURE, UNIV. DU QUEBEC since 1974 also mem. of Bd., Pres. Extve. and Pegagogic Comn.; Dir. Asbestos Corp.; assoc. with mining indust. engn. field and planification (Lamage Mining Co.; Golden Manitou, Canadian Johns-Manville) 1949-70; Adm. Dir. Institut Nat. de la Recherche Scientifique and mem. Extve. Bd. 1970-74; Founder first mining inst. Que. Asbestos 1960; 1st Gov. Univ. du Qué. 1969 (mem. Pres. Comn., Planification Comn., Adm. Comn.); promoted Jr. Achievement Clubs in french schs.; Consultant for the World Bank; named "Man of the Year" Mining Assn. Que. 1968; Scholar Order Engrs. Que. 1947; Hon. Chief Huron Tribe 1968; author many articles, speeches presented to seminars or annual assn. meetings on business or engn. subjects; mem. Bd. Order Engrs. Que. 1964; Pres. Que. Chamber Comm. 1967-68; mem. Extve. Candn. Chamber Comm. 1969-74 (Pres. Research Comte. 1972-73); mem. Engn. Inst. Can.; Candn. Inst. Mining & Metall.; R. Catholic; recreations: golf, skiing, fishing, hunting; Clubs: Canadian; Mount Stephen; Seigniory; Oriskany; Home: 200 De Gaspe, App't 913, Nun's Island, Que.; Office: 180 Ste-Catherine St. E., Montreal, Que. H2X 1K9

DUHAIME, Hon. Yves L., M.N.A., B.A., LL.B.; politician; b. Chicoutimi, Qué. 27 May 1939; s. Gabriel L. and Rose (Gauthier) D.; e. Séminaire Sainte-Marie, Shawinigan B.A. 1959; McGill Univ. LL.B. 1962; Institut d'études politiques Univ. de Paris degree in Internat. Relations 1968; m. Lise d. Albert Racine, Shawinigan 7 Sept. 1963; children: Vincent, Mathieu; MIN. OF ENERGY & RESOURCES, QUE. 1981- and Pres. of Legislation Comte.

1979- ; called to Bar of Québec City and Trois-Rivières 1963; law practice Shawinigan and Grand-Mère 1963-66, 1969-76; cand. riding of Saint-Maurice prov. g.e.1970 and 1973, def.; el. M.N.A. for Saint-Maurice 1976; re-el. since; Min. of Tourism, Fish & Game, Que. 1976; Vice Pres. Conseil exécutif régional Parti Québécois for Mauricie 1973-75, Pres. 1975-76; Depy. Govt. House Leader 1976-81; Min. of Industry, Comm. & Tourism 1979; Parti Québécois; R. Catholic; Home: Saint-Jean des Piles Office: 200, Chemin Sainte-Foy, 6ième étage, Québec, Québec, G1R 4X7

DUHAMEL, Roger, B.A., LL.L., LL.D., F.R.S.C. (1960); b. Hamilton, Ont., 16 April 1916; e. Coll. Sainte-Marie, B.A. 1935; Univ. of Montreal, LL.L. 1938; LL.D. Univ. of Ottawa, 1962; with Municipality of Montreal, 1938-40; Asst. Editor-in-Chief of "Le Canada", 1940-42; Lit. Editor of "LeDevoir," 1942-44; Editor of "La Patrie", 1944-47; Dir., "Montreal Matin", 1947-53; Editor-in-Chief of "La Patrie", 1953-58; Vice Chrmn., Bd. of Broadcast Govs. Can., 1958-60; Queen's Printer 1960-69; Special Advisor to Secy. of State since 1971; Chrmn. Bilingual Districts Adv. Bd. 1970; Candn. Ambassador in Portugal 1972-77; Exec. Dir., La Presse Pub. House; President-Gen. of la Société Sainte-Jean-Baptiste de Montréal, 1943-45; Vice-Pres., du Comité permanent de la Survivance française en Amérique, 1944-45; Pres., la Soc. des Ecrivains canadiens (1955); mem., l'Acad. canadienne-française; l'Alliance française; Prof. of French and French-Candn. Lit., Faculty of Letters, Univ. of Montreal; Publications: "Les Cinq Grands", 1946; "Les Moralistes français", 1947; "Litérature" Vol. 1, 1948; "Bilan provisoire", 1958; "Letters à une provinciale", 1962; "Aux sources du romantisme français", 1964; "Lecture de Montaigne" (1965); "Manuel de littérature canadienne-française" (1967); "L'air du temps" (1968); "Le roman des Bonaparte", 1969; "Histoires galantes des reines de France" 1978; "L'Internationale des rois" 1979; "Témoins de leur temps" 1981; Address: 2810, ch. Ste-Catherine, Montreal, Que. H3T 1B8

DULUDE, Claude,R.C.A.; peintre; né Montréal, Qué. 30 mars 1931; f. Julien et Hélène (Lafleur); é. école Victor-Doré 1949; Chomedey-de-Maisonneuve 1951; Ecole des Beaux Arts de Montréal diplôme 1957; ép. Suzanne f. Guy Bélanger Montréal, Qué. 8 août 1967; enfant: Mathieu; depuis 1957 expose ses oeuvres dans les principales galeries et musées du Can.; Galerie Gilles Corbeil 1976, Musée d'Art contemporaine de Montréal 1964, Galerie Libre de Montréal 1960; livres d'art: "Poésie de'Emile Nelligan" 1967; "Cinquantes contines québécoises" 1970; étude de la gravure chez J. Friedleander à Paris, 1961; étude de l'Histoire de l'Art, Musée du Louvre, Paris, 1961; Exposition: Galerie Frederic Palardy, Montréal, 1981; Dresden Gallery, Halifax, 1981; Forest Art Gallery, Yarmouth, 1981; directeur du Secteur des Arts au cegep du Vieux Montréal 1969-75; mem. Société des Artistes en Arts visuels du Québec; catholique; Adresse: 4020 Adam, Montréal, Qué. H1W 2A3.

DUMAS, Antoine,B.A., R.C.A.; artist; educator; b. Québec City, Qué. 8 Dec. 1932; s. Calixte and Thérèse (Laflamme) D.; e. Séminaire de Qué. 1950; Coll. des Jésuites B.A. 1953; Ecole des Beaux-Arts de Qué. 1954-58 (Lt. Gov.'s Silver Medal); Acad. of Arts San Francisco 1969-70; Galerie Bernard Desroches, Montreal, 1981; m. Marie d. Rodolphe Deschênes, M.D. 7 June 1958; children: Hélène, Caroline, Emilie; PROF. ECOLE DES ARTS VISUELS, UNIV. LAVAL, present Univ. LAVAL. Prof. Ecole des Beaux-Arts de Qué. 1962-69; Dir. Graphic Communication present Univ. 1970-73; Exhns. incl. Galerie Zanettin Québec City 1968, 1971; Galerie Gilles Corbeil Montreal 1973; Art retrospective Québec, Montréal, Rimouski 1973; Consulate Gen. Can. New York 1975; Nancy Poole's Studio Toronto 1977, 1978, 1980; Itinerant Exhn. St. Catharines, Sudbury, London, Sarnia 1980-81 et "Chansons dans la mémoire longtemps" 1981; ; Silk Screen Production

Montréal Graphic Guild 1973-79; rep. various group exhns. incl. Graphic Designers Soc. Qué. 1966; Montreal Museum of Fine Arts 1974, 1975; Forum '76; illustrations for luxury ed. "Kamouraska" 1977; Stamps Design Can. Post 1976, 1978, 1979; author "A l'Enseigne d'Antan" 1970; "Antoine Dumas" 1980; mem. Conseil de la Gravure du Qué.; R. Catholic; Home: 1100 Marguerite-Bourgeoys, Sillery, Qué. G1S 3X9; Office: Pavillon Casault, Univ. Laval. Ste-Foy, Qué. G1K 7P4.

DUMAS, Pierre, B.A., LL.L., M.F.S.; diplomat; b. Montreal, Quebec, 11 July 1920; s. Arthur, M.D. and Angeline (Ferron) D.; e. Jean-de-Brebeuf Coll., Montreal, B.A. 1939; School of Foreign Service, Georgetown Univ., M.F.S. 1941; Sorbonne (Hist. & Lit.), Cert. 1946; Univ. of Montreal, LL.L. 1948; m. Marie Cencelli-Carissimo, d. late A. Carissimo, 14 March 1970; read law with Nadeau and Langis, Montreal; called to the Bar of Quebec 1948; joined Dept. of Ext. Affairs 1948; Third Secy. Paris 1949-43; Adv. Candn. Commrs., I.S.C. Indo-China, 1955; Adviser, Candn. Del., 17th Session U.N. Gen. Assembly, 1957; First Secy. Candn. Perm. Del. to European Office of U.N., Geneva, 1960; First Secy. 1961, Counsellor 1962-63, Belgrade; Head of W. European Sec., European Div., Dept. of External Affairs, 1964-66; Counsellor and Chargé d'affaires a.i. Rome, Min. of Candn. Embassy to Holy See (Rome), 1967-70; Consul Gen. Bordeaux, France, 1970-74; Ambassador to Czechoslovakia 1974-77, and concurrently to Hungary 1974-75; Amb. to Switzerland since 1977; served as writer, Wartime Info. Bd. (Psychol. Warfare Br.), Ottawa, 1943-44; taught (part-time) geog., Coll. Marguerite Bourgeoys, Westmount, Que. 1946-47; mem., Que. Bar Assn.; Prof. Assn. Foreign Service Offrs.; l'Assn. des Anciens du Coll. Jean-de-Brebeuf; Georgetown Univ. Alumni Assn.; Assoc. des Diplômes de l'Univ. de Montreal; R. Catholic; recreations: swimming, skiing, tennis, music, fine arts, reading; Club: Cercle Universitaire; Address: 15, Haspelgasse, Berne, Switzerland.

DUMBRILLE, Dorothy (Mrs. J.T. Smith); novelist; poet; historian; critic; book critic; b. Crysler, Ont., 25 Sept. 1897; d. late Ven. Rupert John and Minnie (Fulton) of U.E.L.; e. Kemptville High Sch., Ont.; Business Coll., Philadelphia, Pa.; m. James Travers Smith, 27 Dec. 1924; served with Dept. of Mil. and Defence, Ottawa, 1916-20; sometime Secy. to M. Albert Linton, Vice-Pres., Provident Mutual Life Ins. Co., Philadelphia; author of "Deep Doorways" 1939; "We Come! We Come!", 1940; "Last Leave", 1942; "Watch The Sun Rise", 1943; "All This Difference" 1945; "Stairway to the Stars", 1946; "Deep Doorways", 1947; "Up and Down the Glens" (the story of Glengarry), 1954; "Braggart In My Step", 1956; "The Battle of Cryslers Farm", 1967; "A Boy at Cryslers Farm", 1967; "Memories of My Father", 1980; in addition has written radio dramas, book reviews, and numerous newspaper and mag., articles; Anglican; mem., St. Lawrence Parks Comm.; hon. mem., Glengarry Historical Soc.; C.N.I.B.; Home: (P.O. Box 522) Alexandria, Ont. K0C 1A0

DUMETT, Clement Wallace Jr., B.Sc.; petroleum executive; b. Tacoma, Wash. 30 Dec. 1927; s. Clement Wallace and Dilma (Arnold) D.; e. Primary Sch. Seattle, Wash.; High Sch. Whittier, Cal.; Stanford Univ. B. Sc.(Petroleum Engn.) 1951; m. Carolyn Jane d Harold Coulthurst 9 March 1957; children: Daniel Wallace, Joanne Margaret, Patricia Jane; PRESIDENT, UNION OIL CO. OF CANADA LTD. since 1975; Dir. Peace Pipe Line Ltd.; Engr. Union Oil Co. of California, Whittier 1951; Engr. present co. Calgary, Alta. 1955, Chief Engr. 1966, Vice Pres. Exploration 1967, Vice Pres. Production 1971; served with US Army Mil. Police Bn. 1945-46; Dir. Calgary Philharmonic Soc.; Candn. Petrol. Assn. (Dir.); Soc. Petrol. Engrs.-Am. Inst. Mining Engrs.; Assn. Prof. Engrs. Prov. Alta.; Anglican; recreations: golf, fishing, hunting, skiing; Clubs: Calgary Petroleum; Canyon Meadows Golf &

Country; Ranchmen's; Calgary Golf & Country; Home: 443 Scarboro Ave. S.W., Calgary, Alta, T3C 2H7; Office: 335 Eighth Ave. S.W., Calgary, Alta. T2P 2K6.

DUMONT, Paul; industriel; né Montreal, Que., 21 mars 1918 f. Wilfrid et Radégonde (Arseneault) D.; B.A. à Montréal; Univ. d'Ottawa (Traduction); Univ. Laval (Espagnol); ép. Françoise, f. Henri St. Jacques, 9 mai 1942; enfants: André, Francois Louis, Michel, Marie; PRESIDENT, PAUL DUMONT, INC., depuis 1956; Chef de la Traduction, Ministère des Munitions et Approvisionnements, Ottawa, 1939-41; Commission des Prix et du Commerce 1946-47; Passé 34 mois en Europe en 2e Guerre; administrateur fondateur CEGEP (Collège) de Lévis-Lauzon; Cndn. Mfrs. Assn. (Que.); Dir., 6 ans, Pres., 19 mois, (Chapitre de la ville de Québec); Administrateur, Fondation VIA pour handicapés; Gestion OPTIMUM; Prés., Brasserie Le Fourquet; Volontaire, SACO (Service adm. canadien outremer); récréations: pêche, natation, ski, voyages; Résidence et Bureau: 162, Fabrique, St-Romuald, Que. G6W 2L4

DUMONTIER, Albert, LL.B., B.A.; judge; b. Lévis, Que., 1 Dec. 1909; s. J. Alphonse and Marie-Luce (Roy) D.; e. Ecole Mariste, Lévis, Que.; Coll. de Lévis, B.A. (Hons.); Univ. Laval, LL.L., 1934; m. Claire, d. Basile Devost, Québec, 21 May 1953; children; Marc, Pierre; CHIEF JUDGE OF THE COURT OF THE SESSIONS OF THE PEACE, since 26 Oct. 1967; apptd. Judge of Sessions of the Peace, 1957; Catholic; Home: 127 Côte du Passage, Lévis, Que. G6V 5T1; Office: Court House, Quebec, Que. G1R 4P6

DuMOULIN, Philip Anthony; insurance broker; b. Victoria, B.C., 8 Feb. 1901; s. Philip and Amy Louisa Theodora (Martin) D.; e. Chesterfield Sch., Kelowna, B.C. (1910-16); Trinity Coll. Sch., Port Hope, Ont. (1917-18); Royal Mill. Coll, Grad. 1921; children: Philippa Agnes Louisa Anne; with Wabasso Cotton Co., Sales Office, Montreal, 1921-22; Cndn. Indust. Alcohol (Sales Office), Montreal, 1921-22; Cndn. Indust. Alcohol (Sales Office), Montreal, 1922-23; Walkerville Hardware (Wholesale), Walkerville, Ont., 1923-29; Brantford Roofing Co., 1929-34; joined DuMoulin, Moore & Duffield Ltd. (est. 1859), now Dale and Co. 1934; served with Royal Candn. Arty., N.P.A.M. 1921-23; Past Pres., London Ins. Agents Assn.; Conservative; Anglican; recreations: fishing, gardening; Clubs: London Hunt & Country; London; Home: 653 Talbot St., London, Ont. N6A 2T6; Office: (P.O. Box 488), London, Ont. N6A 4X4

DUNBAR, Major Angus, Q.C.; b. Guelph, Ont., 27 Dec. 1899; s. C.L., K.C., and Maud (Oxnard) D.; e. Trinity Coll. Sch., Port Hope, Ont.; R.M.C., Kingston, Ont.; Osgoode Hall; m. Amy Grace, d. Dr. Henry Orton Howitt, Guelph, 30 Oct. 1937; has one s. and one d.; PARTNER, DUNBAR, GOETZ & DUNBAR; read law with C.L. Dunbar, K.C.; called to Bar of Ont. 1923; served in 2nd World War 1940-44; Maj., 4th Anti-Tank Regt.; Anglican; recreations: golf, fishing; Clubs: Cutten Fields Golf; Home: 221 Woolwich St., Guelph, Ont.; N1H 3V4; office: 32 Douglas St., Guelph, Ont. N1H 2S9

DUNBAR, (Isobel) Moira, O.C., M.A., F.R.S.C.; glaciologist (retired 1978); b. Edinburgh, Scot. 3 Feb. 1918; d. William and Elizabeth Mary (Robertson) D.; e. Cranley Sch. for Girls, Edinburgh 1935; Oxford Univ. B.A. 1939, M.A. 1948; U.S. Army Lang. Sch. Russian 1958; joined Defence Research Bd. Arctic Research Sec. (later Div. Earth Sciences) 1947, Acting Dir. Earth Sciences 1975-77; mem. Del. to study icebreaker operations in USSR 1964; mem. Comte. on Glaciology, Polar Research Bd., US Nat. Research Council 1976-80; prior to 1947 served in prof. theatre UK; rec'd Centennial Award 1971, Candn. Meteorol. Service; Massey Medal 1972; mem. Candn. Environmental Adv. Council 1972-78; author "Arctic Canada From the Air" (with K. R. Greenaway) 1956; numerous

scient. papers in field sea ice research; Fellow; Arctic Inst. N. Am. (Gov. 1966-69); Fellow Royal Candn. Geog. Soc. (Dir. since 1974); Internat. Glaciol. Soc.; Anglican; recreations: horseback riding, theatre, music, arctic history: Address: R.R. 1 Dunrobin, Ont. K0A 1T0.

DUNBAR, Maxwell John, M.A., Ph.D., F.R.G.S., F.L.S. (Lond.), F.R.S.C. (1954); university professor; b. Edinburgh, Scot. 19 Sept. 1914; s. William and Elizabeth Mary (Robertson) D.; e. Dalhousie Castle and Fettes Coll., Edinburgh; Oxford Univ., 1933-37, B.A., M.A.; Henry Fellow to Yale Univ. from Oxford, 1937-38; McGill Univ., Ph.D. 1941; D. Sc. (Hon.) Memorial Univ. of Nfld., 1979 m. Joan Suzanne, d. Lloyd D. Jackson, Hamilton, Ont., 1 Aug. 1945; m(2) Nancy Jane Wosstroff, Montreal, Que., 14 Dec. 1960; PROF. OF ZOOLOGY, McGILL UNIV., since 1959; Chrmn., Marine Sciences Centre, 1963-77; Gov., Arctic Inst. of N.Am. (Fellow 1947); mem. Que. Wildlife Conservation Assn.; mem. of Oxford Univ. Expdns. to Greenland, 1935 and 1936; to Glacier Bay, Alaska, 1948; mem. of Govt. Party, E. Arctic Patrol, 1939 and 1940; Expdns. to Ungava Bay (marine investigations), 1947, 1949, 1950, 1951, and to Hudson Bay, 1954, 1958; apptd. Asst. Prof. Zool., McGill Univ., 1946, and Assoc. Prof. 1948; Guggenheim Fellowship to Denmark, 1952-53; Candn. Acting Consul to Greenland, Dept. of External Affairs, Ottawa, 1941-46; awarded Bruce Medal for Polar Exploration, 1950 (Royal Soc. of Edin.); Fry Medal, Can. Soc. of Zoologists, 1979; mem., Soc. for Study of Evolution; Fellow, Am. Assn. Advanc. Science; Hon. Fellow (1966), Am. Geog. Soc.; Publications: "Ecological Development in Polar Regions"; "Environment and Good Sense" and about 100 scient. papers; Internat. Convenor-Marine Sec. IBP 1971-75; Scient. Leader, Gulf of St. Lawrence Project, Bedford Inst., Dartmouth, N.S. 1972-73; First Fellows Award, Arctic Inst. of N. Am. 1973: Sigma Xi; Liberal; Protestant; recreations: music, fishing; Clubs: McGill Faculty; Home: 488 Strathcona Ave., Westmount, Que. H3Y 2X1

DUNCAN, Alastair Robert Campbell, M.A.; D.Litt. (Lakehead Univ. 1979); university professor emeritus of philosophy; b. Blackhall, Midlothian, Scot., 12 July 1915; s. Leslie and Jean (Anderson) D.; e. George Watson's Boys' Coll., Edinburgh, 1933; Univ. of Edinburgh, M.A. with 1st Class Hons. in Philos., 1936; Univ. of Marburg, Germany, 1936-37; m. Francoise Anne Marie, d. Emile Pellissier, Vernoux, Ardeche, France, 11 June 1938; three s., Alain Campbell Bruce, Gregor Alastair Francois, Colin Adrien McKinley; PROF. & HEAD, DEPT. OF PHILOSOPHY, QUEEN'S UNIV., 1949-80; Asst. Lect., Univ. of Edinburgh, 1937-38; Lect., Univ. Coll., Univ. of London, 1938-39; Lectr. and Dir. of Studies, Faculty of Arts, Univ. of Edin., 1945-49; Dean, Faculty of Arts & Science, Queen's Univ., 1959-64; served in 2nd World War 1939-45; commd. 2nd Lieut. March 1940, Royal Arty.; promoted Capt., Mar. 1941; seconded to Mil. Intelligence, Sept. 1942; in North Africa and Italy, 1942-44; War Office, 1944-45; mem., Mind Assn.; Aristotelian Soc.; Royal Inst. of Philos.; Candn. Philos. Assn. (Pres. 1961 and 1967); Dante Soc. of N. Am.; Truax Visiting Prof., Hamilton Coll., N.Y. 1974; visiting Prof., Sir Wilfred Greenfell Coll., Nfld. 1982; author of "Practical Reason & Morality", 1957 transl. of "Development of Kantian Thought" by Vleeschauwer, 1962; Moral Philosophy (6 C.B.C. Talks, 1965); and various articles on philos., educ. and Dante; Presbyterian; recreation: sailing; Home: 68 Kensington Ave., Kingston, Ont. K7L 4B5

DUNCAN, G.R., M.Sc.Phm., D.Phil.; educator; b. Windsor, Ont., 22 Feb. 1934; s. Albert and late Edith (Vollans) Brackett; adopted by Mabel Gladys (Vollans) Wright and late Robert Duncan; e. Univ. of Toronto, B.Sc.Phm. 1957, M.Sc.Phm. 1959; Univ. of Basel, D.Phil. 1962; m. Elinor Joan, d. Leo Svirplys, 13 Aug. 1955; two d., Wendy Carolyn, Colleen Suzanne; PROF. OF PHARMACY, UNIV. OF TORONTO and Chrmn., Grad. Programme in Pharm. there; sometime Visiting Prof., Univ. of B.C.; Univ. of Alta.; author of over 16 scient. papers and abstracts; mem., Chem. Inst. Can.; Swiss Chem. Soc.; recreations: gardening, hunting, fishing, carpentry; Home: 2114 Springbank Rd., Mississauga, Ont. L5H 3N6

DUNCAN, Gaylen Rupert, B.Eng.; company executive (retired); b. Ottawa, Ont., 6 Aug. 1914; s. Gaylen Rupert and Florence Benedict (Stewart) D.; e. St. Andrews Coll. (Sr. Matric. 1931); McGill Univ., B.Eng. (Elect.) 1935; Harvard Grad. Sch. of Business Adm., 1935-37; m. Marie Frances, d. late A.P.C. Earle, 1 Nov. 1939; children: John Frederick, Gaylen Arthur, Gordon Alan, Jennifer Jane, James Douglas; Dir. & Treas., Mount St. Hilaire Nature Conservation Centre; Pres. and Dir., Project Residence 65 Inc.; former Vice President and Dir., MSN Industries Ltd.; Appraisal Engr. and Comm. Supt. of Venezuela Power Co., Maracaibo, Venezuela, 1939; Sales Engr., Ont. Mgr., Gen. Sales Mgr. and Dir. of Tamper Ltd., 1940-53; Dir. of Marketing, Canada Iron Foundries Ltd., 1953-57; apptd. Controller and Treas., Mussens Canada Ltd. in 1957; served in Royal Candn. Signals, 2nd Candn. Corps as Lieut.; Delta Kappa Epsilon; Liberal; United Church; recreations: fishing, reading, golf; Clubs: Mount Stephen; Royal Montreal Golf; Home: 2043 Graham Blvd., Town of Mt. Royal, Que. H3R 1H5

DUNCAN, James Stuart, C.M.G., LL.D., Hon. Air Commodore, Chevalier, French Legion of Honour; Croixde Lorraine; King Haakon VII Cross of Liberations; b. Paris, France, 1893; e. Coll. Rollin, Paris; LL.D. Dartmouth, 1957; m. Victoria Martinez Alonzo, Cordoba, Spain, 1936; one s. and two d.; joined Massey-Harris Ltd. Berlin, 1909; came to Can., 1911; served in 1st World War with U.K. forces, 1914-18; rising to Capt. and Adj., 16th Bgde., 16th Irish Div. Arty.; apptd. Gen. Mgr., Massey-Harris Co., 1936, Pres., 1941, Chrmn. and Pres. until resignation, 1956; apptd. Acting Depy. Min. of Defence for Air, 1940, and took over leadership of Brit. Commonwealth Air Training Plan; declined invitation of the Prime Minister to join Fed. Cabinet as Min. of Air, 1940; Chrmn., Combined Agric. & Food Comte., UNRRA, 1941-42; mem., Nat. Research Council, Ottawa, during war years; Chrmn., Hydro-Electric Power Comn. of Ont., 1956-61; Past Chrmn., Toronto Bd. Trade; Toronto Community Chest; Candn. Council Internat. Chambers Comm., Montreal; Hon. Pres., Toronto Sec., "Free Fighting French"; 1st Candn. chosen by Nat. Sales Extve. Organ. as "Canadian Businessman of the Year", June 1956; Chrmn., Nat. Conf. on Engn., Scient. and Tech. Manpower, St. Andrew's, New Brunswick, Sept. 1956; Deputy Chrmn., Candn. Trade Mission to U.K., Dec., 1957; author of various publ. incl. "Russia's Bid For World Supremacy" (1955); "The Great Leap Forward" (1959); "Russia Revisited" (1960); "In the Shadow of the Red Star" (1962); "A Businessman Looks at Red China" (1965); "Not a One-Way Street", (an autobiography) 1971; Clubs: York (Toronto); Royal Bermuda Yacht; Address: Somerset House, Paget, Bermuda.

DUNCANSON, Frank S.; banker; b. 1929; e. Columbia Univ. Extve. Program Business Adm.; Queen's Univ. Extve. Summer Sch. 1963, Perspective for Mang. 1962; m. Joan; children: Marshall, Debbie, Ken; SR. VICE PRES. OIL & GAS DIV., CANADIAN IMPERIAL BANK OF COMMERCE 1980- ; Div. Gen. Mgr. Personnel Div. H.O. present Bank 1965-68, Div. Gen. Mgr. 1968-71, Vice Pres. 1971-73, Vice Pres. & Regional Gen. Mgr. Ont. E. & N., Toronto 1973, Alta. Region 1973-77, Special Projects H.O. 1977-79, Vice Pres. & Gen. Mgr. Corporate Banking 1979-80; Clubs: National; Calgary Petroleum; Ranchmen's; Home: 902 Elizabeth Rd. S.W., Calgary, Alta.; Office: 400, 425 - 1st St. S.W., Calgary, Alta.

DUNELL, Basil Anderson, M.A.Sc., M.A., Ph.D., F.C.I.C.; educator; b. Vancouver, B.C. 5 Apl. 1923; s. Basil and Elizabeth Dodd (Allan) D.; e. Univ. of B.C.,

B.A.Sc. (Chem. Engn.) 1945, M.A.Sc. 1946; Princeton Univ. M.A. 1948, Ph.D. (Phys. Chem.) 1949; PROF. OF CHEMISTRY, UNIV. OF B. C. 1965- ; Textile Research Inst. Fellow, Princeton Univ. 1946-49; Asst. Prof. Univ. of B.C. 1949, Assoc. Prof. 1961; Univ. Fellow Physics Dept. Univ. of Nottingham 1978-79; co-author "Problems for Introductory University Chemistry with Complete Solutions" 1967; scientific articles on polymer rheology and studies in molecular motion in solids by nuclear magnetic resonance; mem. Council, Chem. Inst. Can. 1965-70, Dir. Scient. Affairs 1967-70; Assoc. mem. Royal Soc. Chem. (London); Anglican; Club: Alpine of Canada; Home: 3893 W. 9th Ave., Vancouver, B.C. V6R 2C2; Office: Vancouver, B.C. V6T 1Y6.

DUNLAP, Air Marshal Clarence R., C.B.E., C.D., D.C.L., D.Eng., B.Sc.; Royal Canadian Air Force (retired); b. Sydney Mines, N.S., 1 Jan. 1908; s. late Frank Burns and Flora L. (Whitman) D.; e. Acadia Univ. and N.S. Tech. Coll., B.Sc. in E.E., 1928; D.C.L. Granted Hon. (Acadia 1957); Hon. D. Eng. (N.S.T.C. 1967); m. Hester, d. late Dr. E.A. Cleveland, Vancouver, B.C., 3 Aug. 1935; one s., Dr. David; joined R.C.A.F. in 1928 and commissioned in the rank of Pilot Offr.; for a number of years prior to 2nd World War was engaged in R.C.A.F.'s aerial photographic survey program; later specialized in air armament and attended special training courses in U.K.; at outbreak of war in 1939 was serving as Dir. of Armament at Air Force Hdqrs., Ottawa; early 1942 assumed command of the RCAF Station, Mountain View, Ont., the home of Air Armament School & No. 6 Bombing & Gunner School; late in 1942 posted overseas to become C.O. at R.C.A.F. Stn. at Leeming, Yorks, a station in No. 6 Candn. Bomber Group; in 1943 went to N. Africa as C.O. of No. 331 wing located in Tunisia; R.C.A.F. Sqdns. under his command carried out strategic and tactical bombing in support of campaigns in Sicily, and mainland Italy; returning to U.K. took command of a medium bomber wing (No. 139 Wing) engaged in daylight operations (2nd Tactical Air Force); awarded American Silver Star and Fr. Croix de Guerre; in Jan. 1945 after promotion to Air Commodore, posted back to U.K. taking command of Candn. bomber bases at Middleton-St. George, and Croft; returned to Can., May 1945 and apptd. Depy. Air Member for Air Staff at A.F.H.Q.; in 1946 attended Bikini atomic bomb tests as a Rep. of R.C.A.F., and before his appt. as Air Member for Air Plans in Oct. 1948 was priveledged to attend The Nat. War Coll., Wash., D.C., for one year; in Nov. 1949 assumed duties of A.O.C., N.W. Air Command with hdqrs. at Edmonton, Alta., and was trans. to Air Defence Command, St. Hubert, P.Q., in May 1951 to fill a similar position; apptd. Commandant of Nat. Defence Coll., Kingston, Ont., 1 Aug. 1951; Vice Chief of Air Staff, June 1954; in June 1958 assumed position of Depy. Chief of Staff Operations and was later designated Asst. to the Chief of Staff at Supreme Hdqrs., Allied Powers Europe, Paris, France; Chief of the Air Staff, Canada, 15 Sept. 1962-14 Aug. 1964; Depy. Commdr.-in-Chief, North American Air Defence Command (NORAD), 1964-67; placed on retired list (R.C.A.F.) July 1968; Hon. Pres., RCAF Mem. Fund; Baptist; recreations: golf, fishing, painting, bridge; Clubs: Victoria Golf; Royal Ottawa Golf; Union of B.C.; Home: Apt. 203, 1375 Newport Ave., Victoria, B.C. V8S 5E8

DUNLOP, William Campbell, Q.C.; b. N. Ireland 19 Mar. 1896 s. John Alexander and Elizabeth Ann (Campbell) D.; e. Dalhousie Univ., LL.B. 1922 children: James Hugh, William Bruce, late John Alexander, David Brian; retired Partner, Walker, Dunlop; Chrmn., Halifax Sch. Bd. 1959; called to Bar of N.S. 1922; cr. K.C. 1937; served in World War 1914-19 with C.E.F.; served in France and Belgium 1916-19; Reserve Army in Can. 1939-45; Charter mem. Candn. Legion (Past Pres., Hants Co. and Cornwallis Brs.; Pres., Halifax Dist. Council; served on Prov.

and Dom. Councils); Freemason; United Church; Home: 5860 Pine Hill Drive, Halifax, N.S. B3H 1E5;

DUNN, Albert Wilkerson,D.F.C., A.B.; manufacturer; b. Durham, N.C. 2 March 1921; s. William Burwell and Maude (Wilkerson) D.; e. Durham (N.C.) High Sch. 1939; Duke Univ. A.B. 1943; m. Jane d. late Harold Foote Ballard 23 Oct. 1943; children: Robert R., Stephen R., Christie A. (Mrs. J. P. Miller); PRES. AND CHIEF EXTVE. OFFR., GOODYEAR CANADA INC. 1978- ; Pres. and Dir. Kelly-Springfield Canada Inc.; Dir. Hallmark Auto-Centres Inc.; Seiberling Canada Inc.; joined Pub. Relations Dept., Goodyear Tire & Rubber Co., Akron, Ohio 1946, Mgr. Aviation Products Div. Dayton, Ohio, 1948, Aviation Products Mil. Coordinator 1955; Mgr. Aviation Products Div. Goodyear International Corp. 1957, Sales Dir. Philippines 1959, Vice Pres. and Gen. Mgr. 1961; Mang. Dir. Goodyear-South Africa 1971; served with U.S. Air Force Mediterranean Theatre 48 missions during World War II, rank Lt.; rec'd Air Medal with 3 Oak Leaf Clusters; Distinguished Flying Cross; Past Pres. Am. Chamber Comm. Manila; Am. Sch. Manila; Past Dir. Rotary of Manila; mem. Soc. Automotive Engrs.; Bd. Trade Metrop. Toronto; Candn.-S. Africa Soc.; Sigma Chi; Protestant; recreations: golf, photography; Clubs: Mississauga Golf & Country; Canadian; Home: 446 Copeland Court Oakville, Ont. L6J 4B9; Office: 21 Four Seasons Pl., Islington, Ont. M9B 6G2.

DUNN, Gerald Fitzpatrick, F.C.A. (1957); b. Victoria, B.C., 21 Aug. 1911; s. late Henry Josias and Caroline H.G. (Patten) D.; e. Public and High Schs., Victoria, B.C.; admitted to B.C. Inst. of Chart. Acctounts, 1942; m. late Jean, d. late Alexander MacDonald, 1943; two d., Patricia Ann, Sheelah Jean; retired Partner, Thorne, Riddell & Co.; Dir.; Winthrop Investments Ltd.; Stuart Investments Ltd.; Pres., Ducks Unlimited (Canada); Trustee, Ducks Unlimited (U.S.A.); mem. of Victoria Adv. Bd., National Trust Co.; Past Pres., Victoria Chamber of Comm.; Pres., B.C. Inst. of Chart. Accts., 1953-54, (mem. of Council, 1949-56); B.C. Dir. Candn. Inst. of Chart. Accts., 1952-53-54; Gov., Candn. Tax Foundation; Pres., B.C. Chamber of Comm., 1958-59; Dir., Cedar Lodge Soc.; Freemason; Anglican; recreations: shooting, fishing, golf; Clubs: Union; Victoria Golf; Gyro; Canadian (Past Pres.); Home: 2750 Thorpe Place, Victoria, B.C. V8R 2W4; Office: 2750 Thorpe Ave., Victoria, B.C.

DUNN, Timothy Hibbard, B.Com.; investment executive; b. Quebec City, Que., 26 Aug. 1919; s. late Charles Gwyllym and late Marie Jeanne (Gibaut) D.; e. Quebec High Sch.; Lakefield (Ont.) Coll. Sch.; McGill Univ. B.Com. 1940; m. Osla Jane d. late W.R.G. Holt, Montreal, Que., 18 Nov. 1943; children: Peter, Stuart, Robert, Brian, Debra, Daryl; CHRMN., A.E. OSLER, GENDRON LTD.; served with RCNVR 1939-45, C.O. HMCS "La Malbaie"; Gov. Bishop's Univ.; Gov. and Past Chrmn. Jeffery Hall's Hosp.; Past Pres. McGill Grads. (Que.); Candn. Red Cross; Que. Winter Club; Protestant; recreations: tennis, yachting, golf, squash; Clubs: Quebec Garrison; Mount Royal; Montreal Skeet; Montreal Racket; Lyford Cay (Nassau); Home: 1050 St. Louis Rd., Quebec, Que. G1S 1C7

DUNN, Wesley John, D.D.S., F.A.C.D., F.R.C.D.(C) (Hon.); b. Toronto, Ont., 21 May 1924; s. John James and late Grace Eleanor (Bryan) D.; e. Bloor Coll. Inst., Toronto, 1938-42; Univ. of Toronto, Victoria Coll. 1942-43. Faculty of Dent., D.D.S. 1947 (Student Parlt. Prize, Univ. Honour Award 1947); m. Jean Mildred, d. late George Leclair Nicholls and Ida (Harris) Nicholls, 6 Nov. 1948; three s., Steven Craig, Brian Wesley, Bruce Edward James; private dental practice, Toronto, 1947-56; Registrar-Secy. and Treas., Royal Coll. of Dental Surgs. of Ont., 1956-65; Special Lectr., Univ. of Toronto, Faculty of Dent. 1956-64, Sch. of Hygiene 1957-64; joined Univ. of W. Ont., Faculty of Dent. 1965, Asst. Prof. 1965, Assoc.

Prof. 1966, Prof. 1974, Dean of Faculty 1965-82; mem., Pres.'s Adv. Comte. there and Ex Officio mem., Senate and offr. or mem. of various other univ. Comtes.; Royal Coll. Dent. Surgs. Ont. (Dir. of Coll. 1966-70); Gov., Women's College Hospital, Toronto, 1959-64; Dir., London YMCA-YWCA, 1965-70 (Chrmn. Boys' Dept. Comte 1968-70); mem., Health & Welfare Related Programs Adv. Comte., Fanshawe Coll, 1967-69 and Chrmn., Dent. Assisting Course Adv. Comte.; Dir., Un. Community Services, 1968-70; Chmn., Ont. Council of Univ. Health Sciences, 1974-76; mem., Ont. Council of Health, 1966-71 (Extve. Comte. 1966-69; Chrmn. Comte on Educ. of Health Disciplines 1966); Asst. Ed., Ont. Dent. Assn. Journ., 1948-50; Ed., "Oral Health" 1950-53 and Candn. Dent. Assn. Journ. 1953-59; author of numerous articles for various prof. journs.; Pres., Assoc. of Candn. Fac. of Dentry, 1976-78; Hon. mem. Hamilton Acad. Dent.; mem., Omicron Kappa Upsilon; Candn. Soc. Dent. Children (Organ. Secy. 1951-53); Am. Assn. Dent. Ed's (Pres. 1958); Can. Dent. Assn.; (Chrmn. various comtes.); Fellow Am. Coll. Dents.; Hon. Fellow, Royal Coll. of Dent. of Can.; Candn. Dent. Service Plans Inc. (Dir. and mem. Extve. Comte. 1959-65); Ont. Dent. Nurses' & Asst.'s Assn. (Adv. Bd. 1961-64); Dentists Legal Protective Assn. Ont. (Secy.-Treas. 1956-65); Chrmn., Fluoridation Comte., Health League of Can., 1957-62; United Church; Home: 134 Wychwood Park, London, Ont. N6G 1R7

DUNNIGAN, Gerald George, B.A., M.B.A.; executive; b. Montreal, Que. 12 Dec. 1931; s. John George and Olive Catherine (Brophy) D.; e. Univ. of Montreal B.A. 1954; Labour Coll. Can. Dipl. 1965; McGill Univ. Dipl. Business Mang. 1968; Nat. Defence Coll. 1968-69; Sir George Williams Univ. M.B.A. 1972; m. Constance Barbara d. late Clarence Fleming 22 May 1954; three s. Sean, Paul, Frank; PRESIDENT AND C.E.O., WESTCAN MANUFACTURING LTD.;joined Northern Electric Co. (Northern Telecom Ltd.) Montreal 1951, Product Mgr. Quebec City 1959, Trois Rivieres Mgr. 1961, N.S. Mgr. Halifax 1963, Labour Relations Mgr. 1965, Gen. Mgr. Distribution Sales Div. Montreal 1969, Vice Pres. Product Mang. 1971 and Vice Pres. Marketing Nedco Ltd. 1972; Vice Pres. 1974 and Pres., Distribution Group Steetley Ind. Ltd. 1977; Pres. and C.E.O., Eutectic Can. Ltd. and Pres., Amer. Div. Eutectic Corp. N.Y. 1979; served with RCN (R) 1951-56, rank Lt.; mem. Consultative Comte. to Faculty of Comm. and Adm. Concordia Univ. Montreal; past pres., Cdn. Elec. Distributors Assn. (1977-78); R. Catholic; recreations: golf, skiing, curling, reading; Clubs: Canadian (New York); Metropolitan (N.Y.); Westchester Country Club; Weston Golf & Country; Mount Stephen (Montreal); Home: 1480 Duchess Ave., West Vancouver, B.C. V7T 2W2; Office: 310 Commercial Dr., Vancouver, B.C. V5L 3V6

DUNSMORE, Robert Lionel, M.C., B.Sc., D.C.S., F.E.I.C.; civil engineer; executive; b. Seaforth, Ont., 2 Sept. 1893; s. Robert Johns and Margaret (Paisley) D.; e. St. Thomas (Ont.) Coll. Inst.; Queen's Univ., B.Sc. (Civil Engn.) 1915; Hon. D.C.S. Laval Univ., 1959; Hon. LL.D. Queen's Univ. 1980; m. Rosabel, d. Frederick J. Voaden, 4 May 1916; has one s., R.J.C.; Vice Chrmn. and Dir., B.N.C. (Canada) Ltée 1950-63; Pres. (1963-71) Trafalgar Sch. for Girls; mem. Bd. Trustees, Queen's Univ. 1953-74; Geodetic Survey Canada, Dept. of Public Works of Canada, 1914; joined Imperial Oil Company, Sarnia, Ont., Asst. Engr., 1919, Asst. Master Mechanic 1920, Engr. in charge of Construction, Calgary, Alta. Refinery, 1922, and Asst. Supt. there 1923; Asst. Supt., IOCO Refinery, 1925; Supt., Talara (Peru) Refinery, International Petroleum Co. Ltd. 1926-29, and Gen. Supt. there 1929-30; Supt. at Halifax, Imperial Oil Co., 1930-43; and Mgr., Montreal Refinery, 1944-46; Co-ordinator of Mfg., Internat. Petroleum Co. Ltd., 1946-49; Pres., Champlain Oil Products Ltd., 1949-58; and Dir. 1958-63; served in 1st World War as Maj., R.C.E., awarded M.C.; holds Long Service Decoration; served in 2nd World War as Dir. of

Fuel, Royal Candn. Navy, with rank of Commdr.; Fellow, Engn. Inst. of Can. (Past Vice-Pres., Maritimes; Past Chrmn., Halifax, N.S., Br.; Chrmn., Montreal Br.; Vice-Pres.,Que. Prov.); Dir. and Chrmn. of the Board, Candn. Broadcasting Corp., 1958-63; Past President, Montreal Bd. Trade; mem., Candn. Inst. Internat. Affairs; Protestant; recreation: tennis; Clubs: Forest & Stream; Montreal University (Montreal); Montreal Indoor Tennis; Home: 4 Centre St., Kingston, Ont. K7L 4E6

DUNTON, Arnold Davidson, C.C. (1970), D.Sc., LL.D.; university educator; b. Montreal, P.Q., 4 July 1912; s. Robert Andrew and Elizabeth (Davidson) D.; e. Lower Can. Coll.; Univ. of Grenoble, France; McGill Univ.; Cambridge Univ.; Univ. of Munich; Laval Univ., D.Sc.; LL.D. Univs. Sask., Queen's, B.C., Toronto, McGill, Western Ont., New Brunswick; m. Kathleen, d. T.W. Bingay, Vancouver, B.C., 30 June 1944; children: Darcy, Deborah; FELLOW, INST. OF CANDN. STUDIES, CARLETON UNIV.; Dir. (1973-78) and formerly Pres. (1958-72) of Carleton Univ.; Chrmn. Ont. Press Council; Dir. Reader's Digest Association (Canada) Limited; Shell Canada Ltd.; served on "Montreal Star" as Reporter, 1935-37; Assoc. Ed., 1937-38; Ed., "Montreal Standard", 1938; joined Wartime Information Bd., 1942; apptd. Asst. Gen. Mgr., 1943; Gen. Mgr., 1944-45; apptd. Chrmn. Bd. of Govs., CBC, 1945; apptd. (1963) Co-chairman, Royal Comn. on Bilingualism & Biculturalism; Delta Upsilon; United Church; recreations: skiing, tennis; Clubs: Rideau; Cercle Universitaire d'Ottawa; Home: 410 Maple Lane, Rockcliffe, Ottawa, Ont. K1M 1H9; Office: Carleton University, Ottawa, Ont.

DuPONT, His Hon. Wilfred Roland; judge; b. Foleyet, Ont., 16 Feb. 1926; s. Alexander and Aldea (St. Aubin) D.; e. Osgoode Hall Law Sch., 1950; m. Jeannine, d. Joseph David Levesque, 11 Feb. 1956; children: Linda, Louise, Julie, David, Denise, Richard; JUSTICE, SUPREME COURT OF ONT., EX OFFICO, MEM., ONT. COURT OF APPEAL, since 1977; called to Bar of Ont. 1950; cr. Q.C. 1963; private law practice, Timmins, Ont., 1950-53; Asst. Crown Atty. for Dist. of Cochrane, 1953-66; Crown Atty. for Prov. of Ont., 1966-68; Sr. Judge of Cochrane District Court, 1969-77; served with RCAF 1943-45; rank Flying Offr.; Chrmn. and Trustee, Cochrane High Sch. for 9 yrs. and Lady Minto Hosp. for 10 yrs.; R. Catholic; recreations: flying, hunting; Home: R.R. #3, Caledon East, Ont. L0N 1E0; Office: Osgoode Hall, 130 Queen St. W., Toronto, Ont. M5H 2N5

DUPRE, Joseph Stefan, A.M., Ph.D.; university professor; b. Quebec, Que., 3 Nov. 1936; s. late Hon. Maurice, P.C., K.C. and Anita Arden (Dowd) D.; e. St. Patrick's Sch., Quebec, Que.; Univ. of Ottawa, B.A. 1955; Harvard Univ., A.M. 1957, Ph.D. 1958; Hon. degrees: D.Sc.Soc., Laval, 1976; LL.D., McMaster, 1977; D.U., Univ. of Ottawa, 1977; m. Anne Louise, d. Dr. J. Robert Willson, Philadelphia, Pa., 6 July 1963; children: Daphne, Maurice; PROF. OF POL. SCIENCE UNIV. OF TORONTO since 1966, Chrmn. of the Dept. of Pol. Econ. 1970-74; Dir., Centre for Urban and Community Studies 1966-70; Teaching Fellow in Govt., Harvard Univ., 1956-57; Instr. 1958-61; Asst. Prof. 1961-63; Secy., Grad. Sch. of Pub. Adm., 1960-63; Research Fellow, The Brookings Inst., Washington, D.C., 1957-58; joined present Univ. as Assoc. Prof. of Pol. Science, 1963; Ed. Dir., Ont. Comte. on Taxation, 1964-67; mem., Ont. Civil Service Arbitration Bd., 1965-68; Science Council-Can. Council Study Group on Fed. Support of Univ. Research, 1967-68; Nat. Research Council of Can., 1969-77; Chmn., Ont. Council on Univ. Affairs, 1974-77 and mem. since 1977; author: "Intergovernmental Finance in Ontario: A Provincial-Local Perspective", 1968; co-author "Federalism and Policy Development", 1973; "The Role of the Federal Government in the Support of Research in Canadian Universities", 1969; "Science and the Nation", 1962, Japanese ed. 1965; also numerous contributions to books

and scholarly journs.; mem., Inst. Pub. Adm. Can. (Nat. Vice Pres. 1967-69; Pres. 1969-70); Soc. Sciences and Hum. Research Council of Canada; Council of Trustees, Inst. for Research on Public Policy; Prof. Organizations Comte of the Atty. Gen. of Ont.; Candn. Pol. Science Assn. (Secy.-Treas. 1965-66); Candn. Tax Foundation; R. Catholic; Home: 422 Glencairn, Toronto, Ont. M5N 1V5

DUPUIS, Jacques, B.A., LL.B.; lawyer; b. Montreal, Que., 15 Apl. 1918; s. Pierre-Louis and Carmel (Girouard) D.; e. Coll. de Montréal, B.A. 1937; Univ. of Montreal, LL.B. 1939; Univ. of W. Ont., Business Adm. 1956; m. Jeannine, d. Charles-Auguste Bertrand, 7 Feb. 1948; children: Jacques, Louise, Bertrand; Extve. Vice Pres., The Montreal and Candn. Stock Exchanges, 1969-74; called to the Bar of Que. 1947; on active service 1940-46; served with 4th Medium Regt., R.C.A. in Europe 1942-45; Mentioned in Despatches; Moderator of 39 weekly televised business programs in Montreal, 1961-62; mem., Chambre de Comm. du Dist. de Montréal (Dir. 1958-63); Pres., Assoc. mem. Comte., Que. Wholesale Grocers Assn., 1958-59; mem., Extve. Comte., Candn. Mfrs. Assn. 1960; Dir., Candn. Food Processors Assn., 1959; Dir. and mem. Extve. Comte., Fed. French Charities; Pres. Better Business Bureau; mem., Montreal Bar Assn.; R. Catholic; recreations: swimming, reading; Clubs: Richelieu; St-Denis; Canadian (mem. Extve. Comte. 1960)

DUQUET, Gérard, M.P.; b. Quebec, Que., 17 Apl. 1909; s. Adjutor and Julia (Boucher) D.; e. St-Roch Sch. and St-Vincent de Paul, Quebec; Filiol Acad. of Comm. Quebec; m. Therese, d. Adelard Rodrigue, St-Georges de Beauce, Que., 27 Oct. 1945; Br. Mgr., Peoples Credit Jewellers, Quebec, 1937-65; Vice Pres., Les Entreprises Lairet and RE-NO-VO Inc., 1961-65; Contact Sales Mgr., Mappin's Ltd., 1965-66; el. to H. of C. for Quebec-E.; Parlty. Secy. to Min. of Transport; Vice Pres., Lib. Fed. of Que., 1960-61; Chrmn., Que. Liberal Caucus 1975-77; Pres., Que.-E. Lib. Assn., 1958-61 and "Ligue des Citoyens", 1952; Founder, Pre-scient. Sch., Quebec; Past Pres., Honor Loan to Students, Que.; St-John Baptist Soc., 1951-55; Hon. Pres., Assn. Médicale internationale; awarded Can. Merit Medal; St-Jean Baptiste Soc. Merit Plaque; mem. Chamber Comm. Que.; St-Roch Business Center; Credit Granters Candn. Assn.; Comm. Union Quebec City; Assn. internationale des parlementaires de langue française; Assn. Prop. de Qué. Inc.; Sportifs de Qué; K. of C.; Vice-Chmn. Assn. Can.-Fr.; Vice-Chmn., Management & Mem's Services Comte.; Liberal; R. Catholic: Home: 720 - 19ième Rue, Québec, Qué. G1J 1W5; Office: House of Commons, Ottawa, Ont. K1A 0A6

DUQUET, John Edward Lewis, Q.C., LL.L., LL.D., K.C.S.G.; b. Richmond, Que., 22 June 1904; s. William James and Mary Ellen (Hayes) D.; e. Richmond (Que.) Sch.; St. Charles Semy., Sherbrooke; Univ. of Montreal, B.A., LL.L.; m. Aileen, d.A.L. Caron, Outremont, Que., 1936; two d.; Counsel: Bronstetter, Wilkie, Penhale, Donovan, Giroux and Charbonneau; Dir., Canadair Ltd.; Dir. and Vice Pres., Canada West Indies Molasses Co. Ltd.; Dir., Timmins Investments Ltd.; Gillette of Canada Ltd.; Liquid Carbonic Canadian Corp. Ltd.; Chromasco Ltd.; Wabasso Ltd.; read law with Laflamme, Mitchell, Kearney and Duquet and successors; mem., Montreal Bd. Trade; recreation: golf; Clubs: Mount Royal; Laurentian Golf; Laval-sur-le-Lac Golf; Home: P.O. Box 14, Saint-Agathe-des-Monts, Quebec, J8C 3A1; Office: 3411 Place Ville Marie, Montreal, Que. H3B 3N7

DURHAM, Thompson Seelye, C.D., B.A., M.B.A.; b. Sault Ste. Marie, Ont., 23 Mar. 1930; s. T. Edwin and Jessie (Seelye) D.; e. Queen's Univ., B.A., (Gen.) 1954; M.B.A. Univ. of West. Ont. 1959; m. Leone A., d. Engr Lindstrom, Kenora, Ont., 30 June 1956; MGR., BETTER BUSINESS BUREAU OF WINNIPEG since 1979; engaged in machinery sales, Joy Mfg. Co. (Can.) Ltd. 1954-

1956 & 1959-61; sales, IBM 1961-63; Winnipeg Economic Development Bd., 1966-78; Sr. Bus. Cons., Man. Dept. Ind. & Comm. 1963-66; mem., Winnipeg Chamber of Comm.; Inst. of Assn. Extves.; Conservative; Anglican; Service Affiliation RCNR 1948-66, CAF (NR) 1966-present, Naval Rank CDR (R) - HMCS Chippawa (NRU Winnipeg); recreations: boating, telecommunications; Club: Rotary; Home: 198 Queenston, Winnipeg, Man. R3N 0W7; Office: 204-365 Hargrave St. Winnipeg, Man. R3B 2K3

DURISH, Paul H.; company president; b. Hunta, Ont. 15 Dec. 1935; s. Joseph and Anne (Sernanick) D.; e. Schs. of S. Porcupine, St. Catharines, Merriton, Ont.; Millard Filmore Coll.; m. Carole Ann, d. Gordon Vine, 17 Dec. 1955; three d., Kimberley Ann, Katherine, Karen; PRESIDENT AND DIR., DURISH INVESTMENT CORP. LTD.; commenced with Dana Corp., Thorold, Ont., in Advertising Dept., 1954; joined Studebaker Corp. as Asst. Advertising Mgr., 1959; Dir., Advertising and Pub. Relations, Studebaker Corp. and Mercedes-Benz of Canada Ltd., 1961; Dir. of Advertising, Studebaker Canada, U.S.A., Australia, N.Z., S. Africa, Israel, Belgium, Chile, 1962-64; mem., French Chamber of Comm.; Art Gallery of Ont.; United Ch.; recreations: golf, fishing, photography, travel; Club: Canadian; Home: Las Bisas Farm, Caledon, Ont.

DURNAN, David Frederick, C.A.; publisher; b. Toronto, Ont. 1935; s. James Frederick and Macie (Bowyer) D.; e. Pub. and High Schs., Toronto, Ont.; m. late Victoria Shewchuk 7 June 1957; children: Alison, Catherine; Remarried to: Karen Sue Milne, Feb. 1978; PRESIDENT AND DIR., ENCYCLOPAEDIA BRITANNICA PUBLICATIONS LTD. since 1973; Dir., Encyclopaedia Universalis du Canada Ltée; F.E. Compton of Canada Ltd.; Encyclopaedia Britannica of Canada Ltd.; with Clarkson Gordon & Co., C.A. 1959; joined present Co. as Asst. Controller 1960, Asst. Gen. Mgr. Australia 1961, Internat. Div. Europe 1962-63, Comptroller, Toronto 1964, Asst. Secy. and Comptroller 1966, Vice-Pres. Finance 1971; Inst. Chart. Accts.; Candn. Book Publrs. Assn.; past Chmn., Direct Sellers Assn.; Reference Book Publrs. Adsn.; mem. Bd. Trade Metrop. Toronto; United Church; Kiwanis; recreations: music, tennis; Home: 4 Hartfield Court, Islington, Ont. M9A 3E3; Office: 2 Bloor St. W., Toronto, Ont. M4W 3J1

DUROCHER-JUTRAS, Flore C.M. Durocher-Jutras, C.I.B.; Pres. World Assn. of Women Executives., Canadian Chapter; b. Montreal, Que. d. Eugene Durocher M.P. and Eva (Mercier); e. Univ. of Montreal (Social Service); McGill Univ. Social Service Med. Information; m. late Dr. Fernand Jutras, son of Dr. Jos. A. Jutras; children: Pierre, Agriculture Eng., Prof. and mem. of the Univ. McGill Senate, Guy, B.Sc. B.P.E., Chartered Ins. Broker, Lise (Mrs Ed. Cantin); mem. Nat. Advisory Council on Manpower (to rep. the women of Can.) 1952; Unemployment Ins. Commission, Regional Placement Commitee (to rep. Women's work force 1957; mem. Bd. of Dir. Regie de la Place des Arts 1964; Nat. Vice-Pres. Women's Advisory Comm., 1967 International Exhibition, Montreal; mem. Council Consumers Protection Que. 1972; began prof. career as Social Worker to Dept. of Veterans' Affairs at the Psychiatric Div., on the death of her father in 1944, qualified as first woman in the prov. of Que. as Chartered Ins. Broker and took over family business; Founder-pres. in America (1 Feb. 1956) of the Assn. "FEMMES CHEFS d'ENTREPRISES" created in France in 1946, later in twelve other countries; leader in welfare work, social activities and active in politics since 1939; awarded Centennial of Canada Silver Medal, 1967; Appointed Member of the Order of Canada (Dec. 1979); Address Suite 1612 5999 Monkland Ave., Montreal Que.

DURRANT, Geoffrey Hugh, D. Litt. et Phil., F.R.C.S.; educator; b. Pilsley, Eng. 27 July 1913; s. John and Char-

lotte (Atkinson) D.; e. Chesterfield Sch. Eng.; Jesus Coll. Cambridge Univ. (Open Scholarship 1932-35, Kitchener Scholarship 1932-36) B.A. 1935; King's Coll. Univ. London Ed. Dipl. 1936; Univ. of Tuebingen 1937-39; Univ. of S. Africa D. Litt. et Phil. 1970; m. Barbara Joan d. late John Altson, Natal, S. Africa June 1942; children: John Guy, Catherine Jane; Prof. of Eng. Univ of B.C. 1966-81; Prof. Emeritus 1981; Head Dept. Eng. 1966-69; Head Dept. Eng. Univ. of Natal 1944-60, Univ. of Man. 1965-66; Visiting Prof. Univ. York (Eng.), Univ. of N.Y. Buffalo, Australian Nat. Univ., Univ. of Tuebingen, Univ. of Waterloo; rec'd Carnegie Fellowship 1960; Master Teacher Award U.B.C. 1973; Killam Sr. Fellowship 1976; active in adult educ. and S. African pol. movements 1945-60; Moderator in Eng. Jt. Matric. Bd. S. African Univs. 1948-60; awarded Coronation Medal 1953; served with 1st S. African Div. E. Africa, Egypt 1941-42, S. African Intelligence 1942-44; author 'William Wordsworth' 1969; 'Wordsworth and the Great System' 1970; monographs and articles on Shakespeare, Wordsworth, Malcolm Lowry and on educ. topics; el. Fellow of Royal Soc. of Can. 1977; mem. Assn. Candn. Univ. Teachers Eng.; recreations: fishing, chess; Home: 3994 W. 34th Ave., Vancouver, B.C. V6N 2L5

DUTIL, Marcel; industrial executive; b. Ville St. Georges, Beauce, Que. 17 Aug. 1942; s. Roger and Gilberte (Lacroix) D.; e. St. Georges Primary Sch.; Academie de Qué.; Laval Univ.; m. Helene d. Odule Giguere 1 Feb. 1964; children: Marc, Charles, Marie, Sophie; CHRMN. OF BD., CANAM MANAC INC., Founder 1973; Chrmn. of Bd. Canam Steel Works Inc.; Manac Inc.; Biltrite Furniture Inc.; Treco International Inc.; Canam Steel Corp.; Construction Murox Inc.; Treco Rentals Inc.; Dir. Maritime Life Assurance Co.; Société Inter-Port de Québec; National Bank of Canada; joined Canam Steel Works Inc. 1963, Gen. Mgr. 1966; Founded Manac Inc. 1966; named Business Man of Month, Revue Commerce Oct. 1978; mem. Candn. Inst. Steel Constr.; R. Catholic; recreations: bridge, tennis; Club: Garrison; Home: 10595 Lacroix Blvd., Ville St. Georges, Beauce, Que. G5Y 1K2; Office: 11535 First Ave., Suite 700, Ville St. Georges, Beaucesud, Qué.

DUTOIT, Charles Edouard; conductor; artistic director; b. Lausanne, Switzerland 7 Oct. 1936; s. Edmond and Berthe (Laedermann) D.; e. Conservatory of Lausanne, Acad. Music, Geneva; Academia Musicale Chigiana, Siena; Conserv. Benedetto Marcello, Venice, Italy; m. Marie-Josée Drouin; children: Ivan, Anne-Catherine; ARTISTIC DIR., ORCHESTRE SYMPHONIQUE DE MONTREAL 1977- ; debut with Bern Symphony Orchestra 1963, Assoc. Conductor 1964; Music Dir. 1966-68; invited to conduct Vienna Opera and apptd. Music Dir. Radio-Zurich Orchestra 1964; Music Dir. Mexico's Nat. Orchestra 2 yrs.; regular Conductor Göteborg Orchestra, Sweden 1975-78; regularly conducts London Symphony, London Philharmonic, Royal Philarmonic and New Philharmonia orchestras; guest conductor, Berlin Philharmonic Orchestra 1980, La Scala de Milan 1980, Israel Philharmonic Orchestra 1980, Boston Symphony Orchestra 1981, Philadelphia Orchestra 1981, New York Philharmonic 1982, Cincinnati Orchestra, St. Paul Chamber and Cleveland Orchestras 1982; debut with present Orchestra 1977; has conducted over 1,000 concerts with world's greatest orchestras; tours regularly Europe, S. Am., Japan & Australia; numerous recordings incl. "Histoire du Soldat" by Stravinsky (won Grand Prix du disque); "Le Roi David" by Honegger (Grand Prix spécial du 25e anniversaire de l'Académie du disque français); "Daphnis et Chloé" by Ravel; with present Orchestra toured Can. and Am. W. Coast 1981, played Carnegie Hall 1982 (Internat. Festival of Orchestras); Protestant; recreations: swimming, reading, travel; Address: 200 de Maisonneuve Blvd. W., Montreal, Que. H2X 1Y9.

DUTTON, John Edgar, B.A., B.L.S.; librarian; b. Lethbridge, Alta. 30 Aug. 1924; s. Edgar Evans and Hannah Eleanor (Turner) D.; e. Lethbridge Coll. Inst. 1942; Univ. of Alta. B.A. 1950; Univ. of Toronto B.L.S. 1951; m. Helen Irene d. Frank Dudley Stapley 28 Nov. 1945; children: Corinne Eleanor, Carolyn Ann, Dianne Lillian; DIR., CALGARY PUBLIC LIBRARY 1979- ; joined Univ. of Alta. Lib. 1951-53; Chief Lib. Lethbridge Pub. Lib. 1953-63 and North York Pub. Lib. 1963-77; City Lib. Winnipeg Pub. Lib. 1977-79; served with RCAF 1943-46; author encyclopedia articles, papers on librarianship; mem. Lib. Assn. Alta. (Pres. 1962); Candn. Lib. Assn. (2nd Vice Pres.); Ont. Lib. Assn. (Pres. 1964); P. Conservative; United Church; recreations: canoeing, tennis, skiing, hiking, photography, theatre, reading; Home: 4240 - 40 St. N.W., Calgary, Alta. T2A 0H6; Office: 616 Macleod Trail S.W., Calgary, Alta. T2G 2M2.

DuVAL, Paul Nisbet, B.Com., M.B.A.; b. Winnipeg, Man., 12 May 1928; s. Hon. Paul Guyot and Mary Isabel (Cross) D.; e. Kelvin High Sch., Winnipeg, Man.; Univ. of Man., B. Com. 1949; Harvard Univ., M.B.A. 1951; m. Barbara Jean, d. Norman M. Hall, Winnipeg, Man., 5 Sept. 1950; one daughter and five sons: Margot, Paul Norman, Douglas Bruce, Gordon Robert, James Ian, Bruce John; PRESIDENT, MUTUAL INVESTMENTS LTD.; Dir., Monarch Life Assnce. Co. 1962-78; Financial Analyst, Ford Motor Co. of Can., 1951-53; Manitoba Vice-Pres., Candn. Constr. Assn., 1961-63; Vice-Pres., Arch. Woodwork Inst.; mem., Winnipeg Builders Exchange (Pres. 1959-61); Treas., Man. Conf. United Church; Zeta Psi; Liberal; United Church; recreations: golf, fishing; Club: St. Charles Country; Home: 12 MiddleGate, Winnipeg, Man. R3C 2C4; Office: 285 Smith St., Winnipeg, Man. R3C 1K9

DUVAR, Ivan E.H., P.Eng.; public utility executive; b. Charlottetown, P.E.I., 30 March 1939; e. Prince of wales Coll. Charlottetown 1956; Mt. Allison Univ. Engn. 1960; N.S. Tech. Coll. Elect. Engn. 1962; St. Mary's Univ. Candn. Inst. Mang. 1973; PRESIDENT AND CEO, THE ISLAND TELEPHONE CO. since 1975; Vice Pres. Maritime Telephone and Telegraph Co. Ltd.; Dir. Maritime Computers Ltd.; Trans Canada Telephone System; joined Bell Canada — Engn. 1962-66; Maritime Telephone and Telegraph Co. Ltd. — Engn. 1966-68, Business Information Mgr. 1968-72, Chief Engr. 1973, Vice Pres.-Planning 1975; Asst. Pres. present Co. 1974, Pres. 1975; served with COTC, rank Lt.; Dir. Telecommunications Carriers Assn.; Assn. Prof. Engrs. N.S.; Inst. Elect. & Electronic Engrs.; Candn. Inst. Mang.; Home: 52 Edward Laurie Dr., Halifax, N.S. B3M 2C7; Office: 71 Belvedere Ave., Charlottetown, P.E.I.

DYE, Kenneth M.,M.B.A., C.A., F.C.A.; Offr. of Parliament; b. Vancouver, B.C. 16 Jan. 1936; s. Allan Edward D.; e. Magee and Lord Byng High Schs.; Univ. of B.C.; Simon Fraser Univ. M.B.A. 1971; Inst. of C.A.'s B.C., C.A. 1962; m. Frances Marion d. Ralph Kenneth Johnson, West Vancouver, B.C. 13 Dec. 1958; children: Elizabeth Georgia, Lesleigh Marion, James Kenneth;AUDITOR GEN. OF CANADA1981- ; trained as C.A. with Frederick Field & Co. (later known as Campbell Sharp Chartered Accountants), apptd. Partner 1966-81; Retired Partner, Pannell Kerr Forster Campbell Sharp, Mang. Consultants; served as Flight Cadet 1955-57; Pres. Inst. C.A.'s of B.C. 1979-80; Gov. Candn. Inst. C.A.'s 1977-80; Delta Kappa Epsilon; Anglican; recreations: skiing, hiking, canoeing, curling, reading; Clubs: Hollyburn Country; University (Vancouver); Men's Canadian; The Country; Home: 1907 Highland Terrace, Ottawa, Ont. Office: 240 Sparks St., Ottawa, Ont. K1A 0G6.

DYKES, James Grant, B.Com.; association manager; b. Norwood Grove, Manitoba, 11 May 1920; s. John and Marion (McDonald) D.; e. Univ. of Manitoba, B.Com., 1941; m. Jeanne Elizabeth Wyndels, 27 March 1944; one

d. Jennifer Mary; PRES., MOTOR VEHICLE MFRS. ASSN., since 1954; Foreign Service Offr. (Trade Commr.), Dept. of Trade & Commerce, Ottawa and London, Eng., Jan. 1945-Oct. 1946; with Great-West Life Assnce. Co., Winnipeg, Man., 1946-48; Asst. Dir., Dept. of Industry & Comm., Prov. of Man., 1948-49; Industrial Commr., Windsor, Ont., 1949-54; served in 2nd World War, 1941-45, with R.C.N.; Lieut.-Commdr. (S) R.C.N.(R) retired; United Church; Home: 16 Moorehill Drive, Toronto, Ont. M4G 1A1; Office: 25 Adelaide St. E., Toronto, Ont. M5C 1Y7

DYMOND, William R., M.A., Ph.D.; economist; educator; b. Toronto, Ont., 10 June 1921; s. late John Richardson, F.R.S.C., and late Hilda (Freeman) D.; e. Upper Canada Coll., Toronto, Ont.; Univ. of Toronto, B.A. 1943; M.A. 1946; Cornell Univ., Ph.D. 1950; m.; DEPY. DIR., SOCIAL AFFAIRS, MANPOWER AND EDUC., ORGAN. FOR ECON. CO-OPERATION AND DEVEL.; Asst. Prof. of Econ., Univ. of Mass., 1949-51; Chief of Manpower Div., Econ. & Research Br., Dept. of Labour, Ottawa, 1951-56; Dir., Econ. & Research Br., 1957-61; Asst. Depy. Min. of Labour, 1961-65; Chrmn., Manpower & Social Affairs Comte. of Organ. for Econ. Co-Operation and Devel., Paris 1965-70; Asst. Depy. Min., Manpower and Immigration 1966-70; Chrmn., Dept. Public Adm., Univ. of Ottawa, 1970-74; mem., Indust. Relations Research Assn.; Candn. Econ. Assn.; Club: Ottawa Hunt & Golf; recreation: photography; Home: 14 rue de Petrarque, Paris 75016, France; Office: OECD, 2 Rue André Pascal, Paris 75016, France

DYNES, Henry Edwin; retired finance executive; b. Quebec, P.Q., 2 July 1916; s. Edwin John and Ruth Olive (Conner) D.; m. Gertrude, d. late Joseph Pleau, 10 Sept. 1945; children: Elizabeth Ann, Charles Henry, Helen Gertrude, Lynne; Dir., Country Style Donuts Ltd.; Trustee, First Can. Mortgage Fund; served in 2nd World War with R.C.A.P.C. as Captain; mem. Metrop. Toronto Bd. of Trade; Protestant; recreations: golf, curling; Clubs: Bayview Country; Carlton; Canadian; National; Home: 10 Gustav Cres., Willowdale, Ont. M2M 2C5

E

EAGLES, Blythe Alfred, Ph.D., D.Sc., F.R.S.C. (1952), F.C.I.C. (1958), F.A.I.C.; b. New Westminster, B.C., 23 Apl. 1902; s. John E. and Amelia J. (Johnston) E.; e. U. Brit. Columbia, B.A. 1922 (Gov.-Gen.'s Gold Medal and Research Prize); Univ. of Toronto, M.A. 1924; Ph.D. 1926; Yale Univ. (Sr. Sterling Research Fellow) 1926-28; m. Violet Evelyn, d. John Dunbar, Vancouver, 25 June 1930; Research Chemist, Powell River Pulp & Paper Co., B.C., 1932-33; Assoc. Prof. and Acting Head, Dept. of Dairying, Univ. of B.C., 1933-36, Prof. and Head 1936-67; Dean of Agrc. 1949-67; mem., Burnaby Town Planning Comn., since 1943; Bd. of Mang., B.C. Research Council, 1944-49; Senate, Univ. of B.C., 1936-42 and since 1949; mem., Biochem. Soc.; Candn. Inst. of Chem. (Past pres., Vancouver Br.); B.C. Acad. of Sciences (Pres. 1946); Candn. Microbiol. Soc. (Pres. 1968); Sigma Xi; Phi Gamma Delta; Sigma Tau Upsilon (Past Pres.); Anglican; recreation: gardening; Home: 5655 Sperling Ave., North Burnaby, B.C. V5E 2T2

EAGLESON, R. Alan, Q.C., B.A., LL.B.; b. St. Catharines, Ont., 24 Apl. 1933; s. James Allen E.; e. Mimico (Ont.) High Sch.; Univ. of Toronto, B.A. 1954, LL.B. 1957; Osgoode Hall Law Sch., 1959; m. Nancy d. Melvin Fisk, 1960; children: Allen Jr., Jill Anne; Dir., Hockey Canada; Teledyne Canada Ltd.; read law with J.D.W. Cumberland, Q.C.; called to Bar of Ont. 1959; cr. Q.C. 1972; Counsel for Nat. Hockey League Players' Assn.; directed formation of above Assn. 1967; helped form and direct, Team Canada, World Hockey Champions 1972; el.

M.P.P. for Toronto Lakeshore in prov. g.e. 1963, 1967; el. President, Ontario Progressive Conservative Association 1968; Dir., Big Bros. Metrop. Toronto; mem. Bd. of Govs., Queensway Gen. Hosp.; Etobicoke Gen. Hosp.; Vanier Award Winner 1968; mem., Law Soc. Upper Can.; York Co. Law Assn.; recreations: golf, skiing, tennis, jogging; Clubs: Albany; Empire; Lambton Golf & Country; Toronto Lawn Tennis; Craigleith Ski; Home: Toronto, Ont.; Office: 65 Queen St. W., Toronto, Ont.

EAKIN, William Robert, B.A., B.C.L., transportation executive; b. Montreal, P.Q., 23 Nov. 1909; s. William Robert and Barbara Winning (Hamilton) E.; e. Westmount (P.Q.) Pub. Schs.; Coll. St. Joseph de Berthier, P.Q.; Inst. Mont St. Louis, Montreal; Ashbury Coll., Ottawa, Ont.; McGill Univ., B.A. 1931, B.C.L., 1934; m. Margaret Helen, d. Hon. H.J. Symington, P.C., Q.C., 5 Jan. 1938; children: William Robert Symington, Barbara Gael, Vera Lynn, Margaret Joan; Chmn., McLean Kennedy Ltd.; Dir., Brunterm Limited; C.I. Power Services Ltd.; G. Heyn & Sons Ltd., Belfast; Ulster S.S. Co. Ltd., Belfast; mem. Bd. Govs., McGill Univ.; called to Bar of Que., 1934; left active practice of law in 1938 to become a working dir. in McLean Kennedy Ltd.; joined Victoria Rifles of Can. 1934 and served with that unit in 2nd World War; Overseas on staff of Candn. Army Hdqrs. in Eng., France, Belgium, Holland with rank of Major; Mentioned in Despatches; Pres., Shipping Fed. of Can., 1966-67; mem., Montreal Bd. Trade (Council) 1956-59; Can. Export Assoc. Council 1959-63; Pres., McGill Grads. Soc. 1967-69; Chrmn., Bd. of Gov., McGill Univ. 1975-77; Alpha Delta Phi; Anglican; recreations: skiing, golf; Clubs: University; Mount Bruno Golf; Hermitage; Home: 3940 Cote des Neiges, Montreal, Que. H3H 1W2; Office: 410 St. Nicholas, Montreal, Que. H2Y 2P5

EARLE, Arthur Frederick, B.Sc., Ph.D.; economist; b. Toronto, Ont., 13 Sept. 1921; s. Frederick Charles and Hilda Mary (Brown) E.; e. Univ. of Toronto; London Sch. of Econ., B.Sc. (Econ.), Ph.D.; m. yera Domini, d. late Harry G. Lithgow, 16 Nov. 1946; children: Timothy Arthur Frederick, Michael Nelson Lithgow, Wendy Jacqueline; PRESIDENT, BOYDEN CONSULTING GROUP LTD. since 1974; apptd. Vice Pres. of (parent Co.) Boyden Associates, Inc., Nov. 1976; with Canada Packers Limited, 1946-48; joined Aluminium Limited, British Guiana, West Indies, and Canada, 1948-53; became Treas., Alumina Jamaica Limited, 1953-55; Sales Executive, Aluminium Union, London, 1955-58; apptd. Vice Pres., Aluminium Ltd. Sales Inc., New York, 1958-61; joined Hoover Ltd., Eng., as Depy. Chrmn. and Mang. Dir. (from 1963), 1961-65; Principal, London (U.K.) Grad. Sch. of Business Studies 1965; Pres. International Investment Corp. for Yugoslavia, S.A. 1972; served with R.C.N., rising from Rating to Lieut. Commander, 1939-46; Gov. Ashridge Mang. Coll., Eng., 1962-65; mem., Council of Industrial Design; Gov., The National Institute of Econ. and Social Research; Fellow, Brit. Inst. of Management; mem. Econ. Devel. Comte., Elect. Indust. 1965-71; N.E.D.O. Comte. on Mang. Educ., Training & Devel., 1967-69; Council of Mang., The Ditchley Foundation; Gov.and Hon. Fellow, London Sch. of Econ.; Chairman, Canadian Association of Friends of L.S.E.; Anglican; recreation: hill climbing; Clubs: Travellers (London); National (Toronto); Home: Ste. 1905, High Park Green, 50 Quebec Ave., Toronto, Ont., M6P 4B4; and 144 Regent Street, Niagara-on-the-Lake; Office: P.O. Box 389, Commerce Court N., Toronto, Ont. M5L 1G3

EARLE, Arthur Percival, B.E.; textile engineer; b. Montreal, Que. 23 Apl. 1922; s. Arthur P. and Bernadette (Gosselin) E.; e. Westmount (Que.) High Sch.; Trinity Coll. Sch. Port Hope, Ont.; McGill Univ. B.E. 1949; Harvard Business Sch. Dipl. Business Adm.; m. Muriel Elizabeth d. John G. Vining, Cap-de-la-Madeleine, Que. June 1946; children: Arthur, Richard, Janet; SR. VICE PRES. DOMINION TEXTILE INC. since 1978; joined Shawini-

gan Water & Power Co. 1949-63 serving as Engr., Supt., Asst. Mgr. Production Plant Dept.; Asst. Chief Engr. present Co. 1963, Chief Engr. 1965, Vice Pres. 1969, Group Vice Pres. 1971; Sr. Vice Pres. 1978; Past Pres., Fireside Fabrics; Lana Knit; Elpee Yarns; Jano Ltd.; Fiberworld Ltd.; Past Chrmn., Penmans Ltd.; President, Montreal Bd. Trade 1980-81, Chairman 1981-82; mem. Exec. Comte., Ecole de Technologie Supérieure de l'Université du Qué.; served with RCAF 1941-45; Pilot Offr.; mem. Am. Inst. Elect. Engrs. (Past Sec. Chrmn.); Engn. Inst. Can.; Assn. Prof. Engrs. Prov. Ont.; Ordre des Ingénieurs du Qué.; Anglican; recreations: golf, curling, fishing; Clubs: Mt. Stephen; Royal Montreal Golf; Montreal Thistle Curling (Past Pres.); M.A.A.A.; Home: 63 White Pine Dr., Beaconsfield, Que. H9W 5E4; Office: 1950 Sherbrooke St. W., Montreal, Que. H3H 1E7.

EARLE, Hon. H.R. Valence, M.H.A., (retired); b. Fogo, Nfld., 22 Dec. 1911; s. William A. and Frances Gertrude (White) E.; e. Bishop Feild Coll., St. John's, Nfld.; m. Effie Eugenie, d. Hon. I.R. Randell, 28 Sept. 1939; children: Elizabeth (Mrs. G. Ross Peters), William R.V., V. Randell; MIN. OF FINANCE, NFLD. since 1 Oct. 1974 to Sept. 1975; M.H.A. Fortune Bay 1962; Minister of Educ., Nfld., 1964-67; Min. Pub. Welfare, 1967-68; Min. of Finance, July 1968 till resignation 5 Nov. 1969; re-el. P.C. for Fortune Bay 1972; Min. of Econ. Devel. July 1972, of Public Works & Services Dec. 1972, Municipal Affairs & Housing May 1973; President, Val Earle Ltd. since 1961; 1st Chrmn., Ang. Sch. Bd. of St. John's; mem., Diocesan Synod, Ang. Ch. since 1947; mem., Gen. Synod Ang. Ch. of Can., 1966 and mem., Prov. Synod, 1967; Chrmn., Nfld. Assoc. Fish Exporters Ltd., 1956-61; Pres., Nfld. Fish Trades Assn., 1954; Nfld. Bd. Trade, 1953; Commr. for Can., N.W. Atlantic Fisheries Organ. (Internat.), 1960-61; Candn. Del. to UNESCO, 1966; mem., Royal Commonwealth Soc.; mem., Bd. of Regents, Memorial Univ. of Nfld.; Paul Harris Fellow; P. Conservative; Anglican; recreations: carpentry, gardening, music, fishing; Clubs: Rotary (Past Pres.); Home: 74 Topsail Rd., St. John's, Nfld. A1E 2A8

EARP, Alan, M.A., M.Litt., LL.D.; educator; b. Toronto, Ont., 18 Feb. 1925; s. Rev. William Arthur and Laura (Sloan) E.; e. Cheam Sch., Eng.; Marlborough Coll., Eng.; Trinity Coll., Univ. of Toronto, B.A. 1948; Univ. of Cincinnati (Teaching Fellow), M.A. 1950; Jesus Coll., Cambridge Univ., M.Litt. 1952; Univ. of N.B., LL.D. 1968; two s., Stephen, Jonathan; PRES. & VICE CHANCELLOR, BROCK UNIV. since 1974; (Acting Pres. 1970-71, 1973-74); joined Univ. of Manchester as Asst. Lectr. 1952 = 53; Univ. Coll. of N. Staffordshire (now Keele Univ.) 1953-54; Lectr., Univ. of W. Indies, 1954-55; Dean of Men, Registrar and Assoc. Prof. of Classics, Trinity College, Univ. of Toronto 1955-64; Registrar and Prof. of Classics, Carleton Univ. 1964-65; Princ. and Vice. Chancellor, Univ. of Guyana, 1965-68; served with Argyll & Sutherland Highlanders of Can., 1943-45; N.W. Europe; rank Lt.; author of various articles; Pres., Candn. Bureau Internat. Educ. 1977-79; Pres., Assoc. Univ. and Coll. of Canada, 1979-81; mem. Candn. Delegation to People's Republic of China 1979; Commonwealth Ed. Conference Colombo 1980; Anglican; Home: 473 Johnson St., Niagara-on-the-Lake, Ont. L0S 1J0; Office: St. Catharines, Ont. L2S 3A1

EASTCOTT, Robert Wayne, R.C.A.; artist; b. Trail, B.C. 20 July 1943; s. George Rowland and Annie Spence (Johnson) E.; e. Robson and Rossland, B.C. elem. and high schs.; Vancouver Sch. of Art 1962-66; m. Shirley Lydia d. John Thomas Place, Burnaby, B.C. 6 July 1968; one d. Elizabeth Rose; Lectr., Capilano Coll. N. Vancouver since 1973 (estbd. Print Making Dept. 1975); Graphic Artist, KVOS-TV 12 Vancouver 1967-70; Cascade Electronics 1972; Instr. Vancouver Sch. of Art 1965-74; solo exhns. incl. Mary Frazee Vancouver 1969; Pollock Gallery Toronto 1971; Priestlay Gallery (Equinox) Vancouver 1971;

Gallery Pascal Toronto 1975; Gallery Graphics Ottawa 1976; Fleet Gallery Winnipeg 1977, 1980; Kabutoya, Tokyo 1979; rep. in group exhns. Can., USA, S.Am., Europe, Japan and Hawaii since 1965; rep. in various perm. colls. Can. and USA incl. Can. Council Art Bank, Nat. Gallery Can.; rec'd Can. Council Grant 1968 for research in Print Making utilizing xerox equipment; cited numerous bibliogs.; mem. Soc. Candn. Artists; Soc. Candn. Painters-Etchers & Engravers; Dundarave Print Workshop (Founding mem., Pres. 1972-77); Malaspina Print Soc.; Print & Drawing Council Can.; World Print Council; Presbyterian; recreations: camping, winemaking; Address: 2553 Oxford St., Vancouver, B.C. V5K 1M9.

EASTERBROOK, James Arthur, M.A., Ph.D.; educator; psychologist; b. Spooner, Minn. 10 Apr. 1923; s. William James Arthur and Bertha Lillian (Amorde) E.; e. Dauphin, Man. pub. schs. 1940; St. Mary's Priory; Univ. of Man. sr. matric. 1941 (Gov. Gen.'s Medal); Queen's Univ. B.A. 1949, M.A. 1954; Univ. of London Ph.D. 1963; m. Margaret Pamela Edith d. late James Evans 19 Nov. 1944; children: Christine Susan (Tricoteux), Anthony James, Pamela Jane (Nadeau), Lawrence Arthur, Margaret Ann; PROF. OF PSYCHOL., UNIV. OF N.B. 1967, Head of Dept. 1967-73; Reporter, Dauphin Herald & Press 1940-41; Partner, J. A. Easterbrook & Co., retail trade Dauphin, Man. 1946-49; News Ed. and Assoc. Ed. Queens Journal 1946-49; Research Offr. Inst. Aviation Med. RCAF 1949; Lectr. in Psychol. Queen's Univ. 1949-50; Defence Research Scient. Offr. Fort Churchill, Edmonton, Halifax 1950-57; Research Asst. Inst. of Psychiatry, London, Eng. 1958; Research Psychol. Burden Neurol. Inst. Bristol, Eng. 1959-61; Asst. Prof. of Psychiatry Univ. of Alta. 1961-67; Visiting Lectr. Massey Univ., N.Z. 1976; recipient J. McBeth Milligan Fellowship in Philos. 1949-50; Social Sciences & Humanities Research Council Can. Research Fellowship 1979-80; Chrmn. and Dir. Research Jt. Consultative Comte. Phase Down Coal Mining Minto, N.B. 1968-72; Dir. Social Science Research Inst. N.B. 1970-72; Consultant N.B. Newstart Inc. 1971-74; author "Determinants of Free Will" 1978; over 56 research reports defence science and psychol.; contrib. to various scient. publs.; served with RCAF 1941-45, attached RAF 1942-45, rank Flight Lt.; mem. Brit. Psychol. Soc.; Coll. Psychols. N.B.; Assn. Univ. N.B. Teachers (Vice Pres. 1973-74); N.B. Bd. Examiners Psychol. 1973-79 (Chrmn. 1978-79); United Church; recreations: swimming, gardening, genealogical research; Home: 180 Dunn's Crossing Rd., Fredericton, N.B. E3B 2A6; Office: Fredericton, N.B. E3B 6E4.

EASTERBROOK, William Thomas, M.A., Ph.D., LL.D., F.R.S.C.; university professor (emeritus); b. Winnipeg, Man., 4 Dec. 1907; s. William James and Emily (McKerr) E.; e. Univ. of Manitoba, B.A. 1933, LL.D.; Univ. of Toronto, M.A. 1935, Ph.D. 1938; Guggenheim Fellow, 1940-41; Cambridge Univ., M.A. 1956; m. Dorothy Mary, d. W.T. Walker, Vancouver, B.C., 28 Dec. 1937; children: William Michael, Joel Thomas, Jane Marylin; PROF. OF POLITICAL ECON., UNIV. OF TORONTO; Prof. Emeritus, 1977; Research Assoc., Harvard Univ., 1949; Pitt Prof. of Am. Hist. and Institutions, Cambridge Univ., 1955-56 Professorial Fellow of Jesus College, Cambridge, 1955-56; (Marshall Lectr. there, 1956); Economic Adviser, Min. of Ec. Affairs & Dev. Planning, Tanzania, 1966-67; Visiting Prof., Australia National Univ., 1965; Trustee, Econ. Hist. Assn., 1956-57 (Vice-Pres., 1958-60); Trustee, Business Hist. Foundation, 1959-63; author of "Farm Credit in Canada"; "Canadian Economic History" (with H. Aitken) and "Climate of Enterprise"; "Approaches to Canadian Economic History" (with Mel Watkins), 1968; Home: 50 Prince Arthur, Toronto, Ont. M5R 1B5

EASTMAN, Lieut.-Col. Gerald Ernest, Q.C., C.D.; of U.E.L. descent; b. Ottawa, Ont., 4 May 1906; s. Ernest Roy and Bertha Evelyn (Younghusband) E.; e. Nepean High Sch., Ottawa, Ont.; Osgoode Hall, Toronto, Ont.,

Grad. 1928; m. Elizabeth Maurine, d. Dr. A.E. Rudell, Kitchener, Ont., 8 July 1931; one s. Charles Richard; one d., Marilyn Joyce; COUNSEL, CLEMENT, EASTMAN, DREGER, MARTIN & MEUNIER; read law with Wentworth Greene, K.C., Ottawa, Ont.; called to the Bar of Ont., 1928; cr. K.C. 1945; joined Clement, Hattin & Co., 1928; served in World War, 1939-45; Grad. War Staff Course, 1941; served in Italy as Maj., G.S.O. II 5th Candn. Armoured Divn. and in B.C. Dragoons; wounded, Liri Valley Battle, 1944; mem. of Dir. Staff, Staff Coll., Kingston, Ont., 1945; Commanded 54th Light Anti-Aircraft Regt., Scots. Fusiliers of Can., R.C.A. 1947-51; Vice-Chrmn., Kitchener Sch. Bd., 1952-53; Pres., Waterloo Co. Bar Assn., 1952-53; Dir., Ont. Chamber Comm., 1957-59; Pres., K.W. Art Gallery 1956-58 (Founding Mem. and Dir. since 1956); mem. Gov. Comte., K. & W. Community Foundation since 1967; Pres., Kitchener Chamber of Comm., 1957-59; mem., Candn. Bar Assn.; Royal Candn. Legion; Conservative; Anglican; Clubs: Rotary; Westmount Golf; Home: 194 Claremont Ave., Kitchener, Ont. N2M 2P8; Office: 277 King St. W., Kitchener, Ont. N2G 4J9

EASTMAN, Harry Claude MacColl, A.M., Ph.D.; university professor; b. Vancouver, B.C., 29 July 1923; s. Samuel Mack and Antonia Françoise (Laribe) E.; e. Internat. Sch., Geneva, Switzerland, 1929-36; Dauntsey's Sch., Wilts., Eng., 1936-39; Humberside Coll. Inst., Toronto, Ont., 1939-41; Univ. of Toronto (1941, 1945-47), B.A.; Univ. of Sask., 1942-43; Univ. of Chicago, A.M. 1949, Ph.D. 1952; m. Sheila Baldwin, d. W. N. MacQueen, Toronto, Ont., 9 July 1949; three d. Julia, Alice, Harriet; PROF. OF ECONOMICS, UNIV. OF TORONTO, since 1963 and Vice Pres. Research and Planning 1977-81; mem. of Candn. Nat. Comn. for UNESCO 1957-60; mem., Candn. Pol. Science Assn. (Secy.-Treas. 1955-65); Internat. Econ. Assn. (mem. of Extve. Comte. 1968-74); Candn. Economics Assn. (Pres. 1971-72); elected Fellow, Royal Soc. of Canada 1974; served in 2nd World War with R.C.A.F., 1943-45; Protestant; Home: 41 Hawthorn Ave., Toronto, Ont. M4W 2Z1; Office: 100 St. George St., Toronto, Ont. M5S 1A1

EASTON, Melvin Donald, LL.B.; b. Vancouver, B.C., 9 Feb. 1923; s. Alberta Edward and Mattie (Harrison) E.; e. Cecil Rhodes Jr. Secondary Sch. and Kitsilano High Sch., Vancouver, 1942; Univ. of B.C., LL.B., 1950; m. Elaine Louise; one s. Michael Donald Leary; PARTNER, HARPER, GREY, EASTON & CO.; read law with Hon. Mr. Justice John Groves Gould; called to the bar of British Columbia 1950; Partner, Gould, Thorpe & Easton, 1950-65; joined present firm (then Harper, Gilmour, Grey & Co) 1965, Partner 1966; served with RCAF 1942-45; served overseas with 432 Hvy. Bomber Sqdn.; rank Fly. Offr.; mem. Law Soc. B.C.; Candn. Bar Assn.; Candn. Tax Foundation; Air Force Offrs. Assn.; Phi Gamma Delta; Freemason; Liberal; Anglican; recreations: boating, fishing, shooting; golfing; Clubs: Royal Vancouver Yacht; University; Men's Canadian; Shaughnessy Golf & Country; Home: 450 Greensboro Place, Vancouver, B.C. V5X 4X4; Office: 3100 - 650 West Georgia St., Vancouver, B.C. V6B 4P7

EATON, Fredrik Stefan, B.A.; executive; b. Toronto, Ont. 26 June 1938; s. late John David and Signy Hildur (Stephenson) E.; e. Upper Canada College; Univ. of New Brunswick B.A. 1912; m. Catherine d. of D.A.C. Martin 16 June 1962; one s. and one d.; PRES. EATON'S OF CANADA LTD. AND CHRMN. AND PRES. THE T. EATON CO. LTD.; Pres. The T. Eaton Acceptance Co. Ltd.; The T. Eaton Realty Co. Ltd.; Vice-Pres. & Dir. The Argus Corp. Ltd.; Dir. Baton Broadcasting Inc.; Norcen Energy Resources Ltd.; Hollinger Argus Ltd.; The Toronto-Dominion Bank; Founding mem. The Art Gallery of Ont.; Gov., The Eaton Foundation; York University; Trustee, Toronto Gen. Hosp.; mem. The Ont. Cancer Institute; The Conference Bd. in Canada; Dir. World Wildlife Fund;

Clubs: Royal Canadian Yacht; Caledon Ski; Queen's; Badminton & Racquet; Lyford Cay; York; Office: 1 Dundas St. W., Toronto Ont. M5B 1C8; Home: 104 Forest Hill Rd., Toronto, Ont. M4V 2L7.

EATON, G. Campbell, O.C.; M.C.; C.D.; LL.D., executive; b. St. John's, Nfld., 1 June 1920; s. late William John and Daisy Janet (Bell) E.; e. St. Bonaventures (St. John's, Nfld.); m. Mary Ruth, d. late H. B. Fraser, 26 June 1946; children: Mrs. Janet Ruth O'Dea, C. Fraser, Donald A., David B., Deborah S., Robyn M.; MANG. DIR., NEWFOUNDLAND TRACTOR AND EQUIPMENT CO. LTD.; Dir. Royal Bank of Canada; Chmn., Seabase Ltd.; Chrm., Advisory Committee Arctic Vessel and Marine Research, Nat. Research Council; Dir. R.C. Corps Commrs; Member Economic Council of Canada 1981; Past Chrmn. Gen. Hosp. Corp.; St. John's Hosp. Council; Candn. Assn. Equipment Distributors; St John's Housing Authority; Atlantic Devel. Council; Past Pres. Nfld. Div. Candn. Red Cross; Past Vice Pres. Nfld. Command. R.C. Legion; served R.A., 57 Heavy Regt. and 166th Nfld. Field Regt. in Gt. Brit., N. Africa, Italy, 1940-45; retired as Capt. Commdg. Offr. 166 (Nfld.) Field Regt. R.C.A. 1949-52; Hon. Lieut. Col. Roy. Nfld. Regt. 1971-76; Hon. Col. R.N.R. 1976; Apptd. Officer Order of Canada, 1978; Immediate Award Military Cross, 1944; Hon. Doctor Laws, Memorial Univ., 1978; Presbyterian; Clubs: Rotary; Baly Haly Golf & Country; Home: 15 Dublin Rd., St. John's, Nfld. A1B 2E7; Office: Box 8940, Kenmount Rd., St. John's, Nfld. A1B 3S2

EATON, Gilbert McCrea, M.B.E.; b. Toronto, Ont., 13 June 1915; s. late Sir John Craig and Lady E.; e. Wellington House, Eng.; Stowe, Eng.; m. Marjorie Ann, d. Joseph H. Maston, Wilmington, Del., 21 Jan. 1939; has one s. and one d.; recreations: yachting, riding, motoring; Clubs: R.C.Y.C. (Toronto); York (Toronto); Manitoba; Motor Country; Concordia.

EATON, John Craig; executive; b. Toronto, Ont. 30 May 1937; s. of late John David Eaton and Signy Hildur (Stephenson) E.; e. Upper Canada College; Harvard Univ.; m. 2ndly Sherrill Joan d. Mr. & Mrs. John Howard Taylor Nov. 1975; children: two s. one d. (by previous m.) one d. (by this m.); CHRMN. EATON'S OF CANADA LTD.; Dir. All-View Interphase Systems Inc.; Commerce Capital Corp. Ltd.; Eaton Bay Financial Services Ltd.; Eaton Bay Insurance Co.; Eaton Bay Life Insurance Co.; Inland Publishing Co. Ltd.; Gov., Ont. Society for Crippled Children and mem. Bd. of Trustees, Ont. Crippled Children Centre; Gov., The Eaton Foundation; The Olympic Trust of Canada; Senate mem. Stratford Festival Foundation of Canada; Dir. The John Augustus Soc.; Ducks Unlimited (Canada); Chrmn. Metro Toronto Adv. Bd. The Salvation Army; The Canadian Hearing Soc. Foundation; mem. Canadian Council of Christians & Jews; Bd. of Trade of Metro Toronto; Canadian Section, Canada-United States Comte.; The Canadian Chamber of Commerce; recreations: fishing, music, golf, hockey, deep sea diving; Clubs: Rosedale Golf; Toronto Badminton & Racquet; Toronto; London; York; Caledon Ski; Home: 120 Dunvegan Rd., Toronto, Ont. M4V 2R3; Office: 1 Dundas St. W., Toronto, Ont. M5B 1C8.

EBBS, John Harry, M.D., D.C.H., F.R.C.P.(C), F.R.C.P. (Lond.), M.D. (Birm.), LL.D. (Trent), F.A.A.P.; paediatrician; b. Worksop, Eng., 18 Sept. 1906; s. John Wm. and Clara (Kelk) E.; came to Can. 1912; e. Peterborough (Ont.) Pub. Schs. and Coll. Inst.; Univ. of Toronto, M.D. 1931; Coll. of Phys. & Surgs., Columbia Univ., 1933; Univ. of Birmingham, M.D. 1938; Roy. Coll. Phys. & Surg. (London) D.C.H. 1936; m. Adele Page, d. Taylor Statten, of Toronto, Ont., 16 Mar. 1935; children: Barbara Adele, Alice Susan, John William; Hon. Consultant, Hospital for Sick Children; former Prof. Paediatrics, Univ. of Toronto; Prof. Emeritus, Univ. of Toronto, 1978; Chrmn., Research, Nat. Adv. Council on Fitness and Amateur

Sport Council Can.; Hon. Life mem., Candn. Camping Assn.; Junior Resident Phys., Hosp. for Sick Children, Toronto, 1931, Sr. Residence Phys., 1932; Resident Phys., Babies' Hosp., Columbia Med. Centre, N.Y. City, 1933; Children's Hosp., Birmingham, Eng., 1934, and Path. there 1935; Clinical Teacher, Univ. of Birmingham (Eng.), 1936; Asst. Phys., Hosp. for Sick Children, Toronto, 1938; Clinical Demonst., Univ. of Toronto, 1938; Medical Dir., Taylor Statten Camps, 1938-76; Pres., Brora Research Centre for Children; Mem. of Bd., Neathern Trust; sr. mem., Candn. Med. Assn.; Ont. Med. Assn.; Candn. Paediatric Soc. (Pres.) (Emeritus mem.); Hon. mem., Brit. Paediatric Assn.; Adv. Bd., Care-Medico of Can.; hon. med. advisor, Cdn. Red Cross Soc.; Bd. of Trustees, Rotary-Laughlin Centre; Pediatric Travel Club (Emeritus); Sydenham Medical Club (Past Pres.); Hon. Life mem., Bd. of Govs., Trent Univ.; Duke of Edinburgh Award Scheme; Fellow, Am. Academy Pediatrics; Toronto Academy Med.; Am. Pediatric Soc. (Past Vice Pres.); Pediatric Research Soc. (Emeritus); Can. Centennial Medal, 1967; Queen's Jubilee Medal, 1977; sesquicentennial Hon. award, Univ. of Tor.; Dist. Service Med., Can. Red Cross, 1971; author of 100 med. articles and 14 med. textbook chapters; Phi Delta Theta; Hon. LL.D. Trent Univ. 1975; Rotary International Paul Harris Fellow, 1979; Anglican; recreations: camping, golf, fishing, skiing; Clubs: Arts and Letters; Rotary (Past President), Rosedale Golf; Home: 240 St. Leonard Ave., Toronto M4N 1L1

EBOO PIRBHAI, Count Sir, O.B.E. (1946); corporations director; b. Bombay, India, 25 July 1905; s. late Gangi Pirbhai and Kuverbai P., e. Duke of Gloucester Sch., Nairobi 1912-21; m. Kulsuam d. Karmali Nathoo 1925; two s. and three d.; Representative of His Highness The Aga Khan and Pres. of the Aga Khan's Supreme Council for Europe, Canada, U.S.A. and Africa; mem. of Nairobi City Council 1938-43; Parl. Leg. Council for Kenya 1952-60; Pres., Central Muslim Assn. abd mem. various other official bodies; knighted 1952, given title of Count 1954; awarded Brilliant Star of Zanzibar 1956; Order of Crescent Cross of the Comores 1966; Muslim; recreations: travel, social work; Clubs: Landsdowne; Reform (both U.K.) Royal Commonwealth Soc.; Address; P.O. Box 40898, 12, Naivasha Ave., Muthaiga, Nairobi, Kenya

EBSEN, Alf K., R.C.A.; calligrapher. b. Berlin, Germany 29 July 1908; s. Carl and Minna (Stüber) E.; e. Realschule vor dem Lübeckertor, Hamburg 1926; lithographer apprentice 1927-31; Kunstgewerbeschule, Hamburg 1931-33; m. Florence Irene d. Walter John Bowyer 25 Aug. 1960; one d. Andrea; PROP., EBSEN GRAPHIC ARTS SERVICES LTD. 1962- ; advertising designer for cigarette mfr. prior to war; own design firm from 1947; client Volkswagenwerk AG 1950-54; came to Can. 1954; Dir. of Graphic Arts, Eddy Match Co. Pembroke, Ont. 1955; originator Candn. system of calligraphy and handwriting; author "The Visible Thought" 1982; ed. "The Legible Scribble". Founder Handwriters Guild Toronto; mem. Graphic Designers Can.; Royal Canadian Academy of Arts; recreations: incunabula, sports; Address: 60 Logandale Rd., Willowdale, Ont. M2N 4H4.

ECCLES, William John, M.A., Ph.D.; university professor; author; b. Thirsk, Yorks, Eng., 17 July 1917; s. John and Jane Ellen (Thorpe) E.; came to Can., 1928; e. McGill Univ., B.A. (Hons.) 1949, M.A. 1951, Ph.D. 1955; Sorbonne, Paris, 1951-52; French Govt. Scholar, 1951-52; McGill Univ. Grad. Fellowship, 1952-53; Humanities Research Council Fellowship, 1956; Ewart Foundation Fellowships, 1955, '56, '57, '58; Can. Council Fellowship, 1959, 1964, 1968, 1977-78; m. Margaret Jean Jaffray, d. Arthur Alexander Low, Stratford, Ont., 18 Sept. 1948; children: late Michael John, Robin Christina, Peter Alexander; PROF. OF HISTORY, UNIV. OF TORONTO, since 1963; Lectr., Dept. of Hist., Univ. of Manitoba, 1953-57, Asst. Prof., 1957; Asst. Prof., Dept. of Hist., Univ. of Alberta, 1957-59; Assoc. Prof. 1959-63; rec'd Killam (Fellowship) Award 1969-72; Tyrrell Medal 1979; Senior Connaught Fellow 1980-81; Publications: "Frontenac: The Courtier Governor", 1959 (awarded 1959 prize by Pacific Coast Br., Am. Hist. Assn.); "Canada Under Louis XIV" 1964; "Canadian Society During the French Régime", 1968; "The Canadian Frontier 1534-1760", 1969; "France in America" 1972 (rec'd Inst. Français de Washington Gilbert Chinard Award, 1974); various articles and book reviews; Visiting Prof., Univ. of Chile, Santiago, 1966; McGill Univ., 1966-67; Guest Lectr., Am. Univ. of Beirut, Lebanon, 1967; mem., Council Inst. Early Am. History and Culture 1976-79; club: University (Montreal); Home: 108 Cluny Drive, Toronto, Ont. M4W 2R4

ECKLER, Norman S., C.A.; executive; b. Toronto, Ont. 22 Sept. 1941; e. C.A. 1964; m. Laura; children: Alana Cher, Gregory, Amy Leigh; VICE PRES. FINANCE, NOMA INDUSTRIES LTD. 1978- ; Vice Pres. Finance, Seaway MultiCorp Ltd. 1973-78; Home: 59 Patina Dr., Willowdale, Ont. M2H 1R3; Office: 375 Kennedy Rd., Scarborough, Ont. M1K 2A3.

ECROYD, Lawrence Gerald, M.B.A.; C.A.E.; association executive; b. Montreal, Que., 14 Sept. 1918; s. late George Smith and Marie E. (Guibord) E.; e. High Sch. of Montreal (Que.), 1936; Colscott Sch. of Comm., Montreal, 1940; London Sch. of Econ., 1957-60; Univ. of B.C., 1957-59; Fla. Atlantic Univ., 1970-72; m. Dorothy Gertrude, d. Thomas Albert Howson, Montreal, Que., 26 Dec. 1949; children: Lynn Doreen, Claire Gail, Beverly Ann, Bruce Lawrence; PRES. AND CHIEF OPERATING OFFICER, CANDN. INST. OF PLUMBING AND HEATING since 1973; General Steel Wares Ltd., Montreal, 1936-40; Hinde & Dauch Paper Co., Montreal, 1940-41; Candn. Chamber of Comm., Montreal, Maritimes and B.C., 1946-53; Extve. Dir. and Asst. Publisher, Mitchell Press Ltd., Vancouver, 1953-61; joined Travel Industry Assn. of Can. (then Candn. Tourist Assn.) 1961; served as Gen. Mgr., Extve. Vice Pres.; served with RCN 1941-45; Asst. Naval Secy. 1945; rank Lt. Commdr. (S); mem. Adv. Comte. Ont. Govt. Project on Productivity Improve., 1971; Pres. & Dir., B.C. Borstal Assn., 1952-61; Dir., B.C. Narcotics Addiction Foundation, 1960-61; rec'd Dr. Milton Hersey Gold Medal for Pub. Speaking, 1947; Kenneth R. Wilson Award for Business Journalism, 1954; Award of Merit for Mang. Achievement (Am. Soc. Assn. Extves.), 1971; mem., Am. Soc. Assn. Extves; Cert. Assn. Extve 1973; Past Chmn. of Bd. & Dir., Inst. Assn. Extves; R. Catholic; recreations: reading, philately, fishing; Home: 24 Larose Ave., Unit 4, Weston, Ont. M9P 1A5; Office: Suite 414, 5468 Dundas St. W., Islington, Ont. M9B 6E3

EDEL, (Joseph) Leon, M.A., D.èsL.; writer and professor; b. Pittsburgh, Pa. 9 Sept. 1907; s. Simon and Fannie (Malamud) E.; came to Canada in 1912; e. Pub. and High Sch., Yorkton, Sask.; Yorkton Coll. Inst., 1920-23; McGill Univ., B.A. 1927, M.A. 1928; Univ. of Paris, D.èsL. 1932; D.Litt. Union Coll. 1963; McGill Univ., 1963; Guggenheim Fellow 1936-38 and 1965-66; Bollingen Fellow 1958-60; m. Roberta, d. T. Glen Roberts, Sterling, Neb., 2 Dec. 1950; Henry James Prof., Eng. & American Letters, New York Univ., 1966-73; Emeritus 1973; Citizens Professor of English, Univ. Hawaii, 1971-78; Emeritus 1978-; Teaching Assoc., McGill Univ., 1928-29; Asst. Prof., English, Sir George Williams Coll., Montreal, Que. 1932-34; journalism, broadcasting, and misc. writing, 1934-43; contrib. articles, reviews to "Canadian Forum", 1930-35; present Univ., Assoc. Prof. 1953, Prof. of English, 1955-66; Visiting Prof., Harvard Univ. 1959-60; Visiting Critic, Indiana Univ., 1954-55; Christian Gauss Seminar in Criticism, Princeton Univ., 1953; Univ. of Toronto, The Alexander Lect. 1956; Centenar Prof. 1967; served in 2nd World War, Field Comm., Bronze Star Medal, since 1973; German Occupation 1946-47 (organized News Agency in U.S. Zone); author: "Life of Henry James" Vol. I "The Untried Years" 1953; Vol: II "The Conquest of London" 1962, Vol. III

"The Middle Years" 1962, Vol. IV "The Treacherous Years" 1969, Vol. V "The Master", 1972; co-author, "Willa Cather", 1953; "The Psychological Novel", 1955; "Literary Biography" 1957; "Henry David Thoreau", 1969; Editor: The Complete Plays, Complete Tales, and Selected Letters of Henry James; Ed. The Diary of Alice James, 1964; awarded (1963) Pulitzer Prize for Biography and the (1963) Nat. Book Award for non-fiction; el. mem., Nat. Inst. Arts, Letters 1964 (Secy., 1965-67); Fellow, Am. Acad. Arts & Sciences, 1959, (Council 1970-72); Ed. Bd., P.M.L.A. 1963-68; Hon. mem., W.A. White Psychoanalytic Soc. since 1967; mem. P.E.N. (Pres. U.C. Center, 1957-59); Modern Humanities Research Assn.; Am. Assn. Univ. Prof.; Internat. Assn. of Univ. Prof. of English; Authors' Guild (Pres. 1968-70); Am. Studies Assn.; Internat. Comparative Lit. Assn.; Internat. Fed. for Modern Lit. and Langs.; recreations: music, book collecting; Clubs: Century (N.Y.); Athenaeum (London); Outrigger Canoe (Honolulu); Address: Dept. of English, Univ. of Hawaii, 1733 Donaghho Rd., Honolulu, Hawaii 96882

EDGE, Charles Geoffrey, B.Sc., F.S.S.; federal agency executive; b. Wilmslow, Chesire, Eng. 8 Aug. 1920; s. Charles Edmund E.; e. Varndean Secondary Sch. Brighton, Eng.; Univ. of London B.Sc. (Econ.) 1950; m. Madeline Rita d. Henry Lester Butler Tarrant, M.B.E. 25 May 1940; two d. Christine Dorothy (Clark), Jennifer Wendy (Doyle); CHRMN. NAT. ENERGY BD.; Tax Offr. Brit. Civil Service 1937-39, Higher Extve. Offr. 1946-51; came to Can. 1951; Canadian Industries Ltd. 1951-56; Mgr. Financial Analyses Canadian Chemical & Cellulose Co. Ltd. 1956-59; Asst. Treas. Chemcell Ltd. 1959-62, various sr. positions incl. Vice Pres. Corporate Devel. 1962-70; Dir. Bralorne Oil and Gas Co. Ltd. 1969-70; joined present Bd. 1970 serving as mem., Assoc. Vice Chrmn., Vice Chrmn.; rec'd Queen's Silver Jubilee Medal; author "A Practical Manual in the Appraisal of Capital Expenditure" 1960, revised 1964, 1981; co-author "The Impact of Systems and Computers on Management and on the Accountant" 1966; served with RA 1939-46, rank Lt.; Fellow, Inst. Stats.; Soc. Mang. Accts.; Reg'd Indust. Acct.; mem. Financial Extves. Inst.; Unitarian; Home: 333 Chapel St., Apt. 806, Ottawa, Ont. K1N 8Y8; Office: 473 Albert St., Ottawa, Ont. K1A 0E5.

EDIGER, Nicholas Martin, B.Sc.; mining executive; b. Winnipeg, Man. 25 June 1928; s. Nicholas and Anna (Hamm) E.; e. Univ. of Man. B.Sc. 1950; m. Elizabeth Durden d. Prof. R. E. D. Cattley 18 Sept. 1973; one d. Julia Anne; CHRMN., PRES. AND CHIEF EXTVE. OFFR., ELDORADO NUCLEAR LTD. 1974- ; Chrmn. and Chief Extve. Offr. Eldorado Aviation Ltd.; Eldor Resources Ltd.; joined Gulf Oil Corp. and affiliates 1950-74; Vice Pres. Gulf Minerals Canada Ltd. to 1974; rep. Can. negotiations devel. Syncrude synthetic oil project Alta. 1975; Extve. Dir. Uranium Inst. (London); Dir., Candn. Nuclear Assn.; Mining Assn. Can.; mem. Nat. Council, Candn. Inst. Internat. Affairs; Clubs: Rideau; Glencoe (Calgary); Engineers (Toronto); Home: 20 Crichton St., Ottawa, Ont. K1M 1V4; Office: 400, 255 Albert St., Ottawa, Ont. K1P 6A9.

EDINBOROUGH, Arnold, M.C., M.A., LL.D., Litt. S.D.; b. Donington, Eng., 2 Aug. 1922; s. Frank and Sarah Ann (Clark) E.; e. Spalding (Eng.) Grammar Sch., 1932-40; St. Catharine's Coll., Cambridge, B.A. 1947, M.A. 1949 (Hons. English) 1949; Univ. of Guelph, LL.D. 1966; Litt. S.D., Wycliff Coll. 1980; Hon. Fellow, St. John's College, Winnipeg 1976; m. Letitia Mary, d. late Ralph Henry Woolley, 14 Jan. 1947; children: Christine Ann, Alastair Michael, Sarah Jane; PRES. AND CEO OF THE COUNCIL FOR BUSINESS AND THE ARTS IN CANADA, since 1974; Asst. Prof. of English, Queen's Univ., 1947-54; Visiting Lect., Univ. of Lausanne, 1947; Dir. of Studies in Eng., St. Catharine's Coll., Cambridge, 1952-53; Editor, "Kingston Whig-Standard", 1954-58; Editor, "Saturday Night", 1958-62; Pres. and Publ., Sat. Night Publs. Ltd., 1963-70; Contr. Ed., "The Financial Post"; Columnist, "Canadian Churchman"; Dir. of Sch. of Eng., Queen's Univ., Summer Sch., 1950-53; Special Lectr. Royal Mil. Coll., 1957-58; Special Lectr., in Eng., Royal Mil. College Canada, 1948-52; Candn. Corr. for "Shakespeare Quarterly", and "Shakespeare Survey", 1970; served in 2nd World War; Capt., Royal Arty., with 23rd Field Regt., R.A.; 1st Army, N. Africa, 1942; 5th and 8th Army in Italy, 1942-45; awarded M.C., 1945; extve. mem. of John Howard Soc. of Kingston, 1955-58; Chairman of Bd. of Dir., New Symphony Assn. of Kingston, 1954-58; Chrmn., Eastern Ont. Drama League, 1955-56; former Gov., Dom. Drama Festival; Hon. Dir., John Howard Soc. of Ont.; Senator Stratford Fest. Foundn; Vice Pres., Massey Hall, Toronto; Chrmn., Intern. Scholarship Foundn; Chrmn., Elliot Lake Centre; Chmn. Dyatron (Can.) Ltd.; Deputy-Chairman, Canadian Institute for Radiation Safety; Publications: "One Church, Two Nations", Longman's 1967; "Some Camel, Some Needle", Lester & Orpen 1974; "The Enduring Word", U. of T. Press 1978; "The Festivals of Canada" 1981; Former mem., several national and diocesan comtes., Anglican Church of Canada; Dir. (1963), Nat. Ballet Sch.; mem. (1965) Toronto Planning Bd.; regular Panelist on both C.B.C. and C.T.V. networks; Anglican; recreation: amateur theatricals; Home: 10 Ancroft Place, Toronto, Ont. M4W 1M4; Office: P.O. Box 7, Suite 1507, Simpson Tower, 401 Bay St., Toronto, Ont. M5H 2Y4

EDISON, John Galbraith, Q.C., B.A.; b. Port Hope, Ont., 19 Jan. 1911; s. Rev. Herbert Edison and Georgina (Galbraith) Abraham; e. Upper Canada Coll., Toronto, Ont.; Trinity Coll., Univ. of Toronto, B.A. 1932; Osgoode Hall, Toronto, Ont.; m. Margaret Elizabeth, d. William J. Hill, 27 June 1940; one s. John Robert Churchill; COUNSEL, AIRD & BERLIS; Dir., Lornex Mining Corp. Ltd.; Rio Algom Ltd.; Ash Temple Ltd.; KeepRite Inc.; read law with Smith, Rae, Greer & Cartwright, Toronto, Ont.; called to the Bar of Ont., 1936; cr. Q.C. 1954; served in 2nd World War with R.C.A.F. 1941-45, Sqdn. Leader; Mentioned in Despatches; Croix de Guerre; Presbyterian; Clubs: York; University; Toronto Hunt Badminton and Racquet; Home: 133 Dunvegan Road, Toronto, Ont. M4V 2R2; Office: 145 King St. W., Toronto, Ont. M5H 2J3

EDMISON, John Alexander, Q.C., O.C. 1976; b. Cheltenham, Ont., 12 Nov. 1903; s. Rev. John Hall and Elizabeth Agnes (Fitzgerald) E.; e. Pub. Sch. and Jarvis Coll. Inst.; Queen's Univ., B.A.; McGill Univ. (Law); m. Alice Margaret (B.A.), d. Harold L. Vercoe, B.Sc., Windsor, 28 Aug. 1935; children: Joan, Elizabeth, Nancy; Gov., Queen's Theol. Coll.; mem. Bd. of Govs., Trent Univ.; read law with Brown, Montgomery & McMichael, Montreal; called to Bar of Que., 1932; cr. K.C. 1944; Partner, Creelman, Edmison & Walsh, Montreal, 1934-45; Ald., St. George Ward, Montreal City Council, 1938, and was apptd. to Bd. of Health & Montreal Metropolitan Comn.; sometime Gov. of Shawbridge Boy's Farm & Training Sch. and Chief Legal Counsel, Montreal Legal Aid Bur.; served in World War 1940-45; commnd. in Black Watch (Roy. Highland Regt. of Can.) 1940; served overseas as Offr. in Charge of Legal Aid Bur., Judge Advocate Gen.'s Br., Candn. Mil. Hdqrs., London, Eng.; discharged with rank of Maj., 1945, to assume post of Sr. UNRRA Liaison Offr. to Supreme Hdqrs. Allied Expeditionary Force; received citations from Gen. Dwight Eisenhower and Gen. Charles de Gaulle; on dissolution of Supreme Hdqrs., A.E.F., 1945, made a tour of refugee and concentration camps in Germany and was flown back to U.S. for a lectr. tour of 55 cities under auspices of UNRRA; life-long interest has been Penology and for many yrs. prior to war was Dir. and Hon. Legal Counsel, Prisoner's Aid & Welfare Assn. of Montreal; assoc. with John Howard Soc. of Ont. in various capacities since 1946; retiring as a Dir., 1959, Asst. to Princ., Queen's Univ., 1950-59; mem. Nat. Parole Bd. Can. 1959-69; Prof.,

Dept. of Criminology, Univ. of Ottawa 1969-73; Past Pres., Candn. Club of Ottawa; LL.D. Queen's Univ. 1974; Past Pres., Un. Nations Assn. Ottawa; Past Pres. Internat. House of Ottawa; mem. Fauteux Comte., Dept. of Justice, 1953-56; Phi Delta Theta; United Church; Clubs: Black Watch Assn. (Toronto and Montreal); Home: 239 Engleburn Ave., Asburnham, Peterborough, Ont. K9H 1S5

EDWARD, John Thomas, Ph.D., D.Phil., Sc.D., F.R.S.C., F.C.I.C.; educator; b. London, Eng. 23 March 1919; s. John William and Jessie C. (Simpson) E.; e. Town of Mount Royal (Que.) High Sch. 1935; McGill Univ. B.Sc. 1939, Ph.D. 1942; Iowa State Coll. 1942-43; Oxford Univ. D.Phil. 1949; Trinity Coll. Dublin M.A. 1955, Sc.D. 1972; m. Deirdre Mary d. Cyril Waldron, Birmingham, Eng. 21 March 1953; children: John Valentine, Jeremy Bryan, Julian Kevin; MACDONALD PROF. OF CHEM. McGILL UNIV.; Research Offr. Explosives, Nat. Research Council, Ottawa and C.A.R.D.E. Valcartier 1943-45; Imp. Chem. Ind. Research Fellow in Chem. Univ. of Birmingham 1949-52; Lectr. in Organic Chem. Trinity Coll. Dublin 1952-56; joined McGill Univ. 1956; Visiting Scient. Copenhagen 1953, Stanford 1965, Paris 1972-73, Prague 1977, Sao Paulo 1978; Science Scholar Royal Comn. Exhn. 1851, Oxford 1946-49; author various articles on structures organic molecules, mechanisms organic reactions, conformational effects; mem. Order Chems. Que.; Am. Chem. Soc.; Am. Assn. Advanc. Science; Sigma Xi; recreations: skiing, hiking, gardening; Home: 51 Chesterfield Ave., Westmount, Que. H3Y 2M4; Office: 801 Sherbrooke St. W., Montreal, Que. H3A 2K6.

EDWARDS, Claude Albert, O.C.; b. Toronto, Ont. 8 Jan. 1916; s. late Arthur and Ethel (Large) E.; e. Riverdale Coll. Inst.; Toronto Teachers' Coll. 1935; m. Alice Mildred d. late George Reed 12 Oct. 1945; one s. Robert; MEM. PUBLIC SERVICE STAFF RELATIONS BD. since 1976; Dir. of Welfare Services Dept. of Veterans' Affairs London 1961-62; Pres. Civil Service Fed. Can. 1962-66, Pub. Service Alliance Can. 1966-76; Gov. Carleton Univ.; mem. Ottawa/Carleton Regional Dist. Health Council (Chrmn. since 1978); Nat. Jt. Council (Co-Chrmn. 1969-75, Chrmn. Staff Side 1969-75); Inst. Pub. Adm. Can. 1969-78; Econ. Council Can. 1975-76; Candn. Econ. Policy Comte.; Trilateral Comn.; served with RCAF 1941-45; author various articles on labour relations; Anglican; Home: 2286 Crane St., Ottawa, Ont. K1G 3C7; Office: P.O. Box 1525 Stn. B, Ottawa, Ont. K1P 5V2.

EDWARDS, Clifford Henry Coad, LL.B., Q.C.; educator; b. Jamalpore, India, 8 Nov. 1924; s. George Henry Probyn and Constance Ivy (Coad) E.; came to Canada 1958; e. King's Coll. Sch., Wimbledon, Eng.; King's Coll., Univ. of London, LL.B. (1st Class Hons.) 1945; post-grad work 1946-47; m. Kathleen Mary, d. late Jacob Ernest Faber, 6 Jan. 1951; two s., John Philip and Michael Hugh; two d., Jeanette Marie and Margaret Susan; CHRM., MANITOBA LAW REFORM COMMISSION former Dean, Fac. of Law, Univ. of Manitoba, 1966-79; served articles of Clerkship, London, Eng.; admitted as a Solr., Supreme Court of Eng. 1949; called to Bar of Man. 1964; in practice with firm of Solrs., London, Eng.; 1948; Legal Advisor, Sudan Interior Mission, W. Africa 1952; apptd. Lectr. at Law, Kumasi Coll., Ghana 1956, Sr. Lectr. 1957; apptd. to acad. staff, Manitoba Law Sch. 1958, Sch. Recorder 1960, Assoc. Prof. 1962, Prof. and Dean, Sch. of Law 1964; mem. Exec. Comte. Commonwealth Legal Educ. Assn.; Past Pres., Assn. Candn. Law Teachers; apptd. mem. of the Uniform Law Conf. of Can.; 1979; Publications: "Developments concerning the Criteria of Sex with its Legal Implications" 1959, also various reviews, case comments and articles in leading law journs.; contributor, Casebook on Candn. Law of Contract, 1978; Baptist; recreations: tennis, reading, public speaking;

Home: 53 Agassiz Dr., Winnipeg, Man. R3T 2K9; Office: 521-405 Broadway, Winnipeg, Man. R3C 3L6

EDWARDS, Brig. Gen. Gerard J. J., D.F.C., C.D.; b. Sudbury, Ont., Oct. 1921; e. Ottawa, Ont.; RCAF Staff Coll., 1946; Nat. Defence Coll., 1963; joined RCAF in 1940 and trained as a pilot; served overseas with 428 Heavy Bomber Sqdn. from 1943; later awarded D.F.C. and rose to command 420 Sqdn.; returned to Can. 1945 to serve with Eastern Air Command; posted to staff duties, Directorate of Organ. and Estab., AFHQ, 1946; moved to Candn. Jt. Staff, Washington, attached to U.S. Air Force Planning and Organ. Br., 1948; returned to AFHQ for duties in Chief of Staff Secretariat, 1950; named Commdg. Offr., 435 Sqdn., Edmonton, 1952; trans to Air Transport Command HQ as Sr. Air Staff Offr., 1954; apptd. to Directing Staff, RAF Staff Coll., Eng., 1957; named Chief Staff Offr., Air Transport Command, Trenton, 1959; became Dir. of Postings and Careers, AFHQ, 1964; on integration of Candn. Forces HQ became Dir. of Sr. Appts. (Air); Chief of Staff (Forces Requirement and Doctrine), Mobile Command, 1966; Commdr. 10 Tactical Air Group, 1968; Directing Staff, Nat. Defence Coll. 1969; Sr. Liaison Offr. (AF), Candn. Defence Liaison Staff, Wash., D.C. 1970; apptd. Commandant, Nat. Defence Coll. 1974; Address: National Defence College, Kingston, Ont.

EDWARDS, Commodore Gordon Cheeseman; C.D.; naval officer; b. Toronto, Ont., 24 July 1917; s. Charles and Florence (Paskin) E.; e. Montreal (Que.) High Sch.; RCAF Staff Coll.; Nat. Defence Coll.; m. Rosemary Dorothea Margaret, d. late Lieut. E. W. Bulteel, 22 May, 1942; children: Peter, Steven, Susan, Robert, Jennifer, served as Merchant Navy Cadet; began naval career with RCNVR, Montreal, 1940; loaned to RN engaged on convoy duty on "Dover Run" in Eng. Channel; served in RN aircraft carriers "Unicorn" and "Striker" as Pilot in 824 Sqdn; commanded Sqdn. in 1944 and following yr. apptd. C.O. 769 RN Deck Landing Training Sqdn., Scot. (1st Candn. in World War II to command a Brit. Naval Air Sqdn.); served in N. Atlantic, Arctic and Mediteranean; apptd. Depy. Dir. Naval Aviation and Dir. Naval Air Personnel, Ottawa, 1945-48; served ashore and afloat in destroyers during following 3 yrs.; Commdr. (Air), HMCS Shearwater Naval Air Stn., Dartmouth, N.S., 1951-54; Commdr. HMCS "Stettler" (frigate), 1954; Dir., Naval Aviation, Naval HQ, 1955; Depy. Asst. Chief of Naval Staff (Air and Warfare), HQ, 1958 and subsequently Dir. of Naval Aircraft Requirements; Commdr., Third Candn. Escort Sqdn. and C.O., HMCS "Athabaskan", 1961; C.O., HMCS Shearwater, 1963; apptd. Commodore Personnel Atlantic Coast, Halifax, 1964 (A.D.C. to Gov. Gen. this period); C.O. Naval Divs. and Sr.-Offr.-in-Chief Command Naval Reserves, 1965; Directing Staff, Nat. Defence Coll., Kingston, Ont., 1967; currently Commdr., Candn. Forces Base, Borden, Ont.; Mentioned in Despatches; Anglican; recreations: sailing, skiing, swimming, golf; Clubs: RCYC; Royal Hamilton Yacht; Royal Candn. Naval Sailing.

EDWARDS, John Llewelyn Jones, LL.B., M.A., Ph.D., LL.D., LL.D. (Hon.); university professor; b. Aberystwyth, Cardiganshire, Wales, 16 May, 1918; s. David and Sarah (Jones) E., e. Univ. Coll. of Wales, LL.B. 1939; St. John's Coll., Univ. of Cambridge, B.A. 1947, M.A. 1952, LL.D. 1964; Univ. of London, Ph.D. 1953, and Hon. LL.D. Univ. of Wales, 1976; m. Monica Mary d. Cuthbert and Jessie Haysey, Leigh-on-Sea, Essex, Eng., 24 March 1945; children: Alexandra Mary, Mark Llewelyn John, Stephen Gordon Patrick; PROF. OF LAW, FACULTY OF LAW since 1963, AND FIRST DIR. OF THE CENTRE OF CRIMINOLOGY, UNIV. OF TORONTO, 1963-76; called to Bar at Middle Temple, London, Eng. 1948; Bar of Ont. 1971; Lect., Faculty of Law, Univ. Coll., London.; 1947-51; Queen's Univ. of Belfast (N. Ireland) 1951-53, Reader in Law 1953-58; came to Canada 1958; Sir James Dunn

Prof. of Law, Faculty of Law, Dalhousie Univ., 1958-63; served in 2nd World War, Terr. Army, 1939; served with R.A. in W. Africa; staff appts. with H.Q., Br. Airborne Corps and Directorate of Staff Duties, War Office; Legal Corr., "Manchester Guardian" 1948-52; author: "Mens Rea in Statutory Offences" 1955, "Law Officers of the Crown", 1964, reprinted 1978; "Ministerial Responsibility for National Security", 1980; Founding mem., Conf. of Chief Justices of Canada, 1964-65; Overseas Fellow, Churchill Coll., Cambridge, 1967-68; Ford Foundation Travelling Fellow 1967-69; Visiting Prof,. Fellow, Univ. of Wales, 1974; Commonwealth Prestige Fellow, N.Z. Univers., 1977; Pres. Medico-Legal Soc. of Toronto (1970-71); Special Adviser to McDonald Commission on National Security, 1977-81; Anglican; Home: 66 Baby Pt. Cres., Toronto, Ont. M6S 2C1

EDWARDS, Oliver Edward, B.Sc., M.S., Ph.D., F.R.S.C., F.C.I.C.; organic chemist; b. Wattsville, Wales, 8 Jan. 1920; s. Oliver Edward and Anna E.; came to Canada 1926; e. Univ. of Alberta, Bsc. (Hons. Chem.) 1941; Northwestern Univ., M.S. 1943, Ph.D. 1948; m. Isobel Mary, d. Samuel George Gregg, 4 Aug. 1945; children: Sheryl Anne, Laurel Ruth; PRIN. RESEARCH OFFR., DIV. OF BIOL. SCIENCES, NAT. RESEARCH COUNCIL, which he joined in 1948; served in Candn. Army, 1943-46, retiring with rank of Capt.; mem., Eastview, Ont., Sch. Bd. 1956-58; mem., Am. Chem. Soc.; Chem. Inst. Can.; (1960 Merck, Sharpe & Dohme Award); Chem. Soc. (London); author: over 87 scientific papers; United Church; Home: 678 Portage Ave., Ottawa, Ont. K1G 1T4; Office: 100 Sussex Dr., Ottawa, Ont.

EDWARDS, Stanley Ewart, Q.C., B.A., LL.B., LL.M.; b. Airdrie, Alta., 20 Nov. 1921; s. William Frederick and Anna Lamont (McCracken) E.; e. Public and High Schs., Airdrie, Alta.; Univ. of Alberta (B.A. 1942, LL.B. 1943); Harvard Law School (LL.M. 1947); m. Margaret Jean, d. Frank Duncan Patterson, 11 Nov. 1949; children: Paul Donald, Stanley David, Douglas William, James Richard, John Glen; PARTNER, FRASER & BEATTY; Dir. and Secy., Riverside Yarns Ltd.; Dir., Texas Refinery Corp. of Can. Ltd.; Dir. Schlumberger Canada Ltd.; mem., Edit. Bd. CCH Canadian Tax Reporter, since 1949; Adv. to Royal Comn. on Taxation, 1966-67; Bd. of Govs., St. George's Coll.; served with R.C.N.V.R.; read law with Hannah, Nolan, Chambers, Might and Saucier, Calgary, Alberta; called to the Bar, Alta.; 1946; Ont. 1949; cr. Q.C. 1962; Lectr., Osgoode Hall, Toronto, 1947-49; joined Fraser, Beatty & Co. 1949; Partner 1955; mem., Candn. Bar Assn.; Past Chrmn., Candn. Tax Foundation; Internat Comn. of Jurists; Alta. and Ont. Bar Assns.; Pres. Bd. Trade Metrop. Toronto [Chrmn. Econ. Policy Comte]; Past Pres., Estate Planning Council; United Church; recreations: golf, skiing, Clubs: National; Arts and Letters; Alpine Ski (Past Pres.); Empire; Home: 25 Montressor Dr., Willowdale, Ont. M2P 1Y9; Office: P.O. Box 100, First Canadian Place, Toronto, Ont.

EGBERT, Hon. William Gordon Neil, B.A., LL.B.; judge; b. Calgary, Alta. 21 Dec. 1925; s. William Gordon and Gladys (McKelvie) LL.B., F.R.A.M., Egbert; e. Strathcona Sch. for Boys Calgary 1943; Rideau Park Jr. High Sch. and Central Coll. Inst. Calgary 1947; Univ. of Alta. B.A., LL.B. 1952; m. Margot d. Eugene Burton, Medicine Hat, Alta. 24 May 1952; children: Sherri, Cynthia, Michael, William; JUDGE, COURT OF QUEEN'S BENCY ALTA. 1979- ; called to Bar of Alta. 1953; cr. Q.C. 1969; Assoc. Macleod Dixon 1953-58; Corporate Secy. and Gen. Counsel, Alberta Coal Ltd. 1958-60; Partner, Stack, Egbert & Stack 1960-63; Walsh, Egbert & Harkness 1963-69; Gill Cook 1969-79; Hon. Life Dir., Calgary Exhn. & Stampede; Bencher, Law Soc. Alta. 1970-71, 1974-79; Past Pres. Calgary Bar Assn.; mem. Candn. Bar Assn.; Anglican; recreation: golf; Club: Calgary Golf & Country (Past Pres.); Home: 340, 540 - 14th Ave. S.W., Calgary, Alta.

T2R 0M7; Office: Court House, 611 - 4th St. S.W., Calgary, Alta. T2P 1T5.

EGGLESTON, Anne Elisabeth, Mus. M.; b. Ottawa, Ont., 6 Sept. 1934; d. John Wilfrid and Magdelana (Raskevich) E.; e. Glebe Coll. Inst., Ottawa, 1952; Assoc. of Royal Conserv. of Music of Toronto (piano) 1952; Univ. of Toronto, Artist Dipl. (musical comp.), 1956; Eastman Sch. of Music, Mus.M. 1958; master's thesis, "Autumnal Clouds" (poem for baritone voice and orchestra) performed by Eastman Rochester Symphony Orchestra, 1958; rec'd commission from Ottawa Bd. of Ed. to write, "Lets Celebrate", for S.A.T.B. Recorders and percussion, first performed 1979; arranged "Fifteen Canadian Folk Songs" for piano solo (easy) 1979; arranged "Six variations on the Squid-Jiggin' Ground", dedicated to Ken Prior, 1979; rec'd comns. from Candn. Music Centre to write educ. music (is bilingual) 1963, a work for string orchestra "On Citadel Hill," and from the Charlottetown Festival (1966) an orchestral overture; has orch. and chamber music scores in lib. of Candn. Music Centre; orch. works, chamber music, vocal and instrumental music have been performed over CBC, quartet for piano and strings was performed at Stratford Festival, 1966; concert of compositions given by Musical Arts Club of Ottawa in Nat. Gallery, 1967; "Fanfaron" (for orchestra) performed by Atlantic Symphony over C.B.C. Oct. 1971; "Quartet for Piano and Strings" 1972; "Five Lullabies of Eugene Field" 1972; "Ascent" (for carillon) commmd. by Percival Price and performed by him on Parlty. Bldgs. Peace Tower carillon July 1973; "Quintessence" (for solo cello) performed by Janet Covington, 1975; "Serenade" (for flute, cello, and harpsichord) commissioned by CAMMAC 1975; "Toccata" (for piano) commissioned by and performed by Suzanne Chapin, 1976; "Seven Variations" (for piano) published in "Piano Solos by Ottawa Composers", 1977; "Musical Christmas Cards" for piano 1980; CAPAC; Canadian League of Composers; recreations: yoga, classical guitar, handicrafts; Club: Musical Arts; Address: 234 Clemow Ave., Ottawa, Ont. K1S 2B6

EGGLESTON, Wilfrid, M.B.E. (1943), LL.D., D.Litt.; journalist; b. Lincoln, Eng., 25 Mar. 1901; s. Samuel and Ellen (Cowham) E.; e. Regina Coll. Inst.; Outlook (Sask.) High Sch.; Calgary Normal Sch., 1st Class Cert. 1922; Queen's Univ., B.A. 1926 (English Medallist); Carleton LL.D. 1966; W. Ont. D.Litt. 1967; m. Magdelâna, d. Joseph and Anne Raskevich, Bellevue, Alta., 28 June 1928; one d., Anne Elisabeth; Founding Director (1947-66), currently Prof. Emeritus, School of Journalism, Carleton Univ., Ottawa; Columnist (1966-77), The Ottawa Journal; Rural Teacher, Alta. 1919-20; High Sch. Teacher, 1922-24; entered journalism as Reporter, the Lethbridge "Herald", 1924; contrib. a weekly article to that paper on life and letters, 1920-29; Reporter, Toronto "Star", 1926-27; Asst. to City Ed., 1927-28; Feature Writer, Toronto "Star Weekly", 1929; Ottawa Corr., Toronto "Star", 1929-33; Contrib. to Corr. to numerous periodicals, 1933-37, incl. "Manchester Guardian," "Current Hist.", "Maclean's", etc.; mem. of Secretariat, Roy, Comn. on Dom.-Prov. Relations, 1937-39; Chief Eng. Press Censor, 1940-43; Dir. of Censorship, 1944; broadcast over C.B.C. and internat. short wave on Candn. Affairs; Past Pres., Parlty. Press Gallery, Ottawa; Director, The Candn. Writers' Foundation; author of "Prairie Moonlight and Other Lyrics" (privately printed) 1927; "The High Plains" (novel), 1938; "The Road to Nationhood" (a chronicle of Dominion-Provincial Relations), 1946; "Scientists at War", 1950; "Canada at Work", 1953; "The Frontier and Canadian Letters", 1957; "The Green Gables Letters", 1959; "The Queen's Choice, A Story of Canada's Capital", 1961; "Canada's Nuclear Story", 1965; "While I Still Remember, A Personal Record", 1968; "Newfoundland: The Road to Confederation", 1974; "National Research in Canada: The NRC, 1916-1966", 1978; "Prairie Symphony", a novel, 1978; "Literary

Friends: a book of reminiscence" 1980; rec'd. National Press Club Award in Journalism, 1968; recreation: lawn bowling, curling; Home: 234 Clemow Ave., Ottawa, Ont. K1S 2B6

EGGLETON, Arthur C.; mayor; b. Toronto, Ont. 29 Sept. 1943; m. 2ndly Brenda Louise (Clune) Dec. 1981; children: Stephanie (by first marriage); MAYOR, CITY OF TORONTO 1980- ; first el. to City Council for Ward 4 1969, re-el. since; el. by Council to City of Toronto Extve. Comte. after each re-el. and apptd. each time by the Mayor and Extve. as Budget Chief; served 2 terms as Pres. City Council and Vice Chrmn., Extve. Comte.; Chrmn. Mun. Liaison Comte. 1975; served various comtes. City and Metro; Metro Extve. Comte., Metro Council; 3rd Vice Pres. Candn. Nat. Exhn. several yrs.; Vice Pres. City of Toronto Non-Profit Housing Corp.; Dir. Cath. Children's Aid Soc.; mem. Soc. Mang. Accts.; recreations: skiing, tennis, horseback riding; Office: City Hall, Toronto, Ont. M5H 2N2.

EHRICHT, Horst Hermann, R.C.A.; photojournalist; photographer; b. Berlin-Charlottenburg, Germany 18 Nov. 1928; s. Herman Gottfried Ehricht; e. Staatl. Martin Luther Oberschule, Eisleben, Germany 1948; Ryerson Polytech. Inst. Toronto 1952-55; came to Can. 1951; m. Wilhelmina d. late Jacobus Cornelius van Klaveren, Creemore Ont. 3 Sept. 1955; children: Mark, Lucas, Peter; freelance photojournalist 1955-65; Dir. of Photography "Maclean's" mag. 1965-71; work incls. ed. photography, photographic illustrations, corporate and advertising photography, documentary films; served with German Army 1944-45; mem. Dom. of Can. Rifle Assn.; Ont. Rifle Assn.; Service Rifle Shooting Assn.; P. Conservative; Protestant; recreations: photography, reading, military history, skiing, shooting; Address: Box 253, Kleinburg, Ontario L0J 1C0

EHRMAN, Joachim Benedict, A.M., Ph.D.; educator; b. Nuremberg, Germany 12 Nov. 1929; s. late Dr. Fritz S. and late Ilse (Benedict) E.; e. Univ. of Pa. A.B. 1948; Princeton Univ. A.M. 1949, Ph.D. 1954; m. Gloria Jeanette d. late Stephen Gould 24 Jan. 1961; one s. Carl David; PROF. OF APPLIED MATH., UNIV. OF W. ONT. 1968- ; Research Engr. Atomic Energy Dept. North American Aviation Inc., Downey, Calif. 1951-53; Instr. in Physics Yale Univ. 1954-55; Research Physicist U.S. Naval Research Lab. Washington, D.C. Nucleonics Div. 1955-66, Plasma Physics Div. 1966-68 (part-time Consultant 1969-70); Visiting Staff Theoretical Div. Princeton Univ. Plasma Physics Lab. 1975-76; Assoc. Prof. (part-time) Physics George Washington Univ. 1956-57; part-time lectr. in Physics Univ. of Md. (at U.S. Naval Research Lab. Washington) 1963-64; author or co-author various articles prof. journs.; mem. Am. Phys. Soc. (Plasma Physics Div.); Phi Beta Kappa; Sigma Xi; Pi Mu Epsilon; Jewish; Office: London, Ont. N6A 5B9.

EICHNER, Hans, Ph.D., LL.D.; educator; university professor; b. Vienna, Austria 30 Oct. 1921; s. Alexander and Valerie (Ungar) E.; e. Univ. of London B.A. 1944, B.A. (Hons.) 1946, Ph.D. 1949; Queen's Univ. LL.D. 1974; m. Joan M. d. late James Partridge 29 May 1957; children: Elizabeth Jane, James Alexander; PROF. AND CHRMN. OF GERMAN, UNIV. OF TORONTO since 1975; Asst. Lectr. Bedford Coll. London 1948-50; Asst. Prof. Queen's Univ. 1950, Assoc. Prof. 1956, Prof. 1962-67; Prof. of German present Univ. since 1967, Chrmn. Grad. Dept. German 1967-72; Hon. Prof. of Humanities, Univ. Calgary 1978; author "Thomas Mann" 1953, 2nd rev. ed. 1961; "Reading German for Scientists" 1959; "Four German Authors: Mann-Rilke-Kafka-Brecht" 1964; "Friedrich Schlegel" 1970; Ed. "Friedrich Schlegel: Literary Notebooks 1797-1801" 1957, 2nd (German) ed. 1980; "Kritische Friedrich Schlegel-Ausgabe" Vols. 2-6 and 16, 1959-81; " 'Romantic' and its Cognates: The European History of a Word" 1972; Gen. Ed. "Canadian Studies in

German Language and Literature" 1970 ff.; various articles Thomas Mann, Friedrich Schlegel, Goethe and others; mem. Candn. Assn. Univ. Teachers German (Pres. 1976-78); Fellow of the Royal Society of Canada, since 1967; Jewish; recreation: sailing; Club: Boulevard; Home: 12 Hopperton Dr., Willowdale, Ont. M2L 2S6; Office: 97 St. George St., Toronto, Ont. M5S 1A1.

EIDT, Conrad Harry, B.A.Sc.; municipal engineer; b. Amabel Twp., Bruce Co., Ont. 29 Nov. 1924; s. Alvin Albert and Margaret Caroline (Playford) E.; e. Allan Park, Crawford and Mulock, Bentinck Twp. schs.; Grey Co. Hanover High Sch. 1940; Niagara Parks Comn. Gardening Sch. 1942; Univ. of Toronto B.A.Sc. 1950; m. Nancy Alice James 3 Jan. 1973; children: Andrew G. Reynolds, Alison J. Konyi, C. Jeffrey, Mark Mathew; DIR. OF ENGINEERING, REGIONAL MUNICIPALITY OF NIAGARA 1970- ; Landscape Engr. Hydro Electric Power Comn. Ont. 1950-52; Jr. Engr. Twp. of Stamford 1952-57, Twp. Engr. 1957-63; City Engr. City of Niagara Falls 1963-70; served with RCAF Heavy Bomber Command #4 Group RAF 76 Sqdn., Navig., rank Flying Offr. World War II; author various articles design subdivs., pol. problems establishing sludge disposal facilities Ont., energy from waste Niagara; mem. Engn. Inst. Can.; Assn. Prof. Engrs. Prov. Ont.; Lutheran; Clubs: Niagara Falls; Niagara Falls Rotary; Home: 5710 Robinson St., Niagara Falls, Ont. L2G 2B2; Office: (P.O. Box 3025) 150 Berryman Ave., St. Catharines, Ont. L2R 7E9.

EISEN, Sydney, B.A., Ph.D.; professor and administrator; b. Poland 5 Feb. 1929; s. David and Eva (Singer) E.; e. Orde and Lansdowne Pub. Schs., Harbord Coll. Inst. Toronto 1946; Univ. Education Toronto B.A. 1950; Johns Hopkins Univ. Ph.D. 1957; Cornell Univ. 1950-51; London Sch. of Econ. 1953-54; m. Doris Ruth d. Ben Kirschbaum 22 Jan. 1957; children: Daniel, Robert Joseph, Sarah Anne, Miriam Malka; PROFESSOR OF HISTORY AND HUMANITIES, YORK UNIV. since 1968; Instr. Williams Coll. Williamstown, Mass. 1955, Asst. Prof. 1958-61; Asst. Prof. The City Coll. of New York 1961-65, Acting Asst. Dean 1964-65; Visiting Assoc. Prof. Univ. of Toronto 1965-66; Assoc. Prof. of Hist. and Humanities York Univ. 1965-68, Acting Chrmn. Div. of Humanities 1967-68, Chrmn. Dept. of Hist. 1970-72; Dean, Faculty of Arts 1973-78; Consultant, Reader and Examiner for Coll. Entrance Exam. Bd. and Educ. Testing Service 1959-66; Nat. Humanities Faculty, Concord, MA, since 1972, mem. Bd. Trustees & Extve. Comte. since 1974, Pres. and chrmn. of Bd., 1976-80; mem. Bd. Jewish Educ. Toronto 1970-74; Community Hebrew Acad. Toronto since 1970, Vice Chrmn., Bd. Dirs., Chrmn. Extve. Comte.; Bd. Dirs. Assoc. Hebrew Schs. since 1970; Mgmt. Comm. since 1978, Secretary since 1979; Ont. Inst. for Studies in Educ. 1970-72, Bd. of Govs.; rec'd Louis Rosenfeld (1946), Univ. Coll. Alumni (1948) and John Fraser Gray (1949) Scholarships; Cody Prize 1950; Vincent Fellow 1951-53, and Bissing Fellow 1954-55, Johns Hopkins Univ.; Social Science Research Council of Can. Fellowship 1953-54; Morris Ernst Prize Williams Coll. 1961, 1900 Fund Grant 1961; Can. Council Summer Grant 1967 and Leave Fellowship 1968-69; co-author "The Human Adventure: Readings in World History" 2 vols. 1964; Gen. Ed. "The West and the World" (various books & pamphlets); author various articles and reviews; mem. Am. Jewish Hist. Soc.; Candn. Hist. Assn.; Victorian Studies Assn. Univ.; Conf. on Brit. Studies; Council for Basic Education; Hist. Science Soc.; Am. Hist. Assn.; Home: 5 Renoak Dr., Willowdale, Ont. M2R 2E1; Office: 4700 Keele St., Downsview, Ont. M3J 1P3

ELDON, Walter Donald Ridley, A.M., Ph.D.; economist; b. London, Ont., 9 Aug. 1926; s. Frank Irving, M.A., and Daveda Elinor Louise (Ridley) E.; e. Univ. of Western Ont., B.A. (Gold Medal for highest standing in honour Hist.) 1948; Harvard Univ., A.M. 1951, Ph.D. (Econ.) 1952; m. Jean Elizabeth, d. Donald McLennan,

Brantford, Ont., 12 April 1958; one s. Donald McLennan; one d. Elizabeth Lucinda Louise; SR. ADV., GOV. RELATIONS, IMPERIAL OIL LTD since 1975; Asst. Econ., Candn. Nat. Rlys., Montreal, 1951-55; Dir. of Research, P. Conservative Party of Can., Ottawa, Ont. 1955-58; Asst. Prof. of Econ., Univ. of W. Ont., London, Ont., 1958-61; consultant to various Roy. Comns., 1958-60; mem., Tariff Bd. of Can., 1961-63; Restrictive Trade Practices Comn., 1963-66; Prof. of Econ., Assoc. Dean of Arts & Science and other posts, Trent Univ. 1966-71; Vice Pres., Lakehead Univ. 1971-73; mem., Ont. Energy Bd., 1973-75; Publications: "American Influences in the Canadian Iron & Steel Industry" 1954 & various articles and reports; mem. Royal Econ. Soc.; Am. Econ. Assn.; Candn. Econ. Assn.; Anglican; Home: 281 Watson Ave., Oakville, Ont. L6J 3V3

ELDRIDGE, Robert Huyck, B.A., M.S.; financial consultant; b. New York, N.Y. 13 March 1938; s. William A. and Barbara Franklin (Jones) E.; e. Deerfield (Mass) Acad. 1956; Harvard Univ. B.A. 1961; Mass. Inst. of Technol. Sloane Sch. M.S. 1966; m. Elisabeth B. d. Dr. Walter L. Palmer, Chicago, Ill. 11 Sept. 1965; children: Daniel H., Cynthia B.; independent financial consultant 1980- ; joined Banco de la Republica, Bogota, Colombia 1967-69; Kuhn Loeb & Co. New York 1969-72; Treas. Brascan Ltd. Toronto 1973-79; co-author "La Palma Africana en Colombia" 1968; various articles econ. devel. and Middle E.; Dir. Rosedale Ratepayers Assn. 1973-78; Pres. Lands of Bible Archaeol. Foundation Toronto; service U.S. Marine Corps; Protestant; recreations: long distance running, skiing, fishing; Home: 24 Castle Frank Cres., Toronto, Ont. M4W 3A3; Office: 59 Wynford Dr., Don Mills, Ont. M3C 1K3.

ELGIE, Hon. Robert Goldwin, M.P.P., M.D., F.R.S.C. (Neuro Surgery); politician; b. Toronto, Ont. 22 Jan. 1929; s. Goldwin Corlett and Vivian Granger (McHenry) E.; e. Univ. of Toronto Schools; Univ. of W. Ont.; Osgoode Hall Law Sch.; Univ. of Ottawa; m. Nancy Anne d. Harvey Stewart, London, Ont. 23 June 1956; children: Stewart A.G., William C., Peter G., Allyson G., Catherine A.G.; MIN. OF CONSUMER & COMM. RELATIONS, 1982- ; Min. of Labour, Ont. 1978-82; neurosurgeon; el. M.P.P. for York East prov. g.e. 1977; Parlty. Asst. to Min. of Community & Social Services 1978; P. Conservative; United Church; Clubs: Empire; York Downs Golf & Country; Office: 400 University Ave., Toronto, Ont. M7A 1T7.

ELLEN, Leonard, executive; b. Montreal, Que. 23 Sept. 1925; CHMN., LEONARD ELLEN CANADA INC; Pres. G.A. Grier Inc.; Standard Investments Ltd.; Dir. Central Trust Co.; MICC Investments Ltd.; The Mortgage INsur. Co. of Canada; United Financial Management Ltd.; United Group of Mutual Funds; Enheat Inc.; LifeSurance Corp.; mem. Bd. of Regents, Mr. Allison Univ.; Office: 2 Place Ville Marie, Montreal, Que. H3B 3Y3.

ELLETT, Richard D., B.Sc., F.G.S.A.; geologist; mining executive; b. Seattle, Wash., U.S.A. 14 April 1921; s. Lawrence H. and Agnes (Stevenson) E.; came to Canada 1970; e. Wash. State Univ., B.Sc., 1947; m. Mickey, d. Anton Norman Mikkelsen 8 Mar. 1943; children: Wade, Jenness, Laurel; VICE PRES. OF EXPLORATION, NEWMONT MINING CORP., since 1973; Vice Pres. and Dir., Newmont Exploration Ltd.; Chrmn. and Dir., Newmont Exploration of Canada Ltd.; Dir., O'okiep Copper Co. Ltd.; Tsumeb Corp. Ltd.; Dawn Mining Co.; Idarado Mining Co.; Newmont Proprietary Ltd.; Newmont Oil Co.; Carlin Gold Mining Co.; Geologist, Patino Mines and Enterprises, Sigloxx, Bolivia, 1947-49; Geologist Newmont Mining Corp. Southwestern U.S. 1949-51; Engr. and Geol., National Lead Co. Ltd., Mexico, Australia, Argentina & U.S., 1951-59; Vice-Pres. and Mgr. Utah Development Co. Australia, 1960-69; Vice-Pres., Mining, International Resources Ltd., Denver, Colo., 1969-70;

served with U.S. Army, 1942-45; mem. Am. Mining, Metall. & Petroleum Engrs.; Soc. Econ. Geologists; Australasia Mining & Metall. Engrs.; Geol. Soc. of Australia; Inst. Prof. Geologists; Prof. Engrs. Ont.; Candn. Mining Assn.; Protestant; recreations: golf, fishing; Club: New York Mining; Home: 24 Graenest Ridge Rd., Wilton Conn.; Office: 300 Park Ave., New York, N.Y.

ELLIOT, Alfred Johnston, M.D., D.O.M.S., Med. Sc.D., F.R.C.S.(C); physician; university professor; b. Calgary, Alta., 16 Aug. 1911; s. Laurie Benjamin and late Mary Elizabeth (Howson) E.; e. Univ. of Brit. Columbia, B.A. (Hons.) 1932; Univ. of Toronto, M.D. 1937; Columbia Univ., Med. Sc.D. (Ophthalmol.) 1941; Royal Coll. Phys. and Surgs., London, Eng., Dipl. Ophthalmic Med. and Surg., 1945; m. Jean Kerr, d. Geo. Kerr MacNaughton, Cumberland, B.C., 27 June 1942; children: Mary, Heather, George, Barbara; PROF., OPHTHALMOL., UNIVERSITY OF B.C., since 1961 (and Dept. Head there 1961-73); Prof. and Head, Dept. of Ophthalmology, Univ. of Toronto, 1946-61; Head Dept. Ophthalmology, Tor. Gen. Hosp., 1946-61; Senior Consultant D.V.A. Toronto, 1945-61; practised with Dr. Conrad Berens, New York City, 1941; privately in Toronto, 1945-61; served in World War, 1941-45 with R.C.A.F. as Ophthalmic Specialist, Montreal, 1943; London, Eng., 1944; promoted Flying Offr. and later Flight-Lieut. 1941; Squadron Leader 1943; Wing Commdr. 1944; mem. Am. Ophthal. Soc.; Candn. Med. Assn.; B.C. Med. Assn.; Candn. Ophthalmol. Soc.; Am. Acad. of Ophthalmol. &;Hon. mem., Montreal Ophthalmol. Soc., 1961; Golden Jubilee Award, Candn. Nat. Inst. for the Blind, 1968; Prince of Good Fellows, Vancouver Med. Assn., 1974, 1975; Sen. Mem., Can. Med. Assn., 1977; Hon. Vice Pres., Candn. Nat. Inst. for the Blind, 1978; Award of Merit, Can. Ophth. Soc. 1980; Publications: author and co-author of numerous books on ophthalmic diseases; Nu Sigma Nu.; Protestant; recreations: curling, fishing; Home: #47-6600 Lucas Road, Richmond, B.C. V7C 4T1

ELLIOT, Beverley Vallack, Q.C., b. Norwich, Ont., 11 Feb. 1900; s. Reginald and Jessie (Carling) E.; e. Univ. of Toronto, B.A. 1922; Osgoode Hall, Toronto; m. Iris Elaine, d. Charles E. Lanskail, Toronto, 27 Sept. 1930; PARTNER, BORDEN & ELLIOT; called to Bar of Ont. 1925; cr. Q.C. 1944; practised alone 1926-36; formed partnership with Henry Borden, C.M.G., Q.C., 1936; mem., Law Soc. of Upper Can.; Freemason; Conservative; Anglican; recreations: golf, bridge, fishing; Clubs: National; Rosedale Golf; York; Home: 242 Cortleigh Blvd., Toronto, Ont. M5N 1P7; Office: 250 University Ave., Toronto, Ont. M5H 3E9

ELLIOTT, Rev. Clifford, B.A., B.D., S.T.M., Ph.D., D.D. (Un. Ch.); b. Langham, Sask., 30 March 1919; s. George Wilfred and Annie (Jennings) E.; e. Univ. of Sask., B.A. 1939; St. Andrew's Coll., Saskatoon, B.D. 1944, D.D. 1967; Union Theol. Semy., N.Y., S.T.M. 1945; Columbia Univ., Ph.D. 1950; m. late Margaret Patricia, d. late Walter Kirkpatrick, 15 July 1942; children: Cherry, Kirk, Stuart, Grace (deceased); MINISTER, BLOOR UNITED CHURCH, since 1975; o. by Saskatchewan Conf. 1942; Min., Dundurn (Sask.) 1942-44; Third Ave., N. Battleford, Sask., 1947-52; St. Giles, Hamilton, Ont., 1952-59; Robertson, Edmonton, 1959-66; Metropolitan Un. Ch. 1966-75; has travelled in Far East, Middle East, Europe, Latin America, Africa, USA and China to see missionary and refugee work, social and political conditions, 1960, 1963, 1965, 1979; served for several years as Alberta Consultant on new Hymn Book; served on various national boards of church; Chrmn. of Comte. on Overseas Relief; Pres., Alta. Conf. 1963-64; Lectr. in Homiletics, St. Stephen's Coll., Edmonton for several yrs. and also conducted several workshops there and at Queen's and Centre for Christian Studies; Chrmn., Div. of Ministry Pers. & Ed., Univ. Coll., Univ. of Toronto; Chaplain (part time) of Victoria Univ., 1976-78; Adjct.

Prof., Emmanuel Coll., Toronto; involved in radio and TV broadcasting ch. services devotional programs and educational T.V. courses; children's programs; author: "This is Brazil; "A New Look at Mission"; co-author: "Journey Into Understanding"; "Stewardship Explorations"; contrib. to "United Church Observer" and other papers; columnist for Toronto Star; mem. Family Service Assn.; Social Action Comte.; recreation: music; Home: 417 Brunswick Ave., Toronto, Ont. M4T 2Z2; Office: 300 Bloor St. W., Toronto, Ont. M5S 1W3

ELLIOTT, Donald Campbell, B.A., C.L.U.; executive; b. Napanee, Ont., 23 June 1926; s. Francis Burton and Marion Jane E.; e. Univ. of W. Ont., B.A. (Hons.) 1950; C.L.U. 1957; m. Cornelia, d. Arend Berendse; children: Michael, Margaret, Catherine, Adriana, Robin; PRESIDENT, THE EMPIRE LIFE INSURANCE, CO., MANAGING DIRECTOR, LIFE INSURANCE, THE DOMINION OF CANADA GENERAL INSURANCE CO. since 1981; joined Great-West Life Assurance Co. as Agent, Kingston, Ont. 1950, Mgr. 1953, Agency Asst. 1954, Mgr., Field Training 1956, Asst. Supt. Agencies 1957, Assoc. Supt. Agencies 1962, Br. Mgr., Edmonton 1963, Supt. of Agencies 1966, Regional Dir. 1968, Dir., Marketing (Canada then U.S.) 1969; Vice Pres. Marketing 1981; Vice Pres. Marketing (U.S.) 1976; Zeta Psi; Anglican; recreations: skiing, sailing; Club: Manitoba; Denver; Home: R.R. 2, Kingston, Ont. K7L 5H6. Office: P.O. Box 1000, Kingston, Ont. K7L 4Y4

ELLIOTT, G.A., M.A., LL.D., F.R.S.C.; b. Napier, Ont., 1901; e. Univ. of Manitoba, M.A.; Queen's Univ., LL.D.; m. Mary Stewart Paul, 1929; two children; Head of Dept. of Econ., Univ of Alta., 1929-46; Prof. of Pol. Econ., Univ. of Toronto, 1946-57; mem. Tariff Bd. of Can. 1957-71; mem. Bd. of Dirs., Nat. Bureau of Econ. Research, 1949-57; mem. of Royal Comn. on Co-operatives, 1944-45; former Mang. Editor, "Canadian Journal of Economics & Political Science"; author "Tariff Procedures & Trade Barriers" 1954; Pres., Candn. Pol. Science Assn., 1957-58; mem., Candn. Social Science Research Council, 1944-48 and 1957-61; Home: 356 Mowat Ave., Kingston, Ont. K7M 1L2

ELLIOTT, George Clarence, B.S.A., M.Sc.; retired insurance executive; b. Saskatoon, Sask., 10 June 1910; s. Thomas Arthur and Jessie Ann (Bowes) E.; e. Gideon Pub. Sch. and Bedford Rd. Coll. Inst., Saskatoon, Sask.; Univ. of Sask., B.S.A. 1935, M.Sc. 1937; Cornell Univ., post-grad. studies 1938-39 (Fellowship); m. Olive Mae, d. late Frank Henry Baker, 3 May 1935; children: Allen George, Olive Louise; former Vice-Pres., Invest. Policy, the Great-West Life Assurance Co., 1972-76; Econ. Analyst, Fed. Dept. of Agric., Edmonton, 1939-40; joined present Co. as Farm Inspr., Regina, 1940-43, Invest. Research, Winnipeg, 1943-44; Supvr., Mortgages, Supvr., Motrgages, 1945-46, Mgr., Mortgage Invests., 1947-53, Asst. Treas. 1954-55, Assoc. Treas. 1956-57, Treas. 1968; author, "Why Money Is Tight"; Past Pres., Mortgage Loans Assn. Can.; Appraisal Inst. Can.; Lectr. various seminars Mortgage Bankers Assn. Am.; Liberal; United Church; recreations: curling, golf, reading; Clubs: The Manitoba; Canadian; Granite Curling; Home: One Evergreen Place, Winnipeg, Man. R3L 0E9

ELLIOTT, Harold, M.D.; neurological surgeon; b. Cache Bay, Ont., 22 Dec. 1907; s. William and Ann Isobel (McInnis) E.; m. Helen Doris, d. George Gilbert Gales, 25 July 1937; children: David, Michael, Donald, Timothy, Christopher, Gay, Bonnie; Consultant Neurosurgeon; Montreal General Hospital; Asst. Prof. of McGill Univ.; mem. Parkinson Interdisciplinary Comte. DVA Can., U.S.A.; Edinburgh Univ. 1960; Traffic Accd. Injury Consultant Hon. C. M. Drury, Min. Industry (6 Counties E. Ont. survey) 1965; Donner Can. Foundation Traffic Accd. Comn. 1967-69; Geriatric (Neurovascular) Research Project, Brockville Psychiatric Hosp. 1970; Dir., Royal

Auto. Club; Candn., Rep., Internat. Head Injury Conf., Copenhagen 1965; strong advocate, Can. Accd. Research Foundation; Sigma Chi; Presbyterian; Home: Turtle Pond Farm, Como, Que. J0P 1A0

ELLIOTT, K(enneth) Allan C(aldwell), M.Sc., Ph.D., Sc.D., F.R.S.C. (1963); b. Kimberley, S. Africa, 24 Aug. 1903; s. Kenneth Caldwell and Venetia Mawby (Leppan) E.; e. Christian Brothers Coll., Kimberley, S. Africa; St. Andrew's Coll., Grahamstown, S.A. (Matric. 1920 1st Class); Rhodes Univ., Coll., B.Sc. Physics (1st Class) and Chem., 1923, M.Sc. (Chem. 1st Class) 1924; Selwyn Coll., Cambridge, 1926-33; Ph.D. 1930, Sc.D. 1950; Univ. of Munich, 1931-32 (six mths.); Beit Mem. Fellow for Med. Research, 1929; 4th Year Beit Fellow 1932; Fellow of Selwyn Coll., 1933-36; m. Frances, Ph.D., d. Frank Seaman Howland, 26 Dec. 1936; children: Venetia Caldwell, Joan, Kenneth Howland; Emeritus Prof. of Bio-Chem., McGill Univ., (Honorary); Consultant in Neurochemistry, Montreal Neurological Inst.; before entering Cambridge worked in indust. for two yrs., first as Shift Chem. in Broken Hill, N. Rhodesia, then as Chem. at Moderfontein Dynamite Factory near Johannesburg; went to U.S., 1933; Research Bio-chem., Bio-chem. Research Foundation of Franklin Inst. of Phila., 1933-39 (study of cancer); in charge Biochem. Research Lab., Inst. of the Penna. Hosp. (Psychiatric), Philadelphia and Asst. Prof. of Biochem. in Psychiatry, Univ. of Penna., 1939-44; Assoc. Prof. of Exper. Neurol. and Biochem., McGill Univ., 1944-59, Prof. and Chrmn., Dept. of Biochem., 1959-68; Dir., Donner Lab. of Exper. Neurochem., Montreal Neurol. Inst. 1949-65; CUSO vol.—Prof. of Physio. Chem., Univ. of Nigeria, Fac. of Med., Enugu, 1971-74; CESO vol.—Prof. of Human Chem., Univ. of Jos, Nigeria, 1978; Publications: co-editor, "Neurochemistry, The Chemistry of Brain & Nerve"; approx. 145 scient. articles; former Editor "Canadian Journal of Biochemistry and Physiology"; mem., numerous scient. societies; Sigma Xi; Unitarian; recreations: sailing, fishing, skiing; Home: 2220 Claremont Ave., Apt. 205, Montreal, Que. H3Z 2P8

ELLIOTT, Morley Robinson, O.B.E., M.D., D.P.H.; b. Goodwood, Ont., 1 Aug. 1900; s. John Wesley and Cora Alice (Long) E.; e. Pub. and High Sch., Rapid City, Man.; Wesley Coll., Winnipeg, Man. (pre-med. work); Univ. of Manitoba M.D., 1926; Univ. of Toronto, D.P.H., 1935; m. Ivy Norah Wooller R.N., 7 Dec. 1929; with Manitoba Sanatorium, 1926; in private practice at Wawanesa, Man., 1927-34; Special Investigator for Man. Dept. of Health & Pub. Welfare re Med. Care for Unemployed in Winnipeg, 1935; Municipal Doctor at Erickson, Man., 1935-36; Epidemiol. in charge of field work during polio epidemic of 1936; apptd. Asst. Health Offr. of Winnipeg City, 1936; joined permanent staff, Dept. of Health & Pub. Welfare, Man. as Epidemiologist, 1937; Dir. of Sec. of Extension Health Services, 1947; Acting Dir. of Div. of Health Services, 1948; Dir. Health Survey of Manitoba and Sickness Survey of Manitoba, 1950; Depy. Min. of Health, Manitoba, 1951-1965; served in 2nd World War; M.O. Fort Garry Horse Regt. 1939; Dist. Hygiene Offr., M.D. 10 (Major) 1940; C.O., 10th Candn. Field Hygiene Sec. England, 1941-42; Organized and Commanded Army Sch. of Hygiene, Camp Borden (Lieut.-Col.), 1943; Asst. Dir. Hygiene, H.Q. 1st Candn. Corps in Italy 1944; Asst. Dir. Hygiene, 1st Candn. Army, H.Q. in N.W. Europe, 1945-46; O.B.E.; Mentioned in Despatches; mem., Candn. Med. Assn.; Candn. Pub. Health Assn. (Past Pres.); Am. Pub. Health Assn. (Fellow); Winnipeg Med. Soc.; State & Prov. Health Health Authorities of N. Am. (Pres. 1955); Freemason; Protestant; recreations: curling, golf; Home: 203 - 1035 Belmont, Victoria, B.C. V8S 3T5

ELLIOTT, Robbins L., M.A.; b. Wolfville, N.S., 12 Aug. 1920; s. Malcolm Robertson and Jean Steadman (Haley) E.; e. Wolfville (N.S.) High Sch.; Acadia Univ., B.A. 1941; Univ. of Toronto, M.A. 1947; m. Myfanwy Esther, d. George Frederick Millward, Ottawa, Ont. 9 Sept. 1950;

children: Michael Allan, Shirley Ann, Ruth Barbara, Malcolm Robbins; newspaper Reporter with Halifax and Windsor, Ont., dailies, 1941 and 1946; Editor, Candn. Citizenship Br., Dept. Secy. of State, 1947-48; Extve. Asst. to Min. of Resources & Devel., Ottawa, 1949-53; to Min. of Public Works, 1953-55; Dir. of Property & Building Management, Dept. of Public Works, 1955-56; Dir. of Personnel, Dept. of Pub. Works, 1956-58; Extve. Dir., Arch. Inst. Can. 1958-63; Dir. of Planning Br., Centennial Comn. 1963-68; apptd. Dir., Candn. Govt. Exhn. Comn. 1969-71; Gen. Dir. Office of Design, Dept. of Trade & Comm., 1971-76; Extve. Vice-Pres., Royal Architectural Inst. of Canada; Trustee, Ottawa Bd. of Educ. 1975; served in 2nd World War; Platoon Commdr., North N.S. Highlanders and Field Press Censor, 1st Canadian Army H.Q.; served in U.K. and N.W. Europe; retired with rank of Capt.; mem., Bd. of Dirs., Ont. Heritage Foundation; Past Pres., Ottawa-Hull Chapter, Archaeological Inst. of America; Past Pres., Ottawa Chapter, John Howard Soc.; mem., Bd. of Dirs., Candn. Centenary Council; Baptist; recreations: golf, swimming; Clubs: Rotary (Pres.); Canadian; Rideau; Home: 2325 Georgina Dr., Ottawa, Ont. K2B 7M4; Office: 151 Slater St., Ottawa, Ont. K1P 5H2

ELLIOTT, Roy Fraser, C.M., Q.C., B.Com., M.B.A.; lawyer; b. Ottawa, Ont., 25 Nov. 1921; s. Colin Fraser and Mary Marjorie (Sypher) E.; e. Queen's Univ. B.Com.; Osgoode Hall Law Sch., Toronto, Ont.; Harvard Grad. Sch. of Business Adm., M.B.A.; m. Betty Ann, d. late Roy McNicoll, Westmount, Que., 24 May 1955; PARTNER, STIKEMAN, ELLIOTT, ROBERTS & BOWMAN, Toronto; Stikeman, Elliott, Tamaki, Mercier & Robb, Montreal; Chrmn. of Bd., CAE Industries Ltd.; Standard Paper Box Ltd.; Dir., Montreal Shipping Co. Ltd.; Custom Concrete Ltd.; Canadian Imperial Bank of Commerce; New Providence Development Co. Ltd.; Canada Cement Lafarge Ltd.; Frank W. Horner Ltd.; The Toronto Symphony; Chrm., Can. Cultural Property Export Review Bd.; read law with Borden and Elliot, Toronto, Ont.; called to the Bar of Ont. 1946; Quebec 1948; formerly practised under firm name of Foster, Hannen, Watt, Stikeman & Elliott; author of "Quebec Corporation Manual", 1949; Co-ed, "Doing Business in Canada"; mem., Bd. of Govs.; Trustee, Art Gallery of Ont.; Pres., Art Gallery of Ontario Foundation; President, Canadian Opera Foundation; The Toronto General Hosp.; Anglican; recreations: golf, tennis, swimming; Clubs: Royal Montreal Golf; Mount Royal; Lyford Cay (Nassau); Toronto Golf; Montreal Indoor Tennis; The Hon. Co. of Edinburgh Golfers; Queen's; Toronto; Lost Tree Club; Homes: 110 Dunvegan Rd., Toronto, Ont. and 3450 Drummond St., Apt. 1006A, Montreal, Que.; Offices: Suite 4950, Commerce Court West, Toronto, Ont., and Suite 3900 - 1155 Dorchester Blvd., West, Montreal, Que. H3B 3V2

ELLIOTT, Shirley Burnham, M.A., S.B.; librarian; b. Wolfville, N.S. 4 June 1916; d. Malcolm Robertson and Jean Steadman (Haley) E.; e. Acadia Univ. B.A. 1937, M.A. 1939; Simmons Coll. Boston, S.B. (Lib. Science) 1940; LEGISLATIVE LIBRARIAN, LEGISLATIVE LIBRARY OF N.S. 1954- ; Honorary Librarian, Cambridge Military Library; Reference Asst. Brookline (Mass.) Pub. Lib. 1940-46; Asst. Librarian, Univ. of Rhode Island Library 1946-49; Asst. Ed. "Canadian Index" Candn. Lib. Assn. Ottawa 1949-50; Chief Librarian, Colchester-E. Hants Regional Lib. Truro, N.S. 1950-54; mem. Staff, Duke of Edinburgh's Commonwealth Conf. Can. 1962; author "Nova Scotia in Books, 1752-1967" 1967; "Province House" 1966; "Nova Scotia Book of Days" 1980; Ed. and Compiler, "Atlantic Provinces Checklist, 1957-65" (Atlantic Provs. Econ. Council); contrib. to "Dictionary of Canadian Biography"; Winner, Atlantic Provinces Library Assn. Award, 1981; mem. Royal Commonwealth Soc., N.S. Br.; Candn. Fed. Univ. Women; IODE; Heritage Trust of N.S.; Royal N.S. Hist. Soc.;

Candn. Lib. Assn.; Bibliog. Soc. Can. (Vice Pres. 1970-71); Atlantic Provs. Lib. Assn.; Baptist; recreations: reading, travel; Club: Canadian; Home: Apt. 1501, 5959 Spring Garden Rd., Halifax, N.S. B3H 1Y5; Office: Province House, Halifax, N.S. B3J 2P8.

ELLIOTT, Stephen, F.C.A.; b. London, Eng. 21 Feb. 1920; s. Albert G. and Henrietta E.; came to Canada 1947; e. Ealing Co. Grammar Sch. grad. 1936; m. Lt. Marguerita A.M., d. late Charles and Jane Medforth, Pennant, Sask. 31 Oct. 1944; children: Robert, Derek; Chart. Acct.; C.A. Articled Clerk, B. W. Brixey & Co., London, Eng. 1936-40; F.C.A. (Eng. and Wales) 1947, Ont. 1948, F.C.A. 1968; joined Riddell, Stead, Graham & Hutchison, Toronto 1947, Partner 1954-64; Managing Partner, Canada, Arthur Andersen & Co., 1960-82; served in 2nd World War, Brit. Army 1940-46; Pte. to Maj.; R.A.O.C. 1940; Comnd. R.A.S.C. 1941; service in N. Africa, Italy and Greece; Chrmn. Applications Comte. 1968-70; mem. of Discipline Comte. since 1973; Vice-Chrmn. of same comte. 1976-81, Chrmn. 1981; mem. Que., Alta., B.C., Man., N.S., Jamaican & Bermuda Insts. Chart. Accts.; Candn. Inst. Chart. Accts. (Chrmn. Special Comte., Uniform Code of Ethics 1968-70; Acctg. & Auditing Research Comte. 1968-72, Chrmn. 1970-72); Cdn. rep., Internat. Accounting Standards Comm., Chrmn. Designate 1981, Chrmn. 1982-85, Chmn., Organization and Planning Comm., IASC; Chrmn., Steering Comm. on Rev. Recognition; mem. Assn. Systems Mang. (Pres. Toronto Chapter 1964-65); Bd. Trade Metrop. Toronto; Candn. Chamber Comm.; Chambre de Comm. Franç. au Canada; recreations: golf, curling; Clubs: National; Mississaugua Golf & Country; Beefeater; Empire; Ponte Vedra; Home: 1544 Knareswood Drive, Mississauga, Ont. L5H 2M1; Office: P.O. Box 29 Toronto-Dominion Centre, Toronto, Ont. M5K 1B9

ELLIS, Alfred John; board chairman, company director; b. Montreal, Que., 27 May 1915; s. Robert Louis and Frances Elizabeth (Robinson) E.; e. Argyle School, Westmount, Que.; Lower Can. Coll., Montreal, Que.; m. Christina Joan, d. B. J. Wilson, Marborough, Wilts, Eng., 6 Oct. 1943; children: Elizabeth, Susan, Robert; HON. CHRMN. AND DIR. EMERITUS, CANADA DEVELOPMENT CORP.; Dir., Consolidated Pipe Lines Co., Calgary; Patagonia Corp., Tucson, Ariz., Polysar Ltd.; Bank of Montreal; Consolidated Natural Gas Ltd.; Norland Petroleums Ltd.; Ventures West Capital Ltd., Consolidex Gas and Oil Ltd.; Lougheed Resources Inc.; Sydney Development (1981) Ltd.; Chairman Western Region Advisory Committee Marsh and McLennan Ltd.; mem. Special Committee on Standard-Setting Canadian Inst. of Chartered Accountants; Adv. Bd., The Royal Trust Co., Vancouver; former mem. Acct. Research Bd., Canadian Inst. of C.A.'s; entered Bank of Montreal in 1933 in Montreal subsequently serving from coast to coast in various executive capacities, apptd. Vice-Chrm. of Bd. in 1973; resident in Vancouver from which position he retired in 1976; served in 2nd World War, Inf. and Staff Offr., 1940-45; Staff course at R.M.C.; service in Can., Eng. and Europe; Mentioned in Despatches; Past Pres. & Life Gov., Douglas Hosp.; Dir., B.C. Internat. Trade Fair 1971; mem. Prov. Extve. Comte.; Boy Scouts of Can.; former Chrmn. Internat. & Candn. Trade & Finance Comtes. of Pacific Basin Econ. Council; mem. Adv. Bd. to Div. of Finance, Univ. of B.C.; mem. Extve. Comte., The Asian Centre Fund; mem. Pacific Devel. Group; Past Pres. and Hon. Vice Pres., Canada-Japan Soc. of Vancouver; Past Pres., B.C. Heart Foundation; The Candn. Chamber of Commerce; retired Senate mem. Simon Fraser Univ.; Past Gen. Campaign Chmn., United Appeals Halifax & Vancouver; Anglican; recreations: fishing, hunting, boating, gardening, shooting; Clubs: St. James's; The Vancouver; Vancouver Lawn Tennis & Badminton; Pennask Fish & Game; Home: 3851 Marguerite St., Vancouver,B.C. V6M 3J9; Office: 2272-200 Granville St., Vancouver, B.C. V6C 1S4

ELLIS, James R.; banker; SR. VICE PRES. BANK OF MONTREAL; served with present Bank as Dist. Mgr. W. Ont. Region, Central Ont. Region, Toronto E. Region, Depy. & Sr. Asst. Mgr. Montreal Br., Br. Mgr. Sydney, N.S., Asst. Supt. Atlantic Provs.; mem. Extve. Comte. N.S. Voluntary Econ. Planning Bd.; Gov. and Chrmn. Invest. Comte. Acadia Univ.; Dir. & Treas. Atlantic Provs. Econ. Council; Elder, St. Andrews Un. Ch.; Dir. Halifax Bd. Trade; Clubs: Halifax; Saraguay; Waegwoltic; Ashburn Golf; Halifax Curling; Home: 1158 Dalhousie St., Halifax, N.S. B3H 3W6.

ELLIS, John Firstbrook, M.B.E.; retired jeweller; b. Toronto, Ont., 12 Sept. 1907; s. Arthur William and Ada Louise (Firstbrook) E.; e. Model Sch., Toronto, 1917-21; Upper Can. Coll., 1922-25; Univ. of Toronto, 1926-27; Gemological Inst. of Am., Grad.; m. Phyllis Louise, d. Albert Samuel May, 7 Sept. 1933; children: John Firstbrook, Jr., David Albert Foster; Dir., Acadia Ins. Co.; Acadia Life Ins. Co.; Candn. Dir., The Phoenix of London Group; mem. of Toronto Adv. Bd., The Royal Trust Co.; began career in jewellery bus. with Ellis Bros. 1927; spent yr. 1929 working with Triefus & Co. of London, Eng., studying diamonds; apptd. Asst. Mgr. of Diamond Dept. in 1937 (after merger of Ellis Bros. and Ryrie Birks); apptd. Asst. to Pres. 1946; Dir. 1948, and Mang. Dir. 1950; mem. Am. Gem Soc.; Toronto Bd. of Trade (Pres. 1957-58); mem., N.P.A.M., 1931-38; mem., Bd. of Govs., Toronto Western Hosp.; Chrmn., Parking Authority of Toronto; served in 2nd World War, 1940-46; Lieut.-Col., Toronto Scottish Regt.; Mentioned in Despatches; Zeta Psi; Conservative; Anglican; recreation: golf; Clubs: National; Toronto Hunt; Toronto Golf; Badminton & Racquet; Home: 40 Chestnut Park Rd., Toronto, Ont. M4W 1W8

ELLIS, Roy Gilmore, D.D.S., M.ScD., D.D.Sc. (Adel.) LL.D., F.R.C.D.(C), F.D.S., R.C.S.; b. Peterborough, S. Australia, 10 July 1906; s. Sidney Howard and Mary (Gilmore) E.; e. Univ of Adelaide, B.D.S. 1926; came to Can. 1928; Univ. of Toronto, D.D.S. 1929, B.Sc. 1930; Guy's Hosp., London, Eng., 1934; Univ. of Toronto, M.Sc. 1942; m. Constance, d. Thomas Ferguson, Toronto, 29 June 1935; children; Paul, Brian; Chairman, Health Sciences Council 1970 and its Application to Dentistry"; Zi Psi Phi (Past Depy. Supreme Pres.); Conservative; United Church; recreations: fishing, oil painting; Club: Granite; Home: 426 Glencairn Ave., Toronto, Ont. M59 1V5

EL MAHDY, Wadih; artist-painter; b. Çairo, Egypt, 20 Oct. 1921; e. Italian Acad. of Fine Arts, Leonardo da Vinci Sch., Cairo, dipl. in painting 1939 (studied under Prof. R. Roberti); Egyptian Acad. of Fine Arts, Cairo, 1940-46 (studied under Profs. A. Sabry and B. Huessen) and 1950; Luxor Art Studio; artist painter and arch. draftsman, Dept. of Arch., Cairo Mun., 1946-64; became an Art adviser, newspaper "Al Kahera", 1952; Prof. of Fine Arts, Lycée La Liberté, Cairo, 1962; taught at Univ. of Quebec, Montreal; Acad. of Fine Arts, Paris; Acad. Port Royal, Paris; held one-man exhns. in Ghalion Gallery, Cairo, 1952 and in Cairo, 1962 and 1963; one man shows, Dominion Gallery, Montreal, 1969 and 1973; Kastel Gallery, Montreal, 1976; show with selected artists, Dominion Gallery, Montreal, 1973; exhibited Salon Exhns., Cairo, 1939-65; UNESCO Exhn., Beirut, 1949; Egyptian and Italian Exhn., Cairo, 1952; Egyptian Exhn. in China, 1955; works are incl. in perm. collections of Museum of Modern Art (16 paintings), Min. of Foreign Affairs (2 paintings), Nat. Bank of Egypt, U.A.R. and U.S.A. Educ. Exchange Comn. of Fulbright Comte., Ford Foundation, Min. of Educ. (for sch. libraries), Victoria Art Gallery, B.C., Dominion Gallery, Montreal, Art Museum of Hamilton, Ont., all of Cairo and over 20 paintings are in various private collections; rec'd Luxor Prize, Acad. of Fine Arts, Cairo, 1950; Min. of Comm. Art Competition, Cairo, 1957; Atta Afifi Prize, Cairo Salon, 1958; Internat. Cotton Community Market Award, 1958; Cairo

Salon Prize 1960; Egyptian Min. of Culture Scholarship 1964; Address: 4625 Bourret, #26, Montreal, Que. H3W 1K9

ELMS, Roy Alfred, F.C.I.I.; insurance executive; b. Kingston-Upon-Thames, Surrey, Eng. 25 Nov. 1932; s. late Alfred George and Gladys Louise (North) E.; e. Hampton Wick Endowed Sch. 1944; Hampton Grammar Sch. 1950; m. Eileen Isabel d. late James Rowland Rixon 6 Aug. 1955; EXTVE. VICE PRES. AND DIR., ROYAL INSURANCE CO. OF CANADA THE WESTERN ASSURANCE CO., QUE. ASSURANCE CO., & ROINS HOLDING LTD.; Dir. Seibels Bruce Policy Management Systems Ltd.; joined Royal Insurance in Eng. 1950, trans. to Can. 1959, Underwriting Mgr. for Can. 1971, Sr. Vice Pres. 1974; Past Chrmn. Nuclear Ins. Assn. Can. and Candn. Indust. Risks Insurers; Past Chrmn., Ont. Chamber Comm. United Church; recreations: golf, theatre, travel; Clubs: National; Granite; Board of Trade; Home: 4 Emery Circle, Weston, Ont. M9P 2G6; Office: 10 Wellington St. E., Toronto, Ont. M5E 1L5.

ELOUL, Kosso, R.C.A.; sculptor; b. Moorom, Russia 22 Jan. 1920; s. Leib and Anna (Shapiro) E.; e. Tel-Aviv Hebrew Gimnasia; Chicago Art Inst. 1939-43; m. Rita d. Héliodore Letendre; came to Can. 1964; solo exhns. incl. Tel-Aviv Museum 1951, 1957; Jerusalem Art Pavilion 1957; Galleria Topazia Alliata Rome 1962; Galerie Camille Hébert Montréal 1964; David Stuart Galleries Los Angeles 1965, 1968; Jewish Museum N.Y., 1966; Jerrold Morris Gallery Toronto 1968; Gordon Gallery Tel-Aviv 1969; Galerie Sherbrooke Montréal 1969; O.K. Harris Gallery N.Y. 1971; Dunkelman Gallery Toronto 1971; Galerie de Montréal 1973; Arras Gallery N.Y. 1974, 1976; Marlborough-Godard Toronto 1974, Montréal 1975; West End Gallery Edmonton 1977; Koffler Centre of Arts Toronto 1979; Art Gallery of Hamilton 1980; rep. in many pub., corporate and private colls. Israel, Europe, USA and Can. incl. Montréal Museum of Fine Art; Musée d'Art Contemporain Montréal; Art Gallery Ont.; Smithsonian Inst.; Canada-Mexico friendship sculpture "Signalos" (Invitational 1978); invited to represent Canada at Hakone open-air museum, Japan, 1980; mem. jury Olympic Coin Program '76 Ottawa; 37th Annual Exhn. S. Ont. Art Gallery Windsor 1977; rec'd Can. Council Sr. Art Fellowship 1976; Medal of Accomplishment Mexico City 1978; served with U.S. Navy 1944-45; work cited various publs.; Hon. Fellow, Royal Acad. Fine Art The Hague; Hon. mem. Academia Tiberina Rome; mem. Art & Community Inst.; Sch. for Social Research N.Y. (Adv. Bd. 1977-); Jewish;Address: 288 Sherbourne St., Toronto, Ont. M5A 2S1.

ELTING, Everett E., B.A.; advertising executive; b. New York, N.Y.C. 14 Feb. 1936; came to Can. 1976; s. Everett Ely and Louise (Florsheim) E.; e. Trinity Coll, Hartford, B.A. 1958; m. Judith Lass, 19 June 1960; children: Lynn Elizabeth, Elizabeth Louise; PRES., CHIEF OPERATING OFFR., DIR., GREY ADVERTISING LTD. since 1979; served with U.S. Air Force, 1958-62, rank Cpt.; Dir., Children's Aid Society of Metro Toronto; Chrmn., Bd. of Dir., Children's Aid Society Foundation; Home: 62 Wellesley St. W., Apt. 603, Toronto, Ont. M5S 2X3; Office: 1075 Bay St., Toronto, Ont. M5S 2B1.

ELWORTHY, Arthur B., B.Com.; company executive; b. Victoria, B.C., 18 May 1922; s. Harold B. and Myrta Gladys (MacDonald) E.; e. Sir James Douglas Sch. and Victoria (B.C.) High Sch.; Victoria Coll., 1940-41; Univ. of Brit. Columbia, B.Com. 1948; m. Elizabeth Anne, d. R. S. Laird, Vancouver, B.C., 20 Nov. 1948; children: Mark Barrington, Merrill Anne, Blake Barrington Elworthy; Secy., Straits Towing and Salvage Company Limited, 1942-46; Pres. of Island Tug and Barge Ltd. 1961-70; Chrmn. of Bd., Seaspan Internat. Ltd., 1970-72; Pres. and Gen. Mgr., B.C. Steamship Co. (1975) Ltd., 1976-80; Chrmn. of Bd., International Gulf Marine Training; Pres.

Ramolqus (S.A.) (Mexico); served in 2nd World War with R.C.A.F. as Pilot; discharged Mar. 1946 with rank of Flying Offr.; Phi Delta Theta; Freemason; recreations: golf, fishing; Clubs: Vancouver; Shaughnessy Heights Golf; Union (Victoria); Victoria Yacht; Home: 4172 Yuculta Cres., Vancouver, B.C.; Office: 254 Belleville St., Victoria, B.C. V8V 1W9

EMBLETON, Tony Frederick Wallace, Ph.D., D.Sc., F.R.S.C.; scientist; b. Hornchurch, Essex, Eng. 1 Oct. 1929; s. Frederick William Howard and Lucy Violet Muriel (Wallace) E.; e. Brentwood Sch. Essex, Eng.; Imp. Coll. Univ. of London B.Sc. 1950, Ph.D. 1952, D.Sc. 1964; m. Eileen Loraine Blackall 14 Nov. 1953; one d. Sheila Margaret; PRINC. RESEARCH OFFR. NAT. RESEARCH COUNCIL since 1974; Adjunct Prof. Carleton Univ. since 1978; Fellow, Nat. Research Council 1952-53, Asst. or Assoc. Research Offr. 1954-62, Sr. Research Offr. 1962-74; Visiting Lectr. Univ. of Ottawa 1959-69; Mass. Inst. Technol. 1964, 1967, 1972; mem. Rockcliffe Park Pub. Sch. Bd. 1967-69; Village of Rockcliffe Park, Court of Revision since 1975; Dir. Youth Science Foundation 1969-72, Ed.-in-Chief 1970-72; rec'd Acoustical Soc. Am. Biennial Award 1964; Soc. Automotive Engrs. Arch T. Coldwell Award 1974; Rochester Inst. Technol. John Wiley Jones Award 1976; Founding Ed.-in-Chief "Acoustics and Noise Control in Canada" 1972-75; author chapters "Noise and Vibration Control" 1971; various articles scient. and tech. journs. sound propagation, machinery noise control, acoustical standards; Charter mem. Candn. Acoustical Assn. (Founding Secy. 1961-64); Fellow, Acoustical Soc. Am. (Pres. 1980-81, Vice Pres. 1977-78, Tech. Council 1964-67, Assoc. Ed. 1970-75); Fellow, Royal Society of Canada (Assistant Treasurer 1981-82); Anglican; recreations: gardening, reading and skating; Home: 26 Birch Ave., Ottawa, Ont. K1K 3G6; Office: Montreal Rd., Ottawa, Ont. K1A 0R6.

EMMETT, Martin F.C., B.Sc., M.B.A.; food executive; b. Johannesburg, S.A. Aug. 1934; s. late Cecil Frederik Cheere and Thelma Marie (Ford) E.; e. Univ. of Witswatersrand, B.Sc. (Mech. Engn.) 1957; Queen's Univ., M.B.A. 1962; m. Alice Ellen, d. late Alfred Crispen Lavers 18 Aug. 1956; children: Karen, Robert, Susan; PRES. & CHIEF EXEC. OFFICER & DIR. STANDARD BRANDS, INC. N.Y.C., 1980-; with Alcan Can. Products Ltd., Extrusion Plant, Kingston, Ont. 1962, Dir. Market Res. & Plan, 1965, Gen. Mgr. Wire and Cable 1967, Vice-Pres. 1970; joined Standard Brands Ltd. as Group Vice-Pres. Beverage Div. 1972, Vice-Pres. and Chief Financial Offr. 1973; pres., chief exec. officer, 1973-76; pres., chief exec. officer Internat. Standard Brands, Inc. & Sr. v.p., group exec. Standard Brands, Inc. 1976-79; Pres., & Chief Oper. officer, & dir. Standard Brands, Inc. N.Y.C. 1980; Exec. Vice-Pres., Nabisco Brands, Inc.; Pres. & Chief Oper. Officer Standard Brands Inc.; Exec. Vice-Pres., Nabisco Brands, Inc., Pres. Nabisco Products, Inc. 1981; dir. The Mel Williamson Foundation, Canada; mem. Assn. Prof. Engrs. Ont. Adv. Bd., Univ. of W. Ont.; Adv. Bd., Banff School of Management Studies: Young Presidents' organ,; recreation: golf, skiing, tennis; Clubs: Mount Royal Golf, Winged Foot Golf, Connecticut Golf; The Brook; Mid-Ocean (Bermuda); Canadian Club of New York; Doubles; Deepdale Golf; Home: Frost Rd., Greenwich, Conn. 06830; Office: 625 Madison Ave., New York, NY 10022

EMMONS, Douglas B., B.S.A., M.S., Ph.D.; research scientist; b. Huntington Twp., Hastings Co., Ont., 23 May 1930; s. Thomas Edmund and Margaret Isabelle (Fitchett) E.; e. Univ of Toronto (Ont. Agric. Coll.) B.S.A., 1952; Univ. Wisconsin, M.S., 1953, Ph.D., 1957; m. Mavis Jean, d. late Dr. Phillip Wharton, 19 June 1953; separated; children: Phillip, Peter, Christina, Jennifer, Beryl; RESEARCH SCIENTIST, CAN. DEPT. OF AGRIC., Food Research Inst., Research Br., since 1958; Asst. Prof., Univ. Wisconsin, 1957; awarded "Pfizer

Paul-Lewis Award in Cheese Research" by Am. Dairy Science Assn., 1963; mem., Can. Inst. Food Sci. Technology; Am. Dairy Science Assn.; Agric. Inst. Can.; Ont. Inst. Agrols.; Prof. Inst. Pub. Service of Can.; Protestant; recreations: curling, golf; Home: 1089 Field St., Ottawa, Ont. K2C 2P6

EMORI, Eiko, M.F.A., R.C.A.; graphic designer; b. Dairen, Japan 19 March 1938; d. Morihisa and Fumie (Okura) E.; e. Central Sch. of Arts & Crafts London, Eng. Nat. Dipl. in Design (Graphic) 1958; Yale Univ. Sch. of Art & Arch. M.F.A. 1963; PRES., EIKO EMORI INC. 1967- ; designed E. Algonkian syllabic typefaces and rec'd Can. Council grant for research designing a standardized syllabic typeface for Inuktitut, Algonkian, Athapaskan; Pres. Ottawa Japanese Community Assn. 1980-81; Pres. Ottawa Chapter Soc. Graphic Designers Can. 1980; Office: 2036 Cabot St., Ottawa, Ont. K1H 6J8.

EMORY, Florence H. M., R.N., LL.D.; b. Niagara Falls, Ont., 6 Apl. 1889; d. Rev. Vernon Hope and Margaret Maud (Anderson) E.; e. Coll. Inst., Whitby, Ont.; Grace Hosp., Toronto, Ont. (grad.); Simmons Coll., Mass. Inst. Tech., 1 yr. post-grad. study; LL.D. Toronto, 1970; Hon. Adviser in Nursing, The Candn. Red Cross Soc., 1952-65, and Vice-Pres. since 1965; formerly held staff and supervisory posts, Mun. Dept. Health, Toronto; Assoc. Dir. and Prof., Sch. of Nursing, Univ. of Toronto (named Prof. Emeritus 1954) retiring in 1954; author of textbook: "Public Health Nursing in Canada", 1945; revised ed. 1953; Pres., Candn. Nurses Assn. 1930-34 (Hon. Life mem.1958); Hon. Life mem., Candn. Public Health Assn. (1957); Reg'd Nurses Assn. Ont. (1964); Candn. Conf. of Univ. Schs. of Nursing (1964); awarded Florence Nightingale Medal, 1953, by Internat. Red Cross; United Church; Home: 123 Spadina Rd., Toronto, Ont. M5R 2T1

EMORY, James Vernon, B.Com.; company chairman; b. Montreal, Que., 25 Aug. 1916; s. Arthur Dunham and Annie Louise (Wilkinson) E.; e. Lower Can. Coll., grad. 1934; McGill Univ., B.Com., 1938; m. Wilma Hersey, d. Wilbert H. Howard, Westmount, Que., 28 June 1941; children: Devon, Karen, Verne, James, Arthur; Chairman, United Bond and Share Ltd. (Estbd. 1932); Chrmn. and Dir., RoyFund Ltd.; United Bond & Share Ltd.; RoyFund Distributors Ltd.; RoyFund Income Trust; Director, United Corporations Ltd.; Dir. E-L. Financial Corp. Ltd.; Empire Life Ins. Co.; Dom. of Can. Gen. Ins. Co.; Casualty Co. of Can.; Chrmn. of the Investment Funds Inst. of Can., 1976-78; served in 2nd World War with Roy. Candn. Arty., 1940-46; Anglican; Alpha Delta Phi; Home: 55 Harbour Sq. Suite 2311, Toronto, Ont. M5J 2L1; Office: Suite 2990, South Tower, Royal Bank Plaza, P.O. Box 70, Toronto, Ont. M5J 2J2

EMPEY, Gordon B., B.A., B.C.L.; b. Montreal, Que., 16 Sept. 1929; s. Burton C. and Louise A. (Gordon) E.; e. Bishop's Coll. Sch., Lennoxville, Que.; Ridley Coll., St. Catharines, Ont., 1947; McGill Univ. B.A. 1951, B.C.L. 1954; m. Dorothy Ann, d. late Ralph S. Stephenson, Saint John, N.B., 28 July 1955; children: Mary Ann, Patricia Louise, Susan, Janet, Burton, Elizabeth; MANAGING DIR., ONTARIO SPECIAL OLYMPICS INC. since 1973; called to Bar of Que. 1955; joined present Company as Trust Offr., Montreal, 1957, Mgr., Victoria, B.C., 1962, Montreal, 1969; mem., Bar of Montreal; Candn. Bar Assn.; Delta Sigma Phi; United Church; recreations: gardening, tennis; Club: Union Club, Victoria; Office: 40 St. Clair Ave. W., Toronto, Ont. M4V 1M6

EMPRY, Gino; personal manager; public relations consultant; entertainment director; b. Toronto, Ont. 11 Oct. 1941; s. Arthur and Lucy (Flaminio) Emperatori; e. St. Mary of the Angels Separate Sch. 1953; Oakwood Coll. Inst. 1959; Western Comm. 1961; FOUNDER AND OWNER, GINO EMPRY PUBLIC RELATIONS; Acct., Asst. Office Mgr. Direct Winters Transport 1962; Acct.,

Systems Analyst, Smith Transport 1963; became actor, dir. and producer; Entertainment Dir. and Pub. Relations Royal York Hotel; internat. rep. for Tony Bennett; Personal Mgr. for William Hutt, Sean Mulcahy, Toller Cranston, Robin Ward, Ken James and others; Candn. rep. for Patrick Macnee, Peggy Lee, John Gary, Jack Carter, Craig Russell, and others; Pub. Relations for Best Available Seating System, Royal Alexandra Theatre, Irish Rovers, Johnny Lombardi, Talk of Toronto Dinner Theatre, Sam Shopsowitz Ltd., Candn. Actors' Equity; affiliated with Juno Awards; Candn. rep. for Triumph Theatre Productions, Eng.; mem. Inner City Angels Toronto; Variety Clubs of Ontario; Toronto Rep. for Playboy Magazine; Dir. Actors Fund Can.; Supporter, Famous People Players; author articles theatre, pub. relations various mags.; mem. Candn. Pub. Relations Soc.; Candn. Acad. Recording Arts & Sciences; Liberal; R. Catholic; recreations: gardening, theatre, movies, travel, collecting rare jewelry and artifacts; Clubs: Toronto Men's Press; Variety; Empire; Home: 33 Wood St., Apt. 3006, Toronto, Ont. M4Y 2P8; Office: The Maples, 25 Wood St., Suite 104, Toronto, Ont. M4Y 2P9.

EMSON, Harry Edmund, M.A., B.M., B.Ch., M.D.; FRCP(C) pathologist; educator; b. Swinton, Lancs., Eng. 16 Nov. 1927; s. Edmund E.; e. Manchester (Eng.) Grammar Sch.; Brasenose Coll. Oxford Univ. B.A. 1948, M.A. 1953, B.M., B.Ch. 1952; Univ. of Sask. M.D. 1958; m. Mary Elizabeth Lewis 18 July 1953; children: Jane Margaret, Susan Anne; HEAD OF PATHOLOGY, UNIVERSITY HOSP. since 1975; Prof. and Head, Dept. of Pathol. Univ. of Sask. since 1975; Consultant Pathol. St. Pauls and City Hosps. Saskatoon, Plains, Hosp. Regina; Registrar in Pathol. Birmingham Accident Hosp. 1955-56; Resident in Pathol. St. Pauls Hosp. Saskatoon 1956-57, Univ. Hosp. 1957-58; Asst. Prof. of Pathol. Univ. Hosp. 1958-60; Dir. of Labs. St. Pauls Hosp. 1960-75; served with RAMC 1953-55, rank Capt.; Candn. Forces (Militia) 1965-75, rank Maj.; author 'The Doctor and the Law ' 1979; numerous articles in prof. journs.; Fellow Royal Coll. Phys. & Surgs. Can. (Examiner, Chrmn. Comte. on Gen. Pathol.); mem. Candn. Assn. Pathols. (Past Pres.); Candn. Soc. Forensic Science (Past Pres.); recreations: theatre, hunting, sailing, flying; Office: University Hosp., Saskatoon, Sask. S7N 0X0.

ENFIELD, Frank Arthur, Q.C., B.A.; b. Toronto, Ont., 16 June 1920; s. Ernest Edward and Edith May (Jones) E.; e. Victoria Coll., Univ. of Toronto, B.A. 1948; Osgoode Hall, Toronto, Ont.; m. Jessie Elinor, d. Harry Ferguson Phillips, Hamilton, Ont., 25 Aug. 1945; children: Lawrence Alan, Robert Phillips, Julie Ann; m. 2ndly Esther Lucille, Toronto, Oct. 1980; PARTNER, ENFIELD, HEMMERICK, HENRY, LYONDE & WOOD; Dir., Beer Precast Concrete Ltd.; Gen. Refractories Co. of Canada Ltd.; Gen. Publishing Co. Ltd.; read law with Hon. A. Roebuck, Q.C.; called to Bar of Ont. 1951; Sch. Trustee, Scarborough, Ont., 1949-52; M.P. for York-Scarborough, 1953-57; app'td Queen's Counsel, 1968; served in 2nd World War as Air Navigator; rank of Flt.-Lieut. on discharge, Aug. 1945; Liberal; United Church; Club: Ontario (Toronto); Home: 67 Walmer Rd. Toronto, Ont. M5R 2X6; Office: Royal Trust Tower, (Box 284), Toronto, Ont. M5K 1K2

ENGEL, Marian, M.A.; writer; b. Toronto, Ont., 24 May 1933; Frederick Searle and Mary Elizabeth (Fletcher) Passmore; e. Sarnia Coll. Inst. & Tech. Sch.; McMaster Univ., B.A. 1955; McGill Univ., M.A. 1957; Univ. of Aix-Marseille, France; m. Howard, s. Jack Engel, St. Catharines, Ont., 27 Jan. 1962; div. 1977; children: William Lucas Passmore, Charlotte Helen Arabella; author of "No Clouds of Glory" 1968; "The Honeyman Festival" 1970; "One Way Street" 1973; "Adventure at Moon Bay Towers" 1974; "Joanne" 1975; "Inside the Easter Egg" 1975; 'Bear', 1976; "My Name Is Not Odessa Yarker" 1977; "The Glassy Sea", 1978; "Lunatic Villas" 1981;

"Islands of Canada" 1981; and numerous articles in various mags. and journs.; recipient of Sr. Arts Awards Can. Council, 1968, 1972; mem. ACTRA; City Council Rep., Library Bd. of Toronto (1975-78); was 1st Chrmn., Writer's Union of Can. 1973-74; Gov. Gen. award for "Bear", 1976; Co-winner of City of Toronto Award, 1982, for "Lunatic Villas"; N.D.P.; Home: 70 Marchmount Rd., Toronto, Ont.

ENGLISH, John Thomas, B.A., F.S.A., F.C.I.A.; insurance executive; b. Paris, Ont., 14 Dec. 1928; s. John Thomas and Catherine Elizabeth (Payne) E.; e. McMaster Univ., B.A. (Math.) 1952; m. Edith Evelyn, d. Norman Ghent, Paris, Ont., 26 Sept. 1952; one. d.: Ann Elizabeth; PRESIDENT, TORONTO MUTUAL LIFE INSURANCE CO., since 1972; Actuarial Student, Northern Life Insurance Co., London, Ont., 1952-56; Assoc. Actuary, Commonwealth Life Insurance Co., Louisville, Ky., 1956-61; Vice-Pres. Data Processing, 1961-64; Vice-Pres., and Secy., Boston Mutual Life Insurance Co., 1964-67; joined present Co. as Mang. Dir. and Actuary 1968; mem., Bd. Trade Metrop. Toronto; Anglican; recreations: gardening, wood-working, reading; Clubs: Granite; Home: 77 Barringham Dr., Oakville, Ont. L6J 4B3; Office: 112 St. Clair Ave. W., Toronto, Ont. M4V 2Y3

ENNS, Hon. Harry John, M.L.A.; politician; rancher; b. Winnipeg, Man. 30 Nov. 1931; s. John Herman and Agathe (Unruh) E.; e. matric.; m. Helen H. d. John J. Klassen, Winnipeg, Man. 23 Sept. 1953; two s. Nathan Peter, Andrew J. David; MIN. OF NATURAL RESOURCES, MAN. el. M.L.A. 1966, re-el. since; served as Min. of Agric.; Min. of Highways & Transport.; Min. of Mines & Natural Resources; Min. of Government Services; Responsible for Manitoba Data Serv.; Man. Telephone System; Man. Public Insur. Corp.; P. Conservative; Mennonite; recreations: music, hunting; Home: Double H Ranch, Woodlands, Man. Office: 302 Legislative Bldg., Winnipeg, Man. R3C 0V8.

ENSOR, Arthur John, R.C.A.; industrial designer; b. Llanishen, Wales 2 Jan. 1905; s. Francis Lycett E.; e. Felsted Sch. Eng.; Regent St. Polytechnic London 1923-26; Royal Coll. of Art (Design) 1926-29; Univ. of London Extension Course in Art Hist. 1925-28; Mass. Inst. Technol. summer course 1951; m. Barbara d. Arthur Frederick Wells, Toronto, Ont. 10 Aug. 1963; children: Georgina Frances, John Robert; estbd. ENSOR INDUSTRIAL DESIGN ASSOCIATES 1950, Toronto; Co-owner Wells Gallery Ottawa; travelled Africa collecting visual data for Empire Marketing Bd. producing posters for them and for Imperial Airways 1930-31; Designer Research Dept. Imperial Chemical Industries Plastics Div. 1935-37; estbd. own design consultant office London 1937-39; Design consultant with office of Design, Industry, Trade & Comm. Ottawa 1964-73; has devel. various patents; rec'd various competition awards incl. Stainless Steel Competition 1962; Plastics Horizons Competition 1961; rep. Can. first Indust. Design Conf. Paris 1953; painting selected from Nat. Gallery Coll. for Can. Post Stamp 1967; author various research reports indust. design; mem. Assn. Candn. Indust. Designers (Past Pres.); Indust. Artists (U.K.); served with Royal Engr. Corps UK and N.W. Europe 1940-46, part-time War Artist for Min. of Information; Liberal; Unitarian; recreations: painting, skating, swimming; Club: Arts & Letters (Toronto); Home: 155 Crichton St., Ottawa, Ont. K1M 1W1; Office: 457 Sussex Dr., Ottawa K1N 6Z4.

EPP, Hon. Arthur Jacob (Jake), P.C., M.P., B.A., B.Ed.; politician; b. St. Boniface, Man. 1 Sept. 1939; s. Rev. Jacob Peter and Margaretha (Toews) E.; e. Steinbach, Man. 1957; Univ. of Man. B.A. 1961, B.Ed. 1965; m. Lydia d. Rev. Peter W. Martens, Winkler, Man. 17 Aug. 1961; one d. Lisa Dawn; app'td. MIN. OF INDIAN AND N. AFFAIRS CAN. 1979; Councillor, Town of Steinbach 1970-72; el. to H. of C. for Provencher 1972, re-el. since; mem.

Christian Businessmen of Can.; P. Conservative; Mennonite; recreations: golf, cycling, cross-country skiing; Home: 391 Southwood Dr., Steinbach, Man. R0A 2A0; Office: House of Commons, Ottawa, Ont. K1A 0A7.

EPP, Frank H., B.Th., B.A., M.A., Ph.D., LL.D.; educator; b. Lena, Man., 26 May 1929; s. Henry Martin and Anna (Enns) E.; e. Vancouver Teachers Coll., 1949; Candn. Mennonite Coll., Winnipeg, B.Th. 1953; Bethel Coll., Kans., B.A. 1956; Univ. of Minn., M.A. 1960, Ph.D. 1965; LL.D. Brandon Univ., 1975; m. Helen Louise Dick, 27 June 1953; three d., Marianne Louise, Esther Ruth, Marlene Gay; PRESIDENT; CONRAD GREBEL COLL., UNIV. OF WATERLOO, 1973-79; Prof. of Hist. since 1971; Teacher, Vanderhoof Sch. Dist., 1949-50; Founding Ed., "The Canadian Mennonite", 1953-67; "Mennonite Reporter", 1971-73; part-time pastorates Winnipeg, Minneapolis, Altona and Ottawa; part-time coll. lectr. Winnipeg (1960's); Univ. of Ottawa and St. Paul's Univ., Ottawa, 1967-71; Dir. of Studies, Mennonite Central Comte. Peace Sec. with special assignment in Middle E., 1968-71, Chrmn. 1979-; Extve. mem., Mennonite Central Comte. (Canada); Pres., United Nations Assn. (Waterloo Region) 1980-; mem. Candn. Consult. Council on Multiculturalism, 1981-; Extve., Dir., World Federalists of Can. 1970; mem., Fed. Immigration Adv. Bd.1968-78; Mennonite World Conf. 1972-78; Sch. Trustee, Altona, Man., 1963-65; rec'd Can. Council Awards 1972, 1973, 1975, 1976, 1978, 1979, 1980; Lib. Cand., Waterloo Riding, 1979, 1980; author, "Mennonite Exodus: The Rescue and Resettlement of the Russian Mennonites since the Communist Revolution", 1962; "The Glory and the Shame", 1968; "Your Neighbor as Yourself", 1968; "Whose Land is Palestine: The Middle East Problem in Historical Perspective", 1970; "A Strategy for Peace: Reflections of a Christian Pacifist", 1973; "Mennonites in Canada, 1786-1920: The History of a Separate People", 1974; "Education With a Plus", 1975; "The Palestinians", 1976; "Mennonite Peoplehood", 1977; "Stories with Meaning", 1978; "The Israelis", 1980; mem. Candn. Hist. Assn.; Inst. Mennonite Studies; Home: 361 Craigleith Dr., Waterloo, Ont. N2L 5B5

EPSTEIN, Herbert Bernard, B.A.; executive; b. Brooklyn, N.Y. 26 Nov. 1919; s. Morris Henry and Anne (Gitter) E.; e. Upper Can. Coll. 1938; Univ. of Toronto B.A. 1942; m. Inez Rhoda d. late Louis Budd 20 Jan. 1948; children: Norman James, Jan Linda; CHRMN. OF BD. AND CEO, SILKNIT LTD.; Chrmn. Lovable Brassiere Co. of Canada Ltd.; served with USAF 1942-45, rank Lt.; Governor Baycrest Home for the Aged; Mount Sinai Hosp. Toronto; Dir. Candn. Textile Inst.; P. Conservative; Jewish; recreations: golf, skiing; Clubs: Oakdale Golf and Country; Home: 228 Strathallan Wood, Toronto, Ont. M5N 1T4; Office: 590 King St. W., Toronto, Ont. M5V 1M4.

EPSTEIN, William, B.A., LL.B., LL.D.; UN official; b. Calgary, Alta., 10 July 1912; s. Harry Louis and Masha Belle (Geffen) E.; e. Calgary (Alta.) Pub. and High Schs., 1929; Univ. of Alta., B.A. 1933, LL.B. 1935 (Chief Justice's Gold Medal in Law); London Sch. of Econ. (IODE Overseas Scholarship), Cert. in Internat. Law 1938; Univ. of Calgary, LL.D. 1971; m. Edna Frances, d. Hyman Hyman, 22 Sept. 1946; one. s. Mark Gil; Secy., UN Disarmament Comn. since 1952 and Dir., Disarmament Affairs Div., since 1954; read law with A. L. Smith, K.C., M.P.; called to Bar of Alta. 1936; apptd. to Secretariat of UN as Pol. Offr. 1946; Sr. Pol. Offr., UN Mediator Staff, Palestine; has rep. Secy.-Gen. at various confs. on Nuclear Test Ban and Disarmament and as Tech. Consultant to Comn. for Denuclearization of Latin Am. 1965-67; Chrmn., Internat. Group of Consultant Experts, Report on Chem. & Biol. Weapons for Gen. Assembly, 1967; Mem. Group of Consultant Experts, Report on Comprehensive Nuclear Test Ban for Gen. Assembly, 1980; Special Fellow, U.N. Inst. for Training & Research; Rockefeller Foundation Fellowship "Conflict in Internat.

Relations" 1973-75; Special Consultant on Disarmament to Secy.-Gen. of U.N., 1973-; Cecil H. and Ida Greene Visiting Prof. Univ. of B.C. 1975; Visiting Prof. Univ. of Victoria 1974-78; Visiting Prof. Carleton Univ. 1977-78; Killam Visiting Scholar, Univ. of Calgary 1978-79; Sen. Research Ass., Carleton U., 1979-82; lectr. many organs. and univs. in various countries; served with Candn. Army during World War II; rank Capt.; author, "Disarmament: Twenty-Five Years of Effort", 1971; "The Last Chance: Nuclear Disarmament and Armed Control", 1976; Ed., "United Nations and Disarmament 1945-70"; Ed. "A New Design for Nuclear Disarmament", 1977; Ed., "New Directions in Disarmament", 1981; mem., Alta. Law Soc.; Calgary Bar Assn.; Candn. Inst. Internat. Affairs; Internat. Inst. Strategic Studies; Candn. Delegation to the U.N. Special Session on Disarmament 1978 and to General Assembly of U.N., 1978, 1979, 1980 and 1981; Consultant on Disarmament to Candn. Govt.; Chrmn. Candn. Pugwash Group 1978; organizer of Pugwash Conf. on Science and World Affairs, Banff, Canada, 1981; Arms Control Assocn. (Washington); 1980's Project of Council on Foreign Relations (New York); North Am. Council of the Internat. Peace Acad.; Decorated by Mexican Govt. with Order of Aztec Eagle (Commander) 1977; Rec'd. Peace Hero Award of World Federalists of Canada 1978; recreations: walking, reading, sculpting, art; Home: 400 East 58th St., New York, N.Y. 10022; Office: Unitar, United Nations, New York, N.Y.

ERASMUS, Paul Jacobus, B.Com., C.A.; company extve.; b. Senekal, S. Africa, 16 Feb. 1932; s. Paul Jacobus and Susara Cornelia (Botha) E.; e. Rhodes Univ., B.Com. 1952; C.A., S. Africa, 1956; C.A., Can., 1961; became Candn. Citizen 1964; MANAGING DIR., RUPERT PARTNERSHIP IN INDUSTRY LTD., joined Rothmans International Group 1957; transferred to New York later in that yr.; joined Rothmans of Pall Mall Can. Ltd.; Feb. 1959 and apptd. Treas. in Apl.; Vice Pres., Finance, Nov. 1967; Pres. Candn. Breweries Limited 1969; Chmn., Alpa Industry Ltd. 1972, mem. of Bd., Rembrandt Group Ltd. 1977; mem., Ontario Institute C.A.'s; Protestant; recreations: tennis; Clubs: Toronto Lawn Tennis, Queens; Home: 8 Botany Lane, Bantry Bay, Cape Town 8001, Republic of South Africa; Office: P.O. Box 456, Cape Town 8000, Republic of S.A.

ERESKOVSKY, Alexander Sergeyevich; diplomat; b. USSR 25 Nov. 1936; e. Metall. Inst. Dnepropetrovsk grad. 1960; Diplomatic Acad. Moscow grad. 1967; m. Valentina Y. Oct. 1958; two d. Olga, Natasha; CONSUL-GEN. OF THE SOVIET UNION IN CAN.1980- ; Second Secy. USSR Embassy Washington 1967-72; mem. USSR Strategic Arms Limitation Talks Del. Geneva 1972-75; Pol. Counsellor Washington 1975-80; Office: 3655 Ave. du Musée, Montréal, Qué. H3G 2E1.

ERICKSON, Arthur Charles, O.C. (1973), B.Arch., A.R.C.A., D.Eng., LL.D., F.R.A.I.C., F.A.I.A. (Hon.) M.R.I.B.A.; architect; b. Vancouver, B.C., 14 June 1924; s. Oscar Ludwig and Myrtle (Chatterson) E.; e. Prince of Wales Sch., 1930-43; Univ. of B.C., 1942-44; 520 Japanese Lang. Sch., (Hons.) 1945; McGill Univ., B.Arch. (Hons.) 1950 (Lt. Gov's Bronze Medal, McLennan Travelling Schol.); Nova Scotia Technical Coll., D.Eng. (Honoris Causa) 1971; Simon Fraser Univ., LL.D. (Honoris Causa) 1973; McGill Univ., LL.D. (Honoris Causa) 1975; Univ. of Man., LL.D. (Honoris Causa) 1978; PRINCIPAL, ARTHUR ERICKSON ARCHITECTS, since 1972; Partner, Erickson Massey 1963-72; World War II service in India and Malaya (Capt.), Candn. Army Intelligence Corps; two Hon. Mentions in B.C. Artists Annual, Vancouver Art Gallery, 1941; arch. research in Mid.-East, Mediterranean, Scandinavia, and Britain 1950-53; Asst. Prof., Univ. of Oregon, 1955-56; Univ. of B.C., 1956-61; Assoc. Prof. 1961-64; Massey Medals for houses (with Geoffrey Massey) 1955-58; Western Houses Special Award, 1961; Can.

Council Fellowship, Arch. Research, Japan & Far East, 1961; Pan Pacific Citation, Am. Inst. of Arch. (Hawaiian Chapter) 1963; Winner (with G. Massey) Simon Fraser Univ. Competition, 1963; Nat. Design Awards, Candn. Housing Design Council, 1964; Cert. of Merit, Candn. Wood Designs Awards, 1965; Award, Tokyo Internat. Trade Fair, 1965; Vancouver Citation Awards, 1965-66; pre-Stressed Concrete Inst. Award, 1966-67; three Massey Medals for Simon Fraser Univ., Tokyo Pavilion & Smith House 1967; competition design winner, Candn. Pavilion, Expo '70 in Japan; shared 1967 Molson Award ($15,000); winner, 1971 Royal Bank Award ($50,000); Canadian Housing Design Council Award for two residences, Jan. 1975; Internat. Union of Architects' Auguste Perret Award 1975; Am. Soc. of Landscape Architects, President's Award of Excellence for Robson Square, 1979; numerous articles and examples or work published throughout the world, T.V. series, "Looking at Art," 1956; "The Lively Arts," "House at Comox," 1960; "A Sense of Place" etc., 1966; "The Architecture of Arthur Erickson", 1975; major comms.; Simon Fraser Univ., MacMillan Bloedel Bldg., Man in the Community and Man and His Health (Expo. 1967); Museum of Anthropology, Univ. of B.C.; Robesopn Sq./Law Courts Complex a Founder, Simon Fraser Univ.; Fellow, Royal Arch. Inst. of Can.; mem. Inst. for Research on Public Policy; Hon. Fellow of the Am. Inst. of Architects, 1978; recreations: architecture, travel; Clubs: Univ. of B.C. Faculty Club; University (Vancouver); Offices: 2412 Laurel, Vancouver, B.C. V5Z 3T2 and 80 Bloor St. W., Toronto, Ont. M5S 2V1

ERICSON, Richard Victor, M.A., Ph.D.; sociologist; criminologist; b. Montreal, Que. 20 Sept. 1948; s. John William and Elizabeth Mary (Hinkley) E.; e. Alderwood Coll. Inst. 1967; Univ. of Guelph B.A. 1969; Univ. of Toronto M.A. (Sociol.) 1971; Cambridge Univ. Ph.D. (Criminol./Law) 1974; m. Dianna Lea d. Charles M. McMillan, Toronto, Ont. 31 May 1969; one s. Matthew Simon; PROF. OF SOCIOL. AND CRIMINOLOGY UNIV. OF TORONTO 1982- ; Tutor, Churchill Coll. Cambridge Univ. 1971-73; Asst. Prof. Univ. of Alta. 1973-74; Asst. Prof. Univ. of Toronto 1974, Assoc. Prof. 1979; Visiting Research Assoc., Criminology Univ. of Edinburgh, 1974; Visiting Fellow, Churchill College and Institute of Criminology, Cambridge Univ., 1979; author "Criminal Reactions" 1975; "Young Offenders and their Social Work" 1975; "Making 'Crime'" 1981; "Reproducing Order" 1982; co-author "The Ordering of Justice" 1982; numerous articles various law and social science journs.; co-author research monographs "The Silent System" and "Decarceration and the Economy of Penal Reform"; founding co-ed. "The Canadian Journal of Sociology"; mem. Candn. Assn. Sociol. & Anthrop.; Am. Sociol. Assn.; Am. Soc. Criminol.; recreation: travel; Home: 178 Colin Ave., Toronto, Ont. M5P 2C6; Office: Centre of Criminology, 130 St. George St., Toronto, Ont. M5S 1A5.

ERNST, Frank L.; financial executive; b. Mahone Bay, N.S., 29 Sept. 1903; s. late Arthur L. and Emma L. (Lemcke) E.; m. Stella S. d. late Samuel H. Bryson 3 Sept. 1941; children: James A., Donald B., Patricia Van Boeschoten; CHMN. OF BD., ERNST, LIDDLE & WOLFE LTD.; Pres., Administered Acceptance Corp. Ltd.; Niakawa Investments Ltd.; Dir. Erlow Holdings Ltd.; joined Mutual Life Assurance Co., H.O.; served mang. and supervision brs. life ins. sales various co's; Supvr. Man. and N.W. Ont.; Brit. Columbia Security Comm. during World War II; varied community work incl. Adv. Bd. Curriculum Comte. Dept. Educ. Man.; mem. Winnipeg Real Estate Bd.; Econ. Devel. Bd.; N. Life Museum; Winnipeg Football Club; Better Business Bureau; Property Mang. Assn. (Winnipeg); Mortgage & Loan Assn. of Man.; Chamber Comm.; K. of C.; R. Catholic; recreation: music; Clubs: Winnipeg Winter; Carleton; Home: 232 Moorgate St., Winnipeg, Man. R3J 2L2; Office: 210-387 Broadway Ave., Winnipeg, Man. R3C 0V5

ERNST, Fred H., P.Eng.; b. Brussels, Belgium, 13 Nov. 1924; e. Univ. of Louvain, Metall. Engr. 1950; five children; PRES. OF BG CHECO INTERNATIONAL LTD., ELEC. & MECHAN. CONSTRS. AND MANUFACTURERS since 1977; Research Engr., Cimenteries et Briqueteries Réunies, 1950-54; engn. and constr. of Inland Cement Plant, Edmonton, Alberta; Plant Superintendent, 1955-59; Extve. V. Pres. and Gen. Mgr., Miron Co. Ltd., 1960-70; Dir. and Vice-Pres., "La Société de développement de la Baie James" 1971-77; served in World War II with Belg. Armored Car Regt. 1944-45; Roman Catholic; Home: 270 Appin Ave., Town of Mount Royal, Que. H3P 1V8

EROLA, Hon. Judith A., M.P.; politician; b. Sudbury, Ont. 16 Jan. 1934; d. Niilo M. and Laura (Rauhala) Jacobsen; m. 27 Aug. 1955; two d. Laura Elizabeth, Kelly Ann; MIN. OF STATE FOR MINES; MINS. RESPONSIBLE FOR THE STATUS OF WOMEN 1980- ; Interviewer, Commentator, Performer, CKSO and CKNC TV 1950 to present; Acct. Extve. Radio Stn. CHNO prior to el. to H. of C.; Co-owner and Operator, Marina & Tourist Outfitting Business 1971-72; el. to H. of C. g.e. 1980; Secy.-Treas. Nickel Belt Riding Assn.; former Bd. mem. Mem. Hosp. Sudbury; mem. Advertising Comte. Sudbury Dist. Chamber Comm.; mem. Sudbury Folks Art Council; Founding mem. Sudbury Little Theatre; Liberal; Lutheran; recreations: skiing, swimming, boating; Home: R.R. 1, Whitefish, Ont. P0M 3E0; Office: 707 Confederation Bldg., Ottawa, Ont. K1A 0X2.

ESLER, John Kenneth, B.F.A., B.Ed.; artist; b. Pilot Mound, Man. 11 Jan. 1933; s. late William John and Jennie Mae (Thompson) E.; e. Silver Springs Dist. Sch. La Riviere, Man. 1948; Pilot Mound (Man.) Coll. Inst. 1951; Univ. of Man. Sch. of Art B.F.A. 1960, Dept. of Educ. B.Ed. 1961; m. Annemarie d. late Hans Schmid 26 June 1964; two s. William Sean, John Dererk; Instr. Alta. Coll. of Art, Calgary 1964-68; Prof. of Art Univ. of Calgary 1968-80; prof. artist since 1962; exhibited pub. and private art galleries Can., U.S.A., Europe, Australia, S. Am.; rep. pub. colls. Candn. and foreign galleries incl. Victoria and Albert Museum, London, Eng.; Albright-Knox Museum, Buffalo; Museum of Modern Art, New York; Nat. Gallery Can.; rep. Can. with 4 prints world exhn. fine art prints Florence, Italy 1976; recipient 30 awards for printmaking and painting; mem. Candn. Soc. Painter-Etchers & Engravers; Candn. Soc. Graphic Art; Print & Drawing Council Can. (Chrmn. 1976-78); Liberal; United Church; recreations: skiing, gardening, tree farm; Home: P.O. Box 2, Site 7, S.S.1, Calgary, Alta. T2M 4N3; Studio: 538 24th Ave. N.W., Calgary, Alta. T2M 4R4.

ESTEY, Jack Burton; executive; b. Fredericton, N.B., 18 April 1922; s. Frank Burton and Mary Elizabeth (McCloskey) E.; e. Commercial High Sch., Fredericton, N.B.; m. Lucy Louise, d. Wm. Betts, Millerton, N.B., 2 June 1944; children: Carol, Joyce, Judy; PRESIDENT, A. & R. LOGGIE (1960) COMPANY LIMITED; Pres., Miramichi Cable Ltd.; Dir., L. E. Shaw Limited; National Sea Products Ltd.; Clerk, Royal Bank of Can., 1939-40; Paymaster, Diamond Construction Co. Ltd., 1945-47, and Purchasing Agent there 1947-52; apptd. Gen. Mgr., A. & R. Loggie Co. Ltd., 1952-59, and Monarch Cold Storage Co. (later Eagle Fisheries Ltd.); Exec. V.P. National Sea Products Ltd. 1967-74; served in 2nd World War as Navigator, R.C.A.F. 1940-45; discharged with rank of Flight Lt.; Mentioned in Despatches; Past Chrmn., Loggieville Sch. Bd.; Loggieville Local Improvement Dist.; mem. Candn. Mfrs. Assn. (Extve. Comte.; Chrmn. N.S. Br.); Pres., N.S. Fish Packers' Assn., 1968-69; Pres., Atlantic By-Products Assn.; Past Pres., N.B. Fish Packers Assn.; Pres. Fisheries Council of Canada, 1963-4; mem. Economic Council of Canada, 1964-7; mem. Fisheries Price Support Board, 1969-72; mem., R.C.A.F. Assn.; Royal Candn. Legion; Freemason (Scot. Rite); United Church; recreation: golf; Clubs: Miramichi Golf & Country (Pres.); Chatham

Curling; Home: Loggieville, N.B. E0C 1L0; Office: (Box 338), Chatham, N.B. E1N 3A7

ESTEY, Hon. Willard Zebedee; B.A., LL.B., LL.M.; judge; b. Saskatoon, Sask., 10 Oct. 1919; s. James Wilfred and Muriel (Baldwin) E.; e. Univ. of Sask., Harvard Law Sch.; m. M. Ruth, d. Norman McKinnon, 1946; children: Wilfred M., John W., Eleanor R., Paul N.; JUSTICE OF SUPREME COURT OF CAN., since 1977; called to Bar of Sask. 1942 and of Ont., 1947; QC Ont. 1960. Prof., Coll. of Law, Univ. of Sask., 1946-47; Lectr., Osgoode Law Sch., 1947-51; law practise, Toronto, 1947-72; Mem., Court of Appeal 1973; Chief Justice of High Court, Supr. Court of Ont., 1975; Chief Justice of Ont., 1976; Commr., Steel Profits Inq., Roy. Comn. of Inq., 1974; Air Canada Inq., Roy. Comn. of Inq., 1975; Hon. LL.D., Wilfred Laurier Univ., Waterloo, 1977; Univ. of Toronto, 1979; Univ. of W. Ont., 1980; Law Society of Upper Canada, 1981; served in 2nd World War, Army and R.C.A.F.; Hon. Life mem. Bd. Govs., York-Finch Hosp.; Vice-Pres., Can. Inst. For Advanced Legal Studies; Chrmn., Hockey Canada; Hon. Chrm., Can. Judges Conf.; Chrmn., Foundation for Legal Research; former Bencher, Law Soc. Upper Can.; former Pres. (for Ont.) Candn. Bar Assn.; Home: 575 Prospect Ave., Ottawa, Ont. K1M 0X6; Office: Supreme Court of Canada, Ottawa, Ont. K1A 0J1

ETHERINGTON, Charles Leslie; musician; writer; b. St. Catharines, Ont., 13 Dec. 1903; s. Thomas and Elizabeth (Kirkpatrick) E.; e. Pub. Schs. and Coll. Inst., St. Catharines, Ont.; studied Piano and Organ under Wm. Theodore Thompson (a pupil of Theodor Leschetizky), St. Catharines, Ont.; studied Harmony and Composition under Dr. Alfred Wooler, Buffalo, N.Y., m. Dorothy Beryl, d. late Hugh L. Freeston, 8 Nov. 1930; children: Hugh Richard, James Robert, David Charles; began musical career as Choir Boy at St. George's Ch., St. Catharines, Ont.; successively Organist at Ridley Coll., St. Catharines and Asst. at St. John's Ch., Thorold, Ont.; Organist and Choirmaster, St. John's Ch., Stamford, St. John's Ch., Kitchener; Ch. of the Holy Saviour, Waterloo; Ch. of the Good Shepherd, Kitchener; St. James' Ch., Fergus, Ont.; Organist and Choirmaster, Trinity Ch., St. Thomas, 1962-73; mem. of music faculty, Alma Coll., St. Thomas, 1962-75; now teaching privately; teacher of piano since 1920, specializing in the tech. methods of Leschetizky; during the War joined Beatty Bros. Ltd.; Fergus, Ont. and employed there until 1962; recognizing a need for a gen. improvement in Ch. music, concentrated on problem of smaller parish chs., and is author of "The Organist & Choirmaster", 1952, and "Protestant Worship Music: Its History and Practice," 1962; has composed several organ transcriptions and anthems, incl. "Old Irish Air", 1925, "The Mercy Seat", 1928; "Beloved, let us love One Another", 1928; Past mem., Library Bd., Fergus, Ont.; Candn. Coll. of Organists; Liberal; Anglican; recreation: reading; Address: 41 1/2 John St., St. Thomas, Ont. N5P 2X2

ETIENNE, Errol Herbert Russell, R.C.A.; designer; creative consultant; film maker; b. Edinburgh, Scot. 28 Apl. 1941; s. Russell Earl and Mary (Glover) E.; e. Los Angeles Art Centre 1962-65; various courses all stages of film work and art; m. Shawn Margaret d. Robert James Wigmore 16 Aug. 1975; children: Michelle Alexandria Noel, Nicholas Basileo Errol; PRES., THE FROG AND BISON CREATIVE CONSULTANTS INC.; guest speaker, lectr. on creativity several univs., insts.; painting exhns. various galleries; recipient over 150 awards for design and film work; recreation: sailing; Address: 4670 48B St., Delta, B.C.

ETKIN, Bernard, M.A.Sc., D.Eng., F.R.S.C. (1970); university professor; b. Toronto, Ontario, 7 May 1918, s. Harry and Mary (Goldberg) E.; e. Oakwood Coll. Inst., Toronto, Ont.; Univ. of Toronto, B.A.Sc. 1941, M.A.Sc. 1947, D.Eng. Carleton 1971; m. Maya, d. Samuel Kesselman, Toronto, Ont., 17 May 1942; children: Carol Elizabeth, David Alexander; PROFESSOR, INST. FOR AEROSPACE STUDIES, FACULTY OF APPLIED SCIENCE & ENGN., UNIVERSITY OF TORONTO; joined University of Toronto as Lecturer in Aeronautical Engn., 1942; Asst. Prof. 1948, Assoc. Prof. 1953, Prof. 1957; Chairman, Division of Engineering Science 1967-72; Dean, Faculty of Applied Sci. and Eng. 1973-79; indust. work incl. periods spent as employee and Consultant with various aircraft companies, also Defence Research Bd.; Past Pres. of Aercol (consulting engn. co.); Pres. of Infrasizers Ltd.; Chrmn., Aeronautics Adv. Bd., Transport Can. since 1978; mem., NRC Adv. Comn. on Aerodynamics since 1979; Publications: "Dynamics of Flight", 1959, 2nd ed. 1982; "Dynamics of Atmospheric Flight" 1972; technical papers and reports in sundry journs.; Fellow, Royal Society of Can.; Fellow, Canadian Aero. & Space Institute; Fellow, Am. Inst. of Aero. and Astro.; Assn. of Prof. Engrs. Ont.; Hebrew; recreations: chess, golf; Home: 10 Fashion Roseway, 308N, Willowdale, Ont. M2N 6B6

ETROG, Sorel; sculptor; b. Iasi, Romania; 29 Aug. 1933; s. Moritz Eserick and Toni (Walter) E.; e. High Sch., Jassey, Romania; Tel Aviv Inst., 1953-55; Brooklyn Museum Art Sch., 1958; comns.: Los Angeles Co. Museum, large sculpture; Candn. Pavillion, Expo 67 and Corp. of Expo 67; Olympia York Centre, Toronto; Bow Valley Square, Calgary; 1968 designed "'Canadian Film Awards'"; rep. Candn. sculpture, Venice Bienale, 1966; illustrated and printed 'The Bird That Does Not Exist', poem by Claude Aveline; illustrated "Chocs" by Eugene Ionesco; "Imagination Dead Image" by Samuel Beckett; designed Toronto Symphony 50th Anniversary Coin, produced and directed the film "Spiral" shown on C.B.C., designed sets and costumes for "Celtic Hero" by W. B. Yeats; selected public collections: Nat. Gall. of Can.; Art Gall. of Ont.; Montreal Fine Arts Museum; Tate Gall., London; St. Peter College, Oxford; Kunst Museum, Basel; Musée d'Art Moderne, Paris; Museum of Modern Art, New York; Guggenheim Museum, New York; Fogg Art Gall. & Museum, New York; Hirshhorn Museum, Washington; Jerusalem Museum; Birla Acad., Calcutta; Univ. of Calif. at Los Angeles (U.C.L.A.); Hart House, Univ. of Toronto, Bank of Canada, Ottawa; Selected oneman shows: Montreal, Toronto, New York, Paris, London, Chicago, Los Angeles, Geneva, Amsterdam, Tel Aviv, Venice, Milan, Rome, and many other cities; served with Israeli Army, 1953-55; Hebrew; Club: Arts and Letters; R.C.A. Address: Box 5943, Terminal A, Toronto, Ont. M5W 1P3

ETTINGER, George Harold, M.B.E. (1946), M.D., D.Sc., LL.D., F.R.S.C.; M.D. (Hon., Univ. of Ottawa); retired prof.; b. Kingston, Ont., 9 May, 1896; s. John George and Elizabeth Jane (Watts) E.; e. Kingston Coll. Inst.; Queen's Univ., B.A. 1916; M.D., C.M. 1920; Univ. of Chicago 1923 (post-grad. studies) and Univ. of Edinburgh, 1928-29; m. Pearl Elizabeth, d. William Blyth, Kingston, Ont., 21 Dec. 1920; 2ndly, Margaret Elizabeth (Sawyer), d. Hector H. MacKay, New Glasgow, N.S., 19 Apl. 1969; one d., Barbara (Hinton); Asst. Dir., Divn. of Med. Research, Nat. Research Council 1946-58; Lectr. in Physiol., Queen's Univ., 1920; Asst. Prof. 1929; Assoc. Prof. 1933; Research Assoc., Univ. of Toronto, Dept. of Med. Research, 1931-35; Prof. of Physiol., Queen's Univ., 1937-62 and Dean, Faculty of Med. there, 1949-62; Dir. of Med. Planning for Alcoholism & Drug Addiction Research Foundation of Ont., and Chrmn. of Prof. Adv. Bd., 1962-70; served in World War 1917-18, R.C.A.M.C.; mem., Am. Assn. of Anat.; Am. Phys. Soc.; Candn. Phys. Soc.; Phys. Soc. of Gt. Brit.; Sr. mem., Candn. Med. Assn.; Sigma Nu; United Church; Home: Cartwright's Point, Kingston, Ont. K7K 5E2

EUSTACE, Cecil John; publisher; b. Walton-on-Thames, Surrey, Eng., 5 June 1903; s. John (Dir., Brit. S. Africa Co., in assn. with Cecil Rhodes) and Edith Mary (Cutler) E.; e. Marlborough House, Hove; Felsted Sch., Essex; m. Irene Emily Agnes, d. Richard Van Praagh, 3 June 1930; children: Philip John, Michael Anthony, Elizabeth Mary; farmed in Eng. after leaving Coll. until 1923; with Bank of Montreal, St. Catharines, Ont., 1927; sometime Ed. and Ad. Mgr., "Bookseller and Stationer" Maclean-Hunter Publ. Co., Toronto; Ed., The Eaton Book Club, until 1930; joined J. M. Dent & Sons (Can.) Ltd. 1930; retiring as Pres. 1968; mem. of Gallery of Living Cath. Authors; author of "The Scarlet Gentleman", 1927; "Damaged Lives", 1930; "Romewards", 1933; "Mind and the Mystery", 1937; "Catholicism, Communism and Dictatorship", 1938; "House of Bread", 1943; "An Infinity of Questions", 1946; "A Spring in the Desert", a novel, 1969; "Forgotten Music" (a novel) 1974; former Trustee, North York Pub. Lib. Bd. (Chrmn. 1967); rec'd Centennial Medal; Clubs: Bd. of Trade of Metro. Toronto Country; Knight of the Equestrian Order of the Holy Sepulchre of Jerusalem; Roman Catholic; recreations: golf, writing, fishing, church activities; Home: 22 Anvil Millway, Willowdale, Ont. M2L 1R1

EUSTACE, David F.; company president; b. Dublin, Ireland, 31 Oct. 1931; s. Cecil Rowland Fox and Harriette (Johnson) E.; privately educated overseas; m. Roberta, d. Horace Steeves, Peace River, Alta., 5 June 1954; children: Steven, Gary, James, Talbot; PRESIDENT, HAZLETON MOTION PICTURES INC., since 1978; Pres., Cemasco Management Ltd. 1975-; Dir., Const. Life Assurance Co. of Can.; Salesman, Mutual Life Assurance Co. of Canada, Edmonton, Alta., 1959; H.O. Agency Asst. with Life of Alta., and subsequently rose to Dir. of Agencies and then Asst. Gen. Mgr.; Sr. Consultant to life ins. co's in U.S. with Life Insurance Agency Mang. Assn., 1965-66; returned to Can. as Dir. of Agencies, Global Life Insurance Co., 1966; (subsequently apptd. Vice Pres.); Pres. and Dir., Union Mutual Life Assurance Co., 1970; Past Area Gov., Toastmaster's Internat.; recreations: cinematography, audio, music, writing; Clubs: Ontario; Home: 1551 Pinetree Cres., Mississauga, Ont. L5G 2S9

EVANS, Brig. Gen. Garth Cameron, C.D., D.D.S.; b. Bow Island, Alta., 21 Jan. 1919; s. John Gordon and Cora Evelyn (Thompson) E.; e. Mount Royal Coll., Calgary, Alta.; Univ. of Alta., D.D.S. 1944; U.S. Naval Dental Sch., Operative Dent. 1953; Walter Reed Army Med. Centre, Advanced Dent. 1956; m. (late) Sylvia, d. Matteus B. Ness, Tofield, Alta., 4 June 1944; children: Michael Blake, Annabel Ness, John Howard, Mark Gordon, Kathrine Marea; served with Candn. Army 1943-46; joined Candn. Army (Regular Force) 1947; promoted Capt. 1947; Maj. 1951; Lt.-Col. 1957; Col. 1965; Brig. Gen. 1970; Chief Instr., RCDC Sch., Camp Borden, 1957-59; Sr. Operator, 13 Dental Unit, Trenton, 1959-60; C.O. 4 Field Dental Co., Germany, 1960-63; Dir. of Dental Services, CFHQ, Ottawa, 1964-65; C.O. 11 Dental Unit, Edmonton and Command Dental Offr. W. Command, 1965-70; Dir. Gen. Dental Services, CFHQ, 1970-74; named Queen's Hon. Dental Surg. 1970; rec'd UN Medal; Centennial Medal 1967; Fellow. Internat. Coll. Dents.; mem. Alta. Dent. Soc.; Candn. Dent Assn. (Gov.); Delta Upsilon; Anglican; recreations: flying, curling; Club: Edmonton Flying; Home: 8476-118 St., Windsor Pk., Edmonton, Alta. T6G 1T3; Office: 301 College Plaza W., 8215-112 St., Edmonton, Alta. T6G 2C8

EVANS, Hon. Gregory Thomas, Ph.D., LL.D., K.C.S.G.; judge; b. McAdam, N.B., 13 June 1913; s. Mary Helen (McDade) and late Thomas Vincent E.; e. St. Joseph's Univ., B.A. 1934, and St. Thomas Univ., LL.D. 1963, Fredericton, N.B.; Osgoode Hall Law Sch., Toronto, Ont., grad. 1939; Univ. of Moncton, Ph.D. 1964; m. Zita, d. late Thomas Callon, 1 Oct. 1941; children: Thomas, John, Gregory, Rory, Mary, Kerry, Brendan, Catherine, Erin; CHIEF JUSTICE, HIGH COURT OF ONT. since 1976; Justice, Court of Appeal, Ont., 1965; before appt. to Supreme Court of Ont. in 1963 practised as Sr. Partner,

Evans, Evans, Bragagnolo, Perras & Sullivan, Timmins, Ont.; called to the Bar of Ont. 1939; cr. Q.C. 1953; Bencher, Law Soc. Upper Can., 1961; Vice Chrmn., Can. Judicial Council; Vice Chrm., Ont. Judicial Council; V.P. Can. Inst. for Advanced Legal Studies since 1978; mem., Atty. Gen. Comte. on Adm. of Justice, 1958-63; Ont. Legal Aid Comte., 1962; Vice-Pres., Ont. Candn. Bar Assn., 1962; Pres., Ont. Eng. Catholic Educ. Assn., 1961; Internat. Counsellor, Lions Internat. 1954; Delta Chi; Roman Catholic; Club: University; Home: 44 Charles St. W., Apt. 4704, Toronto, Ont., M4Y 1R8; Office: Osgoode Hall, Toronto, Ont. M5H 2N5

EVANS, James Eric Lloyd; B.Sc. (Hon.), M.A., Ph.D.; geologist; b. Miniota, Man., 25 May 1914; s. James Lloyd and Edith Eleanor (Price) E.; m. Diana Dorothy, d. late Mark Stanley Peacock, 10 Aug. 1940; two d., Susan Louise, Deborah Anne; Prof., Dept. of Geology, Univ. of Toronto, 1980-; Consulting Geologist, 1979-; Dir. of Exploration, Denison Mines Ltd., 1970-79; Geol. Survey Parties, Geol. Survey of Can. 1935-37; Sr. Asst. and Chief for Field Parties, Ont. Dept. of Mines, 1938-41; Research Geol. Falconbridge Nickel Mines Ltd., 1943-45; Exploration Geol., Frobisher Ltd. and Ventures Ltd. (chiefly in Ungava and Labrador) 1945-50; Mgr., Candn. Office, American Metal Co. Ltd., 1950-54; Field Mgr., Technical Mines Consultants Ltd., 1955-56; Chief Geol., Rio Tinto Canadian Exploration Ltd., 1956-70; Mgr. Exploration Planning and Research 1970; B.Sc. (Hon.), Univ. of Man. 1936; M.A. Queen's Univ., Kingston 1942; Ph.D. Columbia Univ., N.Y. 1944; rec'd Centennial Medal 1967; Fellow, Geological Assn. of Can.; Founding mem., Candn. Geol. Foundation; mem., Geol. Assn. Can. (Past Pres. 1967-68); Soc. Econ. Geols.; Assn. Prof. Engrs. Province Ontario; Candn. Inst. Mining & Metall.; Geol. Soc. Am.; Sigma Xi; Anglican; Clubs: Engineers; Bd. Trade Metro Toronto; Empire; Home: 1375 Stavebank Rd., Mississauga, Ont. L5G 2V4

EVANS, John Robert, M.D., D.Phil., F.R.C.P.(C), F.A.C.P. (1960), F.R.C.P. (1980, London Eng.); university president; b. 1 Oct. 1929; e. Univ. of Toronto, M.D. 1952; Rhodes Scholar — interne, Radcliffe Infirmary, Oxford Univ. 1953; Oxford Scholar, 1954; D.Phil. Oxford, 1955; m. Gay Glassco; has four s. and two d.; Dir., Dept. of Population, Health and Nutrition, Internat. Bank for Reconstruction and Development since 1979; President, Univ. of Toronto 1972-78; Def. Lib. Cand. Oct. 1978 by-election, Rosedale riding, Toronto; Dir. Dominion Foundries & Steel Ltd.; Dir., Crown Life Ins. Co.; Jr. interne, Toronto Gen. Hosp., Toronto, Ont. 1952-53; Hon. Registrar, Nat. Heart Hosp., London 1955; Asst. Res., Sunnybrook Hosp., Toronto, Ont. 1956 and Toronto Gen. Hosp. 1957; Ont. Heart Foundation Fellow, Hosp. for Sick Children, Toronto, Ont. 1958 and Chief Res. Phys., Toronto Gen. Hosp., 1959; Research Fellow, Baker Clinic Research Lab., Harvard Med. Sch., 1960-61; and Markle Scholar in Acad. Med., Univ. of Toronto 1960-65; Assoc., Dept. of Med., Faculty of Med., Univ. of Toronto 1961-65; Dean Faculty of Med., McMaster Univ. 1965-72; Pres., Assoc. of Cdn. Med. Colleges 1972; Chrmn., Counc. of Ont. Univers., 1975-77; mem., W.H.O. Adv. Comte. on Med. Research, 1976-80; C.C., 1978; mem. of Task Force on Candn. Unity, 1977; numerous hon. degrees from Candn. univs., Yale and John Hopkins Univ., U.S.A., and Limbourg, Netherlands; apptd. Med. Research Council 1969; mem. council, Inst. of Med., U.S. Nat. Acad. of Sci. 1972-80; Roy. Coll. Phys. and Surgeons 1972-80; recreations: skiing, fishing, farming; Address: 58 Highland Ave., Toronto, Ont. M4W 2A3

EVANS, Hon. Leonard S., M.L.A., M.A.; politician; b. Winnipeg, Man., 19 Aug. 1929; s. David and Gwen (Salusbury) E.; e. Transcona (Man.) Coll. Inst.; Univ. of Winnipeg, B.A. 1951; Univ. of Man., M.A. 1953; postgrad. studies 1968-69; m. Alice Mazinke, 27 June 1953; children: Brenda, Janet, Randall; MIN. OF INDUSTRY

AND COMMERCE, MAN., 1969-77; Economic Critic of Opposition, since 1977; ; Econ., Dom. Bureau of Stat. 1954-62; Central Mortgage & Housing Corp. 1962-64; Prof., Brandon Univ., 1964-69; NDP; Unitarian; Home: 320 Lloyd Cres., Brandon, Manitoba; Office: Room 228, Legislative Bldg., Winnipeg, Man.

EVANS, Paul Charles, B.Sc.; petroleum executive; b. Galesburg, Ill., 13 June 1915; s. Paul Watson and Mae Maude (Nelson) E.; e. Texas A. & M. Coll. B.Sc. (Petroleum Engn.) 1937; m. Sarah Elizabeth Scott d. George Hollingsworth Meason, 26 Dec. 1937; children: Sarah Elizabeth Rogers, Paul Meason, John Charles; DIR., CHAIRMAN OF THE BOARD, PRESIDENT AND CHIEF EXTVE. OFFR., PLACER CEGO PETROLEUM LTD. since 1977; Dir. Canadian Export Gas & Oil (UK); Canadian Export Gas & Oil Inc.; CEGO Asia; Bluewater Oil & Gas Ltd.; Field Aviation Co. Ltd.; Training Engr. Gulf Oil Corp. 1937-42, Dist. Engr. (Hobbs, New Mexico) 1945-49; Chief Engr. Canadian Gulf Oil Co. Calgary, 1949-51; Mgr. W. Canadian Petroleum Ltd. Calgary 1951-54; joined present Co. as Vice Pres.- Production 1954-74; Pres. and Chief Exec. Offr., Can. Export Gas & Oil Ltd., 1974-77; served with US Army 1942-45 (Europe 1943-45), rank Maj. rec'd Bronze Star; mem. Candn. Inst. Mining & Metall.; Protestant; recreations: golf, spectator sports; Clubs: Calgary Petroleum; Calgary Golf & Country; Address: 405, 3204 Rideau Place, SW, Calgary, Alta.T2S 1Z2

EVANS, Trevor A.; retired insurance broker; b. Montreal, Que., 23 Feb. 1925; s. Trevor A. and Dorothy G. (Rhodes) E.; e. Bishop's Coll. Sch., Lennoxville, Que.; McGill Univ.; m. Gillian L., d. late David Murray, 14 June 1947; one s.; David; former Sr. Vice-Pres. and Dir., Marsh & McLennan Ltd. (retired 1975); joined Great American Insurance Co., Montreal, 1946; trans. to Candn. H.O., Toronto, 1948; assumed various positions incl. Supt. of Property Ins. for Can., Supt. of Agencies for Can. and Mgr. of Toronto Office; apptd. Mgr. for Prov. of Que., 1954; joined present firm 1956; apptd. Asst. Vice-Pres. 1957; Vice-Pres. 1959; Dir. 1965; Mgr., Montreal Office 1967; served with R.C.N. in N. Atlantic, 1943-45; Extve. Vice-Pres. 1968; Anglican; recreations: golf, skiing, Great Dane breeding and showing, fishing; Clubs: Beaconsfield Golf (Dir.); St. James's; Whitlock Golf & Country; Hochelaga Kennel (past Pres.); Home: Highway 201, R.R. 1, Hudson, Que. J0P 1H0

EVANS, Walter J.; company director; b. Toronto, Ontario, 3 February 1916; s. Walter E. and Emma (Richey) E.; e. St. Joseph's Sch.; De La Salle Coll., Toronto, Ont. (R.I.A. Degree); m. Mary Dorothy, d. Norman Squire, 3 Aug. 1940; children: Barry M., Paul R., Joan C.; formerly Vice-Pres. and Asst. Gen. Mgr., G. H. Wood & Co. Ltd.; Pres., and Gen. Mgr., S. F. Lawrason Chemicals Ltd.; also Lawrason Holdings Ltd. 1955-72; Dir., S. F. Lawrason & Co. Ltd.; Candn. Nat. Inst. for the Blind; Western Fair Bd.; St. Joseph's Hospital; Multi-Tek Inc., Adrian, Mich.; Pres., Plaza East Assoc.-Florida; Adv. Bd. Huron Coll. Fdn.; Chrmn. of Bd., St. Mary's Hosp., London; Nachurs Plant Food Co., Marion, Ohio and London, Ont.; Dir., St. Joseph's Hosp., mem. Bd. of Govs., 1969-78; Univ. of W. Ont.; Kt. of Malta; Pres., (1963-64) London Chamber Comm.; Trustee, YM-YWCA London, Ont.; Club: London Hunt & Country; Address: 4300 N. Ocean Blvd., Apt. 7L, Fort Lauderdale, Fl. 33308; Home: 1492 Stoneybrook Cresc., London, Ont. N5X 1C5

EVANS, Wilfred Hugo, B.A., D. de l'Un. (Paris); professor emeritus; b. Cardiff, Wales, 18 March 1906; s. David Valentine and Florence Emily (Roberts) E.; e. Cardiff (Wales) High Sch.; Univ. of Wales, B.A. 1927; Univ. of Paris, D. de l'Un. 1931; m. Catherine Mary, d. Harry McLeod Blacklock, Mount Chesney, Ont., 9 Oct. 1969; two d. (by prev. m.) Mrs. John Dossett (Carolyn), Penelope Susan; Fellow, Univ. of Wales, 1931-33; Lectr., Univ. of Liverpool, 1934; Prof. and Head, Dept. of French,

Queen's Univ. 1948, Prof. 1970, Prof. Emeritus of French Lang. and Lit. since 1971; served with R.A.F. in U.K., W. Africa, N.W. Europe, 1941-45: rank Flight Lt.; author "L'Historien Mézeray", 1931; co-author "Sixteenth Century French Verse and Prose", 1938; other writings incl. articles and book reviews in various journs.; rec'd Chevalier dans l'Ordre des Palmes Académiques (France); awarded Jubilee Medal; Hon. mem., Assn. Candn. Univ. Teachers French (Pres. 1966-69); Humanities Assn. (Past Pres. Kingston Br.); Alliance Française (Past Pres. Kingston Br.); Home: 175 Helen St., Kingston, Ont. K7L 4P5

EVELYN, Kenneth Austin, M.D., D.Sc., F.R.C.P.(C), F.A.C.P.; physician; university professor; b. Jamaica, B.W.I., 19 June 1911; s. Rev. Richard Austin and Alice Maude (Shrimpton) E.; e. Munro Coll., Jamaica; McGill Univ., B.Sc. (Hons. Maths. and Physics, with Molson Gold Medal) 1932, M.D., C.M. 1938 (Wood Gold Medallist in Med.), D.Sc. 1971; m. Marjorie Olive, d. John O'Neill, Toronto, 29 July 1939; children: Ronald Geoffrey, Diana Elaine; ERMERITUS PROF. OF MED., UNIV. OF B.C., Chmn., Scientific Advisory Comte.; B.C. Health Care Research Council; Dir. B.C. Science Council; postgrad. training in Med. and Pathol., Roy. Victoria Hosp., Montreal; Research Fellow in Med., Am. Coll. of Phys., 1946; Research Assoc., Harvard Univ. and Mass. Gen. Hosp., 1947; Assoc. Prof. of Med. and Dir., Research Inst. of Biophysics, McGill Univ., Montreal, 1948-54; Dir., B.C. Med. Research Inst., and Research Prof. of Med., Univ. of B.C., 1954-58; served in World War 1940-45 with R.C.A.F. Med. Br. as Commdg. Offr., Biophysics Lab.; held rank of Wing Commdr.; mem., Candn. Med. Assn.; Am. Soc. of Clin. Investigation; Candn. Physiol. Soc.; Vancouver Med. Assn.; B.C. Soc. of Internal. Med.; Candn. Biochem. Soc.; Candn. Soc. for Clinical Investig.; Candn. Cardiovascular Soc.; Alpha Omega Alpha; rec'd Theodore C. Lyster Award for contrib. to Aviation Med., 1952; has written numerous scient. articles on photoelect. colorimetry, decompression sickness, night vision, colour vision, hypertension and radioactivity; inventor of the Evelyn photoelectric colorimeter (1938); Anglican; Home: 5510 Chancellor Blvd., Vancouver, B.C. V6T 1E3

EVERETT, Hon. Douglas Donald, LL.B.; senator; b. Vancouver, B.C., 12 Aug. 1927; s. Horace and Catherine M. (Ritchie) E.; e. Maple Grove (Vancouver), Univ. (Victoria) and Ravenscourt (Winnipeg) Schs., 1943; Royal Candn. Naval Coll., Royal Roads, 1943-45; Osgoode Hall Law Sch., 1947-50; Univ. of Man., LL.B. 1951; m. Patricia G., d. Charles Vince Gladstone, 23 Feb. 1952; 6 children; Chrm. C.E.O., Royal Canadian Securities Ltd.; Dir. Eaton/Bay Mutual Funds; General Foods Ltd.; Canadian Indemnity Co. Ltd.; Versatile Corp.; Continental Bank of Canada; mem., Council of Admin. Studies Faculty, York Univ.; Co-Chrm., Central Region, Can. Counsil Christians and Jews; called to Bars of Ont. 1950, Man. 1951; apptd. to Senate of Can. Nov. 1966; Chairman, Standing Senate Committee on National Finance; Liberal; Anglican; recreations: shooting, skiing, tennis; Clubs: Manitoba; St. Charles Country; York (Toronto); Rideau (Ottawa); Mid Ocean, Bermuda; Home: 514 Wellington Cres., Winnipeg, Man. R3M 0B9; Offices: The Senate, Ottawa, Ont. K1A 0A4 and 252 Fort St., Winnipeg, Man. RC3 1E6

EVERSON, Ronald Gilmour, B.A.; b. Oshawa, Ont., 18 Nov. 1903; s. Thomas Henry and Mary Elizabeth (Farwell) E.; Univ. of Toronto, B.A. 1927; Osgoode Hall, Toronto, 1930; m. Lorna Jean, d. W. R. Austin, The Wilderness, Niagara-on-the-Lake, Ont., 15 Apl. 1931; CHAIRMAN, COMMUNICATIONS 6, INC.; author of "Three Dozen Poems"; "A Lattice for Momos"; "Blind Man's Holiday"; "Wrestle with an Angel"; "The Dark is not So Dark"; "Selected Poems"; "Indian Summer"; "Carnival"; Clubs: Univ. (Montreal); Univ. (Toronto); Beaconfield Golf (Montreal); Montreal Press; Home: 4855 Cote St. Luc Rd., Montreal, Que. H3W 2H5

EVES, Walter Graham, F.A.I.I.E.; manufacturer (retired); b. Regina, Sask., 28 Aug. 1924; s. Walter W. and Marion (Donaldson) E.; e. Pub. & High Schs., Toronto, Ont.; Univ. of Toronto, Indust. Engn. 1950; m. Donna Marie, d. John Wilson, 10 Sept. 1949; children: Dianne, Deborah, Denice, Scott, Grant; Dir., Levy Industries Ltd.; Seaway Multi-Corp.; all employment (1943-71) with Hawker Siddeley Canada Ltd. interests; with Victory Aircraft, Toronto, Time Study 1943-44; Mgr. Indust. Engn., Hawker Siddeley Can. Ltd. 1953, Op. Mgr. 1959, Dir. Indust. Engn. 1963; Op. Mgr., Orenda Engines 1967-69; Gen. Mgr. Canadian Bridge Co. Ltd. 1970; Canadian Car Co. Ltd. 1971; Canadian Acme Screw & Gear 1972; Vice-Pres. Operations, Seaway Multi-Corp. Ltd. and Gen. Mgr. present Co. 1972; mem. Candn. Sporting Goods Association (Dir.); Canadian Mfrs. Association; Am. Mfrs. Association; Candn. Export Assn. (Dir.); Am. Inst. Indust. Engrs.; Anglican; recreations: golf, skiing, minor hockey, oil painting, swimming; Club: Swiss; Home: 6566, 6th Line, R.R. 1, Hornby, Ont. L0P 1E0

EWAN, George Thomson, B.Sc., Ph.D.; physicist; b. Edinburgh, Scot., 6 May 1927; s. Alexander Farmer and Jeannie Young (Taylor) E.; e. Univ. of Edinburgh, B.Sc. (1st Class Hons., Physics) 1948, Ph.D. (Physics) 1952; m. Maureen Louise, d. R. S. Howard, Edinburgh, Scot., 7 Aug. 1952; children: Elizabeth Louise, Robert Alexander; PROF. OF PHYSICS, QUEEN'S UNIV., since 1970; Asst. Lectr., Edinburgh Univ., 1950-52; Research Assoc., McGill Univ., 1952-53 and Nat. Research Council Post doctoral Fellow there 1953-55; Asst. Research Offr., Atomic Energy of Canada Ltd., Chalk River, Ont. 1955-58; Assoc. Research Offr., 1958-62; Sr. Research Offr., 1962-70; Ford Foundation Fellow, Niels Bohr Inst., Copenhagen, 1961-62; Visiting Scientist, Lawrence Radiation Lab., Berkeley, Cal., 1966; Research Associate, CERN, Geneva 1977-78; contrib. author, "Alpha-, Beta- and Gamma-Ray Spectroscopy," 1965 and "Progress in Nuclear Instrumentation and Techniques, Vol. III," 1968; has publ. more than 60 scient. papers on topics in nuclear physics; rec'd Am. Nuclear Soc. Radiation Industry Award 1967 (for pioneering work in devel. of lithium drifted germanium gamma-ray spectrometers); mem., Candn. Assn. Physics; Fellow, Royal Soc. of Canada; Am. Physical Society; Royal Soc. of Arts; Prof. Engrs.; United Church; recreations: golf, skiing, canoeing; Home: 66 Fairway Hill Cres., Kingston, Ont. K7M 2B4

EWEN, Paterson, R.C.A.; artist; educator; b. Montreal, Que. 7 Apl. 1925; s. William Paterson and Edna Mary (Griffis) E.; e. Montreal W. High Sch. 1943; Montreal Museum Sch. of Fine Arts & Design (studied under Goodridge Roberts and Arthur Lismer) Dipl. in Painting, Sculpture and Teaching of Child Art 1950; Asst. Prof. Univ. of W. Ont. since 1952, Asst. Chrmn. Visual Arts Dept. 1978; Advisor to Forest City Gallery, London, Ont.; served with Candn. Army 1943-46, N.W. Europe; recreations: naturalist, walking, reading; Office: University of Western Ontario; London, Ont. N6A 5B7.

EXTON, Eric, A.M.B.; executive; b. Germany 1919; s. late Alvis and Ida E.; e. S. Germany (Indust. Chem.), expelled by Nazis 1938; m. Esther d. Benjamin Friedman; children: Leonard Ralph, Sybil (Mrs. Barry Berenstein); PRES. SEEL MORTGAGE INVESTMENT CORP.; Pres. Seel Enterprises Ltd.; Spartan Realty Management Ltd., and various other affiliates; Dir. Municipal Savings & Loan Corp.; Superior Acceptance Corp.; Can. Geriatrics Research Soc.; Indust. Chem Sandoz Chemical, Toronto until 1946; Dir. Giftcraft Ltd. 1946-54; mem. Comm. Registration Appeal Tribunal for Mortgage Brokers Indust.; Chrmn. Emeritus of the Bd., Baycrest Centre Geriatric Care; Chmn. of Bd. of Canadian Friends of Boys Town Jerusalem; National Pres. Jewish Nat. Fund of Canada; Past Pres. Hillel Adv. Bd. Univ. of Toronto; Toronto B'nai B'rith Regional Council and Eglinton Lodge (Treas.

Youth Inc.); Chrmn. Pension Comte. Un. Jewish Welfare Fund; Founder and Hon. Lifetime Councillor Ilot; Life mem. Bd. and Men's Service Group Baycrest Hosp. and Jewish Home for Aged; Gov. Soc. Fellows League Human Rights; mem. Pres's Council Candn. Opera Co.; mem. Stratford Shakesperian Festival Foundation; Bd. mem. Candn. Foundation Jewish Culture; Mount Sinai Hosp.; Jt. Community Relations Comte.; Jewish Camp Council; Guest Speaker: Alta. Mortgage Brokers Assn.; Real Estate Bd., S. Ont. Region, Queen's Univ., Kingston, various assns. univs. and colls.; twice Chrmn. Adv. Bd. Mortgage Brokers Registration Act Ont. for Dept. Consumer & Comm. Affairs; served as extve. various organs. and conventions; Life mem. Metrop. Zool. Soc.; served with Candn. Fusiliers during World War II; rec'd George Shnier Mem. Award; Peace Award; Negev Award; Past Chrmn. Soc. Accredited Mortgage Brokers Prov. Ont.; mem. Multiple Dwelling Assn.; Ont. Mortgage Brokers Assn.; Inst. of Dirs.; Freemason; B'nai B'rith; Clubs: Primrose; Maple Downs Golf & Country; Royal Candn. Mil. Inst.; Office: 1022—123 Edward St., Toronto, Ont. M5G 1Y4

EYRE, The Hon. Dean Jack; retired diplomat; b. Westport, N.Z., 8 May 1914; e. Hamilton High Sch., N.Z.; Auckland Univ.; m. Patricia Naomi Arnoldson; two s., one d.; High Commissioner for New Zealand, 1968-73, reappointed 1976-80; Mang. Dir. Airco (N.Z.) Ltd., Auckland (founded 1936); M.P. (Nat.) for N. Shore, N.Z., 1949-66; Min. of Customs 1954-56; Min. of Social Security, Min. of Tourist and Health Resorts, 1956-57; Min. of Housing, Min. of Defence 1957, Min. of Police, 1960-63; Min. of Defence 1960-66, Min. of Tourism and Publicity, 1961-66; served with RNVR during World War II; rank Lt.; Pres., Jr. Nat. League, Remuera, Auckland, 1938; recreations: golf, boating, fishing; Clubs: Royal N.Z. Yacht Sqdn.; Northern (N.Z.); Wellington (N.Z.); Officers' (Auckland); United Services (Wellington); Royal Ottawa Golf; Home: Apt. 4, 74 Somerset St. W., Ottawa, Ont. K2P 0H3

EYRE, Ivan, B.F.A., R.C.A.; painter; b. Tullymet, Sask. 15 Apl. 1935; s. Thomas and Katie (Jaworski) E.; e. elem. schs. and Nutana Coll. Inst. Saskatoon 1953; Univ. of Sask. Drawing & Painting 1952; Univ. of Man. Sch. of Art B.F.A. 1957; Univ. of N. Dak. grad. asst. 1958; m. Brenda Yvonne d. Arthur & Alfreda Fenske, Winnipeg, Man. June 1957; two s. Keven Jules, Tyrone Thomas; solo exhns. incl.: Univ. of Man. 1962, 1964, 1976; Montreal Museum of Fine Arts 1964; Winnipeg Art Gallery 1964, 1966, 1969, 1974, 1982; Fleet Gallery Winnipeg 1965, 1969, 1972; Albert White Galleries Toronto 1965; Yellow Door Gallery Winnipeg 1966; Atelier Vincitore Gallery Brighton, Eng. 1967; Mount Allison Univ. 1968; Mendel Art Gallery Saskatoon 1968; Morris Gallery Toronto 1969, 1971, 1973; Frankfurter Kunstkabinett W. Germany 1973; Burnaby Art Gallery 1973; Art Gallery of Greater Victoria 1973; McIntosh Gallery Univ. of W. Ont. 1973; Siemens Werk Erlangen, W. Germany 1974; Playhouse Theatre Fredericton and N.B. Museum Saint John 1976; Nat. Gallery Can. 1978; Mira Godard Gallery Toronto 1978, 1979, 1980; Equinox Gallery Vancouver 1978, 1981; Robert McLaughlin Gallery Oshawa 1980; Rodman's Hall St. Catharines 1980; Art Gallery of Windsor; Beaverbrooke Art Gallery; London Art Gallery; rep. numerous group exhns. since 1956; rep. in various pub., corporate and private colls. incl. Nat. Gallery, Vancouver Art Gallery, Winnipeg Art Gallery, Victoria Art Gallery, Hamilton Art Gallery, Art Gallery of Ont.; works publ. various art journs., books, catalogues; subject of the "Ivan Eyre", by George Woodcock 1981; rec'd Can. Council Sr. Grants 1965, 1971; Queen's Silver Jubilee Medal 1977; Acad. of Italy with Gold Medal 1980; Assoc., Accademia Italia Delle Arti E Del Lavoro; Address: 1098 rue des Trappistes, Winnipeg, Man. R3V 1B8.

EYRE, John Lamarche, LL.B., B.A.; shipping executive; b. Orange, N.J., 30 Oct. 1917; s. John A. and Ethel (Lamarche) E.; e. Millbrook (N.Y.) Sch.; Yale Univ., B.A., 1940; Harvard Business Sch., Naval Supply, 1943; Fordham Law Sch., LL.B., 1949; m. Cornelia, d. Martin LeBoutillier, 17 July 1952; children: Stephen, Martin Banning, Alison; PRESIDENT AND CHRMN., SAGUENAY SHIPPING LTD., Pres. and Dir., Alcan Shipping Services, Ltd., Montreal; Director, Alcan Ore Limited, Montreal; Chaguaramas Terminals Limited (Trinidad) Sprostons (Guyana) Limited; Saguenay Shipping (U.K.) Limited (London, England) 1966-75; United Nation Shipping Advisor, South Pacific 1981-2; Chrmn. Genstar Overseas Ltd. (to 1980); Dir. Oceanic Finance Ltd., 1975-80; mem. The Science Council of Can.; independent shipping consultant 1981; Transportation Comte.; Pacific Basin Economic Co-op. Council; Past Pres., Candn. Transp. Research Forum; Ship's Offr., Grace & Robin Lines, 1940-43; Port of N.Y. Authority, 1945-55; Transp. Consultant, 1955-59; Sr. Transport Consultant, Arthur D. Little Inc., Cambridge, Mass., 1959-66; served as Lieut. during 2nd World War, with U.S. Naval Reserve, in Solomon and Philippine Island campaigns, 1943-45; Pres. 1973-74 Canadian Shipowners Association; mem., Canadian Comte., Lloyd's Register of Shipping; mem. American Bureau of Shipping; Alumni Bd., Yale Univ.; recreations: sailing, beagling, fishing, skiing; Clubs: St. James's; Whitehall; Royal Bermuda Yacht; Address: Chemin Erables, Abercorn, Que. J0E 1B0

EYTON, John Trevor, Q.C., B.A., LL.B.; barrister and solicitor; b. Quebec City, Que. 12 July 1934; s. John and late Dorothy Isabel E.; e. Beaupré (Que.) Pub. Sch.; Jarvis Coll. Inst. Toronto; Univ. of Toronto B.A. 1957 (Victoria Coll.); LL.B. 1960; m. Barbara Jane d. Dr. R.C. Montgomery, Toronto, Ont. 13 Feb. 1955; children: Adam Tudor, Christopher Montgomery, Deborah Jane, Susannah Margaret, Sarah Elizabeth; PRES., CEO AND DIR., BRASCAN LTD.: Partner, Tory, Tory, DesLauriers & Binnington; Chrmn. and C.E.O., Brascade Resources Inc.; Dir., Triarch Corp. Ltd.; National Hees Enterprises Ltd.; Bank of Montreal; CFGM Broadcasting Ltd.; Edper Investments Ltd.; Foodex Ltd.; Foundation of Photographic Arts; Great Lakes Power Corp. Ltd.; Hatleigh Corp.; John Labatt Ltd.; Lacana Mining Ltd.; London Life Insurance Co.; Westmin Resources Ltd.; Noranda Mines Ltd.; North Canadian Oils Ltd.; Radio IWC Ltd.; Scott Paper Co.; The Winnipeg Supply & Fuel Co. Ltd.; Candn. Israel Ch. of Comm.; Candn. Soc. for the Weizmann Inst. of Sci.; The Arthritis Society; Dir. and Shareholder, Astral Bellevue Pathe Ltd.; Carena-Bancorp Inc.; Hume Publishing Ltd.; Trizec Corp. Ltd.; Shareholder Perma-Fleur Ltd.; Gov. U. of Waterloo; read law with Tory, Tory, DesLauriers & Binnington 1960-62, Assoc. 1962-67, Partner 1967-;called to Bar of Ont. 1962; cr. Q.C. 1980; mem. Phi Delta Theta; Upper Can. Law Soc.; Candn. Bar Assn.; P. Conservative; United Church; recreations: tennis skiing, swimming; Clubs: Chinguacousy Golf & Country; RCYC; University; Empire; Caledon Ski; Caledon Riding & Hunt; Caledon Mountain Trout; Toronto Bd. Trade; Coral Beach & Tennis (Bermuda); Home: 15 Elm Ave., Toronto, Ont. M4W 1M9 and Tudorcroft R.R. 1, Caledon, Ont. L0N 1C0; Office: (P.O. Box 48) Commerce Court, Toronto, Ont. M5L 1B7 and (P.O. Box 20) Royal Bank Plaza, Toronto, Ont. M5J 2K1.

EYTON, Rhys T., B.A., C.A., C.L.U.; airline executive; b. Vancouver, B.C. 23 Sept. 1935; s. Geoffrey Tudor; e. Univ. of W. Ont. B.A. 1958; C.A. 1966; Banff Sch. of Advanced Management, 1968; m. Lynn Josephine d. Dr. Russell A. Palmer 7 Dec. 1962; children: Russell, Kathryn, Wendy; PRES. AND CHIEF EXTVE OFFR., PACIFIC WESTERN AIRLINES LTD. since 1976; joined Finance Dept. of Pacific Western 1967; served as Manager, Northern Region, apptd. Vice Pres. 1969; Vice Pres., Trucking Div., 1974-75; apptd. Extve. Vice Pres., Finance and Planning, 1975; Dir., Conference Bd. of Can.; Pacific

Western Airlines and Subsidiary Cos.; Chem-Security Ltd.; mem., Candn. Inst. of C.A.; Past Chrmn., Air Transport Assn. of Can. (1981); also serves on various educational, advisory and alumni assns. and councils; Anglican; Clubs: Calgary Petroleum; Ranchmen's; Calgary Golf and Country; Glencoe; Van. Lawn Tennis and Badminton; recreations: jogging, racquet sports; golf, skiing; Home: 2123 - 7th S.W., Calgary, Alta. T2T 2X3; Office: Ste. 2800, 700 - 2nd St. S.W., Calgary, Alta. T2P 2W2.

EZRIN, Paul V.; financial executive; b. Toronto, Ont. 30 Sept. 1937; e. Forest Hill Coll. Inst. Toronto; Ryerson Polytech. Inst. Business Adm. grad. 1959; m. Judith 22 May 1966; children: Melissa, Melanie, Mark; PRESIDENT & GEN. MGR., CITYCAN FINANCIAL CORP.; Dir. Timeway Credit Ltd.; Pres., Creditway Ltd.; Dir. Manhill Enterprises Ltd.; served as Mortgage Mgr. Young & Biggin Real Estate 3 yers.; Br. Mgr. C.A.C. Acceptance 11 yrs.; Dir. and Pres. Ont. Mortgage Brokers Assn.; Home: 22 Sydnor Rd., Willowdale, Ont. M2M 3A1; Office: 2104 Yonge St., Toronto, Ont. M4S 2A5

F

FACKENHEIM, Emil Ludwig, Ph.D., LL.D., D.D., D.Hu.L., F.R.S.C. (1972); professor; b. Halle, Germany, 22 June 1916; s. Julius and Meta (Schlesinger) F.; e. Univ. of Halle, Germany (1937-38); Aberdeen Univ. (1939-40); Univ. of Toronto (1941-43), Ph.D. 1945; LL.D. Laurentian 1969; Sir George Williams 1971; D.D. St. Andrews Coll. 1972; D.Hu.L. Hebrew Union 1974; m. Rose Komlodi, Calgary, Alberta, 28 December 1957; children: Michael Alexander, Susan Sheila, David Emmanuel, Joseph Jonatan; PROF. OF PHILOSOPHY, UNIV. OF TORONTO, since 1961; Contrib. Editor, "Judaism"; o. as Rabbi, 1939; Rabbi, Cong. Anshe Sholom, Hamilton, Ont., 1943-48; Lectr. in Philos., Univ. of Toronto, 1948-53, Asst. Prof., 1953-56, Assoc. Prof., 1956-61; Guggenheim Fellow, 1957-58; Killam Fellow, 1977-1978; appt. University Professor 1979; author: "Metaphysics and Historicity", 1961; "Paths to Jewish Belief", 1960; "The Religious Dimension in Hegel's Thought', 1968; "Quest for Past and Future: Essays in Jewish Theology" 1968; "God's Presence in History", 1970; "Encounters Between Judaism and Modern Philosophy", 1973; "The Jewish Return Into History", 1978; and many articles and reviews in scholarly journs.; rec'd. Pres.'s Medal of Univ. of W. Ont. for best scholar. article publ. in Can. in 1954; mem., Can. Philos. Assn.; Central Conf. of Am. Rabbis; Jewish; recreations: music, theatre, travel; Home: 563 Briar Hill Ave., Toronto, Ont. M5W 1W1

FAGAN, Hon. Ralph Emerson, LL.B.; judge; b. Kelligrews, Nfld. 5 May 1930; s. late Frank F. and late Hazel (Sheppard) F.; e. St. Alban's Sch. Kelligrews, Nfld; Mem. Univ. Coll. St. John's; Dalhousie Univ. LL.B. 1953; m. Cynthia K. d. (late) Wilfred and Hazel Dawe, Whitbourne, Nfld. 18 Sept. 1956; children: Darroch R., Keith N., Cheryl H., Lisa L., Lida L.; JUDGE, SUPREME COURT OF NFLD. and Presiding Judge of Unified Family Court; called to Bar of Nfld. 1953; cr. Q.C. 1965; Chrmn., Local Improvement Dist. Conception Bay S.; Integrated Sch. Bd. Conception Bay S.; Freemason; Anglican; recreations: motoring, fishing, gardening; Home: Kelligrews, Nfld. A0A 2T0; Office: 21 King's Bridge Rd., St. John's, Nfld.

FAHLGREN, John Edwin Johnston; mining executive; b. Kenora, Ont. 19 July 1913; s. John Johnston and Theresia Anne (Forsstrom) F.; e. Kenora (Ont.) Pub. and High Schs.; Shaw Schs. Ltd., Toronto, Higher Accountancy; m. Helen Amethyst, d. Arthur M. Woodside, Port Arthur, Ont., 11 June 1941; children: John Arthur, Charles Edwin, Peter Thomas, Susan Margaret, Douglas Ian; COMMISSIONER, CHRM., ROYAL COMMISSION ON

THE NORTHERN ENVIRONMENT, ONT; Kenora Sales Division, Kenora Paper Mills Ltd. and Keewatin Lumber Co., 1927-34; Credit Mgr. and Internal Auditor, Starratt Airways & Transportation Ltd., Hudson, Ont., 1935-36; joined Cochenour Willans as Acct. and Office Mgr., 1936-49; Asst. Mgr. 1950; Mgr. 1954; Gen. Mgr. and Asst. to Pres. 1959; Vice Pres. 1960; Pres. 1965; N.P., in and for the Distr. of Kenora; Chrmn., Bi-Munic. Council Comte. Redlake/Balmerton; Commr. (for taking affidavits); Past Pres., P. Cons. Assn., Kenora Riding and Fed. Kenora — Rainy River; Past. Chrmn. and Trustee, Improvement Dist. of Balmertown; Past. Dir., Ont. Chamber Comm.; Dir. and Past Chrmn., Margaret Cochenour Mem. Hosp.; Pres. (twice), Red Lake Dist. Chamber Comm.; Past Chrmn., Red Lake Dist. High Sch.; mem. Bd. of Govs., Lakehead Univ.; Council of Regents, Colls. of Applied Arts and Technol. — Ont.; served as Lt. with Candn. Rangers No. 25 Co., Candn. Army in N. Can.; named Trade & Comm. Man of Month; Town of Red Lake Man of Yr.; Presentation, Chamber Comm., 1963; Assoc., Candn. Inst. Mining & Metall.; mem. Prospectors & Developers Assn.; Freemason (P.M., P.D.D.G.M.); P. Conservative; Lutheran; recreations: hunting, fishing, sailing, music, reading; Clubs: N.S. Order of Good Time; Gyro Internat.; Home: Cochenour Cres., Cochenour, Ont. P0V 1L0; Office: (Box 10), Cochenour, Ont. P0V 1L0

FAHRNI, Walter Harrison, M.D., M.Ch.Orth. (Liverpool 1947), F.R.C.S. (Edin. 1945), F.R.C.S. (Can. 1949), F.R.S.M.; b. Gladstone, Man., 9 May 1916; s. Judge Stanley Harrison and Edith Josephine (Minaker) F.; e. Univ. of Manitoba 1933-39; m. Lana, d. of Yim Quong Lau, Hong Kong; children: Ross Harrison, Josephine Anne, Philip Grant, Jennifer Jean; Asst. in Orthopedics, Univ. of B. C. Med. Sch.; mem., Attending Staff, Vancouver Gen. Hosp. and Vancouver Children's Hosp.; served in 2nd World War 1941-46, Capt., R.C.A.M.C.; author: "Backache: Assessment and Treatment"; mem.; Candn. Med. Assn.; Candn. Orthopaedic Assn.; N. Pacific Orthopaedic Assn.; Protestant; Home: 1309 Tyrol Rd.W., Vancouver, B.C. V7S 2L5; Office: 750 W. Broadway, Vancouver, B. C. V5Z 1H1

FAIR, James Milton, C.A.; agricultural executive; b. Lloydminster, Alta. 14 Apl. 1934; s. James and Evelyn (Warren) F.; e. Paradise Valley and Edmonton, Alta.; C.A. 1958; various courses computer programming and analysis; Participant, Duke of Edinburgh's Study Conf. on Labour-Mang. Relations 1974; Harvard Univ. Advanced Mang. Program, M.A. 1981; m. Joyce d. G. Stanley Dennis, Meeting Creek, Alta. 4 Aug. 1956; children: Dennis, Donna; CHIEF EXTVE. OFFR., SASK. WHEAT POOL 1981- ; Dir. CSP Foods Ltd.; Pacific Elevators Ltd.; Western Pool Terminals Ltd.; XCAN Grain Ltd.; Prince Rupert Grain Ltd.; mem. Pub. Issues Comte. Credit Union Central Sask.; joined Audit Dept. Govt. Alta. after high sch. grad.; participated devel. computer facility Govt. Alta. 1959, Sr. Systems Analyst to 1965; Systems Mgr. Sask. Wheat Pool 1965, Asst. Treas. Systems & Electronic Data Processing 1966, Corporate Treas. 1970, Dir. of Adm. & Depy. Gen. Mgr. 1976, Gen. Mgr.-Operations 1979; Past mem. Sask. Science Council; Co-operative Securities Bd. Govt. Sask.; Loans Comte. Sherwood Credit Union Regina; Adm. Comte. Candn. Co-operative Implements Ltd.; mem. Inst. C.A.'s Alta.; Inst. C.A.'s Sask. (Past Chrmn. Disciplinary Comte.); Gideons Internat. (Past Secy. & Pres. Local Camp); Baptist; recreations: running, physical fitness; Club: Rotary; Home: 2650 Thornicroft Bay, Regina, Sask. S4V 0T8; Office: 2625 Victoria Ave., Regina, Sask. S4P 2Y6.

FAIRBAIRN, Harold Williams, B.Sc., A.M., Ph.D., F.G.S.A., F.M.S.A.; university professor; b. Ottawa, Ont.; 10 July 1906; s. Arthur Edwin and Maria (Spratt) F.; e. Lisgar Coll. Inst., Ottawa, 1919-24; Queen's Univ., B.Sc. (Geol. & Mineralogy) 1929; Univ. of Wisc., grad work 1929-30; Harvard Univ., A.M. 1931, Ph.D. (Geol.)

1932; Innsbruck Univ. (Royal Soc. Can. Fellowship), 1932-34; m. Sheila May, d. late W. P. M. Sargent, 18 April 1939; children: Ann, Patrick, Elspeth, Neil; PROF. OF GEOL., MASS. INST. OF TECHNOL., since 1955, Prof. Emeritus 1972- ; Instr. in Mineralogy, Queen's Univ., 1934-37; joined present Inst. as Asst. Prof. of Geol., 1937-43; Assoc. Prof. 1943-55; Visiting Prof. of Physics 1942-45; Visiting Prof. of Geol., Harvard Univ., 1952; Manhattan Project 1944; Field Surveys (Geol.) 1926-42; Geol. Survey Can., Ont. and Que. Depts. of Mines; attended Internat. Geol. Congresses in Moscow 1937, London, 1948, Algiers 1952, Sydney 1976; author, "Structural Petrology of Deformed Rocks", 1949; other writings incl. numerous short research publs. concerned with geol. mapping, petrofabric analysis, analytical standards, geochronology by radiometric methods; mem., Am. Acad. Arts & Sciences; Protestant; recreations: chamber music, ornithology, medieval architecture; Home: 27 Marcia Rd., Watertown, Mass. 02172

FAIRCLOUGH, Hon. Ellen Louks (Mrs. Gordon Fairclough), P.C. (Can.) 1957, OC, F.C.A., L.L.D; b. Hamilton, Ont., 28 Jan. 1905; d. Norman Ellsworth and Nellie Bell (Louks) Cook; e. Primary and Secondary Schs., Hamilton, Ont., m. David Henry Gordon Fairclough, Hamilton, Ont., 28 Jan. 1931; one. s., Howard Gordon; Chrmn., Hamilton Hydro Electric Comn.; started own acctg. practice in 1935; Life mem., Gen. Accts. Assn. of Can.; Past Pres., Zonta Club of Hamilton; Past Dist. Gov., Zonta Internat.; Past Dom. Secy., U.E.L. Assn.; Past Offr., Prov. and Nat. Chapter, I.O.D.E.; former Vice-Pres. of Young Conservatives of Ont.; served five years on Hamilton City Council as Alderman for four yrs. and Controller for one yr.; def. cand. in Fed. gen. el. June 1949 (def. by Hon. Colin Gibson); 1st el. to H. of C. in by-el. for Hamilton W., 15 May 1950; def. g.e. 1963; Secy. of State, 1957-58; Min. of Citizenship and Immigration, 1958-62; Postmaster-Gen., Aug. 1962 — Apr. 1963; Advisory mem., Candn. Del. to U.N. 1950; del. to Conf. of Parliamentarians from NATO countries, Paris, 1955; Ambassador Extraordinary to Argentina for inauguration of President (1958); apptd. Secy., Hamilton Trust & Savings Corp., Sept. 1963-77 (amalgamated with Canada Permanent Trust); Past Internat. Treas., Zonta Internat. 1972-76; Hon. Treas. and Dir. Chedake-McMaster Medical Centre Found.; Bd. of Gov. Junior Achievement of Hamilton; Coronation Medal, 1953; Centennial Medal, 1967; Jubilee Medal, 1977; among 25 women receiving honours in Ontario for outstanding contributions, 1975; Mem., Hamilton Chamber of Comm.; Bd. of Candn. Council of Christian and Jews; Patron, Huguenot Soc. of Can.; Anglican; Home: 25 Stanley Ave., Hamilton, Ont. L8P 2K9; Office: Hamilton Hydro Electric Comn., 55 John St. N., Hamilton, Ont. L8N 3E4

FAIRFIELD, Robert C., B.Arch., F.R.A.I.C., A.R.I.B.A.; architect; b. St. Catharines, Ont., 31 July 1918; s. Dorothy (Goodman) and late Herbert G.; e. St. Catharines Coll. Inst. 1932-37; Univ. of Toronto, B.Arch. (Hons.); awarded Toronto Arch. Guild Gold Medal for design 1943; m. Joan Mowatt, d. Dr. E. A. Corbett, Toronto, Ont., 22 June 1946; children: Lesley Rae, Michael Stephen, Diana Margaret, Anthony Edward William; commenced practice in Toronto 1945; Massey Gold Medal (with C.F.T. Rounthwaite) for Stratford Festival Theatre, Stratford, Ont. 1958; Partner, Fairfield-Dubois 1963-1975; Massey Medals (with Macy DuBois) for Art Centre, Central Tech. Sch. and Ceterg Office Bldg., Toronto, 1963-67; Hon. Mention, Sao Paulo Brazil Biennial Awards for Arch. 1965; Awards of Excellence from Nat. Concrete Producers Assn.; Ont. Masons Design Council; and Ont. Assn. Archs.; finalist, Amsterdam City Hall Competition (from 803 world entries); other comns. incl. Prov. of Ont. Pavilion and Brewers Assn. of Can. Pavilion, Expo '67; Candn. Ambassador's Residence, Ankara, Turkey; Festival Theatre, Ithaca, N.Y.; New Coll., Univ. of Toronto; Centennial Bldg. for science and adm., Lakehead Univ.;

Residential Coll., Trent Univ.; Albert Campbell Lib., Scarborough, Ont.; design consultant for Kenyon Coll. Theatre, Cultural Centre Red Deer, Alta. and Great Lakes Shakespeare Festival Theatre, Cleveland, Ohio; served in R. N. Fleet Air Arm 1943-45; mem. Bd. Trustees Art Gallery of Ont. 1972-76; recreations: skiing, sailing, painting; Clubs: Reef Boat; Craigleith Ski; Home: R.R. 1, Thornbury, Ont. N0H 2P0

FAIRLEY, Albert L., Jr., B.S.; retired industrialist; b. Jackson, Miss., 28 Dec. 1913; s. Albert Langley and Alethe (Vardaman) F.; e. Phillips High Sch., Birmingham, Ala. (1930); Birmingham-Southern Coll., Birmingham, Ala., B.S. 1934; Johns Hopkins Univ. (Post Grad. work in Geol.) 1935; m. Claire Elizabeth, d. James Barr Haines III, Sewickley, Pa., 20 Aug. 1949; Dir. Canadian Imperial Bank Commerce; Sun Life Assnce. Co. Canada; Sun Life of Canada (U.S.); Trustee, Southern Research Inst., Birmingham Ala.; Edward Norton Business Centre, Birmingham Southern Coll.; Geol. & Foundation Engr., Tennessee Val. Auth., 1935-37; Asst. Geol., Tennessee Coal Iron & Rail. Div., U.S. Steel Corp. at Birmingham, Ala., 1937-41; Asst. Depy. Dir. of Steel Div., U.S. War Prod. Bd., 1941-43; engaged in various Operating and Extve. positions with the Shenango Furnace Co. and subsidiary organizations, Pittsburgh, Pa.; Vice-Pres. and Dir., Shenango Furnace Co., Snyder Mining Co., Lucerne Coke Co., May 1946 — Aug. 1958; apptd. Dir. and Extve. Vice-Pres. of Dom. Steel and Coal Corp. Ltd., Montreal, Que. 1958, and el. Pres. and Dir. 1959-64; Pres., Hollinger Mines Ltd. 1964-78 (ret.); served in 2nd World War with U.S.A.F.; enlisted in 1943 as a Pte., and discharged with rank of Capt., 1946; awarded Letter and Ribbon of Commendation; Emeritus mem., Am. Iron & Steel Inst.; Am. Inst. Mining & Metall. Engrs.; Alpha Tau Omega; Elder, 1st PresbyterianChurch, Birmingham; recreations: swimming, tennis, hunting, fishing; Clubs: Mount Royal; Downtown; The Club, Mountain Brook and Birmingham Country Club (all in Birmingham, Ala.); Allegheny Country (Sewickley); Duquesne (Pittsburgh); Birmingham Country (Ala.); The Toronto (Ont.); York; Home: 3 Ridge Dr., Birmingham, Alabama 35213

FAIRLEY, Barker, F.R.S.C.; professor (emeritus); b. Barnsley, Yorks, Eng., 21 May 1887; s. Barker and Charlotte F.; e. Univ. of Leeds, Eng.; Univ. of Jena; m. Margaret Adele Keeling, Bradford, Yorks, 1914; one s. and two d.; Lektor in Eng., Univ. of Jena, 1907-10; Lect. in German, Univ. of Alberta, Edmonton, 1910-1915; Prof. of German, Univ. of Toronto, 1915-32; Prof. of German and Head of Dept. Victoria Univ., Manchester, Eng., 1932-36; Prof. of German, Univ. Coll. Univ. of Toronto, 1936-57; author of "Charles M. Doughty", 1927, "Goethe as Revealed in His Poetry", 1932; "A Study of Goethe", 1947, "Goethe's Faust, Six Essays", 1953; Heinrich Heine, An "Interpretation", 1954; "Wilhelm Raabe, an introduction to his Novels", 1961; Goethe's "Faust", translated, 1970; Address: University College, Toronto, Ont.

FAIRWEATHER, Rev. Eugene Rathbone, M.A., B.D., S.T.M., Th.D. (Ang.); D.D., F.R.S.C.; b. Ottawa, Ont., 2 Nov. 1920; s. Ernest Eugene and Lulu (Rathbone) F.; e. Mt. Royal High Sch., Montreal, P. Q.; McGill Univ., B.A. 1941; Univ. of Toronto, M.A. 1943; Trinity Coll., Toronto, Ont., B.D. 1945; Union Theol. Semy., S.T.M. 1948, Th.D. 1949; Hon. D.D. McGill Univ., 1971, Huron Coll. 1973, Univ. of King's Coll. 1973; KEBLE PROF. OF DIVINITY, TRINITY COLLEGE Toronto, 1964- ; mem., World Faith & Order Comm., World Council of Chs., 1960-75; Editor, "Canadian Journal of Theology", 1960-70; Bishop Paddock Lect., General Theol. Semy., 1955-56; Visiting Lect., St. Augustine's Coll., Canterbury, 1955; o. Deacon 1943 and Priest 1944; Asst. Curate, St. Matthew's Ch., Toronto, Ont., 1943-47; Fellow and Tutor in Divinity, Trinity Coll., 1944-47; Asst., Cath. of St. John the Divine, New York, 1948-49; Assoc. Prof. of Dogmatic Theol. and Ethics, Trinity Coll., Toronto, 1949-64; Ang. Del. — Observer, Vatican Council II, 1964-65; Examining Chaplain to Bishop of Toronto since 1965; Canon of St. James Cathedral, Toronto, 1969- ; co-author of "Episcopacy and Reunion", 1953; author: "Episcopacy Re-Asserted", 1955; contrib. to "Early Christian Fathers", 1953; Editor, "A Scholastic Miscellany", 1956; author: "The Meaning and Message of Lent", 1962; co-author: "The Voice of the Church' , 1962; Editor, "The Anglican Congress" 1963; "Oxford movement" 1964; co-ed., "The Right to Birth", 1976; articles in various religious journs.; Hale mem. Lectr., Seabury-Western Theol. Semy. 1963; Du Bose Lectr., Univ. of the South, 1963; Keeler mem. Lectr., Univ. of Minnesota, 1968; mem., Candn. Soc. of Biblical Studies (Pres., 1954-55); Pres., Candn. Theol. Soc., 1957-58; mem. Am. Theol. Soc. (Pres. 1973-74); Cdn. Soc. of Patristic Studies (Hon. Pres. 1977-79); recreations: music, swimming, travel; Club: Athenaeum, (London); Address: Trinity College, Hoskin Ave., Toronto,Ont.

FAIRWEATHER, Robert Gordon Lee, O.C., Q.C., B.C.L.; b. Rothesay, N.B., 27 March 1923; s. Jack Hall Alliger Lee and Agnes Charlotte (Mackeen) F.; e. Rothesay (N.B.) Coll. Sch.; Osgoode Hall Law Sch., Toronto, Ont.; Univ. of New Brunswick Law Sch., B.C.L. 1949; m. Nancy Elizabeth, d. late Cyril Hurd Broughall, 1 June 1946; children: Michael Gordon, Wendy Elizabeth, Hugh Alexander; Chief Comm. of Can. Human Rights Comm., 1977; Board of Trustees; Lester B. Pearson Coll. of the Pacific; called to Bar of N.B., June 1949; cr. Q.C. Nov. 1958; practised law with firm of McKelvey, Macaulay, Machum & Fairweather, Saint John, N.B.; served in R.C.N.V.R. 1941-45; rank Lt.-Commandr. (S); 1st el. to N.B. Leg. for Kings 1952; re-el. 1956-60; Atty-Gen. N.B. 1958-60; el. to H. of C. for Royal, g.e. June 1962; re-el. 1963, 65 and for Fundy-Royal 1968, 1972 and 1974; N.B. Barristers Assn.; Candn. Bar Assn.; Anglican; Office: 257 Slater St., 4th Fl., Ottawa, Ont. K1A 1E1

FALCONER, Ian A.; investment dealer; b. Vancouver, B.C., 2 May 1930; s. Alec Pirie and Marion (MacKinnon) F.; m. June Gordenia Matheson, 29 Apl. 1963; 3 children: SR. VICE PRES., DIR. AND MEM. EXEC COMM., MID-LAND DOHERTY LTD.; Chrmn. and Gov., Vancouver Stock Exchange; Dir., Merrit Publishing Ltd.; Irwco Resources Ltd.; P. Conservative; Protestant; recreations: sailing, jogging, handball, tennis; Club: Hollyburn Country; Home: 885 Pyrford Rd., W. Vancouver, B.C. V7S 2A2; Office: 595 Burrard St., Vancouver, B.C.

FALLIS (Albert) Murray, Ph.D., F.R.S.C.; biologist; b. Minto Twp., Ont., 2 Jan. 1907; s. William Robert and Melissa May (Millen) F.; e. Harriston (Ont.) High Sch.; Toronto Normal Sch., 1925-26; Univ. of Toronto, B.A. 1932 and Ph.D. 1937; m. Ada Ruth, d. Hon. Hewitt Bostock (former Speaker of Senate) of Monte Creek, B.C., 21 Sept. 1938; children: Alexander Graham, Hugh Murray, Bruce William; Prof. and Head of Parasitology, Sch. of Hygiene, Univ. of Toronto, 1948-72; Sch. Teacher, 1926-28; Research Fellow, Ont. Research Foundation, 1932-47; Lectr. in Parasitol., Sch. of Hygiene, Univ. of Toronto, 1938-43; Assoc. Prof., 1944-48; Dir., Dept. of Parasitology, Ont. Research Foundation, 1947-66; Conslt. for W.H.O. in Ghana, 1967 and 1971; Assoc. Dean, Div. IV, Sch. of Grad. Studies, Univ. of Toronto, 1967-70; mem., Am. Soc. of Parasitol, (Vice Pres. 1970, Pres. 1979); Am. Soc. of Tropical Med.; emeritus mem., Wilflife Disease Assoc.; hon. mem. Can. Soc. Zoologists; Royal Candn. Inst. (Hon. Ed. 1949-54; Pres., 1954-55); mem. Gov. Council, Univ. of Toronto 1972-73; Erskine Fellow, Univ. of Canterbury Jan. — Apl. 1975; Emeritus Prof. July 1975; Vis. Prof. Memorial Univ. of Nfld., Jan.-Mar. 1978; Freemason (P.M.); Un. Church; Home: RR #1, Caledon East, Ontario L0N 1E0

FALLIS, Fred B., B.A., M.D.; medical educator; b. Vancouver, B.C., 28 March 1921; s. Rev. (Lt. Col.) George Oliver and Mabel Lavinia (Hockin) F.; e. Univ. of Toronto,

B.A. 1942, M.D. 1953; m. Lois Irene, d. late William Henry Bouck, 27 Dec. 1946; children: Mary Louise, George, William, Fred Jr., Lois Anne, Joan Elizabeth; DIR. OF CONTINUING EDUCATION, FACULTY OF MEDICINE, AND PROF. AND CHRMN., DEPT. OF FAMILY AND COMMUNITY MEDICINE, UNIV. OF TORONTO since 1970 and Family Physician-in-Chief, Toronto Gen. Hosp. since 1970; Staff Phys., Med. O.P.D., Toronto Gen. Hosp. and V.D. Clinic 1954, Head, Gen. Practice Clinic, 1966-70; Staff Phys., Addiction Research Foundation, 1954-66; joined the Univ. as Clin. Teacher and Assoc., Dept. of Med., 1966-69; Phys., Bella Coola Gen. Hosp. B.C., 1960, 1963; private practice N. Toronto 1954-70; served with RCAF as Pilot 1941-45; 3rd Secy., Dept. of External Affairs, 1945-47; mem. Dept. of Nat. Health & Welfare Task Force 1971, Comte. on Manpower; Med. Adv. Bd., Toronto Rehabilitation Centre; author of numerous articles in various learned and prof. journs.; Fellow, Coll. Family Phys. Can. (Past Pres.); mem.-at-large Nat. Extve. 1967-68; Chrmn. Nat. Comte. Patterns of Practice & Health Care Delivery 1968-74; Sustaining Fund Comte. 1977-80; Endowment and Awards Cmt. 1980; Pres., N. Toronto Med. Soc. 1967-68; mem. Soc. Teachers Family Med.; former Council mem. Ont. Med. Assn., Toronto Acad. Med. and Family Service Assn.; Trustee, Trinity Un. Ch.; Ed. "Family Practice Manual" 1974; recreations: tree farming, photography, travel; Club: Univ. of Toronto Faculty; Home: Box 67, Bond Head, Ont. L0G 1B0; Office: Room 935, 76 Grenville St., Toronto, Ont. M5S 1B2

FANJOY, Hon. Harold Newton,M.L.A.; politician; b. Saint John, N.B. 1 Nov. 1939; s. Isaac Newton and Muriel Gertrude (Seely) F.; e. Saint John Vocational Sch.; N.B. Inst. of Technol. Accounting Degree; m. Marilyn Dorothy d. Frederick F. Bishop 1 Aug. 1964; two s. Leslie Bennett, Gregory Bishop; MIN. OF SUPPLY AND SERVICES, N.B. 1976- ; el. M.L.A. for Kings Centre prov. g.e. 1974, re-el. 1978; Chrmn. Standing Comte. on Pub. Accounts 1974-75 and of Select Comte. on Rural Life & Land Use; assoc. with invest. firm Pitfield, MacKay, Ross & Co. Ltd. Saint John; Fredericton Hotel Co.; Algonquin Properties Ltd.; former Dir. Fundy-Royal P. Cons. Assn.; mem. and former Treas. Westfield Un. Ch.; Past Dist. Depy. Commr. Boy Scouts Can. Kennebecasis Dist.; served Un. Way Saint John; mem. St. George's Soc.; Hon. mem. Royal Candn. Legion; Freemason; Shriner; P. Conservative; Protestant; Clubs: Kiwanis; Fredericton Golf; Westfield Golf & Country; Address: (P.O. Box 150) Grand Bay, N.B. E0G 1W0;

FARANO, Ronald J., Q.C., B.Com., LL.B.; b. Toronto, Ont., 12 Aug. 1931; s. Vincent and Rose (Lomore) F.; e. De La Salle Oaklands, Toronto, 1949; Univ. of Toronto, B.Com., 1953; Osgoode Hall Law Sch., LL.B. 1957; m. Joan, d. Raymond Engholm, 20 May 1959; children: Gregory, Lisa, Christopher; PARTNER, FARANO, GREEN AND BRANS since 1974; Dir., Seagull Resources Inc.; Dir., Sec., Can. Fed. of Independent Business; chrmn. of Bd.; Italian Cham. of Comm. Toronto (Dir. 1963- 64); read law with Borden, Elliot, Kelley & Palmer; called to Bar of Ont. 1957; cr. Q.C. 1970; in private practice 1957-61; with Goodman & Carr 1961-66; Davies, Ward & Beck 1966-70; mem., Research Staff, Carter Royal Comn. on Taxation and Smith Comn. on Taxation (Ont.), 1963; served with C.O.T.C. summer 1950; author of "Farano's Tax Cases", 1964, 1966, 1968, and 1981; "Handbook on the Business Corporations Act", 1971; "Tax Commentary", Vol. 1, 1977, Vol. 2, 1979; Chr. of Bd., Italian Chamber of Comm. Toronto (Dir. 1963 and 1964); mem., Candn. Bar Assn.; Foundation for Legal Research; Phi Delta Phi; R. Catholic; recreations: skiing, sailing, tennis; Clubs: Albany; R.C.Y.C.; Alpine Ski; Home: 23 Forest View Rd., Etobicoke, Ont. M9C 1W8; Office: 2 St. Clair Ave. E., Suite 1202, Toronto, Ont. M4T 2T5

FARBER, Emmanuel, M.D., Ph.D., F.R.S.C., F.R.C.S.(c); university professor; b. Toronto, Ont., 19 Oct. 1918; s. Morris and Mary (Madorsky) F.; e. Univ. of Toronto, M.D. 1942; Univ. of Cal., Ph.D. (Biochem.) 1949; m. Ruth Wilma, d. late Isaac Diamond, 16 Apl. 1942; one d., Naomi Beth; PROF. AND CHRMN., DEPT. OF PATHOL., UNIV. OF TORONTO since 1975; mem. Surg. Gen.'s Adv. Comte. on Smoking & Health, 1962-64; Chrmn., Pathol. "B" Study Sec., Nat. Insts. of Health, 1964-67; Chrm. Biochem. Carcinogen Rev. Panel, Am. Cancer Soc., 1972-75; mem. Cancer Research Training Grants Comte., Nat. Cancer Inst. 1971-72; mem. Adv. Council, Nat. Cancer Inst., 1967-71; mem. Grants Rev. Panels, Nat. Cancer Inst. Can. 1975-79; mem. Chem. Pathol. Study Sec., Nat. Inst. of Health, 1978-82; served with R.C.A.M.C. 1943-46; rank Capt. on discharge; rec'd Am. Cancer Soc. Fellowship in Cancer Research 1947-50 and Scholarship in Cancer Research 1951-55; Am. Cancer Soc. Research Professorship in Cancer Research, 1959-61, 1970-75; Second Annual Parke-Davis Award in Exper. Pathol., 1958; Fourth Annual Bertha Goldblatt Teplitz Mem. Award, 1961; Samuel R. Noble Foundation Award, 1976; elected Fellow, Royal Soc. of Can., 1980; Assoc. Ed., "Cancer Research"; mem. Ed. Bd., "Am. Journal Pathology"; "Int. Journal/Cancer"; Assoc. Mang. Ed. "Chemico-biological Interactions"; contrib. to nat science journs.; mem., Am. Assn. Advanc. Science; Am. Assn. Cancer Research (Bd. Dir. 1964-67, 1970-73, Pres. 1972-73); American Assn. Pathols. & Bacteriols.; Am. Chem. Soc.; Am. Soc. Biol. Chems.; Am. Soc. Cell Biol.; Am. Soc. Exper. Pathol. (Pres. 1973-74); Biochem. Soc.; Histochem. Soc. (Pres. 1966-67); Internat. Acad. Pathol.; N.Y. Acad. Sciences; Soc. Exper. Biol & Med.; Sigma Xi; Hebrew; Home: 23 Tranby Ave., Toronto, Ont. M5R 1N4

FARGEY, Harold T., B.A.Sc.; company executive; b. Govan, Sask., 26 April 1919; s. Thomas and Hilda Emily (Gimby) F.; e. Pub. and High Schs., Vancouver, B.C.; Univ. of British Columbia, B.A.Sc. (Chem. Engn.) 1942; m. Susan Mona, d. late Albert Asselstine, 15 July 1944; children: Susan Elizabeth, Nancy Louise; EXTVE. VICE PRES. — MARKETING, COMINCO LTD.; Dir., The Canada Metal Co. Ltd.; mem., Candn. Inst. Mining & Metall.; Liberal; Protestant; recreations: swimming, boating, golf; Club: Engineers; Home: 2876 West 49th Ave., Vancouver, B.C. V6N 3S8; Office: 200 Granville Sq., Vancouver, B.C.

FARLEY, James M., LL.B., M.A.; b. Guelph, Ont., 15 Oct. 1940; s. George Albert and Charlotte M. (Thomson) F.; e. Univ. of W. Ont., B.A. 1962; Oxford Univ., B.A. (Juris.) 1964, M.A. 1968; Univ. of Toronto, LL.B. 1966; Osgoode Hall Law School, 1968; m. Sandra Ann, d. L. Douglas Maxwell, Oakville, Ont., 16 July 1966; children: Maxwell Montague George, Michael Douglas Thomson; PARTNER PERRY, FARLEY, & ONYSCHUK since 1974; Chmn. of Bd. of Dir., Belarus Equipment of Can. Ltd.; Stan-Canada Machinery Ltd.; Dir. Candn. Patent Scaffolding Co., Ltd.; Candn-Reserve Oil & Gas Ltd.; Dir., Getty Mines, Ltd.; General Hydrocarbons Ltd.; Lallemand Inc.; Onakawana Development Ltd.; Continental Trust Co.; Belarus Equipment of Canada Ltd.; Stan-Canada Machinery Ltd.; called to Bar of Ont. 1968; Assoc. Lawyer, Thomson, Rogers 1968-70, Partner 1970-74; Secy., Ont. Rhodes Scholarship Selection Comte.; Govnr., George Brown Coll. (Toronto); author of "Corporations" in Canadian Encyclopedic Digest; Club: University; Home: 234 Cardinal Dr., Oakville, Ont. L6J 4P2; Office: (P.O. Box 451) Toronto-Dominion Centre, Toronto, Ont. M5K 1M5

FARLINGER, William Alexander, B.Com., F.C.A.; b. Toronto, Ont. 21 Nov. 1929; s. Alexander William and Allie Margaret (Purves) F.; e. Lawrence Park Collegiate, Toronto, 1947; Univ. of Toronto (Victoria Coll.) B.Com. 1951; C.A. 1954; m. Shirley Ruth Tabb 14 July 1951; children: Brian Allan, William Craig, Leonard Tabb, David

Lloyd, Pamela Ruth (Davenport); CHRM. OF MANAGEMENT COMM., CLARKSON GORDON; joined Clarkson Gordon 1951; mem. Inst. Chart. Accts. Ont. 1954 (Fellow 1976); Phi Kappa Sigma (Pres. 1951); Gov., Roy. Candn. Golf Assn.; Chmn., Candn. Open Golf Championship; Protestant; recreations: skiing, squash, golf, fishing; Clubs: Toronto; University; York; Granite; Caughnawana Fishing & Hunting; Lambton; Saint James's; Royal Montreal Golf; Home: 11 Thornwood Road, Toronto, Ont. M4W 2R8; Office: P.O. Box 251, Toronto-Dominion Centre, Toronto, Ont. M5K 1J7

FARMER, M. Alban, Q.C., B.A., LL.B., LL.D.; b. Kinkora, P.E.I., 27 Sept. 1901; s. Michael and Margaret (Keefe) F.; e. St. Dunstan's Univ., B.A. 1925; Dalhousie Univ., LL.B. 1928; m. Mary Dorothea, d. Dr. W. J. P. MacMillan, 12 Oct. 1932; children: William, Mary Honora (Mrs. Bertrand Plamondon) Michael Alban, Elinor C. (Mrs. Ronald V. Dalzell); Barrister and Solicitor, Farmer, and Farmer; Charlottetown City Council, 1946-52; el. to Prov. Leg., Sept. 1959; re-el., g.e. 1962 and g.e. 1966; Atty. Gen. and Prov. Treas., P.E.I., 1963-66; Bd. of Mang., Charlottetown Hosp.; Chrm. Bd. of Trustees, Maritime Hosp. Service Assn.; Blue Cross; called to the Bar of P.E.I. 1930; cr. Q.C., 1953; mem. Candn. Bar Assn.; P.E.I. Law Soc.; K. of C. (Past State Depy.); P. Conservative; R. Catholic; Home: 25 Rochford Square, Charlottetown, P.E.I.; Office: 83 Queen St., Charlottetown, P.E.I.

FARMILO, Alfred William, M.Sc.; executive; b. Edmonton, Alta., 27 Sept. 1916; s. Alfred, O.B.E. and Ada Louise (Plowman) F.; e. Univ. of Alta., B.Sc. 1941; Univ. of Oklahoma, M.Sc. 1943; m. Grace Maxine, d. James A. McCollum, 1 Oct. 1943; children: Alfred James Farmilo, Carolyn Ann Canny, Mary Margaret Jackson; Chmn. and Dir., Westmin Resources Ltd., Great Lakes Power Corp.; Dir., Brascan Ltd., Lacana Mining Corp., Brascade Holdings; Trustee, E. C. Manning Awards Found.; Geol., California Standard Co. Ltd. and Richmond Exploration, Venezuela 1943-51; Asst. Exploration Mgr., Canadian Fina; Chief Geol., Calvan Consolidated and Western Leaseholds Ltd.; Dir., Calvan Consolidated 1951-64; Vice-Pres., Supertest Petroleum Co. Ltd.; Supertest Investments and Petroleum Co. Ltd.; Pres., Supertest Petroleum Inc.; Vice-Pres. and Dir., Supertest U.K.; Chrmn. Bd., Magnorth Petroleum Ltd. 1964-72; Pres. Mikas Oil Co. Ltd. 1972; mem. Candn. Soc. Petroleum Geols; The Calgary Zoological Soc. (Alta.); Assn. Prof. Engrs., Geols. and Geophysicists; Sigma Xi; Adv. Council, Geology, U. of Oklahoma; Anglican; recreations: golf, lapidarian; Clubs: Glencoe; Earl Grey; Calgary Petroleum; Calgary Ranchmen's; Home: 4515 Coronation Dr. S.W., Calagary Alta. T2F 1M5; Office: Suite 1800, Bow Valley Sq., 255 Fifth Ave. S.W., Calgary, Alta. T2P 3G6

FARMILOE,Dorothy; author; b. Toronto, Ont. 1920; e. Univ. of Windsor M.A. (Eng.) 1969; author "The Lost Island" poetry 1966; "Poems for Apartment Dwellers" 1970; "Winter Orange Mood" 1972 poetry; "Blue is the Colour of Death" poetry 1973; "And Some in Fire" novel 1974; "Creative Communication" 1974, 2nd ed. 1977 textbook; "Elk Lake Diary Poems" 1976; "Adrenalin of Weather" poetry 1978; "How to Write a Better Anything", handbook for creative writers, 1979; "Words for my Weeping Daughter" poetry 1981; co-author "21 X 3" poetry 1967; Ed. "Contraverse" Anthology of Windsor Poets 1971; poems incl. various Candn., Am., Eng. and New Zealand mags.; rep. in 11 anthologies; featured on CBC radio "Anthology"; co-founder and former Ed. "Mainline" mag., "Sesame Press"; Founder and Dir. Windsor Creative Writing Club; founder and publisher the Elk Lake Explorer; rec'd Metrop. Soc. Prize for poem "Heritage" 1975; Can. Council Award 1977; mem. League of Candn. Poets; Writers' Union of Can.; Address: (P.O. Box 94) Elk Lake, Ont. P0J 1G0.

FARNON, Robert Joseph; musician; b. Toronto, Ont. 24 July 1917; from 1934 trumpeter with Toronto dance bands of Bus Browne, Stanley St. John, Bob Shuttleworth and others, also in CRBC (CBC) orchestras of Percy Faith and Geoffrey Waddington; mem. of Happy Gang 1937-43; arranged music for Percy Faith's choral groups and for orchestras of André Kostelanetz and Paul Whiteman; completed first symphony 1940 "Symphonic Suite", premiered by Toronto Symphony Orchestra 1941 and performed several occasions by Philadelphia Orchestra; second symphony "Ottawa" (1942) premiered by TSO 1943 on CBC "Concert Hour"; served overseas during World War II as Music Dir. "The Army Show" and also conducted Candn. band of Allied Expeditionary Forces on BBC; arranged music for various Eng. dance bands incl. Ted Heath and by 1950 had own BBC radio program; in late 1940's began recording commercially under own name and as choral arranger for Vera Lynn; also made several LPs with Queen's Hall Light Orchestra for Chappell & Co. Mood Music; conducted orchestras BBC radio series "Music All the Way" and "Farnon in Concert" mid 1960's; arranged and conducted music for recordings by many performers incl. Tony Bennett, Lena Horne, Peggy Lee, Frank Sinatra, Sarah Vaughan; composed scores "William Comes to Town" and "Spring in Park Lane" 1947, "Just William's Luck" 1948, "Elizabeth of Ladymead" 1949, "Captain Horatio Hornblower" and "Circle of Danger" 1951, "Maytime in Mayfair" 1952, "His Majesty O'Keefe" 1953, "Gentlemen Marry Brunettes" and "Let's Make Up" 1955, "The Little Hut" 1957, "The Sheriff of Fractured Jaw" 1958, "The Road to Hong Kong" 1962, "The Truth About Spring" 1965, "Shalako" 1968; other compositions incl. orchestral setting "A la claire fontaine", suite "Canadian Impressions", theme BBC TV series "Colditz" (Novello Award 1972), "How Beautiful is Night", "Jumping Bean", "Manhattan Playboy", "On the Sea Shore" (Novello Award 1960), "Peanut Polka", "Portrait of a Flirt", "A Star is Born", "Westminster Waltz" (Novello Award 1956); composed "Pleasure of Your Company" for Oscar Peterson, "Scherzo" trumpet and orchestra, "Rhapsody" violin and orchestra, "Prelude and Dance" harmonica and orchestra, "Saxophone Triparti"; appearances CBC TV "Music Makers" 1961, "The Music of Robert Farnon" 1970, 1975, 1976; shared concert with Vera Lynn Maple Leaf Gardens Toronto 1969; cited various bibliogs.; mem. CAPAC.

FARQUHAR, Gordon N., B.A., LL.B.; insurance executive; b. Sandy Spring, Md. 13 Nov. 1923; s. Arthur Douglas and Helen Thomas (Nesbitt) F.; e. Epis. High Sch. of Va.; Yale Univ. B.A. 1948; Univ. of Conn. Sch. of Law LL.B. 1954; Harvard Business Sch. Advanced Mang. Program 1972; m. H. Virginia d. Chester O. Fischer 6 Oct. 1951; two d. Jean, Ellen Brooke; CHRMN. AND PRES., THE EXCELSIOR LIFE INSURANCE CO. 1974- ; Chrmn. and Pres., Aetna Casualty Co. of Canada 1974- ; called to Bar of Conn. 1954; served with U.S. Army 1943-46, 1951-52, rank Capt.; mem. and Chrmn. Govt. Relations Comte.; Candn. Life & Health Ins. Assn.; Dir. Life Office Mang. Assn., Chrmn. Annual Conf. Program Comte. 1982; Trustee, Toronto Symphony; Clarke Inst. Psychiatry; Un. Way Greater Toronto; Past Pres. and Chrmn. Hartford Symphony Soc.; Former Trustee, Hartford Art Sch.; Phi Beta Kappa; Delta Kappa Epsilon; United Church; recreations: tennis, golf, platform tennis, cross-country skiing; Clubs: Toronto; Toronto Golf; Badminton & Racquet; American; Home: 350 Lonsdale Rd., Apt. 204, Toronto, Ont. M5P 1R6; Office: 20 Toronto St., Toronto, Ont. M5C 2C4.

FARQUHAR, Robin Hugh, M.A., Ph.D.; university administrator; b. Victoria, B.C. 1 Dec. 1938; s. Hugh Ernest and Jean (MacIntosh) F.; e. elem. and high schs. Victoria, B.C.; Univ. of B.C., B.A. 1960, M.A. 1964; Univ. of Chicago Ph.D. 1967; m. Frances Harriet d. late Gordon Gladstone Caswell 6 July 1963; three d. Francine Jean, Katherine Lynn, Susan Ann; PRESIDENT AND VICE CHANCELLOR, UNIV. OF WINNIPEG and Univ. Prof. 1981- ; Teaching Asst. in Eng. Univ. of B.C. 1960-62; Teacher, Counselor and Coach, Edward Milne Secondary Sch., Sooke, B.C. 1962-64; Staff Assoc. Midwest Adm. Center Univ. of Chicago 1964-66; Assoc. Dir. Univ. Council for Educ. Adm. 1966-69 (apptd. as Asst. Prof. Ohio State Univ. 1967), Depy. Dir. of Council 1969-71 (Assoc. Prof. of Univ. 1970); Chrmn. of Educ. Adm. and Assoc. Prof. Ont. Inst. for Studies in Educ., Assoc. Prof. Univ. of Toronto Grad. Dept. of Educ. Theory 1971-73, Asst. Dir. Ont. Inst. Studies in Educ. 1973-76, Prof. there and Univ. of Toronto 1974; Dean, Coll. of Educ. and Prof. Univ. of Sask. 1976-81; author "The Humanities in Preparing Educational Administrators" 1970; co-author "Preparing Educational Leaders for the Seventies" 1969; "Preparing Educational Leaders: A Review of Recent Literature" 1972; co-ed. "Social Science Content for Preparing Educational Leaders" 1973; "Educational Administration in Australia and Abroad: Issues and Challenges" 1975; "Canadian and Comparative Educational Administration" 1980; numerous articles, book chapters; Fellow, Commonwealth Council Educ. Adm.; recipient Edward L. Bernays Foundation Award 1968; served with RCN (Reserve); rank Lt.; mem. Candn. Soc. Study Educ. (Pres.); Commonwealth Council Educ. Adm. (Sr. Vice Pres.); Candn. Educ. Assn. (Dir.); Inter-Am. Soc. Educ. Adm. (Dir.); Nat. Acad. Sch. Extves. (Dir.); St. Andrew's Soc.; Beta Theta Pi; United Church; recreations: golf, curling, cross-country skiing; Clubs: Manitoba; Rotary; Home: 49 Oak St., Winnipeg, Man. R3M 3P6; Office: 515 Portage Ave., Winnipeg, Man. R3B 2E9.

FARQUHARSON, Andrew Gray, B.Sc.; company director; b. Dundas, Ont., 4 Oct. 1907; s. Alexander Lockhart and Jessie Elizabeth (Middleton) F.; e. Queen's Univ., B.Sc., 1930; m. Dora Kathleen Bogart, 20 Dec. 1932; children: Douglas Alexander, Mrs. Jane Elizabeth Burland; Ex. Pres. and Chief Extve. Offr., Texaco Canada Inc. Jan 1969 — Nov. 1972; Dir., Texaco Canada Inc.; Regent Refining Canada Ltd.; mem. of Staff of Queen's Univ., 1930-31; joined McColl-Frontenac Oil Co. Ltd. (predecessor Co.) as Lab. Inspr.; subsequently Operating Supv., Maintenance & Construction; Supt. Constr., Toronto Refinery; Asst. Mgr., Refining, 1952; el. a Dir., 1957; mem., Corp. Prof. Engrs. Que.; Engn. Inst. Can.; Freemason (33 degree; Shrine; Scottish Rite); United; recreations: hunting, fishing; Clubs: Mt. Stephen (Past Pres.); Mount Royal; Saint James's; Home: R.R. No. 1, Bainsville, Ont. K0C 1E0

FARQUHARSON, Gordon Mackay, Q.C., B.A.; b. Charlottetown, P.E.I., 12 July 1928; s. late Percy A. and Rachel L. (MacKay) F.; e. W. Kent Sch., Charlottetown; Lawrence Park Coll. Inst.; Toronto; Victoria Coll., Univ. of Toronto, B.A.; Osgoode Hall Law Sch.; m. June Vivienne, d. Harry V. Malabar, Toronto, Ont., 8 Sept. 1954; two s., two d.; m. 2ndly, Judy Lynne, d. George Bridges, St. Thomas, Ont., 10th Oct. 1980; PARTNER, LANG, MICHENER, CRANSTON, FARQUHARSON & WRIGHT; Dir. and Secy., GSW Ltd. — GSW Ltée; Dir., Showerlux Can. Ltd.; Candn. Appliance Manufacturing Co. Ltd.; Dir., Mony Life Insurance Co. of Canada; Valleydene Corp. Ltd.; read law with The Hon. Mr. Justice Willard Z. Estey; called to Bar of Ont. 1954; cr. Q.C. 1965; Pres., Eglinton Lib. Riding Assn. (Prov.) and of Eglinton (Fed.) 1962-67; Don Valley (Fed.) 1966-68; Convention Chrmn. for Mitchell Sharp 1968 Lib. Leadership Convention; Campaign Mgr. for Eglinton Lib. Cand. 1967; Liberal; Protestant; recreations: skiing, canoeing, sailing; Clubs: University; The Toronto; Craigleith Ski; Home: 245 Borden St., Toronto, Ont.; Office: Box 10, First Canadian Place, Toronto, Ont. M5X 1A2

FARR, David M.L., M.A., D.Phil.; b. Vancouver, B.C. 1922; s. A. Morice and Mary Norah (Marlatt) F.; e. Queen

Mary Sch. and Lord Byng High Sch. Vancouver; Univ. of B.C. B.A. 1944; Univ. of Toronto M.A. 1946; Oxford Univ. (New and Nuffield Colls.) D.Phil. 1952; m. Joan Rowena d. J. R. Villiers-Fisher, Victoria, B.C. 5 Sept. 1946; children: David Christopher John, Timothy Robin Wykeham, Jeremy Stuart Talbot; DIR., PATERSON CENTRE FOR INTERNATIONAL PROGRAMS, CARLETON UNIV., 1979- ; Prof. of History, Carleton Univ. since 1961; Lectr. in Hist. Dalhousie Univ. 1946-47; joined present Univ. 1947, Dean of Arts 1963-69; Visiting Lectr. and Assoc. Prof. Univ. of B.C. 1953, 1957-58; Visiting Assoc. Prof. Duke Univ. 1960; served with RCNVR 1944-45; author "The Colonial Office and Canada, 1867-1887" 1955; co-author "Two Democracies" 1963; "The Canadian Experience" 1969; Subj. Ed., History, "Carleton Library" series, 1962-69; Gen. Ed., 1970-72; articles and reviews various journs.; mem. Candn. Hist. Assn. (Eng. Lang. Secy. 1947-50, 1952-57; Pres. 1977-78); mem., Public Records Comte., 1960-67; Adv. Council on Public Records since 1967; Social Science Fed. Can. (Chrmn. Comte. on Publs. 1961-65; Council 1965-69, 1976-80); Candn. Inst. Internat. Affairs (Chrmn. Ottawa Br. 1973-75); Council Deans Arts & Sciences Ont. Univs. (Chrmn. 1967-68); Anglican; Home: 942 Echo Dr., Ottawa, Ont. K1S 5C9

FARRAR, Geoffrey D.;banker; b. Belfast, N. Ireland 9 Mar. 1935; e. Queen's Univ.; Univ. of W. Ont. Banking/Finance; m. Anne Louise 9 July 1962; children: Keith, Roger;PRESIDENT AND C.E.O. AND DIR., BARCLAYS BANK OF CANADA;Canadian Imperial Bank of Commerce 1955-66; Vice Pres. First National City Bank/Mercantile Bank of Canada 1966-75; Fellow, Inst. Candn. Bankers; Clubs: R.C.Y.C.; Cruising Sailors Sqdn. (mem. Comte.); Albany; Home: 312 Douglas Dr., Toronto, Ont. M4W 2C3; Office: 3505 Commerce Court W., Toronto, Ont. M5L 1G2.

FARRAR, John L., B.Sc., M.Sc., Ph.D.; university professor; b. Hamilton, Ont., 31 Dec. 1913; s. Robert Watson and Sarah Wilson (Laird) F.; e. Delta Coll. Inst., Hamilton, Ont.; Univ. of Toronto, B.Sc., (Forestry) 1936; Yale Univ., M.Sc. (Forestry) 1939; Ph.D. 1955; b. Betty Joan, d. Walter May, Woking, Eng., 12 Oct. 1946; PROF. OF FORESTRY, UNIV. OF TORONTO; engaged in general woods work with Canadian Internat. Paper Co., Three Rivers, Que., 1936-37; with Forestry Br., Fed. Govt., 1937-41 and 1945-56 (site classification, tree breeding, silvicultural characteristics of tree species); apptd. Prof. of Forestry, Univ. of Toronto 1956-79; Editor, "Canadian Journal of Forest Research" 1970-81; served in 2nd World War with R.C.A.F., 1941-45; Radar Offr. with R.A.F. in Middle East; mem., Candn. Inst. Forestry; Ont. Prof. Foresters Assn.; Candn. Bot. Assn.; Sigma Xi; Conservative; recreations: bridge, square dancing; Home: 167 Yonge Blvd., Toronto, Ont. M5M 3H3

FARRELL, John Hugh, B.Eng.; executive; b. Cape Breton, N.S. 10 Oct. 1936; e. Sydney Mines, N.S.; N.S. Tech. Coll., B.Eng. (Elect.) 1959; VICE PRES. — COMPUTER COMMUNICATIONS, BELL CANADA 1980- ; Dir., Nfld. Tel. Co. Ltd.; Dir., Bell Canada Int.; Chrmn. of Bd., Bell Communications Systems, Inc.; joined Bell Canada holding various positions engn. depts. Eastern and Montreal Areas 1959-64, Montreal Area Personnel Supvr. 1964, Staff Supvr.-Business Information Systems-Personnel 1965, Gen. Engr.-Customer Equipment Design 1968, Div. Outside Plant Engr. Central Area, Ottawa 1969, Gen. Engr. Systems Planning, Montreal 1971, Asst. Vice Pres.-Regulatory Matters 1972, Asst. Vice President Engn. — W. Region, Toronto 1974; Vice Pres. Regulatory Matters, Bell Canada 1975- ; Order Engrs. Que.; Assn. Prof. Engrs. Ont.; Past Pres. Montreal Brs. St. Francis Xavier Alumni 1965; N.S. Tech. Coll. Alumni 1967; Clubs: Engineer's Club of Toronto; St. James' Club of Montreal; Le Cercle Universit. d'Ottawa; Canadian; Home: 2429 Georgina Dr., Ottawa, Ont. K2B 7N1; Office: 160 Elgin St. F11, Ottawa, Ont. K1G 3J4

FARRELL, Mark, B.Comm., C.A.; retired publisher; b. Montreal, Que., 22 Jan. 1913; s. Gerald William and Eileen (O'Meara) F.; e. Selwyn House Sch., Montreal, P.Q.; Ampleforth Coll., U.K.; McGill Univ., B. Com. 1934, C.A. 1937; m. Joanna Wright, 1939; one d. Sarah Vanessa; m. 2ndly, Florence Wall, 1952; two d. Fiona, Willa; Vice Pres., Southam Press, and Publisher, The Montreal Gazette, 1972-76; Jr. Acct., with McDonald, Currie & Company, Chart. Accountants, Montreal, 1934-36; Managing Editor, "The Canadian Forum", 1936-38; Promotion Mgr., The Montreal Standard Publ. Co. Ltd., 1939-41; Internal Auditor, Brit. Air Comn., 1941-44; Gen. Mgr., Montreal Standard Publishing Co. Ltd., 1945-64; Mang. Dir. 1964-68; Publisher and Dir., Windsor Star, Ont. 1969-72; recreations: skiing, fishing; Clubs: Marden's; University; Home: P.O. Box 976, Stowe, Vermont

FARRILL, Frederick Bryson; investment dealer; b. Trafalgar Twp., Ont. 5 April 1928; e. Kennedy Coll. Inst. and Woodstock (Ont.) Coll. Inst., grad. 1946; Univ. of Toronto, Hons. Degree (Pol. Sc. and Econ.) 1951; children: Robert, Reid, Cynthia; VICE CHRMN., McLEOD, YOUNG, WEIR & CO. LTD. ; Chrmn. McLeod, Young, Weir, Inc.; joined Dawson. Hannaford as Partner 1952, becoming Partner, Greenshields Inc. (on merger) 1961; joined present Co. 1961; Past Chrmn. Ont. Dist. Council, Invest. Dealers Assn. Can.; recreations: golf, skiing, tennis; Clubs: Mississauga Golf; Rosedale; Badminton & Racquet; Dir. & Vice Pres., National; Home: 150 Balmoral Av., Toronto, Ont. M4V 1J4; Office: (Box 433) Toronto-Dominion Centre, Toronto, Ont. M5K 1M2

FARWELL, Charles Franklin, Q.C. (1952); b. Port Perry, Ont., 8 May 1907; s. Charles Franklin, K.C., and Dora (McGill) F.; e. Upper Can. Coll., Toronto, Ont; Burnside Science Scholar, (matric.); Trinity Coll., Univ. of Toronto, B.A. 1929; Harvard Univ. (post-grad. studies, arts) 1930; Osgoode Hall, Toronto, Ont., grad. 1933 (Van Koughnet Scholar. and Silver Medal); m. Margaret, d. Vincent Ashdown, 7 Mar. 1936; children: Peter, Judith; Associate, Fraser & Beatty (Corpn. and Taxation Lawyers) since 1975, partner 1945-75; read law with Rowell, Reid, Wright & McMillan, and George Walsh, K.C.; called to Bar of Ont. 1933; assoc. with firm of Holden, Murdoch, Walton, Finlay & Robinson, 1935-43; Nickle & Nickle, Kingston, Ont., 1934; served with C.O.T.C. (Osgoode Hall) 1940-42; author of "The Law of Succession Duties in Ontario", 1942; asst. W. K. Fraser, in drafting and editing "Canadian Company Forms" 1947; also supplement (3rd) to 4th Ed. "Company Law of Canada", Masten and Fraser, 1945, and 1st supplement to 4th ed., "Handbook on Canadian Company Law", 1946; asst. in compilation of "The Canadian Abridgement", 1935; novice heavyweight champion boxer, Upper Can. Coll., 1923; mem., coll. rugby winning team, Little Big 4, 1924; formerly mem., Trinity Coll. Rugby Team; mem., Candn. Bar Assn.; Phi Kappa Sigma; Conservative; United Church; recreations: golf, photography; Clubs: Muskoka Golf & Country; National; Rosedale Golf; Home: 124 Buckingham Ave., Toronto, M4N 1R6

FAUCHER, Albert, B.A., L.Sc.Soc., M.A.; éducateur; né Beauce, Qué. 20 juillet 1915; f. Joseph et Corinne (Tardif) F.; é. Univ. de Montréal B.A. 1938; Univ. Laval L.Sc.Soc. 1941; Univ. of Toronto M.A. 1945; ép. Louisette f. Pierre-Auguste Couture 10 août 1946; enfants: Louis, Adèle, Antoine, François; PROFESSEUR D'ECONOMIQUE, UNIV. LAVAL; Prix litteraire du Gouverneur Gén. 1974; auteur "Histoire economique et Unité Canadienne" 1970; "Québec en Amérique" 1973; mem. Royal Soc. Can.; Candn. Econ. Assn.; Can. Hist. Assn.; Addresse: 1246 Forget, Sillery, Qué. G1S 3T7; Bureau: Univ. Laval, Québec, Qué. G1K 7P4.

FAULKNER, Hon. (James) Hugh, P.C. (1972), politician; b. Montreal, Que., 9 March 1933; s. George V. and Elizabeth (Baird) F.; e. Lakefield (Ont.) Coll. Sch.; McGill Univ.; Centre d'Etudes Industrielles; Carleton Univ.; Vice-Pres., Alcan Aluminum Ltd.,- ; Visting Prof., Faculty of Administration, Ottawa Univ. 1979-80; 1st el. to H. of C. for Peterborough, g.e. 1965; re-el. since; Depy. Speaker 1969; Parlty. Secy. to Secy. of State 1970; Secy. of State, Can. 1972-76; Min. of State for Science and Tech. 1976-77; Min of Indian Affairs and Northern Development 1977-79; mem. Can. NATO Parlty. Assn.; Candn. Inter-Parlty. Union; Counseil d'Admin., World Film Festival; Candn. Artic Resources Council; Bd. of Gov. Lakefield College School; Liberal; Home: 157 Cap St. Jacques, Pierrefonds, Que.

FAWCUS, Hon. Kenneth Stanley, B.Com.; LL.B.; judge; b. Vancouver, B.C. 3 Jan. 1931; s. Stanley Challoner and May (Sargeant) F.; e. Bayview Elem. and Kitsilano High Sch. 1949 Vancouver; Univ. of B.C. B.Com. 1956, LL.B. 1957; m. Mary Margaret d. late William MacLeod 13 Feb. 1959; children: Susan, Jennifer, Linda, William; JUSTICE, SUPREME COURT OF B.C.; served with RCAF Reserve, rank Flight Lt.; Ald. Dist. of N. Vancouver 1967-71; Dir. Vancouver Bar Assn. 1965-67; Nat. Chrmn. Criminal Justice Sec. 1972-74 Candn. Bar Assn., Pres. B.C. Br. 1975-76; Pres. B.C. Chapter Delta Upsilon, 1955; Anglican; recreations: tennis, skiing, squash; Club: Hollyburn Country; Home: 1282 Rydal Ave., North Vancouver, B.C. V7R 1X8; Office: Court House, Vancouver, B.C.

FEARON, Blair, B.A., M.D., F.R.C.S.(C), F.A.C.S., F.A.A.P.; physician and surgeon; b. Farnham, Que., 26 Jan. 1919; s. John William and Hattie Merrill (Hutchinson) F.; e. Mulgrave (N.S.) pub. and high schs.; Parrsboro (N.S.) High Sch.; Mt. Allison Univ. B.A. 1940; Univ. of Toronto M.D. 1944, post-grad. course Otolaryngol. & Broncho-Esophagol. (also Univ. of Pa.) 1946-50; m. Joyce Doreen d. Dr. Stanley S. Ball 1st June 1946; children: Merrill Ann, Judith Evalie (Mrs. Robert Sheepway), Stanley Blair; SR. SURGEON, HOSP. FOR SICK CHILDREN; Asst. Prof. Dept. Otolaryngol. Univ. of Toronto; First Chief of Otolaryngol. N. York Gen. Hosp.; Consultant Otolaryngol. & Broncho-Esophagol. Women's Coll. Hosp. and Oakville-Trafalgar Mem. Hosp.; served with R.C.A.M.C. 1942-46, rank Capt.; rec'd Chevalier Jackson Award in Broncho-Esophagol. 1976; Chevalier Jackson Award 1980, Philadelphia Laryngologic Soc.; "Honour Award" from Am. Academy Otolarynology (head and neck) Surgery, 1981; author various book chapters and over 50 publs. in nat. and internat. med. journs.; mem. Acad. Med. Toronto; Ont. Med. Assn.; Royal Coll. Phys. & Surgs. (Ont.); Candn.Med. Assn.; Defence Med. Assn.; Candn. Otolaryngol. Soc.; Internat. Broncho-Esophagol. Assn. (Founding mem.); Am. Acad. Opthalmol. & Otolaryngol; Am. Broncho-Esophagol. Assn. (Pres. 1966-67, only Candn.); Am. Triol. Soc.; Am. Laryngol. Assn. (Vice Pres. 1973-74); Pan-Am. Assn. Oto-Rhino-Laryngol. & Broncho-esophagol. (Directive Council); SENTAC; Freemason; Alpha Kappa Kappa; P. Conservative; Protestant; recreation: photography; Clubs: Granite; Naval & Mil.; Rosedale Golf; Home: 13 Douglas Cres., Toronto, Ont. M4W 2E6; Office: 170 St. George St., Toronto, Ont. M5R 2M8

FEAVER, Herbert Frederick Brooks-Hill, B.A., LL.B., LL.M.; b. Glace Bay, N.S., 18 June 1907; s. Rev. Herbert and Marian (Brooks-Hill) F.; e. Chester (N.S.) High Sch.; Kings Coll. Sch.; Univ. of King's Coll., B..A. 1927; Dalhousie Law Sch., LL.B. 1929; Harvard Law Sch., LL.M. 1930; m. Martine Ada Barbara, d. Gerard Martinus del Court van Krimpen, Wassenaar, The Netherlands, 30 Oct. 1945; children: Gerard Martin Julian, Marian Barbara, Charles del Court van Krimpen; Third Secy., Dept. of External Affairs, 1930; Second Secy., Candn. Legation, Tokyo, 1939-41; Head, Prisoner of War Sec., External Affairs, 1942-44; First Secy. of Candn. Legation to the Allied Govts., London, 1945; Candn. Embassy, The Hague, 1945-48; mem. of Candn. Del to the Gen. Assembly of

U.N., Paris, 1948; Head of Commonwealth Div., External Affairs, 1949; Chief of Protocol, 1950-54; Minister, 1954; Ambassador to Denmark, 1956-58; posted to Ottawa, Sept. 1958; Ambassador to Switzerland and also (first) Candn. Ambassador to Tunisia, 1961-64; Ambassador to Mexico, 1964-67, to Greece 1967-70 when retired from the Dept.; Special Adv., Dept. of Secy. of State; read law with W. G. Ernst, M.P.; Anglican; recreations: tennis, golf, skiing, shooting; Home: 90 Park Rd., Rockcliffe Park, Ottawa, Ont. K1M 0B9

FEDOROFF, Sergey, M.A., Ph.D.; educator; b. Daugavpils, Latvia 20 Feb. 1925; e. Univ. of Sask. B.A. 1952 (Hons.) 1953, M.A. 1955, Ph.D. (Histol.) 1958; PROF. AND HEAD OF ANATOMY, UNIV. OF SASK. since 1964; Demonst. in Histol. Univ. of Sask. 1953, Instr. in Anat. 1955, Special Lectr. in Anat. 1957, Asst. Prof. of Anat. 1958, Adm. Asst. to Dean of Med. 1960-62, Assoc. Prof. 1962, Asst. Dean Undergrad. Educ. Coll. of Med. 1970-72; rec'd Lederle Med. Faculty Award 1957-60; Queen's Silver Jubilee Medal 1978; author or co-author numerous scient. publs.; mem. Ed. Bd. "In Vitro" since 1975; Ed., "Advances in Cellular Neurobiology" since 1979; mem. Steering Comte. Study Basic Biol. Research Can., Science Secretariat 1966; mem. Med. Research Council Can. 1973-76 (served on various comtes.); Official Candn. Del. to Pan Am. Cong. Anatomists Caracas 1969, New Orleans 1972, Pres. 4th Cong. Montreal; mem. Bd. Govs., W. Alton Jones Cell Science Center, Lake Placid 1970-72, Vice Chmn of the Bd., since 1980; Chrmn. Internat. Comn. for Estab. Multinat. Training Centers for Anatomists Latin Am. countries since 1973; mem. Internat. Organ. Comte., Internat. Cong. Anat. Mexico 1980 since 1977; Consultant, World Health Organ. in Israel 1977; Vice Chrmn. Candn. Council Animal Care 1979, Chmn., since 1980; mem. Candn. Assn. Anatomists (Council 1963-65, Vice Pres. 1965-66, Pres. 1966-67); Am. Assn. Anatomists (Educ. Affairs Comte. 1968-72, Pan Am. Assn. Anat. (Council since 1966, Pres. 1972-75, Hon. Pres. since 1975); Am. Soc. Cell Biol.; Candn. Soc. Cell Biol.; Tissue Culture Assn. (Vice Pres. 1964-68, Pres. 1968-72); Soc. Exper. Biol. & Med.; Genetics Soc. Can.; Am. Assn. Immunols.; Candn. Soc. Immunol. (Council 1966-71); Soc. for Neuroscience; Candn. Fed. Biol. Socs. (mem. Bd. 1966-67, Vice Chrmn. 1977-78, Pres. 1978-79); New York Academy of Sciences; Corr. mem. Mexican Assn. Anatomists; Hon. mem. Venezuelan Assn. Morphol.; Address: 36 Cantlon Cres., Saskatoon, Sask.

FEDORUK, Sylvia O., M.A., F.C.C.P.M.; physicist; educator; b. Canora, Sask., 5 May 1927; d. Theodore and Annie (Romaniuk) F.; e. Walkerville Coll. Inst., Windsor, Ont., 1942-46; Univ. of Sask., B.A. 1949 (Gov. Gen.'s Gold Medal) M.A. 1951; DIR. OF PHYSICS, SERVICES, SASK. CANCER FOUNDATION, since 1966; a Professor Univ. of Sask., since 1973 and Assoc., Dept. of Physics; Fellow of the Candn. Coll. of Physicists in Med., Jan. 1980; Hon. Consultant, Med. Staff, Univ. Hosp.; mem., Atomic Energy Control Bd. Can.; Sask. member, Science Council of Canada; Past Chrmn. of Bd. of Dirs., Saskatoon Centennial Auditorium Foundation, 1978-79; past mem., Science Council of Can., 1971-74; Assistant Physicist, Saskatoon Cancer Clinic, 1951, Senior Physicist 1957; Assistant Prof., Univ. of Sask., 1956; mem., Adv. Comte. on Clin. Uses of Radioactive Isotopes in Humans to Min. of Nat. Health & Welfare, 1960; mem. Task Group on Scanning, Internat. Comn. on Radiation Units and Measurements, 1962; Consultant, Nuclear Medicine, Internat. Atomic Energy Agency, Vienna, 1966, 1968, 1969; mem., Mayor's Committee Sport Participation Canada; received Citation Saskatoon B&P Club, 1965; author or co-author of over 33 scientific papers and book chapters; Consulting Ed., The Curler Magazine; Pres., Candn. Ladies Curling Assn.; Hon. mem., Peruvian Soc. Nuclear Medicine; mem., Candn. Assn. Physicists (Past Chrmn. Med. & Biol. Phys. Div); Candn. Assn. Radiols. (Council); Hosp. Physicists Assn.; Soc. Nuclear Med. (Past

Trustee & mem. Bd. Dirs.); Health Physics Soc.; Candn. Radiation Protection Assn.; el. a Dir. (1975) Sports Fed. of Canada; Queen's Jubilee Medal, 1977; Sask. Sports Hall of Fame; Ukrainian Greek Orthodox; recreations: curling, golf, fishing; Clubs: Faculty; Granite Curling; Home: 49 Simpson Crescent, Saskatoon, Sask. S7H 3C5; Office: University Hospital, Saskatoon, Sask.

FEENEY, Thomas Gregory, Q.C., B.A., LL.B.; b. Fredericton, N.B., 30 Aug. 1924; s. Gregory Thomas and Doris (Booth) F.; e. Pub. and High Sch., Campbellton, N.B., 1941; Univ. of N.B., 1941-43; Dalhousie Univ., B.A., LL.B. 1946; m. Mary Dorene Steele, 30 Sept. 1946; children: Gregory, Alannah, John, Monica, Ellen, Kathleen; PROF. OF LAW, UNIV. OF OTTAWA, since 1957; read law with G. T. Feeney, Q.C.; called to Bar of N.B. 1950 and of Ont. 1958; cr. Q.C. 1964; Lectr. in Law, Dalhousie Law Sch., 1946-47; Asst. Prof. 1947-50; in gen. law practice with Feeney & Feeney, Campbellton, N.B., 1950-57; Prof. and Dir. of Courses, Common Law Sec., Faculty of Law of present Univ., 1957-62; Dean of Common Law, 1962-73; Pres., Assn. Candn. Law Teachers, 1965-66; mem., Nat. Comte., Candn. Corrections Assn., 1968-73; Co. Law Assn.; Law Soc. Upper Can.; Candn. Bar Assn.; legal advisor, Candn. Soc. of Forensic Science since 1974; author: "The Canadian Law of Wills: Probate", 1975; "The Canadian Law of Wills: Construction", 1978, revised ed. 1981; Liberal; R. Catholic; recreations: golf, curling, bridge; Clubs: Canadian; Home: 1877 Fairmeadow Cres., Ottawa, Ont. K1H 7B8

FEHR, Gordon John; b. Montreal, Que., 6 May 1933; s. John Walter and Rosalie (Fischer) F.; e. Westmount (Que.) High Sch., 1950; McGill Univ., Chem. Engn. 1955; m. Marilyn, d. Larry P. McMahon, 22 June 1957; children: Michael, Kerry, Gary, Mary Clare, Carolyn; PRESIDENT AND DIR., PFIZER CANADA INC., since 1972; Chem. Sales Rep., Shell Oil Co., 1955-56; Tech. Sales Rep., Canadian Analine & Extract, 1956-57; Asst. to Lubricants Mgr., BP Oil Ltd., 1957-58; Consumer Supvr. Que. 1958-59; Consumer Mgr. Can. (Indust. & Farm Sales) 1959-63; joined present Co. as Asst. to Pres. 1963-64; Operations Mgr.-Pharm. 1965-66; Materials & Distribution Mgr. 1966-67; Comptroller & Secy.-Treas. 1967-69; Gen. Mgr. Chem. Div. 1969-72; mem. Finance Comte., City of St. Bruno; Adv. Bd., Extve. Programme, Univ. of Indiana; Warden, Parish St. Augustines, St. Bruno; mem., Montreal Bd. Trade; Corp. Prof. Engrs. Que.; R. Catholic; recreation: sports; Club: Nun's Island Tennis; Home: 156 Fairhaven Ave., Hudson, P.O. Box 291, Que. J0P 1H0; Office: 17300 Trans Canada Hwy., Kirkland, Que. H9I 2M5

FEINBERG, Rabbi Abraham L., B.A., D.D., LL.D.; b. Bellaire, Ohio, 14 Sept. 1899; s. Nathan and Sarah (Abramson) F.; e. Univ. of Cincinnati, B.A. 1921; Hebrew Union Coll., Cincinnati, Ohio, Rabbinical Ordination, 1924, D.D. 1957; Post-Grad work at Univ. of Chicago and Columbia Univ.; American Conservatory of Music, Fontainebleu, France (1930); Univ. of Toronto, LL.D., 1957; m. late Ruth Edith, d. of late Hyman Katsh, 4 Nov. 1930; children: Jonathan Frome, Sarah Jane; Rabbi-Emeritus, Holy Blossom Temple, Toronto; sang as lyric tenor radio personality under name "Anthony Frome", 1932-35, on NBC-WJZ; made a number of theatre appearances, and recorded pop album "I Was So Much Older Then" (Vanguard Records), 1969; retired from Holy Blossom Temple in 1961 to write and campaign for world peace, disarmament, and social justice; Vice Chrmn., Candn. Campaign for Nuclear Disarmament; mem. of Extve. Bd. Central Conf. of American Rabbis; Candn. Jewish Cong., Central Region; Vice-Pres., Assn for Civil Liberties; served as Rabbi in Niagara Falls, N.Y., Wheeling, W. Va., N.Y. City, and Denver, Colo.; selected by mag. poll (Toronto "Saturday Night") as one of Canada's seven greatest preachers; went to N. Vietnam 1967 on peace mission; author of "Storm the Gates of Jericho", "Hanoi Diary",

and "Sex and the Pulpit", 1981; occasional appearances on TV and Radio; frequently writes articles for mags. and newspapers; mem. of Extve. Bd. of many philanthropic, educ. and public welfare organs; Phi Beta Kappa; Pi Lambda Phi; recreations: outdoor summer sport, singing; Clubs: Home: P.O. Box 11574, Reno, Nevada 89510

FEINDEL, William H., B.A., M.Sc., M.D., C.M., D.Phil., D.Sc., F.R.C.S.(C), F.A.C.S., F.R.S.C.; b. Bridgewater, N.S. 12 July 1918; s. Robert Ronald and Annie (Swanburg) G.; e. Acadia Univ. B.A. 1939, D.Sc. 1963; Dalhousie Univ. M.Sc.(Physiol.) 1942 (Banting Foundation Research Grant 1941); McGill Univ., M.D., C.M., 1945; Oxford Univ. D.Phil. (Neuroanat.) 1949 (Rhodes Scholar, Nova Scotia, Merton Coll. Oxford Univ., 1939); Nat. Hosp. London grad. study in Neurol. 1949; m. Dorothy Faith Roswell d. late Lt. Col. Walter E. Lyman 28 July 1945; children: Christopher, Alexander, Patricia, Janet, Michael, Anna; DIR. MONTREAL NEUROLOGICAL INST. and DIR.-GEN. AND DIR. OF PROF. SERVICES, MONTREAL NEUROLOGICAL HOSP. since 1972; Wm. Cone Prof. of Neurosurg. McGill Univ. since 1959, mem. Bd. Curators Osler Lib. since 1963; Founder and Dir. Cone Lab. for Neurosurg. Research since 1960; Neurol. and Neurosurg.-in-Chief Royal Victoria Hosp. since 1972; Neurosurg.-in-Chief Montreal Neurol. Hosp. 1963-72; Neurolog. consultant, Sherbrooke Gen. Hosp., Montreal Gen. Hosp.; Nat. Research Council Grad. Fellowship 1949-50; Research Fellowship in Neuropath., Montreal Neurol. Inst. 1942-44; Research Fellowship in Neurophysiol. Montreal Neuro. Inst., 1951-52; R.C.A.M.C. 1941-45, War Research on brain and nerve injuries for Nat. Research Coun., Dalhousie Univ. and in M.N.I. under Dr. W. Penfield; Reford Postgrad. Fellowship 1953-55; Demonstr. in Biol. Acadia Univ. 1937-39, in Physiol. Dalhousie Univ. 1940-42; Research Asst. & Demonst. in Anat. Oxford Univ. 1946-49; Demonst. in Neurosurg. McGill Univ. 1951, Lectr. 1952-55, Chrmn. of Neurol. & Neurosurg. 1972-77; Prof. of Surg. (Neurosurg.) Univ. of Sask. and Univ. Hosp. Sasktoon 1955-59; Diplomate, Amer. Bd. Neurological Surg., 1955; numerous visiting lectureships and professorships nat. and internat. insts.; Curator, Wilder Penfield Papers, 1976- ; Hon. Lectr. in Hist. of Med. Univ. of B.C.; Editor, Tercentary Edition Thomas Willis's "Anatomy of the Brain", 1964; author or co-author over 270 publs. on neurosurg. and med. topics; ed. or co-ed. various med. publs.; mem. several med. journ. adv. bds.; Dir. Canadn. Assn. Rhodes Scholars 1969-71, 1977; Head, Collaborating Centre for Neurosciences, World Health Organ. 1974- ; mem. Neurosciences Comm., Med. Research Coun. of Can. (M.R.C.) 1975-79; Delegate on 1st Neurosciences Mission to China for World Health Org., 1979; Consul. Scient. to Nat. Inst. of Health, U.S.A., 1979; Chrm., Adv. Bd. Montreal Neurolog. Inst., 1979- ; Chrm. Penfield Pavilion Fund & Bldg. Comm., since 1972; Mem., Conseil de la politique scientifique, Gov. de Qué., 1975-78; Am. Assn. Neurol. Surgs.; Montreal Medico-Chirurgical Soc. (Pres. 1974); Am. Acad. Neurol. Surgs. (Pres. 1976); Soc. Neurol. Surgs. (Vice Pres. 1978); Am. Neurol. Assn. (Vice Pres. 1976); Candn. Med. Assn.; Montreal Neurol. Soc. (Pres. 1962); Assn. Neurosurgs. Prov. Que. (Pres. 1964); Canadn. Neurosurg. Soc. (Pres. 1968); Vancouver Med. Assn. (Hon.); Royal Soc. Med.; Osler Club London (Hon.); Research Soc. Neurol. Surgs.; Candn. & Am. Soc. Hist. Med.; Am. Osler Soc. Inc. and other med. assns.; Bd. of Gov., Acadia U., since 1980; Alpha Omega Alpha; Anglican; recreations: music, history, tennis; Club: University; Montreal Indoor Tennis; McGill Faculty; Home: 4021 Avenue de Vendôme, Montreal, Que. H4A 3N2; Office: 3801 University Street, Montreal, Que. H3A 2B4

FELDBRILL, Victor; conductor and musical director; b. Toronto, Ont., 4 April 1924; s. Nathan and Helen (Lederman) F.; e. Harbord Coll. Inst., Toronto. Ont.; Royal Cons. of Music of Toronto (Artist's Dipl. 1949); studied conducting (under scholarship recommended by Sir Adrian Boult) at Royal Coll. of Music, and Royal Acad. of Music, London, Eng. (1945); also at Hiversum and Salzburg; studied under Pierre Monteux for two yrs.; m. Zelda, d. of M. Mann, Toronto, Ont., 30 Dec. 1945; children: Deborah Geraldine, Aviva Karen; at age 14 conducted sch. performances of Gilbert and Sullivan operas; age 18 apptd. Conductor, Univ. of Toronto Symphony Orchestra; invited (1943) by Sir Ernest MacMillan to conduct Toronto Symphony; on discharge from the Navy in 1946 apptd. Concert-master and Asst. Conductor, Royal Cons. Symphony and Opera till 1949 (when grad.); since 1949 has conducted regularly for C.B.C.; has made annual appearances with Toronto Philharmonic and Toronto Symphony Orchestras; appeared as Conductor for Candn. Ballet Festival, 1952; Conductor for B.B.C. since 1957, Brussels World Fair, 1958; Conductor, Winnipeg Symphony Orchestra, 1958-68; has appeared as Conductor on TV a no. of times; rec'd (with Winnipeg Symphony Orchestra) The Concert Artists Guild of U.S. of Am. Award (first Candn. Conductor and Orchestra so honoured) at Am. Symphony Orchestra League Convention Awards Dinner, Detroit, July 1964; invited to conduct in U.S.S.R., 1963, 1967; conducted World Premiere of Harry Somers Opera "Louis Riel", 1967; first recipient of Candn. League of Composers "Canada Music Citation", 1967; rec'd. Can. Council Sr. Arts Award 1968; rec'd. City of Tokyo Medal 1978; invited by Japanese Ministry of Culture as Conductor at Tokyo Univ. of Fine Arts (Geidai) 1979; served in R.C.N.V.R. 1942-45; appt. (1st) Conductor-in-Residence, Faculty of Music, Univ. of Toronto, 1972; Resident Conductor, Toronto Symphony 1973-77; mem., Musicians Union (Toronto and Winnipeg); Hebrew; recreations: reading, photography; Address: 170 Hillhurst Blvd., Toronto, Ont. M5N 1P2

FELDER, Rabbi Gedalia; Poland; e. Yeshivat Mhram, Keter Torah, Torath CHAIM Toronto Seminary, 1941; m. late Anna Teichner; 3 sons; 2 daughters; 2ndly m. Bat Sheva Brandwein — Liberman, 1980; RABBI, SHOMRAI SHABOTH CHEVRA MISHNAYOTH SYNAGOGUE, since 1949; served previously in Sarnia, Belleville, Brantford; sometime Princ., Bais Yehuda Talmud Torah; Publications "Yesodei Yeshurun", Vols. I (1954) to VI (1970), 2nd ed. of Vol. I with additional Responsa, 1977 (a study of the devel. of the Synagogue, the laws, customs and traditions assoc. with daily prayers, priests of the Temple, the scribes, the Sabbath, etc.), 2nd ed. Vol. II, with additional Responsa, 1980; Sheilat Yeshurum, Responsa vol. 1; Nachlat Tzvi vol. 1-2, (laws of divorce, adoption, conversion etc.)2nd ed. with additional Responsa, 1978; Pri Yeshurum vol. 1, vol. 2, 1979; Abbreviated Otzar Haposkim Israeli; Ed., of Yesode; Yeshurum, 3 vol. (laws of Shabat) pub. 1976, 1978; Siddur (prayer book) Yesodei Yeshurum, Jerusalem, 1981; rec'd. Dr. of Hebrew Letters, Ner Israel Coll., Baltimore, Md. 1972; Mem. of National Beth Din of America (Rabbnic Court) of Rabbinical Council of America; mem. of Agudath Horabonim of Am.; mem. Rabbinical Council of Am., past mem. of Bd.; Former Chrmn. of Ont. Region 1960, 1968; Chrmn. of Rabinnical Vaad Hadashruth, Orthodox Div., Candn. Jewish Congress; life mem., Ner Israel Rabbinical Coll. Bd.; Toronto; Home: 603 Glengrove Ave. W., Toronto, Ont. M6B 2H7; Office: 583 Glengrove W., Toronto, Ont. M6B 2H5

FELICITAS, Sister Mary, R.N., M.Sc., LL.D.; nursing offr.; b. Fife, Sask., 18 Jan. 1916; d. Magdalena (Nickels) and the late Frank Wekel; e. St. Mary's High Sch., Edmonton, Alta. (Sr. Matric.); Providence Hosp., Moose Jaw, Sask., R.N., 1943; Univ. of Ottawa, B.Sc.; Cath. Univ. of Am., M.Sc. (Nursing Educ.) 1953; joined Sisters of Providence of St. Vincent de Paul, and made profession 15 Aug. 1934; apptd. Dir. of Nursing, St. Mary's Hosp., Montreal, and its Nursing Sch., 1945; subsequently (1957) Dir., Nursing Sch. only; President, Candn. Nurses' Assn., 1967-70; 1st Vice-Pres. (1950-53),

Assn. of Nurses of P.Q.; Chrmn., Ed. Bd., Candn. Nurses Journal, 1960-62; Regional Visitor, Special Project for Evaluation of Schs. of Nursing in Can., 1958-60; official del. to Cong. of Internat. Council of Nurses, Melbourne, 1961; attended cong., Germany, 1965; Chrmn., Candn. Conf. of Cath. Schs. of Nursing, 1960-64; served as Gen. Councillor of the Sisters of Providence of St. Vincent de Paul, 1971-77; frequent speaker on prof. and related topics; presently engaged in counselling and spiritual direction; LL.D. Queen's May 1974 (1st Sister and 1st Nurse so honoured); Oi Gamma Mu (U.S.A.), Sigma Theta Tau (Kappa Chapter, Washington, D.C.); recreations: music, crochet, crossword puzzles, reading; Address: Providence Mother House, (Box 427) Kingston, Ontario. K7L 4W4

FELL, Anthony Smithson; investment dealer; b. Toronto, Ont., 23 Feb. 1939; s. Charles Percival and Grace (Matthews) F.; e. St. Andrews Coll., Aurora, Ont., 1959; m. Shari Helen, d. Dr. Allen F. Graham, 12 June 1965; children: Annabelle Elizabeth, Graham Charles, Geoffrey Allen; CHRMN., PRES. AND CEO DOMINION SECURITIES AMES LTD.; Dir., The Candn. Surety Co.; Goodyear Can. Ltd.; Kellogg Salada Can. Ltd.; Ont. Div., Candn. Arthritis & Rheumatism Soc.; Dir., Kellogg Salada Can. Inc.; mem. Bd. pf Govnrs., St. Andrew's Coll.; Baptist; Clubs: Toronto York; Home: 123 Cheltenham Ave., Toronto, Ont. M4N 1R1; Office: (P.O. Box 21) Commerce Court South, Toronto, Ont. M5L 1A7

FELL, Charles Percival, LL.D.; b. Toronto, Ont., 28 Feb. 1894; s. I. C. and Sarah J. (Branton) F.; e. Univ. of Toronto Schs.; McMaster LL.D. 1957; m., first, late Grace E. Matthews, Toronto, Ont.; children: Fraser, Albert, Margaret (Mrs. Mark Y. Marcar), Anthony; second, Marjorie Jane Orr Montgomery; mem. and Hon. Dir., Royal Trust Co.; assoc. with Dillon, Read and Company, New York, 1921-24; with Dominion Securities Corporation, Toronto, Ontario, 1925-29; Pres., Matthews & Co. Ltd., 1950-57; Pres., Empire Life Insurance Co. 1934-67; Chrmn. Bd. of Trustees, National Gallery of Can. 1952-59; mem. of Council and Pres. (1950-53), Art Gallery of Ont.; Hon. Gov., McMaster Univ. (Gov. 1937-60, Chancellor 1960-65); 40 yr. mem., Toronto Bd. Trade; Clubs: York; Toronto; Granite; Home: 52 Park Lane Circle, Don Mills, Ont. M3C 2N2

FELLOWS, Edward Spencer, M.Sc.; forestry and conservation and environment consultant; b. Pulham, Norfolk, Eng., 15 Feb. 1909; s. late Arthur Cecil (a Civil Engr.) and late Alice Margaret (Wallace) F.; e. London Polytech. Inst., 1925-26; Univ. of New Brunswick, B.Sc. (Forestry). 1930 and M.Sc. 1935; D.Sc. (Honorary) 1980); m. late Annie Kathleen, d. late H. W. Woods, 20 Apl. 1935; m. 2ndly, Ersi, d. E. Andreou, 14 Dec. 1967; children: David Michael, Peter Colin; engaged in research work at Forest Products Lab. (Chief of Wood Utilization Divn.), 1930-43; Supt. of Tech. Services, Maritime Lumber Bureau 1943-46; Specialist with Ont. Roy. Comn. on Forestry, 1946-47; private consulting work in B.C., N.B. and Ont., 1947-48; Chief Forester, Eastern Rockies Forest Conservation Board, 1948-55; mem., N.B. Forest Devel. Comn., 1955-57; Regd. Prof. Forester (N.B.); formerly mem., Bd. of Govs. and Senate, Univ. of N.B.; former Chrmn., N.B. Water Authority; Past-Pres. and Fellow, Candn. Inst. Forestry; mem. Am. Assn. Advance. Science; Soc. Am. Frstrs; Assn. Consulting Foresters; Forest Prod. Research Soc.; Commonwealth Forestry Assn.; Woodlands Sec., Candn. Pulp & Paper Assn.; Soil Conservation Soc. of Am.; Chrmn., Fredericton Area Pollution Control Comn.; Past-Pres., Associated Alumni, Univ. of N.B.; Anglican; recreations: music, photography; Home: 157 Parkhurst Dr., Fredericton, N.B. E3B 2J5; Office: P.O. Box 354, Fredericton, N.B. E3B 4Z9

FENN, Anthony Neville; executive; b. Birkenhead, Eng., 14 Dec. 1919; s. Leslie Neville and Lilian (Bind) F.; e.

Bishop Vesey's Grammar Sch., Sutton Coldfield, UK, 1937; Army Sch. of Signals, UK, 1940; Army Sch. Driving & Maintenance, India, 1942; m. Eileen Patricia Erskine Young, 5 Oct. 1946; two s., Ronald Anthony, Giles Patrick; VICE PRES., CANADA WIRE AND CABLE CO. LTD.; Pres. and C.O.O., Canada Wire & Cable (Internat.) Ltd.; Dir., Industrias CM, S.A. (Mexico); Industria de Conductores Electricos S.A.; Metalex Fundicion y Extrusion de Metales C.A.; Representaciones Iconel C.A. (Venezuela); Fabrica de Alambres Tecnicos S.A. (Colombia); Alambres Dominicanos C. por A.; Metales Industriales C.A. (Dominican Republic); Nigerchin Electrical Develop. Co. Ltd. (Nigeria); Tycan Australia Pty. Ltd. (Australia); Tolley Holdings Ltd. (New Zealand); Dir., Transwire (Pty) Ltd. (S. Africa); Ass. Plastics of Ireland Ltd. (Ireland); Mang. Trainee, F. W. Woolworth & Co. Ltd., UK 1938-39, Store Mgr. 1946; Plant Mgr., E. S. Walley, 1947; Mgr. Bland Bros. 1949; Colonial Administrative Service, Nigeria 1950-53; Br. Mgr. to Mang. Dir., Vivian Younger & Bond Ltd., Nigeria 1953-62; also Dir. United Dominions Corp. Nigeria; joined present Co. as Asst. to Vice Pres. Sales & Engn. 1962, Mgr. Internat. Div. 1964, Vice Pres. Internat. Operations 1968; Pres., Canada Wire & Cable (International) Ltd., 1974; served with British Army 1939-46; attached to 1/6 Gurkha Rifles 1942-45; rank Maj.; mem. Bd. Trade Metrop. Toronto; Dir., The Inst. of Dir. in Can.; Fellow, Inst. Dirs. U.K.; Anglican; recreations: swimming, cricket, tennis, golf, reading; Clubs: Granite, Royal Candn. Mil. Inst.; Toronto; Toronto Cricket, Skating & Curling; Office: 147 Laird Dr., Toronto, Ont. M4G 3W1

FENNELL, Doris Pauline, M.Ed., M.L.S.; librarian; education officer; b. Brantford, Ont. 20 Sept. 1925; d. Ernest Hartley and Kathleen (Kingston) Campbell; e. Burtch Pub. Sch. Brant Co. and Brantford Coll. Inst.; Hamilton Teachers' Coll. Elem. Sch. Teaching Cert.; McMaster Univ. B.A. 1951; Univ. of Toronto B.L.S. 1962, M.Ed. 1970, M.L.S. 1973, Secondary Sch. Teaching Cert. 1963; Ont. Ministry of Educ. Certs. in Sch. Librarianship, Primary Educ. and Special Educ.; m. Gordon Stark Fennell 29 Dec. 1954; one s. William Gordon; EDUC. OFFR.-SCH. LIBRARIES, ONT. MINISTRY OF EDUC. 1966- ; Elem. Sch. Teacher, Brant Co., Brantford and Etobicoke 10 yrs.; Secondary Sch. Teacher Etobicoke 1962-64; Co-ordinator of Elem. and Secondary Sch. Libraries, Peel Co. Bd. Educ. 1964-66; Faculty of Educ. Lectr. summer sessions 1963-66; Master, Ont. Teacher Educ. Coll. 1976-77; Chairperson, Learning Materials Program Consultants Ministry of Educ.; Coordinator Ministry of Educ. summer courses 1966-78; conducted survey Media Services for Edmonton Pub. Sch. Bd. 1977; estbd. student lib. resource centre, prof. lib. in Special Educ. and material evaluation centre The Trillium Sch., Milton, Ont. for children with learning disabilities; rec'd Candn. Centennial Medal 1967; co-author "Cataloguing for School Libraries: A Guide to Simplified Form" 1970; "Libraries in Canadian Schools"; "Librarianship in Canada 1946-1967: Essays in Honour of Elizabeth Homer Morton" 1968; "Survey of Media Services" 1978; various publs. Ont. Ministry Educ.; 2 16mm films "As the Need Arises" 1970; "What's in it for us?" 1972; mem. Royal Ont. Museum; Art Gallery of Ont.; Metrop. Toronto Zool. Soc.; Ont. Lib. Assn.; Ont. Sch. Lib. Assn.; Candn. Lib. Assn.; Candn. Sch. Lib. Assn. (Pres. 1979-80); Internat. Assn. Sch. Libs.; Assn. Media & Technol. in Educ. Can.; United Church; recreations: travel, reading, sewing, photography, theatre; Club: Business & Professional Women; Home: 20 Avoca Ave., Apt. 404, Toronto, Ont. M4T 2B8; Office: Ministry of Education, 14th floor, Mowat Block, Queen's Park, Toronto, Ont. M7A 1L2.

FENNELL, Stanley Elmer, Q.C., LL.D.; b. Marlborough Twp., Carleton Co., Ont., 6 Oct. 1909; s. Wm. Henry and Isabella (Macartney) F.; e. Brockville Coll. Inst.; Univ. of Toronto; Osgoode Hall, Toronto, Grad. 1937; m. Anna Isobel, d. James R. Cameron, 26 July 1941; children: Margaret Ann, John Robert; PARTNER, FENNELL, RUDDEN, CAMPBELL AND STEVENSON since 1953; hon. mem., Bd. of Govs., Cornwall Gen. Hosp. (Pres. 1946-55); Life Bencher, Law Soc. of Upper Canada; hon. mem., Candn. Bar Assn. (Pres. 1961-62); Clubs: Cornwall Golf & Country; Cornwall Curling; The Moorings Country Club, Naples, Fla.; Home: 330 Sydney St., Cornwall, Ont. K6H 3H6; Office: 35 Second St. E., Cornwall, Ont. K6H 1Y2

FENNELL, Rev. William Oscar, B.A., S.T.M., D.D., (Un. Ch.); educator; b. Brantford, Ont. 10 Jan. 1916; s. Harry Stark and Wilto Claire (Charters) F.; e. Bellvue Pub. Sch. and Brantford (Ont.) Coll. Inst. 1933; Victoria Coll. Univ. of Toronto B.A. 1939; Emmanuel Coll. Dipl. in Theol. 1942; Union Theol. Semy. N.Y. S.T.M. 1950; research leave Univs. of Strasbourg 1950-51, Freiburg 1961, London 1970-71; Univ. of Winnipeg D.D. 1963; Univ. of Trinity Coll. D.D. 1976; Victoria U. D.D., 1981; Knox College D.D., 1981; m. Jean Louise d. John Henry Birkenshaw, Toronto, Ont. 1 Sept. 1948; children: Paul William, Catherine Louise, Stephen Harry; PRINCIPAL, EMMANUEL COLL. 1971-81, retired; o. 29 May 1942; Pastorate St. John's Un. Ch. Levack, Ont. 1942-44; Lectr. in Christian Doctrine Emmanuel Coll. and Sr. Tutor Victoria Univ. 1946, Prof. of Systematic Theol. 1957, Registrar of Coll. 1956-60, Dir. of Grad. Studies 1962-70, Acting Princ. of Coll. 1971-72; Prof. Em. of Systematic Theology and Past Principal of Emmanuel College, 1981; mem. Staff Internat. Students' Service Seminar Pontigny, France 1950; Chrmn. Nat. Extve. Student Christian Movement Can. 1951-54; Chrmn. Ch. & Univ. Comn. Candn. Council Chs. 1957-59; Un. Ch. Del. N. Am. Conf. on Faith and Order Oberlin, Ohio 1957; Candn. Del. Internat. Assembly World Univ. Service Nigeria (leader of del.) 1959, Germany 1960; rep. N. Am. Sec. World Alliance Reformed Chs. confs. with Lutheran World Fed. 1961-65; Un. Ch. Del. Fourth World Conf. on Faith & Order Montreal 1963; Chrmn. Faith & Order Comn. Candn. Council Chs. 1964-67; Comte. of Direction Toronto Grad. Sch. of Theol. Studies 1966-68; Comte. on Coop. in Theol. Educ. in Toronto 1967-70; Warfield Lectr. Princeton Theol. Semy. 1974; mem. Bd. Fund for Theol. Educ. 1972-75; served as Chaplain RCNVR 1953-57; author "God's Intention for Man: Essays in Christian Anthropology" 1977; also book chapters, articles and reviews; Assoc. Ed. "Canadian Journal of Theology" 1961-68; Fellow (1970), Am. Assn. Theol. Schs.; mem. Candn. Theol. Soc. (Pres. 1962-63); Karl Barth Soc.; recreation: gardening; Home: 71 Old Mill Rd., Apt. 306, Toronto, Ont. M8X 1G9; Summer home: Kingsett Rd., Lake Rosseau, Muskoka, Ont.

FENTON, Byron; company president; b. North Battleford, Sask., 8 Feb. 1917; s. William James and Nina (Williams) F.; e. Buena Vista Pub. Sch. and Nutana Coll., Saskatoon, Sask., 1923-33; Saskatoon Tech. Sch., Business Course 1934; m. Joan Newell, d. late Judge B. M. Wakeling, 24 July 1942; PRESIDENT AND GEN. MGR., TEES & PERSSE LTD., since 1968; Pres. & Dir., Nat. Warehousing Services Ltd., Vancouver; Dir. Thomas E. Paterson Ltd., Vancouver; entered retail business in rural Sask., 1945; rejoined present Co. in Calgary, 1950; apptd. Br. Mgr. in Calgary, 1956-66; Vice-Pres. and Gen. Mgr. and el. a Dir., Winnipeg, 1966; Pres., Alta. Food Brokers Assn., 1957 (Dir. 1955-56); Anglican; recreations: golf, curling; Clubs: St. Charles Golf & Country; Manitoba; Home: 62 Wordsworth Way, Winnipeg, Man. R3K 0J5; Office: 101 Hutchings St., Winnipeg. Man. R2X 2V4

FENWICK, William Roland, R.C.A.; artist; educator; b. Owen Sound, Ont. 4 Feb. 1932; s. Albert William and Marjorie (Patterson) F.; e. Owen Sound Coll. & Vocational Inst. 1950; Mount Allison Univ. 1952-55; m. Phyllis Ann Cregeen 30 June 1956; children: Graeme Scott, Jennifer Lea; ASSOC. PROF. OF VISUAL ARTS, UNIV. OF W. ONT. 1969- ; Art Dir. Simpsons-Sears Co. Ltd. Toronto 1956-66; rep. private and pub. colls.; extensive exhns. incl. restrospective London Regional Art Gallery 1975; designed 2 Candn. book covers publ. 1976; recreation: fishing; Home: 810 Talbot St., London, Ont.; Office: London, Ont.

FERGUSON, George A., B.A., M.Ed., Ph.D., D.Sc.(Hon.), F.R.S.C., professor (emeritus); b. New Glasgow, N.S., 23 July 1914; s. Alexander McNaughton and Jean Smith-Pollock (Dennistoun) F.; e. Dalhousie Univ., B.A. 1936; Univ. of Edinburgh, M.Ed. 1938, Ph.D. 1940; m. Rowena Sheldon, d. Sydney Bellows, Providence, R.I.; children: Claudia, Leith; PROF. OF PSYCHOL., McGILL UNIV., 1949-1981, Chrmn. of the Dept. 1964-75; and Vice Dean for Biol. Sciences 1966-71; Instr., Univ. of Edin., 1939-40; Indust. Consultant, Stevenson & Kellogg Ltd., 1945-47; Asst. Prof., Dept. of Psychol., McGill Univ., 1947-48, Assoc. Prof. 1948-49; Consultant, Social Sciences, UNESCO, Paris, 1954-55; served in 2nd World War with Candn. Army, 1941-45 (Overseas 1942-44); retired with rank of Major; Publications: author of 5 books and monographs and about 40 scient. papers; most recent book: "Statistical Analysis in Psychology and Education" 5th ed. 1981; mem. Candn. Psychol. Assn. (Fellow and Past Pres., Hon. Pres., 1976-78); Am. Psychol. Assn.; Am. Stat. Assn.; Psychometric Soc.; Centennial Medal; Silver Jubilee Medal; Sigma Xi; Liberal; Anglican; recreations: art, gardening; Home: 3003 Cedar Ave., Montreal, Que. H3Y 1Y8

FERGUSON, His Hon. Judge George Stephen Plow; b. Montreal, Que., 23 Aug. 1923; s. William Brophy and Gladys Elizabeth (Plow) F.; e. Univ. of Toronto Schs., grad. 1941; Univ. of Toronto, (Pol. Science and Econ.), 1945; Osgoode Hall, Toronto, 1948; m. Diana, d. Roland C. Steven, Montreal, Que., 28 May 1949; children: George Steven Plow, Michael Taylor, Diana; mem. Bd. of Govs., St. George's Coll., Toronto and Wilfred Laurier Univ., Waterloo; mem., Candn. Bar Assn. (past pres., Ontario branch); called to Bar of Ont., 1948; cr. Q.C. 1959; mem. of the County Court Bench for the Judicial Dist. of York; Alpha Delta Phi (President, Toronto Chapter, 1945); Anglican; recreations: gardening, fishing; Clubs: Lawyers; Advocates Soc.; Caledon Mountain Trout; Toronto Hunt; Home: Apt. 507, 500 Avenue Rd., Toronto, Ont. M4V 2J6

FERGUSON, Harry Stewart; financial executive; b. Glasgow, Scotland Sept. 1933; e. Univ. of Strathclyde; Royal Coll. Science & Technol., Scotland; Univ. of Toronto post-grad. courses;. m. Kathleen Ruth Lowe Sept. 1959; children: Eileen, Evelyn, Kirsten; PRESIDENT, FORBES CAMPBELL (CANADA) LTD.; Pres., Pharos International Ltd.; Britannia Resources Ltd.; Cumberland County Oil and Gas Inc.; Dir., Majesty Resources Ltd.; Ideal Resources Ltd.; Realm Resources Ltd.; Candn. Productivity Council; served as Merchant Banking & Trade Finance Comm. Offr., Ministry of Industry & Tourism, Ont.; Fellow, Internat. Bankers' Assn.; Pres., Sir Walter Scott Soc., Univ. of Toronto; Clubs: Toronto Bd. of Trade Country Club; Adelaide; Oakville Yacht; Home: 1078 Cedar Grove Blvd., Oakville, Ont. L6J 2C4; Office: (P.O. Box 245) Suite 1810, Royal Trust Tower, Toronto-Dominion Centre, Toronto, Ont. M5K 1J5

FERGUSON, Ivan Graeme, B.A., R.C.A.; film director; executive; b. Toronto, Ont. 7 Oct. 1929; s. Frank A. and Grace Irene (Warner) F.; e. Dickson Sch. and Galt (Ont.) Coll. Inst. 1947; Univ. of Toronto B.A. 1952; children: James Norman Munro, Allison June; PRES., IMAX SYSTEMS CORP.; Nat. Secy. World Univ. Service Can. 1953-55; films incl. "The Legend of Rudolph Valentino" (Dir.); "The Days of Dylan Thomas" (Dir.); "The Love Goddesses" (Co-Producer); "The Virgin President" (Co-Producer and Dir.-Cameraman); "Polar Life", multiscreen film Man and the Polar Regions Pavilion Expo '67 (Producer, Dir., Cameraman); "North of Superior" in IMAX (Producer, Dir., Cameraman), Special Jury Prize Candn. Film Awards; "The Question of TV Violence (Dir.); "Man Belongs to the Earth" in IMAX (Co-Producer, Dir., Cameraman); "Snow Job" in IMAX (Producer, Dir.); "Ocean" in OMNIMAX (Producer, Dir., Co-Cameraman); "Nishnawbe-aski" (Co-Producer, Cameraman); developed IMAX and OMNIMAX advanced motion picture systems; Home: 417 Carlton St., Toronto, Ont. M5A 2M3; Office: 38 Isabella St., Toronto, Ont. M4Y 1N1.

FERGUSON, James Bell, B.E.; mechanical engineer; shipbuilder; b. Pictou, N.S., 21 Nov. 1910; s. Allan Andrew and Mary (Bell) F.; e. Pictou, N.S. Acad., 1926-29; Dalhousie Univ., 1929-33; McGill Univ., 1933-35; m. Hazel P., d. Edward Logan, Pictou, N.S., 30 June 1937; children: James Logan, Cherry Grace, Janet Agnew, David John; MARKETING CONSULTANT, FERGUSON INDUSTRIES LTD.; Pres. & Dir. Ferguson Consulting Services Ltd.; Pres. & Dir. Atlantic Inspection Service Ltd.; Pres. and Dir. Gulf Services Ltd.; Pres. Pictou Area Devel. Comm.; Dir. N.S. Heart Found.; Sec. Purov. Acad. Ed. Found.; mem., Engn. Inst. of Can.; Assn. of Prof. Engrs. N.S.; Soc. of Naval Arch.; Sigma Chi; Freemason; Liberal; Protestant; recreations: golf, fishing, skiing, photography; Clubs: Pictou; Rotary; Home: 18 Cottage St., Pictou, N.S. B0K 1H0; Office: 74 Front, Pictou, N.S. B0K 1H0

FERGUSON, James Kenneth Wallace, M.B.E. (1945), M.D., F.R.S.C.; b. Tamsui, Formosa, 18 Mar. 1907; s. Dr. James Young and Harriet Arnold (Wallace) F.; e. George Watson's Coll., Edinburgh, Scot.; Malvern Coll. Inst., Toronto; Univ. of Toronto, B.A. 1928, M.A. 1929, M.D. 1932; m. Mary Frances, d. W. T. Wyndow, Toronto, 30 Aug. 1933; children: Ian, Anne, Brian, Shelagh; Dir., Connaught Med. Research Labs. 1955-72; Research Fellow, National Research Council, Washington, 1933-34; Assistant Professor of Physiol., University. of W. Ont., 1934-36; Ohio State Univ., 1936-38; Univ. of Toronto, Asst. Prof. of Pharm., 1938-41, and Prof. and Head of the Dept., 1945-55; served in World War 1941-45 with R.C.A.F. (Med. Br. Research); mem., Candn. Physiol. Soc. (Pres. 1950-51); Am. Physiol. Soc.; Am. Pharm. Soc.; co-author, "Materia Medica", 1948; has written some 50 papers on respiration, reproduction, and pharm. in scient. journs.; United Church; recreation: boating; Home: 56 Clarkehaven St., Thornhill, Ont. L4J 2B4

FERGUSON, John Thomas, B.Com., C.A.; executive; b. Edmonton, Alta. 21 Dec. 1941; s. Norman Robert and Dorothy Frances (Wigglesworth) F.; e. Univ. of Alta. B.Com. 1964; C.A. (Alta.) 1967; m. Bernice Evelyn McLean 23 June 1966; three s. Robert Brent, Bradley John, Douglas Gordon; PRESIDENT AND CHIEF EXTVE. OFFR., PRINCETON DEVELOPMENTS LTD. 1975- ; Dir. Western Supplies Ltd.; Nu Alta Developments Ltd.; Trans Alta Utilities Corp.; Bellanca Developments Ltd.; Edmonton Broadcasting Ltd.; Acct., Price Waterhouse & Co. 1964-68; Comptroller, Oxford Development Group 1968- ; Vice Pres. and Treas. Numac Oil & Gas Ltd. l968-75; Trustee, Ernest C. Manning Awards Foundation; mem. Alta. Inst. C.A.'s; Protestant; recreations: skiing, golf, squash; Clubs: Mayfair Golf & Country; Edmonton Petroleum; Edmonton Centre; Kappa Sigma; Home: 13011 - 65 Avenue, Edmonton, Alta. T6H 1W9; Office: #1200, 9945 - 108 St., Edmonton, Alta. T5K 1G6.

FERGUSON, Maynard; musician; b. Montreal, Que. 4 May 1928; led own band Montreal area during 1940's; moved to USA 1948 performing in big bands of Boyd Raeburn, Jimmy Dorsey and Charlie Barnet; performed with Stan Kenton 1950-53 winning "Down Beat" readers' polls for trumpet 1950, 1951, 1952; performed Hollywood studio orchestras 1953-56; formed Birdland Dreamland Band to perform at New York jazz club Birdland; performed and recorded at Expo 67 with a big band and a sextet; settled in Eng. 1968 performing with 17 piece band which made N. Am. debut 1971; returned to New York 1973 and reduced band to 13; recorded film themes "Gonna Fly Now" ("Rocky") and "Battlestar Galactica"; appearances in Can. incl. CBC TV "Parade", "In the Mood"; Stratford Festival 1958, Massey Hall, Candn. Stage Band Festival; played solo trumpet opening ceremonies Montreal Olympics 1976; has made numerous recordings; cited various bibliogs.; designed the Firebird (combination slide and valve trumpet) and Superbone (combination slide and valve trombone); Address: P.O. Box 716, Ojai, Calif. 93023

FERGUSON, Robert Bury, M.A., Ph.D., F.R.S.C., F.M.S.A.; educator; b. Cambridge (Galt), Ont. 5 Feb. 1920; s. Alexander Galt and Harriet Henrietta (Bury) F.; e. Central Pub. Sch. and Galt Coll. Inst. 1937; Univ. of Toronto B.A. 1942, M.A. 1943, Ph.D. 1948; m. Margaret Irene Warren 29 Dec. 1948; children: Evelyn Bury, Robert Warren, Marion Galt; PROF. OF MINERALOGY, UNIV. OF MAN. since 1959; Asst. Prof. of Mineralogy Univ. Man. 1947-50, Assoc. Prof. 1951-59; NRC Postdoctoral Fellow, Cambridge 1950-51; Visiting Scient. Oxford 1972-73; Adelaide Univ., 1979-80; Hawley Award, Mineralogical Ass. Canada, 1981; author or co-author about 40 prof. papers mineralogical topics; mem. Mineral. Assn. Can. (Pres. 1977); Mineral. Soc. (London); Am. Crystallographic Assn.; served with RCAF 1945, Flying Offr. (Meteorol.); NDP; Unitarian; recreations: sailing, cross-country and downhill skiing, curling, volleyball, photography, theatre; Home: 184 Wildwood Park, Winnipeg, Man. R3T 0E2; Office: Winnipeg, Man. R3T 2N2.

FERGUSON, Wallace K., M.A., Ph.D., D. Litt., F.R.S.C.; university professor (emeritus); b. Peel County, Ont., 23 May 1902; s. Henry Thomas and Frances (Klippert) F.; e. Univ. of Western Ont., B.A. 1924; Cornell Univ., M.A. 1925, Ph.D. 1927; Univ. of Western Ont., D. Litt., 1954; m. Margaret Wing, 1949; children: Arthur C., Ailsa D.; Professor of Hist., University of Western Ont. 1956-72 and Head of the Dept., 1956-63; Prof. Emeritus, 1972; Instructor, New York Univ., 1928-30; Asst. Prof. 1930-40, Assoc. Prof. 1940-45, Prof. 1945-56; Publications: "Erasmi Opuscula, A Supplement to the Opera Omnia", 1933; "A Survey of European Civilization", Vol. 1 (Vol. 2 by G. Bruun), 1936; "The Renaissance", 1940; "The Renaissance in Historical Thought: Five Centuries of Interpretation", 1948 (French trans., Paris, 1950); "Europe in Transition, 1300-1520" (1962); "Renaissance Studies" (1963); History Editor, "The Collected Works of Erasmus," Vol. I, 1974, Vol. II, 1975); "The Place of Jansenism in French History", in "The Journal of Religion" VII, 1927; "The Attitude of Erasmus toward Toleration", in "Persecution and Liberty, essays in honor of G. L. Burr", 1931; "Humanist Views of the Renaissance", in "American Historical Review", XLV, 1939; "Jacob Burckhardt's Interpretation of the Renaissance" in Bull. Polish Inst. of America, 1943; "The Interpretation of the Renaissance: Suggestions for a Synthesis" in "Journal of the History of Ideas", XII, 1951; "The Church in a Changing World: A Contribution to the Interpretation of the Renaissance" in "American Historical Review", LIX, 1953; "Toward the Modern State" in "The Renaissance, a Symposium", 1953; "Renaissance Tendencies in the Religious Thought of Erasmus" in "Journal of the History of Ideas", XV, 1954; "The Revival of Classical Antiquity or the First Century of Humanism" (Report of the Canadian Hist. Assn.), 1957; "The Interpretation of Italian Humanism: The Contribution of Hans Baron", in "Journal of the History of Ideas", XIX, 1958, etc.; Fellow, Soc. Science Research Council, 1942; Fellow, Guggenheim Foundation, 1939-40; Royal Society of Canada, 1957- ; mem., Candn. Hist. Assn. (Pres. 1960-61); Am. Hist. Assn. (mem. of Council 1963-67); Renaissance Soc. of Am. Pres. 1965-66; Humanities Research Council of Can. (mem. of Council 1960-63); rec'd Can. Council Medal, 1967; Liberal; United Church; Home: 1061 Waterloo St., London, Ont. N6A 3X9

FERGUSSON, Hon. (Mrs.) Muriel MacQueen, O.C. (1976), P.C. (1974), Q.C., D.C.L., LL.D.; has practised her prof. in Grand Falls, N.B.; long interested in Welfare work, and active in Business and Prof. Women's Club; first woman member of Fredericton City Council (former Depy. Mayor); Chairman of Internat. Relations Comte. of Candn. Fed. of Business & Prof. Women's Clubs, former Vice-President and former Educ. Secy. of Prov. Chapter, I.O.D.E.; Past Pres., Prov. Council of Women; Regional Dir. at N.B. Dept. of Nat. Health & Welfare, 1947-53; during 2nd World War connected with W.P.T.B. as Enforcement Counsel for N.B.; summoned to the Senate of Can. 1953; apptd. first woman Speaker of the Senate of Canada 15 Dec. 1972-7 Nov. 1974; retired from Senate May 1975; Hon. D.C.L. Mount Allison 1953, LL.D., New Brunswick 1969; D.C.L. Acadia 1974, St. Thomas 1974; LL.D. W. Ont. 1977; Hon. Pres., Can. Council on Social Development; Can. Fed. of Business and Professional Women's Clubs; Trustee, Forum for Young Canadians; Dir. Prov. of N.B. Safety Council; Dir. du Maurier Council for the Performing Arts; Patron, Lester B. Pearson College of the Pacific; Patroness, Women's Insts. of N.B.; N.B. Assoc. of Hospital Auxiliaries; mem. Candn. Bar Assn.; N.B. Barristers' Soc.; Life mem., N.B. Prov. Chapter I.O.D.E.; apptd. Queen's Counsel 1974; apptd Officer Order of Canada 1976; Address: 102 Waterloo Row, Fredericton, N.B. E3B 1Z1

FERNIE, John Donald, M.Sc., Ph.D., F.R.S.C.; astronomer; educator; b. Pretoria, S. Africa 13 Nov. 1933; s. John Fernie Fernie; e. Univ. of Cape Town B.Sc. 1953; M.Sc. 1955; Ind. Univ. Ph.D. 1958; m. Yvonne Anne Chaney 23 Dec. 1955; two d. Kimberly Jan, Robyn Andrea; PROF. AND CHRMN. OF ASTRONOMY, UNIV. OF TORONTO since 1978, Affiliate Inst. Hist. and Philos. Science & Technol. since 1973, Dir. David Dunlap Observatory since 1978; Lectr. in Physics and Astron. Univ. of Cape Town 1958-61; Asst. Prof. of Astron. Univ. Toronto 1961, Assoc. Prof. 1964, Prof. 1967; author "The Whisper and the Vision" 1976; over 120 tech. papers astron.; mem. Royal Astron. Soc. Can. (Pres. 1974-76); Am. Astron. Soc.; Internat. Astron. Union; recreations: volleyball, swimming; Home: Observatory House, David Dunlap Observatory, Richmond Hill, Ont. L4C 4Y6; Office: David Dunlap Observatory, (P.O. Box 360), Richmond Hill, Ont. L4C 4Y6.

FERNS, Henry Stanley, M.A., Ph.D.; professor (emeritus); b. Calgary, Alta., 16 Dec. 1913; s. Stanley Joseph and Janie (Sing) F.; e. Pub. and High Schs., Calgary, Alta.; St. Johns High Sch., Winnipeg, Man.; Univ. of Manitoba, B.A. (Hons.); Queen's Univ., M.A.; Trinity Coll., Cambridge, M.A., Ph.D. (Distinguished 1st Class, Hist. Tripos, Cambridge; Sr. Scholar and Prizeman, Trinity Coll.; Sr. Research Student of Goldsmith's Co., London); m. Helen Maureen, d. John Jack, 1940; children: Henry John, William Paterson, Christopher Stanley, Eleanor Maureen; EMERITUS PROF. OF POL. SCIENCE, UNIV. OF BIRMINGHAM; temp. Civil Servant, Ottawa, Ont., 1940-44; Asst. Prof. of Hist., United Coll., Winnipeg, Man., 1944-47; Asst. Prof. of Pol. Econ. (Econ. Hist.), Univ. of Manitoba, 1947-49; Research Fellow of Candn. Social Science Research Council, 1949-50; mem. of Labour Conciliation Bd., Prov. of Manitoba, 1947-49; subsequently taught at Univ. of Birmingham, Eng., Dean, Faculty of Commerce and Social Science there, 1961-65; Founder and First Pres. of the Winnipeg Citizen Co-operative Publishing Co. Ltd.; Publications: "The Age of Mackenzie King; the Rise of the Leader" with B. Ostry, 1955; "Britain and Argentina in the Nineteenth Century", 1960; "Argentina", 1969; "Towards an Independent University", 1969; "Teacher-Student Relations" in "University Independence — the Main Questions", 1971; "National Economic History: The Argentine Republic, 1517-1971"; "The Disease of Government", 1978; mem., Pol. Studies Assn. of U.K.; Br. Assn. of Candn.

Studies; Anglican; Home: I. Kesteven Close, Sir Harry's Rd., Birmingham B15 2UT, England.

FERRIER, Ilay Charles, B.Com., C.A.; textile executive; b. 17 Aug. 1927; s. Charles Arthur and Marie Madeleine (Beauvoir) F.; e. St. Patrick's Coll. Ottawa; McGill Univ. B.Com. 1948; C.A. 1952; m. Elizabeth-Jean d. John L. O'Brien, Q.C., Westmount, Que. 6 June 1953; children: Ilay Ian, John James, Catherine Theresa, Andrew Alan, Janet Elizabeth, Mary Alexandra; SR. VICE PRES. FINANCE, DOMINION TEXTILE INC.; with Canron Inc. 1953-75; Vice Pres. Financial Services present Co. 1975; Vice Pres. Finance 1976; Hon. Treas. Que. Br. Candn. Arthritis Soc.; mem. Business Comte. for Nature, Candn. Nature Fed.; Dir., Financial Extves. Inst.; Dir. Vice-Chairman, Financial Extves. Inst. Can. R. Catholic; recreations: ornithology, gardening, squash, tennis; Clubs: University; Montreal Badminton & Squash; Home: 417 Roslyn Ave., Westmount, Que. H3Y 2T6; Office: 1950 Sherbrooke St. W., Montreal, Que. H3H 1E7.

FERRIER, Lee Kenneth, Q.C., LL.B.; barrister; b. Toronto, Ont. 6 Feb. 1937; s. William Gladstone and Hazel Marguerite (Box) F.; e. Cunningham & Mem. Pub. Schs. 1950, Delta Secondary Sch. 1955 Hamilton; McMaster Univ. B.A. 1959; Univ. of Ottawa LL.B. 1962; m. Shannon Miriam d. Ward Bruce Fawcett 11 Oct. 1958; two d. Allison Miriam, Tamara Lynn; PARTNER, MacDONALD & FERRIER; called to Bar of Ont. 1964; cr. Q.C. 1976; former mem. COMSOC Ministry Comte. on Adoption Records; Ont. del. Uniform Law Conf. Can.; Past Bd. mem. Children's Aid Soc. Metrop. Toronto; Visiting Homemaker's Assn., Parkdale Community Legal Services; served as Project Consultant Clarke Inst. Psychiatry; Bar Admission Course Lectr. and Group Instr. 1968- ; Non-bencher Legal Aid Comte. 1972-79; mem. Clin. Funding Comte. 1975-79; Atty.-Gen.'s Comte. on Rep. of Children 1977-79; Trustee Foundation for Legal Research 1978- ; Vice Chrmn. Ont. Legal Aid Plan 1979- ; el. Bencher, Law Soc. Upper Can. 1979; mem. Advocates Soc. (Founding); Candn. Bar Assn. (Past Chrmn. Family Law Sec.; mem. Council 1969-79); York Co. Law Assn.; Trustee Lawyers' Club; co-author "MacDonald and Ferrier: Canadian Divorce Law and Practice" 1969; Ed. "Infants and Children" Candn. Abridgement 1970; Protestant; recreations: skiing, fishing, canoeing, photography, cooking; Club: National Yacht; Home: 304 Keewatin Ave., Toronto, Ont. M4P 2A5; Office: 401 Bay St., Toronto, Ont. M5H 2Y4.

FERRON, Jacques; auteur; médecin; né Louisville, Qué., 20 jan. 1926; f. J. Alphonse et Adrienne (Caron) F.; é. Coll. Jean-de-Brébeuf, Qué.; Univ. Laval; ép. Madeleine Lavallée; enfants: Chaouac, Marie, Martine, Jean-Olivier; médecin à Rivière-Madeleine, Qué. 1946-49, et Longueuil, Qué. depuis 1949; auteur: "Contes d'un pays incertains" (Prix du Gouverneur Gén. 1964); "Le Ciel de Québec"; "Les Grands Soleils"; "Papa Boss"; "Les Roses Sauvages"; Chev. du Mérite de Longueuil; mem. Soc. hist. de Montréal; Parti Québecois; Catholique; Résidence; 931 Bellerive, Longueuil, Qué. J4J 1A5; Bureau: 1285 Chemin de Chambly, Longueuil, Qué. J4J 3W9

FERRON, Marcelle; artist; née Louiseville, Qué., 20 janv. 1924; f. Joseph A. F.; é. Coll. Marguerite-Bourgeois, Montréal, Qué. (dipl. Lettres-Sciences); Ecole des Beaux Arts de Québec; gravure avec S.B. Hayter, lithographie à l'Atelier Desjobert. Paris; 1946-53, participa au "Groupe Automatiste" à Montréal autour de Paul E. Borduas: m. 15 juillet, 1944; 3 d.: Danièle à Paris, Babalou et Diane à Montréal; mem. Ecole des Artistes Canadiens à Paris; Groupe Can. de Peintres et Sculpteurs; depuis 1955, a exposé dans les galleries principales de Paris, Turin, Milan, Spoleto, Zurich, Amsterdam, Londres ainsi qu'au Canada et aux Etats-Unis; expo. pers.; Paris, Bruxelles, Munich, Toronto, Ont., Montréal, Qué., etc.; Prix: médaille d'argent à la Biennale de Sao Paulo, 1961; Boursière du

Conseil des Arts en 1958, 59 et 61; murale de trés grand format exécutée avec J. L. Lapierre, arch., Montréal, 1963; a publié en coll. avec le poète Gilles Hénault "Voyage au pays de mémoire", Paris, 1960; socialiste; récréation: lecture; résidence: 8 rue Louis Dupont, Clamart, Seine, France.

FEWSTER, Leo Blake; actuary; insurance extve.; b. Tillsonburg, Ont., 3 Sept. 1924; s. Anson Oliver and Ada Belle (Sitts) F.; e. Tillsonburg (Ont.) elem. and high schs.; Univ. of W. Ont. 1942-46; m. Mary Josephine, d. late Herve Gerald Davies Humphreys, 27 May 1950; children: Andrea Jane, Mary Patricia, Peter Humphreys, Timothy John; VICE PRES. AND CHIEF ACTUARY, LONDON LIFE INSURANCE CO. since 1974; joined present Co. 1946, Asst. Actuary 1959, Actuary and Administrative Offr. 1970; mem., Soc. Actuaries; Candn. Inst. Actuaries; Delta Upsilon; Anglican; recreations: tennis, wine-making; Club: London Hunt & Country; Home: 70 Elmwood Ave. E., London, Ont. N6C 1J5; Office: 255 Dufferin Ave., London, Ont. N6A 4K1

FIELD, George Sydney, M.B.E. (1946), D.Sc., F.R.S.C.; physicist; b. Wimbledon, Eng., 23 Oct. 1905; s. James and May Edith (Davies) F.; e. Waterville Academy, Que.; Univ. of Alta., B.Sc. 1929, M.Sc. 1930 (received Nat. Research Council Bursary), D.Sc. 1937; m. Jean Olive, d. Jas. A. Richards, Edmonton, Alta., 19 May 1930; children: William James Robert, Gregory George, Marilyn Denise; Physicist, National Research Council, 1930-46; during World War II, spent three months in United Kingdom investigating anti-submarine and anti-mining devices for the National Research Council and the Royal Canadian Navy; also directed a number of researches in the field of underwater warfare and in acoustical aspects of telecommunication systems for the Canadian Armed Forces; mem. Canadian Del. to the Informal Commonwealth Conf. on Defence Science in London, Eng., 1946; Naval Research Adviser to the Defence Research Bd. 1947; Deputy Dir. General of Defence Research, 1948-52; Chief of Div. "A", Defence Research Bd. and Scientific Adv. to the Chief of the Naval Staff, 1952-54; Chief Scientist, Defence Research Bd., 1954-64, Vice Chrmn. 1964-66; Fellow, Acoustical Soc. Am.; has written numerous scient. articles on ultrasonics, vibrations in solids, short elect. waves; Fellow, Inst. of Elect. and Electronics Engrs.; United Church; recreations: gardening, oil painting; Home: Route 4, Box 2607, Bonita Springs, Fla. 33923

FIELDHOUSE, H. Noel, M.A., D.Litt., F.R.S.C., F.I.A.L.; educator; b. Gibraltar, 1900; s. Henry Warwick and Mary (Edwards) F.; e. Univ. of Sheffield, Eng., B.A. with 1st Class Hons. in Hist. 1921, M.A. 1922, and post grad. Dipl. in Educ. (1st Class) 1922; Queen's Coll., Oxford, B.A. with 1st Class Hons. in Modern Hist., 1924; m. Grace, d. Geo. Tinning, Regina, July 1942; KINGSFORD PROF. OF HISTORY, McGILL UNIV., since 1945; Vice-Principal (Acad.) 1961-66; Chrmn. of the Dept. of Hist. 1947-62; Dean of McGill Coll. three months 1942-62; Sen. Research Assoc. (post retirement) 1969-71; Sr. Lect. in Modern Hist., Univ. of Sheffield, 1924-28; Organizer of entire Extension Lect. Scheme there 1926-28; came to Can. 1928; Asst. Prof. of Hist., Univ. of Manitoba, 1928-30, and Prof. and Head of the Dept. 1930-45; sometime Visiting Prof., Queen's Univ., Univ. of B.C., Univ. of Colorado; awarded Coronation Medal, 1953; served in 1st World War with R.A.F., 1918; mem. Candn. Hist. Assn. (Past Pres. and Hon. Life mem.); Candn. Inst. Internat. Affairs; contrib. to leading hist. journs. and to publs. dealing in international affairs in Can., Gt. Britain and U.S.A.; Address: McGill University, Montreal, Que.H3A 1A8

FIERHELLER, George A., B.A., LL.D.; company executive; b. Toronto, Ont., 26 Apl. 1933; s. Harold Parsons and Ruth Hathaway (Bauld) F.; e. Univ. of Toronto Schs.; Univ. of Toronto Trinity Coll. B.A. 1955, post-grad.

work; Concordia Univ. LL.D. 1976; m. Glenna Elaine d. Dr. Walter R. Fletcher, Toronto, Ont., 17 Apl. 1957; two d. Vicki Elaine, Lori Ann; PRES. AND CHIEF EXEC. OFFICER, PREMIER CABLE SYSTEMS LTD., since 1979; Dir. GBC Capital Ltd.; Dominion-Scottish Investments Ltd.; Calsat; Extendicare Ltd.; Datacrown Ltd.; Vice Chrmn. Rogers Cable Systems Inc.; joined IBM 1955 holding various positions Toronto and Ottawa incl. Marketing Mgr. prior to founding Systems Dimensions Ltd.; Chrmn. Data Processing Adv. Comte. Algonquin Coll. Ottawa; Trustee and mem. Extve. Comte. Nat. Arts Centre 1973-79; held various positions Un. Way incl. Campaign Chrmn. 1972, Chrmn. Policy & Planning Comte., First Vice Pres. Bd. Dirs.; Campaign Chrmn. Carleton Univ., Chrmn. of Assoc's, Chrmn. Bd. Govs., 1977-79; trustee, Roy. Ottawa Hosp. 1977-79; mem. Adv. Comte. Paterson Centre Internat. Affairs; has presented papers to many nat. and internat. confs. incl. Jerusalem Conf. 1971, CAN-AM Conf. 1972, OECD Paris 1974; OECD Vienna 1977; mem. Young Pres' Organ.; World Future Soc.; Candn. Information Processing Soc.; Conf. Bd.; Internat. Wine & Food Soc.; Opimian Soc.; Pres. Ottawa Br. Candn. Information Processing Soc. 1967-68, Nat. Pres. 1970-71, Dir. 1972-74; Founding Dir. Candn. Assn. Data Processing Service Organ's 1971; mem. Founding Comte. Inst. Cert. Computer Profs. 1973-74; Bd. of Dir., Vancouver Opera, 1979; Trustee, Vancouver Gen. Hosp. Foundation since 1980; Chm., Council of the 80's 1980- ; Campaign Chmn., United Way of the Lower Mainland 1981; Dir., Cable Telecommunications Research Inst. 1980; Dir. Vancouver Chamber Choir 1980- ; Chmn., Strategie Planning Comte., Candn. Cable T.V. Assn. 1980- ; Sigma Chi; recreations: music, wine, travel; Clubs: Rideau; Vancouver; Cercle Universitaire; Shaughnessy Golf & Country; Home: 4184 Musqueam Dr., Vancouver, B.C. V6N 3R7; Office: #200 1090 W. Georgia St., Vancouver, B.C. V6E 3Z7

FILIATRAULT, Jean, F.R.S.C. (1961); writer; b. Montreal, Que., 14 Dec. 1919; s. Jérôme and Annette (Beaulieu) F.; m. Suzanne, d. Roland Belleau, 9 Aug. 1947; children: Francois, Elise; Past Pres. La Soc. des Ecrivains canadiens; mem., La Société Royale du Canada, sec. 1; author of four novels: ''Terres Stériles'', 1953; ''Chaînes'', 1955 (Cercle du Livre de France Award); ''Le Refuge Impossible'', 1957; ''L'Argent est Odeur de nuit'', 1961; won Nat. Drama Festival in 1954 at Hamilton, Ont. with (play) ''Le Roi David''; awarded Fellowship of Can. Foundation, 1959; recreations: writing and piano; Home: 12,122, Daigle, Montreal, Que. H4J 1S7

FILION, Gerard, C.C.(1970), B.A., M.Com., F.R.S.C.; b. Isle Verte, Que., 18 Aug. 1909; s. Alfred and Philomène (Simard) F.; e. Laval Univ., B.A. 1931; Montreal Univ., M.Com. 1934; m. Françoise, d. Eugène Servètre; 25 Jan. 1937; children: Nicole, Monique, Pierre, Jean, Marcel, Marc-André, Louise, Michel, Claudine; Dir., Canada Life Assurance Co.; Pres., Candian Manufacturers Assn. 1971-72; Vice-Pres., Can. Council, 1962-64; formerly Publisher of ''Le Devoir'' (daily newspaper, estbd. 1910); rec'd. Nat. Newspaper Award for Edit. writing, 1951, '59, '61; Mayor, St. Bruno, Que., 1960-68; mem., Royal Comn. of Inquiry on Educ., Qué. 1961-66; named to Candn. News Hall of Fame by Toronto Men's Press Club, 1966; former President Marine Industries Limited; Roman Catholic; recreations: hunting, fishing; Address: (C.P. 93) La Montagne, St. Bruno de Montarville, Que. J3V 4P8

FILION, Rev. Paul-Emile, S.J., B.A., L.Ph.; L.Th., M.L.S., D.Univ.(Laval), LL.D.(W. Ont.), librarian-bibliothécaire; b. Montreal, 9 Aug. 1922; s. Alfred and Jeanne (Chaput) F.; e. Univ. de Montréal (Colls. Grasset et Brébeuf); B.A., 1948; Coll. de l'Immaculée-Conception, L.Ph., 1949, L.Th., 1955; Columbia Univ., M.S. in L.S., 1957; Laval D.U.L. 1969; W. Ont. LL.D. 1972; ASSISTANT VICE-RECTOR AND DIR. OF LIBRARIES, CONCORDIA UNIV.; Instr. in Science and Dir., Labs.,

Tafari Makonnen High Sch., Addis Ababa, Ethiopia, 1948-51; Consv. bibl., Coll. de l'Immaculée-Conception, 1957-60; Chargé de cours, Ec. de Bibl., Univ. de Montréal, 1957-60; Chief Lib., Laurentian Univ., 1960-70; Coordonnateur aux Communications a l'univ. du Quebec, 1971-76; 2nd Vice-Pres., Candn. Lib. Assn., 1965-66, Councillor 1968-71; Prés. Comité du Projet de loi sur les bibliothèques publiques, Assn. Candn. des Bibliothécaires de langue française, 1958-59; Prés., Sec. régionale de Montréal, 1959-60; Prés., Sec. des bibliothèques universitaires, gouvernementales et spécialisées, 1963-64, 2nd Vice Pres. 1970; Assoc., Survey of Laval Univ., 1962 and 1965; mem. of Bd. (1964-67), Inst. Prof. Librarians Ont.; 2nd Vice-Pres., 1965-66; Councillor, Candn. Assn. Coll. & Univ. Libs., 1963-64; Councillor, Ont. Assn. Coll. & Univ. Libs., 1965-67; Ed., ''Newsletter''of CACUL-ACBCU, 1963-70; mem., Comn. Study Candn. Coll. and Univ. Libs (Downs Survey) 1966-67; Comité d'étude des bibl. gouvernementales du Qué. 1970-71; Ont. Rep., Nat. Lib. of Can. Adv. Council, 1964-67; AUCC Lib. Committee 1974-78; mem., Comité technique d'évaluation des bibl., Univ. Québec, 1978-79; Vice-Prés. Ass. des écrivains canadiens, (1981-2); mem. Advisory Bd., Nat. Library of Canada (1981-4); Prés., Corp. Prof. Librarians of Quebec; R. Catholic; Home: Centre Vimont, 3200 ch. Ste. Catherine, Montreal, Que. H3T 1C1

FILLMORE,Peter Arthur, B.Sc., M.A., Ph.D., F.R.S.C.; educator; b. Moncton, N.B. 28 Oct. 1936; s. Henry Arthur and Jeanne Margaret (Archibald) F.; e. Dalhousie Univ. Dipl. Engn., B.Sc. 1957; Univ. of Minn. M.A. 1960, Ph.D. 1962; m. Anne Ellen d. James W. Garvock, Berwick, N.S. 6 Aug. 1960; children: Jennifer Anne, Julia Margaret, Peter Alexander (Andy); PROF. OF MATH. DALHOUSIE UNIV. since 1976; Instr. Univ. of Chicago 1962-64; Asst. Prof. to Prof. Ind. Univ. 1964-72; Sr. Fellow, Dalhousie Univ. 1972, Killam Research Prof. 1973-76; Visiting Assoc. Prof. Univ. of Toronto 1970-71; Sr. Visiting Fellow, Univ. of Edinburgh 1977; served with RCAF 1953-57, Pilot Offr. (Flying Training); author ''Notes on Operator Theory'' 1970; Ed. ''Proceedings of a Conference on Operator Theory'' 1973; author various research articles functional analysis and operator theory; mem. ed. bds. several prof. journs.; mem. Candn. Math. Soc. (Vice Pres. 1973-75, Council 1975-79); Am. Math. Soc.; Math. Assn. Am.; Edinburgh Math. Soc.; Home: 1348 Robie St., Halifax, N.S. B3H 3E2; Office: Halifax, N.S. B3H 4H8.

FINCH, Robert Duer Claydon, B.A., L.L.D., D.Litt., F.R.S.C.; professor emeritus; b. Freeport, Long Island, N.Y.; 14 May 1900; s. Edward F.; e. Univ. of Toronto B.A. 1925; Univ. of Paris 1928; formerly Prof. of French, Univ. Coll., Univ. of Toronto; awarded Jardine Mem. Prize, 1924, for best Eng. verse; accepted by French Consul-Gen. for Bourse d'Études 1925; awarded Que. Bonne Entente Prize 1925; Hon. Pres., Univ. Coll. Players' Guild 1928; Hon. Pres., Univ. Coll. French Club 1939-40; author of ''Poems'', (Gov. Gen.'s Awd. 1946); ''Dover Beach Revisited and Other Poems'', 1961; ''Acis in Oxford'' (Gov. Gen.'s Awd. 1961); ''Silverthorn Bush and Other Poems'' 1966; ''The Sixth Sense'', a study of Individualism in French Poetry (1686-1760), 1966; ''French Individualist Poetry'', 1971; Saint-Evremond's ''Sir Politick Would-be'', 1978; Saint-Evremond's ''Les Opéra'' (Droz-Paris-Geneva) 1979; ''Variations & Theme,'' 1980; ''Has and Is'' 1981; rec'd. Lorne Pierce Gold Medal Award 1968; held 13th public one-man show of pictures; represented in National Gallery, Ottawa, provincial museums of art and private collections in 5 countries; Address: Massey College, 4 Devonshire Place, Toronto, Ont. M5S 2E1

FINCHAM, Kenneth C., B.Com., F.C.A.; association executive; b. Montreal 1928; e. McGill Univ. B.Com. 1950; C.A. Qué. 1953; rec'd Lt. Gov.'s Silver Medal; m. Alicia Baker; EXTVE. DIR., CANADIAN INSTITUTE OF CHARTERED ACCOUNTANTS 1973- ; articled McDonald, Currie & Co. Montreal; Asst. Comptroller, Canadian National Railways 1956-63; Partner, Touche Ross & Co. and P.S. Ross & Partners, Ottawa 1963-69; Dir. Gen. Audit Services Bureau, Dept. Supply & Services, Ottawa 1969-73; mem. Order C.A.'s Qué.; Inst. C.A.'s Ont.; Inst. C.A.'s Y.T.; Past Hon. Treas. St. John Ambulance Can.; Past Chrmn. Adm. Comte. Nat. Council Boy Scouts Can.; Home: 16 Ancroft Place, Toronto, Ont. M5S 2Y2; Office: 150 Bloor St. W., Toronto, Ont. M4W 1G5.

FINDLAY, Allan, Q.C., B.A., B.C.L.; b. Watson, Sask., 17 Aug. 1914; s. Roy Pattullo and Frances Muriel (Stephens) F.; e. Sydney (N.S.) Acad., 1931; King's Univ., B.A. 1934; Oxford Univ., B.A. (Jurisprudence) 1938, B.C.L. 1939 (Rhodes Scholar); m. Dorothy Graham, d. Ernest Jarvis Smith, 9 Aug. 1947; children: Marion, Carol, Paul, Allan, Donald; PARTNER, TILLEY, CARSON & FINDLAY; Dir., Canadian Pacific Limited; Kerr Addison Mines Limited; called to the Bar of Ont. 1946; cr. Q.C. 1954; served with RCAF 1941-45; mem., Law Soc. Upper Canada; Canadian Bar Association; United Church; recreation: golf; Clubs: The Toronto; Rosedale Golf; Lawyers; Home: 191 Strathgowan Ave., Toronto, Ont. M4N 1C4; Office: 44 King St. W., Toronto, Ont. M5H 1B5

FINDLAY, Earl Charles; Ph.D.; retired company executive; b. Toronto, Ont., 30 Dec. 1915; s. Charles F. and Ethel L. (Van Attan) F.; e. Public and High Schs., Toronto, Ont.; Sir Geo. Williams Univ.; Univ. of Toronto; Cal. Inst. Tech.; McGill Univ. and Univ. of Montreal (Extension); I.C.S.; Brit. Inst. Tech.; m. Norma W., d. William S. Lorenson, June 1939; three d. Willene, (Mrs. Albert James Benson), Sandra, (Mrs. Prather), Trudi (Mrs. Bruce Aston); Vice Pres.-Regional Mgr., Mechanical Drives Div., Zurn Industries Inc.; 1963-80; Dir. of several Am. co's.; with Link Belt Co. Ltd. at Toronto, Montreal, Elmira, N.Y. and Chicago, Ill., 1937-46; Asst. Sales Mgr., United Steel Corp., Montreal, Que., 1946-52; Gen. Sales Mgr., Consol., Engineering & Machinery Co. Ltd., Montreal, 1953-62; joined Zurn Industries Canada Ltd. as Vice Pres. and Tech. Dir., 1962; Vice Pres. and Mang. Dir., 1963; joined Zurn Ind. Inc. U.S.A. as Vice-Pres., 1964; mem., Soc. for Advanc. of Management Engrs.; Soc. of Auto. Engrs.; Am. Soc. Tool & Mfg. Engrs.; Inst. of Power Engrs.; Candn. Inst. Mining & Metall.; Am. Soc. Mech. Engrs.; Bd. Trade Metrop. Toronto; Anglican; recreations: music, skiing, photography, glass etching, foreign cruise travel; Clubs: Lions; Shriners; Home: T-Bar-L Ranch, Long Hill Rd., Raymond N.H. 03077;

FINDLEY, Timothy; writer; b. Toronto, Ont. 30 Oct. 1930; s. Allan Gilmour and Margaret M. (Bull) F.; e. Rosedale Pub. Sch. Toronto; St. Andrew's Coll. Aurora, Ont.; Jarvis Coll. Inst. Toronto; actor and charter mem. Stratford Shakespearean Festival, Stratford, Ont. 1953; extensive appearances in Can., UK and USA in theatre and television; recipient Gov. Gen.'s Award 1977, ACTRA Award, Armstrong Award, Anik Award, Toronto Book Award (1977); Can. Council Award 1968; Sr. Arts 1978; Ont. Arts Council Award 1977-78; author "The Last of the Crazy People" 1967; "Butterfly Plague" 1969; "The Wars" 1977 (being published in 11 langs.) (screenplay, 1981-2) "Famous Last Words" 1981; "Can You See Me Yet?" (play) 1977, performed Nat. Arts Center 1976; "John A. Himself" (play) Theatre London 1979; co-author "The National Dream" CBC TV (Actra Award 1975); "Dieppe 1942" (Anik Award); short fiction various lit. mags.; Novellas include, "Hello Cheeverland, Goodbye" (1974); "Harper's Bazaar" (1980); films incl. 5 film portraits (William Hutt, Kate Reid, Margaret Avison, Raymond Souster, Ulysses Comtois); "The Paper People" "Other People's Children" 1980; interviewed in "Eleven Canadian Novelists"1973, "Conversations with Canadian Novelists" 1973; subject of complete issue of "Canadian Literature", Spring 1982; mem. Assn. Candn. TV & Radio Artists; Writers' Union Can. (Chrmn. 1977-78); Candn. Actors Equity Assn.; recreations: gardening,

music.Address: c/o Nancy Colbert, Nancy Colbert & Assoc. 303 Davenport Rd., Toronto,Ont. M5R 1K5

FINKEL, Henry, R.C.A.; industrial designer; b. London, Eng. 7 Nov. 1910; s. Ben and Jessie (Barkanofsky) F.; e. McGill Univ. Sch. of Arch.; m. Rose d. late Nathan Goldblatt 28 Aug. 1937; children: Jon Darius, Ph.D., Nina Valery; estbd. HENRY FINKEL INDUSTRIAL DESIGN 1947; consultant to many Candn. mfrs. most materials and processes incl. application plastic materials; successful products incl. first Candn.-made hand held calculator; lectr. in indust. design and related subjects McGill Univ., Univ. de Montréal, Univ. of Man., Sir George Williams Univ.; TV and radio interviews; given papers internat. confs. on design; author various articles successful product designs, indust. design; rec'd Candn. Centennial Medal 1967; mem. Bd. Mang. Sadie Bronfman Centre Montreal; mem. Soc. Plastics Engrs. (mem. Bd.); Assn. Candn. Industr. Designers (twice Pres.); Royal Canadian Acad. of Arts; recreations: photography, music, drama, cabinetry, travel; Home: 342 Elm Ave., Westmount, Que. H3Z 1Z5; Office: (P.O. Box 505) Westmount, Que. H3Z 2T6.

FINKELMAN, Jacob, O.C. (1976), Q.C.; b. Poltava, Russia, 17 Jan. 1907; s. Rachmiel and Minnie (Seltser) F.; came to Can. 1907; e. Hamilton, Ont.; Univ. of Toronto, B.A. 1926; Osgoode Hall, Toronto, 1927-30; Univ. of Toronto, M.A. 1932, LL.B. 1933; York Univ. LL.D. 1977; m. Dora, d. David Riskin, Edmonton, Alta., 30 June 1946; 3 sons: Michael, Barry Gordon, Steven Robert; Chrmn., Public Service Staff Relations Bd. 1967-76; read law with J. A. Sweet, K.C., Hamilton; called to Bar of Ont. 1930; cr. K.C. 1946; Lect., Sch. of Law, Univ. of Toronto, 1930-34; Asst. Prof. 1934-39; Assoc. Prof. 1939-44; Prof., 1944-54; Special Lect., Inst. Business Adm., Univ. of Toronto, 1954-1967; Sessional Lect., Carleton Univ. School of Public Admin., 1977-79; McGill Univ. Faculty of Law 1977-79; Editor, Univ. of Toronto Law Journal, 1949-53; Registrar, Labour Court of Ont., 1943-44; Advisor to Select Comte. of Leg. on Collective Bargaining 1943; Chrmn., Ont. Labour Relations Bd., 1944-47 and 1953-67; Nat. Acad. of Arbitrators; Assn. of Labour Relations Agencies; Society of Professionals in Dispute Resolution (Pres. 1976-7); author (with W. P. M. Kennedy) "The Rights to Trade", 1933; Report on Employer-Employee Relations in the Public Service of Canada: Proposals for Legislative Change, 1974; Hebrew; Home: 400 Laurier Ave. E., Apt. 9A, Ottawa, Ont. K1N 8Y2

FINLAY, James Campbell, M.Sc.; museum director; b. Russell, Man. 12 June 1931; s. William Hugh and Grace Muriel (Fleming) F.; e. Brandon (Man.) Coll. Inst. 1949; Univ. of Man. Brandon Campus B.Sc. 1952; Univ. of Alta. M.Sc. 1967; m. Audrey Joy d. Leonard Barton 18 June 1955; children: Barton Brett, Warren Hugh, Rhonda Marie; DIR., JOHN JANZEN NATURE CENTRE 1975- ; Geophysicist 1952-53; Geol. becoming Dist. Geol. 1955-65; Chief Park Naturalist, Biol., Elk Island Nat. Park 1965-66; Dir. Hist. Devel. & Archives City of Edmonton 1967-71; Dir. Hist. & Science Services Edmonton 1971-75; Ed. "A Naturalist Guide to Alberta" 1980; author booklet on outdoor museums, varous ornithol. articles; Founding Dir. Alta. Museums Assn.; Past Dir., Vice Pres. and Pres. Candn. Museums Assn.; Past Pres. Alta. Chapter Candn. Soc. Environmental Biols.; Founding Dir. Fed. Alta. Naturalists; Past Pres. Edmonton Bird Club & Natural Hist. Club; Life mem. Am. Ornothol. Union; el. to Edmonton Hist. Hall of Fame (1st City Civil Servant); Protestant; recreations: ornithology, canoeing, hiking; Home: P.O. Box 7, Site 9, R.R.2, Sherwood Park, Alta. T8A 3K2; Office: Edmonton Parks & Recreation, 10th Floor C.N. Tower, Edmonton, Alta. T5J 0K1.

FINLAY, John Robert, Q.C., B.A., C.F.A., LL.B.; executive; b. Toronto, Ont. 22 Aug. 1939; s. Percy Claire and Elsie (Reppen) F.; e. Upper Can. Coll. Toronto; Univ. of

W. Ont. B.A., LL.B.; Chart. Financial Analysist 1979; Queen's Council, 1981; m. Janet Louise d. Elliot Menzies Little 17 Aug. 1967; children: Sue-Ann, Heather, Shannon; VICE PRES. AND DIR., ARGUS CORP. LTD. 1980- ; Pres., John R. Finlay Ltd. (estbd. 1975); Vice Pres. and Dir. The Ravelston Corp. Ltd.; Dir. Commercial Oil and Gas Ltd.; Hollinger-Argus Ltd.; Industrial Dividend Fund; Industrial Equity Fund; Labrador Mining and Exploration Co. Ltd.; Mackenzie Equity Fund; Mackenzie Financial Corp.; Mackenzie Financial Investment Management Ltd.; Norcen Energy Resources Ltd.; Trustee Industrial Am. Fund; Industrial Growth Fund; Industrial Income Fund; called to Bar of Ont. 1967; read law with Holden, Murdoch, Walton, Finaly, Robinson & Pepall, Toronto; practised with that firm and successor firms until retirement from partnership 1980; Chrmn. Bd. Trustees, Havergal Coll. Foundation; Dir., Children's Aid Society, Metro. Tor.; mem. Law Soc. Upper Can.; Candn. Bar Assn.; Toronto Soc. Financial Analysts; Delta Epsilon; P. Conservative; recreations: golf, tennis, squash, boating; Clubs: Toronto; Toronto Golf; Rosedale Golf; Granite; Cambridge; Home: 6 St. Margaret's Dr., Toronto, Ont. M4N 3E5; Office: 300, 2 Toronto St., Toronto, Ont. M5C 2B3.

FINLAYSON, James Colin, B.A.Sc.; aeronautical engineer; Canadian public service; b. Tignish, P.E.I., 12 Oct. 1918; s. Harold Alexander and Kate (Archer) F.; e. Univ. of Toronto, B.A.Sc. 1940 (Hons., Mech. Engn.; J. A. Findlay Scholar, in 3rd yr.); m. Jean Burwell, d. William F. Moore, Pembroke, Ont., 3 July 1943; children: Harold, Barbara, Judith; former Chief Control Div.; Aerospace Br., Dept. of Supply & Services, retired 1976; Asst. to Factory Supt., Dom. Ammunition Divn., Candn. Industries Ltd., Brownsburg, Que., 1940-41; Aero Engn. course R.C.A.F. Sch. of Aero. Engn., Montreal, Que., 1941-42; Research Aero. Engn. Offr., Test & Devel. Estab., R.C.A.F. Stn., Rockcliffe, Ont., 1942-45 with rank of Flight-Lieut.; Research Engr., Turbo Research Ltd., Leaside, Ont., 1945-46; Engr. in Charge (full scale) Test Plant, A. V. Roe Can. Ltd., Nobel, Ont., 1946-47; Research Aero. Engr., Air Transport Bd., Ottawa, Ont., 1948-49; Acting Chief, Research Aero. Engn. Br., 1949; Aero. Engr., Air Services Bd., Dept. of Transport, 1950-53; Sr. Production Offr., 1953-58; Tech. Adviser, Aircraft Br., 1959; Assoc. Fellow, Candn. Aero. Inst.; mem. Assn. of Prof. Engrs. of Ont.; Anglican; recreations: radio, photography, music; Home: 557 Edison Ave., Ottawa, Ont.; Office: No. 4 Temp Bldg., 56 Lyon St., Ottawa, Ont.

FINLAYSON, J(ock) K(inghorn); banker; b. Nanaimo, B.C., 27 May 1921; s. John Archibald and Elizabeth (Lister) F.; PRES. AND DIR., THE ROYAL BANK OF CANADA, Dir., The Royal Bank and Trust Co., New York; Orion Royal Bank Ltd., London, Eng.; Canadian Reynolds Metals Co.; Miron Inc.; Pan Canadian Petroleum Ltd.; R.J.R.-MacDonald Inc.; Royal Ins. Group; Sun Life Assurance Co. of Canada; United Corps. Ltd.; joined present Bank in Nanaimo, B.C., 1939; served in various branches in that Province and after mil. service was apptd. to the Bank's H.O. Montreal; served in managerial posts in Alta. and Manitoba returning to Montreal in 1960 as Mgr. of the Bank's Main St.; Extve. Offr. at H.O. since 1964; apptd. Gen. Mgr., International 1967, Chief Gen. Mgr. 1969, Vice Pres. and Dir. 1970; Depy. Chrmn. and Extve. Vice Pres. 1972; Vice Pres. Chmn. 1977 Protestant; recreations: golf, fishing; Clubs: Mount Royal; Mount Bruno; Forest & Stream; York (Toronto); The Toronto (Ont.); Granite Overseas Bankers (London, Eng.); Office: Royal Bank Plaza, Toronto, Ont. M5J 2J5

FINLEY, Gerald Eric, Ph.D.; R.C.A.; educator; author; b. Munich, Germany 17 July 1931; s. Frederick James and Winifred Margaret Mackenzie (Barker) F.; came to Can. 1931; e. Univ. of Toronto B.A. 1955, M.A. 1957; Johns Hopkins Univ. Ph.D. 1965; m. Helen Virginia d. Dr. Hawthorne Steele 1961; children: Christopher Frederick,

Heath Christian; PROF. OF HIST. OF ART, QUEEN'S UNIV.; Lectr. in Art & Archaeol. Univ. of Toronto 1959-60; Lectr. in Art Univ. of Sask. Regina 1962-63; Acting Dir., Norman Mackenzie Art Gallery; estbd. Hist. of Art and Art Educ. Programs, Queen's Univ. while Head of Dept. Art Hist. 1963-72; Fellow, Inst. for Advanced Studies in Humanities Univ. of Edinburgh 1979-80; awards: Brit. Council; Can. Council; Social Sciences & Humanities Research Council Can.; Candn. Fed. Humanities; author "In Praise of Older Buildings" 1976; "George Heriot 1759-1839" 1979; "Landscapes of Memory: Turner as Illustrator to Scott" 1980; "Turner and George IV in Edinburgh in 1822" 1981; "George Heriot: Postmaster — Painter of the Canadas", 1982; articles History of Ideas and various aspects of J. M. W. Turner's art and life; exhns. arranged: 3 Am. Painters: Olitski, Noland & Louis, Norman Mackenzie Art Gallery Regina 1963; Decline and Fall: the Arch. of Kingston & Frontenac Co., Agnes Etherington Art Centre Kingston 1976; "George Heriot: Painter of the Canadas, Agnes Etherington Art Centre, Nat. Gallery Can., McCord Museum Montreal, Sigmund Samuels Canadiana Gallery Toronto; 1978, Turner and George IV in Edinburgh, Tate Gallery London, Eng., Nat. Gallery Scot. Edinburgh; 1981; mem. Turner Soc. Gt. Brit. (Vice Pres.); Protestant; Club: Arts & Letters; Home: 53 Earl St., Kingston, Ont. K7L 2G5; Office: Kingston, Ont.

FINN, Donovan Bartley, C.M.G. (1946), M.Sc., Ph.D., F.R.S.C., F.C.I.C.; international official; b. London, Eng., 1900; e. Univ. of Man., B.Sc. 1924, M.Sc. 1926; Cambridge Univ., Eng., Ph.D. 1933; m.; has two d. and one s.; Dir., Fisheries Research Bd. Exper. Station, Prince Rupert, B.C., 1926; Halifax, N.S., 1934; Chrmn., Salt Fish Bd. of Can. 1939; Assoc. Prof. of Biochem., Dalhousie Univ. 1934-39, Chrmn., Candn. Food Requirements Comte. 1943-46; Depy. Min. of Fisheries, Ottawa, 1940-46; apptd. Dir., Fisheries Divn., F.A.O. Un. Nations, 1946 till retired; mem., Biochem. Soc. Gt. Brit.; Home: Castello di Sterpeto, Sterpeto d'Assisi, Perugia, Italy.

FINN, Gilbert, B.A., C.L.U.; b. Inkerman, N.B., 3 Sept. 1920; s. Ephrem and Felicite F.; e. Seminaire de Chicoutimi, B.A.; Univ. of Ottawa (special courses in Life Ins.); Laval Univ., C.L.U.; m. Jeannine, d. Jacques Boudreau, 8 Sept. 1948; nine children; CHRMN. OF BD. AND C.E.O., ASSOMPTION MUTUAL LIFE INSURANCE CO. since 1969; Chrmn. Assomption Place Ltd.; Mother's Own Bakery Ltd.; Rene's Bakery Ltd.; Hôpital Régional Dumont; Acadia Printing (1972) Ltd.; Pres. Assumption Place Ltd.; Pres. Carrefour Assomption Ltd.; Assumption Properties Ltd.; Dir., Brunswick Mining & Smelting Corp. Ltd.; Nat. Bank of Canada; Field Worker, Extension Dept., St. Francis Xavier Univ., 1948-50; joined present firm as Dir. Sales, 1950-62; Vice-Pres., St. Anselme Credit Union, 1961-63; Dir., Conseil Cooperation du Que., 1963; Pres.; 1963-64 and Dir., 1965, Union des Mutuelles-Vie; Dir., St. Enselme Sch. Bd.; George Dumont Hosp.; N.B. Productivity Council; Moncton Univ.; Moncton Connunity Chest Inc.; Pres., Atlantic Provs. Econ. Council; mem., Life Underwriters Assn.; Chart. Life Assn.; R. Catholic; recreation: fishing; Clubs: Richelieu; Beausejour Curling; Home: 884 Amirault St., Dieppe, N.B.; Office: 770 Main St., Moncton, N.B. E1C 1E7

FIRESTONE, O. John ("Jack"), M.A., Ph.D.; professor; b. 17 Jan. 1913; s. Bruce and Regina (Seaman) F.; e. McGill Univ., M.A. (Econ.) 1942; post-grad. studies, London Sch. of Economics; Dr. Juris et Rerum Politicarum, Univ. of Vienna; Dr. of Economics (hon) Hanyang Univ. (Korea) 1975; children: Brenda Ruth, Catherine Paula, Bruce Murray, John Mitchell Peter; 2nd m. Barbara Ann, nee McMahon, 1981; PROF. OF ECONS., UNIV. OF OTTAWA, 1960-78; Prof. Em. since 1978 (Vice Dean, Faculty of Social Sciences, 1964-70); assoc. with Candn. Govt. as Economist 1942-60; 1942-44, research work concerned with post-war planning Advisory Comte. on Reconstr. and Advisory Comte. on Econ. Policy, Privy Council;

1944-46, Research Asst., Econ. Research Br., Dept. of Reconstruction; 1946-48, Dir. of Econ. Research, Dept. of Reconstruction & Supply; 1948-50, Dir. of Econ. Research, Dept. of Trade & Commerce and Econ. Advisor, 1950-60; Econ. Advisor to Central Mortgage & Housing Corp., 1946-54, held concurrently with positions mentioned above; author of a no. of prof. articles and govt. reports, studies and books incl.; "Investment and Inflation, With Special Reference to the Immediate Post-War Period, Canada, 1945-48", monograph prepared for the Royal Comn. on Prices, 1949; "Residential Real Estate in Canada" (book), 1951; "Private and Public Investment in Canada, 1926-1951", govt. report, 1951; "Investment Forecasting in Canada" incl. in "Studies in Income and Wealth", Vol. 17, 1955; "Growth and Future of the Canadian Market, 1900-1975", govt. report, 1956; "Canada's Changing Economy in the Second Half of the 19th Century" (study), 1957; "Canada's Economic Development, 1867-1953" (book); 1958; "The Quebec Dept. of Industry and Commerce", (study), 1961; "Problems of Economic Growth" (book), 1965; "Broadcast Advertising in Canada, Past and Future Growth" (book), 1966; "The Economic Implications of Advertising" (book), 1967; "Industry and Education, A Century of Canadian Development" (book), 1968; "The Public Persuader" (book) 1970; "Economic Implications of Patents", (book), 1971; "Economic Growth Reassessed", (book, editor and contributor), 1972; "Regional Economic Development", (book, editor and contributor) 1974; "Canada's Anti-Inflation Program and Kenneth Galbraith" (book), 1977; "Factory Waste Potential in Sydney", (book & co-author), 1977; "The Other A. Y. Jackson" (book), 1979; apptd. a mem., Royal Comn. (Fed.) on Health Services, July 1961; guest lecturer, Banff School of Advanced Management, 1953-68; vis. Prof., Cambridge Univ., 1972; Australian Nat. Univ., 1975; Univ. of Nevada, 1978; Clubs: Cercle Universitaire d'Ottawa; The Country Club; Rockcliffe Lawn Tennis; Ottawa Athletic; Home: 375 Minto Place, Rockcliffe Park, Ottawa, Ont. K1M 0B1

FIRTH, Edith Grace, B.A., B.L.S.; librarian; b. Lindsay, Ont. 27 Jan. 1927; d. Thomas and Amy Isabelle (Edge) Firth; e. Univ. of Toronto B.A. 1948, B.L.S. 1949; HEAD OF CANDN. HISTORY DEPT., METROPOLITAN TORONTO LIBRARY; joined Reference Div. Toronto Pub. Lib. 1949; in charge of rare Canadiana since 1952; author "The Town of York" 1962-66; various exhn. catalogues, reviews and articles on prof. and hist. subjects; recipient Am. Assn. for State & Local Hist. Cert. of Merit 1963; Candn. Hist. Assn. Cert. of Merit for Local Hist. 1967; Centennial Medal 1967; Toronto Hist. Bd. Award of Merit 1974; mem. Multicultural Hist. Soc. Ont. (Dir.); Champlain Soc. Council and Publs. Comte. (Gen. Ed. Ont. Series 1963-71); Nat. Archival Appraisal Bd.; Presb. Ch. Gen. Assembly Comte. on Hist.; Bibliog. Soc. Can. (Council 1964-67, 1973-77); Ont. Hist. Soc. (Extve Comte. 1965-67, ed. bd. 1972-77); Presbyterian; Home: 6 Glen Murray Dr., Toronto, Ont. M8Y 3H3; Office: 789 Yonge St., Toronto, Ont. M4W 2G8.

FISCH, Gerald Grant, B.Sc., S.B., P.Eng.; management consultant; b. Toronto, Ont., 19 April 1922; s. Arthur F.; e. Guelph (Ont.) Collegiate; McGill Univ., B.Sc. (Bio-Chem. and Econ.); Mass. Inst. of Technol., S.B. (Indust. Mang. and Chem. Engn.); m. Jo-Lee; children: Susan Eleanor, Emily Elizabeth, Michael Gerald; MANAGING PARTNER, PEAT, MARWICK AND PARTNERS since 1968; formerly Managing Partner, P. S. Ross & Partners, and Principal and Director of Management Services, (also Chairman, International Mang. Consulting Comte.), Touche, Ross, Bailey & Smart; for a no. of yrs., was Vice-Pres. and Dir. of a N.Y. management consulting firm; as a Mang. Consultant for past 15 years, has supervised a broad range of assignments; has lectured widely for prof. and educ. organ., incl. Am. Mang. Assn., Am. Marketing Assn. and Amos Tuck Sch. of Business Adm.; Publications: various articles to leading reviews and journs. on

management organisations and promotion; author of "Organization for Profit" 1964 (Am. Acad. of Mang. Award 1966); "Modern Management" 1965; Pres., Management Consultants of Que., 1967; mem., Soc. for Advanc. of Mang.; Candn. Assn. Mang. Consultants (founding mem.); Inst. Management Consultants Que. (Counsellor); Corp. Prof. Engrs. Que.; Assn. Prof. Engrs. Ont.; Montreal Bd. Trade; Bd. Trade Metrop. Toronto; Engn. Inst. Can.; Soc. Indust. & Cost Accts. Can.; Am. Mang. Assn.; recreations: sailing, skiing; Clubs: Canadian (N.Y.); Royal Canadian Yacht; The National; Stamford (Conn.) Yacht; Royal St. Lawrence Yacht; St. James's; University; University (N.Y.); Home: 1455 Sherbrooke St. West, 1403, Montreal, Que. H3G 1L2; Office: 1155 Dorchester Blvd. West, Montreal, Que. H3A 2N3

FISET, Edouard, O.C. (1967), F.R.A.I.C., R.C.A.; architect; town planner; b. Rimouski, Que.; s. Edouard and May (Pouliot) F.; e. Académie de Qué.; Ecole des Beaux-Arts, Que. (Arch.); Ecole Supérieure Nationale des Beaux-Arts, Paris (Arch.); m. Mary-Olga Shewchuk; PARTNER, FISET MILLER VINOIS; Dir., The Mutual Life Assurance. Co. of Canada; Chief Arch., Expo 67; major projects including master plans for Laval University and "Cité Parlementaire" Quebec; plan for Ottawa Region (with Jacques Greber); many new towns; Lectr. on Urbanism, Laval Univ. 1947-48; mem., Hist. Sites & Monuments Bd. of Can., 1955-60; Pres., Que. Bd. Trade, 1959-60; Hon. mem., Canadian Society of Landscape Archs.; mem., Que. and Ont. Assn. Archs.; Town Planning Institute Can.; Soc. des Arch. diplômés par le Gouvernement français; Clubs: Cercle Universitaire (Que.; Pres. 1960-61); Royal Montreal Golf; Home: 406, 5150 MacDonald Ave., Montreal, Que. H3X 2V7; Office: Suite 600, 1980 Sherbrooke W., Montreal, Que. H3H 1E8

FISHER, Alexander David, B.A.Sc.; retired chemical engineer; industrial executive; b. Calgary, Alta., 24 Feb. 1915; s. Dr. Alexander and Sara Jane Vincent (Henderson) F.; e. Univ. of Toronto, B.A.Sc. (Chem. Engn.) 1937; Harvard Grad. Sch. of Business, 1953; m. Evelyn Ruth, d. John Edmund Pett, 30 Nov. 1940; children: John Robert, Katharine Ruth; Vice Pres., Planning, Engn. and Research, Steel Co. Of Canada Ltd., 1965-78; joined company as Metall. 1937; apptd. Foreman, Coke Plant, 1940; Gen. Foreman Coal Chems. Plant, 1941-42; Supt., Coke & Coal Chems. Dept., 1943-49; Asst. Gen. Supt., Hamilton Works, 1950, Gen. Supt., 1951; Mgr., Facilities Planning (corporate-wide), 1963; Past Pres., John Howard Soc. Hamilton; Hon. Dir. John Howard Soc. Ont.; Ont. Bible Coll.; World Vision of Canada; Bd. of Managers, Ont. Bible College; Bd. Chrm., World Vision of Canada; World Vision International; Bd. of Man. The People's Church, Toronto; Bd. of Bibletown, Canada; mem., Assn. Prof. Engrs. Ont.; Toronto Bd. Trade; Conservative; Baptist; recreations: golf, swimming; Home: 2090 Falkway Dr., Mississauga, Ont. L8L 3J9; 6150 Via Tierra Dr., Boca Ratin, Florida 33433

FISHER, Arthur John, professional engineer; b. London, Eng., 13 Sept. 1913; s. John Edward and Elizabeth (Dickinson) F.; e. Eltham Coll., London, Eng.; North Staffordshire Tech. Coll., Eng.; City and Guilds Cert. in Elect. Eng.; m. Dorothy Edith Hipkin, Dec. 1937, four children; CHRMN., BOARD OF DIRECTORS, V.I.L. VERMICULITE INC.; Chmn. of Bd. Fiberglass Can. Inc.; Dir., Great West Steel Ind. Ltd., Vancouver, B.C.; Dir., Koppers International Canada Ltd.; V.I.L. Vermiculite Inc.; Trustee, Southwest Research Inst., Texas; Hon. Vice-Pres., Arthritis Soc.; began with Callenders Cable & Construction Co., Erith, Kent, and Johnson & Phillips Ltd., Charlton, Kent; prior to coming to Canada was Principal Experimental Offr., Atomic Research Estbl., Harwell, Eng.; apptd. Mgr. of Sarnia Plant of present firm in 1948, and Gen. Mgr., 1951; Vice Pres. (Mfg. & Devel.) and Dir., 1955; Pres., 1967, Chrmn. of the Bd. 1978; served in 2nd World War; Lieut.-Col., Royal Arty.; served at War Office, and Brit. Army Staff, Washington and 2nd Brit. Army on the Continent; Legion of Merit (U.S.A.); Chrmn. of Bd., Sandford Fleming Foundation; mem., Inst. of Elect. Engrs., Eng.; Assn. Prof. Engrs. Ont.; Cdn.-Amer. Comm.; Anglican; recreation: sailing; Clubs: Granite; Rosedale Golf; Home: 8 Maytree Road, Willowdale, Ont. M2P 1V8; Office: 3080 Yonge St., Toronto, Ont. M4N 3N1

FISHER, Douglas Mason, B.I.S.; political columnist; b. Sioux Lookout, Ont., 19 Sept. 1919; s. late Roy Waldon and late Eva Pearl (Mason) W.; e. Sioux Lookout Pub. Sch., 1926-30; Fort William, Ont. Collegiate, 1931-37; Univ. of Toronto, B.A. 1949, B.L.S. 1950; m. Barbara Elizabeth, d. late Neil Lamont, 9 Sept. 1948; children: Mark, Matthew, Tobias, John, Luke; former Librarian, Port Arthur Collegiate; Forest Library, Northwestern Ont.; served as Trooper, 18th Armoured Car Regt. (12th Man. Dragoons) 1941-45; el. to H. of C. for Port Arthur 1957; el. Deputy House Leader (N.D.P.) May 1963; def. cand., York Centre to H. of C., g.e. June 1968; former Pol. Columnist for "Toronto Telegram" and now for "Toronto Sun", "Executive Magazine"; "Legion Magazine"; "Mother Truck" (Magazine); In-Site" (Magazine); Commentator and producer for CJOH-TV, Ottawa; author of provincial inquiry "The Policy and Programs of the Ontario Government for Recreation, Sport and Fitness" 1980; Dir., Candn. Forestry Assn; former Chrmn. of Bd., Hockey Canada; mem. Ont. Comn. on the Legislature 1972-75; Unitarian; Address: c/o Parliamentary Press Gallery, Ottawa, Ont. K1A 0A8

FISHER, Edward Joseph, M.A., D.Sc.; optometrist; b. Winnipeg, Man., 25 Nov. 1913; s. Joseph Thomas and Margaret (Cobean) F.; e. Malvern Coll. Inst., Toronto, Ont.; Coll. of Optometry of Ont. (Grad.) 1934; Univ. of Toronto, B.A. 1946 and M.A. (Psychology) 1948; D.Sc. Pennsylvania College of Optometry, 1969; m. Eleanor Jessie Cambridge, d. late Rev. Gordon M. Holmes, 28 Sept. 1936; children: Margaret Eleanor, Gordon Joseph, Barbara Marion; PROF., SCH. OF OPTOMETRY, UNIV. OF WATERLOO; practised as an optometrist in Lindsay, Ont., 1934-37, and in Toronto, Ont., 1937-45 and 1953-67; apptd. part-time Demonst. and Lectr. at the Coll. of Optometry of Ont. 1938 and full-time Lectr. 1945; apptd. Dean 1948-67; Dir., School of Optometry, Univ. of Waterloo 1967-1975; Visting Prof., Univ. of Benin, Nigeria 1976-81; Visting Prof., The City University, London 1976; Organist and Choir Master Highland Bapt. Ch., Kitchener; mem., Optometrical Assn. of Ont.; Nat. Educ. Assn.; Candn. Coll. of Organists; Candn. Psychol. Assn.; Fellow and Councillor and Past Pres. (1st non-resident), Am. Acad. of Optometry; Fellow, Am. Assn. Advanc. Science; rec'd Cert. of Merit, Univ. of Montreal 1961, Centennial Medal 1967; President's Medal, Candn. Assn. of Optometrists 1971, James Cobean Mem. Award 1975; Phi Theta Upsilon; Freemason; Baptist; Address: Univ. of Waterloo, Waterloo, Ont.

FISHER, Gordon Neil, B.Eng.; publisher; b. Montreal, Que., 9 Dec. 1928; s. Philip Sydney and Margaret Linton (Southam) F.; e. Lower Can. Coll., Montreal; Trinity Coll. Sch., Port Hope, Ont.; McGill Univ., B. Eng. (Mech.) 1950; m. Alison Nora, d. William A. Arbuckle, Montreal, 17 June 1955; three s., Derek Arbuckle, Philip Neil, Duncan Southam; PRESIDENT & DIR., SOUTHAM INC.; Dir., Southam Communications Ltd.; Southam Printing Ltd.; Pacific Press Ltd.; Kitchener Waterloo Record Ltd.; Sun Publishing Co. Ltd. (Brandon); Selkirk Communications Ltd.; TV Guide Inc.; Coles Bookstores Ltd.; Trustee, Toronto Gen. Hosp.; mem., Policy Comm., Bus. Council on Nat. Issues; Gov., Trinity Coll. School; Kappa Alpha; Protestant; recreations: sailing, squash; Clubs: Toronto; York; R.C.Y.C.; Mount Royal Club; Badminton & Racquet; Home: 34 Hillholm Road, Toronto, Ont. M5P 1M3; Office: 321 Bloor St. E., Toronto, Ont. M4W 1H3

FISHER, Murray M., B.A., M.D., Ph.D., F.R.C.P.(C); physician; educator; b. Gravenhurst, Ont., 15 Jan. 1934; s. Dr. Murray M. and Martha B. (Rome) F.; e. St. Andrew's Coll., Aurora, Ont., 1947-52 (Head Boy 1952); Univ. of W. Ont., B.A. 1957; Univ. of Toronto, M.D. 1958; Univ. of London, Ph.D. 1963; m. Beverley Frances, d. late Harry Wallace Knight Jr., 1 June 1957; children: Mary Martha, David Malcolm, Suzanne Elizabeth; Assoc. Prof., Dept. of Pathol. and Dept. of Med., Univ. of Toronto; Staff Phys., Dir. of Gastroenterol., Sunnybrook Medical Centre; Residency Program, Toronto Gen. Hosp., 1958-59, 1963-65; MRC Fellow, Univ. Coll. London and Royal Free Hosp., London, Eng., 1959-63; Res. Assoc., Dept. of Pathol., Univ. of Pittsburgh, 1965-68; Dir., Candn. Liver Foundation; rec'd Gold Medal Award, Royal Coll. Phys. & Surgs. 1972; author of various papers relating to liver disease and bile acid metabolism; mem., Acad. Med.; Am. Assn. Study Liver Diseases; Am. Assn. Advanc. Science; A.O.A.; Candn. Assn. Gastroenterol.; Candn. Soc. Clin. Investig.; Internat. Acad. Pathol.; N.Y. Acad. Sciences; Sigma Xi; Zeta Psi; Protestant; recreation: gastronomy; Clubs: Granite; Caledon Mountain; Home: 76 Braeside Dr., Toronto, Ont. M4N 1X7

FISHER, Philip Sydney, O.C. (1967), C.B.E., D.S.O. (1917), D.S.C., D.C.L., LL.D.; company official; b. Montreal, Que., 31 Mar. 1896; s. Roswell Corse and Mary Field (Ritchie) F.; e. Montreal High Sch.; McGill Univ., B.A. 1916; Bishop's D.C.L. 1957; LL.D. McGill 1964, Sir Wilfred Laurier LL.D. 1966; m. Margaret Linton, d. Frederick Neil Southam, Westmount, Que., 8 June 1920; children: Sydney Mary, Guy Southam, Margaret Claire, John Philip, Gordon Neil, Martha June; former Chrmn. of Bd. Southam Inc. Ltd.; Past Pres., Candn. Daily Newspaper Publishers Assn.; Past Pres. Can. Council on Soc. Devel.; Gov., Montreal Gen. and Children's Mem. Hosps.; assoc. with Southam Cos. since 1924; connected with firm of Walter Molson and Co., Montreal, real estate and ins., 1919-20; Stat. Dept., Roy. Securities Corpn., Montreal, 1920-21; private business, 1921-23; served in World War, 1915-19 with R.N.A.S. and R.A.F.; promoted from Sub.-Lieut. to Capt.; wounded 1917; awarded D.S.C.; Delta Upsilon; Clubs: Royal St. Lawrence Yacht; Royal Automobile; St. James's; Home: 3130 Cedar Ave., Montreal, Que. H3Y 1Z1

FISHER, Robert Bill, B.S.F., R.P.F.; forester; b. Yorkton, Sask. 15 Jan. 1926; s. John Alexander and Violet Vivian Victoria (Bill) F.; e. Yorkton (Sask.) Coll. Inst. 1944; Univ. of B.C. B.S.F. 1951; m. Shirley Evlyne d. Ernest Graham Conway 20 Dec. 1948; children: Robert, James, John, Randi, Barri; EXTVE. VICE PRES. AND DIR. L & K LUMBER (NORTH SHORE) LTD.; Dir. Lyttle Bros. Ltd.; Valleau Logging Ltd.; joined B.C. Forest Service Victoria and Vancouver 1951-56; present Co. 1956 serving as Forester, Woodlands Mgr. and Vice Pres.; served with RCNVR 1944-45; Pres. B.C. Loggers Assn. 1966-67; Dir. Council Forest Industs. 1966-67, 1972-81 (Chrmn. 1977-78); mem. Assn. B.C. Foresters; United; Home: 1274 Chartwell Dr., West Vancouver, B.C. V7S 2R3; Office: Ft. Philip Ave., North Vancouver, B.C.

FISK, George Vernon, D.D.S., F.A.C.D., F.I.C.D., F.R.C.D. (Can.); orthodontist (retired); b. Lorneville, Ont. 30 May 1895; s. Frank Mentor and Alberta (Burton) F.; e. Ogden Pub. Sch. and Oakwood Coll. Inst., Toronto; Univ. of Toronto, D.D.S. 1917; m. Olive Athow, d. Rev. John Francis Ockley, 20 June 1923; children: Murray Kent, M.D., Ross Ockley, D.D.S., M.S.; Hon. Consultant in Orthodontics, Hosp. for Sick Children; Capt., R.C.D.C. (Reserve); Hon. Pres., Inter-Am. Orthodontic Cong., 1942; Hon. mem., Mexican Orthodontic Assn.; Costa Rican Orthodontic Assn.; mem., Ont. Dental Assn.; Candn. Dental Assn. (Past Pres.); Am. Dental Assn.; Am. Assn. of Orthodontists (Vice-Pres., 1947); Gr. Lake Soc. of Orthodontists (Past Pres.); Am. Assn. for Advanc. of Science; Hon. Mem., Candn. Soc. Orthodontists, 1962-63; Nat. Geographic Soc.; has written many tech. articles for dent. mags; Xi Psi Phi; Conservative; Protestant; Clubs: Rotary (Toronto), Hon. mem.; Toronto Camera, Hon. mem., (twice past pres.); recreations: bowling, fishing; Home: Apt. 1201 — 880 Lawrence Ave. E., Don Mills, Ont. M3C 1P6

FITCH, Brian Thomas, B.A., Dr.de l'U., F.R.S.C.; educator; b. London, Eng. 19 Nov. 1935; s. Thomas Charles and Hilda (Parish) F.; e. Kings Coll. Univ. of Durham B.A. 1958; Univ. de Strasbourg Dr.de l'U. 1962; m. Josette d. late Aurélien François Jean Albert Ramel 29 Aug. 1959; children: Rafaëlla, Fabrice Julian, Sébastien; GERALD LARKIN PROF. OF FRENCH TRINITY COLL. UNIV. OF TORONTO 1966- ; Lecteur d'Anglais Univ. de Strasbourg 1960-62; Asst. Lectr. in French Manchester Univ. 1962-65; Visiting Assoc. Prof. of French present Coll. 1965-66, Head of French 1971-75, Assoc. Chrmn. Grad. Studies in French present Univ. 1977-81; Visiting Sen. Research Fellow, Merton College, Oxford 1970; Canada Council Leave Fellowships 1970-71, 1976-77; Founding Ed. "Albert Camus" Journal 1968- ; Dir. Littéraire, Lettres Modernes, Paris 1969-; author "Narrateur et narration dans 'L'Etranger' d'Albert Camus" 1960, 2nd ed. 1968; "Les Deux univers romanesques d'André Malraux" 1964; "Le Sentiment d'étrangeté chez Malraux, Sartre, Camus et S. de Beauvoir" 1964; "Essai de bibliographie des études en langue française consacrées à Albert Camus 1937-62" 1965; 2nd ed. (1937-67) 1969, 3rd ed. (1937-70) 1972; "Dimensions et structures chez Bernanos" 1969; "'L'Etranger' de Camus: un texte, ses lecteurs, leurs lectures" 1972; "Dimensions, Structures et textualité dans la trilogie romanesque de Samuel Beckett" 1977; "The Narcissistic Text: A Reading of Camus' Fiction" 1981; "Monde à l'envers/Texte réversible: la fiction de Bataille" 1982; Ed. "Configuration critique de Julien Green" 1964; "Ecrivains de la Modernité" 1981; mem. Modern Lang. Assn. Am.; Candn. Assn. Univ. Teachers; Soc. French Studies (UK); Home: 236 Rose Park Dr., Toronto, Ont. M4T 1R5; Office: Toronto, Ont. M5S 1H8.

FITZPATRICK, John J., Q.C., B.A.; b. Toronto, Ont., 1 Sept. 1914; s. John J. and Agnes (Wray) F.; e. De La Salle Coll.; Univ. of Toronto, B.A. 1939; Osgoode Hall Law Sch., Toronto, Ont.; m. Joan Elizabeth, d. late James Ratchford Cowie, 25 Aug. 1945; children: John, James, Kathleen, Margaret Ann, Moira, Janet, Sheila, Joan; PARTNER, FITZPATRICK & POSS since 1974; Dir., National Sewer Pipe Ltd.; read law with Douglas Haines; practised law with Haines & Haines, Toronto, Ont., 1948-49; Phelan, O'Brien & Fitzpatrick, 1949-55; with Gardiner, Watson Ltd., stockbrokers, Toronto, Ont., 1955-60; Gardiner, Roberts, Anderson, Conlin, Fitzpatrick, O'Donohue & White 1960-74; served in 2nd World War; Pilot, Flight Lieut., R.C.A.F.; mem., Canadian Bar Assn.; mem., Int. Assn. of Insurance Counsel; past Pres., The Advocates' Soc.; Past Chrmn., The Advisory Bd., Sacred Heart Children's Village; Past Chrmn., Bd. of Trustees, Sir William Campbell Foundation; Sigma Chi; Phi Delta Phi; R. Catholic; recreation: tennis; Clubs: Rosedale Golf; Queens; National; Osler Bluff Ski; Muskoka Lakes Golf & Country; Home: 210 Inglewood Drive, Toronto, Ont. M4T 1H9; Office: Commercial Union Tower, Toronto Dominion Centre, Toronto, Ont.

FLAHIFF, His Eminence, George Bernard, Cardinal, C.C. (1974), D.D. (R.C.); b. Paris, Ont., 26 Oct. 1905; s. John James and Eleanor (Fleming) F.; e. St. Michael's Coll., B.A. 1926; St. Basil's Semy. 1926-30; Univ. of Strasbourg 1930-31; Ecole des Chartes and Ecole des Hautes Etudes, Paris, 1931-35; ARCHBISHOP OF WINNIPEG, since March 1961; cr. a Cardinal April 1969; Prof. of Mediaeval Hist., Univ. of Toronto Grad. Sch. and Pontifical Inst. of Mediaeval Studies, 1935-54; Superior-Gen., Basilian Fathers, 1954-61; mem., S. Cong. for Religious, Rome since 1967; Address: 50 Stafford St., Winnipeg, Man. R3M 2V7

FLANAGAN, Edwin Wallace; trust and financial services executive; b. Sacramento, Cal., 18 Dec. 1923; s. Edwin James and Alta Irene (Willard) F.; e. Univ. of S. Cal. 1948; E.D.P. Stanford Grad. Sch. of Business, 1961; m. Nora Clare, d. Francis A. McCabe; children: Frank M., Maureen, Peggy, Tim; PRES. AND DIR., TRADER GROUP LTD.; Dir. & Vice Chrm. Bd., Guaranty Trust Co.; served with U.S. Marine Corps during World War II; Sigma Chi; Roman Catholic; recreations: golf, tennis, skiing; Clubs: Bayview Golf & Country; Pinebrook Golf & C.C. Calgary; Home: 2993 Elbow Dr. S.W., Calgary, Alta. T2S 2J3; Office: 401-9th St. S.W., Calgary, Alta. T2P 3C5

FLANIGAN, His Hon. Keith Allan, B.A.; b. Cornwall, Ont., 19 Oct. 1924; s. Alex Michael and Rita (Colquhoun) F.; e. Queen's Univ., B.A. 1949; Osgoode Hall Law Sch., 1953; m. Shirley Mary; d. Theodore Joseph Miron, 6 Oct. 1945; children: Patricia, Michael, Ted, Sheila, Colleen, Gail, Maureen, Sean; SR. COUNTY COURT JUDGE, JUDICIAL DIST. OTTAWA-CARLETON, 1978; read law with Roberts, Archibald, Seagram & Cole; called to Bar of Ont. 1953; cr. Q.C. 1965; Partner, Gibson Sands & Flanigan, 1954-70; First Chrmn., Tax Review Bd., 1971-78; aptd. to Co. Court Bench, Ont. June 1970; served with R.C.A.F. 1942-45; Chrmn., Capital Fund Campaign, Kingston Y.M.C.A., 1969-70; Pres., Kingston Red Cross; mem. Bd. of Govs., Hotel Dieu Hosp. and St. Mary's of the Lake Hosp., Kingston; mem., Candn. Bar Assn.; Dir., Can. Judges Conference; R. Catholic; recreation: golf; Clubs: University (Toronto); Home: 2481 Regina St., Ottawa, Ont. K2B 6X3; Office: Court House, Ottawa, Ont.

FLECK, James Douglas, B.A., D.B.A.; b. Toronto, Ont. 10 Feb. 1931; s. Robert Douglas and Norma Marie (Byrnes) F.; e. Whitney Pub. Sch. Toronto 1944; Univ. of Toronto Schs. 1949; Univ. of W. Ont. B.A. 1953; Harvard Univ. D.B.A. 1963; m. Margaret Evelyn d. late Robert Humphrys 6 June 1953; children: Robert J., A. Ellen, David A., Christopher C.; PROFESSOR OF MANAGEMENT, UNIVERSITY OF TORONTO Dir. C. N. Tower Co. Ltd.; Pres. Fleck Electrical Mfg. Ltd. Tillsonburg, Ont. 1953-60; Lectr. Harvard Business Sch. 1964-66; Prof. and Assoc. Dean Faculty of Adm. Studies and Dir. M.B.A. Program, York Univ. 1966-70; Extve. Dir. Comte. on Govt. Productivity 1970-71; Chief Extve. Offr. Office of the Premier 1972-73; Secy. to Cabinet 1974-75; Deputy Min. Ind. and Tourism 1976; William Lyon Mackenzie King Visiting Prof. Kennedy Sch. of Govt. Harvard Univ. 1978-79; Visiting Prof. Keio Sch. of Business Tokyo 1964; Univ. of W. Ont. Sch. of Business 1966; European Inst. Business Adm. Fontainebleau, France 1968; Dir, Inst. Research Pub. Policy; Banff Centre for Continuing Educ.; Hauserman Inc. (Cleveland); CN Tower; Gage Publishing Ltd.; Fleck Manufacturing; Multilingual Television Ltd.; Cable Utility Corp. Ltd.; J.C. Hallman Ltd.; Grace Hosp.; Nat. Ballet of Can.; Internat. Pres. Young Pres. Organ. 1972-73; served with RCAF Univ. Reserve 1949-53; author 'Life Insurance Investment Policy' 1969; various reports and articles on business and govt. mang.; Zeta Psi; Anglican; recreations: tennis, art collecting, travel, theatre; Clubs: Donalda; Queens; Home: 20 Wilket Rd., Willowdale, Ont. M2L 1N6; Office: 246 Bloor St. W., Room 435 N, OISE Building, Toronto, Ont. M5S 1V4

FLECK, Paul Duncan, M.A., Ph.D., F.R.S.A.; university professor; college president; b. Montreal, Que. 17 Apl. 1934; s. Robert Douglas & Norma Marie (Byrnes) F.; e. Brown and Whitney Schs. Toronto 1947; Albert Coll. Belleville 1952; Univ. of W. Ont. B.A. 1955, M.A. 1958; Univ. of Edinburgh Dipl. Eng. Studies 1959; Queen's Univ. Belfast Ph.D. 1961; m. Margaret Louise d. late Edward Franklin Pollard 1 Sept. 1956; children: Franklin Conor, John Christopher; PRESIDENT, ONT. COLLEGE OF ART 1975- ; Instr. in Eng. Univ. of W. Ont. 1956, Lectr. 1961, Asst. Prof. 1962, Assoc. Prof. 1965, Prof. 1970, Head and Chrmn. of Eng. 1965-74; rec'd Imp. Oil

Fellowship Award 1958-61; Can. Council Research Awards 1964, 1975; Chrmn. Bd. of Dirs. London French Sch. 1972-73; Chrmn. Educ. Div. Un. Appeal London 1972; Adv. Comte. on Hist. Sites London 1974-75; Adv. Comte. on Arts to Metrop. Toronto since 1976; Bd. of Dir., ARTMAGAZINE; Bd. of Dir. (Chmn.) NDWT Theatre Co.; author articles various learned journs.; mem. Assn. Candn. Univ. Teachers Eng. (Pres. 1974-76); Candn. Assn. Chrmn. Eng. (Pres. 1974); Byron Soc. (Chrmn. since 1974); Candn. Assn. Fine Art Deans. (Pres. 1980-81); United Church; recreations: photography, cooking, boating; Clubs: University; Arts & Letters (Vice Pres. 1980-82); Home: 40 St. Andrew's Gdns., Toronto, Ont. M4W 2E1; Office 100 McCaul St., Toronto, Ont. M5T 1W1.

FLEISCHMANN, George, association executive; b. Budapest, Hungary 31 Oct. 1935; s. Josef and Ella (Schwarcz) F.; e. Univ. of Toronto B.A. 1957, M.A. 1959, Ph.D. (Plant Pathol. & Genetics) 1962; m. Raizi d. Shamai Ogden, Toronto, 3 Sept. 1957; three d. Nira, Elana, Talya; PRESIDENT and C.E.O., GROCERY PRODUCTS MANUFACTURERS OF CANADA 1981- ; Research Scientist, Cereal Diseases Lab., Winnipeg 1962-71; Adj. Prof., Sch. Grad. Studies, Univ. of Man. 1964-71; Director, Chem. & Biol. Research Inst., Ottawa 1972-73; Dir. Gen., Environment Can. 1974-75; Asst. Secy. Program Br. Treasury Bd. 1976-77; Sr. Asst. Depy. Min. (Operations) Agric. Can. 1978-79; Depy. Comptroller Gen (Mang. Practices) 1980; Chmn, Reg. Reform, Privy Counc. Off. 1981; Lectr., Sch. of Business Adm. Univ. of Ottawa 1980-81; NRC Predoctoral Fellow Univ. of Toronto 1960-61; C.D. Howe Mem. Fellow Hebrew Univ. of Jerusalem 1965-66; author over 50 scient. articles rust diseases cereals; CBC freelance commentator pub. affairs and science 1966-73; Residences: 51 Charkay St., Ottawa K2E 5N5 and 1401, 44 Jackes Ave., Toronto M4T 1E5; Offices: 703, 170 Laurier Ave. W., Ottawa K1P 5V5, and 101, 1185 Eglinton Ave. E., Toronto M3C 3C6.

FLEMING, Hon. Donald Methuen, P.C. (Can.) 1957, Q.C., D.C.L., LL.D.; b. Exeter, Ont., 23 May 1905; s. Louis Charles and Maud Margaret (Wright) F.; e. Public Schs. and Coll. Inst., Galt, Ont. (Grad. 1921 with First Carter Scholar. for Waterloo Co.); Univ. of Toronto, B.A. 1925 (Gov. Gen. Gold Medal for Gen. Proficiency and Breuls Gold Medal for Pol. Science), LL.B. 1930; Osgoode Hall 1928 (Silver Medal and Christopher Robinson Mem. Scholar.); Bishop's Univ., D.C.L. 1960; Waterloo Lutheran Univ., LL.D. 1967; m. Alice Mildred, d. Wm. G. Watson, Toronto, 13 May 1933; children: David, Mary, Donald; formerly Mang. Dir., The Bank of Nova Scotia Trust Co. (Bahamas) Ltd.; The Bank of Nova Scotia Trust Co. (Cayman) Ltd.; The Bank of Nova Scotia Trust Co. (Caribbean) Ltd.; Gen. Counsel in extve., financial and other matters to The Bank of Nova Scotia in the Bahamas and the islands of the W. Indies and the Caribbean; Gore Mutual Insurance Co.; Chrmn., M. & G. (Cayman) Ltd.; Chrmn., Solomon Bros. Ltd.; 1st el. to H. of C. for Eglinton, g.e. 1945; re-el. 1949, 1953, 1957, 1958 and 1962; Minister of Finance, 1957-62; Atty.-Gen. and Min. of Justice, Aug. 1962, Apl. 1963; not a cand. in g.e. 1963; Chairman of OECD, 1961-62; candidate for Leadership of Progressive Conservative Party, 1948, 1956, 1967; Chrmn., Commonwealth Trade and Econ. Conf., Montreal, 1958; Headed Canada's Del. to Commonwealth Econ. (Consultative Council), London, Eng., 1959; Gov. Internat. Bank and Internat. Monetary Fund, Internat. Finance Corp. and Internat. Devel. Agency 1957-63; called to Bar of Ont., 1928; cr. K.C. 1944; Ald. Toronto City Council, 1939-44; Trustee Bd. of Educ., Toronto, 1938; Trustee, Toronto Gen. Hosp., 1939-44; Bd. of Dir., Candn. Nat. Exhn., 1941; mem., Univ. of Toronto Senate 1944-8 and Bd. of Govs.; Pres., Upper Canada Bible Society, 1946-49; North Toronto Y.M.C.A., 1944-49; President, Toronto Y.M.C.A., 1966-68; Hon. life member, Canadian Bar Association; Candn. Pol. Science Assn.; contrib. to

"Canadian Encyclopaedic Digest"; Jt. Ed. 5th ed., "Holmested's Judicature Act", 1937; I.O.F.; Freemason (Scot. Rite); P. Conservative; United Church; recreation: sports; Clubs: National; Canadian (Pres. 1964); Rideau (Ottawa); Country (Ottawa); Rosedale Golf; Toronto Cricket Skating & Curling; Empire; Granite (Toronto); Queen's (Toronto); Lyford Cay; Home: Carish House, Nassau, Bahamas; Office: P.O. Box N4267, Nassau, Bahamas.

FLEMING, Hon. James Sydney Clark, M.P., B.A.; politician; b. Kitchener, Ont. 30 Oct. 1939; s. Alexander and Alice Evelyn (McVannel); sons Alexander and John Robert; one d. Skye F.; e. Sheppard Pub. Sch.; Kitchener-Waterloo Coll. Inst.; Eastwood Coll. Inst.; Univ. of Toronto Univ. Coll. B.A.; m. Ilona d. Arnold Snepers, Hamilton, Ont. 30 Nov. 1971; MIN. OF STATE FOR MULTICULTURALISM, CAN. 1980- ; broadcast journalist; Past Pres. Toronto Mun. Press Gallery 1966; Dir. Candn. Soc. Abolition Death Penalty 1971-72; def. cand. Ont. g.e. 1971; el. to H. of C. for Toronto York West 1972, re-el. since; Parlty. Secy. to Min. of Communications 1975 and to Min. of Fisheries & Environment 1976; Liberal; Presbyterian; Home: 69 Ivy Cresc., Ottawa, Ont. Office: House of Commons, Ottawa, Ont. K1A 0A6.

FLEMING, John J., B.Com., C.A.; oil & gas executive; b. Lashburn, Sask. 16 Oct. 1939; e. Univ. of Sask. B.Com. 1960; C.A. 1963; PRESIDENT, BONANZA OIL & GAS LTD.; Dir. Newfoundland Capital Corp.; Campbell Resources Inc.; Dynamic Fund of Canada Ltd.; Summit Oilfield Corp.; mem. Candn. Inst. C.A.'s; Alta. Inst. C.A.'s; Candn. Assn. Petrol. Landmen; Office: 4th Floor, 622 - 5th Ave. S.W., Calgary, Alta. T2P 0M6.

FLEMING, Very Rev. Richard Gordon, B.D., L.Th., M.A., D.D. (Ang.); b. Brockville, Ont., 3 Nov. 1930; s. Edward Charles and Bessie Anna (Rowsome) F.; e. Brockville Public and Montreal High Schs.; McGill Univ., B.Sc. 1951, B.D. 1954; Montreal Diocesan Theol. Coll., L.Th. 1954 and Hon. D.D. 1970; Cambridge Univ., M.A. 1956; m. (Orla) Eileen, d. Clarence J. Green, Lyn, Ont., 2 July, 1955; four children; Rector of Kingston and Dean of Ont., 1964-76; Rector, Marmora, Ont., 1956-62; Christ Ch., Belleville, Ont., 1962-64; mem. Course 25, Nat. Defence Coll. Can. 1971-72; Special Cons., Province of Ont. 1977; Home: 11 Robert Wallace Dr., Kingston, Ont. K7M 1X9

FLEMING, Robert John; government administrator; b. London, Eng. 5 Apl. 1925; s. Austin Lloyd and Helen (Hyde) F.; e. Appleby Coll. Oakville, Ont. 1936; Lakefield (Ont.) Coll. 1941; m. Patricia Carruthers Beeman 16 Dec. 1950; one s. Robert John Carruthers; DIR. OF ADM., ONT. LEGISLATURE; Founder and Ed.-in-Chief, Pace Programs Inc., Los Angeles 1964-70; Extve. Dir. Royal Comn. on Book Publishing, Toronto 1970-72; Extve. Dir. Ont. Comn. on Legislature, Toronto 1972-74; Princ. Secy. (Designate) to Hon. Robert L. Stanfield, Ottawa 1974; author various papers relating to govt.; mem. Inst. Pub. Adm. Can.; Study of Parlt. Group Ottawa; Protestant; recreations: sailing, hiking; Clubs: RCYC; Empire; Kingston Yacht; Home: 51 Boswell Ave., Toronto, Ont. M5R 1M5; Office: Room 188, Legislative Bldg., Parliament Bldgs., Queen's Park, Toronto, Ont.

FLEMING, Robert Percival, B.Arch., F.R.A.I.C., A.R.I.B.A.; b. Cooksville, Ont., 25 Apl. 1914; s. Percival Frederick and Florence Esther (Jones) F.; e. Loyola Prep. Sch., St. Patrick's High Sch., 1928-32, McGill Univ., B.Arch. 1937; m. Helen Florence, d. William Tully, Kenora, Ont., 1940; children: Leo, Paul, William, Roberta; joined office of J. Cecil McDougall, 1938; with Defence Industries 1939-42; Partner, McDougall, Smith & Fleming till 1957; Fleming & Smith, 1957-64; (firm now Robert P. Fleming); Mayor, Town of Barkmere, Que., 1965-66; connected with design: Montreal Gen. Hosp., Jewish Gen.

Hosp., Montreal Children's Hosp., Royal Edward Laurentian Hosp., St. John Gen. Hosp. & Lakeshore Gen. Hosp., McGill Bldgs., New Engineering Bldg., Science Centre, Library, Chemistry & Physics Bldgs., Winter Stadium; various important indust. bldgs.; mem., P.Q., Ont. Arch. Assns.; Catholic; recreations: golf, fishing, hunting; Clubs: Royal Montreal (Pres. 1969-70); Lanthier Fish & Game; Montreal Badminton & Squash; Home: 52 Brock North, Montreal West, Que. H4X 2E9; Office: 1224 St. Catherine W., Montreal, Que. H3G 1P2

FLEMMING, Harry John, B.A., LL.B.; editor; b. Boston, Mass., 8 Oct. 1933; s. late John Albert and Edna Bernice (Tays) F.; e. Colchester Co. Acad., Truro, N.S., 1952; Mount Allison Univ., B.A. 1955; Dalhousie Univ., LL.B. 1958; m. Glen Maureen, d. late Spurgeon H. Perry, Gunningsville, N.B. 28 May 1960; children: Cara Elizabeth, John Andrew, Anne Catherine; read law with Patterson, Smith, Matthews and Grant, Truro, Nova Scotia; editorial writer, Halifax Chronicle-Herald and Mail-Star, 1961 and Toronto Globe & Mail, 1965; information officer, Atlantic Devel. Board and Department of Regional Econ. Expansion, Ottawa, 1966; Extve. Vice Pres., Atlantic Provs. Econ. Council 1970-73; Dec. 1973-77, Policy Adv. to Extve. Council, Prov. Nova Scotia; since 1978, ed. "Barometer" (Halifax weekly newspaper); Lib. cand. for Cumberland-Colchester N g.e. 1968 (def.); author and ed. of numerous reports, submissions, briefs and publ's during various positions held; frequent contrib. to CBC news and pub. affairs productions; mem., N.S. Barristers Soc. (called to Bar of N.S. 1959); Liberal; recreations: reading, golf, bridge; Home: 35 Walton Dr., Halifax, N.S. B3N 1X6.

FLEMMING, Hon. Hugh John, P.C.(Can.), D.C.L., LL.D.; lumberman; b. Peel, Carleton Co., N.B., 1899; m.; two s.; Dir., Flemming Industries Ltd.; North Carleton Land Co.; Caldwell Transport Co.; Juniper Realties Ltd.; Sussex Lumber & Pulpwood Ltd.; Hugh John Flemming Corp.; 1st el. to New Brunswick Leg. for Carleton, g.e. 1944; el. Leader of Conservative Party in N.B. July 1951; Premier and Min. of Pub. Works, Oct. 1952-June 1960 when gov't def. in g.e.; apptd. Min. of Forestry in Diefenbaker Cabinet, 11 Oct. 1960; el. to H. of C. in by-el. (Royal) 31 Oct. 1960; Min. of Forestry Oct. 1960 and Min. of Nat. Revenue, 9 Aug. 1962-Apl. 1963; elec. in General Election 1963 and re-el. 1965 and 1968 retiring from active pol. 1972; Pres., Candn. Good Roads Assn., 1957-58; P. Conservative; United Church; recreations: fishing, baseball; Home: 252 Waterloo Row, Fredericton, N.B. E3B 1Z3

FLEMMING, Paul Brian Nicholas, Q.C., B.Sc., LL.M.; barrister and solicitor; educator; b. Halifax, N.S. 19 Feb. 1939; s. Everett Francis Joseph and Margaret Mary (Meagher) F.; e. Primary and Secondary Schs. Halifax, N.S.; St. Mary's Univ. High Sch.; St. Mary's Univ. B.Sc 1959; Dalhousie Univ. LL.B. 1962; Univ. Coll. London, Eng. LL.M. 1964; Hague Dipl. in Internat. Law 1964; m. Janice Jenifer, d. late Dr. John W. Merritt 25 Aug. 1962; children: Ann Louise, Mark Alexander; Policy Adv. to the Prime Minister, 1976-81; partner, Stewart, Mackeen, & Covert, 1971- ; Vice-Chrmn. and mem. Extve. and Invest. Comtes. The Can. Council; read Law with G. S. Cowan, Q.C.; called to Bar of N.S. 1963 joining present Firm 1964; Free-lance broadcaster for CBC radio and TV since 1965; Lectr. in Law, Dalhousie Law Sch. and Maritime Warfare Sch. CFB Halifax; Lib. cand. for Halifax in 1974 Fed. el.; mem. Assn. Candn. Law Teachers; Am. Soc. Internat. Law; Brit. Inst. Internat. and Comparative Law; Candn. Bar Assn. (Chrmn. Maritime Law Sec.); Internat. Law Assn. (mem. Nat. Council Candn. Br.; Candn. Rep. Helsinki 1966, Buenos Aires 1968); Candn. Council Internat. Law; N.S. Barristers Soc.; Halifax Landmarks Comm.; Adv. Council Procedural Aspects Internat. Law Inst. N.Y.; Extve. Ed., "N.S. Law News"; mem. Candn. Del., UN Law of the Sea Conf., Caracas 1974, Ge-

neva 1975; Bd. Govs. Maritime Conserv. Music; Phi Kappa Theta; R. Catholic; Liberal (Pres. Halifax Fed. Constit.); recreations: travel, reading, swimming, boating; Home: 38 Monkland Ave., Ottawa, Ont.; also Glen Margaret, Nova Scotia (summer); Office: Stewart, Mackeen & Covert, P.O. Box 997, Halifax, Canada B3J 2X2

FLENNIKEN, C. S., B.M.E.; company executive; b. Chickasaw, Ala. (U.S.) 11 Aug. 1925; s. Warren S. and Pearle (Stephenson) F.; e. Georgia Inst. of Technol. B.M.E. 1949; m. Alyce Quince, d. J. P. Parrish, Georgetown, S.C. 15 June 1948; one s., Bruce Phillips; came to Canada 1969; PRES. AND CHIEF EXTVE. OFFR., CIP INC. since 1972; Vice Chrmn. of the Bd. and Chief Extve. Offr., Tahsis Co. Ltd. (Vancouver, B.C.); Dir., Tor. Dom. Bank; Facelle Co. Ltd.; joined International Paper Co. in 1949 serving as Mgr., Pulp and Paper Mills, Pine Bluff, Ark. and the Louisiana Mill at Bastrop, La.; joined present Co. 1969, Vice Pres. 1970, Extve. Vice Pres., Operations, 1971, el. a Dir. 1971; mem. Extve. Bd., Candn. Pulp and Paper Assn.; Trustee, P.I.M.A.; mem., Gen. Council of Industry; mem. Adv. Council, Candn. Mfctrs. Assn.; Beta Theta Pi; Methodist; Clubs: Mount Royal; St. James's; St-Denis; Rideau (Ottawa); Home: 1321 Sherbrooke St. W., Montreal, Que. H3G 1J4; Office: 1155 Metcalfe St., 14th Floor, Montreal, Quebec H3B 2X1

FLOYD, James C., F.R.A.S.; retired aviation consultant; b. England, 20 Oct. 1914; became Candn. Citizen 1951; s. James and Annie Elizabeth (Wilkinson) F.; e. Manchester Coll. of Technol., 1933-36 (Grad. with Associateship of Coll.); m. Irene, d. Edward Habbeshaw, 8 July 1940; children: Anthony David, Colin Noel, Peter Michael, Brian Paul; rec'd early aero training at A. V. Roe Co. and the Hawker Aircraft Co. in Eng.; came to Canada 1946 as Chief Tech. Offr. with Avro Aircraft Ltd.; Chief Design Engr. in charge of the C-102 Jet Airliner project; Vice-Pres. (Engn.), 1955-59; joined the Hawker-Siddeley Aviation Ltd., Eng. to head up an Advance Projects Group (cont. as a Dir., Avro Aircraft Ltd.), 1959; was first non-American to be awarded Wright Bros. Medal (for meritorious contribution to Aero Engn.) by the U.S. in 1950; presented with McCurdy Award by Candn. Aero Inst., 1958; Brit. Commonwealth Lectr., Royal Aero. Soc., 1958; awarded George Taylor Gold Medal by Royal Aero. Soc. for most valuable Aero. paper pub. in 1961; Fellow, Candn. Aero. and Space Inst.; Am. Inst. Aero. and Astronautics; formerly mem. and Past Chrmn., Toronto Sec., Inst. of Aero. Sciences; Regd. Prof. Engr., Ont.; Anglican; recreations: flying, photography; writing; Address: 284 Mill Rd., #A17, Etobicoke, Ont. M9C 4W6.

FLUMERFELT, Joseph Roger, B.Com., C.L.U.; insurance consultant; b. Calgary, Alta. 14 June 1917; s. late Harry Lyman and Alma Elizabeth F.; e. Sunalta Pub. Sch. and Central Coll., Calgary, Alta.; Univ. of Alta., B.Com. 1942, C.L.U. 1949; m. Shirley Jeannette, d. J. Delisle, Calgary, Alta. 29 May 1942; children: Trudy Diane, Roger Gordon, Donald Bruce; PRES., RETIREMENT COUNSELLORS LTD. 1960-81; Chart. Life Underwriter, Vancouver Georgia Agency, London Life Ins. Co.; began career as Clerk, Imp. Bank of Can., Calgary, Alta., 1934; Bookkeeper and Salesman, Simmons Ltd., Calgary, 1934-39; Real Estate Salesman, Lyle Bros. Ltd., Calgary, 1946; joined London Life Ins. Co. as Ins. Consultant, 1946; H.O. Agency Asst., London, Ont. 1957; Assoc. Dist. Mgr., Montreal, 1958; iReg. Mgr & Consultant, & Dist. Mgr. St James Agency to 1981 served in 2nd World War with 8th Field Regt., R.C.A. as Lieut.; 1945; as Capt. (Reserve) 1946-64; Past Dir., Montreal Life Underwriters Assn.; Calgary Life Underwriters Assn. (Pres. 1953); Past Nat. Dir., Life Underwriters Assn. of Can.; mem., Montreal Life Ins. and Trust Offrs. Council; Jr. Chamber of Comm. (Nat. Pres., 1953); Jr. Chamber Internat. (Vice-Pres. 1954); Life mem., Calgary Ch. of Comm., 1981; "Million Dollar Round Table" 1955-57; mem., Montreal Repertory Theatre (Pres. 1962); Mt. Royal Celebrity Concert Sales (Past Dir.); Montreal Bd. of Trade Assn. (Pres. 1962); Mt. Royal Un. Men's Club (Pres. 1962); Upward Trail Camp (Pres. 1959-64, Hon. Chrmn. 1964-68); Montreal Presbytery, Un. Church Men (Pres. 1963-68); Pres., Univ. of Alta. Alumni (Montreal Chapter) 1968-71; Que. Trustee Chart. Life Underwriters Inst. 1974-75, Pres. Montreal Chapter 1977, Life mem. 1978; Hon. Pres. Can. Jaycees 1974-75; Lt. Gov. Champlain Div. Montreal Kiwanis 1975-76; Div. Chrmn., Kiwanis Leaders & Canada Programme; Pres. Les Bonhommes de Gouin 1975; B.C. Dir., Candn. Citizenship Fed.; awarded Queen's Coronation Medal, 1953; Protestant; recreations: golf, curling, music, drama; Hobbies: Youth Welfare and Boys' Work; Clubs: St. James's; The Arts; M.A.A.A.; Kiwanis (Montreal, Pres. 1971-72); Mt. Royal Curling; Hollybeune. Country; Bd. of Trade (Vancouver); Petroleum (Calgary); Office: 3025 Crescent View Dr. North Vancouver, B.C.

FLYNN, Hon. Jacques, P.C., Q.C., B.A., LL.L.; senator; b. St. Hyacinthe, Qué. 22 Aug. 1915; s. late Francis and late Jeanne (Lussier) F.; e. Ste-Anne de la Pocatière, Qué.; Petit Séminaire de Qué. B.A. 1936; Laval Univ. LL.L. 1939; m. Renée d. late Henri des Rivières 14 Feb. 1942; children: Marie (Mrs. Marc André Pey), Francis; LEADER OF GOVT. IN SENATE, MIN. OF JUSTICE AND ATTY. GEN. OF CAN., 1979-80; called to Bar of Que. 1939; cr. Q.C. 1953; Enforcement Counsel E. Que., Wartime Prices & Trade Bd. 1942-45; Prof. of Mun. Law, Laval Univ. 1956-60, Prof. of Bankruptcy Law 1951-62; Sr. Partner, Flynn, Rivard and Associates, Québec City; def. cand. 1957 g.e.; el. to H. of C. for Que. S. g.e. 1958; def. g.e. 1962; Depy. Speaker and Chrmn. of Comtes. H. of C. 1960-61; Min. of Mines & Tech. Surveys 1961-62; summoned to Senate 1962; Leader of Opposition 1967-80; mem. Candn. Bar Assn.; P. Conservative; R. Catholic; recreations: golf, fishing, hunting; Clubs: Cercle Universitaire; Garrison; Home: Sillery, 1086 Parc Thornhill, Québec G1S 3N7; Offices: The Senate, Ottawa, Ont. K1A 0A4; 2 Chauveau C.P. 674 (H-V), Quebec, Q.C. G1R 4S6

FOLEY, Frank Clingan, Ph.D., F.G.S.A.; retired geologist; professor emeritus; b. Hastings Co. (Bayside), Ont., 8 Aug. 1906; s. Rev. Herbert Walter and Annie Laura (Clingan) F.; e. Orillia, Colborne and Cobourg, Ont. Coll. Insts.; Univ. of Toronto, B.A. 1929; Princeton Univ., Ph.D. 1938; m. Adelaide Bowler, d. late George Bowler Kirk, 31 Jan. 1934; one d. Mrs. Barbara Meeker, Ph.D.; Dir. Emeritus and mem. Staff, Kansas Geol., Survey; apptd. Prof. of Geol., Univ. of Kansas, 1954; Field Asst., Geol. Survey of Can. in N. Ont. and Que., summers 1927-31; Chief of Field Party, Nfld. Geol. Survey, N. Nfld., summer 1936; Instr. in Geol., Dartmouth Coll. 1929-30; Grad. Asst., Princeton Univ., 1930-33; Instr. to Prof. of Geol., Univ. of N. Dak., 1933-41 and State Geol. of N. Dak. 1938-41; Dist. Geol., Ground-Water Br., U.S. Geol. Survey, Utah and Wyo., 1941-42 and Wisc. 1946-51; Head, Ground-Water Br., Ill. Geol. Survey Urbana, 1951-54 and Research Prof. of Geol., Univ. of Ill.; overseas studies of ground-water resources conducted in Europe (Am. Battle Monuments Comn.) 1949, W. Africa and Saudi Arabia 1963 to present; Un. Nations expert hydrologist, Uganda, E. Africa 1971; Consultant, Kans. Water Resources Board.; served with Canadian Militia 1925-37; rank Lt.; Corps of Engineers, United States Army in Morocco and Italy, 1942-46; rank Maj.; awarded Bronze Star; International Association Hydro-geols.; Association American State Geologists; Sigma Xi; Lambda Chi Alpha; Republican; Cong.; recreations: gardening, electronics, reading; Home: 2609 W. 24th St., Terrace, Lawrence, Kansas 66044

FOLEY, Joan Eleanor, B.A., Ph.D., F.R.S.A.; educator; b. Sydney, Australia 31 May 1936; d. Alfred Joseph and Bessie Ridgway (Warden) Mason; e. Ravenswood Meth. Ladies Coll. Sydney 1952; Univ. of Sydney B.A. 1957, Ph.D. (Psychol.) 1960; m. Patrick Joseph Foley; two s. Brian Anthony, Colin Andrew; PRINCIPAL, SCARBOR-

OUGH COLL. UNIV. OF TORONTO since 1976 and Prof. of Psychol. there; Scient. Offr. Defence Research Med. Labs. Downsview, Ont. 1960-62; Special Lectr. in Psychol. Univ. of Toronto 1963, Asst. Prof. 1963, Assoc. Prof. 1965, Prof. 1975, Acting Chrmn. Dept. of Psychol. 1969-70, Assoc. Dean Faculty of Arts & Science 1971-74, Chrmn. Div. of Life Science Scarborough Coll. 1975-77; Dir. Donwood Inst. since 1973; author various articles and papers on learning and perception psychol. journs.; mem. and Fellow, Candn. Psychol. Assn.; Australian Psychol. Assn. (Foreign Affiliate); recreations: gardening, etching; skiing; Home: 300 Russell Hill Rd., Toronto, Ont. M4V 2T6; Office: Military Trail, West Hill, Ont.M1C 1A4

FOLINSBEE, Robert Edward, O.C. (1973), M.S., Ph.D., F.R.S.C., F.G.S.A.; professor emeritus; b. Edmonton, Alberta, 16 Apl. 1917; s. Francis John and Elizabeth Irene (Woolverton) F.; e. Univ. of Alta., B.Sc. 1938; Univ. of Minnesota, M.S. 1940, Ph.D. 1942; Harvard Univ., 1945-46; Univ. of Calif. (Berkeley), 1954; m. Catherine Elizabeth, d. late Dr. N. L. Terwillegar, 6 July 1942; children: Robert A., John D., James T., Catherine D.; PROF. EMERITUS, UNIV. OF ALBERTA, since 1978, (Chrmn. of Dept. of Geol. 1955-69); Asst. Geol., Geol. Survey of Can., 1941-43, Assoc. Geol., 1945-46; Asst. Prof., Univ. of Alta., 1946-50, Assoc. Prof., 1950-55, Prof., 1955-59; served in 2nd World War with R.C.A.F. as a Pilot, 1943-45; assisted with the devel. of Potassium argon method of dating rocks & minerals (Univ. of Cal.); Pres., 24th Internat. Geol. Cong., Montreal, 1972; Pres. Science Sec. Royal Soc. Can. 1969-70; awarded Centennial Medal 1967; mem., Candn. Inst. Mining & Metall.; Am. Assn. of Petroleum Geols.; Soc. of Econ. Geols.; Assn. Prof. Engrs., Geols. & Geophysicists, Alta.; Fellow, Geol. Assn. Can.; Pres. Geol. Soc. of Am. 1975-76; Pres. Royal Soc. of Can. 1977-78; Kappa Sigma; Conservative; Anglican; Clubs: Mayfair Golf & Country; Men's Faculty; Home: 1703-11027-87 Ave., Edmonton, Alta. T6G 2P9

FOLKESTONE, Folke Gunnar Sjoberg, C.M.; city councillor; b. West Sallerup, Sweden 21 Nov. 1903; s. August Sjoberg and Ellida Marie (Johnson) F.; e. Malmo Gymnasium Sweden 1922; Newspaper Inst. Am. (correspondence); Inst. Engn. Technol. (correspondence); m. 1stly Christine d. Jakob Schaffer, Yugoslavia; child: Dorothy June (Mrs. Richard Anscomb); m. 2ndly Ann Cecilia d. late Delbert Ball, Yorkton, Sask. 30 Nov. 1971; City Councillor, City of Flin Flon since 1956, Chrmn. Finance Comte. since 1957; Dir. City of Flin Flon Pub. Lib. since inception 1958; former Credit Union Mgr., Flin Flon Credit Union Ltd.; Dir., North of 53 Consumer Co-op. Ltd. 22 yrs. (Secy.-Treas. 1954-70); P. Conservative; Anglican; recreations: gardening, photography, sport fishing; Home: 413 Princess Blvd., Flin Flon, Man. R8A 0L5.

FOOTE, John Benjamin; merchant; b. Grand Bank, Nfld. 23 March 1918; s. Ambrose and Linda (Tibbo) F.; e. Grand Bank Un. Ch. Acad. 1936; m. Joan d. John G. Wilcox, Hearts Content, Nfld. 8 Aug. 1942; PROP. J. B. FOOTE & SONS LTD.; Mang. Dir. Foote Shipping Co. Ltd.; Dir. Newfoundland and Labrador Development Corp. Ltd.; Newfoundland Light and Power Co. Ltd.; Agt. and Distributor Imperial Oil Ltd., Wometco Newfoundland Ltd. (Coca Cola); La Batt Breweries of Nfld. Ltd.; Agt. Steers Insurance Agencies Ltd.; mem. Atlantic Devel. Council 1969-74; former mem. Grand Bank Town Council; Notary Public since 1948; United Church; Club: Lions (Past Pres. Grand Bank-Fortune 1961-62); Home: Camp and Main St., Grand Bank, Nfld. A0E 1W0; Office: Water St., Grand Bank, Nfld. A0E 1W0.

FOOTE, Maj. John Weir, V.C., C.D., LL.D., D.D.; b. Madoc, Ont., 5 May 1904; s. Gordon and Margaret Helena (Weir) F.; e. Univ. of W. Ont., B.A., LL.D.; Presb. Coll., McGill Univ., B.D., D.D.; m. Edith G., d.

Wilson Sheridan, Brockville, Ont., 31 Aug. 1929; mem. of Senate, Presb. Coll., Montreal; awarded Victoria Cross in 1946 for conspicuous gallantry at Dieppe while Regimental Chaplain with Roy. Hamilton Light Inf., 19 Aug. 1942; Command Chaplain, Central Command, prior to appt. as Depy. Chief Commr., Liquor Control Bd. of Ont.; former M.L.A. for Durham; Min. of Reform Inst., Ont.; 1950-57; former Sheriff, Cos. of Northumberland and Durham, Ont.; mem., Candn. Bandmasters' Assn.; Presbyterian; recreations: golf, fishing, music; Clubs: Albany; Royal Cdn. Military Inst.; Home: P.O. Box 7, Cobourg, Ont.

FORAN, William James, B.A.; executive; b. St. James, Man. 14 Apl. 1927; s. Neil J. and Mary (Garthside) F.; e. De La Salle Oaklands Coll. Toronto; Univ. of Toronto B.A. 1947; m. Catherine d. John M. Toorish 27 Nov. 1948; children: Mary Ann, Sean Michael; PRESIDENT AND DIR., CYANAMID CANADA INC. 1977- ; Dir. Shulton Canada Inc.; Sales Rep., Fiberglass Canada Ltd. 1947-53; St. Regis Paper Co. 1953-58; Sales Mgr. present Co. 1958, Dept. Mgr. 1964, Vice Pres. 1975; Past Chrmn., Candn. Chem. Producers Assn.; Indust. Gas Users Assn.; Candn. Fertilizer Inst.; R. Catholic; recreations: golf, skiing; Clubs: Mount Royal; Beaconsfield Golf; University; Home: 117 Alamosa Dr., Willowdale, Ont. M2J 2N8; Office: 2255 Sheppard Ave. E., Willowdale, Ont. M2J 4Y5.

FORBES, Donald Stewart; insurance executive; b. Belfast, N. Ireland, 3 Aug. 1928; s. William Victor John and Mary Agnes (Stewart) F.; e. Methodist Coll., Belfast; m. Joan, d. David Scott; children: Glenn, Janet; Vice-Pres. Marsh and McClennan Ltd.; Executive Vice-Pres. Harry Price, Hilborn Insurance Ltd. since 1960; with Sun Insurance Office, Belfast, 1947; Sun Insurance Office, Toronto, 1953; Geo. McMurrich & Sons Ltd., Toronto, 1955; Osler, Hammond & Nanton Ltd., 1955; joined present Co. through amalgamation of Harry Price, Hilborn Insurance Ltd., 1971; Assoc. Ins. Inst. of Can.; part author of "Legal Aspects of Architectural Practice"; lectd. at Ont. Gen. Constr. Assn., Toronto Constr. Assn., Ont. Assn. of Archs., Candn. Constr. Assn.; recreations: sailing, golf, tennis; Club: Bd. of Trade; Home: 18 Henry Corson Pl., Markham, Ont. L3P 3E9;

FORBES, James Dennis, B.S., M.B.A., Ph.D.; educator and management consultant; b. Ancon, Canal Zone 19 Dec. 1932; s. (late) Raymond Earl and Erma Theo (Caswell) F.; came to Canada 1967 (Citizen 1975); e. Washington State Univ., B.S. (Highest Hons. Agric.) 1954; Harvard Business Sch., M.B.A. 1959; Univ. of Calif. (L.A.) Ph.D. 1967; m. Nancy Currie, d. late Thomas Penman 1 June 1963; children: Susan, Carol, James, Heather; Pres. Forbes Associates, Mang. Consultants and Assoc. Prof. of Comm., Univ. of Brit. Columbia; formerly W. Regional Mgr. Mechrolab Inc., Mt. View, Calif.; joined present Univ. 1967 as Asst. Prof., Assoc. Prof. 1970; served in U.S. Army Signal Corps 1955-57, rank 1st Lt.; Richard D. Irwin Doctoral Fellow 1967; mem. Am. Marketing Assn.; Inst. Mang. Sciences; Consumer's Assn. Can.; author of various articles on agriculture and food policy, distribution, consumer spatial behaviour, consumerism and marketing; author, "Instructions and Influence Groups in the Canadian Food System Policy Process," 1982; co-author "Government Intervention and Regulation in Canadian Agrculture," 1982; "Consumer Interest in Marketing Boards" 1974; Office: Faculty of Commerce, University of British Columbia, Vancouver, B.C. V6T 1Y8

FORBES, William Frederick, Ph.D., D.Sc.; educator; e. Univ. of London, B.Sc. 1947, D.Sc. 1964, Imp. Coll. B.Sc. 1950, Ph.D. (Chem.) 1952, D.I.C.; m. Dr. Margaret Anne (nee Shadbolt); children: Christine Olivia, Alain James, Helena Vivienne; Dean, Faculty of Mathematics, Univ. of Waterloo 1972-80 and PROF. OF STATISTICS there; Lectr., Univ. of Nottingham, Eng., 1952; Assoc. Prof., Memorial Univ. of Nfld., 1953, Prof. 1955; Princ. Re-

search Offr., C.S.I.R.O., Australia, 1959; joined present Univ. as Prof. 1962; Visiting Prof., Univ. of Rochester, 1965-71; Head of World Health Centre for Reference on the Assessment of Smoking Habits; Consultant to U.S. Public Health Service (NICHD) 1965-69; Chrmn., Computer Coordination Bd., Council of Ont. Univs., 1971-73; mem., WHO Expert Adv. Panel on Smoking & Health, 1977-82; served with R.A.F. 1944-47; author of over 200 publs. in fields of gerontol. smoking & health, organic spectral chem.; Assoc., Royal Coll. Science; mem., Candn. Assn. Gerontol. (Pres. 1971-73) (rec. Assn. award for outstanding contributions to Gerontology, 1981); U.S. Gerontol. Soc. (Vice Pres. & Chrmn. Biol. Sciences Sec. 1971-72); Dir., Gerontology Research Council of Ont., recreations: military history, travel, raquet games; Home: 56 Shadywood Cres., Kitchener, Ont. N2M 4J2

FORD, George Harry, M.A., Ph.D.; university professor; author; b. Winnipeg, Man., 21 Dec. 1914; s. Harry and Emma Gertrude (Burgess) F.; e. Kelvin High Sch., Winnipeg, 1932; Univ. of Man., B.A. 1936; Univ. of Toronto, M.A. 1938; Yale Univ., Ph.D. 1942; m. Kathleen Patricia, d. late James Richard Murray, 4 May, 1942; children: Leslie Margaret, Harry Seymour; PROF. OF ENG., UNIV. OF ROCHESTER, since 1958 and Chrmn. of Dept. 1960-72; Lect., Univ. of Man., 1940-42, 1945-46; Assoc. Prof., Univ. of Cincinnati, 1946-55; Prof. 1955-58; Visiting Prof., Univ. of Chicago 1948, Johns Hopkins Univ., 1949, Univ. of B.C. 1953; served with RCA 1942-45; rank Capt.; rec'd John Addison Porter Prize, Yale Univ. 1942; Fellow, Am. Council Learned Socs., 1959; Guggenheim Fellow 1963-64; Huntington Library Fellow 1978; author: "Keats and the Victorians", 1944 reprinted 1945, 1961; "The Pickersgill Letters", 1948; "Dickens and His Readers", 1955 paperback 1961; "Double Measure: A Study of D.H. Lawrence", 1965 paperback 1968; Ed., "Selected Poems of Keats", 1950; "The Dickens Critics", 1961 paperback 1966; "David Copperfield" 1958 and "Hard Times" 1967; "Vanity Fair" 1958; "Bleak House", 1977; "Victorian Fiction: A Second Guide to Research", 1978; "The Making of a Secret Agent", 1978; Co-ed., "The Norton Anthology of English Literature", 1962, 68, 74, 79; mem. Adv. Bd., "Mosaic" (Univ. of Man. mag.) since 1967; Adv. Bd., "Victorian Studies", 1964-67; Adv. Bd., "Thalia" (University of Ottawa Mag.) 1978- ; mem., Eng. Inst. (Supvry. Bd. 1964-66); Modern Lang. Assn (Chrmn., Victorian Lit. Sec., 1965); Pres. (1973-74) Dickens Soc. Am.; Pres. (1975-77) The Dickens Fellowship (London); Pres. (1979); Int. Soc. for Study of Time (Extve. Council 1977); Vice Chrmn., New York Council for Humanities, 1978,79; Consultant, Ontario Council of Graduate Studies 1980-1; Am Acad. of Arts & Sci., 1980; mem., Int. Advisory Bd., Buckingham Univ., England; Delta Upsilon; Democratic; Anglican; recreation: riding; Clubs: Cincinnati Literary; Rochester Pundit; Home: 2230 Clover St., Rochester, N.Y.

FORD, Robert A.D., C.C. (1971), M.A., D.Litt.; diplomat; b. Ottawa, Ont., 8 Jan. 1915; s. late Arthur R. and late Lavinia (Scott) F.; e., Univ. of W. Ont., B.A. 1937; Cornell Univ., M.A. 1940; Univ. of W. Ont., D.Litt. 1965; m. Maria Thereza Gomes, 1946; SPECIAL ADVISOR TO CANDN. GOV'T. ON EAST-WEST RELATIONS; mem. Independent commision on Disarmament and security issues (Palme commision); served on Staff of Cornell Univ., before joining the Dept. of External Affairs in 1940; held appts. in Rio de Janeiro and London before appt. as Second Secy., at Moscow in 1946; again served in London as Secy., later returning to Moscow as Chargé d'Affaires, 1951-54; subsequently Head of European Sec., Ottawa; Ambassador to Colombia, 1956-59; Ambassador to Yugoslavia, Jan. 1959-May 1961; Ambassador to United Arab Republic, 1961-63; Ambassador to U.S.S.R. 1964-80; awarded Gold Medal, Prof. Inst. Pub. Service of Can. 1971; author of: "A Window on the North" (poems), for which rec'd. Gov.-Gen. Award for Poetry

(1956); "The Solitary City"(poems); "Holes in Space" (poems); Address: La Poivrière, Randan, 63310 France

FOREST, L'hon. Joseph-Isai-Yves; judge; b. Sherbrooke, Que., 25 June 1921; s. Lionel, Q.C. and Marie-Alice (Deneault) F.; e. St. Charles Semy., Sherbrooke, Que.; Univ. of Montreal; m. Elizabeth, d. late Napolean St. Martin, 11 Aug. 1947; children: Suzanne, Robert, Barbara, Pierre, Jean; JUSTICE SUPERIOR COURT, QUE.; called to Bar of Que. 1943; cr. Q.C. 1961; served as M.P. 1963-72; Chrmn. of Bd., La Providence Hosp., Magog; R. Catholic; recreations: skiing, golf, fishing; Home: Merry St., Magog, Que.; Office: Court House, Montreal, Que.

FORGET, Nicolle, B. en Sc. Com., L. ès D.; née Saint-Liguori, Qué. 14 mai 1941; f. Léonard et Noella (Desmarais) F.; é. Pensionnat Saint-Joseph, Saint-Liguori, Qué. 1957-58; l'Acad. Maria Goretti, Alexandria, Ont. 1958-59; Ecole des H. E. C. Montréal B. en Sc. Com. 1970; Univ. de Montréal L. ès D.; ép. 28 août 1971; un enfant; mem. du conseil d'administration de Nouveler Inc. 1980- ; mem. du conseil d'adm. de l'Hydro-Québec et de la Soc. d'énergie de la Baie James aussi Hydro-Québec Internat. depuis 1978; mem. Conseil économique du Can. depuis 1978; Antofagasta, Chili, Colegio San José, enseignement du français et de la musique 1960; Séminaire de Joliette, bibliothèque 1961-62; CJLM, Joliette, Service des reportages et émissions féminines 1960-63; Coll. classique Joliette, enseignement du français littéraire 1963; Hôpital psychiâtrique St-Charles, Joliette, enseignement du français aux religieuses espagnoles 1963-64; Comn. scolaire régionale Lanaudière, service d'orientation, secrétaire 1963-65; Etoile du Nord, Joliette (Hebdomadaire) directrice des pages féminines et artistiques 1964-65; Union des Municipalités du Qué. Montréal, secrétaire 1965-67; Conseil de bien-être du Qué. Montréal, chef de secrétariat 1967-68, secrétaire générale intérimaire 1968-69, dir. gén. intérimaire 1970-71; Rédacteur d'une chronique sur la Consommation, Journal de l'Alimentation 1973; Inst. canadien d'éd. des adultes, chargée d'adm. 1973-77; fondateur et dir. de troupe de théâtre "Les deux masques" Joliette 1961-66; mem. du comité des Jeunesses musicales du Can. Joliette 1963-66; dir., comité auxiliaire féminin de la Jeune Chambre de Comm. Joliette 1961-63; mem. Soc. des poètes canadiens-français 1961-66; mem. Conseil gén. de la Féd. des SSJB du Qué. 1964-67 (vice prés. 1966-67, trésorier 1967-69); secrétaire-trésorier de l'Agence Alerte Inc. 1967-69, mem. fondateur et secrétaire de la Féd. des Femmes du Qué. 1967-68; secrétaire francophone de la div. du Qué. de l'Assn. des consommateurs du Can. 1970-71, Vice Prés. 1971-72, trésorier 1972-73, prés. de l'Association des consommateurs du Québec, 1975-78; publié divers articles; Adresse: 1170 Maple, Longueuil, Qué. J4J 4N6.

FORREST, Bruce Wallace, B.Sc., B.E., P.Eng.; b. Halifax, N.S. Feb. 1934; s. Reginald Wallace and Hazel G. (Hall) F.; e. Public and High Schs. Halifax, N.S.; Dalhousie Univ., Dipl. Engn., B.Sc. (Math.) 1955; N.S. Tech. Coll., B.E. (Mech. Engn.) 1959; m. Marilyn, d. Percy Kent Ryan, May 1959; children: Sharon Irene, Carol, Jean; PRESIDENT AND DIR. SNC CONSULTANTS LTD. and of General Engineering Co. Inc. (members of The SNC Group) since 1974; Director SNC Enterprises Ltd.; began as Design Engineer, Integrated Consultants, Montreal 1959; Sr. Mechanical Engineer, Kaiser Engineers 1961; Project Engineer Du Pont of Can. Ltd. 1963; Sr. Mechanical Engineer Asselin, Benoit, Boucher, Ducharme, Lapointe 1965; Sr. Mech. Engr. Surveyer, Nenniger & Chenevert Inc. 1970; Operations Mgr. General Engineering Co. Inc. 1971, Gen. Mgr. Toronto Operations 1971-73; mem. Assn. Prof. Engrs. Ont.; Candn. Inst. Mining & Metall.; Order of Engrs. Que.; Anglican; recreations: golf, swimming; Club: Chinquacousy Golf & Country; Home: 10 Governor Grove Cres., Brampton, Ont. L6Y 1A6;

FORREST, John Russell; forest products executive; b. Port Alberni, B.C. 6 June 1924; s. James Alexander and Elsie (Bigmore) F.; e. Univ. of B.C. Arts Course 1 yr.; m. Jo-Anne 16 Sept. 1977; children: James T., Penny G. Milbrandt; SR. VICE PRES. TIMBER & WOOD PRODUCTS GROUP, BOISE CASCADE CORP. 1977- ; Chrmn. of Bd. Boise Cascade Canada Ltd. 1980- ; Dir. Boise Southern Co.; held various mang. positions sawmill and plywood field and directed pulp and paper complex MacMillan Bloedel Ltd. Vancouver 1942-68, Group Vice Pres. Bldg. Materials 1968-72 and Forestry & Bldg. Materials 1973-77; served with RCAF; mem. Nat. Forest Products Assn. (Dir.; Chrmn. Internat. Trade Comte.); Western Wood Products Assn.; Protestant; recreation: golf; Clubs: Capilano Golf & Country (W. Vancouver); Hillcres Country (Boise); Home: 4215 Country Club Dr., Boise, Idaho 83705; Office: One Jefferson Sq., Boise, Idaho 83728.

FORRESTALL, Thomas DeVany, B.F.A., D.C.L., R.C.A.; artist; b. Middleton, N.S. 11 March 1936; s. Thomas Patrick and Esther Mary (Curphey) F.; e. elem. and high schs. Middleton and Dartmouth, N.S.; Mount Allison Univ. B.F.A. 1958 (studied under Alex Colville and L. P. Harris); travel and study Europe (Can. Council Grant) 1958-59; King's Coll. Halifax D.C.L. 1980; m. Natalie Marie d. Frank LeBlanc, Atholville, N.B. 12 Sept. 1958; 7 children: William, Monica, Renee, John, Curphey, Francis, Colin (d.); Asst. Curator, Beaverbrook Art Gallery, Fredericton 1959; self-employed artist since 1960; began experimenting with panels shaped other than rectangles 1961; completed Kennedy and Churchill Mem. Masks 1964, 1965; solo exhns. incl. Roberts Gallery Toronto 1965, 1970; Dartmouth Coll. Art Gallery Hannover, N.H. 1966; Large Outdoor Sculpture Atlantic Pavilion Expo '67 1967; Walter Klinkhoff Gallery Montreal 1967, 1969; Sir. George Williams Univ. Montreal 1968, 1975; Retrospective "Forrestall High Realism" across Can. 1971; Mendel Art Gallery, Saskatoon 1971, 1979; Art Gallery of Victoria 1971, 1979; Art Gallery of Windsor 1972, 1974; Montreal Museum of Fine Arts 1972; Winnipeg Art Gallery 1972; Candn. Cultural Center Paris, France 1972; Boston City Hall Art Gallery 1972; N.S. Museum of Fine Arts Centennial Gallery 1974; Hart House Univ. of Toronto 1975; Marlborough Godard Gallery Toronto 1975; Tom Thomson Mem. Gallery & Museum of Fine Arts 1975; Robert McLaughlin Gallery 1975; London (Ont.) Pub. Lib.; Art Museum 1975; Marlborough Galleries London (Eng.), Zurich and Rome (individual pieces) 1975-76; Marlborough New York 1976; Mira Godard Gallery Montreal 1977, Toronto 1978; Art Gallery of N.S. tour 1977-78; W.End Gallery Edmonton 1978; Ownes Art Gallery Mount Allison Univ. tour 40 tempera paintings across Can. 1978-79; Evergreen Exhn. 1978; Saidye Bronfman Centre Montreal 1979; Hamilton Art Gallery 1979; Glenbow Inst. Calgary 1979; Beaverbrook Art Gallery Fredericton 1979; Liverpool (Eng.) Acad. 1980; Can. House Gallery London 1980; Cultural Museum Denant, Belgium 1980; Museum of Modern Art Belgrade 1980 and rep. Can. Beograde '80 Internat. Exhn. Plastic Arts; Nat. Museum of Art Sophia, Bulgaria 1980; Nat. Museum of Art of Romania Bucharest 1980; National Museum of Art, CLUJ, Transylvania; Nat. Museum of Art of Hungary, Budapest; Madison Gallery, Toronto, 1981; Bayard Gallery, New York, 1981; rep. various group exhns. Can. and Europe; pub., corporate and private colls.; estbd. Three Oaks Corp. Ltd. 1972, Dir.; N.S. Museum of Fine Arts 1973-75; N.S. Talent Trust 1974-75; Dartmouth Acad. 1979-80; co-judge Series V Olympic Coins '76; rec'd Secy. of State's Citation Commonwealth of Mass. 1972; Royal Arch. Inst. Can. Medal 1975; Queen's Silver Jubilee Medal 1977; author "This Good Looking Land" 1976; co-author "Shaped By This Land" 1972; various catalogues; subject of numerous publs.; mem. St. Vincent de Paul Soc.; Candn. Artists Representation; Candn. Conf. of Arts; Heritage Advisory Council; P. Conservative; R. Catholic; recreations: swimming, outdoors, drawing; Address: 3 Albert St., Dartmouth, N.S. B2Y 3M1

FORRESTER, Maureen (Mrs. Eugene Kash), C.C. (1967), LL.D., D.Litt., D.Mus.; (contralto); b. Montreal Que., 25 July 1930; d. Thomas and Mary Dumican (Arnold) F.; e. Wm. Dawson Sch., Montreal, Que.; private music study; LL.D., Sir George Williams College; D.Litt., York University, Saint Mary's University; D.Mus. Western 1974; m. Eugene Kash, 20 June 1954; children: Paula, Gina, Daniel, Linda, Susanna; rec'd Banff Sch. Fine Arts, Nat. Award in Music 1967; Harriet Cohen Internat. Music Award 1968; Molson Prize 1971; a Fellow, Stong Coll., York Univ.; apptd. mem. Board of Trustees, Nat. Arts Centre Corp. 1973; portrait painted by Miss Jean Primrose; Sigma Alpha Iota; Hebrew; Address: c/o Shaw Concerts Inc., 1995 Broadway, New York City, N.Y. 10023

FORSEY, Eugene Alfred, O.C. (1968), Ph.D., D.C.L., LL.D., D.Litt., F.R.S.C. (1967); retired Senator; b. Grand Bank, Nfld., 29 May 1904; s. Eugene & Florence Elvira (Bowles) F.; e. McGill Univ., B.A. 1925, M.A. 1926, Ph.D. 1941; Rhodes Schl., Que., 1926; Balliol Coll., Oxford, B.A. 1928, M.A. 1932; Guggenheim Fellow 1941; LL.D. Univ. of N.B. 1962, McGill 1966, Sask. 1967, Toronto 1968, Waterloo 1968, Dalhousie 1971, York, 1972, Carleton, 1977, Queen's, 1979; D.Litt., Memorial 1966, Acadia 1967, Trent, 1978; D.C.L., Mt. Allison, 1973; m. Ina Harriet, d. Harry Jewett Roberts, Saint John, N.B., 1935; two d.; def. C.C.F. cand. to H. of C. at by-el. 1948 and g.e. 1949; summoned to Senate of Can. Oct. 1970-79; author of "Economic and Social Aspects of the Nova Scotia Coal Industry", 1926; "The Royal Power of Dissolution of Parliament in the Brit. Commonwealth", 1943; "Social Planning for Canada", 1935 (with others); "Towards the Christian Revolution", (with others) 1936; "Freedom and Order", 1974; "The Canadian Labour Movement 1812-1902", (Booklet) 1975; "How Canadians Govern Themselves" (Booklet) 1979; "Trade Unions in Canada 1812-1902," 1982; mem., Board of Broadcast Govs., Canada, 1958-62; Skelton-Clark Fellow, Queen's Univ., 1962-63; Pres. Candn. Pol. Science Assn. 1961-62; mem. Bd. of Govs., Trent Univ. 1966-73; Chancellor, 1973-77; United Church; Home: 711-315 Holmwood Av., Ottawa, Ont. K1S 2R2

FORSTER, Donald Frederick, B.A., A.M.; educator; b. Toronto, Ont. 1934; s. Frederick E. and Mrs. Forster; e. Primary and Secondary Schs. Toronto; Univ. of Toronto B.A. 1956; Harvard Univ. A.M. 1958; PRESIDENT AND VICE CHANCELLOR, UNIV. OF GUELPH ; Lectr. in Pol. Econ. Univ. of Toronto 1960, Asst. Prof. 1963-65, Prof. 1970-75, Extve. Asst. to Pres. 1965-67, Extve. Asst. to Pres. and Vice Provost 1967-71, Acting Extve. Vice Pres. (Acad.) and Provost 1971-72, Vice Pres. and Provost 1972-75; Pres. present Univ. 1975; Research Asst. Official Biog. W.L.M. King, Laurier House, Ottawa 1958-60; Econ. Adviser Govt. of Tanzania 1970; Econ. Consultant Govt. of Papua, New Guinea 1974; Woodrow Wilson Fellow 1956; Imperial Oil Fellowship 1957; co-author "Economics: Canada" 1963; 3 vols. "Mackenzie King Record"; author numerous articles in field of econ. and pol. science; Review Ed. "Canadian Journal of Economics and Political Science" 1964-67; Asst. Ed. "Canadian Annual Review" 1964-70; mem. Extve. Comte. Council Ont. Univs. 1976-78, 1979-81, 77-79; United Church; Home: President's Residence, Univ. of Guelph, Guelph, Ont. N1G 2W1

FORSTER, Col. Walter Leslie, C.B.E. (1942), B.Sc.; consultant; b. Leeds, England 30 June 1903; s. John Mark F.; e. Leeds Univ., B.Sc. 1925; m. Lorna May Bonstow, 1936; one s.; joined Royal Dutch-Shell Group in 1925, and served in various capacities in exploration and production dept. in Mexico, Venezuela, Roumania, Egypt and elsewhere; Gen. Mgr., Royal-Dutch Shell companies in Colombia, July 1946-Feb. 1947, and Venezuela, Mar. 1947-Nov. 1950 since when has been resident in Canada ; served in 2nd World War; Commissioned in Brit. Army in 1939 and served in various mil. and official capacities

in Middle East countries, the Soviet Union, Burma, Wash., D.C., North Africa, Italy and Roumania; Col. in charge of Econ. Sec. of Brit. Mission on Allied (Soviet) Control Comn. in Roumania (1944-46); awarded C.B.E. for services in Burma 1942; U.S. Legion of Merit (Offr.) for services in N. Africa (1943); Fellow, The Inst. of Petroleum (London); Clubs: St. James's; Mount Royal; Home: 61 Summit Crescent, Westmount, Que. H3Y 1L5

FORSYTH, Rev. Charles Harkness, B.A., B.D., D.D. (Un. Ch.) ; b. Winnipeg, Man., 20 Apr. 1926; s. Charles Harkness and Hazel Margaret (Andison) F.; e. Robert H. Smith Jr. High and Kelvin High Schs., Winnipeg; Un. Coll. (Univ. of Man.), B.A. 1947; B.D. 1950; Univ. of Winnipeg, D.D. 1969; m. Myrna Lee, d. J.J. George, 28 June 1954; children: Charles, Janet Lee, Marcia Gail, Ian Lamont; MIN., FIRST UNITED CH., HAMILTON since Sept. 1978; o. 1950; served at Sioux Lookout, Ont., 1950-54; John Black Mem. Ch., East Kildonan, Man., 1954-60; Supt., Central Winnipeg Parish, 1960-64; Sackville Un. Ch., N.B., 1964-66; Extve. Asst to Premier of N.B. 1966-68; mem., Can. Council 1965-66; Regent Un. Coll., 1963-64; served on various civic and philanthropic bds. 1954-66; Secy., Bd. of Evangelism & Social Service, United Church of Canada 1968-1970; Min., St. Andrew's Ch. 1970-78; mem. Sec. on Aging, Ont. Welfare Council; mem. Sudbury Regional Development Corporation; Hamilton City Central Area Planning Group; Mem. of Bd., Family Services (Hamilton); Victoria Park Community Homes — Strathcona Community Centre; rec'd Centennial Medal 1967; Liberal; recreations: music, camping; Home: 166 Delaware Ave., Hamilton, Ont. L8M 1V6; Office: First United Ch., 350 King Street E., Hamilton, Ont. L8M 3Y3

FORSYTH, Hon. Gregory Rife, B.A., LL.B; judge; b. Calgary, Alta. 15 June 1928; s. Thomas Dalgleish and Marjorie (Rife) F.; e. Univ. of Alta. B.A. 1950, LL.B. 1951; m. Elizabeth Anne d. late H. C. H. Brayfield, K.C. 8 Feb. 1958; children: Douglas, Jane; JUDGE, COURT OF QUEEN'S BENCH ALTA. since 1979; called to Bar of Alta. 1952; cr. Q.C. 1971; joined Canadian Pacific Railway Law Dept. Calgary 1952-55, Toronto 1955-57, Montreal 1957-59; Partner, Howard, Dixon, Mackie, Forsyth 1959-79; served with RCAF (Reserve) 403 City of Calgary Sqdn. 1951-55, 400 City of Toronto Sqdn. 1955, rank Flying Offr.; Anglican; recreations: golf, sailing; Clubs: Ranchmen's; Calgary Golf & Country; Glencoe; Home: 1704—330—26th Ave. S.W., Calgary, Alta. T2S 2T3

FORSYTH, Joseph, M.L.S.; librarian; b. Washington, Co. Durham, Eng. 15 Aug. 1942; s. James Frederick and Maisie (Appleby) F.; e. Stockton Grammar Sch. 1960; Newcastle Sch. of Librarianship A.L.A. 1963; Univ. of London M.L.S. 1976; m. Kay Frances Appleby 3 Oct. 1964; two s. Julian Alastair, Andrew Stuart; DIR. OF LIBRARY SERVICES, PROV. OF ALTA. 1977- ; Coll. Librarian, Easington Tech. Coll. 1963-64; Regional Librarian, N. Yorks. Co. Lib. 1964-66; Reference Librarian, Calgary Pub. Lib. 1960-70; Lib. Devel. Offr., Prov. Alta. 1970-77; author "Bibliography of Government Publications Relating to Alberta" 1971; various articles; Assoc., Lib. Assn. (U.K.); mem. Candn. Lib. Assn.; Lib. Assn. Alta.; Anglican; recreations: gardening, walking, cycling, reading, music, theatre, dog showing; Home: 15211 - 83 Ave., Edmonton, Alta. T5R 3Z5; Office: Alberta Culture, Library Services Branch, 16214-114 Ave., Edmonton, Alta., T5M 2Z5

FORTIER, André; Canadian public servant; b. Montreal, Que., 1927; e. Laval University; Univ. of Montreal, postgrad. math.; PRES., THE SOCIAL SCIENCES AND HUMANITIES RESEARCH COUNCIL OF CAN. since 1978; upon grad. joined Treasury Bd., Ottawa; joined Can. Council as Financial Offr.; subsequently Treas.; Asst. Under Secy., Dept. Secy. of State, 1969-72; Dir., Can. Council, 1972-75; Under Secy. of State, 1975-78; R. Catholic; recreations: skiing, swimming; Office: 255 Albert St. Ottawa, Ont. K1P 6G4

FORTIER, Claude, C.C. (1970) M.D., Ph.D., F.R.C.P.(C), F.R.S.C. (1964), LL.D., D.W.; medical scientist; b. Montreal, Que., 11 June 1921; s. Carolus and Edith (Lanctôt) F.; e. Univ. of Montreal, B.A. 1941, M.A. (Pol. Sciences) 1941, M.D. 1948, Ph.D. (Exper. Med. & Surg.) 1952; post-grad. training Univs. of Lausanne and London, 1952-55; LL.D.; Dalhousie 1977; D.W. (Hon.) U. of Montréal, 1981; U. of Ottawa, 1981; m. Elise, d. Senator Léon-Mercier Gouin, Lausanne, 8 Sept. 1953; children: Anne, Michèle, Nicole, Nathalie; PROF. AND CHRMN., DEPT. OF PHYSIOL., FACULTY OF MEDICINE, LAVAL UNIV., since 1964; Dir., Endocrine Labs.; Pres., Royal Soc. Can. 1974-75; Chrmn. of Bd. of Candn. Fed. of Biol. Socs. 1973-74; Chmn.of Science Council Can. 1978- ; mem. and Vice Chrmn. of Science Council of Can. 1975-78; Chrm., S.C.C. Task Force on Research in Canada, 1976-78; mem. Adv. Council, Order of Can. 1974-75; Bd. Trustees, Inst. for Research on Public Policy 1974-75, 1978- ; Vice Chairman, Med. Research Coordinating and Advisory Committees, Defence Research Bd., 1967-70; Chrmn., Nat. Comte. Internat. Union Physiol. Sciences 1969-72; el. mem. Med. Research Council 1963-68, 1970-72 (Vice Chrmn. 1965-67); Consulting Phys., Centre Hosp. Univ. of Laval since 1969, Lectr. in Neurophysiol., Inst. of Psychol. Univ. of Montreal, 1947-51; Asst. Prof. of Exper. Med. and Surg. 1950-52; Assoc. Prof. of Physiol., Coll. of Med. and Grad. Sch., Baylor Univ., 1955-60; Dir., Neuroendocrinol. Research Lab., Meth. Hosp., Texas Med. Center, Houston 1955-60; joined present Univ. as Dir., Endocrine Lab., 1960; Prof. of Exper. Physiol. 1961; Candn. Foundation for Advanc. Therapeutics, 1964-67; Med. Adv. Bd., Muscular Dystrophy Assn. Can., 1961-65; Scient. Adv. Bd., Inst. de Diagnostic and Rech. Clin. de Montréal, since 1967; Chrmn., Study Group on Med. Research, Govt. of Que., 1968-70; mem. Que. Med. Research Council 1963-70; Killam Comte. of Can. Council 1967-72; Research Fellow: Life Ins. Med. Research Fund 1948-50; Am. Heart Assn. 1950-52, 1953-54; Nat. Research Council Can. 1952-53; Advanced Fellow, Commonwealth Fund 1954-55; mem. Neuroendocrinol. Panel, Internat. Brain Research Organ. (IBRO/UNESCO); Nat. Cancer Inst. Can.; Awards: Archambault Research Award of the French Canadian Association for Advancement of Science 1972; Science Award of Government of Que. 1972; Wightman Award of the Gairdner Foundation, 1979; Marie-Victorin Science Award of the Gov't of Que. 1980; writings, incl. numerous publs. on neurohumoral control of adeno-hypophysial functions , pituitary-thyroid-adrenocortical interactions, bio-statistics, bio-control systems, role of corticosteroid-binding proteins of plasma; Assoc. Ed., "Canadian Journal of Physiology and Pharmacology", 1961-69; Ed. Adv. Bd., "International Journal of Neuro-pharmacology" and "Revue Canadienne de Biologie", 1962-66; mem., Candn. Physiol. Soc. (Pres. 1966-67); Am. Physiol. Soc.; Endocrine Soc.; Am. Thyroid Soc.; Soc. Exper. Biol. and Med.; Am. Assn. Advanc. Science; N.Y. Acad. Science; Candn. Soc. Clin. Invest.; Peripatetic Club; Biomed. Eng. Soc.; Assn. Am. Phys.; Liberal; R. Catholic; recreations: tennis, sailing; Home: 1014 De Grenoble, Ste-Foy, Québec, Qué. G1V 2Z9

FORTIER, d'Iberville, B.A., LL.B., D.S.E.; diplomate; né Montréal, P.Q. 5 fév. 1926; f. Carolus and Flore (Lanctôt) F.; é Coll. Jean-de-Brébeuf; Coll. Stanislas, B.A., 1945; Univ. de Montréal, Lic. en Sciences politiques, 1947, LL.B., 1948; London School of Econ.; Univ. de Paris, Dr. d'Etat ès sciences écon., 1952; ép. Marie-Thérèse, f. Robert Allegret, Boulogne, France, 15 oct., 1968; fils, Sébastien, Valérie; AMBASSADEUR DU CANADA EN BELGIQUE ET AU LUXEMBOURG, 1980- ; reçu avocat (Montréal) 1948; collaboration à Esprit, Ecrits du Canada français et Amérique française; entré aux Ministère des Affaires exterieures, 1952; Washington, D.C. 1953; Conseiller des Commissaires canadien à la CISC en Indochine, 1956; Direction des Affaires econ., Ottawa, 1958; Commissaire canadien suppléant à la CISC au Cambode 1959; Détaché auprès du Secrétariat de l'OTAN 1961; Dir. du Service de Presse et de Liaison du Ministère des Affaires extèrieurs, 1964; Prés du Groupe de travail du Conseil privé sur l'information gouvernementale, 1968; Ambassadeur en Tunisie et en Libye, 1969; Conseil d'Adm. de l'Office national du Film, 1973; Sous-secrétaire d'Etat adjoint, Ministère des Affaires extérieures, Ottawa, Ontario, 1972; Ambassadeur du Canada en Italie et Haut Com. à Malte 1976-80; Catholique; récréations: tennis, ski, litterature, cinema amateur; Résidence: 75 Ave. Franklin D. Roosevelt, Bruxelles, 1050 Belgium

FORTIER, Jean-Marie S.E. (R.C.); Archevêque de Sherbrooke, Que. depuis 1968; né Québec, Que. ler juillet 1920; f. Joseph et Alberta (Jobin) F.; é. Petit Sém. de Québec, Faculté de Théologie, Univ. Laval 1940-45; Louvain University Grégorienne (Rome); Prof. histoire ecclésiastique, Univ. Laval, 1950-60; Evêque aux. La Pocatière, 1961-65; Evêque de Gaspé, 1965-68; auteur: collab., "Dictionnaire d'Histoire et de Géographie ecclésiastiques"; Chevalier de Colomb, Commandeur de l'Ordre du St-Sépulcre (1970); Résidence: 130 de la Cathédrale, Sherbrooke, Que. J1H 4M1

FORTIER, L. Yves, Q.C., B.A., B.C.L., B.Litt. (Oxon.); b. Quebec City, Que., 11 Sept. 1935; s. François and Louise (Turgeon) F.; e. Univ. de Montréal, B.A. 1955; McGill Univ., B.C.L. 1958; Oxford Univ, (Rhodes Scholar), B.Litt. 1960; m. Cynthia Carol, d. John Wallace Eaton, Toronto, Ont., 26 Sept. 1959; children: Michel, Suzanne, Margot; PARTNER OGILVY, RENAULT Dir., The Manufacturers Life Insurance Co.; Mines Patino (Quebec) Ltd.; Jannock Ltd.; Westroc Industries Limited; Westinghouse Can. Inc.; Lemoine Mines Ltd.; Patino Mining Investments Ltd.; Les Entreprises J. René Ouimet Ltée.; Atlantic Sugar Ltd.; read law with predecessor of present firm; called to Bar of Que. 1960; Dir., Candn. Assn. Rhodes Scholars (Prés. 1975-6); Candn. Olympic Assn.; Montreal YMCA; Nat. Youth Orchestra; Montreal Neurological Inst.; Gov., Hôpital Marie-Enfant; McGill Univ.; Montreal Neurological Inst.; Montreal Gen. Hosp.; Gov. and Dir., Nat. Theatre Sch. of Can.; Pres., Jr. Bar Assn. Montreal, 1965-66; Pres., Jr. Bar Sec., Candn. Bar Assn., 1966-67 (Council of Assn. 1968-80) Chrmn. Nat. Mem'ship Comte. and mem. Extve. Comte. 1970-72, 1978-81, Nat. Treasurer 1980-81, Nat. Vice-Pres. 1981-2; mem. Gen Council, Bar Prov. Que 1966-82; Councillor, Bar of Montreal, 1966-67; mem. Council, Candn. Sec., Internat. Comn. of Jurists, 1967-80; Pres. (1975-77) Candn. Assn. of Rhodes Scholars; Pres. (1975-76) Candn. Bar Assn. (Que. Br.); Liberal; R. Catholic; recreations: skiing, tennis, golf, squash; Clubs: University; The Hermitage, Prés. 1980-81; Montreal Badminton and Squash; Canadian (Pres. 1968-69); Home: 19 Rosemount Ave., Westmount, Que. H3Y 2C9; Office: Suite 700, 1 Place Ville Marie, Montreal, Que. H3B 1Z7

FORTIN, Hon. Carrier B.A., LL.L., LL.D.; Judge; b. Beauceville, P.Q., 9 Sept. 1915; s. J. Edouard and Marie Blanche (Carrier) F.; e. Sacred Heart Coll., Beauceville; Semy. of Quebec, B.A. 1937; Laval Univ., LL.L. 1940; Univ. of Sherbrooke, LL.D. 1965; m. Solange, d. Albert Gobeil, Sherbrooke, P.Q., 9 Sept. 1943; children: Jean-Marie, Pierre, Claire; JUSTICE SUPERIOR COURT, QUE. since Nov. 1969; mem. Bd. of Dirs., Law Faculty, Lecturer, Univ. of Sherbrooke; called to Bar of Quebec, 1940; cr. Q.C. 1961; practised law in Asbestos, Que., 1940, moving to Sherbrooke with firm of Desruisseaux, Fortin, et al., 1942; Alderman, City of Sherbrooke and Leader of City Council, 1950-62; el. mem. for Sherbrooke, Nov. 1962; Min. of State Dec. 1962; Min. of Labour, Que., 1963-66;; def. in Que. g.e. 1966; formed Legal Aid Bureau for needy persons, 1957; founded "L'Asbestos" now known as "Le Citoyen", Asbestos, P.Q., 1941; founded, La Coopérative d'Habitation d'Asbestos (first such group in N. Am.) 1941; co-estbd. summer colony for handicapped children of Sherbrooke, 1951; Assurance-Vie Desjardins (Dir. 1958-62); mem. Bd. Examiners, Que. Bar 1954-58; mem., St. Francis District Bar (Treas., 1950; Bâtonnier 1959); Rural Bar Assn., (Dir.); Candn. Bar Assn. (Dir. 1969); Sr. Chamber of Comm. (Sherbrooke); Sherbrooke Co. Liberal Assn.; R. Catholic; Recreations: swimming, yachting, skiing; Clubs: Richelieu; Social de Sherbrooke; Home: 2040 Vermont Ave., Sherbrooke, Que. J1J 1H1; Office: Court House, Sherbrooke, Que. J1H 4R1

FOSTER, Harry Edward, O.C., LL.D. (Hon); F.I.C.A.; advertising executive; b. Toronto, Ont., 1 Mar. 1905; s. D. Harry and Helen (Orr) F.; e. Ridley Coll., St. Catharines, Ont.; m. Kathryn B., d. Percy C. Taylor, Rock Island, P.Q., 27 Jan. 1939; Hon. Chrmn. of Bd., Foster Advertising Co. Ltd.; Pres., The Internat. Productions Ltd.; Harry E. Foster Charitable Foundation; Canadian Special Olympics Inc.; Dir., Canadian General Tower Ltd.; mem. of Bd. of Govs., Ridley Coll.; granted franchise for gen. advertising agency 1944; began career as a pioneer sports broadcaster in Candn. radio, announcing from coast-to-coast commercial football, wrestling, speedboat races, and lacrosse broadcasts; introduced first outdoor radio theatre at Candn. Nat. Exhn. and first combination mobile radio and sound studio in Can.; organ. largest children's radio club in Can.; Dir. of Rallies for Red Cross, Victory Loan and War Savings Comtes. during 2nd World War; organ. Soldier's Field Corpn. Ltd., which became Internat. Productions Ltd. in 1945; Past Pres., Candn. Assn. of Advertising Agencies; mem., Adv. Comte., (past Can. Vice-Pres.) Direct Mail Advertising Assn., N.Y.; Adv. Bd., Boy Scouts Assn. Greater Toronto Region; Hon. life mem. Candn. Assn. for Retarded Children; the first Hon. Life mem. and Hon. Pres. Ont. Assn. for Retarded Children; Hon. life mem. Metro Toronto Assoc. for Retarded; Vice-Chrmn., Retarded Children's Trust; Past Pres. Ridley Coll. Old Boys' Assn.; named "Man of the Year" by Assn. of Candn. Advertisers 1966; Queen's Jubilee Medal, 1977; Chrmn. Canada's Sports Hall of Fame; mem. Bd. of Govs., Oaklands Regional Centre; Founder and Pres., Candn. Special Olympics Inc.; awarded Hon. Doctor of Law by Univ. of Western Ont. for dedicated and voluntary espousal of humanitarian causes over many years, particularly in the provision of assistance for retarded people, 1979; 1981 Royal Bank Award; 1981 Canadian Progress Club Award; Protestant; recreations: riding, fishing, gardening; Clubs: Ad. & Sales; Albany (Past Pres.); Granite; Caughnawana Hunting & Fishing, Que.; Canadian (Toronto); Home: 1416 Lakeshore Rd. East, Oakville, Ont. L6J 1M1; Office: 40 St. Clair Ave. W., Toronto, Ont. M4V 1M2

FOSTER, James Peter, B.A.Sc., M.B.A.; b. Hamilton, Ont., 16 Oct. 1925; s. William Gibbons and Jean Marguerite (Steedman) F.; e. Hillfield Sch. and Westdale Coll. Inst., Hamilton; Univ. of Toronto, B.A.Sc. (Aero. Engn.) 1947; Harvard Univ. Business Sch., M.B.A. 1950; m. Carol Rogers, Portland, Me., 7 July 1950; children: Nancy Jean, Charles Wm., Ellen Rogers; PRESIDENT, LECHAN HOLDINGS INC. since 1980; Dir. Continental Bank of Canada Ltd., Wainbee Ltd., Multi-Trol Corp. Ltd.; Joined Procter & Gamble 1947; served as Indust. Engr. Hamilton Plant, Asst. to Pres. Toronto H.O., Mgr. Forecasting Dept., Compt., Treas., Asst. Mgr. Overseas Finance, Brand Mgr. and Assoc. Adv. Mgr.; Extve. Vice Pres., Robin-Nodwell, 1963; joined Hugh Russel & Sons Ltd. 1965; Vice Pres. Corporate Planning of present firm 1965, Extve. Vice Pres. 1971, President and CEO 1973; Delta Upsilon (Past Treas.); United Church; recreations: cottage, flying; Clubs: Granite; National; Hamilton (Ont.); Home: 305 Rose Park Dr., Toronto, Ont. M4T 1R8; Office: 305 Rose Park Dr., Toronto, Ont. M4T 1R8

FOSTER, Malcolm Burton, M.A.; author; university professor; b. Montreal, Que., 24 Feb. 1931; s. Orval Allison

and Olive Eva (Burton) F.; e. Adelaide Hoodless Sch., Hamilton, Ont., 1943; Howard Sch., Toronto, 1944; Humberside Coll. Inst., Toronto, 1950; Syracuse Univ., B.A. 1955; Univ. of Minn., M.A. 1958; m. Carol Bertha Royce, 2 July 1954 (div. 1978); children: John David, Laura, Victoria Elizabeth, Cynthia Ann; m. 2ndly Anna Weber, 1980; children: Amanda Marie; PROFESSOR OF ENG., CONCORDIA UNIVERSITY since 1968; Asst. Art Ed., "Liberty"(mag.), Toronto, 1955; Teacher, W. Elgin Dist. High Sch., W. Lorne, Ont., 1956; Tech. Asst., Univ. of Minn., 1956-57; Teaching Asst. 1957-58 ; Lectr., Mich. Coll. of Mining & Technol., Sault Ste. Marie, Mich., 1958-60; Lectr., Univ. of Cincinnati, 1960-63; joined present Univ. as Lectr., 1963-65; Asst. Prof. 1965-68; Assoc. Prof. 1968-76; Pres., Julius Richardson Sch. Home & Sch. Assn., 1964-65; Monkland High Sch. Home & Sch. Assn. , 1970-71; rec'd McGraw-Hill Novel Fellowship, 1962; Ind. Univ. Short Story Prize, 1962; Brit. Council Fellowship, 1964; Can. Council Arts Fellowship, 1964, 1965 and Sr. Fellowship 1967-68; Leave Fellowship 1976-77; Houghton Mifflin Lit. Fellowship Award 1967; author. "The Prince with a Hundred Dragons", 1963; "Joyce Cary: A Biography", Am. and Candn. eds. 1968, Brit. ed. 1969; also short stories, lit. articles and book reviews in various mags. and newspapers; mem., Candn. Authors Assn. (former pres., Montreal Br.); recreations: carpentry, painting, boating; Home: 2069 Hampton Ave., Montreal, Que. H4A 2K4; Office: Loyola Campus, Concordia University, Montreal, Que.

FOSTER, Maurice Bryden, M.P., D.V.M., veterinarian; politician; b. Bloomfield, Ont., 8 Sept. 1933; s. Dunam Noxon and Agnes Mary (Anderson) F.; e. Picton(Ont.) Coll. Inst. 1952; Ont. Veterinary Coll. Univ. of Toronto D.V.M. 1957; m. Janet Catherine, d. T. Herb Kerr, 20 Aug. 1955; children: Peter, Andrew, Peggy, James; estbd. veterinary practice Carnduff, Sask. 1957-59; Desbarats, Ont. 1959-68; el. to H. of C. g.e. 1968 as mem. for Algoma; re-el since; served as Chrmn. Veterans Affairs Comte.; Depy. Chief Govt. Whip; Parlty. Secy. Privy Council and Energy, Mines & Resources; del. Inter-Parlty. Union, India 1969, UN(New York) 1971, Special Parlty. Del. to Cuba 1973; Chrmn. of the Commonwealth Parlty. Assn. of Can., 1977; leader of Cdn. Delegation to Int. Conf., Ottawa 1977; Jamaica 1978; N.Z. 1979; Regional Rep., Candn. Br., Commonwealth Parly. Assn., 1980; Vice Chrmn., External Affairs and Nat. Defence Comte., 1977; Chrmn., the Northern Gas Pipeline Comte., 1978; Appointed Chmn., Standing Comte. on Privileges and Elections, 1980; Chrmn. Johnson Twp. Sch. 1964-65; Chrmn. Algoma Dist. Sch. Area 1, 1966-68; Candn. Vet. Med. Assn.; Ont. Vet. Med. Assn. (Dir. 1967); Liberal; United Church; recreations: skiing, sailing; Home: Desbarats, Ont. P0R 1E0; and 3011 Linton Rd., Ottawa, Ont. K1V 8H1; Office: (Box 53) House of Commons, Ottawa, Ont.

FOURNIER, Gerald J., B.A., B.S.W.; insurance executive; b. Windsor, Ont. 8 Aug. 1936; s. Joseph George and Jeannette (McKenty) F.; e. St. Mary's Coll. Brockville, Ont.; Assumption High Sch. Windsor, Ont. 1954; Univ. of Windsor B.A. 1958; Univ. of Ottawa B.S.W. 1959; m. Mary Ethel Nelson 9 May 1959; two s. David, Michael, PRES. AND CHIEF OPERATING OFFR., ALLSTATE INSURANCE COMPANIES OF CANADA 1975- ; Pres., Allstate Foundation of Canada; Traffic Injury Research Foundation; Dir. of Facility Assoc.; Ins. Crime Prevention Bureaux served as Caseworker, Children's Aid Soc. Essex Co. and Cath. Family Service Bureau; Trustee, Art Gallery of Ont.; Dir., Council for Business and the Arts in Canada; Mgr. Ins. Operations, Allstate 1972, Vice Pres. Market Devel. 1973; mem. Young Pres's Organ.; Niagara Inst.; Adv. Bd. mem., Fromkin Van horn Inst.; R. Catholic; recreations: tennis, golf; Club: Bayview Golf & Country; Office: 255 Consumers Rd., Willowdale, Ont. M2J 1R4.

FOURNIER, L. Paul, B. Com., C.A.; pulp and paper executive; b. 1918; e. McGill Univ. B.Com. 1940; m. Mildred Rita Rochette 1943; children: Dr. Paul J.R. Fournier, Dr. Marcel R. Fournier. EXEC. VICE-PRES. & DIR., KRUGER INC.; assoc. with Kruger organ. since 1955; Dir. Chemical Bank of Canada; mem. Que. Inst. C.A.'s; Club: Club Saint-Denis; Home: 250 Clarke Avenue, Apt. 1020, Westmount, Qué.; Office: 3285 Bedford Rd., Montréal, Qué. H3S 1G5.

FOURNIER, Léonard, B.A., M.A.; executive; b. Amos, Que., 13 Oct. 1931; s. J. Albert and Maria (St-Onge) F.; e. Brébeuf and Ste-Marie Colls., Montreal, B.A. 1952; Montreal Univ., B.Sc. (Law and Social Sciences) 1954, M.A. (Industrial Relations) 1956; Univ. of Calif, (Berkeley), Doctoral residence in Indust. Sociology, 1956-58; m. Louise, d. late Alexandre Décarie, 7 May 1960; children: Hélène, Charles, Antoine, Francois; PRÉS. AND CHIEF EXTVE. OFFR., DYNAME CORP. LTD. since 1971; Extve. Vice Pres., SOGRAMCAN (Ltée); Dir. of several other cos.; mem., Candn. Chamber Comm.; Indust. Relations Research Assn.; Candn. Pol. Science Assn.; Am. Sociol. Assn.; recreations: scientific research, athletics; Home: 191 Maplewood Ave. , Outremont, Montreal, Que. H2V 2M6; Office: 800 Dorchester Blvd. W., 11th Fl., Montreal, Que. H3B 1X9

FOWKE, Donald Vernon, B.E., S.M., P.Eng., F.M.C., management consultant; b. Saskatoon, Sask., 22 Sept. 1937; s. Vernon C. and Helen R.(Hilton) F.; e. High School and Univ. of Saskatchewan, B.E. 1959; Mass. Inst. of Tech., S.M. 1963; m. Bonnie McMillan 7 May 1960; children: Barbara, Margaret, Brian; CHAIRMAN AND CHIEF EXECUTIVE OFFICER, HICKLING-JOHNSTON LIMITED since 1975; Engineer with Bearing & Transmission Ltd., Saskatoon, 1960-62; Mang. Consultant, P. S. Ross & Partners, Toronto, Ont. 1963-64; Secy. and Dir. Research, Sask. Royal Comn. on Govt. Adm., Sask. 1964-65; Vice-Pres., Hillis & Partners (Mang. Consultants) Regina 1965-66; apptd. Vice-Pres., Hickling-Johnston Ltd. 1967; Young Presidents' Organization; Dir., Calgary YMCA, Cairnlee Community; recreation: skin-diving; skiing; photography; personal computing; Home: 176 Malibou Rd., S.W., Calgary, Alta.; Office: Bow Valley Square Three, Calgary, Alta. T2P 3G9

FOWKE, Edith Margaret Fulton, C.M., M.A., LL.D., D.Litt.; folklorist; b. Lumsden, Sask., 30 Apr. 1913; d. William Marshall and Margaret (Fyffe) Fulton; e. Pub. and High Schs., Lumsden, Sask.; Regina Coll., Univ. of Sask., B.A. 1933, M.A. (Eng.) 1937; m. Franklin George Fowke, 1 Oct. 1938; prepared and wrote scripts for numerous CBC radio programs from 1950 to present; series incl. "Folk Song Time" , "Folklore and Folk Music" and "Folk Sounds"; items on "Matinee", "Audio", "Assignment"; "Ideas"; contrib. tapes of folk songs collected in Ont. and Que. to archives of Nat. Museum of Can. and Lib. of Congress; author: "Folk Songs of Canada", 1954; "Folk Songs of Quebec", 1957; "Logging with Paul Bunyan" (ed.), 1957; "Songs of Work and Freedom", 1960; "Canada's Story in Song", 1960; "Traditional Singers and Songs from Ontario", 1965; "More Folk Songs of Canada", 1967; "Sally Go Round the Sun" , 1969 (rec'd Medal for Candn. Lib. Assn.'s "Book of the Year for Children", 1970); "Lumbering Songs from the Northern Woods", 1970; "Canadian Vibrations" (ed.), 1972; "Penguin Book of Canadian Folk Songs", 1973; "Folklore of Canada", 1976; "Ring Around The Moon", 1977; "Folktales of French Canada", 1979; "Sea Songs and Ballads from Nineteenth Century Nova Scotia", 1981; "Bibliography of Canadian Folklore in English", 1981; other publs. incl. articles in various folklore and lit. mags.; 8 records of folk songs; pamphlets: Ed., "The Western Teacher", 1938-44; "Food for Thought", 1950-51; "Bulletin of the Indian-Eskimo Association", 1967-70; Assoc. Ed., "Magazine Digest", 1944-49; joined Dept. of Eng., York Univ. as Assoc. Prof.

to teach courses in folklore, 1971; Prof., 1977; (Ed.) "Canadian Folk Music Journal" since 1973; Fellow, Am. Folklore Soc. 1974; LL.D. Brock Univ. 1974; D.Litt., Trent, 1975; C.M., 1978; mem. Writers' Union of Can.; Candn. Folk Music Soc. (Dir.); Candn. Authors' Assn.; mem., Folklore Studies Assn. Can.; ACUTE; recreations: reading mystery stories; walking dogs; travel; Home: 5 Notley Pl., Toronto, Ont. M4B 2M7

FOWKE, Helen Shirley, B.A.; playwright; b. Oshawa, Ont. , 5 Mar. 1914; d. Frederick Luther (former M.P. for S. Ont.) and Flora (Wheeler) F.; e. Bishop Bethune Coll.; Oshawa Coll. Inst.; Univ. Coll., Univ. of Toronto, B.A. (Modern Lang.; Gov. Gen. Medal for Modern Lang.) 1935; studied Ballet and Art for two seasons at Queen's Univ. Summer Sch.; won the Hermit Club Internat. Award in Playwriting, 1946 with a play "Star in the Night"; another play "Mistuh Job" was runner-up in this contest; both these plays were produced in Cleveland, Ohio; two plays have been produced by Dr. Wm. Angus, Dept. of Drama, Queen's Univ., "Devil Take All", 1949 and "Lady in a Maze", 1951; won the Maxwell Anderson Award for a blank verse play in 1952 with "Imperial Wife"; radio production for a one-act play, "The Saving of Socrate Lebel", 1951, by the C.B.C.; "Devil in the Heather", produced Dec. 1952 by St. Francis Xavier Univ. Drama group; author of one-act play "A Wig for My Lady" publ, in "Canadian One-Act Plays", series 1 and in "Book Five Reader"for High Schools; (novel) "Chase of the Black Swan" (pub. in serial form by "Family Herald & Weekly Star" 1954-55); poems have appeared in Toronto "Saturday Night"; "Devil in the Heather" (full length radio play) produced on CBC-Stage-1963; children's TV series, 1958; article in Illustrated London News, 1961; stories read on John Drainie programs and pub. in collection; series of half hour plays produced by C.B.C. Montreal; various stories read on CBC programs, etc.; published "Joe, or A Pair of Corduroy Breeches", (a childrens' book, based on truth) July, 1971; Anglican; recreations: golf, yachting, painting, ballet; Address: Chester, N.S. B0J 1J0

FOWLER, Charles Allison Eugene, B.Sc., B.Eng., B. Arch., D.Eng. (Hon.), F.R.A.I.C., F.A.I.A.(Hon.); arch & engr.; b. Halifax, N.S., 24 Jan. 1921; s. Charles Allison De Witt and Mildred Allison (Crosby) F.; e. Dalhousie Univ., Dipl. in Engin., 1942, B.Sc. 1942; McGill Univ., B.Eng. (Mech.) 1944; Univ. of Manitoba, B.Arch. 1948; D.Eng. (Hon.) N.S. Tech. Coll. 1975; m. Dorothy Christine, d. George Graham, 30 Aug. 1947; children: Beverly Anne, Louise, Graham Allison Douglas; PRESIDENT, C.A. FOWLER, AND CO. LIMITED; Chrmn., Fowler Bauld & Mitchell Ltd.; Dir., Associates Design & Development Limited; Dir., Tidal Power Corp.; mem. N.S. Energy Review Comte.; Voluntary Planning Energy Sector, N.R.C. Standing Comte. on Energy Conservation in Building; served in 2nd World War as 2nd Lieutenant, R.C.O.C. and Lieutenant, R.C.E.M.E. in Canada and N.W. Europe; mem., Engin. Inst. Can.; Assn. Prof. Engrs. N.S.; N.S. Assn. Arch. (Past Pres.); Royal Arch. Inst. Can.; (Past Pres.) N.S. Consulting Engrs. Assn.; United Church; recreations: history, sailing, travel; Clubs: Halifax; North British; R.N.S.Y.S.; Saraguay; Home: 2 Halls Road, Boulderwood, N.S. B3P 1P3; Office: 7001 Mumford Rd., Tower II, Suite 3030, Halifax, N.S. B3L 4R3

FOWLER, John Douglas, B.Sc.; company executive; b. Toronto, Ont., 5 April 1931; s. Joseph and Elizabeth (Douglas) F.; e. Pub. and High Schs., Kingston, Ont.; Queen's Univ., B.Sc. 1955; m. Bette Gray, 8 Sept. 1956; children: Scott, Gray, Heather Ann; PRES. AND DIR., LAKE ONTARIO CEMENT LTD. since 1971; commenced with Cominco Ltd. as Develop. Engr. Montreal and Toronto 1955; Sales Engr., Pennsalt Chemicals of Canada Ltd., Oakville, Ont. 1957; Sales Engr., Saskatchewan Cement Co. Ltd., Saskatoon, Sask. 1958; Sales and Develop. Engr., Inland Cement Industries Ltd., Edmonton, Alta.

1960, Mgr. Marketing Services 1961; joined present Co. as Mgr. Special Projects 1962, Vice Pres., Planning & Develop. 1965, Vice Pres., Marketing 1966, Vice Pres., Marketing and Corporate Planning Offr. 1969, Vice Pres, Marketing and Concrete Products Div., and el. Dir. 1971; Home: 22 Edenbridge Dr., Islington, Ont. M9A 3E9; Office: 2 Carlton St., Toronto, Ont. M5B 1J6

FOWLER, Robert H., O.C. (1975); experimental test pilot; b. Toronto, Ont., 19 Sept. 1922; s. Robert James and Elizabeth (Kitchen) F.; e. Vaughan Road Coll. Inst. Toronto; Univ. of Toronto 1 yr. Law, 4 yrs. Indust. Mang. (Extension); m. Lorna Margaret d. George Hector Ried Phillips, 22 Oct. 1947; children: Robert Stephen, Georgeanne, Patricia Elizabeth, Laurie Jane, Heather Jean; CHIEF EXPER. TEST PILOT, DE HAVILLAND AIRCRAFT OF CANADA since 1959; joined RCAF 1942, rec'd wings and comn. 1943, served in Europe 1944-45 completing 48 B-25 Mitchell missions with 2nd Tactical Airforce of RAF; joined Dominion Gulf Co. of Toronto performing magnetic survey flying N. Ont. and Que. until 1949; engaged in magnetic survey flying and high altitude photo survey Sparton Air Services of Ottawa 1950-52; joined present Co. as Test Pilot 1952, flight testing incl. Caribou, PT-6A, GE-T64, Turbo Beaver, Buffalo, Twin Otter and Dash 7 aircraft; has taken part in all Augmentor Wing simulations at NASA/Ames Flight Research Center and participated as a NASA apptd. test pilot Augmentor Wing Jet Research Aircraft NASA/Ames, Mountainview, Cal.; rec'd Trans Can. McKee Trophy 1974; el. Cdn. Aviation Hall of Fame 1980; Fellow, Candn. Aeronautics & Space Inst.; mem. Soc. Exper. Test Pilots; Candn. Aviation Hist. Soc.; United Church; recreations: skiing, flying; Home: 37 Hibiscus Court, Weston, Ont. M9M 1R9; Office: Garratt Blvd., Downsview, Ont.

FOWLES, Douglas Leonard; real estate developer; b. Toronto, Ont. 18 Nov. 1941; s. George Ernest William F.; e. Humberside Coll. Inst. Toronto 1960; m. Eleanor d. Dixon Kneitl 5 Feb. 1966; children: Cynthia, Paul, Corinne, Douglas; PRES. S.B. McLAUGHLIN ASSOCIATES LTD. 1980- ; joined Deloitte Haskins & Sells 1960-64; Kalmar Realty Ltd. 1964-69; Mgr. Comm. Properties present Co. 1969-73, Extve. Vice Pres. 1978-80; Pres. D. L. Fowles Development Ltd. 1973-78; P. Conservative; Anglican; recreations: tennis, skiing, travel; Home: 3428 Burning Oak Cres., Mississauga, Ont. L4Y 3L5; Office: 77 City Centre Dr., Mississauga, Ont. L5B 1M6.

FOX, Beryl, B.A.; film producer/director; b. Winnipeg, Man., 10 Dec. 1931; d. Meyer and Sipora (Shliefman) F.; e. Univ. of Toronto, B.A. 1958; Co-Dir., "One More River", 1963 (winner Wilderness Award); "Balance of Terror", 1963; "The Chief", 1964 (winner Vancouver Film Festival); Producer/Dir., "The Single Woman & the Double Standard", 1965; "Summer in Mississippi", 1965 (winner, Candn. Film Award, Ohio Film Award Commonwealth Film Festival (Wales) , Vancouver Film Festival, Oberhausen Film Award (Germany), Montreal Festival (Special Mention); "The Mills of the Gods; Viet Nam", 1966 (winner George Polk Mem. Award (U.S.), Wilderness Award, Canadian Film Award, Cert. of Merit and Film of the Year, Vancouver Film Festival Award); "The Honorable René Levesque", 1966; "Youth: in Search of Morality", 1966; "Saigon", 1967; 1967 Woman of the Year Award for Television; "Last Reflections on a War; Bernard Fall", 1968, (winner Atlanta Film Festival Gold Medal for Peace Category 1969); "A view from the 21st Century"; "Martin Luther King Jr.: A Memorial" 1969; "North With The Spring" 1970, Silver Medal for Ecol., Atlanta Film Festival; "Toward the Year 2000 — Jerusalem, Habitat 2000"; "Travel and Leisure"; "Walrus"; "Man Into Superman"; "Wild Refuge"; "Fight Training"; "Take My Hand", "The Visible Woman"; Co-Producer "Here Come the 70's" documentary series 1970-71 (Dir., "The Family", "Cinema", "Race", "The Economy", and "The Human Potential Movement" for this series); "Take

Five" (stage) NFB Producer 1976-78; Producer, "Surfacing" (feature film), 1979; "I'm Getting My Act Together And Taking It On The Road" (Stage Musical), awarded Dora Mavor Moore Award for outstanding production of a musical 1980; "By Design" (Feature Film) 1980; recreation: horses; Address: 43 Britain St., Toronto, Ont.

FOX, Hon. Francis, Q.C., P.C., M.P., M.A., D.E.S., LL.M.; b. Montreal, Que., 2 Dec. 1939; s. Francis Moore and Pauline (Taschereau) F.; e. Jean-de-Brébeuf Coll. B.A. 1959; Univ. de Montréal LL.L 1962, D.E.S. 1964; Harvard Univ. LL.M. 1964; Trinity Coll. Oxford Univ. M.A. 1966 (Rhodes Scholar); SECRETARY OF STATE AND MIN. OF COMMUNICATIONS 1980- Atty. Tansey, De Grandpré & Associates, Montreal 1966-69; Special Asst. to Min. of Consumer and Corporate Affairs Ottawa 1969-70 and to Prime Min. of Can. 1970-72; el. to H. of C. for Argenteuil-Deux-Montagnes g.e. 1972, re-el. 1974; Solicitor-General of Can., 1976-78; Parlty. Dels. to UN and NATO; served with C.A.S.R. rank Capt., Instr. C.O.T.C. Univ. Montréal 1961-63; mem. Que. Bar Assn.; mem., Law Soc. of Upper Can.; Liberal; Address: House of Commons, Ottawa, Ont.

FOX, G. Kingsley, B.A., F.S.A., F.C.I.A.; former insurance executive; b. Winnipeg, Manitoba, 31 March 1913; s. Charles Harry and Ivy (Hind) F.; e. Univ. of Manitoba, B.A. 1935; F.S.A. 1950; m. Hazel Jean, d. Aaron Gore, Prescott, Ont., 9 Aug. 1941; one d. Heather Anne; Former President and Dir., The Imperial Life Assurance Co. of Canada; joined Home Office of the Company in 1935; apptd. Supervisor of Math. Sect. 1949; Asst. Actuary 1950, Extve. Asst. 1951, and Extve. Offr. in 1958; Extve. Vice Pres., 1964; Pres., and Dir., 1967-77; served in 2nd World War in Royal Candn. Navy, 1941-45; Commanding Offr., HMCS "Pictou" (1943-44), HMCS "Winnipeg" (1944-45); mem., Bd. of Insurance Operations, Candn. Foresters Life Insurance Soc.; Past Pres., The Candn. Life Insurance Assocn. 1973-74; Chrmn. West Park Prosthetics Manufacturing Ltd.,; mem. Bd. Trustees, Nat. Sanitarium Assn., West Park Hospital; Past Pres., Kiwanis Music Festival of Greater Toronto; Clubs: Granite; Toronto; Board of Trade; Kiwanis; Muskoka Lakes Golf & Country; Homes: 3 Otter Crescent, Toronto, Ont. M5N 2W1 and R.R. 2, Port Carling, Ont. P0B 1J0

FOX, Thomas Payne; transportation executive; b. Vancouver, B.C., 24 Dec. 1909; s. late Thomas W., and late Sarah (Watson) F.; e. Public Sch., Vancouver, B.C.; m. Clara B., d. late Leroy West, 7 Sept. 1935; children: Mrs. R. J. Limming, Thomas Wm., Barry D.; Pres., C. B. Holdings Ltd.; Fox Investments Ltd.; operated own fuel and trucking business in Vancouver, B.C., 1930-39 (Pilot attached to R.C.A.F. & R.A.F.); formed Associated Airways Ltd., Edmonton, 1945 (sold to Pacific Western Airlines, 1956); served in 2nd World War, Civilian Pilot attached R.C.A.F., 1940-43; No. 45 Group R.A.F. Transport Command (Trans-Atlantic Ferry Pilot) 1943-45; Pres. Edmonton Chamber Comm., 1964; Alta. Quarter Horse Assn. 1964; Edmonton Community Chest 1959-60; Candn. Cutting Horse Assn. 1961-63; Edmonton Quarter Century Aviation Club 1959; Air Industries & Transport Assn. of Can. 1955-56; Alta. Northwest Chamber of Mines & Resources 1954; Freemason (P.M.; Shrine); Protestant; recreations: riding, raising quarter horses; Address 14141 Fox Drive, Edmonton, Alberta. T6H 4P3

FRAIKIN, Leon Arthur, M.Sc., P.Eng.; company president; b. Brussels, Belgium, 4 Feb. 1907; s. Joseph and Marie (Melotte) F.; e. Univ. of Ghent, C.E. 1929; Mass. Inst. Tech., M.Sc. (Civil Engn.) 1931; m. Mary, d. late Maurice Van Ysendyck, 20 Aug. 1930; children: Claire (Mrs. R. Bergman), (Daniel), Eric; Hon. Chrmn. of Bd. Franki Canada Ltd., 1964-79, Hon. Chrmn., 1979- (Pres. 1959-64) (Foundation Engrs. and Contractors, estbd. 1932); Hon. Chrmn. Franki Foundation Co. Ltd., N.Y.; with

Ste. des Pieux Franki, Liege, Belgium, 1931-35; Braithwaite & Co., London, Eng. for British India, 1935-37; McDonald Gibbs & Co., for Mohammed Ali Barrages, Cairo, Egypt, 1937-38; joined present firm in 1938 as Mgr.; served in 2nd World War, 1939-45; Capt. R.A., Belgian Army in Gr. Brit.; Mutual Aid Organ., Brussels; Chargé de Mission, Belgian Econ. Mission, Canada; Offr., Order of Leopold 1st, Belgium; Fellow, Am. Soc. Civil Engrs.; Life mem., Engn. Inst. Can.; Hon. Pres., Belg.-Am. Educational Foundation, New York; Christian Democrat; R. Catholic; recreations: golf, swimming, stamps; Home: "The Rockhill" Apt. B212, 4854 Cote des Neiges, Montreal, Que. H3V 1G7

FRAKES, Rolland George, B.Sc.; executive; b. U.S.A. 12 July 1925; s. Arthur Edward and Glenna (Crandall) F.; e. Walworth (Wisc.) Grade and High Schs. 1943; Univ. of Wisc. B.Sc. (Chem.) 1949; Northwestern Univ. postgrad. studies Math. and Stat.; m. Shirley Anne d. William Campbell 23 Nov. 1973; children: Stephen, Mary Ellen Millward, Timothy; PRES., CHIEF EXTVE. OFFR. AND DIR., ENESCO CHEM LTD. 1981- ; Chem., Ohio Chemical Co. Madison, Wis. 1951; Semi-Works Control Chem., Victor Chemical Co. Chicago 1953, Plant Chem. 1957; Sr. Quality Control Engr. Celanese Fibers, Narrows, Va. 1959, Quality Control Supt. Cumberland, Md. 1960, Dir. Quality Control Newark, N.J. 1960; Plant Mgr. Newark and Belvedere, Celanese Plastics 1961, Vice Pres. Mfg. 1962, Marketing Vice Pres. 1966; Extve. Vice Pres. Celanese Canada, Montreal 1967; Extve. Vice Pres. Stein Hall, Gen. Mgr. and Vice Pres. Specialties Celanese Coatings and Specialties Co. New York 1972; Pres.; Dir. and Chief Operating Offr. Story Chemical Corp. Muskegon, Mich. 1974; Vice Pres. Plastics, Polysar Ltd., Sarnia, Ont. 1975, Group Vice Pres. Chemicals & Plastics 1977, Group Vice Pres. Corporate Devel. and Dir. Petrosar Ltd. 1979; served with U.S. Naval Reserve 1943-46 Atlantic & Pacific Theatres; mem. Am. Chem. Soc.; Soc. Chem. Industry Candn. Sec.; Plastics Industry Can. (Chrmn. and Dir.); P. Conservative; Protestant; recreations: tennis, fishing; Home: 9924 - 114 St., Edmonton, Alta. T5K 1P9; Office: The Executive Building, 10105 - 109 St., Edmonton, Alta. T5J 1M8.

FRAME, Clifford H., B.A.Sc., P.Eng.; company executive; b. Russell, Man., 28 May 1933; s. Hugh MacCallum and Thelma Jean (Setter) F.; e. J.L. Crowe High Sch. Trail, B.C.; Univ. of B.C., B.A.Sc. (Mining Engn.); three d. Wendy A., Kathleen P., Jamie L., three s. Clifford J., Geordie S., Cameron H.; EXTVE. VICE-PRES. DENISON MINES LTD. since 1975; Pres. & Dir., Saxon Coal Ltd.; Denmontan Resources Ltd.; Denmines Coal Ltd.; Quintette Coal Ltd.; Dir., Denison Mines Ltd.; Dentherm Resources Ltd.; Rocklake Coal Ltd.; Dencoke Coal Ltd., Denison Coal Ltd., Denison Mines (Que.) Ltd.; Denison Mines (U.S.) Ltd., Argosy Mining Corp. Ltd.; Consolidated Rexspar Minerals and Chemicals Ltd.; Mine Capt. Consolidated Denison 1957; Chief Mines Planning Engr., International Nickel, Thompson, Man. 1966; Asst. Mgr. Denison Mines Ltd. 1966; Vice-Pres. Operations, International Nickel Australia and P.T. International Nickel Indonesia 1969; Vice-Pres. and Gen. Mgr. Tara Mines Ltd. Ireland 1972-75; Chrmn. (1966) Thompson, Man. City Council; mem. Candn. Inst. Mining & Metall.; Am. Inst. Mining and Metall.; Assn. Prof. Engrs. Ont.; Conservative; Protestant; recreations: fishing, hunting, golf, skiing; Club: Professional Engineers; Home: 1261 Minaki Rd., Mississauga, Ont. L5G 2X5; Office: Suite 3900, South Tower, P.O. Box 40, Royal Bank Plaza, Toronto, Ont. M5J 2K2

FRANCA, Celia (Mrs. James Morton), O.C. (1967), D.C.L., LL.D.; director; choreographer; dancer; narrator; b. London, Eng., 25 June 1921; e. Guildhall School Music, London, England; Royal Academy of Dancing; LL.D., Univ. of Windsor 1959; Mt. Allison 1966; Toronto 1974; D.C.L., Bishop's Univ. 1967; L.L.D., Univ. of Toronto

1974; Molson Award, 1974; Can. Council Senior Grants Award, 1975; D.Litt., Guelph Univ.; LL.D., Dalhousie Univ.; York Univ., 1976; Trent Univ., 1977; m. James Morton, 7 Dec. 1960; Founder (1951) and Artistic Dir. (1951-74) Nat. Ballet of Canada; Co-founder (with Betty Oliphant) Nat. Ballet Sch., Toronto, 1959; made debut in corps de ballet in "Mars" in "The Planets" (Tudor), Mercury Theatre, London, Eng. 1936; Soloist, Ballet Rambert, London 1936-38, lead. dram. dancer 1938-39, guest artist 1950; dancer, Ballet des Trois Arts 1939, Arts Theatre Ballet and The Internat. Ballet, London 1941; leading dramatic dancer, Sadler's Wells Ballet 1941-46; guest artist and choreographer Sadler's Wells Theatre Ballet 1946-47; dancer and teacher, Ballets Jooss, Eng. 1947; ballet mistress and leading dancer, Metrop. Ballet, London 1947-49; dancer, Ballet Workshop, London 1949-51; a princ. dancer Nat. Ballet of Can. 1951-59; princ. roles incl. title role in "Giselle"; Swanilda in "Coppelia"; Young Girl in "Spectre of the Rose"; Operetta Star in "Offenbach in the Underworld"; Woman in His Past in "Lilac Garden"; First Song in "Dark Elegies" ; Black Lady in "Winter Night"; roles originated, Bird in "Peter and the Wolf" (Staff) 1940; Queen in "Hamlet" (Helpmann) 1942; Prostitute in "Miracle in the Gorbals" (Helpmann) 1944; title role in "Le Festin de l'Araignée" (Howard) 1944; "Lady from the Sea" (Leese) 1955; Black Queen in "Swan Lake" (Bruhn) 1967; character roles inc. Madge the Witch in "La Sylphide"; Lady Capulet in "Romeo and Juliet"; Pianist in "The Lesson"; Carabosse in "Sleeping Beauty"; ballets choreographed inc. "Midas" London 1939; "Cancion" 1942; "Khadra" 1946; "Dance of Salome" BBC TV 1949; "The Eve of St. Agnes" BBC 1950; "Afternoon of a Faun" and "Le Pommier" Toronto 1952; "Casse Noisette" 1955; "Princess Aurora" 1960; "The Nutcracker" 1964; "Cinderella" 1968; and choreography for CBC and Canadian Opera Co.; served on jury, 5th Internat. Ballet Competition, Varna, Bulgaria 1970, and 2nd Internat. Ballet Competition, Moscow 1973; 1st woman recipient, Gold Key of City of Washington (D.C.) 1955; rec'd Woman of Year Award, B'nai B'rith 1958; Toronto Telegram Award "for the most outstanding contribution to the arts in Canada" 1965; Hadassah Award of Merit, Toronto, 1967; Centennial Medal 1967; Molson Award 1974; Int. Soc. of Performing Arts Admin.'s Award 1979; Invited by Chinese Govt. to teach & mount full-length "Coppelia" 1980; Author, "The National Ballet of Canada: A Celebration", 1978; Office: 250 Clemow Ave., Ottawa, Ont. K1S 2B6

FRANCIS, Ann — see: Bird, Florence Bayard

FRANCIS, (Cyril) Lloyd, M.P., M.A., Ph.D.; politican; economist; b. Ottawa, Ont. 19 March 1920; s. Frederick Roland and Mary (Dyble) F.; e. Bayview Pub. Sch. and Glebe Coll. Inst. Ottawa 1936; Univ. of Toronto B.A. 1940; M.A. 1946; Univ. of Wis. Ph.D. 1955 (Econ.); m. Margery Elizabeth d. late John Malcolm Miller 23 Dec. 1943; children: John Paul, Donald Lyle, Mary Elaine; DEPY. SPEAKER, HOUSE OF COMMONS 1980- ; Pres., T.F.S. Lands. Ltd.; Special Lectr. Ottawa Real Estate Bd. and Algonquin Coll.; joined Gen. Chems. Div. C.I.L. 1940-41; Lectr. in Econ. and Indust. Relations Univ. of Buffalo 1948-51; Asst. Dir. Div. Research & Statistics, Nat. Health & Welfare 1951-60; Nat. Pres. Prof. Inst. Pub. Service of Can. 1958-59; Ald., Carleton Ward, City of Ottawa 1959-60, Depy. Mayor and Sr. Controller 1960-63, Ald. 1967-68; el. to H. of C. for Carleton 1963, Ottawa West 1968, 1974, 1980; Chrmn. Veterans' Affairs Comte. 1969-70; Chief Govt. Whip and Parlty. Secy. to Min. of Veterans' Affairs 1970-71; Parlty. Secy. to Pres. of Treasury Bd. 1975-76; Vice Chrmn. and Sr. Lib. mem. Pub. Accounts Comte. 1977-79; mem. Special Jt. Comte. Senate & H. of C. Finkelman Report 1968-70, Nat. Capital Region 1976-77; Chrmn. All-Party Comte. on Freedom of Information 1976-77; mem. Candn. Del. to Gen. Assembly U.N. 1967, 1975; Chrmn. Candn. Group Inter-Parlty. Union 1977-79; Visiting Prof. Sch. of Social Work McGill Univ. 1960-61; Dir. Candn. Fed. Mayors & Muns. 1962-63;

mem. Extve. Ottawa Chapter Candn. Council Christians & Jews 1977-79; Trustee Ottawa Civic Hosp. 1960-63; Dir. Children's Aid Soc. 1961-63; served with RCAF 1941-45, Radar Mechanic & Air Navig., attached RAF 1942-43; author several articles on Candn. social welfare expenditures 1955-61; Liberal; Unitarian; recreations: amateur lapsmith, fishing, rock hunting; Clubs: Kiwanis (Charter mem.); Ottawa Lapsmith; Home: 1130 Castle Hill Cres., Ottawa, Ont. K2C 2A8; Office: House of Commons, Ottawa, Ont. K1A 0A6.

FRANCIS, Fred John, B.A.Sc.; company officer; metallurgist; b. Ottawa, Ont., 29 Dec. 1921; s. Samuel Raby and Violet (Hooper) G.; e. Balmy Beach Pub. and Danforth Tech. Sch. (Hons. and Scholarship), Toronto, Ont.; Univ. of Toronto, B.A.Sc. (Metall.); m. Dolores Roslyn (Myers), 1950; children: John, Ronald, Peggy, David; CHAIRMAN, METALS & ALLOYS CO. LTD., since 1972; employed by this Co. since its inception in 1934; Vice-Pres. 1941, Pres. U.S.A. with Aluminum & Magnesium Corpn., Ohio; mem.; Am. Foundrymen's Assn.; Am. Soc. for Metals; Liberal; Protestant; recreations: skiing, golf, movies, canoe trips; Clubs: Granite; Scarborough Golf; Osler Bluffs Ski (Collingwood, Ont.); Home: 25 Tudor Gate, Don Mills, Ont. M2L 1N3; Office: 195 Wicksteed Ave., Leaside, Ont. M4G 2C1

FRANCIS, Jack Peter, B.Com.; retired Canadian public servant; b. Moose Jaw, Sask., 13 May 1918; s. late Ernest Henry and late Rozilla Marion (Fife) F.; e. Runymede Coll. Inst., Toronto, 1938; Univ. of Toronto, B.Com. 1942, post-grad. work 1944; m. Patricia Anne, d. late Philip Ford Townley, 17 Sept. 1955; three d., Margot Susan, Ailsa Jeremy, Michelle Anne; Sr. Asst. Depy. Min., Dept. of Regional Economic Expansion 1974-77; joined Econ. and Research Branch, Dept. of Labour, 1944; apptd. Chief, Manpower Resources Div. of Br., 1957; Dir. of Br. 1961; joined Dept. of Manpower and Immigration, 1965; served as Dir., Planning and Evaluation Br. for 2 yrs.; spent 1 yr. in Quebec City under Govt.'s Bicultural Devel. Program for Sr. Offrs.; apptd. Asst. Depy. Min. (Manpower) of Dept. 1968; Asst. Depy. Min. (Planning), Dept. of Regional Economic Expansion 1969-74; rep. Can. at meetings of Internat. Labour Office and on comtes. of Organ. for Econ. Co-op. and Devel.; mem., Candn. Econ. Assn.; Anglican; Home: 347 Second Ave., Ottawa, Ont. K1S 2J1

FRANCIS, John Drummond, B. Comm., M.S.; advertising executive; b. Calgary, Alta. 30 March 1932; s. Harry and Marjorie (Drummond) F.; e. Univ. of Alta. B. Comm. 1953; Boston Univ. M.S. (Pub. Relations) 1957; m. Lois d. Norman McCutcheon 4 Dec. 1954; two d. Kathryn Joyce, Susan Ann; PRES., FRANCIS, WILLIAMS & JOHNSON LTD.; active in pub. relations since 1954; estbd. present firm 1958; Past Pres., Inside Canada Public Relations Ltd.; Alta. Theatre Projects; Calgary Philharmonic Soc.; Calgary Br. Candn. Pub. Relations Soc.; Vice Chrmn. Strathcona-Tweedsmuir Independent Sch. 1974-79; recreations: golf, curling; Clubs: Earl Grey Golf; Glencoe; Home: 1424 Premier Way S.W., Calgary, Alta. T2T 1L9; Office: #600, 250- 6 Ave. S.W., Calgary, Alta. T2P 3H7.

FRANCIS, Robert M., C.A.; executive; b. Toronto, Ont., 27 Nov. 1935; s. William Bell and Grace (Wilson) F.; e. Pub. and High Sch., Toronto, Ont.; C.A. (Coopers & Lybrand) 1961; m. Marilyn Maguire, 7 June 1957; one s. Andrew; one d. Elizabeth; SR. VICE PRES. — ROGERS CABLESYSTEMS INC., since 1979; Dir., Rogers Radio Broadcasting Ltd.; Cdn. Cablesystems Ltd., TWC Television Ltd. with Phillips Electronics Industries Ltd., Toronto 1961-72 (various positions ending as Pres. of subsidiary Double Diamond Electronics Ltd.); Vice Pres. — Finance, Canada Cycle & Motor Co. Ltd. 1972-75; with Rogers Telecommunications Ltd. 1975-79; mem. Candn. Assn. of Broadcasters; United Church; recreation: swimming; Club: Cambridge; Royal Cdn. Yacht; Home: 38 Fallingbrook Dr., Scarborough, Ont. M5K 1B6; Office: P.O. Box 249, Toronto Dominion Centre, Toronto, Ont. M5K 1J5

FRANCK, August A.; company executive; b. Antwerp, Belgium, 26 Nov. 1910; s. Jules and F. (Van Straeten) F.; e. Notre Dame Coll., Antwerp, B.A.; Institut Supérieur Commerce, Brussels, M.B.A.; m. Hilda, d. late Florent Vandamme, 19 August 1936; children: Dr. Walter A., Dr. Robert E., Greta (Mrs. Vincent Mikolainis); CHRMN., GENSTAR LTD.; Chrmn., Global Terminal & Container Services (N.J.); Wheel Trueing Tool Co. (Columbia, S.C.); Counsellor, Société Générale de Belgique, Brussels; Dir.; Atlantic Overseas Corp. (N.Y.); Belgian American Chamber of Commerce (N.Y.); Chambre de Comm. Belgo Luxembourgeoise au Canada, Montreal; a Chevalier de l'Ordre de la Couronne (Belgium) ; R. Catholic; Home: 2 Westmount Sq., Apt. 1101, Westmount, Que. H3Z 2S4; Office: Suite 4105, 1 Place Ville Marie, Montreal, Que. H3B 3R1

FRANCOEUR, Jacques G.; newspaper publisher; b. Montreal, Que., 15 May 1925; s. Louis and Adèle (Gervais) F.; e. Coll. Notre-Dame; Coll. Saint-Laurent (P.Q.); Cath. High Sch. of Montreal; Sir George Williams Univ.; m. Catherine, d. J. D. Thompson, 6 Oct. 1956; 4 d.: Lyne, Anne, Josée, Louise; PRES. AND PUB., UNIMEDIA INC.; Pres., Dimanche Matin, Hebdos Métropolitains; Chrmn. of Bd. and Publisher, Le Soleil and Le Quotidien, Progres-Dimanche; Vice Pres., La Parole, Dernière-Heure, Montreal-Granby Press, and Distributions Eclair; Dir., Perspectives Inc.; began journalism career as a Reporter for La Patrie, Le Petit Journal, Montreal Star, Ottawa Journal and Montreal Gazette; also was Unit Dir. with Nat. Film Bd.; Purchased Le Guide du Nord (small weekly newspaper), 1950 which subsequently grew into important holding in present Co. (now one of largest newspaper group in French Can.); former mem., Public Safety Comn. of City of Montreal; Past Director and member Executive, The Canadian Press; Past Pres., Candn. Daily Newspaper Assn.; mem. Extve. Candn. Sec., Commonwealth Press Union; former Pres., Que. Daily Newspapers Assn.; mem. Am. Newspaper Assn.; Past Publ. Chrmn., Fed. of French Charities; Past Treas., Que. Div., Candn. Nat. Inst. for Blind; Past Chrmn., Candn. Extve. Service Overseas; Past extve. mem., Internat. Press Inst., London, Engl.; Hon. Vice Pres., St. John's Ambulance Soc., Quebec; mem., Young Pres.'s Organ.; Montreal Chamber of Comm.; R. Catholic; recreations: travel, reading, boating; Clubs: St-Denis; Canadien; Hermitage; Office: 5701 Christophe-Colomb, Montreal, Que. H2S 2E9

FRANKEL, Mrs. Egmont L., C.O.C. (1969); Member of Board of Govs. of Ont. Cancer Treatment and Research Foundation, 1954-79; mem. of Bd., The Ont. Cancer Inst., The Princess Margaret Hosp. until 1979; Gov., The Ryerson Polytech. Inst., 1964-79; Toronto; long interested and active in the field of cancer research and treatment, was formerly Pres., Toronto Br. Candn. Cancer Soc. for 5 yrs. (now Hon. Pres. of Ont. Unit and of the Junior Auxiliary, Toronto Unit); Hon. Life Pres., C.C.S., Auxiliary of the Princess Margaret Hospital & Lodge; in 1949, her Special Women's Comte. within the Candn. Cancer Soc. became the Toronto Br. of the Soc. and she was named Pres.; rec'd Pierre & Marie Curie Medal, 1971 in Paris, France (highest award of the soc.) Feb. 1971; honoured in Eng. by being made a life mem. of the League of Friends by the Duchess of Portland for work in field of cancer and in U.S.A. by The National Inst. of Social Sciences; author of "Three Cheers for Volunteers", 1965; mem., International Assoc. for Volunteer Education of Los Angeles, Cal.; Sustaining mem. of the Women's Comte. of the Art Gallery of Toronto; Toronto Symphony; Candn. Opera Co.; Home: 1 Benvenuto Place, Apt. 401, Toronto, Ont. M4V 2L1

FRANKEL, Saul Jacob, M.A., Ph.D.; educator; b. Montreal, Que., 6 Aug. 1917; s. late Moses Shaya and late Rebecca (Goodman) F.; e. McGill Univ. B.A. 1950, M.A. 1952, Ph.D. 1958; m. Freda Schneyer, 7 Oct. 1939; children: Deborah, Daniel, Naomi; Dean of Social Sciences, McMaster Univ. 1969-76; Lectr. to Prof. of Pol. Science, McGill Univ. 1954-69; full time Bd. mem. Pub. Service Staff Relations Bd., Ottawa, since 1976; Chrmn., Royal Comn. on Employer-Employee Relations in Pub. Services of N.B. 1966-67; served with Candn. Army (Active) 1943-46; Chrmn., Council on Jewish Educ., Hamilton; author of "Municipal Labour Relations in Canada" 1954; "Staff Relations in the Civil Service (Canada)" 1962; other writings incl. "A Model for Negotiation and Arbitration in the Canadian Civil Service" 1962, research report for Royal Comn. on Bilingualism & Biculturalism and articles for various journs.; mem. Inst. Pub. Adm. Can.; Candn. Pol. Science Assn; Hebrew; Home: 400 Laurier Ave. E., Apt 3B, Ottawa, Ont. K1N 8Y2; Office: Public Services Staff Relations Bd., Box 1525, Stn. B., Ottawa, Ont. K1P 5V2

FRANKLIN, Cecil Hammond; company president; b. Toronto, Ont., 5 April 1915; s. Harry Percy and Caroline Frances (Hammond) F.; e. Pub. Sch., Toronto, Ont.; High Sch. of Comm. (Toronto); Toronto Advertising and Sales Club (two year Extension Course); m. Phyllis Lorraine, d. C.C. Tonkin, Toronto. 19 July 1939; children: Sandra Anne, Robert Michael; CHRMN., ALGONQUIN MERCANTILE CORP.; since 1968; Chrmn. of Hardee Farms International Limited; Pres., Minaco Equipment Ltd.; Weiler Machine Co. Ltd.; Tintina Mines Ltd.; Offr. and Dir. of several other Candn. cos.; commenced with Cities Service Oil Ltd., Gen. Accounting Dept., Toronto 1932; Accounting for Prospectors' Airways, Lake Rose (Que.) Mines Ltd. 1938; similar duties at Kerr-Addison Mines Ltd., Virginiatown 1940-41; Chief Acct., Normetal Mining Corp. Ltd. 1942-45; Quemont Mining Corp. Ltd. 1945-51; incorporated Minaco Equipment Ltd. 1951; Pres. (and originally involved in develop.) Tribag Mining Co. Ltd. and Nigadoo River Mines Ltd.; founded Coupco Ltd. 1956 and purchased control of J.M.G. Manufacturing Ltd. 1961, later sold to Vascan Ltd. (now Teledyne Canada Ltd.) 1967, remaining a dir., until Dec. 1971; vice chrmn., Bd. of Govs., Univ. of Guelph; mem., Bd. of Dirs., Scarborough Grace Hosp., Toronto; Bd. Trade of Metrop. Toronto; Candn. Inst. Mining; Prospectors and Developers Assn.; Anglican; recreations: curling, hunting; Clubs: Granite; Goodwood; Rosedale, de Chasse aux Brigands (Ile Reaux); Toronto Engineers; Home: 27 Country Lane, Willowdale, Ont. M2L 1E1; Office: 931 Yonge St., Toronto, Ont. M4W 2H2

FRANKLIN, Gerald, D.D.S., F.A.C.D., F.R.C.D. (Can.), F.I.C.D.; retired orthodontist; b. Montreal, P.Q., 15 May 1899; s. Phillip and Gittel (Burke) F.; e. Montreal High Sch., Jr. Matric. (Murray Prize and Medal and Univ. Exhn. Prize) 1916; McGill Univ., D.D.S. (Stevenson Gold Medal) 1922; m. Sarah Louise Anderson; formerly Prof. of Orthodontics & Head of the Dept., McGill Univ. 1948-60; awarded Cert. by Am. Bd. of Orthodontics, 1935; served in 2nd World War 1939-45; overseas with 1st Divn. R.C.D.C.; No. 1 Plastic and Jaw Surgery Unit, 1939-43; Lieut.-Col., Asst. Dir. Dental Services, N.D.H.Q., Ottawa, 1943-45; mem., Am. Assn. of Orthodontists; Brit. Soc. for Study of Orthodontics; Candn. Dental Assn. (Chrmn. C.D.A. War Mem. Scholar. Comte., 1947-50); Mount Royal Dental Soc.; Order of Dentists of Que.; Past Pres., Candn. Soc. Orthodontists; Chrmn. Bd. of Censors, Northeastern Soc. of Orthodontists, (Pres. 1965-66); Life mem., Northeastern Soc. of Orthodontists; Am. Assn. of Orthodontists; has written numerous articles for prof. journs.; has read papers, given lects. and clinics before prof. groups in U.S.A., Can. and Eng.; Hebrew; recreations: reading, music; Home: 4078 Gage Road, Montreal, Que. H3Y 1R5

FRANKLIN, Ralph A.; banker; b. Grand Rapids, Michigan 16 Nov. 1928; m. Lenore Westlake 31 March 1962; children; Cynthia, Brent; SR. VICE PRES. B.C. DIV., BANK OF MONTREAL; Office: (P.O. Box 49400) Bentall Centre, Vancouver, B.C. V7X 1L5.

FRANKS, Christopher Ralph, L.R.C.P., M.R.C.S., M.B., B.S., MIBiol.,; F.R.S.H.; medical oncologist; educator; b. Bombay, India 1 June 1937; s. Pehin Dato Dr. P. I. Franks, O.B.E.; e. Downside Sch. Somerset, UK; Guy's Hosp. Med. Sch. M.B., B.S. 1973, L.R.C.P., M.R.C.S. 1972; m. Angela Lucy d. M. Malleson, London, Eng. 31 July 1971; children: Timothy Ralph, Richard Christopher, Charlotte Angela; Dir. Cancer Clinic, University Hosp. 1977-79; and Acting Head Dept. Cancer Research Univ. of Sask. 1977-79; stage, TV and comm. film actor UK 1955-64; House Phys. and Surg. Guy's Hosp. London, Eng. 1972-73, Med. Registrar/Clin. Research Fellow I.C.R.F. Breast Unit, Guy's Hosp., 1973-76, Asst. Curator Gordon Museum 1974-76; Speaker and Lectr. Guy's Hosp. Medical School and various scient. meetings Europe, U.S. and Can.; Astley Cooper Student and Greville Student Guy's Hosp. 1974-76; Laura DiSalicetto Student London Univ. 1976; Sask. Cancer Comn. Grant 1977-78; NCI Grant 1978; author numerous publs.; Hon. Vice Pres. Candn. Cancer Soc. Saskatoon Div. 1978; mem. NCIC sub-comte on breast cancer 1978; Brit. Assn. Surg. Oncology; Brit. Assn. Cancer Research; Brit. Soc. Immunology; Brit. Med. Assn.; Candn. Oncology Soc.; R. Catholic; recreations: sculpting, music; Adress: c/o Barclays Bank Ltd., 29 Borough High St., London, SEI ILY, England and Leeds General Infirmary, Leeds, England

FRANKS, Wilbur Rounding, O.B.E. (1944), M.B.; b. Weston, Ont., 4 Mar. 1901; s. Joseph Thompson F.; e. Univ. of Toronto, B.A. 1924, M.A. 1925; M.B. 1928; m. 1st Sarah Ruth, d. Archibald MacLachlan, 14 July 1925, d. 1962; children; two, s. William MacLachlan and Hugh Rounding; 2nd, Janina Polanowska, 1974; served in World War 1941-45 with R.C.A.F. with rank of Wing Commdr.; also with Med. Corps as Head, Inst. of Aviation Med.; Offr., U.S. Legion of Merit 1946; apptd. Assoc. Prof., Univ. of Toronto, 1937; invented anti-blackout flying suit, 1939; Prof., Banting-Best Med. Research Dept. 1945-68; awarded grant by Nat. Cancer Inst. for research, 1947; Theodore C. Lyster Award of Aero Med. Assn. (U.S.) 1948; Liljencrantz Award of the Aerospace Med. Assn. (U.S.) 1962, for outstanding research in Aerospace Med.; Hon. Physician to the Queen, 1970; mem., Internat. Acad. of Astronautics; Internat. Astronaut Fed.; Founders Group Joint Com. Aviat. Pathol.; Hon. Pres., Candn. Soc. Av. Med.; fostered development of "Unigen", Universal Lang. of Air & Space Operations in 1976; Fellow in Aviation Med., Aero Med. Assn.; mem., Founders Group, Am. Bd. of Preventive Med.; Nu Sigma Nu; Publications: "Synthetic Chemo-Antigens against Cancer", 1937; "Biochemical Post-Mortem in Air Accident Investigations", 1952; Home: 186 Hillsdale Ave. E., Toronto, Ont. M4S 1T5

FRAPPIER, Armand, C.C.(1969), O.B.E., M.D., M.S.R.C., F.R.S.M., F.A.P.H.A.; microbiologiste recherches médicales; né Salaberry-de-Valleyfield, Qué., 26 nov. 1904; f. Arthur Alexis et Bernadette (Codebecq) F.; é. Sém. de Valleyfield, B.A. 1924; Univ. de Montréal, M.D. 1930, L.Sc. 1931; Trudeau Sch. of Tuberculosis, N.Y. Dipl. 1932; Cert. Spéc. Bactériol., C.R.M.C.(C) et C.M.C.(P.Q.); boursier Rockefeller, Rochester Univ. et Sanatoriums E.U. et à l'Inst. Pasteur de Paris; ép. Thérèse, f. Noël Ostiguy, 29 juin 1929; enfants: Mme André Davignon, Mme Gilles Des Rochers, Mme Jacques Daignault, Paul; DIRECTEUR FONDATEUR, INST. DE MICROBIOLOGIE ET D'HYGIENE DE MONTREAL (devenu INSTITUT ARMAND-FRAPPIER); Fondateur et doyen, Ecole d'Hygiène 1945-65 Univ. of Montreal; prof. agrégé 1938-50, prof. titulaire de Bactériol. 1950-71 et prof. émérite à la Faculté de Méd. Univ. de Montréal depuis 1971; mem. Comn. d'Hygiène de la Cité de Montréal (Prés. 1959); Tableau d'Experts sur la Tuberculose, OMS; divers comtés et comns. du Min. Santé nat. et du Bien-être (Can.), du CNR, CRM et du Min. de la Défense nat. (Can.), Comité consultatif sur la guerre biologique (1963-68), prés. 1965-68; Conseil Féd. d'Hygiène 1962-68; Comité de Nomenclature et mem. Section Permanente de Standardisation microbiol. Assn. internat. Socs. de Microbiol.; Bureau des Gouvs., Souscription pour les Oeuvres de Santé du Grand Montréal 1967; ancien Prés., Conseil adm., Hôpital-Marie Enfant; mem. Comn. du BCG, Union internat. contre la Tuberculose (Prés. 1957-63); Assn. des Microbiols. de Langue française; Soc. Candn. de la Croix-Rouge (Comité exécutif, Section P.Q. et Comité consultatif nat. sur les recherches); ancien Prés., Soc. de Biol. de Montral; Soc. de Microbiol. P.Q.; Soc. Méd. de Montréal; Soc. Candn. des Microbiols.; mem. hon., Soc. Française de Microbiol.; Soc. Méd. Polonaise; a organisé labs. de plusieurs hôpitaux et institutions; a participé à plusieurs congrès; chargé de missions scient. au Japon, en Inde et en Europe; co-auteur "La Souche du BCG" 1957 et de plus de 100 articles scient. originaux; Dr. (hon. causa) de l'Univ. de Paris 1964; Univ. Laval 1971; Univ. Montréal 1976; Acad. Med. Univ. Cravovie 1978; Univ. du Qué. 1978; Offr. d'Acad. France, 1948; Prix Casgrain & Charbonneau 1945; Prix Ciba 1948; Médaille Archambault de l'Assn. Candn. français pour l'Avanc. des Sc.; Médaille de l'Inst. Pasteur (2 fs.); Médaille de la Soc. Méd. de Montréal; Médaille de l'Acad. Nat. de Med., France 1957; Prix de l'Oeuvre Scient., Assn. des Méd. de Langue française du Can. 1970; Prix Jean Toy de l'Acad. des Sc. 1971. Inst. de France; Prix Eadie, Soc. Roy. Can. 1979; Prix Marie-Victorin, Prov. du Qué 1979; et plusieurs autres; mem. ass., Acad. nat. de Méd. (France); mem. corr., Soc. Méd. des Hôpitaux de Paris; r. catholique; loisirs: musique, jardinage, pêche, chasse; Clubs: Lac d'Argent; La Roue du Roy; résidence: 558 ave. Rockland, Montréal, Que. H2V 2Z3

FRAPPIER, Gilles, B.A., B.Ph., B.L.S.; b. Papineauville, Que., 13 Feb. 1931; s. Roméo and Roma (Robinson) F.; e. Petit Séminaire d'Ottawa; Univ. of Ottawa, Faculty of Philos., Lib. Sch.; McGill Univ., Grad. Sch. Lib. Science; Degrees, B.A., B.Ph., B.L.S.; m. Gertrude, d. Alfred Mainville, Ottawa, Ont., 13 Oct. 1956; children: Raymond, Robert, Joanne; DIR. & SEC. TO THE BOARD, OTTAWA PUBLIC LIBRARY, 1979- ; Assoc. Parlty. Librarian, Library of Parliament, 1970-79; Librarian, Baie Comeau (Que.) Community Assn., 1955-57; Founder, Woodlands Lib., Pulp and Paper Research Inst. Can., Pointe Claire, Que., 1957-59; Librarian, United Aircraft of Canada Ltd., Longueuil, Que., 1959-63; Supvr., Engn. Lib's, Canadair Ltd., St. Laurent, Que., 1963-69; Dir., Science Lib's, Univ. of Montreal, 1969-70; mem., Special Lib's Assn. (Pres. 1973; former Secy., Treas., Bull. Ed., Vice Pres. and Pres., Montreal Chapter; Observer, Internat. Fed. Lib. Assns. Conf., Grenoble, 1973); Corp. Prof. Librarians Que.; Candn. Lib. Assn.; Assn. pour l'avancement des sciences et des techniques de la documentation; Inst. Pub. Adm. Can.; Lib. Assn. Ottawa; Candn. Micrographic Soc. (Scy.-Treas.); (mem., Assn. of Parlty. Librarians in Can.); mem. Cand. Assn. for Information Sci.; Council of Admrs. for Large Urban Public Libraries (Vice Pres. 1981); Chief Extves. of Large Public Libraries, Ont.; L'alliance Française; mem. & Dir. Candn. Writers Foundation; mem. K. of C.; Roman Catholic; recreations: fishing, camping, woodworking, travel; Club: Soc. Chasse & Pêche Laurentien; Home: 423 Carillon St., Gatineau, Que. J8P 3P9; Office: 120 Metcalfe St., Ottawa, Ont. K1P 5M2

FRASER, Hon. Alexander Vaughan, M.L.A.; politician; b. Victoria, B.C. 22 June 1916; s. John Anderson and Lillian (Vaughan) F.; e. Quesnel (B.C.) High Sch.; m. Gertrude Marjorie Watt 8 Aug. 1940; one d. Bonnie Joy; MIN. OF TRANSPORTATION & HIGHWAYS, B.C. 1979- ; Min. Responsible for B.C. Ferry Corp. 1978- ;

Chrmn. Bd. B.C. Steamship Co. (1975) Ltd. 1979- ; Partner, F. & W. Trucking Equipment Ltd.; Chrmn. Village of Quesnel 1951-58, Mayor 1958-69; Chrmn. Regional Dist. Cariboo; el. M.L.A. for Cariboo prov. g.e. 1969, re-el. since; Min. of Highways & Pub. Works 1975; Min. of Transport., Communications & Highways 1978; served with RCASC 1942-46; Life mem. Union B.C. Muns. (Pres. 1963-64); mem. Elks; Royal Candn. Legion; Social Credit; United Church; Office: Parliament Bldgs., Victoria, B.C. V8V 1X4.

FRASER, Alistair Graeme, B.A., LL.B.; Canadian public service; b. Toronto, Ont., 5 Jan. 1923; s. Jane Graeme (Ross) and the late Hon. Alistair F.; e. McGill Univ., B.A. 1946; Univ. of Brit. Columbia, LL.B. 1950; Clerk of the House of Commons, Aug. 1967-Sept. 1979; Lieut., Royal Candn. Artillery, 1942-45; read law with Davis & Co., Vancouver, B.C., 1950; called to Bar of B.C., 1951; engaged in practice of law, Prince Rupert, B.C., 1951-52; Extve. Asst. to Min. of Fisheries, 1952; to Leader of Opposition in Senate, 1959; to Secy. of State, 1963; to Min. of Transport, 1964; apptd. Clerk Asst., H. of C., Jan. 1966; mem., Candn. Bar Assn.; Protestant; Home: 124 Springfield Rd., Ottawa, Ont.

FRASER, Donald Alexander Stuart, Ph.D., F.R.S.C.; statistician; mathematician; educator; b. Toronto, Ont. 29 Apl. 1925; s. Maxwell John and Ailie Jean (Stuart) F.; e. Univ. of Toronto B.A. 1946, M.A. 1947; Princeton Univ. A.M. 1948, Ph.D. 1949; m. Judith Patricia d. Laurence Allen 7 May 1965; children: Maia, Andrea, Ailana; PROF. OF STATISTICS, UNIV. OF TORONTO since 1958; Asst. Prof. Univ. Toronto 1949, Assoc. Prof. 1953; Visiting Prof. Princeton Univ. 1955; Stanford Univ. 1961-62; Univ. of Copenhagen 1964; Univ. of Wis. 1965; Univ. of Hawaii 1969-70; Univ. of Geneva 1978-79; author "Nonparametric Methods in Statistics" 1957; "Statistics An Introduction" 1958; "The Structure of Inference" 1968; "Probability and Statistics" 1976; "Inference and Linear Models" 1978; Fellow, Inst. Math. Stat.; Am. Stat. Soc.; Royal Stat. Soc.; Am. Assn. Advanc. Science; Internat. Stat. Inst.; Home: 4 Old George Pl., Toronto, Ont. M4W 1X9; Office: Toronto, Ont. M5S 1A1.

FRASER, Douglas M. B.A.; retired economist, government official; b. Virden, Manitoba, 1 Aug. 1918; s. Charles Lauchlin and Ethel (Dodds) F.; e. Winnipeg Public and High Schs.; United Coll., B.A. 1940; Univ. of Toronto, 1940-41 (grad. study in econ. and pol. science); m. Margaret, d. late Rev. Clark B. Lawson, 26 Sept. 1942; children: Alastair Hugh Lawson, Alison Margaret; Asst. in Hist. Dept. United Coll., Winnipeg, Man., 1939-40; Asst. to Prices Stat., Dom. Bureau of Stat., 1941-43; Stat. Offr. then Asst. Secy., Wartime Industries Control Bd., 1943-45; in private practice as Consulting Economist, Ottawa, 1945-48, and Econ. Adviser to Royal Comn. on Coal (Carroll Comn.), 1945-46; 1948-52 with Govt. of N.S., first as Asst. to the Vice-Pres., N.S. Research Foundation, later as Chief, Comm. Service Div., Dept. of Trade & Industry; Lectr. in Econ., N.S. Tech. Coll., 1949-51; with Trans-Canada Pipe Lines Ltd. (opened and managed Toronto Office), 1952-55; joined Dept. of Trade & Comm., Ottawa, 1955, first as Acting Assoc. Dir. of Econ. Br., later organized and made Dir. of Energy Studies Br. (during 1957 was also Secy. of Royal Comn. on Employment of Firemen on Diesel Locomotives in Freight & Yard Service on C.P.R. — Kellock Comn.); apptd. mem. Nat. Energy Bd. Can. 1959; Vice Chrmn., Nat. Energy Bd. Can., 1968-76; United Church; recreations: bird watching, fishing, gardening, bridge; Home: 2038 Black Friars Road, Ottawa, Ont. K2A 3K8

FRASER, Duncan Grant Lovat, C.D., M.A.; university professor; b. Halifax, N.S., 3 March 1923; s. Simon MacKay and Gladys Ruth (MacNamara) F.; e. New Glasgow (N.S.) High Sch.; Acadia Univ., B.A. (Hons. Hist.) 1948, M.A. (Hist.) 1949, Sidney Sussex Coll., Univ. of

Cambridge (I.O.D.E. Scholar for N.S.), 1949-51; mem. Inst. Hist. Research and Inst. of Commonwealth Studies Univ. London 1969-70; m. Iris, d. D.S. Watkins, 20 May 1946; children: Janet M., Kathryn E.; PROF., DEPT. OF POL. SCIENCE, ACADIA UNIV. and Head of the Dept., 1961-78; Asst. Lectr. in Constitutional Hist., Univ. Coll. of the West Indies, 1951; promoted Lectr., 1952; apptd. Asst. Prof. of Hist. and Pol. Science, Acadia Univ., 1954, Assoc. Prof., 1956; served in 2nd World War; commnd. in Cape Breton Highlanders, Nov. 1942; served as Lieut. and Capt. in Candn. Army in U.K., Italy (wounded in Liri Valley campaign) and Can.; served in Militia and C.O.T.C. as Maj., 1954-64; Hon. Lieut. Col. West Nova Scotia Regt. since 1975; Pres., Nova Scotia Army Cadet League 1978-80; Dir., Army Museum, The Citadel, Halifax, N.S.; publs: articles, papers broadcasts on Candn. West Indian trade evolution of Brit. Empire and Commonwealth studies on the origins and functions of the Court of Vice-Admiralty in N.S. 1749-83; a frequent contrib. of pol. and social articles to Halifax Chronicle-Herald; has contrib. frequently to C.B.C. since 1956; Contributor to The Candn. Annual Review since 1963; mem., Candn. Inst. Internat. Affairs; Inst. Public Adm. Can.; Candn. Assn. Univ. Teachers; Royal Candn. Military Inst., Toronto; N.S. Adv. Comte. on Constitution; N.S. 1961-70 Del., Confed. of Tomorrow Conf., 1967 and Fed.-Prov. Constitutional Conf., 1968 and 1969; aptd. Special Consultant and Constitutional Adviser to the Office of the Premier of N.S., Oct. 1978; Special Consultant to the Exec. Coun. of N.S., Jan. 1979; Mem. of Delegation, First Ministers Constitutional Conf., Oct. & Nov. 1978 and Feb. 1979; apptd. Sec. of the N.S. House of Assembly Select Comm. on Constitutional Matters, May 1979; September 1980; Presbyterian; Home: Grand Pré, Kings County, N.S.

FRASER, Frank Clarke, B.Sc., M.Sc., Ph.D., M.D., D.Sc., F.R.S.C., F.R.C.P.S.; educator; b. Norwich, Conn. 29 Mar. 1920; s. Frank Wise and Annie Louise (Clarke) F.; came to Can. late 1930's; e. Acadia Univ. B.Sc. 1940; McGill Univ. M.Sc. 1941, Ph.D. 1945, M.D., C.M. 1950; Acadia Univ. D.Sc. 1967; m. Marilyn Preus d. Reidar Preus; children: Noel, Norah, Alan, Scott; PROFESSOR, MEMORIaL UNIV. 1982- ; joined McGill Univ. 1950 as Asst. Prof. of Genetics; Assoc. Prof. of Genetics 1955-60; Prof. of Biology 1960-82; Prof. of Paediatrics 1973-82; Prof., McGill Centre for Human Genetics 1979-82; Dir., Dept. of Medical Genetics 1952-82; MRC Medical Genetics Group 1972-82; Montreal Children's Hosp.; Fellow, Royal Soc. of Can. 1966; Candn. Coll. of Medical Geneticists 1975; Royal Coll. Physicians & Surgeons 1976; Pres., Amer. Soc. of Human Genetics 1961-62; Teratology Soc. 1962-63; Chrmn., Med. Research Council Comte. on Genetics 1971-74; Gen. Chrmn., Fourth Internat. Conference on Birth Defects, Vienna 1973; Vice-Pres., Internat. Birth Defects Congress Ltd. 1972-79; Scientific Officer, Med. Research Counc. on Genetics (Grants Comte.) 1974-80; Vice-Pres., Candn. Coll. of Medical Geneticists, 1975-80; Honorary Pres., Fifth Internat. Conference on Birth Defects, Montreal 1978; Pres., Candn. Coll. of Med. Geneticists 1980- ; rec'd Blackader Award, Candn. Med. Assn. .1968; Honours of the Amer. Cleft Palate Assn. 1974; Medal of Honour, Amer. Assn. of Plastic Surgeons 1975; Allan Award, Amer. Soc. of Human Genetics 1979; Award of Excellence, Genetics Soc. of Can. 1980; mem., Permanent Comte. for Internat. Conferences on Human Genetics 1967-75; Expert Comte. on Occurrence of Congenital Abnormalities, Dept. of Nat. Health & Welfare, Canada 1962-75; Nat. Inst. of Health, Genetics Study Section, U.S.A. 1961-65; Genetics Training Comte., Nat. Inst. of General Med. Sciences, U.S.A. 1971-74; World Health Org. Expert Advisory Comte. on Human Genetics 1963- ; Comte. on Mutagenic Hazards of Environmental Chemicals, Health & Welfare Can. 1977- ; Editorial Board, 'Amer. Journal of Med. Genetics', 'Developmental Pharmacology & Therapeutics', 'Brazilian Journal of Genetics'; co-author (with J.J. Nora) 'Medical Genetics:

Principles and Practice' (1974; 2nd ed. 1981), 'Genetics of Man' (1975); (with J.G. Wilson) 'Handbook of Teratology, Vols. 1-4' (1977); author of numerous scientific papers in Medical Genetics and Teratology; Liberal; Church of England; Clubs: Mount Royal Tennis; Montreal Badminton and Squash; Nu Sigma Nu; Alpha Psi Omega; served in R.C.A.F. 1942-45; recreations: tennis, photography; Home: 5 Forest Ave., St. John's, Nfld.; Office: Health Sciences Centre, Memorial Univ., St. John's, Nfld. A1B 3V6

FRASER, H. Ronald, B.A., B.Econ., M.B.A.; executive; b. Durban, S. Africa, 5 Oct. 1920; s. Andrew Gibson and Mary Margaret (Joyce) F.; e. Natal Univ. Coll., B.A. 1943; Univ. of S. Africa, B.Econ. 1947 (Hons. 1948); Univ. of Pretoria, M.B.A. 1951; m. Betty Wynne, d. late Herbert Barnes,Amberley, Sussex, 26 Dec. 1944; children: Michael, Mary, John, Peter, Elizabeth; PRES. & CHIEF EXEC. OFFICER, MINERALS & RESOURCES CORP. LTD., BERMUDA, since 1979; Dir., Anglo American Corp. of Can. Ltd., Engelhard Minerals & Chemicals Inc., N.Y.; Schoolmaster, Pretoria Boys High Sch., 1944-49; joined South African Iron & Steel Industrial Corp. Ltd. as Administrative Trainee 1949; subsequently Asst. to Chrmn. and Head of Organ. & Method Dept.; joined Anglo American Corp. of South Africa Ltd. 1954; trans. to London,Eng., 1961; became Mang. Dir., Anmercosa Sales Ltd. on its formation 1964; Mgr., Charter Consolidated Ltd. on formation 1965, Dir. 1970; trans. to New York 1970 as Extve. Vice Pres. and apptd. Pres., Anglo American Corp. of South Africa (N.A.) Inc.; apptd. C.E.O. of Anglo A. Corp. of Can. Ltd. (Dir. of Hudson Bay Mining & Smelting Co. Ltd.), Tor. 1973; mem., Am. Inst. Mining & Metall. Engrs.; Mining Assn. of Can.; R. Catholic; recreations: photography, reading, walking; Clubs: York; Mid Ocean, Belmont, Mining Club of N.Y. Home: Bel Horizonte, Warwick Bermuda; Office: Box 650, Hamilton, Bermuda

FRASER, John Anderson, M.A.; journalist; b. Montreal, Que. 5 June 1944; s. John Ramsey and Catherine Margaret (Dickinson) F.; e. Upper Can. Coll. Toronto; Lakefield (Ont.) Coll. Sch.; Mem. Univ. of Nfld. B.A. 1969; Exeter Coll. Oxford Univ. Dipl. 1970; Univ. of E. Anglia M.A. 1971; m. Elizabeth Scott d. Arthur R. MacCallum, Toronto, Ont. 8 March 1975; one d. Jessie MacCallum; NATIONAL COLUMNIST, THE GLOBE AND MAIL 1980- ; Music and Dance Critic, Toronto Telegram 1971-72; Dance Critic and Feature Writer, The Globe and Mail 1972-75, Drama Critic 1975-77, Peking Corr. 1977-79; Visiting Lectr. in Criticism York Univ. 1976-77; rec'd Nat. Newspaper Awards for criticism (dance) 1974, (theatre) 1976, reporting (China coverage) 1978; author "Kain and Augustyn" 1977; "The Chinese: Portrait of a People" 1980 (nominated Gov. Gen.'s Award Nonfiction 1980); articles on politics, arts various nat. and internat. newspapers and mags.; rec'd Queen's Silver Jubilee Medal; mem. Champlain Soc. Toronto; The Writers' Union of Canada; Anglican; recreations: canoeing, piano, reading, tennis; Clubs: Badminton & Racquet; Toronto Arts & Letters; Home: 104 Bernard Ave., Toronto, Ont. M5R 1R9; Office: 444 Front St. W., Toronto, Ont. M5V 2S9.

FRASER, John Foster, B.Com.; executive; b. Saskatoon, Sask. 19 Sept. 1930; s. John Black F.; e. Victoria Sch. and Nutana Coll. Inst. Saskatoon; Univ. of Sask. B.Com. 1952; m. Valerie Georgina d. late George Ryder 21 June 1952; children: John F. Jr., Lisa; PRES. AND CEO FEDERAL INDUSTRIES LTD. since 1978; Chrmn. of Bd. White Pass and Yukon Corp.; Thunder Bay Terminals Ltd.; Citation Industries Ltd.; Dir. Standard Aero Ltd.; Man. Health Sciences Centre; Pres. Empire Freightways Ltd. 1953-61; Empire Oil Ltd. 1961-63; Hanford Drewitt Ltd. 1963-66; Norcom Homes Ltd. 1966-78; Past Pres. Man. Theatre Centre; Candn. Manufactured Housing Inst.; Winnipeg Symphony Orch.; Past Gov. St. John's Ravenscourt Sch.; P. Conservative; Presbyterian; recreations: boating, reading; Clubs: Manitoba; Royal Lake of the Woods Yacht; Home: 119 Handsart Blvd., Winnipeg, Man. R3P 0C4.

FRASER, R. Graeme, K.St.J.; film producer; b. Ottawa, 7 Dec. 1914; s. Robert James and Muriel Gordon (Campbell) F.; m. June Isobel Ferguson; children: (Mrs.) Sonia Hennigar, Rhonda; VICE-PRES., CRAWLEY FILMS LTD.; Vice-Pres., Graphic Films Lab.; Ass., John Doherty & Co. Ltd.; Dir., Robloc Ltd.; Past Chrmn., Conf. on Candn. Information; Red Cross Nat. Pub. Relations Comte.; St. John Ambulance Assn. Nat. Public Relations Comte; Past Chrmn., Ottawa Civic Hosp.; Ottawa United Way; Past Pres., Candn. Adv. & Sales Fed.; Can. Film & Television Assoc; Canada's Capital Visitor's & Convention Bureau; Internat. Quorum of Motion Picture Producers; Ottawa Red Cross; Advertising & Sales Club of Ottawa; Past Vice-Pres., Candn. Pub. Relations Soc.; Former Dir., Ottawa Better Business Bureau; Candn. Film Inst.; Former Depy. Asst. Dir., Supplies & Transport, Candn. Army Overseas, rank Maj.; United Church; recreations: travel, public speaking; Clubs: Rotary (Past Dir.); Bd. of Trade (Past Dir.); Men's Canadian (Past Pres.); Home: 901—370 Dominion Ave., Ottawa, Ont. K2A 3X4; Office: 19 Fairmont, Ottawa, Ont. K1Y 3B5

FRASER, Robert C., B.Com., C.A.; utilities executive; b. Eureka, Pictou County, N.S. 27 Nov. 1929; e. Dalhousie Univ. B.Com. 1952; C.A. (Que.) 1959; m. Josephine, 1953; children: Heather Jane, Allan Eaton; VICE PRES. AND CHIEF FINANCIAL OFFR., NOVA SCOTIA POWER CORP.; Treas., Tidal Power Corp. 1971; Eastern Light & Power Ltd. 1973; Nova Scotia Light & Power Co. Ltd. 1979; Adm. Asst. to Gen. Mgr. present co. 1964, Secy.-Treas. 1965, Treas. & Chief Financial Offr. 1967, Vice Pres. Finance 1972; mem. Inst. C.A.'s N.S. (Past Pres.); Order C.A.'s Que.; Candn. Inst. C.A.'s; Financial Extves. Inst. (Past Pres. Maritime Chapter); Candn. Elect. Assn.; Halifax Bd. Trade; Club: Halifax; Home: 80 Nightingale Dr., Halifax, N.S. B3M 1V6; Office: (P.O. Box 910) Halifax, N.S. B3J 2W5.

FRASER, Ronald Cleveland; broadcasting official; b. Milton, Queens Co., N.S., 14 Mar. 1916; s. Allan Henry and Caroline Maud (Lloyd) F.; e. Pub. Sch., Yarmouth, N.S.; Yarmouth (N.S.) Acad., 1932; m. Gladys Florence, d. A. T. Dauphinee, Yarmouth, N.S., 23 Sept. 1942; has one s., Ronald Ian; SPECIAL ASST. TO THE PRES., C.B.C., 1981; Reporter and Columnist, Yarmouth (N.S.) papers and various pubs. in U.S. and Can., 1934-39; mem. of Staff, Radio Stn. CJLS, Yarmouth, 1939-43; joined C.B.C. 1943 in Halifax as Maritime Farm Broadcast Commentator and inaugurated CBC Fisherman's Broadcast; Producer, CBC Farm Broadcast (Nat. Office), Toronto, 1946-47; Asst. Supv., Press & Information Service, Toronto, 1947, and apptd. Supv. 1948; Nat. Dir. of Press and Information Services, 1949; trans. to Ottawa, 1953; Dir. of Public Relations, 1958; Vice Pres., Corp. Affairs, 1959-64; Vice-Pres. Corp. Affairs and Asst. to the Pres., 1964-81; Dir., Children's Hosp. of Eastern Ont. Foundation, 1981; mem., Ottawa Men's Press Club; United Church; recreation: golf; Home: 544 Hillcrest Ave., Ottawa, Ont. K2A 2M9; Office: 1500 Bronson Ave., Ottawa, Ont.

FRASER, Sylvia Lois, B.A.; author; b. Hamilton, Ont. 8 March 1935; d. George Nicholas and Gladys Olive (Wilson) Meyers; e. Univ. of W. Ont. B.A.; divorced; writer, "Toronto Star Weekly" 1957-68; mag. writing awards incl. Women Press Club Award 1967, 1968; President's Medal 1969; author "Pandora" 1972 novel; "The Candy Factory" 1975 novel; "A Casual Affair" 1978 novel; "The Emperor's Virgin" 1980 novel; guest lect., Banff School of Fine Art, 1973-9; mem. Arts Adv. Panel to Can. Council 1977-81; Writer-in-Residence, U.W.O., 1980; Bd. of Dir., The Writers Development Trust, since 1979; Founding mem. Writers' Union of Can.; Home: 382 Brunswick Ave., Toronto, Ont. M5R 2Y9

FRASER, William Wallace; executive; b. Hamiota, Man. 6 Oct. 1921; e. Hamiota, Man.; m. Dorothy M. McConnell 24 June 1970; PRESIDENT, MANITOBA POOL ELEVATORS; Dir. Dist. 5, Man. Pool Elevators; farmed 1946-78; mem. Royal Candn. Legion; recreations: curling, golf; Club: Lions; Home: 68 Woodlawn Ave., Winnipeg, Man. R2M 2P2; Office: 220 Portage Ave., Winnipeg, Man. R3C 3K7.

FRASTACKY, Rudolf Victor; trust company officer; b. Mosovce, Czechoslovakia, 11 Feb. 1912; s. Andreas and Suzanne (Institoris) F.; came to Canada, 1949; e. Inst. Bratislava, Czech., Grad. in Higher Economics; m. Viera, d. late Joseph Orszagh, 26 Sept. 1942; children: Luba, Fedor, Michael; VICE CHAIRMAN, VICTORIA AND GREY TRUST CO., since 1979; mem. of the Bd., Transohio Financial Corp., Cleveland 1977-79; Secy.-Treas., Minerva Trans-Can. Invests. Ltd.; Vice Pres. & Dir., Five Oaks Holdings Ltd.; with Assn. of Co-operative Banking Socs., 1934-39; Head of Indust. Develop. there 1939-40; Gen. Mgr., Sugar Monopoly, Czech., 1940-44; in politics, 1945-48; Vice Pres. and Pres., European Industrial Products Ltd., 1949-55; Pres. and Gen. Mgr., Allwood Construction Co., 1955-58; real estate invest. business operating through some 30 Cos. in Ont., 1958-62; co-organized present Co., 1962, Pres. 1963; Mem. of Parliament, Czechoslovakia, 1945-48; Min. of Food & Supply, 1945-46; Vice Premier, Govt. of Slovakia, 1946-48; Capt. in Reserve, Czechoslovakian Army; R. Catholic; recreation: skiing; Clubs: Royal Candn. Yacht; National; Home: 338 Cortleigh Blvd., Toronto, Ont. M5N 1R3; Office: 353 Bay St., Toronto, Ont. M5H 2T8

FRAYNE, Mrs. Trent — see: : Callwood, June.

FRAZEE, Rowland Cardwell; banker; b. Halifax, N.S., 12 May 1921; s. Rowland Hill and Callie Jean (Cardwell) F.; e. St. Stephen, N.B.; King's Coll. and Dalhousie Univ.; m. Marie Eileen Tait, 11 June 1949; children: Stephen, Catherine; CHMN. AND CHIEF EXEC. OFFICER, THE ROYAL BANK OF CAN.; served with Carlton & York Regt., 1st Candn. Inf. Div. in Can., UK and Europe during World War II; rank Maj. on retirement 1945; Past. Pres., Candn. Bankers' Assn.; Dir., The Portage Program for Drug Dependencies Inc.; Roosevelt Campobello Internat. Park Comn.; Sports Fund for the Physically Disabled; Council for Canadian Unity; The Conference Bd. of Canada; Gov., McGill Univ.; Phi Kappa Pi; Anglican; recreations: golf, swimming, reading; Clubs: The Toronto; Granite; York (all Toronto); Mount Royal; St. James's; Royal Montreal Golf; Mount Bruno Country; Lyford Cay; Manitoba; Rideau; Office: 1 Place Ville Marie, Montreal, Que. H3B 4A7

FREBOLD, Hans W. L., D.Ph., F.R.S.C. (1955); consulting geologist; b. Hanover, Germany, 31 July 1899; s. Carl and Elizabeth (Denks) F.; e. High Sch., Hanover, Germany, 1906-18; Univ. of Gottingen, D.Ph. 1924; m. Elizabeth (Oster) 1926; children: Fridtjof, Ingeborg, Burkhard, Sigrid, Gudrun; 2ndly, Britta (Bohn) Docent, Geol. and Palaeontol., Univ. Greifswald, Germany 1926-31, Prof. 1931 and Hon. Prof. of Geol. 1945; engaged in Scient. research, Geol. Inst., Univ. of Copenhagen, Denmark 1933-41; Chief of Arctic Div., German Scient. Inst., Copenhagen 1941-45; Consulting Geol., Danish-Am. Prospecting Co., Copenhagen 1947-49; Geol., Geol. Survey of Can., 1949-51; Head. Sec. of Stratigraphic Palaeontology, 1951-59; Sr. Research Palaeontologist, 1959-65, Principal Research Scientist 1965-68; Visiting Prof. Geol., Univ. of Oklahoma, 1963-64; Hon. Prof. Geol., Univ. of Kiel, Germany 1949; Chief, Norwegian Expdn. to Spitzbergen, 1930 and Party Chief, Danish three yrs. Expdn. to N.E. Greenland, 1931; awarded Danish Medal of Merit with Bar; author of "Geologie von Spitzbergen", 1935; "Geologie der Arktis", (vol. I), 1945; numerous articles and reports particularly on the geol. and palaeontol. of the Am. and European Arctic and Canada; mem., Geol.

Soc. of Denmark; Protestant; Home: 265 Patricia Ave., Ottawa, Ont. K1Y 0C6

FRECHETTE, William Dean Howells, B.Com.; association executive; b. Ottawa, Ont., 5 May 1917; s. Howells and Lena (Derick) F.; e. Nepean High Sch., Ottawa, Ont.; Univ. of Toronto, B.Com. 1939; m Jean M. d. Col. Albert E. Dalziel, 21 June 1947; children: Janet Elizabeth; John William; VICE-PRES. & SECY., CANADIAN MANUFACTURERS' ASSN. since 1975; Adm. Trainee, Hudson's Bay Co., Winnipeg and N.W.T., 1939; joined Comm. Intelligence Dept. of present Assn., Toronto 1946; Dept. Mgr. 1955; Gen. Secy. 1966; Etve. Vice Pres. 1972; served in 2nd World War, R.C.O.C. 1940-46; rank at discharge Lieutenant-Colonel & Assistant Director Ordnance Services, 21 Army Group; Roy. Candn. Geographical Soc.; Candn. Forces Logistics Assn. (Life Mem.); Anglican; Clubs: Ontario; Empire Club of Can.; Canadian; Home: 61 Mason Blvd., Toronto, Ont. M5M 3C6; Office: One Yonge St., Toronto, Ont. M5E 1J9

FREDEEN, Howard, B.S.A., M.Sc., Ph.D.; agricultural research scientist; b. Macrorie, Sask., 10 Dec. 1921; s. Alvin Hartley and Olive Arasmith (French) F.; e. Univ. of Sask., B.S.A. 1943, M.Sc. 1947; Iowa State Coll., Ph.D. 1952; m. Audrey Joan, d. John Henry Bryne, Whonock, B.C., 27 Dec. 1954; children: Diane, Lee, John, Gregory, Nancy; Research Scientist, Dept. of Agric., Can., since 1947; Head, Livestock Research, Lacombe, since 1955; Fisheries Research Bd. of Can., 1940-41, 1945-46; Lectr., Animal Science, Univ. of Sask., 1943-44; mem., Commonwealth Agric. Review Conf., 1955; Secy-Treas., Can. Lacombe Breeders Assn., 1959-68; Tech. Advisor, Candn. Swine Council, since 1964; Ed., "Canadian Journal Animal Science", 1966-74; author of over 300 scient. papers and a hist. of Lacombe and dist.; co-Developer of Lacombe breed of swine, 1959, Tech. Developer of new pig carcass grading systems for Candn. (effective Dec. 1968) and beef (effective Sep. 1972); mem., St. Andrews Un. Ch. Bd., 1959 (Chrmn. 1966); Pres., Lacombe Choral Soc., 1955-57; Lacombe Male Chorus, 1952-69; Lacombe Centennial Choir, 1966-68; Pres. Alta. Canoe Assn., 1977; rec'd Pub. Service Merit Award 1969; Fellow, Agric. Inst. Can. 1967; Candn. Soc. Animal Science Cert. of Merit 1976; Genetics Soc. of Canada Award of Excellence 1978, Univ. of Sask., Alumni Award, 1981; mem. Bd. of Dir., Fletchers Fine Foods Ltd., since 1980; mem., Alta. Inst. Agrologists; Candn. Soc. Animal Science (Dir.); Candn. Soc. Genetics & Cytology (Dir.); Am. Soc. Animal Science; Poultry Science; Biometrics Soc.; Am. Soc. Advancement Science; N.Y. Acad. Sciences; Sigma Xi; Protestant; recreations: music, sports, archaeology; Address: Lacombe, Alta. T0C 1S0

FREDEMAN, William Evan, M.A., Ph.D., F.R.S.C., F.R.S.L.; author; educator; b. Pine Bluff, Ark. 19 July 1928; s. Frank Henry and Lucille (Griffiths) F.; e. Subiaco (Ark.) Acad. 1945; Henrix Coll. Ark. B.A. 1948; Univ. of Okla. M.A. 1950, Ph.D. 1956; m. Elta Jane d. Robert J. Cowan, Vancouver, B.C. 25 Apl. 1964; one s. Robert Luke; PROF. OF ENGLISH, UNIV. OF B.C. since 1967; Teacher, Capitol Hill High Sch. Oklahoma City 1948-53; Instr. Univ. of B.C. 1956, Asst. Prof. 1958: Assoc. Prof. 1963; Can. Council Sr. Research Fellow 1959-60, 1970-71, 1978-79; John Simon Guggenheim Mem. Foundation Fellow 1965-66, 1971-72; Killam Sr. Research Fellow 1970-71, 1978-79; S. W. Brooks Visiting Lectr. Univ. of Queensland 1978; served with US Naval Reserve (active) 1945-46, rank Lt., US Army ReServe (inactive) 1948-57; author "Pre-Raphaelitism: A Bibliocritical Study" 1965; "A Pre-Raphaelite Gazette: The Letters of Arthur Hughes" 1967; "Prelude to the Last Decade: Dante Gabriel Rossetti in the Summer of 1872" 1971; "The Letters of Pictor Ignotus: William Bell Scott's Correspondence with Alice Boyd 1859-1884" 1976; ed. "The P.R.B. Journal" 1975; book chapters, articles bibliog., Rossettis, Pre-Raphaelites, Tennyson, Earle Birney; mem. Modern Lang. Assn. Am.;

Bibliog. Soc. (London); Internat. Assn. Univ. Profs. Eng.; P. Conservative; recreation: book collecting; Home: 1649 Allison Rd., Vancouver, B.C. V6T 1S7; Office: 2075 Wesbrook Mall, Vancouver, B.C. V6T 1W5.

FREDERICK, Dolliver H.; industrialist; b. Edmonton, Alta. 2 Apl. 1944; s. Henry and Gladys (Ganske) F.; e. Alta. Coll.; Univ. of Alta.; N. Alta. Inst. Technol. Business Adm. Grad.; m. Joan Beverly d. Lawrence and Luella Dickau 28 Aug. 1965; children: Blayne Jeffrey, Tamara Lea; PRES., CEO AND DIR., FREDERICK INVESTMENT CORP., since 1981; Dir. and Chrmn. Extve. Comte. of Bd., Na-Churs Plant Food Co., Marion, Ohio; Dir. & Chrmn. Exte. Comte. of the Bd., Macleod Stedman Inc., Winnipeg, Toronto, Can.; Sales Rep. Imperial Oil Ltd. Edmonton 1966, Devel. Rep. Red Deer, Alta. 1968, Area Mgr. Regina 1969, Invest. Mgr. Edmonton 1971, Sr. Analyst-Marketing Toronto 1972-73; Corporate Devel. Mgr. Bovis-McNamara Corp. (Now Kesmark/Hatleigh) 1973, Corporate Vice Pres. 1975-79; Pres. and Chief Operating Offr. General Supply Co. of Canada (1973) Ltd. 1975-79; Pres. and Chief Operating Officer Equipment Fédéral Québec Ltée 1975-79; Pres. C.E.O., and Dir., CanWest Investment Corp. 1978-81; Dir. of Membership Cmte. Bd. of Trade of Metrop. Toronto; P. Conservative; recreations: golf, skiing; Clubs: Cambridge; National; Toronto Cricket Skating & Curling; Bd. of Trade Golf; Aurora Highlands; Young Presidents' Organization — Ontario Chapter; Home: 35 Steeplechase, Aurora, Ont. L4G 3G8; Office: (P.O. Box 77) Suite 4650, Toronto-Dominion Bank Tower, Toronto, Ont. M5K 1E7

FREDRICKSON, John Murray, M.D., F.R.C.S.(C), F.A.C.S.; educator; b. Winnipeg, Man. 24 March 1931; s. Frank Sigurdur and Beatrice Sveinross (Peterson) F.; e. Univ. of B.C. B.A. 1953, M.D. 1957 (Surgery Award 1956); Linkoping Univ. Sweden M.D. 1975 (cited for excellence in vestibular research); m. Alix Louise d. late Rae Gordon 12 June 1956; children: Kristin, Lisa, Erik; PROF. OF OTOLARYNGOLOGY, UNIV. OF TORONTO since 1977 and Dir. Clin. Sciences Div. since 1976; Consultant, Hosp. for Sick Children, Princess Margaret Hosp. Toronto; Research and Internship Univ. of B.C., Vancouver Gen. Hosp., Shaughnessy Hosp. Vancouver, Univ. of Chicago (Instr. in Surg. Otolaryngol. 1963-65); Research Fellow, Dept. Clin. Neurophysiol. Univ. of Freiburg 1964-65 (Visiting Investigator 1963-65); Asst. Prof. of Surg. Div. Otolaryngol. Stanford Med. Center 1965-68; Assoc. Prof. of Otolaryngol. Univ. of Toronto, Toronto Gen. Hosp. 1968-77, Asst. Prof. of Physiol. since 1969; Visiting Prof. Linkoping Univ. Sweden 1973; rec'd Medal for film "Laryngeal and Pharngeal Pouches" 49th Annual Clin. Cong. Am. Coll. Surgs. 1963; Research Award 1964 and Award of Merit 1976 Am. Acad. Ophthalmol. & Otolaryngol.; Hodge Mem. Award Candn. Otolaryngol. Soc. 1965; Graham Campbell Prize Univ. of Toronto 1970; served with RCAM Reserve 1956-60, Med. Offr.; Assoc. Ed. several prof. journs.; author or co-author numerous publs., scient. films; inventor of electromagnetic implantable voice box and hearing aid; mem. Bárány Soc.; B.C. and Ont. Coll. Phys. & Surgs.; Ont. Med. Assn.; Pan-Pacific Surg. Assn.; Candn. Otolaryngol. Soc.; Am. Soc. Head & Neck Surg.; Am. Acad. Ophthalmol. & Otolaryngol. Collegium Otolaryngologica and other prof. assns.; Protestant; recreations: racquet sports, skiing, golf, music; Home: 24 Queen Mary's Dr., Toronto, Ont. M8X 1S2; Office: Medical Sciences Bldg., Toronto, Ont. M5S 1A8.

FREEDMAN, Harry; composer; b. Lodz, Poland, 5 Apl. 1922; s. Max and Rose (Nelken) F.; came to Can. 1925; e. St. Johns High Sch., Winnipeg, 1938; Winnipeg Sch. of Art, 1936-39; Royal Conserv. of Music, Toronto, 1945-50; m. Mary Louise, d. late Donald Morrison, 15 Sept. 1951; three d. Karen Liese, Cynthia Jane, Lori Ann; joined Toronto Symphony 1946 and remained playing mem. until appt. as Composer-in-Residence in 1970; won scholarship to study with Aaron Copland, 1949; Host of music segment of CBC's "Junior Roundup", 1960-61; apptd. to Ed. Bd. of "Music Across Canada", 1962; was one of 5 composers who organized Ten Centuries Concerts in Toronto, 1963; asked to rep. Can. at "2nd Festival of Music of the Americas and Spain", Madrid, 1967; Host and Commentator on "CBC Thursday Music", 1968 and 1969; has been assoc. with several Toronto Sch. Bds. in field of educ. music; chosen by Ont. Arts Council to conduct research project on interdisciplinary arts educ.; winner of Canadian Film Awards "ETROG" for best film score, 1970; Candn. Music Council award, "Composer of the Year" 1979; princ. works incl.: 5 Pieces for String Quartet, 1948; Scherzo for Piano, 1949; Nocturne (Orchestra) 1949; 2 Vocalises, 1953; Tableau 1952; Images 1957; Symphony No. 1, 1960 (premiered in Washington 1961); Wind Quintet 1961; Fantasy and Allegro 1962; The Tokaido 1964; Chaconne 1964; Little Symphony 1966; Rose Latulippe (ballet score) 1966; Anerca (3 settings of Eskimo poems for soprano and piano) 1966, Tangents 1967; Toccata (flute and soprano) 1968; Poems of Young People 1968; 5 Over 13 (ballet score) 1969; Scenario 1970; Shining People of Leonard Cohen 1970; Orchestration of Debussy's Preludes, Bk. 1, 1971; Graphic I (". . . Out of Silence"), 1971; Keewaydin (SSA choir), 1971; Pan (flute, sopr., piano), 1972; Graphic II (string quartet), 1972; Tapestry (orch.), 1973; Encounter (violin and piano), 1974; Nocturne 2 (orch.), 1975; Alice in Wonderland (quintet), 1976; Fragments of Alice (chamber orch.), 1976; The Explainer (narrator & chamber ensemble), 1976; Celebration (concerto for Gerry Mulligan), 1977; Green . . . Blue . . . White . . . (choir), 1978; Abracadabra (1-Act Jazz Opera), 1978-79; film and TV scores incl.: Shadow of the City 1956; Where Will They Go 1959; India 1960; 20 Million Shoes 1962; The Dark Did Not Conquer 1963; 700 Million 1964; Pale Horse, Pale Rider 1965; Let Me Count the Ways 1964; Spring Song 1965; China: The Roots of Evil 1966; Romeo and Jeanette 1966; Isabel (film) 1967; The Flame Within (Cantata for film "Act of the Heart") 1968; Night 1970; music for "Much Ado About Nothing" (stage, Stratford 1971); "As You Like It" (stage, Stratford 1972); "Twelfth Night" (stage, Toronto Arts Production, 1972); The Pyx (film), 1973; Romeo and Juliet (ballet), 1973; "1847" (CBC-TV), 1977; "Pyramid of Roses" (1980); Chalumeau (clar. & str. qt.), 1981; served with RCAF 1942-45; mem. Adv. Bd., Pollution Probe (Univ. of Toronto); Advisor, Arts Educ., Prov. of Ont. Council for the Arts; Founding mem. and Pres., (1975-78) Candn. League Composers, Ten Centuries Concerts; Founding mem. & Pres., Guild of Candn. Film Composers (1979-); N.D.P.; recreations: painting (Japanese Sumi), film-making, golf; Address: 35 St. Andrews Gdns., Toronto, Ont. M4W 2C9

FREEDMAN, Hon. Samuel, LL.D., D.Cn.L.; judge; b. Russia, 16 Apl. 1908; s. Nathan and Ada (Foxman) F.; came to Can. 1911; e. Univ. of Man., B.A. (Hons.) 1929; Man. Law Sch., Univ. of Man., LL.B. 1933; Windsor, LL.D. 1960, Hebrew University of Jerusalem, 1964, Toronto, 1965, Man. 1968, Brock 1968, McGill 1968, North Dakota State 1965, Queen's 1969, Dalhousie 1971, York 1971, Trent 1972, Wm. Mitchell Coll. of Law 1973; D.C.L. W. Ont. 1973; St. John's Coll., Winnipeg, D.Cn.L. 1967; m. Claris Brownie Udow, Winnipeg, 29 June 1934; children: Martin Herbert, Susan Ruth, Phyllis Claire; CHIEF JUSTICE OF MAN. since 1971; mem. Bd. Govs., Hebrew Univ., Jerusalem, since 1955; Chancellor, Univ. of Manitoba, 1959-68; a Trustee The John W. Dafoe Foundation, 1955-78; read law with W. D. Lawrence, K.C.; called to Bar of Man. 1933; cr. K.C. 1944; articled law student with Steinkopf & Lawrence 1930-33; Jr. Barrister 1933-35; mem., Steinkopf Lawrence & Freedman, 1935-45; Freedman & Golden 1946-52; Justice, Court of Queen's Bench, Man., 1952-60; Court of Appeal since 1960; Ed., Man. "Bar News", 1942-46; Vice-Pres., Civil Liberties Assn. of Man. 1945-51; League of Nations Soc. of Winnipeg 1941-44; Dir., Family Bur. 1943-47; Vice-Pres., Community Chest 1946-47; Dir., Jewish Welfare Fund 1942-44; mem.,

Man. Bar Assn. (Pres. 1952); Candn. Bar Assn. (mem., Man. Council 1943-44 and 1951-52); Candn. Inst. of Internat. Affairs (Chrmn. Winnipeg Br. 1947-48); mem., Can. Foundation 1948-58; Hon. Pres., Univ. of Man. Students' Union,1949-50; Chrmn., Winnipeg Chapter, Candn. Friends of the Hebrew University, 1953-69; rec'd. Human Relations Award from Candn. Council of Christians and Jews, 1956; served as one-man Indust. Inquiry Comn. investig. the matter of Candn. Nat. Rlys. "run-through" problem, 1964-65; Sigma Alpha Mu (Prior of Sigma Xi Chap., Man., 1930); B'nai B'rith (Pres. 1943-44); Y.M.H.A. (Pres. 1936-37); Jewish; recreations: reading, public speaking;Club: Glendale Country; Canadian (Extve. 1944-45); Home: 425 Cordova St., Winnipeg, Man. R3N 1A5; Office: Court House, Winnipeg, Man. R3C 0V8

FREEDMAN, Samuel Orkin, B.Sc., M.D., C.M., F.R.C.P.(C), F.A.C.P., F.R.S.C.; educator; b. Montreal, Que. 8 May 1928; s. Abraham Orkin Freedman; e. Westmount High Sch. 1945; McGill Univ. B.Sc. 1949, M.D., C.M. 1953; m. Norah Lee d. late Haim Maizel 28 Aug. 1955; children: David Orkin, Daniel Ari, Abraham Edward, Elizabeth Vera; VICE-PR. (ACADEMIC) McGILL UNIV. since 1981; Sr. Phys. Div. Clin. Immunology & Allergy, Dept. Med. Montreal Gen. Hosp.; Prof. of Med. and Dir. Div. Clin. Immunology & Allergy, McGill Univ. 1968-77; Dean of Medicine, McGill Univ. 1977-81; co-discoverer CEA test for cancer; rec'd Queen's Silver Jubilee Medal; Gairdner Award Univ. of Toronto 1978; co-author "Clinical Immunology" 2nd ed. 1976; over 120 scient. articles on topics cancer immunology, clin. allergy and tuberculosis; mem. Internat. Assn. Allergology (Vice-Pres.); Jewish; Club: University; Home: 658 Murray Hill Ave., Montreal, Que. H3Y 2W6; Office: 845 Sherbrooke St. W., Montreal, Que. H3A 2T5.

FREEMAN-ATTWOOD, Edward Carson, F.C.A.; executive; b. Baluchistan, India 20 Aug. 1930; s. Harold Augustus and Jess (Job) F.-A.; e. Marlborough Coll. Wilts., Eng.; m. Marie Marquerite d. late Wilhelm Cavallar von Grabensprung 7 Dec. 1957; EXTVE. VICE PRES.-BRAZIL, BRASCAN LTD. 1979- ; Dir. John Labatt Ltd.; Articled Clk., Honeyman & Co., London, Eng. 1949-55; UN High Commr. for Refugees, Office of Rep. for Austria, Financial and Adm. Offr. 1957-58; joined Clarkson, Gordon & Co. Toronto 1958, Partner 1961-71; Mang. Partner, Arthur Young, Clarkson, Gordon & Co. Brazil 1964-71; Asst. Vice Pres. Finance, Brascan Ltd. 1971-72, Vice Pres. Finance 1972-74, Extve. Vice Pres. 1974-76, Pres. and Chief Operating Offr. 1976-79; Extve. Vice Pres., Brazil, 1979- ; mem. Inst. C.A.'s Ont.; Inst. C.A.'s Nfld.; Club: Ontario; Home: Av. Copacabana, 313-Apt. 651, Rio de Janeiro, Brazil; Offices: Brascan Administraçâo & Investimentos, Av. Presidente Vargas, 642-21 Indar 20.071, Rio de Janeiro, Brazil; (Canada) Box 48 Commerce Court Postal Stn., Toronto, Ont. M5L 1B7.

FREER, (Arthur) Wilfred, M.C.; retired manufacturer; b. Sao Paulo, Brazil, 4 Jan. 1917; s. Arthur Howard and Lily Anne (Beaven) F.; e. Wellington Somerset 1933; Cork Grammar Sch. 1929; m. Jean, d. late Arthur E. Wyles, Horncastle, UK 11 Apl. 1942; children: Mrs. Jill Dodson, Mrs. Wendy Morton, Christopher; joined British United Shoe Machinery Co. Leicester and London 1934-39; Mgr. G. F. Hutchings & Co. Ltd. Bristol, Eng. 1946-52; Head of Quality Control C. & J. Clark Ltd. 1952, Gen. Mgr. various plants 1952, Gen. Mgr. women's mfg. plants 1962, Dir. Clarks Ltd. and Gen. Mgr. Women's Div. 1962, Gen. Mgr. Unbranded Div., Mang. Dir. and Dir. 3 assoc. co's 1970; Group Mang. Dir. Shoe Corp. of Africa Ltd. 1971-75, Dir. BARSARB (Holding Co.) 1972-73, mem. Mang. Dir. Comte. S. African Breweries 1973-75; Pres., Greb Ind. Ltd. 1975; Chrm., Greb Industries, 1977; Pres., A.W. Freer International Inc., 1978; served with 4th Leicester Regt. 1934-40, RA 1941-46, rank Maj.; Past mem. Adv. Bd. Witwatersrand Univ. Business Sch. Johannesburg;

Fellow, Brit. Boot & Shoe Inst.; Freemason; Anglican; recreations: golf, tennis, swimming; Club: Westmount; Rotary; Home: 219 Shakespeare Dr., Waterloo, Ont. N2L 2T5

FREEZE, Roy Allan, F.R.S.C., M.Sc., Ph.D.; hydrologist; educator; b. Edmonton, Alta. 23 May 1939; s. Donald Allan and Beatrice Isobel (Anderson) F.; e. Glebe Coll. Inst. Ottawa 1957; Queen's Univ. B.Sc. 1961; Univ. of Cal. Berkeley M.Sc. 1964, Ph.D. 1966; m. Donna Dorraine d. William B. Davis, Ottawa, Ont. 22 Dec. 1961; children: Geoffrey Allan, Donna Christine, Lori Sandra, Sean Davis; PROF. OF GEOL. SCIENCES, UNIV. OF B.C.; rec'd Horton Award 1972, 1974 and MacElwane Award 1974, Am. Geophys. Union; Meinzer Award, Geol. Soc. Am. 1974; co-author "Groundwater" 1979; author over 50 scient. papers hydrology; mem. Am. Geophys. Union; Geol. Soc. Am.; Candn. Geotech. Soc.; Assn. Prof. Engrs. B.C.; recreations: camping, skiing, reading, duplicate bridge; Home: 5125 Stevens Dr., Delta, B.C.; Office: Vancouver B.C. V6T 1W5.

FREIFELD, Eric, R.C.A.; artist; b. Saratov, Russia 13 March 1919; s. Isaac and Olga (Grodnitsky) F.; e. High Sch. Edmonton, Alta.; St. Martin's Sch. of Art London, Eng. 1938; Art Students League New York 1944-46; m. Gladys Lorrain d. late William H. Sumbling 9 Sept. 1957; one d. Miriam Louise; Instr., Ont. Coll. of Art 1946-80, Chrmn. of Fine Arts 1974-79; solo exhns. incl. Hudson's Bay Co. Edmonton 1937; Brook St. Galleries London, Eng. 1939; Vancouver Art Gallery 1940, 1968; Vancouver Coll. of Art 1941; Ont. Coll. of Art 1946, 1977; Edmonton Art Gallery 1952, 1966; Hart House Univ. of Toronto 1958; Rodman Hall St. Catharines 1966; Univ. of Man. 1968; Saskatoon Art Gallery 1969; Hamilton Art Gallery 1969; London (Ont.) Art Museum 1970; Jerrold Morris Gallery 1971; Yaneff Gallery 1977, 1980; retrospective exhn. 1972 Univ. of N.B. Art Centre, Confederation Art Gallery & Museum Charlottetown, Mem. Univ. Art Gallery, N.B. Museum, Dalhousie Univ. Art Gallery, Univ. of Moncton Art Gallery, Owens Art Gallery Mount Allison Univ.; rep. in many group exhns. Can., Eng. and USA; rep. in numerous pub. and private colls. Can., Europe, USA, Israel, Australia incl. Brit. Fine Art Soc. London, Eng. and Brook St. Galleries, Vancouver, Hamilton and Windsor Art Galleries, Montreal Museum of Fine Arts, Nat. Gallery of Can., Art Gallery of Ont.; Univ. of Alberta; McMaster Univ. Art Gallery; Stratford Art Gallery, Stratford, Ont.; works reproduced various publs.; subject of biog. "Eric Freifeld" by Paul Duval; author forwards to art exhn. catalogues; rec'd Carnegie Trust Fund Scholarship Edmonton 1937; Atla. Soc. Artists Award 1937; Queen's Univ. Travelling Fellowship 1941; C.W. Jeffries Award 1957; Can. Council Sr. Arts Fellowship 1961, Grants 1971-72, 1968, 1970; mem. Gov. Council, Ont. Coll. Art 1971-73, Scholarship founded in his name 1980; served with Candn. Army 1942-44, Artist Candn. Camouflage Sch.; mem. Candn. Soc. Painters in Watercolour, Candn. Soc. Graphic Art (Pres. 1958); recreations: reading, theatre; Address: 48 Eccleston Dr., Toronto, Ont. M4A 1K7.

FREIMAN, Lawrence, O.C. (1967), LL.D.; b. Ottawa, Ont., 4 Feb. 1909; s. Archibald Jacob and Lillian (Bilsky) F.; e. Ottawa Model Sch.; Lisgar Coll. Inst.; McGill Univ.; Harvard Grad. Sch. of Business Adm.; Univ. of Ottawa, LL.D. 1957; m. Audrey Eleanor, d. late Max Steinkopf, K.C., Winnipeg, Man., 25 Mar. 1934; children: Archibald Jacob, Margo; Chrmn. Bd. and Chief Extve. Offr. A. J. Freiman Ltd. until 1971 when sold to Hudson Bay Co.; mem. Bd. of Govs., Weizmann Inst. of Science, Rehovoth, Israel, 1958-77; Hon. Pres., Fed. Zionist Organ. of Can., 1967; mem., Bd. of Dirs., Candn. Writers' Foundation Inc.; began association with A. J. Freiman Ltd., as Vice-Pres., 1931, Pres. and C.E.O. 1944-71; Pres., Canadian Welfare Council, 1953-54; Past Pres., Ottawa Philharmonic Orchestra; Bd. of Gov., The Stratford Shakes-

pearean Fest. Found. of Can., 1956-68; mem. senate, Strat. Shakes. Fest. Found. since 1968; mem. Federal District Commission, 1951-9; First Chrmn., Bd. of Trustees, National Arts Centre 1966-9; Past Vice Chrmn. Bd. of Gov., Univ. of Ottawa, hon. mem. of bd.; Home: 250 Sylvan Rd., Rockcliffe, Ottawa, Ont. K1M 0X1;

FRÉMONT,(Joseph Paul) Claude, B.A., B.A.Sc., M.Sc.,; publisher; b. Québec City, Qué. 18 Aug. 1922; s. Charles and Thaïs (Lacoste) F.; e. Coll. Garnier, Quebec B.A. 1943; Univ. Laval B.A.Sc. 1947, M.Sc. 1948; m. Gabrielle d. Arthur Duval 8 May 1953; children: Jacques, Michèle, Claire; DIR. GEN. LES PRESSES DE L'UNIVERSITE LAVAL since 1971; Lectr. in Physics Laval Univ. 1948, Assoc. Prof. 1952, Prof. 1963, Assoc. Dir. Physics Dept. 1965-71, Dir. Educ. TV Service 1965-69; rec'd Queen's Silver Jubilee Medal; Dir. and former Vice Pres. Conseil Supérieur du Livre; Pres., Assn. Candn. Univ. Presses 1977 and 81; Vice Pres. Assn. Internat. des Presses Univs. de Langue Française since 1976; Sec. Assn. Québécoise des Presses Univs.; Vice Pres. Soc. Développement du Livre et du Périodique; Past Pres. Inst. Canadien de Qué.; R. Catholic; recreations: travel, hobbies; Home: 2970 Longfellow, Sainte-Foy, Qué. G1W 1X7; Office: (C.P. 2447) Québec City, Qué. G1K 7R4.

FRENCH, Carl Burton, B.S., J.D.; company president; b. Burlington, Mich., s. Burton D. and Sarah H. (Stark) F.; e. Northwestern Univ., B.S. 1928; Kent Coll. of Law, Chicago, J.D. 1935; m. Ruth Maretta Arnold; two d., Jean C., Carol M.; PRESIDENT CEEBEE SERVICES LTD.; began with Chicago Daily News on administrative work, 1931; called to Bar of State of Illinois, 1935; practised law, Chicago, Ill., 1935-37; came to Can. 1937 as Secy.-Treas. and Dir., Eldorado Mining and Refining Ltd.; Dir., Giant Yellowknife Mines Ltd., 1938-39; International Uranium Mines Ltd., 1940-45; founded Radium Luminous Industries Ltd. and Dial and Instrument Finishers Ltd. 1942; X-Ray and Radium Industries Ltd. 1945 (all merging in 1959 to become present Co.); Pres., Chrmn. Extve. Comte.; Candn. Cancer Soc., 1953-56; Nat. Cancer Inst., 1957-66; Organizing Chrmn., First Internat. Conf. of Cancer Volunteers, Toronto, Oct. 1965; mem., Internat. Union Against Cancer Comn. for Social Campaigns & Organs.; Sponsoring Comte. on Cancer Control. Santiago, Chile, Nov. 1967; rec'd. in person award Of Vermeil Medal by Soc. d'Encouragement au Progrés, Apl. 1967, at Univ. of Paris (citation referred to his work in utilization of uranium and radium during 1939-42, in assoc. with physicists Enrico Ferme, Leo Szillard and others, and his pioneer work in field of cancer control as former Nat. Pres. Candn. Cancer Soc.; Chrmn. of 1st Internat. Cong. for Volunteers in Can. 1965, and as mem. of Control Comn. of Internat. Union Against Cancer); rec'd. Merit Award, Nthwest. Univ. 1971; Hon. Life mem., Candn. Cancer Soc.; Hon. mem. Liga Colombiana de lucha Contra el Cancer, Colombia, S.A.; Hon. Pres., N. York Unit, Can. Cancer Soc.; Phi Kappa Sigma; Phi Delta Phi; Alpha Kappa Psi; recreations: riding, golfing; Clubs: National; Granite; York Downs Golf; Turf; Eglinton Hunt; Variety; Address: 263 Dawlish Ave., Toronto, Ont. M4N 1J4

FRENCH, Guy Parsons, B.A.; manufacturer; b. Montreal, Que. 6 Apl. 1933; s. George Frederick French; e. Westdale Secondary Sch. Hamilton, Ont. 1951; McMaster Univ. 1952; McGill Univ. B.A. 1954; m. Barbara Ellen d. late Harry Davies 25 June 1955; children: Timothy Guy, Sandra Jane, Mary Ellen, Patrick; PRES. AND CHIEF EXTVE. OFFR., AMERICAN CAN CANADA INC.; Vice Pres., Area Man. Canada and Europe, Am. Can Co.; Dir. PCL Industries Ltd.; Sterling Trust Corp.; former Dir. Central Mortgage & Housing Corp. Ottawa; Dir. Toronto Sch. Theol. (Chrmn. Bd. Trustees 1974-78); mem. Adv. Council Queen's Univ. Sch. of Business; Lay Reader Toronto Diocese Ang. Ch. of Can.; mem. Royal Ont. Museum; Art Gallery of Ont.; Patron, Distress Centre Toronto; author various articles; served with Univ. Naval Training

Div. 1951-53; mem. Grocery Products Mfrs. Assn. Young Pres. Organ.; Business Comte. on Regulatory Reform; Niagara Inst.; Liberal; Anglican; recreations: golf, tennis, gardening; Clubs: Bayview Country; Granite; Rosedale Golf; Wentworth (Surrey); Canadian (Toronto and New York); Home: 139 Teddington Park Ave., Toronto, Ont. M4N 2C7; Office: 1 International Blvd., Rexdale, Ont. M9W 1A1.

FRENCH, John Barry, B.A.Sc., M.Sc., Ph.D., F.R.S.C., F.R.S.A., F.C.A.S.I.; educator; b. Toronto, Ont. 22 Aug. 1931; s. John Edwin and Lilla (Hitchcox) F.; e. Mimico (Ont.) High Sch.; Univ. of Toronto B.A.Sc. (Chem. Engn.) 1955, Ph.D. 1961; Univ. of Birmingham M.Sc. (Thermodynamics) 1957; m. Gloria June Profit; 4 children: PROF. OF AEROSPACE ENGN. SCIENCE, INST. FOR AEROSPACE STUDIES, UNIV. OF TORONTO 1968- ; Chrmn. of Bd. Sciex Inc. 1970- ; Dir. Innovation Foundation Univ. of Toronto; Asst. Prof. present Inst. 1962, Assoc. Prof. 1964, Assoc. Dir. 1973- ; Pres. AER-COL 1969-71; holds several patents on Atmospheric Pressure Chem. Ionization Mass Spectroscopy; recipient Financial Post Best Business Venture Award 1979; I.R. 100 Design Award 1980; Consultant to many U.S. and Candn. firms; author over 40 research papers rarefied gasdynamics, molecular beams, space simulation and instrumentation, trace gas analysis, mass spectroscopy; mem. Assn. Prof. Engrs. Prov. Ont.; recreations: sailing, skiing; Home: 4 Thornbank Rd., Thornhill, Ont. L4J 2A2; Office: 4925 Dufferin St., Downsview, Ont. M3H 5T6.

FRENCH, William, B.A.; literary editor; b. London, Ont., 21 March 1926; s. Harold Edward and Isabel Nimmo (Brash) F.; e. Sir Adam Beck Coll. Inst., London, Ont., 1944; Univ. of W. Ont. B.A. 1948; Harvard Univ. (Nieman Fellow 1955); m. Margaret Jean, d. William C. Rollo, London, Ont., 23 June 1951; children: Jane, Mark, Paul, Susan; LIT. ED., "GLOBE AND MAIL" since 1960; Part-time Lectr. in Journalism, Ryerson Polytech. Inst. since 1955; joined "Globe and Mail" as Gen. Reporter, 1948; covered educ. and City Hall 1949-54; mem. Ed. Bd., 1956-57 and 1959-60; Staff Writer, "The Globe Magazine", 1957-59; author of "A Most Unlikely Village: A Hist. of Forest Hill", 1964; contrib. chapter on Sir Sam Hughes to "The Flamboyant Canadians", 1964; radio documentaries on CBC; awarded President's Medal, Univ. of W. Ont., for Best Gen. Mag. Article Pub. in Can., 1965; won Hon. Mention for ed. writing. Nat. Newspaper Awards, 1957; Winner Nat. Newspaper Award for Crit. Writing, 1977 and 1978; Home: 78 North Hills Terrace, Don Mills, Ont.; Office: 444 Front St. W., Toronto, Ont. M5V 2S9

FRESCHI, Bruno Basilio, B.Arch., R.C.A.; architect; b. Trail, B.C. 18 Apl. 1937; s. Giovanni and Irma (Pagotto) F.; e. J. L. Crown High Sch. Trail, B.C.; Univ. of B.C. B.Arch. 1961; Arch. Assn. London, Eng. postgrad. studies in arch.; children: Dea Rachelle, Anna Nadine, Aaron Basilio, Reuben Alessandro; FOUNDER, BRUNO FRESCHI/ARCHITECTURE.PLANNING.RESEARCH 1970- ; Assoc., Erickson Massey Archs. 1964-70; Assoc. Prof. Univ. of B.C. Sch. Arch. 1968-78, Head of Grad. Studies; Chief Arch. Expo '86; Guest Lectr. Simon Fraser Univ., N.S. Sch. Arch., Univ. of Man., Univ. of B.C. Sch. of Arch. & Centre Human Settlements, Bosman Mont. Sch. Arch.; Vice Pres. & Regional Chrmn. Can. Council Explorations Program 1973-75; Trustee, Vancouver Art Gallery 1973-74; Dir. and Vice Pres., Extve. of Civic Arts Council 1966-71; mem. Civic Design Panel Vancouver 1968-70; mem. Candn. Extve. Service Overseas (volunteer consultant arch. planning for B.C. Indians) 1971-80; mem. Heritage Adv. Comte. City of Vancouver 1980; recipient Royal Arch. Inst. Can. Medal 1961; Pilkington Glass Travelling Fellowship in Arch. 1961; Can. Council Grant - Aspen Internat. Design Conf. 1967; AIBC Design Award 1968; maj. comns. incl. 5 award homes 1964-82, MacMillan Bloedel Research Centre 1983, Burnaby Jamat-

khana 1983, Georgia Pl. 1980, Wickanninish Centre Phase II 1982, Cath. Sq., Civic Centre Trail 1983, Burnaby Mun. Centre 1973-78, B.C. Place Design Consultant Ampitheatre Pier A Victoria 1982-83, Whistler Village Coordination Arch. 1980; author numerous publs.; mem. Arch. Inst. B.C. (Council 1968-71 & Extve. Vancouver Chapter); Royal Arch. Inst. Can.; World Future Soc.; Downtown Vancouver Assn.; recreations: squash, mountain hiking; Home: #1, 1934 Barclay St., Vancouver, B.C. V6G 1L3; Office: 1575 West 7th Ave., Vancouver, B.C. V6J 1S1.

FREYSENG, Willis P., B.A.; executive; b. Toronto, Ont., 1899; s. Edward John and Ida Edith (Hunter) F.; e. Univ. of Toronto Schs.; Univ. of Toronto, B.A. 1926; PRESIDENT, FREYSENG CORK CO. LTD., since 1944; Chrmn., Toronto Br., Candn. Mfrs. Assn., 1951-52; began in family firm (3rd generation) in summer intervals while attending univ.; after grad. joined the Co. as Asst. Secy. and shortly after apptd. Secy.; assumed present position on death of his father; Pres., Candn. Nat. Exhn., (1961 and 1962); mem., Toronto Bd. Trade; Art Gallery of Ontario (Life); Past Pres., John Howard Soc. of Ont.; recreations: golf, swimming, photography; Clubs: National; Toronto Hunt; Eastbourne Golf; Canadian; Empire; Home: 17 Killarney Rd., Toronto, Ont. M5P 1L7; Office: 69 Sumach St., Toronto, Ont. M5P 3J6

FRIDERICHSEN, Blanche Alexia, B.A., B.L.Sc., M.Ed.; education consultant; b. Saskatoon, Sask. 21 March 1925; d. Alexander and Myrtle Jane (Henderson) Irvine; e. Univ. of Sask. B.A. 1948; Univ. of Toronto B.L.S. 1949; Univ. of Alta. M.Ed. 1974; m. Matthias Godske Andreas Friderichsen, Denmark 28 Aug. 1956; PROV. SCH. LIBRARIES CONSULTANT (MEDIA CURRICULUM), ALTA. EDUC. 1966- ; joined Edmonton Pub. Lib. Children's Services 1949-52; initiated children's services Bromley Pub. Lib., Kent, Eng. 1953-55; mem. Acquisitions Dept. Univ. of Toronto, Cataloging Dept. McGill Univ. 1955-56; Head of Circulation Edmonton Pub. Lib. 1957-59; Summer Session Lecturer, Univ. of Alta. 1959-61; Lib. Supvr. Co. of Strathcona, Sherwood Park, Alta. 1959-66; rec'd A.T.A. Learning Resources Council Award of Excellence 1978; author numerous articles sch. lib. services; mem. Lib. Assn. Alta.; Alta. Teachers' Assn. Learning Resources Council (Educ. Rep. 12 years.); Candn. Library Assn.; Int. Assn. of School Librarians; Phi Delta Kappa; Beta Sigma Phi; recreations: golf, reading, crafts, travel; Home: 14703 - 51 Ave., Edmonton, Alta. T6H 5E6; Office: Devonian Bldg., W. Tower, 11160 Jasper Ave., Edmonton, Alta. T5K 0L2.

FRIDMAN, Gerald Henry Louis, M.A., B.C.L., LL.M.; barrister; educator; b. London, Eng., 24 Oct. 1928; s. Henry and Sarah (Cohen) F.; e. Oxford Univ., M.A. 1952, B.C.L. 1949; Univ. of Adelaide, LL.M. 1955; m. Janet Margaret, d. Ellis Blaskey, Sheffield, Eng., 4 Jan. 1959; children: Sara Jayne, Saul Benjamin David, Penelope Louise, Candida Helen; PROF. OF LAW, UNIV. OF WESTERN ONTARIO Prof. and Dean, Faculty of Law, Univ. of Alta., 1969-75; read law with S. Lincoln; called to Bar of Eng. 1950, Bar of Alta. 1972; Bar of Ont. 1977; Barrister-at-Law, Eng., 1950-53; Lectr. and Senior Lectr. in Law, Univ. of Adelaide, 1953-56; Lectr., Sr. Lectr. and Reader in Law, Univ. of Sheffield, 1957-69; author, "Law of Agency", 4th 1976; "Modern Law of Employment" 1963; "Sale of Goods", 1966; "Modern Tort Cases", 1968; "Bankruptcy Law & Practice", 1970; "Studies in Candn. Bus. Law", 1971; "Sale of Goods in Canada", 1973 (2nd ed. 1979); "Law of Contract in Canada" 1976; "Introduction to the Law of Torts" 1978; also numerous essays and articles in various prof. journs.; mem., Soc. Pub. Teachers Law; Assn. Candn. Law Teachers; Law Soc. Upp. Can.; Oxford Union Soc.; Un. Grand Lodge of England; Hadassah; Jewish; recreations: music, theatre, travel; Club: Wig and Pen; Home: 226 Victoria St., London, Ont.; Office: London, Ont. N6A 3K7

FRIEDENBERG, Edgar Z., M.S., Ph.D.; educator; b. New York, N.Y. 18 March 1921; s. Edgar M. and Arline Rai (Zodiag) F.; e. Centenary Coll. Shreveport, La. B.S. 1938; Stanford Univ. M.A. 1939; Univ. of Chicago Ph.D. 1946; Prof. Dalhousie Univ. since 1970; Asst. and Assoc. Prof. Brooklyn Coll. 1953-64; Prof. Univ. of Cal. (Davis) 1964-67; State Univ. of N.Y. Buffalo 1967-70; taught summer sch. Wash. Univ. St. Louis 1962, 1963; Cornell Univ. 1964; Harvard Univ. 1970; served with USNR 1944-45; author "The Vanishing Adolescent" 1959; "Coming of Age in America" 1965; "The Dignity of Youth and Other Atavisms" 1965; "R. D. Laing" 1973; "The Disposal of Liberty and Other Industrial Wastes" 1975; "Deference to Authority: The Case of Canada", 1980; frequent contrib. to various mags. and journs.; mem. Am. Civil Liberties Union; Candn. Civil Liberties Assn.; Am. Sociol. Assn.; Soc. Study Social Problems; Candn. Soc. Study Educ.; Am. Assn. Univ. Profs.; Pres. Dalhousie Univ. Faculty Assn. 1980-81; Candn. Council for Social Devlpt.; Zen Jewish; Home: Conrad's Rd., Hubbards, N.S. B0J 1T0; Office: Dalhousie University, Halifax, N.S. B3H 3J5

FRIEDL, Maj. Gen. Maximilian Theodore, C.D., retired from Canadian armed forces; b. Germany, 28 Jan. 1923; s. Max Julius and Elizabeth (Schlemmer) F.; came to Can. 1928; e. Estevan (Sask.) Coll. Inst.; Univ. of Sask., B.Sc. 1949; Univ. of London, City & Guilds Coll., M.Sc. (Aeronautical Engn.) 1953; m. Ruth Margaret, d. late Lorne Billingsley, 5 Sept. 1947; children: Karen Elizabeth, Catherine Anne; served with RCA 1941-45; joined RCAF 1949 as Engn. Offr.; Flight Test Engr. 1949-51; Devel. Engr., AFHQ, 1953-58 (assoc. with AVRO Arrow and Flight Stimulators); Sr. Aircraft Maintenance Offr., Greenwood, N.S., 1958-60; Tech. Liaison with European Air Forces on F104 Aircraft Program, Bad Godesberg, 1960-64; Base Tech. Services Offr., Bagotville, Que., 1964-67; promoted to Col. and assigned as Depy. Chief of Staff. Tech. Services, Air Transport Command, 1967-68; C.O. Aircraft Maintenance Devel. Unit. Trenton, 1968-70; promoted Brig. Gen. and apptd. Dir. Gen. Maintenance, CFHQ, 1970-72; Dir. Gen. Management Information Systems 1972-73; Dir.-Gen. Aerospace Engn. & Maintenance 1973; promoted Maj. Gen. and apptd. Assoc. Adm. Materiel 1973; mem. of Standards Council of Can., 1977-80; apptd. Chrm. of the Aircraft Accident Review Bd., 1979,; currently business conslt. in private practice; mem.; Candn. Aerospace Inst.; Air Industries Assoc. of Can.; recreation: golf; Club: Ottawa Hunt & Golf; Home: 1634 Amberdale Cres., Ottawa, Ont. K1H 7B3; Office: Suite 101, 56 Sparks St., Ottawa K1P 5A9

FRIEDLAND, Martin Lawrence, Q.C., B.Com., LL.B., Ph.D.; educator; b. Toronto, Ont. 21 Sept. 1932; s. Jack and Mina (Rogul) F.; e. Forest Hill Coll. Inst. Toronto 1951; Univ. of Toronto B.Com. 1955, LL.B. 1958; Cambridge Univ. Ph.D. 1967; m. Judith Fern d. Michael Pless, Toronto, Ont. 19 June 1958; children: Tom, Jenny, Nancy; PROF. OF LAW, UNIV. OF TORONTO; Dean, Faculty of Law 1972-79; Asst. and Assoc. Prof. Osgoode Hall Law Sch. 1961-65; Assoc. Prof. and Prof. Univ. of Toronto since 1965; Visiting Prof., Hebrew Univ. and Tel Aviv Univ., 1979; Visiting Fellow, Clare Hall Cambridge Univ., 1980; assoc. with various Govt. Comtes. and Comns. incl. Atty.-Gen's Comte. on Enforcement of Law Relating to Gambling 1962, Jt. Comte. on Legal Aid 1965, Atty.-Gen's Comte. on Securities Leg. 1965, Min. of Reform Insts. Comte. on Regional Detention Centres 1967, Task Force on Can. Corps. Act 1968, Candn. Comte. on Corrections 1969, Solr.-Gen.'s Task Force on Gun Control Leg. 1975, Comn. of Inq. re Certain Activities of R.C.M.P., 1979, fulltime mem. of Law Reform Comm. of Canada 1971-72; rec'd Angus MacMurchy Gold Medal Faculty of Law Univ. of Toronto; Treas.'s Medal Bar Admission Course Osgoode Hall; called to Bar of Ont. 1960; cr. Federal Q.C. 1975; author "Detention Before Trial" 1965; "Double Jeopardy" 1969; "Courts and Trials" 1975; "Access to the Law" 1975; "Cases and Materials on Crim-

inal Law and Procedure" 5th ed. 1978; "National Security: The Legal Dimensions", 1980; numerous articles; Jewish; Office: Faculty of Law, Univ. of Toronto, Toronto, Ont. M5S 1A1.

FRIEDLAND, Seymour, B.S., M.B.A., Ph.D.; university professor; b. New York, N.Y., 8 Oct. 1928; s. David and Eva (Klausner) F.; e. Boston Univ., B.S. 1950, M.B.A. 1951; Harvard Univ., Ph.D. 1956; m. Gloria Lee, d. late Abraham Tassal, 31 Aug. 1952; children: Randall Roy, Andrew B., Sharon C.; 2ndly m. Eleanor Deborah, d. late Harry Swartzfeldt, April 27, 1980; step children: Lorne E. and Richard N. PROF., YORK UNIV. since 1967; Assoc. Editor, Financial Times of Canada; Dir.; Federal Trust Co. 1971-80; Pres., Camar Consultants Limited; Teaching Fellow, Harvard College, 1952-53; Instructor, Mass. Inst. of Technol., 1955-56; Asst. Prof., Sch. of Business, Boston Univ., 1956-58 and at Rutgers Univ., 1958-60; Prof. and Dept. Chrmn., Business Econ., Claremont Graduate Sch., 1960-66; Visiting Prof., N.Y. Univ. Grad. Business Sch., 1966-67; Sr. Econ., Joel Dean Assoc., 1965-66; served with U.S. Army 1947-48; Dir., Financial Research Inst., 1969-70; Gulf Research Fellow, 1964-65; author, "Employment, Location and Industrial Characteristics of the New Jersey Manufacturing Section", 1960; "Poverty Amidst Plenty", 1960; "Financing Patterns of New Jersey Manufacturing Corporation", 1964; "Economics of Corporate Finance", 1966; "Value, Growth and Taxation", 1970; "Stock Options and Company Performance", 1970; "Principles of Financial Management", 1978; Nat. Business Writing Awd., Royal Bank and Toronto Press Club, 1980; mem., Am. Econ. Assn.; Am. Finance Assn; Jewish; Clubs: Empire; Canadian; Home: #2, 423 Avenue Rd. Toronto, Ont.; Office: 4700 Keele St., Downsview, Ont. M3J 1P3

FRIEDMAN, Sydney M., M.D., C.M., M.Sc., Ph.D., F.R.S.C.; university professor; b. Montreal, Que., 17 Feb. 1916; s. Jack and Minny (Signer) F.; e. McGill Univ., B.A. 1938, M.D., C.M. 1940, M.Sc. 1941, Ph.D. 1946; m. Constance A., d. I. F. Livingstone, Montreal, 23 Sept. 1940; PROF. DEPT. OF ANATOMY, UNIV. OF BRIT. COLUMBIA since 1950; Demonst. in Histol., McGill Univ., 1940-41; Teaching Fellow in Anat. 1941-43; apptd. Asst. Prof., 1944, Assoc. Prof., 1949; Chrmn., Dep't of Anat., U.B.C., 1950-81; served in 2nd World War 1943-44; Flight-Lieut., R.C.A.F. (Med.); rec'd. Ciba Award for Ageing Studies, 1955; Pfizer Trav. Fellow of Clin. Research Inst., Montreal 1971; founding mem. B.C. Heart Foundation; mem., Candn. Assn. of Anats. (Pres 1965-66); Am. Assn. of Anats. (Extve.); Am. Physiol. Soc.; Candn. Physiol. Soc. (Council 1952-54); Am. Heart Assn.; A.O.A.; Council for High Blood Pressure Research; mem. ed. bd., "Blood Vessels"; "Hypertension"; Bd. of Dir., Can Hypertension Soc.; author: "Visual Anatomy", Vols. I and II, Springfield, Ill., 1950 and 1952; "Visual Anatomy", Vols. I, II and III, New York, 1970, 1971, 1972; and papers on endocrinology, anat., kidney function, hypertension and ageing; Sigma Xi; Home: 4916 Chancellor Blvd., Vancouver, B.C. V6T 1E1

FRIEND, Amos Edgar, M.D., C.M., F.A.C.S., F.I.C.S.; otolaryngologist; b. Wolfe Island, Ont., 7 Dec. 1898; s. Thomas and Henrietta (Roadhouse) F.; e. Kingston Coll. Inst.; Queen's Univ., M.D., C.M. 1922; m. Vera Ruth, d. Arthur Lee MacKen, 2 Sept. 1925; children: Hugh, Douglas; Interne, Hotel Dieu Hosp., Kingston, Ont., 1921-22; Med. Dir., Port Simpson Gen. Hosp., 1922-23; Resident, Lutheran Hosp., Brooklyn, N.Y., 1923-25; Sr. Surg. in otolaryngol., Manchester Mem. Hosp.; Consultant in Otolaryngol., Hartford and Rockville City Hosps.; Lic., Med. Council of Can.; Fellow, Am. Acad. Ophthalmol. & Otolaryngol.; Diplomate, Am. Bd. of Otolaryngol.; Past Pres., Hartford Co. Med. Assn. (1954-55); mem., Am. Med. Assn. (Conn.); New Eng. Otol. Soc.; Am. Council of Otolaryngol.; Am. Diopter and Decibel Soc.; Pan-Pacific Surg. Assn.; Manchester Med. Assn. (Past Pres.);

Assoc., Hartford City Med. Soc.; Am. Rhinol. Soc. (chart. mem.); Fellow, Am. Acad. Facial Plastic and Reconstr. Surg.; Am. Assn. Clin. Immunol. & Allergy; Am. Soc. Opthalmic and Otologic Allergy; Am. Coll. Surg.; Internat. Coll. Surg.; Freemason; Republican; Episcopalian; recreations: travel, movie photography; Clubs: Hartford; University; Home: Mt. Sumner Dr., Bolton, Conn.; Office: 36 Haynes St., Manchester, Conn.

FRIESEN, David, Q.C., M.Sc., LL.B., Dr. Oec. (H.S.G.); b. Russia, 16 Nov. 1911; s. David Abram and Aganeta (Driedger) F.; came to Canada, 1924; became naturalized Candn., 1929; e. Univ. of Man., LL.B., 1939; Univ. of Minn., M.Sc. (Business Adm.), 1963; m. Katherine, d. Abraham J. Loewen, 30 Oct. 1943; three d. and one s.; PRESIDENT, QUALICO DEVELOPMENTS LTD.; Sr. Partner, David Friesen & Assoc.; read law with David Laird, Q.C.; called to the Bar of Manitoba, June 1941; cr. Q.C., 1956; mem., Canadian Bar Assn.; Man. Bar Assn.; German-Candn. Business & Prof. Men's Assn. of Man. (Past Pres.); Winnipeg Housebuilders Assn. (Past Pres.); Pres., Mennonite Benevolent Soc.; rec'd Gallen 1973, LL.D. Univ. of Winnipeg, 1981; recreations: swimming, walking; Clubs: St. Charles Country; Y.M.C.A.; Home: 570 Park Blvd. West, Winnipeg, Man. R3P 0H4; Office: 30 Speers Rd., Winnipeg, Man. R2J 1L9 and 711 Notre Dame Chambers, 213 Notre Dame Ave, Winnipeg, Man. R3B 1N3

FRIESEN, Gordon Arthur, LL.D.; health care consultant; b. Rosthern, Sask., 21 Jan. 1909; s. Abraham James and Eliza (Friesen) F.; e. Univ. of W. Ont.; George Washington Univ., LL.D.; m. Jane Helen, d. Oswald W. Fuller, 25 July 1947; two d., Mary Jane, Sarah Elizabeth; Founder, Gordon A. Friesen International, Inc., 1954; Business Mgr., Saskatoon City Hosp., 1929-37; Adm., Belleville (Ont.) Gen. Hosp. 1937-41; Royal Canadian Air Force 1941-46; Mil. Gov., Westphalia, 1944-46; Adm., Kitchener-Waterloo Hosp., 1946-52; Princ. Consultant, Sr. Hosp. Adm., Un. Mine Workers Hosp., Appalachian Region, 1952-54; Lectr.: U.S. Naval Sch. Hosp. Adm., Nat. Naval Medical Center; St. Louis Univ. Grad. Sch., Columbia Grad. Sch. Hosp. Adm., Cornell Univ. Sch. Hotel Adm. and Grad. Sch. Business & Pub. Adm., George Washington Univ., Grad. Sch., Trinity Univ., Xavier Univ., U.S. Army-Baylor Univ., Texas A & M Univ., etc.; Consultant, Surg. Gen. U.S. Navy, 1963-70; Nat. Consultant, U.S.A.F. Hosp. Design & Planning, 1961; mem. Adv. Council, Xavier Univ.; Fellow, Am. Coll. Hosp. Adms.; Fellow, Am. Coll. Hosp. Design & Planning 1961; Fellow, Royal Soc. Health; Fellow, Roy. Soc. for Encouragement of the Arts, Mfr. & Comm.; Hon. Life mem., Sask. Hosp. Assn.; Costa Rican Hosp. Assn. (Hon. Pres.); Gold Medal from Costa Rican Gov't for distinguished services; mem., Internat. Hosp. Fed.; Am. Hosp. Assn. (Life Member); Luther Rice Soc.; Candn. Council of Health Service Extves.; (Life Member); mem. Cosmos Club; Am. Acad. of Med. Administrators (Hon. Fellow); awarded 1st prize in 1971 Gerard B. Lambert Awards; Episcopalian; Home: 24 Croyden Place, Box 45, Arva, Ont. N0M 1C0

FRIESEN, Henry George, B.Sc., M.D., F.R.C.P.(C), F.R.S.C.; endocrinologist; educator; b. Morden, Man. 31 July 1934; s. Frank Henry and Agnes (Unger) F.; e. Univ. of Man. B.Sc. (Med.), M.D. 1958; m. Joyce Marylin d. Gordon MacKinnon, Halifax, N.S. 12 Oct. 1967; children: Mark Henry, Janet Elizabeth; PROF. AND HEAD OF PHYSIOL., UNIV. OF MAN., of Med. since 1973; Intern, Winnipeg Gen. Hosp. 1958-59, Asst. Resident 1959-60 and Royal Victoria Hosp. Montreal 1961-62; Research Fellow Med. and Endocrinol. New England Centre Hosp. Boston 1960-61, 1962-63, Research Assoc. 1963-65; Asst. Prof. of Med. Tufts Univ. Sch. of Med. 1965-66; Asst. Prof. of Med. McGill Univ. 1965, Assoc. Prof. 1968-71, Prof. Exper. Med. 1972-73; Associateship, Med. Research Council Can., McGill Univ. 1965-73; mem. Organ-

izing Comte. VI Internat. Endocrine Cong. Hamburg 1976; Breast Cancer Task Force Exper. Biol. Comte. Nat. Insts. Health Bethesda, Md. 1975-77; Task Force N.I.H. Comte. Evaluation Research Needs Endocrinol. and Metabolic Diseases 1978; Chrmn./mem. various comtes. Med. Research Council; rec'd Eli Lilly Award Endocrine Soc. 1974; Gairdner Foundation Award 1977; Sandoz Lectr. Candn. Soc. Endocrinol. & Metabolism 1978; Izaak Watton Killam Mem. Scholarship, 1979; author or co-author numerous publs. endocrinol. and med.; mem. Am. Physiol. Soc.; Endocrine Soc. (Council 1973-76); Candn. Soc. Clin. Investigation (Council 1974-77, Pres. 1978); Candn. Physiol. Soc.; Am. Fed. Clin. Research; Am. Assn. Advanc. Science; Am. Soc. Clin. Investigation; Candn. Soc. Endocrinol. & Metabolism (Pres. 1974); Internat. Soc. Neuroendocrinol.; mem. various ed. bds. med. journs.; Assoc. Ed. "Canadian Journal of Physiology and Pharmacology" 1974-78; Pres., Can. Soc. for Clinical Investigation, 1978; Mennonite; Office: 770 Bannatyne Ave., Winnipeg, Man. R3E 0W3.

FRITH, Hon. Royce, Q.C., B.A., D.E.S.(D); senator; b. Montreal, Que. 12 Nov. 1923; s. George Harry and Annie Beatrice (Royce) F.; e. Lachine (Que.) High Sch.; Parkdale Coll. Inst. Toronto; Univ. of Toronto Victoria Coll. B.A.; Osgoode Hall Law Sch.; Univ. of Ottawa Dipl. d'études supérieures (droit); m. Elizabeth Mary (d. 1976) d. William E. Davison, Port Credit, Ont. 18 June 1948; children: Valerie Elizabeth, Gregory Royce, (d. 1980); summoned to Senate 1977; DEPUTY LEADER OF GOVERNMENT 1980 served as Councillor and Depy. Reeve Leaside, Ont.; mem. York Co. Council; Royal Comn. on Bilingualism & Biculturalism; Legal Adviser to Commr. of Official Langs.; Past Pres. Ont. Lib. Assn. (1961-62); mem. ACTRA; Liberal; Presbyterian; recreation: squash, hiking; Clubs: Cercle Universitaire; Scarborough Golf; Rideau; Home: 151 Bay, Ottawa, and R.R. 4, Perth, Ont. K7H 3C6; Law Office: S: Perry, Farleyi—Box 451 TD Centre, Toronto M5K 1M5 and 83 Gore St. E., Perth, Ont. K7H 3E7 and The Senate, Ottawa, Ont. K1A 0A4

FRITZ, Irving Bamdas, D.D.S., Ph.D.; cell biol.; scientist; b. Rocky Mount, N.C., 11 Feb. 1927; s. Henry Norman and Rose (Bamdas) F.; e. Univ. of Richmond 1943-47; Med. Coll. of Va. 1945; D.D.S. 1948; Univ. of Chicago, Ph.D. 1951; Univ. of Copenhagen, Post-doctoral fellowship 1953-55; Univ. of Wash. Visiting Scholar Dept. of Biochem. 1963-64; Guggenheim Fellow, ARC Inst. of Animal Physiology, Babraham, Cambridge, 1978-79; Gairdner Award, 1980; m. 1st Helen (d. 1981), d. Ralph Bridgman, N.C., 20 Aug. 1950; 2ndly Angela, d. late William McCourt, 21 Oct. 1972; children: Jonathan Bridgman, Winston Romaine, Rachel Bamdas, Zoë Benedicte McCourt Fritz; PROF. BANTING AND BEST DEPT. MEDICAL RESEARCH, UNIV. OF TORONTO 1978-; Chrm. and Prof. 1968-78; Instr. Harvard Dental Sch. 1951; Asst. Dir. Dept. Metabolism & Endocrinol. Michael Reese Hosp. Chicago 1955; Asst. Prof. Dept. Physiol. Univ. of Mich. 1956,Assoc. Prof. 1960, Prof. 1964; served with US Army, Walter Reed Army Med. Service Grad. Sch. 1951-53; rank 1st Lt.; discovered action of carnitine on fatty acid metabolism and elucidated mechanisms of action; contrib. toward studies on hormone action (adrenal cortical steroids, insulin, gonadotropins, androgens) and understanding of spermatogenesis; author "Insulin Action" 1972 and over 100 publs. and reviews in biol. journs.; mem. Candn. Biochem. Assn.; Am. Physiol. Soc.; Am. Biochem. Soc.; Endocrine Soc.; Soc. for Study of Reproduction; recreations: squash, gardening, writing, hiking; Home: 59 Poplar Plains Rd., Toronto, Ont. M4V 2N1; Office: 112 College St., Toronto, Ont. M5G 1L6

FRITZ, Madeleine Alberta, Ph.D., F.R.S.C., F.G.A.C., F.G.S.A.; palaeontologist; b. Saint John, New Brunswick; d. Edwin John and Jessie Marie (Osborne) F.; e. McGill Univ., B.A. 1919; Univ. of Toronto, M.A. 1923, Ph.D. 1926; Prof. Emeritus, Dept. of Geology, Univ. of Toronto;

Fellow, Palaeontol. Soc. Am.; Research Assoc., Roy. Ont. Museum; Anglican; Home: 70 Delisle, Toronto, Ont. M4V 1S7

FROSST, James E.; pharmaceutical executive; b. Montreal, Que., 4 Jan. 1925; s. Eliot S. and Elizabeth (Ballantyne) F.; e. Pickering Coll., Newmarket, Ont.; McGill Univ.; m. Dorothy Haig; PRESIDENT, CHARLES E. FROSST & CO.; Dir., Intercol Publishing Co. Ltd.; served overseas as Lt. with R.C.N.V.R., 1943-45; United Church; recreations: golf, curling; Clubs: Royal Montreal Golf; Montreal Badminton & Squash, Naval Officers'; Home: 91 Brittany Ave., Montreal, Que. H3P 1A7; Office: 16717 Trans Canada Hwy, Kirkland (Montreal) Que. H9H 3L1

FROST, Col. Charles Sydney Jr., C.D., Q.C., L.L.D.; b. St. John's, Nfld. 21 June 1922; s. Charles Sydney and Gertrude R. (Hains) F.; e. Nutana Coll. Saskatoon, Sask.; Saint John High Sch., N.B.; Royal Mil. Coll. Kingston, grad. 1942; Osgoode Hall grad. 1949; L.L.D., 1976; m. Margaret Alice, d. late Norman Cabeldu, 2 July 1947; one s. Norman, two d. Janet, Catherine; SR. PARTNER, FROST AND REDWAY; Dir., Mercedes-Benz Canada Inc.; Chandris Amer. Lines (Canada) Ltd.; Ithaca Gun Co. (Canada) Ltd.; KNR Concrete Systems Ltd.; Cambridge Thermionic of Canada Ltd.; articled with Tilley, Carson, Morlock and McCrimmon; called to the Bar of Ont. 1949; practised law with Tilley, Carson Morlock and McCrimmon 1949-53; cr. Q.C. 1960; served with P.P.C.L.I. in Italy and N.W. Europe 1942-45; Acting Second in Command 1945; apptd. P.P.C.L.I. Senate, 1978; twice wounded; Royal Regt. of Can. 1947-62, Commdr. 1959-62; Hon. Lt. Col. 1967-74, Hon. Col. since 1974; awarded Can. Forces Decoration and two bars; awarded Candn. Silver Jubilee Medal, 1977; Past Gov. Havergal Coll.; mem. Candn. Scholarship Trust Comte. 1964-77; Canadian Corps of Commissionaires; Pres. Toronto Br. Royal Mil. Coll. Club of Can. 1969-70, Nat. Pres. 1971-72; Hon. Solicitor 1980- ; mem. Candn. Mil. Colls. Adv. Bd. 1975-78; Chrmn. Royal Regt. of Can. Foundation; Trustee, Havergal College Foundation, 1966-69; Hon. Trustee, Havergal Coll. Foundation 1970-78; Soc. for Study of Egyptian Antiquities; Dir. (1965-72) Ft. York Br., Royal Candn. Legion; United Ch.; recreations: golf, flying, tennis, music; Clubs: Toronto; Rosedale Golf; Granite; Ontario; Royal Candn. Mil. Inst.; Empire (Life mem. and Dir. 1958-62); Canadian; Home: 50 Bayview Wood, Toronto, Ont. M4N 1R7; Office: 3080 Yonge St., Toronto, Ont. M4N 3N1

FROST, Rev. Stanley Brice, D.D., Dr.Phil., D.Litt., M.Th. (Un. Ch.); b. London, Eng., 17 Feb. 1913; s. Henry George and Rosa (Goodbody) F.; e. Aske's Haberdashers' Sch., London, Eng. (1924-32); Richmond Coll., London Univ. (1932-36), B.D. 1936; Marburg Univ. (Dr. Williams' Scholar) Dr.Phil. 1938; M.Th. (London) 1943; D.D. Victoria, Univ. of Toronto 1963; Memorial, D.Litt. 1967; m. Margaret Florence, d. George William Bradshaw, London, Eng., 29 July 1939; children: David Brice, Valerie Margaret; o. by Meth. Conference, Great Britain 1939; held pastorates in London, 1939-42, Stoke on Trent, 1942-49; Professor of Old Testament Studies, Didsbury College, Bristol, 1949; Special Lect. in Hebrew, Bristol Univ., 1952; apptd. Prof. of Old Test. Lang. and Lit., McGill Univ., 1956, and Dean of Faculty of Divinity, 1957-63 when apptd. Dean of Grad. Faculty; Min. of Un. Ch. of Can., 1957; Vice Principal, McGill Univ. 1969-74 since when Director, History of McGill Project; Publications: "Die Authoritätslehre in den Werken John Wesleys" 1938; "The Pattern of Methodism", 1948; "Tutors Unto Christ" (Editor) 1949; "Old Testament Apocalyptic" (Fernley-Hartley Lecture) 1952; "The Beginning of the Promise, Eight Lectures on the Book of Genesis", 1960; "Patriarchs and Prophets", 1964; "Standing and Understanding, A Reappraisal of the Christian Faith" (Peake Lecture), 1969, "McGill Universi-

ty: For the Advancement of Learning; Vol I, 1801-1895", 1980; and various articles; mem., Soc. for Old Test. Study; Soc. of Biblical Lit.; Wesley Hist. Soc.; Home: 5 Granville Rd., Hampstead, Que. H3X 3A9

FRUIN, Malcolm G., B.Sc.; management consultant; b. London, Eng. 15 Feb. 1933; e. City of London Freemen's Sch.; Univ. of London B.Sc. 1957; Brunel Coll. of Technol. Post-grad. Business Adm. 1957-58; m. Joan Gilling 20 July 1957; children: Russell, Neal, Sally; PRESIDENT FRUIN CONSULTANTS INC. AND GEN. MGR. ELI LILLY AND CO. (CANADA) LTD. 1980- ; Research Dir. International Surveys Ltd. Montreal 1957-64; Marketing Research Mgr. present Co. Toronto 1964, Dir. Marketing Planning 1965, Mgr. Marketing Research USA 1966 (Eli Lilly & Co.), Dir. Marketing Research Eli Lilly International Corp. Indianapolis 1967, Gen. Mgr. Lilly Laboratories (S.A.) (Proprietary) Ltd. Johannesburg 1969-72, Vice Pres. and Gen. Mgr. Eli Lilly and Co. 1972-80; served with Royal Army Ordnance Corps 1956-57, rank 2-Lt.; Chrmn. Pharm. Mfrs. Assn. Can. 1977-78; Dir. Am. Marketing Assn. Montreal Chapter 1963-64; CDN Found. for Advancement Pharmacy; Pres. Candn. Club Johannesburg 1971-72; recreations: golf, gardening; Club: Scarboro Golf & Country; Office: RR 4 Bowmanville, Ont. L1C 3K5

FRUM, Barbara, B.A.; television host; b. Niagara Falls, N.Y. 8 Sept. 1937; d. Harold and Florence (Hirschowitz) Rosberg; e. Univ. of Toronto B.A. 1959; m. Murray Frum 3 Sept. 1957; children: David, Linda, Matthew; HOST, CBC TV "THE JOURNAL" 1982- ; co-host and interviewer CBC TV series "The Way It Is" (later "Weekday") beginning 1967; host and interviewer radio series "As It Happens" 1971-82; host TV series "The Barbara Frum Journal" 1971-72, "Barbara Frum" 1974, "True North Seris" OECA/CBC and "Quarterly Report" 1978-82; rec'd Media Club Can. Mem. Award top Prize for article writing "One Hundred and Five Potential Women M.P.'s" 1971; Assn. TV and Radio Artists awards for "As It Happens" 1974, 1975, 1979, 1980; author "As It Happened" (interviews) 1976; articles various newspapers and mags.; Office: The Journal (P.O. Box 14000 Station A) Toronto, Ont. M5W 1A0.

FRY, Frederick Ernest Joseph, M.B.E., M.A., Ph.D., D.Sc., F.R.S.C.; university professor; b. Woking, Eng., 17 April 1908; came to Can., 1912; s. Ernest and Mabel Fry; e. Weston (Ont.) High Sch. 1920-25; Univ. of Toronto, B.A. 1933, M.A. 1934, Ph.D. 1937; m. Irene Marguerite d. Henry Stewart, 19 Oct. 1935; PROF. EMERITUS, DEPT. OF ZOOLOGY, UNIV. OF TORONTO; mem. of various profl. assns.; served with R.C.A.F. 1940-45, awarded M.B.E.; Home: 10 Riverlea Rd., Weston, Ont. M9P 2R9

FRY, James Lawrence, B.A., M.A.; Canadian public servant; b. Hartney, Man. July 6 1927; s. James Arthur and Marjorie (McLeish) F.; e. Pub. and High Schs., Hartney, Man.; Univ. of Man. B.A. 1948; Univ. of Toronto, M.A. (Pol. Science) 1950; m. Julie Margaret, d. George Locke, 6 Dec. 1952; children: Julie Anne, James Michael; DEPUTY MIN., NATIONAL HEALTH AND WELFARE 1980- ; Jr. Adm. Offr. 1950; Chief Estab. Offr., Comptroller of the Treas. 1954; Group Chief, Treas. Bd. 1956; Dir., Program Analysis 1965, Asst. Secy. 1969; Asst. Depy. Min., Health Programs Br., Nat. Health & Welfare, 1970-74; Acting Depy. Min. Health 1974-75; Dept. Min., Services, & Depy. Receiver Fen., Dept. of Supply & Services, Can., 1975; mem. Inst. of Pub. Adm.; Anglican; recreations: sailing, skiing, gardening; Home: 1388 Wesmar Dr., Ottawa, Ont. K1H 7T5; Office: Room 2160, Jeanne Mance Building, Tunney's Pasture, Ottawa, Ont. K1A 0K9.

FRYE, Northrop, C.C. (1972), D.D., LL.D., D.Litt., D. de l'U., L.H.D., F.R.S.C.; professor; author; b. Sherbrooke, Que., 14 July 1912; s. Herman and Catharine (Howard)

F.; e. Univ. of Toronto, B.A. 1933; Emmanuel Coll., U. of T., Grad. Theol., 1936; Merton Coll., Oxford Univ., M.A. 1941; m. Helen, d. Stanley Kemp, Toronto, 24 Aug. 1937; Ed., "The Canadian Forum", 1948-54; ordained to Ministry of the United Ch. of Can. 1936; Lectr. in Eng., Victoria Coll., 1939, Asst. Prof. 1942, Assoc. Prof. 1946, Prof. 1948; Chrmn., Dept. of English, 1952-59; Principal, 1959-66; apptd. to new post of Univ. Prof. (allowing to teach anywhere in Univ.) 1967; rec'd. Can. Council Medal. 1967; author of "Fearful Symmetry, A Study of William Blake", 1947; "Anatomy of Criticism", 1957; "The Stubborn Structure", 1970; "The Critical Path", 1971; "The Bush Garden: Essays On the Canadian Imagination" 1971; "Spiritus Mundi", 1976, and 12 other books; awarded Lorne Pierce Medal 1958; Pierre Chauveau Medal 1970; Molson Prize 1971; Hon. Fellow, Merton College, Oxford, 1973; Hon. mem., American Academy and Institute of Arts and Letters, 1981; has contrib. lit. articles to various journs.; Gen. Chrmn. of Comte. for Gov. Gen.'s Lit. Awards 1962-63; Adv. mem. Candn. Radio-Television Telecommunications Comn., 1968-1977; Pres. Mod. Lang. Assn. of Am., 1976; received Royal Bank Award, 1978; apptd. Chancellor of Victoria Univ., Univ. of Toronto, 1978; received 30 Honorary Degrees; Home: 127 Clifton Rd., Toronto, Ont. M4T 2G5

FRYER, John Leslie, B.Sc., M.A., F.R.E.S.; labour executive; b. London, Eng. 6 Oct. 1938; s. Leslie and Mollie (Steele) F.; e. London Sch. of Econ. & Pol. Science B.Sc. (Econ.) 1960; Univ. of Pittsburg M.A. (Labour Econ.) 1962; Univ. of Md. Grad. Seminars 1962; m. Jeanne Crerar; three s. Blair, Darren, Andrew; three daughters Shelli, Lisa, Tanis; GEN. SECY. AND CHIEF ADMINISTRATIVE OFFR., B.C. GOVT. EMPLOYEES' UNION 1969- , presently on leave of absence; mem. Local 1203; Vice Pres., Candn. Labour Congress; Pres., Nat. Union of Prov. govt. Employees; part-time mem., B.C. Labour Relations Bd., 1981- ; Teaching Fellow in Econ. Univ. of Pittsburg 1960-61; Research Dept. AFL/CIO, Washington, D.C. 1961-62; Dir. of Research, United Packinghouse Workers' Union 1962; Asst. Dir. of Research, Labour Cong. 1963, Dir. of Research 1967; Dir. and mem. Extve. Comte. North/South Inst.; Candn. Civil Liberties Assn.; former Extve. mem. Candn. Indust. Relations Research Inst.; mem. Candn. Consumer Council 1968-70; Duke of Edinburgh Fellow 1974; mem. Conf. Council, Duke of Edinburgh's Fifth Commonwealth Study Conf. 1980; rec'd Queen's Silver Jubilee Medal 1977; author numerous articles and presentations on labour econ.; mem. Am. Econ. Assn.; Indust. Relations Research Assn.; London Sch. of Econ. Soc.; Univ. of London (Eng.) Convocation; recreations: cooking, calligraphy, fishing, boating; Home: 3415 Carling St., Ottawa, Ont. K2H 7V5; Office: 204-2841 Riverside Dr., Ottawa, Ont. K1S 8N4.

FULFORD, George Taylor; retired manufacturer; of U.E.L. descent; b. Brockville, Ont., 6 May 1902; s. Hon. Senator George Taylor and Mary Wilder (White) F.; e. Univ. of Toronto, B.A. 1924; Harvard Univ.; m. Judy, d. Jörn Kruse, Hamburg, Germany; children: George Taylor, Martha Charlotte, Dwight Wilder; former Vice-Pres. and Dir., G. T. Fulford Co.; Vice-Pres. and Dir., Fulford-Williams (International) Ltd.; Fulford Dodds Ltd.; el. to Ont. Leg. for Leeds at g.e. 1934; def. g.e. 1937; 1st el. to H. of C. for Leeds, g.e. 1940; def. g.e. 1945 re-el. g.e. 1949, '53; def. g.e. 1957, '58; Gov., Brockville Gen. Hosp. (Pres. 1936); mem., Delta Kappa Epsilon; Freemason; Anglican; Clubs: Brockville Country; Brockville; University (Toronto); Royal Ottawa Golf; Rideau (Ottawa); Home: Fulford Place, Brockville, Ont.
XXX
FULFORD, Patricia (Mrs. R. Spiers), R.C.A.; sculptor; b. Toronto, Ont. 21 March 1935; d. Richard Turner and Muriel Lindsay Broughton (Parsons) Fulford; e. Branksome Hall Sch. Toronto 1953; Ont. Coll. Art. AOCA 1957; Edinburgh Coll. of Art D.A. (Edin.) 1960; m. Raymond Spiers 26 Jan. 1962; teacher, Ont. Coll. of Art

1960-63; Glendon Coll. York Univ. 1970-75; Cariboo Coll. Kamloops 1978-79; solo exhns. incl. Mazelow Gallery Toronto 1972; N.B. Museum 1973; exhns. with R. Spiers incl. Mirvish Gallery 1964, Mazelow Gallery 1967, Toronto; mem. Sculptors Soc. B.C.; recreations: music, gardening; Home: 3852 W. 16th Ave., Vancouver, B.C. V6R 3C7; Office: Harman Sculpture Foundry, 170 Alexander St., Vancouver, B.C.

FULFORD, Robert Marshall Blount; journalist; b. Ottawa, Ont., 13 Feb. 1932; s. Albert Edward and Frances Gertrude (Blount) F.; e. Malvern Collegiate, Toronto; m. Jocelyn Jean, d. late Jeffrey Dingman, 16 June 1956; children: James Marshall, Margaret Frances; divorced 1970; m. Geraldine Patricia Sherman, d. Philip and Helen Sherman, 28 Nov. 1970; children: Rachel Sherman, Sarah Helen; EDITOR, SATURDAY NIGHT, since 1968; Journalist since 1949; Broadcaster since 1955; Reporter, The Globe and Mail, 1949-53, 1956-57; Literary Columnist, The Toronto Star, 1958-62, 1964-68; Asst. Editor, Canadian Homes and Gardens, 1955, Mayfair, 1956, Maclean's, 1962-64; Host of This Is Robert Fulford (CBC radio); contrib. to CBC TV programs; contrib. to Canadian Forum, Canadian Literature, Canadian Art, The Tamarack Review, the New York Times; author "This Was Expo", 1968; "Crisis At The Victory Burlesk", 1968 "Marshall Delaney at the Movies", 1974; "An Introduction to the Arts in Canada", 1977; Office: 70 Bond St., Toronto, Ont. M5B 2J3

FULLERTON, Douglas H., M.Com., LL.D., D.U.C.; economic and financial consultant; b. St. John's, Nfld. 3 Sept. 1917; s. Roy DeMille and Effie (Henderson) F.; e. McGill Univ. B.Com. 1939, M.Com. 1940; Hon. LL.D. Dalhousie 1969, Carleton 1974; Hon. D. Univ. Calgary 1975; m. Charlotte Maude Hickman 20 Nov. 1943; children: Mary Anne, John, Katherine; Dir. Connaught Labs., Potash Corp. of Sask., Fidelity Trust, and other-cos. and organs.; has served on task forces for Que. Govt. incl. takeover of power cos. 1962-3, Comte. on Financial Insts. 1966-69, Montreal Suburban Rail Transit, 1974-77; federal public service 1945-53; Asst. The Research, Royal Comn. on Can.'s Econ. Prospects 1955-57; Treas. and later Consultant, Can. Council 1957-68; Chrmn. Cape Breton Development Corp. 1967-69; syndicated columnist for Toronto Star, Ottawa Citizen, Montreal Gazette and other newspapers 1966-69, 1973-74, 1976-78; Chrmn. Nat. Capital Comn. 1969-73 and subsequent author Special Study "The Capital of Canada: How Should It Be Governed?" 1974; Candn. Army 1941-45, rank Capt.; Hon. Prof. Urbanism, Univ. of Calgary 1979-81; author of "The Bond Market in Canada" 1962; "The Dangerous Delusion: Quebec's Independence Obsession" 1978; Home: 172 Clemow Ave., Ottawa, Ont. K1S 2B4;

FULLERTON, Colonel Herbert R., C.D., RI (BC) FRI; real estate, financial and insurance broker; b. Nelson, B.C., 17 Feb. 1904; s. Herbert Matthew and Marion (Eaton) F.; e. Public Schs. of Victoria and New Westminster, B.C.; Univ. Sch. Victoria, B.C.; m. Minea Elizabeth, d. Carl Milford, Charlottetown, P.E.I.; children: Herbert Michael, Nancy; PRESIDENT, BLANE, FULLERTON & WHITE LTD., which he organ. in 1929; entered real estate and ins. business with Burrard Securities Ltd., 1925; Pres., Candn. Assn. Real Estate Bds. 1961 (Regional Vice-Pres., 1956, 1957); Dir., Nat. Assn. of Real Estate Bds. (U.S.A.) 1961; Pres., Vancouver Real Estate Bd., 1954-55 (Hon. Life mem. 1963); Pres., B.C. Assn. Real Estate Bds., 1956, B.C. Inst. of Real Estate Agents, 1958-59, 1959-60; Pres., Real Estate Council of B.C., 1958-60; Pres., Real Estate Inst. of B.C., 1962 (Hon. Life mem., Realtor Div., 1963; Chrmn., Bd. Govs., Prof. Div., 1960-64); apptd. to Assessment Appeal Bd. for B.C., 1965; Past Pres., Independent Fire Ins. Conf. of B.C.; Independent Auto. Ins. Conf. of B.C.; Hon. Life mem., Westminster Co., Victoria, Vancouver Island, Kootenay and Okanagan Mainline Real Estate Bds.; Hon. Life Mem., Candn. Real Estate Assn. 1976; Real Estate Inst. of Can., 1976; recognized by Real Estate Bd. of Greater Vancouver, for his efforts to improve the Standards of Practice in the Real Estate Vocation, by the establishment of the "Herbert R. Fullerton Chair in Urban Land Policy" at U.B.C., 1979; joined Candn. Militia as mem. Irish Fusiliers of Can., 1924; 2nd World War, 1939-46 with Irish Fusiliers in Can., and with Cape Breton Highlanders in Eng. and Italy; Hon. Col., The Irish Fusiliers of Canada (The Vancouver Regt.) 1949-62; Anglican; recreations: fishing, gardening; Clubs: Vancouver; Union (Victoria); Vancouver Rowing (Life Mem.; el. Hon. Pres. 1971); Home: 4864 Belmont Ave., Vancouver, B.C. V6T 1A9

FULLERTON, R. Donald, B.A.; banker; b. Vancouver, B.C., 7 June 1931; s. late C. G. and late Muriel E.; e. Forest Hill Village High Sch., Toronto; Trinity Coll. Sch., Port Hope, Ont.; Univ. of Toronto, B.A. 1953; VICE-CHMN. & PRES., CANADIAN IMPERIAL BANK OF COMMERCE, and a Dir. since 1974; Dir. American Can of Can. Ltd.; North Am. Life Assurance Co.; California Candn. Bank; Candn. Eastern Finance Ltd.; Amoco Can. Petroleum Co. Ltd.; Massey Ferguson Ltd.; Wellesley Hosp., Toronto; joined Bank in Vancouver, 1953; Agt., New York 1964; Regional Gen. Mgr., Regina, 1966; Regional Gen. Mgr., Internat., 1967; Depy. Chief Gen. Mgr. 1968; Sr. Vice-Pres. & Dep. Chief Gen. Mgr., 1971; Extve. Vice Pres. and Chief Gen. Mgr., 1973; Pres. & Chief Operating Officer, 1976; Vice-Chrmn. and Pres. since 1980; mem., Bd. Trade Metrop. Toronto; Harvard Business Sch. Club; Bd. of Govs., Bishop Strachan School, Toronto; Hon. Treas., Royal Ont. Museum; recreations: golf, skiing; Clubs: Toronto; York; Rosedale Golf; Granite; Caledon Ski; Queen's; Canadian; Empire; Mt. Royal (Montreal); Metropolitan Club (N.Y.); Office: Head Office, Commerce Court West, Toronto, Ont. M5L 1A2

FULTON, Hon. Edmund Davie, P.C. (Can.) 1957, Q.C., LL.D.; b. Kamloops, B.C., 10 Mar. 1916; s. Frederick John, K.C., and Winifred M. (Davie) F.; e. St. Michael's Sch., Victoria, B.C.; Kamloops High Sch.; Univ. of Brit. Columbia, B.A.; St. John's Coll., Oxford, 1937-39 (el. Rhodes Scholar 1937) B.A.; LL.D. Ottawa and Queen's; m. Patricia Mary, d. James M. Macrae, Winnipeg, Man., 7 Sept. 1946; three d., Catherine Mary, Patricia, Cynthia Ann; cr. Q.C. 1957; 1st el. to H. for Kamloops, g.e. 1945; re-el. g.e. 1949, '53, '57, '58, '62, '65; Min. of Justice and Attny-General of Canada 21 June 1957 to 9 Aug. 1962 when appt. Min. of Public Works; mem. of Senate, Univ. of B.C. 1948-57 and 1969-75; first Chrmn. The Law Reform Comn. of B.C. 1969-73; practised law in Kamloops, B.C. 1945-68 and Vancouver, B.C. 1968-73; app'td Judge, Supreme Court of B.C. 1973, resigned 1981; served in 2nd World War with Canadian Army overseas as Company Commdr. with Seaforth Highlanders of Can., and as D.A.A.G. 1st Candn. Inf. Div., 1940-45 incl. both the Italian and N.W. Europe compaigns; Mentioned in Despatches; trans. to R.O. With rank of Maj. 1945; Catholic; Clubs: Vancouver; Shaughnessy Golf & Country; Rideau (Ottawa); Home: 1632 West 40th Ave., Vancouver, B.C. V6M 1V9

FULTON, E(thel) Margaret, M.A., Ph.D.; educator; b. Birtle, Man. 8 Sept. 1922; d. Ernest Bain and Ethel Mary (Futers) F.; e. Winnipeg Normal Sch. First Class Teaching Cert. 1942; Univ. of Minn. Phys. Educ. Dipl. 1946; Univ. of Toronto Ont. Coll. of Educ. Secondary Sch. Eng. Specialist Teaching Cert. 1956, Ont. Secondary Sch. Teacher's Cert. IV 1961; Univ. of B.C. M.A. 1960; Univ. of Toronto Ph.D. 1968; PRES., MOUNT SAINT VINCENT UNIV. and Prof. of Eng. 1978- ; Dir. Fireman's Fund Insurance Co. of Canada; Pub. and Secondary Sch. Teacher, Man. 1942-48; Secondary Sch. Teacher, Ont. 1948-53; Head of Eng. Coll. Inst. Thunder Bay, Ont. 1960-63; Teaching Fellow in Eng. Univ. of Toronto 1963-66; As-

soc. Prof. of Eng. Wilfrid Laurier Univ. 1967-74; Univ. of B.C. 1974-1978; Dean of Women, Univ. of B.C. 1974; rec'd Ont. Grad. Fellowships; Ryerson (Polytech. Inst.); named Honourary class President, 1972 Wilfrid Laurier Univ.; William P. Huffman Scholar-in-Residence, Univ. of Miami, Oxford, Ohio; mem. Interam. Univ. Assn. (Dir.); Candn. Cong. on Learning Opportunities for Women; Candn. Assn. Univ. Teachers; Assn. Candn. Univ. Teachers Eng.; Assn. Univ. & Colls. Can.; Assn. Commonwealth Univs.; Assn. Atlantic Univs.; Assn. Candn. & Que. Lit.; Candn. Council Teachers Eng.; Candn. Soc. Study Higher Educ.; Victorian Studies Assn.; Candn. Research Inst. Advanc. Women; Am. Assn. Higher Educ.; NDP; United Church; recreations: athletics, cultural activities; Clubs: Voice of Women; University Women's; Zonta Internat.; Home: 12A Sherbrooke Dr., Halifax, N.S. B3M 1P6; Office: 166 Bedford Highway, Halifax, N.S. B3M 2J6.

FULTON, Most Rev. Thomas, D.J.C. (R.C.); b. St. Catharines, Ont., 13 Jan. 1918; s. Thomas Francis and Mary Catherine (Jones) F.; e. St. Nicholas Sch., St. Catharines, Ont.; St. Catharines Coll. Inst.; St. Augustine's Semy., Toronto, Ont., 1941; Catholic Univ. of America, D.J.C., 1948; consecrated Aux. Bishop of the Archdiocese of Toronto 1969 by Pope Paul VI in Rome; apptd. Bishop of St. Catherines, 1978; named Domestic Prelate by Pope Pius XII, Nov. 1954; Publication: "The Pre-Nuptial Investigation" (canonical study), 1948; Address: 122 Riverdale Avenue, St. Catherines, Ont. L2R 4C2

FUNASAKA, Shinichi; company president; b. Kyoto, Japan, 30 March 1918; s. Hamachiro and Nobu (Hamaguchi) F.; e. Keio Univ., Japan; grad. in econ. 1942; m. Mari, d. Shuji Yahamoto, 25 March 1948; children: Yutaka, Tom, Mako; PRESIDENT AND DIR., CANDN. MOTOR INDUSTRIES LTD. (TOYOTA CARS) since 1976; Dir., Canadian Motor Industries Holdings Ltd.; commenced as Jr. Extve., Mitsui Tokyo, Japan 1942-56; joined present Co. as Gen. Mgr., Montreal, Que. 1956; Asst. Mgr., Ferrous Faw Materials, Mitsui, Tokyo and Osaka, Japan 1963; Gen. Mgr., Hong Kong 1967; Pres. and Dir., Mitsui & Co. (Can.) Ltd., 1971-76; served in 2nd World War, Japanese Navy 1942-45; rank on discharge Lieut.; recreations: golf, fishing; Club: National; Home: 74 Bayview Ridge, Willowdale, Ont. M2L 1E6; Office: 1291 Bellamy Road N., Scarborough, Ont. M1H 1H9

FUNNELL, Dudley, F.F.A., F.I.A., F.C.I.A.; actuarial executive; b. Godalming, Eng., 5 Aug. 1926; s. Albert E. and Irene M. (Cassell) F.; e. Charterhouse, Eng., 1944; m. Doreen, d. A.B. Hanley, 25 Feb. 1949; children: Alison P., Louise B., Celia M., Eric B.; CHRMN. AND CHIEF ACTUARY, TA ASSOCIATES Actuarial Asst., Scottish Union National Insurance Co., Edinburgh, 1947-53; Asst. Actuary, R. Watson & Sons, Reigate, Eng., 1953-58; Asst. Vice Pres., Wm. M. Mercer, Montreal, 1959-63; Sr. Actuary and Vice Pres., Alexander & Alexander Services Ltd., Montreal, 1963-70, Pres. 1971; Pres., Tomenson-Alexander Ltd. 1972-73; served with Fleet Air Arm 1944-47; Pres., Candn. Pension Conf. 1973-75; Protestant; recreations: gardening, tennis, squash; Clubs: Oakville; Cambridge; Home: 2146 Adair Cres., Oakville, Ont. L6J 5S7; Office: Commercial Union Tower (P.O. Box 439), Toronto-Dominion Centre, Toronto, Ont. M5K 1M3

FUNT, B. Lionel, M.Sc., Ph.D., F.C.I.C.; university professor; b. Halifax, N.S., 20 Jan. 1924; s. Arthur and Rita (Rice) F.; e. Bloomfield High Sch., Halifax, N.S.; Dalhousie Univ., B.Sc. 1944, M.Sc. 1946; McGill Univ., Ph.D. 1949; m. Frances Margaret, d. Henry A. Russell, Amherst, N.S., 20 July 1947; children: Brian Vincent, Gordon Stanley, Warren Henry; PROF. OF CHEMISTRY, SIMON FRASER UNIV. since 1968 (Dean of Science 1968-71); & mem. Bd. of Govs. 1975-78; Dir., Nuclear Enterprises, Ltd.; Nuclear Enterprises (G.B.) Ltd., Edinburgh; Nuclear Enterprises Inc., San Carlos, Cal. 1956-76; Lectr.,

Dalhousie Univ., 1947; Asst. Prof., Univ. of Man., 1950-54, Assoc. Prof. 1954-59, Prof. of Chem. 1959-67, Dean of Grad. Studies 1964-67; author of some 70 publs. in field of polymer chem.; primarily interested in electro-chem. initiation and control of polymerization processes & also in nuclear radiation detection techniques; Chrmn. (1975-76) Chem. Educ., Chemistry Institute of Can.; mem., Universities Grants Commission, Manitoba 1967-69; Vice-President, Canadian Assn. Graduate Studies, 1966-67; Nuffield Travelling Fellowship 1971-72; mem., Am. Chem. Soc.; United Church; recreations: photography, sailing; Home: 1153 Eyremount Dr., West Vancouver, B.C. V7S 2C4

FUREDY, John J., M.A., Ph.D.; educator; b. Budapest, Hungary 30 June 1940; s. Bela Furedy; e. Neutral Bay Boys Primary and North Sydney Boys High Schs. Australia 1957; Univ. of Sydney B.A. 1963 (Univ. Medal), M.A. 1964, Ph.D. 1966; m. Christine P. M. d. W. J. Roche 30 June 1966; PROF. OF PSYCHOL. UNIV. OF TORONTO 1975- ; Visiting Lectr. Ind. Univ. 1965, Visiting Asst. Prof. 1966; Asst. Prof. Univ. of Toronto 1967, Assoc. Prof. 1969-75; Fullbright Scholar; Fellowships Dept. External Affairs Can. and Can.-Hungary Interchange Scheme; author book chapters, over 80 papers scient. journs.; Fellow, Australian Psychol. Soc.; Candn. Psychol. Assn.; Am. Psychol. Soc.; Internat. Coll. Psychosomatic Med.; Internat. Organ. Psychophysiol.; mem. Pavlovian Soc.; Soc. for Psychophys. Research; Psychosomatic Soc.; recreations: tennis, skiing, bridge, body surfing; Clubs: Rosedale Tennis; Jackrabbit Cross-country Ski; Prince Arthur Bridge; Toronto Bridge; Home: 24 Astley Ave., Toronto, Ont. M4W 3B4; Office: Toronto, Ont. M5S 1A6.

FURLONG, David Barry, M.A.; management consultant; b. Leeds, Eng., 11 Jan. 1917; s. John & Ivy (Rogers) F.; e. Swansea (1935); Oxford Univ. M.A. Natural Science (Chem.) 1939; Chemical Engineer, University of Alberta; m. Mary Eileen, d. James W. O'Brien, Elmsdale, P.E.I., 11 Oct. 1947; children: Allannah, Patrice, Kieran, Carla, Shauneen, Nicola, Kilian, Siobhan; PRES., DAVID B. FURLONG CONSULTANTS LTD.; with Calico Printers Assn. of Manchester, U.K. as Res. Chem., 1939-41; Anglo Iranian Oil Co., Iran, 1941-52; Imperial Oil Ltd. (1952-54), Sarnia Products Pipe Line, Toronto and Waterdown, Ont.; Imperial Pipe Line Co. Ltd. (subsidiary of Imperial Oil Ltd.) 1954-59, Edmonton (Asst. Mgr.); Pres. Producers Pipelines Ltd., 1959-65; Sask. Power Corp., Regina 1965-70, Gen. Mgr.; Mang. Dir., Candn Petroleum Assn. 1970-73; mem. Assn. Prof. Engrs. Ont.; Engn. Inst. Can.; Am. Petroleum Inst.; Assn. Pipeline Longitude 75 Ont. Petroleum Inst.; R. Catholic; recreations: reading, fishing; Clubs: Rideau; Edmonton Petroleum; Home: 2118 Thistle Cres., Ottawa, Ont. K1H 5P5; Office: 602-116 Albert St., Ottawa, Ont. K1P 5G3

FURLONG, Patrick Garret, Q.C., LL.B.; barrister; b. Riverside, Ont. 7 Sept. 1926; s. William Henry and Beatrix Elizabeth (Green) F.; e. elem. separate schs.: St. Clair, Notre Dame de Bon Secours, Windsor, Ont.; St. John the Baptist Amherstburg, Ont.; Assumption High Sch. Windsor; Assumption Coll. B.A. 1948; Univ. of W. Ont. Summer Session 1946; Osgoode Hall Law Sch. LL.B. 1952; m. Shirley Day d. John Frederick Waterhouse 20 Aug. 1954; children: Ann Elizabeth, John Garret, Andrew Patrick, Diana Louise, David William; SR. PARTNER, FURLONG & BROWN; Dir. The Lake Erie and Detroit River Railway Co.; read law with Hon. J. Frank Hughes; called to Bar of Ont. 1952; cr. Q.C. 1969; Gov. Univ. of Windsor, mem. Finance Comte. and Nominating Comte.; Dir. Pre-paid Legal Services Program Can.; mem. Essex Co. Dist. Health Council Task Force 1978; Past Dir. former Fed. Co. & Dist. Law Assns. Ont.; Fellow, Foundation for Legal Research Can.; mem. Candn. Inst. Adm. Justice; Windsor Jr. Chamber Comm. 1953-58, Chrmn. Legal Sub-Comtes. Windsor Harbour Devel. and Legal Sub-Comte. Impletement Jr. Achievement Business

Program Windsor; Del. Can. Dept. Justice Nat. Conf. on Law Ottawa 1972; Nat. Conf. on Quality of Legal Services Can. 1978; author various papers; Bencher, Law Soc. of Upper Can.; mem. Candn. Bar Assn. (Pres. Ont. Br. 1968-69, mem. Nat. Extve. Comte. 1972-74); Essex Co. Law Assn. (Pres. 1973-74); Essex Co. Med.-Legal Soc. (Pres. 1970-72); Nat. Assn. Rr. Trial Counsel; Advisory Bd. Windsor-Essex Mediation Centre; Detroit Good Guys; Liberal; R. Catholic; recreations: alpine skiing, tennis, sailing; Clubs: University (Toronto); Windsor Yacht; Windsor; Home: 2035 Willistead Cres., Windsor, Ont. N9A 1K6; Office: Suite 908, 100 Ouellette Ave., Windsor, Ont. N9A 6T3.

FURLONG, Hon. Robert Stafford, M.B.E., Kt. Cdr. of St. Gregory, O.St.J., Lt.Commdr. (S) R.N.V.R.; chief justice; b. St. John's, Nfld., 9 Dec. 1904; s. Martin Williams, K.C. and Mary (McGrath) F.; e. St. Bonaventure's Coll., St. John's; Law Soc. of Nfld.; unm.; CHIEF JUSTICE OF NEWFOUNDLAND, since May 1959; read law with James J. McGrath; called to Bar of Nfld. 1926; cr. K.C. 1944; former Treas. (Pres.), Law Soc. of Nfld.; mem. Nfld. Hist. Soc.; mem., Medico-Legal Soc., London; Royal Commonwealth Soc., London; Law Soc. of Nfld.; Roman Catholic; recreations: motoring, golf; Clubs: Bally Haly Golf & Country; Newfoundland Officers (Crow's Nest); St. John's R.N.V.R. (London); Home: Winter Ave., St. John's, Nfld.; Office: Law Courts, St. John's, Nfld.

FURNIVAL, George Mitchell, B.Sc., M.A., Ph.D., F.R.S.C., F.G.S.A.; mining and petroleum executive; b. Winnipeg, Man. 25 July 1908; s. William George and Grace Una (Rothwell) F.; e. Carleton & Alexander Schs., Kelvin Tech. High Sch. Winnipeg; Univ. of Man. B.Sc. 1929; Queen's Univ. M.A. 1933; Mass. Inst. Technol. Ph.D. 1935; m. Marion Marguerite d. Alexander Dickie Fraser, 8 March 1937; children: William George Fraser F., Mrs. Sharon Grace (Roscoe), Patricia Marion F., Bruce Alexander F; Exec. Vice Pres., Gen. Mgr. and Dir., Westmin Resources Ltd., 1981- ; Pres. and Dir. Western Coal Holdings Inc.; employed by mining companies, 1928-42; Asst. Mine Supt., O'Brien Mining Ltd., 1935-38; Geol. Surv., Canada, 1939-42; served Standard Oil Co. of California Inc., 1942-70, holding various positions incl.: Vice Pres. and Dir. Chevron Standard Co. Alta.; Pres. and Dir. Dominion Oil Ltd. Trinidad, 1942-55; Dir. and Vice Pres. Exploration Chevron Exploration Co. (San Francisco), 1955-63; Asst., Land, to Vice Pres. Exploration and Land Standard Oil San Francisco, Chrmn. Bd. and Mang. Dir. West Australian Petroleum Pty. Ltd. Perth W.A., 1963-70; estbd. consulting practice Calgary 1971; Vice Pres. Operations, Brascan Resources Ltd. 1973, apptd. Dir. and mem. Extve. Comte., Sr. Vice Pres. 1975 also Pres. and Dir. Coalition Mining Ltd., Sr. Consultant 1977; Pres., CEO and Dir., Western Mines Ltd., 1978-80; Secy., Interprovincial Mines' Ministers, Winnipeg Conf., 1947; mem. Policy and Mang. Comte. Earth Resources Data Systems Project; former Dir. of Mines Prov. Man.; rec'd Distinguished Service Award Petroleum Soc. Candn. Inst. Mining & Metall. 1974; rec'd Selwyn G. Blaylock Gold Medal of the Can. Inst. of Mining & Metall. for distinguished service during career in Mining & Petroleum, 1979; author various tech. papers and govt. reports mining and petroleum fields; Fellow, Royal Soc. of Canada since 1947; Geol. Assn. Can.; Hon. Life mem. Candn. Inst. Mining & Metall.; Engn. Inst. of Canada; Australian Petroleum Exploration Assn.; mem. Soc. Econ. Geol.; Alta. Assn. Prof. Engrs., Geols. & Geophysicists; Am. Assn. Petroleum Geols.; P. Conservative; Anglican; Clubs: Ranchmen's; Calgary Petroleum; Calgary Golf & Country; University Club (Vancouver); Home: 1315 Baldwin Cr. S.W., Calgary, Alta. T2V 2B7; Office: 9th Floor Bentall Four, 595 Burrard St., Vancouver, B.C. V7X 1C4.

FURTER, William Frederick, B.A.Sc., S.M., Ph.D., F.C.I.C.; educator; consulting engineer; b. North Bay, Ont., 5 Apl. 1931; s. Alfred Frederick and Eva Margaret (Stinson) F.; e. Royal Mil. Coll., 1949-53; Univ. of Toronto, B.A.Sc. 1954, Ph.D. 1958; Mass. Inst. of Technol., S.M. 1955; Nat. Defence Coll., 1969-70; m. Pamela Margaret, d. H. C. Cooper, Kingston, Ont., 6 Aug. 1966; three d., Lesley Margaret, Jane Elizabeth, Pamela Catharine; DEAN OF THE CAN. FORCES MILITARY COLL., AND CHMN. EXTENSION DIV., ROYAL MIL. COLL., 1980- ; Secy., Grad. Sch. there 1967-80, and Head, Chem. Engn. Div., Dept. of Chem. Engn. there 1960-80, Acting Dean of Grad. Studies & Research 1978-79; Teaching Asst., Mass. Inst. of Technol., 1954-55; Univ. of Toronto 1955-58; Research Engr., Research & Devel. Dept., Du Pont of Canada Ltd., 1958-59; Sr. Tech. Investigator of Dept. 1959-60; joined present Coll. as Special Lectr. in Chem. Engn. (part-time) 1958-60; Asst. Prof. 1960-61; Assoc. Prof. 1961-66; Prof. since 1966; Consulting Engr. to Hexcel Corp., San Francisco, to Union Carbide Corpn., Charleston, W. Va. and to Air Liquide Canada Ltée, Montreal; served with RCE (COTC) 1950-53; militia service with 2nd Field Engr. Regt., Toronto, 1953-57; rank Capt.; rec'd Dom. Scholarship, Gov. Gen. of Can. Bronze and Silver Medals; Lt. Gov. of Ont. Silver Medal; Engn. Inst. Can. Prize; Royal Candn. Sch. Mil. Engn. Prize; 2 M.I.T. Scholarships; 2 N.R.C. Studentships; Defence Research Bd. Grants annually since 1963; Research Grants from Nat. Science Foundation and Petroleum Reseach Fund; Fellow, Chem. Inst. of Can.; mem. Am. Nuclear Soc.; Assn. Prof. Engrs. Prov. Ont.; Candn. Soc. Chem. Engn. (Dir. 1979-); Candn. Nuclear Assn.; Interam. Confed. Chem. Engn.; RMC Club of Can. (Pres., Kingston Br. 1967-68), (Exec. Comm. & Foundation, 1972-75); author of over 90 scient. papers and book contribs.; listed in Who's Who in America, 40th & 41st edn.; United Church; recreations: hunting, music; Home: 406 Elmwood St., Kingston, Ont. K7M 2Z3

FYFE, W. S., M.Sc., Ph.D., F.R.S., F.R.S.C.; geochemist; educator; b. Ashburton, N.Z., 4 June 1927; s. Colin Alexander and Isabella (Pullar) F.; e. Otago (N.Z.) Univ., B.Sc. 1948, M.Sc. 1949, Ph.D. 1952; m. Patricia Jacqueline (Walker), children: Christopher David, Catherine Mary; PROF. AND CHRMN., DEPT. OF GEOLOGY. UNIV. OF WESTERN ONT. since 1972; Fulbright Fellow, U.S.A., 1952-55; Prof. of Chem. in N.Z. 1955-58; Prof. of Geol., Univ. of Cal. Berkeley, 1959-66; Guggenheim Fellow, Cambridge 1964; Royal Soc. Research Prof., Univ. of Manchester, 1966-72; author 5 text books and over 150 research papers; Chrmn., I.C.S.U. committee (continental storage of nuclear waste); Hon. Fellow, Royal Soc. N.Z.; Geol. Soc. Am.; Life Fellow, Mineral. Soc. Am.; Hon. mem., Acad. Science Brazil; mem., Am. Chem. Soc.; Brit. Chem. Soc.; Geol. Assn. Can.; Mineral. Soc. U.K.; Natural Science & Engn. Research Coun., Can.; recreations: travel, swimming; Home: 1197 Richmond St., London, Ont. N6A 3L3; Office: London, Ont.

G

GABOURY, Etienne J., B.A., B.Arch., R.C.A., F.R.A.I.C.; architect; b. Bruxelles, Man. 24 Apl. 1930; s. late Napoleon Joseph and late Valentine (Lafreniere) G.; e. St. Boniface Coll. B.A. 1953; Univ. of Man. B.Arch. 1958; Ecole des Beaux-Arts Paris 1958-59; m. Claire Marie Therese d. late Alberic Breton 1 Sept. 1956; children: Lise Jeanne, Pierre Maurice, Jacques Gabriel, François Adrien; PRINC., E.J. GABOURY AND ASSOCIATES; guest speaker and conf. chrmn. several occasions Can. and USA; mem. Expo '67 Arch. Adv. Comte.; Candn. Housing Design Council 1970-73; Gov., Univ. of Man. 1970-73, Vice Chrmn. 1973; Adv. Comte. Winnipeg Symphony Orchestra Ltd. 1970-72; Adv. Comte. Royal Winnipeg Ballet; Pres. Soc. Franco-Manitobaine 1969-70; Founding

Gov. Heritage Can. 1973-74; Prov. Adv. Comte. on Transport. 1973-74; Man. Arts Council (Chrmn. 1977-78); Candn. Nat. Comte. Habitat 1976 UN Conf.; Studio critiques Sch. of Arch. Univ. of Man. 1965-66; rec'd 5 awards arch. composition Univ. of Man.; French Govt. Scholarship 1958; Massey Awards 1964, 4 bldgs. nominated; Candn. Arch. Yearbook Significant Bldg. Awards 1964, 1966, 1968; Candn. Home Journ. Home of the Yr. 1966; Candn. Housing Council Awards 1967, 1970; Man. Hist. Soc. Centennial Medal of Honor 1970; Man. Assn. Archs. Award 1964; Vincent Massey Awards for Excellence in Urban Environment Special Mention 1971; competition juror on various occasions; author numerous articles, papers; work cited various publs.; major projects, Candn. Embassy in Mexico, 1981; Lycée professionnel hôtelier, Abidjan, 1980; Royal Candn. Mint, Winnipeg, 1973; St. Boniface Cathedral, 1972; St. Boniface Civic Centre, 1963; Precious Blood Church, 1967; E. J. Gaboury residence, 1968; Berney Residence, 1974; mem. Man. Assn. Archs.; Ont. Assn. Archs.; Que. Assn. Archs.; recreations: squash, tennis, golf, reading, music, art; Club: Carleton; Home: 749 South Dr., Winnipeg, Man. R2M 3Z4; Office: 209, 675 Pembina Highway, Winnipeg, Man. R3M 2L6.

GABRIELSE, Hubert, M.A.Sc., Ph.D.; geologist; b. Golden, B.C. 1 March 1926; s. Christian and Lena (Van Hoepen) G.; e. Univ. of B.C., B.A.Sc. 1948, M.A.Sc. 1950; Columbia Univ. Ph.D. 1955; m. Jean Whitehouse d. George C. Freeman, Millington, N.J. 1 Jan. 1955; children: Peter Christian; Nancy Elizabeth; RESEARCH SCIENT.; GEOL. SURVEY OF CAN. 1979- ; Geol., Geol. Survey Can. 1953, Head of Cordilleran Subdiv. 1971-79; author various publs.; mem. Geol. Soc. Am. (Councilor 1981-83); Royal Soc. Can.; N.Y. Acad. Sciences (Geol. Assn. Can.; Candn. Inst. Mining & Metall.; Candn. Soc. Petrol. Geols.; Am. Assn. Advanc. Science; United Church; recreations: skiing, hiking, photography; Home: 693 Alpine Court, North Vancouver, B.C. V7R 2L7; Office: 100 W. Pender St., Vancouver, B.C. V6B 1R8.

GAGE, Frances Marie, R.C.A.; sculptor; b. Windsor, Ont. 22 Aug. 1924; d. Russell and Jean Mildred (Collver) G.; e. Oshawa (Ont.) Coll. & Vocational Inst. 1943; Ont. Coll. of Art (Sculpture) 1951; Art Students League New York 2 yrs. (scholarship); Ecole des Beaux-Arts Paris 2 yrs. (Royal Soc. Scholarship); maj. sculptures incl. twice-life statue and 4 walnut reliefs Fanshaw Coll. London, Ont. 1962; Dr. Bertram Collip portrait relief Univ. of W. Ont. 1963; Kitchener-Waterloo Art Gallery life sized torso 1964; life sized walnut torso Univ. of Guelph 1966; "Bear" ciment fondu Wiszniewski, Newmarket 1965; bronze bust Dr. Andrew Smith Univ. Guelph 1967; 4 bronze portrait reliefs A. Y. Jackson, Fred Varley, Healy Willen, Sir Ernest MacMillan 1967; "Rosamund" twice-life bronze statue Toronto 1968; mem. "Song in the Wind" Music Bldg. Mount Allison Univ. 1968; "Woman" marble statue Women's Coll. Hosp. Toronto 1969; bronze relief mem. Robert Meredith Janes Univ. of Toronto 1969; Memorial, Charles Lake Gundy, Mt. Pleasant Cemetery; commemorative medal Samuel Bronfman 1971, Dr. Jason Hannah Royal Soc. Can. 1973 (also 5 commemorative busts); medal for Jean P. Carriere Award, Standards Council of Canada; Dr. Gordon Mikiforuk bust Univ. of Toronto 1975; bronze "Baby" Mem. Kew Gardens Toronto 1975; rec'd Rothman Purchase Award 1965; served with W.R.C.N.S. during World War II; mem. Council Royal Candn. Acad. Art; recreations: music, conservation; Address: Crosshill, (P.O. Box 55) St. Clements, Ont. N0B 2M0.

GAGLARDI, Philip Arthur; b. Mission City, B.C., 13 January 1913; s. John and Dominica G.; e. Pub. School, Mission City, B.C.; Northwest Bible Coll., Seattle, Wash.; m. Jennie Margurette, d. John Sandin, 8 Dec. 1938; two s.; Robert, William; o. Pentecostal Min., Calvary Temple, Kamloops, B.C. 1939, prior to entering Ministry was Master Mech., A.R. Williams Machinery Company, Vancouver, B.C. and Bloedel, Stewart and Welch, Victoria, B.C.; 1st elected to Brit. Columbia leg. for Kamloops, in g.e. June 1952; Min. of Public Works 1952-55, Min. of Highways 1955 till resignation from Cabinet, March 1968; apptd. Min. of Rehabilitation & Social Improvement 1969; def. in g.e. 1972; conducts daily radio and weekly television services; Chairman, Provincial Alliance of Businessmen; as Minister of Highways was responsible for establishment of B.C. Ferry Service; built one of first sawdust highways in world, first suspension bridge of its kind in Can. at Hudson Hope, and first orthotropic deck used in bridge constr.; founder of "Beautiful British Columbia" publ.; originator of communication system for Dept. of Highways; has travelled extensively in Europe, Asia, Africa, Australia and S. Am.; conducted two-month speaking tour 1949; prominent child and youth worker; Social Credit; Pentecostal; Clubs: Rotary (Hon. mem.); Kiwanis; Lions; recreations: youth work; ranching; pony raising; Home: 514 Strathcona Terrace, Kamloops, B.C. V2C 1B9

GAGNE, Samuel-L., M.A.; b. St.-Fabien de Rimouski, Que., 14 Apr. 1916; s. late Jean-Baptiste and Eva (Bellavance) G.; e. Séminaire de Rimouski; Laval Univ., B.A. 1938; M.A. 1941, Sch. of Social Sciences, Catholic Univ., Washington, D.C.; m. Huguette, d. late Théo Belzile, 22 June 1946; children: Pierre, Madeleine, Claude; PRÉS., REP INC., CONSEILS ET SERVICES EN RELATIONS PUBLIQUES; Pres., Chambre de Commerce du District de Montréal (1968-69); Hon. Trustee Montreal Museum of Fine Arts; Pres., Candn. Public Relations Soc. 1967; Catholic; recreations: reading, travel, fishing; Clubs: St. Denis; Winchester; Home: 3215 Lacombe, Montreal, Que. H3T 1L6

GAGNEBIN, Albert P., M.Sc.; mining executive; b. Torrington, Conn., 23 Jan. 1909; s. Charles A. and Marguerite E. (Huguenin) G.; e. Yale Univ., B.Sc. (Mech. Engn.) 1930, M.Sc. (Metall.) 1932; m. Genevieve Hope, 26 Oct. 1935; children: Anne (Mrs. John D. Coffin), Joan (Mrs. David O. Wicks); MEM., ADVISORY BOARD, INTERNATIONAL NICKEL CO. OF CANADA LTD. (INCO LTD) 1980- ; Trustee, Atlantic Mutual Insurance Co.; Dir., North Am. Adv. Bd. of Swiss Air; ; Abex Corp.; Centennial Ins. Co.; Dir. (emeritus) Illinois Central Indus.; Ingersoll-Rand Co.; Schering-Plough Corp.;joined Internat. Nickel Co. Inc. 1932; successively with Research Lab., Research Ferrous Metall., Devel. Ductile Iron, Devel. and Research Div., 1932-55; Mgr., Primary Nickel Dept., 1956-61; Vice-Pres., 1958-64; Extve. Vice-Pres., 1964-66; mem., Extve. Comte., and Dir., International Nickel Co. Canada Ltd., 1965; Vice-Pres. 1960-64; Extve. Vice-Pres., 1964-67; Pres. 1968-71, Chrmn. of Bd. and Chrmn. of Extve. Comte. 1972-74; el. a Dir., Internat. Nickel Co. Inc. 1967-80; rec'd. Peter L. Simpson Gold Medal, Am. Foundry. Soc., 1952; Annual Award of Ductile Iron Soc. 1965; Grande Medaille d'Honneur, L'Assn. Technique de Fonderie; 1967; Charles F Rand Gold Metal, A.I.M.E. mem., National Academy of Engn.; Yale Engn. Assn.; mem. Am. Inst. Mining & Metall. Engrs.; Am. Soc. Metals; Am. Foundrymen's Soc. (Hon. Life); Mining and Metall. Society of America; American Swiss Assn. (Director); author: "The Fundamentals of Iron and Steel Castings"; co-inventor ductile iron; Sigma Xi; Clubs: Down Town Assn.; Yale; University, N.Y.; Rumson Country (N.J.); Sea Bright Beach (N.J.); Home: 143 Grange Ave., Fair Haven, N.J. 07701; Office: One New York Plaza, New York, N.Y. 10004.

GAGNON, André, O.C.; musician; b. St-Pacôme-de-Kamouraska, Que. 1 Aug. 1942; e. theory lessons with Léon Destroismaisons 1952-53, 1957; CMM 1957-61, piano, composition, solfège (rec'd premier prix harmony 1961); studied in Paris with Yvonne Loriod and took courses in accompanying and conducting 1961 (Que. Govt. Grant); accompanist for Claude Léveillée also music dir., arranger and pianist for most of his recordings 1962-69; some-

time accompanist and arranger for Monique Leyrac and others; soloist Mozart concert Place des Arts 1967; recorded his 4 concertos in the style of Vivaldi "Mes Quatre Saisons" with London Baroque Orchestra 1969; performed Expo 70 Osaka and toured with Quebec Symphony Orchestra in Que. 1970; recorded "Les Turluteries" with Hamburg Philharmonic Orchestra 1972; other recordings incl. "Let It Be Me" and "Projection" 1971, "Saga" 1974, "Neiges" 1975 (Juno Award 1976 best selling LP), "Le Saint-Laurent" (selected instrumental record of yr. ADISQ 1979); rec'd Juno Award for instrumental artist of 1977; performed in France 1975, 1976 and in Mexico 1976; wrote music for Anne Ditchburn's ballet "Mad Shadows" premiered by Nat. Ballet of Can. O'Keefe Centre Toronto 1977; composed music for pas de deux "Nelligan" and for ballet "Adage" performed by Compagnie de Danse Eddy Toussaint at Place des Arts 1977; wrote music for NFB film "Games of the XXI Olympiad", CBS TV movie "Night Fright" and feature film "Running"; performed in concert at Massey Hall and Place des Arts 1978 and toured Can. and USA 1979; host and accompanist CBC TV "Cri-Cri" 1962-64 and Music Dir. "Moie et l'autre" 1966-70; composed music several series incl. "Vivre en ce pays" 1967-71, "Les Forges du St-Maurice" 1972-75 and "Techno-Flash" 1973-77; wrote and performed music children's program "La Souris verte" 1967-76; guest artist "Zoom", "Vedettes en direct", "Dimanshowsoir"; composition "Petit Concerto pour Carignan et orchestre (1976) performed by Carignan & Yehudi Menuhin on CBC TV "The Music of Man" 1978; mem. CAPAC.

GAGNON, Denis J., B.A., B.Pharm., M.Sc., Ph.D.; pharmacologist; educator; b. Quebec City, Que. 3 Sept. 1939; s. Jean-Paul and Alphonsine (Hallé) G.; e. St-Louis Coll. Edmunston, N.B. B.A. 1959; Laval Univ. B.Pharm. 1963; McGill Univ. M.Sc. 1965, Ph.D. 1967; m. Jeannine d. late Louis-Philippe Rheault 26 May 1962; children: François, Josée, Michèle; ASSOC. DEAN OF RESEARCH & GRAD. STUDIES, FACULTY OF MED. LAVAL UNIV. since 1977, Assoc. Prof. and Chrmn. of Pharmacol. 1975-80; Full Prof., 1980; Post doctorate Fellow, Stockholm Univ., Karolinska Inst. 1967-68; Visiting Scient. Royal Coll. Surgs. Eng. 1968; Assoc. Prof. of Pharmacol. Univ. of Sherbrooke 1968, Asst. Prof. 1971-75; co-author 'Introduction to Neurological Sciences' (in French) 1978; author or co-author of numerous articles and scient. papers; mem. Conseil Consultatif de Pharmacologie de la Prov. de Qué. (Pres.); Pharmacol. Soc. Can.; recreations: skiing, biking, sailing; Home: 1401 Gaspard Fauteux, Sillery, Que. G1T 2T7; Office: Quebec City, Que. G1K 7P4.

GAGNON, Emile; industrialist; b. Montreal, Que., 18 April 1928; s. Wilfrid and Yvonne (Senecale) G.; e. Brébeuf Coll., Montreal; Babson Inst. Business Adm., Boston, Mass.; m. Mireille, d. Jacques Fortier, 10 June 1960; two s. Emile Jr., E. Philippe; PRES., LOCATION MINICO LIMITEE since 1978; Pres., Aird Industries Ltd. since 1953; PRESIDENT, AIRD INDUSTRIES LTD. since 1953; Dir., Champlain Oil Products Ltd.; mem. Adv. Council. Ministry of Industry & Comm., Can.; Dir., Hôpital de la Miséricorde; Soc. des Alcools du Qué.; Pres. and Dir., Shoe Mfrs. Assn. Can.; R. Catholic; recreation: sports; Clubs: St. Denis; Laval sur le Lac; Home: 31 Les Sorbiers, Laval sur le Lac, Cité Laval, Que. H7R 1E5;

GAGNON, Jean-Louis, O.C., F.R.S.C. (1971); né Québec, 21 fév. 1913; f. Adhémar et Marie-Elise (Nadeau) G.; é. coll. Ste-Marie et Brébeuf, Montréal; Univ. d'Ottawa; Univ. Laval, Québec, (sc. sociales); ép. Hélène Jobidou, Château d'Eau, Qué., 12 sept. 1936; fondateur, magazine littéraire "Vivre", Qué., 1933, rédact. en chef: "La Voix de l'Est", Granby, Qué., 1935; "L'Evénement-Journal", Qué., 1940; corres. de guerre "Le Soleil", Londres, Angl., 1941; Dir., West African Broadcasting Unit, Accra, Gold Coast, Afrique, 1942; Dir., Agence France-Afrique, Canada, 1943; chef du bureau, Agence France-Presse,

Wash., D.C., 1944; Dir. service d'information et relat. publiques, Brazilian Traction Light and Power Co. Ltd., Rio de Janeiro, Brésil, 1946; Editorialiste, CKAC Montréal, 1949; a lancé "Les Ecrits du Canada Français", Montréal, 1953; Rédact. en chef. "Le Canada", Montréal, 1953; a lancé l'hebdo "La Réforme", Montréal, 1955; Rédact. en chef, "La Presse", Montréal, 1958; a lancé "Le Nouveau Journal", Montréal, 1961; co-président, Comm. Royale d'enquête sur le Bilinguisme et le Biculturalisme; trophée Laflèche "pour la plus grande contribution à la radio canadienne", 1957; Le Grand Prix du Journalisme de l'union can. des journalistes de langue fr., 1962; Trophée des commentaires p. programme "Choc", du Congrès du Spectacle, Union des Artistes, 1963; auteur: Vent du Large, 1944; La Fin des Haricots, 1955; La Mort d'un Nègre, 1961; préface d'album de caricatures de Robert Lapalme, 1950; préface de "Un Monde Fou" de Berthio, 1960; en collaboration: "A Century of Reporting — Un siècle de reportage", 1967; "Le Canada au seuil du siécle de l'abondance" 1969, (collab. Prof. R. Mandrou, Paris, France); Dir.-Gen. Information Canada 1970; Ambassadeur UNESCO, Paris 1972; nommé mem. du Conseil de la radiodiffusion et des telecommunications canadiennes pour sept., ans 1976; Membre: Académie canad.-fr.; Conseil des Arts du Qué.; membre fondateur, Fédérat. Libérale du Qué., 1955; Officier de l'Ordre du Canada, 1980; Bureau: Conseiller, Conseil de la Radio diffusion et des telecommunication canadienne, Ottawa, Ont. K1A 0N2

GAGNON, Marcel-Aimé M.A.; public relations counsel; b. Sherbrooke, Que., 12 Sept. 1918; s. Isaac and Laure-Anna (Thibodeau) G.; e. St. Charles Borromée Classical Coll., Sherbrooke, 1933-38; Univ. of Ottawa, B.A. 1946; Univ. of Montreal, M.A. 1950; m. Lilian, d. William Kugel, Beverley Hills, Cal., 8 March 1947; children: Chantal, Roxane, Alain, Véronique; EXTVE. DIRECTOR, LA FONDATION DE L'UNIVERSITÉ DU QUÉBEC À MONTRÉAL, since 1978; in charge of P.R., same university 1970-78; former President, Marcel-A. Gagnon and Associés Inc.; Les Productions Orleans Ltée and Les Presses Publicitaires Inc.; Reporter, "La Tribune", 1943-46 and "Le Canada", 1947-48; Secy. to Min. of Finance, Que., 1948-50; joined John Price Jones Inc., N.Y. and Brakeley & Co., Montreal; founded weekly paper "Metropole", 1958; author of: "La vie orageuse d'Olivar Asselin", 1962 (rec'd. Grand Jury of Letters Award); "La Lanterne d'Arthur Buies", 1964; "Le ciel et l'enfer d'Arthur Buies", 1965; "Jean-Charles Harvey, Précurseur de la Révolution Tranquille", 1969; "Toute La Vérité (ou presque) sur la drogue" 1970; "Olivar Asselin toujours Vivant" 1974; enlisted in Royal 22nd Regt.; rec'd. hon. discharge 1941 due to illness; Pres., La Société des Ecrivains Canadiens, 1968-69 (Hon. Life mem.); Chrmn. accreditation Bd., Assn. des Relationnistes du Québec; mem. Can. Centre for Philanthropy; accd. mem., Candn. Pub. Relations Soc.; accd. mem. Pub. Relations Soc. of Am.; mem., Candn. Assn. of Univ. Development Officers; CASE: Council for Advancement and Support of Education; Assn. des Ecrivains de langue française d'Outre-mer; Assn. des diplomés, Université de Montréal et d'Ottawa; Roman Catholic; recreations: writing, hunting, fishing, tennis, golf; Clubs: Montréal Press; Cerele de la Place d'Armes; Home: 3808 Grey Ave., Montreal, Que. H4A 3N7

GAIRDNER, John Smith; industrialist; b. Toronto, Ont., 25 July 1925; s. late James Arthur and Norma Ecclestone (Smith) G.; e. Appleby Coll., Oakville, Ont.; Univ. of Toronto 1942-43; m. Ivy Jane, d. Lewis Brothwell, Smiths Falls, Ont., 30 Nov. 1946; two s., John Lewis, Robert Donald; one d., Brenda Leigh; CHRMN. OF THE BD. & PRES., SECURITY TRADING LTD. (formerly Gairdner & Co. Ltd.); President and Dir., Gairdner International Ltd.; Vice Chrmn., The Gairdner Foundation; mem. Bd. of Govs., Appleby Coll., Oakville, Ont.; served in 2nd World War with R.C.A.F. 1943-45; Anglican; recreations: golf, fishing, gardening; Clubs: Toronto Golf; The Hamil-

ton (Ont.); The Oakville; Oakville Golf; St. James's; National; Caughnawana Fishing & Hunting; La Jolla Country; Home: "Edgemere", 1502 Lakeshore Road E., Oakville, Ont. L6J 1M1 and 7599 Caminito Avola, La Jolla, Calif. 92037; Office: Suite 4706, ManuLife Centre, 44 Charles St. W., Toronto, Ont. M4Y 1R8

GALBRAITH, John Kenneth, M.S., Ph.D., LL.D.; economist; b. Iona Station, Ont., 15 Oct. 1908; s. William Archibald and Catherine (Kendall) G.; e. Univ. of Toronto (Ont. Agric. Coll.), B.S.A. 1931; Univ. of California, M.S. 1933 and Ph.D. 1934; Cambridge Univ.; LL.D. Toronto, 1961, W. Ont. 1968; m. Catherine Merriam, d. Charles Atwater of New York, 17 Sept. 1937, three children; Consultant, U.S. Govt. Agencies, Nat. Resources Planning Board; Instr., Harvard Univ., 1934-39; Asst. Prof., Princeton Univ., 1930-40; Depy. Adm., Office of Price Adm. (U.S), 1941-43; Editor of "Fortune" mag., 1943-48 (subject to leaves of absence); Dir., U.S. Strategic Bombing Survey, 1945; Dir., Econ. Security Policy, U.S. Dept. of State, 1946, and other govt. posts; Lectr., Harvard Univ., 1948 and Warburg Prof. of Econ. there since 1949; U.S. Ambassador to India, 1961-63; Visiting Fellow, Trinity Coll., Cambridge Univ., Eng. 1970-71; awarded U.S. Medal of Freedom and President's Cert. of Merit; author of "Modern Competition and Business Policy", 1938; "American Capitalism", 1952; "A Theory of Price Control", 1952; "The Affluent Society"; "The Liberal Hour" (essays) 1960; "The Scotch", 1964; "The New Industrial State", 1967; "The Triumph" (novel) 1968; "Ambassador's Journal" 1969; "Economics and the Public Purpose", 1973; "Money", 1975; "Age of Uncertainty", 1975; and numerous tech., scient. and popular monographs and articles; mem. and past pres., Am. Econ. Assn.; Am. Farm Econ. Assn.; mem. and past chrmn., Americans for Democratic Activity; Democrat; Home: 30 Francis Ave., Cambridge, Mass.

GALE, Charles G., B.Com., F.C.A.; b. Ottawa, Ont., 1 Feb. 1916; s. George Gordon and Marian (Masson) G.; e. Normal Sch., Ottawa, Ont.; Ashbury Coll., Rockcliffe Park, Ont.; McGill Univ., B.Com.; m. Alice Mary, d. Dr. George M. Watt, Brantford, Ont. 20 Sept. 1939; children: Gordon, Georgia, Nancy, Sally; DOMINION SECURITIES LTD. (1977- ;) formerly Partner-in-charge, Ottawa, TOUCHE ROSS & CO., CHARTERED ACCOUNTANTS (ret.), 1951-77; and P.S. Ross & Partners, Management Consultants, 1958-77; joined P.S. Ross & Sons, Montreal 1938; Acct., Dept. of Mun. & Supply, Ottawa, 1941-42; practised his prof. in Ottawa until merging his practice with present firm; served in 2nd World War with R.C.N. 1943-45; rank Lieut.; Past mem. Council, Inst. of Chart. Accts. of Ont. (el. F.C.A. 1965); Past Pres., Ottawa Chart. Accts. Assn.; Past Chrmn., McGill Alma Mater Fund-Ottawa Valley; Past Pres., Ottawa Valley Grads. Soc. of McGill; Past Regional Vice-Pres., McGill Grad. Soc.; Chrmn. Bd. of Govs., Ashbury Coll. 1958-60; Chrmn., Individual Gifts, Carleton Univ. Campaign 1979-80; Delta Upsilon; Anglican; recreations: golf, tennis, swimming, yachting, skiing, fishing; Clubs: Rideau (Past Pres.); Royal Ottawa Golf (Past Pres.); Seigniory (Montebello Que.) (Past Chmn. of Bd.),; Home: 137 Willingdon Rd., Rockcliffe Park, Ottawa, Ont. K1M 0C6

GALE, Hon. George Alexander; C.C., Q.C., LL.D.; retired judge; b. Quebec, P.Q., 24 June 1906; s. Robert Henry and Elma Gertrude (Read) G.; e. Prince of Wales High Sch., Vancouver, B.C.; University of Toronto, B.A. 1929; Osgoode Hall, Toronto 1932; LL.D., McMaster 1968, York 1969, Windsor 1980; m. Hilda Georgina, d. William Arthur Daly, 29 Dec. 1934: children: Robert, Peter, David; VICE CHAIRMAN, ONT. LAW REFORM COMN. 1977-81; read law with Donald, Mason, White & Foulds; called to the Bar of Ont. 1932; cr. K.C. 1945; formerly practised with Mason, Foulds, Davidson & Gale, Toronto; after appt. to High Court of Ont., 1946, elevated to Court of Appeal, Oct. 1963; Chief Justice of the High

Court, 1964-67; Chief Justice of Ont. 1967-76; former Chrmn. of Comte. which deals with Rules of Practice for Prov. of Ont.; mem., Bd. of Govs., Wycliffe Coll., Toronto; former mem. Bd. of Govs., Upper Can. Coll.; formerly mem. of Cdn. Bar Assn., and Council of Cdn. Bar Assn.; former chrmn. Judicial Council for Prov. Judges of Ont.; former mem. of Exec. Cttee of Canadian Judicial Council; Hon. mem., Bar of Georgia; Hon. mem. Cdn. Corps of Commissionaires; Hon. Pres. Ont. Curling Assn.; Hon. Lectr., Osgoode Hall Law Sch. and formerly Faculty of Med. Univ. of Toronto; formerly Chrmn., Rhodes Schol. Selection Comte.; Editor. "Practice and Procedures in Ont." (Holmsted & Gale, 6th ed.); apptd. Companion to the Order of Canada, 1977; Delta Kappa Epsilon; Phi Delta Phi (Hon.); Anglican; recreation: golf, photography; Clubs: Univ. (Vice Pres. 1959); Toronto Curling (Pres. 1956); Lawyers (Pres. 1940, Hon. Pres. 1968); Chippewa Golf; York (Hon. mem.); Home: 2 Brookfield Rd., Willowdale, Ont. M2P 1A9

GALE, Vernon Bruce; manufacturer; b. Eastend, Sask., 2 Feb. 1926; s. William Stanton and Mary (Sloman) G.; e. Britannia High Sch., Vancouver, B.C.; Toronto Training & Rehab. Inst. (1946); Univ. of W. Ont. (Management Training 1959); m. (1), Wilma Grace, one s., William Charles; m. (2), Sue Merril, d. K. M. McAdam; PRESIDENT AND GEN. MGR., GUNTHER MELE (1976) LTD.; joined Farrington Mfg. Co. Ltd. as Sales Mgr., 1952; apptd. Candn. Mgr. of Lektco Products Ltd., Montreal (subsidiary of Remington Rand Corp.), 1955; apptd. Nat. Service Sales Mgr., Elect. Shaver Div., Remington Rand Ltd., 1956; returned to Farrington Bradma in 1957 as Vice-Pres.-Sales and apptd. V.P. and Gen. Mgr. 1957; served in 2nd World War; R.C.A.F., 1944; Candn. Army, 1945-46; mem., Candn. Jewelers Assn. (Pres. 1973-74); Candn. Jewelry Travellers Assn.; Candn. Jewellers 24 Karat Club; Toronto Bd. Trade; Brantford and Region Chamber of Comm. (Pres. 1976); Candn. Jewellery 24 Carat Club, Pres. 1977-78; Freemason; United Church; recreations: golf, tennis, bowling, reading, spectator sports; Clubs: Brantford; Brantford Golf & Country; Rotary (Brantford Pres. 1973-74); National Sales Executive; Home: R.R. #1, Brantford, Ont. Office: 298 Murray St., Brantford Ont. N3S 5T2

GALES, David Lorne, B.A., B.C.L., L.L.D.; educational executive; b. Montreal, P.Q., 6 Jan. 1911; s. George Gilbert and Ada B. (Clarke) G.; e. Lower Can. Coll. 1920-28; McGill Univ. B.A. 1932, B.C.L. 1935; m. Isabel Graham, d. A. O. Dawson, Montreal, P.Q. 5 Jan. 1939; children: Pamela Joan, Robert Lorne, Howard Richard, David Graham; CONSULTANT, McGILL FUND OFFICE; Extve. Dir. and Gen. Secy., Graduates' Soc. of McGill Univ.; read law with Campbell, McMaster, Couture, Kerry & Bruneau, Montreal, P.Q.; called to Bar of Que. 1936; served in 2nd World War with Candn. Armoured Corp at Camp Borden, Ont. with rank of Staff Capt.; following discharge from armed services did not return to the practice of law, but joined Graduates' Soc. of McGill; mem., Am. Alumni Council; Delta Kappa Epsilon; United Church; Clubs: University; Canadian (N.Y.C.); Home: P.O. Box 21, Como, Que. J0P 1A0

GALIPEAULT, André Jacques, B.A., B.C.L.; executive; b. Quebec City, Que. 10 July 1937; s. late Jacques and Jacqueline (Dessaint) G.; e. Jésuits Coll. Quebec City B.L. 1953; Laval Univ. B.A. 1955; McGill Univ. B.C.L. 1959; m. Suzanne d. Charles Valiquette, Montreal, Que. 26 Aug. 1961; children: Nathalie, Eric; VICE PRES. AND GEN. COUNSEL, TEXACO CANADA INC., since 1977; Dir. Regent Refining (Canada) Ltd.; Provincial Construction Co.; read law with Lucien Beauregard, Q.C.; called to Bar of Que. 1960; Assoc. Beauregard Brisset, Reycraft & Chauvin 1960-64; joined present Co. as Solr. 1964, Assoc. Gen. Counsel 1971, Gen. Solr. 1973, Gen. Counsel 1975; Dir. Toronto French Sch.; Pres. of the Nat. Ballet of Can.; Past Chrmn. Bd. of Govs. Nat. Theatre Sch. of Can.;

mem. Assn. France Can.; Past Pres. Chambre de Comm. Française au Can. (Ont.); Vice-Pres. Assn. Candn. Gen. Counsel; mem. Bar Prov. Que.; Bar Montreal; Candn. Bar Assn.; Candn. Maritime Law Assn.; Internat. Law Assn.; Candn. Mfrs. Assn.; Bd. Trade Metrop. Toronto; Liberal; R. Catholic; recreations: tennis, squash; Clubs: mem. Univ. Club of Toronto; Toronto Cricket Skating & Curling; Montreal Racket; Home: 21 Harlington Rd., Don Mills, Ont. M3B 3G3; Office: 90 Wynford Dr., Don Mills, Ont. M3C 1K5

GALLAGHER, Hon. Charles Gunter, M.L.A., B.Sc.; politician; b. Centreville, N.B. 21 Sept. 1925; s. James Isaac and May Irene (Gunter) G.; e. Centreville High Sch.; N.S. Agric. Coll.; Macdonald Coll., McGill Univ.; m. Kathleen Frances Olmstead 7 June 1949; children: Sally, Kathleen, Jane, Isaac, Beth, Patricia, Sam; MIN. OF EDUC., N.B. 1976- ; Min. Responsible for Historical Resources, N.B. 1976- ; Min. of Continuing Educ., N.B. 1980- ; farmer; el. M.L.A. for Carleton North prov. g.e. 1970, re-el. since; Freemason; P. Conservative; United Baptist; Club: Rotary; B.P.O.E.; Office: (P.O. Box 6000) Fredericton, N.B. E3B 5H1.

GALLAGHER, Donald McKenzie, B.Sc.; company executive; b. Saskatoon, Sask., 1915; e. Pub. Sch., Saskatoon, Sask.; High Sch., Sydenham, Ont.; Queen's Univ., B.Sc. (Mining Engn.); m. Margaret Johnston, 1939; children: David, Andrew, Katherine (Mrs. M. Boyes); Extve. Vice President ICI U.S. (ret.), 1972-78 and a Dir. since 1974; Sr. Vice-Pres. and Dir., ICI North America Ltd. 1970-71; joined Defence Industries Ltd., subsidiary of Canadian Industries Ltd., and served in engn. and supervisory capacities 1943-46; held Supv. and Mang. positions in explosives mfg. with Candn. Industries Ltd., 1946-64; apptd. Prod. Mgr., Explosives, 1964-66; Gen. Mgr., Plastic Div., 1966-68, Vice-Pres. 1968; Pres., ICI America Inc. 1969-71 (Extve. Vice Pres., 1972-78); Dir. Delaware State Chamber of Comm.; mem., Soc. Plastics Indust.; Soc. Chem. Industs.; Newcomen Soc.; Assoc. mem., Chem. Inst. Can.; Club: Canadian (N.Y.); Home: 47 Cache Cay Dr., Vero Beach, Fla. 32960

GALLAGHER, John Patrick, B.Sc., geologist and executive; b. Winnipeg, Man., 16 July 1916; s. James and Constance Mary (Burdett) G.; e. Univ. of Manitoba, B.Sc. 1937; Harvard Univ. (Advanced Management) 1948; m. Kathleen Marjorie, d. Norman Stewart, Penhold, Alta., 20 Aug. 1949; children: James Stewart, Thomas Patrick, Frederick Michael; CHRMN. AND C.E.O., DOME PETROLEUM LTD., since 1974; Dir., Hudson's Bay Oil and Gas Co.; Texasgulf Inc.; Dome Mines Ltd.; TransCanada PipeLines Ltd.; Candn. Imperial Bank of Commerce; mem., Artic Inst. of North America; Asst. Geol., Candn. Geol. Survey N. Manitoba and N.W.T., 1936-37; Field Geol., Shell Oil Co. in Cal.and Egypt, 1938-39; Standard Oil Co. (New Jersey), rising from field geologist to Exploration Mgr., 1939-49; Production Mgr., Western Candn. Div., Imperial Oil Ltd., 1949-50; Extve. Vice-Pres. and Gen. Mgr., Dome Petroleum Ltd., Calgary, 1950-53; Pres., Dome Petroleum, 1953-74; Pres., Independent Petroleum Assn. of Canada, 1966; recreations: golf, skiing; Clubs: Calgary Petroleum; Calgary Golf & Country; Office: P.O. Box 200, Calgary, Alta. T2P 2H8

GALLANT, Edgar, M.A.; b. Egmont Bay, P.E.I., 19 Sept. 1924; s. Cyrus P. and Edna (Arsenault) G.; e. Seminaire de Joliette, B.A. 1946; Laval Univ., M.A. (Social Science-Econ.) 1949; LL.D. (honoris causa), Univ. of P.E.I. (1981); m. Annette Louise, d. Wilfrid Perras, Joliette, Que., 3 June 1949; children: Pierre, Louise, Marie, Christel: CHAIRMAN, PUBLIC SERVICE COMMISSION, since July, 1976; Chrmn., Nat. Capital Comn., Sept. 1973 - June 1976; Secy. to Council of Maritime Premiers 1971-73; from 1949 to 1964 served with Federal Treasury Board and the Departments of Finance and Defence Production as well as with NATO International Secretariat in Paris and

Canada's Mission to the European Communities in Brussels; Secy., Economic Council of Can., 1964-65; Dir., Fed.-Prov. Relations Div., Dept. of Finance, Ottawa, 1965-68; Secy. of Constitutional Conf. 1968-69; Depy. Secy. to the Cabinet 1969-71; mem., Bd. Gov., Univ. of Ottawa; Vice-Pres., Ottawa Kidney Foundation (1978); mem., Inst. Pub. Adm. Can.; Officier, Ordre de la Peliade, Association des Parlementaires de Langue Française; Vanier Medal (1978), Institute of Public Administration; R. Catholic; Home: 2257 Bowman Road, Ottawa, Ont. K1H 6V4; Office: Room 1902—West Tower L'Esplanade Laurier, 300 Laurier Ave. W., Ottawa, Ont. K1A 0M7

GALLANT, Mavis; writer; b. Montreal, 1922; e. wide variety of schools; worked for National Film Bd. before joining weekly Montreal Standard as reporter; enjoyed successful career as a feature writer but gave up newspaper work to devote her time to writing fiction; left Canada in 1950 and after extensive travels has made Paris her home; writes short fiction and occasional essays for *The New Yorker*, and *New York Times Book Review*; publications: "Home Truths: Selected Canadian Stories", 1981; "From the Fifteenth District" (short stories) 1980; "The End of the World" (short stories) 1974; "A Fairly Good Time" (novel) 1970; "Green Water, Green Sky" (novel) 1964; "The Pegnitz Junction (short stories) 1973; "My Heart is Broken'" (short stories) 1959; "The Other Paris (short stories) 1956; Writer-in-Residence, Univ. of Toronto, 1982- ; is currently at work on a major study of the Dreyfus case and its impact on French society; Address: c/o MacMillan Co. of Canada, 70 Bond St., Toronto, Ont. M5B 1X3

GALLOP, Richard Kerry Bruce, M.A.; advertising executive; b. U.K. 1 Jan. 1939; s. Kingsley Malcolm Gallop; e. Magdalen Coll. Sch. Oxford 1958; Merton Coll. Oxford M.A. 1961; m. Ruth Margaret d. late Harold Joffre Amiel 1976; three s. Michael Joffre, Stephen Amiel, David Bruce; PRESIDENT, COCKFIELD BROWN INC. 1981- ; joined J. Walter Thompson Ltd. 1970-73, Dir. W. Candn. Operations; Cockfield Brown, Gen. Mgr. Toronto 1975, Extve. Vice Pres. 1979, Chief Operating Offr. 1980; Dir., Candn. Mental Health Assn.; Inst. Candn. Advertising; Anglican; recreations: running; photography, sailing; Club: Leander; Home: 47 Poplar Plains Cres., Toronto, Ont. M4V 1E9; Office: 1 St. Clair Ave. E., Toronto, Ont. M4T 2V9.

GALLOWAY, Col. Andrew Strome Ayers, E.D., C.D.; b. Humboldt, Sask. 29 Nov. 1915; s. Andrew Scott Jubilee and Bertha Maude (Strome) G.; e. High Schs. Que. and Ont.; m. Jean Caroline d. George Alexander Love, Aylmer West, Ont. 29 May 1948; two d, Jean Caroline (Mrs. R. W. Blackburn), Rosemary Dawn; HON. ED., HERALDRY IN CANADA since 1970; commd. 2nd Lt. Candn. Militia (The Elgin Regt.) 1934, trans. to Royal Candn. Regt. 1939 serving Overseas 5 yrs. UK, Tunisia, Sicily and Italy, N.W. Europe; apptd. to Regular Army 1946 rank Maj., Lt. Col. 1951, Col. 1962, retired 1969; mem. Directing Staff Candn. Army Staff Coll. 1951-54, C.O. 4th Bn. Candn. Guards 1955-57, GSO1 HQ 1 Candn. Inf. Div. 1957-59, mem. Nat. Defence Coll. 1961-62, Commdr. Fort Churchill 1962-64, Mil. Naval and Air Attaché Germany 1965-68; Hon. Lt. Col. Gov. Gen.'s Foot Guards 1969-79; Commandant RCAC Bisley Team 1974-76; mem. Fed. Dist. Council St. John Ambulance; Pres. Ottawa Un. Services Inst. 1978; Ottawa Br. Monarchist League 1978-80; Serving Brother, Most Venerable Order of St. John of Jerusalem; Chevalier, Ordre Militaire et Hospitalier de St. Lazare de Jérusalem; rec'd Centennial Medal 1967 and Queen's Jubilee Medal, 1977; Boy Scouts Assn. Can. "Thanks Badge" 1964; Past Pres. P. Cons. Assn. Ottawa-Carleton and def. cand. g.e. 1972; Contrib. Ed. Legion Magazine; author various articles Candn., Brit., Am. and foreign periodicals and newspapers; Hon. Life mem. RCR Assn. London, Ont.; Gov. Gen.'s Foot Guards

Assn. Ottawa; Hon. Pres. Ottawa and District Garrison Sgts' Assoc.; Hon. Vice Pres. N. Am. Br. Grenadier Guards Assn.; Pubs: 'A Regiment at War' 1979, 'The General Who Never Was' 1981, 'Beddoe's Canadian Heraldry' 1981; mem. Royal Candn. Legion (Past Pres. Ottawa Br.); mem. RCMI (Toronto); mem. Cavalry and Guards Club. (London Eng.); Fellow, Heraldy Soc. Can.; Anglican; Address: "Redstones," 1922 Alta Vista Dr., Ottawa, Ont.

GALLOWAY, Charles Thomas Peffers, B.A., F.S.A., F.C.I.A., M.A.A.A.; insurance executive; b. Buckingham, P.Q. 26 April 1927; s. Andrew Scott Jubilee and Bertha Maude (Strome) G.; e. University College (Toronto), B.A. 1950; m. Frances Alice, d. David Mackey, 26 Oct. 1956; children: Charlene Angela, Pamela Frances, Deborah Sue; PRES. AND CHIEF EXTVE. OFFR., THE NAT. LIFE ASSNCE. CO. OF CAN., since 1976; joined present Company as Actuarial Clerk, 1950; apptd. Assistant Actuary, 1953; Associate Actuary, 1955; and Actuary, 1957; Vice-Pres. and Actuary 1963; a Dir. 1973; Pres. 1975; Dir., Dominion Ins. Corp., Continental Ins. Co. of Can.; Pres. Canadian Institute of Actuaries, 1980-81; Protestant; Home: 385 Woburn Ave., Toronto, Ont. M5M 1L4; Office: 522 University Ave., Toronto, Ont. M5G 1Y7

GALT, Thomas Maunsell, F.S.A., F.C.I.A.; company chairman; b. Winnipeg, Manitoba, 1 Aug. 1921; s. late George F. and late Muriel Julyan (Maunsell) Galt (Mrs. R.M. Gemmel); e. Ashbury Coll., Ottawa; Lakefield (Ont.) Prep. Sch.; Arnprior (Ontario) High School; Queen's University; University of Manitoba, B.Comm. 1948; m. Helen W., d. late George Duncan Hyndman, Southboro, Mass., 15 June 1942; children: Lesley Maunsell (Mrs. S.R. Brown), George Hyndman; CHAIRMAN, CHIEF EXTVE. OFFR. & DIR., SUN LIFE ASSURANCE CO. OF CAN. since 1978; Chrmn. and Dir., Sun Life Assur. Co. of Canada (U.K.) Ltd.; Chmn. and Dir., Sun Life Assurance Co. of Canada (U.S.); Dir., Bank of Montreal; Canadian Pacific Enterprises Inc.; Canron Ltd.; Stelco Inc.; Textron Canada Ltd.; Tor. Symphony Orch.; The Can. Club; The Wellesley Hospital Research Foundtn.; joined the Co. as a Clerk, Math. Dept. 1948, Asst. Actuary 1954, Vice-Pres. and Chief Actuary 1963, Extve. Vice-Pres. 1968; el. a Dir. 1970; Pres. and Chief Oper. Offr., 1972; Pres. and Chief Exec. Offr. 1973; served in 2nd World War; Flight Lieut., R.C.A.F. 1941-45; Clubs: Toronto, York, Toronto Golf; Mt. Royal, St. James's, Mt. Bruno Country, Royal and Ancient Golf Club of St. Andrews; Home: 297 Russell Hill Rd., Toronto, Ont. M4V 2T7; Office: P.O. Box 4150, Stn. A, Toronto, Ont. M5W 2C9

GALVIN, Edward Anthony, B.S.; industrialist; b. Richmond, Cal., 10 Jan. 1913; s. William Joseph and Gertrude Anna (Planz) G.; e. Long Beach (Cal.) Polytechnic High Sch.; Univ. of S. Cal., B.S. 1938; m. Frances Esther, d. Percival Merton Bell, 20 Sept. 1938; children: Edward Anthony, Nancy Kathryn Peters; PRES., POCO PETROLEUMS LTD.; POCO OIL LTD.; since 1974; Dir., Norcen Energy Resources Ltd.; Alberta Energy Co. Ltd.; Bathurst Paper Ltd.; Domglas Inc.; Consolidated-Bathurst Inc.; Investors International Mutual Fund; Investors Mutual Fund of Canada; Investors Growth Fund of Canada Ltd.; Coleman Collieries Ltd.; Bonanza Oil and Gas Ltd.; Investors Japanese Mutual Fund Ltd.; Plant Foreman, The Texas Co., Long Beach, Cal., 1933; Supt. Gas Operations, DelValle Gasoline Co. California, 1940; Natural Gas and Natural Gasoline Analyst, Petroleum Adm. for War, Los Angeles, 1942; Chief Petroleum Engr., Western Gulf, Los Angeles, 1945; Canadian Gulf Oil Ltd. 1954; Gen. Mgr., Pathfinder Petroleums Ltd., 1955-59; subsequently Medallion Petroleums Ltd. where apptd. Pres. and Gen. Mgr. 1959; Pres. of present Co. (formed by amalg. Medallion Petroleums) 1965; Chrmn. of Bd. 1973; reg'd Prof. Engr. State. of Cal.; Life mem., Candn. Petrol. Assn. (Chrmn. 1972); Assn. Prof. Engrs. & Geols. Alta.; Sigma

Gamma Epsilon; Protestant; recreations: golf, fishing; Clubs: Calgary Golf & Country (Pres. 1973-74); Ranchmen's; Calgary Petroleum; Home: 4103 Crestview Rd., Calgary, Alta. T2T 2L5; Office: 700, 555-4 Ave. SW, Calgary, Alta. T2P 3E7

GAMPEL, Morison (prof. known as C.M. Gampel); actor; stage director; b. Montreal, P.Q., 19 Feb. 1921; s. Abraham and late Sofie (Matorin) G.; m. Annette Hunt; one d. Abigail; began acting career with Little Theatre in Niagara Falls, Ont.; played in two amateur plays, and num. radio shows over CKTB, St. Catharines, Ont.; joined three prof. cos. in Niagara Falls, N.Y., Buffalo, and Rochester N.Y., playing about 30 rôles within first year; proceeded to N.Y. and scholarship with Neighbourhood Playhouse Sch. of Theatre and then returned to Can. when he joined the Candn. Army; leaving the Army, played stock in Jennerstown, Pa., Milford, Pa., Boston, Newport, East Hampton, Atlantic City, and has played on approx. 2000 TV shows orig. from N.Y.; Broadway debut in Shaw's "Captain Brassbound's Conversion" in support of Edna Best; followed by "Richard II" in support of Maurice Evans; then Tabori's "Flight into Egypt" dir. by Elia Kazan; Arthur Miller's "The Crucible"; Shaw's "Saint Joan"; "Compulsion"; in 1956 was engaged as "standby" for Sir Ralph Richardson in "Waltz of the Toreadors" by Jean Anouilh, subsequently taking over the rôle of Gen. St. Pé for one third of its Broadway run; in Christopher Fry's "The Firstborn", Played on Broadway opposite Katharine Cornell and Anthony Quayle, as the Pharaoh and when the Co. was invited to Israel (10th anniversary of the State); toured 50 cities in leading male rôle of Gibson's "The Miracle Worker", 1962; featured on Broadway in "Girl Who Came to Supper" musical by Noel Coward; revival of Front Page; featured opposite Shirley MacLaine in film "Desperate Characters"; was the Commandant of U.S. Marine Corps in "Hail"; featured as Charles Bronson's boss in "Death Wish", the psychiatrist in "Annie Hall"; film roles in "Fire Power", "The Changeling" (filmed in Vancouver), "The Promise of Love"; played in hundreds of commercials; played on TV series "Guiding Light", "All My Children"; toured in support of Ethel Merman in revival of "Call Me Madam"; was Dr. Chumley opposite Shirley Booth in "Harvey"; played in several off-Broadway productions; served in 2nd World War with Candn. Army, rank of Sgt.; mem., The Players; Actors Equity Assn.; Am. Fed. of TV & Radio Artists; Screen Actors Guild; well known as drama coach with own studio; Hebrew; recreations: chess, golf; Address: 400 W. 43rd St., Apt. 29M, New York, N.Y. 10036.. and care S. Gampel, 5986 Main St., Niagara Falls, Ont. L2G 5Z8

GANONG, David A., B.B.A., M.B.A.; Manufacturer; b. St. Stephen, N.B. 14 Sept. 1943; s. Philip D. and Margaret (Alison) G.; e. High Sch. St. Stephen, N.B. 1961; Univ. of N.B. B.B.A. 1965; Univ. of W. Ont. M.B.A. 1970; m. Diane d. Eugene Simpson, St. Stephen, N.B. 8 July 1972; children: Bryana, Aaron Nicholas; Pres. and Dir. Ganong Bros. Ltd.; Cannem, Hudson Ltd.; Niven M. Jackson (1973) Ltd.; Dir. Print'n Press; New Brunswick and Candn. Railway Co.; Gov. APEC; mem. VACRED, YPO, Confectionery Mfg. Assn. Can. (Past Pres.); Baptist; recreations: skiing, tennis, golf; Home: 44 Union St., St. Stephen, N.B. E3L 2B1; Office: Milltown Blvd., St. Stephen, N.B. E3L 2X5

GANONG, Rendol Whidden; company executive; b. St. Stephen, N.B., 2 Oct., 1906; s. Arthur D. and Berla Frances (Whidden) G.; e. Royal Mil. Coll., Ont., 1924-26; m. Eleanor Katherine Deacon of St. Stephen, N.B., 11 Oct. 1941; CHRMN. GANONG BROS. LTD.; Past Pres., Atlantic Prov. Econ. Council; mem., Bd. of Dirs., C.B.C. 1958-61; Mayor, Town of St. Stephen; entered family firm 1926; served in 2nd World War overseas with R.C.A.F.; mem., Confect. Chocolate and Coca Indust. Can. (Pres.

1947): recreations: farming Home: Water St., St. Stephen, N.B.; Office: 2 St. Croix St., St. Stephen, N.B.

GANSNER, Hon. Leo Simeon, B.A., B.Com.; judge; b. Nelson, B.C. 3 Jan. 1909; s. Christian Gansner; e. Univ. of B.C., B.A., B.Com. 1935; m. Margaret Annette (Netta) d. late John Harvey; 28 Dec. 1939; children: Rosemary Schmidt, Harvey L.; JUDGE, CO. COURT OF FOOTENAY, B.C. 1978- ; called to Bar of B.C. 1938; cr. Q.C. 1964; law practice with Charles Braid Garland, Q.C. 1939-65; apptd. Judge, Co. Court of West Kootenay and Local Judge Supreme Court of B.C. 1965; Chancellor, Notre Dame Univ. of Nelson 1978- ; mem. Pub. Adv. Bd. B.C. Habital Conserv. Fund; mem. W. Kootenay Naturalists; E. Kootenay Hist. Soc.; Kootenay Mountaineering Club; United Church; recreations: back-packing, hiking, skiing, gardening; Home: 2004 - 7th St. S., Cranbrook, B.C. V1C 4L4; Office: Court House, 102 - 11th Ave. S., Cranbrook, B.C. V1C 2P2.

GANT, William George Bruce; executive; b. Vancouver, B.C., 20 Oct. 1927; s. late Alfred George and Emily (Bruce) G.; e. Pub. and High Schs., Medicine Hat, Alta.; Mont. Sch. of Mines; m. Jean Louise, d. late Frank Redmond, 28 Dec. 1950; children: Patricia Lea, Sharon Elizabeth, Nancy Lynn; ASSIST. GEN. MGR. MANCAL LTD. 1980- ; Pres., H. C. Price of Can. Ltd., 1968-77; Engn. Asst., Clk., Office Mgr., Sparling Davis Ltd., Edmonton, 1948-52; Acct. and Office Mgr., Northwest Industries Ltd. and Western Propeller Ltd., Edmonton, 1952-56; joined H. C. Price of Can. Ltd. as Office Mgr. 1957-60; Adm. Mgr. 1961-64; Vice Pres. 1964, Pres. 1968-75; Project Mgr., Price, Potashnik, Codell, Oman, J.V., Alyeska Pipeline 1974-75; Construction Mngr., Beafort Delta Oil Project 1975-76; Sen. Construction Mngr., Cdn. Arctic Gas, 1977; Vice-Pres., Operations, Lorcan Co. Ltd., 1977-79; Vice Pres. Project Management Services, Loram Internat. Ltd., 1979; Past Dir. Calgary Philharmonic Soc.; Dir., Calgary Exhn. & Stampede; Pres., Pipe Line Contractors Assn. Can., 1964 and 1970 (Dir. 1961-75); mem. Labour Comte. 1958-72, Chrmn 1965-68); Chrmn., Candn. Gas Assn., Contractors Sec., 1964 and 1971; mem., Candn. Standards Assn. (Chrmn Z183 and Z184 Jt. Welding subcomte. 1965-75); Pipeline Jt. Adv. Council; Freemason; United Church; recreations: skiing, curling, Club: Rotary; Calgary Petroleum Club; Home: 1416 Craig Rd. S.W., Calgary 9, Alta. T2V 2S8; Office: 840 6th Avenue S.W., Calgary T2P 2M7

GANZ, Sam; manufacturer; b. Czechoslovakia, 22 Oct. 1928; s. late Samuel and late Minge (Yanger) G.; e. Grade Sch. educ. in Europe; m. Gitta, d. late Howard L. Stein, 25 March 1951; children: Howard, Mindy; Founder and Pres., Capitol Textiles Ltd., since 1965; Vice-Pres. and Secy.-Treas., Ganz Bros. Toys; began in toy business in 1950; spent some of war yrs. in German concentration camps; liberated by Am's in Buchenwald, 1944; came to Can. 1948; el. Pres., Candn. Toy Mfrs. Assn., 1968 (Dir., 1965, Vice-Pres. 1966); mem., B'nai B'rith; Hebrew; recreations: golf, fishing; Home: 16 Dorchester St., Downsview, Ont. M3H 3J1; Office: 39 Orfus Rd., Toronto, Ont. M6A 1L7

GARDINER, Frederick Goldwin, Q.C., B.A., LL.D.; b. Toronto, Ont., 21 Jan. 1895; e. Univ. of Toronto, B.A. (Pol. Econ.) 1917 (Alex McKenzie Scholarship); Osgoode Hall (Gold Medallist) 1920; Counsel GARDINER, ROBERTS, Hon. Chrmn., Mack Trucks Mfg. Co. of Can. Ltd.; Hon. Chrmn., Metro Toronto 1979; Amerock Ltd.; A.P. Green Fire Brick Co. Limited; Honorary Director of Canadian National Exhibition; apptd. Chairman (first) Council of Metropolitan Toronto, 1953, retired Dec. 1961; called to the Bar of Ont., 1920; cr, K.C. 1938; served in World War 1916, with C.M.R. and Royal Flying Corps; Past Pres. Children's Aid Soc. of York Co.; Hon. Pres., Toronto Br. Goodwill Industries Inc.; Reeve, Forest Hill Village, 1936-49; Warden, County of York, 1946; Past

Pres., P. Conservative Business Men's Assn.; Past Vice-Pres., Ontario Conservative Assn.; Subject of biography, "Big Daddy": Frederick Gardiner and the building of Metropolitan Toronto, by Tim Colton, 1980; Freemason; United Church; Clubs: Granite, National; Home: 130 Old Forest Hill Rd., Toronto, Ont. M5P 2S1; Office: 5th floor, 120 Adelaide St. W., Toronto, Ont. M5H 1T5

GARDINER, George Ryerson, B.Com., M.B.A.; stockbroker; b. Toronto, Ont., 25 Apl. 1917; s. Percy Ryerson and Gertrude Margaret (Corcoran) G.; e. Univ. of Toronto Schs.; Univ. of Toronto, B.Com. 1939; Harvard Business Sch., M.B.A. 1941; children: Judith, Michael, Christine, CHAIRMAN, GARDINER, WATSON LIMITED Member, Toronto Stock Exchange; C.O.B.; Scott's Hospitality Inc.; Rostland Corp.; Chmn., Commonwealth Holiday Inns; Vice-Pres., The Ontario Jockey Club Limited; Pres., Toronto General Hospital Fdn; Trustee, Toronto Gen. Hosp.; Analyst with Kidder, Peabody and Company, Wall St., New York, 1941-42; Production Planning Supervisor, Chief of Standards Department, Personnel Mgr., Edge Moor Iron Works, Inc., Edge Moor, Delaware, 1942-46; Sigma Chi; Anglican; Clubs: Queen's Club; Badminton & Racquet; Home: 4 Old Forest Hill Rd., Toronto, Ont. M5P 2P7; Office: 11 Adelaide St. W., 12th Floor, Toronto, Ont. M5H 2R4

GARDINER, W.D.H.; retired banker; b. Chatham, Ont., 21 April 1917; s. William Henry and Elsie (Armstrong) G.; e. Kennedy Coll. Inst., Windsor, Ont. (Hon. Matric.); m. Jean Elizabeth, d. Dr. Franklin A. Blatchford, Fort William, Ont., 5 Sept. 1945; children: Donald, Campbell, Gregory; PRES., W. D. H.G. FINANCIAL ASSOC. LTD. Vancouver B.C.; served in Royal Navy, W.W. II, Retired 1946 Lt. Com. R.C.N.V.R.; Retired Vice-Chrmn., The Royal Bank of Canada, 1977-80; Dir., Chmn., Reed Stenhouse Co's Ltd.; B.C. Forest Products Limited; The Enst Asiatic Co. (Canada) Ltd.; Federal Pioneer Ltd.; Hastings West Investment Ltd.; Interprovincial Pipeline Ltd.; Mancal Ltd.; Ni-Cal Developments Ltd.; The Royal Bank of Canada; Scott Paper Ltd.; Shipping Corp. of New Zealand Woodward Stores Ltd.; Federal Pioneer Ltd. Protestant; recreations: golf, fishing, shooting, Clubs: (Toronto) York; Toronto Club; Rosedale Golf; (Vancouver) The Vancouver; Capilano and Shaughnessy Golf. Home: 109-4900 Cartier St., Vancouver, B.C. V6M 4H2; Office: Suite 1600, P.O. Box 11141, 1055 West Georgia St., Vancouver, B.C. V6E 3S5.

GARDINER, David Emmett, M.A.; actor; director; adjudicator; teacher and "Canadian Theatre" historian; b. Toronto, Ont., 4 May 1928, s. David and Madeleine Vera (Cunningham) G.; e. Public Schs., Lawrence Park Coll. Inst. (Valedictorian), Toronto, Ont.; Victoria Coll., Univ. of Toronto, B.A. (Art & Archaeol.) 1950, M.A. 1974 (Theatre); m. Dorothy Rosemary Wood (Kerr) 1965; one d., Jennifer Kathleen; mem. ACTRA; Actor's Equity; Directors' Guild of Canada; Society of Film-makers; Exec. of Assn. Canadian Theatre History; Board of Governors, National Theatre School; Chrmn., Candn. Theatre Centre Comte., which estbd. the "National Theatre Sch. of Canada" (Montreal-Stratford) in 1960, and co-author of the blueprint of sch. aims, curriculum, etc: Past Vice-Pres., Candn. Theatre Centre; former Gov., Dom. Drama Festival; former mem. T.V. Producers Assn.; Actor with original post-war Hart House Theatre group under Robert Gill, performing as Othello, MacBeth, Marc Antony; Asst. to Warden of Hart House, Univ. of Toronto, 1951-52; 1949-59, prof. acting career with Straw Hat Players (4 seasons), Crest Theatre, New Play Society, Jupiter Theatre, Canadian Repertory Theatre (Ottawa), Brae Manor Theatre (Quebec), "Spring Thaw", "Clap Hands"; 1956-57, Canadian Players tour of "Hamlet" (Horatio), and "Peer Gynt" (8 roles) at Stratford Shakespearean Festival, 1955 and 1956 seasons. "Tamburlaine the Great" (N.Y.C.), Edinburgh Festival. (Winner of Tyrone Guthrie Award, 1956); 1957-58. London, Eng., "Requiem for a

Nun" at Royal Court Theatre, and leading role in "Hunter's Moon" by Marc Connelly; with Old Vic Co., played London, Edin. Festival and the 1957-58 N. Am. tour of "Henry V" (Capt. Gower). "Twelfth Night" (Sea Capt.) and "Hamlet" (Fortinbras); created role of John Strang in "Marsh Hay" 1974, and role of Robert Rogers in "Pontiac and the Green Man" 1977; 1950-81, over 200 TV and radio roles with CBC, BBC. Granada, ITV Networks (London), and CBS (NYC) including role of Bellamy in C.B.C.'s "Bethune (1977), Wes McClung in CBC's "Nellie McClung" (1978), Gibson McFarland in C.B.C.'s "Artichoke" (1979), Brian Webster in C.B.C.'s "One of Our Own" (1979) and Larry Greene in 'Home Fires' 1980-2; films incl. role of Reverend Powelly in "Who Has Seen the Wind" (1977) and lead in 'The Field" for U.S. "Navy Log" TV series 1958; "Family Circles" (NFB 1950). "Oedipus Rex" (Stratford 1956); feature films incl. role of psychologist in "Prom Night" (1979), health minister in "Virus" (1979), Dr. Steffen in "If You Could See What I Hear" (1981) and the school principal in 'The Class of 1984' (1982); Cdn. Film Award, Best Sup. Actor, "The Insurance Man from Ingersoll", 1976; Stage Director of a number of plays in Toronto; Crest Theatre, 1960; Candn. Players Ltd. 1961, controversial Arctic "King Lear", "The Lady's Not For Burning", 1959 and "Masterpieces of Comedy"; Hart House productions "Look Back in Anger" 1964. "The Father" 1967; "Rosmersholm", 1972; "Sweet Bird of Youth", 1977; "Under Milk Wood", Neptune Theatre, Halifax, 1966, and "The Ecstasy of Rita Joe" (1st Eng. Prod. at Nat. Arts Centre, 1969); in 1959-69 joined CBC as contract television Drama Producer for such series as "Festival" ("The Applecart" 1962, "Doctor's Dilemma" 1963, "Uncle Vanya" and "Resounding Tinkle" 1964, "Yesterday the Children Were Dancing" 1968, "The Paper People" 1967 — (winner of 1968 Wilderness Award for direction and design), in "The Three Musketeers" (1969); Playdate ("Village Wooing" 1962, "Dear Liar" 1964); "The Serial" ("Jake and the Kid", "Train of Murder", "Reluctant Agent", "Member of Parl.", 1965); Producer/Dir. of "Quentin Durgens, M.P." series, 1966-67-68; Artistic Dir., Vancouver Playhouse 1969-71; Theatre Arts Offr., Canada Council 1971-72; has written many articles for journs. and contrib. chapter on Drama in English-Speaking Canada for "Canadian Annual Review" for 1961, 1962, 1963 and sections on Canada in 4th Ed. of The Oxford Companion to the Theatre; Work in Progress: 3 Vol., History of the Theatre in Canada; Dom. Festival Regional Adjudicator Maritimes (1961), Alta., B.C. (1952), CODL (1965 and 1973), WODL (1968), Simpson's Festival (1963 and 1968); Liberal; United Church; recreations: sports, art; Home: 72 Admiral Road, Toronto, Ont. M5R 2L5

GARDNER, Edwin Alexander, B.Arch., D.Sc., A.R.I.B.A., F.R.A.I.C., R.C.A.; architect; b. Pembroke, Ont. 14 July 1902; s. James Richard and Mary (Chamberlain) G.; e. elem. and high schs. Ottawa; McGill Univ. B.Arch. 1927; Ottawa Univ. D.Sc. 1963; m. Florence Victoria Grace d. William Emerson Calvert, Ottawa, Ont. 29 Sept. 1928; Partner, Burgess and Gardner (Archs.) 1928-40; Chief Arch. of Works & Bldgs. Sec. (civilian) Royal Candn. Naval Service 1940-44; Arch.-in-Charge Hosps. Constr. Dept. Veterans Affairs 1944-46; Asst. Chief Arch. Dept. Pub. Works Can. 1946-50, Chief Arch. 1950-62, Special Advisor to Depy. Min. re bldgs. abroad 1962-4; Designer of Commonwealth Air Training Mem. Green Island, Ottawa; Life Dir. and first Pres. Glebe Centre Inc. 1970- ; Hon. mem. Ont. Assn. Archs.; Freemason 33 Degree; Protestant; Address: Apt. 1003, 2625 Regina St., Ottawa, Ont. K2B 5W8.

GARDNER, J.A.F., M.A., Ph.D., F.C.I.C., F.I.A.W.S.; educator; b. Nakusp, B.C. 17 Aug. 1919; s. George Hunter and Maude (Williams) G.; e. Univ. of B.C. B.A. 1940, M.A. 1942; McGill Univ. Ph.D. 1944; m. Hilda Joyce d. William Harper 3 June 1944; children: Joseph William, Mary Lee Woodworth; DEAN, FACULTY OF FORES-

TRY, UNIV. OF BRIT. COLUMBIA and Prof. there since 1965; Research Assoc. McGill Univ. 1944-45; Research Chem. Howard Smith Paper Mills 1945-47; Head Wood Chem. Forest Products Lab. Vancouver 1947-63; Dir. Western Forest Products Lab. 1963-65; author over 50 publs. mainly in chem. and utilization of wood fields; Fellow, Internat. Acad. Wood Science; Fellow, Chem. Inst. of Canada; mem. Candn. Inst. Forestry; Tech. Assn. Pulp & Paper Indust.; Forest Products Research Soc.; Reg'd. Prof. Forester (Hon.) Phytochem. Soc.; Soc. Wood Science & Technol.; Bd. of Dir., Forintek; Protestant; recreations: fishing, skiing, tennis; Home: 5537 Wallace St., Vancouver, B.C. V6N 2A1; Office: #270-2357 Main Mall, Vancouver, B.C. V6T 1W5

GARDNER, John Milley, B.C.; executive; b. St. John's, Nfld., 27 Feb. 1924; s. Bertie Charles and Jean Elizabeth (Milley) G.; e. Ridley Coll., St. Catharines, Ont. 1941; McGill Univ., B.E. 1949; Centre d'Etudes Industrielles, Geneva, 1950; m. Barbara Ann, d. R.P. Jellett, 18 Apl. 1949; children: Roger Charles, Robin Wye, Julia Elizabeth, Suzanne Charlotte; MANAGER OF METAL PLANNING, ALCAN ALUMINIUM LTD. joined Aluminum Co. of Canada, Montreal, 1949; trans. to Kingston (Ont.) Works; engaged in Sales Engn. and Devel., London (Eng.) and Can. 1950-57; Asst. to Gen. Sales Mgr. 1958 and subsequently apptd. to Export Div. of Co.; returned to London, Eng., 1961 and held appt. Man. Director; served with RCNVR 1942-45; mem., Engn. Inst. Can.; Alpha Delta Phi; Liberal; Anglican; recreation: sailing; Home: Apt. 510, 1250 Pine Ave., Montreal, Que. Office: 1 Place Ville Marie, Montreal, Que.

GARDOM, Hon. Garde Basil, Q.C., M.L.A., B.A., LL.B.; politician; b. Banff, Alta. 17 July 1924; s. Basil and Gabrielle Gwladys (Bell) G.; e. Univ. of B.C., B.A., LL.B.; m. Helen Eileen Mackenzie 11 Feb. 1956; children: Kim, Karen, Edward, Brione, Brita,MIN. OF INTERGOVERNMENTAL RELATIONS, B.C. 1979- ; el. M.L.A. for Vancouver-Point Grey prov. g.e. 1966, re-el. since; Atty. Gen. 1975, 1979; Social Credit; Anglican; Office: 137 Parliament Bldgs., Victoria, B.C. V8V 1X4.

GARIGUE, Philippe, B.Sc., Ph.D., F.R.S.C. (1963), F.R.A.I.; university principal; b. Manchester, England, 13 Oct. 1917; s. Joseph and Giselle (Burke) G.; e. London Sch. of Econ., B.Sc. (Econ.) 1951; Univ. of London, Ph.D. 1953; Diploma of Defense Studies, Nat. Defence College, Kingston, 1973; m. Amalia Maria, d. Giovanni Battista Porcheddu, 11 Oct. 1946; three children: PRINCIPAL, GLENDON COLLEGE, YORK UNIV. Toronto; Chrmn., Family Superior Council of Que. Govt. 1964-71; Pres., Adm. Bd., Inst. of Urban Studies, Univ. of Montreal 1959-67; mem. Bd. Govs., Univ. of Moncton 1967-70; mem. Scient. Comn., Ecole Internat. de Bordeaux, Agence de Cooperation Culturelle et Technique 1971; Pres., Internat. Union of Family Organs. 1969; Vice-Chrmn. Consultative Council, Environment Canada, 1975-80; Lect., National Defence Coll., 1968; Staff School and College, Toronto, 1975; Research Assist., Univ. of Edinburgh 1951-53; Research Fellow, Univ. of London, 1953-54; Asst. Prof., McGill Univ., 1955-57; Full Prof., Pol. Sci., Univ. of Montreal, 1957-80, formerly Dean of Soc. Sci.; Pres., Adm. Council, Inst. for Urbanism, Univ. of Montreal, 1959-67; Comte on Acad. Status 1965-72; mem. Gov. Council Univ. of Moncton 1967-70; mem. Joint Commis. of Univ. Council of Univ. Assembly for the reorgan. of the Univ. of Montreal, 1968-70; mem. Consultative Comte, Centre of Eur. Stu. & Doc. 1975-77; served in 2nd World War; joined Brit. Army, 1939; Sandhurst Royal Mil. Acad.; Commnd. in Royal Fusiliers; Special Air Service (African Campaign, Italy and Austria); attained rank of Captain; Publications: Changing Political Leadership in West Africa (Thesis, 1953); "A Bibliographical Introduction to the Study of French Canada", 1956; "Etudes sur le Canada Français", 1958; "La Vie Familiale des Canadiens Français", 1962, re-ed.

1970; "L'Option politiques des Canadiens Français", 1963; "Analyse du comportement familial", 1967; "Bibliographie de Quebec (1955-65)" 1967; "Science Policy in Canada" 1972; "Famille, Science et Politique", "Famille et Humanisme", "LE temps vivant" all 1973; "L'Humaine Demeure" 1974; "Gueres, Strategies et Societes", 1979; articles on pol. leadership in W. Africa, studies on coloured students in Gt. Brit., on the European family system, Defence Policy, Strategic Studies, etc.; Fellow, Roy. Anthrop. Inst.; Am. Anthrop. Soc.; Am. Sociol. Soc.; mem. Can. Econ. & Pol. Assn. (Vice Pres. 1959-60); Soc. Intern. des soc. de langue française; Am. Pol. Sci. Assn.; Soc. Candn. de Sci. Pol.; Royal Soc. of Can. (mem. of Council, Sect. I., 1975-76; of Comte. of Internat. Rel. 1977-); Acad. des Sci. Morales et Pol.; U.S. Strat. Inst.; Candn. Inst. of Strat. Stu.; Roy. United Services Inst. for Defense Stu. (U.K.); Founding Dir. & Vice-pres. (1965-69), Vanier Inst. of the Family; mem. of Counsel, Internat. Union of Family Org., 1965-75 (Pres. 1969-73); Secty., Council for Social Action, Conf. of Candn. Bishops (1966-70); awarded Knight Grand Cross. and Grand Officer 1972, 1978 and 1979; Hosp. and Mil. Order of St. John of Jerusalem, Rhodes and Malta; Grand Croix, Ordre de Cicernos 1971; plus 5 other military medals and 2 hon. citizenships; Literary Prize Prov. Quebec 1968; Catholic; Address: Glendon College, York Univ., Toronto Ont.

GARLAND, George David, B.A.Sc., M.A., Ph.D., F.R.S.C. (1959); university professor; b. Toronto, Ont., 29 June 1926; s. Nicholas Lowrie and Jean Irene (McPherson) G.; e. Univ. of Toronto Schs. (1937-43); Univ. of Toronto, B.A.Sc. (Engn. Physics) 1947; M.A. 1948; St. Louis Univ., Ph.D. 1951; m. Elizabeth Peat, d. A.S. MacMillan, Schumacher, Ont., 10 June 1949; children: Mary Isabelle, Nicholas, George David, Jr.; PROF. OF GEOPHYSICS, UNIV. OF TORONTO, since 1963; Secy. Gen., Internat. Union of Geodesy & Geophysics since 1963-73; Pres. International Union of Geodesy & Geophys 1979- ; Vice-Pres., Academy of Science, Royal Soc. of Can. 1980- ; Lectr., Physics, Univ. of Toronto, 1949-52; Geophysicist, Dom. Observatory, Ottawa, 1952-54; Prof. of Geophysics, Univ. of Alberta, 1954-63; Fields of Research: structure of the earth's crust, gravity, magnetic variations, geophysical exploration; mem., Assn. Prof. Engrs. Ont.; Am. Geophysical Union; Conservative; Protestant; recreations: camping, photography, collecting of Canadiana; Home: 194 Owen Blvd., Willowdale, Ont. M2P 1G7

GARLICK, Vernon Victor, B.Com., C.A.; executive; b. Toronto, Ont. 29 Jan. 1928; s. late Victor Lisle and late Evelyn Maybel (Farley) G.; e. Univ. of Toronto B.Com. 1951; C.A. 1954; m. Evelyn Elizabeth d. late James Matthew Ellis Mawson 18 Feb. 1950; children: Douglas Michael, Stephen Vernon, Donald Kevin, Melissa Jane; VICE PRES. & TREAS., UNION CARBIDE CANADA LTD. 1980- ; Dir., Consumers' Welding Supplies Ltd., Edmonton; Welders Supplies Ltd., Calgary; Medigas Ltd., Toronto; Campbell Films Ltd.; joined Deloitte Haskins and Sells as Accounting Student 1951; Acct., Union Carbide Canada Ltd. 1955, Asst. Mgr. Gen. Accounting 1958, Asst. to Secy. and Treas. 1960, Asst. Secy. 1964, Business Mgr.-Thermosetting Products, Plastics & Chems. Div. 1967, Div. Controller 1968, Distribution Mgr. 1970, Asst. to Treas. 1972, Asst. Treas. 1973, Controller 1974, Treas. 1976; mem. Ont. Inst. C.A.'s; Financial Extves. Inst.; Bd. Trade Metrop. Toronto; recreations: yachting, reading; Clubs: R.C.Y.C.; Great Lakes Cruising; Home: 95 Thorncliffe Park Dr., Toronto, Ont. M4H 1L7; Office: 123 Eglinton Ave. E., Toronto, Ont. M4P 1J3.

GARNEAU, Brig.-Gen. André, C.D., O. St.J.; army officer (ret.); b. Quebec, Que. 18 Feb. 1921; s. Gérard and late Andrée (de Varennes) G.; e. Univ. of Ottawa; m. Jean Richardson 1946; four s.; COMMISSIONER CANADIAN PENSION COMMISSION 1976- ; joined Gov. Gen.'s Footguards as Guardsman 1938; Regtl. Sgt. Maj.

and Lt., Univ. of Ottawa COTC 1940; trans. C.A. (Active) as Lt., Sept. 1942; served in 2nd World War, Can., U.K., N.W. Europe, with Regt. de Maisonneuve, rank Capt.; Candn. War Staff Course 1945-46; Staff Capt., Mil. H.Q., Montreal 1946, Quebec City 1947; Gen. Staff Offr. 3, H.Q. Central Command, Oakville, Ont. 1951; promoted Maj. and apptd. Gen. Staff Offr. 2 1952; with 2nd Bn. Royal 22e Regt. in Can. and W. Germany 1953; Dir. Mil. Studies, Coll. Mil. Royal, Saint-Jean, Que. 1957; Secy. Army Bd., Mil. Agency for Standardization. NATO, London, Eng. 1961; promoted Lt.-Col. 1962; Commdr. 3rd Bn. Royal 22e Regt. 1964; Head, Combat Arms Sec., Dir. Postings and Careers, Ottawa, Ont. 1966; promoted Col. and apptd. Candn. Forces Attaché, Yugoslavia and Greece 1968; Depy. Commdr. and C.O. Regular Support Staff, Central Mil. Area, Downsview, Ont. 1971; Administrative Secy. to the Gov. Gen. of Can. (ret.), 1972-76; Dir., Red Cross, Ottawa/Hull; R. Catholic; recreations: skiing, curling, tennis, swimming, reading, gardening; Home: 470 Oakhill Rd., Rockcliffe, Ont. K1M 1J6; Office: DVA Memorial Building, Wellington St., Ottawa

GARNER, Fred G.; executive; b. London, Ontario 1925; e. Univ. of Toronto Pol. Science & Econ.; m. Eleanor Dymond, 1950; children: Tom, Jane; PRESIDENT, B. F. GOODRICH CANADA INC. 1979- ; former sr. account extve. Toronto advertising agency; Brand Mgr. Lever Brothers, Toronto; joined B. F. Goodrich Canada Inc. 1962 Mgr. Market Planning, Gen. Marketing Mgr. Tire Div. 1966, Vice Pres. Tire, Marketing Operations 1969, Vice Pres. Internat. Div. Akron, Ohio 1973, Vice Pres. and Gen. Mgr. Indust. Products Kitchener 1977; recreations: tennis, skiing, golf, music, art; Home: 336 Whitmore Dr.; Waterloo, Ont. N2K 1X4; Office: Kitchener, Ont. N2G 4J5.

GARNSWORTHY, Most Rev. Lewis, B.A., L.Th., D.D. (Ang.); b. Edmonton, Alta., 18 July 1922; s. Leonard and Lilian (Kingsland) G.; e. Univ. of Alta., B.A. 1943; Wycliffe Coll., Toronto, L.Th., D.D.; St. Augustine's Coll., Canterbury, Eng.; m. Jean Valence, d. late John Allen, 7 Aug. 1954; children: Peter John, Kathleen Jean; ARCHBISHOP OF TORONTO, and Metropolitan of Ontario; since (Suffragan Bishop 1968) Assistant Curate, St. Paul's Ch., Halifax, 1945; St. John's Norway, Toronto, 1945-48; Rector, St. Nicholas, Birchcliff, 1948-56; Church of the Transfiguration, 1956-60; St. John's, York Mills, 1960-68; recreations: gardening, reading; Clubs: Albany; York; Home: 50 CastleFrank Rd. Toronto, Ont. M4W 2Z6; Office: Synod House, 135 Adelaide St. E., Toronto, Ont. M5C 1L8

GARON, Hon. Jean, M.N.A.; politician; MIN. OF AGRICULTURE, FISHERIES AND FOOD, QUE. 1979- ; el. M.N.A. for Lévis prov. g.e. 1976, re-el. since; Min. of Agric. 1976; economist; lawyer; Parti Quebecois; Office: 200-A, Chemin Ste-Foy, 12th Floor, Québec, Qué. G1R 4X6.

GARON, Roger D.; executive; b. Sherbrooke; Que., 19 May 1930; s. Antoine and Irène (Letarte) G.; m. Thérèsa, d. Joseph Morin, Welland, Ont., 16 Nov. 1952; children: Richard, Michel, Mark; CHAIRMAN OF THE BOARD AND CHIEF EXECUTIVE OFFICER, ARONELLE TEXTILES LTD.; Dir., Domco Industries Ltd.; Paragon Business Forms Ltd.; David Lord Ltée.; National Hees Enterprises Ltd.; Andrès Wines Ltd.; Coll.; Liberal; Roman Catholic; Home: 3970 Maricourt St., St. Hyacinthe, Que. J2S 3S1; Office: 2955 Cartier, St. Hyacinthe, Quebec J2S 1L4

GARRAN, John Richard, B.E.; trade commissioner; b. Hartford, Eng. 19 Apl. 1939; s. Richard Randolph and Kathleen Ida (Boswell) G.; e. Melbourne (Australia) Grammar Sch.; Melbourne Univ. B.E. (Mech.) 1962; m. Irene Wilma d. William Ernest Purnell, Victoria, Australia 28 March 1964; children: Kathy May, Stephen John;

AUSTRALIAN CONSUL GEN. Toronto 1979- ; Asst. Trade Commr. Johannesburg, S. Africa 1969-72; First Secy. (Comm.) Lima, Peru 1973; Consul (Comm.) Sao Paulo, Brazil 1974-75; Comm. Counsellor Berlin 1976-78; mem. Inst. Engrs. Australia; Assoc., Inst. Mech. Engrs. (UK); Anglican; Office: (P.O. Box 69) 2324 Commerce Court W., Toronto, Ont. M5L 1B9.

GARRICK, David Elwood, B.A.; b. Toronto, Ont., 20 Aug. 1939; s. James Marshall and Marjorie Elizabeth (Binkley) G.; e. Swansea Pub. Sch. and Runnymede Coll. Inst., Toronto; Waterloo Univ., B.A.; m. Joy, d. Owen W. Fonger, Thornhill, Ont., 27 June 1964; children: Kimberley, David James; GENERAL MGR., CN TOWER,; joined Cndn. Nat. Exhibition as Asst. Stadium Mgr. 1962; Secy. and Concessions Mgr. 1967; Asst. Gen. Mgr. 1969; Gen. Mgr. 1972; Trustee, Showmen's League of Am.; Pres. Candn. Assn. Exhns.; Dir. Internat. Assn. of Fairs and Exhns.; Dir. Ont. Motor League; Freemason; Shriner; United Church; recreations: skiing, curling, sailing; Club: Rotary; Home: 8 Grenadier Hts. Toronto, Ont. M6S 2W6; Office: 301 Front St. W., Toronto, Ont. M5V 2T6

GARRIGAN, John William, B.Com.; executive; b. Kingston, Ont., 6 May 1934; s. William Joseph and Evelyn Margaret (Jeroy) G.; e. Queen's Univ., B.Com. 1958; m. Marielle, d. Joseph McKenzie, Cap de La Madelaine, Que., 19 June 1962; children: Bruce, Brian, Michelle; CHRMN. OF BOARD, PRICE & PIERCE INTERNATIONAL INC. since 1979; with Canadian Industries Ltd. in various mang. positions 1958-65; with Consolidated-Bathurst Ltd. in various posts incl. Vice-Pres. and Gen. Mgr., Concel Inc. (U.S. subsidiary) 1965-71; Pres. and CEO, Price and Pierce Int. Inc. 1971-79; Vice-Pres., TKM (U.S.A.) Holdings Inc.; R. Catholic; recreations: astronomy, skiing, swimming; Club: Canadian (N.Y.); Sky Club (N.Y.); Home: 60 Pine Brook Rd., Monsey, N.Y. 10952; Office: 522 Fifth Ave., New York, N.Y. 10036

GARRIOCK, Robert Norn, B.S.A.; broadcasting executive; b. Toronto, Ont., 20 Feb. 1922; s. Robert and May Aythleen (Adsheed) G.; e. N. Toronto Coll. Inst.; Ont. Agric. Coll., B.S.A. 1949; m. Orpha Garfield, d. Garfield Laurier Farr, 14 June 1947; children: Roger C., Anne E., Christopher N.F., Robert Kirkwall; MANG. DIR. ENG.-TV, CANDN. BROADCASTING CORP.; Pres., Millwood Investments Ltd.; joined CBC 1949; held various positions incl. Commentator, Producer, Supervising Producer, Regional Producer, Asst. Nat. Supvr., Program Dir. Radio, Asst. Program Dir. TV Network, Dir. of TV; Columnist for former Toronto Telegram; served with RCNVR during World War II; on loan overseas to RN with Motor Torpedo Boats, 65th MTB Flotilla; rank Lt.; Mentioned in Despatches; Councillor and Reeve, Woodbridge, Ont.; mem. York Co. Council for 10 yrs.; Chrmn., Vaughan Twp. Planning Bd. 5 yrs.; mem. Toronto Planning Bd. 4 yrs.; Chrmn. Bd. of Govs., Seneca Community Coll. (Bd. mem. since Coll. formation); mem., Bd. Trade Metrop. Toronto; Agric. Inst. Can. (Past Pres. Toronto Br.); United Church; recreations: gardening, tennis, municipal politics; Club: Celebrity; Home: (Box 54) 9000 Islington Ave., Woodbridge, Ont. L4L 1A9; Office: (Box 500) Terminal A, Toronto, Ont. M5W 1E6

GARRIOCK, William C., B.Com., M.B.A.; manufacturer; b. N. Vancouver, B.C. 11 Aug. 1938; s. Robert and Charlotte (Weeks) G.; e. N. Vancouver High Sch. 1956; Univ. of B.C. B.Com. 1961; Northwestern Univ. M.B.A. 1963; m. Joyce E. McKibbin 4 Nov. 1961; children: Janice, Jeffrey, David, Robert John; PRESIDENT AND DIR. MILES LABORATORIES LTD. since 1975; Pres. and Dir. Household Cleansers Ltd.; The S.O.S. Manufacturing Co. of Canada Ltd.; Product/Sales Mgr. Household Products Div. present co. 1969, also held positions of Business Planning Mgr. and Group Marketing Mgr.; served 6 yrs. in Marketing and Mfg. positions General Foods; mem. Faculty of Business Adm. Univ. of B.C. 1963-64;

Chrmn. of Bd. Proprietary Assn. Can. 1977-78; mem. Young Pres's Organ.; Protestant; recreations: squash, golf, boating; Home: 2 Harfleur Rd., Agincourt, Ont. M1T 2X5; Office: 77 Belfield Rd., Rexdale, Ont. M9W 1G6.

GARSIDE, Clement; forestry executive; e. Burnaby South High Sch.; Sprott-Shaw Business Coll.; SR. VICE PRES. OPERATIONS, CRESTBROOK FOREST INDUSTRIES LTD.; Sales Mgr. Candn. White Pine, MacMillan, Bloedel Ltd. 1947, Plant Mgr. Alberni Plywood 1948, and Alberni Pacific Lumber 1951, Gen. Mgr. W. Dist. Sawmills 1953; Dir. Sawmill Operations, Columbia Cellulose Co. Ltd. 1957, Vice Pres. Interior Operations 1964, Vice Pres. Lumber & Logging Operations 1968-69; Chrmn. Interior Forest Labour Relations Assn.; Clubs: Marine Drive Golf; Cranbrook Golf & Country; Office: (P.O. Box 4600) Cranbrook, B.C. V1C. 4J7

GARTRELL, Rt. Rev. Frederick Roy, B.A., L.Th., B.D., D.D. (Ang.); bishop; (Retired) b. Hamilton, Ont., 27 March 1914; s. William Frederick and Lily Martha (Keeble) G.; e. McMaster Univ., B.A. 1935; Wycliffe Coll. L.Th. 1938, B.D. 1944, D.D. 1962; St. John's Coll., D.D. 1964; m. Grace Elizabeth, d. William Wood, 25 Sept. 1940; children: John, George, Jane, David; since 1970; has held various eccl. positions incl. Dean, Christ Ch. Cath., Ottawa, prior to present appt.; Founding Pres., John Howard and Elizabeth Fry Socs. of Man.; Prolocutor, Provincial Synod, Rupert's Land, 1960, General Synod, 1969; recreations: golf, gardening; Home: 1794 Barrie Rd., Victoria, B.C. V8N 2W7

GARWOOD, Audrey, R.C.A.; painter; printmaker; b. Toronto, Ont. 7 July 1927; d. John H. and Minnie (Robertson) Carwood; e. N. Vocational High Sch. and N. Toronto Coll. Inst.; Ont. Coll. of Art; Rijks Academie Amsterdam; La Grande Chaumiere Paris; m. 5 Feb. 1953; children: Evan Hosie, Spencer Hosie, Graham, Cameron; solo exhns. incl. York Univ. Toronto 1968; Univ. of San Francisco 1974; Lafayette Bank Gallery Uniontown, Pa. 1974; Berkeley (Cal.) City Hall 1975; Lafayette (Cal.) Lib. 1976; Univ. of Cal. Hayward 1978; rep. in various group exhns. incl. Nat. Gallery Can. Drawing & Print Show 1966; Internat. Exhn. Montreal 1971; Candn. Consulate Washington 1971; Contemporary Prints Pratt Inst. 1972; Internat. Print Exhn. Los Angeles 1977; San Francisco Art Festival (invitational) 1974; Palo Alto (Cal.) Invitational 1975; rep. in pub., corporate and private colls. incl. Art Gallery Ont., La Jolla Museum of Contemporary Art Cal.; recipient Print Award Candn. Soc. Printmakers; Sterling Trust Award Candn. Painters & Engravers; Forester Award Ont. Soc. Artists; Purchase Award San Francisco Art Festival; illustrator "Flavors of Southeast Asia" 19 ; "101 Productions San Francisco" 19 ; mem. Ont. Soc. Artists; Candn. Soc. Graphic Art; Candn. Painters & Engravers; Cal. Soc. Printmakers; Artists Equity Assn.; represented by: Gustafson Gallery, 84 Yorkville Ave, Toronto, Ont.; NDP; recreations: dancing, travel; Home: 46 Stephenson Ave., Toronto, Ont.; Office: 401, 109 Niagara St., Toronto, Ont. Toronto, Ont.

GASCON, Jean; C.C. (1975), LL.D.; actor-director; b. Montreal, Qué. 1920; e. LL.D. Western Ont., Queen's, McGill, Bishop's, McMaster, Guelph, Montréal, Ottawa; DIRECTOR, THEATRE FOR NATIONAL ARTS CENTRE, since 1977; formed Le Theatre du Nouveau Monde 1951; Co-Founder and Dir., Nat. Theatre Sch. 1960 and subsequently Gen. Dir. there; directed Shakespeare's "Comedy of Errors", Stratford, Ont. as a consequence of which apptd. Assoc. Dir., Shakespearian Festival Foundation of Can. there 1964; Artistic Dir. of Stratford Festival since 1967; mem. Adm. Council National Film Board; has acted and directed in T.V. and operas; Awards include Molson Award (for promotion of better understanding between French and English cultures in Canada); Canadian Drama Award; $50,000 Royal

Bank Award 1974; named O.C. 1967 and elevated to C.C. 1975; Address: National Arts Centre, Ottawa, Ont.

GATTINGER, Friston Eugene, M.A., B.L.S.; librarian; b. Duff, Sask., 13 Oct. 1920; s. Jacob J. and Amelia (Haberstock) G.; e. Prov. Normal Sch., Regina, Sask. (1st Class Teachers Cert. 1939); Univ. of Sask., B.A. 1949, M.A. (Hon. in Eng.), 1951; McGill Univ., B.L.S. 1952; m. Edith Marguerite, d. Fred E. McAlpine, Nelson, B.C., 21 June 1949; CO-ORD. OF LIBRARY SERVICES, TORONTO BD. OF EDUC. 1980- ; Lectr. Univ. of Toronto (Innis Coll.) on Hist. of Educ.; taught school for approx. two yrs., engaged with Dept. of Nat. Health & Welfare (6 mths.) as Librarian (Cataloguer) 1952; subsequently Librarian & Registrar, Ont. Vet Coll., Guelph, Ont.; Univ. Librarian, Memorial Univ. of Nfld. 1962-67; Asst. Dir. of Lib., York Univ., Toronto 1967-69; Chief Librarian, Toronto Bd. of Educ. 1969-1980; served in 2nd World War with R.C.A.F. as Radar Tech. (3 yrs. on active service overseas), 1941-45; Lectr. in Eng. Lit.; author of: "A Century of Challenge", 1962 and numerous papers, etc.; Editor, A.P.L.A. Bulletin, 1965-67 (vols. XXIX; XXX; XXXI); Pres., Atlantic Provs. Lib. Assn., 1964-65; mem., Candn. Lib. Assn.; Am. Lib. Assn.; Candn. Assn. of Coll. & Univ. Libraries; United Church; recreations: violin, badminton, tennis, handicrafts; Home: 31 George Henry Blvd., Willowdale, Ont. M2J 1E3; Office: 155 College St., Toronto, Ont. M5T 1P6

GATTUSO, Pasquale; company officer; b. Montreal, P.Q., 30 April 1918: s. Paul and the late Lucrezia (Goro) G.; e. Notre-Dame de Mont Carmel Coll.; Univ. of Montreal; m. Lina Pierpaoli, 16 June 1945; children: Peter, Linda, Gloria; CHRMN. BD. GATTUSO CORP. LTD. (food merchants and processors, estbd. 1935) since 1966; Pres., Gattuso Olive Oil Corp. Ltd.; Vice-Pres., Prince-Gattuso Macaroni Co. Ltd.; Extve. Dir., Sogena Inc.; Dir., Prince Macaroni Mfg. Co.; Marc Carrière Ltée.; Buckingham Mills Ltd.; Hon. Life mem., Sons of Italy; served with Les Fusiliers de Mont-Royal, 1941; mem., Candn. Italian Business Men's Assn.; Pres., Italica Football Club; Vice-Pres. and Dir., The Italian Chamber of Comm. of Toronto; Montreal Bd. Trade; Olive Oil Assn. of Am.; Am. Spice Assn.; Candn. Mfrs. Assn.; Candn. Food Processors Assn.; K. of C.; R. Catholic; recreations: travelling, tennis, skiing; Home: 5649 Queen Mary Road, Hampstead, Montreal, P.Q. H3X 1X2; Office: 6694 Papineau St., Montreal, Que. H2G 2X2

GAUDAUR, Jacob Gill; sports manager; b. Orillia, Ont., 5 Oct. 1920; s. Jacob Gill and Alice (Hemming) G.; e. Orillia (Ont.) Coll. Inst., Sr. Matric. 1939; m. Isobel Grace, d. late Joseph Scott, 16 Apl. 1943; three d. Jacqueline, Diane, Janice; COMMR., CANDN. FOOTBALL LEAGUE, since 1968; with Burns Bros. & Co., Toronto, 1946; joined White Motor Co. of Canada as Salesman, 1947-51; Mgr., Hamilton Br., 1952-53; Mgr., Toronto Br. and Ont. Wholesale Mgr., 1954-55; Founder and Pres., Gaudaur Motor Co., 1956 and Jaygil Ltd., 1966; Pres., Hamilton Tiger-Cat Football Club, 1954; Pres. and Gen. Mgr. 1956, principle shareholder 1961; sold interest 1968; Pres., Eastern Football Conf. 1959; Candn. Football League 1962; served with RCAF as Pilot, 1942-45; Chrmn., Downtown Div., Hamilton Un. Appeal, 1967; Chrmn. Bd. of Dir. Candn. Football Hall of Fame; Chrmn. Adv. Bd. Candn. Football League Players' Pension Fund; Chrmn. Rules Cttee., C.F.L.; Freemason; Anglican; recreations: golf, oil painting; Clubs: Albany; Burlington Golf & Country; Hamilton; Variety; Home: 267 Roseland Cres., Burlington, Ont. L7N 1S4; Office: 11 King St. W., Toronto, Ont. M5H 1A3

GAUDEFROY, Henri, D.A.Sc., D.Sc., LL.D., P. Eng.; b. Montreal, P.Q. 18 June 1909; s. Arthur and Lucie (Chopin) G.; e. Mont-Saint-Louis Coll., Ecole Polytech., B.A.Sc. (Civil Engn.) 1933; Mass. Inst. of Tech., B.S. (Elect Engn.), 1934; Hon. D.A.Sc., Laval Univ., 1955;

D.Sc. Sherbrooke Univ., 1958, W. Ont., 1959, Montreal 1973; LL.D. Toronto 1961; m. Berthe Hervieux, 16 Aug. 1937; one s. Pierre; former mem., National Research Council, Ottawa, Reactor Safety Advisory Committee of Atomic Energy Control Board, Ottawa Atomic Energy Control Board, Ottawa; Electrical Engineer with Bell Telephone Co. of Canada, 1935-39; Assistant Professor of Math., Ecole Polytech., 1939, Assoc. Prof. and Asst. to the Dean and Registrar, 1943, Prof. 1946 and Head of the Dept. of Math., 1951, Dean 1953-66; apptd. to Candn. Internat. Devel. Agency, Ottawa, 1966; Dir. Gen. Special Advisors Div. Bilateral Programs Br. 1967; Candn. Ambassador to Tunisia 1972-74; Vice-Pres. i.c. Latin Am., Candn. Extve. Service Overseas 1974, retired June 1979; served in Res. Force (C.O. of Univ. Flight, 1948-53); awarded Coronation Medal, 1952; Queen's Jubilee Medal, 1977; Publications: "Secondary School Mathematics" (in French and used in many French High Schs.), and a no. of papers and other publ. pertaining to engn. educ. and student guidance; mem., Corp. of Prof. Engrs. P.Q.; Fellow and Hon. member, Engn. Inst. Can. (Chrmn. of Montreal Chapter, 1950; mem. of Council, 1951-54); Am. Soc. for Engn. Educ.; Home: 24 Surrey Dr., Town of Mt. Royal, Que. H3P 1B1

GAUDRY, Roger, C.C. (1968), B.A., B.Sc., D.Sc., D.C.L., LL.D., F.R.S.C. (1954), F.C.I.C.; chemist; company director; b. Quebec City, P.Q., 15 Dec. 1913; s. Marc and Marie-Ange (Frenette) G.; e. Laval Univ., B.A. 1933. B.Sc. (Chemistry), 1937, D.Sc. (Chemistry) 1940; Oxford Univ. (Rhodes Scholar) 1937-39; (hon.) D.Sc. Royal Mil. Coll. 1966; (hon.) D.Sc. British Columbia 1967; (hon.) Doctorate Clermont-Ferrand (France); (hon.) LL.D. McGill 1967; (hon.) D.C.L. Brock 1969; (hon.) LL.D., Toronto, 1966 Bishop's (1969), Fredericton (1968); LL.D., Concordia (1980); (hon.) D.Sc., Sask. (1970), Western (1976); m. Madeleine, d. Ivan E. Vallée, Quebec City, P.Q., 19 June 1941; children: Marc, Jean, Hélène, Thérèse, Denise; DIRECTOR, ALCAN ALUMINUM LTD. since 1977; Dir., Corby Distilleries since 1975; Pres. of Internat. Assn. of Univs., 1975-80; Rector, Univ. of Montreal, 1965-75; Vice Chrmn., Science Council of Can. 1966-72; Chrmn. 1972-75; Mem. of Council, United Nations Univ. (Toyko) 1974-80; Chrmn. of Council., U.N. Univ. (Tokyo) 1974-76; Asst. Prof. of Chem., Fac. of Med., Laval Univ., 1940-45, Assoc. Prof., 1945-50; Prof., 1950-54; Guest Lectr., the Sorbonne, Paris, 1954; Asst. Dir. of Research, Ayerst, McKenna & Harrison Ltd., Montreal, 1954-57, Dir., Ayerst, McKenna and Harrison Ltd. and Ayerst Laboratories, N.Y., 1957-65; vice-pres., 1963-65; awarded Pariseau Medal of "Assn. Candn. Française pour l'Advanc. des Sciences", 1958; Medal of Centenary of Can., 1967; Montreal Medal of Chem. Inst. of Can., 1974; also three times recipient of P.Q. Scient. Prize (1942, 46, 50) for publ. work; author or co-author of some 90 papers dealing with the chem. or metabolism of amino acids; mem. of Bd., Bank of Mont.; CDC Life Sciences Inc.; Connaught Labs. Ltd.; Omnimedic Inc.; Hoechst du Can. Ltée; mem. of Bd., S.K.W. Canada Ltd., 1978; mem. Econ. Council of Can. 1970-73; Pres., The Chem. Inst. of Can., 1955-56; R. Catholic; Office: Université de Montréal, Montréal, P.Q. H3C 3J7

GAUTHIER, Charles Arthur, M.P.; marchand; né Mistassini, P.Q. 12 mai 1913; fil de Pierre et Rose (Tremblay) G.; ép Laurette, fille d'Hormias Larouche, 19 juillet 1939; enfants: Francoise, Febienne, Hugues, Thérèse, Jeanne-Mance, Clément, Lola, Jean-Pierre; PROP., C.A. GAUTHIER LTEE (meubles) depuis 1940; Entrepreneur, Pompes funèbres; Député à la Chambre des Communes et Prés., Comn. scolaire; élu pour la première fois à la C. des C. pour Roberval, é.g., 1962; réélu en 1963; Dir. prov., Les Dir. de Funérailles et Embaumeurs de P.Q.; Crédit Social; Catholique r.; récréation: lecture; Clubs: Chevaliers de Colomb; résidence: 122, rue de l'Eglise, Mistassini, P.Q. G0W 2C0; établissement de commerce; 120 rue de l'Eglise, Mistassini, P.Q. G0W 2C0

GAUTHIER, Georges-E., O.C. (1967), M.Com.; federal public servant (retired); b. Sorel, Que., 30 Dec. 1911; s. Edouard and Anna (Cournoyer) G.; e. Univ. Montreal, M.Com., Licencié en Sciences Sociales, Econ. et Pol.; m. Claire, d. Joseph Blondin, 10 June 1940; children: Gilles, Lise, Edouard, Hélène; former Alternate Chrmn., Public Service Arbitration Bd. (1975-6); Public Service Staff Relations Bd., (Vice Chrmn. 1967-74); Asst. Dir. Gauthier, Civil Service Commission, 1952-57; Director Pay Research Bureau, 1957-64; Assoc. Commissioner, Centennial Comn., 1964-67; R. Catholic; recreation: golf; Clubs: Rivermead Golf; Home: 716 - 1833 Riverside Drive, Ottawa, Ont. K1G 0E8

GAUTHIER, Gilles; administrateur; né Palmarolle, Qué.; 28 mars 1935; f. Henri et Adeline (Grenon) G.; é. Primaire Ecole St-Paul 1947; Séminaire D'Amos (classique) 1949; Inst. St. Jean Bosco (comm. sr.) 1952; L'Acad. de Qué. (extention); Univ. Laval (cours corr. Finance et Placements) 1964; ép. Léonne, f. Nérée Aubé, La Sarre, Qué. 19 nov. 1955; enfants: Michelle, Louise, Murielle, Claude; PRES. COURCHESNE MERCURY S&S INC., depuis 1976; Président, Gestion Financiere R.N. Inc.; Place Donavan Inc.; Vice-Président et directeur, Canadian Financial Corporation; Dir., Canadian Affiliated Financial Corp.; Comptable div., Min. de la Voirie, Prov. Qué. 1952; Premier employé fondateur de Continental Discount Corp., à titre de gérant 1955, de dir. gén. adjoint 1960, de vice prés. exécutif 1972, Pres. and Chef de la dir., 1974; Commissaire, Comn. des Loisirs de la Ville de LaSarre; mem. Chambre de Comm. de la Prov. Qué.; ex-prés., Jeune Chambre de Comm. de La Sarre; Catholique r.; recreations: golf, chasse, pêche; Clubs: Richelieu (Prés. 1970); Beattie Golf (Prés. 1968-70); Kiwanis Club of Rouyn, Pres. 1980; Residence: 570 Guertin, Rouyn, Que.; Bureau: 1155 Larivière, Rouyn, Que.

GAUTHIER, Jacques, B.Sc.; pharmaceutical executive; b. Montreal, P.Q., 5 Jan. 1928; s. Antoinette (Morin) and late Henri S.G.; e. Univ. of Montreal, B.Sc. (Chem.), 1949; Univ. of Western Ont., grad., Mang. Adm., 1964; m. Louise, d. late J.A. Lapointe, 30 May 1953; one s. Yves; two d. Danielle, Christiane; VICE PRES., UPJOHN INTERNATIONAL since 1974; Group Vice-Pres. Upjohn International Inc. Sept. 1979- ; joined The Upjohn Co. of Canada as prof. Sales Representative, Sherbrooke and Montreal, P.Q., 1949; Dist. Sales Mgr. for P.Q. 1956; apptd. E. Can. Divn. Sales Mgr., 1961; Asst. Sales Mgr., 1963; Gen. Sales Mgr., 1964; Gen. Mgr., 1968; Pres. and Gen. Mgr. 1969; Gen. Mgr., Labs. Upjohn S.A.R.L., Paris 1971; Roman Catholic; recreations: golf, tennis, skiing, travelling; Office: Upjohn International Inc., 7000 Portage Rd., Kalamazoo, Mich. 49001.

GAUTHIER, Joachim George, R.C.A.; artist; b. North Bay, Ont. 20 Aug. 1897; s. Octave and Clara (Viau) G.; e. St. Mary's R. Cath. Separate Sch. North Bay; Tacoma, Wash. comm. art under V.A. Lewis, draughtsman and sculptor; m. Leonie d. Alfred Quesnel, Sudbury, Ont. 13 May 1924; children: Estelle, Clare, Paul, Edmond, Rosalie; served Art Dept. Sampson-Matthews Ltd. Toronto 37 yrs.; became assoc. with Franklin Carmichael, A. J. Casson and other mems. Group of Seven; numerous solo exhns. Toronto and Montreal incl. retrospective watercolour exhn. Arts & Letters Club 1976, Hal Johnson Gallery Toronto 1978; Libby's Gallery, Toronto, 1980, 1981; rep. in many pub., corporate and private colls. incl. Nat. Gallery Can., Art. Gallery Ont. and the Vatican; comnd. by Robert and Signe McMichael to paint 16 portraits of The Group of Seven and their contemporaries for The Collections Catalogue; mem. Royal Canadian Academy; Ont. Soc. Artists; Candn. Soc. Painters in Watercolour; Liberal; R. Catholic; Club: Arts & Letters; Address: 184 Ranleigh Ave., Toronto, Ont.

GAUTHIER, Robert, C.M., D.Paed., B.A., Ph.B., Ph.L., F.R.S.C.; educator; b. Cap Chat, P.Q., 10 Apl. 1902; s.

Dr. L. P. and Antoinette (Thibault) G.; e. Ottawa Univ., B.A., Ph.B., Ph.L., 1925; Univ. of Toronto Faculty of Educ. 1926; Univ. of Montreal, B.Paed., 1940; Laval D.Paed. 1952; D.Sc.Ed. Montreal, 1958; m. Juliette Roy, 1932; four children; Insp., Elem. Schs., Cochrane, Ont., 1927, Windsor, 1928; Master, Univ. of Ottawa Normal Sch., 1935; Dir. of French Instruction, Ont. Dept. of Educ., 1937-64; mem. of Comm. of Inquiry into Textbooks used by French-speaking pupils; conducted survey of systems of educ., Europe, 1949; UNESCO educ. mission, Burma, 1954; Candn. del., Internat. Conf. on Educ., Geneva, 1959; Lectr. in French Lit., Univ. of W. Indies, Trinidad 1964-65, Barbados 1965-66 for Candn. External Aid; Head of Inspection Br. Sch. of Lang., Public Service of Can. 1966-67; mem., Assn. Candn. des Educ. de Langue française (Past Pres.); Past Pres., Soc. de Confs. of Univ. of Ottawa; mem., Candn. Educ. Assn.; Nat. Adv. Comte. on Educ. Research; Assn. d'Educ. d'Ont.; Hon. mem., Assn. acadienne d'Educ.; awarded Ordre du Mérite scolaire franco-ontarien. 1947; Offr. d'Acad. République française, 1948; de l'Ordre 'Honneur et Mérite'. 1952; Coronation Medal, 1953; Confederation Centenary Medal, 1967; author of: 'Frou-Frou et Fin-Fin' (primer) 1939 and its workbook, 1941: 'Chez Nous', 1949; 'Notre Famille', guide pédagogique, 1950; 'Tan-Gau' (a natural method of learning a second lang.); Clubs: Richelieu (Toronto); Canadian (Ottawa); Home: 2011-400 Stewart, Ottawa, Ont. K1N 6L2

GAUTRIN, Henri F., B.A., C.E., L.Sc.; construction executive; PRESIDENT & CHIEF EXTVE. OFFR., A. JANIN & CO. LTD.; Chrmn. Janin Construction Ltd., Montreal; Janin Building and Civil Works Ltd., Toronto; Janin Western Contractors Ltd., Vancouver, B.C.; Pres. Namur Equipment Ltd.; Turnkey D.E.C.M. Ltd.; Dir., Page Construction Inc.; Regional Asphalt Ltd.; Carrières St. Maurice Inc.; Roy & Trottier Inc.; Sword Contracting Ltd.; Alumicor Ltd. (Toronto); A.D. Ross (Quebec) Inc.; Holding I.H.M. Ltd. (Montreal); Nootka Investments (Vancouver); Serem Ltd.; Industrial Machining Ltd.; Pax Constr. Inc.; mem., Candn. Inst. Mining and Metall.; Engn. Inst. Can.; Corp. Prof. Engrs. Que.; Assn. of Prof. Engrs., Ont.; Quebec Road Builders Assn. (Pres. 1966-68); Chrmn., Bd. of Governors, Candn. Association for Latin America, Cala; Vice-pres., Economic Expansion Council; Catholic; recreation: fishing; Clubs: St. Denis; Mount Stephen Club, Home: 1582 Sioux, Fabreville, Ville Laval, Que., H7P 4R8; Office: 2 Complexe Desjardins, Suite 3218, Montreal, Que.H5B 1B3

GAUVIN, Hon. Jean L., M.L.A., B.A., B.Ed.; politician; b. Inkerman N.B. 15 Nov. 1945; s. Joseph and Helene G.; e. Inkerman Elem. Sch.; Jacquet-River-Don Bosco Intermediate Sch.; Univ. of Moncton B.A., B.Ed.; m. Jacqueline d. Albert Bezeau 7 Oct. 1965; children: Serge, Robert, Rachel; MIN. OF FISHERIES, N.B. 1978- ; professor; el. M.L.A. for Shippegan-Les-Iles prov. g.e. 1978; K. of C.; P. Conservative; R. Catholic; Office: (P.O. Box 6000) King's Place, Fredericton, N.B. E3B 5H1.

GAUVIN, Michel; O.C. (1973), C.V.O. (1976), D.S.O., B.A.; diplomat; b. Quebec, Que., 7 April 1919; s. Stella (MacLean) and late Raymond G.; e. Coll. St. Charles Garnier, Quebec, Que., B.L. 1939; Laval Univ., 1939-40; Carleton Univ., B.A. 1948; m. Nguyen Thi Minh Huong; two s., Jean, Marc., one daugter Kim; AMBASSADOR TO PEOPLE'S REP. OF CHINA, 1980- ; on loan from Candn. Army and Dept. of External Affairs to Prime Minister's Office, 1946-50; Extve. Asst. to Undersecretary of State for External Affairs, 1950-51; postings: Ankara, 1951-53; Lisbon, 1953-55; Saigon, 1955-56; Caracas, 1958-59; Buenos Aires, 1959-60; Leopoldville, 1961-63; Nat. Defence Coll., Kingston, Ont., 1963-64; special assignments: special mission to Kenya, Ethiopia, Congo during Stanleyville crisis Nov. 1964 and to Dominican Republic, May-June 1965; Ambassador to Ethiopia, 1966-69, to Portugal 1969-70, to Greece 1970-75; special assignment:

Head of Candn. Delegation to ICCS at Saigon-Vietnam, 1973; Consul General of Can., Strasbourg, Fr. 1976-78; Ambassador to Morocco, 1978-80; special assignment: Candn. Secy. to Queen and Coordinator of Royal Visits on Occasion of Montreal Olympics 1976 and of Her Majesty's Jubilee, Oct. 1977; Annual Award of Candn. Inst. of Internat. Affairs (Que. Section) 1978; served with Candn. Army in U.K., France, Belgium, Holland and Germany during 2nd World War; commd. 2nd Lt., 1940; discharged as Major, 1947; wounded once; author of 'La Geste du Régiment de la Chaudière' (war hist. of Regt.); mem., Prof. Inst. Pub. Service Can.; L'Assn. des Anciens du Coll. des Jésuites de Qué.; L'Amicale du Régt. de la Chaudière; Carleton Univ. Alumni Assn.; R. Catholic; recreations: golf, hunting; Clubs: Royal Ottawa Golf; Cercle Universitaire; Address: 10 San Li Tun Road, Peking, People's Rep. of China.

GAUVIN, William Henry C.C. (1975), Ph.D., D.Eng., FRSC, FAICHE, FCIC, FICHemE; chemical engineer; b. Paris, France 30 March 1913; s. Hector Gustave and Albertine Marie (Van Halle) G.; e. Paris, Brussels, London schs.; McGill Univ. B.Eng. 1941, M.Eng. 1942, Ph.D 1945; Univ. of Waterloo D.Eng. 1967; m. Dorothy Edna, d. late Horace F. Strong, 23 Aug. 1966; one d. Suzanne (Mrs. S. Schutt); DIR. OF RESEARCH AND DEVELOP., NORANDA MINES LIMITED since 1970; Pres., Advis. Comm., Industrial Materials Research Instit. (Nat'l. Research Council) since 1978; mem., Inst. Nationale de Productivité (since 1979); Past Pres., Interamer. Confed. of Chem. Engineering; Pres., Assoc. de la Recherche du Québec 1980- ; Hon. Pres. II World Congress of Chem. Eng., Montreal (1981); Vice-Chrmn. Can. Research Mgmt. Assn. (1980-81); Sr. Research Assoc. and Dir. Plasma Technol. Group Dept. Chem. Engn. McGill Univ. since 1972; Lectr. Dept. Chem. Engn. McGill Univ. 1942-44, Assoc. Prof. 1947-62, Research Assoc. 1961-72; Plant Supt. F. W. Horner Ltd. Montreal 1944-46; Consultant, Pulp and Paper Research Inst. Can., Montreal 1951-57, Head Chem. Engn. Div. 1957-61; Research Mgr. Noranda Research Centre 1961-70; Délégué-Général, Nat. Research Council Can. 1970-71 (Council 1964-70); mem. Science Council Can. 1966-70, and 1973- ; Candn. Council Weizman Inst. Science; Conseil de la Politique Scientifique du Qué.; Gov. McGill Univ. since 1972; reccipient of Gold Medal of the Société d'Encouragement pour la Recherche et l'Invention (France) 1979; rec'd Distinguished Lectr. Award Candn. Inst. Mining & Metall. 1972,; Decorated Companion Order Canada; Alcan Award 1970; Candn. Soc. Chem. Engn. Award 1968, R. S. Jane Mem. Lecture Award 1963; Médaille Archambault ACFAS 1966; Palladium Medal Chem. Inst. Can. 1966 (Awards for best papers Candn. Journal Chem. Engn. 1960, 1961); Sr. Moulton Medal Inst. Chem. Engrs. 1964; I. H. Weldon Medal Candn. Pulp & Paper Assn. 1958; holds patents in high-temperature chem. processing; author over 135 papers in fields of electrochem., high temperature heat and mass transfer, fluid mech. and particle dynamics; mem. Candn. Soc. Chem. Engn. (Pres. 1966-67); Engn. Inst. Can.; Candn. Nuclear Assn.; Internat. Centre Heat & Mass Transfer (Yugoslavia); Candn. Pulp & Paper Assn. (Tech. Sec.); Order Engrs. Que.; Candn. Inst. Mining & Metall.; Am. Inst. Mining & Metall. Engrs.; Candn. Research Mang. Assn.; Indust. Research Inst. (USA); Brit. Non-Ferrous Metals Research Assn. (UK); Dechema (Germany); La Soc. de Chimie Industrielle (France); La Soc. des Ingenieurs Civils de France; Soc. Chem. Indust. (UK); Am. Mang. Assn. (Research & Devel. Planning Council); Am. Assn. Advanc. Science; Corp. Prof. Engrs. Que.; Sigma Xi and other assns.; Montreal Bd. Trade; recreations: tennis, sailing, chess, piano; Clubs: Royal St. Lawrence Yacht; University; Home: 7 Harrow Pl., Beaconsfield, Que.H9W 5C7; Office: 240 Hymus Blvd., Pointe Claire, Que. H9R 1G5

GAUVREAU, Georges, B.A., L.LL.; utilities executive; b. Québec, Qué. 24 July 1919; e. Ecole des Jésuites, Québec.

Qué.; McGill Univ. Law Sch.; Univ. Laval Law Sch., B.A., L.LL.; m. Thérèse Chapados; children: France, Pierre, Geneviève, Chantal, Bernard, André; COMMISSIONER, HYDRO-QUEBEC since 1961: Dir. Québec Mining and Exploration Co. (SOQUEM and subsidiaries LOUVEM and NIOBEL); commenced practice as Notary, New Carlisle, Qué. 1947; mem. Econ. Planning Council of Qué. 1961; R. Catholic; Office: 75 Dorchester Blvd. W., Montréal, Qué. H2Z 1A3

GEDDES, Eric A., B.Com., F.C.A., L.L.D.; chartered accountant; b. Victoria, B.C. 28 Sept. 1926; s. George and Florrie (Court) G.; e. Victoria High Sch. Edmonton Univ. of Alta. B.Com. 1947; C.A. 1950; m. Frances Jean d. late Russell Stanley 29 Aug. 1947; children: Catherine, Elaine, David, Sheila; CHRMN. OF BD., ALTA. HERITAGE FOUNDATION FOR MEDICAL RESEARCH, Partner in Charge Edmonton Office, Price Waterhouse; joined present firm 1959; Past Chrmn. Bd. of Govs. Univ. Alta.; Founding Chrmn. Old Strathcona Foundation 1975; mem. Council Inst. C.A.'s Alta. 1959-65 and Pres. 1964-65; Past Treas. Alta. P. Cons. Assn.; Past Nat. Vice Pres. for Alta. P. Cons. Assn. Can.; Past Treas. Edmonton Symphony Soc.; Pres. (1981) Edmonton Chamber of Commerce; mem. Business Adv. Council, Fac. of Bus. Admin. and Comm., Univ. of Alta.; Trustee, Univ. of Alta. Foundation; mem., Nat. Council of Duke of Edinburgh Award for Canada; Phi Delta Theta; P. Conservative, Protestant; recreation: golf; Clubs: Edmonton; Mayfair Golf & Country; Derrick Golf & Winter; Faculty Club, Univ. of Alta.; Centre Club; Home: 6631 — 123 St., Edmonton, Alta. T6H 3T3; Office: 2401 Toronto-Dominion Tower, Edmonton Centre, Edmonton, Alta. T5J 2Z1

GELBER, Arthur, O.C.(1972); b. Toronto, Ont. 22 June 1915; s. Louis and Sara Leah (Morris) G.; e. Upper Canada College, Toronto, Ont. (1934); m. Esther, d. late Joseph Salomon, Montreal, P.Q., 17 June 1941; children: Nancy Joan Bjarnason, Patricia Susan Rubin, Judith Ann, Sara Beth; Pres., CHMN. ONT. ARTS COUNCIL 1979-1982; Argel Holdings Ltd.; Past President, Canadian Conf. of the Arts; National Ballet; St. Lawrence Centre; Toronto Arts Productions; apptd. Chrmn. of Bd. of Trustees, Nat. Arts Centre Corp., Ottawa 1977-81; Vice Chrmn., Ont. Arts Council; Board of Governors, York Univ.; Dir., Am. Council for the Arts (N.Y.); Canadian Jewish Cong.; Centenial Medal 1967; Diplome d'Honeur 1978; City of Toronto Award of Merit; Queen's Jubilee Medal; Clubs: Arts & Letters; Home: 166 Roxborough Dr., Toronto, Ont. M4W 1X8; Office: 203 Richmond St. W., Toronto, Ont. M5V 1V5

GELBER, Lionel Morris, B.A., B. Litt., b. Toronto, Ont. 13 Sept. 1907; s. Louis and Sara L. (Morris) G.; e. Upper Can. Coll.; Univ. of Toronto, B.A. 1930, with Maurice Cody Schol. in Mod. Hist. and Rhodes Schol.; Balliol Coll., Oxford, B.Litt. 1933; unm.; resided in London, Eng., 1934-38, most of the 1960s and from 1970-75; Lectr., Dept. of Hist., Univ. of Toronto 1941-43; sometime Lectr. at summer schs., Univs. of Sask. and Alta.; resident in New York, 1945-60; Special Asst. to Prime Min. of Can., Aug. 1960-July 1961; served in W.W. II, Flight Lt., R.C.A.F. Directorate of Education, 1943-45; mem. Canadian Inst. of International Affairs; Institute for Strategic Studies, London; author of "The Rise of Anglo-American Friendship", 1938, 1966; "Peace by Power", 1942; "Reprieve from War", 1950; "The American Anarchy", 1953; "America in Britain's Place", 1961; "The Alliance of Necessity", 1966; "Crisis In The West", 1975; contributions: to Candn., British and American publications and author of pamphlets published in these countries; Club: Brooks's (London); Jewish; Forwarding address: 203 Richmond St. W., Toronto, Ont. M5V 1V3

GELBER, Sylva M., O.C., LL.D., D.Hum.L.; Canadian Gov't official (retired); b. Toronto, Ont. 4 Dec. 1910; d. Louis and Sara (Morris) G.; e. Havergal Coll. Toronto;

Univ. of Toronto; Columbia University; LL.D. Queen's Univ., 1976; LL.D. Mem. Univ. Nfld. 1976; D. Hum. L. Mount St. Vincent Univ. 1976; LL.D. Univ. of Guelph 1977; Govt. of Palestine Dept. of Labour, 1942-48; Govt. of Can., Dept. of Nat. Health and Welfare, Consultant, Health Insur. 1950-68; Can. Dept. of Labour, Dir. Women's Bureau, 1968-75; Special Advisor to Dep. Min. of Labour, 1975-78; mem., Can. Delegation to UN General Assembly 1976, 78; Can. Delegations to ILO Conferences 1969, 71, 75, 76; Can. Rep. UN Commission on Status of Women to 1974; Chrmn., Working Party of OECD 1973-8; mem. Bd. of Governors; Trent Univ., Peterborough; Can. Human Rights Foundation; U.N. Assoc. of Canada; mem. Candn. Inst. Internat. Affairs; Pres., Sylva Gelber Music Foundation; Publications; major reports, papers, articles on labour, health ins., human rights; recreations: music; Home: 77 Placel Rd., Rockcliffe Park, Ottawa, Ont. K1L 5B9

GELDART, Lloyd Philip, M.A., Ph.D.; geophysicist; b. Petitcodiac, N.B., 20 Oct. 1914; s. Oscar David and Edith May (Waterbury) G.; e. High Sch., Petitcodiac, N.B.; Mt. Allison Acad., N.B.; Sydney Acad. (Gov. Gen's Medal); Mt. Allison Univ., B.A. (summa cum laude) 1937; Univ. of Toronto, M.A. 1941; McGill Univ., Ph.D. 1941; Cal. Inst. of Tech., Geophysics Engn., 1949; m. Helena Marie, d. F. C. Burridge, Bridgetown N.S., 4 Sept. 1940; DIRECTOR OF CANADIAN INTERNATIONAL DEVELOPMENT AGENCY, UNIV: FED. da BAHIA, SALVADOR since 1975; Lect. in Math., McGill Univ., 1940; Teacher in Radar Math., R.C.A.F., 1940-41; Teacher, the Cath. High Sch., Montreal, P.Q., 1941-42; Head, Physics Dept., Acadia Univ., 1942-47; Research Geophysicist, Standard Oil Co. of Cal., 1949-52; Chief Geophysicist, Dominion Oil Ltd. (subsidiary of Standard Oil Co. of Cal.), Port-of-Spain, Trinidad, 1952-56; Chief Geophysicist, California Exploration Co., San Francisco, 1956-60; Webster Professor of Applied Geophysics, McGill Univ., 1960-69; Chief Tech. Advisor, UNESCO project to devel. Basic Science at Fed. Univ. of Bahia, Salvador, Brazil, 1968-74; professor of Applied Maths., Univ. Fed. de Bahia, 1974-75; co-author "Applied Geophysics", pub. 1976; Address: Ed. Maria Izabel—601 Av. Princesa Izabel 118 Barra, Salvador, Bahia Brazil

GELINAS, Gratien, O.C. (1967), D.Litt., LL.D., F.R.S.C. (1959); producer; author; director; actor; b. Tite, near Three Rivers, P.Q., 1909; father a French-Candn. and mother (née Davidson) of Scotch-Irish descent; e. Coll. of Brothers, St. Jerome, P. Q.; Coll. de Montreal (Sr. Matric); Sch. of Higher Comm. Studies, Montreal; Univ. of Montreal, Hon. D.Litt. 1949, New Brunswick 1969, Toronto 1951, McGill 1968; LL.D. Sask. 1966; Trent 1970; LL.D. Mount Allison 1973; named "one of 25 great Canadians whose achievements stand out above all others in the Century since Confederation" by Candn. Centennial Lib. 1966; m. 1stly Simone Lalonde, 1935 (d.1967); six children; 2ndly Huguette Oligny, Jan. 1973; designed for a business career, took first job with Dupuis Freres (Dept. Store), Montreal, 1929, and two months later joined La Sauvegarde Ins. Co. as an accountant, remaining with them for nine years, during which period indulged in casual radio and stage acting; at the cabaret "Mon Paris", Montreal, developed the character of "Fridolin" in a series of monologues about Le Bon Petit Garcon and Le Mauvais Petit Garcon; given first opportunity to act his monologues on the stage in "Televise-moi-ça" at St. Denis Theatre, Montreal, 1936, and was an immediate success; resigned from insurance business in 1937 and made radio debut with "Fridolin" (wrote whole show) in "Carrousel de la Gaité" (re-named Le Train de Plaisir following year), 1937; staged his first "Fridolinons Revue", 1938, which extended a one week's engagement to 25 performances, establishing a new record for theatre in Can.; discontinued radio performances in 1941 and engaged in full-time theatre; during 1940-46 wrote, directed, produced and starred in annual reviews playing 75 performances in Montreal and Quebec City, playing to nearly 105,000 theatre-goers per year; scored a hit in "St. Lazare's Pharmacy" (played in Chicago), 1945; sometime called the "Charlie Chaplin" of French Canada; awarded Grand Prix of Dramatists Soc.; his play "Tit-Coq" (1949) mentioned by Prime Min. Hon. St. Laurent in H. of C. as an example of first rate Candn. art, the Montreal premi-ère (May 1948) running for two yrs. to break all Candn. box office records; signed contract to produce Eng. ver-sion for N.Y. stage, 1959; filmed version rec'd "Film of the Year Award", 1952; wrote and starred in T.V. serial "Les Quat'Fers en l'Air", 1954-55; "Fridolinades" (revue) at Orpheum Theatre, Montreal, 1956; appeared as Chas. VI in 1956 presentation of Henry V at Stratford Shakes-pearean Festival; as Pres. and Dir. founded "La Come-die-Canadienne" in Montreal 1 June 1957, after taking over the former Radio City Theatre; dir., first production "L'Alouette" Feb. 1958 and played part of Charles VII in its English adaptation, "The Lark"; mem. Bd. of Govs., Nat. Film Bd. of Can., 1950-52; Chrmn., Candn. Film Devel. Corp. 1969-78; author of "Bousille et les Justes" (Montreal Premiere, 16 Aug. 1959); wrote, produced and starred in "Le Diable à quatre", satirical revue (opening Feb. 1964); author and dir. of play "Hier les enfants dansaient" (Montreal premiere 15 April 1966, and Eng. trans. by Mavor Moore premiere 1966); Founding mem. Nat. Thea-tre Sch. of Can. 1960; Pres., Candn. Theatre Inst. 1959-60; Vice-Pres., Greater Montreal Arts Council, 1957-62; el. Pres., Assn. Canadienne du Theatre Amateur 1950-61; awarded the Victor-Morin Prize for 1967 ("exceptional theatrical talents"), by St. Jean Baptiste Soc., Oct. 1967; makes frequent visits to Candn., European and Am. drama centres; recreations: classical music, boating, ten-nis, skating, travel; Address: 316 Girouard St., OKA, Que. Box 207 J0N 1E0

GELLNER, John, D.F.C., C.D., D.L.; author; educator; b. Trieste 18 May 1907; s. Dr. Gustav and Maria (Tomasi) G.; e. Masaryk Univ. Brno, Czechoslovakia D.L. (Doctor of Law) 1930; m. Lilo d. Wilhelm Mattheis, Essen, Ger-many 14 March 1978; came to Can. 1939; Jr. Partner law firm Brno, Czechoslovakia 1935-39; served with R.C.A.F. 1940-58, Pilot, rank Wing Commdr.; Ed. "Commentator" (Toronto pol. monthly now defunct) 1964-70; Ed. "Canadian Defence Quarterly/Revue canadienne de défense" 1971- ; Visiting Prof. of Pol. Science York Univ. 1970, presently Hon. Prof.; Dir. Atlantic Council Can.; rec'd Czechoslovak Mil. Cross; Czechoslovak Medal for Valour; author "Canada in NATO" 1970; "Bayonets in the Streets: Urban Guerilla at Home and Abroad" 1974; co-author "Climbers' Guide Through the High Tatras" 4 vols. 1936-38; "The Czechs and Slovaks in Canada" 1968; author over 500 publs. incl. articles on internat. relations and defence issues, book chapters; mem. Candn. Inst. Internat. Affairs; Candn. Inst. Strategic Studies; Internat. Inst. Strategic Studies (UK); R. Catholic; Clubs: Royal Candn. Mil. Inst.; Empire; Home: R.R.3, Caledon East, Ont. L0N 1E0; Office: Suite 1300, 100 Adelaide St. W., Toronto, Ont. M5H 1S3.

GENDRON, Hon. François, M.N.A.; politician; b. Val Paradis, Qué. 3 Nov. 1944; s. Odilon and Marguerite (Mercier) G.; e. La Sarre, Berthierville, Amos and Rouyn, Qué. Schs.; m. Madeleine d. Antonio Gagnon, Palma-rolle, Qué. 20 July 1968; children: Nancy, Sylvain, David; MIN. OF STATE FOR LAND USE PLANNING, QUE. 1981- ; professor; Mun. Councillor and Acting Mayor La Sarre 1973-76; Secy. La Sarre Caisse Populaire 1972-76; el. M.N.A. for Abitibi-Ouest prov. g.e. 1976; Min. of Public Service, 1979-81; Parti Quebecois; R. Catholic; Office: 875, Grande-Allée est, Québec, Qué. G1R 4Y8.

GENDRON, Jean-Denis, B.A., L. ès L., doctorat phoné-tique; ne St-Antoine-sur-Richelieu, P. Q. 1er Janv. 1925; f. Antonio et Aldina Langevin; é. Univ. Montréal, B.A. 1946; Univ. Laval, L. ès. L. 1950; Univ. Strasbourg, doc. phon. 1958; ép. Gisèle, f. Dr. Eugène Blouin, 23 âout

1952; enfants: Christiane, Yves, Dominique, Michel; Dir. du Centre International de recherche sur le bilinguisme (Univ. Laval) depuis 1979; Président du Conseil de la lan-gue française du Québec, depuis 1977; Professeur Univ-ersité Laval 1950-74 et depuis 1979; professeur aux. lan-gue française, 1950-55; professeur aux. puis agrégé et titulaire — phonétique, 1958-64; secr. Dép. Linguistique, 1964-67 dir. adjoint, 1967-68; vice-doyen, fac. lettres, 1968-69; prés. Comn. Royale d'Enquête sur la situation de la langue française et sur les droits linguistiques au Québec déc. 1968-72; Vice-prés. de la Régie de la langue française du Qué. 1974-77; Prés. du Conseil de la langue française du Qué., 1977-79; auteur "Tendances phonéti-ques du français parle au Can", 1966; "Phonétique ortho-phonique à l'usage des Canadiens-Français", 1968; co-auteur: "Etudes de linguistiques franco-canadienne", 1967; "Rapport de la Commission royale d'enquête; vol. 1. La langue de travail; vol. 11, Les droits linguistiques; vol. 111, Les groupes ethniques", 1973; "La situation du français comme langue d'usage au Québec", 1974; "Statut des langues et statut des hommes", 1975; "La définition d'une norme de langue parlée au Québec", 1975; "Rapport annuel de la Régie de la langue française", 1975 et 1976; "La situation de la langue fran-çaise et des francophones au Québec et au Canada", 1977; "Fluctuation des frontières ethniques et recrudes-cence des tensions au Canada", 1977; de divers ouvrages et articles sur la phonétique; membre: assn. can. de ling.; assn. internat. de phonétique; soc. de ling. & philologie romanes; conseil internal. langue frse; Catholique; club: cercle universitaire de Québec; Résidence: 2280, rue Mas-son Sillery — Québec, P.Q. G1T 1M8

GENEST, Jacques, C.C. (1967), M.D., LL.D., D.Sc., Dr. Med. Sc., F.R.C.P., F.R.S.C., M.A.C.P.; b. Montreal, Que., 29 May 1919; s. Rosario and Annette (Girouard) G.; e. Coll. Jean de Brébeuf, Montreal B.A. 1937; Univ. of Montreal, M.D. 1942; Harvard Med. Sch. (Surg. Anat.) 1938, (Physiol.) 1939; Harvard Sch. of Chem., 1948; Johns Hopkins Hospital 1945-1948; Rockefeller Inst. 1948-1952; LL.D Toronto 1970; D.Sc., Queen's, D.Med.Sc., Laval, Memorial Univ., McGill; Sherbrooke; Ottawa; m. Estelle, d. Albert Deschamps, 3 Oct. 1953; children: Paul, Suzan-ne, Jacques Jr., Marie Hélène; DIRECTOR, CLINICAL RESEARCH INST. OF MONTREAL; Prof. of Med., Uni-versity of Montreal; Physician Hôtel-Dieu Hospital, Montreal; mem., Bd. of Dir., Merck and Co.; Montreal Trust; rec'd Gairdner Award 1963; Soc. Médicale de Montréal Awards, 1956 and 1959; Assn. Canadienne française pour l'Avanc. des Sciences, Parizeau Award 1965; Flavelle Award, Royal Soc. of Canada; Stouffer award 1969; Marie-Victorin Prize of Quebec 1977; Loyola Medal 1978; Royal Bank of Canada Award 1980; Scientific Prize, Assn. Med. Langue Française du Canada 1980; mem. Peripatetic Club; Am. Clin. & Climatol. Assn.; Assn. Am. Phys.; R. Catholic; Clubs: St-Denis, Montreal, Century, N.Y.; Home: 1171 Blvd. Mont-Royal, Outre-mont, Que. H2V 2H6; Office: 110 Pine Ave. West, Mont-real, Que. H2W 1R7

GENEST, Pierre, Q.C. B.A.; b. Ottawa, Ont. 11 Apl. 1930; s. Hon. Justice Jean and Marie (Rainboth) G.; e. Public and High Schs., Ottawa; Univ. of Ottawa, B.A. 1950; Osgoode Hall Law Sch. 1954; m. Janet, d. Duncan Chisholm 29 Aug. 1953; children: Jean, Michèle, Paul, André, Anne-Louise; PARTNER, CASSELS BROCK; Dir. Power Corp. of Canada Ltd.; deHavilland Aircraft of Can. Ltd.; read Law with McDonald Joyal Fogarty & Mills; called to Bar of Ont. 1954; cr. Q.C. 1968; with Cas-sels Defries DesBrisay 1956; Bell Griffiths Temple & Gen-est 1959; Cassels Brock since 1966; served with RCA, rank 2nd Lt.; Chrmn., Ont. Mental Health Foundation (1975-8); mem, Advocates Soc. (Dir. 1968-71); Candn. Bar Assn.; Co. of York Law Assn.; Med. Legal Soc. Toronto; Lawyers Club Toronto (Pres. 1968-69); Trustee Clarke Inst. of Psychiatry (1975-78); Bencher, Law Soc. of Upper Canada (1979-) (Chrmn., Discipline Cmtee, since 1980);

app't mem. Leg. Council, N.W.T. 1973-75; Liberal (Past Extve. Vice-Pres. Eglinton Fed. Liberal Assn.); R. Catholic; recreations: skiing, golf, fishing, hunting; Clubs: Toronto Golf; Osler Bluff Ski (Pres. 1968-69); University; Lawyers (Pres. 1968-69); Home: 67 Chaplin Cres., Toronto, Ont. M5P 1A2; Office: 130 Adelaide St. West, Toronto, Ont. M5H 3B8

GENT, Michael, M.Sc., F.S.S., F.I.S., F.I.M.A., educator; b. Stanley, Co. Durham, Eng. 4 May 1934; s. John and Winifred Elizabeth (Gibbon) G.; e. Henry VIII Grammar Sch. Coventry 1952; Univ. of Durham B.Sc., M.Sc. 1957; m. Betty d. William Purvis, Tyne-Wear, Eng. 20 July 1957; children: Steven Michael, Heather Margaret; PROF. OF CLIN. EPIDEMIOL. AND BIOSTAT., McMASTER UNIV., AND ASSOC. DEAN (RESEARCH) HEALTH SCIENCES; mem. Scient. Comte. Candn. Heart Foundation 1971-1980; Vice Chrmn. of Comte. 1975-77 and Chrmn. Scient. Review Comte. 1977-80; mem. Med. Research Council Comte. for Assessment Diagnostic & Treatment Procedures 1972-75, Special Adv. Comte. Aorto-Coronary Bypass Surg. 1972; mem. Grants Panel C — Clin. Investigation and Epidemiol. Nat. Cancer Inst. Can. 1973-74; mem. Petch Task Force on Health Research Requirements 1974-75; mem. of Exec. of Council on Thrombosis, Amer. Heart Assn. 1975-77; mem. N.I.H. Workshop Group on Cerebrovascular Disease, 1976; Internat. Comte. on Haemostasis & Thrombosis 1977- ; Subcomte. for Diagnosis, Prophylaxis & Treatment Venous Thromboembolism 1977- ; Co-Chrmn. Subcomte. on Clin. Trials 1978- ; mem. Exec. Comte. Internat. Soc. of Clinical Biostatistics 1978-80; mem. Med. Research Council for Clinical Trials 1979- ; Chrmn. Research Comte., Council of Ont. Faculties of Med. 1980- ; author several book chapters and over 60 scient. articles methodology clin. trials and reports of studies relating to thrombosis; Fellow, Am. Statistical Assn., 1981; mem. Editorial Bd. of Applied Stat. (J.R.S.S. Series C) 1967-69; Review Ed. of Applied Stat., 1968; Secty. Leeds/Bradford Sectn. of Royal Stat. Soc. 1968-69; mem. Biometric Soc.; Am. Stat. Assn.; Am. Pub. Health Assn.; Candn. Pub. Health Assn.; Candn. Soc. Clin. Investigation; Am. Heart Assn.; Internat. Epidemiol. Assn.; Soc. Epidemiol. Research; Candn. Stat. Soc.; Candn. Cardiovascular Soc.; Internat. Soc. Clin. Biostatistics; Internat. Soc. on Thrombosis & Haemostasis; P. Conservative; R. Catholic; recreations: travel, golf; Home: 35 Jerseyville Rd., Ancaster, Ont. L9G 1A1; Office: 1200 Main St. W., Hamilton, Ont. L8N 3Z5.

GENTILCORE, R. Louis, Ph.D.; university professor; b. Welland, Ont., 9 June 1924; s. Carmine and Reparata G.; e. Welland (Ont.) High and Vocational Sch., 1939-43; Univ. of Toronto, B.A. (Geog.) 1947; Univ. of Md., Ph.D. (Geog.) 1950; m. Mary Elizabeth, d. Louis Brajer, Stoney Creek, Ont., 23 July 1960; children: David Carmine, Maria Roxanne, Susan Margaret; PROF. OF GEOG., McMASTER UNIV., since 1968; Lectr., Indiana Univ., 1950-53; Asst. Prof. 1954-56; Visiting Lectr., Univ. Coll. London, Eng., 1953-54; Asst. Prof., Los Angeles State Coll., 1956-58; joined present Univ. as Asst. Prof. 1958-61; Assoc. Prof. 1961-68; rec'd Can. Council Awards 1967, 1968, 1969; author and/or editor of "Canada's Changing Geography", 1967; "Geog. Approaches to Can. Problems", 1971; "Studies in Can. Geog.: Ont.", 1972; (with R. Donkin), "Land Surveys of Southern Ont.", 1973; other writings incl. papers for prof. journs.; mem., Candn. Assn. Geogs.; Assn. Am. Geogs.; Am. Geog. Soc.; R. Catholic; Home: 99 Little John Rd., Dundas, Ont. L9H 4H2

GEORGE, David V., B.Sc., Ph.D., F.C.S., C.Chem.; educator; b. Cardiff, Wales, 14 Feb. 1938; s. David Lewis and Elizabeth Jane (Poole) G.; e. Cathays Grammar Sch., Cardiff, 1955; Univ. of Wales, B.Sc. 1958, Ph.D. 1961; m. Eila Mae, B.A., d. Maurice Connor and Agnes Schommer, Victoria B.C., 13 May 1967; children: Rhiannon Eliz-

abeth, David Maurice, Glenys Myfanwy; PRINCIPAL, NORTHWEST COMMUNITY COLLEGE, since 1976; Dean of Studies, Notre Dame Univ. of Nelson, 1969-75; Princ., Northwest Community Coll., B.C., since 1976; Pres., Notre Dame Univ. of Nelson, 1976, Vice-Pres., 1975; Head of Chem. Dept., Notre Dame Univ. of Nelson, 1964-69; Post-doctoral Research Fellow Univ. of B.C. 1961, Teaching Fellow 1963; mem. Extve. Comte. B.C. Educ. Research Council; Dir. Educ. Research Inst. B.C.; B.C. Council for Leadership in Educ.; Nelson and Dist. Arts Council; mem., Selkirk Coll. Bd., B.C. Fed. Naturalists; Passereau Singers; Royal Inst. Chem.; Pro-Life Society of B.C.; Pres., Nelson and Dist. United Way; Terrace and Dist. Arts Council; mem., Northwest Regional Arts Council; Vice Pres., Terrace Assoc. for Summer School of the Arts; School Trustee, Nelson, B.C.; author "Principles of Quantum Chemistry" 1972 and various papers and articles in prof. journs.; R. Catholic; recreations: hunting, fishing, choral singing; natural history; Address: 4904 Gair Avenue, Terrace, B.C. V8G 2K2

GEORGE, Graham, Mus.D., F.C.C.O., A.R.C.O., F.R.C.C.O. honoris causa 1976; university professor; b. Norwich, Eng., 11 April 1912; s. Alfred Robert and Ethel Elizabeth (Graham) G.; e. Grammar Sch., Birmingham and Dorset, Eng., 1924-28; Oxford Sr. Sch. Cert., and London Matric.; came to Can. 1928; McGill Univ. Arts 1932-33; Univ. of Toronto, Mus.B. 1936; Mus.D. 1939; studied Composition under Alfred Whitehead, Paul Hindemith; Orchestral Conducting under Willem van Otterloo, conductor, Residentie Orkest, The Hague, Hilversum, Holland; m. Tjot, d. late Cornelis Coster, 5 Sept. 1945; children: Charles Robert Brian, Paul Philip Graham, Jan Michael, Derek Norman; PROF. OF MUSIC, QUEEN'S UNIV., Acting Head of Dept. 1968-71; also Res. Musician in charge of extracurricular activities in music; Organist and Choirmaster of churches in Montreal and Sherbrooke, P.Q., Kingston and Gananoque Ont. since 1932; Teacher, Sch. Music, Pub. and High Schs., Sherbrooke, and Montreal, P.Q. 1938-41; Joint Examiner-in-Chief for Music in Gr. XIII, Prov. of Ont., 10 years; Guest Conductor with CBC String Orchestra 1957; served in 2nd World War 1941-45, in 7th Candn. Reconnaissance Regt., in Can., U.K., and N.W. Europe; discharged as G.S.O. (Third Grade) Counter-Intelligence, rank Capt.; served as Arts Faculty rep. to C.O.T.C. (Queen's); retired with rank of Major; Publications: "Canada's Music 1955", "Stratford: Tail of a Comet" 1958; and other contrib. to Candn. Music Journ.; "White Noise and Breaking Crockery" 1960, and other contribs. to "Saturday Night"; various book reviews; paper on songs of B.C. Salish Indians to Journ. of Internat. Folk Music Council Vol. XIV, 1962; "The Structure of Dramatic Music 1607-1909", Musical Quarterly, Oct. 1966; Queen's Quarterly; "Towards a Definition of Romanticism in Music", summer 1965, and "The 'Work-Of-Artness' of a Work of Art", spring 1967; Books: "Tonality and Musical Structure" (Faber 1970); "Twelve Note Tonal Counterpoint" (Frederick Harris 1976); Compositions: opera, ballet, symphony, organ and other church music, stage and radio music; awarded Prix Lallemand (Montreal) 1938; Composers, Authors, and Publishers Assn. of Can. prizes 1943 and 1947; Recordings: "St. John Passion: Alessandro Scarlatti", (first modern performance before conv. of Am. Musicol. Soc. in New Haven, 1952; under dir. of Prof. Howard Boatwright) awarded Grand Prix du Disque (France) 1958; Sec. Gen. Internat. Folk Music Council 1969-80; mem., Candn. Folk Music Soc. (Pres. 1965-68); Council, Coll. Music Soc., 1966-69; Royal Candn. Coll. of Organists (Pres. 1972-4); Candn. Music Council; Am. Musicol. Soc.; recreations: variations within music, family activities, Home: 151 Earl St. Kingston, Ont. K7L 2H3

GERBER, Douglas E., M.A., Ph.D.; educator; b. North Bay, Ont. 14 Sept. 1933; s. Earl Jacob and Bertha Thelma (Cox) G.; e. Univ. of W. Ont. B.A. 1955, M.A. 1956; Univ.

of Toronto Ph.D. 1959; one d. Allison Suzanne; PROF. AND CHRMN. OF CLASSICAL STUDIES, UNIV. OF W. ONT. 1969- , presently holds William Sherwood Fox Chair of Classics; author "A Bibliography of Pindar 1513-1966" 1969; "Euterpe: An Anthology of Early Greek Lyric, Elegiac and Iambic Poetry" 1970; "Emendations in Pindar 1513-1972" 1976; "Pindar's Olympian One: A Commentary" 1982; over 20 articles ancient Greek poetry; mem. Ed. Bd. "Phoenix" 1972-74, 1979-81; mem. Ont. Classical Assn. (Pres. 1968-70); Classical Assn. Can. (Treas. 1960-62); Am. Philol. Assn. (Ed. Transactions 1974-82; mem. Ed. Bd. of Assn. 1974-82, Chrmn. 1978); Corr. mem. Quaderni Urbinati di Cultura Classica; served with RCN (Reserve), rank Lt.; Anglican; Home: 105 Cherryhill Blvd., Apt. 1004, London, Ont. N6H 2L7; Office: London, Ont. N6A 3K7.

GERIN-LAJOIE, Paul, Internat'l lawyer and business consultant; b. Montreal, P.Q., 23 Feb. 1920; s. Henri and Pauline, (Dorion) G-L.; e. Jean-de-Brebeuf Coll.; Univ. of Montreal; Ph.D. (Oxford); m. Andrée Papineau, 1944; children, François, Bernard, Sylvie, Dominique; PRES., GROUP GÉRIN-LAJOIE, 1980; Pres. Projecto International Inc. 1977-80; el. to Que. Leg. for Vaudreuil-Soulanges in g.e. 1960; Min. of Youth, 5 July 1960-64; Min. of Educ. (1st) May 1964-66; re-el. g.e. 1966 (govt. def.); apptd. Vice Chrmn. of Fed. Prices & Incomes Comn. 1969-70; Pres., Candn. Inter. Development Agency (CIDA), 1970-77; Roman Catholic; Office: 101 Amherst Rd., Beaconsfield Quebec, H9W 5Y7

GERLACH, Henry, company executive; b. Hallonquist, Sask., 16 Jan. 1920; s. Adolph and Marie (Bender) G.; e. High Sch. (Grad. 1936) and Manitoba Comm. Coll., Winnipeg, Man. (Grad. 1938); m. Marion Susan Elizabeth d. Alexander Suppes, Winnipeg, Man., 9 July 1949; four s., James Henry, Douglas Robert, Kenneth Lloyd, Donald Alexander; VICE-PRESIDENT, DIR. AND GEN. MGR., WHITE FARM EQUIPMENT LTD.; Public Acct., Winnipeg, Man., 1939-40; Treasury Dept. as Acct., Ottawa, Ont., 1940-41; joined Minneapolis Moline of Canada Ltd. as Acct., Winnipeg, Man. in 1947; apptd. Credit Mgr., 1950; in 1956 went to parent Co. in Indianapolis as Sales Mgr. to help set-up new division of Co.; moved to Harrisburg, Pa. as Div. Mgr. to organ. a new division, 1957; served in 2nd World War with Candn. Army, 1941-46; Lutheran; recreations: golf, curling, fishing; Club: Kiwanis (Past Pres.); Home: 1890 Cowan Cres., Regina, Sask. S4S 4C6; Office: 2201 1st Ave., Regina, Sask.

GERMAN, Neil Victor, B.A., LL.B.; lawyer; b. Hanna, Alta., 29 May 1916; s. Roy Otto and Muriel Eva (Saunders) G.; e. Univ. of Alta., B.A. LL.B. (Rhodes Scholar, 1940 and 17 other scholar. awards); m. Katherine Irene, d. Arthur D. Cuming, Calgary, 27 June 1942, (divorced); children: Gayle Heather, Katherine Wendy Lynn, Arthur Garry; 2ndly Germaine Theresa Hoefle; PARTNER, GERMAN AND COMPANY, President and Director, Arctic Enterprises Ltd.; Katinka Agencies Ltd.; read law with Gerald O'Connor, K.C.; called to the Bar of Alta., 1941; mem., Calgary, Alta. and Candn. Bar Assns.; Past Pres., Calgary N. Lib. Assn. and mem. of Extve. of Alta. Assn.; mem. Calgary Chamber of Comm.; Candn. Chamber Comm., (Nat. Pres. 1971-72); Baptist; recreation: gardening; Club: Optimist; Home: 167 Cardiff Dr., N.W., Calgary Alta. T2P 1K2; Office: main floor 224 9 Ave. S.W., Calgary, Alta. T2P 1K2

GERMAN, Her Honour Judge Patricia Riley, b. St. Catharines, Ont. 2 Jan. 1929; d. George Wilfrid and Mildred K. (Huston) Riley; e. Jarvis Coll. Inst. Toronto; Univ. of Toronto B.A. 1949; Osgoode Hall Law Sch. LL.B. 1966; York Univ. LL.M.; m. John B. German 9 Sept. 1950; children: John Bruce, Jacqueline Green, Timothy R., William M.; JUDGE, CO. COURT ONT.; Alpha Gamma Delta; Anglican; Home: 354 Inglewood Dr., Toronto, Ont. M4T 1J6; Office: 361 University Ave., Toronto, Ont. M5G 1T3.

GERMAN, Vernal C., B.A.Sc., M. Com., P.Eng.; executive; b. Windsor, Ont., 26 Oct. 1922; s. Vernal Albert and Christina (Cameron) G.; e. Univ. of Toronto, B.A.Sc. (Chem. Engn.) 1950. M.Com. (Business Adm.) 1956; m. Barbara Millicent, d. James A. B. Reilly, 3 Sept. 1949; children: Barbara Lynn, Lynda Ann, James Cameron; PAST PRESIDENT, PILKINGTON GLASS INDUSTRIES LTD. 1965-81; Dir., Pilkington Glass Industries Ltd.; Candn. Canners Ltd.; joined Candn. General Electric, Toronto, as Sales Engr., 1951-56; apptd. Vice Pres., Sales, Cochrane Corp. Canada, Rexdale, Ont., 1956-60; Gen. Mgr., Cochrane Div., Crane Co., Philadelphia, Pa., 1960-65; served with R.C.A.F. as Pilot and Flying Offr., 1942-46; Chrmn., Candn. Business & Industry Adv. Comte. for OECD, 1970; Dir. and Vice-Chrmn., 1981, Candn. Mfrs. Assn.; mem., Association Professional Engineers Ont.; Anglican; recreations: flying, photography; Home: 2250 Highriver Court, Mississauga, Ont. L5H 3K4

GERRARD, John Watson, B.A., B.Ch., D.M., F.R.C.P.(C); pediatrician; b. N. Rhodesia, 14 Apl. 1916; s. Herbert Shaw and Doris (Watson) G.; e. Oxford Univ. B.A. 1938; B.M., B.Ch. 1941, D.M. 1951; F.R.C.P. (London) 1947; m. Lilian Elisabeth Whitehead, 28 Aug. 1941; children: Jonathan Michael, Peter, Christopher; PROF. OF PEDIATRICS, UNIV. OF SASK., since 1955; John Scott Award, 1962; served overseas in 2nd World War with R.A.M.C., in N. Africa, Italy, Palestine, 1941-45; United Church; recreation: ornithology; Home: 809 Colony St., Saskatoon, Sask. S7N 0S2

GERRIE, John Wilfrid, D.D.S., M.D., C.M., F.A.C.S.; surgeon; b. Stratford, Ont., 13 Jan. 1905; s. late John Petrie and Martha (Martin) G.; e. Strathcona High Sch., Edmonton, Alta.; Univ. of Alberta, B.A. 1924, D.D.S. 1927; Univ. of Toronto, 1929-30; McGill Univ. M.D., C.M. 1931; m. Mona, d. late Dempster Tredway, Sept. 21, 1929; children: Mrs. Donald Allen, Mrs. Norman Buka, Mrs. Douglas Ackman, Michael Dempster, Mrs. James Butler; Consulting Plastic Surgeon to Montreal Gen. Hosp.; Queen Mary Veteran's Hosp.; Saint Mary's Hosp.; Montreal Children's Hosp.; served in 2nd World War as Major, R.C.A.M.C. with No. 1 Candn. Gen. Hosp. in Eng., 1940-41; Past Pres., Candn. Soc. of Plastic Surgs.; Past Pres., Am. Soc. of Maxillofacial surgs.; mem., Am. Soc. of Plastic Surgs.; Am. Soc. of Plastic & Reconstructive Surgs.; Candn. Soc. of Oral Surgs.; Brit. Assn. of Plastic Surgs.; Diplomate, Am. Bd. of Plastic Surgs.; Dipl. of Plastic Surgery, Royal Coll. of Surgs., Eng.; Publications: with Gurd and Ackman, "Technique in Trauma", 1944; about sixty papers on oral and plastic surgery; produced a Dermatome Cement for skin grafting in collab. with C.I.L., 1944-45; Zeta Psi; Liberal; Protestant; recreations: golf, skiing; Clubs: Faculty; Shawbridge Golf & Country (Pres.): Lac Marois Country (Past Pres.): Home: Lac Marois, R.R. 1, Piedmont, Que. J0R 1K0

GERSON, Wolfgang, F.R.A.I.C., R.C.A.; architect; educator; b. Hamburg, Germany 18 March 1916; s. Oscar Ernst G.; e. Arch. Assn. London, Eng. Dipl. 1940; came to Can. 1941; m. Hildegard J. d. Fritz Aronstein 22 Dec. 1944; children: Martin Sebastian, Ann Charlotte, Erika Eve, Katherine Ruth; Prof. Emeritus of Arch. Univ. of B.C.; arch. practice; author "Patterns of Urban Living" 1970; mem. CAMMAC; Unitarian; recreations: piano, chamber music, drawing, watercolours; Address: 3362 W. 18th Ave., Vancouver, B.C. V6S 1A7.

GERSOVITZ, Sarah Valerie, R.C.A.; artist; b. Montreal, Que. 5 Sept. 1920; d. Solomon and Eva (Gampel) Gamer; e. Macdonald Coll. Sch. for Teachers grad. 1939; Concordia Univ. Dipl. in Communication Studies 1978, presently completing M.A. program in Creative Writing; Art Courses; Montreal Museum of Fine Arts Drawing, Design, Etching, Sculpture; L'Ecole des Arts appliqués Sculpture; Univ. of Alta. Japanese Wood-block Printing; Visual Arts Centre Rochester, N.Y. Photography; Saidye

Bronfman Centre Montreal, Photography; m. Benjamin Gersovitz 22 June 1944; children: Mark, Julia, Jeremy; solo exhns. incl. Montreal Museum of Fine Arts (twice); Art Gallery of Greater Victoria; Univ. of Alta.; Burnaby Art Gallery; Art Gallery of Hamilton; Mount Saint-Vincent Univ.; Coll. Saint-Louis; l'Univ. de Sherbrooke; Saint-Mary's Univ.; Confed. Art Gallery; London Regional Art Gallery; Peter Whyte Gallery; l'Instituto Culturel Peruano, Lima; comm. galleries Bogota, Lima, Montreal, Toronto, Winnipeg, Calgary, Halifax, Hamilton; participated internat. exhns. France, Spain, Korea, Norway, Switzerland, Yugoslavia, Eng., Scot., Australia, Italy, Germany, Brazil, Peru, Colombia, Venezuela, Czechoslovakia, U.S.A., Can.; rep. in various perm. colls. incl. Lib. of Cong., N.Y. Pub. Lib., Nat. Gallery S. Australia, Instituto Culturel Peruano Lima, many Candn. museums, univs. and embassies as well as pub. and private colls. Europe, S.Am., U.S.A., Can.; rec'd First Prize Concours Graphique l'Univ. de Sherbrooke; Hon. Mention Miniature Painters, Sculptors & Gravers, Washington, D.C.; First Prize and Gold Medal Seagram Fine Arts Exhn.; Graphic Art Prize First Winnipeg Show Biennial; Anaconda Award Candn. Painter-Etchers & Engravers (twice); Third Prize Windmill Point Competition; Purchase Awards Dawson Coll., Le Musée du Qué., Thomas More Inst., Nat. Gallery S. Australia, Univ. de Sherbrooke; Hon. Mention Nat. Playwriting Competition Ottawa for 2 one-act plays 1979, 1980; mem. Council, Royal Candn. Acad. Arts; Conseil de la Gravure du Qué.; Print & Drawing Council Can.; Soc. des Artistes en Arts Visuels (Past Extve. mem.); Jewish; recreations: writing plays & short stories, travel, gardening; Address: 5173 Mayfair Ave., Montreal, Que. H4V 2E8.

GERSTEIN, Bertrand, B.A., L.L.D.; merchant; b. Boston, Mass., 11 Feb. 1918; s. Frank and Etta (Wein) G.; came to Canada 1918; e. Univ. of Toronto, B.A. (Pol. Science and Econ.) 1938; m. children: Irving Russell, Ira Mitchael; CHAIRMAN, PEOPLES JEWELLERS LIMITED (Estbd. 1919); former Chrmn., Bd. of Govs., York Univ., Toronto; former Chrmn. of Bd., Mount Sinai Hosp., Toronto; Past Pres., Ont. Div., Candn. Mental Health Assn.; Candn. Jewellers Assn.; Dir., Candn. Imperial Bank of Commerce; mem., Toronto Bd. Trade; City of Toronto Redevel. Adv. Council; Jewish; recreations: tennis, golf, sailing; Clubs: Albany; Ontario; Primrose; Oakdale Golf & Country; Queen's; Home: 82 Oriole Rd., Toronto, Ont. M4V 2G1; Office: 181 Yonge St., Toronto, Ont. M5B 1M6

GERSTEIN, Reva, O.C. (1979)., (1974), M.A., Ph.D., Ont., d. David and Diana (Kraus) Appleby, e. Fern Ave. Sch. and Parkdale Coll. Inst., Toronto; Univ. of Toronto, B.A. 1938; M.A. 1939, Ph.D. 1945; Univ. of W. Ont., LL.D. 1972; D.Litt. Lakehead Univ. 1974; LL.D. Guelph 1975; m. Bertrand Gerstein, 1939; divorced 1971- ; children: Irving Russell, Ira Michael; m. David Raitblat, 1979; Dir. McGraw-Hill Ryerson Ltd., 1974; INCO Ltd., 1976; Avon Products Ltd., 1975; Maritime Life Assnce. Co., 1977; Stratford Shakespearean Festival Inc., 1977 (Hon. Secty., 1979); Niagara Inst., 1978; Inst. for Research and Public Policy, 1978; CJRT-FM Inc.; Fellow Founders Coll., York University; mem. and chrmn., University Affairs Committee 1962-1978; Hall-Dennis Committee; mem. and Ed. Chrmn., Commission on Post-Secondary Educ.; mem., University Affairs Council, 1975-79; Trustee, Can. Studies Foundation; Lectr., Dept. of Psychol., Univ. of Toronto, 1939-49; York Univ. 1965-73; Nat. Dir. of Program, Candn. Mental Health Assn.; Psychol. (first), E. York-Leaside Health Unit; mem. Clinical Education Comm. (Ont. Council on Health) since 1979; mem. Task Force of Council of Health 1971 and Arts Council 1972; Chrmn. Co-ordinator, Social Plan. Council Youth Proj. 1969-71; Chrmn., Adv. on Policy to Leader of Opposition, Ottawa 1977; mem., Prime Minister; Transitional Task Force, 1979; Adv. on Selections and Procedures, Metro. Toronto Police Comn.; Chmn. Solicitor-General's Task force on Policing (Dec. 1979-June 1980); Founder & Past Pres., Hincks Treatment Centre; Nat. Pres., Can. Council on Children & Youth, 1957-65; Nat. Pres., Nat. Council Jewish Women, 1955-59 (Internat. Vice Pres. 1955-59); Trustee, and mem. of Exec. Hosp. for Sick Children; member, Canadian Opera Committee; Art Gallery Ontario; Royal Ontario Museum; named B'nai Brith Woman of the Year 1961; Honorary Life member Ontario Psychiatric Assn. 1967; Centennial Medal 1967; Outstanding Woman Awards of Ont. 1975; mem. Order of Canada 1974; Officer of Order of Canada 1979; life mem. of Ont. Chiefs of Police Assn.; Albert Einstein Coll. of Med. Award 1956; mem., Ont. Psychol. Assn.; Candn. Psychol. Assn.; Am. Psychol. Assn.; Address: 625 Avenue Rd., Apt. 1603, Toronto, Ont. M4V 2K7

GERVAIS, (Rev.) Marc, S.J., Ph.D., M.A., M.F.A., L.Ph., L.Th. (R.C.); university professor; film specialist and critic; b. Sherbrooke, Que., 3 Dec. 1929; s. Césaire and Sylvia (Mullins) G.; e. Loyola Coll., B.A. 1950; L'Immaculée Conception, Montreal, L.Ph. 1956; Cath. Univ. of Am., Washington, M.F.A. (drama) 1960; Regis Coll., Toronto, L.Th. 1964; St. Mary's Univ., M.A. (Theol.) 1964; Sorbonne Univ., Ph.D. (film aesthetics) 1973; PROF. OF FILM, DEPT. OF COMMUNICATION STUDIES, CONCORDIA UNIV., Loyola Campus; mem., Board of Judges Canadian Film Awards; mem. film juries (Cannes, Venice, Oxford, etc.); TV and radio work including TV Specials on Ingmar Bergman for CBC and CTV; received Canada Council Fellowship 1966-67; comm. (parttime) for C.R.T.C. since 1981; author, "Pasolini". 1972; other writings incl. film articles in journals and newspapers in Eng., France, USA, Can., Spain, Sweden, and Italy, and Australia; recreations: sports, arts; Address: 7141 Sherbrooke St. W., Montreal, Que. H4B 1R6

GERVAIS, Hon. Paul M., B.A., LL.L.; judge; b. Sherbrooke, Que., 8 Dec. 1925; s. Hon. Justice Césaire and Sylvia (Mullins) G.; e. St. Charles Semy.; Loyola Coll.; Laval Univ.; m. Hélène Cannon, Quebec City, 14 Nov. 1953; children: Edouard, Charles, Carolyne; JUSTICE, SUPERIOR COURT OF QUE., since 1972; cr. Q.C. 1968; Ald., City of Sherbrooke. 1955-67; el. to H. of C. g.e. 1968; Batonnier, Bar of St. Francis, 1967-68 (Past Secy.); mem. Gen. Council, Que. Bar (Extve. Council); mem. Nat. Council, Candn. Bar Assn., since 1966; Pres., Indust. Comn. Assn. Que., 1965-67; Vice Chrmn. Standing Comte. on Justice & Legal Affairs 1968-70 (Chrmn. 1970-72); Clubs: Social (Hon. mem.); St. George's; Fusiliers de Sherbrooke (Hon. mem.); Réforme (Pres. 1962); Home: 453 Fréchette St., Sherbrooke, Que. J1J 2V5; Office: Court House, Sherbrooke, Que.

GESTRIN, Bengt V., M.A., Ph.D.; banking executive; b. Helsinki, Finland, 12 Jan. 1935; s. Emil Victor and Naimi (Osterberg) G.; e. Univ. of Toronto, M.A. 1963, Ph.D.(Econ.) 1966; m. Carita, d. Edwin George Erlin, March 1957; two s., Michael Victor, Philip George; VICE-PRES-ECON., CANADIAN IMPERIAL BANK OF COMMERCE since 1973; joined the Bank 1957 serving in various capacities; Econ., Bank for Internat. Settlements, Basle, Switzerland, 1966; Monetary Div., OECD, Paris, France, 1967-68, Head of N. Am. Sec. 1971-73; responsible for Econ. Briefings for Prime Min., Privy Council Office, Ottawa, 1968-71; author various financial articles for banking journs.; mem. Am. Econ. Assn.; Candn. Econ. Assm.; Home: 176 Old Yonge St., Willowdale, Ont. M2P 1A2; Office: Commerce Court West, Toronto, Ont. M5L 1P9;

GETTY, Donald, M.L.A., B.A.; businessman; b. Westmount, Que., 30 Aug. 1933; s. Charles Ross and Beatrice (Hampton) G.; e. pub. schs. Montreal, Ottawa and Toronto; high schs. Toronto and London, Ont.; Univ. of W. Ont., B.A. (Business Adm.); m. Margaret Inez Mitchell, 18 June 1955; children: Dale, David, Darin, Derek; PRES., D. GETTY INVESTMENTS LTD., Dir.; Brinco Ltd.; Placer

Devel. Ltd.; Nova Ltd.; Alta. Gas Ethylene Co. Ltd.; C.O.B., Interprovincial Steel and Pipe Co.; Dir., Chrmn., & Chief Exec. Officer, Nortek Energy Co.; Royal Bank of Can.; Dir., Genstar; Pacific Copper Mines; Novacor Ltd.; joined Imperial Oil Ltd. Natural Gas Sec., 1955, Econ. and Co-ordination 1956, Contracts Dept. 1958; joined Midwestern Industrial Gas Ltd. as Land and Contracts Mgr. 1961, Asst. Gen. Mgr. 1963; formed Baldonnel Oil and Gas Ltd. and served as Pres. and Mang. Dir. 1964; Partner, Doherty Roadhouse & McCuaig Ltd., 1967-71; el. M.L.A. for Stratchcona W. prov. g.e. 1967; re-el. M.L.A. for Edmonton Whitemud 1971 and 1975; former Min. of Fed. and Intergovernmental Affairs 1971; former Min. of Energy and Natural Resources, Gov. of Alta.; mem. Edmonton Eskimo Football Team for 10 yrs. (quarterback); named "Outstanding Canadian in Western Canada Football League", 1959; Kappa Alpha; P. Conservative; United Church; recreations: golf, horse-racing; hunting; Clubs: Petroleum (former Gov.); Derrick Golf & Winter (Past Dir.); Office P.O. Box 8202 Stn. F Edmonton, Alta. T6H 4P1

GHADIALLY, Feroze Novroji, M.B., B.S., M.D., Ph.D., D.Sc., F.R.C.P.(C); pathologist; educator; b. Bombay, India 13 Nov. 1920; s. Novroji Bomanji Ghadially; e. Univ. of London M.B., B.S. 1947, M.D. 1949, Ph.D. 1955, D.Sc. 1962; m. Edna May d. late Edward Thomas Bryant 15 Aug. 1950; 4 children; author "Ultrastructural Pathology of the Cell" 1975; co-author "Ultrastructure of Synovial Joints in Health and Disease" 1969; author "Diagnostic Electron Microscopy of Tumours" 1980; author or co-author over 170 med. publs.; author over 50 non-med. papers and books; principal writing on electron microscopy and electron probe x-ray analysis; Fellow, Royal Coll. Pathols.; Royal College of Arts; W.S. Lindsay Prof. of Coll. of Mediane and Prof. of Pathology, U. of Sask.; Izaak Walton Killam Laureate of the Canada Council (1981); recreations: aquariums, music, photography, marquetry pictures; Office: Dept. of Pathology, Health Sciences Bldg., Univ. of Sask., Saskatoon, Sask. S7N 0W0.

GHERT, Bernard Irvin, B.Sc., M.B.A.; real estate executive; b. Lethbridge, Alta.; e. McGill Univ. B.Sc. (Math. & Physics); Univ. of B.C., M.B.A. (Real Estate & Corporate Finance); PRES. AND CHIEF OPERATING OFFICER THE CADILLAC FAIRVIEW CORP. LTD.; Chrmn. and Dir. Continuous Colour Coat Ltd.; Vice Pres. Finance and Dir. The Fairview Corp. Ltd. and mem. Extve. Comte. Bd. Dirs. prior to 1974 merger with Cadillac Development Corp. Ltd. and Canadian Equity and Development Co. Ltd. forming present Co.; Gov., Dir. and Vice Chrmn. Mount Sinai Hosp., Chrmn. Finance & Budget Comte., mem. Extve. Finance and Budget Cmte. and Long Range Planning Comtes.; Dir. and Chrmn., Investment Cmte., Mount Sinai Institute; Dir. Fireman's Fund Ins. Co. of Canada; mem. Adv. Council Faculty of Comm. & Business Adm. Univ. of B.C.; recreations: cycling, photography, reading; Club: National; Office: 1200 Sheppard Ave. E., Willowdale, Ont. M2K 2R8.

GIARRUSSO, Giovanni, B. Com., C.A.; b. Montreal, Que. 22 March 1939; s. Michele and Marie (Ciarlo) G.; e. Ecole St-Philippe-de-Benizi 1953; Ecole Supérieure St-Viateur 1957; Sir George Williams Univ. B. Com. 1961; McGill Univ. Accounting 1961-63; C.A. 1967; m. Suzanne d. Lucien l'Ecuyer, Montreal, Que. 1 Sept.1962; children: Nathalie, Gian Carlo; EXTVE. VICE PRES. AND CHIEF OPERATING OFFICER MONTREAL STOCK EXCHANGE since 1974; Student in Accounts 1961-63 Touche, Ross, Bailey & Smart; joined Exchange as Asst. to Secy. 1963. Dir. of Listings 1964, Vice Pres. and Secy. (Listings) 1969, Vice Pres. and Secy. 1970, Extve. Vice Pres. Adm. 1973; mem. Ordre des Comptables Agréés du Qué.; Chambre de Comm. Française au Can.; Royal Victoria Hospital Centre (Dir.); Cdn. Council of Christians and Jews (Dir.); Italian Chamber Comm. (Pres. and Dir.); Montreal Bd. Trade; Chambre de Commerce du District

de Montréal; R. Catholic; Club: Stock Exchange (Pres. and Dir.); Office: Victoria Sq., Montreal, Que. H4Z 1A9

GIASSON, Jacques J., B.Sc., B.Eng.; manufacturer; b. Montreal, Que., 30 Oct. 1935; s. Georges Léopold and Germaine (St-Onge) G.; e. Loyola Coll., Montreal, B.Sc.; McGill Univ., B.Eng.(Civil); Univ. of Ottawa, Dipl. Business Adm.; Am. Telegraph & Telephone Assn. U.S., Dipl. Operational Research; m. Thérèse, d. Antoine Gagnon, Bedford, Que. 23 April 1960; children: Dominique, Brigitte, Philippe, Patrice, Antoine; CHMN. OF BD. & PRES., GROULX, ROBERTSON LTÉE & CHMN. OF BD., LAURENTIAN WOOD; Pres., St. Lawrence Cement Inc. & subsidiaries, 1973-81; since 1973; with Bell Canada as Supv. Engr. 1959-64; Plant Mgr. Oshawa Plant, Duplate Canada Ltd. 1965, Hawkesbury Plant 1968-69; Gen. Mgr. Mfg., Henry Birks & Sons Ltd. 1970-71; joined St. Lawrence Cement as Asst. to Pres. 1972; Dir., Campbell Soup Co. Ltd.; Black and Decker Mfg. Co.; C.J.A.D. Ltd.; Fondation de l'Université du Québec à Montréal; Dir., l'Université du Quebec à Montreal; Dir., La Laurentienne Insur. Co.; International Paints (Canada) Ltd., National Bank of Canada; Les Prévoyants du Canada, Standard Broadcasting Corp. Ltd.; mem. Candn. Chamber Comm.; Swiss-Candn. Chamber Comm.; Corp. Engrs. Que.; Assn. Prof. Engrs. Ont.; Candn. Operational Research Soc.; Candn., Prov. Que. and Montreal Chambers Comm.; World Wildlife Fund (Can.); Bd. of Govs., Conseil du Patronat du Que.; R. Catholic; recreations: skiing, tennis, swimming, travel, photography, bridge; Clubs: St-Denis; St. James; Laval sur le lac; Mount Royal; Toronto; Home: 633 Laird, Town of Mt. Royal, Que. H3R 1Y5; Office: 365 Cote Vertu, Suite 3, St. Laurent, Que. H4N 1E5

GIBBARD, Harold Allan, Ph.D.; retired university professor: b. Mission City, B.C. 25 Jan. 1912; s. George and Clara Gertrude (Cox) G.; e. Pub. and High Schs., Mission City B.C., 1918-27; Univ. of B.C., B.A. (Econ.) 1932; McGill Univ., M.A. (Sociol.) 1934; Univ. of Mich., Ph.D. (Sociol.) 1938; m. Eleanor Elizabeth. d. late J. Anderson Reid, 8 Sept. 1938; children: Allan Fletcher, Sarah Eleanor (Mrs. A. M. Cook); Instr. and Research Asst. in Sociol., Mich. State Univ., 1937-38; Instr. and Asst. Prof. of Sociol., Brown Univ., 1938-46: Asst. Prof. of Sociol., Univ. of Kansas, 1946-48; Visiting Assoc. Prof. of Sociol., Univ. of Missouri, summer 1947; Prof. of Sociol., West Virginia Univ., 1948-77, Chrmn. Dept. of Sociol. and Anthrop. 1948-69 and 1975-77; Acting Dean, Coll. of Arts and Sciences 1969-70, Asst. to Provost for Instr. 1970-76, Assoc. Provost for Instr. 1976-77, Professor Emeritus 1977; Research Assoc., Makerere Univ. Coll., Kampala, Uganda, 1968; co-author; "Fundamentals of Sociology", 1950; "A Survey of the Educational Programs of the West Virginia Public Schools", 1957; "The Southern Appalachian Region, A Survey", 1962, "Poverty Amid Affluence", 1966; "Retraining the Unemployed", 1968; other writings incl. articles and book reviews; mem., Am. Sociol. Assn.; North Central Sociol. Assn. (Pres. 1960-61); Democrat; Unitarian; Home: 741 Augusta Ave., Morgantown, W. Va. 26505

GIBBS, David George, C.A., M.B.A.; accountant; b. Vancouver, B.C. 5 May 1925; s. Albert Edward and Florence R. (Bedford) G.; e. Magee H.S., Van.; U.B.C., C.A. 1956; Simon Fraser Univ. M.B.A. 1975; m. Lenore Joy d. James Munroe DeGeer 7 Oct. 1949; children: Susan Caroline; VICE PRES., CONTROLLER AND INFORMATION SERVICES, KELLY DOUGLAS AND CO. since 1975; Audit Clerk, Price Waterhouse Co., 1943-46; joined present firm 1946; Controller, 1965; Vice Pres., Inform. Services, 1971; Technical Adv., Langara College; mem., Financial Extve. Inst., Van. Chpt. (Past Dir.); Master Zion 77 Masonic Lodge; Pres., Capilano Lions Club; Order of Kentucky Colonels; Simon Fraser MBA Assn.; Anglican; Club: Lions; recreations: boating, winemaking; Home: 956 Belgrave Ave., N. Van., B.C. V7R 1Z2; Office: 4700

Kingsway, Burnaby, B.C. V5H 2C1 or P.O. Box 2039, Van., B.C. V6B 3S1.

GIBBS, Ronald Darnley, M.Sc., Ph.D., F.R.S.C., F.L.S.; botanist; emeritus professor; b. Ryde, Isle of Wight, Eng., 30 June 1904; s. late Frank Ernest and Edith Beatrice (Wills) G.; e. Univ. Coll., Southampton, Eng.; Univ. of London, B.Sc. 1925, Ph.D. 1933; McGill Univ., M.Sc. 1926; Bd. of Educ. Cert. in Teaching 1923; m. Dr. Avis Patricia Cook 1961; one s.; Macdonald Prof. of Botany, McGill Univ., 1965-71, (Prof. of Botany there 1955-65), Prof. Emeritus, 1971; Pres., Fraser Inst., Montreal, 1955-58; Bio-chemist, Am. Rubber Producers, Salinas, Cal., 1927-28; Fellow, Roy. Soc. Can., 1939 (Pres., Sect. 5, 1953-54); Fellow, Linnean Society of London, 1949; emeritus mem., Am. Soc. Plant Physiol.; author of "A Modern Biology" (with E. J. Holmes), 1937; "Botany: an Evolutionary Approach", 1950; "Chemotaxonomy of Flowering Plants", 1974; has also contrib. about 30 papers and articles to scient. journs.; Sigma Xi (Pres., McGill Chapter, 1944); recreations: gardening; Home: 32 Orchards Way. Southampton SO2 1RE, England.

GIBSON, F. Douglas, Q.C.; b. Toronto, Ont. 18 Nov. 1929; s. Rev. John E. and Lavenia (Rankin) G.; e. Public Sch. Toronto; Ridley Coll. grad. 1949; Univ. of Toronto grad. 1953; Osgoode Hall Law Sch. 1957; m. Anne Elizabeth Pollitt; children: John, Jennifer, Christine, Duncan, Mark, Peter, James; PARTNER, PARTNER FASKEN & CALVIN; read law with Cassels Brock & Kelley; called to Bar of Ont. 1957; cr. Q.C. 1969; with Cassels Brock & Kelley 1959-62 and Fasken & Calvin since 1962; mem. Candn. Bar Assn.; Co. of York Law Assn.; Delta Upsilon; Anglican; Conservative; recreations: fishing, hunting, skiing; Clubs: York; The Toronto Hunt; Albany; Griffith Island; Lawyers; Home: 91 Elm Ave., Toronto, Ont.; Office: (P.O. Box 30) Toronto-Dominion Centre, Toronto, Ont. M5K 1C1

GIBSON, Goodwin, real estate broker and property manager, b. Toronto, Ont., 25 April 1926; s. late Col. Godwin, O.B.E. and Ione Hunter (Heintzman) G.; e. Upper Canada Coll., Toronto, Ont.; Special Courses in Real Estate Appraisal and Property Mang.; m. Sandra, d. Percy B. Williamson, Kelowna, B.C., 27 Nov. 1971; children (by former marriage): Deborah Ruth, Diana Ione, Virginia Adair, Goodwin Jr., J. Patrick; PRESIDENT, GOODWIN GIBSON & CO. LTD.; Dir. and Pres., Clarwin Ltd.; Dir., St. John's Convalescent Hospital, Newtonbrook, Ont.; Lion's Gate Internat. Inc.; Landauer Assoc. Ltd.; joined the firm of Gibson Bros. 1945 and entered into Partnership with late Col. Goodwin Gibson in 1948; upon latter's death in 1954, firm was inc., the ownership remaining unchanged; served in 2nd World War, R.C.N.V.R. 1943-45, serving overseas; mem. Am. Soc. Real Estate Counsellors; Am. Soc. Real Estate Appraisers; Soc. Indust. Realtors; Inst. Real Estate Mang.; Nat. Assn. Real Estate Bds.; Candn. Assn. Real Estate Bds.; Toronto Real Estate Bd.; Young Pres. Organ. Inc.; United Church; recreations: golf, tennis, painting; Clubs: Toronto Golf; Queen's Tennis; Toronto Badminton & Racquet; Cambridge Club; Georgian Peaks; Home: 17 Lamport, Toronto, Ont. M4W 1S7

GIBSON, Graeme C., B.A.; author; b. London, Ont. 9 Aug. 1934; s. Brig. Thomas Graeme and Mary B. (Cameron) G.; e. Univ. of Waterloo 1953-54; Univ. of W. Ont. 1954-55, 1956-58 B.A.; Univ. of Edinburgh 1955-56; children: Thomas Matthew Mann, Graeme Charles Alexander, Eleanor Jess Atwood; author "Five Legs" 1969; "Communion" 1971; "Eleven Canadian Novelists" 1973; "Perpetual Motion" 1982; "As For Me and My House" screenplay (Sinclair Ross) awaiting production; Founding mem. Writers' Union of Can. (Chrmn. 1974-75); Chrmn. Book & Periodical Devel. Council 1976; Chrmn. Writers' Devel. Trust 1977-78; NDP; recreations: birding, travel, nature; Address: 73 Sullivan St., Toronto, Ont. M5T 1C2.

GIBSON, Hon. Hugh F., B.A., B.Com.; judge; b. Kingston, Ont.; 12 Dec. 1916; s. Dr. William and K. Lillian (O'Reilly) G.; m. A. Eileen (Lynn) Barrett e. Queen's Univ. B.A. 1937, B.Com. 1938; Osgoode Hall, Toronto, Ont.; TRIAL DIV., FEDERAL COURT CAN., since 1971 (apptd. Judge of Exchequer Court Can. 1964,; Pres. of Court Martial Appeal Court 1964; called to Bar of Ont. 1942; cr. Q.C. 1960; practised law with Gibson, Sands & Flanigan, Kingston, Ont. 1946-64; Commr. investigation the loss of the M.V. "Fort William" in Montreal harbour 1965; Chrmn. Bd. of Inquiry into crash of Douglas DC-8 Toronto Internat. Airport July 1970; Chrmn., Airport Inquiry Comm. (1973 under Pub. Inquiries Act, re transp. needs of Central Ont. market; Commissioner to Inquire into Certain Allegations Concerning Commercial Practices of the Can. Dairy Comm. (1979); Phi Delta Phi; Clubs: Ontario; University; (Toronto) Cataraqui Golf & Country; Amherstview Golf; Kingston Yacht; (Kingston) Trident Yacht (Thousand Islands); Laurentian; Royal Ottawa Golf; Saint James's (Montreal); Address: 300 the Driveway S., Ottawa, Ont. K1S 3M6

GIBSON, J. Douglas, O.B.E., B.A., LL.D.; economist and banker; b. Toronto, Ont., 3 Sept. 1909; s. late Albert Ralph and late Hannah (Black) G.; e. Upper Canada Coll., Toronto, Ont., Univ. of Toronto, B.A. (Pol. Sc. and Econs.) 1931; m. Mary Margaret (died June 1958) d. late D. H. MacAndrew, Renfrew, Ont., 31 Mar. 1934; two s.; m. 2ndly, Lila Elizabeth, d. late Dr. Fletcher McPhedran, Toronto, Ont., 28 May 1959; two s., one d.; Chrmn., Canadian Reinsurance Co. and Canadian Reassurance Co.; Dir., Imperial Life Assurance Co. of Canada; Harding Carpets Ltd.; Steel Co. of Canada Ltd.; National Trust Co. Ltd.; Bell Canada; Moore Corp., Ltd.; Northern Electric Co. Ltd.; Bank of Nova Scotia as Asst. in Statistical Dept., Sept. 1931; Ed. of Monthly Review, 1935-54; Supvr., Econ. Dept., 1942 lent by Bank to W.P.T.B., Ottawa, Ont., as Chief of Econ. Research, 1942-47; awarded O.B.E. 1946; returned to Bank of Nova Scotia, April 1947; apptd. Asst. Gen. Mgr., Jan. 1954; Gen. Mgr., Dec. 1958; Dir., 1962-65; Chief Gen. Mgr., Sept. 1963; Depy. Chrmn. of Bd. and Extve. Vice-Pres., Dec. 1964; resigned from there Nov. 1965; Pres., Candn. Pol. Sc. Assn., 1955-56; mem., Royal Comn. on Banking and Finance. 1961-64; Candn. Chamber of Comm., Chrmn. Pub. Finance and Taxation Comte. 1955-57, Chrmn. Ont. Regional Comte. 1959-60; Candn. Inst. of Internat. Affairs, Chrmn. Nat. Extve. Comte. 1957-61, Chrmn. Nat. Council 1961-63; mem., Bd. of Trustees, Queen's Univ., 1963-76 and Chrm. 1970-76; Candn. del. on U.N. Ad Hoc Comte. on Finance, 1966; Visiting Prof. York University 1966-73; Publications: Editor, "Canada's Economy in a changing World", 1949, and author of many articles on Candn. econ. and financial subjects; Anglican; Clubs: Toronto; National; University (Toronto); Home: 406 Glenayr Rd., Toronto, Ont. M5P 3C7

GIBSON, J. Kerr, B.Com., F.C.A.; b. Hamilton Ont., 12 Aug. 1924; s. Hon. Colin William George and Florence (Kerr) G.; e. Hillfield Sch. Hamilton, Ont. 1941; Upper Can. Coll. Toronto, Ont. 1942; Univ. of Toronto B. Com. 1948; m. Marion Alison d. Brig. G. R. D. Farmer, Ancaster, Ont., 31 May 1952; children: Marian, Jane, Nancy, James; PARTNER, CLARKSON GORDON & CO. since 1956; joined present firm 1948; served with Candn. Army 1944-45, rank Pte.; Chrmn. Candn. Tax Foundation, 1975-76 (Gov. 1968-71 and 1973-77); Pres. Bd. Trade Metrop. Toronto 1977-78, (mem. Council 1970-79, Dir., Jr. Achievement of Can. (1978-); Dir., Council for Candn. Unity; Kappa Alpha; Liberal; Presbyterian; recreation: tennis; Clubs: University; Queens; Arts and Letters; Tamahaac; Home: 91 Wychwood Park, Toronto, Ont. M6G 2V5; Office: Royal Trust Tower, Toronto, Ont. M5K 1J7

GIBSON, James Alexander, M.A., M.Litt., D. Phil. (Oxon.); LL.D.; president emeritus; b. Ottawa, Ont., 29 Jan. 1912; s. John Wesley, M.A., D.Paed., & Belle Crawford (Magee) G.; e. Public and High Schs. and Victoria Coll., Victoria, B.C.; Univ. of B.C., B.A. 1931; New Coll. Oxford (Rhodes Scholar from B.C. 1931), B.A. 1933, M.Litt. 1934, D.Phil. (Modern History) 1938, M.A. 1953; Carleton Univ., LL.D., 1964; m. Caroline Rauch, d. late Rev. J.R. Stein, D.D., Philadelphia, Pa., 29 Dec. 1938; children: Mrs. Arnold G. Matthews, Peter James, Mrs. Gérald Joly; Emeritus Pres., Brock Univ. 1974 (apptd. Pres. 1963); Lecturer, University of British Columbia, 1937-38; Foreign Service Offr., Dept. of External Affairs, 1938-47 (seconded to office of Prime Min.); mem. Candn. del. to U.N. Conf. on Internat. Organ., San Francisco (1945); Secy to Prime Min. at meeting of Commonwealth Prime Mins., London (1946); mem. Candn. del. Conf. on Peace Treaties, Paris (1946); joined Carleton Univ. as Assoc. Prof. of Hist., 1947; Prof. 1949; Dean, Faculty of Arts & Science, 1951-63; Dean of Arts and Deputy to the Pres., 1963; resigned 1963; Guggenheim Fellow 1953; Visiting Fellow, Princeton Univ., 1953-54; Visiting Scholar, Univ. of Kent at Canterbury, 1972; Visiting Prof. of Candn. Studies, Univ. of Edinburgh, 1976-77; Jules & Gabrielle Léger Fellowship, 1980; Publications: "Sir Edmund Head: A Scholarly Governor" (with D.G.G. Kerr), 1954; contrib. to learned journs.; mem. Bd. Govs. Ridley Coll. (1964); Pres., Candn. Assn. Rhodes Scholars, 1963-65, Secy.-Treas. and Ed., 1977- ; Vice Pres., The Niagara Inst. 1972-76; mem., Canadian Hist. Association; Candn. Inst. Internal. Affairs; Pres., Canadian Writers Foundation, Inc., 1960-63; Vice-Pres., UN Nations Assn. in Can. 1970-72; awarded Medal of Hellenic Red Cross, 1953; Coronation Medal, 1953; Centennial Medal, 1967; Queen Elizabeth II Silver Jubilee Medal, 1977; Unitarian; recreation: gardening; Home: R.R.1, Vineland Stn., Ont. L0R 2E0

GIBSON, John Day; investment mgr. (retired); b. Guelph, Ont., 9 Nov. 1915; s. Leonard and Marion Gertrude (Fox) G.; e. Marchwood W. (Que.) Pub. Sch.; Town of Mt. Royal (Que) Pub. and High Sch.; Montreal (Que.) High Sch.; McGill Univ., 1933-34; Babson Inst. (Gen. Econs.), 1934-36; m. Celo Patricia, d. Eldon P. Racicot, 31 May 1938; two s. John G., David L.; VICE-PRES. & DIR., UNITED NORTH AMERICAN HOLDINGS LTD.; Chrmn., Dir., Candiac Development Corp.; Candiac Nurseries Ltd.; Vice-Pres. & Dir., Sparmont Corp. Ltd.; Dir., Canadian Internat. Investment Trust Ltd.; La Compagnie Foncière du Manitoba (1967), Ltée; Elican Development Co. Ltd.; Combines Estates Corp.; Dir., Combined Mortgage Corp.; Pres. and Dir. French American Management Ltd.; began career as Gen. Clerical and Adm. Asst., Canadian Alliance Corp. Ltd., 1932-40; joined Gairdner & Co. Ltd. as Bond Trader, 1946, Inst. Rep., 1948-50, Sales Mgr., Montreal, Que., 1950-52; admitted to Partnership, 1952; Resident Dir., 1953-60 when retired from the firm; Pres., Norac Finance Corpn. 1961-64; served during 2nd World War with Black Watch of Can. as 2nd Lieut.; retired with rank of Major, 1946; awarded Order of the White Lion (Czech.); Anglican; recreations: bridge, gardening, fishing, hunting; Clubs: Ile aux Saumons Inc.; Dir. Owl's Head Fish and Game Club; Home: Suite 803 40 Baif Blvd., Richmond Hill, ONT. L4C-5M9; Office: Ste. 800, 1420 Sherbrooke, St. W., Montreal, Que. H3G 1K8

GIBSON, Kelly H.; retired: b. Broken Arrow, Okla., 19 March 1912 (Candn. Citizen 1964); s. late Kelly F. and Annie Beatrice (French) G.; e. Oklahoma Mil. Acad., Claremore, Okla.; m. Juliette M., d. late A. V. Robinson, 3 Feb. 1934; two s. James K., Allan S.; Past Dir., Can. Liquid Air Ltd. Genstar Ltd.; Royal Bank of Canada; Past Chrmn. and Dir., Foothills Pipe Lines (Yukon) Ltd., 1974-79; Past Dir., Chrysler Canada Ltd.; Conference Bd. of N.Y.; Pacific Petroleums Ltd.; with Gulf Refining Co. prior to coming to Canada in Aug. 1949 on joining Candn. Gulf Oil Co.; joined Pacific Petroleums Ltd. as Vice-Pres. Nov. 1957; apptd. Extve. Vice-Pres. July 1959; Pres. and Chief Extve. Offr., May 1964, Chrmn. and Chief Extve. Offr. July 1970, retiring as Chrmn. Dec.

1974; Chrmn. and C.E.O. of Westcoast Transmission Co. Ltd., (1970-77); Chrmn. of Board of Westcoast Petroleum Ltd., (1975-78); served in 2nd World War with U.S. Army, 1943-46; Protestant; recreations: reading, Clubs: Calgary Golf & Country; Rotary Club of Calgary; Calgary Petroleum; Ranchmen's; Home: 708 Riverdale Ave. S.W., Calgary, Alta. T2S 0Y3

GIBSON, Shirley; Mann; writer; critic; arts administrator; literary theatre consultant; b. Toronto, Ont., 28 Dec. 1927; d. Charles Stuart and Ivy Grace (Mann) White; e. Howard Park Public School and W. Tech. & Comm. High Sch., Toronto; m. Graeme Cameron Gibson, 1959; two s., Thomas Matthew Mann, Graeme Charles Alexander; divorced 1976; joined Radio Stn. CHUM, Toronto, 1944-45; Asst. to Curator, London (Ont.) Art Museum, 1946-52; founded and managed own retail business 1953-59; Asst. to Ed., "Arts/Canada" mag. 1967-69; joined House of Anansi Press as Mang. Ed. 1970; Pres. Mang. Ed. and Dir. 1972 resigning Dec. 1974; EXEC. DIR. PLAYWRIGHTS CANADA, 1977; 1979, Vice-Pres. Can. Centre of Internat. Theatre Inst.; Pres., Assn. of Cultural Executives, 1981; Assn. of Cultural Exec.; mem. Nat. Joint-Parl. Comte. on Cult. Policy; former mem. Bd. of Govs., Candn. Conf. of the Arts; Past Chrmn. League Can. Poets; author, "I am Watching" (poetry), 1973; "Bloodline and other Poems" 1982; Can. Council Senior Arts Grant (Writing), 1979; Protestant; recreations: books, music; Clubs: Bookman's; Home: 120 South Dr., Toronto, Ont. M4W 1R8

GIBSON, William Carleton, M.D., D.Phil.; b. Ottawa, Ont. 4 Sept. 1913; s. John Wesley and Belle Crawford (Magee) G.; e. Univ. of B.C. B.A. 1933; McGill Univ. M.Sc. 1936, M.D. 1941; Oxford Univ. D.Phil. 1938; m. Barbara Catherine d. late Dr. Walter Stewart Baird 29 Dec. 1946; children: David Baird Penfield, Ian Kenneth, Catherine Ann; Chmn. Univs. Council of B.C. (adv. to Govt. of B.C. on univ. affairs expenditure); Exec. Dir. Terry Fox Med. Res. Fdn.; B.C.; Trustee, Cancer Control Agency of B.C.; Corp. mem. Muscular Dystrophy Assn.; Hon. Dir. Cedar Lodge for Retarded Children, Duncan, B.C.; Kinsmen Prof. of Neurol. Research Univ. of B.C. 1950-60, Prof. Hist. of Med. & Science 1960-78; Dir. of Research, Mental Hosps. of New S. Wales, Sydney 1948-49; Visiting Prof. Neurol. Univ. of Cal. San Francisco 1949, Hist. of Med. Yale 1960; Ald. City of Vancouver 1972-74, 1976-78, Parks Commr. 1974-76; served with RCAF 1941-45, Clin. Investigation Units, Depy. Dir. Med. Research AFHQ 1945, Wing Commdr. 1950-60, Sr. Med. Offr. 19 Wing (Auxiliary) Vancouver; rec'd Centennial Medal 1967; Queen's Silver Jubilee Medal 1977; author 'Young Endeavour' and 'Creative Minds in Medicine' 1959; co-author 'The World of Ramón y Cajal' 1962; 'Sherrington — His Life and Thought' 1978; numerous scient. articles on brain research and med. hist.; Hon. Fellow, Green College, Oxford; Hon. Dir. Kinsmen Foundation; Bot. Gdns. Assn. (Past Pres.); Past Pres. UBC Alumni Assn.; UBC Faculty Assn.; EEG Societies (Can. USA & UK); Pres. Am. Osler Soc.; mem., Council of the Rockefeller Univ. in New York; Hon. mem. Osler Club London; Med. Soc. London; Liberal; United Church; recreation: music; Clubs: University (Past Pres.); Athenaeum (London); Home: 4582 W. 5th Ave., Vancouver, B.C. V6R 1S7; Office: 500 — 805 W. Broadway, Vancouver, B.C. V5Z 1K1.

GIERUSZCZAK, Thaddeus Edward, B.Sc.; P.Eng.; b. Sulkowice, Krakow, Poland 25 Sept. 1923; s. late Albert Wojciech and Anna (Marek) G.; came to Canada 1929; e. Holy Rosary Separate Sch. Hamilton, Ont. 1936; Cathedral High Sch. 1941; McMaster Univ. B.Sc. (Hons.) Chem. and Physics 1945; Univ. of Toronto, M.B.A. course; m. Alda Isabelle, d. late John Torrey 26 July 1958; children: John Albert, Lori Jean, Marianne; VICE-PRES. ADMINISTRATIVE SERVICES, CONSUMERS' GAS CO. 1980- ; joined the Co. as Lab. Asst. Works Div. 1947,

Chief Chem. Works Div. 1952, Staff Asst. to Gen. Supt. Works 1955, Asst. Gen. Supt. Gas Supply 1957, Asst. to Vice-Pres. Gas Supply 1966, Staff Asst. to Pres. and Mgr. Research and Devel. 1968, Asst. to Pres. 1970; Vice-Pres. Research and Special Projects, 1973; First Chrmn. Bd. Dirs. Candn. Gas Research Inst.; Past Pres., Ont. Natural Gas Assn.; Dir. Consumers' Realty Ltd.; mem., Chem. Inst. Can. (Past Treas. Econ. and Business Mang. Div.); Candn. Gas Assn.; Am. Gas Assn. (recipient Award of Merit 1965); Recipient of Queen Elizabeth II Silver Jubilee Medal, 1977, for contributions to the Canadian GAS Industry; Assn. Prof. Engrs. Ont.; United Church; recreations: gardening, fishing, philately, skiing, golfing, curling; Clubs: Engineers; Canadian; Cambridge; Toronto Bd. of Trade; Home: 57 Doonaree Dr., Don Mills, Ont. M3A 1M5; Office: 1 First Canadian Pl., Toronto, Ont.

GIFFIN, Earl Kitchener, B.Sc., C.L.U.; insurance executive; b. Pembroke, Ont., 11 Jan. 1916; s. Gordon Henry and Carrie Maude (Cowan) G.; e. Plattsburg (N.Y.) High Sch.; Ithaca Coll., B.Sc. 1939; m. Sarah Gwen d. Elmer Davies, Lansford, Pa., 22 Nov. 1941; children: Gordon Davies, Gwendolyn Cheryl; REGIONAL VICE PRES., GREATER N.Y. REGION, NEW YORK LIFE INS. CO. since 1976; formerly of East Central Region; Res. Vice-Pres. of Co., Toronto Ont.; Past Pres., Valois Citizens Assn.; Past Chrmn., Lake St. Louis Boy Scouts Council; Past Pres., Montreal Life Managers Assn.; Past Vice Pres., Montreal Kiwanis Club; served in 2nd World War, U.S. Army European Theatre Operation, 1942-46; Member of Am. Army Newspaper "Stars and Stripes"; awarded "The Bronze Star Medal" and Cert. of Conspicuous Service; mem., Life Underwriters Assn.; Life Managers Assn.; Phi Mu Alpha (Pres. and Life mem.); Protestant: Office: Room 2600, 51 Madison Ave., New York, N.Y. 10010

GIFFIN, Hon. Ronald Chapman, M.L.A., LL.B.; politician; b. Windsor, N.S. 1 Dec. 1942; s. Reginald Manning Giffin; e. Windsor Acad. 1959; Acadia Univ. B.A. 1963; Dalhousie Univ. Law Sch. LL.B. 1965; m. Patricia Wade 11 July 1970; two s. Gregory Bennett, Christopher Reginald; CHRMN. OF MANAGEMENT BD., N.S. 1979- , Pres. of Treasury Bd., Min. responsible adm. Civil Service Act and mem. Extve. Council N.S.; called to Bar of N.S. 1966; Partner, Burchell, MacDougall & Gruchy, Truro, N.S. 1966-78; el. M.L.A. for Truro-Bible Hill prov. g.e. 1978, re-elected 1981; Min. of Mun. Affairs and Min. responsible adm. Human Rights Act 1978; Pres. Colchester Barristers Soc. 1978; mem. N.S. Barristers Soc. (Council 1976-78); Candn. Bar Assn.; P. Conservative; Baptist; recreations: curling, swimming, movies, reading, cooking; Club: Truro Men's; Home: 34 Broad St., Truro N.S. B2N 3G2; Office: 1690 Hollis St. (P.O. Box 1619), Halifax, N.S. B3J 2Y3.

GIFFORD, Hilda Gorham, B.A., B.L.S.; librarian; b. Montreal, P.Q., 22 Sept. 1915; d. William Alva and Charlotte Elsie (Hitcham) G.; e. McGill Univ. B.A. 1937, B.L.S. 1938; unm.; COLLECTIONS LIBRARIAN, CARLETON UNIV., 1969-81; with Dalhousie Univ. Library, Halifax, N.S., 1938-43; Postal Censorship, German P.O.W., 1943-45; Internat. Labour Office Lib., 1945-46; Dartmouth Coll. Lib., Hanover, N.H., 1947-48; Chief Lib., Carleton Univ. 1948-69; mem., Candn. Lib. Assn.; Bibliographical Soc. Can.; United Church; recreation: Scottish country dancing; Clubs: Cercle Universitaire (Ottawa); Royal Overseas League (London); Home: 150 Queen Elizabeth Driveway #109, Ottawa, Ont.

GIGNAC, Jacques, B.A., TH.L., L.Sc.S., L. Lettres; diplomate; né Shawinigan, Qué. 24 Juil. 1928; f. James et Jeanne (Gigaire) G.; é. Collège Jean-de-Brébeuf, Montréal, Institut des Sciences Politiques, Paris; Institut Catholique de Paris; La Sorbonne; Etudes post graduées (Sociologie) Univ. de Montréal; ép. Françoise, f. Guilhem Teisserenc, Lodève, France, 19 Juil. 1958; enfants: Guill-

aume, Sébastien, Emmanuel, Marie-Félicité, Marie-Flore; Professeur d'économie au Collège Ste. Marie, Montréal 1957-58; entre au Ministère des Affaires extérieures comme agent du service extérieur, Ottawa 1958; Direction de l'Information 1958; Direction des Affaires d'Asie 1959; Vice-Consul, Boston, Mass. 1960; Deuxième Secrétaire, Paris 1962-65; Adjoint, Direction des Affaires culturelles, Ottawa 1965, puis Chef, (1967-70; Ambassadeur du Canada au Liban, 1970-74, et concurrement en Syrie, 1970, en Jordanie 1970, ainsi qu'en Iraq en 1972 et en Arabie Saoudite en 1973; Ambassadeur en Tunisie 1974-77; Dir. général des Affaires d'Amérique Latine et des Antilles, 1977; Sous-Secrétaire d'Etat adjoint aux Affaires extérieures depuis 1978; Sous-secrétaire d'Etat suppléant, 1981; Cath. romain; recréations: ski, natation, marche, lecture; Bureau: Ministère des Affaires extérieures, Edifice Lester B. Pearson, Ottawa, Ont.

GIGNAC, Jean-Paul, O.C. (1976), B.A., B.Sc.A., P.Eng.; industrial executive; b. Shawinigan, Que. 7 Feb. 1922; s. James and Jeanne (Giguère) G.; e. Coll. Jean-de-Brébeuf, B.A. 1942; Ecole Polytechnique B.Sc.A. (Engn.) 1947; m. Joan Hébert, Shawinigan, Que. 11 Dec. 1947; 7 children; Pres. and C.E.O. Iron and Steel Co. Trinidad & Tobago, Pt. of Spain, Trinidad, W.I.; Former President & C.E.O. Sidbec & Sidbec-Dosco Ltd. 1966-79; Dir. Trans-Canada Corp. Fund; Power Corp. of Canada Ltd.; mem. Bd. of Directors, Pratt, Whitney Aircraft Can. Ltd.; mem. Bd. of Trustees, Clinical Research Inst. of Montréal; mem. Extve. Comte. (1967-70) and mem. Bd. of Govs. (1967-73) Univ. of Montréal; former Dir., Conf. Bd. Can.; Dir. and mem., Extve. Comm. of Candn. Standards Assn., 1963-69; mem. of Natl. Research Council (1968-72); began as Engn. Supvr., Dufresne Engineering 1947-51; apptd. Gen. Mgr. of Albert Gigaire Co. Ltd., Shawinigan, 1951; Commr. of Hydro-Québec 1961-69; Awards: Dr. Applied Science, Univ. Sherbrooke (1968), Montreal (1973); Mérite d'Or, Univ. Montreal; "Man of the Year" York Univ. (1968); Archambault Medal for Advanc. of Sciences; recreations: tennis, golf, skiing; Clubs: Canadian; Cercle de la Place d'Armes; R. Catholic; Home: 3400 rue de la Montagne, Shawinigan, Que. G9N 6V4

GIGUERE, Hon. Louis de G.; senator; administrator; b. Hébertville, Qué., 18 Dec. 1911; s. Joseph and Alexina (Michaud) G.; e. Chicoutimi (Qué.) Coll.; Sherbrooke (Qué.) Coll.; Laval Univ., Law, Social Sciences and Pol. Econ., 1934-37; Secy. Gen., Institut Canadien des Affaires publiques, 1954-61; Dir. and mem. Extve. Comte., Central Mortgage & Housing Corp., 1963-68; mem. Candn. NATO Parlty. Assn. and Candn. World Federalists Parlty. Assn.; summoned to Senate of Can. Sept. 1968; Liberal; recreation: golf; Clubs: Laval sur le Lac Golf; Indian Creek Country (Fla.); Home: 1455 Sherbrooke West, Montreal, Que. H3G 1L2; Office: The Senate, Ottawa, Ont.

GIGUERE, Paul A(ntoine), C.C. (1970), B.A., B.Sc., Ph.D., D.Sc., F.R.S.C., F.C.I.C; chemist; professor (retired); b. Québec, Qué., 13 Jan. 1910; s. Joseph-Emile and Diana (Poitras) G.; e. Séminaire de Québec, B.A. 1930; Laval Univ., B.Sc. 1934; McGill Univ., Ph.D. 1937; (Hon.) D.Sc. Sherbrooke 1970; m. Magdeleine, d. Léandre Lippens, 21 July 1937; with Candn. Industries Ltd., 1937-39; California Inst. of Tech., 1939-41 and 1947-48; Lectr., Laval Univ. 1941-43, Assoc. Prof. 1943-47; Prof. 1947-76; Emeritus Prof. 1978; Dir. of Chem. Dept. 1957-67; mem. Extve. Council 1968-71; Visiting Prof., Univ. of South Florida, Tampa, 1974-78; awarded Nat. Research Council Fellowship, 1935-37; Fellow of the Guggenheim Foundation, 1946-47; Pariseau Medal (ACFAS) 1945; Prix David 1944; Premier lauréat Concours Scient. du Qué. 1967; Palladium Medal, CIC, 1965 Médaille Lavoisier (Soc. chimique de France) 1967; mem. Can. Science Council 1968-71; Dir., Chem. Inst. of Can. 1945-47 (Vice Pres. 1965; Pres. 1966-67); Fellow Roy. Soc. Can.; Chem. Inst. Can., Am. Assn. Advanc. Science; N.Y. Acad. of Sciences; Spectroscopy Soc. Can., Sigma Xi; Liberal; Roman Catholic; Home: 500 - 380 Chemin St-Louis, Québec, Qué. G1S 4M1

GILBERT, Adrian Bradford, Q.C.; b. Gagetown, N.B., 1895; e. Univ. of New Brunswick, B.A. 1916, M.A. 1919; Oxford Univ., B.A. (Juris.) 1921, B.C.L. 1922 (Rhodes Schol. from N.B. 1919) (Hon.) D.C.L. (U.N.B.) 1981; m.; two children; PARTNER, GILBERT, McGLOAN, GILLES, AND JONES; called to the Bar of N.B. 1922; cr. K.C. 1943; practised with Weldon & McLean, Saint John N.B., until 1929; Partner, Gilbert & McGloan, 1929-49: Gilbert, Ritchie & McGloan 1949-50; Ald. of Saint John 1936-40; served in World War 1916-19 with 12th Siege Batty., R.C.A.; World War 1940-44 as G.S.O.2, Mil. Dist. 7, and O.C., 21st Field Regt., R.C.A., with rank of Lieut.-Col.; mem. of Senate, Univ. of New Brunswick, 1936-40 and 1946-50; mem., N.B. Barristers' Soc. (Pres. 1949); Candn. Bar Assn. (mem. of Council; Hon. Treas.); Clubs: Riverside Golf and Country; Union; Canadian; Cliff; Office: 133 Prince William St., Saint John, N.B. E1L 2B5

GILBERT, Most Rev. Arthur Joseph, B.A., B.D. (R.C.); bishop; b. Hedley, B.C. 26 Oct. 1915; s. George Miles and Ethel May (Carter) G.; e. St. Joseph's (N.B.) Coll.; St. Francis Xavier Univ. B.A.; Holy Heart Semy. B.D.; BISHOP OF SAINT JOHN since 1974; o. Priest 1943; served as Curate St. Andrews Parish N.B.; Secy. to Bishop and Chancellor of Diocese Saint John 1943-49; Dir. Silver Falls Orphanage 1949-55; Pastor St. Pius X Parish 1955-69; St. Joseph's Loch Lomond 1969-71, St. Joachim's Saint John 1974; Chancellor & Chrmn. Bd. of Governors, St. Thomas Univ. Fredericton, N.B.; Chrmn. Bd. Dirs. (diocesan newspaper) ''The New Freeman''; K. of C.; Home: 9 Bishop's Dr., Renforth, Saint John, N.B. E2H 2N2; Office: 91 Waterloo, Saint John, N.B. E2L 3P9

GILBERT, Gabriel, LL.L., D.E.S.Jur.; b. Québec, Qué., 13 Jan. 1927; s. Alice (Lamonde) and Hon. J. Oscar Gilbert, c.l.; e. Jésuites Coll., Québec; Laval Univ., B.A., LL.L., D.E.S. Jur.; m. Normande, d. J. Alphonse Allaire, Québec, 25 Sept. 1951; children: Anne, Bernard, Andre; COUNSEL, FLYNN, RIVARD, AND ASSOCIATES; Hon. Life mem. The Canadian Press: mem. of Bd. Le Soleil Ltée (formerly Publisher and Chief Exec.Director); The Price Co. Limited; Dir., La Compagnie d'Assurance du Québec; mem. Qué. Bar Assn.; Candn. Bar Assn.; Roman Catholic; recreations: fishing, golf, skiing, bridge; Clubs: The Garrison: Le Cercle Universitaire de Québec; Home: 1510 Beau-lieu 502 Sillery, Qué G1S 4R3; Office: 2 ave. Chaveau, Quebec, Que. G1R 4J3

GILBERT, Guy, Q.C., B.A., LL.L.; b. Alma, Qué. 19 June 1929; s. Jules and Adrienne (Desjardins) G.; e. St. Charles Garnier Coll. Qué. 1947; Brébeuf Coll. Montréal 1948; Loyola Coll. Montréal B.A. 1951; Univ. of Montréal LL.L. 1955; Univ. of W. Ont. Sch. of Business Adm. 1955-56; m. Lise d. Paul Dufresne, St-Hilaire, Qué. 1 Oct. 1960 children: Frédéric, Philippe, Clément, Bernard; SR. PARTNER, GILBERT AND PARTNERS Sr. Partner, Gilbert, Magnan, Marcotte, Simard, Tremblay & Forget; Dir. Cleyn & Tinker Ltd.; Pierre Gauthier & Fils Ltée; called to Bar of Qué. 1955; cr. Q.C. 1972; law practice Tansey, de Grandpré, Bergeron & Monet 1955-62; estbd. present firm 1963; Pres. Goodholme Investments 1960-61; Pres. Disciplinary Comte. Prof. Corp. Phys. Que. 1974-76; offr. various assns. Brébeuf Coll. 1973-76; Pres. déjeuners-causerie Chambre de Comm. du dist. de Montréal 1974-75; served with UNTD 1950-52, rec'd Strathcona Medal; awarded Bronze Medal Competition Order of Forestry Merit Dept. Lands & Forests Qué. 1975; author various articles; del. legal confs.; Counsel Jr. Bar 1960-62; mem. Montréal Bar (offr. various comtes.; prof. to articling students); Qué. Bar Assn. (Secy. 1964-65); Candn. Bar Assn.; R. Catholic; recreations: arts, agriculture, education; politics; Home: 77 Maplewood, Outremont, Qué.

H2V 2L9; Office: 2020 University, Room 1600, Montréal, Qué. H3A 2A5

GILCHRIST, William McKenzie, B.Sc.; company president; b. Weyburn. Sask., 29 July 1909; s. William A. and Mary Elizabeth (Scott) G.; e. High Schs., Kelvington, Sask., and Chatham, Ont.; Univ. of Manitoba; Queen's Univ., B.Sc. (Mining and Metall.) 1936; PRES., W. M. GILCHRIST & ASSOC. LTD. since 1975; Director, Madawaska Mines Ltd.; New Cinch Uranium Ljtd.; Royal Candn. Geographical Society; Westfield Minerals Ltd.; Aquarius Resources Ltd.; Saskuran Explorations Ltd.; mem. Arctic Inst. of N. Amer. (gov. 1966-71); Atomic Ind. Forum; Candn. Inst. of Mining & Metallurgy (Pres. 1974-75); Candn. Nuclear Assn. (Pres. 1971-72); engaged in various mining operations in Central Man. and N.W. Quebec, 1936-39; Engn. Staff, Preston East Dome Mines Ltd., 1939-41; Efficiency Engr. there, 1945-46; exploration and devel. in N.W. Terr. for Trans American Mining Co. Ltd., 1946-50; Chief Engr. and Underground Supt., Giant Yellowknife Gold Mines Ltd., 1950-51; Vice-Pres. and Mgr. of Mines, Transcontinental Resources Ltd., 1951-52; joined Eldorado Nuclear Ltd. in 1952; Asst. Mgr. of Beaverlodge Operation, 1952-1955; Vice-Pres. in charge of Western Operations, 1958; Pres. and Chrmn. of Bd. of Eldorado Nuclear Ltd. and subsidiaries, 1958-74; retired as Pres. of Eldorado Nuclear Ltd., remaining Chrmn. of Bd.; remained as Pres. of all subsidiaries, 1974; retired from all companies 1975; served in 2nd World War, 1941-45 with Royal Canadian Engrs.; discharged with rank of Staff Capt.; awarded Massey Medal, 1975; Clubs: Engineers (Toronto); Rideau; United Church; Office: Ste. 910, 85 Albert St., Ottawa, Ont. K1P 6A4

GILHOOLY, David James, III, M.A., R.C.A.; artist; b. Auburn, Cal 15 Apl. 1943; s. Dr. David James, Jr. and Gladys Catherine (Schulte) G.; e. Univ. of Cal. Davis B.A. 1965, M.A. 1967; m. Sheila Anne d. late Rodney Allée 10 Oct. 1963; children: David James IV, Andrea Elizabeth, Abigail Margaret, Peter Rodney; Teacher, San Jose State Coll. 1967-69; Univ. of Sask. 1969-71; York Univ. Toronto 1971-75, 1976-77; Univ. of Cal. Davis 1975-76, summers 1971, 1975, 1976; Cal. State Univ. Sacremento summers 1978-79; maj. solo exhns. incl.: San Francisco Museum of Art 1967; M.H. deYoung Mem. Museum San Francisco 1968; Matrix Gallery Wadsworth Atheneum Hartford, Conn. 1976; Museum of Contemporary Art Chicago 1976; Vancouver Art Gallery 1976; ARCO Center for Visual Arts Los Angeles 1977; Traveling Exhn. Candn. maritimes and Ont. 1978-79; St. Louis Ms. of Art 1981 rep. in numerous group exhns. incl.: Berkeley (Cal.) Art Museum, Inst. Contemporary Art Boston 1967; Musée d'art de la Ville Paris 1973; Art. Gallery Ont. and N.Y. Cultural Center 1973; Whitney Museum of Am. Art N.Y. 1974; San Francisco Museum of Art and Nat. Coll. of Fine Art and Nat. Coll. of Fine Art Washington, D.C. 1976-77; Stedelijk Museum Amsterdam 1979; Whitney Mus. of Am. Art, N.Y. 1981; comns. incl. ''Merfrog Family Fountain'' Stanford Univ.; ''Seattle's Own Ark'' Woodland Park Zoo Seattle; ''Bread Wall'' Govt. Can. Bldg. Calgary; ''Performing Frogs'' Eugene (Ore.) Center for Performing Arts; rep. in various perm. colls. incl. Nat. Gallery Can.; Can. Council Art Bank; Stedelijk Museum Amsterdam; Whitney Museum of Am. Art and other colls. Can., USA and Australia; work cited various publs.; came to Can. 1969; Candn. citizen 1976; recreations: collecting; Address: 400 Iris, Davis, Cal. 95616.

GILL, C. Foster; banker; b. Glace Bay, N.S. 4 Dec. 1927; e. Windsor N.S. High Sch; m. Wanda Mounce, 11 Feb. 1950; children: Michael, Patricia, Jennifer; SR. VICE PRES. AND GEN. MGR., THE BANK OF NOVA SCOTIA; Dir. Scotia-Toronto Dominion Leasing Ltd.; Clubs: National; St. George's Golf & Country; Home: 2143 Devon Rd., Oakville, Ont.; Office: 44 King St. W., Toronto, Ont. M5H 1H1.

GILLAN, T. M.; company executive; b. Toronto Ont., 20 April 1912; s. Robert Smith and Elizabeth (McBryde) G.; e. Pub. Sch. and Oakwood Coll. Inst. Toronto, Ont.; Dominion Bus. Coll.; m. Geraldine Eva, d. David F. McLay, Winnipeg, Man., 22 June 1940; children: Mary Louise, Robert David; DIRECTOR OF BD. CORNING CANADA LTD., since 1967; Dir., Four-Phase Systems Ltd.; Dir., Four-Phase Finance Inc.; began as Sales Rep., Colgate-Palmolive-Peet, 1930-33; joined John A. Huston Co. Ltd. as Sales Rep., 1934; Westn. Sales Supervisor, 1939-46; Sales Mgr., 1946-52; Vice-Pres., 1952-53; Extve. Vice-Pres., 1953-60; President, Corning Canada 1960; Chrmn. of Bd. P. Conservative; Presbyterian; recreations: boy's work and youth service; shooting; Home: "Openwood", R.R. l, Caledon East, Ont. L0N 1E0; Office: 135 Vanderhoof Ave., Leaside, Ont. M4G 2J3

GILLEN, Ralph L., M.A.; executive; b. New York City, N.Y., 3 May 1928; s. Benjamin and Rose (Kalner) G.; e. Queens Coll'., N.Y., B.A. 1949; Fletcher Sch. of Law and Diplomacy (Tufts and Harvard Univs.), M.A. 1950; Univ. of Liverpool, 1950-51 (Fulbright Fellow); m. Ruth Irene Sperling, 29 Apl. 1956; two s., Gerald Roy, Jay Michael; PRES. AND CEO, CANADIAN COMMERCIAL CORP. since 1978; Chrmn. of Bd., Ins. Corp. of B.C., 1978-1980; joined International Marketing Division, R.C.A., New York, 1950; Securities Analyst, E. F. Hutton and Co., New York, 1951; Management Consultant, McKinsey and Co., Inc., Washington, D.C. 1954, Cleveland 1963, Partner, 1961-68; joined Macmillan Bloedel Ltd. as Vice Pres., Marketing, Pulp and Paper, 1969, Vice Pres., Pulp & Paper Group 1970, Vice Pres., Strategic Planning and Devel. 1971-78 Instr. in Econ., Tufts Univ. 1949-50; served with U.S. Naval Reserve 1945-47; U.S. Naval Intelligence 1951-53; rank Lt.; mem. Extve. Comte., Nat. Marketing Adv. Bd., U.S. Dept. of Comm., 1967-68; Regional Expansion Council, U.S. Dept. of Commerce, 1965-6; Secy.-Treas., Fed. Stat. Users Conf., 1957-64; Bd. mem., Community Services Div., Cleveland Welfare Fed. 1965-68; mem. Adv. Council, Cleveland Inst. of Music (Trustee & Chmn. Finance Comte 1965-69); Chmn. Arts Review Comte (Cleveland) 1966; Citizens League Candidate Evaluation Comte. (Cleveland 1967; mem. Univ. Council of B.C. 1976-79; Vice Chrmn. Bd. of Trustees, Vancouver Academy of Music 1970-78; Adv. Council, Multiple Sclerosis Soc. of B.C., 1976-80; Trustee Hudson Institute of Can. 1975- ; author, "Needed: A Marketing Concept for Labor" 1965; co-author, "The Business Representatives in Washington" 1961; contrib. to various business mang. publs.; mem., Nat. Assn. Business Econs.; Am. Marketing Assn. (Pres. Washington Chapter 1962-63); recreations: bridge, opera; Clubs: Vancouver; University (Vancouver); St. James's (Montreal); Home: 28 Belvedere Cres., Ottawa, Ont. K1M 2E4; Office: Tower B, 112 Kent St., Ottawa, Ont. K1A 1E9

GILLESPIE, Hon. Alastair William, P.C., M.P.; M.A.; M.Com.; b. Victoria, B.C., 1 May 1922; s. Erroll Pilkington and Catherine Beatrice (Oliver) G.; e. Brentwood Coll. Inst., 1941; Univ. of B.C. 1941; McGill Univ., B. Com. 1947; Oxford Univ., M.A. 1949; Univ. of Toronto, M.Com.; m. Diana Christie, d. Christie T. Clark, 17 June 1947; children: Cynthia, Ian; Min. of Energy, Mines and resources; Science & Technology, 1978-79; formerly Pres., Welmet Industries Ltd.; Canadian Chromalox Co.; Vice Pres. and Dir., Canadian Corporate Mang. Co. Ltd.; Dir. and Vice Pres. Operations, W. J. Gage Ltd.; Dir., Richardson, Bond and Wright Ltd.; International Equipment Co. Ltd.; Mechanics for Electronics Inc.; The Larkin Lumber Co.; Extve. Lib. Party in Ont. 1965-68; el. to H. of C. for Etobicoke in g.e. 1968, 72, 74; defeated g.e. 1979; Min. of Ind. Trade & Commerce (1972-75); Min. of State for Sci. & Technology (1971-72); Partly. Secy. to Pres. of Treasury Bd. 1970; mem. Med. Policy Comte. and Budget Comte. Hosp. for Sick Children, 1965-68; Nat. Ballet Sch.; Chrmn., Candn. Inst. Pub. Affairs, 1962-64 (Dir. 1954-65); served with RCNVR Air Arm 1941-45; rank Lt. (Pi-

lot); rec'd Centennial Medal 1967; Liberal; Anglican; recreations: skiing, squash, tennis, golf; Clubs: Toronto; University; Badminton & Racquet; Toronto Golf; Osler Bluff Ski.

GILLESPIE, Robert Douglas (Sid), B.A.Sc., M.B.A.; engineering and consulting executive; b. Colborne, Ont. 10 Nov. 1931; s. William Stanley and Ruby Mary (Grant) G.; e. Royal Mil. Coll. Kingston 1955; Univ. of Toronto B.A.Sc. (Mech. Engn.) 1956, M.B.A. 1961; m. Marion Elaine d. Robert Erle MacMurdo 23 May 1955; two d. Susan Elizabeth, Cynthia Margaret; PRES., CHIEF OPERATING OFFR. AND DIR., MACLAREN ENGINEERS, PLANNERS & SCIENTISTS, INC.; joined MacLaren 1956 serving as Mech. Engr., Partners' Asst.; apptd. Dir. and Secy.-Treas. 1962, Vice Pres. Adm. 1969, Extve. Vice Pres. 1971; Consultant to World Health Organ. (water & sewerage) Kabul, Afghanistan and Nassau 1966; dir. various studies incl. Toronto dist. heating study; Chrmn. Research & Devel. Comte. Assn. Consulting Engrs. Can. 1971-75; mem. Consulting Engrs. Ont. Interprof. Comte. 1977-78; Dir. Cndn. Nuclear Assoc. (1979-83); Assoc. Consulting Engineers of Canada (1979-83); Project Dir. Lepreau Nuclear Generating Stn. N.B. Electric Power Comn.; site selection Atomic Energy Organization of Iran nuclear generating stn.; Eldorado Nuclear Ltd. uranium hexafluoride plant, Water & Agric. Devel. Studies - Arabian Shield South in Saudi Arabia; qualified as Navig. RCAF; author or co-author various tech. papers; mem. Assn. Prof. Engrs. Prov. Ont.; Am. Soc. Mech. Engrs.; Engn. Inst. Can.; Am. Water Works Assn.; Pollution Control Assn. Ont.; Internat. Dist. Heating Assn.; Air Pollution Control Assn.; Candn. Soc. Mech. Engrs.; Water Pollution Control Fed.; Prof. Services Business Mang. Assn.; Clk. of Session Timothy Eaton Mem. Ch. 1972-77; United Church; recreations: golf, curling; Club: Thornhill Country (Pres. 1975-76); Home: 12 King Maple Place, Willowdale, Ont. M2K 1X6; Office: 1220 Sheppard Ave. E., Willowdale, Ont. M2K 2T8.

GILLESPIE, Robert James, B.Sc., B.Eng., M.S.I.A.; exec-utive; b. Halifax, N.S. 16 July 1942; s. Robert Leo and Pearl (Wincek) G.; e. Royal Candn. Elect. & Mech. Engrs. Sch. 1961-62; St. Mary's Univ. B.Sc. 1962; N.S. Tech. Coll. B.Eng. (Mech.) 1964; Purdue Univ. M.S.I.A. 1965; m. Carol Ann d. Frank M. Caliendo, Bronxville, N.Y. 16 Nov. 1968; children: Erica Christine, Brooke Caroline; PRES. CORN PRODUCTS UNIT, CPC INTERNAT. INC.; Chmn. of Bd., Canada Starch; Dir., Corn Products and Best Foods Units, CPC International Inc.; Dural Products Ltd.; Mgr. Facilities Planning, CPC International Inc., Englewood Cliffs, N.J. 1967, Asst. to Vice Pres. Finance Devel. Div. 1969, Product Mgr. Indust. Div. 1970, Group Product Mgr. Indust. Div. 1972, Vice Pres. Business Mang. Indust. Div. 1973; Pres. and Chief Operating Offr. Canada Starch Co. 1979-81; served with Candn. Army 1960-64, W. Germany 1963, Halifax 1964; author "Selection of Engineering Materials and Their Use in A Marine Environment" 1966; "Merger and Acquisition Factbook" 1970; Dir. Montreal Metrop. YMCA; Dir. Dalhousie Univ. School of Business Advisory Bd., recreations: tennis, squash, skiing; Clubs: Montreal Badminton & Squash; St. James's; Home: 473 Cote St. Antoine, Westmount, Que. H3Y 2K3; Office: 1 Place du Commerce, Montreal, Que. H3E 1A7.

GILLESPIE, Ronald James, B.Sc., Ph.D., D.Sc., F.R.S., F.R.S.C., F.R.I.C., F.C.I.C.; educator; b. London, Eng. 21 Aug. 1924; s. James Andrew and Miriam Grace (Kirk) G.; e. Harrow Co. Sch. Middlesex, UK 1942; Univ. Coll. London B.Sc. 1944, Ph.D. 1949; m. Madge Ena d. William Garner 24 June 1951; two d. Ann Hilary, Lynn Judith; PROF. OF CHEMISTRY, McMASTER UNIV. 1958- ; author "Molecular Geometry" 1972; over 300 articles inorganic chem. and chem. educ. prof. journs.; recipient Ramsay Medal Univ. Coll. London 1949; Commonwealth Fund Fellowship Brown Univ. 1953-54; Harrison Mem.

Medal Chem. Soc. 1954; Noranda Award Chem. Inst. Can. 1966; Candn. Centennial Medal 1967; Am. Chem. Soc. N.E. Region Award Phys. Chem. 1971; Mfg. Chems. Assn. Coll. Chem. Teacher Award 1972; Prof. Associé, Univ. des Sciences et Techniques de Languedoc, Montpellier, France 1972-73; Am. Chem. Soc. Award Distinguished Service Advanc. Inorganic Chem. 1973; Chem. Inst. Can. Union Carbide Award Chem. Educ. 1976; Chem. Inst. Can. Medal 1977; Chem. Soc. Nyholm Lectureship 1978-79; Am. Chem. Soc. Award Creative Work Fluorine Chem. 1981; recreations: sailing, skiing, travel; Office: Hamilton, Ont. L8S 4M1.

GILLESPIE, Thomas Stuart, B.A., B.C.L.; advocate; b. Montreal, Que. 18 July 1939; s. Alexander Robert and Lois Tully (O'Brien) G.; e. McGill Univ. B.A. 1959, B.C.L. 1963; m. Caroline Pierce d. William George Herbert Doyle, Boca Grande, Fla. 28 June 1963; children: Caroline Alexandra, Alexandra Olivia, Vanessa Margaret, Joshua William; PARTNER, OGILVY, RENAULT 1973- ; Dir. H. H. Brown Shoe Co. (Canada) Ltd.; Guerlain Canada Ltd.; Bouverie Investments Ltd.; called to Bar of Que. 1964; Gov., Bishop's Coll. Sch.; Pres. and Dir. Montreal Transition Houses Inc.; Trustee, Study Endowment Fund; Counsel to Standing Senate Comte. on Banking, Trade & Comm. income tax matters; mem. Candn. Bar Assn.; Que. Bar Assn.; Candn. Tax Foundation; Internat. Fiscal Assn.; Tax Adv. Comte. Montreal Bd. Trade and Comité de Promotion Economique de Montréal; R. Catholic; recreations: skiing, jogging, fishing, golf, reading; Clubs: Orleans Fish & Game; Mount Bruno Country; Tarratine; Home: 48 Aberdeen Ave., Westmount, Que. H3Y 3A4; Office: 1981 McGill College Ave., Montreal, Que. H3A 3C1.

GILLETT, Margaret, M.A., Ed.D.; university professor; b. Wingham, N.S.W., Australia, 1 Feb. 1930; d. Leslie Frank and Janet Alene (Vickers) G.; e. Univ. of Sydney, B.A. (Eng., Hist., Anthrop.) 1950, Dipl. Educ. 1951; Univ. of Copenhagen, summer 1953; Russell Sage Coll., M.A. (Eng., Sociol.) 1958; Columbia Univ., Ed.D. (Social & Philos. Foundations of Educ.) 1961; PROF. OF EDUC., McGill Univ., since 1967; High Sch. Teacher, N.S.W., Aust., 1951-53; Educ. offr. (Research & Adm.), Commonwealth Office of Educ., Sydney, 1954-57; Asst. Prof. of Educ., Dalhousie Univ., 1961-62 and Visiting Prof., 1967; Registrar, Haile Selaissie I Univ., Addis Ababa, Ethiopia, 1962-64; Assoc. Prof. of Educ., McGill Univ., 1964-67 and Chrmn., Dept. of Hist. & Philos. of Educ., 1965-9; Chrmn. Dep't Social Found. of Educ., 1979-80; Founding Ed., ''McGill Journal of Education'', 1966-77; author of ''A History of Education: Thought and Practice'', 1966; ''Readings in the History of Education'', 1968; ''Educational Technology: Toward Demystification'', 1973; author, 'We Walked Very Warily, A History of Women at McGill' 1981; co-author, ''The Laurel and the Poppy'', 1967 (chosen by Catholic Digest Book Club as selection for March '68); Contributor, ''Plot Outlines'', 1962; Consulting Ed., ''Educational Studies'', (Journ. of Am. Educ. Studies Assn.); co-ed. ''Foundation Studies in Education: Justifications and New Directions'' 1973; Ed. Bd., Journal of International Education; has written numerous articles for learned journs. and read papers at many prof. conferences; active in Women's Studies; first chairperson of McGill Senate Comte. on Women; rec'd. Canada Council grants for research and writing; mem., Canadian Association University Teachers; Candn. Assn. Profs. of Educ.; Comparative Educ. Soc. (U.S.): Comparative & Internat. Educ. Soc. Can. (Founding Secy., Pres., 1977-79); Hist. of Educ. Soc.; Foundations of Educ. Soc.; Australian Coll. of Educ.; recreations: tennis, skiing, theatre; Home: 4800 De Maisonneuve Blvd. W. Westmount Que. H3Z 1M2 Office: 3700 McTavish St., Montreal, Que. H3A 1Y2

GILLHAM, P. Michael, B.E., P.Eng.; executive; consulting engineer; b. Montreal, Que., 3 Dec. 1934; s. Harry and Emily Avernia (Hinton) G.; e. West Hill High Sch. Montreal 1952; Mount Allison Univ. Dipl. in Engn. 1957; N.S. Tech. Coll. B.E. 1959, post-grad. courses; m. Ann, d. late Leonard Crane, 27 Aug. 1966; children: Liseanne Kathryn, Jeffrey Michael, Andrew James; PRESIDENT, WHITMAN, BENN & ASSOCIATES LTD. since 1969; Extve. Vice Pres. Integrated Survey Systems Ltd.; Dir. Keltic Savings Corp.; joined present firm as Jr. Design Engr. 1959; served as Project Engr. and Project Mgr.; mem. Halifax Bd. Trade; Assn. Prof. Engrs. N.S.; Perm. Assn. Navig. Cong's; N.S. Consulting Engrs. Assn. (Past Pres.); Design Constr. Inst. N.S. (Past Dir.); Assn. Consulting Engrs. Can., Past Pres.; Anglican; recreations: sailing, skating, skiing; Clubs: N.S. Yacht Sqdn.; Waegwoltic; Halifax; Saraguay Home: 1223 Cromwell Rd., Halifax, N.S. B3H 4L1; Office: 5251 Duke St. Tower, Halifax, N.S. B3J 1N9

GILLIATT, Brig.-Gen. Courtney Spurr S., D.F.C., C.D., B.Sc., (AGR), M.A.; b. Annapolis Royal, N.S., 19 Aug. 1921; s. Frederick Courtney and Hortense (Spurr) G.; e. Annapolis Acad. 1938; N.S. Agric. Coll., grad. 1941; Macdonald Coll., McGill Univ., B.Sc. (AGR) 1947; M.A. (International Affairs) Carleton Univ., 1978; m. Helen Wilhelmina, d. W. F. L. Edwards, 1 May 1948; children: Victoria, Christopher, Catherine; joined RCAF 1941; grad. as Pilot and commnd. 1942; completed tour of operations in Europe on Mosquito Fighter Bomber Aircraft (107 Sqdn. RAF); awarded Distinguished Flying Cross and Mentioned in Dispatches; retired 1945; rejoined 1947; promoted to Brigadier General 1971 and apptd. Dir. Gen. Air Force; retired 1976; Anglican; recreations: skiing, swimming; Home: 618 Denbury Ave., Ottawa, Ont. K2A 2P1

GILLIES, Gordon R., B. Com.; printing executive; b. Toronto, Ont., 17 Oct. 1914; s. Kenneth S. and Margaret J. (Amos) G.; e. Brown Pub. Sch., Toronto; Univ. of Toronto Schs.; Univ. of Toronto, B. Com. 1939; m. Evelyn Frances, d. Frank Jacklin, Chesley, Ont., Feb. 1943; DIRECTOR, PHOTO ENGRAVERS AND ELECTROTYPERS LTD., since 1976; joined Robt. Simpson Co. as Acct., 1940-46; apptd. Acct. with present firm, 1946; Mgr. Comm. Div. 1952; Gen. Mgr. 1956, Vice Pres. 1958; Pres., 1966; served with Candn. Army as Lt., 1942-45; mem., Rotary Club of Rexdale; Bd. Trade Metrop. Toronto; Gravure Tech. Assn.; Gravure Research Inst. (Dir.); Protestant; recreations: gardening, machine shop, travelling; Club: Carlton; Home: 29 Wimpole Dr., Toronto, Ont. M2L 2L1

GILLIES, James, M.A., Ph.D., M.P.; educator; b. Teeswater, Ont., 2 Nov. 1924; s. John Midford and Gladys Irene (Macpherson) G.; e. Univ. of W. Ont., B.A. (Econ.); Brown Univ., M.A. (Econ.); Indiana Univ., Ph.D. (Econ.); m. Elizabeth Louise, d. Harry Etienne Matson, 30 Dec. 1953; children: David, Catherine, James, Edward; PROF. OF POLICY, AND DIRECTOR, MAX BELL BUSINESS GOV'T STUDIES PROGRAM FAC. OF ADM. STUDIES, YORK UNIV.; former Dean, Fac. of Adm. Studies 1965-72; formerly Dir. of a no. of important industrial and comm. companies; former mem., Hellyer Task Force; Dir., Senate Comte. on Growth Employment & Price Stability; Prof., Univ. of Calif., 1961-65; served with R.C.A.F. during 2nd World War; former mem. Candn. Civil Libs. Assn.; Humber Mem. Hos.; mem. Export Adv. Council; served as Vice Chrmn., Redevel. Agency of City of Los Angeles and Adviser to Calif. Comn. on Metrop. Problems; author of ''Management in the Light Construction Industry'', 1962; ''Metropolis: Values in Conflict'', 1964; contrib. to ''Federal Credit Programs in the Housing Sector of the Economy'', 1963; ''Essays in Urban Land Economics'', 1966; mem. and Dir., Am. Finance Assn.; Am. Real Estate & Urban Econ. Assn.; el. M.P. for Don Valley 1972, re-el. 1974; Sr. Policy Adviser to Prime Minister, 1979-80; Protestant; Clubs:

University; Bayview Country; Home: 73 Fairway Heights Dr., Thornhill, Ont. L3T 3A7

GILLIS, Duncan Hugh, B.A., Ph.D.; educator; b. Glen Alpine, Antigonish Co., N.S., 11 Aug. 1918; s. John J. and Catherine Ann G.; e. St. Francis Xavier Univ., B.A. 1939; London Sch. of Econ., Ph.D. 1948; post-doctoral studies Fribourg and Laval Univs.; m. Celia Antoinette, d. late Alfred Hamilton, Edinburgh and London, 21 June 1952; children: Rosemary, Anthony, Paulina; ACADEMIC VICE PRES., SAINT MARY'S UNIV. and Secy, to Bd. of Govs. there since 1972; Asst. Prof., St. Francis Xavier Univ. 1948-50; Research Writer Encyclopedia Canadiana and Ed., Labour Journal, Cape Breton 1952; Assoc. Prof., Marymount Coll., N.Y. 1953; Program Organizer and Asst. Nat. Supvr. Pub. Affairs Dept., CBC, 1955; Prof. and Div. Chrmn., Boston Univ. 1959-70; Dir., Sch. of Adult Learning, Univ. of Botswana, Lesotho and Swaziland 1968-70; Dir., Coady Internat. Inst., Antigonish, 1970-72; Dir., Candn. Broadcasting League; served with RCA Italy and N.W. Europe during World War II; RCHA Korean War; militia 1957-59; rank Lt. Col.; Mentioned in Despatches (Korea); P. Conservative cand. g.e. 1965, 1968; author "Democracy in the Canadas", 1951; also prof. and popular writings in various print media; Dir., Candn. Bureau of Internat. Educ.; Progressive Conservative: R. Catholic; recreations: walking, travel; Home: 5920 Gorsebrook Ave., Halifax, N.S. B3H 1G2; Office: Halifax, N.S.

GILLMORE, Allan K., B.A. university administrator; b. London, Ont. 20 Aug. 1923; s. John Joseph and Ruby Florence (Gregory) G.; e. Sir Adam Beck Coll. Inst. London, Ont. 1939; McMaster Univ. B.A. 1943; m. Hilda Jean, d. late William Adams, 20 May 1944; children: Donald Alan, Marilyn Jean (Mrs. J. Cavill); EXECUTIVE DIR. ASSOC. COLLEGES and UNIVERSITIES of CANADA, Sept. 1980- ; Vice-Rector, Univ. of Ottawa 1966-1980; mem. Adv. Bd. Guaranty Trust Co.; mem. Bd. Dir. and Chrmn. Exec. Comte. of Ottawa Health Sciences Centre, Inc.; mem. Wascana Centre Adv. Bd.; Wascana Centre Authority; Extve. Dir. Sarnia Y.M.-Y.W.C.A. 1948; Dir. Sask. House, Centre for Continuing Educ. Regina, 1960; Asst. to Min. of Educ. Sask. 1961; Extve. Dir. Wascana Centre Authority, Regina, 1962; mem. Candn. Assn. Univ. Business Offrs.; Anglican; recreations: gardening, photography; Home: Unit 4B - 300 Queen Elizabeth Dr., Ottawa, Ont. K1S 3M6

GILLMOURE, L. E., banker; b. 2 Sept. 1924; SR. VICE PRES. OPERATIONS & SYSTEMS, THE ROYAL BANK OF CANADA 1979- ; Dir. Group Services Ltd. (Nassau, Bahamas); Computer Service & Programming Ltd. (Jamaica); joined present Bank 1941, Spencerville, Ont.; served various brs. Ont., N.B. and Que.; Inspr.'s Asst. H.O. Inspector's Dept. Montreal 1953, H.O. Inspector Dept. 1954, Personnel Staff Offr. Que. Dist. 1956, Asst. Inspr. Ont. Inspr.'s Dept. Toronto 1961, Mgr. Barrie, Ont. 1965, Project Mgr. Organ. Planning H.O. Montreal 1968, Dist. Inspr. Que. Dist. 1969, Chief Inspr. 1973, Vice Pres. Systems & Processing Operations 1978; Club: Summerlea Golf & Country; Home: 149 Bexhill Dr., Beaconsfield, Que. H9W 3A6; Office: (P.O. Box 6001) Montreal, Que. H3C 3A9.

GILMER, John Capill, F.C.A. (ret.); transportation executive; b. Chester, Eng., 6 Jan. 1910; s. Victor Watters and Rose (Capill) G.; came to Can. Aug. 1914; e. Univ. of Manitoba, C.A. degree; President and Chief Extve. Offr., CP Air (Can. Pacific Air Lines Ltd.), 1965-76, Chrmn. and Dir., Insurance Corp. of B.C.; Dir. Fraser Inst.; Chrmn. of the Bd. of Man. St. Vincent's Hospital; joined C.P.R. Company, Montreal, 1937-49 becoming General Auditor; transferred to C.P. Air, Vancouver, B.C. as Asst. Comptroller, 1949; apptd. Comptroller 1956; Vice Pres. and Comptroller 1962; Extve. Vice Pres., 1963; mem., Candn. Inst. C.A.s; Protestant; Clubs: Vancouver; Shaughnessy

Golf & Country; Home: Apt. 503, 2055 Pendrell St., Vancouver V6G 1T9

GILMORE, James P., O.C. (1981) D. Mang.Sc., broadcasting executive (ret.); b. Regina, Sask., 13 Feb. 1917; s. James J. and Laura (Barden) G.; e. Vancouver (B.C.) Coll. to 1936; Univ. of British Columbia, 1936-37; Wireless Cert. 1937; D. Mang.Sc. Ottawa 1970; m. Mercedes Walker, 6 Oct. 1943; children: Katherine Ann (Goodings), Bernard James, Mary Carol (Webb), Patrick John (deceased 1967); Sr. Vice Pres., CBC (ret.); engaged in broadcasting operations, 1937-41 with Vancouver private stns. CKMO and CJOR; production and operations 1941-48 with Vancouver studios of CBC; Supv. of Studio Operations with Montreal Eng. H.Q. of CBC, 1948-51 (Engn. Hdqrs.); Engn. Hdqrs. Management, 1951-52; Corp. Extve. Asst. Positions, Ottawa 1952-59; Vice Pres., Engn. and Operations, 1959-61; Vice-Pres., Personnel and Operations, 1961-64; Vice Pres., Planning 1964-67; Vice Pres., Planning and Acting Chief Operating Offr. Feb.-Dec. 1967; Pres., Dec. 1967-Jan. 1968; Vice Pres.-Planning and Asst. Chief Operating Offr. Feb. 1968-May 1969; Vice Pres.-Planning 1969-74 (Sr. Vice-Pres. 1974-75); mem. Board Governors, Univ. of Ottawa 1965-69 and from 1972 (Hon. Mem. 1979); Trustee, Ottawa Separate Sch. Bd., 1961-64; mem., Research & Devel. Adv. Council of American Mang. Assn. 1962-67; All-AMA Planning Council; member, Institute Elect. & Electronic Engrs.; Candn. Inst. Public Adm.; Candn. Overseas Inst.; awarded Coronation and Centennial Medals; Amer. Mgt. Assoc. President's Gold Medal 1970; Officer of the Order of Canada, July, 1981; R. Catholic; Home: 976 Inverness Rd. #306, Victoria, B.C. V8X 2R9

GILMOUR, Eric Herbert, e. Alleyn's Sch., Eng. and Queen's Univ. (B.A.) (1934); m. Isabella MacLaren, 1938; after a brief period in journalism in Toronto, Ont., several yrs. in business in Brockville, Ont., and 4 yrs. in Cdn. Army with rank of Major; joined Dept. of External Affairs in 1947; postings: First Secy. at Candn. Embassy, Washington; Candn. Commr., I.C.S.C. Cambodia; Counsellor of Embassy, Brussels; High Commr. to Trinidad and Tobago; successively Dir. Consular Div., Dir. Gen., Bureau of Consular Affairs (retired 1975); Vice Pres., Internat. Soc. Serv., Can. Address: 2032 Fairbanks Ave., Ottawa K1H 5Z1and Chelsea, Que.

GIMLIN, Robert Charles, B.Sc.; pulp and paper executive; b. Chicago, Ill. 11 Jan. 1921; s. Guy M. and Corrine (Koch) G.; e. Purdue Univ. B.Sc. (Mech. Engn.) 1942; m. Jane Elizabeth Haltom 19 Apl. 1942; children: Hal, Gail; PRES. AND CHIEF EXTVE. OFFR., DIR., ABITIBI-PRICE INC. 1979- ; Dir. The Price Co. Ltd.; Interprovincial Pipe Line Ltd.; Mang. to Vice Pres. Merchandising, United States Gypsum Co., Chicago 1946-66; Vice Pres. Abitibi Paper Co. Ltd. Toronto 1966-69, Pres. Abitibi Corp., Birmingham, Mich. 1969-74; Group Vice Pres. 1974-76, Chrmn. Abitibi-Price Sales Corp., New York, 1976-8; Pres. and Chief Operating Offr. 1978-79; served with U.S. Navy 1942-45, rank Lt. Sr. Gr.; recreations: golf, hunting, fishing; Clubs: Toronto; York; Toronto Hunt; Mount Royal; Pinehurst Golf & Country (N.C.); Home: 31 McKenzie Ave., Toronto, Ont. M4W 1K1; Office: Toronto-Dominion Centre, Toronto, Ont. M5K 1B3.

GINGRAS, Gustave, C.C., K.St.J., Q.H.P., M.D., D.M., LL.D. D.C.L., D.Sc., F.R.S.A., F.R.C.P.(C); physician; b. Montreal, Que. 18 Jan. 1918; e. Coll. Bourget, Rigaud, Que. B.A. 1938; Univ. de Montréal M.D. 1941; Sir George Williams Univ., Univ. of Winnipeg and Univ. of W. Ont. LL.D. 1967, 1970, 1971; Univ. de Sherbrooke D.M. 1973; Bishop's Univ. D.C.L. 1974; McMaster Univ. D.Sc. 1982; Chancellor, Univ. of P.E.I. 1974- ; Hon. Pres. Nat. Council Candn. Human Rights Foundation 1978- ; mem. Candn. Forces Med. Council 1973- , Consultant 1954-59, 1968-71; Hon. Vice Pres. Candn. Nat. Inst. Blind 1975- , mem. Bd. Mang. Que. Div. 1965-67; Dir. Abbott Laboratories Ltd. 1975- ; mem. Social Sciences & Humanities Research Council 1978- , Extve. 1981- ; Extve. Dir. Rehabilitation Inst. Montreal 1949-76; Prof. of Phys. Med. & Rehabilitation Univ. de Montréal 1954-76, Dir. Sch. Rehabilitation 1954-76, Chrmn. Extve. Council Geriatric Inst. 1961-65, Prof. Emeritus 1976- ; Chief of Service, Phys. Med. & Rehabilitation, Queen Mary Veterans Hosp. and D.V.A. Montreal Dist. 1945-76; Consultant, World Health Organ. on Med. Rehabilitation 1955-80; Phys. Med. & Rehabilitation War Amputations Can.; Centre de reéduc. des Handicapés de Yaoundé, Cardinal Léger and His Endeavours Organ; UN. Tech. Assistance Div. 1953-59; mem. Nat. Adv. Bd. Rehabilitation. Disabled Persons 1954-65; Dir. Ecole de Réadaptation Univ. Laval 1964-69; Head, Dept. Phys. Med. & Rehabilitation Pasteur Hosp. Montreal 1947-57; mem. Nat. Med. Adv. Comte. Candn. Rehabilitation Council Disabled 1960-68; Dir. Rehabilitation Services Dept. Health P.E.I. 1977-80 and Med. Dir. Rehabilitation Centre; recipient Royal Bank of Can. Award 1972; Medal of Honour Pharm. Mfrs. Assn. Can. 1973; Albert Lasker Award Internat. Soc. Rehabilitation Disabled 1969; Can. Centennial Medal 1967; Silver Medal Internat. Coop. 1965; Rabbi Dr. Harry J. Stern Award 1974 (co-recipient); Outstanding Citizen Award Montreal Citizenship Council 1970; B'nai B'rith Humanitarian Award 1966; Cavaliere Order St. Agathe Repub. San Marino 1968; Order Cedar of Lebanon 1972; Chuong My Medal Repub. S. Viet Nam 1973; Medal of Merit Veterans Ministry S. Viet Nam 1969; F.N.G. Starr Award Candn. Med. Assn.; 1978; Que. Hosp. Assn. Award 1980; George Findlay Stephens Mem. Award of Merit Candn. Hosp. Assn. 1981; Queen's Hon. Physician 1982; author "Combats pour la survie" 1975, Eng. transl. "Feet Was I To The Lame" 1977; co-author "Human Rights for the Physically Handicapped and Aged" 1977; numerous articles; Pres., P.E.I. Hosp. Assn. 1980- ; Candn. Med. Assn. 1972-73; Internat. Fed. Phys. Med. 1968-72; Que. Prof. Corp. Phys. 1966-72; Candn. Assn. Phys. Med. & Rehabilitation 2 terms; Que. Physiatrists Assn. 1959-60; Hon. Pres. Candn. Physiotherapy Assn. 1973-75: Hon. Vice Pres. Order St. John Que. Council; Fellow, Am. Acad. Phys. Med. & Rehabilitation; Internat. Coll. Surgs.; Am. Geriatric Soc.; Hon. mem. Que. Med. Assn.; Am. Med. Assn. and various internat. med./scient. assns.; Candn. Red Cross Soc.; mem. Royal Soc. Med.; Internat. Med. Soc. Paraplegia; Internat. Rehabilitation Med. Assn.; Heraldry Soc. Can.; Candn. Railroad Hist. Assn.; UN in Can.; Candn.-S.African Soc. (Dir.); Steamship Hist. Assn. Can.; served with R.C.A.M.C. Can. and Overseas 1942-46; Address: Monticello R.R. 5, Souris, P.E.I. C0A 2B0.

GIRARD, Alice M., O.C. (1968), R.N., B.Sc.N., M.A., D.Sc., LL.D., O.St.J.; administrateur, professeur émérite; né. Waterbury, Conn., 11 Nov. 1907; f. Philippe et Rose (Joyal) G.; venue au Canada avril 1918; é. école normale, brevet superieur en pedagogie 1925; diplôme d'infirmière l'Hôpital St. Vincent de Paul, Sherbrooke, P.Q. 1931; diplôme en hygiène publique, Univ. of Toronto 1939; B.Sc.N. Catholic Univ. of America, Washington, D.C. 1942; M.A. Columbia Univ. 1944; cours d'adm. hospitaliere (Fellow de la Fondation Kellogg) Johns Hopkins Univ. 1954; LL.D. Univ. of Toronto 1968; D.Sc. Univ. de Montréal 1975; PROF. FACULTE DE NURSING, UNIV. DE MONTREAL depuis 1962; doyen 1962-73 (fondatrice de la faculté et première femme doyen de l'Univ. de Montréal); infirmière hygeniste 1931-38; dir. l'Ecole d'infirmières hygiènistes de l'Univ. de Montréal 1942-48; dir. nat. du nursing la Cie. d'assurance-vie Metropolitan 1949-53; dir. et asst. admn. l'Hopital St. Luc a Montréal 1956-62; mem. la Commission Royale d'Enquête sur les services de santé au Can. 1961-64; nomée mem. hon. de la Registered Nurses Assn. of Ont., Sask. Registered Nurses Assn.; citoyenne hon. de la Ville de Montréal; reçue la médaille du Centenaire; la médaille Florence Nightingale (la Ligue de la Croix Rouge Internat.); pres.; l'Assn. des Infirmières Candnnes. (1958-60); Pres. la Fon-

dation des Infirmières Candnnes.; Pres. Nat. du Victorian Order of Nurses (1975-77); 1ᵉʳᵉ pres. candnne. Conseil Internat. des Infirmières (1965-69); Comité Rélations Publiques P.E.M.P. (1974); mem. bureau des govs. du Conseil Candn. du Bien-être; Fed. internat. des Hôpitaux; American Coll. of Hospital Administrators; recue Commander de l'Ordre de St. Jean (1977); résidence: 2966 Fendall, Montreal, P.Q. H3T 1N1

GIRARD, Claude, R.C.A.; painter; stage designer; b. Chicoutimi, Que. 30 Nov. 1938; s. Armand and Yvette (Tremblay) G.; e. Ecole des Beaux-Arts du Qué.; Academia of Venice, Italy; Dean of Art Dept. Coll. Brébeuf, Montréal; collab. with over 50 theatrical groups incl. Les Grands Ballets Canadiens, Nat. Ballet of Can., Opera de Nancy (France), Opera de Wallonie (Liège), Palais des Congrès, Paris (France) Place des Arts Montréal; paintings in colls. maj. Candn. galleries; Address: 4077 St. Hubert Montreal, Que. H2L 4A7

GIRARDIN, Joseph-C.-Emile, C.C. (1969); C.C.S.S., K.C.L.J., éducateur; cooperateur; né Yamachiche, Qué.; 28 Nov. 1895; f. Dionis et Flora (Lamothe) G.; e. l'Acad. Ste.-Anne, Yamachiche; Sém. des Trois Rivières; l'Ecole Normale Jacques-Cartier, brevèt acad. d'enseignement 1913; "Docteur honoris cause", l'Univ. de Montréal, 1970; ép. Aline, f. d'Arcadius et Eleonora (Gendron) Descoteaux; enfants: Denyse, Guy, Rolande, Louise; PRES. HON. DE LA CONFÉDÉRATION DES CAISSES POPULAIRES ET D'ÉCONOMIE DESJARDINS DU QUEBEC; La Fédération des Caisses populaires Desjardins de Montreal et de l'Ouest du Quebec; La Caisse populaire Notre Dame de Grace de Montreal; Pres. Caisse Populaire de Terre des Hommes; Assn. Cooperatif Desjardins; Ex-Vice-prés. Caisse Populaire de Notre Dame de Grâce de Montréal; Ex-Adm. Union Régionale de Montréal; Principal de l'école St.-Irenée, 1923-29; organisateur du premier bgde. de sécurité dans une école française; princ. de l'école Olier, 1929-39; mem. du Conseil pédagogique, 1937; dir. de district, 1939; dir. adjoint du personnel en 1947; fond le premier cercle d'une école primaire à s'affilier à la Soc. du Bon Parler Français; décerné Chevalier du Bon Parler Français; contributeur dans le domaine des choeurs et de chants scolaires; réorganisateur des caisses d'épargnes scolaires, 1949; Directeur générale adjoint des Services des Etudes 1949-60; depuis 1919, actif à l'organisation des Caisses populaires Desjardins; gérant de la Caisse populaire Ste.-Clothilde, 1919-1934; Secrétaire-gérant de l'Union régionale de Montréal des Caisses populaires Desjardins, 1934-63; gérant de la Caisse centrale de Montréal, 1936-44; devint prés. de l'Union régionale et de la Caisse centrale de Montréal, 1954; élu vice-prés. de la Fed. de Qué. des Caisses populaires, et de l'Assnce-vie Desjardins, 1955; il est aussi prés. de la Caisse populaire Notre Dame de Grâce; recu médaille de l'Ordre du Mérite scolaire (dept. de l'Instr. publique); médaille du Jubilé d'argent du roi George V, médaille du Couronnement, 1954; Chevalier de l'Ordre Equestre du Saint-Sepulchre de Jérusalem, 1956; Chevalier de l'Ordre St. Lazare de Jérusalem, 1969; Chevalier Commandeur du S. Sépulcre (par le Cardinal Tisserant), 1970; Ex-prés. de la section Jean-Baptiste-Meilleur, de la Soc. St.-Jean Baptiste de Montréal; résidence: 4014 ave Melrose, Montréal, Qué. H4A 2S4

GIRDWOOD, Charles P., B. Eng.; mining engineer, company executive; b. Montreal, P.Q., 23 Feb. 1910; s. late Edward P. and Florence (Matthews) G.; e. Public and High Schs., Victoria B.C.; McGill Univ., B. Eng. 1933; m. Edna Florence, d. late J. H. A. Mackay, Montreal, P.Q., 19 Sept. 1936; children: Allan, Margaret; CONSULTANT, DOME MINES LTD., 1978; Gen. Manager. Vice-Pres. and Dir., 1954-78; former Commr., Ontario Northland Railway; former Director, Sigma Mines (Quebec) Ltd.; Pres., Porcupine (Ont.) Gen. Hosp. Board 1954-73; Plant Operator, Consol. Mining & Smelting Co. of Can. Ltd., Trail B.C., 1930-31; engaged in mining various prospects in N.W. Quebec 1933-34; Engr., Canadian Malartic Gold Mines 1934-35; Asst. Mgr., O'Brien Mine, Cobalt, Ont., 1936; Asst. to Gen. Mgr., M. J. O'Brien Ltd., Ottawa, Ont., 1936-39; Asst. Engr., Dome Mines Ltd., 1939-42; Chief Engr. 1942-47, Gen. Supt. 1947-54, Gen. Mgr. 1954-73; Past Pres., Mines Accident Prev. Assn. Ont.; former Dir., Ont. Mining Assn. (Pres. 1966-67); Dir., Porcupine Chamber of Comm. 1960-63; mem., Adv. Council on Engn., Queen's Univ., 1961-64; Hon. Pres., Porcupine Div., St. John Ambulance Soc.; 1950-72; Past Chairman of Metal Mine Div. Candn. Inst. Mining & Metall. (Past V. Pres.; awarded Distinguished Service Medal 1972); Hon. Pres., Porcupine Div., Candn. Cancer Soc. 1955-72; Dir., Ont. Hosp. Assn. (Past V. Pres. 1962-72); Pres. and Dir. Children's Aid Soc. of Leeds and Grenville; mem. Am. Inst. Mining & Metall. Engrs.; Assn. Prof. Engrs. Ont.; Delta Sigma Phi; Conservative; Protestant; recreations: golf, gardening; Club: Prescott Golf; Home: River Rd. W., R.R. 1, Prescott, Ont. K0E 1T0; Office: Dome Mines Ltd., South Porcupine, Ont.

GIROUX, Roland, C.C. (1972); pub. utility executive; b. 15 Jan. 1913; s. Edouard and Florida Blanche (Girard) G.; e. Coll. Saint-Césaire; m. Yvette Blain, Montreal 6 Sept. 1936; children: Pierre Michèle (Mrs. Albert G. Urbina), François, CHRMN. OF BD., CONSOLIDATED-BA-THURST Inc.; BATHURST PAPER LTD., since 1977; Pres., Hydro-Quebec 1969-77; Chrmn. of Bd., James Bay Energy Corp. (1972); Dir., James Bay Development Corp. (1971); Churchill Falls (Labrador) Corp. Ltd.; Sales Manager, L. G. Beaubien Ltée. 1946; Gen. Manager 1951; Pres. 1961; Vice-Pres., L. G. Beaubien & J. L. Lévesque Inc., 1963, Pres. 1965; Vice-Pres., General Investment Corp. of Que., 1966; Econ. Adviser, Govt. of Que., 1966; mem. Olympic Installations Bd. (1975); Dir. Bank of Montreal (1977); Power Corp. of Can. (1977); Candn. Commercial Corp. (1978); Chmn. of Bd. of First Canadian Investments Ltd. (1979), mem. Candn. Chamber Comm.; Catholic; recreation: St. Denis, Canadien de Montréal; Home: 1250, Pine Ave. West, Montreal, P.Q. H3G 2P5 Office: 800 Dorchester Blvd. W., Montreal H3B 1Y9

GISHLER, Paul Ernest, M.Sc., Ph.D., F.R.S.C., F.C.I.C.; research chemist (retired, 1980); b. Golden Lake, Ont., 30 July 1904; s. Ernst Magnus and Emma (Oetzel) G.; e. Univ. of Alberta, B.Sc. 1929, M.Sc. 1931; McGill Univ., Ph.D. 1935; previously with National Research Council, Ottawa, dir. research on new petrochemicals; with Atomic Energy Project at Chalk River, Ont.; devel. recovery method of oil from Alta. oil sands; devel. spouted bed technique; determined heat transfer value for fluidized solids systems; Consultant, Alta. Research Council (1971-75); mem., Alta. Oil Sands Tech. and Research Authority, 1975-78; consultant on Energy; mem. Can. Soc. for Chem. Eng.; Protestant; Home: 8735-118 St., Edmonton, Alta. T6G 1TA

GLASS, Charles Lapslie Ogden, M.A., D.C.L., D.d'U.; b. Montreal, P.Q., 26 July 1913; s. Louis Gordon and Sallie (Judah) G.; e. Bishop's Coll. Sch.; Bishop's Univ., B.A. 1935 (Rhodes Schol., Prov. of Que.); Oxford Univ., B.A. 1938, M.A. 1941; D.C.L. Bishop's 1960; D.d'U., Univ. of Sherbrooke 1967; m. Janet Wright, d. H.F. McNeil, Boston, Mass., 9 Sept. 1939; children: Nancy Ogden, Janet Diana, Charles Philip Gordon, Frederick Richard Ogden; Vice-President, Montreal City and District Trustees Ltd.; Trustee of the Elizabeth T. Greenshields Mem. Foundation; Assoc. mem., former Prof. Comte. of Council of Educ. P.Q.; Dir., Montreal City & District Savings Bank; mem. (apptd. 1965), Fed. Electoral Boundaries Comn. for P.Q.; Bishop's Coll. Sch. Assn.; Gov., Sherbrooke Hosp.; Reporter, Montreal "Gazette", 1938-39; Asst. Master, Bishop's Coll. Sch., Lennoxville, P.Q., 1939-41; Headmaster, Ashbury Coll., Ottawa, Ont., 1945-50; Headmaster, Bishop's Coll. Sch. 1950-60; Principal and Vice Chancellor Bishop's Univ. 1960-69; served in World War 1941-45 with R.C.N.V.R. as Lieut.; Hon. mem., Headmasters

Assn. Can. (Pres. 1949-50; Recording Secy., 1947); Candn. Educ. Assn.; Candn. Hist. Assn.; Champlain Soc.; Candn. Inst. Internat. Affairs; Candn. Pol. Science Assn.; Am. Acad. Pol. & Soc. Sciences; Hon. Life Trustee, Corp. of Bishop's Univ.; mem., Corp. King's Hall, Compton, P.Q.; Anglican; recreations: lawn tennis, golf, boating; Clubs: Royal Poinciana Golf and Country (Naples, Fla.); Rideau (Ottawa); St. George's (Sherbrooke); Mount Royal (Montreal); Mount Bruno Country (Montreal); Naples Bath & Tennis; Address: (Box 390) North Hatley, Que. J0B 2C0 and Apt. 301, 2875 Gulf Shore Blvd., Naples, Fla. 33940.

GLASS, Irvine Israel, M.A.Sc., Ph.D., F.R.S.C.; professor; b. Poland, 23 Feb. 1918; s. Samuel Solomon and Gitel (Helfand) G.; came to Canada 1930; e: Ogden Pub. Sch. and Central Tech. Sch., Toronto, Ont.; Univ. of Toronto, B.A.Sc. (Engn. Physics), M.A.Sc. (Aero. Engn.) Ph.D. (Aerophysics) 1950; m. Anne, d. Israel Medres, Montreal, P.Q., 30 Aug. 1942; children: Vivian, Judith (Mrs. Shimon Felsen), Ruth Miriam (Mrs. Robt. Moses), Susan Hinda: WITH INST. FOR AEROSPACE STUDIES, UNIV. OF TORONTO since 1950, PROF. OF AEROSPACE SCIENCE & ENGINEERING since 1953 and Asst. Dir. (Education); Consultant for Candn. and U.S. industry; held positions as Stress Analyst and Aerodynamicist with Canadair, Canadian Car & Foundry, A. V. Roe and Canadian Armament Research and Devel. Establishment; Chrm., Dept. of Aerospace Studies, Sch. of Grad. Studies, Univ. of Toronto, 1961-66; served in 2nd World War with R.C.A.F. rank Fl. Lt., 1942-45; spent sabbatical leave at the Imp. Coll. of Science and Tech., research in high-temperature gas flows; invited by Soviet Acad. of Sciences to lect. on high-temperature gas flows at Moscow Univ. and other Insts., 1961 and 1969; Chrmn., Astronautics Sec. (CASI), 1961; mem. Assoc. Comte. on Space Research, Nat. Research Council, 1962-65; mem. Assoc. Comte. on Aerodynamics and Chrmn., Standing Subcomte. on High Speed Aerodynamics, Nat. Research Council; mem., NASA Basic Research Adv. Subcomte., on Fluid Mech.; mem., Extve. Comte., Div. of Fluid Dynamics Am. Phys. Soc.; Assoc. Ed. "Physics of Fluids"; mem., Bd. of Editors, "Progress in Aerospace Sciences"; mem., Assn. Prof. Engrs. Ontario; Fellow, Am. Inst. of Aero. and Astronautics; Am. Assn. Advanc. Science; Candn. Aeronautics and Space Inst.; Am. Phys. Soc.; Vice Pres. (Engineering), Comte. of Concerned Scientists (U.S.A.) 1978- ; author and editor of books and over 100 scient. papers on gasdynamics, shockwave phenomena and aerophysics; W. Rupert Turnbull Lectr. for 1967; First G. N. Patterson Lecturer (1974); Royal Candn. Inst. Lect. 1965 and 1976; premier Paul Vieille Lecturer at 13th International Symposium on Shock Tubes and Waves Niagara Falls, N.Y. 1981; gave invited lectures in many countries; Chrmn., 7th Internat. Shock Tube Symposium, June 1969, Toronto; Lady Davis Fellow, Technion-Israel Inst. of Technology, Haifa, sabbatical leave, 1974-75; Visiting Prof., Japan Soc. for Promotion of Science, Kyoto Univ., 1975; supervised numerous Master's, Ph.D.'s, Postdoctoral Fellows and visiting Professors on research problems in unique facilities conceived by him; recent book, "Shock Waves and Man" transl. into Russian, Moscow, 1977, Polish ed., Warsaw, 1980, and Chinese edition, Peking, forthcoming; U. of T. Sesquicentennial Long Service Honour Award 1977; Invited by Chinese Academy of Sciences to lecture in a number of institutions 1980; named distinguished 'University Professor,' University of Toronto, 1981; Hebrew; recreations: swimming, photography, music; Home: 31 Heathdale Rd., Toronto, Ont. M6C 1M7

GLASSCO, Colin Stinson; company officer; b. Hamilton, Ont., 24 Jan. 1909; s. Gerald Stinson, M.D., and Constance Ewart (Lucas) G.; e. Highfield Sch., Hamilton, Ont.; Trinity Coll. Sch., Port Hope, Ont.; m. Alice Mary, d. St. Clair Balfour, Hamilton, Ont., 31 Jan. 1942; children: Colin Balfour, Roger Stinson; Dir., Balfours Ltd.;

Barcast Ltd.; The G. W. Robinson Co. Limited 1959-78; Chedoke Securities Limited; Frost Metal Products Limited; Gov., Trinity Coll. Sch., Port Hope, Ont.; Pres., Hamilton Theatre Auditorium Foundation-1965-75; joined Brown Forest Industries Ltd. 1926; in charge of Br. Factory in Montreal, 1930-36; Comptroller of Parent Co., Hamilton, Ont., 1936, Vice-Pres. (Mfg.) 1950; Vice-Pres. and Gen. Mgr., Appleford Operations of Co. 1953; apptd. a Dir. of Southam Printing Co. Ltd. 1967, Vice-Chrmn. & Chief Extve. Offr. 1969, Chrmn. of Bd. 1972-74 (retired 1974); former Dir. (retired 1974) Southam Inc.; Drummond & McCall Inc.; Union Gas Co. Ltd.; Canada Trust Co.; comml. Lt., R.C.N., 1940 and served in World War 1941-46; held rank of Cmdr.; Former Pres., Extve., Candn. Red Cross Soc., Hamilton Br.; Conservative; Anglican; recreations: golf, tennis; Clubs: Hamilton Golf and Country; Hamilton; Tamahaac; Muskoka Lakes Golf & Country; Home: 58 Markland St., Hamilton, Ont. L8P 2J7

GLASSFORD, Jack Stewart, B.Sc.; Canadian public service (ret.); b. Arkona, Ont., 29 Aug. 1920; s. James Ross and Margaret (Thomas) G.; e. Queen's Univ., B.Sc. 1950; m. Kathleen E. Moore, 24 Apt. 1948; one d. Elizabeth Ann; Pres., Crown Assets Disposal Corp. 1974-77; Pres., Candn. Commercial Corp.; Canadian Arsenals Ltd.; Dir. Radio Engineering Products Ltd.; Dir., Electronics Branch Dept. of Supply & Services 1962-67; subsequently Asst. Depy. Min. (Engn. Procurement); served with Royal Canadian Signal Corps, 1939-57; mem. Assn. Prof. Engrs. Ont.; recreations: fishing, curling; Club: Rideau; Home: 2327 Hillary Ave., Ottawa, Ont. K1H 7J2

GLAZEBROOK, George Parkin de Twenebrokes, M.A.; b. London, Ont., 1899, father a banker; e. Upper Canada Coll.; Univ. of Toronto, B.A. 1922; Oxford Univ., M.A. 1930; mem., staff, Dept. of History, Univ. of Toronto, 1924-41, 1946-48; Special Wartime Asst., Dept. of External Affairs, 1942-46; mem. Dept. of External Affairs, 1949-63; Candn. Minister to the U.S. 1953-56; author of "A History of Transportation in Canada", 1938; "Canadian External Relations", 1950; "Life in Ontario", 1968; and other works on Candn. hist.; Special Lectr. in Hist., Univ. of Toronto 1963-67; Home: 45 Glen Road, Toronto, Ont. M4W 2V2

GLAZIER, Kenneth MacLean, B.D., M.A., M.L.S., Ph.D., F.C.B.A.; librarian; b. Carnduff, Sask., 21 Sept. 1912; s. late Harry MacLean and Martha Elizabeth (Heslip) G.; e. Queen's Univ., F.C.B.A. 1932; Univ. of Toronto, B.A. 1936; Union Theol. Semy., N.Y.C., B.D. 1939; Yale Univ., M.A. 1942, Ph.D. 1944; Univ. of Calif., Berkeley, M.L.S. 1962; m. Teresa, d. late Clement J. Ferster, 2 Aug. 1940; children: Gretchen Elizabeth, Christopher Ferster, Kenneth MacLean; joined Bank of Montreal 1929-33; Min., Glenview Presb. Ch., Toronto, 1946-59; Mgr., Candn. Mission Schs., Guyana, 1961-62; Depy. Curator, Hoover Inst., Stanford Univ., 1962-65 and Librarian there 1965-71; Chief Librarian, Univ. of Calgary, 1971-78; author, "Africa South of the Sahara: A Select and Annotated Bibliography 1964-68", 1969; co-author, "A Checklist of Serials for African Studies", 1963; numerous articles in scholarly journs.; mem., Candn. Lib. Assn.; Candn. Assn. Research Libs.; Am. Soc. Information Science; Soc. Am. Archivists; Candn. Assn. Am. Studies; Assn. Candn. Studies U.S.; Liberal; Presbyterian; recreations: golf, skiing; Club: Canadian; Home: 2936 University Pl., Calgary, Alta. T2N 4H5

GLEN, Rev. John Stanley, M.A., B.Ed., Ph.D., B.D., Th.D., D.D. (Presb.); college principal (retired); b. Briercrest, Sask., 1907; s. John and Minabel (Wyatt) G.; e. Univ. of Toronto, B.A. 1930, M.A. 1933, Ph.D. 1937; Univ. of Sask., B.Ed (McColl Scholar.) 1931; Knox Coll., Toronto, Grad 1937; Victoria Coll., Toronto, B.D. 1941, Th.D. 1945; Presbyterian Coll., Montreal, D.D. 1955; m. Winifred MacDougall 1931; children: Eleanor, Gwyn-

neth, Catherine; Mem. Central Exec. of World All. of Reformed and Presbyterian Churches 1954-59; Chrmn N.A. Area of the Alliance 1957-58; Principal Emeritus, Principal, Knox Coll., Univ. of Toronto 1952-76; Instr. in Pyschol., Univ. of Toronto 1932-34 and 1935-37; Min. Glenview Presb. Ch., Toronto, 1938-45; Prof. of New Test. Lit. & Exegesis, Knox Coll. 1945-77; Publications: "Recovery of the Teaching Ministry;" "Parables of Conflict in Luke;" "Pastoral Problems in First Corinthians;" "Erich Fromm. A Protestant Critique;" "Justification by Success: The Invisible Captivity of the Church;" Home: 1507 21st St. N.W., Calgary, Alta. T2N 2M3

GLEN, Robert, O.C. (1967), M.Sc., Ph.D., LL.D., D.Sc., F.A.I.C., F.R.S.C. (1960); entomologist; b. Paisley, Scot., 20 June 1905; s. James Allison and Jeanie Blackwood (Barr) G.; e. Univ. of Sask., B.Sc., 1929, M.Sc. 1931; Univ. of Minnesota (1931-33), Ph.D. 1940; m. Margaret Helen, d. late Rev. J. C. Cameron, 30 June 1931; has two s., Robert Cameron, Ian Robert; Junior and Assistant Entomologist, Dom. Entomol. Lab., Saskatoon, Sask., 1929-35; in charge of Wire-Worm Investigations, Saskatoon, Sask., 1935-45; Research Co-ordinator, Divn. of Entomol., Ottawa, 1945-50, and Chief of the Div., 1950-57; Assoc. Dir., Science Service, 1957-59; Dir. Gen. Research Br., Dept. of Agric., 1959-62; Asst. Dep. Min. (Research) 1962-68; Secy., Commonwealth Scientific Comte. (London, Eng.) 1968-72; Outstanding Achievement Award, Univ. of Minnesota (1960); Gold Medal, Entom. Soc. of Can. (1964); Foreign Assoc., U.S. Nat. Acad. Sciences (1967); Fellow Entom. Soc. of Ont.; Hon. Fellow Entom. Soc. of Am.; Fellow Entom. Soc. of Can.; Hon. Mem. Entom. Soc. Can.; Hon. Life Mem. Candn. Seed Growers' Assoc.; mem. Agric. Inst. of Can.; Entomol. Soc. of Am.; Entomol. Soc. Can.; Entomol. Soc. B.C.; Protestant; Home: 4523 Juniper Place, Victoria, B.C. V8N 3K1

GLOUTNEY, Pierre, B.A.; stockbroker; b. Montreal, Que. 5 March 1940; e. McGill Univ. B.A. 1961; m. Dorothy 26 August 1961; children: Mark, Louise, Lisa; PRES., REYNOLDS SECURITIES (CANADA) LTD.; EXEC. VICE-PRES., DEAN WITTER REYNOLDS (CANADA) INC.; Club: Montreal Badminton & Squash Club; Home: 147-1st Blvd., Terrasse Vaudreuil, Que. J5V 5T2; Office: Suite 1300, 635 Dorchester Blvd. West, Montreal, Que. H3B 1S1.

GLOVER, William Elwood; radio and television broadcaster; b. Moose Jaw, Sask., 11 May 1915; s. William J. A. and Emma (Speirs) G.; e. Junior Coll., Univ. of Sask., Assoc. in Arts 1934; Davidson's Business Coll., Moose Jaw, 1935-36; m. Violet, d. John Sharpe of Moose Jaw, Sask., 3 Mar. 1939; two d. Sharon L., Barbara L.; STAFF ANNOUNCER, CANADA ALL NEWS RADIO, CKO-FM since 1979; joined staff CHAB, Moose Jaw, Sask., as an Announcer 1936 and was successively Tech. Operator, Salesman, Sales Mgr. until Mar. 1938; joined CBC Apr. 1938; took part in Royal Tour 1939; acted as Chief Announcer during war years: Master of Ceremonies of several "Victory Star Shows" during Victory Bond Drives 1941-45; associated with programs "Musically Yours", "Glover's Lane", "At Ease with Elwood Glover" on radio 1946-71; originated and hosted "Luncheon Date with Elwood Glover" on CBC-TV, 1963-75; retired from CBC 1975; Staff Announcer, CKEY 1975-79; Free Lanee Broadcaster at Multicultural Television Channel 47; 1979-80; rec'd. "Beaver Award" for distinguished service to radio, 1945, and "Radio World Trophy" by "Radio World" (popularity poll) 1947; recreations: movies, history, modelling in plastics; Home: 39 Foxwarren Dr., Willowdale, Ont. M2K 1C1

GLUBE, Hon. Constance R., B.A., LL.B.; b. Ottawa, Ont. 23 Nov. 1931; d. Samuel, Q.C. and Pearl (Slonomsky) Lepofsky; e. Mutchmore and Hopewell Ave. Pub. Schs., Glebe Coll. Inst. 1948 Ottawa; McGill Univ. B.A. 1952; Dalhousie Univ. LL.B. 1955; m. Richard H. Glube 6

July 1952; children: John B., Erica D., Harry S., B. Joseph CHIEF JUSTICE, TRIAL DIV. SUPREME COURT OF N.S. since 1977; called to Bar of N.S. 1956; cr. Q.C. 1974; Solr. Kitz & Matheson, Halifax 1964-66; Partner Fitzgerald & Glube 1966-68; Solr. Legal Dept. City of Halifax 1969-74; City Mgr. City of Halifax 1974-77; mem. Court House Comn. 1972-74; Metro Centre Bd. 1975-77; Halifax Grammar Sch. Bd. Trustees 2 terms; mem. Extve. and Bd. Candn. Council Christians & Jews (Atlantic Provs.) 1977-79, Co-chrmn. 1980- ; mem. Bd. of Dir. Candn. Judges Conference 1979, 2nd Vice-Chrmn. 1980- ; mem. Bd. of Dir. Candn. Inst. for the Adm. of Justice, 1979- ; Extve. and Bd. Candn. Assn. Mun. Adm. 1975-77; Inst. Pub. Adm. Can. Extve. 1975-77; Internat. City Mgrs. Assn.; N.S. Bar Soc.; Candn. Bar Assn.; Hebrew; recreations: sailing, swimming; Clubs: RNSYS; Saraguay; Home: 404 Francklyn St., Halifax, N.S. B3H 1A8; Office: Law Courts, 1815 Upper Water St., Halifax, N.S. B3J 3C8.

GLYDE, Henry George, R.C.A. (1949); artist; teacher; b. Luton, Eng., 18 June 1906; e. Hastings (Eng.) Sch. of Art & Science; Royal Coll. of Art, London, Eng.; formerly Student Demonst., Royal Coll. of Art, London, Eng. 1930; Instr., Borough Polytech., London, Eng.; Croydon Sch. of Art and High Wycombe Sch. of Art; Head of Art Dept., Inst. of Tech. & Art. Calgary, Alta., 1936-46; Head Dept. of Art. Univ. of Alta., 1946 till apptd. Prof. Emeritus; rep. in Nat. Gallery of Can.; Art Gallery of Toronto; exhibited: Royal Acad., London; Royal Candn. Acad.; O.S.A., Candn. Group, etc.; Past Pres., Alta. Soc. of Artists; mem., Candn. Soc. of Graphic Arts; Past Nat. Pres. (1954), Fed. Candn. Artists; Can. Council Sr. Fellowship 1958; rec'd. Univ. of Alta. Nat. Banff Medal 1966; Address: R.R. One, Pender Island, B.C. V0N 2M0

GOAD, John Lawrence, B.A.Sc.; investment dealer; b. Toronto, Ont., 3 Dec. 1927; s. J. Lawrence and Mary (Barclay) G.; e. Upper Canada Coll., Toronto; Univ. of Toronto, B.A.Sc. 1949; m. Diana, d. John R. Jacob, 4 Oct. 1952; children: Geoffry, Laurie, Jennifer, Martha, Allison; PRESIDENT. ST. LAWRENCE SECURITIES LTD. since 1971; Pres. and Dir. J. L. Goad & Co. Ltd.; Engr., Canadian Westinghouse Co. Ltd., 1949-53; with Dominion Securities Corp. Ltd. (Sales and Trading Divns.), 1950-53; joined J. L. Goad and Co. Ltd., Brokers, 1953; Pres., 1966; Dir., Boys Home, Toronto (past Chrmn.); mem., Toronto Stock Exchange; Investment Dealers Assn. Can.; Anglican; recreations: golf, squash, sailing; Clubs: National; Badminton; Lake Joseph Yacht; Granite; Home: 34 Bay View Wood, Toronto 12, Ont.; Office: Suite 2315, The Simpson Tower, 401 Bay St., Toronto, Ont. M5H 2Y4

GOBEIL, Denis, B.A.; judge; b. Baie St-Paul, Charlevoix, Que., 10 Feb. 1927; s. Jules and Albertine (Danais) G.; e. Séminaire de Nicolet (Que.), Université de Laval, Licence en Droit; m. Marguerite, d. Roméo Tremblay, Baie St-Paul, Que., 7 Apl. 1958; children: Anne, Simon, Luce, Valérie, Christine; JUDGE, PROV. COURT OF QUE., since Aug. 1967; called to Bar of Qué. 1955; R. Catholic; Home: rue Mont-Joli, Ste.-Foy, Que.; Office: Court House, Quebec, Que.

GODBEHERE, Walter, manufacturer; b. Montreal, Que. 8 June 1924; s. late Horace William and Elsie (Scott) G.; e. Riverside Pub. Sch.; Strathearn Comm.; Sir George Williams Univ. Extension; McGill Univ. 1 yr.; C.G.A. 1954; m. Frances Mary d. late Oswald Willett 2 June 1945; children Walter Wayne, Ann Frances; PRESIDENT, AND DIRECTOR, CEO ENHEAT INC. since 1977; Pres. and Dir. Airco Products; Dir.; Thompson and Sutherland Ltd.; Cdn. Foundry Assn. served Northern Telecom 1940-74 holding middle and sr. mang. positions from 1956, latterly Mang. Dir. subsidiary co. Istanbul, Turkey; Sr. Vice Pres. Operations, BXK Machinery International Ltd. 1974-77; served with Candn. Army 1942-45, rank Sgt.; Fellow, Cert. Gen. Accts. Assn. (Life mem. Past Pres. Que. Assn. & Montreal Chapter); Liberal; Anglican; re-

creations: fishing, golf, woodworking: Home: 283 Orleans St., Dieppe, N.B. E1A 1W8; Office: Lusby St., Amherst, N.S. B4H 3Y7, and Main St., Sackville, N.B. E0A 3C0

GODBOUT, Jacques, M.A.; écrivain, cinéaste; né Montréal, 27 nov., 1933; f. Fernand et Mariette (Daoust) G.; é. Univ. de Montréal, B.A., M.A., 1954; ép. Ghislaine, f. Henri Reiher, 31 juil. 1954; enfants: Alain, Sylvie: SCENARISTE ET REALISATEUR, OFFICE NATIONAL DU FILM; Prof. asst., Univ. Coll. d'Addis Abeba, Ethiopie, 1954; Publicitaire, McLaren Advertising Agency, Montréal, 1957; Réalisateur aux versions françaises, Office National du Film, Montréal, 1958, scénariste, réalisateur et monteur, 1961, Dir. de la prod. française, 1969, scénariste et réalisateur, 1970; chargé de cours a l'Univ. de Montréal, 1969; écritures cinématiques: "Les Dieux", 1961; "Pour quelques Arpents de Neige", 1962 (1er prix. 17e Festival internat. du Film documentaire, Salernes, Italie; "A Saint-Henri", 1962; "Rose et Landry", 1963 (Prix du Centre de la Culture et de la Civilisation, de La Fondation G. Cini, Venise, 1963; Plaque du Lion de St-Marc, Expn. intern. du film documentaire, Venise, 1963; 1er prix, Festival du film du Mid-West, Chicago, 1964; Mention, Festival du film documentaire, Cordoba, Argentine, 1964); "Paul-Emile Borduas", 1963; "Le Monde va nous prendre pour des Sauvages", 1964 (diplôme, 16e Palmarès du film canadien, Toronto, 1965); "Fabien-ne sans son Jules", 1964 (Grand prix, 2e semaine internat. du film 16mm, Evian, France, 1964); "Huit Témoins", 1965 (Prix, Palmarès du film canadien, Toronto); "Yul 871", 1966 (Meilleure réalisation, 2e Festival internat. du film Chicago, 1966); "Kid Sentiment", 1968; "Les vrais Cousins", 1970; "Le Roman d'Ixe-13", 1972; "Les Troubbes de Johny" 1973; "La Gammick" 1974; "Aimez-vous Les Chiens" 1975; "Arsenal", 1976; "L'Invasion", 1977; "Derrière L'Image", 1978; "Feu L'objectivite", 1978; "Deux Épisodes Dans La Vie d'Hubert Aquin", 1979; 'Distorsions', 1981 (Prix du Publique, Nyon, Suisse); écriture lit.: "Carton-Pâte" (poèmes), 1956; "Les Pavés secs" (poèmes), 1958; "La chair est un commencement" (poèmes), 1959; "C'est la chaude Loi des Hommes" (poèmes), 1960; "l'Aquarium" (roman), 1962 (Prix France-Canada, 1962); "le Couteau sur la Table" (roman), 1965 (prix de l'Acad. française, 1965); "le Mouvement du 8 avril" (pamphlet), 1966; "Salut Galarneau" (roman), 1967 (Prix du Gouverneur-Général, 1968); "la grande Muraille de Chine" (poèmes, en collab. avec J. R. Colombo), 1969; "d'Amour P.Q." (roman), 1972; "L'Interview" (théâtre) 1973; "Le Réformiste" (essai) 1975; "L'Isle au Dragon" (roman) 1976; 'Les Têtes à Papineau' (Roman) 1981; éd. anthol., "Poésie-poetry 62/64"; Résidence: 815 Pratt, (Outremont), Montréal, P.Q. H2V 2T7; Bureau: B.P. 6100, Montréal, P.Q.

GODBOUT, Roland Guy; company executive; b. Edmonton, Alta., 27 Nov. 1922; s. Raoul and Irene (Racicot) G.; e. Mont St. Louis; course on Industry, Sales and Adm. in U.S. 1946-47; m. Yvonne, d. Calix LeBeuf, 3 Aug. 1946; s. Pierre; Chrmn. of the Board, Cogan Wire and Metal Prod. (1974) Ltd.; Superior Concrete Accessories. Pres., Tempo Associates Inc. Gestion Prego; Dir. SNC Group; VS Services Ltd.; Menasco Manufacturing of Canada Ltd.; SLM Inc.; Bow Valley Ind. Ltd.; served overseas, Candn. Army Inf., 1941-46; discharged with rank of Major; mem. Young Pres. Organ.; Floor Covering Club (Montreal), Past-Pres.; La Chambre de Comm. Française au Can.; La Légion Canadienne; Candn. Cham. of Comm.; Hon. Col. Le Regiment de la Chaudière; Club: Mt. Royal, Laval sur le Lac Golf Club; Catholic; recreations: fishing, hunting, Home: 3980 Cote des neiges #B76 Montreal. Que. H3H 1W2 Office: 1390 Sherbrooke W., #240, Montreal H3G 1J9

GODFREY, Bert; company president; b. Toronto, Ont., 1 June 1908: s. Solomon and Minnie (Reisman) G.; e. Pub. and High Schs., Toronto Ont.; m. Ruth Grossman, 26

Jan. 1934; children: Corine L. (m. Prof. Baruch Levine), Sheldon J. (m. Judy Cole); PRESIDENT, S. GODFREY CO. LTD., Wool Importers; Dir., Candn. Foundation for Jewish Culture; mem., Toronto Citizens' Centenary Comte.; Candn. Camp Ramah; Bd. Dirs., New Mount Sinai Hosp., Toronto, Ont.; Jewish Home for the Aged and Baycrest Hosp.; Un. Jewish Welfare Fund of Toronto; World Council of Synagogues (1964); Associated Hebrew Schs. of Toronto; Bd. Overseers, Jewish Theol. Semy. of Am.; mem., Extve. Comte., Candn. Jewish Cong.; Bd. Govs., State of Israel Bond Organ. of Toronto; Pres., Jewish Pub. Library of Toronto; Past Pres. (1960-62), Bureau of Jewish Educ. of Toronto; Goel Tzedec Synagogue (1948-52); Founding Pres., Beth Tzedec Synagogue (amalg.), 1952-55 (Hon. Pres. since 1956); Ont. Region, Un. Synagogue of Am. (now Hon. Pres.); Founding Chrmn., Un. Synagogue Day Sch. of Toronto, 1961-62; Gen. Campaign Chrmn., Israel Bond Comte. of Toronto, 1964-65; Nat. Vice-Pres., Un. Synagogue of Am., 1957-61; Toronto Co-Chrmn., Brotherhood Week, 1954; mem., Extve. Comte., Candn. Council Christians & Jews (winner Nat. Human Relations Award, 1964); recipient, Louis Marshall Award, Jewish Theol. Semy. of Am., 1961; Negev Dinner-Jewish Nat. Fund, 1966; "Tower of David" award for participation in Israel Bond effort, 1969; Hebrew; Clubs: Canadian; Primrose; Oakdale; B'nai Brith; Home: 325 Glenayr, Toronto, Ont. M5P 3C6; Office: 49 Front St. E., Toronto, Ont. M5E 1B3

GODFREY, John Ferguson, D. Phil.; university president; b. Toronto, Ont. 1942; e. Upper Can. Coll. Toronto 1960; Neuchatel Jr. Coll. Switzerland 1961; Trinity Coll. Univ. of Toronto B.A. 1965; Balliol Coll. Oxford Univ. M.Phil. 1967, St. Antony's Coll. D.Phil. 1975; PRES. AND VICE CHANCELLOR, UNIV. OF KING'S COLL. since 1977; Can. Council Doctoral Fellowship 1968-69 (Nat. Archives Paris 1 yr.); Asst. Prof. of Hist. Dalhousie Univ. 1970-75, Assoc. Prof. 1980; mem. Senate; Carnegie Prof. of Hist. and Don Univ. of King's Coll. 1975-76, mem. Tenure & Appts. Comte.; mem. Bd. Atlantic Sch. of Theol.; chrmn., Dalhousie Art Gallery Comm.; Health, Education, and Social Services Division, United Way; Dir., National Film Bd.; mem. Gov. Gen. Study Conference; Can. Council of Christians and Jews; numerous book reviews, commentaries on hist. events, educ. matters and current events CBC radio and TV; author various publs. prof. journs. and mags.; Council for Candn. Unity; Bd. Trade Halifax; N. Brit. Soc.; St. George's Soc. Halifax; Lunenburg Chamber Comm.; Assn. of Atlantic Universities; Assn. of Univs. and Coll. of Can.; Assn. of Commonwealth Univ.; chrmn. Soc. French Hist. Studies; Atlantic Assn. Historians; chrmn., N.S. Comm.; HRM Duke of Edinburgh's 1980 study conference; Address: President's Lodge, Univ. of King's Coll., Halifax, N.S. B3H 2A1.

GODFREY, Hon. John Morrow, Q.C.; senator; b. Port Credit, Ont., 28 June 1912; s. Hon. Mr. Justice John Milton and Lily (Connon) G.; e. Univ. of Toronto Schs.; Royal Mil. Coll.; Osgoode Hall Law Sch. (Silver Medalist 1939); m. Mary Burwell d. Hector Ferguson, Toronto, Ont., 10 Sept. 1940; children: John, Sally (Mrs. Nickolas Forrest), Anne, Stephen; Counsel, CAMPBELL, GODFREY & LEWTAS; Dir. Montreal Trust Co.; Dover Industries Ltd.; read law with Macdonald & Macintosh; called to Bar of Ont. 1939; cr. Q.C. 1954; summoned to Senate 1973; served with RCAF 1940-45, pilot; Hon. Vice-Pres. Candn. Council on Social Devel.; mem. Extve. & Invest. Comtes. Can. Council 1970-73; Pres. Nat. Ballet of Can. 1968-70; Chrmn. Candn. Tax Foundation 1968-69; Pres. Candn. Mutual Funds Assn. 1969-70; mem. Candn. Bar Assn.; Zeta Psi; Liberal; Unitarian; recreations: golf, tennis, skiing; Clubs: Toronto; Toronto Golf; Osler Bluff Ski; Home: 99 Elm Ave., Toronto, Ont. M4W 1N9 Office: Toronto-Dominion Centre, Toronto, Ont. and Senate, Ottawa, Ont. K1A 1A4

GODFREY, Paul Victor, B.A.Sc., P.Eng.; b. Toronto, Ont., 12 Jan. 1939; s. Philip and Bess (Greenbaum) G.; e. Univ. of Toronto, B.A.Sc. (Chem. Engn.) 1962; m. Regina, d. Irving Bowman, Willowdale, Ont., 19 Nov. 1967; three s. Robin James, Noah Adam, Joshua Jay; Chrmn., Metrop. Toronto Council since 1973; Ald. and Controller, Borough N. York, 1965-73; Commr., Toronto Transit Comn. since 1973; Comm. Metro Board of Commissioners of Police 1973- ; Dir., Toronto Area Transit Operating Authority; Crusade Against Leukemia; Ont. Foundation of Visually Impaired Children Inc., 1980; mem. Assn. Prof. Engrs. Ont.; B'nai B'rith; Mason; P. Conservative; Jewish; Home: 25 Leacock Cresc., Don Mills, Ont. M3B 1N8; Office: 2nd Floor, City Hall, Toronto, Ont. M5H 2N1

GODFREY, William Harry, company president; b. Russell, North Dakota, 12 Feb. 1912; s. William Harry and Corinne (McCarthy) G.; came to Canada 1922; m. Esme Elizabeth, d. Frederick H. Lytle, 10 May 1947; children: Patrick, Timothy, Nicholas; CHRMN. AND DIR., NORTHWAY GESTALT INC. (formerly Lockwood) since 1978; Extve. Consultant, Hickling Smith Inc.; commenced with Goodyear Tire and Rubber Company in Sales and Service Dept., London, Ont. 1931; operated own business as road contractor 1946; Sales Dept., Percival Aircraft 1947; Gen. Mgr., Photographic Survey Corpn. 1948, becoming Internat. Marketing Vice-Pres. when Co. name changed to Hunting Associates Ltd. 1955; Vice-Pres., Lockwood, Kessler & Bartlett Inc. (N.Y.) 1962; joined Northway Consultants Ltd as Extve. Vice-Pres. 1965; Pres., 1967-78; served in 2nd World War, R.C.A.F. 1939-45; rank Pilot, Flight Lieut.; awarded D.F.C. and Croix de Guerre for service in French Liberation; Past Chrmn., Red Cross Blood Bank; mem. Am. Soc. Photogrammetry; Candn. Inst. Surveys & Mapping; Bd. Trade of Metrop. Toronto; Anglican; recreation: golfing; Clubs: Granite; Toronto Golf; University; Home: 63 St. Clair Ave. W.; Office: 625 Church St., Toronto, Ont. M4Y 2G1

GODIN, Jean-Cléo, B.A., L.Lett., Dr. de l'U.; professeur; né Petit-Rocher, N.B., 13 août, 1936; f. Nicolas et Anastasie (Doucet) G.; é. Coll. Ste. Marie, 1949-55; Boston Coll., B.A., 1961; Univ. de Montréal, L.Lett., 1964; Dr. de l'U. d'Aix-Marseille, 1966; ép. Michèle, f. Hermann Gervais, 3 août, 1963; enfants: François, Christian, Isabelle, Nicolas; PROF. TITULAIRE, DEPT. D'ETUDES FRANCAIS, Université de Montréal; Boursier du Conseil des Arts, 1962 et 1964; Boursier du Ministère de l'Education de Qué. 1963 et 1965; mem., Modern Language Assn.; Assoc. Profs. de Français des Univs. Canada; Assoc. Québécoise des Professeurs de Français; Société d'histoire du Théâtre du Québec; l'auteur du livre "Henri Bosco: une poétique du mystère", 1968; Prix littéraire du Québec 1969; l'auteur en collaboration avec Laurent Mailhot, des. livres "Le Théâtre québécois", 1970; Théâtre québécois II (1980); l'auteur de nombreaux articles; Catholique; récréations: tennis, natation; Résidence: 3769 avenue Melrose, Montréal, Qué. H4A 2S3; Bureau: C.P. 6128, Montréal, Qué.

GODIN, John Kenneth; mining consultant; b. Eganville, Ont., 21 June 1911; s. late Edward and late Catherine Anne (Power) G.; e. Eganville (Ont.) R.C. High Sch.; Renfrew (Ont.) Dist. Coll. Inst.; St. Michael's Coll., Univ. of Toronto; m. Margaret Mary, d. late Dr. M.J. Maloney; children: Catherine Anne, Margaret Mary, Edward, Martin James, Arthur Kiernan, Jane Eleanor, John Kenneth, Jr.; Dir., National Trust Co. Ltd.; Madeleine Mines Ltd.; joined McIntyre Porcupine Mines Ltd. as Miner, 1933; apptd. Shift Boss and Safety Inspr. by 1938; trans. to Belleterre Mines as Mine Supt., 1938, Mgr. 1951; trans. to Toronto as Asst. Gen. Mgr. of McIntyre, 1959; Gen. Mgr. 1963; Extve. Vice-Pres. and Dir., 1967; Pres. and Chief Extve. Offr. 1969; Commr. of Appeals, Ont. Workmen's Comp. Bd. 1976; Mayor, Town of Belleterre, Que., 1952-59; Past Pres., Que. Metal Mining Assn.; Dir., Mining

Assn. of Can.; mem. Candn. Inst. Mining & Metall. (Chrmn., Toronto Br. 1966-67); Assn. Prof. Engrs. Ont.; Royal Candn. Inst.; Bd. Trade Metrop. Toronto; R. Catholic; recreations: fishing, music; Clubs: St. George's Golf & Country; Home: 50 Ravensbourne Cres., Islington, Ont. M9A 2A8

GODREAU, Lt. Col. Jean Yves, C.D., A.D.C.; manufacturers' agent; b. Quebec, 1 Aug. 1921; s. Col. J. P., E.D., and Jeanne (Gagnon) G.; e. Séminaire de Québec; m. Monette, d. J.I. Samson, Lauzon, Que.; child: Guy, Lawyer; PRES., LES EXPLOSIFS CHAMPLAIN, INC.; served overseas in 2nd World War in Candn. Intelligence Corps in Germany; promoted Lt.-Col. Feb. 1963 and apptd. C.O., Le Régt. de la Chaudière; apptd. A.D.C. to Lt.-Gov. of Que., March 1966; Past Pres., Cercle, Goethe de Qué.; Soc. de Généalogie de Qué; mem. Chambre de Commerce; and Cercle Cervantes; recreation: International Radio (Amateur) VE 2 DMG; geneology; Roman Catholic; Home: 1287 Ave. Allard, Ste.-Foy, Que. G1W 3G3; Office: 1990 Ouest, boul. Charest, Ste. Foy, Qué.

GODSON, Warren Lehman, M.A., Ph.D., F.R.S.C.; atmospheric physicist; b. Victoria, B.C. 4 May 1920; s. Walter Ernest Henry and Mary Edna (Lehman) G.; e. Victoria, B.C. pub., high schs. and coll. 1937; Univ. of B.C. B.A. 1939, M.A. 1941; Univ. of Toronto M.A. 1944, Ph.D. 1948; m. 1stly Merl Ellen Hotson (d.) Dec. 1942; m. 2ndly Ruth Margaret Clarke Sept. 1967; m. thirdly Harriet Rosalie Burke Dec. 1977; children: Elliott, Marilyn Henderson, Murray, Ralph, Ellen; step-children: Alan Bloom, Alison Bloom, Stephen Bloom; DIR. GEN. ATMOSPHERIC RESEARCH DIRECTORATE, ATMOSPHERIC ENVIRONMENT SERVICE since 1973; Hon. Prof. Inst. Environmental Sciences, Univ. of Toronto since 1975; Gen. Research and Lecturing post, Candn. Meteorological Service (became Atmospheric Environment Service) 1943-54, Supt. Atmospheric Research Sec. 1954-71, Dir. Atmospheric Processes Research Br. 1971-73; Pres. Can. for Atmospheric Sciences (UN) 1973-77; rec'd IMO Prize 1975, Patterson Medal 1968; Buchan Prize 1964; co-author "Atmospheric Thermodynamics" 1974 and 1981; over 100 scient. articles meteorol. research; Fellow, Am. Meteorol. Soc. (former Councillor); mem., Candn. Meteorol. & Oceanographic Soc. (Pres. 1957-59); Internat. Assn. Meteorol. & Atmospheric Physics (Secy. 1960-75, Vice Pres. 1975-79, Pres. 1979-1983,); Anglican; recreation: colour photography; Home: 39 Dove Hawkway, City of North York, Willowdale, Ont. M2R 3M8; Office: 4905 Dufferin St., Downsview, Ont. M3H 5T4.

GODWIN, Ted, R.C.A.; artist; educator; b. Calgary, Alta. 13 Aug. 1933; s. John Griffin and Hilda (Sirett) G.; e. S. Alta. Inst. of Technol. & Art Calgary 1951-55; m. Phyllis Wanda d. Walter Goota, Prince Albert, Sask. 24 Dec. 1955; children: Teddi Ruth, Tammi Lynn; PROF. OF ART, UNIV. OF REGINA; art dir.-TV, Ad Agency work, store display, sign writer, neon sign designer 1955-61, 1963-64; solo exhns. incl. Allied Arts Centre Calgary 1958, 1967; Norman MacKenzie Art Gallery Regina 1965; Univ. of Man. 1966; Ont. Art Circuit 1966; Atlantic Art Circuit 1967; Blue Barn Gallery 1967 Ottawa (2 man show 1962); Dunlop Art Gallery 1968, 1976; York Univ. Toronto 1971; Bau-Xi Gallery Vancouver 1971, 1979, 1980, Victoria 1974, Toronto 1977, 1978, 1979; Edmonton Art Gallery 1971; Perry's Art Centre Regina 1974; Moose Jaw Art Museum, Mendel Art Gallery Saskatoon, Art Gallery of Greater Victoria 1975 (Recent Landscapes); Subway Art Gallery Winnipeg 1976 (Survey 1964-74; Rocks, Flowers, Scissors), 1977; Candn. Art Galleries Calgary 1977 (2 exhns.), 1978, 1980; Lefebvre Gallery Edmonton 1977; Glenbow Art Museum Calgary 1980; rep. in various group shows incl. Young Contemporaries (nat. tour) 1955; 3rd Biennial Candn. Art Nat. Gallery (nat. tour) 1959; 5 Painters from Regina (nat. tour) 1961; 4th Biennial Candn. Art 1961, 6th Biennial 1965; Candn. Pavillion

Expo '67; Painting 68 Art Gallery Ont.; Selected Sask. Painters Waddington Art Galleries Montreal 1968; 2 man exhn. Kenny's Art Gallery Galway, Eire 1972; 9 out of 10 (nat. tour) 1974; Survey of Candn. Painting since 1776 Art Gallery Ont. 1975; Hist. Suvey of Watercolour Alta. Glenbow Art Museum, Calgary 1980 and other exhns.; rep. in various pub., corporate and private colls. incl. Nat. Gallery Can., Art Gallery Ont., Can. Council Art Bank; recipient 2nd Prize Internat. Neon Design Competition 1958; Merit Award Winnipeg Biennial 1964; Winnipeg Show Purchase Award 1968; Can. Council Grant (Greece) 1962-63; Queen's Silver Jubilee Medal 1978; featured various bibliogs.; Home: 65 Hamlet Rd. S.W., Calgary, Alta. T2V 3C9; Office: Regina, Sask.

GOETZ, Peter, artist; b. Slavgorod, Russia, 8 Sept. 1917; s. Henry Peter and Justina (Friesen) G.; came to Can., 1929; e. grad Kitchener-Waterloo Collegiate, 1938; studied art with F.H. Varley (1947); Waterloo Coll. (1944); Doon Sch. Fine Art, (1946); m. Helena Warkentin, 9 Aug. 1941; children: Jean Margot, Peter Andrew; paints and teaches art to adult educ. groups; has exhibited with Royal Candn. Acad., Ont. Soc. of Artists, Candn. Soc. of Painters in Watercolour, Montreal Museum of Fine Arts, National Gallery, Winnipeg Show, Western Art League; exhibited one-man shows annually since 1957; Fellow, International Institute Arts and Letters; International Platform Association; Centro Studie Scambi Internat., Rome; mem. Ont. Soc. Artists; Candn. Soc. Painters in Watercolour; Candn. Soc. of Artists; Address: 784 Avondale Ave., Kitchener, Ont. N2M 2W8

GIROUX, Robert E., B.A.Sc., C.A.; executive; e. Univ. of Toronto B.A.Sc. 1960; C.A. 1963; DIR. OF FINANCE & ADM., TORSTAR CORP. 1981; joined Clarkson Gordon 1960-69; Treas. Maple Leaf Gardens Ltd. 1969 Secy.-Treas. Hayhoe Foods Ltd. 1971; Extve. Vice Pres. Can-Sports Inc. 1973; Extve. Vice Pres. Toronto Hockey 1974; Corporate Controller, Torstar Corp. 1977, Dir. of Finance & Adm. 1978, Vice Pres. & Gen. Mgr. Nielsen-Ferns International Ltd. (subsidiary) 1980-81; Club: Lambton Golf & Country; Home: 8 Orland Court, Weston, Ont. M9R 3H4; Office: One Yonge St., Toronto, Ont. M5E 1P9.

GOFFART, Walter André, A.M., Ph.D.; educator; b. Berlin, Germany (Belgian citizen by birth) 22 Feb. 1934; s. Francis Léo and Andrée (Steinberg) G.; e. Phillips Acad. Andover, Mass. 1951; Harvard Univ. A.B. 1955, A.M. 1956, Ph.D. 1961; Ecole normale supérieure, Paris 1957-58 (concurrently Ecole pratique des Hautes étudies, sciences historiques); m. Roberta d. Norman Frank, Bronx, N.Y. 31 Dec. 1977; children (by first marriage): Vivian, Andrea Judith; PROF. OF MEDIEVAL HIST. UNIV. OF TORONTO 1971- ; Lectr. present Univ. 1960, Asst. Prof. 1963, Assoc. Prof. 1966-71, Acting Dir. Centre for Medieval Studies 1971-72; Visiting Asst. Prof. Univ. of Calif. Berkeley 1965-66; Visiting Fellow, Inst. Advanced Study, Princeton 1967-68; Dumbarton Oaks Center for Byzantine Studies, Washington, D.C. 1973-74; recipient Can. Council Leave Fellowship 1967-68; Am. Council Learned Socs. Fellowship 1973-74; Guggenheim Fellowship 1979-80; author "The Le Mans Forgeries" 1966; "Caput and Colonate" 1974; "Barbarians and Romans A.D. 418-584" 1980; co-translator "The Origin of the Idea of Crusade" 1978; numerous articles late Roman & early medieval subjects; mem. Am. Hist. Assn.; Fellow, Medieval Acad. Am. (Councillor 1978-80); Home: 24 Chicora Ave., Toronto, Ont. M5R 1T6; Office: Toronto, Ont. M5S 1A1.

GOHEEN, Duncan S., B.A., M.S.; financial executive; e. Graceland Coll. Iowa B.A. 1966; Univ. of Mo. M.S. 1968; PRESIDENT AND CHIEF EXTVE. OFFR., SUN FINANCIAL CORP. LTD.; Pres. and Chief Extve. Offr. Gohoon Ltd. 1975-78; recreations: flying, hunting, fishing, camping, hockey, singing; Office: 205 Northland Professional Bldg., 4600 Crowchild Trail N.W., Calgary, Alta. T3A 2L6.

GOLD, Abe; company executive; b. Montreal, Que., 31 July 1920; s. Louis and Goldie (Shapiro) G.; e. Strathcona High Sch., Montreal; m. Hannah (deceased), d. Louis Aron, Toronto, Ont., 12 July 1941; children: Sari, David; PRES. & CHIEF EXECUTIVE OFFICER, PEOPLES DEPARTMENT STORES LTD.; Pres. D'Allard's Ltd.; Walkers Holdings Ltd.; Walkers Stores Ltd.; St. Michael Shops of Can. Ltd.; Dir., Marks & Spencer, London, Eng.; recreations: golf; Home: 5500 MacDonald, Apt. 1707, Montreal Que.; Office: 5590 Royalmount, Town of Mount Royal, Que. H3X 2W5

GOLD, Joseph, B.A., Ph.D., university professor; b. London, Eng. 30 June 1933; e. Univ. of Birmingham, Eng. B.A. 1955; Univ. of Wisconsin, Ph.D. 1959; PROF. OF ENGLISH, UNIV. OF WATERLOO; Univ. of Wisconsin, Dept. of Eng., 1955-59; Whitewater State Coll, Wis., Dept. of Eng., 1959-60; Univ. of Man., Dept. of Eng., 1960-70; El. to Senate, Univ. of Man., 1968-71; El. Pres., Assn. of Chrmn. of Eng. of Ont. 1971-72; Re-el. 1972-73; Chrmn. & Prof. Eng., Univ. of Waterloo, 1970-73; Chrmn. ACUTE Cmte. on Professional concerns, 1974-76; Grad. Extve. Cmte., Univ. of Waterloo, 1981- ; has taken part in panel discussions, delivered public lectrs. and addresses, presented papers, chaired workshops, etc.; author of "William Faulkner: A Study in Humanism from Metaphor to Discourse", 1966; Ed., "King of Beasts and Other Stories", 1967; author, "The Stature of Dickens: A Centenary Bibliography", 1971; "Charles Dickens: Radical Moralist", 1972; other writings incl. articles on Ivy Compton-Burnett, Faulkner and Dickens; awarded Best Director, Univ. of Birmingham Drama Festival, 1954; Trustee, Dickens Soc. of Am., 1971-73; Apptd. to Man. Censor Appeal Bd., 1969; Bd. of Gov. Man. Theatre Centre, 1969; Pres., Temple Shalom Reform Congreg., 1978; Extve. Mem. Candn. Assn. for Am. Studies, 1964-73; Ed. Bd. "Forester Newsletter", Writers' Union of Can.; mem., ACUTE, ACTRA; Jewish; Clubs: Celebrity Club, Toronto; recreations: Nordic skiing, fishing, acting, photography, canoeing, acting and directing student dramas; Home: 97 Morse St., Toronto, Ont., M4M 2P7; Office: Waterloo, Ont. N2L 3G1.

GOLD, Phil, O.C., M.Sc., M.D., C.M., Ph.D., F.R.C.P.(C), F.R.S.C., F.A.C.P.; medical scientist; educator; b. Montreal, Que. 17 Sept. 1936; s. Jack Gold; e. McGill Univ. B.Sc. 1957, M.Sc. 1961, M.D., C.M. 1961, Ph.D. (Physiol.) 1965; m. Evelyn Katz 21 Aug. 1960; children: Ian Jeffrey, Joselyn Sue, Joel Todd; PROF. OF MED., McGILL UNIV. since 1973, Prof. of Physiol. since 1974, Dir. Cancer Centre since 1978; Physician-in-Chief Montreal Gen. Hosp. since 1980, Dir. McGill Univ. Med. Clinic and Sr. Investigator Montreal Gen. Hosp. Research Inst. since 1972; Consultant in Allergy & Immunol. Mount Sinai Hosp. Ste. Agathe des Monts, Que.; internship and residency Montreal Gen. Hosp. 1961-62, 1965-66; Career Investigator, Med. Research Council Can. (Fellow 1963-65, Assoc. 1968, Chrmn. Grants Panel for Cancer Research 1972-77); Pres. Med. Adv. Bd. Cancer Research Soc. Inc. Montreal 1975-77; Founding mem. and mem. Constitution Comte. Internat. Research Group for Carcinoembryonic Proteins since 1976; Pres. Scient. Adv. Bd. Israel Cancer Research Fund; mem. Cancer Grants Panel B, Nat. Cancer Inst. Can.; Dir. Mount Sinai Inst. Toronto; mem., Medical Advisory Bd., Gairdner Foundation, 1979; Pres. Ninth Ann. Meeting of International Soc. for Oncodevelopment Biology and Medicine, Alta., 1981; Chrmn. Medical Research Council Grants Cmtee. for Cancer, 1981-2; Inaugural Terry Fox Scient. 1981; Visiting Scient. Pub. Health Research Inst. N.Y. City 1967-68; rec'd numerous univ. scholarships and awards; Royal Coll. Phys. & Surgs. Can. Medal in Med. 1965; E. W. R. Steacie Prize for Science, NRC 1973; Outstanding Scientist Award (Inaugural) Internat. Research Group Carcinoembryonic Proteins 1976; Queen's Silver Jubilee Medal 1977; Award Internat. Conf. on Clin. Uses Carcinoembryonic Antigen 1977; Johann-Georg-Zimmer-

mann Prize for Cancer Research, Medizinische Hochschule, Hannover 1978; Gairdner Foundation Annual Award 1978; Gold Medal Award of Merit, Grad. Soc. McGill Univ. 1979; first recipient Terry Fox Medal, B.C. Medical Assoc., 1981 Chair in Science, Weizmann Inst. of Sc., Israel; Officer of the Order of Canada, 1978; Member, Med. Adv. Bd., Gairdner Foundation, 1980; Heath Mem. Award of the M.D. Anderson Hospital & Texas Inst. of the Univ. of Texas Cancer Centre, 1980; mem. various med. journ. ed. bds., Assoc. Ed. "Cancer Research" 1973; co-ed. and co-author "Clinical Immunology" 2nd ed. 1975; over 100 papers scient. journs.; mem. Am. Acad. Allergy; Am. Assn. Advanc. Science; Am. Assn. Cancer Research; Am. Assn. Immunols.; Am. Fed. Clin. Research; Am. and Candn. Soc. Clin. Investigation; Candn. Fed. Biol. Sciences; Candn. Med. Assoc.; Candn. Oncology Soc. (Founding mem.); Candn. Soc. Allergy & Clin. Immunol.; Candn. Soc. Immunol. (Pres. 1975-77) and other med. and scient. socs.; Alpha Omega Alpha; Hebrew; recreations: photography, music, lapidary, sailing, cross-country skiing; Club: Explorers; Home: 5705 Parkhaven Ave., Côte St. Luc, Montreal, Que. H4W 1X6; Office: 7135 Montreal Gen. Hosp., 1650 Cedar Ave., Montreal, Que. H3G 1A4.

GOLDBERG, David Myer, M.B., Ch.B., Ph.D., M.D.; educator; b. Glasgow, Scot. 30 Aug. 1933; e. Univ. of Glasgow B.Sc. 1958, M.B., Ch.B. 1959, Ph.D. 1965, M.R.C. Path. 1970, F.R.I.C. 1972, M.D. 1974, F.R.C. Path. 1979; m. 9 March 1964; children: Susan, Tanya; came to Can. 1975; HEAD OF BIOCHEM., RESEARCH INST., HOSP. FOR SICK CHILDREN; Prof. and Chrmn. of Clin. Biochem. Univ. of Toronto; mem. World Health Organ. Expert Panel on Biochem. Indicators of Radiation Damage, Paris; 1970, and Expert Panel on Enzymes in Clinical Diagnosis, Tutzing, Bavaria 1973 and Munich 1974; Organ. Comte. 6th (1974), 7th (1976), 8th (1978) and 9th (1980) Internat. Cong. on Clin. Enzymol.; Foundation Comte. Internat. Soc. Clin. Enzymol. 1974-76, Extve. since 1976, Vice Pres. 1978- ; mem. Am. Assn. Clin. Chems.; Candn. Assn. Clin. Chems.; Candn. Assn. Med. Biochem.; Candn. Soc. Clin. Invest.; author over 160 scient. Papers and reviews, 60 abstracts diagnostic enzymol., gastroenterol. and biochem. of cancer; Editor of "Annual Review of Clinical Biochemistry" and "Progress in Clinical Enzymology"; recreations: squash, music, theatre; Home: 9 Harrison Rd., Willowdale, Ont. M2L 1V3; Office: 555 University Ave., Toronto, Ont. M5G 1X8.

GOLDBERG, Nathan Ralph; writer; b. Montreal, Que., 11 June 1919; s. Strul and Gertie (Lazarovitch) G.; e. Stanstead Acad.; Strathcona Acad.; Sir George Williams Coll.; Univ. of Toronto; m. Dvora, d. Shloime Wiseman, Montreal, 18 Apl. 1942; served in World War 1942-45 with R.C.A.F. overseas; author of "Twelve Poems", 1941; "History of the City of Edmonton Squadron", 1945; "Coffee and Bitters", 1947; "Those Ills We Have", (play); Left Wing; Hebrew; recreations: cinema, swimming, chess, travelling; Club: Modern Writers; Home: 192 Combe St., Toronto, Ont. M3H 4K5

GOLDBERG, Simon Abraham, M.A., Ph.D.; statistician; b. Poland, 4 Dec. 1914; s. Isaiah and Helen (Pachter) G.; came to Canada, Oct. 1927; e. Public and High Schs., Montreal, Que.; McGill Univ., B.A. 1939; M.A. 1940; Harvard Univ., M.A. 1942, Ph.D. 1954; Co-Ordinator, U.N. Nat. Household Survey Capability Programme, U.N. Stat. Offc. since 1979; Dir., Statistical Office, U.N., 1972-9; Asst. Chief Statistician of Can., Statistics Canada, 1954-72; National Income Statistician there, 1945-50, Director of Research and Development Division, 1950-54; mem., International Stat. Inst.; Internat. Assn. for Research into Income and Wealth; Conf. on Research in Income and Wealth; Am. Stat. Assn.; hon. F.S.S.; fellow, Amer. Statistical Assn.; served in 2nd World War with R.C.A.F., 1942-45; Home: 400 E. 54th St., Apt. 19C, New

York, N.Y.; Office: Statistical Office, United Nations, New York, N.Y.

GOLDBLOOM, Richard B., B.Sc. M.D., C.M., F.R.C.P. & S. (C); physician; university professor; b. Montreal, Que., 16 Dec. 1924; s. Alton, M.D. and Anne E. (Ballon) G.; e. Selwyn House Sch. and Lower Can. Coll., Montreal; McGill Univ., B.Sc. 1945, M.D., C.M. 1949; postgrad. med. educ. Royal Victoria Hosp., Montreal, Montreal Children's Hosp. and Children's Med. Centre, Boston; m. Ruth Miriam, d. Abraham Schwartz, New Waterford, N.S., 25 June 1946; children: Dr. Alan, Barbara (Mrs. Robert Issenman), David; PROFESSOR AND HEAD OF PAEDIATRICS, DALHOUSIE UNIVERSITY: Physician-in-Chief & Director of Research, The Izaak Walton Killam Hospital for Children, Halifax; Teaching Fellow, Dept. of Paediatrics, Harvard Med. Sch., 1951-52; Hosmer Teaching Fellow in Paediatrics, McGill Univ., 1953-56; Assoc. Prof. McGill and Phys., Montreal Children's Hosp., 1964-67; rec'd Lederle Med. Faculty Award 1962; el. mem., Med. Research Council, 1970-72; Pres., Atlantic Symphony Orchestra, 1976-79; Vice Pres., Assoc. of Candn. Orchestras, 1978-9; Dir., Atlantic Trust Co., 1977-79; Atlantic Research Centre for Mental Retardation; Chrm., Comte. on Career Investigatorships, Med. Research Council; Bd. of Trustees, Queen Elizabeth II Fund for Research in Diseases of Children; mem., Soc. Paediatric Research; Am. Pediatric Soc.; Am. Acad. Paediatrics: Comte on Areas of National Concern, Medical Research Council; Killam Awards Comte. Canada Council 1977-80; Bd. Chrm. Waterfront Devel. Corp., Halifax, 1976-80; Assn. Med. Sch. Paediatric Dept. Chrmn. Alpha Omega Alpha; Liberal; Jewish; recreations: music, sailing; Clubs: Royal Nova Scotia Yacht Squadron; Saraguay; Home: 324 Purcell's Cove Rd., Boulderwood, Halifax, N.S. B3P 1C7

GOLDBLOOM, Hon. Victor Charles, M.N.A.,M.D.; politician; pediatrician; b. Montreal, Que., 31 July 1923; s. Dr. Alton and Annie (Ballon) G.; e. Selwyn House and Lower Can. Coll., Montreal; McGill Univ., M.D. 1945; m. Sheila, d. late Jacob Saul Barshay, New York, 15 June 1948; children: Susan, Michael, Jonathan; PRES. CANADIAN COUNCIL OF CHRISTIANS AND JEWS Lecturer in Pediatrics, McGill University; spokesman for Quebec medical profession before Royal Commission on Health Services; Advisor, Canadian Assn. Occupational Therapists and Candn. Assn. Physiotherapists; former Min. of Municipal Affairs, Quebec; mem. Prov. Govt's. Comte. on Nursing; named as arbiter in conflict between nurses and adm. St. Justine's Hosp.; Pediatrician Bureau, Montreal; Candn. rep., Seminar on Health Objectives for Developing Soc., Duke Univ., 1964; mem. Adv. Del. for Min. of Health, Que. to Fed.-Prov. Conf. of Health Mins., 1965; served with RCAMC 1944-46; Vice Pres., Coll. Phys. & Surgs. Prov. Que.; Chrmn. Nat. Comte. on Med. Econ., Candn. Med. Assn.; Zeta Beta Tau; Liberal; Hebrew; recreations: opera, lieder singing; Home: 5 Grove Park, Montreal, Que. H3Y 3E6; Office: Parliament Bldgs., Quebec City, Que.

GOLDEN, David A., O.C., LL.B., LL.D.; executive; b. 1920; e. University of Manitoba (Law); Rhodes Scholar, 1940; Oxford Univ.; m. Molly Berger, Estevan, Sask, Sept. 1946; two s. and one d. CHRMN. OF BD., TELESAT CANADA since 1980; Chrmn. of Bd., Computel Ltd.; C.C.M. Inc.; Dir., Atomic Energy of Can. Ltd.; Provigo Inc.; Pratt and Whitney Aircraft of Canada Ltd.; Conference Bd. of Canada mem. Ottawa Adv. Bd., Royal Trust Co.; joined the Dept. of Defence Production in 1951 as Dir. of Legal Br., after practising law in Winnipeg, Man., with (now) the Hon. Chief Justice Samuel Freedman; apptd. Asst. Depy. Min. and Gen. Counsel, Feb. 1953 and promoted to Depy. Min. 1954; Depy. Min., Dept. of Industry, 1963-64; Pres., Air Industries Assn. Can. 1964-69; Pres., Telesat Canada, 1969-80; enlisted in Candn. Army in 1941 and served overseas; prisoner of war in Hong Kong 1941-45; discharged Dec. 1945 with rank of Capt.; named an Offr. of Order of Canada, 1977; Home: Apt. 2405, 900 Dynes Rd., Ottawa, Ont. K2C 3L6 Office: 333 River Rd., Ottawa, Ont. K1L 8B9

GOLDENBERG, Gerald Joseph, M.D., Ph.D., F.R.C.P. & S.(C); educator; b. Brandon, Man. 27 Nov. 1933; s. Jacob and Fanny (Walker) G.; e. Univ. of Man. M.D. 1957; Univ. of Minn. Ph.D. 1965; m. Sheila Claire d. Henry Melmed, Winnipeg, Man. 4 Jan. 1959; children: Lesley Peace, Jacob Allan, Suzanne Elise, Ellen Rachel; DIR., MANITOBA INST. OF CELL BIOL. 1973- ; Prof. of Med. Univ. of Man. 1975- ; Lectr. in Med. present Univ. 1964, Asst. Prof. 1966, Assoc. Prof. 1970-75; Research Asst. Man. Cancer Foundation 1964-73; Physician to Winnipeg Munc. Hosps. 1964-67 and to Winnipeg Gen. Hosp. 1965- ; Consultant in Oncology Winnipeg Children's Hosp. 1967- ; recipient Univ. of Man. Gold Medal Faculty Med., Dr. Charlotte Ross Gold Medal 1957; Fellow, Am. Cancer Soc. 1959-61; McEachern Fellow Candn. Cancer Soc. 1961-62; Fellow, Nat. Cancer Inst. 1962-63, Clin. Research Assoc. 1967-73, Candn. Hadassah Cancer Research Fellow 1963-64; author over 80 scient. publs.; mem. Am. Assn. Cancer Research; Am. Soc. Exper. Pathol.; Candn. Soc. Clin. Investigation; Candn. Oncology Soc.; Sigma Alpha Mu; Y.M.H.A.; Freemason; Jewish; recreations: golf, tennis, swimming, skiing, chess; Home: 700 Oak St., Winnipeg, Man. R3M 3R7; Office: 100 Olivia St., Winnipeg, Man. R3E 0V9.

GOLDENBERG, Hon. H. Carl, O.C., O.B.E., Q.C., M.A., B.C.L., LL.D.; senator; b. Montreal, Que., 20 October 1907; s. Maurice and Adela (Gradinger) G.; e. McGill Univ., B.A. 1928, M.A. 1929, B.C.L. 1932; Gold Medal in Econ. amd Pol. Science 1928, in Law 1932; LL.D. of McGill, Montréal, Toronto and B.C. Univs.; m. Shirley Claire, d. Myer Block, Montreal, Que., Feb. 1945; children: Edward Stephen, Ann Helen Bergman; Special Counsel on the Constitution to the Prime Minister of Canada 1968-71; summoned to the Senate of Canada 4 Nov. 1971 (Chrmn. Standing Senate Comte. on Legal and Const. Affairs); mem. Joint Senate-House of Commons Comte. on Proposals for Patriation of the Constitution of Canada, 1980; called to the Bar of Que. 1932; Q.C. 1952; Sessional Lecturer in Economics and Political science, McGill University 1932-36; Adviser to Royal Commission on Dominion-Prov. Relations 1937-38; Chairman, Royal Comn. on Finances and Adm. of Winnipeg 1938-39; Commr., Man. Govt. Comm. Enterprises Enquiry 1939-40; Adviser to Que. Tax Revision Bd. (Montpetit Comn.) 1940; Chrmn., Prov. Bd. of Arbitration, Women's Apparel Indust. in Que. 1940; apptd. to Can's. War Organ., Sept. 1940; and occupied posts: Dir.-Gen., Econ. and Stat. Br. and mem. of Production Bd., Dept. of Mun. and Supply; Chrmn., Indust. Production Co-operation Bd.; mem., Nat. Selective Service Advisory Bd.; Extve. Asst. to Chrmn., Joint War Production Comte. of Can. and U.S.A. (Candn. Sec.); as a special Fed. Commr., settled Montreal Tramways Co. employees strike, 1943 and Great Lakes Shipping Strike, 1956; Rept. Min. of Mun. & Supply at War Production meetings in London, Eng., 1943; Adviser to Candn. Govt. Del. to Internat. Labour Conf., Philadelphia, 1944; Labour Adviser, Dept. of Reconstruction, 1945-46; Roy. Commr. on Prov.-Mun. Relations in B.C., 1946-47; Special Commr. under Combines Act to investigate Baking Indust. in W. Can., 1948; Special Counsel for B.C. (1950-56), N.B. (1960-61) and Nfld. 1957-65, at Fed.-Prov. Confs.; Special Commr. under Combines Act to investigate Wire & Cable Industry 1952-53; Counsel for Nfld. on Revision of Financial Terms of Union with Canada, 1954-58; Commr. on Mun. Taxation in Winnipeg, 1957-58; Chrmn. Comn. of Enquiry into the sugar industry of Jamaica, 1959 and of Trinidad, 1960 and 1962; Roy. Commr. on constr. indust. strikes in Vancouver, 1958; Royal Commr. on Labour-Mang. Relations in Constr. Industry Ont., 1961-62; settled year old Royal York Hotel strike in 1962; Vice-Chrmn., Prov. Que. Royal

Comn. of Enquiry into Prov., Mun. and Sch. Bd. sources of Revenue, 1963; Vice-Chrmn., Quebec Econ. Adv. Council, 1962-68; Royal Comn. on Metropolitan Saint John, N.B., 1963, on Greater Fredericton, N.B. 1970-71, on Greater Moncton, N.B. 1970-71; Royal Comn. on Metrop. Toronto, 1963-65; Royal Commr. on Mail Transport in Montreal 1970; Impartial Chrmn. and Arbitrator, Women's Dress Industry, Women's Coat & Suit Industry, and Men's Clothing Industry, Montreal; Impartial Umpire of Juris. Disputes, Candn. Labour Cong.; Arbitrator, Ont. Hydro Employees' Dispute 1962; Federal Mediator in national railway dispute following settlement of 1966 railway strike; settled nat. strike in meat-packing industry 1966, and strike at Sydney Steel Corp., N.S. 1972; Mediator in Man. Hydro Employees' dispute 1973; Arbitrator, Nfld. Hosp. Employees' dispute 1973; Chrmn. Bd. of Arbitration, Windsor, Ont. separate sch. teachers' dispute 1974; Arbitrator, Toronto Transit Comn. Employees' strike 1974; Arbitrator, Univ. of Man. Faculty Assoc. Dispute 1976; settled Vanier College Teachers' strike, 1978; Arbitrator, Acadia University Faculty Assoc. Dispute 1979," Chrmn., Tri-Level Confs. of Fed., Prov. and Mun. govts. 1972 and 1973; Chrmn. First Nat. Conf. on Multiculturalism, 1973; Gov. Emeritus McGill Univ., Hon. mem. Bd. Adm. Montreal Jewish General Hospital; author: "The Law of Delicts Under the Quebec Civil Code", 1935, "Municipal Finance in Canada", 1939; Co-Ed "Construction Labour Relations", 1969; mem., Candn. Pol. Science Assn.; Candn. Bar Assn.; recreations: reading, music; Club: McGill Faculty; Home: 566 Roslyn Ave., Westmount, Que. H3Y 2T8; Office: 1010 St. Catherine St. W., Montreal, Que.

GOLDFARB, Leo; Real Estate Exec./Financier; b. Warsaw, Poland, 8 May 1925; s. Max and Helen (Haberman) G.; e. Baron Byng H.S., Sir George Williams Univ.; m. Rita (d), d. Sam Steinberg, 19 Nov. 1950; children: Eileen, Robert, Gail; 2ndly Shirley Greenfeld Hitzig 26 Jan. 1973; PRESIDENT RINGOLD ENTERPRISES LTD.; Mgr.-Real Estate, Steinberg Ltd., 1954-68; Dir. and Exec. Vice. Pres. Corp. Affairs, Trizec Corp. 1969-79, Vice Pres. Retail Operations; Dir., Exec. Vice-Pres. and Chief Operating Officer Pres. and Dir., Place Bonaventure Inc.; Dir., Morgan Trust Co.; Dir., Jewish Gen. Hosp.; Clubs: Elmridge Golf and Country, Mount Royal Tennis, Montefiore, Home: Apt. 1611, 3 Westmount Sq., Westmount, Que. H3Z 2S5; Office: Place Bonaventure, Level 2, P.O. Box 1000, Montreal, Que. H5A 1G1

GOLDHAMER, Charles; painter; b. Philadelphia, Pa., 21 August 1903; s. Albert and Margaret G.; e. Pub. Sch. and Coll. Inst., Toronto, Ont.; Ont. Coll. of Art, A.O.C.A. 1928; Instr. Ont. Coll. of Art 1926-28; Dir. of Art, Cen. Tech. Sch., Toronto 1928-70; Instr., Ont. Coll.; Official War Artist overseas with R.C.A.F. 1943-46; co-author (with Tom Stone) "Lithographs of Ontario", 1933; mem., Candn. Soc. Painters in Water Colour; Ont. Soc. Artists; Clubs: Arts and Letters; Art Directors; Home: 1 Brule Gardens, Toronto, Ont. M6S 4J1

GOLDHART, Irwin; executive; b. Toronto, Ont. 5 Jan. 1911; s. late Joseph and late Sarah G.; PRESIDENT, AUTOMOTIVE HARDWARE LTD.; Chrmn., Arrow Head Metals Ltd.; R.B. & W. Mentor Ohio; Dir. Niagara Structural Steel Co. Ltd.; Dayton-Walther Corp.; recreation: fishing; Home: 922 Mississauga Heights Dr., Mississauga, Ont. L5C 1A6; Office: 55 Brown's Line, Toronto, Ont. M8W 3S4.

GOLDIE, David Michael Mills, B. Com., LL.B., Q.C. (1972); b. Toronto, Ont., 1 July 1924; s. Edward Crosby and Margaret Mostyn (Mills) G.; e. Pub. and High Schs. Bowen Island, Vancouver and Westmount, Que.; Univ. of B.C., B.Com. 1946; Harvard Law Sch., LL.B. 1949; m. Lorraine Catherine, d. J.J. Conway, 27 March 1948; children: Diana, David, Mary, Christopher; PARTNER RUSSELL & DUMOULIN, since 1964; called to Bar of

B.C. 1950; Assoc., MacDougall, Morrison & Jestley, 1950-52; Partner, Jestley, Morrison, Eckardt & Goldie, 1952-56; Solr., British Columbia Electric Co. Ltd., 1956-59; Gen. Solr., 1959-61; Vice Pres. and Secy., British Columbia Power Corp. Ltd., 1961-64; served with Candn. Artillery 1943-45 and 1952-62 (reserve); mem. B.C. Cancer Foundation; Vancouver Bar Assn.; Candn. Bar Assn.; Cdn. Inst. for Advanced Legal Studies; Internat. Law Assn.; recreations: reading, walking, sailing; Clubs: Vancouver; Royal Vancouver Yacht; Home: 1443 W. 54th Ave., Vancouver, B.C. V6P 1N8; Office: 1075 W. Georgia, Vancouver, B.C. V6E 3C9

GOLDRING, Charles Warren, B.A.; investment counsel; b. Toronto, Ont., 21 Oct. 1927; s. Cecil Charles and Helen Beatrice (Mitchell) G.; e. Lawrence Pk. Coll. Inst., Toronto, 1945; Univ. of Toronto, B.A. (Pol. Science & Econ.) 1949; London Sch. of Econ., 1953-54; m. Dorothy Barbara, d. Kenneth E. Dowd, Town of Mount Royal, Que., 10 Sept. 1953; children: Jill, Blake, Jane, Bryce, Judith; PRES., AGF MANAGEMENT LTD.; Dir. or Gov.; Growth Equity Fund Ltd.; AGF Special Fund Ltd.; Corporate Investors Ltd.; Corporate Investors Stock Fund Ltd.; American Growth Fund Ltd.; Canadian Gas & Energy Fund Ltd.; Canadian Security Growth Fund Ltd.; AGF Japan Fund Ltd.; AGF Money Market Fund; AGF Option Equity Fund; Gov., Canadian Trusteed Income Fund; Past Chrmn., Canadian Mutual Funds Assn.; Analyst, Sun Life Assurance Co. of Canada, Montreal, 1949-53; joined Fry & Co. Ltd., Toronto, 1954; author, "How to Invest for Bigger Profits", 1957; "Your Guide to Investing for Bigger Profits", 1975; Past Pres., Toronto Soc. Financial Analysts; Anglican; recreation: fishing; Clubs: Granite; National; Empire; Ticker; Home: 41 Montressor Dr., Willowdale, Ont. M2P 1Y9; Office: (P.O. Box 50), Toronto-Dominion Centre, Toronto, Ont. M5K 1E9

GOLDRING, Gvirol, M.Sc., Ph.D.; nuclear physcist; b. 6 Feb. 1926; s. Pessach and Dora (Seligman) G.; e. Gymnasia Ivrit, Jerusalem 1944; Hebrew Univ. Jerusalem, M.Sc. 1949; Imperial Coll. Science & Tech., Ph.D., D.I.C. 1953; m. Hanna, d. Rafael Kohn, 15 March 1950; children: Alon Pessach, Noa; LADY DAVIS PROFESSOR OF EXPER. PHYSICS, CANDN. CENTRE OF NUCLEAR PHYSICS, WEIZMANN INST. OF SCIENCE; at Hebrew Univ., Jerusalem 1953; joined present Inst. 1954 and Head, Heineman Accelerator Lab. there since 1964; mem. Israel Physical Soc.; Am. Physical Soc.; Co-Ed. (with R. Kalish) "Hyperfine Interactions in Excited Nuclei" (Proceedings of Rehobot Conf.) 1970; author of numerous papers on nuclear structure, nuclear electromagnetic moments and transition probabilities; awarded Landau Prize 1973; Jewish; Address: Rehovot, Israel.

GOLDSMITH, Gerald Ethelbert; manufacturer; b. Montreal, Que., 26 Aug. 1911; s. William Donald and Ann (McGillis) G.; e. Loyola Coll.; m. Margaret Laura, d. Charles Starr Carrick, 5 Feb. 1949; children: Mary, William, Margaret, Katherine, Barbara, Elizabeth; PAST PRESIDENT, NATIONAL NUT & CONFECTION CO.; Past Pres., Johnson Nut & Confection Co.; Ovaltine Food Products Co.; Past Pres. and Chief Extve. Offr., Sandoz-Foods, North America; Dir. of Bd., Sandoz (Canada) Ltd.; Chrmn. of Bd. The Wander Co. of Can.; served in 2nd World War with Canadian Army (Infantry), 1940-45; Roman Catholic; recreations: fishing, reading, boating; Clubs: Granite; Bayview Golf & Country; Toronto Bd. Trade; Vancouver (B.C.); Peterborough Golf & Country; National (Toronto); M.A.A.A. (Montreal); Home: 74 Glengowan Rd., Toronto, Ont. M4N 1G4; Office: 1377 Lawrence Ave. E., Don Mills, Ont. M3A 3M4

GONDER, Douglas Vivian; of U.E.L. descent; b. Pingyao, Shansi, N. China, 4 Jan. 1908; s. Rev. Roy K., missy. in China for 18 yrs., and Ruby Lorraine (Dodds) G.; came to Can. 1922; e. China Inland Mission Schs., Chefoo. N. China; Listowel and Stratford (Ont.) High Schs.;

Univ. of Toronto (extra mural); McGill Univ. (night classes); m. Doris Esther, d. late Jas. J. Poole, Brantford, Ont., 28 Oct. 1933; children: Joan Rose (Dacord) Montreal, Eleanor Anne (Eller) M.D. Alabama, Dorothy Ruby (Messenger) Moncton, Margaret Louise (Moore) Toronto; Dir., The Citadel Life Assnce. Co.; Dir. Citadel Gen. Assne Co.; with Royal Bank of Can., 1924-25; with CN Railways since 1925; successively, Machinist Apprentice, Draughtsman, Inspr., Foreman, Locomotive Foreman, Supt. Montreal Shops, Gen. Supv. Motive Power and Car Equipment at Moncton. Gen Mgr. Winnipeg; Asst. Vice-Pres., Montreal Hdgrs., 1950-57; Vice-Pres. and Gen. Mgr., Atlantic Region, 1957-60; Vice-Pres., Atlantic Region, 1960-61; Vice-Pres., Prairie Region, 1962-63, Great Lakes Region 1964 till retired; worked as Volunteer Consultant with Can. Exec. Service Overseas (CESO) for 7 months in W. Malaysia (1976-77) and 6 months in Sabah (1978-79); A.S.M.E.; McGill Assn.; Clubs: Canadian; Canadian Railway (Montreal); York Downs Golf and Country; National; Home: 95 Thorncliffe Park Drive, Toronto, Ont. M4H 1L7

GONTHIER, Hon. Charles Joseph Doherty, B.C.L; judge; b. Montreal, Que., 1 Aug. 1928; s. Georges and Kathleen (Doherty) G.; e. Ecole Garneau, Ottawa, 1939; Coll. Stanislas, Montreal, 1947; Univ. of Paris, B.A., 1947; McGill Univ. B.C.L. 1951; m. Mariette Morin, M.D., M.Sc., F.R.C.S. (c) children: Georges, François, Pierre, Jean-Charles, Yves; JUSTICE, SUPERIOR COURT OF QUE. since 1974; read law with Senator John T. Hackett, Q.C.; called to Bar of Que. 1952; Q.C. 1971; practised law Hackett, Mulvena & Laverty, Montreal 1952-57; Hugessen, Macklaier, Chisholm, Smith & Davis subsequently Laing, Weldon, Courtois, Clarkson, Parsons, Gonthier & Tetrault 1957-74; Dir. McCord Museum; Hon. Councillor Montreal Museum of Fine Arts; Gov. Société Pro Musica; Dir. Montreal Legal Aid Bureau 1959-69; mem. Discipline Comm. Que. Bar 1973-74; Candn. Judges Conference (Dir.) 1963-4); Candn. Inst. for Adm. of Justice; Candn. Bar Assn. (Pres. Jr. Sec. 1961-62 & Secy. Que. Br. 1963-4); Candn. Inst. Internat. Affairs (Montreal Br.); R. Catholic; Clubs: University; Home: 221 Outremont Ave., Montreal, Que. H2V 3L9; Office: 10 St. Antoine St. E., Montreal, Que.

GOOCH, Bryan Niel Shirley, M.A., Ph.D., A.R.C.T., F.T.C.L.; educator, administrator, performing artist (pianist and conductor); b. Vancouver, B.C., 31 Dec. 1937; s. Commdr. Niel Cyril Shirley and Mary Adeline Bryan (Williams) G.; e. (external) Roy. Conservatory of Music, Toronto, A.R.C.T. 1957; Trinity Coll. of Music, London, Engl. L.T.C.L. 1959; F.T.C.L. 1961; e. (internal) Univ. of B.C., B.A., 1959, M.A. 1962; Univ. of London, Ph.D. 1968; m. Dr. Jane Lytton Tryon, 1974; Son: Arthur FACULTY MEM., UNIV. OF VICTORIA and Asst. Dean from 1972 to 1975; Instr., Dept. of English, Univ. of Victoria, 1964; Asst. Prof., 1968; Assoc. Prof., 1976; Res. Fellow, Craigdarroch Coll., 1968-69; Master of Lansdowne Coll. 1969-72; Faculty, Victoria Conservatory of Music, 1967-70; Musical Dir. and Conductor, Nanaimo Symphony, 1968-71; New Westminster Symphony, 1975-77; served with R.C.S.C., 1957-62 as Div. Offr. and Instr., rank Lt.; numerous awards and scholarships, including IODE Second War Memorial Post-Grad. 1962-64; Can. Council Research Grant, 1973, 1974, 1975-78; SSHRCC Research Grant, 1978-80, 1980-81; Can. Council Leave Fellowship, 1976-77; co-editor "Poetry is for People"; "Musical Settings of Late Victorian and Modern British Literature: A Catalogue"; "Musical Settings of Early and Mid-Victorian Lit.: A Catalogue"; and author of articles in learned journs.; frequent concerts, recitals, and broadcasts; mem., Advisory Academic Panel, SSHRCC, 1978-81; Am. Musicological Soc.; Modern Lang. Assn.; Renaissance Soc. of Am.; Life Fellow of Roy. Commonwealth Soc.; Anglican; recreations: climbing, hiking, tennis, sailing, model railways, watercolours; Home: 2791 W. 43 Ave.,

Vancouver, B.C. V6N 3H8; Office: Univ. of Victoria, Victoria, B.C. V8W 2Y2

GOOCH, Peter William, M.A.Sc.; industrialist; b. Toronto, Ont., 18 Feb. 1915; s. John William, and Winifred Margaret (Griffiths) G.; e. Upper Can. Coll.; Univ. of Toronto, B.A.Sc., 1936, M.A.Sc. 1937; m. Evelyn Rosamonde, d. late Thomas Hodgson, 24 May 1939; children: Diana Judith, John Gregory, Philip William, Eric Paul; PRESIDENT AND DIR. FLUIDYNAMIC DEVICES LTD.; 1937-39, joined Haviland Aircraft of Canada, Toronto as Design Engr. and parent Co. in England 1939-41; 1941-47 Candian Vickers Ltd., Aircraft Div. (later Canadair Ltd.), various positions in Engn. Dept. finishing as Chief Engr.; 1947-61 Canadian Vickers Ltd., indust. Div. starting as Special Projects Engr., finally Chief Engr.; apptd. Vice-Pres. of the Div. 1961; Pres. and Dir., Canadian Vickers Industries Ltd., 1964-68; mem. Engn. Institute Canada; Assn. of Prof. Engineers of Ont.; Am. Soc. Mech. Engrs.; Am. Inst. Aero. & Astronautics; Air Pollution Control Assn.; Instrument Soc. of Amer.; Un. Church, recreations: golf, swimming, skiing, curling; Clubs: Rotary; Lambton Golf & Country; Office: 3216 Lenworth Drive, Mississauga, Ont. L4X 2G1

GOODENOUGH, Laurence George, Q.C., B.A., LL.B.; b. England, 8 Apl. 1909; s. George Edward and Elizabeth (Mantell) G.; e. Humberside and Bloor Coll. Insts., Toronto, Ont.; Univ. of Toronto, B.A. (Arts, Law and Econ.) 1931; LL.B. 1936; Osgoode Hall, Grad. 1934; m. Lillian Eileen, d. John Alexander Buchanan, Toronto, Ont., 25 June 1938, children: Laureen Frances, Brenda Gail, Robert Laurence; PARTNER, GOODENOUGH, McDONNELL & ANDERSON; read law with Angus M. Dewar, K.C.; called to Bar of Ont. 1934; cr. Q.C. 1953; assoc. with Angus M. Dewar, Q.C., 1934-46; Leonard & Leonard 1937-45; Clubs: United Toronto Lawyers'; Engineer's; Runnymede; Bd. of Trade; Boulevard; Home: 4 Waller Ave., Toronto, Ont. M6S 1B7; Office: 320 Bay St., Toronto, Ont. M5H 2P6

GOODERHAM, Peter S.; investment dealer; b. Toronto, Ont., 23 March 1926; s. Henry Stephen and Dorothy F. (Mulkern) G.; e. Upper Canada Coll., Toronto, Ont.; Ridley Coll., St. Catharines, Ont.; m. Jane Graeme, d. Robert Hay, Toronto, Ont., 4 Oct. 1950; children: Sarah Craeme, Peter Hay, Margaret Frances; Chrmn., Casualty Co. of Canada; Dominion of Canada General Insurance Co.; Dir., Empire Life Insurance Co.; E-L Financial Corp. Ltd.; served in Royal Candn. Navey, 1944-45; Presbyterian; recreations: fishing, tennis, Clubs: Badminton & Racquet; Toronto; York; Toronto; Home: 66 Garfield Ave., Toronto Ont. M4T 1E9; Office: Ste. 702, 110 Yonge St., Toronto, Ont. M5C 1V9

GOODLAD, John Inkster, Ph.D., L.H.D., LL.D.; educator; dean; b. N. Vancouver, B.C., 19 August 1920; s. William James and Mary (Inkster) G.; e. Vancouver Normal Sch., Teaching Cert. 1939; Univ. of B.C., B.A. 1945, M.A. 1946; Univ. of Chicago, Ph.D. 1949; Nat. Coll. of Educ., L.H.D. 1967; Univ. of Louisville, L.H.D. 1968; Kent State Univ., LL.D. 1974; Pepperdine Univ., L.L.D. 1976; m. Evalene M. d. Harry and Edith Pearson, White Rock, B.C., 23 Aug. 1945; children: Stephen John, Mary Paula; PROF. OF EDUC., UNIV. OF CALIFORNIA, LOS ANGELES and Dean Grad. Sch. of Educ. there since 1967; also Prof. and Dir., Univ. Elem. Sch. of Univ. since 1960; Dir., Research Div. Inst. for Devel. of Educ. Activities Inc. since 1966; former Teacher and Princ., Surrey Schs., B.C.; Past Dir. of Educ. Prov. Indust. Sch. for (Delinquent) Boys, B.C.; Consultant in Curriculum, Atlanta (Ga.) Area Teacher Educ. Service, 1947-49; Assoc. Prof., Emory Univ. and Agnes Scott Coll., 1949-50; Dir., Teacher Educ. Program there and Prof. and Dir., Div. of Teacher Educ., Emory Univ., 1950-56; Professor and dir. Center for Teacher Educ., Univ. of Chicago, 1956-60; Chrmn., Bd. of Dirs., Council for Study of Mankind (Bd.

of Dirs. 1965-69); mem., Curriculum Theory Network, Ont. Inst. for Studies in Educ., Toronto; also mem. of numerous bds. and comtes. in field of educ. in U.S. incl. mem. Pres. Task Force on Early Educ. 1966-67 and on Educ. of the Gifted 1967-68; survey participant and educ. consultant to schs. and colls. in most states and consultant to educ. foundations; author: "Planning and Organizing for Teaching", 1963; "School Curriculum Reform in the United States" 1964; "School Curriculum and the Individual" 1966; "The Changing School Curriculum", 1966; "The Dynamics of Educational Change", 1975; "Facing the Future: Issues in Education and Schooling 1975; "What Schools are for" 1979; co-author: "The Elementary School", 1956; "Educational Leadership and the Elementary School Principal", 1956; "The Nongraded Elementary School", 1959, revised ed. 1963; "Computers and Information Systems in Education", 1966; "The Development of a Conceptual System for Dealing with Problems of Curriculum and Instruction", 1966; "Behind the Classroom Door", 1970; "Early Schooling in the United States", 1973; "Early Schooling in England & Israel", 1973; "Toward a Mankind School: An Adventure in Humanistic Education", 1974; "The Conventional and the Alternative in Education", 1975; "Curriculum Inquiry: The Study of Curriculum Practice" 1979; Ed., "The Changing American School", 1966; Co-ed., "The Elementary School in the United States", 1973; Chrmn., Ed. Adv. Bd., "New Standard Encyclopedia", since 1953; mem., Ed. Adv. Bd., "Child's World"; "The Education Digest"; Editorial consultant, "Journ. of Curriculum Studies" Univ. of Birmingham (Engl.); mem. Ed. Bd. "The Educational Forum" 1969-71; mem. Bd. of Eds. "Internat. Review of Education", since 1972; past mem. of numerous other ed. bds. of prof. journs.; other writings incl. chapters and papers in over 35 books and yearbooks, numerous articles in prof. journs. and encyclopedias: Kappa Phi Kappa Fellow 1946-47; Ford Foundation Fellow 1952-53; Fellow, Internat. Inst. Arts & Letters; Charter mem., Nat. Acad. Educ., Sec.-Treas. 1972-5; Past Pres. (1962-63) Nat. Soc. Coll. Teachers of Educ.; Am. Educ. Research Assn. (1967-68); mem., Gov. Bd., UNESCO Instit. for Educ., Hamburg, Germany, 1968-79; Chmn., Prof. Advis. Council, Internat'l. Learning Cooperative, Oslo, Norway since 1978; Home: 3235 Rambla Pacifico, Malibu, Cal. 90265.

GOODMAN, Hon. Allan, B.A.; b. Hamilton, Ont. 22 Feb. 1921; s. Samuel and Fanny (Swircz) G.; e. Delta Coll. Inst., Hamilton 1937; McMaster Univ. B.A. 1940; Osgoode Hall Law Sch.; Gold Medalist, Osgoode Hall, 1943; m. Rhoda Katzman 24 Dec. 1950; children: Frances, Susanne, Daniel; JUSTICE SUPREME COURT OF ONT. and Ex Officio mem. Court of Appeal, Ont. since 1973; called to the Bar of Ont. 1944, cr. Q.C. 1963; Sr. Partner, Goodman, Gowan and Fleury, Welland, Ont. 1946-73; Ald., City of Welland 1953-60, Water Commr. 1961-66, Chrmn., Bd. of Water Commrs. 1964-65; served in R.C.A.F. 1943-45; mem. Candn. Bar Assn.; Jewish; Home: 23 Snowshoe Millway, Willowdale, Ont. M2L 1T4 Office: Osgoode Hall, Toronto, Ont.

GOODMAN, Aubrey Wildrige, C.A.; b. Halifax, N.S. 17 Nov. 1917; s. F. Ivo C. Goodman; e. McGill Univ.; m. Joan Audrey Savage; three s; CHRMN. AND CEO, MORGAN BANCORP INC. since 1975; CHAIRMAN AND CEO MORGAN TRUST CO. OF CANADA, TORONTO AND THE MORGAN TRUST CO. MONTREAL; Dir. Morgan's Rockland Centre Inc.; Morgan Intercapital Inc., Montréal; Edfilan Investment Corp. S.A., Panama; Edfilan Capital Consultants Ltd., London, England; IMAG, Switzerland; Cheyenne Petroleum Corp., Calgary; Dir., Fort Norman Explorations Inc., Calgary; Sec'y Treas. The Guarantee Co. of North America, Montreal 1952-60; Vice Pres. and Chairman Dean Witter International 1960-75; served with RCA 1940-46; mem. Candn. Ski Instrs. Alliance; Canadian Alpine Club; Clubs: Mount Royal; Royal Montreal; Home: P.O. Box 1554 Station B,

Montreal, Quebec H3B 3L2; Office: 1 Place Ville Marie, Montreal, Que. H3B 2B4.

GOODMAN, Edwin A., Q.C., B.A.; b. Toronto, Ont., 1918; s. David Bertram and Dorothy (Soble) G.; e. Harbord Coll. Inst., Toronto, Ont.; Univ. of Toronto (Hon. Law) B.A.; Osgoode Hall Law Sch., Toronto, Ont.; m. Suzanne Dorothy, d. late Selig Gross, 21 Dec. 1953; two d. Joanne Ruth, Dianne Selena; PARTNER, GOODMAN & GOODMAN, Estbd. 1917; Directorships: Dir., John Labatt Ltd.; Cadillac Fairview Corp. Ltd.; Baton Broadcasting Inc.; Ogilvie Foods Ltd.; Midland Doherty Financial Corp.; Past President and Director, National Ballet Guild of Canada; mem. Shaw Festival; Director, Baycrest Hospital; United Jewish Welfare Fund; Past President, Toronto Chapter, Canadian Friends of the Hebrew Univ.; Dir. Toronto Y.M.H.A.; Past Pres., Univ. Coll. Alumni Assn. of Univ. of Toronto; P. Cons. Cand. in St. Andrew's Riding, Toronto, Prov. g.e. 1945; former Chrmn. of Organ. and Vice Pres. of P. Conservative Party of Canada; Former Vice Pres. of P. Conservative Party of Ont.; Former Chairman of Comte. for an Independent Canada; read law with David B. Goodman, Q.C.; called to the Bar of Ont., June 1947; cr. Q.C. Dec. 1954; Bencher, Law Soc. of Upper Can.; mem., Candn. Bar Assn. (mem. of Council); served in 2nd World War on active service, 1940-45: Major, Fort Garry Horse; twice wounded in N.W. Europe; Mentioned in Despatches; Past Pres., Gen. Wingate Chapter, Royal Candn. Legion; Dir., New Mount Sinai Hosp.; Trustee, Ontario Jockey Club Tau Epsilon Rho; Pi Lamda Phi (Rex); P. Conservative; Hebrew; recreations: tennis, riding; Clubs: Queen's; Empire; Albany; Primrose; Home: 402 Glenayr Road, Toronto, Ont. M5P 3C7; Office: Suite 3000, P.O. Box 30, Toronto, Ont. M5H 1V5

GOODRIDGE, Hon. Noel Herbert Alan, B.A., LL.B.; judge; b. St. John's, Nfld. 18 Dec. 1930; s. William Prout and Freda Dorothy (Hayward) G.; e. Rockford Sch., Bishop Field Coll., St. John's, Nfld.; King's Coll. Sch. Windsor, N.S.; Bishop's Coll. Sch. Lennoxville, Que.; Dalhousie Univ. B.A. 1951, LL.B. 1953; m. Isabelle Galway, 23 April 1956; four children, Alan, William, Douglas, Maria; TRIAL JUDGE, SUPREME COURT OF NFLD. apptd. Nov. 14, 1975; Judge of the Ct. Martial Appeal Ct., apptd. July 22 1981; called to Bar of Nfld. 1953; Q.C. 1974; practiced law with Stirling Ryan and Goodridge; Past Gov. and Life mem. Kinsmen Clubs Can.; Past Councillor, Nfld. Bd. Trade; Past Secy. Nfld. Law Soc.; Past exec. mem., Nfld. Assn. Help Retarded Children; past. exec. mem. Candn. Bar Assn. (Past Pres. Nfld. Br.); Past Chrmn., St. John's Transportation Commission; Can. Bar Assoc.; Dir. Candn. Judges Conf.; Candn. Inst. for the Adm. of Justice; Zeta Psi; Rotary Club; Anglican; recreations: golf, tennis, skiing, swimming, bridge, walking; Club: Bally Haly Golf & Country (Past Pres.); Home: 71 Rennies Mill Rd., St. John's, Nfld. A1C 3P9; Office: (P.O. Box 937) St. John's, Nfld. A1C 5M3.

GOODSON, William A.; publisher; b. Toronto, Ont., 4 Sept. 1923; e. Toronto Schs.; m. Marianne Birchall, 29 Apr. 1955; children: Gregg Wm., Derek Robt., Lynne Christine; Publisher and President, Chief Executive Officer the Montreal Star Ltd. 1977-80; Pres. and Dir., The Montreal Standard Ltd. since 1968; Pres. and Dir., Optimum Publishing Co. Ltd./Les Editions Optimum Ltée.; Pres. and Dir., Canada Wide Feature Service Ltd.; Dir., Houbigant Ltée.; joined present Co., Toronto, 1940, Ad. Dept., 1945; Asst. Ad. Mgr., Toronto, 1952; apptd. Asst. Publisher and Gen. Mgr., "Family Herald" (Montreal), 1956; rejoined Montreal Standard as Vice-Pres., Advertising, of Weekend Mag./Perspectives, 1959; apptd. Vice-Pres. and Gen. Mgr. 1967 and el. Pres. and Dir. 1968; apptd. Pres. and Dir., The Montreal Star Ltd. 1973; served in 2nd World War, RCAF, 1942-45. discharged as a Pilot; Post-War Auxiliary Flight Lieutenant, 1951-52; Hon. Colonel, 401 Squadron, Can. Air Reserve Group;

United Church; recreations: skiing, tennis, squash; Clubs: St. James Club; Montreal Badminton & Squash; Mt. Mansfield Ski; The Stowe Country Club; Advertising & Sales Executives, Montreal; Home: 1390 McGregor Ave., Montreal, Que. H3G 1B7; Office: 245 rue St-Jacques, Montreal, Que. H2Y 1M6

GORDON, Douglas James, B.Sc., P.Eng.: public utilities executive; b. Brockville, Ont., 30 July 1920: s. late Claude Lester and Edna Irene (McLaughlin) G.; m. Yvonne e. Victoria Pub. Sch. and Kingston (Ont.) Coll. Vocational Inst.: Queen's Univ., B.Sc. 1943; Nat. Defence Coll. 1957-58: Pres. Ont. Hydro 1974-80; joined former Comm. 1945; Gen. Mgr. June, 1970; served with RCN 1943-45; rank Lieutenant; mem. Assn. Prof. Engrs. Prov. Ont.; Candn. Elect. Assn. (Pres., 1971-72); Bd. Trade Metrop. Toronto: United Church; recreations: golf, sailing, skiing; Dir. Canada Wire and Cable Co. Ltd., Tran Alta Utilities Corp. Home: 41 Wentworth Ave., Willowdale, Ont. M2N 1T5

GORDON, Duncan Lockhart, M.B.E., F.C.A., D.S. Litt.; b. Toronto, Ont., 14 Sept. 1914; s. late Col. H. D. Lockhart and Kathleen Hamilton (Cassels) G.; e. Upper Canada Coll., Toronto, Ontario.; Appleby Coll.; Oakville, Ont.; Royal Mil. Coll.; Kingston, Ontario.; Chairman, Board of Trustees, The Hospital for Sick children; Dir., Torstar Corp.; Cdn. Corp. Management Co. Ltd.; Joined CLARKSON, GORDON & CO. after graduation from Royal Military College in 1936 and was admitted to partnership in the Firm in 1947. Retired 1979. Partner, Woods, Gordon & Co., 1952, Retired 1979. In 2nd World War with Royal Canadian Artillery, 1939-45; awarded M.B.E.; President (1963) Institute Chart. Accts. Ont.; Recreation; fishing Clubs: The Toronto; Toronto Golf; University; York; Home 90 Glen Edyth Drive Toronto, Ont. M4V 2V9 Office: Suite 2055 Commerce Court West, Toronto, Ont. M5L 1E2

GORDON, Howard Scott, B.A., A.M., Ph.D.; university professor; b. Halifax, N.S., 14 Aug. 1924; s. Ely and Dorothy (Shabbes) G.; e. Dalhousie Univ., B.A. 1944; Columbia Univ., A.M. 1947; McGill Univ., Ph.D. 1964; Cambridge Univ., 1954-55; m. Barbara, d. late William Rowe, Coaticook, Que., 27 Aug. 1945; children: Geoffrey William, Paul Maxwell Ivan, James Marshall; PROF. OF ECON., INDIANA UNIV., since 1966 (also Prof. of Econ., Queen's Univ. Kingston, since 1970); Lectr., McGill Univ., 1947-48; Asst. Prof., Carleton Univ., 1948-53, Assoc. Prof. 1953-57, Prof. 1957-66; Visiting Prof., Univ. of Chicago, 1956-57; Guggenheim Foundation Fellow, 1965; Pres., Candn. Economics Assn. 1976-77; Pres., Western Economics Assn. 1976-77; F.R.S.C. 1975; Home: 314 Arbutus Ave., Bloomington, Ind. 47401.

GORDON, John Mitchell, B.Sc., P.Eng.; mining executive; b. Sydney, N.S. 31 Oct. 1929; s. Harold Cowan Morton and Dorothy Elizabeth (Ross) G.; e. Westville (N.S.) Pub. and High Schs. and Argyle Pub. Sch. Sydney, N.S. (1941-42) 1946; Queen's Univ. B.Sc. (Mining) 1952; m. Irene Meriam d. late John Nieminen 16 May 1959; children: Dorothy Lynn, Stephen Harold; VICE PRES.- MINES CENTRAL CAN., NORANDA MINES LTD. 1980- ; Vice Pres. and Dir., Hopewell Land Corp.; Alberta Sulphate Ltd.; Pamour Porcupine Mines Ltd.; Dir., Granview Industries Ltd.; Mining Engr. Dominion Steel and Coal Corp. 1952-56 (Nova Scotian Coal Mines 1952-54 and 1956, on loan to Nat. Coal Bd. Eng. 1955); Mine Supvr. Horne Mine, Noranda Mines, Noranda, Que. 1956-58; Mine Supt. Hallnor Mines Ltd. Timmins, Ont. 1959-62, Mine Mgr. 1962-65; Mine Mgr. Aunor Gold Mines Ltd. Timmins 1965-67; Mine Supt. Potash Div. Noranda Mines Ltd. Saskatoon 1967-70; Gen. Supt. Central Canada Potash, Saskatoon 1970-71, Mine Mgr. 1971-76; Gen. Mgr. Mines, Noranda Mines Ltd. 1976-80; Dir. (1961-64) and Chrmn. (1963) Victorian Order of Nurses Timmins; Dir. (1975) Sask. Chamber Comm.; mem. Adv.

Comte. Haileybury Sch. of Mines 1965; mem. (1963-65) and Vice Chrmn. (1964-65) Porcupine Sch. Bd. Timmins; mem. Assn. Prof. Engrs. Prov. Ont.; Candn. Inst. Mining & Metall.; Ont. Mining Assn., Dir. 1965-66; mem. Comte. on Occupational Health, Mines, Accident Prevention Assn. 1974-75, 1975-76; United Church; recreations: tennis, swimming, skiing, reading, gardening; Clubs: Saskatoon; Riverside Tennis; Canadian (Timmins, Dir. 1962-65); Home: 1707 Shannon Cres., Saskatoon, Sask. S7H 2T8; Office: 801-230-22nd St. E., Saskatoon, Sask. S7K 0E9

GORDON, John Peter George, B.Sc.; industrial executive; b. Toronto, Ont. 14 Nov. 1920; e. Central Coll. and Westdale Secondary Sch., Hamilton, Ont.; Univ. of Toronto, B.Sc. (Mech. Eng.) 1943; Harvard Univ., Advanced Mang. Program 1966; York Univ., Hon. LL.D., 1980; m. former Joan Muriel MacPherson; two children: one s. and one d.; 4 grandchildren; CHRMN. AND CHIEF EXTIVE. OFFR., STELCO. INC., since 1976, Dir. since 1970; Dir., Bank of Montreal; Gulf Oil Corp., (Pittsburgh); the Molson Co.s; Sun Life Assurance Co. of Can.; entire career since 1946 with present Co.; Superintendent 1963; General Supt., Flat Rolled Div. 1964; apptd. Vice-Pres., Mfg., Tubular & Finishing Plants 1964; Vice-Pres., Operating Div. (Div. Head) 1966; Sr. Vice-Pres. 1970; apptd. Pres. 19 April 1971; apptd. chief executive officer, 1973; served with RCEME in Can., Eng. and in N.W. Europe 1942-46; rank of Capt.; a Gov., McMaster Univ.; Gov., Olympic Trust of Can.; a Dir., Candn. Council of Christians & Jews; Dir. Jr. Achievement of Can.; N. Amer. Advisory Bd. of Swissair; mem. Assn. Prof. Engrs. of Ont.; Iron Steel Inst. (Eng.); Am. Iron & Steel Inst. (Dir.); Internat. Iron & Steel Inst.; (Dir.); Adm. Comte., Nat. Council of Can. Y.M.C.A.; Pres., Hamilton Chapter, Ont. Heart Foundation; Vice-Chrmn. Business Council on Nat. Issues; Dir., Jr. Achievement of Can.; Natl. Adv. Council Boys' and Girls' Clubs of Can.; recipient Benjamin F. Fairless Award, Am. Inst. of MIning, Metalurg. & Petrol. Eng. St. Andrews Presb. Church, Port Credit, Ont.; Mem. of Bd., Wellesley Hosp., Tor.; Schenley Football Awards; Delta Upsilon; recreations: curling, golf; Clubs: York; Mount Royal (Montreal); Tamahaac (Ancaster); Rideau (Ottawa) Toronto Rotary; Union (Cleveland); Board of Trade of Metro. Toronto; Toronto; Hamilton; Hamilton Golf & Country; Mississauga Golf and Country; Canadian; Harvard Business Sch. of Toronto; Rideau (Ottawa); Home: "Stonecrest", 1343 Blythe Rd., Mississauga, Ont. L5H 2C2; Office: P.O. Box 205, Toronto-Dominion Centre, Toronto, Ont. M5K 1J4

GORDON, John R. M., B.A.Sc., M.B.A., Ph.D.; educator; b. Toronto, Ont. 3 Feb. 1935; s. late Russell Charles Gordon; e. Trinity Coll. Sch. Port Hope, Ont. 1953; Univ. of B.C. B.A.Sc. 1958; Queen's Univ. M.B.A. 1963; Mass. Inst. Technol. Ph.D. 1966; m. Virginia d. late Walter E. Huckvale, Lethbridge, Alta. 3 Jan. 1959; children: Jane, Charles, Ian; PROF. AND DEAN, SCH. OF BUSINESS, QUEEN'S UNIV. since 1978; mem. Adv. Comte. Institut pour l'Etude des Methodes de Direction de l'Enterprise, Lausanne, Switzerland since 1976, Chrmn. MBA Program 1973-75, Dir. of Research 1973-74, Prof. 1970-75; Chrmn. Can. Fed. of Deans of Mang. & Adm. Studies; Dir. Am. Can. of Can. Ltd.; Dye & Chemical of Can. Ltd.; Rama Dev. Corp.; Vicom Ltd.; Lectr. in Mech. Engn. Royal Mil. Coll. 1959-63; Lectr. Sloan Sch. of Mang. Mass. Inst. Technol. 1965-66; Asst. Prof. Sch. of Business Adm. Univ. of W. Ont. 1966-68, Assoc. Prof. 1968-73, Dir. Production/Operations Mang. Course 1970-72, Chrmn. Undergrad. Program in Business Adm. 1968-69; Assoc. Prof. Sch. of Business Queen's Univ. 1975-78, Chrmn. Continuing Educ. 1976-78, Dir. Small Business Consulting Program 1976-78; Gov., Inst. of Cndn. Bankers (ICB) since 1981; Pilot Offr. Aircrew Training RCAF 1954-57; Design Offr. Canadian Pacific Airlines Repairs Ltd. Calgary 1957; Engn. Offr. Dept. Nat. Defence Ottawa 1958-59; Gen. Mgr. Vicom Ltd. Kingston 1976-77;

rec'd various research grants and fellowships incl. Ford Foundation Doctoral Fellowship 1963-66; consulting and seminar mang. devel. activities various univ., govt. and business programs; Trustee, Commonwealth Am. Sch. Lausanne; author various publs.; mem. Inst. Mang. Sciences; Am. Inst. Indust. Engrs.; Am. Inst. Decisions Sciences; Acad. Mang.; Candn. Assn. Adm. Studies; Am. Production & Inventory Control Soc.; Dir. Junior Achievement (Kingston & Dist.); P. Conservative; Anglican; recreations: tennis, skiing, sailing; Clubs: Kingston Yacht; Kingston Tennis; University (Toronto); Home: 154 Earl St., Kingston, Ont. K7L 2H2; Office: Kingston, Ont.

GORDON, L. Lamont; investment executive; b. Harriston, Ont., 29 April 1932; s. Ernest Francis and Katharine Walker (Brown) G.; e. High Sch. Harriston, Ont.; Univ. of Western Ont., Sch. Business Adm., B.A. 1955; m. Barbara Warren children: Katharine Elizabeth, Deborah Joane, James Neil, Pamela Suzan, Jennifer Brook; PRES. ALMARK RESOURCES LTD. Chrmn. and Dir., Gordon, Lloyd Price Investments since 1979; Dir.; Seel Mortgage Invest. Corp.; Westgrowth Petroleums Ltd.; Br. Candn. Resources Ltd.; Pres., Orion Petroleum Ltd.; Westgrowth Petroleums Ltd.; Frontier Mud Logging; began with Nesbitt Thomson and Co. Ltd. 1957, Dir. 1964; resigned 1969 and founded Gordon Securities Ltd.; served with R.C.N.R. as Lieut. 1951-57; Zeta Psi; Presbyterian; Clubs: St. James's; Montreal Badminton & Squash; St. Moritz Tobogganing; Canadian Club (New York); Candn. Amateur Bobsleigh & Luge Assn. (Dir. and Vice-Pres.); Candn. Olympic Comte.; Home: 55 Avenue Rd., Apt. 405W, Toronto Ont. M5R 2E2; Office: 11 Adelaide St. W., Toronto, Ont.

GORDON, Myron J., M.A., Ph.D.; educator; b. New York, N.Y. 15 Oct. 1920; s. Joseph G.; e. Univ. of Wis. B.A. 1941; Harvard Univ. M.A. 1947, Ph.D. 1952; m. Helen Elizabeth Taylor 14 March 1945; children: Joseph, David; PROF. OF FINANCE, FACULTY OF MANG. STUDIES, UNIV. OF TORONTO; served with US Army World War II, rank 2nd Lt.; author 'The Drug Industry: A Case Study in Foreign Control' 1981; 'Accounting: A Management Approach' 6th ed. 1979; 'The Cost of Capital to a Public Utility' 1974; "The Investment Framing and Valuation of the Corporation" 1962; Pres. Am. Finance Assn. 1975; recreation: tennis; Home: 33 Elmhurst Ave, Apt # 1009, Willowdale, Ont. M2N 6E8; Office: 246 Bloor St. W., Toronto, Ont. M5S 1V4

GORDON, Philip, P.Eng.; company director and Industrial Consultant; b. Montreal Que., 7 Nov. 1917; e. McGill Univ. B.Eng. (Chem. Engn.) 1939; m. Rachel Winer, 22 March 1942; children: David, Penny; Sr. Vice-Pres. and Dir., Shell Can. Ltd.; (ret. 1977); Dir., Boise-Cascade Co. Ltd.; Cont. Colour Co. Ltd.; Mem. Fed. Gov't Energy Supply Allocation Board; Cont. Council for Univ. Affairs; Medallist, Brit. Assn. for Advance. Science; Assn. Prof. Eng. Ont.; Club: Donalda; Home: No. 3 Royal Oak Dr., Don Mills, Ont. M3C 2M1

GORDON, Roderick Angus, C.D., B.Sc., M.D., F.R.C.P.(C), F.F.A.R.C.S., F.W.A.C.S., Hon. F.F.A.R.C.S.; physician; educator; b. Watrous, Sask., 2 Aug. 1911; s. Alexander James, Q.C. and Mabel Margaret (Richardson) G.; e. Toronto Conservatory of Music, L.T.C.M. 1929; Univ. of Sask., B.Sc. 1934; Univ. of Toronto, M.D. 1937, postgrad. training Anaesthesia 1937-39; Dipl. in Anaesthesia, Conjoint Bd., London, Eng. 1940 Cert. R.C.P. & S. Can. 1944; Dipl. Am. Bd. Anaesthesiol. 1948; F.R.C.P. (c) 1952; m. Ruth Anna Catherine d. Albert L. Breithaupt, Kitchener, Ont. 30 June 1939; children: Catherine Anne (Mrs. E. L. Wilson), Janet Elizabeth, Roderick Arthur James; PROF. EMERITUS, DEPT. OF ANAESTHESIA, UNIV. OF TORONTO since 1977; Prof. and Chrmn. of Anaesthesia, U. of T., 1961-77; Anaesthetist in Chief, Toronto Gen. Hosp. 1961-77; Pres. and Dir., Candn. Anaesthetists' Mutual Accumulating

Fund; Interne, Toronto Gen. Hosp. 1937, Resident Anaesthetist 1938-39, Anaesthetist 1945; joined present Univ. as Clin. Teacher, Faculty of Med. 1945, Asst. Prof. 1954: served with RCAMC (Active Force) 1939-45; 15 Candn. Gen. Hosp. and Basingstoke Neurol. & Plastic Surg. Hosp.; Candn. Rep., Inter-allied consultants Comte. in Anaesthesia, UK 1944-45; rank Maj.; Anaesthetist, Special Treatment Unit, Christie St. Hosp., Toronto 1945; Lt.-Col. O.C. 7 Field Ambulance (Reserve) 1945-49; Col., A.D.M.S., Med. Adv. Staff 1949-52; mem. Defence Med. Assn. Can. Council 1946-59 (Pres. 1959-61); Vice Pres., World Fed. Soc's Anaesthesiols, 1968-72 (Extve. Comte. 1955-68; former Trustee and Co-Chrmn. Educ. & Relief Fund); rec'd Coronation Medal 1953; Centennial Medal 1967; Candn. Anaesthetists' Soc. Medal 1969; Queen's Jubilee Medal 1977; U. of T. Hon. Sesquicentennial Award, 1977; Kt. Cmdr. St. Lazarus of Jerusalem; ed. "Anaesthesia for Thoracic Surgery", 1963; Ed. "Anaesthesia and Resuscitation — A Manual for Medical Students" 1967, 2nd ed. 1973; co-ed. "Malignant Hyperthermia" 1973; Hon. Fellow, W. African Coll. Surgs.; mem. Candn. and Ont. Med. Assns.; Candn. Anaesthetists' Soc. (Trustee & Chrmn. Anaesthesia Training Fund; Council since 1945; Secy. 1946-61; Vice Pres. 1961-63; Pres. 1963-64; Ed. of Journ. since 1954); Acad. Med. Toronto; Acad. Anaesthesiol. (Pres. 1961-62); Assn. Anaesthetists Gt. Brit. & Ireland; Assn. Anaesthetists W. Africa (Hon Pres. 1965-67); Liberal; United Church; recreations: boating, music; Clubs: University; Aesculapian; Home: 44 Charles St. W., Toronto, Ont.

GORDON, Hon. Walter Lockhart, P.C., C.C., F.C.A., LL.D., D.LiH.; b. Toronto, Ont., 27 Jan. 1906; s. late H. D. Lockhart and late Kathleen (Cassels) G.; e. Upper Can. Coll.; Royal Mil. Coll., Kingston, Ont.; m. Elizabeth Marjorie Leith, d. late J. L. Counsell, K.C. and late Marjorie Counsell, 1932; children: Kyra, Jane, John; began as a student with Clarkson, Gordon & Co., Chartered Accountants, in 1927; Partner 1935-1963; Partner, Woods, Gordon & Co., Management Consultants, 1940-1963; Hon. Chairman of the Board, Canadian Corporate Management Co. Ltd.; Chrmn., Cdn. Inst. for Econ. Policy; Special Assistant to the Deputy Minister of Finance, 1940-42; Chrmn., Royal Comn. on Canada's Economic Prospects, 1955; Chrmn., Nat. Campaign Comte. of Liberal Party, 1962, 1963 and 1965; el. to H. of C. for Toronto-Davenport g.e., 1962, 1963, 1965; apptd. Min. of Finance April 1963; resigned from Cabinet, 9 Nov. 1965; apptd. President of the Privy Council, May 1967; resigned from the Cabinet, 11 March 1968; former Gov. (1945-63), Univ. of Toronto; Chancellor, York Univ. (1973-77); Sr. Fellow, Massey Coll. (Univ. of Toronto) 1973-78, elected Assoc. Fellow 1978-83; author: "Troubled Canada — The Need for New Domestic Policies", 1961, "A Choice for Canada — Independence or Colonial Status", 1966, "Storm Signals — New Economic Policies for Canada", 1975, "A Political Memoir", 1977, "What is Happening to Canada", 1978; Home: 22 Chestnut Park Rd., Toronto, Ont. M4W 1W6; Office: P.O. Box 131, Commerce Court Postal Station, Toronto, Ont. M5L 1E6

GORDON, Wilferd, Q.C., B.A., Ph.B., M.H.L.; b. Toronto, Ont., 21 Aug. 1909; s. late Rabbi Jacob and Lena (Sobol) G.; e. McMaster Univ., B.A. 1931; Univ. of Chicago, Ph.B. 1931; Osgoode Hall, Toronto, Ont. (1935); M.H.L. 1963; o. Rabbi by Rabbi Saul Silber, Pres. of Hebrew Theol. Coll., Chicago, Ill.; Dr. of Rabbinic Studies, Ner Israel Rabbinical Coll., Baltimore, 1972; m. Balfoura, d. late Dr. Joseph Feldman, Palm Beach, Fla., 30 June 1952; children: Jared, Daniel T., Phyllis L.; PARTNER, GORDON, TRAUB AND ROTENBERG;Twenty-Seven Wellington West Ltd.; Cloverdale Park Ltd.; Terry Investments Ltd.; Keygor Investments Ltd.; Hallgor Investments Ltd.; Newgor Land Group Ltd.; Vice-Pres., Abgor Investments Ltd.; Mountain Theatre Ltd.; Keswick Construction Ltd.; Bellgor Mang. Ltd.; Secy-Treas. Belhill Construction Ltd.; Yorkleigh Investments Ltd.; Yorkville

Financiers Ltd.; Gen. Mgr., One Hundred Simcoe St. Ltd.; Queen City Leaseholds Ltd.; Dir., Tower-Chisholm Ferguson Ltd.; Martingrove Homes Ltd.; Partition Holdings Ltd.; Torlease Properties Ltd.; mem., Toronto Adv. Bd., the Metropolitan Trust Co.; read law with Roebuck & Bagwell, Toronto, Ont.; called to the Bar of Ont., 1935; cr. Q.C. 1954; Rabbi, McCaul St. Synagogue, Toronto, Ont., 1935-36 and 1942-44; Chaplain (part-time civilian) Camp Borden, Ont., 1942-43; Chaplain, R.C.A.F., 1944-46; Dir., J. Wolinsky, J. B. Goldhar and H. Abramsky Charitable Foundations; Pres., Camp Massad of Ont., 1954-61; Pres. Hebrew Day Sch. of Toronto, 1962; Past Pres., Assoc Hebrew Schs. of Toronto; Nat. Vice-Pres., Candn. Friends Bar-Ilan Univ., Natl. Vice Pres., 1961; Chrmn., Negev Dinner, 1962; Chrmn., Ner Israel Yeshiva Coll. of Toronto; Extve. mem., Central Fund for Traditional Insts., 1961-62; United Jewish Welfare of Toronto; Keren Hatarbut of Canada; mem., Nat. Extve. Council, Zionist Organization of Can.; Jewish Nat. Fund; Candn. Jewish Cong.; mem., Ont. Housing Adv. Comte., 1962; Advisory Comm., Metro. Trust Co. 1962; mem. Exec. Ont. men's ORT.; Exec. mem. Can. Friends of Boys Town Jerusalem 1974- ; Bd. of Hillel Foundation (Univ. of Toronto); Bd. of Govs., State of Israel Bonds (Canada-Israel Securities Ltd.); mem. Bd. of Govs., Candn. Friends of Yeshiva Univ. and Bd. of Trustees, Emet Rabbi Herzog World Acad. 1966; Regional Vice Pres., Nat. Comm. on Torah Educ., 1970; Nat. Extve. Mizrachi Organization of Can., 1970; Dir., Candn. Friends of Bar. Ilan Univ. since 1975; Home: 200 Dunvegan Rd., Toronto, Ont. M5P 2P2; Office: 390 Bay St., Toronto, Ont. M5H 2Y2

GORHAM, Paul Raymond, B.A., M.S., PhD., F.R.S.C. (1961); biologist; educator; b. Fredericton, N.B., 16 April 1918; s. Raymond Paddock and Marie Jeanette (Tanner) G.; e. Univ. of New Brunsick, B.A. 1938; Univ. of Maine, M.S. 1940; Cal. Inst. of Tech., Ph.D. 1943; Univ. N.B., D.Sc., 1973; m. Evelyn Ruth, d. late Lewis Greene Woods, 8 July 1943; children: John Henry, Arthur Raymond, Harriet Ruth; PROFESSOR OF BOTANY, UNIV. OF ALBERTA since 1969; formerly Princ. Research Offr., Div. of Biol., Nat. Research Council; Agric. Assistant, Div. Botany and Plant Path., Dept. of Agric., Ottawa, Ont., 1943-45; joined N.R.C. as Jr. Research Offr., Div. of Applied Biol., 1945; Asst. Research Offr., 1946-50, Assoc., 1950-57; Sr., 1957-65 Princ. Research Officer 1965-69; Chrmn., Dept. Botany, Univ. of Alberta, 1971-79; Assoc. Dir., U. of A. Devonian Botanic Garden since 1976; Adjunct Prof., W.K. Kellogg Bio. Sta., Mich. State U. 1976; Visiting Scientist, Agr. Can. Res. Sta., Lethbridge, Alta. 1977; Academic Relations Lecturer, Can. Embassy to Japan, 1977; Publications: author or co-author of some 66 papers in the field of plant physiol. and aquatic ecology; mem. Canadian Society Plant Physiologists (first Pres., 1958-59); Am. Soc. Plant Physiols. (Edit. Bd. Plant Physiology since 1973); Bot. Soc. Am.; Am. Soc. Agron; Candn. Biochem. Soc.; Internat. Assn. for Plant Physiol. (Council mem. 1959-69); Candn. Botanical Assn. (pres. 1977-78); Phycological Soc. Am. (Vice-Pres. 1966, Ed. Bd. Journ. Phycology 1967-69); Internat. Phycological Soc.; Soc. Internat. Limnologiae; Am. Assn. Adv. Science; Secy., Candn. Comte. for Internat. Biol. Programme 1968-69; received Centennial Medal (1967); Silver Jubilee Medal (1978); Can. Bot. Assoc., Mary E. Elliot Award (1979); mem. Bd of Trustees, Friends of Univ. of Alta. Devonian Bot. Garden; Bd of Trustees, Edmonton Art Gallery (secy. 1981-3); recreations: swimming, skiing; Office: Edmonton, Alta. T6G 2E9

GORING, David Arthur Ingham, B.Sc., Ph.D., F.C.I.C., F.R.S.C.; scientist; b. Toronto, Ont. 26 Nov. 1920; s. George Ingham and Susan Edna Hill (Jones) G.; e. Queen's Coll. Brit. Guiana 1939; Univ. Coll. London B.Sc. 1942; McGill Univ. Ph.D. 1949; Cambridge Univ. Ph.D. 1953 (Merck Postdoctoral Fellow 1949-51); Univ. of W. Ont. Business Mang. 1976; m. Elizabeth Dodds d. late

William Rochester Haswell 24 Aug. 1948; children: James Haswell Ingham, Rosemary Jane Erskine, Christopher David Gowland; VICE PRES. SCIENT., PULP AND PAPER RESEARCH INST. OF CAN., joined Inst. 1955; joined Chem. Dept. McGill Univ. 1955, presently Sr. Research Assoc.; Maritime Regional Lab. Nat. Research Council, Halifax 1951-55; rec'd Anselme Payen Award 1973 Am. Chem. Soc.; author or co-author over 150 scient. publs.; Fellow, Internat. Acad. Wood Science; mem. Tech. Sec. Candn. Pulp & Paper Assn.; Tech. Assn. Pulp & Paper Industry; Brit. Paper & Bd. Industry Fed.; Cellulose, Paper & Textile Div. Am. Chem. Soc.; Anglican; recreations: badminton, fishing, music; Home: 237 Strathearn Ave., Montreal West, Que. H4X 1Y1; Office: 570 St. John's Blvd., Pointe Claire, Que. H9R 3J9.

GORMAN, Eugene Michael, B.A.; Consultant Sea Fisheries; b. Welland, Ont. 21 Feb. 1914; s. George Earl and Mary (McKenna) G.; e. St. John Evangelist High Sch., N. Cambridge, Mass.; Boston Coll.; St. Dunstans Univ. B.A.; Business Mang. Courses; m. Vera Ruby, d. Joseph Barnett, Sept. 1945; children: Ian Earl, Mary Terasa, Eugene Michael; Special Asst. To Dir. Gen. Atlantic Region, FISHERIES AND MARINE SERVICE, ENVIRONMENT CANADA 1974-78; Dir. Extension Services, St. Dunstans Univ. 1947-50; Chrmn. (1st) Fishermen's Loan Bd. P.E.I 1949-57; Dir. (1st) Fisheries Div. Dept. Indust. and Natural Resources 1950-57; Depy. Min. P.E.I. Dept. Mun. Affairs 1965-66 and Depy. Min. (1st) P.E.I. Dept. of Fisheries 1957-74; served in 2nd World War U.K., Italy and N.W. Europe, citation from Field Marshal Montgomery; mem. Internat. Oceanog.; Candn. Inst. Food Science Technol.; R. Catholic; recreations: boating, diving; Home: 191 Mt. Edward Rd., Charlottetown, P.E.I. C1A 5T1; Office: Box 2264, Charlottetown, P.E.I.

GORMAN, Ruth, O.C. (1968), B.A., LL.B., LL.D., lawyer and writer; b. Calgary, Alta., 14 Feb. 1914; d. late Col. M.B. (Q.C.) and Fleda (Pattyson) P.; e. Calgary Pub. Sch.; Strathcona Lodge Sch., B.C.; Univ. of Alberta; m. (JUDGE) John C. (K.C.), 14 Sept. 1940; one d., Linda I.F. Gorman; called to date 1940; Publisher "Golden West" mag. 1965-70, editor until 1975; named Calgary's "Woman of the Year" by Local Council of Women 1960; "Citizen of the Year" by Calgary Jr. Chamber of Comm. 1961; awarded "Alberta Woman of the Century Medal", Nat. Council of Jewish Women 1968; Past Hon. Convenor of Laws to Canada's Nat. Council of Women; mem. and on Founding Bd. Tweedsmuir Sch., Calgary; past Chrmn. Civil Liberties Sec. of Candn. Bar on Indian Law; Queen Mother of Cree and Princess of the Stony Indian Tribe of Alberta; winner of three Calgary Br., Candn. Women's Press Club Award, 1966 and 1968; Anglican; Pi Beta Phi; Home: 203 Roxboro Rd. S.W., Calgary, Alta. T2S 0R2

GORNALL, Allan Godfrey, B.A., Ph.D., D.Sc., F.R.S.C., (1966); university professor; b. River Hébert, N.S., 28 Aug. 1914; s. Late Rev. Dr. Herbert Thomas and Lucy Amy (Markham) G.; e. High Sch., Saint John, N.B.; Mount Allison Univ. B.A. (cum laude) (Hon. Chem.) 1936; Univ. of Toronto, Ph.D. 1941; m. Mary Elizabeth Sheila, d. late Dr. Herbert Leslie Stewart, 27 Dec. 1941; children: William Stewart, Douglas Allan, Thomas Herbert, Catherine Anne; PROF. OF CLIN. BIOCHEM., UNIV. OF TORONTO since 1963 and Chrmn. of Dept. 1966-76; joined present Univ. as Asst. Prof., Dept. of Pathol. Chem., 1946-52; Assoc. Prof., 1952-63; Nuffield Scholar, Edinburgh, Scot. and London, Eng.; 1949; served with R.C.N.V.R. (Special Br.), 1942-46; retired as Lt. Commdr.; author or co-author of 75 scient. articles; awarded Reeve Prize 1941; The Ames Award, 1977; mem., Toronto Bichem. Biophys. Soc. (Pres. 1954); Am. Chem. Soc.; Am. Physiol. Soc.; Candn. Physiol. Soc. (Treas. 1954-57); Biochem Soc. (Gt. Brit.); Endocrine Soc.; Candn. Soc. Clin. Investigation; Candn. Biochem. Soc.; Candn. Fed. Biol. Socs. (Hon. Treas. 1957-62); Candn.

Soc. Clin. Chem. (certified, 1964); Candn. Soc. Endocr. Metab.; Academy Clin. Labor. Physicians and Scientists; Roy. Soc. of Can.; United Church; recreations: sailing, skating, tennis; Clubs: Toronto Cricket Skating & Curling; Lunenburg (N.S.) Yacht; Home: 135 Hanna Rd., Toronto, Ont. M4G 3N6; Office: 100 College St., Toronto, Ont. M5G 1L5

GOSE, Elliott Bickley, Jr., M.A., Ph.D.; educator; b. Nogales, Ariz. 3 May 1926; s. Elliott Bickley and Eleanor (Paulding) G.; e. Univ. of Colo. B.A. 1949, A.M. 1950; Cornell Univ. Ph.D. 1954; m. Kathleen Kavanaugh Brittain 1950; children: Peter C., Sarah E.; PROF. OF ENGLISH, UNIV. OF B.C. 1967- ; Instr. in Eng. present Univ. 1956, Asst. Prof. 1958, Assoc. Prof. 1963; rec'd Can. Council Travel Grants research Dublin 1970-71 and Sr. Fellowship 1971-72; grant-in-aid of publ. 1972, 1978; Chrmn. Comte. Symposium Centenaries James Joyce and Virginia Woolf 1982; Founding mem. New Sch. 1960-62, Pres. of Bd. 1962-63, 1965-66, Vancouver; Trustee, Vancouver Sch. Bd. 1973-76, Vice Chrmn. 1975-76; author "Imagination Indulged: The Irrational in the Nineteenth-Century Novel" 1972; "The Transformation Process in Joyce's 'Ulysses' " 1980; numerous articles; served with U.S. Army 1946-47, Counter-Intelligence Corps; Phi Beta Kappa; recreations: cycling, hiking, weaving; Home: 2956 Blanca St., Vancouver, B.C. V6R 4G1; Office: 397 - 1873 East Mall, Vancouver, B.C. V6T 1W5.

GOSS, Maj. Gen. (Ret.) Denys William, C.D., B.A.Sc., M.Sc. FCASI, P. Eng.; b. Hamilton, Ont., 18 June 1922; e. Queen's Univ., B.A.Sc. (Mech. Engn.) 1949; Univ. of Michigan, M.Sc. (Aeronaut. and instrumentation Engn.) 1956; Air Force Coll., Toronto, 1962; PRES. HOVEYAND ASSOC. (1979) LTD. and CEO D.S. FRASER & CO. LTD.; since 1980; joined R.C.A.F. 1941 and trained as a pilot; served as Flying Instructor in Canada until 1944 when assigned to a Mosquito sqdn.; was selected to attend guided missile course in U.S.A., 1949; seconded to Defence Research Bd., 1950; apptd. to staff duties with directorate of armament engn., AFHQ, 1952; attended special armament course with R.A.F. in Eng., 1953; apptd. to directorate of aircraft engn., AFHQ, 1956; posted to No. 3 Fighter Wing, Zweibrucken, Germany as Chief Tech. Services Offr., 1963; Sr. Tech. Staff Offr., Air Defence Command HQ, St. Hubert, Que., 1964; posted to Material Command HQ as Sr. Staff Offr., Aircraft, 1965; Depy. Chief of Staff, Logistics Materiel Command, 1966; Dir. Gen., Maintenance 1968-69; Depy. Chief of Staff, Logistics & Adm. NATO, Fourth Tactical Air Force HQ, Ramstein, Germany, 1969-71; Dir. Gen. Aerospace Systems 1971; Chief of Logistics 1972; Chief of Eng. and Maint. 1973; Ret. Can. Forces 1976; Vice Pres. ONEX Holdings 1976-78; Assist. Dean and Registrar, Fac. of Eng., Sch. of Indust. Design, Sch. of Archit., Carleton Univ., 1978-80; Address: 2378 Holly Lane, Ottawa, Ont. K1V 7P1

GOSSAGE, Stevenson Milne, M.Sc.; b. London, Eng., 6 Dec. 1905; s. Alfred Milne, C.B.E., M.D., and Bertha Pillans (Stevenson) G.; e. Hilderham House, Broadstairs, Eng.; Rugby Sch., Eng. (1923); Univ. Coll., Univ. of London, B.Sc., (Engn.) 1926; Yale Univ., M.Sc. (Transportation), 1934; m. Edith, d. Frederick Chatfield, New Haven, Conn., 6 May 1935; children: Jonathan Frederick Milne, Edith Abigail; 2ndly, Eva Maria, d. Kurt Huldschinsky, M.D., Berlin, Germany, 19 April 1958; PRINCIPAL CONSULTANT, CANADIAN PACIFIC CONSULTING SERVICES, since 1977; Chrmn., Metric Comn. Can. 1971-76; (Sr. Extve. Offr. CP Rail, 1969-71); came to Can. 1926; Trucker, Clerk, Steno., Freight Office, Three Rivers, Que., 1926-28 (Candn. Pac. Rly. Co.); Steno, Supts. Office, Montreal, 1929-30; Steno-Clerk, Vice-Pres. and Gen. Mgrs. Office, Montreal, 1930-34; Statistician, Vice-Pres. and Gen. Mgrs. Office, Montreal, 1935-37, and at Toronto, 1937-41; Asst. to the Vice-Pres. and Gen. Mgr., Toronto, 1941-45; Asst. Mgr. of Personnel, Montreal, 1945-46;

Mgr., Labour Relations, 1956-58; Vice-Pres., E. Region, Toronto, 1958-62, and of Prairie Region, Winnipeg, Man., 1962-64; Vice Pres., Co. Svaes, Montréal, 1964-66, Vice-Pres., Dir., and mem. Extve. Comte., 1966-71; Anglican; Clubs: University: Canadian Railway; Home: 6 Hilltop Crest P.O. Box 248 Sutton Quebec. J0E 2K0,

GOSTLING, Brig. Guy Standish Noakes, C.B.E., E.D., C.D.; b. Lyme Regis, England, 13 Aug. 1901; s. Charles Richard and Millicent (Noakes) G.; e. Public Sch., Eustis, Fla.; High Sch., England; Univ. of Toronto Extension, A.C.I., 1928; m. Frances Margaret, d. Col. Royal Burritt, D.S.O., V.D., Winnipeg, Man., 14 Sept. 1929; children: Mrs. David B. Gill, G.S.N., Jr., Brenda M. (Mrs. K. Eric Rogers); began as Bookkeeper and later Asst. Supt. of Grounds, Nitrate of Soda Mines, Chili, S.A., 1919-22; Acct. and Invest. Depts. of Monarch Life Assurance Co., Winnipeg, Man., 1922-27; with predecessor co's. of Moore Corp. Ltd., 1927-46 (except for war service), becoming Mgr. at Vancouver 1931, Sales Mgr. for Can. at Toronto, 1933, Market Devel. Mgr. of Moore Corp. Ltd. for U.S.A. and Can., 1945; Mang. Dir. for Canada of Eversharp International, Toronto, Ont., 1946-51; founded and became Pres. of Pakfold Continuous Forms Ltd. and assoc. Co's. 1952 till sold interests Oct. 1971; served in Candn. Militia, Lieut., Winnipeg Grenadiers, 1925; Lieut. to Major, The Royal Regt. of Can., 1933-39; served in 2nd World War 1939-45, Capt. to Brig. (May 1943); Commanded Toronto Scottish Regt., 1942; C.B.E.; Mentioned in Despatches; Free French Croix de Guerre with Palme de Vermeil (1942); Hon. Lieut.-Col., The Toronto Scottish Regt. 1949-64; Nat. Pres., Graphic Arts Industries Assn. 1959-62; Hon. Dir., Niagara Peninsular Graphic Arts Assn.; Anglican; recreations: travelling, reading; Clubs: Niagara Falls Club Canada.; Royal Canadian Military Inst.; Home: 40 Hillcrest Ave., St Catharines. Ont. L2R 4Y1

GOTLIEB, Allan E., LL.B., M.A., B.C.L.; public servant; b. Winnipeg, Man., 28 Feb. 1928; s. David Phillip and Sarah (Schiller) G.; e. Univ. of Cal., B.A. 1949; Harvard Law Sch., LL.B 1954 (Ed., "Harvard Law Review", 1950-51); Oxford Univ., M.A., B.C.L. (Vinerian Law Scholar, 1954-56); m. Sondra, d. David Kaufman, 20 Dec. 1955; children: Rebecca, Marcus, Rachel; Ambassador of Canada to the United States 1981- ; Member of the National Film Board; Canadian member of the Permanent Court of Arbitration; Called to the Bar of Eng. (Inner Temple) 1956; Fellow, Wadham Coll. and Univ. Lectr. in Law, Oxford Univ., 1954-56; joined Department of External Affairs 1957; 2nd Secy., Candn. Mission to UN, Geneva, 1960-62; 1st Secy., Candn. Del. to Eighteen Nation Disarmament Conf., 1962-64; Head of Legal Div., Dept. External Affairs, 1965-66; Asst. Under Secy of State for External Affairs and Legal Adviser, 1967-68; Depy. Min. of Communications (1968-73); Depy. Min. of Manpower & Immigration, 1973-76; Chrmn. of Can. Employment and Imm. Comn., 1976-77; Under-Sec. of State for External Affairs, 1977-81; Special Lectr. on Disarmament, Queen's Univ., 1965-66; Visiting Prof. of Pol. Science, Carleton Univ., 1966-71; Adjunct Prof. Internat. Relations, Carleton Univ., 1975-78; Visiting Fellow, All Souls Coll., Oxford, 1975-76; author of "Disarmament and International Law", 1965; "Canadian Treaty-Making", 1968 and numerous articles on Internat. Law; Ed., "Human Rights Federalism and Minorities", 1970; Jewish; Address: Canadian Embassy, 1746 Massachusetts Ave. N.W. Washington, C.C. 20036

GOTLIEB, Calvin Carl, M.A., Ph.D., D.M., F.R.S.C.; computer scientist; univ. professor; b. Toronto, Ont., 27 March 1921; s. late Israel and Jennie (Sherman) G.; e. Harbord Coll. Inst., Toronto, Ont. (1933-38); Univ. of Toronto, B.A. (Physics and Chem.) 1942, M.A. (Physics) 1944, Ph.D. (Physics) 1947; D.M. Waterloo 1968; m. Phyllis Fay, d. late Leo Bloom, 12 June 1949; children: Leo, Margaret, Jane; PROF. IN COMPUTER SCIENCE, UNIV.

OF TORONTO; worked with proximity fuse group in Can., U.S. and U.K.; Consultant to Aero. Labs., R.C.A.F. and Defence Research Bd. of Can. 1948-52; interested in electronic computers since 1948; appointed Lecturer in Physics, Univ. of Toronto, 1949; Candn. Rep. to Internat. Fed. Information Processing (known as IFIP) 1960-65; Chrmn. IFIP Technical Comte., (Relationships between Computer and Society), 1975-81; Pres., C.C. Gotlieb Consulting Ltd.; Consultant to UN, Can. and other govts., industry; Publications: "High Speed Data Processing" (with J. N. P. Hume) 1958, "Social Issues in Computing" (with A. Borodin) 1973, "Data Types and Structures" (with L. R. Gotlieb) 1978, over 70 articles on all phases of electronic digital computers; mem. Candn. Information Processing Society (which helped organize in 1958; Pres. 1960-61); Assn. for Computing Machinery (ACM); Brit. Computer Soc.; Editor-in-chief Communications of ACM 1962-65, Journ. 1966-68; Editor, Annals of History of Computing of Amer. Fed. of Information Processing Socs. (AFIPS) 1977- ; Jewish; recreations: sailing, swimming, chess; Address: University of Toronto, Toronto M5S 1A7

GOTLIEB, Phyllis Fay Bloom, M.A.; writer; b. Toronto, Ont. 25 May 1926; d. Leo and Mary (Kates) Bloom; e. Public Schs., Toronto, Ont.; Victoria and Univ. Colls., Univ. of Toronto, B.A. 1948, M.A. 1950; m. Calvin Carl, s. Israel G. 12 June 1949; children: Leo, Margaret, Jane; author of "Within the Zodiac" (poems) 1964; "Sunburst" (science fiction novel) 1964; "Why Should I have all the Grief?" (novel) 1969; "Ordinary, Moving" (poems) 1969; "Doctor Umlaut's Earthly Kingdom" (poems) 1974; "O Master Caliban!" (science fiction novel) 1976; "The Works" (collected poems) 1978; "A Judgement of Dragons" (science fiction novel) 1980; poems and stories publ. in mags. and anthologies in Can. and U.S.; poetry-dramas broadcast on CBC; mem. Science Fiction Writers of Am.; Jewish; Home: 29 Ridgevale Dr., Toronto, Ont. M6A 1K9

GOTTSCHALK, Fritz, R.C.A.; graphic designer; b. Zurich, Switzerland 30 Dec. 1937; s. Friedrich and Hermine (Schmid) G.; e. elem. and high schs. Zurich; Coll. of Design Zurich; Art Inst. Orell Fussli Zurich apprenticeship 1954-58; Gewerbeschule Basel post grad. course Coll. of Design 1962-63; PRES., GOTTSCHALK & ASH INTER-NATIONAL 1977- ; Founder (1964) and Dir. Gottschalk & Ash Int'l Tor.; Dir. Gottschalk & Ash Int'l, Montréal; Gottschalk & Ash Int'l. New York; exhns. of firm's work in Montreal, Chicago; cited various Swiss, Canadian, USA, German and Japanese publs.; author numerous articles and lectures on design in Can. and USA; mem. Alliance Graphic Internat.; Assn. Suisse des Graphistes; Protestant; recreations: skiing, swimming; Office: Sonnhaldenstrasse 3, 8032 Zurich, Switzerland.

GOUDGE, T. A., M.A., Ph.D., LL.D., F.R.S.C. (1955); university professor; b. Halifax, N.S., 19 Jan. 1910; s. Thomas Norman and Effie (Anderson) G.; e. Halifax (N.S.) Acad., Grad. 1927; Dalhousie Univ., B.A. 1931 and M.A. 1932; Univ. of Toronto, Ph.D. 1937; Harvard Univ., 1936-37; m. Helen Beryl, d. H. B. Christilaw, Blind River, Ont., 23 June 1936; one s. Stephen T.; PROF. EMERITUS OF PHILOSOPHY, UNIV. OF TORONTO, since 1976; Interim Lect. in Philos., Waterloo Coll., Ont., 1934; Fellow and Tutor in Philos. and later Lect., Queen's Univ., 1935-38; Lect. in Philos., Univ., of Toronto, 1938-40; Asst. Prof. 1940-45, Assoc. Prof. 1945-49; Prof. 1949-75 and Chrmn. of Dept. 1963-69; Special Lect. 1975-76; mem. of Editorial Comte., "University of Toronto Quarterly", since 1951 (Acting Editor, 1955); served in 2nd World War; joined R.C.N.V.R., 1943, with rank of Sub-Lieut. (S.B.); discharged 1945, Lieut.-Commdr. (S.B.); author of "Bergson's Introduction to Metaphysics", 1949; "The Thought of C. S. Peirce", 1950; "The Ascent of Life", 1961 (Governor General's award winner, 1961); more than 50 articles on philos. subjects, logic, epistemology, philos.

of science, etc. in learned journs.; Pres., Candn. Philos. Assn. (1964); mem. Editorial Board, Ency. of Phil.; mem. Editorial Board, The Monist; mem., Am. Philos Assn.; Mind Assn.; Humanities Assn. of Can.; Pres., Charles S. Peirce Soc., 1957-59; mem. Acad. Panel, Can. Council 1965-68; received Centennial Medal, 1967; Canada Council Sr. Fellowship, 1970-71; 'Pragmatism and Purpose: Essays Presented to Thomas A. Goudge, 1981; recreation: oil painting; Home: 244 Glenrose Ave., Toronto, Ont. M4T 1K9

GOUDIE, Hon. Denzil Joseph, M.H.A.; politician; b. Mud Lake, Labrador 4 Apl. 1939; s. James and Elizabeth (Blake) G.; e. North Star Primary & High Schs. Happy Valley, Labrador; m. Mona d. James Squires, St. Philips, Nfld. 24 Dec. 1966; children: James Scott, Jason Trevor; MIN. OF RURAL, AGRICULTURAL AND NORTHERN DEVELOPMENT, NFLD. 1979- ; el. M.H.A. for Naskaupi prov. g.e. 1975, re-el. 1979; mem. Labrador Heritage Soc. (Pres. 1973-75); Northern Co-ordinating Comte. Un. Ch.; former mem. RCMP Auxiliary; mem. Co. of Young Candns. Happy Valley 1973-75; Announcer-Operator CBC Happy Valley 1964-73; Mgr. Maritime Accessories Happy Valley 1963-64; Town Clk. and Town Mgr. Happy Valley 1959-63; P. Conservative; United Church; Office: Atlantic Place, Water St., St. John's, Nfld. A1C 5T7.

GOUDIE, John E.; gas company executive; b. Calgary, Alberta 3 March 1924; e. R.I.A. 1961; m. Audrey, 1948; EXTVE. VICE PRES. AND DIR., ALBERTA & SOUTH-ERN GAS CO. LTD.; Extve. Vice Pres. and Dir., Alberta Natural Gas Co. Ltd.; Address: E. Tower, Esso Plaza, 425 - 1st St. S.W., Calgary, Alta. T2P 3L8

GOUDIE, Stuart Russel, B.A.; company executive; b. Kitchener, Ont. 26 Oct. 1911; s. Arthur Russel and Alice M. (Weseloh) G.; e. Waterloo Coll. and Vocational Sch. (Grad. 1931); Univ. of W. Ont., B.A. 1935 with Hons. in Business Adm.; m. L. Louise, d. William Anderson, 16 Sept. 1947; PRESIDENT, GOUDIES LTD. since 1960; Pres., Goudie Bldgs. Ltd.; mem., Kitchener Parking Authority, 1956-65; joined firm as Buyer 1935; Asst. Mgr., 1939, Vice-Pres. 1940; served in World War 1942-45; Lieut., R.C.O.C.; Alpha Kappa Psi (Beta Kappa Chapter, Pres. 1934-35); Sec.-Treasurer, Norse Yachtsmen Ltd.; United Church; recreations: boating, golf, skiing; Clubs: Granite; K. & W. Gyro; Westmount; Home: 197 Lincoln Rd., Waterloo, Ont N2J 2P2; Office: 22 King W., Kitchener, Ont. N2G 3Y9

GOUGH, Barry Morton, B.Ed., M.A., Ph.D., F.R.H.S.; educator; b. Victoria, B.C. 17 Sept. 1938; e. Univ. of Victoria; Univ. of B.C., B.Ed. 1962; Univ. of Mont. M.A. 1966; King's Coll. Univ. of London Ph.D. 1969; m. Barbara Louise Kerr (div.); 2ndly Marilyn Joy Morris 1981; children: Melinda Jane, Jason Jeremy; PROF. OF HISTO-RY, WILFRID LAURIER UNIV. 1978- ; taught high sch. B.C. 3 yrs.; lectr. in hist. Western Wash. Univ., co-founder Candn. Studies Program. co-dir. and archivist Pacific Northwest Studies Centre also teacher Northwest Interinstitutional Council on Study Abroad and served as Financial Dir. London, Eng. program (1970), 1968-72; joined present univ. as Assoc. Prof. 1972, Founding Co-ordinator Candn. Studies 1973-79, served as mem. Senate, Senate Extve. and Univ. Rep. to Humanities Council Can., mem. ed. bd. Wilfrid Laurier Univ. Press 1973-80; visiting lectr. Duke Univ., Univ. of Victoria, Univ. of Me., Simon Fraser Univ., Univ. of B.C.; Adjunct Prof. of Hist. Univ. of Waterloo 1972-77; author "The Royal Navy and the Northwest Coast of North America 1810-1914: A Study of British Maritime Ascendancy" 1971; "To the Arctic and Pacific with Beechey: Lieutenant George Peard's Journal of the Voyage of H.M.S. Blossom 1925-8" 1973; "Canada" 1975; "Distant Dominion: Britain and the Northwest Coast of North America 1579-1809" 1980; recipient Can. Council Koerner Foundation and other awards for research; John Lyman Prize N. Atlantic Soc.

for Oceanic Hist. 1980; European Comn. and European Parlt. Visiting Fellowship 1980; Chrmn. Jt. Comte. Candn. Hist. Assn.-Am. Hist. Assn. 1972-73; mem. Council Champlain Soc. 1975; Chrmn. Kitchener-Waterloo Br. Candn. Inst. Internat. Affairs 1978; mem. Nat. Council Candn. Human Rights Foundation; Home: 37 Ahrens St. W., Kitchener, Ont. N2H 4B6; Office: Waterloo, Ont. N2L 3C5.

GOUGH, Denis Ian, M.Sc., Ph.D., F.R.S.C., F.R.A.S.; educator; b. Port Elizabeth, S. Africa 20 June 1922; s. Frederick William and Ivy Catherine (Hingle) G.; e. Selborne Coll. East London, S. Africa 1938; Rhodes Univ. B.Sc. 1943, M.Sc. 1947; Univ. of Witwatersrand Ph.D. 1953; m. Winifred Irving d. late William Irving Nelson 1 June 1945; children: Catherine Veronica, Stephen William Cyprian; PROF. OF PHYSICS, UNIV. OF ALTA. since 1966 and Dir. Inst. Earth & Planetary Physics 1975-80; Research Offr. and Sr. Research Offr. S. African Council for Scient. and Indust. Research 1947-58; Lectr. and Sr. Lectr. Univ. Coll. of Rhodesia and Nyasaland 1958-63; Assoc. Prof. Southwest Center for Advanced Studies Dallas, Texas 1964-66; served with S. African Corps of Signals 1943-45; Hugh Kelly Fellow, Rhodes Univ. 1977; Visiting Fellow, Churchill Coll. Cambridge 1978; author numerous papers geophys. research; Fellow Am. Geophys. Union mem., Candn. Geophys. Union (Past Chrmn.), Geol. Assoc. of Can.; Anglican; recreations: reading, gardening, cross-country skiing; music; Home: 11747 - 83 Ave., Edmonton, Alta. T6G 0V2; Office: Edmonton, Alta. T6G 2J1.

GOUGH, Douglas W., B.B.A. (Hon.), M.B.A.; banker; b. Montreal, Que. 14 Oct. 1947; e. York Univ. M.B.A. 1973; m. Karen 8 Dec. 1978; children: Laura; SR. VICE-PRES., NORTH AMER. REAL ESTATE, BANK OF MONTREAL; previously Financial Analyst, Confederation Life; Account Mgr., Internat. Banking Group, Citicorp Ltd.; Clubs: Granite; Cambridge; Home: 23 Glenbrae Ave., Toronto, Ont. M4G 3R4; Office: (P.O. Box 1) First Canadian Place, Toronto, Ont. M5X 1A1

GOUIN, Hon. Léon Mercier, Q.C., LL.D., F.R.S.C.; senator, lawyer (ret. 1980); b. Montreal, P.Q., 24 Dec. 1891; s. Sir Lomer, K.C.M.G., and Eliza (Mercier) G.; e. St. Mary's Coll., Montreal, P.Q.; Loyola Coll.; Laval Univ., B.A.; Univ. of Montreal, LL.D.; Oxford Univ.; Queen's Univ. (Dipl. in Econ.); m. Yvette, d. Nazaire Olivier, 20 Nov. 1917; children: Lisette M., Thérèse M., Olivier M.; Advocate, 1915; created K.C. 1925; practised law in father's office, later in partnership with David Murphy, formerly one of his father's partners, 1915-22; summoned to the Senate, 7 Nov. 1940; Legion of Hon. (France), 1947; Liberal; Roman Catholic; Club: Cercle Universitaire; Home: Apt. 5, 2174 Sherbrooke St. West, Montreal, Que. H3H 1G7

GOULD, George Edward; grain merchant; b. Winnipeg, Man., 19 July 1914; s. William George and Jennie (Thompson) G.; e. Norwood and St. Boniface, Man. Grade and High Schs.; Univ. of Manitoba (two yrs. Accountancy); m. Bette Jane, d. Frederick Thibedeau, 4 May 1946; three children; Dir. and Sr. Consultant, Cargill Grain Co., Ltd.; Sr. Advisor, Prince Rup. Grain Ltd.; Freemason (Shrine); Conservative Protestant; recreations: golf, woodworking; Clubs: Manitoba; St. Charles Country; Winnipeg Winter; Home: 120 Mountbatten Ave., Winnipeg, Man. R3P 0P6; Office: 500 Grain Exchange, Bldg. 6, Winnipeg, Man.

GOULD, Glenn Herbert; pianist; composer; b. Toronto, Ont., 25 Sept. 1932; s. Russell Herbert and Florence (Greig) G.; e. Williamson Road Public Sch., and Malvern Coll. Inst., Toronto, Ont.; Royal Conservatory of Music of Toronto where he studied Piano under Alberto Guerrero, Organ under Frederick Silvester, and Composition under Leo Smith; received his A.R.C.T. at age twelve; is largely selftaught since the age of nineteen; made his prof. debut at age fourteen with the Toronto Symphony Orchestra, and began concert tours at age nineteen; made New York debut at Town Hall in 1955, since when has won international fame; appeared with Berlin Philharmonic, New York Philharmonic, Symphony Orchestras of Detroit, Pittsburgh, Montreal, Dallas, Vancouver, St. Louis, San Francisco, Cleveland; engaged in a two weeks concert tour in U.S.S.R., incl. Moscow 1957; made debut at the Salsburg Festival as Soloist with Concertgebouw Orchestra of Amsterdam under Demitri Mitropoulos, performing the Bach D Minor piano concerto, Aug. 1958; awarded the Bach Medal for Pianists by Comte. of the Harriet Cohen Music Awards, London, Eng., Feb. 1959; LL.D., Univ. of Toronto, 1964; Publications: (a quartet) Bach's "Goldberg Variations" (recording); his favourite composers for concert work: Bach, Beethoven, Brahms; his interests lie "more in the literature of music, in composition, in conducting"; received Molson Prize from Can. Council, 1968;

GOULD, John Howard, R.C.A.; artist; filmmaker; jazz musician; b. Toronto, Ont. 14 Aug. 1929; s. Graham and Mona (MacTavish) G.; e. Ont. Coll. Art A.O.C.A. 1952; m. Ingi Bergman; children: Maria, Ellen; solo exhns. incl.: Here and Now Gallery 1961; Agnes Lefort Gallery Montreal 1962; Dorothy Cameron Gallery Toronto 1963; Arwin Gallery Detroit 1963, 1964, 1966, 1968, 1970, 1972, 1975; Hart House Univ. of Toronto 1965; Roberts Gallery Toronto 1966, 1968, 1970, 1971, 1972, 1974; Galerie Sherbrooke Montreal 1969; Art Gallery Ont., Whitby Art Centre, Tom Thomson Gallery Owen Sound, Algoma Festival Sault Ste. Marie, Art Gallery of Brant, Lynwood Arts Centre Simcoe 1974-76; Robert McLaughlin Gallery Oshawa 1976; rep. nat. and internat. group exhns.; filmmaker since 1965; pioneered technique of drawn documentary for TV; works incl. "Pikangikum" 1968 (Nat. Film Bd.); "Marceau on Mime" 1971; "Waubaushene Faces" 1975; rep. Can. Venice Biennale 1968 (short films); Instr. in Life Drawing Ont. Coll. of Art; author "The Drawn Image" 1978; "What a Piece of Work is Man" 1980; work incl. in "The Nude in Canadian Painting"; "One Hundred Years of Canadian Drawings"; "Great Canadian Painting: A Century of Art"; "Art in Architecture"; mem. Toronto Musicians Assn.; recreations: cross-country skiing, biking, swimming; Address: Waubaushene P.O., Ont. L0K 2C0.

GOULET, Robert G.; singer; b. Lawrence, Mass., 26 Nov. 1933; s. Joseph and Jeanette (Gauthier) G.; Royal Conservatory of Music, Toronto, Ont.; m.; one d., Nicolette; sometime Radio Announcer, Edmonton, Alta.; host weekly TV program, Canada; Broadway debut in Camelot, 1961; numerous TV appearances

GOURDEAU, Jean-Paul, M.Sc.; engineer; b. Québec, Qué., 29 June 1925; s. Alexandre and Lucienne (Cloutier) G.; e. Laval Univ., 1949; École Polytechique, Univ. of Montréal, 1951; Harvard Univ., M.Sc. 1952; Robert A. Taft Sanitary Engn. Center, Cincinnati, 1953; m. Jeannine, d. Gérard Lamarre, Rivière Bleue, Qué., 13 Sept. 1952; children: Pierre, Lucie, Louis, Joanne; PRESIDENT AND CHIEF OPERATING OFFICER, SNC GROUP OF COMPANIES; since 1975; Dir. SNC Enterprises Ltd.; École de Technologie Supérieure de l'Université du Quebéc; Ducros Meilleur, Roy et Associés Ltée; Didier Refractories Corporation; tech. consultant to mun. authorities on waste treatment and water supply, constr. of aqueducts, filtration plants, sewage systems and sewage treatment plants in E. Que., Dept. of Health, Prov. of Qué., 1951; joined present firm as Chief Engr. of Mun. Div. 1961, Dir. of Engn. 1965, Vice-Pres.-Operations 1966; Exec. Vice-Pres., 1972-75 Asst. Prof. (part-time) in Sanitary Engn., Laval Univ.; rec'd Arthur Sidney Bedell Award, Water Pollution Control Fed. of Washington, D.C. 1971; mem. Assn. Consulting Engrs. Can. (Pres. 1973-74); Engn. Inst. Can.; Ordre des ingénieurs du Quebéc; Am. Water Works Assn.; Water Pollution Control Fed.; Assn. Québécoise des Techniques de l'Eau (Past Pres.); Internat. Fed. Consulting Engrs. (Extve. Comte 1971-79.) (Vice-Pres., 1978-79); Science Council of Can.; Advisory Bd., Comm. d'initiative et de développement économiques de Montréal; R. Catholic; recreation: golf; Clubs: Richelieu Valley Golf; St-Denis; Home: 878 Isle de France, St. Lambert, Qué. J4S 1T7; Office: 1, Complexe Desjardins, P.O. Box 10, Desjardins P.O., Montréal Qué. H5B 1C8

GOURLAY, Hon. Douglas MacLeod, M.L.A., B.Sc.A.; politician; agrologist; b. Brandon, Man. 1 Dec. 1929; s. late Andrew Judson and Catherine MacLeod (Rammage) G.; e. White Bank Lea Elem. Sch. 1943; Cardale High Sch. 1947; Univ. of Man. B.Sc.A. 1952; m. Audrey May d. late William Thomas Porter 27 Sept. 1952; children: Diane, Joan, Gerald, Robert; MIN. OF MUNICIPAL AFFAIRS AND MIN. OF NORTHERN AFFAIRS, MAN. 1979- , Min. Responsible for Community Econ. Devel. Fund; Owner Roadrunner Drive-In Ltd. Swan River, Man.; Charter Dir. Mantex Holding Co. Inc. Texas; Westwood Inn Ltd. Swan River; Settlement Offr. Fed. Dept. Immigration 1952-56; Agric. Rep. Prov. Man. pilot Mound 1956-63, The Pas 1963-66, Swan River 1966-77; Councillor Town of Swan River 1972-75, Mayor 1975-77; el. M.L.A. for Swan River 1977, mem. Agric. Inst. Can.; Man. Inst. Agrols.; P. Conservative; United Church; Clubs: Rotary; Home: (P.O. Box 387) Swan River, Man. R0L 1Z0; Office: 330 Legislative Bldg., Winnipeg, Man. R3C 0V8.

GOVIER, George W., M.Sc., Sc.D., F.C.I.C.; professional engineer; b. Nanton, Alberta, 15 June 1917; s. George Arthur and Gertrude (Wheeler) G.; e. Univ. of British Columbia, B.A.Sc. (Chem. Engn.) 1939; Univ. of Alberta, M.Sc. (Phys. Chem.) 1945; Univ. of Michigan, Sc.D. (Chem. Engn.) 1949; m. Doris Eda, d. Henry Kemp, 23 Feb. 1940; children: Gertrude Rose, Katherine Mary, Susan Elizabeth; PRES., GOVIER CONSULTING SERVICES LTD. since 1978; 1940-48, Instr., Lectr., Asst. Prof., Assoc. Prof. of Chem. Engn., Univ. of Alta.; Prof. of Chem. Engn., 1948-54; Head of the Dept. of Chem. and Petroleum Engn., 1948-59; Dean of Faculty of Engn. and Prof. of Chem. Engn. 1959-1963 Chrmn., Energy Resources Conservation Bd., Alta. 1962-78 (mem. since 1948; Deputy Chrmn. 1959-62); Chief Deputy Minister of Energy and Natural Resources, Gov't of Alta. 1975-77; Publications: approx. 60 scient. and tech. papers; Fellow, Chem. Inst. Can. (Chrmn., Chem. Engn. Div., 1948-49, and Vice-Chrmn., 1959-60); Councillor, 1951-52); Foreign Assoc., Nat. Acad. of Eng. of U.S.; Chrmn., Sci. Programme Comm., World Petroleum Congresses since 1975; Fellow, Engn. Inst. Can. (Chrmn., Chem. Engn. Div., 1961-63); mem. Candn. Nat. Comte. for World Petroleum Cong.; Candn. Inst. Mining & Metall. (Chrmn., Petroleum and Natural Gas Div. 1950-51; Pres. 1966); Assn. Prof. Engrs. Alta. (Pres., 1958-59; mem. Council, 1959-60); Fellow, Am. Inst. Chem. Engrs.; Dir. 1966-79, Vice Pres., 1976-79, Petroleum Recovery Inst.; Chrmn. Policy Comte 1977-78; Vice Pres. 1978-79 Coal Mining Research Centre; Chrmn. of Bd., Alberta Helium Ltd.; Dir Canadian Foremost Ltd.; Texaco Can. Inc.; Combustion Engineering-Superheater Ltd.; Candn.-Montana Gas Co. Ltd; Candn.-Montana Pipeline Co.; Roan Resources Ltd.; Raylo Chemicals Ltd. 1980-1; Stone & Webster Can. Ltd.; Bow Valley Resource Services Ltd.; recreations: swimming, skiing, dancing; Club: Calgary Petroleum; Ranchman's; Home: 1507 Cavanaugh Pl., Calgary, Alta. T2L 0M8; Office: 24th Floor, Royal Bank Bldg., 335-8th Ave. S.W., Calgary, Alta. T2P 1C9

GOWDEY, Charles Willis, B.A., M.Sc., D.Phil.; educator; b. St. Thomas, Ont. 3 Sept. 1920; s. William Charles and Myrtle (Craford) G.; e. St. Thomas Coll. Inst. 1940; Univ. of W. Ont. B.A. 1944, M.Sc. 1946; Oxford Univ. D.Phil. 1948; m. Madelon Craig d. late Clarence E. Gilmour, London, Ont. Sept. 1946; children: David, Kathe-

rine, Kevin, Sheila; PROF. AND HEAD OF PHARMACOL. UNIV. OF W. ONT. since 1960; Demonst. Oxford Univ. 1946-48; Lectr. present Univ. 1948, Asst. Prof. 1950, Assoc. Prof. 1952-60; served with RCAF Auxiliary 1951-64; mem. Defence Research Bd. Panel on Aviation Med. 1955-68; Candn. Drug Adv. Comte. to Min. of Nat. Health & Welfare 1962-69; Special Comte. on Compulsory Licensing 1965; Nat. Research Council, Assoc. Comte. on Dental Research 1965-68, Assoc. Comte. on Space Research 1967-69; author various research papers; mem. Pharmacol. Soc. Can. (Pres. 1964-65); Brit. Pharmacol. Soc.; Am. Soc. Pharmacol. & Exper. Therapeutics; Candn. Assn. Research Toxicology; Undersea Med. Soc.; Alpha Omega Alpha; Club: Harvey; Home: 428 Wortley Rd., London, Ont. N6C 3S8; Office: London, Ont. N6A 5C1.

GOWDY, Samuel James, B.A.; insurance executive; b. Toronto, Ont. 5 Feb. 1926; s. late Angus Bannerman and Gertrude May G.; e. Parkdale Coll. Inst. Toronto; Univ. of Toronto B.A. 1949; m. Helen Bernice Maw 15 March 1952; three d. Mary Elizabeth (Mrs. J. R. Pryde), Patricia Anne (Mrs. D. Higgins), Barbara Jean; SR. VICE PRES. GEN. ADM., SUN LIFE ASSURANCE CO. OF CANADA 1979- ; joined present Co. Toronto Br. Office 1949, Br. Secy. Philippines Br. Office 1957, Br. Office Inspr. 1957, Asst. Personnel Offr. 1962, Personnel Offr. 1967, Extve. Offr. Personnel 1968, Vice Pres. Personnel 1972; Freemason; Clubs: National; Granite; Home: 251 Banbury Rd., Don Mills, Ont. M3B 3C7; Office: (P.O. Box 4150 Stn. A) Toronto, Ont. M5W 2C9.

GOWLING, Ernest Gordon, Q.C., LL.D.; patent counsel; b. Ottawa, Ont., 7 June 1903; e. Pub. and High Schs.; Ottawa; Osgoode Hall, Toronto; Queen's Univ., LL.D.; m. Aileen Isabel, d. William A. Harston, Toronto, 12 Oct. 1929; one s., William Gordon; COUNSEL, GOWLING & HENDERSON; read law with the late Geo. F. Henderson; Past Pres. and Life mem., Candn. Bar Assn.; Hon. mem., Am. Bar Assn.; Freemason; United Church; Club: Country; Home: 305 Clemow Ave., Ottawa, Ont. K1S 2B7; Office: 160 Elgin St., Ottawa, Ont. K2P 2C4

GOYER, Hon. Jean-Pierre, P.C., Q.C. (1976), M.P., B.A., LL.B.; b. St. Laurent, Que., 17 Jan. 1932; s. Gilbert and Marie-Ange G.; e. Notre Dame des Neiges and Beaudet Schs.; St. Laurent (Que.) Coll.; Ste-Marie Coll.; Univ. of Montreal; m. Michelle, d. Charles-Auguste Gascon, Montreal, Que., 24 June 1960; children: Christine, Sophie, Julie; Min. of Supply and Services and Receiver General for Can. 1972-78; 1st el. to H. of C. for Dollard, g.e. 1965; re-el. 1968, 72, 74; apptd. Parlty. Secy. to Secy. of State for External Affairs 1968; Solr. Gen. of Can. 1970; resigned seat in House of Commons, Jan 1979; recreations: tennis, skiing, squash; Liberal; R. Catholic; Club: Reform

GOYETTE, Bernard Jean, B.A., B.Sc.C., M.Sc.C., F.C.B.A.; banker; b. Montreal, Que. 18 May 1940; s. Louis and Annette (Blondin) G.; e. Laval Univ. B.A., B.Sc.C., M.Sc.C. 1964; m. Rachelle M. d. Paul Jauvin 28 Oct. 1967; two d. Isabelle Christine, Cybèle Chantal; EXEC. VICE PRES.- MARKETING., THE MERCANTILE BANK OF CANADA since 1980, Sr. Vice Pres. 1977-1980; joined Royal Bank of Canada, Montreal 1964, trans. to Paris, France 1965; assigned to Bank Reorganization Team 1966; assignments Invests. and Foreign Exchange 1967; Credit Supvr. 1968, Asst. Mgr. Montreal 1969; joined present Bank as Asst. Mgr. 1970 Montreal, Mgr. Montreal 1971, Vice Pres. H.O. Montreal 1973, Vice Pres. Invest. and Exchange 1974, Sr. Vice Pres. Invest. and Exchange 1976; R. Catholic; recreations: hunting, fishing, trap, skeet; Clubs: St. Denis; Club Laval-sur-le-Lac; La Roue du Roy; Home: 3057 Lacombe, Montreal, Que.; Office: 625 Dorchester Blvd. West, Montréal, Que. H3B 1R3

GRACE, John William, M.A., Ph.D.; journalist; b. Ottawa, Ont., 6 Jan. 1927; s. Archibald William and Beatrice (O'Connor) G.; e. Holy Cross Convent, Ottawa, Ont. 1934; Corpus Christi Sch., Ottawa, 1939; St. Patrick's Coll. High Sch., Ottawa 1941; St. Patrick's Coll., Ottawa, B.A. 1949; Catholic Univ. of Am., M.A. 1952; Univ. of Mich., Ph.D. 1958; m. Ruth Ellen, d. John Allen Herbert, Newport, Md., 8 Sept. 1954; children: James, Ellen, John, Christopher, Elizabeth, Anne; COMMISSIONER, C.R.T.C.; Editor-in-chief, Ottawa Journal 1959-80; Instructor, Department English, Univ. of Michigan 1956; mem. Bd. Governors, University of Ottawa (Vice Chairman, Extve. Comte. 1970); mem. Canada Council 1971-77; Ottawa Welfare Council; Dir., Catholic Family Service; mem. Coll. Inst. Bd. of Ottawa 1963-69 (Chrmn. 1967); R. Catholic; recreations: gardening, skiing, boating; Clubs: Rideau; Country Club; Gatineau Fish & Game; Home: 291 Clemow Ave., Ottawa, Ont. K1S 2B7

GRAEFE, Christian Wilhelm Arnold, C.M.; investment consultant; consul of Finland; b. Helsinki, Finland 29 Nov. 1932; s. David Andreas Herman Arnold and Astrid Margareta Sunniva (Sandroos) G.; e. Finland and Germany; came to Can. 1952; divorced; children: Mathias Maximillian Arnold, Victoria Sunniva Alexandra; PRES., CHRISTIAN GRAEFE AND CO. INVESTMENT CONSULTANTS LTD. Pres., Internat. Candn. Petroleum Exhn. & Conf. Ltd. 1978-80; International Can. Trade Fair Management Corp. Ltd., 1979- ; Hon. Consul of Finland for N. Alta. 1975- ; joined Agric. Can. and Ford Motor Co. Oakville 1952-54; served with Royal Candn. Dragoons 1954-56; W. Command H.Q. Edmonton 1956-57; Weber Bros. Real Estate Co. Residential Div. Edmonton 1957-64, Comm. Invest. Div. 1964-67 Dir. Internat. Div. 1967-69; Founding Pres. and Past Dir., German Candn. Business & Prof. Assn. Alta.; Past Chrmn. W. Comm., Candn. German Chamber Indust. & Comm. Inc.; Past Dir. Edmonton Real Estate Bd.; Scandinavian Centre Edmonton and Edmonton Exhn. Assn.; Mission Organizer, City of Edmonton Indust. Devel. Mission to Europe 1965; Mission Coordinator, Prov. Alta. Ministerial Tour Europe 1971; Knight-Commander, Hospitaller Order of Saint John of Jerusalem, 1980; Knight Military and Hospitaller Order of St. Lazarus of Jerusalem, 1981; mem. City of Edmonton Brit. Commonwealth Games Del. to Olympics, Munich 1972; Sponsor, Scandinavian Businessmen's Club; Home: #1207, 11135 - 83 Ave., Edmonton, Alta. Office: Main Floor, Hotel Macdonald, Edmonton, Alta.

GRAFFTEY, Heward, B.A., B.C.L.; b. Montreal, P.Q., 5 August 1928; s. William A. and H. R. (Heward) G.; e. Mount Allison Univ., B.A.; McGill Univ., B.C.L.; m. Alida Grace, d. Mattheus Visser, San Francisco, Cal. 28 Dec. 1961; children: Arthur Heward, Clement Tai Yong, Leah; Chrmn. of Bd., Montreal Lumber Co. Ltd.; Dir., Steamship Supply Lumber Co. Ltd.; Pres., Missisquoi Realties Ltd.; Past Dir., John Howard Soc. (1958); read law with Heward, Holden & Co.; called to the Bar of Que., 1955; 1st el. to H. of C. for Brome-Missisquoi in g.e. 1958; Parlty. Secy. to Min. of Finance, 1962-63; re-el. in g.e. 1968; re-el g.e. 1972, 74, 79; Min. of State (Social Programs) 1979; Candn. Delegate to U.N., 1958 and 1966; author, "The Senseless Sacrifice — A Black Paper on Medicine"; P. Conservative; Anglican; Home: Victoria St., Knowlton, Que. J0E 1V0

GRAHAM, Angus Frederick, M.A.Sc., Ph.D., D.Sc., F.R.S.C.; scientist; educator; b. Toronto, Ont. 28 March 1916; s. Frederick James and Mary Ann (Ball) G.; e. Univ. of Toronto B.A.Sc. 1938, M.A.Sc. 1939; Univ. of Edinburgh Ph.D. 1942, D.Sc. 1952; m. Jacqueline Françoise d. Joseph Poirier 3 July 1954; three s. Robert James, Andrew Donald, Paul Frederick; GILMAN CHENEY PROF. OF BIOCHEM., McGILL UNIV. 1970- , Chrmn. of Biochem 1970-80; mem. Scient. Adv. Bd. Inst. for Cancer Research Philadelphia 1974- ; Assoc. Prof. of Microbiol. Univ. of Toronto 1956-58; mem. Wistar Inst. of Anat. & Biol. Phil-

adelphia and Wistar Inst. of Anat. & Biol. Philadelphia and Wistar Prof. of Microbiol. Univ. of Pa. 1958-70; Eleanor Roosevelt Internat. Cancer Fellow, l'Institut du Radium, Paris 1964-65; Josiah Macy Jr. Foundation Faculty Scholar, Imp. Cancer Research Fund Labs.; London, Eng. 1977; author over 100 research papers aspects cell biol. and virology various scient. journs.; Ed.-in-Chief "Journal of Cellular Physiology" 1965-70; mem. various scient. journ. adv. bds.; mem. Am. Assn. Advanc. Science; Am. Soc. Microbiols.; recreations: skiing, sailing, tennis, poker; Home: 447 Strathcona Ave., Westmount, Que. H3Y 2X2; Office: McIntyre Medical Sciences Bldg., 3655 Drummond St., Montreal, Que.

GRAHAM, Hon. (Bernard Alasdair) Al, B.A.; senator; b. Dominion, N.S., 21 May 1929; s. John, D.D.S. and Genevieve (MacDonald) G.; e. St. Anne's High Sch. Glace Bay, N.S.; St. Francis Xavier Univ. B.A. 1950, post-grad. studies in Eng. and Educ.; m. Jean Elizabeth d. Hadley MacDonald, Antigonish, N.S., 30 June 1952; children: Patricia, Alasdair, John, David, Eileen, William, Daniel, Mary, Jean, Anne Marie; summoned to Senate 1972; Chrmn. Bd. Dirs. Darr (C.B.) Ltd.; Dir. Canadian Engineering Co. Ltd.; teacher N.S. schs. 1951-55; Broadcaster/Journalist N.S. 1955-63; Special Asst. Fed. Min. of Labour 1964-65; Extve. Asst. Fed. Min. Health & Welfare 1965-66; Extve. Vice Pres. and Gen. Mgr. Middlesex Broadcasters Ltd. London, Ont. 1967-68; Extve. Secy. Cape Breton Development Corp. Sydney 1968-71, Vice Pres. and Extve. Secy. 1971-72; def. cand. Fed. el. 1958; Pres. Lib. Party of Can.; Gov. Coll. of Cape Breton; Dir. St. Rita Hosp.; N.S. Heart Foundation; Resi-Care (C.B.) Assn.; mem. Candn. Inst. Mining & Metall.; N.S. Mining Soc.; Liberal; R. Catholic; Club: Royal Cape Breton Yacht; Home: 93 Whitney Ave., Sydney, N.S. B1P 4Z8; Office: The Senate, Ottawa, Ont. K1A 0A4

GRAHAM, David R., B.A., M.B.A.; broadcasting executive; b. Ottawa, Ont. 14 Feb. 1937; s. John and Susan C. (Hill) G.; e. Public and Ashbury Coll., Ottawa; Waterloo Coll., B.A. 1962; Harvard Univ., M.B.A. 1964; A.M.P., 1975; CHRMN., CABLE AMERICA INC. Pres. and Dir., Cablecasting Ltd., 1969-80; Dir. Cable Atlanta, Inc.; Cable Los Angeles, Inc.; Home: 16 Eaton Place, London, S.W., England

GRAHAM, Hon. Douglas Roy, M.L.A.; politician; b. Fort Assinaboine, Alta. 29 Dec. 1949; s. Gordon Russell and Alma Jean (Whitney) G.; e. F. H. Collins Secondary Sch. Whitehorse, Yukon 1967; Univ. of Alaska Elect. Engn. 1968-70; B.C.I.T. Vancouver Dipl. in Business Adm. 1973; m. Mayvor Louise d. Helge Engren, Whitehorse, Yukon 30 Oct. 1970; children: Melanie Kim, Richard Douglas; MIN. OF EDUC., JUSTICE INFORMATION RESOURCES, GOVT. SERVICES, CONSUMER & CORPORATE AFFAIRS, WORKERS' COMPENSATION BD., Y.T. 1978- ; el. M.L.A. for Porter Creek W. 1978; P. Conservative; Anglican; recreations: hockey, badminton, baseball; Home: 43 Wann Rd., Whitehorse, Yukon; Office: (P.O. Box 2703) Whitehorse, Yukon Y1A 2C6.

GRAHAM, Eric Richard, B.Com., C.A.; company executive; b. Montreal, P.Q., 31 May 1912; s. James F. and A. (Farley) G.; e. McGill Univ., B.Com. 1933; C.A. 1942; m. late Vera E. Cowan, 25 Sept. 1937; children: Sandra Joan, Verda Lynn, David Eric, Susan; 2ndly, Jacqueline D. Galipeault, 29 Nov. 1958; VICE-PRES. (FINANCE) SECY. AND DIR., PILKINGTON BROTHERS (CANADA) LTD.; Dir. and Secy. Treas., Pilkington Glass Mfg. Co. Ltd.; Vitrerie Franklin Ltée; Dir., Pilkington Glass Ltd.; Duplate (Canada) Ltd.; R. Catholic; Clubs: Rotary; University; Home: 44 Charles St. W., Toronto, Ont.; Office: 101 Richmond St. W., Toronto, Ont. M5H 1T1

GRAHAM, Eric Stanley, M.Sc., Ph.D., F.C.S.; university administrator; b. Kingston, Ont. 31 Dec. 1921; s. Stanley Newlands and Beatrice Deacon (Birch) G.; e.

Queen's Univ. B.Sc. 1942, M.Sc. 1946; Mass. Inst. Technol. Ph.D. 1950; m. Barbara Frances d. late Laurence G. Herchmer 5 Sept. 1945; two s. Ian Stanley, David Laurence; PRINCIPAL, ROYAL ROADS MILITARY COLL. since 1961; Assoc. Prof. Kenyon Coll. Gambier, Ohio 1950, Prof. 1956, Head Chem. Dept. 1957-61; Research Assoc. Univ. of London (Ford Foundation Faculty Fellow) 1954-55; Coll. Entrance Exam. Bd. Advanced Placement Program (Chief Reader 1959-61) 1958-61; Am. Chem. Soc. Visiting Scientists Program 1958-64 (Visiting Scient. 1958-64; Dir. H.S. Visits 1959-61); Asia Foundation Visiting Prof. Univ. of Dacca 1961 (summer); Visiting Prof. Univ. of Redlands (Cal.) summers 1962, 1963, 1965; served with Royal Candn. Corps Signals 1942-45 Eng., N.W. Europe; Past Dir. Service for Admission to Coll. and Univ.; Fellow, Ohio Acad. Sciences; Sigma Xi; Anglican; recreations: fishing, golf, gardening; Home: 3065 Uplands Rd., Victoria, B.C. V8R 6B3

GRAHAM, Francis Ronald; investment dealer; b. Toronto, Ont., 6 May 1920; s. Francis Ronald and Helen Marguerite (Phelan) G.; e. St. Michael's Coll. Sch., Toronto, Ont. (1938)); m. Renee Beatrice, d. Rene Moncel, Montreal, P.Q., 10 Mar. 1942; children: Susan, (Mrs. David Wild) Ronald, Robert, Margot, Anthony, Ian; Chrmn and Dir., Graymont Ltd.; Grayron Industries Ltd.; Domlim Inc.; Vice-Chrmn. and Dir., Scott's Hospitality Inc.; Dir., Dickenson Mines Ltd.; Panagaea Petroleum; Sulconam Inc.; Levesque, Beaubien Inc.; with Bank of Nova Scotia, 1939-41; Chrmn., Capital Wire Cloth & Mfg. Co. Ltd., 1946-60; served in 2nd World War, 1941-46, with Royal Candn. Armoured Corps, 14th Candn. Armoured Regt.; R. Catholic; Clubs: St. James's; Montreal; Seigniory; Home: Apt. 1, 40 South Dr., Toronto Ont. M4W 1R1; Office: Suite 1414, 401 Bay St., Toronto Ont. M5H 2Y4

GRAHAM, George Edwin, B.Sc., P.Eng.; communications executive; b. Worcester, Mass., s. Roy Sayers and Gladys Isabel (Fisher) G.; e. Moncton (N.B.) High Sch.; Univ. of N.B., B.Sc. (Engn.) 1946; m. Marion Aileen, d. Harold Milner Steeves; one s., Roger Stief; VICE PRES., PLANNING, THE NEW BRUNSWICK TELEPHONE CO. LTD., since 1970; joined present Co. as Engn. Asst. 1946; Chief Engr. 1958; Gen. Staff Engr. 1962; Vice Pres. Operations 1966; Saint John Bd. Trade (Pres. 1969-70); Engn. Inst. Can.; Assn. Prof. Engrs. N.B.; Past Pres. Can. Standards. Assoc.; Mem and Past Pres. Atlantic Prov. Chamber of Commerce; Dir. Ganong Bros Ltd., N.B. Coal Ltd.; mem. N.B. Development Inst.; Pres. Bd of Comm. St John Regional Hosp; Protestant; Home: 121 Beach Cres., Saint John, N.B. E2K 2E5; Office: One Brunswick Sq., Saint John, N.B. E2L 4K2

GRAHAM, Gerald Sandford, M.A., Ph.D., D.Litt., LL.D.; professor (retired); historian; b. Sudbury, Ont., 27 Apl. 1903; s. Henry Sandford and Florence Marian G.; e. Queen's Univ., M.A. 1925; Cambridge Univ., Ph.D 1929; m. Winifred Emily, d. late Charles Ware, London, Eng., 1929 (m. dissolved); one s.; 2ndly, Constance Mary, d. late John Greey, Toronto, Ont.; 1950; two d.; one s.; Queen's Travelling Fellowship to Harvard Univ., 1926-27; Sir Geo. Parkin Schol. to Trinity Coll., Cambridge, 1927-29; Rockefeller Fellowship to Germany, 1929-30; Instr. in Hist., Harvard Univ., 1930-36; Asst. Prof. of Hist., and later Prof., Queen's Univ., 1936-46; Guggenheim Fellowship to the U.S. 1941; Rhodes Prof. of Imp. Hist., Univ. London 1949-70; R.C.N.V.R. 1942-45; mem., Inst. for Advanced Study, Princeton, 1952; author of "British Policy in Canada, 1774-91", 1930; "Sea Power and British North America, 1783-1820", 1941; "Empire of the North Atlantic", 2nd ed. 1958; "Canada: A Short History", 1950; "The Walker Expedition to Quebec, 1711" (Champlain Soc.) 1953; "The Navy and South America 1807-1823" (with R. A. Humphreys), 1962; "The Politics of Naval Supremacy", 1965; "Great Britain in the Indian Ocean 1810-1850", 1967; "A Concise History of Canada", 1968; "A Concise History of the British Empire" 1970; "Tides of Empire", 1972; contributor to "Newfoundland, Economic, Diplomatic & Strategic Studies", 1946; "The Royal Navy in the War of American Independence" 1976; "The China Station: War and Diplomacy, 1830-60" 1978; various articles on hist. subjects; Kemper K. Knapp Prof., Univ. of Wisconsin, 1962; Visiting Prof., Univ. of Hong Kong, 1966; Visiting Prof. of Strategic Studies, Univ. of Western Ont., 1970-72; Montague Burton Visiting Prof. of Internat. Relations, Univ. of Edinburgh, 1974; Protestant; recreations: travel, walking; Address: Hobbs Cottage, Beckley, Rye, Sussex, Eng.

GRAHAM, Lieut.-Gen. Howard D., O.C. (1967), C.V.O., C.B.E., D.S.O. and Bar, E.D., C.D., Q.C.; Army Offr. (ret.); b. 1898; e. Osgoode Hall, Toronto, Ont., Grad. 1922; read law with Mowat, Maclennan & Co., Toronto; called to Bar of Ont., 1923; cr. K.C. 1933; served in 1st World War, 1916, going Overseas with the 155th Bn., and served in France and Germany as an N.C.O. till the end of the war; Commissioned in the Hastings and Prince Edward Regt. (N.P.A.M.) in 1923, was second-in-command of that unit when it was mobilized in 1939, and took command of it overseas a year later; promoted to the command of the 7th Bgde. of the 3rd Div. in 1942, and in 1943 took Command of the 1st Candn. Inf. Bgde., heading it during the Sicilian and part of the Italian Campaigns; apptd. Deputy Chief of the Gen. Staff in charge of Training, 1944; Sr. Candn. Army Liaison Offr. in London, and Army Advisor to the Candn. High Commr. in London, Eng., 1946-48; successively Vice Chief of the Gen. Staff and O.C., Central Command, Oakville, Ont., 1948-55; Chief of the Gen. Staff, 1 Sept. 1955 — 31 Aug. 1958; after retirement from Candn. Army became Assoc. Counsel, McCarthy & McCarthy, Toronto, Ont.; agreed to undertake, on behalf of the Government, a comprehensive survey of all aspects of Canada's Civil Defence policy and programme; apptd. Commr. (1958) for Royal Visit of 1959; apptd. Pres. and Gen. Mgr., Great Lakes Waterways Devel. Assn., Nov. 1959; Pres., Toronto Stock Exchange 1961-66; apptd. Co-ordinator for Royal Visits 1967, and Candn. Temp. Secy. to H.M. the Queen; el. Hon. Nat. Pres., Boy Scouts of Can., May 1964; Home: 33 Colonial Cr., Oakville, Ont. L6J 4K8

GRAHAM, James Edmund; executive; b. Coboconk, Ont. 24 Dec. 1933; s. Henry Archibald Roy and Etta Isobel (Jackson) G.; e. Lindsay (Ont.) Coll. Inst. Sr. Matric.; m. Lorna Margaret d. late Elmer Christian 8 Nov. 1950; children: Deborah Louise, Catherine, Jeffrey Edmund, Stephanie, Meredith; PRES., CHIEF EXTVE. OFFR. AND DIR., VS SERVICES LTD.; Vice Pres. and Dir. La Societe VS; Dir., Major Foods Limited, N.S.; joined Northern Electric 1952-61; Procter & Gamble 1961-75; Gen. Mgr. Shopsy Foods 1976-78; VS Services Ltd. since 1978; Anglican; recreations: squash, tennis; Home: Oakhill Rd., Mississauga Ont. M1P 3L9; Office: (Box 950) Station U, Toronto, Ont. M8Z 5Y7

GRAHAM, John Finlayson, A.M., Ph.D., F.R.S.C. (1968), university professor; b. Calgary, Alta., 31 May 1924; s. William and Hazel Marie (Lund) G.; e. King Edward High Sch., Vancouver, B.C., 1943; Univ. of B.C., B.A. (Hons. in Econ.) 1947; Columbia Univ., A.M. (Econ.) 1948, Ph.D. (Econ.) 1959; m. Hermioni, d. Theodore Sederis, Halifax, N.S., 30 Apl. 1956; children: Andrew Thomas, James Theodore, Johanna Hermione, Nicholas Lund; PROF. DEPT. OF ECON., DALHOUSIE UNIV., since 1960 (Dept. Chairman, 1960-70); Past Chrmn., Acad. Panel of Can. Council; Gen. Ed., "Atlantic Province Studies," since 1959; past mem., Soc. Science Research Council of Can.; Asst. Prof. of Econ., Dalhousie Univ., 1949-60, Assoc. Prof. 1960; served as Econ. Affairs Offr., Internat. Comn. and Financial Relations Sec., U.N., summers 1949 and 1950; Skelton-Clark Visiting Research Fellow, Queen's Univ., 1963-64; Visiting Prof., Inst. for Higher Studies, Vienna, March 1964; devel. formula for prov.-mun. grants adopted by Govt.

of N.B. on recommendation of Royal Comn. on Finance and Mun. Taxation (Byrne Comn.) 1964; Consultant in educ. finance to Royal Comn. on Educ. and Youth in Nfld., 1967; Chrmn. Nova Scotia Royal Comn. on Educ., Public Services & Prov.-Mun. Relations 1971-74; Pres., Acad. of Humanities and Social Sciences, Royal Soc. of Can., 1977-78; Vice-Chrmn., Bd. of Dir., Art Gallery of Nova Scotia, 1977-78; mem. Adv. Comte. to B.C. Comn. of Inquiry on Property Assessment and Taxation, 1975-76; served with Candn. Army in Arty. and Inf. Corps, 1943-45; attained rank of 2nd-Lt.; author of "Fiscal Adjustment and Economic Development: A Case Study of Nova Scotia," 1963 and numerous articles in learned journs. on intergovt. fiscal relations, econ. devel. and public policy; Past Chrmn., Pub. Accts. Bd. of Prov. of N.S.; mem., Canadian Econ. Assn. (Pres. 1970-71); Candn. Tax Foundation; Candn. Inst. Internat. Affairs (Past Chrmn., Halifax Br.); Home: 6606 South St., Halifax, N.S. B3H 1V2

GRAHAM, John Phelan; executive; b. Toronto, Ontario, 2 April 1928; s. Francis Ronald and Helen Marguerite (Phelan) G.; e. Newman House Sch., Montreal; St. George's Sch., Vancouver, B.C.; Royal Candn. Naval Coll., Royal Roads, B.C., grad. 1947; Univ. of B.C., arts course, 1947-51; m. Mary D., d. John R. Newton, 6 Feb. 1954; children: Boyd, Sally, Vice-President and Director, Graymont Ltd.; President, OCR Concepts Limited; Dir., Dominion Lime Limited; Director, All Canadian Venture Fund; Information Resources Inc.; Journalist, "Daily Mail", London, England, 1952-57; with Greenshields Inc., Montreal, Que., 1958-67; mem. Montreal Museum of Fine Arts; Montreal Soc. of Financial Analysts; recreations: skiing, gardening; Clubs: Montreal Badminton & Squash; London Press; Home: 702 Upper Roslyn, Montreal, Que. H3Y 1H9 H3Z 2P9

GRAHAM, John Webb, E.D., Q.C., B.A. D.S. Litt.; b. Toronto, Ont., 10 Sept. 1912; s. George Wilbur and Rosaline Campbell (Webb) G.; e. Upper Canada Coll., Toronto; Univ. of Toronto; Osgoode Hall Law Sch.; m. Velma Melissa, d. William J. Taylor, 19 June 1941 (deceased 1971); m. Natalia Nikolaevna, d. Nikolaj A. Popov, 15 July 1976; one step-s. Edward Samuel Rogers, one d. Ann Taylor Calderis; PARTNER, CASSELS, BROCK since 1977; Chrmn., Rogers Cablesystems Inc.; Rogers Radio Broad. Ltd.; Rogers Cable TV Ltd.; Travcan Ltd.; Travelers Indemnity Co. of Canada; Travelers Life Insurance Co. of Canada; Rogers Telecommunications Ltd.; TWC Television Ltd.; Pres.; Bridle Park Investments Ltd.; Hendeles Developments Ltd.; Travelers Canada Corp.; Dir.; Charter Oak Fire Insurance Co.; Natomas of Canada Ltd.; Phoenix Insurance Co.; Travelers Corp.; Travelers Indemnity Co. of Am., also of Illinois, of Rhode Isl.; Travelers Insurance Company of Illinois; Travelers Life Insurance Company; Victoria and Grey Trust Co.; Victoria and Grey Trustco Ltd; Premier Communications Ltd.; read law with Peter White, K.C. 1933-36; called to Bar of Ont. 1936; cr. Q.C. 1956; with Toronto General Trusts Corp. as Corporate Trust Offr. 1936-39; Solr., Daly, Thistle, Judson & McTaggart 1946-48; Gen. Counsel, Imperial Life Assurance Co. of Canada 1949-58; Partner, Payton, Biggs & Graham, 1958-77; served with Gov. Gen.'s Body Guard 1930-36, Gov. Gen.'s Horse Guards 1936-39; 2nd World War in Can., U.K., and N.W. Europe with R.C.A.C. 1939-46; retired with rank Maj.; Hon. Lt. Col., Gov. Gen.'s Horse Guards 1970-75; Registrar, Inc. Synod, Diocese Toronto; Chrmn., Extve. Comte., Corp. of Trinity Coll. 1966-69; Pres. (1957-61) St. Paul's P. Conservative Assn.; Vice-Pres. (1966-69) P. Conservative Business Men's Club Toronto; mem. Candn. Bar Assn.; County of York Law Assn.; Assn. Life Ins. Counsel; Candn. Tax Foundation; Bd. Trade Metrop. Toronto; Estate Planning Council Toronto; Sigma Chi (Internat. Pres. 1971-73); Conservative; Anglican; Clubs: Mid Ocean; Tuckers Town (Bermuda); Empire Club of Canada; The Toronto Hunt; The York; Albany; Muskoka Lakes Golf &

Country; The Hartford (Conn.); Royal Canadian Military Institute; Home: 2 Wood Ave., Toronto, Ont. M4N 1P4; Office: 130 Adelaide St W., Suite 2300, Toronto, Ont.

GRAHAM, Kathleen Margaret, B.A., R.C.A.; painter; b. Hamilton, Ont. 13 Sept. 1913; d. Charles and Blanche (Leitch) Howitt; e. Trinity Coll. Univ. of Toronto B.A.; m. Dr. J. Wallace Graham 17 Dec. 1938; children: Dr. John Wallace, Janet Howitt; solo exhns. incl.; Carmen Lamanna Gallery Toronto 1967; Trinity Coll. Univ. of Toronto 1968; Heliconium Club Toronto 1970; York Univ. Founders Coll. Toronto 1970; Pollock Gallery Toronto 1971, 1973, 1975; Art Gallery of Cobourg 1972; City Hall Toronto 1974; David Mirvish Gallery Toronto 1976; Klonaridis Inc. Toronto 1979, 1981; Frans Wynans Gallery Vancouver 1979; Watson Willour Gallery, Houston, Texas 1980; Downstairs Gallery, Edmonton, 1980; Lillian Heidenberg Gallery New York 1981; maj. group exhns. incl. "Canada X Ten" 1974-75, "The Canadian Canvas" 1975, "Changing Visions, The Canadian Landscape" 1976-77 (all toured maj. pub. galleries Can.); "Four Toronto Painters" Washington 1977; "14 Canadians" Hirshhorn Museum Washington 1977; "Certain Traditions" toured Can. and Gt. Brit. 1978-80; Anglican; Home: 26 Boswell Ave., Toronto, Ont. M5R 1M4; Office: Klonaridis Inc., Suite 600, 144 Front St., Toronto, Ontario M5T 1G2.

GRAHAM, Philip H., M.B.A.; executive; b. London, Eng. 30 Jan. 1936; s. Leonard George and Marjorie (Holmes) G.; e. St. Edwards Public Sch., Oxford, Eng.; Royal Air Force Coll. 1958; City of London Coll. M.B.A. 1962; m. Jane, d. George Griffin, 16 May 1969; one d. Deborah-Elizabeth; PRES. AND DIR., OGILVY AND MATHER (CANADA) LTD., since 1975; with Shell International Petroleum, Eng. 1958-65; Trainee, Ogilvy and Mather U.S.A., New York 1965; Sr. Vice Pres., Ogilvy and Mather, Houston, Texas 1972, Mang. Dir., Admsterdam, Holland 1974; served in Royal Air Force 1957-58; mem. Inst. Candn. Advertising; Candn. Chamber of Comm.; Anglican; recreations: tennis, golf, sailing, flying, squash; Office: 80-100 University Ave., Toronto, Ont.

GRAHAM, Robert Grant, B.Com.; b. Ottawa, Ont., 8 April 1931; s. Wilmer A. and Lylian (Wiltsie) G.; e. McGill Univ.; m. Diane K., d. Charles T. Wilson, Town of Mount Royal, Que., 28 May 1953; d. Susan Diane; s. Bruce Wilson; PRESIDENT AND CHIEF EXEC. OFFICER, INTER-CITY GAS LIMITED; Dir., Cdn. Gen. Ins. Co. (Exec. Comm); Moffat Communications Ltd.; Winnipeg Foundation; Winnipeg Jets Hockey Club (Chmn. of the Bd.); Manitoba Theatre Centre (Bd. of Trustees); Federal Industries Ltd.; Guaranty Trust Co. (Exec. Comm.); The Conference Board in Canada; Traders Group Ltd.; Exec. Comte. Great-West Life Assnce. Co.; United Church; Clubs: Manitoba; Winnipeg Squash Racquet; Home: Townhouse 3-277 Wellington Cres., Winnipeg, Man. R3M 0A3; Office: 444 St. Mary Ave., Winnipeg, Man. R3C 3T7

GRAHAM, Robert James, A.M.A.; executive; b. Toronto, Ont. 13 June 1936; s. Gawn and Mary E. (Stephenson) G.; e. Toronto Pub. Sch.; Leaside High Sch., Meisterschaft Coll.; Univ. of Toronto A.M.A.; Harvard Univ. Sr. Financial Mang.; m. Evelyn E. d. W.H. Ferguson, Hudson, Que. 21 Sept. 1963; children: Sean W., Joel T., Toby H.; EXECUTIVE VICE-PRESIDENT, FIRST CITY TRUST CO. since 1978; Dir. First City Mort. Co.; Fid-mor Mortgage Investors Corp. 1981; Pres., Arnham Investment; Seajot Inc.; Mgr. 1967, Vice Pres. Sales 1971, Sr. Vice Pres. 1973, Pres. and Dir. 1976, Candn.-Dom. Leasing Corp.; mem. Bd. Trade Vancouver P. Conservative; Presbyterian; recreations: hunting, reading, antique cars; Clubs: Boulevard; University Club; Canadian; National; Home: 5524 Parthenon Place, West Vancouver, B.C.

GRAHAM, Victor Ernest, M.A., D.Litt., Ph.D., F.R.S.C.; educator; author; musician; b. Calgary, Alta. 31 May 1920; s. William John and Mary Ethel (Wark) G.; e. Univ. of Alta. B.A. 1946; Oxford Univ. (Rhodes Scholar) B.A. 1948, M.A. 1952, D.Litt. 1968; Columbia Univ. (Open Fellowship) Ph.D. 1953; m. Mary Helena d. late Joseph Michael Faunt 1 Aug. 1946; children: Ian Robert, Gordon Keith, Miriam Elizabeth, Ross William; PROF. OF FRENCH, UNIV. COLL. UNIV. OF TORONTO since 1960; Asst. Prof. of French and Eng. Univ. Alta. 1948, Assoc. Prof. of French 1953, Prof. 1958; Assoc. Prof. of French present univ. 1958, Chrmn. Grad. Dept. French 1965-67, Assoc. Dean Sch. of Grad. Studies 1967-69, Vice Princ. Univ. Coll. 1969-70; mem. Gov. Council 1973-76; Can. Council Fellow 1963; Guggenheim Fellow 1970; Connaught Sr. Fellowship in Humanities 1978; Organist & Choirmaster, First Bapt. Ch. Calgary 1948-49, Grace Presb. Ch. Calgary 1950-58, Park Rd. Bapt. Ch. Toronto 1959-61, Yorkminster Park Bapt. Ch. Toronto 1961-62; Organist, First Ch. of Christ Scientist Toronto 1964-74; pub. recitals and concerts Calgary, Edmonton, Ottawa, Toronto, CBC; mem. Extve. Royal Candn. Coll. Organists; editor, Philippe Desportes, 'Cartels et Masquarades, Epitaphes' 1958; 'Les Amours de Diane' I 1959; 'Les Amours de Diane' II 1959; 'Les Amours d'Hippolyte' 1960; 'Les Elégies, 1961; 'Cléonice Dernières Amours' 1962; 'Diverses Amours," 1963; editor, 'Representative French Poetry' 1962, 2nd ed. 1965; 'Sixteenth Century French Poetry' 1964; author 'How to Learn French in Canada' 1965; editor, André Chamson, 'Le Chiffre de nos jours' 1965; author 'The Imagery of Proust' 1966; editor, Pernette du Guillet, 'Rymes' 1968; author 'Bibliographie des études sur Marcel Proust et Son Oeuvre' 1976; co-author 'Le Recueil des Inscriptions 1558' 1972; 'The Paris Entries of Charles IX and Elisabeth of Austria 1571' 1974; "The Royal Tour of France by Charles IX and Catherine de Medici 1564-1566" 1979; numerous articles prof. journs. and newspapers, book reviews; Presbyterian; Home: 100 Glenview Ave., Toronto, Ont. M4R 1P8; Office: Toronto, Ont. M5S 1A1.

GRAHAM, William A.; executive; b. Edmonton, Alta., 2 June 1917; s. Thornton A. and Grace G. (Montgomery) G.; e. Strathcona High Sch. and Alberta Coll., Edmonton; m. Olwyn A., d. Oliver C. Johnston 22 Nov. 1941; one s. Thomas A.; one d. Brenda M. Trendel; PRESIDENT, WESTERN SUPPLIES LTD. since 1960; Pres., Quality Utilities Ltd.; Westlund Industrial Supplies Ltd.; Dir., Edcan Enterprises Ltd.; started with present Co. in 1937 progressing from warehouse through accounting, sales and management; served in R.C.N.V.R. 1941-45, rank Lieut.; rec'd North Atlantic Star; Past Pres., Candn. Inst. of Plumbing & Heating; Anglican; recreations: golf, hunting, sailing; Club: Mayfair Golf & Country (Past Pres.); Home: 7627 Saskatchewan Drive, Edmonton, Alta. T6G 2A6; Office: 14940 — 121A Ave., Edmonton, Alta. T5V 1A3

GRAHAM, William Hugh, B.A.; b. Winnipeg, Man., 18 May 1912; s. Robert Blackwood Whidden and Louisa (Ramwell) G.; e. St. John's Coll. Sch. 1929; Univ. of Manitoba, B.A. 1934; m. Catherine Eleanor Godfrey, 29 March 1940; child: William Hugh; Chrmn., Tarragan Theatre 1974-79; mem. extve. Nat. Theatre School of Can. (Pres. 1971-74); formerly Extve. Vice Pres. and Dir., MacLaren Advertising Co. Ltd.; served in 2nd World War 1940-45; Toronto Scot. 2nd Bn.; Queen's Own Cameron Highlanders of Can.; Staff, 6th Candn. Inf. Bgde.; II Candn. Inf. Div.; II Candn. Corps; author: "The Tiger of Canada West", biog. of Dr. William Dunlop, (Univ. of B.C. Award for Popular Biog.); Home: Belleview Farm, Greenbank, Ont. L0C 1B0

GRAINGER, Jack Kirby, M.A.; newspaper publisher; b. Toronto, Ont., 15 Jan. 1912; s. Alfred Henry and Mildred (Kirby) G.; e. Mount Allison Univ., B.A. 1934, M.A. 1935; m. Jean Martell, d. Stuart J. Macleod, Moncton, N.B., 1

Sept. 1939; children: Peter, Nancy; PRESIDENT AND MANG. DIR., MONCTON PUBLISHING CO. LTD. (Estbd. 1877; publishers of "Moncton Daily Times" and "Moncton Transcript"); mem. of Advisory Bd., Eastern Trust Co.; Dir., Moncton Community Chest; Reporter with "Moncton Transcript", 1930; Advertising Mgr., 1936; Gen. Mgr., 1938; Publisher, 1940; Vice-Pres., Moncton Publishing Co. Ltd., 1945 and Pres. and Mang. Dir., 1951; mem., 8th Reserve Field Batty., R.C.A.; mem., The Candn. Press; Candn. Daily Newspaper Publishers Assn.; United Church; recreations: golf, curling, swimming; Clubs: Moncton Golf; Beaver Curling; Moncton Curling; Moncton City; Home: 150 Bonaccord St., Moncton, N.B. E1C 5L6; Office: Main St., Moncton, N.B.

GRANATSTEIN, Jack Lawrence, M.A., Ph.D.; educator; b. Toronto, Ont. 21 May 1939; s. Benjamin and Shirley (Geller) G.; e. Coll. Militaire Royal de St-Jean 1959; Royal Mil. Coll. Kingston B.A. 1961; Univ. of Toronto M.A. 1962; Duke Univ. Ph.D. 1966; m. Elaine d. Percy Hitchcock 29 Nov. 1961; children: Carole, Michael; PROF. OF HIST., YORK UNIV. 1966-; Historian, Directorate of Hist. Nat. Defence HQ Ottawa 1964-66; Ed. "Canadian Historical Review" 1981-; author "The Politics of Survival" 1967; "Canada's War" 1975; "Ties that Bind" 1975; "Broken Promises: A History of Conscription in Canada" 1977; "American Dollars-Canadian Prosperity" 1978; "A Man of Influence" 1981; various articles pol. hist., defence and foreign policy in scholarly and popular journs.; served with Candn. Army 1956-66; mem. Candn. Hist. Assn.; Candn. Inst. Internat. Affairs; Home: 53 Marlborough Ave., Toronto, Ont. M5R 1X5; Office: 4700 Keele St., Downsview, Ont. M3J 1P3.

GRANDE, George Kinnear, B.A.; businessman; b. Montreal, Que., 21 Aug. 1919; s. Albert Edward and Marion Harriet (Kinnear) G.; e. Guy Drummond Sch. (1925-32) and Strathcona Acad. (1932-36), Outremont, Que.; McGill Univ., B.A. 1940; Osgoode Hall Sch., 1940-41; m. Margaret Sutherland Yule, d. late Robert Yule Pagan, 14 Feb. 1947; children: Robert, Susan, John, Donald; m. Diane Dekens, 13 Sept. 1975; served with War Assets Corps., 1945-46; joined Department of External Affairs 1946; served in Dipl. Div., Consular Div. and Under Secy's Office, 1946-47; Secy. to Candn. Del. to U.N. Atomic Energy Comn. and of Perm. Del. of Can. to U.N.; 1947-50; served on Candn. Dels. to U.N. Gen. Assembly 1947, 1948 (Paris) and 1949; served in U.N. and Legal Divs., Ottawa, 1950-52; 1st Secy. and Chargé d'Affaires, Athens, 1952-54; served in Far E. Div., Defence Liaison Div. and as Depy. Head of Consular Div., Ottawa, 1954-57; Depy. Head and Consul, Candn. Mil. Mission, W. Berlin, 1957-60; Depy. Head, Defence Liaison (2) Div. and later Head, then served as Head, Inspection Service, Ottawa, 1960-64; High Commr. to Ceylon 1964-66; External Affairs mem.; Directing Staff, Nat. Defence Coll., Kingston, Ont., 1966-68; Ambassador to Norway and Iceland 1968-72; Head Candn. Del. and Ambassador, Mutual and Balanced Force Reduction Talks, Vienna 1972-76; Ambassador to S. Africa, and concurrently High Commr. in Botswana, Lesotho and Swaziland, 1976-79; Appointed Assistant to Pres., Later Chemicals Ltd., 1979; Appointed Vice Pres. International Operations 1980; appointed Dir. Haagsche Smederij, The Hague, 1980; joined RCAF 1941; comnd. Pilot Offr. 1942; served in U.K., India and Ceylon; discharged as Flight Lt. 1945; mem., McGill Univ. Grads.' Soc.; Delta Sigma Phi; United Church; recreations: golf, international affairs; Address: Haagsche Smederij en Constructiewerk plaatsen B.V., 2501-CZ Den Haag, Nikkelwerf 11-13, The Netherlands.

GRANDY, James Frederick, B.A., B.Phil.; business advisor; b. Ft. William, Ont., 24 Nov. 1919; s. Clarence Wood and Anne (Adams) G.; e. Univ. of Western Ont. (Econ. & Pol. Science), B.A. 1941; Oxford Univ. (Econ.), B.Phil. 1948; m. Alexandra, d. late Norman Shaw, 18 Aug. 1945;

children: David, John, Kathleen; PRES., REISMAN & GRANDY LTD.; Chrmn. of the Board, Cdn. Marconi Co.; Dir., Brascan Ltd.; Monsanto Can. Inc.; Trustee, Royal Ottawa Hospital; joined Dept. of External Affairs, Sept. 1948; trans. to Dept. of Finance 1957; Asst. Secy. to the Cabinet, Privy Council Office, 1963-64; Asst. Depy. Min. of Finance, 1964-67; Deputy minister Consumer and Corporate Affairs Dec. 1967 — Sept. 1971; Depy. Min., Dept. of Industry, Trade and Comm. 1971-1975; attended various internat. conferences and meetings of General Agreement on Tariffs and Trade; served in 2nd World War with rank of Maj., R.C.A., 1941-46; United Church; Home: 920 Muskoka Ave., Ottawa, Ont. K2A 3H9; Office: Suite 401, 275 Slater St., Ottawa, Ont. K1P 5H9

GRANGE, Hon. Samuel George McDougall; judge; b. London, Ont. 19 March 1920; s. Edward Wilkinson and Marion Osborne (McDougall) G.; e. Univ. of Toronto 1937-39; Osgoode Hall 1946-48; children: Alice Alexandra, Robert Morris McDougall; JUDGE, SUPREME COURT OF ONT. since Dec. 1974; read law with T. H. Wickett, Q.C. and A. C. Heighington, Q.C.; called to the Bar of Ont. 1948; cr. Q.C. 1963; practised law with Heighington, Symons & Grange 1948-61; McMillan, Binch 1961-74; Chrmn., Min. Comte. on Franchising 1969-70; Chrmn., Min. Comte. on Hosp. Privileges 1970-71; Chrmn. Inq. into Legal Aid Clinical Funding, 1978; Commissioner, Mississauga Railway Accident Inq. 1980; served in 4th Candn. Field Regt. R.C.A. 1940-45, rec'd. Croix de Guerre avec Etoile de Vermeille, France 1944; Bencher, Law Soc. of Upper Can. 1971-75 (Vice Chrmn., Legal Educ. Comte. 1973-75); Clubs: UniVersity; Lawyers (Pres. 1967); Home: 24 College View Ave., Toronto, Ont. M5P 1J4; Office: Osgoode Hall, Toronto, Ont. M5H 2N5

GRANT, Alexander Marshall, C.B.E. (1965); ballet director, dancer; b. Wellington, New Zealand, 22 Feb. 1925; s. Alexander Gibb and Eleather May (Marshall) G.; e. Wellington (N.Z.) Coll.; Royal Ballet Sch., London, Eng., joined Royal Ballet, London, Eng. 1946; Dir. Ballet for All, Eng. since 1970; ARTISTIC DIR. NATIONAL BALLET OF CANADA as of July 1976; Anglican; recreation: country matters; Office: 157 King St. E., Toronto, Ont. M5C 1G9

GRANT, Carl T., Q.C.; b. Ottawa, Ont. 20 June 1933; s. Archibald Joseph and Patricia (Cormier) G.; e. Lisgar Coll. Inst., 1951; Carleton Coll., B.A. 1955; Osgoode Hall Law Sch., 1959; m. Estelle Jacqueline, d. A. deWilde, Hoogstraten, Belgium, 1 June 1957; children: Michèle, Gregory, Nadine; PARTNER, AIRD & BERLIS; President & Dir. no. of real estate devel. and invest. co.'s; called to Bar of Ont. 1959; cr. Q.C. 1971; has practised law in Toronto since 1959; Lectr., Osgoode Hall Law Sch.; legal editor, "Business and Securities Valuations" 1972; also several articles on business valuation; legal; Founding Dir. and Secy., Candn. Liver Foundation; Dir.; Candn. Assn. Business Valuators; mem. Law Soc. Upper Can.; Delta Chi; Liberal; Anglican; recreations: tennis, skiing; Home: 109 Dawlish Ave., Toronto, Ont. M4N 1H4; Office: 145 King St. W., Toronto, Ont. M5H 2J3

GRANT, Rev. Daniel Murdoch, B.A., D.D. (Un. Ch.); minister (ret.) b. Boularderie, N.S., 5 Jan. 1900; s. Duncan and Elizabeth (Corbett) G.; e. Dalhousie Univ., B.A. 1923; Pine Hill Divinity Hall, Halifax, L.Th. 1925, D.D. 1956; New Coll., Edinburgh, 1928-29; m. Jean, d. James H. Stewart, Antigonish, N.S., 22 June 1932; children: James Daniel, Hugh David; recreations: curling, gardening, walking; Home: 225 Olivier Ave., Apt. 105, Westmount, Montreal, P.Q. H3Z 2CM

GRANT, Donald Gordon, LL.B.; lawyer; b. Bridgeville, N.S., 7 Feb. 1909; s. John Albert and Margaret (Holmes) G.; e. Dalhousie Univ., B.A. 1930, LL.B. 1932; m. Edith, d. F. G. G. Cottle, 21 Sept. 1934; children: Elizabeth, John, Heather; mem., Royal Comn. on Taxation (1962);

Dir., Pictou County Bus Services Ltd.; Maritime Steel & Foundries Ltd.; Past Pres., Bd. of Mang., The Children's Hosp.; read law with Hon. Mr. Justice Doull; called to Bar of N.S.; practised law in Halifax 1932-37; Mgr., Sydney Br. of The Nova Scotia Trust Co. 1937-42; Mgr., Halifax office 1945-47; Vice Pres., Gen. Mgr. and Dir. 1947-66, Pres. 1966-71; served in World War 1942-45 with Candn. Army; held rank of Maj., Judge Advocate Gen. Br.; Prov. Chrmn., Candn. Red Cross Campaign 1947-48; Pres., Trust Co's Assn. of Can., 1956-57; Past Pres., North Brit. Soc. of Halifax; mem., N.S. Bar Soc.; Candn. Bar Assn; United Church; recreations: golf, curling, farming; Clubs: Halifax; Halifax Golf & Country; Commercial; Rotary; Home: 384 Purcells Cove, Halifax, N.S. B3P 2E6

GRANT, James Anderson; mining executive; b. Richmond Hill, Ont., 11 Feb. 1902; s. late Rev. James Anderson and Jessie (Mackay) G.; e. Upper Can. Coll., Toronto, 1918-22; m. Isabel Sutherland Langmuir, 1928; children: Gordon Mackay, Janet Elizabeth Love; HON. CHRMN. AND DIR., TOMBILL MINES LTD.; has been actively interested in mining exploration since 1933 and holds Ont. complimentary miner's lic. (40 yrs.); service incls. Vice Pres. and Dir., Gulch Resources Ltd.; Francana Minerals Ltd.; Manitoba Chromium Ltd.; Hudson Yukon Mining Co. Ltd. Dir., Anglo-American Corp. of Canada Ltd.; Craskie Mines Ltd.; served in mfg. industry for 12 yrs.; became assoc. with financial firm Aird & McLeod, 1933 and Playfair & Co., 1934 (apptd. Partner in latter firm 1955); Vice Pres. until 1966; served with RCAF 1940-44; rank Sqdn. Leader; Hon. Vice Pres., Upper Can. Coll. Old Boys' Assn. (Pres. and mem. Bd. of Govs. 1939-40); Presbyterian; mem. Bd. Trade Metrop. Toronto; Clubs: Toronto Hunt; Home: Grantwood, Shanty Bay, Ont. L0L 2L0; Office: P.O. Box 28, Toronto-Dominion Centre, Toronto, Ont. M5K 1B8

GRANT, John, B.A. Ph.D.; investment dealer; b. Thunder Bay, Ont. 23 May 1938; s. Norman Stewart and Margaret Glenn (Stevenson) G.; e. Kapuskasing (Ont.) High Sch. 1955; Univ. of Toronto B.A. 1959; Univ. of London (London Sch. of Econ.) Ph.D. 1964; m. Judith Ann, d. Sydney R. Skelton 28 Sept. 1963; children: Adam, Hamish; DIR. AND CHIEF ECON. WOOD GUNDY LTD. since 1973; began as Lectr. Monetary Econ., London Sch. of Econ. 1960; Asst. Prof. of Econ., Univ. of Toronto 1964; mem. Toronto Soc. Financial Analysts; Home: 17 Admiral Rd., Toronto, Ont. M5R 2L4; Office: Royal Trust Tower, Toronto-Dominion Centre, Toronto, Ont. M5K 1M7

GRANT, John Sutton, B. Com., F.C.A.; b. London, Ont., 13 July 1916; e. Univ. Toronto, B.Com. 1937; Inst. of Chart. Accts. of Ont., C.A. 1942, F.C.A. 1956; Order of C.A.'s Que., 1958; m. Merrill Claire, d. William Jardine, Toronto, Ont., 8 Sept. 1950; children: Georgina Kathleen, John William Jardine; Retired PARTNER (1979), PEAT, MARWICK, MITCHELL AND CO.; Anglican; Clubs: St. James's; London Hunt; Royal Montreal Golf; Home: 1001 Hunt Club Mews, London Ont. N6H 4R7

GRANT, Rev. John Webster, M.A. D.Phil., D.D. (Un. Ch.); university professor; b. Truro, N.S., 27 June 1919; s. late Rev. William P. and Margaret Dorothy (Waddell) G.; e. Dalhousie Univ., B.A. (Eric Dennis Scholarship in Pol. Science) 1938 and M.A. 1941; Rhodes Scholar from N.S., 1941; Princeton Univ. (Grad. Sch., Dept. of Politics) 1938-39; Pine Hill Divinity Hall, Halifax, N.S., Cert. in Theol. (Travelling Scholarship) 1943; Oxford Univ., D.Phil. 1948; m. Gwendolen Margaret, d. late John s. Irwin, 3 June 1944; Professor of Church History, Emmanuel College, University of Toronto, since 1963; Pres., Pacific Coast Theol. Conf., 1951-52; o. 1943; Minister, West Bay, N.S., 1943; Director of Religious Information to non-R.C. Churches, Wartime Information Bd. 1943-45; Lectr. in Systematic Theol. Pine Hill Divinity Hall, N.S., 1945-46; Woodward Foundation Prof. of Ch. Hist., Union Coll. of B.C., 1949-59; Editor-in-Chief, The Ryerson Press, 1959-

63; Editor, "Dalhousie Gazette", 1941-42 and "Canadian Churches and the War", 1943-45; managing editor SR. 1972-77; Publications: "Free Churchmanship in England, 1870-1940", 1955; "God Speaks XXX We Answer", 1965; "The Canadian Experience of Church Union", 1967; Ed. "Salvation! O the Joyful Sound: the Selected Writing of John Carroll", 1967; Ed. "Die Unierten Kirchen", 1973; author "God's People in India" 1959; "George Pidgeon: a Biography" 1962, "The Church in the Canadian Era" 1972; served in 2nd World War as Chaplain with R.C.N.; Office: Emmanuel College, Toronto, Ont.M5S 1K7

GRANT, Jon K., executive; b. Toronto, Ont., 25 Apl. 1935; s. John King and Rita May (Loney) G.; e. Humberside Coll. Inst. Toronto 1954; Univ. of W. Ont. Sch. of Business Adm. 1959; m. Shelagh Dawn d. late Donald I. Adams, 10 June 1960; children: Susan Whitney, Deborah Lynne, David Adams; PRESIDENT, DIR. AND CEO, QUAKER OATS OF CANADA LTD. since 1976; Vice-Pres., Quaker Oats Co., Chicago; Dir.; Hiram Walker Resources Ltd.; Gov. Trent Univ.; Trustee St. Joseph's Hosp. Peterborough; Director Grocery Products Mfrs. Can.; Zeta Psi; Protestant; recreations: skiing, sailing, tennis; Clubs: Granite (Toronto), Toronto; Peterborough; Home: 581 Weller St., Peterborough, Ont. K9H 2N9; Office: Quaker Park, Peterborough, Ont.

GRANT, Marion Elder, M.A., D.Paed., LL.D., D.C.L.; psychologist; educator; b. Quebec, Que., 16 March, 1900; d. Donald and Alice (Fitch) G.; e. Wolfville (N.S.) Elem. and High Schs., 1916; Acadia Ladies Semy., 1917; Acadia Univ., B.A. 1921, D.C.L. 1964; Univ. of Toronto, M.A. 1924, D.Paed. 1931; Univ. Coll., Univ. of London, post-doctoral study 1931-32; Harvard Univ., Univ. of Cal. (Berkeley) and Univ. of Chicago summer courses; Univ. of N.B., LL.D. 1950; taught Branksome Hall, Toronto, 1922-26; Assoc. Prof. of Educ., Baylor Coll. for Women, Belton Texas (later Mary-Hardin-Baylor Univ.), 1926-31; Dean of Women and Prof. 1932-36; Asst. Prof. of Educ. (later Psychol.) and Dean of Women, Acadia Univ., Wolfville, N.S., 1936-60; Prof. and Head, Dept. of Psychol., 1960-63; part-time Psychol., Fundy Mental Health Centre, Wolfville, 1955-75 (retired); rec'd centennial Medal 1967; mem. Candn. Commonwealth Scholarship & Fellowship Comte. for 6 yrs.; Del., Commonwealth Educ. Conf., New Delhi 1962, Ottawa 1964; Pres., Candn. Fed. Univ. Women, 1949-52; Bd. of Gov., Acadia Univ., 1976-82; Hon. Fellow, Candn. Psychol. Assn.; mem. Am. Psychol. Assn.; IODE; P. Conservative; Baptist; recreations: travel, swimming, yoga, music; Club: University Women's; Home: 9 Prospect St., Wolfville, N.S. B0P 1X0

GRANT, William Frederick, M.A., Ph.D., F.L.S. (1962); university professor; b. Hamilton, Ont., 20 Oct. 1924; s. William Aitken and Myrtle Irene (Taylor) G.; e. McMaster Univ., B.A. (Science) 1947, M.A. (Botany) 1949; Univ. of Virginia, Ph.D. (Biol.) 1953; m. Phyllis Kemp, d. William John Harshaw, 23 July 1949; one s., William Taylor; PROF. OF GENETICS, McGILL UNIV., since 1967; Blandy Research Fellow. Univ. of Virginia, 1949-53 (awarded Andrew Ellgen Prize, 1953); Botanist to Dept. of Agric., Kuala Lumpur, Malaya, 1953-55 under tech. co-op. prog. of Colombo Plan; Asst. Prof. Genetics, McGill Univ., 1955-61, Assoc. Prof. 1961-66; appointed Hon. mem. of Morgan Aboretum and Woodlot Devel. Assn. of Macdonald Coll. of McGill Univ., 1960; Specialist in plants of genus "Lotus"; mem., Am. Genetic Assn.; Am. Soc. Plant Taxonomists; Genetics Soc. Can. (Pres. 1974-75, Life member, 1979); Am. Inst. Biol. Science; Crop Science Soc. of Am.; Environmental Mutagen Soc.; Phytochem. Soc. of N. Am.; Bot. Soc. Am.; Genetic Soc. Am.; Internat. Assn. Plant Taxonomists; Am. Soc. Cell Biol.; Candn. Bot. Assn.; Candn. Soc. Cell Biol.; Pres., Internat. Organ. Plant Biosystematics, 1981-; Internat. Comte. on Chemotaxonomy; Treas., Biol. Council Can. 1974-78; Fellow, Am. Assn. Advanc. Science; Linnean Soc. London; Consultant to UN Environmental Program;

Rec'd. Silver Jubilee medal; Sigma Xi (Pres., McGill Chapter 1975-76); Soc. Study Evolution (Vice-Pres. 1972); Editor, Candn. Journ. of Genetics and Cytology since 1974 and Lotus Newsletter since 1970; Home: 43 St. Andrews Rd., Baie d'Urfe, Que. H9X 2T9; Office: Genetics Lab., Box 282 Macdonald Campus, McGill Univ., Ste. Anne de Bellevue, Que. H9X 1C0

GRANT, William Neil, B.Ed.; food manufacturer; b. New Westminster, B.C. 13 July 1942; s. William Albert and Dorothy Patricia (Neilson) G.; e. Como Lake High Sch. 1960; Univ. of B.C.B.Ed.; m. Sue J. two s. W. Douglas, R. Brian, one d. Cheryl Ann; President, C.E.O. Vitality Products Ltd., and Chmn., C.E.O., Guardian Knight Financial Corp.; Sales Rep. and Dist. Field Asst. Procter & Gamble 1967-69; joined Standard Brands 1970, Gen. Mgr. Hygrade Packers 1971, Regional Sales Mgr. B.C. 1972, Div. Mgr. 1972, Vice Pres. and Gen. Mgr. Consumer Products Div. 1975, Pres. Food Service Div. 1976; Pres., C.E.O., Nabob Foods Ltd., 1976-78; mem., Young President's Org.; Executive Cmte., B.C., Div. Candn. Mfrs. Assn.; Delta Kappa Epsilon; Protestant; recreations: golf, skiing, photography; Clubs: M.A.A.A.; Vancouver Golf; Summerlass Golf & Country; Terminal City; Westminster; Home: 730 Dansey Ave., Coquitlam, B.C. V3K 3G5; Office: 8036 Enterprise St., Burnaby, B.C. V5A 1V7.

GRAPKO, Michael Frederic, M.A., Ph.D.; educator; b. Stuartburn, Man. 4 Feb. 1921; s. Gregory and Helen (Morell) G.; e. St. Paul's Coll. Winnipeg; United Coll. Winnipeg, Univ. of Man. B.A. 1944; Univ. of Toronto M.A. 1948, Ph.D. 1953; m. Tillie d. late Nicholas Stefanik 18 Sept. 1948; two d. Deborah Anne, Janice Ellen; PROF. OF EDUC. ADM. FACULTY OF EDUC. & INST. OF CHILD STUDY, UNIV. OF TORONTO 1980- ; Asst. Prof. of Psychol. and Inst. of Child Study present Univ. 1960-64, Assoc. Prof. 1964-71, Prof. and Dir. 1971-80; Co-ordinator of Educ. Services Thistletown Regional Centre 1964-71; Psychol. Consultant, Kenora Bd. Educ. 1965-72, Grey Co. Bd. Educ. 1968- ; Faculty Rep. Governing Council Univ. Toronto 1971-75, mem. Planning & Resources Sub-comte. 1979-80; Chrmn. Faculty Assn. 1967-69; Candn. Rep. to White House Conf. 1971; Dir. Internat. Fed. Parent Educ. 1967-82; Dir. Toronto YMCA; recipient grants Ont. Mental Health Foundation and Ministry of Educ. Ont. 1962-79; author numerous publs., papers, addresses; mem. Ont. Psychol. Assn. (Dir. and Secy. Treas. 1978-80); Candn. Psychol. Assn.; Am. Psychol. Assn.; Soc. Research Child Devel.; served with RCNVR 1944-45; R. Catholic; Home: 2045 Lakeshore Blvd. W., Toronto, Ont. M8V 2Z6; Office: 45 Walmer Rd., Toronto, Ont. M5R 2X2.

GRATON, Yves, B.A., B.Com.; company president; b. Montreal, Que., 31 Dec. 1932; s. Doris and Hélène (Quesnel) G.; e. Coll. Sainte-Marie, Montréal, B.A. 1953; Ecole des Hautes Etudes Comm., Univ. de Montréal, B.Com. 1955; Univ. of Pittsburgh, Master's Degree in Retailing 1956; m. Micheline, d. Lucien Lalonde, 6 Sept. 1958; children: Marie-Josée, Julie, Pierre-Yves, Véronique, Isabelle; CHIEF EXECUTIVE OFFICER, DELTA DES GOUVERNEURS INC. 1981- ; Vice Dir. Société Générale de Financement du Québec; Artopex Inc.; Gax Intercité de Quebec Inc.; mem. Quebec Chapter, Young Presidents' Organ. Inc.; Chambre de Comm. R. Catholic; recreation: golf; Clubs: St. Denis; Vallée du Richelieu-Ste Julie; Home: 1815 Montpellier, St-Bruno, Qué. J3V 4P4; Office: 3050 Laurier Blvd., Sainte-Foy, Que. G1V 3Z4

GRATTON, Robert, LL.L., LL.M., M.B.A.; financial executive; b. Montreal, Que. 1943; e. Univ. de Montréal LL.L.; London Sch. of Econ. & Pol. Science LL.M.; Harvard Business Sch. M.B.A.; PRESIDENT, CHIEF EXTVE. OFFR. AND DIR., CREDIT FONCIER 1979- ; Dir. Allstate Insurance Co. of Canada; Montreal City & District Savings Bank; Francana Oil & Gas Ltd.; called to Bar of Que.

1967; Asst. to Hon. Paul Gérin-Lajoie, Quebec City 2 yrs.; joined Credit Foncier 1971, Co-Gen. Mgr. 1975, Extve. Vice Pres. 1976, Dir. 1977; Dir. Soc. Générale de financement; Candn. Inst. Internat. Affairs; Clubs: Mount Royal; St-James's; St-Denis; Home: 105 Maplewood Ave., Outremont, Qué. H2V 2M2; Office: 612 rue St-Jacques, Montréal, Qué. H3C 1E1.

GRATWICK, John, B.Sc.; transportation executive; b. Langley, Eng., 2 March 1923; s. Ernest Frank and Doris Hilda (Shepherd) G.; e. St. Clement Danes Grammar Sch., London, Eng., 1941; King's Coll., Univ. of London, B.Sc. 1948; Northwestern Univ., ATMP 1968; m. Gwendoline S., d. Percy Johnston, 23 Mar. 1957; one s. Adrian; VICE-PRES., EXECUTIVE, Cndn. Nat. 1981 VICE-PRES., CORPORATE AFFAIRS CANADIAN NATIONAL 1980; served with RAF Tech. Sigs. (Radar) Br. 1942-46; Scient. Offr., Brit. Colonial Office, Gambia, 1948-50; Exper. Offr. and subsequently Sr. Scient. Offr., UK Dept. of Scient. Adv. to Air Ministry, 1950-57; Depy. Dir. of Mang. Engn. RCAF 1957-60; joined CNR as Sr. Operational Research Analyst, Research & Devel., 1960-63; Sr. Tech. Adv. to Head Express Services 1963-70; Co-Chrmn., Ministry of Transport Task Force on Objectives and Structure for fed. transport., 1969; Chrmn., Transport. Devel. Agency, Montreal (Fed. Govt.) 1970-72; Vice-Pres., Research and Devel., CN, 1972-76; Pres. and CEO, CN Marine, 1976-79 Vice Pres. Corporate Policy and Development 1979; Dir., Candn. Organ. for Simplification Trade Procedures (Chrmn. 1971-77); Candn. Inst. Guided Ground Transport, Queen's Univ. (Dir. 1970-72; Chrmn. 1972-74; Dir. 1974-76); Dir., CNM Inc.; Dir. C.N. Marine Inc.; Dir. Halifax Industries Ltd.; mem., Royal Stat. Soc. (Cert. 1954); Candn. Operational Research Soc. (Nat. Pres. 1969-70); Operations Research Soc. Am.; Candn. Transport. Research Forum (Pres. 1971-72); Sigma Xi; recreations: puppetry, food, theatre; Club: University; Home: 7400 de Roquancourt, Montreal, Que. H3R 3C9; Office: P.O. Box 8100, Montreal, Que. H3C 3N4

GRATZER, George A., Ph.D.; educator; b. Hungary 2 Aug. 1936; s. Jozsef and Maria (Herzog) G.; e. L. Eötvös Univ. Budapest Bachelor's Degree 1959, Master's Degree 1960; Hungarian Acad. of Sciences Ph.D. 1960; m. Catherine Zahony 25 Jan. 1961; children: Thomas, David; PROF. OF MATH. UNIV. OF MAN. since 1967; Postdoctoral Fellow, Queen's Univ. 1961; Visiting Asst. Prof., Assoc. Prof. and Prof., Pa. State Univ. 1963-67; rec'd Steacie Prize in Natural Sciences 1971; Zubek Mem. Award for Excellence in Research and Scholarship 1974; author "Universal Algebra" 1968; "Lattice Theory: First Concepts and Distributive Lattices" 1971; "General Lattice Theory" 1978 (rev. and expanded ed., Russian, 1981); "Universal Algebra", 2nd Ed., 1979; "Super BASIC for the TRS-80," 1981; over 150 papers on algebra, especially universal and lattice theory; mem. Royal Soc. Can.; Am. Math. Soc.; Candn. Math. Soc.; recreations: skiing, cottage; Home: 75 Laval Dr., Winnipeg, Man. R3T 2X8; Office: Winnipeg, Man. R3T 2N2.

GRAUER, Sherry, B.F.A., R.C.A.; artist; b. Toronto, Ont. 20 Feb. 1939; d. Albert Edward and Shirley (Woodward) Grauer; e. York House Sch. Vancouver 1955; Wellesley (Mass.) Coll. 3 yrs., 3rd yr. as exchange student Ecole du Louvre, Ecole de Science Politique, Paris; Atelier Ziegler Paris 1958-59; San Francisco Art Inst. B.F.A. 1964; m. John Keith-King 12 Feb 1971; children: Callum, Jonathan, Max; solo exhns. incl. Mary Frazee Gallery West Vancouver 1964; Bau-Xi Gallery 1965, 1967, 1968, 1970, 1975, 1976, 1978; Loyola Bonsecours Centre Montreal 1968; Jerrold Morris Gallery Toronto 1969; Véhicule Art Inc. Montreal 1973; Surrey (B.C.) Art Gallery (retrospective) 1980; rep. in various group exhns. since 1964 incl. The Candn. Group of Painters Travelling Exhn. 1965-68; Montreal Museum of Fine Arts and Candn. Pavilion Expo '67 1967; Nine out of Ten Hamilton Art Gallery 1973; Nat. Gallery Can. Some Candn. Women Artists

1975; B.C. Prov. Coll. Travelling Exhn. Europe 1978-79; comns. incl. World Wide Internat. Travel Office Vancouver wall mural 1969; Univ. of B.C. sculpture "Swimmers" 1972; Centennial Hotel Lounge Vancouver sculpture "Football Star" 1973; Dept. Pub. Works Ottawa for Fed. Bldg. Powell River, B.C. ceiling sculpture 1976; Habitat Banners for Burrard Bridge Vancouver 1976; Candn. Training Inst. Cornwall sculpture "Brave Birdmen" 1978-80; rep. in various pub. and private colls. incl. Can. Council Art Bank, Musée d'Art Contemporain Montreal, Nat. Gallery Can.; cited numerous articles, reviews; Dir. Freen Screen Co. Ltd.; Arts & Sciences Centre Vancouver; Trustee Vancouver Art Gallery 1974-76 (Hon. Secy. 1975-76); mem. Candn. Conf. Arts; recreations: sailing, reading, work; Clubs: Royal Vancouver Yacht; Arbutus; Home: 4794 Belmont Ave., Vancouver, B.C. V6T 1A9; Office: 3F, 1206 Homer St., Vancouver V6B 2Y5.

GRAVES, Mervyn Gilmore, F.C.A.; b. Calgary, Alta., 24 Jan. 1907; s. Arthur G. and Harriet (Gilmore) G.; e. High Sch. and Business Coll., Calgary; C.A. 1931; m. Dorothy, d. Charles Westley, 3 Sept. 1938; children: Donald, Robert, Linda; C.A., Clarkson, Gordon & Co.; Chrmn., Alta. Children's Hosp., 1952-69; Dir., F. R. Reeves Foundation; mem., Candn. Inst. C.A.'s (Pres. 1968-69); Inst. C.A.'s Alta. (Pres. 1941); Shriner; Anglican; recreations: gardening, curling; Clubs: Ranchmen's; Glencoe; Petroleum; Home: 1028 Hillcrest Ave., Calgary, Alta. T2T 0Z2

GRAY, Gordon C., B.Com., F.C.A.; real estate broker; b. Copper Cliff, Ont., 24 Oct. 1927; s. Robin and Corinne (Muir) G.; e. Pub. and High Schs., Copper Cliff, Ont.; Queen's Univ., B.Com.; m. Patricia d. R. G. Godson; children: Donald, David, Diane, Douglas, Deborah; CHMN. AND C.E.O. AND DIR., A.E. LePAGE LTD., since 1978; Dir. and mem. Extve. Comte., Markborough Properties Ltd.; Dir. and mem. Extve. Comte., Rio Algom Ltd.; Dir. Canadian Gypsum Co. Ltd.; Hiram Walker Resources Ltd., Crown Life Ins. Co.; Toronto-Dominion Bank; Rogers Cablesystems Inc.; McDonald's Restaurants of Canada Ltd.; ROYAL INSURANCE CANADA; Consumers' Gas Co. Ltd.; Hospital for Sick Children; Queen's Univ., Art Gallery of Ontario Found.; with Price, Waterhouse & Co., 1950-55; Controller, A. E. LePage Ltd., 1955-57; Vice-Pres. and Dir., 1957-68; Extve. Vice-Pres. 1968-69; Pres., 1970-78; Chmn. and C.E.O., 1978; mem. Inst. C.As. Ont.; Roman Catholic; recreations: golf, fishing, boating; Clubs: Toronto Golf; Toronto; Rosedale Golf & Country; York, Granite; Lambton Golf; Lost Tree (Palm Beach, Fla); Muirfield (Ohio); Home: Drynoch Farms, Jefferson Side Rd., R.R. No. 1, Richmond Hill, Ont. L4C 4X7; Office: P.O. Box 100, Toronto Dominion Centre, Toronto, Ont. M5K 1G8

GRAY, Hon. Herbert Eser, P.C., Q.C., M.P.; b. Windsor, Ont., 25 May 1931; s. Harry and Fannie G.; e. Victoria Sch. and Kennedy Coll. Inst., Windsor; McGill Univ., Grad. Sch. of Comm.; Osgoode Hall Law Sch., Toronto; m. Sharon, d. S. Sholzberg, Ville St. Laurent, Que. 23 July 1967; children: Jonathan, Elizabeth; el. to H. of C. for Windsor W. in g.e. 1962; re-el. since; MINISTER OF INDUSTRY. TRADE AND COMMERCE 1980- ; served as Parlty. Secy. to Min. of Finance, 1968-69; named Min. Without Portfolio 1969; Min. of National Revenue 1970-72, Min. of Consumer & Corporate Affairs 1972-74; Appointed Critic on Finance, Chmn., Comm. on Fiscal and Monetary Affairs for Official Opposition, 1979; Chairman, House of Commons Standing Committee on Finance, Trade and Economic Affairs, 1966-68; has served as mem. of Candn. dels. to various internat. confs. on econ. and other matters; Del. Internat. Monetary Fund and World Bank meetings 1967, 69, 70; Co-Chrmn., Candn. Del to OECD Ministerial meeting 1970; Leader, Candn. Del. to Commonwealth Finance Mins. meeting 1970; Windsor Pres., Jaycees, 1961-62; Home: 1253 Victoria Ave., Windsor, Ont. N8X 1N8; Office: House of Commons, Ottawa, Ont. K1A 0A6

GRAY, Jack, playwright; author; b. Detroit, Mich., 7 Dec. 1927; s. John Russell and Jessie Parsons (Paterson) G.; e. Queen's Univ.; Univ. of Toronto; m. Araby, d. James W. Lockhart, 4 Dec. 1952; children: John, Nicholas, Rebecca, Susannah, Felix; Asst. Ed., "Maclean's Magazine", 1953-57; freelance writer since 1957; Pres., John Gray Productions Ltd.; Secy. Gen., Candn. Theatre Centre 1971-73; Prof., Dept. of Integrated Studies, Univ. of Waterloo, 1969-71; plays produced incl.; "Bright Sun at Midnight", Crest Theatre, Toronto, 1957; "Ride a Pink Horse" (musical with Louis Applebaum), Crest Theatre, 1958; "The Teacher", Stratford, Ont., 1960; "Chevalier Johnstone", Neptune Theatre, Halifax, 1964; "Emannuel Xoc", Crest Theatre, 1965; "Godiva!", Belgrade Theatre, Coventry, 1967; "Striker Schneiderman", St. Lawrence Centre, Toronto, 1970; extensive work in radio, TV, film and journalism; mem., Writers Guild Gt. Brit.; Assn. Candn. TV & Radio Artists Pres.; Pres., Internat. Writers Guild; Home: 32 Binscarth Rd., Toronto, Ont. M4W 1Y1

GRAY, James, M.A., Ph.D., F.R.S.A., F.R.S.C.; university professor; b. Montrose, Scot., 11 May 1923; s. James and Matilda (Smythe) G.; e. Montrose (Scot.) Acad., Sr. Leaving Cert. 1940; Univ. of Aberdeen, M.A. 1946; UniV. of Oxford, B.A. (Hons.) 1948, M.A. 1951; Univ. of Montreal, Ph.D. 1970; Yale Univ., Columbia Univ. and Univ. of Montreal, Grad. and Research Work; m. Pamela Doris, d. Reginald Knight, Milford-on-Sea, Hants., Eng., 26 July 1947; one d.: Caroline Gordon; Dean, Faculty of Arts & Science, Dalhousie Univ., 1975-1980; joined Bishop's University as Lecturer in English, 1948; Assistant Professor 1951, Associate Professor 1955; Prof. and Head of Dept. 1958-71; Chrmn., Div. of Humanities 1971-72; Prof. of English, Dalhousie Univ. 1972; appointed Thomas McCulloch Prof. of Eng. Lit. 1980; Visiting Professor, Queen's University, summer 1954, 1970, and Univ. of B.C., summer 1958; Part-time Lectr., Bureau of Current Affairs, 1955-58; mem. of Faculty, Candn. Nat. Rlys. summer staff Training Course 1959-70; Educ. Advisor to Inst. of Candn. Bankers, 1966; Trustee, Corp. of Bishop's Univ. and mem. of Senate, 1966; mem., Adv. Bd., Candn. Scholarship Trust; Comn. on Higher Educ., Prov. of Que.; served with Brit. and Indian Armies in India and Burma, 1943-46; rank Maj.; C.O., Bishop's Univ. C.O.T.C., 1952-60; rec'd Coronation Medal, 1953; Jubilee Medal, 1977; Co-editor, "The Sermons of Samuel Johnson," 1978; author "Johnson's Sermons: A Study" 1972; author of numerous articles in fields of Aesthetics, Lit. Criticism and Biog. and has written scripts and broadcast for the C.B.C.; mem., Executive Comm., Yale Univ. Press Ed. of Works of Samuel Johnson; mem., Candn. Inst. Internat. Affairs (Past Pres., Sherbrooke-LennoxVille Br.); Royal Philatelic Soc. Can.; Humanities Assn. Can. (Nat. Pres. 1958-60); Humanities Research Council Can. (Chrmn., Publ. Comte., 1966-68); Assn. Candn. Univ. Teachers of Eng. (mem. Extve. 1960-61, Vice-Pres., since 1981); mem. of Bd. Candn. Federation of the Humanities, 1980- ; Modern Lang. Assn.; Eng. Inst.; Assn. Eng. Dept. Chrmn.; Internat. Assn. Soc. for 18th Century Studies; Candn. Assn. of Chairmen of English Depts. (Nat. Pres. 1974-75); Liberal; Presbyterian; recreations: golf, travel, philately, rare book collecting; Club: Dalhousie Faculty; Address: Halifax, N.S.

GRAY, James Henry, LL.D., D.Lit.; author; b. Whitemouth, Man. 31 Aug. 1906; s. Harry and Maria (Sargent) G.; e. Winnipeg, Man. 1921; Univ. of Man. LL.D. 1974; Univ. of Brandon D.Lit. 1974; Univ. of Calgary D.Lit. 1975; m. Kathleen Burns 28 Dec. 1926; children: Patricia, Alan, Linda; Office Boy, Winnipeg Grain Exchange 1922, Margin Clk. 1925-29; Mgr., Stockbroker's Office Lethbridge 1930; on relief Winnipeg 1931-33; Reporter, "Winnipeg Free Press" 1935-42, Ed. Writer 1942-46, Ottawa Corr. 1947; Ed., "Farm and Ranch Review" Calgary 1947-55; "Western Oil Examiner" 1955-58; Pub. Relations Mgr. Home Oil Co. 1958-64; author "The Winter Years" 1966; "Men Against the Desert" 1967; "The Boy From

Winnipeg" 1970; "Red Lights on the Prairies" 1971; "Booze" 1972; "The Roar of the Twenties" 1975; "Troublemaker!" 1978; "Boomtime" 1979; rec'd Candn. Hist. Soc. Award 1967; Alta. Hist. Soc. Award 1968, 1975; Margaret McWilliams Medal 1967; Univ. of B.C. Silver Medal 1971; recreation: horse riding; Club: Calgary Petroleum; Address: 11 Strandell Cres. S.W. Calgary Alta. T3H 1K8

GRAY, James Lorne, C.C.(1969), M.Sc., LL.D., D.Sc.; retired from Canadian public service, 1974; b. Brandon, Man., 2 March 1913; s. James Bruce and Sarah Edna (Elder) G.; e. Pub. Sch., Winnipeg, Man. and Pub. and High Schs., Winnipeg, Man. and Saskatoon, Sask.; Univ. of Sask., B.E., 1935, M.Sc. 1938, LL.D., 1961; Univ. of Brit. Columbia, D.Sc., 1961; Carlton Univ. D.Sc. 1975 Honours, Gold Medal, Assoc. of Prof. Engineers, Province of Ontario 1973; m. Anne Evelyn Lawrence, 1 June 1940; one s. James Michael; President, Atomic Energy of Canada Limited, 1958-1974 (ret.); Candn. Gen. Electric Co. Test Course, 1938-39; Lect.; Univ. of Sask., 1939; Assoc. Dir.-Gen., Dept. of Reconstruction & Supply, 1945-46; Asst. to the Pres., Montreal Armature Works Ltd., Montreal, P.Q., 1946-47; Scientific Asst. to the Pres., Nat. Research Council, Ottawa, 1947-49; Chief of Adm., Chalk River, N.R.C., 1949-52; Gen. Mgr., Atomic Energy of Can. Ltd., 1952-53; Vice-Pres. (Adm. & Operations) 1954-58; served in 2nd World War for over five yrs. with R.C.A.F. (Air-crew); retired with rank of Wing Commdr.; mem., Engn. Inst. Can.; Assn. of Prof. Engrs. Ont.; Freemason; United Church; recreations: golf, curling, gardening, woodworking; Clubs: Royal Ottawa Golf; Rideau; Deep River Golf; Deep River Curling; Royal Automobile Country (London, Eng.); St. George's Hill Golf (London, Eng.); Home: 25 Beach Ave., Deep River, Ont. K0J 1P0; Office: P.O. Box 1510, Deep River, Ont. K0J 1P0

GRAY, Kenneth John, D.F.C., B.Eng.; company chairman; b. Goulburn, N.S.W., Australia, 6 Apl. 1919; e. Univ. of Sydney, 1949; Univ. of London, 1951; m. Eileen McInteer; one s. Ian; CHAIRMAN AND DIR., SHAWINIGAN GROUP INC., since 1979 Dir. and Pres., Shenco Holdings Ltd.; Dir. Shawinigan Energy Consultants Ltd.; ShawMont Nfld. Ltd., Teshmont Consultants Inc.; SBR Offshore Ltd.; Dir. and Chrmn., CIPM Can. Internat. Project Managers Ltd.; Engr., Hydro-Electric Comn. of Tasmania, 1951; Design Engr. Shawinigan Engineering, 1957, Mgr. of Engn. 1961, Vice Pres. 1964, Dir. and Pres. 1970; served with Royal Australian Air Force 1940-45; rank Sqdn. Leader; mem., Engn. Inst. Can.; Order Engrs. Que.; Assn. Prof. Engrs., Geols. & Geophys. Alta.; Candn. Nuclear Assn.; Assn. Consulting Engrs. Can.; Am. Soc. Civil Engrs.; Club: St. James', Lambton Golf & Country; Home: Apt. 435, 21 Dale Ave. Rosedale, Ont. M4W 1K3; Office: 620 University Ave., Toronto, Ont. M5G 2C1

GRAY, Nigel George Davidson, B.Sc., LL.B.; b. Chakrata, U.P., India 16 June 1935; s. Dr. James D. Gray; e. St. Paul's Sch. London, Eng. 1952; Coll. Militaire Royal, St. Jean, Que. 1955; Dalhousie Univ. B.Sc. 1959, LL.B. 1964; Lincoln Coll. Oxford Univ. post-grad. studies Comparative Law 1964-65; m. Barbara Johnston d. Allan A. Ferguson, Pictou, N.S. 22 Aug. 1964; two s. Nicholas, Christopher; VICE PRES. AND GEN. COUNSEL, CANADA DEVELOPMENT CORP. 1978- ; Geol.; Canadian Pacific Rly. 1959-61; read law with Stewart, McKeen & Covert; called to Bar of N.S. 1966, Bar of Que. 1969; Asst. Secy. and Asst. Counsel, Petrofina Canada Ltd. 1966-69; Legal Counsel and Secy., Capital Management Ltd. 1969-72; Asst. Gen. Counsel, Brinco Ltd. 1972-75, Assoc. Gen. Counsel 1975-78; Assoc. Gen. Counsel, Canada Development Corp. 1975; mem. N.S. Barristers Soc.; Barreau du Québec; Candn. Bar Assn.; Assn. Prof. Engrs. Alta.; Fellow, Geol. Assn. Can.; Phi Delta Theta; Anglican; Clubs: Oakville; Montreal Badminton & Squash; University (Toronto); Home: 506 Lakeshore E., Oakville, Ont. L6J 1K5; Office: 444 Yonge St., Suite 200, Toronto, Ont. M5B 2H4.

GRAY, Timothy E., B.A.; banker; b. 1951; e. Univ. of Man. B.A.; m. Andrea E. Kristof; PRES. GRINDLAYS BANK OF CANADA; joined Grindlays Bank Ltd., London, 1972, Personal Asst. to Charmn. 1973, Resident Rep. for Middle East Beirut 1974, Mgr. Business Devel. Middle East Bahrain 1976, Mgr. Bahrain 1978-80; Clubs: Granite, Adelaide, Board of Trade of Metropolitan Toronto; Home: 283 St. Leonard's Ave., Toronto, Ont. M4N 1K9; Office: (P.O. Box 145) Royal Bank Plaza, North Tower, Toronto, Ont. M5J 2J3.

GRAYDON, Alexander Simpson, B.A., B.C.L.; company executive; b. London, Ont., 20 Nov. 1915; s. Ismena Archange (Labatt) and late Alexander Henry Marshall Graydon, K.C.; e. Ridley Coll., St. Catharines, Ont.; La Villa, Lausanne, Switzerland (1929-30); Trinity Coll. Sch., Port Hope, Ont. (1930-32); Inst. Sillig, Vevey, Switzerland (1932-33); McGill Univ., B.A. 1937, B.C.L. 1949; Wahl-Henius Inst., Chicago, Ill. 1938-39); Univ. of Western Ont. (Management Training 1950); m. 2ndly, Madeleine Labonté, 7 July, 1967; two s. Alexander Peter, Derek Marshall; PRESIDENT AND DIR., PARHAM INVESTMENTS LTD.; Chrmn., Talisman Ski Resort Ltd.; Dir., John Labatt Ltd.; served in 2nd World War, Capt. in Candn. Army, 1940-45; service in Aleutians, Can., U.K. and N.W. Europe; Kappa Alpha; Anglican; recreation: golf, tennis, sailing, skiing; Club: The London; Home: R.R. 4, Meaford, Ont. N0H 1Y0

GRAYDON, Kenneth Rubert, M.S.A.; association executive; b. Toronto, Ont. 23 Sept. 1934; s. Rubert and Helen (Eland) G.; e. Public and High Schs. Toronto; Univ. of Toronto, B.S.A. (Agric.) 1956, M.S.A. (Agric.) 1958; m. Phyllis, d. Kenneth MacDougall 8 June 1957; children: Catherine, Sheila; EXECUTIVE VICE-PRESIDENT, FEDERATION OF AUTOMOBILE DEALER ASSNS. OF CAN., since 1977; Pres. Rubber Assn. of Can. 1973-76; joined C.B.C. Radio and TV Broadcasting 1957; advertising Dept. Massey Ferguson Industries Ltd. 1959; Dir. Public Relations, Meat Packers Council of Can. 1960-66; Gen. Mgr. Cdn. Farm and Industrial Equipment Inst. 1966-72; mem. Inst. Assn. Extves.; Amer. Soc. of Assn. Extves; Agric. Inst. of Can.; Ont. Inst. of Agric.; mem. Metrop. Toronto Bd. Trade; Presbyterian; recreations: music, gardening, fishing, photography; Home: R.R.4, Bolton, Ont. L0P 1A0; Office: Suite 1902, 2 Shepherd Ave. E., Willowdale, Ont. M2N 5Y7

GRAYDON, William Frederick, M.A.Sc., Ph.D., F.C.I.C.; engineer; educator; b. Toronto, Ont., 27 June 1919; s. Walter and Josephine (Hamilton) G.; e. Univ. of Toronto, B.A.Sc. (Chem. Engn.) 1942, M.A.Sc. 1945; Univ. of Minnesota, Ph.D. 1949; m. Evelyn Crouch, 28 May 1945; children: John William, Mary Evelyn, Jane Hamilton, Elizabeth Ann, Catherine Ruth; PROFESSOR OF CHEMICAL ENGINEERING, UNIV. OF TORONTO since 1960; Pres., Chemical Engineering Research Consultants Ltd.; Asst. Prof. of Chem. Engn., Univ. of Toronto, 1949; Prof. 1960; Assoc. Dean, Faculty of Applied Science and Engn. 1966-70; el. to Etobicoke Bd. of Educ. since 1958 (Chrmn. 1963, 1966); mem. Bd. of Govs.; Humber Coll. of Applied Arts and Tech.; author of over 50 research publs. in field of applied surface chem.; Conservative; Presbyterian; recreation: sailing; Club: T.S. & C.C.; Home: 3 Mossom Pl., Toronto, Ont. M6S 1G4

GRAYSON, Henry Wesley, M.A., Ph.D., professor emeritus (ret.); b. Moose Jaw, Sask., 24 May 1910; s. Albert Kirk and Mary Alice (Simpson) G.; e. Univ. of Saskatchewan, Hon. B.A. 1937; Univ. of Toronto, M.A. 1947, Ph.D. 1950; m. Helen Mary, d. E. B. Galloway, Medicine Hat, Alta., 30 Apl. 1942; children: David Kirk, Geraldine Helen; formerly Chrmn., Dept. of Business Econ., Univ. of Hawaii; Teacher in Saskatchewan High Schools, 1928-

40; Research Economist, Department of Trade & Commerce, Ottawa, 1947-49; Prof. of Econ., Univ. of Maryland, 1949-62; served as Educ. Offr. in R.C.A.F.; Publications: "Economic Planning Under Free Enterprise", 1954; "The Crisis of the Middle Class", 1955; "Principles of Economics" (with Philipp H. Lohman), 1958; "Price Theory in a Changing Economy", 1964; "This World", 1967; "The Theory of a Discrete Finite and Nonsimultaneous Universe" 1972; papers in relativistic physics and gravitation in Eng. & Europ. journs. 1973-75; "The Theory of Relativity Revisited", 1978; mem., Am. Econ. Assn.; Candn. Pol. Science Assn.; Economic Soc.; Unitarian; recreations: golf, swimming, fishing, hiking; Address: Rte. 2, Box 715, Harpers Ferry, W. Va. 25425.

GREB, Harry D., LL.D.; industrialist; b. Kitchener, Ont., 4 Oct. 1915; s. Erwin C. and Clara M. (Miller) G.; e. Pub. and High Schs., Kitchener, Ont.; LL.D. Waterloo Lutheran 1971; m. Dorothy M., d. John C. Spain, Galt, Ont., 10 Sept. 1938; Pres., Metro Marine Ltd., Dir. and 2nd Vice Pres., Equitable Life Ins. Co. of Can.; Clk., Greb Shoe Co. Ltd. 1933; Dir. and Vice-Pres. 1936, Pres. 1954, retired 1975; mem. Bd of Pensions, Lutheran Church in America; Freemason; Lutheran; recreation: yachting; Clubs: Royal Canadian Yacht (Toronto); Scottish Rite (Hamilton); Royal Hamilton Yacht; Lighthouse Point Yacht (Florida); Westmount Golf & Country (Kitchener) Rotary; Home: 292 Pilgrim Circle, Waterloo, Ont. N2K 1Y4

GREEN, Alton Joseph, B.A.Sc., P.Eng.; b. Calgary, Alta. 14 May 1929; s. Walter Alton and Martha Josephine (Martin) G.; e. Mt. View High Sch. and Victoria (B.C.) Coll. 1947; Univ. of B.C. B.A.Sc. (Civil Engn.) 1952; m. Mary Elizabeth d. Julius Varanai, Kamloops, B.C. 27 Dec. 1954; children: Duane Alton, Valerie Elizabeth; VICE PRES. AND DIR., WESTCOAST TRANSMISSION CO. LTD.; Dir. Foothills Pipe Lines (North B.C.) Ltd.; joined Bechtel Corp. as Engr. in varying capacities 1952-56, Chief Engr. Pembina Pipeline Ltd. 1956-61, Westcoast Transmission Co. Ltd., 1970-73, Adm. Asst. 1961-62, Asst. Chief Engr. 1962-64, Chief Engr. 1964-70, Mgr. of Engn. 1970-73, Group Mgr. Supply & Sales 1973-75, Vice Pres. Supply & Sales 1975-78, Dir. and mem. Extve. Comte. 1977, Vice Pres. and Northern Pipelines Co-ordinator 1978; mem. Engn. Inst. Can.; Assn. Prof. Engrs. B.C. and Alta.; Alpha Delta Phi; Protestant; recreations: skiing, hiking, fishing; Club: Terminal City; Home: 3965 Viewridge Pl., West Vancouver, B.C. V7V 3K7; Office: 1333 West Georgia St., Vancouver, B.C. V6E 3K9.

GREEN, Bremner B., company executive; b. Toronto, Ont. 4 July 1925; s. Charles C. Duncan and Marion W. (Baillie) G.; e. Appleby Coll., Oakville, Ont. 1943; m. Margaret, d. Harold W. Scruton, Oct. 1954; children: Bremner, Thomas, David; CHRMN. OF BD., C.E.O., BOWES CO. LTD. since 1981; with J. D. Woods & Gordon, Toronto, 1948-51; The Clarkson Co. Ltd., Toronto, 1955; Vice-Pres., Dominion Building Materials Ltd., Ottawa, 1955; joined present Co. as Extve. Asst. to Pres., 1960; Pres. and Gen. Man. 1967-81; served in 2nd World War, R.C.A.F., rank Pilot Offr., 1943-45; Gov., Appleby Coll.; mem. Bd. Trade of Metro Toronto; Anglican; recreations: golf, tennis; Clubs: Oakville; Toronto Golf; Oakville Golf; Home: 1355 Cambridge Drive, Oakville, Ont; Office: 75 Vickers Rd., Islington, Ont. M9B 6B6

GREEN, Donald Mackenzie, C.M.; executive; b. Hamilton, Ont. 8 Oct. 1932; s. Victor and Isabelle G.; e. Westdale Secondary Sch. Hamilton; Ryerson Inst. Technol. Toronto; m. Sandra Little 13 July 1957; children: Stephen, Sharon; CHRMN. AND CHIEF EXTVE. OFFR., THE TRIDON COMPANIES; Chrmn., Stearn Sailing Systems; Bay Marine Inventory Inc.; Gov., Olympic Trust of Canada; Dir. Laidlaw Transportation Ltd.; Thomson-Gordon Ltd.; Victor Equipment Co. of Canada Ltd.; North Sails Fogh Ltd.; Gov., Ont. Research Foundation; mem. Extve.

Comte. Ont. Research Foundation; Dir. Candn. Nat. Sportsmen's Shows; mem. Business Adv. Council Faculty of Business McMaster Univ.; Offr., Ont. Emergency Supply Planning Br. Dept. Nat. Production; former Chrmn. and Dir. Hamilton Civic Hosps., Chrmn. Sch. Nursing; Chrmn. Hamilton-Wentworth Dist. Health Council; Pres., Burlington Chamber Comm.; Greater YMCA; Candn. Cancer Soc. Hamilton Unit; Dir. Jr. Achievement Hamilton; rec'd Ryerson Fellowship 1979; named Young Man of Yr. Burlington 1969; One of Ten Outstanding Men Ont. 1969; author "White Wings Around the World" 1953; winner Can.'s Cup races Bayview, Mich. as owner racing yacht "Evergreen" 1978; mem. Hamilton Chamber Comm.; Young Pres. Organ.; Clubs: Royal Hamilton Yacht (Past Commodore); Burlington Golf & Country; Holimont Ski; Hamilton; Home: 682 North Shore Blvd. E., Burlington, Ont. L7T 1X2; Office: Stelco Tower, 100 King St. W., Hamilton, Ont. L8P 1A2.

GREEN, H. Gordon, B.Sc., M.A., Ph.D.; author; teacher; b. Anderson, Ind., 8 May 1912; s. Henry & Mabel Lola (Jensen) G.; e. Arthur (Ont.) Public and High Schs.; Stratford (Ont.) Normal Sch., 1931-32; Univ. of Michigan, B.Sc. 1942, M.A. 1949; Ont. Coll. of Educ., 1946; Florida State, Ph.D. 1972; children: Lowell E., Mrs. Phyllis German, Marielle A., Joy I., Barry I., Laura Dawn; mem. Teaching Staff, Kahnawake Survival School, Caughnawaga, Que.; Pres., Candn. Authors' Assn., 1958-59; Chrmn., Bois-des-Filions (Que.) Prot. Sch. Bd. 1952-57; served in U.S. Army Med. Dept., 1943-45; Candn. Army, 1945; introduced Landrace Swine to America, 1953; Mag. Ed. "The Family Herald" 1948-68; Publications" "The Praying Mantis" (novel,) 1953; "The Silver Dart" (biography of Hon. J. A. D. McCurdy), 1959; "A Time to Pass Over" (novel), 1962; "Behind the Cheering" (a hist. of hockey with Frank Selke Sr.), 1963; "Stories to Read Again" (anthology), 1964; "The Faith of Our Father" (novel), 1965' "A Countryman's Christmas" (essays), 1965; "Headlining a Century with the Montreal Star (a hist. of the Montreal Star), 1966; "Professor Go Home" (essays), 1968; "Goodbye Little Town" (novel), 1970; "Don't Have Your Baby in the Dory" (biog. of Myra Bennett M.B.E.) 1974; "Diary of a Dirty Old Man" (novel) 1974; "God and the Rooster" (collection) 1975; "With My Sock Feet on the Oven Door" (collection) 1975; num. short stories and articles in Candn. & Am. periodicals; Ed. Eng. lang. sec. of Centennial Comte.'s survey of Candn. Lit. 1867-1967; "A Century of Candn. Lit.", 1967; a frequent contrib. to "Reader's Digest"; CBC television and radio; daily radio commentary "The Old Cynic"; awarded Centennial Medal, 1967; Silver Jubilee medal, 1978; Unitarian; Clubs: Lions (Past Pres.); Royal Canadian Legion; Home and Farm: Ormstown, Que.

GREEN, Hon. Howard Charles, P.C. (Can.) 1957, Q.C., LL.D. (retired); b. Kaslo, B.C., 5 Nov. 1895; of U.E.L. descent; s. Samuel Howard, a pioneer of Kootenay district, B.C., and Flora Isabel (Goodwin) G.; e. Kaslo, B.C.; Univ. Coll., Univ. of Toronto, B.A. 1915; Osgoode Hall, Toronto, Grad. as silver medalist, 1920; Univ. of B.C., LL.D. 1960; m. the late Marion Jean, d. late Lewis Alfred Mounce, Vancouver, B.C., 7 Aug. 1923; children: Lewis Howard, John Willison; 2ndly, Donna Enid, d. late Dr. D. E. Kerr, Duncan, B.C., 29 March 1956; practised law with firm of Collins, Green, Eades & Collins, Vancouver, B.C.; read law with Mowat, Maclennan, Hunter and Parkinson, Toronto, and Ladner and Cantelon, Vancouver, B.C.; called to Bar of B.C. Jan. 1922; served in World War 1915-19 with 54th Kootenay Bn., C.E.F.; also as Instr., Candn. Corps. Infantry School and with 6th Candn. Inf. Bgde., and after Armistice attached to Candn. section, G.H.Q.; Mentioned in Despatches; discharged as Staff Captain; 1st el. to H. of C. for Vancouver S. at g.e. 1935; re-el. g.e. 1940 and 1945; el. for Vancouver-Quadra in g.e. 1949; and re-el. g.e. 1953, 1957, 1958 and 1962; def. g.e. Apl. 1963; apptd. Minister of Public Works, 22 June

1957 and was Acting Min. of Defence Production to May 1958; Secy. of State for External Affairs, 1959-63; Govt. House Leader 1957-59; Deputy to Prime Min. 1957-63; Head, Candn. Dels. to U.N. General Assembly, N.Y., and to N.A.T.O., 1959-62; Special Ambassador for Can. at the 150th anniversary of Argentinian Independence, Buenos Aires, 1960; named Freeman of City of Trail, B.C., 1961 and of Vancouver, 1972; Hon. Life mem. Royal Candn. Legion, Candn. Inst. of Internat. Affairs, Vancouver Board of Trade, and Men's Candn. Club of Vancouver; Hon. Vice Pres., United Nations Assn. of Canada; Conservative; United Church; Clubs: Terminal City; Home: 4160 West 8th Ave.; Vancouver, B.C. V6R 1Z6

GREEN, John Joseph, M.B.E., B.Sc., A.R.C.S., D.I.C., Ph.D., C.Eng., F.R.Ae.S., F.A.I.A.A., Hon. F.C.A.S.I.; b. Portsmouth, Eng., Nov. 1905; s. George Edward and Elizabeth (Jarmey) G.; e. London, Eng.; Roy. Coll. of Science, London Univ., B.Sc. (Physics) and A.R.C.S. (Physics) 1928, D.I.C. (Aeronautics) 1929; Busk Student in Aeronautics 1928-29; Beit Scient. Research Fellow 1929-30; Imperial Coll. Govs. Prize in Physics 1928; m. Winifred Maud, d. Silas John Pascoe, Portsmouth, England, 31 May 1930; children: Lorna, Janet; Consultant since 1971; Past Pres. and mem. of Exec. Bd., Internat. Council Aero Sciences; Aero. Research, Nat. Research Council 1930; Chief Research Engr., R.C.A.F. Test Devel. Estab. 1943; Chief Research Aero. Engr., Air Transport Bd. 1945; Chief, Div. "B", Defence Research Board and Scient. Adv. to Chief of Air Staff, R.C.A.F. 1949; Defence Research mem., Candn. Joint Staff and Defence Research Attaché, Candn. Embassy, Washington, D.C. 1955; Chief Supt., Candn. Armament Research & Devel. Estab., Valcartier, Que. 1959; apptd. Dir. Research Litton Systems (Can.) Ltd. 1963, Director Govt. Relations 1968, Consultant 1970, 71; Dir., Leigh Instruments Ltd. 1970-79 served in 2nd World War, R.C.A.F. 1943-45; retired with rank of Sqdn. Leader; 1st Pres., C.A.I. 1954-55; Pres., C.A.S.I. 1962-63; awarded M.B.E. 1943, King's Commendation for Valuable Service in the Air 1945; Hon. Life mem., Am. Assn. Airport Extves.; Pres., Internat. Council Aero. Sciences 1972-78; Rep. of Can. on Commonwealth Adv. Aero. Research Council (1949); Founding mem. and rep. of Can. on Council of Adv. Group on Aero. Research & Devel. to NATO (1952); mem. Bds. of Award, Daniel Guggenheim Medal (1963-73), Laura Taber Barbour Flight Safety Award (1961-73); apptd. to Corresponding Membership of the Deutsche Gesellschaft für Luft-und Raumfahrt e.V., 1977; principal author, Science Council Report on Aero Research & Devel. in Can. (1970); mem. Internat. Bd. Trustees, Asian Inst. of Technol., Bangkok since 1973; mem. Adv. Comte. on Science & Tech., Govt. of N.B. since 1973; recreations: swimming, golf, music, photography, writing; Clubs: Rotary Club of Toronto; Lambton Golf & Country; Address: 45 La Rose Ave., Apt. 608, Weston, Ont. M9P 1A8

GREEN, Joseph G., M.A., Ph.D.; educator; b. Philadelphia, Pa., 24 June 1934; s. late Herman I. and Anna M. (Brantz) G.; e. Temple Univ., B.A. 1956; Ind. Univ., M.A. 1959, Ph.D. 1964; m. Rhoda Arlene, d. Morris Rabinowitz, Camden, N.J., 23 Dec. 1956; two s., Michael, Marc; Dean, Faculty of Fine Arts, York Univ. 1980; Mgr., Louisville Little Theatre, 1959-60; Dir. of Theatre, Ind. Univ., and Asst. Prof. of Theatre 1961-65; Theatre Co-ordinator and Asst. Prof., Hunter Coll., 1965-68; Visiting Prof. of Theatre, Columbia Univ. Teachers Coll., 1967; joined present Univ. as Asst. Dean of Fine Arts and Dir. of Theatre 1968-71; Dean of Fine Arts and Prof. of Theatres York Univ., 1973-80; writings incl. numerous book reviews and articles; CBC radio critic for Summer 1970; Lectr., Stratford Shakespeare Seminar Summer 1971; Chrmn., Candn. Assoc. of Fine Arts Deans; Bd. mem., Co-opera Theatre Co.; Chrmn. of Bd., Candn. Theatre Review; Bd. mem., Can.-Israel Cultural Foundation; mem. Exec. Comm., Internat. Council Fine Arts Deans; Candn.

Assn. Univ. Teachers; Am. Theatre Assn.; Jewish; Home: 625 Vesta Dr., Toronto, Ont. M5N 1J2

GREEN, Stewart Edward, B.Com., LL.B.; executive; b. Toronto, Ont. 1 Aug. 1944; s. Robert Edward Stewart Green; e. Univ. of Toronto B.Com., LL.B.; SECY., GEORGE WESTON LTD.; Ass't-Sec., Loblaw Cos. Ltd.; recreations: sailing, skiing; Home: 133 Sherwood Ave., Toronto, Ont; Office: 22 St. Clair Ave. E., Suite 1901, Toronto, Ont. M4T 2S7.

GREENE, Lorne, O.C. (1971), B.A., D.H.L., LL.D.; actor, broadcaster; b. Ottawa, Ont., 12 Feb. 1915; s. Daniel and Dora G.; e. Queen's Univ., B.A.; Fellowship to the Neighbourhood Playhouse Sch. of the Theatre, m. 1st Rita, d. Mark Hands, Toronto, Ont.; children: Charles, Linda; 2nd, Nancy Ann Deale; children: Gillian; Founder & Dir., Acad. of Radio Arts 1946-53; Nat. Newscaster, C.B.C., 1939-42; Commentator on National Film Bd. Series, "Carry on Canada", and "The World in Action"; served in 2nd World War with Candn. Army (Active); Vice-Chrmn., Amer. Horse Protection Assn.; Hon. Chrmn. Medic Alert Foundation International; Bd. member, Pritikin Research Foundation only Candn. to win the NBC H.P. Davis Award for the Best Announcer in his field; made debut as a Broadway (N.Y.) actor in "The Prescott Proposals (opposite Katharine Cornell), 1953; has acted in N.B.C. TV production of "Bonanza", since 1959; Numerous mini-series, including ABC-TV's "Roots" & "Battlestar Galactica," "Last of the World" series; appeared in many films incl.: "Autumn Leaves" "The Buccaneers", "Tight Spot," Silver Chalice, "Peyton Place", "Earthquake"

GREENE, Nancy Catherine (Mrs. Al Raine), O.C. (1968); ski champion; b. Ottawa, Ont., 11 May 1943; d. Robert Kenneth Wollaston and Helen Catherine (Sutherland) G.; e. Rossland (B.C.) Pub. and High Schs.; Trail (B.C.) Business Coll.; Notre Dame Univ. of Nelson; m. Al Raine, Apl. 1969; twin s. Charles, William; mem. Nat. Ski Team 1959-68; Olympic Team, 1960, 1964 and 1968; World Championship Team, 1962 and 1966; winner of Gold Medal for Giant Slalom and Silver Medal for Slalom, Olympic Games 1968; winner of 1967 and 1968 World Cup for Skiing; named Canada's Woman Athlete of the Year, 1967; Lou Marsh Trophy for Athlete of the Year (twice) 1967, 1968; Dir., Nat. Recreation and Sport Centre; Vice-pres. and mem., Candn. Ski Assn.; Candn. Ski Instrs. Alliance; Beta Sigma Phi (Hon.); recreations: skiing, reading, music, tennis; Clubs: Whistler Ski; Soroptomist (Hon.); Address: 3010 Arbutus Dr., Whistler, B.C. VON 1B0

GREENHILL, Stanley, The Lord Greenhill M.D., D.P.H., F.R.C.P.(C), F.A.C.P., F.F.C.M.(U.K.); physician; educator; b. Glasgow, Scot. 17 July 1917; e. Kelvinside Acad. Glasgow, Scot.; Glasgow Univ.; Univ. of Cal. Berkeley; Univ. of Toronto; Degrees: M.D. 1944, D.P.H. 1947, M.F.C.M. (London) 1975; m. Margaret Jean d. late Thomas J. Newlands, Hamilton, Ont. 17 Aug. 1946; children: Catherine Elizabeth Youngren, Sheila Anne Davidson; PROF. OF COMMUNITY MED., UNIV. OF ALTA. since 1959; Consultant, W.H.O. India, Thailand, Nepal, Sri Lanka; C.I.D.A. Swaziland, Pakistan; Dept. of Environment Alta.; N. Med. Services Ottawa; contributor to 'Health Care' 1976; reports for internat., nat., prov. and mun. govts.; prof. papers various med. journs.; mem. Candn. and internat. med. socs.; recreations: photography, internat. travel as related to work; Home: 10223 — 137 St., Edmonton, Alta. T5N 2G8; Office: 13-108 Clinical Sciences Bldg., Univ. of Alta., Edmonton, Alta. T6G 2G3.

GREENIAUS, H. John, B.Com.; food company executive; b. Toronto, Ont. 12 Feb. 1945; e. McGill Univ. B.Com. 1966; PRESIDENT, STANDARD BRANDS FOOD CO.; formerly assoc. with Procter & Gamble, Pepsi-Cola; joined Standard Brands 1977 as Vice Pres.

Marketing, Wines & Spirits Div.; Home: 359 Lonsdale Rd., Toronto, Ont. M5P 1R3; Office: 1 Dundas St. W., Suite 2800, Toronto, Ont. M5G 2A9.

GREENWAY, Michael Charles, B.Com., M.B.A., C.A.; executive; e. Rondebosch Boys' High Sch. 1957; Univ. of S. Africa B.Com. 1961; C.A. South Africa 1963, B.C. 1969; Simon Fraser Univ. M.B.A. 1972; Univ. of S. Calif. Summer Extve. Program 1978; VICE PRES. CORPORATE DEVEL., BALFOUR GUTHRIE (CANADA) LTD. 1980- ; C.A. and Mang. Consultant, Deloitte, Haskins & Sells, London, Eng. 1963-68; Corporate Financial Analyst & Financial Mgr., MacMillan Bloedel Ltd. 1968-75; Dir. of Planning & Devel., Weldwood of Canada Ltd. 1976-80; Lectr. in Business Policy Simon Fraser Univ.; mem. N. Am. Soc. Corporate Planning; recreations: swimming, boating, fishing; Clubs: University; Canadian; Home: 1102 Hillside Rd., West Vancouver, B.C. V7S 2E9; Office: 740 Nicola St., Vancouver, B.C. V6G 2C2.

GREENWOOD, Hugh John, M.A.Sc., Ph.D., F.G.S.A., F.M.S.A., F.R.S.C.; geologist; educator; b. Vancouver, B.C. 17 March 1931; s. John Marshall and Joan (Sampson) G.; e. N. Vancouver High Sch. 1949; Univ. of B.C. B.A.Sc. 1954 (F.J. Nicholson Scholarship 1954), M.A.Sc. 1956; Princeton Univ. Ph.D. 1960 (Siscoe Fellowship 1959, Porter Ogden Jacobus Fellowship 1958); Carnegie Inst. of Washington Predoctoral Fellow (Geophys. Lab. 1959); m. Mary Sylvia d. late John Proudfoot Ledingham 5 Oct. 1955; children: Stuart Bruce, Kelly Louise, Barbara Lynn; PROF. AND HEAD OF GEOL. SCIENCES, UNIV. OF B.C. since 1977; Geol. Ventures Ltd. Lake Dufault Mines, Que. 1956-57; Phys. Chem., Geophys. Lab. Carnegie Inst. of Washington 1960-63; Assoc. Prof. of Geol. Princeton Univ. 1963-67; Assoc. Prof. Univ. of B.C. 1967, Prof. 1969; rec'd Steacie Prize Nat. Research Council; author or co-author numerous publs. petrology, metamorphism, phys. chem., thermodynamics; mem. Geochem. Soc. (Pres.); Geol. Assn. Can.; Mineral. Assn. Can.; Assn. Prof. Engrs. B.C.; Am. Geophys. Union; recreations: skiing, sailing, mountain climbing, music; Home: 6262 Blenheim St. Vancouver, B.C. V6N 1R4; Office: Vancouver, B.C. V6T 1W5.

GREENWOOD, James Ward, B.Sc., M.A.; physicist; b. Winnipeg, Man., 13 May 1925; s. late James Arthur and Marion C. (Evans) G.; e. Univ. of Manitoba, B.Sc. 1946; Univ. of Minnesota, M.A. 1953; m. Dorothy F., d. late Joseph E. Swancar, 4 June 1949; children: Nancy Jean, Douglas James; INTERNATIONAL DIVISION, MINISTRY OF STATE FOR SCIENCE & TECHNOLOGY, OTTAWA; (Science Counsellor, Candn. High Comm., Lond, 1972-77, same post at Candn. Embassy, Wash., D.C. 1967-72); Lecturer Physics, University of Manitoba, 1946-49; Atomic Energy of Canada Ltd., Chalk River, Ont., 1954-59; Head, Internat. Affairs, Atomic Energy of Canada, Ottawa, 1959-67; loaned to Candn. Embassy as Alternate Gov. for Canada, Internat. Atomic Energy Agency, 1964-65; Club: Savile (London); Office: MOSST, 270 Albert St., Ottawa K1A 1A1

GREENWOOD, Lawrence George; banker; b. Briercrest, Sask., 16 June 1921; s. late George Tuckfield and Mildred Jane (Greenwood) G.; e. Regina Central Collegiate, grad. 1938; m. Margaret, d. Wm. Purser, Winnipeg, Man., 28 June 1947; Dir., Kinross Mortgage Corp.; Pres., Edifice Dorchester-Commerce Inc.; Dir., Imp. Life Assnce. Co. of Can.; Candn. Imp. Bank of Commerce; Cdn. Reinsurance Co and Cdn. Reassurance Co; Blue Jays Baseball Club; mem., Candn. Adv. Bd., Liberty Mutual Ins. Co.; mem. Bd. Trustees Queen's Univ.; The Hospital for Sick Children; dir. Multiple Sclerosis Society of Can. Ont. Div.; joined Candn. Bank of Commerce, 1938; Asst. Mgr., Toronto Br., 1953; Mgr., Seattle (Wash.) Br. 1956; Supt. H. O. Toronto, March, 1958; Mgr., Toronto Br., Sept. 1958; Asst. Gen. Mgr., H.O., 1962; Regional Gen. Mgr., Internat., 1963; Depy. Chief Gen. Mgr., H.O.,

1964, and Chief Gen. Mgr., Dec. 1964; el. a Dir., Nov. 1967, Pres. 1968-71; Vice-Chrmn. of Bd., 1971-76; Extve. Vice-Pres. 1978-81 Chrmn. and Pres., Dominion Realty Co. Ltd. and Imbank Realty Co. Ltd. 1976-81; served in 2nd World War overseas in North Africa and Europe with R.C.A.F., 1941-45; Candn. Council, Internat. Chamber of Comm.; mem. Candn. Chamber of Comm.; mem., Board of Trade, Metropolitan Toronto; Nat. Trust for Scotland; Patron, Toronto French School; United Church; recreations: tennis, fishing; Clubs: York, Toronto; Home: 7 Tudor Gate, Willowdale Ont. M2L 1N3 Office: Ste. 2090, Commerce Court West, P.O. Box 63, Commerce Court Postal Stn., Toronto, Ont. M5L 1B9

GREENWOOD, Russell James; retired company president; b. Saskatoon, Sask., 15 Feb. 1920; s. late Robert Arthur and late Julia Maud (Kidd) G.; e. Central Coll. High Sch., Regina, Sask., 1937; Queen's Univ., Mang. Course; m. Mabel June, d. late Chester Mastin, Regina, 24 Feb. 1942; children: Clarence James, Mrs. Linda Joyce Walker; Dir., Dominion Dairies Ltd.; joined Kraft Foods Ltd., as Salesman, 1944; Br. Mgr., Regina, 1948, B.C. 1953 and Ont. 1956; Cheese Products Sales Mgr. for Can., 1960; Marketing Dir., Kraft Foods Ltd.-Eng., 1967; Pres., and Gen. Mgr., 1968-81; Dir., Nat. Dairy Council; Grocery Products Mfrs.; Protestant; recreations: golf, curling; Club: Summerlea Golf; Home: 401 Church St., Beaconsfield, Que. H9W 3R5; Office: 8600 Devonshire Rd., Town of Mount Royal, Que. H4O 2K9

GREER, William Newton, B.Arch., M.S., F.R.A.I.C.; R.C.A.; architect; b. Kingston, Ont. 21 Feb. 1925; s. Lt. Col. George Garnet and Mamie Louisa (Garrett) G.; e. Crescent Sch. Toronto 1937; Trinity Coll. Sch. Port Hope 1943; Univ. of Toronto B.Arch. 1948; Ill. Inst. of Technol. M.S. (Product Design) 1951 (Nat. Indust. Design Council Scholarship); m. Rina Claire d. Sydney Sussman, Long Island, New York 7 Nov. 1973; children: Jonathan Newton, Simon Garnet; STAFF ARCH., TORONTO HISTORICAL BD. 1976- ; joined Shore & Moffat, Archs. 1950, Assoc. 1955, Partner of Shore & Moffat and Partners, Archs., Engrs., Site Planners 1962-72; Sole Princ., William N. Greer, Arch. 1972-76; mem. Extve. Comte. Corp. of Trinity Coll. Univ. of Toronto 1958-63; Vice Chrmn. 1966, Adm. Comte. 1965-75, Chrmn. 1965-69, Bldg. Comte. 1960-65, 1980-81; mem. Adv. Bd. Cath. Ch. of St. James 1967-76; Adv. Bd. St. James Cemetary 1968- ; Dir., Friends of Old City Hall Toronto 1972-75; Adv. Comte. to Adv. Task Force on Housing Policy Prov. Ont. 1973; served with RCN 1944-45; mem. Ont. Assn. Archs.; Toronto Soc. Archs.; Arch. Conservancy Ont.; Soc. Study Arch. Can.; Kappa Alpha; P. Conservative; Anglican; recreations: skiing, sailing, photography, sk&tching; Clubs: R.C.Y.C.; Osler Bluff Ski; Home: 155 Hudson Dr., Toronto, Ont. M4T 2K4; Office: Marine Museum, Exhibition Place, Toronto, Ont. M6K 3C3.

GREGOIRE, Mt. Rev. Paul, M.A., Ph.D., L. es L., S.T.L. O.C. (R.C.); b. Verdun, Que., 24 Oct. 1911; s. Albert and Marie (Lavoie) G; e. Ecole Supérieure Richard, Verdun, Que.; Séminaire de Ste-Thérèse (Que.); Grand Seminary of Montreal; ordained priest 1937. Univ. of Montreal; ARCHBISHOP OF MONTREAL, since 23 Apl. 1968; o. 1937; successively Dir., Séminaire de Ste-Thérèse, Prof. of Philos. of Educ., l'Ecole Normale Secondaire and l'Institut Pédagogique and Students' Chaplain, Univ. of Montreal (1950-61); consecrated Bishop 196l with title of Bishop of Curubi and became Auxiliary Bishop of Montreal; named Vicar Gen. and Dir. of Office for the Clergy; apptd. Pres., Epis. Comn. on Ecumenism (French Sector), 1965; presided over Salary Comn., 1965; Apostolic Adm., Archdiocese of Montreal, Dec. 1967 Archbishop 1968; mem. Exec. of Bishops Assembly of Quebec; board of CCCB; pres. Episcopal Assembly of Bishops of Montreal Region; Rec'd Hon. PH.D. from U. Montreal 1969; Hon. PH.D. Winooski Park, Vermont, U.S.A. 1970; mem. of Can. del. to Bishop's Synod in Rome, 1971, to Inter-American Episcopal meeting in Chateauguay 1972, in Brazil 1973, to Cuba 1976; Apptd. mem. of Sacred Congregation officer for the Clergy by Pope John Paul II 1978; Office of the Order of Canada 1979; Address: 2000 Sherbrooke St. W., Montreal, Que. H3H lG4

GREGOR, Helen Frances, R.C.A.; artist; b. Prague, Czechoslovakia, 28 June 192l; d. Fred and Lily (Leipen) Lorenz; e. Royal Coll. of Art, London, Eng.; m. T.P. Gregor; children: Jan Michael, Charlotte Anne; has exhibited widely in local, nat. and internat. exhns. incl. Art Gallery Ont., Museum of Fine Arts Montreal, Music de l'Art Contemporaire, 4th and 8th Internat. Biennale of Tapestry Lausanne, Switzerland, Lisbon, Portugal, Mobilier National, Paris, Internat. Craft Show Stuttgart, Nat. Gallery Can., Surrey Univ. and Can. House London, Eng., Jacques Baruch Gallery Chicago, Museum of Modern Art Kyoto and Tokyo, Candn. Cultural Centre, Paris, Fr., Royal Ont. Museum; solo show at Nancy Poole's Studio, Toronto, 1981; 3 fibre-artist show, Art Gallery of Windsor, 1981 (with N. American tour); recent comns. incl. J. J. Deutsch Memorial Tapestry, Queen's Univ. (1977), Hamilton (Ont.) Auditorium, "Meeting Place", Toronto Bd. of Trade 1979, Ebco Co., Columbus, Ohio, U.S.A., 3 tapestries Ont. Hydro H.O. and other corporate, univ. and private comns.; rep. colls. Queen's Univ., Nat. Gallery Can., Candn. Dept. of External Affairs, Royal Ont. Museum, Centre de la Tapisserie Brussels, Coll. of World Tapestry, Lausanne, Switzerland, Osler Hoskin & Harcourt coll., Hyatt Regency Hotel in Jedda (Saudi Arabia) and other educ., comm. and private colls.; Head of Textiles Ont. Coll. of Art; Visiting Lectr. various art galleries and museums incl. Agnes Etherington, Queen's Univ., Hamilton, Saskatoon Univ., Halifax Coll. of Art; participant extension programmes Art Gallery Ont., Kitchener, Windsor Art Gallery; frequent seminars on tapestry and textiles incl. Vancouver Fine Art Dept., Univ. of Wis.; special project serialized tapestry with design group Zurich; comnd. to execute John J. Deutsch Mem. Tapestry Queen's Univ. 1976; mem. Ont. Coll. Art Selection Comte. of Art Gallery Exhn. 100th Retrospect Art Gallery Ont.; rec'd Can. Council Awards 1965 (Sweden) and 1969 (Lausanne); Founder mem., International Tapestry Council "Assoc. Pierre Pauli", work in 1st World Collection of Tapestry, Lausanne; author various writings Assoc. Royal Coll. Art; mem. Council R.C.A. 1976-78, 1980-82; Art Advis. Comte. City Hall, 1979-80, Toronto; Com. Programs & Relations Comte, A.G.O. 1980-82; Built in Art Comte., Visual Art Ont.; Address: 218 Glen Rd., Toronto, Ont. M4W 2X3

GREGORY, Gordon F., Q.C., B.C.L., LL.M.; government administrator; b. Saint John, N.B., 25 Nov. 1938; s. Robert Alexander and Gertrude B. (Deakin) G.; e. Univ. of N.B., B.B.A. 196l, B.C.L. 1963; Harvard Univ. LL.M. 1965; m. Carol A., d. Elston L. Reid, Fredericton, N.B., 8 Aug. 1964; children: Andrew R., Kathryn A., DEPUTY MINISTER OF JUSTICE, N.B., since 1971; read law with Benjamin R. Guss, Q.C.; called to Bar of N.B. 1963; mem., Candn. Bar Assn.; Barristers Soc. N.B.; Fredericton Law Soc,; United Church; Home: 365 Wright St., Fredericton N.B. E3B 2E3; Office: Centennial Bldg., Fredericton, N.B.

GREGORY, John H., B.E.; manufacturer; b. Windsor, Ont., 15 June 1913; s. Ernest Henry and Margaret Jane (Mann) G.; e. Kelvin Tech. High Sch., Winnipeg; Univ. of Man., 1929-32; McGill Univ., B.E. (Mech.) 1934; m. Kathleen Mary, d. Peter H. Winstanley, 7 September 1937; children: Peter, Elizabeth, Barbara; CHRMN. OF THE BD., CANDN. BLOWER/CAN. PUMPS LTD., Buffalo, N.Y.; Compair Canada Inc.; mem., Assn. of Prof. Engrs. Ont.; United Church; Home: 243 Lydia St., Kitchener N2H lW4; Office: 90 Woodside Ave., Kitchener, Ont. N2M 3S1

GREICIUS, Mrs. Vincent — see: Hagen Betty-Jean.

GREGORY, Hon. Milton E. C.(Bud), M.P.P.; politician; b. Toronto, Ont. 9 March 1926; s. Thomas and Myrtle (Truman) G.; e. Gen. Mercer Pub. Sch. and W. Tech. & Comm. Sch. Toronto 1945; m. Shirley Isobel d. William Rusk 3 Oct. 1947; two d. Judith Ann Atkinson, Martinne Louise; MIN. WITHOUT PORTFOLIO AND CHIEF GOVT. WHIP, ONT. 1975- ; Life Underwriter, Mutual of Canada 1957; Br. Mgr. Empire Life 1965, Equitable Life 1967; estbd. Bud Gregory Insurance 1970; Town Councillor, Mississauga 1971-73, City Councillor 1974-75; Peel Regional Councillor 1974-75; el. M.P.P. 1975; mem. Commonwealth Parlty. Assn. (Rep. Ont. at Lusaka, Zambia); mem. Ont. Extve. Council; Bd. Trade Mississauga; P. Conservative; Anglican; recreations: music, golf, art; Club: Mississauga Golf and Country Club, Albany Club, Mississauga Optimist Club; Home: 3500 Silverplains Dr., Mississauga, Ont. L4X 2P4; Office: Room 251 Parliament Bldgs., Queen's Park, Toronto, Ont. M7A 1A2.

GREINER, Peter Charles, B.Sc., M.A., Ph.D., F.R.S.C.; educator; b. Budapest, Hungary 1 Nov. 1938; Dr. Anthony Charles and Ildiko (Willoner) G.; e. Univ. of B.C. B.Sc. 1960; Yale Univ. M.A. 1962, Ph.D. 1964; m. Kathryn Suzanne d. Dr. Wayne S. Dewald, Cohasset, Mass. 3 July 1965; children: Michael Anthony, Melissa Suzanne; PROF. OF MATH. UNIV. OF TORONTO since 1977; Instr. Princeton Univ. 1964-65; Asst. Prof. Univ. of Toronto 1965, Assoc. Prof. 1970; mem. Inst. for Advanced Study, Princeton, N.J. 1973-74; rec'd Steacie Prize in Natural Sciences 1977; co-author "Estimates for the XXX Neumann Problem" 1977; various math. articles; mem. Candn. Math. Soc.; Am. Math. Soc.; R. Catholic; Home: 121 Rose Park Dr., Toronto, Ont. M4T 1R6; Office: Toronto, Ont. M5S 1A1.

GRENDLER, Paul Frederick, M.A., Ph.D.; educator; b. Armstrong; Iowa 24 May 1936; s. August and Josephine (Girres) G.; e. Oberlin Coll. A.B. 1959; Univ. of Wisc. M.A. 1961, Ph.D. 1964; m. Marcella T. d. Peter J. McCann, Chicago, Ill. 16 June 1962; children: Peter, Jean; PROF. OF HISTORY, UNIV. OF TORONTO 1973- ; Instr. in Hist. Univ. of Pittsburgh 1963-64; Lectr. in Hist. present Univ. 1964, Asst. Prof. 1965, Assoc. Prof. 1969-73; Postdoctoral Fellow, Inst. Research in Humanities Univ. of Wisc. 1967-68; Can. Council Leave Fellowship 1970-71; Am. Council Learned Socs. Fellowship 1971-72; I Tatti Fellow (Harvard Univ. Center for Italian Renaissance Studies) Florence, Italy 1970-72; Sr. Fellow, Soc. for Humanities Cornell Univ. 1973-74; Guggenheim Mem. Fellowship 1978-79; Social Sciences & Humanities Research Council Can. Leave Fellowship 1979-80; Fellow, Woodrow Wilson Internat. Center for Scholars, Washington, D.C. 1982-83; author "Critics of the Italian World 1530-1560" 1969; "The Roman Inquisition and the Venetian Press 1540-1605" 1977 (Howard R. Marraro Prize, Am. Cath. Hist. Assn. 1978); "Culture and Censorship in Late Renaissance Italy and France" 1981; numerous articles and reviews learned journs.; mem. Ed. Bd. and Extve. Comte. "Collected Works of Erasmus" 1976- ; mem. Toronto Renaissance & Reformation Colloquium; Renaissance Soc. Am.; Am. Cath. Hist. Assn.; Soc. Italian Hist. Studies; recreations: piano playing, watching baseball; Home: 115 Sheldrake Blvd., Toronto, Ont. M4P 2B1; Office: Toronto, Ont. M5S 1A1.

GRENIER, Pierre, B.A., B.Sc.A., M.S.; ingénieurchimiste: né Québec, Qué., 15 août, 1922; f. Joachim et Corinne (Koenig) G.; é. Univ. Laval, B.A., 1942, B.Sc.A., 1946; Columbia Univ., M.S., 1947; ép. Thérèse, f. Ivan E. Vallée, 3 sept. 1949; enfants: Lucie, Ivan, François, DOYEN DE LA FACULTE DES SCIENCES ET DE GENIE, UNIV. LAVAL 1969-77; Prof. adjoint de Génie chimique, Univ. Laval, 1947; Prof. agrégé, 1950; Prof. titulaire, 1955; Prof. associé, Univ. de Nancy 1963-64; Dir. Dépt. de Génie chimique, Univ. Laval, 1965-69; publ.

divers articles techniques, Candn. Journ. Chem. Engn.; mem. Ordre des Ingénieurs du Qué.; Inst. de Chimie du Can. (Prés. 1972-73); Bureau Canadien d'accréditation (Pres. 1979-80); Conseil Nat. de Reserches du Can., 1972-78 apptd. Offr. of Order of Canada, 1976; Catholique; récréations: musique, jardinage, ornithologie; Résidence: 1575 Msgr. Taché, Québec, Qué.; Bureau: Québec, Qué.9

GRENON, Jean-Yves, B.A., L.L.D., Dr.jur.; diplomate; né St-Jovite, Qué. 3 septembre 1925; f. Paul-Emile et Aurore (Grégoire) G.; é. coll. des Frères du Sacré Coeur, St-Jovite; coll. Jean-de-Brébeuf, Montréal B.A. 1947; Univ. de Montréal L.L.D. 1950; Cambridge Univ. Diplôme en droit internat. 1953; Univ. de Paris Certificat de l'Institut d'Etudes politiques 1952, Dr.jur. (internat.) 1952; ép. Françoise Petit, Bordeaux, France 5 novembre 1952; enfants: Brigitte, Nathalie, Jean-François, Anne-Sylvie; AMBASSADEUR EN BOLIVIE ET AU PEROU 1979- ;entré au Ministère des Affaires extérieures 1953; Troisième secrétaire et vice-consul Rome 1955, deuxième secrétaire 1956; Chef du Service des traités Ottawa 1959-62; Premier secrétaire et consul Santiago 1962, Caracas 1965-67; Conseiller, Dakar 1967-69; Directeur d'Afrique francophone Ottawa 1969-71; diplomate en résidence et prof. invité Univ. de Montréal 1971-72; Premier conseiller Bruxelles et Luxembourg 1972, Chargé d'affaires a.i. 1974; Dir. des relations avec universités Ottawa 1976-77; diplomate en résidence et prof. invité Univ. Laval 1977-79; a participé à plusieurs conférences internat., colloques et congrés; mem. du comité du lexique de terminologie diplomatique 1969-70 et du Comité du bilinguisme des affaires extérieures; fréquentes missions au Conseil de l'Europe (Strasbourg) 1973-76; auteur nombreuses publs.; mem. Comité de rédaction de "Perspectives internationales"; Conseil canadien de Droit internat.; institut canadien des Affaires internat. et du Centre québécois de Relations internat.; R. Catholique; récréations: voile, ski, vol-à-voile, natation; Bureau: 130 Calle Libertad, Miraflores, Lima, Peru.

GRETZKY, Wayne; hockey player; b. Brantford, Ont. 26 Jan 1961, oldest of 4 boys and one girl; s. of Walter and Phyllis Gretzky; coached from childhood by his father and widely publicized as a ten-year old scoring sensation; played Junior hockey with Sault Ste. Marie Greyhounds; played with Indianapolis Racers in WHA 1978-79; scored 110 points in WHA at age seventeen; played with Edmonton Oilers in WHA and then in NHL in 1979-80 season; tied Marcel Dionne for scoring championship first season with 51 goals, 86 assists, and 137 total points; assaulted the record books in 2nd NHL season: most points in one season, 164, breaking Phil Esposito's record of 152 (1970-71); most points in one season, incl. playoffs, 185, again breaking Esposito's record of 162 (1970-71); most assists in one season, 109, breaking Bobby Orr's record of 102 (1970-71); most assists in one season, incl. playoffs, 123, again breaking Orr's record of 109 (1970-71); youngest player in league history to win scoring championship; in 1981-82 season demolished all his own records, scoring a phenomenal 92 goals in regular season play, with 120 assists, amassing a staggering 212 total points; reached the 50 goal plateau in 39 games; winner of practically every award in hockey, incl. The Hart Trophy, The Ross Trophy, Lady Byng Trophy; chosen for All-Star Team in each of 3 yrs in NHL; Player of the Year for 3 seasons; played for Team Canada Helsinki, 1982 (Bronze Medal); and winner of many other awards too numerous to mention; recreations: tennis, baseball, golf; Address: The Northlands Coliseum, Edmonton, Alberta.

GRIER, James C., B.A.; executive; b. Owen Sound, Ont.; e. Owen Sound Public and High Schs.; Univ. of Toronto, B.A. 1926; m.; President, Parker Imperial Ltd., 1971; Pres., Candn. Jewelers Assn., 1957-58; began career in the stationery dept. of a Toronto dept. store after which he joined Parker Pen Co. Ltd. in 1928; successively Sales Rep. in Ont. and Quebec till apptd. Sales Mgr., 1938; apptd. Sales and Advertising Mgr., 1942, Vice-Pres.,

1956, Pres. 1961, Chrmn. 1969-74; Pres., Candn. Jewellers Twenty-four Karat Club, 1963-64; Gov., Candn. Jewellers Inst. 1955-65; Home: Apt. 509, 70 Delisle Ave., Tor. M4V 1S7 Office:

GRIEW, Stephen, B.Sc., Ph.D., F.B.Ps.S.; b. London, Eng. 13 Sept. 1928; s. Harry and Sylvia (Wetstein) G.; e. Univ. of London, Univ. Coll. B.Sc. 1949, Birkbeck Coll. Postgrad. Dipl. in Psychol. 1951; Univ. of Bristol Ph.D. 1958; m. Eva Margareta Ursula d. late Dr. Joannes Ramberg, Stockholm, Sweden 7 May 1977; one s. and two d. from previous marriage, one d., one step-s.; PRES. ATHABASCA UNIV., EDMONTON, ALTA. 1981- ; Vocational Offr. Ministry of Labour and Nat. Service UK 1951-55; Research Worker and Lectr. Univ. of Bristol 1955-63; Consultant O.E.C.D. Paris 1963; Prof. and Head of Psychol. Univ. of Otago (N.Z.) 1964-68; Consultant I.L.O. Geneva 1966-67; Dean of Science Otago 1967-68; Prof. and Head of Psychol. Univ. of Dundee 1968-72; Consultant Dept. Employment UK 1969-71; Visiting Prof. San Diego State Coll. 1969, Univ. of W. Ont. 1970, 1971; Vice Chancellor, Murdoch Univ. Perth, W. Australia 1972-77; Australian Vice Chancellors' Comte. 1972-77; W. A. Tertiary Educ. Comte. 1972-76; Prof. & Chrmn. of Behavioural Sc., Univ. of Toronto, 1977-80; rec'd Kenneth Craik Research Award St. John's Coll. Cambridge Univ. 1960; Gov. Bayfield High Sch. Dunedin, N.Z. 1965-67; Bd. Mang. Dundee N. Hosp. Group 1968-72; Extve. W. A. Br. Australian Council for Rehabilitation of Disabled 1974-77; Vice Pres. Australian Council on Aging 1975-76; mem. Ed. Adv. Bd. "Occupational Psychology" 1969-73; author "Job Re-design: The Application of Biological Data on Aging to the Design of Equipment and the Organization of Work" 1964; "The Adaptation of Jobs for the Handicapped" 1969; co-author "Workers' Attitudes and the Acceptability of Shift Work in New Zealand Manufacturing Industry" 1969; articles and chapters on educ. planning, aging, human skilled performance, indust. psychol. in prof. and scient. books and journs.; Fellow, Gerontological Soc.; mem. Eng.-Speaking Union; recreations: music, tennis, travel; Office: Athabasca Univ., 12352-149 St., Edmonton, Alta., T5V 1G9

GRIFFIN, Anthony George Scott; company director; b. Lovehill, Langley; Bucks, England, l5 Aug. 1911; g.s. of Sir William Mackenzie; s. (Edward) Scott and Mabel Hannora (Mackenzie) G.; e. Appleby Sch., Oakville, Ont., 1922-29; Univ. of Toronto (Arts) 1929-30; Royal Mil. Coll., Kingston, Ont., 1930-31; m. Kathleen Lockhart, d. Col. H.D. Lockhart Gordon, Toronto, Ont., 12 June 1937; children: Scott, Ian Gordon, Margaret Ann McCall, Peter Mackenzie Gordon, Timothy Kirkfield; Chrmn. of the Bd., Commercial Life Assurance Co. of Canada; The Halifax Insurance Co.; Dir., C.I.L. Inc.; Hiram Walker Resources Ltd.; The Consumers' Gas Co. Ltd.; Scurry-Rainbow Oil Ltd.; United Dominions Corp. (Can.) Ltd.; Raymond International Inc.; Victoria & Grey Trustco Ltd.; ICI Americas Inc.; Candn. Corporate Management Co. Ltd.; S. G. Warburg & Co. Internat. Holdings Ltd.; Meridian Concepts Ltd.; Chrmn. St. Michael's Hosp.; mem. Adv. Council Nat. Ballet Can. (Pres. 1955-58); Mgr., Standard Life Assce. Co., Hamilton, Ont., 1935-40; Secy., W.P.T.B., 1945-47; Dept. of Ext. Affrs. 1948-51; Secy., Royal Comn. on Prices, 1948-49; Secy., Dollar-Sterling Trade Bd., 1949-51; served in 2nd World War with R.C.N., 1940-45; Commanded Corvette and Frigate; Staff Offr. (operations); to Flag Offr., Nfld. with rank of Cdr.; Mentioned in Despatches; mem., Candn. Inst. of Internat. Affairs; mgr. Candn. Olympic Sailing Team 1976; Commodore (1972-3) Canadian Albacore Assoc.; Pres. (1975-77); Internat. Albacore Assn. R. Catholic; recreations: tennis, sailing, skiing; Clubs: Toronto; Toronto Racquet; Badminton & Racquet; R.C.Y.C.; Osler Bluff Ski; Home: 2l Dunvegan Road, Toronto, Ont. M4V 2P5; Office: Suite 2540, First Candn. Place, P.O. Box 45, Toronto, Ont. M5X 1A9

GRIFFIN, John Douglas Morecroft, M.A., M.D., F.R.C.P.(C); psychiatric specialist; b. Hamilton, Ont. 3 June 1906; s. Herbert Spohn Griffin and Edith Moore (Robinson) G.; e. Hamilton Coll. Inst. 1924; Univ. of Toronto B.A. 1929, M.A. 1933, M.D. 1932; Dipl. in Psychol. Med. (Eng.) 1936; m. 1stly Erica Maude Withrow 22 Sept. 1934 (d. 1981); children: Charles Peter Morecroft, John David Anthony; m. 2ndly Barbara Mary Solandt 12 March 1982; Consultant, Candn. Mental Health Assn. 1972- ; post-grad. training Hosp. for Sick Children Toronto; Butler Hosp. Providence, R.I.; Nat. Hosp. Queens Square, London, Eng. (Rockefeller Fellow) 1934-36; Dir. of Educ. Candn. Mental Health Assn. 1936-41, Med. Dir. 1945-52, Gen. Dir. 1952-72; served with RCAMC 1941-45, rank Col.; mem. Extve. Comte. Ont. Mental Health Foundation 1975-81; rec'd Bowis Award Am. Coll. Psychiatry 1974; Hon. mem. Ont. Sch. Counsellors Assn.; Candn. Coll. Family Physicians; Sr. mem. Candn. Med. Assn.; Life mem. Ont. Med. Assn.; Toronto Acad. of Med.; Am. Psychiatric Assn.; Candn. Psychiatric Assn.; Ont. Psychiatric Assn.; author or co-author numerous publs.; Liberal; recreations: sailing, woodwork, travel; Club: National Yacht; Home: 18 Bracondale Hill Rd., Toronto, Ont. M6G 3P4; Office: 2160 Yonge St., Toronto, Ont. M4S 2Z3.

GRIFFIN, Melvin William, B.Sc., P.Eng.; company executive; b. Winnipeg, Man. 16 March 1923; s. late Aylmer & Elma (Hand) G.; e. Univ. of Manitoba; Queen's Univ.: m. Kathleen, d. late Lorne and Kathleen Devine, 27 Oct. 1947; children: Lorna (Mrs. Roger Smith), Patrick, Richard, Bruce, David; EXTVE. VICE-PRES., MFG., SEAGRAM CO. LTD. since 1978; Dir., The Seagram Co. Ltd.; Montreal Baseball Club Ltd.; Rowett Legge & Co. Ltd. Joseph E Seagram & Sons Ltd.; Seagram Distillers Ltd; Glenlivet Distillers Ltd.; The Donwood Inst.; Concordia Center For Management Studies; with Defence Industries Ltd. 1944; joined Distillers Corp. Ltd. 1945, serving in Jamaica ; until 1963 apptd. Dir. Candn. Operations 1963, Vice-Pres. and Dir. 1967; Exec. Vice-Pres. and Chief Operating Officer 1970; Pres. House of Seagram Ltd. 1975; Exec Vice-Pres Manufacturing, the Seagram Co. Ltd., 1978; Pres. Jos. E. Seagram & Sons, Inc., Chief Exec. Officer, 1980; 1978 mem., Prov. of Que. Chamber of Commerce; Chambre du Commerce du District du Montréal; Winnipeg Chamber of Commerce; Can. Council, International Chamber of Commerce; The Montreal Bd. of Trade; Queen's Univ. Alum.; Clubs: Royal Montreal Golf; Montreal Amateur Athletic Assoc; recreations: curling, golf, swimming; R. Catholic; Home: 3460 Simpson St., Apt. 905, Montreal, Que. H3G 2J4; Office: 1430 Peel St., Montreal, Que. H3A 1S9

GRIFFIS, Arthur Thomas, M.A., Ph.D.; geologist; b. Fort William, Ont., 29 Dec. 1912; s. Arthur Hatton and Ida Elizabeth (Thomas) G.; e. Primary and Secondary Schs., Fort William, Collingwood and Colborne, Ont.; Univ. of Toronto, B.A. 1934, M.A. (Geology), 1937; Cornell Univ., Ph.D. (Geology), 1939; m. Jean Elizabeth, d. David Darling, 27 Dec. 1937; children: Robert J., Maj. A.T.D., Elizabeth; Sen. Geological Consultant, WATTS, GRIFFIS AND McOUAT LTD., President Canadian Magnesite Mines Ltd.; Camino Gold Mines Ltd.; Field Engr., Hollinger Consolidated Gold Mines, 1939-47; Chief Geol., Tsumeb Corp., S.W. Africa, 1947-50; Field Mgr., Exploration Miniére au Congo, French Equatorial Africa, 1950-52; self-employed Geol., S. Ont. and Que., 1952-55; Mgr., Oceanic Iron Ore of Canada, Ungava, Que., 1955-58; Research Geol., McIntyre Porcupine Mines, Timmins, Ont., 1958-62; Fellow, Geol. Assn. Can.; Senior mem. Soc. Econ. Geols.; life mem., Candn. Inst. Mining & Metall.; mem. Am. Inst. Mining Engn.; Assn. Prof. Engrs. Ont.; Liberal; Presbyterian; Office: 159 Bay St., Toronto, Ont. M5J 1J7

GRIFFITH, Rev. A. Leonard, D.D. (Ang. Ch.); b. Preston, Lancs., Eng., 19 Mar. 1920; s. Thomas Mostyn and

Sarah Jane (Taylor) G.; both parents were prof. opera singers with companies touring the Brit. Isles; e. Wesley Coll., Dublin, Ireland; Brockville (Ont.) Coll. Inst.; McGill Univ., B.A. 1942; United Theol. Coll., B.D. 1945, D.D. 1962; ordained U.C. of Can. 1945; Ang. Church, 1975; m. Anne Merelie, d. Stanley B. Cayford of Montreal, Que., 17 June 1947; two d.; ASSOCIATE MINISTER ST. PAUL'S CHURCH, since 1975; Asst. Min., St. Andrew's-Westmount Ch., Montreal, Que., 1941-44; Dominion-Douglas Ch., Montreal, Que., 1944-45; Min., Arden-Mountain Grove (Ont.), 1945-47; Trinity Ch., Grimsby, Ont., 1947-50; Chalmers Ch. Ottawa, Ont., 1950-60; City Temple, London, Eng. 1960-66; Deer Park United Church, Toronto 1966-75; Lecturer in Homiletics, Toronto School of Theology; Organist when at Divinity Hall, McGill Univ.; has been interested in theatre as actor and organizer with Brockville Theatre Guild, McGill Players, Montreal Repertory Theatre, C.B.C., Montreal and Grimsby Players' Guild; Publications: "Take Hold of the Treasure"; "Reactions to God"; "Gospel Characters"; "We Have This Ministry"; "Ephesians: A Positive Affirmation"; "Hang on to the Lord's Prayer"; "The Need to Preach"; and others; recreations: gardening, fishing, jogging; Address: 102 Arjay Cres., Willowdale, Ont. M2L 1C7

GRIFFITH, Harold M.; industrial executive (ret.); b. Clinton, Ill., 4 July 1904; s. Melvin May and Anna (McGaw) G.; e. Missouri Sch. of Mines; Chicago Tech. Inst., Elect. Engn. Grad.; Harvard Business Sch., 1949; m. Fredrica, d. late John Schneider, 14 Sept. 1927; two d. Gretchen (Mrs. H.R. Skeels), Shirley (Mrs. G.R. Russell); Dir., Toronto, Hamilton and Buffalo Railway Co.; mem. Bd. Govs., Bethlehem Steel Corp., Johnston, Pa., 1926-30; Jones & Laughlin Steel Corp. 1931-36; joined present co. as Metall. Engr. 1936; subsequently became Asst. Open Hearth Supt., Open Hearth Supt., Asst. Works Mgr. (Hilton Works), Works Mgr., Asst. to the Pres.; apptd. Vice Pres., Operations, 1953-63; Extve. Vice Pres. 1964-66; Pres., 1966; Dir., 1967; Chrmn., 1971; Retired from Stelco Inc., 1976; Past Chrmn., Hamil-Commerce; mem., American Iron & Steel Institute (Past Chrmn. Comte. Mfg. Problems); Am. Inst. Mining & Metall. Engrs. (Past Chrmn. Nat. Open Hearth Comte.); rec'd Am. Soc. for Metallurgists Medal for Advanc. of Research, Oct. 1969; Presbyterian; recreations: hunting, fishing, golf; Clubs: Seigniory (Montebello, Que.); St. James's (Montreal); Rotary; The Toronto; Tamahaac (Ancaster); Union (Cleveland); Hamilton Golf and Country (Ltd.); Home: 2304 Old Mill Towers, 39 Old Mill Road, Toronto, Ont. M8X lG6; Office: Royal Trust Tower, (P.O. Box 205), Toronto-Dominion Centre, Toronto, Ont. M5K 1J4

GRIFFITH, Harold Randall, O.C. (1974), M.D., C.M., LL.D., F.F.A., R.C.S.(Eng.), F.R.C.P.(C), F.A.C.A.; anaesthetist; b. Montreal, Que., 25 July 1894; s. Alexander Randall, M.D., and Mary Euphemia (Milne) G.; e. McGill Univ., B.A. 1914; M.D., C.M. 1922; Hahnemann Med. Coll., M.D. 1923; m. Linda May, d. W.W. Aylen, M.D., Westmount, Que., 27 June 1922; Anaes.-in-Chief & Med. Supt., Queen Elizabeth Hosp. of Montreal 1924 to 1964; Emeritus Prof. of Anaesthesia, McGill Univ., since 1957; joined staff of McGill Univ. in 1946 as Lectr. in Anaesthesia; served in 1st World War 1914-18; Sgt., No. 6 Canda. Field Ambulance, 1914-17; Surg. Sub-Lieut., R.N.V.R. 1917-18; awarded Mil. Medal, 1917 (Vimy Ridge); served in 2nd World War 1944-46; Hon. Wing Commdr., R.C.A.F., Consultant in Anaesthesia; Registrar, Coll. Homeopathic Phys. and Surgs. of Montreal, since 1933; Gov., Queen Elizabeth Hosp. of Montreal; introduced "Curare" into clinical use in anaesthesia, 1942; Pres., World Fed. of Societies of Anaesthesiologists, 1955; awarded Feltrinelli Prize in Med. of Accademia Nazionale Dei Lincei, Rome, 1954; Henry Hill Hickman Medal, Royal Soc. of Med., London, 1956; mem., Candn. Anaesthesia Soc. (Pres. 1942-45); Am. Soc. Anaesthesiol-

ogists (Vice-Pres. 1948); Internat. Anaesthesia Research Soc. (Pres. 1948); Assn. Anaesthetists of U.S. and Can. (Pres. 1933); Candn. Med. Assn., Montreal Medico-Chirurg. Soc.; el. Fellow, Royal Coll. of Surgs. Faculty of Anaesthetists, London (1st Candn.), July 1959; author of about sixty articles in various Candn., Am. and Eng. med. journ., dealing particularly with endotrocheal anaesthesia, cyclo-propane anaesthesia, curare and other anaesthesia agents and methods; Hon. LL.D. Sask. 1975; Nu Sigma Nu; Baptist; recreation: curling; Clubs: McGill Faculty; University; Heather Curling (Pres. 1947-48); Home: Apt. 1301, 4998 de Maisonneuve Blvd. W., Montreal, Westmount, Que. H3Z 1N2

GRIFFITHS, Anthony F., , B.A., M.B.A.; company executive; b. Rangoon, Burma, 19 July 1930; s. David Thomas and Margaret (Tompkins) G.; McDonogh Sch., Baltimore, Md.; Williams Coll., Mass.; McGill Univ., B.A. 1954; Harvard Grad. Sch. of Business Adm., M.B.A. 1956; m. Dorothy, d. John B. Richardson, 15 Aug. 1959; children: Jennifer, Stephanie, David, Michael; VICE-CHRMN. AND PRES., HARDING CARPETS LTD. Dir. Harding Carpets Ltd.; Confederation Life Show Industries Ltd., Capital Cable TV Ltd., Meridian Concepts Ltd., Rous Mann & Brigdens Ltd.; Assoc., Connor, Clark & Co. Ltd.; joined Candn. Resins & Chem. Ltd., Montreal, Que., 1956; Candn. Curtiss Wright, 1958-59; P.S. Ross & Partners, Management Consultants, Montreal and Toronto, 1959-60; joined Consumers Glass Co. Ltd. as Marketing Mgr., 1960; apptd. Vice-Pres., 1965, Extve. Vice-Pres., 1968, Extve. Vice-Pres. and Dir. 1969-71; Pres., Candn. Cablesystems Ltd. 1971-76; served as Lieut., R.C.A. (Supplementary Reserve); mem. Soc. Financial Analysts; Zeta Psi; Anglican; recreations: tennis, squash, skiing; Clubs: Badminton & Racquet; Toronto Club; Queen's Club; Home: 53 Rowanwood Ave., Toronto, Ont. M4W 1Y8; Office: Connor, Clark & Co. Ltd., 390 Bay St., Suite 2318, Toronto, Ont. M5H 2Y2

GRIFFITHS, Donald John; banker; b. Dudley, Eng., 24 Aug. 1920; s. Donald Cecil and Doris Rosalind (Purnell) G.; e. Dudley (Eng.) Grammar Sch., 1937; Oxford Univ., Honours Dipl. Econ. Studies, 1945; Carnegie Mellon Univ., Extve. course, 1970; m. Celia Doreen, d. James Carpenter, 15 March 1952; children: Peter John, Elaine, Joan Margaret; VICE PRES. INTERNATIONAL BANKING, CANDN. IMPERIAL BANK OF COMMERCE, since 1973; Dir., United Dominions Corp. (Canada); Ontario Educational Services Corp., Bank of Commerce Jamaica Ltd., Kuwait Pacific Finance Corp., Hong Kong, California Canadian Bank; joined Barclays Bank Ltd. 1937; Barclays Bank (Can.), Montreal 1947-56; Imperial Bank of Can. 1956-62; joined present company as Asst. Mgr. Montreal Br. 1962, Mgr. 265 St. James St. W., Montreal, 1966, Regional (Que.) Gen. Mgr. 1969, Vice Pres. and Regional (Que.) Gen. Mgr. 1970; served with RAF 1940-45; attached RCAF 419 Sqdn. 1943-45; Fellow, Inst. Candn. Bankers; Fellow, Inst. Bankers, Eng.; Anglican; recreations: golf, skiing; Clubs: National, Toronto Overseas Bankers Club (London, Eng.); Home: 1284 Minaki Rd., Mississauga, Ont. N5G 2X4; Office: Commerce Ct. West, Toronto, Ont.

GRIFFITHS, Franklyn John Charles, Ph.D.; educator; b. Edinburgh, Scot. 8 Sept. 1935; s. John Francis and Tamara Juliana (Wender) G.; e. Ridley Coll. St. Catharines, Ont. 1953; Trinity Coll. Univ. of Toronto B.A. 1958; Columbia Univ. Sch. of Internat. Affairs M.I.A. 1962, Dept. Pub. Law & Govt. Ph.D. 1972; m. Margaret Reva d. late James Hogarth 18 Oct. 1958; children: Tamara Juliana, Rudyard John Francis; PROF. OF POL. ECON. UNIV. OF TORONTO 1973- ; Ed., Pergamon Press, London and Oxford 1958-60; Researcher, Candn. Peace Research Inst. Toronto 1962-63 and M.I.T. Center for Internat. Studies Cambridge, Mass. 1963-64; Asst. Prof. of Pol. Econ. Univ. Toronto 1966, Dir. Centre for Russian & E. European Studies 1975-79; recipient Ford Foundation Award arms control 1976; Fellow, Woodrow Wilson Internat. Center, Smithsonian Inst. 1979; commentator on pub. affairs incl. Candn. foreign policy, internat. security affairs, arctic internat. relations; author "Khrushchev and the Arms Race" 1966; co-ed. and contrib. "Interest Groups in Soviet Politics" 1971; "The Dangers of Nuclear War" 1979; author various articles, short studies; mem. Nat. Council Candn. Inst. Internat. Affairs; Candn. Pol. Science Assn.; Candn. Assn. Slavists (Pres. 1978-79); Arms Control Assn.; Candn. Pugwash Group; Comite Arctique; recreations: squash, guitar, farming; Home; 360 Brunswick Ave., Toronto, Ont. M5R 2Y9; Office: 100 St. George St.; Toronto, Ont. M5S 1A1.

GRIFFITHS, Naomi E.S., M.A., Ph.D.; b. Hove, Eng., 20 Apl. 1934; d. Robert Lewis and Agnes Mary (Saunders) G.; e. Lewes Co. Grammar Sch. for Girls; London Univ. Bedford Coll. B.A. 1956, Ph.D. 1969; Univ. of N.B., M.A. 1957; DEAN, FACULTY OF ARTS, CARLETON UNIV. since 1979 and Prof. of Hist. since 1978; Lectr. Coll. Maillet 1957-58; joined present Univ. as Instr. in Hist. 1961, Lectr. 1962, Asst. Prof. 1964, mem. Senate since 1971 (Extve. 1973-75), Pres. Acad. Staff Assn. 1971-72; rec'd State Scholarship 1953-56, Goldsmith Travelling Scholarship 1956, Univ. N.B. Grad. Fellowship 1956-57, Lord Beaverbrook Overseas Travelling Fellowship 1958-60, Can. Council post-doctoral research grant 1971, 1972, 1973; Chairwoman CAUT Comte. on Status Acad. Women in Can. 1973; author "The Acadian Deportation: Deliberate Perfidy or Cruel Necessity" 1969, "The Acadians: Creation of a People" 1973, "Penelope's Web, Some Perceptions of Women in European and Canadian Society" 1976; also pamphlets, articles and reviews; TV programmes various topics and script for ETV "1755"; mem. Candn. Research Inst. for Advanc. Women (mem. Bd. of Dirs.) 1975-78; NDP; R. Catholic; recreations: music, science fiction, cooking, cross-country skiing; Home: 141 Southern, Ottawa, Ont. K1S 0P4

GRIFFITHS, Hon. Wilson David; b. Owen Sound, Ont. 28 May 1925; s. Leonard Whitney and Jean Mearns (Davidson) G.; e. Pub. and High Schs., Owen Sound; Univ. of Toronto, Victoria Coll. B.A. Law (Hons.) 1948, Post Grad. LL.B. 1950; Gold Key, Osgoode Hall 1951; m. Doris Jean, d. late Aylmer Plowright 4 Sept. 1948; children: Pamela Read, Brenda, Bradley, Wilson; JUSTICE, SUPREME COURT OF ONT.; read law with Haines and Haines 1948-49 and Fraser Beatty Tucker & McIntosh 1950-51; called to the Bar of Ont. 1951; cr. Q.C. 1962; Jr. Solr. J. Donald Bell, Toronto 1951-53; Partner, Bell Keith Gangong & Griffiths, Toronto 1953-56; Bell Griffiths Temple & Genest 1956-66; Sr. Partner, Cassels Brock 1966-75; served as Wireless Navig. 1943-44, with Candn. Army 1944-45, rank Lt.; Past Bencher, Law Soc. Upper Can. (Lectr. and Instr., Head of Civil Procedure, Bar Admission Course 1959-75; Lectr., panelist, sometime Chrmn. 16 Cont. Legal Educ. series; Vice Chrmn., Ont. Legal Aid Plan 1971-75; Chrmn., Prepaid Legal Services Comte.; Errors & Omissions Ins. Comte. 1971-75); Chrmn., (1960-71) Civil Justice Sec., Co. of York Law Assn.; Chrmn. (1963-74) Ins. Sec., Candn. Bar Assn.; mem. Council (1972-75) Medico-Legal Soc. of Toronto; Hon. mem. Am. Trial Lawyer Assn.; Dir. (1968-71. Pres. 1971-72) The Advocates' Soc.; Chrmn. (1956-57) Building Comte., W. Ellesmere United Ch.; Hon. Life Mem., Guildwood Community Assn.; United Ch.; recreations: skiing, fishing, sailing, golf; Clubs: Royal Candn. Mil. Inst.; Scarboro Golf & Country; Home: 19 Somerdale St., Scarborough, Ont. M1E 1M9; Office: Osgoode Hall, Toronto, Ont. M5H 2N5

GRILLS, Richard Michael, B.A.; investment dealer; b. Toronto, Ont., 3 July 1929; s. Thomas Oliver and Dorothy Mary (Leroy) G.; e. Forest Hill Coll. Inst., Toronto, 1946; Univ. of Toronto, Trinity Coll., B.A. 1951; m. Joan Stuart, d. late Lindsay Stuart Mackersy, 16 Sept. 1953; two s., Jeffrey, Peter; VICE-PRES. AND DIR., McLEOD YOUNG

WEIR LTD.; Dir., C.S. Computer Leasing of Canada Ltd.; Reg'd. Rep. of present firm, Toronto, 1953, Sales Mgr., Montreal 1960, Inst'al Mgr., Toronto 1962, Resident Dir. and Vice Pres., Montreal 1968; Trustee and Campaign Chrmn. (1975), Un. Community Fund Metrop. Toronto; Hon. Gov. Trent Univ.; mem. of Bd., Toronto Symphony Orchestra; Boys and Girls Clubs of Canada; North York Hospital; mem. Invest. Dealers Assn. Can.; Zeta Psi; Anglican; recreations: hunting, fishing, reading; Clubs: Toronto; Granite; Home: 93 Mona Dr., Toronto, Ont. M5N 2R3; Office: Commercial Union Tower, T.D. Centre, Toronto, Ont. M5K 1N2

GRIMLEY, Peter H., B.Sc., Ph.D.; exploration geologist; b. Blackpool, Eng., 18 Oct. 1933; s. Hugh & Ruth (Greenwood) G.; e. Royal Sch. of Mines, B.Sc. (Min. Geol.) 1955, ARSM 1955; Imp. Coll. Dipl. (DIC) 1958; Univ. of London, Ph.D. (Mining Geol.) 1958; m. Patricia Harriet, d. Stephen William Still, 29 Sept. 1961; children: Simon Jonathon, Judith Sarah; VICE PRES., CORPORATE BANKING BANK OF MONTREAL since 1981; field work E. Africa 1955-58; Geol. on expdn. to Karakoram Himalayas, W. Pakistan, 1957; exploration activities in Can. 1959; geol. & topographical exploration in Antarctica 1959-61; Exploration Mgr. various exploration activities, Argentina, 1961-66; joined Brinco Ltd. 1966; Vice-Pres. and Exploration Mgr., Brinex 1972-81; Vice-Pres. and Gen. Mgr., Brinco Ltd.; exploration activities in Can. and U.S.A.; awarded Polar Medal; Assoc. mem., Inst. Mining & Metall., London; mem., Candan. Inst. Mining & Metall.; Trustee Candn. Outward Bound Wilderness School; Anglican; recreations: mountaineering, fishing; Clubs: Antarctic, Engineers; Home: 64 Truman Rd., Toronto, Ont. M2L 2L6; Office: Bank of Montreal, First Canadian Place, Toronto, Ont. M5X 1A1

GRINDLEY, Thomas V.; banker; b. Chester, U.K. 1929; m. Edith (Nyland) 1956; children: Robin and Toby SR. VICE PRES. CORPORATE BANKING DIV., CANADIAN IMPERIAL BANK OF COMMERCE; Dir. Canlea Ltd.; Delta Hotels Ltd.; prior to joining present Bank 1953 with Mercantile Bank of India 2 yrs.; Depy. Mgr. present Bank London, Eng. 1966, Area Mgr. Trinidad & Tobago 1967, Area Extve. W. Indies & Far E. 1971, Asst. Gen. Mgr. Project Financing 1976, Vice Pres. Corporate Banking Main Br. Toronto 1979; recreation: tennis; Club: Ontario; Home: 109 Valecrest Drive, Toronto, Ont. M9A 4P5; Office: Commerce Court W., Toronto, Ont. M5L 1A2.

GRISDALE, John Hiram, B.Sc.; executive; b. Olds, Alta. 21 Aug. 1923; s. Frank S. Grisdale; e. McGill Univ. B.Sc. (Agric.) 1949; m. Mary (Lu) Kennedy d. William Connell, Wingham, Ont.; children: John Hiram Jr., Paul D., Jill; SR. VICE PRES. ADM. AND DIR., CAMPBELL SOUP CO. LTD.; Pres. CanVin Products Ltd.; Dir. Candn. Food Processors Assn.; served with Candn. Army 1941-45; recreation: golf; Club: St. George's Golf & Country; Home: 22 Abilene Dr., Islington, Ont. M9A 2M8; Office: 409 Evans Ave., Toronto, Ont. M8Z 1L1.

GRONDIN, Pierre, O.C. (1968), M.D., F.R.C.S.(C), F.A.C.S.; né Québec, 18 août 1925, f. G. Antoine et Germaine (Fortier) G.; é. Univ. Laval, Québec, B.A., magna cum laude, 1945; M.D., magna cum laude, 1951; Conseil Nat. de. Méd. du Canada, L.M.C.C., 1951; Univ. de Pennsylvanie, chirurgie, 1955; Calif. Board of Med. Examiners, licence, 1956; Coll. Royal du Canada, F.R.C.S. (chirurgie); Coll. des Méd. et Chirurgiens du Qué., C.S.P.Q., 1959; F.A.C.S., 1960; Univ. Baylor, Houston, Texas, chirurgie thoracique cardiaque, 1961-62; enfants: Louis, Jean; MEDECIN-CHIRURGIEN, INSTITUT DE CARDIOLOGIE de MONTREAL, depuis 1963; méd. gén., Trois-Rivières, Qué., 1951; pratique chirurgie gén., Trois-Rivières, 1960-62; consultant, Hôpital Ste-Marie, Trois Rivières et Cloutier, Cap de la Madeleine; Prof. associé de chirurgie clinique, Univ. Laval, Qué., 1961; Chef résident, chirurgie cardiaque et vasculaire, Children et St. Lukes Hospitals, Houston, Texas, 1962; Chef du départ. de chirurgie cardiaque et vasculaire et du départ. de chirurgie expérimentale, Inst. de Cardiologie de Montréal, 1963; Consultant en chirurgie cariovasculaire, Hôpital Jean-Talon, Montreal et Hôpital St-Joseph, Trois-Rivières, 1963; Membre associé, chirurgie cardio-vasculaire, Hôpital Jean-Talon, Montréal, 1965; Consultant chirurgie thoracique et cardio vasculaire, Hôpital Fleury, Montréal, 1966; et Hôpital, Bellechasse, Montréal, 1967; Membre fondateur, The Society of Thoracic Surgery, 1966; Membre: Soc. Can. de Cardiologie; Soc. de Cardiologie de Montréal, Assoc. des Méd. de Langue Fr.; Soc. Méd. Can., Assoc. de Chirurgie Thoraciques et Cardiovasculaire de la Prov. de Qué.; Soc. Française de Chirurgie Thoracique; Soc. Espagnole de Cardiologie; decoré de Lords de Christophe Colomb (Republique Dominicaine); Auteur de plus de 125 articles sur la chirurgie cardio-vasculaire et la greffe du coeur humain; Prix Bergeron, Univ. Laval et le Laval Méd., 1961; Médaille Bene Merenti de Patria, Soc. St-Jean Baptiste, 1968; Personalité de l'Année 1968, Assoc. des Hommes d'Affaires et Prof. Can.-Italiens Inc.; Catholique; Loisirs: sports d'hiver et d'été; Résidence: 32, Les Bouleaux, Laval, Qué. H7R 1E2;

GROOME, Reginald K.; O.C.; hotel executive; b. Montreal, Que., 18 Dec. 1927; s. late Muriel Harbord (Forbes-Toby) and Cyril Thomas G.; e. Willingdon Elem. Sch., Montreal; Montreal High Sch.; McGill Univ., Montreal; Cornell Univ., Ithaca, N.Y.; m. Christina Marie Florence, d. Alfred George Walker, 20 June 1953; CHRMN. AND PRES., HILTON CANADA INC., since Dec. 1972; Dir., Crum & Forster (New York); U.S. Fire Ins. Co.; Westchester Fire Ins. Co.; Internat. Ins. Co.; North River Ins. Co.; Crum and Forster of Can. Ltd.; Herald Insurance Co.; Alliance Compagnie Mutuelle d'Assurance-Vie, Dustbane Enterprises Ltd.; started career as journalist with Montreal Publishing Co., Montreal, served as overseas correspondent 1951; began hotel career at Sheraton-Mount Royal Hotel, Montreal, 1953; joined present firm at Queen Élizabeth Hotel 1957; now in charge of Hilton's Canadian operations; invested with Silver Acorn 1964 (Boy Scouts of Can.) by Gov. Gen. Vanier; Outstanding Citizen Award by Montreal Citizenship Council, 1976; Queen's Jubilee Medal, 1977 B'nai B'rith Inaugural Award of Merit, 1978; Invested with Silver Wolf (Boy Scouts of Can.) by Gov. Gen. Léger 1978; Meritorious Citizen's Award from Lt. Gov. Jean-Pierre Coté, Quebec 1980; invested as Officer, Order of Can. by Gen. Schreyer, 1980; free lance broadcaster since 1946, now with CFQR-FM (Montreal); Past Pres. Montreal Bd. of Trade; Vice Pres., Chambre de Com. de la Prov. de Qué.; mem. 12-man World Scout Comte., Geneva; Gov., Concordia Univ., Montreal; Life Gov. Montreal Gen. Hosp.; Internat. Commis. Boy Scouts of Can.; recreations: golf, water skiing, boating; Clubs: Mount Royal; St. Denis; M.A.A.A.; Mount Bruno Golf & Country; Royal Montreal Golf; Ocean Reef (Key Largo, Fla.); Office The Queen Elizabeth Hotel, 900 Dorchester, Montreal, Que. H3B 4A5

GROSART, Hon. Allister, P.C.; B.A.; (1962-82) senator; b. Dublin, Ireland, 13 Dec. 1906; s. Herbert Montgomery and Elizabeth (Mackey) G.; e. Chefoo, China, 1915-23; Univ. of Toronto, B.A. 1927; Carnegie Fellow of Internat. Law, 1928; m. (2nd) Thelma Anna Galbraith, 1978; daughters; Mrs. Geraldene Hubble, Mrs. Victoria Stoney, Miss Jane Galbraith; Pres., Creative Arts Co.; Grosart & Co. Ltd.; Dir. First City Financial Corp. (Vancouver); Chrmn. Audit Committee and Dir. First City Trust Co. (Calgary); Toronto Daily Star, 1928-34; Consultant, Toronto Globe and Toronto Globe & Mail, 1935-37; formed Canadian Publicity Bureau, 1932; 1944, formed Southern Music Publishing Co. (Can.) Ltd., Peer International (Can.) Ltd., Editions Sud Ltd., 1948; Public Relations Consultant to P. Conservative Party (Ont.) 1948-57; Public Relations Consultant to P. Conservative Party in By-elections, 1948-56, Nat. Dir. of the Party and Campaign

Mgr., 1957-62; summoned to the Senate of Can., 25 Sept. 1962; Candn. Delegate to International Conferences (1960-80) in Europe, Caribbean, U.K., Washington D.C., Ottawa, Mauritius, Australia, Malaysia, S. Korea, India, Zambia, Egypt, Cyprus, Malawi, Kenya, Somalia, etc.; Vice-Pres. and Dir., McKim Advertising Ltd., 1952-57; created War Effort Radio programs for C.B.C.; Lieut. to Major, 2nd Bn. Irish Regt. of Can. (C.A.R.), 1940-45; Chrmn. Senate Steering Comm. on Nat. Sci. Policy 1968-76; Pres., Parliamentary and Scientists Comm.; former V. Chrmn. Senate Finance Comm. and Senate Foreign Affairs Comm.; former Dep. Leader of Opposition and Govt in Senate; Speaker. of Senate 1979-80; summoned to Queen's Privy Council for CAn. 1981; Clubs: Albany; Rideau (Ottawa); National Press; Home: 1400 Dixie Rd., Mississauga, Ont. L5E 3E1; Office: 1240 Bay St., Suite 401, Toronto, Ont. M5R 2A7

GROSMAN, Brian Allen, Q.C. B.A., LL.B., LL.M.; b. Toronto, Ont. 20 May 1935; s. Morris and Bessie Celia (Benson) G.; e. Forest Hill Coll. Inst. Toronto 1954; Univ. of Toronto B.A. 1957, LL.B. 1960; Osgoode Hall 1961; McGill Univ. LL.M. 1967; m. Penny-Lynn d. Arthur George Cookson, Calgary, Alta. Verna Cookson, Saskatoon, Sask. 1 Sept. 1967; one s. John Shain; PARTNER, GREENGLASS AND GROSMAN, Barristers at Law, Toronto, since 1979; Prof. of Law, Coll. of Law Univ. of Sask., 1971-79; Founding Chrmn. Law Reform Comn. Sask. 1974-1978; read law with Harries, Houser, Brown & Houlden, Toronto; called to Bar of Ont. 1962, Bar of Sask. 1971; private law practice Toronto 1962-66 in assn. with Burrell M. Singer; assoc. with firm Greenberg, Gorsky & Greenberg, Ottawa 1966; Special Prosecutor to Ministry of Justice (part-time) 1964-65; Teaching Fellow McGill Univ. 1966; Fellow N.Y. Univ. Inst. Comparative Criminal Law 1966; Asst. Prof. McGill Univ. 1966-68, Assoc. Prof. 1969-71; Visiting Prof. Univ. of Free Berlin 1968; Russell Sage Fellow Univ. of Denver 1969; Consultant: Royal Comn. on Status of Women in Can. 1970; Law Reform Comn. of Can. Project on Criminal Procedure 1972-73; Canadian Wildlife Service, A Survey of Resource Sharing Agreements (3 Vols.); Ont. Task Force on Policing 1972; City of Winnipeg Comte. Studying Unification Police Forces Greater Winnipeg 1972; Nat. Adv. Comte. Task Force on Disorders and Terrorism Washington 1976; apptd. one-man Comn. Inquiry into Police Organ. and Structure P.E.I. 1974; Candn. del. Conf. Centre Internat. de Criminologie Comparee Versailles, France 1971; Candn. Rep. l'Indice Penale Internat. Criminol. Quarterly Univ. of Milan; Sask. Commr. Uniformity Conf. Can. 1974-77; Chrmn. Conf. Indians and the Law McGill Univ. 1970 and Que. Conf. on Crime and Delinquency 1969; Moderator Unitel Univ. of Sask. Educ. TV 1972-73; Chrmn. Senate Discrimination as to Sex at Univ. McGill 1970; Chrmn. Conf. on Human Rights and the Adm. of Justice, 1980-81; rec'd. Candn. Bar Foundation Award for Legal Research 1966; author "The Prosecutor, An Inquiry into the Exercise of Discretion" 1969; "Police Command: Decisions and Discretion" 1975; "New Directions in Sentencing" 1980; "The Executive Firing Line: Wrongful Dismissal and the Law", 1982; Contributor to "Employment Law Report", 1981-82, and "Conflict Quarterly", 1980-82; Contributing editor, Executive Magazine, 1982; also various articles, book chapters, booklets, surveys and reports including "The Grosman Report on Policing in PEI" 1974; ; Assoc. Secy. Gen. Que. Soc. Criminol. 1968-69 (Vice Pres. 1969-70); Life mem. Internat. Soc. Study Comparative Law: mem. Am. Judicature Soc.; Internat. Assn. De Droit Penale; Internat. Conf. Criminal Law; Am. Soc. Criminol. (Extve. 1973; rec'd Presidential Citation 1975); Am. Law Inst.; Advocate's Soc. of Ont.; Candn. Assn. Law Teachers; mem. Adv. Council, Candn. Human Rights Foundation (1975-81); Law Soc. Upper Can.; Ont. Bar Assn.; Law Soc. Sask.; Sask. Bar Assn.; Candn. Bar Assn. (Council 1974-76); Jewish; recreations: tennis, skiing, riding; Clubs: University; Albany; North Toronto Lawn & Tennis; Cambridge; Home:

Grante Pl., 61 St. Clair Ave. W., Apt. 907, Toronto, Ont. M4V 2Y9 Office: Ste. 2000, 390 Bay St., Toronto, Ont. M5H 2Y2

GROSS, Hon. Reginald John, M.L.A.; politician; b. Vanguard, Sask. 3 Oct. 1948; s. Edward W. and Emilia T. (Biesek) G.; e. Glen Bain (Sask.) Elem. Sch.; Kincaid (Sask.) Central High Sch.; m. Debra d. Alan McDonald, Wapella, Sask. 4 May 1974; children: Jeffrey, Theodore, Taylore; MIN. OF GOVT. SERVICES AND MIN. OF TOURISM & RENEWABLE RESOURCES, SASK. 1979- ; el. M.L.A. for Gravelbourg 1971, def. 1974, re-el. 1978; Chrmn. of Bd., Sask. Minerals; Sask. Fur Marketing Service; Secy.-Treas. Glenwood Co-op; mem. Nat. Farmers Union; NDP; R. Catholic; recreation: skiing; Home: (P.O. Box 9) Glen Bain, Sask. S0N 0X0; Office: 43 Legislative Bldg., Regina, Sask. S4S 0B3.

GROSS, William Harvey, B.A.Sc., M.A., Ph.D.; geologist; b. New Westminster, B.C. 5 Dec. 1917; s. William Palmer and Leila (Harvey) G.; e. Univ. of B.C. B.A.Sc. 1940; Univ. of Toronto M.A. 1947, Ph.D. 1950; m. Shirley d. late Gordon S. Wismer 19 Apl. 1943; children: Stephen William, John Harvey; CHAIRMAN AND CHIEF EXECUTIVE, LACANA MINING CORP. since 1968; Prof. of Mineral Econ. Univ. of Toronto 1950-68; served with RCAF Bomber Command Europe during World War II, Pilot; author numerous scient. papers and articles; Fellow, S.E.G.; mem. C.I.M.; G.S.A.; G.A.C.; Assn. Prof. Engrs. Prov. Ont.; Phi Delta Theta; recreation: golf; Home: No. 10, 1900 Palmira, Cuernevaca, Mexico; Office: Suite 3701 Royal Trust Tower, Toronto, Ont.

GROSSKURTH, Phyllis, M.A., Ph.D.; educator; author; b. Toronto, Ont., 16 March 1924; d. Milton Palmer and Winifred Agnes (Owen) Langstaff; e. St. Clement's Sch., Toronto, Ont.; Univ. of Toronto, B.A. 1946; Univ. of Ottawa, M.A. 1960; Univ. of London, Ph.D. 1962; m.; children: Christopher, Brian, Ann; author of "John Addington Symonds" (biography), 1964 (Gov. Gen. Lit. Award for 1965); "Havelock Ellis", 1980; articles in "Review of English Literature", "Review of English Studies", "Modern Language Review", "University of Toronto Quarterly", etc.; Prof., Dept. of English, Univ. of Toronto; mem., Nat. Film Bd. Can. 1968-74; Anglican; Hon. Research Fellow, University College, London, 1978-82; Address: University of Toronto, Toronto, Ont.

GROSSMAN, Alfred B.; manufacturer; (retired, 1977) b. Eagle Pass, Texas, 18 Oct. 1912; s. Sam and Jessie (Stark) G.; e. Univ. of Texas; Univ. of N.Y.; came to Can. 1932; m. Margaret Lea, d. Wilfred Menard, Granby, Que., 3 Dec. 1945; two d. Leslie Diane, Denise Jeanne; served with RCA during World War II; a Founder, Candn. Heart Foundation; Dir., Que. Heart Foundation; former Trustee, Temple Emmanu-El; Dir., Candn. Textile Inst.; recreations: golf; Clubs: Montefiore; Elmridge Country; Home: 1610 St. Clare, Town of Mount Royal, Que. H3R 2P1;

GROSSMAN, Allan, Can. Govt. official; b. Toronto, Ont., 25 Dec. 1910; s. late Morris and late Sarah (Pilsmaker) G.; e. Toronto Pub. and High Schs.; D. Crim. (Hon.), University of Ottawa, 1971; C.L.U. (Chartered Life Underwriter); m. Ethel Audrey, d. late Mr. and Mrs. O. Starkman, 12 Jan. 1936; children: Hon. Larry, Denise Irene (Mrs. Jay Davis), Susan Joy (Mrs. Rodger Fletcher); CHRMN. OF CRIMINAL INJURIES COMPENSATION BD. since 1976; Alderman, Toronto City Council, 1952-55; charter mem., Metrop. Toronto Council, 1952-55; M.L.A. (Ontario) 1955-75; Min. without Portfolio, (1st P. Conservative Cab. mem. of Jewish faith in Candn. History) 1960-63 and Chief Commr. of the Liquor Control Bd. of Ont., 1961-63; Min. of Correctional Services 1963-71; Min. of Trade & Devel. and responsible for Housing, 1971-72; Min. of Revenue and responsible for Housing, 1972-74; Vice-Chrmn. Treas. Bd. and Mang. Bd. of Cabinet, 1972-

75; Prov. Secy. for Resources Devel. and Sci. Policy, 1974-75; mem. Policy and Priorities Bd. of Cabinet; resigned from Govt., Oct. 1975; Dir., Jewish Nat. Fund; Past Reg. and Nat. Pres., Jewish Immigrant Aid Services; St. Alban's Boys' Club; Mt. Sinai Hosp.; Candn. Foundation Jewish Culture; Jewish Vocational Service; Baycrest Centre for Geriatric Care; mem., Assoc. Chartered Life Underwriters; B'nai B'rith (Past Pres. Toronto Lodge); Past Pres., Toronto Branch, Candn. Assoc. of the Ben-Gurion Univ. of the Negev, Trustee of Candn. Friends of Haifa Univ.; mem. of Extve., Central Region Candn. Jewish Congress; mem. of Bd., United Jewish Welfare Fund; mem. of Bd., Candn. Jewish Congress; mem. of ORT; Dir. Migraine Foundation; Dir. Doctors' Hospital mem. Nat. Council Candn. Human Rights Foundation; mem. John Howard Soc.; Clubs: Primrose; Candn.; R.A.M.; Mount Sinai Lodge A.F. and A.M.; P. Conservative; Hebrew; recreation: boating, fishing; Home: 325 Rosemary Rd. Toronto, Ont. M5P 3E4; Office: 439 University Ave., 17th Floor, Toronto, Ont. M5G 1Y8

GROSSMAN, Emanuel; executive; b. Toronto, Ont., 29 May 1918; s. Annie (Applebaum) and late Samuel Grossman; e. Ryerson Pub. Sch., Toronto; Harbord Coll. Inst., Toronto; Central Tech. Sch., Toronto; Univ. of Toronto (Extension), m. Dorothy, d. late Samuel Kerzner, 16 June 1940; one d. Elisa Ellen (Mrs. Jeffrey E. Friedman); PRESIDENT, MANDOR RESEARCH AND MARKETING SERVICES LTD. since 1972; with Reliable Toy Company Limited 1934-51; joined Dee & Cee Toy Co. Ltd., 1951; apptd. Treas. 1954-56; Vice-Pres. and Treas. 1957-58; Pres. and Gen. Mgr., 1959-61 (Co. sold to Mattel, Inc., Calif., 1962); apptd. Pres. and Gen. Mgr., Dee & Cee Toy Co. Ltd. (Div. of Mattel, Inc.), 1962; resigned 1963; Man. Consultant 1964; Dir. of Marketing, Noma Lites Canada Ltd., 1965-66; re-joined Reliable Toy Co. Ltd. 1966-72; Dir., Jewish Home for the Aged; Baycrest Hosp.; Charter mem. N. Toronto Y.M.H.A.; member, Society of Mfg. Engrs.; Liberal; Hebrew; recreations: fishing, golf, curling, photography, reading; Clubs: Maple Downs Golf & Country; Primrose; Home: 1555 Finch Ave. E. Apt. 1105, Willowdale, Ont. M2J 4X9; Office: 1210 Sheppard Ave E., Suite 304, Willowdale, Ont. M2K 1E3

GROSSMAN, Irving, B.Arch., F.R.A.I.C.; b. Toronto, Ont., 7 Dec. 1926, s. Benny and Mrs. (Appel) G.; e. Harbord Coll. Inst., Toronto, 1945; Sch. of Arch., Univ. of Toronto, B.Arch. 1950; m. Helena Derwinger, 28 Feb. 1970; two s.; arch. practice, Toronto, since 1954; as an arch.-planner has been responsible for several large scale residential projects, maj. urban renewal, pub. housing units, condominium units, pub. schs., residences and other facilities in Can. and U.S. most recently mixed use building, St. Lawrence neighbourhood, Toronto (1979); lectr., Sch. of Arch. for 8 yrs.; has participated in numerous confs., seminars, lectures in Can. and U.S.; mem. Housing Comte. of Candn. Council on Social Devel.; since 1959-has been primarily concerned with residential environment; presented 13 weeks radio series on subject for CBC; author of numerous articles for Candn. and foreign publs.; TV appearances; rec'd various scholarships and prizes at univ. incl. Arch. Guild Medal 1950 and Pilkington Glass Fellowship 1950; won Regional Housing Design Award, Candn. Housing Design Council, 1957 (Nat. Design Award 1962, 1971); Can. Council Research Award 1959; Massey Finalist 1961, 1964, Massey Medal 1967; Ont. Assn. Archs. Design Award 1967; Candn. Centennial Medal 1967; Award of excellence, Candn. Arch's Yearbook, 1970, 1971, 1978; Ont. Mason's Relations Award, 1970; Design Award, Scarborough Planning Bd., 1972; Ont. Mason's Relations Award, 1973; Fellow of Royal Cdn. Academy, 1973; mem., Ont. Assn. Archs.; Jewish, recreations: sailing, tennis, skiing, climbing; Home: 21 Chestnut Park Rd., Toronto, Ont. M4W 1W4; Office: 7 Sultan St., Toronto, Ont. M5S 1L6

GROSSMAN, Hon. Lawrence S. (Larry), Q.C., M.P.P., B.A., LL.B.; Lawyer; b. Toronto, Ont. 2 Dec. 1943; s. Allan and Ethel (Starkman) G.; e. McMurrich Pub. Sch.; Forest Hill Jr. High and Coll. Inst.; Univ. of Toronto B.A. 1964; Osgoode Hall Law Sch. LL.B. 1967; m. Carole Amelia d. Murray and Joan Freeman, Toronto, Ont. 20 June 1968; children: Melissa, Jaimie, Robbie; MIN. OF HEALTH 1982- ; Min. of Industry and Tourism Ont. 1978-82; called to Bar of Ont. 1969; cr. Q.C. 1978; el. M.P.P. for St. Andrew-St. Patrick Sept. 1975; Parlty. Asst. to Atty. Gen. Oct. 1976; re-el. June 1977; Min. of Consumer and Comm. Relations, 1977-78; Dir. Mount Sinai Hosp. Bd.; League of Human Rights; Jewish Vocational Services; Jewish Immigrant Aid Services; former Vice Chrmn., mem. Bd. Doctors Hosp.; Gov. Ben Gurion Univ.; former Dir. Ont. Assn. Corrections & Criminology; former Dir. and mem. Extve. Comte. Metro Toronto Zool. Soc.; mem. Family Service Assn.; Scadding Court Adv. Bd.; hon. mem., Alumni Federation, George Brown College; hon. Dir., Kidney Fndn. of Can.; Founding mem. Forest Hill Residents' Assn.; Vice Pres. N.W. Forest Hill Home Owners' Assn.; mem. Extve. Comte. Candn.-Jewish Cong. Central Region and Toronto Jewish Cong.; Teacher of Eng. to new Candns.; Mun. Law Lectures Candn. Bar Assn.; P. Conservative; Jewish; recreations: tennis, squash, skiing; Office: Hearst Block, Queen's Park, Ont. M7A 2E2

GROTTEROD, Knut, executive; b. Sarpsborg, Norway 12 Feb. 1922; s. Klaus and Maria Magdelena (Thoresen) G.; e. Sarpsborg (Norway) High Sch. 1941; Horten (Norway) Tech. Sch. 1945; McGill Univ. 1949; m. Isabel Edwina d. late Donald G. MacMaster 25 Feb. 1950; children: Ingrid, Christopher, Karen, EXEC. VICE PRES. AND DIR. FRASER INC. since 1976; held various mang. positions incl. Asst. to Vice Pres.-Mfg. 1951-70 Consolidated-Bathurst and predecessor Co's; Vice Pres. and Gen. Mgr. Nova Scotia Forest Industries 1970-73; joined present Co. as Vice Pres. Mfg. 1973; mem. Norwegian Underground Army 1941-45; Pres. Candn. Scandinavian Foundation 1977-78; mem. Candn. Pulp & Paper Assn.; Paper Indus. Mang. Assn.; Tech. Assn. Pump & Paper Indus.; Order Engrs. Que.; Protestant; Home: 28 Lawson St., Edmundston, N.B. E3V 1Z4; Office: 27 Rice St., Edmundston, N.B. E3V 1S9

GROUND, John Dawson, Q.C., B.A., LL.B.; b. Toronto, Ont. 20 June 1932; s. William J. and Mildred (Dawson) G.; e. Public and High Schs. Toronto, Ont.; Univ. of Toronto, B.A. (Pol. Sc.) 1954, LL.B. 1957; m. Helen, d. Dr. Wilfred H. Taylor 11 Sept. 1959; children: Derek, Alison, Colin; PARTNER, OSLER, HOSKIN & HARCOURT; Dir. Doulton Can. Inc.; Trucena Investments Ltd.; Cascade Hydraulics (Canada) Ltd.; Donn Can. Ltd.; Mastorak Ltd.; Bencher, Law Soc. Upper Can.; Chrmn., Professional Conduct Comm., Law Society of Upper Can.; mem. of Session, Timothy Eaton Mem. Church; Past-Pres., Federation of Law Societies of Can.; mem. Ont. and Nat. Council, Candn. Bar Assn.; recreations: skiing, art; Home: 142 Alexandra Blvd., Toronto, Ont. M4R 1M2; Office: First Canadian Place, P.O. Box 50, Toronto, Ont. M5X 1B8

GRUBE, George Maximilian Anthony, F.R.S.C. M.A., LL.D.; classical scholar; retired professor; b. Antwerp, Belgium 2 Aug. 1899; s. Antoine and Marie (Reiners) G.; e. King Edwards Sch. Birmingham, Eng.; Emmanuel Coll. Cambridge M.A. 1925; Univ. of Victoria LL.D.; m. Gwenyth d. Charles Macintosh 7 Aug. 1924; children: Mrs. Antonia Swalgen, John Deen, Mrs. Jennifer Podlecki; retired Prof. of Classics Trinity Coll. Univ. of Toronto; held many extve. positions CCF and NDP 1935-70 incl. Prov. Pres.; author "Plato's Thought" 1935, new ed. 1980; "The Drama of Euripides" 1941; "Greek and Roman Critics" 1965 (rec'd Am. Philol. Assn. Award); numerous classical transls.; over 30 articles in learned journs.; many pol. booklets and pamphlets; Ed. "Canadian Forum"

1937-41; Bd. of Educ. Trustee 1941-43; served as Interpreter 1918, rank Sgt.; mem. Candn. Classical Assn. (Pres.); Am. Philol. Assn.; NDP; recreation: chess; Home: 158 Crescent Rd., Apt. 309, Toronto, Ont. M4W 1V2.

GRUBEL, Herbert G., B.A., Ph.D.; economist; educator; b. Frankfurt, Germany, 26 Feb. 1934; s. Ernst and Elisabeth (Hessler) G.; e. Abitur 1954, Germany; Rutgers Univ., B.A. 1958; Yale Univ., Ph.D. 1962; m. Joan A. Andrews, 20 July 1958; children: Eric, Heidi; PROF. OF ECONOMICS, SIMON FRASER UNIV. since 1971; Instr., Yale Univ., 1961-62; Asst. Prof., Stanford Univ., 1962-63 and Univ. of Chicago, 1963-66; Visiting Fellow, Australian Nat. Univ. 1969; Asoc. Prof. of Econ., Univ. of Pa. 1967-70; Sr. Policy Adviser, US Treasury, Washington, D.C., 1970-71; Visiting Fellow, Nuffield Coll., Oxford, 1974-75; Visiting Prof., Univ. of Nairobi, Kenya, 1978-79; author, "Forward Exchange", 1966; "The International Mcnetary System", 1969; "International Economics", 1977; co-author, "Intra-Industry Trade", 1975; "The Brain Drain"; Editor "International Monetary Reform", 1964; Co-editor, "Effective Protection", 1971; "Exchange Rate Policies in South East Asia", 1973; other writings incl. over 60 papers and notes in prof. journs. and colls.; mem., Candn. Econ. Assn.; Am. Assn.; Royal Econ. Soc.; recreations: skiing, tennis, hiking; Home: 1180 Renton Pl., W. Vancouver, B.C. V7S 2K7; Office: Burnaby, B.C.

GUERIN, Anthony Morris, M.B.A., M.P.A.; federal civil servant; b. Lincoln Park, Mich., 2 Aug. 1928; s. Arthur and Marie (Lapointe) G.; e. Sturgeon Falls (Ont.) High Sch. 1946; St. Hyacinthe Textile Inst. 1950; Univ. of Toronto M.B.A. 1972, York Univ. M.P.A. 1972; m. Marie-Anne Jacqueline d. Sosthène Gladu, Hull, Que., 25 Sept. 1954; children: Dominique Marie-Claire, Anthony Morris Jr.; ASST DEPY. MIN. INDUST. DEVEL., DEPT. IN-DUST. TRADE AND COMM. since 1974; Dir., Canadair; De Havilland Aircraft Co.; Uranium Canada; Indust. Engr. Dominion Textile Co. Ltd. 1950-54 and P.O. Dept. 1954-56; Production Mgr. Tooke Bros. Ltd. 1956-59; Vice Pres. Canadian Textile Consultants Ltd. 1959-64; Dir. Textile and Clothing Br. Fed. Dept. of Indust. 1964-68; Gen. Dir. Textiles and Consumer Products Br. Dept. Indust. Trade and Comm. 1968-74; Fellow Massey Coll.; mem. Textile Grads. Soc.; Am. Inst. Indust. Engrs.; R. Catholic; recreation: farming; Home: 85 Range Rd., Ottawa, Ont. K1N 8J6; Office: 235 Queen St., Ottawa, Ont. K1A 0H5

GUERIN, Hon. Claude; judge; b. Montreal, Que. 23 March 1930; s. Judge Charles Edouard and Antoinette (Foucreault) G.; e. Coll. Stanislas, Outremont, Que.; Univ. de Montréal; Univ. of Toronto; m. Henriette d. Arthur Clement 11 Aug. 1967; children: Charles Edouard, Michel, Julie; JUDGE, SUPERIOR COURT OF QUE. 1980- ; called to Bar of Que. 1954; cr. Q.C. 1972; Partner, Johnson & Tormey 1954-64; Sr. Partner, Bruneau, Dulude, Guerin 1964-80; Crown Prosecutor 1957-60, 1966-70 (Special Cases); P. Conservative; R. Catholic; recreations: golf, tennis, skiing, jogging, fishing; Club: Laval-sur-le-Lac Golf & Country; Home: 25 Beloeil Ave., Outremont, Que. Office: Court House, Montreal, Que.

GUIDON, Hubert, B.A., B.Ph., L.Ph., M.A.; sociologist; educator; b. Bourget, Ont. 10 Oct. 1929; s. Pascal and Josephine (Lalonde) G.; e. Ottawa Univ. B.A., B.Ph. 1949, L.Ph. 1950, M.A. 1951; Univ. of Chicago 1951-54; PROF. OF SOCIOL. CONCORDIA UNIV. since 1970; Asst. Prof. of Sociol. Univ. de Montréal 1954-60; Assoc. Prof. of Sociol. Sir George Williams Univ. 1964-67, Prof. 1967-69; Prof. of Sociol. and Visiting Prof. Inst. Candn. Studies, Carleton Univ. 1969-70; co-ed. "Modernization and the Canadian State" 1978; author various articles, book chapters; mem. Royal Soc. Can.; Candn. Assn. Sociol. & Anthrop. (Pres. 1971); Internat. Sociol. Assn. (Extve. 1970-74); mem. Task Force on Urbanization, Que. 1974-77; Re-

search Sociol., Task Force on Candn. Unity 1978; R. Catholic; Home: 1280 St. Marc, Montreal, Que. H3H 2G1; Office: Montreal, Que.

GUILBAULT, Jacques, B.Ph., M.Sc.Soc.; b. St-Jacques
de Montcalm, Que., 1 Nov. 1928; s. Rolland and Made-
leine (Dugas) G., e. St. Viateur (Que.) High Sch., 1946;
Laval Univ., B.Ph. 1947, M.Sc.Soc. 1950; Columbia
Univ., Sch. of Business Adm., 1951; m. Andrée, d. late
Roger Valiquette, 15 June 1958; children: Jean, Bernard;
DIR. OF INDUST. RELATIONS, MONTREAL URBAN
COMMUNITY TRANSIT COMN., since Oct. 1966; In-
vited Prof., School of Indus Relations, Laval Univ.; Lec-
turer at Sch. of Indust. Rel., Montréal Univ.; Employer
Rep., Can. Labour Relations Board, July 1966-73; Pub.
Staff Relations Bd., Apl. 1967-Oct. 1970; joined Que.
Dept. of Labour as a Conciliator, 1951 and also worked
for Fed. Dept. of Labour as Indust. Relations Offr.; joined
Candn. British Aluminium Co. Ltd., Baie Comeau, Que.,
as Mgr., Indust. Relations, 1962; R. Catholic; recreations:
golf, fishing, curling; Home: 5026 Grosvenor Ave., Montreal, Que. H3W 2M1; Office: 159 St-Antoine St., Montreal, Que. H2Z 1H3

GUIRY, James Duncan, B.Sc., P.Eng.; industrial executive; b. Chatham, Ont. 11 Oct. 1933; s. Emmett David
and Beatrice Mary (Duncan) G.; e. St. Joseph's Chatham
1946; Assumption High Sch. Windsor 1951; Univ. of
Windsor 1951-52; Univ. of Detroit B.Sc. (Civil Engr.)
1955; m. Barbara Jane d. late Ernest Hector Predhomme 1
Oct. 1954; children: Shawne Marie Pehar, James Paul,
Timmothy David; PRES., INCO TECH 1979- ; Vice Pres.
responsible for Engineering, Environment, Energy, Inco
Metals, 1980- ; Dir. Engn., Inco Metals 1972- ; Dir., Inco
Gulf, Bahrain; Eximbal, Guatemala; Engr. Trainee, West-
inghouse Canada Ltd., Hamilton 1955-56; Design Engr.
Steep Rock Iron Mines 1956-63; Project Engr. Fenco, To-
ronto 1963-65; Mgr. Project Engn. Rio Algom Mines 1965-
71; Asst. to Vice Pres. Engn., Inco Metals 1971-72; mem.
Assn. Prof. Engrs. Prov. Ont.; Candn. Inst. Mining &
Metall.; P. Conservative; R. Catholic; Club: Engineers'
Club of Toronto; Home: 6 Kylemore Cres., Weston, Ont.
M9P 1C9; Office: 1 First Canadian Place, Toronto, Ont.
M5X 1C4.

GUITE, Harold Frederick, M.A.; educator; b. Clayworth,
Notts., Eng. 12 March 1920; s. Frederick William and
Amy Hetty Eliza (White) G.; e. Abbeydale Council Sch.
Sheffield, Eng. 1931; Scholar, King Edward VII Sch. Shef-
field 1939; Open Exhibitioner in Classics, St. Catharine's
Coll. Cambridge 1939-40; B.A. (London External) 1946;
Arthur Platt Student in Classics, univ. of London (held at
St. Catharine's Coll. Cambridge) 1946-47; M.A. (London
External) 1952; m. Janetta Inglis Keith d. late John Hay
Murray 26 March 1951; children: Candace Jane Elizabeth,
Ayodeji Malcolm; PROF. OF CLASSICS, McMASTER
UNIV. 1967- ; Coll. Supvr. in Classics St. Catharine's and
Downing Colls. Cambridge 1946-47; Asst. Lectr. in Latin
and Lectr. in Classics Univ. of Manchester 1947-56, Gov.
Hartley Victoria Coll. 1952-56; Lectr. and Sr. Lectr. in
Classics Univ. of Ibadan, Nigeria 1956-63; Her Majesty's
Inspr. of Educ. (Hon.) W. Region, Nigeria 1958-63; Prof.
and Head of Classics, Univ. of Zimbabwe 1963-67, Dean
of Arts and mem. Bd. Govs. Extve. 1964-66; Local
Preacher Meth. Ch. Eng. since 1943; Sr. Friend, Student
Christian Movement 1947-67; Chrmn. Youth Comte. In-
ternat. Fellowship of Reconciliation 1951-56; mem. Nige-
rian Comte. World Univ. Service 1957-63; Rhodesian
Govt. Adv. Comte. on Teacher Training Colls. 1964-67;
Co-Chrmn. Un. Way Campaign 1978; Gov. Waddilove
Training Inst. Zimbabwe 1964-67; author various publs.;
Life mem. Youth Hostels Assn.; Asia Christian Colls.
Assn.; Hugenot Soc. Can.; Sir Walter Scott Club Toronto;
Methodist; recreations: theatre, walking, gardening;
Home: 100 Victoria Ave., Hamilton, Ont. L8L 5E5; Office:
Hamilton, Ont. L8S 4M2.

GULDEN, Simon, B.A., LL.L.; executive; b. Montreal,
Que. 7 Jan. 1938; s. David and Zelda (Long) G.; e. High
Sch. of Montreal 1955; McGill Univ. B.A. 1959; Univ. de
Rennes, St. Malo, France Cert. 1961; Univ. de Montréal
LL.L. 1962; m. Ellen Lee d. late Samuel Alexander Barb-
our Jr. 12 June 1977; VICE PRES., GEN. COUNSEL AND
SECY., STANDARD BRANDS LTD. 1975- ; Dir. Acadian
Distillers Ltd.; Calona Wines Ltd.; Dickson's Food Serv-
ices Ltd.; Lowney Inc.; McGuiness Distillers Ltd.; Mimico
Warehousing Co. Ltd.; Standard Brands Canada Ltd.;
called to Bar of Que. 1963; Partner, Genser, Phillips,
Friedman & Gulden, Montreal 1963-68; Secy. and Legal
Counsel, Place Bonaventure Inc. Montreal 1969-72; Legal
Counsel Real Estate, Steinberg Inc. Montreal 1972-74; Legal Counsel and Prime Atty. Bell Canada, Montreal HQ
1975; mem. Candn. Bar Assn.; Internat. Bar Assn.; Internat. Assn. Lawyers & Jurists; Lord Reading Law Soc.; Internat. Fiscal Assn.; Bd. Trade Metrop. Toronto; Assn.
des conseil en francisation du Qué.; Advertising & Sales
Extve. Club; Am. Mang. Assn.; B'Nai B'Rith; Liberal;
Jewish; recreations: sailing, skiing, horseback riding, ka-
rate, numismatics, philately, music, literature, theatre,
travel, politics, community organs; Clubs: Island Yacht;
Cambridge; Equestrian Guards Riding; Canadian Power
Squadron; Canadian; Home: 15 Morning Gloryway, Willowdale, Ont. M2H 3M1; Office: 1 Dundas St. W., Suite
2900, Toronto, Ont. M5G 2A9.

GUNDY, Henry Pearson, M.A.; professor emeritus; b.
Toronto, Ont., 1 June 1905; s. Henry Wentworth & Gra-
cey (Mackay) G.; e. Univ. of Toronto Schs.; Univ. of To-
ronto, B.A. 1928, M.A. 1930; Univ. of Chicago; Columbia
Univ. Library Sch. (summer session) 1944; m. Dorothy
Diamond (deceased 28 Dec. 1967), d. Very Rev. Dr.
James Endicott, 31 Aug. 1929; children: Joyce, Carolyn;
Fellow in Eng., Victoria Coll., Toronto, 1929-31; Lectr. in
Eng., McMaster Univ., 1931-35; Instr. in Eng., Univ. of
Chicago, 1936-37; Asst. and Assoc. Prof. Mt. Allison
Univ., 1937-42; Joseph Allison Prof. of Eng., Head of
Dept., and Dir. of Library Service, 1942-47; Librarian,
Queen's Univ., 1947-65; Prof. of Eng. Lang. and Lit.
1966-70; Editor "Queen's Quarterly" 1967-71; Assoc. Dir.
and Sr. Ed. McGill-Queen's Univ. Press 1969-71; Ed.,
"Historic Kingston" 1959-75; Ed. Letters of Bliss Carman;
1981; mem., Candn. Hist. Assn.; Ontario Hist. Society;
Bibliographical Society of Can.; United Church; amateur
artist; Home and studio: Apt. 6, 650 Woodbine Ave., Toronto, Ont. M4E 2J1

GUNN, Edward James Hamilton; b. Prince Albert,
Sask., 2 Feb. 1915; e. Upper Canada Coll., grad. 1932;
VICE-PRES. AND DIR., DOMINION SECURITIES
CORP. LTD., N.Y. since 1972; Dir., Dominion Securities
Corp. Ltd.; served during 2nd World War with R.C.A.F.
and R.A.F., in Eng. and on the Continent; discharged
with rank of Sqdn. Ldr., 1945; former Chrmn., Candn.
Comte., Invest. Bankers Assn. of Am.; Un. Church; rec-
reation: golf; Clubs: Toronto; Rosedale Golf; Royal Cana-
dian Military Institute; Canadian (N.Y.); Office: 100 Wall
St., New York, N.Y.

GUNN, Nigel Hamilton; investment dealer; b. Edin-
burgh, Scotland, 19 July 1910; s. James Hamilton and
Agnes Cecilia (Mackenzie) g.; e. Pub. and High Schs.,
British Columbia; grad. 1925 Brentwood Coll., Victoria
B.C.; m. Eleanor Jessie, 8 Oct. 1938; children: Patricia H.,
Neil H.; HON. CHAIRMAN, BELL, GOUINLOCK LTD.
Dir., Bell, Gouinlock & Co. Inc., N.Y.; Pres., Invest.
Dealers' Assn. of Can., 1956-57; Vice-Pres., Ont. Dist.
Extve. Comte., Invest. Dealers' Assn. of Can., 1954-56;
Pres., Visiting Homemakers Assn.; Vice Pres. & Chrm.,
Finance Comte., Toronto East General & Orthopaedic
Hosp.; joined present firm in 1932 at Toronto; Vice-Pres.,
1951, Pres. 1957; C.O.B., 1972; recreation: golf; Clubs:
National; Rosedale Golf; Home: 255 Glencairn Ave., To-
ronto, Ont. M5N 1T8; Office: P.O. Box 110, First Candn.
Place, Toronto, Ont. M5X 1B6

GUNNING, Harry Emmet, M.A., Ph.D., D.Sc., F.R.S.C., F.C.I.C., Hon. D.Sc. Univ. of Guelph and Queen's, Hon. LL.D. Univ. of Victoria; university professor; b. Toronto, Ont. 16 Dec. 1916; s. Lorenzo Edward and Ledo Beryl (Shangraw) G.; e. Riverdale Coll. Inst. Toronto, Ont. (Sr. Matric. 1935); Univ. of Toronto, B.A. (Hons. Chem. First Class) 1939, M.A. (Phys. Chem.) 1940, Ph.D. (Phys. Chem.) 1942; D.Sc. Guelph; m. Donna Marie, d. late William Beahan, 30 Jan. 1943; one d. Judith Beryl; PROF. AND HEAD, DEPT. OF CHEM., UNIV. OF ALBERTA, since 1957, Pres., Univ. of Alberta; Killam Mem. Prof.; Consultant in Industrial Chem; Dir., Steacie Mem. Trust Fund; U.S. Nat. Research Council Post-Doctoral Fellow, Harvard Univ. 1942-43; Research Chemist, Pure Chem. Div., Nat. Research Council Can., 1943-46; Asst. Prof., Univ. of Rochester, 1946-48; Ill. Inst. of Tech., 1948-52 and Assoc. Prof. there 1952-55, Prof. 1955-57; Publications: Contrib. author to "Advances in Photochemistry" (Vol. 1 1963, Vol. 4 1965); over 139 research papers in various scient. journs. on photochem. kinetics, free radical chem., isotope separation, spectroscopy and thermodynamics; mem. Hon. Adv. Comte., Nat. Research Council; Chrmn. of Adv. Comte. on Chem. Research, Defence Research Bd.; mem., Edit. Bd., Candn. Journal of Research; mem., Am. Assn. Advanc. Science; N.Y. Acad. Sciences; Chem. Inst. Can. (Pres.-elect. 1972-73); Am. Chem. Soc.; Faraday Soc.; Am. Phys. Soc.; Candn. Assn. Univ. Teachers; Sigma Xi; Protestant; recreations: music, literature, languages; Clubs: Derrick Golf & Country; Mayfair Golf and Country; Home: 13119 Grandview Ave., Edmonton, Alberta. T6H 4K7

GUNNING, Henry Cecil, B.A.Sc., Ph.D., F.R.S.C., F.G.S.A.; retired consulting geologist; b. Belfast, N. Ireland, 9 Sept. 1901; s. Samuel and Margaret Elizabeth (Hewitt) G.; came to Can. 1907; e. Univ. of Brit. Columbia, B.A.Sc. 1923; Mass. Inst. Tech. S.M. 1926; Ph.D. 1929 (Geol.); Hon. D.Sc., Univ. of B.C. 1965; m. Edith Frances, (deceased, 1963) d. Ernest V. Fitts of Braintree; Mass., 1 Dec. 1928; children: Donald Fitts, Patricia; m. 2ndly, Marion Wilcox Moberg, 14 Jan. 1964; practical mining experience, B.C. 1923-24; Geol. Instr., Mass. Inst. Tech., 1926-27; Asst. Geol., Geol. Survey of Can., 1928-29, Assoc. Geol. 1929-36, Geol. 1936-39; Prof., Dept. of Geol. and Geog., Univ. of Brit. Columbia, 1939-59 (Head of Dept. and R.W. Brock Prof. 1949-59; Dean, Faculty of Applied Science, 1953-59); Vice Pres. Curriculum for B.C.I.T., 1962-64; Consulting Geol. since 1939; Consulting Geol., Anglo-American Corpn. of S. Africa (Rhodesia), 1959-61; Assoc. Editor, "Canadian Journal of Earth Sciences", 1964-67; mem., Candn. Inst. of Mining and Metall., (Barlow Mem. Prize 1937) (Inst. Medal for Distinguished Serv.); Assn. Prof. Engrs. of B.C. (Pres. 1955); Geol. Assn. of Can. (Pres. 1956), Logan Medal; Soc. of Econ. Geols. (Pres. 1965); Anglican; recreations: gardening, reading; Home: Suite 302, 1437 Foster St., White Rock, B.C. V4B 3X6

GUNNING, Kenneth Samuel, B.A., F.C.A.; b. Vancouver, B.C. 6 Apl. 1930; s. Basil Hewitt and Olive May (Laffere) G.; e. Pub. and High Schs. Vancouver 1948; Univ. of B.C. B.A. 1952; Brandon Coll. Univ. of Man. 1952-53; Assoc. Royal Conserv. of Music Toronto; m. Flora Marie d. Hans Johnson 2 July 1954; children: Laureen Elizabeth, Lynda Marie, Karen Jane, Kevin John; EXTVE. PARTNER, THORNE RIDDELL since 1977; articled Helliwell Maclachlan & Co. Vancouver 1953, C.A. 1957, Partner 1966; Dir. of Research and Training Thorne Gunn Helliwell & Christenson, Toronto 1970; Adm. Partner Thorne Gunn & Co. 1972, Extve. Partner 1973; Depy. Extve. Partner present firm 1974; mem., Central Mgmt. Comm., Klynveld Main Goerdeler (International firm); mem. Financial Disclosure Advisory Bd. to Ontario Securities Comm.; Exec. Comm., Can. Academic Accounting Assoc.; Bd. of Gov., Can. Comprehensive Auditing Foun.; past Chrmn. CICA Auditing Standards Comte; mem. CICA Special Comte to Examine the Role of the Auditor (1977-78); author several articles in prof. accounting journs.; rec'd Queen's Silver Jubilee Medal 1978; Fellow, Inst. C.A.'s Ont. (1976) and B.C. (1977); Beta Theta Pi; Protestant; recreations: squash, curling, tennis, golf, music; Clubs: Toronto; Granite; Vancouver Lawn Tennis & Badminton; Vancouver Racquets; Home: 539 Blythwood Rd., Toronto, Ont. M4N 1B4; Office: (P.O. Box 262) Toronto-Dominion Centre, Toronto, Ont. M5K 1J9.

GUOLLA, Louis, Q.C., B.A., b. Sault Ste. Marie, Ont. 2 Feb. 1917; s. Vincent and Elvira (Ceccol) G.; e. High Sch. Timmins, Ont; Univ. of Toronto, Ont. B.A. (Hon. Law) 1939; Osgoode Hall Law Sch., Toronto, 1943; m. Eleanor, d. John Pariselli 29 June 1944; A SR. PARTNER, DALY, COOPER, GUOLLA AND O'GORMAN; Dir., Continental Can Co. of Canada Ltd.; Stoffel Seals of Canada Ltd.; Soudronic of Canada Ltd., Visirecord Systems of Canada Ltd.; read law with Wilfred Wolman, Q.C., Toronto, Ont.; called to the Bar of Ont. 1943; created Q.C. 1962; practised with Daly, Hamilton and Thistle and successor firms since 1943; mem., Candn. Bar Assn.; York Co. Law Assn.; Bd. Trade Metrop. Toronto; Golf Assn. of Toronto Bar (Past Pres.); Roman Catholic; recreations: golf, fishing, hunting; Clubs: Canadian; St. George's Golf & Country (Pres.); Home: 70 Prince George Drive, Islington, Ont. M9A 1Y6; Office: (Box 141) Commerce Court N., Toronto, Ont. M5L 1E2

GURD, Fraser Newman, M.D., C.M., M.Sc., D.A.B.S.; surgeon (retired, 1979); b. Montreal, Que., 19 Mar. 1914; s. Jessie Gibson (Newman) and Fraser Baillie G., M.D.; e. Selwyn House, Montreal, 1920-27; Westmount High Sch., Montreal, 1927-29; Inst. Sillig, Vevey, Switzerland, 1929-30; McGill Univ., B.A. 1934, M.D., C.M., 1934-36 and 1937-39; Univ. of Munich, 1936-37; Jr. Intern, Johns Hopkins Hosp., 1939-40; Asst. Res., Montreal Gen. Hosp., 1940-41; Research Fellow, Univ. of Penna., M.Sc. (Med.) 1946-47; Res., Royal Victoria & Montreal Gen. Hosps., 1947-48; m. Mary Louise, d. Harold Willis Moore, Denver, Colo., 19 Dec. 1938; children: Patricia Pryde, Katharine Chaplin, Mary Goss, Susan Bexton, Deborah Gregorash; CONSULTANT R.C.P.&S. OF CAN. since 1976; Gov., Un. Theol. Coll., Montreal 1958-72; Jr. Asst., Montreal Gen. Hosp., 1948, Sr. Surg. 1959; Surg.-in-Chief, Reddy Mem. Hosp., 1952-59, Consultant 1959; Hon. Consultant in Surg., Jewish Gen. Hosp., 1964; Consultant in Surg., Queen Elizabeth Hospital, 1964 (all Montreal); Demonstrator in Surg., McGill Univ., 1948; Research Asst. Dept. Exper. Surg., 1948-52; Asst. Prof., Surg., 1955, Assoc. Prof. 1959; Prof. and Chrmn. of the Dept. 1963-71; Emeritus Prof., McGill Univ., 1980- ; Surgeon-in-Chief, Montreal Gen. Hosp. 1963-71; Assoc. Dir., McGill-Montreal Gen. Hosp. Univ. Surg. Clinic, 1959-63, Dir., 1963-71; Assoc. Secy., R.C.P. & S. of Can., 1972-75; has lectured at many N. Am. univs.; served as Capt., R.C.A.M.C. in Can., U.K., Italy and Holland, 1941-46; Publications: Chapter on shock in "Complications in Surgery and Their Management" by Artz and Hardy, 1967; over 70 articles in prof. journs.; Assoc. Ed., "Journal of Trauma"; Ed. Comte., "British Journal of Surgery"; Ed. Bd. "Canadian Journal of Surgery"; "Annals of Surgery"; F.R.C.S.(C); mem., Council and Comtes.; F.A.C.S.; mem., Board of Regents and Comtes.; mem., American Association Surg Trauma (Pres.); Central Surg. Assn. (Pres.); Canadian Assn. Clin. Surgs. (Pres.); Am. Surg. Assn. (Vice Pres.); Assn. Surgs. Que.; C.M.A.; Candn. Physiol. Soc.; Candn. Soc. Clin. Investigation; Internat. Fed. Surg. Colls. (Research Comte.); James IV Assn. Surgs. Inc. (Pres.); Montreal Medico-Chirurgical Soc.; Montreal Physiol. Soc.; Surg. Travel Club; Soc. Univ. Surgs.; Internat. Surg. Group (Treas.); Soc. for Surg. of the Alimentary Tract (Trustee); Delta Upsilon; Alpha Kappa Kappa; Alpha Omega Alpha; Un. Ch.; recreations: history, writing travel; Home. 85 Range Road, Apt. 801, Ottawa, Ont. K1N 8J6;

GUSHUE, Hon. James Randell, M.A.; judge; b. St. John's, Nfld. 4 June 1933; s. Raymond and Phyllis (Randell) G.; e. Prince of Wales Coll. St. John's 1950; Mem. Univ. of Nfld. B.A. 1955; Oxford Univ. (Rhodes Scholar Nfld.) M.A. (Jurisprudence) 1959; m. Gail Allison d. Hubert C. Herder, Topsail, Conception Bay, Nfld. 11 June 1970; one s. Jonathan; JUDGE, COURT OF APPEAL, SUPREME COURT OF NFLD. since 1976; called to Bar of Nfld. 1960; cr. Q.C. 1975; practiced law with Hon. P. J. Lewis, Q.C. St. John's 1960-61; joined Food & Agric. Organ. of UN, Rome 1961-62; practiced law St. John's 1963-76; Partner, Stirling, Ryan & Goodridge (latterly Stirling, Ryan & Gushue); Commr., Royal Comn. on Health & Safety Standards and Standard of Care in Nursing Homes and Homes for Special Care in Prov. Nfld. 1977-78; United Church; recreations: curling, walking; Clubs: Bally Haly Golf & Country; St. John's Curling; Royal Nfld. Yacht; Home: 144 Elizabeth Ave., St. John's, Nfld. A1B 1S3; Office: St. John's, Nfld. A1C 5P5.

GUSS, His Hon. Benjamin Rex, B.A., LL.B.; judge; b. Saint John, N.B., 15 July 1905; s. Morris and Celia Gertrude G.; e. Saint John Pub. and High Schs.; Dalhousie Univ., B.A. 1928, LL.B. 1930; read law with Hon. John B. M. Baxter, Q.C., D.C.L., LL.D., late Chief Justice of Supreme Court of N.B., 1930; called to Bar of N.B. 1931; m. Mildred Ruth, B.A., d. T. Davis Bassen, 2 Dec. 1938; children: Keren Sarah Jane, Judith Mary, Faith Gabrielle, Jonathan Joseph Enman; JUDGE, PROBATE COURT, SAINT JOHN CO., N.B., and First Judge, Prov. Court, Family Div.; Appt'd Administrator of Deregulation for New Birnswick 1980; Administrator (Saint John Dist.) Fed. Court of Can.; Chief Judicial Offr. for Saint John, Kings and Charlotte Cos.; Master of Supreme Court of N.B.; for many years head of legal firms of Guss & Guss, then Guss & Baxter, then Guss, Taylor & Gregory; Extve. of the Fellows and Trustee, Candn. Foundation for Legal Research; Founding Nat. Chrmn., Legal Aid Comte.; Former Nat. Chrmn., Mun. Law Sec., mem. Council, and Past Vice-Pres. for N.B., Candn. Bar Assn.; Chrmn., Defence Research Inst. for Atlantic Provs.; Royal Comn. for Free Hosp. Services for N.B.; Hon. Solr., Animal Resuce League and many other local organs.; Vice-Pres. and mem. Prov. Directorate, Saint John Tuberculosis Assn.; Hon. Life mem. and a Founder, N.B. Competitive Festival of Music; Life mem., Candn. Music Festivals; mem. Bd., Atlantic Symphony Orchestra Assn.; Chrmn. Finance Comte., Saint John Tuberculosis Assn.; N.B. Hist. Soc.; Life mem. N.B. Museum; Saint John Art Club; Consul in N.B. and P.E.I. for the Netherlands; a Founder, Vice-Pres., and Pres. College Devel. Corp. and Comte. on Continuing Educ., St. John; Founder, Assn. for Children with Learning Disabilities; pioneered Legal Aid, First Founder of Legal Aid Comte of Candn. Bar Assn.; Founding Chrmn. Young Lawyers Comte. of Candn. Bar Assn.; Founder, Vice Pres., Pres. of Young Conservatives of Can.; rep. Port of St. John before Internat. Waterways Comn.; mem. Candn. Council on Social Development; Candn. Forestry Assn.; Regional Administrator Fed. Court of Can.; past Counsel, Municipality of County of St. John; Counsel, St. John Gen. Hosp.; Chrmn., St. John Harbour Bridge Authority; lifetime Hon. Mem. of N.B. Prov. Judge's Assoc.; St. John City Brotherhood award; C.H.S.J.-"I Care Award"; Man of Year Award (twice); received medal on occas. of 25th Anniversary of Queen's ascension to the throne; Freemason; recreation: music; Clubs: Westfield Golf & Country; Union; I.O.O.F.; K. of P.; Rotary (Past Pres; Past Dist. Gov.; Past Dir. Rotary Internat.); Young Conservatives of Canada (Past Nat. Pres.); Zionist (Nat. Hon. Vice-Pres); Home: 61 Rocky Terrace, St. John, N.B.; Office: City Hall, St. John, N.B. or Regional Prov. Centre, 300 St. Mary's St., Fredericton, N.B.

GUSSOW, William Carruthers, M.Sc., Ph.D., F.R.S.C. (1955), F.G.S., F.G.S.A.; consulting geologist and engineer; b. London, Eng., 25 April 1908; s. Hans Theodor

and Jenny Maria (Hitzigrath) G.; e. Pub. and High Schs., Ottawa, Ont.; Queen's Univ., B.Sc. 1933, M.Sc., 1935; Mass. Inst. of Tech., Ph.D. 1938; m. Margaret Blackett, d. late Christopher Blackett Robinson, 24 Sept. 1936; children: Christopher H., David William, James Frederick Robinson; Map Draughtsman, Geological Survey of Can., 1927-29; ten field seasons on geol. mapping with Fed. and Prov. Geol. Surveys in Ont., Que., and N.W.T., 1930-39; travelled extensively in U.S., Mexico, Panama, Japan, Philippines, Malay, Burma, India, Ceylon, N. Africa, Italy, Sicily, Austria, Germany, Holland, England 1937-38; Geol. Royal Mil. Coll. staff, Kingston, Ont., 1938-39; Cost Engr., Office Engr. and Resident Engr. on Shipshaw Hydro-Elect. Power Devel. and Arvida Works Que., 1939-44; Chief Geol. and Exploration Mgr., Shell Oil Co. of Can. Ltd., and Shell Inc. in Okla. and Texas, 1945-52; Consulting Geol. and Engr., 1953-55; Staff Geol., Union Oil Co. of Calif. 1956-62, Sr. Research Assoc., 1962-71; Consultant, Japan Petroleum Development Corp., 1972-74; awarded Royal Soc. of Can. Research Fellowship, 1936; discovered principle of differential entrapment of oil and gas; has publ. numerous articles on geol. and related subjects; mem., Geol. Assn. Can.; Soc. of Econ. Geols; Am. Assn. of Petroleum Geols. (mem. Pacific Sect.), (Distinguished lectr. 1955); Internat. Assoc. Sedimentol.; Candn. Inst. Mining & Metall. (Chrmn., Calgary Br. 1954-55); Engn. Inst. Can. (Program Chrmn., Calgary Br. 1953-54); Alta. Soc. of Petroleum Geols. (Pres. 1959); Assn. Prof. Engrs. Alta. (mem. Council 1955-56); Fellow, Am. Assn. Advanc. Science; Charter mem., Am. Inst. Prof. Geol. (Secy.-Treas., Cal. Sec., 1967-68); mem., Nat. Adv. Comte. on Research in Geol. Sciences, Ottawa, 1957-59; House of Soc. Reps., Am. Geol. Inst., (1963-65); Nat. Acad. of Sciences Observatio Adv. to U.S. Geol. Survey, 1966-72; Hon. mem. Candn. Soc. of Petroleum Geol., 1980; Guest, Accademia Nazionale dei Lincei, Italy, 1957; Guest Lectr., Lomonosov Univ., Moscow, USSR, 1960; U.N. Expert to Research & Training Inst., Oil & Natural Gas Comn., Dehra Dun, India, 1967; Guest, People's Republic of China, to discuss Taching oilfield, Oct. 1977; recreations: geological field work; Home: 188 Dufferin Rd., Ottawa, Ont. K1M 2A6

GUSTAFSON, Ralph Barker, M.A., D. Litt., D.C.L.; poet; b. Lime Ridge, Que., 16 Aug. 1909; s. Carl Otto and Gertrude Ella (Barker) G.; e. Bishop's Univ., B.A. 1929 (1st Class Hons. in Hist. and Eng., winner of Gov.-Gen's. Medal, Chancellor's Prize, Ven. Archdeacon Scott's Prize for Poetry, Mackie Eng. Essay, and 1st Class Aggregate Prize), M.A. 1930 (Thesis on "Sensuous Imagery in Shelley and Keats", winner of Ven. Archdeacon Scott's Prize for Poetry again); Oxford Univ., B.A. 1933 (Hons. in Eng. Lit. and Lang.), M.A. 1963; D.Litt. Mt. Allison 1973; D.C.L. Bishop's Univ., 1977; m. Elisabeth, d. Francis X. Renninger; Prof. and Poet in Residence, 1963-1979. Bishop's Univ.; music critic, C.B.C. since 1960; Mus. Master, Bishop's Coll. Sch. 1930; Master St. Alban's Sch., Brockville, Ont., 1934; thereafter lived in London, Eng., until return to Can. 1938; with Brit. Inf. Servs. 1942-46; author of following books of poems: 'The Golden Chalice', 1935 (awarded Prix David By Que. Govt. 1935); "Alfred the Great" (a play in blank verse), 1937; "Epithalamium in Time of War", 1941; "Lyrics Unromantic", 1942; "Flight into Darkness", 1944; "Rivers Among Rocks", 1960; "Rocky Mountain Poems", 1960; "Sift in an Hourglass", 1966; "Ixion's Wheel", 1969; "Selected Poems", 1972; "Theme & Variations for Sounding Brass", 1972; "Fire on Stone", 1974, winner of Gov. Gen.'s Award for poetry 1974, and winner of A.J.M. Smith Award of Internat. Studies Program, Michigan State Univ. 1974; "Corners in the Glass", 1977; Soviet Poems, 1978; "Sequences", 1979; "Gradations of Grandeur", 1979; "Landscape with Rain", 1980; 'Conflicts of Spring' 1981; 'At the Ocean's Verge' 1982; "The Brazen Tower", (short stories) 1974; "The Vivid Air" (short stories), 1980; wrote "Poetry and Canada" for

Candn. Legion Educ. Services, 1945; his short stories and crit. articles have appeared in foremost lit. journs. in Can. and abroad, incl. "The Best American Short Stories", 1948 and 1950; "Canadian Short Stories", 1960; "A Book of Canadian Stories", 1962; and in foremost poetry anthologies up to the present; Ed. of "Anthology of Canadian Poetry", 1942; "Canadian Accent", 1944 (contemporary Candn. poetry and prose); "A Little Anthology of Canadian Poets", 1943; Candn. poetry issue of "Voices", 1943; "Penguin Book of Candn. Verse" 1958; revised ed. 1967, 1975; awarded Sr. Fellowship of Canada Council, 1959-60, Can. Council Award 1971; Arts Award, 1980; Queen's Silver Jubilee Medal, 1978; poetry delegate to U.K. 1972, to U.S.S.R. 1976, to Washington, D.C. 1977, to Italy 1981; Founding mem., League of Candn. Poets; Keble Coll. Assn., Oxford (Life); Home: North Hatley, Que. J0B 2C0

GUTELIUS, John Robert, B.A., M.D., C.M., F.R.C.S.(C), F.A.C.S.; surgeon; educator; b. Montreal, Que. 18 Jan. 1929; s. Nelson Edward and Gertrude (Regina) G.; e. Univ. of Montreal (Loyola Coll.) B.A. 1950; McGill Univ. M.D., C.M. 1955, Dipl. Surg. 1961; m. Elizabeth Ann Timmins 23 July 1955; children: Charles, Julie, Ann, John, Joan, Peter, Matthew, Kathryn; SURGEON-IN-CHIEF, KINGSTON GEN. HOSP., Prof. and Head of Surgery Queen's Univ. 1973- ; Intern Royal Victoria Hosp. Montreal 1955-56; Resident McGill Univ. Teaching Hosp. 1956-61, Assoc. Prof. of Surgery McGill Univ. 1965-69, Assoc. Dean 1968-69; Prof. and Head of Surgery Univ. of Saskatoon 1969-73, Dean Coll. of Med. 1970-73; practice specializing in Surgery Kingston, Ont. 1973- ;James IV Traveller in Surgery 1973; Markle Scholar in Acad. Med. 1963-68; mem. Am. Coll. Chest Physicians; Royal Soc. Arts; Assn. Candn. Med. Colls. (Pres. 1973-74); Am. Surg. Assn.; Candn. Assn. Clin. Surgs. (Pres. 1979-80); Candn. Soc. Vascular Surg. (Pres. 1980-81); R. Catholic; Home: R.R. #1, Kingston, Ont. K7L 4V1; Office: Kingston, Ont. K7L 3N6.

GUTHRIE, Hugh, Q.C., B.Com.; solicitor; b. Toronto, Ont. 3 Feb. 1931; s. Hugh Comyn and Margaret (Murray) G.; e. elem. and high schs. Guelph; Univ. of Toronto B.Com. 1952; Osgoode Hall Law Sch. 1956; m. Lorna Jean Ellen d. Harold A. Knight, Guelph, Ont. 4 Aug. 1961; two d. Lorna Margaret, Patricia Ann; PARTNER, HUNGERFORD, GUTHRIE & BERRY; Dir. The Homewood Sanitarium of Guelph Ltd.; Omark Canada Ltd.; called to Bar of Ont. 1956; cr. Q.C. 1968; sometime lectr. Univ. of Guelph; mem. Dental Technols. Adv. Comte. 1972; Past Pres. Guelph Y.M.-Y.W.C.A.; served with C.O.T.C. 1950-52; Bencher, Law Soc. Upper Can.; Fellow, Foundation for Legal Research; Past Pres. Wellington Law Assn.; mem. Waverley Lodge Guelph; Delta Kappa Epsilon; P. Conservative; Presbyterian; recreation: golf; Clubs: Albany (Toronto); University (Toronto); Home: 49 Edinburgh Rd., Guelph, Ont. N1H 5P2; Office: 15 Douglas St., Guelph, Ont. N1H 2J7.

GUTHRIE, Richard Hamilton, B.Sc.; b. London, Ont., 15 Nov. 1916; s. Hamilton and Bernice J. (Meldrum) G.; e. London Central Collegiate, Sr. Matric., 1934; McGill Univ., Sch. of Arch., 1934-36; Mass. Inst. Tech., B.Sc. (Aero Engn.) 1939; m. Isobelle Ruth, d. Brainard Carlyle, Oshawa, Ont., Dec. 1942; children: Richard, Barbara, Susan, Carolyn, JoAnn; PRES., SCAN MARINE INC., AND VICE-PRES., PRATT AND WHITNEY AIRCRAFT OF CANADA LTD.; since 1980; began career with National Research Council, Ottawa, 1940-42; Turbo Research Ltd., 1945; DeHavilland Aircraft, 1946-50; Hussman Refrigerator Co. Ltd., 1951; joined present Co., 1951; Engn. Mgr. until 1962; Planning Mgr. until 1966 when apptd. Mgr., Indust. & Marine Div.; served as Flt. Lieut., R.C.A.F., 1942-45; AFHQ Engineering Officer; Fellow, Candn. Aero. & Space Inst. (Founding mem. and Chrmn., Planning Comte.); mem., Corp. Prof. Engrs. Que.; United Church; recreations: swimming, canoeing, tennis, gar-

dening, skiing, sailing; Club Lake Brulé Country; Homes: 123 Beacon Hill Rd., Beaconsfield, Que. H9W 1S8; Lac Brulé, Terrebonne, Que.; Office: (P.O. Box 80) Longueuil, Que. J4K 5C6

GUY, Claude; stockbroker; b. Montreal, Que., 15 May 1930; s. Roméo and Marguerite (Lapointe) G.; e. St. Charles Garnier Coll., Quebec City; coll. Ste. Marie and Loyola Coll. (Comm.), Montreal; m. Laure, d. Paul Dufresne, Westmount, Que., Sept. 1958; children: Geneviève, Charles, Sylvain; CHRMN. OF THE BOARD, MOLSON, ROUSSEAU AND CIE LTÉE; Dir., Canagex Mutual Fund; Clk., Montreal Refrigerating and Storage, The Sun Life Assurance Co. and Canadian Alliance Corp. for 1 yr. each; Salesman, W.C. Pitfield & Co. Ltd. for 8 yrs.; Partner, Brault & Chaput, 1959; Extve. Vice-Pres. and Dir., Brault, Guy, Chaput Inc.; mem. Bd. of Mang., Candn. Stock Exchange, 1963 (Chrmn. 1968); Dir., Montreal Br., Jr. Invest. Dealers' Assn. Can., 1954-55 (Pres. 1957-58); Hon. Pres. 1958-59); Gov., Montreal Stock Exchange 1969; R. Catholic; recreations: skiing, swimming, golf; Clubs: St-Denis; Laval-sur-le-Lac; Home: 1550 McGregor St., Montreal, Que. H3G 1C2; Office: Place Victoria, Montreal, Que.

GUY, Hon. Robert DuVal, LL.B.; retired judge; b. Winnipeg, Man., 1 Jan. 1912; s. Robert Dunbar and Anna Corinne (DuVal) G.; e. Pub. and High Schs., Winnipeg; Univ. of Man., B.A. 1932; Manitoba Law Sch., LL.B. 1936; m. Helen Patricia, d. J.J. Gibbons, Toronto, 27 Dec. 1941; children: Monica Jane, Nancy Victoria, Ralph DuVal, Robert Jonathan, Patrick Gibbons; JUSTICE COURT OF APPEAL, MAN., 1961-80; formerly a Partner, Guy, Chappell, Guy, Wilson & Coughlin; Lectr. in Law, Univ. of Manitoba; Pres., Man. Progressive Cons. Assn. 1948-52; called to Bar of Man. 1936; Delta Upsilon; Freemason; United Church; Clubs: Manitoba; Motor Country; Home: 135 East Gate, Winnipeg, Man. R3C 2C2;

GWYN, Quintin Peter Thorsby Jermy, C.D., M.A.; Grand Chancellor Sov. Milit. Order of St. John of Jerusalem, of Rhodes, & of Malta, 1968-78; retired 1978 b. Norwich, England, 4 Feb. 1906; s. Maj. R.P. Jermy and Isabel Mary (Nicholson) G.; e. Stonyhurst Coll., Lancs., Eng., 1915-23; Balliol Coll., Oxford, B.A. 1927, M.A. 1930; qualified for Foreign Office in Civil Service exams, 1930; m. Barbara Desgrand, d. late Percy José Mitchell 10 May 1933; children: Nicholas Rhys, Peter José, Julian, Caroline, Quintin Hugh, Isabel, Robin, Rosemary; Dir., Seagram Overseas Corp. Ltd., Montreal; Casa Vinicola Barone Ricasoli, Florence; Noilly Prat Torino S.p.A., Turin; Bersano S.p.A., Nizza, Monferrato; Corporate mem. Inst. of Export (London); with Law Fire Ins. Co. Ltd., London, Eng., 1930-31; Cadbury Fry Co., Export Dept., 1931-38; trans. to Can., 1938, as Dir. and Sales Mgr., Fry-Cadbury Ltd., Montreal, Que.; joined House of Seagram as Asst. to the Gen. Mgr., 1946; Asst. Dir. Of Export, 1948; Dir. of Export, 1953; Vice-Pres. and Dir., Asst. to the Pres., Seagram Overseas Corp. Ltd., 1956-68; served in O.T.C., Stonyhurst Coll., 1918-23; McGill C.O.T.C., May-July 1940; served with 2nd (Reserve) Bn., Royal Montreal Regt., 1950-51; Maj. 2nd in Command, R.M.R. (R), 1949-51; Pres. and Hon. Life Mem., Candn. Export-ers Assn. 1950-51; Gov., Candn. Inter-Am. Assn. 1965-68; Chrmn., Montreal Italian Chamber of Comm. 1966-68; Vice-Pres., Candn. Comn. of Internat. Chamber of Comm. 1964-68; Bailiff Grand Cross of Obedience, Sovereign and Military Order of Malta (Grand Cross of Merit 1961; President Canadian Association 1961-68, Honorary President 1968); Kt. Order of St. John 1966, Offr. 1953; rec'd. Coronation Medal 1953; Centenary Medal 1967; Commdr., Order of Isabel la Catolica (Spain) 1957; Grand Cross Orden de Mayo (Argentine), 1968; Gr.Cr. do Cruzeiro do Sul, 1969-Brazil; Gr.Cr. de Boyacà, 1969-Colombia; Bailiff Gr.Cr. of Justice Constantinian Order of St. George, 1969; Gran Cruz Placa de Plata de la Orden de Ruben Dario, 1969-Nicaragua; Gran Cruz de la Orden al

Merito de Chile, 1970; Gran Cruz de la Orden Nacional al Merito, 1970-Ecuador; Gran Cruz de la Orden El Sol del Perù, 1970; Grand-Croix de l'Ordre au Mérite, 1970-Niger; Grand Officer National Order of Senegal, 1970; Gr.Cruz Order of Isabel La Catolica, 1971-Spain; Gran Croce al Merito della Repubblica Italianna, 1971; Grosskreuz Verdiensordens-1971, German Federal Republic; Grand Cross of Merit, Gabon, 1972; DATU Order of Sikatuna, Philippines, 1972; Grand Cross Placa au Plata Orden "Francisco Morazan", Honduras, 1972; Grand Cross Orden del Quetzal, Guatemala, 1972; Gran Cordone Orden Libertador, Venezuela, 1973; Gran Cruz Extraordinaria Orden Nacional del Merito, Paraguay, 1973; Condecoration Honor el Merito de Salud Publica, Paraguay, 1973; Grand Croix au Merite, Dahomey, 1974; Gold Grand Cross of Merit, Austria, 1977; Grand Officier Ordre National, Côte d'Ivoire, 1977; Liberal; Roman Catholic; Clubs: University (Montreal); Travellers (London); Home: Champlain Towers Apt. 1306 - 200 Rideau terr. Ottawa L1M 0Z2

GYLES, Cedric G.E.; insurance executive; b. Vancouver, B.C. 23 Dec. 1926; s. Cedric Harold and Vera (Rider) G.; e. Public and High Schs., Vancouver, B.C.; m. Barbara, I. Martin, 18 Feb. 1949; children: Peter David, Cedric James, Patricia Catherine, Marti Ann, John Phillip, George Edward; PRESIDENT AND CHIEF EXTVE. OFFR., REED STENHOUSE LTD. since 1975; with Price Waterhouse, Vancouver, B.C. 1947-50; Prof. Football Player with Calgary Stampeders 1948-51; Godfrey Investments Ltd., Calgary, 1950-53; Reed Stenhouse Limited & Predecessor Companies - Calgary and Edmonton 1953-61; Winnipeg Mgr 1961-71; Sr. Vice-Pres. Toronto 1971-74; Exec. Vice-Pres. 1974-75; Appointed to the Board and Exec. Committee of Reed Stenhouse Companies limited 1980. Clubs: Royal Canadian Yacht; Royal Vancouver Yacht; Ontario; Griffith Is.; Winnipeg Football (Life mem., Pres. 1968-69); Home: 65 Harbour Square, Apt 1480 Toronto, Ont. M5J 2L4 Office: Royal Trust Tower (Box 250) Toronto-Dominion Centre, Toronto, Ont. M5K 1J6

H

HABER, David; impresario; theatre manager and producer; b. Montreal, Que., 15 July 1927; s. Louis and Molly (Nahamovitz) H.; e. Bancroft Sch. and Baron Byng High Sch., Montreal; Quebec (Que.) High Sch., 1945; various theatre, dance and music schs.; PRESIDENT, DAVID HABER ARTISTS MANAGEMENT INC. founded 1975, inc. 1976, represents Canadian performing artists internationally, also tour direction and touring productions, consultancy; Production, Stage and General Mgr.; Brae Manor (summer) Theatre, Knowlton, Que., 1948-56; Production Stage Mgr.; Candn. Repertory Theatre, Ottawa, 1949-51; Nat. Ballet of Can., Toronto, 1951-56; Indust. productions in Can. and U.S.A., Nat. Film Bd., Montreal, 1956-58, Assoc. Producer "The Drylanders" 1961; personal and tour mgr. to various performers incl.: Sir John Gielgud "Ages of Man", Stanley Holloway "Laughs and Other Events", Mahalia Jackson World Tour, 1958-61; Personal Agt. and Mgr., William Morris Agency, N.Y. (incl. Mahalia Jackson, Basil Rathbone, Celeste Holm); Producer of Theatre Presentations for World Festival of Expo 67, Montreal, 1964-67; Dir. of Programming, Nat. Arts Centre, Ottawa 1968-73; Artistic Dir., Nat. Ballet of Can. 1973-75; rec'd Centennial Medal 1967; Queen's Jubilee Medal, 1976; organizes tours abroad for Dept. of External Affairs and tours in Can. for Candn. and foreign co.'s; mem., Internat. Soc. Performing Arts Administrators, Vice Pres. of Entertainment, Consultant & Producer of World Festival for 1982 World's Fair, Knoxville Tenn.; Consultant, Southwest Arts Foundation, Houston; Tel-Pro Prods., L.A.; Jubilee Festival, Toronto; mem. Bd., Internat. Soc. of Performing Arts Administrators; mem.

Assn. of Coll., Univ. and Community Arts Adm.; Candn. Assn. of Artists Managements (Past Pres.); Candn. Music Council; Candn. Conf. of the Arts (Bd. Govs.); Assn. of Theatrical Press Agents and Mgrs.; Dance Can. Assn.; Can.-Israel Cultural Fdns. (Adv. Bd.); Hebrew; recreation: swimming; Address: 553 Queen St. W., Toronto, Ont. M5V 2B6

HACHEY, Henry Benedict, M.B.E., E.D., LL.D., F.R.S.C.; oceanographer (retired); b. W. Bathurst, N.B., 7 June 1901; s. Joseph Bennet and Sarah (Kelly) H.; e. St. Thomas Univ., Chatham, N.B.; St. Francis Xavier Univ., B.Sc., 1922; McGill Univ., M.Sc., 1925; St. Thomas Univ., LL.D. and St. Francis Xavier; m. Katherine Avis, d. late Dr. Philip Cox, Fredericton, N.B. 18 Oct. 1930; children: Philip Osmund, Mary Isabel (Mrs. Anthony R. Oland), John Henry, Jane Elizabeth (Mrs. Patrick Sullivan); Lectr., Univ. of St. Francis Xavier, 1922-23; Demonst. and Tutor, McGill Univ., 1925-26; Prof. of Physics, Univ. of N.B., 1926-28; Oceanographer, Fisheries Research Bd., 1928-46, and Chief Oceanographer, 1946-64; and Consulting Oceanographer, 1964-68 Secy. Candn. Comte. on Oceanography 1946-66; Candn. del. to various meetings of Internat. Council for Exploration of Sea; Internat. Union of Geodesy & Geophysics; Internat. Oceanographic Comte.; Scient. Comte. on Oceanic Research; Commonwealth meeting on Oceanography; joined N.P. A.M. 1921; Commd. 1923; active duty with North Shore Regt. Aug. 1940, Capt. and Adjt.; Major "D" Co. overseas, 3rd Div.; G.S.O., Directorate Staff Duties (weapons); Lieut.-Col. with Army Operational Research Group: seconded to Royal Candn. Navy Apl. 1944; retired to Reserve March 1946; Mayor of St. Andrews, N.B. (13 terms); mem., Charlotte Co. Council (8 terms); author of numerous publs. in field of oceanography; mem., Bd. Govs., St. Francis Xavier Univ. (6 years); Coronation medal 1937; Queen's Jubilee medal 1977; K. of C.; R. Catholic; recreations, gardening, hunting, fishing, curling; Address: St. Andrews, N.B. E0G 2X0

HACKETT, William Thomas Gould; LL.D. (Concordia Univ.) 1980; former banker; b. Carbonear, Nfld., 30 May 1906; s. Charles and Jane Maber (Gould) H.; e. Guelph (Ont.) Coll. Inst. (Grad. 1924); Univ. of Toronto (Grad. 1927; Econ. and Pol. Science); m. Alice, d. Geo. A. Scroggie, Guelph, Ont., 1 July 1936; one son, David; Executive in Residence, Dept. of Finance, Faculty of Comm. and Admin., Concordia Univ.; entered firm of Fry, Mills, Spence & Co. Ltd., Invest. Dealers, Toronto, Ont., 1928; with Mills, Spence & Co. Ltd., 1935-41; in 1941 apptd. Secy. of Ont. Extve. Comte. of Nat. War Finance Comte. and later that year Secy. of Wartime Industries Control Bd., Ottawa; joined Bank of Montreal as Econ. Adviser, 1943; apptd. Asst. Gen., Manager, 1952; Vice Pres. Money Mang. 1968-70; author of: "A Background of Banking Theory", and has publ. articles on econ. and banking subjects; mem., Candn. Inst. of Internat. Affairs; LL.D. (Honoris Causa); Concordia Univ. 1980; Anglican; recreations: music, tennis, curling; Clubs: University; Royal Montreal Curling; Mount Royal Tennis; Home: 448 Argyle Ave., Westmount, Montreal, P.Q. H3P 3B4

HADDAD, Hon. William Joseph, B.A., LL.B.; judge; b. Meyronne, Sask. 26 Nov. 1915; s. late Abdelnour Farhat and Sophia Mary (Ead) H.; e. Univ. of Alta. B.A., LL.B. 1941; m. Frances Margaret d. late Peter Assaly 14 May 1944; children: Gayle Frances Blake, Ronald William, Kenneth Peter; JUDGE, COURT OF APPEAL, ALTA. 1979- ; read law with Nelles V. Buchanan, K.C.; called to Bar of Alta. 1942; cr. Q.C. 1957; law practice Marks and Haddad 1946-51; Partner, Wood, Haddad, Moir & Hope 1952; Partner, Haddad, Cavanagh & Buchanan 1961, merged with Simpson, Henning & Co. 1962 under name Simpson, Haddad, Cavanagh, Henning, Buchanan & Kerr, became Sr. Partner; apptd. to Dist. Court Dist. of N. Alta. 1965; apptd. to Appellate Div. Supreme Court of Alta. 1974 (became present Court 1979); served with

RCN1942-46, rank Lt. (SB), legal offr. Staff C.O. Pacific Coast 1943-46; Dir., Vice Pres. and mem. Mang. Comte. Edmonton Eskimo Football Club 1958-64, Dir. and Secy. Touchdown Club 1956-57; Secy.-Treas. Edmonton Lib. Assn. 1962-63; Chrmn. Edmonton Bd. Police Commrs. 1966-71; mem. Alta. Securities Comn. 1966-74, Vice Chrmn. 1974-78; Pres., Men's Candn. Club Edmonton 1954; Edmonton Kinsmen Club 1955-56; Pres. Edmonton Bar Assn. 1955; mem. Royal Candn. Legion; Candn. Bar Assn.; Anglican; recreation: golf; Clubs: Mayfair Golf & Country (Pres. 1973); Royal Glenora; mem. 6507 Grandview Dr., Edmonton, Alta. T6H 4K2; Office: Law Courts, 1A Sir Winston Churchill Sq., Edmonton, Alta. T5J 0R2.

HADWEN, John Gaylard, M.A.; public servant; b. Ottawa, Ont., 18 April 1923; s. Dr. Seymour and Estelle Alden (Godwin) H.; e. Brown Pub. Sch., Toronto 1935; Univ. of Toronto Schs. 1941; Trinity Coll., Univ. of Toronto, B.A. 1948, M.A. 1949; London Sch. of Econ. 1950; Inst. Universitaire des Hautes Etudes Internats., Genève, Switzerland, 1971; HIGH COMMISSIONER TO INDIA AND AMBASSADOR TO NEPAL since 1979; joined Dept. External Affairs as Foreign Service Offr., 1950 Ottawa; Pakistan 1952-54, New York 1956-59, Oslo 1961-64; Special Asst. to SSEA and to P.M. 1964-67; High Commr., Malaysia and Singapore and Ambassador to Burma 1967-71; Ambassador to Pakistan and Afghanistan, 1972-74; served in R.C.A., enlisted Cadet, discharged Lance Sgt.; perm. rank Lt.; co-author of "How United Nations Decisions Are Made"; United Church; recreations: golf, tennis, philately; Clubs: East India and Sports (London, Eng.); Royal Selangor Golf (Kuala Lumpur); Office: P.O. Box 500 (NDI), General Post Office, Ottawa, Ont. K1N 8T7

HAERING, Rudolph Roland, O.C. (1976), M.A., Ph.D., FRSC; educator; b. Basle, Switzerland, 27 Feb. 1934; s. Rudolph and Selma (Tschudin) H.; e. Univ. of B.C., B.A. 1954, M.A. 1955; McGill Univ. Ph.D. 1957; m. Mary Patricia, d. late Edward Peatfield 6 Aug. 1954; two d. Susan Jane, Linda Jean; DIR., MOLI ENERGY LTD. 1977.; Prof. of Physics, Univ. of Brit. Columbia 1973; post-doctoral Fellow Univ. of Birmingham 1957-58 (NRC Fellowship); Asst. Prof. of Theoretical Physics McMaster Univ. 1958-60; Research Staff mem. IBM Research Center, Yorktown Heights, N.Y. 1960, Group Leader 1961-63; Prof. of Physics Univ. of Waterloo 1963-64; Prof. and Head Dept. of Physics Simon Fraser Univ. 1964, Acting Acad. Vice Pres. 1968-69, Prof. of Physics 1969-72; Visiting Prof. Univ. of B.C. 1964-65; Consultant IBM Research Labs. Poughkeepsie 1959-66; United Mineral and Chemical Corp. N.Y. 1963-64; Lear Siegler Corp. Grand Rapids 1964-65; Editor, Can. Journal of Physics, 1968-73; Pres. Candn. Thin Films Ltd. 1970-73; Pres., Can. Assn. Physicists, 1978; mem. Nat. Research Council 1974-77; Adv. Council B.C. Inst. Technol. 1965-72; Bd. of Mang. B.C. Research Council 1968-74; Adv. Comte. for Physics Defence Research Bd. 1969-75; Bd. of Mang. TRIUMF 1973-76; Centennial Medal 1967; C.A.P. Herzberg Medal 1970; Queen's Jubilee Medal 1978; Ed. "Canadian Journal of Physics" 1968-72; Chrmn. Theoretical Physics Div. Candn. Assn. Physicists 1965-67; recreation: outdoor sports; Home: 647 Croydon Pl., North Vancouver, B.C. V7N 3A2

HAGEN, Betty-Jean (Mrs. Vincent Greicius); musician; b. Edmonton, Alta., 1930; e. studied in Edmonton, Calgary, Alta., Chicago, then moved with family to Toronto; Royal Conservatory of Music, Toronto, Ont. (studied under Geza de Kresz); Grad. 1951; post-grad. study with Ivan Galamian in New York; winner of Toronto Women's Musical Club Scholarship, 1950; Walter W. Naumburg Musical Foundation Award, 1950; m. Vincent Greicius, New York, July 1954; made N.Y. debut, Town Hall 15 Nov. 1950; winner of Pathé Marconi Prize at Thibaud Internat. Competition, Paris, 1951; Winner of Naumburg Award; won Eaton Graduate Award of $1,000 at Royal Conservatory of Music, Toronto, 1951; engaged in European tour, 1951-52 and European and Am. tours; made London debut, Jan. 1952; awarded Harriet Cohen Medal, 1952 (as the outstanding woman in the Brit. Commonwealth); named, "Woman of the Year" in Canadian music, 1953; gave 400th Concert in the History of Hart House, Univ. of Toronto, 1974; winner of Carl Flesch Medal, London, Nov. 1953; Leventritt Foundation Award, N.Y., Apl. 1955; engagements as Soloist: N.Y. Philharmonic, London Philharmonic, etc.; Now Teaches and coaches chamber ensembles in New York, specializing in teenage students; recorded for Beaver Records, Canada.

HAGEN, George Leon, B.S.; chemical engineer; b. Bancroft, Idaho, 8 Sept. 1924; s. George William and Mabel (Waddell) H.; e. Boise (Idaho) High Sch.; Boise Jr. Coll.; Montana Sch. of Mines, Butte, Mon.; Univ. of Washington, B.S. (Chem. and Indust. Engn.); m. Anita Louise, d. Arthur O. Rowe, 31 Aug. 1946; three s., one d.; PRESIDENT, G.L. HAGEN ASSOC. INC., BUSINESS CONSULTANT 1981- ; President and Chief Extve. Offr., Reichhold Ltd. 1966-81; Indust. Engr., Methods, Boeing Airplane Company, Seattle, Wash., 1948-51; Plant Engr., Reichhold Chemicals Inc., 1951-56, Sales Representative 1956-61; Division Manager, Western Division, Reichhold Chemicals (Canada) Ltd., Vancouver, B.C., 1961-63; Vice-Pres. and Gen. Mgr., 1963-64, Extve. Vice-Pres., 1964-66; el. Dir. 1963, el. Pres. 1966; served as Lt. with U.S. Naval Reserve, Aviation Br.; private airplane Pilot; mem., Tappi; former Prof. Engr., State of Washington and B.C.; Am. Mang. Assn.; Toronto Bd. of Trade; Pres. Assn.; Advncd. Mang. Research; Candn. Chem. Prod. Assn.; author of: "Patent on Formaldehyde Manufacturing"; Phi Kappa Psi; recreations: skiing, swimming, tennis, fishing, hunting, reading, golf, squash; photography; Clubs: Markland Woods Country; Mississauga Golf and Country; Home: 296 Mill Rd., E8, Etobicoke, Ont., M9C 4X8

HAGER, Roger T.; company director; b. Vancouver, B.C.; Stanford Univ. (Grad.); DIR., THE CANADIAN FISHING CO. LTD.; Domtar Ltd.; British Pacific Properties Ltd.; Park Roval Shopping Centre Ltd.; Dir., Western Resources Ltd.; began business career in 1930 when he joined The Canadian Fishing Co. Ltd., retiring as Chrmn. of Bd. and Chief Extve. Offr.; served in 2nd World War with R.C.N.V.R. and discharged with rank of Lieut.-Commdr.; Home: 6895 Balsam St., Vancouver, B.C. V6P 5W9

HAGEY, J. Gerald, B.A., LL.D.; b. Hamilton, Ont., 28 Sept. 1904; s. Menno and Esther (Hagey) H.; e. Public and High Schs., Hamilton, Ont.; Waterloo Coll. (in affiliation with Univ. of W. Ont.), B.A. 1928; Susquehanna LL.D., Sir Geo. Williams; Waterloo Lutheran (1970); Univ. of Waterloo, 1971; Univ. of Western Ont., 1975; m. late Minota Margaret Weichel, 15 June 1929; children: Robert Gerald, John Edward; m. 2ndly, Mrs. Eleanor Ford Duff, 16 June 1967; Founding Pres., Univ. of Waterloo 1957-69, Pres. Emeritus 1970; Dir. and Pres., The Speech Foundation of Ont.; Past Pres. & Dir., Assn. of Candn. Advs.; with Sales Dept., B.F. Goodrich Canada Ltd., Kitchener, Ont., 1928-33; Sales Rep., Brigden's Ltd., Toronto, Ont., 1933-34; Merchant's Printing Co., Kitchener, Ont., 1934-35; Nat. Advertising and Public Relations Mgr., B. F. Goodrich Canada Ltd., Kitchener, Ont., 1935-53; Pres., Waterloo Lutheran Univ. 1954-59; recreations: gardening, photography, woodworking; Clubs: Kitchener Rotary; Granite; Home: 637 Westmount Rd. West, Kitchener, Ont. N2M 1R7

HAGGETT, William Stanley; company executive; b. Newport, England, 26 May 1920; s. James Henry and Maude H.; e. Jones' West Monmouth, Newport, Eng.; m. Betty, d. George William Brown, E. Yorks, England, 23 Feb. 1943; one d. Susan; PRESIDENT, GENERAL AVIA-

TION SERVICES LTD.; General Aviation Sales Ltd.; General Aviation Jetways Ltd.; formerly President of The Bristol Aeroplane Company of Canada Ltd. which company he joined in 1938 and resigned in 1967; served eight years on outside Tech. Liaison with R.A.F.; Sr. Tech. Rep. in Paris, 1946; Sales Manager, The Bristol Aeroplane Co. of Can. Ltd. Montreal, 1950; Gen. Mgr. MacDonald Bros. Aircraft Ltd. 1954; Sr. Vice-President, The Bristol Aeroplane Co. of Can. Ltd. 1958; Dir. and Past Chrmn., Air Industries Assn. Can.; mem., Candn. Aero & Space Inst.; Am. Inst. of Mang.; McGill Associates; Anglican; recreations: tennis, squash, skiing; Clubs: Rideau (Ottawa); Manitoba; M.A.Á.A.; St. James's; Home: 1212 Pine Ave. W., Apt. 1804, Montreal, Que. H3G 1A8

HAGUE, John Brian, B.A.; executive; b. Lethbridge, Alta. 15 Aug. 1944; s. Rev. John Rayson and Rose (Knowlden) H.; e. Univ. of B.C., B.A. 1965; Univ. of Minn. grad. work Econ. 1965-66; EXTVE. VICE PRES., CANADA DEVELOPMENT CORP. 1979- ; Dir. Polysar Ltd.; Canterra Energy Ltd.; Kidd Creek Mines Ltd.; Business Analyst Pacific Region Office Imperial Oil Ltd. 1966; Asst. Dir. Price Review Div. Fed. Prices & Incomes Comn. 1969-72; Financial Analyst present Corp. 1972-75; Dir. Gen. Prices & Profits Br. Fed. Anti-Inflation Bd. 1975-76 (leave of absence from CDC); Mgr. Financial Analysis becoming Vice Pres. present Corp. 1976; Anglican; recreations: travel, backpacking; Home: Suite 10, 423 Avenue Rd., Toronto, Ont. M4V 2H7; Office: Suite 200, 444 Yonge St., Toronto, Ont. M5B 2H4.

HAHN, Jack, B.Eng.; electrical engineer; b. Hersfeld Germany, 21 June 1920; s. Adolph and Rosa (Nussbaum) H.; e. McMaster Univ., pre-engn. 1941-42; McGill, B.Eng. (Elect.) 1947; m. Freda, d. Max Handman, 14 Dec. 1947; children: Alan, Norman, Rosanne; CONSULTANT, PRES., JACK HAHN ASSOCIATES Toronto; Dir., S.N.C. Group, 1966-80; Chrmn., SNC/GECO Can. Inc. (Toronto) 1977-80; joined S.N.C. 1946; Project Engr., 1952; Dir. of Engn., 1956; Partner 1959; mem., Corp. Engrs. of Que.; Assoc. Prof. Eng. of Ont.; Fellow & Pres., Engn. Inst. of Can.; Am. Inst. of Mining, Metall. & Petroleum Engrs.; Candn. Inst. of Mining & Metall.; Assn. of Consulting Engrs. of Can.; Candn. Soc. of Mech. Engrs.; Conservative; Jewish; recreations: gardening, sailing; Clubs: National; Montefiore; Home: 1 Benvenuto Place, Toronto, Ont. M4V 2L1; Office: 1867 Yonge St., Toronto, Ont. M4S 1Y5

HAIDASZ, Hon. Stanley, P.C. (1972), Senator, M.D.; b. Toronto, Ont., 4 Mar. 1923; s. Peter and Josephine (Justynski) H.; e. St. Mary's Sch., Toronto, Ont. 1929-36; St. Michael's College., Toronto, 1936-41; Univ. of Ottawa, B.Ph. 1944, L.Ph. 1945; Univ. of Toronto, M.D. 1951; Course in Electro-cardiog., Cook Co. Post Grad. Sch. of Medicine, 1955; m. Natalie, d. Stanley Gugala, Toronto, 26 Aug. 1950; children: Marie, Walter, Barbara, Joanne; el. to H. of C. for Trinity g.e. 1957; re-el. for Parkdale until 1974 election; Ont. Vice Pres., Nat. Liberal Federation, 1958-61; Parlty. Secy. to Min. of Health & Welfare, 1963; Parlty. Secy. to Secretary of State for External Affairs, 1964-65; Parlty. Secy., to Min. of Indian Affairs and Northern Development, 1966-67; Parlty. Secy., to Minister Consumer & Corporate Affairs, 1968; to Min. Nat. Health and Welfare 1969-70; Min. of State for Multiculturalism 1972-74; Head, Canadian Del., World Food Program, Geneva 1964; Del., U.N. Gen. Assembly 1964-65; mem. Candn. Del., WHO, Geneva 1970, and 1972; Head of Candn. del. to Inter-Am. Health Social Security Congress, Santo Domingo 1969 and Bogota 1970; accompanied Prime Minister, Pierre E. Trudeau on official visit to U.S.S.R., 1971; Queen's Privy Council, 1972; apptd. first Min. of State Responsible for Multiculturalism; Can. Delegation, Inter-Parliamentary Union meetings on Human Rights, Belgrade, 1976 and Vienna, 1978; appt. to Senate 1978; member, Senate Standing Committees on Foreign Rel., and Health, Sci. & Welfare; Past Bd. Dirs., Council

on Drug Abuse; Assoc. in Surgery, Shouldice Clinic, Toronto, 1952-55; Staff, St. Joseph's Hospital, Toronto; Past Pres., Toronto Br., Candn. Polish Cong.; former Nat. Chrmn., Candn. Polish Millenium Fund; Bd. Dirs., Copernicus Sen. Citizens Lodge; Coll. of Family Phys. of Can.; Pro merito medal citation of Latvian Fed. of Can.; Can. Inst. of International Affairs; Assoc., Soviet & E. European Studies, Carleton Univ., Ottawa 1964-72; Hon. citizen of Winnipeg; Hon Life Mem., Polish Alliance Friendly Soc. of Can.; Knight Commander of the Sovereign Order of St. John of Jerusalem, (Knights of Malta) and Chancellor of its Priory in Canada; Liberal; R. Catholic; recreations: gardening, swimming, badminton; Office: 514 Lansdowne Ave., Toronto, Ont. M6H 3Y3

HAIG, Graeme Thomson, M.C., C.D., Q.C.; b. Moose Jaw, Sask., 7 Aug. 1923; s. Gordon Stuart and Catherine Margaret (Thomson) H.; e. elem. and high schs. Moose Jaw (Sask.) 1931 and Winnipeg (Man.) 1940; Univ. of Man. 1940-42; Man. Law Sch. LL.B. 1949; m. Patricia Joyce d. John Jackson, 28 May 1949; children: Gordon, Briony, Margot, Angela; PARTNER, D'ARCY & DEACON since 1965; Chrmn. of Bd. Settlers Savings & Mortgage Corp.; Dir. Polaris Leasing Co. Ltd.; Dir., Wawanesa Mutual Insce. Co.; called to Bar of Man. 1949; cr. Q.C. 1964; practised law Winnipeg, Man. 1950-61 in partnership with A.L. Campbell, Q.C.; Chrmn. Man. Law Sch. Foundation; Pres. Winnipeg Humane Soc.; Pres. Man. P. Cons. Assns. 1970-74; Pres. Un. Way of Winnipeg 1977-78; served in N.W. Europe 1943-46; Fort Garry Horse Militia 1949-61, Hon. Lt. Col.; mem. Winnipeg Chamber Comm. (Past Pres.); Man. Chamber Comm. (Past Pres.); Candn. Chamber Comm. (Dir.); Man. Bar Assn. (Past Pres.); Candn. Bar Assn. Past Vice Pres.; Nat. Council); Candn. Foundation on Alcohol & Drug Dependencies (Past Pres. and Hon. Life mem.); Presbyterian; P. Conservative; recreations: golf, curling, music, reading; Clubs: Manitoba; St. Charles Country; Home: 191 Oakdean Blvd., St. James, Man.; Office: 300 - 286 Smith St., Winnipeg, Man. R3C 1K6

HAIG, John Douglas, D.F.C.; banker; b. Winnipeg, Man. 27 Jan. 1921; s. John Thomas and Josephine (Dickie) H.; m. Dorene Grace d. Fred Decker 24 Aug. 1946; three s. Douglas Decker, John Cameron, James David; VICE PRES. AND REGIONAL GEN. MGR. CANADIAN IMPERIAL BANK OF COMMERCE; Dir. Victoria Gen. Hospital; served with RCAF during World War II, Pilot; P. Conservative; United Church; recreations: curling, golf, Clubs: St. Charles Country; Manitoba; Winnipeg Winter; Home: 412 Park Blvd., Winnipeg, Man. R3P 0G9; Office: 1 Lombard Place, Winnipeg, Man. R3C 2P3

HAILEY, Arthur; writer; b. Luton, Eng. 5 April 1920; came to Canada 1947; s. (late) George Wellington and (late) Elsei Mary (Wright) H.; e. British Elem. Sch.; m. 2ndly Sheila Marjorie d. (late) James Watt Dunlop 28 July 1951; children: Jane, Steven, Diane (and by previous m.) Roger, John, Mark; author of "Runway Zero-Eight", (with John Castle) 1958; "The Final Diagnosis", 1959; "In High Places", 1962; "Hotel", 1965; "Airport", 1968; "Wheels", 1971; "The Moneychangers", 1975; "Overload", 1979; (collected plays) "Close-Up on Writing for Television", 1960; motion pictures include: "Zero Hour", 1956; "Time Lock", 1957; "The Young Doctors", 1961: "Hotel", 1966; "Airport", 1970; "The Moneychangers", 1976; "Wheels", 1978;."Overload" (in progress); television plays include: "Flight into Danger" 1956; and 11 others; Pres., Seaway Authors Ltd.; served as Pilot with RAF 1939-47, rank Flight Lieut.; mem. Assn. of Candn. Tel. and Radio Artists (hon. life member); Authors League of Am.; Writers Guild of America; Independent Conservative; Clubs: Lyford Cay, Bahamas; River, N.Y.; recreations: boating, fishing, enology, music; Home: Lyford Cay, P.O. Box N-7776, Nassau, Bahamas; Office: First Canadian Pl., 6400-Box 130, Toronto, Ont. M5X 1A4

HAINES, Hon. Edson Livingstone; judge; b. Hamilton, Ont., 26 Mar. 1907; s. Charles Frederick and Evelyn Eliza (Douglas) H.; e. Pub. and High Schs., Hamilton, Ont.; Osgoode Hall, Toronto, Ont.; m. Vera Lorraine Jones, 25 Nov. 1932; children: Barbara Elaine, Paul and Bruce (twins); JUSTICE, SUPREME COURT OF ONT., since Nov. 1962; Bencher, Law Soc. of Upper Canada, 1951-62; called to the Bar of Ont. 1930; cr. K.C. 1942; practised his prof. with Thos. N. Phelan, K.C., 1930-32; practised alone 1933-37 when became Sr. Partner, Haines, Thompson, Rodgers, Howie & Freeman, upon its formation; Chrmn., Lt. Gov.'s Adv. Review Bd. under The Ont. Mental Health Act; Hon. Pres., Toronto Med.-Legal Soc.; Hon. Life mem., Ont. Med. Assn.; Ont. Psychiatric Assn.; Acad. of Med. of Toronto; mem. Am. Law Inst.; National Council for Administration of Justice; United Church; recreations: golf, fishing; Club: Granite; Royal Can. Military Inst.; Home: 500 Avenue Road, Toronto, Ont. M4V 2J6; Office: Osgoode Hall, Toronto, Ont. M5H 2N5

HAINS, Rt. Rev. Gaston, L.Ph., D. Sc.soc. et pol.; né St.-Frédéric de Drummondville, Qué., 10 sept. 1921; f. Hormidas et Germaine (Gauthier) H.; é. Séminaire de St.-Hyacinthe, Qué., B.A., 1941; Angelicum, Rome, Italie, L. Ph., 1950; Institut Catholique de Lille, France, D. ès Sc. soc. et pol., 1952; EVEQUE D'AMOS, QUE. depuis 31 oct. 1968; Prof., Séminaire de St.-Hyacinthe, 1946-49; Aumônier d'Action Catholique et Apostolat laï*que, 1952-64; chanoine titulaire, Cathédrale St-Hyacinthe, 1956-64; Evêque auxiliaire de St-Hyacinthe, 1964-67; Adm. Apostolique du diocèse d'Amos, 13 juin 1967-31 oct. 1968; Auteur: "Notes sociales et pastorales", 1959; Résidence: 67-77 Curé de St.André de la Sarre 230, Principale La Sarre, Qué. J9Z 1Y6

HAIST, Reginald Evan, B.A., M.D., M.A., Ph.D., F.R.S.C.; professor; b. Hamilton, Ont., 14 Jan. 1910; s. Oscar Wesley and Anna (Leppert) H.; e. Hamilton (Ont.) Central Coll. Inst.; Univ. of Toronto, B.A. 1933, M.D. 1936, M.A. 1937, Ph.D. 1940; m. Margaret Scott, d. Winford G. Milne, Hamilton, Ont., 7 Aug. 1936; children: Lynda Margaret, David Winford, Stephen Richard, Margaret Catherine, Frances Elizabeth; Geo. Brown Mem. Fellowship, Univ. of Toronto, 1936-37; Research Asst. in Physiol., 1937-38; Demonst. 1938-40; Asst. Prof. of Physiol. Hygiene 1940-41 and also Applied Physiol. 1941-42; Asst. Prof. of Physiol., Applied Physiol. and Physiol. Hygiene, 1942-43; Asst. Prof. of Physiol. and Applied Physiol., 1943-45; Assoc. Prof. of Physiol., 1945-49, Professor 1949 (Chrmn. of Dept. 1965-75), Emeritus Prof. 1975; mem., Am. Diabetes Assn.; Am. Physiol. Soc.; Candn. Physiol. Soc.; The Physiol. Soc.; Alpha Omega Alpha; United Church; recreation: painting; Home: 56 Cheltenham Ave., Toronto, Ont. M4N 1P7

HALDENBY, Lieut. Col. Douglas Charles, C.D., B.Arch., F.R.A.I.C. (1968); architect; b. Toronto, Ont., 3 March 1925; s. Eric Wilson and Shirley Margaret (Hamilton) H.; e. Rosedale Pub. Sch.; Upper Can. Coll.; Univ. of Toronto, B.Arch.; m. Muriel Ross, d. Ross MacDonald, 14 Feb. 1948; children: Eric Ross MacDonald, David Douglas, James Charles, Margot Shirley; SR. PARTNER, MATHERS & HALDENBY; Chrmn., Arch. Div., Un. Appeal, 1967; Vice-Chrmn., Corporate Group, Un. Appeal, 1964; commenced prof. career with present firm; Supv. Arch. on projects in Toronto, Ont., Cuba, Vancouver, B.C., Calgary, Alta., Regina & Saskatoon, Sask., Montreal & Quebec City, Que.; served with Upper Can. Coll. Cadet Corps; enlisted in the Candn. Army Active in 1943; commd. in March 1945 and served until Sept. 1945; joined 48th Highlanders of Can. as Lieut. in 1946 and retired as C.O. 1964; mem., Ont. Assn. of Arch.; Royal Arch. Inst. Can.; Zeta Psi (Toronto); Anglican; recreations: tennis, squash, sailing; Clubs: University; Badminton & Racquet; R.C.Y.C.; Home: 226 Rosedale Heights

Drive, Toronto, Ont. M4T 1E1; Office: 10 St. Mary St., Toronto, Ont. M4Y 1P7

HALE, G. Douglas, B.S.; industrialist; b. Syracuse, N.Y., 14 Aug. 1929; s. George T. and Hazel T. (Snyder) H.; e. Primary and Secondary Schs., East Syracuse, N.Y.; Univ. of Ill., B.S. (Marketing), 1951; m. Margaret E., d. Chas. A. Smith, Syracuse, NY., 17 May 1952; two s., Kevin C., G. Douglas; PRES. CHIEF EXEC. OFFC. & DIR. BLACK & DECKER (U.S.) INC.; Dir., Black & Decker Can. Inc., First Maryland Bank Corp.; Monumental Corp.; Monumental Life Ins. Co.; Sales Engineer, U.S. Radiator Corporation, 1953-55; Porter Cable Co., 1953-61; joined present Co. as Gen. Sales Mgr., 1961: Vice-Pres., Marketing-Adm., 1963-66; Chrmn. of Bd., Black & Decker Can. Inc., 1967-1975; when apptd. to present position; served with U.S. Army, 1951-53, rank Capt.; Maj. U.S. Army Reserve, 1953-63; Dir., Mercy Hospital; Baltimore Symphony; Phi Kappa Theta; Conservative; Roman Catholic; recreations: golf, fishing, boating; Clubs: Baltimore; Brockville Golf & Country; Candn. Club of N.Y.; Home: P.O. Box 238, Athens, Ont.; Office: 100 Central Ave., Brockville, Ont. K6V 4N8

HALE, Grete, B.J.; food company executive; b. Ottawa, Ont. 1929; e. Carleton Univ. B.J. 19..; m. Reginald B. Hale 1957; PRESIDENT, MORRISON LAMOTHE INC.; Dir. North American Life Assurance Co.; Key Radio Ltd.; Dir. Rideauwood Inst.; PC Can. Fund; Ottawa-Carleton Regional Hosp. Food Services Inc.; mem. Bd. Mang. Bequests & Endowments Program Un. Way Ottawa-Carleton, Past Dir.; Vice Senechale de la Chaîne des Rôtisseurs; Chrmn. MacDonald Cartier Lib.; mem. Grace Gen. Hosp. Bd. Mang.; Ont. Council Regents; after grad. rec'd 10 yrs. catering experience Eng., France, Scandinavia, Switzerland and U.S.A.; first woman Pres., Bakery Council Can.; formerly Vice Pres. Ottawa Council Women; Corr. Secy. Nat. Council Women in Can.; Dir. Alliance for Bilingualism in Can.'s Capital Region; Women's Adv. Council (5 yrs.) Ministry of Industry & Tourism; Councillor Ottawa Bd. Trade; Chrmn. Comte. Nat. Unity; Dir. Centre Hospitaler Order St. Lazarus Jerusalem; mem. Royal Candn. Geog. Soc. (Dir.); Home: 40 Fuller St., Ottawa, Ont. K1Y 3R8; Office: 275 Slater St., Ottawa, Ont. K1P 5H9.

HALE, John H., M.A.; executive; b. London, Eng., 8 July 1924; s. John and Elsie Ledbroke (Coles) H.; e. Eton Coll., Eng., (Open Scholar in Math.) 1942; Magdalene Coll., Cambridge Univ. M.A. (Mech. Science Tripos) 1948; Harvard Grad. Sch. of Business Adm. (Henry Fellow) 1948-49; m.(2) Nancy Ryrie Birks, 9 Oct. 1980; children: Susan, Jonathan, Anne; DIRECTOR, SR. VICE PRESIDENT, CHIEF FINANCIAL OFFICER, ALCAN ALUMINIUM LIMITED 1970- ; Chmn., Aluminum Co. of Can. Ltd.; Dir. of various Alcan group co's; joined Alcan group of co's 1949; Alcan Finances Ltd., Montreal, 1949-60; Vice Pres., Aluminium Ltd., Inc., New York, 1960-62; Chief Financial Offr., Alcan Industries Ltd. (became Alcan Booth Industries Ltd. in 1970), London, 1964-67; Mang. Dir. 1967-70; Dir., Scovill Inc., Waterbury, Conn., U.S.A.; mem. Allendale Mutual Ins. Co., Candn. Adv. Bd.; Chrmn. Accounting Res. Adv. Bd. of C.I.C.A.; Pres. Mont St. Hilaire, Nature Conservancy; served with RAF and RN 1943-46; qualified pilot, final rank Lt. (A) RNVR; Home: 3117 Daulac Rd., Montreal, Que. H3Y 2A1; Office: 1 Place Ville Marie, Montreal, Que. H3C 3H2

HALL, Albert Earl; banker; b. Grey County, Ont., 12 Aug. 1913; s. Wilfred and Margaret Ellen (Todd) M.; e. Schs., Grey Co., Ont.; m. Mildred Lucille Echlin, 5 April 1941; two d. Nancy, Sharon; Dir. and Adviser, Bank of British Columbia; entered service with Toronto-Dominion Bank in Thornbury, Ont., June 1930, and subsequently served in Hamilton, Galt, Meaford and Toronto, Ont.; became Mgr. of Queensway & Royal York Road Br., Toronto, March 1947; Eglinton & Bathurst Br., Feb.

1949; apptd. to Inspection Dept., H.O., Feb. 1951; Mgr. Sarnia, Ont., 1952; Supervisor, Western Div., Winnipeg, Oct. 1955; Supt., Alta. Div., Nov. 1956; apptd. Gen. Mgr., Dec. 1960, Vice-Pres. and Dir. 1962; Chrm. and Pres., Bank of B.C. 1968-74; Chrmn. and C.E.O., Bank of B.C. 1974-77; Chrmn. of Bd. and Chrmn. of Extve. Comte., Bank of B.C., 1977-78; United Church; Dir., and 2nd Vice-Pres., P.A. Woodward Fdn.; recreation: golf; Clubs: Vancouver; Shaughnessy Golf & Country; Home: 5276 Connaught Dr., Vancouver, B.C. V6M 3G4; Office: Suite 1725, Two Bentall Centre, 555 Burrard St. Vancouver, B.C. V7X 1K1

HALL, Sir Arnold A., B.A., F.R.S., F.R.Ae.S.; engineer and administrator; b. Liverpool, Eng. 23 April 1915; s. Robert and Ellen (Parkinson) H.; e. Alsop High Sch., Liverpool, Eng.; Cambridge Univ. M.A. 1936; m. Dione Sykes; CHAIRMAN HAWKER SIDDELEY CANADA LIMITED 1981- ; Dir., Lloyds Bank Ltd.; Lloyd; Bank UK Management Ltd.; Phoenix Assurance Co. Ltd.; I.C.I. Ltd.; Prof. of Aeronautics, Univ. of London 1945-51; Dir. Royal Aircraft Estab., Farnborough, Eng. 1951-55; Tech. Dir., Hawker Siddeley Ltd. Group 1955-58; Dir., 1958-63; Managing Dir. 1963-81; Chmn. and Mang. Dir., Bristol Siddeley Engines Ltd. 1959-63; Mang. Dir., 1967-81; Pres., Brit. Elect. and Allied Mfrs. Assn. 1967-68; Locomotive and Allied Mfrs. Assn. 1968-70; Soc. Brit. Aerospace Cos. 1972-73; Hon. Fellow, Inst. Mech. Engrs. (U.K.); Inst. Elec. Engrs. (U.K.); Royal Aeronautical Soc. (U.K.); U.S. Academy of Eng.; Foreign Assoc., Am. Inst. Aeronautics & Astronautics; Hon. Mem., Am. Soc. Mech. Eng.; Clare Coll., Cambridge; Fellow, Imp. Coll. of Science & Tch., London Univ.; Chrmn., Fasco Industries Inc. (U.S.A.); Anglican; recreation: boats; Clubs: Atheneum; London; Home: Wakehams Dorney, Windsor, Eng.; Base: 18 St. James Sq., London, S.W: Y., England.

HALL, (Charles) Denis, B.Eng., M.Sc., Ph.D., P. Eng.; b. Sherbrooke, Que., 1 July 1938; s. Charles Wayne and Grace Elizabeth (Hall) H.; e. Lennoxville (Que.) High Sch.; Macdonald High Sch., Ste. Anne de Bellevue, Que., 1955; McGill Univ., B.Eng. 1960; Univ. of Sask., M.Sc. 1961, Ph.D. 1964; m. Florence May Falkingham, 23 Nov. 1963; Exec. Vice-Pres., Marketing & Technology, Northern Telecom Canada Ltd.; Pres. Bell-Northern Research 1976-81; Extve. Vice Pres., Development, 1974-76; joined Research and Devel. Div., Northern Electric Co. Ltd. 1964, Vice Pres., Switching Devel., 1973; mem. Engn. Inst. Can.; Assn. Prof. Engrs. Prov. Ont.; Inst. Elect. & Electronic Engrs.; Christian Scientist; Office: 304 The East Mall, Islington, Ont. M9B 6E4

HALL, (Charles) Wayne, M.A., D.C.L. (Bishop's Univ., 1978); educator; b. Lennoxville, Que., 1 March 1910; s. Charles Loring and Sadie Jane (McMurray) H.; e. Lennoxville High Sch.; Bishop's Coll., B.A. 1931 and M.A., 1932; Ont. Coll. of Educ. post-grad. work in Psychol., 1933; m. Grace Elizabeth, d. A. A. Hall, Coaticook, P.Q., 1936; children: Denis, Mary, Jane, Christopher; PROF. EMERITUS, McGILL UNIV., since 1975; Dean, Fac. of Educ., 1965-75; Dir., Inst. of Education, McGill Univ., since 1964; Teacher, Sherbrooke High Sch., 1932-34; Principal, Coaticook High Sch., 1934-36 and St. Francis Coll. High Sch., 1936-37; Inspector of Schs. for Dept. of Educ. (Que.), 1937-40; Supervisor of English in Prot. Schs. of Que., 1940-49; Assoc. Prof., Macdonald Coll., 1949-52; Pres., Prov. Assn. of Prot. Teachers, 1947; Tech. Adv. to Nigerian Gov. in teacher training, 1960-61; Secy., UNESCO Comn. on the Univ. of Lagos, 1961; Dir., Nat. Council of Teachers of English (Am.); Fellow, Candn. Coll. of Teachers; Publication: "Growth Through the Language Arts", 1955; Order of Scholastic Merit (3rd Degree) 1956; Anglican; recreations: gardening, camping; Home: 12 Belvidere St., Lennoxville, Que. J1M 1T9

HALL, Fernau, B.Comm., A.I. Chor.; dance critic; author; lecturer; radio commentator; b. Victoria, B.C., 5 February 1913; s. Henry Charles and Elena Margarita (Fernau) H.; e. Central High Sch. and Victoria Coll., Victoria, B.C.; Univ. of B.C., B.Comm. (Hons.) 1932; m. Marianne Alma, d. late Henry Balchin, Nov. 1949 (divorced Nov. 1953); Statistician, Imp. Econ. Comte., London, Eng., 1933-39; Actor, 1933-35; Dancer, 1936-39 and 1946-50; Stage Dir. and Business Mgr. of ballet companies and dance groups, 1946 onwards, incl. Dance Theatre, Nritya Darpana (New Indian Ballet), Imp. Ballet of Japan, Azuma Kabuki Dancers; one of founding fathers of schools television in U.K., and worked in this field 1957-73; stage dir. for Indian and Japanese classical dancers; critic of dance, mime and puppets, "Daily Telegraph", London, 1969- ; ballet criticism: "The Dancing Times", London (1937-39); New Statesman, London (1966-68); chief critic, "Ballet Today", London, 1958-71; currently dance etc. critic, "Daily Telegraph"; mem. Council, Benesh Inst. of Choreology; Br. Soc. of Aesthetics; Critic's Circle, London; author of "Ballet", 1949; "Modern Eng. Ballet", 1950; "An Anatomy of Ballet", 1953; "World Dance" (Am. ed. of "An Anatomy of Ballet"), 1954; "The World of Ballet and Dance" 1970, 2nd edition 1972; (with Elvira Roné) "Olga Preobrazhenskaya: A Portrait", 1978; "Antony Tudor: Choreographer of Genius", in prep.; articles on dance in a wide variety of magazines; served in 2nd World War with Brit. Army, 1940-46 (Radar Expert); Address: 44 South Hill Park, London, NW3 2SJ England.

HALL, Hon. Gordon Clarke, LL.B.; judge; b. Cranbrook, B.C., 3 Oct. 1921; s. Watson Smythe and Mary Ellen (Leitch) H.; e. Primary Schs., Moose Jaw, Sask., Winnipeg and Brandon, Man. 1937; Kelvin High Sch., Winnipeg, Man. 1938; Univ. of Manitoba, Faculty of Agric. 1941; Univ. of Manitoba Law Sch., LL.B. 1948; m. Agnes Margaret, d. late Clarence White Rife, 26 June 1944; children: Nancy Margaret, David Malcolm, Douglas Rife; JUSTICE, COURT OF APPEAL, MAN. since 1971; read law with Paul G. DuVal; called to Bar of Man. 1948; cr. Q.C. 1959; with law firm of Guy, Chappel & Co., Winnipeg 1948; mem. Thompson, Dilts, Jones, Hall & Dewar 1956; Justice, Court of Queen's Bench Jan 1965; Lectr., Univ. of Man. Med. Sch. (Juris.) 1954-65; served in R.C.A. 1942-45; Lt. (Inf.) and Candn. Parachute Bn.; served Overseas; Chrmn., Adv. Bd. Winnipeg Fdn.; Past Chrmn., Bd. of Mang. Inst. of Cell Biol.; Dir., Man. Forestry Assn.; Justice of the Court of Appeal for Man., since 1971; Past Chrmn., Jt. Senate Comte., Univ. of Winnipeg and Man. on Jt. Masters Programs; has held many positions in Lib. Party of Can. and Man. 1948-65; mem. Man. Bar Assn. (Past Secy.-Treas., Past Vice-Pres. and Hon. Past Pres.); Candn. Bar Assn.; Law Soc. of Man.; United Church; recreations: golf, farming; Clubs: St. Charles Country; Home: 322 Kingsway Ave., Winnipeg, Man. R3M 0H4; Office: Law Courts, Winnipeg, Man.

HALL, John Alexander; artist; teacher; designer; illustrator; typographer; b. Toronto, Ont., 10 Oct. 1914; s. Alexander G. and Dorothy B. (Hughes) H.; e. Upper Canada Coll.; Ont. Coll. of Art, 1937; m. 1stly, Joan Margaret, d. Barker Fairley, Toronto, 29 May 1937; children: Susan Jane, Margaret Gillian, Rebecca Ann, Jennifer Ruth; 2ndly Pauline Hooton, 27 April 1968; Assoc. Prof. in Drawing & Colour, Faculty of Architecture and Landscape Architectures, Univ. of Toronto 1946-80; Teacher, Upper Can. Coll. (Art) 1936-43 and 1945-47, (acad. subjects) 1938-43; Sat. morning classes, Art Gallery of Toronto, 1936-37; York Twp. Schs., 1938-42; teachers' summer courses in art, Ont. Dept. of Educ., 1938-39, 1946-52, and 1958-73; rec'd. Canada Council award (1 yr.) 1963; instr. in Art and Campcraft, Taylor Statten Camps, for 11 summers; has exhibited with Ont. Soc. of Artists, Roy. Candn. Acad., Candn. Soc. of Graphic Art, Contemp. Art Soc., Candn. Group of Painters, Montreal Art Assn.; Nat. Gallery of Can., Candn. Soc. of Painters in Watercolour, and in the U.S.A. and S. Am.; works purchased by Nat. Gallery, Ottawa, Toronto Art Gallery, Brazilian Govt.; mem., Print and Drawing Council of Can. (old Candn. Soc. of Graphic Art, Pres. 1947-48 and 1959); Ont. Soc. of Artists; Anglican; Home: Glencroft, R.R. 2, Newmarket, Ont. L3Y 4V9

HALL, Monty, B.Sc. television performer and producer; b. Winnipeg, Man., 25 Aug. 1924; s. Maurice and late Rose (Rusen) Halparin; e. Univ. of Man., B.Sc. 1944 (Pres. Student Body 1944); m. Marilyn Doreen, d. Joseph Plottel, Vancouver, B.C., 28 Sept. 1947; children: Joanna, Richard, Sharon; producer and performer on TV and radio in Can. and U.S. for over 25 yrs.; singer-actor-sportscaster-M.C. on nationally broadcast programs in Can. 1940-55 and in U.S. from 1955; t.v. show, "Let's Make a Deal" (Producer-M.C.), has run for 17 years; has received over 500 awards in U.S. and Canada for charitable and philanthropic contributions; read into United States Cong.-Record by Congressman Thos. Rees, Feb. 1971 "for outstanding humanitarianism"; also several awards for TV performances; rec'd Variety Club "Heart" Award, Toronto, 1954; Variety Club "Star of the Year", Hollywood, Cal. 1971; Dir., Anti-Defamation League; Guardians of Courage; Israel Bonds; Technion Univ.; Hebrew Univ.; Variety Boys Club; United Jewish Welfare Fund; UCLA Monty Hall Children's Centre; Cedars-Sinai Hosp.; Dir., Far West Financial Corp.; Spon., Monty Hall Celebrity Tennis for Diabetes; author "Emcee Monty Hall"; mem., Am. TV & Radio Artists; Nat. Acad. TV Arts & Science; Screen Actors Guild; el. Internat. Pres. of Variety Clubs in London, Eng. 1975; honoured by "Hollywood Walk of Fame" star in cement 1973; recreations: golf, tennis,; Clubs: Variety International; Hillcrest Country; Home: 519 N. Arden Dr., Beverly Hills, Cal.; Office: Monty Hall Enterprises, 7833 Sunset Blvd., Los Angeles, Cal.

HALL, Per, M.Sc., P.Eng.; consulting engineer; b. Denmark, 29 June 1911; s. Gunnar Lykke and Karen Margarethe (Aksel-Hansen) H.; e. Lyngby Statsskole; Royal Tech. Coll. of Denmark (M.Sc. Civil 1935); Univ. of Toronto (Post-Grad Studies); m. Nina, d. William Monsted, 17 Dec. 1937; children: Peter William, Karen Agnete, Ingrid Marianne; DIR., KAMPSAX PERHALL LTD., HONG KONG. Pres., Per Hall Assoc. Ltd., since 1969; Pres. Per Hall Consultants Ltd., Hong Kong; began career as Project Engineer, A.S. Manniche and Hartmann, Copenhagen, Denmark, 1935-37; Manager, A. B. ASA Stockholm and Gotenberg, Sweden, 1937-38; Designing Engineer, Christiani & Nielsen, London, Eng., 1939; arrived in Canada, 1940; joined Aluminium Co. of Canada Ltd. later that year as Project Engr., Can. and W. Indies, 1940-46; Designing Engr., The Foundation Co. of Canada Ltd., Montreal, P.Q., 1946-49; apptd. Asst. Chief Engr., 1949; el. Vice-Pres. of Foundation of Canada Engineering Corpn. Ltd., 1953; el. Extve. Vice-Pres., 1957 and Pres., 1958; Sr. Partner, Per Hall Associates 1962-69; Pres., General Engineering Co. Ltd. 1963-70; mem. Engn. Inst. Can.; Corp. Prof. Engrs. Que.; Dansk Ingenior Forening; Fellow Am. Soc. Danish Engrs.; Fellow, Institution of Civil Engrs. (U.K.); Fellow, Am. Soc. of Civil Engrs.; Lutheran Church; recreations: skiing, yachting; Clubs: University; Royal St. Lawrence Yacht; Royal Hong Kong Yacht; The Hong Kong; Home: Flat 7, 125 Repulse Rd., Hong Kong; Office: Kampsax Perhall Ltd., Centre Point, 11th Floor, 184 Gloucester Rd., Hong Kong

HALLE, Maurice, E.D., B.A., L.Ph.; b. Sherbrooke, P.Q., 26 Feb. 1906; s. N. A. and M. L. (Joncas) H.; e. St. Hyacinthe Coll., B.A.; Univ. of Montreal, L.Ph.; m. Raymonde, d. G. Rainville, Farnham, P.Q., 1942; former Pres., Canadian Nat. Livestock Records; Canadian Cattle Breeders Assn. and Que. Agric. Marketing Bd.; el. to H. of C. for Brome-Missisquoi, g.e. 1940; re-el. g.e. 1945; served in World War 1940-45 with R. C. Arty. in U.K. and Italy; held rank of Lieut.-Col.; Liberal; Roman Catholic; Home: (P.O. Box 100), Cowansville, Que. J2K 3H1

HALLETT, Archibald Cameron Hollis, B.A., Ph.D.; b. Paget Parish, Bermuda, 5 Feb. 1927; s. late Hon. Rupert Carlyle Hollis, D.C.L., and Jessie Wales (Cameron) H.; e. Saltus Grammar Sch., Bermuda, 1931-44; Univ. of Toronto, B.A. 1948, King's Coll., Univ. of Cambridge, Ph.D. 1951; m. Clara Frances Edith, d. late Rev. Charles Langton Gilbert, Gravenhurst, Ont., 5 Sept. 1950; children: William Langton Hollis, Mary Frances Hollis, James Archibald Hollis; Principal, Univ. Coll., Univ. of Toronto 1970-77; C.E.O. Bermuda College since 1977; joined Univ. of Toronto as a Lectr., Dept. of Physics, 1951; apptd. Asst. Prof., 1952; Assoc. Prof. 1958; Prof. 1963; Assoc. Dean, Faculty of Arts & Science 1966-70; mem., Am. Physical Soc.; Candn. Assn. Physicists; Comm. 1, Institut. Internat. du Froid; Anglican; recreations: music, cabinet-making. Office: Bermuda College, Prospect, Devonshire, Bermuda.

HALLIWELL,Dean Wright, M.A., B.L.S.; librarian, b. Estevan, Sask. 26 July 1924; s. late John and Gladys May (Wright) H.; e. Univ. of Sask. B.A. 1948; Univ. of Toronto B.L.S. 1949; m. Marjory Allen d. late George Lawson Robertson, Wapella, Sask. 29 Oct. 1949; children: Kathryn Allen, John Robertson; UNIV. LIBRARIAN, UNIV. OF VICTORIA 1960- ; Bookmobile Librarian, Cuyahoga Co. Pub. Lib. Cleveland, Ohio 1949-52, Coordinator of Reference Services 1952-55; Canadiana Librarian, Univ. of Sask. 1955-57, Asst. Librarian 1957-60; Dir., Un. Way Greater Victoria 1978-84; served with RCAF 1943-45, Pilot Offr. (Navig.), Reserve 1957-60, 1961-64, rank Flight Lt.; rec'd Queen's Silver Jubilee Medal 1977; mem. Candn. Lib. Assn. (Pres. 1971-72); Candn. Assn. Coll. & Univ. Libs. (Pres. 1967-68); B. C. Lib. Assn. (Pres. 1965-66); Am. Lib. Assn. (Dir. 1980-84); United Church; recreations: golf, travel; Club: Uplands Golf (Dir. 1978-81); Home: 1828 St. Ann St., Victoria B.C. V8R 5W1; Office: (P.O. Box 1800) McPherson Library, Victoria, B.C. V8W 3H5.

HALLMAN, Rev. Errol Emerson, B.A., B.D., D.D., (United Church of Can.); b. Rosenthal, Ont., 6 May 1902; s. Orlando Groff and Arby Tena (Snyder) H.; e. Pub. Sch., Arnprior, Ont.; High Sch., Chesley, Ont.; N. Central Coll., Naperville, Ill., B.A., 1929; Evangelical Theol. Semy., Naperville, Ill., B.D. 1932; Chicago Divinity Sch. (Grad. study); m. Hilda Mae, d. Edward Hamel, Waterloo, Ont., 19 Oct. 1932; children: Catherine Ann, Donald Emerson, Errol Douglas; CANADA CONFERENCE SUPT., E.U.B., 1959-68; Trustee, Evangelical Theol. Semy., Naperville, Ill.; Pres. (1952-54) Candn. Council of Churches; Pres., The Religious Educ. Council of Can., 1938-39; Pres., Social Service Workers' Council (Kitchener-Waterloo); o. 1932; Assoc. Min., and Dir. of Christian Educ., Zion Ch., Kitchener, Ont., 1932-41; Minister, Salem Ch., Hanover, Ont., 1941-44; Sr. Minister, Zion Ch., Kitchener, Ont., 1944-53; Min., Emmanuel Ch., Waterloo, Ont. 1953-59; Dir. of Christian Educ., The Canada Conf. of the E.U.B. Ch., 1935-45 and Pres. of Cdn. Conference Corp. since 1968; Dir. of Youth Camps, 1936-51; Supt. of Cdn. Conference of Evangelical United Brethren Ch., 1959-68; Home Mission Supt. United Ch. of Can. 1968-70 and Extve. Secy., Hamilton Conf. — United Church 1970-72; Dir., Alma Coll. 1968-77; Dir., Five Oaks Christian Training Centre since 1968; Dir., Kitchener-Waterloo Y.M.C.A. since 1945; Dir., Kitchener-Waterloo Federated Appeal 1975-79; Dir., U.C. Archives since 1977; Dir., John Milton Soc. for the Blind in Can., since 1978; Assoc. Minister, Dublin St. U.C., Guelph 1972-80; D.D. Victoria Univ. Toronto 1964; Confederation Medal 1967; Liberal; recreations: curling, gardening; Home: 398 Union Blvd., Kitchener, Ont. N2M 2T4

HALLUM, B. C.; fraternity executive; b. N. Dakota, 5 May 1913; s. Charles B. and Jennie C. (Dahl) H.; e. Univ. of S. Calif.; m. Florence M., d. Allan English, 16 Nov. 1940; children: Roger, Peggy Sue; PRES. AND CHIEF SU-

PREME RANGER, INDEPENDENT ORDER OF FORESTERS 1972- ; with the Order as Depy. 1939, Dist. Mgr., S. Calif. 1950, Head Great Lakes Div. 1954, apptd. mem. Supreme Extve. Council 1966; Past Pres., Can. Fraternal Assn.; Nat. Fraternal Congress of Am.; mem., Nat. Adv. Council; Big Brothers/Big Sisters of Amer.; Illinois Fraternal Congress; formerly with U.S. Coast Guard; rec'd. Grand Cross, Legion of Honor; recreations: golf, fishing; Clubs: Toronto Hunt; Caledon Mountain Trout; Home: Leaside Towers, Thorncliffe Park Drive, Toronto, Ontario; Office: 789 Don Mills Rd., Don Mills, Ont. M3C 1T9

HALPENNY, Francess Georgina, O.C., M.A., LL.D., F.R.S.C.; editor, professor; b. Ottawa, Ont., 27 May 1919; d. James Leroy and Viola Gertrude (Westman) H.; e. Oakwood Coll. Inst., Toronto, 1936; Univ. of Toronto, B.A. 1940, M.A. 1941; Univ. of Guelph, LL.D. 1968; Dalhousie Univ., LL.D., 1978; Dean, Faculty of Library Science, Univ. of Toronto 1972-78; Prof. of Library Sc., Univ. of Toronto, 1972- ; Assoc. Dir. (Academic) Univ. of Toronto Press, 1979- ; Gen. Ed., "Dictionary of Canadian Biography" 1969- ; joined Ed. Dept., Univ. of Toronto Press, 1941, Ed. 1957-65; Mang. Ed. 1965-69; served with Womens Div., RCAF, as Meteorol. Observer in Nfld. and P.E.I., 1942-45; Past Pres., Univ. Alumnae Dramatic Club; mem. Ed. Bd., "Scholarly Publishing"; author of articles on publishing and editing in various journs.; mem., Candn. Hist. Assn. (Council 1968-70); Candn. Lib. Assn. (Chrmn. Comte. on Edit. and Publications Policy 1973-75); Nat. Lib. Adv. Bd., 1976- (Chrmn. 1979-) Chrmn., Comte. on Bibliog. Services for Can., 1977-9; mem., Commitee on Library Info., Cdn. Book and Periodical Devel. Council 1974- ; (Chrmn. 1979-); Univ. of Toronto Research Bd. (Chmn., Humanities and Social Sciences Res. Comte 1979-); Fellow, Royal Soc. of Canada, 1977 (Chmn., Awards Comte. 1980-); Officer, Order of Canada, 1979; Collected Works John Stuart Mill (Ed. Comte.); recreation: theatre group; Clubs: Heliconian (Past Pres.); Home: 32 Glenbrae Ave., Toronto, Ont. M4G 3R5; Office: Univ. of Toronto Press, Toronto, Ont. M5S 1A6

HALPERIN, Maurice, A.M., D. de l'Un.; educator; b. Boston, Mass., 3 March 1906; s. Philip and Ethel (Summer) H.; e. Harvard Univ., A.B. 1927; Univ. of Okla., A.M. 1929; Sorbonne, D. de l'Un. 1931; m. Edith, d. late Herman Frisch, 5 Sept. 1926; children: David, Judith (Mrs. Hillel Gamoran); PROF. OF POL. SCIENCE, SIMON FRASER UNIV. since 1968; Prof. Emeritus since 1979; univ. teaching in various insts. in N.Am., Europe and Latin Am. since 1931; served with U.S. Office of Strategic Services 1942-45; rec'd. Order of the S. Cross, Brazil, 1952; author, "The Rise and Decline of Fidel Castro: An Essay in Contemporary History", 1972; "The Taming of Fidel Castro", 1981; also numerous articles in acad. journs.; mem., Candn. Assn. Latin Am. Studies; Jewish; recreation: music; Home: 131 - 600 Smith Ave., Coquitlam, B.C. V3J 2W4; Office: Burnaby, B.C. V5A 1S6

HALPERN, Ida, C.M., Ph.D., LL.D.; musicologist; critic; adjudicator; b. Vienna, Austria 17 July 1910; d. Heinrich and Sabine (Weinstock) Ruhdoerfer; e. Reform Real Gymnasium Vienna 1929; Univ. of Vienna Ph.D. 1938; Simon Fraser Univ. LL.D. 1978; m. George R. Halpern, Ph.D., F.C.I.C. 19 Nov. 1936; came to Can. 1939; Music Critic "Fremden Presse" Vienna 1937; Lectr. in Music Shanghai Univ. China 1938-39; Lectr. in Music Univ. of B.C. 1942-64, Author, Correspondence Course in Music, U.B.C., 1943, Lectr. in Ethnomusicology 1964-66; Music Critic "Vancouver Province" 1952-58, "Musical Courier" 1953-62 (N.Y.); Simon Fraser Univ. Convocation Founder 1965 and Hon. Assoc. in ethnomusicology 1965-68; Chrmn. and initiator Internat. Centennial Workshop on Ethnomusicology contributor Proceedings 1968; Complete Discussions, co-ed., pub. by B.C. gov't.; 1978; Hon. Dir. Vancouver Symphony Soc.; Hon. Life Pres. New

Artists Assn.; Acoustic Consultant Civic Theatre Comte. Vancouver 1959; Dir. Brock House; Vice Chrmn. and Trustee, Community Music Sch. Greater Vancouver; Consultant in Ethnomusicology Univ. of Victoria; Chrmn. and Dir. Metrop. Opera Auditions for W. Can.; Dir. Festival Concerts Soc., Chrmn. Artistic Comte.; Hon. Pres., Founder and Past Pres. Friends of Chamber Music; Chrmn. Research Comte. Candn. Folk Music Soc.; elected mem. Oesterreichische Musikwissenschaft; Consultant, Community Arts Council Vancouver (Vice Pres. Music Sec.); adjudicator many music festivals and competitions Can. and USA; collected over 500 N.W. Indian hereditary songs, catalogued Lib. Congress; Nat. Museum of Canada, Ottawa; numerous radio and TV broadcasts CBC, BBC, RAVAG, RIAS; own musical program "Musical Mailbox" CBC; and supplied Indian songs for many films Westcoast Indian topics incl. "Legend of the Magic Knives" 1971; Encyclopedia Brittanica and National Film Bd.; Contributed Indian music through Educ. Service Programs Inc. for use at Smithsonian Instit. and Milwaukee Public Meseum 1969; Consultant, and supplied Indian songs for "The World of the Wonderful Dark" Vancouver Int. Festival, 1956; "Winter Dances", Phoenix Theatre, N.Y. 1979; records and books incl. "Kwakiutl Indian Music of the Pacific Northwest" 1981; "Nootka Indian Music of the Pacific Northwest" 1974; "Indian Music of the Pacific Northwest" 1967 (Folkways Records, N.Y.); "B.C. Indian Songs, World Library of Folk and Primitive Music", 1952-53 (Columbia Recordings); numerous papers and articles on Northwest Indian Music for journs., newspapers, museums, edc. confs.; Supplied Indian music to Canadian composers (A. Pavk, T. Goldberg, I. Raminsh), commissioned by C.B.C. and "Habitat"; 2 U.B.C. Music theses based on Indian music research, educational book, pub. U.B.C.; elected Councellor Soc. for Ethnomusicology, U.S.A. 1979; Printer, Prov. of B.C., U.B.C. and Folkways Records, N.Y.; Columbia Records; awarded Order of Canada, 1978; recreations: bridge, riding, theatre; Clubs: Women's Musical (Hon. Life mem. and Past Pres., Dir. Mem. Trust Fund Vancouver); University Women's; Georgian; Soroptimist; Address: 2505 Wallace Cres., Vancouver, B.C. V6R 3V3.

HALSTEAD, John G. H., B.A., B.Sc.; foreign service officer; b. Vancouver, B.C. 27 Jan. 1922; s. Frank Henry and Minnie Williams (Horler) H.; e. Prince of Wales High Sch. Vancouver 1939, John Oliver High Sch. 1940; Univ. of B.C. B.A. 1943; London Sch. of Econ. B.Sc. 1950; m. Jean McAllister, d. late Paul Gemmill 20 June 1953; children: Ian, Christopher; AMBASSADOR AND PERMANENT REP. OF CANADA TO NORTH ATLANTIC COUNCIL since 1980; served with RCNVR 1943-46, rank Lt. (S.B.); Ambassador to Fed. Republic of Germany 1975.80; mem. Prof. Assn. Foreign Service Offrs.; Candn. Inst. Internat. Affairs; International Institute of Strategic Studies; Zeta Psi; United Church; recreations: tennis, swimming, sailing; Home: 187 Billings Ave., Ottawa, Ont.; Office: Canadian Delegation to NATO, Léopold III Blvd., 1110 Brussels, Belgium.

HALTON, David Campbell, B.A.; broadcast journalist; b. Beaconsfield, U.K. 28 May 1940; s. Mathew Henry and Jean Joslin (Campbell) H.; e. King's Sch. Canterbury, U.K. 1957; Sorbonne, Paris, Dipl. D'Etudes De Civilisation Française 1958; Trinity Coll. Univ. of Toronto B.A. 1962; Inst. D'Etudes Politiques, Paris Cert. d'Etudes Politiques 1963; m. Zoia Titova 12 Sept. 1968; two s. Julian Alexander, Daniel Andrew; CHIEF POL. CORR. OTTAWA, CBC TV 1978- ; contrib. ed. Time Magazine (Candn. Ed.) 1964-65; Paris Corr. CBC 1965-67, 1969-71; Moscow Corr. 1967-68; Que. Nat. Reporter CBC TV News 1971-73; London Corr. 1974-78; rec'd Anik Award Host-Narration documentary "The October Crisis" 1975; Anglican; recreations: tennis, sailing; Club: National Press; Home: 275 Cloverdale Rd., Rockcliffe Park, Ottawa, Ont. K1M 0Y3; Office: 150 Wellington St., Ottawa, Ont. K1P 5A4.

HALVORSON, Hon. Kenneth R., B.A., LL.B.; judge; b. Sask. 28 Nov. 1937; s. Melvin Halvorson; e. Flin Flon (Man.) Coll. Inst. 1956; Univ. of Sask. B.A., LL.B. 1962; m. Carol Ann d. late Joseph Harrison 6 Oct. 1962; children: Bonnie, Becky, Peter; JUDGE, COURT OF QUEEN'S BENCH SASK.; called to Bar of Sask. 1963; Extve. Offr., Candn. W. Agribition Assn.; mem. Candn. Inst. Adm. Justice; Protestant; recreation: athletics; Home: 77 Calder Cres., Regina, Sask. S4S 4A5; Office: 2425 Victoria Ave., Regina, Sask. S4P 0S8.

HAM, Arthur Worth, M.B., D.Sc., F.R.S.C.; b. Brantford, Ont., 20 Feb. 1902; s. John Taylor and Isabelle (Anderson) H.; e. Univ. of Toronto, M.B. 1926; m. Dorothy Carlotta Ross (deceased), 18 Aug. 1925; one s. John A. D.; secondly, m. Lotta Dempsey Fisher 27 Feb. 1981; Prof. emeritus of Anat., Univ. of Toronto; author of: "Doctor in the Making" (with M. B. Salter); "Histology" 8 editions, 1950-79 (last ed. with D. H. Cormack) over 50 papers in scient. journs.; mem., Candn. Davis Cup teams, 1926-28; Psi Upsilon; Conservative; Home: R.R. 2, Markham, Ont. L3P 3J3

HAM, James Milton, O.C. B.A.Sc., S.M., ScD.; b. Coboconk, Ont., 21 Sept. 1920; s. James Arthur and Harriet Boomer (Gandier) H.; e. Runnymede Coll. Inst., Toronto, Ont., 1936-39; Univ. of Toronto, B.A.Sc. 1943; Mass. Inst. of Tech., S.M. 1947, ScD. 1952; D.A.Sc., Montreal, 1973; D. Sc., Queen's 1974; D. Sc. New Brunswick 1979; D. Sc. McGill 1979; D.Sc. McMaster, 1980; N.S. Tech Univ., 1980; LL.D. Man., 1980; m. Mary Caroline, d. Albert William Augustine, Kitchener, Ont., 4 June 1955; children: Peter Stace, Mary Martha, Jane Elizabeth; PRES., UNIV. OF TORONTO since 1978; Dean of Grad. Studies, 1976-78; Chrmn. Research Bd., 1974-76; Dean, Faculty of Applied Sc. & Engn. 1966-73; Chrmn., Royal Comn. on Health and Safety of Workers in Mines, Ont., 1974-76; mem. Nat. Research Council 1969-75; Bd. of Govs., Ont. Research Foundation; Lectr. & Housemaster, Ajax Div., Univ. of Toronto, 1945-46; Research Assoc., Mass. Inst. of Tech., 1949-51; Asst. Prof. of Elect. Engn. 1951-52; Assoc. Prof. of Elect. Engn., Univ. of Toronto 1952-59; Prof. since 1959; Chrmn., Assoc. Comte. on Automatic Control, Nat. Research Council, 1959-65; Visiting Scientist, Cambridge Univ., and U.S.S.R., 1960-61; Head, Dept. of Elect. Engn., Univ. of Toronto, 1964-66; served with R.C.N.V.R. as Elect. Lt. 1944-45; awarded Brit. Assn. for Advanc. of Science Medal, 1943; Research Fellowship in Electronics, Mass. Inst. Tech. 1950; Fellow of New Coll., Univ. of Toronto, 1963; Chrmn. of Comte. on Engn. Educ. of World Fed. of Engn. Organs. 1970-74; author of "Scientific Basis of Electrical Engineering" (with G. R. Slemon), 1961 and some 15 papers for scient. journs.; patented (U.S.) "Apparatus for Electronic Integration", 1955; Fellow, Inst. Elect. & Electronic Engrs.; mem., Assn. Prof. Engineers Ontario; F.E.I.C.; awarded Centennial Medal; Engn. Medal, Assn. Prof. Engrs. Ont. 1974; Engr. Alumni Medal, Univ. of Toronto, 1974; McNaughton Medal, I.E.E.E. 1977; Silver Jubilee Medal, 1977; Officer of the Order of Canada, 1980; Sigma Xi; Anglican; recreations: sailing, skiing; Home: 93 Highland Ave., Toronto, Ont. M4W 2A4

HAM, Leslie Gilmer, B.A., B.Comm., M.B.A., C.A.; beverage company executive; b. Winnipeg, Man. 3 March 1930; s. Arthur Leslie and Frances Irene (Gilmer) H.; e. McGill Univ. B.A. 1951, B.Comm. 1953; Univ. of W. Ont. M.B.A. 1956; m. Anne Corris d. Charles Adrian Dinsmore, Toronto, Ont. 12 June 1954; children: Charles Keith, Susan Lesley, Cynthia Anne; ZONE VICE PRES., CAN. FAR EAST, PEPSICO INTERNAT. 1981- ; Auditor, Peat Marwick Mitchell, Montreal 1953-55; Brand Mgr. Proctor & Gamble Co. of Canada, Toronto 1956-58; Extve. Vice Pres. Seven Up Montreal Ltd. 1958-70; Vice Pres. Operations Pepsi-Cola Canada Ltd., Toronto 1970-74; Pres., Soc. Internationale de Produits Alimentaires, Paris 1974-75; Extve. Vice Pres. Sales, Pepsi-Cola Bottling

Group, Purchase, N.Y. 1975-78; Pres., C.E.O., and Dir., Pepsi-Cola Can. Ltd. 1978-81; Pres. Theta Delta Chi 1951; Anglican; Clubs: Mississauga Golf, St. George's Golf; Granite; Royal Montreal Golf; Red Birds Ski (Montreal); Darien (Conn.) Country; Home: 43 The Kingsway, Toronto, Ont. M8X 2S9; Office: 1255 Bay St., Toronto, Ont. M5R 2A9.

HAMANN, George Frederick, B.Arch., OAA, MRAIC, F.R.I.B.A.; architect; b. Toronto, Ont., 14 June 1928; e. Central Tech. Sch. and Riverdale Coll. Inst., Toronto, Ont.; Univ. of Toronto, Sch. of Arch., Hon. Grad., 1951; awarded George T. Goulestone Fellowship in Arch. (Post-Grad. studies in London, Eng., and Europe); m. Isabelle, d. Archibald Charles MacKinnon, 12 Oct. 1957; children: David George and Diane Lee; SENIOR PARTNER, BREGMAN & HAMANN, since 1953; Vice-Pres., Associated Professional Consultants; prior to present partnership, while living in London, Eng., was employed by Sir John Burnet Tait and Partners to develop designs for a postwar housing and apartment project in the Greater London area; mem. Royal Arch. Inst. Can.; Bd. Trade Metrop. Toronto; Rotary Club of Toronto; recreations: farming, tennis, squash, golf; skiing; Clubs: Donalda; Queen's Granite; Devils Glen; Home: 181 The Bridle Path, Don Mills, Ont. M3C 2P3; Office: 50 Gervais Dr., Toronto, Ont. M3C 1Z3

HAMBLETON, Hugh George, M.A., Dr. de l'U. (Paris), Ph.D.; university professor; b. Ottawa, Ont. 4 May 1922; s. George and Bessie Josephine (McKenna) H.; e. Khaki Univ. of Can. 1945; Univ. of Ottawa, 1946-48; Univ. of Americas, Mexico, M.A. 1949; Univ. of Paris, Dr. de l'U. (Paris) 1956; Univ. of London, Ph.D. 1964; Institut d'Etudes de Développement Economique et Sociale, France, Certificat d'Études Supérieur 1960; m. Fiorella Anna, d. Filippo Marzi, Rome, Italy, 4 Apl. 1959; children: Ricardo, Sonia, George William; ASSOC. PROF. OF ECONOMICS, LAVAL UNIV., since 1968; Comm. Div., Nat. Film Bd. of Can., 1950-51; Econ. Directorate, NATO 1956-61; joined present Univ. as Asst. Prof. of Econ. 1964-68; served with Allied Armies 1943-45; mem. Board of Advisors, American Pre-Coll. Pro gram in Paris, 1964-66, Dean 1967-69, Pres. 1973-75; author: "The Petroleum Industry in Latin America", 1949; "Les Idées monétaires en Espagne du XVIe au début du XIXe siècle", 1955; "The Economic Decline of Spain in the Seventeenth Century", 1964; other writings incl. various articles and reviews in prof. journs.; Econ. Adviser, Govt. of Peru 1971; Dir.; Course to Formulate and Evaluate Projects, Haiti 1973-75; mem., Candn. Assn. Latin Am. Studies (Vice-Pres. 1969-71, Pres. 1971-73); Soc. of St. George; Royal Yachting Assn.; Federacion Española de Vela.; recreation: Sailing; Home "La Mariposa", Mijas, Spain

HAMBLEY, J. Mervyn, B.Sc., D.Eng., D.Sc.; consultant; b. Copper Cliff, Ont., 26 May 1905; s. William John and Ella (Harris) H.; e. Public Sch., Copper Cliff, Ont.; High Sch., Sudbury, Ont.; Queen's Univ., B.Sc. (Elect. Engn.) 1929, D.Sc. 1967; Univ. of W. Ont. (Mang. Training) 1952; Waterloo Univ., D.Eng. 1965; m. Leonia Jule, d. Edward Joyner, Kingston, Ont. 26 Dec. 1933; one s.: E. John; Dir.; Steag Coal Power Ltd., joined Ont. Hydro in 1930 as Asst. Dist. Operating Engr., Georgian Bay Divn. and N. Ont. properties; Dir. of Operations, Toronto, Ont., 1947-53; Deputy Asst. Gen. Mgr. (Adm.), 1953-55; Asst. Gen. Mgr.-Adm., 1955-59; Depy. Gen. Mgr. 1959; Gen. Mgr. 1960-70; mem., Assn. of Prof. Engrs. of Ont.; Candn. Elect. Assn. (Pres. 1964-65); Fellow Engn. Inst. of Can. (Pres., 1966-67); Fellow, Inst. of Elect. & Electronic Engrs.; United Church; recreations: gardening, fishing; Clubs: Granite; Rotary; Canadian; Electric; Home: 28 Arjay Cres., Willowdale, Ont. M2L 1C7

HAMEL, Alfred; transportation executive; b. St-Félicien, Qué. 20 Feb. 1924; s. Émile and Martine (Dallaire) H.; e. Coll. des Frères Maristes, St-Félicien; Special studies in

Eng. and Business Adm.; m. Rolande d. Wilfred Perron, St-Félicien, Qué 6 July 1948; six s. Rénald, Jacques, Guy, André, Luc, Sylvain; one d. Normande; PRES. AND CHIEF OPERATING OFFR., QUEBECAIR; Pres. Expeditex Ltd.; Hamel Transport Ltd.; Les Immeubles Hamel Inc.; Vice Pres. Cartier Transport Inc.; Magny Transport Inc.; Cartier Moving Inc.; Côté Moving (1977) Ltd.; Northern Express Ltd. (Nfld.); Dir. Imperial Trust Co.; Windsor Hotel (Montreal); Distribution Sentinelle Inc.; Gov., Quebec Tariffs Bureau Inc.; Official Candn. Del. to World Cong. Internat. Union Highway Transporters biannually 1964-76; Que. Govt. Official Del. to Écon. Mission, France 1971; Ald. St-Félicien 1957-60, Mayor 1960-77; Gov. and Faculty mem. in Transport, Sherbrooke Univ.; named Businessman of Yr. 1978-79 Saguenay Lake St. John Chibougamau Region; Transport. Personality of Yr. 1979; Past Pres. (1959-67, 1968) and Life Gov. Candn. Trucking Assn.; Pres., Que. Trucking Assn. (Lake St. John Saguenay & N. Shore Region); Hon. Treas. and mem. Extve. Council, Que. Chamber Comm.; K. of C.; R. Catholic; recreations: golf, yachting, photography, sport fishing; Home: 580 Blvd. Sacré Coeur, St-Félicien, Qué. G0W 2N0; Office: (P.O. Box 490) Dorval Airport, Dorval, Qué. H4Y 1B5.

HAMEL, Jean-Marc, M.Com., M.P.A.; b. Lotbinière, Que., 19 Feb. 1925; s. Lorenzo and Hermine (Leclerc) H.; e. Lotbinière and Ste-Croix, Que., Pub. Schs.; La Pointe de Lac, Que., High Sch.; Laval Univ., B.Com. 1948, M.Com. 1949; Syracuse Univ., M.P.A. 1956; m. Jacqueline, d. late Emile Lapointe, 11 July 1953; children: Pierre, Denis; CHIEF ELECTORAL OFFR., CANADA, since 1966; with Industrial Life Ins. Co. as Asst. Chief, Selection of Risks Dept., 1949-50; joined Civil Service Comn. 1950, Regional Rep. in Quebec City, 1950-53; Asst. Regional Dir. for Prov. of Que., 1953-57; Personnel Selection Offr., 1957-58; Organ. and Classification Offr., 1958-60; Asst. Secy. to Comn. 1960; Secy. 1960-63; Co-ordinator of Lang. Training for Pub. Service, 1963-64; apptd. Dir. of Adm., H. of C. 1964-65; Asst. to Under-Secy. of State, 1965-66; sec. Can.-Fr. Interpartly. Assn. 1965-66; Mem. Coll. d'Enseignement Gen. et Prof., Hull, Que. 1967-72; v.p. 1971; medal of merit, Fr. Nat. Assembly 1965; Centennial Medal 1967; Silver Jubilee Medal 1977; Chevalier de la Légion d'Honneur 1981; mem. Inst. Pub. Adm. Can.; Candn. Pol. Science Assn.; Pub. Personnel Assn. (Past Pres., Ottawa Chapter); R.Catholic; recreations: music, swimming, travel; Club: Richelieu de Hull Inc.; Cercle universitaire d'Ottawa; Home: 2376 Wyndale Cres., Ottawa, Ont. K1H 7A6; Office: 440 Coventry Road, Ottawa, Ont. K1A 0M6

HAMELIN, Louis-Edmond, Ordre du Can. (1974), F.R.S.C.; prof. d'univ.; ses ancêtres sont arrivés de France au Can. au 18e siècle; né St-Didace, Comté de Maskinongé, Qué.; f. Antonio et Maria (Désy) H.; 21 mars 1923; e. Séminaire de Joliette, P.Q. B.A. 1945; Univ. Laval M.A. (Econ.) 1948; McGill Geography Summer Sch. 1947; Univ. de Grenoble, France, Cert. d'études supérieures en géographie, histoire, économie politique, 1949-50; D. en Géog. 1951; Univ. de Paris, recherches 1956-57; Scott Polar Research Institute, Cambridge, 1964; Doctorat d'Etat (France), 1975; ép. Colette, prof., fille de Gaston Lafay, Grenoble, France, 11 août 1951; enfants: Philippe, Anne-Marie; RECTEUR, UNIVERSITE* DU QUEBEC, 1978- ; mem. N.W. Terr. Council 1971-75; prof. de géographie, 1951; premier directeur de l'Institut de Géographie, 1955; dir. jusqu'en 1962; dir.-fondateur du Centre d'Etudes Nordique, Univ. Laval 1961-72; participation à des congrès internat. de geographie et du Quaternaire; voyages d'études dans les zones arctiques et subarctiques; professeur invité à Montréal, Ottawa, Toulouse, Abidjan; Publications: "Recueil de travaux sur l'histoire de la géographie dans le Québec", 1961; "Sables et Mer aux Iles-de-la Madeleine" 1959; "Périglaciaire par l'image — Illus. Glossary of Periglacial Phenomena" 1967 (avec Frank A. Cook); "Le Canada", 1969; "Canada: a ge-

ographical perspective", 1973; "Nordicité canadienne", 1975; "Population of the NWT", 1978; "Canadian Nordicity", 1979; mem., Roy. Canadian Geog. Society (Ottawa); Association Canadienne des Géographes (Ottawa, President 1972); Société de Géographie de Québec (President 1952-56); Union Géographique Internat.; Arctic Inst. of N. Am., Gouverneur, 1964-68; Catholique R.; récréation: voyage; photographie; Résidence: 1244, rue Albert-Lozeau, Sillery, Que. G1T 1H4

HAMELIN, Marcel, D.ès L.; educator; b. Saint-Narcisse, Que. 18 Sept. 1937; e. Séminaire Ste-Marie, Shawinigan 1958; Univ. Laval L.és L. 1961, D.ès L. 1972; m. Judith Purcell 18 Aug. 1962; children: Danielle, Christine, Marc; DEAN OF ARTS, UNIV. OF OTTAWA 1974- , Prof. of Hist. 1966- ; Chrm. of Hist. 1968-70, Vice Dean Sch. of Grad. Studies 1972-74; author "Les premières années du parlementarisme québécois: 1867-1878" 1975; co-author "Les élections provinciales dans le Québec" 1969; "Les moeurs électorales dans le Québec, de 1791 à nos jours". 1962; "Aperçu de la politique canadienne au XIXᵉ siècle" 1965; "Confédération 1867" 1966; éd. "Les mémoires de l'honorable Raoul Dandurand" 1967; "Les débats de l'Assemblée legislative de la province de Québec 1867-1870" 1974; (vol. I-IV); "Les débats de l'Assemblée législative de la province de Québec 1871-1875" 1976 (vol. V-VIII); "Les débats de l'Assemblée legislative de la province de Québec 1875-1878" 1977; (vol. IX-XI); mem. Assn. canadienne-française pour l'avancement des Sciences; Candn. Hist. Assn.; Candn. Hist. Assn.; Royal Soc. Can.; Home: 33 Woodlawn Ave., Ottawa, Ont. K1S 2S8; Office: 165 Waller St., Ottawa, Ont. K1N 6N5.

HAMER, Ian M., B.A.Sc., F.R.Ae.S., F.C.A.S.I.; professional engineer; consultant; b. Ottawa, Ont., 1914; s. late Roy Stokes (C.B.E.) and Mary Isabel (Hope) H.; e. Public and High Schs., Ottawa, Ont.; Univ. of Toronto. B.A.Sc. (Mech. Engn. and one year teaching fellowship in Aeronautics), 1937; m. Gladys Gertrude, d. H. S. Johnston, Lindsay, Ont., 1941; children: Kathryn Eryl (Mrs. P. J. Edwards), Mary Margot (Mrs. D. B. Muir), David Ian Wallace; mem. Staff, Univ. of Toronto 1937-38; Design Office, Handley Page Ltd., London, England, 1938-40; Stress Office, and Staff Assistant to Managing Director, Dowty Equipment Limited, Cheltenham, England, 1940-41; Chief Engineer, Dowty Equipment of Canada Limited, Montreal and Ajax, 1941-51; Tech. Dir., 1951-56; Dir., Vice-Pres. and Gen. Mgr., 1956-60; Pres., Cametoid Ltd., 1956-60; Consultant to Roy. Comn. on Govt. Organ. (Glassco), 1961-62; Co-ordinator, External Aid/CIDA Student Services, Univ. of Toronto 1968-69; mem., Engn. Inst. Can.; A.P.E.O.; C.Eng. (U.K.); mem. Steering Comte. and Interim Council leading to founding of Candn. Aero Inst. 1954; mem. Indust. Council and Chrmn., Assoc. Mfrs. Comte., Air. Indust. & Transport Assn. 1958-60; C.A.S.I. del. at Anglo-American Aero. Conference, London, England 1973; United Church; recreations: reading, photography, gardening, woodworking; Clubs: Univ. (Toronto); Home: "Westlea", 701 King St., Whitby, Ont. L1N 5A2

HAMER, Keith L., B.A., F.C.I.S.; retired company executive; b. Aurora, Ont.; s. Thomas A. and Bertha A. (Howard) H.; e. Aurora Public and High Schs.; Univ. of Toronto, B.A.; m. Dorothy Chapman, 14 Sept. 1940; children: Gordon, Nancy; student, Thorne, Mulholland, Howson & McPherson, Chart. Accts., Toronto, Ont., 1934-37; joined A.M. International Inc. in 1939; Office Mgr., 1940-46, Secy.-Treas. 1946-56; apptd. Mang. Dir. 1956; Vice-Pres., Treas. and Dir., until 1977; United Church; Home: 14 Banstock Drive, Willowdale, Ont. M2K 2H6.

HAMILTON, Albert Charles, M.A., Ph.D., F.R.S.C.; educator; b. Winnipeg, Man. 20 July 1921; s. George Ford and Mary (Briggs) H.; e. Univ. of Man. B.A. 1945; Univ. of Toronto M.A. 1948; Cambridge Univ. Ph.D. 1953; m.

Mary McFarlane 1950; four s. Ian, Malcolm, Peter, Ross; PROF. OF ENGLISH, QUEEN'S UNIV. since 1968; Prof. of Eng. Univ. of Wash. 1952-68; Fellow, St. John's Coll. Cambridge 1974-75; Excellence in Research Award, Queen's Univ. 1981; author "The Structure of Allegory in 'The Faerie Queene' " 1961; "The Early Shakespeare" 1967; "Sir Philip Sidney: A Study of His Life and Works' 1977; "Edmund Spenser's 'Faerie Queene' " 1977, critical studies in Renaissance lit.; mem. Ed. Bd. "English Literary Renaissance"; Duquesne Studies in English; mem. Modern Langs. Assn. Am.; Renaissance Soc. Am.; Assn. Candn. Univ. Teachers Eng.; Spenser Soc. Am. (Extve. Comte.); Sr. Ed., "The Spenser Encyclopedia''; Candn. Soc. Renaissance Studies; Protestant; recreations: canoeing, hiking; Home: 50 Edgehill St., Kingston, Ont. K7L 2T5; Office: Kingston, Ont. K7L 3N6.

HAMILTON, Alexander Daniel, B.Eng.; industrialist; b. Montreal, Que., 13 Nov. 1917; s. Daniel Evoy and Isobel (Stewart) H.; e. Elem. and High Schs., Westmount, Que.; McGill Univ., B.Eng. (Chem.) 1940; m. Frances McLeod, 25 Feb. 1942; children: Joanne, Sandra, Stewart, Kirk, Alexander, Jr.; CHMN. OF BOARD AND CHIEF EXTVE. OFFR., DOMTAR INC. 1981- ; Dir., Inco Ltd., Domtar Inc.; Mount Royal Club; Canadian Imperial Bank of Commerce; Drummond McCall Inc.; Total Petroleum (North America) Ltd.; Dominion Textile Inc., with Ontario Paper Co., Thorold, Ont., 1946; Supt., Quebec North Shore Paper Co., 1955; Asst. Div. Mgr., Ontario Paper Co., 1960; Vice Pres., Brit. Columbia Forest Products Ltd. 1961; Pres., 1964; Pres. & Chief Extve. Offr., 1967-68; Pres., Domtar Pulp and Paper Prod. Ltd., 1968-74; Pres. and C.E.O., Domtar Inc. 1974-81; mem., Bd. of Mgmt., Montreal Gen. Hospital; mem. Gov. Body, Trinity Col. Sch.; Bd. Govs., McGill Univ.; Conseil du Patronat du Quebec; Douglas Hospital Corp.; Jr. Achievement of Que.; served with Tech. Br., R.C.A.F. Canada 1941, Overseas 1942-45; Mentioned in Despatches; Delta Upsilon; recreations: golf, fishing, skiing, tennis; Home: 3 Murray Ave., Westmount, Que. H3Y 2X9; Office: Domtar House, 395 de Maisonneuve Blvd. West, Montreal, Que. H3A 1L6

HAMILTON, Hon. Alvin, P.C. (Can.) 1957; M.P.; b. Kenora, Ont., 30 Mar. 1912; s. Francis Robert and Alice May (Jamieson) H; e. Public Sch., Kenora, Ont.; High Sch., Delisle, Sask. (Grad. 1930); Normal Sch., Saskatoon, Sask., 1930-31; taught school 1931-34; Univ. of Saskatchewan, B.A. 1937, B.A. (Hons. in Hist. and Econ.) 1938; m. Constance Beulah Florence, d. late William John Major, 14 Nov. 1936; two s. Robert Alexander, William Alvin; def. cand. for Rosetown-Biggar to H. of C., g.e. 1945 and 1949; Prov. cand. for Rosetown (def.) 1948, and for Lumsden, 1952; def. cand. for Qu'Appelle to H. of C., 1953; Prov. cand. (def.) for Saskatoon, 1956; 1st el. to H. of C. for Qu'Appelle, g.e. June 1957; apptd. Min. of Northern Affairs & Nat. Resources, 22 Aug. 1957; Min. of Agric. 11 Oct. 1960-Apl. 1963; def. cand. for Regina E. g.e. June 1968; el. for Qu'Appelle-Moose Mt. g.e. Oct. 1972; re-el. since; Prov. Organizer for Conservative Party in Sask., 1948-57; Prov. Ldr. of Conservative Party in Sask., 1949-57; served in 2nd World War with R.C.A.F., 1941-45, Navigator, Flight-Lieut.; mem., Royal Canadian Legion; R.C.A.F. Assn.; Conservative; Protestant; recreations: outdoor activities, historical reading; Home: 4 Kitoman Crescent, Manotick, Ont. K0A 2N0; Office: House of Commons, Ottawa, Ont. K1A 0A6

HAMILTON, Hon. Alvin Chown, LL.B.; judge; b. Winnipeg, Man., 14 Aug. 1926; s. Judge Frank A. E. and Mary Aleda (Chown) H.; e. Kelvin High School, Winnipeg; Un. Coll.; University of Man., LL.B. 1950; m. Lorna, d. late Charles Hasselfield, Deloraine, Man., 24 Oct. 1951; one d., three s.; JUSTICE, COURT OF QUEEN'S BENCH, MANITOBA, since 1972; read law with B.C. Parker, K.C., C.T. Wyrzykowski, K.C. and E.N. McGirr, K.C.; called to Bar of Man. 1951; cr. Q.C. 1968; private law practice Roblin, Man. 1951-54; Winnipeg 1954-55;

Melita, Man., 1955-58; Brandon, Man. 1958-72; served with Candn. Army during World War II; rank Cpl.; Past Pres., Man. Assn. Sch. Trustees; John Howard Soc. (Brandon Br.); former sch. bd. mem. and Chrmn.; Lib. cand. in Brandon-Souris 1963; Past Pres., Brandon Chamber Comm.; Bencher, Law Soc. of Man.; mem., Candn. Bar Assn.; Man. Bar Assn.; Freemason; United Church; recreations: sailing, golf, skiing; Home: 4585 Roblin Blvd., Winnipeg, Man. R3R 0G2; Office: Court House, Winnipeg, Manitoba.

HAMILTON, D. G., B.Sc., M.S., Ph.D.; Canadian public service, retired; b. Fredericton, N.B., 22 July 1917; s. Charles and Mary Jane (Scott) H.; e. McGill Univ., B.Sc. 1938; Univ. of Wisconsin, M.S. 1940, Ph.D. 1947; m. Helen Easley, d. James K. Hewett, Omaha, Neb., 22 March 1947; children: James Hewett, Douglas Scott; Consultant, Agric. Research Council and internat. development agencies, 1978-79; Dir.-Gen. (Planning and Eval.) Research Br., Dept. of Agric., 1975-77; Asst. Dir.-Gen., 1964-75; joined present service in 1938; Asst. in Oatbreeding, 1938-42 and 1945-49; Offr. in Charge of Barley Breeding Unit, 1949-55; Chief, Cereal Crops Div., Exper. Farms Service, 1955-59; Dir. of Program (Crops) Research Br., 1959-64; served in 2nd World War Overseas with Royal Candn. Arty., 1942-45; demobilized with rank of Capt.; Fellow Agric. Inst. Can. (Pres., Eastern Ont. Br., 1950-51; Hon. Sec. 1951-53; Vice Pres., 1953-54); mem. Am. Soc. of Agronomy; Fellow, Am. Assn. Advanc. Science; Sigma Xi; Gamma Alpha; Anglican; Home: 911 Parkhaven Avenue, Ottawa, Ont. K2B 5K4

HAMILTON, Frank Fletcher, M.P.; b. Mazenod, Sask. 1921; e. Univ. of Sask.; m. the late May Olga Barlow; one s. and one d.; m. 2ndly Wanda Fern Jones 1972; farmed before entering university; joined R.C.A.F. 1940; served first with R.A.F. then with R.C.A.F. in bombing raids; awarded D.F.C., D.F.M., C.D. and promotion to Flight Lieut.; remained with RCAF flying transports and as Instr. till 1951 when returned to farming; subsequently Asst. Grain Commr. at Saskatoon for 18 mos.; former mem. of Sask. Wheat Pool and Dir. of Mazenod Telephone Co.; Chrmn. and Chief Commr., Bd. of Grain Commrs. for Can. 1962-71; 1st el. to H. of C. for Swift Current-Maple Creek, g.e. 30 Oct. 1972; re-el. 1974, 1979 and 1980; Dir., Hudson Bay Route Assn.; P. Conservative; Address: House of Commons, Ottawa, Ont. K1A 0A6

HAMILTON, John Drennan, M.D.; pathologist, retired; b. Revelstoke, B.C., 22 Sept. 1911; s. James Henry and Mary Stearns (Edwards) H.; e. Univ. of B.C.; Univ. of Toronto, M.D. 1935; Cambridge Univ. 1937-39; Johns Hopkins Univ., 1939-40; m. Frances Doone, d. Maj.-Gen. C. F. Constantine, Kingston, Ont.; 6 Sept. 1947; children: John Charles Douglas, Suzanne Margery, Alice Jane, Maria Doone; Vice Provost, Univ. of Toronto, 1972-76; Dean, Faculty of Med. there 1961-66, Vice-Pres., Health Sciences 1966-72; former Dir., Connlab Holdings; and Connaught Laboratories Ltd. 1972-79; former Trustee, Toronto General Hosp., Sunnybrook Med. Centre, Clarke Inst. of Psychiatry, Princess Margaret Hosp., Addiction Research Foundation; Prof. of Pathol. & Head of Dept., Univ. of Toronto & Pathologist-in-Chief, Toronto Gen. Hosp., 1951-61; Asst. Prof. of Path., McGill Univ. 1945-46; Prof. of Path. and Head of Dept., Queen's Univ. 1946-51; served in 2nd World War with R.C.A.M.C., No. 1 Research Lab., 1940-45; mem. of Ont., Candn. Assns. of Path.; has published articles on arteriosclerosis, immunology, wound infection experimental glomerulo-nephritis; Home: Apt. 211, 955 Humboldt St., Victoria, B.C. V8V 2Z9

HAMILTON, Margaret Letitia; publishing executive; b. Galt, Ont.; d. Norman and Venetia (Townley) H.; e. Galt (Ont.) Coll. Inst. & Vocational Sch.; PRES., CHIEF OPERATING OFFR. AND DIR., THOMSON

NEWSPAPERS LTD. 1981- ; Pres., Chief Operating Offr. and Dir. Thomson B.C. Newspapers Ltd.; Canadian Newspapers Co. Ltd.; Replacement Sales Co. Ltd.; St. John's Publishing Co. Ltd.; Western Publishers Ltd.; Extve. Vice Pres. and Dir. Thomson Newspapers Inc.; Thomson Brush-Moore Newspapers Publishing Co. Inc.; Thomson Newspapers (Alabama) Inc.; Thomson Newspaper Inc.; Thomson Newspapers (Florida) Inc.; Thomson Newspapers (Illinois) Inc.; Thomson Newspapers (Kentucky) Inc.; Thomson Newspapers (Michigan) Inc.; Thomson Newspapers (Minnesota) Inc.; Thomson Newspapers (Missouri) Inc.; Thomson Newspapers (New Hampshire) Inc.; Thomson Newspapers (Ohio) Inc.; Thompson Newspapers (Oklahoma) Inc.; Thomson Newspapers (Pennsylvania) Inc.; Thomson Newspapers (Wisconsin) Inc.; Thomson Publications of New York Inc.; Chew Newspapers of Ohio Inc.; Douglas Dispatch Inc.; Greenville Newspapers Inc.; Humboldt Newspapers Inc.; The Independent Inc.; Key West Newspaper Corp.; Lock Haven Express Printing Co.; Oxnard Publishing Co.; Phenix-Citizen Inc.; The Punta Gorda Herald Inc.; The San Gabriel Valley Tribune Inc.; Rocky Mount Publishing Co. Inc.; Dir. The Advocate Co. Barbados; joined "The Evening Reporter", Galt, Ont. 1949-54 becoming Assoc. Publisher and Gen. Mgr.; Extve. Asst. to Mang. Dir. Thomson Newspapers Ltd. 1955-69; Vice Pres., Asst. to Mang. Dir. Thomson Newspapers Ltd. and Thomson Newspapers Inc. 1969-75, Sr. Vice Pres. 1975-78, Extve. Vice Pres. 1979-80; Vice Pres. and Dir. Candn. Press; 2nd Vice Chrmn. and Dir. Advertising Bureau Candn. Daily Newspapers; Co-Chrmn. Taskforce Women in Advertising; Dir. Candn. Advertising Adv. Bd.; mem. Associated Press; Internat. Press Inst.; Inter-Am. Press Inst.; Am. Newspapers Publishers Assn. (Dir.); Candn. Daily Newspapers Assn.; Ont. Prov. Dailies Assn.; Commonwealth Press Union; Bd. Trade Metrop. Toronto (Dir.); Ont. Council Univ. Affairs; Adv. Comte. to Secy. State on Status of Women; Adv. Comte. Sch. Business Adm. Univ. W. Ont.; Zonta Internat.; United Church; recreations: golf, tennis, music, photography; Clubs: Galt Country; Granite (Toronto); Home: 64 Blair Rd., Cambridge, Ont. N1S 2J1; Office: 65 Queen St. W., Toronto, Ont. M5H 2M8.

HAMILTON, Peter Williamson, M.Arch., M.R.A.I.C., R.C.A.; architect; b. Toronto, Ont. 15 July 1941; s. John Williamson and Dorothy Clarkson (Hogg) H.; e. Upper Can. Coll. Toronto 1959; Univ. of Toronto B.Arch. 1963; Harvard Univ. Grad. Sch. of Design M.Arch. 1969; m. Linda Deb Kasen, d. George Kasen, N.Y.C., 8 Jan. 1967; two d. Jennifer Kara, Alissa Anne; PARTNER, HAMILTON KEMP ARCHITECTS; rec'd Jvaskyla, Finland New Town First Prize with Bengt Lundsten Arch. 1964; Candn. Housing Design Council Award 1974; Ont. Assn. Archs. Design Prize 1978, Heritage Can. Nat. Award of Honour 1979 with Hamilton Ridgely & Bennett Archs.; EDEE Award Nomination for Cantelevered Child; High Chair; mem. Ont. Assn. Archs.; Royal Arch. Inst. Can.; Royal Canadian Academy of Arts; recreations: sailing, skiing, squash; Clubs: Badminton & Racquet; Rosedale Golf Club; Craigleigh Ski Club; Toronto Lawn Tennis; Harvard; Home: 71 Tranby Ave., Toronto, Ont. M5E 1N4; Office: 47 Colborne St., Toronto, Ont. M5E 1P8.

HAMILTON, Robert McLean Prior, B.Sc.; industrial engineer (retired); b. Anaconda, Montana, 24 Sept. 1903; s. Edward Henry and Ethel Mary (Prior) H.; e. High Schs. of Trail, B.C. and Salt Lake City, Utah; Bishop's Coll. Sch.; Lennoxville, P.Q.; McGill Univ., B.Sc. 1925; m. Elizabeth Miriam, d. Charles S. Parsons, 8 June 1935; children: John McLean Parsons, Susan Elizabeth; joined The Gen. Engn. Co. in Salt Lake City, Utah, 1927; Field Rep. in E. Can. 1929-33; apptd. Pres., General Engineering Co., 1933; Chrmn. of Bd., 1963-67; Dir. of several mining and industrial companies between 1945 and 1976; Chrmn., Confed. of Churches and Business People, 1977-80; mem. Candn. Inst. Mining & Metall.; Am. Inst.

Mining & Metall.; Assn. Prof. Engrs. of Ont. Corp. Prof. Engrs. of Que.; Theta Delta Chi; Anglican; recreations: farming; Clubs: Engineers; National; Granite; Home: 333 Cortleigh Blvd., Toronto, Ont. M5N 1R2

HAMILTON, Robert Morris, B.A., B.L.S.; librarian, retired; b. Lachine, Que., 25 March 1912; s. Andrew McWhirter and Agnes (Morris) H.; e. McGill Univ., B.A. 1934, B.L.S. 1935; Columbia Univ. (Carnegie Fellow, 1936-37); m. Anne Louise, d. late John H. Harrington, 30 July 1938; children: John, Robert, Louise; Asst. Univ. Librarian, Univ. of Brit. Columbia, 1964-77; entered the Civil Services of Can. 1937; apptd. Asst. Librarian (English), Library of Parliament, Ottawa, 1946; Assoc. Prof. Sch. of Librarianship, Univ. of B.C., 1961-64; Pres. (1961-62), Canadian Lib. Association; Publications: "Canadian Quotations and Phrases", 1952; "Canadian Book-prices Current, 1950-55", 1957; "Canadian Book-prices Current, 1956-58", 1959; "Orchid Flower Index, 1736-1979", 1979; "Dictionary of Canadian quotations" (with D. Shields), 2nd ed., 1979; Home: 9211 Beckwith Rd., Richmond, B.C. V6X 1V7

HAMILTON, Hon. William M., O.C., P.C. (Can.), B.Sc.; executive; b. Montreal, P.Q., 23 Feb. 1919; s. Ernest Samuel and Alice Amanda (Beaman)H.; e. Montreal High Sch. (Matric.); Sir. Geo. Williams Coll., B.Sc.Com., 1943; m. Ruth Isabel Seeman, Ottawa, Ont.; PRES. AND CHIEF EXTVE. OFFR., EMPLOYERS' COUNCIL OF B.C.; Chrmn., Fidelity Life Assce. Co.; Century Ins. Co. of Can.; City Councillor, Montreal, 1950-57; Treas., Royal Victoria Hotel, Nassau, Bahamas 1943-45; with W.P.T.B. 1945-47; Extve. Asst. to Pres., McFarlane Son & Hodgson Ltd., 1947-49; Extve. Dir., Fed. of Candn. Adv. & Sales Clubs, Montreal, 1949-57; el. to H. of C. for Notre Dame de Grace (Montreal) g.e. 1953; Postmaster General of Can., 1957-63; Pres. (1971-72) Vancouver Bd. Trade; Dir., Phoenix Assnce. Co., 1976; Conservative; Anglican; Home: 6212 Wiltshire St., Vancouver, B.C. V6M 3M2;

HAMLIN, John Haig, B.A., LL.B.; company executive; b. Winnipeg, Man., 18 Apl. 1918; s. Robert Henry and Evelyn Gertrude (Bradshaw) H.; e. St. John's Coll. Sch., Winnipeg, 1934; Univ. of Man., B.A. 1938; Man. Law Sch., LL.B. 1942; m. Mary Elizabeth, d. late Charles Cecil Irvine, 13 July, 1946; children: Lynn Cecil, John David, Deborah Catherine, Laurel Ruth; SR. VICE PRES. AND DIR., ESSO RESOURCES CAN., since 1979; Dir., Interprovincial Pipe Line Ltd.; read law with Ben C. Parker, Q.C.; called to Bars of Man. 1942, Alta. 1950; Law Partner, Parker, Parker & Hamlin, 1945-49; joined Imperial Oil as Solr. 1949-50; W. Div. Solr. 1950-51; various mang. positions 1951-62; Creole Petroleum Corp., Venezuela, 1962-63; Standard Oil Co. (N.J.) 1963-64; Pres., Esso Exploration Inc. (Australia), 1964-69; Chrmn., Esso Standard Oil (Australia) 1969-70; Vice Pres., Esso Europe Inc., 1970-71; Dir., Imperial Oil Ltd., 1971-79; served with RCNVR 1942-45; rank Lieut. (n); mem. Am. Petroleum Inst.; Candn. Chamber of Comm.; Conference Board, Inc.; 25 Year Club of the Petroleum Industry; Phi Kappa Pi; Anglican; recreations: golf, fishing; Clubs: National (Toronto); Calgary Golf and Country; Calgary Petroleum American National (Australia); Canadian; Home: 8959 Bay Ridge Dr. S.W., Calgary, Alta. T2V 3N1; Office: 237-4th Ave. S.W., Calgary, Alta. T2P 0H6

HAMMARSKJOLD, Knut, F.C.A.S.I.; association executive; b. Geneva, Switzerland, 16 Jan. 1922; s. Ake and Britte (Wahlgren) H.; e. Internat. Sch., The Hague, 1928-35; Sigtunaskolan, Sigtuna, 1935-40; Stockhom Univ., 1941-46 (Filosofie Kandidat 1944); m. Margrit, d. Henry Meyer, Lübeck, W. Germany, 14 Nov. 1969; four children; DIR. GEN. AND CHMN. OF EXTVE. COMMITTEE, INTERNAT. AIR TRANSPORT ASSN., since 1966; Min. Plenipotentiary; Dir., Sydsvenska Dagbladet AB, Sweden; A.T.I. Ltd.; Bermuda; Inst. Air Transport, Paris; joined Foreign Service 1946; Attaché, Paris 1947; Foreign

Office, Stockholm, 1949; Vienna 1951; Second Secy., Moscow (with Bucharest, Sofia and Kabul), 1952; First Secy. 1954; First Secy. Foreign Office, Stockholm, 1955; Head of Foreign Relations Dept. of Swedish Civil Aeronautics Bd. 1957; Counsellor of Swedish Embassy and Depy. Head of Swedish Del. to OEEC, Paris, 1959; Depy. Secy. Gen., European Free Trade Assn., Geneva, 1960; served as Arty. Offr. during World War II; awarded Commdr. First Class Order of the North Star (Sweden); NOR (Sweden); Grand Cross of the Order of Civil Merit (Spain); Grand Offr., Order of Al-Istiqlal (Jordan); Commdr. Order of Lion (Finland); Commdr. Order of Nassau (Netherlands); Order of the Falcon First Class (Iceland); Order of the Black Star (France); author of articles in pol. econ. and aviation fields; mem., Inst. Transport, London; Acad., Mexican Acad. Internat. Law; Protestant; Club: NYA Sällskapet (Stockholm); Home: Le Manoir, Sézegnin/GE, Switzerland; Office: 2000 Peel St., Montreal, Que. H3A 2R4. and 26, Chemin de Joinville, B.P. 160, 1210 Cointrin-Geneva, Switzerland.

HAMMERSMITH, Hon. Jerry, M.L.A., M.Ed.; politician; educator; b. Melfort, Sask. 10 Oct. 1938; s. Alvin Marcy and Molly Beatrice (Byers) H.; e. Melfort Coll. Inst. 1955; Sask. Teachers Coll. 1961-62; Univ. of Sask B.Ed. 1968, MEd. 1971; m. Bernice Michelle Jacobson; children: Renée, Jody, Jamie; MIN. OF NORTHERN SASK., SASK. 1979- ; Vice Chrmn. of Bd. Sask. Mining Development Corp.; Sask. Forest Products Corp.; Mgr Bulk Oil Dealership, Gronlid, Sask 1956-58; Lineman, Sask. Power Corp. 1958-61; Princ., Stony Rapids, Sask. 1962-63; Teacher, Hinton, Alta. 1963-64; Teacher and Vice Princ. Frobisher Bay, N.W.T. 1964-66; owner and operator Cree Lake (Sask.) Lodge and Kasba Lake (N.W.T.) Lodge, also comm. bush pilot 1966-72; Lectr. Univ. of Sask. 1970-72; Co-ordinator, Community Devel. Dept. N. Sask., La Ronge, Sask. 1972-73; Princ., James Smith Community Sch. Kinistino, Sask. 1973-75; Consultant Fed. Sask. Indians Prince Albert, Sask. 1975-79; el. M.L.A. for Prince Albert-Duck Lake 1978; rec'd Fed. Co-ops. Scholarship 1967-68; Inst. N. Studies Musk Ox Scholarship and Grad. Student Bursary 1968-69; former Dir. and Pres. N. Sask. Outfitters Ass.; former Dir. Sask. Tourist Assn.; mem. Prince Albert Chamber Comm.; served with R.O.T.P. 1955-56; NDP; recreations: skiing, fishing, reading; Club: Optimist; Home: 513 Bennett Dr., Prince Albert, Sask.; Office: 132 Legislative Bldg., Regina, Sask. S4S 0B3.

HAMMOND, John Allan, administrator; b. St. Lambert, Que., 13 Oct. 1920; s. Frederick Peter and Mary Anne Elizabeth (Callan) H.; e. St. Lambert (Que.) High Sch., 1938; m. Elizabeth Grace, d. Arthur Douglas Cooke, 15 Sept. 1945; two s. Peter Wallace, Michael Douglas; EXTVE. DIR., GRANVILLE ISLAND since 1978; Radio Announcer, CFCF, Montreal, 1945; Mgr., CFCF, 1950; Broadcasting Mgr., Canadian Marconi Co., 1953; Gen. Sales Mgr., Comm. Products Div., 1956; Mgr., CKRC, Winnipeg, 1959; Dir. of Adm., St. John's-Ravenscourt Sch., Winnipeg, 1962; Extve. Vice Pres., Glenbow Alberta Inst., Calgary, 1970; served with RCAF 1941-45; Past Dir. Royal Winnipeg Ballet; Candn. Assn. Broadcasters; Central Can. Assn. Broadcasters; Bureau Broadcast Measurement; former mem., Adv. Comte. on Broadcasting, Ryerson Inst. Technol.; former mem. of Senate Univ. of Calgary; Past President, Museum Directors Association Can.; mem., Candn. Museums Assn.; Alta. Hist. Soc.; past Chrmn. Candn. Comte., Internat. Council of Museums; Liberal; Protestant; Home: 1194 West 40th Ave., Vancouver, B.C. V6M 1V2; Office: Granville Island, Vancouver V6H 3M5

HAMPSON, H. Anthony, M.A. (Econ.); corporate executive; b. Montreal, Que., 18 Aug. 1930; s. Harold Ralph and Geraldine Mary (Smith) H.; e. Selwyn House Sch., Montreal; Westmount (Que.) Pub. Schs.; Bishops Coll. Sch., Lennoxville, Que.; McGill Univ., B.A. 1950; Cam-

bridge Univ., M.A. (Econ.) 1952; m.; children: Terence, Greville, Hilary, Alexandra; PRESIDENT AND CHIEF EXECUTIVE OFFICER, CANADA DEVELOPMENT CORPORATION, since 1972; Dir Texasgulf Inc.; Polysar Ltd.; CDC Oil & Gas Ltd.; Petrosar Limited; CDC Life Sci. Inc; Connaught Labs. Ltd.; Omnimedic Inc.; AES Ltd; Ventures West Capital Ltd.; Secy.,with Bank of Montreal, Credit Analyst, H.O. 1952; Department Finance, Ottawa, Econ. Policy Div. (on loan for 2 years to Royal Comn. on Can.'s Econ. Prospects (The Gordon Comn.) and co-authored study on Can.'s Secondary Mfg. Indust.) 1953; Dir., Research and Underwriting, Burns Bros. & Denton, Toronto 1957-64; Secy., Royal Comn. on Banking and Finance (The Porter Comn.) 1961-64; Vice-Pres., Power Corp. of Canada Ltd. 1964-68; Pres., Capital Management Ltd. 1965, (full time) 1968-72; Past Chrmn., Gen. Adjustment Assistance Bd., Dept. of Industry, Ottawa; Pharm. Industry Devel. Adv. Comte.; Office: Suite 200, 444 Young St., Toronto, Ont. N5B 2H4

HANBIDGE, R(obert) Walter D., B.S.A.; b. Peterborough, Ont., 5 April 1925; s. Hazel Elizabeth (Dawson) and the late George Burnham H.; e. Peterborough Coll. Inst., 1939-44; Ont. Agric. Coll., B.S.A. (Econ.) 1948; m. Mary Elizabeth, d. late Dr. H. J. Vallentyne, 25 July 1946; children: Catherine Anne, Val Elizabeth (deceased), Mary Ellen, Robert John; PRES., CEO, AND DIR., BP CANADA INC.; Dir., BP Canadian Holdings Ltd.; Pres. and Dir., BP Oil Ltd.; BP Properties Ltd.; Dir., BP Minerals Ltd.; Pres. and Dir., BP Exploration Canada Ltd.; Dir., BP Oil & Gas Invest. Ltd.; British Columbia Oil Lands Ltd.; Sukunka Mines Ltd.; Chatelaine Restaurants Ltd.; BP Invest. Can. Ltd.; Mem., Bd. of Gov., Univ. of Guelph; Advertising Supervisor, various Product Accounts, Canadian Industries Limited, 1948-53; Advertising Promotion Manager, Reader's Digest Assn. (Can.) Ltd., Toronto, 1953-54; Advertising Supvr., Gen. Co. and Merchandising Mgr. of Textile Fibres, Candn. Industries (1954) Ltd., 1954-58; Dir. of Marketing Services, Leethan Simpson Ltd., 1958-61; joined present Co. as Comm. Mgr., 1961; apptd. Gen. Mgr., Marketing, 1963; Vice-Pres., Marketing, 1964; Extve. Vice Pres., 1966; Pres., 1977; Offr., Royal Comn. on Govt. Organ., 1961; recreations: farming; photography; restoration of Canadian antiques; Clubs: National (Toronto) Mount Royal, Canadian; Home: 14 Salvi Court, Toronto, Ont M4A 1P7 Office: First Canadian Place, P.O. Box 79. Toronto Ont. M5X 1G8

HANCOX, Ralph; journalist, editor; b. Hampstead, Eng., 23 Aug. 1929; s. Harold Barnsley and Ada Frances (Smith) H.; e. Harrow Co. Grammar Sch. for Boys; R.A.F. Flying Coll.; Heany, S. Rhodesia Sch. of Modern Languages; Regent St. Polytech., grad. 1954; m. Margaret Gilmour, d. George Chisholm Frier, 5 June 1954; children: Linda Elaine (Carlsson), Kenrick Guy, Alison Janet, Julian Roderick Rufus; PRES., THE READER'S DIGEST ASSOCIATION (CANADA) LTD.; Pegatex Inc.; former Ed., Can. edition, The Reader's Digest; Peterborough (Ontario) Examiner; former Vice-Pres., Op.-Customer Serv., Book Pubs., Produc., Readers Digest Asoc., (Can.) sometime News Editor, Weekly Post, London, Eng.; Daily Columnist, Kingston "Whig-Standard", Ont.; Correspondent Candn. Affairs, Observer Foreign News Service, London; articles in numerous papers incl. "The Scotsman", Edinburgh, "The Jerusalem Post", Israel and many papers in U.S.A.; served with R.A.F., 1947-52; discharged with rank of Sgt. Pilot; Trustee, Peterborough Bd. Educ. 1964-66; Nieman Fellow, Harvard Univ., 1965-66; Winner, Nat. Newspaper Award for Edit. Writing, 1966; recreations: reading, anthropology, writing, travel; Home: 624 Habitat '67, Cité du Havre, Montreal, Que. H3C 3R6 Office: 215 Redfern Ave., Montreal, Que. H3Z 2V9

HANDLEY, Thomas G., C.A., M.B.A.; organization consultant; b. Pretoria, South Africa 3 March 1943; e. Univ.

of W. Ont. M.B.A.; m. Dr. Allyson Hughes 15 Aug. 1969; children: Vanessa, Stephen, Rachael; PARTNER, FROMKIN VAN HORN HANDLEY, 1982- ; formerly Sr. Vice Pres., Corporate Human Resources, Bank of Montreal; Home: 253 Russell Hill Road, Toronto, Ont. M4V 2T3; Office: 1 Yonge St., Suite 2208, Toronto, Ont. M5E 1E5

HANES, Charles Samuel, Ph.D., Sc.D., F.R.S., F.R.S.C.; biochemist; biologist; b. Toronto, Ont. 21 May 1903; s. late Carmi Addison and late Anastasia (Kavanagh) H.; e. Oakwood Coll. Inst. Toronto 1919; Univ. of Toronto B.A. 1925; Cambridge Univ. Ph.D. 1931, Sc.D. 1953; m. Theodora Burleigh Auret, Johannesburg, S. Africa 7 March 1931; one d. Ursula Ann; Prof. Emerit of Biochem. Univ. of Toronto since 1968; Overseas Scholar Exhn. of 1851 1925-27, Sr. Scholar 1928-31; Lectr. in Biol. Queen's Univ. 1927-28; Scient. Offr. Low Temperature Research Stn. for Research in Biochem. and Biophys., D.S.I.R. and Cambridge Univ. 1934-44; seconded to Scient. Advs. Div., Ministry of Food and apptd. Scient. mem. Brit. Food Mission to N. Am. 1941-44; Dir. of Food Investigation UK 1943-47, Reader in Biochem. Cambridge Univ. and Dir. Unit of Plant Biochem. Agric. Research Council 1947-51; Hon. Fellow, Downing Coll. since 1951, Fellow 1947-51; Prof. of Biochem. Univ. of Toronto 1951-68; has served on numerous comtes. and bds., UK, USA and Can.; Sec. Chrmn. Plant Biochem. 1st Internat. Cong. Biochem., Cambridge 1950; Hon. co-Pres. of 11th Internal. Congress Biochem., Toronto, 1979, rec'd Flavelle Medal Royal Soc. Can. 1955; author numerous publs. interpretation structure starch from mode of attack by different amylases; postulation of 1st helical structure for a macromolecule; discovered amylose phosphorylase of higher plants and by its action produced first example of a synthesized macromolecule identifiable with a natural product; discovered various other enzymes; co-devel. unrestricted kinetic theory enzyme action; recreations: carpentry, furniture design, language study; Home: 60 Beech Ave., Toronto, Ont. M4E 3H4.

HANES, Ursula Ann, (Ursula Hanes Guthrie) A.R.C.A.; sculptor; b. Toronto, Ont., 18 Jan. 1932; d. Prof. Charles Samuel, Ph.D., F.R.S. F.R.S.C., and Theodora Burleigh (Auret), H., Ch.D.; e. Perse Sch. for girls, Cambridge, U.K., 1949. Cambridge Sch. of Art, 1951; Art Student's League, N.Y.C., 1953 (studied under Wm. Zorach, John Hovannes); Dept. of Fine Arts, Columbia Univ., N.Y.C., 1953 (studied under Oronzio Malderelli); Inst. of Child Study, Univ. of Toronto, (Dipl.) 1954; m. David John, C.D., M.A. s. Harold Fry, Toronto, Ont., 30 Aug. 1956; divorced 1968; m. D. Peter Guthrie 1976; divorced 1981; children: Rachel Sabina, Simon David, Tanya Amanda, Timothy Jeremy John; has exhibited at Columbia Univ., 1953, New Eng. Soc. Artists, 1953, O.S.A., 1954-62, R.C.A., 1955, 1957, 1959-62, Stratford Festival, 1955, Young Candn. Contemporaries, 1957, Candn. Nat. Ex., 1956, 1959-60; several sculpting and batik exhibitions in Lanzarotte, Canary Islands, Spain, 1969-75; Audio-Visual Consultant for I.D.R.C. (Ottawa) in Rep. Dumali, West Africa, 1971-72; Exhibition, Sara Gallery, Toronto, 1980; also various civic art galleries in Can.; Commissions incl.: bust of Dr. Tyrone Guthrie, Evan McCowan, Dr. Margaret McCready and various murals and fountains; mem., Sculptors' Soc. Can. (Pres. 1964-65); Ont. Soc. Artists; Agnostic; recreations: reading, theatre, arts; Address: Box 224, Arroyo Grande, Calif. 93420

HANIGAN, Lawrence,; executive; b. Notre-dame de Stanbridge, Que. 3 April 1925; s. John H. and Alice (Lareau) H.; m. Anita d. Joseph O. Martin 20 July 1946; children: Carmen, Doris, Guy, Patricia, Michael; CHRMN. AND GEN. MANAGER, COMMISSION DE TRANSPORT DE LA COMMUNAUTE URBAIN DE MONTREAL: Pres., Agence de Voyage Gray Line de Montreal Inc.; Vice Pres. Candn. Urban Transit Assn.; Mem., Montreal City Council, 1960-78; Mem., Extve. Comte., City of Montreal, 1970-78; Chrmn., Extve. Cmte., Mont-

real Urban Community, 1972-78; R. Catholic; Club: Saint-Denis; Home: 2360 Charles-Gill St., Montreal, Que. H3M 1V7; Office: 159 St. Antoine W., Montreal, Que. H2Z 1H3.

HANINGTON, Rear Admiral Daniel Lionel, D.S.C., C.D.; marine consultant; b. London, Eng., 10 July 1921; s. Charles Lionel and Mary Arbuthnot (Willet) H.; e. Rothesay (N.B.) Coll. Sch., 1940; Royal Naval Staff Coll., psc 1961; m. Margot Rita, d. H. V. Wallace, Ottawa, Ont. 1 Mar. 1943; children: Gillian, Mark, Brian, Felicity; VICE PRES. PROGRAMS, TRANSPOLAR SHIPPING INC.; joined RCNVR as Midshipman, 1940; sunk in HMS "Rajputana", Denmark Strait, 1941; trans. to RCN 1944; promoted Cdr. 1955; C.O., HMCS "Iroquois", 1955-57; Offr.-in-Charge, Navig.-Direction Sch., 1958; promoted Capt. 1961; Cdr., 3rd Candn. Escort Sqdn. 1965-66; promoted Commodore 1966 and apptd. Commandant, Candn. Maritime Warfare Sch.; subsequently Depy. Commdr., Candn. Defence Educ. Estab., Ottawa; Dir.-Gen. Program Vice Chief of Defence Staff Br.; promoted Rear Adm. 1973 as Chief of Program; trans. to staff of Supreme Allied Command Atlantic 1974 as D/COS (Support) (ret. 1976); spec. marine navig. offr. & fighter control; qual. Clearance Diving Offr. (ship); Clubs: Chesapeake (founding mem.); Master Foreign Going Steamships; Anglican; Bytown Seagull; recreations: swimming, skiing, scuba diving, philately; Home: 908 Bay Colony Dr., Virginia Beach, Va.;

HANLEY, Rev. Msgr. John Gerald, B.A., D.D.; priest; b. Read, Ont. 21 Feb. 1907; s. Denis and Jessie Elizabeth (Bryson) H.; e. Regiopolis Coll. Kingston; St. Michael's Coll. Univ. of Toronto B.A. 1927; Queen's Univ. D.D. 1973; Msgr. Archdiocese of Kingston; Dir. Hotel Dieu Hosp. Kingston; mem. Bd. Mang. Queen's Theol. Coll. Kingston; Ed. The Canadian Register 1942-70; Teacher, Jr. Semy. Christ the King, Ladner, B.C. 1932-34; named Prelate of Honor 1955; Protonotary Apostolic 1976; author "Across Canada with Newman" 1953; mem. Cath. Press Assn. U.S. & Can. (Secy. 1962-68); Candn. Fed. Newman Clubs (Nat. Chaplain 1944-45, 1952-55); Address: 279 Johnson St., Kingston, Ont. K7L 1Y5.

HANNA, Geoffrey Chalmers, M.A., F.R.S.C.; physicist; b. Stretford, Lancs., England, 5 Oct. 1920; s. Walter and Dorothy (Cross) H.; e. Manchester Grammar Sch. (1931-38); Trinity Coll., Cambridge, B.A., M.A.; m. Barbara Helen, d. late Harry Scott, 7 April 1951; three s. Christopher Scott, David Scott, Jeremy Scott; RESEARCH DIRECTOR, CHALK RIVER NUCLEAR LABS., ATOMIC ENERGY OF CANADA LTD.; engaged in nuclear physics research, since 1952; with British Min. of Supply, radar research and devel., 1940-45; Nat. Research Council of Can., Montreal and Chalk River, nuclear physics research, 1945-52; Publications: part-author, "Experimental Nuclear Physics" (edited E. Segrè), 1959; various papers in scient. journs.; mem., Candn. Assn. Physicists; Anglican; Home: 5 Tweedsmuir Place, Deep River, Ont. K0J1P0; Office: Chalk River, Ont. K0J 1J0

HANNON, Matthew S., Q.C., B.A.Sc., B.C.L.; b. Toronto, Ont., 19 Sept. 1921; s. Matthew Stuart and Sarah Gertrude (Bingham) H.; e. De La Salle Coll. "Oaklands," Toronto; Univ. of Toronto, B.A.Sc. (Civil Engn.) 1944; McGill Univ., B.C.L. 1950; m. Janet Laura, d. Harry J. Renaud, Montreal, 4 Jan. 1950; children: Matthew, Sally, Jane, Gregory, Kathryn; SENIOR PARTNER, OGILVY, RENAULT, Chrmn. Extve. Comte., Montreal Trust Co.; Dir., Standard Brands Ltd.; Daks Canada Ltd.; Lowney Inc.; TV Guide Inc.; called to Bar of Que. 1950; cr. Q.C. 1968; has practised law since that date specializing in corp. financing, real estate and banking law; served with R.C.E.M.E., 1944-46; Dir. and Treas., The Priory Sch. Inc., 1960-65; mem., Assn. Prof. Engrs. Ont.; Engn. Inst. Can.; Candn. Bar Assn; Delta Tau Delta (Past Pres.); R. Catholic; recreations: golf, skiing; Clubs: Mount Royal;

Montreal Badminton & Squash; Royal Montreal Golf (Dir.; Pres. 1965-66); Mt. Bruno Golf; Engineers'; Home: 579 Roslyn Ave., Westmount, Que. H3Y 2T7; Office: Ste 700, 1Place Ville Marie, Montreal, Que.H3B 1Z7

HANSARD, Hugh Gerard Hazen, Q.C.; b. Saint John, N.B., 3 Dec. 1904; s. Hugh Hazen (lawyer) and Annie Maud (Burpee) H.; e. Ridley Coll., St. Catharines, Ont.; McGill Univ., B.A. 1926; B.C.L. 1928; m. Marguerite Jessie, d. Arthur Barry, Westmount, P.Q., 27 Sept, 1930; children: Hugh, Philippa; retired Partner, Ogilvy, Cope, Montgomery and Co.; Gov. Ridley Coll.; Montreal Gen. Hosp.; Douglas Hosp.; read law with George H. Montgomery, K.C.; called to Bar of P.Q. 1928; Ont. 1953; cr. K.C. 1943; has been in practice since 1928 with present firm and predecessor, Brown, Montgomery & McMichael; Pres., Candn. Bar Assn. 1964-65; Hon. Life mem., Am. Bar Assn.; mem., New York State Bar Assn.; Montreal Museum of Fine Arts; Zeta Psi; Freemason; Liberal; Anglican; Clubs: University; Laurentian; Forest & Stream; Home: 17 Edgehill Rd., Westmount, Montreal. P.Q. H3Y 1E8

HANSEN, Frank, B.Sc.; civil engineer; b. Aklavik, N.W.T., 29 Dec. 1944; s. Hans Pedersen and Kathleen (Nutik) H.; e. Schs. in Aklavik and Inuvik, N.W.T.; Univ. of Alta., B.Sc. (Engn.) 1969; m. Sandra Arlene, d. John Welch, Calgary, Alta., 19 Dec. 1970; OWNER HANSEN PETROLEUM PRODUCTS since 1874; Pres. and Part., Aklak Air Ltd.; Resident Engr., Williams Bros. Canada Ltd. since 1971-72; PastDir., Canadian Broadcasting Corp.; with Govt. of N.W.T. as Asst. Regional Engr., Inuvik 1969; Town Councillor, Inuvik 1970, 1972-73; mem. First N.W.T. Science Adv. Bd. 1976-81; mem. Assn. Prof. Engrs., Yukon and N.W.T.; Anglican; recreations: all sports, music; Home: (Box 1037) Inuvik, N.W.T. X0E 0T0

HANSON, Christilot; writer; dressage rider; b. Batavia, Indonesia, 12 Apl. 1947; d. Linden Lawrence and Willy Jeanne (Blok) H.; e. Branksome Hall, Toronto; m. James A Boylen 1972; two d. Christa-Dora, Billie Jeanne; dressage training and private tutoring langs., regular curriculum, Hanover, Germany, 1961-63; as a child did extensive amount of dancing and acting work incl. some dance tours on behalf of the Ont. Govt. (mem. Willy Blok Hanson Dance Group); series role in children's programme "Howdy Doody"; youngest equestrian in hist. of Olympic Games to compete in Grand Prix de Dressage Event, Tokyo, 1964; mem. Bronze Medal Team, Pan Am. Games, Winnipeg, 1967; mem. Mexico Olympic Team, 1968; winner of 2 classes at Aachen Internat. Horse Show, 1970 (first N. Am. to win "Coupe Carven" as Leading Lady Rider); holds many other dressage titles incl. Candn. Dressage Champion (7 times) and E. U.S. Dressage Champion (2 times); only Canadian and youngest competitor in U.S. Nat. Championships winning the Championship (aboard Bonne Annee) at Far Hills, N.J., Oct. 1970; Pan Am. Games Double Gold Medallist, 1971; placed 8th in Munich Olympics 1972; Indiv. Gold Medallist Dressage, Pan Am Games, 1975; placed 7th in Grand Prix Dressage, Olympics, 1976; author, "Canadian Entry", 1965; "Basic Dressage for North America", 1977; also many equestrian articles; Exec.-Vice Pres., International Equestrian Sports Services Ltd. 1981; Dir., Candn. Dressage Owners and Riders Assn. (CA-DORA Inc.); mem., P. Cons. Assn.; Assn. TV & Radio Artists; Club: Toronto & N. York Pony; Address: Bonacres Farm, R.R. #1, Cedar Valley, Ont. L0G 1E0

HANSON, Eric J., M.A., Ph.D., F.R.S.C., F.R.S.H.; economist; professor emeritus; b. Alfta, Sweden, 14 Oct. 1912, s. August P. and Brita (Erickson) H.; came to Canada 1925; e. Camrose Normal School, Alberta, 1931; Queen's University B.A. 1942; Univ. of Alta. M.A. 1946; Clark Univ., Ph.D. 1952; m. Helen D., d. John C. Sutherland, 13 June 1936; Pres., Hanson Economic Surveys Ltd.; Dir., Alberta Municipal Financing Corp.; began

teaching in Alta. Schs. 1932; joined Univ. of Alberta as Lectr. 1946, Adm. Offr. Dept. Political Econ. 1952, Head Dept. 1957, Prof. of Econ. 1957-74, Assoc. Dean Grad. Studies 1964-67, mem. Bd. Govs. 1968-71; NATO Visiting Prof. (Can.) Norwegian Sch. of Econ. and Business, Bergen, Norway 1962; mem. Candn. Econ. Assn.; Royal Econ. Soc.; Am. Econ. Assn.; author of "Local Government in Alberta" 1956; "Dynamic Decade" 1958; also other books, papers and articles in fields of pub, finance and petroleum industry; recreations: reading, music, golf, bridge; Home: 302-12207 Jasper Ave., Edmonton, Alta. T5N 3K2

HANSON, Horace A., M.B.E., Q.C., B.A., LL.B.; b. Boston, Mass., 28 Feb. 1909; s. Benjamin Menzies and Henrietta Marian (Allen) H.; came to Canada, 1915; e. Public Schs. of Boston and St. Andrews; Univ. of New Brunswick, B.A. 1930; Dalhousie Law Sch., LL.B. 1935; m. Marian Hill, d. Luke S. Morrison, 17 Sept. 1940: children: John Morrison, Patricia Ruth, Richard Burpee, Elizabeth Gay; COUNSEL, HANSON, GILBERT & HASHEY; Ret. as Dir. and Vice-Pres., Central and Eastern Trust Co. 1979; read law with William J. West, Q.C.; called to the Bar of N.B. 1935; cr. Q.C. 1953; practised law as an assoc. of Hanson, Dougherty & West, 1935-40; organ. the firm of Hanson & Smith, 1948 (present firm successor); served in 2nd World War; enlisted in 1940 and served abroad till 1945; held staff appts. with Fourth Candn. Armoured Div. and other formations; discharged with rank of Major; M.B.E.; Solr. for City of Fredericton, 1945-52; Chrmn., N.B. Labour Relations Bd., Minimum Wage Bd. and Apprenticeship Comte., 1952-60; mem., N.B. Barristers Soc.; Candn. Bar Assn. (Vice-Pres., 1959-60); Candn. Tax Foundation (Past Gov.); Bd. of Gov. of Beaverbrook Art Gallery, Fredericton, N.B.; Freemason (P.M. Scot. Rite); recreations: hunting, fishing; Club: Fredericton Curling; Home: 296 Church St., Fredericton, N.B. E3B4E4; Office: 61 Carleton St., Fredericton, N.B. E3B 3T2

HANSON, Jean; artist; b. Toronto, Ont., 27 Sept. 1933; d. Walter John and Ursula (Gallagher) H.; e. St. Joseph's Coll. Sch., Toronto; Ont. Coll. Art; Artists' Workshop, Toronto; m. John A. Elphick, Art Dir., 1966; one d., Shanna; has exhibited widely in Can. and U.S.A., incl. Washington Watercolour Club, 1956; Nat. Gallery (Ottawa) Travelling Exhn., 1955; Montreal Museum of Fine Arts, 1956, 1962; Ont. Soc. Artists, 1957; Royal Ont. Museum, 1958; Toronto Art Gallery, 1963; Candn. Soc. of Painters in Watercolour 1954-69; mem. Candn. Soc. Painters in Watercolour; Ont. Soc. Artists; Liberal; R. Catholic; recreation: photography.

HANSON, Telfer R.; retired investment dealer; b. Toronto, Ont. 10 Aug. 1910; s. Frederick Charles and Jessie B. (Telfer) H.; e. Upper Canada Coll., Toronto, Ont. (1920-24 and 1927-29); Lower Canada Coll., Montreal, P.Q. (1925-26); m. Elizabeth Kendall, d. late Herbert K. Patterson, 6 Dec. 1936; children: Gordon Telfer, Robert Kendall, David Charles, Jane Elizabeth; was Dir. R. A. Daly & Co. Ltd.; was Dir., Productive Land Enterprises; Lyman Tube & Bearings Ltd.; Chrmn. of Invest. Comte., United Community Fund; mem. of Extve. Comte., Boy Scouts Assn.; Candn. Red Cross Soc.; Upper Can. Coll. Old Boys' Assn.; during 2nd World War, Supervisor of Nat. War Finance Comte., Ottawa Valley; Freemason; Anglican; recreations: hunting, fishing, golf; Clubs: Rosedale Golf; Badminton & Racquet; Caledon Mountain Trout; Home: 345 Lonsdale Rd., Apt. 601, Toronto, Ont. M5P 1R5

HANTHO, Charles Harold, B.Sc.; company executive; b. Lethbridge, Alta. 1931; e. Pub. and High Schs., Calgary, Alta.; Univ. of Alta., B.Sc. (Chem. Engn.); m. Phyllis Mae Weir 1957; children: Karl Alan, Mark Albert, Jon Andrew, Heather Gale; VICE-PRES., CANADIAN INDUSTRIES LTD. since 1978; joined the Co. as Tech. Assistant,

Edmonton, Alberta, 1953, Prod. Engineer. 1954, various positions in plastics prod. 1958-59; Sales Rep., Plastics Div., Toronto, Ont.; Sales Devel. Supv., Brampton, Ont. and Montreal; Sales Devel. Mgr., Plastics 1965; Mgr., Packaging 1967; Gen. Mgr., Plastics Div. 1968; Vice Pres., 1971; seconded to Imp. Chem. Indust. as Dep. Chrmn., Petro-Chem. Div., Teeside, Eng. 1976-78; mem. Mfg. Chem. Assn.; Candn. Chem. Producers Assn.; recreations: golf, skiing, water sports; Club: Whitlock Golf; Office: 630 Dorchester Blvd. W., CIL House, Box 10, Montreal, Que. H3C 2R3

HANUSCHAK, Hon. Ben, M.L.A., LL.B., B.Ed.; politician; b. Earl Grey, Sask., 29 April 1930; s. John and Anna (Bartkiw) H.; e. St. Joseph's Coll., Yorkton, Sask. 1947; Man. Normal Sch., Winnipeg, Man. 1951; Manitoba Law Sch., LL.B. 1956; Univ. of Manitoba, B.Ed. 1961; m. Nadia, d. W.F. Stechkewich, Winnipeg, Man. 22 Aug. 1953; one d., Nadine Sonia; Min. of Continuing Ed. and Manpower, and Min. of Tourism, Recreation & Cultural Affairs, 1976-77; Minister of Educ., MAN. 1971 and Min. of Colls. and Univs. Affairs 1973-76; Chrmn., Mang. Comte. of the Cabinet 1972-75; Teacher, Winnipeg 1959-66 and 1968-70; 1st el. to Man. Leg. for Burrows Constit. 1966, re-el. 1969; el. Speaker of House 1969; Min.; Consumer & Corporate Affairs 1970; Prov. Secy., Man. N.D.P. 1966-68; Pres., Red River Co-op. 1965-68; Winnipeg Teachers' Assn. 1965; mem. Council of Exceptional Children; Man. Educ. Assn.; Man. Teachers' Soc.; Guidance Counsellors' Club; N.D.P.; recreations: painting, photography, gardening; Home: 11 Aster Ave., Winnipeg, Man. R2V2K5; Office: Legislative Bldg., Winnipeg, Man.

HARBINSON, Vincent Noble, B.Com., C.A.; proprietor; b. Toronto, Ont. 30 March 1919; s. Vincent David and Ida Irene (Noble) H.; e. Univ. of Toronto Schs.; Univ. of Toronto B.Com; C.A.; children: John Noble, Hugh David, Bruce Frederick, Shirley Karon, Anne Irene; OWNER, PROFESSIONAL MANAGEMENT SERVICES and THE HARBINSON MINING GROUP: Chrmn. and Chief Extve. Offr. and/or Pres. and Dir., The Harbinson Mining Group; Chapcoe Investment Corp. Ltd.; Spooner Mines and Oils Ltd.; Consolidated Durham Mines & Resources Ltd.; N.B.U. Mines Ltd.; Noble Mines & Oils Ltd.; CAM Mines Ltd.; Dominion Explorers Ltd.; O'Brien Energy & Resources Ltd.; Onaping Mines Ltd.; Share Mines & Oils Ltd.; Silvermaque Mining Ltd.; Tex-Sol Explorations Ltd.; Homestake Explorations Ltd.; Tipacanoe Co. Ltd.; Joutel Copper Mines Ltd.; Partner, Harbinson, Glover & Co., C.A.'s Toronto 1949-57; Owner Professional Management Services 1957- ; served with Royal Candn. Ordnance Corps 1941-45, rank Capt.; mem. Candn. Inst. Mining & Metall.; St. George's Soc. (Life mem.); Theta Delta Chi; Anglican; recreations: fishing, golf, hunting, swimming; Clubs: Engineers; Petroleum (Calgary); Ontario; Beaver Brook Golf & Country; Home: R.R. 1, Kinmount, Ont. K0M 2A0; Office: 916, 111 Richmond St. W., Toronto, Ont. M5H 2G4.

HARBOTTLE, Merry Deirdre, B.A., M.L.S.; librarian; b. Regina, Sask. 25 Nov. 1948; d. Wilson James and Helen Jane (Clarke) Harper; e. Sarnia (Ont.) N. Coll. Inst. 1967; Univ. of W. Ont. B.A. 1971, M.L.S. 1976; Univ. of Sask. grad. teaching fellowship in pol. science 1972; m. Robert Éric Harbottle 1 Sept. 1972; one d. Anne Deirdre; PROV. LIBRARIAN OF SASK. 1981- ; Asst. Clk. Leg. Assembly Sask. 1972-74; Dir. of Adm. Dept. Extve. Council 1978-80; Asst. to Depy. Min. of Urban Affairs 1980; Dir., Regina YWCA; mem. Women's Healthsharing of Regina; Sask. Lib. Assn.; Candn. Lib. Assn.; Parlty. Assn. Clks.-at-the-Table (Secy. for Can.); Pi Beta Phi (Secy.); Protestant; recreations: swimming, cross-country skiing, racketball; Home: 35 Lincoln Dr., Regina, Sask. S4S 2V7; Office: 1352 Wimmipeg St., Regina, Sask. S4P 3V7.

HARBRON, John Davison, M.A., F.R.S.A.; b. Toronto, Ont., 15 Sept. 1924; s. Tom and Sara Lillian (Peace) H.; e. Lawrence Park Coll. Inst., Toronto; Univ. of Toronto, B.A. 1946, M.A. 1948; post graduate studies, University of Havana 1947-48; m. Sheila Elizabeth. d. late Egerton Lester, 20 Sept. 1950; children: Patrick John, Christopher Tom, Ann Kathryn; Chairman, Department of Hist. and Econ., Canadian Services College, Royal Roads, Victoria, B.C., 1948-51; Candn, Ed. "Business Week", N.Y., 1956-60; Ed., "Executive" Magazine, 1961-66; Associate Editor, The Toronto Telegram, 1966-71; served in Royal Canadian Navy during Korean War, 1951-53; Lieutenant-Commander RCN(R) retired; mem. Board Govs., St. George's College, Toronto; author of "Communist Ships and Shipping", 1963; "Canada without Quebec", 1977; Commdr., Order of Isabella the Catholic (Spain); presented with Maria Moors Cabot Medal, Columbia Univ., N.Y., 1970; Pres.; Couchiching Inst. on Public Affairs, 1979; awarded Silver Jubilee Medal, 1977; now Foreign Affairs Analyst, Thomson Newspapers, Toronto; recreations: sailing, philately; Clubs: Royal Canadian Military Institute; Barrie Yacht; Home: 4 Élstree Rd., Islington, Ont. M9A 3Z1

HARDER, Rolf, R.C.A.; graphic designer; b. Hamburg, Germany 10 July 1929; s. Henry and Henriette (Loeffler) H.; e. Christianeum (High Sch.) Hamburg 1948; Hamburg Acad. of Fine Arts 1948-52; m. Maria-Inger d. Karl Rumberg 3 May 1958; children: Christopher, Vivian; self-employed ROLF HARDER & ASSOC.; travelling exhn. with Ernst Roch sponsored by Candn. Govt. in Can., U.S.A., Germany and Yugoslavia; rep. in group exhns. Can., U.S.A., Europe, S.Am., Japan; participant 36th Venice Biennale Exper. Graphic Design Sec. 1973; rec'd over 80 nat. and internat. design awards; work publ. in prof. mags. Can., U.S.A., Eng., Austria, Germany, Switzerland, Italy, France, Japan; mem. Alliance Graphique Internationale (Pres. Candn. Group); Internat. Centre for Typographic Arts; Soc. Graphic Designers Can.; Am. Inst. Graphic Arts; recreations: tennis, skiing, swimming; Home: 43 Lakeshore Rd., Beaconsfield, Que. H9W 4H6; Office: 1350 Sherbrooke St. W., Suite 1000, Montreal, Que. H3G 1J1.

HARDING, Col. Charles Malim, O.B.E., B.A., L.L.D.; industrialist; b. Toronto, Ont., 13 May 1911; s. Charles Victor Malim and Minnie Flavelle H.; e. Univ. of Toronto Sch.; Univ. of Toronto, B.A. 1931; m. Constance Hope Magee, 10 Sept. 1947; children: Stephanie Constance Hope Magee Brady, Charles Malim Victor, Debora Mary Malim; CHRMN., HARDING CARPETS Ltd.; Dir., Toronto Dominion Bank; Confederation Life Insurance Co.; at start of 2nd World War joined 54th R.C.A. Batty. as Lieutenant, serving overseas in England, France and Italy with 1st Candn. Divn., 4th Candn. Armoured Divn., 1st Candn. Corps; and in Can. as Chief Instr., R.M.C., Kingston, Ont., retiring with rank Col. 1945; Past Pres., Candn. Carpet Inst.; Past Chrmn., Candn. Textiles Inst.; Governing Council, Univ. of Toronto; mem., Past Chrm., Kappa Alpha; Anglican; recreations: skiing, fishing, shooting, tennis; Clubs: Toronto; Toronto Golf; York; Queen's; Badminton & Racquet; Big Point; Home: 48 Rosedale Road, Toronto, Ont. M4W2P6; Office: 35 Worcester Rd., Rexdale, Ont. M9W 1K9

HARDING, Herbert Holt; executive; b. Montreal, P.Q., 16 Dec. 1915; s. Howard and Sarah (Holt) H.; e. Pub. & High Schs., Montreal, P.Q.; Montreal Tech. Inst.; Sir Geo. Williams Univ.; McGill Univ.; m. late Jessie Morris, 14 Aug. 1943; children: John, Patricia; 2ndly, Jean Thelma Doe, 27 Apl. 1974; PRES. & GEN. MGR., CANDN. CARDWELL CO. since 1 Dec. 1963; assoc. with Cardwell Westinghouse Co., and Universal Railway Devices, Chicago, Ill.; joined present Co. in 1937; apptd. Vice-Pres., 1949; mem., Am. Soc. Mech. Engrs.; Am. Soc. Testing Metals; Anglican; Freemason (Karnak Temple); recreations: swimming, golf, curling; Clubs: St. George Kiwanis; Engineers (Montreal); Candn. Railway; Home: 1432 de la Montagne St., Apt. 1801, Montreal, Que. H3G 2M4; Office: 1875 46 Ave., Lachine, Que., H8T 2N8

HARDISTY, A. Pamela, B.A., M.L.S.; library consultant; b. Winnipeg, Man., 1 Nov. 1919; d. late Freda (Priestley) and Reginald H.; e. Univ. of Manitoba, B.A. 1941; Univ. of Toronto, B.L.S. 1947, M.L.S. 1954; unm.; ASST. PARLTY LIBRARIAN 1962-80; previously, to which was Assistant Director of Reference Services, National Library 1958-62; Ref. Librarian there, 1953-58; with Toronto Public Library, Reference Division, 1947-53; Publication: "Publications of the Canadian Parliament"; contrib. to prof. journals; member Canadian Association of Law Libraries (President 1975-77); Canadian Library Association; Beta Phi Mu; United Church; recreations: reading, photography, travel; Club: Chelsea Zonta; Office: 3340 Albion Rd., Ottawa, Ont. K1A 0A9

HARDMAN, Gilbert James, F.R.I.C.S.; company president; b. Manchester, Eng., 4 Dec. 1923; s. Arthur and Mary Elizabeth (Delaney) H.; m. Audrie, d. Alfred Small, W. Vancouver, B.C., 7 March 1953; two d., Amanda Jane, Stephanie Ann; President, British Columbia Place Ltd.; served with R.E. and Queen Victoria's Own Madras Sappers and Miners, in India, Burma, Malaya, Java, 1942-46; comnd. 1943; mem., The Nat. Design Council; Anglican; recreations: golf, swimming, scuba diving, sailing; Clubs: Capilano Golf; Vancouver; Pacific Union (San Francisco); Home: 4490 Marine Dr., West Vancouver, B.C. V7W 2N9;

HARDWICK, David Francis, M.D.; educator; b. Vancouver, B.C. 24 Jan. 1934; s. late Walter Henry Wilmot and Iris Lillian (Hyndman) H.; e. Univ. of B.C. M.D. 1957; Cert. Pathol. 1965; m. Margaret McArthur d. late Robert Lang, Vancouver, B.C. 22 Aug. 1956; children: Margaret Frances, Heather Iris, David James; PROF. AND HEAD OF PATHOL. UNIV. OF B.C. since 1976; Dir. Labs. Vancouver Gen. Hosp. since 1976; Chief of Med. Staff Children's Hosp. since 1969; residencies Montreal Gen., Vancouver Gen., Children's Los Angeles 1957-65; Clin. Instr. Univ. S. Cal. and Univ. of B.C. 1960-64; Asst. Prof. Univ. of B.C. 1965, Assoc. Prof. 1969, Prof. of Pathol. 1974; Pediatric Pathol. Vancouver Gen. Hosp. and Children's Hosp. 1965-69; Dir. Children's Hosp. and Pediatric Pathol. Vancouver Gen. Hosp. 1969-76; rec'd Queen's Silver Jubilee Medal 1978; publisher B.C. Geog. Series, Candn. Culture Series, Tantalus Research Ltd.; co-ed. 'Intermediary Metabolism of the Liver' 1973; author or co-author numerous articles prof. journs.; Founding mem., Dir. Electors' Action Movement 1964-71; Past Pres. Pediatric Pathol.; mem. Candn. Med. Assn.; B.C. Med. Assn. and other med. assns.; Protestant; recreations: backpacking, skiing; Home: 1260 W. King Edward Ave., Vancouver, B.C. V6H 1Z7; Office: 2075 Wesbrook Pl., Vancouver, B.C. V6T 1W5.

HARDY, Christian, B.A., M.Soc.Sc.; diplomat; b. Montreal, Que., 7 May 1923; s. Alphonse and Augustine (D'Auteuil) H.; e. Jesuits Coll., Quebec City, 1936-43; Laval Univ., B.A. 1943, B.Soc.Sc. 1945, M.Soc.Sc. (Sociol.) 1946; m. Henriette, d. late Dr. H. A. Houle, 4 Sept. 1948; three d., Christiane, Micheline, Marie-Josée; joined Dept. of External Affairs as Foreign Service Offr., 1947; Vice-Consul, Chicago, 1951-54; 2nd Secy. and subsequently 1st Secy., Rio de Janeiro, 1954-57; 1st Secy. and then Counsellor, Paris, 1960-63; Head, Personnel Operations Div. of Dept., Ottawa, 1963-67; Ambassador to Lebanon, Syria and Jordan, 1967; Ambassador to Brazil 1970; Ambassador to Algeria 1971; Dir., Bureau of Personnel, Dept. of External Affairs; Depy. High Commr., London 1975; Ambassador to Spain 1981; Chrmn., Bd. of Trustees St. Gabriel's Sch., Gloucester Twp., Ont., 1959-60; mem. Bd. of Trustees, Gloucester Twp. High Sch. Bd., 1964-67; mem., Prof. Assn. Foreign Service Offrs.; R. Catholic; recreations: reading, collecting antique books and maps,

music; Office: Embajada de Canada, Aparatado 587, Spain.

HARDY, (Norman E.) Peter; company officer; b. Toronto, Ont., 4 Jan. 1917; s. George and Myrtle (Dunsmore) H.; e. Public Schs., Toronto, Ont.; Pickering Coll., Newmarket, Ont.; m. Dorothy, d. John Walter, 6 April 1939; two d. Eleanor Gayle, Beverley Georgine; CHRMN. OF BD., JOHN LABATT LTD. (former Pres.); Dir., Brascan Ltd.; Noma Ind. Ltd.; Vice Chrm., Toronto Blue Jays Baseball Club; Chrmn., Ont. Racing Commission; began career with Hardy Cartage Co. Ltd., 1935; Brewers' Warehousing Co. Ltd., 1948-49; joined present firm in May 1949 as Mgr. of Toronto Brewery; apptd. Gen. Mgr. (Ont. Div.) 1956 and Vice-Pres. Beverages Div., 1959; served in 2nd World War with R.C.N.V.R., Lieut.; mem. St. Georges Soc.; recreation: golf; Clubs: The London; Mississauga Golf & Country; London Hunt & Country; Granite; Primrose; Home: 597 Cranbrook Rd., #52, London, Ont. N6K 2Y4; Office: 451 Ridout St. N., London, Ont.

HARDY, Robert Macdonald, O.C. (1974), D.Sc., F.R.S.C.; consulting civil engr.; b. Winnipeg, Man., 25 Sept. 1906; s. Robert and Winnifred H.; e. Univ. of Man., B.Sc. (C.E.) 1929, D.Sc., 1957; McGill Univ., M.Sc. 1930; Univ. of Mich. (summer session) 1932-33; Harvard Univ. 1939-40; Royal Military Col. of Can., D.Sc., 1972; m. France V., d. H. De Savoye, 23 Aug. 1939; children: Robert, George, John; CHRMN. OF BD., HARDY ASSOC. (1978) LTD.; Prof. Emeritus, Univ. of Alberta; Dean of Engineering and Prof. of Civil Engn., Univ. of Alberta, 1944-59, 1963-71; mem., Research Council of Alta.; temporarily with Candn. Indust. Ltd., Montreal, 1937; Defence Indust. Ltd., there 1940; Aluminum Co. of Can. Ltd., 1941-42; served in Reserve Army with Roy. Candn. Engrs. 1938-41, with rank of Capt.; with R.C.A.F.; Sqdn. Ldr. (Non-Active) 1942-45; Univ. of Alberta, LL.D. 1957; mem., Assn. Prof. Engrs. Geol. and Geoph. of Alta. (Past Pres. and Assn.); Alta. Land Surveyors' Assn. (Past Pres.); Am. Soc. of Civil Engrs. (M.); Fellow Engr. Instit. of Can.; Assoc. Prof. Engrs. of Man.; Assoc. Consulting Engrs. of Can.; Officer of Order of Can. 1974; Gold Medal of Can. Council of Prof. Engrs. 1973; Achievemend Awd. of Prov. of Alta. 1974; A.F. Legget Awd. of Can. Geot. Soc. 1971; Centennial Medal of Can. 1967; Centennial Awd. of Assoc. Prof. Engrs. Geol. and Geoph. of Alta. 1968; Julian C Smith Medal of Engr. Inst. of Can. 1977; numerous articles in Can. Prof. journalsl dealing with Geotechnical Engr.; Freemason; Unitarian; Club: Mayfair Golf & Country; Home: 11615 Edinboro Rd., Edmonton, Alta. T6G 1Z7

HARE, Frederick Kenneth, B. Sc., Ph.D., O.C., F.R.S.C. (1968), Hon. LL.D. (Queen's Univ. 1964, Univ. of Western Ont. 1968, and Trent Univ., 1979), Hon. D.Sc. (McGill 1969, Adelaide 1974, Yort Univ., 1978); b. Wylye, England, 5 Feb. 1919; s. Frederick Eli and Irene (Smith) H.; e. Windsor Sch., Eng.; King's Coll., Univ. of London, B.Sc. (Special) (1st Class Hons. in Geog.) 1939; Univ. of Montreal, Ph.D. (Geog.) 1950; two s., Christopher, Robin; one d. Elissa Beatrice: PROF. OF GEOG. AND PHYSICS, UNIV. OF TORONTO, since 1969 and Provost of Trinity Coll. 1979- ; Chrmn. Cdn. Climate Planning Bd. 1979- ; Dir., Resources for the Future Inc. 1968-80; Dir.-Gen. of Research Coordination, Environment-Canada (on leave from U. of T. 1972-73); Lectr. Univ. of Manchester 1940-41; Operational Forecaster in Air Min., 1941-45; Asst. Prof. of Geog., McGill Univ., 1946, and subsequently Prof. and Chrmn., Dept. of Geog. and Meteorology; Warden of Peterson Residences, 1946-50; Dean, Faculty of Arts & Science, 1962-64; Prof. of Geog., King's Coll., Univ. of London, 1964-66; Master of Birkbeck Coll. there, 1966-68; Pres., Univ. of B.C. 1968 resigning 1969; Dir., Inst. for Environmental Studies, Univ. of Toronto, 1974-79; author of "The Restless Atmosphere" (textbook on climatology), 1953; "On University Freedom", co-author of "Climate Canada" (2nd ed., 1979); 1968; many articles on climatol., meteorol, and geog. in scient. journs.; Co-Chmn., Nat. Acad. of Sci. (U.S.A.); Roy. Soc. Can., Study of Acid Precipitation, 1980- ; mem., Bd. of Gov., Trinity Coll. Sch. 1979- ; mem., Nat. Research Council of Can., 1962-64; Am. Meteorol. Soc. (Council); Chrmn. of Bd., Arctic Inst. of N. Am., 1963; Hon. Fellow, Am. Geog. Soc., 1962; Councillor, Assn. of Am. Geogs. and Candn. Assn. of Geogs., 1964; Chrmn. Adv. Comte. on Canadian Urban Demonstration Program; Special Program on the Ecosciences, NATO, 1975; awards: Fellow, King's Coll. 1967; Patterson Medal, Canadian Meteorological Service 1973; Massey Medal, Roy. Candn. Geog. Soc. 1974; Patron's Medal of Royal Geog. Soc. of U.K. 1977; Sigma Xi; Anglican; recreations: music, photography; Address: Provost's Lodge, Trinity Coll., 6 Hoskin Ave., Toronto, Ont. M5S 1H8

HARE, George E., B.Sc., M.A., Ph.D.; banker; b. Truro, N.S. 17 May 1941; e. Mount Allison Univ.; S. Ill. Univ.; B.Sc. 1963, M.A. 1965, Ph.D. 1970; m. Mary Joyce Crosby 7 June 1969; children: Rebecca, David; GEN. MGR. OPERATIONS, THE BANK OF NOVA SCOTIA; Dir., Hospital Computing Services of Ontario Inc.; Consultant, Canada Systems Group 1971-73; Mang. Consultant, Peat, Marwick & Partners 1974-77; joined present Bank 1977; Sigma Xi; Home: 51 Belvedere Blvd., Toronto, Ont. M8X 1K3; Office: 44 King St. W., Toronto, Ont. M5H 1H1

HARKNESS, Lieut.-Col. the Hon. Douglas Scott, P.C. (Can.) 1957, O.C.G.M., E.D., B.A.; farmer; b. Toronto, Ont., 29 Mar. 1903; s. William Keefer and Janet Douglas (Scott) H.; e. Central Coll., Calgary; Univ. of Alta., B.A.; m. Frances Elizabeth, d. James Blair MacMillan, Charlottetown and Calgary, 3 Aug. 1932; had one s. Kenneth Blair (deceased); served overseas (Italy and N.W. Europe) in World War 1940-45; Maj. and Lieut.-Col., Roy Candn. Arty.; R.O. 1945; with Reserve Army, Commdg. Offr., 41st Anti-Tank Regt. (S.P.), Roy. Candn. Arty.; 1st el. H. of C. for Calgary East, g.e. 1945, re-el. g.e. 1949; re-el. for Calgary N., g.e. 1953, 57, 58, 62, 63, 65 and for Calgary Centre g.e. 1968; Minister of Northern Affairs & Nat. Resources, June-Aug. 1957; Min. of Agric., Aug. 1957-Oct. 1960; apptd. Min. of Nat. Defence, 11 Oct. 1960; and resigned from Cabinet 4 Feb. 1963; past Chmn. Bd. Govs., Glenbow-Alberta Institute; P. Conservative; Presbyterian; Clubs: Ranchmen's (Calgary); Calgary Petroleum; Alberta Military Institute; Home: 716 Imperial Way S.W. Calgary, Alta. T2S 1N7

HARLAND, Harry Edward, B.S.Sc., F.S.A., insurance executive; b. Minnedosa, Man., 24 Sept. 1927; s. Thomas Edward and Florence Mabel (Millward) H.; e. Moorepark (Man.) High Sch.; Univ. of Man., B.Sc. 1951; m. Edith Phyllis Catherine, d. Herbert Budgen, Winnipeg, Man., 20 Jan. 1953; children: Carol Louise, Shelley Ruth, Mary Edith, Thomas Edward; SR. VICE PRESIDENT, CORPORATE RESOURCES GREAT-WEST LIFE ASSURANCE COMPANY, since 1980; joined present firm 1952; apptd. Supvr., Actuarial Gen., 1956; Actuarial Asst. 1956; Asst. Actuary 1957; Assoc. Actuary, Reports and Stat., 1961; Assoc. Actuary, 1965, Actuary 1970, Vice Pres. and Actuary 1970-73; Sr. Vice Pres., 1973-80; Fellow, Soc. of Actuaries; Candn. Inst. of Actuaries; mem. Internat. Actuarial Assoc.; Am. Acad. of Actuaries; Candn. Inst. Actuaries; Anglican; recreations: tennis, skiing, golf, canoeing; Clubs: St. Charles Country; Manitoba; Winnipeg Tennis; Home: 106 Aldershot Blvd., Winnipeg, Man. R3P 0E1; Office: 60 Osborne St., Winnipeg, Man. R3C 3A5

HARMAN, Eleanor, M.A.; publisher; retired; b. North Battleford, Sask., 14 Dec. 1909; d. J. Howard and Lily (Teskey) Harman; e. North Battleford Coll. Inst.; Regina Coll.; Univ. of Sask., B.A. 1929; University of Toronto, M.A. 1930; entered the publishing business with Clarke, Irwin and Company Limited, Toronto, Ontario, and served in various capacities on the editorial, promotional and business sides; was Edit. Asst. to the Pres. (Clarke,

Irwin), and to the Mgr. (Oxford University Press) before leaving to become Asst. Editor at Copp Clark Co.; joined Univ. of Toronto Press as Assoc. Editor and Production Mgr., 1946; Asst. Mgr., 1952; Asst. Dir. 1953; Assoc. Dir. 1970-75; Editor of "Scholarly Publishing", 1969-79; Publications: co-author "A Student's Workbook in Canadian History" 1946; "The Story of Canada" 1950; "Teacher's Manual to The Story of Canada" 1951; "Canada in N. America to 1800" 1960; "Canada in North America, 1800-1901" 1961; "The University as Publisher" (editor) 1961; "Canada in North America Since 1800" (co-author) 1967; "The Thesis and The Book" (co-editor) 1976; Queen's Jubilee Medal; Liberal; recreations: boating, swimming, hifi recordings; Address: Box 141, King City, Ont. L0G 1K0

HARNETTY, Peter, A.M., Ph.D.; educator; b. Eng. 6 June 1927; s. Edward and Anita (McKeon) H.; e. Univ. of B.C., B.A. 1953; Harvard Univ. A.M. 1954, Ph.D. 1958; m. Claire d. Ovide Demers 5 Sept. 1956; one s. Richard; PROF OF ASIAN STUDIES AND HIST., UNIV. OF B.C. 1971- ; Instr. in Hist. and Internat. Studies present Univ. 1958-61, Asst. Prof. 1961, Asst. Prof. of Asian Studies & Hist. 1962-65, Assoc. Prof. 1965-71, Head of Asian Studies 1975-80; Author "Imperialism and Free Trade: Lancashire and India in the Mid-Nineteenth Century" 1972; numerous articles learned journs.; served with Brit. and Indian Armies 1944-49; mem. Assn. Asian Studies; Econ. Hist. Assn.; Hist. Assn.; Shastri Indo-Candn. Inst. (Pres. 1970-71); recreations: hiking, skiing; Home: 3026 W. 34th Ave., Vancouver, B.C. V6N 2K2; Office: 1871 West Mall, Vancouver, B.C. V6T 1W5.

HARPER, Alex M., B.Sc., M.Sc., Ph.D.; research scientist; b. Lethbridge, Alta. 10 March 1926; e. Lethbridge (Alta.) Coll. Inst.; Univ. of Alta. (Gold Ring Extve. A Award 1948); Wash. State Univ.; m. Georgean Hirst; children: Bradley, Shawna, Paula, Liana; Research Officer, Sc. Service, Agric. Can. 1948-59; Research Scient. Research Br. Agric. Can. since 1959; Research Offr. Science Service Labs. Can. Dept. of Agric.; Dir. Lethbridge YMCA 1967-68; Lethbridge Boy Scout Comte. 1972-74; author numerous scient. and tech. papers; Pres. S. Alta. Br. Prof. Inst. Pub. Service of Can. 1967-68 (Secy.-Treas. 1966-67); mem. Entomol. Soc. Can.; Entomol. Soc. Am.; Entomol. Soc. Alta. (Secy. 1960, Dir. 1963, Treas. 1966, Secy. Treas. 1972-73, Vice Pres. 1974, Pres. 1975); Candn. Nature Assn.; Southern Alta. Art Gallery Assoc.; The Cdn. Club of Lethbridge; Writers' Guild of Alta; Dir., Lethbridge and District Japanese Garden Society; recreations: skiing, hiking, writing, reading; Home: 1127.— 29 St. 'A' South, Lethbridge, Alta. T1K 2Y2; Office: Research Station, Canada Agriculture, Lethbridge, Alta.

HARPER, Col. J. Ralph, O.B.E., C.St.J., T.D., K.L.J., F.R.S.A., F.S.A. Scot; consultant; b. Tientsin, N. China, 23 July 1907; e. Tientsin Grammar Sch., China; Rose Hill, Tunbridge Wells and Bedford, Eng.; m. Dorothy Ailsie Jean Coghlin (deceased), Montreal 1956; former Corp. Secy., Macdonald Tobacco Inc.; comnd. in Bedfordshire & Hertfordshire Regt., 16th Regt. Foot, Aug. 1926; to France 1939 in 4th Div.; Lt. Col. 1942 commanded 54 Div. Battle Sch. and 2nd Bn. Hertfordshire Regt.; Normandy D Day 1944 in command 9 Beach Assault group with 50 Div.; posted to command 101 Beach, Group Combined Operations. Apptd. Col. Commandant, C.T.C. Dundonald and commanded 22 Beach Bgde.; to Reserve 1954; Decorations incl. Ordre de la Liberation; Croix de Guerre avec Palme; Twice Mentioned in Despatches; Offr., Legion d'Honneur; Dir., T.C.F of Canada 1954 then with Distillers Co. (Edinburgh) Ltd. till retired 1968; Pres., Un. Services Club 1966-67; Montreal Un. Services Inst. 1967; Montreal Mil. & Maritime Museum 1966-69; St. Andrew's Soc., Montreal 1967-68; Citoyen d'Hon. de Ver-sur-Mer; Dir., Antiq. & Numis. Soc. Montreal; raised the old 78th Fraser Highlanders 1961, The Fort, St. Helen's Island (now Col. Cmdt. of the Regt.); author of "The Fighting Frasers" 1966; "The Fraser Highlanders" 1979; Clubs: Naval & Military (London, Eng.); Canadian; United Services; Forest & Stream; Home: 3425 Redpath St., Montreal, Que. H3G 2G2; Office: 1195 Sherbrooke St. West, Montreal, Que. H3A 1H9

HARPER, J. Russell, O.C. (1975), M.A., D.Litt., F.R.S.C.; art historian; b. Caledonia, Ont., 15 April 1914; s. Alexander T. and J. Evelyn (Taylor) H.; e. Hamilton (Ont.) Teachers Coll. (1932); McMaster Univ. (1934); Ont. Coll. of Art (evenings) 1938-42; Victoria Coll., Univ. of Toronto, B.A. 1947; Univ. of Toronto Grad School, M.A. 1949; D.Litt., Guelph; m. M. Elizabeth, d. Rev. John Goodchild, Cambridge, Eng., 12 May 1945; one d. Jennifer E.; Curator of Lee Coll., Hart House, Univ. of Toronto, 1947-50; Chief Cataloguer, Royal Ont. Museum, 1948-52; Archivist of N.B. Museum, Saint John, N.B., 1952-56; Curator of Lord Beaverbrook Art Coll., N.B., 1957-59; Apptd. Curator of Candn. Art, Nat. Gallery of Can., 1959; McCord Museum, McGill Univ., 1963-66; Prof., Sir George Williams Univ. 1967-79; winner of Royal Soc. Can. Fellowship for Research in Paris, 1956; Publications: "Portland Point, 4,000 Years of New Brunswick History"; "The Hart House Collections of Paintings"; "New Brunswick Newspaper Bibliography"; "Everyman's Canada"; "Painting in Canada: A History", 1966; "Portrait of a Period: The Notman Collection", 1967; "Early Painters and Engravers in Canada", 1970; "Paul Kane's Frontier", 1971; "A People's Art", 1974; "Wm. G.R. Hind", 1976; "Krieghoff" 1979; and numerous articles; served in 2nd World War with R.C.A.F., 1942-46; mem., Royal Soc. of Can.; Presbyterian; recreations: philately, print collecting; Home: P.O. Box 61, South Lancaster, Ont. K0C 2C0

HARPER, Robert J.C., M.A., Ph.D., F.R.S.A. 1975; educator; b. Greenock, Scot., 29 March 1927; s. Abram Craig and Anne (Berryman) H.; e. Holmscroft Sch. and Greenock High Sch., 1945; St. Andrews Univ., M.A. 1951; Edinburgh Univ., M.A. 1953, Ph.D. 1964; m. Margaret Everilde, d. late Thomas Kirk, 22 Dec. 1953 four s., Paul, Alan, David, Michael; PROF., DEPT. OF COMMUNICATION STUDIES, SIMON FRASER UNIV. since 1973 and Senator there 1966-71; Clin. Psychol., Prov. Mental Hosp., Alta., 1953-54, Lectr. and Dir., Educ. Clinic, Univ. of Alta., 1954, Asst. Prof. 1956, Assoc. Prof. 1962; Consulting Clin. Psychol., Dept. of Veterans' Affairs, Univ. Hosp., Edmonton, 1954; Prof. and Dir. of Studies, Behavioral Science Foundations, Simon Fraser Univ., 1965, Chrmn. of Dept. 1965 till resigned 1972; Hon. Lectr. and Examiner in Psychol. and Ethics, Royal Coll. of Nursing, London and Edinburgh, 1959-60; served with R.A.F. 1945-48; R.A.F.V.R. St. Andrews Univ. Air Sqdn. 1949-51, Edinburgh Univ. Air Sqdn, 1951-53; author, "Cognitive Processes", 1964; also numerous prof. papers, articles and addresses; mem. Candn. Assn. Univ. Teachers; Presbyterian; recreations: skiing, fishing, golf; Office: Burnaby, B.C.

HARRIES, Hu, M.S., M.A., Ph.D., F.R.E.S.; economist; educator; b. Strathmore, Alta., 8 Dec. 1921; s. Thomas Batin and Marion Emily (Osborne) H.; e. Univ. of Alta., B.Sc.; Univ. of Iowa, M.S., Ph.D.; Univ. of Toronto, M.A.; m. Joyce Maxine, d. late B. T. Farrell, 8 Aug., 1948; children: Bruce F., Jody Anne, Lori J., Jeffrey K., Daniel H.; PRESIDENT, HU HARRIES & ASSOC. LTD. (estbd. 1950); Pres., Ehrlick Transport Ltd.; Western Turf Express Ltd.; Stampede Cattle Station Ltd.; Hidden Bar Ranch; Consultant, World Bank (missions to Korea, Algeria, Iran, Tunisia, Pakistan), Govts. of Alta., B.C., Man. and to several Candn. firms; Ald., City of Edmonton, 1952-58; M.P. 1968-72; Prof. and former Dean, Faculty of Business, Univ. of Alta.; mem., Extve. Financial Inst.; Am. Econ. Assn.; Protestant; recreations: riding, hunting; Clubs: Ranchmen's (Calgary); Petroleum; Home: 8727 — 120 St., Edmonton, Alta. T6G 1X4; Office: 1418 — 10025 Jasper Ave., Edmonton, Alta. T5J 1S6

HARRIGAN, Kenneth William James, B.A.; executive; b. Chatham, Ont. 27 Sept. 1927; s. Charles Angus and Olga Jean (Wallace) H.; e. Univ. of W. Ont. B.A. 1951; m. Margaret Jean Macpherson 18 June 1955; children: Tara Lynne, Stephen Charles; PRESIDENT, CHIEF EXTVE. OFFR. AND DIR., FORD MOTOR CO. OF CANADA LTD. 1981- ; Dir. Ford Motor Co. of Australia Ltd.; Ford Sales Co. of Australia Ltd.; Ford Motor Co. of N.Z. Ltd.; Ford Motor Co. of South Africa (Proprietary) Ltd.; joined present Co. 1951; Gen. Field Mgr. Edmonton 1962, Regional City Mgr. Vancouver 1963, Asst. Regional Mgr. Toronto 1964, Regional Mgr. Toronto 1965, Gen. Sales Mgr. Central Office Oakville 1968, Staff Dir. Sales & Marketing Ford Asia-Pacific Inc. Australia 1972-73, Group Dir. S. European Sales Ford of Europe, 1973, Vice Pres. Truck Sales & Marketing Ford of Europe 1977, Vice Pres., Gen. Mgr. Sales, Ford of Canada, Oakville 1978-81; mem. Business Council on Nat. Issues; Gov. Council Gov. Gen.'s First Candn. Study Conf. 1983; Dir. Motor Vehicle Mfrs.' Assn.; mem. Candn. Chamber Comm.; Clubs: Mississauga Golf & Country; Canadian; Empire; Home: One Maple Grove Dr., Oakville, Ont. L6J 4T8; Office: The Canadian Rd., Oakville, Ont. L6J 5E4.

HARRINGTON, Arthur Russell, B.Eng., D.Eng., D.C.L.; b. Sydney, N.S., 28 June 1914; s. Arthur Lloyd and Ethel Tryphena (Cunningham) H.; e. Halifax (N.S.) Acad., grad. 1931; Dalhousie Univ., (Engn.), 1934; N.S. Tech. Coll., B.Eng., 1936, D.Eng. 1968; m. Beatrice Marian, d. late Harry Dean, Halifax, N.S., 17 Sept. 1938; one s. Arthur Gordon; Vice Pres. and Dir., N.S. Savings and Loan Co.; Eastern Halifax Developments Ltd.; Dir., Central & Nova Scotia Trust Co.; Durham Leaseholds Ltd.; Chrmn., Atlantic Region Man Training Center Ltd.; Vice Chrmn., Atlantic Industrial Research Institute; joined Nova Scotia Light and Power Company Limited as Jr. Engr., 1936; apptd. Asst. Mgr., 1951, Mgr., 1958; apptd. to Bd. of Dir., 1960; Vice Pres., 1961; Pres. and Gen. Mgr. 1962-72; Gov., Nova Scotia Tech. College; Director, Maritimes Div., Candn. Nat. Inst. for the Blind; Halifax Adv. Council, Salvation Army; Past Pres. and Dir., Halifax Y.M.C.A. (now Trustee); Dir., N.S. Labour Relations Bd.; Chrmn., N.S. Vol. Planning Bd.; Chrmn., Atlantic Region Mgmt. Training Center; mem. Assn. Prof. Engrs. N.S.; Fellow, Engn. Inst. Can.; D.C.L. Acadia 1969; Baptist; recreations: fishing, swimming; Clubs: Halifax; Waegwoltic; Home: 2350 Armcrescent West, Halifax, N.S. B3L 3E3

HARRINGTON, Conrad F., C.D., B.A., B.C.L., KStJ, C.T.C.I.; company executive; b. Montreal, Que., 8 Aug. 1912; s. late Conrad Dawson and Muriel Theodora (Fetherstonhaugh) H.; e. Selwyn House, Montreal; Trinity Coll. Sch., Port Hope, Ont.; McGill Univ., B.A. 1933, B.C.L. 1936; Univ. of Besancon (France), 1936-37; m. Joan Roy, d. late John O. Hastings, Montreal, Que., 6 Aug. 1940; one s. Conrad; two d., Jill, Susan; FORMER CHRMN. OF EXTVE. COMTE., THE ROYAL TRUST CO.; Chrmn., Redpath Industries Ltd.; Glaxo Canada Ltd.; Dir., The Royal Trust Co. and subsidiaries; Gerling Global Gen. Ins. Co.; Gerling Global Reins. Co.; Gerling Global Life Insurance Co.; R. L. Crain Limited; Consumers Glass Company Ltd.; MPG Investment Corp. Ltd.; Stone and Webster Canada Limited; Governor, Montreal Gen. Hosp.; practised law in Montreal with Phelan, Fleet, Robertson & Abott, 1937-39; called to the Bar of Que. 1937; joined Estates Dept. of Royal Trust Co. 1945; apptd. Mgr., Business Devel. Dept., 1946-50; Asst. to Gen. Mgr., 1951-52; Mgr., Toronto Br., 1952; Asst. Gen. Mgr. at Toronto, 1954; Supvr. of Ont. Brs., 1955; Vice Pres. 1957; el. a Dir. 1960; Vice-Pres. and Gen. Mgr. 1963; Extve. Vice-Pres. 1965; served in 2nd World War with R.C.A., 1940-45; U.K., Italy, N.W. Europe, with 5, 2, 17 Candn. Field Regts., twice Mentioned in Despatches; Reserve Army, 1945-51; O.C. 37 Candn. Field Regt.; Hon. Lt. Col., 2nd Field Regt. RCA (M); Life Gov., Trinity Coll. Sch., Port Hope, Ont.; Gov., Candn.

Welfare Council; Apptd. Chancellor of McGill Univ. 1976; Hon. Dir., Que. Council, St. John Ambulance; Hon. Vice-Pres., Montreal Regional Council, Boy Scouts of Can.; Past Pres., McGill Grads. Soc.; Councillor, Montreal Museum of Fine Arts; Chmn., McCord Museum; Chrmn. Toronto United Appeal Campaign, 1958; Pres., Trust Co.'s Assn. Can., 1958-59, 1970-71; Zeta Psi; Anglican; recreations: golf, reading, painting; Clubs: York (Toronto); Toronto; Toronto Golf; University (Montreal); St. James's; Mt. Bruno Golf; Mount Royal; Forest & Stream; Home: 556 Lansdowne Ave., Westmount, Que. H3Y 2V6; Office: 630 Dorchester Blvd. W., Montreal, Que. H3B 1S6

HARRINGTON, John Eric; industrialist; b. Montreal, P.Q., 28 Aug. 1914; s. late Conrad Dawson and late Muriel Theodora (Featherstonhaugh) H.; e. Selwyn House Sch., Montreal; Trinity Coll. Sch., Port Hope, Ont.; L'Institution Sillig, Switzerland; Royal Mil. Coll.; m. Hazel Peace, d. John Ogilvy Hastings, Montreal. P.Q., 2 Nov. 1939; three d.; DIR., GRANADA TV RENTAL LTD. Dir., Vickers Limited, London; Lloyd's Register of Shipping; Chrmn., Crabtree-Vickers (Canada) Ltd., Toronto; Vickers America Inv.; served in 2nd World War, 1939-45 with Royal Candn. Navy, commanding several ships; retired with rank of Lieut.-Commdr.; mem., Engn. Inst. of Can.; Bd. of Mang., Montreal Children's Hosp.; Anglican; recreations: golf, fishing; Clubs: St. James's; Mount Royal; Mount Bruno Country; Home: 3030 Trafalgar Ave., Montreal, Que. H3Y 1H4; Office: 5000 Notre Dame St. E., Montreal, Que. H1V 2B4

HARRINGTON, John Maurice, M.A., M.Sc. (Econ.); diplomat; b. Cromer, Eng., 14 March 1924; s. late Maurice Joseph and Dorothy Deacon (Hollyman) H.; e. St. Illtyd's Coll., Cardiff, Wales; Central Coll., London, Ont.; Univ. of W. Ont., B.A. 1946, M.A. 1947; London Sch. of Econ. and Pol. Science, M.Sc. (Econ.) 1949; m. Dorothy Irene, d. late Sylvester Pocock 1950; one s. Douglas John; DIRECTOR, ACADEMIC RELATIONS, DEPT. OF EXTERNAL AFFAIRS OTTAWA since 1979; Asst. Prof. Econ., St. Francis Xavier Univ. 1949; joined Dept. External Affairs 1950, Third Secy., Belgrade 1952, Second Secy. 1954; Econ. Div., Ottawa 1955-57; attended ICAO Assembly, Caracas 1956 (Adviser); Second Secy., Candn. High Comn., London 1958, First Secy. 1960-62; Candn. Observer, First Session U.N. Econ. Comn. for Africa, Tangier, Morocco 1960, Second Session, Addis Ababa 1961; with Econ. Div., Head Comm. Policy Sec., Ottawa 1962-65; Adviser, U.N. Gen. Assembly, N.Y. 1962; Counsellor, Candn. Embassy Tokyo 1965-68; mem. Del. to Inaugural Meeting, Asian Development Bank, Tokyo 1966 and to U.N. Econ. Comn. for Asia and Far E. Sept. 1966; Special Ambassador, Inauguration of Pres. Park, Republic of Korea, Seoul 1967; Depy. Head, Far E. Div. 1968, Dir. Pacific Div. 1970; mem. Science and Tech. Mission to Japan, Feb. 1972; High Commr. to Jamaica 1972-76; Foreign Service Visitor, Univ. of Toronto (Trinity Coll.) 1976-77; Depy. Cmdt., Nat. Defence, Coll., 1977-79; R. Catholic; recreations: photography, swimming, gardening; Home: 37 Belvedere Cres., Ottawa, Ont. K1M 0E5; Office: Lester B. Pearson Bldg. 1 Sussex Dr., Ottawa, Ont. K1M 0G2

HARRIS, Charles Alexander, B.A.; public affairs consultant; b. Toronto, Ontario, 10 March 1920; s. Charles Alexander and Arline (Rouget) H.; e. University of Toronto, B.A. (Modern History) 1947; m. Bernice, d. G. L. Adam, Toronto, Ont., 9 Oct. 1942; children: David, Robert, Reed; PRESIDENT CHAIRMAN, HARRIS HEAL LTD. since 1980; Reporter, Toronto "Globe & Mail", 1937-41; joined C.B.C. as a Producer in Talks and Public Affairs Dept., May 1947; apptd. Asst. to Dir., of Television, C.B.C. Toronto, 1950; joined Candn. Mfrs. Assn. as Public Relations Offr. 1951; Asst. to Dir. of Public Relations, Candn. Nat. Railways, Montreal, 1952, Asst. Dir., 1956, Dir. 1959, Vice-President 1970; joined Bell Canada as

Vice-Pres., Public Relations, Montreal, 1972; Vice-Pres., Public and Environmental Affairs, 1973; served in R.C.A.F., 1941-45, rank Flying Offr.; Past Pres., Candn. Public Relations Soc. (rec'd. Nat. Award of Attainment 1966); Pub. Relations Soc. Am.; mem. emeritus, Conf. Bd. of Canada Council of Public Affairs Executives; recreations: sailing, photography; Clubs: St. James's; Toronto Press; Advertising & Sales Executives; Home: 1400 Dixie Rd., Ste. 601, Mississauga, Ont., L5E 3E1; Office: 1 Yonge St., Ste. 2106, Toronto Ont, M5E 1E5

HARRIS, Geoffrey Thomas; retired life insurance executive; b. Edmonton, Alta., 16 Sept. 1912; s. Thomas and Florence A. (Young) H.; e. Queen Alexandra Elem. and Strathcona High Schs., Edmonton, Alta.; Candn. Army Staff Coll., 1945; Univ. of W. Ont., Mang. Training Course 1967; m. Norma Amelia, d. Verner Winfield Smith, 15 Aug. 1947; children: Thomas Claude, Leslie Margaret, Beverley Ann, Terry Kathleen, Nancy Elizabeth; Rep. of Mutual Life of Can. 1937-46; Mgr. 1947-50; Supt. of Field Training 1951-52; Supt. of Agencies 1953-64; Sr. Supt. Agency Operations 1965-68; Vice-Pres., K.-W. I/C Agencies 1968; Symphony Orchestra; Sr. Vice Pres. and Dir. of Marketing, Mutual Life of Can. 1969-78 (ret.); Dir., Guelph Spring Festival; Gov., Renison college (Univ. of Waterloo); enlisted as Private in Inf. 1939; rank Maj. 1945; P. Conservative; Anglican; recreations: golf, curling, swimming, photography; Club: Westmount Golf & Country; Home: 266 Stanley Dr., Waterloo, Ont. N2L 1J1

HARRIS, Henry Silton, M.A., Ph.D.; university professor; b. Brighton, England, 11 April 1926; s. Henry and Amy Adelaide (Sampson) H.; e. Hove (Sussex) Co. Sch.; Lancing Coll., Shoreham, Sussex; St. Edmund Hall, Oxford, B.A. 1949, M.A. 1952; Northwestern Univ.; Univ. of Illinois, Ph.D. 1954; m. Ruth Evalene, d. Henry A. Koski, Chassell, Mich., 20 June 1952; children: Carol Elizabeth, David Neville Silton, Peter Geoffrey, Anne Cassandra; PROF. OF PHILOS., YORK UNIV., since 1965; Instr. in Philos., Ohio State Univ., 1954-57; Asst. and Assoc. Prof. of Philos., Univ. of Illinois, 1957-62; Assoc. Prof. of Philos., York Univ., 1962; served in 2nd World War with Brit. Army; Signalman, Royal Signals, 1944-45; Publications: "The Social Philosophy of Giovanni Gentile", 1960; "Hegel's Development I", 1972; mem., Am. Philos. Assn.; Candn. Philos. Assn.; Hegel Soc. of Am.; Int. Hegel Vereinigung; Home: 429 Glencairn Ave., Toronto, Ont. M5N 1V4

HARRIS, Milton E., B.Com.; construction executive; b. Detroit, Mich. 26 July 1927; s. Sam Harris; e. St. George's Sch. and Central Coll. Inst. London, Ont. 1945; Univ. of Toronto B.Com. 1949; m. d. of Joseph Brody 4 Sept. 1949; children: Judith Rachel, Naomi Ruth, David Eli; PRES., HARRIS STEEL GROUP INC.; Pres. Milton Harris Investments Ltd.; Livingston Industries; Air Canada; Pres. London Lib. Assn.; Chrmn. Finance Comte. Nat. Lib. Extve.; mem. London Bd. Educ.; Pres. London Jewish Community Council; Toronto Jewish Cong.; Chrmn. Ont. Jewish Cong.; Vice Pres. Candn. Jewish Cong.; mem. Senate Univ. of W. Ont.; Dir. Mount Sinai Hosp.; Pres. Reinforcing Steel Inst. Ont.; Internat. Pres. Upsilon Lambda Phi; Toronto Pres. Beta Sigma Rho; Liberal; Jewish; recreations: squash, sailing, reading, history; Home: 28 Fifeshire Rd., Toronto, Ont. M2L 2G5; Office: 1 First Canadian Place (P.O. Box 163), Suite 6455, Toronto, Ont. M5X 1C7.

HARRIS, Nicholas George; publisher; b. Salisbury, Eng. 8 Sept. 1939; s. George Ivan and Phyllis Dorothy (Porter) H.; e. Bishop Wordsworths Sch. Salisbury, Eng. 1957; m. Margaret Jane d. Lewis Townsend Darling, Hammond River, N.B. 3 Feb. 1968; children: Nicola Jane, Gregory Jack; PRESIDENT, CHRMN. AND CHIEF EXTVE. OFFR., COLLINS PUBLISHERS 1975- ; Dir., Pan Books; Sales Rep. present Co. London, Eng. 1963, Montreal

1967, Sales Mgr. Montreal 1970, Sales Dir. Toronto 1973, Extve. Vice Pres. 1974-75; served with Brit. Army 1958-63, rank Lt.; mem. Candn. Book Publishers Council; Anglican; recreations: skiing, tennis; Club: Donalda; Office: 100 Lesmill Rd., Don Mills, Ont. M3B 2T5.

HARRIS, Richard Colebrook, B.A., M.Sc., Ph.D.; educator; b. Vancouver, B.C. 4 July 1936; s. Richard Colebrook and Ellen Gertrude (Code) H.; e. Univ. of B.C. B.A. 1958; Univ. of Wis. M.Sc. 1962, Ph.D. 1964; m. Muriel Joyce d. Douglas Watney, Vancouver, B.C. 6 June 1964; children: Douglas, Colin, Rachel; PROF. OF GEOG., UNIV. OF B.C.; author "The Seigneurial System in Early Canada" 1966; "Canada Before Confederation" 1974; numerous articles on European settlement in early Can. particularly Que. and B.C.; Home: 6660 Wiltshire St., Vancouver, B.C. V6P 5G7; Office: 2075 Wesbrook Mall, Vancouver, B.C. V6T 1W5

HARRIS, Richard Eugene, B.Sc.; petroleum executive; b. Edmonton, Alta., 16 Aug. 1921; s. Thomas and Florence (Young) H.; e. Univ. of Alta., B.Sc. (Chem. Engn.) 1944; m. Marjorie E. Aylward, 2 Dec. 1978; children: (by previous m.) Ann, Audrey, David; VICE PRES., HUMAN RESOURCES DEPT. & REALTY DEPT., GULF CANADA LTD.,since 1975; Dir.; Sulconam Inc. joined present Co. (then B.A. Oil Co. Ltd.) as Asst. Chem., Calgary Refinery, 1944; process Engr., Mfg. Dept., Toronto H.O., 1948; Asst. Mgr., Moose Jaw Refinery, 1954; Mgr.; Edmonton Refinery, 1957; Mfg. Dept., Toronto H.O., 1961; Gen. Mgr. of Dept., 1963 and of Crude & Products Supply Dept., 1965; Vice Pres., Crude & Products, Supply, Pipelines, Transport. 1966; Vice Pres., Refining Dept., 1970-75; mem., Engn. Inst. Can.; Assn. Prof. Engrs. Prov. Ont.; recreations: golf, curling, skiing; Clubs: Thornhill Country; Engineers'; Home: 31 Danville Dr., Willowdale, Ont. M2P 1H7; Office: 130 Adelaide St. W., Toronto, Ont. M5H 3R6

HARRIS, Richard William; executive; b. Aylesford, N.S., 13 Oct. 1899; s. Frederick E. and Agnes M. (MacIntyre) H.; e. Pub. Schs. and Maritime Business Coll., m. Helen M. Outhit; children: Helen, Elizabeth, Richard B.; PRESIDENT AND DIR., ALLIED INVESTMENTS LTD.; Dir., Amalgamated Investments Ltd.; Dir., Can-Amera Oil Sands Develop. Co.; mem., Halifax Bd. of Trade; Clubs: Lauderdale Yacht (Fla.); Homes: Tantallon, N.S., B0J 3J0 and 1922 S. Ocean Lane, Ft. Lauderdale, Fla. 33316

HARRIS, Roland Allen, O.B.E., B.A.; management consultant; b. Toronto, Ont., 20 Nov. 1906; s. Roland Caldwell and Alice Mary (Ingram) H.; e. Univ. of Toronto Schs., Sr. Matric. 1923; Univ. Coll., Univ. of Toronto, B.A. (Pol. Sci.) 1928; Imperial Staff Coll., Camberley, Eng., 1943; m. Dae, d. late F.H.B. Lyon, 23 Sept. 1933; children: Molly Dae, John Roland; Dir., Canadian General Tower Ltd.; Davis and Henderson Ltd.; Whitman Golden Ltd.; joined A. McKim Ltd. as Asst. Acct. Extve., 1928; apptd. Salesman, Pub. Dir. & Adv. Mgr., DeForest Crosley Ltd., Toronto, 1929; Asst. to Sales Mgr., Woods Underwear Co. (Toronto), 1933; Sales Mgr., Dent. Allcroft & Co. Ltd. (Eng.), 1937; Gen. Mgr., C. H. Smith Co. Ltd., Windsor, 1945, Mang. Dir. 1949; Dir., Gordon Mackay and Stores Ltd., 1949 and Dir. i/c Retail Divs., 1954; Vice Pres., 1955; Pres., Walker Stores Ltd., 1957; Pres., Canada Cycle & Motor Co. Ltd. 1959-61; Vice-Pres., Marketing B.F. Goodrich Canada Ltd., 1961-67; served with Q.O.R. of C., 1940-45; held staff appts. with HQ 8th Candn. Inf. Bgde., HQ 1st Candn. Corps, HQ 1st Candn. Army, HQ S.E. Command and Candn. Planning Staff; Mil. Asst. to Lt. Gen. Sir Frederick E. Morgan (planned Normandy Invasion); returned to HQ 1st Candn. Army 1945 and attached to HQ 30th Brit. Corps; discharged Oct. 1945 with rank Lt. Col.; awarded O.B.E.; Mentioned in Despatches; Pres., Ont. Chamber Comm., 1957-58; ad hoc Magistrate and Police Commr., Windsor,

Ont., 1950; Phi Delta Theta; Conservative; Anglican; recreations: fishing, golf; Clubs: University (Toronto); Toronto Racquet; Westmount Golf & Country; Home: 10 Westgate Walk, Kitchener, Ont. N2M 2T8

HARRIS, Walter Edgar, M.Sc., Ph.D., FCIC, F.R.S.C. 1977, FAAAS 1980; retired educator; b. Wetaskiwin, Alta., 9 June 1915; s. Ernest William and Emma Louise (Humbke) H.; e. Wetaskiwin (Alta.) High Sch., 1934; Univ. of Alta., B.Sc. 1938, M.Sc. 1939; Univ. of Minn., Ph.D. 1944; m. Phyllis, d. Samuel Pangburn, Northwood, Iowa, 14 June 1942; children: Margaret Anne, William Edgar; Prof. of Analytical Chem., Univ. of Alberta, 1946-80; Chmn. Dept. of Chem. there 1974-80 (ret.); rec'd Fisher Scient. Lecture Award, Chem. Inst. Can., 1969; Outstanding Achievement Award for Univ. of Minn. Alumni, 1973; Chem. Educ. Award of Chem. Inst. of Can., 1975; co-author, "Programmed Temperature Gas Chromatography", 1966; "Chemical Separations and Measurements", 1974; "Chemical Analysis", 1975; "An Introduction to Chemical Analysis", 1981; author over 80 articles in scient. journs.; Ed., Candn. Journ. Chem.; Councillor, Chem. Inst. Canada; mem., Am. Chem. Soc.; rec'd Alberta Outstanding Achievement Award 1974; Sigma Xi; Protestant; recreations: curling, badminton, bridge, ballroom dancing; Home: 9212 — 118 St., Edmonton, Alta. T6G 1T9.

HARRIS, Hon. Walter Edward, P.C. (Can.), Q.C., D.C.L.; b. Kimberley, Ont., 14 Jan. 1904; s. Melvin and Helen (Carruthers) H.; m. Grace Elma, d. J. J. Morrison, Toronto, Ont.; children: Fern, Margaret Helen, Robert Walter; member, firm of Harris & Dunlop, Barristers, Markdale, Ont.; Homewood Sanitarium Limited; 1st s. to H. of C. for Grey-Bruce, g.e. 1940; apptd. Parlty, Asst. to Secy. of State for External Affairs (Hon. L. S. St. Laurent) 1947, and Parlty. Asst. to the Prime Min., 1948; Minister of Citizenship & Immigration, 1950-54; Min. of Finance, 1954-57; served in 2nd World War (five yrs.); Freemason (P.M.); Liberal; Baptist; Clubs: Ontario (Toronto); Home: 32 Wellington St., Markdale, Ont. N0C 1H0; Office: Main St., Markdale, Ont. N0C 1H0

HARRIS, William Albert; retired manufacturer; b. Toronto, Ont., 1909; e. Howard Park Pub. Sch.; Humberside and Parkdale Coll. Insts.; m. Margaret King; one s. and three d.; Past President, Aristocrat Mfg. Co. Ltd.; Past Pres., Wilmar Mgf. Co. Ltd.; Can. Nat. Exhn. (1955-56); Roy. Winter Fair, Toronto (1972-73); began bus. career with family firm of Canada Metals Ltd.; mem., Candn. Equestrian Federation; Am. Horse Shows Assn.; Candn. Hackney Soc.; recreations: photography, woodworking; Clubs: Toronto; Home: (Box 578) Erin, Ont. N0B 1T0

HARRIS, William Bowles, M.A.; financier; b. Toronto, Ontario, 17 August 1930; s. William Cranfield and Ethel Mary (Bowles) H.; e. Upper Can. Coll.; Univ. of Toronto, B.A. 1953, Oxford Univ. (Christ Ch.), M.A. 1955; m. M. Patricia, d. Rev. Canon F. Arthur Smith, 22 May 1957; children: Diana, Virginia; William A.; Chrmn., Mercantile & General Reinsurance Co. of Can. Ltd.; Barclays Bank of Canada; Dir., E-L Financial Corp. Ltd.; Key Publishers Ltd.; joined Harris & Partners Ltd. 1955; apptd. Dir., 1960; Vice-President, 1964; Pres. 1966-73; Co-Chrmn., Dominion Securities Harris 1973-74; mem. Candn. Econ. Policy Comte.; former Chmn. Exec. Comm., Trinity Coll., Univ. of Toronto; former Chrmn. Bd. Govs., Univ. of Toronto; Alpha Delta Phi; Anglican; recreations: farming; Clubs: Toronto; York; Mount Royal (Montreal); Links (N.Y.); Home: 56 Cluny Drive, Toronto, Ont. M4W 2R2; Office: 141 Adelaide St. W., Toronto, Ont. M5H 3N2

HARRISON, James M., C.C.(1971), B.Sc., M.A., Ph.D., F.R.S.C., F.G.S.A.; geologist; b. Regina, Sask., 20 Sept. 1915; s. Roland O. and Vera Frances (Merritt) H.; e. High

Sch., Winnipeg, Man.; Univ. of Manitoba, B.Sc. 1935; Queen's Univ., M.A. 1941, Ph.D. 1943; m. Herta Boehmer Sliter, 5 May 1944; one step-son, N.E. Sliter; CONSULTANT, NAT. RESOURCES, SCIENCE POLICY; for six seasons prior to joining the Geol. Survey of Canada, was Asst. on Geol. Survey Parties of Fed. and Prov. Govts. and of mining companies; since 1943, with Geol. Survey of Can. engaged on general and special studies of the Candn. Shield up to and incl. 1954; in 1955 apptd. Chief of Precambrian Div., and in Nov. 1956 made Dir. of the Geol. Survey of Can.; apptd. Asst. Depy. Min. (Research), Dept. of Mines and Tech. Surveys 1964, Asst. Depy. Min., Science & Technol. 1964-71; Sr. Asst. Depy. Min., Dept. Energy, Mines & Resources, 1972; Del. of Candn. Govt. to Internat. Geol. Cong., Algiers, 1952; awarded Gold Medal by Prof. Inst. Pub. Service Can., 1966; Foreign Assoc. Nat. Acad. Sciences, USA, 1965; Blaylock Medal, Candn. Inst. Min. & Met., 1967; Logan Medal, Geol. Assn., Can., 1969; Kemp Medal, Columbia Univ., 1962; Fellow, Geol. Assn. of Can., Pres. 1960-61; Internat. Union Geol. Sciences (1st Pres. 1961-64); Candn. Inst. of Mining & Metall. (Pres. 1969-70); Soc. of Econ. Geol. (Regional Vice-Pres. for N.A. 1962-64); Pres., Internat. Council Scientific Unions 1966-68; named 1970 winner of outstanding achievement award of Fed. Public Service; Companion, Order of Canada, 1971; 1973-76 leave of absence from Candn. Govt. to act as Asst. Dir.-Gen. for Science Unesco, Paris; recreations: golf, colour photography; Home: 4 Kippewa Drive, Ottawa, Ont. K1S 3G4; Office: 5 Kippewa Dr., Ottawa, Ont.

HARRISON, Mark, B.A.; newspaper editor; b. 10 Aug. 1924; s. Harry and late Sonia (Doduck) H.; e. Univ. of Toronto B.A. 1948, one yr. grad. studies Pol. Science & Econ.; m. Isabel Cliften'd. late Frederick George and Zaidee Maude (Smith) Hay-Roe, Toronto, Ont. 24 Feb. 1950; children: Steven, Timothy, Judith, Nancy; EDITOR, MONTREAL GAZETTE since 1977; joined Toronto Star 1949, Ottawa Bureau Chief 1958-59, European Corr. 1963-66, Ed. Page Ed. 1959-63 and 1966-69, Extve. Ed. 1969-77; served with R.C.A.F. 1943-46, Flying Offr. (Navig.), RAF No. 78 Bomber Sqdn. U.K.; recreations: sailing, skiing, golf, reading; Club: Royal Montreal Golf; Office: The Gazette, St. Antoine St., Montreal, Que.

HARRISON, Michael A., B.A.Sc., D.B.A., P.Eng., F.I.C.B., F. Inst. D.; executive; b. Toronto, Ont. 24 Apl. 1930; s. James Arthur and Thekla Rothschild (Pineo) H.; e. Univ. of Toronto, B.A.Sc. 1952; London Sch. Econs., Dipl. in Business Adm. 1958; Inst. of Cdn. Bankers, F.I.C.B., 1981; m. Elizabeth Marshall (Ramsden), 2 June 1956; children: Michael Scott, Mark Marshall, Nancy Elizabeth; Pres. and Dir., Mgt. Consultants Internat., Inc.; with C.B.C. 1952-56 (Toronto) as TV Tech., Indust. Relations Asst., Adm. Asst. to Regional Dir.; (Ottawa) Asst. Mgr., Indust. Relations and Mgr. Indust. Relations 1958-61; Extve. Asst. to Pres. 1962-64; Project Offr., Royal Comn. on Govt. Organ. 1961; Planning Offr., Royal Comn. Implementation, Treas. Bd. 1965; Extve. Asst. to Pres. and Marketing Offr., Denison Mines Ltd., 1965-67; Vice Pres., Broadcasting, Tele-Information, Computers/-Communications, Southam Press Ltd. 1967-75; Exec. Dir., Canadian Bankers Assn. 1975-80; Dir.; Scriptonics Corp.; Dir. and Exec. Vice-Pres., Council on Drug Abuse; Dir., Toronto Arts Productions; Blue Mt. Ratepayers Assn.; Awards: Athlone Fellow, 1956-58; Fellow, Inst. of Directors, 1981; Fellow, Inst. of Cdn. Bankers (honours), 1981; Fellow, Huguenot Soc. of Can.; Inst. of Directors in Can.; Cdn. Information Industry Assn.; Publications: Cdn. Business Mgt. Devel., CCH Cdn. Ltd.; Issues in Internat. Banking, Inst. for Research on Public Policy; mem., Can. Nat. Exhibition Assn.; Reg'd. Prof. Engr. Ont.; recreations: swimming, tennis, squash, skiing, bridge, billiards, theatre, films; Clubs: Royal Canadian Yacht; University Club of Toronto; Home: 1702 Ruscombe Close, Mississauga, Ont. L5J 1Y5; Office: Ste. 303, 56 The Esplanade, Toronto, Ont. M5E 1A7

HARRISON, Russell Edward; banker; b. Grandview, Man., 31 May 1921; s. Edward Smith and Annie L. (Purvis) H.; m. Nancy Doreen Bell, 18 Oct. 1944; one s., one d.; CHRMN. & CHIEF EXTVE. OFFR., CANADIAN IMPERIAL BANK OF COMMERCE since 1976; Dir., Cdn. Eastern Finance Ltd.; Cdn. Exec. Service Overseas; The Dominion Realty Co., Ltd.; Edifice Dorchester Commerce Inc.; Imbank Realty Co. Ltd.; Royal Ins. Co. of Can.; Can. Life Assnce. Co.; TransCan. Pipe Lines; Falconbridge Nickel Mines Ltd.; The Western Assurance Co.; California Candn. Bank; MacMillan Bloedel Ltd.; mem., Business Council on Nat. Issues; Gov. Council, Gov. Gen.; First Can. Study Conf., 1983 Hon. Comm., Stanford Research Inst.; Advis. Bd., Business School, Univ. of Western Ont.; Finance and General Purposes Comm., ROINS Holding Ltd.; Development Board, Univ. of New Brunswick, Centre for Conflict Studies; Can. Advisory Committee, Amer. Assn. for the Advancement of Science; Reg. mem., Comm. The Conference Bd. Inc.; Bd. of Dir., C.D. Howe Research Inst.; Conference Bd. in Can.; Gov., Adela Investm. Co. S.A.; Olympic Trust of Can.; Nat. Chmn., Ministries Enrichment Progrm, The Salvation Army; Vice-Chmn. Finance Comm. and Gov., Massey Hall; Chmn., Adv. Council, West Park Hospital fund-raising campaign; hon. Bd. of Dir., Can. Jaycees 1981-82; joined the Bank, Winnipeg, Man. 1945; Asst. Mgr., Hamilton, Ont. 1953 and Toronto, Ont. 1956; Head of Banks Operations in Que., Dec. 1956; Extve. Vice-Pres. and Chief Gen. Manager, Head Office, 1969; elected a Dir. 1970; Pres. and Chief Operating Offr., 1973; served in W.W.II; Clubs: Toronto; Albany; Mount Royal; St. James's (Both Montreal, Que.); The Ranchmen's (Calgary); Rosedale Golf; Ont. Jockey; Ontario; York (Toronto); Office: Commerce Court West, Toronto, Ont. M5L 1A2

HARRISON, William Allan; painter; b. Montreal, Que. 27 Dec. 1911; s. William Tate and Janet (Jessie) (Allan) H.; e. Fairmount Sch. Montreal 1926; Ecole des Beaux-Arts 1929-30; Art Students League New York 1931; Atelier, Montreal 1932-33; Paris, France 1933, 1947-48, 1956; Art Dir., J. Walter Thompson Montreal 1941-46, Rio de Janeiro 1946-47; residence abroad: France, Eng. 1933-36; Brazil 1946-47; France, Italy 1947-49, 1956-57; New York 1950-54, 1957-59; has lectured at Sch. of Architecture, McGill Univ., Mount Allison Univ., and Alta. Coll. of Art (Calgary); founding mem., Contemporary Art Soc., Montreal 1939-48; designer book jackets McGill Queens Univ. Press 1960-73, also Harvest House Montreal; solo exhns. incl. Montreal Museum of Fine Arts 1945, 1978 (Retrospective); Instituto dos Arquitetos Rio de Janeiro 1947; Galerie de Montréal 1973; Macdonald Coll. McGill Univ. 1957; Galerie Agnes Lefort 1957; Galerie l'Art françáis 1976; Nancy Poole's Studio Toronto 1980 and 1981; rep. various colls. incl. Museum Bezaleí Jerusalem, Musée du Qué., Montreal Museum of Fine Arts., Montefiore Club (Montreal), Shell Can. Art Collection (Calgary), Can. Council Art Bank, CBC/Radio Can. (Montreal); Address: 201 Metcalfe Ave., Westmount, Que. H3Z 2H7

HARRON, Donald, B.A.; actor; writer; b. Toronto, Ont., 19 Sept. 1924; s. Lionel William, and Delsia Ada (Hunter) H.; e. Univ. of Toronto, B.A. 1948 (Sanford Gold Medal in Philos. 1948; Regent's Silver Medal 1948); m. Catherine McKinnon, 12 March 1969; children: Martha, Mary (both by previous marriage), Kelley; as an actor has starred on Broadway ("Tenth Man"), London, Eng. ("Mary, Mary"); first 3 seasons with Stratford, Ont. Festival; one season with Bristol Old Vic, one with New York Shakespeare Festival; 6 shows on Broadway, 4 in London's W. End; T.V. appearances in Can., U.S. and Eng. incl. guest star on most U.S. drama series, comedy star role in CBS series "Hee Haw"; played title role in 2 TV specials "Reddick I" and "Reddick II" now sold to Am. and Brit. TV; has appeared opposite such actresses as Katherine Hepburn, Catherine Cornell, Maggie Smith, Irene Worth, Zoe Caldwell, Joanne Woodward, Rosemary Harris, Ann Todd; helped create first ed. of "Spring Thaw",

1948 and wrote and performed in subsequent yrs. culminating in writing entire show for "Spring Thaw '67"; has written for BBC radio and TV incl. regular writing assignment on "Bedtime with Braden"; wrote musical comedy "Ann of Green Gables" with Norman Campbell (6 seasons in Charlottetown Summer Festival; 1967 tour of Can.; productions in Kenya and Sweden; 10 months at New Theatre, London; rec'd London Theatre Critics "Best Musical of 1969"); also wrote "Private Turvey's War" (musical comedy), "Broken Jug" (farce, played in New York Phoenix Theatre 1959), "Once" (original screenplay), "Here Lies Sarah Binks" (musical comedy), "And That's the News Good Night" (TV special 1969); Host of CBC Radio's "Morningside"; author of "Charlie Farquharson's History of Canada" 1972; "Charlie Farquharson's Joyfree of Canada, the Wild and Other Places" 1974; "Charlie Farquharson's Korn Almanac" 1976; "Olde Charlie Farquharson's Testament" 1978; Stage Musical, "Wonder of It All" (Life of Emily Carr) 1980; Film, "Once" (CBC TV) 1981; served as Pilot Offr. with RCAF 1943-45; recreation: football; Club: Arts & Letters; Address: c/o Morningside, P.O. Box 500, Stn. A., Toronto, Ont. M5W 1E6

HARROWER, George Alexander, M.Sc., Ph.D.; university professor: b. Flesherton, Ont. 15 May 1924; s. Joseph and Edith Winnifred (McCann) H.; e. Univ. of W. Ont., B.Sc. (Physics) 1949: McGill Univ., M.Sc., 1950, Ph.D., 1952; m. late Ruth Marie, d. W. L. Boyce, London, Ont., 26 June, 1948; children: Timothy Douglas, Lisa Catherine; m. 2ndly Judith Lynne, d. D. W. Bollman, Pittsburgh, Pa., 19 Sept. 1969; children: David Andrew, Kardi Lynne, Mark Alexander; PRES., LAKEHEAD UNIV. since 1978, Prof. of Physics, Queen's Univ., since 1955 (Vice-Princ. 1969-76; Dean, Faculty of Arts and Science 1964-69; Asst. Dean 1962-64); with Bell Telephone Labs., Murray Hill, N.J., 1952-55; served in 2nd World War with R.C.A.F., 1943-45; Publications: papers on electronics and radio astron. to scient. journs.; mem. Candn. Astron. Soc.; Internat. Astron. Union; Protestant; Address: Lakehead Univ., Thunder Bay Ont. P7B 5E1

HART, Alexander H., Q.C., LL.B.; agent general; b. Regina, Sask., 17 July 1918; s. Alexander and Mary (Davidson) H.; e. Dalhousie Law Sch., LL.B.; m. Janet MacMillan, d. Colin Mackay, Rothesay, N.B., 5 June 1948; children: Mary, Colin, Sandy, John; AGENT GENERAL FOR PROV. OF B.C. IN LONDON ENGLAND since 1981; Sr. Vice-President, Canadian Nat. RLYS., 1971-81 previously Vice Pres., Marketing 1967-71; Pres., Past Vancouver Bd. Trade; Past Pres., Can.-Japan Soc.; read law with McInnis, McQuarrie and Cooper, called to the Bar of Nova Scotia 1947; served in 2nd World War with Royal Canadian Artillery, 1939-45; retired with rank of Major; mem., Candn. Comte.; Can. Japan Business Co-op. Comte.; N.S. Barristers Soc.; International Phi Kappa Pi; Presbyterian; Clubs: Vancouver; Men's Canadian; Pine Valley Golf; Shaughnessy Golf & Country; Roy. Automobile; The East India; Home: and Office: 1 Regent St., London SW1Y 4NS, England.

HART, Anthony M. B.; executive; b. Newport, Wales 31 May 1945; e. Univ. of Birmingham Dipl. in Metall. 1966; m. Maria Bodziona 1 August 1970; children: Ashley St. John, Alexandra Leila; PRESIDENT & DIR., JOHNSON MATTHEY LTD.; Dir. Johnson Matthey & Co. (Canada) Ltd.; Johnson Matthey Jewellery, Fla.; Johnson Matthey Inc., Pa.; Metall., INCO 1962-66; Product Devel. Johnson Matthey (U.K.) 1966-70; Johnson Matthey Canada since 1970; Home: 40 Cedar Dr., R.R. 2, Caledon, Ont. L0N 1C0; Office: 110 Industry St., Toronto, Ont. M6M 4M1.

HART, George Arnold, M.B.E., D.C.L., LL.D., D.C.Sc.; retired banker; b. Toronto, Ont., 2 April, 1913; s. George Sanderson and Laura Mary (Harrison) H.; e. Pub. Schools and Oakwood Coll. Inst., Toronto, Ont.; Fellow, The Canadian Inst. of Bankers, 1936; LL.D., Univ. of

Sask. 1961; Univ. of Montreal 1962; D.C.L., Bishop's Univ. 1963; Acadia Univ. 1970; D.C.Sc., Univ. of Sherbrooke 1965; m. late Jean C. Gilbert, 2 Sept. 1939; one d., Diane (Mrs. Edwin S. Keeling); m. 2ndly Patricia I. Hart, 8 Dec., 1961. Bank of Montreal: Chmn., of the Exec. Comte 1964-77; Chmn. of the Bd. 1964-75; Chief Exec. Officer 1959-74; Pres. 1959-67. Dir. Bank of Montreal (Executive Comte); Canadian Pacific Limited; Consolidated-Bathurst Inc. (Executive Comte); Bathurst Paper Limited; Domglas Inc.; Inco Limited (Executive Comte); Pratt & Whitney Aircraft of Canada Ltd.; Sun Life Assur. Co. of Canada (Exec. Comte); Uniroyal, Inc. (Exec. Comte.); Canadian Fund, Inc. (Chmn.); Canadian Invest. Fund, Ltd. (Chmn.). Board of Governors, Royal Victoria Hospitals; Canadian Export Assoc.; Institut de Cardiologie de Montreal; Mem., Cdn. Econ. Policy Comte.; Adv. Bd., Concordia Univ.; Hon. Dir., C.D. Howe Research Inst.; Joined Bank of Montreal, Toronto, 1931. Served with Canadian Army 1941-46; discharged with rank Major. Anglican. Recreation: golf. Clubs: Mount Royal; Forest and Stream; Mount Bruno Country. Home: R.R. 2, Mountain, Ont. K0E 1S0 Office: 129 St. James St. West, Montreal, Que. H2Y 1L6.

HART, Hon. Gordon Leavitt Shaw, LL.B.; judge; b. Halifax, N.S., 23 Dec. 1924; s. Gilbert Shaw and Jean Thompson (Leavitt) H.; e. Halifax (N.S.) Co. Acad. 1942; King's Univ. B.A. 1946; Dalhousie Law Sch., LL.B. 1948; m. Catherine, d. Dr. Hugh MacKinnon, 1 Jan. 1949; children: Christine Ellen, Thomas E., Norah, Gordon G., Hugh A., Jonathan L.; JUDGE, SUPREME COURT OF N.S. and mem. of Appeal Division Court; called to the Bar of N.S. 1948; cr. Q.C. 1963; Ald., City of Dartmouth 1956-60; M.L.A. 1960-63, 1967-68; apptd. Royal Comn. to conduct inquiry into pollution of Candn. waters by steam tanker "Arrow" 1970; served in R.C.N. 1944-45, rank Sub. Lt.; Pres., N.S. Assn. Urban & Mun. Sch. Bds. 1958-59; mem. and Chrmn., Dartmouth Sch. Bd. 1954-60; Vice-Pres., Candn. Sch. Trustees Assn. 1959; mem. Bd. Govs., Dartmouth Acad. 1968-70; apptd. a Mem. of Court Martial Appeal Court, 1972; apptd. to Appeal Div. of Supreme Court of N.S., 1978; United Church; Home: 18 Clearview Cres., Dartmouth, N.S. B3A 2M8; Office: Court House, Halifax, N.S.

HART, Howard, B.Com.; association executive; b. Montreal, Que., 12 July 1930; s. William Henry and Alice (Howard) H.; e. Queen's Univ., B.Com., 1953; m. Elinor Diane, d. C. E. Goodwin, Picton, Ont., 1954; children: William, Peter, Suzanne, Caroline; PRES., CANDN. PULP AND PAPER ASSN., since 1972; joined present Assn. 1954; Secy. of the Assn. and Asst. to Pres., 1962-67; Vice Pres. 1967; Extve. Vice Pres. 1970-72; Club: St. James's; Home: 18 Kirkwood Ave., Beaconsfield, Que.; Office: 2300 Sun Life Bldg., Montreal, Que.

HART, Ian C., Q.C., B.A.; b. Toronto, Ont., 28 Sept. 1925; s. Alfred Purvis and Katherine (Crichton) H.; e. Univ. of Toronto Schs., Toronto; Univ. of Toronto, B.A. 1946; Osgoode Hall Law Sch.; m. Patricia Ann, d. late Avery Clifton Turner, 29 Aug. 1951; children: Stephen Peter, Sheila Ann Sisley, Derek Alfred; PARTNER, COATSWORTH, RICHARDSON & HART.; Dir., Zurich Life Insurance Co. of Canada; read law with H. A. Coon, Q.C.; called to Bar of Ont., 1949; cr. Q.C. 1961; served with R.C.N.V.R.; Councillor, Toronto Twp., 1953-54; mem., Toronto Twp. Pub. Utilities Comn., 1955-57; mem., Metrop. Toronto Bd. of Trade; Alpha Delta Phi; Protestant; recreations: golf.; Club: Toronto Golf; Home: 53 Edenvale Cres., Islington, Ont. M9A 4A5; Office: 85 Richmond St. W., Toronto, Ont. M5H 2C9

HARTFORD, Donald Harold; executive, b. Edmonton, Alta., 24 Jan. 1919; s. Harold Hunter and Mabel Irene (Younge) H.; e. W. Canada Schs.; m. Jean Emilie Skogland, 1973; children from previous marriage: Donald Leigh, Douglas Wayne, Diane Leslie; stepchildren: Fred,

Kari Skogland; PRES. CFRB LIMITED; Pres., Radio Div., Standard Broadcasting Corp. Ltd.; CJAD Inc.; St. Clair Prod. Ltd.; Eastern Sound Co. Ltd.; Dir., and Vice-Pres., Standard Broadcast Productions; Standard Broadcasting Corp. Ltd.; Standard Sound Systems Co. Ltd.; served with Calgary Regt. Tanks, later with R.C.A.F.; discharged with rank of Flying Offr.; Past Pres. Western Assn. of Broadcasters,; Ont. Safety League; Advtsg. and Sales Club, Calgary; Vice-Chrmn., Candn. Assn. of Broadcasters; Dir., and mem., Candn. Nat. Sportsmen's Show; Dir., Ontario Place; Fndg. Dir., Radio Bur. of Can.; Fndg. mem., Broadcast Extve. Soc.; Past Council mem. Bd. Trade Metrop. Toronto; Past Dir., Can. Nat. Exhibition; Mem., Candn. team, Internat. Tuna Cup Match, 1970; Advis. Bd., Cdn. Friends of Tel Aviv Univ.; Salvation Army; Past Dir., Alta. Heart Foundation, Clarke Instit. of Psychiatry; Past Assoc. Dir., Calgary Stampede; Past Vice-Chmn., United Appeal, Calgary; Past Zone Chmn., United Appeal, Toronto; Awards, Humanitarian Award of International B'nai B'rith, 1978; "Broadcaster of Yr." Award, Central Can. Broadcasters Assn., 1981; recreations: fishing, hunting, boating,; Clubs: Granite; Variety; Bd. of Trade Metro Toronto; Goodwood; Home: 1204-65 Harbour Sq., Toronto, Ont. M5J 2L4; Office: 2 St. Clair Ave. W., Toronto, Ont. M4V 1L6

HARTLE, Douglas Graham, M.A., Ph.D., F.R.S.C.; economist and educator; b. Winnipeg, Manitoba, 10 March 1927; s. Francis Stewart and Elsie (Perry) H.; e. Pub. and High Schs., Winnipeg, Ottawa and Montreal; Carleton Univ., B.A.; Duke Univ., M.A., Ph.D.; m. Lexia Weir, d. late Harry J. Clark, 5 Sept. 1955; children: Sandra, Paul, Martha, Geoffrey; PROF. OF ECONOMICS, UNIV. OF TORONTO and Assoc., Inst. for Policy Analysis there since 1973; Research Dir., Extve. Secy., Ont. Econ. Council; Pres., Can. Econ. Assn.; Dir., National Bureau of Econ. Research, N.Y. City; Dir., Manpower Div., Research Br., Dept. of Labour, Ottawa, 1955-57; Prof. of Econ., Univ. of Toronto, 1957-62 and Dir., Inst. for Quantitative Analysis of Social and Econ. Policy, 1967-69; Research Dir., Royal Comn. on Taxation, 1962-67; Deputy-Secretary — Planning, Treasury Bd. 1969-73; former mem. Bd. of Govs., Carleton Univ.; mem., Candn. Econ. Assn.; Royal Econ. Soc.; Am. Econ. Assn.; Anglican; Home: 14 South Drive, Toronto, Ont. M4W 1R1; Office: 150 St. George St., Toronto, Ont. M5S 2E9

HARTLEY, Eric Llewellyn, M.B.E., OStJ, E.D., C.D., F.R.S.A., F.E.I.C., P. Eng.; civil engineer; b. Liverpool, England, 19 March 1912; s. Frederick Llewellyn and Lila (Roberts) H.; e. Liverpool (Eng.) Inst. Sch., 1930; Queen's Univ., B.Sc. 1933; m. Audrey Grace, d. late Frederick James Ralston, Vancouver, B.C., 5 Nov. 1937; children: Sydney Frederick, Eric Robert, Timothy James; Retired 1975 as Chrmn. of Bd. and Chief Extve. Offr., Frankel Steel Construction Ltd.; Pres. (1972-73) and Hon. Life mem., Canadian Construction Association; in 1934 entered the Properties Department of Jas. Richardson and Sons Limited in Winnipeg and two years later joined W. G. Swan Engineering Co. Limited in Vancouver; in 1937 apptd. Engr. in Charge of construction of the Canada Packers Ltd. Vancouver plant, serving also during this period as Asst. Estimating Engr. for the Western Bridge Co.; in 1938 was assoc. with B.C. Appraisal Co. Ltd., also with Dom. Bridge Co. Ltd. during the construction of the Lions Gate Bridge; joined Western Bridge & Steel Fabricators Ltd. in 1945 as Design Engr.; apptd. Contract Engr. 1947 and Asst. Gen. Mgr. 1951, Gen. Mgr. 1955; subsequently Vice-Pres. and Gen. Mgr., Dom. Structural Steel Div. of Canada Iron Foundries, Ltd., having been Pres., of Dom. Structural Steel Ltd.; served in 2nd World War; Major, Royal Candn. Engrs. on staff of Chief Engr., First Candn. Army in U.K. and N.W. Europe; M.B.E.; Offr., Order of Orange-Nassau; Mentioned in Despatches; Offr., OStJ Hon. Colonel, 2nd Field Engineer, Regt. R.C.E.; mem., Assn. of Prof. Engrs. of Ont. and B.C.;

Engn. Inst. of Can. (Life mem. and Fellow); Can. Past Pres. and Chmn. of Bd., Inst. of Steel Construction (Past Chrmn. of Bd.; Past President, Ontario Fed. of Constr. Assns.; Vice. pres. and mem., extve. comte., Ont. council, St. John Ambulance; United Church; Clubs: Terminal City (Vancouver); Seigniory (Montebello); Granite; York; Empire; Roy. Candn. Mil. Inst.; Home: 355 St. Clair Ave. W., Apt. 2406, Toronto, Ont. M5P 1N5

HARTLEY, Fred Lloyd, B.A.Sc.; company president; b. Vancouver, B.C., 16 Jan. 1917; s. late John William and late Hannah (Mitchell) H.; e. Pub. and High Schs., Vancouver; Univ. of B.C., B.A.Sc. (Chem. Engn.) 1939; m. Margaret Alice, d. late Joseph W. R. Murphy, 2 Nov. 1940; children: Margaret Ann, Fred L., Jr., CHRMN. AND PRES., UNION OIL CO. OF CALIFORNIA; Chrmn. of Bd., Union Oil Co. of Canada Ltd., Calgary; Dir., Union Bank; Rockwell Corp.; joined present Co. 1939; held following positions: Chem. Engr., various refineries of Co.; Vice Pres., Research Dept.; Sr. Vice Pres., Marketing, Sr. Vice Pres., Refining and Marketing; Extve. Vice Pres.; Assoc., Univ. of S. Cal.; Trustee, Cal. Inst. of Technol.; U.S. Council of the Internat. Chamber of Comm., Inc.; Pres. (1972) Cal. Chamber of Comm.; Dir., L.A. Philharmonic; mem. Council on Foreign Relations; Trustee. Tax Foundation; Eisenhower Exchange Fellowships; Dir., Los Angeles World Affairs Council; Chrm., Am. Petrol. Inst.; mem., Candn. Soc. Los Angeles; Am. Chem. Soc.; Am. Inst. Chem. Engrs.; N.Y. Acad. Sciences; Soc. Automotive Engrs.; Nat. Petrol. Council; Independent Petrol. Assn. Am.; Episcopal; recreations: tennis, swimming, golf, piano; Office: P.O. Box 7600, Los Angeles, Cal. 90051

HARTOG, Robbert, M.A.; manufacturer; b. Nijmegen, Netherlands 28 Jan. 1919; s. Arthur and J. S. E. (Catz) H.; e. Secondary Sch. The Hague; Dipl. Ecole Libre des Sciences Politiques, Paris; Univ. of Toronto M.A. 1942; PRESIDENT AND CEO, WALTEC ENTERPRISES LTD.; Pres. and Dir. Foreign Investment Trust Inc.; Kindred Industries Ltd.; Waltec Industries Ltd.; Waltec Forgings Ltd., Dalex Co. Ltd.; Markle Community Newspapers Ltd.; served with Royal Netherlands Army during World War II, rank Acting Maj.; Gov. Georgian Coll. Barrie, Ont.; author "De L'Utilite du Controle de Change en Temps du Guerre"; mem. Candn. Pol. Science Assn.; Royal Econ. Soc.; United Church; Clubs: canoeing, boating; Club: Granite; Home: R.R. 1, Perkinsfield, Ont.; Office (P.O. Box 936) Cambridge, Ont. N1R 5X9.

HARTROFT, Walter Stanley, B.Sc., M.D., Ph.D. LL.D., F.R.C.P.(C), F.R.S.C.; professor; b. Calgary, Alta., 5 Aug. 1916; s. Samuel Munroe and Myrtle Pearl (Coons) H.; e. Univ. of Alta., B.Sc. (Med., Anat.) 1941 and M.D. 1941; Univ. of Toronto, Ph.D. (Path.) 1949; Univ. of Alta. LL.D. 1961; PROF., EXPER. PATHOL., UNIV. OF HAWAII, Sch. of Med.; Research Asst. to Prof. C. C. Macklin, Dept. of Histol., Univ. of W. Ont. 1940-43; joined Banting & Best Dept. of Med. Research as Research Assoc., 1946; Asst. Prof., 1947-49, Assoc. Prof., 1949-52, Prof., 1952-54; Mallinckrodt Prof. and Chrmn., Dept. of Pathology, Washington Univ. Sch. of Med., Pathol.-in-Chief, Barnes and Allied Hosps. and St. Louis Children's Hosp., St. Louis, 1954-61; apptd. Dir., The Research Inst., Hosp. for Sick Children, Toronto, Ont., 1961; awarded Royal Coll. of Phys. & Surg. of Can. Prize for Research, 1949; served in 2nd World War as Specialist in Path., R.C.A.M.C., with rank of Major; service in Holland and Germany and with Candn. Army of Occupation in Germany, 1945-46; engaged for past several years in basic med. research on problems related to exper. and clinical liver disease; exper. and clinical kidney disease; exper. and clinical arterial disease and hypertension exper. and clinical diabetes; has contrib. articles to scient. journals on these subjects; mem., Ont. Assn. Pathols.; Candn. Assn. Pathols.; Am. Assn. of Pathols. & Bacteriols.; Am. Assn. of Anat. Gerontol. Soc.; Histochem.

Soc.; Am. Soc. for Exper. Pathol.; Candn. Physiol. Soc.; Anat. Soc. of Gt. Brit. & Ireland; Am. Assn. Study Liver Diseases; Am. Bd. Nutrition; Am. Diabetes Assn.; Candn. Diabetic Assn.; Coll. Am. Pathols; Council Arter. of Am. Heart Assn.; N.Y. Acad. Sciences; Ont. Diabetes Assn.; Roy. Soc. Promotion Health; Soc. Exper. Biol. & Med.; Toronto Diabetes Assn.; Am. Assn. Advancement Science; Am. Inst. Nutrition; Am. Med. Assn.; Am. Soc. Clin. Nutrition; Am. Thoracic Soc. etc.; Burton Soc. Electron Microscopy; Candn. Fed. Biol. Soc.; Candn. Med. Assn.; Candn. Soc. for Clin. Investigation; Internat. Assn. for Study of Liver; Nutrition Soc. Can.; Pluto Club; Royal Soc. Med.; Toronto Acad. Med.; Toronto Physiol. Soc.; Delta Kappa Epsilon; Atheist; recreation: music; Address: Honolulu, Hawaii, 96822

HARTZ, Paul F., B.Com., C.P.A.; manufacturer; b. Hastendal, Denmark, 20 Aug. 1921; s. Ernest Ferdinand and Clara (Folden) H.; came to Canada 1941; e. Univ. of Toronto, B.Com., 1949; C.P.A., 1953; m. Stella, d. Ralph Duncanson, Falmouth, N.S., 16 Dec. 1943; children: Jo Ann, Peter; PRESIDENT AND CHRMN. BD., FRAM CORPN.; Fram Canada Ltd.; Dir. and Vice Pres., The Bendix Corp. (Mich.); Rhode Island Hospital Trust National Bank; Outlet Co. (R.I.); Jamesbury Corp. (Mass.); Friona Industries, Texas; Student Acct., Anton Jenset Co., Toronto, 1949-51; Acct., Aladdin Industries Products of Canada Ltd., 1951-52; joined Fram Canada Ltd. 1953, Pres. 1959; Extve. Vice-Pres., Fram Corpn., 1964-66; served with R.C.A.F., 1941-45; Home: 32 Nayatt Rd., Barrington, R.I. 02806; Office: 105 Pawtucket Ave., Providence, R.I. 02916

HARVEY, Alan, B.A.; newspaper correspondent; b. Toronto, Ont., 11 Apl. 1919; s. late Dorothy Margaret (Collins) and late Percy Elton H.; e. Harbord Coll. Inst., Toronto, Ont.; Univ. Coll., Univ. of Toronto, B.A. 1940; m. Annick Francine, d. Marcel Miel, St. Malo, France, 10 Sept. 1949; children: Malo, Christine; worked for The Candn. Press news agency in Toronto, Ottawa, New York and London, Eng.; covered variety of events incl. funeral of King Geo. VI, Feb. 1952 and Coronation of Queen Elizabeth, 2 June 1953; visited Spain, Yugoslavia, Poland, USSR, France and W. Germany on assignments ranging from 10 days to one mth.; sometime London Editor-Corr., Toronto Globe & Mail; freelance for Ottawa Journal, Winnipeg Free Press, Edmonton Journal and Financial Post Magazine; joined Reuters News Agency covering pol. and diplomatic field Sept. 1968; served as London corres. for Maclean's magazine; wrote stories for Maclean's and The Canadian Magazine; served in 2nd World War with Royal Candn. Navy, 1944-45; recreations: golf, racing; Club: Press (London); Home: 114 Burns Way, Heston, Middlesex, Eng.; Office: Reuters, 85 Fleet St., London, E.C.4

HARVEY, Donald, R.C.A.; artist; educator; b. Walthamston, Eng. 14 June 1930; s. Henry Guy and Annie Dorothy (Sawell) H.; e. Worthing (Eng.) High Sch. 1946; W. Sussex Coll. of Art Worthing, Eng. Nat. Dipl. of Design, Nat. Dipl. of Painting 1950; Brighton Coll. of Art Eng., Art Teachers Dipl. 1952; m. Elizabeth d. Albert James Clark 9 Aug. 1952; children: David Jonathon, Shan Mary; PROF. OF FINE ARTS, UNIV. OF VICTORIA 1961- ; Art Master, Ardwyn Grammar Sch. Wales 1952-56; Extve. Secy. to Sask. Arts Bd. 1958-61; rep. in various pub. and private colls. incl. Nat. Gallery Can., Montreal Museum Fine Arts, Charlottetown Confed. Gallery, Art Gallery Greater Victoria, Albert Knox Gallery Chicago, Seattle Art Museum; rec'd Sr. Can. Council Fellowship 1966; mem. Candn. Group Painters; Candn. Painters & Etchers; N.D.P.; recreations: movies, music, tennis; Home: 1025 Joan Cres., Victoria, B.C. V8S 3L3; Office: Victoria, B.C.

HARVEY, Hon. Gerald, accountant; b. Jonquière, Que., 1 March 1928; s. late Charles E. and Cécile Ida (Girard)

H.; e. St. Michel Acad., Jonquière; Sacred-Heart Coll., Victoriaville; Goyetch Business Coll., Jonquière, 2 yrs. lang. course; Internat. Soc. of Accounting, 3 yrs. Corr. course; m. Nora, d. James Northon, Kenogami, Que., 29 Aug. 1955; children: Louise, Johanne; EXTVE. VICE PRES. PROV. AUTOMOBILE DEALERS ASSOC. OF QUE. LTD. since June 1978; served in various positions Stores Dept., Candn. Nat. Rly. Co., 1944-59; Accounting Dept., Price Bros. & Co. Ltd., 1959; el. M.I.A. for Jonquière Constit. in prov. g.e. 1960; re-el. since; apptd. Parlty Asst. to Min. of Social Welfare 1962; apptd. Co-ordinator of Labour Comtes. 1966; rep. Que. Govt. at Internat. Labour Congress, Geneva, 1968; apptd. State Min. for Dept. of Social Welfare May 1970; apptd. Min. of Revenue, Que., Oct. 1970; apptd. Min. of Labour & Manpower, Que., Aug. 1975; retired from politics, 1976; sabbatical yr., 1977; rec'd. Centennial Medal 1967; Hon. mem., Jonquière Community Coll.; mem., Internat. Union Clks. & Accts.; Bd. of Dir. of Foundation of Que. Univ. of Chicoutimi; K. of C.; Liberal; R. Catholic; recreations: fishing, hunting, curling; Home: 3346, Chemin St-Louis, Ste-Foy, Que. G1W 1S4

HARVEY, Patrick Joseph, F.R.I., S.I.R., C.R.B.; Ontario land economist; realtor; b. Dublin Ireland, 1914; s. James F. and Kathleen M. (Kelly) H.; came to Can., June, 1923; e. Public and High Schs., Toronto, Ont., De La Salle Coll., Toronto, Ont.; m. Margaret E., d. Thomas Knight, 28 October, 1943; PRESIDENT, P. J. HARVEY REALTIES LTD.; moved from Toronto to Brantford, Ontario, 1939; Mgr. Continental Credit Adjusters, 1939-40, and then purchased the agency; operated as sole owner a gen. real estate brokerage office from 1942, inc. it under present style, 1960; Past Pres., Candn. Real Estate Assn.; Ont. Real Estate Assn.; Real Estate Institute Can.; Past Pres. Brantford Regional Real Estate Assn; Past Gov., Nat. Marketing Inst., (U.S.A.); mem. and past Dir., Nat. Assn. of Realtors; mem. Soc. of Ind. Realtors; served in extve. capacities in Candn. and Ont. real state assns. for over 30 yrs.; Past Pres., Brantford Community Council; Past Chrmn., Brantford and Suburban Planning Board; Past Dir., Brantford Regional Chamber of Comm.; Past Chrmn., Brantford Comte. of Adjustment; Catholic; recreation: golf; Clubs: Optimist (Past Pres.); Past Pres., Brantford Club; Brantford Golf & Country; Home: 37 Westmount Blvd., Brantford, Ont. N3T 5J1; Office: P.O. Box 1148 Brantford, Ont. N3T 5T3

HARVEY, William Sutherland, F.C.I.S.; retired association executive; b. Winnipeg, Manitoba, 29 Sept. 1913; s. William Henry-Howard and Mary Harrold (Sutherland) H.; e. Winnipeg, Man., Pub. Schs.; m. Jean MacDonald, d. late John McArthur, 27 April 1939; one d. Mrs. M. J. Rouse; joined Acct. Dept., Canadian Nat. Rlys., Western Region, 1929; trans. to Air Canada (then Trans Canada Airlines) Winnipeg, when first organized. Oct. 1937; Disbursement Acct., System, 1941, Asst. Auditor 1945, Auditor 1947, Gen. Auditor 1948, Comptroller 1952; Sr. Vice-Pres., Finance 1962; Asst. Dir. Gen.-Adm. & Finance, Internat. Air Transport Assn. 1971-72; United Church; recreations: golf, curling, reading; Club: St. James's; Home: 2045 Graham Blvd., Town of Mount Royal, Que. H3R 1H5

HARVIE, Donald Southam; professional engineer; petroleum executive; b. Calgary, Alta., 16 March 1924; s. Eric Lafferty and Dorothy Janet (Southam) H.; m. Mary, d. J. J. Soper, Victoria, B.C., 10 Sept. 1949; children: Dorothy Janet, Ian Soper, Patrick Neil, Mary Ann; Dir., Molson Industries Limited; Bank of Montreal; Northern Telecom Ltd.; B.C. Resources Investment Corp.; Chairman, The Devonian Group of Charitable Foundations; Anglican; Clubs: Ranchmen's; Calgary Golf and Country; Home: 4119 Crestview Rd. S.W., Calgary, Alberta T2T 2L5; Office: 770, 999 Eighth St. S.W., Calgary, Alta. T2R 1J5

HASKAYNE, Richard Francis, B.Com., C.A.; petroleum executive; b. Calgary, Alta. 18 Dec. 1934; s. Robert S. and Bertha (Hesketh) H.; e. Univ. of Alta. B.Com. 1956; C.A. 1959; Univ. of W. Ont. Mang. Training Program 1968; m. Lee Mary d. Matthew W. Murray, Gleichen, Alta. 25 June 1958; PRES. AND C.E.O., HOME OIL CO. LTD. 1981- ; Dir., Hiram Walker Resources Ltd.; Articling Student and Staff Acct. Riddell, Stead, Graham & Hutchison, Calgary 1956-60; Corporate Accounting Supvr., Mgr. Treasury, Chief Acct., Controller, Vice Pres. Treas. and Controller Hudson's Bay Oil and Gas Co. Ltd. 1960-73, Sr. Vice Pres. 1975, Extve. Vice Pres. 1977, Dir. 1977, Pres. 1980; Comptroller, Canadian Arctic Gas Study Ltd. Calgary 1973-75; Dir. Alta. Children's Hosp. Foundation; Alta. Children's Research Centre; mem. Financial Extve. Inst.; Inst. C.A.'s; C. D. Howe Research Inst.; Kappa Sigma; Calgary Chamber Comm. (Dir.); P. Conservative; Anglican; recreations: golf, weekend farming; Clubs: Calgary Petroleum; Ranchmen's; Calgary Golf & Country; Earl Grey Golf; Univ. of Calgary Chancellor's, Lib.; Home: 6942 Leaside Dr. S.W., Calgary, Alta. T3E 6H5; Office: 700 Second St. S.W., Calgary, Alta. T2P 0X5.

HASLAM, Phyllis Georgie, O.C., B.Sc., D.S.Litt.; social worker; b. Dharmsala, Punjab, India 24 May 1913; d. Robert Henry Albert and Mildred Jean (Hoylls) H.; came to Can. 1916; e. Havergal Coll. Toronto 1919-22, 1927-30; Albert & Victoria Schs. Saskatoon 1922-26; Nutana Coll. Inst. Saskatoon 1926-27; Univ. of Sask. B.Sc. 1934; Univ. of Toronto Dipl. in Social Work 1936, Trinity Coll. D.S.Litt. 1980; Camp Dir. and Program Asst. Montreal YWCA 1936-41; Extve. Dir. Cornwall YWCA 1941-43; Extve. Dir. (First) YWCA Trinidad, W.I. 1943-48; Personnel and Training Secy. Nat. YWCA 1948-53; Extve. Dir. (First) Elizabeth Fry Soc. Toronto 1953-78; mem. Nat. Adv. Comte. on Female Offender 1976; Del., 4th UN Cong. on Prevention Crime & Treatment of Offender, Kyoto 1970; Chrmn. Central Council, Centre Christian Studies 2 yrs.; mem. Can.'s Swimming Team Brit. Empire Games, Eng. 1934, rec'd Gold and Silver Medals; admitted Candn. Aquatic Hall of Fame, Winnipeg and Sask. Sport's Hall of Fame; recipient John Howard Soc. Award 1970; St. Leonard's Soc. Can. Cody Award 1976; Ont. Assn. Prof. Social Workers Outstanding Achievement Award 1978; Toronto Soroptimist Club "Women Helping Women" Award 1979; Candn. Centennial Medal 1967; Queen's Silver Jubilee Medal 1977; mem. Ont. Assn. Prof. Social Workers (Chrmn. Toronto Br. 2 yrs); Candn. Assn. Prevention Crime (Bd. 1 term); York Co. Area Comte. (Chrmn. 2 yrs.); Anglican; recreations: swimming, walking, camping, reading; Address: 13 Washington Ave., Toronto, Ont. M5S 1L1.

HASSELL, Hilton MacDonald, R.C.A.; artist; b. Lachine, Que. 14 March 1910; s. Hilton George Samuel and Elizabeth (Cooper) H.; e. Ont. Coll. of Art; Heatherly's Sch. of Fine Art, Eng.; m. Valerie Ariel Richardson 2 Aug. 1914; children: Dr. Christopher Hilton, Laurel Ann; solo exhns. annually Eaton's Gallery 1961-71; Mem. Univ. of Nfld. 1963; Univ. of Toronto 1964; Laurentian Univ. 1971; Kensington Fine Art Gallery Calgary 1973, 1979; Manuge Galleries Halifax 1977; Wallack Galleries Ottawa 1978; mem. Ont. Soc. Artists; Club: Arts & Letters; Address: 32 Inglewood Drive, Toronto, Ontario M4T 1G8

HASTINGS, Hon. Earl Adam; senator; b. Regina, Sask., 7 Jan. 1924; s. Clarence Beverly and Eva Pearl (Winter) H.; e. Wetmore & Strathcona Pub. Schs., Regina; Balfour Tech. Sch., Regina; Regina Coll.; m. Evelyn Audrey, d. late John Andrew Kain, 19 Apl. 1952; children: David Telfer, Donald Earl, Leslie-Lynn; Asst. to Leader of Opposition and Leader of Sask. Lib. Party, 1948-52; also Asst. Secy., Sask. Lib. Assn.; Land Adm.; Dept. of Agric., Sask., 1952-57; Petroleum Landman, Sun Oil Co., Calgary, 1957-66; summoned to the Senate of Can., 1966; served with RCAF, 1942-45; Pres., Calgary Lib. Assn.,

1958 and 1959 and Alta. Lib. Assn., 1960, 1961 and 1962; Liberal; United Church; recreations: swimming, curling, hunting; Home: 3419 Utah Crescent, Calgary, Alta. T2N 4A9

HASTINGS, Thomas Roy, B.A., M.Sc.; company executive; b. 13 Feb. 1923; s. J. Ogilvie and Hazel M. (Ekers) H.; e. McGill Univ., B.A. 1946; N. Carolina State Univ., M.Sc. 1949; m. Ann, d. J. D. Finch, Iuka, Miss., 8 Oct. 1949; children: W. Roy, Melinda Ann, John O.; VICE-PRES. DIR. AND GEN. MGR. CALDWELL LINEN MILLS LTD. since 1969; commenced with Canadian Cottons Ltd., Quality Controller, 1955; subsequently Asst. Plant Mgr. and Plant Mgr.; Product Sales Mgr., Dominion Textile Ltd. 1955; subsequently Div. Sales Mgr. and Asst. to Vice-Pres. Marketing; served with R.C.N.V.R. 1942-45 in minesweepers and corvettes; rank Sub-Lt.; recreations: tennis, skiing, golf; Address: Iroquois, Ont. K0E 1K0

HATCH, Gerald Gordon, B.Eng., Sc.D.; consulting engineer; b. Brockville, Ont., 30 July 1922; s. Earle Clifton and Ethel Helen (Goodfellow) H.; e. McGill Univ., B.Eng. 1944; Mass. Inst. Of Technol., Sc.D. 1948; m. Sheila Pamela, d. John S. Baillie, 4 Sept. 1946; children: Linda, Douglas, Christopher, Joan; PRESIDENT HATCH ASSOCIATES LTD., since 1965; Research Engr., Shawinigan Water & Power Co. Ltd., 1944-45; Research Engr., Armour Research Foundation, Chicago, Ill., 1948-52, engaged on devel. of processes for prod. of titanium metal; joined Quebec Iron & Titanium Corp., Sorel, Que., as Dir. of Research & Devel., 1952-54; apptd. Works Mgr., 1954-58; became Pres., W. S. Atkins & Associates Ltd., 1958-65; awarded 1st President's Gold Medal by Candn. Inst. Mining & Metal., 1961; mem., Am. Inst. Mining & Metall. Engrs.; Ordre des Ingrs. du Que.; Sigma Xi; Anglican; recreation: golf, gardening; Clubs: University (Montreal); National (Toronto); Engineers'; St. George's Golf & Country; Home: 421 The Kingsway, Islington, Ont. M9A 3W1; Office: 21 St. Clair Ave. E., Toronto, Ont. M4T 1L8

HATCH, H. Clifford; executive; b. Toronto, Ont., 30 April 1916; s. Harry Clifford and Elizabeth (Carr) H.; m. Joan, d. late E. G. Ferriss, 1 May 1940; children: Henry Clifford, Gail Elizabeth, Sheila M., Richard F.; CHAIRMAN AND DIRECTOR, HIRAM WALKER RESOURCES LTD., since 1980, Chrmn. and CEO Hiram Walker-Gooderham & Worts Ltd. 1978-80; Pres., 1964-78; Dir. & Offr. of subsidiary companies; Dir., T. G. Bright & Co. Ltd., Niagara Falls, Ont.; Toronto-Dominion Bank; Bell Canada; R. Angus (Alta.) Ltd., Edmonton, Alta.; London Life Ins. Co., London, Ont.; Commdr., Royal Candn. Navy, 1940-45; Roman Catholic; Clubs: Essex Golf & Country (Windsor); Rosedale Golf (Toronto); Detroit Athletic (Detroit, Mich.); Home: 7130 Riverside Drive East, Windsor, Ont. N8S 1C3; Office: Ste. 4200, P.O. Box 90, 1 First Canadian Place, Toronto, Ont. M5X 1C5

HATCH, Laurence Edward "Ted"; company executive; b. Quebec, Que. 17 Dec. 1922; s. John Valiant and Louise (Capell) H.; e. Que. City High Sch.; m. Ruth Catherine, d. James Hanrahan 20 Sept. 1947; children: Brian, John, Bruce, Timothy; PRESIDENT, SEIKO TIME CANADA LTD. since 1975; joined Hatch & Co. Ltd. as Trainee, Quebec City 1939, Office Mgr. 1944, Watch Buyer 1947-71, Sales Co-ord. 1960, Gen. Mgr. 1962, Vice-Pres. 1965-71; Pres. Hatchcraft Ltd. 1948-51; joined present Co. as Candn. Sales Mgr. 1971, Vice-Pres. Can. Sales 1973; mem. Bd. Trade Metrop. Toronto; Candn. Jewellers Assn.; Protestant; recreations: golf, sailing; Club: Oakville Golf; Home: 2036 Ardleigh Rd., Oakville, Ont. L6J 1V5; Office: 235 Yorkland Blvd., Willowdale, Ont. M2J 1S8

HATCH, Roger Eugene, B.Sc.; company executive; b. Strasbourg, France, 11 June 1919; s. Eugene and Amandine H.; e. Mount Allison Univ., B.Sc. (Hons. Chem.; Eng. Cert.) 1941; McGill Univ. 1942; Harvard Univ. (Adv. Mgt.) 1959; m. Betsy (Gay) G., d. Graham Wanless, Sarnia, Ont., 5 May 1945; one d. Barbara; PRES., CANPOTEX LTD. (exporters of Candn. potash) since 1972; Pres., Canpotex Shipping Services Ltd.; Dir., Dresdner Bank; Past Chrmn., Candn. Export Assn.; mem. Advisory Council to Minister of Dept. of Ind., Trade and Comm.; Chrmn., Fed. gov't. Export Promotion Review Comte.; Chrmn., Export Trade Dev. Bd.; mem. Can. Japan Business Cooperation Comte.; Can.-China Trade Council; Dir. and past Pres., La Chambre de Commerce Française au Canada (Ont. Section); joined Polysar Ltd. (formerly Polymer Corp.) as Chem. Engr., 1942; Mgr., Sales & Tech. Service Div., 1948; Gen. Sales Mgr., 1954; Vice-Pres., Marketing, 1957; Dir. and C.E.O. of numerous subsidiary companies, including Pres. of Polymer Corp. (France) and Polysar Internat. (Switzerland) 1960-69; Group Vice Pres. 1971-72; Lieut., R.C.E. (inactive); Protestant; Clubs: Harvard Business School Club of Toronto; Ontario; Granite; Rideau; Rosedale; Home: 9 Bayview Ridge Crescent, Willowdale, Ont. M2L 1E8; Office: Box 233, Commerce Court W., Toronto, Ont. M5L 1E8

HATCH, William Douglas; vintner; b. Montreal, Que., 26 Dec. 1923; s. Elizabeth Catharine (Carr) and late Harry Clifford H.; e. Whitney Public Sch., Toronto (Ont.) 1929-37; Coll. Mont-St-Louis, Montreal (Que.) 1937-40; St. Michael's Coll., Toronto, 1940-42; Univ. of Toronto, 1946; m. Irene Frances, d. late Frank McLaughlin, 29 June 1946; children: Harry Clifford II, Carr; CHRM., T. G. BRIGHT & CO. LTD. (Estbd. 1874) since 1978; Dir., Canada Malting Co. Ltd.; Canada Permanent Trust Co.; Can. Permanent Mortgage Corp.; joined present Co. as Lab. Asst., 1947; apptd. Export Mgr., 1948, Asst. to Vice-Pres., Sales and Ad. Mgr., 1949; el. Dir. 1952; apptd. Secy. 1952; Vice-Pres., Sales, 1959; Pres. 1963-78; mem. Adv. Council, Hotel Dieu Hosp., St. Catharines (Ont.); Past Pres. Candn. Wine Inst.; served in 2nd World War RCNVR l942; active service, Sub-Lieut. 1943, Lieut. 1944-45; mem. Internat. Oceanographic Foundation, Miami (Fla.); Naval Offrs. Assn. (Toronto Bd.); Knight Of Malta; Chevalier de l'Ordre des Coteaux de Champagne, Rheims, France; Past Chrmn., Wine Council of Ont.; R. Catholic; recreations: golf, thoroughbred horses, curling, yachting; Clubs: Granite; RCYC; Rosedale Golf; Ontario Jockey; St. Catharines; St. Catharines Golf & Country; Cherry Hill (Ridgeway, Ont.); Niagara Falls; Home: 173 Highland Ave., St. Catharines, Ont. L2R 4J9; Office: (P.O. Box 510) Niagara Falls, Ont. L2E 6V4

HATCHER, James Donald, M.D.; PhD.; university professor; b. St. Thomas, Ont., 22 June 1923; s. Fred Thomas and Cora Pearl (Rooke) H.; e. Univ. of Western Ont., M.D. 1946, Ph.D. 1951; F.R.C.P.(C) 1977; m. Helen Edith, d. James Roberts, 14 June 1946; two d.: Janet Louise, Carolyn Elizabeth; PROF. OF PHYSIOL., DALHOUSIE UNIV. and Dean, Faculty of Med., since 1976; Instr. in Med., Boston Univ. Sch. of Med. and Research Fellow, Robert Dawson Evan's Mem. Hosp., Boston, 1950-52; Asst. Prof. of Physiol., Queen's Univ., 1952-55, Assoc. Prof. 1955-59; Prof. and Chrmn. of Dept. of Physiol. 1959-62; Assoc. Dean, Faculty of Med. 1968-71; Visiting Prof. of Physiol. and Visiting Research Assoc., Cardiovascular Research Inst., Univ. of Cal. 1971-72; Prof. of Physiol. and Head of Dept., Queen's Univ. 1962-76; served with R.C.A.M.C. 1944-46 and with Reserve 1947-50 (Lt., 15th Field Ambulance); mem., Nat'l Research Council Comm., Internat. Sc. and Tech. Affiliations, 1981; Advisory Comm. on Research, Royal Coll. Phys. and Surg. of Can., 1981; Bd. of Dir., Connaught Laboratories, 1981; Chrmn., Tertiary Care Comm., Min. of Health, Prov. of N.B. 1981; ex-officio mem., Bd. of Dir., Dalhousie Univ., Med. Research Fdn., 1979; Dir., Ont. Heart Foundation 1967-71 (mem. Medical Adv. Comte. 1966-71); mem., Arctic Panel, Defence Research Bd., 1957-62 (mem., Med. Adv. Comte. 1962-67; Candn.

Forces Adv. Group on Operational Effectiveness of Personnel, 1966-68; Chrmn., Panel on Arctic Med. & Climatic Physiol., 1962-67); mem., Surg. Gen.'s Adv. Comte., 1964-66; Panel mem., Med. Research Council of Canada, 1964-81 and since 1977; (mem. Council 1967-70); Chmn. Fellowship Comm., Med. Research Council of Can. 1967-72 Rep. of Assn. Candn. Med. Colls. on Nat. Research Council Comte. in Care of Exper. Animals, 1964-66; Queen's Univ. Rep. to Consultative Comte., Med. Research Council 1970-71; Candn. Physiol. Soc. Rep. to Biol. Council of Can. 1968-71; Med. Research Council Rep. on Candn. Council on Animal Care 1968-71; Markle Scholar in Medicine, Queen's Univ., 1952-57; Nuffield Travelling Fellowship 1956; Fellow, Ont. Heart Foundation 1957-59; Sr. Research Assoc., Nat. Heart Foundation 1959-60; Fellow of the Royal Coll. of Phys. and Surg. of Can. 1977; Contrib. to "Physiology of Human Survival," 1965; Coed., "International Symposium on the Cardiovascular and Respiratory Effects of Hypoxia," 1965; author of over 35 papers on research related to physiol. of cardiovascular system; mem., Candn. Physiol. Soc. (mem. Council 1961-65; Treas. 1965-68; Vice Pres. 1969-70, Pres. 1970-71); United Church; recreation: oil painting; Home: 24 Rockwood, Halifax, N.S.

HATFIELD, Hon. Richard Bennett, M.L.A., B.A., LL.B., LL.D.; politician; b. Woodstock, N.B., 9 Apl. 1931; s. Heber Harold and Dora Fern (Robinson) H.; e. Acadia Univ., B.A., 1952; Dalhousie Univ., LL.B., 1956; (Hon. Causa) L.L.D., Univ. of Moncton (1971); Univ. of N.B. (1972); St. Thomas Univ. (1973); Mount Allison Univ. (1975); PREMIER OF NEW BRUNSWICK since Nov. 1970; admit. to Bar of N.S., 1956; practiced law 1957; Sales Mgr., Hatfield Industries, 1958-65; Extve. Asst. to Min. of Trade and Comm., Ottawa 1957-58; first el. to N.B. Leg. for Carleton in by-el. 1961; re-el. since; el. Leader of N.B. P. Cons. Party, 1969; El. to form Govt. of N.B. (Oct. 1970); sworn in as Premire Nov. 1970; P.C. party returned as govt. in prov. el. Nov. 1974 and Oct. 1978; Dir., Cdn. Council of Children and Jews, Atlantic Div.; Hon. Chief of Micmac-Maliseet, 1970; rec'd. Can.-Israel Friendship Award 1973; Hon. mem. Extve., N.B. Div., Candn. Red Cross Soc. and Prov. Council, Boy Scouts of Can.; P. Conservative; Protestant; Home: Hartland, N.B.; Office: Premier's Office, P.O. Box 6000 Centennial Bldg., Fredericton, N.B. E3B 5H1

HATTERSLEY, John Martin, M.A., LL.B.; b. Swinton, Yorkshire, Eng., 10 Nov. 1932; s. Charles Marshall and Ethel Vera (Chambers) H.; e. Repton Sch., Derbyshire, Eng. 1946-50; Clare Coll., Cambridge 1952-56, B.A. (Econ. and Law) 1955, LL.B. (Pub. and Adm. Law) 1956, M.A. 1959; m. Florence Anne, d. Frederick William Stilwell, 14 Sept. 1957; three d. Catherine Rose, Nancy Jane, Janet Marie; PARTNER, HATTERSLEY & HENDRICKSON; Pres.,; Greno Holdings Ltd.; Pres., Christian Family Life Foundation of Alta. 1970-80; Dir., Jr. Achievement of Edmonton; Edmonton Volunteer Action Centre; emigrated to Can. 1956; articled with Milner & Steer, Edmonton, Alta.; read law with Ronald Martland, Q.C.; called to Bar of Alta. 1957; 1962-64 served as Personal Secy. to Robert Thompson, M.P., Nat. Leader of Social Credit Party, becoming also Dir. of Research and Editor of "Focus" for S.C. Assn. of Can.; served as Offr. in Royal Arty. 1951-56, rank on discharge Lieut.; Nat. Pres., Social Credit Party of Can. 1973-78 (Vice Pres. Alta. League 1966-67, 1979-80; Alta. Br. of Party 1969-73, Nat'l Leader, 1980-); former Vice Pres., Sorrento Centre for Human Devel.; former mem. Doctrine & Worship Comte., Gen. Synod, Ang. Ch. Can.; Hon. Asst. Priest, St. Peter's Anglican Ch., Edmonton, since 1974; mem. Edmonton Chamber Comm. (Vice Pres., Gov't. Dept., 1977, 1979-; Law Soc. Alta.; Edmonton and Candn. Bar Assns.; Royal Candn. Legion; I.O.F.; Mensa; Publications: "Human Rights-The New Political Direction" and "Monetary Reform for Canada" 1980; Social Credit; Anglican; recreations: music, yoga, badminton, photography; Club: The Edmonton; Home: 8112-144A St., Edmonton, Alta. T5R 0S2; Office: 1200-10015,-10015, 103 Ave., Edmonton, Alta. T5J 0H1

HAUSER, Alexis; conductor; b. Vienna, Austria 25 May 1947; s. Willibald and Elenore (Kern) H.; e. Conserv. of Music Vienna Dipl. in Conducting and Composition 1968; Academie fur Musik und Darstellende Kunst grad. Conducting 1970; Salzburg Mozarteum Akademie Dipl. in Conducting 1970 (Princ. teacher Herbert von Karajan); Siena (Italy) Accademia-Chigiana Dipl. in Conducting 1969; Conducting Seminar New York Philharmonic with Erich Leinsdorf; CONDUCTOR AND MUSIC DIR., LONDON-CANADA SYMPHONY ORCHESTRA 1981- ; internat. guest conductor with maj. orchestras and opera companies Europe and Am. since 1970 incl. Vienna Symphony, RIAS-Symphony Orchestra Berlin, Belgrad Philharmonic, Philharmonia Hungarica, Orchestre Capitol de Toulouse-France, Biennale Venice, Montreal Symphony Orchestra, Atlanta, San Francisco and Toledo Symphony Orchestras, Rochester Philharmonic, New York City Opera, Washington Opera House-Kennedy Center, Chicago Opera and Civic Orchestra, St. Louis Philharmonic; summer festival Tanglewood; Orquesta Sinfonica Mexico City; Orquesta Nat. Lima; rec'd Koussevitzky-Conducting Prize 1974; prize 1st Internat. Hans Swarowsky-Conducting Competition Vienna 1977; many broadcasts Europe and Am., TV and film participation; author various articles and essays on music of Gustav Mahler; mem. Internat. Gustavemahler-Gesellschaft Vienna; Am. Gustav Mahler Soc.; recreations: arts, literature, jogging, yoga, calisthenics, swimming, oriental cooking; Home: Beethovengasse 8/4, A-1090 Vienna, Austria

HAVEL, Jean Eugène Martial, Dr. ès L.; university professor; b. Le Havre, France, 16 June 1928; s. Marc Louis Gustave and Suzanne Céline Marie (Doré) H.; e. Univ. de Paris, Faculté de Droit, Lic. 1950; Institut des Etudes Politiques Diplôme, 1952; Institut des Etudes Scandinaves 1953, Faculté des Lettres Dr. ès L. 1956; Univ. of Oslo Sch. of Law 1953-54; m. late Anne Marie, d. Georg Robert Mauritz Luhr, Djursholm, Sweden 22 Aug. 1955; children: Jean Guillaume, Frédérik, Mathilde Sophie, Ingrid Lucie; PROF. OF POL. SCIENCE, LAURENTIAN UNIV., since 1969; Part-time Teacher of French, Univ. of Stockholm, 1956-59; Asst. Prof. of Pol. Science, Univ. de Montréal, 1959-62; political commentator for Radio-Canada, 1961-71; Asst. Prof. of Pol. Science, Laurentian Univ., 1962, Assoc. Prof. 1964, Acting Head of Dept. 1967-70; mem. Extve. Social Science Research Council, 1968-69; rec'd Norwegian Govt., Swedish Inst. and Council of Europe Scholarships; 2nd Prize, Carnegie Endowment for Internat. Peace — European Center, 1958; Acad. des Sciences Morales et Politiques "mention," 1962; Guest speaker, Univ. New Brunswick 1968, Caen, Helsinki, London, Padova and Rouen 1969; Liége, 1981; author of "La Finlande et la Suède", 1978; "Les états scandinaves et l'intégration européenne", 1970; "Les citoyens de Sudbury et la politique," 1966 (Eng. transl. 1966); "La condition de la femme," 1961 (Italian translation 1962, Spanish translation 1965, Japanese trans. 1970); "Habitat et Logement," 1957, 1964, 1967, and 1974 (Spanish translation 1961); "La fabrication du journal" 1957; "Cours de journalisme: la rédaction," 1957; 5 pamphlets and numerous articles and reviews for learned journs.; corres. of Nordic Council since 1969; mem. Canadian Political Science Association; Learned Journal Jury of Can. Council, 1976, 1977; Adjudicating Panel, Soc. Sc. and Humanities Research Council of Can., Special M.A. Scholarships (Ont. area) 1981; Fellow of Internat. University Seminar on Armed Forces and Society 1979; scholarship from Salzburg Seminar on Am. Studies, 1957; grants from Can. Council, 1968, 1975-76 and Social Science Research Council of Can., 1979-80; awarded Centennial Medal; Can. Council Fellowship Award 1968 and 1975; recreations: travel, fine arts, music; Home: 175 Boland Ave., Sudbury, Ont. P3E 1Y1

HAVLIK, Jaroslav Jan; manufacturer; b. Prague, Czechoslovakia, 13 Sept. 1903; s. Jan and Jana (Savrdova) H.; e. grad. eng.; PRESIDENT AND GEN. MGR., HAVLIK ENTERPRISES LTD. since 1959; Pres., Williams Machines Ltd.; True Forge Ltd.; Material Processing; came to Canada 1951; took over father's business, Prague 1930; left Czechoslovakia 1938 for U.S. then U.K. 1939 where joined Allied Underground movement; mem. Exile Czech Govt. and Czechoslovakian Intelligence Service 1939-44; captured 1944 by Gestapo and interned till 1945; formed machine tool business in Ireland 1946; joined Williams Machines Ltd. as Mgr., 1951 purchasing that Co. in 1959; Pres., Candn. Machine Builders Assn.; mem. Canadian Czechoslovakian Legion; Prog. Conservative; Protestant; recreations: tennis, bowling, swimming; Clubs: Rotary; Albany; Home: 952 Hamilton St., Cambridge, Cambridge, Ont.; Office: 695 Bishop St., Preston, Ont.

HAWEY, Ghislain, M.Com., C.A.; b. Quebec, Que., 16 Aug. 1931; s. Arthur and Juliette (Lajeunesse) H.; e. Laval Univ., B.Com. 1952, M.Com. 1953, Master in Accounting Sciences 1955; children: Steven Bernard, Douglas, Michael; PARTNER, TOUCHE ROSS & CO. and Charette, Fortier, Hawey & Cie. and P.S. Ross & Partners and Charette Fortier Hawey & Associés; Pres., Que. Planning and Devel. Council 1974-78; Dir. Industrial Development Corp. of Que.; 1973-78 Dir. Touche Ross & Co. (Canada) and managing Partner of the Quebec Practice Unit; Prof. of Accounting, Faculty Adm. Sciences, Laval Univ. 1962-63; Pres., Que. Chamber Comm. 1971-72; Pres., Rotary Club of Quebec E., 1967; Gov., Laval Univ. Found.; mem. Candn. Inst. Chart. Accts.; Que. Order Chart. Accts.; Que. Inst. Mang. Consultants; R. Catholic; recreations: swimming, fishing, tennis, golf; Clubs: Garrison; Cercle Universitaire; Home: 3336 Arthur Grenier St., Beauport, Quebec, Que. G1E 1G8, and 1115 Sherbrooke W., Montreal, Que. H3A 1H3; Office: 880 Chemin Ste-Foy, Quebec, Que. G1S 2L2 and Royal Bank Bldg., 1 Place Ville Marie, Montreal, Que. H3B 2A1

HAWKE, John Howard, B.A.; company chairman; b. St. Catharines, Ont., 14 April 1926; s. Edith Moore (Magee) and the late Charles W. Hawke; e. St. Catharines Coll. Inst.; Univ. of Toronto, B.A.; m. Aileen Gwendolyn Demont, Toronto, Ont., 29 Jan. 1960; children: Laurien, Martha, Charles, Gordon, Kelly; CHRMN. AND CHIEF EXTVE. OFFR., BACHE HALSEY STUART CAN. LTD. since 1975; Pres., Hawke-Lea Holdings Ltd.; Chrmn., Fletcher Golf Enterprises Ltd.; Dir. and mem. Extve. Comte., Canadian Occidental Petroleum Ltd.; Dir., Jannock Ltd.; Carswell Co. Ltd.; with Gairdner & Co. Ltd. 1949 till resignation as Pres. 1970; mem. Bd. Govs., St. Andrew's Coll. (Aurora, Ont.); served overseas during 2nd World War with R.C.N.V.R. as Sub-Lieut., N.A.C., 1943-45; Delta Upsilon; United Church; recreations: golf, tennis, skiing; Clubs: Ontario; Empire; Canadian; Badminton and Raquet; Rosedale Golf; St. Andrews; Delray Beach, Fla.; Home: 10 Castlefrank Rd. Toronto, Ont. M4W 2Z4; Office: 18 King St.E., Toronto, Ont. M5C 1E3

HAWKES, Robert H., Q.C.; executive; b. Toronto, Ont., 9 March 1930; s. Agnes (Howie) and late Robert Kelvin H.; m. Joan May, d. late Earl Lepard, 6 May 1960; one s. Robert Scott; PRESIDENT, AND CEO, ROTHMANS OF PALL MALL CANADA LIMITED; United Church; recreations: sailing; skiing; Home: 94 Elm Ave., Toronto, Ont. M4W 1P2; Office: 1500 Don Mills Rd., Don Mills, Ont. M3B 3L1

HAWKINS, Dallas Euel, II; petroleum executive; b. Houston, Texas, 29 May 1923; s. Dallas Euel and Loretta (O'Reilly) H.; e. Rice Univ.; Univ. of Mich.; m. Mary Ann, d. Franklin Pierce Wood, Dallas, Texas, 27 Apl. 1951; children: Kathleen, Dallas O'Reilly, Robert Pierce; CHMN., C.E.O. AND DIR., OAKWOOD PETROLEUMS LTD. (estbl. 1925) and its subsidiaries Dir., Commercial Oil & Gas Ltd.; Audican Eagle Petroleum Ltd.; Conven-

tives Ltd.; Roustabout, Illinois Oil Fields, 1936-40: Field Engr., Magnolia Petroleum Co., Victoria, Texas 1944; Chief Engr., Commanche Corp., Dallas, Tex., 1947-50; came to Can., 1951; Supt. i/c Operations, Candn. Delhi Oil & Gas Ltd., Calgary, Alta., 1951; Gen. Mgr., Scandia Drilling Co. Ltd. 1952-53; Asst. Supt., Sun Oil Co., 1954-56; Vice Pres. Gen. Mgr. and Dir., Fargo Oils Ltd., 1956-62; Dir., British Columbia Oil Transmission Co. Ltd., 1960-62; Chrmn. of Bd., Am. Eagle Petroleums Ltd.; mem., Assn. Prof. Engrs. Alta., Man., Texas; Am. Inst. Mech. Engrs.; Am. Inst. Chem. Engrs; Alta. Oil Field Tech. Soc.; Am. Petroleum Inst.; served overseas in 2nd World War with U.S.N. in Pacific with Underwater Demolition Team 12, Jt. Intell. Command, Tokyo, Japan, Iwo Jima, Okinawa invasions; Tau Beta Pi; Sigma Xi; Phi Lambda Upsilon; Anglican; recreations: skiing, golf; Clubs: Calgary Golf & Country; Calgary Petroleum; Northwood (Dallas); Home: 302-3204 Rideau Place S.W., Calgary Alta. T2S 1Z2 Office: 1800-311 6th Ave. S.W., Calgary, Alta. T2P 3H2

HAWKINS, Hon. John, M.L.A., M.A.; politician; b. Halifax, N.S., 5 May 1932; s. Walter John and Dorothy M. H.; e. E. H. Horne Sch., Enfield, N.S.; Dalhousie Univ.; St. Mary's Univ. B.A. (Lit. Award, French Grad. Award); Univ. of N.B., M.A.; m. Monique Marie Roach, May 1956; children: John, Eleanor, Mary Ann; former Min. of Agric. & Marketing, N.S.; Min. of the Environment & Min. for Emergency Measures Organ. 1976; Chmn., Treasury Bd. 1976-78; N.S. Liberal Caucus 1981- ; served with Candn. Army Halifax, Germany 1954-60, rank Lt.; Dir. of Recreation Mun. of E. Hants, Enfield 1961-63; el. M.L.A. 1970, re-el. since; rec'd N.S. Playwriting Award 1960, 1962; author "Life and Times of Angus L. Macdonald", 1969, "Dear Hunting in Eastern Canada" 1981 and various articles in learned journs.; mem. Univ. Teachers Eng.; Commonwealth Party. Assn.; Royal Candn. Legion; Liberal; recreations: hunting, fishing; Home: Enfield, Hants Co., N.S. B0N 1N0;

HAWKINS, John; real estate executive; b. London, Eng. 15 March 1918; s. George and Maude Hope (Freeman) H.; e. Sir Richard Ackland, London, Eng.; m. Lucy d. George Brown, Cayton Bay, Yorks., Eng. 26 Oct. 1946; CHRMN. AND DIR. MACAULAY NICOLLS MAITLAND & CO. since 1977; Dir. Wardley Canada Ltd.; Hastings West Investments Ltd.; International Land Ltd.; Granville Savings & Mortgage; Selkirk Mortgage; served with Brit. Army 1939-46, Mentioned in Despatches; Fellow, Real Estate Inst. Can (Past Gov. and Pres.); mem. Internat. Real Estate Fed.; Vancouver Real Estate Bd.; Pres., Arthritis Soc. (B.C.); Anglican; recreations: golf, bridge; Clubs: Vancouver; Capilano Golf & Country; Home: PH 3, 955 Marine Dr., West Vancouver, B.C. V7T 1A9; Office: 16th Floor, 200 Granville St., Vancouver, B.C. V6C 2R6

HAWKRIGG, Melvin Michael, B.A., C.A.; financial services executive; b. Toronto, Ont. 26 Aug. 1930; s. Harry and Ida May (Cornish) H.; e. Islington Pub. Sch.; Etobicoke Coll. Inst.; McMaster Univ., B.A.; C.A. 1956; m. Marilyn, d. Jack Field, 4 June 1954; children: Elizabeth Jane, John Michael, Peter Alan, Mary Ann, John Richard; EXTVE. VICE-PRESIDENT, FINANCIAL SERVICES GROUP/BRASCAM LTD.; joined Clarkson, Gordon & Company 1952; joined Fuller Brush Co. Ltd. 1959; Comptroller, 1961; Comptroller and Gen. Mgr., 1963 and subsequently Pres.; Past Chrmn. of Bd. of Jr. Achievement of Can.; mem., Extve. Comte., McMaster Univ. Alumni Assn.; Home & Sch. Assn. Waterdown Ont. (Pres.); Candn. Inst. Chart. Accts.; Chrmn. and C.E.O., Candn. Depository for Securities; Candn. Curtiss Wright Ltd.; Candn. Mfrs. Assn.; Direct Sellers Assn. (Pres.); mem. of Council, Metrop. Toronto Bd. of Trade; Anglican; recreations: golf, curling; Club: Toronto; Burlington Golf & Country; Home: First St., Waterdown, Ont.; Office: Box 48, Commerce Court Postal Stn., Toronto, Ont. M5L 1B7

HAWORTH, Mrs. Bobs Cogill, R.C.A., O.S.A. artist; painter in water colour and oils; b. Queenstown, S. Africa; e. Royal Coll. of Art, London, Eng.; Specialist in Ceramics; came to Can., 1923; m. Peter Haworth, artist; in charge of Ceramics, Central Tech. Sch., Toronto, Ont.; Represented in Nat. Gallery of S. Africa, Nat. Gallery Can., Art Galleries of Ontario, Art Galleries of Hamilton, Art Galleries of Windsor, London, and many private collections; mem., Ont. Soc. of Artists; Candn. Group of Painters; Royal Cdn. Academy; Candn. Soc. of Painters in Water Colour (Pres. 1954-56); Candn. Guild of Potters; winner of Jessie Dow Prize for Water Colour (R.C.A.), 1953; Home: 111 Cluny Drive, Rosedale, Toronto, Ont. M4W 2R5

HAWORTH, Lawrence Lindley, M.A., Ph.D.; educator; b. Chicago, Ill. 14 Dec. 1926; s. Lawrence and Ruth (Johnson) H.; e. Rollins Coll. Fla. B.A. 1949; Univ. of Ill. M.A. 1950, Ph.D. 1952; m. Alison Mindea d. Graham Pedlar, Lincoln, Eng. 24 Dec. 1977; children: Lawrence III, Ruth; PROF. OF PHILOS., UNIV. OF WATERLOO 1965- , Assoc. Dean Grad. Studies 1975-81, Chrmn. of Philos. 1967-70; served with U.S. Army 1944-46; author "The Good City" 1963; "Decadence and Objectivity" 1977; numerous papers prof. journs.; mem. Candn. Philos. Assn.; Phi Beta Kappa; recreations: cross-country skiing, jogging; Home: R.R.1, St. Agatha, Ont. N0B 2L0; Office: Waterloo, Ont.

HAWORTH, Peter, D.F.C., R.C.A. (1954), F.R.S.A.; artist; e. Roy. Coll. Art (London) A.R.C.A.; Past Pres. and mem., Candn. Soc. of Painters in Water-Colour; mem., Candn. Group of Painters; men. and Past Pres., Ont. Soc. of Artists; Dir. of Art, Central Tech. Sch., Toronto, Ont., 1929-55 (retired); Painter represented in Nat. Gallery of Can., Art Galleries of Ont., London, Hamilton, Windsor and public galleries in U.S.A., Australia, N. Zealand, Brazil, and many private collections; Designer of many stained glass windows in churches and buildings across Can.; Military record: Flying Offr. in 1st World War; awarded D.F.C.; Home: 111 Cluny Drive, Toronto, Ont. M4W 2R5

HAWTHORN, Harry, O.C. (1972), B.A., M.Sc., PhD., F.R.S.C. (1956); retired univ. prof.; b. Wellington, N.Z., 15 Oct. 1910; s. Henry Josiah and Henrietta Louisa (Hansen) M.; e. Wellington Coll., 1924-27; Univ. of N.Z., B.Sc. 1932, M.Sc. 1934, B.A. 1937; Univ. of Hawaii, 1938-39; Yale Univ., Ph.D. 1941; LL.D.(Hon.) Univ. of B.C., Brandon Univ. and McMaster Univ.; m. Audrey Genevieve, d. Dr. E. T. Engle, New York, N.Y., 1941; Research Asst., Inst. of Human Relations, Yale Univ., 1939-42; study in Bolivia, 1942: mem. of Faculty, Sarah Lawrence Coll., 1942-47; Emeritus Prof. of Anthropol., Univ. of B.C., 1947-76, and Head of the Department 1956-68; Director Museum of Anthropology 1948-74; Publications: "The Maori: A Study in Acculturation" (memoir) 1944; Ed., "The Doukhobors of British Columbia" 1955; Ed. and co-author, "The Indians of British Columbia", 1957; Ed., "A Survey of the Contemporary Indians Of Canada", 1967; some 20 articles in various journs. of science and opinion; Home: Riverlea Rd. 2, Kumeu, New Zealand

HAY, Rev. David William, D.D. (Presb.); b. Capetown, South Africa, 18 August 1905; s. David and Elizabeth (Hendry) H.; e. Royal High School, Edinburgh; University of Edinburgh and New Coll., M.A. 1929 (Hons.); Queen's Univ., D.D. 1949; Trinity Coll., D.D. 1973; King's Coll., D.D. 1977; St. Michael's Coll., D.D. 1979 (Hon.); m. Christina Crawford, d. Sir Charles C. Reid, 29 April 1936; children: Olive, Alastair; MODERATOR, PRESBYTERIAN CHURCH IN CANADA, 1975; formerly Prof. of Systematic Theol., Knox Coll. Univ. of Toronto; Pollok Lecturer, Pinehill Divinity Hall, 1939; Assoc. Editor, Candn. Journal of Theology 1958-70; Pres., Candn. Council of Churches, 1960-62; Birks Lecturer, McGill Univ. 1974; recreations: golf, fishing; Home: The Manse,

St. David's Ont. L0S 1P0; Office: Knox College, Univ. of Toronto, Ont. M5S 2E6

HAY, George Edward, Ph.D.; mathematician; b. Durham, Ont. 11 June 1914; s. Edward Alexander and Frances Annetta (Scarr) H.; e. Durham (Ont.) Pub. and High Schs., 1919-28; Brampton (Ont.) High Sch., 1928-31; Univ. of Toronto, B.A. 1935, M.A. 1936, Ph.D. 1939; m. Lillian Edith Parker, d. late Thomas Herbert Howl. 28 May 1943; children: Edward James, John Robert, Kathryn Ann; PROF. OF MATH., UNIV. OF MICHIGAN, since 1955 and Assoc. Dean Grad. Sch. 1967-76; Instr., Ill. Inst. of Technol., 1939-40; joined present Univ. as Instr., 1940-42; Asst. Prof. 1942-47; Assoc. Prof. 1947-55; Chrmn., Math. Dept., 1957-67; Assoc. Dean Grad. School, 1967-76; Consultant, U.S. Health, Educ. and Welfare, since 1964; during World War II Research Assoc., U.S. Govt. Office of Scient. Research and Devel., 1944-45; author: "Vector and Tensor Analysis", 1953; other writings incl. several scient. papers on Mech. of a Continuum; mem., London Math. Soc.; Am. Math. Soc.; Math. Assn. Am.; Soc. Indust. & Applied Math.; Indust. Math. Soc.; Sigma Xi; Democrat; Protestant; recreation: golf; Club: Rotary; Home: 1714 Morton Ave., Ann Arbor, Mich. 48104

HAY, James Miller, B.E., M.P.E., Ph.D., F.C.I.C.; chemical executive; b. Regina, Sask. 9 July 1929; s. Charles Cecil Hay; e. Univ. of Sask. B.E. (Chem. Engn.) 1950; Univ. of Tulsa M.P.E. 1954; Univ. of Toronto Ph.D. 1957; m. d. of Ralph M. Cantlon 28 Oct. 1950; PRES., CHIEF EXTVE. OFFR. AND DIR. DOW CHEMICAL OF CANADA LTD. 1980- ; joined Refinery Engineering Co. Tulsa, Okla. and Toronto 1950-54; Process Engn. and Devel. in various supervisory positions Dow Chemical of Canada Ltd., Sarnia 1957-65, Mgr. Devel. Sarnia 1965-68; Business Mang., Corporate Planning, Dir. Information Systems & Technol. Adm. The Dow Chemical Co. Midland, Mich. 1968-73; Vice Pres. Operations and Dir. present Co. 1973-80; mem. Assn. Prof. Engrs. Prov. Ont.; Candn. Chem. Producers Assn. (Dir.); United Church; recreations: sports, music; Office: (P.O. Box 1012) Sarnia, Ont. N7T 7H6.

HAYCOCK, Kenneth Roy, M.A., M.Ed.; librarian; educator; b. Hamilton, Ont. 15 Feb. 1948; s. Bruce Frederick Travis and Doris Marion Page (Downham) H.; e. Univ. of W. Ont. B.A. 1968, Dipl. in Educ. 1969; Univ. of Toronto Specialist Cert. in Sch. Librarianship 1971; Univ. of Ottawa M.Ed. 1973; Univ. of Mich. M.A. (Lib. Science) 1974; m. Carol-Ann Low 31 July 1979; COORDINATOR OF LIB. SERVICES, VANCOUVER SCH. BD. 1976- ; Hist. Teacher and Head Librarian, Glebe Coll. Inst. Ottawa 1969-70; Head, Learning Media Centre, Colonel By Secondary Sch. Ottawa 1970-72; Educ. Media Consultant (K-13), Wellington Co. Bd. Educ. Guelph 1972-76; mem. Cultural Services Br. Publishing Assistance Comte., B.C. Ministry of Prov. Secy. and Govt. Services 1979- ; B.C. Arts Bd. Lit. Arts Comte., 1980- ; Can. Council Book and Periodicals Promotion Comte., 1980- ; Lib. Tech. Program Adv. Comte., Vancouver Community Coll. 1979; Council, Sch. of Librarianship, Univ. of B.C. 1978- ; Trustee, Guelph Pub. Lib. 1975-76; sometime sessional instr. in Sch. Librarianship, Educ., Univs. of Toronto and B.C. 1975- ; guest lectr., workshops, addresses; author "Free Magazines for Teachers and Libraries" 1974, 2nd ed. 1977; "Index to the Contents of Moccasin Telegraph" 1975; "Security - Secondary School Resource Centres" 1975; "Sears List of Subject Headings: Canadian Companion" 1978; book chapters, pamphlets, articles, reports; Ed. "Free! The Newsletter of Free Materials and Services" 1979- ; Co-Ed. "Emergency Librarian" 1979- ; mem. various advisory and ed. bds.; rec'd Wilson Lib. Bulletin "Front-Liner" 1974; Beta Phi Mu Award Univ. of Mich. 1976; Queen's Silver Jubilee Medal 1977; Margaret B. Scott Award of Merit, Candn. Sch. Lib. Assn. 1979; Phi Delta Kappa Leaders in Education Award, 1980; mem. Am. Lib. Assn.; Am. Assn. Sch. Librarians (Dir. 1974-75); Assn. for Media & Technol. in Educ. Can.; B.C.

Council for Leadership Educ. Adm.; B.C. Lib. Assn. (Extve. 1981-); B.C. Teachers' Fed.; B.C. Primary Teachers' Assn.; B.C. Sch. Librarians Assn.; B.C. Sch. Supvrs. of Instruction; Candn. Lib. Assn. (Pres. 1977-78, Dir. 1974-75, 1976-79, Council 1974-81); Candn. Lib. Trustees Assn.; Candn. Sch. Lib. Assn. (Pres. 1974-75); Ont. Sch. Lib. Assn.; Ont. Lib. Assn.; Pacific Instructional Media Assn.; Vancouver Schs. Coordinators Assn. (Treas. 1978-79, Pres. 1979-80); Internat. Assn. Sch. Librarianship; Candn. Coll. Teachers; Beta Phi Mu; Phi Delta Kappa; Home: 6871 Shawnigan Pl., Richmond, B.C. V7E 4W9; Office: 1595 W. 10th Ave., Vancouver, B.C. V6J 1Z8.

HAYCRAFT, Alan Finch, S.M.; company executive; b. Renfrew, Ont. 7 May 1925; s. Mr. and Mrs. C. C. Haycraft; e. Public and High Schs., Renfrew, Ont.; Queen's Univ., B.Sc. (Elect. Engn.) 1946; Mass. Inst. Tech., S.M. (Mang.) Sloan Fellow 1968; m. Joyce Maxwell, 4 June 1949; children: Janice, Paul, Barbara; CHRMN. OF BD. & GEN. MGR. CONSUMER & SERVICE PRODUCTS DIV., KIMBERLY-CLARK OF CANADA LTD. since 1974; joined Spruce Falls Power and Paper Company Limited, Kapuskasing 1946; served successively as Industrial Engr., Chief Indust. Engineer and Personnel Manager; apptd. Mgr., Kimberly-Clark of Canada mill, Niagara Falls, Ont. 1960; Asst. Gen. Mgr. Operations, Kimberly-Clark of Canada Ltd., Toronto, Ont. 1963; Vice-Pres. Operations, Kimberly-Clark Corp, International Div., Neenah, Wis. 1968; apptd. Extve. Vice-Pres. present Cos. 1970, Pres. 1971; mem. Assn. Prof. Engrs. Ont.; Candn. Pulp & Paper Assn.; Anglican; recreations: sailing, music; Clubs: National; Port Credit Yacht; Home: 2238 Highriver Court, Mississauga, Ont. L5H 3K4; Office: 365 Bloor St., East Toronto Ont. M4W 3L9

HAYDEN, Gerald Francis, Q.C.; b. Toronto, Ont., 14 Dec. 1924; s. Hon. Salter Adrian and Ethel Gwendolyn (Connolly) H.; e. Allenby Pub. Sch. and De La Salle Coll., Toronto, Ont.; Univ. of Toronto; Osgoode Hall Law Sch., Toronto, Ont.; m. Mary Louise, d. Lauren Drake Mayer, Toronto, Ont., 19 Aug. 1953; children: Gerald Francis, Judith Louise, Richard Drake Laird, Andrew Crashley; SR. PARTNER, McCARTHY & McCARTHY; Secy. & Dir., Kearney-National (Canada) Ltd.; Dir., Engineered Yarns of Canada Ltd.; Chmn. of Bd., Orthopaedic and Arthritic Hosp.; President and Director, Nelson Arthur Hyland Foundation; Dir. and Secty., T. Donald Miller Fndtn.; Orthopaedic and Arthritic Hospital Fndtn; Gov., Crescent Sch., Toronto; mem., Nat. Council of Boy Scouts; read law with Beaton, Bell & Pond, Toronto, Ont.; called to Bar of Ont., June 1950; cr. Q.C., 1 Jan. 1965; Liberal; R. Catholic; recreations: golf, swimming; Club: Rosedale Golf; Home: 29 Oriole Road, Toronto, Ont. M4V 2E6; Office: Toronto-Dominion Centre, Box 48, Toronto, Ont. M5K 1E6

HAYDEN, Melissa (Mrs. Donald H. Coleman); ballerina; b. Toronto, Ont., 25 April 1923; d. Jacob and Kate (Weinberg) Herman; m. Donald Hugh Coleman, Feb. 1959; children: Stuart H., Jennifer H.; began as student of Boris Volkoff Ballet Sch., Toronto, Ont.; Sch. of Am. Ballet, Vilzak-Shollar; Member, Ford Foundation Nat. Scholarship Comte.; Member, N.Y. State Arts Council; mem. of Corps de Ballet, Radio City N.Y., 1945; Soloist, Ballet Theatre, tours U.S. and Europe, 1946-55; Prima Ballerina on tour, 1953; toured S. Am. with Ballet Alicia Alonzo; with N.Y.C. Ballet, 1949-53 and since 1955; appeared in Ballet Pas de Trois, The Cage, The Duel, Illuminations, Age of Anxiety, Miraculous Mandarin, Firebird, Ivesiana; appeared in motion picture, Limelight; received Merit Award "Mademoiselle", 1952; retired from N.Y.C. Ballet 1973 (gala in her honour including her final Ballet "Cortege Hongrois" choreographed for her by G. Balanchine; presented by Mayor John Lindsay with Handel Medallion (highest cultural award of N.Y.C.); mem. Bd.

of Trustees, Brandeis Univ.; Home: 171 West 79th St., New York, N.Y. 10024

HAYDEN, Hon. Salter Adrian, Q.C., M.A., Ph.M., LL.D.; senator; b. Ottawa, Ont., 31 May 1896; s. late Patrick J. and Helen Elizabeth (Salter) H.; e. Ottawa Univ. (M.A., Ph.M., LL.D.); Osgoode Hall; m.; three s.; ASSOCIATE COUNSEL McCARTHY & McCARTHY, Barristers & Solrs., former Sr. Partner; mem.i, Senate of Can.; Chrm. Bd. of Dirs., Nelson Arthur Hyland Foundation; read law with the late Edw. J. Daly, Ottawa; joined Foy, Knox, Monahan & Keogh on graduation; called to the Bar of Ont. Sept. 1922; cr. K.C. 1934; joined the firm of McCarthy & McCarthy, 1923 and became Partner, 1929; def. Lib. cand. for St. Paul's Riding, Toronto, Oct. 1935; summoned to the Senate of Can. 9 Feb. 1940; Liberal; R. Catholic; recreation: golf; Clubs: R.C.Y.C.; University; Rosedale Golf; Granite; Home: Ste. 1705, 63 St. Clair Ave. W., Toronto, Ont. M4V 2Y9; Office: (Box 48) Toronto-Dominion Centre, Toronto, Ont. M5K 1E6

HAYDON, Harold Emerson, Ph.B., M.A., university professor; artist; b. Fort William, Ont. 22 April 1909; s. Prof. Albert Eustace and Edith Elizabeth (Jones) H.; e. Univ. of Chicago, Ph.B. 1930, M.A. 1931; Sch. of Art Inst. of Chicago; m. Virginia Elnore, d. James Sherwood, Toledo, Ohio, 4 July 1937; PROFESSOR EMERITUS OF ART, UNIV. OF CHICAGO; Adjunct Prof. of Fine Art, Indiana Univ. Northwest since 1975; Visiting Lecturer, School of Art Inst. of Chicago 1975-81; Art Critic, Chicago Sun-Times since 1963; Resident Artist, Pickering Coll., Newmarket, Ont., 1933-34 (Mural painting there); Instr. and Asst. Prof. of Art, George Williams Coll., Chicago, 1934-44; apptd. Asst. Prof. of Art, Univ. of Chicago, 1944 exhibiting art since 1934; illustrator; Tapestry Ark Cover and Mosaic Mural (1958), Temple Shalom, Chicago; Mosaic Murals, Temple Beth Israel, Hammond, Ind.; 5 mural projects in Shankman Orthogenic School of Univ. of Chicago; stained glass windows for Rockefeller Memorial Chapel, Univ. of Chicago; and other commissions in U.S.A.; author: "Great Art Treasures in America's Smaller Museums", 1967; mem., Am. Assn. of Univ. Profs.; Artists Equity Assn.; Chicago Soc. Artists; National Society Mural Painters; Alumni Citation for Public Service, Univ. of Chicago, 1978; Phi Beta Kappa; Psi Upsilon; Order of "C"; Home: 5009 Greenwood Ave., Chicago, Ill. 60615.

HAYES, Derek Cumberland, LL.M.; lawyer; executive; b. Toronto, Ont. 27 Sept. 1936; s. Charles Walter and Phyllis (Cumberland) H.; e. Upper Can. Coll. Toronto 1950; Trinity Coll. Sch. Port Hope, Ont. 1954; Univ. of Toronto, Trinity Coll. B.A. 1958, LL.B. 1961; Univ. Coll. Univ. of London LL.M. 1966; m. Susan Howard Bennett 15 July 1963; children: Sean, Kate, Stewart; VICE PRES., GEN. COUNSEL AND SECY., SHELL CANADA LTD. 1980- ; called to Bar of Ont. 1963; Solr. McCarthy & McCarthy 1963-67; Solr. Massey-Ferguson Ltd. 1967-71; Sr. Solr. The T. Eaton Co. Ltd. 1971-73; Legal Advisor, Atty. Gen.'s Chambers, Republic of Tanzania 1973-74; Asst. Secy. Massey-Ferguson Ltd. 1974-77, Secy. 1977-80; Vice Pres. and Dir. John Howard Soc. Ont.; Dir. Inst. Citizenship; mem. Extve. Comte. Trinity Coll. Univ. of Toronto; mem. Law Soc. Upper Can.; Candn. Bar Assn.; recreations: skiing, music, woodworking; Clubs: University; Arts & Letters; Home: 47 Oriole Parkway, Toronto, Ont. M4V 2E2; Office: 505 University Ave., Toronto, Ont. M5G 1X4.

HAYES, Mt. Rev. James M., J.C.D., D.D. (R.C.); b. Halifax, N.S., 27 May 1924; s. Leonard J. and Rita G. (Bates) H.; e. St. Thomas Aquinas Sch. and St. Mary's Coll. High Sch., Halifax; St. Mary's Univ., B.A. 1943; Angelicum Univ., Rome, J.C.D. 1957; Hon. D.D. Univ. of King's Coll. 1967; ARCHBISHOP OF HALIFAX; Address: P.O. Box 1527, Halifax, N.S. B3J 2Y3

HAYES, Meredith S.; executive; b. New York, N.Y., 10 Sept. 1914; s. Meredith and Roberta (Rajotte) H.; e. Lower Can. Coll. 1939; m. Marjorie Ella, d. late Harry Hall, 7 March 1941; three children; PRES. M.S. HAYES, CONSULTANTS INC.; Dir., Seaway International Bridge Corp. Ltd.; Past Pres. Canadian Machine Tool Distributors Assn.; mem. Soc. Mech. Engrs.; mem. of Numerical Control Soc.; Dir., Que. Soc. for Crippled Children; Past Chrmn., Internat. Material Mang. Soc.; Protestant; recreations: fishing, photography; Clubs: Mount Stephen; Canadian; Montreal Kiwanis; Home: 514 Stanstead Ave. Montreal, Que. H3R 1X7; Office: 514 Stanstead Ave., Montreal, Que. H3R 1X7

HAYHURST, William Palmer; advertising executive, retired; consultant; b. Galt, Ont., 21 Dec. 1902; s. F. H. and Fannie Ann (Palmer) H.; e. Univ. of Toronto Schs.; Univ. of Toronto (undergrad.); m. Jean Eleanor, d. James Hunniseth, 30 Sept. 1939; children: James Frederick Palmer, George Wilson Palmer, Douglas Palmer; Chrmn. of the Bd. and Chief Extve. Offr., F. H. Hayhurst Co. Ltd. 1964-76; with Baker Advertising Agency, Toronto, Ont., 1925, becoming Account Extve., 1928; joined with his father 1928 to form the present company; apptd. Pres., 1940-64; served in 2nd World War 1940-41 as Lieut., Toronto Scottish Regt.; Pres.; Candn. Assn. of Advertising Agencies, 1959-60; Theta Delta Chi; Conservative; United Church; recreations: fishing, golf; Clubs: University; Caledon Mountain Trout; Toronto Hunt; The Moorings Golf & Country, Naples, Fla.; Home: Granite Place, 63 St. Clair Ave. W., Apt. 1604, Toronto, Ont. M4V 2Y9; Office: 55 Eglinton Ave. E., Toronto, Ont. M4P 1G8

HAYNE, David M., M.A., Ph.D., F.R.S.C. (1970); university professor; b. Toronto, Ont., 12 Aug. 1921; s. Herbert George and Elizabeth (Mackness) H.; e. Norway Public Sch. and Malvern Coll. Inst., Toronto, Ont.; Univ. Coll., Univ. of Toronto, B.A. 1942; Univ. of Ottawa, M.A. 1944, Ph.D. 1945; m. Madge Hood Robertson, d. David P. Niven, St. Andrews, Scotland, 20 Dec. 1955; one d. Heather Elizabeth; two s., Frederick Steven, Bruce Jonathan; PROF. OF FRENCH, UNIV. OF TORONTO, since 1961; Research Offr., Nat. Research Council, Ottawa, 1942-45; attached to Directorate of Mil. Intelligence, N.D.H.Q., 1943-45; joined Univ. Coll., Univ. of Toronto as Lectr. in French, 1945; Asst. Prof. 1950, Assoc. Prof. 1956, Prof. 1961; Registrar of University Coll., 1956-61; Visiting Prof. of Fr., U.B.C. 1970-71; mem., Pres., Bibliographical Soc. Can.; Candn. Assn. Univ. Teachers; Internat. Comparative Lit. Assn., etc.; Anglican; Home: R.R. 2, Claremont, Ont. L0H 1E0

HAYNES, Arden R., B.Com.; petroleum executive; b. Sask. 7 Aug. 1927; e. Univ. of Manitoba, B.Com.; m. Helen Beverly Henderson; children: Richard J., Leslie A.; EXTVE. VICE PRES., IMPERIAL OIL LTD., TORONTO 1978-81; joined Imperial Oil at Winnipeg 1951, held various marketing positions across Can., and with Standard Oil (N.J.) to 1972; Vice-Pres. and Gen. Mgr. Imperial Oil Ltd., Toronto, 1973; Sr. Vice Pres. and Dir. 1974; Pres. and C.E.O., Esso Resources Corp. 1978-81; recreations: golf, fishing, skiing; Clubs: York Downs Golf and Country; Granite; Office: 111 St. Clair Ave. W., Toronto, Ont. M5W 1K3

HAYS, Daniel Philip, B.A., LL.B.; lawyer; livestock breeder; b. Calgary, Alta. 24 Apl. 1939; s. Hon. H. W. Hays, P.C.; e. W. Can. High Sch. Calgary 1958; Univ. of Alta. B.A. 1962; Univ. of Toronto LL.B. 1965; m. Linda Janette d. John W. Jolly; three d. Carol E., Janet M., Sarah L.; PARTNER, MACLEOD DIXON 1974- ; Dir. Eaton Bay Trust Co. (Alta.); Inter City Papers Ltd.; Canadian Broadcasting Corp.; called to Bar of Alta. 1966; breeder purebreed sheep and cattle since 1956; former Dir. Calgary YMCA; Calgary & Dist. Foundation; mem. Alta. Law Soc.; Candn. Bar Assn.; Calgary Bar Assn.; Liberal; Clubs: Rotary; Glencoe; Calgary Golf & Country;

Ranchmen's; Home: 1106 Frontenac Ave. S.W., Calgary, Alta. T2T 1B6; Office: 1500 Home Oil Tower, 324 - 8th Ave. S.W., Calgary, Alta. T2P 2Z2.

HAYS, Hon. Harry, P.C. (1963); senator; auctioneer; cattle breeder; b. Carstairs, Alberta, 25 Dec. 1909; s. Dr. T. E. Hays; e. Elem. and High Sch.; m. Muriel Alice, d. Ernest Bigland, Calgary, Alta., 28 Feb. 1934; one s. Daniel P.; Dir., Canada Permanent Mortgage Corp. and Canada Permanent Trust Co.; Home Oil Ltd. interest in cattle export business began in 1932 when became Alta. Fieldman with Holstein-Friesian Assn. of Alta.; in 1933 became first Candn. to ship purebred dairy cattle to Britain, and in foll. yrs. to 21 other countries; in 1945 as Pres. of Hays Farms Ltd. in Ontario, became first cattle exporter to ship by air and his Co. was first in N. Am. to export cattle to Spain and Italy; Mayor, City of Calgary, 1959-63 prior to which travelled an average of 35 thousand miles a year in selling 2 million worth of livestock; relinquished interests in Ont. farm to a brother, and in 1943 purchased the family farm business, Hays and Co. in Alberta of which he became Pres. inaugurated "Sale of Stars" at Royal Winter Fair, Toronto, Ont.; active for many yrs. in agric., business and community affairs; has served on Extve. of Holstein-Friesian Assn. of Can., and Alta. Cattle & Sheep Breeders' Assns.; was Pres. of Candn. Swine Breeders' Assn. during 2nd World War when producers supplied 600 million pounds of bacon for export to Britain; Past Pres., Southern Egg & Poultry Producers' Assn., and Alta. Holstein-Friesian Assn.; Life Dir., Calgary Exhn. & Stampede Bd.; Heritage Park, Calgary; Lakeside Cattle Fund; Can. Studies Foundation; Roy. Winter Fair, Toronto; CARE-Can.; life mem., Alta. Dairyman's Assoc.; Dairy Club of Amer.; Can. Charolais Assoc.; Agric. Inst. of Can.; el. to H. of C. for Calgary g.e. 1963; Min. of Agric., 1963-65; summoned to the Senate Feb. 1966; former mem., Bd. of Govs., William Roper Hull Home, Calgary; Candn. Council of Christians & Jews; Clubs: Calgary Golf & Country; Rotary (Gov. Dist. 536, 1963-64); Office: The Senate, Ottawa, Ont. K1A 0A4

HAYWOOD, Leslie Rupert, B.A., M.Sc., P.Eng.; nuclear energy consultant; b. Sask., 18 Mar. 1919; s. Arthur Stanley & late Evelyn Theresa (Castle) H.; e. Univ. of Sask., B.A., B.Sc. (Engn.), M.Sc. (Engn.); m. Joyce Vivian, d. late Angus McNaughton, 23 June 1943; children: Linda, Carol, Lois; Pres., 5215 Inc. (formerly Vice Pres. Heavy Water Projects, Atomic Energy of Can. Ltd. 1972-74); joined Atomic Energy as Supv., Elect. & Instr. Br. 1947; with Pacific Naval Lab., Defence Research Bd. in work on underwater sound 1954; Mgr., Instrumentation and Control, Canadian General Electric Co. Ltd. 1955; Mgr., Reactor Devel. Projects, Atomic Energy of Canada Ltd. 1961, Vice-Pres., Engn. 1963, Vice-Pres., Chalk River Nuclear Labs. 1967; served in R.N.V.R. 1942-45; Protestant; Home: (Box 995) Deep River, Ont. K0J 1P0; Office: (Box 286) Chalk River, Ont. K0J 1J0

HEAD, (George) Bruce, R.C.A.; artist; b. St. Boniface, Man. 14 Feb. 1931; s. George Melborne and Ellen (Ingram) H.; e. Univ. of Man. Dipl. in Fine Arts 1953; m. Verona Sadella Orchard; divorced; children: Glenn Roland, Grant Coleman, Ian Bruce, Toni Eileen, Tara Nadine; graphic designer CBC Winnipeg; paintings, designs, sculptures rep. in numerous group and solo exhns. incl. Nat. Gallery Can.; Art Gallery of Ont.; Montreal Museum of Fine Arts; Commonwealth Arts Festival Cardiff, Wales; Dirs. Choice Traveling Exhn. 1967-68; 150 yrs. of Art in Man.; Spectrum Can. RCA 1976 Olympic Exhn. and other maj. exhns. Can. and USA; rep. in various pub., corporate and private colls. incl. Nat. Gallery Can., Montreal Museum of Fine Arts, Can. Council Art Bank, Govt. Man. Dept. Pub. Works; work cited maj. publs.; awards incl.: Monsanto Candn. Art Exhn. 1957; 5th, 6th and 7th Winnipeg Shows; 20th W. Ont. Exhn.; Eaton Graphics Award Manisphere 1969; Haddassah Art Exhibit 1st 1973; CBC Banner Competition Vancouver 1975;

comns. incl. Man. Teachers' Coll. Mural 1959; Benson & Hedges Art Walls Winnipeg 1972; Woodworth Bldg. Main Wall Man. Govt. 1976; City of Winnipeg Portage & Main Concourse 1980; Address: 18 St. Michael Rd., Winnipeg, Man. R2M 2K6.

HEAD, Ivan Leigh, Q.C., B.A., LL.M.; b. Calgary, Alta., 28 July 1930; e. Elem. and High Schs., Calgary and Edmonton, Alta.; Univ. of Alta., B.A. 1951, LL.B. 1952; Harvard Law Sch., LL.M. 1960 (Frank Knox Mem. Fellow); m. 1) Barbara Spence Eagle; 2) Ann Marie Price; four children; called to Bar of Alta. 1953; cr. Q.C. (Can.) 1974; practised law in partnership with S. J. Helman, Q.C. and R. H. Barron, Q.C., Calgary 1953-59; Foreign Service Offr., Dept. of External Affairs serving in Ottawa, Kuala Lumpur, Rangoon and Bangkok 1960; Assoc. Prof. of Law, Univ. of Alta. 1963, Prof. 1967 (on leave 1967-1973); Assoc. Counsel to Min. of Justice Can. for constitutional matters 1967; Leg. Asst. to Prime Min. of Can. 1968; named Special Asst. 1970 (special responsibility for advice on foreign policy and conduct of foreign relations); mem. Candn. Dels. to Commonwealth Heads of Govt. meetings London 1969, Singapore 1971, Ottawa 1973, Kingston 1975, London 1977; Sr. Advisor to Prime Min. on official visits to UN 1968, 1969; USA 1969, 1971, 1974, 1977; Britain 1969, 1972, 1975; Soviet Union 1971; People's Republic of China 1973 and other countries; Special emissary of Prime Minister in consultations with Heads of numerous countries including Nigeria, Britain, India, Japan; mem. North Am. Sponsoring and Policy Review Council, World Law Fund, World Order Models Project; Organizer and Chrmn., Banff Conf. on Law & Order in Internat. Community 1965; Secy. to Fed. Electoral Boundaries Comn. for Alta. 1965-66; Extve. mem. Banff Conf. On World Affairs 1964-68; Extve. Comte. The Atlantic Conference since 1971; co-author, "International Law, National Tribunals and the Rights of Aliens" 1971; Ed. and Contrib., "This Fire-Proof House" 1966; Ed. "Pierre Elliott Trudeau, Conversation with Canadians" 1972; mem. Bd. of Eds., "Canadian Yearbook of International Law" since 1965; Adv. Comte., "University of Toronto Law Journal" 1966-70; mem. Can. Council on Internat. Law; Law Soc. Alta. (Secy. to Benchers' Special Comte. on Mineral Titles 1955-56); Candn. Bar Assn. (Extve. Comte. Internat. & Constitutional Law Sec. 1968-74; Candn. Br. Internat. Law Assn. (Nat. Council 1966-68, Vice Pres. since 1968); Candn. Inst. Internat. Affairs; Am. Soc. Internat. Law (Extve. Council 1968-71); Bd. of Trustees, Inter. Food Policy Research Inst., 1979- ; Fellow, World Acad. of Art and Sci. 1981- ; Pres. and mem., Bd. of Govs., Internat. Dev. Research Centre since 1978; Office: Internat. Devel. Research Centre, 60 Queen St., Ottawa, Ont. K1G 3M9

HEALD, Hon. Darrel Verner, B.A., LL.B.; judge; b. Regina, Sask., 27 Aug. 1919; s. Herbert Verner and Lottie (Knudson) H.; e. Univ. of Sask., B.A. 1938, LL.B. 1940; m. Doris Rose, d. A. P. Hessey, Regina, Sask., 30 June 1951; children: Lynn Doris, Brian Darrel; JUSTICE, APPEAL DIV., FEDERAL COURT OF CANADA since 1975; Co-Commr. re. bilingual IFR Air Traffic Services in Que. 1976; formerly Atty. Gen. and Prov. Secy. of Sask.; el. to Sask. Leg. for Lumsden, g.e. 22 April 1964; Dir. for 16 yrs. of Sask. Roughrider Football Club; Past Pres., Regina Bonspiel Assn.; read law with A. B. Gerein; called to Bar of Sask. 1941; cr. Q.C. Dec. 1964; apptd. Justice, Trial Div., Fed. Court of Can. 1971; served in 2nd World War as Radar Tech. with R.C.A.F., 1941-45; Freemason; United Church; recreation: curling; Home: 44 Aleutian Rd., Ottawa, Ont. K2H 7C8; Office: Supreme Court Bldg., Ottawa, Ont.

HEARN, John, C.A.; management consultant; b. London, Eng. 22 Feb. 1930; s. Jackson and Elizabeth (Potter) H.; came to Canada 1957; e. Grammar Sch., Bucks. Eng.; London Sch. of Econ., Post-Grad. Studies; m. Agnes, d. John Young Boyd, May 1953; children: Steven, Deborah,

Jackson; CHRMN. & C.E.O. PERFORMANCE SAIL-CRAFT INTERNAT. LTD. AND LASER INTERNAT. HOLDINGS, INC.: 1975- ; Francis F. King & Son, C.A. London Eng. 1947-52; Exvte. Asst. to Mang. Dir., Suntex Safety Glass Industries Ltd. 1952-54; Consultant, R. F. Fraser, Mang. Consultants 1954-56; joined Peat, Marwick, Mitchell & Co. as Consultant, Toronto 1957, Regional Dir. - W. Can. 1958-63, Partner 1963-75; 1970-75; Managing Partner, Peat Marwick & Partners, Toronto 1970-75; Man. Dir., Lamshoert Import Co. Ltd.; Dir., Long Range Invest., Nife-Powertronic Corp., Onward Manufacturing Co.; Infinitum Growth Fund Inc.; mem. The Shipping Corp. of New Zealand (Canada) Inc. Insts. Chart. Accts. Ont., B.C., Eng. and Wales; Anglican: re-creations: golf, squash, bridge; Clubs: Capilano Golf (Vancouver); Rosedale Golf; Toronto Cricket; Homes: 29 Swansdown Dr., Willowdale, Ont. M2L 2N2 and Lake of Bays, Muskoka, Ont;

HEARN, Richard Lankaster, O.C. (1973), B.A.Sc., D.Eng., LL.D.; consulting engr.; b. Toronto, Ont., 18 May 1890; s. Dr. Richard and Ellen Jane (French) H.; e. St. Alban's Cathedral Sch., Toronto; Univ. of Toronto, B.A.Sc. 1913, D.Eng. 1952; m. late Ethel, d. James Macdonald, Smiths Falls, Ont., 11 June 1923; one d., Ellen Marie; installed as First Chancellor, Brock University, May 1967; Hydro-Electric Power Comn. of Ont., 1913-18; Asst. Engineer on Constr. 1918-21; Assistant Chief. Engr., Wash. Water Power Co., Spokane, Wash., 1921-24; Chief Engr. and Secy.-Treas., H. G. Acres & Co. Ltd., Niagara Falls, Ont., 1924-30; Consult. Engr., Dom. Constr. Co. and H. F. McLean Ltd. 1930-34, Chief Engr. 1934-42; Extve. Asst. to Chrmn., Hydro-Eect. Power Comn. of Ont. 1942-44; on loan to Polymer Corpn. to direct and supervise constr. of Synthetic Rubber Plant, Sarnia, Ont., 1942-44, serving as Chief Engr.; on loan from H.E.P.C. to act as Candn. Tech. Advisor to Publ. Utilities Div., Combined Prod. & Resources Bd., Wash., D.C., 1944-45; Chief Engr., Design and Constr., H.E.P.C., 1945-47; Gen. Mgr. and Chief Engr., 1947-55, Chrmn., 1955-56; consulting engr. 1956-76; Hearn lectures sponsored by Inst. of Elec. Engrs., (Eng.); assoc. on design and constr. of: Sir Adam Beck-Niagara G.S. No. 1, Niagara Falls; Abitibi Power Devel.; Duplicate Water Supply, City of Toronto; Ottawa River Power Project; St. Lawrence Power Project; Chelan Power Project, Chelan, Wash. etc.; Hon. mem. CANCOLD (Candn. Nat. Comte. Internat. Comn. on Large Dams); Fellow, Candn. Geog. Soc.; mem. Am. Soc. Civil Engrs. (mem. Golden Jubilee Hon. Comte. 1975); American Institute Electrical Engineers; Engineering Inst. Can. (awarded Julian C. Smith Medal 1954; Sir John Kennedy Medal, 1957; and now Hon. mem.); Newcomen Soc. of N.A.; Ont. Assn. Prof. Engrs. (Medal 1956); Roy. Soc. Arts; Am. Soc. Civil Engrs.; Hon. mem., The Moles; Inst. Elect. Engineers (Eng.); el. to Engn. Alumni Hall of Distinction, Univ. of Toronto, 1978; Freemason (50-year Pin, University Lodge 1974); Anglican; recreation: photography; reading; Clubs: Toronto; Granite; Niagara Falls (Ontario); Home: (P.O. Box 135), Niagara Parkway, Queenston, Ont. L0S 1L0

HEARNDEN, Kenneth W., B.Sc.F.; professional forester; b. Toronto, Ont., 11 May 1923; s. Arthur William and Elsie Hutchinson (Monk) H.; e. Parkdale Coll. Inst., Toronto, Ont.; Univ. of Toronto, B.Sc.F. (1st Class Hons.); m. Sheilagh Jean, d. Rev. E. C. McCullagh, Dunnville, Ont., 7 Oct. 1950; children: James Stanley, John; PROF. & DIR. SCH. OF FORESTRY, LAKEHEAD UNIV. since 1969; Dean of Students, 1980- ; Chrmn., Lakehead Region Conservation Authority 1968-73; mem., Candn. Inst. Forestry (Pres. 1964-65); Ont. Prof. Foresters Assn. (Pres. 1969-71); Ont. Forestry Assn.; Freemason (Scot. Rite); mem., Bd. of Dir., Thunder Bay Temple Bldgs. Ltd., (Pres., 1974-77); Vice-Chmn., Municipality of Shuniah Planning Bd.; Secy-Treas., Assn. of University Forestry School of Can. 1973-80; Presbyterian; recreations:

photography, carpentry, music listening; Address: 8-328 River St., Thunder Bay, Ont. P7A 3R2

HEASLIP, William Thomas, B.A.Sc.; professional engineer; b. Toronto, 13 Oct. 1920; s. William Henry and Eva Louise (Moody) H.; e. W. Tech. Sch., Toronto, 1933-38; Univ. of Toronto, 1938-40 and 1945-47, B.A.Sc. (Aero. Engn.); m. Jean Phyllis d. L. G. Myatt of Hamilton, 12 Sept. 1947; children: William David, James Edward, Anne Marie, John Leonard, Patricia Jean, Robert Vernon, Kathleen Carol, Paul Douglas; VICE-PRES., SPECIAL PROJECTS, THE de HAVILLAND AIRCRAFT OF CAN. LTD.; joined Co. in May 1947; employed in various capacities in aerodynamics, stress analysis and design; spent 3 yrs. with Parent Co. in Hatfield, Eng.; apptd. Depy. Chief, Design Engr., 1955; Chrmn., Engn. Directorate, 1961; Chief Engr. (Product) 1962; Depy. Vice-Pres., Engn., 1965, Vice Pres., Engn. 1966, Dir. 1970, Vice Pres., Special Project, 1977; served with R.N. & R.C.N. 1941-45 as Radar Offr. in Mediterranean & N. Atlantic with rank of Elect. Lt. RCNVR; Trustee, King (Ont.) School Bd., 1962-65 (Chrmn., 1964-65); Bd. of Dir., French Chamber of Commerce in Canada, 1980; mem. Assn. Prof. Engrs. Ont.; Fellow, Candn. Aero & Space Inst. (Pres. 1972-73); mem. Steering Comte. and Dir. of City of North York Bus. Assn., 1980; Vice-Pres. 1981; Aircraft Operators Comte, Transportation Research Bd. (U.S.) 1980- ; Conservative; United Church; recreations: golf, camping; Home: 108 Confederation Way, Thornhill, Ont. L3T 5R5; Office: Downsview, Ont. M3K 1Y5

HEASMAN, George Robert, O.B.E. B.Com.; b. Ottawa Ont., 22 Dec. 1898; s. George and Rose (Cawdron) H.; e. Queen's Univ., B.Com. 1925; m. Audrey Beatrice, d. Charles Cooke, New Carlisle, Que., 18 Sept. 1930; children: Robert George, Rosemary Louise; Wayagamack Pulp & Qaper Co., Three Rivers, Que., 1923-27; Asst. Trade Commr. to Batavia, Java, N.E.I., 1928; Trade Commr. 1930; Trade Commr. in S. Africa, London and Chicago; Chief, Export Permit Br., Trade & Commerce and Asst. Dir. of Mutual Aid Adm., Ottawa, 1941-45; Director, Trade Commissioner Service, 1946-53; Candn. Ambassador to Indonesia, 1953-57; Candn. High Commr. to New Zealand, 1958-63; retired 1964; Freemason; Anglican; recreations: golf, fishing; Club: Royal Ottawa; Address: 356 Roger Rd., Ottawa, Ont. K1H 5C4

HEATHCOTE, Lesley Muriel, B.S., M.A.; librarian (retired); b. Edmonton, Alta., 12 May 1904; d. Henry Walter and Annie Selina (Hilton) H.; e. Westmount Grade Sch. and Victoria High Sch., 1921, Edmonton, Alta.; Univ. of Alta., B.A. 1924, M.A. 1928; Univ. of Wash., B.S. (Lib. Science) 1929, grad. work in hist. 1939-51; Hon. D. Hum. L., Montana State Univ. 1981; Asst. to Registrar, Univ. of Alta., 1924-28; Serials Librarian, Univ. of Wash., 1929-44; Research Asst., Internat. Labour Office, Montreal, 1945-46; Lib. Asst., Montana State Univ. (then Mont. State Coll.), 1946-47; Assoc. Prof. and Librarian, 1947-52; Prof. and Librarian, 1952-65; Prof. and Dir. of Libraries 1965-70 (during tenure of Office at Univ. Lib. has grown from some 75,000 vols. to nearly 500,000 and two lib. bldgs. have been erected); one of founders & incorporators, Bozeman Symphony Soc. Inc.; Secy. 1968-70; author of numerous articles for prof. periodicals in lib. field; mem., Pacific N.W. Lib. Assn. (Pres. 1951-52); Mont. Lib. Assn. (Pres. 1953-54); Am. Lib. Assn.; Agric. Hist. Soc.; Am. Assn. Univ. Profs.; chosen Librarian of the Year for Montana 1969; Montana State Univ. Blue and Gold Award, 1978; recreations: hiking, riding, gardening, flute playing; Club: Alpine of Can.; Home: 9236 SE 33rd Place, Mercer Island, Wash. 98040

HEBB, Donald O., M.A., Ph.D., D.Sc., D.H.L., D.C.L., LL.D., F.R.S., F.R.S.C., (1959); educator; b. Chester, N.S., 22 July 1904; s. Arthur Morrison and Mary Clara (Olding) H.; e. Dalhousie Univ., B.A. 1925, LL.D. 1965; McGill Univ., M.A. 1932; Harvard Univ., Ph.D. 1936;

Univ. of Chicago, Sc.D.; Univ. of Waterloo, D.Sc. 1963; Northeastern Univ., D.H.L. 1963; LL.D., Queen's 1967, Western 1968; D.Sc., York 1966, McMaster 1967, D.Sc., St. Lawrence Univ.; McGill 1975; D.Sc., Trent Univ.; D.Sc., Memorial Univ., 1977; LL.D., Concordia Univ., 1975; D.C.L., Bishop's Univ., 1977; m. Marion Isabel Clark, 1931 (d. 1933); m. 2ndly, Elizabeth Nichols Donovan (d. 1962); m. 3rdly, Margaret Doreen Williamson (Wright) 1966; two d., Jane Nichols, Mary Ellen; Chancellor, McGill University (1st appt. from Faculty) 1970-74; Research Fellow, Montreal Neurol. Institute, 1937-39; Lecturer Queen's University 1939-42; Research Fellow, Yerkes Laboratories of Primate Biol., Orange Park, Fla., 1942-47; Prof. of Psychol., McGill University 1947-72; Professor emeritus, 1975; Hon. Prof., Dalhousie Univ., 1978- ; Pres., Candn. Psychol. Assn., 1953; Pres. Am. Psychol. Assn., 1960; author: "Organization of Behavior", 1949; "Textbook of Psychology", 1958, revised (3rd. ed.) 1972; "Essay on Mind", 1980; also some 70 tech. papers; Address: R.R.1, Chester Basin, N.S. B0J 1K0

HEBERT, Anne; author; b. Rossamberg, Que. 1916; novels incl. "Wooden Rooms" ("Les Chambres de Nois"); "Torrents" and "Kamouraska" 1971 (awarded French Prix des Libraries); "Children of the Black Sabbath", 1977; Address: Paris, France

HEBERT, J. Claude, D.F.C.; consultant; b. Magog, Que., 28 Jan. 1914; s. Napoleon and Anne (Boisonneault) H.; Grad. from War Staff Coll., Toronto, Ont.; m. Madeleine, d. S. Ouilimar, 1 Sept. 1945; children: Pierre, George, Louise, Daniel; DEPUTY CHAIRMAN, PETRO-CAN.; Dir., Alliance Mutuelle-Vie; Carena-Bancorp Inc.; Eastern Prov. Airways (1963) Ltd.; Dominion Textile Co. Ltd.; mem., Adv. Comte., Business Sch. Adm., Univ. of W. Ont.; recreations: fishing, golf, hunting; Clubs: Mount Bruno; Hermitage (Magog); Mount Royal; Home: Apt. 1301, 2 Westmount Sq., Montreal, Que H3Z 2S4; Office: 1 Place Ville Marie, Suite 1725, Montreal, Que. H3B 4A9

HEBERT, Jacques, M.Com.; publisher; b. Montreal, Que., 21 June 1923; s. Dr. Louis-Philippe and Denise (Saint-Onge) H.; e. Coll. Ste-Marie, Montreal; St. Dunstan's Coll, Charlottetown, P.E.I.; Ecole des Hautes Etudes Commerciales, M.Com. 1945; m. Thérèse, d. Dr. Desjardins, Beloeil, Que., 21 Oct. 1951; children: Michel, Pascale, Isabelle, Bruno, Sophie; FOUNDER, PRESIDENT CANADA WORLD YOUTH, co-Chrmn., Katimavik; Co-Chrmn. Fed. Cultural Policy Review Comte.; Founder and Publisher, VRAI (weekly newspaper), 1954-59; Founder and Dir., Editions de l'Homme, 1959-61; Founder, Pres. and Gen. Mgr., Editions du Jour, 1961-74; author: "Autour des trois Ameriques", 1948; "Autour de l'Afrique", 1950; "Aicha l'Africaine", 1950; "Aventure autour du Monde", 1952; "Nouvelle aventure en Afrique", 1953; "Coffin était innocent", 1958; "Scandale à Bordeaux", 1959; "J'accuse les assassins de Coffin", 1963; "Trois jours en prison", 1965; "Les ecoeurants", 1966; "The Temple on the River", 1967; "Ah! mes Aieux!", 1968; "Obscénité et Liberté", 1970; BlaBlaBla du Bout du Monde", 1971; co author with Pierre Elliott Trudeau, "Deux innocents en Chine rouge", 1960 (Engl. transl. 1968); "The World is Round", 1977; "Have Them Build a Tower Together", 1979; "L'Affaire Coffin", 1980; "The Great Building Bee", 1980; Offr. O.C.; R. Catholic; Home: 3480 Prud'Homme, Montréal, Qué. H4A 3H4; Office: 2500 ave. Pierre Dupuys, Cité de Havre, Montréal, Qué. H2X 3K4

HEBERT, Louis; O.C.; banker, retired; b. Laprairie, Que., 3 May, 1908; s. Alphonse and Elvina (Picard) H.; e. Ecole Supérieure St-Louis; International Accountants Soc.; m. Simone, d. L. E. Loiselle, 29 May 1940; one d. Louise; former Chrmn. of Bd. and Chief Extve. Offr., Banque Canadienne Nationale, Dir., Roy-Nat. Ltd.; Compagnie Immobilière BCN Ltée; Banque Can. Nat.

(Europe); la Soc. de la Caisse de Retraite de la Banque Can. Nat.; Sun Life Assurance Company of Canada; Wabasso Limited; Noranda Mines Ltd.; Gaspé Copper Mines Limited; La Compagnie des Ciments du St-Laurent; Secretary-Treasurer, Service Social des Sourdes Muettes; Governor, Hôpital Notre-Dame; began as Jr., Banque Canadienne Nationale, Mont Laurier, Que., 1925-33; Acct. Dept. H.O., Montreal, 1933-49; Chief Acct., H.O., Montreal, 1949-54; Asst. Gen. Mgr., H.O. 1954-60; apptd. Gen. Mgr., 1960; Vice-Pres. 1963, President, 1964; Chairman and President, 1969; Roman Catholic; recreation: golf; Clubs: Laval-sur-le-Lac; Mount Royal; St. James's; Mount Bruno Country; Office: 500 Place d'Armes, Montreal, Que. H2Y 2W2

HEDDON, Kenneth Frederick, B.A.Sc.; retired company executive; b. Columbus, Ont., 27 Aug. 1912; s. Frederick John and Elsie (Orchard) H.; e. Oshawa Collegiate, Oshawa, Ont.; Univ. of Toronto, B.A.Sc., 1933; m. Doris B., d. Luther Bone, July 1939; Asst. Chassis Engr., General Motors Ltd., 1933-36; financial interest in Chrysler-Plymouth Dealership, 1936-38; Rep. Indust. & Wholesale Products, Sun Oil Co. Ltd.; 1938-40; Tech. Rep., 1940-44; Mgr., Indust. Products & Wholesale Div., 1944-58; Dist. Mgr., London, Ont., 1958-59; Asst. Regional Mgr. (Western Region U.S.) Detroit, 1959-62; General Sales Manager, 1962-64; Pres., 1964; Vice Pres., Great Candn. Oil Sands Ltd. 1967; Pres., Great Can. Oil Sands Ltd., 1967; Chrm. of Bd. of Dir., Great Can. Oil Sands Ltd., 1977; Chrmn. of Bd. of Dirs., Sun Oil Ltd. 1972; retired from Sun Oil Co. Ltd., Aug. 1977; retired as Chrm., Great Can. Oil Sands Ltd., Aug. 1979; Dir., Acres Inc. and Acres Davy McKee Ltd., Can. Automotive Museum; mem., Association Prof. Engineers Ontario; United Ch.; recreations: fishing, photography, music; Clubs: Granite; The Franklin; Home: 10 Daleberry Pl., Don Mills, Ont. M3B 2A6;

HEDGEWICK, Peter; industrialist; b. Montreal, Que., 30 Apl. 1915; s. Ivan Hatrick and Tekla (Sokolowski) H.; e. Windsor (Ont.)-Walkerville Tech. Sch., 1929-32; m. Anne, d. late Harry Mereszczak, 23 Dec. 1936; children: Kenneth Peter, (Mrs.) Carol Ann Briese, CHAIRMAN, I.T.L. INDUSTRIES LIMITED; served as Private in Canadian Army, Barriefield Unit, 1942-43; mem., Soc. Automotive Engineers (Detroit Branch); Society Plastic Engineers; American Tool and Mfg. Engrs.; Founding mem., Windsor Chapter, Nat. Tool & Die Mfrs.; Charter mem., Renaissance Club (Detroit); mem., Royal Candn. Legion; Protestant; recreations: golf, music, fishing; Clubs: Essex Golf; Windsor; Home: 3691 Victoria Blvd., Windsor Ont. N9E 3L6; Office: 3805 Malden Rd., Windsor, Ont. N9C 3Y8

HEENEY, Edwin H., B.A.; company officer, retired; b. Aylwin, P.Q., 30 June 1910; s. H. A. and Elizabeth (Carruthers) H.; e. Jarvis Coll. Inst., Toronto, Ont.; Victoria Coll., Univ. of Toronto, B.A. 1935; m. Beatrice, d. W. S. Sterne, 17 Dec. 1938; children: Stephen, Shelagh; Dir., Moore Corp. Ltd.; National Trust Co. Ltd. 1972-77 (past Chmn.); past Hon. Chrmn. of Bd., Munich Reins. Co. of Can.; began as Asst. to Ed. of "Monthly Review", Bank of Nova Scotia, 1935; joined present Co. 1937, becoming Trust Offr., Investment Dept.; Treas., 1946-54; Asst. Gen. Mgr. 1954; later Vice-Pres.; Extve. Vice-Pres. 1965-67; Pres. 1967-72; served in 2nd World War 1942-46 as Capt., Royal Candn. Arty., 6th Anti-Tank Regt.; Mentioned in Despatches; Anglican; recreations: golf; Clubs: National; York; Toronto; Toronto Golf; Office: 21 King Ste. E., Toronto, Ont. M5C 1B3

HEES, Hon. George Harris, P.C. (Can.) 1957, M.P. b. Toronto, Ont., 17 June 1910; s. Harris Lincoln and Mabel Mills (Good) H.; e. Trinity Coll. Sch., Port Hope, Ont.; Roy. Mil. Coll., 1927-31; Univ. of Toronto, 1931-33; Cambridge Univ., Eng., 1933-34; m. Mabel Ferguson, d. Hon. E. A. Dunlop, 30 June 1934; children: Catherine Mabel,

Martha Ann, Roslyn Georgia; Dir., Industrial Life Ins. Co.; def. cand. for Spadina to H. of C. at g.e. 1945; 1st el. to H. of C. for Toronto-Broadview, byel., May 1950; not a cand. in g.e. Apl. 1963; apptd. Min. of Transport, 22 June 1957, Min. of Trade & Comm. 11 Oct. 1960; resigned from Diefenbaker Cabinet 9 Feb. 1963; former Pres., P. Cons. Assn. of Canada (el. 1954); apptd. Pres., Montreal and Canadian Stock Exchanges, Apl. 1964, resigning to re-enter active politics, Sept. 1965; el. to 16th H. of C. for Northumberland, g.e. 8 Nov.1965 and for Prince Edward-Hastings in g.e. June 1968, 1972, 1974; 1979 and 1980; Chrmn. of Candn. Sect. of Can.-U.S. Permanent Joint Bd. on Defense, Oct. 1979- ; served in World War, 1939-45; Bgde. Maj., 5th Inf. Bgde.; wounded in Holland, Nov. 1944; Zeta Psi; P. Conservative; Anglican; recreations: skiing, golf, tennis; Clubs: Toronto Golf; Badminton & Racquet; Royal Ottawa Golf; Home: Rathbunwood, Cobourg, Ont. and 7 Coltrin Place, Rockcliffe Park, Ottawa, Ont.

HEFFELFINGER, George, B.A.; company officer; b. Minneapolis, Minn., 15 Oct. 1926; s. George W. P. and Ruth J. H.; e. Blake Sch., Minneapolis; Univ. of Minn., B.A.; m. Jane, d. Henry Glenn Sayler, Fargo, N. Dakota, 22 July 1949; children: Totton, Park, Adam, Lisa, Amanda; PRES., HIGHCROFT ENTERPRISES LTD., Vice-Pres., Monday Publications Ltd.; Dir., Peavey Co., Minn.; Peavey Ind. Ltd., Red Deer; Mega Enterprises Ltd.; Broughton Investment Group Ltd. of Victoria; N. American Life Assurance Co.; began as Elevator Helper, National Grain Co., Grenfell, Sask. 1949, Div. Mgr. 1955, Pres. 1960, Chrmn. 1974; served with U.S. Navy as Seaman 1944-45; S. Pacific Theatre; Dir., and Pres., Pacific Opera Assn. of Victoria; Home: 3155 Rutland Rd., Victoria, B.C. V8R 3R7 Office: 823 Broughton St., Victoria, B.C., V8W 1E5

HEFFERNAN, Gerald R., B.Sc., P.Eng.; industrialist; b. Edmonton, Alta., 12 July 1919; s. William Samuel and Elsie Winnifred (Graves) H.; e. Univ. of Toronto, B.Sc. (Metall.) 1943 (Gold Key Honor Award); Univ. of B.C., post-grad. work in Metall. and Indust. Mang. 1945-46; m. Geraldine Joan, d. Joseph P. O'Leary, 18 Dec. 1943; children: Joseph John, Mary Clare, Mark Gregory, Helen Louise, Shelagh Agnes, Tracey Frances, Teresa Jane, Virginia Rae; PRESIDENT AND DIR., CO-STEEL INTERNATIONAL LTD. since 1970; Chrmn. Raritan River Steel Co.; Chrmn. and Dir., Lake Ontario Steel Co.; Dir., Corod Mfg. Ltd.; Corod Mfg. Ltd.; Ferr Co. Engineering Ltd.; Sheerness Steel Co.; Steep Rock Iron Mines Ltd.; Chapparral Steel Company; Staff, Dept. of Metall., Univ. of B.C. 1945; Metall. Asst. Mgr., Westland Iron & Steel Foundries 1946; Supt. and Gen. Supt., Western Canada Steel 1948-53; Mang. Dir., Premier Steel Mills 1954-62; Pres., Lake Ontario Steel Co. Ltd. 1963; served with RCE during World War II; rank Lt.; Fellow, Am. Soc. for Metals; mem. Assn. Prof. Engrs., Alta., B.C., Ont.; Assn. Iron & Steel Engrs.; Candn. Inst. Mining & Metall.; Am. Inst. Mining, Metall. & Petroleum Engrs.; Royal Automobile Club; R. Catholic; recreations: golf, swimming, skiing, fishing, theatre; Club: Oshawa Golf; Home: Ringwood Farm, RR 2, Whitby, Ont. L1N 5R5; Office: Hopkins St., Whitby, Ont.

HEFFERNAN, Joseph James, M.A., Sc., consulting engr.; b. Windsor, Ont., 20 May 1922; s. late Harry Aloysius and Eleanor (Brooks) H.; e. Assumption Coll. High Sch., Windsor, Ont.; Univ. of Toronto, B.A.Sc. (Mech. Engn.) 1948, M.A.Sc. (Civil Engn.) 1953; m. Gwendolyn Joan, d. late Thomas Roach, 7 July 1945; children: Anne Elizabeth, James Harry; VICE PRES. DEVEL., M. M. DILLON LTD.; left Dept. of Nat. Defence to join present Co., London, Ont., 1954; successively Project Mgr., Assoc.; trans. to Toronto, 1956; served with R.C.E. 1943-54; rank Capt.; Fellow, Am. Soc. Civil Engrs.; Eng. Inst. Can.; mem., Assn. Prof. Engrs. Ont.; Assn. Consulting Engrs. Can. (Pres. 1977-78); Roman Catholic; recreation: tennis;

Club: Donalda; Home: 5 Eastview Cres., Toronto, Ont. M5M 2W4; Office: 50 Holly St., Toronto, Ont. M4S 2E6

HEGGTVEIT, Halvor Alexander, M.D., F.R.C.P. (C), F.C.A.P., M.R.C. Path., F.A.C.A., F.I.C.A., F.C.C.P., F.A.C.C., D.A.B.Path.; educator; consultant; b. Montreal, Que. 3 March 1933; e. Lisgar Collegiate Inst., Ottawa, Ont.; Univ. of Ottawa M.D. 1957; m. Mary Jane Catherine Bonfield; children: John Halvor, Mary Anne; PROF. OF PATHOL., UNIV. OF OTTAWA since 1972; Acting Head of Dept. since 1973; Path. and Acting Dir. Labs., Ottawa Gen. Hosp. since 1962; Regional Pathol., Mun. Ottawa-Carleton, Solr. Gen. Dept. since 1963; Consultant Pathol., Nat. Research Council; Nat. Defence Med. Centre; Food and Drug Directorate; Ottawa Civic Hosp.; mem. World Health Organ. Expert Adv. Panel on Cardiovascular Diseases; Scient. Subcomte. Candn. Heart Foundation; Research Assoc., Ont. Heart Foundation; Resident in Pathol. Kings Co. Hosp., Brooklyn, N.Y. 1959-60; Chief Resident and Asst. Instr., New York Downstate Med. Centre, Brooklyn 1960-61; Instr., 1961-62; Lectr. in Pathol., Univ. of Ottawa 1962-63, Asst. Prof. 1964-67, Assoc. Prof. 1968-72; served in R.C.N.(R) 1951-59; rank on retirement, Surg.-Lt.; author of over 60 invited lectures, 2 scient. exhibits shown at 10 meetings and 75 papers publ. in learned journs.; Examiner, R.C.P. & S.; Depy. Registrar (1967-71) Med. Council Can.; Consulting Ed., Univ. of Ottawa Med. Journ. 1963-70; mem. Ont. Med. Assn.; Candn. Med. Assn.; Ont. Assn. Pathols. (mem. Council 1967-70, Vice Pres. 1972-73, Pres. 1973-74); Candn. Assn. Pathols. (mem. Council 1973-74); Internat. Acad. Pathol.; Am. Assn. Pathols. & Bacteriols.; Am. Assn. Advanc. Sc.; Am. Geriatrics Soc.; Candn. Cardiovascular Soc.; Candn. Soc. Forensic Science; Am Soc. Clin. Pathols.; Am. Coll. Angiology; Am. Coll. Chest Phys. (Internat. Comte. on Coronary Disease); Ottawa Biochem. and Biol. Soc.; Internat. Study Group for Research in Cardiac Metabolism (Extve. Comte.); Candn. Assn. Univ. Teachers; Medical Lit. Club of Ottawa; Home: 550 Fairview Ave., Ottawa, Ont. K1M 0X5

HEIMBECKER, Raymond, M.D., M.A., M. Surg., F.R.C.S.(C.), F.A.C.S.; b. Calgary, Alta., 29 Nov. 1922; s. Harry O. and Dorothy A. (Turner) H.; e. Univ. of Sask., B.A., 1944; Univ. of Toronto, M.D., 1947, M.A., 1950, M. Surg., 1957; m. Kathleen Jensen, 18 Nov. 1950; children: Kathleen, Raymond, Harry, Anita, Constance; Surgeon, Univ. Hosp., London, Ont.; CHIEF OF CARDIOVASC. AND THORACIC SURG., UNIV. HOSP., PROF. OF SURG., UNIV. OF WEST. ONT.; formerly Asst. Professor, Dept. of Surgery, Univ. Toronto & Surgeon, Toronto Gen. Hosp.; mem., Bishop Strachan Sch. Foundation; served in C.O.T.C., 1941-45; Cardiovascular Ed. "Modern Medicine of Canada"; Assoc. ed., "European Surg. Research"; Publications: over 140 med. articles; Gov. for Ont., Am. Coll. of Chest Phys. and member presidential committee 1980; mem., Soc. Univ. Surgs.; Internat. Cardiovascular Soc.; Soc. for Vascular Surg.; Am. Assn. Thoracic Surg.; Soc. for Thoracic Surg.; Candn. Cardiovascular Soc.; C.N.A.S.C. (Council); Am. Heart Assn.; Candn. Soc. Microcirculation (Former Pres.); Am. Surg. Assn.; rec'd George Armstrong Peters Award (Exper. Surg.) 1950, Lister Award (Exper. Surg.) 1957; Gold Medal, Royal Coll. of Phys. and Surg., 1967; Special Award from Rose Fndn. of India, 1976; First Golden Murray Memorial Lectureship, Univ. of Toronto, 1981; Anglican; recreations: sailing, fishing, farming, flying; Clubs: Badminton & Raquet (Toronto); Hunt (London); R.C.Y.C.; Nut Island Shooting; Hopetown Sailing Club; Office: University Hospital, London, Ont.

HEINE, William Colborne, B.A.; newspaper editor; b. Saint John, N.B., 21 Nov. 1919; s. Roland Wallace and Winnifred Beatrice (Trider) H.; e. Saint John, Norton (N.B.) Schs., 1937; Univ. of W. Ont., B.A., 1949; m. Vivian Noreen Scribner, 17 May 1944; EDITOR, THE LONDON FREE PRESS since 1967; served with Candn. Army,

1939-42; R.C.A.F. 1942-45; publications: "The Last Canadian", 1974; "Historic Ships of the World", 1977; and others; Independent; Un. Church; Clubs: London; Hunt; Home: 647 Hillcrest Dr., London, Ont. N6K 1A8; Office: 369 York, London, Ont. N6A 1B2

HEINRICH, Hon. John Herbert, M.L.A., B.A., LL.B.; politician; b. Mission City, B.C. 20 Dec. 1936; e. Mission City High Sch.; Univ. of B.C., B.A., LL.B.; m. Linda Strachan 7 July 1962; children: Paul, Kim; MIN. OF LABOUR, B.C. 1979- ; el. M.L.A. for Prince George North prov. g.e. 1979; Social Credit; Office: Parliament Bldgs., Victoria, B.C. V8V 1X4.

HELLEINER, Christopher Walter, B.A., Ph.D.; educator; b. Vienna, Austria 21 March 1930; s. Karl Ferdinand Maria and Grethe (Deutsch) H.; e. Brown Sch. and Oakwood Coll. Inst. Toronto 1948; Univ. of Toronto B.A. 1952, Ph.D. 1955; Oxford Univ. postdoctoral 1955-57; m. Mary Margaret d. late Frederick Harold Burbidge, Toronto, Ont. 20 May 1955; children: Edith Caroline, Margaret Hope; PROF. OF BIOCHEM., FACULTY MED. DALHOUSIE UNIV. since 1965; Research Scient. Princess Margaret Hosp. Toronto 1957-63; Asst. Prof. of Med. Biophysics Univ. of Toronto 1959-63; Asst. Prof. of Biochem. Dalhousie Univ. 1963, Assoc. Prof. 1964-65; Prof. and Head of Biochem. 1965-1979; former mem. Bd. Halifax Grammar Sch.; mem. Halifax Chamber Choir; N.S. Bird Soc.; Candn. Biochem. Soc.; Soc. Gen. Microbiol. (UK); numerous articles in scient. journs.; Club: Waegwoltic; Home: 834 Marlborough Ave., Halifax, N.S. B3H 3G6; Office: Sir Charles Tupper Med. Bldg., Halifax, N.S. B3H 4H7.

HELLEINER, Karl Ferdinand Maria, Ph.D., LL.D. (hon. causa), F.R.S.C.; emeritus professor; b. Vienna, Austria, 19 April 1902; s. Karl and Karoline (Fischer) H.; e. Univ. of Vienna, Ph.D. 1925; m. Grethe, d. Dr. Julius Deutsch, Vienna, Austria, 2 July 1929; children: Christopher Walter, Frederick M., Gerald K.; Research Fellow, "Monumenta Germaniae Historica", 1925-28; Archivist of City of St. Pölten, Austria, 1927-38; came to Can. and joined Staff of Univ. of Toronto; Asst. Prof., Dept. of Pol. Econ., 1948, Assoc. Prof. 1953, Prof. of Economics 1959-70; Publications: "Readings in European Economic History", 1946; "The Imperial Loans", 1965; "Free Trade and Frustration", 1973; Econ. Hist. Assn.; Fellow, Austrian Inst. Hist. Research; recreation: music appreciation; Home: 317 Warren Ave., Toronto, Ont. M5P 2M7

HELLER, Jules, M.A., Ph.D.; univ. professor; b. New York City, N.Y., 16 Nov. 1919; s. Jacob Kenneth and Goldie (Lassar) H.; e. Ariz. State Coll., B.A. 1939; Columbia Univ., M.A. 1940; Univ. of S. Calif., Los Angeles, Ph.D. 1948; m. Gloria, d. Jack Spiegel, Hallandale, Fla., 11 June 1947; two d., Nancy Gale, Jill Kay; DEAN, COLL. OF FINE ARTS, York Univ., 1973-76 (Founding Dean 1968-73); Special Art Instr., 8th St. Sch., Tempe, Ariz., 1938-39; Dir. Art, Music, Union Neighborhood House, Auburn, N.Y., 1940-41; Prof. of Fine Arts & Head of Dept., Univ. of S. Cal., 1946-61; Visit. Assoc. Prof. of Fine Arts, Penn. State Univ., summers 1955, 1957; Dir. Sch. of Arts there 1961-63; Founding Dean, Coll. Arts & Arch., 1963-68; served U.S. Army Air Force, 1941-45; mem., Commonwealth Pa. Council on Arts 1966-68; author: "Problems in Art Judgment", 1946; "Print-making Today", 1958, 1959, rev. 1972; "Papermaking", 1978; contrib. artist: "Prints by California Artists", 1954; "Estampas de la Revolucion Mexicana", 1948; illustrator, "Canciones de Mexico", 1948; exhns. incl.: Santa Monica Art Gallery; Martha Jacabson Gallery, N.Y.; Los Angeles Co. Museum; Philadelphia Print Club; Seattle Art Museum; Landau Gallery; Kennedy & Co. Gallery; Brooklyn Museum; Cincinnati Art Museum; Dallas Museum of Fine Arts; Butler Art Inst.; Oakland Art Museum; Pa. Acad. Fine Arts; rep. in perm. colls. of Long Beach Museum of Art; Tamarind

Inst., Univ. of New Mexico; Allan R. Hite Inst.; Univ. of Louisville; Ariz. State Univ. and many private colls.; Pres., Internat. Council Fine Arts Deans, 1968; mem., Internat. Council of Fine Arts Deans 1963- ; Coll. Art Assn.; Dir., Nat. Council of the Arts in Educ. 1968-69; mem. Bd., The Toronto Symphony; Coll. Art Assn.; mem. Univ. Art Assn. Can.; Arizona-Mexico Comm. 1980- ; Art Consultant, Toronto-Dominion Centre 1968-70; Authors League; Internat. Assoc. of Paper Historians; Alpha Rho Chi.

HELLIWELL, David Leedom, B.A., C.A., F.C.A.; b. Vancouver, B.C. 26 July 1935; s. John Leedom and Kathleen B. (Kerby) H.; e. Prince of Wales High Sch. Vancouver 1953; Univ. of B.C., B.A. 1957, 1st yr. Law 1958; C.A. 1962; F.C.A. 1979; m. Margaret Jeanette d. late J. Cowan Adam 2 June 1961; children: Kerby C., Wendy J., Catherine J., Marnie L., John A.; PRESIDENT TRACTOR HOLDINGS LTD. 1981- ; Dir. Barbecon Inc.; Concord Development Ltd.; Great West Steel Ltd.; Swiss Bank Corp. (Can.); Steel Brothers Canada Ltd.; Fidelity Life Assnce. Co.; Westcoast Transmission Co. Ltd.; joined Thorne Riddell & Co. as C.A. 1962-65; Div. Mgr. Steel Brothers Canada Ltd. 1965, Vice Pres. and Gen. Mgr. for B.C. 1967, for Alta. 1969, Extve. Vice Pres. 1971, Pres. 1973; Pres., B.C. Resources 1978; Chmn. 1980 Anglican; Clubs: Vancouver; Vancouver Lawn Tennis & Badminton; Arbutus; Home: 6288 Macdonald St., Vancouver, B.C. V6N 1E6; Office: 400-601 Cordova St., Vancouver, B.C. V6B 1G1.

HELLIWELL, John Forbes, B.Com., B.A., D.Phil., F.R.S.C.; educator; b. Vancouver, B.C. 15 Aug. 1937; s. John Leedom and Kathleen Birnie (Kerby) H.; e. Prince of Wales High Sch. Vancouver 1954; Univ. of B.C. B.Com. 1959; Oxford Univ. (Rhodes Scholar) St. John's Coll. B.A. 1961, Nuffield Coll. D.Phil. 1966; m. Judith Isobel d. late E. A. Millsap, London, Ont. Oct. 1969; children: David Forbes, James Allen; PROF. OF ECON. UNIV. OF B.C. since 1971; Econ. Research Consultant Bank of Can. since 1965; mem. Research Staff Royal Comn. on Banking & Finance 1962-63, Royal Comn. on Taxation 1963-64; Lectr. in Econ. St. Peter's Coll. Oxford Univ. 1964-65, Research Fellow Nuffield Coll. 1965-67; Assoc. Prof. of Econ. Univ. of B.C. 1967-71; Managing Ed., Canadian Journal of Economics 1979-82; author 'Public Policies and Private Investment' 1968; co-author 'The Structure of RDX2' 1971; Ed. and contrib. 'Aggregate Investment' 1976; various articles; Anglican; Home: 4659 Simpson Ave., Vancouver, B.C. V6R 1C2; Office: Dept. of Econ., Rm 997, 1873 East Mall, Vancouver, B.C. V6T 1Y2.

HELLYER, Paul T., P.C. (Can.) 1957, B.A., F.R.S.A.; b. Waterford, Ontario, 6 August 1923; s. Audrey Samuel and Lulla Maud (Anderson) H.; e. High Schs., Waterford; Curtiss-Wright Tech. Inst. of Aeronautics, Glendale, Cal., Dipl. in Aeronautical Engn., 1941; Univ. of Toronto, B.A. 1949; m. Ellen Jean, d. late Henry Ralph, 1 June 1945; children: Mary Elizabeth, Peter Lawrence, David Ralph; with Fleet Aircraft Ltd., Fort Erie, Ont. 1942-44, commencing as Jr. Draughtsman, later becoming Group Leader in Engn. Dept.; estbd. Mari-Jane Fashions in 1945; became Pres. of Curran Hall Ltd., Bldrs. & Contractors, and of Trepil Realty Ltd.; served in 2nd World War 1944-46; Aircrew R.C.A.F., 1944; R.C.A. Active, 1945-46; 1st el. to H. of C. for Toronto Davenport in e. 1949; re-el. g.e. 1953; appt. Parlty. Asst. to Min. of Nat. Defence, 9 Feb. 1956; Assoc. Min. of Nat. Defence, 26 April 1957; def. in g.e. June 1957 and March 1958; el. for Toronto Trinity in by-el. Dec. 1958 and G.E.'s of 1962, 63, 65, 68 and 72; Min. of Nat. Defence, 1963-67; apptd. Min. of Transport, Sept. 1967; Min. responsible for Central Mortgage & Housing Corp., Apl. 1968; Chrmn., Task Force on Housing and Urban Devel., 1968-69; resigned from Cabinet 1969; joined Canadian Parlty. Press Gallery as syndicated Columnist for the Toronto Sun, 1974; Distinguished visitor, Grad. Faculty of Environmental Studies, York University 1969-70; author of "AGENDA: A Plan for Action", 1971; "Exit Inflation", 1981; United Church; recreations: singing, gardening, stamp collecting; Address: Ste. 506, 66 Harbour Sq., Toronto Ont. M5J 2L4

HELMERICKS, Constance, B.A.; author; lecturer; explorer; b. Binghamton, N.Y. 4 Jan. 1918; d. Arthur Smith, M.D. and Winifred (Browning) Chittenden; e. Univ. of Ariz. B.A. 1954; m. 1stly Harmon Helmericks 27 Apl. 1941; div. 1956; m. 2ndly Gilbert Doyle Bertie Kitchener Barrett 2 July 1969; div. 1970; children: Constance Jean, Carol Ann; comprehensive studies Arctic population and animals Can. and Alaska 1941-56; field researcher in sociol. Univ. of Ariz. 1956-72; came to Can. 1972; collector small mammal specimens for Cornell Univ. and Smithsonian Inst. 1947-52; nat. lectr. 1947-56 incl. Carnegie Hall, N.Y. Town Hall, Explorers Club, Am. Museum Nat. Hist., Philadelphia Acad. Arts, Detroit Art Inst.; producer TV films Jack Douglas Studios Hollywood; enrichment lectr. Royal Viking Line cruise ship 1974; author "We Live in Alaska" 1944; "We Live in the Arctic" 1947; "Summer with the Eskimos" 1948; "Our Alaskan Winter" 1949; "The Flight of the Arctic Tern" 1951; "Hunting in North America" 1957; "Down the Wild River North" 1968; "Australian Adventure" 1972; articles various mags., reports; film subjects incl. Arctic of Alaska & Can., Mexico, Honduras & Nicaragua, jungle rivers by raft and canoe, Australia; Charter mem. Arctic Inst. N. Am.; Assn. Mental Health (Pima Co. Ariz.); mem. Internat. Press Club; recreations: hiking, camping, backpacking, canoeing maj. river systems Alaska & Candn. N., movies; Home: 3863 Parker St., N. Burnaby, B.C. V5C 3B5.

HELWIG, David Gordon, M.A.; author, educator, b. Toronto, Ont. 5 Apl. 1938; s. William Gordon and Ivy Lorraine (Abbott) H.; e. Stamford Coll. Inst. 1956; Univ. of Toronto B.A. 1960; Univ. of Liverpool M.A. 1962; m. Nancy Mary d. James Henry Keeling 19 Sept. 1959; two d. Sarah Magdalen, Kathleen Rebecca; educ. in Eng. Queen's Univ. 1962-80; author "Figures in a Landscape" 1968; "The Sign of the Gunman" 1969; "The Streets of Summer" 1969; "The Day Before Tomorrow" 1971; "A Book About Billie" 1972; "The Best Name of Silence" 1972; "Atlantic Crossings" 1974; "The Glass Knight" 1976; "A Book of the Hours" 1979; "Jennifer" 1979; "The King's Evil, 1981; "Itl. Always Summer" 1982; mem. ACTRA; Writers' Union Can.; Address: 73 Baiden St., Kingston, Ont.

HEMENS, Henry John, Q.C., B.A., B.C.L.; b. Montreal, Que. 16 June 1913; s. Sidney John and Margaret Ann (O'Brien) H.; e. Loyola Coll. B.A. 1932; McGill Univ. B.C.L. 1935; Univ. de Paris 1935-36; m. Sarah Ann Wright 4 Nov. 1939; children: Mary-Margaret, John, Paul, Eileen; Counsel for Hemens, Harris, Thomas, Mason, Schweitzer & McNeill, Montreal since 1977; Dir. Dennison Manufacturing Canada Inc.; Quebec Distillers CorO.; Chancellor and mem. Bd. of Govs. Concordia Univ. 1974-81; called to Bar of Que. 1935; cr. Q.C. 1956; Mgr. Legal Dept. Du Pont of Canada Ltd. 1939, Gen. Counsel 1954, Secy. 1962, Vice Pres. and Secy. 1969-77; Dir., Du Pont, 1971-78; Mayor of Rosemere, Que. 1955-59; Mun. Judge of Rosemere 1965-76; Order of Malta; mem. Financial Adm. Comte. Diocese St. Jerome; mem. Bar Que.*; Assn. Candn. Gen. Counsel (Past Pres.); Candn. Mfrs.' Assn. (Past mem. Extve. Comte.); Candn. Chamber Comm. (Past Chrmn. Comte. Combines & Competition Policy); R. Catholic; recreations: golf, reading, swimming; Clubs: St. James's; Lorraine Golf; Home: 214 Rose Alma, Rosemere, Que. J7A 3B6; Office: 505 Dorchester Blvd. West, Montreal, Que H27 1A8

HEMLOW, Joyce, M.A., Ph.D., LL.D., F.R.S.C. (1960); professor; author; b. 31 July 1906; d. William and Rosalinda (Redmond) H.; e. Queen's Univ., B.A. 1941, M.A. 1942, LL.D. 1967; Radcliffe Coll., A.M. 1944, Ph.D. 1948; Marty Travelling Fellow, Queen's, 1942-43; Candn. Fed. of Univ. Women Fellow, 1943-44; Gugenheim Mem. Foundation Fellow, 1951, 1967; Nuffield Fellow (summer), 1954; Greenshields Prof. of English Lang. & Lit., McGill Univ.; Ll.D. Dalhousie Univ., 1972; Prof. Emerita, 1975- ; mem. of Humanities Research Council of Canada, 1957-61; Publications: "The History of Fanny Burney", 1958 (rec'd. Gov-Gen. Award for Acad. Non-fiction 1958, Rose Mary Crawshay Prize, and James Tait Black memorial book prize for the best biography in the U.K. in 1958;); "A Catalogue of the Burney Family Correspondence, 1749-1878", (1971); 10 volumes of an edition "The Journals and Letters of Fanny Burney (Madame d'Arblay) 1791-1840", 1972- ; and various articles mainly about the Burney's; awarded Grad. Achievement Medal by Radcliffe Grad. Soc. 1969; Phi Beta Kappa; Protestant; Address: Apt. 106, 3555 Atwater Ave., Montreal, Que. H3H 1G3 or Liscomb, Nova Scotia

HEMMANS, George E. W.; retired banking executive; b. Regina, Sask. 19 July 1914; s. George W. and Mary (Carthew) H.; e. Public Sch. Regina, Sask.; High Sch. Vancouver, B.C.; Harvard Univ. Advanced Mang. Program; m. Gwendolyn, d. Lawrence Haskins 1 Sept. 1942; children: Gayden, Barbara P.; joined Toronto-Dominion Bank (then Bank of Toronto) 1934, Sr. Offr. in various capacities Div. and H.O. Vancouver and Toronto 1949-57, Br. Mgr. Toronto 1957, Vancouver Supt. Pacific Div. 1963 and Vice-Pres. Pacific Div. 1965, Vice-Pres. Corp. Credit, H.O. 1970 Pres. T.D. Realty Inv. 1972; served in 2nd World War, Candn. Armed Forces 1941-46, rank on discharge Lt.; Anglican; recreations: golf, tennis, badminton, curling; Club: St. George's Golf and Country; Home 26 Ridgevalley Cres., Islington, Ont. M9A 3J6; Office: Toronto Dominion Bank, International Banking Group Head Office, P.O. Box 1, Toronto-Dominionn Centre, Toronto, Ont. M5K 1A2

HEMPHILL, Brig. Gen. William Howard, C.D., A.D.C.; company extve.; b. Hensall, Ont., 25 March 1916; s. Alvin Wilfred Ethelbert and Sarah Alice Etta (Davis) H.; e. Hensall (Ont.) Pub. Sch.; Exeter (Ont.) High Sch.; Univ. of Toronto; Univ. of W. Ont., B.A. (Hon. Business Adm.) 1938; Royal Mil. Coll., Kingston, Ont.; m. Elizabeth Helen, d. Gordon John Ingram, London, Ont., 22 Feb. 1941; children: Nancy, Gordon, Mary, Daphne; CHRM. AND DIR., KRUG FURNITURE INC. (Estbd. 1880); Dir., The Ellis-Don Limited; Canada Trust; past Gov., University of Western Ontario; Stratford Shakespearean Festival; Past Chairman, Stratford, Ont., Indust. Comn.; Past Pres., Stratford, Ont., Chamber of Comm.; Past Chrmn., Furniture Mfrs. Assn.; served in 2nd World War; Major, D.A.A. & Q.M.G., Candn. Liaison Sec., H.Q. 6 Airborne Div., to 1945; Lt.-Col. in Command of Perth Regt., N.P.A.M. till 1953; commanding 18 Militia Group, till 1962; Delta Upsilon; Anglican; recreations: golf, swimming; Clubs: Rotary (Past Pres.) National (Toronto); Home: 126 John St., Stratford, Ont. N5A 6K9; Office: 93 Trinity St., Stratford, Ont. N5A 6K9

HENDERSON, (Andrew) Maxwell, O.B.E., F.C.A., L.L.D.; chartered accountant; b. Carshalton, Surrey, Eng., 24 March 1908; s. Andrew Louis and Eva Gertrude H.; e. Mill Hill Sch., London, Eng.; Rollins Coll., Fla.; m. Beatrice Johnstone, d. Charles L. Maltby, Toronto, Ont. 1 June 1935; one s., David J.; Auditor Gen. of Can., 1960-73; joined Harvey E. Crowell, F.C.A., Halifax, 1924-29; Price Waterhouse & Co., Toronto, 1929-36; Comptroller, Hiram Walker-Gooderham and Worts Ltd., Walkerville, Ont., 1936-40; Foreign Exchange Control Bd. and Asst. to Chrmn. and Comptroller of W.P.T.B., Ottawa, 1940-46; Secy.-Treas., Distillers Corp.-Seagrams Ltd., Montreal, 1946-56; Comptroller, Candn. Broadcasting Corp., Ottawa, 1957-60; mem. Inst. C.A.'s Que. and Ont.; Anglican; Home: 17 Coulson Ave., Toronto, Ont. M4V 1Y3

HENDERSON, George Milne; executive; b. Black Cape, Que., 8 Oct. 1915; s. Hastie Milne and Pearl (Steel) H.; e. Public School Black Cape, Qué.; Sir George Williams College, Montreal; Monument National; m. Mary Rosella Jones, 23 June 1939; children: Milne Lawrence, John Brooke, Clinton Ross, Robert Howard, Catherine Anne; PRESIDENT AND DIR., MARTIN & STEWART LTD., owner, Martin & Stewart of New Eng. Inc.; Pres., Martin & Stewart (N.Y.) Inc.; Martin and Stewart (B.C.) Ltd.; McCordick Leathers Ltd.; La Tannerie Can. Inc.; River Market Commodities Inc.; Polar Quick Freezing Co. Ltd.; Henderson Lumber Co. Ltd.; Wilson Hide & Skin Co. Ltd.; Inhuma B.V. (Rotterdam); Black Cape Holdings Ltd.; Elesnar Realities Ltd.; Hendeck Holdings Ltd.; Pres. and Dir., P.E.I. Produce Co. Ltd.; J. W. Macdonald & Co. Ltd.; Vice Pres., Dominion Metals Ltd.; Crowley-Henderson Inc.; Financial Adv., Simpson & Lea Hides Ltd.; Great Plains Processing; Chmn. of Bd., Green Gables Fine Foods Stores Ltd.; Green Gables Realty Ltd.; owner, Glencoe Horse Farms and Glen Brae Farms, Howick, Que.; Argyle Farms, Cambelville, Ont.; began as Apprentice, Martin & Stewart, Montreal, Que. 1933; Buyer & Traveller, 1936; Mgr., 1942; acquired interest in firm in 1946 & formed partnership with Mr. A. A. Dectar, bought out Mr. Dectar's interest 1964; Alderman, Town of Mount Royal, Que., 1954 re-e. 1957-60-73-75-79; Nat. Vice-Pres., Candn. Jr. Chamber of Comm., 1948-49, Regional Pres., 1949-50; Pres. Downtown Citizens' Assn. of Montreal 1968-70; re-el. Councillor Town of Mount Royal 1973; United Ch.; recreations: fishing, hunting, horse-racing; Clubs: Montreal; Mount Stephen; M.A.A.A.; Home: 95 Fernlea Cres., Town of Mount Royal, Montreal, Que; Office: 316 Bridge, Montreal, Que. H3K 2C4

HENDERSON, Gordon Fripp, O.C., Q.C., B.A., LL.D.; b. Ottawa, Ont., 17 April 1912; s. Gordon Smith and Charlotte (Stratton) H.; e. Ottawa Model Sch.; Lisgar Coll. Inst.; Univ. of Toronto, B.A. 1934; Osgoode Hall, Toronto, Ont.; m. Joan, d. late John Parkins, 15 Aug. 1942; children: Joanne Gail, Gordon Stuart, Robert John; PARTNER, GOWLING & HENDERSON; called to the Bar of Ont., June 1937, and of Que. 1952; cr. Q.C. 1953; Apptd. O.C. 1977; LL.D. (Univ. of Ottawa) 1979; Bencher, Law Soc. of Upper Canada; Hon. Vice-Consul for Liberia; Trustee, Schenley Awards; Immediate Past Pres., Cdn. Bar Assn. 1979.80; Pres. Performing Rights Organization of Can. Ltd.; Ottawa Cablevision Ltd.; Vice Pres., Cdn. Bar Foundation; Fellow, Am. College of Trial Lawyers; Dir., CKOY Ltd.; Sandvik Candn. Ltd.; Sandvik Conveyor Can. Ltd.; Mechron Engineering Ltd.; Huron Chemicals Ltd.; Selkirk Communications; Candn. Writers' Foundation Inc.; Columbia Artists Mgmt. Can. Ltd.; Bradley Air Services Ltd.; NIFE-Powertronic Equipment Ltd.; Burlec Ltd.; Flakt Can. Ltd.; Disston (Can.); Vice Pres. and Dir., Leimark Farms Ltd.; Music Promotion Foundation; Mem., Bd. of Gov., Univ. of Ottawa; mem. Ottawa Adv. Bd., Royal Trust Co.; Past mem. Bd. of Govs., Stratford Shakespearean Festival mem. Advocates Society; Internat. Bar Assn. (Council, Business Law Section); Adv. Bd., Ottawa Boys & Girls Club; Foundation; Editor, Canadian Patent Reporter; Past Pres. (1953-65) Patent & Trade Mark Inst. Can.; Royal Canadian Flying Clubs assn.; Canadian Citizenship Council; Trustee, Cdn. Figure Skating Assn.; Delta Kappa Epsilon; United Church; Clubs: Rideau; Country; Royal Ottawa Golf & Country; Canadian (New York); Home: 190 Acacia, Rockcliffe Park, Ottawa, Ont. K1M 0L5; Office: 160 Elgin St., Ottawa, Ont. K1N 8S3

HENDERSON, Hon. Lorne Charles, M.P.P.; politician; farmer; b. Enniskillen Twp. Lambton Co. Ont. 31 Oct. 1920; s. David Howard and Elizabeth Lomena (Robinson) H.; m. Reta Pearl d. late Floyd Sackrider, Norwich, Ont. and Lula Maw, Petrolia, Ont. 21 Aug. 1947; children: Shirley Pearl Phillips, David, Marian Elizabeth; PROV. SEC. FOR RESOURCES DEVELOPMENT, ONT. 1982-; Min. of Agriculture and Food, Ont. 1979-82; Min. of

Govt. Services Ont. 1978-79; mem. Enniskillen Twp. Council 1946-49; Depy. Reeve 1950-51; Reeve 1952-57; Warden Lambton Co. 1957; Assessor Enniskillen Twp. 1958-63; el. to Ont. Leg. g.e. 1963, re-el. since; Chrmn. Select Comte. on Land Drainage; served on all Standing Comtes., Chrmn. of several; Min. without Portfolio 1975; Chrmn. of Cabinet 1977; has operated gen. mixed farming operation Enniskillen Twp.; Past Pres. St. Clair Dist. Boy Scout Assn.; Five Co.'s Trustees & Ratepayers Assn.; Lambton Rural Game Conserv. Assn.; Lambton Trustees & Ratepayers Assn.; Petrolia & Enniskillen Agric. Soc.; Past Dir. Ont. Mun. Assn.; named Hon. mem. Walpole Island Indian Band 1968; P. Conservative; United Church; Home: R.R. 3, Oil Springs, Ont. N0N 1P0; Office: Parliament Bldgs., Queen's Park, Toronto, Ont.

HENDERSON, Lyman George, B.A.; company executive, prof. speaker and writer; b. Toronto, Ont., 12 Aug. 1920; s. Marion Joy (Ryan) and the late Lyman Abraham H.; e. Whitney Pub. Sch., and Univ. of Toronto Schs., Toronto, Ont.; Trinity Coll., Univ. of Toronto, B.A. 1942; m. Ann Elizabeth L.M.Z., d. late Capt. E. W. Buchanan, R.N., London, Eng., 3 March 1945; children: Buchanan Lyman M., Victoria Ann Z., Antonia Joy Z.; CHRMN., DAVIS AND HENDERSON LIMITED (Graphic Communications., Estbd. 1875) since 1974; joined firm in 1946; Pres., 1959-74; served in 2nd World War, 1942-46; Captain, R.C.A. (Overseas 1943-46); Chrmn., Reilly, Rennie, Campbell Ltd. (Commercial Artists); Hon. Life mem. Candn. Cancer Soc. (Past Pres. Ont. Div.); Past Chairman, Good Neighbour Club; Past Pres. (1972-73) Graphic Arts Industries Assn.; Past Pres. Nat. Ballet of Canada; mem. of Bd., Visual Arts Ontario; Alpha Delta Phi (Past Pres.); Presb. (Elder, Woodbridge Ch.); recreations: home computer, the arts, skiing, travel, tennis; Clubs: University; Donalda; Arts & Letters; Home: Windborne, R.R. No. 3, Woodbridge, Ont. L4L 1A7; Office: 41 Scarsdale, Don Mills, Ont. M3B 2R2

HENDERSON, Mary Elizabeth Park, B.L.S.; M.A., LL.D.; b. Kindersley, Sask. 12 April 1921; d. James Archibald and Elizabeth Jane (Park) H.; e. Elem. Schs. rural Sask 1933; Airdrie (Scot.) Acad. 1938; Univ. of B.C., B.A. 1941, M.A. 1943; Univ. of Toronto B.L.S. 1944; LL.D. Univ. of P.E.I. 1975; PROF., FACULTY OF LIBRARY SCIENCE, UNIV. OF ALBERTA since 1974; Jr. Cataloguer and Reference Lib., Univ. of B.C. Lib., 1944-49; Cataloguer, Univ. of Wales Lib. Aberystwyth 1950-51; Tech. Services Lib., Govt. of Sask. Prov. Lib., Regina 1952-59; Chief Lib. Regina Campus, Univ. of Sask. 1960-66; Asst. Lib. i.c. tech. services - experiments in lib. technol., Prince of Wales Coll., Charlottetown, P.E.I. 1967-69; Assoc. Prof. Fac. of Lib. Science, Univ. of Alta. 1970-74 and Acting Dir. 1971-72; Dir./Dean, 1972-76; mem. Univ. Senate, 1975-77; Nat. Lib. Adv. Bd., 1975-78; Candn. Lib. Assn. (Pres. 1974-75); Am. Lib. Assn.; Candn. Assn. Lib. Schs.; Am. Assn. Lib. Schs.; Candn. Assn. Univ. Teachers; Can. Research Inst. for the Advancement of Women; author of "Planning the Future by the Past" 1969; Ed. Sask. Lib. Bull. 1954-57; judge for Leacock Medal for Humour from 1978-80; has contrib. numerous articles and book reviews to various newspapers, learned and prof. journs.; recreations: books, art, record collecting, travel; Home: 906-11111 - 87 Ave., Edmonton, Alta., T6G 0X9; Office: Edmonton, Alta.

HENDERSON, Wesley E., B.S.A.; agrologist; b. Swan River, Man., 18 Nov. 1928; s. Nelson and Eunice Hazel (Watson) H.; e. Public and High Schs., Swan River, Man.; Normal Sch. 1948; Univ. Man., B.S.A. 1955; m. Eleanor Rose Atwood, 11 July 1964; children: Lisa Marie, Jennifer Anne; GEN. MANAGER, AGRICULTURAL INSTITUTE OF CANADA since 1966; Teacher, rural sch. 1946-47, Jr. High Sch., Boissevain, Man., 1948-50; Agric. Rep., Man. Dept. of Agric., Carberry, Man., 1955-56; Information Offr. Candn. Seed Growers Assn., Ottawa, 1956-62; Program Organizer and then Asst. Radio Network Supv., Farm Broadcasts, CBC, Toronto, Ont., 1966; Dir., Candn. Council 4H Clubs; mem., Candn. Farm Writers Fed.; Ont. Inst. of Agrols.; Candn. Soc. of Rural Extension; Inst. of Assn. Extves. (Ottawa Chapter); Hon. Secy.-Treas., Commonwealth Assn. of Scientific Agr. Soc.; United Church; recreations: curling, golf, skiing, boating, reading; Club: Men's Church; Home: 24 Seymour Ave., Nepean, Ont. K2E 6P2; Office: Suite 907, 151 Slater St., Ottawa, Ont. K1P 5H4

HENDERSON, Hon. William J., M.B.E.; retired judge; b. Empress, Alta., 13 Oct. 1916; s. John Albert and Leita (Davey) H.; e. Queen's Univ., B.A. 1938; Osgoode Hall Law Sch., Toronto, 1942; m. Helen, d. late Dr. Lorne MacDougall, New York, 13 March 1943; two d., Margaret Rose, Judith Anne; read law with J.M. Hickey, Q.C., Kingston, Ont.; called to Bar of Ont. 1942; cr. Q.C., 1961; Justice, Supreme Court of Ont. 1965-79 (ret.); estbd. law firm 1945, later known as Henderson & Woods, engaged in general practice; estbd. Loyalist Farms Ltd. for dairy products and reg'd. Holstein cattle; served with Candn. Army 1942-45 in Eng., Italy, France, Belgium, Holland and Germany; mem. Order of the British Empire el. M.P. for Kingston, 1949-58; Pres., Ont. Lib. Assn., 1958-60; mem., Candn. Bar Assn.; Judicial Conf. of Can.; Dir., Can. Inst. for the Adm. of Justice; mem. of Bd. Hotel Dieu Hospital, 1974- ; Bd. of St. Mary's on the Lake Hospital, 1954- ; Gen. Chrmn., Hotel Dieu Hospital-Kingston General Hospital Capital Appeal Fund Raising Campaign; United Church; recreations: farming, golf, curling, sailing; Clubs: University; Cataraqui Golf & Country; Trident Yacht; Home: 4567 Bath Rd., Kingston, Ont. K7N 1A8

HENDRICK, Air Vice Marshal Max Morton, O.B.E., C.D., B.A.Sc.; b. Portland, Oregon, 28 April 1910; s. Max William and Laura Esther (Phillips) H.; came to Canada, 1912; e. Lisgar Coll., Ottawa; Montreal High Sch.; Univ. of Toronto, B.A.Sc. (Mech Engn.), 1932; McGill Univ. (Rockefeller Scholar.) 1934; m. Dorothy Somerville Stratton Cameron, Toronto, 24 July 1940; permanent R.C.A.F. 1934-65; trained as a General List Pilot; Army co-operation sqdn. duties and Wireless Sch. Instr. until war; signals duties with No. 3 Wireless Sch. and Candn. Jt. Staff, Wash., D.C., until 1943; signals duties with SHAEF and 2nd Tactical Air Force, 1944; Tiger Force, 1945; Dir. of Signals, R.C.A.F. until 1947; Northwest Air Command, Edmonton, Stn. Commdr. and Sr. Air Staff Offr. until 1950; Air Attache, Wash, D.C., 1950-51; Imp. Defence Coll., London, Eng., 1952; N.D.H.Q., Ottawa, Chief of Telecommunications until 1955; Air mem. for Tech. Services until 1958, Chrmn., Candn. Jt. Staff, and Cdn. Rep. on N.A.T.O. Mil. Ctee. in Permanent Session, Wash., D.C., 1959-62 A.O.C. Air Defence Command, St. Hubert, Que., 1963-64; retired 1965; apptd. Consultant, Allied Chemical Corp., Dec. 1964; Extve. Vice-Pres. and Dir., Allied Chemical Canada Ltd., Montreal, 1965-68, Pres. and Chief Extve. Offr. 1968-72, Consult. Extve. 1973-74, ret'd. May 1975; Wing Commdr. 1941, Group Capt. 1943; Air Commodore 1949, Air Vice Marshal 1955; mem., Nat. Extve. Comte., Candn. Chamber Comm. 1968-72; Que. Dir., Nat. Extve. Comte., Candn. Mfrs. Assn. 1970-72; Dir., Montreal Bd. of Trade, 1966-68; Fellow, Candn. Aero Space Inst.; Life mem., Engn. Inst. Can.; mem. Cdn. Club of Montreal, 1965-72 (Pres., 1971). Protestant; recreations: sailing, golf; Clubs: R.A.F. (London, Eng.); University (Toronto); Mt. Royal; Mt. Bruno; St. James's Montreal; Mission Valley Golf(Sarasota); Residence (summer); Box 652 Lakefield, Ont., K0L 2H0; (winter): 5141 Sandy Cove Ave., Sarasota, Fla., 33581

HENDRY, Noel W., B.A.Sc., M.Sc.; geologist; company executive; e. Univ. mmof British Columbia, B.A.Sc. (Engn. and Geol.) 1937; Cal. Inst. Tech., M.Sc. 1939; VICE-PRES., JOHNS MANVILLE SALES CORP.; after grad. entered the mining exploration field; joined present Co. in 1949 as Sr. Mining Engr. at Jeffrey Mine; Chief Ge-

ologist in Exploration Dept. of the Divn., 1950-53; Exploration Mgr., 1953-59; Gen. Sales Mgr., A.F.D., 1959-76; Gen. Mgr., Mining Div., 1976-77; Gen. Mgr., Filtration and Minerals Div., 1977-80; Home; 31 Wedge Way, Littleton, Colo. 80123; Office: Ken Caryl, P.O. Box 5108, Denver, Colo. 80217

HENDRY, Thomas Best, C.A.; playwright; producer; b. Winnipeg, Man. 7 June 1929; s. Donald and Martha (Best) H.; e. Bishop Taché Sch. and Norwood Coll. Inst. St. Boniface, Man. 1945; Kelvin High Sch. Winnipeg 1947; C.A. (Man.) 1955; m. Judith d. late George Hubert Sherriff Carr 22 Nov. 1963; children: Thomas John, Christopher Stefan Carr, Ashleigh Elizabeth Jane; PRES., TORONTO FREE THEATRE INC. 1971- ; Treas. Playwrights Can.; co-founder Hendry & Evans, C.A.'s 1955-61; co-founder Theatre 77 Winnipeg 1957; Man. Theatre Centre 1958 (Gen. Mgr. 1958-63); re-organized Rainbow Stage 1958 (Gen. Mgr. 1958-61); Candn. Players Foundation 1964; Candn. Centre Internat. Theatre Inst. 1964 (Secy.-Gen. 1964-68); Literary Mgr. Stratford Festival 1969-70; co-founder Playwrights Can. and Toronto Free Theatre 1971, Banff Playwrights Colony 1974; Fellow, Bethune Coll. York Univ.; MacDowell Colony Peterborough, N.H.; Candn. del. World Theatre Congs. 1965, 1967, 1981; author "15 Miles of Broken Glass" 1965 comedydrama; "Gravediggers of 1942" 1977 musical; "How are Things with the Walking Wounded" 1972, drama; "Dr. Selavy's Magic Theatre" musical (original cast LP United Artists)1972; "Satyricon," (musical) 1969; various book chapters, articles; rec'd Centennial Medal 1967; Lt. Gov. of Ont's Medal 1969; Queen Elizabeth's Silver Jubilee Medal 1977; Chrmn. Elgin-Lowther Ratepayers Assn. 1977- ; mem. Man. Inst. C.A.'s; Ont. Inst. C.A.'s; Guild Candn. Playwrights; Candn. Actors Equity Assn.; Assn. Candn. TV & Radio Artists: Assn. Cultural Extves.; Anglican; recreations: building World War I and II model aircraft, reading, collecting Canadian prints; Home: 34 Elgin Ave., Toronto M5R 1G6; Office:26 Berkeley St., Toronto, Ont. M5A 2W3.

HENDY, Robert Ian, V.R.D., C.D., Q.C.; b. Toronto, Ont., 4 Dec. 1916; s. Harold Robert and Isabel (Reid) H.; e. Upper Canada Coll., Toronto, 1930-35; Trinity Coll., Univ. of Toronto, B.A. 1939; Osgoode Hall Law Sch., Toronto, 1945-48; m. Margaret Elizabeth, d. Cecil M. Corkett, 26 Oct. 1940; children: Thomas C., Beverly Joan, Julia M., Susan I; PARTNER, BIGELOW, HENDY, SHIRER & UUKKIVI, since 1964; Dir., Sterling Trust Corp.; Independent Order of Forresters; Gen. Solr., I.O.F, since 1963; read law with Maxwell C. Purvis, Q.C.; called to Bar of Ont. 1948; cr. Q.C. 1959; joined Sommerville, Purvis & Bigelow, 1949 (predecessor firm); served with RCNVR and RCNR, 1936-62, on active service 1939-45; Chrmn., Conf. of Defence Assns., 1962; former C.O., HMCS York, Sr. Naval Offr., Toronto; retired as Commodore; Hon. ADC to Gov. Gen. of Can., 1952-67; Chrmn., Comte. on Naval Reserve, 1964; Gov., Candn. Corps Commissionaires (E. Can.) since 1951 (Chrmn. of Bd. 1965-66); mem. Bd. Govs., Upper Canada Coll., 1960-64; Nat. Council, Navy League of Can. (Pres., 1976-78) and mem. Ont. Mang. Comte. 1951-74; mem., Law Society Upper Can.; Candn. Bar Assn.; Candn. Tax Foundation; Co. of York Law Assn.; Royal Candn. Legion (Past Pres., Fort York Br.); St. George's Soc.; St.Andrews Soc.; Naval Offrs. Assn.; Royal Candn. Naval Assn. (Hon. Pres. 1959-74); Toronto Brigantine Inc.; Haida Inc. (mem. Adv. Comte.); Zeta Psi; Conservative; Protestant; recreations: squash, tennis, skiing; Clubs: Badminton & Racquet; Caledon Ski; Empire; Royal Candn. Mil. Inst.; Naval; Home: 179 Dunvegan Rd., Toronto, Ont., M5P 2P1; Office: 789 Don Mills Rd., Don Mills, Ont., M3C 1T5

HENLEY, Hon. David Lloyd George, M.L.A.; druggist; b. Roslin, N.S. 11 Jan. 1917; s. Bickford and Estella Marie (Murphy) H.; e. Roslin, N.S.; N.S. C.V.T.S. Pictou, N.S.; Dalhousie Univ.; m. Muriel Pearl (d.) d. Ralph Douglas

Russell, Oxford, N.S. 6 Sept. 1946; children: Terrence, Richard, Nancy, Michael, Gregory, Kevin, William, Thomas; MIN. OF LANDS & FORESTS, N.S. 1978– and Min. Responsible for Adm. Liquor Control Act; retail druggist; el. M.L.A. for Cumberland West prov. g.e. 1963, re-el. since; Freemason; mem. Royal Candn. Legion; Office: (P.O. Box 698) Toronto-Dominion Bank Bldg., 1791 Barrington St., Halifax, N.S. B3J 2T9.

HENEAULT, Robert Edmond, B.A.; manufacturer; b. Danielson, Conn. 5 July 1926; s. George J. and Rose Alma H.; e. Univ. of Notre Dame B.A. (Econ.); m. Mary Theresa d. late John J. Keenan 31 May 1952; children: Robert George, Suzanne Mary, Pamela Rose, John Keenan, Thomas Maurice, Kathryn Anne; VICE PRES. ADM., STELCO INC. 1976– ; Chrmn., Technical Service Council; Dir. St. Lawrence Cement Co.; The Canada Systems Group; came to Can. 1952; Personnel Mgr. Singer Manufacturing Co. St. Jean, Que. 1952-54; Supt. of Indust. Relations Montreal Works, Stelco Inc. 1954, Personnel & Indust. Relations Adm. E. Region 1959, Supt. of Indust. Relations Hilton Works Hamilton, Ont. 1960, Mgr. of Production Planning 1962, Mgr. of Field Sales Central Region 1964, Mgr. Sheet & Strip Sales 1965, Vice Pres. Personnel 1972; served with U.S. Navy S. Pacific Amphibian Forces 1944-46; mem. Internat. Iron & Steel Inst.; Am. Iron & Steel Inst.; Candn. Mfrs. Assn.; Gov., Stratford Shakespearean Festival Foundation Can.; R. Catholic; Club: Ontario; Home2174 Oneida Cres., Mississauga, Ont. L5C 1V6; Office: (P.O. Box 205) Toronto-Dominion Centre, Toronto, Ont. M5K 1J4.

HENNEN, Brian Kenneth Edward, M.D., M.A.; family physician; educator; b. Hamilton, Ont. 14 June 1937; s. Albert Victor Hennen; e. Queen's Univ. M.D. 1962; Mich. State Univ. M.A. 1969; m. Mary Margaret d. Fred R. Barnum 20 Aug. 1960; children: Albert, Leslie, Nancy; PROF. AND HEAD OF FAMILY MED., DALHOUSIE UNIV. 1977- ; internship and residency Kingston Gen. Hosp.; Teaching Fellow in Family Med. McMaster Univ. 1967-68; Fellow in Med. Educ. and Instr. in Med. Mich. State Univ. 1968-69; Family Practitioner, Harvie Clinic, Orillia, Ont. 1963-65; Lectr. in Community Med. Univ. of W. Ont. 1969, Asst. Prof. of Family Med. 1970, Assoc. Prof. 1973; Prof. and Head, Dept. of Family Med. Dalhousie Univ. 1974; Visiting Prof., Univ. of Newcastle 1981-82; co-author "Family Medicine — A Guidebook for Practitioners of the Art" 1980; author or co-author numerous articles med. journs.; mem. Med. Soc. N.S.; Coll. Family Phys. Can.; Alpha Omega Alpha; P. Conservative; Protestant; recreation: music; Home: 112 Crichton Ave., Dartmouth, N.S. B3A 3R5; Office 5599 Fenwick St., Halifax, N.S. B3H 1R2.

HENNESSY, Vice-Admiral Ralph L., D.S.C. (1942), C.D.; b. Edinburgh, Scot., 5 Sept. 1918; s. Col. Patrick and Ellen Dorothy (Robb) H.; e. George Watsons, Edinburgh; Pub. Sch., Winnipeg, Man. and Esquimalt, B.C.; Univ. of Toronto Schs.; RCAF Staff Coll., 1947; Nat. Defence Coll., 1954; m. Mary Constance, d. J. T. O'Neil, Ottawa, 9 May 1944; children: Diana, Michael, Terence, Timothy; EXECUTIVE DIRECTOR. STANDARDS COUNCIL OF CANADA, since Jan. 1971; joined RCN 1936; service afloat in World War II and subsequently; Senior Staff appointments Canada and abroad; Vice-Admiral June 1966; Comptroller-General, Candn. Forces 1966-68; Chief of Personnel, 1969-70; Vice Pres. of Internat. Organ. for Standardization from 1976; Fellow, Standards Eng. Soc.; Bd. of Govs., Ottawa Div., Can. Corps of Commissionaires; Knight Commander, Military and Hospitallers Order of St. Lazarus of Jerusalem; Anglican: recreations: golf, swimming; Home: 2627 - 200 Clearview Ave., Ottawa, Ont., K1Z 8M2; Office: 350 Sparks St., Ottawa, Ont.,K1R 7S8

HENNIGAR, Ross A., B.Sc.; company executive; b. Halifax, N.S. 14 June 1929; s. Carl V. and Harriet (Anderson)

H.; e. Mount Royal High Sch.; MacDonald Coll., McGill Univ. B.Sc. 1951; Certificate in Personnel Adm., McMaster Univ.; m. Nancy Jane, d. Margaret G. Stephens, Collingwood, Ont. 2 Oct. 1954; children: Mary Catherine, Robert Grant, John Ross; PRESIDENT C.E.O. AND DIRECTOR, SUNCOR INC.; Pres. and Dir., Sunoco Inc.; Dir., Storwal Internat. Ltd.; Div., Ont. Chamber of Comm.; Pres., Greater Toronto Region, Boy Scouts of Can.; Dir., Toronto Bd. of Trade Bd. of Gov., Rosseau Lake School; recreations: sailing, do-it-yourself projects; Clubs: Granite; Toronto; Home: Toronto, Ont. Office: 20 Eglinton Ave. W., Toronto, Ont.; M4R 1K8

HENNING, Doug; illusionist; b. Ft. Garry, Man. 1947; grad. in Physiol. Psychology, McMaster Univ.; m. Barbara De Angelis, Dec. 1977; created star in rock magic musical "Spellbound," Toronto 1973-74; co-creator, star rock magic musical "The Magi-Show," N.Y.C., 1974-75; TV specials "Doug Henning's World of Magic," 1975, 76, 77, 78; lecture tour on magic and consciousness expansion, univs. U.S. and Canada, 1977-78; appeared casino shows, Las Vegas and Lake Tahoe; recipient Las Vegas best spl. attraction of yr. award, 1978; "Appeared on Night of a Hundred Stars", 1982; author (with Charles Reynolds) "Houdini, His Legend and His Magic", 1977

HENNING, Commodore R. V., C.D., retired naval officer; b. Kerrobert, Sask., 13 March 1918; s. Maj. Roy Massey and Jean Wylie H.; e. Kerrobert (Sask.) Pub. and High Schs.; Saskatoon (Sask.) Success Business Coll. 1936; Univ. of Alberta 1941, Mining Engineering; m. Mary Julia, d. George F. Baldwin, Vancouver, B.C., 21 Aug. 1943; children: Christopher Roy, James Andrew, Mary Jane; Commissioner, N.E. Alta. Region since 1974; served in 2nd World War on HMS Shropshire and Cardiff and HMCS Ontario; shore appts. E. and W. Coasts, N.D.H.Q. Ottawa, and Candn. Jt. Staffs, Wash. and London; Base Commdr. Candn. Forces Base, Esquimalt and Commdr. Tech. Services Pacific till retired 1973; Extve. Dir. Banff Sch. Advanced Mang. 1973-74; Chrmn., Un. Appeal Campaign, Gtr. Victoria 1970; mem. Assn. Prof. Engrs. Ont. and Alta.; Anglican; recreations: tennis, golf; Clubs: Mayfair Golf and Country; Garneau Lawn Tennis Club, Edmonton; Office: 609, 8215 - 112 St., Edmonton, Alta. T6G 2L9

HENNING, William James McKay, Q.C., B.A., LL.B; b. Kerrobert, Sask., 6 Aug. 1927; e. Elem. Sch., Kerrobert, Sask. and Edmonton, Alta.; High Sch., Edmonton, Alta. (grad. with hons. 1946); Univ. of Alberta B.A. 1950, LL.B. 1951; SR. PARTNER, PARLEE, IRVING, HENNING, MUSTARD & RODNEY since 1971; Pres. and Dir., Fidelity Mgmt. Edmonton Ltd.; Femco Financial Corp. Ltd.; Dir., VGM Trustco; Star Oil and Gas Ltd.; Ed-Mon Developments Ltd.; Sr. Solr. for the Bank of Montreal in N. Alta.; apptd. Hon. Consul of Belgium July 1974; entered law practice with firm of W. E. Simpson, Q.C. 1952; formed partnership with Wm. J. Haddad, Q.C. (now Justice of Court of Appeal of Alta.) and with Jas. C. Cavanagh, Q.C. (now a Justice of Court of Queen's Bench) 1962; cr. Q.C. Jan. 1, 1968; practises mainly in corp. finance and related fields; Pub. Sch. Bd. Trustee 1957-59; Alderman City of Edmonton 1959-62; Pres., Edmonton Exhn. Assn. 1966-67 and a Dir. since 1962; recreations: tennis, badminton, racquet ball, curling (mem. Alta. Briar team 1954-56-57); Clubs: Mayfair Golf & Country; The Edmonton; Royal Glenora; Home: Apt. 1502, 11920 —100 Ave., Edmonton, Alta; T5K 0K5; Office: 1800 Standard Life Centre, 10405 Jasper Ave., Edmonton Alta. T5J 3N4

HENRIPIN, Jacques, L. ès Sc., Dr. de l'U. (Paris); éducateur; né Lachine, Qué. 31 août 1926; f. Gérard et Gertrude (Poitras) H.; é. Univ. de Montréal, L. ès Sc. (sociales économiques et politiques) 1951; Dr. de l'U. (Paris) sciences économiques 1953; ép. Marthe f. Albert Pinel 18 août 1951; enfants: Catherine, Natalie, Sophie; PROF. DE

DEMOGRAPHIE, UNIV. DE MONTREAL; enseigne et fait de la recherche à l'Univ. de Montréal depuis 1954; a fondé et dirigé le Dépt. de démographie de cette univ. 1964-73; Médaille Innis-Gérin de la Soc. royale du Can.; auteur, "La population canadienne au début du XVIIIᵉ" 1954; "Tendances et facteurs de la fécondité au Canada" 1968; "Le coût de la croissance démographique" 1968; co-auteur, "Perspectives d'accroissement de la population de la province de Québec et de ses régions et prévision des effectifs scolaires 1961-1981" 1962; "La population du Québec et de ses régions 1961-1981" 1964; "Evolution démographique du Québec et de ses régions 1966-1986" 1969; "La fin de la revanche des berceaux: qu'en pensent les Québécoises?" 1974; "La Situation demolinguistique au Canada" 1980; "Les Enfants qu'on n'a isius au Quebec" 1981; a écrit une cinquantaine d'articles scientifiques et de nombreux autres articles de vulgarisation dans divers journaux et revues; auteur de plusieurs rapports pour divers gouvernements; mem. Féd. canadienne de démographie (prés. depuis 1978); Assn. des démographes du Qué.; Population Assn. Am.; Union internat. pour l'étude scientifique de la population; Assn. internat. des démographes de langue française (vice-prés. depuis 1977); Soc. royale du Can.; Inst. canadien des affaires publiques (prés. 1966-67); récreations: sports, musique; adresse: 2935 rue Fendall, Montreal, Qué. H3T 1N2; bureau: C.P. 6128, Succursale A, Montréal, Qué. H3C 3J7.

HENRIQUEZ, Richard G., M.Arch., R.C.A.; architect; b. Jamaica, W.I. 5 Feb. 1941; s. Alfred George and Essie (Silvera) H.; e. Calabar High Sch. Kingston, Jamaica 1956; Univ. of Man. B.Arch. 1964; Mass. Inst. of Technol. M.Arch. (Urban Design) 1967; m. Carol Gail d. Isidor Aaron, Vancouver, B.C. 3 Sept. 1962; children: Alfred Gregory, Alisa Ruth Gay; PARTNER, HENRIQUEZ & PARTNERS 1979- ; Pres., Henriquez Production Ltd.; Partner, Henriquez & Todd 1969-1977; Henriquez Associates 1977-79; Lectr. in Design Univ. of B.C. Sch. of Arch. 1968-70; mem. Vancouver Urban Design Panel; Past Vice Chrmn. Vancouver Heritage Adv. Bd.; former mem. Gastown Hist. Area Adv. Comte.; rec'd various undergrad. scholarships and prizes incl. Royal Arch. Inst. Can. Gold Medal 1964; Avalon Foundation Post Grad. Fellowship 1966; R.A.I.C. Festival of Arch. 2 Honour Awards, 2 Awards of Merit 1980; author various articles relating to arch.; mem. Royal Arch. Inst. Can.; Arch. Inst. B.C.; Jewish; recreations: tennis, art-printmaking, boating; Club: Western Indoor Tennis; Home: 1443 W. 47th Ave., Vancouver, B.C. V5M 1M4; Office: 322 Water St., Vancouver, B.C. V6B 1B6.

HENRY, His. Hon. Charles J.; judge; b. Toronto, Ont., 5 July 1911; s. John J. and Eileen (McCrohan) H.; e. Tor. pub. schs, St. Michael's Coll., Univ. of Toronto, B.A. 1932; Osgoode Hall Law School; m. Geraldine, d. late D. J. and Cecil O'Brien, 21 May 1941; children: John Daniel, Mary Christine; JUDGE, CO. COURT OF THE JUDICIAL DIST. OF YORK, since 1965; read law with Hon. Frank J. Hughes, Q.C.; called to Bar of Ont. 1937; cr. Q.C. 1957; assoc. with Sims, McIntosh, Schofield & Sims of Kitchener, Ont.; rep. inter alia the Mutual Life Assnce. Co. of Can.; Legal Adviser in Armed Services Divn., Dept. of Labour (Ottawa), i/c legal matters affecting the mobilization of manpower in Can., 1942-44; apptd. Secy. to the Prime Min. of Canada, 1944; 1st el. to H. of C. in the Liberal interest for Toronto-Rosedale, g.e. 1949; re-el. in 1953 and def. in g.e. 1957; served on Parlty. Comtes. having to do with External Affairs, Banking and Comm., as well as Radio and TV; Past Chrmn. of Adm. Law Sec., Candn. Bar Assn.; Past Hon. Chrmn., Inter-Faith Comte.; Un. Community Fund Metrop. Toronto; Past Pres., Candn. Cath. Hist. Association; Roman Catholic; Clubs: Lawyers'; Empire; Canadian; Home: 113 Hudson Dr., Toronto, Ont., M4T 2K4; Office: Courthouse, University Ave., Toronto, Ont. M5G 1T3

HENRY, Hon. David (Howard Woodhouse), B.A.; judge; b. London, England, 30 October 1916; s. Howard Robert Lawrence and Mabel Marion Josephine (Woodhouse) H.; came to Canada, 1921; e. Ottawa Normal Model Sch.; Lisgar Coll. Inst., Ottawa; Queen's Univ., B.A. 1939 (Econ. and Hist.); Osgoode Hall Law Sch., Toronto, Ont.; m. Elizabeth Elaine, d. Emile A. Pequegnat, Stratford, Ont., 24 March 1945; one d. Janice Elizabeth; JUSTICE, SUPREME COURT OF ONT. since 1973; Lectr. in Adm. Law, Univ. of Ottawa 1961-73; Visiting Lectr. in Law, McGill Univ., 1962-73; Chrmn., Comte. of Experts on Restrictive Business Practices, O.E.C.D., Paris, 1966-72; read law with Mason, Foulds, Davidson and Kellock, Toronto, Ontario, called to the Bar of Ont., June 1942; cr. Q.C. (Dom.) 1955; practised law 1943 with Mason, Foulds, Davidson & Kellock, and with Fleming, Smoke & Mulholland, Toronto; apptd. Jr. Advisory Counsel, Dept. Of Justice, Oct. 1945; Solr. to the Treas., Nov. 1949; Dir., Advisory Sec., JulY 1953; Acting Dir. Criminal Law Section, 1958; Dir. of Investig. and Research, Combines Investig. Act, Ottawa 1960; served in 2nd World War; Commissioned, 1941 in 2nd Bn., Royal Regiment of Canada; Overseas, 1943-44 with 1st Bn. (England and Normandy); wounded at Falaise; transferred to Judge Advocate General Branch, Ottawa, with rank of Captain, Nov. 1944; Past Pres., Fed. Lawyers' Club; Clubs: Rideau Club, Ottawa; University Club of Toronto; Faculty Club, McGill Univ.; Anglican; recreations: wood-working, photography, clock repairing; Office: Osgoode Hall, Toronto, Ont., M5H 2N5

HENRY, Keith Austen, B.Sc., P.Eng,; consulting engineer; b. Winnipeg, Man., 18 Oct. 1923; s. Austen Percival and Greta Madeleine (Humphries) H.; e. Consort (Alta.) High Sch., 1943; Univ. of Alta., B.Sc. 1948; m. Marguerite Irene, d. James A. Hayes, 2 June 1945; children: Margaret Jeanne (Wilson), Kathleen Elizabeth (Corrigan), James Patrick, William Keith; PRESIDENT, CHIEF EXTVE. OFFR. AND DIR., CBA ENGINEERING LTD. since 1969; Dir. and Vice Pres., Crippen Consultants; Dir., Alberta Dam Engn. Co. Ltd.; Commr., Internat. Jt. Comn. 1972-78; joined Ontario Hydro 1948, Design Engr. 1948-51, Hydraulic Model Engr., Toronto, 1951-56, River Control Engr., St. Lawrence Power Project, 1956-61; joined present Co. as Cheif Mech. and Hydraulic Engr., Hugh Keenleyside Dam, 1961-63, Extve. Vice Pres., Operations and Project Mgr. there 1963-69; served with Candn. Army 1943-45; rank Lt.; Fellow, Am. Soc. Civil Engrs.; mem., Engn. Inst. Can.; B.C., Alta. & Ont. Assns. Prof. Engrs.; Assn. Consulting Engrs. Can. (Dir.); recreations: badminton, tennis, ornithology; Clubs: Vancouver; Terminal City; Hollyburn Country; Engineers; Home: 1110 Millstream Rd., W. Vancouver, B.C., V7S 2C7 Office: 1425 W. Pender, Vancouver, B.C. V6G 2S3

HENRY, Stewart Ward, B.A., M.B.A., C.A.; banker; b. Montreal, Que. 20 Feb. 1942; e. Bishop's Univ. B.A. 1963; Wharton, Univ. of Pa. M.B.A. 1970; C.A. 1968; m. Marie Elise Vaillancourt 1978; children: SR. VICE PRES. WORLD CORPORATE FINANCE BANK OF MONTREAL; Dir. Bank of Montreal (Bahamas & Caribbean) Ltd.; BM-RT Ltd.; articled with Price Waterhouse remaining until 1969 (Audit Sr.); Vice Pres. Bank of America (N.Y.) 1971-73; Asst. Treas. Crown Zellerbach Corp. San Francisco 1973-75; Treas. Northern Telecom Ltd. 1975-78; Dir. Financial Extves. Inst.; Club: Montreal Badminton & Squash; Home: 187 Montclair Ave., Toronto Ont. M5P 1R1 Office: First Canadian Pl., Toronto, Ont.

HENTHORN, George Leslie, B.Com.; telephone executive; b. Montreal, Que., 22 Jan. 1923; e. Huntingdon, Que.; McGill Univ., B.Com. 1949; VICE PRES. AND COMPTROLLER, BELL CANADA 1969- ; Vice-Pres., Bell Canada 1973- ; Dir., Tele-Direct Ltd.; Newfoundland Telephone Co.; Bell Canada International; FEI Can.; joined present Co. 1941; various mang. positions in Treasury Dept., Montreal, 1945-58; Am. Telephone &

Telegraph Co., N.Y. 1958-60; returned to Bell Canada 1960; named Gen. Supvr. — Financial Studies, 1964; Regional Accounting Mgr. 1967; served with RCN in N. Atlantic 1942-45; mem., Montreal Soc. of Financial Analysts; Montreal Chapter Financial Extves. Inst.; Frederick Johnson Council — Telephone Pioneers Am.; Home: 115 Charnwood Rd., Beaurepaire, Que., H9W 4Z5; Office: 1050 Beaver Hall Hill, Montreal, Que., H2Z 1S3

HEPHER, Michael Leslie, F.I.A., F.C.I.A.; A.S.A.; insurance executive; b. Maidstone, Eng. 17 Jan. 1944; s. Leslie and Edna M. (Day) H.; e. Kingston Grammar Sch. Eng. 1961; m. Janice Earla d Earl R. J. Morton, Halifax, N.S. 6 Nov. 1971; children: Kelly Lynn, Erin Lesley; President, Maritime Life Assurance Co. 1975-79; Dir. Industrial Estates Ltd.; Maritime Life (Caribbean) Ltd.; Actuary, Commercial Life Assurance Co. of Canada 1967-70; Actuary present co. 1970, Vice Pres. Sales 1972, Extve. Vice Pres. 1974; Pres. Halifax Bd. Trade; Anglican; recreation: reading; Clubs: Halifax, Saraguay; Home: 18 Botany Terr., Halifax, N.S. B3N 2Z7

HERBERT, John (John Herbert Brundage); author; educator; b. Toronto, Ont. 13 Oct. 1926; s. Claude Herbert and Gladys Rebecca (Kirk) Brundage; e. York Mem. Coll. Inst. Toronto 1944; Ont. Coll. Art 1948-50; Nat. Ballet Sch. 1954-57; Boris Volkoff Ballet Sch. 1953-57; New Play Soc. Theatre Sch. 1956-59; Artistic Dir.: Adventure Theatre Co. Toronto 1960-62; New Venture Players Toronto 1963-65; Garret Theatre Studio 1965-71; Medusa Theatre Co. Toronto 1972-74; Teacher of Drama and Writing, Three Schs. of Art 1975-81; Assoc. Ed. Arteditorial Co. Toronto 1975-82; Guest Lectr. Ryerson Inst., York Univ., Univ. of Waterloo and others 1969-82; rec'd Chalmers Award 1975 (Best Candn. Play Performed on Stage); named Life mem. Actors Studio New York 1967; author "Fortune and Men's Eyes" play 1967 (rec'd Special Honour Lib. of Cong. USA 1969); "Some Angry Summer Songs" 4 plays 1976; "Omphale and the Hero" play 1974; various book chapters, articles, essays and critiques since 1967; John Herbert papers purchased by Univ. of Waterloo Archives; Hon. mem. Bd. Fortune Soc. Am. (prison reform organ. founded 1967 as result of play "Fortune and Men's Eyes"); Dir. Comte. Candn. Playwrights Coop 1974-75; mem. Dramatists Guild Am.; Soc. des Auteurs et Compositeurs Dramatiques (France); NDP; Address: Suite B1, 1050 Yonge St., Toronto, Ont. M4W 2L1.

HERDER, Stephen Rendell, newspaper publisher, b. St. John's Nfld., 15 July 1928; s. Ralph Barnes and Mary (Rendell) H.; e. King's Coll. Sch., Windsor, N.S. 1938-44; Mount Allison Acad., Sackville, N.B. 1944-45; m. Lillian Joan, d. late W. J. Bursey, 9 Sept. 1949; children: Arthur Daniel, R.I.A., Stephanie Lynn, M.D.; VICE PRES., DIR., GEN. MGR. AND CHIEF EXTVE. OFFR., ST. JOHN'S PUBLISHING CO. LTD., since Aug. 1970; joined the Evening Telegram, St. John's, Nfld., as apprentice, 1945; reporter daily newspapers Sarnia and Woodstock, Ont. 1949; rejoined the Evening Telegram 1950, Mang. Ed. 1954, Dir. 1958, Vice Pres. and Gen. Mgr. 1967, till assets bought by present Co.; Dir. Western Printing and Publishing Co. Ltd. 1954-70; mem. External Adv. Comte. on Educ., Govt. Nfld. 1972; Gen. Chrmn., Candn. Sch.; Curling Championships, St. John's Nfld. 1966; mem. St. John's Comte. Candn. Curling Championships 1972; United Church; recreations: fly fishing; Home: 5 Pringle Pl., St. John's, Nfld. A1B 1A2; Office: Topsail Rd., St. John's, Nfld. A1C 5X7

HERISSON, Charles Daniel, D.Jur.Econ., L.ès L., M.A. F.R.S.C. (1962); university professor; b. Toulouse, France, 2 October 1906; s. Daniel and Marie (Molinier) H.; e. Baccalauréat, lycée de Toulouse, 1924; L.ès. L. (Toulouse) 1929; Lafayette Univ. (U.S.A.) M.A., 1935; D.jur. (Sciences Econ.) cum laude, Toulouse, 1932; Dipl. (Ecole Libres des Sciences Pol.) Paris, 1933; m. Mary Gertrude, B.A., M.B., Ch.B., D.C.H., d. John Southern-

Holt, 4 Apl. 1941; two s.: Michel R. P., Martin C. C.; PROF. OF FRENCH, CARLETON UNIV., since 1967; Lectr., Sociol., Inst. d'Etudes Supérieures, Paris, 1932-34; Fellow and Instr., French, Lafayette Univ. Coll., 1934-35; Resident, "Maison de l'Inst. de France" and research worker, London Sch. of Econ. and Pol. Science, 1936; Asst. Prof., French, Univ. of Cape Town, S.A., 1937-39, 1941-44; Prof. of French, Head, Dept. of French, Rhodes Univ., S.A., 1945-57; Prof. of French, Univ. of N.B., 1957-67; Offr., Linguistic Div., European Sec. of U.N., Geneva, 1956; S. African Corr. and contrib. to "Le Temps", Paris, 1938-41; co-ed., "France", 1942-44; S.A. Corr. for Belgian Congo newspapers, 1941-44; Publications: "Le Contrôle du Crédit par la Banque d'Angleterre", 1932; "Les Nations Anglo Saxon-nes et la Paix", 1936, "Autarcie Economie Complexe et Politique Commerciale Rationnelle", 1937; "Les Problèmes économiques et raciaux de l'Union Sud-Africaine", 1940; "La Politique Economique Internat. des Etats-Unis après la Guerre", 1939; "Je suis un Noir (transl.), 1950; "Kim", 1968; "Le Temps de Vivre" 1973; Commentator for Radio-Canada, 1959-61; served in 2nd World War on staff of French Air Force, 1939-40; cr. Chev. de la Légion d'Honneur (Fr.) 1959; recreations: tennis, skiing, swimming;16 rue du 14 Juillet, Cannes 06400, France

HERMAN, William Bernard, Q.C.; barrister; executive; b. Toronto, Ont. 31 March 1911; s. Joseph and Rose (Scop) H.; e. Grace St. Pub. Sch., Harbord & Oakwood Coll. Insts. Toronto; Univ. of Toronto Univ. Coll. B.A. 1931; Osgoode Hall Law Sch. Toronto grad. 1934; m. Alice Blanche Suroff 6 July 1933; two d.; CHRMN. CITI-COM INC. 1979- ; Secy. Wilson Century Theatres Ltd. 1952- ; Dir. First City Trust Co.; First City Financial; Utilities & Funding; Mortgage Investment Corp. of Canadn. Comm. Bank; called to Bar of Ont. 1934; cr. Q.C. 1962; Chmn., Citicom Inc.; Gov. Univ. of Toronto; Dir. and Past Chrmn. York-Finch Gen. Hosp. Toronto; winner Class A, S. Ocean Racing Conf. 1972 with yacht Bonaventure IV; repeatedly winner Freeman Cup Lake Ont. Internat. with yachts Inishfree, Bonaventure II and V; Yacht of the Yr. between 1962 and 1980; mem. Pi Lamda Phi; P. Conservative; Hebrew; recreations: yacht racing, golf, tennis, squash; Clubs: Oakdale Golf & Country (Past Pres.); Island Yacht (Past Commodore); Primrose; Palm Beach Country (Fla.); Home: 34 High Point Rd., Don Mllls, Ont. M3C 2R3; Office: 11 Adelaide St. W., Toronto, Ont. M5H 3P8.

HERMANIUK, Mt. Rev. Maxim; theologian; (Ukrainian Cath.); b. Nove Selo, W. Ukraine, 30 Oct. 1911; s. Mykyta and Anna (Monchuk) H.; e. Louvain, Belgium, Philos. 1933-35, Dr. Theol. 1943, Maitre Agregé Theol. 1947; Beauplateau, Belgium, Theol. 1935-39; came to Can. 1948; joined Redemptorist Cong. 1933; o. Priest 1938; Supvr. Vice-Prov. of Can. and U.S.A. 1948-51; Auxiliary Bishop Winnipeg 1951; Apostolic Adm. 1956; Archbishop-Metrop. 1956; mem. Vatican II Council 1962-65; mem. Secretariat for Promoting Christian Unity, Rome, 1963; mem. Jt. Working Group (World Council Chs.) 1969; mem. Council to the Secretariat of the Synod of Bishops, Rome, 1977; Prof. of Moral Theol.; Sociol. and Hebrew, Beauplateau, Belgium, 1943-45; Prof. Moral Theol. and Holy Scripture, Redemptor Semy., Waterford, Ont., 1949-51, Co-founder mem. Ukrainian Relief Comte., Belgium, 1942-48; Co-founder and first Pres., Ukrainian Cultural Soc., Belgium, 1947; Organizer Ukrainian Univ. Students Organ., Obnova, Belgium 1946-48 and Can. 1953; mem. World Congress of Free Ukrainians since 1967; Taras Shevchenko Scient. Soc.; Hon. mem. Mark Twain Soc. 1972; mem. Ukrainian Hist. Assn.; author: "La Parabole Evangélique", 1957; "Our Duty", 1960; First Ed., Logos Ukrainian Theol. Review, 1950-51; K. of C.; Address: 235 Scotia St., Winnipeg, Man. R2V 1V7

HERMANT, Sydney, B.A., LL.D.; company chairman; b. Toronto, Ont., 27 Dec. 1912; s. Percy and Dorothy

(Morris) H.; e. Upper Can. Coll. (Grad. 1930); Univ. of Toronto (Grad. in Hon. Law) 1935; m. Margaret Lewis Marshall, d. Prof. James Eustace Shaw of Toronto, Ont., 26 Oct. 1938; children: Peter Morris, John Duer, Adam Brodo Thomas, Andrew Shaw; CHMN., IMPERIAL OPTICAL CO. LTD.; Dir., Candn. Imp. Bank of Commerce; North American Life Assurance Co.; Peoples Jewellers Ltd.; Pres., Empire Club of Canada 1950-51; mem., Toronto Board Trade (President 1959-60) Chrmn. Bd. of Trustees, ROM; Conservative; Jewish; recreation: tennis; Clubs: Hamilton (Ontario) Thistle; Albany; National; Granite; Toronto Cricket, Skating & Curling; Queen's; Montreal Amateur Athletic Association; Home: 154 Glen Road, Toronto, Ont., M4W 2W6; Office: 21 Dundas Sq., Toronto, Ont. M5B 1B7

HERRICK, John Dennis, B.A.; company chairman; b. St. Paul, Minn., 8 Oct. 1932; s. late Willard R. and Gertrude (O'Connor) H.; e. Cretin High Sch., St. Paul, Minn,; Coll. of St. Thomas, B.A. 1954; CHRMN. OF BD.... GENERAL MILLS CANADA INC., 1971- ; Chrmn., Grocery Products Div., and Lancia-Bravo Foods Div.; Field Auditor, General Mills, Minneapolis, 1954-59; Accounting Supvr., Chem. Div., Kankakee, Ill., 1959-61; Adm. Mgr., S. Chicago Plant, 1961-62; Mgr. of Auditing, Minneapolis, 1962-65; Mgr., New Business Devel., 1965-66; Dir. Adm. and Controller, Smiths Food Group (subsidiary), London, Eng., 1966-68; Pres., General Mills Cereals Ltd., Toronto, 1969-71; Chrmn. of Bd., General Mills Can. 1971; served with USAF 1954-57; rank Capt.; mem. Grocery Products Mfrs. Can.; Young Pres.'s org.; Pres., Junior Achievement of Toronto 1970-1971, of Can. 1971-72, (Can.); mem. Pres. Council, Coll. of St. Thomas, 1971- ; Gov., Soc. of Goodwill Services, 1974-81; Dir., The Empire Club & The Empire Club Foundation; Pres. The Empire Ind. Dev. Bd.; Gov., Queensway Gen. Hosp.; Dir., Emmanuel Convalescent Foundation; mem. of Council, Bd. of Trade of Metrop. Toronto; Past Pres., Am. Club; 3rd Vice Pres., Nat. Macaroni Mfrs. Assn.; recreations: golf, boating, flying; Clubs: Lambton Golf & Country; American; Canadian; Empire; K. of C.; Rotary; R. Catholic; Office: 1330 Martin Grove Rd., Rexdale, Ont. M9A 4M6

HERRON, H. Raymond, B.Sc., A.M.; telecommunications executive; b. Selkirk, Man. 6 Oct. 1920; s. Harold H. and Evelyn P. (Smith) H.; e. Univ. of B.C. B.Sc. (EE); Harvard Sch. of Business Adm. A.M. (P); m. Dorothy G. d. Harry B. Pugh 11 Sept. 1950; children: Murray L., Robert D., James A., Laurie J.; PRES. AND CHIEF EXTVE. OFFR., AEL MICROTEL LTD. 1979- ; Successor Co. of GTE Automatic Electric (Canada) Ltd. and GTE Lenkurt Electric (Canada) Ltd; joined GTE Lenkurt Electric (Canada) Ltd. 1952, Mgr. Sales 1957, Vice Pres. Marketing 1959, Pres. and Gen. Mgr. 1966; Pres. and Chief Extve. Offr. GTE Automatic Electric Canada Ltd. Brockville, Ont. 1977-79; served with RCAF during World War II, Radar Offr.; mem. Prof. Engrs. Assn. B.C.; Sigma Phi Delta; recreation: boating; Clubs: West Vancouver Yacht; Brockville Yacht; Home5865 Mayview Circle, Burnaby, B.C. V5E 4B7; Office: 108, 4664 Lougheed Highway, Burnaby, B.C. V5C 5T5.

HERSENHOREN, Samuel; musical conductor and director; b. Toronto, Ont., 2 July 1908; s. Louis and Celia (Fruitman) H.; e. Pub. Schs., Toronto, Ont.; Hambourg Conservatory of Music; m. Jeanie Gibbard, 1947; one d., Suzi; travelled about Europe for 5 yrs. studying under Jan Hambourg in Eng., France, Italy and Germany; began radio career as Violinist; joined Toronto Symphony Orchestra 1927, and played in 1st Violin Sec. till 1944; Founder and Conductor of New World Orchestra, 1930; Founder and Violinist, Canadian Artists Trio; Violinist, Parlow String Quartet, 1942-51; Conductor, C.B.C. musical and dramatic programs and features; Guest-Conductor, Toronto Symphony Orchestra, Buffalo Philharmonic and Toronto Philharmonic; Conductor, commercial radio broadcasts, "Wayne & Shuster Show", "House Party",

"Music for Canadians", etc.; Musical Dir. of two Candn. Ballet Festivals; Conductor, C.B.C. Television shows; winner of LaFleche Trophy for the most important contrib. to Candn. radio in field of music, each year Trophy awarded; recreations: gardening, theatre, boating; Clubs: Arts and Letters; Variety; Home: 41 Spadina Rd., Apt. 6, Toronto, Ont. M5R 2S9

HERTZMAN, Lewis, Ph.D.; university professor; historian; author; b. Toronto, Ont., 7 July 1927; s. late Harry and Pauline (Hertanu) H.; e. Univ. of Toronto, B.A. 1949; Harvard Univ., A.M. 1950, Ph.D. 1955; Univ. de Paris, 1950-51; PROF. OF HISTORY, YORK UNIV., since 1968 and Chrmn. of Dept. 1967-70; Teaching Fellow in Gen. Educ., Harvard Univ., 1953-55; Instr. in Social Science, Drake Univ., 1955-56; Instr. in Hist., Princeton Univ., 1956-59; Asst. Prof. of Hist., Univ. of Alta., 1959-63; Assoc. Prof. 1963-65; joined present Univ. as Assoc. Prof. of Hist., 1965; Mellon post-doctoral fellow, Univ. of Pittsburgh, 1963-64; Visiting Assoc. Prof. of Hist., Univ. of Toronto, 1965-66; Univ. of Guyana, ext. examiner, 1968-73; Dir. Grad. Prog. in Hist., York Univ., 1973-74; author: "DNVP: Right-Wing Opposition in the Weimar Republic", 1963; co-author; "Alliances & Illusions: Canada and the NATO-NORAD Question", 1969; other writings incl. articles in various journs. and newspapers; mem. Extve., Comité Internat. des Sciences Hist.; membre assesseur du Bureau, since 1970; mem. Candn. Hist. Assn.; Can. Comte. of Hist. Sc. of the Candn. Hist. Assn.; Soc. d'Histoire Moderne; Comn. internat. d'histoire des mouvements sociaux et des structures sociales; Conf. Group on Central European Hist.; Conf. Group on German Politics; Study Group on Internat. Labour and Working-class History; Immigration History Soc.; del., Can. Comn. for UNESCO, 1972-75; Chrmn., York Univ. Faculty Assn., 1967-68; recreations: running, swimming, travel; Home: 102 Mildenhall Rd., Toronto, Ont. M4N 3H5

HERZ, Carl Samuel, Ph.D.; educator; b. New York City, N.Y. 10 Apl. 1930; s. Michael and Natalie (Hyman) H.; e. Cornell Univ. B.A. 1950; Princeton Univ. Ph.D. 1953; m. Judith d. Philip Scherer 28 Feb. 1960; children: Rachel, Nathaniel; PROF. OF MATH., McGILL UNIV. 1970- ; Instr., Cornell Univ. 1953, Asst. Prof. 1956, Assoc. Prof. 1958, Prof. 1963-70; mem. Inst. Advanced Study 1957-58; Visiting Prof. Brandeis Univ. 1969-70; Prof. associé, Univ. de Paris 1964-65, 1968; Alfred P. Sloan Fellow 1962-63; author various publs. harmonic analysis; mem. Candn. Math Soc. (Vice Pres.); Am. Math. Soc.; Royal Soc. Can.; Home: 228 Simcoe, Montreal, Que. H3P 1W9; Office: Burnside Hall, 805 Sherbrooke St. W., Montreal, Que. H3A 2K6.

HERZ, Charles Karel, D.P.Sc.; J.U.Dr. B. Uzhorod, Czechoslovakia, 5 July 1907; s. Alexander and Cecilia (Muller) H.; e. High Sch.-Jr. Coll., Uzhorod; Hochschule für Welthandel, Vienna (Diplomkaufmann) 1927; Univ. of Trieste, D.P.Sc. 1928; Univ. of Prague, Jur.utr.Dr. 1935; came to Can. 1938; m. Mary Jean Strath, 26 Aug. 1975; DIR. EMERITUS & CONSULTANT, BATA IND. LTD. 1974- ; Ret. Pres. (1970) Tiga Trading Co. Ltd.; Bata Shoe Co. of Can. Ltd.; joined Export Div., Bata A.S., Zlin, Czech. 1929-32; N. Am. Export Div. 1936-37; started Can. Operations as Gen. Mgr. Bata Exports & Imports Ltd. (predecessor of Bata Shoe Co. of Can. Ltd.) 1938-41; Vice Pres. & Marketing Mgr., Bata Shoe Co. Can. Ltd. 1941-47; Vice Pres. & Mang. Dir. 1942-47; Pres. 1947-70; also starting 1947, Vice Pres. & Dir., Kent Shoes Ltd.; Pres., Tiga Trading Co. Ltd.; Batawa Commun. Corp. Ltd.; Candn. Commerc. Enterprises Ltd., Reg. Co-ord., Bata Ltd. for Australia, N.Z., Pacific Reg.; Caribbean Reg.; U.S.A. & Can.; World Trade Counsellor, 1969-70; mem. Exploration Comte. for Internat. Trade, Govt. Ont., 1972; Chrmn. Joint Fed. Govt. and Ind. Task Force for estab. of Footwear & Leather Inst. of Can., 1975, Adv. 1976-81; Dir., Que. corp. representing Enterprise Dev.

Bd., Ottawa (Dept. of Ind. Trade & Commerce) 1979; Past Chrmn. Footwear Bureau Can.; Candn. Shoe Fair, 1961-62; Shoe & Leather Council, Can.; Past Pres. Shoe Mfrs. Assn. Can., 1968-69; Candn. Council of Walking, 1967-72; Can. Council of Distribution, 1966-68; Past Dir. Candn. Shoe Retailers Assn.; John Howard Soc.; Past Vice Pres. Candn. Tourist Assn.; Past mem. Prov. Bd. Boy Scouts Can.; Candn. Ind. Preparedness Assn.; Machinery & Equipment Mfrs. Assn. Can.; Candn. Exports Assn.; Belleville, Trenton C. of C.; mem. Nat. Footwear Conf. Can.; Bd of Trade of Metrop. Toronto; received "Shoe Person of the Year" Award from Nat. Footwear Council of Can., 1979; R. Catholic; recreations: outdoor sports, collector objects of art; Club: Belleville Golf & Country; Empire; Canadian; Trenton Country; Home 561 Avenue Rd., Toronto, Ont., M4V 2J8

HERZBERG, Gerhard, C.C. (1968), D.Sc., LL.D., F.R.S. (1951), F.R.S.C.; scientist; b. Hamburg, Germany 25 Dec. 1904; s. Albin and Ella (Biber) H.; e. Darmstadt Inst. of Tech., Dr. Ing. 1928; Univ of Goettingen, 1928-29, and Univ. of Bristol, 1929-30, post-grad. studies; children: Paul Albin, Agnes Margaret (by late 1st wife); m. 2ndly Monika Tenthoff 1972; DISTINGUISHED RESEARCH SCIENTIST, NATIONAL RESEARCH COUNCIL, since 1969; Chancellor, Carleton Univ. 1973-80; Lecturer and Chief Asst., Physics Dept., Darmstadt Inst. of Technol. 1930-35; Research Prof. of Physics, Univ. of Sask., 1935-45; Prof. of Spectroscopy, Yerkes Observatory, Univ. of Chicago, 1945-48; Princ. Research Officer, Nat. Research Council, Ottawa, Ont., 1948-49 and Dir., Div. of Pure Physics there 1949-69; George Fisher Baker Non-Res. Lectr. in Chem., Cornell Univ. 1968; mem., Am. Chem. Soc.; Am. Astron. Soc.; Faraday Soc.; Am. Phys. Soc.; Optical Soc. Am.; Hon. Fellow, Indian Acad. of Sciences, 1954; author of "Atomic Spectra and Atomic Structure", 1936, 2nd ed. 1944; "Molecular Spectra and Molecular Structure", Vol. 1, "Diatomic Molecules", 1939, 2nd ed. 1950, Vol. 2, "Infra-red and Raman Spectra of Polyatomic Molecules", 1945, Vol. 3, "Electronic Spectra and Electronic Structure of Polyatomic Molecules" 1966; "The Spectra and Structures of Simple Free Radicals: An Introduction to Molecular Spectroscopy" 1971; "Constants of Diatomic Molecules" (with K. P. Huber) 1979;more than 200 original papers on problems of atomic and molecular structure, chem. and astrophys. applications; awarded Henry Marshall Tory Medal by Roy. Soc. Can., 1953; LL.D. Sask. 1953; Toronto 1958; Dalhousie 1960; Alta. 1961; St. Francis Xavier 1972; Simon Fraser 1972; D.Sc. McMaster 1954; Nat. Univ. of Ireland, 1956; Oxford 1960; Brit. Columbia 1964; Queen's 1965; New Brunswick 1966; Chicago 1967; Carleton 1967; Memorial 1968; York 1969; Windsor 1970; Roy. Mil. Coll. 1971; Drexel 1972; Montreal 1972; Sherbrooke 1972; Cambridge 1972; McGill 1972; Manitoba 1973; Bristol 1975; Andhra 1975; Osmania 1976; Delhi 1976; Laval 1979; Ph.D., Weizmann Inst. of Science 1976; Dr., rer. nat., Göttingen 1968; Hamburg 1974; Fil. Hed. Dr., Stockholm 1966; Pres., Candn. Assn. Physicists, 1956-57; Vice-President, International Union of Pure and Applied Physics, 1957-63; President, Royal Society Canada, 1966; awarded Chair Francqui at University of Liege 1960; Frederic Ives Medal, Optical Soc. Am. 1964; Academician, Pontifical Acad. of Sciences 1964; Willard Gibbs Medal, Am. Chem. Soc. 1969; Gold Medal, Prof Inst. of Public Service of Can. 1969; Faraday Medal, Chem Soc. of London 1970; Linus Pauling Medal, Am. Chem. Soc. 1971; Royal Medal, Roy. Soc. London, 1971; Chem. Inst. Canada Medal 1972; Nobel Prize in Chemistry 1971 for "his contributions to the knowledge of electronic structure and geometry of molecules, particularly free radicals"; Hon. mem., Optical Society of Am.; Spectroscopy Society of Canada; Japan Acad. 1976; Chem. Soc. of Japan 1978; Honorary Fellow, Chem. Society of London; Chem. Institute of Can.; mem., Hungarian Acad. Science, 1964; Hon. Foreign mem., Am. Acad. Arts & Sciences, 1965; Foreign mem. (Physics), Roy. Swedish Acad. of Sci. 1981; Bakerian Lecture, Royal Soc.

London, 1960; named Foreign Assoc., U.S. Nat. Acad. of Sciences, 1968; Office: 100 Sussex Dr., Ottawa, Ont., K1A 0R6

HERZOG, John P., B.Sc., Ph.D.: educator; b. Canton, Ohio, 28 Aug., 1931; s. Phil Charles and Frances Lillian (Norris) H.; e. Univ. of Cal. Berkeley, B.Sc. 1958; Ph.D (Business Adm.) 1962 m. Sharon Lee Prosser, 26 June 1969; one d., Lisa M.; PROF., SCH. of BUS. ADM. AND ECON., ... SIMON FRASER UNIV. since 1969; Acting Chrmn., Dept. of Econ. & Comm. 1969-71; Asst. Prof., Univ. of Wis. Sch. of Comm., 1961; Assoc. Prof., Claremont Grad. Sch., Dept. of Business Econ., 1965; served with U.S. Air Force 1950-54; Russian Translator /Interpreter; rank Staff/Sgt.; author, "The Dynamics of Large-Scale Housebuilding", 1963; "Home Mortgage Delinquency and Foreclosure", 1970; also articles in various prof. journs.; mem. Am. Finance Assn.; Am. Econ. Assn.; Am. Real Estate and Urban Econ. Assn.; W. Finance Assn. (Pres. 1975); W. Econ. Assn.; Phi Beta Kappa; Beta Gamma Sigma; Protestant; Office: Burnaby B.C.

HESELTINE, Gilbert F. D., B.A., L.M.C.C., D. Psych. F.R.C.P.(C), F.R.C. (Psych.), F.A.P.A.; psychiatrist; educator; b. Winnipeg, Man. 15 Nov. 1928; s. Charles D. and Freda Mary H.; e. Univ. of Man. B.A. (Indust. Psychol.) 1952; West London Med. Sch. L.M.S.A. 1958; L.M.C.C. 1960; McGill Univ. Dipl. in Psychiatry 1964; m. Ethel d. William Jack McKeag 20 Sept. 1952; children: Geoffrey, Christopher, Pamela; PROF. AND CHRMN. OF PSYCHIATRY, UNIV. OF W. ONT. since 1971; Chief of Psychiatry, Univ. Hosp. Health Sciences Centre, London since 1971; Consultant Psychiatrist various London, Ont. and Regional hosps.; Chrmn. London Area Health Council Comte. on Psychiatry 1973; Dir. N. Health Services Comte., Univ. of W. Ont. and Fed. Govt.; Ont. Council of Health Task Force on jt. research review 1976; McLaughlin Travelling Fellow 1962-63 (Clin. Research Asst. Middlesex Hosp. Acad. Unit, Dept. Psychiatry London Univ.); Consultant Psychiatrist, Am. Embassy London and later Am. Consulate Montreal 1963-71; Asst. Prof. of Psychiatry, McGill Univ. 1967, Assoc. Prof. 1969-71; Assoc. Clin. Dir. Allan Mem. Inst. Montreal 1969-71; Sr. Psychiatrist Royal Victoria Hosp., Allan Mem. Inst. 1970-71; Vice Chrmn. Ont. Mental Health Foundation 1973-75, Chrmn. Adv. Bd. 1976; rec'd Med. Research Council and Nat. Inst. Mental Health Research Grants for research Univ. of Vt. 1971-75; Labatt Research Grant 1969-70; 1st recipient Prov. of Ont. Ministry of Health Travelling Fellowship 1977 — 78; Visiting Lectr. and Consultant to various hosps. and univs N. Am. and overseas; produced psychiatric films for McGill Univ. and Univ. of W. Ont.; mem. numerous bds. volunteer, govt. and community agencies; Dir., Northern Health Services, U.W.O.; Ed., author or co-author numerous med. publs.; Chrmn. Health Adv. Bd. Brewers' Assn. Can. 1977; Dir., Northern Health Sciences Programme, U.W.O.; Health Planning consultant; Fellow, Am. Psychiatric Assn.; Royal Coll. of Psychiatrists; mem. Candn. Med. Assn.; Que. Med. Assn.; Ont. Med. Assn.; Ont. Psychiatric Assn.; Que. Psychiatric Assn.; Candn. Psychiatric Assn. (Chrmn. Scient. Council 1972); Royal Med. Psychol. Assn.; Royal Soc. Med.; Am. Psychosomatic Soc.; Internat. Coll. Psychosomatic Med.; Invited Assoc. mem. Pan-African Assn. Psychiatrists World Fed. Mental Health; Protestant; International Hospital Foundation; Pres., Internat. Health Services Consortium Ltd.; Home: P.O. Box 21, 33 Northcrest Dr., London, Ont.; Office: 10th Floor, University Hospital, 339 Windermere Rd., London, Ont. N6G 2K3.

HESLER, Ronald John; association executive; b. Montreal, Que. 26 Feb. 1921; s. Dr. Norman Arthur and Nelda Elizabeth (Roos) H.; e. Valley Forge Mil. Acad., Wayne, Pa.; Mount Allison Univ.; 1) m. Donna d. Donald Graham 1966 (deceased); m. 2) Elva Hooper, 16 May 1981; PRES., THE CANDN. RADIO RELAY LEAGUE INC.;

Pres., Amherst Stove and Furnace Co. Ltd.; Atlantic Industries Ltd.; Airco Products Ltd.; Fundy Recording Co. Ltd.; Vice Pres., Collyer Advertising Ltd.; Enamel & Heating Products Ltd.; Humberstone Mgmt. Ltd.; Dir., Am. Radio Relay League Inc.; Ald., Town of Sackville; N.B. mem. Lib. Fed.; mem. Boys Work Comte.; Nat. Design Council; Y.M.C.A.; served with Royal Candn. Elect. & Mech. Engrs. 1941-45, rank Capt. and Tech. Staff Offr.; mem. Audio Engn. Soc.; Radio Soc. Gt. Brit.; Quarter Century Wireless Assn.; Freemason; Shriner; Liberal; Anglican; recreations: photography, amateur radio, audio recording, yachting, private flying; Club: Royal St. Lawrence Yacht (Montreal); Home: 5 Pickard Pl., Sackville, N.B. E0A 3C0; Office: P.O. Box 418, Sackville, N.B. E0A 3C0.

HESSION, Raymond Vincent, B.A.; executive; b. Regina, Sask., 27 June 1940; s. Edmund Gilbert and Marion Elizabeth (Lawlor) H.; e. elem. and secondary schs. Ont. and N.B.; Coll. Militaire Royal de Saint-Jean; Royal Mil. Coll. B.A. 1962; m. Louise d. Jean Gérard Richard, 20 Apl. 1963; children: Natalie, Brian, Raymond, Adèle; PRESIDENT, CANADA MORTGAGE AND HOUSING CORP. since 1976; served with Candn. Army 1962-65, rank Capt.; held mang. positions IBM Canada Ltd. and Multiple Access Ltd. 1965-74 incl. Gen. Sales Mgr. Toronto latter Co. and Marketing Mgr. (IBM); joined present Corp. as Extve. Dir. Data and Systems 1974, Vice Pres. Adm. and Finance, Extve. Vice Pres. 1975; R. Catholic; recreation: golf; Clubs: Royal Mil. Coll.; Golf Outaouais; Ottawa Athletic Club; Cercle Universitaire; Home: 308 Cathcart St., Ottawa, Ont. K1N 5C4; Office: Montreal Rd., Ottawa, Ont. K1A 0P7

HETENYI, Geza Joseph, M.D., Ph.D.; educator; b. Budapest, Hungary 26 Sept. 1923; s. Geza Joseph and Margaret (Wabrosch) H.; e. Univ. of Budapest M.D. 1947; Univ. of Toronto Ph.D. 1960; m. Caroline E., M.D., F.R.C.P.(C) d. late Geza Scossa; 15 July 1947; VICE DEAN, FACULTY OF HEALTH SCIENCES UNIV. OF OTTAWA since 1979; joined Dept. of Physiol. Univ. of Toronto 1957, Asst. Prof. 1960, Assoc. Prof. 1964, Prof. 1967; Prof. and Head of Physiol., Univ. of Ottawa 1970-79; cross appts. Inst. Clin. Science and Inst. Biomed. Engn.; co-author 'The Story of Insulin' 1962, German trans. 1963, Dutch 1964, Japanese 1965; 110 papers in Am. Candn. Brit. German and other scient. journs.; mem. Candn. Physiol. Soc. (Vice Pres. 1975-76, Pres. 1976-77); Candn. Soc. Clin. Investigation (Sr. mem.); Candn. Diabetic Assn. (Chrmn. Grants Comte. 1975-79); Candn. Soc. Endocrinol. & Metabolism; Am. Physiol. Soc.; Am. Diabetes Assn.; Club: Cercle Universitaire; Home: 417 Crestview Rd., Ottawa, Ont. K1H 5G7; Office: 275 Nicholas St., Ottawa, Ont. K1N 9A9.

HETHERINGTON, Charles R., B.S., M.S., Sc.D.; company president; b. Norman, Oklahoma, 19 Dec. 1919; s. William Leslie and Helen Rowena (Hudgens) H.; e. Univ. of Oklahoma, B.S. 1940, M.S. 1941; Mass. Inst. of Tech., Sc.D. 1943; m. 1stly Jane Helen, d. Stanton F. Childs, 28 Aug. 1943; children: William Leslie II, Childs Pratt, Helen Jane, Gail Ann; 2ndly, Rose Cosco Scurlock, 17 July 1967; stepchildren: Robert H., Donald S.; PRESIDENT AND CHIEF EXTVE. OFFR., PANARCTIC OILS LTD. since 1970; Pres., Chas. R. Hetherington & Co. Ltd.; Cancrude Oil & Gas Co. Ltd.; Dir., Panarctic Oils Ltd.; Greyhound Lines of Canada Ltd.; Hetherington Panches Ltd.; obtained field and other experience during summers while at college; Research Engr. with Research and Devel. Dept. of Standard Oil Co. of Cal. and subsequently California Research Corpn., Richmond, Cal., Sept. 1942- Aug. 1943; Engr. with Ford, Bacon & Davis, Inc., New York City engaged in prof. consulting engn. with particular emphasis on petroleum and natural gas technol., becoming Sr. Engr. of the Co., 1946-52; apptd. Vice-Pres. of Westcoast Transmission Co. Ltd. in charge of all engn. functions 1952; Vice-Pres. for Production and

Mfg., Pacific Petroleums Ltd., while maintaining the position with Westcoast Transmission Co. 1956; subsequently Mang., Dir., Pacific Petroleums Ltd.; during 2nd World War, retained as a civilian in the Office of Nat. Defense Research Comte. of the Office of Scient. Research & Devel., U.S.A.; mem., Am. Chem. Soc.; Am. Gas Assn.; Candn. Gas Assn.; Anglican; recreations: polo, fishing, hunting, amateur radio; Clubs: Calgary Petroleum; Calgary Golf & Country; Mount Pleasant Racquet; Calgary Polo; El Dorado Country; El Dorado Polo; Home: 1001 - 300 Meredith Rd. N.E., Calgary, Alta. T2E 7A8; Office: 703 - 6th Ave. S.W., Calgary, Alta., T2P 0T9

HEULE, Robert Kneeland, P.Eng.; pipeline executive; b. Duluth, Minn. 9 Aug. 1925; e. Univ. of Minn. B.S.M.E. 1945; m. Dorothy Jane Johnson 2 July 1949; children: Mark K., Michael D., Laurie J.; PRES. C.E.O. AND DIRECTOR, INTERPROVINCIAL PIPE LINE LTD. since 1978; Pres. and Dir. Lakehead Pipe Line Co. Inc.; joined Lakehead Pipe Line, Superior, Wisc. 1950; held various positions becoming Gen. Mgr. Interprovincial and Lakehead 1966, Vice Pres. and Gen. Mgr. 1970, Dir. 1975, Pres. 1977; served with U.S. Naval Reserve, active duty 1943-46, 1951-53, rank Lt.; mem. Am. Petrol. Inst.; Candn. Petrol. Assn.; Assn. Prof. Engrs. Prov. Ont.; Bd. Trade Metrop. Toronto; Freemason; Shriner; United Church; recreation: skiing; Clubs: National; Edmonton; Canadian; Home: 1142 Morrison Heights Dr., Oakville, Ont. L6J 4J1; Office: (P.O. Box 48) 1 First Canadian Place, Toronto, Ont. M5X 1A9.

HEWARD, Arthur Brian Augustus, M.A.; stock broker; b. Brockville, Ont., 15 July 1900; s. Arthur Richard Graves and Sarah Efa (Jones) H.; e. Lower Can. Coll.; St. John's Coll., Cambridge, Eng., B.A. 1921, M.A.; m. Anna Barbara Lauderdale, d. Hon. Mr. Justice W. A. Logie; children: Barbara, Chilion, Efa (Mrs. Donald Greenwood), Faith (Mrs. William Berghuis); CHRMN. OF BD. AND CHIEF EXTVE. OFFR., JONES HEWARD & CO. LTD., estbd. 1925; Chrmn. Bd. & Dir., Consumers Glass Co. Ltd.; served in World War with R.N.V.R.; Anglican; recreations: golf, tennis, rowing, swimming; Clubs: Mount Royal; University; Mount Bruno Country; Brockville Country (Brockville, Ont.); Leander (London, Eng.); Royal & Ancient Golf (St. Andrews, Scotland); Home: 11 Anwoth Rd., Westmount, Que., H3Y 2E6; Office: 249 St. James St. W., Montreal, Que. H2Y 1M8

HEWETT, F. Robert; executive; b. Toronto, Ont. 11 Oct. 1945; s. Frank Victor Charles and Irene T. (Petersen) H.; e. Blythwood Pub. Sch., Upper Can. Coll., Oakwood Coll. Inst. Toronto; Lakefield (Ont.) Coll. Sch.; m. Lynn Ellen, d. Frank A. Hardy, Tucson, Ariz. 29 June 1968; children: Frank Gregory, Jeffrey Robert, Dana Ellen; PRES. & CHIEF EXTVE. OFFR., COMMERCIAL FINANCE CORP. LTD.; Dir. Investors Finance Corp.; Northridge Investments Ltd.; PCL Industries Ltd.; Sterling Trust Corp.; Trust General du Can.; P. Conservative ; Anglican; recreations: golf, hunting, fishing; Clubs: Osler Bluff Ski; National; York Downs; Nicholson's Island; Franklin Fishing; Home: R.R.2, Aurora, Ont., L4G 3G8; Office: 55 University Ave., Ste. 707, Toronto, Ont., M5J 2H7

HEWITT, Foster William, O.C. (1972); b. Toronto, Ont., 21 Nov. 1903; s. William Arthur and the late Flora Morrison (Foster) H.; e. Upper Can. Coll.; Univ. of Toronto; m.; children: Bill, Wendy, Ann (deceased); Pres., Hewittdale Productions Ltd.; Vice Pres., CFTO-TV, Toronto; Baton Broadcasting Ltd.; I.P.D. Holdings Ltd.; Glenwarren Prods.; Dir.,; Radio CFGO (Ottawa); CKLW Radio Broadcasting Ltd.; CKLW Radio Sales Inc.; Glen-Warren Productions Ltd.; Agincourt Productions Ltd.; ABF Automated Business Forms Ltd.; ABF Automated Business Forms (Western) Ltd.; ABF Formules D'Affaires Ltée.; C.F. Haughton Ltd.; Telfer Packaging Ltd.; broadcast 1st hockey broadcast in Can. 1923; other events: arrival at

Montreal of Brit. Airship R34 and R-100; Empress of Britain at Que. on maiden voyage; visit of H.R.H. the Prince of Wales to Toronto; first 8-game series Can.-U.S.S.R. from Can. and Moscow, 1972; author of "Down the Ice", 1934; "He Shoots. . . He Scores", 1949; "Hello Canada", 1950; "Along Olympia Road", 1951; "Hockey Night in Canada", 1953; has contrib. articles on sports to various mags., e.g. "Readers Digest"; "Maclean's"; "Liberty"; "T.V. Guide"; "Sport"; and to "Toronto Star Weekly"; winner of Candn. Inter-Coll. Boxing Champ., 1921-22; boxed 8 yrs. at Upper Can. Coll. & Univ. of Toronto and remained undefeated; Beta Theta Pi; Eta Delta Sigma; mem., Hockey Hall of Fame, 1965; Sports Hall of Fame, 1972; Corp. of Toronto Award of Merit; Ont. Achievement Award; Official Opening of C.N.E., 1980; Broadcaster of the Year, Candn. Radio & TV Exec. Club; New York Hockey Writers' Award for excellence in sports broadcasting; Charlie Conacher Res. Fund Citation for outstanding record of over 50 yrs. in broadcasting; CTV-CBC special award for Can.-Rus. 1st TV network Hockey World Series, 1972; Sportsman of the Year (B'Nai Brith); Anglican; Clubs: Toronto Hunt; Granite; Rosedale Golf; Cedarhurst Golf; Home: 205 Lytton Blvd., Toronto, Ont., M4R 1L6; Office: 2 Carlton St., Ste. 908, Toronto, Ont. M5B 1J3

HEWITT, Hon. James J., M.L.A., R.I.A.; politician; b. Toronto, Ont. 28 Jan. 1933; s. James Henry and Mary (Harrison) H.; e. Toronto and Vancouver; m. Dorothy children: James Russell, Catherine Lee, Robert Allen, Ronald William; MIN. OF AGRICULTURE & FOOD, B.C. 1980- ; Credit Union Gen. Mgr.; Ald. City of Penticton 1971-76; Dir. Regional Dist. Okanagan-Similkameen 1972-74 and Union of B.C. Muns. 1974-76; el. M.L.A. for Boundary-Similkameen prov. g.e. 1975, re-el. 1979; Min. of Agric. 1976-78; Min. of Energy, Mines & Petroleum Resources 1978-79; Min. of Agriculture 1979; Social Credit; United Church; Office: Parliament Bldgs., Victoria, B.C. V8W 2Z7.

HEWSON, Edgar Wendell, M.A., D.I.C., Ph.D., F.R.S.C., F.A.M.S., F.R.Met.S; meteorologist; b. Amherst, N.S., 12 July 1910; s. Edgar Ellis and Helen Clarissa (Bell) H.; e. Cumberland Co. Acad., Amherst, N.S.; Mt. Allison Univ., B.A. 1932; Dalhousie Univ., M.A. 1933; Univ. of Toronto, M.A. 1935; Imperial Coll. of Science and Technol., D.I.C. 1937; (Beit Scient. Research Fellow) Univ. of London, Ph.D.1937; m. Julia Elizabeth, d. Dr. G. W. O'Brien, Amherst, N.S., 17 Aug. 1935; children: David Garnet, Barbara Elizabeth; PROF. EMERITUS, DEPT. ATMOSPHERIC SCIENCES, OREGON STATE UNIV.; Research Meteorol., Meteorol. Service of Can., 1938-39 and 1941-47; Dir. of Diffusion Project, Mass. Inst. of Tech. 1948-53; Consult Meteorol., Consol. Mining & Smelting Co. of Can. Ltd., 1939-46; U.S. Bur. of Mines, 1939-40 and 1945-46; Asst. Controller for Training and Research Services, Meteorol. Service Of Can., 1947-48; formerly Prof. of Meteorol., Univ. of Mich.; established Dept. of Atmospheric Sci.; Oregon State Univ. 1969; Chmn. 1969-76; Prof. 1969-81; holder of Roy. Soc. of Can. Fellowship, Imperial Coll., London, Eng., 1938; awarded Buchan Prize of the Roy. Meteorol. Soc. 1939; author (with R. W. Longley), "Meteorology, Theoretical and Applied", 1944; contrib. articles to Encycl. Brit., 1946-47; publ. over 70 articles on a wide range of meteorology subjects; held numerous consult. pos'ns; Prof. mem., Comte. on Climatology, Nat. Acad. of Sci., 1957-61; Am. Meteorol. Soc. (Assoc. Ed., "Journ. of Meteorol", 1944-54, Councillor, 1945-47 and 1952-54, Publ. Comte. 1946-57; Chrmn., Bd. of Reviewing Eds., "Meteorol. Monographs", 1948-58; Chrmn., Air Pollution Abatement Comte., 1951-56, rec'd Award for Outstand. Contrib. to the Advancement of Applied Meteorology 1969; Chrm. Nom. Comte., 1971; mem., Nom. Comte. of Fellows and Hon. Mem., 1972-73); mem., Soc. of Friends; Am. Geophysical Union; Physical Soc.; Am. Int. Soc. of Biometeorol; Int. Solar Energy Soc.; recreations: canoeing, hiking; Address: Corvallis, Oregon, 97331.

HEYWOOD, J(ohn) C(arl), R.C.A., O.S.A.; artist; educator; b. Toronto, Ont. 6 June 1941; s. John William and Margaret Wight (Downs) H.; e. Ont. Coll. of Art Toronto A.O.C.A. 1963; Atelier 17 Paris, France 1967-69; m. Renate Antonie d. Anton Laxgang, West Germany 18 Aug. 1969; PROF. OF ART, QUEEN'S UNIV. 1974- ; High Sch. Teacher Ont. 1966-67; Master Printmaking Sheridan Coll. 1969-71; mem. Art Adv. Bd. St. Lawrence Coll. Kingston; Visiting Lectr., N.S. Coll. of Art, Univ. of Ottawa, London Art Gallery, Univ. of Guelph, Univ. of Victoria, Ont. Coll. of Art, Museum of Holography, N.Y.C.; New Jersey State Coll.; Univ. of Alta.; Univ. of Sask.; Univ. of West. Ont.; Mem. Univ. Nfld. and other univs. and colls. Can and USA; solo exhibitions incl. Mira Godard Gallery 1975, 76, 78, 81; Art Gallery of Ontario touring exhibitions 1974-76, 77-78; Canadian Cultural Centre, Paris 1973; Musee de Chartres 1972; Universities of Manitoba 1970, Toronto 1974, Guelph 1974, 1978, Western Ontario 1979, Alberta 1980, Dalhousie 1970, Memorial 1977; Agnes Etherington Art Centre Kingston 1975; 26 other One-Man exhibitions at public and private galleries in Canada between 1969 and 1981. Participated in every major international print biennale since 1970, notably Crakow, Ljubljana, Britain, Norway, Switzerland, Germany, etc. (winning 16 Print Awards); prints incl. 37 maj. pub. colls. Can., USA, W. and E. Europe, Gt. Brit.; maj. print publs.: "The Venus Suite" 1968-71; "The Disparates" 1970-71; "Understatements" 1971-72; "Opus IV" 1971-73; "Pages From My Notebook" 1973-74; "Small Needles" 1974; "Retinal Pieces" 1975-78; "Barbershops" 1977; "Defunct Modes" 1977-79 Can. Council Grant for vectograph 1976; for Colour Prints 1978; Ont. Arts Council Grants to train Apprentice Printmakers 1977, 78, 81; mem. Ont. Soc. Artists; Royal Candn. Acad.; Print & Drawing Council Can.; recreations: canoeing, hiking Canada, Switzerland, Nepal; Office: Queen's Univ., Dept of Art, Kingston, Ont. K7L 3N6.

HIBBARD, George Richard, M.A.; educator; b. Notts., Eng. 31 May 1915; s. George Henry and Sydney Ann (Eaton) H.; e. Southwell Minster Grammar Sch. Notts. 1933; Univ. Coll. Nottingham 1933-38; Univ. of London B.A. 1936, M.A. 1938; Zurich Univ. 1938-39; m. Louise Allen Higgitt 4 Nov. 1939; one d. Sophia Josephine; PROF. OF ENG., UNIV. OF WATERLOO 1970- ; Asst. Lectr. in Eng. Univ. Coll. Southampton 1939-40; Lectr., Sr. Lectr. and Reader in Eng. Univ. of Nottingham 1946-70; author "Thomas Nashe" 1962; "The Making of Shakespeare's Dramatic Poetry" 1981; Ed. Shakespeare's "Coriolanus" 1967; "The Taming of the Shrew" 1968; "Timon of Athens" 1970; "The Merry Wives of Windsor" 1973; Jonson's "Bartholmew Fair" 1977; Ed. "The Elizabethan Theatre" IV, V, VII; contrib. to "The New Cambridge Bibliography of English Literature" Vol. I; various articles; served with Brit. Army 1940-46; mem. Internat. Shakespeare Assn.; Shakespeare Soc. Am.; Renaissance Soc. Am.; Modern Humanities Research Assn.; Assn. Candn. Univ. Teachers Eng.; recreations: walking, gardening; Home: 90 Empire St., Waterloo, Ont. N2L 2M2; Office: Waterloo, Ont. N2L 3G1.

HIBBARD, Rear Admiral James Calcutt, D.S.C.; Royal Canadian Navy (retired); b. Hemison, Ste-Malachie, Que., 26 Mar. 1908; s. late Rev. Gerald Fitzmaurice and Elfreda H.; e. Hemison (Que.) Pte. Sch.; (summer training) with R.C.N.V.R., 1924-26; Cadet, R.C.N., 1926; Royal Naval Training 1926-31; m. Inez Jessie, d. late David R. Ker, Victoria, British Columbia, 25 March 1933; children: Richard James, William Robert; mem., Advisory Bd., Victoria, Royal Trust Co.; entered R.C.N. in 1926 and in same year went overseas for training in H.M.S. "Erebus" and R.N. Coll., Greenwich; promoted Midshipman while serving in Battleship "Emperor of India"; returned to Can. in 1931 and saw service in the destroyers

"Vancouver" and "Champlain"; returned overseas in 1936 and later became Extve. Offr. of the Brit. destroyer "Ambuscade"; later held similar post in H.M.S. "Bulldog" and served on Non-Intervention Patrol off coast of Spain during Spanish Civil War; apptd. to Halifax, 1938 joining training schooner "Venture"; in 2nd World War was serving on destroyer "Restigouche", but joined "Assiniboine" in Eng., Oct. 1939; Commanded destroyer "Skeena", 1940-42 in battle of Atlantic; D.S.C and Bar; apptd. to Staff of Capt. (D) as Training Commdr. for ships engaged in battle of Atlantic; apptd. to Command of H.M.C.S. "Iroquois", July 1943; awarded Bar to D.S.C. 1944; Legion d'Honneur (France); Croix de Guerre (avec Palmes); King Haaken Cross of Liberation (Norway); Depy. Chief of Navy Personnel, Ottawa, 1945-47; C.O., H.M.C.S "Ontario" 1947-49; Nat. War Coll., Wash., D.C., 1949-50; Chief of Naval Personnel and mem. of the Naval Bd., Ottawa, 1950-53; Flag Offr., Pacific Coast, 1953-56; Hon. Citizen, City of Victoria; Life mem. Hon. and Treas., Cancer Foundation of B.C.; Hon. Gov., Corps of Commrs. of Van. Is.; Hon. Trust., Maritime Museum of B.C.; mem. Anglican; Home: #206—1211 Beach Drive, Victoria, B.C. V8S 2N4

HICKEY, Hon. Thomas V., M.H.A.; politician; b. Outer Cove, Nfld. 15 Feb. 1933; s. Thomas and Mary H.; e. St. Francis Sch. Outer Cove; Mem. Univ. of Nfld.; m. Dorothy Grace Wall; one d.; MIN. OF SOCIAL SERVICES, NFLD.1979- ; el. M.H.A. for St. John's East Extern prov. g.e. 1966, re-el. since; Min. of Social Services & Rehabilitation 1972; Min. of Prov. Affairs & Environment 1972; Min. of Transport. & Communications 1973; Min. of Tourism 1975; former mem. Placentia Town Council; Hon. Pres. Placentia Regatta Comte. (Pres. and Founder 1964); mem. Lions; Star of the Sea Assn.; P. Conservative; R. Catholic; Office: (P.O. Box 4750) Confederation Bldg., St. John's, Nfld. A1C 5T7.

HICKEY, Winston Edward, B.Sc., B.Eng., LL.D.; professional engineer; company executive; b. Alma, N.B., 6 June 1912; s. Frederick John and Annie Ermina (Connely) H.; e. Public Schs.; Great Salmon River and Alma, N.B. (1918-28); Mount Allison Acad. (Matric. 1929); Mount Allison Univ., B.Sc. 1933, LL.D. 1966; N.S. Tech. Coll., B.Eng. (Civil) 1938; m. Louise Gladys, d. William Thomas Murray, Coverdale, N.B., 4 Jan. 1941; children: David William, Linda Louise; PRES. AND DIR., McNAMARA ENGINEERING LTD., since Oct. 1968; Pres., Tantramar Contractors Ltd.; engaged in various capacities with Strayhorne & Hickey Lumber Co., 1933-36; New Brunswick Department of Highways, 1936-39; Field Engineer, Hydro-Electric Power Commission of Ont., 1939-40, Design Engr. in Hydraulic Dept., 1940-42 and 1945-46; joined the Foundation Group in 1946 as Supervisor Structural Design; District Engr., Design Office, 1949-51; Div. Engr. in charge of Design Office and Field Engn., 1951-54; apptd. Vice-Pres. in charge of Toronto Office, Foundation of Canada Engineering Corp. Ltd., 1954-58, then in successively Vice-Pres. and Chief Engr., Exec. Vice-Pres. and Dir. of Engn. and Chrmn., Foundation Co. of Can. Ltd.; mem., Assn. Prof. Engrs. Ont.; Fellow, Engn. Inst. Can.; served in 2nd World War with Royal Candn. Engrs., 1942-45; Overseas July 1943-Nov. 1945; N.W. Europe July 1944-Oct. 1945 with rank of Lieutenant; Dir. and Vice Pres., Canadian Institute of Arbitrators, Past Pres.; United Church; Clubs: National; Home: 15 Ridgegate Crescent, Toronto, Ont., M8Y 2C9; Office: 759 Warden Ave., Scarborough, Ont. M1L 4B5

HICKINGBOTTOM, Donald George; company president; b. Toronto, Ont., 1 July 1932; s. George Lane and Williamette (Le Drew) H.; e. Sch. of Comm., Toronto, Ont. 1952; m. Audrey Joyce, d. Clifford Webb, Toronto, Ont. 22 Oct. 1955; children: Stephen Donald, Karen Anne, Wendy Lynn; PRESIDENT, C.E.O. AND DIR., EASTERN BAKERIES LTD. since 1971; Dir., Barbour Fs Ltd.; Chan Foods Ltd.; Barnes-Hopkins Ltd.; Manage-

ment positions Corporate Foods Ltd., 1951-71; Conservative; United Church; recreations: golf, reading, travelling; Club: Union; Home: 90 Horton Rd., Country Club Heights, East Riverside, Saint John, N.B.; Office: (P.O.Box 308), Saint John, N.B. E2L 3Z2

HICKLING, David, M.A., P.Eng.; b. London, Eng. 8 Feb. 1933; s. Richard Anderson and Betha Joy (Winterbotham) H.; e. Felsted Sch. Essex, Eng. 1951; Cambridge Univ. B.A. 1956, M.A. 1960; m. Elizabeth A. S. Rogers 25 July 1959; children: Richard Anderson, Heather Mary; PRESIDENT, ECODYNE LTD. since 1977; Service Engr. Permutit Co. Ltd. London, Eng. 1956-59; Sales Engr. present co. 1959, Div. Mgr. 1966, Vice Pres. 1972; served with RA, rank Lt.; mem. Assn. Prof. Engrs. Prov. Ont.; Am. Water-Works Assn.; Candn. Pulp & Paper Assn.; P. Conservative; United Church; recreations: sailing, squash, tennis; Clubs: Oakville; Port Credit Yacht; Caledon Ski; "The Club" Oakville; Home: 55 Howard Ave., Oakville, Ont. L6J 3Y4; Office: 2201 Speers Rd., Oakville, Ont. L6L 2X9.

HICKMAN, George Albert, M.A., Ed. D.; emeritus dean; b. Fortune, Nfld., 9 January 1909; s. John Robert and Mary Frances (Parsons) H.; e. Mount Allison Univ., B.A. 1937; Acadia Univ., M.A. 1941; Columbia Univ., Ed.D. 1954; m. Mary Martin, 5 June 1946; two s. Albert John, William George; Teacher in one-room schools in Newfoundland for 3 years; Princ., four-room schools for 4 years; Master, Grand Falls Acad., Nfld., for 4 yrs. and Head Master for 4 yrs.; Head, Dept. of Educ., Memorial Univ. of Nfld., 1944-48, Dean 1949-74; LL.D. Mt. Allison, 1972; Memorial, 1974; Queen Elizabeth Coronation Medal; Centennial Medal; Silver Jubilee Medal 1977; mem. Nat. Soc. for the Study of Educ.; Atlantic Prov. Conf. on Teacher Educ. (Pres. 1955); writer of many articles on educ.; United Church; Home: 7 Bideford Place, St. John's, Nfld. A1B 2W5

HICKMAN, Hon. Chief Justice Thomas Alexander, Q.C., LL.B.; judge; b. Grand Bank, Nfld. 19 Oct. 1925; e. Un. Ch. Acad. Grand Bank 1942; Memorial Univ. of Nfld. 1944; Dalhousie Univ. LL.B. 1947; m. Nancy J. d. Mayor H. G. R. Mews 4 July 1953; children: Alexander, Peter, Harry, and Heather; CHIEF JUSTICE, SUPREME COURT OF NEWFOUNDLAND, TRIAL DIV. called to Bar of Nfld. 1948; cr. Q.C. practised law St. John's 1948-66; Min. of Health 1968-69; Min. of Justice and Atty. Gen., 1966-69, 1972-79; Min. of Finance 1978-79; also Govt. House Leader; Chrmn. Un. Ch. Sch. Bd. for St. John's 1959-66; served as Vice Pres. Candn. Bar Assn.; Bencher and Hon. Secy. Law Assn. Nfld.; mem. Bars of N.S. and Nfld.; United Church; Clubs: Bally Hally Golf and Country; Murray's Pond Fishing; Kiwanis (Past Pres.); Home: 62 Carpasian Rd., St. John's, Nfld. A1B 2R4; Office: Judges' Chambers, Supreme Court of Newfoundland, Trial Division Court House, Duckworth St., St. John's, Nfld. A1C 5M3.

HICKS, Douglas Barcham, B.A.; diplomat; b. Kingston, Ont. 27 Dec. 1917; s. Rivers Keith and Marjorie (Edgar) H.; e. Univ. of Toronto Schs.; Univ. Coll. Univ. of Toronto B.A. 1939; m. Elizabeth Maud d. late John Douglas Stone 12 Sept. 1944; children: Deborah, Gillian, Graham, Elisabeth; joined Dept. External Affairs 1944 serving in London, Dublin, Oslo, New Delhi and Ottawa, High Commr. to Ghana 1968-70, Dir. Information Div. External Affairs Ottawa 1971-74, Dir. S. Asia Div. 1974-75, Ambassador to Ethiopia 1975-78; served with RCNVR 1940-44, N. Atlantic and UK, rank Lt.; rec'd Centennial Medal 1967; Anglican; recreations: golf, swimming, Dir., Ottawa Branch, Can. Red Cross Soc.; Club: Ottawa Y.M.C.A. Health; Home: 467 Wilbrod St. Apt. 2, Ottawa, Ont. K1N 6N1;

HICKS, Edward James; utilities executive; b. Halifax Co., N.S. 3 Nov. 1939; s. late Charles Edward H.; e. St. Patricks High Sch. Halifax 1957; Cooc. Mang. Accts. Can. 1965; m. Dorothy Elizabeth d. Duncan Isner, Halifax Co., N.S. 23 July 1962; children: Colin E., Jacqueline A., Catherine L.; VICE PRES. FINANCE, MARITIME TELEGRAPH & TELEPHONE CO. LTD. 1975- ; Vice Pres. Finance and Dir. The Island Telephone Co. Ltd.; Pres. and Dir. Maritime Computers Ltd.; joined present Co. 1969, Secy.-Treas. 1974; Prov. Treas. Boy Scouts of Can.; Fellow, Soc. Mang. Accts. Can. (Prov. Pres. 1972-73); mem. Inst. Internal Auditors (Hon. Gov. Halifax Chapter); Halifax Bd. Trade; Telephone Pioneers Am.; R. Catholic; Club: Halifax; Home: 3143 Mayfield Ave., Halifax, N.S. B3L 4B3; Office: Maritime Centre, 1505 Barrington St., Halifax, N.S. B3J 3K5.

HICKS, Hon. Henry Davies, C.C.(1970), Q.C., B.Sc., B.C.L., M.A., D.C.L., D.Ed., LL.D.; senator; university president; ex-premier; b. Bridgetown, Annapolis Co., N.S., 5 Mar. 1915; s. Henry Brandon and Annie May (Kinney) H.; e. Bridgetown (N.S.) High Sch.; Mount Allison Univ., B.A. 1936; Dalhousie Univ., B.Sc. 1937; Exeter Coll., Oxford, B.A. (Juris.) 1939; B.C.L. 1940, M.A. 1944; St. Anne's Coll., D.Ed. 1952; King's Coll., D.C.L. 1954; Mount Allison, LL.D. 1956; Univ. of New Brunswick, D.C.L. 1963; Acadia Univ., D. Litt. 1979; Dalhousie Univ., L.L.D., 1980; Mount St. Vincent Univ., D. Hum. L. 1981; m. Paulene Agnes (d. Feb. 1964), d. George E. Banks, Caledonia, Queens Co., N.S., 28 Dec. 1945; children: Catherine Kinney, Henry Randolph Harlow, John George Herbert, Paulene Jane Francess; m. 2ndly. Margaret Gene MacGregor, d. late Norman Morison, 15 April 1965; PRESIDENT, DALHOUSIE UNIV., 1963-80; Member of The Canada Council (apptd. 1963); read law with Stewart, Smith, MacKeen & Rogers, Halifax, N.S.; called to the Bar of N.S. 1941; practised law on discharge from the Army (1946) in Bridgetown, N.S.; formed partnership with J. D. Orlando 1948; served in 2nd World War as Capt. Royal Candn. Arty.; saw service in Can., U.K., Belgium, Holland and Germany; 1st el. to N.S. Leg. for Annapolis Co., g.e. 1945; re-el. g.e. 1949, 1953, and 1956; apptd. Min. of Educ., Sept. 1949, Prov. Secy., Jan. 1954, Premier, Sept. 1954 to Oct. 1956 when Govt. defeated; Leader of Opposition in N.S. Leg. 1956-60, and Leader of Liberal Party in N.S.; def. in Prov. g.e. June 1960; resigned as Leader of Lib. Party in N.S. and apptd. Dean of Arts & Science, Dalhousie Univ., Nov. 1960, Vice-Pres., 1961-63; called to Senate of Can., April 1972; Freemason (Scot. Rite); Liberal; United Church; recreations: fishing, philately; Home: 6446 Coburg Rd., Halifax, N.S. B3H 2A7

HICKS, Robert Allen; manufacturer; b. Toronto, Ont., 4 May 1919; s. late William Rowland and late Gertrude (Pringle) H.; e. Parkdale Coll. Inst., grad. 1938; m. Doris, d. late Rhys Lint, March 1948; two s., James Robert, William Rhys.; PRESIDENT, BENJAMIN MOORE & CO. LTD., since 1965; Pres., Technical Coatings Co. Ltd.; joined present Co., 1939, served in various managerial positions; served with R.C.A.S.C., 1941-45, rank Lt.; Dir. and mem. Extve. Comte., Candn. Paint & Coatings Assn.; mem. Bd. Trade Metrop. Toronto; United Church; recreation: golf; Club: Islington Golf; Home: 4 Swindon Rd., Islington, Ont., M9A 3Y7; Office: 15 Lloyd Ave., Toronto, Ont. M6N 1G9

HIGGINBOTHAM, David Crichton, B.Com., F.C.A.; chartered accountant; b. Chatham, Ont. 24 Jan. 1928; s. Hubert C. and Bessie H. (McKeough) H.; e. Trinity Coll. Sch., Port Hope, Ont. 1939-44; Trinity Coll., Univ. of Toronto, B.Com. 1948; m. Mary A., d. late Dr. A. M. McFaul, 9 Aug. 1952; children: Anne, John, Ted; SR. PARTNER, PRICE WATERHOUSE & CO., since 1975; joined the Co. 1948, admitted to partnerhsip 1960; (Past) Dir. and Pres., Nat. Ballet Sch. of Can.; mem. Extve. Comte.; Bd. of Gov., Trinity Coll. Sch.; mem., Adv. Comte., Sch. of Business Admin., Univ. of Western Ont., London; Clubs: The Toronto; Toronto Golf; Bad-

minton & Racquet; Craigleith Ski; Home: 98 Garfield Ave., Toronto, Ont., M4T 1G1; Office: Toronto-Dominion Centre, Toronto, Ont.

HIGGINS, Benjamin Howard, M.A., M.Sc., Ph.D., F.R.S.C.; educator; consultant; b. London, Ont. 18 Aug. 1912; s. Benjamin H. and Ruth (Holway) H.; e. Univ. of W. Ont. B.A. 1933; London Sch. of Econ. M.Sc. 1935; Harvard Univ. M.P.A. 1939; Univ. of Minn. Ph.D. 1941; Melbourne Univ. M.A. (Hon.) 1949; m. Agnes Charlotte d. E. G. Quamme, Minneapolis 1 June 1936; children: Holway, Benjamin, Edward; m. 2ndly Jean Downing Sept. 1955; children: Ean, Alain; DIR., CENTRE FOR APPLIED STUDIES IN DEVELOPMENT, THE UNIV. OF THE SOUTH PACIFIC 1981- ; Prof. Emeritus, Univ. of Ottawa 1978- ; Instr. in Econ. Univ. of Sask. 1935, Univ. of Minn. 1936-38; Littauer Fellow and Asst. in Fiscal Policy, Harvard Univ. 1938-39, Instr. in Econ. 1939-41; Bronfman Prof. of Econ. McGill Univ. 1942-52; Prof. of Econ. Yale Univ. summer 1946; Ritchie Prof. of Econ. Research Melbourne Univ. 1948-49; Prof. of Econ. Center Internat. Studies Mass. Inst. of Technol. 1954-59, Dir. of Indonesia Project 1954-59; Prof. of Econ. and Chrmn. of Dept. Univ. of Texas 1959-61, Ashbel Smith Prof. of Econ. 1961-67, Dir. RFF Project 1961-63, Dir. Center for Econ. Devel. & Planning 1967; Prof. titulaire en science économique, Univ. de Montréal 1967-73, Univ. d'Ottawa 1973-79 and Vice Dean for Research Faculty of Social Sciences there; Visiting Prof.: ECLA Inst. for Econ. Devel. & Planning Santiago 1961; Getulio Vargas Foundation Rio de Janeiro 1961; Centro Estudios Monetarios Latino-Americano Mexico City 1961; Di Tella Inst. CAFADE and Ministry of Econ. Affairs Buenos Aires 1961; Univ. of Cal. Berkeley 1963; AEA-IIE Econ. Boulder, Colo. 1963; AEA-IIE Inst. (Chrmn. Adv. Comte. AEA Econ. Inst.) 1965; Murdoch Univ. Perth, Australia 1979; Univ. of New England, Australia 1981; Sr. Specialist, East-West Center Univ. of Hawaii 1967; Sr. Consultant Project on Unified Appeoach to Devel. Planning UN Research Inst. for Social Devel. 1971-73; Dir. du projet CRDE/UNDP, Projet de planification Mauritanie 1971-73; Visiting Fellow, Centre for Research in Federal Financial Relations 1980-81 and Development Studies Centre 1980, Australian Nat. Univ.; special consultant various agencies incl. UNESCO for econ. and social devel. S.Am., Africa, Southeast Asia; Chrmn. Adv. Comte. UN Centre for Regional Devel. 1978- ; advisor various OECD and CIDA projects; author "Economic Development: Problems, Principles and Policies" 1959, 2nd ed. 1968; "Indonesia: The Crisis of the Millstones" 1963; co-author "Japan and Southeast Asia" 1968; "Economic Development of a Small Planet" 1979; numerous reports, book chapters, papers and articles; Delta Upsilon; Protestant; recreations: art, music, sports; Address: P.O. Box 1168, Suva, Fiji.

HIGGINS, Paul; food processor; b. Collingwood, Ont.; s. Stafford and Belinda (Byrnes) H.; e. St. Michael's Coll., Toronto; m. Evelyn, d. P.D. Bowlen, Tyler, Texas, 25 Nov. 1939; children: Sandra McKenna, Patty-Anne, Shelagh, Paul Jr., Michael; PRES., MOTHER PARKER'S FOOD LIMITED; Pres., Higgins & Burke Ltd.; Sandra Instant Coffee Co. Ltd.; Dannemiller (Canada) Ltd.; Vice-Pres., Lounsbury Foods Ltd.; since leaving school in 1929 has been continuously in the food business; Dir., St. Bernard's Hospital, Toronto; Treas., Tea Council of Can.; Dir., Grocery Products Mfrs. of Can.; Roman Catholic; recreations: golf, shooting, riding; Clubs: Granite; Lambton Golf & Country; Briars Golf; Office: 2530 Stanfield Road, Cooksville, Ont., L4Y 1S4

HILBORN, Colonel Robert Harvey, M.V.O., M.B.E., C.D.; co. pres.; b. Preston, Ont., 20 July 1917; s. Gordon Verne and Sadie Winifred (Devitt) H.; e. Preston Public Sch., Galt (Ont.) Coll. Inst.; m. Mary Elizabeth, d. Frank Pattinson, Preston, Ont., 16 Oct. 1946; children: David Hedley, Lynn Irving; SR. ASSOC., BEECH, AND PARTNERS LTD.; Chrmn. Zarex Equity Ltd.; Pres., Hilborn

Holdings Ltd.; Dir., Savage Shoes Ltd.; Champlain Estates of Whitby Ltd.;joined Bank of Toronto as a Jr. in 1935; estb. his own Gen. Ins. Agency 1938; Vice Pres. and Gen. Magr., George Pattinson & Co. Ltd. (Textile Mfrs.), 1948; Vice-Pres. and Gen. Mgr., Farlinger Development Ltd. (Constr. and Land Devel.), 1956; Vice-Pres. and Gen. Mgr., Gibson Brothers Ltd. (Real Estate), 1958; Pres., Harry Price, Hilborn Ins. Ltd., 1963; Sr. Vice Pres. and Dir., Marsh and McLennan Ltd. 1971; Chrmn. of Bd., Exchequer Trust Co., 1977; Lieut., The Highland Light Inf. of Can., 1937; mobilized 1940; proceeded overseas, 1941; Staff Capt., 9 Candn. Inf. Bgde., 1942; p.s.c. Camberley, 1943; G.S.O. 2, Hdqrs. 1 Candn. Corps (Italy and N.W. Europe) 1944-45; Bgde. Major, 10 Candn. Inf. Bgde., 1945; M.B.E.; Mentioned twice in Despatches; promoted Lt.-Col. to command Toronto Scottish Regt. 1960; Hon. Lt. Col. 1968-71, Hon. Col. 1971-77, Candn. Equerry to H.M. Queen Elizabeth the Queen Mother, 1965, 74; 79 and 80; Gov., Candn. Corps of Commissionaires; Hon. Dir., Royal Agric. Winter Fair; Vice-Pres., Empire Club Toronto; Past Pres., Empire Club of Can.; Duke of Edinburgh's Award in Can.; Preston Ch. of Comm.; Fort York Br., Royal Candn. Legion; Bd. of Trade, Metrop. Toronto; Nat. Assn. Surety Bond Producers (U.S.); Anglican; recreations: cattle breeding; Clubs: Toronto; Empire; Bd. of Trade (Toronto); Royal Can. Mil. Inst.; Home: Greenbrae Farm, R.R. 1, Oshawa, Ont. L1H 7K4; Office: 80 Bloor St. W. Toronto, Ont. M5S 2V1

HILDEBRAND, Henry Peter, C.M., M.A., D.D.; educator; b. Steinfeld, S. Russia 16 Nov. 1911; s. Peter and Anna (Froese) H.; came to Can. 1925; e. Winnipeg Bible Coll. Grad. Dipl. 1933, Postgrad. Dipl. 1934; Wheaton Coll., Winona Lake Sch. of Theol. B.A. 1964, M.A. 1966; Winnipeg Theol. Semy. D.D. 1975; m. Inger d. Olaf Soyland, Norway 12 Aug. 1937; children: Marcia (Mrs. P. Leskewich), Évelyn (Mrs. R. Moore), David, Paul, Glen; CHANCELLOR AND DIR., BRIERCREST BIBLE INST. since 1977, Founder and Pres. 1935-77; Dir. Candn. Sunday Sch. Mission since 1945; Pres. Assn. Candn. Bible Colls. 1976-80; Dir. Africa Inland Mission since 1979; Radio Pastor, Briercrest Bible Hour 1937-78; rec'd Queen's Silver Jubilee Medal 1977; Order of Canada, 1979; Interdenominational; recreations: golf, gardening, fishing; Address: Caronport, Sask. S0H 0S0.

HILDES, John A., C.M., M.D., F.R.C.P. (Lond.), F.R.C.P.(C); physician; educator; b. Toronto, Ont. 1918; e. Univ. of Toronto M.D. 1940; Post-grad. Med. Sch. of London 1946-49; PROF. OF MED., UNIV. OF MAN. since 1960, Assoc. Dean, Div. of Community Med. since 1975 and Dir. N. Med. Unit; Asst. and Assoc. Prof. of Physiol. Univ. of Man. 1949-60; Med. Dir. Winnipeg Mun. Hosps. 1951-54; Attending Phys. and sometime Chief of Gastroenterol., Health Sciences Gen. Centre Winnipeg 1949-77; mem. Bd. Churchill Health Centre and Seven Oaks Gen. Hosp.; served with R.C.A.M.C. 1941-45, UK and S.E. Asia, rank Lt. Col.; Mentioned in dispatches; co-ed. "Studies in Physiology" 1969; author or co-author over 90 scient. publs. gastrointestinal & hepatic physiol. studies, bulbar and respiratory poliomyelitis, human tolerance to cold, epidemiol. circumpolar diseases, health care delivery for remote n. communities; mem. Am. Physiol. Soc.; Candn. Physiol. Soc.; Man. Med. Assn.; Candn. Med. Assn.; Home: 130 Waterloo St., Winnipeg, Man. R3N 0S2; Office: 61 Emily St., Winnipeg, Man. R3E 1Y9.

HILL, Frederick Walter, D.F.C., B.A., M.B.A.; executive; b. Regina, Sask., 2 Sept. 1921; s. Walter H. A. and Grace E. Hill; e. Lakeview Pub. Sch.; Campion High Sch.; Univ. of Sask. B.A.; Harvard Grad. Sch. of Business Adm. M.B.A.; m. Margaret Shirley d. Patrick J. Mulvihill, 1 Feb. 1944; children: Paul J., Terrence F., Daniel W., Colleen P., Marylyn A.; Chrm. and Dir., McCallum Hill Ltd; Western Surety Co.; Pres. and Dir., Harvard Developments Ltd.; Harvard Resources Ltd.; Harvard Oil & Gas;

Marathon Investments Ltd.; Dir. Sask. Roughriders; Can. Imp. Bank of Commerce; mem. Council of Canada West Foundation Ltd.; Chancellor, The Athol Murray College of Notre Dame, Wilcox, Sask.; Ald. City of Regina 1954-55; served with RCAF 1941 (med. discharge), US Army Air Force 1942-45, pilot heavy bombers 15th Air Force Italy and 8th Air Force Eng.; awarded Air Medal with 3 oak leaf clusters; Distinguished Flying Cross; Sustaining mem. Urban Land Inst., Washington, D.C.; mem., Newcomen (N.Y.); Knights of Columbus 3rd and 4th Degree; recreations: golf, swimming; Clubs: Assiniboia; Wascana Country; Un. Services Inst.; Home: 1032 Gryphons Walk, Regina, Sask. S4S 6X1; Office: Tenth Floor, McCallum Hill Bldg., 1874 Scarth St., P.O. Box 527 Regina, Sask. S4P 3A2

HILL,Graham Roderick, M.A., M.L.S.; university librarian; b. Richmond, Surrey, Eng. 4 Apl. 1946; s. Herbert Edgar and Elsie (Davies) H.; e. Univ. of Newcastle-on-Tyne B.A. 1968; Univ. of Lancaster M.A. 1969; Univ. of W. Ont. M.L.S. 1970; m. Penelope Mary d. Maj. John Potts 31 Aug. 1968; one d. Lindsay; UNIV. LIBRARIAN, McMASTER UNIV. 1979- ; Mang. Ed. and Treas., Cromlech Press Inc.; Councillor, The Hamilton Assn. 1979-82; Secy.-Treas., Can. Assn. of Research Libraries Secy., Ont. Council Univ. Libs. 1980-81; Bd. of Gov., Hillfield-Strathllan. Coll.; joined present lib. 1971 holding various positions incl. Assoc. Univ. Lib. (Collections Dev.); Council on Lib. Resources Acad. Lib. Mang. Intern, Ind. Univ. Lib. 1977-78; Home: 40 Roanoke Rd., Hamilton, Ont. L8S 3P7; Office: 1280 Main St. W., Hamilton, Ont. L8S 4L6.

HILL, James Jay; retired executive; b. Tyvan Sask., 22 Jan. 1912; s. John and Mary C. (Wilson) H.; e. Pub. and High Schs., Tyvan, Sask.; Univ. of Sask. (Agric. Engn.); m. Juanita Mae Kettering; two s., James Jay Jr., Richard Charles; Pres. Gen. Mgr. and Dir., Diamond National of Can. Ltd., June 1966-77; with Cockshutt Plow Co., 1935-45 as Serviceman, Salesman, Sales Supv. in Sask., E. U.S.A. and Ont.; operated own retail Cockshutt farm equipment business in St. Catharines, Ont., 1946-49, Gen. Sales Mgr., Cockshutt Farm Equipment, Brantford, Ont., 1949-55; Gen. Mgr. and Dir., Scarfe & Co., Brantford 1955-59; Gen. Mgr., Diamond National of Can. Ltd., 1959-66; Part time Consultant, Screen Print Display Advtg. Ltd. 1977-79; mem., Candn. Jr. Chamber of Comm. (Pres., Brantford, 1945, Pres., Ont. 1946, Vice-Pres., Can. 1947, Senator 1961); Brantford Chamber of Comm. (Dir. 1953-54); Ont. Retail Farm Equipment Assn. (Pres. 1947-48); Rotary Club of Brantford (Pres. 1963-64 mem. Adv. Bd., 1964-69); Indust. A, Brantford Community Chest (Past Chrmn.); Brantford Community Chest (Past Chrmn. Budget Comte.); Brantford and Brant Co. Community Chest (Past Campaign Chrmn.); Community Chest Bd. of Dirs. (Past Pres.); Community Welfare Council of Brantford (Past mem. of Bd.); Community Welfare Council of Brantford and Co. (Past Pres.); Jr. Achievement of Brantford (Past Pres.); Jr. Achievement of Can. (Dir.); Past Comte. Chrmn., Brantford Capital Appeal for Brantford Gen. Hosp., Y.M.C.A.-Y.W.C.A., Salvation Army; Capital Appeal, Brantford Civic Centre; Prot. (Past. Chrmn. Bd. of Mang., Zoin United Ch.); recreations: golf, curling; Clubs: Brant Curling; Brantford Golf & Country (Dir. 1966-70); Home: 105 St. Paul Ave., Brantford, Ont., N3T 4G1; Office: 505 - 301 Fairview Dr., Brantford Ont. N3S 5A1

HILL, James Thomas, H.B.A., C.A.; insurance executive; b. Hamilton, Ont. 13 Dec. 1932; e. Univ. of W. Ont. H.B.A. 1956; C.A.; m. Jane Gretchen Reid 9 Aug. 1958; children: Jeffery, Christopher, Andrea; PRES. AND GEN. MGR., ECONOMICAL MUTUAL INSURANCE CO.; Dir. Canada Trustco Mortgage Co.; Dir. The Canada Trust Company; Club: Westmount Golf & Country; Home: 44 Rusholme Rd., Kitchener, Ont. N2M 2T6; Office: (P.O. Box 700) Kitchener, Ont. N2G 4C1

HILL, Peter B., D.F.C., B.Eng.; manufacturer; b. Toronto, Ont., 1 March 1923; s. Clarence Bruce and Charlotte Muriel (Allen) H.; e. Ridley Coll., St. Catharines, Ont. (1932-36); St. Catharines Coll. Inst. (1936-41) m; McGill Univ., B.Eng. 1949; Mang. course, Univ. of W. Ont. (1959); m. Marjorie Gertrude, d. R. A. Hanright, St. Catharines, Ont., 26 Dec. 1944; children: Derek Peter Bruce, Susan Virginia; PRES. AND DIR., ETF TOOLS LTD., since 1962; Dir., Mott Mfg. Ltd.; joined present Co., May 1949; apptd. Vice-Pres., Sales, 1951; served in 2nd World War, enlisting with R.C.A.F., May 1941; Grad. as Sgt. Air Observer, Feb. 1942; Overseas, 1942 attached to R.A.F.; Commissioned 1943; repatriated July 1944; discharged with rank of Flight Lt.; D.F.C.; Operations Wing & Bar; mem., Engn. Inst. Can.; McGill Grad. Soc.; St. Catharines Chamber Comm.; Candn. Automotive Parts Mfrs. Assn.; Niagara Peninsula Armed Forces Inst.; Pres. (1971-72) St. Catharines & Dist. Chamber of Comm.; Conservative; Anglican; recreations: fishing, hunting, skiing; Clubs: St. Catharines (Past Pres.) Niagara Hardy Hunt (Secy. Treas.); Home: 189 Lockhart Dr., St. Catharines, Ont., L2T 1W8; Office: 21 Woodburn, P.O. Box 128, St. Catharines, Ont. L2R 6R4

HILLER, Arthur Garfin, M.A.; film director; b. Edmonton, Alta., 22 Nov. 1923; s. late Harry and late Rose (Garfin) H.; e. Victoria High Sch., Edmonton; Univ. of Toronto, B.A. 1947, M.A. (Psychol.) 1950; Univ. of B.C., 1 Yr. law; Victoria Coll., Glasgow, F.V.Ch.C.; m. Gwen, d. late Mayer Pechet, 14 Feb. 1948; children: Henryk Jay, Erica Liba; Producer-Dir., CBC Radio, 1949-53; Dir., CBC TV, 1953-54; Dir.; Matinee Theatre, NBC, 1955-56; Playhouse 90, CBS, 1956-58; various other TV and film shows incl. Alfred Hitchcock Presents, Gunsmoke, Naked City, Route 66, Playhouse 90, 1958-64; films incl. The Americanization of Emily, Popi, Out of Towners, Love Story, Plaza Suite, Man of La Mancha, Hospital, The Man in the Glass Booth, Silver Streak, The In-laws; Academy of TV Arts & Science Nomination Best Director 1962; Golden Globe Award Best Director and Best Film 1970; Academy Award Nomination Best Director 1970; Dirs. Guild of Am. Nomination Best Dir. 1970; N.Y. Foreign Press Award Best Dir. 1970; Dr. Lauriate, Imp. Order of Constantine, Brussels 1972; Dr. Letters, London Inst. for Applied Research 1973; Commdr. Surzam Corda, Belgium 1972; served with RCAF Overseas; Navig. 1942-45; rank Flying Offr.; mem., Dirs. Guild Am. (Bd.); Acad. Motion Picture Arts & Sciences (Bd.); Address: 1218 Benedict Canon Dr., Beverly Hills, Cal. 90210

HILLIARD, Irwin M., M.D.; university professor; b. Morrisburg. Ont.; e. Univ. of Toronto; m. Agnes Magee; children: Ann, Dr. Robert, John, Barbara; PROF. EMERITUS, DEPT. OF MED., UNIV. OF TORONTO; Physician-in-Chief at Candn. Mission Hosp. in Fowling Szechuan, China, 1939-45; after 3 yrs. at Toronto Gen. and Toronto Western Hosps., became Staff mem. of Univ. of Toronto till 1954 when joined Univ. of Sask. as Head of Dept. of Med.; returned to Univ. of Toronto 1962; Prof. of Med., Univ. of Toronto, 1962-73; Phys. In Chief, Toronto Western Hospital, 1962-73; Prof. Emeritus, Dept. of Medicine, 1976; Pres., American Geriatrics Society, 1980; Home: 123 Sylvan, Scarborough, Ont., M1M 1J9; Office: 3070 Ellesmere Road, Suite #305, Scarborough, Ont., M1E 4C3

HILLIER, James, M.A., Ph.D., F.A.P.S.; retired research executive; pioneer in electron microscopy; b. Brantford, Ont., 22 Aug. 1915; s. James and Ethel Anne (Cooke) H.; e. Univ. of Toronto, B.A. 1937 (Math. and Physics), M.A.(Physics) 1938, Ph.D. (Physics) 1941; D.Sc. (Hon.) Univ. of Toronto 1978; D.Sc. (Hon.) New Jersey Inst. of Tech. 1981; m. Florence Marjorie, d. William Wynship Bell, 24 Oct. 1936; two s., James Robert, William Wynship; Extve. Vice Pres., Research & Engn., RCA Corp., 1969-76; Research Asst., Banting Inst. of Univ. of Toronto Med. Sch., 1939-40; designer and builder (with Albert Prebus) 1st successful high-resolution electron microscope in W. Hemisphere, 1937-40; Research Physicist and Engr., RCA, 1940-53; Dir. of Research Dept., Melpar, Inc., 1953; Adm. Engr., Research & Engn., RCA 1954; Chief Engr., RCA Comm. Electronics Products, Nov. 1955-57; Gen. Mgr., RCA Laboratories 1957; Vice-Pres., RCA Laboratories, 1958-68; Vice-Pres., Research & Engn. 1968-69; Extve. Vice Pres., Research and Engn. 1969-76; Extve. Vice Pres. and Sr. Scientist 1976-77 (ret.); mem. of Nat. Acad. of Engineering; Fellow, Am. Assn. Advance. Science; Fellow, Inst. Elect. & Electronic Engrs., Fellow, Am. Phys. Soc.; Eminent mem., Eta Kapp Nu; Past Pres., Electron Microscope Soc. of Am.; mem., Am. Management Assn.; Am. Public Health Assn. (Albert Lasker Award, 1960); Pres., Indust. Research Inst. 1963-64; Pres., Indust. Reactor Labs., 1964-65; Comm. Tech. Adv. Bd., U.S. Dept. Comm.; Chrmn., Adv. Council to Dept. Elect. Engn., Princeton Univ., 1965; Gov. Bd., Am. Inst. Physics; mem., Adv. Council, Coll. of Eng., Cornell Univ. since 1966; mem., N.J. Higher Educ. Study Comte., 1963-64; Sigma Xi; Publications: co-author of "Electron Optics and the Electron Miscroscope", 1938; about 150 papers dealing mainly with fields of electron microscopy and research management; holds 41 patents in his name; medalist, Ind. Research Inst. 1975; inducted Nat. Inventors Hall of Fame (U.S.) 1980; Founders Medal Inst., Electric & Electronic Engrs. 1981; Protestant; Home: 22 Arreton Rd., Princeton, N.J., 08540;

HILLIKER, John Arthur Charles, B.A.; banker; b. Toronto, Ont. 17 Feb. 1928; s. Arthur Ellwood and Kathleen (Keyes) H.; e. Univ. of Toronto B.A. 1951; Univ. of Alta. Banff Sch. Advanced Mang.; Harvard Univ. Advanced Mang. Program; m. Barbara Doreen d. Russell E. Kenny, Almonte, Ont. 20 Feb. 1954; children: Nancy Lynne, David John; VICE CHRMN. AND DIR., CANADIAN IMPERIAL BANK OF COMMERCE 1980- ; Chrmn. and Dir. Kinross Mortgage Corp.; Chmn. and Dir. United Dominion Corp. (Canada) Ltd.; Mgr. present Bank Montego Bay, Jamaica 1960, Ottawa 1964; Asst. Gen. Mgr. and Mgr. Main Br. Toronto 1965-70; Vice Pres. H.O. 1971; Sr. Vice Pres. and Regional Gen. Mgr. B.C. 1973; Sr. Vice Pres. Domestic Regions 1976 and Extve. Vice Pres. 1978; Gov. St. George's Coll.; Hon. Treas. Columbus Centre Toronto; Phi Delta Theta (Past Pres.); recreations: boating, swimming, skiing, gardening; Clubs: Toronto; Granite; Rideau (Ottawa); Vancouver; Home: 180 Fenn Ave., Willowdale, Ont. M2P 1X9; Office: Commerce Court, Toronto, Ont. M5L 1A2.

HILLMAN, Donald Arthur, M.D.; b. Montreal, Que. 25 June 1925; s. Daniel and Bertha Jean H.; m. Elizabeth d. Fred Sloman, Clinton, Ont. 29 Dec. 1955; 5 children; PROF. OF PEDIATRICS, MEMORIAL UNIV. OF NFLD.: Phys.-in-Chief, Janeway Child Health Center; served with RCA Overseas 1943-46; Anglican; Home: 102 New Cove Rd., St. John's, Nfld.; Office: Janeway Child Health Center, St. John's, Nfld. A1B 3V6.

HIMMS-HAGEN, Jean, B.Sc., D.Phil.; educator; b. Oxford, Eng. 18 Dec. 1933; s. Frederick Hubert and Margaret Mary (Deadman) Himms; e. Milham Ford Sch. Oxford 1949; Univ. London B.Sc. 1955; Oxford Univ. D.Phil. 1958; m. Paul Beo Hagen 29 Sept. 1956; children: Anna Jean, Nina Jean; PROF AND CHRMN. OF BIOCHEM. UNIV. OF OTTAWA since 1977; Asst. Prof. Univ. of Man. 1959-64; Assoc. Prof. Queen's Univ. 1964-67; Assoc. Prof. present Univ. 1967, Prof. 1971, Acting Chrmn. 1975-77; rec'd Bond Award Am. Oil Chemists, Soc. 1972; Ayerst Award Candn. Biochem. Soc. 1973; elected to Royal Soc. of Can., 1980; author various research publs.; scient. reviews, book chapters; mem. Candn. Biochem. Soc.; Candn. Physiol. Soc.; Endocrine Soc. (US); Candn. Soc. Endocrinol. & Metabolism; Biochem. Soc. (UK); Am. Soc. Pharmacol. & Exper. Therapeutics; Am. Assn. Advanc. Science; recreations: swimming, sailing, cross-country skiing; Home: 235 Tudor Pl., Ottawa, Ont. K1L 7Y1; Office: 275 Nicholas St., Ottawa, Ont. K1N 9A9.

HINES, William James; transportation executive; b. Toronto, Ont., 16 Sept. 1911; s. late William Albert and late Annie Francis (Beatty(H.; e. N. Toronto Coll. Inst., 1929; War Staff Coll., Royal Mil. Coll., 1945; Univ. of Toronto; m. Gunda, d. late Henry Herbert Mason, 17 Feb. 1935; two s., William Henry Charles, John Anthony; CONSULTANT, LAND TRANSPORT, CANADA STEAMSHIP LINES LTD. since 1976, formerly Vice-Pres. (1973-76); Past Pres., Kingsway Transports Ltd.; Kingsway Freight Lines Ltd.; Kingsway Dalewood Ltd.; Bennet & Elliott Co. Ltd.; Laurentide Transport Ltd.; Drummond Transit Ltd.; Past Vice Pres. and Dir., Provincial Transport Enterprises Ltd.; Past Dir., John N. Brocklesby Transport Ltd.; Chmr. of Bd., Peelco Mfg. Ltd.; Dir., Floor Trader and Office Mgr., Hambly, Peaker & Trent (now Alfred G. Bunting & Co.) 1934; Acct. and Office Mgr., Atlas Polar Co. Ltd., 1940-42; Acct. and subsequently Secy.-Treas. and Dir., Webster Air Equipment Ltd., London, Ont., 1945; Vice Pres., Gen. Mgr. and Dir., Husband Transport Ltd., 1949; Asst. Gen. Mgr., Kingsway Transports Ltd., 1952; Gen. Mgr. 1961; Vice Pres. and Pres. subsidiary co's 1969; joined present co. as Vice Pres.-Land Transport., 1969; served with R.C.A. Service Corps in Can., Eng. and N.W. Europe 1942-45; rank Maj. on discharge; Trustee, Elder, Kingsway Lambton Un. Ch.; Dir. and Past Pres., Ont. Trucking Assn.; Beta Theta Pi; P. Conservative; United Church; recreations: golf, boating; Clubs: St. George's Golf & Country; RCYC; Carlton; Royal St. Lawrence Yacht (Montreal); Beaconsfield Golf (Montreal); Home: 39 Old Mill Rd., Apt. 2103, Toronto Ont. M8X 1G5; Office: 123 Rexdale Blvd., Rexdale, Ont. M9W 1P1

HIRSCH, John, O.C. (1967), Litt.D., LL.D.; theatre director; b. Siofok, Hungary, 1 May 1930; s. Joseph and Ilona (Horvath) H.; e. Jewish Gymnasium, Budapest; St. John's Tech. High Sch., Winnipeg; Univ. of Man.; Hon. Fellow of Univ. Coll., Litt.D. 1966; University of Toronto, LL.D. 1967; ARTISTIC DIR., STRATFORD FESTIVAL THEATRE, 1980- ; Head of CBC T.V. Drama 1972-74; mem. of Bd., Theatre Communication Group, U.S.A.; Consulting Artistic Dir., Seattle Repertory Theatre (1979-80); Founder, Rainbow Stage, Winnipeg; Theatre 77; Manitoba Theatre Centre; T.V. Producer, CBC Winnipeg and Toronto; Crest Theatre, Toronto; Theatre Nouveau Monde, Montreal; Lincoln Centre Repertory Theatre, N.Y.; Broadway, N.Y.; Theatre of the Deaf, U.S.A.; Stratford (Ont.) Festival Theatre; Habimah-National Theatre (Israel); Guthrie Theatre, Minneapolis; New York City Opera, N.Y.; Mark Taper Forum, L.A.; St. Lawrence Centre, Toronto; named New Candn. of the Yr.; Outer Circle Critics Award; L.A. Drama Critics Circle Award; "Obie" Award; Molson prize; writings incl. essays for "Architects of Modern Thought" (CBC Publ.); poems in "Northern Review" and "Alphabet"; children's plays incl.: "Box of Smiles"; "Saaurkringle"; "Destination Planet Dee"; "Rupert the Great"; Office: Stratford Festival Theatre, P.O. Box 520 Stratford, Ont. N5A 6V2

HIRST, Peter C., M.A., F.I.A., F.C.I.A.; actuary; b. Nairobi, Kenya 22 Aug. 1943; e. Oxford Univ. M.A. 1965; m. Audrey 27 July 1968; children: Phillipa Anne, Sara Elizabeth; PRESIDENT, TILLINGHAST, NELSON & WARREN INC.: Supvr. Group Pension Dept. Imperial Life 1968; Consulting Actuary, Kates Peat Marwick & Co. 1971; Sr. Consulting Actuary, Johnson & Higgins, Willis Faber Ltd. 1974, Asst. Vice Pres. 1975; Founder Hirst Consultants Ltd. 1976, merged with present co. 1980; Assoc., Soc. Actuaries; mem. Conf. Actuaries Pub. Practice; Candn. Pension Conf. Personnel Assn.; Assn. Candn. Pension Mang. (Policy Comte.); Bd. Trade Metrop. Toronto; Squash Acad.; Clubs: Rotary; Mississauga Golf & Country; Chinguacousy Country; recreations: sports, theatre, reading; Home: 1381 Queen Victoria Ave., Mis-

sissauga, Ont. L5H 3H2; Office: 808, 390 Bay St., Toronto, Ont. M5H 2W9.

HISCOCKS, Richard Duncan, M.B.E., B.A.Sc., P.Eng.; b. Toronto, Ont., 4 June 1914; s. William Duncan and Elizabeth Gertrude (Barnes) H.; e. Pub. and High Schs., Toronto; Univ. of Toronto, B.A.Sc. 1938; Hon. degrees: McGill and McMaster 1971; m. Bettie Eileen, d. Wilfred S. Jacobs, 22 Aug. 1942; children: Peter, Susan, Patricia, David Christopher; former Vice-Pres. (Engineering), DeHavilland Aircraft of Can. Ltd.; Pres., Canadian Patents & Development Ltd.; Scientific Consultant, Univ. of Toronto; with Nat. Research Council, Ottawa, 1940-46; Vice Pres. (Ind.) 1969-77 De Havilland Aircraft of Canada Ltd., 1946-68; Vice Pres. (Eng.) 1977-79; Consultant 1980- ; Hon. Fellow, Candn. Aero. Inst.; Fellow Engn. Inst. Canada; Home: 14818 Thrift Ave., White Rock, B.C. V4B 2J7

HITCHMAN, George C.; b. Toronto, Ont., 10 Aug. 1914; s. Percy R. and Effie (Roger) H.; e. Pub. and High Sch., Tottenham, Ont.; m. Muriel Robinson, New York, 14 June 1942; one d. Barbara Ann; DIR., THE BANK OF NOVA SCOTIA, since 1974; Dir., Algoma Central Railway; Can. Bus. Health Research Inst.; Canborough Corp.; Canborough Limited; William Collins Sons & Co. (Canada Ltd.); Constellation Hotel Corp. Ltd.; Husky Injection Moulding Systems Ltd.; Insmor Holdings Ltd.; Insmor Mortgage Ins. Co.; The Mortgage Ins. Co. of Canada Relaty Ltdd.; MICC Investments Ltd.; Standard Brands Ltd.; Ontario Energy; Robert Bosch (Canada) Ltd.; Scotia Toronto Dominion Leasing Ltd.; joined present Bank, Woodbridge, Ont., 1931; held various positions at London, Ont., Toronto (Danforth & Greenwood Br.), New York Agency; apptd. Asst. Mgr., Montreal Br. 1946; Mgr., London, Eng., 1948; London, Ont., 1951; Edmonton 1952; Supvr. of Que. Brs., 1954; Asst. Gen. Mgr. 1957; Depy. Gen. Mgr. 1963; Joint Gen. Mgr. 1966; Executive Vice President 1972; served with the 104th U.S. Infantry in France, Belgium, Holland and Germany, 1942-45; rank of Staff Sergeant; Anglican; recreation: golf; Clubs: National; Toronto; Lambton Golf & Country; Home: 60 Old Mill Rd., Toronto, Ont. M8X 1G7; Office: 44 King St. W., Toronto, Ont. M5H 1E2

HITSCHFELD, Walter, B.A.Sc., Ph. D.; meteorologist; physicist; educator; b. Vienna, Austria, 25 April 1922; s. Alois H. and Amélie (Brahms) H.; e. Elem. and Secondary Schs., Vienna; McGill Univ. Jr. Matric.; St. Michael's, Toronto, Ont., Sr. Matric.; Univ. of Toronto, B.A.Sc. (Engn. Physics) 1946; McGill Univ., Ph.D. (Atmospheric Physics) 1950; came to Canada 1941; m. Irma, d. late N.W. ("Paul") Morissette, Haileybury, Ont. 1947; children: Paul Alois, Charles Philip; VICE PRINC. (RESEARCH) AND DEAN, GRADUATE STUDIES, McGILL UNIVERSITY, 1971-80; Dir., McGill Internat. 1981- ; Professor of Physics and Meteorology there since 1961 and Canada Steamship Lines Professor since 1962; started in field of Radar Meteorology with Professor J. S. Marshall, branching out into several areas of atmospheric physics, notably physics of hail and radiative transfer; under former heading played part in building of Alta. Hail Studies (jt. enterprise of Nat. Research Council, McGill Univ. and Research Council of Alta.); Chrmn., Dept. Meteorol., McGill Univ. 1964-67, Vice-Dean, Physical Sciences 1964-71; mem. National (U.S.) Hail Research Experiment; Dir., Expo-Sciences de Montréal 1961-66 (Prés. 1965); Comn. de l'enseignement secondaire du Conseil supérieur de l'éduc. 1965-70; Comn. de la recherche universitaire 1971-78; Pres., Candn. Assn. of Grad. Schs.; Pres., Candn. Assn. Univ. Research Admin. 1977-78; Fellow, Am. Meteorol. Soc.; Royal Meteorol. Soc.; Candn. Meteorol. Soc. (Pres. 1973-74); Royal Soc. of Can.; recipient of Darton Prizes 1960, 62, 63 for meteorol. research; Patterson Medal, Atmos. Envir. Serv.; author of over 20 articles on cloud physics and related subjects; farms near Sutton, Que.; Home: Notre Dame-de-Grâce, Montreal, Que.; Office: Montreal, Que. H3A 2T6

HLECK, Paul, Q.C., B.A., LL.B.; b. Englefeld, Sask., 7 July 1931; e. Englefeld Pub. and High Schs.; Univ. of Sask. B.A. 1953, LL.B. 1956; m. Mary Lou; children: Mary Ann, Peter; SR. PARTNER, HLECK, KANUKA, THURINGER, SEMENCHUCK SANDOMIRSKY, BOYD & BAKER; Dir. Nu West Development Corp.; Cairns Homes Ltd.; read law with MacPherson, Neuman & Pierce; called to Bar of Sask. 1957; cr. Q.C. 1974; served 5 yrs. on City of Regina Planning Comn.; mem. Community Planning Assn. Can.—Regina Br. (Extve. 1961-69);— Housing and Urban Devel. Assn. Regina; active Ukrainian Greek Orthodox Ch. (Extve. Regina Parish 10 yrs.; Nat. Extve. Lay Organ.; Dir. Mohyla Ukrainian Student Residence Saskatoon 10 yrs.) ; mem. Regina and Candn. Bar Assns.; Regina Chamber Comm.; Clubs: Assiniboia; Candn. Men's; Kiwanis (Pres. 1968; Lt. Gov. Div. 4 W Can. Dist. 1970); Home: 118 Patterson Dr., Regina, Sask., S4S 3W9; Office: 1500 Chestmere Plaza, 2500 Victoria Ave., Regina, Sask. S4P 3X2

HNATYSHYN, Hon. Ramon John, M.P., B.A., LL.B., Q.C.; b. Saskatoon, Sask. 16 March 1934; s. Sen. John, Q.C. and Helen Constance (Pitts) H.; e. Victoria Pub. Sch. and Nutana Coll. Inst. Saskatoon; Univ. of Sask. B.A. 1954, LL.B. 1956; m. Karen Gerda d. George Andreasen, Saskatoon, Sask. 9 Jan. 1960; two s. John Georg, Carl Andrew; Min. of Energy, Mines & Resources and Min. of State for Science & Technol. 1979-80; called to Bar of Sask. 1957; cr. Q.C. 1973; law practice Saskatoon 1956-58; Private Secy. and Extve. Asst. to Govt. Leader in Senate 1958-60; rtn'd to law practice 1960 Saskatoon; Lectr. in Law, Univ. of Sask. 1966-74; el. to H. of C. for Saskatoon-Biggar g.e. 1974, re-el. g.e. 1979 for Saskatoon West; apptd. Depy. House Leader of Official Opposition and co-ordinator of Question Period 1976; former mem. RCAF 23 Wing (Auxiliary) Saskatoon; Past Pres. UN Assn. Can. (N. Sask. Br.); Pres. Law Soc. Sask. 1973-74; Bencher Law Soc. 1970-74; Pres. Saskatoon Gallery and Conserv. Corp. 1974; Past Vice Pres., Dir. and mem. Extve. Comte. Saskatoon YMCA; Court Depy. Independent Order Foresters; Past Dir. Un. Community Funds Sask., Chrmn. Saskatoon Un. Way Campaign 1972; mem. Saskatoon Bar Assn.; Candn. Bar Assn.; P. Conservative; Ukrainian Greek Orthodox; Home: 724 Saskatchewan Cres. E., Saskatoon, Sask.; Office: House of Commons, Ottawa, Ont. K1A 0A6.

HOAR, William Stewart, O.C., M.A., Ph.D., D.Sc., L.L.D., F.R.S.C. (1955); professor emeritus; b. Moncton, N.B., 31 Aug. 1913; s. George W. and Nina B. (Steeves) H.; e. Univ. of New Brunswick (Beaverbrook Schol.), B.A. 1934; Univ. of W. Ont. M.A. 1936; Boston Univ., Ph.D. 1939; D.Sc., Univ. of N.B. 1965, Memorial Univ. 1967; St. Francis Xavier 1976; Univ. West. Ontario 1978; L.L.D. Simon Fraser 1980; m. Margaret M., d. Angus MacKenzie, Thamesville, Ont., 13 Aug. 1941; children: Stewart, David, Kenzie, Melanie; PROF. OF ZOOLOGY, UNIV. OF BRIT. COLUMBIA, (Head of Dept. 1964-71); onetime mem., Nat. Research Council and Fish. Res. Bd. Can.; Demonst. in Zool., Univ. of W. Ont., 1934-36; Asst. in Histol. & Embryol., Boston Univ., 1936-39; Asst. Prof. of Biol., Univ. of N.B., 1939-42; Research Assoc. in Physiol., Univ. of Toronto, 1942-43; Prof. of Zool., Univ. of N.B., 1943-45; apptd. Prof. in present Univ. 1945; John Simon Guggenheim Mem. Foundation Fellowship, Oxford Univ., 1958-59; Flavelle Medal, RSC 1968; Fry Medal, CSZ 1974; Hon. Life mem. Pacific Sc. Assn., 1979; United Church; Home: 3561 W. 27th. Ave. W., Vancouver, B.C. V6S 1P9

HOBBS, Clement Francis, B.Sc., F.I.S., F.S.S.; mathematician; b. London, Eng., 8 March 1927; s. Francis Walter James and Margaret (Pearmine) H.; e. William Ellis Secondary Sch.; Norwood Tech. Coll., 1948-49; Birbeck Coll. (London Univ.), B.Sc. 1955; came to Canada 1955; m. Marie-Marguerite Sonia, d. Roland Rousseau, Nicolet, Que., 9 Dec. 1960; children: Frances Margaret, Clement Francis,

Jr.; DIR.-GEN., PLANNING & SYSTEMS SECY. OF STATE, CAN., since 1974; Director General, Post Office Dept.; with Medical Research Council, England, 1949-53; Fairey Aviation Company Weapons Div., U.K., 1953-55; Sr. Ballistics Offr., Inspection Services, Dept. of Nat. Defence, Ottawa, 1955-59; Chief of Systems Analysis, Army Equip. Engn. Estab., Dept. of Nat. Defence, 1959-65; Supt. Systems Engn., P.O. Dept., 1965; Director of Operational Research 1966; Vice Pres. Finance, Adm. & Personnel, Canadian International Development Agency 1972-74; co -author of "Tables for Inspection by Attributes", 1962 (first statistical standard publ. by Canadn. Govt.); author or co- author of a number of systems and methods studies; served with British Army 1944-48; mem. Assn. Prof. Engrs. Ont., Anglican; recreations: swimming; sailing, skating, judo; Home: (P.O. Box 118) Manotick, Ont., K0A 2N0; Office: Secy. of State Dept., Ottawa, Ont. K0A 0M5

HOBBS, George P., B.Eng.; industrialist; b. Hearts Content, Nfld., 22 June 1917; s. Stephen and Rebecca (Pugh) H.; e. Memorial Univ., 1934-37 (Engn. Diploma); McGill Univ., B.Eng., 1940; m. Fanny Irene, d. Thomas G. Hudson, 26 Sept. 1939; children: Marion Evelyn, John William, Robert Stephen, Evelyn Elizabeth; Dir., Churchill Falls (Labrador) Corp.; Elect. Engr., Defence Industries Ltd., 1940-45; Marathon Paper Ltd., 1945-46; Bowater's Nfld. Pulp & Paper Co. Ltd., 1946-47; Asst. Chief Engr. 1947-54, Chief Engr. 1954-56; Mill Mgr., 1956-60; Pres. and Dir., Bowater's Engn. & Devel. Corp. Inc., Calhoun, Tenn. and Dir., Bowater's Southern Paper Corp. and then Bowater's Carolina Corp., 1960-63; Chrmn. Nfld. & Labr. Power Comm. 1964-70; mem., Engn. Inst. Can.; Am. Inst. Elect. Engrs.; Assn. Prof. Engrs Nfld.; Bd. of Regents, Memorial Univ.; Freemason (P.M.); Grand Marshal, Grand Lodge of Scotland); Liberal; Anglican; recreations: fishing, swimming; Home: (Box 4265) Pouch Cove, St. John's East, Nfld., A1A 2X8; Office: (Box 9100) Philip Place, St. John's, Nfld. A0A 3L0

HOBBS, Gerald Henry Danby; private investor; b. Vancouver, B.C. 11 March 1921; s. Charles D. and Victoria M. (Danby) H.; e. Vancouver Coll.; m. Phyllis Rae Nicolson 1 May 1947; children: David, Leslie, Janet, Philip; Dir. The Bank of Nova Soctia; British Columbia Telephone Co.; Dillingham Corp. Honolulu; MacMillan Bloedel Ltd.; North American Life Assurance Co.; Okanagan Helicopters Ltd.; Suncor Inc.; Discovery Parks Inc.; Dir. Emeritus, Hawaiian Western Steel; Sales Mgr. Pacific Bolt Manufacturing Co. 1946-54; Gen. Mgr. Western Canada Steel Ltd. 1955, Pres. 1964, Chrmn. and Chief Extve. Offr. 1968-72; Vice Pres. Vancouver, Cominco Ltd. 1968, Vice Pres. Pacific Region 1969, Extve. Vice Pres. 1972, Pres. 1973, Chrmn. 1978-80; Chrmn. West Kootenay Power and Light 1978-80; Gov. Univ. of B.C.; Chrmn. Mang. Comte. Health Sciences Centre; Dir. B.C. Health Assn.; Dir. and mem. Extve. Council St. John Ambulance Assn.; mem. Greater Vancouver Adv. Bd. Salvation Army; named Commdr. Order of St. John; served with Royal Candn. Army Service Corps 1940-46; Anglican; Clubs: Vancouver; Shaughnessy Golf & Country; Home: 3803 Marguerite St., Vancouver, B.C. V6J 4E8; Office: 1112 West Pender St., Suite 910, Vancouver, B.C. V6E 2S1.

HOBBS, Richard John, B.A., M.Sc.; executive; b. Toronto, Ont. 11 Feb. 1931; s. Cecil and Isobel (Mitchell) H.; e. Danforth Tech. Sch. Toronto 1950; Univ. of W. Ont. B.A. 1956; Columbia Univ. M.Sc. 1957 (Samuel Bronfman Fellowship in Democratic Business Enterprise); m. Phyllis Mitsuye d. Diagoro Toyota; 3 children; PRES., C.E.O. & DIR. MACLEOD-STEDMAN INC. 1980- ; Vice Pres., and Dir., Candn. Tire Corp. Ltd., 1967-79; Pres.-Owner Cavalier Beverages Ltd. Orillia since 1976; Pres. Cantire Realty & Construction 1977-79; Dir. McGraw-Hill Ryerson Ltd.; Grandma Lee's Inc.; Lectr. Univ. of W. Ont. Sch. of Business Adm. 1957-58; Mgr. Canadian Tire Associate Store, Sault Ste. Marie, Ont. 1958-60, Dealer-Owner Orangeville, Ont. 1960-62 and Hamilton, Ont. 1962-67; Dir. of Merchandising & Retail Operations Candn. Tire 1965, Vice Pres. 1966; Vice Pres. & Dir. 1967-79; Past Dir. Bishop Strachan Sch.; Past Pres. Candn. Council Distribution; P. Conservative; recreations: squash, skiing, tennis; Clubs: Granite; Talisman Ski; Cambridge; Winnipeg Squash; Home: 93 Dunvegan Rd., Toronto, Ont. M4V 2P8; Offices: 1530 Gamble Place, Winnipeg, Man. R3T 1N6; 7622 Keele St., Toronto, Ont. L4K 1C4.

HOCKIN, Alan Bond, M.A.; finance executive; b. Winnipeg, Man., 7 Nov. 1923; s. Harold and Jean (Bond) M.; e. Univ. of Manitoba, B.A. (Hons.) 1944; Univ. of Toronto, M.A. 1946; children: Jeremy, Gillian, Nicholas, Jonathan; EXECUTIVE VICE PRESIDENT, INVESTMENTS, TORONTO-DOMINION BANK since Sept. 1972; joined Dept. of Finance, Ottawa in 1946; Financial Attaché, Canada House, London, 1951-52; Second Secy. (Finance), Permanent Candn. Del. to NATO & OEEC, Paris, 1952-53; Alternate Extve. Dir., on the Internat. Monetary Fund, Internat. Bank for Reconstr. & Devel., and Internat. Finance Corp., and Financial Counsellor; Candn. Embassy, Washington, 1957-59; Dir., Financial Affairs & Econ. Analysis Div., Dept. of Finance, Ottawa, 1959-64; Asst. Depy. Min., Dept. of Finance 1964-69; Alternate Governor for Canada of Internat. Bank for Reconstr. And Development, and later of Internat. Monetary Fund; with Morgan Stanley & Co. 1970-71; Deputy Chief General Manager Investment Division; Toronto-Dominion Bank 1971-72; Extve. Vice-Pres., Invest. Div., 1972; Trustee, Tor. General Burying Grounds; European & Pacific Management Ltd.; TD Realty Invests.; Dir.; Phoenix Assur. Co.; Acadia Life Ins.; The Tor.-Dominion Bank Pension Fund Soc.; Tordom Corp.; Leamor Holdings Ltd.; Regtor Investments; Tor. Dominion Leasing Ltd.; Nat. Council mem., Ont. Bus. Adv. Council; Industry Trade & Commerce Adv. Comte.; Canada Council Investment Comte.; Canada Safety Council; Nat. Cancer Inst. of Canada; Clubs: Tor. Club; Royal Candn Yacht; Office: Toronto-Dominion Bank Tower, Toronto, Ont. M5K 1A2

HODGETTS, Alfred Birnie, O.C. (1976), B.A., LL.D.; educator; b. Omemee, Ont., 20 May 1911; s. Alfred Clark and Mary Elsie (Birnie) H.; e. Ont. schs. to Sr. Matric.; Univ. of Toronto, B.A. (Pol. Science) 1933; Queen's Univ., LL.D. 1974; m. Helen Nicoll, d. William David Ross, Midland, Ont. 12 Aug. 1939; children: Ross, David, Pauline (Marston); Trustee, Canada Studies Foundation; founder (1949) and owner Hurontario Camp Co. Ltd.; taught hist. and coached team games Pickering Coll. 1933-39; Lakefield Coll. Sch. 1939-42; Trinity Coll. Sch. 1942-66; granted leave to direct Nat. Hist. Project (2 yr. study of civil educ. in Can. at elem. and secondary sch. level); co-estbd. Can. Studies Foundation 1968-70 (designed to improve quality of Candn. studies in Candn. schs.); served as Dir. 1970-75; Chrmn. 1975-81; Past Pres., Georgian Bay Assn.; author 'Decisive Decades' 1960; "What Culture? What Heritage?" 1968; co-author 'Teaching Canada in the 1980's", 1978; also various articles in journs. and mags.; Anglican; recreations: fly-fishing, conservation; Home: 1 Rose Glen Rd., Port Hope, Ont.;

HODGETTS, John Edwin, M.A., Ph.D., LL.D., D.Litt., F.R.S.C.; b. Omemee, Ontario, 28 May 1917; s. late Alfred Clark and Mary Elsie (Birnie) H.; e. Cobourg, (Ont.) Coll. Inst.; Univ. of Toronto, B.A. 1939 (Gold Medallist); M.A. 1940; Univ. of Chicago (Fellowship 1940-43); Ph.D. 1946; Rhodes Scholar, Ont., 1939; LL.D., Mount Allison 1970; Queen's 1970; D.Litt., Memorial Univ. 1971; m. Ella Ruth, d. late Rev. W. P. Woodger, 26 June 1943; children: Edwin Clark, Peter Geoffrey, Eleanor Anne; PROF. OF POL. SCIENCE, UNIV. OF TORONTO; Principal of Victoria College 1967-70 and Pres. 1970-72; Lecturer in Political Science, University of Toronto, 1943-45; successively Lectr., Assistant Prof., Associate

Prof. and Professor of Pol. Science, apptd. to the Hardy Chair of Pol. Science (1961-62) all at Queen's Univ.; Nuffield Travelling Fellow in Social Sciences, Oxford Univ., 1949-50; Skelton-Clark Research Fellow, Queen's Univ., 1954-55; Editorial Dir., Royal Comn. on Govt. Organization, 1960-62; Can. Council Sr. Research Fellow (sabbatical leave in Oxford Univ., Nuffield Coll. Visiting Fellow) 1962-63; Editor, "Queen's Quarterly", 1956-58; mem., Acad. Adv. Panel, Canada Council, 1966-69; Visiting Prof., Northwestern Univ., 1975; Dalhousie, 1975-76; Memorial, 1976-77; Publications: "An Administrative History of the United Canadas", 1956; (with J. A. Corry) 3rd ed. of "Democratic Government and Politics"; (with D. C. Corbett) "Canadian Public Administration: A Book of Readings"; "Administering the Atom for Peace"; "The Candn. Public Service, 1867-1970"; (jt. author) "The Biog. of an Inst.: The Civil Service Comn. of Can., 1908-1967; "Prov. Gov'ts as Employers"; numerous articles in scholarly journs.; mem., Candn. Pol. Science Assn. (Pres. 1971-72); Inst. Public Adm. Can.; Internat. Pol. Science Assn. (mem. Extve. Comte. 1961-64); mem, Royal Comn. on Financial Mang. and Accountability 1976-79; Awarded Vanier Gold Medal by Inst. of Public Administration of Canada, for a lasting and significant contribution to Canadian Public Administration; Phi Delta Theta; United Church; recreations: sailing, fishing, wood-carving; Home: R.R. No. 1, Newtonville, Ont. L0A 1J0

HODGINS, Jack Stanley, B.Ed.; writer; b. Comox, B.C. 3 Oct. 1938; s. Stanley and Reta (Blakely) H.; e. Univ. of B.C. B.Ed.(Sec.) 1961; m. Dianne Child Dec. 1960; children: Shannon, Gavin, Tyler; VISITING PROFESSOR, UNIVERSITY OF OTTAWA, 1981- ; Teacher of High School English, Nanaimo, B.C. 1961-80; Writer-in-Residence, Simon Fraser Univ., 1977; Writer-in-Residence, Univ. of Ottawa, 1979; Workshop Instructor, Sask. Summer School of the Arts, 1979, 1980, 1981, 1982; author 'Spit Delaney's Island' 1976; 'The Invention of the World' 1977; 'The Resurrection of Joseph Bourne' 1979; 'The Barclay Family Theatre' 1981; editor 'The Frontier Experience' 1975; 'The West Coast Experience' 1976; mem. Writers' Union of Can.; rec'd President's Medal, Univ. of W. Ont., 1973; Eaton's B.C. Book Award, 1977; Gibson's First Novel Award, 1978; Governor General's Award, 1980; recreations: canoeing, reading; Address: c/o Macmillan of Canada, 146 Front St. W., Toronto, Ont. M5J 1G5

HODGINS, John Willard, B.'A.Sc., Ph.D., F.R.S.C., F.C.I.C.; univ. dean; b. St. Catharines, Ont., 29 Sept. 1917; s. James Willard and Lucy (Howell) H.; e. Thorold (Ont.) High Sch.; Univ. of Toronto, B.A.Sc. (Chem. Engn.) 1938, Ph.D. (Phys. Chem.) 1947; hon. D.Eng., Corleton; hon. D.Sc., McMaster, R.M.C.; m. Jean Wallace, d. Gavin Russell, Ottawa, Ont., 15 July 1944; one d. Susan Ann; PRES., JOHN W. HODGINS, INC., since May 1980; and Assoc., Nordicom Technology, Inc.; Chrmn., Centre for Applied Research & Engn. Design; Metall. Chemist, Algoma Steel Co., Sault Ste. Marie, Ont., 1938-40; Research Chemist, Chem. Warfare Labs., Ottawa 1940-45; Head Phys. Chem. Sec., Defence Research Chem. Labs., Ottawa, 1947-50; Prof. of Chem. Engn., Royal Mill. Coll. of Can., 1950-56; McMaster Univ. to 1975 (Dean of Engn., 1958-69); Dir. of Research, Domtar 1975-77; Vice-Pres., Research and Environmental Technol. of Domtar Inc. 1977-80; Prof., Florida Atlantic Univ. 1980- ; served in Candn. Active Army, 1942-45, discharged with rank Capt.; mem., Adv. Comte. on Science and Med., Expo '67; Chrmn. (1962) Chem. Engn. Div., Chem. Inst. Can.; mem., Assn. Prof. Engrs. Ont.; Bd. of Govs., McMaster Univ.; Bd. of Govs., Mohawk Coll.; Bd. of Govs., John Abbott College; M.O.E.Q. (Order of Engn., Que.); Anglican; recreations: sketching, golf, photography; Club: Whitlock Golf & Country; St. James (Montreal) Home: 80 Côte St. Charles Rd., Hudson Heights, Que.

HODGKINSON, Lloyd Morley; publisher; b. Toronto, Ont., 1 Dec. 1920; s. Allen Morley and Violet May (Still) H.; e. Runnymede Coll. Inst. (Toronto, Ont.) 1933-39; m. Lucie Rita, d. Gérard N. Pratte, Montreal, Que., 9 Nov. 1948; two s., Robert Lloyd, Charles André; VICE-PRES., MAGAZINE DIV., MACLEAN-HUNTER LTD. since 1972; Publisher, "Macleans" and "L'Actualité" since 1971, and Dir., Maclean-Hunter Ltd. since 1964; Dir.; Mag. Advertising Bureau of Can.; Candn. Opera Co.; Co-Founder and Publisher "Canadian High News" (newspaper for Secondary Sch. students), 1939-43; joined present firm as Advertising Mgr., 'Plant Administration", 1943-46; joined Consolidated Press Ltd., apptd. Montreal Mgr. "Saturday Night", 1946-51 and Advertising Mgr., 1951-54; Dir. of Advertising, "Saturday Night" and "Canadian Home Journal", 1954-58; Publisher, "Chatelaine" Mags. and "Miss Chatelaine" 1958-71; Pres.; Periodical Press Association; Magazine Publishers Association; Canadian Tourist Assn.; Vice Chrmn., Audit Bureau of Circulations (Dir.); Dir., Candn. Opera Co.; R. Catholic; recreations: golf, theatre, music; Clubs: Rotary; Mississauga Golf & Country (Past Pres.); Home: 1202 Cloverbrae Cr., Mississauga, Ont. L5H 2Z8; Office: 481 University Ave., Toronto, Ont. M5G 1W8

HODGSON, Gordon Wesley, B. Sc., M.Sc., Ph.D., F.C.I.C.; educator; b. Islay, Alta., 25 May 1924; s. Wesley White and Olive (Trevithick) H.; e. Univ. of Alta., B.Sc. 1946, M.Sc. 1947; McGill Univ., Ph.D. 1949; m. Jeannette F. Doull, 25 May 1953; children: Patricia, Kathryn, Robin, Lauren, Shannon; DIR., KANANASKIS CENTRE FOR ENVIRONMENTAL RESEARCH, UNIV. OF CALGARY, since 1973; with Research Council of Alta., Edmonton, 1949-67; latterly Head, Petroleum Research; Visiting Prof., Tohoku Univ., Sendai, Japan, 1962; NASA Ames Research Center, Moffett Field, Calif., 1967; Stanford Univ. Med. Center, 1968; joined present Univ. 1969; invented capsule pipe lining; author of over 150 articles in various prof. journs.; mem. Chem. Inst. Can.; Am. Chem. Soc.; Geochem. Soc.; Astron. Soc. Am.; Presbyterian; Home: 18 Varbay Pl. N.W., Calgary, Alta. T3A 0C8

HODGSON, John Humphrey, B.A., M.A., Ph.D., F.R.S.C. (1958); scientist; b. Toronto, Ontario 24 September 1913; s. Ernest A. and Elizabeth (Humphrey) H.; e. University of Toronto, B.A. (Maths. and Physics) 1940, M.A. (Geophysics) 1946, Ph.D. (Geophysics) 1951; m. Helen W., d. late Ernest Baines, 16 Dec. 1940; children: Michael John, Peter Baines, Julie Margaret; Consultant in Earthquake Seismology;engaged in petroleum exploration and exploitation by geophys. means in S. & W. U.S.A., 1940-45; Asst. Prof. of Geophysics, Univ. of Toronto, 1945-59; Seismologist. Dept. of Mines & Tech. Surveys. Ottawa, 1949-52; Chief, Div. of Seismology, 1952-64; Dir. Earth Physics Br., Dept. of Energy, Mines and Resources 1964-73; Chief Seismologist, UNESCO Seismological Prog. for S.E. Asia, 1973-9; mem. Seismological Society of America (Director of 1951-1964); Associate Comte. on Geodesy and Geophysics, National Research Council (Chrmn. 1968-71); Internat. Assn. of Seismology & Physics of the Earth's Interior (Pres. 1963-67); Foreign & Commonwealth mem., Geol. Soc. of London (1968); Home: 268 Daniel Ave., Ottawa, Ont. K1Y 0C8

HODGSON, John Murray, Q.C., B.A.; b. Toronto, Ont., 21 Sept. 1921; s. Gregory Sanderson and Isabel (Murray) H.; e. Brown Sch. and Upper Can. Coll., Toronto; Trinity Coll., Univ. of Toronto, B.A. 1943; Osgoode Hall Law Sch.; m. Joan Weir, d. late James Walter Morris, 11 Oct. 1952; children: James Sanderson, John Matthew Russell, Barbara Morris; read law with Blake, Cassels & Graydon; called to Bar of Ont. 1949; cr. Q.C. 1968; law practice with Blake, Cassels & Graydon; Lectr. on Estate Tax, Osgoode Hall Law Sch., 1958-63; served with Candn. Forces 1943-46 (Italy 1944-45); Chmn., Can. Centre for Philanthropy; Dir., Laidlaw Foundation; Agora Foundation; Trustee,

Neathern Trust; mem., Candn. Bar Assn. (Ont. Pres., 1971); Candn. Tax Foundation, Estate Planning Council Toronto; Kappa Alpha; United Church; Club: University; Home: 129 Strathallan Boulevard, Toronto, Ont. M5N 1S9; Office: Blakes, Box 25, Commerce Court W., Toronto, Ont. M5L 1A9

HODGSON, Stuart Milton, O.C. (1970); Commissioner; b. Vancouver, B.C., 1 Apr. 1924; s. Allen Jay and Mary Louise (Allen) H.; e. John Oliver High Sch.; m. Pearl d. Harry Kereliuk, Edmonton, 28 July 1951; children: Lynne Mary, Eugene Allen; COB, BRITISH COLUMBIA FERRY CORP., VICTORIA, B.C. since 1981; after school worked one yr. in B.C. Plywood Div., H. R. MacMillan Co., Vancouver; returned after war service; became Internat. Organ., Internat. Woodworkers of Am. 1948; el. Financial Secy., Local 1-217, I.W.A., 1949; spent 2 yrs., as mem., I.W.A. Extve. Bd., Portland, Ore.; 8 yrs., Vice-Pres., W. Can. Regional Council No. 1, I.W.A.; 6 yrs., mem., Extve. Council, former Candn. Cong. of Lab.; mem., Candn. Cong. of Lab. Del. to 4th World Cong., I.C.F.T.U., Vienna; Del. to I.L.O. Geneva 1955; el. for 2 yrs. term as mem., B.C. Fed. of Lab. Extve. Council, 1956; Chrmn., Internat. Affairs Comte. from inception to 1964; concurrently mem., Candn. Lab. Cong. Standing Comte. on Internat. Affairs; apptd. to Council, N.W.T. 1964; Depy. Commr., 1965; Commr., 1967; Chrmn., Cdn. Section Internat. and Joint Commission Can. and the U.S. 1979-81; served with R.C.N. overseas, 1942-45; with H.M.C.S. "Monnow", escort frigate, on antisubmarine patrol in N. Atlantic; formerly mem., Publicity Comte., Brit. Empire Games; Dir., B.C. Round Table Athletic Soc.; John Howard Soc.; W. Can. Council of Christians and Jews; awarded Knight of Grace of St. John of Jerusalem Nov. 1971; Order of Can. (1978; Order of St. Lazarus (1980); Order of St. Hubert (1980); Public Serv. Achievement Award; Hon. LL.D., Univ. of Calgary 1977; Home: 4253 Thornhill Cres., Victoria, B.C. V8N 3G6; Office: c/o Ferry Corp., Victoria, B.C.

HOEMBERG, (Mrs.) Elisabeth, M.A.; author; university lecturer; b. Toronto, Ont., 31 Aug. 1909; d. Rev. Robert Arthur and Beatrice Alberta (Atkinson) Sims; e. Havergal Coll., Toronto, Ont.; Univ. of Toronto, B.A. 1931 and M.A. 1934; Sorbonne (Paris) 1931-32; Ont. Coll. of Educ., 1932-33; Gertrude Davis Exchange Schol., Univ. of Berlin, 1934-35; m. late Dr. Albert Hoemberg, 3 Sept. 1938; children: Philip, Peter, Beata; Reader on the British Dominions, Univ. of Toronto, 1936-38; Civilian Interpreter, B.A.-O.R., 1945-46; author of "Thy People, My People" (a diary of the war inside Germany), 1950; Address: Halfmoon Bay, B.C. V0N 1Y0

HOENIG, Julius, M.D.; educator; b. Prague, Czechoslovakia 11 Apl. 1916; s. Josua and Berta (Graz) H.; m. Inge d. late Ernst Greve 31 Jan. 1942; children: Elisabeth, Peter; PROF. AND CHRMN. OF PSYCHIATRY, MEMORIAL UNIV. OF NFLD. since 1969; co-author 'The Desegregation of the Mentally Ill' 1969; co-translator, "General Psychopathology" (1963) and "The Nature of Psychopathy" (1964) by K. Jaspers; served with RAMC 1943-46; Fellow, Royal Coll. Phys. (UK); Royal Coll. Psychiatrists (UK); Office: Health Sciences Centre, St. John's, Nfld. A1B 3V6.

HOENIGER, Frederick J. David, M.A., Ph.D.; educator; b. Goerlitz, Germany 25 Apl. 1921; s. George J. and Elli (Dohne) H.; e. Quaker Sch. Eerde, Ommen, Holland, Oxford Sch. Cert. 1938; Univ. of Toronto, Victoria Coll. B.A. 1946, M.A. 1948; Univ. of London Ph.D. 1954; m. Judith F. M. d. Guy Whitaker 13 Sept. 1954; children: Brian, Cathleen; PROF. OF CLASSICS, VICTORIA COLL., UNIV. OF TORONTO 1963- ; Lectr. Univ. of Sask. 1946-47; Lectr. present Coll. 1948-51, 1953-55, Asst. Prof. 1955, Assoc. Prof. 1961, Chrmn. of Classics 1969-72, Dir. Centre for Reformation & Renaissance Studies 1964-69, 1975-

79; Brit. Council Scholar 1951-53; Guggenheim Fellow 1964-65; Gen. Ed. "The Revels Plays" 1971- ; ed. or co-ed. various publs.; mem. North-Central Br. Renaissance Soc. Am. (Co-ordinating Secy. 1965-73); Candn. Soc. Renaissance Studies (Pres. 1976-78); Internat. Shakespeare Assn.; Toronto Field Naturalists (Pres. 1960-62); recreations: ornithology, book collecting, travel; Home: 133 Roxborough Dr., Toronto, Ont. M4W 1X5; Office: 315 Pratt Library, Victoria Coll., Toronto, Ont. M5S 1K7.

HOFFMEISTER, Maj-Gen. Bertram Meryl, C.B. (1945), C.B.E. (1944), D.S.O. (1943), E.D.; b. Vancouver, B.C., 15 May, 1907; s. Louis George and Flora Elizabeth (Rodway) H.; e. Pub. and High Schs., Vancouver, B.C.; m. Donalda Strauss 1935; commissioned in N.P.A.M. 1927 with Seaforth Highlanders Can.; promoted Capt. in 1934, Maj. 1939 and given command of a company; served in 2nd World War with great distinction: Commdr., Seaforth Highlanders Can. in Eng., 1939-40; returned to Can. and attended Jr. War Staff Course 1942; promoted Lieut.-Col. 1942 and O.C. Seaforth Highlanders Can.; led his regt. in assault on Sicily, July 1943 (D.S.O.); promoted Brig. and in command of 2nd Inf. Brig., Oct. 1943, taking part in Battle of Ortona 1943 (Bar to D.S.O.); promoted to Maj.-Gen., and apptd. to command 5th Armoured Divn. 1943 and took part in Liri Valley operation in 1944, terminating in smashing of Gustav and Hitler Lines (2nd Bar to D.S.O. and C.B.E.); took 5th Armoured Divn. into action in N.W. Europe, March 1945, into the campaigns around Nimegen and Arnheim; assigned to assault on the heavily fortified Frisian Islands when war ended (C.B.); apptd. Commdr. 6th Candn. Divn. (for operations in the Pacific) May 1945; retired from active service in September 1946; apptd. to command 15th Inf. Bgde. (Reserve) 1946; prior to war was Sales Mgr., Candn. White Pine Co. Ltd., Vancouver, B.C.; Commdr., U.S. Legion of Merit 1947; apptd. Vice-Pres. (Production), H. R. MacMillan Export Co. Ltd. (predecessor Co.) 1949; Pres., MacMillan & Bloedel Ltd., 1949, Chrmn., 1956-58; Agt. Gen. in London (Eng.) for B.C., 1958-61; Pres., Council of Forest Industries of Brit. Columbia 1961-68; recreations: shooting, skiing; Clubs: Vancouver; Capilano Golf & Country; Vancouver Rowing; Canadian; Address: 3040 Proctor, West Vancouver, B.C. V7V 1G1

HOFMANN, Theo, D.Sc.; educator; b. Zurich, Switzerland 20 Feb. 1924; s. Edwin and Hedwig (Moos) H.; e. Evangelische Mittelschule Schiers, Switzerland 1943; Swiss Fed. Inst. of Technol Dipl. Chem. Engn. 1947; D.Sc. 1950; m. Doris Topham d. late John Forbes 15 July 1953; three s. Martin Ian, Tony David, Peter Adrian; PROF. OF BIOCHEM. UNIV. OF TORONTO 1964- ; Post-doctoral Fellow, Univ. of Aberdeen 1950-52; Scient. Offr. Hannah Dairy Research Inst. 1952-56; Lectr. Univ. of Sheffield 1956-64; Visiting Sr. Scient. C.S.I.R.O., Animal Genetics Div. Sydney, Australia 1972; Visiting Prof. Univ. of Calif. Santa Cruz 1981; mem. Grants Comte. Med. Research Council Can. 1970-74; Assoc. Ed. "Canadian Journal of Biochemistry" 1970-72; author over 90 articles and reviews structure & function of proteins scient. journs. and books; mem. Candn. Biochem. Soc.; Biochem. Soc. (UK); Am. Soc. Biol. Chems.; Treas. 1977-78, Univ. of Toronto Faculty Assn.; NDP; recreations: ornithology, canoeing, Scottish country dancing, photography, hiking, skiing; Home: 199 Arnold Ave., Thornhill, Ont. L4J 1C1; Office: Toronto, Ont. M5S 1A8.

HOFSESS, John Leonard; film director; writer; b. Hamilton, Ont. 27 May 1938; s. Jack Leonard and Gladys May (Van Valkenburg) H.; e. McMaster Univ. 1965; Asst. Ed., Maclean's Magazine; film critic and author of monthly columns and features since 1970; Contrib. Ed., "Take One" Canadian Film Magazine, 1967-72; Writer-Dir. feature film "Palace of Pleasure", 1967 (1st Prize Vancouver Internat. Film Festival 1967 and Candn. Artists' Exhn., Art Gallery of Ont. 1968); writer, "Issues

and Episodes in Canadian History" and "Ontario Arts Seen", CICA TV, 1971; Writer and Interviewer, Andrew McLaglen, CICA TV, 1971; writer, feature film "Columbus of Sex", 1969; author, "Mocking the Afflicted", 1974; "How to Survive Middle Age", 1975; 'Inner Views: Ten Canadian Film-makers', 1975; "Lay of the Land", 1975; past contrib. to various newspapers and mags.; Home: 115 Main St. E., Apt. 1204, Hamilton, Ont. L8N 1G5; Office: 481 University Ave., Toronto, Ont. M5G 1W8

HOGG, Benjamin G., B.Sc., M.A., Ph.D., F.R.S.C.; physicist; b. Winnipeg, Man., 26 July 1924; s. David Cochrane and Harriet (Olwen) H.; e. Univ. of Man., B.Sc. 1946; Wesleyan Univ. (Conn.), M.A. 1947; McMaster Univ., Ph.D. 1953; m. Emilie (d) d. Anton Shipel, June 1949; children: David, Kristine; PROF. OF PHYSICS, UNIV. OF WINNIPEG since 1972; Research Scientist, Defence Research Bd., 1949-51; Royal Mil. Coll. 1954-57; Prof., Univ. of Man., 1957-72 and Grad. Dean there 1969-72; Vice Pres. (Academic), Univ. of Winnipeg, 1972-78; Prof. of Physics, Univ. of Winnipeg, 1972- ; Gast Prof., Max Planck Inst., 1964; NCR Exchange Scientist. Inst. Chem. Physics, USSR Acad. of Sciences, 1970; Visiting Scientist NRC-CNRS Exchange 1978-79, Saclay, France; author of over 65 research papers on mass spectroscopy and positron annihilation; mem., Candn. Assn. Physicists (Past. Dir.; Past. Councillor); Sigma Xi (Pres., Univ. of Man. cap. 1978); awarded Silver Jubilee Medal, 1977; recreations: sailing, skiing; Home: 1587 Wolseley Ave., Winnipeg, Man. R3G 1J2

HOGG, Mrs. Helen Battles Sawyer, O.C. (1968), C. C. (1976), A.M., Ph.D., D.Sc., F.R.S.C.; astronomer; her ancestors played an important role in the hist. of New Eng.; b. Lowell, Mass. 1 Aug. 1905; d. Edward Everett (former Vice-Pres. Union Nat. Bank, Lowell, Mass.) and Carrie Myra (Sprague) S.; e. Charles W. Morey Sch., Lowell, Mass.; Lowell High Sch.; Mount Holyoke Coll., A.B. (Hons.) 1926, D.Sc. 1958; D.Sc., McMaster Univ. 1976; Univ. of Toronto 1977; D.Litt., St. Mary's Univ. 1981; Radcliffe Coll., A.M. 1928, Ph.D. 1931; D.Sc. Waterloo 1962; m. Frank Scott (d. 1951), s. Dr. Jas. Scott Hogg, 6 Sept. 1930; children: Sarah, David, James; PROF. EMERITUS, UNIVERSITY OF TORONTO since 1976 (Asst. Prof. 1951, Assoc. Prof. 1955, Prof. 1957); Pickering Fellow, Harvard Coll. Observ. 1926-30; Lectr., Smith Coll. 1927, Mount Holyoke Coll. 1930-31; Research Assoc., Dom. Astrophys. Observ. 1931-34; Research Assoc. and Lectr., David Dunlap Observ., Univ. of Toronto, since 1936; Research (Nat. Acad. of Sciences) Steward Observ., Univ. of Arizona, 1939; later Asst. Prof. and Acting Chrmn., Dept. of Astron., Mt. Holyoke Coll.; mem., Am. Astron. Soc. (awarded Annie J. Cannon Prize, 1949); Roy. Astron. Soc. of Can. (Pres. 1957-59, recd. Service Medal 1967, Hon. Pres. 1977-78); Internat. Astron. Union; Am. Assn. of Variable Star Observers (Pres. 1940-41); Pres., Sec. III, Royal Soc. Can. 1960-61; Visiting Prof., Harvard Univ. Summer Sch. 1952; given leave of absence to serve with Nat. Science Foundation, Washington, D.C., as Program Dir. for Astronomy, Aug. 1955; rec'd. Citation, Mount Holyoke Coll., 1952; el. Pres. (1st Woman), Royal Candn. Inst., 1964; rec'd Radcliffe Grad. Achievement Medal 1967; Centennial Medal; Rittenhouse Silver Medal (1st Candn.) 1967; Silver Jubilee Medal, 1977; D.Sc., McMaster Univ. 1976; Univ. of Toronto1977; mem., Bd. of Dirs., Bell Canada, 1968-78; 1st President, Candn. Astron. Soc. (1971-72); Astron. Columnist, Toronto Star, since 1951-81; has contributed numerous papers on globular star clusters and variable stars to various tech. journs.; Phi Beta Kappa; Sigma Xi; Protestant; recreations: stamps, handiwork; Home: 98 Richmond St., Richmond Hill, Ont. L4C 3Y4; Office: David Dunlap Observatory, Richmond Hill, Ont.L4C 4Y6

HOGG, William MacDougall, C.M., B.A.Sc., M.E.I.C., P.Engn.; civil engineer; corporation executive; b. Chippewa, Ont.; s. late William and late Cecilia (MacDougall) H.; e. Chippewa (Ont.) Public Sch.; Niagara Falls (Ont.) Coll. Inst.; Univ. of Toronto, B.A.Sc. 1939; m. late Mona E., d. late John Angus MacPherson, Niagara Falls, Ont., 1 June 1940; children: Carolyn (Mrs. J. Philip Harrington), Eleanor (Mrs. M. Kuntz, M.D.), William R.; DIR., GREAT LAKES POWER CORP. LTD.; Dir., St. Mary's Bridge Co.; Butchawana Band Industries; mem., Adv. Bd., Royal Trust Co.; prior to grad. with Ont. Hydro as Surveyor and Engr. on survey and constr. work throughout Ont.; with Ont. Hydro as Design Engr., 1939, Project Engr., 1946, Sr. Resident Engr., Des Joachims Power Development, 1949, Field Project Engr., Sir Adam Beck Power Devel., 1951; St. Lawrence Power Development, 1954; in 1957 joined Great Lakes Power Corpn. Ltd. as Vice-Pres. and Chief Engr.; mem. (Pres. 1959, Chrmn. 1971), Elect. Utilities Safety Assn.; Dir., & Past Pres., Y.M.C.A.; Candn. Rep., Internat. Bridge Authority of Mich.; Chrmn., Algoma Dist. Homes for Aged; Trustee & Past Pres., United Way; founder Dir. of Algoma Coll., & mem. of Adv. Bd., Algoma Coll.; Dir., Art Gallery of Algoma; Pres. of Bd. Plummer Memorial Hospital; member Operations Action, Upper Peninsula Mich.; Engn. Inst. of Can.; Assn. of Prof. Engrs. Ont.; Am. Soc. for Metals; Past Pres., Sault Ste. Marie Chamber of Comm.; mem. of the Bd. of Trustees Central Un. Ch.; Adv. Council Salvation Army; Algoma Health Council Committee on Aging; Recip. Order of Can.; Centennial Medal; Jubilee Medal; City of Sault Ste Marie Medal of Merit; Assn. of Prof. Eng. Ont. Citizenship Award; Sons of Martha Medal; Freemason; Anglican; recreations: gardening, athletics; Clubs: Kiwanis; Algo Club; Niagara Falls; Home: 62 Oak Park Crescent, Sault Ste. Marie, Ont. P6A 5A9; Office: 122 East St., Box 100, Sault Ste. Marie, Ont. P6A 5L4

HOHOL, Hon. Albert Edward, M.L.A., B.Ed., M.Ed., Ph.D.; b. Two Hills, Alta., 27 Dec. 1922; s. George Harry and Mary (Ruptash) H.; e. Univ. of Alta., B.Ed. 1950, M.Ed. 1954; Univ. of Ore., Ph.D. 1967; m. Katherine, d. late John Chrapko, 1 Sept. 1946; children: Milton David, Barbara Lynn; Mem., Workers Compensation Board, Edmonton, Alta.; Min. of Alta. Advanced Education and Manpower, 1975-79; former Min. of Manpower & Labour; Teacher and Princ., Clover Bar Sch. Dist., 1947; Sch. Princ., Two Hills, Alta., 1955; Asst. Princ., W. Jasper Pl. Sch. Dist., 1957, Supt. of Jr. High Schs. there 1959, Adm. Asst. of Dist. 1960, Supt. of Schs. 1963; Asst. Supt. of Pupil Personnel Services, Edmonton Pub. Sch. Bd. 1964-68; Assoc. Supt.-Educ. Adm. 1969-71; served with RCAF during World War II; el. MLA for Edmonton-Belmont prov. g.e. 1971 and apptd. Min. of Labour, Alta.; has been active mem. of Candn. Mental Health Assn.; Boys' Club of Edmonton; also served on Prov. Adv. Comte. on Juvenile Delinquency; H.R.D.A. Comte. on Misuse of Drugs & Narcotics; Juvenile Corrections Implementation Comte.; mem., W.C.B. of Alberta; mem., Internat. Assn. Govt'al Labour Officials (Extve. Bd.); mem; Extve. Bd. of Dirs., Alberta College; Educ. Soc.; Phi Delta Kappa (Charter mem.); co-author (with SafrAn and Zingle) "Decision Making"; mem. Bd. of Dirs., British Commonwealth Games Comte.; mem., Bd. of Stewards, Robertson United Church; Fellow, Royal Soc. of Arts; P. Conservative; Protestant; recreations: reading, golf, music; Office: 9912-107 St., Edmonton, Alta.

HOLBROOK, Elizabeth Bradford, R.C.A.; sculptor; b. Hamilton, Ont. 7 Nov. 1913; d. William Ashford and Alma Victoria (Carpenter) Bradford; e. elem. schs. Hamilton; Hamilton Tech. Sch. (Art) and Hamilton Conserv. of Music (Piano) 1929; Ont. Coll. of Art (Sculpture) 1934, postgrad. work with E. Hahn 1935 (Lt. Gov.'s Silver Medal for Sculpture; Royal Coll. of Art London, Eng. 1936; Cranbrook Acad. of Art Bloomfield Hills, Mich. 1948; m. John Grant Holbrook, D.D.S. 3 Aug. 1936; children: John David, M.D., Elizabeth Jane, William Howard (d.); Assoc. and Alumnist, Ont. Coll. of Art; stone sculpture Royal Bot. Gdns. Hamilton 1937; 2 stone panels

Hamilton Fed. Bldg. 1955; bronze portrait Emanuel Hahn Nat. Gallery Can. 1957; Ellen M. Fairclough Parlt. Bldgs. 1967; Rabbi Bernard Baskin, Anshe Shalom Temple Hamilton, Ont. 1969; Dr. Charles Comfort, Royal Candn. Acad. 1971; Carl Schaefer Art Gallery of Ont. 1974; Frank Panabaker Art Gallery of Hamilton, also Emanuel Hahn #2 1974; James Babcock Hamilton Golf & Country Club 1976; bronze plaque former Mayor Lloyd Jackson Hamilton 1979; liturgical sculpture Altar Frontal St. John's Ang. Ch. Ancaster 1978, St. Mark's Ch. Kitsilane 1980-81 (both oak); bronze portrait Hon. John Diefenbaker 1980; struck medal of Ambassador Kenneth D. Taylor 1980; solo sculpture exhns. Art Gallery of Hamilton 1974; Sisler Gallery Toronto 1976; McMaster Med. Centre Gallery 1978; rep. in Fed. of Internat. Medallists Prague, Cologne, Helsinki, Cracow, Lisbon; Women Medallists of Can. Pub. Archives Ottawa 1980; rec'd Gold Medal for Portraiture, Nat. Sculpture Soc. New York 1969; mem. Candn. Hunter Improvement Soc. (Hon. Dir., Past Pres. 1968-69); Candn. Pony Club (Adv. Bd.); Ont. Soc. Artists; Sculptors Soc. Can.; Candn. Equestrian Fed. (retired Sr. Judge Ont. Div.); Liberal; Anglican; recreation: equestrian; Clubs: Zonta Internat.; Hamilton Hunt; Home: "Brookford" 1177 Mineral Springs Rd., R.R.3, Dundas, Ont. L9H 5E3.

HOLBROOK, George W., M.Sc., Ph.D.; retired Canadian public servant; b. Asquith, Sask. 16 Dec. 1917; s. Alfred and Florence (Cutler) H.; e. Hastings Private Sch., Eng.; London Univ.; Eng., B.Sc. 1938, Ph.D. 1956; Queen's Univ. 1948-49, M.Sc. Elec. Engn.; D.Sc. (H.C.) Royal Mil. Coll. Can. 1980; m. Frances Mary (Fletcher) 22 Nov. 1944; children: John Adam Duncan, Peter George, Mary Jane Louise; CONSULTANT; joined Transmission and Devel. Lab., Standard Telephone & Cables (London, Eng.); served Brit. Terr. Army Feb. 1939; Royal Corps of Signals, armoured and airborne formations until demob. rank of Major, Feb. 1946; joined Candn. Army as Chief Instr., Royal Candn. Sch. of Signals 1946; promoted Lieut. Col., posted to Dept. of Elect. Engn., Royal Mil. Coll. 1950; Head of Dept. 1952; retired Candn. Army to become Prof. of Elect. Engn. Jan. 1952; Pres. and Vice-Chrmn., Nova Scotia Tech. Coll. 1961-71; Dir.-Gen. Communications Research Centre, Dept. of Communications to July 1975; Adjunct Prof., Tech. Univ. of N.S., Nov. 1977; mem., Inst. of Elect. Engrs.; Fellow, Engn. Inst. Can.; Assn. Prof. Engrs., N.S.; Anglican; recreation: sailing; Office: Tantallon, Halifax County, N.S. B0J 3J0

HOLLAND, Hon. John, B.A.; judge; b. Toronto, Ont., 4 Oct. 1917; s. late John and late' Hannah Clark (Christie) H.; e. Univ. of W. Ont. B.A. 1941; Osgoode Hall Law Sch. 1948; m. Mary Agnes d. Courtney Chick, 24 Feb. 1944; children: Nan Polleys, John C., Melissa Costigan, Mary Agnes, Dan; JUSTICE, SUPREME COURT OF ONT. since 1975; called to Bar of Ont. 1948; cr. Q.C. 1958; Assoc. McTague law firm 1945-58, Partner 1948-75; served with RCNVR 1940-45; mem. Candn. Bar Assn.; Advocates Soc.; Essex Co. Med. Legal Soc.; Essex Law Assn.; Internat. Assn. Ins. Counsel; mem. Royal Candn. Mil. Inst.; Anglican; recreations: swimming, golf; Clubs: Windsor; Beach Grove Golf; Windsor Yacht; Home: 57 Widdicombe Hill Blvd., Weston, Ont. M9R 1Y4; Office: Osgoode Hall, Toronto, Ont. M5H 2N6

HOLLAND, Hon. Richard Estcourt, B.A.; judge; b. London, Eng., 9 Sept. 1925; s. Percy Estcourt and Nesta (Owen) H.; e. Primary Schs., France and Eng.; Univ. of Toronto, B.A. 1947; Osgoode Hall Law Sch., 1950; m. Nancy Margaret, d. John Milford Wyatt, 28 Aug. 1948; two d., Anne Estcourt, Suzanne Estcourt; JUSTICE, SUPREME COURT OF ONTARIO, since 1972; called to Bar of Ont. 1950; cr. Q.C. 1962; practised with Hughes, Agar, Amys & Steen, Toronto for 4 yrs.; assisted in forming firm of Bassel, Sullivan, Holland & Lawson continuing practice in partnership until present appt.; served with Candn. Army 1943-45; Past Pres., Cdn. Inst. for Administration of Justice; Anglican; recreations: fishing, shooting; Clubs: Caledon Mountain Trout; Canard Gun; Home: 86 Dunloe Rd., Toronto, Ont. M4V 2Y9; Office: 130 Queen St. W., Toronto, Ont. M5H 2N5

HOLLANDER, Samuel, B.Sc.Econ., A.M., Ph.D., F.R.S.C.; b. London, Eng. 6 Apl. 1937; s. Jacob and Rachel Lily (Bornstein) H.; e. Letchworth Grammar Sch. Eng. 1951; Hendon Co. Sch. London, Eng. 1953; Gateshead (Eng.) Talmudical Acad. 1954; Hendon Tech. Sch. London 1955; Kilburn Polytech. London 1956; London Sch. of Econ. B.Sc. (Econ.) 1959; Princeton Univ. A.M. 1961, Ph.D. 1963; m. Perlette d. late Elie Kéroub 20 July 1959 in Paris, France; children: Frances, Isaac; PROF. OF ECON. UNIV. OF TORONTO; rec'd Sir Edward Gonner Prize 1959; Guggenheim Fellowship 1968-69; Killam Fellowship 1973-75; author "The Sources of Increased Efficiency" 1965; "The Economics of Adam Smith" 1973; "The Economics of David Ricardo". 1979; various articles prof. journs.; recreation: travel; Home: 87 Searle Ave., Downsview, Ont. M3H 4A6; Office: 100 St. George St., Toronto, Ont. M5S 1A1.

HOLLING, Crawford Stanley, M.A., Ph.D., F.R.S.C.; scientist; b. Theresa. N.Y. 6 Dec. 1930; s. Dr. Stanley Arnold and Claude Anne (Guichard) H.; came to Can. 1935; e. Univ. of Toronto B.A. 1952, M.A. 1954; Univ. of B.C. Ph.D. (Zool.) 1957; m. Ilse Artner 26 Aug. 1978; children: Christopher, Nancy, James; DIR., INTERNAT. INST. FOR APPLIED SYSTEMS ANALYSIS 1981- ; Project Leader Ecology & Environment 1973-75, Hon. Fellow 1975; Consultant: U.S. Fish & Wildlife Service, Office of Biol. Services, Washington, D.C. 1978- ; Environment Can. Planning & Finance Ottawa 1975-77; Ford Foundation, N.Y. 1967-74 (Ecology); Research Offr., Forest Insect Lab., Can. Dept. Forestry, Sault Ste. Marie, Ont. 1952-64, Scient. 4, Forest Research Lab. Victoria, B.C. 1965-67; Visiting Colleague Univ. of Hawaii and Bureau of Comm. Fisheries Honolulu 1964-65; Visiting Prof. of Entomol. & Parasitol. Univ. of Calif. Berkeley 1965; Prof. Inst. Animal Resource Ecol. and Dept. Zool. Univ. of B.C. 1967-81, Hon. Prof. of Community & Regional Planning 1969- , Dir. Inst. Animal Resource Ecol. 1969-73; Affiliate Prof. Univ. of Idaho and Univ. of Wash.; Assoc., Natural Resource Inst. Univ. of Man.; mem. Candn. Ad Hoc Adv. Group NATO Science Comte. 1977-81, mem. Special Program on Eco-sciences 1976-80, Chrmn. Eco-Science Panel 1978-80; Visiting Distinguished Prof. of Econ. Univ. of Colo.; mem. Nat. Adv. Bd. Ecosystems Research Center Cornell Univ.; author, co-author, ed. and mem. ed. bds. various publs.; Fellow, Am. Assn. Advanc. Science; mem. Ecol. Soc. Am.; Brit. Ecol. Soc.; Japanese Ecol. Soc.; Candn. Ecol. Soc. Zools.; Candn. Entomol. Soc.; mem. Bd. Internat. Stat. Ecol. Program; recipient Anne Shepard Mem. Scholarship in Biol. 1951 and Gold Medal Biol. 1952; Nat. Research Council Can. Scholarship 1953; George Mercer Award Ecol. Soc. Am. 1966; Gold Medal Entomol. Soc. Can. 1969-70; Home: Schweizertalstrasse 24, 1130 Vienna, Austria; Office: Schlossplatz 1, 2361 Laxenburg, Austria.

HOLMAN, Donald Morison, C.D., B.Sc., M.Eng.; teacher (ret.); b. Pittsburgh, Pa., 15 Feb. 1916; s. late Prof. William Ludlow and Mary (Morison) H.; e. Univ. of Toronto Schs.; Royal Mil. Coll., Dipl. (Hons.); Univ. of Toronto, B.Sc. (Aeronautical-Hons.); Royal Mil. Coll., M.Eng.; RCAF Staff Coll.; Nat. Defence Coll.; m. Frances Margaret, d. late Donald Macdonald, 15 June 1940; children: Donald Fraser, Susan Ellen, Robert Alan; during World War II served with Air Force HQ (Aero Engr.); Test and Devel. Estab. (Chief Project Engr.); RCAF Overseas HQ (Aero Engr.); various Candn. bomber bases in U.K.; ended War as Chief Tech. Offr., RCAF Stn. Wombleton; Field Information Agency (Tech.), Germany; mem., Candn. Jt. Staff, Washington, D.C. and RCAF Resident Engn. Offr., Avro (Canada) Ltd., 1946-48; held various staff appts. RCAF Air Material Command, 1950-

58; RCAF Air Div. Europe, Planning Team and Staff Offr. Aeronautical Engn., 1952-53; Dir. of Instrument & Elect. Engn. Air Force HQ, 1959-60; Depy. Chief, Logistics Div., Air Material Comd., becoming Chief, 1960-65; Depy. Chief of Staff Logistics, Candn. Forces Material Command, 1965-66; Air Force mem., Dir. Staff, Nat. Defence Coll. 1966-68, Commandant 1968-69; retired from armed forces, rank Air Commodore; Associate Professor Mechanical Engineering, Royal Military College 1970-1980; Fellow, Canadian Aero. and Space Inst.; Alpha Delta Phi; Anglican; recreations: sailing, skiing, music; Clubs: Kingston Yacht; RMC Ex Cadet; Home: Lot 3, Milton-on-the-St. Lawrence, R.R. 1, Kingston, Ont. K7L 4V1;

HOLMAN, Donald R., B.F.A., R.C.A.; printmaker; b. Kansas City, Mo. 20 May 1946; s. Thomas C. and Vanida (Ball) H.; e. Allen Sch. and Westport High Sch. Kansas City; Kansas City Art Inst. B.F.A. 1968; came to Can. 1968; m. Elizabeth Louise d. Arnold Zetlin 7 Aug. 1979; children: Chiah, Ira Zingraff; Dir. of Lithography, Open Studio; Sr. Tutor, Scarborough Coll. Univ. of Toronto; rep. in exhns. Can., USA, Europe, Mexico, Hong Kong; rep. nat. and internat. pub. colls.; mem. Ont. Soc. Artists; Print & Drawing Council Can.; Address: 44 Spruce St., Toronto, Ont. M5A 5L9.

HOLMES, A. Bruce, C.L.U.; insurance executive; b. Newton, Ont. 5 Nov. 1928; s. Alexander E. and Mary Stuart (Magwood) H.; e. Listowel High Sch.; m. Grace d. John Harris 1949; children: Linda, Deborah, Pamela, Paul, Mark; VICE PRES. PERSONAL INS. OPERATIONS & PLANNING, METROPOLITAN LIFE INSURANCE CO. 1980- ; joined H.O. Manufacturers Life Insurance Co. 1946; Loblaws Ltd. 1950; Agt. present Co. 1951, Asst. Mgr. Scarborough Dist. 1952, Field Training Instr. CHO 1955, Territorial Field Supvr. CHO 1955, Dist. Mgr. London 1959, Regional Sales Mgr. Toronto 1969; Area Chrmn. Red Feather London; Campaign Chrmn. Riverside Un. Ch. London; mem. Bd. Trade Metrop. Toronto: Life Underwriters Assn. Can.; Candn. Life & Health Ins. Assn.; Life Mgrs. Assn. (Toronto); recreations: sports, canoeing, reading, gardening, jogging; Club: Mississauga Canoe (Commodore); 38 The Masters Dr., Ottawa, Ont. K1V 9Y4; Office: 99 Bank St., Ottawa, Ont. K1P 5A3.

HOLMES, James, B.Sc.; executive; b. Stacksteads, Lancashire, Eng. 24 Oct. 1919; came to Can. 1949; s. David Thomas and Emily (Hill) H.; e. Univ. of London B Sc., 1949; m. Mildred Alice d. John David Deans 14 July 1943; children: David Caird, Barbara Mary; CHRMN. AND CHIEF EXTVE. OFFR., HOMEWARE INDUSTRIES LTD. since 1981; Dir., Candn. Manuf. Assoc.; Homeware Industries Ltd.; Homeware Ltd.; Ronyx Corp. Ltd.; Vulcan Industrial Packaging Ltd.; Gen. Aluminum Forgings (U.S.) Ltd.; held various positions with Canadian Pacific incl. Sr. Research Econ., mem. of planning team in the office of Chrmn. and Pres., Treasurer of C.P. Ltd. and C.P. Investments Ltd., 1949-69; Vice Pres., Finance, Falconbridge Nickel Mines Ltd. (Toronto) and Falconbridge Dominicana (Santa Domingo, D.R.), 1970-76; Chrmn. and Chief Extve. Offr., Electrohome Ltd., Kitchener, 1977-80; Chrmn. Central Ont. Telev. Ltd., Kitchener, 1977-80; served with RAF, 1940-46; mem., Finance Council, Am. Management Assn.; Anglican; Club: Oakville; recreations: squash, tennis, skiing; Home: 149 Suffolk Ave., Oakville, Ont. L6K 2L5; Office: 945 Wilson Ave., Downsview, Ont. M3K 1E8.

HOLMES, James Murray, B.Sc., M.A., Ph.D.; chemist; university professor; b. Doaktown, N.B. 30 Sept. 1919; s. Akeley and Elsie Jean McKay (Murray) H.; e. pub. sch. Doaktown, N.G. 1925-35; High Sch. Newcastle N.B. 1935-36; Univ. of N.B. B.Sc. 1936-40; Univ. of W. Ont. M.A. 1940-42; McGill Univ. Ph.D. 1942-44; m. Helen Hargrave d. late John Hill 6 Sept. 1946; children: Janet Murray, John Akeley, Jean Elizabeth; PROF. OF CHEMIS-

TRY, CARLETON UNIV. since 1961 (Chrmn. 1957-69, 1970-73); Chrmn. East. Ont. Sci. Ed. Council; Chrmn. Bd. Dir. Triangle Treelands Ltd.; Sess. Lectr. McGill Univ. 1946-48; came to Carleton Univ. as Lectr. 1948-49; Asst. Prof. 1949-53; Assoc. Prof. 1953-61; Sabbatical leave Univ. of Washington 1960-61; Univ. of Bristol, Eng. 1969-70; N.R.C., Ottawa 1981-82; Candn. Offr. Training Corps, rank Lt., 1936-42; Candn. Army, Reg. rank Lt. Chemical Warfare Serv., 1944-46; Carleton Univ. Contingent COTC, rank Capt., sec. in command, 1952-55; as Major, Officer Commanding, 1955-60; Supp. reserve as major 1968; rec'd Centennial Medal 1967; C.D. and bar; rec'd Beaverbrook Scholarship Univ. of N.B. 1936-40; Chem. Ed. Award, Chem. Inst. of Can. 1973; Chrmn. Gordon Res. Conf. on Interfaces 1963; Chrmn. local arrangements 37th and 47th Natl. Colloid Symp. 1963, 1973; Ont. Cmte. Student Awards 1965-69 (Chrmn. 1968-69); Cmte. on Univ. Affairs 1972-74; Chrmn. Conf. comte. Annual Conf. of Chem. Inst. of Can. 1980; Bd. of Gov. Carleton Univ. 1972-81; author of twenty research papers on adsorption of gases at low temps.; preparation and surface properties of precipitated calcium phosphates; mem., Chem. Inst. of Can.; Am. Chem. Soc.; Royal Soc. of Chem. (Engl.); Can. Assoc. of Univ. Teachers; Science Teacher's Assoc. of Ont.; Sigma Xi; P. Conservative; United Church; Clubs: Carleton Univ. Faculty; Ottawa Hunt and Golf; recreations: golf, photography, fishing, travel; Home: 60 Grove Ave., Ottawa, Ont. K1S 3A8:Office: Colonel By Drive, Ottawa, Ont. K1S 5B6.

HOLMES, John Wendell, O.C. (1969), LL.D., D.C.L., D.Litt., F.R.S.C., M.A.; b. London, Ont., 18 June 1910; s. Wendell and Helen (Morton) H.; e. Univ. of Western Ont., B.A. 1932; Univ. of Toronto, M.A. 1933; Univ. of London (Eng.) 1938-40; CLAUDE T. BISSELL PROF. OF CAN.-AM. RELATIONS, UNIV. OF TORONTO 1980-81; PROF. OF INTERNAT. REL., UNIVERSITY OF TORONTO 1981- ; Counsellor, Candn. Inst. of Internat. Affairs; mem., U.N. Advisory Bd. on Disarmament Studies; Visiting Prof. of Modern Commonwealth History, Univ. of Leeds, Eng. 1979; Bd. of Dirs., Internat. Peace Acad.; English Master, Pickering College, Ontario 1933-38; Information Secretary, Canadian Inst. of International Affairs, Toronto, Ont., 1940-41, and National Secy. there 1941-43; joined Dept. of External Affairs, Ottawa, 1943; 1st Secy., Canada House, London, 1944-47; Chargé d'affaires, Candn. Embassy, Moscow, 1947-48; Head of U.N. Div., Dept. of External Affairs, Ottawa, 1949-51; Acting Permanent Rep. of Can. to U.N., 1950-51; mem., Directing Staff, Nat. Defence Coll., 1951-53; Asst. Under-Secy. of State for External Affairs, Ottawa, 1953-60; retired from pub. service, 1960; Visiting Prof., Univ. of Leeds, Eng. 1979; Claude T. Bissell Prof., Univ. of Toronto 1980-81;author of: "The Better Part of Valour: Essays on Canadian Diplomacy", 1970; "Canada: A Middle-Aged Power"; "The Shaping of Peace: Canada and the Search for World Order, 1943-57"; vol. 1, 1979, vol. 2 (forthcoming); "Life with Uncle: The Canadian American Relationship; Home: 36 Castle Frank Rd., Toronto, Ont. M4W 2Z6; Office: 15 King's College Circle, Toronto, Ont. M5S 2V9

HOLMES, Philip D. Pemberton, , D.F.C., K.L.J., F.R.I., R.I. (B.C.); realtor; b. Victoria, B.C., 2 Feb. 1924; s. Henry Cuthbert and Philippa Despard (Pemberton) H.; e. Brentwood Coll., Victoria, 1935-40; Univ. of Victoria, 1940-41; m. 1stly 4 June 1946; m. 2ndly Catherine Cecily Anne, d. late Cecil John Webb, 22 Aug. 1964; children: Diana Joan, Susan Philippa, Jennifer Cicely: PRESIDENT AND DIR., PEMBERTON, HOLMES LTD. since 1965; Pres., Pemberton Parkade Ltd.; Fort Mortgage Corp.; Pres. Internat. Real Estate Fed., F.I.A.B.C.I., 1975-77; Pres., Victoria Ins. Agents Assn., 1958; Victoria Real Estate Bd., 1960; B.C. Assn. Real Estate Bds., 1961; joined present firm (4th generation) 1945; mem., Council of Ins. Agents of B.C., 1959; Dir., Soc. Residential Appraisers (Victoria Chapter # 48), 1950; Real Estate Inst. B.C., 1961, (Gov. of Div.

1961-65); Pres., Candn. Assn. Real Estate Bds., 1966; Dir., National Assn. of Real Estate Bds. (U.S.A.) 1966; Chrmn., Candn. Chapter, Internat. Real Estate Fed. 1974-75; mem., Real Estate Council of B.C., 1962-68; apptd. to Canadian Housing Design Council 1967; to Saanich Adv. Planning Comn. 1967; Dir., Victoria Visitors Bureau, 1968; Vice-Pres., MacPherson Playhouse Fdn. 1980-82; Pres., Victoria Downtown Business Assn. 1979-81; Greater Victoria Chamber Comm. 1970; Pres., Assoc. Chamber Comm. of Van. Is. 1973; served with 433 Sqd., # 6 Bomber Grp. RCAF in Europe, 1941-45; retired as Sqdn. Leader; 1st C.O., # 2455 A.C. & W Sqdn. (Auxiliary), 1950; Pres., Air Force Offrs. Assn. of Vancouver Island, 1950; App't Hon. Lt.-Colonel #11 (Victoria) Service Battalion 1981; Gov., Brentwood Coll. Sch. 1972-82; Extve., Candn. Council of Christians and Jews; Hon. Citizen, City of Victoria; Hon. A. de C. to Lt. Gov. of B.C., 1978-82; Appt. to Provincial Capital Comm., 1980; Bd. of Gov., Univ. of Victoria 1980-83; P. Conservative; Protestant; recreation: sailing; Clubs: Union; Royal Victoria Yacht: Home: 488 Beach Dr., Victoria, B.C. V8S 2M5; Office: 1000 Government, Victoria, B.C. V8W 1X8

HOLMES, Raymond Henry Lavergne, M.Sc., A.M., Ph.D., F.R.S.C.; retired research chemist; b. Ottawa, Ont., 28 June 1911; s. Charles William and Addie (Crisp) H.; e. Queen's Univ., B.Sc., 1934, M.Sc. 1935; Harvard Univ., M.A. 1937, Ph.D. 1938; Med. Inst., Graz Univ., Austria (Dipl.) 1938; Oxford Univ., Visiting Prof. (1938-39); Mass. Inst. Tech., Research Asst. (1939-40); Harvard Univ., Private Asst. (1940-41); Asst. and Assoc. Prof., Univ. of Sask., 1941-47; Assoc. Prof., Univ. of B.C., 1947-49; Harvard Fellow, 1949-50; Dir. Organic Research, Riker Chemical Co., 1950-53; Mass. Inst. Tech., 1953-54; Lincoln Laboratories, 1954-56; Research Chemist, Defense Research Bd. 1960-79 (ret.); Protestant; Address: 156 Third St. N.E., Medicine Hat, Alta. T1A 5M1.

HOLMES, Richard Brian, M.D., M.Sc., FRCPS(C); educator; b. London, Ont. 11 Dec. 1919; s. Dr. L. Seale and Haroldine (Goble) H.; e. Univ. W. Ont. M.D. 1943, M.Sc 1949, LL.D. 1978; m. Barbara Louise, d. Hubert H. Reid, 28 Apl. 1945; children: Richard Seale, Diane Elizabeth, Erin Louise, Katherine Jane; Dean of Medicine, Univ. of Toronto 1973-80; Prof. and Chrmn. Dept. of Radiol. 1965-72; Radiologist-in-Chief, Toronto Gen. Hosp. 1965; served with RCAMC during World War II; rank Capt.; Chrmn., ONTARIO COUNCIL HEALTH 1981; Fellow, Am. Coll. Radiol. 1956 Gold Medallist 1980; mem. Candn. Assn. Radiols. (Past Pres.); Bd. of Dirs., Gairdner Fdn.; Radiol. Soc. N. Am. (Pres. 1976, Gold Medallist 1981); Am. Roentgen Ray Soc.; Ont. & Candn. Med. Assns.; Assn. Candn. Med. Coll. (Pres. 1977); Silver Jubilee Award; recreations: golf, philately, rural retreat; Home: 44 Charles St. W., Apt. 3609, Toronto, Ont. M4Y 1R5; Office: c/o Ont. Council of Health, 700 Bay St., Toronto Ont. M5G 1Z6

HOLMES, Thomas Edward; insurance executive; b. Regina, Sask. 10 Nov. 1932; s. Edward Sloan and Mary Ulah (McFadden) H.; e. Magee High Sch. Vancouver, B.C.; m. Cecilia Theresa d. Henry Karl Linnhoff 4 Sept. 1954; children: Karen Teresa, Paul Karl; PRES. AND CHIEF EXTVE. OFFR., INSURANCE CORP. OF BRITISH COLUMBIA 1980- ; Prop., T.E. Holmes Insurance Agency Ltd. Vancouver 1961-66; Gen. Mgr. B.C. Motorists Insurance Co. and B.C.A.A. Holdings Ltd. 1966-76; Sr. Vice Pres. Autoplan, Insurance Corp. of B.C. 1976-80; Anglican; recreations: numismatics, golf, curling, racketball; Office: Box 11131 Royal Centre, 1055 W. Georgia St., Vancouver, B.C. V6E 3R4.

HOLTBY, Philip Norman; investment dealer; b. Toronto, Ont. 1931; e. Ridley Coll. St. Catharines, Ont., Ont. Coll. Art Toronto; m. Evalon Schury; children: Caren, Ann, Christopher, Markus; VICE CHRMN. AND PRES., MIDLAND DOHERTY LTD.: Dir. Unicorp Financial

Corp.; joined Matthews & Co. 1951; Doherty Roadhouse & Co. 1959; Mem. of the Bd of Governors, Toronto Stock Exchange, 1976-1978; recreations: gardening, art, skiing; Club: Badminton & Racquet; Office: (P.O. Box 25) Commercial Union Tower, Toronto-Dominion Centre, Toronto, Ont. M5K 1B5.

HOMBURGER, Walter; concert manager; b. Karlsruhe, Germany, 22 Jan. 1924; s. Victor and Lotte (Fruehberg) H.; came to Canada 1941; e. Schs. in Germany; Eastbourne Coll., Eng. 1939-40; Central Technical School 1941-42. Central Coll., Toronto (Sr. Matric.) 1943; m. Emmy Schmid, 23 June 1961; children: Michael, Lisa; Mgr., Toronto Symphony Orchestra since Jan. 1962; Founder and Pres. since inception 1946 of International Artists Concert Agency; Mgr., National Ballet of Can. 1951-55; over past 25 yrs. has been Mgr. of various artists incl. Glenn Gould, Jan Rubes, Victor Conrad Braun, Donald Bell, Alfred Brendel and Louis Lortie; served in Cdn. Army 1943-45; Jewish; Club: Variety; Home: 278 Heath St. E., Toronto, Ont. M4T 1T4; Office: 178 Victoria St., Toronto, Ont. M5B 1T7

HONDERICH, Beland Hugh; newspaper officer; b. Kitchener, Ont., 25 Nov. 1918; s. John William and Rae Laura (Armstrong) H.; e. Pub. Sch., Baden, Ont.; Hon. LL.D. York Univ., 1976; Wilfrid Laurier Univ., 1977; m. Florence Irene, d. William H. Wilkinson, 15 Oct. 1943; children: John Allen, Mary Elizabeth, David Beland; 2ndly Agnes Janet Hutchinson, Oct. 24, 1969; CHRM. AND PUBLISHER, TORONTO STAR NEWSPAPERS LTD., since 1976; CHRM. AND PRES., TORSTAR CORP., 1977-; joined editorial staff of Kitchener "Record", 1935; resigned to become reporter with Toronto "Star", 1943; Financial Editor, 1945, Editor-in-Chief 1955; el. a Dir., 1957; Pres. and Publisher, 1966; Home: 6 Bluejay Place, Don Mills, Ont. M3B 1V9; Office: One Yonge St., Toronto, Ont. M5E 1E6

HOO, Sing; A.R.C.A. (1948), R.C.A. (1965); sculptor: b. Canton, China, 15 May 1911; s. Kin and Lili (Chow) H.: came to Canada, 1922; m. Norah, d. late Dr. W. J. Chambers, 7 Dec. 1937; one d. Catherine: e. Ont. Coll. of Art (Grad. 1933); Slade Sch., London, Eng. (1937); mem., Ont. Soc. of Artists (1938); Sculptors Soc. Can. (1952); Fellow, Internat. Arts & Letters, Geneva, 1959; Men of Achievement, Internat. Biog. Centre, Cambridge, Eng. 1975; mem., Academia Italia Delle Artie Del Lavoro, Italy, 1980; Conservative; United Church; Address: 139 Livingstone Ave., Toronto, Ont. M6E 2L9

HOOD, Hugh, M.A., Ph.D.; writer; university professor; b. Toronto, Ont., 30 Apl. 1928; s. Alexander Bridport and Margaret Cecile (Blagdon) H.; e. De La Salle Coll. "Oaklands", Toronto, 1945; Univ. of Toronto, B.A. 1950, M.A. 1952, Ph.D. 1955; m. Ruth Noreen, d. Dwight Harcourt Mallory, D.D.S., 22 Apl. 1957; children: Sarah Barbara, Dwight Alexander, John Arthur Mallory. Alexandra Mary; Teaching Fellow, Univ. of Toronto, 1951-55; Asst. and Assoc. Prof., Saint Joseph Coll., Hartford, Conn., 1955-61; Prof. asst., puis agrégé, enfin prof. titulaire, Univ. de Montréal, since 1961; rec'd Pres.'s Medal, Univ. of W. Ont., 1962, 1969; Sr. Artists Award, Can. Council, 1971; author: "Flying A Red Kite", stories, 1962; "White Figure, White Ground", novel, 1964; "Around the Mountain: Scenes From Montreal Life" (short stories) 1967; "The Camera Always Lies", novel, 1967; "Strength Down Centre", sports, 1970; "A Game of Touch", novel, 1970; "The Fruit Man, The Meat Man And The Manager", stories, 1971; "You Can't Get There From Here", novel, 1972; "The Governor's Bridge is Closed", essays, 1973; The New Age/Le nouveau siècle, Vol. I, "The Swing in the Garden", novel, 1975; "Dark Glasses", short stories, 1976; the New Age/Le nouveau siècle, Vol. II, "A New Athens", novel, 1977; "Selected Stories", short stories, 1978; "Scoring: Seymour Segal's Art of Hockey", art criticism, 1978; The New Age/Le nouveau

siècle, Vol. III, "Reservoir Ravine", novel, 1979; "None Genuine Without This Signature", short stories, 1980; The New Age/Le nouveau siècle, Vol. IV, "Black and White Keys" 1982; also many stories and articles in Candn., Am. and European mags. and anthols.; mem., Candn. Assn. Univ. Teachers; Sr. Artists Award, Can. Council, 1974 and 1978; City of Toronto Literary Prize, 1975; recreations: music, sports; Home: 4242 Hampton Ave., Montreal, Que. H4A 2K9

HOOD, William Clarence, M.A., Ph.D., LL.D., F.R.S.C.; Canadian public servant; economist; b. Yarmouth, N.S., 13 Sept. 1921; s. Percy Alexander and Vida Barr (Webster) H.; e. Mount Allison Univ., B.A. (Hons. in Econ.) 1941, LL.D. 1970; Univ. of Toronto, M.A. (Econ.) 1943, Ph.D. (Econ.) 1948; Univ. of Chicago Fellow 1949-50; m. Alville Mary Lennox, 4 June 1948; children: Ronald Douglas, Nancy Anne; ECONOMIC COUNSELLOR AND DIR. OF RESEARCH, INT. MONETARY FUND 1980- ; Depy. Min. of Finance 1979; Associate Depy. Min. of Finance, 1975-78; (Assistant Deputy Minister 1970-74); taught Econ. at University of Sask., 1944-46; apptd. to Staff of Dept. of Pol. Econ., Univ. of Toronto. 1946; Prof. 1959; Advisor, Bank of Canada 1964-69; Research Assoc. at Cowles Comn. for Research in Econs. Univ. of Chicago, 1949-50; has served on a number of special assignments for Candn. Govt.; Publications: "Studies in Econometric Method", 1953, "Output Labour and Capital in the Canadian Economy" (with A. D. Scott), 1958; "Financing of Economic Activity in Canada", 1959; many articles on econ. theory and stat.; mem., Royal Econ. Soc.; Econometric Soc.; Candn. Pol. Science Assn.; Am. Econ. Assn.; Am. Stat. Assn.; engaged in special meterol. work during part of war period; Head of special UNESCO 3-mth. mission to Sierra Leone to study educ. and econ. devel. 1961; on partial 2-yr. leave as Econ. Adv. and Dir. of Research for Royal Comn. on Banking & Finance 1961; Named Alternate Gov. for Can. of the I.M.F., 1970; Dir., CMHC, 1977; United Church;

HOOLEY, Joseph Gilbert, M.A., Ph.D., F.C.I.C.; university professor; b. Vancouver, B.C., 26 Sept. 1914; s. Joseph S. and Cecilia Mary (Frisby) H.; e. Univ. of Brit. Columbia, B.A. 1934, and M.A. 1936; Mass. Inst. of Tech., Ph.D. 1939; m. Agnes Schroeder, d. J. J. Irwin of Parkesville, Vancouver, B.C., 1939; PROF. EMERITUS OF CHEMISTRY, UNIV. OF B.C.; Research Chemist, Corning Glass Works, New York, 1939-42; Asst. Prof. of Chem., Univ. of B.C., 1942, Assoc. Prof. 1947; Prof. and Chrmn. of the Dept. 1949-55; research career concerned with low temp. heat capacity studies and atomic weight determination (accepted by Internat. Comn. 1936); patents (3) on special phosphate glass compositions and present work on intercalation in graphite; recreations: skiing, music, sailing; Club: Varsity Outdoor; Home: 4769 West 7th Ave., Vancouver, B.C. V6T 1C7

HOOPER, Cleeve Francis Wilfrid, B.A., A.M., B.Litt.; diplomat; b. Toronto, Ont. 29 Nov. 1924; s. late Mortimer Cleeve, Q.C. and Irene Mildred (Wood) H.; e. Lawrence Park Coll. Inst. Toronto; Univ. of Toronto B.A. 1947; Harvard Univ. A.M. 1948; Oxford Univ. B.Litt. 1950 (Nuffield Student); m. Katherine Patricia d. late Robert S. Ingram, Orillia, Ont. 18 March 1950; children: Alison Mary, Jonathan Thomas, Jeremy Cleeve; DIR.-GEN. BUREAU OF INTELLIGENCE ANALYSIS AND SECURITY Ottawa, 1978; joined Dept. of External Affairs 1950, Vice Consul Caracas 1952, Third Secy. Buenos Aires 1953, Second Secy. 1955, Ottawa 1956 (Information Div.), Second Secy. New Delhi 1958, Ottawa 1961, First Secy. Dar Es Salaam 1964, London 1966, Counsellor 1967, Ottawa 1970 (Depy. Dir. E. European Div.), Co-ordinator for Candn. participation in Conf. on Security and Co-op. in Europe 1972-76, Dir. E. European Div. 1974-76, High Commr. Jamaica with concurrent accreditation to Bahamas and Belize 1976-78; served with RCNVR 1944-45; Baptist; recreations: shooting, walking; Home: 92 Stanley Ave., Ottawa, Ont. K1M 1P4; Office: (Dept. of Extn. Affrs., Ottawa, Ont. K1A 0G2

HOPKINS, George W.; banker; b. Thunder Bay, Ont. 27 Feb. 1938; e. Univ. of Toronto B.Sc. 1961; RMC 1960; m. Marion C., Dec. 1960; children: Todd, Lisa; SR. VICE PRES. OPERATIONS & SYSTEMS, BANK OF MONTREAL; Office: Box 7000, Scarborough, Ont. M1S 4M5

HOPKINS, Leonard, M.P., B.A.; b. Argyle, Ont., 12 June 1930; s. John James and Victoria Maude (Brown) H.; e. Argyle (Ont.) Pub. Sch.; Woodville (Ont.) Cont. Sch.; Ryerson Inst. of Technol.; Queen's Univ., B.A.; North Bay (Ont.) Teachers Coll.; Ont. Coll. of Educ., Univ. of Toronto; m. Lois Mary, d. William Albert Gust and Lena (Mohns) Petawawa, Ont., 28 June 1958; children: Sherri Lynne, Douglas Leonard; Elem. Sch. Teacher for 7 yrs. and Princ. for 4 yrs.; High Sch. Teacher for 5 1/2½ yrs. and Vice-Princ. 1964-65; mem. Petawawa Twp. Council 1963-65; Charter Pres., Rotary Club of Petawawa, 1961; el. to H. of C. in g.e. 1965; re-el 1968, 1972, 1974, 1979, 1980; Vice Chrmn., H. of C. Standing Comte. on Industry, Energy & Mines 1966-68; Chrmn., H. of C. Standing Comte. on National Resources & Pub. Works 1968-72; apptd. Parlty. Secy. for Defence 1972; Hon. mem., Royal Candn. Legion Branch 72, Pembroke and Branch 517, Petawawa; Hon. Mem., Lanark and Renfrew Scottish Regiment; Freemason; Charter Mem. of Tunis Temple Shrine in Ottawa; Liberal; Presbyterian; recreations: skating, fishing, camping; Club: Rotary; Home: 33 Sunset Cres., Petawawa, Ont. K8H 2L8; Office: House of Commons, Ottawa, Ont. K1A 0A6

HOPPE, Robert H., F.C.I.S.; company executive; b. Montreal, P.Q., 16 Dec. 1916; s. John Charles and Emily Sophie (Tomkinson) H.; e. High Sch. of Montreal, Matric. 1934; Sir George Williams Coll., Montreal, Que.; Assoc. in Commerce, 1938; m. Shirley Eugenie, d. Henry E. Bell, J.P., Montreal, Que., 1 May 1943; children: Elizabeth Diane, John David; CHAIRMAN, GIVAUDAN LTD.; Chrmn. Stuart Brothers (West Indies) Ltd.; Trinidad Lime Products Ltd.; Stuart Brothers Jamaica Ltd.; Dir., Finlayson Enterprises Ltd.; Fire Insurance Co. of Canada; Advisory Bd. Concordia Univ.; joined Dom. Rubber Co., Montreal, in 1935 as Clerk at Papineau factory, later becoming Foreman, then Buyer; Chief Clerk, Montreal Br. Indust. Sales, 1940: Purchasing Agt. and Mgr. Material Planning, Production Planning, Stores & Traffic, Dom. Rubber Munitions Ltd., Cap-de-la-Madeleine, Que., 1942; Purchasing Agt., etc., Papineau factory, Montreal, 1945; Purchasing Agt. and Asst. to Pres., M. Steiner Co. Ltd. and Flyfast Ltd., Montreal, 1947; joined predecessor firm of Stuart Bros. Co. Ltd. as Secy.-Treas. 1948; moved to Toronto, 1954, Montreal, 1958; Past Pres. Y.M.C.A., Montreal; Past Councillor Montreal Bd. of Trade; Freemason; Anglican; recreation: golf; Clubs: St. James's; Montreal Badminton & Squash; Hermitage (Lake Memphramagog); Home: 4000 de Maisonneuve W., Westmount, Que. H3Y 3C5; Office: 4131 Sherbrooke St. W., Montreal, Que. H3Z 1B7

HOPPER, Wilbert H. (Bill), B.Sc., M.B.A.; petroleum executive; b. Ottawa, Ont. 1937; e. American Univ. Washington, D.C. B.Sc. (Geol.) 19..; Univ. of W. Ont. M.B.A. 19..; m. Patricia Marguerite 12 Aug. 1957; children: Sean Wilbert, Christopher Mark; CHRMN. OF BD. AND CHIEF EXTVE. OFFR., PETRO-CANADA; Dir. Panarctic Oils Ltd.; Syncrude Canada Ltd.; Polar Gas; Westcoast Transmission Co. Ltd.; Canada China Trade Council; Canertech Inc.; Petro-Canada International Assistance Corp.; Petrofina Canada Inc.; Petroleum Geol. Imperial Oil Ltd.; Petroleum Econ. Foster Associates; Sr. Energy Econ. Nat. Energy Bd. 1961-65; Sr. Petroleum Consultant, Arthur D. Little Inc. Cambridge, Mass. 1965-72; Sr. Advisor on Energy Policy Dept. Energy, Mines & Resources becoming Asst. Depy. Min. for Energy Policy

1974; Chrmn. Internat. Energy Agency's Standing Comte. on Internat. Oil Markets 1976; Office: (P.O. Box 2844) 407 Second St. S.W., Calgary, Alta. T2P 3E3.

HOPPER, William David, B.Sc., Ph.D.; scientist: b. Ottawa, Ont. 22 Feb. 1927; s. late Wilbert C. and Eva Luella (Hill) H.; e. Lisgar Coll. Inst., Ottawa; Macdonald Coll., McGill Univ., B.Sc. (Agr.), 1950; Cornell Univ., Ph.D. 1957; D.Sc. (Hon.) McGill Univ., 1976; Orissa 1980; m. Jessie Dodds Hebron 1951; d. 1973; children: Ann Elizabeth, David Ian; m. 2nd., Ruth Kramer, 1974; VICE-PRES. (SOUTH ASIA) INTERNAT. BANK FOR RECONSTRUCTION AND DEVELOPMENT since 1978; Grad. Asst., Dept. of Agric. Econ., Cornell Univ., 1950-53 and 1955-57; Social Science Research Council Area Research and Training Fellowship to study organ. of village in N.-Central India, 1953-55; Assoc. Prof. of Agric. Econ., Ont. Agric. Coll., Guelph, 1957-59; Asst. Prof. of Econ., Univ. of Chicago, 1959-62; Evaluation Offr., Intensive Agric. Dists. Programme, Ford Foundation, New Delhi, India, 1962-65: Agric. Econ. and Assoc. Field Dir., Indian Agric. Program, Rockefeller Found., New Delhi and visiting Prof. of Agric. Econ., Indian Agric. Research Inst., New Delhi 1965-70; Pres. Internat. Dev. Research Centre, 1970-77; former mem., Soc. Sci. Research Council of Can. 1970-76; OECD-DAC Expert Planning Group on Application of Sci. and Tech. to Dev. Problems of Low Income Countries 1970-77; Council and Exec. Comte. of Soc. for Internat. Dev., 1971-76; Technical Advisory Comte. to Consultative Grp. for Internat. Agr. Research 1976-78; former Trustee, Internat. Agric. Dev. Serv. 1976-77; foreign Hon. mem., Amer. Academy of Arts and Sci; Hon. mem., Roy. Agric. Soc.; mem., Governing Body; Inst. of Dev. Studies, Sussex, Eng. since 1971; Dir., Appropriate Tech. Internat., Washington D.C. since 1978; Vice Chmn. of Bd. of Trustees, Internat. Fertilizer Development Centre, Muscle Shoals, Alabama; Trustee and Chrmn. of Exec. Comte., Population Council, N.Y., since 1971; Office: 1818 "h" St., N.W., Washington D.C. 20433

HORLICK, Louis, M.Sc., M.D., C.M.; university professor; b. Montreal, Que., 2 Dec. 1921; s. Philip and Sophie (Katz) H.; e. McGill Univ., B.Sc. 1944, M.D., C.M. 1945, M.Sc. 1952; m. Ruth Lenore, d. late Garfield George Hood, 1953; children: Jonathan, Andrew, Allan, Simon; PROF. OF MEDICINE, COLL. OF MEDICINE, UNIV. OF SASK.; Pres., Sask. Heart Foundation; mem. of Bd. Candn. Heart Fdn.; mem. Candn. Council on Hosp. Accreditation; Sask. Health Res. Bd.; Hebrew; recreation: music; Home: 1215 Elliott St., Saskatoon, Sask. S7N 0V5

HORNE, Arthur Edward Cleeve, R.C.A.; painter; sculptor; b. Jamaica, B.W.I., 9 Jan. 1912; s. Arthur Charles Washington and Gladys Lillian (Grant) H.; e. Ont. Coll. of Art (Lieut-Gov's Medal, painting) 1934; sculpture, D. Dick of Eng., 1927-28; painting, J. W. Beatty and John Russell, 1932-34, Europe 1936; m. Jean Mildred, d. William Thomas Harris, 11 Feb. 1939; children: Robert Cleeve, Arthur William, Richard Rowley; served World War, 1943-46, C.I., Cam. Wing, C.E.T.C., retired with rank of Capt.; paintings include portraits of people prominent in industry, law, gov't, banking, educ., etc.; sculpture comns. incl., Alexander Graham Bell, Brantford, Ont., 1948; William Shakespeare, Stratford, Ont., 1950; War Memorial, Law Soc. of Upper Can., Osgoode Hall, Toronto, 1951; Bank of Can., Toronto, 1958; R. S. McLaughlin R.O.M. Planetarium, Toronto, 1970; artist consultant, Imperial Oil Building, Toronto, 1953-58; St. Lawrence Power Project Adm. Bldg., 1957-59; Canadian Imperial Bank of Commerce H.O., Montreal, 1960-62; Commerce Court, Toronto, 1970-73; Chairman R.C.A. Art Consultant Committee to Ont. Government Queens Park Project, 1968-70; Ont. Hydro H.O., Toronto, 1974-76; R.A.I.C. Allied Art Award, 1963; Centennial Medal; Silver Jubilee Medal; mem. Ont. Soc. of Artists (Pres. 1949-51); Sculptors' Soc. of Can.; Anglican; Clubs: Arts and Letters (Pres. 1955-57); York; Studio Home: 181 Balmoral Ave., Toronto, Ont. M4V 1J8

HORNE, Joicey Mary; b. Carnduff, Sask., 20 Nov. 1906; d. Gilbert and Rosa (Harris) H.; e. Wheatland Pub. and High Sch. Carnduff, Sask.; Regina Normal Sch.; Ont. Coll. of Art, Grad. 1933; Univ. of Toronto (Extension); unm.; Teacher, Toronto Pub. Schs. for a no. of yrs.; Art Master, Toronto Teachers' Coll., 1937-70: mem., Ont. Educ. Assn. (Pres., Training Sec. 1947-48); Publications: "The Art Class in Action", 1941; "Young Artists", 1961: has contrib. numerous articles to educ. journs.; Protestant; recreations: arts and crafts; Home: c/o 102 Lexington Ave., Rexdale, Ont. M9V 2G8

HORNE, Mercèdés, R.C.A.; artist; b. Birmingham, Eng. 23 May 1925; d. Herbert Edward and Janet (Hayton) Deeley; e. Kings Norton Grammar Sch. Birmingham 1941; m. David Ernest Horne 15 June 1957; one d. Janet Mercèdés Sidey; solo exhns. incl. Pollock Gallery Toronto (5 exhns.); Shaw-Rimmington Gallery Toronto (3 exhns.); Ont. Assn. Archs. Toronto; Garret Gallery St. Catharines; Albert White Gallery Toronto; Merton Gallery Toronto; Rebecca Sisler Gallery; Gallery Brand Oakville; Sarnia Pub. Art Gallery; Prince Arthur Galleries; rep. various group exhns. incl. Nat. Gallery Can., Art Gallery of Ont. "100 Years: Ontario Society of Artists", "50 Years: Canadian Society of Painters in Water Colour"; "Canadian Visions" Albright-Knox Gallery Buffalo; Exchange Exhn. Candn. & Japanese Water Colour Soc's; Montreal Museum of Fine Arts; comns.: large mural for Ont. Jockey Club; mural for Rubin Corp.; rep. various maj. pub., corporate and private colls.; rec'd Aviva Art Auction 1961; Hadassah Award 1963; Candn. Soc. Painters Watercolour Award 1971, 1972; Ont. Soc. Artists 2 awards 1972; Queen's Silver Jubilee Medal 1977; mem. Candn. Soc. Painters in Watercolour (Vice Pres. and Treas., mem. Extve. Bd.-Retired); Ont. Soc. Artists; mem. Council Royal Candn. Acad. 1980-81; P. Conservative; Anglican; Home: 421 Chartwell Rd., Oakville, Ont. L6J 4A4.

HORNER, Hon. Jack H., P.C. (1977), rancher; farmer; b. Blaine Lake, Sask. 20 July 1927; s. Senator Ralph Byron and Mac (Macarthur) H.; m. Leola Funnell, 11 April, 1950; children: Blaine, Craig, Brent; First elected to H. of C. 1958; re-elected, 1962, 63, 65, 68, 72, 74; Joined Lib. Party 1977; Apptd. Min. of Industry Trade & Commerce, 1977; Def. g. e. 1979; author: "My Own Brand" (autobiography) 1980; United Church; Home: Pollockville, Alta. T0J 2L0

HORNSTEIN, Reuben Aaron, M.B.E. (1946), M.A.; retired public servant; meteorologist; radio and television artist; b. London, Ont., 18 Dec. 1912; s. Morris and Sophia (Rosenthal) H.; e. London Central Coll.; Univ. of W. Ont., B.A. 1934 (Gold Medal in Hon. Physics), M.A. 1936; Univ. of Toronto, M.A. 1938; m. Helen Christina MacDonald, 1956; Demonst. in Physics, Univ. of W. Ont., 1934-37; joined Meteorol. Br., Dept. of Transport and served at St. Hubert and Malton Airports 1938-40; placed in charge of Halifax Office, serving all three Brs. of Armed Forces 1940-46; in charge of Halifax Atlantic Weather Central 1946-72; author of (booklets) "Weather Facts and Fancies", 1949; "It's in The Wind", 1950; "Weather and Why", 1954; "The Weather Book", 1980; awarded The Patterson Medal for distinguished Service to Candn. meteorol., 1962; Special Merit Award, Fed. Inst. of Mang., 1977; Hon. Big Brother, Big Brothers of Dartmouth-Halifax, 1976-77; Fellow, Roy. Meteorol. Soc.; mem., N.S. Inst. of Science; Candn. Meteorol. and Oceanographic Soc.; Candn. Assn. Physicists; Roman Catholic; recreations: golf, bridge; Clubs: Ashburn Golf & Country; Saraguay; Home: 1074 Wellington St., Apt. 301, Halifax, N.S. B3H 2Z8

HOROWITZ, Myer, B.A., M.Ed., Ed.D., LL.D.; educator; b. Montreal, Que., 27 Dec. 1932; s. Philip and Fanny (Cotler) H.; e. Comm. High Sch., Montreal, 1949; Sch. for Teachers, Macdonald Coll., Teacher's Cert. 1952; Sir George Williams Univ., B.A. 1956; Univ. of Alta., M.Ed. 1959; Stanford Univ., Ed.D. 1965; Hon. LL.D., McGill Univ. 1979; m. Barbara, d. Samuel Rosen, Montreal, 3 Oct. 1956; two d.: Carol Anne, Deborah Ellen; PRESIDENT, UNIV. OF ALBERTA since 1979; Teacher, Elem. and High Schs., Prot. Sch. Bd. of Greater Montreal, 1952-60; joined McGill Univ. as Lectr. in Educ., 1960-62; Asst. Prof. 1963-65, Assoc. Prof. 1965-67, Asst. to the Dir., 1964-65; Prof. of Educ., 1967-69; and Asst. Dean 1965-69; Prof. and Chrmn., Dept. Elementary Educ., Univ. of Alta. 1969; Dean of Educ., 1972-75; Vice Pres. (Acad.) 1975-79; Research and Teaching Asst., Stanford Univ., Chrmn., Candn. Comte. on Early Childhood; Pres., Early Childhood Educ. Council, Alta. Teachers' Assn.; Chrmn. Adv. Comte., Study of Mental Retardation, Univ. of Alta.; Pres., Edmonton Chapter, Candn. Coll. of Teachers; Project Dir., Tanzania Educ. Project; contrib. several articles to prof. and educ. mags. and journs.; Fellow, Candn. Coll. of Teachers; Life mem., Prov. Assn. of Prot. Teachers of Que.; Hon. mem. Alta Teachers' Assn.; Jewish; Home: 14319, 60 Ave., Edmonton, Alta. T6H 1J7

HORROCKS, Norman, B.A., M.L.S., Ph.D., F.L.A., A.L.A.A.; librarian; educator; b. Manchester, Eng. 18 Oct. 1927; s. Edward Henry and Annie (Barnes) H.; e. Burnage High Sch. Manchester 1939-1943; Manchester Coll. of Science & Technol. Sch. of Librarianship 1948-50; Univ. of W. Australia 1957-61; Univ. of Pittsburgh 1963-70; m. Sandra d. Roy and Helen Sheriff, Pittsburgh, Pa.; children: Julie Carol, Carl Scott, Gina Louise, Anne Patricia, Sarah Helen; PROF. AND DIR., SCH. OF LIB. SERVICE, DALHOUSIE UNIV. 1972- ; asst. Librarian, Manchester Pub. Lib. Eng. 1943-45, 1948-53; Librarian, Brit. Council, Cyprus 1954-55; Tech. Librarian, State Lib. of W. Australia 1956-63; Part-time Lectr. in Librarianship, Perth Tech. Coll. 1961-63; Teaching Fellow, Instr., Asst. Prof., Grad. Sch. of Lib. & Information Science, Univ. of Pittsburgh 1963-71; Summer Sch. Faculty, Grad Sch. of Lib. Studies, Univ. of Hawaii 1969; Extension Lectr. Program for Certification of Lib. Assts., State Lib. of Pa. 1966-71; Assoc. Prof. and Asst. Dir. Sch. of Lib. Service, Dalhousie Univ. 1971; External Examiner, Dept. Lib. Studies, Univ. of W. Indies 1976- ; served with Brit. Army Intelligence Corps 1945-48, Egypt, Palestine, Cyprus; rec'd W. H. Brown Prize 1949; Atlantic Provs. Lib. Assn. Merit Award 1979; Series Ed., "The Great Bibliographers" 1974- ; Contrib. Ed. "Quill & Quire"; regular contrib. to lib. press Can. and U.S.; mem. various journ. adv. bds.; mem. Am. Lib. Assn. (Extve. Bd. 1977-81); Assn. Am. Lib. Schs. (Chrmn. Ed. Bd. 1971-76, Ex-Officio mem. Extve. Bd. 1971-76); Atlantic Provs. Lib. Assn.; Atlantic Publishers Assn.; Atlantic Booksellers Assn.; Candn. Assn. Lib. Schs.; Candn. Assn. Univ. Teachers; Candn. Council Lib. Schs.; Candn. Lib. Assn. (2nd Vice Pres. Council & Bd. Dirs. 1978-80); Lib. Assn. Australia (Assoc.); Nat. Book League (London); N.S. Lib. Assn.; N.S. Sch. Lib. Assn.; Nat. Research Council Can.; Adv. Bd. of Sci. and Technological Infor.; Nat. Library Advisory Bd. Committee on Soc. Sc. and Humanities, Bibliographic and Information Services; Beta Phi Mu (Nat. Treas. 1968-71); Chrmn. Overseas Book Centre (Halifax Br.) 1980- ; United Church; recreations: parliamentary procedures, editing, publishing, spy stories; Club: Banook Canoe; Home: 14 Cleveland Cres., Dartmouth, N.S. 2L6; Office: Halifax, N.S. B3H 4H8.

HORSEY, (William) Grant, B.Com.; industrialist; b. Buffalo, New York, 17 Oct. 1915; s. John William and Clara (Banford) H.; came to Canada 1920; e. Pub. Schs. of Buffalo, Toronto and Montreal; McGill Univ., B.Com. 1938; m. Eleanor Mae, d. H. J. Child, Montreal, P.Q., 17 Feb. 1940; one d. Mrs. Susan H. Dees; PRESIDENT, WILGRAN CORP. LTD., since 1962; Chairman of the Board,

DRG Limited; Dir., Gage Research Inst.; Pilot Insurance Co.; National Trust Co. Ltd.; Trustee, The Toronto Western Hosp.; Route Salesman, Standard Brands Ltd., Toronto, Ont., 1938; Jr. Audit Clerk, McDonald, Currie & Co., Montreal, P.Q., 1938; Asst. Dist. Mgr., Dominion Stores Ltd., Halifax, N.S., 1939; Sr. Audit Clerk, McDonald Currie & Co., Montreal, P.Q., 1941; Treas., Apte Canning Sales Corp., Tampa, Fla., 1946; Vice-Pres., J. William Horsey Corp., Plant City, Fla., 1946, Pres., 1950; Pres., Shirriff-Horsey Corp. Ltd., Toronto, Ont., 1955; Pres., Salada Foods Ltd. (formerly Salada-Shirriff-Horsey Ltd.) & Salada Foods Inc. (formerly Salada-Shirriff-Horsey Inc.) 1957; Chrmn. Bd., Salada Foods Ltd. & Salada Foods Inc., 1964-67; Lieut., Candn. Army Overseas, R.C.A., 1943-46; Presbyterian; Theta Delta Chi; Clubs: The Toronto; Tampa Yacht & Country (Fla.); University (Tampa, Fla.); Donalda; Granite; Home: 70 Cluny Drive, Toronto, Ont. M4W 2R3; Office: 3080 Yonge St., Ste. 5044, Toronto, Ont. M4N 3N1

HORSMAN, Hon. James Deverell, Q.C., M.L.A., B.Com., LL.B.; politician; b. Camrose, Alta. 29 July 1935; s. George Cornwall and Kathleen (Deverell) H.; e. Meeting Creek, Alta.; Alexandra Pub. Sch. and Central Coll. Inst. Moose Jaw, Sask.; Univ. of B.C., B. Com., LL.B.; m. Elizabeth Marian d. Thompson and Marian Whitney, Medicine Hat, Alta. 4 July 1964; children: Catherine Anne, Diana Lynn, Susan Marian; MIN. OF ADVANCED EDUC. AND MANPOWER, ALTA. and Depy. Govt. House Leader 1979- ; cr. Q.C. 1980; Cand. prov. g.e. 1967, 1971 def.; el. M.L.A. for Medicine Hat prov. g.e. 1975, re-el. 1979; mem., Alta. Delegation to First Ministers Conference on Constitution 1982; Chmn., Prov. Ministers Responsible for Manpower 1982; mem. and Chrmn. Bd. Govs. Medicine Hat Coll. 1972-74; Pres. Medicine Hat Chamber Comm. 1971-72; Elder St. John's Ch. Medicine Hat; Shriner; Conservative; Presbyterian; Clubs: Kinsmen (Past Pres., Past Dist. Offr.); Cypress; Office: 130 Legislative Bldg., Edmonton, Alta. T5K 2B6.

HORTE, Vernon L., B.Sc.; company president; b. Kingman, Alta., 12 July 1925; s. Thor and Marit (Haugen) H.; e. Univ. of Alta., B.Sc. (Chem. Engn.) 1949; m. Thelma Margaret Boness, 18 Feb. 1950; children: Joan, Robert, Douglas; PRES. V. L. HORTE ASSOC. LTD., since 1977; Dir., National Trust Co. Ltd.; Total Petroleum (N.Amer.) Ltd.; Gen. Accident Assnce. Co. Can.; Can. Utilities Ltd.; ProGas Ltd.; Engr., Chem. and Geol. Labs., Edmonton, Alta., 1949-50; Gas Engr., The Alta. Petroleum Natural Gas Conserv. Bd., Calgary, 1950-52; Petroleum Engr., DeGolyer & MacNaughton, Consulting Petroleum Engrs., Dallas, Texas, 1952-57; joined TransCanada PipeLines, Chief Gas Supply Engr., 1957; Mgr. of Gas Supply 1959; Vice Pres., Gas Supply 1961; Group Vice Pres., 1966; Pres. 1968; Pres., Candn. Arctic Gas Study Ltd., 1972-77; served as Navig. with RCAF 1943-45; mem., Candn. Gas Assn.; Am. Gas Assn.; Am. Inst. Mining, Metall. & Petroleum Engrs.; Assn. Prof. Engrs. Alta.; Assn. Prof. Engrs. Texas; Candn. Inst. Mining & Metall.; Candn. Soc. Petroleum Geols.; recreations: skiing, golf, hunting; Clubs: National; Rideau (Ottawa); Earl Grey Golf; Glencoe; Bayview Country; Home: Apt. 305-3204 Rideau Place S.W., Calgary, Alta. T2S 1Z2; Office: 910 Selkirk House, 555-4th Ave. S.W., Calgary, Alta. T2P 3E7

HORWOOD, Harold Andrew, C.M.; author; b. St. John's, Nfld. 2 Nov. 1923; s. Andrew and Vina (Maidment) H.; m. Cornelia Lindismith 1 July 1973; children: Andrew, Leah; taught creative writing Mem. Univ. of Nfld. and Univ. of W. Ont.; Writer in Residence Univ. W. Ont. 1976-77; Univ. of Waterloo, 1980-81; mem. Arts Adv. Panel Can. Council 1977-80; Lib. mem. for Labrador, House of Assembly Nfld. 1949-51; def. NDP cand. for Trinity-Conception; author "Tomorrow Will Be Sunday" 1966 (Beta Sigma Phi Novel for 1966); "The Foxes of Beachy Cove" 1967 (Best Scient. Book 1967);

"Newfoundland" (travel) 1969, 1977; "White Eskimo" (novel) 1972; "Voices Underground" (poetry ed.) 1972; "Beyond the Road" (travel) 1976; "Bartlett, the Great Canadian Explorer" (biog.) 1977, 1979; "The Colonial Dream" (hist.) 1979; "Only the Gods Speak" (fiction) 1979; numerous articles for mags. and lit. journs.; mem. Writers Union Can. (Vice Chrmn. 3 times, Chrmn. 1980-81); recreations: music, mathematics, boating, ornithology, gardening; Address: (P.O. Box 489) Annapolis Royal, N.S. B0S 1A0.

HOTCLKISS, Harley Norman, B.Sc.; geologist; b. Tillsonburg, Ont. 10 July 1927; s. Morley R. and Carrie E. (Todd) H.; e. Mich. State Univ. B.Sc. (Geol.) 1951; m. Norma Rebecca d. Gordon A. Boyd 33Oct. 1951; children: Paul A., Brenda E., John S., J. Richard, Jeffrey A.; self-employed personal invests. oil and gas, real estate and agric. since 1976; Dir. Nova; Conwest Exploration Co. Ltd.; Bluewater Oil & Gas Ltd.; Calgary Flames Hockey Club; Gov. Banff Centre for Continuing Educ.; Geol. Canadian Superior Oil Ltd. 1951-53; Geol. and Asst.Mgr. Oil & Gas Dept. Canadian Imperial Bank of Commerce 1953-59; Pres., Alcon Petroleums Ltd. 1959-67 and Sabre Petroleums Ltd. 1967-76; served with Canadian Merchant Marine 1944-45; Fellow, Geol. Assn. Can.; mem. Candn. Soc. Petrol. Geols.; Am. Assn. Petrol. Geols.; Candn. Inst. Mining & Metall.; Soc. Petrol. Engrs. (A.I.M.E.); Phi Kappa Phi; President's Club Mich. State Univ.; recreations: sports, reading, travel; Clubs: Ranchmen's; Griffith Island; Calgary Petroleum; Calgary Golf & Country; Home: 40 Eagle Ridge Pl. S.W., Calgary, Alta. T2V 2V8; Office: 1206 Dome Tower, Toronto-Dominion Sq., 333 - 7th Ave. S.W., Calgary, Alta. T2P 2Z1.

HOUGH, Michael, R.C.A.; landscape architect; b. Nice, France 5 Aug. 1928; s. William and Hortense (Rocher) H.; e. Bradfield Coll. Pub. Sch. Eng. 1947; Edinburgh Coll. of Art Dipl. Arch. 1955; Univ. of Pa. Master of Landscape Arch. 1958; m. Bridget d. Richard Woodhams, Sedbergh, U.K. 26 July 1956; children: Timothy, Adrian, Fiona; SECIAL CONSULTANT, HOUGH, STANSBURY & MICHALSKI LTD. 1979- ; Assoc. Prof. of Environment Studies, York Univ. 1970- ; Asst. Arch., Basil Spence & Partners, Edinburgh 1955-56; Landscape Arch.; various U.S. landscape arch. practices 1958-59; Project Planning Associates Ltd. Toronto 1959-62; Planning Office Univ. of Toronto 1962-65; Princ. and Dir. of Design. Hough, Stansbury & Associates Ltd. 1964-79; Assoc. Prof. of Landscape Arch. Univ. of Toronto 1963-70, Acting Head Div. Landscape Arch. 1966-67; recipient Am. Soc. Landscape Archs. Honor Award (Inst. Planning - Scarborough Coll.) 1967, Merit Award (Parks & Recreational Planning - Ont. Place) 1975, Honor Award (Design Guidelines for Forest Mang.) 1978; Am. Assn. Sch. Adms. Exhns. Sch. Arch. Award (Site Devel. Elem. Schs. K-6) 1970; Am. Soc. Interior Designers Internat. Design Award (Ont. Place) 1975; author "The Urban Landscape" 1971; co-author "Design Guidelines for Forest Management" 1972; "In Celebration of Play" 1980; served with Brit. Army (Dorset Regt.) 1947-49, Malay and Singapore 1948-49; mem. Inst. Assn. Landscape Archs.; Candn. Soc. Landscape Archs.; Anglican; recreations: music, painting, carpentry, gardening; Home: 29 Cornish Rd., Toronto, Ont. M4T 2E3; Office: 63 Galaxy Blvd., Unit 1, Rexdale, Ont. M9W 5R7.

HOULDEN, Hon. Lloyd William; judge; b. Toronto, Ont., 16 Sept. 1922; s. Everett Bruce and Mary Jane (Ball) H.; e. Humbercrest Pub. Sch. and Runnymede Coll. Inst., Toronto; Victoria Coll., Univ. of Toronto, B.A. 1944; Osgoode Hall Law Sch., Toronto, 1948; m. Joyce Beryl, d. Marshall Peter Laing Wood, 30 Sept. 1950; children: Pauline Jane, Brent Marshall Wood, Robyn Leslie; JUSTICE, COURT OF APPEAL, ONT., since 1974; read law with I. E. Houser, Toronto; called to Bar of Ont. 1948; cr. Q.C. 1962; Special Lectr. for Law Soc. of Upper Can., 1954, 1956, 1965; apptd. a Justice, Supreme Court of Ont. 1969; served with R.C.N.V.R. 1944-45; author of

"Houlden & Morawetz — Bankruptcy Law of Canada"; mem., Bd. Trade Metrop. Toronto (Bankruptcy Comte.): Phi Delta Phi; Presbyterian (Elder); recreations: gardening, reading, travelling; Home: 48 Anglesey Blvd., Islington, Ont. M9A 3B5; Office: Osgoode Hall, Toronto, Ont M5H 2N6

HOULDING, John Draper, B.A.; executive; b. London, Ont., 26 Nov. 1921; s. late Rev. Lloyd Milton and Muriel Lorena (Draper) H.; e. Leamington (Ont.) High Sch.; Ridley Coll., St. Catharines, Ont.; London S. Coll. Inst.; Univ. of Western Ont., B.A. (Hons. Physics and Chem.); m. Margaret Gordon, d. late David Thompson, Alyth, Perthshire, Scotland, 11 July 1945; children: Anne, David, John: PRESIDENT AND CHIEF EXTVE. OFFR., POLAR GAS PROJECT; Dir., Allied Chem. Can. Ltd.; Canada Wire & Cable Co. Ltd.; Canron Inc.; Crown Zellerbach Can. Ltd.; Spar Aerospace Ltd.; C.D. Howe Inst.; Ont. Research Foundation National Ballet of Can.; held Engineering and Sales posts with Canadian Westinghouse Company, 1945-51; Sales Manager, then Div. Mgr. of Electronics Div., 1952-53; promoted to Div. Mgr., Indust. Prod. Div., 1953-55; Div. Mgr., Atomic Energy Div., 1955-57; joined RCA Victor Co. Ltd. as Vice-President, Tech. Products 1957-58; Vice-Pres., Gen. Mgr. and Dir., 1958; Pres. 1960; loaned to Dept. of Defence Prod., Ottawa as Radar Production Offr., 1951; served in 2nd World War; Lieut. (Electrical) R.C.N.V.R.; on loan to Royal Navy as Radar Offr.; served in N. Atlantic and Mediterranean area; Past Pres. and Dir., Electronic Industries Assn.; Past mem., Defence Research Bd.; Past mem., Science Council of Can.; United Church; recreations: golf, fishing, tennis; Clubs: Mount Royal; Forest & Stream; York (Toronto); Queen's (Toronto); Rideau (Ottawa); Home: 136 Dunvegan Rd., Toronto, Ont. M4V 2R3; Office: (Box 90) Commerce Court W., Toronto, Ont. M5L 1H3

HOULE, Guy, B.A., LL.L.; public utilities executive; b. Montreal, Que., 6 Apl. 1935; s. late Lucien and Jeanne (Morin) H.; e. Ste. Marie Coll., B.A. 1955; Univ. of Montreal, LL.L. 1958; McGill Univ. 1959; m. Celine. d. Herve Bienvenu, Montreal, Que. 24 Dec. 1960; children: Sylvie, Marie-Josee, Christine, Jean; CORPORATE SECRETARY, BELL CANADA 1980- ; Dir., Bell Can. Internat.; Tele-Direct Ltd.; The Capital Telephone Co. Limited; The North American Telegraph Co. Ltd.; Ronalds-Federated Ltd.; read law with Lacoste, Lacoste, Savoie & Laniel; called to Bar of Que. 1959; private law practice Lacoste, Lacoste, Savoie & Laniel, Montreal, 1959-61; Legal Counsel to Royal Comn. of Inquiry on Educ. (Parent Comn.) 1961-66; Secy. and Legal Counsel to General Investment Corp. of Quebec, 1964-67; joined present Co. as Asst. Vice Pres. (Law), 1967-68, General Counsel, 1968-80; Mun. Judge St. Bruno; St. Bruno Chamber Commerce; Dir., Quebec Soc. Crippled Children; Chrmn., Can. Student Exchange Program and Que. Student Intra-Exchange Program Inc.; Quebec Student Intra-Exchange Program Inc.; mem., Can. Bar Assn.; Bar Prov. Que.; Internat. Law Assn.; Assn. Candn. Gen. Counsel; Montreal Bd. Trade; Can. Chamber of Commerce; Intl. Assoc., Am. Bar Assn.; Am. Soc. of Corp. Secretaries, Inc.; R. Catholic; recreations: music, travel, history, golf; Clubs: Richelieu Golf & Country; St.-Denis; Ville Marie Squash; Home: 1895 de la Duchesse St., St. Bruno de Montarville, Que.; Office: 1050 Beaver Hall Hill, Montreal, Que. H3C 3G4

HOUSDEN, Warwick Henry George, B.Arch. Hons., A.R.I.B.A., M.R.A.I.C.; architect; b. Eastbourne, Sussex Eng. 30 Mar. 1931; s. John E. Collins and Gladys Eva Collins; Lodge Farm, Barningham, Suffolk, Eng.; e. Culford Sch., Suffolk, Eng.; Liverpool (Eng.) Sch. Arch., (B.Arch. 1st Class Hons.); Charles Minorio Scholarship; Holt Travelling Scholarship; m. Lynn Anne Kenny; three d. Jane, Lisa, Andrea; CHMN. OF BOARD, WZMH GROUP INC. U.S. 1981- ; began career with Derbyshire Co.

Schools; joined Peter Dickinson Assocs., Toronto, Ont. 1957-61; founding Partner, Webb Zerafa Menky Housden; mem., Royal Arch. Inst. of Can.; Ont. Assn. Archs.; Prov. Que. Assn. Archs.; Clubs: Summit Golf & Country; Canyon Creek Country (Texas); Home: 5925 Colhurst, Dallas, Texas, 75230; Offices: 2050 Mansfield St., Suite 301, Montreal, Que. H3A 1Y9; 1901 N. Akard, Ste 730, Dallas, Texas, 75201; 99 Yorkville Ave., Toronto, Ont. M5R 3K5

HOUSE, Hon. Herbert Wallace, M.H.A., B.A., M.Ed.; politician; b. Bellburns, Nfld. 17 Dec. 1929; s. Herbert and Jessie (Moss) H.; e. Bellburns Sch. 1951; Memorial Univ. of Nfld. B.A.(Ed.) 1957; Boston Univ. M.Ed. 1965; Univ. of N.B. courses 1966; m. Winnifred Mildred d. late Alonzo Bannister, Port Rexton, Nfld. 29 Aug. 1963; children: Pamela Rae, William Baxter, Andrew Wallace; MIN. OF HEALTH, NFLD. 1979- ; Min. of Education, 1975-79; Min. of Labour and Manpower, 1978-79 (Double Portfolio); fisherman and constr. worker prior to 1950; Teacher 1952-53; Princ. 1957-65; Dir. Educ. 1966-69; Supt. of Educ. 1969-75; Mayor Town of Deer Lake 1969-75; el. M.H.A. 1975; has served as Br. Pres. Nfld. Teachers Assn., Pres. Sch. Adms., Dist. Supts. Assn., Vice Pres. Nfld. Fed. Muns.; rec'd Queen's Silver Jubilee Medal 1977; mem. Candn. Council Mins. Educ.; Hon. mem. Royal Candn. Legion; P. Conservative; Anglican; recreations: hiking, fishing, reading; Home: 18 Borden St., St. John's, Nfld.; Office: Confederation Bldg., St. John's, Nfld. A1C 5R9.

HOUSE, Robert J., B.S., M.B.A., Ph.D.; educator; b. Toledo, Ohio, 16 June 1932; s. Louis H. and Mary M. (Kinn) H.; e. Univ. of Detroit B.S. 1955, M.B.A. 1958; Ohio State Univ., Ph.D. 1960; children: Daniel, Timothy, Mary Kathleen; SHELL PROF. OF ORGANIZATION BEHAVIOUR, UNIV. OF TORONTO. Faculty of Mang. Studies since 1973; Sr. Mang. Training Specialist, North American Aviation Inc., Columbus, Ohio 1958; Instr. and Asst. Prof. Dept. Business Organ., Ohio State Univ. 1959; Research Assoc., Bureau of Industrial Relations, Univ. of Mich. 1963; Extve. Dir., McKinsey Foundation for Management Research Inc. and Assoc. Prof. of Mang., Bernard M. Baruch Coll., City Univ. of N.Y. 1965, Assoc. Prof. 1968, Prof. 1970; mem. Bd. Govs., Acad. of Mang.; E. Acad. of Mang.; Edit. Review Bd., Acad. of Mang. Review; Edit. Bd. Adm. Science Quarterly; fellow, Acad. of Mang.; fellow, Amer. Psych. Assn.; author of "Management Development: Design, Evaluation and Implementation" 1967; "Managerial Process and Organizational Behavior" 1969, revised ed. 1976; "Studies in Managerial Process and Organizational Behaviour" 1972; "Managerial Motivation and Compensation" 1972; also numerous articles and reviews in various learned and prof. journs.; mem. Edit. Review Bd., Journ. of Candn. Behavioral Science (1975); Home: 44 Charles St. W., Toronto, Ont.

HOUSTON, Donald P.; company president; b. Toronto, Ont., 13 Dec. 1933; s. John Arthur and Margaret (Airhart) H.; e. Toronto (Ont.) Schs.; m. Rose, d. John Gagne, 8 Nov. 1976; children: Linda, Susan, Christopher, Kimberlee; PRES., GEN. MGR. AND DIR., CHESEBROUGH-POND'S (CAN.) LTD. since 1971; commenced with Pond's Extract Co. of Canada Ltd. (name changed to present) as Acctg. Clerk 1954, Office Mgr. 1960. Chief Acct. 1962, Controller 1967, Treas. Sept. 1969, Vice Pres. and Treas. Dec. 1969; Past Pres., mem., of Adv. Bd. Candn. Cosmetics, Toiletries & Fragrance Assn.; United Church; recreations: golf, swimming; Home: 129 Fincham Ave., Markham, Ont. L3P 4A8; Office: 150 Bullock Dr., Markham, Ont. L3P 1W3

HOUSTON, Col. Robert Laird, C.D., B.Sc., P.Eng., LL.D., KLJ, MMLJ; trade Consultant; b. Melville, Sask., 3 Nov., 1911; s. Thomas Harrison and Frances Henrietta (Semark) H.; e. Clarkson Coll. of Technol. Potsdam,

N.U., B.Sc. (Elect. Engn.); Brit. Army Staff Coll. Camberley; U.S. Armed Forces Staff Coll. Norfolk; Nat. Defence Coll. Can.; Univ. of Sask. LL.D. 1979; m. Edna Caroline d. Arnot Glassup Vivian Leishman, M.D. 16 March 1951; two s. Thomas Arnot, John Alfred; Pres., Can.-Japan Trade Council 1967-81; Life Dr. Western Transport. Adv. Council; Dir. Royal Candn. Geog. Soc.; Ottawa Orthopaedic Fdn.; The John G Diefenbaker Memorial Fdn.; served with Candn. Army during World War II; C.O. 4th Candn. Armoured Div. Signals 1945; wounded during campaign France; awarded French Croix de Guerre; formed and commanded 3rd Candn. Div. Signals, Candn. Army Occupation Force, Germany; Dir. of Operations and Plans Candn. Army co-ordinating planning for Can.'s tri-service participation UN Emergency Force Middle E. 1956; later served as Depy. Mil. Adviser to Internat. Control Comn. Vietnam; attended U.S. Nuclear Trials Pacific, 1958; served on various internat. comtes. incl. U.S.-Can. Perm. Jt. Bd. of Defence, Chrmn. Planning Sub-comte. of that body; former Instr. Candn. Army Staff Coll. Kingston and NATO Defence Coll. Paris; resigned Candn. Armed Forces 1963; Extve. Secy. Can.-Japan Trade Council 1963, Extve. Dir. 1965-67; rec'd Gold Key to City of Osaka 1970; has lectured widely Can., Japan and U.S.; Past Chrmn. Candn. Nat. Comte. Un. World Colls.; Past Patron, Lester B. Pearson Coll. of the Pacific and Un. World Colls. (Can.) Inc.; Past Chrmn. Nat. Comte., The Rt. Hon. John G. Diefenbaker Centre, Univ. of Sask.; mem. Extve. Comte. Asian Centre Fund, Univ. of B.C.; Hon. mem. Can.-Japan Soc. of Japan; mem. Past Pres. Clarkson Coll. Alumni Assn. Bd. Govs. (rec'd Distinguished Service Award 1969); Arnold H. Barben Award, 1981; Past Pres. NATO Defence Coll. Assn. Can.; mem. Assn. Prof. Engrs. Prov. Ont.; 1st Pres., Candn. Maritime Football League 1947; made Kt. Grace Mil. & Hospitaller Order St. Lazarus Jerusalem; Mem., Companionate of Merit; Delta Upsilon; Anglican; recreations: golf, shooting, fishing; Clubs: Rideau; Royal Ottawa Golf; Canadian; Home: 2061 Cabot St., Ottawa, Ont. K1H 6J7; Office: Suite 903, 75 Albert St., Ottawa, Ont. K1P 5E7.

HOW, Douglas George, B.A.; b. Winnipeg, Man., 5 Feb. 1919; s. George Herbert and Althea (Dobson) H., e. Dorchester (N.B.) High Sch. (Grad. 1936); Sir George Williams Univ.; Mount Allison Univ., B.A. 1971; children: Patricia, Susan, Dwight; joined Moncton, N.B. "Daily Times" as a Reporter, 1937; Canadian Press, Halifax Bureau 1940-41; after war service became War Corr., edited CP News, then went to Italy; with Candn. Press in Parl'ty. Press Gallery, Ottawa, 1945-53; free-lanced as a writer in N.S. 1953-55; Extve. Asst. to Hon. Robert Winters, Min. of Public Works, Ottawa, 1955-57; with "Time" mag. in Ottawa, Toronto and N.Y., 1957-59; Mang. Ed. in Can., The Reader's Digest 1959-69; Dir. of Extension, Mount Allison University, 1973-76; now writing on his own; served in Canadian Army (Lieut., Cape Breton Highlanders), 1941-43; author of "The 8th Hussars", a regimental hist.; comnd. biog. of financier Izaak Walton Killam; ed. "The Canadians at War, 1939-45", 1969; Anglican; recreations: reading, golf; Address: R.R. 1, Parrsboro, N.S.

HOW, Hon. Henry (Harry) W., Q.C., M.L.A., B.Sc., B.C.L.; politician; b. 29 Sept. 1920; m.; 2 children; ATTORNEY GEN. OF N.S., Prov. Secy. and Min. Responsible for Adm. Regulations Act 1978-; el. M.L.A. for Kings South prov. g.e. 1970, re-el. since; Office: (P.O. Box 7) Provincial Bldg., Halifax, N.S. B3J 2L6.

HOWARD, Albert Warren, B.A.Sc.; electrical engineer, company executive; b. Calgary, Alta., 27 Nov. 1913; s. Horace Arnold and Elizabeth (Johnson) H.; e. Earl Grey Sch., Calgary, Alta.; Central High Sch., Calgary, Alta.; Univ. of Toronto, B.A.Sc. (Engn.) 1935; m. Mary Susan, d. William Davidson, 29 Sept. 1940; two s. Daryl, John; CHMN., TRANSALTA. UTILITIES CORP.; Dir. Monenco Ltd.; Dir., Maritime Electric Company Ltd.; Pres., Ottawa Valley Power Co.; joined Calgary Power Co. Ltd. as Apprentice Engr., 1935; Jr. Engr., Montreal Engineering Co. Ltd., 1939-49; Extve. Asst., Calgary Power Ltd., 1949-52; Gen. Mgr., 1952-59; Vice-Pres., 1959-65; Pres. 1965-73; mem., Candn. Elec. Assn. (Pres. 1954); Engn. Inst. Can. (Treas. 1963-64); Inst. Elect. & Electronic Engrs.; Can. National Committee/World Energy Conference; Assn. Prof. Engrs. Alta. and Que.; Protestant; recreations: golf, skiing; Home: 209 Eagle Ridge Dr. S.W., Calgary, Alta. T2V 2V6; Office: (Box 1900) Calgary, Alta. T2P 2M1

HOWARD, Helen Barbara, R.C.A.; artist; b. Long Branch, Ont. 10 March 1926; d. Thomas Edmund and Helen Margaret (MacIntosh) H.; e. elem. schs. Toronto, Thunder Bay, Chatham; Chatham Coll. Inst.; W. Tech. & Comm. Sch. Toronto; Ont. Coll. of Art A.O.C.A. 1951 (Silver Medal for Drawing & Painting); m. Richard Daley Outram 13 Apl. 1957; co-founder and proprieter with husband The Gauntlet Press 1960- ; solo exhns. incl. Picture Loan Soc. Toronto 1957, 1958, 1960, 1965; Towne Cinema, Internat. Cinema Toronto 1962; Wells Gallery 1966; Fleet Gallery Winnipeg 1966; Victoria Coll. Toronto 1966; Sisler Gallery Toronto 1974, 1976; Prince Arthur Galleries Toronto 1980; rep. in group exhns. Art Gallery of Ont. 1958, 1960, 1961 (Toronto Collects), 1976 (Drawings & Sculpture); Nat. Gallery of Can. (Candn. Watercolours, Drawings & Prints) 1966 and other exhns.; rep. numerous pub. and private colls. Can., Eng. and USA incl. Nat. Gallery of Can.; Art Gallery of Ont.; Nat. Lib. Can.; Brit. Museum; Bodleian Lib. Oxford; Am. Lib. Cong.; Univ. of Toronto Rare Books Coll.; books designed and/or illustrated: "Creatures" 1972; "Seer" 1973; "Thresholds"1973; "Locus" 1974; "Turns and Other Poems" 1975; "Arbor" 1976; "The Promise of Light" 1980, all by Richard Outram; "The Bass Saxophone" Josef Skvorecky 1977; "Whale Sound" 1977; rep. in various bibliogs.; mem. Extve. Council Royal Candn. Acad. Arts 1980-82; recreations: music, gardening, bookbinding; Address: Prince Arthur Galleries, 33 Prince Arthur Ave., Toronto, Ont. M5R 1B2.

HOWARD, Kenneth S., Q.C., B.A.; b. Montreal, Que., 24 May 1924; s. Wilbert Harvard, Q.C. and Annie Olive Partridge (Simpson) H.; e. Bishop's Coll. Sch., Lennoxville, Que., 1937-41; McGill Univ., B.A. 1946, Law 1949; m. Marie Elizabeth, d. late Knud Iversen, 25 Oct. 1950; children: Todd, Erika, Brett: PARTNER, OGILVY, RENAULT; Dir., United Corporations Ltd.; Drummond McCall Inc.: Robert Mitchell Inc.; KHD Can. Inc.; Can. Starch Co. Inc.; Halco Inc.; RoyMor Mortgage Corp.; read law with Montgomery, McMichael, Common and Howard; called to the Bar of Quebec, 1949; cr. Q.C. 1964; served as Pilot Offr. with RCAF and as Sub-Lt. with R.N. Fleet Air Arm during World War II; Unitarian; recreations: boating, golf; Clubs: Mount Bruno Country; Home: 1289 Caledonia Rd., Town of Mount Royal, Que. H3R 2V7; Office: 1981 McGill College Ave., Montreal, Que. H3A 3C1.

HOWARD, Thomas Palmer, Q.C., B.A., B.C.L.; b. Montreal, Que., 19 Aug. 1910; e. Thomas Palmer and E. Daisy (Taylor) H.; e. Selwyn House Sch. and Lower Can. Coll., Montreal, Que.; McGill Univ., B.A. 1931, B.C.L. 1934; m. Katharine, d. Charles Chipman Pineo, 22 Dec. 1934; children: Mrs. Anne Howard Osterholm, Thomas P. (C.A.); COUNSEL, McMASTER MEIGHEN; Vice Pres. and Dir., Lygon Investment Services Ltd.; Dir., Supreca Inc.; Iron Cat Inc.; Life Gov., Montreal Gen. Hosp.; read law with Lafleur, MacDougall, Macfarlane & Barclay; called to Bar of Que. 1934; cr. Q.C. 1960; Sr. Partner, Howard, McDougall, and Graham & Hannan; served in 2nd World War, R.C.A.F. 1942-46; rank Squadron Leader, Capacity Senior Judicial Officer; Hon. Solr., Weredale Foundation; Life Governor (Past President Bd. Govs. and Past Chrmn. Bd. Trustees) Martlet Foundation; mem.

R.C.A.F Benevolent Fund (Past Chrmn. and Hon. Solr. Montreal Br.); Anglican; Clubs: St. James's; Montreal; Montreal Badminton & Squash; Coral Beach & Tennis (Bermuda); Royal Bermuda Yacht; Home: Apt. 804, 4300 De Maisonneuve West, Westmount, Montreal, Que. H3Z 1K8; Office: 630 Dorchester Blvd. W., Montreal, Que. H3B 4H7

HOWARD, William Arnold, C.M.M., C.D., Q.C.; b. Calgary Alta. 19 Oct. 1918; s. late Horace Arnold and Elizabeth (Johnson) H.; e. Earl Grey Pub. Sch., King Edward High and W. Can. High Schs. Calgary 1936; Univ. of Alta. B.A., LL.B. 1941; m. Margaret, Elizabeth d. late George A. Hannah 8 Apl. 1950; children: Mary Louise, John Arnold, Barbara Joan; PARTNER, HOWARD, MACKIE; Dir. Bow Valley Industries Ltd.; Nova, an Alberta Corp.; Alberta-National Drug Co. Ltd.; Ranchmen's Resources (1976) Ltd.; Villacentres Ltd.; Magnorth Petroleum Ltd.; Itvco Resources Ltd. read law with W.H. McLaws, Q.C.; called to Bar of Alta. 1942; cr. Q.C. 1955; joined McLaws, Cairns & McLaws, Calgary 1946; Cairns & Howard 1947-51; Mahaffy & Howard 1951-57; present firm since 1957; joined Cdn. Army 1942 as Lt. serving overseas, C.O. King's Own Calgary Regt. rank Lt. Col. 1955-57, Brig. 22nd Militia Group, Militia Advisor (W. Can.) rank Brig. Gen., Depy. Chief (Reserves) CFHQ 1966, Maj. Gen. Reserves, Advisor on Reserves to Chief of Defence Staff 1970-73, Col. Commandent Royal Candn. Army Cadets 1973-8, and Hon. Col. King's Own Calgary Regt. 1973; Chrmn. Calgary Police Comm. since 1976; Chrmn. Devel. Comte.; Faculty of Law, Univ. of Calgary; Gov. Cdn. Corps of Commissionaires (S. Alta); mem. Calgary Bar Assn. (Past Pres.); Candn. Bar Assn.; Law Soc. Alta.; United Church; recreation: golf; Clubs: Ranchmen's; Calgary Golf & Country; Glencoe; Royal Candn. Mil. Inst.; Royal Alta. United Services Insti.; Home: 1232 Belavista Cres. S.W., Calgary, Alta. T2V 2B1; Office: 330 — 5th Ave. S.W., Calgary, Alta. T2P 0L4

HOWARTH, E. Michael, M.A.; association executive; b. Brighton, Eng., 26 Aug. 1918; s. William and Clara Florence (Barry) H.; came to Can. 1920; e. Pub. and High Schs., Verdun, Que.; Queen's Univ., B.A. (Econ.) 1949; Oxford Univ. (Ont. Rhodes Scholar, 1949), M.A., 1951; m. Joy Edwyna, d. E.J. Delo, Montreal, Que., 2 Nov. 1940; one s. Barry William; SR. CONSULTANT, R.W. NEAL & ASSOC.; Sales Clerk, Robert Simpson Co. Ltd., Montreal, P.Q., 1935-36; Acct. Clk., Sun Life Assurance Co. of Can., Montreal, 1936-40, and Investment Analyst there 1951-52; Office Supervisor, Charles E. Frosst & Co., Montreal, P.Q. 1952-55; Secy., Candn. Inst. of Chart. Accts., 1955-60; Extve. Vice-Pres., Fed. Council of Sales Finance Co.'s, 1960-65; Dean of Men, Univ. of Coll., Univ. of Toronto 1965-74; Nat. Dir., Assn. of Can. Clubs 1974-80; served in 2nd World War with RCAF 1940-45 as Flying Instr.; discharged with rank of Flying Offr.; Past Asst. Gen. Secy. for Rhodes Scholarships in Can.; Candn. Assn. of Rhodes Scholars (Secy.-Treas. 1955-65; Pres. 1973-75); Liberal; Anglican; recreations: badminton, swimming, bridge; Office: Ste. 602, 350 Sparks St., Ottawa, Ont. K1R 7S8

HOWARTH, J. E. Gorse, M.B.E., M.A.; Canadian public servant; b. Bradford, Eng., 10 Oct. 1921; s. James and Lilian (Oliver) H.; e. Archbishop Holgates York, Eng.; St. Edmund Hall Oxford Univ. M.A. (Oxon) 1947; m. Audrey d. Harry Holmes, 14 July 1950; one s. Jeremy Peter Gorse; COMMR. FOREIGN INVESTMENT REVIEW AGENCY since 1976; Asst. Merchandise Mgr. Tootal Ltd. Manchester, Eng. 1947-51; Asst. Mang. Dir. Baerlein Bros. Ltd. Manchester 1951-53; Mgr. Product Devel. Dominion Textile Ltd. 1953-60; Merchandise Mgr. United Merchants & Manufacturers Ltd. 1960-64; Depy. Br. Dir. and Br. Dir. Dept. Industry Ottawa 1965-67, Dir. Internat. Econ. Relations Dept. Finance 1967-70; Pres. Howarth & Co. Ottawa 1971-74; Depy. Commr. present Agency 1974; served with Royal Marines 1941-46, No. 3

Commando Bgde., rank Maj.; Anglican; Home: Cascades R.R. # 3, Wakefield, Que. J0X 3G0; Office: 240 Sparks St., Ottawa, Ont. K1P 6A5

HOWE, Bruce Iver; executive; b. Dryden, Ont. 19 May 1936; s. Norman I. and Laura A. (Locking) H.; e. Queen's Univ. Chem. Engn. 1958; Harvard Univ. Mang. Devel. 1961; m. Elsie Evelyn Ann Ferguson 25 Aug. 1962; children: Karen, Norman, Kristina; PRES., CHIEF EXTVE. OFFR. AND DIR., BRITISH COLUMBIA RESOURCES INVESTMENT CORP. 1980- ; Chmn. of Bd., B.C. Coal and B.C. Timber 1980- ; Dir., Bank of Montreal; B.C. Place; joined MacMillan Bloedel 1963, Group Vice Pres., Pulp & Paper 1971, Sr. Vice Pres. Operations 1977-79; Pres., C.O.O. and Dir., 1979-80; Trustee, Queen's Univ.; Gov., Vancouver Pub. Aquarium; Extve. Bd. YMCA; author various articles pulp and paper prof. mags.; mem. City & Guilds; London Inst. (Insignia Award); Assn. Prof. Engrs. Prov. B.C.; Am. Mang. Assn.; Brit. Paper & Bd. Makers Assn.; recreations: diving, tennis, squash; Clubs: Vancouver; Vancouver Lawn Tennis; Past Pres., Canadian Club of Vancouver.; Home: 4715 W. 2nd Ave., Vancouver, B.C. V6T 1C1; Office: 1176 West Georgia St., Ste. 1900 Vancouver, B.C. V6E 4B9.

HOWE, Gordon, O.C. (1971); hockey player; b. Saskatoon, Sask., 31 March 1928; s. Albert Clarence and Katherine (Schultz) H.; e. Westmount and King George Schs., Saskatoon, Sask. 1944; m. Colleen Janet, d. Valerian Mark, Joffa, 15 April 1953; children: Marty Gordon, Mark Steven, Cathleen Jill, Murray Albert; Pres., Gordon Howe Enterprises; Breeder Reg'd. Polled Hereford & Simmental cattle, Jackson, Mich.; commenced prof. hockey for Galt (Ont.) 1944-45, and Omaha (Neb.) 1945-46; joined Detroit Hockey Club 1946 and with that Organ. until retirement 1971 when joined World Hockey Assn. (Houston Oilers and later Hartford Whalers); scored 1000 NHL career goal, 1979-80; Awards incl., Hart Memorial Trophy; Art Ross Trophy; Lester Patrick Trophy; mem. 1st All Star Team 12 times and 2nd All Star Team 9 times; named Candn. Athlete of the Yr. 1963; mem. Hockey Hall of Fame; Sports Hall of Fame; co-author of "Hockey, Here's Howe" 1963; co-author, "Gordie Howe, No. 9"; also numerous articles for sports publs.; mem. Hockey Hall of Fame; Protestant; recreations: golf, fishing; Club: Plum Hollow Golf.

HOWE, John Wallace, M.S., Ph.D.; b. Greenwood, B.C., 18 Dec. 1901; s. William Wallace and Eva Elizabeth (Abbott) H.; e. Westward Ho! Sch., Edmonton, Alta., 1918; Olds (Alta.) Sch. of Agric., 1920-21: Univ. of Alta., B.S. 1925; Iowa State Coll., M.S. 1928; Iowa State Univ., Ph.D. 1946; Cambridge Univ., 1935; m. Bessie Isabel, d. Thomas Gourlay Bell, Portgage La Prairie, Man., 26 June 1931; children: Joan Isabel, John Vernon Wallace; Dean Emeritus, Sch. of Agric. Texas A&I Univ., since 1967; Dist. 4-H Club Agt., Mitchell, S.Dak., 1928-30; Agric. Rep., Camrose, Alta., 1930; Instr., Animal Science Univ. of Alta., 1930-31; Asst. Prof. 1945-48; Princ., Sch. of Agric. and Supt., Govt. Stock Farm, Jamaica 1931-39; Dir., Div. of Agric., Texas Coll. of Arts and Industries, 1948-65; Dean, Sch. of Agric. 1965-72; retired 1972; served with Jamaica Engr. Corps, 1932-45; retired with rank Maj.; rec'd. Kings Jubilee Medal; Kings Coronation Medal; Silver Beaver Award Boy Scouts of Am.; author of series of articles on Dairy Farming for "Journal Jamaica Agricultural Society", 1933-40; mem. Am. Soc. Animal Prod.; Am. Soc. Advanc. Science; Am. Soc. Range Mang.; building Texas A & I Univ. Campus named in his honour; Freemason; Alpha Tau Alpha; Alpha Gamma Rho; Gamma Sigma Delta; Sigma Xi; Episcopalian; recreation: amateur radio; Club: Rotary; Home: 1630 Santa Maria Dr., Kingsville, Texas 78363.

HOWES, Frederick Stanley, M.Sc., Ph.D.; emeritus professor Elec. Eng., McGill Univ.; b. Paris, Ont., 25 July

1896, s. Alfred and Martha Alberta (Adamson) H.; e. Windsor (Ont.) Coll. Inst.; McGill Univ., B.Sc. (Elec. Engn.) 1924, M.Sc. 1926; Imperial Coll., Dipl. 1928; Univ. of London, Ph.D. 1929; m. Margaret Isobel, d. James Andrew Kinney, 24 Apl. 1943; Lectr., Dept. of Engn., McGill Univ., 1929-43, Asst. Prof. 1943-46, Assoc. Prof. 1946; Prof. 1956-64; Dir. of Univ. Extension, 1949-60; served in World War 1916-19; enlisted with 241st Candn. Scot.; served in France with 75th Bn. Signals; discharged 1919; Hon. Life mem. or Fellow of a no. of learned socs.; mem., Corp. of Engrs. Que.; Home: 3375 Ridgewood Ave., Apt. 412, Montreal, P.Q. H3V 1B5

HOWICK, Wilfrid, C.M.; O.St.J.; industrialist; b. Tripoli, Lebanon 20 Jan. 1909; s. Louis D. and Mariana (Haddad) H.; came to Can. 1909; e. St. Mary's Pub. Sch. and Comm. High Sch. Montreal; Montreal Tech. Sch.; Sir George Williams Coll.; McGill Univ.; m. Najla d. Assaf Aziz 19 Oct. 1937; children: John David, Stephen Andrew, Suzanne Mary, Peter Douglas; founded W. Howick Ltd. 1938 (now Howick Apparel Ltd.); Founder (1959) and Dir. Lloyd Shirt Inc.; Founding Pres., Children's Apparel Mfrs. Assn; Middle East Immigrant Aid Society; Dir. Big Blue Inc.; Manoir Knitting Inc.; Mona Knit Inc.; Domaine Distributors; founded Town Girl Wear Ltd. 1946; Salesman 1929-38; Gov., Montreal Children's Hosp.; Montreal Gen. Hosp.; Notre Dame Hosp.; Royal Victoria Hosp.; Cedars Cancer Fund; Hon. Life Gov., Candn. Apparel Mfrs. Assn.; mem. La Loge des Couers Unis; Club: Kanawaki Golf; Home: 51 Vivian Ave., Town of Mount Royal, Que. H3P 1N5; Office: 1400 Antonio Barbeau, Montreal, Que. H4N 1H5.

HOWISON, Alan G.; executive; b. London, Eng. 9 June 1932; s. James Condie and Molly Beatrice H.; e. Loretto Sch., Musselburgh, Scot. 1950; m. Nancy Louise d. C. Gordon Smith, Winnipeg, Man. 1 Oct. 1955; children: Tricia, Jamie, Bruce; EXTVE. DIR. THE WINNIPEG FOUNDATION since 1976; Dir. Tees and Persse Ltd.; The Canadian Indemnity Co.; United Canadian Shares Ltd.; joined Oldfield Kirby & Gardner Ltd. 1956-67; Partner Invest. Div. 1961-67; Br. Mgr. Winnipeg Office, Francis I. Du Pont & Co. 1967-70; Richardson Securities of Canada 1970-75, Resident Mgr. Winnipeg Br. 1974-75; served with The Black Watch (R.H.R) 1950-53, attached 1st Bn. Kings African Rifles 1951-52, service in E. Africa and Malaya, Queen's Own Cameron Highlanders (Reserve) 1953-55, rank Lt.; mem. of Bd., Winnipeg Bible Coll.; Sinking Fund Trustee, City of Winnipeg and Winnipeg Sch. Divis. No. 1.; Presbyterian; recreations: golf, cross-country skiing, gardening; Clubs: Manitoba; St. Charles Country (Dir. 1966-73); Winnipeg Squash; Home: 2850 Assiniboine Ave., Winnipeg, Man. R3J 0B1; Office: 800 — 305 Broadway, Winnipeg, Man. R3C 3J7

HOWISON, Jean-Pierre; B.Com.; executive; b. Montreal, Que. 25 Jan. 1933; s. Alfred and Cécile (Racette) H.; e. Loyola Coll. B.Com. 1956; McGill Univ. C.A. 1959; m. Dorothy d. Harris 14 Nov. 1959; children: Robert, Nathalie; VICE PRES. (FINANCE & PLANNING) & TREASURER, SIDBEC/DOSCO LTD.; Dir. Sidbec-Normines Inc.; Asst. Treas. Davie Shipbuilding Ltd. Lauzon, Que. 1959-66; joined Sidbec 1966 serving as Chief Acct., Treas. and Comptroller, Vice Pres. Finance; Dir. Inst. Charlemagne; mem. Candn. Inst. C.A.'s; Financial Extve. Inst.; R. Catholic; recreation: skiing; Home: 4 Hazel Dr., Dollard-des-Ormeaux, Que. H9B 1C5; Office: 507 Place d'Armes, Montreal, Que. H2Y 2W8

HOWLAND, Robert Dudley, Ph.D.; economist; b. Bexley, Kent, England, 1 June 1909; s. Sidney James and Kate (Holmes) H.; came to Canada 1926; e. Queen Elizabeth's Grammar Sch., Faversham, Kent, Eng.; Brandon (Man.) Coll.; London Sch. of Econ. Ph.D. (Econ.); m. 1st, late Gertrude Adelaide, d. late Ernest Bruder, Winnipeg, Man., Sept. 1943; children: Roger Douglas, Charles Robert, Janet Doreen; m. 2ndly, Kathleen Dorothy Kier-

ans, 1967; ENERGY CONSULTANT; Special Asst. to Deputy Minister of Labour, Ottawa, Ont., 1943-47; Secy., Royal Comn. on Coal (Justice Carroll), 1944-46; Vice-Pres., N.S. Research Foundation 1947-50; Depy. Min. of Trade & Industry, N.S., 1950-53; Econ. Advisor to N.S. Govt., 1950-55; Economist Royal Comn. on Canada's Econ. Prospects, 1955-57; mem., Royal Comn. on Energy, 1957-59; member & Vice-Chairman, National Energy Board, Canada, 1959-68, Chairman 1968-73; member, Royal Commission on Saskatchewan Coal Mining Indust., 1949; mem., N.S. Institute of Science; Institute of Pub. Adm.; Baptist; recreations: sheep breeding, beekeeping, gardening, golf; Home: R.R. No. 1, Dunrobin, Ont. K0A 1T0

HOWLAND, Hon. William Goldwin Carrington, B.A., LL.B., LL.D.; b. Toronto, Ont., 7 Marc. 1915; s. Dr. Goldwin William and Margaret Christian (Carrington) H.; e. Upper Canada Coll., Toronto, 1923-32; University of Toronto, B.A. (Law) 1936, LL.B. 1939; Osgoode Hall Law Sch. (Silver Medallist); m. Margaret Patricia, d. late Kenneth Alfred Greene, 20 Aug. 1966; CHIEF JUSTICE OF ONT. since 1977; Advisory Council, The Toronto Symphony; read law with Rowell Reid Wright & McMillan; called to Bar of Ont. 1939; cr. Q.C. 1955; has practised law with McMillan, Binch 1939-75; Justice, Court of Appeal, Ont., 1975-77; Lectr. in Mortgages, Osgoode Hall Law School, 1950-67; served with Canadian Army 1942-45; Captain RCASC; appointed Staff Captain, Canadian Army Pacific Force; National Pres., U.N. Assn. in Canada, 1959-60 Pres., Univ. Coll. Alumni Assn., 1958; Churchwarden, Grace Church on-the-Hill, 1959-61; Extve., Council for Social Service, Ang. Ch. of Can. for many yrs. to 1967; mem., Bd. of Govs., Upper Can. Coll. 1968-70, 1977- ; mem. of Senate, York Univ. 1968-69; el. Bencher, Law Soc. Upper Can. 1961 and 1966 (Treas. 1968-70); Chrmn., Legal Educ. Comte. 1964-68; mem., Candn. Bar Assn. (Council 1959-62); Pres., Fed. of Law Socs. of Can. 1973-74; Trust., Wycliffe Coll.; Hon. LL.D. Queen's Univ. 1972; Univ. of Toronto 1981; Phi Delta Phi (Hon. mem.); Delta Upsilon (Pres. 1936); Anglican; recreation: travel; Clubs: Toronto; Toronto Hunt; Canadian; Empire; Home: 2 Bayview Wood, Toronto, Ont. M4N 1R7; Office: Osgoode Hall, Toronto, Ont. M5H 2N5

HOWLETT, Leslie Ernest, M.B.E., M.A., Ph.D., F.R.S.C. (1946); b. London, Eng., 29 Oct. 1903; s. Ernest William and Gertrude Miriam (Whyman) H.; e. Univ. of Brit. Columbia, B.A. 1927; Univ. of Toronto, M.A. 1928; McGill Univ., Ph.D. 1931; m. Kathleen Ruby, d. Harold Sankey Hammond, 10 Oct. 1947; three s. William, John, Keith; Demonst., Dept. of Physics, Univ. of Toronto, 1927-28; held Nat. Research Council Bursary, 1928, Studentship 1929 and Fellowship 1930; Head, Optics Lab., Nat. Research Council, 1931-48; Chief Scient. Liaison Offr., Nat. Research Council, London, Eng., on interchange of scient. information between the U.K. and Can., 1941-42; Co-Dir., Divn. of Physics, Nat. Research Council, 1948-52; Dir., Div. of Applied Physics, 1952-68; Ed.-in-Chief, "Metrologia" 1965-68; Pres., Space Optic Ltd. 1968; Fellow, Optical Society of Am.; mem. and Vice Pres., Internat. Comn. of Optics 1966-69; Am. Soc. Photogrammetry; Candn. Nat. Comte. for Physics 1950-68; Hon. Treas., Roy. Soc. of Can., 1947-53; mem. Internat. Comte. of Weights & Measures 1954-68 (Vice Pres. 1960-64, Pres. 1964-68); Pres., Adv. Comte. for Definition of the Metre 1954-68; Hon. mem., Internat. Comte. of Weights and Measures since 1969; Hon. mem., Candn. Inst. Surveying; Alpha Delta Phi; recreations: tennis, swimming, painting, sailing; Home: 1702 - 71 Somerset St. W., Ottawa, Ont. K2P 2G2

HOWSAM, Air Vice Marshal George Roberts, C.B. (1945), M.C.; b. Port Perry, Ont., 29 Jan. 1895; s. George Roberts and Mary Ida (Cutting) H.; e. Port Perry Pub. and High Schs.; R.A.F. Staff Coll., Andover, Eng., P.S.A. 1930; m. 1stly Lillian Isobel (d. 1970) d. William

Mitchell Somerville, 18 June 1918; one s., Peter Somerville; 2ndly Marion Isobel, d. Clarence Albert Mitchell and Mary Blanche McCurdy, Nova Scotia, 1972; joined C.E.F. 1916 and R.F.C. 1917; served in France 1917-18; twice wounded; awarded M.C.; with Army of Occupation in Germany; returned to R.C.A.F. in Can. 1921; engaged R.C.A.F Aerial Survey, N.W. Can.; mem. of first R.C.A.F. Siskin Team, Cleveland Air Races, 1929; Staff member CGAO Operations AFHQ 1931-32; Air Staff Offr., M.D. 2, Toronto, 1933-36; O.C. 2 Army Co-op. Sqdn., Ottawa, 1937; Director of Training, Air Force Headquarters, Canada 1938-40; England and France, 1940; in charge of Organization and Training, No. 4 Training Command, Western Canada, late 1940; Commanded No. 11 Service Flying Training Sch., Yorkton, Sask., 1941; Air O.C., No. 4 Training Command, Calgary, Alberta, 1942-44, and also simultaneously commanded Operational Air Staging Route from U.S. through N.W. Canada to Alaska (double command for 2 years), 1942-43; Chairman, Organ. Comte., Air Force Hdqrs, Ottawa, 1945; retired 1946; entered business, Dir., Sicks' Breweries Ltd., 1946-58; Dom. Dir., Air Cadet League, 1946-47 (Sask. Prov. Chrmn., 1946); Pres., Regina Flying Club, 1946; Alta. Chrmn., R.C.A.F. Assn., 1958-59; Pres. Edmonton Un. Services Inst., 1948; Commdr., Legion of Merit (U.S.) 1945; Commandeur de l'Ordre de la Couronne (Belgium), 1948; Order of the White Lion (Czechoslovakia), 1946; Alta. Co-ordinator for Civil Defence 1950-57 on one-dollar-a-year basis, and on salary basis, 1957-Dec. 1959 when resigned; Candn. Del. to Emergency Measures, NATO Assembly, Paris, 1960; Freemason; Conservative; Anglican; recreations: gardening, writing, shooting; Clubs: Ranchmen's (Calgary); Union of B.C.; Empire (Toronto); Canadian: Victoria Golf; Address: 2040 Paul's Terrace, Victoria, B.C. V8N 2Z3

HOWSE, Claude Kilborn, D.Sc.; geologist; b. Burin, Nfld. 7 Nov. 1907; s. Rev. Dr. Charles and Elfrida (Palmer) H.; e. Grand Bank (Nfld.) Acad.; Meth. Coll., St. John's, Nfld.; Dalhousie Univ., Memorial Univ. B.Sc., 1933, one yr. post-grad. studies; Mem. Univ. of Nfld., D.Sc. 1974; m. (Mary) Phyllis, d. William King Mercer, 4 Oct. 1937; two d. Claudia Florence (Temple), Barbara Jean (Shaffer) Nfld. Rep., Iron Ore Co. of Canada, 1959-74; Consult., Iron Ore Co. of Can., 1974- ; Dir., Carol Lake Co.; Asst. Govt. Geol., Geol. Survey of Nfld., 1934-37; Assoc. Govt. Geol. 1937-42; Govt. Geol. 1943-49; Depy. Min. of Mines, Dept. of Mines, Nfld. 1950-55; St. John's Rep., British Newfoundland Corp. 1955-59; mem. Un. Ch. Bd. of Educ., St. John's 1939-64; Bd. of Regents, Mem. Univ. of Nfld. 1950-69; United Church; recreation: golf; Club: Lindsay Golf & Country; Address: 147 Albert St. N., Lindsay, Ont. K9V 4V1

HOWSE, Rev. Ernest Marshall Frazer, S.T.M., Ph.D., D.D., Litt.D., (Un. Ch.); retired; b. Twillingate, Nfld., 29 Sept. 1902; s. Rev. Charles (D.D.) and Elfreda (Palmer) H.; e. Meth. Coll., St. John's, Nfld.; Albert Coll., Belleville, Ont.; Dalhousie Univ., B.A. 1929; Pine Hill Divinity Hall, Halifax (Grad. Theol., Hon. Ch. Hist.) 1931; Union Theol. Semy., N.Y., S.T.M. 1932; Univ. of Edin., Ph.D 1934; United Coll., Winnipeg, Man., D.D. 1948; Laurentian Univ., D.D. 1964; Univ. of Toronto, D.D. 1967; Memorial Univ. of Nfld., Litt.D. 1965; m. Esther Lilian, d. David Black of Pasadena, Cal., 17 Sept. 1932; children: Margery (Mrs. Raymond Dyer), David, George; Min., Beverly Hills Pres. Ch., Cal., 1934-35; Westminster Un. Ch., Winnipeg, 1935-48; Pres., Toronto Conf. Un. Ch. Can., 1961-62; Commr., Gen. Council Un. Ch., Belleville, 1942, Montreal 1946, Toronto 1950, Sackville, N.B. 1954, Windsor 1956, Edmonton 1960, London, 1962, St. John's, Nfld., 1964; Min., Bloor St. United Ch., Toronto 1948-70; Moderator, United Ch. of Can. 1964-66; Accredited Visitor and Newspaper Corr., 1st Assembly World Council of Chs., Amsterdam 1948, 2nd Assembly, Evanston, Ill., 1954, 3rd Assembly, New Delhi 1961; 4th Assembly,

Uppsala 1968; 5th Assembly, Nairobe 1974; given Key to City and made Hon. Citizen of Soeul, Korea, 1965; one of 25 Christians invited, 1954 to Bhamdoun, Lebanon for first Muslim Christian Convocation; el. in Cairo, Egypt, 1955, Christian Co-Pres. of Continuing Comt. on Muslim-Christian Co-operation; Candn. Del. to 1st World Conf. on Religion & Peace, Kyoto, Japan 1970; author of "Our Prophetic Heritage", 1945; "The Law and the Prophets", 1947; "Saints in Politics", 1955, 2nd Eng. ed. 1960, 3rd 1971; l"Spiritual Values in Shakespeare," 1955; "The Lively Oracles", 1956; "People and Provocations", 1965; many articles and reviews; weekly Columnist for Toronto Star 1970-79; rec'd Toronto's annual Award of Merit, 1980; recreations: carpentry, boating, fishing; Home: 31 Eastbourne Ave., Toronto, Ont. M5P 2E8

HOYT, George C., M.A., Ph.D.; educator; b. N.J., 5 Oct. 1924; s. George Stanley and Annie Elizabeth (Wright) H.; e. Stanford Univ., A.B. 1950; Univ. of Chicago, M.A. 1954; Univ. of Cal. Berkeley, Ph.D. 1962; m. Eugenia, d. late Peter Zappas, 26 March 1951; children: David, Barbara, Riley, Carl: PROF. AND CHRM., BUSINESS ADM., SIMON FRASER UNIV.; served with Edwin S. Hewitt Assoc. as Consultant; Bechtel Corp.; Univ. of Cal.; Univ. of Iowa; Mass. Inst. of Technol.; Consultant to various firms in Can. and U.S.; Commendation; author of numerous articles on community study, organ. leadership and decision making, indust. retirement policy; mem., Am. Econ. Assn.; Candn. Econ. Assn.; Candn. Assn. Administrative Sciences; Am. Sociol. Assn.; Gamma Beta Sigma; Omicron Delta Epsilon; recreations: fishing, hiking, horses; Club: University; Home: 10128 McKinnon Cres., Fort Langley, B.C. V0X 1J0; Office: Burnaby, B.C.

HRABOWSKY, Ivan, D.D.S., F.A.G.D.; dentist; b. Toronto Ont., 2 Aug. 1931; s. late Nestor and Klimentia (Semen) H.; e. King Edward Pub. Sch., Toronto 1944; Harbord Coll. Inst., Toronto 1949; Univ. of Toront, Faculty of Dent., D.D.S. 1954; m. Vlada, d. late Petras Karvelis and Rose Zukus, 12 Sept. 1953; children: Ivan Mark, Michael Peter, Yvonna Vladislava; Pres. (1970-71), Ont. Dental Assn. (mem. Bd. Govs. 1967-72, mem. Extve. Council 1967-72); Pres., Denpropco Ltd.; Praxiscomputer Inc.; Gov., Candn. Dental Assn. (mem. Extve. Council); C.O.T.C. 1951-54; rank 2/Lt.; P. Conservative; recreations: travel, photography, philately, skiing; Address: 203 - 431 St. Paul St., St. Catharines, Ont. L2R 3N4

HUBBARD, Robert Hamilton, O.C., M.A., Ph.D., LL.D., F.R.S.C.; art historian; b. Hamilton, Ont., 17 June 1916; s. Charles Robert and Mary Elizabeth (Strattan) H.; e. McMaster Univ., B.A. 1937; Inst. d'Art et d'Archéologie, Univ. of Paris, Summer School 1938; Musées royaux de Belgique, Brussels, Summer School 1939; Univ. of Wis., M.A. 1940; Ph.D. 1942; Mount Allison. LL.D. 1965; HONORARY HISTORIAN AND ARCHIVIST TO GOVERNOR GENERAL OF CAN., since 1981; and Adjunct Prof. Carleton Univ. since 1974; Fellow, Art Hist., Univ. of Wis., 1939-41; Asst. there 1941-42; Chrmn., Dept. of Art., Univ. of Kansas City, 1942-44; Special Lectr., Nat. Gallery of Can., 1944-45; joined staff of Nat. Gallery, 1946; apptd. Curator of Candn. Art, 1947; Chief Curator, 1954-78; Cultural Adv. to Gov. Gen. of Can. 1978-81; Lectr. in Art and Archaeol., Univ. of Toronto, 1945-46; has lect. at McMaster Univ., Carleton Coll., Ottawa, and at various museums and soc.; author of "The Colonial Tradition in French Canadian Sculpture" (Ph.D. thesis), 1942; also many exhibition catalogues, articles, etc. on art and architecture and the Nat. Gallery Collection in "Arch. Review" (London), "Connoisseur" (London). "Art Quarterly" (Detroit). "Art in America" (N.Y.), "Canadian Art", and "Oxford Companion to Art"; "Dictionary of Canadian Biography"; "Growth in Canadian Art" in "The Culture of Contemporary Canada", 1957; "Viceregal Influences on Canadian Society" in W.L. Morton's "The Shield of Achilles",

1968; Books: "The National Gallery Catalogues", Vol. 1; "Older Schools", 1957; Vol. 2: "Modern European Schools", 1959; Vol. 3: "Canadian School", 1959; "An Anthology of Canadian Art" 1959; "European Paintings in Canadian Collections", 2 vol., 1956-62; "Tom Thomson", 1962; "The Development of Canadian Art" 1963; "Rideau Hall", 1967; "Scholarship in Canada" (ed.), 1968; "Cathedral in the Capital" 1972; "Thomas Davies in Early Canada" 1973; "Rideau Hall, an Illustrated History", 1977; mem., Royal Soc. of Arts; Fellow, Royal Canadian Geog. Society; mem., Internat. Council of Museums: Candn. Hist. Assn.; Hon. Secy., Roy. Soc. of Can., 1969-71, Hon. Librarian 1971-75, Pres. of Acad. of Humanities and Social Sciences, 1977-78; Clubs: Rideau; Athenaeum (London); Home: 916, The Champlain Towers, 200 Rideau Terrace, Ottawa K1M 0Z3, Ont.; Office: Rideau Hall, Ottawa, Ont.K1A 0A1

HUBBS,George James, A.B., M.B.A.; computer company executive; b. San Francisco, Cal. 9 Oct. 1938; s. Ronald Marion and Margaret Stewart (Jamie) H.; e. St. Paul (Minn.) Acad. 1956; Yale Univ. A.B. 1960; Harvard Univ. M.B.A. 1963; m. Ann Fraser d. C. L. Granquist, Hadley, Mass. 19 Aug. 1961; children: James Fraser, Robin Stewart, Jennifer Ann; CHRMN. OF BD. AND PRES., CONTROL DATA CANADA LTD. 1977- ; Dist. Mgr. Applications Analysis, Control Data Corp. 1968-70; Dist. Sales Mgr. 1970-73; Gen. Mgr. Cybernet Services Div. 1973, Gen. Mgr. Educ. & Med. Industry Mgmt. Offices 1973-75; Vice Pres. Financial & Comm. Group 1975-76; mem. Ont. Business Adv. Council 1978- ; First Vice Pres. and Dir. Candn. Business Equipment Mfrs. Assn. 1979- ; mem. Ont. Global Product Mandate Adv. Comte. 1980- ; served with U.S. Army 1964-66, rank Sgt.; Chi Phi, P. Conservative; Anglican; recreations: skiing, tennis, numismatics, reading; Clubs: Sir Winston Churchill Tennis; Mississauga Racquet; Sankaty Head Golf; Home: 74 Ardwold Gate, Toronto, Ont. M5R 2W2; Office: 1855 Minnesota Court, Mississauga, Ont. L5N 1K7.

HUBEL, Vello, R.C.A.; industrial designer; artist; educator; b. Tallinn, Estonia 6 July 1927; s. Gustav and Hilda (Kunkman) H.; came to Can. 1947; e. Ont. Coll. of Art Indust. Design A.O.C.A. 1955; Mass. Inst. of Technol. summer 1962, 1971, 1973 (Nat. Design Council Scholarships); m. Nelly d. Anton Gustavson, Toronto, Ont. 10 Apl. 1965; two d. Kalli Ann, Tiina Katrin; PROP., VELL HUBEL DESIGNS 1958- ; indust. design consultant to Candn. mfrs.; designer many wood, plastic and metal products, comm. interiors and exhibits; consultant to fed. and various prov. govts. on design; initiated and directed no. of design based symposiums and events; served on various design and art juries; part-time teacher Ont. Coll. of Art since 1965; prepared over 300 coloured drawings of old Toronto houses 1970-76; recipient numerous design awards; City of Toronto Medal of Service; exmem. Art Adv. Comte. Toronto City Hall; Hon. Treas. Royal Candn. Acad. Arts 1978-81; mem. Assn. Candn. Indust. Designers (Vice Pres. 1965-67, Ont. Chapter Pres. 1970-72); Candn. Power Sqdn.; Estonian Fed. in Can. (Pres. 1979-); Protestant; recreations: cross-country skiing, sailing, drawing, painting; Address: 531 Soudan Ave., Toronto, Ont. M4S 1X1.

HUDECKI, Stanley Michael, M.P., M.D., F.R.C.S.(C); politician; orthopedic surgeon; b. Hamilton, Ont. 22 Apl. 1916; s. Michael and Mary (Marcisz) H.; e. Cathedral High Sch. Hamilton; Univ. of Toronto M.D. 1940; Postgrad. Surg. Training Hamilton Gen., Toronto Gen. and Sick Children's Hosps.; m. Mary Leona d. Henry Johnson 24 Oct. 1945; children: Bernard, John, Mary Ann Thompson, Helen Daly, Peter, Catherine, Steven, Stanley and Richard; mem. Active Staff St. Joseph's Hosp. Hamilton; Assoc. Prof. of Surg. McMaster Med. Sch.; el. to H. of C. for Hamilton W. by-el. 1980; Trustee, Rygiel Home; Participation House; named Sertoma Man. of Yr.; rec'd Glen Sawyer Award for Community Service, Ont.

Med. Assn.; Queen's Silver Jubilee Medal; served with Royal Candn. Med. Corps 1942-46; Past Pres. Newman Alumni and Candn. Club; Med. Legal Soc. (Hamilton); mem. Candn. Orthopedic Assn.; Am. Acad. for Cerebral Palsy; Candn. Med. Assn.; Toronto & Hamilton Acad. Med.; Liberal; R. Catholic; recreations: tennis, reading; Home: 290 Caroline St. S., Hamilton, Ont. L8P 3L9; Office: House of Commons, Ottawa, Ont. K1A 0A6 and 987 King St. E., Hamilton, Ont.

HUDON, Albert V., B.A., B.Com., M.B.A.; b. Montreal, Que. 11 Jan 1932; s. Dr. Maurice and Alexina (Beaudry) H.; e. Bourget Coll., Rigaud, Que. 1950; Sir George Williams Univ. B.A., B.Com. 1954; Babson Inst., M.B.A. 1955; Centre d'études industrielles, Geneva, Cert. in Internat. Adm. 1956; m. late Victoria, d. Daniel de Ytturalde 6 Aug. 1955; children: Maurice, François, Danielle; Principal-Charette Fortier Hawey-Tucheross & Partners; former Pres. and Chief Extve. Offr., Miron Co. Ltd. commenced as Jr. Analyst, Northern Aluminium, Banbury, Eng. 1956; Sr. Programmer-Analyst Alcan Aluminum Co. Ltd., Montreal 1960; Secy.-Treas. Constr. Industry Joint Comte. 1963, Gen. Mgr. 1965; Corp. Secy. Atlas Construction Co. Ltd. 1969; Extve. Vice-Pres. Miron Co. Ltd. 1973; R. Catholic; recreations: golf, swimming; Clubs: St. Denis; Mount Bruno Golf & Country; Home: 424 Wood Ave., Westmount, Que. H3Y 3J2

HUDON,Yves; exécutif; né Montréal, Qué. 11 mai 1925; f. Paul et Evelyne (Lefaivre) H.; é Académie Saint-Léon de Westmount; McGill Univ.; ép. Claire f. Alphonse Bélanger 24 février 1953; enfants: François, André, Marie, Martine; PRES., LES ALIMENTS IMASCO LTÉE 1979- ; Prés. dir. gén., Les Aliments Grissol Ltée; Viau Ltée; Aliments Loney Ltée; Taillefer & Fils Inc.; mem. du Conseil d'adm., Modern Plastics Co. Ltd.; Les Industries John Lewis Ltés; Les Constructions Sofidel Inc.; Gérant du bureau et du service de crédit, Hudon & Orsali 1948-52, administrateur 1952-56; asst.-directeur du service des achats, Shop & Save 1957-58; prés. et gérant gén. Loney Foods 1959-61; prés. et gérant gén. Les Aliments Grissol 1961- ; Gouverneur, Univ. de Sherbrooke, Faculté Adm.; mem. Ex-Young Pres.' Organ. (Y.P.Q.); Adresse: 1403 Boul. Mont-Royal, Outremont, P.Q. H2V 2J5 Bureau: 4 square Westmount, Montréal, Qué. H3Z 2S8.

HUDSON, Alan Roy, M.B., Ch.B., F.R.C.S.(C); neurosurgeon; educator; b. Cape Town, S. Africa 16 March 1938; s. John George H.; e. Rondebosch Boys'' High Sch.; Univ. of Cape Town; Univ. of Toronto; Oxford Univ.; M.B.Ch.B. 1960; F.R.C.S. Ed. 1964; L.M.C.C. 1965; F.R.C.S. (C.) 1968; came to Can.; m. Susan Elizabeth d. Roy Hurd 1962; children: Jean, Katherine, Erin, Roy; PROF. OF NEUROSURGERY UNIV. OF TORONTO; author numerous papers and chapters on peripheral nerve injuries; mem. Council Candn. Neurosurgical Soc.; recreation: yachting; Home: 40 Bannatyne Dr., Willowdale, Ont. M2L 2N9; Office: St. Michael's Hospital, 38 Shuter St., Toronto, Ont. M5B 1A6.

HUDSON, George Wharton, E.D., F.C.A., R.I.A.; b. Grenada, B.W.I., 25 Jan. 1899; s. Horace and Georgina (Ross) H.; e. Pub., Private and Grenada Boys' Secondary Sch., Grenada, B.W.I.; Jarvis Coll. Inst., Toronto, Ont. (night classes); corr. course with Queen's Univ., for C.A. degree; m. Leslie Stewart, d. Lieut.-Col. Stewart S. Skinner, M.D., 11 June 1930; children: Stewart Wharton, Leslie Claire; former Partner, Hudson, McMackin & Co. (Chart. Accts.); Jr. Bookkeeper, Willard Chocolates Ltd. 1917-18; articled Clk., Oscar Hudson & Co., 1918; later trans. to offices in Montreal, P.Q. and St. John, N.B.; opened Brs. of Hudson, McMackin & Co. in Moncton 1932, Halifax 1937, Montreal 1949; Offr., Candn. Mil., 26th Bn., St. John Fusiliers, 1927; Adj., 1929-31; trans. to N.B. Rangers, 1932; commanded "C" Co. with H.Q. at Moncton, N.B.; served in 2nd World War, 1939-45, in Active Army; rank of Lt. Col.; Pres. (1961-62) Candn. Inst.

Chart. Accts.; mem., Inst. of Chart Accts. of N.B. (Pres. 1950-51); Inst. of Chartered Accts. of P.E.I. and N.S.; Pres. Moncton Br., Royal Canadian Legion, 1949; mem., Soc. of Indust. & Cost Accts. of N.B.; Candn. Extve. Service Overseas; author: "History of The New Brunswick Institute of Chartered Accountants — 1916 to 1966"; life mem., Moncton City Club; B.P.O. Elks Club; N.B. Inst. C.A.; Moncton Br., Royal Candn. Legion; Freemason; Anglican; recreations: tennis (N.B. Champion, 1923), golf, swimming, fishing, shooting; Home: "Capeview", Shediac Cape, N.B. E0A 3G0Address in Winter: Apt. 103 Centennial Towers, 141 Cameron St., Moncton, N.B. E1C 5Y7

HUDSON, James William, B.Com., C.A., company executive; b. Victoria, B.C., 8 Sept. 1917; s. James William and Nora Mary Elizabeth (Gray) H.; e. Sir James Douglas Sch., Victoria, 1924-30; Victoria High Sch., 1930-34; Victoria Coll., Victoria, B.C., 1934-36; Univ. of Brit Columbia, B.Com., 1938; Inst. of Chart. Accts. of B.C., C.A. 1948; m. Margaret Olive, d. late William T. Birney, 12 March 1946; children: James William, Jr., Alan Birney, Margot Elizabeth, Kathleen Rosetta; PRES., CHIEF EXTVE. OFFICER & DIR. BURRARD YARROWS CORP.; Past-Pres. and Dir., Candn. Shipbuilding & Ship Repairing Assn.; articled with Helliwell, Maclachlan & Co., Chart. Accts., Vancouver, B.C., 1938, leaving in 1953 when apptd. Secy-Treas. and Comptroller of present firm; served in 2nd World War; enlisted as Gunner, 1942; trans. to inf. and served in Can., U.K. and N.W. Europe; discharged in 1946 with rank of Lieut; mem., Inst. of Chart. Accts. of B.C.; Past Pres., United Way of Greater Vancouver; Vancouver Board of Trade; Past Chrmn. and Gov., Employers Council of B.C.; Zeta Psi: United Church; recreations: golf, fishing; Clubs: Vancouver; Shaughnessy Golf & Country; Union (Victoria) Pennask Lake Fishing and Game; Home: 4900 Cartier St., Vancouver, B.C. V6M 4H2; Office: 109 Esplanade E., North Vancouver, B.C. V7L 1A1

HUDSON, Hon. R. Fisher, Q.C., M.L.A., LL.B.; politician; b. Country Harbour, N.S. 16 May 1920; s. Harold V. and Sarah E. (Fisher) H.; e. Country Harbour Sch.; Mount Allison Acad.; Mount Allison Univ.; Dalhousie Univ.; m. Noreen Edith d. Wilfred Ward, Eureka, N.S. 31 Jan. 1946; children: Brian, Sandy, Stewart, Graham, Elaine, June; MIN. OF THE ENVIRONMENT, N.S. and Min. Responsible for EMO (NS) Act & Regulations and for Adm. of Housing Devel. Act 1980-; Cand. prov. g.e. 1967, 1974, def.; el. M.L.A. for Victoria prov. by-el. 1980, re-el. 1981; P. Conservative; United Church; Office: (P.O. Box 2107) Howe Bldg., Halifax, N.S. B3J 3B7.

HUGESSEN, Hon. James K., M.A., B.C.L., judge; b. Montreal, Que., 26 July 1933; s. Adrian Knatchbull and Margaret Cecelia Ross (Duggan) H.; e. Bishop's Coll. Sch., Lennoxville, Que.; Oxford Univ., B.A. 1954, M.A. 1958; McGill Univ., B.C.L. 1957; m. Mary Rosamond, d. R. E. Stavert, Montreal, Que., 12 Sept. 1958; children: Jaime William, Kathleen Jill, Alicia Mary, Alexander Ewart, Ross Adrian; JUSTICE, SUPERIOR COURT OF QUEBEC, since 1972 and Associate Chief Justice since 1973; Anglican; recreations: skiing, sailing, curling; Clubs: Royal St. Lawrence Yacht; Royal Montreal Curling; Red Birds Ski; Home: 4480 deMaisonneuve Blvd. W., Westmount, Que. H3Z 1L7; Office: Court House, Montreal, Que. H2Y 1B6

HUGGINS, Charles B., B.A., M.Sc., M.D., D.Sc., LL.D., F.R.C.S.(Edin. & Eng.) F.A.C.S.; surgeon; cancer researcher; b. Halifax, N.S., 22 Sept. 1901; s. Charles Edward and Bessie (Spencer) H.; e. Acadia Univ., B.A. 1920, D.Sc. 1946; Harvard Univ., M.D. 1924; Yale Univ., M.Sc. 1947; D.Sc.i, Washington Univ. 1950, Leeds Univ. 1953, Turin Univ. 1957, Trinity Coll. 1965, Wales 1967, Univ. of Cal. 1968, Univ. of Mich. 1968; Gustavus Adolphus Coll., 1975; Med. Coll. of Ohio (Toledo), 1973;

Univ. of Louisville, 1980; D.Sc., Wilmington College, Wilmington, Ohio, 1980; LL.D., Univ. of Aberdeen 1966, York Univ. 1968; D.P.S., George Washington Univ. 1967; Sigillum Magnum, Bologna Univ. 1964; Hon. Prof., Madrid Univ. 1956; m. Margaret Wellman, 29 July 1927; children; Charles Edward, Emily Fine; Prof. of Surg., Univ. of Chicago, since 1936; Dir., The Ben May Lab. for Cancer Research, 1951-69; William B. Ogden Distinguished Service Prof., 1962; Intern in Surg., Univ. of Mich., 1924-26; Instr. in Surg. 1926-27; joined Univ. of Chicago as Instr. in Surg., 1927-29; Asst. Prof. 1929-33; Assoc. Prof. 1933-36; rec'd. Nobel Prize for Med. and Physiol. 1966; other honors incl.: Am. Med. Assn. for Scient. Exhibits Gold Medal, 1936 and 1940; Katherine Berkan Judd Award for Cancer Research 1942; Charles L. Mayer Award 1944; Gold Medal (Prix Fenwick) 1947; Francis Amory Prize 1948; Am. Urology Assn. Award 1948; Meyer Bodansky Lecture, Univ. of Texas, 1952; Ramon Guiteras Lecture, Am. Urology Assn. 1952 and Medal and Award 1966; Judd Lecture, Univ. of Minn., 1953; Bertner Lecture, M. D. Anderson Hosp., Houston, Texas, 1953; Am. Pharm. Mfrs. Assn. Research Award 1953; Wolbach Mem. Lecture, Harvard Univ. 1955; Am. Assn. Genito-Urinary Surgs. Gold Medal 1955; Assn. Am. Med. Colls., Borden Award and Gold Medal 1955: Order "Pour le Merite" by German Fed. Republic 1958; Comfort Crookshank Prize for Cancer Research 1958; Charles Mickle Fellowship 1958; Cameron Prize in Practical Therapeutics 1958; City of Hope Award 1958; MacEwen Mem. Lecture, Univ. of Glasgow 1958; Centennial Lecture, Gesellschaft deutscher Naturforscher u. Aerzte, Wiesbaden, 1958; Marnoch Lecture, Univ. of Aberdeen, 1959; Orden "El Sol del Peru", Class Grand Offr., 1961; Walker Prize for 1955-60 awarded by Royal Coll. of Surgs. of Eng., 1961 and Moynihan Lecture there, 1963; Oscar B. Hunter Award 1962; First Ferdinand Valentine Award 1962: Albert Lasker Award for Clin. Research 1963; Rudolf Virchow Med. Soc. Gold Medal 1964; Markle Lecture 1965; Passano Foundation Award 1965; The Worshipful Soc. Apothecaries London Gold Medal in Therapeutics 1966; Gairdner Award, Toronto, 1966; Chicago Med. Soc. Award 1967: Acadia Univ. Centennial Medal 1967; Hamilton Award 1967; Bigelow Medal 1967; Univ. of Mich. Sesquicentennial Award 1967: Lincoln Acad. Medal 1967: St. Louis Univ. Silver Medal 1968; Chancellor Acadia Univ., 1972-79; I. S. Ravdin Lect. (Am. Coll. Surgs.) 1974; Tracy O. Powell Lecture. (Los Angeles Urol. Soc.) 1975; Lucy Wortham James Lect. of the James Ewing Soc. 1975; Robt. V. Day Lect. (Am. Urol. Assn., Portland) 1975; author of over 200 articles in sc. & med.; Hon. Fellowship Inst. of Med. of Chicago, 1968; mem., Royal Soc. Med. (Hon.): Candn. Med. Assn. (Hon.); Nat. Acad. Sciences: Am. Philos. Soc.; Am. Assn. Cancer Research (Hon.): Alpha Omega Alpha; Home: 5807 Dorchester Ave., Chicago, Ill. 60637; Office: 950 E. 59th St., Chicago, Ill. 60637.

HUGHES, Campbell Bannerman; publisher; b. Stroud, Ont., 30 Sept. 1913; s. Harvey Edwin and Bessie Helen (Johnson) H.; e. Barrie (Ont.) Coll. Inst.; Toronto Teachers Coll.; McMaster Univ., 1946; Ont. Coll. of Educ., 1947; m. Patricia Margaret, d. John R. Zieman, Toronto, Ont., 22 Dec. 1942; four d., Ann, Margaret, Mary, Janet; Educational Rep., The Ryerson Press, Toronto, 1947-52; Textbook Ed. 1952-60; Ed. in Chief and Vice Pres., Charles F. Merrill Books Inc., Columbus, Ohio 1960-65; re-joined Ryerson Press as Dir. of Textbook Publishing, 1965-67; Dir. of Publishing 1967-68; Gen. Mgr. 1968-70; Pres., Van Nostrand Reinhold Ltd., 1970-78; Pres. Beaufort Books (N.Y.) 1980; Dir., Victoria Day Care Services; Managing Dir., Beta Assoc.; Chrmn., Book and Periodical Development Council; mem. Candn. Book Publishers' Council (Pres. 1970-71); Comm. Travellers Assn.; Liberal; United Church; recreations: music, Canadian history; Clubs: Arts and Letters, Toronto; Empire; Home: 55 Bannantyne Dr., Willowdale, Ont.M2L 2P2

HUGHES, Hon. Charles Joseph Arthur, B.A., LL.D., judge; b. Fredericton, N.B., 2 March 1909; s. James Austin and Mary Eveleen (McMahon) H.; e. St. Dunstan's Sch., Fredericton 1923; Fredericton (N.B.) High Sch. 1926; Univ. of N.B., B.A. 1930 L.L.D. 1973; Saint Thomas Univ., LL.D. 1972; m. Edith Barbara, d. Charles E. Atwater, 19 Aug. 1937; children: Richard Atwater, Charles David, Barbara Helen; CHIEF JUSTICE OF N.B.; read law with Hon. Mr. Justice P. J. Hughes; called to Bar of N.B. 1933; cr. Q.C. 1952; Judge of County Courts of York, Sunbury and Queen's Cos., 1965-68; apptd. Justice of Appeals Div., Supreme Court 1968; R. Catholic; recreations: gardening, golf; Club: Garrison; Home: 186 Waterloo Row, Fredericton, N.B. E3B 1Z2; Office: Justice Bldg., Fredericton, N.B. E3B 1Z2

HUGHES, Edward John, R.C.A.; artist-painter; b. N. Vancouver, B.C., 17 Feb. 1913; e. Vancouver Sch. of Art (teachers incl. F. H. Varley and J. W. G. MacDonald), 1929-35; free-lance comm. artist in Vancouver 1935-39; collab. on murals for First Un. Ch. and W. K. Oriental Gardens, Vancouver; Malaspina Hotel, Nanaimo and B.C. display in W. States Bldg., Golden Gate Expn., San Francisco, 1939; el. mem., Candn. Group of Painters, 1948 (later resigned); comnd. by Standard Oil Co. to travel on tanker to paint series of B.C. coast, 1954; cross-country trip to paint Candn. cities, 1956; rec'd Can. Council grants to travel and sketch on coast and in interior of B.C., 1958, 1963; painted covers for B.C. telephone directory, 1958-61; mural for Royal York hotel, "View from Qualicum Beach", 1958; one-man exhn., Vancouver Art Gallery and York Univ., Toronto, 1967; Victoria Art Gallery, 1978; group exhn., Stratford Art Gallery, Stratford, Ont., 1978; Work in permanent colls. of Nat. Gallery Can., Montreal Museum of Fine Art, Art Gallery of Ont., Vancouver and Victoria Art Galleries, Hart House, Toronto, Beaverbrook coll. and other pub. and pte. colls.; enlisted R.C.A. as Gunner 1939; became Army artist (Sgt.) 1940; official Army War Artist (Capt.) in Can., Gt. Brit. and Aleutians, 1942-46; awarded Emily Carr Scholarship 1947; Can. Council Award 1967 and 1970; Address: c/o Dominion Gallery, 1438 Sherbrooke St. W. Montreal, Que. H3G 1K4

HUGHES, Everett Cherrington, B.A., Ph.D., LL.D.; sociologist; b. Beaver, Ohio, 30 Nov. 1897; s. Charles Anderson and Jessamine Blanche (Roberts) H.; e. Ohio Wesleyan Univ., B.A. 1918; Univ. of Chicago, Ph.D. 1928; McGill Univ., LL.D. 1970; m. Helen Gregory MacGill, 18 Aug. 1927; two d., Helen Cherrington Brock, Elizabeth Gregory Schneewind; PROF EMERITUS., BOSTON COLL., since 1977; Prof. Emeritus, Brandeis Univ., since 1968; Asst. Prof., McGill Univ., 1927-38; Asst. Prof., Assoc. Prof. and Prof., Univ. of Chicago, 1938-61; Chrmn., Dept. of Sociol., 1952-56; Prof. of Sociol., Brandeis Univ., 1961-68; Post-doctoral Fellow, Social Science Research Council, 1931-32; Visiting Prof.: Laval Univ. 1942-43; Univ. Frankfurt/Main, 1948, 1953, 1968; Columbia Univ. summer 1951; Radcliffe Coll. 1957-58; Univ. of Kansas (Rose Morgan Prof.) 1959, 1961; Stanford Univ., summer 1963; Am. Studies Seminar, Kyoto, summer 1962; Seminar on Research Methods, Univ. of Vienna, 1964 summer; McGill Univ. and Univ. of Montreal 1965; Prof. of Sociol., Boston Coll., 1968-77; awarded Dr. Sci. Soc., Univ. of Laval 1977; Dr. ès Lettres, univ. de Montréal 1978; has served on following research and adv. comtes., Am. Nurses' Foundation 1953-60; Pub. Health and Nursing Study Sec., Nat. Insts. of Health; Co-op. Research Br., U.S. Office of Educ., UNESCO Mission on Co-op. of Social Scientists of E. and W. (Geneva, Moscow, Prague); Citizens' Comn. on Med. Educ., Am. Med. Assn., 1963-67; Assoc. Ed., "American Journal of Sociology", 1941-52 (Ed. 1952-60); author: "Where Peoples Meet: Racial and Ethnic Frontiers", 1952; "Men and Their Work", 1958; "French Canada in Transition", 1943, Phoenix ed. 1963; The Sociological Eye: Papers on Institutions, Race, Work, and The Study of Society, 1971; " Rencontre de Deux Mondes: La Crise D'Industrialisation Du Canada Français", Montreal, 1945, 1972; Fellow, Am. Sociol. Assn. (Pres. 1962-63); Am. Anthrop. Assn.; Am. Assn. Advanc. Science; mem.; Soc. Applied Anthrop. (Pres. 1951-52); Soc. Study Social Problems; Candn. Anthrop-Sociol. Soc. (Hon. Life Pres.); E. Sociol. Soc. (Pres. 1968-69); Democrat; Episcopal; Home: 27 Shepard St., Cambridge, Mass.

HUGHES, Francis Norman, B.S., Phm.B., M.A., LL.D.; dean emeritus; b. Dresden, Ontario., 23 Jan. 1908; s. Charles Harvey Norman and Ella May (McKim) H.; e. Sarnia (Ont.) Coll. Inst.; Ont. Coll. of Pharmacy (Univ. of Toronto), Phm.B. 1929; Purdue Univ., B.S. (Pharm.), 1940, and Hon. LL.D., 1954; Univ. of Toronto, M.A. 1944 LL.D. (Hon. caus.) 1980; m. 1st Helen Laird Hamilton (died 11 Apl. 1953), 2 Sept. 1935; 2ndly, Lorna Felice Roberts Hunt, 25 June 1954; children: Judith, Mary, Margaret, Elizabeth, David, Donald, Linda; DEAN EMERITUS, FACULTY OF PHARMACY, UNIV. OF TORONTO, since 1973i; Dean upon estab. of the Faculty 1953-73; Apprentice in Ingersoll Bros. Pharmacy, Sarnia, Ont., 1924-27 and Partner there, 1930-37; mem., Bd. of Examiners, Ont. Coll. of Pharm., Toronto, 1930-37; apptd. Asst. Prof. of Materia Medica, Ont. Coll. of Pharm. 1938, Prof. 1946, Asst. Dean 1948 and Dean 1952; mem. of Diocesan Bd. of Religious Educ., Toronto Diocese, 1948-56; Publications: "New Products Index", Vols. 1 to 13, 1951-58; "Compendium of Pharmaceutical Specialties", 1960, 1963, 1967-79,; Pres. 1956-57 Can. Foundation for Adv. Pharm. and Chrmn. of Comte. on Pharm. Educ. and Research; mem., Council, Ont. Coll. of Pharmacy 1953-73; Pres., Can. Conference Ph. Fac. 1952-53; Pres., Assoc. Fac. Ph. of Can: 1970; Assoc. Deans Ph. of Can. 1966-69; Pharm. Examining Bd. Can. 1964-66; mem. of Ed. Bd., Applied Therapeutics (1959-65); Contrib. Ed., "Canadian Pharmaceutical Journal"; Registrar-Treas., Pharmacy Examining Bd. Can., 1973-81; Hon. Life mem., Candn. Pharm. Assn.; Candn. Soc. Hosp. Pharm.; Ont. Pharm. Assn.; Assn. of Fac. of Pharm. of Can.; Assn. of Deans of Pharm. of Can.; Hon. LL.D., Purdue 1954; Dalhousie 1973; Toronto 1980; Kappa Psi; Rho Pi Phi (Rokeah; Chapter, Hon. Chancellor); Conservative; Anglican; Home: 56 Alexandra Blvd., Toronto, Ont. M4R 1L9

HUGHES, Gordon Frederick; O.C.; executive; b. Windsor, N.S., 30 March 1924; s. John Frederick and Annie Margaret H.; e. Windsor (N.S.) Acad.; m. Barbara Dorothy Pope, 10 June 1950; one s., Trevor Ian; PRESIDENT OCEAN CO. LTD.; Pres., Evangeline Savings and Mortgage Co.; Partner, Scotia Bond Co. Ltd.; Dir., Annapolis Travel Ltd.; Can. Devel. Corp.; John Labatt Ltd.; Olands Breweries (1971) Ltd.; Sobey Leased Properties Ltd.; Fid-Mor Mortgage Investors Corp.; Fisheries Products Ltd.; served with RCAF as Wireless Airgunner 1943-46; Part-time mem. Candn. Radio TV Comn. 1968-74; Founding Dir., "Windsor Elms" Un. Ch. Sr. Citizens Home; Recreation: tennis; Home: Hampshire Court, 1049 King St., Windsor, N.S. B0N 2T0; Office: (Box 10) King St., Windsor, N.S.

HUGHES, John Noel; investment dealer; b. Jamaica, W. Indies, 5 Jan. 1930; s. Noel W. and Mary (Crosse) H.; e. De Carteret Prep. Sch. and Munro Coll., Jamaica; Trinity Coll. Sch. Port Hope, Ont.; m. Janice, d. Lawrence Jackson, 12 Sept. 1958; children: Peter, Sarah; PRESIDENT AND DIR., BURGESS GRAHAM SECURITIES LTD. since 1975; Dir. J. L. Graham & Co. Ltd. (now present firm) 1958, Pres. 1968; mem. Toronto Stock Exchange; Invest. Dealers' Assn.; Anglican; recreations: golf, tennis, fishing, hunting, skiing; Club: Badminton & Racquet; Home: 37 Elderwood Dr., Toronto, Ont. M5P 1W8; Office: 44 King St. W., Toronto, Ont. M5H 1E6

HUGHES, Patrick Joseph; industrialist; b. N. Ireland, 1924; came to Canada 1949; e. Haileybury Sch. of Mines; m. Loretta McConville; has five children; CHRM., NOR-

THGATE EXPLORATION LTD.; Chrmn. and Pres., West-field Minerals Ltd.; Chmn., Northgate Patino Mines Inc.; Irish Base Metals Ltd.; Dir., Anglo United Development Ltd.; Tara Exploration and Development Co. Ltd.; Chmn., Whim Creek Consolidated N.L.; commenced exploration in Ireland 1959; for some time engaged in construction, Port Radium. N.W.T.; R. Catholic; Home: Dublin, Ireland; Office: P.O. Box 143, 1 First Canadian Place, Toronto, Ont. M5X 1C7

HUGHES, Samuel Frederick; investment finance; b. Toronto, Ont. 25 Aug. 1929; s. Samuel Ashfield and Alice Lamson (Mann) H.; e. Upper Canada Coll.; Univ. of Western Ont. Business Adm.; m. Joan L., d. F. D. Sasse 12 April 1958; children: Stephen, Heather, Cynthia; CHRMN. OF BD., HUGHES, KING & CO. LTD.; Past Pres. Candn. Chamber of Comm.; Past Chrmn. Bd. Trustees, Upper Can. Coll. Foundation; United Church; Clubs: Toronto; Offices: 390 Bay St., Toronto, Ont. M5H 2Y2

HUGHES, Hon. Samuel Harvey Shirecliffe, M.A.; judge; b. Victoria, B.C., 24 Oct. 1913; s. Maj.-Gen. Garnet Burk, C.B., C.M.G., D.S.O., and Elizabeth Irene Bayliss (Newling) H.; e. Stowe Sch., (England); Upper Canada Coll., Toronto, Ont.; Univ. of Toronto, B.A. 1934; Oxford Univ., B.A. 1936, M.A. 1951; Osgoode Hall, Toronto, Ont.; m. Helen Beatrice, d. late L. B. Spencer, Q.C., 27 July 1940; children: Lynn Spencer (Mrs. John H. Clappison), Samuel Garnet Spencer; JUSTICE, SUPREME COURT OF ONT., since 1962; read law with L. B. Spencer, Q.C., Welland, Ont.; called to the Bar of Ont. 1947; cr. Q.C. 1955; History Master, Ridley Coll., St. Catharines, Ont., 1936-39; practised law with Raymond Spencer Law & MacInnes, Welland, Ont., 1947-55; Chrmn. of Ont. Highway Transport Bd., 1955-58; Justice, Supreme Court of Ont., 1958-59; Chrmn. Civil Service Comn. Can., July 1959-62; apptd. to conduct Roy. Comn. on Atlantic Acceptance Corp. 1965 (reported to Ont. Govt. 1969); apptd. to conduct Roy. Comn. on Waste Mang. Inc. 1977 (reported to Ont. Govt. 1978); Alderman, City of Welland, 1953, 54, 55; served in 2nd World War; Overseas with Gov. Gen. Horse Guards as Lieut., 1941; trans. to Candn. Intelligence Corps, 1942; Italy (1st Candn. Inf. Div.) 1943-44; Historical Sec., Gen. Staff; Lieut.-Col. on retirement, Apl. 1946; Zeta Psi; Protestant; Clubs: University; Rideau (Ottawa); Toronto Hunt; Office: Osgoode Hall, Toronto, Ont. M5H 2N5

HUGHES, Stanley John, D.Sc., F.R.S.C.; mycologist; b. Llanelli, Dyfed, Wales 17 Sept. 1918; s. John Thomas and Gertrude (Roberts) H.; e. Llanelli Grammar Sch. 1938; Univ. Coll. of Wales B.Sc. 1941, M.Sc. 1943, D.Sc. 1954; m. Lyndell Anne d. late Wilfred Conway Rutherford 11 Oct. 1958; children: Robert Conway, Glenys Anne, David Stanley; PRINC. MYCOLOGIST, BIOSYSTEMATICS RESEARCH INST. CENTRAL EXPER. FARM since 1962; Asst. to Adv. Mycologist, Nat. Agric. Adv. Service, Univ. Colls. of Wales, Aberystwyth and Cardiff 1941-45; Asst. Mycologist, Commonwealth Mycological Inst., Kew, Eng. 1945-52; Mycologist, Central Exper. Farm, Agric. Can. Ottawa 1952-58, Sr. Mycologist 1958-62; invited scient. Univ. of Ghana 1949; tour of Herbaria univs. and museums of Europe 1955; Sr. Research Fellow, DSIR, Auckland, N.Z. 1963; Nat. Research Councils of Can. and Brazil Exchange Scient. Univ. of Pernambuco, Recife 1974; rec'd Jakob Eriksson Gold Medal 1969; George Lawson Medal (Can. Bot. Assn.) 1981; author over 100 publs.; Assoc. Ed. "Canadian Journal of Botany" 1968-79; Ed. "Fungi Canadenses" since 1973; Fellow, Linnean Soc. of London; mem. Brit. Mycol. Soc.; Mycol. Soc. Am. (Pres. 1975); Internat. Mycol. Assn. (Vice Pres.); United Church; Home: 360 Hamilton Ave., Ottawa, Ont. K1Y 1C5; Office: Ottawa, Ont. K1A 0C6.

HUGO, John Robert Yeomans, B.P.H.E., B.A.; barrister; b. Newmarket, Ont., 18 Dec. 1932; s. Howard Victor and

Georgia (Hewitt) H.; e. Pub. and High Sch., Newmarket; Univ. of Toronto, B.P.H.E. 1955, B.A. 1956; Osgoode Hall Law Sch., 1960; m. Gloria Dianne, d. Charles Noakes, 26 May 1978; children: Michael John, Tracy; SOLE PRACTITIONER; read law with Fraser, Beatty, Tucker, McIntosh & Stewart, 1958-62, McDonald, Davies & Ward, 1962, Partner, 1963; Partner, McDonald & Zimmerman, 1966; mem., Candn. Bar Assn.; Candn. Tax Foundation; United Church; recreations: golf, squash, tennis, swimming; skiing; Clubs: Cambridge; Lambton Golf & Country; Home: 727 Avenue Rd., Toronto, Ont.; Office: Ste. 1104, 20 Queen St. W., Toronto, Ont. M5H 3R3

HULBERT, Richard Elliott, F.R.A.I.C. M.Arch., R.C.A.; architect; b. St. Louis, Mo. 25 Dec. 1945; s. Sidney and Lillian (Waisman) H.; e. Univ. of Ariz. B.Arch. 1969 (Silver Medal Am. Inst. Archs.); Univ. of Calif. Berkeley M.Arch. 1970; m. Tina Paul 20 Aug. 1967; one s. Zachary; PRINCIPAL, R. E. HULBERT AND PARTNERS 1974- ; joined GRV Design Group 1970, Pres. Los Angeles Div. 1972-74; Fellow, Royal Arch. Inst. of Can.; Chrmn., Candn. Housing Design Council; awards incl. City of Calgary Award of Merit 1981, First Annual Urban Design Award 1979; Edmonton City Hall Competition Award of Merit 1980; Arch. Inst. B.C. 2 Housing Awards 1979; Arch. Record Award Design Excellence 1978; Candn. Arch. Yearbook Award Design Excellence 1977, 1975; Winner, Ltd. Design Competition Housing Corp. B.C. 1977; First Runner-up Prize Design Culture Centre & Lib. Prince George, B.C. 1976; jury mem. various award programs; rep. Can. 1981 Can./Hapan Housing Meetings Tokyo; frequent guest speaker innovative design and planning nat. and internat. meetings; author over 50 articles; mem. Arch. Inst. B.C.; Royal Can. Acad. of the Arts; Man. Inst. Archs.; Housing & Urban Devel. Assn. Can.; Urban Devel. Inst. Pacific Region (Dir.); Office: 215-14th St., West Vancouver, B.C. V7T 2P9.

HULL, Hon. Leslie Irvine, M.L.A.; politician; b. Springfield, N.B. 21 Dec. 1935; s. John and Helen H.; e. Fredericton High Sch.; Prov. Teachers Coll.; St. Thomas Univ.; m. Eva Elizabeth d. Roy Jackson, Scott's Lake, N.B. 5 Apl. 1958; children: Richard James, Lawrence Edward, David Leslie, Mary Lynn; MIN. OF SOCIAL SERVICES, N.B.1974- ; Physical Educ. Instr.; Extve. Secy. N.B. Basketball Assn. 1973-75; Pres. Silverwood Home & Sch. 1973; Mayor of Silverwood; Councillor City of Fredericton; el. M.L.A. for York South prov. g.e. 1974, re-el. 1978; P. Conservative; Baptist; Club: Capital Winter Curling (Assoc. mem.); Office: (P.O. Box 6000) Fredericton, N.B. E3B 5H1.

HULL, Robert (Bobby) Marvin, O.C.; hockey player (retired) farmer; b. Pointe Anne, Ont., 3 Jan. 1939; s. Robert Edward and Lena (Cook) H.; m. Joanne McKay, 1960 (div.); children: Bobby Jr., Blake, Brett, Bart; Commentator, Hockey Night in Canada, 1982- ; turned pro with Chicago Black Hawks 1957-58 season playing left wing in NHL through 1971-72 campaign before shifting to Winnipeg Jets of WHA 1972-79; briefly player-coach before returning to playing only; second to Gordie Howe in goals, points scored; in 15 NHL seasons played in 1,036 regular schedule games scoring 604 goals, 67 assists for 129 points and 102 penalty minutes; in four WHA seasons played in 330 games, scored 255 goals, 261 assists, 516 points 160 penalty minutes; five 50-plus goal seasons with Chicago; first team all-star NHL 10 times, WHA four times; second team NHL twice; Lady Byng Trophy (most gentlemanly NHL) 1964-65; Lester Patrick Award (service to hockey in US) 1969; Gary Davidson Trophy (WHA MVP) 1973, 1975; nickname Golden Jet; fastest left-handed slap shot 118.3 mph, fastest skater 29.7 mph; author "Hockey is My Game" Pres., Boby Hull Enterprises, 1966- ;

HUME, James Nairn Patterson, M.A., Ph.D., F.R.S.C.; educator; b. Brooklyn, N.Y. 17 March 1923; s. James Smith and Jean Frances (Nairn) H. (both Candn.); e. Goderich, Ont. pub. and high schs.; Univ. of Toronto B.A. (Math. & Physics) 1945, M.A. (Physics) 1946, Ph.D. (Theoretical Atomic Spectroscopy) 1949; m. Patricia d. H. A. S. Molyneux, Toronto, Ont. 8 Aug. 1953; children: Stephen, Philip, Harriet, Mark; MASTER, MASSEY COLL., UNIV. OF TORONTO 1981- ; Prof. of Physics and of Computer Science Univ. of Toronto 1963- ; Demonst. in Physics present Univ. 1945, Instr. in Math. (Ajax) 1946-49, Asst. Prof. of Physics 1950, Assoc. Prof. 1957, Assoc. Dean (Physical Sciences) Sch. of Grad. Studies 1968-72, Chrmn. of Computer Science 1975-80; Instr. in Physics Rutgers Univ. 1949-50; CBC TV programs incl.: "Focus on Physics" 1958; "Two for Physics" 1959; 15 short programs on Physics for children Can. and U.S. 1960; 'The Nature of Things" 1960-65; "The Ideas of Physics" 1962; "The Nature of Physics" 1963; "The Constants of Physics" 1966; co-writer 4 films produced by Phys. Science Study Comte. U.S.A.; audio tape with slides lectures "Fortran"; recipient Special Citation Edison Foundation for best science educ. film 1962 ('Frames of Reference'); Scient. Inst. Rome Silver Medal "Random Events"; Ohio State Award for "Count on Me" from 1962 "Nature of Things" and for "Order or Chaos?" from 1962 "Ideas of Physics" series; Centennial Medal 1967; Silver Core Award Internat. Fed. for Information Processing, Stockholm 1974; Sesquicentennial Long Service Honour Award Univ. of Toronto 1977; Distinguished Service Citation Assn. Physics Teachers, N.Y. 1979; author "Programmers' Guide" 1963; "Programmers' Guide (Fortran IV)" 1966; "Relativity, Electromagnetism and Quantum Physics" Vol. II of "Physics in Two Volumes" 1974; co-author "Trancode Manual" 1955; "High-speed Data Processing" 1958; "Structured Programming Using PL/1 and SP/k" 1975; Fundamentals of Structured Programming Using Fortran with SF/k and Watfiv-S'' 1977; "Programming Fortran 77" 1979; "Programming Standard Pascal" 1980; "UCSD Pascal: A Beginner's Guide to Programming Microcomputers" 1982; author or co-author numerous articles; mem. Cand. Information Processing Soc.; Assn. Computing Machinery; Am. Phys. Soc.; Sigma Xi; recreations: theatre, painting; Club: Arts & Letters; Home: 4 Devonshire Place, Toronto, Ont. M5S 2E1; Office: 255 Huron St., Toronto, Ont. M5S 1A7.

HUMPHREY, John Peters, O.C. (1974), B.C.L., Ph.D., D.Sc.Soc.; LL.D., D.C.L., D.Litt.; b. Hampton, N.B., 30 April 1905; s. Frank M. & Nellie (Peters) H.; e. Rothesay Coll.; Mt. Allison Univ.; McGill Univ., B.Comm. 1925, B.A. 1927, B.C.L. 1929, Ph.D. 1945; Dr. of Univ. of Algiers (hon. causa 1944); Dr. of Soc. Sciences, Ottawa 1966; LL.D., Carleton 1968, St. Thomas 1971, Dalhousie 1975, McGill 1976; D.C.L., Mt. Allison 1977; D.Litt., Acadia 1980; Macdonald Travelling Schol. in law, University of Paris, France 1929-30; m. 1) Jeanne Marie Louise (deceased), d. Albert Godreau, 3 September 1929; 2) Dr. Margaret Koustler, 21 June 1981; called to the Bar 1929; practised law with Wainwright, Elder and McDougall, Montreal, 1930-36; appointed Lectr. in Roman Law, McGill University,1936; awarded Fellowship by Carnegie Foundation for Internat. Peace to pursue studies in internat. law at Univ. of Paris, 1936-37; Secy., Faculty of Law, McGill Univ., 1937-46; apptd. Gale Prof. of Roman Law and Dean of Law Faculty, McGill Univ., 1946; Prof. Law and Political Science, 1966-71; Dir., Div. of Human Rights, U.N. Secretariat, 1946-66; author of "The Inter-American System: A Canadian View", 1942; many articles in Am., Brit. and Candn. periodicals on internat. pol. and legal subjects; mem., Candn. Inst. Internat. Affairs (Vice-Chrmn. Montreal Br. 1943-44; Chrmn. N.Y. Br., 1961-66); U.N. Assn. in Can. (Nat. Pres. 1968), Hon. Nat. Vice-Pres. 1967-68, Hon. Pres. Montreal Br. 1966-68, Pres. Montreal Br. 1945-46); Pres., Candn. Comn. Internat. Year for Human Rights; mem., U.N. Sub-Comn. on Prevention of Discrimination and Protection of Minorities

(Chairman, 1970); mem., Bd. of Dirs., Internat. League for Human Rights; mem., Royal Comn. on Status of Women in Can.; Extve. Secy., U.N. Conf. on Freedom of Information, Geneva, 1948; U.N. Conf. on Refugees and Stateless Persons, Geneva, 1951; U.N. Conf. on Status of Stateless Persons, 1954; Principal Secy. to U.N. Mission to Viet Nam, 1963; Internat. Cooperation Year Citation (Can. 1965); World Jewish Cong. Citation 1966; Rapporteur, Internat. Law Assn. Comte. on Human Rights; Rapporteur, U.N. Seminar on Human Rights (Jamaica) 1967; Vice-Chrmn., U.N. Seminar on Racial Discrimination (New Delhi) 1968; "World Legal Scholar" award, World Peace through Law Centre (1973); John Reid Medal (Canadian Council of Internat. Law, 1973); Visiting Prof., Univ. of Toronto, 1971-72; Univ. of Western Ont. 1981-82; Past Pres., Amnesty Internat. (Canada); Pres., Canadian Human Rights Foundation; mem. Internat. Comn. of Jurists; International Law Assn. (Rapporteur on Human Rights); Candn. Council of International Law; Clubs: University (Montreal); McGill Fac.; University (London); Home (summer): Brackley Beach, P.E.I. Address: 30 Tharlow Rd., Montreal, P.Q. H3X 3G6

HUMPHREY, William A., B.S.; mining engineer; b. Potrerillos, Chile 12 Jan. 1927; s. Thomas Zenas and Ethel Katherine (Kolbe) H.; e. Rutgers Univ. 1946-47; Univ. of Ariz. B.S. 1950; m. Edna Lillian Joule 20 Dec. 1947; children: Patricia, Nancy, Katherine, William; VICE PRES.- OPERATIONS NEWMONT MINING CORP. since 1975; Vice Pres. and Dir. Carlin Gold Mining Corp.; Idarado Mining Co.; Vekol Copper Mining Co.; Vice Pres. Dawn Mining Co.; Dir. Sheritt Gordon Mines Ltd.; Resurrection Mining Co.; Newmont Mines Ltd.; Magma Copper Co.; Geol. Cananea Consolidated Copper Co. Sonora, Mexico 1950-55, Foreman Underground Div. 1955, Planning Engr. 1959, Asst. to Mgr. 1965, Gen. Supt. 1968, Vice Pres. and Asst. Gen. Mgr. 1968, Extve. Vice Pres. Gen. Mgr. and Dir. 1971-75; Vice Pres. Planning Ment. Div. Anaconda Co. Butte 1975; served with USNR 1945-46; mem. Am. Inst. Mining Engrs.; Tau Beta Phi; Protestant; Home: 28 Chicken St., Wilton, Conn.; Office: 300 Park Ave., New York, N.Y.

HUMPHREYS, Russell Dodsley, Q.C.; b. Toronto, Ont., 18 Feb. 1905; s. John Russell and Emma (Mellow) H.; e. Model Sch., and Univ. of Toronto Schs., Toronto, Ont.; Osgoode Hall 1928; m. Margaret Hyney, 12 Sept. 1930; children: Donna Jean, John Dodsley; COUNSEL, HUMPHREYS & HILLMAN; read law with Saunders, Kingsmill & Price; called to Bar of Ont., 1928; cr. K.C. 1945; Capt., Ont. Regt. (Reserve); Ald., City of Oshawa, Ont., 1938-43 and 1954-53; Freemason; Conservative; Anglican; recreations: golf, hunting; Clubs: University; Ex-Officers Ontario Regiment; Oshawa Golf; Home: 136 Alexandra St., Oshawa, Ont. L1G 2C4; Office: 36 1/2 King St. E., Oshawa, Ont. L1H 7L1

HUMPHRIES, George Edward, M.B.E., P.Eng.; b. Wolverhampton, England, 31 Dec. 1907; s. Walter William and Clara Louise (Whitcomb) H.; e. Elem. Schs. and Tech. Coll., Eng., and at various Colls. (Extension courses); m. Margaret Merle, d. John Stewart, 25 May 1940; two s., David George, Walter John; SR. CONSULTANT, M. M. DILLON LTD. (former Chrmn. & Chief Engr.); Sr. Partner, Transport. Plan. Assoc., Birmingham, Eng.; Dir., Cities Heating Co. Ltd.; came to Can. 1928 after having worked on steam power plant design in Eng. (1926); with Hamilton Bridge Co. Ltd., Hamilton, Ont., as Structural Draftsman, 1928; with Hydro-Elect. Power Comn. of Ont., 1929-30; McClintic Marshall Corp., Pittsburgh, 1930-31; engaged as Engr. in N. Ont. gold fields 1932-40; with M. Murray Dillon estbd. present firm, 1945; served in 2nd World War with R.C.E., U.K. and N.W. Europe, 1940-45; awarded M.B.E.; Mentioned in Despatches; Offr., Candn. Army (R) 1946-56; retired with rank of Lieut.-Col.; Hon. mem. Assn. Consulting Engrs. Can. (Pres. 1963); Assn. of Consult. Engrs., U.K.; Fellow,

Engn. Inst. Can. (Pres. 1964-65); Institution of Civil Engineers; mem., Royal Canadian Legion (Vimy Branch); Assns. Prof. Engrs., Provs. of Ont., Man.: Candn. Inst. Mining & Metall.; Anglican; recreations: fishing, gardening; Club: The London; Home: 421 Wortley Road, London, Ont. N6C 3S7; Office: 495 Richmond St., London, Ont. N6A 5A9

HUMPHRYS, Richard, B.A., F.S.A., F.C.I.A.; civil servant; b. Jasmin, Sask., 27 March 1917; s. William and Olive Mary (Maher) H.; e. Public and High Sch., Kelliher, Sask.; Univ. of Manitoba, B.A. 1937; F.S.A. 1944; m. Wilma Kay Grant, 3 Oct. 1942; SUPT. OF INSURANCE CAN., since Oct. 1964; joined Great-West Life as Actuarial Clerk, 1939; apptd. to Fed. Dept. of Ins. as Actuarial Asst., 1940; Assoc. Actuary, 1944; joined Teachers Ins. & Annuity Assn. in New York as Asst. Actuary, 1947 and promoted Assoc. Actuary in 1948; rejoined Fed. Dept. of Ins. as Chief Actuary, 1948 and promoted Asst. Supt. of Ins., 1956; fellow, Soc. of Actuaries (Vice-Pres., 1979-81); mem. Conseil de Dir., Internat. Actuarial Assn.; fellow, Candn. Inst. of Actuaries (Pres. 1965-66); recreations: golf, skiing, music, reading; Club: Ottawa Hunt & Golf; Home: 50 Rothwell Drive, Ottawa, Ont. K1J 7G6; Office: L'Esplanade Laurier, 140 O'Connor, Ottawa, Ont. K1A 0H2

HUNGERFORD, John G., Q.C.; retired company officer; executive; b. London, Ont., 15 Nov. 1905; s. Walter Francis and Maude Margaret (MacLaren) H.; e. Univ. of Western Ont., B.A. (Hon. Pol. Econ.) 1926; Osgoode Hall, Toronto, Ont.; m. Persis Stephanie, d. Norman Seagram of Toronto, Ont., 21 April 1934; children: Lorna, Mary, Nancy; Past Chmn., National Trust Co. Ltd.; Past Chmn. of Bd., Canada Life Assnce. Co.; Hon. Trustee, Hosp. for Sick Children, Toronto; called to the Bar of Ont. 1929; joined present Co. as Trust Offr., 1929; apptd. Mgr. Trust Dept. 1944; Asst. Gen. Mgr., 1948, Gen. Mgr. 1949; el. a Dir. and Extve. Vice-Pres., 1951, Pres. 1954-64, Chmn. 1964-72; Zeta Psi; Anglican; Clubs: Toronto; York; Toronto Golf; Home: 252 Forest Hill Rd., Toronto, Ont. M5P 2N5; Office: 21 King St. E., Toronto, Ont. M5C 1B3

HUNT, D. Earl, M.D.; physician; surgeon; b. Honeywood, Ont., 16 March 1915; s. John and Myrtle (Lockhart) H.; e. Univ. of Toronto, M.D. 1946; m. Jean M., d. Charles Blundell, St. Catharines, Ont., 26 July 1944; children: Margaret, Elizabeth, John, Douglas; Pres. (1966) Coll. of General Practice of Can.; post-grad. work, St. Michael's Hosp., Toronto; while at univ. was on staff of Dept. of Anatomy and assisted with research for R.C.A.F. for 3 yrs; Lectr., St. John's Ambulance for several yrs.; ACTIVE STAFF, ST. CATHARINES GEN. AND HOTEL DIEU HOSPITALS St. Catharines; former Chief, Sec. of Gen. Practice, St. Catharines Gen. Hosp., Past Dir., Out Patient Dept., there; former Lectr. in Hematology, Mack Training Sch.; Past Chief Family Physicians Hotel Dieu Hosp., St. Catharines; taught sch., Melancthon, Simcoe, Muskoka for 4 yrs.; during 2nd World War served with C.O.T.C., Univ. of Toronto; on Active Service 1 1/2 yrs.; Med. Dir., Niagara District Diabetic Assn.; mem., Am. Geriatrics Soc.; N. Am. Acad. of Manipulative Med.; Fellow, Coll. of Family Physicians of Can.; mem. Candn. Med. Assn. (Past Secy., Sec. Gen. Practice); Ont. Med. Assn. (Past Chrmn., Educ. Comte., Sec. Gen. Practice; mem., Tariff Comte.); Coll. of Gen. Practice (Past Pres., Ont. Chapter; Past Chrmn., Bd. Dirs.); Lincoln Co. Acad. Med.; Past Pres., Talent Invest.; Freemason °; United Church; recreations: skeet shooting, hunting, fishing, flytying, coin and gun collecting; Clubs: Niagara Arms Collectors; St. Catharines Game & Fish Assn.; St. Catharines Coin (Hon. mem.); Address: 58 Yates St., St. Catharines, Ont. L2R 5R8

HUNT, Rt. Rev. Desmond Charles (Ang.); b. Toronto, Ont., 14 Sept. 1918; s. George Pfeilitzer and Kathleen Ulrica (Phillips) H.; e. Public Sch. and Vaughan Road Coll.

Inst., Toronto, Ont.; Univ. Coll., Univ. of Toronto (1939); Wycliffe Coll., Toronto (1942); Hon. D. Div., Wycliffe Coll. (1978); m. Naomi Florence, d. Willis Naylor, Toronto, Ont., 17 June 1944; children: Christopher, Pamela, Jonathan, Rachel; BISHOP, DIOCESE OF TORONTO, 1980- ; Canon, Diocese of Toronto, 1978-80; named Archdeacon of Kingston, since 1959; past Pres., Candn. Ang. Evangelical Fellowship; o. Deacon in 1942, and Priest in 1943; Curate of All Saints Ch., Toronto, Ont., 1943; Rector of Trinity Ch., Quebec City 1943-49; St. John's, Johnston, N.Y., 1949-53; St. James's Ch., Kingston, Ont. 1953-69; Ch. of the Messiah, 1969-81; Suffragan Bishop of Toronto, 1981; recreation: music (piano); Home: Box 1150, Lakefield, Ont. K0L 2HO

HUNT, Keith E., B.Sc.; retired transportation executive; b. Frome, Ont., 12 Sept. 1923; s. Percy Edward and Thelma Pauline (Daugherty) H.; e. Pub. and High Schs., Talbotville and London, Ont., 1940; Queen's Univ., B.Sc. 1951; m. Marion Elsie Jack, 25 Aug. 1951; three d., Lynn, Dawn, Vicki; can. National joined as apprentice electrician, London, Ontario, 1940; Special Engr., Montreal, 1952; Mech. Engr. 1955; Gen. Foreman 1955; Asst. Supt. Motive Power 1956; Asst. Supt. Econ. Br. 1956; Asst. Gen. Supt., M.P. & C.E. (GTW), Battle Creek, 1957; Chief Budget Offr., Montreal, 1959; Chief of Budgets & Engn. Econ., 1960; Gen. Supt. Equipment 1961; Area Mgr., Belleville 1963 and London 1965; Gen. Mgr., Toronto, 1967; Vice Pres., Great Lakes Reg., 1974; Vice Pres., Ind. Relations and Organization, 1976; Corp. Vice Pres. 1979-81 (ret.) served with RCAF 1942-46; mem., Engn. Inst. Can.; Candn. Rr. Hist. Assn.; Conf. Bd. of Can.; Protestant; recreations: golf, woodworking; gardening; Clubs: Bd. of Trade (Montreal); Toronto Railway; Canadian Railway; Home: Conway, RR #1, Bath, Ont. K0H 1G0

HUNT, Roy Thomas; company exec.; b. Toronto, Ont., 27 Apl. 1925; s. Alfred T. and Ada (Howard) H.; e. Upper Canada Coll., Toronto; m. Violet, d. Harry Brooks, 30 Sept. 1950; two s. Bryan, Howard; PRESIDENT GESTETNER INC., since Oct. 1965; worked with Gestetner as a Driver during summer vacations; prior to grad.; then with this Co. in various capacities and in machine selling, 1945; formed Am. Co. in 1950; worked as Field Supv., Yonkers, N.Y., 1950-55; Mgr., Toronto Br., 1956; Asst. Gen. Mgr., 1957-59; Gen. Mgr., 1959-63; Mang. Dir. 1963-65; served during 2nd World War with R.C.A.F., 1943-45; mem., Candn. Business Equipment Mfrs. Assn.; Bd. Trade Metrop. Toronto; Anglican; recreations: flying, swimming; Clubs: Granite; Home: 16 Saintfield Ave., Don Mills, Ont. M3C 2M5; Office: 849 Don Mills Rd., Don Mills, Ont.M3C 1W1

HUNTER, George Richard, M.B.E., Q.C., B.A., LL.B., b. Edmonton, Alberta, 15 Dec. 1917; s. Roy Butler and Lena Mitton (Young) H.; e. Public and High Schs., Winnipeg, Man.; Univ. of Manitoba, B.A. 1937, LL.B. 1941; m. Constance Anita, d. R. D. Guy, Q.C., Tuxedo, Man., 4 Oct. 1941; children: Heather, Patricia, Gail; PARTNER, PITBLADO; Dir., Hudson's Bay Co.; Metropolitan Stores of Canada Ltd.; Canadian Imperial Bank of Commerce; General Distributors of Canada Ltd.; read law with Isaac Pitblado, Q.C.; called to the Bar of Manitoba 3 Nov. 1943, and to Bar of Ont., 20 Oct. 1955; cr. Q.C. 28 Dec. 1957; served in 2nd World War with Candn. Army, May 1941-Oct. 1945, retired as Lieut.-Col.; awarded M.B.E.; Extve. Asst. to Min. of Nat. Defence (Hon. D. C. Abbott), Ottawa, Oct. 1945-Dec. 1946, and to Min. of Finance (Hon. D. C. Abbott), Dec. 1946-Oct. 1947; returned to law practice with Pitblado, Hoskin & Co., Winnipeg, 1947-49; Secy., Royal Comn. on Transportation, Ottawa, 1948-51, returning then to Pitblado, Hoskin & Co.; Past Pres., Winnipeg Chamber Comm.; Winnipeg Canadian Club; Delta Upsilon; Protestant; recreations: hunting, curling; Clubs: Manitoba; St. Charles Country; Winnipeg Winter; Home: 49 Aldershot, Tuxedo, Winnipeg, Man. R3P 0C9; Office: Suite 1900, One Lombard Place, Winnipeg, Man. R3B 2L8

HUNTER, Gordon W., B.A., C.A.; Canadian public service; b. Winnipeg, Man., 5 Nov. 1914; s. Gordon E. and Katharine (Ward) H.; e. St. Johns Coll., Winnipeg, Man.; Univ. of Manitoba, B.A. 1935 and C.A. 1941; m. Evelyne Anne, d. John J. Fahlgren, Kenora, Ont., 2 June 1945; children: Kathryn, Gordon, Richard; Vice President, Canadian Arsenals Limited 1948-75; with Peat, Marwick, Mitchell & Company, 1935-41; Secretary-Treasurer, Cutting Tools & Gauges Ltd., (Crown Corp.) 1942-45; Asst. Comptroller, Dept. of Munitions & Supply, 1945-46; Extve. Asst. to Depy. Min. of Reconstruction & Supply, 1947-48; Trade & Commerce 1948-51; Defence Production 1951-52; Financial Adviser in that Dept. 1953-54; Asst. Depy. Min. 1954-62; Depy. Min. 1962-69; Depy. Min. of Supply 1969-70; Master, Royal Candn. Mint, Jan. 1970-June 1975; Pres. G.W. Hunter Consultants Ltd.; mem., Inst. C.A.'s Man. & Ont.; Can. Inst. C.A.'s; Inst. Pub. Adm. Can.; United Church; recreation: golf; Clubs: Rideau; Ottawa Hunt and Golf; Home: 840 Dunlevie Ave., Ottawa, Ont. K2A 2Z3

HUNTER, John William Gordon, M.C., Q.C.; b. Toronto, Ont. 28 Jan. 1909; s. late Col. Alfred Taylour and Olive May (Jeffrey) H.; e. Univ. of Toronto Schs.; Univ. of Toronto, B.A. 1931; Osgoode Hall, 1931-34; m. Margaret Agnes, d. late Thomas Patrick Culhane, 21 June 1941; one d. Shelagh Mary; Director of a number of comm. and indust. companies; read law with McMaster, Montgomery, Fleury & Co.; called to Bar of Ont. 1934; cr. K.C. 1948; served in 2nd World War; saw action with 7th Bn. Green Howards. 69 Bgde., 50th (Northumbrian) Divn., on loan from Candn. Army; began as 2nd Lieut., retiring to supplementary R.O. as Lieut.-Col.; def. cand. to H. of C. for Parkdale, by-el. 1946, and 1st el. there in g.e. 1949; re-el. g.e. 1953; def. in g.e. 1957; apptd. Chairman, Banking & Comm. Comte.; mem., County of York Law Assn.; Candn. Bar Assn.; Law Soc. of Upper Can.; Phi Kappa Sigma; Liberal; Anglican; recreations: reading, golf, gardening, curling, sailing; Clubs: Lawyer's; Eastbourne Golf; Royal Canadian Military Inst.; Roches Point Yacht; Home: 855 Lake Drive North, R.R. 2 Keswick, Ont. L4P 3E9 Office: Suite 422, 131 Bloor St. W., Toronto, Ont. M5S 1S2

HUNTER, Maj.-Gen. Kenneth Adams, O.B.E., C.D., Q.H.P. (1954), M.D., C. of St. J.; Canadian Army (retired); b. London, Ont., 28 Aug. 1904; s. William Allan and Eva (Durdin) H.; e. Central Coll. Int., London, Ont. (Grad. 1924); Univ. of Western Ont. Med. Sch., M.D. 1930; Lic., Med. Council of Can. 1930; m. Lorna Alberta, B.A., d. Francis Studley Ashplant, London, Ont., 10 Sept. 1932; children: Ruth St. Leger, K. Michael Francis; in ranks, N.P.A.M., Candn. Machine Gun Corps., 1922-26; Lieut., C.M.G.C., 1927-30; Lieut. R.C.A.M.C.(PF) 1930; Capt. 1931, Major 1939; Lt.-Col. 1940; Col. 1943; Brig. 1952; Maj.-Gen. 1958; operational service with Candn. Army in U.K., 1940-43; Mentioned in Despatches; Dieppe, 1942, Sicily, 1943, Italy, 1944, Holland and Germany, 1945, Korea 1951 and 1953; subsequently Dir. Gen. of Med. Services, then (1958-59) Surgeon-Gen. Commanding Med. Services of Candn. Armed Forces; a noted school athlete; Individual Track & Field Champion, Central Collegiate, London, Ont., 1923, and Univ. of W. Ont., 1924; Univ. Letter for Football, 1924-30; granted Freedom of City of London, Ontario 1961; mem., Canadian Med. Assn.; Sigma Kappa Sigma; United Church; recreation: golf; Club: London Hunt & Country; Home: 66 Rollingwood Circle, London, Ont. N6G 1P7

HUNTER, Peter William, C.D.; advertising executive; b. Toronto, Ont., 26 July 1930; s. Howard W. and Maple Elizabeth H.; e. Univ. of Toronto (Ont.) Schs.; Royal Mil. Coll., grad. 1953; children: Geoffrey William, Elizabeth Hope; CHRM., CEO AND DIR., McCONNELL ADVERTISING CO. LTD., since 1965; Pres. and Dir., Signum Communications Inc.; Dir., SCP Producers Services Limited; Roberts Ketchum International Limited; Foster Ad-

vertising Limited, 1951-55, appointed Account Executive; joined McConnell Eastman & Co. Ltd., as Account Extve., Toronto, 1955-58; Vice Pres. W. Ont., London, Ont., 1958-60; Vice Pres. and Account Supvr., Toronto, 1960-65; Lt. Col. and former C.O., Gov. Gen.'s Horse Guards; former Aide de Camp to Gov. Gen.; awarded Centennial Medal; CJRT-FM; Bd. of Gov., York-Finch Hospital; mem., Inst. Candn. Advertising; Candn. Advertising Adv. Bd.; Am. Marketing Assn.; Pres. Can. Liver Foundation; P. Conservative; Presbyterian; recreations: skiing, golf, reading; Clubs: Rosedale Golf, Canadian; Empire; London (Ont.); PC Business Men's; Home: Maple Ridge Farm, R.R. #2, Tottenham, Ont. L0G 1W0; Office: 234 Eglinton Ave. E., Toronto, Ont. M4P 1K7

HUNTER, Robert Lloyd, B.Com.; lawyer; investment dealer; b. Toronto, Ont., 29 Aug. 1914; s. late Cecil and Josephine (Sipprel) H.; e. Ridley Coll., 1931; Univ. of Toronto, B.Com. 1941; Osgoode Hall Law Sch., 1947; m. Hope Hazen, d. late Hugh Mackay, 22 Jan. 1944; three d. Susan, Kate, Hope; Vice Chmn. and Dir., Cleyn & Tinker Ltd.; Dir., QCTV Ltd.; called to Bar of Ont. 1947; Jr. Solr.; Fraser & Beatty, 1947-49; joined Pitfield, Mackay, Ross as Mgr., Underwriting Dept., 1950, el. a Dir. 1957; Sr. Vice Pres. 1963-78 (ret. as Dir. & Vice Pres.) Cadet COTC 1939-40; comnd. 2nd Lt. 1940; served with 7th Toronto Regt. Reserve 1941-42; Active Duty 26th Field Regt. & Arty. 1942-45; Past Pres., Westmount P. Cons. Assn.; Westmount Mun. Assn.; mem. Law Soc. Upper Can.; Anglican; recreations: skiing, tennis, swimming, gardening; Clubs: Forest and Stream; Toronto; Albany; Toronto; RCYC; Home: 501 Russell Hill Rd., Toronto, Ont. M5P 2T1; Office: (P.O. Box 54) Royal Bank Plaza, Toronto, Ont. M5J 2K5

HUNTER, Robin C.A., M.D., C.M., F.R.C.P. (C); psychiatrist; professor; b. Jamaica, B.W.I., 2 March 1919; s. James Wood and Mary Anne (Parsons) H.; e. Calabar High Sch., Jamaica, 1938; Univ. of London (extra-mural), 1942-45; McGill Univ., M.D., C.M., 1950, Dipl. Psychiatry, 1955; C.R.C.P. (C.), 1956; m. Philippa Doane d. late Dr. Philip Doane McLaren, Halifax, N.S., 16 June 1951; children: Leith Adair, Robin McLaren, Jonathan Joel; Dir., Clarke Inst. of Psych. 1967-74; Rotating Interne, Royal Victoria Hosp., 1950-51; Res., Allan Mem. Inst., 1951-53; Registrar, Maudsley Hosp., London, Eng., 1953-55; Demonst., McGill Univ., 1955-56; Lectr., 1956-58, Asst. Prof., 1958-64; Prof. and Head, Dept. of Psychiatry, Queen's Univ., 1964-67; apptd. Chrmn. and Prof., Dept. of Psychiatry, Univ. of Toronto, 1967; Assoc. Dean, Clinical Sciences, Faculty of Med., Univ. of Toronto, 1974-78; served with R.C.A.F. in European theatre, 1940-45; author of over 50 papers publ. in prof. journs.; Fellow, Am. Psychiatric Assn.; Am. Coll. of Psychiatrists; mem., Canadian Psychiatric Assn.; Candn. Inst. Psychoanalysis; recreations: fishing, swimming, tennis; Home: 29 Alcina Ave., Toronto, Ont. M6G 2E7; Office: Sunnybrook Medical Centre, 2075 Bayview Ave., Toronto, Ont. M4N 3W5

HUNTER, Roderick Oliver Alexander, B.A., LL.B., LL.D.; retired company executive; b. Mather, Manitoba, 12 Dec. 1915; s. John Oliver and Ida Bessie May (Maclean) H.; e. United Coll., and Un. of Man., B.A. 1937; Man. Law Sch., LL.B. 1941; m. Doris Audrey, d. George S. Moffat, Winnipeg, Man., 26 Dec. 1942; three s. Roderick G. M., John David, Richard Craig; CHANCELLOR, UNIV. OF WINNIPEG; Past Chmn., Man. Civil Serv. Comn.; Dir., The Great West Life Assurance Co.; Dir., Ducks Unlimited (Canada); Dir., Dominion Textiles Inc.; The Investors Group Trust Co. Ltd.; Inv. Mutual of Can. Ltd.; Inv. Growth Fund of Can. Ltd.; Inv. Internat. Mutual Funds Ltd.; Inv. Dividend Fund Ltd.; Provident Stock Fund Ltd.; Dir. Gold Circle Ins. Co.; Harriott & Assoc. of Can. (1974) Ltd.; read law with Benjamin C. Parker, K.C., Esten K. Williams, K.C.; called to the Bar of Manitoba, 1942; Barrister & Solicitor, Parker, Parker, Hunter and Hamlin, 1945-46; joined Great West Life Assurance Company, 1946; appointed Asst. Secy., 1947, Asst. Secy. and Legal Offr., 1952; Secy., 1953; Vice Pres. 1962; Vice-Pres., Secy. and Dir. 1969; Vice Pres., James Richardson & Sons, Ltd., 1971-77; Past Chrmn., Bd. of Regents, United Coll.; served in 2nd World War with R.C.N., 1941-45; discharged with rank of Lt.-Commdr.; mem., Law Soc. of Man.; Man. Bar Assn.; Pres., Assn. Life Ins. Counsel (1st Candn.) 1966-67; Phi Kappa Pi; United Church; recreations: golf, curling, hunting; Clubs: Deer Lodge Curling; St. Charles Country; Manitoba; Home: 346 Oxford St., Winnipeg, Man. R3M 3J7

HUNTINGTON, Hon. (Arthur) Ronald, P.C., M.P., B.S.A.; politician; b. Vancouver, B.C. 13 Feb. 1921; s. Samuel Clegg and Winifred Ethel (McIntyre) H.; e. Lord Byng High Sch. Vancouver; Univ. of B.C., B.S.A.; m. (Sydney) Jean d. late John R. Christie 13 Apl. 1943; children: Victoria Jean, Ronald Miles; Min. of State for Small Business and Industry 1979-80; Chrmn., Service Packing Co. Ltd. 1976-79, Spraying and Dusting Contractor, Pest Control (Canada) Ltd. and Weed Control Service Inc. (USA) 1946-51; Mgr. and Dir. Western Appraisal & Farm Management Ltd. 1952-54; Pres. Ronco Pole Structures Ltd. 1953-57; Pres. Service Packing Co. Ltd. 1957; P. Cons. cand. for Capilano g.e. 1972, el. to H. of C. 1974, re-el. 1979 & 1980, Chrmn. Standing Comte. on Pub. Accts. 1977-79; former Mem. at Large, Narcotic Addiction Foundation B.C.; former mem. B.C. Inst. Agrols.; served with RCN 1941-45, Battle of Atlantic and Mediterranean, mem. staff Royal Roads Naval Coll. 1944-45, rank Lt. Commdr. (retired); rec'd Queen's Silver Jubilee Medal; Dir., Bd. P. Cons. Can. Fund; Boys' & Girls' Club Greater Vancouver; mem. Vancouver Bd. Trade; Candn. Mfrs. Assn. B.C. (Extve. Comte.); Naval Offrs. Assn. Can.; Royal Candn. Legion; author "View from the Street" 1976; various articles; Anglican; recreations: yachting, fishing, reading; Clubs: Kiwanis (Pres. 1971-72); West Vancouver Yacht (Commodore 1967); Hollyburn Yacht (Hon. mem.); University (Past Dir.); Home: 1752 Ottawa Pl., West Vancouver, B.C. V7V 2T7; Office: House of Commons, Ottawa, Ont. K1A 0A6.

HURD, Edwin Cecil, B.A., B.Sc.; company director (retired); b. Marquis, Sask., 3 July 1914; s. Francis Edwin and Hattie D. (Tanner) H.; e. Public and High Schs., Marquis, Sask.; High Sch., Moose Jaw, Sask. (Matric.); Univ. of Sask., B.A. 1932; B.Sc. (Chem. Engn.) 1934; Harvard Advanced Mang. Program, 1960; m. Helen Z., d. Francis Edick, 29 May 1937; children: Randall Eugene, Frances Pat, Penelope Jane; joined British American Oil Co. Ltd. in 1934 at Moose Jaw, Sask., later trans. to offices in Toronto and Montreal, and subsequently apptd. Refinery Mgr. and Asst. to Mgr. of Refineries; self employed from Feb. 1949 to Oct. 1950; Industrial Engr., Co-operative Refinery Assn., Kansas City, Mo., Oct. 1950-July 1951; Refinery Supt., Mercury Oil Refinery Co., Oklahoma City, Okla., Aug. 1951-Dec. 1952; joined Trans Mountain Pipe Line Co. Ltd. 1953; successively Mgr. of Oil Movements, Adm. Mgr.; appt. Vice-Pres., 1958, Pres. 1960; Chrmn., retired 1979; mem., Engn. Inst. Can.; Am. Petroleum Inst.; Assn. of Oil Pipe Lines; Candn. Power Sqdns.; Anglican; recreations: golf, curling, yachting; Clubs: Shaughnessy Golf & Country; Marpole Curling; Home: Apt. 120, 4675 Valley Dr., Vancouver, B.C.

HURDON, Lloyd George; department store operator; b. Port Arthur, Ont., 16 Oct. 1917; e. Pub. and High Schs., Port Arthur, Ont.; s. Nicholas Dyer Freer and Annabelle Grace (Anderson) H.; m. Edna Catherine Jones, 6 Oct. 1948; three s. David, Jonathan, Charles; PRES., CHAPPLES LIMITED; Chapmont Investments Limited; mem., Bd. of Dirs., Central Ont. Industrial Relations Inst., Toronto; Retail Council of Can.; United Church; Clubs: Gyro; Fort William Golf & Country; Home: 32 Scott Rd., Amethyst Heights McGregor Township; Office: Box 1400, Thunder Bay, Ont. P7C 4Y3

HURLBUT, Robert St. Clair, B.Com.; company president; b. Toronto, Ont. 10 June 1924; s. St. Clair and Maude I. (Burleigh) H.; e. Earl Haig Collegiate, Toronto, Ont., (Sr. Matric.); Univ. of Toronto, B.Com. 1948; Osgoode Hall Law Sch., 1948-51; m. Anne Marilyn, d. Walter T. Moffat, 2 May 1953; two s. David, Andrew; PRESIDENT, GENERAL FOODS, LTD., since 1967; Chrmn., General Foods Limited; Hostess Food Products Ltd.; White Spot Limited; Canterbury Foods Ltd.; Industrial Catering Ltd.; Vice-Pres., General Foods Corp., White Plains, N.Y.; read law with Robert Pringle, Q.C.; called to the Bar of Ontario 1951; practised law with Daly, Thistle, Judson and McTaggart, Toronto, Ontario 1951-52; joined Colgate-Palmolive, Toronto, as Salesman, 1952; Brand Manager, 1953-54; Group Manager, 1954-55; joined General Foods, Limited, as Product Mgr., 1956-59; Product Group Mgr. 1959-62; Mgr. Sales Operations, Mar.-Nov. 1962; Devel. Mgr. 1962-63, Adv. and Merch. Mgr. 1963-65, Nat. Sales Mgr. 1965-66, Marketing Mgr. May-Nov. 1966; Vice-Pres., Marketing, 1966-67; Ordinary Seaman Apl. 1943-Dec. 1943 when commissioned; discharged Sept. 1945 as Lieut. R.C.N.(R.); Dir., North Amer. Life Assnce Co.; Hiram Walker Resources Ltd.; Rio Algom Ltd., Northern Telecom Ltd.; Northern Telecom Ltd.; Dir., The Conf. Bd. in Can.; Exec. Comte., Grocery Prod. Mfrs. of Can. (Past Chrmn.); Sr. mem., Business Council on Nat. Issues; Ont. Govt. Adv. Comte. on Quality of Working Life; Ont. Govt. Adv. Comte. on Econ. Future; Bd. of Gov., Crescent Sch.; Bd. of Gov. York Univ.; Bd. of Dir., Junior Achievement of Canada; Nat. Exec. Council, Cdn. Manufacturers Assoc.; Gov., Olympic Trust of Can.; Bd. of Gov., Guelph Univ. 1970-76; Dir. Assoc. of Cdn. Advertisers 1964-68; mem. Law Society Upper Canada; Sigma Nu; Conservative; Anglican; Clubs: Granite; Rosedale Golf; National; Board of Trade; recreations: sailing, photography, golf, tennis; Home: 18 Sandfield Rd., Don Mills, Ont. M3B 2B6; Office: 2200 Yonge St., Toronto, Ont. M4S 2C6

HURLY, Cyril Oswald; company executive (retired); b. Toronto, Ont. 4 Aug. 1914; s. late Samuel J. and Elizabeth (Day) H.; e. Pub. Sch. and Collegiate, Willowdale, Ont.; m. Mildred L., d. late Charles F. Wright, 12 August 1955; Dir., Guaranty Trust Company of Canada; F. Jos. Lamb (Can.) Ltd.; joined Chrysler Can. Ltd. in 1936 and previously in various sales capacities; Asst. to the Vice-Pres. in charge of Sales, 1954; Dir. of Sales, 1955; Dir. and Vice Pres., Marketing 1956; Extve. Vice-Pres. 1974; Pres. and Dir., 1975-79; Anglican; Clubs: Windsor; Beach Grove Golf; Renaissance (Detroit Mich.) Residence 279 Eastlawn Blvd., Windsor, Ont. N8S 3H1

HURST, Andre, B.Sc., M.Sc., Ph.D.; microbiologist; educator; b. Dej. Romania 2 Aug. 1918; came to Can. 1968; e. Univ. of Reading, U.K., B.Sc. 1942, Ph.D. 1947, M.Sc. 1964; m. Betty Anne d. late Wm. Green 14 Sept. 1942; children: Catherine Ann, Peter Francis, Nicholas Wm. and Suzanne Hilary, Christopher Paul; RESEARCH SCIENTIST, HEALTH AND WELFARE CAN. since 1968; PROF., UNIV. OF OTTAWA; Sr. Scientific Offr.; Natl. Inst. for Research in Dairying, Shinfield, U.K., 1943-52; Dir., Microbiology Lab., Unilever Research Lab., Sharnbrook, U.K., 1952-68; co-author of "The Bacterial Spore", 1909; "Microbial Foodborne Infections and Intoxications," 1973; Ed., "Candn. Jnl. of Microbiology", 1975-80; other writings incl. about 100 scientific articles, chpts. and reviews concerning food microbiol.; discovered and patented the antibiotic nisin process (the only antibiotic used in food preservation); rec'd. Prix Gorini, 1952; Harrison Prize of the Royal Soc. of Can., 1979; Award winner of the Ottawa Biol. and Biochem. Soc., 1980; Fellow, Inst. of Biol., U.K., 1968; mem., Soc. for Applied Bacteriology, U.K.; Candn. Soc. for microbiologists; Quaker; Clubs: Ottawa Bacteriology; recreations: music, jogging, cycling, skiing, carpentry; Office: Sir Fredrick Banting Research Centre, Tunney's Pasture, Ottawa, Ont. K1A 0L2.

HURST, D.G., M.Sc., Ph.D., F.R.S.C.; physicist; b. St. Austell, England, 19 March 1911; s. George Leopold and Sarah Ellen (Inns) H.; e. McGill Univ., B.Sc. 1933, M.Sc. 1934, Ph.D. 1936; Univ. of Cal. 1936-37; Cavendish Lab., Cambridge Univ. (1851 Exhn. Scholar.) 1937-39; m. Margaret Christina, d. D. A. McCuaig, 23 Dec. 1939; children: Dorothy June, David Alan; with Division of Physics, National Research Council, Ottawa, 1939-44; Montreal Lab., N.R.C., 1944-45; joined Chalk River Lab., 1945, Dir., Div. of Reactor Research & Devel.; 1965-67 on leave as Dir., Nuclear Power and Reactors Div., I.A.E.A., Vienna, Austria; Dir., Applied Research and Develop., Chalk River Nuclear Labs. 1967-70; Pres., Atomic Energy Control Bd. 1970-74; Fellow and Hon. Extve. Dir., Royal Soc. of Can.; Fellow, Am. Nuclear Soc.; mem., Candn. Assn. of Physicists; United Church; Address: 160 Leopolds Dr., Ottawa, Ont. K1V 7E3

HURST, F(rederick) Warren, B.Com., M.B.A., F.C.A.; executive; b. Toronto, Ont. 4 May 1926; s. Frederick Clarence, F.C.A. and Alice (Moody) H.; e. Univ. of Toronto Schs. Matric. 1943; Univ. of Toronto, Trinity Coll., B.Com. 1947; Harvard Grad. Sch. of Business Adm., M.B.A. 1949; Inst. of Chart Accts. of Ont. C.A. 1953, Fellow 1965; m. Cynthia Masson d. Cyril M. Smith, Q.C. 24 Jan. 1953; children: David Warren, Wendy Ann, Graham John Britton; and VICE-CHRMN. AND DIR., F. H. DEACON HODGSON INC., Dir., Northstar Res. Ltd.; Fairbank Lumber Co. Ltd.; White Rose Nurseries Ltd.; Paderno Can. Ltd.; with Mang. Adv. Services Sec. of Price Waterhouse & Co. 1949-55; joined The Consumers' Gas Co. in 1955 as Comptroller and was chief financial offr. till 1972 when apptd. Extve. V.P., Commercial Operations (Dir. of the Co. 1971-73); Dir., Extve. Comte., Home Oil 1972-73; Extve. Dir., The Ontario Comte. on Taxation, 1963-67; Treas., Candn. Inst. of Chart. Accts. 1965-68; Pres., Bureau of Mun. Research of Metro Toronto 1965-70; Vice Chrmn., Metrop. Toronto Planning Bd. 1970-76; Delta Kappa Epsilon; Anglican; Clubs: Donalda; National; Ranchmens; Osler Bluff Ski; Home: 3 Vyner Road, Willowdale, Ont. M2L 2N3; Office: Box 414, Ste. 2700, 2 First Canadian Place, Toronto, Ont. M5X 1J4

HURST, William Donald, C.M. (1972), M.S.C.E., P.Eng.; b. Winnipeg. Man., 15 Mar. 1908; s. William and Magdalene (Unger) H.; e. Laura Secord Pub. Sch.; Greenway Jr. High Sch.; Kelvin Tech. High Sch., Winnipeg, Man., Matric. 1925; Univ. of Manitoba, B.Sc. (in C.E.) 1930; Virginia Polytechnic. Inst., and State Univ. M.S.C.E. 1931; m. Gytha Johnson, Winnipeg, Man., 2 June 1934; children: Marilyn Ragna, William Helgi Donald; Consulting Civil Engr. since 1972; City Engr. and Commr. of Bldgs., Winnipeg (retired) 1944-72; Chrmn. of Commrs., Greater Winnipeg Water Dist. & Greater Winnipeg Sanitary Dist. 1959-60; Chrmn., River & Streams Protection Authority 1951-72; Chairman, Winnipeg Building Comn. 1944-60; Sr. Research Assoc., Am. Public Works Assn., Chicago, 1972 to present; Pres., Winnipeg Symphony Orchestra, 1955-56; joined staff Hurst Engn. & Construction Co. Ltd., Winnipeg, as Jr. Engr., 1925-29; apptd. Inspr. Reservoir Construction, City of Winnipeg Engn. Dept.; 1930; Teaching Fellow, Civil Engn., Virginia Polytechnic. Inst., Blacksburg, Va., 1930-31; rejoined Engn. Dept., Winnipeg, as Resident Engr., 1931-32; Office Engr., 1932-34; Engr. of Water Works, 1934-44; Asst. City Engr., 1944; served as Secy.-Engr., Bd. of Engrs., Greater Winnipeg Sanitary Dist., 1935-39; apptd. Commr., Winnipeg-St. Boniface Harbour Comn., 1946; Commr., Nat. Capital Comn., Ottawa, 1971-76; mem. Exec. Comte., Chrmn., Land Comte.; mem., Assoc. Comn. on Geotech. Research, NRC, Ottawa, 1967-71; served in 2nd World War, 10th (Reserve) Dist. Engrs., R.C.E., Capt. O/C 1st Workshop and Park Co.; mem., Assn. of Prof. Engrs., Man. (Pres. 1950 and 1951); Engn. Inst. of Can. (Chrmn., Winnipeg Br., 1938 and 1951); Am. Water Works Assn. (Chrmn., Minnesota Sec., 1947-48; Chrmn. Candn. Sec., 1952-53; Dir., 1952-55; Nat. Vice

Pres. 1961-62; Nat. Pres., 1962-63); Am. Pub. Works Assn. (Pres. 1958-59); Candn. Inst. on Pollution Control; Hon. Fellow, Inst. of Water Engrs. & Scientists (U.K.); Chart. Engr. (U.K.); Fellow, American Society of Civil Engineers; Vice-Chairman, Research Foundation, American Public Works Association; President, Institute for Mun. Engn., 1966-67; Brit. N. Am. Philatelic Soc.; Reg'd. Prof. Engr., Man. and Minn.; Hon. Reg'd Architect, Manitoba; Hon. mem., Assn. of Prof. Engrs., Manitoba, 1977; awarded George Warren Fuller Award, Am. Water Works Assn.; Pub. Works Man of the Year, 1962, Kiwanis Internat. and Am. Pub. Works Assn., Samuel Greeley Service Award; author of many technical papers; Phi Delta Theta; Golden Legion; Freemason (Scot Rite 33°); A.A.O.N.M.S. (Khartum Temple); United Church; recreations: golf; philately; Clubs: Manitoba; Carleton; Scientific; Collectors (New York); Home: 67 Kingsway, Winnipeg, Man. R3M 0G2

HURTER, Alfred Max, B.Eng.; company president; consulting engineer, b. Bucharest Rumania, 19 July 1921; s. Alfred Theodore and Olga Hedwig (Egli) H.; came to Canada, 1923; e. St. Andrew's Coll., Aurora, Ont., McGill Univ., B.Eng. (Chem. Eng.) 1946; m. Agnes Marguerite Violette d. A. H. Cadieux, Montreal, Que., 16 Oct. 1948; children: Alfred Timothy, Robert Walter, Hedy-Anne Marguerite, Agnes Maxine Adele; PRESIDENT, HURTERFIBER CONSULTANTS LTD.; mem., Engineering Institute Canada; Chemical Institute Canada; Association Consulting Engrs. Can.; Corp. Engrs. Que.; Assn. Prof. Engr. of Ont.; Assn. Prof. Chemists Que.; Sr. mem., Tech. Sec., Candn. Pulp & Paper Assn.; mem., Tech. Sec., Am. Pulp & Paper Assn.; Lutheran; recreations: fishing, bridge, collecting; Club: St. James's; Home: 165 Frobisher Dr., Apt. 1006, Pointe Claire, Que. H9R 4R8; Office: 85 St. Catherine St. W., Montreal, Que. H2X 3P4

HURTIG, Mel, O.C.; L.L.D.; book publisher; b. Edmonton, Alta., 24 June 1932; m. Kay Eleanor Studer, 18 Nov. 1981; children: Barbara, Gillian, Jane Anne, Leslie; PRESIDENT, NEW CANADIAN ENCYCLOPEDIA PUBLISHING LTD. AND HURTIG PUBLISHERS; estbd. bookstore Edmonton 1956 subsequently expanding to three; sold retail book operations 1972 to concentrate on publishing Can. books; named Can. Book Publisher of the Yr. 1974 and 1981; former Pres. Edmonton Art Gallery; former mem. Univ. of Alta. Senate; served on Bd. Team Products, City of Edmonton's Grants Comte.; served in adv. capacity Can. Council, Pollution Probe, Can. Council on Social Devel.; helped found Pub. Petroleum Assn. Can. 1975; founding mem. Comte. for an Independent Can. (Past Nat. Chrmn.); former mem. Ed. Bd. "Journal of Canadian Studies"; Past Chmn. Bd. Can. Booksellers' Assn.; mem. Assn. Can. Publishers; Order of Can. 1980; L.L.D. York Univ., 1980; Home: #1202, 9908 - 114 St., Edmonton, Alta., T5K 1R1; Office: 10560 - 105 St., Edmonton, Alta. T5H 2W7

HURTUBISE, René, B. ès A., LL.L., M.A.; avocat et éducateur; né Montréal Qué., 1 avril 1933; fils Louis-Vincent et Bernadette (Brunet) H.; é. Univ. de Montréal, B. ès A., 1954; LL.L., 1957; Univ. d'Oxford, M.A. (Jurisprudence), 1960; Univ. de Montréal, M.A. (Droit), 1961; ép Jeannine, f. Fortunat Carrier, 10 août 1957; enfants: Patrice, Martin, Frederic; JUGE À LA COUR SUPÉRIEURE DU QUÉBEC; a contribué des articles à plusieurs revues; co-auteur de (Les mécanismes de législation d'administration et et d'interprétation de la fiscalité fédérale) "Legislation, Administration and Interpretation Processes in Federal Taxation"; L'Université-La Société et Le Gouvernement" 1970, "L'Université Quebecoise du Proche Avenir" 1973; ex membre du Conseil, des Universites du Qué.; ex Prés., du Comté sur les Objectifs de l'Enseignement Supérieur du Conseil des Univs.; Conseiller auprès du représentant permanent du Can. lors de la 33ème Sess. de la Comm. des droits de l'homme des Nations-Unies

(1977); Pres. de l'Assoc. Can. des organismes statutaires pour la protetion des droits de l'homme (1977-78); invité à titre d'expert par l'UNESCO au colloque "L'Homme et la Paix", à Paris, Oct. 1977, et à Montréal, Comme expert et rapporteur, en juillet 1978, "Le Racisme et l'Histoire"; Pres. de la Comm. des Droits de la personne du Quebec 1975 a 1980; ant. Dir. gén. de la Conférence des recteurs et des principaux des univ. du Québ. Catholique: résidence: 3546, ave Marcil, Montréal, Qué. H4A 2Z3; Bureau: 360 St-Jacques - #611, Montréal, Qué. H2Y 1P5

HUSBAND, Harold; company president; b. Troy, N.Y., 1905; became a naturalized Candn. 1929; s. late John Husband; e. New York and Montreal Schs.; m. Margaret Kay Lindsay, 1937; three d.; PRES., HUSWEST ENTERPRISES CORP.; Hon. Dir., The Royal Trust Company; Director, Victoria Chamber Comm.; worked for C.P.R., particularly in connection to constr. of hotels at Banff and Lake Louise; worked with the late J. S. H. Matson, organ. and buying bus lines on Vancouver Island; later became Gen. Mgr. of Vancouver Island Transportation Co. and Vancouver Island Coach Lines Ltd., subsequently buying these co's from C.P. Rly. Co.; for many yrs. was active in publishing business and was Mang. Dir. of "Victoria Colonist", a Dir. of Candn. Daily Newspapers Assn. and a mem. of The Candn. Press; owned and op. Victoria Machinery Depot Co. Ltd. 1947-81; Pres., Candn. Ship Building and Ship Repairing Assn. 1957-60, B.C.; mem., Victoria Chamber of Comm. (Past Pres.); Victoria and Island Publicity Bureau (Past Pres.); recreation: golf; Clubs: Victoria Golf; Union; Vancouver; Home: 3150 Rutland Rd., Uplands, Victoria, B.C. V8R 3R8; Office: (Box 1117) 343 Bay St., Victoria, B.C. V8W 2S6

HUSTON, M.J., M.Sc., Ph.D., retired university dean; b. Ashcroft, B.C., 4 Sept. 1912; s. William Mervyn and Irene Mary (Gray) H.; e. Univ. of Alberta, B.Sc. (Pharm.) 1934, M.Sc. (Biochem.) 1938; Univ. of Wash., Ph.D. (Pharm.) 1941; m. Helen Margaret McBryan, 18 Dec. 1939; children: Bryan Mervyn, Dorna Helen; joined staff of Univ. as Lect. 1939, Asst. Prof. 1943, Acting Dir. Sch. of Pharm., 1946, Dir., 1948; Dean, Faculty of Pharmacy and Pharmaceutical Sciences, Univ. of Alberta, 1955-78; Pres. (1970), Candn. Foundation for Advanc. of Pharm.; Candn. Pharm. Assn. 1968-69; mem., Alta. Pharm. Assn.; Am. Pharm. Assn.; Candn. Conf. of Pharm. Faculties (Chrmn. 1948-49); author of "The Great Canadian Lover", 1964; "Toast to the Dollar" 1969; "Canada Eh to Zed" 1973; "Great Golf Humour", 1977; "Golf and Murphy's Law" 1981 Ed.-in-Chief, Candn. Journ. of Pharm. Science 1965-78; has publ. two textbooks and written many papers for tech. journs.; rec'd. Dr. E. R. Squibb Award 1971; Alberta Achievement Award Medal 1971; Hon. Life Mem.: Can. Pharmaceutical Assoc., 1977; Alta. Pharmaceutical Assoc., 1978; Man. Pharmaceutical Assoc., 1978; B.C. Pharm. Assn. 1978; Sask Pharm. Assn. 1978; Sigma Xi; Phi Sigma; Phi Delta Theta (Adv. 1948-50); Rho Chi; Freemason (32°); Conservative; United Church; recreations: music, sports; Club: Kiwanis (Pres. 1956); Home: 11562-80 Ave., Edmonton, Alta. T6G 0R9

HUTCHEON, Hon. Henry Ernest, B.A., LL.B.; b. Brantford, Ont., 26 July 1920; s. James and Florence (Carey) H.; e. Univ. of Toronto, B.A. 1948; Univ. of B.C., LL.B. 1950; m. Valerie Marie, d. Albert John McCullagh, 9 March 1955; children: Bruce, Craig, Kerry; JUSTICE, SUPREME COURT OF B.C. 1974-80; Justice, Court of Appeal for B.C., 1980- ; read law with R. N. Shakespeare; called to the Bar of B.C. 1951; cr. Q.C. 1967; Partner, Shakespeare & Hutcheon, 1958-68; Guild, Yule, Schmitt, Lane, Hutcheon & Collier 1968-73; apptd. Judge Co. Court 1973; served with the Royal Canadian Corps of Signals 1939-45; Protestant; recreation: golf; Club: Point Grey Golf & Country; Home: 2327 W. 35th St., Vancouver, B.C. V6M 1J7; Office: Court House, Vancouver, B.C.

HUTCHESON, Francis Wilson; of Scottish-Irish descent; 3rd generation of family engaged in lumber industry; b. Huntsville, Ont., 25 Mar. 1893; s. Robert James (pioneer lumberman and Founder of The Muskoka Wood Mfg. Co. Ltd.) and Martha Isabel (Wood) H.; e. Elem. Schs., Huntsville, Ont.; Univ. of Toronto, class of 1914; m. Emily Agnes, d. W. A. Cockburn, Toronto, Ont.; children: Robert, Gerald; formerly for some years Pres., Muskoka Wood Products Ltd.; disposed of his interests in 1955; now engaged in invest. and mang.; Pres., Lake Vernon Realty Ltd.; Past Pres., Hon. Dir. and mem. permanent Extve., National Hardwood Lumber Assn., Chicago; Director, Veneer Log Supply Co. (Crown Company), 1943-44; D.C.L. (honoris causa) Thornloe Univ., Nov. 1974; served in 1st World War 1914-18 as Lt., R.N.V.R., attached to Roy. Navy in European Waters; Phi Delta Theta; Anglican; recreations: fishing, shooting, golf; Clubs: Granite; University (Toronto); Toronto Hunt; Home: 1 Elm St., Huntsville, Ont. P0A 1K0

HUTCHESON, James Robert MacLeod, B.A.Sc.; retired executive; b. Huntsville, Ont., 17 May 1922; s. John George and Carmen Annie (Miller) H.; e. Earl Haig Coll. Inst., Willowdale, Ont.; Univ. of Toronto, B.A.Sc. 1949; Univ. of W. Ont., Mang. Training Course, 1968; m. Charlotte d. Walter Reck, Zurich, Switzerland, 12 Apr. 1980; children: Pamela Stewart Bacon, James Phillip Nase, Robert John George; Vice-Pres., Asbestos Fibre, Johns-Manville Corp; Dir., Advocate Mines Ltd.; Kingsey Falls Paper Co.; during World War II served with RCNVR; Anti-Submarine; rank Lt.; Gov., The Wales Home, Richmond, Que.; Dir., Candn. Mineral Indust. Educ. Foundation; author of various presentation papers; mem. Mining Assn. Can. (Dir.); Que. Asbestos Mining Assn. (Dir.); Assn. Engrs. Que.; Candn. Inst. Mining & Metall.; Am. Inst. Mining, Metall. & Petrol. Engrs.; Am. Soc. Testing & Materials (Past Chrmn. Asbestos & Naturally Occurring Fibres Comte.); Gov., Quebec Hosp. Assn.; Gov. Whales Home Richmond Crt.; Phi Kappa Pi (Pres.); Protestant; recreations: hunting, skiing, tree farming; Clubs: St. James's (Montreal); Home: 3450 Drummond St., Montreal, Que. H3G 1Y2

HUTCHINGS, Harold Ross, M.D.; pharmaceutical executive; b. Brantford, Ont., 3 Apl. 1935; s. Arthur R. and May (Topping) H.; e. Pub. and High Schs. Hamilton, Ont.; Univ. Western Ont., M.D. 1960; m. Gertrude, d. Francis Quinlan, 21 June 1961; 2 d., Barbara Lyn and Kathryn Mary; VICE PRES., SYNTEX PHARMACEUTICALS DIVISION, of Syntex Corp. since Oct. 1974; commenced in private practice 1961-64; joined G. D. Searle & Co. of Canada Ltd. as Med. Dir. 1964; Vice-Pres. and Gen. Mgr. 1967; Dir. 1968, Pres. 1971-73; Area Dir., N.W. Europe, Searle International 1973-74; mem. Coll. of Family Physicians; Candn. Med. APsn.; Ont. Med. Assn.; Pharm. Mfrs. Assn. Can. (Hon. mem. Med. Sec.); Alpha Kappa Kappa; Protestant; Home: 2 Abbots Dr., Virginia Water, Surrey, GUZ54QS Eng.; Office: Syntex Corp. U.K. Branch Office, 23/25 Marlow Rd., Maidenhead, Berks., Eng.

HUTCHISON, Hamish Rodney, B.Com.; investment management executive; b. England, 1931; e. McGill Univ. B.Com. 1956; CHRMN., TORONTO INVESTMENT MANAGEMENT INC. 1976- ; Vice Chrmn. The International Trust Co.; Partner and Mgr. Bond Dept. Greenshields Inc. 1957-63; Vice Pres. and Dir. Research, Loomis, Sayles & Co. (Canada) Ltd. 1964-72; Vice Pres. and Dir. AGF Management Ltd. 1964-72; Pres., AGF Toronto Investment Management 1973-76; Dir. Children's Aid Soc. Metrop. Toronto Foundation; mem. Ed. Adv. Bd., Benefits Can.; Home: 52 High Park Ave., Toronto, Ont. M6P 2R9; Office: (P.O. Box 75) Royal Bank Plaza, Toronto, Ont. M5J 2J2.

HUTCHISON, (William) Bruce, O.C. (1967); author; journalist; b. Prescott, Ont., 5 June 1901; e. Pub. Schs.,

Victoria, B.C.; Hon. degree, Yale, 1968; m. Dorothy Kidd McDiarmid, 1925; children: Joan Edith, Robert Bruce; Editor (Emeritus) Vancouver Sun, 1979- ; Edit. Dir., 1963-79; Dir., Sun Publishing Co.; Pol. Reporter, Ottawa, 1925; Assoc. Ed., Winnipeg "Free Press" 1944-50; Editor, Victoria "Daily Times", 1950-63; has travelled extensively throughout the Dom.; at Imperial Conference 1937: considered one of Can.'s foremost authorities on pol. and econ. affairs; well-known in Wash., D.C., journalistic circles; author of "The Unknown Country", 1943 (winner of Gov.-Gen.'s Award); "The Hollow Men", 1944; "The Fraser" (42nd in "Rivers of America Series"), 1950; "The Incredible Canadian", 1952 (biography of Rt. Hon. W.L.M. King); "The Struggle for the Border" (novel), 1955; "Canada: Tomorrow's Giant", 1957; "Mr. Prime Minister'. (hist.), 1964; "Western Windows" (essays), 1967; "The Far Side of the Street", 1976 (C.A.A. Award, 1977); "Uncle Perey's Wonderful Town" 1981 has written numerous short stories publ. in "Saturday Evening Post", "Colliers ", "Cosmopolitan", "American", "Liberty"; first winner of new award for Distinguished Journalism in the Commonwealth, given by Royal Soc. of Arts, London, 1961; Home: 810 Rogers Ave., Victoria, B.C. V8X 3P9; Office: 2250 Granville St., Vancouver, B.C. V6H 3G2

HUTCHISON, William Leslie, B. Eng., P.Eng.; b. Ottawa, Ont. 18 July 1911; s. George Norman and Amelia Maria (Schneider) H.; e. Public Schs. and Glebe Coll. Inst., Ottawa; McGill Univ., B.Eng. 1934; m. Ellen Milne, d. F. O. Weeks, Ottawa, 5 Sept. 1936; children: William G., Mrs. Norman Hawkins; PRES. W.L. HUTCHISON ASSOCIATES LTD. Mang. Consultants, since 1962; Secy. Treas. Telnor Holdings Ltd. & its subsidiaries; after grad. joined Wabi Iron Works Ltd. in N. Ont. as Jr. Draftsman remained until 1942 when he left as Mgr.; Works Mgr., Hamilton Bridge Co., Hamilton, Ont. 1942-45, engaged in extensive ordnance and govt. contracts; joined Remington Rand Ltd. in 1946 as Gen. Mgr. of Mfg. in Can.; trans. to Europe as Dir. of Mfg. for U.K. and Asst. Dir. for Europe, 1952-55; joined Moffats Ltd., Weston, Ont., in 1955 as Vice Pres. until 1962 engaged in the establishment of internat. businesses and responsible for the setting up of a Brit. subsidiary and mfg. unit in Scotland; Dir., Fluid Power Ltd., from inception 1960, Vice-Pres. 1962; Pres., 1964; Chrmn. 1976-79 (ret.); Dir. Baxter Energy Systems Ltd.; Telnor Holdings Ltd.; Past Pres., Engr. Inst. of Can.; Chrmn. Internat. Comte., Standards Council of Can.; Dir., Rotary Club of Toronto; mem., Ont. Assn. Prof. Engrs.; Club: St. George's Golf & Country; Home: 14 Edenbridge Dr., Islington, Ont. M9A 3E9

HUTT, Frederick Bruce, Ph.D., D.Sc.; emeritus professor; b. Guelph, Ont. 20 Aug. 1897; s. Howard Laing and Annie (Pook) H.; e. Ont. Agric. Coll., B.S.A. 1923; Univ. of Wis., M.S. 1925; Univ. of Manitoba, M.A. 1927; Univ. of Edinburgh, Ph.D. 1929, D.Sc. 1939; Univ. of Agric., Brno, Czechoslovakia, D.Sc. (h.c.) 1965; Univ. of Guelph, D.Sc. (h.c.) 1974; m. Alice Jean, d. Dr. L. C. Bacon, St. Paul, Minn., 30 June 1930; children: Frederick Bruce, Jr., Robert Bacon, Margaret Ann; Lectr. in Poultry Husbandry, Univ. of Man. and Extension Poultryman, Dept. of Agric., 1923-27; Asst. Prof. of Poultry Husbandry, Univ. of Minn., 1928-29; Assoc. Prof. 1929-31; Prof. of Animal Genetics and Poultry Husbandry, 1931-34; Prof. of Poultry Husbandry and Animal Genetics and Head of Dept. of Poultry Husbandry, Cornell Univ., 1934-40; Prof. of Zool. and Chrmn. of the Dept., 1939-44; Prof. of Animal Genetics, 1940-65; Prof. Emeritus since 1965; Collab., U.S. Dept. of Agric., 1938-46; mem., Advisory Comte., Regional Poultry Lab., East Lansing, Mich., 1939-45; mem., Comte. on Fellowships in Biol. and Agric., Nat. Research Council (Wash.), 1946-49; Visiting Prof., N.C. State Coll., 1956; Visiting Scholar, Va. Polytech. Inst. 1966; Guest Prof. in Genetics, Oregon State Univ. 1966; mem., Ed. Bd., Journal of Heredity, since 1957; Geo. Scott Robertson Mem. Lectr., Queen's Univ.,

Belfast, 1957; Halpin Mem. Lectr. Univ. of Wisconsin, 1978; Newman Trust Internat. Poultry Award (1961); winner of Research Prize of Poultry Science Assn., 1929; Borden Award for Research, 1946; Pres., Poultry Science Assn., 1933; mem., Genetics Soc. Am.; Am. Genetic Assn. (mem. of Adv. Comte., 1952-57; Ed. Bd. since 1957); Am. Soc. Human Genetics; Fellow, Poultry Science Assn.; mem., Fellow, Am. Assn. Advanc. Science; mem., Poultry Science Assn.; Sigma Xi; author: "Genetics of the Fowl", 1949; "Genetic Resistance to Disease in Domestic Animals", 1958; "Animal Genetics", 1964, 2nd Ed. 1982; "Genetics for Dog Breeders" 1979; papers on genetics in scient. journs.; Hon. mem. Cong. on Genetics Applied to Livestock Production, Madrid 1974; Hon. Fellow, Roy. Soc. of Edin. 1975; Poultry Hall of Fame, 1980; recreations: nature study, gardening, stamps; Home: 107 Woodcrest Terrace, Ithaca, N.Y. 14850.

HUTT, William, C.C. (1969), M.M., D.F.A., LL.D.; actor-director; b. Toronto, Ont. 2 May 1920; s. Edward DeWitt and Caroline Frances Havergal (Wood) H.; e. Vaughan Road Coll. Inst., Toronto, Ont.; N. Toronto Coll. Inst. (1941); Trinity Coll., Univ. of Toronto, B.A. 1949; Ottawa, D.F.A. 1969; Guelph, LL.D. 1973; Univ. of Western Ontario, LL.D. (L.C.) 1981; unm.; began prof. field in 1947 with a summer stock co. in Bracebridge, Ont.; spent a season as Asst. Mgr. & leading man with Candn. Repertory Theatre, Ottawa; also directed Little Theatre groups throughout Ont. and adjudicated for W. Ont. Drama League; from 1948-52 was with various summer stock theatres before joining the Stratford Shakespearen Festival Co. in its first year (1953) taking the roles of Sir Robert Brackenbury and Capt. Blunt in "Richard III", and Minister of State in "All's Well That Ends Well"; in 1954 acted Froth in "Measure for Measure", Hortensio in "The Taming of the Shrew", and the leader of the Chorus in "Oedipus Rex" (became 1st recipient of Tyrone Guthrie Award); in 1955 acted Ligarius and Cinna the Poet in "Julius Caesar". Old Gobbo in "The Merchant of Venice", Chorus Leader in "Oedipus Rex"; in 1956, Leader of the Chorus in "Oedipus Rex" for the filmed version, Canterbury in "Henry V" and Ford in "The Merry Wives of Windsor"; 1957 Polonius in "Hamlet"; 1958, Worcester in "Henry IV Part I", and Don Pedro in "Much Ado About Nothing"; 1959, Lodovico in "Othello" and Jaques in "As You Like It"; has also appeared in several Canadian Players tours in various Shakespearean parts and lead in Noel Coward's "Private Lives", 1963-64; has often appeared on CBC-TV and ABC-TV in Britain; in Eng. starred at Bristol Old Vic in "Long Day's Journey Into Night" playing James Tyrone; was also in Noel Coward's "Waiting in the Wings", and in several films on TV for BBC; on tour in U.S. in "Sail Away" (Coward) which he left in Boston to tour with Canadian Players as Lear in "King Lear" and Thomas Mendip in "The Lady's Not For Burning"; returned to the Stratford Festival for 10th Season to play Prospero in "The Tempest", Banquo in "Macbeth" and Carson de Castel-Jaloux in "Cyrano de Bergerac"; has appeared in three Broadway productions; toured with Candn. Players across Can. playing lead in Noel Coward's "Private Lives", 1963-64; originated role of Tsar Nicholas II in world premiere of "Nicholas Romanov", Man. Theatre Centre; at Stratford (Ont.) Festival played Pandarus in "Troilus and Cressida", 1963; title role in "Richard II" and Sparkish in "The Country Wife", 1964; Brutus in "Julius Caesar", Justice Shallow in "Henry IV Pt. II" and Gaev in "The Cherry Orchard", 1965; Chorus in "Henry V", Warwick in "Henry VI", Grand Duke Michael in world premiere of "Last of the Tsars", 1966; Khlestakov in "The Government Inspector" (repeated at Expo in Oct. 1967), Clarence in "Richard III". Enobarbus in "Antony and Cleopatra", (repeated at Expo), 1967; played title role in "Tartuffe" (later recorded for Caedmon Records), Trigorin in "Seagull", and directed "Waiting for Godot", 1968; with Nat. Theatre (special engagement), Chichester, Eng., played Don Adriano de Armado in "Loves Labours Lost" and Alcibiades in "Timon of Athens". 1964; on Broadway played Lawyer in Edward Albee's "Tiny Alice" opposite John Gielgud and Irene Worth, 1964; played Tsar Nicholas in the MGM film "The Fixer", 1967; played Warwick in Shaw's "St. Joan", Lincoln Centre, N.Y., 1968; played title role in Moliére's "Tartuffe" 1968-69; apptd. Assoc.-Dir., Stratford Nat. Theatre 1970-71, directing "Much Ado About Nothing" and playing title role in "Volpone" there; dir., "As You Like It" and played title role in "King Lear" 1971-72; played Epicure Mammon in "The Alchemist" 1968-69, and again at Chichester Festival, Eng., 1970; led Stratford Nat. Theatre as "King Lear" on tour of European capitals incl. Moscow, Leningrad, Warsaw, 1973; led Stratford Nat. Theatre in title role "The Imaginary Invalid" on tour of Australia, repeated role in Stratford summer season, 1974; as Dir., Festival Stage under artistic directorship of Robin Phillips, played Duke of Vienna "Measure for Measure", in "Captain Brazen", "Trumpets and Drums", and Lady Bracknell in "The Importance of Being Earnest"; also directed "St. Joan" for Festival Stage and "Oscar Remembered" for The Third Stage, Stratford 1975; awarded Earl Grey A.C.T.R.A. for best performance on television as Sir John A. MacDonald in "The National Dream" 1975; (won E TROG — Best Actor in Can. films); won Prix Anik for performance of Bernard Shaw in CBC TV production, "First Night of Pygmalian", 1975; apptd. Artistic Dir., Theatre London (Ont.) and Dir., Festival Stage, Stratford, 1976; with Theatre London has directed "Candida" (Bernard Shaw), and played James Tyrone opposite Jessica Tandy in "Long Day's Journey into Night", dir. by Robin Phillips; played Pastor Manders in "Ghosts", King of France in "All's Well that Ends Well" and David in "Hay Fever" at Stratford, 1977; played title role in "Uncle Vanya", title role in "Titus Andronicus" and Falstaff in "Merry Wives of Windsor", at Stratford, 1978; Title Role, "Titus Andronicus" (Revived Stratford 1980; "Feste" in "Twelfth Night"; "Dorn" in "Seagull" (with Maggie Smith); "Fool" in "Lear" (with Peter Ustinov); "James Tyrone" in "Long Day's Journey into Night" (with Jessica Tandy); "Schill" in "The Visit" (with Alexis Smith); Starred in "The Wars", a film of Timothy Findley's novel, directed by Robin Phillips, and in "Models", a film directed by Jean Claude Lord, both in 1981; served in 2nd World War, 1941-46 with 7th Canadian Light Field Ambulance (front-line service in Italy, France, Belgium, Holland); awarded Military Medal; member, "The Players", New York; Actor's Equity Association; Assn. Canadian TV and Radio Artists; Liberal; Anglican; recreations: fishing, golf, swimming, playing piano; Address: 4 Waterloo St. N., Stratford, Ont. N5A 5H4

HUTTON, James Rookes Smeaton, B.Sc.; company executive; b. Greenock, Scot., 18 Sept., 1922; s. James Smeaton and Annie Banks (Rookes) H.; e. Lairdsland Sch., Kirkintilloch, Scot., 1927-34; High Sch. Glasgow, Scot., 1934-40; Royal Tech. Coll. (Dipl.) and Glasgow Univ., B.Sc. (Mech. Engn.) 1943; m. Marguerite S. Gauthier, d. Arthur Gauthier, Dorval, May 1974; came to Canada 5 May 1949; PRES. AND DIR., MAN ASHTON INC. since 1967; Senior Vice Pres., M.A.N. WOOD INC., Middlesex, N.J.; joined Rolls-Royce Ltd., Glasgow, Scot. as Tech. Engr., 1943-46, Engr., Derby, Eng., 1946-49, Sr. Tech. Rep., Can., 1949-51; joined Bristol Aero-Industries Ltd., Montreal, Que., as Quality Mgr., 1951; Sales and Service Mgr., 1952-53; Mgr. Engn., 1953-56; Asst. Gen. Mgr., Vancouver, B.C., 1957-59; Gen. Mgr. there 1959-60; Vice-Pres., Gen. Mgr. and Dir., 1960-67; also Extve. Vice-Pres. and Dir., present Co. 1964-67; Liberal; Protestant; recreations: golfing; Home: 4911 Cote des Neiges Rd., Montreal, Que. H3V 1H7; Office: 7875 Trans Canada Hwy., Montreal, Que. H4S 1L3

HUXLEY, Herbert H., M.A., F.I.A.L.; university professor; b. Brooklands, Cheshire, Eng., 29 July 1916; s. Henry and Amy (Bland) H.; e. Sale High Sch., Cheshire, Eng., 1927-29; Manchester (Eng.) Grammar Sch., 1929-35; St. John's Coll., Cambridge Univ., B.A. 1939, M.A. 1942; Trinity Coll., Dublin, M.A. 1961; m. Joan Mary, d. late Rev. Thomas Peers, 30 Aug. 1941; two s., Martin Neil, Ph.D., Andrew David, B.A., B.C.L.; Joan Mary d., Oct. 22 1974; 2ndly m. Margaret Elizabeth, d. Rev. G. E. P. Cox; PROF. OF CLASSICS, UNIV. OF VICTORIA, 1968-79; Supervisor of Classics of St. John's & Queen's Colleges, Cambridge, 1979- ; el. mem. of Classical Fac., Univ. of Cambridge, 1980; Lectr. in Classics, Leeds Univ., Eng., 1944-51; Sr. Lectr. in Latin, Univ. of Manchester, Eng., 1951-62; Reader in Latin 1962-68; Visiting Lectr. in Classics, Dublin Univ., 1961; Visiting Assoc. Prof. of Classics, Brown Univ., 1966-67; Visiting Fellow of Univ. Coll., Cambridge Univ., 1970-71; Visiting Fellow of St. Cross Coll., Oxford 1978-79; Visiting Fellow of St. Edmund's House, Cambridge, 1980; Past Pres., N.W. Naturalists' Union, Eng.; Ed., "Claudian: The Rape of Proserpine" (translated by Leonard Digges; an ed. of a book publ. 1617), 1959; Virgil, Georgics I & IV", 1963, 1965 and 1979; "Carmina MCMLXIII", 1963; "Corolla Camenae", 1969; other writings incl. over 250 Latin poems publ. in over 30 different metres; contrib. to "Fifty Years of Classical Scholarship" and many classical journs.; Ed., "North Western Naturalists' Union Handbook", 1961-69; Fellow, "Latinitas" Fdn. (Vatican) 1977; Fdn. Life Mem., The Cambridge Society 1977; mem., Classical Assn. Can.; The Oxford Society; Classical Assn. (GB); Classical Assn., Manchester & Dist. Br. (Ed., MAMVCIVM 1963-69); Virgil Soc.; Cambridge Philol. Soc.; Oxford Philol. Soc.; Leeds Lit. & Philol. Soc.; Orbilian Soc. (Pres. 1969; Vice Pres. 1970); Ouidianum (Romania); Assn. for the Reform of Latin Teaching (Vice Pres.); Anglican; recreations: walking, swimming, music; Home: 12 Derwent Close, Cambridge, CB1 4DZ England

HUYCKE, F. A. M., Q.C.; b. Toronto, Ont. Oct. 1924; s. George Meredith and Ottilie (Avery) H.; e. Toronto Public Schs.; Trinity Coll. Sch. 1943; Trinity Coll., Toronto, 1948; Osgoode Hall, Toronto, 1951; m. Catherine, d. John LeBel 1952; children: Catherine, Mary, Margot, Graeme, Jennifer; Dir., Norcen Energy Resources Ltd., and Northern and Central Gas Corp. Ltd.; Trustee and mem. Investment Comte. T.D. Realty Investments; Dir., Morgan Bank of Canada Ltd.; served in R.C.A. 1943-45; called to the Bar of Ont. 1951; mem. Can. Bar Assn.; County of York Law Soc.; Anglican; recreations: skiing, golf; Clubs: The Toronto; Toronto Golf; Badminton and Racquet; Osler Bluff Ski; Home: 39 Rosedale Hts. Dr., Toronto, Ont M4T 1C2

HYDE, Hon. G. Miller, Q.C., C.D., B.A., B.C.L.; ex-judge; b. Sewickley, Pa., 25 March 1905; s. George Taylor and Mary (Reppert) H.; e. Selwyn House Sch.; Lower Can. Coll.; McGill Univ., B.A. 1926; B.C.L. 1929; m. N. E. Anne, d. B. W. P. Coghlin, Montreal, 17 Oct. 1938; children: Peter, Christopher; read law with Lawrence Macfarlane, K.C.; Advocate 1929; cr. K.C. 1949; practised with firm of Lafleur, MacDougall, Macfarlane & Barclay, later known as Scott, Hugessen, Macklaier, Chisholm & Hyde; Justice, Court of Appeal, Que. 1950-73; Hon. Pres. and Dir. Montreal Gen. Hosp. Research Inst. and mem. Bd. of Mang., Montreal General Hosp.; Governor, (Emeritus) McGill Univ. and Trinity Coll. Sch., Port Hope, Ont.; Hon. Vice Pres., Mount St. Hilaire Nature Conservation Centre; Dir., McCord Museum; Secy.-Gen. Anglo-French Purchasing Bd., 1939; served as Dir. and Hon. Legal Advisor to Fed. Aircraft Ltd., 1940-46; C.O.T.C. (McGill Univ.) as Paymaster, 1940-46; retired with rank of Maj.; Pres., McGill Graduates Soc. 1961-62; St. Andrews Soc.; Delta Upsilon; Presbyterian; recreations: golf, fishing; Clubs: Mount Royal Club; Mount Bruno Country; Knowlton Golf; University; Canadian; Home: 3066 Trafalgar Ave., Montreal, Que. H3Y 1H4

HYDE, Ralph Ernest, Judge, B.A., LL.B.; b. Edmonton, Alta., 27 June 1922; s. Ernest Elmer and Mildred Mary (Jolliffe) H.; e. Highlands Pub. and Eastwood High Schs. Edmonton; Royal Mil. Coll.-Kingston 1940-42; Univ. of Alta. B.A. 1949, LL.B. 1950; m. Marion Webster d. late William Alexander Milroy, 8 Aug. 1945; children: Jill, Marion, Pamela, John; JUDGE OF THE PROVINCIAL COURT since 1978; Dir. Opto Investments Ltd.; read law with Nelles Victor Buchanan; called to Bar of Alta. 1951, Bar of N.W.T. 1964; cr. Q.C. 1968; articled Wood Buchanan Campbell 1950-51, assoc. 1951; Partner Wood Haddad Moir Hyde & Ross 1953; senior partner, Newson Hyde, 1973-77; served with Royal Candn. Armoured Corps 1942-46 UK, Sicily, Italy, N.W. Europe; Reserve Army 1946-57, A.D.C. Lt. Gov. of Alta.; mem. Adv. Bd. St. Johns Sch. of Alta. 1971-74; Adv. Comte. NAIT Court Reporting; mem. Edmonton Bar Assn.; Law Soc. Alta.; Candn. Bar Assn.; Loyal Order Blue Goose Internat.; P. Conservative; Anglican; recreations: golf, skiing, hunting, fishing; Clubs: Kiwanis Internat.; Crestwood Curling; Edmonton Ski; RMC; Garrison Officers; Mil. Inst.; Glendale Golf & Country (Dir. 1973-74); Home: 66 St. Georges Cres., Edmonton, Alta. T5N 3M7; Office: Provincial Court Judges' Chambers, 700 Century Place, 9803 - 102A Ave., Edmonton, Alta. T5J 3A3

HYLAND, Frances; actress, educator; b. Regina, Sask.; e. Royal Acad. Dramatic Art (Eng.) under Sir Kenneth Barnes; m. George McCowan (divorced); one s., Evan McCowan; Head, Dept. of Drama, Univ. of Sask., 1975; first prof. performance Stella in "A Streetcar Named Desire" London, Eng.; others incl. "The Winter's Tale" with Sir John Gielgud, directed by Peter Brooks; "Crime and Punishment"; "The Idiot"; "A Woman of No Importance"; "The Dark Is Light Enough"; invited to Stratford Festival (Can.) by Tyrone Guthrie, 1954; played Isabella in "Measure for Measure" opposite James Mason, Portia opposite Frederick Valk; Ophelia opposite Christopher Plummer etc.; toured with winter co., The Canadian Players; appeared in "Look Homeward Angel" New York; "A Time to Laugh" London, Eng. Under the direction of Tyrone Guthrie; helped pioneer regional theatres in Can. such as Man. Theatre Centre, Vancouver Playhouse; apptd. mem. Can. Council 1974; Winner of the Drainie Award for Distinguished Contribution to Braodcasting, 1981;

HYLAND, J(ames) Norman, B.Com.; company officer; b. Vancouver, B.C., 1913; e. Vernon, (B.C.) Pub. Schs.; Univ. of Brit. Columbia, B.Com. 1934; m.; has two children; Chrmn., Pacific Press Ltd.; Dir., MacMillan Bloedel Ltd.; Southam Inc.; Selkirk Communications Ltd.; Woodward Stores Ltd.; Inland Nat. Gas Co. Ltd.; former Chrmn. and Chief Exec. Offr., British Columbia Packers Ltd. (retired 1969); Past Pres., Fisheries Council of Canada; Chmn. of Bd., B.C. Railway; United Church; Club: Shaughnessy Heights Golf. 4350 Valley Dr.; Vancouver, B.C. V6L 3B5

HYNDMAN, Frederick Eardley; insurance executive; b. Charlottetown, P.E.I. 5 Feb. 1939; s. Hon. Frederick Walter and N. Cecile (Shannon) H.; e. Charlottetown elem. schs.; Kings Coll. Sch. Windsor, N.S.; Dalhousie Univ.; m. Shirley Lillian d. B. Guy Gamester, Charlottetown, P.E.I. 6 July 1966; two d. Helen Elizabeth, Norah Joanne; MANG. DIR., HYNDMAN & CO. LTD.; Pres., Charlottetown Area Development Corp.; joined gen. ins. industry Montreal 1960; trans. to Halifax 1962 as life ins. sales rep.; joined present family firm following 9 yr. Sales Office, Summerside, P.E.I.; assumed mang. role H.O. 1970; comnd. Candn. Army (Reserve) 1960, served 2 yrs. Royal Candn. Hussars, Montreal; active supporter P. Cons. Party local level; Past Prov. Pres. Jaycees; Past Dir. Chamber Comm.; mem. Planning Comte. and first Bd. Govs. (1968-73) Holland Coll.; Dir. and mem. Extve. Comte. P.E.I. Centennial Comn.; Chrmn. Local Adv. Comte. Heritage Can.; Fellow, Ins. Inst. Can.; mem. Ins.

Inst. P.E.I. (Past Pres. and mem. Nat. Council); Ins. Agts. Assn. P.E.I. (Past Pres. and Dir. Nat. Body); Candn. Fed. Ins. Agts. & Brokers (Past Dir.); P. Conservative; Anglican; recreation: sailing; Clubs: Charlottetown Yacht; United Services Officers'; Home: 10 Goodwill Ave., Charlottetown, P.E.I. C1A 3C7; Office: 57 Queen St., Charlottetown, P.E.I. C1A 7L9.

HYNDMAN, Hon. Louis Davies, M.L.A., B.A., LL.B.; politician; b. Edmonton, Alta. 1 July 1935; s. Louis Davies, Q.C. and Muriel (MacKintosh) H.; e. Glenora, Oliver & West Glen P.S. Edmonton; Univ. of Alta. B.A., LL.B.; m. Mary Evelyn d. Dr. A. H. Maclennan, Edmonton, Alta. 2 June 1962; children: Mary Jennifer, Bruce Louis Davies, Peter; PROV. TREASURER, ALTA. 1979- ; Hon. Aide-de-Camp to Lt. Gov. Alta. 1960-62; service R.C.N. (Reserve) rank Ltd., retired 1962; Extve. Asst. to Min. of Citizenship & Immigration Ottawa 1962-63; el. M.L.A. for Edmonton Glenora prov. g.e. 1967, re-el. since; Min. of Educ. 1971-75; Min. of Fed. & Intergovernmental Affairs and Govt. House Leader 1975; P. Conservative; Anglican; Office: 323 Legislative Bldg., Edmonton, Alta. T5K 2B6.

HYNDMAN, Margaret Paton, O.C. (1973), Q.C. (1938), D.C.L. (1976); b. Palmerston, Ontario; d. Hugh and Agnes (Wilkie) H.; e. Pub. Schs., Palmerston, Ont.; Listowel (Ont.) High Sch.; Osgoode Hall, Toronto; D.C.L.; Acadia Univ. 1976; COUNSEL, BLACKWELL, LAW, SPRATT, ARMSTRONG AND GRASS; Dir. Emeritus, GSW Inc.; Dir. Harry Hamilton Construction Ltd.; Viwat Cleda Fine Fashion Ltd.; Viwat Corp. Ltd.; articled to Alfred Bicknell, K.C., later to F. W. Wegenast, K.C.; called to Bar of Ont. 1926; cr. K.C. 1938 (2nd woman in Brit. Empire to receive this hon.); was mem., Wegenast, Hyndman & Kemp; practised under her own name for some years; has done legal work in most Candn. provs.; Dir. of several indust. organs. & has taken active part in mang. of these firms; 1st woman in Can. to become Dir. of a Trust Co.; was 1st Vice-Pres., Women's Coll. Hosp.; Toronto, for a number of years; Pres., Zonta Club, Toronto, 1936-37; organ. the vol. registration of Candn. women and was a mem. of and Hon. Counsel to C.W.V.S. during 2nd World War; organ. Ont. Wartime Legal Services Comte., Candn. Bar Assn. (Chrmn. for five yrs.); Pres., Internat. Fed. of Business & Prof. Women, 1956-59 (el. "Woman of the Year", 1952); mem., Advocates' Soc. of Ont.; Trustee Sir William Campbell Foundation; author in collab. with F. W. Wegenast, K.C., of "Canadian Companies" 1931, reprinted 1979; Nat. Exec. Council, C.N.I.B.; Presbyterian; recreation: gardening; Club: Toronto Ladies'; Home: 21 Winchester St., Toronto, Ont. M4X 1A6; Office: Suite 1501, 110 Yonge St., Toronto, Ont. M5C 1V2

HYNES, Hugh Bernard Noel, Ph.D., D.Sc., F.R.S.C.; educator; b. Devizes, Eng. 20 Dec. 1917; s. Harry George Claude and Anna Minnie Lucy (Meyer) H.; e. Prices Sch. Fareham, Eng. 1934; Royal Coll. of Science, Univ. of London, ARCS 1938, B.Sc. 1938, Ph.D. 1941, D.Sc. 1958 (External Research Student Fresh. Biol. Assn. Windermere 1938-40); Imp. Coll. of Tropical Agric. Trinidad, Colonial Service Cadet 1941-42; m. Mary Elizabeth d. late Edward Hinks 24 Oct. 1942; children: Richard Olding, Elisabeth Anne Grant, Andrew John, Julian David; PROF. OF BIOL. UNIV. OF WATERLOO since 1964, Chrmn. of Biol. 1964-71; Colonial Agric. Service special Anti-Locust work Ethiopia, Kenya and Somalia 1942-46; Faculty mem. Dept. Zool. Univ. of Liverpool 1946-64; Visiting Prof. of Zool. Ind. Univ. 1960, Monash Univ. Melbourne 1971-72; Visiting Research Assoc. in Bot. Univ. of Tasmania 1978; Distinguished Visiting Scholar in Zool., Univ. of Adelaide, 1979; mem. Technical Advisory Committee, Atomic Energy of Can. Ltd.; Fisheries and Oceans Research Adv. Council, Govt. of Can.; mem. Ecological Group of Onchocerciasis Control Program, World Health Organ., W. Africa; served various Nat. Research Council comtes.; Internat. Biol. Program; mem. and Candn. Chrmn. (2 yrs.) Bd. Govs. group of schs. Educ. Dept. Liverpool 1960-64; rec'd Centennial Medal 1967; author "The Biology of Polluted Waters" 1960; "The Ecology of Running Waters" 1970; over 150 articles scient. journs.; Fellow, Am. Assn. Advanc. Science; mem. Brit. Ecol. Soc.; Freshwater Biol. Assn.; Internat. Assn. Great Lakes Research; Internat. Assn. Limnology; Am. Soc. Limnology & Oceanog.; N. Am. Benthol. Soc.; Candn. Soc. Zool.; recreations: camping, canoeing, nordic skiing; Home: 127 Iroquois Pl., Waterloo, Ont. N2L 2S6; Office: Waterloo, Ont. N2L 3G1.

I

IACOBUCCI, Frank, B.Com., LL.B.; educator; b. Vancouver, B.C. 29 June 1937; s. Gabriel and Rosina (Pirillo) I.; e. Britannia High Sch. Vancouver 1955; Univ. of B.C. B.Com. 1959, LL.B. 1962; Cambridge Univ. LL.B. 1964, Dipl. in Internat. Law 1966; m. Nancy Elizabeth d. late James S. Eastham 31 Oct. 1964; children: Andrew Eastham, Edward Michael, Catherine Elizabeth; DEAN OF LAW, UNIV. OF TORONTO 1979-; Prof. of Law, Univ. of Toronto, 1971-; Dir. Decision Systems Inc.; Supvr. in Internat. Law, St. John's Coll. Cambridge 1963-64; Assoc., Dewey, Ballantine, Bushby, Palmer & Wood, New York 1964-67; Assoc. Prof. of Law, Univ. of Toronto 1967-71, Prof. of Law, Univ. of Toronto 1971-, Assoc. Dean 1973-75, Vice. Pres. Internal Affairs 1975-78 Dean. of Law 1979-; Visiting Fellow, Wolfson Coll. Cambridge Univ. 1978-79; Consultant, Select Comte. on Co. Law, Ont. Leg. 1968-70; Dept. Consumer & Corporate Affairs 1974-78; Dept. Consumer Affairs Alta. 1974-75; called to Bar of Ont. 1970; mem. Islington Residents & Ratepayers Assn; Dir., Multicultural Hist. Soc. Ont.; 1st Vice Pres., Nat. Congress of Italian-Canadians; Vice-Pres. and mem., Bd. of Govs. Candn. Inst. of Advanced Legal Studies; co-author "Business Associations Casebook" 1979; "Canadian Business Corporations" 1977; co-ed. "Materials on Canadian Income Tax" 1973, 1974, 1976, 1979, Supplement 1977; author book chapters, articles, reports and papers; mem. Law Soc. Upper Can; Candn. Assn. Univ. Teachers; Candn. Assn. Law Teachers; Phi Gamma Delta; Sigma Alpha Tau; United Church; recreations: sports, coaching (baseball, soccer), reading; Home: 172 Royalavon Cres., Islington, Ont. M9A 2G6; Office: 78 Queen's Park Cres., Toronto, Ont. M5S 1A1.

IACURTO, Francesco, R.C.A.; painter; b. Montreal, Que. 1 Sept. 1908; s Joseph and Angelica (Cappabianco) I.; e. Notre Dame du Mont. Carmel Montreal; Beaux-Arts Montreal Dipl. 1928; Académie de la Grande Chaumière Paris 1929; Art Gallery Montreal 1926-29; m. Laurette Asselin, Ottawa, Ont. 8 Apl. 1968; rep. in Qué. Museum, Nat. Gallery Can. (portrait), The Senate Ottawa (portrait), Qué. Parlt. (portrait); biog. "Iacurto" by Alain Stanké; R. Catholic; Address: 1232 La Vigerie, Ste-Foy, Qué. G1W 3W7.

IBEY, Frederick Eldridge; communications executive; b. Campbellford, Ont., 2 Nov. 1922; s. Bennett McLeod and Ethel Maude (Long); e. Riverdale Coll. Inst., Toronto, 1941; Univ. of Toronto 1945-46; m. Betty Eileen, d. Charles Henry Tugwell, 21 August 1943; children: Christopher, Bennett, Carol, Ellen; Exec. Vice-Pres., Bell Canada since 1976; joined present Company as Coin Box Collector, 1946; held a no. of operating and staff management positions in Toronto and Montreal; formerly Area Coml. Mgr., Toronto, 1963, Asst. Vice-Pres.-Coml., Mtl, 1967; Asst. Vice-Pres.-Reg. Matters, Mtl., 1968; Vice-Pres Public Relations, Mtl. 1970; Vice-Pres.-Operations Staff, Toronto, 1972; Dir. Maritime Tel. & Tel.; Bell Northern Research; Ont. Chamber of Commerce; served with RCAF as Navig. Inst. in World War II, rank Flying Officer; recreations: golf; curling; clubs: St.

James's; Forest & Stream Club; Ontario Club; Lambton Golf & Country, Tor.; Home: 2010 Islington Ave. Apt. 1804, Weston, Ont. M9P 3S8; Office: 393 University Ave., Toronto, Ont. M5G 1W9

IDE, Frederick Palmer, M.A., Ph.D.; b. Ottawa, Ont., 4 Sept. 1904; s. William and Helen Winnifred (Masson) I.; e. Ottawa Collegiate Inst., grad. 1924; Univ. of Toronto, B.A. 1928, M.A. 1930, Ph.D. 1934; Instr., Dept. of Zoology, Univ. of Toronto, 1930-33, Lectr., 1933-39, Asst. Prof., 1939-50, Assoc. Prof. 1950-62, Prof. 1962-70, now emeritus; Consultant, Ont., Dept. of Planning & Development, 1946-54; mem., Entomol. Research Panel, Defence Research Bd. of Can., 1948-51; Consultant, Fisheries Research Bd. of Can., 1955-62; mem., Adv. Comte. on Fisheries and Wildlife of the Research Comn. Ont., 1946-55; Assoc., Great Lakes Inst., Univ. of Toronto, 1960; Wartime Meteorol., Dept. of Transport, Can., 1943-45; Publications: numerous papers on entomol. and limnol. topics in prof. and scient. journs,; Fellow, Entomol. Soc. Am.; Am. Assoc. Advanc. Science; mem., Ont. Soc. Biols. (Pres., 1957-58); Toronto Field Naturalists Club (Pres., 1937-38); Entomol. Socs. of Ont., Can., and Am.; N.Y. Acad. Science; Limnol. & Oceanographic Soc. Am.; Ecol. Soc. Am.; Am. Fisheries Soc.; Internat. Assn. for Great Lakes Research; North Am. Benthological Soc.; Research Assoc., Can. Soc. of Zoologists; Roy. Ont. Museum since 1970 Hon Chrmn., 3rd Int. Conf. Ephemeropt., 1979; P. Conservative; Anglican; recreations: photography, skiing, boating; Clubs: Hart House (U. of T.); Toronto Ski; Home: (P.O. Box 10) Washago, Ont. L0K 2B0

IDE, (Thomas) Ranald, C.M., B.A., L.L.D.; b. Ottawa, Ont., 20 Feb. 1919; s. Richard and Lola (Scharfe) I.; e. elem. sch. Ottawa; high sch. Saint John, N.B.; Mount Allison Univ. B.A. 1940; L.L.D., Queen's Univ., Kingston Ont., 1978; L.L.D., Univ. of Waterloo, Waterloo, Ont., 1978; m. 1st. Eleanor (d. 1965) d. late Dr. F. A. Aylesworth, 18 June 1942; m. 2nd. Arlene d. late Maj. Hugh G. Miles, 14 Apl. 1967; three s. Richard, John, Douglas; PRES., T.R.IDE CONSULTANTS INC. Chrmn. Sc. Council of Can., Comte. on Computers & Inf. Soc.; Vice Chrmn. Canadian Videotex Cmte., Dept. of Commun., Chrmn. Communications Research Advisory Board; Chrmn. & Dir. The Donwood Inst.; Teacher, Vice-Prin. and Prin. Port Arthur (Ont.) Coll. Inst. 1947-62; Dist. Inspr. of Secondary Schs. N.W. Ont., 1963-65; Supt. of Secondary Schs. Port Arthur 1965-66; Dir. Educ. Television Br. Ont. Dept. Educ. 1966-70; served with RCAF as Navig. in Can. and UK during World War II, rank Flying Offr.; Gov. Ont. Teachers' Fed. 1959-61 (Chrmn. Audio-Visual Comte. 1961-62) Vice Chrmn. Ont. Educ. Television Assn. 1959-62; Dir. of Courses on Educ. Television Ryerson Polytech. Inst. 1960-62; mem. Planning Comte. on Scope and Organ. Ont. Curriculum Inst. 1964-66, mem. Curriculum Comte. to revise courses of study for Student Occupations; Candn. Rep. Third E.B.U. Internat. Conf. on Educ. Radio and TV, Paris 1967; Chrmn. E.T.V. sub-comte. Educ. Media Comte. Council Mins Educ. 1969; mem. Media & Communications Standing Comte. Ont. Inst. for Studies in Educ. 1973; Mem. Steering Comte. for a Nat. (U.S.) Conf. on the new Literacy 1977; Chrmn. and CEO, Ont. Educ. Commun. Authority, 1970-79; Dir. Agency for Instructional Television 1973-79; Dir. Ont. Educ. Research Council 1976-78; author various articles in prof. journs,; Fellow, Ont, Inst. for Studies in Educ,; mem. Candn. Assn. for the Club of Rome, Candn. Commun. Assn.; World Future Studies Fed. Nat. Assn. Educ. Broadcasters; Assn. Educ. Communications & Technol.; Assn. Scient. Engn. & Technol. Community Can.; Club of Rome; Queen's Silver Jubilee Medal, 1967; Col. Watson Award, 1979; Anglican; recreations tennis, music; Club: Celebrity; Home: 307 Chartland Blvd. South, Scarborough, Ont. M1S 3P4 Office: 307 Chartland Blvd. S., Scarborough, Ont. M1S 3P4

IDLER, David Richard, D.F.C., Ph.D., F.R.S.C.; scientist; educator; b. Winnipeg, Man. 13 March 1923; s. Ernest and Alice (Lydon) I.; e. Univ. of B.C. B.A. 1949, M.A. 1950; Univ. of Wis. Ph.D. 1954 (Babcock Fellowship 1952-53); m. Myrtle Mary Betteridge 12 Dec. 1956; children: Louise, Mark; DIR. MARINE SCIENCES RESEARCH LAB. and Prof. of Biochem. Memorial Univ. of Nfld.; served as mem. Nat. Research Council of Can. Grants Selection Comte. for Animal Biol., past Chrmn. of Comte.; served with RCAF 1942-45, rank Flying Offr.; Ed. "Steroids in Nonmammalian Vertebrates" 1972; author over 200 publs.; mem. ed. bds. various scient. journs.; Steroids and Pituitary Hormones; Founding mem. European Soc. Comparative Endocrinol.; mem. Candn. Biochem. Soc.; Am. Chem. Soc.; Am. Assn. Advanc. Science; Am. Zool. Soc.; Endocrine Soc.; N.Y. Acad. Sciences; Anglican; interest: philately; Home: 44 Slattery Rd., St. John's, Nfld. A1A 1Z8; Office: St. John's, Nfld. A1C 5S7.

IGNATIEFF, George, C.C. (Dec. 1973), M.A. (Oxon), LL.D., D.C.L., D.Litt.S; b. St. Petersburg, Russia, 16 Dec. 1913; s. Count Paul and Princess Natalie (Mestchersky) I.; e. Lower Canada College., Montreal, 1928-30; Central Tech. School and Jarvis Coll. Inst., Toronto, Ont.; Univ. of Toronto (Trinity Coll.), B.A. 1935; Rhodes Scholar, Ont., 1935; Oxford Univ., M.A. 1938; LL.D. Toronto, Guelph, Brock, Saskatchewan, Mount A. & York Univs.; D.C.I. Bishops 1973, D.Litt.S. Vict. College, m. Alison; d. William L. Grant, LL.D., 17 Nov. 1945; two s., Michael Grant, Andrew Grant; CHANCELLOR, UNIV. OF TORONTO 1980-; Pres., United Nations Assoc. in Can.; joined Department of External Affairs, Ottawa, Ontario, 1940; 3rd Secretary, Canada House, London, 1940-44; promoted 2nd Secy. and returned to Ottawa, 1944-45; Diplomatic Advisor, Candn. Del., U.N. Atomic Energy Comn., 1946; Adviser with a Candn. Del., U.N. Assembly, 1946-47; Candn. Alternate Rep., U.N. Security Council, 1948-49, and also Interim Comte. of Gen. Assembly; el. Rapporteur, Interim Comte., Jan. 1949; Candn. Alternate to Gen. Assembly (2nd part, 3rd Session, 1949); el. Chrmn. of Adm. and Budgetary Comte. of Gen. Assembly, 1949; apptd. Counsellor, Candn. Embassy, Washington, Aug. 1949; attended Imp. Defence Coll., London, 1953-54; apptd. Head of Defence Liaison (1) Div., Dept. of External Affairs, 1955; Ambassador to Yugoslavia, 1956-58; Depy. High Commr. to U.K. 1959; Asst. Under Secy. of State for External Affairs, 1960-62; Perm. Rep. of Can. to NATO, 1963; Ambassador to U.N., 1966-69; Candn. Ambassador, Disarmament Comte., Geneva, 1969-71; Pres., U.N. Security Council, Apl. 1967 and Sept. 1968; Perm. Rep. of Can. to European Office of U.N., Geneva 1970-72 Provost, Trinity Coll., Univ. of Toronto, 1972-79; Chrmn. Bd. of Trustees, National Museums of Can., 1973-78; Nowlan Lecturer (Memorial Univ.) 1979; Author of Spectrum No. 4 "Canadian Foreign Policy in an Interdependent World" (pub. C.I.B.C.) Russian Orthodox; Address: 18 Palmerstone Gardens, Toronto, Ont. M6G 1V9

IMLAH, Albert Henry, A.M., Ph.D.; professor emeritus; b. New Westminster, B.C., 30 Jan. 1901; s. John Mackie and Mary Ann (Richardson) I.; e. Duke of Connaught High Sch., New Westminster, 1915-18; Univ. of B.C., B.A. 1922; Clark Univ., A.M. 1923; Harvard Univ., Ph.D. 1931; Tufts Univ., Litt. D. 1981; m. 1stly Helen (d. 1954), d. Prof. S. H. Woodbridge, 2 April 1925; 2ndly Miriam, d. Carl G. Beede, 4 Apl. 1955; two d., Ann Gordon (Mrs. Ann I. Schneider), Janet Gay (Mrs. T. S. Collett); Instr. in Hist., Univ. of Maine, 1923-26; joined Tufts Univ. as Instr. in Hist., 1927-29; Asst. Prof. 1929-35; Prof. 1935-70 and Prof. of Dipl. Hist., The Fletcher Sch. there 1944-70; taught Summer Sch., Univ. of B.C. 1937 and Harvard Univ. 1965; Visiting Lectr. in Hist. 1948-49 and in Econ. 1957-58 and Visiting Prof. in Econ. 1965-66, Harvard Univ.; author of "Life of Lord Ellenborough". 1939; "Economic Elements in the Pax Britannica". 1958; other writings incl. articles on Brit. foreign trade in 19th Century for various journs. also articles and reports on instr. salaries in selected U.S. colls. and univs; mem., Am. Hist. Assn.; Am. Econ. Hist. Assn.; Am. Assn. Univ. Profs. (Nat. Council 1947-51; Chrmn., Comte. Z, 1948-58); Phi Beta Kappa (Pres., Delta Chapter of Mass. 1958-60); Congregational; recreations: travel, gardening; Home: 19 Sawyer Ave., Medford, Mass. 02155

IMRIE, Ross Cooper; executive; b. Toronto, Ont. 18 Sept. 1916; s. James Hamilton and Bertha May (Cooper) I.; e. Univ. of Man. Business Adm. 1962-63; m. Janet Foster d. Rev. John Hardwick 27 May 1938; children: Sandra Jean, Janet Holly Elvins, Lynda Karen Paul, Ross J. J., Charles Gordon, William Michael, Stephen Scott; PRES., VICE CHRMN. AND DIR., LAWSON & JONES LTD.; Pres., and Dir., Lawson & Jones Manufacturing Div.; Lawson Graphics Atlantic; Pres. and Dir., Lawson Graphics Manitoba Ltd.; Lawson Graphics Western Ltd.; Lawson Graphics Pacific Ltd.; Lawson Business Forms Manitoba; Chrmn. and Dir., Lawson & Jones Inc.; Vice Pres. and Dir. Lawson Packaging Ltd.; Dir. Lawson Flexible Packaging; Montreal Lithographing Ltd.; R.B.T. Printing and Litho Co. Ltd.; Lawson Business Forms Ltd.; Lawson Business Forms Alberta; Oxford Paper Boxes Ltd.; Pres., Packagemaster Ltd.; served with RCNVR 1943-46; Shriner; P. Conservative; United Church; recreations: swimming, golf, hockey; Clubs: Manitoba; Ontario; London; London Hunt; Rotary; Home: 431 Lawson Rd., London, Ont. N6G 1X7;office: 395 Wellington Rd. S., London, Ont. N6C 4P9.

INGOLD, Keith U., B.Sc., D.Phil., F.R.S.C. (1969), F.R.S. (1979), F.C.I.C.;research chemist; b. Leeds, Eng., 31 May 1929; s. Sir Christopher Kelk and Lady Edith Hilda (Usherwood) Ingold; e. Univ. Coll., Univ. of London, B.Sc. (Hon. Chem.) 1949; Oxford Univ., D.Phil. 1951; m. Carmen Cairine, d. Frank G. Hodgkin, Ottawa, Ont., 7 Apl. 1956; children: Christopher Frank, John Hilary, Diana Hilda; Assoc. Dir Div. of Chem; Nat. Research Council since 1977 Research Offr., Div. of Applied Chem., Nat. Research Council, 1955; post-doctoral fellow, Div. of Pure Chem. of Council, 1951-53; Defense Research Council post-doctoral Fellow, Chem. Dept., Univ. of B.C., 1953-55; Visiting Prof., Chevron Research Co., Richmond, Cal., 1966; Univ. Coll., London 1969 and 1972; rec'd Petroleum Chem. 1968 Award; rec'd Queen's Jubilee medal, 1977; mem. Am. Chem. Soc.; Chem. Soc. (London); Carnegie Fellow of Univ. of St. Andrews. Scotland; rec'd. Chem. Soc. (London) Award in Kinetics and Mechanism, 1978; The Chem. Inst. of Can. Medal 1981; recreations: skiing, surfing, scuba diving; Home: (Box 712) R.R. #5, Ottawa, Ont.; Office: National Research Council, Sussex Dr., Ottawa, Ont., K1A 0R6

INNES, Ian Rome, Ch.B., M.D.; medical educator; b. Portgordon, Scot., 14 July 1916; s. Rome and Evelyn Ann (Downie) I.; e. Buckie High Sch., Scot. 1932; Univ. of Aberdeen, M.B., Ch.B. 1937, M.D. 1955; m. Rodway, d. Frederick Amos, Winterbourne, Eng. 20 July 1940; children: Ian Rome, Valerie Rome; PROF. AND HEAD, DEPT. OF PHARMACOLOGY & THERAPEUTICS, UNIV. OF MANITOBA since 1967; Surg. Offr., Prince of Wales Gen. Hosp., London 1938; gen. med. practice 1940; Lectr. in Physiol., Univ. of Aberdeen 1947-58; Research Assoc. in Pharmacol., Harvard Univ. 1957; joined present Univ. as Asst. Prof. subsequently becoming Prof. 1964-67; mem. Med. Research Council Comte. on Pharm. Sciences 1968-70 and Comte. on Physiol. & Pharmacol. 1967-72 (Chrmn. 1970-72); Chrmn., Man. Drug Standards & Therapeutics Comte., 1971-; mem. Pharmacol. Soc. Can. (Pres. 1968); Brit. Pharmacol. Soc.; Physiol. Soc. (UK); Am. Soc. Pharmacol. & Exper. Therapeutics; Home: 575 Elm St., Winnipeg, Man. R3M 3N7; Office: Winnipeg. Man. R3E 0W3

INNES, Robert Thompson Livingstone, B.A., Q.C.; b. Simcoe, Ont., 25 Oct. 1904; s. (Judge) Hugh Paterson and Mabel Margaret (Livingstone) I.; e. Simcoe Pub. and High Schs.; Upper Can. Coll.; Univ. of Toronto, B.A. 1927; Osgoode Hall 1930; m. Lauretta Frances Dowling, d. Dr. F. W. Landymore, Brantford, Ont., 30 June 1948; children: Joan Frances (Hoffman), Robert Hugh Landymore, Philip Scott; retired Partner, Read, Innes, Verity & Gregory; read law with Kilmer, Irving & Davis; called to Bar of Ont. 1930; cr. K.C. 1945; Past Pres., Brantford P. Cons. Assn.; Ald., City of Brantford, 1934; former mem., Brant Law Assn. (Past Pres.); former mem., Brantford Bd. Trade (Past Pres.); mem. Royal Order of Scotland; Psi Upsilon; Murton Lodge of Perfection, Hamiton Chapt. of Rose Croix & Moore Sovereign Consistory; Elder, Central Presbyterian Church Freemason (Scot. Rite; 33°) Mocha Temple Shrine; P. Conservative; Presbyterian; recreation: gardening; Clubs: Brantford Golf & Country; Brant. Curling (hon. life mem.); Home: 181 Dufferin Ave., Brantford, Ont. N3T 4R4;

INNS, Gordon Ellis, B.A.Sc.; telecomunications executive; b. Wiarton, Ont., 27 Feb. 1926; e. Waterford & Burford, Ont.; Univ. of Toronto, B.A.Sc. 1948; EXTVE. VICE PRES. BELL CANADA, since 1974; joined the Co. St. Catharines, Ont., 1948; various mang positions in Engn. 1948-68; Chief Engr. Toll Area, Montreal 1968; Dir. Engn. Comte. Trans-Canada Telephone System 1966-69; Vice-Pres. Engr. Montreal 1966, Engn. and Planning 1970; Vice-Pres. Computer Communications, Ottawa 1971; Chief Tech. Coordinator, Telephone Assn. of Can. 1969-71; served with Candn. Army 1943-45; Sr. mem., Inst. Elect. & Electronics Engrs.; mem. Assn. Prof. Engrs. Ont.; Fellow, Engn. Inst. of Can.; Rep. on the Bd. of Mang. Trans-Can. Tel. System; Dir; Candn. Enterprise Devel. Corp.; N. Telecom-Can. Ltd.; Northern Telecom Internat'l Ltd.; Bell Northern Research; Northern Telecom Inc.; BNR Inc.; Nat. Bd., Jr. Achievement of Can.; mem. Adv. Bd., Sal. Army Metro Toronto; Bd. of Gov., Ryerson Polytech. Inst.; Chrmn., Fund Raising Campaign for Ryerson Polytech. Inst.; Clubs: Toronto, Donalda; Home: 39 Longwood Dr., Don Mills, Ont. M3B 1T9; Office: 145 King St. W., Toronto, Ont. M5G 1W9

IRVING, Edward, M.A., Sc.D., F.R.A.S., F.R.S.C. F.R.S.(1979); research scientist; b. Colne, Eng. 27 May 1927; s. George Edward and Nellie (Petty) I.; e. Colne Grammar Sch. 1945; Univ. of Cambridge B.A. 1950, M.A. 1957, Sc.D. 1965; Carleton Univ. D.Sc. 1979; m. Sheila Ann d. William Arthur Irwin, Victoria, B.C. 23 Sept. 1957; children: Kathryn Jean, Susan Patricia, Martin Edward, George Andrew; RESEARCH SCIENT. EARTH PHYSICS BR. DEPT. ENERGY MINES AND RESOURCES Pacific Geoscience Centre, Sidney, B.C. since 1981; Adjunct Prof. and Part-time Lectr. 1967-81 Carleton Univ.; Research Fellow, Fellow and Sr. Fellow Dept. of Geophysics Australian National University 1954-64; Research Offr. Mines and Tech. Surveys, Ottawa 1964-66; Prof. of Geophysics, Univ. of Leeds 1966-67; Research Scientist, Earth Physics Br.; Dept. Energy, Mines and Resources, Ottawa, 1967-81; served with Brit. Army 1945-48, 2 yrs. Middle E.; rec'd Christien Mica Gondwanaland Medal, Mining Geol. & Metall. Inst. of India 1960-62; Logan Medal Geol. Assn. Can. 1975; Walter H. Bucher Medal of American Geophysical Union 1979; author "Paleomagnetism and Its Application to Geological and Geophysical Problems" 1964; Assoc. Ed. International Journals "Tectonophysics"; "Physcs of the Earth and Planetary Interiors"; author numerous articles scient. journs.; Fellow, Am. Geophys. Union; Fellow, Royal Soc.Am.; Fellow, Geological Soc. of London; mem. Geol. Assn. Can.; Candn. Geophys. Union; United Church; recreations: gardening, singing, carpentry; Home: 2130 Central Ave., Victoria, B.C. V8S 2R3; Office: Pacific Geoscience Centre, 9860 West Saanich Rd., P.O. Box 6000, Sidney, B.C. V8L 4B2

IRWIN, Grace Lillian, M.A., D.Litt. (Hon.); speaker, writer; b. Toronto, Ont., 14 July 1907; d. John and Martha (Fortune) Irwin; e. Parkdale Coll. Inst., Toronto, Ont.; Victoria Coll., Univ. of Toronto, B.A. 1929 and M.A. 1932; unm.; Teacher of Latin, English, Hist. at Humberside Coll. Inst., Toronto, Ont., 1931-42 and Head of Latin and Greek Dept. there 1942-69; Co-pastor, Emmanuel Christian Congregational Ch., since 1974; Pastor, ordained 1980; author of "Least of All Saints", (novel) 1952; "Andrew Connington" (novel), 1954; "In Little Place" (novel), 1959; "Servant of Slaves" (biog. novel), 1961; "Contend With Horses", (novel), 1968; "The Seventh Earl" (biog. novel) 1976; contrib. of poems in "Little Songs for Little People" and of occasional poems and articles to mags.; Past Pres., Toronto Classical Club; mem. of Extve. Comte., Ont. Classical Assn.; Candn. Classical Assn.; mem. of Senate, Univ. of Toronto, 1952-56; awarded Centennial Medal 1968; Christian; Home: 33 Glenwood Ave., Toronto, Ont. M6P 3C7

IRWIN, John Arnold, B.A.; diplomat; b. Watrous, Sask. 4 July 1917; s. James and Margaret I.; e. Meacham, Sask. elem. and high schs.; Univ. of Sask. B.A. 1940; MINISTER, CANADIAN EMBASSY, TOKYO Since 1979; joined Dept. External Affairs 1945, 3rd Secy. Dublin 1945, 3rd Secy. Dublin 1947, 2nd Secy. Prague 1948, Ottawa 1950, 1st Secy. Jakarta 1953, Candn. Rep. to ICAO 1954, Ottawa 1957, Counsellor Cairo 1959, Ambassador Warsaw 1963, Ottawa 1965, High Commr. Dar-es-Salaam 1965, High Commissioner to Tanzania, Zambia and Mauritius 1967; Ottawa 1971; Ambassador to the Philippines, 1975-79; served with RCAF 1941-45; United Church3-38 Akasaka 7-chome, Minato-Ku, Tokyo 107, Japan

IRWIN, Neal Alexander, B.A.Sc., P.Eng.; consulting engineer; b. Toronto, Ont. 2 Jan. 1932; s. William Arthur and Jean Olivia (Smith) I.; e. N. Toronto Coll. Inst. 1950; Univ. of Toronto, B.A.Sc. (Engn.-Physics) 1955; m. Carol Anne, d. Dr. J. H. Howson; children: Christine Alice, Anne Olivia, Arthur Campion, Alexander James Howard; MANAGING DIR., IBI GROUP; Chrmn. InterBase Inc.; Partner, Beinhaker/Irwin Assocs.; Pres. Neal A. Irwin Ltd.; Nuclear Power Stn. Designer, English Electric Co., U.K. 1955-57; Nuclear Power Design Engr. Atomic Energy of Can. Ltd. and several other Candn. cos. 1957-60; Sr. Project Engr., Traffic Research Corp.; Vice-Pres. i.c. U.S. operations Traffic Research Corp. (subsidiary co.) 1961-66; Extve. Vice-Pres. KCS Ltd. 1966; Sr. Partner, Kates, Peat, Marwick & Co. (merger) 1967-74; formed own firm of Neal A. Irwin Ltd. and apptd. Sr. Partner, IBI Group 1974-75; with Univ. Naval Training Div. 1950-53, Acting Sub-Lt. RCN(R); Fellow, Inst. Traffic Engrs.; Councillor Bureau of Mun. Research; mem. Assn. Prof. Engrs. Ont.; Engn. Inst. Can.; Candn. Operational Research Soc.; Phi Gamma Delta (Pres. 1955); recreations: music, athletics, building; Club: Granite; Home: 18 Lawrence Cres., Toronto, Ont. M4N 1N1; Office: 156 Front St., Toronto, Ont. M5J 1G6

IRWIN, Richard Arnold, B.A.Sc., LL.D.; b. Tara, Ont., 5 Apl. 1909; s. Alexander James and Amelia Jane (Hassard) I.; e. Univ. of Toronto (S.P.S.), B.A.Sc. (Chem.) 1931; m. Catherine Janet, d. F. W. Moffat of Weston, Ont., 4 Sept. 1937; children: Richard Moffat, Judith Catherine, Catherine Jane, Margaret Elizabeth; HON. DIR. CONSOLIDATED BATHURST LTD., Dir., T.I.W. Industries Ltd. Maritime Paper Products Ltd.; Rolland Paper Co. Ltd.; Past Pres.; with Ontario Department of Health, 1931-32; National Carbon Co., 1932-33; Somerville, London, Ont., 1934-57; Vice-President and Dir., Somerville, 1945-53, and Pres., 1953-57; Pres., Eddy Paper, Hull, Que., 1954-57; joined present Co. in 1957 as Vice-Pres.; became a Dir., 1958; Pres. 1967 Chrmn. 1971; mem., Candn. Pulp & Paper Assn. (Chrmn. Extve. Bd. 1964-65); Phi Delta Theta; Protestant; recreations: golf, curling; Clubs: Mount Royal; Mount Bruno; London Hunt & Country (London, Ont.); National (Toronto);

London Club; Home: 597 Cranbrook Rd., London, Ont. N6K 2Y4

IRWIN, William Arthur, O.C., LL.D.; b. Ayr, Ont., 27 May 1898; s. Rev. Alexander J., B.A., B.D., D.D., and Amelia J. (Hassard) I.; e. Univ. of Manitoba; Univ. of Toronto, B.A. (Pol. Science) 1921; Univ. of Victoria, LL.D. (Hon.) 1977; m. 1st, Jean Olive (died Oct. 1948), d. Rev. W. E. Smith, M.D., Toronto, Ont.; children: Neal A., Sheila A. Irving, Patricia J. Morley; 2nd, Patricia K., d. late Maj.-Gen. L. F. Page, Dec. 1950; sometime Rodman, Candn. Northern Rly. construction; later Reporter, Toronto "Mail & Empire" and subsequently Reporter, Corr. (Parlty. Press Gallery, Ottawa) and Ed. Writer, Toronto "Globe"; Assoc. Ed., Maclean's Mag., 1925-42, Mang. Ed. 1943-45 and Editor 1945-50; Commr. and Chrmn., Nat. Film Bd. Can. 1950-53; High Commr. for Can. in Australia, 1953-56; Ambassador to Brazil, 1956-59; Ambassador to Mexico, 1960-64; Ambassador to Guatemala, 1961-64; Publisher, Victoria Daily Times, and Vice-Pres., Victoria Press Ltd. 1964-71; served in 1st World War with C.E.F., 10th Batty., Candn. Garrison Arty., France; former Pres., Toronto Writers' Club; former mem., Nat. Extve. and Research Comte., Candn. Inst. of Internat. Affairs; "Candn. Writers' Market Survey", 1931; author of "The Wheat Pool", brochure reprinted from "Maclean's Mag.", 1929; author, Motor Vehicle Transportation Briefs A Royal Comn. on Railways & Transportation 1932; Royal Comn. of Transp. in Ont., 1937; Candn. Del. to Brit. Commonwealth Relations Conf., London, Eng., 1945; mem., Candn. del. to U.N. Conf. on Freedom of Information, Geneva, 1948; Candn. Alternate Del. to XIV and XV Gen. Assemblies of U.N., 1959 and 1960; co-author "The Machine", an ice ballet, 1939; Address: 3260 Exeter Road, Victoria, B.C. V8R 6H6

IRWIN, Mrs. William Arthur — see: Page, Patricia Kathleen.

ISAAC, Philip Kenneth, B.Sc., Ph.D.; educator; b. E. Suffolk, Eng. 23 Jan. 1928; s. late Kenneth James and Janet Mary (Quayle) I.; e. Northgate Grammar Sch. (Ipswich, UK); Imp. Coll. B.Sc. 1949, D.I.C., Ph.D. 1952; m. Evelyn, d. W. Foster-Thornton, Burringham, UK, 3 Aug. 1950; children: Peter W. P., Jane E., Wendy H., Sarah A.; PROF. OF BOTANY, UNIV. OF MANITOBA since 1965 joined present Univ. as Research Fellow 1952, Assoc. Prof. 1955, Assoc. Dean of Science and Chrmn. Div. Biol. 1970, Acting Dean of Science 1973-74; co-inventor automatic, rotary, rabbit-powered lawn mower 1961; served with Royal Winnipeg Rifles (Militia), RCAMC (Militia); rank Lt.; mem. Bd. Man. Inst. Cell Biology, Winnipeg; author over 20 papers in scient. journs.; mem. Man. Rifle Team 1953-65 (Commandant 1965); Past Council mem. Dom. Can. Rifle Assn. (Bronze Cross), Man. Prov. Rifle Assn.; mem. Candn. Bisley Rifle Team 1958, 1961; Nat. Rifle Assn. (Silver Medal, Bronze Cross); other rifle awards incl. H.M. Queen's Hundred Badges 1958, 1961, 1964, St. George's Cross and Lt. Gov. Man. Gold Medal; Fellow, Roy. Microscop. Soc.; mem. Candn. Yachting Assn. (Past Dir.); Man. Sailing Assn. (Past Vice Pres.); Inst. Biol.; Candn. Soc. Plant Physiols. (Plant Vice Pres.) Soc.; Winnipeg Scient. Club (Past Pres.); Candn. Microscop. Soc.; recreations: gardening, curling, sailing, full bore rifle shooting; Club: Gimli Yacht (Past Commodore); Home: 1194 Kildonan Dr., Winnipeg, Man. R2G 1T6; Office: Winnipeg, Man.

ISAUTIER, Bernard François; mining engineer; executive; b. Saint-Symphorien, Indre et Loire, France 19 Sept. 1942; s. François and Geneviève (Roy) I.; e. Ecole Polytechnique, Paris 1963; Ecole des Mines, Paris 1966; Institut d'Etudes Politiques, Paris 1968; m. Charlotte Roche; children: Anne-Caroline, Armelle, François; PRES., CANTERRA ENERGY LTD. 1978-; Dir., Al-Aquitaine Exploration Ltd.; Aquitaine Pennsylvania Inc.; Candn. Petroleum Assn.; Cansulex Ltd.; Universal Gas; Westacc

N.V.; The Sulphur Inst.; Advisor (Uranium) to Pres., Repub. of Niger, Africa 1968-70; Head-Mining Exploration Dept. Ministry of Industry, Paris 1970-73, Advisor to Min. of Industry for Energy & Raw Materials 1973-75; Gen. Mgr. of SEREPT, Tunisia 1976-78; rec'd Chevalier de l'Ordre du Mérite (France); mem. Calgary Chamber Comm.; Chambre de Comm. Française au Can.; L'Alliance Française de Calgary; Univ. of Calgary Chancellor's Club; Clubs: Calgary Petroleum; Ranchmen's (Calgary); Home: 4619 Coronation Dr. S.W., Calgary, Alta. T2S 1M5; Office: 505 - 5th St. S.W., Calgary, Alta. T2P 3J2.

ISBISTER, Claude Malcolm, B.A., Ph.D.; economist; Consultant on management strategies; b. Winnipeg, Man. 15 Jan. 1914; s. Claude and Margaret Ethel (McKechnie) I.; e. Univ. of Man. B.A. 1934; Univ. of Toronto grad. work in Econ. 1938-39; Harvard Univ. Ph.D. 1946; m. Ruth d. late William Cunningham 18 June 1938; children: John William, Alex James, Kathryn Ruth; CONSULTANT since 1978; joined Publ. Service of Can. 1945, served successively as Asst. Dom. Stat., Asst. Depy. Min. Trade & Comm. and of Finance, Depy. Min. Citizenship and Immigration, Mines and Tech. Surveys and Energy Mines & Resources, Chrmn. Dominion Coal Bd., Dir. Canadian National (West Indies) Steamships Ltd.; Extve. Dir. World Bank Group Washington and Chrmn. Jt. Audit Comte. 1970-75; Royal Commr. on Petroleum Products Pricing Prov. Ont. 1975-76; Consulting Partner, Currie, Coopers & Lybrand, 1976-78 Unitarian; recreations: public affairs, golf, swimming; Club: Rideau (Ottawa); Address: Suite 1432, 33 Harbour Square, Toronto, Ont., M5J 2G2

ISELER, Elmer Walter, O.C., B.Mus., LL.D.; choir conductor; choral editor; b. Port Colborne, Ont. 14 Oct. 1927; e. Waterloo Lutheran Univ. (now Wilfrid Laurier) organ and church music with Ulrich Leupold; Univ. of Toronto B.Mus. 1950; Ont. Coll. of Educ. 1951; Dalhousie Univ. LL.D. 1971; Brock Univ. LL.D. 1972; CONDUCTOR, ELMER ISELER SINGERS 1978-; conducted Univ. of Toronto Symphony Orchestra and All-Varsity Mixed Chorus 1950-51; Asst. Rehearsal Conductor, Toronto Mendelssohn Choir 1951-52 becoming Conductor 1964; taught orchestral and choral music Toronto high schs. 1952-64; helped found Toronto Festival Singers 1954 serving as Conductor 3 yrs.; taught choral music Univ. of Toronto 1965-68; began editing "Festival Singers of Canada Choral Series" 1968; rec'd City of Toronto gold Civic Award of Merti 1973; Société d'Encouragement et d'Education de Paris silver medal 1973; Candn. Music Council Medal 1975.

ISHWARAN, Karigoudar, Ph.D., D. Litt.; university professor; b. India, 1 Nov. 1922; s. Channappa and Basamma Patil; e. Univ. of Bombay, M.A. 1947; Univ. of Karnatak, Ph.D. 1954; Oxford Univ., B. Litt. 1956; Univ. of The Hague, M.S.S. 1957; Univ. of Leiden, D.Litt. 1959; m. Wobine, May 1960; children: Arundhati, Hemant, Shivakumar; PROF. OF SOCIOL., YORK UNIV.; Lectr., J. G. Coll. of Comm. and S. K. Art Coll., Hubli, India, 1947-52; Princ., Sangameshivar Coll., Sholapur, India, 1953-54; Research Fellow of the Netherlands' Univs. Foundation for Internat. Cooperation, The Hague, 1956-59; Reader and Chrmn., Dept. of Grad. Studies in Social Anthrop., Karnatak Univ., Dharwar, India, 1959-62; Univ. Prof. and Chrmn. of Dept., 1962-64; Visiting Prof., Memorial Univ. of Nfld., 1964-65; author of "Family Life in the Netherlands", 1959; "Tradition and Economy in Village India", 1966; "Politics and Change", 1967; "Shivapur — a South Indian Village", 1968; "Change and Continuity in India's Villages", 1969; "The Canadian Family", 1971, rev. 1976; co-author of "Urban Sociology", 1965; "Family, Kinship and Community: A Study of Dutch-Canadians", 1977; "A Populistic Community and Modernization in India", 1977; "Childhood and Adolescence in Canada", 1979; "Canadian Families: Ethnic Variations", 1980; ed. no. of bks. and written papers for internat. journs.; Ed. "International Journal of Comparative Sociology"; "Journal of Asian and African Studies"; "Contributions to Asian Studies"; recreations: reading, writing, travelling; Home: 374 Woodsworth Rd., Toronto, Ont. M2L 2T6

ISRAEL, Charles Edward, B.A. B.H.L.; writer; b. Evansville, Ind. 15 Nov. 1920; s. Edward Leopold and Amelia (Dryer) I.; e. Baltimore City Coll. 1937; Univ. of N.C.; Univ. of Cincinnati B.A. 1942; Hebrew Union Coll. B.H.L. 1943; m. Gloria Isabel Varley; staff mem. UN Relief & Rehabilitation Adm. and successor Internat. Refugee Organ. 1946-50, European program; fulltime prof. writer since 1950; accumulated over 550 credits Candn. and U.S. radio, TV and film work; author "How Many Angels" 1956; "The Mark" 1958; "Rizpah" 1961; "Who Was Then the Gentleman?" 1963; "Shadows on a Wall" 1965; "The Hostages" 1966; "Five Ships West" 1966; co-author "The True North" 1957; monthly column and numerous features on wines and spirits "Toronto Calendar Magazine" 1979-82; recipient Prix Italia City of Genoa Award for TV Drama 1964 (nominated 1965, 1969); Best Scenario Prague TV Film Festival 1965; Best Screenplay Yorkton Internat. Film Festival 1973; served with U.S. Merchant Marine 1943-45; mem. Acad. TV Arts & Sciences (US); Acad. Candn. Cinema; ACTRA; Writers Guild Am. (US); Writers' Union Can.; Periodical Writers' Assn. Can. (Nat. Treas. 1980-82); Jewish; recreations: wine-tasting, cooking, cross-country skiing, jogging; Address: 31 Walmer Rd., Townhouse 6, Toronto, Ont. M5R 2W7.

ISRAEL, Milton, M.A., Ph.D.; educator; b. Hartford, Conn., 27 July 1936; s. Archie and Jean (Tulin) I.; e. Bristol (Conn.) High Sch., 1954; Trinity Coll., Hartford, B.A. 1958; Univ. of Mich., M.A. 1959, Ph.D. 1965; Fulbright Fellow in India 1963-64; Internat. Studies Fellow (Univ. of Toronto) in India 1970-71; m. Beverly, d. Arthur Stein, Springfield, Mass., 22 Aug. 1959; children: Lauren Beth, Andrew Shale; RESIDENT DIRECTOR IN INDIA, SHASTRI INDO-CANADIAN INST.; Pres. 1976-79; Assoc. Prof. of Hist., Univ. of Toronto; joined present Univ. as Lectr. 1964, Assoc. Prof. of Hist. 1972, Asst. to Dean, Sch. of Grad. Studies, 1967-70, Assoc. Chrmn. Dept. of Hist. 1972-74; Vice Provost, U. of T., 1974-79; Ed., "Pax Britannica" 1968; "Studies in Islam's History and Society in Honour of Professor Aziz Ahmad" 1981; author of articles and reviews for various journs.; mem. Assn. Asian Studies; Candn. Soc. Asian Studies; Pi Kappa Alpha (Past Pres.); Jewish; recreation: antiques; Home: 156, Golf Links, New Delhi - 110003, India

ISRAEL, Werner, M.Sc., Ph.D.; educator; b. Berlin, Germany 4 Oct. 1931; s. Arthur Israel; e. Cape Town High Sch. 1948; Univ. of Cape Town B.Sc. 1951, M.Sc. 1954; Dublin Inst. for Advanced Studies 1956-58; Trinity Coll. Dublin Ph.D. 1960; m. Inge d. late Lionel V. Margulies 26 Jan. 1958; children: Pia Lee, Mark; came to Can. 1958; PROF. OF THEORETICAL PHYSICS, UNIV. OF ALTA.; Visiting Prof. Dublin Inst. for Advanced Studies 1966-68; Sherman Fairchild Distinguished Scholar, Cal. Inst. of Technol. 1974-75; Sr. Visitor, Dept. Applied Math. and Theoretical Physics Univ. Cambridge 1975-76; Maitré de Recherche Associé, Institut Henri Poincaré, Paris 1976-77; Visiting Prof., Univ. of Berne 1980; Ed. "Relativity, Astrophysics and Cosmology" 1973; co-ed. "General Relativity: An Einstein Centenary Survey" 1979; various papers black hole physics, relativistic stat. mechanics and gen. relativity; mem. Royal Soc. Can.; Internat. Astron. Union; Candn. Assn. Physicists (Chrmn. Theoretical Physics Div. 1971-72) (Medal foent in Physics 1981); Jewish; recreation: music; Home: #1403, 11027 87th Ave., Edmonton, Alta. T6G 2P9; Office: Edmonton, Alta. T6G 2J1.

ISSENMAN, Bernard, B.Sc.; executive; b. Montreal, Que., 16 March 1921; s. John and Mary (Frank) I.; e. Queen's Univ., B.Sc. 1943; m. Ruth, d. late Reuben Garmaise, 9 July 1943; children: Philip Alan, Robert Malcolm, Candy Deborah, Tina May; Pres., Bric Holdings; Dir., Dominion Electric Protection Co.; Imported Delicacies Ltd.; Vice-Pres. (1968), Lighting Equipment Mfrs. Assn. Can.; mem. Engn. Soc. of Quebec; Jewish; recreations: skiing, golf; Club: Elm Ridge Country; Home: 2181 Lakeshore Rd., Burlington, Ont. L7R 1A5; Office: 3015 Kennedy Rd., Agincourt, Ont. M1S 3I2

IVANIER, Isin; industrialist; b. Vijnita, Romania, 9 Apl. 1906; s. Jacob and Perl (Weintraub) I.; m. Francia, d. David Herling, Feb. 1929; children: Paul, Sydney; came to Can. 1949; CHMN. & DIR.; IVACO INC.; Dir. and Officer (Chmn.) New York Wire Mills Corp.; S.W. Transport Inc.; Dir. and Officer (Pres.) Infatool Ltd.; Dir. Atlantic Steel Co.; Ingersoll Machine & Tool Co., Ltd.; Niagara Lockport Industries, Inc.; Niagara Lockport Industries Quebec, Inc.; Capitol Wire & Fence Co., Inc.; Florida Wire and Cable Co.; P.C. DropForgins Ltd.; Wrights Can. Ropes Ltd.; Nat. Wire Products Corp. of Md.; Bakermet Inc.; Hebrew; Club: Montefiore; Home: 5509 Westbourne Ave., Cote St. Luc, Que. H4V 2G9; Office: 800 Ouellette St., Marieville, Que. J0L 1J0

IVEY, Donald Glenn, M.A., Ph.D.; physicist and educator; b. Clanwilliam, Manitoba, 6 Feb. 1922; s. Carle R. and Bessie Luella (Reid) I.; e. Univ. of British Columbia, B.A. 1944, M.A. 1946; Univ. of Notre Dame, Ph.D. 1949; m. Marjorie Eileen Frisby, 1944; children: Donna Marleen, Sharon Eileen, David Donald Glenn; PROF. OF PHYSICS, UNIVERSITY OF TORONTO; Principal of New Coll., Univ. of Toronto, 1963-74; Assoc. Chmn., Dept. of Physics, 1978-80; Vice Pres. Inst. Rel., 1980-; engaged also in preparation and presentation of educ. television programmes for C.B.C.; Publications: "Physics", 1954; "Classical Mechanics and Introductory Statistical Mechanics" 1974; tech. articles to journals; mem., Canadian Assn. Physicists; Canadian Association University Teachers; Am. Phys. Soc.; Am. Assn. of Physics Teachers; Anglican; recreation: tennis; Clubs: Queens; Toronto Cricket, Skating & Curling; Home: 34 Yewfield Crescent, Don Mills, Ont. M3B 2Y6

IVEY, Peter John; industrialist; b. London, Ont., 2 Feb. 1919; s. Charles H. and Ethel (Jamieson) I.; e. Univ. of W. Ont. (1939-40); Harvard Business Sch.; m. Barbara Campbell, d. E. V. Smith, 1946; Former Emm. & Chief Extve. Officer, Emco Limited (1969-74); Pres., Benmiller Estates Corp.; Cambarex Investments Ltd.; served in 2nd World War with Candn. Army Overseas, 1941-45; mem., Candn. Inst. Plumbing & Heating (Pres. 1970-71); Anglican; Home: 1132 Richmond St., London, Ont. N6A 3K8; Office: 784 Richmond Street, London, Ont. N6A 3H5

IVEY, Richard Macaulay, Q.C., LL.D.; b. London, Ont., 26 Oct. 1925; s. Richard Green and Jean (Macaulay) I.; e. Ridley Coll., St. Catharines, 1943; Univ. of W. Ont., B.A., 1947; Osgoode Hall, Toronto, Ont., 1950; Univ. of W. Ont., Hon. LL.D., 1979; m. Beryl Marcia, d. Col. W. I. Nurse, Chatham, Ont., 6 Aug. 1949; children: Richard William, Jennifer Louise, Rosamond Ann, Susanne Elizabeth; CHRMN., ALLPAK LTD.; Livingston Ind. Ltd.; Chippewa — Camcor, Inc.; Dir., The Northern Life Assnce. Co. of Can.; Bank of Montreal; Eaton Yale Ltd.; Dashwood Industries Ltd.; T.I. Industries Ltd.; Timberjack Inc. (Can.); F. W. Woolworth Co. Ltd.; Union Gas Ltd.; Pres., The Richard Ivey Foundation; Chancellor, Univ. of W. Ont.; Trustee, World Wildlife fund (Int.); Mem. of Council, The Wildlife Trust (U.K.); Dir. World Wildlife Fund (Can.); The Richard and Jean Ivey Fund; Hon. Trustee, Royal Ont. Museum; mem. Adv. Bd., Sch. of Business Adm. Univ. W. Ont.; St. Joseph's Hospital, London, Ont.; Ridley College, St. Catharines, Ont. Theatre London, London, Ont.; read law with Robertson,

Lane, Perrett, Frankish & Estey, Toronto, Ont.; called to the Bar of Ont., 1950; cr. Q.C., 1963; Partner, Ivey, Livermore & Dowler, 1960-64; Ivey & Dowler, since 1964; mem. Candn. Bar Assn.; Clubs: London; London Hunt & Country; Toronto; Home: 990 Wellington St., London, Ont. N6A 3T2; Office: Suite 1701, 380 Wellington St., London, Ont. N6A 5C3

IVEY, Richard William, B.A., LL.B.; lawyer; b. London, Ont. 15 Aug. 1950; s. Richard Macaulay and Beryl Marcia (Nurse) I.; e. Ridley Coll. St. Catharines, Ont. 1968; Univ. of W. Ont. Sch. of Business Adm. B.A. 1972; Univ. of Toronto Law Sch. LL.B. 1975; m. Donna Lois Smith, 6 Sept. 1980; ASSOC., TORY, TORY, DESLAURIERS & BINNINGTON, 1977-81; read law with above firm; called to Bar of Ont. 1977; Dir., Allpak Ltd.; Livingston Internat. Inc.; Chippewa - Camcor Inc.; recreations: skiing, tennis; Club: London Hunt & Country; Home: 101 Hazelton Ave., Toronto, Ont. M5R 2E4; office: Ste. 171, Northern Life Tower, 380 Wellington St., London, Ont. N6A 5C3

IVISON, Donald A.S., B.A., M.B.A.; executive; b. Ottawa, Ont. 1932; e. McMaster Univ. B.A. 1953; Univ. of W. Ont. M.B.A. 1955; m. M. Elizabeth Mann 1955; children: Deborah A., Robert S., Duncan M.; SR. VICE PRES., DU PONT CANADA INC. 1980- ; joined present co. Accounting Dept., Montreal 1955; held various positions in accounting, sales, market research, extve. office, becoming Mgr. Corporate Planning 1968, First Asst. Treas. 1973, Vice Pres. and Treas. 1975, Vice Pres. and Chief Financial Offr. 1979; mem. Financial Extves. Inst. Can.; recreations: gardening, music; Home: 68 Baby Point Road, Toronto, Ont. M6S 2G3; Office: Box 2200, Streetsville Postal Stn. (6700 Century Ave.), Mississauga, Ont. L5M 2H3

IZUMI, Kiyoshi, B. Arch., R.C.A., F.R.A.I.C.; educator; environmental design consultant; b. Vancouver, B.C. 24 March 1921; s. Tojiro and Kin (Fujii) I.; e. Vancouver Tech. Sch. 1939; Regina (Sask.) Coll. 1943; Univ. of Man. B.Arch. 1948; AA Sch. of London, Eng. 1949; London Sch. of Econ. 1949; Mass. Inst. of Technol. M.C.P. 1952; Harvard Univ. 1952; m. Amy Nomura 11 Apl. 1950; children: James Kiyoharu, Gordon Satoshi, Mary Kiyoko; PROF. OF URBAN & REGIONAL PLANNING, UNIV. OF WATERLOO 1972- ; Environmental Design & Planning Consultant 1968- ; private arch. practice Izumi, Arnott & Sugiyama, Regina, Sask. 1953-68; Chrmn. Human Information and Ecology Program Univ. of Sask. Regina 1968-71; Resident Consultant Ministry of State for Urban Affairs Ottawa 1971-72; Trustee, Nat. Museums Can. 1968-74; Chrmn. Visiting Comte. Nat. Gallery Can. 1970-74; mem. various comtes. devel. and review Nat. Bldg. Code Govt. Can. 1954-74; Chrmn. Comn. Prof. Status Teachers Sask. 1962; mem. Health & Environment Research Comte. Nat. Health & Welfare Can.; Mental Health Survey Comte. State of Colo., Nat. Inst. Mental Health Govt. U.S.A. 1962; rec'd Can. Council Killam Fellowship 1968-71; author "Psychiatric Hospital Design and Planning Standards" 1965; various articles, papers; mem., Acad. Orthomolecular Psychiatry; recreation: golf; Home: 289 Hiawatha Dr., Waterloo, Ont. N2L 2V9; Office: Univ. of Waterloo, Waterloo, Ont. N2L 3G1.

J

JACKETT, Hon. Wilbur Roy, D.C.L.; b. Tompkins, Sask., 27 June 1912; s. William Henry and Frances Victoria (Sweet) J.; e. Univ. of Sask., B.A. 1931, LL.B. 1933, D.C.L. 1958; Rhodes Scholar from Sask. 1934; Oxford

Univ., B.A. 1936, B.C.L. 1937, and M.A. 1949; m. Kathleen, d. Robert Robertson, 5 Sept. 1939; Chief Justice Federal Court of Canada, June 1971-Sept. 79; (previously Pres. of predecessor Exchequer Court of Can. 1964-71); joined the Dept. of Justice, 1939, leaving as Depy. Min. and Depy. Atty. Gen. of Can. (1957-60); drafted revision of the Income Tax Act in 1948 in addition to other govt. leg.; Gen. Counsel, Candn. Pacific Railway, 1960-64; author of "Chart of Privy Council Decisions with Reference to the B.N.A. Act" (pub. privately, 1946); read law with H. M. Stewart of Kamsack, Sask., and G. H. Yule, K.C., of Saskatoon, Sask.; called to the Bar of Sask. 1938, Ont. 1952, Que. 1960, B.C. 1964; cr. K.C. (Dom.) 1949; Protestant; Club: Cercle Universitaire d'Ottawa; Home: 150 Queen Elizabeth Drive, Ottawa, Ont.

JACKMAN, Frederic (Eric) Langford Rowell, B.A., M.A., Ph.D., C. Psych.; executive; psychologist; b. Toronto, Ont. 17 May 1934; s. late Henry Rutherford, O.C., K.St.J., Q.C. and Mary Coyne (Rowell) J.; e. Rosedale Pub. Sch. Toronto; Trinity Coll. Sch. Port Hope 1952; Univ. of B.C. 1952-53; Univ. of Toronto B.A. (Econ.) Trinity Coll. 1957, M.A. Psychol. 1962; Univ. of Chicago Ph.D. (Human Devel.) 1980; m. Sara Ellyn 4 Nov. 1978; children: by previous marriage Tara Griffith, Thomas Frederic Rowell; PRES. AND DIR. INVICTA INVESTMENTS INCORPORATED 1980- ; Pres. and Dir. Resource Conservation Products Ltd.; Easy Fill Products Ltd.; Vice Chrmn. International Power Development Corp.; Atlantic Energy and Development Corp.; Invest. Dealer Burns Bros. and Denton Ltd. Toronto 1958-60; Psychol. Intern Ont. Hosp. Toronto 1962; Psychol. Clk. Neuropsychiatric Inst. Univ. of Ill. 1962-63; Clin. Psychol. Researcher, Ill. Mental Health Insts. 1965-66, Clin. Psychol. Univ. of Chicago Service, IMHI 1966-70; extensive prof. teaching and consulting services to Youth Enrichment Services Inc. Chicago 1978; Chicago Lighthouse for the Blind 1971-78; Ill. Mental Health Insts. 1976-78; Lettuce Entertain You Enterprises Restaurants Chicago 1976-78; Mount Sinai Hosp. Dept. Psychiatry Chicago 1976-78; Circuit Court Cook Co. Juvenile Div. Ill. 1972-76; George J. London Mem. Hosp. Chicago 1972-73; Edison Park Home Park Ridge, Ill. 1969-73; Illinois Bell Telephone Chicago 1972-73; P. Cons. Cand. Fed. Riding of Spadina g.e. 1980; mem. Adv. Bd. Tarragon Theatre Toronto; Cabbagetown Youth & Boxing Club; Trustee, Jackman Foundation; recipient Am. Group Psychotherapy Assn. Cert. of Award 1975; Ill. Group Psychotherapy Soc. Award of Distinction 1977; Ill. Psychol. Assn. Special Award 1978; Founding mem. Candn. Group Psychotherapy Soc.; mem. Ont. Psychol. Assn.; Ill. Group Psychotherapy Soc. (Past Pres.); Ill. Psychol. Assn. (Past Chrmn. Clin. Sec.); Am. Group Psychotherapy Assn.; Am. Psychol. Assn.; Candn. Mental Health Assn.; World Federalists Can.; Cand. Inst. Internat. Affairs; Zeta Psi; P. Conservative; United Church; recreations: skiing, boating, gardening, tennis, photography, travel; Clubs: Albany; Empire of Can.; Canadian; Toronto Bd. of Trade; Osler Bluff Ski; Toronto Golf; University; Quadrangle (Chicago); Home: 9 Drumsnab Rd., Toronto, Ont. M4W 3A4. Office: Ste. 200, 60 Yonge St., Toronto, Ont.

JACKMAN, Henry Newton Rowell, B.A., LL.B.; executive; b. Toronto, Ont. 10 June 1932; s. Henry Rutherford, O.C., K.St.J., Q.C. and Mary (Rowell) J.; e. Upper Can. Coll. Toronto; Univ. of Toronto Schs.; Univ. of Toronto B.A. 1953, LL.B. 1956; London Sch. of Econ.; m. Maruja Trinidad d. James Stuart Duncan, C.M.G., LL.D. 14 Aug. 1964; children: Henry, Duncan, Maria Victoria, Consuelo, Trinity; CHRMN. BD. OF DIRS., THE EMPIRE LIFE INSURANCE CO.; Chrmn. of Bd., Economic Investment Trust Ltd.; Victoria & Grey Trustco.; Algoma Central Railway; United Corporations; Vice Chrmn., The Dominion of Canada General Insurance Co.; The Casualty Co. of Canada; Victoria Grey Trust Co.; Pres., Canadian and Foreign Securities Co. Ltd.; Canadian Northern Prairie Lands Co. Ltd.; E-L Financial Corp. Ltd.; The Debenture and Securities Corp. of Canada Ltd.; Dominion and Anglo Investment Corp. Ltd.; Vice Pres., Dir. and mem. Extve. Comte., Argus Corp.; Dir. and mem. Extve. Comte., Standard Broadcasting Ltd.; Dir., Fulcrum Investment Co. Ltd.; Mercantile & General Reinsurance Co. of Canada Ltd.; E-L Investment Management Ltd.; Electra Investments (Canada) Ltd.; Hiram Walker-Resources Ltd.; Hollinger-Argus Ltd.; The Ravelston Corp. Ltd.; Trans Ohio Fin. Corp. Inc.; Hon. Trustee, Toronto Western Hosp.; Gov., St. Andrew's Coll. Aurora, Ont.; Stratford Shakespearean Festifal; mem. Toronto Soc. Financial Analysts (Treas. 1958-59); Metrop. Toronto Adv. Bd. Salvation Army; Adv. Bd. Toronto Old Aged Men's & Women's Homes (Past Chrmn.); Atlantic Council Can. (Dir.); Nat. Council, Candn. Inst. Internat. Affairs; Extve. Asst. to Min. of Pub. Works Can. and Min. in Charge of Central Mortgage & Housing Corp. Ottawa 1959-61; Pres., Rosedale Riding P. Cons. Assn. 1963-65 and P. Cons. Businessmen's Club Metrop. Toronto 1968-70; former cand. for H. of C., Rosedale Riding; mem. Bd. Trade Metrop. Toronto; Phi Gamma Delta; P. Conservative; United Church; Clubs: Toronto; York; Albany, R.C.Y.C.; Canadian; Empire (Pres. 1971-72); Home: 19 Rosedale Rd., Toronto, Ont. M4W 2P1; Office: 165 University Ave., Toronto, Ont. M5H 3B8.

JACKMAN, Sydney W., B.S., M.A., Ph.D., F.S.A., F.R.Hist.S.; historian; educator; b. U.S.A., 25 March, 1925; s. Ensleigh Ellsworth and Dorothy (Anfield) J.; came to Can. 1925; e. Victoria (B.C.) High Sch.; Univ. of Wash., B.S. 1946, M.A. 1947; Harvard Univ., M.A. 1948, Ph.D. 1953; PROF. OF HISTORY, UNIV. OF VICTORIA, B.C. since 1963; Instr., Phillips Exeter, 1952-56; Asst. and Assoc. Prof., Bates Coll., 1956-62; served with U.S. Army; mem. Bd. Dirs., Art Gallery of Greater Victoria, 1965-73; Humanities Research Council, 1976-81; Adv. Comte., Maltwood Museum; mem. Prov. Jt. Bd. of Teacher Educ., 1972-73; corresp. mem., Council Soc. for Army Hist. Res.; Woodbury-Lowry Mem. Scholar; Rockefeller Fellow; Penrose Fellow; Visiting Fellow, Aust. Nat. Univ.; Visiting Prof., Univ. of Tasmania; Univ. of Mich.; Univ. of Papua, New Guinea; Visiting Scholar, Trinity Hall, Cambridge 1978-79; author, "Galloping Head", 1958; "Man. of Mercury", 1965; "Portraits of the Premiers", 1969; "Men at Cary Castle", 1972; "Vancouver Island", 1972; "Tasmania", 1974; "Nicholas Cardinal Wiseman", 1977; "A Slave to Duty", 1979; Ed., F. Marryat "Diary in America", 1962; "With Burgoyne From Quebec", 1963; "English Reform Tradition", 1963; "American Voyageur", 1969; "Romanov Relations", 1969; "The Journal of William Sturgis", 1978; Ed., "Acton in America" 1979; "A Curious Cage", 1981; mem. Ed. Adv. Bd., "American Neptune"; other writings incl. articles in various scholarly journs.; Fellow, Roy. Irish Soc. Antiquaries; Roy. Soc. Arts; Society of Antiquaries (London); Royal Hist. Soc.; mem. Colonial Soc. Mass.; Mass. Hist. Soc.; Am. Antiquarian Soc.; Soc. Army Hist. Research; Royal Soc. Tasmania; Royal Commonwealth Soc.; Hasty Pudding Inst. 1770; Century Assn. (N.Y.); recreations: travel, collecting pictures; Clubs: Union (Victoria); Atheneum (London); Authors (London); Home: 1065 Deal St., Victoria, B.C. V8S 5G6

JACKSON, Andrew Sander, F.C.A.; executive; b. Winnipeg, Man., 15 June 1925; s. Esther Secelia (Lindgren) and late Alfred Sander J.; e. Daniel McIntyre Coll.; Univ. of Manitoba, C.A. 1948; F.C.A. 1970; m. Elsie Mary, d. late William Edmund Collicut, 12 June 1948; children: Brian, Barbara, Sandra; EXECUTIVE VICE PRESIDENT, INVESTORS GROUP since 1979; Dir., Investors Syndicate Ltd.; Investors Group Trust Co. Ltd.; Winpak Ltd.; Apprentice, Glendinning, Gray & Roberts 1942; Income Tax Dept. 1948-50; with Peat, Marwick, Mitchell & Co. 1950;

Comptroller, Investors Syndicate of Canada Ltd. 1955, Asst. Gen. Mgr. and Treas. 1963, Vice-Pres. and Treas. 1964, Exec. Vice-Pres. 1970; President, Investors Syndicate Ltd. 1974; served in R.C.N.V.R. 1943-45; mem. Bd. Dirs., Children's Hosp. of Winnipeg Research Found. Inc.; Rainbow Stage Inc.; mem. Inst. Chart. Accts. of Man.; Anglican; recreations: golf, curling, painting; Clubs: The Manitoba; Winnipeg Winter; Granite Curling; St. Charles Country; Home: 476 South Drive, Winnipeg, Man. R3T 0B1; Office: 280 Broadway, Winnipeg, Manitoba. R3C 0R8

JACKSON, Donald K., B.A., M.B.A.; transportation executive; b. Castor, Alta. 6 April 1944; e. Univ. of Alta. B.A. 1965; Univ. of W. Ont. M.B.A. 1967; m. Erin Sloan 2 Sept. 1973; children: Andrea, Sara; PRESIDENT, TRIMAC TRANSPORTATION GROUP LTD. 1977- ; Dir. Trimac Ltd. 1981- ; Partner & Gen. Mgr. Rentway 1968 (acquired by Trimac Ltd. 1970); Pres., Transport Acceptance Corp. Ltd. (affiliated Trimac) 1971- ; Vice Pres. Trimac Ltd., Toronto 1973, also Pres., Tricil Ltd.; Group Vice Pres. Trimac Ltd., Calgary 1976; mem. Young Pres.' Organ.; Calgary Chamber Comm.; Home: 1021 Sydenham Rd. S.W., Calgary, Alta. Office: (P.O. Box 3500) Calgary, Alta, T2P 2P9.

JACKSON, Douglas Northrop, M.Sc., Ph.D.; psychologist; educator; b. Merrick, N.Y. 14 Aug. 1929; s. Douglas N. and Caya (Cramer) J.; e. Cornell Univ. B.Sc. 1951; Purdue Univ. M.Sc. 1952, Ph.D. 1955; Menninger Foundation Topeka, Kans. postdoctoral fellow 1955-56; m. Lorraine J. d. late Jacob Morlock 28 June 1962; children: Douglas III, Lori, Charles Theodore; SR. PROF. OF PSYCHOL., UNIV. OF W. ONT. 1964- ; Ed. Research Psychologists Press Inc.; Chrmn. Can. Council Fellowship Comte. (Psychol.) 1976-78; Special Research Review Comte. U.S. Pub. Health Service 1971- ; Scient. Adv. Comte. Psych. Systems Inc. 1981- ; Mang. Adv. Comte. Applied Psychological Measurement 1980- , mem. Bd. Eds.; Psychol., U.S. Veterans Adm. 1951-52, 1953-55; Research Psychol. Menninger Foundation 1952-53, U.S. Pub. Health Service postdoctoral Fellow 1955-56; Asst. and Assoc. Prof. Pa. State Univ. 1956-63, Visiting Prof. 1978-79; Consultant, Educ. Testing Service 1958-64, Visiting Scholar 1971-72; Research Consultant Family Services London (Ont.); Consultant London Police Dept.; Dir. London (Ont.) French Sch. 1970-71; co-ed. "Problems in Human Assessment" 1967, 1977; over 125 scient. articles; mem. bd. eds. various journs.; Fellow, Candn. Psychol. Assn.; Am. Psychol. Assn.; mem. Psychometric Soc.; Soc. Multivariate Exper. Psychol. (Pres. 1975-76); recreations: fishing, boating, music; Home: 29 Maldon Rd., London, Ont. N6C 1W2;Office: London, Ont. N6A 5C2.

JACKSON, Edwin Sydney, B. Com., F.S.A.,F.C.I.A.; actuary; b. Regina, Sask., 17 May 1922; s. late Dorothy Hazel (Bell) and late Edwin J.; e. Univ. of Man., B.Com. 1947; m. Nancy Joyce, d. late Gordon Stovel, Winnipeg, 19 May 1948; three d., Patricia, Barbara, Catherine; PRESIDENT AND C.E.O., MANUFACTURERS LIFE INSURANCE CO., since 1972; joined present co. 1948; Asst. Actuary 1952; Actuary 1956; Actuarial Vice Pres. 1964; Sr. Vice Pres. 1969; Exec. Vice Pres. & Dir., 1970; Pres. (1966-67) Candn. Inst. Actuaries; Chrmn., Candn. Life Ins. Assn., 1977-78; Vice Pres., Arthritis and Rheumatism Soc. (Ont. Div.); Dir. Bus. Council on National Issues; Vice Chmn., Life Office Mngt. Assn.; United Church; recreations: skiing, curling; Clubs: Toronto; Granite; Rosedale Golf Home: 101 Stratford Cres., Toronto, Ont. M4N 1C7; Office: 200 Bloor St. E., Toronto, Ont. M4W 1E5

JACKSON, G. Ernest; insurance executive; b. Toronto, Ont., 2 Feb. 1921; s. George Ernest and Jean Tinsely (McNeil) J.; e. London (Ont.) S. Coll. Inst.; SR. VICE PRES. AND DIR. REED SHAW STENHOUSE LTD. since 1973; Dir. National Travellers Ltd.; Reed Stenhouse Ltd.; Hiram Walker-Consumers Home Ltd.; Lake Ont. Cement

Ltd.; Monarch Investments Ltd.; Winston's Restaurant Ltd.; Br. Mgr. Canadian Pittsburgh Industries 1946; Partner Cronyn Pocock & Robinson 1948; Dir. Reed Shaw Osler 1968; served with Royal Candn. Regt. Eng. Sicily and Italy 1939-45, rank Capt.; el. M.P.P. for London S. 1955-59; Campaign Mgr. for Hon. J.P. Robarts Leadership Campaign 1961 and for Ont. prov. g.e.'s 1963, 1967; Shriner; P. Conservative; Anglican; recreations: sailing, fishing, hunting; Clubs: Griffith Island; Albany; London Hunt; The London; Home: 78 Cluny Drive, Toronto, Ont. M4W 2R3; Office: P.O. Box 250 Toronto-Dominion Centre, Toronto, Ont.M5K 1J6

JACKSON, Mt. Rev. George Frederic C., D.D., B.A. L.Th. (Ang.); retired archbishop; b. Peterborough, Ont., 5 July 1907; s. James Sandiford and Agnes Nina (Sweet) J.; e. Teacher Training Coll., Peterborough, Ont. (1927); Univ. Coll., Univ. of Toronto, B.A. 1932; Wycliffe Coll., Toronto, L.Th. 1935, D.D. 1959; m. Eileen deMontfort Wellborne, 14 Sept. 1939; children: David Michael, Elizabeth Mary, Peter Ian, Catherine Ann; Archbishop of Qu'Appelle and Metropolitan Rupert's Land, 1970-77; Bishop Ordinary, Candn. Forces, 1977-80; o. Deacon 1934, Priest 1935; Rector of Hornby 1935; Asst. Curate, Holy Trinity, Toronto, 1936-37; Sr. Asst. Curate, St. Paul's, Tranmere, Birkenhead, Eng., 1938-40; Vicar, St. John, Egremont, Wallasey, Cheshire, Eng., 1940-46; Rector, Lowville and Nassagaweya (Niagara Diocese), 1947; St-Judes, Oakville, Ont., 1947-58; Rector and Dean St. Paul's Pro-Cath., Regina, Sask., 1958-60; Bishop of Qu'appelle 1960; Hon. Canon, Christ's Ch. Cath., Hamilton, Ont., 1952; Chaplain, Candn. Legion, Provincial Command, Sask.; Chaplain R.C.M.P., Regina, 1959-77; Mayor, Kaptewa Beach Village; mem. The Fishing Lakes Planning Comm. (Sask.) 1980; recreation: skiing, gardening; Address: Box 519, Fort Qu'Appelle, Sask. S0G 1S0

JACKSON, Harold J. G., B.Com.; company president; b. Windsor, Ont., 18 June 1910; s. John Alfred and Josephine (Woodiwiss) J.; e. Windsor, Ont. Coll. Inst.; Univ. of Toronto, B.Com. 1933; m. Hazel M., d. late James G. Stuart, 24 June 1939; PRESIDENT AND GEN. MGR., W. L. WEBSTER MFG. LTD., since 1961; Dir. of Advertising & Public Relations, Chrysler Corp. of Canada Ltd., 1945-54; Vice-Pres. and Gen. Mgr., Ross Roy of Canada Ltd. 1954-59; Dir. of Operations, Fairview Shopping Centres Ltd., 1959-60; Pres., Assn. Candn. Advertisers, 1947-48; Presbyterian; Clubs: Detroit Boat; Renaissance (Detroit); New Windsor; Beach Grove Golf; Essex Golf; Windsor Curling; Ontario (Toronto); Home: 1715 Ypres Blvd., Windsor, Ont. N8W 1S3; Office: 10150 Riverside Dr. E., Windsor, Ont. N8P 1A1

JACKSON, J. T. Blair, B.A., FRI, RI (B.C.), CAE; corporate; executive; b. Vernon, B.C. 9 Aug. 1931; s. George T. and Kathleen (Galbraith) J.; e. Public and High Schs., Ottawa, Ont.; Carleton Univ.; Univ. of Brit. Columbia, F.R.I. 1961; m. . 1954; children: Suzanne, Todd, Mark; PRES. AND GEN. MGR., JACKSON, DORAN AND ASSOC. LTD., SR. VICE PRES., CENTURY 21 REAL ESTATE CAN. LTD.; with Household Finance Corp., Br. Mgr. Ottawa 1951; Credit Mgr.; Galbraith & Sons Ltd., Vernon, B.C. 1954, Gen. Mgr. 1956-58; Pres., Verndale Devel. Ltd., Vancouver, B.C. 1959-; Pres. and Gen. Mgr., Verndale Const. Ltd. 1961; Reg. Mgr., Capitol Holdings Ltd., Vancouver 1963; Mortgage Appraisal Mgr., Wolstencroft Corp., New Westminster B.C. 1965, Vice-Pres. and Asst. Gen. Mgr. 1968; Dir. Research and Public Relations, Candn. Assn. Real Estate Bds., Toronto, Ont. 1968-70; EXEC. VICE-PRES. & GEN. MGR., CAN. REAL ESTATE ASSN., 1971-79; Sr. Vice Pres., Century 21 Real Estate Can. Ltd. 1980; served with R.C.A.F. as Flying Offr. 1950-51; mem. Soc. Real Estate Appraisers; Internat. Council Shopping Centres; Urban Devel. Inst.; Housing and Urban Devel. Assn. Can.; Real Estate Inst. Can.; Real Estate Inst. B.C.; Candn. Real Estate Assn.; Internat. Real Estae Fed.; Inst. of Assn. Exec., Can. Cham-

ber of Commerce; Un. Church; recreations: tennis, riding, skiing, boating, photography; Home: 8631 Demorest Dr., Richmond, B.C. V7A 4P8; Office: Suite 135, 10551 Shellbridge Way, Richmond, B.C. V6X 2W9.

JACKSON, Mary Victoria, M.D.; physician; b. Toronto, Ont., 20 March 1905; d. John Henry and Victoria Celia (Honsberger) J.; e. Brown Sch. and Oakwood Coll. Inst., Toronto; Univ. of Toronto, M.D. 1929; Cert. in Psychiatry, Can., 1945, F.R.C.P.(C) 1974; Cert. Mental Hosp. Adm., Am. Psych. Assn., 1955; Consult. in Psychiatry, Metro Toronto Geriatric Centre, since 1970; rotating internship, Toronto Gen. Hosp., 1929-30; served with Toronto Psychiatric & Ont. Mental Hosps., 1930-34; apptd. Staff Phys. (Women's Serv.), Toronto Psych. Hosp. 1934-40; Sr. Psychiatrist, 1940-66; Acting Dir. (Adm.), 1965-66; Assoc. Prof., Dept. of Psychiatry, 1966-69; Asst. Dir. (Med.) and Consultant Psychiatrist, Clarke Inst. of Psychiatry 1966-69; Consultant in Psychiatry Metro Toronto Geriatric Centre, 1970-; mem. Hon. Council and Hon. mem. Candn. Assn. Occupational Therapists; Life Fellow, Am. Psychiatric Assn. & Acad. of Med. Toronto; Life Mem., Candn. and Ont. Psychiatric Assns.; mem., American Geriatric Society; Candn. and Ontario Medical Associations; Ontario Psychogeriatric Assn.; Medico-Legal Soc. Toronto; Alpha Phi; Clubs: Granite; Home: 77 St. Clair Ave. E., Apt. 1811, Toronto, Ont. M4T 1M5; Office: 351 Christie St., Toronto, Ont. MG6 3C3

JACKSON, Sarah Jeanette, M.A.; artist; b. Detroit, Mich. 13 Nov. 1924; e. Wayne State Univ. B.A. 1946, M.A. 1948; m. Anthony Jackson 1949; children: Timothy, Melanie; ARTIST-IN-RESIDENCE, TECHNICAL UNIV. OF N.S. 1978- ; Dir., Art & Tech. Program and accompanying annual Festivals; solo exhns. sculpture, drawings and xerography incl.; Apollinaire Gallery London 1951; New Bision Gallery London 1956; Arts Club Montreal 1956; Montreal Museum Gallery Twelve 1957; Robertson Galleries Ottawa 1959; Here & Now Gallery Toronto 1960; Roberts Gallery Toronto 1961; Jerrold Morris Internat. Gallery Toronto 1963; Galerie Libre Montreal 1964, 1966, 1968; Dalhousie Univ. 1965; Mt. St. Vincent Univ. 1967, 1968, 1981; Zwicker's Gallery Halifax 1971; St. Mary's Univ. 1973; Gallery Danielli Toronto 1975, 1976; Tech. Univ. N.S. 1976, 1979; Gallerie Scollard Toronto 1976; Pa. State Univ. 1978; Gadatsy Gallery Toronto 1979; numerous group exhns. Can., Europe, U.S.A.; rep. perm. colls. incl. Hirshorn Museum & Sculpture Garden; Nat. Coll. Fine Arts (Smithsonian Inst.); Nat. Gallery Can.; Art Gallery Ont.; musée des Beaux-arts de Montréal; Musée d'Art Contemporain Montréal; subject of film "Sarah Jackson Halifax 1980" (sponsored by Nat. Film Bd.); lectr. many colls. and galleries incl. Mexico City Coll. 1948, Tate Gallery London, Eng. 1954-55, Nat. Gallery Can. 1957; Address: (P.O. Box 1000) Halifax, N.S. B3J 2X4.

JACKSON, William Robert; hospital administrator; b. Stonewall, Man. 15 June 1945; s. William Jackson; e. Univ. of Winnipeg; Ryerson Polytech. Inst. Cert. in Pub. Health Inspection 1966; Red River Community Coll. Winnipeg; m. Betty Helen d. Henry Haak, Clearbrook, B.C. 25 March 1973; children: Heidi Karen, William David John; EXEC. DIR., HOPITAL ALBERT SCHWEITZER, Deschapelles, Haiti 1981-; Pres. and CEO, Nat. Union of Prov. Govt. Employees 1979-81; Vice Pres. 1976-79; Pres., Man. Govt. Employees' Assn. 1976-79; Vice Pres., man. Fed. of Labour 1976-78; mem. Candn. Inst. Pub. Health Insprs.; Protestant; recreations: curling, golf; Home: 45 Waxwing Dr., Ottawa, Ont. K1V 9H1; Address: P.O. Box 1744, Port-au-Prince, Haiti, W.I.

JACOBS, John Arthur, M.A., Ph.D., D.Sc., F.R.S.C., F.R.A.S.; b. London, Eng., 13 April 1916; s. Arthur George and Elfrida Malvine (Boeck) J.; e. Dorking High Sch., Surrey, Eng. (1927-34); Univ. of London, B.A. 1937, M.A. 1939, Ph.D. 1949, D.Sc. 1961; m. Daisy Sarah Ann, d. late J. Montgomerie, 7 Nov. 1941 (d. 1974); two d.

Coral Elizabeth, Margaret Ann.; m. 2nd Margaret Jones, 4 Oct. 1974; PROF: OF GEOPHYSICS, UNIV: OF CAMBRIDGE since 1974; Sr. Lectr. in Applied Maths., Royal Naval Engn. Coll., Devonport, Eng. (also Depy. Training Commdr.) 1944-46; Lectr. in Applied Maths., Univ. of London, 1946-51; Assoc Prof., Applied Maths., Univ. of Toronto, 1951-54 and Assoc. Prof. of Geophysics there 1954-57; Prof. of Geophysics, Univ. of Brit. Columbia, 1957-61; Dir., Inst. of Earth Sciences, Univ. of Brit. Columbia, 1961-67; Killam Mem. Prof. of Sciences, Univ. of Alberta, 1967-74; Dir. of the Inst. of Earth & Planetary Physics, Univ. of Alta 1970-74; Lieut.-Commdr., R.N.V.R., 1941-46; Publications: more than 150 scient. papers in tech. journs.; Author of 5 books, Cent. Medal of Can. 1967; Gold medal of Candn. Assoc. of Physicists, 1975; recreations: walking, music; Home: The Old Manor House, Hinxton, Cambs., Eng.

JAEGER, Leslie Gordon, M.A., Ph.D., F.R.S.E., P. Eng.; educator; b. Southport, Eng. 28 Jan. 1926; s. late Henry and late Beatrice Alice (Highton) J.; e. King George V Sch. Southport, Eng. 1943; Gonville & Caius Coll. Cambridge Univ. B.A. 1946, M.A. 1950 (State Scholar 1943-45, Scholar of Coll. and Prizeman 1944-45); Univ. of London Ph.D. 1955; m. Annie Sylvia d. late William Arthur Dyson 3 Apl. 1948; two d. Valerie Ann, Hilary Frances; SPECIAL ASSIST. TO THE PRES., TECHNICAL UNIV. OF NOVA SCOTIA 1980-; Vice Presdent Atlantic Access Ltd.; President Jaeger and Muft: Research Associates; Dir. Comstock Premises Ltd. & Comstock Internat. Ltd.; Fellow, Magdalene Coll. Cambridge 1959-62; Prof. of Civil Engn. and Applied Mech. McGill Univ. 1962-64 and 1966-70; Regius Prof. of Engn. and Head of Dept. Edinburgh Univ. 1964-66; Dean of Engn. Univ. of N.B. 1970-75; Vice Pres. (Acad.) Acadia Univ. 1975-80; Consultant to various firms incl. Rolls Royce Ltd.; United Aircraft of Canada Ltd.; co-leader team structural design theme bldgs. Expo 67; Consultant design hwy. bridges Ont. Govt.; N.B. Electric Power Comn.; Chrmn. 1975 Candn. Congress Applied Mech.; mem. Candn. Nat. Comte. on Earthquake Engn. 1973-76; served with RN 1945-48, rank Lt.; Dir. N.B. Prot. Orphans Home 1973-75; mem. Maritime Provs. Higher Educ. Comn. 1974-78; author "The Analysis of Grid Frameworks and Related Structures" 1958; "Elementary Theory of Elastic Plates" 1962; "Cartesian Tensors in Engineering Science" 1964; also over 50 papers mainly in field of structural engn. with emphasis on behaviour of tall bldgs. and nuclear power stns. in earthquakes; Fellow, Inst. Civil Engrs. (London); Past Fellow, Inst. Structural Engrs. (London); mem. Engn. Inst. Can.; Candn. Standards Assn.; Freemason; Liberal; United Church; recreations: golf, curling, contract bridge; Clubs: Halifax; Home: 73 Tangmere Cres., Clayton Park, Halifax N.S. B3M 1K2

JAGGER, Kenneth, B.Sc., P.Eng.; executive; b. Birmingham, Eng., 17 Sept. 1925; s. David Haigh and Jessie J.; e. Coastbridge Secondary Sch.; Glasgow Univ., B.Sc.; m. Katherine, d. Frederick Read, Bear River, N.S., 10 Nov. 1956; one s. Douglas Charles, one d. Lynn Carol; PRES. AND DIR., PROCOR LTD.; Pres. and Dir., Procor (U.K.) Ltd.; Dir., Can. Oxygen Ltd.; Compair (Can.) Ltd.; Slough Estates Ltd.; Wagon Repairs (U.K.) Ltd.; Trustee, Toronto Western Hospital; commenced as Field Engr., R. McAlpine & Sons Ltd., Eng. 1950; with Defence Construction Ltd., Kingston, Ont. 1952; Sales Engr., Standard Iron & Steel Ltd., Toronto 1954; Asst. Sales Mgr., Anthes Steel Products Ltd. 1959, Gen. Sales Mgr. 1961; joined present Co. as Vice-Pres. 1966; served in Fleet Air Arm 1944-47; Conservative; Presbyterian; recreations: golf, swimming, tennis; Clubs: Toronto Golf; Ont. Racquet; Home: 2068 Tenoga Drive, Mississauga, Ont. L5H 3K2; Office: 2001 Speers Rd., Oakville, Ont. L6J 5E1

JAMES, Albert J., B.S.; executive; b. Somers Point, N.J. 28 Oct. 1936; s. Leonard Robert and Helen (Ingersoll) J.; came to Can. Aug. 1981; e. Univ. of Rochester, N.Y., B.S.

(Chem. Eng.) 1958; m. Louise A. Winkler-Prins d. Antony Winkler-Prins 23 Aug. 1958; children: Elizabeth L., Catherine A.; PRES., CANDN. CANNERS LTD., 1981-; Dir., St. Williams Preservers; Aylmer Foods Warehousing Ltd.; Vice-Pres., Luck's Inc. (Div. of Amer. Home Foods) 1968-75; Sr. Dir., R.J.R. Foods Inc. 1975-80; Vice-Pres., Prepared Foods & Beverage Group, Del Monte Corp. 1980; served in U.S. Navy 1958-61; Lt. U.S.N.R. (retired); Delta Upsilon (Pres.); Presbyterian; Clubs: Hamilton; Burlington Golf & Country; recreations: fishing, snorkeling, tennis, racquetball, cross-country skiing; Office: 44 Hughson St. S., Hamilton, Ont. L8N 3K6

JAMES, Brian Robert, M.A., D.Phil., F.C.I.C., C. Chem. F.R.S.C. (U.K.); F.R.S.C.; educator; b. Birmingham, Eng. 21 Apl. 1936; s. Herbert Arthur J.; e. Handsworth Grammar Sch. Birmingham 1954 (State & Open Scholarships); Oxford Univ. B.A. 1958, M.A., D.Phil. 1960; m. Mary Jane d. Howard Edward Thompson, Mississauga, Ont. 6 Oct. 1962; children: Jennifer Ann, Peter Edward, Sarah Elizabeth, Andrew Francis; PROF. OF CHEM., UNIV. OF B.C. 1974- ; Sr. Scient. Offr. U.K. Atomic Energy Authority Harwell 1962-64; Asst. Prof. present Univ. 1964, Assoc. Prof. 1969; Visiting Lectr. Univ. of Sussex 1970; Visiting Prof. Univ. of Waterloo 1971; Visiting NATO Prof. Univ. of Pisa 1979; Consultant, Rayonier, MacMillan Bloedell, Cominco 1968-73; Fellow, Roy. Soc. of Can. (1982); mem. Inco Grad. Research Fellowships Comte. 1974-77 (Chrmn. 1976-77); Nat. Research Council Chem. Comte 1974-76; Noranda Lectr. Chem. Inst. Can. 1975; Allied Chemicals Distinguished Lectr. 1976; Inorganic Lectureship Univ. of W. Ont. 1980; Consultant, Ont. Council on Grad. Studies 1975, invited lectr. Eng., U.S.A., Japan, Italy, Hungary, Portugal, Greece, France; author "Homogeneous Hydrogenation" 1973, Russian transl. 1976; book chapters, over 130 research papers nat. and internat. journs.; rec'd Royal Soc. Bursarship (London) 1970; mem. Am. Chem. Soc.; N.Y. Acad. Sciences; Wadham Coll. Soc.; Liberal; Anglican; recreations: sports, music, coaching soccer and cricket; Home: 4010 Blenheim St., Vancouver, B.C. V6L 2Y9; Office: Vancouver, B.C. V6T 1Y6.

JAMES, Christopher Robert, M.A.Sc., Ph.D.; university professor; b. Vancouver, B.C., 15 Nov. 1935; s. Christopher Robert and Lillian Bernice (Shaw) J.; e. Univ. of Brit. Columbia, B.A.Sc. 1960, M.A.Sc. 1961, Ph.D. 1964; Oxford Univ., Post Doctoral Fellow 1964-65; m. Arline Sigrid, d. Alwyn Fox, 21 April 1956; children: Alison Elaine, Margo Arline, Heather Gail, Cheryl Kirstin, Maureen Beth; PROF. OF ELECT. ENGN., UNIV. OF ALBERTA since 1971 and Chairman of Dept. since 1974; joined the University as Asst. Prof. 1965, Assoc. Prof. 1967; apptd. Dir., Nat. Research Council Negotiated Devel. Grant in Laser-Plasma Tech. 1972; Mem., Am. Assn. Advanc. Science; mem. Assn. Prof. Engrs., Geols. and Geophysicists of Alta.; Candn. Assn. Physicists; Eng. Inst. of Can. Am. Physical Soc.; rec'd Assn. Prof. Engrs. Gold Medal for Engn. in B.C. 1960; Publications: "Plasma Laser Pulse Amplifier Using Induced Ramon or Brillomin Processes"; also numerous articles in leading prof. and tech. journs.; mem. Am. Assn. Advance. Science; recreations: hunting, gardening, climbing, skiing, fishing; Clubs: Alpine; Alberta Fish & Game; Edmonton Sporting Dog Club; Home: 4B36-122 A St., Edmonton, Alta. T6H 3S7

JAMES, Edward Douglas, O.B.E.; company president; b. Edmonton, Alberta, 2 May 1914; s. Stanley Edward and Jessie (Corbet) J.; e. Public and High Schs., Vancouver, B.C.; Univ. of British Columbia (1930-34); General Motors Inst., Flint, Mich., Grad. (1934-36); m. Helen d. William Jardine, Toronto, Ont., 8 Nov. 1941; has three d; Pres., J. Spencer Turner Co. Ltd., Estd. 1924, since 1960; served in 2nd World War with Candn. Army, 1939-45; Col.-Dir. of Mechanization, 1943-45; awarded O.B.E.; Beta Theta Pi; Anglican Church; Clubs: The Hamilton; Home: 1704, 130

St. Joseph's Dir., Hamilton, Ont. L8N 2E8; Office: (P.O. Box 147) Ancaster, Ont. L9G 3L4

JAMES, William, M.A., Ph.D.; mining executive; b. Ottawa, Ont., 5 Feb. 1929; s. William Fleming and Lenore (McEvoy) J.; e. pub. and high schs. Toronto; Univ. of Toronto B.A. 1954, M.A. 1954, Ph.D. 1957; m. Joanna d. Fred T. Watson, 15 Sept. 1954; children: Paul, William, Anne, Mary, George, John; EXTVE. VICE PRES, AND DIR., NORANDA MINES LIMITED; Pres. and Dir., Agnew Lake Mines Ltd.; Brunswick Mining and Smelting Corporation Ltd.; Empresa de El Setentrion; Empresa Fluorspar Mines Ltd.; Keradamex Inc.; Kerr Addison Mines Ltd.; Kerramerican Inc.; Western Barite Mines Ltd.; Vice-Pres. and Dir., Garon Lake Mines Ltd.; Noranda Lakeshore Mines Inc.; Brenda Inc.; Dir. Brenda Mines Ltd.; Canada Permanent Mortgage Corp., Canada Permanent Trust Co.; Canadian Electrolytic Zinc Ltd.; Canadian Gypsum Company Ltd.; Canadian Hunter Exploration Ltd.; Compania Minera Las Cuevas; Morrison Petroleums Ltd.; Craigmont Mines Ltd.; Inversiones Mexicanas Industriales S.A.; Mattabi Mines Ltd.; Mogul of Ireland Ltd.; The Mutual Life of Canada; Noranda Sales Corp. Ltd.; Placer Development Ltd.; Tara Mines Ltd.; Noranda Exploration Co. Ltd.; Electrolyser Inc.; Geol. Rio Algom Mines 1958-60; Hopewell Land Corp.; Les Mines Gallen Ltd.; Pacific (Northern) Gold Mines Ltd.; Tara Exploration & Dev. Co., Ltd.; Mining Corp. of Canada Ltd.; Noranda Mining Ltd.; James & Buffam 1961-67, Partner 1967-73; Dir., Mining Assn. Can.; Assn. Prof. Engrs. Ont.; R. Catholic; Clubs: Engineers: York; Home: 41 St. Leonards Ave., Toronto, Ont. M4N 1K1; Office: Suite 4500, Commerce Court West, Toronto, Ont. M5L 1B6

JAMES, William Fleming, Ph.D., F.R.S.C. (1954), D.Sc., LL.D.; consulting geologist; Dir., Campbell Red Lake Mines Ltd.; Dome Mines Ltd.; Falconbridge Nickel Mines Ltd.; Falconbridge Dominicana C. por A; Giant Yellowknife Mines Ltd.; Grafton Group Ltd.; Lolor Mines Ltd.; Templeton Growth Fund Ltd.; Templeton World Fund; rec'd. Award from Candn. Inst. Mining & Metall. for contrib. to mineral industry, 1964; Home: 300 Vesta Dr., Toronto, Ont. M5P 3A3; Office: P.O. Box 39, Suite 2920, Commerce Court North, Toronto, Ont. M5L 1A1.

JAMIESON, Hon. Donald Campbell (Don), P.C., LL.D.; b. St. John's, Nfld., 30 Apl. 1921; s. Charles and Isabelle (Bennett) J.; e. Prince of Wales Coll., St. John's; LL.D., Memorial Univ. 1970; m. Barbara Elizabeth, d. late Kenneth Oakley, 20 Dec. 1946; children: Donna, Heather, Roger, Debbie; first elected to Nfld. Legis. g.e. 1979; Chosen leader of the Lib. Party in Nfld., May 1979; Leader of the Opposition, 1979-80; served as mem., Consultative Comte. on Private Broadcasting, Bd. of Broadcast Govs.; Past Dir. of Broadcast News and Past Chrmn. of Affiliates Sec., Network Adv. Comte. of CBC; former mem., "Troika" Comte. on broadcasting estbd. by Fed. Govt., 1963; el. to H. of C. for Burin-Burgeo in by-el., Sept. 1966, re-elected 1968, 72, 74; Minister of Defense Production, 1968; Min. of Transport, 1969; (Min. of Regional Economic Expansion, 1972-75; Min. of Ind. Trade and Comm., 1975-76; Minister of External Affairs, 1976-79; resigned H. of C. June 18, 1979; Past Chrmn., Financial Campaign, Candn. Cancer Soc.; author of "The Troubled Air," 1966; Pres.(1961-64) Candn. Assn. of Broadcasters; Liberal; Presbyterian; recreation: fishing; Club: City; Home: 4 Winter Pl., St. John's, Nfld.;

JAMIESON, John Kenneth; company director; b. Medicine Hat, Alta., 28 Aug. 1910; s. John Locke and Kate (Herron) J.; e. Univ. of Alta.; Mass. Inst. of Tech., Grad.; m. Ethel May Burns, 23 Dec. 1937; children: John Burns, Anne Frances; Dir., Exxon Corp.; Equitable Life Asssurance Soc.; Raychem. Corp.; Chmn. of the Board Crutcher Resources Corp.; has been engaged in the oil industry since 1931; el. a Dir. of Imperial Oil Co., Ltd., To-

ronto, Ont., 1952; Vice Pres. 1953; Pres., International Petroleum Co., Ltd., 1959-61; Vice President and Dir., Exxon Co. (U.S.) 1961-62; Extve. Vice Pres. 1962-63; Pres. 1963; el. Extve. Vice Pres. and Dir. Exxon Corp. 1964, Pres. 1965-69; Chrmn. and Chief Extve. Offr. 1969-75; mem., Association of Prof. Engrs. Ont.; Lambda Chi Alpha; Episcopalian; Clubs: Houston (Texas) Country; Augusta National Golf; Office: 1100 Milam Bldg., Suite 4601, Houston, Texas 77002

JAMIESON, Stewart Edgar, B. Eng.; metallurgical engineer; company executive; b. Passmore, B.C., 11 Oct. 1917; s. William James Edgar and Lillian Hope (Dockendorf) J.; e. Univ. of British Columbia, 1935-38; McGill Univ., B.Eng. (Metall.) 1939-41 and post-grad. study there, 1946-47; m. Margaret Eugenie, d. Adolphus William Brown, Montreal, Que., 15 July 1942; children: Glen, Brian, Bruce, Heather, John; CHAIRMAN, CHIEF EXTVE. OFFR. AND DIR., BRITISH METAL CORP. (CANADA) LTD. and of Amalgamet Canada Ltd.; (internat. marketing of metals and natural resource commodities); Dir., Amalgamet Inc., New York; British Metal International Ltd., Bermuda; Drew Brown; Conwest Exploration Co. Ltd.; Chance Mining and Exploration Co. Ltd.; Metall. Engr. at Battelle Memorial Institute, Columbus, Ohio, 1947-48; Westcoast Petroleum Ltd.; joined present interests in 1948; served in 2nd World War with R.C.E.M.E. N.W. Europe; discharged with rank of Major, 1946; mem. Candn. Inst. Mining & Metall.; United Church; Clubs: National; Engineers; Home: 484 Blythwood Rd., Toronto, Ont. M4N 1A9; Office: (P.O. Box 95) Commerce Court W., Toronto, Ont. M5L 1C9

JANISCH, Andrew, B.Sc.; petroleum executive; b. Wallern, Austria 7 Nov. 1931; s. Joseph and Anna (Summer) J.; came to Can. 1935; e. Univ. of Man. B.Sc. (Civil Engn.) 1953; m. Jessie Patterson d. Thomas Dickson 26 Aug. 1953; children: Stephen Alexander, Gregory Joseph, Mark Richard, Matthew Lawrence; PRES. AND CHIEF OPERATING OFFR., DIR., PETRO-CANADA since 1979; Dir. Panarctic Oils Ltd.; Dir., Westcoast Transmission Co. Ltd.; joined Gulf Oil Canada Ltd. 1953; Vice Pres. and Gen. Mgr., Gulf Minerals Canada Ltd., Pres. 1975; Sr. Vice Pres. Petro-Canada 1977; mem. Alta. Assn. Petrol. Geols.; Am. Petrol. Inst.; Alta.-N.W. Chamber Mines & Resources; Soc. Petrol. Engrs. of A.I.M.E.; Candn. Inst. Mining & Metall.; R. Catholic; recreations: golf, curling; Clubs: Engineer's (Toronto); Pinebrook Golf & Winter; Ranchmen's; Calgary Petroleum; Home: 116 Pump Hill Bay S.W., Calgary, Alta. T2V 4L6; Office: 407 —2nd St. S.W., Calgary, Alta. T2P 2M7.

JANISS, Eugene, D. Arch.; architect; b. Latvia. 29 June 1911; e. Elem. and High Schs., Riga, Latvia; Univ. of Riga, Latvia, B. Arch. (Hons.) 1943; Univ. of Hanover, Germany, D. Arch., 1947 (earned); m. Mirdza, d. late J. Veilands, 10 April 1939; one d. Vija, B.Sc.; PRINCIPAL & CHIEF DESIGNER, EUGENE JANISS, ARCHITECTS; also Arch. Consultant, Mental Health Div., Ont., Dept. of Health; began practice of his prof. in Latvia, 1940; moved to Germany in 1945; Member of the Research Team for the rebuilding of Germany in Hanover, Germany, 1945-48; came to Can., 1948, joining firm of Page & Steele, Archs., Toronto, Ont.; started practice under own name, 1956; in partnership with Wm. H. Gilleland as Partner, i/c Design, 1960-68; Publications: "Standardization of floor plans adapted to Small Suites in Multi-storey Apartment Buildings in German Cities", 1947; "Objective Evaluation of Floor Plans for Residential Buildings", 1948; responsible for many ccmm., indust., educ. insts. and other bldgs., hosps., churches and residences; among outstanding designs are: American Motors Plant in Brampton, Ont., Shoppers World Shopping Centre, Toronto, Prof. Bldg. for doctors and dentists, Toronto; Psychiatric Hosp., Penetanguishene, Ont.; commended for design for Vancouver Civic Auditorium Competition 1955, Alcan Dist. Sales Office Competition,

Toronto, 1957, Toronto City Hall and Sq. Internat. Competition, 1958; mem., Royal Arch. Inst. Can.; Ont. Assn. Arch.; Selonia; Protestant; recreations: photography, travelling, boating; Club: Toronto Cricket Skating & Curling; Home: 209 St. Clements, Toronto, Ont. M4R 1H3; 443 Mt. Pleasant Rd., Toronto, Ont. M4S 2L8

JAQUES, Louis B., M.A., Ph.D., D.Sc., F.R.S.C.; professor; b. Toronto, Ontario, 10 July 1911; s. late Robert Herbert and Ann Bella (Shepherd) J.; e. Univ. of Toronto (Trinity Coll.), B.A. 1933, M.A. 1935, Ph.D. 1941; m. Helen Evelyn, d. late Thomas J. Delane, Huntsville, Ont., 15 May 1937; one d., Catherine Mary Ann (Hall); EMERITUS PROF. PHYSIOLOGY AND RESEARCH ASSC. OF DENTISTRY, UNIV. OF SASK., 1979; Hon. Lay Canon, Ang. Deoc. of Saskatoon, 1981; Surgery (under a grant from Banting Foundation) Univ. of Toronto, 1934-35; Fellow, Dept. of Physiology 1936-38 and Research Asst., 1938-42; Research Asst., Dept. of Physiol. Hygiene, 1939-42; Lectr and Research Assoc., Dept. of Physiol., 1943-44; Asst. Prof., 1944-46; Prof. and Head Dept. of Physiol. Pharmacol., Univ. of Sask., 1946-71; Prof. of Physiology, Univ. of Sask, and Head of Haemostasis — Thrombosis Unit, 1971-79; Lindsay Prof., 1972-79; author of "The Prayer Book Companion", 1963; "Anticoagulant Therapy", 1965; numerous articles in scient. journ.; mem., New York Acad. Sciences; Med. Research Council, 1960-61; Gen. Synod, Ang. Ch. Can., 1952-59; Gen. Comn. on Union, Ang.-Un. Ch. of Can. 1967-73-; Adv. Comte., Med. Div., Nat. Research Council, 1952-55, 1958-60; Internat. Comte. for Standardization of Nomenclature of the Blood Clotting Factors 1954-66; mem., Candn. Physiol. Soc.; Pharmacol. Soc. Can.; Am. Soc. of Hematol.; Anglican; Home: 682 University Drive, Saskatoon, Sask. S7N 0J2

JARISLOWSKY, Stephen A., B.Sc., M.A., M.B.A.; investment counsel; b. Berlin, Germany, 9 Sept. 1925; s. Alfred and Kaethe (Gassmann) J.; e. Ecole du Moncel, Jouy-en-Josas, France; Asheville (N.C.) Sch., 1942; Cornell Univ., B.Sc. 1944; Univ. of Chicago, M.A. 1947 (Phi Beta Kappa); Harvard Univ., M.B.A. 1949; m. Margaret Gail, d. late Harold Merilees, 11 Apl. 1968; children: Stephen Alfred, Michael Andrew, Alexandra Cecile, Marika Ann; PRESIDENT, JARISLOWSKY, FRASER & COMPANY LTD.; Dir., Phénix Mills; Prefab Concrete; Office Equipment Co. Canada; Fraser Bros.; Canadian Computerized Information; President & Director Didier Refractories Canada Ltd.; Dir. Growth Oil & Gas Investment Fund; Inter City Papers Ltd.; SNC Group; Goodfellow Lumber Co.; Steinberg Foods; Swiss Bank Corp. (Canada); Chambre de Comm. de Montréal; Past Chrmn. Qué. MBA Assn.; Past Extve. Council, Candn. Chamber of Comm.; served with Alcan Aluminum Ltd. as Plant Engr., Sales Adm., Finance Adm. and Area Supvr., Asia, Africa and Australia, 1949-52; The Twin Editions, Art Publishing, New York, 1952-55; estbd. Growth Oil & Gas Investment Fund, 1952; General Impact Extrusions Ltd. 1953; estbd. present firm 1955; has reorganized various other firms and served as extve. incl. Vice Pres. and Dir., Phénix Mills (1966); taught invest. analysis, Dept. of Comm., McGill Univ., 1956-60; consultant to various banks and corps.; frequent contrib. to newspapers on econ. topics; served with US Army 1944-46, Japan; Counter Intelligence Corps; rec'd Order of Chrysanthemum (4th Class) Japan; Unit Citation Medal; Trustee, Asheville Sch. 1955-60; mem., Chamber Comm. Finance Comte.; Candn. Econ. Policy Comte.; Financial Analyst Soc.; Protestant; recreations: hiking, tennis, swimming, music, gardening; Clubs: University; Mt. Royal; Home: 9 Murray Ave., Westmount, Que. H3Y 2X9; Office: 1110 Sherbrooke St. W., Montreal, Que. H3A 1G8

JARMAIN, William Edwin Charles, M.Sc., P.Eng.; company president; b. London, Ont., 25 May 1938; s. Edwin Roper and Ruth Winifred (Secord) J.; e. Mass. Inst. of Technol., B.Sc. (Elect. Engn.) 1961, M.Sc. (Elect. Engn.)

1964, M.Sc. (Indust. Mang.) 1964; m. Patricia Catherine, d. Edmund T. Carroll, 29 Feb. 1964; three d. Catherine Carroll, Ellen Ruth, Anne Beatrice; PRESIDNT, JARMAIN COMMUNICATIONS INC.; CHRMN., NORTHSTAR HOME THEATRE INC.; formerly Pres., Canadian Cablesystems Ltd.; Staff mem., Sch. of Indust. Mang., Mass. Inst. of Technol., 1961-64; Assoc., McKinsey & Co., Inc. (mang. consultants), New York, 1964-66; Visiting Lectr. in Business Adm., Univ. of W. Ont., 1967; mem., Assn. Prof. Engrs. Prov. Ont.; Inst. Elect. & Electronics Engrs.; Candn. Cable TV Assn. (Dir. 1968-73; Chairman 1970-72); Dir., Ont. Development Corp. 1972-80; Dir. Ont. Energy Corp., 1980-; The Inst. for Political Involvement, 1980-; recreations: skiing, sailing, reading; Home: 412 Russell HillRd., Toronto, Ont., M4V 2V2; Office: Suite 738, 40 University Ave., Toronto, Ont., M5J 1T1;

JARVIS, William Esmond, M.Sc.A.; agrologist; b. Gladstone, Man. 10 Dec. 1931; s. Frederick Roberts and Dorothy Welles (Tuckwell) J.; e. Univ. of Man. B.Sc.A. 1955; Mich. State Univ. M.Sc.A. 1960; m. 9 May 1953; children: Cheryl, Darrell, Dennis; CHIEF COMMR. THE CANDN. WHEAT BD. 1977- ; joined Dept. Agric. Man. 1955, Depy. Min. of Agric. 1962-67; Asst. Depy. Min. of Agric. Can. and Assoc. Depy. Min. 1967-77; rec'd Nuffield Foundation Travelling Research Fellowship, Univ. of Man. Alumni Assn. Jubilee Award 1981; mem. Agric. Inst. Can.; Man. Inst. Agrols.; United Church; recreations: sporting and outdoor activities; Club: Gyro; Home: 2-311, 65 Swindon Way, Winnipeg, Man. R3P 0T8; Office: 423 Main St., Winnipeg, Man. R3C 2P5.

JARVIS, Hon. William Herbert, Q.C. (1979) B.A., LL.B.; politician; b. Hamilton, Ont. 15 Aug. 1930; s. Garfield and Nina (McBean) J.; e. Univ. of W. Ont. B.A. 1953, LL.B. 1962; children: Elizabeth, Richard; MIN. OF STATE FOR FED.-PROV. RELATIONS since 1979; el. to H. of C. g.e. 1972, re-el. since; P. Conservative; Protestant; Office: House of Commons, Ottawa, Ont. K1A 0X2.

JASMIN, Gaëtan, B.A., M.D., Ph.D. F.R.C.P.(C); educator; b. Montreal, Que. 24 Nov. 1924; s. Horace and Antoinette (Piquette) J.; e. Coll. St-Laurent B.A. 1945; Univ. de Montréal M.D. 1951, Ph.D. 1956; C.S.P.Q. 1968; F.R.C.P.(C), 1978; m. Suzanne Dupont 8 Oct. 1952; children: Eve, Luc, Pierre; CHRMN. DEPT. DE PATHOLGIE, UNIV. DE MONTREAL; affiliated Hôpital Site-Justine; Ed. 'Mechanism of Inflammation' 1953; 'Endocrine Aspects of Disease Processes' 1968; 'Methods and Achievements in Experimental Pathology' Vols. 1-10, 1966; author numerous publs.; mem. Assn. Pathols. Qué.; Assn. Médecins Spécialistes Qué.; Internat. Acad. Pathol.; Soc. Exper. Biol. & Med.; Fed. Am. Biol. Socs.; Candn. Fed. Biol. Socs.; Histochem. Soc.; Soc. Française de Microscopie électronique; Assn. Pathology Chairmen (Am.); Can. Assn. Pathology Chairmen; Assn. internat. de pédagogie universitaire; Goups for Research in pthology Eeuc.; Assn. Can. française pour l'avancement des sciences; Soc. de physiologie de Montreal; N.Y. Academy of Sc.; Internat. Soc. for Heart Research; Am. Physolog. Soc.; Am. Fed. for Clinical Research; Can. Soc. for Clinical Investigation; Muscular Dystrophy Assn. of Can.; Soc. Can. de physiologie; Am. Assn. for Advancement of Sc.; R. Catholic; Home: 189 Glengarry, Mont-Royal, Qué. H3R 1A3; Office: (P.O. Box 6128) Montréal, Qué. H3C 3J7.

JASPER, Herbert H., O.C. (1972); M.D., Ph.D., D.ès.Sc., F.R.S.C.; neurophysiologist; b. La Grande, Oregon, 27 July 1906; s. Franklin M. and Lina (Dupertuis) J.; e. Reed College, Portland (Oregon) B.A. 1927; University of Oregon (Eugene), M.A. 1929; University of Iowa, Ph.D. 1931; Laureat of Acad. Sciences, Paris, 1933; University of Paris, D.ès.Sc. 1935; McGill University, M.D.C.M. 1943; Doctorat, honoris causa, Université de Bordeaux, 1949; Univ. d'Aix Marseille, 1960; McGill, 1971; Western, 1977; Queens, 1979 m. Margaret E., d.

Hon. Lincoln Goldie, Guelph, Ont., Aug. 1940; children: Stephen, Joan; PROF. EMERITUS, Centre de Recherche en Sciences Neurologiques, DEPT. DE PHYSIOL., UNIV. DE MONTREAL since 1976; Prof. Neurophysiology, 1965-76; Acting Dir., Dept. of Physiol., 1971-72; Nat. Research Council Fellow, Paris, 1931-33; Asst. Prof., Brown Univ., 1933-38; joined McGill Univ. as Asst. Prof. in 1938; Prof. Exper. Neurol., 1946-64; Dir., Labs of Neurophysiology and Electroencephalography of the Montreal Neurol. Inst.; 1st Extve. Secy., Internat. Brain Research Organization; published numerous papers in scient. and med. journs.; mem., Am. Physiol. Soc.; Hon. mem. Am. Neurol. Soc.; Assoc. mem. Am. Med. Assn.; mem. Candn. Neurol. Soc.; Hon. mem., First Pres., Am EEG Soc.; First Pres., Internat. Fed. of Soc. for EEG & Clin. Neurophysiol.; served in 2nd World War with R.C.A.M.C., 1943-45; Liberal; United Church; recreations: skiing, sailing; Home: 4501 Sherbrooke St. West, Apt. 1F, Westmount, Que. H3Z 1E7

JAWORKSA, Tamara, M.F.A., R.C.A.; painter; tapestry maker; b. Archangielsk, Russia; d. Antoni Jankowski; came to Can. 1969; e. State Acad. Fine Arts, Lodz, B.F.A. (Hons.) 1950, M.F.A. (art weaving) 1952; m. Tadeusz, s. Zygmunt J. 1957; children: Eva, Pyotr; Asst. Prof., Sr. Asst. Prof. and Lect., State Acad. Fine Arts, Poland 1952-58; Artistic Dir., Artist Guild "Lad" Poland 1954-59, "Cepelia" Polish Guild for arts and crafts 1963-68; Artistic Dir. (Lab.) design, Linen Indust. Poland 1959-63; exhns. incl. Warsaw and Lodz Art Galleries 1965; Pushkin Museum, European Art Gallery, Moscow 1966; Radom Art Museum 1966; Richard Demarco Gallery, Edinburgh and Scot. Woolen Art Gallery, Galashields, Scot. 1968; Fine Art Museum, Plymouth, Eng. 1968; Merton Gallery, Toronto; McLaughlin Gallery, Oshawa, Ont., Ont. Assn. Archs., Toronto; Holy Blossom Art Gallery, Toronto; Rothman's Art Gallery, Stratford, Ont. (all 1970); Hermitage Leningrad, USSR 1968; Nat. Art Gallery, Teheran, Iran 1968; Museum Modern Art, Mexico City 1969; Art Gallery of Ont. 1971 and 73; one-woman exhns. in Art Galleries of London & Windsor Ont. 1971; Glendon Art Gall., Toronto 1972; major solo exh. Art Gall. of Hamilton 1980; Academia Italia delle Arti e del Lavoro, Academitian of Italy 1980; solo exhib. France, West Germany, Belgium, Switzerland, Luxemburg 1982; rep. by Centre National de la Tapisserie D'Aubusson Galerie Inard, Paris, Boulevard St. Germain, France; exhn. later travelled to major Museums & Galleries in Madrid, Barcelona, Valencia, San Sebastian, Tarragona, Malaga 1980-81 & Paris 1981; tapestries owned by museums, galleries, public and private collectors in U.S., USSR, Poland, U.K., Switzerland, Sweden and Can.; comns. incl. "Unity" (32x22 ft.), Place Bell Canada, Ottawa 1972; IDS-Finch-1000, Metropolitan Life H.O., tapestry (18x9 ft.) 1974-75; "Quartet Modern" (4 tapestries, ea. 15x9 ft.), Bank of Montreal, First Canadian Place, Toronto; Gold Medallist, Internat. Exhn. Interior Design and Arch., Triennale de Milano 1957; Award for Excellence "Wool Gathering 73" Montreal 1973; Fellow, R.C.A.; mem. Candn. Guild of Craft; Home: 49 Don River Blvd., City of North York, Willowdale, Ont. M2N 2M8

JAWORSKI, Tad, M.F.A., R.C.A. film and TV producer-director; b. Poland, 20 Feb. 1926; s. Zygmunt and Teofila (Wroblewska) J.; came to Canada 1969; e. Gymnasium and Lyceum, Lodz, Poland 1945; Univ. of Lodz 1947; L. Schiller Acad. of Film & Theatre, Lodz, B.F.A. 1950, M.F.A. and Film Producer-Director Diploma 1952; m. Tamara, d. Antoni Jankowski, Warsaw, Poland 1957; children: Eva, Pyotr; Film Prod., Dir., Scriptwriter, Polish National Film Board 1952-68; TV Drama Producer, Polish National TV 1967-68; Documentary Film Producer and Dir., U.N., WHO Geneva, Switzerland 1964-68; Feature Film Producer-Director "Kamera" Group, Polish National Film Board 1967-68; writer, producer and dir. of numerous documentaries, features films, radio and TV dramas incl. "Africa '60" (best radio documentary award,

ZAIKS) 1960; "The Source 1962 (Warsaw Mermaid Critics Prize; Min. Culture & Art Great Prize; Bronze Dove, Leipzig Film Festival; Grand Prix & Golden Dragon Prize, Cracow Film Festival); "The Secretary" 1966 (Silver Laikon Award, Cracow Film Festival); "I was Capo" (Special Prize, Oberhausen Internat. Film Festival) 1963; "The Boys" 1966 (numerous awards incl. Golden Screen Independent Prize); "A Cry in the Emptiness of the World" 1967 (Best Stage Production and Most Outstanding TV Drama Award, Polish Min. Broadcasting & TV); recent Candn. works incl. "Miniatures" CBC 1970; "Selling Out" (feature documentary, Golden Etrog. Best Candn. Film 1972 & Academy Award "Oscar" Nomination 1973) 1972; "Canadian Artists" CBC 1972; also several documentary feature films in assoc. with CBC and private Candn. film cos.; Prod., dir. and co-author of documentary drama series, "The Jesus Trial", for TV Ont. 1977-78; Tutorial Film Leader, Stong Coll. York Univ.; Master of Cinematog. and Resident Film Producer, Humber Coll.; Fellow, Academic, Royal Canadian Acaemy of Arts, 1978; Producer Director, Feature Film "Betrayals", ITV, England and TV Ontario, 1979; Producer/Director, TV Series "World Shakers", TV Ontario and U.K., U.S. Networks, 1979; awards incl. Laureate of State Prize, Min. Culture and Art, Poland 1967; Cavalier Order Cross "Polonia Restituta" 1967; mem. Internat. Film Makers Assn.; Internat. Authors Assn.; author of numerous articles on aesthetic problems in film and TV; Lecturer in film and TV subjects at Canadian univs. and colls. since 1970; Home: 49 Don River Blvd., City of North York Willowdale, Ont. M2N 2M8

JAY, Charles Douglas, B.D., M.A., Ph.D., D.D. (United Church); educator; b. Monticello, Ont., 10 Oct. 1925; s. Rev. Charles Arthur and Luella Gertrude (McPherson) J.; e. Humberside Coll. Inst., Toronto, 1942; Univ. of Toronto, B.A. (Victoria Coll.) 1946, M.A. 1948, B.D. (Emmanuel Coll.) 1950; Univ. of Edinburgh, Ph.D. 1952; Queen's Univ., D.D. 1971; Wycliffe Coll., D.D. 1976; Regis Coll. D.D. 1980; m. Ruth Helen, d. late Mervyn Arthur Crooker, 30 Jan. 1948; three s. David, Ian, Garth; Principal-elect, Emmanuel Coll., Univ. of Toronto (1981); Philos. of Religion & Ethics, Emmanuel Coll., Univ. of Toronto, since 1963; Dept. of Philos., Queens Univ., 1946-47; o. 1950; Min., Elk Lake-Matachewan, 1952-54 and Trafalgar-Sheridan, 1954-55; joined Emmanuel Coll. as Asst. Prof., exhn. of Religion & Christian Ethics, 1955; Registrar 1958-64; AATS Fellow 1963; founding Dir., Toronto School of Theology, 1969-80; sabbatical leave spent in India and Far E.; served on Comn. on Accreditation, Am. Assn. Theol. Schs., 1962-68; R. P. McKay Mem. Lectr. various univs. and colls. across Can., 1966-67; Special Lectr. at Hankuk Theological Seminary, Seoul, Korea, 1978; mem. Working Group, Dialogue with People of Living Faith and Ideologies, World Council of Churches, since 1970; Chrm., Division of World Outreach, United Church of Canada, 1975-; writings incl. various book chapters; served with COTC 1943-45; Chaplain, RCN (R), 1956-59; Vice-Pres., Assn. of Theol. Schs. in U.S. and Can., 1976-78; mem., Am. Soc. Christian Ethics; Candn. Theol. Soc.; Candn. Soc. Study Religion; recreations: skiing, gardening; Home: 1606 Watersedge Rd., Mississauga, Ont. L5J 1A4; Office: Emmanuel Coll., 75 Queen's Park Cres., Toronto, Ont. M5S 1K7;

JAY, Rev. Eric George, M.A., B.D., M.Th., Ph.D. (Ang.), D.D. (Hon.); university professor; b. Colchester, England, 1 March 1907; s. Henry and Maude (Lucking) J.; e. High Sch. Colchester, Eng. 1917-24; Coll. of Resurrection, Mirfield Yorks, Eng. 1924-26, 1929-31; Leeds Univ. B.A. 1929, M.A. 1930; London Univ. B.D. 1937, M.Th. 1940, Ph.D. 1951; Hon. D.D., Montreal Diocesan Theol. Coll., 1964; Trinity Coll., Toronto, 1975; United Theol. Coll., Montreal, 1976; m. Margaret, d. Rev. Alfred Webb, Ashton Hayes, Cheshire, Eng., 22 July 1937; children: Christine, Susan, Peter; Prof. of Systematic Theol., McGill Univ., 1958-75; Prof. Emeritus, 1977; Dean, Faculty of Divinity there 1963-70; o. Deacon 1931 and Priest 1932; Asst. Curate, St. Augustine's, Stockport, Eng., 1931-34; Lect. in Theol. King's Coll., London, 1934-47; Asst. Curate, St. Andrew Undershaft, London, 1935-40; Rector, St. Mary-le-Strand, 1945-47; Dean of Nassau, Bahamas, 1948-51; Sr. Chaplain to Archbishop of Canterbury, 1951-58; came to Canada 1958; Princ., Montreal Diocesan Theol. College, 1958-64; served in 2nd World War as Chaplain, R.A.F., 1940-45; Fellow of King's College, London, 1958; author: "The Existence of God" 1948; "Origen's Treatise on Prayer" 1954; "New Testament Greek: an introductory Grammar" 1958; "Friendship with God" 1959; "Son of Man, Son of God", 1965; "The Church: Its Changing Image through Twenty Centuries", 2 vols. 1977-78; contrib. to "Church Quarterly Review", "Theology", "Candn. Journ. of Theol."; mem., Candn. Theol. Soc. (Pres. 1964-65); Home: 570 Milton St., Montreal, Que. H2X 1W4

JAY, R(aymond) Harry, B.A., B.C.L.; diplomat; b. Lachine, Que., 13 Aug. 1919; s. Lincoln P. and Mary Higginson (Dilworth) J.; e. St. Albans Sch., Brockville, Ont.; Northwestern High Sch., Detroit, Mich.; Wayne Univ.; McGill Univ., B.A. 1941, B.C.L. 1947; m. Dorothy V., d. Rev. (Maj.) Harry Andrews, M.B.E., E.D., 7 Sept. 1945; three s: Lincoln A., Michael H., Stèphen D.; joined Dept. of External Affairs 1948; served in Ottawa, India (1950-52), Indochina (1955), Geneva (1956-59); Depy. Perm. Rep., Candn. Del. to NATO, Paris, 1963-65; High Commr. in Jamaica, 1965-68; External Affairs Rep., Candn. Nat. Defence Coll., 1968; Dir. Gen., Bureau of U.N. Affairs 1968-73; Ambas. to Sweden 1973-76; Ambas. & Permanent Rep. to U.N.; Disarmament & GATT in Geneva 1976-79; Chief Air Negotiator, 1980-; has attended numerous internat. confs.; negotiated and signed for Can. U.N. Anti-Slavery Convention; Chmn. Exec. Cmte., U.N. Comm. for Refugees 1978-79; ret. from Dept. External Affairs, 1981; Exec. Sec., Xth World Congress on Prevention of Occupational Accidents and Diseases, 1981; served with RCAF 1941-45; P.O.W. Germany 1943-45; Sigma Chi; Anglican; recreations: golf, swimming, tennis, boating, flying, travel, music, theatre; Clubs: Caymanas Golf & Country; Jamaica; Liguanea; Royal Ottawa Golf; Address: Home: 806-20 Driveway Ottawa, Ont. Office: 500 - 300 Slater St., Ottawa, Ont.

JEAN, Hon. Bernard A., M.A.; judge; b. Lameque, N.B. 2 March 1925; s. Azade and Esther (Duguay) J.; e. Couvent Jesus Marie, Lameque, N.B.; Univ. St. Joseph B.A. 1946; Laval Univ. M.A. 1949; m. Corinne d. late Majorique Lanteigne, Caraquet, N.B. 3 Sept. 1955; children: Suzanne, Rodrigue, Maurice, Monique, Françoise, Isabelle; JUDGE, COURT OF QUEEN'S BENCH N.B.; el. M.L.A. N.B. 1960-72, Speaker of Legislature 1963-66, Min. of Justice 1966-70; mem. Candn. Centennial Comn. 1963-67; Bd. Govs. Univ. of N.B. 1965-71; called to Bar of N.B. 1951; cr. Q.C. 1966; R. Catholic; Home: (P.O. Box 267) Caraquet, N.B. E0B 1K0; Office: Queen's Bench Chambers, Court House, Bathurst, N.B.

JEANNERET, Marsh, O.C., B.A., LL.D., D.Litt., D.U.; publisher; author; b. Toronto, Ont., 9 Feb. 1917; s. François Charles Archile and Evelyn Frances Mildred (Geikie) J.; e. Univ. of Toronto Schs. (1934); Univ. of Toronto, B.A. 1938 (Hon. Law); McGill Univ., LL.D. 1966; Memoril Univ. of Nfld., D.Litt 1977; Laval Univ., D.U. 1978; m. Ethel Beatrice Mellon, 31 Dec. 1938; children: David Kenneth, Keith Marsh; Director, Univ. of Toronto Press, 1953-77 (ret.); formerly Dir., Copp Clark Co. Ltd. (publishing); President, Canadian Copyright Institute 1965-67; Pres. Candn. Book Publishers' Council, 1968; Special Consultant on Scholarly Publishing, Australian National Univ., Canberra, 1965; author of "Story of Canada", 1947; "Notre Histoire", 1949; "Canada in North America", 1961; various articles on publishing, educ., etc.; mem. Royal Comn. on Book Publishing (Ont.) 1970-73; mem. Cons. Group on Scholarly Publishing (Soc. Sci.

Res. Council) 1976-79; apptd. O.C. 1978; el. Pres. (first Candn.) of Assn. of Am. Univ. Presses, 1970; Pres., Internat. Assn. of Scholarly Publishers 1976-78; United Church; recreations: cruising, photography, classical recordings, amateur radio (VE3 EMJ); Club: Board of Trade; Home: R.R. 1, King City, Ont. L0G 1K0; Office: 5201 Dufferin St., Downsview, Ont. M3H 5T8

JEFFERIS, Jeffrey Douglas, M.A., Ph.D., D.C.L.; emeritus professor; b. London, Eng., 10 Feb. 1906; s. Percy William and Lillian (Douglas) J.; e. Christ's Hosp., Horsham, Eng.; Bishop's Univ., B.A. 1927; McGill Univ., M.A. 1929; Univ. of Toronto, Ph.D. 1934; Bishop's Univ., D.C.L. 1968; Fellow, Candn. Coll. of Teachers; m. Elizabeth (d. 1974), d. Frank Spooner, Cobourg, Ont., 1938; Asst. Master, Mount Royal High Sch., 1927-30; Crescent Sch., Toronto, 1930-31, 1936-38; Lectr. in Classics, Queen's Univ., 1932-33; Sr. Classical Master, Trinity Coll. Sch., Port Hope, Ont., 1934-36; Prof. of Classics, Waterloo Coll., Univ. of W. Ont., 1936-44; Prof. of Educ., Bishop's Univ., 1944-68; Reserve Army, 1940-45, with Univ. C.O.T.C.; author: "An Introduction to Educational Psychology", 1958; Anglican; Address: 12 Glendale, Lennoxville, Que. J1M 1Y3

JEFFERY, Alexander Haley, Q.C., B.A.; b. London, Ont., 29 Jan. 1909; s. James Edgar and Gertrude (Dumaresq) J.; e. Victoria Pub. Sch. and London S. Coll. Inst.; Univ. of W. Ont., B.A. (Hon. Econ. and Pol. Science) 1931; Osgoode Hall, Toronto, 1934; m. Eulalie E., d. William G. Murray, 29 June 1934; children: Alexander, Judith; PARTNER, JEFFERY & JEFFERY (estbd. 1890); Deputy Bd. Chrmn. London Life Ins. Co.; Pres. and Dir., Forest City Investments Ltd.; Director, Canada Trust-Huron and Erie; Thames Valley Investments Ltd.; London Realty Management and Rentals Ltd.; London Winery Ltd.; read law with Jeffery & Jeffery; called to Bar of Ont. 1934, and has since practised law with present firm; mem., H. of C. for London, 1949-53; mem., Candn. Bar Assn.; Assn. of Life Ins. Counsel (U.S.); Liberal; Anglican; recreations: yachting, sailing; Clubs: R.C.Y.C., (Toronto); Sarnia (Ont.) Yacht; Windsor (Ont.) Yacht; Port Stanley Sailing Squadron (Port Stanley); London Hunt & Country; London; London Curling; University (Toronto); Great Lakes Cruising; Home: 104 Commissioners Rd. E., London, Ont. N6C 2T1; Office: (P.O. Box 2095) London, Ont. N6A 4E1

JEFFERY, Cecil James; company executive (ret.); b. Sault Ste. Marie, Ont., 15 Sept. 1914; s. William James and Annie Hazel (Purdy) J.; e. Public and High Schs., Sault Ste. Marie, Ont. (Sr. Matric.); Corr. course in Engn.; m. Marjorie Leatha, d. Bartholomew Gordon Gray, Sault Ste. Marie, Ont., 25 Oct. 1947; employed in Groundwood Mill of Spruce Falls Power & Paper Co., 1931-37; left for New Zealand in Jan. 1938 to assist in opening the Whakatane Paper Mills; believed to be responsible for the operation of the first Groundwood Mill in S. Hemisphere; helped to conduct experiments in producing groundwood out of Aust. Eucalyptus wood in 1939, Melbourne, Aust.; after return from Melbourne became Asst. Mill Supt., of Whatkatane Paper Mills, N.Z.; served in 2nd World War; W.O.1, 2 N.Z. E.F. 27th Machine Gun Bn.; with 8th Army, N. Africa and Italy; rejoined Whakatane Paper Mills after leaving for Can., May 1946; joined Kalamazoo Vegetable Parchment Co., Espanola, Ont. to assist in opening mill; joined Great Lakes Paper Co. Ltd. Nov. 1947 as Asst. Groundwood Supt. and two mths. later promoted to Supt.; Mill Night Supt., 1952; Mill Mgr., 1954; Vice Pres.-Mfg. 1959 Board of Directors, 1966; Extve.Vice Pres., 1971-77; mem. of Extve. Council, Candn. Pulp & Paper Assn.; Ft. William Chamber Comm.; Freemason (32°); Protestant; recreations: golf, curling; Clubs: Gyro; Ft. William Country; Home: 1745 Murray Ave., Thunder Bay, Ont. P7E 5A9; Office: (P.O. Box 430), Thunder Bay, Ont. P7C 4W3

JEFFERY, Gordon Dumaresq, B.A., F.R.C.O., F.T.C.L.; barrister; b. London, Ont., 15 July 1919; s. James Edgar, K.C., and Gertrude (Dumaresq) J.; e. Pub. Schs. and South Coll. Inst., London, Ont.; Univ. of Western Ont., B.A. 1939; Osgoode Hall, Toronto, Ont.; read law with Fennell, Porter & Davis, Toronto; called to Bar of Ont. 1942; PARTNER, JEFFERY & JEFFERY; Dir., London Life Ins. Co.; began his practice with Jeffery in Jeffery in 1942; Past Pres., Royal Candn. Coll. of Organists; Liberal; Anglican; recreation: music; Clubs: London Hunt and Country; R.C.Y.C. (Toronto); Office: 174 King St., London, Ont. N6A 1C6

JEFFERY, Joseph, O.B.E. (1946), C.D. (1976), Q.C. (1955), LL.D. (1975); b. London, Ont., 1 Sept. 1907; s. James Edgar and Gertrude (Dumaresq) J.; e. London Pub. and Secondary Schs.; Osgoode Hall, Toronto, Ont.; Hon.LLD, U.W.O.; m. Nora Alicia, d. Rev. John Morris, St. Williams, Ont. 19 Oct. 1949; d. Elizabeth (by former m.); two s., Joseph and John Gordon; three d., Alicia, Jennifer, Deborah; PARTNER, JEFFERY & JEFFERY; Chrmn. Bd. London Life Ins. Co.; Chmn. Bd, Lonvest Corp.; Chrmn. Bd. and Dir., Duffwell Realties; Lonlife Data Services Ltd.; President and Dir., London Winery Ltd.; London Hunt Kennels Ltd.; Tobermory Islands Development Limited; Covent Garden Building Inc.; Vice-President and Director, Forest City Investment Limited; London Realty Management & Rentals Ltd.; Chrmn. and Dir., Lonlife Financial Services Ltd.; Secy.Treasurer and Lonvest Corp.; Secy. and Dir., London Broadcasters Ltd.; Secy. T Dir. Lonwin Holdings Ltd.; Treasurer and Dir., Dunwell Holdings Ltd.; Hagor Holdings Ltd.; Kilworth Holdings (London) Ltd.; Thames Valley Inv. Ltd.; Chrmn. Invst. cmte. and Dir., London Life Ins. Co.; Vice Chrmn., Exec. Cmte. Mem. and Resources Comte. mem., Thames Valley Dist. Health Council; Past. Gov. U.W.O.; Dir. Hiram Walker-Gooderham & Worts Ltd.; Hiram Walker Resources Ltd.; Past Dr., London Health Assoc.; Dir., Markborough Properties Ltd.; Lonwin Holdings Ltd.; Kilworth Holdings Ltd.; Canadian Enterprise Development Corporation Limited; Past Dir., Toronto-Dominion Bank Two Hundred Queens Ave. Ltd.; Boug Realty Ltd.; read law with Phelan and Richardson and with Jeffery and Jeffery; called to the Bar of Ont. 1930; cr. Q.C. 1955; served with R.C.N. 1940-46, retiring with rank of Captain; also acted as Secretary and mem., Naval Board of Canada; Past Hon. Col., London Service Bn.; Hon. Past Pres., Ont. Business & Comm. Teachers' Assn.; Hon. Vice-Pres., Candn. Arthritis & Rheumatism Soc.; London United Services Inst. (Past Pres.); Trustee, Y.M.C.A.-Y.W.C.A. Dir. Extve. Comte. Candn. Council of Christians & Jews; Candn. Extve. Service Overseas; Can.-Israel Chamber Comm. and Indust.; Can. Comte.; Life mem., and Past Pres., V.O.N.; mem., Extve. Comte. of Adv. Comte. of Sch. Business Adm., University of Western Ontario; former Vice-Chairman, Canadian Council, International Chamber Commerce; member Advisory Board, London Little Theatre; mem., Inst. Radio Engrs.; Law Soc. of Upper Can. London Cham. Commerce; Advis. Comte. Royal Cdn. Naval Benev. Fund; Past Bd. of Manage. and Invest, and Finance Cmte, V.O.N.; Newcomen Soc. in N. Am.; Candn. Business & Indust. Adv. Comte. for Organ. for Econ. Co-op. and Devel.; Candn. Chamber Comm. (mem. Adv. Comte. and past Pres.); U.N. Assn., London Br.; Club of Rome, Candn. Sec.); St. John Ambulance Assoc. (London Br.); Past Vice-Pres. and mem., Candn. Bar Assn. (mem. Council Ont. 1956-57, Vice-Pres. Ont. 1958-59); Candn. Inst. Internat. Affairs; Candn. Inst. Public Affairs; Ont.-Jamaica Partnership Foundation; Middlesex Law Assn.; rec'd. Human Relations Award, Candn. Council Christians & Jews 1956; Freemason; Liberal; Anglican; recreations: riding, fishing, yachting, amateur radio; Clubs: London Hunt & Country; Sarnia Yacht; Great Lakes Cruising; London Baconian; London City Press; The London; The Toronto (Ont.); St. Denis (Montreal, Que.); Royal Canadian Naval Sailing Assn.; Home: Black Acre

Place, R.R. 3, London, Ont. N6A 4B7; Office: 174-180 King St. (P.O. Box 2095), London, Ont. N6A 4E1

JEFFREY, Arnold H.; company president; b. Orford, Ont. 18 Aug. 1939; s. Harold R. and Irene (Griffith) J.; e. Pub. Schs., Windsor, Ont.; m. Gail d. Garfield Preston, 30 July 1960; Children: Craig, Susan, Peter, Andrea, Sean; CHAIRMAN & C.E.O., FIRST CITY TRUST COMPANY appt. Dec. 1980; Dir. & Sr. Vice Pres., First City Financial Corp. Ltd.; Dir. Endeavour Soc. of Vancouver; Aurora Czar Energy Co. Ltd., Chrmn., Pacific Northwest Equipment Leasing Corp.; Secy. & Dir., Mortifee Munshaw Ltd.; with Candn. Imp. Bank of Commerce, Toronto, 1956; Vice-Pres. and Dir., California Canadian Bank, San Francisco, 1964; joined Candn. Dom. Leasing Corp. Ltd. 1967 as Vice-Pres. and Treas.; Pres., 1969; Pres. & Dir., First City Trust Co., 1976; Catholic; recreations: reading, tennis, skiing; Clubs: Caledon Ski; Ontario; Bd. of Trade; Terminal City; Capilano Golf and Country; Holyburn Country; Home: 450 Southborough Dr., W. Vancouver, B.C. V7S 1M2; Office: First City Building, 777 Hornby St., Vancouver, B.C. V6Z 1S4

JEFFREY, James George, B.S.P., M.Sc., Ph.D.; university professor; b. Scott, Sask., 3 May 1917; s. George Jordan and Bertha Janie (Porteous) J.; e. Univ. of Sask., B.S.P. 1943, M.Sc. 1946; Univ. of Wisc., Ph.D. 1955; m. Joyce Dick, d. Peter L. McQuaker, Saskatoon, Sask., 3 July 1948; children: Ian G., Neil J., Alan P., Keith D., Jean A.; PROF. OF PHARMACY, UNIV. OF SASK. since 1956; served Pharm. apprenticeship with Moose Jaw Drug & Stationery Co. Ltd., 1936-39; joined staff of present Univ. as Instr. in Pharm., 1945; apptd. Asst. Prof. 1946; Assoc. Prof. 1948; served in 2nd World War, 1943-44; with C.O.T.C., 1942, and commd. Lieut.; Instr. Offr. in Candn. Active Army, June 1943; mem., Sask. Pharm. Assn.; Candn. Pharm. Assn.; Am. Pharm. Assn.; Assn. of Faculties of Pharm. of Can.; Baptist; recreations: woodworking, reading; Home: 22 Weir Crescent, Saskatoon, Sask. S7H 3A9

JEFFREY, Paul Goforth; business consultant; pres. and dir. P.G. Jeffrey and Co. Ltd.; b. Toronto, Ont., 12 Feb. 1926; s. David Ivory (missionary) and Ruth (Goforth, d. of Dr. Jonathan Goforth, a pioneer Presb. missionary in China from 1888-1938) J.; e. Chefoo, N. China; French Indo-China; Kimball Union Acad., Meriden, N.H.; Queen's Univ., B.A. (Econ.) 1949; m. Jane, d. J. Worden Edwards, 17 June 1950; children: Mary Elisabeth, Jennifer Susan, John Stephen David; DIR., F. H. DEACON HODGSON INC.; Mem. Advis. Bd., Bloorview Children's Hosp.; Council Ont. College of Art; after graduation spent five years with U.S. and Export Divs. of Massey-Ferguson Ltd.; Marketing Consultant, J. D. Woods and Gordon, 1954-57; Vice-Pres. and Mang. Service Dir., McCann-Erickson Canada Ltd., 1957-61; Extve. Vice-Pres., Sayvette Ltd., 1961; Pres. 1962-67; Pres. and C.E.O. of Sterisystems Ltd. 1967-77;served in 2nd World War with 1st Candn. Parachute Bn., 6th (U.K.) Airborne Div.; interned (as a civilian) by Japanese in French Indo-China, Dec. 1941-Aug. 1942; Anglican; recreations: golf, chess, military history; Clubs: University; Toronto Golf; GoodwoodHome: Wentworth Woodhouse, R.R. 3, Uxbridge, Ont. L0C 1K0; Office: Suite 600, 55 University Ave., Toronto, Ont.

JEFFRIES, Terence David; industrialist; b. Toronto, Ont., 18 Nov. 1921; s. Harold Clayton and Gladys Irene (White) J.; e. Runnymede Coll. Inst., Toronto, Ont.; Univ. of Toronto (1939-40); m. Ruth Amelia Dillon, 8 Sept. 1945; children: John Hugh, Mary Susan, Shirley Jane; 2ndly Shirley Grace McNally, 31 Jan. 1966; children: Nancy Louella, Linda Ruth; PRESIDENT VICEROY MFG. CO. LTD.; Pres., Viceroy Plastic Packages Ltd.; Candn. Concord Limited; Clerk, Viceroy Mfg. Co. Limited, 1940-42; Fruit Grower, Grimsby, Ont., 1945-50; rejoined present Co. as Clerk, 1950; Extve. Asst., 1951-52;

Manager, Canadian Concord Limited, St. Catharines, Ont., 1952-60; Manager of Canadian Vineyards Limited, Niagara Fruit Orchards Limited, and Pres. of T. D. Jeffries & Co. Ltd., 1955-60; served in 2nd World War with R.C.A.F. 1942-45 as Pilot; discharged with rank of Flying Offr.; recreation: boating; Home: 34 Castle Frank Rd., Toronto, Ont.; c/o General Delivery, Port Carling, Ont. P0B 1J0; Office: 1655 Dupont, Toronto, Ont. M3P 3S9

JELETZKY, Jurij (George) Alexander, F.G.S.A., F.R.S.C. (1970); geologist; b. Pensa, Russia, 18 June 1915; s. Alexander Grigorii and Halina Nicolas (Romanov) J.; e. High Sch., Ssaratov, Russia, 1932; State Univ., Kiev, Russia, 1938 (grad. as Geol.); Inst. of Geol. Sciences. Ukrainian Acad. of Sciences, Kiev (grad. studies), 1941; m. Tamara Fedorovna, d. Prof. F. P. Bohatirchuk, Ottawa, Ont., 22 June 1941; children: Alex, Olga, Theodore, Halina; GEOLOGIST (RESEARCH SCIENTIST), GEOL. SURVEY OF CANADA, since 1948; Scientist (palaeontol), Inst. of Geol. Sciences, Ukrainian Acad. of Sciences, Kiev, 1941-43; since present appt. has been engaged in research of cretacoeus (principally) jurassic, triassic and tertiary palaeontology and stratigraphy of W. and Arctic Can.; rec'd Willet G. Miller Medal of Royal Soc. Can. for outstanding research of basic nature in geol. (palaeontol and stratigraphy), 1969; Elkanah Billings Medal of Geological Assn. Can. for research in feld of Cndn Paleontology, 1978; author of about 130 scient. papers, reports and monographs published in Can. and abroad; mem., Palaeontol. Soc. Am.; Palaeontol. Assn. (Eng.); Greek-Orthodox; recreation: outdoor sports; Home: 500 Queen Elizabeth Drive, Ottawa, Ont., K1S 3N4; Office: 601 Booth St., Ottawa, Ont. K1A 0E8

JENKINS, Frederick Lionel; company president; b. London, Ont., 26 Jan. 1913; s. William Alexander Hunt and Katherine Edna (Elliott) J.; e. Lord Roberts Pub. Sch.; London (Ont.) Central Coll. Inst.; Ont. Agric. Coll.; m. the late Eleanor Noble, d. late John Kent Campbell, 12 Sept. 1934; children: William Alexander Kent, Judith May Burns; PRESIDENT, W. A. JENKINS MFG. CO. LTD. (Estbd. 1904, Mfr. of Feeds, Distr. of Seeds); Dir., Upper Thames Valley Conservation Authority; Chrmn., London Planning Bd., Dir., London Chamber of Comm.; Victoria Hosp. Corp.; Westminster Hosp. Co-ordinating Bd.; Middlesex Court Centre Corp.; member Ontario Assessment Review Court; London Jt. Parks Comte.; Central Middlesex Planning Bd.; Chrmn. (1959-70) London Housing Authority; Dir. (1962-65) Candn. Broadcasting Corp.; Candn. Mfrs. Assn.; Freemason (32° Scot. Rite; Past Potentate Mocha Temple Shrine); P. Conservative; Protestant; recreations: fishing, hunting; Clubs: The London; London Hunt & Country; Home: 465 Everglade Cres., London, Ont. N6H 4M8; Office: 359 Ridout St.N., London N6A 2N8

JENKINS, William, M.Sc., Dr. P.A.; association executive; b. New York City, 17 Oct. 1916; s. Hugh Alexander and Florence Ann (MacInnis) J.; e. N.S. Agric. Coll. (1938); Macdonald Coll., McGill Univ., B.Sc. (Agric.) 1942; M.Sc. 1947, Cornell Univ.; Harvard Univ. (1952-53); Dr. P.A. 1961; m. Rebecca Jean, d. William Retson, 1 July 1943; two d. Catherine Faye, Heather Jo; GOVERNOR, ATLANTIC PROVS. ECON. COUNCIL, ret. as Extve. Vice-Pres. 1977; Director, Atlantic Provinces, Canadian Executive Service Overseas, 1979-; formerly Princ. N.S. Agric. Coll.; Chrmn. Maritime Provinces Higher Euduc. Comm; Assoc. Dir., Extension N.S. Dept. of Agric., 1951-61; Chrmn., N.S. Land Settlement Bd., 1961-64; served in 2nd World War, Offr., 1st Candn. Parachute Bn.; mem., Agric. Inst. Can.; Candn. Agric. Econ. Soc.; N.S. Inst. Agrols.; Inst. of Assn. Extves.; Freemason; Baptist; Clubs: Golden K, Truro; Home: 165 Ryland Ave., Truro, N.S. B2N 2V5

JENNEKENS, Jon Hubert Felix, B.Sc., P.Eng.; b. Toronto, Ont. 21 Oct. 1932; s. Hubert Joseph and Laura Sessla

(Thorvaldson) J.; e. Royal Mil. Coll. Can. 1954 (Ridout-Van der Smissen Award 1954); Queen's Univ. B.Sc. 1956; m. Norah Margaret Aylesworth Magee 5 June 1954; children: Sandra Ellen, Jon Darren, Jennifer Norah; MEM., ATOMIC ENERGY CONTROL BD. since 1962; served with Royal Can. Elect. & Mech. Engrs. 1954-58, U.N. Forces S. Korea 1954-55, rank Lt.; mem. Chalk River Nuclear Labs. 1958-62; Hockey Coach, Alta Vista Recreational Assn. 1968-77; mem. Can. Progress Club (Past Pres., Past Regional Gov.); Bd. Stewards, Un. Ch. of Can.; mem. Assn. Prof. Engrs. Prov. Ont.; Assn. Scient. Engn. & Technol. Community Can.; United Church; recreations: skiing, boating, swimming; Home: 1815 Dorset Dr., Ottawa, Ont. K1H 5T7; Office: 270 Albert St., Ottawa, Ont. K1P 5S9.

JENNISON, George Leslie; financial consultant; b. New Glasgow, N.S., 19 June 1906; s. John Leslie and Florence (Des Barres) J.; e. Univ. of Toronto, 1923-25; m. Frances McPherson, d. S. B. Playfair of Toronto, Ont., 12 Oct. 1929; children: Joan (Mrs. Robert Wright), Elizabeth (Mrs. Wilson Mclean); Chrmn., Bd. of Govs., Toronto Stock Exchange, 1953-55; Dir., Canada Permanent Mortgage Corp.; Canada Permanent Trust Co.; mem., Bd. of Govs., Queen Elizabeth Hosp. Research Institute, Toronto; Past mem. of Council, Art Gallery of Ont.; Trustee, Un. Community Fund of Greater Toronto; Dir. of Priorites Br., Dept. of Munitions & Supply, 1941-45; Wills, Bickle & Co. Ltd., Partner 1945-57, Pres. 1957-66, Chrmn. of Bd. 1966-68; mem., Delta Kappa Epsilon (Pres., Alumni Assn. 1935-37); mem., Bd. of Trade Metrop. Toronto; Conservative; Anglican; recreations: hunting, fishing; Clubs: Toronto; Rosedale Golf; Canadian; York; St. Andrews Club (Florida); Home: 243 Warren Road, Toronto, Ont. M4V 2S7; Office: Suite 2350, South Tower, Royal Bank Plaza, P.O. Box 60, Toronto, Ont. M5J 2K6

JEROME, Harry W., O.C. (1970), M.Sc.; athlete; teacher; b. Prince Albert, Sask., 30 Sept. 1940; s. Harry Vincent and Elsie Ellen J.; e. N. Vancouver (B.C.) High Sch.; Univ. of Ore., B.Sc. 1964, M.Sc. 1968; one d., Deborah Catherine; teacher, Richmond Sch. Bd. 1964-65 and Vancouver Sch. Bd. 1965-67, B.C.; Research Asst., Univ. of Ore., 1967-68; Cross Can. Sports Demonstration, sponsored by Fitness and Amateur Sport Directorate, Dept. of Nat. Health & Welfare, 1968-70; Sport Consultant to Fitness & Amateur Sport, Ottawa, 1970-75; Sport Consultant, Sport B.C., 1975-80; mem. B.C. Sports Adv. Council 1968; Dir. Pacific Nat. Exhib. Bd., 1975-79 World Records; 100 meters (10.0), 100 yds. (9.1, 9.2, 9.2, 9.3), 4 x 100 yds. (40.0) mem. Univ. of Ore.; Candn. Records: 60 yds. (6.0), 100 yds. (9.1), 220 yds. (20.4), 100 meters (10.0), 200 meters (20.4); mem. of various Candn. teams 1959-68 incl.; Olympics Tokyo (3rd 100 m., 4th 200 m.) 1964; Univ. Games Budapest, 1965 (3rd 100 m.); Commonwealth Games 1966 (1st 100 yds.); Pan. Am. Games 1967 (1st 100 m.); won 20 Sr. Candn. Championships 1959-69; 5 times all Am. Coll. Track & Field Team, Univ. of Ore.; rec'd "Tait McKenzie" Service Award presented by Royal Candn. Legion 1967; mem. B.C. and Candn. Sports Hall of Fame; recreations: jogging, touch football, ice hockey, skiing; Home: 5998 Larch, Vancouver, B.C. V6M 4E4

JEROME, Hon. Mr. Justice James, P.C.; Judge b. Kingston, Ont., 4 March 1933; s. Joseph Leonard and Phyllis (Devlin) J.; e. St. Michael's Coll. High Sch., Toronto Univ. of Toronto, B.A. 1954; Osgoode Hall Law Sch., grad. 1958; m. Barry Karen Hodgins, 7 June 1958; children: Mary Lou, Paul, Jim Jr., Joey, Megan Phyllis; ASSOC. CHIEF JUSTICE, FEDERAL COURT OF CANADA 1980-; Privy Councillor 1981-; Elected to Sudbury City Council, 1965; el. to H. of C. for Sudbury in g.e. 1968; re-el., 72, 74 & 79; Vice Chrmn., Standing Comte. on Privileges and Els.; Chrmn., Special Committee on El. Expenses, 1970; Parlty. Secy. to Pres. of Privy Council and Govt. House Leader, 1970; mem. Can. delegation to NATO, 1972; Chmn., Standing Comte on Justice and Legal Affairs, 1972-74; elected Speaker of the House of Commons, 1974, and in 1979 became the first Speaker to be re-elected after a change of government; el. Pres. of the Commonwealth Parliamentry Assn., 1976; Liberal; R. Catholic; recreations: golf; music; Home: 22 Eisenhower Cres., Nepean, Ont.; Office: Supreme Court of Canada Building, Ottawa, Ont.

JESSUP, Hon. Arthur R.; judge; b. Montreal, Que., 13 Nov. 1914; s. John Arthur and Margaret Ethel (Cassidy) J.; e. Univ. of Toronto, B.A. 1936; Osgoode Hall Law Sch., Toronto, Ont.; m. Vera M., d. Kenneth Halladay, Toronto, Ont., 25 Jan. 1946; children: Mary, John, Colleen, Ann Catherine, Margaret; JUSTICE, COURT OF APPEAL ONT., since Sept. 1967 (apptd. to Supreme Court, Aug. 1964); read law with T. N. Phelan, Q.C.; called to the Bar of Ont., 1939; cr. Q.C. 1959; served in 2nd World War with Candn. Army, 1942-46, N.W. European Campaign;retired with rank of Major 21 C.A.R. (G.G.F.G.); Mentioned in Despatches; rec'd. Order of Leopold II, Croix de Guerre, 1940; Anglican; recreations: fishing, golf, reading; Clubs: Essex Golf & Country (Windsor); The Windsor (Ont.); Home: 96 The Kingsway, Toronto, Ont. M8X 2T8; Office: Osgoode Hall, Toronto, Ont. M5H 2N7

JEWISON, Norman Frederick, B.A., LL.D.; film producer and director; b. Toronto, Ontario, 21 July 1926; s. Percy Joseph and Irene (Weaver) J.; e. Malvern Coll. Inst., Toronto, Ont. (Matric.); Victoria Coll., B.A. 1940-44; Univ. of Toronto, 1950; LL.D. Western Ont. 1974; m. Margaret Ann, d. James Nelson Dixon, 11 July 1953; children: Kevin Jefferie, Michael Philip, Jennifer Ann; joined CBC, 1952-58; CBS, 1958-61; Universal Studios, 1961-64, where he directed the motion pictures "40 Pounds of Trouble", "The Thrill of It All", (1963); "Send Me No Flowers", (1964); as a Free Lance, 1964-68; directed "Art of Love", "The Cincinnati Kid", (1965); produced and dir. "The Russians Are Coming", (1966); dir., "In The Heat of the Night", produced and dir. "The Thomas Crown Affair", (1967); dir. "Gaily, Gaily", (1968); produced "The Landlord" (1969); produced and directed "Fiddler on The Roof" (1970); "Jesus Christ Superstar" (1972); produced "Billy Two Hats" (1972); "Rollerball" (1974); produced & dir. "F.I.S.T." (1977); "And Justice for All" (1979); Exec. producer "Dogs of Warù", 1980; mem. Bd., Festival of Festivals, Toronto 1981; presenter of C.N.E. student film award, 1980 and 1981; directed Belafonte, Jackie Gleason, Andy Williams, Judy Garland, Danny Kaye TV shows; produced 1981 Academy Awards; rec'd. Academy Award Nominations 1966-67, 72, 74; Directors Guild Nominations 1966-67; Golden Globe Award (Foreign Press) 1966; Emmy Award 1960; Emmy Nominations, 1961 and 1962; TV Directors Award, 1961; Candn. Liberty Award, 1958; Judge of Monte Carlo Internat. TV Festival, 1966; Faculty mem., Inst. for America Studies 1969, Salzburg, Austria; served as Pres. of Jury, Avoriaz Film Festival (France) 1981; served with R.C.N., 1945-46; Liberal; Protestant; recreations: skiing, yachting, tennis; Office: Knightsbridge Films Ltd., 18 Gloucester St., 5th floor, Toronto, Ont. M4Y 1L5.

JOBIN, Pierre, M.D., F.R.C.S.(C); retired university professor; b. Que. 8 Sept. 1907; s. Albert and Julie-Anna (Delage) J.; e. Que. Semy.; Laval Univ., B.A. 1927, M.D. 1932; post-grad. studies in France and Eng., 1934-37; m. Blanche C. de Lery, Quebec, 6 Feb. 1970; one s., Pierre; Prof. of Anatomy, Laval Univ., 1944-75; Asst. étranger en Chir. de Lyon, France, 1935; Asst. Surg., Hotel-Dieu Hosp., Que., 1937; Lectr. in Anat., Laval Univ., 1938, Assoc. Prof. 1940, Dir. Continuing Med. Educ. 1963; apptd. Med. Consultant to Roy. Comn. on Health Service, July 1961; mem., Soc. Méd. des Hôpitaux Univ.; Assn. des Méd. de Langue Française de Can.; Am. Assn. Anat.; Assn. French-speaking Doctors (Pres. 1960); Liberal; Roman Catholic; recreations: fishing, golf, singing; Clubs:

Richelieu; Home: 610 Chemin St-Louis, Quebec, Que. G1S 1B8

JODREY, John J.; industrialist; PRES., MINAS BASIN PULP & POWER CO. LTD.; Pres. and Dir., Avon Foods Ltd.; Chrmn., Scotia Investments Ltd.; Pres. & -Dir., Canadian Keyes Fibre Co. Ltd.; Dir., Maritime Paper Products Ltd.; Crown Life Insurance Co.; L. E. Shaw Ltd.; Bank of Nova Scotia; Algoma Central Railway; Extendicare Ltd.; Chairman of Board and Director, Halifax Developments Limited; Freemason (Scot. Rite); Baptist; recreations: golf, boating; Clubs: Halifax (N.S.); National (Toronto); Chester Golf (Chester, N.S.); Office: Prince St., Hantsport, N.S. B0P 1P0

JOHNS, Charles Frederick (Air Vice Marshal, RCAF, ret.), M.B.E., E.D., C.D., B.Sc., LL.D., P.Eng.; b. Portsmouth, Eng., 24 Nov., 1903; s. Reuben and Elizabeth Ann (Slocombe) J.; e. Royal Tech. Coll., Portsmouth (1916-19); H.M. Dockyard Sch., Bermuda (1919-24); Mount Allison Univ., B.Sc. 1930; m. late Cecil Record, d. late Frank R. Brown, Wells, Eng., 28 July 1930; children: Beatrice Elizabeth, (Mrs. T.D. Peters, Ottawa), Deborah Lue (Mrs. J.G. Fauquier, Ottawa) m. Bette L. Morrison, d. late H.C. Morrison, Q.C., Oct. 1973; ; Pres., Oromocto Development Corp. (Crown Co.) since March 1969; Special Adv. to Min. of Nat. Defence (Planning) 1963-68; Chief Engr., Enterprise Foundry Co. Ltd., Sackville, N.B., 1930-39, and Chief Engr. and Asst. Sales and Adv. Mgr. there, 1946-50; Dir. Constr. Engn., RCAF, Ottawa (Group Capt.), 1950-51; Chief of Constr. Engn. RCAF Overseas, 1951-53; Special Asst. to Minister of Nat. Defence, 1953-55 (Air Commodore); Asst. Dept. Min. of Nat. Defence, 1955-63; served in O.T.C., 1926-30; Princess Louise 8th (N.B.) Hussars, 1930-39; 2nd World War, 1939-46; Constr. Engn. Offr., RCAF (Sqdn. Leader), 1939-42; Dir. of Mech. and Elect. Engn., 1942-45 (Wing Commdr.); Chief of Constr. Engn., 1945-46 (Group Capt.); awarded M.B.E.; mem. of Town Council, Sackville, N.B., 1947-50, and Sch. Bd., 1947-50; mem. of Extve. Comte. and Bd. of Regents, Mount Allison Univ., 1947-52 and 1963-76; mem., Engn. Inst. Can.; Reg'd. Prof. Engr. since 1931; Anglican; recreation: boating; horseback riding Clubs: Royal Bermuda Yacht Club; Royal Can. Military Inst.; University; Home: 59 Russell Ave. (Apt. 1), Ottawa, Ont. K1N 7W9 and Brooking Cottage, Somerset Bridge, Bermuda.

JOHNS, Harold Elford, O.C., Ph.D., LL.D., F.R.S.C. (1951); university professor; b. Chengtu, West China, 4 July 1915; s. Alfred Edward and Myrtle Madge J.; e. McMaster Univ., B.A. 1936; Univ. of Toronto, M.A. 1937, Ph.D. 1939; Univ. of Sask., LL.D. 1959; McMaster 1970; D. Sc. Carleton Univ., 1976; D.Sc. Univ. of Western Ont., 1978; m. Alice Sybil, d. late Stonewall Jackson Hawkins, 15 June 1940; children: Gwyneth, Claire, Marilyn; PROF. OF MED. BIOPHYSICS, UNIV. OF TORONTO, since 1962; Head, Physics Div., Ont. Cancer Inst. 1956-80; Prof., Dept. of Physics, Univ. of Toronto, since 1956; Lectr. in Physics, Univ. of Alberta, 1939-45; during 2nd World War, Lectr. in radar to Air Force and Navy Personnel, Univ. of Alberta, 1939-45; Official Radiographer of aircraft casting for W. Can., 1942-45; Asst., Assoc. Prof. of Physics, Univ. of Sask., 1945-56 (also Physicist, Sask. Cancer Comn.); named Saskatoon's (Sask.) Citizen of the Year, 1952; Roentgen Award, Brit. Inst. of Radiology, 1953; Henry Marshall Tory Medal, Royal Royal Soc. Can.; Gairdner International Award 1973; Offr. Order of Can. 1977; Gold Medalist, Am. Coll. of Radiology, 1980; author of: "The Physics of Radiation Therapy", 1953; "The Physics of Radiology", 1961 (3rd edition 1970); also over 200 papers in scientific journals; holds a number of patents on the design of Cobalt 60 units for treatment of cancer; Chrmn., Healing Arts Radiation Protection Cmte., 1981-; mem., British Institute of Radiol.; Candn. Assn. Radiol.; Candn. Assn. Physicists; Candn. Assn. Med. Physicists (Pres. 1962); Am. Phys. Soc.; Am. Radium

Soc.; Am. Assn. of Physicists in Med.; Soc. of Photographic Scientists & Engrs.; Radiation Research Soc.; United Church; Home: 4 Boxbury Rd., Etobicoke, Ont. M9C 2W2; Office: 500 Sherbourne St., Toronto, Ont. M4X 1L1

JOHNS, Martin Wesley, M.A., Ph.D., F.R.S.C. (1958); physicist; retired university professor; b. Chengtu, Szechuan, W. China, 23 March 1913; s. Rev. Alfred Edward and Myrtle Madge J.; e. Canadian Sch., W. China; High Schs. in Tacoma, Wash., Vancouver, Brandon and Exeter, Ont.; Brandon Coll. (1928-31); McMaster Univ., B.A. 1932, M.A. 1934; Univ. of Toronto, Ph.D. 1938; m. late Margaret Mary, d. Edwin Hilborn, Hamilton, Ont., 15 July 1939; children: Robert, Elizabeth, Kenneth and Kathryn (twins); re-married, Elaine North, 1981; Prof. of Physics, McMaster Univ., 1953-81; Co-ordin., Part-time Degree Studies in Adult Educ., 1977-81; Chrmn. of Dept. of Physics, 1961-67 and 1970-76; Lectr. in Physics; Brandon Coll., 1937-38; Prof. of Physics there, 1938-46; Assoc. Research Physicist, Nat. Research Council, Chalk River, Ont., 1946-47; Asst. Prof., McMaster Univ., 1947-48, Assoc. Prof., 1948-53; Visiting Prof., Oxford Univ., 1959-60; Colombo Plan "expert" sent to Pakistan, 1960; Visiting Scientist Chalk River Nuclear Labs., 1967-68; served in C.O.T.C., 1940-41; research concerned with neutron physics (Chalk River), nuclear spectroscopy (McMaster); Publications: 100 papers in these fields; actively interested in Un. Ch. as Layman, and has served on many Ch. Comtes. at Local and Nat. level; Co-Chrmn., Family Life Comte. of Un. Ch. 1954-67; Dir., Family Services of Hamilton -Wentworth, 1977-79; Pres. Ontario Assn. of Family Service Agencies, 1979-81; United Church; recreations: swimming, hiking, gardening; Home: 116 Sterling St., Hamilton, Ont. L8S 4J5

JOHNS, Walter H., O.C., B.A., Ph.D., LL.D., D. ès L.; professor emeritus; b. Exeter, Ont., 10 Nov. 1908; s. William Charles and Martha (Hern) J.; e. High Schs., Exeter and Goderich, Ont.; Univ. of Western Ont., B.A. (Hons. Classics) 1930, LL.D. 1959; Cornell Univ., Ph.D. (Classics and Ancient Hist.) 1934; Laval Univ., D. ès L. 1964; LL.D. Sask. 1968, Waterloo Lutheran 1968, Alberta 1970; m. Helen Elizabeth, d. late Robert N. Merritt, Waterloo, Ont., 9 Jan. 1937; two d., Barbara Ann (Mrs. Dennis Hutchins), Mary Elinor (Mrs. P.M. Bentley), 4 grand children; PROF. OF CLASSICS, UNIV. OF ALBERTA 1969-73; Lecturer in Classics, Waterloo Coll., Waterloo, Ont.; 1934-38; joined staff of Univ. of Alberta in 1938 as Lectr. in Classics; Asst. to the Dean of Arts and Science, 1945; Asst. to the Pres., 1947; Dean of Arts & Science, 1952; Vice-Pres., 1957; Pres. 1959-69; served on Senate of St. Stephen's Coll., Edmonton for several yrs. to 1958; Offr. Order of Can. 1978; Pres., Assn. of Univs. and Colls. Can., 1966-67; mem. of Council, Assn. of Commonwealth Univs.; mem. Adv. Selection Comte. for the Order of Canada; assoc. with various church, sch. and community services; Alta. Achievement Award. 1977; City of Edmonton Cultural Award, 1978; City of Edmonton 75th Aniversary "Builder of the Community" Award 1979; mem., Am. Philol. Assn.; Classical Assn. Can. (mem. of Council for several terms); served in C.O.T.C., Univ. of Alta., 1941-45; United Church; recreation: golf; Club: Mayfair; Home: 103 Fairway Dr., Edmonton, Alta. T6J 2C2

JOHNSON, Albert Wesley, M.A., M.P.A., Ph.D., O.C.; Canadian Broadcasting Corp.; b. Insinger, Sask., 18 Oct. 1923; s. Rev. Thomas William and Louise Lillian (Croft) J.; e. Wilcox (Sask.) Secondary Sch.; Univ. of Sask., B.A.; Univ. of Toronto, M.A.; Harvard Univ., M.P.A., Ph.D.; L.L.D. (H.C.) Univ. of Regina, 1977; L.L.D. Univ. of Regina, 1978; m. Ruth Elinor, d. Rev. R. W. Hardy, 27 June, 1946; children: Andrew, Frances, Jane, Geoffrey; PRESIDENT, C.B.C. since 1975; formerly Depy. Min. of Welfare 1973-75, Secy. Treasury Bd. 1970-73, and Assist. Depy. Min. Finance 1964-68, Gov. of Can.; Econ. Advisor

to Prime Minister on the Constitution, 1968-70; served with Candn. Army 1942; Depy. Prov. Treas. & Secy. to the Treas. Bd., Govt. of Sask., 1952-64; mem. Bd. of Dirs., Nat. Film Bd.; Nat. Arts Centre; rec'd. Gold Medal, Prof. Inst. of Pub. Service of Can.; Vanier Medal; mem., Commonwealth Broadcasting Assn.; Candn. Pol. Science Assn. (Extve. Council 1963-64); Inst. of Pub. Adm. Can.; has contrib. articles to prof. publs.; mem. Bd., Univ. of Sask. Hospital, 1957-64; United Church; Home: 1042 Castle Hill Cres., Ottawa, Ont.; Office: 1500 Bronson Ave., Ottawa, Ont. K2C 2A8

JOHNSON, Allison Heartz, M.A., Ph.D., D.Litt., F.R.S.C.; professor; b. Vancouver, B.C., 12 December 1910; s. Arthur Livingstone and Lena Harrison (Heartz) J.; e. Mt. Allison Univ., B.A. 1931; Univ. of Toronto, M.A. 1932, Ph.D. 1937; Univ. of Chicago, 1934-35; Harvard Univ., 1936-37; m. Helen Margaret, d. Adam H. Bolender, Rockford, Ill., 1 July 1935; two d.; Sandra Margaret (Mrs. Albert H. Oosterhoff), Sheila Elizabeth (Mrs. Hugh M. Kindred); Sr. Prof. of Philos., Univ. of Western Ont., 1964-76, now Prof. Emeritus; Acting Prof., Philos., Waterloo Coll., 1936; Instr., Philos. and Psychol., Univ. of W. Ont., 1937; Prof. and Head of Dept. of Philos., 1948-64; Publications: "Whitehead's Theory of Reality", 1952; "Whitehead's Philosophy of Civilization", 1958; "Experiential Realism", 1973; "Philosophers in Action", 1977; "Modes of Value", 1978; also editor of several books on philos.; numerous articles in prof. journs.; mem., Candn. Philos. Assn. (Pres. 1962-63): Am. Philos. Assn.; Mind Assn.; Aristotelian Soc.; D.Litt. Mount Allison 1972; Univ. of W. Ont., 1979; United Church; recreations: music, gardening; Club: University; Home: 1639 Richmond St. N., London, Ont. N6G 2M9

JOHNSON, Arthur Joseph Fynney, M.B.E., C.D., Q.C., M.A., B.C.L.; b. Vancouver, B.C., 15 Feb. 1915; s. Joseph Fynney and Alice Gertrude (Jones) J.; e. Sir William Van Horne Pub. Sch. and John Oliver Secondary Sch., Vancouver, 1931; Univ. of B.C., B.A. 1935, M.A. 1936; Oxford Univ. (Rhodes Scholar for B.C. 1936), B.A. 1938, B.C.L. 1939, M.A. 1942; m. Catharina, d. late H. W. van der Ploeg, Holland, 10 Jan. 1946; children: Harold M. G., Nelie Catharina, Philip D. A.; PARTNER, DAVIS & COMPANY; read law with E. Slade, St. John's Coll., Oxford; called to Bar of B.C. 1939; cr. Q.C. 1969; Asst. to Supvr. for B.C. Foreign Exchange Control Bd., 1939-41; Second Secy., Dept. of External Affairs, Ottawa, 1946-47; served with Candn. Army Overseas 1941-46; Lt. Col. Commdg. B.C. Regt., Candn. Militia, 1951-54; mem. Vancouver Sch. Bd. 1964-68 (Chrmn. 1968); mem. Vancouver Police Commission 1970-74; Governor, St. George's Sch., Vancouver; mem., Candn. and Vancouver Bar Assns.; Un. Services Inst. Vancouver (Past Pres.); Psi Upsilon; Anglican; recreations: golf, hiking, gardening; Clubs: Vancouver; Shaughnessy Golf & Country; Home: 1550 Laurier Ave., Vancouver, B.C. V6J 2V3; Office: 1030 W. Georgia, Vancouver, B.C. V6E 3C2

JOHNSON, Bernard T., B.A.Sc.; business executive; b. Toronto, Ont., 31 July 1921; s. Reuben and Nellie Louise (Gallois) J.; e. Univ. of Toronto Schs., 1939; Univ. of Toronto, B.A.Sc. (Chem Engn.) 1943; m. Shirley Marie Tait; children: Susan, Carol, Jane, Liane, Steven, Mark, James; EXEC. VICE-PRES. GENSTAR LTD.; joined Sogemines Ltd. (Genstar predecessor) as Project Engr., 1956; Vice Pres., Brockville Chemical Industries Ltd. (Genstar subsidiary, 1963; Vice Pres., Genstar Ltd. and Pres.; Iroquois Glass Ltd. (Genstar subsidiary), 1966; Chmn. & C.E.O., Genstar Chem. Ltd. 1970; served with RCAF as Pilot Offr. (Navig.) 1943-45; Past Chrmn. Extve. Council, Candn. Chamber of Comm.; Candn. Fertilizer Inst.; mem., Assn. Prof. Engrs. Prov. Ont.; Chem. Inst. Can.; Soc. Chem. Indust.; Theta Delta Chi; Anglican; recreations: skiing, tennis. Home: 2486 Butternut Dr., Hillsborough, Calif. 94010; Office: 3 Embarcadero Center, San Francisco, Calif. 94111

JOHNSON, Bradley R., B.F.A., M.L.A., R.C.A.; landscape architect; b. Toronto, Ont. 9 Oct. 1936; s. Robert Theodore and Ethel Isabel (Lisk) J.; e. Univ. of Ill. B.F.A. 1958 (Edward L. Ryerson Fellow); Harvard Univ. Grad. Sch. of Design, Master of Landscape Arch. 1963 (Charles Elliot Fellow); m. Mary d. Wallace Irl Johnston 28 Feb. 1959; two d. Lisa, Brooke; PARTNER AND DIR., JOHNSON SUSTRONK WEINSTEIN & ASSOCIATES, TORONTO 1966- ; Dir. Heine Johnson Sustronk Weinstein & Associates Ltd. Edmonton; Brad Johnson & Associates Ltd.; joined Project Planning Associates Ltd. Toronto 1958-66, Chief Landscape Arch. 1965-66; planning and design of land devel., incl. new communities in Toronto, Oakville, Edmonton and Fort Worth, Texas; Waterfront devel. incl. Harbour City Etobicoke Sector Toronto Waterfront; consultant to municipal, prov. and fed. agencies for numerous park and recreation studies and designs in Ont. and West. Can. incl. the master plan for the Metro Toronto Zoo, Humber Arboretum, Little River Corridor, Windsor; designs for various priv. and pub. proj. incl. IBM, Bank of Montreal, American Express head off., Bell Trinity, Art Gallery of Ont. and the Grange, Atmospheric Environment, Royal Ont. Museum re-development, Rideau Centre Complex and Major's Hill Park Ottawa, Chubb Cay Bahamas; Market Square, Toronto; Adjunct Prof. of Landscape Arch. Univ. of Toronto; Univ. of Guelph; mem. Bd. Stratford Seminar on Civic Design 1965-66; Foundation for Aggregate Studies; author various articles landscape arch.; Fellow, Candn. Soc. Landscape Archs.; mem. Ont. Assn. Landscape Archs.; Royal Candn Academy of Art; Am. Soc. Landscape Archs.; Delta Upsilon; Scarab; recreations: golf, tennis, sailing, skiing; Home: 21 Dale Ave., Apt. 516, Toronto, Ont. M4W 1K3; Office: 290 Merton St., Toronto, Ont.

JOHNSON, Clifford Henry, B.S.; manufacturer; b. Minneapolis, Minn. 31 March 1925; s. late Henry J. and Ethel I. Johnson; e. Barron, Wisc.; Univ. of Wisc. B.S. (M.E.); m. Rose d. Robert Hermann 28 Aug. 1949; children: Clifford Jr., Mrs. Mary Eymann, Mrs. Pamela Ehrlich; PRES., CHIEF EXTVE. OFFR. AND DIR. GOODYEAR CANADA INC. 1981- ; Pres. and Dir. Kelly-Springfield Canada Inc.; Dir. Hallmark Auto Centres; Seiberling Canada Inc.; Production Sqdn. Trainee, Goodyear Tire & Rubber Co. Akron, Ohio 1951, held various sales and mang. positions in U.S. prior to appt. as Vice Pres. Gen. Products Goodyear Canada Inc. Toronto 1977, apptd. Vice Pres. Tire Sales 1979, Extve. Vice Pres. and Chief Operating Offr. 1980; mem. Bd. Trade Metrop. Toronto; Automotive Sales Council; Freemason; Shriner; Protestant; Club: Mississauga Golf & Country; served with U.S. Navy 1943-47, rank Lt.; Home: 458 Linden Lane, Oakville, Ont. L5H 3K1; Office: 21 Four Seasons Place, Islington, Ont. M9B 6G2.

JOHNSON, F. Ross, B.Comm., M.B.A.; industrialist; b. Winnipeg, Man., 13 Dec. 1931; s. Frederick Hamilton and Caroline (Green) J.; e. Univ. of Manitoba, B.Com.; Univ. of Toronto, M.B.A.; LL.D. (Hons.) Univ. St. Francis Xavier (Antigonish N.S.) 1978; LL.D. (Hons.) Memorial Univ. of Newfoundland, 1980; two s. Bruce, Neil; m. (2nd) Laurie Ann, d. Robert A. Graumann, Mar. 1979; two s. Bruce, Neil; PRES. & C.E.O., NABISCO BRANDS INC. 1977-81; Dir., Wosk's Ltd. Vancouver; Bank of Nova Scotia, Toronto; joined Standard Brands Ltd. (Can.) 1971 Pres. 1971; joined Standard Brands Inc. 1973; Sr. Vice-Pres. and Dir. 1974; Pres. 1975; Chrmn. and Chief Operating Offr. 1976; Vice Chmn., Adv. Council, Columbia Univ. business school (New York); The Economic Club of New York; Chrmn., The Nat. Multiple Sclerosis Soc. (New York City Chapter); New York City Geographic Soc. (New York City Chapter); Phi Delta Theta (Pres. 1951); recreations: golf, skiing, tennis; Clubs: The Brook; The Links; Blind Brook; Deepdale Connecticut Golf (Easton Conn.); Home: 210 East Mountain Rd., Sparta, N.J. 07871; Office: 9 West 57th St., New York, N.Y. 10019.

JOHNSON, Frederick Paul, B.Sc., P.Eng.; retired executive b. Edmonton, Alta.; s. late Francis James and Clara M. (Fyle) J.; e. Pub. and High Schs., Edmonton; Univ. of Alberta, B.Sc. (Elect. Engn.) 1939; m. Jacqueline Mary, d. late Fraser M. Johnston, 29 May 1943; one d., Paula Jacqueline; joined C.B.C. in 1939 as Transmitter Engr. at CBK, Watrous, Sask.; served C.B.C. as War Corr. with Candn. forces in Eng., N. Africa, Sicily, Italy, France, 1942-44; returned to Can. 1944 and apptd. Asst. Sr. Engr., Internat. Service C.B.C. (Radio Can. Internat.); Sr. Engr. 1948; Asst. to Dir. of Engn. 1954; Dir. of Special projects (Engn), C.B.C. 1962 mem. Assn. of Prof. Engrs. of Ont.; Protestant; recreations: gardening, boating, travel, woodworking, music; Home: 1217 Field St., Ottawa, Ont. K2C 2P9;

JOHNSON, Hon. Frederick William, B.A., LL.B.; judge; b. Sedgley, Staffordshire, Eng. 13 Feb. 1917; s. Edwin Priestley and Laura (Caddick) J.; e. Univ. of Sask., B.A. 1947, LL.B. 1949; m. Joyce Marilyn d. William Laing, Stockholm, Sask. 30 July 1949; children: William Frederick, Dr. Royce Laing Caddick, Sheila Frederika; CHIEF JUSTICE, COURT OF QUEEN'S BENCH SASK. since 1977; called to Bar of Sask. 1950; cr. Q.C. 1963; law practice Johnson, Bayda, Trudelle & Beke; apptd. Justice, Court of Queen's Bench Sask. 1965; served with RCA 1941-46 UK and W. Europe; Trustee Regina Pub. Sch. Bd. 1956-60; Chrmn. Royal Comn. on Govt. Adm. (Sask.) 1964-65; Bencher, Law Soc. Sask. 1960-65; United Church; Clubs: Assiniboia; United Services Inst.; Home: 121 Leopold Cres., Regina, Sask. S4T 6N5; Office: Court House, Regina, Sask. S4P 3V7

JOHNSON, Ven. George Harold, M.A., B.D., D.D. (Ang.); retired; b. Sunderland, Ont., 8 Dec. 1909; s. Rev. George Isaac Bray and Alice Stuart (Curry) J.; e. Public and High Schs., Toronto, Ont.; Univ. of Toronto, B.A. 1930, M.A. 1932; Trinity Coll., Toronto, Ont., B.D. 1936, D.D. 1944; m. Margaret Katherine, d. late Horace Gravenor, 31 Oct. 1936; one d. Joanne Margaret; o. Deacon, 1932, Priest, 1933; Asst., St. Clement's Ch., Toronto, Ont., 1932-36; Rector, Omemee, Ont., 1936-40; Newmarket, Ont., 1941-45; Rector, St. Chad's, Toronto, 1945-62; Archdeacon of Toronto West, 1956-62; Archdeacon of Urban Parishes, 1962-66; Archdeacon of the Diocese, 1966-77, and Extve. Assistant to the Bishop of Toronto and Chaplain to the Chapel of St. Peter & St. Paul, 1973-77; mem., Trinity Coll. Clerical Alumni Assn.; P. Conservative; recreations: sports, baseball, hockey, travel; Club: Albany; Home: P.O. Box 1027, Bracebridge, Ont. P0B 1C0

JOHNSON, Gordon Edward, B.Sc.Phm., M.A., Ph.D.; educator; b. Welland, Ont. 21 Sept. 1934; s. Edward and Dorothy (Williams) J.; e. Univ. of Toronto B.Sc.Phm. 1957, M.A. 1959, Ph.D. 1961; m. Mary-Jane Graham d. Graham Bowles, Toronto, Ont. 20 Sept. 1958; children: Dorothy, Ian, Warren, Louise, Edward, Rebecca; PROF. AND HEAD OF PHARMACOL. UNIV. OF SASK. since 1973; Chrmn. Drug Quality Assessment Comte. Sask. Prescription Drug Plan; Asst. Prof. Univ. of Toronto 1963, Assoc. Prof. 1966, Prof. 1971-73; Visiting Prof. Med. Research Council Can., Drug Metabolism Labs. CIBA Ltd. Basel, Switzerland 1968-69; author over 50 scient. articles; Fellow, Am. Coll. Clin. Pharmacol.; mem. Pharmacol. Soc. Can.; Am. Soc. Pharmacol. & Exper. Therapeutics; mem. Am. Soc. Clin. Pharmacol. Therapeutics; Lambda Chi Alpha; Protestant; recreations: music; farming; Home: R.R.5, Saskatoon, Sask. S7K 3J8; Office: Univ. of Sask., Saskatoon, Sask. S7N 0W0.

JOHNSON, Irene, M.A.; Canadian public service; b. Winnipeg, Man., 5 March 1925; d. Charles and Irene Alyea (LaBerge) Flint; e. Univ. of Toronto, B.A. (Law) 1947, M.A. (Econ.) 1949; London Sch. of Econ., post-grad studies in Econ.; m. Geoffrey Phipps Johnson, Dec. 1953, div. 1973; one s., Blaine; ASST. DEP. MIN., PERSON-

NEL AND MNGT. PRACTICES, ENERGY, MINES AND RESOURCES CAN., since 1981; Cdn. High Commissioner, Wellington, N.Z., Dept. External Affairs with Accreditation to Fiji, Western Samoa, Tonea, Kiribati and Tuvalu; 1978-81; Lectr., Sch. of Business Adm., Univ. of W. Ont., 1952-54; Econ., N.S. Dept. Trade & Indust., Halifax, 1956-62; Econ. & Research Br., Dept. of Labour, Ottawa, 1962-64; Econ., Area Devel. Agency, Dept. of Indust., 1964-67; Finance Officer, Econ. Devel. Div., Dept. of Finance, 1967-69; Chief, Analysis & Devel. Sec., Dom. Bureau of Stat., 1969-71; Group Chief, Manpower Group, Social & Cultural Div., Treas. Bd., 1971; Commn., Pub. Service Comn. of Can., 1971-76; Ex: Dir., Employment Training, Can. Employment & Immig. Comn, 1976-78 N.V.R. since 1952, rank Sub-Lt.; former Dir., Civil Service Recreational Assn.; mem. Candn. Inst. Internat. Affairs (Chrmn. 1967-68); Candn. Econ. Assn.; Inst. of Pub. Adm. of Canada (Extve. Comte); Internat. Personnel Mang. Assn.; Am. Economic Assn; Civil Service Co-op. Credit Soc. (Mem. of Exec. 197-8); Board of Gov. Carleton Univ. (1976-78); recreations: theatre, music, skiing, golf, cycling, wilderness canoeing; Home: 205 Irving Pl., Ottawa, Ont. K1Y 1Z7; Office: 580 Booth St., Ottawa, Ont.

JOHNSON, John Thomas, Q.C., B.A.; b. Toronto, Ont., 6 Aug. 1913; s. John and Charlotte (Southwell) J.; e. Univ. of Toronto, B.A. 1935; Osgoode Hall Law Sch., Toronto, 1938; m. the late Marie Valentine, d. late Emile Darte, Welland, Ont., 28 June 1947; children: John Emile, Marie-Jeanne, Michael Charles, Marie-Suzanne; PARTNER, BORDEN & ELLIOT; Dir., Stanton Pipes Ltd.; Mercantile Bank of Can.; Standard Brands Ltd.; read law with Jos. Sedgwick, Q.C.; called to Bar of Ont. 1938; cr. Q.C. 1953; practiced with Grierson, Creighton & Fraser, Oshawa, Ont., 1939-42; joined Borden, Elliot, Sankey & Kelley (now present firm), 1942; admitted to partnership 1956; Club: University; Home: 98 Bedford Rd., Toronto, Ont. M5R 2K2; Office: 250 University Ave., Toronto, Ont. M5H 3E9

JOHNSON, Patrick Trench, M.A.; headmaster; b. Kalacherra, Assam, India, 4 April 1926; s. Francis Richard, D.F.C. and Phyllis Mary (Wilkinson) J., e. Emscote Lawn Prep. Sch., Warwick, Eng., 1930-39; Rossall Sch., Fleetwood,Eng., 1939-44; Queen's Coll., Oxford Univ., B.A. 1951, M.A. 1956, m. Eleanor Jean, d. Andrew D. McCain, Florenceville, N.B., 21 Aug. 1954; children: Patrick Trench, Jr., Derek Wallace McCain; GEN. MGR., THE SPENCER HALL FOUNDATION Asst. Gen. Mgr., Corporate Personnel, The Bank of Nova Scotia 1975-81; Principal, Upper Canada College, Sept. 1965-Jan. 1975; Master, Graham-Eckes Sch., Palm Beach, Fla., 1951-53; Rossall Sch., Fleetwood, Eng., 1953-58; Upper Can. Coll., since 1958 and Housemaster from 1960; Pres., Can. Securities Inst.; served as Capt. and Adj. with 3rd Bn. 9th Gurkha Rifles, Indian Army, 1944-48; Anglican; recreations: tennis, swimming, walking, bridge, theatre; Address: 116 Dunvegan Rd., Toronto, Ont.

JOHNSON, Hon. Pierre Marc, M.N.A., B.A., LL.L., M.D.; politician; b. Montreal, Qué. 5 July 1946; s. late Daniel (Prime Min. of Qué. 1966-68) and Reine (Gagné) J.; e. Coll. Jean-Bréboeuf Montréal B.A. 1967; Univ. de Montréal LL.L. 1970; Univ. de Sherbrooke M.D. 1975; m. Marie-Louise d. Douglas Parent 30 June 1973; children: Marc Olivier, Marie-Claude; MIN. OF SOCIAL AFFAIRS, QUÉ. 1981- ; called to Bar of Qué. 1971; admitted Qué. Coll. of Phys. & Surgs. 1976; mem. Bd. and various comtes. Oxfam Can. and Oxfam Qué. 1969-76; el. M.N.A. for Anjou 1976; mem. Nat. Extve. Council Parti Québécois 1977-79; Min. of Labour and Manpower 1977-80; R. Catholic; recreations: swimming, music; Home: 16 Roskilde St., Outremont, Qué. H2V 2N5; Office: Parliament Bldgs., Québec City, Qué.

JOHNSON, Richard Golding, B.A., LL.B.; b. Calgary, Alta., 3 Mar. 1913; s. Percy Wilfrid and Lottie May (Gold-

ing) J.; e. Pub. Schs., Calgary, Alta.; Strathcona High Sch., Edmonton, Alta., Univ. of Alberta, B.A. 1933; LL.B. 1935; m. Emily Irene, d. C. W. Loney, Owen Sound, Ont., 1940; has one s., Robert Golding; CONSULTANT TO C.I.S.C. Chrmn. Can. Construction Mngt. Inst.; admitted to the Bar of Alta., 1936; articled at law and practised with Milner, Steer & Co., Edmonton, Alta., 1935-37; Estates Offr., London & Western Trusts Co. Ltd., Toronto, and Trusts Offr. at the Co's. H.O., London, Ont., 1937-40; Solr.; Legal Br., Dept. of Mun. & Supply, 1940-41; Contracts Offr., Asst. Dir. and Dir., Defence Projects Br., Dept. of Mun. & Supply, 1941-44; Secty. Dept of Reconstruction and Supply, 1944-45; Gen. Mgr., Candn. Construction Assn., 1945-55; loaned to Candn. Govt. as Constr. Consultant, Candn. Commercial Corpn., Oct. 1950; Pres. and Gen. Mgr., Defence Construction (1951) Ltd. (Crown Co.) 1950-63 (on loan from Candn. Construction Assn., 1950-55); Extve. Vice-pres., Canadn Inst. of Steel Construction, 1963-66; Pres. of C.I.S.C., 1966-78; recreations: golf, swimming; Club: Rideau; Home: 21 Dale Ave., Toronto, Ont. M4W 1K3; Office: 201 Consumers Rd., Willowdale, Ont. M2J 4G8

JOHNSON, S. Ross, B.Com., C.L.U.; life insurance executive; b. Calgary, Alta., 18 Apl. 1929; s. Stanley C. and Margaret C. (Fisher) J.; e. King Edward Pub. Sch. and W. Can. High Sch., Calgary; Univ. of B.C., B.Com.; m. Muriel Helen, d. Henry G. Fairley, Calgary Alta., 15 July 1953; 4 children; Susan Kim, Judy Lynn, Grant Ross, Warren Scott; EXEC. VICE PRES., THE NATIONAL LIFE ASSURANCE CO. OF CAN. 1979-; joined present company as Exec. Vice President in 1979. Prior to that spent 27 years with New York Life Insurance Co.; Past Secy. Bd. of Govs., Alta. Coll.; Edmonton; mem., Bd. of Dir., Nat. Life, 1980; Continental Ins. Co. of Can., 1981; Dominion Ins. Corp., 1981; Life Underwriters Assn. Can.; Univ. Club, Toronto; Delta Upsilon; Freemason; P. Conservative; United Ch. (St. John's, Oakville); recreation: fishing; Home: 1312 Cleaver Dr., Ennisclair Park, Oakville, Ont. L6J 1W4; Office: 522 University Ave., Toronto, Ont. M5G 1Y7

JOHNSTON, Archibald Frederick, B.Com.; executive; b. Peter's Rd., P.E.I. 9 March 1919; s. Frederick William and Christy Annie (MacLeod) J.; e. elem. and high schs. Murray River and Charlottetown, P.E.I. 1937; Prince of Wales Coll. Charlottetown 1945-46; Queen's Univ. B.Com. 1949; m. 1stly Frances Ann d. James Haunts, Kingston, Ont. 20 Feb. 1945 (d.); children: James Archibald Frederick, Heather Ann Ellen, Alexandra Frances, Margaret Ellen MacLeod; m. 2ndly Elizabeth d. Ferdinand Van Siclen Parr, Morristown, N.J. 6 March 1982; VICE PRES. PUBLIC AFFAIRS & GOVT. RELATIONS, CANADIAN GENERAL ELECTRIC CO. LTD. 1979- ; joined present Co. as Consultant to Appliance Dealers 1949, Mgr. Operations W. Ont. Dist. 1953 and W. Dist. B.C. & Alta. 1955, Mgr. Finance Wholesale Dept. 1957, Mgr. Que. Dist. Wholesale Dept. 1960, Mgr. Corporate Planning Services 1966, Mgr. Corporate Relations 1968, Vice Pres. & Gen. Mgr. Supply Sales & Distribution Dept. 1970 and Gescan Business Dept. 1974-79; named Elect. Man. of Yr., Elect. News & Engn. 1970; served with Royal Candn. Corps Signals 1939-45 Can. & Overseas, rank Capt., Reserve Army 1945-52; Dir., Inst. Pol. Involvement; Jr. Achievement Metrop. Toronto; Queen's Univ. Alumni; mem. Elect. & Electronic Mfrs. Assn. Can. (Dir.); P. Conservative; Anglican; recreations: sailing, golf, cross-country skiing, reading; Clubs: Royal Candn. Mil. Inst.; Port Credit Yacht; Summerlea Golf & Country (Montreal); Home: 58 Glencairn Ave., Toronto, Ont. M4R 1M8; Office: (P.O. Box 417) Commerce Court, Toronto, Ont. M5L 1V2.

JOHNSTON, Bruce F., B.Eng.; b. Schnectady, N.Y., 4 Sept. 1924; s. Bruce Henry and Lillian Emma (Fraser) J.; e. Lower Canada Coll., Montreal, Que.; McGill Univ., B.Eng.; m. Bunty Jessie, d. John M. Moffat, 28 July 1956;

children: Scott Fraser, Lisa Ewen, Sandra Moffat; CHRMN. BOARD & PRESIDENT THE SPECTRUM GROUP LTD. Pres. & Dir. Kimlease Ltd.; Sanlisco Ltd.; Dir. Case Assoc. Advertising Ltd.; Jean Léveillé & Associés Inc.; McKim Advertising Ltd.; Vrlak Robinson Advertising Ltd.; commenced as International Management Trainee, Lever Bros. Limited, Can. & U.K. 1948, Brand Mgr., Toronto 1950; joined McKim Advertising Ltd., Montreal 1952, Vice-Pres. 1956, el. a Dir. 1958, Extve. Vice-Pres. 1964, Pres., 1966-74 Chrmn. Exec. Cmte. And C.E.O. 1975-77; served in R.C.A.F. during 2nd World War; 417 Sqdn.; Pilot, Flying Offr.; Past Pres. & Gov., Inst. Candn. Advertising; recreations: golf, skiing; Clubs: Mississauga Golf; Royal Montreal Golf; Home: 1368 Ravine Dr., Mississauga, Ont. L5J 3E7; Office: P.O. Box 305, Commerce Court E., Toronto, Ont. M5L 1G1

JOHNSTON, Charles Bernie, Jr., B.A., M.B.A., educator; b. Sudbury, Ont. 3 June 1931; s. Charles Bernie and Beatrice Eileen (Gilpin) J.; e. Sch. of Business Adm. Univ. of W. Ont. B.A. 1954, M.B.A. 1957; m. Carol Jean d. Ernst T. Querney, Sudbury, Ont. 22 Aug. 1953; children: Charles David, Jeffrey Philip, Craig Matthew, Laura Myerling, Nancy Anne Beatrice; PROF. AND DEAN OF BUSINESS ADM., UNIV. OF W. ONT. also Chrmn. Continuing Educ. and Dir. Mang. Training Course since 1972; Dir. Pathex (Canada) Ltd.; Photochemical Research Associates Inc.; The Quaker Oats Co. of Canada Ltd.; Promotion Co-ordinator, Proctor and Gamble Co. of Canada Ltd. 1954; Gen. Mgr. C. B. Johnston Ltd. 1955; joined Univ. W. Ont. 1957, Assoc. Dean of Business Adm. 1975-78; Visiting Prof. IMEDE Mang. Devel. Inst. Lausanne, Switzerland 1967-68; co-author "How Industry Buys" 1959; Contrib. 2nd Ed. 1965 and co-author 3rd Ed. 1972 "Canadian Problems in Marketing"; author numerous cases in Marketing; Chrmn. of Bd. London (Ont.) French Sch. 1970-71; mem. Am. Marketing Assn.; Administrative Sciences Assn. Can.; Delta Upsilon; Protestant; Home: 165 Hunt Club Dr., London, Ont. N6H 3Y8; Office: London, Ont. N6A 3K7.

JOHNSTON, Hon. Dick, B.A., M.B.A., C.A.; politician; b. Lethbridge, Alta. 5 March 1940; s. Archibald Stewart J.; e. Lethbridge sch. system; Univ. of Alta.; Univ. of Calgary B.A., M.B.A.; m. Janice Lynn d. Douglas T. Phillips, Lethbridge, Alta. 16 May 1964; children: Carolyn Jane, Suzanne Marie, Barbara Boyne, David R. M.; MIN. OF FEDERAL AND INTERGOVERNMENTAL AFFAIRS, 1979-; Min. of Mun. Affairs, Alta. since 1975-79; C.A. practice Johnston & Associates, Lethbridge, Alta. 1969-75; Mang. Consultant, D. Johnston Management Consultants, Lethbridge 1969-75; el. M.L.A. for Lethbridge E. 1975; re-el. M.L.A. for Lethbridge E., March, 1979; app. Minister of Federal and Intergovernmental Affairs, Gov't of Alta, March, 1979; mem. Bd. Lethbridge Community Coll.; Dir. Victorian Order Nurses Lethbridge Br.; mem. Alta. Inst. C.A.'s; P. Conservative; United Church; recreations: skiing, mountain climbing; Home: 3223 105th St., Edmonton, Alta. T6J 2Z9; Office: 127 Legislative Bldg., Edmonton, Alta. T5K 2B6.

JOHNSTON, Hon. Donald James, P.C., B.A., B.C.L.; politician; b. Ottawa, Ont. 26 June 1936; s. Wilbur Austin and Florence Jean Moffat (Tucker) J.; e. Montreal High Sch.; McGill Univ.; Grenoble Univ.; m. Heather Bell d. James MacLaren, Halifax, N.S. 11 Dec. 1965; children: Kristina, Allison, Rachel, Sara; PRES. OF TREASURY BD. 1980- ; el. to H. of C. for Montréal St-Henri-Westmount by-el. 1978, re-el. since; Clubs: St. James's; Montreal Indoor Tennis; Liberal; Protestant; Home: 4080 Highland Ave., Montreal, Que. H3Y 1R3; Office: House of Commons, Ottawa, Ont. K1A 0A6.

JOHNSTON, Frances-Anne, R.C.A. 1963 (Mrs. Franklin Arbuckle); b. Toronto, Ont., 9 Oct. 1910; d. Francis Hans (Frank H.) and Florence (Jamieson) J.; e. Ont. Coll. Art; m. Franklin s. George Lyon Arbuckle, 15 June 1934; children: Candace (Mrs. David Shaw), Robin (Mrs. Peter N. Quinlan); mem., Ont. Soc. Artists; R.C.A. (1948); R. Catholic; Address: 278 Lawrence Ave. E., Toronto, Ont. M5M 4M1

JOHNSTON, George, M.A., Ph.D., D.D., LL.D.; educator, Minister, United Church, Can.; b. Clydebank, Scotland, 9 June 1913; s. William George and Jennie (McKeown) J.; e. Glasgow Univ., M.A. (Hons.), 1935 and B.D. (with Distinction) 1938, D.D. 1960; Marburg Univ., 1938; Cambridge Univ., Ph.D. 1941; United Theological Coll., D.D. 1974; Montreal Diocesan Theological Coll., D.D. 1975; Mt. Allison Univ., LL.D. 1974; Brown Downie Fellow in New Testament, 1937; Black Theol. Fellow, Glasgow Univ., 1938; Maxwell Forsyth Fellow, Trinity Coll., Glasgow, 1938; Cleland & Rae Wilson Gold Medals in New Test. & Divinity; A.A.T.S. Faculty Fellowship, 1967; Canada Council Leave Fellowship, 1975-76; m. Alexandra, d. late John Gardner, M.D., 6 Aug. 1941; children: Christine, Ronald, Janet; PROFESSOR, NEW TESTAMENT, McGILL UNIVERSITY 1959-81 (Dean, Faculty of Religious Studies 1970-75); Fac. Lecturer, Christian Theology, 1981-82; Gov., McGill Univ. 1971-75; Bruce Lectr., Trinity Coll., Glasgow, 1940-43; Min. of Martyrs' Ch., St. Andrews, Fife, Scot., 1940-47; Pres., Ch. of Scot. Young Men's Guild, 1942-45; Assoc. Prof. of Ch. Hist. & New Testament, Hartford (Conn.) Semy. Foundation, 1947-52; Kellner Mem. Lectr. in New Testament, Episcopal Theol. Sch., Cambridge, Mass.; 1951; Prof. of New Testament Lit. and Exegesis, Emmanuel Coll., Victoria Univ., Toronto, Ont., 1952-59; Principal, United Theol. Coll., Montreal, 1959-70, Prof. 1976-; R.T. Orr Visitor, Huron Coll., London, Ont., 1971; served in 2nd World War; Acting Chaplain, 7th Black Watch, 51st Highland Div., 1945; author of: "The Doctrine of the Church in the New Testament", 1943; "The Secrets of the Kingdom", 1954; "Ephesians-Philippians-Colossians-Philemon" (The New Century Bible), 1967; "The Spirit-Paraclete in the Gospel of John" 1970; Ed. "The Church in the Modern World" (with W. Roth), 1967; contrib. "Peake's Commentary", 1962; "Interpreter's Dict. of the Bible", 1962; "Hastings' Dict. of the Bible", 1963; several composite vols. and Festschriften, and various religious journs.; Commr. Un. Ch. Gen.-Council, 1958, 1966, 1968; mem., Soc. of Biblical Lit.; recreations: music, early Christian art & Celtic archaeology; Address: 39 Clarke Ave., Apt. 1C, Montreal, Que. H3Z 2E7

JOHNSTON, B. Gen. Ian Strachan, C.B.E. (1945), D.S.O. (1943), E.D., C.D.(1967), Q.C., LL.D.(1973); b. Toronto, Ont. 12 Aug. 1908; s. Strachan and May Murray (Walker) J.; e. Upper Can. Coll.; Ridley Coll.; Roy. Mil. Coll., 1930; Osgoode Hall, 1933; m. Debora Elizabeth Coulson Armstrong, d. John L. Coulson, 18 Feb. 1947; Hon. Dir., Candn. Paraplegic Assn.; Past Pres., Candn. Red Cross Soc.; R.M.C. Club of Can.; read law with Tilley, Johnston, Thomson & Parmenter; called to the Bar of Ont. 1933; cr. K.C. 1947; served in World War, 1939-45; with 48th Highlanders 1939; Lieut.-Col. in Command, in Sicily and Italy, 1943; Commdr., 11th Candn. Inf. Bgde., 1944; N.W. Europe 1944; Commdr., 5th Candn. Armoured Divn., 1945; Commdr., 4th Inf. Bgde. (Reserve) with rank of Brig., 1946; awarded Bar to D.S.O. 1944; Mentioned in Despatches; Chevalier, Legion d'Honneur; Croix de Guerre avec Palme; Hon. Col., 48th Highland, 1967-71; served in Candn. Mil., 1930-39; Lieut., 48th Highlanders; Anglican; Clubs: York; Homes: 24 Chestnut Park Rd., Toronto, Ont. and "Brackmont", RR2, Aurora, Ont.; Office: P.O. Box 11 Royal Bank Plaza, Toronto, Ont. M5J 2J1

JOHNSTON, Hon. John Franklin, M.L.A.; politician; MIN. OF ECON. DEVELOPMENT, MAN. 1978- AND OF TOURISM 1979- ; el. M.L.A. for Sturgeon Creek prov. g.e. 1969, re-el. since; Min. without Portfolio 1977-78; Min. Responsible for Man. Housing & Renewal Corp.

1977-80; P. Conservative; Office: 358 Legislative Bldg., Winnipeg, Man. R3C 0V8

JOHNSTON, Lawrence Hugh, B.Com., F.C.A.; manufacturer; b. Hamilton, Ont., 4 May 1918; s. Lawrence Bastedo and Aleda Pearl (Neil) J.; e. Queen's Univ., B.Com. 1940; m. Mildred Kathleen, d. John C. Wright, 9 Apl. 1949; three children; CHMN., DIR. AND CHIEF EXTVE. OFFR., CANADIAN CANNERS LTD.; joined Price Waterhouse & Co., Toronto, 1940-51; trans. to Hamilton, Ont., 1951-58; served with R.C.N.V.R. 1941-45; Pres., Hamilton Chapter, Financial Extves. Inst., 1965-66; Chrmn., Hamilton & Dist. C.A.'s Assn., 1958-59 Pres. Cndn. Food Processors Assn., 1972-3; Chrmn. McMaster University Medical Centre, 1978-9; Bd. of Gov., McMaster Univ.; Dir. Fireman's Fund Ins. of Can, Fidmore Mortgage Investors Corp.; Chmn. Bd. of Trustees and Exc. Comm., Chedoke-McMaster Hospitals; United Church; recreations: golf, curling, fishing; Clubs: Hamilton; Hamilton Golf & Country; Hamilton Thistle; Home: 311 Golf Links Rd., Ancaster, Ont. L9G 2N6; Office: 44 Hughson St. S., Hamilton, Ont. L8N 2A7

JOHNSTON, Patricia Cherie, B.A.; economist; b. Tillsonburg, Ont. 20 March 1950; d. William Pitcher and Rosemary (McInerny) J.; e. Annandale High Sch. Tillsonburg; Trent Univ. B.A. (Pol. Econ.) 1973; VICE PRES. LEGISLATIVE AFFAIRS, CANDN. FED. OF INDEP. BUSINESS; Dir. Candn. Inst. for Econ. Policy; mem. Long-range Planning Adv. Council, Ont. Educ. Communications Authority; Research Assoc., Bureau of Mun. Research Toronto 1973; Ont. N.D.P. Queen's Park 1974; independent econ. policy consultant 1977; Dir. of Policy and Research, Candn. Fed. of Independent Business 1978; Dir., Econ. & Pub. Affairs, Toronto Stock Exchange, 1979; author, various monograms & articles; mem. Toronto Assn. Business Econs.; Innovation Mang. Inst. Can.; recreations: canoe trips, snowshoeing, running; Home: 90 Kilbarry Rd., Toronto, Ont. M5P 1K7; Office: 4141 Yonge St., Toronto, Ont. M2P 2A6

JOHNSTON, Peter Arthur Edward, B.A.; diplomat; b. Toronto, Ont., 18 Sept. 1921; s. George Arthur, Q.C. and Gladys Madeleine (Baker) J.; e. Univ. of Toronto, B.A. 1948; m. Rosanne d. Rupert Hughes, 15 Sept. 1973; children: Celia, Stuart, Geoffrey, Sarah; joined Nat. Research Council Ottawa 1948-57; Dept. of External Affairs 1957, First Secy. London 1962, Counsellor Dar-Es-Salaam 1966, Dir. Security and Intelligence Liaison Div. Ottawa 1968, Min. Tokyo 1972, Ambassador to Indonesia 1974-77; Amb. to Czechoslovakia 1977-81; Ambassador to Venezuela and Dominican Republic, 1981-; served with Candn. Army UK, Sicily, Italy, France, Holland 1940-45, Mentioned in Despatches; recreations: tennis, squash, golf; Address: Canadian Embassy, Venezuela

JOHNSTON, Randolph Wardell, sculptor; graphic artist; writer; b. Toronto, Ont., 23 Feb. 1904; s. Howard Addison and Gertrude (Wardell) J.; e. Central Tech. Sch., Toronto, Ont.; Univ. of Toronto; Ont. Coll. of Art, Toronto; Central Sch. of Arts & Crafts, London, Eng.; independent study in France, Italy, Mexico; m. Muriel Grace Norman (died 1927), 1926; one d., Mrs. A. F. Galarneaux; 2ndly, Margaret Kate, d. Wm. Broxton, DeLand, Fla., 19 June 1937; children: William Wardell, Paul Dennithorne, Jeremy Peter; taught at Central and Riverdale Tech. Schs., Toronto, Ont., 1927-31; Cummington Sch., Mass., (summers) 1931, 1932; Eaglebrook Sch., Bement Sch., and Deerfield Acad., Mass., 1933-40; Dir. Deerfield Studios, 1933-37; Asst. Prof., Smith Coll., 1940-50; Assoc. Prof., Univ. of Mass., 1950; Pres., Turnip Yard Bronze Co. Inc., Deerfield, Mass., 1947-49; Mgr., Chelsea Pottery Nassau, Bahamas, 1959-60; has exhibited at O.S.A. and R.C.A. shows, Toronto, Montreal, Nat. Gallery, Ottawa, Whitney Museum of Am. Art, N.Y., Metrop. Museum, N.Y.; Penna Acad., Soc. of Ind. Artists, N.Y., Soc. of Audubon Artists, Tate Gallery, London, etc.; one-man

shows, Toronto, Boston, Springfield (Mass.), New York, Cleveland, Providence (R.I.), etc.; Bust, Lorne Pierce, Queen's Univ., Kingston, Ont-1925; Bronze groups: "Five that Escaped", Univ. of Nebraska, 1945; "Panic" 1949 Comnd. and purchased sculptures in several Candn. and Am. cities; Publications: "The Country Craft Book", 1937; "The Practice of Direct Casting", 1940; "The Direct Casting of Figures", 1941; "Escapists Notebook" in "The Rudder", 1956; "Mexican Indian Pottery" in "Leisure", "The Book of Country Crafts", 1965; "Artist on his Island" 1975; est. Little Harbour Press, 1976; "Survive Man! or Perish," 1980; subject of TV documentary by Curt Clausen QCTV (Edmonton) 1975; Comns. incl.: Monument to Chief Mettawanpe, 1950; portrait bust Mrs. Julie Lauer-Leonardi, N.Y., 1960; "The Kiss" (life size terra cotta group); "Old Woman Who Never Dies" (bronze group), St. Thomas, Virgin Is., 1964; Crucifix (bronze and buttonwood), Cathedral St. Francis Xavier, Nassau, 1965; heroic size monumental bust of Sir George Roberts, 2 bronze casts, House of Assembly, Nassau, and Sir George Roberts Mem. Park, Harbour Island 1965; Merman and Mermaid capitals, French Bldg., Nassau; Bronze groups: "World at War", "Death and Everyman", "Nine Ages of Man", for California collection, 1969-74; "Springtime", "Birth of Aphrodite", "Razor's Edge" in limited editions for private collectors; in Montreal, Peterborough, Ont. and other cities, 1970-78; Bronze, "Undine", Atlanta, Ga. 1965; 20 bronze portrait busts and heads in New York, Chicago, Miami, Minneapolis, St. Louis, etc. 1966-75; Life size casuarina nude, "Daphne", Toledo, O., 1972; "Effort to Evolve", St. Eustasius, (N.W.I.), 1972; heroic size "Fisherman and Wife", Jumbey Village, Nassau, 1973; "Monument to Bahamian Woman", Nassau, 1974; "Poise and Counterpoise", 1976-78; "We are All Brothers" Woodstock, Ont. (also in Col.) Okla., Cal.) 1976-79; "Flame of Life" 1975-79; "Springtime", "Aphrodite" 1975-77; "Burden of Evil" and "Man With the Burden" 1976-79; bronzes for collectors in Toronto, Edmonton, Germany, France, 1974-9; Portrait heads and reliefs 1975-78; "Orpheus and Eurydice," 1979; "Joy of Youth," 1979; "Life an Ocean — Time a Wave," 1980; monument to Gov.-Gen. of Bahamas, Sir Milio Butler, 1977-79; Bronze figures and groups: Endangered Species; St. Peter as Fisher of Men; Thou Art Fair My Love; Joy of Youth; Black Venus; Pursuit; Black Madonna; for collections in Toronto, Sarnia, Boston, New York, Ohio, Texas, Calif., Venezuela, 1980-81; Address: Box 530, Marsh Harbour, Bahamas.

JOHNSTON, Ray H., C.A.; financial executive; b. Edmonton, Alta. 10 June 1947; e. Univ. of Alta. Faculty Business Adm.; C.A. Alta. 1973; m. Wendy 21 May 1967; children: Stephanie, Aaron, Amanda; PRESIDENT AND DIR., SHERWOOD FINANCIAL SERVICES LTD. 1979- ; Staff Acct. Thorne Riddell 1969-73; Jr. Consultant Thorne Group 1973; sole prop. R. H. Johnston, C.A. 1973-82 and R. H. Johnston & Associates 1973-77; Dir. Sherwood Park & Dist. Chamber Comm. (Pres. 1980); Kiwanis Sherwood Park (Pres. 1981); mem. Econ. Soc. Alta.; Candn. Tax Foundation; Trustee, Co. Strathcona Bd. Educ.; author "Incentives to Small Business" 19..; "Management Problems?-Consult Your Chartered Accountant" 1975; "16.8% Yield on 1978-79 Canada Savings Bonds" 1978; "Financial Planning for Retirement" 1981; Office: 2012 Garland Court, Sherwood Park, Alta. T8A 2P1.

JOHNSTON, Robert Stanley, Q.C.; of U.E.L. descent; b. Hamilton, Ont., 13 Sept. 1905; s. Robert Lawrence and Emma Matilda (Martindale) J. e. Osgoode Hall, Toronto, Ont.; m. Marjorie Lloyd, d. H. A. Webber, 26 Sept. 1936; has one s., Robert Douglas, and one d., Roseanne M.; read law with Mortimer Clark & Co., Toronto, Ont.; called to Bar of Ont. 1930; cr. Q.C. 1958; Hon. Life mem., V.O.N. Canada (Pres., Prov. Ont. Br. and Hamilton Br. 1957); Past Chrmn. and Hon. Solr., Royal Candn. Humane Assn.; mem., Estate Planners Council, Hamilton; Pres., Dom. Council, U.E.L. Assn. Can., 1939-49; mem.,

Hamilton Art Gallery; Candn. Bar Assn.; Chamber of Comm., Hamilton; Freemason 32° (mem. of all Scot. Rite bodies); Past Chrmn., Scottish Rite Club (Hamilton); Treas. and Trustee, St. Giles United Church; pastmen., Exec. Gen. Council, United Church of Can.; recreation: gardening; Clubs: Lawyer's; Canadian; Hamilton Thistle; Scottish Rite; Home: 1202-136 Bay St. S., Hamilton, Ont. L8P 3H5; Office: 403-20 Hughson St. S., Hamilton, Ont. L8N 3C8

JOHNSTON, Stewart A., M.Sc., Ph.D.; chemist; b. Fort William, Ont., 22 Aug. 1911; s. Thomas Stewart and Ada Emily Eva Gill (Murchison) J.; e. Kelvin Tech. High Sch., Winnipeg, 1925-27; Univ. of Man., B.Sc. (Hons.) 1932, Teaching Cert. 1934, M.Sc. (Physics) 1937; Stanford Univ., Ph.D. 1940; m. late Amelia Alice, d. late Walter Alston, Motherwell, Scot., 4 Feb. 1932; three d., Shirley (Mrs. Milan Merhaut), Betty, Suzanne (Mrs. Ronald Reddall); PROF. OF CHEM., CALIF. STATE UNIV., LOS ANGELES 1964-76; Consultant Aerospace Cos. (1954-72); Instr., U. Coll., Winnipeg, 1934-38; Teaching Asst., Stanford Univ., 1938-39; Research Fellow 1939-40; Research Chemist, Virgina Chemical Corp., Piney River, Va., 1940-41; Engr., Western Electric Co., Kearney, N.J., 1941-42; Asst. Prof., Univ. of S. Cal., Los Angeles 1944; Research Chemist and Chief, Chem. Sec., Jet Propulsion Lab., Cal. Inst. of Technol., Pasadena, 1944-46; Staff Engr. 1952-53; Head, Dept. of Math., W. Wash. State Coll., Bellingham, 1946-52; Joined present Univ. 1953 and has served as Head, Dept. of Phys. Science (1 yr.), Chrmn., Div. of Science & Math. (10 yrs.) and Dir., Govt. Research (2 yrs.); writings incl. several articles for learned journs. and many classified reports; performed some of early research in rocket propellants; was responsible for 1st rocket motors in U.S. to use concentrated hydrogen peroxide and also for introduction of hydrazine as a rocket fuel; later was responsible for writing specifications for fuel for Atlas Missile; rec'd Univ. Gold Medal in Science, Univ. of Man.; mem., Am. Assn. Univ. Profs.; Am. Chem. Soc.; Am. Assn. Advance. Science; Nat. Educ. Assn.; Gamma Alpha; Sigma Xi; Phi Lamda Upsilon; Presbyterian; recreations: chess, swimming, ping pong, bridge; Home: 181 White Oak Drive, Arcadia, Cal. 91006;

JOHNSTON, W. Ritchie, B.Sc.; retired company executive; b. Montreal, P.Q., 24 May 1921; e. Montreal High Sch., grad. 1938; McGill Univ., B.Sc. 1946; m. Anna Edith Davidson, 1947; children: Nancy Mary, Robert Walter; joined Northern Electric Co. Ltd. as Equipment Engr., 1946; Asst. Supt., Trans. Systems Engn., 1955; Bell-Northern Engn. Co.-Ord. studies, 1957; Supt., Communications Systems Engn., 1958; Sales Mgr., Communications Equipment Div., 1960; Vice Pres. and Gen. Mgr., Sales Div., 1962, Marketing Service Div. 1963; Vice-Pres. Research & Devel. 1968, Switching Marketing 1969; Group and Extve-Vice Pres. 1971-73; Sr. Staff Vice Pres. 1974-75 (ret.) served overseas in 2nd World War with R.C.A.F. in U.K., Gibraltar, N. Africa; discharged with rank of Flight Lieut.; O.E.Q.; Bd. of Gov., United Theological Coll.; recreations: photography, curling, carpentry, church and community work; Club: Lachine Curling; Home: 410 Caledonia Ave., Dorval, Que. H9S 2Y2

JOLLIFFE, Alfred Walton, Ph.D., F.R.S.C., F.G.S.A., F.M.S.A.; b. Winnipeg, Man., 8 May 1907; s. Richard Orlando and Mary Ethel (Frost) J.; e. Queen's Univ., B.A. (Chem.) 1929, M.A. 1931; Princeton Univ., Ph.D. (Geol.) 1935; m. Catherine Bell, d. George Sterling Peabody, Woodstock, N.B., 23 oct. 1937; children: Leslie Ann, Mary Catherine, Peter Alfred, Thomas Sterling; PROF. OF GEOLOGICAL SCIENCES, QUEEN'S UNIV., 1950-72; Prof. Emeritus, 1972-; Geol. Consultant for various mining cos.; Field Asst., Geol. Survey of Can., in various parts of Man., Ont. and N.W.T., 1928-34; Asst. Geol., 1935-36; Assoc. Geol., 1936-45; Geol., 1945; joined McGill Univ. as Assoc. Prof., Dept. of Geol. Sciences, 1946;

rec'd. Barlow Award, Candn. Inst. of Mining and Metall., 1938; mem., Geol. Assn. of Can.; Candn. Inst. of Mining and Metall.; has written numerous govt. reports and techn. papers, dealing mainly with the geol. and mineral deposits of N.W.Y., also uranium and iron ore deposits; made some of the early gold discoveries at Yellowknife, N.W.T., and some of the early uranium discoveries at Great Bear Lake, N.W.T., and Lake Athabaska, Sask.; Hon. Life mem., Prospectors & Developers Assn. Can.; recreation: gardening; golf; Home: 68 Collingwood, Kingston, Ont. K7L 3X4

JOLLIFFE, Edward Bigelow, Q.C., M.A.; arbitrator; b. Luchow, China, 2 March 1909; s. Rev. Charles and Gertrude (Bigelow) J.; e. Rockwood Pub. Sch. 1922; Candn. Sch., Chengtu, 1924; W. China Union Univ. 1925; Guelph Coll. Inst., Ont. 1927; Victoria Coll., Toronto, (Rhodes Schol. 1931); Christ Ch., Oxford, 1934; Gray's Inn, London (Arden Schol.); called to the English Bar 1934; Ontario. 1936; K.C. 1944; m. Ruth Conger, d. Charles Herbert Moore, Dundas, Ont., 26 October 1935; children: Naomi, John, Nancy, Thomas; VICE CHAIRMAN, ONT. PUBLIC SERVICE GRIEVANCE SETTLEMENT BD., appt. 1980; from time to time with The Candn. Press as Reporter, Cable Ed. and Counsel, Toronto, Montreal, N.Y., 1930-43; def. cand. to H. of C. for Toronto St. Paul's g.e. 1935, and York E., g.e. 1940; Ont. C.C.F. Leader 1942-53; Leader of the Official Opposition in the Leg. 1943-45 and 1948-51; practiced law with Lang and Michener, Toronto, 1936-43; Jolliffe, Lewis, and Osler, 1945-69 Candn. gen. counsel for United Steelworkers and other internat. and nat. unions and prof. organizations; apptd. Chief Adjudicator under Public Service Staff Relations Act, 1969, also Depy. Chrmn. P.S.S.R. Bd. 1975; retired 1978; contributed to Candn. Bar Review, American Administrative Law Review, McGill Law Journ., MacLean's and other U.S. and Candn. periodicals; co-author "Witness to a Generation" (history) 1966; author "The First Hundred" (novel) 1972; mem., Candn. Bar Assn.; Nat. Acad. Arbitrators; Life mem. Assn. of Candn. Television & Radio Artists; Hon. mem. Candn. Veterinary Med. Assn.; Vice-Chrmn. of Bd., Central Hosp., Toronto 1967-69; Chrmn. Atai Arctic Creative Devel. Foundation 1975; Pres., Empire Club of Canada, 1968-69; Clubs: University; Rideau; Home: Rockwood Hill Farm, Office: Box 136, Rockwood, Ont. N0B 2K0.

JOLY, Jean-Marie, M.A., Ph.D.; éducateur et administrateur; né Cap St-Ignace, Qué. 28 déc. 1925; f. François R. J. et Wilhelmine (Leclerc) J.; é. Univ. Laval, B.A. 1946; Univ. d'Ottawa, M.A. 1949; Syracuse Univ., Ph.D. 1957; ép. Mariette, f. J. E. Bélanger (décédé) 13 juin 1953; enfants: Mathieu, Dominique, Elisabeth, Martine, Michèle; PROFESSEUR TITULAIRE, FACULTÉ d'EDUCATION, UNIV. D'OTTAWA depuis 1971; enseignement: univ. d'Ottawa 1949, Syracuse Univ. 1953, Univ. Miami 1955, Univ. Laval 1956; Dir. gen. des Programmes et des Examens, Min. de l'Educ. Qué. 1964; Dir. Inst. de Recherche pédagogique, Min. de l'Educ. Qué. 1967; Vice-recteur adjoint, Univ. of Ottawa, 1971-77; mem. Soc. candn. pour l'étude de l'éduc. (Vice-Prés. 1974-75); Assn. Inst. Research; Assn. candn. des chercheurs en éduc.; auteur de plusieurs articles; reçu Whitworth Award, Conseil candn. de la recherche en éduc. 1970; Catholique r.; loisirs: musique, lecture, ski, jardinage; résidence: 2520 Alta Vista, Ottawa, Ont. K1V 7T1

JONAS, George; writer; b. Budapest, Hungary, 15 June 1935; s. Dr. George M. Hubsch and Magda (Klug) J.; e. Lutheran Gymnasium, Budapest; studied theatre and film arts under F. Hont, Budapest; m. Barbara Amiel; (by 1st m.) one s., Alexander; came to Can. 1956; author, "The Absolute Smile" (poems), 1967; "The Happy Hungry man" (poems), 1970; "Cities" (poems) 1973; co-author "By Persons Unknown" (non-fiction) 1977; "Pushkin" (stage play commissioned by Theatre Plus, 1978); "Final Decree", (novel) 1981; Can. Council Grants

1968, 1971; other writings incl. numerous radio & TV plays; librettos for operas by Tibor Polgar, "The European Lover" (toured Canada 1966) and "The Glove" (commissioned by Canadian Opera Company 1973); contributed poems, articles and reviews to various journals; regular columnist, Toronto Life Magazine; films include "Robert Fulford in Conversation with George Jonas", 1968; "Dennis Lee in Conversation with George Jonas", 1970; "Adrienne Clarkson Talks with George Jonas", 1970; winner, Edgar Allan Poe Award for Best Fact Crime Book, 1977; mem., Writers Union of Can.; League Candn. Poets; Assn. TV Producers & Dirs.; Composers, Authors & Publishers Assn. Can.; Poets & Writers, N.Y. State Council on Arts; recreation: motorcycle riding; Address: c/o CBC (Box 500) Terminal "A", Toronto, Ont. M5W 1E6

JONES, Mrs. Colin Edward — see: Seymour, Lynn.

JONES, D. Carlton, B. Eng.; oil and gas consultant; b. Calgary, Alta., 14 Dec. 1914; s. David Charles and Norah Elizabeth (Browne) J.; e. S. Alta. Inst. of Technol., Calgary, Dipl. 1933; Univ. of Alta., 1935; McGill Univ., B.Eng. 1937; Harvard Univ., Advanced Mang. Program 1963; m. Marian Lilian, d. Thomas Sydney Glover, Calgary, 30 Nov. 1940; two d., Donna Marian (Mrs. J. K. Motherwell), Linda Noreen (Mrs. M. E. Feddersen); PRESIDENT, CARLTON RESOURCE MANAGEMENT since 1977; Pres. and Dir.; Hudson's Bay Oil and Gas Co. Ltd., 1970-77; DuPont of Canada Ltd.; Polysar Ltd.; Aquitaine Company of Canada; CDC Oil and Gas Co.; Ranchmen's Exploration Ltd. Instructor, Southern Alberta Inst. of Technol., Calgary, 1937-39; Riverside Iron Co., Calgary, 1945; Engr., Canadian Western Natural Gas Co., Calgary 1946-51; Consulting Engr., Denton Spencer Co., Calgary, 1951-53; joined Hudson's Bay Oil and Gas as Engr. 1954-57; Asst. Mgr. Production 1958-60; Vice Pres. Production 1960-66; Extve. Vice Pres. 1966-70; served with RCAF 1940-44; Calgary Adv. Bd., Nat. Trust Co. Ltd. since 1976; mem. Bd. of Mang., Foothills Gen. Hosp., Calgary 1969-76; mem., Alta. Assn. Prof. Engrs. (Past Pres.) Candn. Inst. Mining & Metall.; Anglican; recreations: golf, skiing, fishing; Clubs: Calgary Petroleum (Past Pres.); Calgary Golf & Country; Home: 1411 Beverley Pl., Calgary, Alta. T2V2C7; Office: 1400 Elveden House, Calgary, Alta. T2P 0Z3

JONES, David Haney, Q.C.; commissioner; b. Winnipeg, Manitoba, 13 Mar. 1925; s. late Stanley Neville Kennedy and Miriam Margaret (Haney) J.; e. Pub. Schs. and St. John's-Ravenscourt Sch., Winnipeg, grad. 1942; Univ. of Man., Faculty of Arts, 1942-43 and Law Sch., LL.B. 1948; Univ. of Cambridge, Dipl. in Comparative Legal Studies 1950; m. Kathleen Elizabeth, d. late Robert Barry, 2 Sept. 1950; children: Sarah Kennedy, Andrew Robert O'Neil; CHRMN. WATER TRANSPORT COMTE. 1979-; read law with th late Hon. E. K. Williams and Chief Justice Samuel Freedman; called to Bar of Man. 1949; cr. Q.C. (Fed.) 1972; served in Office of Econ. Adv. to Premier, Govt. of Man., 1949-50; Solr., Dilts, Baker, Laidlaw & Shepard, Winnipeg, 1950-53; Partner of law firm Thompson, Dilts and Co., Winnipeg, 1953-67; Lectr., Man. Law Sch., Univ. of Man., 1952-66; Commr., Candn. Transport Comn. and Chrmn., Rly. Transport Comte., 1967-79; served with R.C.N.V.R. 1943-45; demobilized with rank Sub-Lt.; R.C.N. (Reserve) 1950-56; retired with rank Lt.; mem., Man. Bar Assn. (Extve. Council 1952-67); Candn. Bar Assn. (Council, Man. Sec. 1964-67); Law Soc. of Man.; Zeta Psi; United Church; recreations: reading, swimming, railway history, boating; Club: Winnipeg Squash Racquet; Home: No.6 Dufferin House, 174 Dufferin Rd., Ottawa, Ont. K1M 2A6; Office: 15 Eddy, Hull, Québec

JONES, Frederick W.P., B.A.; financial consultant, educator, corporate director; b. London, Ontario, 17 August 1910; s. Joseph W. P. and Gertrude R. (Whittaker) J.; e.

University of Western Ontario, B.A. (Business Adm.) 1934, LL.D. (Hon.) 1977; m. Elsie A., d. C. H. Dearborn, Saint John, N.B., Aug. 1936; two d. Deborah and Gwyneth; 2ndly, Aileen Tyrrell (Douglas), August 1967; Dir., AVCO Corp.; AVCO Financial Services Can. Ltd.; Candn. Liquid Air Corp. Ltd.; Economic Investment Trust; Ellis Don Ltd.; EMCO Ltd.; Royal Trustco; Royal Trust Corp.; SNC Enterprises; Taurus Fund; Union Gas Ltd.; engaged in own business, 1934-37; General Sales Mgr., Mang. Dir. and Pres., Hobbs Glass Co. Ltd., 1937-52; Mang. Service, Fed. Govt., Ottawa, 1942-43; Ont. Econ. Council, Thunder Bay Study; Chrmn., Ont. Govt. Roy. Comn. Agric. Marketing, 1959-62; Dean, Sch. of Bus. Adm., Univ. of W. Ont. 1954-63, Prof. 1963-74; United Church; Clubs: London Hunt & Country; The London; Caledon Mountain Trout; Home: 35 Doncaster Ave., London, Ont. N6G 2A1

JONES, John Hugh Mowbray, B.Sc., D.Eng.; retired company executive; b. Sault Ste. Marie, Ont., 24 Aug. 1905; s. late Col. Charles Hugh le Pailleur (pioneer) pulp and paper mfr.) and Elisabeth (Kennedy) J.; e. Sault Ste. Marie Pub. Schs.; Upper Canada Coll., Toronto, 1918-23; Univ. of Toronto, B.Sc. in Mech. Engn. (Hons.) 1927; Hon. D.Eng., N.S. Tech. Coll., 1959; m. Phyllis Lucille, d. Thomas Hodges, Santa Barbara, U.S.A., 7 Apl. 1934; has two s. and three d.; Dir., Chrmn. and Pres., Maritime Coastal Containers Ltd.; Dir. and Chrmn., White Point Estates Ltd.; Chrmn. White Point Beach Lodge Ltd.; Pres., Glencannon Corp.; Chateau Bonne Entente, Inc.; Dir., Hermes Electronics Ltd.; Ben's Holdings Ltd.; Halifax Developments Ltd.; began career in Engn. Dept., Spanish River Pulp & Paper Co. Ltd., 1928; Resident Engr., Mersey Paper Co. Ltd., 1928-35, Chief Engr. 1935-59, Mill Mgr., 1939-47, Vice-Pres. and Dir., 1947-58; Pres. and Dir., Bowaters Massey and Bowaters Nfld., 1958-61; Bowaters N. Amer., 1962; Pres., Bowaters Can., 1965-66; retired, 1967; Lieut.-Col. Maritime Div., Kiwanis Internat. 1937; Serving Brother, Order of St. John of Jerusalem; Chrmn. of Bd., Queens Gen. Hosp. Assn., Liverpool, N.S.; mem. Engn. Inst. Can.; Assn. Prof. Engrs. N.S. (Pres. 1944); served in Reserve Army 1943-45 as Maj. and O.C. 20th (R) Field Co., R.C.E.; Delta Kappa Epsilon; Conservative; Anglican; Clubs: Halifax (Halifax); Liverpool Golf & Country (N.S.); Home: PH5 Spring Garden Terrace Apts., Halifax, N.S.;

JONES, Llewellyn Petley; painter; artist; b. Edmonton, Alta., 23 Aug. 1908; grands. of John Matthew J., one of the original Fellows of Roy. Soc. of Can. and a Founder of the Nova Scotia Inst. of Nat. Science (sometime Pres.); s. Arthur Hurdis and Elizabeth (Petley) J.; e. Edmonton (Alta.) Pub. and High Schs.; exhibitor, Salon d'Automne, Paris, Waddington Galleries, London (1957) and Dominion Gallery, Montreal (1958); recreations: cricket, tennis; Address: c/o Dominion Gallery, 1438 Sherbrooke W., Montreal, Que. H3G 1K4

JONES, Hon. Malachi C., B.A., LL.B.; judge; b. Rockingham, N.S., 2 Sept. 1929; s. late Alexander William, K.C. and Lillian Agatha (Lyons) J.; e. Rockingham (N.S.) Pub. Sch. and St. Patrick's High Sch., 1946; St. Mary's Univ., 1946-48, B.A. 1970; Dalhousie Univ., LL.B. 1951; m. Catherine Ann Marie, d. late Dugald MacDonald, 2 Aug. 1952; children: Roseanne, Barbara, Maureen, Sheila, Colleen, Monica, Jennifer, Stephanie, Stephen; JUSTICE, SUPREME COURT OF N.S., since 1970; appointed to the Appeal Division, 1979; read law with Walter Barss, K.C. and John A. Y. MacDonald, K.C., Depy. Atty. Gen. N.S.; called to Bar of N.S. 1952; cr. Q.C. 1967; cont. to practice with Dept. of Atty. Gen. N.S. after receiving law degree; Leg. Counsel for N.S. 1966-67; apptd. Asst. Depy. Atty. Gen. 1967, Assoc. 1969; has appeared on numerous occasions before Supreme Courts of N.S. and Can. and various prov. adm. bds.; rep. of N.S. on Conf. of Commrs. on Uniformity of Leg. in Can.; has lectered at St. Mary's and Dalhousie Univs.; Past Vice

Chrmn., Halifax Housing Authority; mem. Bd. of Govs., St. Mary's Univ., 1966-70 (Pres. Alumni Assn. 1963-65); past mem. Bd., Home of the Good Shepherd, Halifax; mem. N.S. Barristers' Soc.; Candn. Bar Assn.; R. Catholic; recreations: sailing, swimming, walking; Clubs: Waegwoltic; Armdale Yacht; Home: 2339 Armcrescent W., Halifax, N.S. B3L 3E4; Office: The Law Courts, 1815 Upper Water Street, Halifax, N.S. B3J 3C8

JONES, Peter, Ph.L., S.T.L., Ph.D.; b. Warwickshire, Eng. 10 Dec. 1938; s. William Edward and Doris Ellen (Simpson) J.; e. St. Philips Grammar Sch. Eng.; Gregorian Univ. Rome Ph.L. 1960, S.T.L. 1964; Oxford Univ. 1972-73; McGill Univ. Ph.D. 1973; m. Elizabeth Margaret d. G.D. Meredith, San Francisco, Cal. 27 Dec. 1968; children: Martin David, Marc Andrew, Simon Francis; Exec. Dir., Univ. of B.C. Alumni Assoc., 1979-; President, Candn. Council of Christians and Jews 1976-79 Lectr. Marianopolis Coll. (Univ. de Montréal) 1964-65; Asst. Prof. and Dir. Dept. Interdisciplinary Studies, mem. Senate Loyola Coll. Montreal 1065-74; Pacific Region Dir. Candn. Council of Christians & Jews Vancouver 1974-75, Asst. to Pres. 1975-76; mem. Acad. Council Sch. of Continuing Studies Univ. of Toronto 1977-79; Bd. of Dir., Tibetan Refugee Aid Soc., Candn. Ecumenical Action, Vancouver Inst. R. Catholic; recreations: gardening, camping; Clubs: Canadian; University (Vancouver), U.B.C. Faculty; Home: 5000 8A Avenue, Delta, B.C.

JONES, Phyllis Edith, B.Sc.N., M.Sc., R.N., F.A.P H.A.; nursing administrator; b. Barrie, Ont. 16 Sept. 1924; d. Colston Graham and E. (Shand) J.; e. Barrie Coll. Inst. 1943; Univ. of Toronto B.Sc.N. 1950; M.Sc. 1969; DEAN, FACULTY OF NURSING, UNIV. OF TORONTO since 1979; Co-Chairperson Candn. Public Health Assn. Comte. to develop "A Statement of Functions and Qualifications for the Practice of Public Health Nursing in Canada", 1964-66; Mem. Bd. Dir. Victorian Order of Nurses, 1971-79; of Ont. Council of Health Task Force on Evaluation of Primary Health Care Settings, 1975; of Task Force Coll. of Nurses of Ont., 1978-80; of Advisory Comte. Toronto Gen. Hosp. Patient Classification Study, 1978-80; of George Brown Advisory Comte. to Diploma Nursing programme, 1981-; of Metro. Toronto Dist. Health Council, 1981-; author of various articles with reference to the primary health care sector and nursing diagnoses; mem., Candn. Public Health Assn.; Ont. Public Health Assn.; Candn. Assn. of Univ. Schs. of Nursing (Council member); Candn. Council of Social Development; Candn. Nurses Assn.; R.N. Assn. of Ont.; Protestant; recreations: skiing, reading, walking, cooking; Home: 81 Sutherland Dr., Toronto, Ont. M4G 1H6; Office: 50 St. George St., Toronto, Ont. M5S 1A1.

JONES, Rev. Richard Ditzel, O.C. (1972), M.A., B.S.T., LL.D.; b. Elizabeth, N.J. 17 Sept. 1907; s. John Richard and Hannah M. (Ditzel) J.; e. Elizabeth, N.J.; Wesleyan Univ., B.A. 1928; Boston Univ., Sch. of Theol., M.A. 1932 and B.S.T. 1933; Windsor Univ., LL.D. 1968; York Univ. 1975; m. Evelyn A., d. John M. Allen of Gladstone, N.J., 26 June, 1937; children: Richard, Nancy; PRES., CANADIAN COUNCIL OF CHRISTIANS AND JEWS, 1967-76; Pres. Emeritus, 1976; mem. Newark, N.J., Conf. of the Meth. Ch.; taught Latin and English at Athens Coll. Athens, Greece, 1928-31; Pastor, Gladstone (N.J.) Meth. Ch., 1934-37; Grace Meth. Ch., Kearny, N.J., 1937-47; Dir., Canadian Council of Christians and Jews, 1947-67; attended World Brotherhood Conf. at UNESCO House, Paris, June 1950, and 2nd Conf. in Brussels, 1955; Past Chrmn., West Hudson Am. Cancer Soc.; has travelled and lectured in many countries; toured Iraq and Iran with Richard Haliburton; served in 2nd World War with U.S. Marine Corps; contributed various articles on human relations to numerous journs.; recipient of Beth Sholom Brotherhood Award; Award of Merit, Corp. of City of Toronto 1972; Candian Citizen October 1957; apptd. Chaplain, Metrop. Toronto Police, 1968; Exec. Cmte., St. Al-

bans Boys and Girls Club; Finance Chmn., John G. Diefenbaker Memorial Fdn.; Bd. Dir., Council for Can. Unity; Delta Tau Delta; recreations: fishing, travelling; Clubs: Rotary (Hon.); Kiwanis; Home: 2466 Shepard Ave., Mississauga, Ont.; Office: 180 Yorkland Blvd., Willowdale, Ont.

JONES, Richard Norman, Ph.D., D.Sc., F.R.S.C.; research scientist; b. Manchester, Eng., 20 March 1913; s. late Richard Leonard and Blanche (Mason) J.; e. Manchester Univ., B.Sc., M.Sc., Ph.D., D.Sc.; m. Magda, d. late Eugene Kemeny, 11 July 1939; two s.; Richard Kemeny, David Leonard; DISTINGUISHED VISITOR, DEPT. OF CHEM., UNIV. OF ALTA., 1982-83; Guest Prof., Dept. of Chemistry, Tokyo Inst. of Technology, 1979-82; Commonwealth Fund Fellow, Harvard Univ., 1939-42; Lectr. and Asst. Prof., Dept. of Chem., Queen's Univ., 1942-46; Principal Research Offr., Div. of Chem., Nat. Research Council Can., 1946-78; author of three books and tech. papers in chem. and spectroscopic journs.; mem., Chem. Inst. Can.; Am. Chem. Soc.; Royal Soc. Chem. (London); Internat. Union Pure & Applied Chem. (Past Pres.), Phys. Chem. Div.); I.C.S.U. Comn. on Data for Science and Tech.; recreations: travel, photography, computer programming; Home: Ann Manor, Apt. 601, 71 Somerset St. W., Ottawa, Ont. K2P 2G2; Office: Dept. Chem., Univ. of Alta., Edmonton, Alta. T6G 2G2

JONES, Robert Leslie, Ph.D.; college professor; b. Cobden, Ont., 4 Apl. 1907; s. Robert and Martha (Caswell) J.; e. Renfrew (Ont.) Coll. Inst., 1919-24; Queen's Univ., B.A. 1927; M.A. 1928; Ont. Coll. of Educ., 1929; Harvard Univ., M.A. 1932, Ph.D. 1938; m. Maude, d. George Cook Lacey, Chesterville, Ont., 25 Dec. 1939(d. Aug. 1975); 2nd m. Irene Dorothy, d. Frederick Francis Neu, Mount Healthy, Ohio, 25 Nov. 1976; two d. Constance Helen, Natalie Ruth; PROFESSOR EMERITUS OF HISTORY, MARIETTA COLLEGE SINCE 1975; Head, Depts. of Hist. and Pol. Science, 1945-72; Teacher, Lindsay (Ont.) Coll. Inst. 1929-30; Napanee (Ont.) Coll. Inst. 1930-31; Pembroke (Ont.) Coll. Inst., 1933-34; joined present Coll. as Instr. in Hist., 1938; Asst. Prof. 1943-45, Prof. 1945-66 Andrew U. Thomas Prof. of Hist., 1966-75; author: "History of Agriculture in Ohio, 1750-1880", 1980; "History of Agriculture in Ontario 1613-1880", 1946; Contrib. to: "Books for College Libraries", 1967; "The Old Northwest", 1969; also articles for various journs.; mem., Candn. Hist. Assn.; Organ. Am. Historians; Ohio Acad. Hist. (Pres. 1953-54); Agric. Hist. Soc.; received Distinuished Service Award of Ohio Academy of History, 1979 Delta Tau Delta; Omicron Delta Kappa; United Church of Christ; Home: 206 Brentwood St., Marietta, Ohio, 45750

JONES, Robert Orville, O.C. (1981), M.D., C.M., D.Eng. (Hon.), F.A.P.A., F.R.C.P.(C) 1963, F.A.C.P. 1965; university professor; psychiatrist; b. Digby, N.S., 31 Mar. 1914, of English parentage; e. Dalhousie Univ., B.Sc., 1933 and M.D., C.M. 1939; post-grad. study in Psychiatry, Maudsley Hosp., London, Eng.; Rockefeller Fellow in Psychiatry, Henry Phipps Psychiatric Clinic, Johns Hopkins Hosp.; N.S. Tech. Coll., D.Eng. 1970; m. Mary Eleanor Allen, 1937; children: David R., Louisa E.; PROF. EMERITUS OF PSYCHIATRY, DALHOUSIE UNIV.; Consultant in Psychiatry, Victoria Gen. Hosp., Halifax, N.S.; joined Dept. of Psychiatry, Dalhousie Univ., 1941; Hon. mem., Candn. Psychiatric Assn.; Charter Fellow (1965), Am. Coll. of Psychiatry; Life Fellow, Am. Psychiatric Assn.; mem. Extve. Comte. (Can.), World Psychiatric Assn.; mem., Nova Scotia Med. Soc.; Candn. Med. Assn. (Pres. 1965-66; Past Pres., N.S. Div.); Am. Assn. for Advanc. of Science; Nova Scotia Hist. Soc.; Candn. Inst. Internat. Affairs; Centennial Medal, 1967; Queen's Jubilee Medal, 1978; Club: Rotary; Home: 6504 Jubilee Road, Halifax, N.S. B3H 2H4; Office: 1362 Robie St., Halifax, Nova Scotia. B3H 3E2

JONSSON, Douglas William, F.R.A.I.C. Architect and Planner; b. Saskatoon, Sask., 30 Nov. 1918; s. Junius and Eleanor Elizabeth (Mighton) J.; e. Univ. of Manitoba, B.Arch.; m. Audrey Grace, d. Harry Richardson, Fredericton, N.B., 26 Apl. 1950; PROV. ARCHITECT, NEW BRUNSWICK; with Prov. Arch. of B.C., 1946; Chief Arch., Wartime Housing Corpn., 1946; Project Designer and Arch. with Central Mortgage & Housing Corpn., 1947; selected the site and laid out the original town plan for Imperial Oil's Alta. Leduc field town of Devon, 1947; laid out Vancouver's 500 House Project "Renfrew Heights"; estbd. Prov. Arch. office for N.B., 1948; served in 2nd World War for 5 years in Candn. Army as Lieut., R.C.E.; mem., Arch. Assn. of N.B. (Pres. 1951); Fellow, Royal Architectural Institute of Canada 1974; Mil. Engrs. Assn. of Can. (Chrmn., N.B. Br.); Fredericton Chamber of Comm.; Protestant; Clubs: Fredericton Curling; Fredericton Tennis; Fredericton Golf; Address: 173 Edinburgh, Fredericton, N.B. E3B 2C8

JOPLIN, Albert Frederick, B.Ap.Sc., P.Eng.; transportation executive; b. Victoria, B.C., 22 Feb. 1919; s. Albert Edward and Emily Eliza (Norford) J.; e. Univ. of B.C., B.A.Sc. (Civil Engn.) 1948); m. the late Margaret McMorragh-Kavanaugh, 26 May 1947; one d. Mary Lynn Barbara; 2nd. m. Dorothy Anne Cook, 29 July 1977; PRES. & C.E.O. CANADIAN PACIFIC (BERMUDA) LTD. since 1976; Dir., Canadian Pacific Consulting Services Ltd.; Director, Shaw Industries Ltd.; Pres. & Dir., Arion Shipping Corp.; Dir., Arion Ins. Co. Ltd.; Britannia Steamship Ins. Assoc. Ltd.; Dir. Expo Oil, N.L.; Candn. Pacific Internat. Freight Services Ltd.; Pres. & Dir., Candn. Pacific Shipmanagement (Hong Kong) Ltd.; joined Canadian Pacific as Transitman, Roadmaster, Div. Engr., B.C. 1947-62, Special Engineer, Calgary 1962-65, Development Engineer Vancouver 1965; Manager, Special Projects, Canadian Pacific Investments Ltd. and Gen Mgr., Marathon Realty, Vancouver, 1966; initiated Project 200 devel. scheme for Downtown Vancouver; System Mgr. Planning & Devel., Canadian Pacific Ltd., Montreal 1968, Dir. Devel. Planning 1969; Vice Pres., Marketing & Sales, CP Rail 1971; Vice-Pres, Operation and Maintenance, CP Rail 1974; served with RCAF 1941-45; rank Flight Lt.; mem. Assn. Prof. Engrs. Prov. B.C.; Candn. Soc. for Civil Engr.; Engn. Inst. Can.; N. Am. Soc. Corporate Planning; Rly. Assn. Can. Clubs: Mount Stephen; Canadian Railway; Royal Montreal Golf; Traffic; Mid Ocean; Hamilton Rotary; Order of St John; Beta Theta Pi; Office: P.O. Box 1260 Hamilton 5, Bermuda

JOPLING, Samuel Haigh, B.E., M.Sc., D.Phil.; educator; b. Kingston, N.Y. 6 Sept. 1928; s. late Samuel Haigh and Nellie (Bennett) J.; e. Georgia Inst. Technol. B.E. (Mech. Engn.) 1950; Pa. State Univ. M.Sc. 1965, D.Phil. 1975; m. Anneliese d. Frederick F. Schmitz, Germany 1 Aug. 1959; children: Mary Louise, Frederick Haigh; DEAN OF COMM. SAINT MARY'S UNIV. since 1976; joined US Army 1950, held various command, staff and gen. staff assignments Europe, Asia and N. Am. 1950-66, Comptroller USA Center for Mil. Assistance 1966-68. Chief Budget Systems Br. Office of Comptroller HQ US Army Europe (Heidelberg, Germany) 1968-70, rank Lt. Col. (Inf.), Sr. Parachutist; joined Cal. State Univ. Los Angeles 1972, Assoc. Dean (1973-76) and Accounting faculty mem. Sch. of Business & Econ.; Founder (1975) and first Mang. Ed. "Los Angeles Business and Economics" mag.; awarded Legion of Merit, Bronze Star Medal, Army Commendation Medal; Dir. Atlantic Mang. Inst.; mem. Council Deans Faculties Mang. & Business Adm. Can.; Financial Executives Inst. (Pres. Maritime Provs. Chapter); Candn. Acad. Accts. Assn.; Halifax Bd. Trade; Canadian Institute of Management (Nat. Educ. Advisory Council); Nat. Assn. Accts.; Phi Tau Sigma; Beta Alpha Psi; recreations: swimming, hiking, camping; Home: 1038 Robie St., Halifax, N.S. B3H 3C5; Office: Halifax, N.S. B3H 3C3.

JORDAN, Edward Conrad, M.Sc., Ph.D.; professor; b. Edmonton, Alta., 31 Dec. 1910; s. Conrad E. H. and Erna Elizabeth (Penk) J.; e. Victoria High Sch., Edmonton, Alta., 1927; Univ. of Alta., B.Sc. 1934, M.Sc. 1936; Ohio State Univ., Ph.D. 1940; m. Mary Helen, d. Thomas Walker, Edmonton, 3 Sept. 1941; three s., Robert E., David W., Thomas C.; PROF. AND HEAD, DEPT. OF ELECT. ENGN., UNIV. OF ILLINOIS, 1954-79; Prof. Emeritus 1979-; Control Operator, Radio Stn. CKUA, Edmonton, 1928-35; Elect. Engr., International Nickel Co., Sudbury, Ont., 1936-37; Instr. in Elect. Engn., Worcester (Mass.) Polytechnic Inst., 1940-41; Instr. and Asst. Prof., Ohio State Univ., 1941-45; joined present Univ. as Assoc. Prof. 1945; Trustee, Bolljahn Mem. Foundation; rec'd Educ. Medal, Inst. Elect. and Electronics Engrs., 1968; author: "Fundamentals of Radio", 1942; "Electromagnetic Waves and Radiating Systems", 1950, 2nd ed. 1968; "Fundamentals of Radio and Electronics", 1958; "Foundations of Future Electronics", 1961; Ed.; "Antennas and Electromagnetic Theory", 2 vols., 1963; other writings incl. numerous tech. articles in field of elect. engn.; Fellow, Inst. Elect. & Electronics Engrs.; Past Chrmn., Prof. Group on Antennas & Propagation; Past Chrmn., U.S. Nat. Comte., Internat. Union of Radio Science; mem. Nat. Acad. of Engn.; Eta Kappa Nu; Tau Beta Pi; Sigma Xi; recreations: handball, golf; Home: 415 W. Indiana, Urbana, Ill.

JORDAN, Patricia Jane, M.L.A. R.N.; Min. of Tourism; b. Vernon, B.C., 7 Dec. 1930; d. late John William and late Eva Maud (Wiseman) Laidman; e. Vernon (B.C.) Pub. Schs.; Univ. of B.C.; Vancouver Gen. Hosp. Sch. of Nursing; San Antonio State Coll.; Univ. of Minn.; m. Laurance Theodore Jordan, M.D., s. late Laurance Edward Jordan, 4 Sept. 1954; two s.; James David Edward, Laurance Henry Phillips; former Min. without Portfolio, B.C.; post-graduate in open-heart surg. ward, St. Mary's Hosp., Rochester, Minn.; Teacher, Aldridge Mem. Nursery Sch., Rochester, Minn.; el. Miss Vernon 1945; mem., B.C. Interior Basketball Championships Team, 1946; Vernon (B.C.) Singles Badminton Champion 1947; Past Pres., Mayo Clinic-Fellow Wives Assn.; Hon. mem., 4-H Club; B.C. Rep. for Fed. Govt's. "Fashions Canada"; author of "Laws and Rights of Women in British Columbia"; mem., Vancouver Art Gallery; Vernon Arts Soc.; Past mem., Minneapolis R.N. Assn.; Texas R.N. Assn.; R.N. Assn. B.C.; Social Credit; Anglican; recreations: painting, swimming, tennis, fishing, gardening; Home: c/o 3311-30th Ave., Vernon B.C. V1T 2G6; Office: Parliament Bldgs., Victoria, B.C.

JORGENSEN, Erik, M.F.; educator; b. Haderslev, Denmark, 28 Oct. 1921; s. Johannes and Eva Bromberg (Hansen) J.; e. Akad. Aarhus (Denmark), 1940; Royal Veterinary and Agric. Coll., M.F. 1946; m. Grete, d. Osvald Moller, Fredericia, Denmark, 13 June 1946; children: Marianne, Birthe; DIR., UNIV. OF GUELPH ARBORETUM AND PROF., ENVIRONMENTAL BIOL., since 1978; Research Offr., Danish Forest Exper. Stn., Springforbi, Denmark, 1946; Forest Pathol., Royal Veterinary and Agric. Coll., 1949; Research Offr., Forest Pathol. Lab., Science Service, Can. Dept. of Agric., Maple, Ont., 1955; Asst. Prof., Faculty of Forestry, Univ. of Toronto, 1959-63, mem. Grad. Dept. of Bot., 1959-73; i.c. Shade Tree Research Lab. 1962-72, Assoc. Prof. 1963, Prof. 1967; Assoc., Inst. of Environmental Sciences & Engn., 1971-73; Chief, Urban Forestry Program, Forest Mang. Inst. Candn. Forestry Service, Dept. of the Environment, 1973-78; served with Danish Army 1946-48; rank 2nd Lt.; consultant govt. agencies, private individuals and firms 1959-73; participated in devel. of urban forestry concept in Can. and in devel. of techniques for study and control of Dutch Elm Disease and other tree diseases; Founding mem. Dutch Elm. Disease Control Comte. for Metrop. Toronto & Region (forerunner Ont. Shade Tree Council), 1961; rep. for S. Ont. Sec., Candn. Inst. Forestry on Conserv. Council of Ont., 1966-69; mem. Bd. of Examiners,

Ont. Inst. Parks Extves., 1967-70; mem., Ont. Ornamentals Research Comte.; author of over 60 articles and scient. papers on urban forestry and tree diseases; rec'd "Author's Citation", Internat. Shade Tree Conf., Inc., 1970; mem., Candn. Inst. Forestry (Dir. 1967, Chrmn. Bd. Examiners 1970) Chrmn. S. Ont. Sec. 1966); Ont. Prof. Foresters Assn.; Danske Forstkandidaters Forening; Internat. Shade Tree Conf., Inc. (Gov. 1966-72, Pres. Candn. Chapter 1967-68); Ont. Shade Tree Council (Pres. 1970-71); Hon. Dir.; Rose Soc.; Vice-Pres., Guelph Arts Council; Ed. Bd., Agricultural Journal, The Internat. of Urban Forestry; Candn. Phytopathol. Soc.; Phytochem. Soc. N. Am.; Am. Assn. Advanc. Science; N.Y. Acad. Sciences; Sigma Xi; Danish Lutheran; Home: 47 Sherwood Dr., Guelph, Ont. N1E 6E6; Office: Guelph, Ont. N1G 2W1

JORGENSON, Frederick Charles, B.Ed.; educator; b. Cereal, Alta., 27 May 1923; s. Alfred Adolph and Vera Vandecar (Garbutt) J.; e. McConnell Sch., New Brigden, Alta., 1929-38; Dept. of Educ. Corr. Sch. (High Sch. Sec.), Edmonton, 1938-41; Calgary (Alta.) Normal Sch., 1943-44; Univ. of London, Univ. of Sask. and Univ. of Alta. extension courses leading to B.Ed. from latter Univ. 1958; Univ. of B.C.; m. Margaret Mary, d. T. H. McKim, Lethbridge, Alta., 6 Oct. 1951; children: Charles, Anne, Keith, Lynn, Gale; PRESIDENT, S. ALBERTA INST. OF TECH., since 1969; Teacher, Acadia Sch. Div., Oyen, 1944-47; Instr. and Dean of Men, Olds Sch. of Agric. and Home Econ., 1947-56; Instr. of Eng. and Math., Southern Alta. Inst. of Tech., Calgary, 1956-58; Head of Eng. Dept. and Information Offr., 1958-62; Vice Princ. Apl.-Aug. 1962; Princ. 1962-66; Princ. of Ryerson Polytech. Inst., Toronto, Ont. 1966-67 and Pres. 1967-69; Dir. (1969-75) and Chrmn. of Bd. (1973-75), Vocational and Rehab. Research Inst. Calgary; Chrmn., Habitat and Beyond, Calgary, 1977-8; mem., Ad. Council Alta. Dental Research Found., since 1977; Nat. Extve. Comte., Inst. of Pub. Adm. Can., 1977-8; mem., Candn. Nat. Comte., Un. World Colls., 1969-76 and currently Patron, Lester B. Pearson Coll. of the Pacific; Banff Centre Council, 1970-77; former mem. Senate of Univ. of Alta. (1962-66); Patron, Calgary Sch. Science Fairs; Extve. mem., Candn. Vocational Assn. (1965-68); mem. Senate, Univ. of Calgary; Alta. Educ. Communications Authority, incl. Program Policy Adv. Comte. (1970-74) and Alta. Educ. Communications Corp. (1974-77); Epsilon Pi Tau, Inc.; Adv. Council, Alta. Dental Research Fdn.; Patron's Council, Toronto French School; Bd. Dir., Old Sun Coll.; Anglican; Recreations: music, reading, photography, travel; Club: Canadian; Educ. Progress; Office: 1301 - 16 Ave. N.W., Calgary, Alberta T2M 0L4.

JORGENSON, Hon. Warner H., M.L.A.; politician; b. Canora, Sask. 26 March 1918; s. George and Hilma (Naslund) J.; e. St. Elizabeth elem. and Dominion City High Sch.; m. Corrine d. H. Ansell, Hove, Sussex, Eng. 16 Sept. 1945; children: Linda, Patricia, Christopher; MIN. OF GOVT. SERV., MAN. 1981- ; Min. of Consumer & Corporate Affairs and Environment, Man. 1979-81 Min. Responsible for Rent Stabilization Bd. and Office of Supt. of Ins. 1978-81; farmer; el. to H. of C. g.e. 1957, re-el. g.e. 1958, 1962, 1963, 1965, def. 1968; el. M.L.A. for Morris prov. by-el. 1969, re-el. since g.e. 1969; Min. without Portfolio and Govt. House Leader 1977; served with Candn. Army 1940-46; Hon. Pres. Valley Agric. Soc.; mem. Royal Candn. Legion; Lions; P. Conservative; Protestant; Club: Riverview Golf & Country (Pres.); Office: 141 Legislative Bldg., Winnipeg, Man. R3C 0V8.

JORON, Hon. Guy, M.N.A., B.A., B.Sc.; politician; b. Montréal, Qué. 2 June 1940; s. C. Conrad and Blanche (Moreau) J.; e. St. Lawrence Coll.; Loyola Coll.; Univ. of Montréal; MIN. OF CONSUMER AFFAIRS, CO-OPERATIVES & FINANCIAL INSTITUTIONS, QUE. 1979- ; financial advisor; el. M.N.A. for Mille-Iles prov. g.e. 1970, def. 1973, re-el. 1976, 1981; Min. Responsible for

Energy 1976; Parti Quebecois; Office: 800 Place d'Youville, Québec, Qué. G1R 4Y5.

JOSEPHSON, Joseph Edward, M.D., C.M., B.Sc. (Med.), F.R.C.P.(C); F.A.C.P.; pathologist; educator; b. Hamilton, Ont., 1 Nov. 1911; s. Samuel Ellis and Katherine (Wolkin) J.; e. Hamilton (Ont.) Central Coll. Inst.; Queen's Univ., M.D. 1934; Univ. of Toronto, B.Sc. (Medicine) 1936; m. Vivian Mary, d. Sir John Charles and Lady Puddester, 22 Mar. 1948; two s., Clayton Glenn, Dr. Bruce; CLINICAL PROF. OF PATHOL., FACULTY OF MED., MEMORIAL UNIV. OF NFLD.; Recipient of Queen's Jubilee Medal; Hon. Consultant, St. John's Gen. Hospital in Health Sciences Complex; Consultant Pathol., Waterford Hosp., St. Clares Hosp., Grace Hosp., Janeway Children's Hosp.; Consultant, Red Cross Blood Transfusion Service, St. John's, Nfld. Centre; served as M.O. (Capt.) to Nfld. Regt. 1942-45; Major, R.C.A.M.C. (R); holds Specialist Cert., R.C.P. & S. (Can.) in Path., Bacteriol. and Internal Med.; Past Pres., Nfld. Med. Assn. (1957); Past Pres. Med. Council of Can. (Pres. 1966); Past President, Candn. Assn. of Pathols.; Past Pres., Nfld. Assn. of Pathols.; Ret. Chmn., Dep't of Lab. Med. ad Chief Pathologist, St. John's Gen. Hosp.; Ret. Dir. Nfld. Pub. Health Labs and Prov. Pathologist, Nfld.; Past Pres. Med. Staff, mem. of Adv. Council, St. John's General Hospital; former mem. Bd. of Mang., Nfld. Div., C.N.I.B.; Extve. mem. Nfld. Div., Candn. Cancer Soc.; Freemason; recreations: fishing, hunting; Clubs: St. John's Curling; Bally Haly Golf; Murray's Pond Fishing (former director); Royal Newfoundland Yacht; Home: 189 Waterford Bridge Rd., St. John's, Nfld. A1E 1E4; Office: Waterford Hospital, St. John's, Nfld.

JOTCHAM, Thomas Denis; advertising executive; b. Llandudno, Wales, 21 Feb. 1918; s. late George James and Marion Alice Helen (Brand) J.; came to Canada, 1926; e. Lower Canada Coll., Montreal, P.Q. (Grad. 1936); McGill Univ. (Science) 1937-38; m. Margaret Jean, d. late M. W. Thirlwell, Winnipeg, Man., 10 Aug. 1940; children: Patricia, Douglas, Joy, Candace; VICE CHMN.., SHERWOOD COMMUNICATIONS GROUP LTD.; FOSTER ADVERTISING LTD.; Pres. 1977-81; Vice pres. 1956-73; Extve. Vice Pres. 1973-76; Sales Rep., Montreal Lithographing Co. Ltd., 1945; Sales Mgr., Wesco Waterpaints Canada Ltd., 1947; Advertising Mgr., Pepsi-Cola Co. of Canada Ltd., 1948, Montreal Mgr. for the Co., 1952; Asst. Advertising Mgr., Reader's Digest Assn. (Canada) Ltd., 1954; Chmn. PromoVision Communications Ltd., 1979-81; Pres., 1973-79; Pres., Foster, Young, Ross and Anthony Ltd., 1979-81; Dir., Western Display Services Ltd. 1979-81; served in 2nd World War, 1939-45 with P.P.C.L.I. and R.C.R.; demob. with rank of Major; Mentioned in Despatches, Italy 1944; Past Vice-pres. and Hon. mem., N.D.G. Cons. Assn. (N.D.G. Organizer 1957-62); Co-ordinator of Publ., Eng. Ridings, Montreal 1957-62; Past Dir., P.C. Assn. Mt. Royal; Past Pres. and Hon. Pres., Jr. Adv. & Sales Club, Montreal; Past Pres., Adv. & Sales Extves. Club, Montreal (Marketing Personality of the Year 1971); Past Pres., Candn. Adv. & Sales Assn. (Advertising Man of the Year 1971); Past Pres., Inst. Candn. Advertising (Fellow 1971); Past Pres. Adv. Agency Council of Que.; Past Pres., Montreal Bd. of Trade 1979-80; Founding Co-Chrmn., Montreal Economic Promotion Comte., 1979-80; Past Dir., Les Grands Ballets Canadiens; Past Hon. Pres. West Is. Jaycees, 1980-81, Hon. mem., 1981-; Pres. Grace Dart Hosp. Centre; Dir., Can. Council of Christians and Jews. Quebec Div.; recipient of ACA Gold Medal Award 1978; Charter recipient of McGill Management Achievement Award, 1981; Psi Upsilon; Conservative; Baptist; recreations: golf, curling; Clubs: Saint James's; Mount Stephen (Past Pres.); Montreal Thistle Curling (Past Pres.) Royal Montreal Golf Club; Home: 80 St. Clair Ave. E., Apt. 503, Toronto, Ont. M4T 1N6; Office 14th floor, 80 St. Clair Ave. W., Toronto, Ont. M4V 1M6

JOUBIN, Franc R., M.A., D.Sc.; mining geologist; technical mine consultant; b. San Francisco, Cal., 15 Nov. 1911; s. Auguste and Marthe Jeanne (Renault) J.; e. Pub. and High Sch., Victoria, B.C. (Matric. 1929); Victoria Coll., 1931-32; Univ. of Brit. Columbia, B.A. (Chem. and Geol.) 1936, M.A. (Geol.), 1942, D.Sc. 1958; m. Mary Toine Torvinen, 21 Dec. 1938; one d., Marion Frances; PRESIDENT, FRANC R. JOUBIN & ASSOCIATES; Mining Exploration Dept., Pioneer Gold Mines of B.C., Western Can. Divn.; 1936-43; in charge of E. Can. Exploration, 1948-52; self-employed Geol. Consultant for Candn. and American clients (travelled extensively throughout Can. and Central. Am.), 1948-52; publicly regarded as one of Canada's Specialists in uranium exploration through discoveries in the Blind River Dist. of Ont., the Beaverlodge Dist. of Sask. and in B.C.; Consultant to U.N. Tech. Assistance Programs since 1962; author of many tech. papers on mining exploration topics for tech. journs. in Can., U.S.A. and U.K.; mem., Candn. Inst. Mining & Metall. (Chrmn. of various sub-comte's.); Am. Inst. Mining & Metall.; Geol. Assn. of Can.; awarded Leonard Medal by Engn. Inst. of Can., 1956; Blaylock Medal by Candn. Inst. Mining & Metall., 1957; apptd. to serve on Nat. Adv. Comte. on Research in Geol. Sciences (1958); Protestant; recreations: reading, writing, painting; Clubs: Engineers; University; Arts & Letters; Home: 500 Avenue Road, Toronto, Ontario M4V 2J6; Office: 170 Bloor St. W., Toronto, Ont. M5S 1T9

JOUDRY, Patricia, playwright; b. Spirit River, Alberta, 18 October 1921; m. 1st, Delmar Dinsdale (divorced 1952); two d.; 2ndly, John Steele, Toronto (divorced 1975); three d.; author of plays, radio & TV scripts "Teach Me How To Cry" (play; Dom. Drama Festival Best-play Award, 1956) produced off-broadway theatre; script writing incl. the "Henry Aldrich Show" for four years, and "Penny's Diary" both radio serials; other works: "The Sand Castle" (comedy); "Three Rings for Michele" (play); "The Song of Louise in the Morning" (one act drama); "Stranger in My House" (play); "Walk Alone Together", (comedy; prize winner, Stratford-Globe playwriting competition and London West End 1959); "Semi-Detached" (drama, Broadway theatre 1960); "Valerie" (comedy); "Don The Dinted Armour" (comedy; 1st Prize Winner, Nat. Playwriting Seminar, London, Ont.); "God Goes Heathen" (drama); "Think Again" (comedy) 1969; "Now" (science-fiction, multi-media drama) 1970; "I Ching" (drama) 1971; "The Dweller on the Threshold" (novel) 1973; "And the Children Played" (non-fiction) 1975; "Spirit River to Angels' Roost" (Non-fiction) 1977; "The Selena Tree," (NOVEL) 1980; "A Very Modest Orgy", (Play) 1981; Address: C.P. 78, St Denis, Sask. S0K 3W0

JOUSSE, Albin T., O.C. (1969), B.A., M.D., LL.D., FRP-C(C); physician; university professor; b. Van-Kleek Hill, Ont., 21 July 1910; s. Paul Théophile Felix and Alice Edith (Raney) J.; e. VanKleek Hill (Ont.) Pub. and Coll. Inst., 1928; Coll. of Optometry, Toronto, Diploma 1930; McMaster Univ., B.A. 1937; Univ. of Toronto, M.D. 1942; Queen's Univ., LL.D. 1967; Dalhousie Univ., LL.D. 1981; m. Mary Margaret, d. Andrew and Katherine (Doyle) McCarthy, Montreal, Que., 19 Aug. 1944; two d. Eileen Elizabeth Woloshyn, Sheila Katharine Avery; Prof. Emeritus, Division of Rehab. Med., University of Toronto (Dir., 1953-72); Med. Dir. Lyndhurst Lodge Hosp., 1945-74; Med. Dir. Lyndurst Hospital, 1974-75; Appointed to Ont. Human Rights Commission, 1979; awarded Coronation Medal 1952; Centennial Medal 1967; Award of Merit, Montreal Rehab. Institute, 1975 E.R. 25th Anniversary Medal, 1952-77; Tenth Anniversary Medal of Order of Canada, 1967-77; Keith Armstrong Award by Cndn. Rehab. Council for the Disabled, 1979; author of over 40 papers for various journs. and assns. in Can., Brit., W. Europe and U.S.A.; mem., Candn. Med. Assn.; Ont. Med. Assn.; Candn. Assn. Phys. Med. & Rehab.; Candn. Neurol. Soc.; Liberal; recreations: sailing, travel, reading;

Home: 66 Willowbank Blvd., Toronto, Ont. M5N 1G6; Office: Lyndhurst Hospital, 520 Sutherland Dr., Toronto, Ont., M4G 3V9

JOY, Nancy Jean Hannah Grahame; medical illustrator; educator; b. Toronto, Ont. 15 Jan. 1920; d. Ernst Grahame and Dorothy Ewart (Primrose) J.; e. St. Clement's Private Sch. for Girls, Toronto; Ont. Coll. Art Dept. Drawing & Painting 1942 (Hughes Owens Prize), night courses Life Drawing & Water Colour 1963-65; Univ. of Toronto Special Student Anat., Histol., Pathol. Embryol., Neuroanat. 1942-44; Univ. of Ill. Pupil Apprentice Med. Illustration 1944-47; Ryerson Polytech. Inst. TV Studio Production Cert. 1971; PROF. AND CHRMN. OF ART AS APPLIED TO MED., UNIV. OF TORONTO since 1973, Dir. program of study since 1962; Illustrator, Dept. Anat. Univ. of Toronto 1947-52, 1954-56 (also Dept. Radiol.); freelance med. illustrator Eng. and Scot. 1952-54; Med. Illustrator Dept. Surg. Univ. of Man. 1956-59, Asst. Prof. of Med. Illustration 1959-62; Assoc. Prof. and Chrmn. of Art as applied to Med. Univ. of Toronto 1962-73, Dir. of AAM Services 1962-69; author or co-author numerous articles, reviews, bibliogs., reports, monographs-vocational guidance; scholarly addresses and seminar panels; illustrations contrib. to numerous med. books, films, projection slides; co-inventor Constudium Carrel 1969, Avisars 1975; production co-ordinator and/or designer med. exhibits, film "Dizziness" 1969 (Med. Educ. Award and one other Biocommunications '70 Houston 1970, Internat. Med. Videotape & Film Festival Williamsburg 2nd place 1970); mem. Candn. Acad. Med. Illustrators; mem. Ont. Coll. Art Alummi Assn.; Assoc. mem. Acad. Med.; mem. Assn. Med. Illustrators; Candn. Science Film Assn.; Anglican; recreations: skiing, camping; Club: Heliconian; Home: Apt. 905, 565 Avenue Rd., Toronto, Ont. M4V 2J9; Office: 256 McCaul St., Toronto, Ont. M5T 1W5.

JOYCE, Douglas; industrialist; b. Armathwaite, Cumberland, Eng., 17 Jan. 1917; s. Thomas Royter and Helen (MacAskill) J.; e. St. Bees College, 1928-34; m. Zena May, d. A. C. Watkiss, Appleby, Lincs., Eng., 28 Oct. 1939; children: Gordon Patrick, Patricia Anne; DIR., MILLCRAFT INDUSTRIES AND TECH. ASST. TO CHMN., since 1981; College Apprentice, United Steel Companies (Eng.) 1934-38 serving in various depts, in various works; Staff Asst., Richard Thomas & Baldwin's, 1938-39; Asst. Supt., Blast Furnaces, R. T. & B., 1939-43; Asst. Supt., Blast Furnaces, Millom Askam Hematite Iron Co. (Cumberland) 1943 and promoted to Supt. 1944; Supt., Blast Furnaces, Consett Iron Co. (Co. Durham), 1946-49; joined Algoma Steel as Asst. Supt., Blast Furnaces, 1949; promoted to Supt. 1953, Gen. Supt. 1956; Mgr. of Operations, Dec. 1956; Vice-Pres.-Operations 1957; el. a Dir. 1962; Sr. Vice-Pres. and Dir. 1970-82; Capt., 7th Bn., Home Guard, 1942-47; Offr. Training Corps, 1928-34; mem., Am. Iron & Steel Inst.; Iron and Steel Engrs.; Am. Mining & Metall. Engrs.; Hon. Colonel 49th (Sault Ste. Marie) Regiment 1965; Anglican; recreation: sport; Office: Bailey Hoogovens Canada Inc., 3050 Harvester Rd., Burlington, Ont. L7N 3J1

JOYCE, Hugh Kirkpatrick, B.B.A.; paper company executive president; b. Toronto, Ont., 19 March 1921; s. Thomas Wolsey and Lail Kirkpatrick (Hyslop) J.; e. Upper Canada Coll., grad. 1938; Univ. of W. Ont., B.B.A. (Univ. Gold Medalist; Hons.) 1949; m. Nancy Jane, d. B. J. Waters, Fort Point, Liverpool, N.S., 6 Jan. 1943; children: Richard Kirkpatrick, John Waters; PRESIDENT, CHIEF EXTVE. OFFR. AND DIRECTOR, BOWATER NORTH AMERICAN CORP. since 1972; Dir., Bowater America Corp. (formerly Bowater Holdings Inc.); Catawba Newsprint Co.; Bowater Corp. Ltd., London; Bowater China Ltd., London; Bowater Mersey Paper Co. Ltd.; Chrmn. and Dir., Bowater Canadian Ltd.; Terrain Enterprises (N.S.) Ltd.; Chrmn. Terrain Inc.; Dir., Kay Corp.; State Nat. Bank of Conn.; State Nat. BANCORP;

joined Mersey Paper Co. Ltd., Liverpool, N.S. 1949, Personnel Mgr. 1950, Asst. to Gen. Mgr. 1955, Asst. Gen. Mgr. 1960-62; Asst. Gen. Mgr., Bowaters Newfoundland Ltd. Corner Brook Nfld.; 1962, Vice-Pres. 1962-65, Pres. and Gen. Mgr. 1965-68; Dir., 1966-80; President & Dir., Bowater Sales Company, 1970-72; served with R.C.N.V.R. 1939-45, discharged with rank of Lieutenant Commdr.; Vice-Chmn., Southwestern Area Comm. & Ind. Assn. of Conn. Inc.; Chrmn., Bd. Trustees, Holderness Sch., Plymouth, N.H.; Trustee, Conn. Publ. Expenditure Council Inc.; mem. Extve. Bd. Candn. Pulp & Paper Assn. (sr. mem.); Dir. Am. Paper Inst.; Atlantic Prov. Econ. Council (Past Vice Pres. 1965-66); Candn. Mfctrs Assn. (Past Vice Pres.-Nfld.); Anglican; recreations: sailing, golf, skiing, reading, photography; Clubs: Blomidon Country, Corner Brook, Nfld. (Past Pres.); Greenwich Country; Canadian Soc. of New York; Metropolitan (N.Y.C.); Montserrat Yacht (W.I.); Home: Birch Lane, Greenwich, Conn. 06830; Office: 1500 E. Putnam Ave., Old Greenwich, Conn. 06870.

JOYCE, James Herbert, B.Com.; Ont. public service; b. Cranbrook, B.C., 20 Nov. 1913; s. James & Edith Edna (Armitage) J.; e. Pub. Schs. and Western Can. High Sch., Calgary, Alta.; Univ. of Toronto, B. Com. 1934; unm.; CHAIRMAN, ONTARIO DEVELOPMENT CORP. since 1973 and DIRECTOR NODC AND EODC 1976-80; with Confederation Life Association, Bond & Stock Invest. Dept., 1934-44; Investments Ed., "The Financial Post", Toronto, 1944-52; apptd. Treas., Crown Trust Co., 1952-54; Assist. Gen. Mgr. & Treas., 1954-63; Asst. Gen. Mgr. 1963-64; Extve. Vice-Pres. 1965-73; Vice-Pres. (Special Assignments) 1973; Chief Extve. Offr., Ontario Development Corp, 1975-79; mem. Univ. Coll. Comte. of Bd. of Govs. of Univ. of Toronto 1971-72; Senate, Univ. of Toronto 1962-68 College of Electors 1972; Governing Council 1972-79; Trustee & Mem; Council, Wycliffe Coll. since 1959; Extve. Univ. Coll. Alumni Assn. since 1956 (V.P. 1960-61; Pres. 1961-62); Dir. & Treas., Moore Pk. Ratepayers Assn. 1955-71; Hon. Treas., St. Paul's Ch., since 1961; mem. Comte. for local Organs. United Community Fund Greater Toronto, 1953-65; mem. Dom. Mortgage & Investments Assn. (2nd Vice Pres. 1962-63; 1st Vice Pres. 1963-64; Pres. 1964-65); mem., St. George's Soc.; Eng. Speaking Union; Advisory Board Bloorview Children's Hosp. (Chrmn. 1966-69, 1972-74); Conservative; Anglican; recreations: curling, sailing, golf; Clubs: Granite (Hon. Dir. 1970-, Pres. 1964-65; Chairman of Board 1966-67; Hon. President 1968-70, Dir. 1952-70); R.C.Y.C.; Univ. of Toronto Alumni Assn (treas. 1979-80, Pres. 1980-81); Rosedale Golf; Empire (Pres. 1954-55); Canadian; Home: 306 Rose Park Dr., Toronto, Ont. M4T 1R7; Office: 1200 Bay St., Queen's Park, Toronto, Ont. M7A 2E7

JOYCE, John Thomas, Q.C., B.A., LL.B.; b. Rochdale, Lancashire, Eng., 5 May 1921; s. John and Jane (Slater) J.; came to Canada 1922; e. Univ. of Alberta, B.A. 1951, LL.B. 1952; m. Nora Evelyn, d. Harry Moss, 13 June 1953; children: Anthony Slater, Peter Lindsell, Jennifer Ann; SR. PARTNER, WEEKS, JOYCE; Dir., Panel Investments Ltd.; Margna Holdings Ltd.; called to the Bar of Alta. 1953; cr. Q.C. 1972; served in R.C.A.F. 1942-46; Chrmn. of Legal Aid Soc. of Alta.; mem. Law Soc. Alta.; mem., Lloyd's of London; Zeta Psi; P. Conservative; R. Catholic; recreations: golf, hiking, camping, reading; Clubs: The Edmonton Club; Mayfair Golf & Country Club; Home: 5123 Lansdowne Drive, Edmonton, Alta. T6H 4L1; Office: 2700 CN Tower, 10004-104 Ave., Edmonton, Alta. T5J 0K1

JUNEAU, Denis, R.C.A.; artiste; né Montréal, Qué. 30 Sept. 1925; f. Laurent Edmond et Marguerite (Angrignon) J.; é. Institution des Sourds de Montréal, diplômé 1942; Ecole des Beaux-Arts de Montréal 1943-50 (prix du Ministre, peinture); Stage chez Georges Delrue, orfèvre de Montréal 1951-52; Chez Gilles Beaugrand, orfèvre d'église de Montréal 1952-53; Centro Studi Arte Industria

de Novara (Italie), études sur l'esthétique industrielle, diplômé 1956; L'Atelier Jean Ouellet, architecte de Montréal 1963-65; expositions - solo: Galerie Denise Delrue Montréal 1958, 1963; Musée des Beaux-Arts Montréal 1962 (Galerie Norton), 1970; Galerie Nova et Vetera Montréal (rétrospective, peintures, sculptures et dessins) 1962; Galerie du Siècle Montréal 1967; Galeria Carmen Lamanna Toronto 1968, 1973; Galerie le Gobelet Montréal 1969; Musée Provincial de Québec 1970; Centre Culturel de Trois-Rivières 1971; Centre audio-Visuel de l'Université de Montréal 1971; Symposium des Arts Plastiques, Centre Culturel de Drummondville 1971; Galerie de Montréal 1973; Galerie Bourguignon Montréal (58 dessins de 1954-66) 1974; Galerie Optica Montréal (perspective des oeuvres de 1969-78) 1979; Galerie le Groupe de Somerville Montréal 1981; Galerie Treize Montréal 1981; expositions itinerante: Consulat Général du Can. New York, Centre Culturel Canadien à Paris, Centre Culturel de l'Ambassada du Can. à Bruxelles, Can. House à Londres, 1975-76; expositions nombreaux - groupe, collections publiques et privées (comprenant Musée d'Art Contemporain et Musée des Beaux-Arts Montréal, Conseil des Arts du Can. et Galerie Nationale du Can. Ottawa); prix: Boursier du Conseil des Arts du Can. 1961-62, 1962-63, 1968-69, 1969-70, 1972-73, 1974-75; Mention honorable, Concours Nat. de l'arch. du Can., Alcan 1957; Grand prix du concours du trophée pour le grand prix de l'urbanisme de la prov. de Qué. 1965; Mention, concours artistiques du Qué. 1967, 1971; Mention, Show Winnipeg 1968; Subvention du service de l'aide à la recherche et à la création du ministère des affaires culturelles du Qué. 1970;

JUNEAU, Pierre, O.C. (1975), LL.D.; public servant; b. Verdun, P.Q., 17 Oct. 1922; s. Laurent Edmond & Marguerite (Angrignon) J.; e. Coll. Ste-Marie, Montréal, B.A.; Inst. Cathol., Paris, L.Ph.; m. Fernande, d. Hector Martin, 17 March 1947; children: André, Martin, Isabelle; DEPUTY MINISTER OF COMMUNICATION April 1980; joined Nat. Film Bd. in 1949 as Montreal Dist. Rep.; apptd. Asst. Regional Supervisor, P.Q., 1950; Chief, Internat. Distribution, 1951; Head of European Office, 1952; Secretary, 1954; Sr. Asst. to Commr. and Extve. Dir., 1957; Sr. Asst. to Commr. and Dir. of French Lang. Prod., 1964; Vice Chrmn. Bd. of Govs. 1966; Chrmn. Candn. Radio-TV Comn. 1968; Pres. Montreal International Film Festival, 1959-68; Min. of Communications 1975; joined Prime Minister's staff as special policy advisor 1975; def. in by-el. to H. of C. Oct. 1975; joined Prime Minister's staff as special policy advisor Nov. 1975; apptd. mem. and Chrmn. of Nat. Captial Comn. 1976; Under Secretary of State, Feb. 1978; Officer of the Order of Canada; member, Royal Society of Canada, Hon. LL.D. York Univ.; Roman Catholic; recreations: tennis, music, reading; Office: Journal Tower North, 300 Slater St., Ottawa, Ont.

JUNEJA, Diljit S., M.A., FIA, FCIA; company executive; b. Peshawar, India, 14 Nov. 1922; s. Kartar Singh and Rawel (Ahuja) J.; e. Panjab Univ., Edwards Coll., B.A. 1943; Islamia Coll., M.A. 1945; m. Gulshan Raj, d. Ishar Chug, 10 Oct. 1943; children: Ravinder Singh, Vinita M.; PRES., W.M. MERCER LTD. Elected to Bd. of Dir. of William M. Mercer Ltd., 1971; taught math at Brijinda Coll., Panjab University, Head of Math. Dept. and Dean of Arts Faculty, 1945-51; Head, Dept. of Math., S.G.T.B. Coll., Delhi Univ., 1951-52; Actuary, New India Insurance Co. Ltd., 1953 and on nationalization of life ins. worked for Life Insurance Corp. of India in various capacities incl. Prof. of Life Office Mang. at Offrs. Training Coll.; Adviser to and assisted in organ. of Insurance Corp. of Ceylon, 1961-65; joined present Co. as an Actuary, 1965; apptd. Vice Pres. 1968; Director 1971; Extve. Vice-Pres. 1976; Bd. of Dir., William M. Mercer Inc., N.Y. 1979; Pres. William M. Mercer Ltd., 1980-; Extve. Vice Pres., William M. Mercer Inc., N.Y. City., Feb. 1981; Consultant to various co's and univs.; Assoc., Soc. Actuaries; Acad. of Act.; Can. Inst. Act.; Intnl. Assoc. Consulting Act.; Cndn. mem. IACA'S Int. Cmte.; Sikh; recreation: golf; Clubs: Granite; National; Home: 2 Breen Crescent, Willowdale, Ont. M2P 1Z7; Office: P.O. box 59, 1 First Canadian Place, Toronto, Ont. M5X 1G3

JUTRA, Claude, M.D.; actor; film-maker; b. Montreal, Que. 1930; e. Univ. of Montreal, M.D. (never practised); student/actor Théâtre du Nouveau Monde, Montreal and Cours Simon, Paris; 1st film "Mouvement perpetuel" 1949 rec'd Candn. Film Award (Amateur category) 1949 and a prize Cannes Film Festival 1950; TV series "L'Ecole de la peur" 1950 won Prix Frignon; joined Nat. Film Bd. Can. 1955 and made several prize-winning films incl. "Les mains nettes" 1958, "A tout prendre" 1963, "Comment savoir" 1966; "Mon oncle Antoine" rec'd 8 Etrogs, Candn. Film Awards 1971 and judged best picture Chicago Film Festival; made "Kamouraska" 1975; declined O.C. 1972; rec'd Victor Morin Prize, St. Jean Baptiste Soc., Montreal 1972.

K

KADLEC, James Daniel, LL.B., M.B.A.; insurance exe-cutive; b. e. Man. Law Sch. LL.B. 1952; Stanford Univ. M.B.A. 1954 CHRMN. OF THE BD., THE FAMILY LIFE INSURANCE GROUP; Chrmn. and Dir. Sovereign General Assurance Co.; Sovereign Life Assurance Co.; Family Life Assurance Co.; Pres. and Dir. Kadco Consultants Ltd.; Chrmn. of the Bd., First Calgary Petroleums Ltd.; Dir. First Calgary Petroleum Corp. Ltd.; Victoria Mortgage Corp.; Lectr. in Corporate Finance McGill Univ. Extension 1955-63; Chrmn. Extve. Comte., Prudential Trust Co. Ltd.; Champion Saving Corp. Ltd.; Champion Mutual Fund of Canada Ltd. 1957-60; Consultant, Towers, Perrin, Forster & Crosby (Canada) Ltd. 1960-62; Special Consultant, Invest. Dealers' Assn. Can. 1962; Vice Pres. and Secy. Sogemines Consultants Ltd. (now Genstar) 1962-65; Mang. Dir. Cape Flattery Silica Mines Pty. Ltd. Australia 1968; Dir. of Special Projects The Patino Mining Corp. Toronto 1965-67; Pres. Great Pacific Industries Ltd. Vancouver 1969-70; Chrmn. of Bd. and Chief Extve. Offr. Pan Pacific Group 1970-74; Dir. WAGI S.p.a. Rome; Vice Chrmn. Steel Alberta Ltd.; Extve. Vice Pres. A.G. Industries International Inc., Del. 1955-77; Vice Pres. The Alberta Gas Trunk Line Co. Calgary 1974-77; mem. Sir Winston Churchill Soc.; Financial Extves. Inst.; recreations: hunting, camping, gun collecting; Clubs: Calgary Golf & Country; Capilano Golf & Country; Home: 4563 Woodgreen Court, West Vancouver, B.C. V2S 2V8; Office: (P.O. Box 210 Main Depot) Calgary, Alta. T2P 2H6.

KAEDING, Hon. Edgar, M.L.A.; politician; b. Church-bridge, Sask. 16 June 1920; s. Emil E. and Katie K.; m. Alva Boreen 12 Oct. 1943; children: Jerome E., Harold E., Heather, Debora; MIN. OF RURAL AFFAIRS 1979-; farmer; el. M.L.A. for Saltcoats prov. g.e. 1971, re-el. since; Del. Interprov. visit Commonwealth Parlty. Ass. Nfld. 1973; Ottawa 1974; Del. to World Food and Agricultural conf., Rome 1975; Del. to Commonweath Agricultural Soc. conf., Regina and Jamaica, 1978; Min. of Agric. 1975-79; mem. Royal Candn. Legion; NDP; Lutheran; Office: Legislative Bldg., Regina, Sask. S4S 0B3.

KAIN, Karen; ballerina; b. Hamilton; Ont.; 28 March 1951; d. Charles A. and Winifred Mary (Kelly) K.; e. Fessenden Pub. Sch., Ancaster, Ont.; Springfield Pub. Sch., Erindale, Ont.; Nat. Ballet Sch., Toronto, Ont.; joined Corps de Ballet, Nat. Ballet Co. of Can., 1969; became princ. dancer 1970; rec'd Ont. Arts Foundation, Can. Council and Ford Motor Co. Scholarships 1964-69; Hon. Awards, Prov. of Ont., Cities of Mississauga and Toronto, 1973; Silver Medalist, Internat. Competition Moscow, 1973; apptd. Offr. Order of Can. June 1976; Protestant; recreations: reading, swimming, theatre, music; Address:

c/o The National Ballet of Canada, 157 King St. E., Toronto, Ont. M5C 1G9

KAISER, Edgar F., Jr., B.A., M.B.A.; industrialist; b. Portland, Ore., 5 July 1942; s. Edgar Fosburgh and late Sue (Mead) K.; e. Governor Dummer Acad.; Stanford Univ. B.A. 1965; Harvard Univ. M.B.A. 1967; CHRM., C.E.O. AND CHRM. EXTVE. COMTE., KAISER RESOURCES LTD. 1978- ; served as Pres. and C.E.O. 1973-78; Chrm. and C.E.O. Kaiser Oil Ltd.; Dir., DAON Develop. Corp.; The Toronto-Dominion Bank; served Agency for Internat. Devel. Vietnam 1967-68; White House Fellow (Asst. to Pres. Johnson) 1968; Special Asst. to Secy. US Dept. of Interior 1969; joined present Co. as Mgr. Corporate Planning and Devel. 1970, Mgr. Resources Devel. Kaiser Steel Corp. 1970; Pres. and C.E.O. 1979- ; Vice Pres. and Treas. Kaiser Resources Ltd. 1971, Extve. Vice Pres.-Operations 1972; mem., Candn.-Am. Comte.; Can-Japan Business Co-Op Conte.; Nat. Adv. Comte. on Mining Indust.; Candn. Comte. Pacific Basin Econ. Council; Trilateral Comn.; U.S. Council on Foreign Relations; Hon. Dir. Boys' and Girls' Clubs Vancouver; Trustee Henry J. Kaiser Family Foundation; California Inst. of Technology; Governor Dummer Acad.; Nat. Choral Arts Soc. Washington; Past Pres. Coal Assn. Can.; mem. Am. Iron & Steel Inst.; mem., Council on Foreign Rel.;Young Pres.' Organ.; Can.-Asia Conf. Planning Comte.; Bus. Council on Nat. Issues; H.R.H. The Duke of Edinburgh's Fifth Commonwealth Study Conf. Can., 1980; White House Fellows Assn.; awarded Am. Acad. of Achievement 1978 Golden Plate Award; Office: Kaiser Resources Ltd., 1500 West Georgia St., Vancouver, B.C. V6G 2Z8

KALHOK, Anthony Ignatius, B.Sc., M.B.A.; executive; b. Mor, Hungary, 25 July 1941; s. Frank and Maria (Negle) K.; came to Canada 1949; e. Univ. of Toronto B.Sc. 1962; McGill Univ. M.B.A. 1969; m. Barbara Marie Burke 3 Oct. 1964; two children; PRES. AND CHIEF EXTVE. OFFR., IMASCO RETAIL INC. 1980- ; Dir. Imasco Ltd.; held various mfg. and marketing positions Imperial Tobacco Ltd. Montreal 1962-75, Vice Pres. Marketing and Dir. 1976-79; R. Catholic; recreations: skiing, golf; Clubs: National; York Downs Golf & Country; Royal Montreal Golf; Home: 74 Glengowan Rd., Toronto, Ont. M4N 1G4; Office: (P.O. Box 84) Royal Bank Plaza, Toronto, Ont. M5J 2J2.

KALISKI, Stephan Felix, M.A., Ph.D.; educator; b. Warsaw, Poland 4 Nov. 1928; s. late Jacob and late Ludwika (Romanus) K.; e. Univ. of B.C. B.A. 1952; Univ. of Toronto M.A. 1953 (Alexander Mackenzie Research Fellow 1953-54); Cambridge Univ. Ph.D. 1959 (Research Fellow Social Science Research Council 1956-57, Fellow Candn. Social Science Research Council 1957-58); m. Marian Ieleen d. late Abel J. Nelson, and Hilda N. Clyde, Alta. 6 Oct. 1960; one d. Susan Maria; PROF. OF ECON. QUEEN'S UNIV. since 1969; Stat. Dom. Bureau of Stat. 1951-52; Lectr. Queen's Univ. 1954-56; Research Fellow in Econ. Stat. Manchester Univ. 1958-59; Asst. Prof. Carleton Univ. 1959, Assoc. Prof. 1962, Prof. 1965-69, Chrmn. Econ. Dept. 1962-63, 1964-66; Research Supvr. Royal Comn. on Taxation 1963-64; Research Assoc. Univ. of Cal. Berkeley 1966-67 (Can. Council Sr. Fellowship, Dept. of Labour Univs. Research Comte. Grant); Hon. Research Assoc. in Econ. Harvard 1973-74 (Can. Council Leave Fellowship); Mang. Ed. 'Canadian Journal of Economics' 1976-79; Director, McGill — Queen's Univ. Press, 1978-80; Dir. Nat. Bureau Econ. Research, (U.S.A.), 1979- ; author or co-author numerous publs. on applied econ., internat. econ., unemployment, inflation; mem. Candn. Econ. Assn.; Am. Econ. Assn.; Royal Soc. Can.; Home: 72 Fairway Hill Cres., Kingston, Ont. K7M 2B4; Office: Kingston, Ont. K7L 3N6

KALLER, Cecil Louis, B.A., B.Ed., M.A., Ph.D.; educator; b. Humboldt, Sask., 26 March 1930; s. Frank Joseph and Cecilia Johanna (Hinz) K.; e. Elem. and High Schs. Sask.; Sask. Normal Sch., Saskatoon; Univ. of Sask., B.A. 1954, B.Ed. 1954, M.A. 1956; Purdue Univ., Ph.D. (Math. Stat.) 1960; m. Theresa Ann, d. Clarence Fricke, Ohio, 26 May 1962; four s. Kevin Paul, Damon Michael, Brian Francis, Alan Matthew; Teacher, Elem. and High Schs. 1948-52; Asst. Research Stat. Educ. Div., Dom. Bureau of Stat., Ottawa 1955; Research Stat., Upjohn Co., Kalamazoo, summers 1958-60; Asst. Prof. of math., Univ. of Sask. 1960, Assoc. Prof. 1964, trans. Regina campus as Assoc. Prof. and Chrmn. Dept. of Math. 1965, Prof. and Chrmn. of Math. 1967-70; President, Notre Dame Univ. of Nelson, also Prof. of Math. and mem. Bd. of Govs. 1970-76; Instructor of Mathematics, Okanagan Coll., Kelowna, B.C. 1976- ; author articles in various prof. and scholarly journs.; Vice Pres. Computer Science Assn. 1963-70; Assn. Computing Machinery 1967-70; Biometric Soc. 1959-70; Inst. Math. Stat. 1959-68; Trustee St. Joseph's Sch. Nelson 1973-75; Dir., Kelowna Minor Hockey Assoc. 1976-78; Vice-Pres., Catholic School Trustees Assoc. of B.C. 1977-80; Vice Pres., Faculty Assn. of Okanagan College, 1979- ; Trustee St. Joseph's & Immaculata School 1978-80; B.C. Dir. on Cdn. Catholic School Trustees Assn., 1980- ; Chrm., 4th Kelowna Boy Scout Assn., 1978-81; St. Thomas More Coll. Corp., 1982- ; mem. Am. Math. Soc.; Math. Assn. Am.; Candn. Math. Congress; Am. Stat. Assn.; Sigma Xi; Humanities Assn. Can.; R. Catholic; Home: 2056 Pandosy Kelowna, B.C. V1Y 1S3

KALLMANN, Helmut, B.Mus., LL.D.; music librarian and historian; b. Berlin, Germany, 7 Aug., 1922; s. late Dr. Arthur and late Fanny (Paradies) K.; e. Elem. and High Schs., Berlin, 1928-39; Sr. Matric., Toronto, 1946; Royal Conserv. of Music, Grade X Piano 1948; Univ. of Toronto, B.Mus. 1949, LL.D. 1971; m. Ruth, d. late Israel Singer, Toronto, 31 Dec. 1950; one step-d., Lynn Proctor (Mrs. R. Salter); CHIEF OF MUSIC DIV., NAT. LIBRARY CAN., since 1970; CBC Toronto Music Lib. 1950-70; Music Clk. 1950-51, Music Lib. 1951-61, Sr. Music Lib. 1961-62, Supvr. of Music Lib. 1962-70; author, "Catalogue of Canadian Composers" (rev. ed. only), 1952; "A History of Music in Canada 1534-1914", 1960 (reprint and paperback 1969); co-ed., "Encyclopedia of Music in Canada", 1981; other writings including book chapters, dict. and music journ. articles; collab. in various bibliog. publs.; Candn. Music Council Medal for "outstanding service to Candn. musical life", 1977; mem., Candn. Music Council (Vice Pres. 1971-76); Candn. Assn. Music. Libs.; Internat. Assn. Music Libs.; Candn. Folk Music Soc.; Bibliog. Soc. Can.; Assoc. pour l'advancement de la recherche en musique du Québec; recreations: music, travel; Home: 38 Foothills Dr., Nepean, Ont. K2H 6K3; Office: 395 Wellington St., Ottawa, Ont.

KALSNER, Stanley, B.A., Ph.D.; scientist; university professor; b. New York 21 Aug. 1936; came to Can. 1967; s. Wm. Louis and Sadie K.; e. N.Y. Univ. B.A. 1954-58; State Univ. N.Y. Pharmaco. 1960-62; Univ. of Manitoba Ph.D. 1963-66; Cambridge Univ. postdoctoral 1966-67; m. Jenny d. Max and Anna Book 4 Aug. 1963; children: Lydia, Pamela, Louisa; FULL PROF. OF PHARMACOLOGY, UNIV. OF OTTAWA; Dir. Grad. training prog. in Pharm.; mem. Council of Grad. Studies; Prof. Assn. (grievance Comte.); Teaching personnel Comte. (pharm.); Ed. Bd. of Candn. Jnl. of Physiol. and Pharm.; of Blood Vessels; Jnl. of Autonomic Pharm.; on-going research prog. on heart disease and nerve control mechanisms; ed. "Trends in Autonomic Pharmacology", Volumes I and II 1979, 1982, "The Coronary Artery" 1982; author over sixty scientific papers in professional jnls. on heart and blood vessel disease; rec'd grant from Candn. Heart Found.; NRCC; Med. Res. Coun. of Can.; meritorious research award Can. S. Physiol. and Pharm.; Consultant Natl. Inst. of Health; mem., Candn. Pharm. Soc.; Am. Pharm. Soc.; N.Y. Academy of Sciences; Am. Assn. for Advancement of Science; Candn. Hypertension Soc.;

Conservative; Jewish; recreations: painting, writing, jogging; Home: 994 Bronson Ave., Ottawa, Ont. K1S 4H1;Office: 275 Nicholas St., Ottawa, Ont. K1N 9A9

KAMAL, Musa Rasim, B.S., M.Eng., Ph.D.; educator; b. Tulkarm, Jordan 8 Dec. 1934; s. Rasim Kamal Ismail and Aminah Adu Hadbah; e. Univ. of Ill. B.S. 1958; Carnegie-Mellon Univ., Pittsburgh, Pa. M.Eng. 1959, Ph.D. (Chem. Eng.) 1961; Columbia Univ., N.Y. Grad. studies in Economics; m. Nancy Joan d. Arthur Edgar 23 Dec. 1961; children: Rammie, Basim; PROFESSOR, CHEM. ENG. DEPT., MCGILL UNIV. 1973- ; Pres., Tulkarm Enterprises Ltd. (Consultants & Planners); Research Chem. Eng., Central Research Lab, Amer. Cyanamid Co., Stamford, Conn. 1961-65; Research Group Leader, Plastics & Resins Divn., Amer. Cyanamid, Wallinford, Conn. 1965-67; joined present Univ. as Assoc. Prof. of Chem. Eng. in 1967; Head Micro-Economics & Sectoral Studies Grp., Morocco 5-Year Ind. Devt. Plan, Rabat, Morocco 1978-82; author "Weatherability of Plastics Materials" 1967; over 60 publications in fields of Chem. Eng. and Polymer Technology; 13 patents; mem. Advisory Bd., "Polymer Engineering and Sci. Journal"; Ed. Bd., "Advances in Polymer Tech. Journal"; mem., Que. Order of Engineers; Can. Soc. of Chem. Engrs. (past Treas.); Chem. Inst. of Can. (past mem. Finance Comte.); Soc. of Plastics Engrs. (past Dir., Plastics Analysis & Engineering Structure & Properties Divns.); Plastics Inst. of Amer. (past Dir.); Amer. Chem. Soc.; Amer. Inst. of Chem. Eng.; Amer. Inst. of Physics; Amer. Assn. for Advancement of Sci.; Amer. Acad. of Mechanics; Soc. of Rheology; U.N. Assn. of Can; McGill Assn. of Univ. Tchrs.; Tau Beta Pi; Phi Lamda Epsilon; Pi Mu Epsilon; Sigma Xi; various academic & admin. comtes., McGill Univ.; Progm. Chrmn., 2nd World Congress of Chem. Engrs. 1981; Annual Technical Conf., Soc. of Plastics Engrs. 1973; Muslim; Clubs: Montreal Amateur Athletics Assn.; McGill Univ. Faculty; recreations: tennis, reading, travel; Home: 338 Roslyn Ave., Westmount, Que. H3Z 2L6; Office: 3480 University St., Montreal, Que. H3A 2A7

KANE, Hugh P.; book publisher; b. Belfast, N. Ireland, 13 Sept. 1911; s. Hugh Smiley and Alice Harvey (Pyper) K.; e. Rothesay (N.B.) Coll. Sch., 1922-28; m. Lorna Elizabeth, d. Harry Would, 15 Apl. 1955; children: Sean Hugh Whitford, Maire Elizabeth; PRES. & MANG. Dir., NSL Natural Science of Canada Ltd., 1976-80; Pres., The Macmillan Co. of Canada Ltd., 1969-72; Vice-Chrmn. & Dir. 1972-76; Extve. Vice Pres., McClelland and Stewart Ltd., 1955-69; Chrmn., Book Publishers' Assn. of Can., 1962-63; Pres., Co-Operative Book Centre of Canada Ltd., 1963-66; Pres., Canadian Book Publishers' Council, 1966-67; served with R.C.A. 1942-46; Protestant; recreations: reading, travel; Home: 14 Summerhill Gardens, Toronto, Ont. M4T 1B4;

KANE, Hon. Joseph C.; judge; b. Stratford, Ont. 19 Oct. 1928; s. Frederick H. and Lillian May (Jones) K.; e. Oakwood Coll. Inst. Toronto 1948; Univ. of Toronto Victoria Coll. B.A. 1951; Ont. Coll. of Educ. 1952; Osgoode Hall Law Sch. 1957; m. Janet Wylie d. Ernest Henry Perkins 30 June 1956; children: Terrance, Wendy, Timothy, Steven, Christopher; JUDGE, CO. COURT JUDICIAL DIST. OF YORK; called to Bar of Ont. 1957; cr. Q.C. 1974; Protestant; home: 169 Munro Blvd., Willowdale, Ont. M2P 1C9; Office: Court House, 361 University Ave., Toronto, Ont. M5G 1T3.

KANE, R. James, B.Com., F.C.A.; b. Toronto, Ont., 28 Oct. 1917; s. Thomas and Anne (Pennell) K.; e. Univ. of Toronto, B.Com. 1940; C.A. 1948 (el. F.C.A. 1959); m. Mary, d. late G. Cecil Ames, 13 June 1947; children: Thomas Douglas, Lawrence Ames, Cynthia Mary, Rodger James; CHRMN., THORNE RIDDELL; joined Thorne, Mulholland, Howson & McPherson as student in accounts 1940; rejoined 1946; Past Pres. and Hon. Vice-Pres., Candn. Red Cross Soc.; Vice Pres., League of Red

Cross Soc., Geneva; Wycliffe Coll.; served in R.C.A. 1941-46; Major, 23rd Candn. Field Regt.; awarded Centennial Medal 1967; Queen's Jubilee Medal 1977; mem. Inst. Chart. Accts., Ont., Que., and Bahamas Anglican; recreations: golf, curling, bridge; Clubs: Toronto Cricket, Skating & Curling; Toronto; Rosedale Golf; University; Rotary; Home: 21 Mason Blvd., Toronto, Ont. M5M 3C6; Office: Commercial Union Tower, (Box 262) Toronto-Dominion Centre, Toronto, Ont. M5K 1J9

KANEE, Sol, O.C., B.A., LL.B., LL.D.; executive; b. Melville, Sask., 1 June 1909; s. Sam and Rose (Lercher) K.; e. Univ. of Man., B.A. 1929, LL.D. 1974; Univ. of Sask., LL.B. 1932; m. Florence Barish, 10 Apl. 1935; one s., Stephen Charles; CHAIRMAN, SOO LINE MILLS (1969) LTD.; Chrmn., G III Ltd.; McCarthy Milling Co. Ltd.; Dir., Bank of Canada; Kanee Grain Co. Ltd.; Grant Park Plaza Ltd.; Weston Bakeries Ltd.; Mony Life Ins. Co. Can.; Pacific Western Airlines; read law with J. W. Estey, K.C., Saskatoon; called to Bar of Sask. 1933; with law firm Kanee & Deroche, Melville, Sask., 1933-40; Shinbane, Dorfman & Kanee, Winnipeg, 1945-65; served with RCA in Europe and S. Pacific 1940-45; rank Maj.; Past Pres., Candn. Jewish Cong.; Un. Way of Greater Winnipeg; Community Welfare Planning Council; Royal Winnipeg Ballet; Services for Handicapped (Man.) Inc.; Vice Pres., Social Service Audit Inc.; Chrmn., North Am. Br., World Jewish Cong.; Past Chrmn., Bd. Govs., Univ. of Man.; Candn. Nat. Millers Assn.; Offr. Order of Can. 1977; Liberal; Jewish; recreation: fishing; Club: Glendale Golf & Country; Office: 7 Higgins Ave., Winnipeg, Man.

KANFER, Julian Norman, M.Sc., Ph.D.; biochemist; educator; b. Brooklyn, N.Y. 23 May 1930; s. Benjamin N. and Clara (Lichtenberger) K.; e. Brooklyn Coll. B.Sc. 1954; George Washington Univ. M.Sc. 1958, Ph.D. 1961; children: Brian, Rachel; PROF. AND HEAD OF BIOCHEM., UNIV. OF MAN. 1975- ; Consultant, Health Sciences Center Winnipeg 1976- ; mem. Med. Adv. Bd. Nat. Tay-Sachs Foundation New York 1970- ; mem. Study Sec. on Pathobiol. Chem. Nat. Insts. Health 1974- ; recipient Am. Soc. Biol. Chems. Travel Award 1967; Med. Research Council Can. Visiting Scient. Award 1980; Tokyo Soc. Med. Sciences and Faculty of Med. Univ. of Tokyo Award; author "Sphingolipid Biochemistry" 1982; mem. Am. Soc. Biol. Chem.; Am. Neurochem. Soc.; Internat. Neurochem. Soc.; Am. Chem. Soc.; Am. Assn. Advanc. Science; Soc. Complex Carbohydrates; Fed. Am. Socs. Exper. Biol. (Nat. Corr.); Candn. Fed. Biol. Socs.; Multiple Sclerosis Soc. Can. (Dir. Winnipeg Chapter); Home: 116 Kingsway St., Winnipeg, Man. R3M 0G9; Office: 770 Bannatyne Ave., Winnipeg, Man. R3E 0W3.

KAPLAN, J. Gordin, M.A., Ph.D., D.Sc.; educator; b. New York City, N.Y. 26 Nov. 1922; s. Michael and Nadia (Gordin) K.; e. Coll. of City of New York B.A. 1943; Columbia Univ. M.A. 1948, Ph.D. 1950; Concordia Univ. D.Sc. 1978; m. Sylvia Leadbeater 31 Aug. 1949; 2 children; PROF. OF BIOCHEM., AND VICE-PRES. (RESEARCH), UNIV. OF ALTA., 1981- ; Prof. of Biol., Univ. of Ottawa, 1966- and Chrmn. of Biol. there 1975-81 ; Prof. of Physiol. & Biophysics, Dalhousie Univ. 1950-66; Founder and Past Chrmn. Bd. Dirs. (1961-62) Halifax Grammar Sch.; Dir., N.S. Rehabilitation Hosp.; Pres., XI Internat. Cong. of Biochem., Toronto 1979; Ed. "The Molecular Basis of Immune Cell Function" 1979; Co-Ed. "Canadian Journal of Biochemistry"; author over 100 papers molecular biol.; served with U.S. Army Med. Dept. 1943-46, Europe 1944-46, Surg. Tech. rank Cpl.; mem., Can. Assoc. of Univ. Teachers (Pres. 1970-71); Candn. Soc. Cell Biol. (Pres. 1971-72); Candn. Fed. Biol. Socs. (Pres. 1975-76); Candn. Biochem. Socs. (Pres. 1978-79); recreation: chamber music; Home: 8922-119th St., Edmonton, Alta. T6G 1W9; Office: 3-2 Univ. Hall, Univ. of Edmonton, Edmonton, Alta. T6G 1J9.

KAPLAN, Robert Phillip, P.C., Q.C., M.P., B.A., LL.B.; b. Toronto, Ont., 27 Dec. 1936; s. Solomon Charles and Pearl (Grafstein) K.; e. Univ. of Toronto B.A. (Univ. Coll.) 1958, LL.B. 1961; m. Estherelke, d. Joseph Tanenbaum, Toronto, Ont., 10 Oct. 1961; children: Jennifer Mia, John David, Raquel Katherine; SOLICITOR GENERAL OF CANADA 1980- ; called to Bar of Ont. 1963; practised law Toronto; el. to H. of C. for Don Valley g.e. 1968, def. g.e. 1972, def. M.P. for York Centre 1974; Official Opposition Critic: Immigration and Citizenship; Past Chrmn. H. of C. Standing Comte. on Finance, Trade & Econ. Affairs; Past mem. Candn. Del. to UN Gen. Assembly; mem. Can.-US Parlty. Group; Past Parlty. Secy. to Min. of Nat. Health & Welfare; Past Parlty Secy. to Min. of Finance; served as Consultant on Candn. Affairs Hudson Inst. of N.Y. lecturing on this subject at Inst. confs. in N. Am. and abroad; co-author "Bicycling in Toronto" 1971; mem. Candn. Bar Assn.; The Law Society of Upper Canada; Candn. Civil Liberties Assn.; Liberal; Jewish; Home: 28 Kendal Ave., Toronto, Ont. Office: House of Commons, Ottawa, Ont.

KAPLANSKY, Irving, M.A., Ph.D., D.Math., D.Sc.; university professor; b. Toronto, Ont., 22 March 1917; s. Samuel and Anna (Zuckerman) K.; e. Univ. of Toronto, B.A. 1938, M.A. 1939; Harvard Univ., Ph.D. 1941; Waterloo, D.Math. 1968; Queen's D.Sc. 1969; m. Rachelle, d. late Nathaniel Brenner, 16 March 1951; children: Steven, Daniel, Lucille; PROF. OF MATH., UNIV. OF CHICAGO, since 1956; Instr., Harvard Univ. 1941-44; Math., Columbia Univ. 1944-45; joined present Univ. as Instr., 1945-47; Asst. Prof. 1947-52, Assoc. Prof. 1952-56, Chrmn. of Math. Dept. 1962-67; author of "Infinite Abelian Groups", 1954, 2nd ed. 1969; "Introduction to Differential Algebra", 1957; "Rings of Operators", 1968; "Fields and Rings", 1969; other writings incl. approximately 100 papers for math. journs.; mem., Math. Assn. Am.; Math. Soc.; Nat. Acad. Sciences; Am. Acad. Arts & Sciences; Jewish (Reform); recreations: music, sports; Home: 5825 S. Dorchester, Chicago, Ill. 60637.

KAPLANSKY, Kalmen; C.M.; labour consultant; b. Bialystok, Poland, 5 Jan. 1912; s. late Abraham and Masha (Wisotsky) K.; e. High Sch., Poland (Matric. 1929); m. Esther, d. late Nathan Kositsky, 21 June 1945; children: Marsha Anne, Frances F.; DIR. OF CAN. BR. OFFICE AND SPECIAL ADV. TO DIR.-GEN., INTERNAT. LABOUR OFFICE, 1967-80; mem., Econ. Counc. of Can.; Refugee Status Adv. Comte., Employment and Immigration Comn.; Bd. Govs., Carleton Univ.; Gov. Body, ILO 1960-66; Typesetter and Linotype Operator, 1932-43; Nat. Dir., Jewish Labour Comte. of Can., 1946-57; Secy. Publications Comte., Candn. Labour Reports, 1946-57; Dir., Dept. of Internat. Affairs, Candn. Labour Congress, and Secy. Nat. Comte. for Human Rights, 1957-66; served in 2nd World War with Candn. Army (Active) 1943-46; def. cand. to Quebec Leg. (C.C.F.) 1944, and Fed. by-el. for Cartier, 1950; Chrmn. of Montreal Organ. of Work-Circle (1940-43); mem., Internat. Typographical Union since 1932; substitute mem., Extve. Bd., ICFTU, 1957-66; Alternate mem., Candn. Nat. Comn. on UNESCO, 1957-66; mem. Candn. del. to 10th Session of Gen. Conf. of UNESCO, Paris, 1958 and to 18th General Assembly of the United Nations (1963); Advisor to Worker's Del. of Can. to 40th, 42nd, 43rd, 44th, 45th, 46th, 47th, 48th, 49th and 50th sessions, I.L.O., Geneva (1957-66); Sr. Fellow, Human Rights Inst., Univ. of Ottawa; Vice Chrmn., Douglas-Coldwell Foundation; Chrmn. Special Staff Group on Employment and Econ. Opportunities for Native Northerners, Dept. Indian & N. Affairs 1970-74; Hebrew; recreation: reading; Home: 771 Eastbourne Ave., Manor Park, Ottawa, Ont. K1K 0H8;

KARDISH, Laurence ("Larry"), M.F.A.; curator; author; film maker; b. Ottawa, Ont., 5 Jan. 1945; s. Samuel and Tillie (Steinberg) K.; e. Lisgar Coll. Inst., Ottawa, 1962; Carleton Univ., B.A. 1966; Columbia Univ., M.F.A. 1968;

(divorced); one d., Naomi Frances; ASSOC. CURATOR, MUSEUM OF MODERN ART, N.Y.; founded Carleton Univ. Cine Club 1964; New Am. Cinema Group; Filmmakers' Distribution Center; one of maj. retrospectives mounted at present museum "New Cinema From Quebec", 1972; "Senegal: Fifteen Years of an African Cinema, 1962-1977, 1978" and "Cinema Quebecois, 1972-78";rec'd Art Gallery of Ont. award "Best Narrative — Canadian Film", 1969; author "Reel Plastic Magic", 1972; other writings incl. "Brussels Sprouts" (play) 1969; "Bronx Lullaby"; "Slow Run" (film), 1968; "Soft Passions" (screenplay) 1973; "Egg Cream" (play) 1975; mem. Nat. Film Theatre (Ottawa); Candn. Film Inst.; Candn. Fed. Film Socs.; Comité d'honneur of the festival Internat. du film de la critique quebecoise Montreal Home: 165 Christopher St., New York, N.Y. 10014; Office: 21 W. 53rd St., New York, N.Y.

KARFILIS, James, B.A., LL.B.; barrister; b. Greece, 15 Oct. 1928; s. Daniel and Rose (Koroloff) K.; came to Canada 1936; e. Pub. and High Schs., Toronto, Ont.; Univ. of Toronto, B.A. 1947, LL.B. 1964; Ont. Teachers' Coll., Cert. 1949; Osgoode Hall Law Sch. 1964; m. Elsie, d. Samuel Kurtis, 7 Sept. 1947; children: Jane Ellen, Peggie Anne Thomas, Nancy Lynn, Richard James; Founder and Legal Counsel, Pollution Probe, Univ. of Toronto and Lectr. on Pollution to all Sr. Grade Schs., Toronto; read law with Justice Patrick Hartt and G. Arthur Martin, Q.C.; called to Bar of Ont. 1965; Teacher, Ogden St. Pub. Sch., Toronto 1948 and Bloor Coll. Inst., Toronto 1953-54; founded present practice 1966; mem. Co. York Law Assn.; Candn. Bar Assn.; Upper Can. Law Soc.; sometime Asst. Counsel to Mr. Justice Arthur Kelly on Roy. Comn. on Windfall Mines & Oils Ltd.; has contrib. articles on environment to various mags.; Greek Orthodox; Home: 35 Kingsway Cres., The Kingsway, Toronto, Ont. M8X 2S9; Office: 85 Richmond St. W., Toronto, Ont. M5H 2G2

KARSH, Yousuf, O.C. (1967), D.C.L., LL.D., D.H.L., F.R.P.S., R.C.A.; portraitist; photographer; b. Armenia-in-Turkey, 23 Dec. 1908; s. Amsih and Bahia (Nakash) K.; came to Canada, 1924, and naturalized, 1947; e. LL.D., Carleton Univ., Queen's Univ., Emerson Coll., Boston; D.H.L., Dartmouth Coll.; Mt. Allison and Ohio Univs. 1968; D.C.L. Bishop's 1969; D.H.L., Univ. of Detroit 1978; D.F.A. Amherst College, 1979; D.H.L. Univ. of Hartford, 1980; D.F.A. Tufts Univ., 1981; m. 1st Solange Gautier, (d. 1961), 1939; 2nd., Estrellita, d. late Philip Nachbar, Chicago, Ill., 28 Aug. 1962; studied photography under his uncle in Sherbrooke, Que., and in Boston with John Garo; settled in Ottawa in 1932, and shortly after estbd. his studio there; has since established an internat. reputation for his portraits of famous men and women, notably Sir Winston Churchill (1941), and many others throughout the world; Fellow, Royal Photographic Soc. (Eng.); Photo. Soc. of Am.; mem., Candn. Photo. Soc. (Hon. Life); Candn. Armenian Congress (Hon. Pres.); Publications: "Faces of Destiny", 1947; "This is the Mass", 1958; "This is Rome", 1959; "Portraits of Greatness", 1959; "This is the Holy Land", 1960; "These are the Sacraments", 1963; "The Warren Court" (Frank and Karsh) 1964; "Karsh Portfolio", 1967; "Faces of Our Time" 1971; "Karsh Portraits", 1975; Karsh Canadians, 1978; awarded Can. Council Medal, 1965; Centennial Medal; one-man exhibitions: Canadian Pavilion, Expo '67; Montreal Museum Fine Arts; Boston Museum Fine Arts; Corning Museum, 1968; Corcoran Gallery; Detroit Art Museum; Seattle Art Museum 1969-70; Kalamazoo Inst. of Arts; Philadelphia Civic Centre; Grand Rapids Art Museum; Hackley Art Gallery 1971; Nelson Gallery of Art; Sedona Arts Centre; Reading Museum; St. Petersburg Museum of Arts 1972; Palm Springs Desert Museum; Albright-Knox Art Gallery; Santa Barbara Art Museum; Toledo Museum of Art 1973; Flint Inst. of Arts; State Univ. of N.Y.; Ulbrich Art Gallery (Wichita) 1974; Loch Haven Art Center (Orlando); Honolulu Contemporary

Arts Center 1975; Kenosha Pub. Museum (Wis.) 1976; Ulbrich Art Gallery (Wichita) 1977; Museum of Science and Indust. (Chicago) 1978; Albrecht Museum, (St. Joseph, Missouri); Evansville Art Gallery, (Evansville, Ind.) 1979; Palm Springs De Soit Museum, 1981; one-man exhn.: "Men Who Make Our World" acquired by Nat. Gallery Australia, Museum Contemporary Arts, Tokyo and Prov. of Alta.; Guest of Hon., Arles, (France) Arts Festival & Exhn. 1975; Visiting Prof. of Photog. Art. Ohio Univ. 1967-68; Emerson Coll. 1970-72; el. R.C.A. 1975; Achievement in Life Award, Encyclopaedia Brittanica, 1980; Office: Chateau Laurier Hotel, Suite 660, Ottawa, Ont. K1N 8S7

KASDORF, Gerhard, B.Sc., P.Eng.; petroleum executive; b. Bassano, Alta., 4 Nov. 1933; s. David D. and Helen (Zacharias) K.; e. Rosemary (Alta.) High Sch.; Mount Royal Coll. 1954-55; Okla. Univ. B.Sc. (Petrol. Engn.) 1957; m. Leona Helen d. late Jacob Daniel Heyde, 27 Dec. 1956; children: at home, Lindsey Lee, Julie Ann Michelle; one married daughter, Mrs. Robert J.F. Romney; PRESIDENT AND DIR., PROLUD PETROLEUMS INC., 1981- ; and Pres., Astral Energy Systems Ltd., 1978- ; joined Gulf Oil Corp. of Can. 1957-63 serving principally as reservoir engr.; Dist. Production Engr. S. M. Huber Corp. 1963, Production Mgr.-Candn. Operations 1967-71; Pres. and Dir., Am. Eagle, 1972-81; Vice Pres. and Dir. Oakwood, 1971-80; mem. Am. Inst. Mining Engrs. Socs. Alta. and Sask.; P. Conservative; United Church; recreations: golf, curling, tennis; Clubs: Club 400; Canyon Meadows Golf & Country; Kelowna Golf & Country; Calgary Winter (Past Pres. and Dir.); Home: 3344 Barrett Pl. N.W., Calgary, Alta. T2L 1W6; Office: 330 Elveden House, 717-7th Ave. S.W., Calgary, Alta. T2P 0Z3

KASHTAN, William; political leader; b. Montreal, Que. 27 June 1909; e. Public Sch., Montreal, Que.; m. 31 Dec. 1937; one d.; NAT. LEADER & GEN. SECY., COMMUNIST PARTY OF CANADA: joined Young Communist League at 18; came to Toronto, Ont., as Southern Organizer, 1928; became Nat. Secy., 1931; worked towards formation of indust. unions in Can.; took active part in formation of Candn. Youth Congress in 1930's; del. to World Youth Congress, Geneva, sponsored by League of Nations; assisted in formation of McKenzie-Papineau Bn., Internat. Bgdes., for support of Loyalist Govt. in Spain; since 2nd World War has served in Party as Toronto Organizer, Labour Secy., Extve. Secy.; has been cand. in federal els.; served in Reserve Army; has participated in World Confs. of Communist and Workers Parties; has written numerous pol. pamphlets and articles for journs. incl. "World Marxist Review" (Prague); author of weekly column for "Canadian Tribune"; recreations: reading, music, gardening, sports, carpentry; Office: 24 Cecil St., Toronto, Ont. M5T 1N2

KATES, Josef, B.A., M.A., Ph.D., LL.D., P.Eng.; F.E.I.C.; consultant; b. Vienna, Austria, 5 May 1921; s. Baruch and Anna (Entenberg) Katz; e. Goethe Real Schule, Vienna 1938; Internat. Corr. Schs. Radio Engn. Course 1942; Univ. of Toronto B.A. 1948, M.A. 1949, Ph.D. (Physics) 1951; m. Lillian S., d. late Louis Kroch 24 Dec. 1944; children: Louis, Naomi, Celina, Philip; PRESIDENT, JOSEF KATES ASSOCIATES, INC. since 1974; Pres. SETAK Computer Services Corp. Ltd. (formerly KCS Ltd.) since 1954; Teleride Corp., 1977- ; joined Imperial Optical Co. Toronto 1942 in charge of precision optics for naval equipment; Special Projects Engr. Rogers Electronics Tubes (now Philips Electronics Ltd.) 1944-48; joined Computation Centre, Univ. of Toronto 1948; designed and built first pilot model (UTEC) of Electronic Computer in Can.; also designed first electronic game playing machine (Bertie the Brain), exhibited Candn. Nat. Exhn. 1950; served as computer consultant to numerous Candn. and Am. firms and organs.; estbd. KCS Ltd. Toronto 1954 subsidiary Traffic Research Corp., subsequently expanded to other Candn., Am. and UK centres; designed world's first computer controlled signal system in Metrop. Toronto, capacity improvement of Welland Canal, computer models for urban and regional transport. and land use planning utilized by numerous cities and regions in N. Am. and Europe; consulting operations KCS Ltd. in 1967 merged with consulting div. Peat, Marwick, Mitchell & Co. in Can. to form Kates, Peat, Marwick & Co. (Can.), Peat, Marwick, Kates & Co. (Eng.) and Peat, Marwick & Livingstone & Co. (US), remained Depy. Mang. Partner of Candn. firm until 1968; computer operations of KCS Ltd. continued by SETAK Computer Services Corp. Ltd. from 1967; mem. Science Council Can. 1968-74; Chrmn. Science Council Can. 1975-78; mem. Bd. Candn. Weitzmann Inst. of Science; Candn. Technion Soc.; New Mount Sinai Hosp.; past mem. bd., Hospital Computing Services of Ont. Inc.; Past Pres. Operations Research Soc.; Past Chrmn. Operations Research Comte. Candn. Indust. Traffic League; former mem. Nat. Research Council Adv. Comte. on Computers; Past. Vice Pres. Candn. Assn. Data Processing Service Organs.; Ont. Inst. Mang. Consultants; Fellow, Engn. Inst. Can. (Past Chrmn. Mang. Sec. Toronto Region); elected Ch Univ. of Waterloo, 1979-82; re-elected 1982-85; recreations: tennis, skiing; Clubs: Donalda and University; Home: 17 Fifeshire Rd., Willowdale, Ont. M2L 2G4; Office: 156 Front St. West, Toronto, Ont. M5J 2L6

KATES, Morris, M.A., Ph.D.; educator and researcher; b. Galati, Romania 30 Sept. 1923, s. Samuel and Tobe (Cohen) K.; e. Parkdale Coll. Inst. Toronto 1941; Univ. of Toronto B.A. 1945, M.A. 1946, Ph.D. 1948; m. Pirkko Helena Sofia d. Urho Makinen, Korso, Finland, 14 June 1957; children: Anna-Lisa, Marja Helena, Ilona Sylvia; VICE DEAN (RESEARCH), UNIV. OF OTTAWA since 1978; Prof. of Biochem. since 1968; Nat. Research Council Postdoctoral Fellow 1949-51, Research Offr. Ottawa 1951-68; Visiting Scient. Nat. Inst. for Med. Research, London, Eng. 1959-60; Visiting Prof. Univ. of Helsinki 1975, Japanese Soc. for Promotion of Science 1975; rec'd Ottawa Biol. and Biochem. Soc. Prize for Scient. Achievement 1977; awarded Univ. of Ottawa Staff Research Lectureship; author "Techniques of Lipidology" 1972; co-ed. "Metabolic Inhibitors" Vol. III 1972, Vol. IV 1973; "Canadian Journal of Biochemistry" since 1974; over 150 scient. articles original research lipid biochem. and metabolism; mem. Chem. Inst. Can. (Councillor 1966-69); Candn. Biochem. Soc. (Councillor 1971-74); Royal Soc. Can.; Am. Chem. Soc.; Am. Soc. Biol. Chems.; Biochem. Soc. (London); Ottawa Biol. & Biochem. Soc. (Pres. 1974-75); recreations: music composition, chamber music playing (violin, viola) swimming, skiing; Home: 1723 Rhodes Cres., Ottawa, Ont. K1H 5T1; Office: Ottawa, Ont. K1N 6N5.

KATES, Paul Allan; insurance executive; b. Toronto, Ont. 3 Feb. 1926; e. Toronto Schs.; m. Claire Gelfond 15 Aug. 1955; children: Kathryn, Valerie; PRESIDENT, KATES-DUNCAN AND ASSOCS. LTD.; Sr. Partner, Creative Planning Insurance Agencies Ltd.; Dir. Standard Trust Co.; mem. Pension Comn. Ont.; Pres. Coronet Insurance Agencies Ltd. 1954-61; served in Candn. Intelligence Corp (R) 1948-49; mem. (Life) Million Dollar Round Table; P. Conservative (Campaign Chrmn. for Metrop. Toronto, Fed. P. Conservative Party 1972-74); Jewish (Past Pres. Temple Emmanuel); recreations: calisthenics, history, classical music, walking; Club: Albany; Home: 62 Bannatyne Dr., Willowdale, Ont. M2L 2P1; Office: 50 Gervais Dr., Suite 501, Don Mills, Ont. M3C 1Z3

KATO, Laszlo, M.D.; microbiologist; educator; b. Medgyes, Hungary, 5 July 1914; s. Denes and Gizella (Panczel) K.; e. Univ. Pazmany Peter, Budapest, M.D. 1939; Research Training Courses in Biochem., Bacteriol. and Serol. 1940, in Clin. Pathol. 1944; m. Vilma Dombos, 29

June 1941; children: Laszlo, Gabor; DIR. RESEARCH, THE SALVATION ARMY, CATHERINE BOOTH HOSPITAL CENTRE, MONTREAL Aug. 1, 1979- ; Prof., Hansen Chair of Research, Inst. Armand Frappier, Univ. Que. (in collab. with W.H.O.); Asst. Prof., Exper. Pathol., Univ. Pazmany Peter, Budapest 1942; Med. Offr., UNRRA Operations, Germany 1944-48; came to Can. 1951 as Head, Lab. of Exper. Pathol., Univ. of Montreal; Assoc., Candn. Extve. Service Overseas for Brazil 1969, for Brazil, Senegal and Cameroon 1972; Head, Hansen Lab. 1970; served in 2nd World War, Lieutenant Medical Corps; service with combatting troops, Royal Hungarian Army, Eastern Front 1942-43; awarded Fire Cross 1st Class with Swords; Order for Heroism; Expert, W.H.O. Communicable Diseases, Leprosy Sec., H.Q. Geneva; Hon. mem. Argentinian Soc. Biochems.; Brazilian Soc. of Leprol.; mem. Am. Pavlovian Soc.; Am. Coll. Neuropsychopharmacol.; Coll. Phys. and Surgs. P.Q.; Internat. Leprosy Assn.; Candn. Assn. Microbiols.; Assn. Internat. Léprologues de langue française; Adv. Comte., Candn. Leprosy Council; Kt., Mil. and Hosp. Order St. Lazarus of Jerusalem; Cross of Merit, Sovereign Order of Malta; Publications: "Horn, Clapper and Bell" 1972; "Studies on phagocytic stimulation" 1957 and "Acute Inflammation" 1970 (both with B. Gözsy); Ed. Monography Series, Inst. Microbiol. and Hygiene; author of over 268 original publs. in field of exper. pathol. and leprosy and the iconography and hist. of leprosy; Presbyterian; recreations: cabinetmaking; mosiacs; Home: 6 Kilburn Cres., Hampstead, Que. H3X 3B9; Office: Dept. of Research, The Salvation Army, Catherine Booth Hospital Centre, 4375 Montclair Ave., Montreal, Que. H4B 2J5

KATTAN, Naim; author; public institution executive; b. Bagdad, Iraq 26 Aug. 1928; s. late Nessim and Hela (Saleh) K.; e. Alliance Israélite Universelle Bagdad 1943; Tafayoudh (Coll.) Bagdad 1943-45; Univ. de Bagdad Faculté de Droit 1945-47, Sorbonne 1947-51; m. Gaëtane d. late Avila Laniel July 1961; one s. Emmanuel; HEAD OF WRITING AND PUBLICATION SEC., CANADA COUNCIL; author: Essai critique, "Le réel et le théâtral" 1970 (Prix France-Can. 1971); La mémoire et la promesse" 1978; "Ecrivains des Amériques" Tome I Les États-Unis, Tome II Le Canada Anglais, Tome III L'Amérique latine 1980; nouvelles, "La discrétion et autres pièces" 1974; Roman nouvelles, "Dans le désert" 1975; "La Traversée" 1977; "Le Rivage" 1979; "Adieu Babylone" 1976; "Les Fruits Arrachés" 1978; "Le Sable de l'île" 1981; numerous articles various publs.; mem. Royal Sco. Can.; Société des Cent Associés; Jewish; Home: 4803 rue Mira, Montreal, Que. H3W 2B5; Office: 255 Albert St., Ottawa, Ont. K1P 5V8.

KATZ, Leon, O.C. (1974), M.Sc., Ph.D., F.R.S.C.; educator; b. Russia, 9 Aug. 1909; s. Jacob and Malka K.; came to Can. 1920; e. Queen's Univ., B.Sc., M.Sc. 1936; Calif. Inst. of Tech., Ph.D. 1942; m. Georgina May Caverly, 4 Jan. 1941; children: Sylvan, Zender, David, Malka Faye; consultant; formerly Dir. Science Policy Secretariat, Govt. of Sask. formerly Head, Physics Dept., Univ of Sask and Dir., Accelerator Lab.; has written over 60 scient. papers on thermodynamics and nuclear physics; Univ. of Sask. Rep., Candn. Research Mang. Assn.; mem. (Founding) Candn. Assn. for Club of Rome; Council Trustees, Institute for Research on Public Policy; mem., Science Council of Can. 1966-72; mem. Canadian Assn. Physicists (Past Pres.); Fellow, Am. Phys. Soc.; Hebrew; Home: 203 Ball Cresc., Saskatoon, Sask. S7K 6E1

KAUFMAN, Hon. Fred, B.Sc., B.A., B.C.L., D.C.L.; judge; b. Vienna, Austria, 7 May 1924; s. late Richard and Alice (Singer) K.; e. Bishop's Univ., B.Sc. 1946; Univ. de Montréal, B.A. 1953; McGill Univ., B.C.L. 1954; Bishop's Univ., D.C.L. (Hon.) 1976; m. Donna Joy, d. late Kenneth D. Soble, Hamilton, Ont., 9 Apl. 1967; children: Leslie Ann, David Richard; JUSTICE, QUE. COURT OF APPEAL since 1973; former Sr. Partner, Kaufman, Yarosky & Fish; read law with Joseph Cohen, Q.C.; called to Bars of Que. 1955, N.W.T. 1961, Alta. 1968; cr. Q.C. 1971; Lectr. in Criminal Law, McGill Univ. 1962-68, Asst. Prof., Med. Jurisprudence 1968-73; mem. of Corp. and Chrmn., Extve. Comte. (1973-76) Bishop's Univ.; author, "The Admissibility of Confessions in Criminal Matters" 1960, 3rd ed. 1979; mem. and Que. Chrmn. Criminal Justice Sec. (1969-71), Candn. Bar Assn.; Candn. Soc. Forensic Science; Medico-Legal Soc. (Eng.); Vice-Pres.Reué Cassin Fdn. of Can., 1981- ; Clubs: University; Montefiore; Knowlton Golf; Home: 3 Westmount Sq., Westmount, Que. H3Z 2S5; Office: Court House, Montreal, Que. H2Y 1A2

KAUFMAN, Nathan, M.B.E., M.D., C.M.; pathologist; professor; b. Lachine, Que., 3 Aug. 1915; s. Solomon and Anna (Sabesinsky) K.; e. McGill Univ., B.Sc. 1937, M.D., C.M., 1941; Intern., Royal Victoria Hosp., Montreal, 1941-42; Jewish Gen. Hosp., Montreal, Res. in Path., 1946-47; Cleveland City Hosp., Asst. Res. in Path., 1947-48; m. Rita, d. Jack Friendly, 1946; children: Naomi Friendly, Michael David, Miriam Elizabeth, Hannah Esther, Judith Anne; SECY. TREASURER (U.S.) CAN. DIV. OF INTER. ACADEMY OF PATHOLOGY 1979- ; Prof. And Head, Dept. of Path., Queen's Univ., 1967-79; Prof. Emeritus, Queen's Univ., 1981- ; Attending Staff, Kingston Gen. Hosp., 1967-81; Honourary Staff 1981- ; Pathologist-in-Chief, Kingston (Ont.) Gen. Hosp., 1967-79; Consultant, Hotel Dieu Hospital; Chrmn., Med. Research Council Grants Comte. for Pathol. and Morphol., 1971-74; mem., Med. Research Council and Extve., 1971-77; Clinical Prof. of Humanities, Medical Coll. of Georgia, 1980-; began teaching at Western Reserve Univ. Med. Sch.; Instr. in Path., 1948, Sr. Instr. 1951, Asst. Prof. 1952, Assoc. Prof. 1954; Prof., Duke Univ. Sch. of Med., 1960-67; Dir., Grad. Studies, Dept. of Path., there 1965-67; at Cleveland City Hosp. (later Cleveland Metrop. Gen. Hosp.); Asst. Pathol., 1948-52, Pathol., i/c, 1952-60, Dir., Sch. of Cytol., 1955-60; Consulting Pathol., Marymount Hosp., Cleveland; Assoc. Ed., Lab. Investig., 1952-66 and Ed. 1972-75, Edit. Bd. 1975- ; mem. Edit. Bd. Am. Journ. Path., 1967-71; served as Capt., R.C.A.M.C., 1942-46; M.B.E., Mentioned in Despatches; mem., Amer. Medical Assn.; Internat. Acad. of Path. (Pres. 1976-78, Pres. U.S.-Candn. Division 1973-74); Publications: numerous scient. articles on iron metabolism and nutrition in major scient. and med. journs.; mem., Am. Soc. Clin. Pathols.; Am. Assn. Pathols.; Candn. Med. Assn.; Cleveland Soc. Pathols. (Pres., 1958-59); Internat. Acad. Path. (mem., Council 1967-70); Am. Assn. Advanc. Science; Soc. Exper. Biol. and Med.; Am. Assn. Cancer Research; N.Y. Acad. Sciences; Medical Assn. of Georgia; Candn. Assn. Pathols.; Candn. and Am. Socs. Cytology; Candn. Assn. Pathols.; Sigma Xi; Jewish; Address: United States. Canadian Division of the Inter. Academy of Pathology, 1003 Chafee Ave., Augusta, Ga., U.S.A. 30904

KAVANAGH, Kevin Patrick, B.Com.; insurance executive; b. Brandon, Man. 27 Sept. 1932; s. Martin and Katherine (Power) K.; e. Brandon Coll. Inst.; Univ. of Man. B.Com. 1953; m. Elisabeth M. Mesman July 1963; children: Sean K., Jennifer T.; PRES. AND C.E.O., THE GREAT-WEST LIFE ASSURANCE CO.; recreations: tennis, boating, skiing; Clubs: Manitoba; Winnipeg Winter Club; Home: 131 Grenfell Blvd., Winnipeg, Man. R3P 0B6; Office: 60 Osborne St. N., Winnipeg, Man. R3C 3A5.

KAVANAGH, Paul M., B.A., Ph.D.; executive; b. Ottawa, Ont., 2 Jan. 1928; s. Alfred Byron and Monica Margaret (McEvoy) K.; e. St. Patrick's High Sch., Ottawa, Ont.; Univ. of Toronto, B.A. 1950; Univ. of B.C. (Geol.), 1950-51; Princeton Univ., Ph.D. (Geol.) 1954; m. Marcia Ann, d. Mrs. M. Sorber, Willow Grove, Pa., 3 Nov. 1973; children: Janet Mary, Paul Edward, Gerret William; VICE PRES. — EXPLORATION, RIO ALGOM LTD. since 1975; with Cyprus Mines Corp., 1954-56; Chief Geol., Asbestos Corp., 1956-57; joined Yukon Consol. Gold Corp.

Ltd., 1957 first as Devel. Engr., then Asst. Mgr. and finally (1959-60) as Gen. Mgr.; apptd. Chief Geol. Kerr Addison Mines Ltd. 1960; Vice President Exploration 1967, Vice President & Director 1970; Pres., Newmont Mining Corp. of Can., 1973-75; mem., Geol. Assn. of Can.; Candn. Inst. Mining & Metall.; Prosp. & Devel. Assn.; Roman Catholic; recreations: tennis, skiing; photography; Home: 463 Lytton Blvd., Toronto, Ont. M5N 1S5; Office: Suite 2400, 120 Adelaide St. W., Toronto, Ont. M5H 1W5

KAVANAGH, Richard Jack; banker; b. Dartmouth, N.S. 26 Dec. 1934; e. Public School, Dartmouth, Parrsboro and Halifax, N.S.; m. Carol Anne Wiseman 1957; children: Kathryn, Janet, Elizabeth; SR. VICE PRES. & GEN. MGR. W. CAN. DIV., THE BANK OF NOVA SCOTIA; joined present Bank Dartmouth, N.S. 1951; served at various Maritime Branches; transferred London, Ont. and appointed Accountant 1959; General Office Personnel 1961; Asst. Supvr. N.S. 1963; Asst. Supvr. Staff, Quebec 1965; Asst. Supvr. Credit, Quebec 1966; Sen. Asst. Mgr., Montreal Main Branch 1968; Depy. Mgr. Kingston, Jamaica 1970; Mgr. Kingston, Jamaica 1971; Gen. Mgr., B.C. & Yukon Region 1974; Vice-Pres. & Gen Mgr., B.C. & Yukon Region 1976; Sen. Vice-Pres. & Gen. Mgr. W. Can. Div. 1979; Fellow, Inst. Candn. Bankers; Clubs: National; St. George's Golf & Country; Vancouver; Shaughnessy Golf & Country; Office: 44 King St. W., Toronto, Ont. M5H 1H1

KAWANA, Yoshikazu (Ken), B.A.; automobile executive; b. Tokyo, Japan 19 Dec. 1936; e. Keio Univ. B.A. 1959; m. Toyoko Yasukawa 1967; two s., one d.; EXTVE. VICE PRES., GEN. MGR. AND CHIEF OPERATING OFFR., NISSAN AUTOMOBILE CO. (CANADA) LTD. since 1978; various mang. positions Nissan Motor Co. Ltd. 1959-65, Mgr. N. Am. Export Dept. 1973-78; Vice Pres. Adm. and Finance present Co. 1965-72; mem. Can.-Japan Soc. Vancouver; Japanese Businessmen's Assn. Vancouver; recreations: golf, music; Home: 5094 Marguerite St., Vancouver, B.C. V6M 3K1; Office: (P.O. Box 2501) New Westminster, B.C. V3L 5A1.

KAY, Cyril Max, Ph.D., F.R.S.C.; educator; b. Calgary, Alta. 3 Oct. 1931; s. Louis and Fanny (Pearlmutter) K.; e. Central Coll. Inst. Calgary 1949; McGill Univ. B.Sc. 1952; Harvard Univ. Ph.D. 1956; m.Faye d. Alter Bloomenthal, Calgary, Alta. 30 Dec. 1953; children: Lewis Edward, Lisa Franci; PROF. OF BIOCHEM. UNIV. OF ALTA. since 1958; Co-dir., Med. Research Council Group in Protein Structure and Function, 1974- ; Postdoctoral Fellow in Biochem. Cambridge Univ. 1956-57; Research Physical Biochem. Eli Lilly & Co. Indianapolis 1957-58; Med. Research Council of Can. Visiting Scient. Weizmann Inst. of Science, Israel 1969-70; Visiting Prof., Weizmann Ins. of Science, Rehovot, Israel, Summers of 1973, 75, 77, 80; rec'd Ayerst Award in Biochem., Candn. Biochem. Soc. 1970; co-author "Muscle" 1964; over 100 research publs. phys. biochem., protein chem. and muscle biochem.; Ed.-in-Chief, Pan American Assn. Biochem. Socs. Review; Assoc. Ed. Candn. Journ. Biochem.; Fellow, N.Y. Acad. Sciences; mem. Candn. Biochem. Soc. (Pres. 1977-78); Am. Soc. Biol. Chems.; Biophys. Soc. Med. Adv. Bd., Gairdner Foundation, 1980-84; mem., Bd. of Dir., Can. Soc. for Weizmann Inst. of Sc.; Sigma Xi; Jewish; Home: 9408-143 St., Edmonton, Alta. T5R 0P7; Office: Edmonton, Alta. T6G 2H7.

KAYLER, Reginald L., Q.C., LL.B., C.L.U.; association executive; b. Napanee, Ont., 2 July 1919; s. late Pansy Mary (Spafford) and late Harold Wray K.; e. Osgoode Hall Law Sch., Toronto, Ont. (Bronze Medal Award) 1943; Inst. of Chart. Life Underwriters of Can., C.L.U. 1949; Q.C. 1972; m. Phyllis Marie, d. late Edward G. Brisley, 5 Aug. 1944; children: Catherine, Douglas, Grant; EXTVE. VICE PRES. AND GEN. COUNSEL, THE LIFE UNDERWRITERS ASSN. OF CANADA; read law with

Malone, Malone & Montgomery, Toronto, Ont.; called to the Bar of Ont. 1943; entered life ins. business as Rep. of Standard Life Assurance Co., Toronto, Ont. 1946; became assoc. with Excelsior Life Insurance Co., Toronto, 1949 as a Partner in firm of Barton & Kayler; joined Extve. Staff of present Assn. as Gen. Counsel and Dir. of Educ., 1957, having previously served as an el. mem. of the Bd. of Dirs. for five yrs. in the capacities of Chrmn. of Taxation Comte. and Hon. Secy.; became Chief Extve. Offr. of the present Assn. with the title of Extve. Dir. and Gen. Counsel, cont. as Dir. of Educ., Feb. 1961; served during 2nd World War with R.C.N. in N. Atlantic, 1943-45; discharged with rank of Lt.; mem. Candn. Bar Assn.; Lawyers' Club of Toronto; Estate Planning Council of Toronto; Candn. Inst. Internat. Affairs; Inst. of Chart. Life Life Underwriters of Can.; United Church; recreations: golf, skiing; Club: Scarborough Golf and Country; Home: 259 Lytton Blvd., Toronto, Ont. M5N 1R7; Office: 41 Lesmill Rd., Don Mills, Ont. M3B 2T3

KEARNS, Frederick R.; company executive; b. Quyon, Que., 1924; e. St. Patricks Coll., Ottawa; McGill Univ. (Comm.); m. E. Black; three s. and two d.; PRES.C.E.O., CANADAIR LTD., since 1965; Dir., Asbestos Corp. Ltd.; joined Canadair 1949 in Acct. Sec.; successively Chief Acct., Asst. to the Pres., and Vice-Pres. & Comptroller; Extve. Vice Pres., Finance and Sales, 1960-63; Extve. Vice Pres., 1963-65; served in 2nd World War with R.C.A.F. as Fighter Pilot 1942-45; served with the 443rd Squadron; joined 401 City of Westmount Reserve Sqdn. 1946-52; mem., Life Gov., Douglas Hosp.; Dir., Air Industries Assn. Can. Ltd.; Canada-China Trade Council; St. Mary's Hospital Fdn; Gen. Comte. of the Mt. Royal Club; recreations: golf, skiing, hunting, fishing; Clubs: Mount Bruno Country; Roy; Ottawa Golf; Mount Royal; Rideau (Ottawa); Office: (P.O. Box 6087) Montreal, Que. H3C 3G9

KEATE, James Stuart, O.C., B.A.; publisher; journalist; b. Vancouver, B.C., 13 Oct. 1913; s. William Lewis and Ethel May (Anderson) K.; e. Prince of Wales High Sch., Vancouver, B.C.; Univ. of Brit. Columbia, B.A. 1935; m. Letha Katherine, d. Hugo E. Meilicke, Vancouver, B.C., 22 July 1939; children: Richard Stuart, Kathryn Jane; Publisher, The Vancouver Sun 1964-1973; Past mem. Senate, Bd. Govs., Univ. of Brit. Columbia; Reporter, Vancouver "Province" and "Toronto Daily Star" 1935-42; Contrib. Ed., Time Inc., N.Y. 1945-46, Bureau Chief. Montreal 1947-50; Publisher "Victoria Daily Times" 1950-64; served with R.C.N.V.R. 1942-45, Lt. Commdr.; Hon. Life mem. and Past Pres. Canadian Press; Past President, Canadian Daily Newspaper Publishers Assn.; Canadian Club of Vancouver; mem., Canada Council 1963-69; Vancouver Advisory Board; Salvation Army; Past Dir., Candn. Comte., Internat. Press Inst.; Past Pres. Prov. Council, Boy Scouts Assn.; rec'd Centennial Medal 1967; Offr. Order of Can. 1976; author of, "Paper Boy", memoir, 1980; "Press and Public" (Candn. Club lect. 1955 and 1968); "State of the University" (report to Univ. of B.C. 1960); Nat. mag. articles in Maclean's, Saturday Night, N.Y. Times Book Review and London Times "Canada" supplement; report on CBC Programme "This Hour Has Seven Days" for Candn. Govt.; elected Candn. News Hall of Fame 1974; rec'd. Nat. Press Award 1967; Psi Upsilon; Liberal; Anglican; recreations: golf, swimming; Clubs: Union (Victoria, B.C.); Faculty (Univ. of B.C.); Capilano Golf & Country; Shaughnessy Golf & Country; The Vancouver; Home: 3455 Marpole Ave., Vancouver, B.C. V6J 2S3

KEATES, George A.; company executive; b. Toronto, Ont., 9 June 1898; s. William James and Margaret Jane K.; e. Dufferin Sch., Toronto; Shaw Business Coll. and Sheldon Sch. Psychology, Toronto; m. Mary Dalzelle, d. Samuel A. Keers, 6 Sept. 1930; one s. Geo. Warren; Employers' Representative, Manitoba Labour Bd.; Hon. Life Mem., Winnipeg Chamber of Commerce; with Fair-

weathers Ltd., Toronto, Ont., 1919-27; Asst. Treas., Terminal Warehouses Ltd., Toronto, 1927-38; Gen. Mgr., 1939-44; Vice-Pres. and Mang. Dir., 1944; acquired interest in Manitoba Cartage and Storage Ltd. and assumed management 1944; Pres. from 1955; served in 1st World War 1916-19 with 43rd Batty., C.F.A., C.E.F.; Elected Capt. of the Hunt, Order of the Buffalo Hunt, Prov. of Man., 1979; Freemason; P. Conservative; Protestant; recreations: golf, riding, fishing; Clubs: Manitoba; Winnipeg Winter; Winnipeg Horsemen's (Honorary); Rotary (Past Pres.); St. Charles Country; Home: 125 Lamont Blvd., Tuxedo, Man. R3P 0E7; Office: 324 Lizzie St., Winnipeg, Man.

KEATING, Ronald R.; manufacturer; b. Johannesburg, S. Africa, 1 Nov. 1929; s. late David William and Martha (Louw) K.; e. Coll. of Accountancy, Johannesburg; m. Mary Elizabeth, d. late George Beyl, 4 Feb. 1950; two d.; PRESIDENT, LITTON SYSTEMS CANADA LTD.; Protestant; recreations: squash, tennis, swimming; Home: 2255 Otami Trail, Mississauga, Ont. L5H 3N2; Office: 25 Cityview Dr., Rexdale, Ont. M9W 5A7

KEBARLE, Paul, Ph.D., F.C.I.C., F.R.S.C.; educator; b. Sofia, Bulgaria 21 Sept. 1926; s. Paul and Kathryn (Mihailov) K.; e. Gymnasium Sofia, Bulgaria 1944; Eth, Zurich, Switzerland Dipl. Chem. 1952; Univ. of B.C. Ph.D. 1956; m. Bevery Jean d. Walter Harris, North Vancouver, B.C. 14 Jan. 1955; children: Kathy, Karen, Paula; PROF. OF CHEM. UNIV. OF ALTA. since 1966; Postdoctoral Fellow Nat. Research Council, Ottawa 1956-58; Asst. Prof. Univ. of Alta. 1958, Assoc. Prof. 1962; developed method of ion equilibria studies in gases; author over 125 research articles Candn. and internat. science journs.; elected fellow, Royal Society (Canada) 1978, Alberta Achievement Award, 1980; mem. Am. Chem. Soc.; Am. Soc. for Mass Spectrometry (Dir. 1976-77); recreations: sailing, canoeing, scuba diving, backpacking, skiing; Home: 7816-119 St., Edmonton, Alta. T6G 2L4; Office: Edmonton, Alta. T6G 2G2

KEEFLER, Maj. Gen. Ralph Holley, C.B.E., D.S.O., E.D., B.A.Sc., LL.D.; industrialist (retired); b. Weston, Ont., 12 Sept. 1902; s. Lt.-Col. Joseph and Margaret Isabel (Holley) K.; e. Schs. in W. Can., Eng. and Toronto, Ont.; Univ. of Toronto (S.P.S.), B.A.Sc. (Mech. Engn.) Hons., 1924; LL.D., Queen's Univ., May 1965; m. late Beatrice Louise, d. Robert Taschereau, 14 Sept. 1927; one s. Robert, one d. Lois (Kehoe); 2ndly, Pauline H. Chapman; joined Bell Telephone Co. of Canada, 1924; apptd. Dist. Mgr., Kingston, Ont., 1929; E. Div. Mgr., Feb. 1946; Asst. to Pres., Ottawa, Ont., 1949; Gen. Mgr., E. Area, 1953; successively apptd. Vice-Pres., Pub. Relations, Operations Staff, Finance; resigned July 1961, to become Pres., Northern Electric Co. Ltd.; Pres. and Chrmn. of Bd. 1963-1967, Chrmn. of Bd. 1967-70; served in 2nd World War, 1940-45; apptd. to staff of 2nd Candn. Inf. Div., 1940 and posted overseas to attend Staff Coll. at Camberley; returned to Can. 1942, becoming Dir. of Mil. Training with rank of Col.; reverted to Lt.-Col., 1943 and posted overseas to command 12th Field Regt., R.C.A.; landed in Normandy as Brig. commandg. 2nd Div. Arty. and took part in fighting around Caen and Falaise; temporarily commanded 2nd Inf. Div. during fight for Scheldt Estuary; commanded 6th Candn. Inf. Bgde. at Neimegen and during battles of Reichwald and Hochwald, 1944-45; promoted to Maj. Gen. 1945, as Commdr. 3rd Candn. Inf. Div., during advance through Holland and Germany; C.B.E. (Falaise); D.S.O. (Immediate) (South Beveland); Chevalier, Legion d'Honneur (France); Croix de Guerre, avec Palme (France); twice Mentioned in Despatches; Commdr. Brother, Venerable Order of St. John of Jerusalem; Delta Kappa Epsilon; recreations: outdoor sports; Clubs: St. James's (Montreal); R.B.Y.C., Riddell's Bay Golf, Coral Beach (Bermuda); Home: "Cappagarriff" and Oughterard, Co. Galway, Ireland

KEEN, Michael John, Ph.D.; geophysicist; b. Sussex, Eng. 1 Jan. 1935; s. John and Susanah (Bedwell) K.; e. Haberdashers' Aske's Hampstead 1953; Oxford Univ. B.A. 1957; Cambridge Univ. Ph.D. 1961; m. Susan Jane Atkinson 1976; children: Alison Lindsey, Rebecca Jane, Jonathan Atkinson; DIR. ATLANTIC GEOSCIENCE CENTRE, GEOL. SURVEY OF CAN. since 1977; Prof. of Geol. Dalhousie Univ. 1961-77, Chrmn. of Geol. 1968-72, 1975-77, Asst. Dean of Arts & Science 1973-74; author "Introduction to Marine Geology" 1968; numerous scient. publs. geol. and geophysics; mem. Geol. Assn. Can. (Pres. 1974-75); Royal Soc. Can.; recreations: skiing, sailing; Home: 1591 Chestnut St., Halifax, N.S. B3H 3S9; Office: Bedford Inst. of Oceanography, Dartmouth, N.S. B2Y 4A2

KEENAN, Patrick John, B.Com., C.A.; b. Montreal, Que. 7 Jan. 1932; s. Thomas Philip and Kathleen (Collins) K.; e. D'Arcy McGee High Sch. Montreal; McGill Univ. B.Com. 1954 (Laddie Millen Mem. Scholarship 1952); C.A., Chart. Secy. 1956; m. Barbara Gwendolyn d. Charles Douglas Fraser, Oakville, Ont. 14 Feb. 1959; children: Sean Patrick, Gwendolyn Mary, Katharine Ann, Christina Fraser; CHMN. OF BD., BARNES WINES LTD.; Pres., CEO & Dir., Patino International N.V.; Dir. compagnie Française D'Enterprises Minieres, Metal et D'Invest. (France); Brascan Ltd.; Westmin Resources Ltd. Great Lakes Power Corp. Ltd.; Hatleigh Corp.; Foodex Corp.; London Life Insurance Co.; Lonvest Corp.; Lada Cars of Canada Inc.; Keewhit Investments Ltd.; rec'd Inst. Chart. Secy's Gold Medal 1962; Inst. C.A.'s Ont.; Order C.A.'s Que.; Inst. Chart. Secy's; Bd. Trade Metrop. Toronto; Delta Sigma Phi; R. Catholic; recreations: skiing, golf, sheep farming; Club: National; Mid Ocean Bermuda); Home: 16 Whitney Ave., Toronto, Ont. M4W 2A8; Office: Suite 2, Armadale Bldg., Toronto-Buttonville Airport, Markham, Ont. L3P 3J9.

KEENLEYSIDE, Donald William, B.A., M.D., C.M.; b. Port Colborne, Ont., 7 Sept. 1930; s. James Ord and Ida Pearl (La Fortune) K.; e. Queen's Univ., B.A. 1954, M.D., C.M. 1956; m. Anna Veronica, d. late John Finn, 17 July 1954; children: Laura, David, Timothy; Pres., Dir., Goldlund Mines; mem. Council, Queen's Univ.; P. Conservative; Anglican; recreations: golf, curling; Club: Cataraqui Golf & Curling; Home: 180 Victoria St., Kingston, Ont. K7L 3Y8; Office: 800 Princess St., Kingston, Ont. K7L 5E4

KEENLEYSIDE, Brig. Hubert Brock, C.B.E. (1944), B.A.Sc.; b. London, Ont.; 5 July 1900; s. John Dawson and Mary Elizabeth (Brock) K.; e. London, Ont.; Univ. of Toronto, B.A.Sc. Mech. Engineering 1923; m. Margaret Anne (d. 1945), d. of late Rev. W. R. McIntosh, D.D., 3 July 1926; three sons: H. B. Keenleyside, Jr., M.D., F.R.C.P., J. G. Keenleyside, M.D., F.R.C.P., D. A. Keenleyside, B.A.Sc., P.Eng.; 2ndly Mary Olive Wall (d. Aug. 1968), d. of late E. Cotteril, Montreal, Que., 27 June, 1951; Dir., Robt. Simpson Co. Ltd., 1948-66; Union Gas Ltd., Chatham, Ont., 1948-76; Pres. and Mang. Dir., Photo Engravers & Electrotypers Ltd., 1946-66; retired from active business 1966; served in 2nd World War 1941-45 with Candn. Overseas in the U.K., Italy and N.W. Europe (Col. 1941, Brig. 1942); Dir. of Ordnance Services, Ottawa 1941 and at Candn. Mil. Hdqrs. London, Eng., 1941-43; A.D.Q.M.G., there, 1943-45; Depy. Q.M.G. 1945; held rank of Brig.; Hon. Col. Commandant, Royal Candn. Ordnance Corps., 1957-62; Phi Gamma Delta; Anglican; Clubs: National (Toronto); Muskoka Lakes Golf & Country (Port Carling, Ont.) Home: 10 Avoca Ave., Apt. 1503, Toronto, Ont., M4T 2B7

KEENLEYSIDE, Hugh Llewellyn, C.C. (1969), Ph.D., D.Sc., LL.D.; b. Toronto, Ont., 7 July 1898; s. Ellis William and Margaret Louise (Irvine) K.; e. Pub. Schs. and Langara Sch., Vancouver, B.C.; Univ. of B.C., B.A. 1920; Clark Univ., M.A. 1921, Ph.D. 1923; m. Katherine Hall, d. J. H. Pillsbury, Prince Rupert, B.C., 11 Aug. 1924; has four children; Chancellor, Notre Dame Univ. of Nelson, 1969-77; Dir., Resources for the Future; Trustee, Clark Univ., 1953-56; mem. of Senate, Univ. of B.C., 1962-68; Vice-Chrmn., Bd. Govs., Carleton Univ., 1942-50; Instr. and Special Lectr. in Hist. at various U.S. univ's. and at the Univ. of B.C. 1923-27; 3rd Secy., Dept. of External Affairs, 1928; 2nd Secy., 1929; 1st Secy., Candn. Leg., Tokyo, Japan, 1929-36; Counsellor, Dept. of External Affairs, Ottawa, Ont., 1940; Asst. Under-Secy. of State for External Affairs, 1941; Candn. Ambassador to Mexico, 1944-47; Depy. Min. of Mines & Resources and Commr. of the N.W.T., 1947-50; Depy. Min. of Resources & Devel., Jan.-Oct. 1950; Dir.-Gen., U.N. Tech. Assistance Adm., 1950-58; Under-Secy. General for Pub. Adm., 1959; Chrmn., B.C. Power Comn. 1959-62, and of B.C. Hydro and Power Authority 1962-69; Assoc. Commr. Gen., U.N. Habitat Conference, Vancouver, 1975-76; author of three books and many articles on econ., social and internat. affairs; served during 1st World War with C.F.A. and 2nd Candn. Tank Bn., 1918; Secy., Inter-Dept. Comte. which handled arrangements for Roy. Tour, 1939; Chrmn., Bd. of Review investigating charges of illegal entry of Orientals in B.C., 1938; mem., N.W.T. Council, 1941-45; Candn.-U.S. Jt. Econ. Comte's., 1940-44; mem. and Secy., Can.-U.S. Permanent Jt. Bd. on Defence, 1940-45, and Acting Chrmn., 1944; mem., Nat. Jt. Council on the Pub. Service, 1948-50; Head of Candn. Del. to the first U.N. Scient. Conf. on Conserv. and Utilisation of Resources, Lake Success, 1949; a Founder and mem., Bd. Govs., Arctic Inst. of N. Am.; mem., Assn. Candn. Clubs (Pres. 1948-50); Pres., Horticultural Centre of the Pacific, 1979- ; Life Fellow, Asiatic Soc. of Japan; awarded Haldane Medal, Roy Inst. Pub. Adm., 1954; first recipient of Vanier Medal, Inst. Pub. Adm. Can., 1962; Companion, Order of Can. 1969; Home: 3470 Mayfair Drive, Victoria, B.C. V8P 1P8

KEEP, John Leslie Howard, Ph.D.; educator; b. Orpington, UK 21 Jan. 1926; s. Norman Marion Howard and Phyllis Mary Rolls (Austin) K.; e. Univ. of London B.A. 1950, Ph.D. 1954; m. Ann Elizabeth 17 Dec. 1948; PROF. OF RUSSIAN HISTORY, UNIV. OF TORONTO 1970- ; Lectr., Reader in Russian Hist. Sch. of Slavonic & E. European Studies Univ. of London 1954-70; John S. Guggenheim Fellow 1978-79; Connaught Fellow 1981; author "The Rise of Social Democracy in Russia" 1963; "The Russian Revolution: A Study in Mass Mobilization" 1976; ed. and trans. "The Debate on Soviet Power" 1979; various articles Russian hist., politics; served with Brit. Army 1943-47, rank Capt.; mem. Candn. Assn. Slavists; Am. Assn. Advanc. Slavic Studies; Home: 75 Oriole Rd., Apt. 1, Toronto, Ont. M4V 2E9; Office: Toronto, Ont. M5S 1A1.

KEESAL, Norman J., B.A., M.B.A.; company executive; b. Chicago, Ill., 5 Oct. 1927; s. Harry Edward and Celia (Gordon) K.; e. Harvard Univ., B.A. (Econ.) 1950; Harvard Grad. Sch. of Business Adm., M.B.A., 1952; m. Miriam, d. late Samuel Shapiro, 15 Feb. 1959; children: Sheldon Ian, Brenda Joy, Nancy Beth; VICE-PRES. AND GEN. MGR., CARTIER CHEMICALS LIMITED, since 1960; Invest. Counsellor and Analyst, Stein, Roe & Farnham, Chicago, 1952-54; Vice-Pres., Red Comet (Canada) Ltd. of Montreal, 1954-60; Lectr., McGill Univ. since 1957; Extve. Devel. Inst. since 1958; Queen's Univ. 1964-66; served with U.S. Air Force during 2nd World War; Chief Air Inspr. 103 Weather Group; author of numerous articles for prof. journs.; Pres., Reconstructionist Synagogue of Montreal; past mem. Extve. Comte. and Bd. Trustees, Allied Jewish Community Services of Greater Montreal; Vice-Pres. YM-YWHA; Dir, Extve. Devel. Inst.; Jewish Peoples of Peretz Schs.; mem., Harvard Business Sch. Club of Montreal; Montreal Bd. Trade; K of P.; Hebrew; recreations: public speaking, teaching; Home: 5611 Hartwell, Cote St. Luc, Que. H4W 1T5; Office: 445 21st St., Lachine, Que. H8S 3T8

KEEVIL, Norman B. Jr., B.A.Sc., Ph.D., P.Eng.; b. Mass. 28 Feb. 1938 (came to Can. 1939); s. Norman Bell and Verna Ruth (Bond) K.; e. Univ. of Toronto B.A.Sc. (Applied Geol.) 1959; Univ. of Cal. Berkeley Ph.D. 1964; m. Catherine Elizabeth d. Thomas Taylor, Toronto, Ont. 1969; children: Scott, Laura, Jill, Norman II; EXTVE. VICE PRES. TECK CORP. LTD. since 1970; Chrmn. Newfoundland Zinc Mines Ltd.; mem. Soc. Exploration Geophysics; Candn. Inst. Mining & Metall.; Nat. Adv. Committee on the Mining Ind.; Dir., Mining Assn. of Can.; Discovery Parks Foundation; Copperfields Mining Corp.; Lorney Mining Corp. Ltd.; Southam Inc.; Protestant; recreations: golf, tennis, fishing, phoptography; Clubs: Vancouver; Shaughnessy Golf & Country; University; Home: 4706 Drummond Dr. at Blanca, Vancouver, B.C. V6T 1B4; Office: 1199 W. Hastings St., Vancouver, B.C.

KEFFER, James Fennell, M.A.Sc., Ph.D.; educator; b. Toronto, Ont. 15 Dec. 1933; s. James Wellington and Helen McKim (Fennell) K.; e. Univ. of Toronto B.A.Sc. (Mech. Engn.) 1956, M.A.Sc. 1958, Ph.D. 1962; Cavendish Lab. Cambridge Univ. Post Doctoral Fellow 1962-64; m. Anne Rosemary d. John Floyd Hooper, Cambridge, Ont. 24 Sept. 1955; two s. James David, John Wellington; ASSOC. DEAN OF SCHOOL OF GRADUATE STUDIES AND PROF. OF MECH. ENGN., UNIV. OF TORONTO; Partner, Atmospheric Environment Research; consulting engr. for industry and govt.; Visiting Prof. Institut de Mécanique Statistique de la Turbulence, Marseille, France; Univ. of Barcelona, Tarragona, Spain; author approx. 100 papers on fluid mechanics and turbulent flows; mem. Soc. Automotive Engrs.; Assn. Prof. Engrs. Prov. Ont.; recreations: sailing, skiing, squash; Clubs: Oakville Yacht Squadron; Lemon Squash; Home: 247 Riverside Dr., Oakville, Ont. L6K 3N1; Office: King's College Rd., Toronto, Ont. M5S 1A4.

KEITH, Agnes Newton; writer; b. Oak Park, Ill., 6 July 1905; d. Joseph Gilbert and Grace Darlington (Goodwillie) Newton; e. Univ. of California, B.A. 1924; m. 1934; children: Jean Alison, Henry George Newton; author of "Land Below the Wind", 1939 (Borneo); "Three Came Home", 1947 (story of internment by Japanese); "White Man Returns", 1951; "Bare Feet in the Palace", 1955 (story of the Philippines); "Children of Allah", 1965 (story of Muslem Libya); "Beloved Exiles", 1972 (novel of Borneo); "Before the Blossoms Fall", 1975 (return to Japan); Episcopalian; Address: 785 Island Rd., Oak Bay, Victoria, B.C. V8S 2T8

KEITH, Lieut.-Col. the Hon. Donald Allayne, M.B.E., B.A.; b. Toronto, Ont., 12 May 1911; s. George Walter and Edith Louise (Jones) K.; e. Bloor Coll. Inst., Toronto, Ont.; Univ. of Toronto, B.A. 1931; Osgoode Hall, Toronto, Ont., 1931-34; m. Laura Margaret, d. late Charles Matthew Coquhoun, K.C., 19 Oct., 1935; children: Charles Anthony, Janet Louise, Margaret Elizabeth; JUSTICE, HIGH COURT OF ONT., since 1967; read law with City of Toronto Legal Dept.; called to the Bar of Ont., June 1934; cr. Q.C. 1952; served in 2nd World War, with Queen's Own Rifles of Can. in various Staff appts.; served Overseas finally as A.A.G., H.Q. 1st Candn. Army; awarded M.B.E.; Chevalier, Order of Leopold (Belgium); Croix de Guerre (Belgium); Mentioned in Despatches; Presbyterian; Clubs: Ontario; Toronto Hunt; Home: Toronto, Ont.; Office: Osgoode Hall, Toronto, Ont. M5H 2N5

KEITH, Gordon Layng, B.A.Sc., F.C.I.S.; retired company executive; b. Toronto, Ont., 3 Jan. 1913; s. Gordon Campbell and Lillian (Layng) K.; e. Clinton St. and McMurrich Pub. Schs. and Oakwood Coll., Toronto, Ont.; Univ. of Toronto, B.A.Sc. (Chem. Engn.) 1935; m. Mary G., d. Dr. A. M. Rolls, 11 Jan. 1941; children: Gordon A., Margaret I., David M.; Vice-President, Nuodex Canada Ltd., 1947-76; with J. T. Donald Co. Ltd., Mont-real, Que., 1935; Vultex Chem. Co. Ltd., St-Remi, Que., 1936; mem., Assn. Prof. Engrs. of Ont.; Pres., N. York Br. C.P.A.'s, 1956-57; United Church; recreations: golf, bridge, philately, photography; Club: Rotary; Home: 32 Biggar Ave., Toronto, Ont. M6H 2N4

KEITH, Haddow MacDonnell, M.D.; paediatrician; b. Toronto, Ont., 20 May 1899; s. George Alexander and Bessie (Haddow) K.; e. Univ. of Toronto, Faculty of Med. 1924; m. 1stly Marion Fraser (d. 1956) 20 Aug. 1927; m. 2ndly Katherine Roberts, 31 Aug. 1957; children: Fraser, Alison; Prof. Emeritus, Mayo Clinic, since 1964; Intern. and Asst., Henry Ford Hosp., 1924-26; Resident, Strong Mem. Hosp., Rochester, N.Y., 1926-28; joined Mayo Clinic as Asst. and Staff mem., 1928-32; Asst. Prof. and Prof., 1939-64; Montreal Neurol. Inst. 1933-39; Travelling Fellow, 1935-36; private practice Montreal 1932-39; served with R.N.A.S. and R.A.F. 1917-19; served in various positions on Boy Scout Council for 15 yrs.; author, "Convulsive Disorders in Children", 1963; other writings incl. over 85 med. papers; mem., Am. and Minn. Med. Socs.; Am. Pediatric Soc.; Candn. Pediatric Soc.; Fellow, Am. Acad. of Pediatrics; mem., Northwest Pediatric Soc.; Am. Epilepsy Soc. (Past Pres.); Nu Sigma Nu; Democrat; Congregationalist; recreations: tennis, fishing, camping; Home: 924-9th Ave. S.W., Rochester, Minn. 55901

KEITH, William John, M.A., Ph.D., F.R.S.C.; educator; literary critic; b. London, Eng. 9 May 1934; s. late William Henry and late Elna Mary (Harpham) K.; e. Brentwood Sch. Essex, Eng. 1952; Jesus Coll. Cambridge B.A. 1958; Univ. of Toronto M.A. 1959, Ph.D. 1961; m. Hiroko Teresa d. late Norio Sato 26 Dec. 1965; PROF. OF ENG., UNIV. COLL. UNIV. OF TORONTO 1971- ; Lectr. in Eng. McMaster Univ. 1961-62, Asst. Prof. 1962-66; Assoc. Prof. Univ. of Toronto 1966-71; served with Royal Army Educ. Corps 1953-55; author "Richard Jefferies: A Critical Study" 1965; "Charles G. D. Roberts" 1969; "The Rural Tradition" 1974; "The Poetry of Nature" 1980; "Epic Fiction: The Art of Rudy Wiebe" 1981; Ed. "Charles G. D. Roberts: Selected Poetry and Critical Prose" 1974; "A Voice in the Land: Essays by and about Rudy Wiebe" 1981; coed. "The Arts in Canada: The Last Fifty Years" 1980; author numerous articles Eng. and Candn. lit.; Fellow, Royal Soc. of Can.; Hon. Pres. Richard Jefferies Soc. (Swindon, Eng.); mem. Assn. Candn. Univ. Teachers Eng.; Ed. "University of Toronto Quarterly" 1976- ; recreations: walking, ornithology; Home: 142 Hilton Ave., Toronto, Ont. M5R 3E9; Office: Toronto, Ont. M5S 1A1.

KELLY, Hon. Arthur, LL.D., K.C.S.G.; b. Toronto, Ont., Dec. 1900; s. Hon. Hugh Thomas (K.C.S.G., formerly Justice of Supreme Court of Ont.) and Mary (Hynes) K.; e. St. Michaels Coll.; Univ. of Toronto, B.A. 1920; Osgoode Hall, Grad. 1923; m. Aileen, D.D.S., d. Andrew J. McDonagh, D.D.S., 24 Oct. 1928; children: Carol, Miriam, Hugh, Kevin; Justice, Court of Appeal, Ont., 1960-75; Dep. Justice, Fed. Crt. of Can., 1977- ; formerly mem., Day, Wilson, Kelly, Martin & Campbell, Toronto, Ont.; read law with Osler, Hoskin & Harcourt and with T. N. Phelan, K.C.; called to Bar of Ont. 1923; cr. K.C. 1944; Pres., County of York Law Assoc., 1944; Candn. Bar Assn. 1957-58; former mem., Roy. Comn. on Educ., Prov. of Ont., 1945-50; Gov., Univ. of Toronto, 1945-70; Chrmn. Alcoholism Research Fdn., 1951-55; Ont. Mental Health Foundation 1961-68; United Welfare Fund of Toronto; Theta Delta Chi; Catholic; recreation: sailing; Clubs: National; R.C.Y.C.; Home: 3 McKenzie Ave., Toronto, Ont. M4W 1K1

KELLY, Burton Vincent, B.Com.; banker; b. Woodstock N.B. 16 June 1932; s. late Burton Murrant K.; e. Woodstock (N.B.) High Sch.; Sir George Williams Univ. B.Com.; m. Mary Pamela Ludford d. late John B. L. Taylor, St. Andrew, Jamaica 31 Aug. 1957; one s. John B. V.; SR. VICE-PRES., INTERNAT., ROYAL BANK OF CANADA since 1979; Career: joined the Bank at Woodstock,

N.B. 1950; numerous postings throughout Latin America and Caribbean. Exec. Dir. & Sen. Rep. of the Bank, seconded to Orion Banking Group and Orion Multinational Serv. Ltd.; apptd. Asst. Gen. Mgr. of the Royal Bank & Chmn. and Mng. Dir., Orion Multinational Serv. 1975; Asst. Gen. Mgr. for Latin America & Caribbean at Montreal, Internat. Div. 1977; Vice-Pres. & Gen. Mgr. 1978; Sen. Vice Pres., Internat. Assoc., Inst. Cdn. Bankers; Dir., Roy West Group, Nassau, Bahamas; Clubs: Royal Montreal Curling; Royal Montreal Golf; St. Jame's; Royal Nassau Sailing; Overseas Bankers (London, Eng.); Home: 341 Redfern Ave., Westmount, Que. H3Z 2G4; Office: (P.O. Box 6001) Montreal, Que. H3C 3A9.

KELLY, (Howard) Garfield, M.D., C.M., F.R.C.P.(C), F.A.C.P.; medical consultant administrator; b. Kingston, Ont. 16 Aug. 1917; s. Howard and Hazel Dell (Lewis) K.; e. Queen's Univ. M.D., C.M. 1940; postgrad. studies Queen's Univ. Kingston Gen. Hosp., McGill Univ. Royal Victoria Hosp. Montreal Neurol. Inst., Univ. of Toronto Banting Inst. Toronto Gen. Hosp., Post-grad. Med. Sch. London, Eng.; m. Grace Ellen d. David Southall, Kingston, Ont. 17 Oct. 1941; two d. Diane Grace Burkom, Joan Champ; VICE PRINCIPAL HEALTH SCIENCES, QUEEN'S UNIV. and Prof. of Med. there; served with RCAF 1941-46, rank Sqdn. Leader, Med. Services; Fellow, Am. Coll. Cardiol.; mem. of Bd, Physicians Services Inc. Foundation; Chrmn., Ont. Council of University Health Sciences; Hon. Life Mem., Can. Arthritis Soc.; Pres., Kingston Branch of Can. Arthritis Soc.; Mem. of Bd., Alcoholism and Drug Addiction Research Inst.; recreation: swimming, photography; Home: 77 Alwington Ave., Kingston, Ont. K7L 4R4

KELLY, Howard Lloyd, B.A., M.B.A.; trust company executive; b. Huntingdon, Que., 30 Dec. 1929; s. Douglas Lloyd and Ruth Stewart (Gardner) K.; e. Huntingdon (Que.) High Sch.; Stanstead (Que.) Coll.; Bishop's Univ. B.A. 1951; Univ. of W. Ont. M.B.A. 1953; two s., Peter William, John Gardner; PRESIDENT, DIR., AND C.E.O., GUARDIAN TRUSTCO INC. since 1980 and of Guardian Trust Co. since 1975; Pres. and Dir. Victoria Square Corp.; Vice-Pres. and Dir., Morgan and Dilworth Inc.; Dir. and Secy. Lynch-Transcom Inc.; Hemlu Placements Inc.; Dir. Gama Toy Ltd.; Hunt and Moscrop (Can.) Inc.; Kindermann (Can.) Ltd.; joined Guardian Trust Co. as Gen. Mgr. 1969, Vice Pres. and Dir. 1972; recreations: curling, hunting, gardening, water skiing; Clubs: Pointe Claire Curling (Past Pres.); Canadian; Office: 618 St. James St. W., Montreal, Que.

KELLY, J. Howard, Q.C.; corporation executive; b. Wingham, Ont.; s. Thomas J. and Mary E. (Cliford) K.; e. Univ. of Alberta (Arts and Law); m. Leona A., d. Edward J. Lemieux, Calgary, Alta., 14 Sept. 1933; two children; Dir., Burns Foods Ltd.; Zurich Life Ins. Company; Revelstoke Building Materials Ltd.; Canadian Hydro Carbons Ltd.; mem., Calgary Adv. Bd., Canada Perm. Trust Co.; read law with Jones, Pescod & Adams, Calgary; called to the Bar of Alta., 1928; cr. K.C. 1952; mem., Calgary Chamber Comm. (Past Pres. 1954 Pres. 1954); Gov., Univ. of Alta.; Chrmn., Holy Cross Hosp. Bd.; mem. Candn. Council Duke of Edinburgh Awards; Bd. Trustees, Alta. Med. Research & Educ. Foundation; Candn. Council, Internat. Chamber Comm.; Roman Catholic; recreations: golf, gardening; Clubs: Ranchmen's; Calgary Golf & Country; Glencoe; Home: 4219 Britannia Dr., Calgary, Alta. T2S 1J4; Office: 901-610 8th Ave. W., Calgary, Alta. T2P 1G4

KELLY, Rev. John M., C.S.B., M.A., Ph.D., LL.D., D.D. (Hon.), D.S. Litt. (Hon.); university president; b. Scranton, Pa., 27 July 1911; s. John and Mary Agnes (McAndrew) K.; e. St. John's Sch., Scranton, Pa.; St. Michael's Coll., Univ. of Toronto, B.A. 1932; Univ. of Toronto, M.A. 1935, Ph.D. 1947; St. Basil's Semy., 1933-37; D.D. Victoria Univ., Toronto; D.S. Litt. TrinityColl., Toronto;

LL.D. St. Thomas Univ., St. John Fisher College (Rochester), Univ. of Toronto; PRES. EMERITUS, UNIV. OF ST. MICHAEL'S COLLEGE 1978; and Dir. of Alumni Affairs and Development Chrmn. Finance Comte., Toronto School of Theology, Kelly Comte., Univ. of Toronto; Dir. and men. Adv. Bd., Assn Medical Services Inc.; Adv. Bd. Mem. Ont. Min of Correctional Services; entered Cong. of St. Basil, 1932; o. 1936; Instr., Cath. Central High Sch., Detroit, Mich., 1937-38; Aquinas Inst., Rochester, N.Y., 1938-39; Inst. in Philos., Assumption Coll., Windsor, Ont., 1939-40; Asst. Prof., Assoc. Prof. and Prof. of Philos., St. Michael's Coll., Toronto, Ont., since 1940, and Head of the Dept. of Philos. 1950-61; Pres, St. Michael's College, 1958-78; awarded the Georgetown Univ. 175th Anniversary Medal of Hon., Oct. 1963; Sesquicentennial Medal (Univ. of Tor.); Citation, School of Continuing Studies, U. of T. 1980; mem., (Hon.) Paris Foreign Missions Soc. of Paris, 1981; Address: 50 St. Joseph St., Toronto, Ont. M5S 1J4

KELLY, Milton Terrence, B.A., B.Ed.; writer; poet; b. Toronto, Ont. 30 Nov. 1947; s. Milton Thomas and Sybil Lucy (Preston-Vores) K.; e. York Univ. B.A. 1970; Univ. of Toronto B.Ed. 1976; Gen. reporter, "The Scotsman", Edinburgh, 1973-74; City Hall reporter, Moose Jaw Times Herald, 1974-75; Publicity writer, Ont. Educ. Communications Authority, "Outreach Ontario", 1975; Teacher of Eng., Sudbury Bd. of Ed., 1976-77; Columnist, "Between the Sexes", The Globe and Mail, 1979-80; Publications: "I Do Remember the Fall," 1978 (a finalist in the Books In Can. competition, 1978); "Country You Can't Walk In" (poetry), 1979; "The More Loving One" (a novel and 3 stories), 1980; has also published in several Candn. and American jnls., reviews and quarterlies; Ont Truckers' Assn. Bursary; Ont. Arts Council grants; Can. Council grants; mem., Writers' Union of Can.; Federation of Ont. naturalists; Bruce Trail Assn.; Clubs: YMCA; Metro Toronto Road Runners; Canoe Ont.; recreations: canoeing, running, cross country skiing, fishing; Home/Office: 286 Major St., Toronto, Ont. M5S 2L6.

KELLY, Nora Hickson; author; b. Burton-on-Trent, Staffordshire, Eng., 8 Mar. 1910; d. Samuel Charles and Kate Elizabeth (Bagnall) Hickson; e. Pub. and High Sch., North Battleford, Sask.; Saskatoon Normal Sch., 1st Class Teacher's Diploma, 1929; m. William Henry, R.C.M.P., s. William George Kelly, 10 July 1940; taught pub. sch. in rural and urban Sask., for about nine yrs.; author, "Highroads to Singing", a book of children's songs; "The Men of the Mounted", 1949; Co-author, "The Royal Canadian Mounted Police: A Century of History" 1973; "Policing in Canada" 1976; contributor "The Americana Annual" (American Encyclopedia Yearbook) 1974; "The Academia American Encyclopedia", 1980; "Canadian Geographical Journal"; "Canadian Red Cross Junior"; has publ. children's plays and songs; sch. help work books in health, citizenship; operettas; Talks for C.B.C.; shadow plays; stories, articles and plays in school readers; pre-school "Look and Learn"; teacher's manuals in lit.; mem., Writers' Union of Can.; Life mem., Nat. Assn. for Advancement of Coloured People; Vol. Exit (Euthanasia Soc. of Gr. Brit.); Rationalist Press Assn. (Gr. Brit.); recreation: music; Home: 2079 Woodcrest Rd., Ottawa, Ont. K1H 6H9

KEMP, Anthony Leslie, B.Arch., MRAIC, ARIBA, RCA; architect; b. Kingston-On-Thames, Eng. 9 July 1936; s. Leslie Hagger and Louise (Winter) K.; e. Sherborne Sch. Dorset; Ridley Coll. St. Catharines, Ont.; Univ. of Toronto B.Arch.; came to Can. 1947; m. Patricia Ann Fraser July 1968; one d. Katharine Nicole; PARTNER, HAMILTON, KEMP ARCHITECTS 1978- ; Extve. Asst. to John C. Parkin, Parkin Architects and Engineers 1964-69; Sole Princ., Anthony Kemp Architects, Toronto 1969-78; Gov., Ridley Coll.; Dir., Toronto Symphony Sustaining Fund; Past Pres. Associates of Toronto Symphony; recipient various design awards incl. Candn. Housing Design

Council, Ont. Masonry Council, Candn. Arch. Yearbook; mem. Ont. Assn. Archs.; Royal Arch. Inst. Can.; Toronto Soc. Archs.; Arch. Conservancy Ont.; Royal Soc. Arts UK; Hon. Co. Freeman City of London in N. Am. (Master); Worshipful Co. of Gardners London, Eng.; Delta Upsilon; Anglican; recreation: sailing; Club: RCYC; Home: 104 Balmoral Ave., Toronto, Ont. M4V 1J4;Office: 47 Colborne St., Toronto, Ont. M5E 1P8.

KEMP, John Patrick Gordon, B.A.Sc.; retired company executive; b. London, Eng., 2 March 1919; s. James Colin and Elsie Marion (Blackader) K.; came to Canada 1921; e. Selwyn House Sch., Montreal, Que.; Bishop's Coll. Sch., Lennoxville, Que., 1933-36; McGill Univ., 1936-39 and 1947-48, B.A.Sc. (Mech. Engn.), 1948; m. Hazel Patricia, d. late Col. E. Gerald Hanson and Florence Ekers, Montreal, Que., 20 May 1948; children: James Patrick Hanson, Penelope Anne, Sarah Patricia; Dir., Atlas Copco Canada Ltd.; Chmn., FLAKT Can. Ltd.; Dir., Can. Malting Co. Ltd., Computel Systems Ltd.; PHH Services (Can.) Ltd.; Chrm., Knox Vicars Mclean Ont. Ltd.; mem. Toronto Adv. Board, The Royal Trust Company; mem., Advisory Comm. Mitsubishi Canada Ltd.; Governor, McGill University; joined Mount Royal Rice Mills Ltd., Montreal, Que., as Mill Engineer, Production Mgr., 1948-53; Mgr. Engn. Dept., Molson's Brewery Ltd., Montreal, Que. 1954; Vice-Pres. and Gen. Mgr. of Molson's Brewery (Ont.) Ltd., 1955, Extve. Vice-Pres., 1956-61; Vice-Pres. and Gen. Mgr., Molson's Brewery Quebec Ltd., 1961, Pres. and Dir. 1966-71; Sr. Vice-Pres, The Molsen Co. Ltd., 1971-78 served in 2nd World War; with The Black Watch of Can. 1939-45; Overseas 1940-45; wounded July 1944; discharged with rank of Major; member, Board of Trustees, Hosp. for Sick Children (Toronto); Corp. Engrs. of P.Q.; Alpha Delta Phi; Anglican; recreation: golf; Clubs: Toronto; University (Montreal); Royal Montreal Golf; Toronto Golf; Badminton & Racquet; Mt. Bruno Golf (Montreal); Royal; Ancient Golf, St. Andrews, Scotland; Home: Apt. 1205, 500 Avenue Rd., Toronto, Ont. M4V 2J6; Office: Suite 1420, 390 Bay St., Toronto, Ont. M5H 2Y2

KENDALL, Douglas Neville, O.B.E., F.R.G.S.; company executive; b. Oporto, Portugal, 18 Sept. 1914; s. Edward Neville and Cecilia (Burns) K.; e. Ampleforth College, Yorkshire, Eng., 1924-32; Oxford Univ. (Christ Church) 1933-34; m. Joan Mary, d. late Charles Hollis, 16 Apl. 1938; children: Jeremy Neville, David Edward, Nicola Mary; Chrmn., Enterprise Dev. Bd.; Dir. Connaught Laboratories; Connlab Holdings Ltd.; Eucalyptus Pulp Mills Ltd.; Acadia Life Insurance Co.; The Acadia Insurance Co.; deHavilland Aircraft of Can. Ltd.; Canadian General Investments Ltd.; Can. Development Corp.; mem. Candn. Bd., Phoenix Assurance Co. Ltd.; Dir. Fisheries Research Bd.; Chrmn. Enterprise Devel. Bd.; mem., Ontario Conservation Council; course in surveying at Royal Geo. Society 1935; Pilot's Licence 1935; engaged air survey operations South and East Africa 1936-39; after 2nd World War moved permanently to Canada; served in 2nd World War 1939-46 as Wing Commander R.A.F.; awarded O.B.E. and U.S. Legion of Merit; Fellow, Candn. Aerospace Inst.; Trustee, Quetico Foundation; mem., Canadian Inst. Surveying; American Society of Photogrammetry; Arctic Institute; Roman Catholic; recreations: fishing, tennis, riding; Clubs: Bath (London, Eng.); Caledon; Home: Hedgerow Farm, R.R. 2, Caledon, Ont. L0N 1E0; Office: 47 Colborne St., Toronto, Ont. M5E 1P8

KENDLE, John Edward, M.A., Ph.D.; educator; b. London, Eng. 14 Apl. 1937; s. Arthur and Sybil Violet Mary (Jordan) K.; e. Lord Roberts Jr. High and Gordon Bell High Schs. Winnipeg 1955; Univ. of Man., Un. Col. B.A. 1958, M.A. work 1959-61; King's Coll. Univ. of London Ph.D. 1965; m. Judith Ann d. late Charles Halsey 3 Aug. 1963; children: John Stephen, Andrew Bruce, Nancy Elizabeth; PROF. OF HIST. ST. JOHN'S COLL. UNIV. OF

MAN. 1965- ; IODE Doctoral Fellow 1961-63; Can. Council Doctoral Fellowship 1964-65, Leave Fellowship 1971-72, 1978-79, Post-doctoral Fellowship 1967-68; Tutorial Studentship in Imp. Hist. Univ. London 1964-65; Margaret McWilliams Medal Man. Hist. Soc. 1980; Visiting Research Fellow, Australian Nat. Univ. and Auckland Univ. 1967-68; mem. ed. bd. Candn. Hist. Assn. Papers 1973-78; author "The Colonial and Imperial Conferences 1887-1911" 1967; "The British Empire-Commonwealth 1897-1931" 1972; "The Round Table Movement and Imperial Union" 1975; "John Bracken: A Political Biography" 1979; various articles imp. fed., fed. and devolution in UK; mem. Candn. Hist. Assn. (Vice Pres. 1980-81, Pres. 1981-82); Am. Comte. Irish Studies; Candn. Assn. Irish Studies; Royal Commonwealth Soc.; recreations: curling, cycling, reading; Home: 149 The Glen, Winnipeg, Man. R2M 0B5;Office: Winnipeg, Man. R3T 2M5.

KENNEDY, Anthony A., C.A., textile manufacturer; b. Belfast, N. Ireland, 6 June 1931; s. Robert Henry and Norah Teresa K.; e. St. Mary's Coll., Dundalk, Ireland, 1948; McGill Univ., C.A. 1961; m. Mary Cherry, d. William Miller Dunn, 5 May 1953; two s. Matthew, Nicholas; PRESIDENT, MALIBU FABRICS OF CANADA LTD., since 1968; Clarkson Gordon & Co., 1954-61; Industrial Development Bank, 1961-62; joined Collins & Aikman Ltd. as Secy. 1962; apptd. Secy.-Treas. 1963; Dir. 1964; Vice-Pres. and Gen. Mgr. 1966; mem., Inst. C.A.'s Que.; Financial Extves. Inst.; R. Catholic; recreations: reading, music; Club: St. James's, Home: 266 Macaulay Ave., St. Lambert, Que. J4R 2G9

KENNEDY, Betty (Mrs. G. Allan Burton); b. Ottawa, Ont. 4 Jan. 1926; d. late Walter Herbert and Janet Kincaid (McPhee) Styran; e. Lisgar Coll. Inst.; m. lstly Gerhard William Thomas Kennedy (d. 1975); children: Mark, Shawn, D'Arcy, Tracy; m. 2ndly G. Allan Burton 1976; Broadcast Journalist and Pub. Affairs Ed. Radio Stn. CFRB since 1959; Panelist CBC-TV 'Front Page Challenge' since 1962; Dir. Simpsons Ltd. 1974-79; Bank of Montreal; Akzona Inc.; mem. Metrop. Toronto Hosp. Planning Council 1965-70; Gov. Council Univ. of Toronto and mem. various comtes. incl. Extve. Comte. and Chrmn. External Affairs Comte. 1972-77; first non med. mem. Coll. Phys. & Surgs. Ont. Complaints Comte. 1970-75; Adv. Comte. on Communications, Comte. on Govt. Planning Ont., Adv. Comte. Special Study regarding med. prof. in Ont. comnd. by Ont. Med. Assn. (Pickering Report 1972-73), mem. Citizens Adv. Comte. of Assn. 1973-76; served on Special Program Review Comte. to recommend efficiencies in Prov. spendings 1975; first woman Chrmn. Nat. Brotherhood Week, Candn. Council Christians & Jews 1975; mem. of Bd., Toronto Western Hospital; mem. Selection Comte. for Outstanding Achievement Award in Pub. Service of Can. 1972 (Chrmn. 1973); mem. Adv. Comtes. for Ont. Educ. Communications Authority, Ryerson Polytech. Inst. (Radio, TV Arts), Univ. of W. Ont. (Sch. of Journalism); author 'Gerhard' 1976; "Hurricane Hazel," 1979; Office: CFRB, 2 St. Clair Ave. W., Toronto, Ont.

KENNEDY, Jack William, Q.C., B.A., LL.B.; b. Toronto, Ont., 26 Apl. 1926; s. John and Mary (Strong) K.; e. St. Andrew's Coll., Aurora, Ont., 1938-44; Univ. of Alta., B.A. 1950, LL.B. 1951; m. Maryalice, d. Alexander I. Millar, 12 Aug. 1950; children: Sandra, William, Marylee, Elizabeth; PARTNER, CORMIE KENNEDY, since 1953; Dir.; Collective MutualFund; Principal Venture Fund; Principal Certificate Series Inc.; Chmn., Bd. of Dir., Churchill Devel. Corp. Ltd.; read law with The Hon. Mr. Justice C. W. Clement, Q.C.; called to Bar of Alta. 1952; cr. Q.C. 1969; served as Lt. (retired) RCN Reserve; mem., Bd. of Gov., Univ. of Alta.; Past Pres., Edmonton Symphony Soc.; Past mem. of Council, Candn. Bar Assn.(Alta.Sec.); Past Chrmn., Comparative Law Subcomte. for Alta., Candn. Bar Assn.; Delta Kappa Epsilon;

mem. of Council and Chmn., Gen. Practice Sec. Internat. Bar Assn; Past Chmn, N. Alta Adv. Comte., Salvation Army; P. Conservative; Protestant; recreations: golf, swimming, gardening; Clubs: Edmonton; Mayfair Golf Home: 6203 Grandview Dr., Edmonton, Alta. T6H 4K2; Office: 1600 Cambridge Bldg., Edmonton, Alta.

KENNEDY, James Macoun, B.A., M.A., Ph.D.; professor; university administrator; b. Ottawa, Ont. 25 Apr. 1928; s. Howard and Mary (Macoun) K.; e. Univ. of Toronto B.A. 1949, M.A. 1950; Princeton Univ. Ph.D. 1953; m. Norah Hilda d. Harold Arthur Leake 9 Sept. 1950; PROFESSOR, DEPT. OF COMPUTER SCIENCE, UNIV. OF B.C. 1968- ; Vice-Pres., Univ. Services 1980- ; Research Offr., Atomic Energy of Can. Ltd. 1952; joined Univ. of B.C. 1966 as Dir. of Computing Ctr., Acting Head of Dept. 1968-69 and 1973-74); author of many articles and addresses on technical & social aspects of computers; Bd. Mem., Vancouver Community Coll. 1976-80 (Chrmn. 1976-78); mem. Candn. Information Processing Soc. (Pres. 1971-72); Candn. Assn. of Physicists; Candn Mathematics Assn.; Can. Applied Math. Assn.; Anglican; Club: U.B.C. Faculty; recreation: music; Home: 1891 Acadia Rd., Vancouver, B.C. V6T 1R2; Office: President's Office, 6328 Memorial Rd., Vancouver, B.C. V6T 2B3

KENNEDY, Taylor, M.Eng.; retired industrialist; b. Montreal, Que., 15 March 1916; s. W. Alan and Gladys (Taylor) K.; e. McGill Univ., B.Eng. 1938, M.Eng. 1939; m. Eleanore, d. late H. V. Book, Detroit, Mich., 27 Jan. 1940; children: James T., Frederick B., Mrs. Iain Mackay (Cynthia); since May 1970; Dir., Montreal Trust Company; joined predecessor Co. (Can. Cement Co. Ltd.) as Plant Eng.,1940-45; Project Engr., 1955-56; Gen. Supt. 1956-62; Vice-Pres. and Asst. Gen. Mgr., 1963-67; Vice-Pres. and Gen. Mgr., 1967-68; Pres. and Gen. Mgr. 1968-70; Dir. Pres & C.E.O., Can. Cement Lafarge Ltd., 1970-77; Pres., Montreal Neurological Hospital, 1977- ; Bd. of Gov., McGill Univ., 1970- ; Chmn., Athletic Bd., McGill, 1975- ; Lt. Col., Royal Montreal Regt., 1957-60; Trustee, Westmount Armoury Memorial Assoc.; Life Gov., Notre Dame Hosp. and Montreal Gen. Hosp.; mem., Indust. Accident Prevention Assn.; Que. Safety League (Pres. 1968); Candn. Mfrs. Assn. (Pres. 1977-78) (Extve. Comte.); Candn. Chamber Comm.; recreations: golf, squash, sailing, skiing; Clubs: Montreal Badminton & Squash; Mount Royal; University; Royal Montreal Golf; Laurentian Golf & Country; Rideau (Ottawa); Que. Garrison; Gator Creek Golf Club, Sarasota, Florida; Home: 3488 Cotes des Neiges Rd., Apt. 1613, Montreal, Quebec H3H 2M6

KENNETT, William A., B.A., M.Sc.; Canadian public servant; b. Toronto, Ont. 4 Sept. 1932; s. late Horace and Lena (Thorburn) K.; e. Univ. of Toronto, B.A.1955; London Sch. of Econ. M.Sc. 1957; m. Valerie Cosby d. late Frank S. Spence Jan. 1958; children: Steven, Brenda; INSPR. GEN. OF BANKS since 1977; Dir. Royal Candn. Mint; Can. Deposit Insurance Corp.; Inst. Citizenship; Ottawa YM YWCA; Home: 395 Huron Ave., Ottawa, Ont. K1Y 0X2; Office: 240 Sparks St., Ottawa, Ont. K1A 0G5.

KENNEY, R. Martin, C.D., B.A., M.Ed.; educator; b. Vancouver, B.C. 8 Jan. 1932; s. H. Martin Kenney; e. Appleby Coll. Oakville, Ont. 1952 (Head Boy); McMaster Univ. B.A. 1966; State Univ. of N.Y. (Buffalo) M.Ed. 1970; m. Lynne Tunbridge 13 Feb. 1959; children: Martin Steven, David John, Jason Thomas; PRES., ATHOL MURRAY COLL. OF NOTRE DAME since 1976 and mem. Bd. Regents; Master (Hist.) and Housemaster, Appleby Coll. Oakville 1962-73; Headmaster, Balmoral Hall Sch. Winnipeg 1973-76; Dir. Winnipeg Un. Appeal 1973; served with RCAF 1956-62, Flying Offr., Jet Pilot; Reserve Force, Maj., C.O. Appleby Coll. Cadet Corps; protestant; recreations: hunting, fishing, golf, squash, reading history; Club: Lakeshore Estate Tennis; Home: P.O. Box 219,

Wilcox, Sask. S0G 5E0; Office: P.O. Box 220, Wilcox, Sask. S0G 5E0.

KENNY, Charles W.; pulp and paper executive; b. Buckingham, Que. 26 Feb. 1922; s. Robert MacLaren and Jessie R. (MacLaren) K.; e. Buckingham (Que.) Elem. Sch. 1930; Bishops Coll. Sch. Lennoxville, Que. 1940; Univ. of W. Ont. Mang. Training Course 1963; m. Mary Suzanne d. Sydney Dion, Ottawa, Ont. 6 Dec. 1947; two s. John Alexander, Charles Alan; VICE PRES. AND GEN. MGR., THE JAMES MACLAREN CO. LTD.; Vice Pres. MacLaren Power & Paper Co.; MacLaren Quebec Power; Dir. MacLaren Newsprint Sales; served with RCAF 1942-46; mem. Candn. Pulp & Paper Assn.; United Church; recreations: golf, curling, fishing, hunting; Clubs: Seigniory; Ottawa Curling; Buckingham Curling; Buckingham Golf; Home: 591 Main St., Buckingham, Que. J8L 2H2; Office: Buckingham, Que. J8L 2X2.

KENNY, Douglas T., M.A., Ph.D.; educator; b. Victoria, B.C. 1923; e. Univ. of B.C. B.A. 1945, M.A. 1947, Univ. of Wash. Ph.D. (Psychol.); m.; two children; PRESIDENT, UNIV. OF BRIT. COLUMBIA since 1975 and Prof. of Psychol. there; joined Dept. of Psychol. present Univ. 1950, Head of Dept. 1965-69, Acting Dean of Arts 1969-70, Dean 1970-75; has taught psychol. Univ. of Wash., Wash. State Univ. and Harvard Univ.; apptd. to Can. Council 1978; Trustee, Soc. Sciences & Humanities Research Council, 1978; since 1950 has participated Univ. and Senate Comtes. regarding Univ. affairs; author numerous articles in Candn. and US learned journs.; mem. several Candn. Eng. and Am. learned socs.; Pres. B.C. Psychol. Assn. 1961; Pres., Faculty Assn. 1962; Address: Univ. of British Columbia, Vancouver, B.C.

KENNY, R. Timothy, B.Sc. Forestry; manufacturer; b. Buckingham, Que. 26 Sept. 1929; s. late Robert Maclaren and late Jessie Robertson (Maclaren) K.; e. Buckingham Consol. Elem. Sch. 1940; Ashbury Coll. Ottawa 1948; Univ. of N.B., B.Sc. Forestry 1952; m. Audrey Joyce d. late Albert Cutting Wilson 24 Oct. 1953; children: Robert M., E. Ann, Patricia J., Mary J.; PRES. AND CEO MACLAREN POWER & PAPER CO. since 1979; Pres., Thurso Pulp and Paper Co.; Macdev Enterprises Ltd.; Quebec Hardwoods Inc.; Canadian Hardwoods Ltd.; The James Maclaren Co. Ltd.; The Thurso Railway Co.; Sogefor Ltée; Dir., Lumonics Research Inc.; Northwood Mills Ltd.; Norpak Ltd.; Forestry Engr. 1952; Dir. present Co. 1962; mem. Order Forestry Engrs. Que.; Candn. Pulp & Paper Assn.; Pulp & Paper Research Inst. Can.; Protestant; recreations: swimming, curling, cross-country skiing; Club: Buckingham Curling; Home: 585 Main St., Buckingham, Que. J8L 2H2; Office: Buckingham, Que. J8L 2X3.

KENT, Charles Deane, B.A., B.L.S., retired librarian; b. Ottawa, Ont., 30 Aug. 1915; s. Herbert John and Adelyne Merle (Cone) K.; e. Glebe Coll. Inst., Ottawa, Ont.; McMaster Univ. B.A. 1939; McGill Univ., B.L.S. 1945; Univ. of Mich. (summer sch.) 1955-56; Univ. of Maryland (Summer Sch.) 1967; m. Barbara Elaine, d. Reginald James Russell, St. James, Manitoba, 11 Dec. 1942; children: Judith Ann (Grant), Susan Elizabeth d) Nicholas Russell Cone, James Anthony; Director and Secretary Treasurer, Board of the Lake Erie Regional Library System, 1968-76 (Director & Secretary 1964-67); with W.P.T.B. 1939-41; Inspection Bd. of United Kingdom and Can., 1941-42; joined present interest as Asst. Librarian, 1945; Chief Librarian, Regina (Sask.) Public Library, 1945-48; Asst. Dir., London Public Library and Art Museum, 1948-61, Director and Secretary-Treasurer 1961-73; with C.O.T.C. University of Ottawa, 1941-42, C.A.A.F. (RCASC) 1942-44; A.D.C. to Maj.-Gen. J. H. Roberts, C.B., D.S.O., 1944; Publications: "Libraries & Museums in Scandinavia To-day", 1960 and "Improving your Reading", 1961 (both occasional papers contrib. to Candn. Lib. Assn.); numerous writings and articles on local hist. and lib. work in various journs.; awarded Can. Council Fellowship, 1958 and travel grant, 1963, CAAE Award 1958; Brit. Council Visitor, 1963, 1972; Chrmn., London local Council of International Reading Assn., 1963-64; Pres., London Council for Adult Educ., 1959-60; Pres., London Film Soc., 1951-52; Chrmn., Inst. of Prof. Librarians of Ont., 1957-58; Chrmn., London Arts Council, 1962-63, 1963-64; mem. of Extve., Ont. Curriculum Devel. Assn.; Life mem., Ont. Lib. Assn. (Pres. 1959-60); Life mem., Candn. Lib. Assn.; mem. Am. Lib. Assn.; Sask. Lib. Assn. (Vice-Pres. 1947-48); Regina Lib. Assn. (Pres. 1947-48); mem., McMaster Univ. Senate 1965-73; mem., Executive Committee, Baconian Club of London (Pres. 73-74); toured German libraries as guest of West German Government 1964; toured fr. maison de la culture as guest of Fr. Govt., 1969 UNESCO mission to Uganda, 1970, to draft plan for library service in that country; recreations: skating, philately, travel; Clubs: Canadian 1438 Bradshaw Cr., Gloucester, Ont. K1B 562

KENT, Lionel Pelham, F.C.A.; b. N. Vancouver, B.C., 13 Oct. 1914; s. Gerald Aldwyn and Ethel Mary (Felton) K.; e. Lynn Valley Pub. Sch., 1920-26; Churchers Coll., Hants., Eng., 1927-31 (grad. with Hons. Sr. Cambridge Sch. Cert.; London Matric.); m. Josephine Hope, d. late Henry Brealey (Dec'd), 2 March 1939; children: Judith Hope (Mrs. Robert J. Cowling), Michael Pelham, Brian Brealey, (dec'd) Lionel Richard, David Pelham, Patrick Henry; DIR., ALCAN ALUMINUM LTD. 1979- ; Chmn, Bd of Management, McLintock Main Lafrentz & Co: 1977-79; Chrmn. Thorne Riddell Assocs. Ltd. 1974-77; articled Clerk with Riddell, Stead, Graham & Hutchison, Vancouver, 1931-38; C.A. 1938; Partner 1945, Partner i.c. Vancouver Office 1955; Extve. Partner Riddell Stead & Co. Montreal 1959-74 (Chrmn. Mang. Comte. 1963-67); Chrmn. Riddell Stead & Assocs. Ltd. 1973-74;Extve. Partner, Thorne Riddell & Co., 1974-77 Financial Advisor to Counsel for British Columbia in series of freight rate cases, 1946-50; Financial Advisor to Board of Transport Commissioners for Can., 1950-57; served in 2nd World War with R.C.A.F. 1940-45 (Dir. of Accts. & Finance, Overseas); discharged with rank of Group Capt., mem., Inst. of Chart. Accts. of B.C. (mem. Council 1946-47), Que., Ont.; Governor, Crofton House School, 1947-59 (Chairman 1957-59); St. George's School, 1957-59 (Director, 1958-59); Trinity College School, Director 1965, Life Gov. 1966; Trustee Bisops University, 1980; mem., Air Force Offrs. Assn. (Dir., 1956-57); Candn. Chamber Comm. (Chrmn. Extve Council 1968-69, Nat. Dir.); Pacific Basin Economic Council (Chrmn. Candn. Comte. 1971-72); Can. Japan Business Co-op Comte; Anglican; recreations: shooting, fishing, golf, bridge, horses; Clubs: Vancouver; Capilano Golf & Country; Mount Royal; Mount Bruno Country; Canadian; York; Forest & Stream; Toronto; Toronto Golf; Ontario Jockey; Royal Candn. Mil. Inst.; Home: R.R. #3, Ayer's Cliff, Que., J0B 1C0; Office: Suite 2500, 630 Dorchester Blvd., West, Montreal. Que. H3B 1W2

KENT, Thomas Worrall, O.C., M.A.; executive and writer; b. Stafford, Eng., 3 April 1922; s. John Thomas and Frances (Worrall) K.; e. Wolstanton (Eng.) Grammar Sch.; Corpus Christi Coll., Oxford, B.A. 1941 (1st Class Hons. in Modern Greats); Univ. of Oxford, M.A. 1950; m. Phyllida Anne, d. M. R. Cross, Aston Tirrold, Eng., 3 June 1944; children: Duncan M. S., Oliver R. T., Andrew J. F.; DEAN, FACULTY OF ADMINISTRATIVE STUDIES, DALHOUSIE UNIV. 1980- ; Ed. of "Policy Options" and Chrm. of Editorial Bd., Inst. for Research on Public Policy; Pres., TWK Associated Consulting Ltd.; Gov. Atlantic Provinces Economic Council; Trustee, Bell Inst. of Coll. of Cape Breton; Patron, Lester B. Pearson Coll. of the Pacific; mem. of Council, Inst. of Public Affairs of Dalhousie Univ.; engaged in intelligence service for U.K. War Office and Foreign Office, 1942-45; Edit. Writer for the "Manchester Guardian", 1946-50; Asst. Editor, "London Economist", 1950-54; Editor, "Winnipeg Free Press", 1954-59; Vice-Pres., Chemcell Ltd., Montreal, Que., 1959-61; Special Consultant to late Rt. Hon. Lester B. Pearson, P.C. 1961-63; def. cand. to H. of C. for Burnaby-Coquitlam in g.e. 1963; Co-ordinator of Programming & Policy Secy. to Prime Min., 1963-65; Dir. of Special Planning Secretariat, P. Council Office, 1965; Deputy Min., Dept. of Manpower and Immigration, 1966-68; Deputy Min., Dept. of Regional Econ. Expansion, 1968-71; Pres. & Chief Exec. Offcr., Cape Breton Devel. Corp., 1971-77; Pres. and C.E.O., Sydney Steel Corp., 1977-79; Chmn. of Royal Comm. on Newspaper, 1980-81; author of "Social Policy for Canada", 1962; contrib. to various periodicals on pol. and econ. subjects; Invested as Officer of the Order of Canada, 1979; Home: Mabou, Inverness County, N.S.; Office: Box 3670, Halifax South, N.S. B3J 3K6

KEON, Wilbert Joseph, M.D., M.Sc., F.R.C.S.(C), F.A.C.S.; surgeon; b. Sheenboro, Que. 17 May 1935; e. St. Paul's High Sch. Sheenboro, Que. and St. Patrick's Coll. High Sch. Ottawa; Univ. of Ottawa, St. Patrick's Coll. B.Sc. 1957, M.D. 1961; McGill Univ. M.Sc. (Exper. Surg.) 1963; children: Claudia, Ryan, Neil; SURGEON-IN-CHIEF, OTTAWA CIVIC HOSP. since 1977, Chief Div. Cardiothoracic Surg. since 1969; Prof. and Chrmn. of Surg. Univ. of Ottawa ince 1976, Chrmn. Div. Cardiothoracic Surg. since 1974, Dir. Cardiac Unit since 1969; Co-chairman, Medical Advisory Committee, C.H.F.; Surgical Traveler, James IV Assoc. of Surgeons Inc., 1979; post-grad. training Ottawa Civic Hosp., Montreal Gen. Hosp., Toronto Gen. Hosp., Toronto Hosp. for Sick Children, Peter Bent Brigham Hosp. and Harvard Med. Centre, 1961-69; Dir. Ont. Heart Foundation; rec'd Peter Ballantine Ewing Gold Medal-Surgery; McLaughlin Fellowship; Ont. Heart Foundation Sr. Fellowship; Man of the Yr. Award, Ottawa Knockers Club; Univ. of Ottawa Staff Research Award 1975; Carleton Univ. Outstanding Alumnus Award 1977; author or co-author numerous publs.; frequent speaker; Fellow, Am. Heart Assn. Council on Clin. Cardiol.; Am. Coll. Cardiol.; Affiliate, Royal Soc. Med.; mem. Ont. Med. Assn.; Candn. Med. Assn.; Acad. Med. Ottawa; Candn. Cardiovascular Soc.; Candn. Heart Foundation (Past Chrmn. Scient. Sub-comte.); Med. Research Council (Grants Comte. for Heart & Lung); Internat. Cardiovascular Soc.; Am. Assn. Thoracic Surg.; Soc. Thoracic Surgs.; Ont. Cancer Treatment & Research Foundation (Adv. Med. Bd.); Candn. Assn. Clin. Surgs.; Candn. Soc. Clin. Investigation; Soc. Vascular Surg.; Alpha Omega Alpha (Hon. mem.); Home: 2298 Bowman Rd., Ottawa Ont.Office: 1053 Carling Ave., Ottawa, Ont. K1Y4E9

KER, John William, B.A.Sc., M.F., D.For., D.Sc.; forester; university dean; b. Chilliwack, B.C., 27 Aug. 1915; s. John and Ellen (Fitz-Gibbon) K.; e. Univ. of British Columbia, B.A.Sc. (Forestry) 1941, D.Sc. 1971; Yale Sch. of Forestry, M.F. 1951, D.For. 1957; m. Marguerite Frances, d. late Seth Witton, 26 April 1943; children: John Gerald, Kerry Ann, Wendy Rena; DEAN, FACULTY FORESTRY, UNIV. OF NEW BRUNSWICK; formerly a Prof., Faculty of Forestry, Univ. of British Columbia, mem., Science Council of Can., 1966-68; mem., Candn. Inst. of Forestry (Pres. 1971-72); Candn. Forestry Advisory Council 1970-81; mem. (Forestry), B.C. Natural Resources Conf., 1955-57; Pacific Science Cong. (Del. to Tenth Cong., Honolulu, 1961); Assn. of B.C. Foresters (Chrmn. of Bd. of Examiners, 1955; mem. of Council, 1956); assn. of Reg'd. Prof. Foresters of N.B.; Forest Engr. (P.Eng.) admitted into Assn. Prof. Engrs. of N.B. 1971; mem. Candn. Council Rural Devel. 1972-73; Natural Sciences and Engineering Research Council of Can., 1980-83; C.I.D.A. expert, Agric. University Malaysia 1973-74; Publications: co-author of a number of books related to forestry; many articles in prof. journs.; Anglican; recreations: outdoor sports, camping, curling; Home: 760 Golf Club Road, Fredericton, N.B. E3B 4X4

KERGIN, Dorothy Jean, B.S.N., M.P.H., Ph.D., F.A.P.H.A.; university professor; nurse; b. Prince Rupert, B.C., 5 Sept. 1928; d. Louis Wellington and Mina Mary (McCaffrey) K.; e. Univ. of B.C., B.S.N. 1952; Univ. of Mich., M.P.H. 1962, Ph.D. 1968; DIR. AND PROF., SCH. OF NURSING, UNIV. OF VICTORIA, Jan. 1980- ; Dir. and Prof., Sch. of Nursing McMaster Univ., 1970-79; Pub. Health Nurse for 7 yrs., B.C. Dept. of Health, Princeton, Kitimat and Port Alberni; Occupational Health Nurse 3 yrs. Aluminum Co. of Canada, Kitimat, B.C.; Instr. in Pub. Health Nursing 3 yrs. Univ. of Mich.; Assoc. Dir., Assoc. Prof. at McMaster Univ. 1968-70; Chrmn., Comte. on Clin. Training of Nurses for Med. Services in N., Dept. of Nat. Health & Welfare, 1970; Consultant, Assn. of Atlantic Universities (Masters Program in Nursing) 1972; mem., Candn. Nurses Assn. (Chrmn. ad hoc Comte. on Nursing Research 1970); Candn. Pub. Health Assn.; Delta Omega Soc.; Med. Research Council 1972-77; Consultant, AGA Khan Foundation, Pakistan, 1979; mem., Addiction Research Foundation, Ont. 1978-79; Pres., Candn. Univ. Schools of Nursing 1976-80; Chmn., Nursing Ed. Council of B.C. 1980-82; mem., Capital Region Hospital and Health Planning Comm. 1981- ; Steering Comte, Operation Bootstrap, Can. Nurses Assn. 1980- ; Review Comte. 47, Health Services and Promotion Br., Health and Welfare Can., 1981- ; Protestant; Home: 3815 Campus Cres., Victoria, B.C.; Office: Sedgewick Bldg., Univ. of Victoria, P.O. Box 1700, Victoria, B.C., V8W 2Y2

KERMAN, Arthur, B.Sc., Ph.D., F.A.P.S.; professor; b. Montreal, Que., 3 May 1929; e. Strathcona Acad., Outremont, Que. (1942-46); McGill Univ., B.Sc. 1950; Mass. Inst. Tech., Ph.D. 1953; m. Enid, d. Irving Ehrlich, New York, N.Y., 21 Dec. 1952; five children; DIR., CENTRE FOR THEORETICAL PHYSICS, MASS. INST. OF TECH., since 1977, and Prof. of Physics at M.I.T. since 1964; Adjunct Prof. of Physics, Brooklyn Coll., 1971-76; Consultant, Argonne Nat. Lab.; Brookhaven Nat. Lab.; Lawrence Radiation Lab.; Los Alamos Scient. Lab.; Oak Ridge Nat. Lab.; Teaching Fellow, Mass. Inst. Tech., 1950-53; N.R.C. (U.S.) Postdoctoral Fellow at Cal. Inst. of Tech., 1954; N.R.C. (Can.) Overseas Fellow at Inst. of Theoretical Physics, Copenhagen, 1955; Asst. Prof. of Physics, Mass. Inst. Tech., 1956-60, Assoc. Prof. 1960-64; Guggenheim Fellow, University of Paris, 1961-62; Visiting Prof. Physics, State Univ. of N.Y. 1970-71; mem. Visiting Comte., Bartol Research Foundation; Physics Div., Argonne Nat. Lab.; Princeton Penn Accelerator; mem. Programme Adv. Comte., LAMPF; Mass. Inst. Tech., Electron Linac; mem. Nat. Acad. Science panels on Nuclear Data, Heavy Ion Physics; Physics Survey Comte., Nuclear Physics Panel; Extve. Comte., Nuclear Physics Div., Am. Phys. Soc.; mem. Visiting Comte. Physics Dept. & High Energy Adv. Comte. AGS, Brookhaven Nat. Lab.; Chrmn. Program Adv. Comte. BEVLAC, Lawrence Berkeley Lab.; Assoc. Ed., "Reviews of Modern Physics" 1968-71; Home: 37 Rangeley Road, Winchester, Mass.

KERN, Rolf Robert, Dr. rer. pol.; insurance executive; b. Freiburg, Germany, 5 Aug. 1927; s. Friedrich Albert and Lina (Mattmueller) K.; e. Elem. and High Schs., Freiburg, Germany; Univ. of Freiburg, Dipl. rer. pol. 1953, Dr. rer. pol. 1955; post grad. work univs. France and U.S.; m. Inge Elizabeth, d. Emil Schmidt, 26 Aug. 1958; children: Rona Elizabeth Lina, Barbara Diana, Petra Ruth; PRES. AND DIR., GERLING GLOBAL REINSURANCE CO. since 1980; Pres. and Dir., Gerling Global General Insurance Co. since 1980; commenced in market research Radische Anilin & Sodafabrik A.G., Ludwigshafen, Germany 1955; Jr. Extve., Gerling-Konzern, Cologne 1957; joined present Co. as Mgr. and Secy.-Treas. 1958, Vice-Pres. 1968, Sr. Vice-Pres. and Secy.-Treas. 1971; Adm. Mgr., Gerling Global General Insurance Co. 1964, Sr. Vice-Pres. and Secy.-Treas. 1971; Vice-Pres. and Secy., Gerling Service Corp. Ltd. 1969; Extve. Vice-Pres. and Secy. Treas.,

Gerling Global Reinsurance 1976-80; Extve. Vice-Pres. and Secy., Gerling Global General Ins. Co., 1976-80; mem. Bd. Trade Metrop. Toronto; Ins. Accounting and Stat. Assn.; Reinsurance Research Council (Pres. and Dir.); Protestant; recreations: swimming, yoga, tennis; Clubs: Bayview Country; Granite; Office: 480 University Ave., Toronto, Ont. M5G 1V6

KERNAGHAN, Kenneth Watt, Q.C., B.A.; b. Toronto, Ont., 6 March 1916; s. Hugh and Lucy (Watt) K.; e. Humberside Coll. Inst., Toronto, Ont.; Trinity Coll., Univ. of Toronto, B.A. 1937; Osgoode Hall Law Sch., Toronto, Ont. 1940; m. Edna Mortley, d. Clarence Percival Button, Toronto, Ont., 4 Oct. 1941; COUNSEL-ARMSTRONG, KEMP, YOUNG, BURROWS & GRANT, BARRISTERS & SOLICITORS 1980- ; Vice-Pres. and Secy., Simpsons, Limited, Apl. 1968-Jan. 1980; Dir., Greenridge Investments Ltd., Pape Investments Ltd.; Plum Investments Ltd.; read law with John S. Macfarlane, Q.C.; called to the Bar of Ont., 1940; cr. Q.C. Dec. 1958; Trust Offr. in Toronto for The London & Western Trust Co. Ltd., 1940-41, and at London, Ont., 1942-44; Mgr. of Toronto Office, 1944-45; joined The Robert Simpson Co. Ltd. in June 1945 as Solr., and Asst. to Secy.; apptd. Asst. Secy., 1953 and Secy., 1958-68; mem., Bd. Trade of Metrop. Toronto; Co. of York Law Assn.; Candn. Bar Assn.; Phi Delta Phi; P. Conservative; Anglican; Clubs: University; Granite; Home: Apt. 704, 625 Avenue Rd., Toronto, Ont. M4V 2K7; Office: Suite 1606, 141 Adelaide St., West, Toronto, Ont. M5H 1V7

KERNER, Fred, B.A.; publisher; b. Montreal, Que., 15 Feb. 1921; s. Sam and Vera (Goldman) K.; e. Sir George Williams Univ., B.A. 1942; m. Sally Dee, d. Fred Stouten, Valley Stream, N.Y., 18 May 1959; children: David, Diane, Jon; VICE-PRES. AND PUBLISHING DIR., Book Division of HARLEQUIN ENTERPRISES LTD. since 1975; Dir., Colophon Publishing Inc.; Centaur House, Inc.; National Mint Inc.; Publitex International Corp.; Publishing Projects; Personalized Services, Inc.; Peter Kent, Inc.; Ed. Writer, Saskatoon Star-Phoenix, 1942; Asst. Sports Ed., Montreal Gazette, 1942-44; News-Ed., The Candn. Press, Montreal, Toronto & N.Y., 1944-50; Night City Ed. and roving corr., The Associated Press, N.Y., 1951-56; Sr. Ed., Hawthorn Books, 1957-58; Extve. Ed., Fawcett World Lib., New York, 1959-62; Ed.-in-Chief 1962-64; Pres. and Ed.-in-Chief, Hawthorn Books, Inc., N.Y., 1964-67; Pres., Centaur House, Inc., New York, 1964-79; Pres., Paramount Security Corp. 1965-68; Vice-Pres., Publitex International Corp., Pa., 1967-78; Mang. Dir., Publishing Projects, New York, 1967-78; Publishing Director, Books and Educ. Divisions, Reader's Digest Assn. (Canada) Limited 1969-75; mem. Local Sch. Bd., Dist. 4, New York, 1968; author "Stress and Your Heart", 1961; "A Treasury of Lincoln Quotations", 1965; "Love Is a Man's Affair", 1958; "Watch Your Weight Go Down" (pseudonym: Frederick Kerr), 1962; "It's Fun to Fondue" (pseudonym: M. N. Thaler), 1968; co-author: "Eat, Think and Be Slender", 1954; "The Magic Power of Your Mind", 1956; "Ten Days to a Successful Memory", 1957; "Secrets of Your Supraconscious", 1965; "Buy High, Sell Higher", 1966; "What's Best for Your Child — and You", 1966; "Nadia", 1976; contributed to "Chambers's Encyclopedia", "The Overseas Press Club Cookbook", "Successful Writers and How They Work" and various mags.; mem. Bd. Govs. Concordia Univ.; Trustee, Benson & Hedges Lit. Awards; Gibson Lit. Awards; Candn. Authors Association Lit. Awards; Judge, Cobalt National Poetry Contest 1975; Pres. Assn. of Alumni, Sir George Williams Univ. 1971-74; Chrmn. (1973) Sch. Comte. (ombudsman) Westmount (Que.) High Sch.; (Bd. of Dir., Canadian Book Publishers Council (Chrm. Copyright Committee) 1977-78; Bd. of Gov., Canadian Copyright Inst., 1977-81; Organization of Can. Authors and Publishers, 1977-81; Pres., Can. Assoc. for the Restoration of Lost Positives, 1969- ; Chrmn. (1965) Internat. Affairs Conf. for Coll. Editors; mem., Mystery Writers Am. (Ed. "Third

Degree" bulletin; Co-chrmn., Awards Comte.); Candn. Authors Assn. (Nat. Vice-Pres. 1972-78, Pres. Montreal Br. 1974-75 Chrm. Awards Comm. 1972-81; Founder Chrm. Toronto Literary Luncheon program); Am. Mang. Assn.; Author's League; Author's Guild; Candn. Soc. of Prof. Journalists; Sigma Delta Chi; recreations: music, skating, walking; Clubs: Author's (London); Dutch Treat (N.Y.); Overseas Press, N.Y. (Chrmn., Election Comte., Lib. Comte., Book Night Comte., Awards Comte.); Toronto Men's Press; Candn. Soc. N.Y.; Deadline (N.Y.); Home: 25 Farmview Cres., Willowdale, Ont. M2J 1G5; Office: 225 Duncan Mill Rd., Don Mills, Ont. M3B 3K9

KERR, Byron Thomas, B.E., F.E.I.C.; management consultant; b. Campbellton, N.B. 28 Dec. 1924; s. Thomas F. and late Isobel (Butler) K.; e. Mount Allison Univ. 1942-45; N.S. Tech. Coll. B.E. (Civil) 1947; m. Shirley B. d. late Stanley M. Bulmer 27 Dec. 1947; children: Peter T., Patricia Ann, Susan W.; PRESIDENT, CHIEF EXTVE. OFFR. AND DIR., KERR AND ASSOCIATES LTD. 1980- ; Dir. Canadian Stebbins Engineering and Manufacturing Co. Ltd.; B.B.FK.. Consultant Ltd.; BURCAN Industries Ltd.; Resident Engr. Shawinigan Engineering Co. Ltd. 1947-51; Aircraft Indust. of Can; Autair Ltd.; Timmins Aviation Ltd; Crombie Advertising Ltd., P. Lawson Travel; International Bronze Powders Ltd; Henderson Furniture Ltd; Pres. and Dir.: North American Trust Ltd. 1965-69; Watnock Hersey Management Consultants Ltd. 1960-69; Warnock Hersey Soils Investigations Ltd., Warnock Hersey Caribbean Ltd., The Warnock Hersey Appraisal Co. Ltd., 1955-65; Pres., The Warnock Hersey Co. Ltd. 1966-65, Extve. Vice Pres. and Dir. Warnock Hersey International Ltd. 1965-70, Pres., Chief Extve. Offr. and Dir. Warnock Hersey Professional Services Ltd. 1977-80; Pres. Purdy & Henderson Co. Ltd 1950-55; Pres. Kerr & Associates Ltd. 1970-72 Gen. Mgr. and Chief Extve. Offr. Engn. Inst. Can. 1972-77; mem. C.S.A. Comte on Nondestructive Testing, 1963-69; Nat. Research Council on Internat. Scientific & Technical Applications; Ald. St. Lambert 1957-61, Mayor 1961-64; active prov. and fed. politics 1957-72; Dir. and Secy. Treas. Julian C. Smith Mem. Fund, Brace Request Fund; Publisher and Ed. "Engineering Journal" 1972-78; author numerous tech. papers engn. publs.; served with RCN, rank Lt. Commdr. (Engn.); rec'd Queen's Silver Jubilee Medal; Fellow, Am. Inst. Mang.; mem. Order Engrs. Que.; Assn. Prof. Engrs. Ont., Alta., N.S., N.B., Nfld.; Newcomen Soc. Am.; Am. Soc. Civil Engrs.; Am. Soc. Mech. Engrs.; Candn. Soc. Civil Engrs.; Candn. Dir. Pan Am. Union Engn. Organs. 1975-81; Liberal; United Church; recreations: sports, photography Clubs: Mount Stephen; Cercle Universitaire (Ottawa); Country Montreal; St.Lambert Curling;Office: 240 First St., St. Lambert, Que. J4R 1B5.

KERR, Howard Hillen, B.Paed., B.A.Sc., LL.D.; b. Seaforth, Ont., 24 Dec. 1900; s. late James and Martha Jane (Hillen) K.; e. Univ. of Toronto, Mech. Engn., 1922, B.Paed., 1932; LL.D., Toronto 1963, W. Ont. 1967; m. Beatrice Jean, d. late Dr. F. H. Larkin, 26 Aug. 1926; children: Mrs. Ian G. Walker (dec'd.), Dr. James Ian, Mrs. J. H. Martin; after grad. worked in engn. positions and business for five yrs. before entering the teaching prof.; taught at Galt (Ont.) Coll. & Vocational Sch., Western-Tech. Comm. Sch., Toronto, Oshawa (Ont.) Coll. & Vocational Inst. (10 yrs.); apptd. Regional Dir. for Ont., War Emergency Training Program (operated by Fed. Dept. of Labour), 1940; Regional Director (Ontario), Canadian Vocational Train. Prog. (rehab. training for veterans discharged from Armed Forces) 1944-48; found. Princ. Ryerson Polytech. Inst.; Toronto, 1948-66; Chrmn., Council of Regents, Ont. Colleges of Applied Arts and Technology 1966-70; mem., Assn. Prof. Engrs. Ont.; Engn. Inst. Can.; Chrmn., Tech. Inst. Div., Am. Soc. for Engn. Educ., 1961-63; Canada Defence Research Bd., 1965-68; mem. Bd. Govs., Ryerson Polytechnical Inst.; founding mem., Board Trustees, Ontario Science Centre; awarded

Queen's Coronation Medal; Gold Medal, Prof. Inst. Public Service of Can., 1959; Centennial Medal; Queen's Jubilee Medal 1977; Fellow, Ont. Inst. for Studies in Ed., 1981; Freemason; Presbyterian; Home: 227-11 Elm Ave., Toronto, Ont. M4W 1N2

KERR, Illingworth H.; artist; illustrator; fiction writer; b. Lumsden, Sask., 20 Aug. 1905; s. William Hugh and Florence Amelia Kemp (Nurse) K.; e. Pub. Schs., Sask.; Central Tech. Sch., Toronto; Ont. Coll. of Art, Toronto; Westminster Sch. of Art, London, Eng., 1936; m. Mary, d. John Thomas Spice, Yorkton, Sask., 3 Aug. 1938; exhibited landscape paintings with western and eastern socs., Lumsden, Sask., 1927-34; Asst. Dir. of Documentary Films, London, Eng., 1936; wrote Candn. fiction for Brit. mags. in Scot., 1937; an artist with Empire Show, Glasgow, Scot.; with Candn. Exhn. for N.Y. World Fair; held one-man show in Regina, 1939; employed at Boeing's Aircraft, Vancouver, B.C., Production Illustration Dept., 1942; won award for best water colour, B.C. Artists' show, 1942; painting of Qu'Appelle Valley purchased by Grand Central Galleries, N.Y. City, 1945; Instr., Vancouver Sch. of Art, 1945-46; author and illustrator "Gay Dogs and Dark Horses" 1946; illustrated "The Story of Our Canadian Northland" 1946; "The Saskatchewan", Rivers of America Series, 1949; "The NorWesters", 1954; "Willowdale" 1956; "Travellers West" 1956; apptd. Head of Alta. Coll. of Art, 1947-67; Art Dept., Inst. of Technol. & Art, Calgary, Alta., 1947 (designed as Alta. Coll. of Art since 1961), S. Alta, Inst. of Technol., 1947; Sr. Fellowship, Can. Council, 1960-61, to investigate teaching of Indust. Design in U.S. and Brit.; one man shows of oils and water colours: A.C.A. Gallery,Calgary, 1962, 1968; Calgary Allied Arts Council, 1963; Edmonton Art Gallery, 1964; Maritimes galleries, 1968; major retrospective exhn. "Fifty Years a Painter", A.C.A. Gallery, Calgary; Saskatoon Art Gallery; Norman MacKenzie Gallery, Regina, 1974; paintings in many collections incl. Can. Council Art Bank; Alta. Art Foundation; Law Courts Bldg., Edmonton; Convention Centre, Calgary; publications: "Gay Dogs & Dark Horses", 1946; also many Candn. short stories publ. in "Blackwood's Mag.", Edinburgh, Scot.; actively engaged as a painter, chiefly landscapes; executed portraits of Lieut.-Gov. Grant MacEwan, John C. Bowen and Premier Harry Strom for the Alberta Leg. Bldgs., also portraits for Univs., Alberta, Edmonton, Calgary; Achievement Award, Alta. Govt. 1973; Gold Medal, Nat. Award for Painting and Realted Arts, Univ. of Alta., 1975; rec'd. Hon. Doct. Univ. Calgary 1974; mem., Alta. Soc. of Artists; recreations: camping, hunting, swimming; Home: 1723 — 10 St., S.W., Calgary, Alta. T2T 3E9

KERR, James W., B.Sc.; company executive; b. Hamilton, Ont., 11 March 1914; s. George Robert and Helen Robertson (Bews) K.; e. Pub. Sch. and Delta Coll. Inst., Hamilton, Ont.; Univ. of Toronto, B.Sc. (Applied Sc. & Engn.) 1937; m. Ruth Eleanor, d. Charles H. Marrs, Hamilton, Ont., 5 Oct. 1940; children: David, Barbara; CONSULTANT & DIR., TRANS-CANADA PIPELINES 1979- ; formerly Chrm. and Chief Exec. Officer, 1968-79; Dir., Canadian Imperial Bank of Commerce; Manufacturers Life Ins. Co.; Bell Canada; Great Lakes Gas Transmission Co.; Lehndorff Corp.; Internat. Minerals & Chem. Corp. (Can.) Ltd.; Maple Leaf Mills Ltd.; commenced work with Canadian Westinghouse Company Limited, Hamilton, Ont. 1937, in various positions, becoming Vice-Pres. and Gen. Mgr., Apparatus Products Group 1956; joined present Co. as Pres. and Chief Extve. Offr. 1958, Chrmn. Bd. and Pres. 1961, Chrm. and CEO 1968; served in 2nd World War, R.C.A.F.; rank Sqdn. Ldr.; mem., Bd. Govs., Queen Elizabeth Hosp.; Depy. Chrm., Bd. of Trustees, Timothy Easton Mem. Church; Chmn., Nat. Advisory Bd. Exec., The Salvation Army; Bd. Govs., Ont. Research Foundation; Past Pres., Candn. Gas Assn.; Bd. Trade Metrop. Toronto; Hon. Pres. Internat. Gas Union; mem., McMaster Univ. Med. Centre Found;

Engn. Inst. Can.; Assn. Prof. Engrs. Ont.; Theta Delta Chi; recreations: golf, gardening; Clubs: The Toronto; York; The Hamilton; Rideau (Ottawa); Rosedale Golf; Mount Royal (Montreal); Home: 3 Highland Ave., Toronto, Ont. M4W 2A2; Office: (Box 54) Commerce Court W., Toronto, Ont. M5L 1C2

KERR, Hon. John Gregory, M.L.A., B.A., B.Ed.; politician; b. Annapolis Royal, N.S. 8 Oct. 1947; s. John Roland K.; e. Annapolis Royal Regional Acad. 1966; Mount Allison Univ. B.A. 1970, B.Ed. 1971; m. Marcia Lee d. Bernard Longmire, Hillsburn, N.S. 22 Aug. 1970; children: Gillian Loring, Megan Bernice; MIN. OF CULTURE, RECREATION AND FITNESS, N.S. 1980- ; el. M.L.A. for Annapolis West prov. g.e. 1978; Caucus Chrmn. P. Cons. Party 1979-81; Trustee, Granville Ferry Consolidated (Elem.); Historic Restoration Soc. Annapolis Co.; Gov. Heritage Foundation Annapolis Royal; P. Conservative; Anglican; recreations: squash, racketball, farming; Home: R.R. 1, Granville Ferry, Annapolis Co., N.S. BOS 1K0; Office: (P.O. Box 864) Halifax, N.S. B3J 2V2.

KERR, Hon. Roderick, B.A., LL.B.; judge; b. Louisbourg, N.S.; 16 Jan. 1902; s. Roderick and Mary (MacDonald) K.; e. Louisbourg and Glace Bay, N.S., High Sch.; Dalhousie Univ., B.A. 1923, LL.B. 1925; m. Myra, d. Alexander MacDougall, Glace Bay, N.S., 12 Jan. 1946; two d.: Phylli, Valerie; DEPUTY JUDGE, FED. COURT OF APPEAL retired Justice, Fed. Court of Appeal Can.; called to Bar of N.S. 1926; cr. K.C. 1949; practiced law in Sydney and Glace Bay, N.S., 1926-40; entered Fed. Civil Service as Legal Adviser to Unemployment Ins. Comn., Ottawa, 1946-49; apptd. Asst. Counsel, Bd. of Transport Commrs., 1949 and Gen. Counsel, 1952; Commr. Oct. — Nov. 1958, Asst. Chief Commr. Nov. — Dec. 1958; Chief Commr. 1959-67; apptd. Puisne Judge Exchequer Court of Canada 1967, Judge, Federal Court of Canada 1971; served in 2nd World War; enlisted with Cape Breton Highlanders, 1940; proceeded overseas 1941; trans. to Candn. Mil. Hdqrs., Judge Advocate Gen.'s Br., 1942, serving there and with Claims Br., C.M.H.Q., London, till end of war; retired with rank Maj. 1945; United Church; Home: 2430 Island Park Towers, 200 Clearview Ave., Ottawa, Ont. K1Z 8M2; Office: The Federal Court, Wellington St., Ottawa, Ont.

KERRIGAN, Harold Fleming, D.S.O., D.F.C.; trust company officer; b. Sandwich, Ont., 10 June 1917; s. Harold George and Frances Maud (Fleming) K.; e. Public and High Schs., London, Ont.; m. Virginia Ernestine, d. Ernest Albee Porter, Brookline, Mass., 12 Aug. 1944; children: Geoffrey Blair, Stephen Frederic, Lesley Meredith; DIR., CHMN. OF BD. AND CHIEF EXTVE. OFFR., CROWN TRUST CO. since 1969; Pres., The Trust Buildings Ltd.; Dir., Prudential Growth Fund Canada Ltd.; with Midland Securities Corp. Limited, London and Toronto, Ont., 1937-40; joined present Co. in 1945; appt. Mgr. of Montreal Office, 1947; Asst. Gen. Mgr., 1954; Vice Pres. and Gen. Mgr. 1965; served in 2nd World War, 1940-45 with R.C.A.F.; attached to R.A.F. on Overseas Operations and Staff; awarded from R.A.F., D.S.O. (immediate), D.F.C.; discharged with rank of Sqdn. Ldr.; Pres., Life Ins. & Trust Council of Montreal, 1954-55; Pres., Trust Co.'s Assn. of P.Q., 1957; Pres., Trust Co.'s Assn. Can. 1971-72; Trustee, Prudential Income Fund of Canada; Dir. Boys Clubs of Can.; mem. Extve. Comte., Candn. Corps of Commissionaires (E.Can.); Past Pres. Rotary Club, Montreal; mem., 1st President & Chrmn., Combined Health Appeal Gr. Montreal; Anglican; recreations: curling, golf; Clubs: Toronto Golf; Toronto; Royal Candn. Mil. Inst., Nat; Granite; R.A.J. (London), St. James's (Montreal); Royal Montreal Golf; Mount Royal (Montreal); Royal and Ancient Golf (St. Andrew's Scotland); Home: 366 Russell Hill Rd., Toronto, Ont. M4V 2V2; Office: 302 Bay St., Toronto, Ont. M5H 2P4

KERSHAW, Derrick Frederick, CBE (1976), F.C.C.A.; b. Edmonton, Eng., 19 May 1917; s. Frederick Deeks and May Unsworth (Fryers) K.; e. Elem. Sch. and Latymer Grammar Sch. Edmonton, Eng.; m. Olga Patricia d. late George Swan 1939; children: Michael Patrick, Susan Elizabeth Finley, Philip John; PRESIDENT, WOLF POWER TOOLS LTD. since 1960; joined Basil Hallett & Co. (Chart. Accts.) London, Eng. 1933-39; Murphy Radio 1939-41; Asst. Secy. and Sales Mgr. B. Elliott and Co. Ltd. London 1946-54, Dir. and Gen. Mgr. B. Elliott (Canada) Ltd. Ont. 1954-60; served with RNVR 1941-46, rank Lt.; Fellow Cert. & Corporate Accts. (UK); Freemason (UK); Anglican; recreations: swimming, theatre; Club: Toronto Bd. of Trade; Home: Suite 1808, 1300 Bloor St., Mississauga, Ont. L4Y 3Z2; Office: 93 Advance Rd., Toronto, Ont. M8Z 2T1

KERWIN, Claire, R.C.A.; artist; b. Chatelet, Belgium; d. Emile and Elisabeth (Fremersdorf) Roland; e. Belgium; came to Can. 1947; m. 1 Feb. 1947; children: Michael, Shawn; rec'd Medal of Merit City of Toronto; mem. Ont. Soc. Artists; Print & Drawing Council Can.; Royal Canadian Academy; recreations: tennis, squash, farming; Club: Toronto Lawn Tennis; Address: 20 Monteith St., Toronto, Ont. M4Y 1K7.

KERWIN, Larkin, C.C., M.Sc., D.Sc., LL.D., F.R.S.C., D.C.L., F.R.S.A., K.G.C.H.S.; physicist; b. Quebec, Que., 22 June 1924; s. Timothy John and Catherine (Lonergan) K.; e. St. Patrick's High Sch., Quebec, 1941; St. Francis Xavier Univ., B.Sc. 1944; Univ. of Toronto, 1944-45; Mass. Inst. of Technol., 1946-47; Univ. Laval, D.Sc. 1949; LL.D., St. Francis Xavier 1970; D.Sc. B.C. 1973, Toronto 1973, McGill 1974; LL.D., Concordia 1976; D.Sc., Memorial 1978; D.C.L., Bishop's 1978; D.Sc., Univ. Ottawa, 1981; m. Maria Guadalupe, d. André Turcot, Sillery, Que., 10 June 1950; children: Lupita, Alan, Larkin, Terence, Rosa-Maria, Gregory, Timothy, Guillermina; PRESIDENT, NATIONAL RESEARCH COUNCIL OF CANADA 1980, rector, univ. laval, 1972-77, and Prof. of Physics; joined present University as Assistant Professor 1946; Chairman, Physics Dept., 1961-69; Vice Dean, Faculty of Science, 1968-69; mem. various scholarship and grants committees of Prov. of Que.; Nat. Research Council and Defence Research Bd., Secy. — Gen. Internat. Union Pure and Applied Physics; Pres. du Conseil, Univ. Laval; Vice Pres., Que. Br., U.N. Assn. Can., 1958-59; Vice-Pres., Natural Sciences & Eng. Research Council, Canada, 1978-80; Pres. Assn. Univs. and Colls. of Can. 1974; Vice-Pres. Royal Soc. of Can. 1974, Pres. 1976; Pres. Acad. of Sc., Royal Soc. of Can. 1973; awarded Prix David 1951; Médaille Pariseau 1964; Centenary Medal 1967; Medal of Canadian Association Physicists 1969; M.s.; Order of Holy Sepulchre, 1969; Queen's Jubilee Medal 1977; Officer, Order of Canada, 1978, Companion, 1981; Medal "Gloire del'Escolle" of the Anciens de Laval, 1978; contrib. to prof. new devices for focusing ion and electron beams, the discovery of phosphorous — 8 molecule, of various excited states of atmospheric gases; author: "Atomic Physics — an Introduction", 1963; "Introduction à la physique atomique", 1964; "Introduction a la Fisica Atomica", 1968; other writings incl. chapters for prof. books and over 50 scient. papers on atomic physics; mem., Grand Magisterium Equestrian Order of Holy Sepulchre; Assn. Canadienne Française pour l'Avance. des Sciences; Candn. Assn. Phys. (Pres. 1955); Am. Phys. Soc.; Mexican Phys. Soc.; Royal Astron. Soc. Can.; Order des engénieurs du Québec; R. Catholic; recreations: skiing, sailing, canoeing, history; Home: 2166 Bourbonnière Park, Sillery, Quebec, Que. G1T 1B4

KEY, Archibald Frederic, C.M., F.R.S.A.; fine art; museum consultant; author; b. Huddersfield, Eng. 19 Jan. 1894; s. Frederic Charles and Edith Ann (Proctor) K.; e. taught privately; Hon. Dr. Univ. of Calgary 1968; m. Marjorie Elaine d. late Henry Sidenius 24 Dec. 1952; one child, Chapin, M.D.; came to Can. 1922; Ed., Timmins

Weekly and Mining Corr., Toronto Globe & Mail and other dailies 1925; Ed., The Drumheller (Alta.) Mail 1926-34; mem. Ad Hoc comte. which founded summer sch. of drama (later Banff Sch. of Fine Arts) 1931-32; Publisher and Ed., The Plaindealer 1935-40; served in Candn. Armed Forces as Instr., later posted to Educ. Div. 1940-46; Founding mem. and 1st Dir., The Calgary Allied Arts Centre 1946-64; Hon. Adm., The W. Can. Art Circuit 1947-60; one hour classical record program radio stn. CKXL "The Lively Arts" 1953-59; 3rd W. Vice Pres. Candn. Arts Council 1949-66; wrote brochure on organ. and adm. of cultural centres, comnd. by Can. Council 1957-58; Hon. Assessor of Visual Arts Applications for Can. Council Scholarship & Fellowship Grants 1958-67; served as mem. 1st museums' training program sponsored by Candn. Museums Assn.; worked actively in organ. and adm. travelling performing arts co's sponsored by Can. Council and helped organ. w. tours for internat. co's under Can.'s cultural relations exchange programs with Europe and China 1961-67; apptd. 1st Dir., Candn. Museums Assn. 1965-68; mem. and Vice Chrmn., Calgary Allied Arts Foundation since 1971; recalled by Candn. Museums Assn. as Interim Dir. 1974; Dir. of Information and Research Centre, Calgary and also served as Consultant, Nat. Museums Corp. 1975-76; part-time Consultant, Shell Resources (Western) 1976-78; Hon. Tech. Consultant, Calgary Lib. Bd. 1977-78; rec'd Can. Council grant 1977; rec'd Candn. Council Citation 1967; Candn. Centennial Medal 1967; Queen's Silver Jubilee Medal 1978; Alta. Achievement Award 1978; Royal Candn. Acad. Arts Gold Medal 1977; author "Mother Lode" (play); "Canada's Museum Explosion" 1967; "Museum Guide Lines" 1968; "Beyond Four Walls" (hist. of museums) 1972; compiled and ed. "Canadian Museums and Related Institutions" 1968; various articles, prose and poetry in journs. and mags.; awaiting publ.: co-author "Alberta's Bloodless Revolution—The Aberhart Years"; "Strawberry Bee"; "Once-Over Lightly" (memoirs); Fellow, Candn. Museums Assn.; mem. Candn. Conf. Arts; recreations: visual arts, theatre, music; Address: Apt. 605, 104 Twenty-sixth Ave. S.W., Calgary, Alta. T2S 0L9.

KEYES, Gordon Lincoln, B.A., M.A., Ph.D.; university professor; b. Kearney, Ont. 5 March 1920; s. Rev. Arthur Beverly and Edna Grace (File) K.; e. Perth Coll. Inst. 1937; Vic. Coll. Univ. of Toronto B.A. 1941; Univ. of Toronto, M.A. 1942; Princeton Univ. Ph.D. 1944; m. Mary d. Wm. Stanley Ferguson 9 June 1945; children: Katherine Mary (Ewing), John Thomas David; PROF. OF CLASSICS, VICTORIA UNIVERSITY; Lectr. (part-time) Greek, McMaster Univ., 1941-42; Asst. Prof. Latin and Greek, Birmingham Southern Coll, Birmingham, Ala., 1945-47; came to Victoria Coll. as Lectr. 1947-49; Asst. Prof. 1949-57; Assoc. Prof. 1957-63; Can. Council Research Fellow, 1959-60; Prof. 1963-68; Nelles Prof. of Ancient Hist., 1968; Chrmn. combined Depts. of Classics, Univ. of Toronto, 1967-69; Visiting Prof. U. of Victoria, B.C., 1969; Chrmn. Vic. Coll. Council, 1970; Chrmn. Dept. of Classics, Vic. Coll., 1971-74; Principal, Vic. Coll. 1976-81; author of "Christian Faith and the Interpretation of History". A Study of St. Augustine's Philosophy of History", 1966, other writings incl. philosophy of hist., religious experience in the Roman Empire; mem., Am. Philological Assn.; Society for the Promotion of Roman Studies; Classical Assn. of Can.; Medieval Academy of Am.; Anglican; recreations: reading, music, travel; Home: 122 Orchard Dr., Thornbury, Ont. N0H 2P0; Office: Victoria University, 73 Queen's Park Cresc. E., Toronto, Ont. M5S 1K7.

KEYFITZ, Nathan, Ph.D., LL.D., F.R.S.C.; professor; b. Westmount, P.Q., 29 June 1913; s. Arthur and Anna (Gerstein) K.; e. McGill University, B.Sc. 1934; University of Chicago, Ph.D. 1952; Univ. of N. Carolina, 1946; m. Beatrice, d. Henry Orkin, Oct. 1939; children: Barbara, Robert; CHRMN., DEPT. OF SOCIOLOGY, HARVARD

UNIV., 1978-1980; Prof. since 1972; engaged in Census, Soc. Analysis, External Trade Department, 1936-46; Math Advisor, Central Research and Development Staff, Dominion Bureau of Statistics, 1946-50; Senior Research Stat., Dom. Bureau of Statistics, 1950-59; Dir., Colombo Plan Bureau. 1956-7; Gold medal, Professional Inst. of the Civil Service of Canada, 1957; Teach., Asst. missions Burma, 1951; Indonesia, 1952-3; Argentina, 1960; Chile, 1963; Vienna, 1981; Beijing, 1981; others, Prof., Dept. Pol. Econ., Univ. of Toronto, 1959-63; Univ. of Montreal, 1962-3; Prof., Dept. of Sociol., Univ. of Chicago, 1963-68 Chmn., 1965-7; Prof. of Demography, Univ. of Cal., Berkeley 1968-72; Lectr. in Demography, Univ. of Moscow 1978; apptd. Acad. Adv., Royal Comn. on Biling. & Bicult., Feb. 1964; mem., Bd. of Dirs., Social Science Research Council, 1959-64; Ll.D., Univ. of Western Ont., 1972; Publications: "World Population: An Analysis of Vital Data", 1968; "An Introduction to the Mathematics of Population", 1968; "Applied Mathematical Demography" 1977; "Population Change and Social Policy", 1982; papers in scient. journs.; Fellow, Am. Stat. Assn.; el. to Royal Society of Canada, 1959; Nat. Acad. of Sciences (U.S.) 1977; mem., Internat. Stat. Inst.; Population Assn. of Am. (Pres. 1970-71); Candn. Pol. Science Assn. (Vice-Pres. 1962); Address: 1580 Massachusetts Ave., Apt. 7C, Cambridge, Mass. 02138

KEYS, John David, M.Sc., Ph.D.; Canadian public servant; b. Toronto, Ont., 30 Sept. 1922; s. David Arnold and May Irene (Freeze) K.; e. Montreal West (Que.) and Lower Can. Coll. Montreal, 1939; McGill Univ., B.Sc. 1947, M.Sc. 1948, Ph.D. (Nuclear Physics) 1951; m. Ruth Olivet, d. George Henry Harris, 23 Oct. 1945; children: Susan Irene, David George; CONSULTANT since 1976; Prof. of Physics and subsequently Head of Dept., Candn. Services Coll., Royal Roads, 1951-58; joined Dept. of Mines and Tech. Surveys, Mines Br., Mineral Sciences Div. as Research Scientist, 1958; apptd. Head, Mineral Physics Sec., 1963; Chief, Hydrologic Sciences Div., Inland Waters Br., Dept. of Energy, Mines and Resources, 1967-70; Science Adv., Treasury Bd. Secretariat 1970-71; Asst. Vice Pres. (Labs.) Nat. Research Council 1971-76; Assistant Deputy Min. (Science & technol.) Dept. of Energy, Mines & Resources 1976-81; served with RCNVR attached to RN (Combined Operations), 1941-45; mostly Mediterranean Theatre 1942-44; rank Lt.(n) on discharge; spent 5 months at Semiconductor Inst., Leningrad and research estabs. in Moscow, Baku and Tashkent under auspices of Nat. Research Council — Soviet Acad. of Sciences Exchange Program, 1963; mem., Am. Assn. Advanc. Science; Am. Phys. Soc.; Candn. Assn. Physicists; Royal Astron. Soc.; Sigma Xi; Psi Upsilon (Pres., McGill Chapter, 1945); Protestant; recreations: skiing, squash, tennis; Home: 22 Oaklands Ave., Toronto, Ont. M4V 2E5;

KEYSER, J. James, B.A.; management consultant; b. Toronto, Ont., 1 Sept. 1936; s. James M. and Laura K.; e. Univ. of Toronto B.A. 1960, post-grad. work 1961; m. Mary H., d. Dr. W. D. Harding, 1 July 1962; children: Murray, Ellen, Nancy; PARTNER IN CURRIE, COOPERS AND LYBRAND; Personnel Mgr. Traders Group Ltd. 1966, Dir. of Personnel 1971, Vice Pres. — Personnel and Organ. 1973; Personnel Supvr. Bank of Nova Scotia 1969; Vice Pres. Personnel Assn. Toronto; mem. Ont. Soc. Training & Devel. (Bd.); Phi Kappa Sigma (Vice Pres.); Club: RCYC; Home: 66 Silverbirch Ave., Toronto, Ont. M4E 3K9; Office: 145 King St. W., Toronto, Ont. M5H 1J8

KEYSER, Walter Alan, B.A.; commercial property investment; b. London, Ont. 1 Aug. 1936; s. Walter Davidson and Edna May (Skinner) K.; e. Univ. of W. Ont., B.A. (Hons. Business Adm.) 1958; PRES., W.A. KEYSER & ASSOC. LTD. and W.A. Keyser Investment Co. of Canada Ltd., an NHA approed lender and mortgage correspondent for pension funds and financial institutions;

with Bank of Canada, special assignment, Can. Conversion Loan 1958; joined Gairdner & Co. Ltd., Toronto, Invest. Dealers to estab. Money Market Dept. 1959; el. a Dir. 1965; retired from Co. as Sr. Vice-Pres. March 1973; to assist in forming Heitman Canadian Realty Investors, a public real estate investment trust; served in RCASC rank Lt.; Dir., AGF Management Ltd., Tor.; mem. Internat. Council of Shopping Centres; Beta Theta Pi; P. Conservative (Past Pres. UWO Young P. Cons. Assn.); Un. Church; recreations: golf, skiing; Home: R.R. 1, Terra Cotta, Ont. Office: Box 82, Toronto-Dominion Centre, Toronto, Ont.

KEYSERLINGK, Robert Wendelin Henry, B.A., LL.D., K.M.; journalist; publisher; b. St. Petersburg, Russia, 29 Nov. 1905; s. Count Henry Jeannot and Baroness (Haaren) K.; e. St. Joseph's Coll., Yokohama, Japan; Canadian Acad., Kobe, Japan; Shanghai Pub. Sch.; Univ. of Brit. Columbia, B.A. (Hons. Econ) 1929; Univ. of Zurich and Berlin, post-grad. studies; Univ. of Ottawa, LL.D. 1954; m. Sigrid, Baroness von der Recke, 1 Dec. 1931; children: Robert, Edward, Cecile, Alexander, Henry, John; PRES. AND MANG. DIR. PALM PUBLISHERS (CAN.)LTD.; joined Un. Pres. 1930 and assigned to Berlin Bureau; Mgr. for Switzerland with hdqrs. at Zurich, 1932; Mgr. for N.W. Europe of Continental Dept., with hdqrs. in Berlin, 1934; Gen. Mgr. for Europe, London, 1935; Gen. Mgr. of B.U.P., with hdqrs. in Montreal, 1938-48; Man. Dir., British United Press, 1942-62; Publisher, "The Ensign", 1948-57; Publications: "Unfinished History", 1947; "Fathers of Europe" 1972; "The Dragon's Wrath" 1981; Ed., "The Iron Curtain" by Igor Couzenko; has world pub. rights on Prof. M. Klotchko's book on China; mem. of Chapter General Sovereign, Order of Malta (1st Candn.) July 1967; Pres. of Extve. Council of the Candn. Assn. of the Order, of Malta 1973; Roman Catholic; recreations: farming; riding; Clubs: University (Montreal); Royal Automobile (London); Home: Apt. 501 Le Carrefour, 450 Racine Ave., Dorval, Que. Office: 1949 — P.O. Box 2267 Dorval, P.Q.

KIDD, George Pirkis, M.A.; retired diplomat; b. Glasgow, Scotland, 6 June 1917; s. George Watson and Mary Hood (McIntyre) K.; came to Canada, 1922; e. St. Michaels Sch. (1928-32) and Brentwood Coll., Victoria, B.C. (1932-36); Univ. of British Columbia, B.A. 1939; Univ. of Illinois, (Fellowship) M.A. 1941; m. Lola M., d. R. H. Calverley, Loveland, Colo., 1949; joined Dept. of External Affairs, 1946; Candn. Legation, Warsaw, 1947-49; Candn. Embassy, Paris, 1949-51; student at Nat. Defence Coll., 1951-52; with the Dept. at Ottawa, 1952-54; Charge d'Affaires, Candn. Embassy, Tel Aviv, 1954-57; returned to the Dept. at Ottawa, 1957-59; mem. of Directing Staff, Nat. Defence Coll., 1959-61; Ambassador to Cuba & Haiti, 1961-64; Minister Candn. Embassy, Washington, 1964-67; Vice-Pres., Canadian Inter. Development Agency, 1967-71; Asst. Secretary — General, Commonwealth Secretariat, London, 1971-74; High Commr. Nigeria and concurrently Sierra Leone, 1974-77; served in 2nd World War with Candn. Army, 1941-46; served overseas with Queens Own Cameron Highlanders of Can. in U.K. and France; wounded in action; Pres., Vancouver Island Branch, Royal Commonwealth Soc.; mem., Bd. of Gov., Univ. of Victoria; mem., Bd. of Trustees, Art Gallery of Greater Victoria; Anglican; Address: 3150 Ripon Rd., Victoria, B.C. V8R 6G5

KIDD, James Robbins, M.A., Ed.D., LL.D.; educationalist; b. Wapella, Sask., 4 May 1915; s. John and Muriel (Robbins) K.; e. Sir George Williams Univ., B.A. 1938; McGill Univ., M.A. 1943; Columbia Univ., Ed.D. 1947; Univ. of B.C., LL.D. 1961; Concordia Univ., 1970; Trent Univ., LL.D., 1975; McGill Univ., LL.D., 199; Laurentian Univ., LL.D., 1980; York Univ., LL.D., 1981; m. Margaret Edith, d. late George Frederick Easto, 18 Aug. 1941; children: Bruce, Ross, Alice, David, Dorothy; PROF. COMPARATIVE STUDIES DEPT. ADULT EDUC., ONT.

INST. FOR STUDIES IN EDUC. since 1971; Y.M.C.A. Secy., Montreal, P.Q., 1935-43, Ottawa, 1943-45; Veteran's Counselor, N.Y. 1945-47; Assoc. Dir., Candn. Assn. for Adult Educ. 1947-50, Dir. 1960-61; Secy. Treas., Social Science Council of Can. and Secy. Treas. Humanities Research Council of Can. 1961-66; Chrmn., Dept. Adult Educ. of present Inst. 1966; Publications; "Look, Listen and Learn", 1947; "Film Utilization", 1952; "Adult Education in the Canadian University", 1956; "Adult Education in the Caribbean", 1958; "How Adults Learn", 1959; "18 — 80", 1960; "Continuing Education in Alaska", 1962; "Financing Continuing Education", 1962; "A Tale of Three Cities: Elsinore — Montreal — Tokyo" 1974; "Whilst Time is Burning" 1974; "Comparative Studies in Adult Education: An Anthology", 1976; "Coming of Age", Ed., 1978; "Adult Learning: A Design for Development", Ed., 1978; also articles and pamphlets on group work, camping, recreations, education, etc.; Pres., World Conference on Adult Education, 1960; Chairman, Internat. Comte. for Advancement of Adult Educ., 1961; Secy. Gen., Internat. Council for Adult Educ.; Protestant; Office: 252 Bloor St. W., Toronto, Ont. M5S 1V6

KIDD, Kenneth E., M.A.; university professor; b. Barrie, Ont. 21 July 1906; s. D. Ferguson and Florence May (Jebb) K.; e. Univ. of Toronto (Victoria Coll.) B.A. 1931, M.A. 1937; Univ. of Chicago, 1939-40; m. Martha Ann, d. late O. V. Maurer, Oct. 1943; PROF. OF ANTHROPOL., TRENT UNIV., since 1968; Prof. Emeritus, 1973 (Chrmn. of Dept. 1967-70; 1st Chrmn., Indian — Eskimo Studies 1969-70); joined staff of Royal Ont. Museum, 1935; Asst., Dept. of Ethnol., 1942, Jt. Curator, 1956, at present is Honorary Curator (Ethnology); in charge of numerous archaeol. excavations; as Ste. Marie I (site of Jesuit mission of 1639-49), Huron Indian ossuary, Ossassané, 1947-48; Publications: "The Excavation of Ste. Marie I", 1949; "Canadians of Long Ago", 1951; "Indian Rock Paintings of the Great Lakes" (with S. Dewdney), 1961; "A classification for glass beads for the use of field archaeologists" (with M.A. Kidd) 1977; "Glass bead-making from the middle ages to the early 19th century" 1979; awarded Guggenheim Mem. Fellowship, 1951-52; awarded the Cornplanter Medal, 1970; Fellow, Am. Anthropol. Assn.; Royal Anthrop. Inst. of Gt. Britain & Ireland; mem., Soc. Am. Archaeol. (Past Vice-Pres.); Am. Indian Ethnohist. Conf. (Extve. Comte.); Internat. Cong. of Americanists; Am. Ethol. Soc.; Am. Soc. for Ethnohist.; Soc. for Hist. Arch.; British Museum Soc.; Candn. Rock Art Research Assocs.; Candn. Sociol. & Anthrop. Soc.; Indian — Eskimo Assn. Can.; Ont. Archeol. Soc.; Ont. Hist. Soc.; Candn. Archaeological Assn.; Hon. Life mem. R.O.M. since 1964; mem. Scient. Adv. Comte. of Quetico Foundation; elected mem. of Explorers' Club of N.Y., 1979; Protestant; recreation: travel; Office: Trent University, Peterborough, Ont.

KIDD, Paul James Garland, Q.C., B.A.; b. Kingston, Ont., 25 June 1913; s. late the Rev. Charles Edward and the late Mary (Youngson) K.; e. Gananoque High Sch.; Queen's Univ., B.A. 1932; Osgoode Hall Law Sch., Toronto, Ont. (1936), Columbia Grad. Sch. of Business Extve. Program (1955); m. Elizabeth, d. late George T. Dixon, 23 May 1940; two d. Virginia, Ruth; Dir., Hiram Walker Resources Ltd. and DIR., HIRAM WALKER — GOODERHAM & WORTS LTD.; Liquid Carbonic Canada Ltd.; Trustee, Nature Conservancy of Canada; joined Hiram Walker & Sons Ltd. (Distillers. Estbd. 1858) Legal Dept. in 1936; read law with Coatsworth & Richardson, Toronto, Ont.; called to the Bar of Ont., 1936; cr. Q.C. 1954; Delta Chi; Presbyterian; Home: 7080 Riverside Dr., East Windsor, Ont. N8S 1C3; Office: Walkerville — Box 2518, Windsor, Ont. N8Y 4S5

KIDDER, Margot; actress; b. Yellowknife, N.W.T. 17 Oct. 1948; e. Univ. of B.C.; m. 1stly Tom McGuane (divorced); one d. Maggie; m. 2ndly John Heard (divorced); began career Candn. theatre and TV; film debut "Gaily,

Gaily" 1969; other films incl. "Quackser Fortune Has a Cousin in the Bronx" 1970; "Sisters" 1972; "Gravy Train" 1974; "The Great Waldo Pepper" 1975; "The Reincarnation of Peter Proud" 1975; "92 in the Shade" 1977; "Superman" 1978; "The Amityville Horror" 1979; starred TV series "Nichols" 1972; other TV appearances incl. "Switch", "Baretta", "Barnaby Jones", "Hawaii Five-O, Mod Squad"; TV movie "Honky Tonk" 1974; Address: c/. William Morris Agency, 1350 Ave. of Americas, New York, N.Y. 10019.

KIERAN, Sheila Harriet; writer; b. Toronto, Ont. 4 May 1930; d. Seymour Robert and Ida (Schulman) Ginzler; e. elem. and high schs. Toronto and New York City; Columbia Univ. Sch. of Extension; Univ. of Toronto Dept. of Extension; m. 24 Aug. 1951; divorced 1968; children: Susan Elizabeth, Michael Robert, Patricia Regis, Mark William John, Jon William Anthony, Frances Mary Therese, Andrew Robert Charles; Extve. Dir., Multiple Sclerosis Soc. of Can. 1980-81; joined Radio Stn. CKEY 1950-51; freelance mag. and newspaper writing 1955-64, 1966-68; Reporter, Toronto Globe and Mail 1964-66; staff writer, The Canadian Magazine 1968-71; Host and Producer The Consumer Show, City-TV Toronto 1972-73; Dir. of Pub. Participation, Royal Comn. on Violence in Communications Industry 1975-77; Extve. Dir., Book and Periodical Devel. Council 1977-79; Depy. Extve. Dir. MS 1979-80; Bd. mem. Humber Bay Child and Family Clinic; Founder, Foundation for Women in Crisis; Chrmn. Journalism Adv. Bd. Centennial Coll. 1979-80; author "The Non-Deductible Woman" 1970; contrib. "Encyclopedia Canadiana" 1974; numerous articles mags. and newspapers; Freedom of Choice Comte.; France-Can. Assn.; Assn. Candn. Radio & TV Artists; Hebrew; Club: 21 McGill; Home: 66 Badgerow Ave., Toronto, Ont. M4M 1V4; Home: 66 Badgerow Ave., Toronto, Ont. M4M 1V4

KIERANS, Hon. Eric William, P.C., B.A., LL.D. (Hon.); economist; executive; b. Montreal, P.Q., 2 February 1914; s. Hugh and Lena (Schmidt) K.; e. Loyola Coll., B.A. 1935; McGill Univ. (1947-51) Grad. Research in Econ.; St. Thomas Univ., LL.D. (Hon.), 1979; m. Teresa Catherine, d. late Edw. P. Whelan, 12 Nov. 1938; children: Thomas Edward, Catherine Anne; formerly Dir., Sch. of Comm., McGill Univ., and Prof. of Comm. and Finance there, 1953-60; Pres., Montreal and Canadian Stock Exchanges 1960-63; el. to Que. Leg. for Notre Dame de Grace, by-el. Sept. 1963; Minister of Revenue, Que., 1963-65; Min. of Health, Que., 1965-66; Pres., Que. Lib. Fed., 1966-68; a candidate for Fed. Liberal leadership 1968; el. to H. of C. June 1968; apptd. Postmaster General (also Min. responsible for Dept. of Communications); resigned from the Cabinet 29 April 1971; Prof. of Econ., McGill Univ. 1972; apptd. (first) Dir., Savings & Trust Corp. of B.C. 1975; Apptd Dir. of Sidbec-Dosco Ltée. 1978; Dir., Caisse de Dépot et Placement du Qué.; Chrm., Canadian Adhesives Ltd.; engaged by Manitoba Govt. as a Consultant on Resources Policy, April 1972; author: "Challenge of Confidence: Kierans on Canada", 1967; "Report on Natural Resources Policy in Manitoba"; Independent; Roman Catholic; recreation: sports; Clubs: M.A.A.A. (Past Pres.); Faculty (McGill); University (Montreal); Coral Beach and Tennis (Bermuda); Home: 5631 Queen Mary Rd., Hampstead, Que. H3X 1W8

KIERANS, P. Emmet, Q.C., B.A., B.C.L.; lawyer; b. Montreal, Que., 23 March 1915; s. late Thomas and Margaret (McAran) K.; e. St. Patrick's and D'Arcy McGee High Sch., Montreal; Univ. of Montreal; Sir George Williams Univ.; Queen's Univ., B.A. 1945; McGill Univ., B.C.L. 1948; m. Doris May, d. Joseph Daigle, Edmundston, N.B., 7 May 1949; children: Patrick, David, Mark, Elaine, Louise, Renée; SR. PARTNER, KIERANS & GUAY, since 1973; Dir. inter alia: Hilton Canada Inc.; Burlington Canada Inc.; read law with Dixon, Claxton, Senécal, Turnbull & Mitchell; called to Bar of Que. 1948; cr. Q.C. 1963; Partner, Dixon, Senécal, Turnbull, Mitch-

ell, Stairs, Culver & Kierans, 1956; Senécal, Kierans & Stairs, 1963; Kierans & Guay, 1964; Kierans, Kisilenko & Guay, 1967-73; Lectr. in Civil Law, McGill Univ., 1957-63; served as Civil Math. Instr., RCAF, St. Hubert during World War II; Vice-Pres., Que. Lib. Fed. 1956-58; Westmount Lib. Assn. 1967-69; N.D.G. Lib Assn. 1952-58; Vice Pres. and Hon. Legal Counsel of Boy Scouts of Canada, Qué. Prov. Council; Rental Commr. of Que., 1960-66; mem. Council of Montreal Bd. Trade, 1976-81; Secy. and Charter mem., Fed. Eng. Speaking Cath. Teachers Inc. 1939-41; Secy., Jr. Bar Assn. Montreal, 1951-53; Life mem., St. Patrick's Soc. Montreal; mem., Montreal, Que. and Candn. Bar Assns; Liberal; R. Catholic; recreations: Canadian history, art, antiques, fishing, Clubs: St. James's Club (Montreal); Garrison (Quebec); Weectigo Fish & Game; Home: 3548 Ave. de Vendome, Montreal Que. H4A 3M7; Office: Suite 440, Canada Cement Bldg. 606 Cathcart St., Montreal, Que. H3B 1K9

KIERANS, Thomas E., B.A., M.B.A.; stockbroker; e. McGill Univ. B.A. 1961; Univ. of Chicago M.B.A. 1963 (Dean's Honours List); PRESIDENT, McLEOD YOUNG WEIR LTD. 1980- Dir. Canadian Adhesives Ltd.; Vice Pres., Dir. and Princ., Nesbitt, Thomson & Co. Ltd. 1963-74; Sr. Vice Pres. and Dir., Pitfield Mackay Ross Ltd. 1974-80; Chrmn. Ont. Econ. Council; mem. Council Trustees, Inst. for Research on Pub. Policy; Adv. Comte. Ont.'s Econ. Future; recreations: literature, shooting, trekking; Clubs: Albany; Griffith Island; University (Montreal): Ontario; Granite; Cambridge; Home: 229 Dunvegan Rd., Toronto, Ont. M5P 2P3; Office: (P.O. Box 433) Toront0-Dominion Centre, Toronto, Ont. M5K 1M2.

KILBOURN, William Morley, A.M., Ph.D., F.R.S.C.; university professor; writer; b. Toronto, Ont., 18 Dec. 1926; s. Kenneth Morley and May Rae (Fawcett) K.; e. Upper Can. Coll., Toronto, Ont. (1937-44); Trinity Coll., Univ. of Toronto, B.A. 1948; Harvard Univ. A.M. 1949, Ph.D. 1957; Oxford Univ. (1949-51), B.A. 1952, M.A. 1956; m. Mary Elizabeth, d. late Rev. Philip Sawyer, Guelph, Ont., 10 Sept. 1949; children: Philippa, Hilary, Nicholas, Timothy, Michael; WRITER, AND PROF. OF HISTORY AND HUMANITIES, YORK UNIV. since 1962; (Chrmn. of Humanities Div., 1962-67); mem., Dept. of Hist., McMaster Univ., 1951-62; Teaching Fellow, Harvard Univ., 1953-55; Publications: "The Firebrand: William Lyon Mackenzie and the Rebellion in Upper Canada" 1956 (2nd ed. 1960; London, 1958), winner of Univ. of B.C. President's Medal for Biog., 1956; "The Elements Combined: A History of the Steel Company of Canada", 1960; "The Writing of Canadian History" in "The Literary History of Canada", 1965 (revised ed. 1976); "The Restless Church", 1966; "The Making of the Nation", 1966, rev. ed. 1973; "Religion in Canada", 1968; "Pipeline: TransCanada, and the Great Debate", 1970; "Canada: A Guide to the Peaceable Kingdom", 1970; "Inside City Hall: The Years of the Opposition", 1972 (co-auth. D. Crombie, K. Jaffary, J. Sewell); "The Toronto Book" (an anthology) 1976; "Toronto" (essays and photography) 1977; "C.D. Howe: A Biography" 1979 (co-author Robert Bothwell); "Canada in the 1880's's"m 1980; Winner of Corey Prize awarded jointly by the Canadian and the American Historical Associations; and articles and reviews in various books, newspapers, encycs., and journs.; mem., Canada Council and its executive committee and its representative on the executive of the Can. Nat. Comm. for UNESCO; Trustee, Toronto General Hosp.; Adv. Panel, Toronto Historical Bd.; CJRT-FM; Chmn., Toronto Arts Council; Dir., Niagara Institute; mem., Candn. Hist. Assn.; Isaacs Gallery Ensemble for performance of mixed media compositions; alderman, City of Toronto 1970-76; mem. Metrop. Council and City of Toronto Extve. Comte. 1973-76; mem., Trinity Square Devel. Comte., Holy Trinity Church; Liberal; Anglican; recreations: piano, art, tennis; Home: 67 Glen Rd., Toronto, Ont. M4W 2V5

KILBURN, Peter, B.A.; investment dealer; b. Lloydminster, Alta., 15 July 1908; s. late Hilda May (Mantle) and Nicholas Arthur K.; e. Pub. and High Schs., Edmonton, Alta.; Univ. of Alta., B.A. 1929; m. Helen Elizabeth, d. W. A. Morris of Montreal, P.Q., 24 Feb. 1936; HON. CHRMN. AND DIR., GREENSHIELDS INC., Investment Dealers; Chmn., Shieldings Ltd.; Ritz — Carlton Hotel Co. of Montreal Ltd.; Paccar of Canada Ltd.; Imasco Ltd.; Weyerhaeuser Canada Ltd.; Stanton Pipes Ltd.; Past Pres., Invest. Dealers' Assn. Can.; Montreal Symphony Orchestra; mem., Bd. of Management, Montreal Gen. Hosp.; Anglican; recreations: shooting, fishing, riding; Clubs: University; Mount Royal; Montreal Indoor Tennis; Mt. Bruno Golf; Home: 3555 Côte des Neiges Rd., Montreal, Que. H3H 1V2; Office: 4 Place Ville Marie, Montreal, Que. H3B 2E7

KILLAM, G. Douglas, B.A., Ph.D.; educator; b. New Westminster, B.C. 26 Aug. 1930; s. Harry and Margaret Marion (Currie) K.; e. Univ. of B.C. B.A. 1954; Univ. of London Ph.D. 1964; m. Helen Shelagh d. H.C. Anderson, Creston, B.C. 22 Aug. 1959; children: Christopher, Sarah; Prof. of Eng. Univ. of Guelph since 1977; taught in Sierra Leone 1963-65; Nigeria 1967-68, Tanzania 1970-72, Edmonton (Alta) York Univ. Toronto 1968-73, Acadia Univ. 1974-77 (Head Dept. Eng. 1974-76, Dean of Arts 1976-77); held Prof'ship and Chair of Lit. Dar Es Salaam, Tanzania; author "Africa in English Fiction" 1968; "Novels of Chinua Achebe" 1968 (republished as "The Writings of Chinua Achebe" 1977); "African Writers on African Writing" 1972; "An Introduction to the Writings of Ngugi" 1980; "Contexts of African Criticism"; also articles on Can. literature and new lits. in Eng.; "Critical Perspectives on Ngugi," Ed., "East and Central African Literatures in English," Ed., "World Literature Written in English," Co-editor, "Canadian Journal of African Studies"; Pres., The Assoc. of Commonwealth Literature and Language Studies (ACLALS) 1980-83; mem. Assn. Candn. Univ. Teachers Eng. (Extve.); Candn. Assn. African Studies (Past Pres.); Internat. Assn. of Univ. Professors of English; Protestant; recreations: gardening, dogs, aviculture; Home: 108 Glasgow St., Guelph, Ont. N1H 4W3

KING,A. Douglas, B.A., M.B.A.; banker; b. Toronto, Ont. 13 Feb. 1941; s. Francis G. King; e. Univ. of Toronto B.A. 1963, M.B.A. 1965; m. Patricia Anne MacLea 9 July 1965; three s. Andrew, Edward, Peter; VICE PRES. AND GEN. MGR. EUROPE, MIDDLE EAST, AFRICA DIV., LONDON, ENG., THE TORONTO-DOMINION BANK 1980- ; Dir. Midland & Internat. Banks Ltd.; Vice-Chrmn., Toronto Dominion Internat. Bank Ltd.; Agt., N.Y. Agency, The Toronto-Dominion Bank 1967, Mgr. Internat. Div. Toronto 1970, Asst. Gen. Mgr. Far E., Hong Kong 1972, Singapore 1974, Asst. Gen. Mgr. Can./USA Toronto 1976, Gen. Mgr. 1978, Vice-Pres & Gen. Mgr. 1979; Theta Delta Chi; United Church; recreations: skiing, tennis, golf; Club: Ontario; Office: 55 King St. W., Toronto, Ont. M5K 1A2.

KING, Allan, B.A.; film producer and director; b. Vancouver, B.C., 6 Feb. 1930; s. John Owen and Kathleen Mary (Keegan) Winton; e. Univ. of B.C. B.A. (Philos.) 1954; m. Phyllis April, d. Douglas M. Leiterman, Pickering, Ont. 10 May 1952; one d. Anna Augusta; 2ndly Patricia Watson 30 June 1970; one d. Maggie Amanita, one s. Robert Alexander; formed Allan King Associates Ltd. 1961 and later Allan King Associates England Ltd.; films incl. "Skidrow" (documentary), 1956 (won 3 awards in Can. and U.S.); "The Yukoners", 1956; "Pemberton Valley", 1957; "Rickshaw", 1960 (won awards at Leipzig and Vancouver Festivals, 1961); "Dreams", 1961; "Warrendale" (won 2 awards at 1967 Cannes Festival, top Candn. film of 1967, shared Brit. critics' Best Foreign Film award 1967, won 2 prizes in Austrialia and was named Best Documentary of 1968 by U.S. film critics); has directed and produced works ranging from TV com-mercials to documentary features; credits incl.: "Lynn Seymour" (ballerina), 1964; "Bjorn's Inferno", 1964 (shown by invitation at 9th Annual San Francisco Film Festival); "Running Away Backwards", 1964 (won awards at 1966 San Francisco and Sydney Film Festivals and was screened by invitation at Venice, Montreal, Vancouver and Mannheim Festivals); recent films (1974-78) incl.: TV dramas "A Bird in the House" (four Candn. Film Awards), "Baptising" (Best Drama Yorkton Festival), "Red Emma" and "Six War Years"; and feature films "Who Has Seen the Wind" (Grand Prix Paris Film Festival), "One Night Stand", "Silence of the North"; three; retrospectives of his work have been shown by Cinematheque Canadienne, Montreal; Commonwealth Film Festival, London; Mea Roma el. R.C.A. 1975; mem. Dirs. Guild Can.; Assn. Cinematograph & TV Techs. (U.K.); Candn. Assn. of Motion Picture Producers; Candn. Council Film Makers; recreations: music, reading; Address: 397 Carlton St., Toronto, Ont. M5A 2M3

KING, Charles; journalist; communications consultant; b. Vancouver, B.C., 27 Nov. 1926; s. late Eileen Edith (Arnoldi) and Harold George K.; e. Pub. and High Schs., Vancouver, B.C.; Univ. of Brit. Columbia; m. Pauline Ida, d. late J. J. Trueb, Campbell River, B.C., 1 June 1948; children: John C. P., Terry E.; PRES., CHARLES KING CONSULTING LTD., Ottawa; joined Circulation Dept., "Vancouver Sun", 1941; Reporter, "Vancouver Daily Province", 1944, and after several positions became Assistant News Editor, 1956; apptd. to Ottawa Bureau, Southam News Services, March 1957-62 and became Chief of Ottawa Bureau, July 1960; Dir., Candn. Parlty. Press Gallery, 1960-62; Broadcaster and Commentator, Stn. CFCF and CFCF-TV Montreal, 1958-62; apptd. Chief of London Bur., Southam News Services, 1962-67; Assoc. Editor, The Citizen, Ottawa, 1967-77; Vice Pres. and Editor, Ottawa TODAY 1977-78; formed own company 1978; contrib. to CBC as Commentator on gov't. affairs; free-lance commentator CBC and BBC, 1962 to present; has covered news assign. in Candn. Arctic, Japan, Africa, Britain and W. Europe, U.S. and Can. from coast — to — coast; served in 2nd World War with Candn. Army Active as Pte., 1945; Nat. Newspaper Award, 1961; Home and Office: 128 Lisgar Rd., Rockcliffe Pk., Ottawa, Ont. K1M 0E6

KING, Hon. David Thomas, M.L.A.; politician; b. Perth, Ont. 22 June 1946; s. Rev. Dr. Albert Edward and Ethel (Dickson) K.; e. Univ. of Victoria 1964-65; Univ. of Alta. 1965-67, 1969-70; m. Clare Elaine Ann d. late Oliver Piven 19 Oct. 1968; two s. Troy Oliver Albert, Jason Darren Tod; MIN. OF EDUC., ALTA. since 1979; el. to Leg. Assembly Alta. 1971, re-el. since; P. Conservative; United Church; Home: 11248—63rd St., Edmonton, Alta. T5W 4E6; Office: 319 Legislative Bldg., Edmonton, Alta. T5K 2B6.

KING, Donald N., B.Com.; lumber executive; b. Calgary, Alta. 13 June 1926; s. Norman Stanley and Hazel Lillian (MacFarlane) K.; e. Univ. of B.C., B.Com. 1948; m. Dianne Elizabeth, d. Thomas R. Fyfe, W. Vancouver, B.C., 15 May 1954; children: Thomas Norman, Tracey Elizabeth; PRESIDENT, EACOM TIMBER SALES LTD. since 1973; Dir. Terminal Sawmills Ltd.; joined H. R. MacMillan Export Co. after grad.; later joined East Asiatic Co. (Canada) Ltd.; co-estbd. co. 1960; merged with lumber interests of East Asiatic Co. (Canada) Ltd. to form present Co.; became Extve. Vice Pres.; Phi Gamma Delta; Protestant; recreation: horseback riding, Sailing; Clubs: Vancouver; Terminal City (Past Pres.); Shaughnessy Golf & Country; Royal Vancouver Yacht; Home: 1641 West 57th Ave., Vancouver, B.C. V6P 1T3; Office: 900-1111 Melville Street Vancouver, B.C. V6E 3V6

KING, Egerton Warren, B.Sc., P.Eng.; utilities executive; b. Calgary, Alta., 19 May 1919; e. Univ. of Alta., B.Sc. (Elect. Engn.); m. 1943; four s., one d.; PRESIDENT,

C.E.O. AND DIRECTOR, CANADIAN UTILITIES LTD. and subsidiary companies; Director, Echo Bay Mines Ltd.; Pacific Western Airlines; C-I-L Inc. Royal Trustco; Atco Ltd.; mem. Edmonton Adv. Bd., Royal Trust Co.; began career in elect. industry as Test Engr., Canadian General Electric Co. Ltd., Peterborough, Ont. 1942; Elect. Engr., East Kootenay Power Co. Ltd., Fernie, B.C. 1945; Mgr., McGregor Telephone & Power Construction Co. Ltd., Edmonton, Alta. 1955; joined present Co. as Transmission and Distribution Supt. 1956; Gen. Mgr., Yukon Electrical Co. Ltd. and Yukon Hydro Co. Ltd. 1958; Vice-Pres., Northland Utilities Ltd., Edmonton 1961; Gen. Mgr., Canadian Utilities Ltd. 1966; Pres., Northland Utilities Ltd. and Canadian Utilities Ltd. 1968; apptd. Pres. and Dir., present Co. on merger of mem. cos. in group 1969; became C.E.O. 1981; served in 2nd World War, Elect. Lt., R.C.N. 1943-45; Overseas service on landing craft and at Naval Service H.Q., Ottawa; Past Pres., Candn. Elect. Assn.; Past Chrmn., Candn. Gas Assn.; Assn. Prof. Engrs., Alta., B.C. and Yukon; Past Pres., Edmonton Chamber of Commerce; Northwest Electric, Light and Power Association; Alta. N.W. Chamber of Mines; Delta Upsilon; United Church; Clubs: Edmonton Flying; Ranchmen's (Calgary); The Edmonton; Edmonton Petroleum; Mayfair Golf and Country; Derrick Golf & Winter; Home: 46 Marlboro Rd., Edmonton, Alta. T6J 2V6; Office: 10040 — 104th St., Edmonton, Alta. T5J 0Z2

KING, Gerald Wilfrid, Ph.D., D.Sc., F.R.S.C., F.C.I.C., C.Chem., F.R.S.C. (U.K.); educator; b. West Hartlepool, Eng. 22 Jan. 1928; s. Wilfrid James and Doris Amelia (Jackson) K.; e. Highgate Sch. London 1943-45; Univ. Coll. London B.Sc. 1949, Ph.D. 1952; Univ. of London D.Sc. 1970; m. Gwyneth d. David Emrys Jones, Gwynedd, Wales 27 March 1954; children: Richard James, Juliette Mary, Jennifer Wyn, Gillian Clare; PROF. OF CHEM. McMASTER UNIV. since 1964; Scient. Offr. Atomic Weapons Research Estab. Aldermaston, Eng. 1952-54; Lectr. Univ. Coll. London 1954-57; Asst. Prof. McMaster Univ. 1957, Assoc. Prof. 1959-64; rec'd Sir William Ramsay Medal 1952; author "Spectroscopy and Molecular Structure" 1964; numerous papers and articles phys. chem. especially spectroscopy, molecular structure and laser applications; Chrmn. Phys. Chem. Div. Chem. Inst. Can. 1963-64, Vice Chrmn. 1962-63; Pres. McMaster Faculty Assn. 1973-74; Chrm., Chemistry Dept., McMaster Univ., 1979- ; mem. Optical Soc. Am.; Ed."Canadian Journal of Chemistry" 1974-79; mem. several ed. bds. prof. journs.; received Gerhard Hertzberg Award of the Spectroscopy Soc. of Can., 1981; Anglican; Home: 674 Northland Ave., Burlington, Ont. L7T 3J7; Office: Hamilton, Ont. L8S 4M1

KING, John Erlin, B.A.; retired oil company executive; b. Napinka, Manitoba, 10 Feb. 1911; s. Amos Warne and Rietta (Hawthorne) K.; e. Grammar and High Sch., Winnipeg, Man.; Univ. of Manitoba, B.A. 1933; m. Phyllis, d. William Stanley Evans, Winnipeg, Man., 20 March 1940; children: William Warne, Roberta Jean, Conlin Ann; Vice-Pres. and Dir., Regent Refining (Canada) Ltd., joined Texaco Ltd. (formerly McColl — Frontenac Oil Co. Ltd.) as Salesman, Winnipeg, Man., 1935; Sales Promotion Mgr., Calgary, Alta., 1941-45; District Mgr., Vancouver, B.C., 1945-47; Asst. Div. Mgr., Calgary, 1947-49; Mgr. of Adv. and Sales Promotion, Montreal, 1949-53; Div. Mgr., Calgary, 1953-56, Toronto, 1956-59; Gen. Sales Mgr., 1959-61; Vice-Pres. Sales, 1961-71; Vice-Pres Public Affairs, Ont. Texaco Can. Ltd. 1971-76; Pres., Candn. C. of C. 1973-74; currently Counsellor for C.A.S.E. (counselling assistance for small enterprises); United Church; recreations: golf, fishing; Home: 255 Ridge Road East, Grimsby, Ont. L3M 4E7

KING, Lyle Evans, Mrs., B.A., B.L.S., M.S.; professor; b. Briercrest, Sask.; d. Thomas Harris and Lydia Lucinda Ann (Gilbert) E.; e. Univ. of Sask., B.A. 1940; Univ. of Toronto, B.L.S. 1942; Columbia Univ., M.S. 1952; m. Dr.

Carlyle King, 1977; ASSOC. PROF. COLL. OF EDUC., UNIV. OF SASK.; taught in Sask. elem and high schs. for 8 yrs.; Librarian in Toronto, Ont. Public Libraries for three yrs.; for one year Lib. at Graham-Eckes Pte. Sch., Palm Beach, Fla.; Prov. Supv. of Sch. Libraries, Dept. of Educ., Sask., (apptd. 1946); former mem. of Council (4 yrs.), Am. Lib. Assn.; Bd. of Dirs., Am. Assn. of Sch. Lib. (2 yrs.); mem. Sask. Lib. Assn. (Past Pres.); Candn. Lib. Assn. (Pres. of Young People's Sec. for one yr.); Regina Lib. Assn.; Sask. Assn of Sch. Librarians; Assn. of State Supervisors of Sch. Libs., Secy. 1959-60; Pres. 1960-61; Pres. Candn. Sch. Libs. Assn.; Ass. Prof., Fac. of Ed., Univ. of Regina, 1964-76; Prof. Emeritus; N.D.P.; recreations: reading, opera, theatre, golf; Home: 1830 College Ave., #1201, Regina, Sask. S4P 1C2; Office: Regina, Sask.

KINGAN, Ted, N.D.D., A.T.D. (MANC.), R.C.A.; artist; educator; b. Lytham-St-Annes, Lancs., Eng. 12 Oct. 1927; s. James Edward and Elsie (Charnley) K.; e. Bluecoat Sch. for Boys Stamford, Eng. 1938; St. John's Sch. Lytham-St-Annes, Eng. 1941; Blackpool (Eng.) Sch. of Art Nat. Dipl. in Design 1952; Regional Coll. of Art Manchester, Eng. Art Teacher's Dipl. 1953; Victoria Univ. Manchester Art Teacher's Cert. 1953; m. Nelly d. late John Snow 11 July 1948; one s. Randolph Paul; CHMN., STUDIO ART PROGRAM and Lectr. in Painting, Capilano Coll. 1973- ; conducts painting and design workshops through Emily Carr Coll. of Art Outreach Program; art teacher secondary schs. Eng. and Can. 1953-73; solo exhn. Bau-Xi Gallery Vancouver 1970; group exhns. inc. Surrealist Group Show Swindon 1948; B.C. Soc. Artists and several juried annual shows Vancouver Art Gallery 1960-70; Galerie Allen Vancouver 1971-75; Alma Mater Gallery Univ. of B.C. 1975; Gallery Move Vancouver 1975-80; Internat. Surrealist Exhn. Camden Arts Centre London, Eng. 1978; Agnes Etherington Art Centre Queen's Univ., Can. House London and Centre Culturel Canadien Paris 1979; West Coast Surrealists, Group Exhib., Gallery Move, Vancouver, 1980; "Collaborations", Robson Sq. Media Centre, Vancouver, 1981; R.C.A. Group Exhib., Kenneth Heffel Gallery, Vancouver, 1981; rec'd Can. Council Project Grant 1978, Travel Grant 1978; rep. in B.C. Govt. Perm. Coll. and various private colls. Eng., Can. and USA; served with Royal Signals Eng. and Germany 1946-48; mem. Prison Arts Foundation (B.C.); recreations: magic (especially card manipulation), reading, underwater photography, travel; Club: Vancouver Magic Circle; Home: #202, 2020 Fullerton Ave., North Vancouver, B.C. V7P 3G3; Office: 2055 Purcell Way, North Vancouver, B.C. V7J 3H5.

KINGSMILL, Ardagh Sidney, Q.C.; b. Cambridge, Mass., 17 June 1927; e. Univ. of W. Ont., Business Adm. grad. 1950; Osgoode Hall Law Sch., 1954; m. Alva Marjorie Coles, 7 July 1956; two s., Andrew Winnett, David Ardagh; PARTNER, TILLEY, CARSON & FINDLAY; Dir., Ampex Canada Inc.; FBM Distillery Co. Ltd.; Magnetic Metals Ltd.; Suncor Inc.; Sunoco Inc.; Cummins Diesel of Can. Ltd.; The Tapecoat Co. of Canada, Ltd.; Velsicol Corp. of Canada Ltd.; A. W. Chesterton Co. Ltd.; called to Bar of Ont. 1954; cr. Q.C. 1968; mem., Candn. Bar Assn. (Past Chrmn. Ont. Taxation Subsec.); Candn. Tax Foundation; Internat. Fiscal Assoc.; Internat. Bar Assn.; Phi Delta Phi; Protestant; recreations: sailing, badminton, swimming; Clubs: Toronto; Granite; Home: 322 Lytton Blvd., Toronto, Ont. M5N 1R8; Office: 44 King St. W., Toronto, Ont. M5H 1E2

KINGSTON, Robert Arnold, Q.C., B.A.; b. Prescott, Ont., 17 Sept. 1915; s. Paul and Elizabeth Theresa (Coughlin) K.; e. Trinity Coll., Univ. of Toronto, B.A. 1936; Osgoode Hall, Toronto, Ont. (Gold Medallist); m. Jeanne Elizabeth, d. Percy McFarlane, Toronto, Ont., 8 Sept. 1944; children: Susan, Barbara, John, Judith; PARTNER, BLAKE, CASSELS & GRAYDON; Chmn. of Bd., Rockwell Internat. of Canada Ltd.; Dir., Associates Capital Corp.; Caterpillar of Canada Ltd.; Sotheby Parke Bernet (Can.) Inc.; Peoples Jewellers Ltd.; mem. of Senate, Univ. of Toronto, 1952-56; Chrmn. of Convocation, Trinity Coll., 1950-52; read law with Fennell, Porter & Davis, Toronto, Ont.; called to Bar of Ont., 1940; cr. Q.C. 1955; author, "Ontario Corporation Manual", 1949; "Canada Corporation Manual", 1950; mem. Candn. Bar Assn; Delta Chi; Freemason; Anglican; recreations: curling, golf; Clubs: Toronto; Granite; Ticker; Home: 500 Duplex Ave., Toronto, Ont. M4R 1V6; Office: (Box 25) Commerce Court W., Toronto, Ont. M5L 1A9

KINNEAR, David; executive; b. Co. Down, N. Ireland 25 Nov. 1909; s. Thomas A. and Annie (Dickson) K.; e. Downpatrick (N. Ireland) Pub. Sch.; Business Coll. Belfast; m. Millicent Elizabeth d. F. A. Wilson, Hamilton, Ont. 2 June 1937; two s. David Wilson, Wayne Dickson; VICE PRES. AND DIR A. E. LePAGE LTD. since 1976; Eaton's of Canada; Eaton-Bay Funds Group; T.R.I.S.A.; T. Eaton Acceptance Co.; Uniroyal Ltd.; Trustee Canadian Realty Investment Trust; Irish Corp. Management Ltd.; Energex Minerals Ltd.; joined T. Eaton Co. Ltd. Toronto 1928, held various mang. positions Hamilton 1932-48, Asst. Gen Mgr. B.C. 1948, Gen. Mgr. B.C. 1952, Dir. and Controller H.O. 1961, Vice Pres. Operations 1963, Chief Extve. Offr. 1965, Chrmn. 1969-73; Vice Chrmn. Bank of Montreal 1973-75; served with Argyle & Sutherland Highlanders Reserve 1941-45, rank Lt.; Chrmn., Candn. Geriatric Research Soc.; Past Pres. Vancouver Bd. Trade; Vancouver Downtown Business Assn.; P. Conservative; United Church; recreations: golf, racing, hockey; Clubs: Jockey Club of Canada; York; Rosedale Golf; Vancouver; Home: 561 Avenue Rd., Toronto, Ont. M4V 2J8; Office: (P.O. Box 100) Toronto-Dominion Centre, Toronto, Ont. M5K 1G8

KINNEY, Samuel Marks, Jr., J.D.; lawyer; b. Jenkintown, Pa. 10 July 1925; s. Samuel Marks and Margaret (Rennie) K.; e. Lawrenceville (N.J.) Sch. 1942; Allegheny Coll. Pa. 1942-43; Pa. State Univ. B.A. 1946; Rutgers Univ. Sch. of Law J.D. 1948; m. Nora Kathryn d. Ross Canton Clouser 21 Sept. 1946; children: Lee Kinney Anthony, Samuel Marks III, Brian S.; PARTNER, HANNOCH, WEISMAN, STERN, BESSER, BERKOWITZ & KINNEY; Dir. and mem. Extve. Comte., First National State Bank (Newark)1973- ; Dir., First National State Bancorp, 1973- ; Canada Cement Lafarge Ltd. 1979- ; Citadel Cement Corp. (Ga.) 1979- ; mem. Conseil Consultatif Internat. Lafarge, Paris 1979- ; called to U.S. Bar 1949; Assoc. of law firm Martin & Reiley, Newark 1949-51; held various positions Daystrom Inc., Murray Hill N.J. 1951-62 becoming Vice Pres. and Gen. Counsel; various positions Union Camp Corp. incl. Pres. and Vice Chrmn., 1962-79; Dir. and mem. Extve. Comte. 1972-79; served in various civic and pol. (Repub.) positions; Trustee, Overlook Hosp. 1976- ; Overseer, Rutgers Univ. Foundation 1977- ; served with U.S. Marine Corps 1943-45; rec'd Distinguished Alumnus Award Pa. State Univ. 1977; author various articles and papers corporate devel., mergers and acquisitions; mem. U.S. Supreme Court Bar; N.J. Bar Assn.; Am. Bar Assn.; Phi Delta Theta (Warden); Episcopalian; recreations: golf, bridge, sailing; Clubs: Union League (N.Y.); Economic (N.Y.); Baltusrol Golf (Springfield, N.J.); Echo Lake Country (Westfield, N.J.); Essex (Newark, N.J.); Home: 109 Golf Edge, Westfield, N.J. 07090; Office: 744 Broad St., Newark, N.J. 07102.

KINSLEY, Kenneth Charles, , B.A., C.A.; executive; b. Simpson, Sask., 25 Feb. 1932; s. Justin Henry and late Gladys Maude (David) K.; e. Bedford Rd. Coll. 1950; Colo. Coll. B.A. (Business Adm.) 1954; m. Barbara Jean d. Joseph Henigsman, Pueblo, Colo., 28 Nov. 1954; two s. David Ross, Jon Todd; VICE-PRES., ADMINISTRATION FEDERAL INDUSTRIES INC. since 1980; Acct. Edmonton Br. Dominion Bridge Co. Ltd. 1959, Controller Alta. Br. (Calgary) 1963-64; Controller Constr. Div. B.A.C.M. Ltd. 1965, Treas. 1967, Vice-Pres.-Finance

1971, Extve. Vice-Pres. Constr. Operations 1974-76; Pres. and C.E.O. Genstar Construction Ltd. 1976-80; C.A. Alta. 1958, Man. 1967; United Church; recreations: golf, swimming, skiing; Clubs: Niakwa Golf & Country; Winnipeg Winter; Home: 1176 Kildonan Dr., Winnipeg, Man. R2G 1J4; Office: 2400 One Lombard Place, Winnipeg, Man. R3B 0X3

KIPP, Robert Angus; company president; b. Moose Jaw, Sask., 24 Aug. 1912; s. Theodore and Jessie McKay (Ross) K.; e. Public Schs. and Kelvin High Sch., Winnipeg, Man.; St. John's Coll., Winnipeg, Man.; Univ. of Alberta (1930-32); m. Donalda Catherine, d. Oscar Johnston, Winnipeg, Man., 25 Oct. 1939; children: Catherine Theodora, Deborah Margareta, Roberta Donalda; PRESIDENT AND MANG. DIR., KIPP — KELLY LTD. (Manufacturing & Sales Engrs.) since 1941; Pres. and Mang. Dir., Kipp — Kelly (London) Ltd., London, Eng.; joined the Co. in Nov. 1932 as a Shop Apprentice; apptd. Export Mgr., 1936; moved to England in 1937 and became Mang. Dir. of Separation Engineering Ltd. (which subsequently became Kipp — Kelly (London) Ltd.); returned to Winnipeg in Aug. 1939; went to Egypt in 1940 to install a large mining plant; Plant Supt. and subsequently Indust. Relations Mgr. De Haviland Aircraft, Toronto, Ont. 1943-45; Pres., Royal Winnipeg Ballet, 1954-56; Unitarian; recreation: golf; Clubs: Manitoba; St. Charles Country; Home: 8 Fulham Crescent, Winnipeg, Man. R3N 0G2; Office: 68 Higgins, Winnipeg, Man. R3B 0A5

KIPPEN, Walter Bruce, B.Com.; oil executive; b. Montreal, Que., 30 Jan. 1926; s. Col. Eric Douglas Bruce, O.B.E., and Marguerite Beresford (Stetham) K.; e. Lower Canada College, Westmount High Sch., Montreal, Que.; McGill Univ., B.Com. 1949; m. Claire Elfride Audley, 1 May 1958; children: Alexander Bruce, Ciulia Francesca, Winston David Bruce; PRES., PETROKIPP CAPITAL CORP. INC.; Chrm. and Pres., First Calgary Petroleums Ltd., since 1975; Sr. Vice Pres. and Dir., Bongard, Leslie & Co. Ltd. 1974-75; CHRM. AND C.E.O., KIPPEN & CO. INC., INVESTMENT DEALERS, 1964-74; Dir., Kippen & Co. Inc., 1958-64; mem., Montreal, Toronto Can. and Midwest (Chicago) Stock Exchanges and Investment Dealers Assoc. of Canada; Gov., Can. Stock Exchange, 1962-63; Montreal Y.M.C.A. 1965-69; Vice-Pres., Canada Comm. 1965-72 (now called Council for Canadian Unity); moved to Calgary, Alta. in 1967 and engaged as Pres. of Westcan Corp. Inc. and Jiffy Auto Ltd. and oil exploration & petroleum management till 1956; Dir., Jetoils Ltd., Pathfinder Petroleums Ltd., Canadian Diamond Coring Ltd.; formed and acquired control of several oil companies resulting in consol. into Medaillon Petroleums Ltd. (later absorbed into Norcen Energy Resources Ltd.); served in 2nd World War with R.C.A.F.; discharged as Pilot Offr.; Gov., Council for Canadian Unity, 1972- ; mem., Am. Metal Mining Assn.; Independent Petroleum Assn. of Can. (I.P.A.C.); co-author and sponsor of "Option Canada", published in 1966, an analysis of the Economic Consequences of Separatism; received Queen's Jubilee Medal from Gov. Gen. for efforts re developing Council for Cdn. Unity; Alpha Delta Phi; Anglican; recreations: shooting, skiing, golf, tennis; Clubs: St. James's; M.A.A.A.; Hillside Tennis; Calgary Petroleum; The Leash (N.Y.); Home: 478 Mount Pleasant Ave., Westmount, Montreal, Que. H3Y 3H3; Office 5th Floor, 444 5th Ave. S.W., Calgary, Alta

KIPPING, Hon. Eric John, M.L.A., B.A., B.Ed.; politician; b. Glace Bay, N.S. 16 March 1925; s. John Henry and Alfreda (King) K.; e. Glace Bay High Sch.; Acadia Univ. B.A., B.Ed.; m. Isabel Christina d. William W. Nicholson, Baddeck, N.S. 1 Sept. 1951; children: Patricia Linda, John Eric, Christopher William, Carl Erwin, Jonathan Edmund; MIN. OF THE ENVIRONMENT, N.B. and Min. Responsible for Housing Policy 1978- ; mgr. N.B. Telephone Co. Ltd.; Supt. P.E.I. Nat. Park 1958-63; Councillor City of Saint John 1971-77; served with RCCS

1942-46 and comnd. RCN(R) 1951; el. M.L.A. for Saint John North prov. g.e. 1978; mem. St. Georges Soc.; Un. Services Inst.; P. Conservative; United Church; Club: Union; Office: (P.O. Box 6000) Fredericton, N.B. E3B 5H1.

KIRBY, Hon. William John Cameron, C.D., B.A.; judge; b. Calgary, Alta., 12 Jan. 1909; s. William John and Catherine Georgina (Gray) K.; e. Rocky Mountain House (Alta.) Pub. Sch.; Hanna (Alta.) High Sch.; Univ. of B.C., B.A. 1930; Univ. of Alta., Grad. Sch. of Educ., 1931-32; Vancouver Law Sch. 1938-41; m. Marion Jean, d. Stanley Floyd Torrance, Calgary, Alta., 10 Apl. 1954; children: William John Torrance, Catherine Elaine; JUSTICE, COURT OF QUEEN'S BENCH OF ALBERTA; read law with Dugald Donaghy, K.C., Vancouver, B.C.; called to Bar of B.C. 1943, Alta. 1945; High Sch. Teacher, Hussar, Alta., 1932-35; Princ., Okotoks (Alta.) Schs., 1935-38; practised law in Red Deer, Alta., 1945-60 (Partner, McClure & Kirby, 1945-47; Kirby, Murphy, Armstrong, Beames & Chapmen, 1947-60) apptd. Chrmn. Review Bd. to Study Alta. Prov. Court System 1973; served with Candn. Army Active Service 1941-45; Inst., Offrs. Training Centre, Victoria, B.C., 1941-43; Troop Commdr., 25th and 24th Field Regts. RCA 1943-44; Legal Offr., Pacific Command HQ, 1944-45; M.L.A. Alta. 1954-59; Prov. Leader, P. Cons. Party of Alta., 1958-59; Pres., Red Deer Br., Royal Candn. Legion, 1950-53; Freemason; Anglican; recreations: golf, gardening, bridge; Club: Ranchmen's; Home: 246 Eagle Ridge Dr., Calgary, Alta. T2V 2V7; Office: Court House, Calgary, Alta. T2P 1T5

KIRCHMANN, Neville Walter, P.M.D., C.A.; b. Johannesburg, S. Africa 16 Nov. 1938; s. Frederick and Thelma Eileen (Elliott) K.; e. Marist Brothers Coll. 1955; Univ. of Witwatersrand C.A. 1961; Harvard Univ. Business Sch. P.M.D. 1972; m. Edith Irene d. George France, S. Africa 22 Apl. 1968; children: David, Jillian; PRES.; C.E.O. AND DIR. COCA-COLA LTD. — CAN. since 1976; Dir. Grandale Co. Ltd.; articled George Beaton & Co. Johannesburg 1956-60; Secy. and Chief Acct. Hippo Holding Group H.O. Johannesburg 1960-64; Asst. to Gen. Mgr. Bottling Operations Coca-Cola Export Corp. Johannesburg 1964; Gen. Mgr. Coca-Cola Bottling Co. of Durban 1968-71, Coca-Cola Bottling Co. of Johannesburg 1972-73 and Co. Bottling Operations S. Africa 1974-75, Vice Pres. and Gen. Mgr. Co. Bottling Operations Coca-Cola Ltd. Can. 1975-76; mem. Candn. Soft Drink Assn. Board; Can. Soft Drink Assoc. Advisory Council; Patron of the Ronald McDonald House; Past Chrmn. Can Diabetes Assoc. Mem. Exec. Comte. Bd of Gous-Variety Village Sport Training and Fitness Centre; Bd. Trade Metrop. Toronto; Anglican; recreations: squash, golf; Club: Donalda; Granite; Griffith Island; Home: 33 Hudson Drive, Toronto, Ont. M4T 2K1; Office: 42 Overlea Blvd., Toronto, Ont. M4H 1B8

KIRKBRIDE, David Spencer, M.Sc.; civil engineer; b. Calgary, Alta., 15 Aug. 1913; s. late John Frederick and Idabelle (Spencer) K.; e. Victoria Pub. Shc. and Central Coll. High Sch., Regina, Sask.; Univ. of Sask., M.Sc. (Engn.) 1937; Harvard Univ., M.Sc. (Engn.) 1939; m. Muereta, d. late Ernest Alexander Turnbull, 1937; one s.: John Michael; Past Consultant Western Canada Canadian Industries Limited; Dir. Raylo Chem. Ltd.; Education Research and Devel. Park Authority; Structural Design and Jr. Res. Engr., Fed. Dept. of Pub. Works, Sask., 1935-37; Structural Designer, Canadian Industries Ltd., 1937; Structural Designer, Project Engr. and Res. Engr., Defence Industries Ltd., 1939; Works Engr., Small Arms Ammunition Plant Montreal, 1943; Res. Engr. in charge of Constr., Atomic Energy Plant and Village, Chalk River, Ont., 1944; Engr., Devel. Dept., Canadian Industries Ltd., 1947; Mgr. of Dept. 1954; Asst. Gen. Mgr., "Fabrikoid" Div., New Toronto, 1957; Gen. Mgr. of Div. 1958; Employee Relations Mgr., Montreal, 1964; Pres. and Dir., Milhaven Fibres Ltd. (subsidiary) 1967-69; Vice

pres. 1969-1978; mem. Occupational Health and Safety Council, Alta. 197-80; past Pres. and dir, Construction Owners Assn. of Alta.; mem., Soc. Chem. Indust. (Chrmn., 1972-73); Engn. Inst. Can.; Protestant; recreations: curling, golf; Clubs: Montreal; Engineers' (Dir. 1973-75); Edmonton, Mayfair Golf & Country; Mount Royal Curling (Dir. 1967-68); Home: 103-14810-51 Ave., Edmonton, Alberta T6H 5G5.

KIRKHAM, Peter Gilbert, B.A.Sc., M.B.A., M.A., Ph.D.; economist; Canadian public servant; b. Red Deer, Alta. 24 Oct. 1934; s. Norman Kennedy K.; e. Royal Mil. Coll., Kingston, Ont. 1957; Univ. of Brit. Columbia, B.A.Sc. 1958; Univ. of Western Ont. M.B.A. 1963, M.A. (Econ.) 1964; Princeton Univ. Ph.D. (Econ.) 1970; m.; SR. VICE-PRES AND CHIEF ECONOMIST, BANK OF MONTREAL Chief Statistician, Statistics Canada 1975-80; Prof. of Econ., Univ. of Western Ont. 1964-65, 1969-73; Asst. Chief Stat., Statistics Can. 1973; served in Royal Candn. Engrs. 1953-60; rank on retirement Capt.; mem. Candn. Econ. Assn.; Am. Econ. Assn.; Office: Head Office, P.O. Box 6002, Montreal, Que. H3C 3B1

KIRKLAND — CASGRAIN, Hon. Marie Claire, B.A., LL.D. (Hon.); b. Palmer, Mass., U.S.A., 8 Sept.; d. Rose A. (Demers) and late Dr. Charles Aimé Kirkland (former M.L.A. for Jacques — Cartier, 1939-61); e. Villa — Maria Convent; McGill Univ., B.A. 1947; McGill Univ. Law Sch. (Grad. 1950); LL.D. (Hon.), Moncton Univ. 1965; Glendon Coll., York Univ. 1975; m. P. Casgrain; children: Lynne-Marie, Kirkland, Marc; JUDGE, PROV. COURT OF QUE.; with law firm of Cerini, Jamieson 1952; cr. Q.C. 1969; first el. to Que. Leg. in by-el. for Jacques-Cartier, Dec. 1961 (1st woman to sit in Que. Leg.); re-el for Marguerite-Bourgeoys g.e. April 1970; Min. of Tourism, Fish and Game 1970; Min. of Cultural Affairs 1972 until retired 1973; Judge (1st woman), Prov. Court of Que. 1973; seconded the address in reply to speech from the Throne at 1st session of Leg.; first woman to plead before the private bills comte. in Que.; Founder and Pres. Candn. Chapter, Internat. Alliance of Women; mem. Candn. Bar Assn.; Montreal Bar Assn.; Kappa Alpha Theta; Roman Catholic; recreations: golf, fishing, travels; Home: 45 Northridge Rd., Ile Bizard, Que. H9E 1A8; Office: 1 est, Notre Dame St., Montreal, Que. H2Y 1B6

KIRKPATRICK, James Balfour, Ed.D.; retired university dean; b. Saskatoon, Sask., 20 Apl. 1909; s. Wilbur Allan and Elizabeth (Balfour) K.; e. Univ. of Sask., B.A. 1929, B.Ed. 1930, M. Ed. 1935; Teachers' Coll., Columbia Univ., Ed.D. (Physical Educ.) 1944; m. Mary d. late John Convey, 30 Oct. 1943; eight children; served as High Sch. Instr., Melfort, Sask., 1930-33; Instr., Bedford Rd. Coll., Saskatoon, 1934-39; Physical Educ. Instr., Edmonton (Alta.) Normal Sch., 1939-42; Dir. of Physical Fitness and Recreation, Dept. of Educ., Regina, Sask., 1944-48; Dir., McGill Sch. of Physical Educ., Montreal, P.Q., 1948-56; Dean of Education, Univ. of Sask., 1956-76; rep. Candn. Conf. on Educ., 1956, 1962; Pres., W. Can. Regional Conf. on Teacher Educ., 1960-61; served in 2nd World War 1942-44; P.T. and Drill Offr., R.C.A.F.; co-author, "Physical Fitness", 1944; Catholic; Address: 1410 Main St., Saskatoon, Sask., S7H 0L6.

KIRKPATRICK, John Gildersleeve, Q.C., B.Sc., B.C.L.; lawyer; b. Toronto, Ont., 28 Jan. 1917; s. Herbert Rutherfoord and Edna Margaret (Nelles) K.; e. Westmount (P.Q.) Public Schs.; Trinity Coll. Sch., Port Hope, Ont.; McGill Univ., B.Sc. 1939, B.C.L. 1942; m. Irena, d. William Groten, 24 June 1944; children: Xenia, Kathleen, Patricia; PARTNER, OGILVY, RENAULT, chrmn., Anaconda-Ericsson Communications Inc.; Vice Chrmn. and Dir., MoDoMekan (Canada) Ltd.; Dir., Canron Inc.; Domtar Inc.; RoyFund (Equity) Ltd.; Volvo Canada Ltd.; Krupp Canada Inc.; Colt Canada Inc.; Moldcast Inc.; Ludvig Svensson (Canada) Ltd.; Trustee, Royfund Income Trust; called to the Bar of Quebec, 1943; cr. Q.C.,

1961; practised with present firm and its predecessors since 1943; Anglican; Club: St. James's, Mount Royal; Home: 1321 Sherbrooke St. W., Montreal, Que. H3G 1J4; Office: Suite 700, 1 Place Ville Marie, Montreal, Que. H3B 1Z7

KIRKPATRICK, Lesmere Forrest, D.S.O., D.Eng., F.E.I.C.; public utility executive; b. Parrsboro, N.S., 19 Oct. 1916; s. Rupert Edwin and Vera Lavina (Ward) K.; e. Parrsboro High Sch.; Mount Allison Univ. (Engn. Cert. 1936); N.S. Tech. Coll., B.Eng., 1938; Atlantic Sch. of Business Adm., June — July, 1957; m. Eva Katherine, d. Augustus P. Gavin, 25 Sept. 1948; children: Kathie Jane, Mary Leslie; PRES., CHIEF EXEC. OFFICER, AND DIR., N.S. POWER CORP. 1978- ; Pres. and Gen. Mgr. N.S. Power Corp. since 1973; Vice-Pres. and Dir., Nova Scotia Tidal Power Corp.; mem. Bd. of Dir. and Past Pres., Can. Electrical Assn.; Dir., Can. Nuclear Assn.; Nova Scotia Energy Council; Dir. and Vice-Pres., Blue Cross Atlantic Canada; Atlantic Mutual Life; Dir., Nova Scotia General Ins. Co.; Supt., Parrsboro Mun. Elect. Light System, 1938-40; Constr. Engr., Canada Electric, March — Dec. 1946, and Res. Engr., 1947-49, Steam Plant Supt., Amherst, N.S., 1949-55; Comm. Supt., N.S. Power Comn., 1955; Asst. Mgr., 1959; Gen. Mgr., N.S. Power Comn., Dec. 1959; served in 2nd World War, 1940-42; with 2nd R.C.A., Halifax, Lieut.; promoted Capt. 1942 and trans. to 106th Coast Batty., Nfld.; Overseas, Oct. 1943; posted to 12th Candn. Field Regt., France, June 1944; promoted to Major i/c 16th Field Batty., 1945; awarded D.S.O.; mem. and Past Dir., Halifax YMCA; Past Pres., Candn. Council of Prof. Engrs.; mem., Assn. of Prof. Engrs. of N.S.; Halifax Bd. Trade (past dir.); Bd. mem. Mt. St. Vincent Un.; Bd. of Gov. and Exec. Comte., St. Mary's Un.; mem. Eng. Inst. of Can.; past Dir. and Chmn., Atlantic Industrial Research Inst.; past Dir., Halifax Children's Hospital; Freemason; United Church; recreations: curling, golfing, fishing, tennis; Clubs: Halifax (Pres.); Halifax Curling; Parrsboro Golf; Halifax Rotary; Ashburn Golf & Country; Burnside Tennis; Waegwoltic; Home: 2259 Macdonald St., Halifax, N.S. B3L 3G2; Office: c/o D.W. Flemming, P.O. Box 910, Halifax, N.S. B3J 2W5

KIRKWOOD, David Herbert Waddington, M.A.; Canadian public servant; b. Toronto, Ont., 8 Aug. 1924; s. late Dr. William Alexander and Dr. Mossie May (Waddington) K.; e. Univ. of Toronto Schs., 1941; Univ. of Toronto, B.A. (Physics & Chem.) 1945, M.A. (Pol. Science) 1950; m. Diana Thistle, d. late Henry R. T. Gill, Ottawa, Ont., 6 June 1953; children: Peter Henry Alexander, Gill David William, Melissa Macdonald Thistle, John Robert Waddington; DEP. MIN., SERVICES, DEPT. OF SUPPLY AND SERVICES AND DEPUTY RECEIVER GENERAL FOR CANADA since 1980; Research Physicist, Atomic Energy Council, Chalk River, Ont., 1945-48; Asst., Dept. of Pol. Econ., Univ. of Toronto, 1949-50; Foreign Service Offr., Dept. of External Affairs, 1950-69; Ottawa 1950-52; 2nd Secy., Candn. NATO Del., 1952-55; Ottawa 1955-58; 1st Secy., Canadian Embassy, Athens, 1958-60; Councillor, Candn. Embassy, Bonn, 1960-63; Ottawa 1963-69 (Head, Office of Econ. Affairs, 1966-69); Asst. Secy. to the Cabinet, Privy Council Office, 1969-72; Asst. Depy. Min. Policy Dept. Nat. Defence, 1972-75; Sr. Asst. Depy. Min. Transport Canada, 1975-77; Chmn. Anti-Dumping Tribunal 1978-80; Anglican; recreations: skiing, fishing, tennis, sailing; Home: 572 Manor Ave., Ottawa, Ont. K1M 0J7; Office: Hull, Qué. K1A 0S5

KIRSCHBAUM, James L., B.S., M.B.A.; insurance executive; b. San Francisco, Cal. 5 July 1926; s. John D. and Sadie (McLennan) K.; e. Univ. of Cal. Berkley B.S. 1949; Golden Gate Univ. M.B.A. 1951; Chart. Property Casualty Underwriter 1951; Univ. of Mich. Mang. of Mgrs. Program 1973; m. Beverly d. E. B. Hardman 28 March 1947; children: James Lawrence, Carol, John, Scott, Jean; PRES., CHIEF EXTVE. OFFR. AND DIR. FIREMAN'S FUND INSURANCE CO. OF CANADA 1980- ; Dir. Shaw

& Begg; served Fireman's Fund Insurance Co. holding various positions incl. 17 yrs. as Resident Vice Pres., Vice Pres. and Gen. Mgr. Famex (marketing subsidiary) 3 yrs., Field Operations Extve. W. States (U.S.) 2 yrs.; Secy.-Treas. Nat. Soc. Chart. Property & Casualty Underwriters; Dir. Insurers Adv. Organ.; Past Chrmn. State of Pa. Chamber Comm. Ins. Comte.; Past Pres. Ins. Soc. Philadelphia; author numerous articles and speeches on tech. ins. subjects, sales, marketing, mang.; Pres. Toronto Stake Ch. Jesus Christ Latter Day Saints (Mormon); served with U.S. Navy S. Pacific World War II, Electronics Tech.; P. Conservative; Mormon; recreations: golf, camping, hiking; Club: Lambton Golf & Country; Home: 5 Edenbrook Hill, Islington, Ont. M9A 3Z5;Office: 350 Bloor St. E., Toronto, Ont. M4W 1H4.

KISSICK, (William) Norman, B.A.Sc.; executive; b. Toronto, Ont. 3 Oct. 1930; s. late William John and late Evelyn Elizabeth (Hayes) K.; e. Bloor Coll. Inst. Toronto 1948; Univ. of Toronto B.A.Sc. 1952; m. Lois Elizabeth d. late John Joseph Caddell 2 June 1956; three s. James Stephen, John David, William Peter; PRESIDENT AND CHIEF OPERATING OFFR. UNION CARBIDE CANADA LTD. 1981- ; Dir. Pétromont Inc.; Process Engr. Dominion Tar & Chemicals, Toronto 1952-53 and Montreal E. 1954; Dept. Head Chemicals, Carbide Chemical Co. Montreal E. 1955-61, Dept. Head Olefins 1961-63; Area Supvr. Olefins, Union Carbide Canada Ltd. 1963-65, Asst. Plant Mgr. 1965-69, Business Mgr. Chemicals 1969-73 and Gen. Mgr. Businesses 1974-75 Plastics & Chemicals Toronto, Vice Pres. 1975-81, Dir. 1975- ; mem. Candn. Chem. Producers' Assn. (Chrmn. 1977-78; Dir. 1975-); Soc. Chem. Industry (Can.) (Chrmn. 1978-79; Dir. 1977-80); Soc. Plastics Industry (Dir. 1980-); Ont. Chamber Comm. (Dir. 1979-81); Candn. Soc. Chem. Engrs.; Protestant; Home: 40 Wakefield Cres., Agincourt, Ont. M1W 2C2;Office: 123 Eglinton Ave. E., Toronto, Ont. M4P 1J3.

KITCHING, Maj. — Gen. George, C.B.E. (1945), D.S.O. (1943); Canadian Army retired; b. Canton, China, 19 Sept. 1910; s. George Charlesworth and Florence Dagmar (Rowe) K.; e. Cranleigh Sch., Eng.; Roy. Mil. Coll., Sandhurst; m. Audrey Katherine Calhoun, Oct. 1946; children: George, Katherine; served in 2nd World War 1939-45; Royal Candn. Regt. 1939-40; G.S.O. III, H.Q. 1st Candn. Divn. 1941; Staff Coll., 1941-42; G.S.O. II, H.Q. 1st Candn. Corps 1942; Lieut. — Col. commdg. Loyal Edmonton Regt. 1942; G.S.O. I, 1st Candn. Divn., 1943; Brig. Commdg. 11th Candn. Inf. Bgde. 1943-44; G.O.C., 4th Candn. Armoured Divn. (Acting Maj. — Gen.) 1944; B.G.S. and C. of S., 1st Candn. Corps 1944-45; on return from overseas Aug. 1945 apptd. Vice-Q.M.G., at N.D.H.Q.; in Washington D.C., Nat. War College, 1947-48; Brig. Gen. Staff (Plans) Army Hdqrs. 1948-51; subsequently Commandant, Candn. Staff Coll. and Commdr., B.C. Area; apptd. Vice-Chief of the Gen. Staff, Ottawa, 1956 and later Chrmn., Candn. Jt. Staff, London; G.O.C. Central Command, 1962-65; Chief Commr., L.C.B.O., 1970-76; Colonel Commandant, Royal Canadian Infantry Corps, 1974-78; mem. Nat. Council, Duke of Edinburgh's Award in Can.; Legion of Merit (U.S.); Commander, Order Orange Nassau (Netherlands); Commander, Military Order of Italy; mem. Candn. Nat. Comte., Un. World Colleges; mem., Inst. Internat. Affairs; Chmn. Gurkha Welfare Appeal (Can.) 1974-77; Patron, Old Fort York 1975; Sir Edmund Hillary foundation; Pearson College & United World Colleges; Anglican; recreations: golf, gardening, stamps; Clubs: National; Rideau Golf; Empire; Home: 3434 Bonair Place, Victoria, B.C., Victoria, B.C. V8P 4V4

KITTS, Dean Carson, Q.C., B.A.Sc., LL.B.; lawyer; executive; b. Matheson, Ont. 9 Dec. 1934; s. James and Evelyn (Carson) K.; e. Univ. of Toronto B.A.Sc. (Chem. Engn.) 1958; Osgoode Hall Law Sch. LL.B. 1963; m. Elizabeth Ann d. James Brawley, St. Thomas, Ont. 24 May

1958; children: Dean, Robert, Mary; VICE PRES. ADM. AND GEN. COUNSEL, JOHN LABATT LTD. 1981- ; called to Bar of Ont. 1963; cr. Q.C. 1979; joined Cavanagh & Norman, Patent Agts. Toronto 1963-64; Corporate Counsel present Co. 1966, Vice Pres. and Secy. 1971; mem. Assn. Prof. Engrs. Prov. Ont.; Candn. Bar Assn.; Am. Bar Assn.; Patent & Trade Mark Inst. Can.; Delta Chi; Clubs: London; St. Thomas Golf & Country; Home: 18 Applewood Cres., St. Thomas, Ont. N5R 1H2;Office: (P.O. Box 5050 Stn. A) 451 Ridout St. N., London, Ont. N6A 4M3

KITZ, Leonard Arthur, Q.C., LL.B., D.C.L.; b. Halifax, N.S., 9 Apr. 1916; s. Harry and Yetta (Lesser) K.; e. Dalhousie Univ., LL.B.; m. 1stly Alice Duff, d. Robert Findlay, 17 Oct. 1945; children: Hilary Ann, John Findlay, Alan Lawrence; 2ndly Janet Brownlee, 18 Dec. 1971; SR. PARTNER, KITZ, MATHESON, GREEN & MacISAAC; Pres.; The Provincial Realty Co.; 1st Vice-Pres., Halifax Developments Ltd.; Dir. Grand Hotel Ltd.; mem. Halifax Adv. Bd., Royal Trust Co.; read law with Pearson, Rutledge and Donald; called to Bar of N.S. 1939; cr. Q.C., 1959; served with Princess Louise Fusiliers as Capt.; 12th Candn. Light Brigade as Staff Offr.; mem., Bd. Technical Univ. of N.S. 1973-81; former Chrmn. Atlantic Industrial Research Inst.; Mayor of Halifax, 1955-57; Past Pres., The John Howard Soc. of N.S.; Chrmn., N.S., Candn., Inst. of Internat. Affairs; Trustee, National Arts Centre, 1967-73; Pres., N.S. Barristers Soc., 1968-69; Prov. Vice-Pres., Candn. Bar Assn. 1969-71; Liberal; Jewish; recreations: greenhouse, fishing, bridge, gardening; Clubs: Halifax; R.N.S.Y.S.; Saraguay; Home: 1110 Rockcliffe Street, Halifax, N.S. B3H 3Y6; Office: Suite 1600, 5151 George St., Halifax, N.S. B3J 1M5

KIVES, Philip; merchandise executive; b. Oungre, Sask., 12 Feb. 1930; s. Kiva and Lily (Wiener) K.; m. Ellie d. Dr. H. Corman, Winnipeg, Man., 24 May 1971; two d. Samantha Ruth, kelly; PRESIDENT, K — TEL INTERNATIONAL LTD.; Dir. Flair Travel Ltd.; Capri Carpets Ltd.; National Developments Ltd.; Hebrew; recreations: tennis, skiing; Home: Office: 1670 Inkster Blvd., Winnipeg, Man. R2X 2W8

KLEINERT, Theodor Niklaus, D.Sc.; chemist; b. Vienna, Austria, 25 March 1897; s. Theodor and Amalia (Herusch) K.; e. Low Sch., Vienna and High School there; Tech. University, Vienna (Engn.) Diploma, 1921, and D.Sc. 1924; children: Eva Lieselotte, Diane Susanne; Chemist in charge of Production at Saltpetre Plant, ERWA, 1921-22; Asst. Prof., Tech. Univ., Vienna, 1924-30; Co-Consultant with Prof. L. Jaloustre of the Sorbonne, Paris, 1930-36; independent Consultant, Vienna, 1937-39; Research Chemist in Schlesische, Zellulose-u. Papierfabriken E. Schoeller & Co., 1941-42; Dir. of Research in Zellwolle Lenzing A.G., 1943-53; Assoc. Prof of Wood and Cellulose Chem., Tech. Univ., Vienna, 1948-53; Sr. Scientist, Pulp & Paper Research Inst. of Can., 1954-62; Principal Scientist, there, 1960-62; served in World War I; Lieut. in Austrian — Hungarian Army; Publications: 200 in the field of wood, cellulose and textile chem.; mem., Am. Tech, Assn. of Pulp & Paper Industry; awarded Karl Kellner Gold Honor Medal, Austrian Assn. of Pulp & Paper Chemists & Tech., 1955; I. H. Weldon Medal, Tech. Sec. Candn. Pulp & Paper Assn., 1965; Grand Medal of Honor for Services to the Republic of Austria, 1968; TAPPI — Fellow, 1970; Alexander Mitscherlick Medal, German Assn. of the Pulp & Paper. Chemist 1976; Roman Catholic; Address: 120 Embleton Crescent, Pointe Claire, Que. H9R 3N2

KLIBANSKY, Raymond, M.A., D.Phil., F.R.H.S., F.R.S.C. (1970); university professor; b. Paris, France, 15 Oct. 1905; s. Armand and Rose (Scheidt) K.; e. Univs. Heidelberg, Kiel, Hamburg; D.Phil., Heidelberg, 1928; Oxford Univ., M.A. (by decree) 1935; FROTHINGHAM PROF. OF LOGIC AND METAPHYSICS, McGILL UNIV., since 1946; pres., Inst. Internat. de Philos., Paris, since 1966; Prof. invité, Inst. d'Etudes Médiévales, Univ. de Montréal; Hon. Fellow, The Warburg Inst., Univ. of London; Asst. Heidelberg Acad. of Science & Letters 1927-33; and Univ. Lect. in Philos., 1931-33; Lectr. in Philos., King's Coll., Univ. of London, 1934-36; Oriel Coll., Oxford, 1936-48; Dir. of Studies, The Warburg Inst., Univ. of London, 1947-48; Mahlon Powell Prof. of Philos., Univ. of Indiana, 1949-50; served as Temporary Civil Servant, P.I.D., Foreign Office, London, 1941-46; Cardinal Mercier Prof. of Philos., Univ. of Louvain, 1956; Foundation Lectr., Univ. of Rome, 1957; Visiting Prof., Faculty of Philos., Univ. of Rome, 1961; Univ. of Genoa, 1964; Guggenheim Foundation Fellow, 1954, 1965; mem. of Dir. Council, Internat. Centre of Humanist Studies, Rome; Gen. Ed., Corpus Platonicum Medii Aevi, Brit. Acad.; "Philosophical Texts"; Joint Ed., "Mediaeval and Renaissance Studies"; author, "Ein Proklos — Fund und seine Bedeutung", 1929; "Nicolai de Cusa Opera omnia", vols. I and II, 1932; "Magistri Eckardi Opera Latina", 1934-36; "Philosophy and History" (ed. jointly with H. J. Paton), 1936; "The Continuity of the Platoric Tradition", 1939; "Leibniz' Unknown Corr. with Eng. Scholars and Men of Letters", 1941; "Plato's Parmenides in the Middle ages and the Renaissance", 1943; edited "Mussolini's Memoirs, 1942-43", 1949; el. Fellow, Internat. Acad. for the Hist. of Science, Paris, 1960; Pres., Candn. Soc. for the Hist. and Philos. of Science; mem. Comte. Dir. (Candn. rep.), Fed. Internat. Socs. Philos.; Nat. Research Council, mem. Candn. Nat. Comte. for Hist. and Philos. of Science and Candn. Nat. Comte. for Internat. Council of Scient. Unions; Candn. Secy., Union Internat. Philos. and Hist. of Sciences; mem., Extve. Comte., Am. Philos. Assn.; Jewish; recreations: music, old books and manuscripts; Home: 3660 Peel St., Apt. 29, Montreal, Que.

KLINCK, Carl Frederick, O.C. (1973), Ph.D., D.Litt., F.R.S.C., (1961); emeritus professor; b. Elmira, Ont., 24 Mar. 1908; s. John and Anna (Milhausen) K.; e. Waterloo Coll., Univ. of W. Ont., B.A. 1927, D.Litt. 1974; Columbia Univ., M.A. 1929, Ph.D. 1943; m. Margaret Elizabeth, d. William A. Witzel, Kitchener, Ont., 27 Feb. 1934; has one s. David Michael; Prof. of Eng., Waterloo Coll., 1928-47; Dean, Faculty of Arts, there, 1942-47; Assoc. Prof. of English, Univ. of W. Ont., 1947-49; Prof. 1949-73; since when emeritus; Head Of Dept., 1949-56; Prof. Candn. Lit. 1956-73; publications: 'Wilfred Campbell, A Study in Late Provincial Victorianism', 1942; 'Edwin J. Pratt, The Man and His Poetry', (with Henry W. Wells) 1947; 'Canadian Anthology' (ed. with R. E. Watters), 1955, rev. 1974; 'William 'Tiger' Dunlop', 1958; 'Tecumseh', 1961; 'Canadian Writers/Ecrivains Canadiens' (edited with Guy Sylvestre and Brandon Conron), 1964; General Editor of 'Literary History of Canada', 1965, 2nd edit 1976; 'Robert Service, A Biography', 1976; 'The Journal of Major John Norton,' (edited with James J. Talman), 1970; awarded the Lorne Pierce Medal (of the Royal Soc. of Can.) 1978; Anglican; Address: 8 Grosvenor St., London, Ont. N6A 1Y4

KNELMAN, Fred H., B.A.Sc., M.Eng., Ph.D.; university professor; b. Winnipeg, Man., 9 Oct. 1919; s. Morris J. and Betsy D. K.; e. Univ. of Man., 1936-39; Univ. of Toronto, B.A.Sc. (Chem. Engn.) 1943; McGill Univ., M.Eng. 1950; Imp. Coll. of Science, Dipl. 1953; Univ. of London, Ph.D., Post-Doctoral Fellow Inst. of Educ. 1960-61; divorced; children: Kevin M., Linda M.; PROF. OF SCIENCE & HUMAN AFFAIRS, CONCORDIA UNIV.; Chem. Engr., Prod. Control, Monarch Battery Co., Kingston, Ont., 1945-46; Tech. and Research Dir., Stuart Brothers Ltd., 1953-63; Consultant to Food Indust. 1963; Visiting Prof. Cal. Inst. of Arts 1973-74; Visiting Prof. Environmental Studies, Univ. of Cal., Santa Barbara 1977-78; served with RCE 1943-45; rank Lt.; appearances on various CBC and CTV programs; Consultant, Science Council of Can.; Nat. Film Bd.; Dept. of Environment; Rensselaer Polytech. Inst.; Dir., Inovan Consulting

Corp., Toronto; received various scholarships, fellowships and research grants 1936-81; rec'd. White Owl Conservation Prize 1972; World Wildlife Prize, 1970; Candn. del., World Conf. on Human Environment, Stockholm, 1972; Ed., "Flavour", 1962; sometimes edit. writer, Montreal Gazette and Toronto Star; author, books and monographs: "1984 and All That", 1971; "Nuclear Energy; The Unforgiving Technology", Hurtig, 1976; "Anti-Nation: Transition to Sustainability", Mosaic Press, 1979; "Energy Conservation", Background Study No. 33, Science Council of Canada other writings include over 200 articles in areas of environment, engineering, sociol. of science; Past Chairman, UN Montreal; Past Chairman, Montreal Committee for Control of Radiation Hazards and Citizens for Social Responsibility in Science; mem., Engn. Inst. Can.; Candn. Inst. Food Technol. (Chrmn. 1958); Am. Assn. Advanc. Science; Internat. Ozone Inst.; World Future Soc.; Can. Future Society; Am. Public Health Assoc.; Can. Peace Res. & ED. Assoc.; Mexican Inst. of Chemical Engrs; Internat. Epidemiological Assoc.; New York Academy of Sciences; recreations: music, tennis, card games; Home: 3492 Dorian, Montreal, Que.; Office: 2010 Mackay, Montreal, Que. H3G 2M1

KNIEWASSER, Andrew Graham, O.C. (1967), B.A.; association executive; b. Ottawa, Ont., 9 Sept. 1926; s. Andrew Vernon and Helen Graham (Cooch) K.; e. Lisgar Coll., Ottawa, Ont.; Queens Univ., B.A. (Hon. Econ.); m. Jacqueline Marie, d. late Wilfred Delaney, 3 Aug. 1951; children: Andrew Peter, James David, John Hugh, Andréa Hélène; PRESIDENT, INVESTMENT DEALERS ASSN. CAN. since 1972; Dir., Can. Securities Inst.; Atlantic Inst.; Atlantic Council of Can.; Queen Elizabeth Hospital; Econ., Economics Research and Devel. Br. Dept. of Trade and Comm., Ottawa, 1949; Econ., Dept. of Defence Prod., Ottawa, 1950; Trade Commr. service 1951; Asst. Trade Commr., Candn. Embassy, Athens, 1952; Candn. Acting Trade Commr. a.i., Beirut, 1953, Cairo 1954; Asst. Comm. Secy., Candn. Embassy, Caracas, 1955, Comm. Secy., 1957; Area Trade Offr. for Latin Am., Dept. Trade and Comm., Ottawa, 1957; Extve. Asst. to the Depy. Min. of Trade and Comm., 1958; Comm. Counsellor, Candn. Embassy, Paris and Centre. Del. to Bureau of Internat. Exhns., 1960; Gen. Mgr., Expo '67, 1963-67; Asst. Dep. Min. (Trade Promotion), Dept. Trade and Comm., Ottawa, 1967; Export Credits Ins. Corp., 1968; Sr. Asst. Depy. Min., Dept. Indust., Trade and Comm., Can 1970; served with Candn. Inf. Corps 1945; Dir., Donwood Inst.; Queen's Fund Council; Dir. and Treas., Futures Secretariat; United Church; recreations: hunting, fishing, Clubs: National White Pine Fishing (Dir.); Eglinton Equestrian (Dir.); Canadian (Dir.); Goodwood; Home: 304 St. Clair Ave East, Toronto, Ont. M4T 1P4; Office: (P.O. Box 217) Commerce Court S., Toronto, Ont. M5L 1E8

KNOTT, Leonard L., B.A.; b. Winnipeg, Man., 30 March 1905; s. John Albert and Emily Edith (Stephens) K.; e. Univ. of Manitoba, B.A. 1927; m. Lilian, d. Philip King-Hill, 20 Sept. 1930; one s. Leonard L., Jr.; Pres., Candn. Public Relations Soc., 1956-57; Chairman, Third World Cong. of Public Relations (Montreal, 1964); Feature Writer and Editor, Toronto "Star", Montreal "Gazette", 1926-36; Co-ordinator, Consumer information, Wartime Information Bd., Ottawa, 1942-43; Publications: "PR in PRofit: a Guide to Successful Public Relations in Canada", 1955; a cont. series of children's books about Canada; "Plain Talk About Public Relations", 1961; "Montreal — The Golden Years", 1966; "Montreal 1900-1930", 1976; "Rally Round the Jack" (novel), 1976; "Next — A practical how-to-do-it book about dying.", 1981; Lectr. in Public Relations, Harvard, Toronto, McGill; Dir., Public Relations Soc. of Am., 1957-60; Pres., Architectural Conservancy of Ont. 1973-74; recreation: collecting Canadiana; Home: 321 Lanthier Ave., Pointe Claire, Que. H9S 5K6

KNOWLES, Arthur Neville; executive; b. London, Ont. 31 July 1927; e. Appleby Coll. Oakville, Ont.; m. Verna June 1954; children: Peter Allen, Arthur Neville, James Laurie, Elizabeth June; EXTVE. VICE PRES., LONDON WINERY LTD.; Dir. Knowlwin Holdings Ltd.; Westminster Transport Ltd.; Home: 617 Wharncliffe Rd. South, London, Ont. N6A 2N7; Office: 560 Wharncliffe Rd. South, London, Ont. N6J 2N5

KNOWLES, Henry Joseph, Q.C., LL.M., M.B.A.; b. London, Ont. 22 Jan. 1932; e. London S. Coll. Inst. 1952; Univ. of W. Ont. Sch. Business Adm. B.A. 1956; Osgoode Hall Law Sch. 1960; Yale Univ. Law Sch. LL.M. 1961; Univ. of Toronto Sch. of Business M.B.A. 1962; m. Marilyn Anne Radcliffe 1960; 2 children; CHRMN., ONT. SECURITIES COMN. 1980- ; called to Bar of Ont. 1960; cr. Q.C. 1978; law practice Borden & Elliot 1961-64; Smith, Lyon, Torrance, Stevenson & Mayer 1965-68, Partner 1969-80; Seminar Instr. in Corporate Law 1966-69 and in Income Tax Law 1974, 1976, 1977, Osgoode Hall Bar Admission Course; author "Partnership" (statutory annotation) 1978; mem. Candn. Bar Assn.; Candn. Tax Foundation; Co. York Law Assn.; Inst. Law Clks. Ont. (Hon. mem. 1978); Delta Upsilon; Phi Delta Phi; recreations: skiing, jogging; Clubs: Granite; Cambridge; Home: 6 Doon Rd., Willowdale, Ont. M2L 1L9; Office: Suite 1700, P.O. Box 55, 20 Queen St. W., Toronto, Ont. M5H 3S8

KNOWLES, Hon. Stanley Howard, P.C., M.P., B.A., B.D., LL.D.; b. Los Angeles, Cal., 18 June 1908; s. Stanley Ernest and Margaret Blanche (Murdock) K. (both born in Canada); e. Elem. and High Sch., Los Angeles; Brandon Coll., Man., B.A. 1930 (Gen. Prof. Medal); Univ. of Man. (Theol. and post grad. studies in Philos. and Econ. 1930-34); B.D. 1934 (Gen. Prof. Medal); Brandon, LL.D. 1967; McMaster, LL.D., 1973; Queen's, LL.D., 1976; Toronto, LL.D., 1976; Trent, LL.D., 1978; York, LL.D., 1979; m. late Vida Claire, d. Chas. Gordon Cruikshank, Winnipeg, Man., 9 Nov. 1936; one son (m.) and one d. (m.); Ald., City of Winnipeg 1941-42; 1st el. to H. of C. for Winnipeg N. Centre, 1942, in by-el. to succeed late J. S. Woodsworth; re-el. g.e. 1945, 1949, 1953, 1957; def. g.e. 1958; re-elected, g.e. 1962 and since; Chief C.C.F. Whip 1944-57; C.C.F. Depy. Leader, 1957-58; Extve. Vice-Pres., The Candn. Labour Cong., 1958-62; Chrmn., C.C.F. Nat. Convention, 1948, '50, '52, '54, '56, '58, active in formation of N.D.P.; Chrmn., Nat. Comte. for New Party, 1958-61; House Leader, N.D.P. Caucus in H. of C.; Candn. Del. to U.N. Gen. Assembly (1st session) 1946; Workers' Del. for Canada at I.L.O. Conf., Geneva, 1959, '60 and '61; mem. of 1st Bd. of Dirs. of Red River Co-operative Supply Ltd., Winnipeg; mem., Winnipeg Local No. 191 of Internat. Typographical Union; Candn. Inst. of Internat. Affairs (Winnipeg Br.); Nat. Council and Nat. Extve. of C.C.F. (Man. Prov. Chrmn. 1935-36 and 1939-41; el. Nat. Vice-Chrmn. 1954); mem., Fed. Council, N.D.P.; named Chancellor of Brandon Univ., Manitoba, 1970; author of: "The New Party" ("Le Nouveau Parti"), 1961; sworn in as Mem. of Queen's Privy Council for Canada, 1979; N.D.P.; United Church; Club: Canadian; Address: 359 Elm St., Winnipeg, Man. R3M 3N6; Office: House of Commons, Ottawa, Ont. K1A 0A6

KNOWLTON, Gerald Loree, B.A.; real estate executive; b. Calgary, Alta. 10 March 1933; s. Frederic Demille and Dorothy Faye (Pringle) K.; e. Univ. of Alberta; Univ. of W. Ont. B.A. 1955; Postgrad. studies, Administrative Practices in European Industry, Univ. of W. Ont., 1955-57; Candn. Inst. Realtor's Course; m. Mary Janet d. late Harry M. Jarvis 17 May 1957; children: Mary Catherine, Barbara, Kelly, Nancy, Jean; PRES. CONGRESS RESOURCES LTD., Chrmn. Knowlton Realty Ltd. (Calgary, Edmonton, Vancouver); Chrmn. Knowlton Realty Ltd. (Denver, Colo.); Chrmn. Knowlton Realty Ltd. (Calif.); Chrmn. Knowlton Realty (Ontario) Ltd.; Pres. and

Chrmn. of the Bd., The Knowlton Corp., Texas; Chrmn. Congress Developments Ltd.; Dir. Napili Kai Beach Club, Maui, Hawaii; Dir. Regina Pats Hockey Club Ltd.; Vice Chrmn. Alta. Ventures Fund; Fellow, Real Estate Inst.; Mem., Adv. Cmte. Sch. of Bus. Admin., Univ. of W. Ont.; mem., Chevalier Chateau Montlabert, Bordeaux, France; Adv. Council, Men's Candn. Club of Calgary; Conservative; United Church; Clubs: Ranchmen's'; Calgary Petroleum; Glencoe; Earl Grey Golf; Calgary Golf and Club; recreations: hunting, golfing, tennis, badminton, travelling; Home: 1031 Durham Ave. S.W., Calgary, Alta. T2P 0P8; Office: #2350, 444 - 5th Ave. S.W., Calgary, Alta. T2P 2T8.

KNOWLTON, W. Leo., Q.C.; executive; b. Toronto, Ont., 1905; e. St. Michael's Coll. Sch.; Univ. of Toronto, B.A. (Gold Medal in Philos.): Osgoode Hall Law Sch., Toronto, Ont.; m. Mary Teaffe, Ottawa, Ont., 1931; two d., Mary, Adele; Director, Lake Erie Tobacco Co. Ltd.; CFRB Limited; Standard Broadcasting Corp. Ltd.; called to the Bar of Ontario, 1930; cr. Q.C. 1948; joined Can. Permanent Trust Company as a Trust Offr. 1930; Mgr. of Toronto Br. of the Co., 1940-54; apptd. Asst. Gen. Mgr., 1955, Gen. Mgr. 1956 and Vice Pres. 1961, Extve. Vice Pres. 1965; Pres., Trust Co.'s Assn. Can., 1962-63; Dir., Ont. Cancer Inst.; Princess Margaret Hosp.; mem., Toronto Bd. Trade; Clubs: National; Lawyers; Granite; Toronto Hunt; Home: 53 Widdicombe Hill Blvd., Weston, Ont. M9R 1Y3; Office: 320 Bay St., Toronto, Ont. M5H 2P2

KNOX, James Wilson, M.B.E., E.D.; chartered insurance broker; b. Westmount, P.Q., 17 Apl. 1915; s. Frank John and Mary Luceneth (Jones) K.; e. Lower Canada Coll., Montreal, P.Q.; m. Georgina W., d. George W. Grier, Montreal, Que., 17 Feb. 1945; children: Victoria W., Frances J., Georgina M., Alexandra J.; CHMN., KNOX VICARS MCLEAN INC. (estbd. 1908), since 1953; Dir., Knox Vicars McLean (Ont.) Ltd.; Knox Vicars McLean Agency Inc. (Ohio); Inscon Consultants Ltd.; began with the Royal — Liverpool Group of Ins. Co's at Candn. H.O., Montreal 1933; joined present Interests 1938 and apptd. Vice-Pres. and Dir., 1951; joined N.P.A.M., The Black Watch (RHR) of Can., 1934 with rank of Lieut.; served in 2nd World War with 1st Bn. of this Unit, 1939-45 in U.K., and on General Staff, N.W. Europe; Dir., Staff, Staff Coll., Camberley; awarded M.B.E.; 1946-53, The Black Watch (Militia) retired Lieut. — Col. Commanding; 1960-65 Col. of the Regt., mem., Ins. Brokers Assn. of Que.; Reg. Ins. Brokers of Ont.; Life Underwriters Assn.; Ins. Inst. of Can; Montreal Bd. of Trade; Candn. Chamber Comm.; Candn. Red Cross Soc., Que Div. (Hon. Vice-Pres., Trustee, Audit Board and Past Pres.); St. Andrews Soc. of Montreal (Past Pres.); Fellow, Royal Commonwealth Soc.; Gov., Douglas Hosp.; Montreal Gen. Hosp.; Royal Victoria Hospital; Presbyterian (Elder and Former Trustee); recreations: yachting; music; amateur radio (VE3AAP and J3AAP); Clubs: St. James's; Royal St. Lawrence Yacht; Great Lakes Cruising; Canadian Power Squadrons; Canadian Legion; The Pistol of Montreal; The Highland Montreal, Kingston and Granada, W.I., Amateur Radio Brigade; St. Lawrence Cruising Assn.; Home: 165 Ontario St., Kingston, Ont. K7L 2Y6; Office: Suite 800, Place Université, 1255 University, Montreal, Que. H3B 3W3

KNOX, Olive Elsie; author; b. Fort Stewart, Ont.; d. Rev. George David and Elsie Anne (Le Beau) Robinson; e. Univ. of Man., Grad. 1931; B.Ed. 1961; m. Harold C. Knox, 25 Dec. 1924; has one d. Eileen Joy and 2 grandsons Jeff and Jay Davis; 2 yrs. in Germany; 7 yrs. of teaching, 1957-66 (Churchill High Sch. 1959-66); author of "By Paddle and Saddle", 1943, 2nd ed. 1945, 3rd ed. 1946; "Red River Shadows", 1948; "Little Giant", 1951-52; "Black Falcon", 1954; "Young Surveyor", 1956; "Mrs. Minister", 1956; "John Black of Old Kildonan" (biog. novel), 1958; also publ. six Macmillan radio plays 1945;

short stories in Am., Candn. mags.; CBC radio plays, "Science on the March" series; has given radio addresses; mem., Candn. Authors' Assn.; Manitoba Hist. Soc.; United Church; Address: 1705 — 55 Nassau, Winnipeg. Man. R3L 2G8

KNOX, William Alexander; actor; author; a collat. descendant of John Knox, celebrated Scot. Divine, and David Livingstone, Explorer; b. Strathroy, Ont., 16 Jan. 1907; s. Rev. William John (M.A.); Min., First Presb. Ch., London, Ont.) and Jean (Crozier) K.; e. Pub. and High Schs., London, Ont.; Univ. of Western Ont.; played repertoire in Boston for two and a half yrs.; played in Edgar Wallace's plays in London, "On the Spot" and "The Smokey Cell"; gave up the stage for four yrs. to write, then returned to play a half — season at The Old Vic.; among his prof. appearances after his return to the stage in 1937 were, Bernard Shaw's "Geneva"; Benn Levy's play, "The Jealous God"; James Bridle's "King of Nowhere", and "Babes in the Wood", all in London; in N.Y. played in Cronin's "Jupiter Laughs" and the Theatre Guild's production of "Somewhere in France"; "Jason"; "Three Sisters"; film engagements include "The Ringer" and "The Sea Wolf"; "Wilson"; "Over 21"; "Sister Kenny"; "Indian Summer"; author of "The Bride of Quietness"; "Old Master" (play produced at Malvern Festival, 1929); "The Closing Door" (melodrama), 1949; collab. on screen play of "Sister Kenny" and "Indian Summer"; has contrib. to "Christian Science Monitor", New York "Times", Boston "Post", London "Times Literary Supplement", "Willison's Monthly", "Saturday Night" and "Hollywood Quarterly"; his portrait painted by Elizabeth Montgomery, Dame Laura Knight; recreations: chess, tennis, fishing; Address: c/o L. J. Deak, 170 S. Beverly Dr., Beverly Hills, Cal.

KNUDSEN,Conrad Calvert, B.A., LL.B.; executive; b. Tacoma, Wash. 3 Oct. 1923; s. Conrad and Annabelle (Callison) K.; e. Univ. of Wash. B.A. 1948, LL.B. 1950; Columbia Univ. Fellow in Law 1951; m. Julia Lee d. David Morgan Roderick 22 Nov. 1950; children: Calvert Jr., Elizabeth Page, Colin Roderick, David Callison; CHRMN., CEO AND DIR., MacMILLAN BLOEDEL LTD. 1976- ; Dir. Cascade Corp.; Castle & Cooke Inc.; Koninklijke Nederlandsche Papierfabrieken N.V.; Rainier Bank/Rainier Bancorp.; Termicold Corp.; Safeco Corp.; Celupal, S.A.; West Fraser Timber Co. Ltd.; called to Bar of Wash. 1950; Assoc. and Partner, Bogle, Bogle & Gates, Seattle 1951-61; Extve. Vice Pres. and Dir., Aberdeen Plywood & Veneer Inc., Aberdeen, Ore. 1961-63; Pres. and Chief Adm. Offr., Vice Chrmn., Evans Products Co., Portland, Ore. 1963-68; Sr. Vice Pres. Corporate Growth, Weyerhaeuser Co., Tacoma, Wash. 1969-76; served with U.S. Army 1942-46; mem. Am. and Wash. State Bar Assns.; recreations: tennis, jogging, winery/vineyards, skiing; Clubs: Vancouver; Vancouver Lawn Tennis & Badminton; Terminal City; Men's Canadian; Rainier (Seattle); Seattle Tennis; University (Seattle); Arlington (Portland); Multnomah Athletic (Portland); Racquet (Portland); Home: 1589 Matthews Ave., Vancouver, B.C. V6J 2T1; Office: 1075 West Georgia St., Vancouver, B.C. V6E 3R9.

KNUTSON, Harry L.; financial executive; b. Prince Rupert, B.C. 18 Jan. 1946; e. Simon Fraser Univ. (Econ. & Commerc.); m. Judith Oatman; children: Harry Louis, Todd Murray James; PRESIDENT AND DIR., POCKLINGTON FINANCIAL CORP. LTD.: Dir. Fidelity Trustco; Fidelity Trust; Canadian Realty Investors; Westown Ford Sales Ltd.; joined Aetna Life & Casualty, Hartford, Conn. 1969; Dir. of Pensions & Financial Services, Excelsior Life Insurance Co. 1971; Vice Pres. and Dir. AGF Toronto Investment Management Inc. 1972; Pres. and Trustee Canadian Realty Investors 1975; recreation: hunting; Home: (P.O. Box 22, Site 11) R.R.5, Edmonton, Alta. T5P 4B7;Office: 2500 Sun Life Place, 10123-99 St., Edmonton, Alta. T5J 3H1.

KOCH, Norris Gale, M.Sc.; petroleum geologist; b. Lomond, Alta. 10 Jan. 1934; s. Christian Frederick and Gladys Verneda (Kellogg) K.; e. elem. and high schs. Lomond and Calgary, Alta. 1952; Univ. of Alta. B.Sc. 1956, M.Sc. 1959; m. Joan Carol d. William Edward Ferguson 19 Sept. 1959; children: Daniel Edward, Katherine Joan; EXPLORATION MGR., PETRO-CANADA 1979- ; Sr. Geol. Amoco Canada Petroleum, Calgary and Tulsa 1956-67; Chief Geol. Dome Petroleum, Calgary 1967-77; Sr. Evaluation Geol., Geol. Survey of Can. 1977-79; recipient Mobil Oil Scholarship Geol. 1955; Amoco Can. Fellowship in Geol. 1958; Candn. Soc. Petroleum Geols. Grad. Student Award 1959; author various scient. articles; mem. Candn. Soc. Petroleum Geols. (Treas.; Chrmn. Tech. Program, Membership); Am. Assn. Petroleum Geols.; Assn. Prof. Engrs., Geols. and Geophysicists Alta.; Kappa Sigma; P. Conservative; Unitarian; recreations: hiking, curling, badminton, tennis, gardening; Clubs: Calgary Winter; 400; Home: 4839 Nelson Rd. N.W., Calgary, Alta. T2K 2M1; Office: (P.O. Box 2844) Calgary, Alta. T2P 3E3.

KOCH, Lt. Col. Robert; international executive; b. Luterbach, Switzerland, 17 Feb. 1909; s. Ernest Casper and Emmy (de Vigier) K.; e. Swiss High Sch. of Technol. Zurich; children: Beat, Fernand, Janine, Thomas; Chmn. Vigier Cement Luterbach/Switzerland since 1943; Alamo Cement Co., San Antonio, Texas since 1979; A. Bangerter & Co. Ltd.; Construvit Ltd.; G. Hunziker Ltd.; Franzetti Ltd.; Dir. various internat. co's; Asst. to Mgr. Soc. Anonyme des Ciments Libanais, Chekka, Libanon 1935-36; Tech. Mgr. Soc. Egyptienne des Ciments Portland Tourah, Tourah Le Caire 1936-37; Tech. Mgr. Vigier Cement Luterbach CH 1939-43; Pres. St. Lawrence Cement Co. Montreal 1953-63; Clubs: York (Toronto); Golf & Country (Basel); Home: Wylihof CH — 4708 Luterbach, Switzerland; Que.

KOERNER, Iby (Mrs. Otto), O.C. (1971); b. Budapest, Hungary, 28 July 1899; d. Dr. Eugene Molnar; e. High Sch. and Secretarial Sch.; studied Violin and Singing, Conserv. of Budapest; m. Otto Koerner, Vienna, 30 Oct. 1921; CHMN. AND FOUNDER, VANCOUVER ACADEMY OF MUSIC; came to Can. 1939; naturalized Candn. 1943; served during Second World War with Women's Auxiliary to Seaforth Highlanders; Shaughnessy Mil. Hosp. Red Cross Lodge; Founder, Vancouver Internat. Festival Soc., 1954-69; mem., Sitefinding Comte., Queen Elizabeth Theatre, Vancouver, 1955; Gov., Candn. Nat. Sch. of Theatre, Montreal, since 1962; Trustee, Nat. Gallery of Can., 1963-68; Dir. Conf. of Arts, Toronto, since 1962 (rec'd Diplome d'Honneur, 1962); rec'd Queen's Jubilee Medal; mem., Art Selection Comte., Charlottetown Confed. Mem. Art Gallery, since 1963; Hon. Pres., Vancouver Internat. Film Festival 1963-70; Past Pres., Vancouver Art Gallery Woman's Auxiliary Comte.; (Hon. Vice Pres. of Gallery since 1963); Dir., Community Arts Council since foundation; Dir., Soc. Incorp. for Welfare of Arts, Sciences and Health 1963-69; mem. Adv. Council, Vancouver Opera Assn. 1963; Vancouver Symphony Soc. 1964; Pres., Candn. Handicraft Guild 1966-68, presently Hon. Vice-Pres.; mem., Adv. Comte., Vancouver Art Sch.; Anthropology Museum, U.B.C.; Centennial Museum of Vancouver Dir., Vancouver Alliance Française; former Dir., Jeunesse Musicale, Vancouver; Sustaining mem., Vancouver Chamber Music Assn.; mem., Stratford Festival Soc. Can.; Candn. Opera Guild; mem. of Senate, Simon Fraser Univ. (Convocation Founder 1964) L.L.D., Honoris Causa, 1980; Founder and Chmn. Vancouver Academy of Music, since 1969; mem., Cultural Adv. Committee to the Vancouver Foundation, since 1972; Hon. mem., Faculty Club, Univ. B.C.; Alliance française; Vancouver Chamber Music Assn.; Candn. Opera Assn.; Am. Museum Assn.; Am. Fed. Arts; Metropolitan Museum of Art; Metropolitan Opera Guild; Seattle Art Museum; Victoria Art Gallery; United Church; Clubs: Vancouver Lawn Tennis & Badminton; Patron of

the Arts Club Theatre; Home: 1838 Matthews Ave., Vancouver, B.C. V6J 2T5

KOERNER, Michael Milan, S.B., M.B.A.; executive; b. Prague, Czechoslovakia 26 Aug. 1928; s. Walter Charles and Marianne (Hikl) K.; e. Cheltenham (Eng.) Jr. Sch.; St. George's Sch. Vancouver; King Edward High Sch. 1945; Mass. Inst. of Technol. S.B. 1949; Harvard Grad. Sch. of Business Adm. M.B.A. 1952; m. Sonja d. Enrique Novak, Lima, Peru 18 Dec. 1951; children: Alexandra Maria, Jacqueline Laura, Michelle Diane; PRES., CANADA OVERSEAS INVESTMENTS LTD.; Dir. CAE Industries Ltd.; CUC Ltd.; Canadian Enterprise Development Corp. Ltd.; Commercial Union of Canada Holdings Ltd.; Corod Manufacturing Ltd.; Co-Steel International Ltd.; Finning Tractor & Equipment Co. Ltd.; Helix Investments Ltd.; Huron Chemicals Ltd.; Lake Ontario Steel Co. Ltd.; Pratt & Whitney Aircraft of Canada Ltd.; Scan Marine Inc.; Suncor Inc.; Taurus Fund Ltd.; Dir. Art Gallery Ont.; Vice Chrmn. York Univ.; mem. Assn. Prof. Engrs. Prov. Ont.; Anglican; recreations: music, tennis, squash; Clubs: Badminton & Racquet; National; Granite; Home: 14 Ridgefield Rd., Toronto, Ont. M4N 3H8; Office: (P.O. Box 62) 2901 Royal Bank Plaza, South Tower, Toronto, Ont. M5J 2J2.

KOFFLER, Murray Bernard; C.M., Phm.B., Ph.C., Ph.D. (Hon.); executive; b. Toronto, Ont., 22 Jan. 1924; s. late Leon and Tiana K.; e. Oakwood Coll.; Faculty of Pharm., Univ. of Toronto, Phm.B. 1946; m. Marvelle, d. Irving Seligman; 3 s.: Leon, Tom, Adam; 2 d.: Theo, Tiana; CHAIRMAN KOFFLER STORES LTD., since 1971; Vice Pres. and Dir., Four Seasons Hotels Ltd.; Dir., Can. Devel. Corp. 1976; Imasco, 1978; operates Shoppers Drug Mart and Embassy Cleaners chains; Pharmacist, Koffler Drug Stores (estbd. 1921), Toronto, 1946, later Prop.; Pres., Koffler Stores Ltd., 1968-71; Dir., Toronto Symphony until 1978; Dir., Mt. Sinai Hosp.; Candn. Jewish News; Candn. Council of Christians and Jews; Un. Jewish Welfare Fund; World Wildlife Fund; Jerusalem Found.; Hon. Chrm., Toronto Outdoor Art Show; Gov., Massey Hall; Olympic Trust; Weizmann Inst. of Science; Chrmn., Candn. Soc. for Weizmann Inst. of Science; Hon. Chrmn. and Dir., Council on Drug Abuse; Pres., Jokers Hill Horse Trials; Patron, Lester B. Pearson Coll. of Pacific; mem., Bd. of Trade of Metrop. Toronto; Candn., Ont. and Rokeah Pharm. Assns.; Candn. Found. for Advancement of Pharm.; Candn. Hotel Assn.; Candn. Equestrian Team; mem. Order of Can. 1977; Pi Lambda Phi; Rho Pi Phi; recreations: skiing; sailing; golf; tennis; Clubs: Canadian; Empire; Toronto & North York Hunt; Craigleith Ski; York Tennis; Homes: 23 Beechwood Ave., Willowdale, Ont. M2L 1J2; Jokers Hill, R.R. No. 3, King, Ont. L0G 1K0; Office: 225 Yorkland Blvd., Willowdale, Ont. M2J 4Y7

KOFFMAN, Moe (Morris): musician; b. Toronto, Ont. 28 Dec. 1928; e. began studying violin at 9 and alto saxaphone at 13; Toronto Conserv. of Music clarinet, theory; studied with Gordon Delamont during 1940's and during 1950's in New York with Harold Bennett (flute) and Leon Russianoff (clarinet); winner CBC "Jazz Unlimited" poll as best alto saxophonist 1948; made first recording in Buffalo 1948; moved to USA 1950 playing in big bands of Sonny Dunham, Jimmy Dorsey and others; returned to Toronto 1955 dividing career between his jazz group and studio work; first Toronto appearance at House of Hambourg; became booking agent George's Spaghetti House 1956, remaining in this capacity over 20 years, also appears there monthly with own band; recording of "Swinging Shepherd Blues" brought Candn. and US recognition as flutist (1958); appearances in mid 1960's incl. NBC TV "Tonight Show"; became member and featured soloist Boss Brass in 1972 and has played in Candn. orchestras led by Benny Goodman, Woody Herman and Quincy Jones at Candn. Nat. Exhn; recordings during 1970's include arrangements of music by various classical composers Bach, Berlioz, Debussy, Gluck, Grieg, Mozart, Vivaldi; also recorded "Solar Explorations", led own big band as music dir. Global TV "Everything Goes" 1974; recorded "Live at George's" 1975, "Musuem Pieces" 1977, tours Canada regularly; performed at many festivals including Expo 67, Shaw Festival 1975, CBC festival series W. Can. 1978, Ontario Place Jazz Festival 1979 and 80; various appearances with symphony orchestras incl. Toronto, Hamilton, Sudbury, London, Kitchener/Waterloo 1975-81; performed Lewiston, N.Y. (Artpark) and Monterey Jazz Festival 1979; Bracknell Festival, London, England, Montreux Jazz Festival, UCLA, toured Australia, and gave special concerts for Her Majesty Queen Elizabeth II, and for Chancellor of West Germany at request of Canadian Prime Minister's Office 1981; Montreux Jazz Festival, Chamber Music with Orford String Quartet 1981; soloist many pop recordings and has played in various jazz-oriented TV orchestras; winner of the 1981 Harold H. Moon award for outstanding contribution to Canadian music; affiliate PRO Canada; Address: c/o 471 Queen Street East, Toronto, Canada M5A 1T9.

KOLBER, Ernest Leo, B.A., B.C.L.; financier; b. Montreal, Que., 18 Jan. 1929; s. late Moses and Luba (Kahan) K.; (now Mrs. P. Lassar); e. Westhill (Que.) High Sch.; McGill Univ., B.A. 1949, B.C.L. 1952; m. Sandra, d. Haim Maizel, Montreal, Que., 8 Sept. 1957; children: Marna Lynne, Jonathan; PRESIDENT, CEMP INVESTMENTS LTD., since 1971; Vice-Chrmn. and Chrm. of Investment Committee, The Cadillac Fairview Corp. Ltd.; Dir., Bow Valley Industries Ltd.; Pres. and Dir., Toronto-Dominion Centre Ltd.; Claridge Investments Ltd.; Dir., Super-Sol Ltd.; The Seagram Company Ltd.; Warrington Products Limited; The Toronto-Dominion Bank; Pacific Centre Ltd.; read law with Mendelsohn, Rosentzveig, Shacter & Taviss; called to Bar of Que. 1952; Dir., Montreal Baseball Club; Royal Victoria Hosp.; Gov., Y.M. — Y.W.H.A. of Montreal; United Talmud Torahs; Jewish Hosp. of Hope; Hebrew Free Loan Association; Jewish General Hospital; mem., Shaar Hashomayim Synagogue; Hebrew; recreation: golf; Clubs: Montefiore; Elm Ridge Golf & Country; Mount Royal; Mount Royal Tennis; Palm Beach Country; Home: Summit Circle, Westmount, Que.; Office: 630 Dorchester Blvd. W., 32nd Floor, Montreal, Que. H3B 1X5

KOLISNYK, Peter, R.C.A.; artist; b. Toronto, Ont., 30 Nov. 1934; s. Fred and Mary (Koszlok) K.; e. Western Tech. and Comm. Sch.; m. Anne Bernadette, d. T. B. Buckley, Mimico, Ont., 20 June 1960; children: Peter, Beth; Curator, Cobourg Art Gallery, 1964-69; teaching assignments: Elliott Lake Centre for Continuing Educ.; McMaster Univ.; Rothman Art Gallery, Stratford, Ont.; Brock Univ.; Trent Univ.; Ont. Dept. Educ. Community Programmes; Glendon Coll., York Univ.; Whitby Art Gallery; exhns. incl.: Montreal Museum of Fine Art's Spring Shows; Royal Candn. Acad.; Ont. Soc. Artists; Candn. Soc. Painters Watercolour; Nat. Gallery IV Candn. Biennial; 1st Winnipeg Biennial; St. Catharines Spring Shows — Rodman Hall; Art Inst., Centennial Travelling Exhn.; Jerrold Morris Gallery, 1967; Hart House, Univ. of Toronto. 1961; Albright Knox Museum, 1968; "A Plastic Presence", Jewish Museum, N.Y., Milwaukee Art Centre, San Francisco Museum of Art, 1969; "3D into the 70's", Art Gallery Ont.; "Transparent and Translucent Art", St. Petersburg Museum Fine Arts and Jacksonville Art Museum, Fla. 1971; "49th Parallels — New Canadian Art", Museum Contemp. Art, Chicago, Ill. 1971; Jeunesses Musicales du Canada, Orford Arts Centre 1971; Ont. Soc. Artists — 100 Years 1872-1972; "5 Candn. Artists" Ukrainian Inst. Modern Art 1972; "Plastic Fantastic" London Art Gallery 1972; Kitchener-Waterloo Art Gallery, Hamilton Art Gallery, Art Gallery Ont., 1975-76; Harbour Front Gallery, Toronto, The Gallery, Stratford, Cobourg Art Gallery, Whitby Art Gallery, Quinte Arts Council, Belleville, Queen's Silver Jubilee Exhn., Toronto, 1977; 50 years — The Canadian Society

of Painters in Watercolour; Ontario Now — A Survey of Contemporary Art, Art Gallery of Hamilton; Limits, Lines, Prosections — The Gallery Stratford; Rehearsal, An Exhibition of Sculpture — Harbourfront Gallery, 1977; The Winnipeg Perspective — The Winnipeg Art Gallery; 4 Sculptors — The Ukrainian Inst. of Modern Art; Performance, An Exhibition of Sculpture — The Harbourfront Art Gallery, Toronto; Monmumental Sculpture — Tor. Dominion Centre; Sculpture Out of Doors — Agnes Etherington Art Centre, 1978; Ails by Artists — Harbourfront Gallery — Tor., 1979; Art Toronto '80 — Outdoor Sculpture on the Waterfront, 1980; Group Exhibitions: — Down Under —, Harbour Front Gallery, 1981; First Purchase Art Gallery at Harbourfront, 1981; — The Constructivist Heritage —, Art Gallery at Harbourfront, 1981; — White Snow —, Harbourfront Gallery, 1981; one-man exhns. incl.: Pollock Gallery, Toronto, 1965, 1968, 1969, 1970; York Univ. Glendon Coll. 1970; "Inventory", Robert McLaughlin Gallery, Oshawa; Art Gallery of Brantford 1973; Ukrainian Inst. Modern Art, Chicago 1975; "Artist with his Work", Art Gallery Ont., Univ. of Toronto 1975; "Peter Kolisnyk", Art Gallery Ont., Art Gallery of Windsor, Sir George Williams Galleries, Dalhousie Art Gallery, 1977; Alta. Coll. Art Gallery, Artists with their works circ. by Art Gallery of Ont., Art Gallery of Lindsay, 1980; "Peter Kolisnyk Drawings", The Gallery Stratford; Glendon Gallery, York Univ.; MacIntosh Gallery, Univ. of Western Ont.; The Nickle Arts Museum, Univ. of Calgary; Ukrainian Inst. of Modern Art, Chicago; incl. in perm. colls. of Art Gallery Ont., Cobourg Art Gallery; Robert McLaughlin Gallery; Can. Council — Art Bank; Ont. Council for the Arts Centennial Collection; Queen's Silver Jubilee Art Collection; Ukrainian Inst. Modern Art, Chicago; rep. in private collections in Canada, U.S.A. and Eng., The Winnipeg Art Gallery and The Gallery Stratford; Agnes Etherington Gallery, Queen's Univ.; theatre design for: "Fortune and Men's Eyes", Kingston; "Creeps", Toronto; "The Odd Couple", Cobourg; "Branch Plant", Toronto; rec'd C.S.P.W. Watercolour Award 1962; Candn. Artists '68 Sculpture Award; Ont. Soc. Artists Sculpture Award; Canada Council Senior Arts Grant, 1975-76; Province of Ont. Council for the Arts Grant. 1975-77 and 78-79; Appt. Qcquisition Comte. of the Art Gallery of Ont. for the Purchase of Contemporary Art; Art Advisor to the Prison Arts Fdn. 1979-80; mem., Ont. Soc. Artists; Roy. Candn. Acad. Arts; C.A.R.O.; Candn. Soc. Painters Watercolour; Home and Studio: 247 King St. E., Box 971, Cobourg, Ont. K9A 1L7

KONG, Shiu Loon, C.M., B.A., M.Ed., Ph.D., LL.D.; psychologist, educator; b. Hong Kong 1 May 1934; s. Shiu-Ying and (Cheung) Yuk Kong; e. Wah Yan Coll. Hong Kong Dipl. 1953; Hua Kiu Univ. B.A. 1958; Univ. of Ottawa M.Ed. 1959, Ph.D. 1961; m. Maggie Yuk Ping Chan d. Chan See 19 Sept. 1959; children: Lana Ann, Raymond Tao, Norman Holt; PROF. OF EDUC., UNIV. OF TORONTO since 1976; Assoc. Prof. Nanyang Univ. Singapore 1961; Tutor, Queen's Univ. 1961-62; Asst. Prof. Brandon Univ. 1962-64; Dir. Research Dept. North York Bd. Educ. 1964-67; Assoc. Prof. Univ. of Toronto 1967-72; Dean and Chair Prof. Sch. of Educ., The Chinese Univ. of Hong Kong 1972-75; Bd. Chrmn., York Herbart Sch. Toronto; Pres., Toronto Chinese Community Services Assn.; Multiheritage Community Alliance of Toronto; author "Learning from Teaching" 1957; "Summer Sixteen" 1958; "Humanistic Psychology and Personalized Teaching" 1970; "Cognitive Processes Applied to Education" 1973; "An English-Chinese Glossary of Social Sciences and Education" 1975; "The Foundation of Modern Mathematics" 1975, 2nd ed. 1979; "Psychological Considerations in Personalized Teaching" 1979; co-ed. "Unity Within Diversity" 1978; "The Development of American Seconday and Higher Education" 1980; Pres., Comparative and Internat. Educ. Soc. Can.; mem. Candn. Soc. Studies in Educ.; Candn. Univ. Teachers' Assn.; Am. Educ. Research Assn.; Internat. Assn. Applied Psychol.; Internat. Assn. Advanc. Educ. Research; Internat. Council Educ. for Teaching; Phi Delta Kappa; recreations: painting, swimming, music appreciation; Home: 50 Larkfield Dr., Don Mills, Ont. M3B 2H1; Office: Toronto, Ont.

KORCHINSKI, Stanley, M.P.; farmer; b. Rama, Sask., 29 Jan. 1929; s. Joseph and Doris (Doroshenko) K.; e. Pub. and High Schs., Sask., 1935-47; Univ. of Sask. (Arts) 1947-48; m. Marcella Ron; four children; Dir., local Petroleum Co-op.; Pres., local Wheat Pool Organ.; served on Canora Union Hospital Bd.; Secy. — Treas. Village of Rama, 1951-58; Reeve, Mun. of Invermay, Sask., 1952-58; el. to H. of C. for Mackenzie since 1958; re-el. since; Del. C.P.A. to Poland 1966, to I.P.U. Meeting, New Delhi 1969; K. of C.; P. Conservative; Roman Catholic; Home: Rama, Sask.

KOREY-KRZECZOWSKI, George, D.Sc.Econ., LL.M., LL.D., C.M.C., F.R.E.S.; college administrator; b. Kielce, Poland, 13 July 1921; s. Antoni — Marian Kniaz, Judge of the Castle Court and Zofia Emilia Wanda (Chmielewska) Korczak — Krzeczowski; e. State High Sch. and State Coll., Kielce, Poland; Dept. of Law and Adm., Jagellonian Univ., Cracow, Poland, LL.M. 1945; Post Grad. studies at Acad. of Pol. and Social Science, Warsaw, Poland; Dept. of Internat. Law, Univ. of Bucharest, Rumania; Inst. of Internat. Law, and Dept. of Law and Pol. Science, Univ. of Fribourg, W. Germany, LL.D. 1949; Dept. of Econ. Science, Univ. of Tuebingen, W. Germany, D.Sc. (Econ.) 1950; grad. Inst. of Educat. Mgmt., Harvard Univ. 1975; m. Irene Marie, d. Wladyslaw Latacz, 15 July 1944; one s. Andrew George; PRES., CANDN. SCH. OF MANAGEMENT AND NORTHLAND OPEN UNIVERSITY; mem. Bd. of Trustees, Union Grad. Sch. (Cincinnati, Ohio) and Pres., Univ. Without Walls Internat. Council; formerly Exec. Vice Pres. and Dean of Business, Ryerson Polytechnical Inst., 1971-77; former Chrmn., Ont. Adv. Council on Multiculturalism; Vice-Pres. and Dir. York — Ryerson Computing Centre; President Ryerson Applied Research Limited; President; Korey International Ltd., Toronto; Director, Canadian Operations, Canadian Textile Consultants Ltd.; Dir., Werner Management Consultants (Canada) Ltd.; Div. Mgr., Werner Assoc., Inc.; Dir., Indust. & Econ. Devel. Div. Mang. Consultants Inc. (N.Y.); Dir. of Dept. Min. of Culture and Arts, Poland, 1945; Vice-Pres., Council of Arts and Sciences, Kielce, Poland, 1945; Press Attaché, Polish Embassy, Bucharest, Rumania; Vice-Consul of Poland; Cultural Counsellor of Embassy, 1946; also Dir. and Prof. of Polish Inst.; Bucharest and Consul of Poland in Bucharest, Rumania; Econ. Adv. of Embassy; Counsellor, Min. of Foreign Affairs, Warsaw, Poland, 1947; Consul of Poland in Berlin, Germany; Consul of Poland in Baden — Baden, W. Germany, 1948-50; Head of Econ. and Restitution Mission, 1949-50; in these capacities often took part in internat. negotiations; resigned diplomatic career for pol. reasons and came to Can. 1951; Assistant Supervisor, Indust. Engn. Dept and Contract Estimating Dept. Canadair Ltd.; Asst. Mang. Dir. and Controller, Damar Products of Canada Ltd., and Around — the — World Shoppers Club (Canada) Ltd.; Vice-Pres. and Mang. Dir., Schlemm Assoc. Ltd., Mang. Consultant on own account; Pres., Pan-American Mang. Ltd.; apptd. Dean of Business and Vice-President, Ryerson Polytech. Inst. 1971, Extve. Vice-Pres. and Dean, External Programmes 1973-77; Acting President 1974; Publications: "Siedemnasta Wiosna", 1938; "Rytm Serca"; 1938; "Goloborze", 1939; "Pamietnik Poetycki", 1939; "Internationale Rechtsverhaeltnisse Polens Im Gebiete des Strafrechts", 1949; "Plannung in der Polnischen Landwirtschaft", 1950; "Liryki Nostalgiczne", 1974; Lunch Sodomie", 1976; "Korey's Stubborn Thoughts", 1980; "New Role for the Cdn. Economy in the Age of World Food Shortage", 1975; "Attitudes in the Business and Health Care sectors towards Nontraditional Management Education" 1980; "University Without Walls" 1981;

numerous articles on mang., econ. planning, internat. affairs, foreign markets, and marketing; publ. a series on European Common Market and Canada's Econ. Policies in "Industrial Canada" and "Canadian Textile Journal", a market mang. series in "Marketing", mang. consulting series in "Canadian Textile Journal"; Guest Lectr. on radio and T.V. talks and interviews; has had mang. consulting experience on over 50 countries in many types of industries; Fellow, Roy. Econ. Soc.; Acad. Marketing Sc. (U.S.A.); Knight -Commander of Justice, Sovereign Order of St. John of Jerusalem; Knight, Military Constantinian Order of St. George; Knight-Commander, Sovereign Order of Cyprus; Kt. Grand Cross, Military Order of St. Agatha di Paterno; decorated with the Cross of Polish Home Army (1939-45), awarded Polish Military Medal for W.W.II; Queen's Jubilee Medal; mem. Inst. Mang. Consultants Que. and Ont.; Fellow N.Y. Acad. Sc.; Fellow, Royal Society of Arts; Pres. & Fellow, Can. Inter. Acad. of Humanities and Social Sc.; Am. Mang. Assn.; Acad. of Mang. U.S.A.; Inter — Am. Research Inst.; Acad. Internat. Business; Candn. Council for Internat. Co-op (Dir.); Candn. Inst. Public Affairs; European Foundation Mang. Devel.; Internat. Inventors Assn.; Polish Institute (U.K.); Candn. Assn. Univ. Business Offrs. and mem. several other assns. and comtes.; Pres. (1966) Nat. Council, Candn. Polish Cong.; mem., World Council of Poles (1978-81); Hon. Citizen, City of Winnipeg; Roman Catholic; recreations: swimming, skiing; Home: 55 Tanbark Cres., Don Mills, Ont. M3B 1N7; Office: S-425, 252 Bloor St. W., Toronto, Ont. M5S 1V5

KORTHALS, Robert W., B.Sc., M.B.A.; banker; b. 7 June 1933; e. Univ. of Toronto B.Sc. (Chem. Engn.) 1955; Harvard Business Sch. M.B.A. 1961; PRES., TORONTO DOMINION BANK since 1981; Chrmn. TD Realty Investments Ltd.; Vice Pres. and Dir. Tordom Corp.; TDRI Ltd.; Dir. Toronto Dominion Leasing Ltd.; Co-Steel International Ltd.; Talcorp Associates Ltd.; Supt. Term Financing Internat. Div. of Bank 1967, Supt. Nat. Accts. Div. 1968, Asst. Gen. Mgr. of Nat. Accts. Div. 1969, Gen. Mgr. of Nat. Accts. Div. 1972, Vice Pres. Adm. 1972, Sr. Vice Pres. 1976; Gov. Central Hosp. Toronto; mem., Ont. Economic Council; Office: (P.O. Box 1) Toronto-Dominion Centre, Toronto, Ont. M5K 1A2.

KOSKIE, Hon. Murray James, M.L.A., B.Ed., LL.B.; politician; b. 5 Nov. 1929; s. Frank and Mary K.; e. Humboldt Coll.; Univ. of Sask.; m. Shirley Ann 24 June 1961; children: Maury, Douglas, Lisa; MINISTER OF CONSUMER AND COMMERCIAL AFFAIRS SASK. 1980- ; Min. of Social Services, 1979-80; el. M.L.A. for Quill Lakes prov. g.e. 1975, re-el. 1978; Del. Interprov. visit Commonwealth Parlty. Assn. Fredericton 1976; NDP.; R. Catholic; Office: 315 Legislative Bldg., Regina, Sask. S4S 0B3.

KOSTUIK, John, B.Sc.; mining executive; b. Poland, 4 July 1911 (came to Can. with parents same yr.); e. Primary and Sec. Schs., Cobalt, Ont.; Queen's Univ., B.Sc. 1934; Post-Grad. 1935, Mine Ventilation and Silicosis; m. Anne; children: John P., M.D.; Paul S., B.Sc., M.Sc., David E., B.Sc., M.Sc., MBA, Margaret Rose, B.A., DIR.AND CONSULTANT, DENISON MINES LTD.; Dir., Joy Manufacturing Co.; Denison Mines Ltd.; Roman Corpn. Ltd.; Northgate Exploration Ltd.; Rayrock Mines Ltd.; prior to grad., spent five summers with O'Brien Mines in Ont. and Que., two summers at Hollinger; spent eighteen yrs. after grad. in N.W. Ont and Que. as Mine Supt. and Mgr. for various mining co's; almost four yrs. Tech. Advisor to French Co., Morocco — Algeria for Newmont Mining Corpn. in a lead — zinc mining and smelting complex; returned to Can. 1955 to join present Co.; Past Chrmn. The Uranium Inst.; Dir. and Past Pres., Mining Assn. of Can.; mem., Ontario Mining Association (Past Pres.); Candn. Institute of Mining and Metall.; Am. Inst. Mining Engrs.; Roman Catholic; recreations: golf, fishing; Clubs: National; Engineers; York Downs

Golf; Home: 14 Briancliff Drive, Don Mills, Ont. M3B 2G2; Office: P.O. Box 40, Royal Bank Plaza, Toronto, Ont. M5J 2K2

KOSTYNIUK, Ronald P., M.S., M.F.A., R.C.A.; artist; educator; b. Wakaw, Sask. 8 July 1941; s. George and Ann (Shutter) K.; e. Univ. of Sask. B.A. (Biol.) 1963, B.Ed. 1963; Univ. of Alta. B.F.A. 1969; Univ. of Wis. (Fellowship) M.S. 1970, M.F.A. 1971; m. Jeanette d. Jack Pellizzari 1963; one s. Christopher; ASSOC. PROF. OF ART, UNIV. OF CALGARY 1978- , Chrmn. of Div. of Design 1971-76; Co-ordinator of Graduate Studies, Dept. of Art 1976- ; Teacher of Biol. Brandon, Man. and Edmonton High Schs. 1963-68; joined Univ. of Calgary Art Dept. 1971; solo exhns, incl. Brandon Allied Arts Centre 1965 and Univ. 1966; Edmonton Art Gallery 1969; Bradley Gallery Milwaukee 1970; Univ. of Man. 1971, 1979; Univ. Alta. 1971; Mendel Art Gallery Saskatoon 1971; Univ. of Calgary 1972, 1978; Glenbow Art Foundation Calgary 1972; York Univ. Toronto 1973; Beaverbrook Art Gallery Fredericton 1973; Dalhousie Univ. 1973; Mem. Univ. of Nfld. 1973; Inst. Modern Art Chicago 1973; Gallery Oseredok Winnipeg 1974; Sarnia Art Gallery 1974; Univ. of Moncton 1974; Mt. St. Vincent Univ. 1975; rep. numerous group exhns. incl. 7th Biennial of Candn. Painting Nat. Gallery Can. 1968; Museum of Contemporary Art Chicago and Herron Museum Indianapolis 1969; 5 Candn. Artists Inst. Modern Art Chicago 1972 and Evanston Art Centre (Ill.); Alta. Art Japan tour 1979; Evolution of Constructed Relief 1913-1979 W. Can. tour 1979-80; Harbourfront Art Gallery, Toronto 1981; rep. various pub., corporate and private colls. incl. Alta. Govt. Art Foundation, Can. Council Art Bank; participant various radio and TV programs; Visiting Artist, Univ. of Man. 1970, 1979; Visiting Speaker, Mendel Art Gallery Saskatoon 1980; Univ. of Alta. 1980; recipient numerous awards incl. Alta. Govt. Visual Arts Grant 1968, Culture Project Grant 1978, 1979; Winnipeg Biannual Prize 1968; Can. Council Art Bursary 1969, Grants 1975, 1976, 1978, 1979, 1980; Univ. of Calgary Research Grant 1976-77; External Affairs Foreign Exchange Scholar Can.-USSR 1978; Killam Resident Fellowship Univ. Calgary 1979; Lipschultz Foundation for the Arts Grant 1979; Univ. of Calgary Special Projects Grant 1979, 1981; subject numerous bibliogs.; author various publs. including "The Evolution of the Constructed Relief" 1913-1979; mem. Candn. Assn. Univ. Teachers; Univ. Art Assn. Can.; Coll. Art Assn. Am.; Alta. Soc. Artists; Home: 4907 Viceroy Dr., Calgary, Alta. T3A 0V2; Office: Calgary Alta. T2N 1N4.

KOTAITE, Assad, Docteur en Droit (Paris); barrister; b. Hasbaya, Lebanon, 6 Nov. 1924; s. Adib and Kamlé Abou (Samra) K.; e. French Univ. of Beirut, law grad. 1948; Univ. of Paris, Docteur en Droit 1952, Inst. des hautes études internat.; Acad. of Internat. Law, The Hague; PRES. OF COUNCIL, INTERNAT. CIVIL AVIATION ORGAN., since 1976; Secy. Gen. 1970-76; barrister at law Beirut 1948-49; Chief, Legal Services, Ministry of Pub. Works, Lebanon, 1953-56; Rep. of Lebanon on Council of present organ. 1956-70; Home: 1455 Sherbrooke St. W., Apt. 2207, Montreal, Que. H3G 1L2; Office: 1000 Sherbrooke St. W., Montreal, Que. H3A 2R2

KOTCHEFF, William Theodore, (Ted); director; b. Toronto, Ont. 1931; joined CBC 1952-57; ABC TV London 1957; dir. plays incl. "Of Mice and Men", "Desparate Hours", "Progress in the Park", "Luv", "Maggie May"; dir. films incl. "Life at the Top" 1965; "Two Gentleman Sharing" 1970; "Outback" 1971; "Billy Two Hats" 1973; "The Apprenticeship of Duddy Kravits" 1974; "Fun with Dick and Jane" 1977; "Who is Killing the Great Chefs of Europe" 1978; dir., writer film "North Dallas Forty" 1979; Office: c/o International Creative Management, 8899 Beverly Blvd., Hollywood, Calif. 90048.

KOUWENHOVEN, Simon; banker; b. Delft, The Netherlands 24 Oct. 1932; e. School of Commerce, The Nether-

lands; m. Martha 6 Sept. 1955; children: Wendy, Stephen John, Joanne D., Franciska A.; SR. VICE PRÉS. ALTA. DIV., BANK OF MONTREAL: Fellow, Institute of Candn. Bankers; Home: 531 - Willow Brook Drive S.E., Calgary, Alta. T2J 1N6; Office: (P.O. Box 850) Calgary, Alta. T2P 2N1

KOVITZ, Muriel, C. M. (1977); LL.D.; b. Calgary, Alta. 20 Feb. 1926; d. Norman and Ethel Rose (Shapiro) Libin; e. Calgary pub. and high schs.; Univ. of Toronto 1944-45; London Royal Schs. of Music LRSM 1944; m. David M. Kovitz 2 Aug. 1945; children: Jeffrey Wayne, Ronald Stephen, Ethel Rose; Chancellor (Emeritus), Univ. of Calgary, 1978- ; Chancellor, Univ. of Calgary 1974-78; Chrmn. Senate Extve. Comte. and Senate, mem. Extve. Comte. Bd. of Govs. there; Dir. Centennial Packers of Canada Ltd.; Imperial Oil Ltd.; Alberta Investments Ltd.; The Reader's Digest Ass. (Can.) Ltd.; Inst. of Donations and Publics Affairs Research; mem. Extve. Bd. Dirs. Candn. Council Christians and Jews (W. Region); Co-Chrmn. 3rd Internat. Banff Conf. on Man and His Environment 1978; mem. Fed. Govt. Task Force on Candn. Unity; Pres. Calgary Sec. Nat. Council Jewish Women of Can. 1959-61 (Nat. Extve. Comte. 1961-73, Nat. Program Chrmn. 1963-67, Nat. Chrmn. Sch. for Citizen Participation 1967-73); mem. City Calgary Recreation Bd. 1966-69; Pres. Calgary Social Planning Council 1967-69; mem. Bd. Vocational & Rehabilitation Research Inst. Calgary 1968-69; Calgary Housing Authority 1968-72; participant various nat. confs. and seminars 1959-73; el. to Senate Univ. of Calgary 1970, apptd. to Bd. of Govs. 1972, served on various univ. comtes.; Dir. Calgary and Dist. Foundation; mem. Alta. Rhodes Scholarship Selection Comte. 1976; received Alberta Achievement Award Oct. 1977; Clubs: Canyon Meadows Golf & Country; Glenmore Racquet; Home: 4708 Britannia Dr. S.W., Calgary, Alta. T2S 1J7

KOVRIG, Bennett, M.A., Ph.D.; educator; b. Budapest, Hungary 8 Sept. 1940; s. John and Clara Radoczi Mattyok K.; e. Jarvis Coll. Inst. Toronto 1958; Univ. Coll. London 1959-60; Univ. of Toronto B.A. 1962, M.A. 1963; London Sch. of Econ. & Pol. Science Ph.D. (Internat. Relations) 1967; m. Marina d. Joseph Kuchar, . Mont Tremblant, Que. 10June 1967; children: Michael John, Ariana Julia; PROF. OF POL. SCIENCE 1974- AND CHRMN. OF POL. ECON. 1979- UNIV. OF TORONTO; Dir. Recochem Inc.; Group Relations, Candn. Corp. 1967 World Exposition, Montreal 1966-67; Asst. Prof. Queen's Univ. 1967-68; Asst. Prof. of Pol. Science present Univ. 1968, Assoc. Prof. 1970-74, mem. Governing Council 1975-78, cross-appt. Trinity Coll. 1975; Dir., Candn. Scene; St. Lawrence Centre Productions; author "The Hungarian People's Republic" 1970; "The Myth of Liberation: East-Central Europe in U.S. Diplomacy and Politics Since 1941" 1973; "Communism in Hungary from Kun to Kadar" 1979; numerous articles East-West relations, E. European politics and hist.; mem. Candn. Pol. Science Assn.; Candn. Inst. Internat. Affairs; Home: 48 Wilgar Rd., Toronto, Ont. M8X 1J5; Office: Toronto, Ont. M5S 1A1.

KOYL, Donald H., A.A.C.I., F.R.I., C.R.E.; Realtor; appraiser; b. Saskatoon, Sask., 27 Dec. 1918; s. late Arthur Leon and Josephine Elizabeth (Eckstein) K.; m. Doris, d. late A. P. Moodycliffe, 27 Sept. 1941; children: Donald Gavin, Mary Lee Morrow; CHRMN. OF THE BD. AND DIR., KOYL AGENCIES LTD. (Estbd. 1909); Pres., Home Properties Ltd.; Koyl Brunsdon Appraisals Ltd.; Dir., Standard Trust Company; joined present Co. in 1937, rejoining in present position 1945; served in 2nd World War, R.C.A.F. as Pilot in 1940; discharged 1945 with rank of Sqdn. Leader; Founding Treas., Saskatoon Auditorium Foundation; Founding Pres. Saskatoon Gallery Corporation (Mendel Gallery); served 20 years as member and Chrmn., Assessment Bd., City of Saskatoon; Alderman, City of Saskatoon, 1962-64, 1967-73; Past Pres. and Life

Mem., Candn. (Real Estate) Assn. (1959); Pres. and Life Mem., Saskatoon Real Estate Bd., 1950-51; Past Pres. and Fellow, Real Estate Inst. Can. 1962; Exchange Dir., Nat. Association of Real Estate Bds. (U.S.A.) 1959; mem. Am. Soc. Real Estate Counselors; United Church; Clubs: The Saskatoon; Riverside Country; Home: 1333 Temperance St., Saskatoon, Sask. S7N 0P4; Office: 116-103rd St., Saskatoon, Sask. S7N 1Y7

KOYL, Jack Eardley, D.S.C.; company executive; b. Saskatoon, Sask., 14 May 1916; s. Arthur Leon and Josephine Elizabeth (Eckstein) K.; e. Nutana Coll., Saskatoon, Sask.; Univ. of Saskatchewan (1934); Univ. of W. Ont. (Chem. and Business Adm.); m. Edith Jessie Morrow, 16 Nov. 1968; children: Gregory, Jacqueline, Paul, Glenn Morrow, Mrs. Trevor Alexander; Vice-President, The Bird — Archer Co. Ltd., since 1958-72; Dir., The Bird — Archer Co. Ltd.; Partner, Koyl Agencies Ltd., Saskatoon, Sask., 1934-36 (Real Estate); Hockey Player, Madison Square Garden Corp., 1936-37; with W. H. Bosley & Co. in 1937; Service Engr., London, Ont. and Montreal, P.Q., 1937-38; Field Engr., W. Can., 1938-41, Dist. Mgr. 1946-51; Mgr., Railway Service Dept., 1951-53; Mgr., Railway Service Dept. and Mgr. of Gen. Chem. Div., 1953-57; served in 2nd World War; Commissioned Sub. — Lieut., June 1941, Royal Roads Naval Coll.; Lieut., Sept. 1942; Lieut. — Commdr., R.C.N.R. 1945; D.S.C.; Mentioned in Despatches; mem., Navy League of Can., Past Pres. Ont. Div., Pres. Nat. Council; Pres., Naval Offrs. Assn., Vancouver Island Div.; Dir., Royal United Services Institute; Freemason (R.A.M.; K.T.K.M.) United Church of Canada; recreations: golf, boating, bridge; Clubs: Canadian Railway; Toronto Railway; Home: 2073 Pauls Terr., Victoria, B.C.

KOZIAK, Hon. Julian G. J., M.L.A., LL.B.; politician; b. Edmonton, Alta. 16 Sept. 1940; s. John H. and Marie (Woytkiw) K.; e. Univ. of Alta. B.A. 1962; LL.B. 1963; m. Barbara Lee d. late Joseph Melnychuk 19 Aug. 1961; children: Leanne, Donald, Deborah, Susan, Julian; MIN. OF CONSUMER & CORPORATE AFFAIRS, ALTA. 1979-; called to Bar of Alta. 1964; Partner, Kosowan & Wachowich 1964-75; el. M.L.A. for Edmonton Strathcona 1971, re-el. since; Min. of Educ. 1975-79; Pres., St. Basil's Sr. Citizens Residence 1969-71; St. Basil's Men's Club 1969; St. Thomas More Lawyers Guild 1968-69; mem. Law Soc. Alta.; Kappa Sigma; K. of C.; Ukrainian Prof. & Business Fed.; Malmo Community League; P. Conservative; Ukrainian Catholic; recreations: music (instrumental & choral singing), skiing; Home: 4715 Malmo Rd., Edmonton, Alta. T6H 4L7; Office: 224 Legislature Bldg., Edmonton, Alta. T5K 2B6.

KRAFT, Charles Hall, M.A., Ph.D.; educator; b. Chicago, Ill. 20 March 1924; s. Robert Hollo and Fanny (Hall) K.; e. Mich. State Coll. B.A. 1947, M.A. 1949; Univ. of Calif. Berkeley Ph.D. 1954; m. Constance d. late Willem van Eeden 8 Dec. 1960; children: Kathleen, Sally, Harry, Penny, Kari van Eeden; PROF. OF MATH. AND STAT., UNIV. DE MONTREAL 1965-; served with U.S. Air Force 1942-45; co-author "Nonparametric Introduction to Statistics" 1968; mem. Inst. Math. Stat.; Am. Stat. Assn.; Candn. Math. Soc.; Stat. Soc. Can.; Home: 4854 Cote des Neiges, Apt. 1207, Montreal, Que. H3V 1G7;Office: Montreal, Que.

KRAINTZ, Leon, M.A., Ph.D.; educator; b. Johnstown, Pa. 3 Oct. 1924; s. late Franz and late Marie (Peterlin) K.; e. Harvard Univ. A.B. 1950; Rice Inst. M.A. 1952, Ph.D. 1954; Oak Ridge Inst. for Nuclear Studies, Radioisotope techniques in Biochem. Cert. 1952; m. Frances Draper d. late Warren Draper Whitcomb, Waltham, Mass. 29 Aug. 1949; children: Dona Sturmanis, Erika Collins, Franz Peterlin; PROF. AND HEAD OF ORAL BIOL., UNIV. OF B.C. 1970-, Hon. Prof. of Physiol. 1966-; Research Asst. in Psychiatry Boston Psychopathic Hosp. 1947-48; Research Asst. in Clin. Investigation, Sloan-Kettering Inst.

for Cancer Research and Cornell Univ. 1948-50; Research Asst. in Exper. Med. Univ. of Texas M.D. Anderson Hosp. for Cancer Research Houston 1950-51; Instr. in Radiobiol., Edocrinol., Physiol. and Micro-biol. Rice Inst. Houston 1950-54, Research Assoc. in Biol. (U.S. Atomic Energy Comn. Grant) 1951-52; Visiting Lectr. and Instr. in Physiol. Baylor Univ. 1956-64; Visiting Prof. of Biol. Univ. of St. Thomas, Houston 1958-64; Prof. of Biol. and Assoc. Dir., Nat. Inst. Dental Research Training Grant, Rice Univ. 1962-64; Visiting Assoc. Clin. Prof. of Physiol. & Curriculum Consultant, Univ. of Texas Dental Br. 1962-64, Visiting Prof. Dental Science Inst. 1981-82; Visiting Prof. of Physiol. Emory Univ. Sch. of Med. 1964-68; Visiting Scient. Physiol. Dept. Univ. of Melbourne 1969-70; Sr. Research Fellow, Nat. Insts. of Health U.S. 1969-70; mem. Independent Assessors Panel, Nat. Health & Med. Research Council, Australia 1972- ; served with U.S. Navy 1942-45, Reserve 1945-48, N. Atlantic, N. Africa, Mediterranean, Sicily, Italy invasions; rec'd Unit Commendations N. Africa, Sicily; author over 80 publs. scient. journs., book chapters physiol., endocrinol. and mineral metabolism; Fellow, Am. Assn. Advanc. Science; mem. Soc. Exper. Biol. & Med. (Councilor 1975-77); Internat. Assn. Dental Research (Councilor 1975-78, Pres. B.C. Sec. 1966-69, 1980); Endocrine Soc.; Am. Physiol. Soc.; Candn. Physiol. Soc.; Soc. Neurosciences; Sigma Xi (Pres. 1978- , Nat. Del. 1975, 1978-80, Dir. 1974-); Pres., Texas Med. Center Research Soc. 1960-62; Quaker; recreations: music, gardening, cross-country skiing, camping, enology; Club: Harvard; Home: 6478 Dunbar St., Vancouver, B.C. V6N 1X6; Office: 2199 Wesbrook Mall, Vancouver, B.C. V6T 1W5.

KRAL, Dennis Z.; hotel executive; b. Czechoslovakia, 20 Sept. 1928; s. Josef and Marie K.; Candn. citizen; e. completed in Europe; m. Eva, d. Ulrich E. Hladik, 21 Jan. 1950; two s. Martin, Michael; PRES., ATLIFIC INC.; Vice-Chrmn., Wendy's Restaurants of Can., Inc.; Offr. and Dir., Atlific Group of Cos. since 1962; R. Catholic; Clubs: Royal Montreal; Montreal; Ontario; Home: 484 Avenue Rd., Toronto, Ont.; Office: 6550 Côte de Liesse, Montreal, Que. H4T 1S7

KRAMER, Burton, M.F.A., B.Sc., R.C.A., A.G.I., F.G.D.C.; graphic designer; educator; b. New York City, N.Y. 25 June 1932; s. Sam and Ida (Moore) K.; e. Bronx High Sch. of Science Dipl. 1949; State Univ. of New York Oswego 1949-51; Inst. of Design of IIT Chicago B.Sc. in Graphic Design 1954; Royal Coll. of Art London, Eng. Fullbright Scholar Design 1955-56; Yale Univ. Sch. of Art & Arch. M.F.A. (Graphic Design) 1957; m. Irène Margarite Thérèse d. late Johann Jacob Mayer 24 Feb. 1960; children: Gabrielle Kimberly, Jeremy Jacques; PRES. AND CREATIVE DIR., BURTON KRAMER ASSOCIATES LTD. 1967- ; Instr. in Design Ont. Coll. of Art 1978- ; Designer, Geigy Chemical Corp. New York 1959-61; Chief Designer, Halpern Advertising Zurich 1961-65; Dir. Corporate Graphics, Clairtone Sound Corp. Toronto 1967; Guest Lectr. in Graphic Design Rochester Inst. of Technol. 1976 and Lectr. Cincinnatti Univ. 1980; Guest Lectr. "Designer-in-Residence" 1981; Visiting Lectr. Cincinnatti Univ. 1980; Guest Speaker ICO-GRADA Edmonton 1975; maj. works incl. Visual Identity Programs for CBC, Ont. Educ. Communications Authority, Candn. Crafts Council, Ont. Guild of Crafts; Design of Exterior Graphics Candn. Discovery Train; Signage System for Eaton Centre Toronto, Hosp. for Sick Children Toronto, Erin Mills New Town Mississauga; Graphic Design Program for Royal Ont. Museum; Map-Directory System & Graphics Expo 67 Montreal; rep. many nat. and internat. design exhns.; rec'd Gold Medal Internat. Typographic Composition Assn. 1971, Art Dirs. Club Toronto 1973; numerous awards for Design Excellence; designed Candn. art book "The Art of Norval Morrisseau" 1979; "Passionate Spirits" (hist of Royal Candn. Acad. Arts) 1980; author Candn. sec. "Trademarks and Symbols of the World"; co-author "Report on Canadian Road Sign Graphics" Transport

Can.; author various articles and editor of special issue on Canadian graphic design "Idea" mag. Tokyo; work published by numerous nat. and internat. annuals, books and journals.; Fellow, Soc. Graphic Designers Can. (Past Pres.); mem. Alliance Graphique Internat.; Am. Inst. Graphic Arts; Swiss Graphic Designers Soc.; Toronto Folk Festival (Bd. mem.); recreations: music, sailing, cross-country skiing, books, art; Home: 101 Roxborough St. W., Toronto, Ont. M5R 1T9; Office: 20 Prince Arthur Ave., Suite 1E, Toronto, Ont. M5R 1B1.

KRAMER, Hon. Eiling, retired politician; rancher; auctioneer; b. North Battleford, Sask., 14 July 1914; s. Minne Douwe and Jacobina (Kopinga) K.; e. Pub. and High Schs., North Battleford, Sask., New York Sch. Journalism (Corr.); m. Dorothy Augusta, d. Leslie Warwick Johnston, 15 Dec. 1944; two s., six d., twogrndsns., two grndds.; Dir., Crown Investments Corp.; founder of Round Hill Ranch 1942 and Kramer Auctions 1949; 1st el. M.L.A. for Battlefords Constit. 1952, re-el. since and retired 1980; Min., Highways & Transport, Sask. 1972-80; Min.-in-charge, Hwy. Traffic Bd. 1979-80; Min., Natural Resources, Sask. 1962-64; Min., Depts. Natural Resources & Co-op. 1971-72; Dir., Dist. 16, Sask. Farmers' Union and Vice-Pres. 1951-52; I.O.O.F.; New Democrat; United Church; recreations: hunting, fishing; Clubs: Cosmopolitan; Wildlife Federation; Home: 1429 Parker St., Regina, Sask. S4S 4R7

KRANCK, Ernst Hakan, D.Sc., F.R.C.S., F.G.S.A.; b. Birkala, Finland, 7 Nov. 1898; s. Ernst Albin and Alexandra (Lisizin) K.; e. Univ. of Helsingfors, D.Sc. 1933; m. Valborg Maria, d. Hilding M. Meinander, 9 July 1930; children: Svante Hakan, Elisabeth Maria, Kate Margaretha; Asst. Prof., Univ. of Helsingfors, 1930-45; Prof. at Comm. Coll. of Helsingfors, 1932-40; Chief Geologist of Wuoksenniska Co., Finland, 1940-45; Prof. Univ. of Neuchâtel, Switzerland, 1945-48; Prof. of Geol., McGill Univ. 1948-70; Publications: three travel books and over 90 papers publ. in scient. journs.; mem. of Research Expdns. to Lapland, Siberia, Tierra del Fuego, Greenland, Canadian Arctic, etc.; mem., Geol. Assn. Can.; Soc. Scientiarum Fennica; Geol. Soc. Am.; Geol. Soc. Finland; Royal Society Canada; Geographic Soc. Finland; Lutheran; Home: 28 Brookdale Cres., Dartmouth, N.S. B3A 2R5

KRAVIS, Janis, B.Arch.; architect; interior and industrial designer; b. Riga, Latvia, 20 Oct. 1935; s. Arvids Ludvigs and Laima (Mednis) K.; e. Sweden 1944-50; Bloor and Earl Haig Coll. Insts.; Univ. of Toronto Sch. of Arch. B.Arch 1959; m. Helga Milda d. late Herbert Braslis, 23 Apl. 1960; children: Leif, Nils, Guntar; PRESIDENT, JANIS KRAVIS ARCHITECT since 1963; Pres. Janis Kravis Consultants Ltd. (estbd. 1969); estbd. Karelia Studio Ltd. 1959; architectural, interior, graphic and indust. designs incl.: Three Small Rooms (awarded Ont. Tourism Award 1967) and Number Twenty-two Lounge Windsor Arms Hotel, Credit Valley and York Regional Schs. of Nursing, Richview Lib., Etobicoke Hydro H.O. Bldg., Inn on the Park Athletic Club, Univ. Centre Carleton Univ., Four Seasons Hotel (Belleville), Aurora (Ont.) Highlands Golf Club, Young & Rubicam Ltd., Constellation Hotel, North Albion Lib., and other indust. pub. and residential bldgs.; founded Karelia International 1969; opened Karelia store Vancouver 1973; rec'd Eedee Award in Lounge Seating category furniture design 1967; mem. Museum of Modern Art; Art Gallery of Ont.; Heritage Can.; mem. Ont. Assn. Archs.; Royal Arch. Inst. Can.; Assn. Candn. Indust. Designers — Ont.; Royal Candn. Acad.; Faculty mem., Dept. of Design, Ontario Coll. of Arts; recreations: farming, sailing, tennis; Club: Boulevard; Home: 38 Cedarbank Cres., Don Mills, Ont. M3B 3A4

KREISEL, Henry, M.A., Ph.D., F.R.S.A.; educator; author; b. Vienna, Austria, 5 June 1922; s. David Leo and Helene (Schreier) K.; e. Zirkus Gymnasium, Vienna,

1932-38; Harbord Coll. Inst., Toronto, Ont., 1941-42; Univ. of Toronto, B.A. 1946; M.A. 1947 (Reuben Wells Leonard Fellow); Univ. of London, Ph.D. 1954 (Royal Soc. Can. Travelling Fellowship); m. Esther, d. late Aaron Lazerson, 22 June 1947; one s., Philip; PROF. OF ENGLISH, UNIV. OF ALBERTA, since 1959; joined present Univ. as Lectr. in Eng., 1947-50; Asst. Prof. 1950-55; Assoc. Prof. 1955-59; Head, Dept. of Eng., 1961-67; Sr. Assoc. Dean of Grad. Studies 1967-69; Acting Dean 1969-70; Vice Pres. (Academic) 1970-75; Univ. Prof., 1975- ; Chrm., Can. Studies Program, Univ. of Alta., 1979- ; Visiting Prof. of Eng., Univ. of B.C., 1951; Visit. Fellow, Wolfson Coll., Cambridge Univ. 1975-76; mem., Adv. Comte. on Fine Arts, Dept. of Transport, 1959; Can. Council Post-grad. Scholarship Comte. (Chrmn., Eng. Panel 1963-65); Gov. — Gen.'s Awards Jury for Lit., 1966-69; Bd. of Govs., Univ. of Alta., 1966-69; Council of Edmonton Art Gallery 1967-70 Pres., Edmonton Chamber Music Soc., 1980- ; rec'd Pres. Medal for Lit. (short story), Univ. of W. Ont., 1959; author: "The Rich Man" (novel) 1948; "The Betrayal" (novel), 1964; "The Almost Meeting", (short stories) 1981; Ed., "Aphrodite and Other Poems" by John Heath, 1959; other writings incl. short stories in many mags. and reprinted in 'The Best American Short Stories 1966", "A Book of Canadian Stories", "Modern Canadian Stories" and other anthols.; plays for radio performed on CBC "Stage" and "Wednesday Night"; "The Broken Globe" (play) performed in Edmonton and on CBC TV, 1976; el. Fellow, Internat. Inst. Arts & Letters, Geneva, 1961; Roy. Soc. Arts 1974; Pres., Assn. Acad. Staff Univ. of Alta., 1960-61 (Vice-Pres. 1959-60); Pres., Assn. Candn. Univ. Teachers Eng., 1962-63; Nat. Extve. Humanities Assn. Can., 1964-66; Pres., Philos. Soc. Univ. of Alta., 1955-56; Jewish; recreations: art collecting, music, travel; Home: 12516 — 66 Ave., Edmonton, Alta. T6H 1Y5

KREVER, Hon. Horace, B.A., LL.B.; judge; b. Montreal, Que., 17 Feb. 1929; s. Morris and Leah (Levy) K.; e. Harbord and N. Toronto Coll. Insts.; Univ. of Toronto, Univ. Coll. B.A. 1951, LL.B. 1954; Osgoode Hall Law Sch. 1956; m. Elizabeth Mardane, d. late Herbert Wiggin, 15 Oct. 1954; children: Catherine, Susan, Barbara, Bruce; JUSTICE, SUPREME COURT OF ONT. since 1975; read law with Goodman & Goodman, Toronto; called to Bar of Ont. 1956; cr. Q.C. 1970; law practice Kimber & Dubin 1956-64; part-time Lectr. in Law Univ. of Toronto 1962-64, Prof. 1964-68; Prof. of Law and Special Lectr. Faculty of Med. Univ. of W. Ont. 1969-74, Prof. of Law and Prof. of Community Med. Univ. of Toronto, 1974-75; mem. Univ. of Toronto Senate 1960-64; Comte. on Healing Arts (Ont.) 1966-70; Fed. Community Health Centre Project (Hastings Comte.) 1971-72; Bencher Law Soc. of Upper Can. 1970-75 (Chrmn. Legal Educ. Comte 1974-75); mem. Rules Comte. under Judicature Act (Ont.) 1972-75 and since 1977; Ont. Council of Health (Extve. Comte. and Chrmn. Comte. on Human Resources) 1971-75; Commr., Royal Comn. on The Confidentiality of Health Records in Ont. 1977-80; Adv. Council, Medal for Good Citizenship Prov. of Ont., 1972-76; Alternate Chrm., Ontario Advisory Review Bd., 1976- ; mem., Comte. on Accreditation of Canadian Medical Schools, 1979- ; Comte. on Human Exper. Research Inst. Hosp. for Sick Children Toronto 1966-75; Arbitrator Ont. Labour — Mang. Arbitration Comn. 1973-75; rec'd Univ. of Toronto Alumni Assn.'s Faculty Award 1975; Ed. — in — Chief Dominion Law Reports, Ontario Reports, Canadian Criminal Cases, 1967-75 (Ed. 1965-67); mem. Candn. Bar Assn.; Co. York Law Assn.; Medico — Legal Soc. Toronto (Pres., 1976-77) Chrmn. Special Comte. Human Tissue Gift Act 1971-75); Candn. Pol. Science Assn.; Am. Judicature Soc.; Hebrew; Home: 134 Roxborough Dr., Toronto, Ont. M4W 1X4; Office: Osgoode Hall, Toronto, Ont.

KRISTJANSON, Kristjan, C.M., M.Sc., Ph.D.; insurance executive; b. Gimli, Man. 4 Jan. 1921; s. late Hannes and Elin Thordis (Magnusdottir) K.; e. Univ. of Man.

1939-42; Univ. of Alta. B.Sc. 1943; Univ. of Toronto M.Sc. 1946; Univ. of Chicago summer 1946; Univ. of Wis. Ph.D. 1954; m. Lois d. late Hugh Hill 24 Dec. 1952; children: Ruth, Helga, Ingrid, Stefan; VICE PRES. CORPORATE PLANNING & PERSONNEL, GREAT-WEST LIFE ASSURANCE CO. since 1971; Research Econ. Dominion Econ. Div. Saskatoon 1943-44; Lectr. in Econ. Univ. of Guelph 1945-46; Research Econ. and Teaching Asst. U.S. Forest Service & Univ. of Wis. 1946-48; Research Econ. U.S. Dept. Agric. Brookings, S.D. 1949-53; Assoc. Prof. Univ. of Neb. 1953-56; Sr. Administrator Govt. Can. Ottawa 1956-61; Dir. Econ. Div. Man. Hydro Electric Bd. Winnipeg 1961-66, Asst. Gen. Mgr. Adm. Man. Hydro 1966-71; Dir. Museum of Man & Nature; Winnipeg Chamber Comm.; Chrmn. Med. Research Council Biohazards Comte.; Pres. Can. Iceland Foundation; mem. Inst. Pub. Adm. Can. (Pres. 1967-68); P. Conservative; recreations: swimming, tennis, golf, billiards; Home289 Queenston St., Winnipeg, Man. R3N 0W9; Office: 60 Osborne St. N., Winnipeg, Man. R3C 3A5.

KRISTJANSON, Leo Friman, M.A., Ph.D.; educator; economist; b. Gimli, Man. 28 Feb. 1932; s. Hannes and Elin Thordis (Magnusdottir) K.; e. Un. coll. Winnipeg B.A. 1954; Univ. of Man. M.A. 1959; Univ. of Wis. Ph.D. 1963; Univ. of Winnipeg, LL.D. 1980; m. Jean Evelyn d. Hector M. Cameron, Moorepark, Man. 29 June 1957; children: Terri Elin, Darryl Cameron, Brenda Jean, Johanne Alda; PRES. UNIV. OF SASKATCHEWAN;Chrmn. Sask. Natural Products Marketing Council; has served on several adv. comtes. to govt.; author various articles in fields of co-operatives, demography and agric. policy; mem. Candn. Econ. Assn.; Candn. Agric. Econ. Assn.; Candn. Pol. Science Assn.; President's Residence, Univ. of Sask., Saskatoon, Sask.; Office: Saskatoon, Sask. S7N 0W0.

KRNJEVIC, Kresimir Ivan, M.B., Ch.B., B.Sc., Ph.D., F.R.S.C.; neurophysiologist; b. Zagreb, Croatia, Yugoslavia 7 Sept. 1927; s. Juraj and Nada (Hirsl) K.; e. Primary Sch. Geneva, Switzerland 1935-39; High Sch. Realna Gimnazija, Zagreb 1939-41; Wynberg Boys' High Sch. Capetown, S. Africa 1941-43; Edinburgh Univ. M.B., Ch.B. 1949, B.Sc. (Physiol.) 1951, Ph.D. 1953; m. Jeanne W. d. late John Herbert Bowyer 27 Sept. 1954; two s. Peter Juraj, Nicholas John; DIR. OF ANAESTHESIA RESEARCH DEPT. McGILL UNIV. since 1965; JOSEPH MORLEY DRAKE PROF. OF PHYSIOL. and CHRMN. OF PHYSIOL. DEPT. since 1978; Goodsir Mem. Fellow 1950-52; Beit Mem. Fellow 1952-54; Demonst. in Physiol. Edinburgh Univ. 1950-54; Research Assoc. and Asst. Prof. of Physiol. & Biophysics, Univ. of Wash. 1954-56; Visiting Fellow, John Curtin Sch. of Med. Research, Australian Nat. Univ., Canberra 1956-58; Princ. becoming Sr. Princ. Scient. Research Offr., A.R.C. Inst. Animal Physiol., Babraham, Cambs., Eng. 1959-65; Visiting Prof. of Physiol. McGill Univ. 1964-65; Forbes Lectr. Woods Hole 1978; mem. Conseil de la Recherche en Santé du Qué. 1974-79; Ed. "Canadian Journal of Physiology and Pharmacology" 1972-78; author numerous articles in physiol. and neuroscient. journs.; Hon. mem. Soc. royale de medecine mentale de Belgique 1969; mem. Physiol. Soc. (U.K.); Am. Physiol. Soc.; Internat. Brain Research Organ.; Internat. Soc. Neurochem.; Soc. for Neuroscience (Pres. E. Candn. Chapter 1973-74); Candn. Physiol. Soc. (Pres. 1979-80); Montreal Physiol. Soc. (Pres. 1977-78); recreations: mountaineering, skiing, swimming, reading, music; Home: 653 Belmont Ave., Westmount, Que. H3Y 2W3; Office: 3655 Drummond St., Montreal, Que. H3G 1Y6.

KROEGER, Arthur, M.A.; Canadian public servant; b. Naco, Alta. 7 Sept. 1932; s. Heinrich and Helena (Rempel) K.; e. Consort (Alta.) High Sch. 1950; Univ. of Alta. B.A. 1955; Pembroke Coll. Oxford Univ. (Rhodes Scholar) M.A. 1958; m. late Gabrielle Jane Sellers, Toronto, Ont. 7 May 1966; two d., Nina Alexandra, Kate Megan Jane; DEPY. MIN. OF TRANSPORT 1979- ; former Depy.

Min. of Indian Affairs and Northern Development; former Dir., Petro Canada; Northern Transportation Company Ltd.; Sessional Instr. Univ. of Alta. 1954-55; Master, St. Johns — Ravenscourt Sch., Winnipeg 1955-56; joined Dept. External Affairs 1958 becoming Secy. GATT Del. Geneva 1960, Second Secy. New Delhi 1961, Ottawa 1964 (seconded to Dept. Nat. Defence 1967-68), Counsellor Washington 1968; Treasury Bd. Secretariat, Program Br., Dir. External Affairs and Defence 1971, Asst. Secy. 1972, Depy. Secy. 1972; served as Sub — Lt. RCN(R) 1954; Club: Five Lakes Fishing; Home: 245 Springfield Rd., Ottawa, Ont. K1M 0L1; Office: Transport Canada Bldg., Place de Ville, Ottawa

KROEGER, Hon. Henry, M.L.A.; politician; b. Moscow, Russia 28 March 1918; s. Henry Kroeger; came to Can. 1926; m. Cleona Elora d. Harvey Kelts, Consort, Alta. 9 Apl. 1939; children: Thomas Brent, Brian Harvey, Debora Anna; MIN. OF TRANSPORTATION, ALTA. since 1979; el. M.L.A. g.e. 1975; re-el. since; Pres., Kroeger Bros. Farm Equipment Ltd. since 1944; Past Pres., Stettler Rotary; P. Conservative; United Church; recreation: curling; Home: (P.O. Box 370) Hanna, Alta.; Office: 418 Legislature Bldg., Edmonton, Alta. T5K 2B6.

KROETSCH, Robert, M.A., Ph.D.; writer; university professor; b. Alta., 26 June 1927; Paul and Hilda (Weller); e. Heisler (Alta.) Pub. Sch.; Red Deer (Alta.) High Sch. 1945; University of Alta., B.A. 1948; McGill Univ. 1954-55; Middlebury Coll., M.A. 1956; Univ. of Iowa, Ph.D. 1961; m. Mary Jane, d. George Clinton Lewis, Wilmington, N.C., 13 January 1956; two d., Laura Caroline, Margaret Ann; PROF. OF ENGLISH, UNIV. OF MANITOBA, since 1978; Purser on Mackenzie River riverboats, 1948-50; Dir. of Information and Educ., U.S. Air Force, Goose Bay, Labrador, 1951-54; joined State Univ. of N.Y. as Asst. Prof. of Eng. 1961; Assoc. Prof. 1965-68; Prof. 1968-78; Fellow, Univ. of Iowa, 1960-61; Fellow Bread Loaf Writers Conf., 1966; rec'd. Gov. Gen.'s Lit. Award (novel) for 1969 ("The Studhorse Man"); author of the following novels: "But We Are Exiles", 1965; "The Words of My Roaring", 1966; "The Studhorse Man" 1969; "Gone Indian" 1973; "Badlands" 1975; "What the Crown Said" 1978; poetry: "The Stone Hammer Poems" 1975; "Seed Catalogue" 1977; "The Sad Phoenician" 1979; "Field Notes" 1981; travel: "Alberta" 1968; journal: "The Crow Journals" 1980; other writings incl. short stories, poems and book chapters in various mags. and journs.; Office: Winnipeg, Man.

KROFT, Hon. Guy Joseph, LL.B.; judge; b. St. Boniface, Man. 27 May 1934; s. Charles and Heloise (Cohn) K.; e. Univ. of Man. B.A. 1955, LL.B. 1959; m. Hester Lee d. late A. Montague Israels, Q.C. 10 June 1956; children: Jonathan Barry, Deborah Faith, David Joseph, Sarah Lynn; JUDGE, COURT OF QUEEN'S BENCH, MAN.; called to Bar of Man. 1959; cr. Q.C. 1978; former Partner, Thompson, Dorfman, Sweatman; Dir., Can. Judges Conf.; Gov., Can.-Israel Fdn. for Academic Exchangers; Past Pres.: Man. Div. Red Cross Soc.; Candn. Club Winnipeg; Lib. Party of Man.; Secy.-Treas. Winnipeg Jewish Community Council, Vice Pres.; former mem. Nat. Bd. Can. Israel Comte.; mem., Nat. Extve. Candn. Jewish Cong.; Nat. Red Cross Budget Comte.; former Bencher, Law Soc. Man.; mem. Nat. Council, Candn. Bar Assn. (Past Vice Pres. Man. Sec.); Sigma Alpha Mu; Jewish; recreations: cross-country skiing, tennis; Home: 352 Oxford St., Winnipeg, Man. R3M 3J7;Office: Judges Chambers, Law Courts Bldg., Winnipeg, Man. R3C 0V8.

KROPP, Benjamin Nathan, S.B., A.M., Ph.D.; anatomist; b. Boston, Mass., 24 May 1899; s. Nathan and Hannah — Bayla (Wise) K.; e. Harvard Coll., S.B. 1923; Harvard Univ., A.M. 1924, Ph.D. 1927; Parmenter Scholar, 1921; Sheldon Travelling Fellow, 1929; m. Laurette Germaine, d. Dr. J. H. Choquette, Adams, Mass., 24 July 1934; children: Mary Esther, Jonatha Elisabeth, Laura

Anne, Josefa Hannah — Bayla; Austin Teaching Fellow, Harvard Univ., 1926-27; Inst. in Zool., 1927-29; mem., Bd. of Tutors in Biol. Sciences, 1925-29; Guest Investigator, Kaiser Wilhelm Inst., Für Biologie, Germany, 1929-31, and at Stazione Zoölogica, Naples, Italy, 1930; Research Fellow in Gen. Physiol., Harvard Univ., 1932; Instr. in Anatomy, Boston Univ. Med. Sch., 1935-36; Research Fellow in Anat. and Obstetrics, Instr. in Anat., Harvard Med. Sch., 1934-38; joined Queen's Univ. 1938, as Lectr. and retired as Emeritus Prof. of Anatomy, Faculty of Med. 1964; Guest Lectr., Sorbonne, Paris, 1960; Prof. of Anat., Louisiana State Univ. Sch. of Med., 1964-65; Prof. of Anat. and Head of Dept., Ghana Med. Sch., Accra, Ghana, 1965-67; visiting Prof. of Anat., Univ. of West Indies, Kingston, Jamaica, 1967-72; Adv. in Med. Educ., Canadian International Development Agency, Ottawa, since 1965; served in 1st World War 1918; Student A.T.C. (Tufts Coll. Unit.) U.S. Army; Fellow, Am. Assn. Advance. Science; Life mem., N.Y. Acad. Sciences; mem., Assn. of Anats.; Am. Soc. Zools.; Candn. Physiol. Soc.; Am. Assn. Physical Anthropol.; Candn. Assn. Anats.; Home: 385 Bath Road, Kingston, Ont. K7M 2Y1

KRUEGER, Peter J., M.Sc. D.Phil., F.C.I.C., F.R.S.C. (UK); educator; university administrator; b. Altona, Man. 11 Nov. 1934; s. Jacob J. and Elisabeth (Friesen) K.; e. Mennonite Coll. Inst. Gretna, Man. 1951; Univ. of Man. B.Sc. 1955, M.Sc. 1956 (Nat. Research Council Can. Bursary); St. John's Coll. Oxford Univ. D.Phil 1958 (Univ. of Man. Travelling Fellowship, Shell Commonwealth Scholarship); m. Dorothy Isabel d. late Lawrence Lashley, Lanark, Ont. 18 July 1959; children: Kathryn, Vivian, Jonathan; VICE PRES. (ACAD.) UNIV. OF CALGARY since 1976 and Prof. of Chem. there since 1966; Post — doctoral Research Fellow Nat. Research Council of Can. Ottawa 1958-59; Asst. Prof. of Chem. Univ. of Alberta, Calgary 1959, Assoc. Prof. Univ. of Alta, Calgary 1964-66; Head, Dept. of Chem. present Univ. 1966-70, Vice Dean (Budget and Phys. Planning) Faculty of Arts and Science 1970-72, mem. Bd. of Govs. 1970-73, Senate (ex officio) since 1976, Vice Chrmn. Gen. Faculties Council (ex officio) since 1976; Visiting Scient. Nat. Research Council Can. Ottawa 1966-67; Brit. Council Visitorship 1974; NRC/CNRS Scient. Exchange Programme (France) 1974; rec'd Coblentz Soc. Award in Spectroscopy 1967 (1st Candn.); Gerhard Herzberg Award in Spectroscopy 1973; Alta. Achievement Award 1974; past and present mem. educ./scient. comtes. univ., prov. and nat. levels; author over 70 research publs. in scient. journs.; mem., Ed. Adv. Bd., "Canadian Journal of Spectroscopy"; Chart. Chem., Royal Soc. of Chem.; mem. Spectroscopy Soc. Can.; Coblentz Soc.; Am. Chem. Soc.; Am. Assn. Advanc. Science; Sigma Xi; Baptist; recreation: squash; Home: 88 Brown Cres. N.W., Calgary, Alta. T2L 1N5; Office: 2500 University Dr. N.W., Calgary, Alta. T2N 1N4

KRUEGER, Ralph R., M.A., Ph.D.; educator; b. Huron Co., Ont. 10 March 1927; s. late Elmer G. and Myrtle M. (Horner) K.; e. London (Ont.) Normal Sch.; Univ. of W. Ont. B.A. 1952, M.A. 1955; Ind. Univ. Ph.D. 1959; m. B. June d. late J. Everet Hambly 30 June 1949; two d. Karen, Colleen; PROF. OF GEOG. UNIV. OF WATERLOO 1962- ; mem. Faculty Wayne State Univ. 1957-59; Waterloo Lutheran Univ. 1959-62; Chrmn. of Geog. and Planning present Univ. 1962-70; mem. Kitchener Planning Bd. 1960-72; Waterloo Co. Area Planning Bd. 1966-72; author "Canada: A New Geography" 1969; "Urban Problems" 1970; "Managing Canada's Renewable Resources" 1977; numerous articles and book chapters Can.'s agric. land base particularly urbanization orchard lands; mem. Candn. Assn. Geographers (Pres. 1978-79); Am. Assn. Geographers; recreation: skiing; Home: 743 Glasgow St., Kitchener, Ont. N2M 2N7;Office: Waterloo, Ont. N2L 3G1.

KRUGER, Arthur M., Ph.D.; educator; b. Toronto, Ont. 4 Nov. 1932; s. Joseph and Anna Martha (Barron) K.; e.

Univ. of Toronto B.A. 1955; Mass. Inst. of Technol. Ph.D. 1959; m. Betty Mina d. Levy Jacober 19 Aug. 1958; children: Sarah Anne, Helen Nina, Gerald Zev, Naomi Vered; DEAN OF ARTS & SCIENCE, UNIV. OF TORONTO 1977- and Prof. of Pol. Econ.; Asst. Prof. Wharton Sch. Univ. of Pa. 1959-61; joined present Univ. 1961, Chrmn. Div. of Social Sciences Scarborough Coll. 1969-70, Assoc. Chrmn. of Pol. Econ. 1970-74, Princ. Woodsworth Coll. 1974-77; Dir. Assoc. Hebrew Schs.; Or Chaim and Ulpanat Orot Schs.; arbitrator and mediator in labour disputes; author "The Canadian Labour Market" 1968; various articles related to labour; mem. Am. Econ. Assn.; Indust. & Labour Relations Assn.; Candn. Econ. Assn.; Jewish; Home: 34 Shallmar Blvd., Toronto, Ont. M6C 2J9; Office: Toronto, Ont. M5S 1A1.

KRUGER,Gene Henry, hon. D.SC.; pulp and paper executive; b. Borough of Manhattan, New York City, N.Y. 21 May 1902; s. Joseph Kruger; came to Can. 1904; e. Westmount (Que.) High Sch.; McGill Univ.; children: Carlyn Dodds, Joan Robinson, Joseph Kruger II; CHRMN. OF BD., KRUGER INC.; Freemason; mem. Atlantic Salmon Assn.; Home: Apartado 6413, Panama 5, Republic of Panama; Office: 3285 Bedford Rd., Montreal, Que. H3S 1G5.

KRUPSKI, Zbigniew Henry, B.Sc.; retired executive; b. Pressbaum, Austria, 1 Sept. 1910; s. Henry and Sophy (Schramm) K.; e. Vienna Tech. Univ. Dipl. Engn. (B.Sc.) Elect. Engn. 1935; m. Barbara Jean, d. late Dr. Wesley Bourne, 29 Sept. 1951; one d. Anne; joined Bell Can. as Asst. Engr., Montreal, 1948; served in various engn. mang. positions, Montreal, 1948-54 and 1956-60; Radio Systems Engr. 1954; Area Chief Engr., Toll Area, Montreal, 1961; Vice-Pres. Bell Canada and Chrm. Trans-Canada Telephone System 1964-71; 1964; Extve. Vice-Pres., Bell Can 1971-75; served with RAF (Polish Unit) in N.W. Europe and UK 1940-48; rank Flight Lt. (A/Sqdn. Leader); mem., Engn. Inst. Can.; Royal Ottawa Golf; Home: 447 Roger Road, Ottawa, Ont. K1H 5B7;

KUBRYK, David, C.D., C.St.J., M.D., D.P.H., F.A.P.H.A., F.R.S.H.; ret. Canadian public servant; b. Cluj, Roumania, 5 April 1912; s. Herman and Mina (Turner) K.; e. Liceul Mihaiu Viteazul, Bucharest, B.A. 1929; Ecole des Sciences, Rouen, France, B.Sc. 1931; Ecole de Médecine, Rouen, France; Faculté de Médecine, Paris. Univ. di Bologna, Italy, M.D. 1936; Univ. of Montreal, D.P.H. 1956; m. Marion, d. John Charles Willey, Exeter, Eng., 14 Feb. 1953; children: Geoffrey Charles, Giselle Ruth, Gillian Helen; Med. offr. (part time) London Heathrow Airport, 1977- ; Med. offr. i.c. Med. Services, Health & Welfare Can.; Embassy Paris, France 1974-77; Asst. in Surg., Policlinico Umberto 1, Rome, Italy, 1936-39; gen. practice in U.K. 1943-52; Med. Offr. with Candn. Army, Can & Korea, 1952-57; Med. Consultant, Epidemiol. Div., Dept. Nat. Health & Welfare, 1957-61; Public Health Med. Consultant, Emergency Health Services, Dept. Nat. Health & Welfare 1961-70, Chief Emergency Health Services 1970-72; Med. Offr. i.c. Med. Services, Health and Welfare Can., Candn. High Comn., New Delhi, India 1972-74; Lt. — Col., R.C.A.M.C. (ret.); served in 2nd World War with French Army, Foreign Leg. (1939-41) & Brit. Army, 1942; mem., Brit. Med. Assn.; Royal Soc. of Health; Candn. Public Health Assn.; Assn. Mil. Surgs. of U.S.; Defence Med. Assn. Can.; Assn. des méd. de langue française; Home: 27 Oakland Drive, Dawlish, Devon, England, EX7 9RW

KULKA, Marshall, M.Sc., Ph.D., F.C.I.C., F.R.S.C.; chemist; b. Warspite, Alta. 1 March 1911; s. William and Anna (Zukewich) K.; e. Eastwood High Sch. Edmonton, Alta.; Univ. of Alta. B.Sc. 1935, M.Sc. 1936; Sch. of Educ. High Sch. Teacher's Dipl. 1937; McGill Univ. Ph.D. 1942; m. Sophia d. David Danyluk, Vegreville, Alta. 23 Dec. 1939; children: Maria Louise, David William; Consultant, Uniroyal Research Labs. since 1976; taught high sch.

Hairy Hill, Alta. 1937-40; postdoctoral studies 1942-43; Research Chem. Dominion Rubber Co. Ltd. 1943-63; Sr. Research Chem. and Leader of Organic Chem. Group, Uniroyal Research Labs. 1963-69, Mgr. Organic Research 1969-76, retired 1976; discoverer agric. chems. to combat fungal pathogens; rec'd Thomas W. Eadie Medal, Royal Soc. Can. 1975; author over 80 scient. papers incl. patents and book chapters; Vice Chrmn. Guelph Presto Music Club; Chrmn. Wellington-Waterloo Sec. Chem. Inst. Can.; recreation: curling; Home: 65 Metcalfe, Guelph, Ont. N1E 4X7; Office: 120 Huron St., Guelph, Ont. N1H 6N3.

KUPSCH, Walter Oscar, M.Sc., Ph.D., F.R.S.C., F.A.I.N.A., F.G.A.C., F.G.S.A.; b. Amsterdam, Netherlands, 2 March 1919; s. Richard Leopold and Elizabeth (Heuser) K.; e. Univ. of Amsterdam, B.Sc. 1946; Univ. of Michigan, M.Sc. 1948; Ph.D. 1950; m. Emmy Hélène d. C. B. de Jong, Amsterdam, 2 Oct. 1945; children: Helen Elizabeth, Yvonne Irene, Richard Christopher; PROFESSOR OF GEOL., UNIV. OF SASK. Petroleum Advisor, N.W.T. Government since 1980; Dir., Institute for Northern Studies 1965-73; University of Michigan, 1948-49; joined teaching staff, University of Saskatchewan, 1950; Consultant, Saskatchewan Dept. Mineral Resources and Gulf Oil Corp., 1957-58; with J. C. Sproule, Consulting Engrs., 1959-65; Extv. Dir., Adv. Comm. on Devel. of Govt. in N.W.T., 1965-66; Dir., Churchill River Study, 1973-76; served in Netherlands Army, 1939; principal or co-author of over 30 scient. papers on geol.; Vice-Chrmn., Science Adv. Bd. N.W.T. since 1976; mem., Science Council Can. since 1976; Am. Assn. Petroleum Geols.; Liberal; Home: 319 Bate Cr., Saskatoon, Sask. S7H 3A6

KUSHNER, Eva, M.A., Ph.D., F.R.S.C.; educator; author; b. Prague, Czechoslovakia 18 June 1929; d. Josef and Anna (Kafková) Dubský; e. elem. sch. Prague 1935-39; Coll. classique de jeunes filles, Cognac, Charente, France 1939-45; Coll. Marie de France, Montreal B.Ph. 1946; McGill Univ. B.A. 1948, M.A. (Philos.) 1950, Ph.D. (French Lit.) 1956; m. Donn Jean Kushner, Lake Charles, La. 15 Sept. 1949; children: Daniel Peter, Roland Joseph, Paul Joel; PROF. OF FRENCH LANG. AND LIT., McGILL UNIV. since 1976; Hon. Adjunct Prof. of Comparative Lit., Carleton Univ. 1976-79; Sessional Lectr. in Philos. Sir George Williams Univ. 1952-53; Sessional Lectr. in French, McGill Univ. 1952-55; Instr. McGill French Summer Sch. 1956, 1958, 1961, 1962, 1967, 1968, 1969; Lectr. Univ. Coll. London, Eng. 1958-59; Lectr. Carleton Univ. 1961, Asst. Prof. 1963, Assoc. Prof. 1965, Prof. of French & Comparative Lit. 1969-76, Chrmn. of Comparative Lit. 1965-69, 1970-72, 1975-76; elected to Académie Européene des lettres, des science et des Arts (1980); Royal Society of Can. (1971); Pres. of Academie des lettres et sciences humaines and Vice-Pres. of the Royal Society of Canada; mem. Can. Council 1975-81 and of Executive Comm. of the Canada Council; mem., Comité-Conseil F.C.A.C., Dept. of Education Québec; Council d'administration, fond de soutien et aide à la recherche; Adv. Bd. Nat. Lib. of Can.; Pres. Humanities Research Council Can. 1970-72; author, "Patrice de La Tour du Pin" 1961; "Le mythe d'Orphée dans la littérature française contemporaine" 1961; "Chants de Bohème" 1963; "Rina Lasnier" coll. "Ecrivains canadiens d'aujourd'hui" 1964; "Poètes d'aujourd'hui" 1969; "Saint-Denys Garneau" 1967; "François Mauriac" 1972, Japanese transl. 1976; co-author of an anthology of Quebec poetry, translated into Hungarian; co-editor, "Proceedings of the VIIth Congress of the Internat. Comparative Lit. Assn"; Vol IV (Evolution of the Novel) of the IX ICLA Congress; numerous articles and papers on 16th Century French Lit., 20th Century poets of France and Québec, comparative lit. and comparative lit. theory; co-dir. of research Renaissance vols. "Histoire comparée des littératures de langues européennes"; mem. ed. comte. "Canadian Comparative

Literature Review"; Internat. Adv. Bd. "Comparative Literature Studies"; mem. Am. Comparative Lit. Assn. (Adv. Bd.); Internat. Comparative Lit. Assn. (Vice Pres. 1973-78; President 1979-82); Modern Lang. Assn. Am. (mem. Del. Assembly, twice Chrmn. 16th century French Lit. Div.); Assn. internat. des études françaises; Assn. des profs. de français des univs. canadiennes; Assn. canadienne de littérature comparée (Vice Pres. 1969-71); Internat'l Assoc. for Neo-Latin Studies; Soc. canadienne d'études de la Renaissance; Assn. des littératures canadienne et québecoise; Candn. Soc. Semiotic Research; N.D.P.; United Church; Home: 289 Clemow Ave., Ottawa, Ont. K1S 2B7; Office: 3460 McTavish St., Montréal, Qué. H3A 1X9.

KUTNEY, Peter Ray, B.Sc.; executive; b. Lethbridge, Alta., 12 July 1931; s. Harry and Helen K.; e. Lethbridge Secondary Schs.; Univ. of Alta., B.Sc. (Chem. Engn.); m. Laura Mae Stillings, 14 Aug. 1959 (divorced); one s. Peter Douglas; m. Irene Ruth Brooks, 3 Dec. 1972; PRESIDENT AND DIR., COSEKA RESOURCES LTD. since 1972; President and Director, Wharf Resources Limited; formerly Vice-Pres., Westcoast Transmission Co. Ltd.; Comnd. as Flying Offr., R.C.A.F. (R); Clubs: The Vancouver; Vancouver Lawn Tennis; Home: 802-300 Meredith Rd. N.E., Calgary, Alta. T2E 7A8

KUWABARA, (Mrs.) Seisho Kina, C.M.; b. Sendai, Japan 12 Apl. 1899; d. Koji and Ju (Sakurada) Takeuchi; e. Kyoritsu Women's Coll. in Konda, Tokyo, Japan, Dipl. in Home-Making (Kateika); Takeya Sch. of Moribana, Nageire and Bonkei; Kado Takeya Sch. of Japan, Cert. 1940; m. Peter Eiichi Kuwabara May 1923; four children; organ. Sunday Sch. for Japanese children, St. Augustine Ch. of Eng. in Can. and served on Women's Auxiliary, Holy Cross Mission for 10 yrs.; evacuated to Sandon, B.C. 1942 and came to Montreal in 1945; helped estb. a Japanese kindergarten, Sisters of Christ the King 1952; founded Montreal Br. of Kado Takeya Sch. and became an advisor of Seisho-Kai Club 1951; named Counsellor of Hdqrs., Kado Takeya Sch. of Japan 1961; estbd. Candn. Hdqrs. of Kado Takeya Sch. 1970; has served as judge for Fête des Fleurs, Museum of Fine Arts on several occasions as well as being a prize winner on other occasions; has been involved with Japanese flower arrangement demonstrations Montreal Bot. Gdn. and held numerous Ikebana exhns. Montreal, Three Rivers, Ottawa, Quebec City, Massena (N.Y.), Va. Beach, Cal. and Fla. as well as making appearances on Eng. and French TV; has given various demonstrations Que. Dept. Cultural Affairs, Handicapped groups, Ladies' Clubs, Church groups, Hortic. Soc's and rehabilitating prisoners; rec'd Queen's Silver Jubilee Medal; Japanese Cath. Women's Assn's Gold Medal; "Women of the Year" Award for community services; author "Ikebana and I" 1977; mem. Museum of Fine Arts Montreal; Internat. Ikebana (Montreal Br.); Anglican; Address: 2417 Mariette Ave., Montreal, Que. H4B 2E7.

L

LABERGE, Paul-Andre, M.A.; university professor; b. Quebec, Que., 14 March 1917; s. Andreas and Florida (Levesque) L.; e. Seminaire de Que. (Coll.), B.A. 1937; Laval Univ., L'èsL. 1941, M.A. 1940; m. Rita, d. Ernest Menard, 1 July 1943; children: Lise, Michèle, Francine, Marie, Claire, Jacques, Louise; taught at Rimouski, Que., 1940-43; Ed., "Notre Revue" (employee mag. of Que. Power Co.), 1943-44; taught at Le Séminaire de Que. 1944-57; joined Laval Univ. as Secy. of Curriculum Comte., Faculty of Arts, 1957-60; apptd. Secy., Faculty of Arts, 1960; mem. La Commission politique de la Féd. Libérale du Que., 1960-63; Sect.-Treas., Mun. of Le Village de l'Ancienne-Lorette; former Secy. (8 yrs.) and Pres. (2 yrs.), l'Assn. des prof. de l'enseignement secondaire classique de la P.Q.; Secy-Gen. Laval Univ. 1962-75; mem., Candn. Assn. Univ. Registrars (Past Pres.); has written articles for educ. mags.; R. Catholic; recreations: tennis, swimming, skiing; Home: 862 Bellevue St., Quebec, Que. G1V 2R5

LABERGE-COLAS, Hon. Rejane, B.A., LL.L., D.C.L.; judge; b. Montreal, Que., 23 Oct. 1923; d. Dr. Louis Xiste and Isabelle (Lefebvre) Laberge; e. Villa-Maria Convent, Montreal, 1940; Coll. Marguerite-Bourgeois, Westmount, B.A. 1943 (cum laude); Univ of Montreal, LL.L. 1951 (cum laude), D.C.L. Bishop's 1971; m. Emile Jules Colas, Q.C., 25 Oct. 1958; children: Bernard, Hubert, Francois; JUSTICE, SUPERIOR COURT, QUE., since 1969; called to Bar of Que. 1952; cr. Q.C. 1968; legal Dept., The Aluminum Co. of Canada Ltd., Montreal, 1952-57; mem. of firm Geoffrion & Prud-homme, Montreal, 1957-69; former mem., Jr. Bar Council, 1955-56; Vice Chrmn. Candn. Consumers Council 1968-70; specialized in corp. law; Founding Pres. Féd. des Femmes du Québec; mem. Montreal Pub. Safety Comn. 1960-64; toured Europe with Montreal Bach Choir (contralto) singing at Edinburgh Festival, Brussels, Basel, London and Paris, 1958; Dame Magistral Grace, Order of Malta; Roman Catholic; recreations: music, golf, skiing, tennis, swimming; Club: University Women's; Home: 1 Summerhill Terrace, Montreal, Que. H3H 1B8Office: Judges' Chambers, Superior Court, 1, East Notre-Dame St., Montreal, Que. H2Y 1B6

LaBROSSE, Guy; pharmaceuticals executive; b. Montreal, Que. 28 Nov. 1922; s. Joseph E. and Hortense (Crevier) LaB.; e. Public and High Schs., Montreal, Que.; Sir George Williams Univ.; m. Lucile, d. Henri Guay 21 June 1947; children: Francine, Diane, Louise, Guy; EXTVE. VICE PRES. AND GEN. MGR., PHARMACEUTICAL/CONSUMERS PRODUCTS GROUP, since 1977; cont. Dir. of Candn. subsid.; joined present Co. as Med. Service Rep. 1951, Mgr. French Dist. Que. 1957, Mgr. E. Dist. Que. and Maritimes 1960, Nat. Sales Mgr. 1965, Vice-Pres. and Dist. Mgr. Marketing 1970; Div. Vice-Pres., Searle Pharmaceuticals 1972; Pres. and Dir., G. D. Searle & Co. of Can. Ltd., 1973; Home: 541 Turicum Rd., Lake Forest, Ill.; Office: 4901 Searle Parkway, Skokie, Ill. 60680

LABROSSE, Hon. Jean-Marc, B.A., LL.B.; judge; b. Masson, Que. 2 June 1935; s. Olida and Gracia (Pilon) L.; e. Ecole St. Charles Ottawa 1949; Univ. of Ottawa High Sch. 1953; Univ. of Ottawa B.A. 1957, LL.B. 1960; m. Louise d. Armand Dumas, Malartic, Que. 1 Dec. 1962; children: Danielle, Michèle, Marc; JUDGE, SUPREME COURT OF ONT.; called to Bar of Ont. 1962; law practice Sudbury, Ont. 1962-75; served with U.N.T.D., comnd. as Sub-Lt. 1960, retired 1961; while in Sudbury actively engaged in Jr. Hockey and served as Dir. of Sudbury Wolves Jr. Hockey Club; Dir. Sudbury Dist. Boys Home; mem. Candn. Bar Assn.; Advocates' Soc.; R. Catholic; recreations: golf, skiing, fishing, hunting; Office: 130 Queen St. W., Toronto, Ont. M5H 2N5.

LABROSSE, Leo E.,., B.Com.; company executive; b. Montreal, Que., 20 Nov. 1925; s. Eddy Joseph and Hortense (Crevier) L.; e. Sir George Williams Coll., B. Com. 1956; m. Claire, d. late Georges Lesage, 24 June 1950; children: Pierre, Johanne; PRES., ATLANTIC SUGAR LTD.; mem., Montreal Board Trade; Roman Catholic; recreations: skiing, golf, swimming, tennis reading; Home: 1580 Markham Rd., Town of Mount Royal, Que. H3P 3B2; Office: 5660 Ferrier, Montreal, Que. H4P 1M7

LACE, Francis Dwyer, D.S.O., O.B.E., E.D.; investment dealer; b. Qu'Appelle, Sask., 20 Nov. 1911; s. Algernon Francis Doyne and Marion Edith (Leonard) L.; e. Upper Can. Coll., Toronto, Ont., 1922-28 (Sr. Matric.); Royal Mil. Coll., Kingston, Ont. Grad. 1932; m. Barbara Lynne, d. W. Boyd Caldwell, Toronto, Ont., 12 Sept. 1939; children: Roger Dwyer, Catherine Anne; Hon. Dir., Domin-

ion Securities Ames Ltd.; Algonquin Mercantile Corp.; Harding Carpets Ltd.; Hardee Farms Ltd.; Trustee, Toronto Western Hospital; Jr. with A. E. Ames & Co. Ltd., Invest. Dealers, Toronto, Ont., 1932-37; joined Matthews and Co. Ltd. in 1937 as Salesman; admitted a Partner, 1946, and apptd. Vice-Pres. in 1952, Pres. 1960; Dir. 1972-75; served with Candn. Militia, 1932-39; Candn. Army Active, Overseas, 1939-45; promoted to rank of Brig. on active service, Oct. 1944, C.R.A. 2 Candn. Div.; awarded D.S.O., O.B.E.; Chrmn. of Ont. Dist., Invest. Dealers Assn. Can., 1958-59; Anglican; recreations: golf, tennis; Clubs: Toronto Golf; Toronto; Badminton & Racquet; Home: 15 Hillholm Road, Toronto, Ont. M5P 1M1; Office: 320 Bay St., Toronto, Ont. M5H 2P7

LACHANCE, Gustave, C.M., B. ès L., D.D.S.; educator; b. Quebec City, Que. 20 Dec. 1912; s. late Joseph Michel Eusebe and late Edith Pritchard (Guité); e. Hist. Guide of Que. Cert. 1928; Que. Little Semy. B. ès L. 1930; Univ. Montreal, Certificate of B.C.P. 1933; Univ. Montreal Bachelor of Dental Surg. 1935, D.D.S. 1937; m. Jeanne d. late Pierre Poirier, Bonaventure Cty., Que. 16 Oct. 1937; children: Jacques (m. Rita Dorion), Odette (m. François Labrousse), Louis de Gaspé (m. Nicole Talbot), Andre; PROF. OF DENTAL MED., LAVAL UNIV., Dir. of Clinics since 1972 and Archivist since 1974; dental practice New Richmond, Que. 1937-50, Quebec City 1950-72; Asst. Prof. of Dental Med., Laval Univ. 1972, Assoc. Prof. 1978, Life mem. Laval Univ. Foundation 1975; Special Counsellor, Laval Univ. Service of Expansion B.; 1980, Past Pres. Inst. Canadien de Que. 1966-69; La Croix Rouge Canadienne, New Richmond Dist. 1946-49; La Caisse Populaire Desjardins New Richmond 1948-50; La Soc. Dentaire de Qué. 1954-55; Le Congrès Internat. Richelieu, Que. 1961-62; Poly-Glot (1963) Inc. Que. 1963-68; Bibliothèque Municipale de Qué. 1966-69; Jeunesses Musicales du Can. Que. Sec. 1967-68; Gov., Ordre des Dentistes du Qué. 1968-72; Consulting Dentist, Qué. Workmen's Compens. Bd., 1969-72; Qué. Symphonic Orchestra, 1979-; Past Dir. Assn. des Medecins et Dentistes de la Gaspésie 1939-50; Corp. du Theatre du Vieux-Que. 1967-68; Corp. du Theatre Le Trident Inc. Que. 1970-71; Ordre des Dentistes du Que. 1968-72; Assn. Dentaire Canadienne (Exécutif des Congrès Nat. Toronto) 1968-69; Corp. de l'Opéra du Qué. 1971-75; Gov., Que. Symphonic Orchestra since 1980; Corp. du Pavillon des Jeunes Inc. St. Damien since 1975; Adm., Laval Hospital Inst. of Cardiology; rec'd Order of Merit, Univ. of Montreal 1936; Centennial Medal 1967; Order of Canada 1978; mem. emeritus 1977 Inst. Canadien de Que.; mem. Canadian Opera Guild 1974-; Heritage Canada 1975-; Can. Dental Assn.; Order Dentists Que. (Gov. 1968-72); Am. Assn. Dental Faculties; Que. City Dental Club (Past Pres.); Can. Soc. of History of Med., Quebec City Sect.; Advisory Board of "Les Presses" de l'Université Laval 1979-; Liberal; R. Catholic; recreations: music, reading, writing, travel; Home: 1695 Parc des Sources, Sillery, Que. G1S 4B6;

LACHAPELLE, Roger; b. Montreal, Que., 5 Apr. 1925; e. Lachine (Que.) High Sch.; Sir George Williams Coll.; McGill Univ.; m. Jeanne Carey, 29 Aug. 1953; children: Robert, Marc, Marie-Josée, Lucie; CHAIRMAN OF THE BOARD, MEAGHER'S DISTILLERY LTD.; Pres. and C.E.O. Corby Distilleries Ltd., 1979-; Dir., BNP Canada Inc.; Meagher's Distillery Ltd.; Corby Distilleries Ltd.; Dir. Club St. Denis; Assoc. of Can. Distillers; Alliance Mutuelle-Vie; joined Transparent Paper Products Ltd., as Secy. Treas., 1949-60, Extve. Vice-Pres., 1960-66; Pres. and Mang. Dir., 1966; served in 2nd World War with RCAF, 1943-45; recreations: boating, fishing, hunting, skiing; Clubs: St. Denis; Forest & Stream; Mount-Royal; Home: 11807 de Meulles, Cartierville, Que. H4J 2E4; Office: 1201 Sherbrooke St.W. Montreal, Que. H3A 1J1

LACOSTE, Gérald Alexandre, B.A., LL.L., LL.M., b. Lac Lacoste, Labelle Co. Que., 18 July 1943; s. Judge

Marc and Jacqueline (Barsalou) L.; e. Coll. St-Viateur d'Outremont B.A. 1963; Univ. of Montreal LL.L. 1966; Univ. of London LL.M. 1968, L.S.E. (Pub. Adm.) 1969; m. Fernande d. W. Boutin, 2 Sept. 1967; children: Marie-Catherine, Alexandra, Hugo; called to Bar of Que. 1967; mem. Extve. Comte. and Gen. Council Bar Prov. Que. 1975-76; Counsellor Bar of Montréal 1975-77 (Secy. Jr. Bar 1972-73); R. Catholic; recreations: fishing, hunting; Home: 44 ave. Thornton, Ville Mont-Royal, Qué. H3P 1H4;

LACOSTE, Paul, O.C., LL.L., Ph.D.; lawyer, professor; b. Montreal, P.Q., 24 April 1923; s. Juliette (Boucher) and the late Wing Commdr. Emile L., C.G.A.; e. Univ. of Montreal, B.A. 1943, M.A. 1944, L. Ph. 1946, LL.L. 1960; Univ. of Chicago, 1946-47; Univ. of Paris, Ph.D. 1948; m. Louise Marcil, 31 Aug. 1973; one d., Helene; one s., Paul-André; RECTOR, UNIV. OF MONTREAL; Prof. of Philos. (1946-), and Law (1962-70), Univ. of Montreal; Partner, Lalande, Brière, Reeves, Lacoste & Paquette, 1964-66; Commentator and Moderator on C.B.C. Radio and Television, 1948-63; mem. Royal Comn. on Biling. & Biculturalism (1963-71); mem. Superior Council of Educ., Qué. 1964-68; Que. Univs. Council (1969-77); Council of City of Montreal and of Montreal Urban Community (1970-74); Mem. of Bd., Ecole polytechnique de Montréal (1975-); Institut de recherches cliniques de Montréal (1975-); Association des universités partiellement ou entièrement de langue française (1975-)Pres. 1978-81; Fonds international de coopération universitaire (1975-81); Association of Commonwealth Universities (1977-80); Vice-Pres., Canada Studies Foundation (1972-79); Officer of the Order of Canada (1977); Hon. Doctor of Laws, McGill Univ., 1975, Univ. of Toronto, 1978; Human Relations Award, Cdn. Council of Christians and Jews, 1981; Pres., Soc. de Philosophie de Montréal, 1951-57; Vice Rector, Univ. of Montreal 1966; Extve. Vice Rector, 1968-75; Pres., Conf. of Rectors & Principals of Que. Univs., 1977-79; Pres., Association of Universities & Colleges f Canada, 1978-79; Candn. Philos. Assn.; Candn. Assn. of Univ. Teachers; Montreal Museum of Fine Arts; Publications (with others): "Justice et paix scolaire", 1962; "A Place of Liberty", 1964; "Principes de gestion universitaire", 1970; "Education permanente et potentiel universitaire", 1977; Club: Saint Denis; Office: Univ. de Montréal, 2900 boul. Edouard-Montpetit, Montréal, Qué. H3C 3J7

LACOURCIERE, Hon. Maurice-Norbert; judge; b. Montmartre, Sask., 8 Oct. 1920; s. Joseph-Emile Q.C. and Atala (Fortin) L.; e. Coll. Mathieu, Gravelbourg, Sask., Univ. of Ottawa, B.A. 1940; Osgoode Hall Law Sch.; m. 7 April 1956; children: Luc, Marc, Brigitte, François, Chantal, Michel; JUSTICE, COURT OF APPEAL, ONT., since 1974; read law with Phelan, O'Brien & Phelan, Toronto, and J. E. Lacourciere, Q.C., Sudbury; called to Bar of Ont. 1949; served 1 yr. with H.O. Crown Life Ins. Co., Toronto after call to Bar; thereafter in partnership with father, J. E. Lacourciere, Q.C., in Sudbury; apptd. Judge of Co. Court, Nipissing District, 1964; Justice, Supreme Court of Ontario 1967; served with the R.C.A.F. 1941-45, rank Flying Offr.; (mem., Bd. of Govs., Laurentian Univ. 1962-69); Past Gen. Chrmn., Sudbury & Dist. Un. Welfare Fund; Pres., Sudbury Law Assn., 1955; Past Dist. Gov. (1956), N. Ont. Richelieu Soc.; Past Pres., Société Historique du Nouvel Ont.; Chmn., Editorial Advisory Bd., Cdn. Bar Review; mem. (1968-72) Bd. of Govs., Univ. of Toronto; Inst. of Judicial Admin.; R. Catholic; recreations: golf, swimming; Club: York Downs Golf & Country; Office: Osgoode Hall, Toronto, Ont. M5H 2N5

LACROIX, Benoît; éducateur; né St-Michel de Bellechasse, Qué. 8 septembre 1915; f. Caius et Rose-Anna (Blais) L.; é. Lectorat en Théologie Ottawa 1941; Maîtrise ès sciences médiévales, Toronto 1946, Doctorat ès sciences médiévales Toronto 1951; Harvard Univ. 1959-60

(Bourse Guggenheim); PROFESSEUR, INSTITUT d'ETUDES MÉDIEVALES, UNIV. DE MONTREAL depuis 1960; Directeur-fondateur de Vie des Lettres Canadiennes 1956-75; Professeur invité aux Universités de Kyoto, Butare et de Caen; Directeur, Institut d'Etudes Médiévales, Univ. de Montréal 1962-68; Centre d'études des Religions populaires (Montréal) depuis 1970; Prof. invité au Dept. d'histoire (CELAT), Univ. Laval, 1978-; Dir. de l'Édition critique Lionel Groulx, Montréal, 1979; Chercher & mem. du Comte. Scient. de l'Inst. québ. de recherche sur la culture, Qué., 1979; auteur "Pourquoi aimer le moyen âge?" 1950; "Les débuts de l'historiographie chrétienne" 1951; "L'histoire dans l'antiquité" 1951; "Vie des Lettres et histoire canadienne" 1954; "Compagnons de Dieu" 1961; "Le P'tit Train" 1964; "Orose et ses idées" 1965; "Le Japon entrevu" 1966; "Le Rwanda: au pays des mille collines" 1966; "L'historien au moyen âge" 1971; "Les cloches" 1974; en collaboration "The Development of Historiography" 1954; "Classiques canadiens" ("Saint Denys Garneau" 1956, "Lionel Groulx" 1967); "Edition critique des Oeuvres de Saint Denys Garneau" 1971; "Folklore de la mer et religion", 1980; "Les Pèlerinages au Québec" 1980; "Célébration des saisons" 1981; articles nombreux; mem. Société Royale du Can.; Académie des Sciences Morales et Politiques; Catholique; Adresse: 2715 Côte Sainte-Catherine, Montréal, Qué. H3T 1B6;

LACROIX, Mt. Rev. Fernand, C.J.M. (R.C.); bishop of Edmundston; b. Quebec City, Que., 16 Oct. 1919; s. Jean-Charles and Cécile (Doré) L.; e. Ecole Morissette, Que.; Coll. du Sacre-Coeur, Bathurst, N.B.; Scolasticat des Eudistes, Charlesbourg, Que.; Univ. "Angelicum", Rome, Licence en Droit Canon 1949; Address: Centre Diocésain, Edmundston, N.B.

LACROIX, Georgette; auteur et journaliste; née Québec, Que. 6 avril 1921; f. Jean Baptiste et Alice (Mercier) L.; é. Congrégation Notre Dame St. Malo; Inst. Jean Thomas; cours privés pour l'espagnol et l'italien; une f. Hélène; 24 années de radio CHRC à 2 années de journ. à "L'Action Québec; collaboration à 'Echos-Vedettes", "Québec en Bref" et "Audace" (revue belge); Dir. de la revue "Poésie" de la Soc. des Poètes Candn.-Français; depuis 1972 à l'emploi du Gouv. du Que., Min. des Affaires culturelles; d'abord comme attaché de presse du min., puis agent d'information au Service des Lettres, agent culturel au Service de la Recherche; rédatrice du bulletin d'information "Archives en tête", des Archives nationales du Qué. 1978-81; archiviste au Centre de la Capitale; auteur de "Mortes Saisons" 1967; "Entre Nous . . . Ce Pays" 1970 (Prix France Que. 1971); "Le Creux de la Vague" 1972; "Aussi Loin que Demain" 1973; "Dans L'Instant de ton Age" 1974; "Au large d'Eros" 1975; "Vivre l'automne" 1976; "Québec 1608-1978" (1978); "Québec, Capitale de la Neige", (1979); 'Québec', 1979; "Faire un enfant", 1980; "Hommage au Québec, Eugène Kedl Photographe", 1980; "Artistes du Quebec", 1980; à mérité 2 prix de poésie de la Soc. du Bon Parler Francais, Montreal 1963, 1969; prix des Arts et Poésie de Touraine (France) 1972; membre du bureau de direction de la Soc. des Ecrivains Can.; Salon internat du livre de Qué; mem. du comité de la collection Civilisation du Qué du min. des Aff. culturelle; Dir., concours litt. pour le Prix Air Can. 1981; catholique; é. récréations: lecture, natation, cinéma, voyages; residence: 694 rue St-Jean, Québec, Que. G1R 1P8; bureau: Archives Nationales du Qué. 1210 ave. du Séminaire, C.P. 10450, Sainte-Foy, Que. G1V 4N1

LACROIX, Marcel, P.Eng.; company president; b. Ste. Marie, Beauce Co., Que., 13 March 1930; s. Charles and Marie (Giroux) L.; e. Laval Univ., Civil Engn., 1953; m. Louise, d. Fernand Boutin, Quebec City, Que., 9 Oct. 1954; children: Monique, Charles, Camille; PRES., Corp. Marcel Lacroix; Dir., Candn. Union Ins. Ltd.; Resource Service Group Ltd.; mem., Corp. Prof. Engrs. Que.;

Engn. Inst. Can.; K. of C.; Roman Catholic; recreations: golfing, skiing; Home: 2140 Parc Gomin, Sillery, Que. G1T 1A5; Office: 2125 boul. Charest ouest, St.-Foy, Québec, G1N 2G2

LACROIX, Richard; painter-engraver-sculptor; b. Montreal, Que., 14 July 1939; s. Simon and Reine (Despres) L.; e. Inst. of Graphic Arts of Prov. of Que., Montreal, Dipl. 1960; Montreal Sch. of Fine Arts, Cert. of Pedagogy and Methodology, 1960; Inst. of Applied Arts, Montreal, Cert. of Aesthetics and Art Hist., 1960; rec'd Can. Council Award to study engraving in various European studios, 1961-64; with help of Que. Ministry of Cultural Affairs founded Atelier Libre De Recherches Graphiques for graphic research; co-founder of Fusion Des Arts, Inc., 1964; with aid of Min. of Cultural Affairs, Que., and Can. Council founded The Graphic Guild, dedicated to publishing original Candn. prints 1966; further scholarships, 1968, 1971, and 1978, from Qué. Min. of Cultural Affairs; scholarship for free work from Prov. Bank of Can., 1978; directed environment design for 7th Montreal Film Festival, 1966; designed plastic program and poster for "Festival du Quebec" 1967; directed kinetic sculpture "Fusion des Arts" Expo; "Frappez la Cocotte" Mus. Contemp. Art, Montreal, 1967; kinetic sculptures for Montreal Internat. Airport, Radio-Quebec 1968; Invited Teacher, Dept. of Art History, Univ. Que., Montreal 1969-70; designed cloth banner for Confederation Museum, Charlottetown, P.E.I., 1970 murals Pie-X School, Montreal, Cath. Sch. Bd. 1971; supv. organ. Graphic Guild 1972; mem. of Jury, 10th Salon Internat. de la Caricature 1973; one man shows: Gallerie l'Art Francais, Montreal, 1961; Maison du Can., Paris, 1962-63; Dorothy Cameron Gallery, Toronto, 1963; Gallerie Agnes Lefort, Montreal, 1963; Gallery XIII, Montreal Mus. of Fine Arts, 1964; Art Centre of Jeunesse Musicules, Mont-Orford, 1966; Fleet Gallery, Winnipeg, 1966; Triangle Gallery, San Francisco, 1968; Dunkelman Gallery, Toronto, 1968; Univ. of Sask. 1969; Boutique Soleil, Montreal, 1969; Open House, 4677 St. Denis, Montreal, 1970; Mont-Orford, Que., 1978; Place des Arts, Montreal, 1978; Galerie "A", Montreal, 1980; has exhibited in group shows in Can., Europe, S. Am., U.S. and Asia including Internat. Biennal of Engraving; Internat. Triennal of Engravings; Bienal Americanna de grabado/Am. Biennal of Engraving; Québec Pavillion, Osaka, Japan, 1970; author of deluxe portfolios "Sept Eaux-Fortes", 1959; "Pierres du Soleil", poems and lithos, 1960; "Bestiaire", etchings, 1961; "Metamorphose de la Pitoune" 1969; "Poems d'Alain Grandbois", (illus.), 1970; "Mutations" 1970; "Cristaux" 1971; "Danses Carrées" 1973; "Keys", 1975; "Kamis", 1977; films & documentaries, "LaGraveur", C.B.C. TV; "La Fougere et La Rouille", N.F.B. Can.; "Il Ne Faut Pas se Couper l'Orielle pour Ca", N.F.B. Can; "Il Faut Que l'Itippopotame Poursuive sa Demarche", Que. Film Bd.; received First Prize, Fête des Fleurs, 1960 and Purchase Award, Spring Show, 1962, Montreal Museum of Fine Arts; Prize, Second Burnaby Nat. Print Show, 1963; Candn. Graphic Assn., 1964; Internat. Biennale of Graphic Art, Lugano, Switzerland, 1964; First Prize, Painting Sec., Hadassah Exhn., Montreal, 1965, 2nd Prize, 1966; Purchase Award 10th Annual Print Exhn., Calgary 1970; 1st choise, Montreal Catholic Sch. Bd. contest for murals, 1971; 1st Prize, Graphics, Hadassah Auction, Montreal 1974; Prize, Que. Engraving concourse, Cult. Centre, Sherbrooke Univ., 1977; lectures & seminars on engraving & sculpling, Montreal Mus. F.A.; Univ. of Qué.; U.B.C., Vancouver; Studio of Graphic Guild, Montreal; rep. in collections in Can. & abroad, incl. Montreal Mus. Fine Arts, Nat. Gallery of Can., Art Gallery of Ont., Victoria & Albert Museum (London, Eng.), Museum of Modern Art (N.Y.), Cabinet des Estampes, Bibliothèque Nationale de Paris; Canada Council; Radio-Canada, Montreal; mem., Cinématheque canadienne; Soc. des Artistes prof. du Que.; Candn. Soc. of Graphic Art; Home: 4273 Fabre, Montreal, Que. H2J 3T5; Studio & Office: La Guilde Graphique, 9 St. Paul Ouest, Old Montreal, H2Y 1Y6

LADLY, Frederick Bernard, B.A.; food processing executive; b. Toronto, Ont. 14 July 1930; s. John Bernard and Olivia Montgomery (Fennimore) L.; e. Univ. of Toronto B.A. 1951; m. Sharon Mary Davidson children: Martha Jane, Patricia Anne, Lois Elizabeth, Katharine Olivia, Sarah Jane; EXTVE. VICE PRES. and Dir. CANADA PACKERS INC. since 1978; Pres. and Dir., William Davies Co. Inc. (USA); Chrmn. and Dir., Canada Packers (Japan) Inc.; Dir., Canada Packers GmbH (Germany); Fleischwarenfabrik Waltner GmbH & Co. Ltd. (Germany); Dir., Canada Packers (Australia) Pty. Ltd.; Canada Packers (U.K.); Teys Bros. (Beenleigh) Holdings Pty. Ltd. (Australia); Haverhill Meat Products Ltd. (U.K.); John Loudon and Co. Ltd; (U.K.); Vice Pres. Canada Packers Ltd. 1975; Home: 48 Burnhamthorpe Park Blvd., Islington, Ont. M9A 1J1; Office: 95 St. Clair Ave. W., Toronto, Ont. M4V 1P2.

LADOUCEUR, Roland J.,M. Com.; film executive; b. Trois-Rivières, Qué. 2 March 1929; s. Elzéar and Yvonne (Landry) L.; e. Laval Univ. Sch. of Adm. B.Com. 1951, M.Com. 1952; Univ. of Ottawa Sch. of Pol. Sciences Dipl. 1953; m. Henriette d. late Paul Martel 19 June 1954; EXTVE. DIR. FILM CANADA CENTER 1980- ; joined Nat. Film Bd. Can. 1953 serving as Assoc. Dir. of Distribution and Cost Acct.; Asst. Govt. Film Commr. Montreal 1966-68; Dir. for Europe, Middle East and Africa Nat. Film Bd. Paris 1968-74, U.S. Gen. Mgr. N.Y. 1974-78, Dir. of Pub. Relations Montreal 1978-80; recipient Queen's Silver Jubilee Medal 1977; Accredited mem. Candn. Pub. Relation Soc.; mem. Candn. Cultural Extves.; Conf. on Candn. Information (Vice Chrmn.); Acad. Candn. Cinema; Candn. Soc. Los Angeles; R. Catholic; recreations: cinema, arts and cultural activities, travel, golf, new cuisine; Club: Canadian; Home: 256 South Spalding Dr., Beverly Hills, Cal. 90212; Office: Suite 400, 144 S. Beverly Dr., Beverly Hills, CA 90212.

LAFLEUR, Guy Damien; hockey player; b. Thurso, Que., 20 Sept. 1951; s. Rejean and Pierrette L.; m. Lise (Barre), 16 June 1973; children: one. s. Martin; spotted by scouts while leading Thurso team to class C title in 1962 Quebec international peewee tournament; at 14 joined Quebec City junior B team; following year played eight junior A games scoring first of 315 junior A goals with Quebec Ramparts; in first full junior campaign scored 30 goals, added 50 next year, 103 third season; scored 130 goals, 79 assists for 209 points in final junior season; Montreal's first choice and first overall in 1971 amateur draft; scored 29 goals as rookie and in six years three times has cleared 50 goals; through 1971-77 in 445 games scoring 243 goals, 312 assists for 555 points, 221 penalty minutes, plus 67 playoff games scoring 32 goals, 44 assists for 76 points, 38 penalty minutes; three times first team all-star right winger; Art Ross Trophy 1976, 1977; Lester B. Pearson Trophy 1976, 1977; Hart Trophy 1977; Conn Smythe Trophy 1977; Sport Magazine playoff MVP award 1977; mem., Team Canada 1976, 1981; Home; 15 Magnolia Rd., Baie D'Urfe, Que. H9X 3K7; Office: 2313 St. Catherine St. W., Montreal, Que. H3H 1N2

LAFLEUR, Henri Grier, Q.C.; b. Montreal, Que., 17 June 1908; s. Henri Amedee and Olive Masson (Grier) L.; e. Selwyn House Prep. Sch., Montreal, 1922; Lower Can. Coll., Montreal, 1925; McGill Univ., B.A. 1929; Rhodes Scholar, Quebec, 1929; Oxford Univ., B.A. 1931, B.C.L. 1932; m. Celia Frances Cantlie; two s. by 1st m.; COUNSEL, LAFLEUR, BROWN, DE GRANDPRÉ; called to Bar at the Inner Temple, London, Eng. 1932; Quebec 1933; cr. K.C. 1946; practised law with Cook & Magee, Montreal, 1933-37; Mann, Lafleur & Brown, 1938; City Councillor, Montreal, 1939-45; Zeta Psi; Presbyterian; Clubs: Mount Royal; Metropolitan, New York; Montreal Racket; Orleans Fish & Game; Home: 337 Metcalfe Ave., Westmount, Que. H3Z 2J2; Office: Ste. 720, P.O. Box 214, Stock Exchange Tower Montreal, Que. H4Z 1E4

LA FOREST, Gerard V. J., Q.C., B.C.L., M.A., LL.M., J.S.D., LL.D., F.R.S.C. (1975); Judge; b. Grand Falls, N.B. 1 Apl. 1926; s. J. Alfred and Philomene (Lajoie) La F.; e. Grand Falls (N.B.) Pub. and High Schs.; St. Francis Xavier Univ., 1946-48; Univ. of N.B., B.C.L. 1949; St. John's Coll., Oxford Univ. (Rhodes Scholar), B.A. Juris. 1951, M.A. 1956; Yale Univ. (Yale Grad. Fellow), LL.M. 1965, J.S.D. 1966; LL.D. (Ba), 1981; m. D. Marie, d. William Warner, 27 Dec. 1952; children: Marie, Kathleen, Anne, Elizabeth, Sarah; JUSTICE, NEW BRUNSWICK COURT OF APPEAL, 1981-; Prof. Law and Dir. Legislative Drafting Prog., Faculty of Law (Common Law Section) Ottawa, 1979-81; called to the Bar of N.B. 1949; cr. Q.C. 1968; law practice Grand Falls, N.B. 1951-52; Adv. Counsel, Legal Br., Dept. of Justice, Ottawa, 1952-55; Legal Advisor, Irving Oil, Saint John, N.B., 1955-56; Assoc. Prof. Univ. of N.B. 1956-63; Prof. 1963-68; Dean of Law, Univ. of Alberta, 1968-70; Asst. Depy. Atty. Gen. of Can. (Research & Planning) 1970-74; Commissioner, Law Reform Com. of Canada, 1974-79; frequent consultant to federal and provincial governments including appearances in Constitutional Law cases before the Supreme Court of Canada; served on Glassco Royal Commission and Royal Comn. on Pilotage; Adviser to Special Counsel on Constitution to Min. of Justice and Prime Min. 1967-70; Chrmn., Fed.-Prov. Inquiry on Kouchibouquac Nat. Park; publs. incl. ''Disallowance and Reservation of Provincial Legislation''; ''Extradition to and from Canada''; ''Natural Resources and Public Property under the Canadian Constitution''; ''The Allocation of Taxing Powers under the Canadian Constitution''; ''Water Law in Canada''; co-author ''Le Territoire Quebecois''; also numerous articles; Extve. Vice Chrmn., Candn. Bar Assn. Comte on the Constitution of Can., 1977-78; mem., N.B. Bar; Assn. Candn. Law Teachers; R. Catholic; Home: 115 Church St., Fredericton, N.B. E3B 4C8; Office: Justice Bldg., P.O. Box 6000, Fredericton, N.B. E3B 5H1

LAFORTUNE, Gerald Daniel; manufacturer; b. Hull, Que. 10 June 1925; s. Gerald Lafortune; e. Notre Dame Coll. Hull; Holy Ghost Fathers, Ironsides, Que.; m. Yolande; children: Anne, Marc, Guy; PRES., CEO. AND SHAREHOLDER WITH CONTROLLING INTEREST, DUSTBANE ENTERPRISES LTD. since 1960; joined Dustbane as Jr. Bookeeper 1946 becoming Acct., Chief Acct., Secy.-Treas.; apptd. Pres. Modern Building Cleaning Div. 1959; R. Catholic; recreations: tennis, fishing, hand-ball; Clubs: Laurentian; Seigniory (Montebello); Aylmer Country; Home: 85 Range Rd., Ottawa, Ont. K1N 8J6; Office: 250 Tremblay Rd., Ottawa, Ont. K1G 3K1

LAFRAMBOISE, G. Guy, M.D., F.R.C.S.(C); otolaryngologist; educator; b. Ottawa, Ont. 24 Aug. 1927; s. George Etienne and Marie Antoinette (Smith) L.; e. Loyola Coll. Montreal B.A. 1948; Univ. of Ottawa L.B., L.M.C.C. 1954; Johns Hopkin's Hosp. Postgrad. Residency Training Otolaryngol. 1954-59; m. Mary Anne d. John Darcy Coulson 6 Oct. 1951; children: Lise Anne, Lorainne, Julie, Estelle, Moira, Guy Jr., Deirde, Nicole; CHRMN. OF OTOLARYNGOLOGY, UNIV. OF OTTAWA MED. SCH. since 1964; Chrm. of Otolaryngol. Ottawa Gen. Hosp.; Consultant Otolaryngol. Riverside Hosp., Ottawa Civic Hosp., St. Louis Marie De Monfort Hosp., Hôpital Sacré Coeur of Hull, Centre Hospitalier de Buckingham, Centre Hospitalier de Maniwaki, Nat. Defence Med. Centre; has contributed and organized Rhinoseptoplasty courses Univ. of Toronto, Univ. of Montreal; service with Hull Regt. Armoured Corps (Reserve); has presented papers on Rhinoseptoplasty in Children; mem. Ottawa Acad. Med.; Candn. and Ont. Med. Assns.; Liberal; R. Catholic; recreations: fly fishing, upland bird shooting, white water canoeing, farming, riding; Home: Luskville, Que.; Office: Ottawa General Hospital, 501 Smyth Rd., Ottawa, K1H 8L6

LAGACE, Hon. Maurice E., B.A., LL.L.; judge; b. Montreal, Que. 29 Oct. 1931; s. Omer and Blanche (Legault) L.; e. Coll. Ste.-Marie Montréal B.A. 1952; Univ. of Montreal LL.L. 1956; m. Louise d. Lt. Col. Paul Lambert, Montreal, Que. 5 Aug. 1961; children: Pascale, Janique, Marie-Claire; JUDGE, SUPERIOR COURT MONTREAL; called to Bar of Que. 1956; cr. Q.C. 1972; former Sr. Assoc. Martineau, Walker, Allison, Beaulieu & Associates; R. Catholic; Home: 4150 Trafalgar Rd., Montreal Que. H3Y 1R2.

LAGASSE, Jacques; notary; b. St-Hyacinthe, Que., 24 Aug. 1916; s. Joseph Arsene and Yvonne (Cadorette) L.; e. Acad. of Sacred Heart, Windsor, Que.; St. Charles Semy., Sherbrooke, Que.; Univ. of Montreal; Notary 1939; LL.D. (hon.c.) Univ. of Sherbrooke; m. Suzanne, d. Dr. Jean Marcoux, Sherbrooke, Que., 22 Feb. 1941; children: Françoise L. (Mrs. Pierre Boily), Jacques, Pierre, Louis; MEM., LAGASSE, LAGASSE & LAGASSE (established 1939); Pres., CJRS Radio Sherbrooke Inc.; Dir. and Mem. of Extve. Counc. of Banque Canadienne Nationale 1972-80; Sec. of Enterprises Rimac, Inc.; Dir. Economic-Mutuelle Assn.-Vie; Past Pres., Bd. of Notaries Que.; Memb. Admin. Counc. Univ. of Sherbrooke Liberal; Roman Catholic; recreations: golf, skiing; Clubs: Sherbrooke Country; Social; Golf Longchamp Inc.; Reform; Mount Royal; Home: 245 Heneker St., Sherbrooke, Que. J1J 3G5; Office: 32 Wellington St. N., Sherbrooke, Que.

LAHEY, Rev. Raymond John, M.Th., Ph.D.; clergyman b. St. John's, Nfld. 29 May 1940; s. Raymond John and Marguerite Mary (Murphy) L.; e. St. Bonaventure's Coll. St. John's Nfld.; Univ. of Ottawa B.Th. 1961, M.Th. 1963, Ph.D. 1966; Gregorian Univ. Rome and Cambridge Univ. post-doctoral studies; VICAR-GEN., ARCHDIOCESE OF ST. JOHN'S, NFLD 1981-; Principal, St. John's Coll. Mem. Univ. of Nfld. 1968-81; Prof. (1980) and Head (1977) of Religious Studies; Chrmn. of the Senate, Archdiocese of St. John's; Asst. Prof. of Religious Studies present Univ. 1968, Assoc. Prof. 1972, Acting Head of Dept. 1974-75; coauthor ''Bishops and Writers: Aspects of the Evolution of Modern English Catholicism'' 1977; various articles religious hist.; contrib. to ''Dictionary of Canadian Biography''; R. Catholic; Home: Basilica Residence, Box 1363, St. John's Nfld. A1C 5N5; Office: St. John's, Nfld. A1C 5S7.

LAHN, Mervyn Lloyd, B.A.; trust company executive; b. Hanover, Ont., 24 June 1933; s. Charles Henry and Emma Wilhelmine Frederika (Leifso) L.; e. Hanover (Ont.) Pub. and High Schs., 1951; Waterloo Coll., Univ. of W. Ont., B.A. 1954, Grad. Mang. Training Course 1964; m. Myra Ann Helen, d. late J. Herbert Smith, 17 Sept. 1960; two s.: John Geoffrey, Pearce Alexander, one d. Margaret Ann; PRES. AND CHIEF EXEC. OFFR., THE CANADA TRUST CO. & Can. Trustco Mortgage Co., Dir., The Dominion Life Assurance Co.; Union Gas Ltd.; Heritage Group Inc.; Hayes-Dana Ltd.; Can. Trust Co.; John Labatt Ltd.; joined Waterloo Trust and Savings Co. 1955; apptd. Asst. Treas. 1958, Treas. 1959, Asst. Gen. Mgr. and Treas. 1967; Asst. Gen. Mgr., Canada Trust 1968, Depy. Gen. Mgr. 1972, Sr. Vice Pres. & Gen. Mgr. 1973; Extve. Vice Pres. 1974; Pres. and Chief Operating Officer, 1978; Pres. & C.E.O. Dec. 1979; P. Conservative; Lutheran; recreations: curling, golf; Clubs: London Hunt; The London; Toronto; Westmount Golf & Country, Home: 1597 Ryersie Rd., London, Ont. N6G 2S2; Office: Canada Trust Tower, City Centre, London, Ont.

LAIDLER, Keith James, M.A., Ph.D., D.Sc., F.C.I.C., F.R.S.C., university professor; b. Liverpool, Eng., 3 Jan. 1916; s. George James and Hilda (Findon) L.; e. Liverpool Coll., 1929-34; Trinity Coll., Oxford (1934-38), B.A., M.A., D.Sc.; Commonwealth Fellow, Princeton Univ. (1938-40), Ph.D. 1940; m. Mary Cabell, d. late John Auchincloss, 22 June 1943; children: late Margaret Cabell (Mrs. Paul McGaw), Audrey Auchincloss (Mrs. Peter

Bunting), James Reid; PROF. EMERITUS OF CHEMIS-TRY, UNIV. OF OTTAWA, since 1981; Prof. of Chem. 1955-81; Chairman of Dept., 1961-66; Vice-Dean, Faculty of Pure and Applied Science, 1963-66; Research Scientist, N.R.C. (Ottawa), 1940-42; Scient. Offr., Inspection Bd. of U.K., 1942-44; Chief Scient. Offr. Candn. Armaments Research & Devel. Estab., 1944-46; Assoc. Prof. Cath. Univ. of Am., 1946-55; Commonwealth Visiting Prof., Univ. of Sussex, 1966-67; Chairman, Comte on Symposia, Royal Soc'y of Can., since 1971; Chairman, Committee on Chemical Kinetics, International Union of Pure and Applied Chemistry, since 1977; Publications: "Theory of Rate Processes", 1941; "Chemical Kinetics", 1950; "Chemistry of Enzymes", 1954; "Chemical Kinetics of Excited States", 1955; "Chemical Kinetics of Enzyme Action", 1958; "Principles of Chemistry", 1966; "Reaction Kinetics", Vols. I and II, 1963; "Theories of Chemical Reaction Rates", 1969; "The Chemical Elements", 1970; " Physical Chem. with Biological Applications", 1978; "Physical Chemistry" (with J.H. Meiser), 1982; over 250 articles in scient. journs.; mem., Chem. Soc. of London; Am. Assn. Advanc. Sc.; Chem. Inst. of Canada Medallist, 1971; Chem. Educ. Award, Chem. Inst. of Canada 1974; Chem. Teacher Award, Mfg. Chem. Assn. 1975; Queen's Jubilee Medal, 1977; Boomer Lectr., Univ. of Alberta, 1978; Robert A. Welch Lectr., 1982; recreations: painting, acting; Club: Cercle Universitaire; Home: 551 Mariposa Ave., Rockcliffe Park, Ottawa, Ont. K1M 0S5

LAIDLEY, Charles Munroe, B. Com.; business consultant; b. Lindsay, Ont. 18 Jan. 1931; s. Clifford Munroe L.; e. Lindsay Coll. Inst.; Univ. of Toronto B. Com.; Mass. Inst. Technol. (S.M.I.M.); m. Barbara Helen Clark 7 May 1954; 3 s.; Dir., Misener Holdings Ltd.; mem. Bd. Queen Elizabeth Hosp.; Clubs: Albany; York Downs Golf & Country; Home: 3 Green Valley Rd., Willowdale, Ont. M2P 1A4.

LAING, Gertrude M., O.C. (1972); b. Tunbridge Wells, Kent, Eng., 13 Feb. 1905; d. Arthur George and Mary Elizabeth (Williams) Amies; e. Univ. of Man., B.A. 1925; Sorbonne, post-grad. studies 1927; m. 16 June 1930; two s.: Colin D. B., Alan R. B.; Teacher, Riverbend Sch. for Girls, Winnipeg, 1928-32; Lectr. in French, Univ. of Man., 1945-50; served as Extve. Secy., War Services Bd. and Central Volunteer Bureau, Winnipeg, 1942-45; apptd. Commr., Royal Comn. on Bilingualism & Biculturalism, 1963; appt. part-time mem., Candn. Radio-Television Comn., 1968; W. Regional Vice-Pres., Candn. Welfare Council, 1964-70; Pres., YWCA, Winnipeg, 1941-43; Central Volunteer Bureau, Winnipeg, 1951-52; Social Planning Council, Calgary, 1957-59; mem. Canada Council; named Chrmn. of Canada Council, 1975-78; extve. mem. Candn. Comn. for UNESCO, 1974-75; mem. Candn. Del. UNESCO Gen. Assembly 1974; Lecturer, Univ. of Calgary 1977; Hon. D. Univ., Calgary 1973; U.B.C. 1977; Univ. of Ottawa 1978; Univ. of Man., 1980; Liberal; recreation: music; Clubs: Ranchmen's; Calgary Golf & Country; Address: 1223-38th Ave. S.W., Calgary, Alta. T2T 2J3

LAING, Peter Marshall, Q.C.; b. Montreal, Que., 24 March 1916; s. Campbell and Hazel (Marshall) L.; e. Marlborough Coll., Wiltshire, Eng., 1929-32; McGill Univ., B.A. 1935; Oxford (Univ. Coll.), B.A. 1938; Lun. LL.D., McGill Univ. m. Kathleen Griffith, d. J. W. McConnell, 12 May 1945; children: Murdoch, David; MEMBER, COURTOIS, CLARKSON, PARSONS AND TETRAULT; Emeritus Governor, McGill Univ.; admitted to the Bar of England, 1939; Bar of Que. 1944; cr. Q.C. 1958; served in 2nd World War, 9th Lancers; Anglican; Clubs: University; Montreal Racket; Home: 1291 Redpath Crescent, Montreal, H3G 1A1; Office: 630 Dorchester Blvd. W., Montreal, Que. H3B 1V7

LAIRD, William Warring, LL.B., Q.C.; lawyer; b. Regina, Sask. 2 March 1918; s. William Clarence and Cora (Williamson) L.; e. John Ross Pub. Sch. and N. Toronto Coll. Inst., Toronto 1936; Univ. of Toronto B.A. 1940; Osgoode Hall Law Sch. LL.B. 1943; m. Gertrude d. Vanamber Kenneth Greer, Toronto, Ont. 5 June 1943; children: William Kenneth, Katherine Greer, Robert Warring; estbd. private law practice WILLIAM W. LAIRD, Q.C. 1964; Chrmn. Bd. Dirs. Riverside Yarns Ltd.; Dir. Mollenhauer Ltd.; Miles Laboratories Ltd.; Marks & Spencer Canada Inc.; called to Bar of Ont. 1943; cr. Q.C. 1957; Partner, Urquhart & Urquhart, Toronto 1943-46; joined Loblaw Groceterias Co. Toronto 1946-64, Vice Pres. 1956, Vice Pres. Extve. Div. and Asst. Gen. Mgr. 1959; served with Candn. Army 1939-40; mem. Law Soc. Upper Can.; Delta Upsilon; Anglican; recreations: golf, philately, bridge, chess, swimming; Clubs: Lambton Golf & Country; Coral Ridge Country; Home: apt. 1704W, 57 Widdicombe Hill Blvd., Weston, Ont. M9R 1Y4; Office: 99 Avenue Rd., Suite 202, Toronto, Ont. M5R 2G5.

LAJEUNESSE, Claude, M.Sc.A., Ph.D., P.Eng.; association executive; b. Quebec City, Que. 20 June 1941; s. Paul-Henri and Marie-Ange (Rousseau) L.; e. Ecole Polytechnique Montreal B.Sc.A. 1965; Rensselaer Polytechnic Inst. Troy, N.Y. M.Sc.A. 1967, Ph.D. (Nuclear Engn.) 1969; m. Nicole d. Emile Morin, Quebec City, Que. 23 Dec. 1961; children: Christine, France, Marc, Nathalie, Pascale, François; EXTVE. DIR., CANDN. COUNCIL OF PROF. ENGRS. 1978-; Sr. Staff Physicist, Combustion Engineering Co., Windsor, Conn. 1969-70; Asst. Prof. of Engn. Physics, Univ. of Qué. Trois-Rivières 1970, Head of Engn. Physics 1971, Head of Engn. Faculty 1972-74; Syndic and Head of Legal Affairs Dept., Ordre des ingénieurs du Qué. 1974-78; author or co-author various scient. publs.; mem. Assn. Prof. Engrs. Prov. Ont.; Ordre des ingénieurs du Qué.; Bd. of Dir. Youth Science Foundation; Comte. Internat. Scientific & Technol. Affiliations-Nat. Res. Council; Fellow, Engn. Inst. Can.; recreations: tennis, badminton, squash; Clubs: Ottawa Athletic, Cercle Universitaire, Ottawa; Home: 17 Malden Sq., Ottawa, Ont. K1V 9T2; Office: 116 Albert St. Suite 401, Ottawa, Ont. K1P 5G3.

LAJOIE, Hon. François, B.A., LL.L; judge; b. Trois-Rivières, Que., 12 Apl. 1922; s. François Lajoie. Q.C. and Annette (Nobert) L.; e. Jardin de l'Enfance, Trois-Rivières, 1933; Coll. Jean de Brébeuf, Montréal, B.A. 1941; Laval Univ., LL.L. 1944; m. Thérèse, d. Léon Lamothe, Q.C., 8 May 1948; children: François III, Marc, Marie, Lucie, Anne, Bernard; JUSTICE, QUÉBEC COURT OF APPEALS since 1970; called to Bar of Que. 1944; cr. Q.C. 1957; practised law with father 1944-59 and with brother 1957-66; Sr. Partner, Lajoie, Lajoie, Gouin, Vigeant & Désaulniers, 1966-70; Bâtonnier of Trois-Rivières, May 1967; Bâtonnier of Bar of Prov. of Que. 1967-68; mem. various comtes., Bar Prov. Que., 1967-70; mem. and Pres., Bd. of Bar Examiners, 1960-66; mem., Candn. Bar Assn.; Pres., Trois-Rivières Chamber Comm., 1964-65; R. Catholic; recreations: hunting, fishing, swimming; Home: 170 De Bernières, Quebec G1R 2L7; Office: Court House, Quebec, Que.

LAKIE, David, M.B.A.; executive; b. Scotland, 19 Dec. 1924; s. James Irons and Agnes Naismith (Kennedy) L.; came to Can. 1947; e. Dalziel High Sch., Scotland; Harvard Univ., M.B.A. 1955; m. June, d. Charles E. Hunt, Q.C., Oct. 1949; children: David, Bruce, Jennifer: Sr. Vice Pres., Corporate Relations, Molson Companies, Ltd. 1975-1978; Sr. Vice-Pres. Retail Merchandising Group, The Molson Companies Ltd., since 1971; joined Procter & Gamble Sales Department, Sydney, N.S. and served at St. John's, Nfld. and Halifax, N.S., 1947-50; Sales Manager, Wm. Stairs, Son & Morrow Ltd., Halifax, N.S., 1951-53; McKim Advertising Ltd., Toronto and Montreal, 1955-61; Vice-Pres., Marketing, Office Specialty Ltd. (Div. of Anthes Imperial Ltd.) 1961-62, Vice-Pres. and Gen. Mgr., 1962-66; Vice-Pres., Anthes Imperial Ltd., 1966-68; joined Molson Industries Ltd. as Sr. Vice-Pres.,

Candn. Indust. Group 1968; Sr. Vice-Pres., Retail Merchandising and Dir. 1971; Pres. and Dir., Beaver Lumber Co. Ltd. 1972-75; served as Radio Offr., Merchant Navy, 1941-43 and as Lt. (A), R.N.V.R., 1943-46; Dir., Candn. Business Equip. Mfrs. Assn. (Pres. 1968-69); P. Conservative; Presb.; recreations: golf, reading, music, curling; Clubs: National; Granite; Rosedale Golf; Manitoba (Winnipeg); St. James's (Montreal); Home: 1 Dunbar Rd., Toronto, Ont. M4W 1X5; Office: 2 International Blvd. Toronto, Ont. M9W 1A2

LALONDE, Jacques; hotel executive; b. Mont-Laurier, Que., 18 Sept. 1929; s. His Hon. Judge Maurice and Eleanore (Côte) L.; e. Coll. Mont-Laurier (Que.); Coll. St-Jean; Univ. of Ottawa; Univ. of Montreal; McGill Univ.; m. Denise, d. Dr. J. H. Charbonneau, 4 May 1957; children: Louise, Francine, Guy; CHRMN. OF BD., ATLIFIC INC. AND ATPRO INC. AND WENDY'S RESTAURANTS OF CAN. INC.; called to Bar of Que. 1955; mem. Montreal Bar Assn.; Roman Catholic; recreations: tennis, skiing; Home: 50 Linwood Cres., Town of Mount Royal, Que. H3P 1J2; Office: 6550 Côte de Liesse, Montreal, Que. H4T 1S7

LALONDE, Jean-Louis, B.A., R.C.A.; architect; b. Coteau Station, Que., 17 June 1923; s. Charles and Marie-Ann (LeFebvre) L.; e. Coll. St. Marie (Montreal); Univ. of Montreal, B.A. 1944; Beaux Art 1950; Architectural Assn. Sch. of Arch. (London, Eng.), Dipl. in Arch. 1951; m. Gisele, d. Trancrede Bissonnette, 8 July 1950; children: Pier, Marc; PARTNER, HEBERT AND LALONDE since 1968; with Fry and Drew, Architects, London, Eng. 1951-52; then Breuer-Nervi-Zehrfuss, Paris, France 1952-56; joined Rother-Bland & Trudeau, Architects, Montreal 1957, prior to commencement in private practice, 1960; Chrmn., Adv. Comte. on Design, Nat. Capital Comn.; mem. Prov. Que. Assn. of Arch. (Past Pres.); R.A.I.C. (Pres. 1971); Arch. and Planning Comn., City of Westmount; Extve. Bd. Internat. Union of Archs.; Jacques Viger Comn. (Hist. Monuments), Montreal; Roman Catholic; recreations: tennis, Clubs: Mount-Royal Tennis, Montreal Badminton & Squash; Home: 4328 Montrose Ave., Westmount, Que. H3Y 2A9; Office: 1980 Sherbrooke St. W., Montreal, Que. H3H 1E8

LALONDE, Hon. Marc, P.C. (Can.), Q.C., M.P., LL.L., M.A.; politician; b. Ile Perrot, Quebec, 26 July 1929; s. J. Albert and Nora (St. Aubin) L.; e. St. Laurent College, Montreal, B.A. 1950; University of Montreal, LL.L 1954, M.A. (Law) 1955; Oxford University (Econ. & Political Science), M.A. (Oxon) 1957; Ottawa Univ., Dipl. of Superior Studies in Law, 1960; m. Claire, d. J. Georges Tétreau, Montreal, Que., 8 Sept. 1955; children: Marie, Luc, Paul, Catherine; Min. of Justice 1978-79; Min. of State for Fed.-Prov. Relations 1977-78 and Min. Resp. for Status of Women, 1975-78; called to Bar of Que. 1955; Prof. of Comm. Law and Econ., Univ. of Montreal, 1957-59; Special Asst. to Min. of Justice, Ottawa, 1959-60; Partner, Gelinas, Bourque, Lalonde & Benoit, Montreal, 1960-68; Lectr. in Adm. Law for Doctorate Students, Univ. of Ottawa and Univ. of Montreal, 1961-62; Policy Adviser to Prime Min. 1967; Princ. Secy. to Prime Min. 1968-72; el. to H. of C. for Montreal-Outremont g.e. 30 Oct. 1972-77; MINISTER OF ENERGY, MINES & RESOURCES 1980-; sworn of the P.C. and appointed Minister National Health and Welfare 1972; mem. Bd. Dirs., Inst. of Pub. Law, Univ. of Montreal; Dir., Cand. Citizenship Council; mem. Comte. on Broadcasting, 1964; Counsel before several Royal Comns. incl. Norris Comn. and Royal Comn. on Pilotage; mem., Chambre de Comm. de Montreal; Institut Canadien des Affaires Publiques; Liberal; R. Catholic; recreations: tennis, skiing, swimming, reading; Club: Home: 5440 Legaré, Montreal, Que. H3T 1Z4; Office: Room 515-S, House of Commons, Ottawa, Ont. K1A 0A3

LAMARRE, Charles Jules, M.D.; university professor; b. Quebec City, Que., 18 April 1930; s. Charles Arthur and

Hombéline (Ferlatte) L.; e. Coll. St. Jean Eudes (Que.); Univ. Laval, London Univ., Univ. of Sask., McGill Univ.; m. Claire Chalifour, 13 Aug. 1956; children: Anne, Martine, Catherine, Charles; PROF., DEPT. OF PSYCHIATRY, MED. SCH., UNIV. DE SHERBROOKE: Dir. and Sr. Res. in Psychiatry, Sask. Hosp., North Battleford, 1960-61; Curriculum Instr. and Res. in Psychiatry, Univ. of Sask., 1962; Asst. Prof., 1963; Assoc. Prof., Univ. de Sherbrooke, 1966; rec'd. Prix de la République Française at end of jr. internship; author, "Integration d'un Departement de Psychiatrie dans un nouveau centre hôpitalier Universitaire," France, 1967; mem., Que. Psychiatric Assn.; Candn. Psychiatric Assn.; Sask. Psychiatric Assn.; Sask. Assn. for Maladjusted; Président de l'Association Générale des Etudiants de Laval, 1954-1955; Roman Catholic; recreation: swimming.

LAMB, William Kaye, O.C. (1969), Ph.D., LL.D., D.S. Litt., F.R.S.C.; librarian and archivist (retired); b. New Westminster, B.C., 11 May 1904; s. Alexander and Barbara S. (McDougall) L.; e. Univ. of Brit. Columbia, B.A. 1927, M.A. 1930; Univ. of Paris (Sorbonne), sessions 1928-29, 1930-32; Univ. of London, Eng., Ph.D. 1933; LL.D., Univ. of B.C. 1948; Manitoba 1953; Toronto 1954; Sask. 1956; Assumption 1958; McMaster 1966; LL.D., Univ. of Victoria 1966; New Brunswick 1967; York 1968; D.S.Litt. Victoria (Toronto), 1961; m. Wessie M. Tipping, 15 May 1939; one d. Barbara Elizabeth; Prov. Librarian and Archivist of B.C. 1934-40; Supt., B.C. Pub. Lib. Comn., 1936-40; Librarian, Univ. of B.C. 1940-48; apptd. Dom. Archivist, 1948-69; Nat. Librarian 1953-68; mem., B.C. Pub. Library Comn. 1943-48; The Champlain Soc. (Past Pres.); B.C. Library Association (Past Pres.); B.C. Hist. Assn. (Past Pres.); Candn. Library Assn. (Pres. 1947-48); Steamship Hist. Soc. of Am.; Soc. of Archivists (Past Pres.); Am. Soc. of Archivists (Past Pres.); Fellow, Roy. Soc. Can. (Past Pres.); mem. Mass. Hist. Soc.; Am. Antiq. Soc.; Ed., "B.C. Hist. Quarterly", 1937-46; contrib. hist. introductions to "Letters of John McLoughlin" (three series) 1942-45; edited "Journal of Daniel Williams Harmon", 1957; "The Letters and Journals of Simon Fraser, 1806-1808", 1960; "Journal of Gabriel Franchère", 1969; author of "Journals and Letters of Sir Alexander MacKenzie" 1970; "Canada's Five Centuries: From Discovery to Present Day" 1971; (with N. R. Hacking) "The Princess Story" 1974; "History of the CPR", 1977; numerous articles in hist., library, and marine journs.; Awarded Tyrrell Medal (Roy. Soc. of Can.), 1965; Psi Upsilon; Address: #2105-2055 Pendrell St., Vancouver, B.C. V6G 1T9

LAMBART, Evelyn Mary, R.C.A.; film maker; b. Ottawa, Ont. 23 July 1914; d. Frederick Howard John and Helen Marianne (Wallbridge) L.; e. Ottawa Model Sch.; Lisgar Coll. Inst. Ottawa; Ont. Coll. of Art grad. 1937; retired film maker Nat. Film Bd. Can.; recreations: gardening, embroidery; Address: R.R. 4, Sutton, Que. J0E 2K0.

LAMBERT, Allen Thomas, banker (retired), O.C.; b. Regina, Sask., 28 Dec. 1911; s. Willison Andrew and Sarah (Barber) L.; e. Victoria (B.C.) Pub. and High Schs.; m. Marion Grace, d. William G. Kotchapaw, Winnipeg, Man., 20 May 1950; children: William A., Anne B.; Chrmn. of Toronto-Dominion Bank, 1961-78; Dir., Raritan River Steel Co.; Rolls-Royce Holdings, N.A., Ltd.; Tahsis Co. Ltd.; Toronto-Dominion Bank; R. Angus (Alberta) Ltd.; Cyprus Anvil Mining Corp.; INCO Ltd.; Lonvest Corp.; Private Invest. Corp. for Asia (PICA), S.A.; The Continental Corporation; Hudson Bay Mining & Smelting Co. Ltd.; IBM Canada Ltd.; Westinghouse Canada Ltd.; Hiram Walker Resources; Hiram Walker-Gooderham & Worts Ltd.; The Continental Insurance Cos.; Dome Mines Ltd.; The London Life Ins. Co.; Western Broadcasting Co. Ltd.; Pan American Banks; Past Pres. Internat. Monetary Conf.; Hon. Trust.; Upper Can. Coll. Fdn.; apptd. Head, Roy. Comm. on Financial Mang. and Accountability, 1976; entered service of the Bank at Victoria, B.C., 1927 and subsequently served in Vancouver,

Brockville and Montreal; became Mgr. at Yellowknife, N.W.T., 1946; Insp., Winnipeg, Man., 1947; Supv., H.O., Toronto, 1949; Asst. Mgr., Main Office, Montreal 1950; Supt. H.O., Toronto 1953; Asst. Gen. Mgr., 1953; apptd. General Manager, 1956; Vice-President and Director, 1956; President 1960; Chairman of Board 1961; served during the 2nd World War with R.C.N., 1943-45; discharged with the rank of Lieutenant; United Church; recreations: golf, fishing, curling; Clubs: Toronto; Toronto Hunt; Toronto Golf; Granite; York; Home: 483 Russell Hill Road, Toronto, Ont. M5P 2S8; Office: P.O. Box l, Toronto-Dominion Centre, Toronto, Ont. M5K 1A2

LAMBERT, Hon. John Douglas, B.A., LL.B.; judge; b. Ardrossan, Scot. 30 June 1930; s. James Edward and Jane Grierson (Todd) L.; e. Ardrossan (Scot.) Acad. 1944; Trinity Coll. Glenalmond, Scot. 1948; St. Andrews Univ. 1948-52; Queen's Univ. B.A. 1955; Univ. of B.C. LL.B. 1958; m. Barbara-Rose d. late Adolf George Schwenk 31 Dec. 1956; children: James Matthew, Sheena Louise, John Andrew Bowman; JUDGE, B.C. COURT OF APPEAL AND YUKON TERRITORY COURT OF APPEAL since 1978; Lectr. in Law Univ. of Victoria 1977-81 and Univ. of B.C. 1979-81; called to Bar of B.C. 1959, Ont. 1963; Counsel, Dept. of Justice 1959-65; Solr. B.C. Hydro & Power Authority 1964-67, 1968-69; Advisor, External Aid Program, Barbados 1967-68; Assoc. Davis and Co. Vancouver 1969-71, Partner 1971-78; mem. Law Reform Comn. Vancouver 1967-78, Chrmn. 1978; mem. Candn. Bar Assn.; Presbyterian; recreation: walking; Club: Vancouver; Home: 6435 Wellington Ave., West Vancouver, B.C. V7W 2H7; Office: 800 Smithe St., Vancouver, B.C. V6Z 2E1.

LAMBERT, Hon. Marcel Joseph Aime, P.C. (Can.), Q.C., M.P., B.Com., B.C.L., M.A.; barrister; b. Edmonton, Alta., 21 Aug. 1919; s. late Joseph Edward and Marie (Kiwit) L.; e. St. Joseph's High Sch., Edmonton, Alta.; Univ. of Alberta, B.Com. (Hons. Econ.) 1947; Rhodes Scholar for Alta. 1947; Oxford Univ., B.A. (Juris), 1948, B.C.L. 1950 M.A. 1956; m. Olive Margaret, d. late Arthur Wm. Lowles, Seaford, Sussex, Eng., 30 June 1945; Children: Adrian M. J., Christopher John, Peter; ASSOC., EMERY, JAMIESON, AGRIOS, BERCOV, LEWIS & DREWRY; read law with F. A. Ford, Q.C.; called to the Bar of Alta., Sept. 1951; served in 2nd World War as Lieut., King's Own Calgary Regt. (Tank); Dieppe Raid, 1942; P.O.W., 1942-45; def. cand. for Alta. Leg. 1952; el. to H. of C. for Edmonton W., 1957; re-el. since; apptd. Parlty. Secy. to Min. of Nat. Defence, 1957, Nat. Revenue, 1959; Speaker of H. of C., Sept. 1962-Feb. 1963; apptd. Min. of Veterans Affairs, Feb. '63 resigning with the def. Govt., Apl. 1963; Trustee, St. Mary's Home & Tech. Sch. for Boys, Edmonton, Alta.; mem., Edmonton Bar Assn.; Alta. Law Soc.; Candn. Bar Assn.; P. Conservative; Roman Catholic; K. of C. (4th Degree); recreations: gardening, sports; Office: M4-9509 — 156th St., Edmonton, Alta. T5P 4J5

LAMBERT, Phyllis, B.A., M.S., O.A.A., O.A.Q., R.A.I.C., R.C.A.; architect; b. Montreal, Que. 24 Jan. 1927; d. Samuel and Saidye (Rosner) Bronfman; e. The Study Montreal 1944; Vassar Coll. B.A. 1948; Ill. Inst. of Technol. M.S. (Arch.) 1963; m. Jean Lambert 1949; divorced; PRINC., PHYLLIS LAMBERT ARCH.; projects incl. Dir. of Planning Seagram Bldg. N.Y. 1954-58; Consultant to Fairview and Toronto-Dominion Bank re Toronto-Dominion Centre 1962; Arch., Saidye Bronfman Centre YM-YWHA Montreal in assn. 1963-68; Planning studies for Douglas Community Organ. Chicago 1968-69; Communications Arts Center Study for Vassar Coll. 1970; Fogg Museum Space Study 1972; Consultant to Cadillac-Fairview for design arch. Eaton Centre 1972; Dir. Groupe de recherche sur les bâtiments en pierre grise de Montréal 1973- ; Consultant to Cadillac-Fairview for design arch. Les Promenades St.-Bruno (Que.) Shopping Centre 1974; Arch., Jane Tate House renovation Montreal 1974-

76; Dir. Seagram Bicentennial Project 1974-79; Arch., cinema in private home, Montreal, 1976; Arch.-Developer Biltmore Hotel renovation Los Angeles 1976; Developer renovation 8 housing units St-Hubert St. Montreal 1978; Founder/Dir. Candn. Centre for Arch. Montreal 1979; exhns. incl. McCord Museum 1975, 1980; Fourth Floor Gallery, Seagram Bldg., N.Y., 1977; awards: Massey Medal for Arch. 1970; Robinson's Design Award (Biltmore Hotel) 1977; W. Art Dirs. Club Award of Merit 1977; Am. Inst. Archs. S. Cal. Chapter Award of Honour 1978; Am. Jewish Cong. Nat. Women's Div. N.Y. Award 1978; Printing Industries of America Inc. Cert. of Award Graphic Arts Award Competition 1978; Am. Inst. Archs. Design Award 1979; Am. Inst. Graphic Arts Cert. of Excellence 1979; Am. Soc. Interior Designers Internat. Design Award 1980; Médaille de Mérite Ordre des Architectes du Qué., 1981 co-recipient Am. Inst. Archs. Nat. Honor Award 1980; Nat. Preservation Award, 1981; frequent guest lectr.; author or co-author various publs.; work cited various articles; mem. Candn. Arctic Resources Comte.; Inst. Fine Arts N.Y. Univ. (Trustee); Save Montreal (Dir.); Adv. Bd. Mies van der Rohe Archive Museum of Modern Art N.Y. (Chrmn.); Heritage Montreal (Founding Pres.); Visiting Comte to Nat. Gallery Can.; Academician, Royal Cdn. Acad. of Arts; Internat. Confed. Arch. Museums (Commr.); Bd. of Dir., Intnl. Confed. of Architectural Museums; Soc. du Patrimoine Urbain de Montréal (Pres.); mem., Comiatrimoine, Ordre des Arch. du Qué.; Adv. Bd., Centre for Study of Amer. Arch., Columbia Univ.; Architectural Magazine Society, TRACE (Dir.); National Building Museum (Dir.); Office: 2e étage, 1440 ouest rue Ste-Catherine, Montreal, Que. H3G 1R8.

LAMBERT, Ronald Dick, M.A., Ph.D.; social psychologist; educator; b. Sophiasburg Twp., Prince Edward Co., Ont., 6 April 1936; s. Wilfred Morley and Edith Marjory (Dick) L.; e. Sudbury (Ont.) High Sch. 1954; McMaster Univ., B.A. 1959, M.A. 1961; Univ. of Mich., Ann Arbor, Ph.D. 1966; m. Marilyn Ruth, d. Emmett Gordon Black, 15 June 1964; three d.; ASSOC. PROF. OF SOCIOL., UNIV. OF WATERLOO since 1970; joined the Univ. as Asst. Prof. of Sociol. (with cross-appt. in Dept. of Psychol.) 1966; mem. Candn. Sociol. & Anthropol. Assn.; Am. Sociol. Assn.; Assn. Candn. des sociologues et anthropologues de lanque francaise (ACSALF); Cdn. Ethnic Studies Assn.; Publications: "Sex Role Imagery in Children: Social Origins of Mind" 1971; "Social Process and Institution: The Canadian Case" (text-reader with J. E. Gallagher) 1971; "The Sociology of Contemporary Quebec Nationalism: An Annotated Bibliography and Review", 1981; articles in "Candn. Journ. of Pol. Science"; "Candn. Review of Sociology and Anthropology" and elsewhere; Home: 11 Ellen St.W., Kitchener, Ont. N2H 4K1

LAMBRECHT, Anton Frank; retired distillery executive; b. Regina, Sask., 1 Aug. 1916; s. N. J. and Theresa (Mayer) L.; e. Balfour High Sch., Regina, Sask.; Commercial Coll. of Regina; m. Emily Romund, 27 Sept. 1941; children: Penny (Mrs. Neil MacInnes), Patricia (Mrs. Richard Jeffries), Jane (Mrs. Clayton Folkart); Vice-Pres. and Dir., Park and Tilford, Can. Inc. Public Relations Dir., Sask. Brewers' Assn., 1933-46; Asst. Prov. Liquor Commr., Liquor Bd. of Sask., 1946-56; Vice-Pres., Operations and Dir. of Schenley Can. Inc. 1956-69; Sr. Vice Pres. and Dir. 1969-81 (ret.) Roman Catholic; recreations: gardening, wood crafts; Club: Mt. Stephen; Home: 430 Elmridge Ave., Dorval, Que. H9S 2Z9

LAMER, Hon. Antonio, LL.D., LL.L.; judge; b. Montreal, Que., 8 July 1933; s. Antonio and Florence (Storey) L.; e. Coll. St-Laurent, Montreal 1952; Univ. de Montréal, LL.L 1956; LL.D.; Univ. of Moncton, 1981; m. Suzanne, d. Emile Bonin, 4 March 1961; one s. Stéphane; JUSTICE, SUPREME COURT OF CANADA since 1980; Justice Superior Court Que., 1969-78; Justice, Que. Court of Appeal, 1978-80; Vice-Chrmn. Nat. Law Reform Comn., since 1971; Prof. agrégé, Univ. de Montréal since 1967; read law with Cutler, Lamer, Bellemare & Assoc.; called to Bar of Que. 1957; Lectr. for many years, Faculty of Law and Sch. of Criminol., Univ. de Montréal; Lectr., Candn. Judicial Conf.; formerly a Sr. Partner, Cutler, Lamer, Bellemare & Assoc.; Que. Bar Rep. on Govt. Inter-disciplinary Comte. on Structures to be given the new Univ. du Québec; Chrmn. Candn. Law Reform Comm., 1975; served in R.C.A. (R) 1952; Past Pres. (1960) Montreal Dist. Young Libs.; Secy. (1961-66) Montreal Men's Reform Club; Founder Defence Attorneys' Association Quebec; Past Nat. Chrmn., Criminal Justice Sec., Candn. Bar Assn.; Pres., Quebec Criminology Soc., 1978; R. Catholic; recreations: fox hunt, gun hunt, riding, flying; Clubs: Montreal Hunt; La Roue du Roi; Le Cercle Universitaire (Ottawa); Office: Supreme Court of Canada, Ottawa, Ont. K1A 0J1

LAMONT, Campbell Thompson, M.D. C.C.F.P.; D.A.B.F.P.; F.A.A.F.P.; Physician; educator; b. Mount Brydges, Ont. 19 March 1922; s. late Alexander and late Evelyn Marie (Thompson) L.; e. Strathroy Coll. Inst. 1940; Univ. of W. Ont. M.D. 1946; m. Patricia Joan d. late Alfred Hartley MacRobert 23 March 1949; children: John, Mary; PROF. OF FAMILY MED. UNIV. OF OTTAWA since 1975; private practice Bothwell and Thamesville, Ont. 1949-67; Lectr. in Family Med. Univ. of W. Ont. 1967, Asst. Prof. 1969, Assoc. Prof. 1971; Prof. and Chrmn. of Family Med. Sch. of Med. State Univ. of N.Y. Stony Brook 1971-75; Chrmn. of Family Med., Univ. of Ottawa, 1975-81; served with RCAMC 1945-46; author or co-author various med. publs.; Fellow, Am. Acad. Family Phys.; Mem. Bd. of Examiners, College of Family Physicians of Canada 1978-; Mem. Comte on Examinations and Evaluations WONCA (World Org'n. of Nat'l Colleges and Academies of Family and General Practice, 1979-; Chrmn, Task Force on Palliative Care, Ottawa-Carleton Dist. Health Counc., 1979; Visiting Prof., Div. of Geriatrics, Dept. of Med., U.C.L.A., 1981-82; mem. Candn. Med. Assn.; Ont. Med. Assn.; Coll. Family Phys. Can.; Delta Upsilon; Freemason; Protestant; recreations: biking, skating; Home: Apt. 301, 370 Dominion Ave., Ottawa, Ont. K2A 3X4; Office: Children's Hosp. of E. Ont., 385 Smyth Rd., Ottawa, Ont. K1H 8L2.

LAMONT, Francis B., M.A. (Oxon), LL.B.; financier; b. Winnipeg, Man., 23 March 1933; s. John Salmon and May (Bastin) L.; e. Univ. of Man. B.A. 1953; Oxford Univ. Jesus Coll. (Rhodes Scholar) B.A. 1958, M.A. 1972; Man. Law Sch. LL.B. 1960; m. Judith d. Robert Barrett, 27 July 1963; children: John R. T., Dougald F., Alexandra M., Laura J.; MANG. PARTNER, RICHARDSON SECURITIES OF CANADA 1976-; read law with Thorvaldson, Eggertson, Bastin & Stringer; called to Bar of Man. 1960; Barrister and Solr. Thorvaldson, Eggertson, Bastin, Saunders & Mauro, Winnipeg, 1960-63; joined Legal Dept. present firm 1963, Secy. and Gen. Counsel 1966-76, Partner 1972-; Lt., Winnipeg Grenadiers (Militia) 1960-65; has held Constit. and Prov. Extve. positions Lib. Party of Man.; Liberal; recreations: rowing, cross-country skiing; Clubs: Vincents; Leander; Isis; Winnipeg Winter; Manitoba; St. Charles Country; Winnipeg Rowing; Home: 47 Harvard Ave., Winnipeg, Man. R3M 0J6; Office: Richardson Bldg., One Lombard Pl., Winnipeg, Man. R3B 0Y2

LAMONT, Vincent G.; construction executive; b. Orillia, Ont., 8 June 1924; s. Victor E. and Mary Ann (Cooper) L.; e. Pub. and High Schs., Orillia, Ont.; m. Margaret, d. George Thomas Haw, 20 April 1946; two s. Robert James, two d. Patricia, Janis; President, Bridge and Tank Co. of canada Ltd. 1971-1975; Pres. and Dir., Bridge and Tank Western Ltd.; Ford-Smith Machine Co. Ltd.; with E. Long Ltd., Jr. Draughtsman 1942, subsequently Mgr., Sales Div.; joined John Bertram & Sons, Dundas, Ont. as Gen. Sales Mgr. 1961; Gen. Sales Mgr. of present Co.

1963, Vice-Pres., Sales 1964; served in 2nd World War, R.C.N. 1944-47 on cruise "Ontario" in S. Pacific; mem. Social Services Devel. Council of Ancaster (Dir.); Candn. Inst. Steel Constr.; United Church; recreations: fishing, golf, flying; Clubs: Hamilton Golf & Country; Hamilton Flying; The Hamilton; Home: 30 Park Lane, Ancaster, Ont. L9G 1K8; Office: 390 Gage Ave. N., Hamilton, Ont. L8L 7B2

LAMONTAGNE, Hon. J.-Gilles, P.C., M.P., B.A.; politician; b. Montreal, Que. 17 Apl. 1919; s. Trefflé and Anna (Kieffer) L.; e. Jean-de-Brébeuf Coll. Montreal B.A.; m. Mary Katherine d. Joseph Schaefer, Dayton, Ohio 23 Apl. 1949; children: Michel, André, Pierre, Marie; MIN. OF NAT. DEFENCE 1980-; mem. Que. City Council 1962-65, Mayor 1965-68; mem. Econ. Council of Can. 1974-77; former mem. Planning Council Prov. of Que.; Pres., Union of Muns. of Que. 1974-77; Past Extve. mem. and Vice Pres., Fed. of Muns.; Founding mem. "Le Progrès civique de Québec" mun. party; el. to H. of C. for Langelier by-el. 1977, re-el. since; Sworn of Privy Council and apptd. Min. without Portfolio 1978; Postmaster Gen. 1978; Min. of Nat. Defence 1980; Acting Min. for Veterans Affairs, 1980-81; served with RCAF 1941-45, rank Ltd.; Clubs: Royal Golf; Garrison; Cercle Universitaire; Liberal; R. Catholic; Home: 1040 Moncton Ave., Quebec, Que. Office: House of Commons, Ottawa, Ont. K1A 0A6.

LAMONTAGNE, Lieut.-Col. Leopold, C.D., B.A., Ph.D., D.èsL., F.R.S.C.; writer; b. Mont-Joli, Quebec, 8 July 1910; s. Alphonse and Marie (Joncas) L.; e. Laval Univ., B.A. 1931, L.èsL. 1934; Ottawa Univ. Ph.D. (Lettres) 1944; D.èL., Paris, 1955; m. Cécile d. late Auguste Lepage, 31 Aug. 1940; children: Denis, Marie, André, Marc; Prof., Séminaire de Rimouski, Que., 1934-40; Capt.-Adj., Mil. Instr. Centre, Rimouski, Que., 1940-42; Bureau of Translation, Candn. Army, Ottawa, 1942-48; Assoc. Prof. of French, R.M.C., Kingston, Ont., 1948-52; Dir., Dept. of French, C.M.R., St-Jean, Que., 1952-54; became Prof. and Head Dept. of Modern Lang., Royal Mil. Coll., 1955, Dean, Faculty of Letters, Laval Univ., Quebec, 1963-67; Executive Director, Service for Admission to College and University; President, TRIC Translating Service; awarded Royal Society Candn. Overseas Fellowship (Sorbonne) 1954-55; Publications: "La Gaspésie", 1936; "Les Archives régimentaires des Fusiliers du St-Laurent" 1943; "Arthur Buies, homme de lettres", 1957; "Royal Fort Frontenac" (co-ed. Dr. R. A. Preston), 1958; "Histoire du 22e Regiment", 1964; "Visages de la civilisation au Canada français", ed. RSC, 1970; "Le Canada français d'aujourd'hui", ed. RSC, 1970; many hist. and other articles in journs. and bulls. incl. "Queen's Quarterly", "London Illustrated", "Revue d'histoire d'Amerique française", etc.; awarded P.Q. Literary Prize, 1958; mem., Candn. Hist. Assn. (Ed. annual report 1950); Humanities Assn. Can. (Council 1954-55); Humanities Assn. St-Jean (Qué.) Br. Pres. 1953-54); Humanities Assn. Kingston, Ont., Br. Pres. 1957); Alliance Française, Kingston, Ont., Br. (Vice-Pres. since 1958); Modern Lang. Assn. Am., Sec. VIII (Secy. 1954-56, Pres. 1956-57); R. Catholic; Address: 2238 Lilac Lane, Ottawa, Ont. K1H 6H7

LAMONTAGNE, Mary S., C.M. (1976), B.Sc.A., B.Ph.; b. Dayton, Ohio 1 Nov. 1926; d. Joseph J. and Mary (Kette) Schaefer; e. Ravenhill Acad. Philadelphia 1943; Coll. de Bellevue, Que. 1944; Univ. Laval B.Sc.A. (Chem.) 1948, B.Ph. 1974; m. Joseph Gilles Lamontagne 23 Apl. 1949; children: Michel, Andre, Pierre, Marie; Dir. National Bank of Canada; North American Life Assurance; Canada Development Corp.; Quaker Oats Co. of Canada; mem. Nat. Comte. on Educ. Candn. Univ. Women 1962; Bd. of Adv., Centre for Bioethics, Clinical Research Inst. of Montreal; Founding mem. Que. Sec. UN Assn.; Treas. Symphonic Matinees 1960-65; Pres. Alumni Assn. Laval Univ. 1971-72, mem. Council 1970-

74; Pres. Comte. 125th Anniversary Institut Canadien de Que.; Dir. United Way, 1979 (Qué. city and region), Chrmn., fund-raising drive, United Way, Qué., -1979. Mem. Ethics Review Comte., Faculty of Medicine Laval University; Pres. Candn. Foundation on Alcohol & Drug Abuse 1974-75; mem. Bd. of Dir. CHVL, Laval Univ. Hospital Centre; Founding Pres. S.O.S. Grossesse; mem. Med. Research Council Can. 1975-80 (Chrmn. Centennial Fellowship Comte., mem. Task Force on Ethics of Human Experimentation); R. Catholic; Address: 1040 Moncton Ave., Quebec City, Que. G1S 2Y8

LAMONTAGNE, Hon. Maurice, P.C., M.Sc., F.R.S.C. (1956), F.R.S.A.; economist; senator; b. Mont Joli, Que., 7 Sept. 1917; s. Alphonse and Sophronie (Joncas) L.; e. Rimouski (Que.) Sémy.: Laval Univ., M.Sc. (Social Science) 1941; Harvard Univ. M.Sc. (Econs.); m. Jeannette Morin, Quebec City, 9 Feb. 1943; children: Hélène (Mrs. Lucien Binet), Pierre, Bernard; Dir., Canadian Corporate Management Co. Ltd.; Candn. General Electric; in 1943 asst. in organ. Faculty of Social Sciences at Laval Univ. and became Prof. of Écons. there; Dir., Dept. of Econs. 1949; apptd. Asst. Depy. Min., Dept. of Northern Affairs & Nat. Resources, Ottawa, May 1954; Econ. Advisor to the Privy Council, 1955; resigned in 1957 to become Prof. of Econs. at Ottawa Univ.; apptd. Econ. Advisor to Hon. Lester B. Pearson, then Leader of the Opposition, 1958 and concomitantly Asst. Dean of Faculty of Social Sciences at Ottawa Univ.; 1st el. to H. of C. for Outremont-Saint-Jean. g.e. 8 Apl. 1963; sworn to the P.C. and apptd. Pres. of the Queen's P.C. for Can., 22 Apl. 1963; apptd. Secy. of State and Registrar Gen. of Can., 3 Feb. 1964; resigned from the Cabinet 16 Dec. 1965; summoned to the Senate of Can. Apl. 1967; apptd. Chrmn., Senate Special Comte. on Science Policy 1970; Liberal: Roman Catholic; Office: The Senate, Ottawa, Ont. K1A 0A4

LAMOUREUX, Hon. Lucien, Q.C., M.A., L.Ph., LL.D.; diplomat; b. Ottawa, Ont., 3 Aug. 1920; s. Prime and Graziella (Madore) L.; e. Univ. Ottawa, B.A., L.Ph., M.A., LL.D.; m. Claire, d. Achille Coture, Hull, Que., 22 Sept. 1945; children: Michel, Sylvie, Adèle, Claude; CANADIAN AMBASSADOR TO PORTUGAL; Sept 1980-; Senior Partner in law firm Lamoureux, Rouleau and Forget, 1954-74; after grad. apptd. Extve. Asst. to Min. of Transport; first el. to H. of C. as Lib. mem. for Stormont g.e. 1962; el. as an Independent for Stormont-Dundas in g.e. 1968; apptd. Depy. Speaker of H. of C. and Chrmn. of Comtes. of the Whole for 26th Parlt.; Speaker, H. of C. 1965-74; Candn. Ambas. to Belgium & Luxembourg, 1974-80; former Director, Children's Aid Society, Community Chest, Service Club Council; Past President, Board of Trustees, Ottawa General Hosp.; Visiting Prof. of Parlty. Law (Grad. Studies), Faculty of Law, Univ. of Ottawa; Past Hon. Pres., Alumnae Assn., Univ. of Ottawa; Past Chrmn., Can. Council of Commonwealth Parlty. Assn.; Past Pres., Can-France Inter-parlty. Group; apptd. Chancellor, Univ. of Windsor, May 1971-78; Hon. Lt.-Col., Stormont, Dundas and Glengarry; R. Catholic; Club: Richelieu (Past Dir.); Office: Canadian Embassy, Rua Rosa Araujo 2-69, 1200 Lisboa, Portugal

LAMY, André; officier du gouvernement; né à Montréal, Que. 19 juillet 1932; f. Adélard et Marie-Antoinette (Crépeau) L.; e. Ecole de technol. méd., Univ. de Montréal 1952-55; Internat, quatres hôpitaux 1955-56; Faculté des Scs., McGill 1956-57; Cours d'adm. de l'entretien, Ecole des Hautes Études comm., Montréal 1969-71; ép. Françoise, f. J. Hector Martin, Outremont, Que. 1958; enfants: Mathieu, Marc, Philippe; VICE PRES. RELATIONS AVEC L'AUDITOIRE RÁDIO CANADA, OTTAWA, 1979; COMMISSAIRE DU GOUVERNEMENT A LA CINEMATOGRAPHIE CANADIENNE ET PRESIDENT OFFICE NAT. DU FILM — National Film Board 1975-79; Commissaire-Adjoint Office Nat. du Film, 1970-75; Directeur-Executif de la Soc. de Devel. cinematographique Canadienne, depuis 1980; Rep. méd., The Upjohn Co. of

Canada 1957-62; Dir. des ventes, Producteur, Niagara Films, Montreal 1962-64; Vice-prés. fondateur, Producteur réalisateur, Dir. de la Production et Adm., Onyx Films, 1964-70; Commissaire adjoint et Dir. gén., Office nat. du film du Can. 1970-75; Adm. de la Soc. des Amis de l'Enfance Ecole Nouvelle Querbes, Outremont 1965-75; Memb. du Cons. d'admin. de Radio- Canada/CBC., Mem. du Cons. d'admin. de Centre national des Arts/Nat'l Arts Centre; Membre du conseil d'admin. de l'Institut Canadien du film (Canadian Film Inst.); Membre du Cons. d'admin. de la Société de développement de l'industrie cinématographique Canadienne/CFCD. New Western Film and Television Foundation; Conseil d'admin. de Participaction; catholique romain; résidence: 245 rue Outremont, Outremont, Qué. H2V 3L9;

LANCASTER, Peter, B.Sc., M.Sc., Ph.D.; mathematician; b. Appleby, Eng. 14 Nov. 1929; came to Can. 1962; s. John Thomas and Emily (Kellett) L.; e. elem. sch. Northwich, Eng. 1940-46; Liverpool Coll. Sch. 1946-48; Univ. of Liverpool B.Sc. 1952, M. Sc. 1956; Univ. of Singapore Ph.D. 1964; m. Edna Lavinia d. Robert J. Hutchinson 3 Sept. 1962; children: Jane, Jill, Joy; Prof. of MATH, UNIV. OF CALGARY 1967- ; author of "Labda-Matrices and Vibrating Systems", 1966; "Theory of Matrices", 1969; "Mathematics: Models of the Real World", 1973; co-author "Matrix Polynomials", 1982; many published articles in scholarly jnls. on math. and its application; Comte. work for Nat. Science and Engn. Research Council, 1976- ; Pres., Can. Math. Society, 1979-81; recreations: music, squash, hiking, skiing; Home: 3052 Conrad Dr., Calgary, Alta. T2L 1B4; Office: Dept. of Math., Univ. of Calgary, Calgary, Alta. T2N 1N4.

LANCTOT, Laurent-Lépold, B.A., Ph.L., Th.L., C.L.L.; priest; publisher; b. Montreal, Que. 30 May 1911; s. Roland-Laurent and Marie-Louise (Perreault) L.; e. Ecole supérieure St-Louis Montreal 1927; Univ. of Ottawa B.A., Ph.L. 1932, Th.L. 1936, C.L.L. 1939; DIR. UNIV. OF OTTAWA PRESS since 1946; entered Order of Missy. Oblates of Mary Immaculate 1930; o. Priest 1935; Asst. Dir. Univ. of Ottawa Press 1936-46; Chaplain, French Speaking Girl Guides; co-author 'Sors de ta Ouache-Carnet Nature' 1975; many articles on nat. hist.; mem. Assn. Candn. Univ. Presses (Treas.); Internat. Assn. Scholarly Publishers; Assn. Editeurs canadiens; R. Catholic; recreations: canoeing, ornithology, botany, entomology; Home: 305 Nelson St., Ottawa, Ont. K1N 7S5; Office: 65 Hastey Ave., Ottawa, Ont. K1N 6N5.

LAND, Reginald Brian, M.A., M.L.S.; Library administrator and library educator; b. Niagara Falls, Ont., 29 July 1927; s. Allan Reginald and Beatrice Beryl (Boyle) L.; e. Oakwood Coll. Inst. (Toronto, Ont.) 1945; Univ. of Toronto (Univ. Coll.), B.A. (Pol. Science & Econ.) 1949, B.L.S. 1953, M.L.S. 1956, M.A. (Pol. Science) 1963; m. Edith Wyndham Eddis, 29 Aug. 1953; Children: Mary, John; DIR., ONT. LEGIS. LIB., RESEARCH AND INFO. SERVICES, since 1978; Commr., Candn. Radio-Television and Telecommunications Comn. 1973-78; with T. Eaton Co. Ltd. as Copy Editor, Mail Order Advertising, 1949-50; became Reference Librarian, Toronto Public Library, 1953-55; joined University of Toronto Library as Cataloguer, 1955-56 becoming Assistant Chief Librarian 1959-63 and Assoc. Lib. 1963; apptd. Head, Business & Indust. Div., Windsor Pub. Lib. 1956-57; joined "Canadian Business" magazine, Montreal, as Asst. Ed. 1957-59 (Assoc. Ed. 1959-62); apptd. Extve. Asst. to Min. of Finance, Ottawa, 1963-64; Prof., Faculty of Library Science, University of Toronto, 1964- ; Dean, Fac. of Libr. Sci., 1964-72; rec'd Kenneth R. Wilson Mem. Award, Bus. Newspapers Assn. of Can., 1959; Distinguished Achievement Award, Ont. Lib. Trustees' Assn. for contribs. to advance. of lib. services in Ont., 1968; Silver Jubilee Medal, 1977; author of: "Directory of Business, Trade and Professional Associations in Canada", 1962; "Eglinton: The Election Study of a Federal

Constituency", 1955; "Directory of Associations in Can." ed. 1981; "Sources of Info. for Candn. Business", 3rd ed. 1978; has contrib. articles and researches to business and library journs.; mem., Candn. Council of Lib. Schs. (Chrmn. 1971-72); Am. Lib. Assn. Comte. on Accreditation (Chrmn. 1973-74); Ont. Comte. Deans & Dirs. of Lib. Schs. (Chrmn. 1967-71); Inst. Prof. Lib. Ont. (Pres. 1961-62); Candn. Lib. Assn. (Pres. 1975-76); Am. Lib. Assn.; Ont. Lib. Assn. (Vice President 1962-63); Special Libs. Assn. (Toronto); Assn. Am. Lib. Schs. (Pres. 1973-74); Candn. Assn. of Lib. Schs. (Pres. 1966-67); Candn. Lib. Research and Devel. Council (Vice-Pres. 1965-67); Ont. Prov. Lib. Council (1967-70); Bibliog. Soc. Can.; Ont. Genealog. Soc.; Beta Phi Mu; Anglican; Home: 18 Kirkton Rd., Downsview, Ont. M3H 1K7; Office: Legis. Library, Legislative Bldg., Queen's Park, Toronto, Ont. M7A 1A2

LANDE, Lawrence M., O.C. (1967), LL.B., D.Litt., F.R.S.A.; notary; writer; b. Ottawa, Ont., 11 Nov. 1906; s. Nathan and Rachel Ray (Freiman) L.; e. Westmount (Que.) High Sch., grad. 1924; McGill Univ., B.A. 1928; Univ. of Montreal, LL.B. 1931; Univ. of Grenoble, Dipl. in Philos. 1928; m. late Helen Vera, d. Meyer Leon Prentis, 14 June 1939; children: Denise (Mrs. Walter Farber), Nelson; remarried, to Helen Ackerman Rogal, 6 Dec. 1975; served with Civil Protection Comte. during 2nd World War; Hon. Past Chrmn. Herzl Health Centre; Dir., Candn. Writer's Foundation Inc.; author of "The Lawrence Lande Collection of Canadiana", 1965; "Old Lamps Aglow" (an appreciation of early Candn. poetry), 1957; "The 3rd Duke of Richmond" (hist.), 1956; "Toward the Quiet Mind", 1954; "Psalms Intimate and Familiar", 1945; "Experience" (Poetry written jointly with Prof. T. Greenwood), 1963; "L'Accent" 1970; "Rare & Unusual Canadiana, 1st Supplement to Lande Bibliog." McGill University 1971; "Adventures in Collecting", McGill 1977; "Can. Historical Documents and Manuscripts", Montreal 1977-82 (5 vols.); has made 35 long-playing records; composes for piano; Past Pres., Montreal Centre of Canadian Friends of Hebrew Univ.; Past Pres., Candn. Centre P.E.N. Internat.; Past Chrmn. & Pres., Jewish Hist. Soc. Can. (1968); Hon. Corr. mem. for Que. Royal Soc. of Arts (1968); Sigma Alpha Mu; Liberal; Hebrew; recreations: travel, apple trees; Clubs: Grolier (N.Y.); University; Beaver; Montefiore; Elm Ridge Golf; St. James Lit. Soc.; Home: 4870 Cedar Cr., Montreal Que. H3W 2H9; Office: Lande Room, 3rd fl. McLennan Library of McGill University;

LANDER, Jack Robert, M.A., M.Litt., F.R.H.S., F.R.S.C.; historian; educator; b. Hinckley, Eng. 15 Feb. 1921; s. Robert Arthur and Hilda Mary (Goodman) L.; e. Alderman Newton's Sch. Leicester, Eng. 1940; Pembroke Coll. Cambridge B.A. 1942, M.A. 1945, M.Litt. 1950; J. B. SMALLMAN PROF. UNIV. OF W. ONT. since 1970; Lectr. and Sr. Lectr. Univ. of Ghana 1950-63; Assoc. Prof. Dalhousie Univ. 1963-65; Prof. present Univ. 1965-70; author "The Wars of the Roses" 1965; "Conflict and Stability in Fifteenth Century England" 1969; "Crown and Nobility 1450-1509" 1976; "Crown and Community: England 1450-1509", 1980; articles on fifteenth and early sixteenth century Eng. in various learned journs.; Liberal; recreations: travel, swimming, biking; Club: Reform (London, Eng.); Home: Apt. 1701 The Whitehall, 1265 Richmond St., London, Ont. N6A 3M1; Office: London, Ont. N6A 5C2.

LANDRETH, Wallace Johnstone, C.D., B.A.; Canadian public servant; b. Benough, Sask., 2 Oct. 1913; s. late Walter Anderson and Margaret White (Johnstone) L.; e. Pub. and High Schs., Lauder and Hartney, Man., 1928; Univ. of Man., B.A. 1933; Candn. War Staff Coll. 1944; m. late Marjorie Louise, d. late Robert Ingram Bradley, Winnipeg., 1941; children: Cameron Roy, Robert Anderson, Lauris Ann, Frances Margaret, Douglas Bradley; m. Clothilde d. late Joseph and Malvina Côté, Cap Chat, Que. 1978; Vice Chrmn., Tariff Bd., 1971-79; served with

Hudsons Bay Co. 1936-41; Extve. Secy., Man. Fed. of Agric., 1946; Asst. Mgr., Canadian Poultry Sales Ltd., 1947, Gen. Mgr. 1957; Pres., Edmonton Produce (1962) Ltd., 1962-66; Gen. Mgr., Produce Div., Ogilvie Flour Mills Co., 1962-66; Mang. Secy., Alta. Poultry Meat Marketing Bds., 1966; joined Candn. Army Reserve as Trooper, 12 Man. Dragoons, 1940; served in Can., UK and N.W. Europe 1941-45; present rank Lt. Col.; Councillor, R.M. of Fort Garry, 1950-51; mem. Prov. Extve., Lib. Party of Man., 1961-62; Chrmn. GP Comte., Boy Scouts & Girl Guides; served on numerous comtes. for Community Chest, Community Club or welfare activities: Past Chrmn. or Past Pres., Candn. Produce Council; Candn. Poultry Council; Poultry Products Inst. Can.; W. Can. Produce Assn.; Alta. & Man. Div., W. Can. Produce Assn.; Produce Sec., Winnipeg Chamber Comm.; Freemason; Liberal; Unitarian; recreations: boating, hunting, shooting, fishing, handloading; Home: 7911-145 St., Edmonton, Alberta T5R 0S7

LANDRY, Alfred R., Q.C., M.A., B.Com., D.C.L.; barrister and solicitor; b. Robichaud, N.B., 21 Apl. 1936; s. Albert and Agnes (Thibodeau) L.; e. Notre-Dame des Victoires High Sch., Barachois, N.B. 1953; Coll. l'Assomption, Moncton, 1955; St-Joseph Univ., B.A. 1957; Univ. of Ottawa, B.Com. 1958; Univ. of N.B. Law Sch., 1958-60; Rhodes Scholar, Oxford Univ., M.A. (Juris.) 1962; St. Thomas Univ., D.C.L. 1973; Univ. de Moncton, (Hon.) D.C.L. 1977; m. Alfreda Hazel, d. Albenie J. Leger, Shediac, N.B., 4 July 1964; children: Christian and Chantal; SR. PARTNER, LANDRY, & McINTYRE; Dir., Mother's Own Bakery Ltd., New Brunswick Telephone Company Limited; Natgas Ltd.; Can. Council of Christians and Jews; N.B. Heart Foundation; Chmn., Bd. of Trustees, N.B. Extra-Mural Hospital; Past Vice President, N.B. Young P. Cons. Assn.; Past President (Past Treas), N.B. P. Cons. Party; Mayor of Shediac 1966-71; Past Secy., N.B. Union of Towns; Founding Co-Pres., N.B. Assn. Nursing Homes; Past Vice Pres., S.E. Tourist Bureau; Past Chrmn., Bd. of Govs. and Extve. Comte. Univ of Moncton; Past Chrmn., N.B. Liquor Corp.; N.B. Rep., Uniform Law Comn.; mem., N.B. Rhodes Scholarship Selection Comte.; Candn. Council on Admin. of Justice; mem. Bd. Dirs., Georges-L. Dumont Hosp. (Pres. Constr. Comte.); read law with Judge C.I.L. Leger; called to Bar of N.B. 1964; mem., Candn. Bar Assn.; N.B. Barristers' Soc.; Moncton Barristers' Soc. (Past Secy.); Assn. Ins. Atty's; Moncton Bd. Trade; Shediac Chamber Comm.; P. Conservative; R. Catholic; recreations: fishing, hunting, gardening, snowmobiling; Clubs: Shediac Lyons (Past Secy.); Moncton Rotary; Home: 44 Sackville St., Shediac, N.B. E0A 3G0; Office: 19th Floor, Assumption Pl., 770 Main St., Moncton, N.B. E1C 1E7

LANDRY, Hon. Bernard, M.N.A.; politician; b. St-Jacques de Montcalm, Qué. 9 March 1937; s. Bernard and Thérèse (Granger) L.; e. Univ. of Montréal; Univ. of Paris; m. Lorraine d. Donat Laporte, Montréal 6 Aug. 1963; children: Julie, Philippe, Pascale; MIN. OF STATE FOR ECONOMIC DEVELOPMENT, QUE. 1976-; lawyer; Extve. mem. Parti Quebecois 1974 and 1981; el. M.N.A. for Fabre prov. g.e. 1976, re-el. M.N.A. for Laval-Des-Rapides 1981; Economic Development Publictions: "Challenges for Quebec", 1979; "Report on Savings", 1980; Parti Quebecois; R. Catholic; Office: Edifice H. 875 est, Grand-Allée, Québec, Qué. G1A 1A2.

LANDRY, Louis E.; businessman; b. Cap Pelé, N.B. 7 Nov. 1927; s. Edvard E. and Edith (Leblanc) L.; e. N.B.; m. Rita d. Domenique Cormier 1 Sept. 1951; children: Guy, Joanne, Janice, Yvette, Jacqueline; PRES., MALL CENTRE-VILLE LTD. 1973- ; Vice Chrmn. N.B. Electric Power Comn. 1970- ; Pres. Atlantic Industrial Ltd.; L. E. Landry Ltd.; Vice Pres. Villa du Repos Inc.; Secy.-Treas. Marina Beach Ltd.; Dir. L'evangeline newspaper; Villa Providence Inc.; Cité d'age d'or Inc.; Villa Heritage Inc.; Shediac Medical Centre Ltd.; farm implement dealer

1949-55; furniture retailer 1953-80; maritime snowmobile distributor 1965-73; real estate 1960- ; jewellry store 1975- and restaurant 1976- owner; P. Cons. cand. 3 prov. els.; Co-Chrmn. 2 N.B. prov. els.; served as Vice Pres., Treas. local and prov. P. Cons. organs.; Co-Chrmn. organ. Fed. P. Cons. for N.B.; Ald. Shediac Town Council; P. Conservative; R. Catholic; recreations: hunting, fishing, snowmobiling; Clubs: Rotary; Richelieu (Past Pres.); Chamber of Comm.; Past Pres. Shediac Lobster Festival Inc.; Home: Riverside Dr., Shediac, N.B. E0A 3G0; Office: P.O. Box 250, Shediac, N.B. E0A 3G0.

LANDRY, Hon. Louis-Philippe, B.A., B.Ph., LL.L.; judge; b. Hull, Que. 29 Apl. 1935; s. Ulysse and Marie-Rose (Duval) L.; e. Ottawa, Ont. Semy. 1953; Univ. of Ottawa Inst. of Philos. B.A., B.Ph. 1955, LL.L. 1958; m. Lise d. Antoine Deveault, Hull, Que. 31 May 1958; children: Marc, Suzanne, Hélène, Sylvain; JUDGE, SUPERIOR COURT PROV. OF QUE. since 1979; Lectr. in Law, Univ. Ottawa since 1971; called to Bar of Que. 1959; cr. Q.C. 1969; Legal Offr., Combines Br., Dept. Justice 1959-61 and Criminal Law Sec. 1961-63; Prov. Crown Atty. Montreal 1963-65; Dir. Regional Office, Fed. Dept. Justice Montreal 1965-75; Asst. Dept. Atty. Gen. (Criminal Law) Dept. Justice Ottawa 1975-79; lectr. in Criminal Law, Bar Admission Course Prov. Que. and sometime lectr. Univs. Sherbrooke, Montreal, McGill and Laval; recreations: tennis, fishing, music; R. Catholic; Home: 36 Cannes St., Gatineau, Que. J8T 5M5; Office: Courthouse, 17 Laurier St., Hull, Que. J8X 4C1.

LANDYMORE, Rear Adm. William Moss, O.B.E., C.D.; b. Brantford, Ont., 31 July 1916; s. Dr. Frederick William and Gladys (Moss) L.; e. Brantford Coll. Inst.; Royal Mil. Coll., Kingston, Ont.; m. Joan Lenore, d. late John Hall, Staffordshire, Eng., 14 Sept., 1940; children: Lauretta Jean, Roderick William, John Frederick; joined R.C.N. in Aug. 1936; trained in R.N. as a Cadet and Midshipman in H.M.S. "Frobisher", "Emerald" and "Glasgow"; in World War II served in H.M.S. "Windsor", H.M.C.S. "Fraser", "Margaree", "Restigouche" in Atlantic operations; served in H.M.S. "Belfast" and "Grenville" in Arctic patrols and in H.M.C.S. "Uganda" in the Pacific; O.B.E.; twice Mentioned in Despatches; after war, Deputy Dir., Warfare and Training, Ottawa; Dir. of Manning and Dir. of Plans and Operations; during Korean War served in command of H.M.C.S. "Iroquois" and as Sr. Offr. Candn. Destroyer Forces Far East, rank of Capt.; grad. of Naval Staff Coll., Jt. Services Staff Coll., and Imp. Defence Coll.; Commander aircraft carrier H.M.C.S. "Bonaventure" rank of Capt.; served as Chief of Staff to Flag Offr., Atlantic Coast and as Sr. Offr. Afloat Atlantic in rank of Commodore; promoted to Rear Adm., 1963; Flag Offr., Pac. Coast and Maritime Commdr. Pacific, 1963; OC Maritime Command June 1965-July 1966; mem., Naval Offrs. Assn.; Royal Commonwealth Soc.; Chmn., Bd. of Mgmt., Salvation Army Grace Maternity Hospital Halifax; recreations: golf; Club: Brightwood Golf & Country; Home: Rainbow Ridge Farm, RR #2, Porters Lake, Halifax County, N.S. B0J 2S0

LANE, Elizabeth, A. (Mrs. William T.), C.M. (1979), B.A., LL.D. (S.F.U. 1977); (Elizabeth Ann Greer); b. Vancouver, B.C. 30 Jan. 1928; d. Thomas Hyland and Bettie Maud (Beattie) Greer; e. Prince of Wales Sch., Vancouver; Univ. of B.C., B.A. (Chem.) 1949; m. William Tierney Lane, 1 Dec. 1956; one d. Naomi Elizabeth; one s. Thomas Wallace; served as research chem. with: Nat. Research Council Atomic Energy Project, Chalk River, 1949-50; B.C. Research Council, Vancouver, 1951-52, 1954-56; Royal Sch. of Mines, London, Eng., 1952-53; el. mem. Can. Council 1970-73; Dir., Community Arts Council of Vancouver since 1959 (Pres. 1964-65); Chrmn., Vancouver Br. Extve., Community Planning Assn. Can., 1963-64; Chrmn., Cultural Activities Sub-comte., Vancouver Centennial Committee, 1966-68; President Vancouver Museums Association, 1968-70; President, Jr. League of

Vancouver, 1965-67; also served as Dir., Playhouse Theatre Co.; Vancouver Festival Soc.; Vancouver Housing Assn., Vancouver Art Gallery; mem. Fed. Cultural Policy Review Comte., 1979-81; Convocation mem. of Senate, Univ. of B.C. 1969-78; Pres. Candn. Conf. of the Arts 1976-78; Chrmn. B.C. Arts Bd. 1974-78; Extve. Comte., Candn. Comn. for UNESCO, 1978-81; Delta Gamma; Home: 4438 Marguerite St., Vancouver, B.C. V6J 4G6

LANE, George Stewart, B.Com., M.A., Ph.D.; educator; b. Nanton, Alta. 21 May 1937; s. George Birtle Irving and Gwendolyn Rachael (Stewart) L.; e. Parkland and Lindsay Thurber Composite High Schs. Alta.; Univ. of Alta. B.Com. 1960; Univ. of Wash. M.A. 1965, Ph.D. 1969; Soc. Mang. Accts. Can. R.I.A. 1965; m. Marcia d. Milton Eliasoph 15 May 1970; two s. Michael, David; PROF. FAC. OF MANAGEMENT, UNIV. OF CALGARY 1976- ; (Dean, 1976-81); Instr. Sask. Tech. Inst. 1960-64, Chrmn. 1962-64; Lectr. Univ. of Alta. 1964-66, Acting Faculty Secy. 1965-66; Predoctoral Lectr. Univ. of Wash. 1966-69; Assoc. Prof. and Consultant Sir George Williams 1972-73; Assoc. Prof. and Acting Dean Univ. of Calgary 1974-76, 1975-76; author "Ralph Nader is a Marketing Man" 1969; "Festival of Waste Revisted" 1971; "Being Made Aware of Your Rights" 1971; "Marketing in the Canadian Environment" 1973; "A Canadian Replication of Mason Haire's Shopping List Study" 1975; "Environmental Forecasting: A New Dimension of Marketing Planning" 1975; recipient Queen Elizabeth Scholarship 1959-60; Can. Council Doctoral Fellowship 1967-69; Edna Benson Dissertation Fellowship 1969; Prov. of Que. Scholarship 1973; Brit. Council Visitorship 1973; mem. Acad. Mang.; Am. Marketing Assn.; Internat. Communication Assn.; Soc. Indust. Accts.; Acad. Marketing Sciences; Candn. Assn. Adm. Sciences; Clubs: Canadian Men's; Glencoe; Home: 2917-10 St. S.W., Calgary, Alta. T2T 3H4;Office: 2500 University Dr. N.W., Calgary, Alta. T2N 1N4.

LANG, Arthur Hamilton, M.A., Ph.D., F.R.S.C.; geologist (ret.); b. Peachland, B.C., 3 July 1905; s. Hamilton and Gertrude Lena (Pope) L.; e. Univ. of B.C., 1923-28, B.A. (1st class Hons.), M.A., Princeton Univ., Ph.D. 1930; Carleton Univ. (evening classes) 1959-68; Geologist, Geol. Survey of Canada, 1930-70; Chief Radioactive Resources Div., 1952-55, Mineral Deposits Div., 1955-60; Special Projects, 1960-70; retired 1979; author of "Canadian Deposits of Uranium and Thorium" 1952, 2nd ed. 1962; "Prospecting in Canada", 1956, 2nd ed. 1970; "La Prospection au Canada", 1961, 2nd ed. 1976; "Preliminary Study of Canadian Metallogenic Provinces", 1961; laymen's geol. guidebooks to four Candn. nat. parks, 1974-75; about 100 published reports and papers in scient. and engn. journs.; fel., Geol. Soc. Am.; mem., Candn. Inst. Mining & Metall. (Life); Freemason; Protestant; recreations: golf, skiing; Clubs: Royal Ottawa Golf: Laurentian; Address: 130 Somerset St. W., Apt. 909, Ottawa, Ont. K2P 0H9

LANG, Hon. Daniel Aiken, Q.C.; senator; barrister and solicitor; b. Toronto, Ont., 13 June 1919; s. the late Daniel W., Q.C., and Edna (Aiken) L.; e. Upper Canada Coll.; Trinity Coll., Univ. of Toronto; Osgoode Hall Law Sch., 1941 and 1945-47; m. Frances, d. late Dr. H. J. Shields and Cecil (Oatman) S., 24 Sept. 1948; children: Daniel, David, Nancy, Janet: COUNSEL, LANG, MICHENER, CRANSTON, FARQUHARSON & WRIGHT; read law with Lang & Michener; called to Bar of Ontario 1947; joined firm of Lang, Michener & Cranston; with same firm to date; summoned to the Sen. of Can. 1964; former mem., Bd. of Govs., Univ. of Toronto; Dep. Chmn., Bd. of Trustees, Sunnybrook Hosp.; served in 2nd World War with R.C.N.V.R., 1941-45; Liberal; Protestant; Home: 43 Hillholm Rd., Toronto, Ont. M5P 1M4; Office: Box 10, First Candn. Place, Toronto, Ont. M5X 1A2

LANG, Frederick Andrew, F.C.A., LL.D.; Chartered accountant, investment consultant; insurance executive: b.

Dunrea, Man., 8 June 1910; s. George Frederick and Margaret Elizabeth (Bissett) L.; e. John M. King Sch., Winnipeg, 1918-25; Daniel McIntyre Coll. Inst., 1926-28; Univ. of Man. (Extension), C.A. 1934; Hon. LL.D., Univ. of Manitoba 1978; m. Ruth Hay, d. late Alexander Noble, 6 June 1936; children: Mrs. R. J. Gooding (Charon Ruth), Frederick Stuart, Douglas Andrew; Pres., Candn. Funding Services Ltd., 1975; Student in Acct., William Gray & Co., 1928-34; C.A. 1934; Assessor, Income Tax Dept., Govt. of Man., 1935-38; Corpn. Assessor, Income Tax Dept., Gov. of Can., 1938-41; Secy.-Treas., Systems Equipment Ltd., 1941-55; Pres. & Mang. Dir., Candn. Premier Life Ins. Co. 1955-75; Fellow of Chartered Accts. (Man. Inst.), 1975; mem., B.C. Inst. Chart Accts. 1975; Mem. Bd. of Dir. Citadel Life Assce. Co.; Citadel General Assurance Co.; Chrmn., Bd. of Govs., Regent Coll. Van.; Hon. mem., Bd. of Dir., Man. Inst. of Mang. Inc.; Protestant; recreations: golf, music; Clubs: Manitoba; Vancouver; Home: 680 Fairmile Rd., West Vancouver, B.C. V7S 1R2; Office: 722-601 W. Broadway, Vancouver, B.C., V5Z 4CZ

LANG, Hon. (Hector) Daniel; politician; b. Dawson Creek, B.C. 3 Apl. 1948; s. Hector Craig and Margaret (Campbell) L.; e. F. H. Collins High Sch. Whitehorse, Y.T.; Univ. of Alaska; m. Augusta Marie Almstrom 19 May 1972; children: Danielle Marie, Hector Ian, Molly Stewart; MIN. OF TOURISM & ECON. DEVEL. AND RENEWABLE RESOURCES, Y.T. 1980- ; 1st el. to Yukon Leg. 1974, re-el. 1978; Min. of Educ. 1975; Min. of Highways & Pub. Works, Mun. & Community Affairs and Housing Corp. 1978; co-founder Soc. for N. Land Research; P. Conservative; Presbyterian; recreation: bagpipes; Home: 39 Cedar Cres., Whitehorse, Y.T. Y1A 4P2; Office: (P.O. Box 2703) Whitehorse, Y.T. Y1A 2C6.

LANG, Howard Jerome, B. Eng.; industrialist; b. Galt, Ont., 15 June 1912; s. Louis LaCourse and Gertrude O. (Dietrich) L.; e. Galt Coll. Inst., Galt, Ontario; McGill Univ., B.Eng.; (Chem.) 1935; m. Helen Mary, d. George S. Grant, Vancouver, B.C., 29 Oct. 1938; children: David L., Christopher H., Michael J., Martha H., Jennifer M.; DIRECTOR, CANRON INC.; Vice President and Director, Canadian Imperial Bank of Commerce; Dir., Sun Life Assurance Co. of Canada; Canadian Pacific Ltd.; Canadian Marconi Co.; Dofasco Inc.; Texaco Canada Inc.; Canadian Fund, Inc.; Canadian Investment Fund Ltd.; Drummond McCall Inc.; mem., Govs. Appleby Coll., Oakville, Ont.; Gov., Univ. of Waterloo, Waterloo, Ont.; The Conf. Bd.; with Canadian Industries Ltd., 1935-45; Asst. to the Pres., National Steel Car Corpn. Ltd., Hamilton, Ont. 1945, and apptd. Vice-Pres. in 1951, Pres. and Dir. 1953; resigned from National Steel Car and assoc. Cos., July 1960; el. a Dir. Pres. and C.E.O. of Canada Iron Foundries Ltd. (now Canron) July 1960; mem., Assn. Prof. Engrs. of Ont.; Newcomen Soc. of Eng.; Delta Kappa Epsilon; Catholic; recreations: fishing, shooting, golf; Clubs: Mt. Royal, St. James's (Montreal); Mount Bruno Country (St. Bruno, Que.) York, Toronto, Toronto Golf; Hamilton; Home: 13 Rosedale Heights Dr., Toronto, Ont. M4T 1C2; Office: First Canadian Place, P.O. Box 134, Toronto, Ont. M5X 1A4

LANG, Hon. Otto E., P.C., Q.C., B.A., LL.B., B.C.L.; b. Handel, Sask., 14 May 1932; s. Otto T. and Marie (Wurm) L.; e. Humboldt (Sask.) Coll. Inst.; Univ. of Sask., B.A. 1951, LL.B. 1953; Oxford Univ. (Rhodes Scholar) 1953, B.C.L. 1955; m. Adrian Ann Merchant, 21 Dec. 1963; children: Maria, Timothy, Gregory, Andrew, Elisabeth, Amanda, Adrian; EXEC. VICE-PRES., PIONEER GRAIN CO. LTD. AND ASS'T GEN. MGR., GRAIN MERCHANDISING, JAMES RICHARDSON AND SONS LTD., since 1979; read law with W. B. Francis, Q.C.; called to the Bar of Sask., 1956; Secy., Rhodes Scholar. Selection Comte. for Sask. 1962-68; prior to political engagement was Dean and Prof. of Law, Univ. of Sask.; el. to H. of C. for Saskatoon-Humboldt g.e. June 1968; apptd. Min. without Port-

folio July 1968; Acting Minister Energy, Mines and Resources 1969; Min. of Manpower and Immigration 1970; Min. of Justice 1972; cr. Q.C. 1972; Min. of Transport 1975-79; Min. responsible for Cdn. Wheat Bd. 1969-79; publications: "Contemporary Problems of Public Law in Canada" 1967 and numerous articles on labour law, torts, & no-fault auto. ins.; Pres., Assn. of Candn. Law Teachers, 1962; Liberal; Roman Catholic; Knight of Malta; Home: 12 Kingsway, Winnipeg, Man.; Office: 25th floor, 1 Lombard Place, Winnipeg, Man. R3B 0X8

LANG, Ronald William, M.A., Ph.D.; trade union researcher; b. St. Mary's, Ont., 26 Apl. 1933; s. Judge Harold DeFoe and Marion Christine (Grieve) L.; e. Stratford (Ont.) Secondary Sch. 1950; Ont. Agric. Coll. 1950-52; Labour Coll. Can. 1964; Univ. of Waterloo B.A. 1968, M.A. 1969; London Sch. of Econ. and Pol. Science Ph.D. 1974; m. Birthe Anna d. Simon Simonsen, Denmark, 5 June 1954; children: Harold DeFoe, Heather Anne, Stephen Ronald, John Douglas, Christopher Simon, Sheldon; DIR. OF RESEARCH AND LEGISLATION CANDN. LABOUR CONGRESS; farm labourer 1952-53; independent farmer St. Mary's Ont. 1953-63; Shop Steward Local 368 Un. Cement, Lime and Gypsum Workers Internat. Union 1959, Secy. 1960, Pres. 1961-64, Secy.-Treas. Dist. Council No. 10 1964; Pres. Woodstock, Ingersoll Dist. Labour Council 1963 (Hon. Life mem.); Asst. Prof. of Candn. Govt. Politics Glendon Coll. York Univ. 1971-72; Bd. of Dir., Canada Post Corp.; Adv. Bd. Sch. of Public & Community Affairs, Concordia Univ.; rec'd Can. Council Doctoral Fellowship 1969; author "The Politics of Drugs" 1975; Freemason; NDP; United Church; recreations: gardening; antique boat, Home: 293 John St. N., Arnprior, Ont. K7S 2P5; Office: 2841 Riverside Dr., Ottawa, Ont. K1V 8X7

LANG, T. E., B.Sc.; food executive; b. Osage, Iowa, 16 May 1919; s. Elmer P. and Martha (Hartnell) L.; e. State Univ. of Iowa, B.Sc. 1941; Harvard Business Sch., 1958; m. Hanne; children: Dr. R. T., Jori, Janelle; PRESIDENT, CARNATION INC., since Jan. 1971; joined present co. 1941; held various positions from Plant Supt. to Gen. Supt. of all Plants, 1950; apptd. Asst. Vice Pres., Sales 1953, Vice Pres. 1965; served during 2nd World War as Lt. with U.S.N.; Pres., Cont. Processing Council, 1959; Pres., Candn. Frozen French Fry Assn.; Dir., Nat. Dairy Council; Chrmn., Grocery Products Mfrs. Can.; United Church; recreations: fishing, hunting, gardening, skiing, bridge; Clubs: Hunt; Toronto Rotary; Islington Sportsmen Club (Pres.); Home: R.R. 3, Georgetown, Ont.; Office: 4174 Dundas St. W., Toronto, Ont. M8X 1X3

LANG, William Smithson MacKenzie, B.A.; retired insurance executive; b. Long Beach, Cal., 5 Feb. 1912; s. Lisgar L. and Reathea L.; e. Bishop Ridley Coll., 1928-29; Univ. of Man., B.A. 1933; joined Great-West Life Assurance Co., Invest. Dept., 1933-41, 1945-47; Supvr., Security Adm., 1947-48, Mgr., Bond Invests., 1948-52, Asst. Treas. 1952-56, Assoc. 1956-68, Sr. Assoc. 1968-72; vice pres. and Treas. 1972-78; served with Candn. Army (Inf.) in Can., Eng. and Europe 1941-45; rank Lt.; Hon. Treas., Community Chest Greater Winnipeg, 1952-54; mem. Bd., V.O.N.; mem. Adm. and Finance Comte., Diocese of Rupert's Land, since 1961; mem., Standing Comte. on Securities, C.L.I.A. of Invest. Sec.; Trustee Sinking Fund, Bd. Trustees Winnipeg Sch. Div. No. 1; Anglican; recreation: golf; Clubs: Winnipeg Winter; Manitoba; St. Charles Country; Home: Apt. 901-200 Tuxedo Blvd., Winnipeg, Man. R3P 0R3; Office: 60 Osborne St. N., Winnipeg, Man. R3C 1V3

LANGER, H. Peter; real estate executive; b. Vienna, Austria, 25 March 1916; s. Viktor and Margarete (Wachsmann); e. High Sch., Vienna, Austria (Sr. Matric. 1934); Vienna Agric. Coll.; Reading Univ. Eng. (Intermediate Science) 1939; m. Lillian, d. late Henry Patterson, Toronto, Ont., 3 Sept. 1941; children: Ann, Peter, Paul;

CHMN. AND CEO, MARKBOROUGH PROPERTIES LTD., previously Extve. Vice Pres., then Pres. and Dir. emigrated to Canada after discharge from U.K. forces in Sept. 1946; joined real estate firm of A. W. Farlinger, Toronto, Ont. 1947; apptd. Mgr. of East End Office, 1949, Gen. Mgr. in 1951, and Extve. Vice-Pres. in 1953 (firm name changed to Farlinger and Langer Ltd., 1954); joined A. E. LePage Ltd. as Vice-Pres. and Dir. 1960; served in 2nd World War joining U.K. forces in Feb. 1940; served in France Eng., N. Africa, Italy; final appt. Depy. Asst. Dir of Labour, N. Italy with rank of Staff Major; discharged with Hon. rank of Major, Sept. 1946; mem., Soc. of Indust. Realtors; Appraisal Inst. Can.; Community Planning Assn. Can.; Past Pres., Urban Devel. Inst.; Past Pres. and Hon. Life mem., Toronto Real Estate Bd.; former Vice-Pres., Ont. Assn. of Real Estate Bds.; mem. Assn. Ont. Land Econs.; has written articles and lect. on real estate matters; appeared as speaker, moderator and panel mem. on real estate and allied subjects on many occasions; Past Pres., Downtown Club, Candn. Legion; mem., Royal Candn. Mil. Inst.; Fellow of the Real Estate Inst. of Can.; Lambda Alpha; Anglican; Clubs: National; Donalda; Empire; Home: 4 Prince Hal Cres., Agincourt, Ont. M1T 2V8; Office: 90 Eglinton Ave. West, Toronto, Ont. M4R 2E7

LANGFORD, Arthur Nicol, M.A., PH.D.; botanist; b. Ingersoll, Ont., 30 July 1910; s. Thomas Eli and Bertha Alexandra (Nicol) L.; e. Queen's Univ., B.A. (Hons. Biol. and Chem.) 1931; Univ. of Toronto; M.A. (Bot.) 1933, Ph.D. (Plant Path.), 1936; m. ABNE B. d. GEORGE BRODIE, July 1938; m. Marjorie A. d. William Gilbert, 12 June 1976; children: Mrs. E. G. Cone, Peter Arthur, John Stephen; EMERITUS PROF. OF BIOLOGY, BISHOP'S UNIV.: began there as Lectr., 1937; Visiting Prof. of Biology, Univ. of Botswana and Swaziland, Kwaluseni, Sd. 1976-80; Candn. Bot. Assn.; Presbyterian; recreations: photography, nature study, philately; Home: 41 Clough Ave., Lennoxville, P.Q. J1M 1W4

LANGFORD, Henry Eden, Q.C., B.A.; b. Toronto, Ont., 25 May 1903; s. Frederick and Annie (Burwash) L.; e. Secondary Schs., Calgary, Alta.; Univ. of Toronto, B.A. (Commerce) 1925; Osgoode Hall, Toronto; m. Helen, d. Rev. Herbert Uren, 1930; children: Alexander, Elizabeth; called to the Bar of Ont. 1928; cr. Q.C. 1958; with Rowell, Reid, Wright & McMillan and successor firms 1928-40; with R.C.A.F. 1940-44; W.P.T.B. 1944-45; Gen. Mgr., Chartered Trust 1945-58; Pres. Eastern & Chartered Trust Co., 1959-67; Chrmn., Ont. Securities Comn., 1967-69; Pres., Toronto Iron Works 1969-71; Pres., Trust Co's. Assn. of Can. 1964-65; Pres., Dom. Mortgage & Invest. Assn., 1950-51; former Dir., Empire Life Ins. Co.; E.L. Financial Corp.; Home Oil Co.; Consumer Gas Co.; Scurry Rainbow Oil Co.; Victoria & Grey Trust Co.; Candn. Inst. Internat. Affairs; Freemason; Liberal; United Church; Clubs: R.C.M.I.; Can. Legion; Granite; Rotary; Canadian (Pres. 1957-58); Home: 484 Avenue Rd., Apt. 709, Toronto, Ont. M4V 2J4

LANGFORD, J. Alex, Q.C.; b. Toronto, Ont., 7 Dec. 1931; s. Henry E., Q.C. and Helen Elizabeth (Uren) L.; e. Univ. of Toronto Schs. 1950; Univ. of Toronto, B.A. 1954; Osgoode Hall Law Sch., 1958; m. Marion Grace, d. late Elzwood Barker, 20 Apl. 1957; children: Mary, Sarah, Anne, John, Jane: PARTNER, MILLER, THOMSON; Dir., E-L financial Corp., VGM Trust Co., Victoria Grey Trust Co.; The Debentures & Securities Corp. of Canada; Secy., Magna Internat. Inc.; read law in Toronto; called to Bar of Ont. 1958; cr. Q.C. 1971; Chrmn., Ont. Adv. Comte. on Succession Duties 1972-73; comnd.; Hon. Solr., Candn. Inst. Internat. Affairs; mem. Candn. Bar Assn.; Phi Gamma Delta; P. Conservative; United Church; recreations: reading, tennis, skiing, hiking, sailing; Clubs: National; Albany; Granite; Caledon Ski; Home: 129 Coldstream Ave., Toronto, Ont.; Office: P.O. Box 27, 20 Queen St. W., Toronto, Ont. M5H 3S1

LANGFORD, James Alfred, B.Arch.; Canadian public servant; b. Winnipeg, Man., 30 Jan. 1928; s. James Alfred and Laura (Willis) L.; e. Daniel McIntyre Collegiate, Winnipeg, Man.; Univ. of Manitoba, Sch. of Arch., B.Arch., 1951; m. Audrey Jean, d. late W. J. Oliver, Calgary, Alta., 27 Nov. 1953; children: Lorie Jean, William James, Janet Leigh, Leslie Ann, Mary Joan; MGR. DESIGN & CONSTRUCTION, 1979- ; Arch. with Rule, Wynn and Rule, Calgary, Alberta, after articling with them; later associated with J. A. Cawston in Calgary; moved to Kindersley, Sask. in 1953 to become resident Arch. responsible for design and supervision of numerous schools in the area and outside, as well as community hosp. and home for aged projects; Depy. Min. of Public Works Dept. of Sask., 1956-63; Chief Arch., Dept. Pub. Works, Can. 1963-66; Asst. Depy. Min. (Design) 1966-72; Asst. Depy. Min. (Technol. Research and Devel.) 1972-74; Secy., Adv. Comte. on Parlty. Accommodation, 1974-78; Programme Mgr. Lower Energy Bldg. Design, 1978-79; former mem., Community Planning Comn. for Regina, Sask.; member, Royal Arch. Institute Can.; Ont. Assn. of Arch.; Freemason; Protestant; recreations: golf, skiing, fishing, photography; Address: 140 O'Connor St., Ottawa, Ont. K1A 0M3

LANGHAM, Michael, L.Litt., D.Litt., LL.D.; theatrical producer; director; b. Bridgewater, Somerset, England, 1919; e. Radley Coll.; Univ. of London; m. Helen Burns (actress); one s. Christopher; DIR. OF THEATRE CENTRE, THE JUILLIARD SCHOOL 1980- ; completed formal educ. as a student-at-law; L.Litt., McMaster 1962; LL.D. Toronto 1966; D. Litt. Wellington 1967, Coll. of St. Scholastica 1972; served in 2nd World War going to France in 1940 where taken P.O.W. for five yrs.; on return to Eng., engaged as Assoc. Dir. of Arts Council 1946, directing "Twelfth Night", and Midland Theatre Co. in Conventry, Eng., taking over Directorship after two mths.; subsequently became one of England's best-known directors while working at Old Vic and Stratford-on-Avon Mem. Theatre; Dir. of production, Birmingham Repertory Theatre, 1948-50; Memorial Theatre, Stratford, 1950, directing "Julius Caesar; Dir. "The Gay Invalid (Moliere's LaMalade Imaginaire) The Garrick Theatre, London, 1951; Theatre des Galeries, Brussels, 1951 (French adapt. "Richard III"); Dir. Old Vic. Co. production "Othello" at Berlin Festival, 1951, and Old Vic, London; Dir. "The Merry Wives of Windsor (Dutch trans.), Haagsche Comedie, The Hage, 1952; Dir. of productins, Citizens' Theatre, Glasglow, 1953-54; worked with Tyrone Guthrie at Old Vic, directing "Othello" with Douglas Campbell and Irene Worth (1952); came to Stratford Festival, Canada, 1955 and directed "Julius Caesar", apptd. Artistic Dir. 1955-1967, directing an average of 2 plays per year, and building the company from a summer group to a year-round ensemble of international stature; Chief of Stratford Festival Foundation's Acting Sch., 1955-58; directed "Two Gentlemen of Verona" at Old Vic., 1957; has directed plays at the Crest Theatre, Toronto, Ont.; in 1960 (Apl.) staged "The Merchant of Venice" at Eng. Stratford; directed "Romeo and Juliet" at Stratford Festival Can., and "A Midsummer Night's Dream" at Old Vic, Eng., 1960; "Much Ado About Nothing" at Stratford-upon-Avon, Eng., and "Coriolanus" and "Loves Labour's Lost" at Stratford Festival, Can. 1961; 1962, planned and directed the two parts of the Stratford Festival Universities Tour; also directed Stratford Festival Company, Canada in "The Taming of the Shrew", "Cyrano de Bergerac", 1962; "The Affliction of Love" (N.B.C., T.V., N.Y.C.); "Troilus and Cressida", "Timon of Athens", 1963; "Love's Labour's Lost", and "Timon of Athens" (Chichester Festival Theatre Shakespeare Birthday Season); "King Lear", "The Country Wife", 1964; "Andorra" (Biltmore Theatre, N.Y.C.), 1963; "The Prime of Miss Jean Brodie", Helen Hayes Theatre, N.Y.C. 1967; "A Play by Aleksandr Solzhenitsyn", 1970; "Cyrano de Bergerac", "The Taming of the Shrew", "The Diary of a Scoundrel" 1971 (all at The Guthrie Theater Minneapolis); Artistic Dir., The Guthrie Theatre, 1971-79; Michael Langham Theatre Fund (for young actors, directors & designers) est. by Guthrie Theatre Foundation to honour his contributions in artistic direction & financing; Address: c/o The Juilliard School, Lincoln Centre, New York, N.Y. 10023

L'ANGLAIS, Paul, O.C. (1971), C.D., B.A.; b. Quebec City, 22 Oct. 1907; s. Judge Romeo and Marguerite (Hamel) L.; e. Que. High Sch.; Coll. Ste. Marie, Montreal; Univ. of Montreal, B.A. 1927; McGill Univ. (Arch.) 1927-28, (Law) 1928-30; m. Violet, d. T. L. H. Saunderson, 14 Dec. 1934; children: Constance (Mrs. Peter W. Barnes), Marguerite (Mrs. John D. Cowans), Anne (Mrs. John Rosiak Jr.); past Pres., Paul L'Anglais Inc.; past Chrmn. Bd., now Dir. and Consult., Tele-Metropole Inc.; past Dir., JPL Productions Inc.; CJPM-TV Chicoutimi; Publicist, Seigniory Club, 1930-31; Editor, A.O.A. Bulletin, 1931-32; Producer, Stn. CHLP 1932; Co-Founder of Radio Programme Producers with late Ivan F. Tyler; Co-Founder and Pres. of La Comedie d'Montreal, 1941; Que. Production Corpn., 1946; Dir.-Producer of Lux Theatre; Lieut. in 6th C.B.C.A., Levis, 1925-29; attached McGill C.O.T.C., Lt. Cavalry, 1929-30; served in Gen. Offrs. Reserve 1930-42; with 2nd Fusiliers Mont Royal since 1942 and holds rank of Lieut-Col. (retired); Dir., Buckshee Fund, 1944-45; Jean Brillant Br., Candn. Legion, 1944-45; Pres., Radio Guild 1945-46; former Vice-Pres., Better Business Bureau of Montreal Inc.; former Dir., Candn. Assn. of Broadcasters; C.A.A.B.; Pres., A.C.R.T.F. 1967-70; Chrmn. Nat. Bd. of Dir. of Can. Comte., 1969-72; Dir. and Past Pres., Que. Council, St. John Ambulance; Dir., C.B.I. (Toronto); awarded Radiomonde Production Trophy, 1943 and Candn. Beaver Award 1944, L'Hommage au mérite 1977; publications: articles entitled "What Gives With Jean Baptist", Toronto Ad Club 1945; "How to Get the Most Out of the Quebec Market", 1945; Extve. Producer of "Whispering City — La Fortresse", first bilingual film produced in Can., 1946; author of autobiog., "Ma Belle Epoque", 1977; Kappa Chi; Roman Catholic; Kt. Order of St. John; Kt. Malta; Kt. St. Lazarus; recreations: curling, riding, writing; Clubs: St. Denis; University; Montreal; Advertising and Sales (Dir., 1946-47); Pointe Claire Curling; Address: 354 Beaconsfield Blvd., Beaconsfield, Que. H9W 49A

LANGLEY, Rev. Abner James, B.Th., M.A., B.D., D.D. (Bapt.); educator (retired); b. Goldboro, N.S., 9 May 1910; s. T. Sandford and Geraldine (Giffin) L.; e. Gordon Coll., Boston, B.Th. 1934; Boston Univ., M.A. 1935; Acadia Univ., B.D. 1936, D.D. 1961; m. Thelma Irene, d. Earl S. Damon, North Abington, Mass., 14 Oct. 1936; children: Wayne D., Donna D. (Mrs. Norman Jeffrey), Miriam (Mrs. Gregory Cook), Dianne J. (Mrs. Gordon Brown); Dean of Theology, Acadia Univ. and mem. of Senate, 1971-75; Gov. 1952-67; Princ., Acadia Divinity Coll. 1971-75, Trustee, 1967-75; Lecturer, A.D.C 1971-75, and Head of Dep't of pastoral Theology; Field Super. for Dr. of Min. program for South. Bapt. Theol. Seminary, Louisville, Kentucky, since 1975; o. 1935; Acting Asst. Pastor, Tremont Temple, Boston, 1934-35; Min., Immanuel Bapt. Ch., Truro, N.S., 1936, Central Bapt. Ch., Saint John, N.B., 1940, W. End Bapt. Ch., Halifax 1950, First Bapt. Ch. Moncton, 1956; Assoc. Princ. Acadia Divinity Coll., 1968-71; mem. Extve., Candn. Bapt. Foreign Mission Bd., 1960-66 (Vice Chrmn. 1965-67); Chrmn., Candn. Bapt. Overseas Mission Bd., 1967-70 and made official visits to Africa etc. on behalf of Board; Vice Pres., Lord's Day Alliance. Can.; mem. Bd., Candn. Bible Soc., N.B.; Extve. Comte., Bapt. World Alliance Comn. on Religious Liberty & Human Rights 1971-75; Chrmn., Union Jubilee Comte., Atlantic Un. Bapt. Convention, 1965-68; Pres., Bapt. Fed. Can. 1962-64; Del., Bapt. World Cong., Atlanta 1939, London (Eng.) 1955, Rio de Janeiro 1960, Miami Beach 1965; Del. Bapt. World Congress, Stockholm, 1975; Official Del., World Cong. on Evangelism, Berlin, 1966; Candn. Rep., N. Am. Bapt. Fellowship Comte.

1966-70; Pres., Moncton Min. Assn., 1966; Chrmn., Bd. of Dirs. Atlantic Bapt. Coll., 1957-60; official Del. to Internat. Cong. on World Evangelization, Lausanne, 1974; 2 visits to U.S.S.R., (1966, 1972) official visitor from Can. Baptist Churches and guests of Baptist Churches in Russia. Preached and lectured in Moscow, Leningrad, Riga and Minsk; also preached and lectured in S. America, Europe, Asia, Africa; author of articles in various mags.; mem., Am. Acad. Homiletics; Humanities Assn. Can.; recreation: travel; Home: 3 Sunset Terrace, Wolfville, N.S. B0P 1X0; Office: Acadia Divinity Coll., Wolfville, N.S. B0P 1X0

LANGLEY, George Ross, B.A., M.D., C.M., F.R.C.P.(C), F.A.C.P., F.R.C.P. (Edin); Physician and University professor; b. Sydney, N.S. 6 Oct. 1931; s. John George Elmer Langley; e. Port Hawkesbury Elem. and New Glasgow High Schs. N.S. 1948; Mt. Allison Univ. B.A. 1952; Dalhousie Univ. M.D., C.M. 1957 F.R.C.P. (C), 1961; m. Jean Marie d. Ernest Pitblado Ballantyne, Ballantyne's Cove, N.S. 22 June 1957; children: Joanne Marie, Mark Ross, Richard Graham; PROF. AND HEAD OF MED. DALHOUSIE UNIV. since 1974; Head of Med. Victoria Gen. Hosp. since 1974; Lectr. in Med. Dalhousie Univ. 1962, Asst. Prof. 1964, Assoc. Prof. 1966, Prof. 1968; Chief of Service Med. Camp Hill Hosp. 1969-74; Vice Pres. (Medicine), Royal College of Physicians and Surgeons of Can., 1980-82; mem. Nat. Cancer Inst. Can. (Professional Awards Panel 1981, Chmn., Comte. on Priorities, mem. 1981-; Clin. Adv. Comte. 1973-76, Clin. & Epid. Research Adv. Comte. 1978; Chmn. 1981-; Clinical and Epid. Research Grants Panel mem. 1973-78, Chmn. 1978-81; John and Mary Markle Scholar in Acad. Med. 1963-68; rec'd Queen's Silver Jubilee Medal; author over 60 scient. articles red cell metabolism, leukemia, med. educ.; Fellow, Royal Coll. Physic. & Surg. Can.; Fellow, Am. Coll. Physic.; Royal coll. of Physics of Edinborough; Internat. Soc. Hematology; mem. Am. Soc. Hematology; Council mem. Royal Coll. Phys. & Surgs. 1978-82; Chrmn. Hematology Specialty Comte., 1974-80; Chrmn., Examinations Comm. 1980-; Gov. Am. Coll. Phys. 1974-78; mem. Candn. Soc. Clin. Investigation (Council 1966-69, Chrmn. Awards Comte. 1968-69); Med. Research Council Can. (Grants Comte. Clin. Investigation 1974-78, Chrmn. 1976-78); Candn. Hematology Soc. (Pres. 1976-78, Vice Pres. 1974-76); Med. Soc. N.S. (Chrmn. Sec. Internal Med. 1971); N.S. Soc. Internal Med. (Vice Pres. 1970, Pres. 1971); Dalhousie Med. Alumni (Pres. 1973-75, Vice Pres. 1971-73, Secy. Treas. 1967-71); Alpha Omega Alpha; Phi Rho Sigma; United Church; recreations: gardening, reading skiing,; Clubs: Wentworth Valley Ski; Waegwaltic; Home: 6025 Oakland Rd., Halifax, N.S. B3H 1N9; Office: Victoria Gen. Hosp., Halifax, N.S. B3H 2Y9.

LANGLOIS, Hon. J. G. Léopold, Q.C., B.A., LL.L.; senator; b. Ste. Anne des Monts, Que., 2 Oct. 1913; s. Capt. Octave and Amanda (Fournier) L.; e. Gaspe Semy.; Rimouski Semy.; Laval Univ., B.A., LL.L.; m. Ginette Fournier, Ste. Anne des Monts, Que.; one s. Raynold; SR. PARTNER, LANGLOIS, DROUIN AND ASSOCIATES: Dir., Canadian Foundation Company Limited; K.H.B. Can. Inc.; Group Degagnes Inc.; Montreal Life Ins. Co.; Les Armateurs du St-Laurent Inc.; specialized in Marine Law; served in World War 1940-45 with R.C.N., Lieut-Commdr. R.C.N.(R); Master Mariner, Foreign Going; el. to H. of C. for Gaspe, g.e. 1945, '49, '53; apptd. Parlty. Asst. to Postmaster Gen. Jan. 1951; re-apptd. Parlty. Asst. to the Min. of Transport, Oct. 1953; def. g.e. 1957; summoned to the Senate July 1966; Hon. Pres., Que. Branch, Navy League of Can.; Prs. Bureau des Gouverneurs de la "Société musicale Le mouvement Vivaldi"; L'Association des marins de la Vallée du St-Laurent Inc.; SOUVERNEUR, Fondation Univ. Laval; mem., Internat. Parlty. Union; Commonwealth Parlty. Assn. (Candn. Br.); Candn. NATO Parlty Assn.; Candn. Bar Assn.; Bar of Prov. of Que.; Royal Canadian Legion; St. Lawrence Shipowners Assn. Inc.; Prov. of Que. Board of Trade; Bureau de l'Industrie et du Comm. du Que. Métropolican Inc.; Groupe Maritime de Quv. Inc.; rec'd. 1939-45 Star, Atlantic Star, Voluntary Service Medal with clasp, General Service Medal; Coronation Medal 1953, Centenary Medal 1967; Queen's Jubilee Medal, 1978; K. of C.; Roman Catholic; Clubs: Quebec Yacht; Quebec Garrison; Reforme Inc. de Que.; Silmère Inc.; Home: Le Montmorency, (1003) 165, Grande Allée East, Quebec, Que. G1R 2H8; Office: 126 St. Peter St., Quebec, Que.

LANGLOIS, Yves, B.A., M.Com., M.B.A.; telecommunications executive; b. Plessisville, Que. 2 Nov. 1933; s. Jean and Pauline (Houde) L.; e. Univ. Laval B.A. 1954, M.Com. 1957; Harvard Grad. Sch. of Business M.B.A. 1960; EXTVE. VICE PRES. FINANCE & ADM. TELE-GLOBE CANADA since 1978; Mang. Consultant, Price Waterhouse and Associates 1964-69; Vice Pres. Finance Bellevue-Pathe 1969-72; Dir. Financial Services Teleglobe Canada 1972-76, Vice Pres. Finance 1976-77; recreations: tennis, music, reading; Home: 511 Sherbrooke St. E., Montreal, Que. H1T 3V4; Office: 680 Sherbrooke St. W., Montreal, Que. H3A 2S4.

LANGS, John Gauld, Q.C.; b. Hamilton, Ont., 22 Feb. 1909; s. late Cecil Vanroy and late Edith Erie (Perney) L.; e. Highfield Sch., Hamilton; McMaster Univ. 1934; Osgoode Hall Law Sch., 1937; m. Ann Wilhelmina, d. late John Inglis McLaren, 22 Dec. 1934; children: Wendy Ann Johnson, John McLaren; PARTNER, LANGS BINKLEY O'NEAL & SMITH; read law with Saunders Kingsmill Mills & Price and Day Wilson, Ferguson & Kelly; called to Bar of Ont. 1937; cr. Q.C. 1959; Past Pres., Hamilton W. Riding, Lib. Assn.; Finance Chmn., Advisor and mem. Extve., Hamilton Dist. Lib. Assn.; Past Pres., Hamilton & Dist. Un. Appeal (Hon. Solr., mem. Exctve. Comte. and Dir.); Past Dir., Social Planning Council Hamilton & Dist.; mem. Finance Comte, YMCA (Hamilton) Foundation; Dir., Royal Bot. Gdns. (Chmn. Nominations Comte.; mem. Property & Finance Comte.); Past Pres., Hamilton Dist. Cancer Soc.; past Chmn., Honours & Awards Comte., Ont. Div., Candn. Cancer Soc. (mem. Exctve. & Finance Comtes., Bd. mem.; Life mem., Nat. Body); Hon. Solr., Big Sister Assn. Hamilton Inc.; Girl Guides Can., Hamilton Area; Past Pres., Hamilton Law Assn.; Past Chmn. Bd. of Stewards and presently Vice Chmn., Cong. Bd., Melrose Un. Ch.; Chmn. Property Comte., Hamilton Presby., Un. Ch. of Can.; Phi Gamma Delta; Liberal; United Church; Clubs: Hamilton (Chrmn. 1973); Home: 165 Aberdeen Ave., Hamilton, Ont. L8P 2P8; Office: 8 Main St.E., Hamilton, Ont.

LANGSTON, Charles Ewing; banker; b. Montreal, Que. 7 Sept. 1924; s. John Charles and Isobel Mary (Ewing) L.; e. Westmount (Que.) High Sch. 1943; m. Margery Emily d. Charles Henry Armstrong, Montreal, Que. 10 May 1947; one d. Susan Joan; SENIOR VICE PRES. , CANADIAN IMPERIAL BANK OF COMMERCE; joined present Bank 1945 serving in Que., Man. and N.Y.; assigned to Internat. Dept. Regional Office Toronto 1960, appts. incl. Asst. Gen. Mgr. and Mgr., Vice Pres. Money Market and Internat. Services, Vice Pres. and Gen. Mgr., Internat; Dir., Candn. Imperial Bank of Commerce Trust Co. (Bahamas) Ltd.; Bank of Commerce Trust Co. Barbados Ltd.; C.I.B.C. Trust Co. (Cayman) Ltd.; Martin Corp. Group Ltd., Australia; served with RCNVR 1943-45, HMCS Mayflower, HMCS Quinte, telegraphist; mem. Bd. Trade Metrop. Toronto; Forex Assn. Can.; Royal Arcanium; P. Conservative; Anglican; recreations: model railroading, gardening; Club: Albany; Home: 7 Cherryhill Avenue, Scarborough, Ont. M1C 1W9; Office: Commerce Court West, Toronto, Ont. M5L 1A2.

LANGSTON, John F., B.Sc.; consulting petroleum engineer, retired; b. Calgary, Alta., 11 Mar 1911; s. Frederick Francis and Cora (Roberts) L.; e. Univ. of Alta., B.Sc. (Engn.) with distinction, 1937; m. Kathleen Ann, d. Mark F. Canning, Calgary, 15 Jan. 1940; children: Margaret

Ann, Frederick Francis, Gordon Charles; DIR. SCURRY-RAINBOW OIL LTD.; served as Apprentice Engr. with Calgary Power Co. Ltd., 1937-38; Field Engr., Lane-Wells Co., Calgary, 1938-41; Petroleum Engr., Gen. Petroleums Ltd. and Denton & Spencer, 1941-45; becoming Mang. Dir., Denton Spencer Co. Ltd. 1945; Life mem.; Assn. of Prof. Engrs. of Alta.; Engn. Inst. of Can. (Regional Councillor); Oilfield Tech. Soc.; Candn. Inst. Mining & Metall. (Chrmn. Calgary Br. 1968-69); Anglican; recreations: photography, hiking, swimming; Home: 1622 Scotland St., Calgary, Alta. T3C 2L5; Office: 2300 Home Oil Tower, 324-Eighth Ave. S.W., Calgary, Alta. T2P 2Z5

LANK, Herbert H., D.C.L. (Bishop's). L.H.D. (Delaware), LL.D. (Montreal); b. Seaford, Delaware, 7 Jan. 1904; s. Albert J. and Elizabeth (Hayman) L.; e. Univ. of Delaware; Univ. de Nancy; La Sorbonne; Ecole Libre des Sciences Politiques; m. Oriana, d. Prof. A. E. Bailey, Worcester, Mass., 19 Mar. 1927; children: Raymond, Alden, David; HON. DIR., DU PONT CANADA INC.; Hon. Dir. Candn. Enterprise Development Corp. Limited; Dir., Pratt and Whitney Aircraft of Canada Ltd.; Chrmn., Candn. Chem. Producers' Assn. 1966-67; Chrmn. of Extve. Council Candn. Chamber of Comm. 1951-52 (Candn. Chrmn., Can.-U.S. Comte. 1955-56); mem., Defence Research Bd. 1956-59; Pres., Montreal Symphony Orchestra, 1955-56; Pres., Candn. Inst. of Internat. Affairs 1968; awarded Canada Medal by Soc. Chem. Indust., 1966; prior to coming to Canada in 1942, was associated with the Du Pont Co., La Société Française Duco, and Industrias Quimicas Argentinas Duperial, working in North and South America and Europe; Kappa Alpha; United Church; Clubs: St. James's; Mount Royal; Forest & Stream; Union Interalliée (Paris); University; Chemists' (N.Y.); Home: 168 Edgehill Rd., Westmount, Que. H3Y 1E9; Office: 555 Dorchester Blvd. W., Montreal, Que. H3C 2V1

LANSDOWNE, James Fenwick, O.C., LL.D.; artist; b. Hong Kong 8 Aug. 1937; s. Ernest Lansdowne; e. St. Michael's Sch. and Victoria High Sch., B.C.; Univ. of Victoria LL.D. 1974; author/artist "Birds of the Northern Forest" 1966; "Birds of the Eastern Forest" vol. I 1968, vol. II 1970 (co-author); "Birds of the West Coast" Part I 1976, Part II 1980; Fellow, Explorers Club; Anglican; recreations: antiques, book collecting, ornithology; Home: 681 Transit Rd., Victoria, B.C.; Office: 941 Victoria Ave., Victoria, B.C. V8S 4N6.

LANSKAIL, Donald A.S., B.A., LL.B.; forestry executive; b. Regina, Sask. 21 Oct. 1917; s. George Joseph Alexander and Catherine (Ross) L.; e. Regina elem. and high schs.; Univ. of B.C. B.A., LL.B.; m. Marjorie Anne Brownlie 19 Dec. 1953; children: John, Bruce, Anne; PRESIDENT AND CHIEF EXECUTIVE OFFICER, COUNCIL OF FOREST INDUSTRIES OF B.C. since 1976; Dir., Canada Past Corp. 1981-; law practice 1950-54; Legal Counsel and Asst. Mgr. Forest Industrial Relations 1954-68; Pres. Pulp and Paper Indust. Relations Bureau 1968-76; Pres. Forest Indust. Relations 1973-76; comnd. offr. Royal Candn. Signals 1941-45 serving in Pacific Command and N.W. Europe; Ald. W. Vancouver since 1962; Chrmn. Lower Mainland Regional Planning Bd. 1967-69; GVRD Regional Park Comte. 1971-74; Dir. Central Mortgage and Housing Corp. 1962-69; mem. Adv. Comte. to Prime Min.'s Task Force on Labour Mang. Relations 1967-68; Gov. B.C. Lions Football Club; Liberal; Anglican; recreations: golf, fishing; Clubs: Vancouver; Capilano Golf & Country; Home: 2465 Rosebery Ave., West Vancouver, B.C. V7V 2Z8; Office: 1500 - 1055 West Hastings St., Vancouver, B.C. V6E 2H1

LANTHIER, André, B.A., M.D.; physician; professor; b. Montreal, Que. 13 Apr. 1928; s. late Eugène and Blanche (Paquette) L.; e. Univ. of Montreal B.A. 1948, M.D. 1953; Notre Dame Hosp., Montreal intern & resident, 1952-55; Harvard Med. Sch. Research Fellow 1958; m. Ghislaine d.

Sylvio Matte 15 Dec. 1956; children: Francois, Gilbert, Stéphane; PROFESSOR, DEPT. OF MEDICINE, UNIV. OF MONTREAL 1968- ; Assoc. Dir. (Research) 1972- ; Dir., Research Ctr., Notre Dame Hosp. 1978- ; Chief, Endocrinology Lab., Notre Dame Hosp. 1959- ; joined present Univ. in 1954 as Asst. Prof, Dept. of Med.; Assoc. Prof. 1964; Chrmn. of Dept. 1968-72; Physician-in-chief, Notre Dame Hosp. 1967-72; author over 100 articles in scientific journals on biomedical research; mem. and Past Pres. Candn. Soc. for Clinical Investigation; mem. Endocrine Soc. (U.S.); Amer. Federation for Clinical Research; Royal Coll. of Phys. of Can.; Amer. Coll. of Physics; awarded Medal of the Lt.-Gov. (Qué.) 1953; recreations: swimming; boating, fishing, duck hunting; Home: 1880 de la Duchesse, St-Bruno (Chambly), Qué. J3V 3L9; Office: Laboratoire d'endocrinologie, Hôpital Notre-Dame, 1560 est, rue Sherbrooke, Montreal, Qué. H2L 4K8

LaPALME, Robert, O.C., R.C.A.; caricaturist; b. Montreal, Que. 14 Apl. 1908; s. Tancrede and Elodie (Beauchamp) L.; e. autodidact; m. Annette (d. 1978) d. Alphonse Demers, Montreal, Que. 14 Jan. 1935; one s. Pierre; pol. cartoonist Montreal and New York since 1933; FOUNDER AND DIR., INTERNAT. PAVILION OF HUMOUR; Pres. Gaboriau & Associés Ltée; Founder and Dir. Internat. Salon of Cartoons 1964; Founder Qué. Mun. Art Gallery; exhns. incl. New York, Montréal (4), Toronto, Rio de Janeiro (2), Sao Paolo, Rome, Paris, Nat. Gallery Can.; painted 3 murals Expo '67 (now in Montreal metro); large tapestry Place des Arts; mural Place Crémazie; Prof. Faculty of Sciences Laval Univ. 5 years.; cited in many books; R. Catholic; recreation: reading; Club: Montreal Press (Hon. Life mem.); Home: 2055 St-Mathieu, s/1502, Montréal, Qué. H3H 2J2; Office: Man & His World, Ste-Helene Island, Montréal, Qué. H3C 1A0.

La PIERRE, Laurier L., M.A., Ph.D., LL.D.; university professor; b. Lac Mégantic, Que., 21 Nov. 1929; s. Lionel and Aldora (Bilodeau) L.; e. Univ. of Toronto, B.A. 1955, M.A. 1957, Ph.D. 1962: LL.D., Prince Edward Island 1970; m. Paula, d. late C.H.A. Armstrong, Toronto, 28 May 1960; children: Dominic, Thomas; Assoc. Prof. of Hist., McGill Univ., 1965; Dir., French Can. Studies Programme, McGill; Pres., Comn. of Inquiry into Educ. of Young Children in Ont.; Dir. of the collection. "La Saberdache Québécoise"; Lectr., Univ. of Western Ont., 1960-62; Asst. Prof., Loyola Coll., 1962-63; McGill Univ., 1963-64; T.V. and Radio Commentator; served as Co-Host, "This Hour Has Seven Days"; Host, C.B.C. television show "La Pierre"; Moderator, Radio-Québec television series "En se racontant l'histoire d'ici"; Commentator and Programmer for C.K.V.U., Vancouver; has written numerous articles for mags. & learned journs.; mem., Candn. Hist. Assn.; Candn. Assn. Univ. Teachers; ACTRA.

LA PIERRE, Tom, R.C.A.; artist; educator; b. Toronto, Ont. 28 Dec. 1930; s. Romeo Paul and Catherine (White) La P.; e. Ont. Coll. of Art 1955; Ecole des Beaux-Arts Paris; La Grande Ohaumierr Paris; Atelier 17 Paris; m. Patricia Clemes 28 Apl. 1958; children: Armand, David; Art Instr. Ont. Coll. of Art; rep. nat. and internat. exhns. incl. USA, France, Italy, Japan, S. Am.; recipient various arts awards, scholarships, Can. Council grants; mem. Candn. Soc. Painters in Watercolour; recreations: music, film, literature, theatre, nature; Address: 2067 Proverbs Dr., Mississauga, Ont. L4X 1G3.

LAPLANTE, André; concert pianist; b. Rimouski, Que. 12 Nov. 1949; s. Roger and Anne-Marie (Demers) L.; e. Coll. Ste-Marie and Coll. Notre-Dame, Montreal 1969; Vincent D'Indy Ecole de Musique, Montreal 1969; Juilliard Sch. of Music, N.Y. 1976-79; m. France d. Henri de Guise, Montreal, Que. 21 Aug. 1976; has toured Europe, Orient, Australia, Russia and N. Am. as prof. pianist; performed Carnegie Hall 1978, 1980; rec'd Silver Medal

Tchaikowsky Internat. Competition 1978 (1st Candn. to win prize) Moscow; named Candn. Interpreter of Yr., Candn. Music Council 1978; R. Catholic; recreations: swimming, photography, cinema; Home: 155 W. 68th St., #1017, New York City, N.Y. 10023 and 166 Blvd. Inberville, Repentigny, Que.; Office: Columbia Artists Management, 165 W. 57th St., New York City, N.Y.

LAPOINTE, Hon. Charles, M.P.; politician; b. Tadoussac, Que. 17 July 1944; s. Pierre and Emilienne (Gingras) L.; e. Tadoussac elem. sch.; Hauterive Coll.; Laval Univ. of Que.; MIN. OF STATE FOR SMALL BUSINESS AND TOURISM, CAN. 1980- ; former prof. and foreign service officer; el. to H. of C. for Charlevoix g.e. 1974, re-el. since; Parlty. Secy. to Min. of Transport 1977; Liberal; R. Catholic; Home: Tadoussac, Que. Office: House of Commons, Ottawa, Ont. K1A 0A6.

LAPOINTE, Col. the Hon. Hugues, P.C. (Can.), O.C. Q.C., B.A., LL.L., LL.D., K.G.StJ.; b. Rivière du Loup, Que., 3 Mar. 1911; s. Rt. Hon. Ernest, P.C., and E. (Pratte) L.; e. Univ. of Ottawa; Laval Univ., LL.L.; LL.D. Ottawa 1954, R.M.C. 1967; m. Lucette, d. Dr. R. E. Valin, Ottawa, 15 Oct. 1938; BARRISTER, 1978;served in 2nd World War 1939-45 with Le Régt. de la Chaudière; called to Bar of Que. 1935; cr. K.C. 1949; 1st el. Liberal mem. H. of C. for Lotbinière, g.e. 1940; apptd. Parlty. Asst. to Min. of Nat. Defence 1945, and to Secy. of State for External Affairs, Jan. 1949; sworn of the P.C. and apptd. Solr.-Gen. of Can., Aug. 1949; Minister of Veterans' Affairs, Aug. 1950, and Postmaster-Gen., Nov. 1955; Del. to Gen. Assembly of Un. Nations, Paris, Sept. 1948, Lake Success, Apl. 1949 and Sept. 1950; re-el. to H. of C. in g.e. 1953; def. g.e. 1957; Agent-Gen. for Que. in U.K., 1961-66; Lieut. Gov., Prov. of Que., 1966-78; Roman Catholic; Officer of the Order of Canada; Kt. Grand Cross of Magistral Grace, Sovereign and Mil. Order of Malta; Hon. Col., Régt. de la Chaudière (1971); Clubs: Garrison (Quebec); Home: 135 W. Grande Allée, apt. 1005, Quebec City; Office: Goodwin, De Blois et Associes, 2, Place Quebec, #602 Quebec City.

LAPOINTE, Marc C., Q.C., M.C.L.; labour relations lawyer; b. Montreal, Que. 18 Apl. 1923; s. Edouard Charles and Antoinette (Trudeau) L.; e. St. Vincent Ferrier Pub. Sch. and Coll. André-Grasset; Univ. de Montréal B.A.; McGill Univ. B.C.L., M.C.L. (Labour Relations); Inst. of World Affairs, Cert. in Internat. Law; m. Thérèse Gallant 11 June 1951; children: Luc, Judith, Marc Jr., Anne; CHRMN., CAN. LABOUR RELATIONS BD. since 1973; called to Bar of Que. 1947; cr. Q.C. 1964; mem. law firm Desaulniers, Lapointe, Lussier 1948; Sr. of law firm Lapointe, O'Brien & Associates 1948-51 and of Lapointe and Levesque & Associates 1951-73; specialist, lectr. (McGill Law Faculty 12 yrs.) and speaker on labour law, leg. and relations; author numerous articles various law reviews; mem. Internat. Bar Assn.; Candn. Bar Assn.; Que. Bar Assn.; Candn. Indust. Relations Assn. (Extve. Bd.); R. Catholic; recreations: boating, tennis, fishing, painting, sculpting; Home: 31 Chemin des Capucines, Hull, Que. J9A 1S8; Office: Lester B. Pearson Bldg., 125 Sussex Dr., Ottawa, Ont. K1A 0X8.

LAPOINTE, Hon. (Louise Marguerite) Renaude, P.C., senator; b. Disraeli, Que. 3 Jan. 1912; d. Joseph-Alphonse and Marie-Louise (Poulin) L.; e. Stanstead Convent; Laval Univ.; Dominion Coll. of Music, Lic. Mus. 1927: SPEAKER, SENATE OF CANADA 1974-79; Journalist with Le Soleil, La Presse, Le Nouveau Journal Que. and Montreal, Corr. for Time and Life Mag. and for CBC Internat. Service (Fr. Sec.) 1939-70; apptd. Senator of Can. 1971; Candn. Del. to 25th, 26th and 27th Sessions of U.N. Gen. Assembly N.Y.; mem. Bd. Dirs., Candn. Human Rights Fdn.; CRIAW (Candn. Research Inst. for the Advance of Women); MATCH (Internat. Centre); Candn. Hunger Foundation; mem. Internat. Parlty. Union; Commonwealth Parlty. Assn.; Candn. Assn. of NATO Parliamentarians; Assn. des Parlts. de langue française; World Fed. Parlty. Assn.; author of "L'histoire bouleversante de Monseigneur Charbonneau"; R. Catholic; Liberal; recreations: movies, theatre; Clubs: Media; Cercle des Femmes Journalistes; Home: 180 Maclaren Apt.1109, Ottawa, Ont. K2P 0L3; Office: Senate of Canada, Ottawa, Ont. K1A 0A4

LAPONCE, Jean Antoine, Ph.D.; educator; b. Decize, France 4 Nov. 1925; s. Fernand and Fernande (Ramond) L.; e. Institut d'Etudes Politiques Paris, Dipl. 1947; Univ. of Cal. Los Angeles Ph.D. 1956; m. Iza d. Stanislaw Fiszhaut 7 Apl. 1971; children: Jean-Antoine, Marc, Patrice (from 1st marriage), Danielle (from 2nd marriage); PROF. OF POL. SCIENCE, UNIV. OF B.C.; author "The Protection of Minorities" 1961; "The Government of France Under the Fifth Republic" 1962; "People vs Politics" 1970; forthcoming "Left and Right" (1981); various articles comparative politics, ethnic relations; mem. Candn. Pol. Science Assn. (Pres. 1972-73); Internat. Pol. Science Assn. (Pres. 1973-76); Royal Soc. Can.; Home: 604 4101 Yew St., Vancouver, B.C. Office: Dept. of Pol. Sci., U.B.C., Vancouver, B.C. V6T 1W5.

LaQUE, Francis Laurence, B.Sc., LL.D.; chemical and metallurgical engineer; b. Gananoque, Ont., 21 July 1904; s. Wilfred Francis and Mary Agnes (O'Neill) L.; e. Queen's Univ., B.Sc. 1927, LL.D. 1964; m. Kate Winton, d. John Winton Clark, Muirkirk, Ont., 8 November 1930; children: Mary, Katherine; joined International Nickel Company Inc. 1927; apptd. Engineer in Charge Corrosion Engineering Sec., Devel. & Research Div., 1946-54; Mgr., Devel. & Research Div., 1954-62; Vice Pres. Extve. Dept. 1962-69; Pres. Internat. Organ. for Standardization 1971-73; Depy. Asst. Secy., U.S. Dept. of Commerce 1974; Sr. Lect., Scripps Inst. of Oceanog., Univ. of Calif. 1975; Adjunct Prof., Univ. of Hawaii 1979; hon. mem., Electrochem. Soc. (Pres. 1962-63); Nat. Assn. Corrosion Engrs. (Pres. 1949); Am. Soc. Test and Materials (Pres. 1959-60); Fellow/; Standards Eng. Soc.; Am. soc. Metals; Past Chrmn. of Corrosion Research Council, 1957-59; received F.N. Speller Award in Corrosion Engn., Nat. Assn. Corrosion Engrs., 1949; Acheson Medal of Electrochem. Soc. 1968; Howard Coonley Medal, Am. Standards Assn., 1962; Astin-Polk Int. Standardization Medal, Amer. Nat. Standards Inst., 1976; Leo B. Moore Medal, Standards Eng. Soc. 1975; A. T. Colwell Medal, Soc. of Auto Eng. 1979; delivered Edgar Marburg Lect., Am. Soc. for Testing Materials, 1951; Pres., Am. Nat. Standards Inst., 1969-70, Hon. Life mem., 1974; Roman Catholic; recreation: sailing; Address: Harbour Placesuite 707, 1850 Ontario St., Kingston, Ont. K7L 2Y7

LARDER, David Frederic, C. Chem., B.Sc., Ph.D., F.R.S.C.(U.K.); educator; b. Lowestoft, Eng. 20 Feb. 1935; s. late Frederic Robert Arthur and Lilian Wray (Hadfield) L.; e. Notwich School and Norwich (Eng.) City Coll. 1945-1954; Univ. of Edinburgh, B.Sc. 1958; Univ. of Strathclyde, B.Sc. 1959; Univ. of Alta. 1959-61; Univ. of Aberdeen, Ph.D. 1968; m. Corrine, d. late Patrick O'Donnell, 27 Dec. 1961; children: Andrew Frederic, Yvette Marie, Leona Jane, Debra Ann; EXECUTIVE DIR. SASK. UNIV. COMM. since 1980; Teaching Asst. Univ. of Alta. 1959; Dept. Head, Notre Dame Univ. Coll. 1961; Dean Acad. Studies, Notre Dame Univ. of Nelson 1963; Acting Pres. and Vice Chancellor 1969; Prof. (Chem. and Hist. of Science) 1970-72; Vice Pres. (Acad.) and Registrar 1972-75; Sr. Research Offr. (Univ. Affairs) and Leg. Offc., Dept. of Continuing Educ., Govt. of Sask. 1975-78; Prog. Planner, Sask. Univ. Comm. 1978-80; Gov. 1969-70, 1971-73; Trustee, Nelson Dist. (No. 7) Sch. Bd. 1970-71, 1972-73; Chrmn. Educ. Comte. 1971-73; mem. City of Nelson Adv. Planning Comn. 1970-71; Selkirk Coll. Council 1972-73; Prof. Adv. Comte. on Research of Educ. Research Inst. B.C.1972-75; Chrmn. Med. Record Science Consultative Comte., 1972-75; Sask. Bd. of teachers training & Certification; Adv. Council to W. Coll. of Vet.

Med.; Adv. Council to Coll. of Agric., Univ. of Sask.; 1975-78; Grad. Studies & Research Adv. Comte. (Chmn. from 1978) to Sask Univ. Comm. since 1976; Agric. Services & Research Review Comte., 1978; Dir. International Educational Services Corp 1979-; rec'd. Can. Council Humanities & Social Sciences Research Grant 1970 and Internat. Conf. Travel Grant 1971; author numerous prof. and newspaper articles, radio talks; mem. Soc. for Study Alchemy & Early Chem.; Brit. Soc. for Hist. Science; Internat. Cong. Hist. Science; recreations: swimming, camping, writing; Home: 17 Stephenson Cres., Saskatoon, Sask. S7H 3L6

LARGE, Hon. Frederic Alfred; judge; b. Bradalbane, P.E.I. 7 Dec. 1913; s. Ernest Alfred and Georgie Eliza (Leard) L.; e. Mount Allison Acad.; Prince of Wales Coll.; m. Mildred Grace d. late Chester Morgan Cox 7 Nov. 1939; children: David Frederic Holland, M.D., Susan Ruth (Mrs. B. L. Brennan), Donald Philip, LL.B.; JUDGE, SUPREME COURT OF P.E.I.; called to Bar of P.E.I. 1937; cr. K.C. 1944; practiced law Charlottetown 1937-39 and 1944-75; Crown Prosecutor 1937-39; Partner, Large & Large 1973-75; Atty. Gen. of P.E.I. 1944-49; Min. of Educ. P.E.I. 1949-53; served with RCNVR 1937-39, rank Lt., R.C.N. 1939-44 overseas and at sea in H.M.C.S. Niagara, also bases Saint John, Halifax and Gaspé, rank Lt. Commdr.; Past Pres., Law Soc. P.E.I.; P.E.I. Lib. Assn.; Past Prov. Vice Pres. Candn. Bar Assn.; mem. Royal Commonwealth Soc. (Treas.); Fort La Joye French Club; United Church; recreations: yachting, travel; Club: Charlottetown Yacht; Home: 205 North River Rd., Charlottetown, P.E.I. C1A 3L4; Office: (P.O. Box 1797) Law Courts Bldg., Charlottetown, P.E.I. C1A 7N4.

LARGE, Richard Geddes, M.B., F.A.C.S., F.I.C.S., F.R.C.S. (C.), F.R.G.S.; b. Bella Bella, B.C., 21 Oct. 1901; s. Richard Whitfield and Isabella Matilda (Geddes) L.; e. Univ. Toronto, M.B. 1923; m. Annie Beatrice, d. I.C. Wilson, Oakville, Ont., 18 Sept. 1923; children: Allan, Margaret, Richard; Consulting Surgeon, Miller Bay Indian Hosp.; Interne, Vancouver Gen. Hosp., 1923-24; Asst. Med. Offr., Hazelton (B.C.) Hosp., 1924-26; Med. Supt., Port Simpson Gen. Hosp. 1926-31; Publications: "Blended Fish Oils for Med. Purposes" in "Candn. Med. Assn. Journ.", 1935, and "A Hypoglycemic Substance from the Roots of the Devil's Club" in "Candn. Med. Assn. Journ.", 1938; "Soogwilis"; "The Skeena-River of Destiny"; "Prince Rupert: A Gateway to Alaska"; "Drums and Scalpel"; mem., Candn. Med. Assn. (Past Pres., B.C. Div. 1953-54); Prince Rupert Med. Assn.; Ex. Alderman, City of Prince Rupert; Past Pres., Prince Rupert Chamber of Comm.; Chrmn., Prince Rupert School Board 1945-56; President, Museum of Northern B.C.; Freeman, City of Prince Rupert, 1977; Freemason (G.M., G.L. of B.C. 1955-56); P. Conservative; United Church; recreation: music; Club: Gyro (Past Pres.); Address: (P.O. Box 487), Prince Rupert, B.C. V8J 3R2

LARKIN, Leo Paul, Jr., A.B., LL.B.; attorney; b. Ithaca, N.Y. 19 June 1925; s. Leo Paul and Juanita (Wade) L.; e. Cornell Univ. A.B. 1948, LL.B. 1950; Assoc. Atty. and Partner, Rogers & Wells and predecessor firms since 1950; Dir., Indal Ltd.; served with U.S. Army Europe 1943-45; mem. Bd. Eds. "Cornell Law Quarterly"; mem. Am. and N.Y. State Bar Assns.; Assn. Bar City N.Y.; Fed. Bar Council; Union Internationale des Avocats; Delta Phi (Trustee Educ. Fund); Phi Beta Kappa; Phi Kappa Phi; Theta Delta Phi; R. Catholic; recreations: theatre, music, magic; Clubs: University, Sky (N.Y.); Home: 200 E. 66th St., New York, N.Y. 10021; Office: 200 Park Ave., Suite 5200, New York, N.Y. 10166.

LARKIN, Peter Anthony, M.A., D.Phil., F.R.S.C.; biologist; university professor; b. Auckland, N.Z., 11 Dec. 1924; s. Frank Wilfrid and Caroline Jane (Knapp) L.; e. Balfour Tech. Sch., Regina, Sask.; Regina Coll., 1941-42; Univ. of Sask., B.A., M.A. 1946 (Gov. Gen.'s Gold Medal); Oxford Univ., Exeter Coll. (Rhodes Scholar), D.Phil. 1948; m. Lois Boughton, d. late John G. Rayner, Saskatoon, Sask., 21 Aug. 1948; five d. Barbara, Kathleen, Patricia, Margaret, Gillian; ASSOC. VICE PRES. OF RESEARCH, UNIV. OF B.C. 1980- ; Dean, Fac. of Grad. Studies, 1975-; and Professor, since 1966; Bubonic Plague Survey, Sask. Govt., 1942-43; N.W. Fisheries Investigation, Fisheries Research Bd. of Can., 1944-46; Chief Fisheries Biol., B.C. Game Comn., 1948-55; joined present Univ. as Asst. Prof. 1948-55; Prof. 1959-63 and since 1966; Dir., Inst. of Fisheries at Univ. 1955-63 and 1966-69; Dir., Biol. Stn., Fisheries Research Bd., Nanaimo, 1963-66; el. mem. of Bd. of Dir., B.C. Packers Ltd, 1980; Acting Head, Dept. of Zool., UBC, 1969-70; Head Dept. of Zool., U.B.C., 1972-75 Hon. Life Gov., Vancouver Pub. Aquarium; mem. Science Council of Can.; 1971-77 Senate UBC since 1956; mem. Can. Com. Int. Biological Program, (B.C. co-chrmn 1967-73 Subcomte CT, 1967-73; Chrmn P.M. Subcomte 1968-73); fish. Res. Bd. Can. since 1972; Exec. Bd. 1972-79; Nat'l Chrmn. Can. Com. for Man & the Biosphere; int. Centre for Living Aquatic Resource Mgmt. since 1977; Candn. Assn. Grad Studies; Candn. Comte. for Freshwater Fisheries Research; Program; Fisheries Devel. Council; Pres. Can. Assoc. Univ. Research Administrators 1979-80; rec'd Candn. Centennial Medal 1967; Master Teacher Award UBC 1970; Nuffield Foundation Fellow 1961-62; Queen's Jubilee Medal, 1977; Fry Medal, Can. Soc. of Zoo. 1978; Can. Sports Fishing Inst. Award 1979; author, co-author and ed. of numerous publs.; mem., Internat. Limnol. Assn.; Am. Fisheries Soc.; Candn. Assn. Rhodes Scholars.; Pacific Fish Biol. Assn.; Royal Soc. Can. 1965; Candn. Soc. Wildlife & Fisheries Biols. (Vice President 1961); Candn. Soc. Zools. (Vice Pres. 1971); Home: 4166 Crown Cres., Vancouver, B.C. V6R 2A9

LAROSE, Roger, O.C. (1973), B.A., B.Pharm.; industrialist; b. Montreal, P.Q., 28 July 1910; s. Alfred Fervac & Anna (Contant) L.; e. Coll. Ste. Marie, Montreal; Univ. of Montreal, B.A., B.Pharm. and a degree in Social Pol. & Econ. Sciences; m. Julienne Bégin, 3 Aug. 1961; one d. (by prior m.) Louise; CHRMN. OF THE BD., CIBA-GEIGY CANADA LTD., since 1978; Vice Chrmn. of Bd., mem. Extve. Comte., Banque Canadienne Nationale 1969-80; Pres. of the OSM 1978; Pres. and Managing Dir., 1979-81; apptd. (first) Vice Rector (Adm.) Univ. de Montréal (1969-79); Pres., Candn. Pharm. Mfrs. Assn., 1961-62; joined Ciba Co. Ltd., 1936 where he successively held positions of Med. Rep., Production Mgr., Asst. Mgr., Mgr. of Pharm. Div.; el. a Vice-Pres., 1958; el. a Dir. 1967, Pres. 1968-73; Dean, Faculty of Pharm., Univ. of Montreal, 1960-65; Governor, Canadian Bankers Institute 1973-80; appointed officer of Ord. of Can. 1973; Roman Catholic; Clubs: St. Denis; Forest & Stream; Home: Le Tournesol, Apt. 404, 205 Chemin de la Cote Ste. Catherine, Montreal, Que. H2V 2A9; Office: 6860 Century Ave., Mississauga, Ont. L5N 2W5

LAROUCHE, Gérard-Ludger, B.A., M.D., L.M.C.C., F.R.C.P.(C); physician; b. Cacouna, Quebec, 24 Jan. 1918; s. Ernest and Eva (Lamoureaux) L.; e. Coll. Ste-Anne de la Pocatière (1932-40); Laval Univ., M.D., L.M.C.C. 1944; Asst. étranger des Hôpitaux de Paris (1947); F.R.C.P.(C) 1956; m. Luce, d. Euchariste Michel, 3 June 1950; Prof., Faculty of Med. Sherbrooke Univ. (Dean of the Faculty of Med. 1961-64); mem., Candn. Med. Assn.; L'Assn. des Méd. de Lang. Française du Can. (Councillor 1960-68); Nat. Geog. Soc.; Roman Catholic; Home: 430, rue Denonville, Sherbrooke, Que. J1J 2K2

LARSEN, Arnold, B.A. (Econ.), M.B.A.; company executive; (ret.) b. Lakeview, Mich., U.S.A. 12 July 1917; s. Nels Otto and Julia Rebecca (Peterson) L.; e. Univ. of Mich. B.A. (Econ.), M.B.A.; m. Maxine Patricia Delaurante, Cody, Wyoming, 23 June 1951; children: Jon, Gregg, Mark, Rande, Julie Kay; Corp. Advisor, Alta. Energy Co. Ltd.; Past Pres. and Dir., Northern Natural Gas

Co. Ltd.; Past Vice Pres., Husky Oil Exploration, Inc.; Husky Petroleum Corp.; Husky (Netherlands) Oil Inc.; Husky (Germany) Oil Inc.; Husky Pipeline Co. and other Husky subsidiaries; Frontier Oil & Refining Co., Frontier Research Co.; Past Vice Pres. & Dir., Husky Oil (Alta.) Ltd.; Lloydminster Pipeline Ltd.; Husky Pipeline Ltd.; Husky Oil Leasing Ltd.; Past Dir., Peace Pipe Line Ltd.; Husky Leasebacks Ltd.; Gate City Steel Corp.; Past Mang. Dir. Husky Finance Co. N.Y.; Dir., Interprovincial Steel and Pipe Corp. Ltd.; C.O.B., Dir and Pres., Steel Alta. Ltd.; Maynard Exploration Comp.; British Columbia Resources Ltd.; C.O.B. and Dir., AEC Power Ltd., began career with White, Bower & Prevo, C.P.A.'s Detroit, Mich. 1947; Peat, Marwick, Mitchell & Co., Billings, Montana, 1948; came to Canada in 1953 joining present Husky as Secretary-Treasurer; Sr. Vice-Pres., Husky Oil Ltd. until 1974; served in 2nd World War as Captain in U.S. Army Artillery; mem., Canadian Chamber of Commerce; Ind. Petroleum Assn. of Can.; Candn. Petroleum Assn.; Wyoming Inst. of C.P.A.'s; Methodist; recreations: golf, swimming; Clubs: Calgary Petroleum; Calgary Golf & Country; Ranchmen's; Glencoe; Home: 68 Massey Place, Calgary, Alta. T2V 2G8Office: 2400, 639-5th Ave. S.W., Calgary Alta. T2P 0M9

LARSEN, Edward Reynolds, M.A.; headmaster; b. Vancouver, B.C., 1 Apl. 1925; s. late Thorleif and Irene (Reynolds) L.; e. Shawnigan Lake Sch. (B.C.), 1938-43 (Head Boy); Woodward and Pringle Scholar. to Univ. of B.C., B.A. (Hon. Math.) 1948; (Pres., Hon. Frat., Pres. Big Block Club); I.O.D.E. Scholar. to Oxford Univ., B.A. (Hon. Hist.) 1953, M.A. (Oxford Soc. Prize, Quarrel Read Prize, Pres., Exeter Coll. J.C.R.; Oxford "Blue" for squash, badminton and basketball); m. Patricia, d. W.E. Smith, 4 Oct. 1980; children: Thomas Geoffrey, Brenda Fraser, Sandra Rene; HEADMASTER, ROTHESAY COLLEGIATE SCH., 1981-; Extve. Asst. to Min. of Nat. Defence, Can. 1957-58; Headmaster, Shawnigan Lake Sch., 1958-67; Asst. Headmaster, St. Stephen's Sch., Rome, 1967-68; Headmaster, Appleby Coll., 1968-80; Master at Lansing Coll. (Sussex Eng.) 1980-81; served with RCNVR 1943-45; Founder and Gov., Strathcona Lodge Sch. and Cliffside Prep. Sch., Vancouver Is., B.C.; rep. Can. in squash on tour to Eng., 1955 and in field hockey at World Tournament, Lyon, France, 1963; Pres., Independent Schs. Assn. B.C., 1962-64; Founder and 1st Pres., Fed. Independent Sch. Assns. B.C., 1966-67; Twice Pres., Candn. Headmasters' Assn. 1966-67, 72-73; Founder and 1st ed. Candn. Independ. Sch. Journal; Duke of Edinburgh Leadership Award, 1977; Queen's Silver Jubilee Award, 1978; Christian; recreations: squash, tennis, drama; Club: Oakville; Address: Rothesay, N.B. E0G 2W0

LaSALLE, Gérald, B.A., M.D., D.H.A.; university officer; b. Que. 15 Dec. 1915; s. J. Pierre and Mabel (Ryan) L.; e. Univ. of Montreal, B.A.; Laval Univ., M.D.; Univ. of Toronto, D.H.A.; m. Jeanne, d. J. P. Ménard, Oct. 1941; nine children; VICE-PRES. i/c MED. AFFAIRS, UNIV. OF SHERBROOKE, and Founder and Dir. Inst. Superieur d'Adm. Hop. de l'Univ. de Montréal; Dean, Sch. of Med., Univ. of Sherbrooke; Founder and first Extve. Dir., Que. Hosp. Assn.; Les Artisans (Coop. Life Ins. Co.); Chrmn. Unity Bank of Can.; Extve. Fund of Can.; Dir., Sandoz (Canada) Ltd.; mem. of Royal Commission on Hospital Problems (Favreau Commission); mem. of Hospital Committee of Ministry of Health, Que., 1956-60; Past Pres., Assn. of Univ. Programs in Hosp. Assn. and Candn. Council on Hosp. Accreditation; Past Registrar of Coll. of Phys. & Surgs. of Que.; Pres., Fourth Internat. Oceanography, St-Malo (France); Roman Catholic; Address: 10 Driveway, Ottawa, Ont. K2P 1C7

LASKIN, Rt. Hon. Bora, M.A., LL.M., D.D.L., LL.D., F.R.S.C. (1964); b. Fort William, Ont., 5 Oct. 1912; s. late Max and Bluma (Singel) L.; e. Fort William Coll. Inst., 1930; Univ. of Toronto, B.A., 1933, M.A. 1935; LL.B.

1936; Osgoode Hall Law Sch.; Harvard Law Sch., LL.M. 1937; LL.D.: Queen's, 1965; Edinburgh, 1966; Trent, 1967; Toronto, 1968; Dalhousie, 1971; Law Soc. of Upper Can. 1971; Alberta, 1972; Manitoba, 1972; York, 1972; McGill, 1974; Ottawa, 1974; Simon Fraser, 1975; OISE, 1975; Victoria, 1976; Yeshiva, 1977; L.L.D. Carleton, 1978; Harvard, 1979; U.B.C., 1981; D.C.L. New Brunswick, 1968; Windsor, 1970; West. Ont., 1972; ?D.Phil., Hebrew U. of Jerusalem, 1976; D.Hu.L., Hebrew Union Coll., 1977; m. Peggy Tenenbaum, 1938; children: John, Barbara; CHIEF JUSTICE, SUPREME COURT OF CAN. since 1973; Chancellor, Lakehead University 1970-1980; Bd. of Govs., Carleton Univ. 1970-73; Chrmn., Bd. of Govs., Ont. Inst. for Studies in Educ. 1965-69; Bd. of Govs., York Univ. 1966-70; read law with W. C. Davidson, Q.C.; called to Bar of Ont., 1937; cr. Q.C., 1956; Lectr. in Law, Univ. of Toronto, 1940-43; Asst. Prof. 1943-45; Lectr., Osgoode Hall Law Sch., 1945-49; Prof., Univ. of Toronto, 1949-65; Lab. Arbitrator and Conciliator, 1942-65; Assoc. Ed., Dom. Law Reports and Candn. Criminal Cases, 1942-65; Justice, Court of Appeal of Ont. 1965-70; Puisne Judge, Supreme Court of Canada 1970; Publications: "Canadian Constitutional Law", 3rd edition 1966; "Cases and Notes on Land Law", new ed. 1964; articles in legal journals; member, Assn. Candn. Law Teachers (Pres. 1953-54); Candn. Assn. of Univ. Teachers (Pres. 1964-65); Nat. Acad. Arbitrators; presented with Candn. Assn. of Univ. Teachers (first) Milner Award (in cause of Acad. Freedom) 1971; Hon. Bencher, Lincoln's Inn; Office: Supreme Court Bldg., Ottawa, Ont. K1A 0J1

LASNIER, Rina; writer; poet; b. St.-Grégoire, d'Iberville, Que., 6 Aug.; d. Moise and Laura (Galipeau) Lasnier; e. Collège Marguerite Bourgeoys; Univ. of Montréal; author of "Féerie indienne", 1939; "Le Jeu de la Voyagère", 1941; "Madones canadiennes", 1944; "Escales", "Le Chant de la Montée", 1947; "Les Trois Rivières", 1950; "Présence de l'Absence", 1956; Mémoire sans jours, Ed. de l'Atelier, 1960; Miroirs, E. de. l'Atlier, 1960; L'arbre blanc" 1966; "Poèmes" 1968; "Ces Visages qui sont un pays"; "La Salle des Rêve" poems 1971; 'l'Échelle des Anges" (proses), 1975; "L'Invisible" poems; "Les Signes" poèmes, 1976; "Matin d'oiseaux", 1978; "Paliers de Paroles", 1978; "LeSoleil Noir" (drame poétique), 1981; "Le Choix de Rina Lasnier" (anthologie), "Le Rêve du Quart Jour" 1973; made record of poems 1970; contrib. to many reviews and journs.; awarded Prix David 1943; Bourse de la Soc. Royale du Canada, 1953; Prix Duvernay, 1957; Prix Molson, Jan. 1972; Lorne Pierce Prize and Medal, Royal Soc. of Can. 1974; Prix France-Can. 1973-74; Prix David du Qué. 1974; Médaille Commémorative de la Reine, 1978; Prix A.J.M. Smith, Univérsité du Michigan; Prix Edgar-Poe, Paris, 1979; L'Assoc. des femmes diplômées des Univ., Mont., 1978; l'union des Ecrivains Quebecois, 1976; l'Inst. Gracian, 1977; Doctorat Honoris Causa, Univ. de Mont., 1977; mem., Acad., canadiennefrançaise; Address: 299 sud., rue Lavaltrie, Joliette, Que. J6E 5X6

LATHAM, Arthur Russell, B.A.Sc., M.B.A.; b. Moose Jaw, Sask., 16 Apr. 1927; s. Arthur and Beulah (Hogarth) L.; e. Univ. of B.C., B.A.Sc. (Chem. Engn.) 1950; Stanford Univ., M.B.A. 1952; m. Anne Katherine, d. W. J. R. Peers, 18 Aug. 1950; children: Jane, Brant, Garth, Brenda, Ian; PRES. and CHIEF EXEC. OFFICER ALLIED CHEMICAL CANADA, LTD., 1980-; Technical Assistant, Canadian Industries Ltd., 1952-54; Extve. Asst., Brunner Mond Canada Sales, Ltd., 1954-58; joined present Co. as Asst. Dir. of Sales, 1958; Dir. of Sales, 1961-64; Dir., Marketing, 1964-67; Vice-President Marketing 1967; Pres., 1974; 1974-77 Pres. Alied Chem. Can. Ltd.; 1977-79 Exec. Vice Pres. Industrial Chemical Div. Allied Corp. N.J.; mem., Beta Theta Pi; Club: St. George's Golf & Country; Chmn., Soc. of Chem. Ind.; Can. Chem. Producers Ass.; Home: 2254 Shawanaga Trail, Mississauga, Ont. L5H 3X8; Office: 201 City Centre Drive, Mississauga, Ont. L5B 2T4

LATIMER, Radcliffe Robertson, B.Sc., M.B.A.; pipeline co. executive; b. Florence, Ont. 2 Oct. 1933; s. Rev. Canon Ralph and Grace (Dinsmore) L.; e. McGill Univ., B.Sc. (Math.) 1953; Univ. of Western Ont., M.B.A. 1956; m. Barbara Bernice, d. late John Henry Bastion, 15 June 1957; PRES. AND C.E.O., TRANSCANADA PIPELINES; 1979- ; Dir., TransCanada Pipelines; Great Lakes Transmission Co.; Trans Qué. & Maritimes Pipeline; Prudential Assurance Co. Ltd.; joined CN Rail as Adm. Asst. Traffic Dept. Montreal 1956; Mgr. of Research, Royal Securities Corp. 1962; Extve. Vice-Pres. Algoma Central Railroad, Sault Ste. Marie 1963; Vice-Pres. Operations, White Pass & Yukon Corp. Vancouver 1969-70; System Vice-Pres. Marketing, CN Rail 1974; Vice-Pres. and Sr. Exec. Officer, CN Rail, 1976; Pres. CN Rail, 1979; Pres. and C.E.O., TransCanada PipeLines, 1979; recreation: skiing, golf; Clubs: St. James's; Mt. Bruno Country; Cdn. Chamber of Commerce; Bayview Golf and Country; Toronto; Rideau; P.O. Box 54, Commerce Crt. W., Toronto, Ont. M5L 1C2

LATT, Richard Harry, D.V.M; veterinarian; b. Montreal, Que. 29 March 1944; s. Bernard and Bernice (Solomon) L.; e. Ont. Veterinary Coll. Univ. of Guelph D.V.M. 1969; Johns Hopkins Univ. Sch. of Med. Postdoctoral Fellow Div. Lab. Animal Med. 1969-72, Dept. Pathol. 1972; Diplomate Am. Coll. Lab. Animal Med.; DIR., McINTYRE ANIMAL CENTRE, McGILL UNIV. since 1977, Prof. of Pathol. and Univ. Animal Care Offr.; member, Council on Accreditation, Am. Assn. for Accreditation of Lab. Animal Care, Joilet, Ill.; author "Drug Dosages For Laboratory Animals" in "Handbook of Laboratory Animal Science" 1976; mem. Candn. Assn. Lab. Animal Science (Dir.); Am. Vet. Med. Assn.; Am. Assn. for Lab. Animal Science; Office: 3655 Drummond St., Montreal, Que. H3G 1Y6.

LATTER, His Excellency Edward Gale, M.B.E., E.D.; diplomat; b. Kaikoura, N.Z. 29 Feb. 1928; e. Christ's Coll. Christchurch, N.Z.; m. Anne Morton Ollivier 1952; two d., one s.; HIGH COMMR. FOR N.Z. TO CANADA, BARBADOS, GUYANA, JAMAICA, TRINIDAD & TOBAGO 1980- ; sheep farmer N.Z.; MP (Nat.) for Marlborough, N.Z. 1975-78; Brig. Gen. (Ret'd) N.Z. Army Territorial Force, MBE, ED and Bar; recreations: gardening, tramping; Clubs: Officers (Christchurch, N.Z.); Marlborough (Blenheim, N.Z.); Rideau (Ottawa); National Press (Ottawa); Board of Trade (Ottawa); Office: 801, 99 Bank St., Ottawa, Ont. K1P 6G3

LATTIN, Hon. E. Geoffrey, M.T.C.; politician; b. Edmonton, Alta. 9 May 1920; s. E. C. and Mary (Whittaker) L.; e. Berwyn, Alta. and Vancouver, B.C.; Univ. of B.C.; m. Patricia Zaiser 1953; two d. Colleen, Dianne; MIN. OF MUNICIPAL & COMMUNITY AFFAIRS AND MIN. OF HIGHWAYS & PUBLIC WORKS, Y.T. 1980- ; el. M.T.C. for Whitehorse North Centre g.e. 1978; Depy. Speaker 1978-80; P. Conservative; Anglican; Office: (P.O. Box 2703) Whitehorse, Y.T. Y1A 2C6.

LAUNAY, Jean E. L., B.A., L.ès L., professor; b. Bourges, France, 19 Feb. 1913; s. Eugène and Anne (Danjon) L.; e. Univ. of Paris, B.A. 1930, L.ès L. 1932; Dipl. Etudes Supérieures, Univ. of Paris, 1933; Agrégé de L'Univ. de France, 1937; m. Simone, d. late Alix Salmon, 26 Dec. 1936; children: Marc Pierre, Viviane Françoise; formerly Prof. of French Lang. & Lit., McGill Univ., Chrmn. Romance Langs. 1946-66; Chrmn. Humanities Group 1957-64; Dir., French Summer Sch., McGill 1947-63, Transl. Courses 1946-76; Prof., Lycée de Rennes, France, 1936-38; Lect., Univ. de Rennes, 1945; served with the French Army, 1935-36; French Liaison Offr. with Brit. Expdn. Force, Sept. 1939-July 1940; joined Brit. Army, Royal East Kent Regt. (The Buffs), Aug. 1940-Sept. 1945; commissioned, 1942, Temp. Capt. 1944; Staff Offr., 12 Corps; Chevalier Order of Leopold (Belgium); Croix de Guerre; cr. an Offr. d'Académie, 1954; Publications: "Jean-Paul des Laurentides", a French translation of Helen Guiton's "The Country Lover", 1954; "Précis de Littérature française", 1959; mem., Modern Lang. Assn. of Am.; Am. Assn. of Teachers of French; Humanities Assn. of Can.; Amicale Prof. Francais Au Can. (Pres. 1950-52); Candn. Assn. Univ. Teachers of French; Chevalier de la Legion d'honneur, 1962; Roman Catholic; recreations: fly-fishing, philately; Home: 4003 Oxford Ave., Montreal, Que. H4A 2Y3

LAUNAY-ELBAZ, Viviane Françoise, M.A.; association executive; b. Montreal, Que. 30 July 1947; d. Jean E. L. and Simone (Salmon) Launay; e. Coll. Marie de France, Montreal; Acad. de Caen, France Baccaularéat en philosophie 1966; McGill Univ.; Carleton Univ. B.A. 1969, M.A. 1970; Univ. d'Ottawa; Univ. de Paris X-Nanterre; Centre de recherche en néologie lexicale, C.N.R.S., Paris; children: Michael, Arielle; EXTVE. DIR., CANDN. FED. FOR THE HUMANITIES 1979- ; Instr. French Summer Sch. McGill Univ. 1966, 1967; Teaching Asst. Univ. d'Ottawa 1970-71; Offr., Aid to Scholarly Publs. Program, Humanities Research Council Can. and Social Science Research Council Can. 1974-75, Dir. above Program 1975-79; rec'd Carleton Univ. Fellowship 1969-70; Ont. Grad. Fellowships 1969-70, 1970-71; France-Qué. Fellowship 1971-72; Can. Council Doctoral Fellowships 1972-73, 1973-74; mem. Assn. Candn. & Que. Lits.; Assn. Candn. Univ. Teachers French; Candn. Comparative Lit. Assn.; Candn. Linguistic Assn.; Candn. Semiotics Assn.; Candn. Univ. Music Soc.; Classical Assn. Can.; Humanities Assn. Can.; Soc. Study Egyptian Antiquities; Candn. Assn. Univ. Research Adms.; Inst. Assn. Extves.; recreations: music, antiques, bibliography; Club: Cercle Universitaire d'Ottawa; Home: 290 Buchan Rd., Rockcliffe Park, Ont. K1M 0W5; Office: 151 Slater St., Ottawa, Ont. K1P 5H3.

LAURENCE, George Craig, M.B.E. (1945), Ph.D., LL.D., D.Sc., F.R.S.C. (1941); physicist; b. Charlottetown, P.E.I., 21 Jan. 1905; s. Harold Forbes and Florence Ethel (Dexter) L.; e. Dalhousie Univ., B.Sc. 1925, M.Sc. 1927; Cambridge Univ. Ph.D. 1931 (Student of Lord Rutherford, 1927-30); D.Sc. Sask. 1964, Queen's 1965; LL.D. Dalhousie 1967; m. Elfreda Elizabeth, d. E. H. Blois, Halifax, N.S., 21 Jan. 1930; children: Mrs. Patricia Buchanan, Mrs. Judith Jost; joined Nat. Research Council as Physicist in radium and X-ray research, 1930; engaged in nuclear energy research, 1940; in jt. Brit.-Candn. Atomic Energy Research Lab., Montreal, 1942; mem., Candn. Del. to U.N. Atomic Energy Comn., 1946-47; Dir., Reactor Research and Devel. Div., Atomic Energy of Canada Ltd. until 1961; Pres., Atomic Energy Control Bd. Can. 1961 till retired; rec'd Candn. Assn. Physicists Medal for Achievement in Physics (1966); mem., Candn. Assn. Physicists; Radiological Soc. N. Am.; Am. Nuclear Soc.; Am. Coll. Radiology; Club: Rideau; Home: 1 Beach Ave., Deep River, Ont. K0J 1P0

LAURENCE, Margaret, C.C. (1972), B.A., D.Litt., LL.D. F.R.S.C. (1977); novelist; b. Neepawa, Manitoba, 18 July 1926; d. Robert Harrison and Margaret Campbell (Simpson) Wemyss; e. United Coll., (now Univ. of Manitoba,) B.A. 1947; D.Litt. McMaster 1971; m. John Fergus Laurence 1947 (div. 1969) two children; Publications: "A Tree for Poverty" (trans. "This Side Jordan", 1960; "The Prophet's Camel Bell", 1963; "The Tomorrow-Tamer", 1963; "The Stone Angel", 1964; "A Jest of God" 1966; "Long Drums and Cannons" (essays on Nigerian lit.) 1968; "The Fire Dwellers", 1969; "Jason's Quest" (children's fiction) 1969; "A Bird in the House", 1970; "The Diviners", 1974, "Heart of a Stranger" (essays) 1976; "The Olden Days Coat" (children's) 1979; "Six Darn Cows" (children's) 1979; "The Christmas Birthday Story" (children's) 1980; short stories publ. in "Prism", "Tamarack Review", "Saturday Evening Post", "Ladies Home Journal", "Chatelaine", "Atlantic Monthly", "Argosy", "Winter's Tales"; articles in "Holiday Magazine"; rec'd. Beta Sigma Phi Award for best first novel by a Candn., 1960; Univ. of W. Ont. President's Medal for best Candn. short story, 1961, 1962, 1964; Gov. Gen. Award for fiction (English) (A Jest of God) 1966, for Lit. (The Diviners) 1974; Companion, Order of Canada, 1971; Molson Award 1975; Periodical Distributor's Award, 1977; B'Nai B'rith (Toronto Women's Br.) Woman of the Year, 1976; City of Toronto Award of Merit, 1978; Honorary Degrees: United Coll., 1966; D. Litt. McMaster 1970, Trent 1971, Toronto, 1971, Carleton 1974, Brandon, 1975, U.W.O. 1975, Mount Allison 1976, Simon Fraser 1977, York 1980; L.L.D. Dalhousie 1971, Queen's 1975; Writer-in-Residence, Univ. of Toronto, 1969-70; Univ. Western Ont. 1973; Trent Univ. 1974; Home: P.O. Box 609 Lakefield Ont.; Address: c/o Writers' Union, 24 Ryerson St., Toronto, Ont.

LAURIN, Hon. Camille, M.N.A.; politician; b. Montréal, Qué. 6 May 1922; s. Eloi and Mary (Morin) L.; e. Univ. of Montréal, M.D. 1949; Boston State Hosp., Specializing in Psychiatry; and then in Psycho Analysis in Paris; practiced at the Albert Trevost Institute in Montreal 1957; appointed Scietific director 1959; Dir. Dept of Psychiatry, 1958; Founding mem. de l'Association des Psychothérapeutes catholiques, 1956; Pres., l'Association des Psychiatres du Quebec, 1964; MIN. OF EDUCATION, QUÉ. 1980- ; Min. of State of Cultural Developments, 1976-81; which ministry became Min. of Cultural & Scientific Development; Chief Parti Quebecois 1970-73, Vice Pres. 1971-77; el. M.N.A. for Bourget prov. g.e. 1976, re-el. 1981; Parti Quebecois; Office: Édifice 1035, de la Chevrotiére, Quebec G1R 5A5

LAURIN, Cyrille Joseph, O.B.E., B.A.; b. Montreal, Que., 25 March 1912; s. Joseph Antoine and Lillian Beatrice (Sheppard) L.; e. St. Andrews Coll., Aurora, Ont.; Univ. of Toronto, B.A. 1934; m. Elaine Roche, d. Fuller Claflin, Detroit, Mich., 2 Oct. 1946; joined Maclean-Hunter Ltd., Montreal 1934; returning from war service was publisher of each of Maclean-Hunter Consumer mags.; apptd. a Dir. 1958, Vice-Pres. and Dir., 1960; Head Mag. Div. 1958-64, Financial Post Div. 1964-68; retired 1968; served in 2nd World War returning to Canada as Deputy Adj. Gen. with rank of Brig., 1945; awarded O.B.E.; Mentioned in Despatches; Past Pres., Periodical Press Assn.; Mag. Publishing Assn.; Chrmn. Metro Toronto Planning Bd. 1965-67; Dir., Audit Bur. of Circulations 1965-68; Pres., Candn. Club Toronto 1968; Consult. to Organ. Comte., 1976 Olympics; Commr. Metric Comn.; past Pres., St. John Ambulance; Boy Scout Medal of Merit; Centennial Medal 1967; Jubilee Medal 1977; Candn. Lifestyle Award 1978; Awarded Grand Cross St. John, 1980; author of "Help Yourself"; recreation: golf; Clubs: Bayview and National, Toronto; Tequesta Country and Jupiter Hills, Tequesta, Florida; Canadian; Homes: 95 Thorncliffe Park Dr., Toronto, Ont. M4H 1L7 and 375 Beach Rd., Penthouse A, Tequesta, Fla. 33458

LAURIN, J(oseph) W(ilfred) Paul; association executive; b. Ottawa, Ont. 24 Apl. 1938; s. Wilfred and Rose-Anna (Lafrance) L.; e. Eastview High Sch. Ottawa; Univ. of W. Ont. I.A.E. Sch. of Assn. Mang.; RCAF Sch. of Instructional Techniques; m. Florence Ann d. late William Coey 2 Aug. 1958; two d. Suzanne Irene, Yvonne Marie; EXTVE. DIR., CANDN. ASSN. CHIEFS OF POLICE 19 - ; joined RCAF 1955-63; served as Pilot, Pilot Instr. (Moose Jaw, Sask.), Ground Sch. Instr., C.O. Flight Simulator Sec., Pub. Information Offr., Commentator and Pub. Relations Offr. to Golden Hawks, Pub. Relations Offr. Coll. militaire royal de Saint-Jean; Co-ordinator Pub. Relations and Advertising in French lang. Bank of Montreal H.O.; Regional Dir. of Pub. Relations, Candn. Bankers' Assn.; Dir. of Communications, Montreal Urban Community; Dir. Laurin Enterprises Inc.; author many promotional brochures, folders, reports, news releases; articles mil. hist. aircraft Candn. Armed Forces; mem. Candn. Pub. Relations Soc.; Inst. Assn. Extves.; Air Cadet League

Can. (Dir. Sponsoring Comte.); RCAF Offrs.' Mess Ottawa; RCMP Offrs. Mess N. Div.; Anglican; recreations: fishing, curling, photography, working with sports & recreational youth groups; Clubs: Royal Candn. Mil. Inst. (Toronto); National Press; Admac Fish & Game (Dir. & Secy.-Treas.); Home: 1575 Senio Ave., Ottawa, Ont. K2C 1T7; Office: 1002, 116 Albert St., Ottawa, Ont.K1P 5G3.

LAURIN, Pierre, B.A., L.Sc.Com., D.B.A.; b. Charlemagne, Que., 11 Aug. 1939; s. Eloi and Mary (Morin) L.; e. Seminaire de Philosophie B.A. 1960; Ecole des Hautes Etudes Commerciales L.Sc.Com. 1963; Harvard Business Sch. D.B.A. 1970; m. Jacqueline d. Jean-Jacques Cardinal, 24 Apl. 1965; children: Pierre-Eloi, Philippe, Anne-Marie; DIRECTEUR, ECOLE DES HAUTES ETUDES COMMERCIALES; Co-Founder C.E.G.I.R. (Mang. Consultants); author: "Facteurs Humains de la Croissance des P.M.E." 1976; co-author "Orientation and Conflict in Career" 1970; "Le Management, Textes et Cas" 1973; author various articles; Founder & Editor of "Gestion" (Business review); mem. Econ. Council of Can. and various boards of private and public corporations, notably: Aluminum Co. of Can.; Alliance Mutual Life; Sandoz Co. of Can; J.R. Ouimet Ltd.; McLaren Paper & Power Co.; SNC Group, etc.; recreations: tennis, skiing; Clubs: St-Denis; Joyce; St-Laurent; Home: 28 Ave. Kelvin, Outremont, Que. H2V 1T2; Office: 5255 Ave. Decelles, Montreal, Que. H3T 1V6

LAUTENS, Gary, B.A.; journalist; b. Fort William, Ont. 3 Nov. 1928; s. Joseph and Bertha (George) L.; e. McMaster Univ. B.A. 1950; m. Jacqueline Joan d. Edward Lane, St. Sauveur, Que. 6 Apl. 1957; children: Stephen, Jane, Richard; EXEC. MANAGING ED., TORONTO STAR, 1982- ; Columnist, Toronto Star 1962-82; Columnist, Hamilton Spectator 1950-62; writer CBC-TV "Front Page Challenge" and writer, performer various other TV and radio shows; recipient Nat. Newspaper Award (Sports) 1965; Leacock Medal for Humour 1981; author "Laughing With Lautens" 1965; "Take My Family—Please!" 1980; over 8,000 newspaper columns, various mag. articles; United Church; Home: 80 Asquith Ave., Toronto, Ont. M4W 1J8;Office: 1 Yonge St., Toronto, Ont. M5E 1E6.

LAUTENSCHLAEGER, Gerhardt, Dr. Econ.; investment and finance (insurance) executive; b. Gefell, Germany, 3 May 1927; s. Friedrich and Martha (Hofmann) L.; e. Elem. and High Schs., Hirschberg, Germany, Sch. of Econ., Mannheim-Heidelberg, Dr. Econ., 1953; Univ. of Wisconsin (Fulbright Scholarship) 1954; m. Ursula Erna, d. Erich Walther, 11 July 1955; children: Frank, Christine, Gabriele; EXTVE. VICE-PRES. AND GEN. MGR., GERLING GLOBAL GROUP HEAD OFFICE, and Global Investment Corp. Ltd. since 1970; Dir. and Exec. Vice Pres. (Finance) & Secy.-Treas., Gerling Global General Insurance Co.; Gerling Global Reinsur. Co.; Gerling Global Life Ins. Co.; Dir. & Sr. Vice Pres., Gerling Global Offices Inc., New York; Mgr., Gerling-Konzern Globale Rueckversicherungs A. G., Cologne, Germany; after employ. with Dresdner Bank, Frankfurt, Mannheim & Heidelberg, Germany, joined Internat. Dept. of Gerling Global Group, Cologne, 1954; commissioned to Canada and immigrated, April 1956, to become assoc. with Gerling Global Group, Toronto, Ont. since its inception, with multiple functions and capacities; mem., Candn. German Chamber of Indus. and Comm.; Swiss Candn. Bus. Assoc. Inc.; Lutheran; recreation: tennis; Clubs: National; Canadian; Granite; Home: 114 Donwoods Drive, Toronto, Ont. M4N 2G8; Office: 480 University Ave., Toronto, Ont. M5G 1V6

LAVERDIERE, Jacques; executive; b. Beaurivage, Que., 18 Dec. 1930; s. Albert and Eva (Croteau) L.; e. Coll. Sacré-Coeur, Victoriaville, Que., Comm. Dipl. 1949; Candn. Credit Inst. Dipl. 1958; M.C.I.; Laval Univ., Degree Credit Course 1958; Univ. of Western Ont. Business Mang. Course 1966; VICE PRES. ROCK CITY TOBACCO

CO. LTD., since 1975; Civil Service, 1950-51; Credit Dept., Rock City Tobacco Co. Ltd., Quebec City, 1951-60; Rothmans of Pall Mall Can. Ltd., Budget Offr., 1960-63; Asst. Gen. Mr., Que. Div., 1967; Rothmans of Pall Mall Can Ltd., Vice Pres., Finance, 1968-75; mem., Chambre de Commerce (Montreal); Chambre de Commerce Française; Pres., Cdn. Red Cross Soc. (Que.); R. Catholic; recreation: golf; Clubs: Advertising and Sales Executives, Canadian; Donalda; Quebec Garrison; St.-Denis; Home: Office: 6855 Chemin Côte de Liesse, Montreal, Quebec H4T 1E5

LAVERY, Kenneth R., B.A., R.I.A., C.M.C., F.C.A., C.A.E.; association executive; b. London, Ont., 29 Jan. 1930; s. Ernest Anderson and Norma Loretta (Reid) L.; e. Westdale Coll. Inst., Hamilton, Ont.; Univ. of Toronto, B.A.; m. Joan Elizabeth, d. Wilfred Charles Langford, Hamilton, Ont., 28 June 1958; children: Shawn, Stephen, Joanne, Kathryn; PRESIDENT AND CHIEF EXTVE. OFFR., BREWERS ASSN. OF CAN., since 1971; Riddell Stead, Graham & Hutchison, Toronto, 1954-55; J. T. Symons, C.A., Toronto, 1956-58; Consultant, P. S. Ross & Partners, Toronto, 1958-64; Partner, Montreal, 1964-71; Dir. Internat. Consulting Services and Mang. Partner; Partner, Touche Ross & Co., Montreal, 1964-71; Project Offr. Glassco Comn.; has participated in mang. devel. programs at seminars and confs. for univs., govt., prof. assns., industry groups, organs.; served with 79th Field Arty. Regt. and 27 Candn. Inf. Bgde. 1950-53; author, "Selective Inventory Management"; also articles for various journs.; mem., Inst. C.A.'s Ont.; Inst. Mang. Consultants Ont.; Candn. Tax Foundation; Inst. for Future; Soc. Indust. & Cost Accts. Can.; Candn. Operational Research Soc.; Inst. Assn. Extves.; Anglican; recreations: golf, fishing, skiing, boating, philately; Clubs: Rideau; Country; St. James's (Montreal); Royal Ottawa Golf; Montreal Badminton & Squash; National (Toronto); Mississauga Golf & Country (Toronto); Hardy Bay Fishing (Toronto); Home: 155 Acacia Ave., Ottawa, Ont. K1M 0R4; Office: 151 Sparks St., Ste. 805, Ottawa, Ont. K1P 5E3

LAVIGUEUR, Guy, M.Sc.C., M.B.A., C.A.; Canadian public service; b. Montreal, Que., 4 March 1937; s. Paul Émile and Alice (Sicotte) L.; e. Mont St-Louis Coll. Montreal B.A. 1955; Laval Univ. B.Com., L.Sc.Comp., M.Sc.C. 1960; Conserv. of Que. Dipl. Music 1961; Columbia Univ. M.B.A. 1962; PRES. FED. BUSINESS DEVELOPMENT BANK since 1978; Pres. Fed. Inst. of Mang.; Dir. Walzwerk G.M.B.H.; N. Lemichka; mem. Review Comn. on Mirabel Airport; Sr. Assoc. Lavigueur & Associés 1963; Prof. Montreal Univ. Hautes Etudes Commerciales 1963; mem. Lavigueur & Lavigueur Inc. (Consultants) 1965; Advisor Pro Gestuib 1967; Mem., Review Commission on Mirabel Airport and Lemay Comn. on Fusion of Mun's; joined Candn. Pub. Service 1972, Extve. Dir. Policy & Planning Unemployment Ins. Comn. 1972; Asst. Depy. Min. (Finance) Dept. Transport 1973; Sr. Assistant Deputy Min. of Ind., Trade & Comm., 1975; Dir. Candn. Dev. Corp., 1975; Pres. Fed. Inst. of Mgmt., 1976; Ex. Vice-Pres. F.B.D.B, 1977; Dir., Canadair Ltd., Export Devel. Corp.; mem. Public Relations Comte. Inst. C.A.'s Que. 1967; Montreal Chamber Comm.; recreations: music, theatre, golf, tennis, sailing; Clubs: Montreal Country; St-Denis; Mount-Royal; Home: 1321 Sherbrooke W., Montreal, Que. H3G 1J4; Office: 901 Victoria Sq., Montreal, Quebec H2Z 1R1

LAVIGUEUR, J. Bernard, B.A.Sc., P.Eng.; engr. sch. pres. & principal; b. Montreal, P.Q., 1 Mar. 1918; s. Marie H. (Charron) and late Joseph R. L.; e. Mont Saint-Louis Coll.; Univ. of Montreal, Ecole Polytechnique, B.A.Sc., Civil Eng.; m. Moira L., d. late J. P. McKeown, Montreal, two s., Marc, Philippe; PRES. & PRINCIPAL, LA CORP. DE L'ECOLE POLYTECHNIQUE DE MONTREAL; since 1969; Chrmn., Technology Development Centre of Ecole Polytechnique; Northern Engineering Centre of Ecole Polytechnique; Industrial Innovation Centre (Montreal); Vice-chmn. Sidbec; Sidbec-Dosco; Vice-Pres., Canadian Engineering Manpower Council (Canadian Council of Professional Engineers); Dir., Comm. d'Initiative et de Développement Economiques de Montréal (CIDEM); Mem., Corp. Ste-Justine Hospital; Roads and Transportation Ass'n. of Canada; Association Québécoise du Transport et des Routes; Engineering Inst. of Canada; Order of Engineers of Que.; Can. Inst. of Mining and Metallurgy; Society of Automotive Engineers; Association des Diplômés de Polytechnique; Les Diplômés de l'Univ. de Montréal; Les Associés de l'Univ. de Montréal; Montreal Chamber of Commerce; joined Sicard Inc. as Production Engr. 1945, Asst. Gen. Mgr. and Chief Engr. 1949, Gen. Mgr. and Chief Engr. 1952, Extve. Vice-Pres. and Gen. Mgr. 1959., Pres. and Gen. Mgr. 1962, Chairman of the Board 1968-76; R. Catholic; Knight of the Sovereign and Military Order of Malta; recreations: golf, fishing, music; Clubs: Saint-Denis; Home: 74 Maplewood Ave, Outremont, Montreal, Que. H2V 2M1; Office: University of Montreal Campus, P.O. Box 6079, Station A, Montreal, Que. H3C 3A7.

LAVOIE, Léo, Dr. Com. Sc.; banker; b. Notre-Dame-du-Lac, P.Q., 18 March 1913; s. Phydime and the late Caroline (Viel) L.; e. St-François-Xavier Coll., Rivière-du-Loup, Que. (Comm. Course); Harvard Univ. (Adv. Mang. Program, grad. 1954); Dr. Com. Sc., Montreal 1970, L'Ecole des Hautes Etudes Commerce 1970; m. Claire, d. Ernest Maranda, Rivière-du-Loup, Que., 10 June 1940; one d. Mrs. Léon Courville; CHRMN. AND PRES. THE PROVINCIAL BANK OF CAN., since 1974; Chrmn. of Bd., Canadair Ltd. since 1976; with the Bank as Jr. Clk. at Rivière-du-Loup, Que., 1930; Main Office, Montreal, 1953; Asst. to the Pres., Jan. 1955; Asst. Gen. Mgr., June 1955, Gen. Mgr., 1957; el. Dir., 1960; Vice-Pres. and Gen. Mgr., Oct. 1966; President and Chief Executive Officer 1967; awarded Hon. Cert., Inst. Candn. Bankers 1970; Office: 221 St. James St. W., Montreal, Que.

LAVOIE, Roger; banker; b. Montreal, Que. 26 Sept. 1928; s. late Hector and late Cécile (Théoret) L.; e. Coll. Supérieur St-Stanislas Montreal; Ecole des Hautes Etudes Commerciales Montreal 1970; Post University courses; m. Huguette d. late Maurice Mousseau and Cécile Decelles, 3 Oct. 1953; children: Michel, Daniel; VICE-CHAIRMAN OF THE BOARD, THE MONTREAL CITY AND DISTRICT SAVINGS BANK since 1981; joined City and Dist. Savings Bank 1946, Asst. Chief Inspr. 1960, Founding Mgr. Methods and Procedures Dept. 1961-67, Founding Mgr. Marketing Dept. 1967-73, Asst. Gen. Mgr. 1973; Gen. Mgr. The Montreal City and District Trustees 1973-76, Extve. Comte. and Dir. 1974; mem. Mang. Comte. present Bank 1973, Gen. Mgr. and Chief Operating Offr. and mem. Extve. Comte. 1976, Vice Pres., Gen. Mgr. and Chief Operating Offr. 1976, Extve. Vice Pres. 1978; Vice-Pres., The Montreal City and District Trustees Ltd., 1978; Pres. and Chief Operating Off'r., The Montreal City and District Savings Bank, 1979; Dir., Credit Foncier Franco-Canadian, 1979; lectr. in Mang., Le Coll. du Gésu 1964; Founder, Mun. of Repentigny Lib. 1963; Dir. Le Gardeur Regional Sch. Bd. 1963 (Pres. Planning Comte. 1964); Pres. Repentigny Sch. Bd. 1966; Dir., Lake Raymond Country & Boating Club, 1966; rec'd Merit Award Internat. System Meeting St. Louis 1968; Hon. Pres., Multiple Sclerosis Soc. 1979; Decorated Hon. mem. Order Sons of Italy in Can. 1979; Pres. Assn. of counsels in Methods & Procedures, 1966; nominated Gov., La Jeune Chambre de Montréal 1977; author various articles; recipient of Award for outstanding service as Pres., Ville Marie Chapt., Systems & Procedures Assn., 1966/67; R. Catholic; recreations: skiing, tennis, travel; Clubs: Canadian; St-James's; St-Denis; Laval-sur-le-Lac; Cercle de la Place d'Armes; Home: 3135 Cap-à-l'aigle, Duvernay, Laval, Que. H7E 1C8; Office: 266 St. James St., Montreal, Que. H2Y 1N1.

LAWLESS, Ronald Edward; transportation executive; b. Toronto, Ont. 28 Apl. 1924; e. elem. and high schs. Toronto; Univ. of Toronto, McGill Univ. and Sir George Williams Extension Courses; m. Marion Steen; 3 children; PRES., CN RAIL 1979- ; Dir. Halterm Ltd.; Autoport Ltd.; Thunder Bay Terminals Ltd.; Canaven; joined CN Express Dept. Toronto 1941, Employee Relations Offr. HQ 1961, Gen. Supt. Express, Great Lakes Region, Toronto 1962, System Mgr. Container Dept. Montreal 1969, Gen. Mgr. Express and Intermodal Systems 1970, Vice Pres. Freight Sales 1972, Vice Pres. Marketing 1974; served with RCAF 1943-46; mem. Northern Alberta Railway Co.; The Shawinigan Falls Terminal Railway Co.; The Toronto Terminals Railway Co.; CANAC Consultants Ltd.; CANAC Distribution Ltd.; Canalog Logistics Ltd.; N.Y. Traffic Club; Toronto Railway Club; Transportation Club Toronto; Candn. Railway Club; Traffic Club Montreal; Nat. Freight Assn.; Montreal Bd. Trade; recreations: golf, reading; Clubs: M.A.A.A.; Beaconsfield Golf; Home: 337 Penn Rd., Beaconsfield, Que. H9W 1B5; Office: (P.O. Box 8100) Montreal, Que. H3C 3N4.

LAWRENCE, Albert Benjamin Rutter, M.C., Q.C.; barrister and solicitor; b. Calgary, Alta., 31 March 1923; s. Charles Albert Rutter and Myrtle (Benjamin) L.; e. Hopewell Ave. Pub. Sch. and Ashbury Coll., Ottawa, 1940; Royal Mil. Coll., grad. 1942; Osgoode Hall Law Sch., grad. 1948; m. Lois, d. E. Keith Davidson, 8 Oct. 1949; children: Paula, John, David, Andrea; called to Bar of Ont. 1948; cr. Q.C. 1959; gen. practice of law 1948-68; Partner, Honeywell, Wotherspoon, Ottawa; mem. Gloucester Twp. Council 4 yrs.; el. M.P.P. for Russell in prov. g.e. 1963; re-el. for Carleton East 1967; apptd. Min. Without Portfolio 1969; Min. of Financial and Comm. Affairs 1970; Min. of Health 1971; Prov. Secy. for Resources Devel. 1972; resigned from the Cabinet Feb. 1974 and apptd. Chrmn. Ont. Heritage Foundation; resigned from Leg. Oct. 1974; served with the Royal Candn. Armoured Corps 1942-46; rec'd. M.C. 1944; mem., Law Soc. Upper Canada; Candn. Bar Assn.; Royal Candn. Legion; P. Conservative; Anglican; recreations: skiing, sailing, tennis; Clubs: Rideau; Albany; Canadian; Royal Mil. Coll.; Home: 23 Davidson Dr., Ottawa, Ont. K1J 6L7

LAWRENCE, Hon. Allan Frederick, Q.C., M.P.; b. Toronto, Ont., 8 Nov. 1925; s. Frederick Charles and Elizabeth Anne L.; e. Jarvis Coll. Inst., Toronto; Victoria Coll., Univ. of Toronto, B.A. 1949; Osgoode Hall Law Sch.; m. Moira Patricia McGuffin, 1 Sept. 1949; children: Sean, Alison; Partner, McLaughlin, May, Soward, Morden and Bales, 1955-68; read law with Roberts, Archibald, Seagram and Cole; called to the Bar of Ont. 1954; cr. Q.C. 1963; el. M.P.P. for Toronto-St-George in Prov. g.e. 1958; named Min. of Mines, Feb. 1968, Min. of Mines and Northern Affairs, 1970; Min. of Justice and Atty. Gen., March 1971, Prov. Secy. for Justice 1972, resigning Sept. 1972; el. to H. of C. Oct. 1972; re-el. since; M.P. for Durham-Northumberland; named Solicitor Gen. of Can. and Min. of Consumer and Corporate Affairs, June 1979; served with RCNVR as Seaman 1944-45; mem., Bd. of Govs., Central Hosp., Toronto; P. Conservative; Anglican; Clubs: Albany; University; Home: R.R. 1, Janetville, Ont. L0B 1K0; Office: House of Commons, Ottawa, Ont. K1A 0A6

LAWRENCE, Hon. Gerald A.(Jerry), M.L.A.; politician; b. Halifax, N.S. 26 July 1939; s. Eate Joseph and Evelyn L.; e. Halifax schs.; m. Sheila Wooden 1963; children: Michael, Peter, Patrick; MIN. OF GOVT. SERVICES,N.S. 1980- ; Broadcast Extve. CHFX-FM Morning Show; former Ald. City of Halifax; rec'd Vanier Award 1976; Candn. Paraplegic Assn. Award of Merit, 1980; el. M.L.A. for Halifax-St. Margaret's prov. g.e. 1978, re-el. 1981; mem. Candn. Paraplegic Assn.; Candn. Diabetic Assn.; Halifax Antique Car Club; P. Conservative; R. Catholic; Office: 9th Floor, Maritime Centre, Halifax, N.S. B3J 2L4.

LAWRENCE, Lionel H., M.A.; educator; b. Scot. 1936; e. Loretto Sch. Scot. 1954; Queen's Univ. B.A. 1962; Univ. of Ill. M.A. (theatre) 1963; 3 children: DEAN, FACULTY OF FINE ARTS, YORK UNIV. and Prof. of Theatre 1980- ; Business Mgr. Univ. Theatre, Univ. of Ill. 1963-65; Asst. Prof. Drama Div. Eng. Dept. Dalhousie Univ. 1965, Assoc. Prof. Theatre Dept. 1969, Chrmn. of Theatre 1972-80; Gov., Bd. Candn. Conf. Arts 1978, 1981; Adv. Bd. mem. Arts Admin. Program, Lakehead Community College Thunder Bay, 1981- ; Adv. Bd. mem. Etobicoke High Sch. For the Performing Arts, 1981- ; Co-Chrmn. Candn. Conf. Arts Prov. Task Force Arts & Educ. 1977; mem. N.S. Drama Task Force Curriculum Dept. Educ. 1975; Candn. Theatre Hist. Nat. Comte. 1976; Ed. Adv. Bd. "Canadian Theatre Review" 1972-75; Candn. Del. Internat. Research Inst. Quadrennial Conf. Prague 1973; Pres. Atlantic Educ. Drama Council 1966-68; dir., producer, actor numerous plays; adjudicator, participant various theatre festivals, confs.; Perm. Adjudicator Cape Breton Theatre Festival; theatre critic "The Fourth Estate" 1968-71, "The Mail Star" 1966-68; theatre critic and commentator CBC Radio and TV N.S. regional theatre 1966-79; Tech. Dir. Dom. Drama Festival finals (regional) 1967, mem. N.S. Extve. 1966-67; served with RN 1954-56; Home: 47 Stephanie St., Toronto, Ont. M6T 1X8; Office: 4700 Keele, Downsview, Ont. M3J 1L2.

LAWRENCE, Richard John (Jack), B.A.; investment dealer; b. Orangeville, Ont. 23 Apl. 1934; s. Albert and Reta (Fenton) L.; e. Etobicoke High Sch. Toronto 1952; Univ. of W. Ont. B.A. 1956; m. Janice Letitia d. John Boyd; children: Brian, Judy, Wendy, Debbie, Carolyn; PRES., BURNS FRY LTD. 1970- ; Money Market Specialist, Equitable Securities 1956; joined Fry Mills Spence Ltd. 1961, Dir. and Mgr. Money Market & Bond Dept. 1964, Vice Pres. 1967; mem. Young Pres.'s Organ.; Zeta Psi; United Church; recreations: golf, squash, skiing, flying; Clubs: Lambton Golf; Cambridge; Home: 2 Cluny Dr., Toronto, Ont. M4W 2P7; Office: P. O. Box 150, One First Canadian Place, Toronto, Ontario M5X 1H3.

LAWRENCE, Air Vice Marshal Thomas Albert, C.B., C.D.; R.C.A.F. (retired); b. Creemore, Ont.; m. (late) Claudine, d. late John A. Jamieson; served in 1st World War 1914-18, Overseas with 76th Bn.; trans. to 4th Bn. in France; subsequently Flight Cadet, R.F.C., later with 24 Fighter Sqdn., R.A.F.; after War joined Candn. Air Bd. as Pilot-Navigator employed on survey, air photog. and forest fire patrol; was one of original group of offrs. comnd. into permanent R.C.A.F. 1924; commanded Hudson Strait Expdn. 1927 and spent 16 months on Air Survey of ice and navigation conditions there; Liaison Offr., R.C.A.F., Air Min., London 1932-35; Commdr., Sch. of Army Coop., Camp Borden and Trenton, Ont. 1935; O.C. No. 2 A.C. Sqdn., Rockcliffe, Ont.; took Sqdn. to Atlantic Coast for defence duties during Munich crisis 1938; posted to Air Force Hdqrs. as Dir. Plans and Operations 1939; apptd. C. O. Trenton, Ont. 1940; posted to Winnipeg and promoted to Air Vice Marshal A.O.C. No. 2 Training Command 1942; A.O.C. Northwest Air Command, Edmonton 1944; retired from R.C.A.F. 1947; Mgr., E. Region of the Dewline 1956-58; Commdr., Legion of Merit (U.S.A.); inducted into-Candn. Aviation Hall of Fame (Edmonton) and awarded the Hall's Medal, June 1980; City of Edmonton's Companion of Flight; Yukon Territory's Member of Order of Polaris; Home: 581 Avenue Rd., Toronto, Ont. M4V 2K4

LAWSON, Donald G.; stock broker; b. Toronto, Ont., 11 Oct. 1928; s. Frank Gordon and Janet Waters (Ross) L.; e. Blythwood Pub. Sch., Toronto, Ont.; Univ. of Toronto Schs. (Matric. 1947); Univ. of Toronto (Comm. and Finance) 1948-50; m. Lorraine Marilyn Forbes, 10 May 1957; children: Douglas Forbes, Elizabeth Anne, David Andrew, Bruce Gordon; PRESIDENT AND DIR., MOSS LAWSON & CO. LTD.: Dir., Broulan Reef Gold Mines Ltd.; Hugh-Pam Porcupine Mines Ltd.; Standard Indus-

tries Ltd.; Chrmn (1971-72), Bd. of Govs., Toronto Stock Ex.; joined predecessor Co., Moss, Lawson & Co. in June 1950 becoming a Partner in Nov. 1950; Past Pres., Metrop. Toronto YMCA; United Church; recreation: golf; Clubs: National; Granite; Rosedale Golf; Briars Golf & Country; Home: 36 Daneswood Rd., Toronto, Ont. M4N 3J8; Office: 48 Yonge St., Suite 1100, Toronto, Ont. M5E 1G6

LAWSON, Gordon, LL.D., F.C.I.S.; b. Dominion City, Man., 1 Oct. 1904; s. Henry and Catherine (Renwick) L.; e. Kelvin High Sch., Winnipeg, 1920, m. Cathrine Margaret, d. T. G. McIntosh, Winnipeg, Man., 28 May 1948; children: James Renwick, Laura Anne, Catherine Jane; Dir., Bristol Aerospace Ltd.; James Richardson & Sons Ltd.; Intercolonial Trading Corp. Ltd.; Interprovincial Trading Corp. Ltd.; Rolls Royce Holdings North America Ltd.; fellow, Man. Inst. of Mang.; Pres. Conservative; United Church; Clubs: Manitoba; St. Charles Country; Home: P.O. Box 273 St. Norbet, Man., R3V 1L6; Office: 30th Floor, One Lombard Place, Winnipeg, Man. R3B 0Y3

LAWSON, Harold R., F.S.A. (1933); insurance executive; b. Toronto, Ont., 21 Feb. 1908; s. Ernest H. and Margaret J. (Little) L.; e. N. Toronto Coll. Inst. (Hon. Matric.); m. late Emily S. Stewart, 17 Oct. 1933; children: Barbara Anne, Mary Elizabeth; 2ndly late Margaret B. Hamlin; Chrmn., National Life Assnce. Co.; with Crown Life Ins. Co. 1926-44; Dir., Vice-Pres. and Actuary, Mass. Protective Assn. Inc. of Worcester, Mass., 1945-52; Dir., Vice-Pres. and Mang. Dir., Nat. Life Assnce. Co., 1952-55; el. Pres. 1955, Vice Chrmn. 1969, Chrmn. 1970; Pres., Glen Falls Insurance Co., 1966; Vice Chrmn. 1968-70; Protestant; Clubs: Granite; Glen Falls Country; Lake George; Home: 40 North Road, Glens Falls, N.Y.

LAWSON, John Barker, Q.C.; b. Toronto, Ont., 18 June 1926; s. Hugh Hutchinson and Muriel Maud (Rogers) L.; e. Upper Can. Coll., Toronto, 1944; Trinity Coll., Univ. of Toronto, B.A. 1948; Osgoode Hall Law Sch., 1951; PARTNER, McCARTHY & McCARTHY; Chrmn. of Bd., Toronto Mendelssohn Choir; Vice-Pres. and mem. Bd. Govs. Massey Hall; read law with McCarthy & McCarthy; called to the Bar of Ontario 1951; cr. Q.C. 1965; mem., Candn. Bar Assn.; Delta Kappa Epsilon; Anglican; recreation: music; Clubs: University; Toronto; Arts & Letters; Home: 28 Elgin Ave., Toronto, Ont. M5R 1G6; Office: TorontoDominion Bank Tower, Toronto-Dominion Centre, Toronto, Ont. M5K 1E6

LAWSON, R(uston) William, M.A., LL.D.; economist; banker; b. Glenboro, Man., 19 Oct. 1917; s. Rev. Dr. Clarke B. and Florence Martha (Ruston) L.; e. United Coll.; Univ. of Manitoba, B.A. 1938; Oxford Univ., B.A. 1940, M.A. 1945; LL.D. Winnipeg 1975; m. Katharine, d. Hon. J. M. Macdonnell, 1 Aug. 1964; one d. Anne; SR. DEPUTY GOV., BANK OF CANADA since 1973; mem. of Statistics and Research Section, Foreign Exchange Control Board, 1940-42 and 1947-50; Economist, Royal Comn. on Coal, 1945-47; joined Research Dept., Bank of Can., 1950, and Chief of Dept., 1956-62; Extve. assn. to Gov. 1962-64; Depy. Gov. 1964-73; served in 2nd World War with Candn. Army 1942-45; served in Can., U.K., Belgium, Germany, Holland; Lieut., 2nd Candn. Arty. Survey Regt.; United Church; Home: 158 Carleton St., Rockcliffe, Ont.; Office: Bank of Canada, Wellington St., Ottawa, Ont. K1A 0G9

LAWSON, Col. Thomas, C.D., D.C.L., L.L.D. B.A.; executive; b. London, Ont., 12 Nov. 1915; s. Hon. Ray and (late) Helen (Newton) L.; e. Ryerson Pub. and London Central Coll. Inst., London, Ont.; Upper Can. Coll., Toronto, 1932; Westervelt Business Coll., 1932; Univ. of W. Ont., B.A. 1935; m. Margaret, d. George Otton, Woodstock, Ont., 10 Sept. 1938; children: Constance, Joan, Tom Jr., Marilyn, Tim, Peter; HON. CHAIRMAN, LAW-

SON AND JONES LIMITED (Established 1882; Printing and Lithographing), since 1953; Vice-Pres. and Dir., The Canada Trust Co.; served in 2nd World War with Candn. Fusiliers (City of London Regt.), Royal Cdn. Regt., Eng. in the Aleutians, Lincoln, Welland, Holland and Germany; Col., Roy. Can. Regiment; Pres., London, Ont. Chamber of Comm., 1951-52; Pres., Ont. Chamber of Comm., 1953-54; Pres., Candn. Lithographers Assn., 1953-54; D.C.L. King's Univ., 1977; L.L.D., Univ. of W. Ont., 1980; Chmn., Salvation Army Advisord Bd. (London); Delta Upsilon; Liberal; Anglican; recreation: farming; Clubs: London; Rotary (Pres. 1949-50); Home: 1384 Hutton St., London, Ont. N6G 2C1; Office: 395 Wellington Rd. S., London, Ont. N6C 4P9

LAWSON, Walter Reynolds, B.Sc.; company executive; b. Amherst, N.S., 11 Feb. 1918; s. Gerald and Rose (Smith) L.; e. Saint John (N.B.) High Sch.; Dalhousie Univ., B.Sc. 1940; m. Harriet Jane, d. late Harry Senior, 22 June 1946; children: Cecily, Walter Geoff, Tim, Heather; EXEC. VICE-PRES., DOMTAR INC. since 1979; Plant Engineer, Toronto Works, Dominion Tar and Chemical Limited, 1945; Plant Manager, Sifto Salt Co., Sarnia, Ontario, 1947; Works Manager, Domtar Ltd., Toronto, 1950; Plant Manager, Manistee (Mich.) Salt Works, 1951-52; Project Engr., Domtar Engineering Department 1953-54; General Sales Mgr. and Asst. Gen. Mgr., Sifto Salt Div. of Dom. Tar & Chemical Co. Ltd., 1955-56; Vice-Pres. and Gen. Mgr., Sifto Salt 1957-62; Vice-Pres. and Gen. Mgr., Bell Kilgour Div. of Domtar Packaging, 1963-65; Corp. Vice-Pres. Purchasing and Transport., 1966-70; Vice-Pres. and Gen. Mgr. Domtar Packaging 1970-77; Pres., Domtar Packaging 1977-79; served in 2nd World War with Candn. Army, 1940-45; discharged with rank of Maj.; served in Eng., N.W. Europe, Philippines, Okinawa; p.s.c.; mem., Chem. Inst. Can.; mem. Business and Industry Advisory Committee to O.E.C.D; Bd. of Govs., Montreal Gen. Hosp.; Candn. Mfrs. Assn. (Nat. Pres., 1974-75, Chrmn., Que. Div. 1964-65); Inst. of App. Econ. Research (Bd. of Govs. 1975-79); Dir., St. James's Club, 1976-79, Chrmn., 1979; Roman Catholic; recreations: golf, shooting, skiing; Clubs: St. James's; Royal Montreal Golf (Dir., 1964-67); Granite; Home: 224 Senneville Rd., Senneville, Que. H9X 3L2; Office: 395 de Maisonneuve Blvd. W., Montreal, Que. H3A 1L6

LAYCRAFT, Hon. James Herbert, B.A., LL.B.; judge; b. Veteran, Alta. 5 Jan. 1924; s. George Edward and Hattie (Cogswell) L.; e. High River (Alta.) High Sch.; Univ. of Alta. B.A., LL.B. 1951; m. Helen Elizabeth d. late Percy Bradley 1 May 1948; children: Anne Loreen MacKay, James Bradley; JUDGE, COURT OF APPEAL ALTA. since 1979; called to Bar of Alta. 1952; cr. Q.C. 1964; Partner, Jones Black Gain & Laycraft until apptd. to Trial Div. Supreme Court of Alta. 1975; served with RCA 1941-46, seconded Australian Imp. Forces 1944-46, S.W. Pacific Theatre of Operations; mem. Candn. Bar Assn.; United Church; recreations: hiking, fishing, skiing; Club: Ranchmen's; Home: 8952 Bayridge Dr. S.W., Calgary, Alta. T2V 3M8; Office: 611-4th St. S.W., Calgary, Alta. T2P 1T5.

LAYNE, Donald S., M.Sc., Ph.D., F.R.S.C.; scientist administrator; b. Marbleton, Que. 5 Apl. 1931; s. John Graham L.; e. Harrison Coll. Barbados, High Sch.; McGill Univ. B.Sc. 1953, M.Sc. 1955, Ph.D. 1957; Univ. of Edinburgh Postdoctoral 1957-58; m. Alice Edith Common d. Dr. Robert H. Common, Ste. Anne de Bellevue, Que. 25 Apl. 1959; children: Donald Graham, Kathleen Renate, Geoffrey Haddon; VICE-PRESIDENT, RESEARCH AND TECHNOLOGY, CONNAUGHT LABORATORIES since 1979; Dir., Connaught Research Insti; Research Assoc. Queen's Univ. 1958-59; Scient. Worcester Foundation, Mass. 1959-64; Assoc. Prof. of Biol. Clark Univ., Worcester, Mass. 1964-66; Chief, Pharmacol. Div. Food & Drug Labs Nat. Health & Welfare Ottawa 1966-68; Chrmn. of Biochem. Univ. of Ottawa 1969-75; Vice-Dean, Health

Sciences, Univ. of Ottawa 1975-79; author, "Metabolic Conjugation and Metabolic Hydrolysis" 1970; "Advances in Sex Hormone Research" 1974; over 80 scient. articles various journs.; mem. Candn. Bioch. Soc. (Pres. 1976-77); Am. Soc. Biol. Chems.; Am. Assn. Advanc. Science; Liberal; Anglican; recreations: squash, tennis, sailing; Home: 15 Allenwood Cresc. Willowdale, Ont. M2J 2R1; Office: 1755 Steeles Ave. W., Willowdale, Ont. M2R 3T4.

LAYTON, Irving, O.C. M.A., D.C.L.; poet; teacher; b. Neamtz, Rumania, 12 Mar. 1912; s. Moses Lazarovitch and Klara (Moscovitch) L.; came to Canada, Apl. 1913; e. Alexandra Public Sch. and Baron Byng High Sch., Montreal, P.Q.; Macdonald Coll., B.Sc. (Agric.) 1939; McGill Univ., M.A. 1946; D.C.L. Bishop's 1970; D. Lih., York U., 1979; m. Betty Frances, d. Fred Sutherland, Bridgewater, N.S., 13 Sept. 1946; children: Max Rubin, Naomi Parker; 2ndly Aviva, d. George Cantor, Sydney, Australia, 13 Sept. 1961; one s. David Herschel; 3rdly, Harriet Bernstein, Nov. 23, 1978, d. of Jack and Mary Bernstein; one d., Samantha Clara; Teacher, York Univ., formerly Poet-in-Residence Sir Geo. Williams Univ., Montreal; Lieut. in R.C.A., 2nd World War; discharged in 1943; Publications: "Here and Now", 1945; "Now Is the Place", 1948; "The Black Huntsmen", 1951; "Love the Conqueror Worm", 1953; "In the Midst of My Fever", 1954; "The Long Pea-Shooter", 1954; "The Cold Green Element", 1955; "The Blue Propeller", 1955; "The Bull Calf and Other Poems", 1956; "Music On a Kazoo", 1956; "A Laughter in the Mind", 1958; "Red Carpet for the Sun", 1959 (Gov.-Gen. Award for English Poetry 1960); "The Swinging Flesh", 1961; "Balls For a One-Armed Juggler", 1963; "The Laughing Rooster", 1964; "Collected Poems", 1965; Ed. "Love Where The Nights Are Long" (Candn. love lyrics) 1963; Prix Littéraire de Québec, First Prize, 1963; "Periods of the Moon", (Poems) 1967; "The Shattered Plinths", (poetry) 1968; "The Whole Bloody Bird" (prose and poetry) 1969; "Selected Poems", 1969; "Nail Polish", 1971; "Collected Poems", 1971; "Lovers and Lesser Men", 1973; "The Pole Vaulter", 1974; "Seventy-Five Greek Poems", 1974; "The Darkening Fire" (Selected Poems, 1945-68), 1975; Il freddo Verde Elemento (Giulio Einaudi, Torino) "The Unwavering Eye: Selected Poems 1969-75", 1975; "For My Brother Jesus", 1976; "The Covenant", 1977; "Taking Sides" (prose), 1977; "Selected Poems, New Directions", 1977; "The Tightrope Dancer", 1978; "The Love Poems of Irving Layton," (deluxe edition), 1978; Irving Layton, Carlo Mattioli (Edition Trentadue), 1978; Irving Layton-Aligi Sassu Portfolio, Milan, 1978; "Droppings from Heaven," 1979; "An Unlikely Affair: Layton-Rath Correspondence", 1979; "For My Neighbour in Hell' 1980; "in un'etadi ghiaccio" ("In An Ice Age-Bilingual Selected Poems, 1981; Europe and Other Bad News; co-ed. with L. Dudek of "Canadian Poems 1850-1952", 1953; rec'd Can. Council Award 1959; his poems have appeared in translation in Roumanian, Polish, Russian, Korean and in Spanish, Italian in Argentine lit. papers and journs.; in 1956 an American ed. of his selected poems under title "The Improved Binoculars" with foreword by William Carlos Williams, appeared under the imprint of Jargon Press; awarded a Canada Foundation Fellowship, 1957; D.C.L. Concordia Univ. 1976; rec'd. Can. Council Special Arts Award, 1967; Canada Council Arts Award 1979-1981, Long Term Award; Poet-in-Residence, Univ. of Guelph, 1969; Univ. of Ottawa, 1978; Visiting Professor, Concordia University, 1978; Writer-in-Residence, Univ. of Toronto 1981; N.D.P.; Freethinker; recreations: handball, swimming, chess; Address: c/o McClelland & Stewart, 25 Hollinger Rd., Toronto, Ont. M4B or, P.O. Box 1349 Niagara-on-the-Lake, Ont., L0S 1S0

LAYTON, Robert Edward John, B.Eng.; engineering executive; b. Montreal, Que. 25 Dec. 1925; s. Gilbert and Norah Lestelle (England) L.; e. Lower Can. Coll. Montreal; Montreal W. High Sch.; McGill Univ. B.Eng. (Mech.) 1947, Mang. Inst. 1970; Insead Exec. Inst. Fontain bleau 1978; m. Doris Elizabeth d. late J.T.R. Steeves 6 March 1948; children: John Gilbert, Robert Steeves, David Ross, Nancy Jean; CHMN. OF THE BD., T. PRINGLE & SON LTD. since 1976; Chmn. Gaucher Pringle Carrier Inc.; Pringle Zambia Ltd.; Pringle U.S.A. Inc.; LAS Corp.; Layton Holdings Ltd.; Rucam Realties Ltd.; joined present Co. as Mech. Design Engr. 1947, Chief Mech./Élect. Engr. 1952, Vice Pres. Marketing Operations 1960, Pres. and CEO 1962; served with RCA 1943-44; Gov. and Past Pres. John Abbott CEGEP; Chrmn. Montreal Assn. for Blind; Past Chrmn. Hudson YMCA.; Past Chrmn. McGill Alma Fund; Dir., Que. Soc. for Handicapped Children; mem.; Engn. Inst. Can.; Order Engrs. Que.; Assn. Consulting Engrs. Can. (also Que.); Candn. Constr. Assn.; Candn. Chamber Comm. (also Que.); Montreal Bd. Trade; Am. Soc. Plant Engrs.; recreations: golf, curling, gardening; Clubs: St. James's; Royal Montrea Golf; Rotary Westmount (Past Pres.); Home: 225 Olivier Ave. Westmount, Que. H3Z 2C7; Office: 245 Victoria, Montreal, Que. H3Z 2M6

LAZURE, Hon. Denis, M.L.A., M.D.; politicoen; né Napierville, Qué. 12 oct. 1925; f. Thomas et Berthe (Durivage) L.; é. Coll. Jean-de-Brébeuf Montréal B.A. 1946; Univ. de Montréal M.D. 1952; Adm. hospitalière certificat 1965; Univ. of Pa. Dipl. in Child Psychiatry 1957; ép. Anne Marie f. Paul Lalande 22 avril 1977; enfants: Gabrielle, Michel, Catherine, Eric-René; DEPUTÉ de BERTRAND, ASSEMBLÉE NATIONAL DU QUEBEC 1981-; Fondateur et dir. Dépt. de Psychiatrie Infantile, Hôpital Ste-Justine Montréal 1957-69; Dir. général Hôpital Rivière-des-Prairies Montréal 1969-74 et Hôpital Louis-H. Lafontaine Montréal 1974-76; Min. d'État au Développement Social 1976-81; député de Chambly 1976 Assemblée Nationale Qué.; auteur "One Million Children" 1970; Parti Québecois; récreations: tennis, skiing, natation; Adresse: 2068, Bellevue, St-Bruno, Qué. Bureau: 1075, chemin Ste-Foy, Québec, Qué. G1S 2M1.

LEACH, Augustus Searle, Jr., A.B., M.B.A.; executive; b. Winnipeg, Man., 6 March 1939; s. Augustus Searle and Frances Conway (Gilman) L.; e. Dartmouth Coll., A.B. 1960; Univ. of W. Ont., M.B.A. 1962; m. Heather Gail, d. Samuel M. Allman, Winnipeg, 8 Sept. 1962; children: Barbara, Tannis, Margo; VICE PRES. AND DIR., FEDERAL INDUSTRIES LTD. since 1973, and Pres. and Dir., Thunder Bay Terminals Ltd., since 1974; Dir. The White Pass and Yukon Corp. Ltd.; Ventures West Capital Ltd.; mem., Winnipeg Adv. Bd., Royal Trust Corp. Can.; held various operating and accounting positions with Searle Grain Co. Ltd. 1962-66 and upon merger with Federal Grain Ltd. 1966-73 incl. Div. Mgr. 1965, Dir. of Mang. Information 1966, of Finance & Control 1968, of Corporate Devel. 1972; name changed to present Co. 1973; Past President and mem. Bd. of Govs., Winnipeg Art Gallery; mem., Bd. of Dirs, Winnipeg Football Club; Jr. Achievement of Manitoba; Delta Kappa Epsilon; Anglican; recreations: tennis, skiing, sailing; Clubs: Manitoba; St. Charles Country; Winnipeg Winter; Winnipeg Squash Racquet; Home: 139 Grenfell Blvd., Winnipeg, Man. R3P 0B6; Office: 2400 One Lombard Pl., Winnipeg, Man. R3B 0X3

LEAL, Herbert Allan Borden, Q.C., B.A., LL.M., LL.D.; b. Beloeil, P.Q., 15 June 1917; s. Frederick William and Marie Ange (Ranger) L.; e. Tweed (Ont.) High Sch.; McMaster Univ., B.A. (Hons. Hist.) 1940 (O.H.A. Scholar, 1936; Gov. Gen. Medal 1939; A. G. Alexander Scholar, 1939); Rhodes Scholar for Ont. 1940; Osgoode Hall Law Sch. 1945-48; Harvard Law Sch., LL.M. 1957; m. Muriel Isobel, d. Rothsay Eugene Clemens, Hamilton, Ont., 21 March 1942; children: Kathleen Mary (Mrs. Malcolm A. Clark), Allan Ross, James Frederick; SPECIAL ADVISOR TO PREMIER OF ONT. CONSTITUTIONAL LAW 1981; Chancellor, McMaster Univ., 1977- ; read law with Frank Erichsen-Brown, Q.C., Toronto, Ontario; called to the Bar of Ontario 1948; practised with Erichsen-Brown and

Leal, Toronto 1948-50; Lecturer, Osgoode Hall Law School 1950; Vice-Dean and Professor 1956, Dean and Prof. 1958-66; Chmn., Ont. Law Reform Comm., 1966-77; Special Lectr., Law Soc. of Upper Can. 1951, 1957, 1960, 1966 and 1977; Special Lectr., Property Law, Faculty of Law, Univ. of Toronto 1972-77; Prov. of Ont. Atty.-Gen.'s Adv. Comte. on Adm. of Justice 1958-64; mem. Council, Medico-Legal Soc. of Toronto (1st Vice-Pres. 1968; Pres. 1969); mem. Extve. Comte., Toronto Br., Candn. Red Cross Soc. 1959-64; Co-Chrmn. Special Comte., Assn. Am. Law Schs. and Assn. Candn. Law Teachers on Candn.-Am. Co-operation 1962-66; Commr. for Ont., Uniform Law Conf. of Can. since 1963, Pres. 1977-78; mem. Adv. Comte., Candn. Civil Liberties Assn. Ont. 1965-66; mem. Faculty, Candn. Judicial Conf. 1969-73 (Dir. 1969-70); mem. Canadian delegation to The Hague Conference on Private International Law 1968, 1972, 1976, 1980; Chief of Can. Del. and Vice Pres., Hague Conf. on Private Internat. Law, 1980; mem. Can. Del., Special Commission on the Civil Aspects of Internat. Child Abduction, 1979; Chief of Can. Del, Int. Diplomatic Conf. on Wills, Washington, 1973; Chairman, Special Committee of Uniform Law Conference, on International Conventions on Private Internat. Law; served in 2nd World War, R.C.A. 1943-45 in Can., England and U.S.; grad. War Staff Gunnery Coll., Royal Sch. Arty., Larkhill, England and Royal Coll. Science; retired with rank of Capt.; Publications incl. articles in several legal and prof. journs.; mem. Law Soc. Upper Can.; Candn. Bar Assn. (mem. Council); Toronto Arty. Offrs. Assn.; Past Pres., Assn. Candn. Law Teachers; Past Chrmn. Nat. Scholar. Comte. and former Dir., African Students Foundation; Freemason; recreations: sailing, fishing, golf; Clubs: Lawyers; Empire (Pres. 1975); Home: 77 Ternhill Crescent, Don Mills, Ontario M3C 2E4; Office: 18 King Street E., Toronto, Ont. M5C 1C5

LEAMY, Cameron J. D.; insurance executive; b. Montreal, Que. 26 Sept. 1932; s. late Andrew and late Gladys (Cameron) L.; e. Sir George Williams High Sch.; m. Joan Ghent 19 Apl. 1958; children: Andrew, Sharon; SR. VICE PRES. MARKETING, SUN LIFE ASSURANCE CO. OF CANADA 1981- ; joined present Co. as Agt. 1953, Unit Mgr. 1956, Inspr. of Agencies E. Candn. Div. 1963, Inspr. of Agencies Central U.S. Div. 1964, Asst. Supt. Agencies 1965 and Supt. Agencies 1968 Central U.S. Div., Supt. Agencies E. U.S. Div. 1971, Br. Mgr. 1973; Home: 67 Edenville Cres., Toronto, Ont. M9A 4A5;Office: (P.O. Box 4150 Stn. A) Toronto, Ont. M5W 2C9.

LEARNING, Walter J., M.A., D. Litt.; theatre and drama director; b. Quidi Vidi, Nfld., 16 Nov. 1938; s. Edwin James and Maud (Maheal) L.; e. Bishop Feild Coll., St. John's, Nfld., 1957; Univ. of N.B., B.A. 1961, M.A. 1963; Australian Nat. Univ., 1963-66; D.Litt. (Hon) U.N.B. 1968; m. Lea, d. James A. Mersereau, Fredericton, N.B., 14 Feb. 1962; one s., James Warwick Christopher; HD. OF THEATRE FOR THE CANADA COUNCIL, since 1978; Founder, Theatre New Brunswick (productions tour prov.), 1968; Teaching Fellow, Univ. of N.B., 1961-63; Dir. of Drama, summer seasons 1966-67; Sessional Lectr., Mem. Univ., 1966-67; Lectr. 1967-68; Artistic Dir. and Gen. Mgr., The Beaverbrook Playhouse, 1968-78; theatrical experience in N.B. 1957-63 incl. Miller in "Journey's End" (Dom. Drama Festival final), Marco in "A View from the Bridge" (Dom. Drama Festival Hon. mention) and Roo, "Summer of the Seventeenth Doll" (Dom. Drama Festival Hon. mention) during this period also involved in design, direction and production; other theatrical experience incls. Toronto summer 1961 and Canberra, Aust., 1963-66 (leading stage roles and Dir. no. of plays); also TV and drama critic, book reviewer during latter period; formed production group Prompt Theatre, Fredericton, 1966; Production Mgr., Playhouse, Fredericton, summer 1967; Asst. Dir. and Dir. several plays and stage roles St. John's, Nfld., 1966-67; Pres. N.B. Drama Soc.; Extve. Offr. N.B. Drama League for 5 yrs., Secy. 2

yrs.; Extve. Offr., Canberra Repertory Theatre, 3 yrs.; Moderator, 1967 Dom. Drama Festival theatre conf. (Nat. Vice Pres. of Festival; has served also as Gov. and Extve. Offr.); Gov., Nat. Theatre School, 1973; Founder, Theatre New Brunswick Young Company, 1974; Pres. and Gen. Mgr., Learning Productions Ltd.; co-author (with Alden Nowlan) "Frankenstein — The Man Who Became God" 1974 (produced by four major Candn. theatres and C.B.C. radio); "The Dollar Woman", 1977; "The Incredible Murder of Cardinal Tosca", 1978; writer and dir., Story editor TV series, "Up at Ours", 1978-79; received Graduate Fellowship 1961-63; Commonwealth Scholarship 1963-66; awarded D.Litt. from Univ. of N.B., 1978; Recipients of Queen's Jubilee Medal, 1978; Dir., Candn. Conf. of the Arts; Candn. Theatre Centre; Home: 151 Bay St., Apt. 1103, Ottawa, Ont. K1R 5Y3; Office: The Canada Council, 255 Albert St., Ottawa, Ont.

LEATHER, Sir Edwin H. C., K.C.M.G., K.C.V.O., K.St.J., LL.D.; b. Toronto, Ontario, 22 May 1919; s. Harold H., M.B.E. and Grace C. (Holmes) L.; e. Hillfield School, Hamilton, Ontario; Trinity Coll. School, Port Hope, Ontario; R.M.C., Grad 1939; m. Sheila A. A., d. Major Greenlees, Hamilton, Ont., 9 March 1940; two d., Hope A., Sarah A. G.; Dir., N.M. Rothschild Bermuda; mem. Extve. Comte. and Bd. of Finance, Conservative Party Nat. Comte. 1965-71, Chmn. 1970-71; Gov. Yehudi Menuhin Sch.; served in 2nd World War 1939-45; commd. to R.C.H.A.; served Overseas, 1940-45; cand. for S. Bristol, 1945; el. to H. of C. for N. Somerest in g.e. 1950; re-el. to H. of C. g.e. 1951, '55, '59; sometime Depy. Chrmn. Commonwealth Affairs Comte.; mem. Extve. Comte., Brit. Commonwealth Ex-Services League, 1953-63; Chrmn., Bath Festival Soc., 1960-65; Pres., Inst. of Marketing, U.K. 1960-65; Gov. & Commdr.-in-chief, Bermuda, 1973-77 (ret.); rec'd. Meritorious Service Medal of Royal Candn. Legion; mem., Extve. Comte., Brit. Commonwealth Producers Organ.; regular Broadcaster; cr. Kt. Bachelor, 1962; Hon. F.R.S.A. 1972; K.C.M.G. 1973, K.St.J. 1974; K.C.V.O. 1975; Hon LL.D., Bath Univ. 1975; mem. Council, Imp. Soc. of Kts. Bachelor; Hon. Mem. Nat. Inst. of Social Sciences, New York; Author, "The Vienna Elephant" 1977; "The Mozart Score" 1978; "The Duveen Letter" 1980; Conservative; Anglican; Clubs: Carlton; Canadian (New York); York (Toronto); Royal Bermuda Yacht; Hamilton, (Ont.). Address: Mangrove View Paget, Bermuda

LEATHERS, Winston Lyle, R.C.A.; artist; educator; b. Miami, Man. 29 Dec. 1932; s. Almer Leathers; e. Miami Coll. Inst. 1952; Univ. of Man. Fine Arts grad. 1956, Art Educ. 1960-61; post-grad. art educ. Mexico 1957; Man. Teachers Coll. maj. in Art Educ. 1959; Univ. of B.C. Festival of the Arts Scholarship student 1962; m. Kathleen Dawn Wilson 30 Jan. 1978; one s. Paul William; ASSOC. PROF. OF ENVIRONMENTAL STUDIES, UNIV. OF MAN.; Design Consultant, Haid and Jesson Architects, Winnipeg; mem. Bd. Govs. Winnipeg Art Gallery; numerous comtes. on art educ.; solo exhns. incl. Mexico City 1957; Alty Gallery Winnipeg 1960, Toronto 1962; Univ. of B.C. 1961; Point Gallery Victoria 1963; Grant Gallery Winnipeg 1964; W. Candn. Art Circuit 1966-67; Yellow Door Gallery 1967; London, Eng. 1968; Brandon Univ. 1969; Grant Univ. 1969; Upstairs Gallery 1969; Mem. Art Gallery St. John's, Nfld. 1972; Beau-xi Gallery Vancouver 1973; Univ. of Man. Faculty of Arch. 1973; Winnipeg Art Gallery 1974; Albert Whyte Gallery 1975; rep. in numerous maj. group exhns. incl. 69th Internat. Exhn. Prints, Inst. of Contemporary Arts, Washington, D.C.; Xylon V Internat. Graphics Zurich 1971; Paris Internat. Print Exhn. 1972; Monaco and Bermuda Biennial Internat. Print Exhns. 1972; Brit. Fed. Internat. Argentina 1972; Graphics Can. Art Gallery Ont. and Nat. Travel Show 1973-74; Internat. Print Exhns. Zurich, Lucerne, London, Paris, Japan 1974; rep. in various pub., corporate and private colls. Can. USA, Europe, Mexico, S.Am.; maj. awards incl. Winnipeg Show 2nd Prize in Oils 1960;

Calgary Graphics Purchase Prize 1964; Winnipeg Biennial Purchase Price 1964; Sr. Can. Council Fellowship 1967-68, Grant 1970; Soc. Painter, Etchers & Engravers 1973; Internat. Print Exhn. Zurich 1974; mem. Candn. Artists Representation (Pres. Man.); Man. Soc. Arts (Pres.); Brit. Fed. Arts; Print & Drawing Council Can.; Teacher Indust. Design Dept. Winnipeg Tech. Vocational High Sch. 1958-68; Liberal; recreations: sailing, skiing; clubs: Winnipeg Ski; Gimili Yacht; Home: #1215, 2080 Pembine Hwy., Winnipeg, Man. R3T 2G9; Office: Univ. of Man., Faculty of Arch., Winnipeg, Man.

LEAVITT, Alfred D.; financier; b. St. Lambert, Que., 25 Feb. 1924; s. Robert Douglas and Gertrude (Cope) L.; e. Consol. Schs., Wellington, Ont.; Queen's Univ.; m. Glenna, d. Kenneth Reade, 11 June 1949; two d. Carolyn, Jane; PRES. & DIR., ASSOCIATED FINANCIAL SERVICES CO. LTD. since 1972; Pres. & Dir., Associates Finance Co. Ltd.; commenced career in Marketing, H. J. Heintz Co. 1945-47; Mgr., Household Finance Corp. of Canada 1949; Supv., Citizens Finance Co., Toronto, Ont. 1958; Supv., Associates Acceptance Co. Ltd. 1962, Dir. of Supvs. 1965, Asst. Vice-Pres. 1968, Vice-Pres. 1969, Sr. Vice-Pres., U.S. 1970; served with R.C.A.F. 1942-44; rank on discharge Pilot Offr.; mem. Bd. Trade Metrop. Toronto; Fed. Councilof Sales Finance Cos.; Anglican (Rector's Warden, Ch. St. Andrew, Toronto); recreations: golf, music, reading; Club: North Halton Country (Georgetown, Ont.); Home: 4 Morningdale Cres., Agincourt, Ont.; Office: 40 Wynford Drive, Don Mills, Ont. M3C 1J5

LEBEL, J. Louis, Q.C. B.A., LL.B.; Counsel with McLaws & Co. (Calgary); b. Longueil, Que. 17 Oct. 1918; s. Alfred U. and Margaret Jean (Ivany) L.; e. Laval Univ. B.A. 1940; Univ. of Alta. LL.B. 1943; Harvard Sch. of Business Adm. 1947-48; Stanford Univ. Extve. Devel. Program 1963; m. Therese Marguerite d. Charles Edmond Barry, Edmonton, Alta. 18 Nov. 1950; children: Robert, Pierre, Charles, Marguerite, Louise, Simone; RETIRED VICE PRES. AND DIR. CHEVRON STANDARD LTD. Oct. 1980; Dir., Calgary Cable Television Ltd.; Canadian Arsenals Ltd.; Imperial Life Assurance Co.; Cherokee Resources Ltd.; Credit Foncier Trust Co.; Noreen Energy Resources Ltd.; called to Bar of Alta. 1947; appointed Queen's Council, 1979; served with Candn. Inf. Corps 1943-46, rank Lt.; Vice Pres. Lib. Party of Can. (Alta.); Dir., Candn. Inst. for Child Health; mem. Senate Univ. of Calgary (Chancellor 1978-82); Past Pres. Calgary Un. Appeal and Alta. Heart Foundation; Past Treas. Candn. Petroleum Law Foundation; former Chrmn. Candn. Petrol. Assn.; mem. Law Soc. Alta.; Candn. Assn. Petrol. Landmen; Am. Assn. Petrol. Landmen; R. Catholic; recreations: golf, skiing; Clubs: Calgary Petroleum; Calgary Golf & Country; Glencoe; Home: 1011 Elizabeth Rd. S.W., Calgary, Alta. T2S 1N2; Office: 6th Floor, 407-8th Ave. W.W., Calgary, Alta. T2P 1E6.

LEBEL, M. Maurice, O.C. (1967), M.A., L. LèsL., Ph.D., D.Litt., D.C.L., F.R.S.C. (1947); educator; b. St. Lin, Can., 23 Dec. 1909; s. André and Eugénie (Robichaud) L.; e. Univ. of Montreal, B.A. 1928; Laval Univ., M.A. 1930; Sorbonne, Dipl. d'études Supérieures en lang. et. lit. classiques 1931; Univ. of London, B.A. (Hons.); Ph.D. (Educ.) 1952; D.Litt., Athens 1957, Hon degrees from the following Universities; Birmingham, Memorial, Dalhousie, McMaster, Saskatchewan, Rennes.; m. Eva Sophia, d. Reginald Batt, Camberley, Eng., 7 July 1938; children: Andrew, Mark, Michael; PROF. OF ANCIENT STUDIES, LAVAL UNIV., Faculty of Letters; attended numerous educ. and scient. cong. 1936-39 and 1947; travelled throughout Europe and Russia, touring univs., 1930-39; studied classical antiquity for two summers in Greece, 1932-33; Prof. of Greek Lit., Laval Univ. 1937-75; Dean Faculty of Letters, 1957-63 (Secy. 1938-52); winner of Prix David 1945 and Prix Théodore Reinach (France) 1947; Pres., Classical Assn. of Can., 1955-56; mem., Candn. Authors Assn.; Classical Assn. of U.S.A.; l'assn. des

Etudes Grecques de France; author of "L'étude et l'enseignement de l'Anglais", 1942; "Suggestions pratiques pour notre Enseignement", 1939; "Les Humanités classiques dans la Société Contemporaine",1944; "L'Enseignement et l'étude du grec", 1944; "Life et le Canada Francais", 1944; "Natural Law in Greece"; "Pourquoi apprend-on le grec", 1952; "Explications de Textes français et anglais", 1953; "Le Conseil Canadien de recherches sur les Humanités", 1954; "Lettres de Grèce", 1955; "L'Explication des Textes Littéraires", 1957; "Recheres sur les Images dans la Poésie de Sophocle", 1957; "Images de la Turquie", 1957; "Considérations sur le rôle de l'Université au XXe Siècle", 1958; "Humanisme et Technique", 1959; "La Langue parlée", 1959; 2nd ed. 1960; "Trois Cultures et Sagesse", 1960; "Le mirage des États-Unis et de la Russie dans l'enseignement supérieur au Canada", 1961; "La Tradition du nouveau", 1962; "Propos inédits et interdits sur l'Éducation", 1963; "d'Octave Cremazie à Alain Grandbois", 1963; "De Saint François de Sales à Alphonse Daudet", 1964; "De René Bazin à Saint-Exupéry", 1964; "Sir Philip Sidney Un Plaidoyer pour la Poésie", 1965; "Éducation et Humanisme", 1966; "Les Humanités classiques au Québec" 1967; Pages choisies d'Eugenio Maria de Hostos" 1969; La Grèce et Nous" 1969; "Histoire Littéraire du Canada 1970; "Mgr. Jean Calvet De la Faculté des Lettres au Pro-Rectorat 1939-45" 1970 (Bibliographie); "Images de Chypre" 1972; "Académie des Sciences morales et politiques Montréal" 1973; "De transitu hellenismi ad christianismum de Guillaume Budé" 1974; "État présent des travaux sur Platon "1975; "Iacurto Souvenirs" 1976; "Regards sur la Grèce d'hier et d'aujourdh'hui" 1977; "Mythes anciens et drame moderne", 1977; "Mutation de la culture, de l'éducation et de l'enseignement" 1978; "La Composition Stylistique" de Denys d'Halicarnasse, 1981; awarded P.J.O. Chauveau Medal 1962; Prix Venizelos, 1962; Prix de l'Académie française; Past Pres., Royal Soc. of Can.; Roman Catholic; Home: 2007, rue Bourbonniere, Québec, Que. G1T 1A9

LeBLANC, Conrad; insurance executive; b. North Bay, Ont. 18 Nov. 1924; s. late Arthur and Alma (Renaud) L.; e. Sch. of Beaupré: Institut Thomas de Qué.; Academie of Quebec; Ins. Inst. Can.; m. Lucille d. late Pierre Duval 12 June 1948; children: Michèle, Alain; PRES. AND CHIEF EXEC. OFFICER, DIR. AND EXEC. COMM., LE, GROUPE DESJARDIERES ASSURANCES GÉNÉRALES AND LA SECURITÉ CIE D'ASSURANCES GÉNÉRALES DU CANADA; Dir. Confédération des Caisses Populaires et d'èconomie Des Jardins du Quèbec; Dir., Insurers' Adv. Organ.; Dir. of I.B.C.; Fellow, Ins. Inst. Can.; Past Dir. Bd. Trade Quebec; R. Catholic; recreations: tennis, squash, swimming, travel, music; Club: Kiwanis (Past Pres.); Garrison; Home: 2125 Marillac, Sillery, Que. G1T 1L3; Office: 100 Route Trans Canada E., Lévis and Complexe Desjardins, Dorchester Blvd. W., Montreal, Qué.

LEBLANC, Fernand E., M. Comm., C.A.; Senator; b. Montreal, Que.; 1 July 1917; s. Ulric and Aglaée (Guindon) L.; e. St. Stanislas Primary Sch. Montreal; Montreal Coll.; Univ. of Montreal B.Sc., L.S.C., C.A. 1945; m. Claire d. Hon. J. Eugène Lefrançois. St-Laurent, Que. 16 June 1945; children: Daniel, François; el. to H. of C. by-el. 1964, re-el. until 1979; summoned to the Senate, 1979; Liberal; R. Catholic; Home: 350 Côte Vertu, Apt. 522, St-Laurent, Que. H4N 1E2; Office: The Senate of Canada, Ottawa, Ont. K1A 0A4.

LeBLANC, Jean-Paul; b. College Bridge, N.B., 16 August 1923; s. Edgar T. and Anna (Landry) LeB.; e. Moncton (N.B.) Schools; St. Joseph's College, Memramcook, N.B. 1937-41; St. Francis Xavier University, 1941-42 and 1946-47; m. late Isabel, d. Laughlin McLellan, Antigonish, N.S., 31 May 1948; children: Anne-Marie (Mrs. Gerald Arsenault), Pauline (Mrs. Marc Theriault), Donald, Bernice, Mark, Owen, Claire (deceased); Claude; CHRMN.,

CIVIL SERVICE COMN. N.B. since 1974; former President, Moncton Plumbing & Supply Co. Ltd.; served with RCNVR as Able Seaman Radar Operator, 1943-45; Moncton City Council, 1959-63 and 1967-70 (Depy. Mayor); Chrmn., Treas. Bd., Min. Tourism, and Min. Municipal Affairs, N.B. 1970-74; Past Nat. Dir., Candn. Plumb. & Mech. Contractors' Assn.; Candn. Constr. Assn.; Past Chmn., Bd. of Dir., Insitut de Memramcook Inst.; mem., Inst. Pub. Admn. Can.; Internat. Personnel Mang. Assn.; Roman Catholic: Home: Apt. 815, 700 Forest Hill Rd., Fredericton, N.B. E3B 5X9; Office: Centennial Building, Fredericton, N.B. E3B 4X6

LeBLANC, Hon. Roméo A., P.C., M.P., B.A., B.Ed.; politician; b. L'Anse-aux-Cormier, Memramcook, N.B. 18 Dec. 1927; s. Philias and Lucie L.; e. St-Joseph Univ.; Univ. of Paris; m. Joslyn Carter, Montreal, Que. 17 Dec. 1966; children: Dominic, Geneviève; MIN. OF FISHERIES AND OCEANS, CAN. 1980- ; former prof. and journalist; Press Secy. to Prime Min. of Can. 1967-71; el. to H. of C. for Westmorland-Kent g.e. 1972, re-el. since; Sworn of Privy Council and apptd. Min. of State for Fisheries 1974; Min. of Fisheries and Environment 1976; Liberal; R. Catholic; Home: (P.O. Box 93) Grand Digue, N.B.; Office: House of Commons, Ottawa, Ont. K1A 0A6.

LEBLOND, Charles Philippe, M.D., Ph.D., D.Sc., F.R.S. (1965), F.R.S.C. (1951), O.C. (1977); university professor; b. Lille, France, 5 Feb. 1910; s. Oscar and Jeanne (Desmarchelier) L.; e. Univ. of Lille, Lic.-ès-Sciences 1932; Univ. of Paris, M.D. 1934, D.Sc. Sorbonne, 1945; Univ. of Montreal, Ph.D. 1942; m. Gertrude, d. L. W. Sternschuss, New Haven, Conn., 22 Oct. 1936; children: Philippe, Paul, Pierre, Marie Pascale; PROF. OF ANATOMY, McGILL UNIV., since 1948; Lectr. in Anat. and Histol., Univs. of Lille and Paris, 1934-35; Rockefeller Fellow, Yale Univ., Dept. of Anat., 1935-37; Dir. of the Biol. Divn., Lab. de Synthèse Atomique, Paris, 1937-40; Research Fellow in Anat., Rochester Univ., 1940-41; Lectr. in Histol., McGill Univ., 1941-42; apptd. Asst. Prof., 1943; Assoc. Prof. of Anat., 1946; Prof. of Anatomy 1948-; Chrmn. of Dept. M'gill U., 1957-74; organ. "Selection of Personnel" in Free French Army, 1944-45; Pres., The Histochem. Soc. (1955-56); Pres., Am. Assn. Anats. 1962-63; Pres., Candn. Assn. Anats, 1966; mem., Am. Assn. for Cancer Research; Soc. of Exper. Biol. & Med.; Biol. Stain Comn.; Amer. Soc. for Cell Biology; Research Adv. Group, Nat. Cancer Inst. of Can. 1953-63; author, "L'Acide Ascorbique dans les Tissus et sa Detection", 1936; "Iodine Metabolism", in "Advances in Biological and Medical Physics", 1948; about three hundred articles of original research work in biol. and med.; rec'd the following Special Honours; Prix Saintour, French Academy 1935, Iodine Education Bureau Award 1951, NATO Professor, University of Louvain, Belgium 1959, Flavelle Medal, Royal Society of Canada 1961, Medal Leo Pariseau, Assoc, Canadienne-Française pour l'Avancement des Sciences 1962, Fellow of the Royal Society, London 1965, Gairdner Fdn. Award 1965, Am. Coll. Phys. Award for distinguished contrib. in med. science 1966, Province of Quebec Biology Prize 1968, Honorary Member of the American Academy of Arts and Sciences 1970, Honorary Degree of Doctor of Science, Acadia University, Wolfville, Nova Scotia 1972, Isaac Schour Award of the International Association for Dental Research 1974, Fogarty Scholar of the National Institutes of Health (January to July) 1975, Prix Scientifique de l'Association Canadienne des Médecins de Langue Française 1976, Officer of the Order of Canada 1977, Henry Gray Award of the American Association of Anatomists 1978, J.C.B. Grant Award of the Cdn. Assoc. of Anatomists 1979; Roman Catholic; Club: Faculty; Home: 68 Chesterfield Ave., Westmount, Que. H3Y 2M5

LeBLOND, Sylvio, E.D., M.D.; b. Thetford-Mines, Que., 17 Dec. 1901; s. Moise and Henrietta (Rousseau) L.; e. Que. Semy., B.A. 1923; Laval Univ., M.D. 1928; Internship, St. Sacrament Hosp., Quebec (two Yrs.); Post Grad.; Ecole de Méd. and Hosps. Bichat, Vaugirard, Tenon and La Salapatrière, Paris, France, 1929-31; Specialist, Internal Med., Royal Coll., and Coll. Phys. & Surg., Qué., 1950; m. Jeanne, d. Dr. Eugène Lacerte, Thetford-Mines, Que., 28 May 1936; children: Paul H. (Ph. D. Physic.; Prof., Inst. of Oceanography U.B.C.), Pierre F. (M.D., Haematol.; Prof. Laval Univ.); Assoc. Prof., Laval Univ. Med. Sch., 1934; Prof. of Clinical Med. 1946-67 and History of Medicine 1939-54, Emeritus Prof. 1970; served with Candn. Militia, 1928-39; promoted Capt. 1934; served in 2nd World War 1940-45; O.C., Valcartier Mil. Hosp., 1940-43; promoted Major 1940, Lt.-Col. 1941; Med. Consultant, Que. Area, 1943-45; E.D. 1945; Chief of Med., Quebec Veterans Hosp., 1946-51; Chief of Med., Hôtel-Dieu St-Vallier de Chicoutimi Hosp., affiliated Laval Med. Sch., 1951-67; Med. Consultant, Quebec Pension Plan since 1972; Past Pres., Soc. Méd. des Hôpitaux Univ. de Laval 1955; Can. Med. Assn. Que. Div. 1959-60; mem. Am. Assn. for Hist. of Med.; Soc. Internat. d'Hist. de Méd.; Soc. d'Hist. de Méd. Qué.; Life mem. and Past Pres., Can. Soc. for History of Medicine; Sr. mem. (1968) Can. Med. Assn.; Roman Catholic; recreations: driving, golfing, reading, travelling; Home: 2590 Sillery Plaza, Apt. 420, Sillery Quebec, Que. G1T 1X2

LEBRUN, François, B.A. LL.L., L.Sc.Pol. M.Sc.; né Montréal, Qué. 28 janvier 1940; f. Henri et Marie (Hêtu) L.; é. Coll. Jean-de-Brébeuf, Montréal B.A.; Univ. de Montréal LL.L. 1964; Barreau du Qué., 1965; Inst. d'Etudes Politiques de Paris Dipl. 1968; London Sch. of Econ. M.Sc. 1969; ép. Claudette Poulin; enfants: Simon, Olivier; PRÉSIDENT DE LA SOCIÉTÉ DE DEVELOPPEMENT INDUSTRIEL DU QUÉBEC depuis 1981; chargé de cours sur les relations intergouvernementales, Univ. de Montréal 1977; Conseiller à la direction des affaires fédérales et provinciales du Ministère des Affaires intergouvernementales 1969-70; chargé du secteur des Affaires educatives et culturelles 1970-74; directeur général des relations fédérales et provinciales 1974-77; Delegue general du Quebec à Toronto, 1977-81; dir. de Thémis 1963-64; vice prés. de la Promotion 1964; prés. des résidents de la Maison canadienne, Paris 1965-66; secrétaire de l'Assn. générale des étudiants du Quebec en france, 1966-67; .memb. Comm. permanente Ont.-Qué. 1970-80; de l'Institut d'administration publique du Can.; du comité consultatif sur les relations intergouvernementales de l'Université Queen's 1977-80; du Centre québecois de relations internationales et de l'Inst. canadien des affaires internationales 1969-77; Bureau: Tour de la Bourse, suite 4205, C.P. 276, Montreal, Que. H4Z 1E8et 1126, Chemin St.-Louis, bureau 700, Québec, Qué. G1S 1E5

LECERF,Olivier Maurice Marie, B.A., LL.M.; industrialist; b. Merville-Franceville (Calvados), France 2 Aug. 1929; s. late Maurice and Colette (Lainé) L.; e. Coll. St. Louis de Gonzague, Paris B.A. (Philos.) 1946; Ecole des Sciences Politiques, Paris Dipl. 1950; Univ. of Paris LL.M. 1950; Univ. of Geneva Centre d'Etudes Industrielles grad. 1960; m. Aline Marie-Anne (Annie) d. R. Bazin de Jessey, Paris, France 11 Jan. 1958; children: Christophe, Véronique, Nicolas, Patricia; CHRMN. AND CEO. LAFARGE COPPÉE, 1974- ; Dir., Ciments Lafarge France; La Farge Réfractaires; Canada Cement Lafarge Ltd.; Canadian Imperial Bank of Commerce; Crédit Commercial de France; Veuve Clicquot-Ponsardin; Société Nat. E.L.F. Aquitaine; mem. AGREF; Chrmn. CEI Foundation Bd. Geneva; Internat. Counsellor of Conf. Bd.; mem. CNPF, politique économique générale, conseil exécutif; mem. Adv. Bd., Volvo International; Banque de France; Asst. Mgr. Omnium for Importation and Exportation, Paris 1951-56; joined Ciments Lafarge, Paris 1956, Asst. Mgr. 1956-60 (serving in Can. 1956-57, Brazil 1958-59); Asst. Mgr. Foreign Dept. 1961, Asst. Comm. Mgr. Paris 1962-64; Gen. Mgr. and Pres. Lafarge Cement of North America, Vancouver 1965; Pres. Ciments Lafarge Quebec,

Montreal 1968 becoming Lafarge Canada Ltd. 1969; Gen. Mgr. Canada Cement Lafarge 1970; Extve. Gen. Mgr. Ciments Lafarge Paris 1971-73; named Chevalier Legion of Honour; Off., Order Nat. du Merité; R. Catholic; recreations: tennis, skiing, swimming; Clubs: Automobile de Paris; Polo de Paris; Home: 8, rue Guy de Maupassant, 75116 Paris, France; Office: 28, rue Emile Menier, 75116 Paris, France.

LECKIE, Robin B., B.A., F.S.A. (1957); insurance executive; b. Vancouver, B.C., 30 June 1931; s. G. Duncan and Margaret S. (Brooks) L.; e. Univ. of Brit. Columbia, B.A. (Hons. Math) 1953; m. Rosemary D., d. J. Basil Topp, 6 Nov. 1959; children: Barbara, Stephen, Edward, Roseann; SR. VICE-PRES. & CHIEF ACTUARY, MANUFACTURER'S LIFE INSURANCE CO. since 1977; formerly Actuary i/c Actuarial Dept., Research and Devel. Dept.; commenced with the Co. as Actuarial Clerk 1953, Vice-Pres. U.S. Operations 1970, Vice-Pres. Planning and Control 1973; Vice-Pres & Chief Actuary, 1974-77; mem. Candn. Inst. of Actuaries (Pres. 1975-76); mem. Soc. of Acturaries, Pres. 1980-81; Conservative; United Church; Home: 171 Dawlish Ave., Toronto, Ont. M4N 1H6; Office: 200 Bloor St. E., Toronto, Ont. M4W 1E4

LeCLAIR, J. Maurice, B.Sc., M.D., C.M., M.Sc. (Medicine), L.L.D., D.Sc.(Hon.c.) F.R.C.P.(C), F.A.C.P., Transportation Executive; b. Sayabec, Que., 19 June 1927; s. Francois and Rose-Anna (Chassé) LeC.; e. McGill Univ., B.Sc. 1947, M.D., C.M. 1951; Univ. of Minn., M.Sc. (Medicine) 1958; m. Pauline, d. Eugène Héroux, Shawinigan, Que., 22 Nov. 1952; children: Suzanne, Marie, François, Manon, Nathalie Guy SENIOR CORPORATE VICE PRES. CANADIAN NATIONAL, 1981; formerly Corp. Vice Pres. 1979 Secy. of Treasury Board 1976; Secy. Min. of Science and Technol. (1974); Depy. Min. of Health and Welfare (1970); Dean, Faculty of Med., Univ. of Sherbrooke, 1968; Head, Dept. of Med., 1965; Vice Dean, Fac. of Med., Univ. of Montréal, 1962; Consulting Internist, Notre Dame Hospital, Montreal, 1958; Fellow, Mayo Clinic, Minn., 1955; G.P., Shawinigan, 1953; Vice Pres., Med. Research Council of Can. 1968-70; author of over 30 publications in Med. & Admin.; Roman Catholic; recreation: collecting antiques; Home: 53 Maplewood Ave., Outremont, Que. H2V 2L9 Office: P.O. Box 8100, Montreal, Que. H3C 3N4

LECLERC, Marc, B.A., M.Com., manufacturer; b. Granby, P.Q., 2 June 1915; s. J. H. and Clara (Messier) L.; e. Ecole Sacré-Coeur, Granby, P.Q.; Coll. St. Laurent, Ville St. Laurent, B.A. (cum laude) 1935; Ecole des Hautes Etudes Commerciale de l'Univ. de Montréal, M.Com. 1939; m. Jeanne Mercier, 14 Oct. 1944; children: Martine, Sylvie, Jean; Executive Vice President, Quebec-Lait Inc.; Dir., Les Laiteries Leclerc Inc.; mem. Internat. Assn. Ice Cream Mfrs.; (Dir. then Vice-President and President 1952-54); Province of Quebec Milk Dealers' Association Inc. (Dir. 1952-56, President 1956-59); Milk Industry Foundation, Washington, D.C. (mem. of Bd. to rep. E. Can. 1954-60); appted. by the Prov. Govt. as rep. of mfrs. on the Dairy Industry Inquest Comte. (Nov. 1960); Pres. Catholic Sch. Bd., Granby, Que., 1956-60 and 1961-62; Regional Sch. Planning Bd., 1964-66; Chrmn. Bd., Sherbrooke Coll., Chmn. Sherbrooke Univ. Hosp.; past mem. Extve. Council, Candn. Chamber of Comm.; Pres. Nat. Dairy Council Can. 1967-69; Dir., Quebec Hosp. Assn.; Dir., Can Hosp. Assn.; Dir Voyages Travel Inc.; Catholic; recreation: skiing; Home: 97 Ėlm St., Granby, Que. J2G 2H7; Office: 10 Laval St., Granby, P.Q. J2G 7G1

L'ECUYER, Philibert G., B.Sc., D.Phil., F.R.S.C.; retired professor; b. St. Bonaventure, Yamaska, Que., 3 Oct. 1908; s. Georges and Rosanna (Caron) L.; e. Semys. of St. Hyacinthe and Nicolet; Laval Univ., B.Sc.A. 1933; Rhodes Schol. for Que. 1933-36; Oxford Univ., B.Sc. 1935; D. Phil. 1936; m. 1st, Maria Holler (d. 1946) of Germany, 25 July 1936; children: Rosanne, Gisele, Gilles; 2ndly, Ida

Fradette, 26 May 1947; two s., Paul, Charles; retired Prof. of Organic Chem., Laval Univ.; mem., Roy. Soc. of Can.; former Mem., Candn. Inst. of Chem.; Professeur Émérite, Laval Univ. 1979; Médaille "La Gloire de L'Escolle", Anciens de Laval, 1979; Roman Catholic; recreations: cross-country skiing, bridge; Home: 815 Ave. Bellevue, Quebec, Que. G1V 2R4

Le DAIN, Hon. Gerald Eric, B.C.L., D. de l'Univ., D.C.L., LL.D.; judge; b. Montreal, Que., 27 Nov. 1924; s. Eric George Bryant and Antoinette Louise (Whithard) Le D.; e. West Hill High Sch., 1942; William A. Birks and Sir William Macdonald Schols. to McGill Univ., (Arts), 1942-43; Candn. Army Univ. Course ("With Distinction"), McGill Univ., 1943; Khaki University, Eng., 1946; McGill University, B.C.L., 1949; Univ. Scholar; Elizabeth Torrance Gold Medal; Macdonald Travelling Scholarship; Université de Lyon, Docteur de l'Université ("Mention Très Bien"), 1950; Hon. LL.D.'s, York Univ. 1976; Concordia Univ. 1976; Hon. D.C.L., Acadia Univ. 1978; m. Cynthia Moira Emily, d. late Colin Ian Roy, 13 Sept. 1947; children: Jacqueline, Catherine, Barbara, Caroline, Eric, Jennifer; JUSTICE, FEDERAL COURT OF APPEAL since Sept. 1975; called to the Bar of Quebec, 1949; cr. Q.C., 1961; practised law with Walker, Martineau, Chauvin, Walker & Allison, 1950-53; Associate Professor and Secy., Faculty of Law, McGill Univ., 1953-59; Legal Dept., Canadian International Paper Co., 1959-61; Partner, Riel, Le Dain, Bissonnette Vermette & Ryan, 1961-66; a counsel to the Attorney General for Quebec in constitutional cases, 1963-67; Prof., Constitutional and Adm. Law, McGill Univ., 1966-67; Prof. of Law, Osgoode Hall Law Sch. York Univ. 1967-75 and Dean of Law there 1967-72; called to the Bar of Ont. 1968; served with Canadian Army, 1943-46; Gunner, N.W. Theatre, with 7th Medium Regt., R.C.A., 1944-45; Army of Occupation, 1945-46; published several articles on constitutional adm. comm. and civil law and legal educ.; Consultant to Royal Comn. on Bilingualism and Biculturalism; Adv. to Special Counsel on the Constitution to the Min. of Justice 1967; Chrmn., Comn. of Inquiry into Non-Medical Use of Drugs 1969-73; Anglican; Club: Rideau; Home: 263 Island Park Drive, Ottawa, Ont. K1Y 0A5; Office: The Federal Court of Canada, Ottawa, Ont. K1A 0H8

LEDDY, (John) Francis, O.C. (1972), M.A., M.Litt., D.Phil., D.Litt., D.ès L., D.C.L., LL.D., K.C.S.G. (1964), F.R.S.A. (1971); F.R.S.Hist. (1972); former university president; b. Ottawa, Ont., 16 April 1911; s. late John Joseph and Teresa Frances (Dwyer) L.; e. University of Saskatchewan, B.A. (Hons. in Latin and French) 1930, M.A. (Latin) 1931, LL.D. 1965; University of Chicago (Grad. Sch.) 1932-33; Oxford Univ., 1933-36; (Sask. Rhodes Schol. at Exeter Coll.), B. Litt. 1935, D.Phil. (for research in Ancient Hist.) 1938 and M. Litt. 1980; D. Litt., St. Francis Xavier 1953; Ottawa 1957; D.ès L., Laval 1957; LL.D., Assumption, 1958; D.C.L., St. Mary's 1960; LL.D. Toronto 1966; Hanyang (Korea) 1971; Notre Dame (Nelson, B.C.) 1971; Waterloo Lutheran 1972; West. Ontario 1975; m. Kathleen Beatrice, d. late W. T. White, 7 May 1938; PRESIDENT AND VICE-CHANCELLOR, UNIV. OF WINDSOR, 1964-78; Instr. in Classics. Univ. of Sask., 1936-39, Asst. Prof. 1939-45 and Assoc. Prof. 1945-46; Prof. and Head of Dept., 1946-64; Dean Coll. of Arts and Science, 1949-64; Vice-Pres. (Academic), 1961-64; Dir., Univ. of Sask. Summer Sch., 1942-49; Chrmn., Educ. Council, Prov. of Sask., 1945-63; mem. of Senate, Univ. of Sask., 1945-64; Extve. mem., Nat. Conf. of Candn. Univs., 1948-50, 1956-57 (Secy. Treas 1953-56); Hon. Life mem., Sask. Alumni Assn. (Pres., 1940-43); mem. Humanities Research Council of Can. 1943-64 (Chrmn., 1949, 1955); Humanities Assn. of Can. (first Chrmn. 1950-52); Classical Assn. of Can. (Pres., 1956-58); Candn. Inst. Internat. Affairs (Pres. Saskatoon Br. 1943; mem. of Nat. Council 1944 and 1951-55); Pres., Candn. Assn. Rhodes Scholars, 1957-59; President, Candn. Nat. Comn. for UNESCO, 1960-62; mem., Candn. Cath. Hist. Assn. (Presi-

dent General 1960-61); Adv. Bd., CARE of Canada; Candn. Del., Internat. Union of Acads., Brussels, 1953, 1955, 1958, Rome 1956, Stockholm, 1961 Vienna, 1963; Candn. mem., Extve. Council, Assn. of Univs. of Brit. Commonwealth, Melbourne, Aust., Aug. 1955; Hon. Pres., Nat. Fed. of Candn. Univ. Students, 1961-62; Candn. Del., East-West UNESCO Conf., Calcutta, 1961; mem., Bd. of Dirs., Assn. Univ. Coll. of Can.1966-69; mem., Prov. Comte. on Aims and Objectives of Educ. in Schs. of Ont., 1965-68; Pres., Candn. Service for Overseas Students and Trainees, 1967-70; Pres. Gen., Eng. Cath. Educ. Assn. of Ont., 1967-69; Vice-Pres., Internat. Extve., World Univ. Service, 1964-68; Hon. Pres., Candn. Univ. Service Overseas (Chrmn. 1962-65); Vice Chrmn. The Can. Council, 1964-69, 1957-60; mem., Nat. Conf. on Centennial1963-67; Chrmn., Organizing Comte., Co. of Young Candns.1965; mem., Council, Candn. Soc. for Asian Studies 1970-72; Hon. Pres., Candn. Assn., The Order of Malta 1981, Pres 1978-81; Pres. World Federalists of Canada, 1981; mem. Council, World Assn. of World Federalists, 1980; Human Relations Award, Candn. Council Christians and Jews, 1953; Univ. of Sask., Alumni Assn. Award for Achievement, 1980; Papal Medal, "Pro Ecclesia et Pontifice", 1956; Knight of Malta, 1956; Knight of the Holy Sepulchre, 1959; Cardinal Newman Award, Candn. Fed. Newman Clubs, 1958; Lateran Cross, 1963; Gentleman of His Holiness, Pope Paul VI, 1969; and of Pope John Paul I, 1978; and of Pope John Paul II, since 1978; Roman Catholic; Address: The Leddy Library, University of Windsor, Windsor, Ont. N9B 3P4

LEDUC, André, B.A., M.D.; né Montréal, Que., 7 Déc. 1915; p. Joseph A. et Blanche (Vaillancourt) L.; é. Coll. Jean de Bréboeuf, Montréal, B.A. 1936; Univ. de Montréal, M.D. 1942 et Cert. supér. en microbiol. 1948; Institut Pasteur, Paris, France (microbiol.) 1949; certifié spécialiste en Microbiol. de la P.Q. 1951; ep. Ginette, p. Marcel Langlois, 26 Fév. 1948; enfants: Nicole, Elaine; Chef du Service de Microbiol., Hôpital Notre-Dame, Montréal 1959-77; Prof. Agrégé en Microbiol., Univ. de Montréal; Officier Médical, R.C.A.F., Canada et outre-mer, 1942-46; Médailles de service et du centenaire; Médaille du 25ème anniversaire du couronnement; Auteur de plus de vingt articles d'intérêt scient. dans journaux médicaux; Prés. (1968-69), Assn. des Méd. de Langue Française du Canada; membre. Can. Soc. of Microbiol.; Am. Soc. of Microbiol.; Can. Med. Assn.; Ass. Med. du Que.; Can. Public Health Assn.; Can. Assn. of Med. Microbiols.; Assn. des Méd. Bactériols. du Qué.; Catholique; loisirs: golf, chasse, pêche; Résidence: 25 Vincent D'Indy, Outremont, Que. H2V 2S8 Bureau: Hôpital Notre-Dame, 1560 est, rue Sherbrooke, Montréal, Que. H2L 4M1

LEDUC, Gilles Germain, B.A., M.D., F.A.C.C., F.A.H.A.; cardiologist; educator; b. Montreal, Que. 14 Oct. 1923; s. Joseph Octave and Elise Marie (Lussier) L.; e. Univ. of Ottawa B.A. 1944; Univ. of Montreal M.D. 1950; m. Francine d. Oscar Mercier 12 Sept. 1959; children: Bertrand, Martin; CARDIOLOGIST, INSTITUT DE RECHERCHES CLINIQUES; Intern, Hôtel-Dieu de Montreal 1950; Resident 1951-52; Resident (Cardiology) St. Luke's Hosp., N.Y.C. 1952-54; Hôpital Foucicaut, Paris 1954-55; Attending Physician, Hôtel-Dieu Hosp. 1955; private practice specializing in internal medicine and cardiology, Montreal, 1955- ; Consulting Physician, St. Justine Hosp. 1956- ; Prof. of Medicine, Univ. of Montreal 1956- ; Sen. Mem., Inst. Research, Montreal; Fellow, Amer. Heart Assn.; Amer. Coll. of Cardiology; mem. Montreal Cardiac Soc. (past Pres.); Acad. Religion and Mental Health (mem. Adv. Council); Candn. Cardiovascular Soc.; author several scientific papers; Home: 82 Lockhart St., Town of Mont Royal, Que. H3P 1X8; Office: 110 Pine Ave. W., Montreal, Que. H2W 1R7

LEE, Alvin A., B.A., B.D., M.A., Ph.D.; university officer and educator; b. Woodville, Ont. 30 Sept. 1930; s. Norman Osborne and Susanna Elizabeth (Found) L.; e.

Lindsay Coll. Inst., Lindsay, Ont.; Victoria Coll., Univ. of Toronto, B.A. 1953; Emmanuel Coll. B.D. 1957, Sch. of Grad. Studies M.A. (Eng.) 1958, Ph.D. 1961; m. Annie Hope, d. George Arnott 21 Dec. 1957 children: Joanna, Monika, Fiona, Alison, Margaret; PRES: and VICE CHANCELLOR, McMASTER UNIV. 1980-; and a prof. there since 1960; Teaching Fellow, Univ. Coll. Univ. of Toronto 1957-59; Asst. Prof. of English, Assoc. and Full Prof., McMaster Univ. 1960 to present, Asst. Dean, Grad. Studies 1968-71, Dean, Grad Studies 1971-73; Vice Pres. (Academic) 1974-79 author: "James Reaney" 1968; "The Guest-Hall of Eden" 1972; co-author (with Hope Lee): "Wish and Nightmare" 1972; "Circle of Stories One" 1972; "Circle of Stories Two" 1972; "The Garden and the Wilderness" 1973; "The Temple and the Ruin" 1973; "The Peaceable Kingdom" 1974; contrib. articles in scholarly journals on Old English poetry and Candn. lit., awarded Sanford Gold Medal in Divinity, Victoria Univ.; Canada Council Pre-doctoral Fellowship, Sr. Fellowship, Leave Fellowship (twice); mem. Assn. Candn. Univ. Teachers of Eng.; Mediaeval Acad. Am.; Modern Lang. Assn.; Assn. of Univ. & Coll. Can.; Council of Univ. Pres. 1980-; Community Educ. Coordinating Comm.; Centre for Applied Res. & Eng. Design, Inc.; Dir. & Chrmn., Can. Inst. of Metalworking, 1980-; mem. Bd. of Trustees & Exec. comte., Chedoke-McMaster Hospital, 1980-; Council of Ont. Univ. 1981-82, mem. Council 1980-; Hon. Pres., Hamilton Assoc. for the Advancem. of Lit., Sc., and Art 1980-; Hon. Mem. of the Bd., Operation Lifeline, 1980-; Hon. Pres., McMaster Univ. Alumni Council, 1980-; McMaster Univ. Eng. Soc., Pres. 1981-; Hamilton-Wentworth, Extve Comm. 1980-; mem. Health Sci. Liasion Centre 1980-; Dir., Nuclear Activation Services, 1980-; mem. Bd. & Exec. Comte., Royal Botanical Gardens, 1980-; Vice Chrmn. of the Bd., Chrmn. of the Prov. and Fed. Relations Comm.; Mem. of the Scientific and Educ. Comm.; Mem. of the Nominating Comm.; United Church; recreations: gardening, swimming, hiking, canoeing, running, theatre, music, reading; Home: Stormont, West Flamborough, Ont. Office: President's Office, McMaster Univ., 1280 Main St. W., Hamilton, Ont. L8S 4L8

LEE, Betty, journalist; b. Sydney, Australia, 18 Dec. 1921; d. Albert George and Violet (Haffenden) L.; e. Sydney (Aust.) High Sch.; Univ. of Sydney; Columbia Univ.; began career in Sydney, Australia as Script Writer, Radio 2UE, 1944-46; Feature Writer and Ed., K. G. Murray Publ. Co., Sydney; Argus (morning newspaper), Melbourne, 1949-51; Reporter, Daily Mirror in London, Eng., 1951-52; Press Offr., Wembley (Eng.) Stadium, 1952-53; came to Can., Oct. 1953 as Sr. Reporter, Ed. Writer, Globe & Mail, Toronto, 1953; in 1954 became freelance writer for various U.S. publs. and later Staff Writer with Street and Smith Publs., N.Y.; returned to Globe & Mail, Toronto, as Reporter and Feature Writer, 1957; joined Maclean-Hunter Ltd. as Sr. Editor of Chatelaine, 1978; Freelance contributor to various Candn. publs. and editorial & communications consultant, 1980; joined Canadian Business, Sr. Editor 1981- author of "The Stock Market Story", "The Borrowers", "Insurance: The Magic of Averages", in Globe & Mail; "Love and Whisky, The Story of the Dominion Drama Festival" (1973); "Lutiapik" (1975); rec'd. Candn. Women's Press Club Nat. Award for Spot News Reporting (1965); Nat. Newspaper Award for Feature Writing (1966); Southam Fellow, Univ. of Toronto 1972-73; Home: Toronto, Ont.; Office: c/o Writers' Union of Canada, 24 Ryerson Ave., Toronto, Ont.

LEE, Charles Stirling, B.Sc., F.G.S.; petroleum executive; b. London, Eng., 2 Aug. 1910; s. Ethel Mary (Hartley) and late John Stevens L.; e. Cheltenham Coll., Eng.; Royal Sch. of Mines, London Univ., B.Sc. 1932, A.R.S.M. (Petroleum Technol.) 1932; m. Margery Marie, d. late W. F. Thompson, 15 July 1939; four d.; Pres., New Brunswick Oilfields Ltd.; Decalta International Corp.; The Pe-

trol Oil & Gas Co. Ltd.; Vice-Pres., Petrorep (Can.) Ltd.; Corexal Inc.; Dir., The Guaranty Trust Co. of Canada; Hudson Bay Mining and Smelting Company Limited; Pembina Pipeline Ltd.; Traders Group; with Trinidad Leaseholds Limited as Field Geol., Trinidad, B.W.I. 1933; engaged in geol. and geophysical exploration in Venezuela and B.W.I. for several years; Manager or Field Manager, numerous oil fields, Trinidad Leaseholds Ltd. 1939-45; Pres. & Dir. (1952-71) and Chmn. of Bd. and Chief Extve. Offr. (1971-77) of Western Decalta Petroleum Ltd.; Pres. of present Co. 1977; mem. Candn. Inst. Internat. Affairs (Past Pres. Calgary Br.); Independent Petroleum Assn. Can (Past Pres.); Chrmn., United Way Campaign Calgary 1978; Trustee, Fraser Institute; Calgary Chamber Comm. (Past Vice-Pres.); Kt. Round Table (Past Pres.); Y.W.C.A. Calgary (Hon. Pres.); Fellow, Geological Society of London, Eng.; Episcopalian; recreations: fishing, skiing, documentary films, woodworking; Clubs: Glencoe; Calgary Petroleum; Ranchmen's; Home: 4015 Crestview Rd. S. W., Calgary, Alta. T2T 2L5;

LEE, Dennis Beynon, M.A.; author; editor; b. Toronto, Ont., 31 August 1939, s. Walter Edgar Lorne and Jetret Emma Louise (Garbutt) L.; e. University of Toronto, B.A. 1962, M.A. 1964; m. Donna Alberta, d. Albert Youngblut, 20 May 1961; children: Kevyn, Hilary; div. 1976; former Pres. House of Anansi Press; author: "Kingdom of Absence", 1967; "Civil Elegies", 1968, rev. ed. 1972; "Wiggle to the Laundromat", 1970; "Alligator Pie", 1974; "Nicholas Knock and Other People", 1974; "The Death of Harold Ladoo", 1976; "Garbage Delight", 1977; "Savage Fields: An Essay in Literature and Cosmology", 1977; "The Gods", 1979; "The Ordinary Bath", 1979; Ed., "T.O. Now; 1968; Co-ed., "An Anthology of Verse", 1965; "Second Century Anthology of Verse", 1967; "The University Game", 1968; Address: c/o Macmillan of Can., 146 Front St. W., Toronto, Ont. M5J 1G2

LEE, Hon. James M., M.L.A.; politician; b. Charlottetown, P.E.I. 26 March 1937; s. late James Matthew and Catherine (Blanchard) L.; e. Queens Square Sch.; St. Dunstan's Univ.; m. Patricia d. late Ivan Laurie 2 July 1960; 3 children; PREMIER OF P.E.I., 1981- ; Min. of Health and Social Service, el. M.L.A. by-el. 1975, re-el. since; P. Conservative; R. Catholic; Home: 41 Centennial Dr., Sherwood, P.E.I. C1A 6C6; Premier's Office, Shaw Bldg., Box 2000, Charlottetown, P.E.I.

LEE, Leonard G., B.A.; economist; association executive; company president; b. Wadena, Sask., 17 July 1938; s. William Henry Edwin Morley and Winnifred Marcella (O'Farrel) L.; e. Archerwill High Sch., Sask., 1956; Royal Roads Mil. Coll., Dipl. Civil Engn. 1960; Royal Mil. Coll., 1961 (apptd. Cadet Wing Commdr.); Queen's Univ., B.A. (Econ.) 1963; m. Lillian Lorraine, d. Frank King, Ottawa, Ont., 9 March 1961; two s., Robin, James; PRES. LEE VALLEY TOOLS LTD. since 1978; extve. dir., nat. dairy council since 1971; Asst. Trade Commr., Ottawa, 1963-64; Consul and Asst. Trade Commr., Chicago, 1964-67; First Secy. and Head of Comm. Div., Lima, Peru, 1967-68; Extve. Asst. to Asst. Depy. Min., Dept. Indust. Trade & Comm., 1968-69; Extve. Asst. to Depy. Min., Dept. of Consumer & Corporate Affairs, 1969-70; Dir. Candn. Consumer Council, 1970-71; RCAF Flight Cadet 1968-71; nominated for Agrarian Medal of Peru 1968; Alcuin Soc.; United Church; recreations: duplicate bridge, golf, skiing, Clubs: Rideau; Home: 517 Westminster Ave., Ottawa, Ont. K2A 1T4; Office: 2680 Queensview Dr., Ottawa, Ont. K2B 8J9

LEECH, Geoffrey Bosdin, B.A.Sc., M.Sc., Ph.D., F.R.S.C.; geologist; b. Montreal, Que., 28 Aug. 1918; s. Daniel Herbert and Olive Roberta (Shepherd) L.; e. Univ. of B.C., B.A.Sc. (Geol. Engn.) 1942; Queen's Univ., M.Sc., 1943; Princeton Univ., Ph.D. (Petrol., Econ. Geol.) 1949; m. Mary Jean, d. Roy Winters, Pembroke, Ont., 1 Oct. 1946; one d. Joan Elizabeth; Dir., Econ. Geol., Geol.

Survey of Can.; Geol. Internat. Nickel Co. of Can. Ltd., 1943-46; B.C. Dept. of Mines, 1947-48; Geol., Geol. Survey of Canada 1949; investigations concerned with the mechanics of origin of Rocky Mts., genesis of mineral deposits and evaluation of mineral resources; author of over 25 articles in scient. journs.; mem., Geol. Soc. Am.; Candn. Inst. Mining & Metall.; Soc. Econ. Geol.; Comn. on Metallogenic Map of N. Am.; Geol. Assn. Can.; Assoc. Secy. Gen., Internat. Assn. on Genesis of Ore Deposits; Sigma Xi; Unitarian; Home: 1113 Greenlawn Cres., Ottawa, Ont. K2C 1Z4; Office: 601 Booth St., Ottawa, Ont. K1A 0E8

LEESON, Thomas Sydney, M.A., M.D., Ph.D., F.R.S.H.; b. Halifax, Eng., 26 Jan. 1926; s. Charles Ernest and Gladys (Stott) L.; e. Cambridgeshire High Sch., Higher Sch. Cert.; St. Catharines Coll., Cambridge, B.A., 1946, M.A. 1947, Ph.D. 1971; King's Coll. Hosp. Med. Sch., London, M.B.B. Chir. 1950; Cambridge, M.D. (by thesis) 1959; m. Catherine Mary, d. Thomas Witcomb, Newent, Glos., U.K., 6 Sept. 1952; children: Roland Paul, Susan Gillian, Helen Clare; PROF. OF ANAT., UNIV. OF ALBERTA and Chrmn. of the Dept.; Demonst. in Anat., Cambridge Univ. 1950; Lectr. in Anat., Univ. of Wales, 1955-57; Asst. Prof. in Anat., Univ. of Toronto 1957-60, Assoc. Prof. 1960; served in R.A.F.-V.R. G/D Pilot, 1945-50; R.A.F. Med. Br., 1951-55; Sqdn. Ldr., 1955-57; Med. Offr. 1957-59; co-author: "Histology" (with C. R. Leeson) 4th ed. 1981; "Human Structure" (with C. R. Leeson) 1972; "A Brief Atlas of Histology" (with C. R. Leeson) 1979; has written some 130 articles in med. and scient. journs. mainly in respect of electron microscopy; Part Inventor of Sims-Leeson Ultramicrotome 1956; Anglican; recreations: hunting, angling, rock-climbing; Address: Univ. of Alberta, Edmonton, Alta.

LEFEBVRE, Jean, B.A., B.Sc., F.S.A., F.C.I.A.; insurance executive; b. Valleyfield, Que., 25 Dec. 1934; s. Rodrigue and Marie (Perron) L.; e. Univ. de Montréal, B.A. 1953, B.Sc. 1956; F.S.A. 1964; m. Marcelle, d. Rolland Allard, 12 April 1969; one s., Jean Marc, one d. France; VICE-PRES., ACTUARY, MERCER LTD.; Dir., Excellence Life Insurance Co.; Home: 88 Burns, Beaconsfield, Que. H9W 3X4; Office: 1801 McGill College, Montreal, Que.

LEFEBVRE, Jean-Jacques, B.Litt., F.R.S.C., F.R.S.A.; writer; historian; b. St.-Philippe-de-Laprairie, Que., 4 Aug. 1905; s. late Jean and Ernestine (Poissant) L.; e. Coll. Bourget, Rigaud Qué. 1919-24; under private tutors at Montreal in philos. & sciences, 1925-26; Fac. of Philos., Univ. of Montréal, 1927-29 (Cert. of Study); B. Litt. (h.c.); unm.; Chief Archivist, Superior Court, Montreal 1947-71; Prothonotary, Dept. of Civil Status & Archives, Montreal, 1927; Depy. Prothonotary, 1929; Sr. Depy. 1940; Head Librarian & Custodian, St. Sulpice (Prov.) Library Montreal, 1944-47; Biographer, Bench and Bar of Que; 1941-76; in la "Revue du Barreau", and of Notaries in "Revue du Notariat", 1961-78; Treas. Candn. Arts Council, 1950-51; mem., Soc. Hist. de Montréal, 1928, Councillor 1936, Secy., 1938-50, and Vice-Pres. 1950-54; Antiq. and Numismat. Soc. of Montreal (Trustees of the Chateau Ramezay), Vice-Pres. 1950, Benefactor, 1962; Quebec Lib. Assn. (Pres. 1947-48; rep. at Conv. at Vancouver and San Francisco, 1947); Charter mem., Union Culturelle Française (Dir., Candn. Comte., 1954); F.R.S.C. 1956 (Pres., Sec. I, 1965); Pen & Pencil Club (Pres. 1959); P.E.N. Club, Montreal Centre (Pres. 1961-63, Del. to Internat. Cong., N.Y., 1966); Pol. Acad. N.Y.; Roy. Soc. of Arts (London), 1968-77; Soc. des Ecrivains Candn. (Treas. 1949-55, Pres. 1967, Hon. mem. 1968); Candn. Library Assn.; Candn. Hist. Assn. (Dir. 1954-56); mem., Hist. Sites and Monuments Bd. of Can., 1963-74; Pub. Records Committee of Canada 1947-54; Inst. of Translation, Univ. of Montreal (Dir.); Soc. Can. d'Hist. de l'Eglise (Dir. 1957); with Candn. del. to 10th Conv. of NATO, London, 1959; mem., Places and Streets Naming

Comte., City of Montreal, 1960; mem., Candn. Inst. of Pub. Adm., 1966; Life and Emeritus mem., Soc. Généalogique C.-F., 1968; Comte. des descendants de Sainte-Marie des Hurons, Midland, Ont.; a Lecturer; author; French translation, Wilfrid Bovey's "The French Canadians Today", 1940; "William Smith (1769-1847), His History of Canada," 1946; "Saint-Constant et Saint-Philippe de Laprairie, 1744-1946", 1947; "La Descendance de Pierre Lefèvre, de Rouen, marié à Laprairie en 1673 à Margerite Gagné", 1947; "Voyage-Eclair dans l'Ouest canadien et américain", 1948; "Le Canada, L'Amérique, Geographie, Histoire"; 8,000 art. in "Larousse Canadien", Montréal, 1954 (10th printing 1966), revised, 11,200 art., Beauchemin, Montreal, 1968, 20,000 copies (out of print 1979); "La Vie sociale du Grand Papineau" 1958; French Catalogue, Château de Ramezay", 1962; "De quelques Testaments"(from Papineau to Chapleau), 1963; "Sir Louis-H. La Fontaine, Bart. (+ 1864) Ses ascendants, ses alliés . . ." 1964; "La Famille Cartier — Sir George-Etienne Cartier", 1965; "Quelques Officiers de 1812", 1967; "La Famille Laurier, Sir Wilfrid Laurier" 1968; "Les Officiers de Milice de Laprairie en 1745" 1969; "La lignée Canadienne de Sir Thos. Chapais" 1975; 1970; "La Famille Bourassa, de Laprairie" 1971; "Le très hon. Louis S. St. Laurent, 1882-1973" 1974; "Félix-Gabriel Marchand, Premier Ministre du Québec, 1897", 1978; "Ancêtres et Contemporains", 1979; R.C.; recreations: reading, travel, meditation; Home: 3540 Durocher, Montreal, P.Q. H2X 2E5

LEFFEK, Kenneth Thomas, B.Sc., Ph.D., F.R.S. Chem., F.C.I.C., F.R.S.A.; educator; b. Nottingham, Eng. 15 Oct. 1934; s. Thomas and Ivy Louise (Pye) L.; e. Clacton Co. High Sch. 1951; Univ. Coll. London Univ. B.Sc. (Chem.) 1956, Ph.D. 1959; m. Janet Marilyn d. J. C. M. Wallace, Grimsby, Ont. 26 Sept. 1958; children: Katharine, Geoffrey; DEAN OF GRAD. STUDIES, DALHOUSIE UNIV. and Prof. of Chem. there since 1972; Postdoctoral Research Fellow Nat. Research Council Ottawa 1959-61; Asst. Prof. of Chem. present Univ. 1961, Assoc. Prof. 1967; Leverhulme Visiting Research Fellow Univ. of Kent, Canterbury, Eng. 1967-68; author over 40 research papers in phys.-organic chem.; mem. Candn. Assn. Univ. Teachers; Nat. Council Chem. Inst. Can.; recreation: camping; Club: Waegwoltic; Home: 1155 Belmont-on-the-Arm, Halifax, N.S. B3H 1J2

LEFRANCOIS, Roger, R.I.A., C.G.A., F.S.M.A.C., university executive; b. Québec City, Qué. 3 Oct. 1931; s. Philéas and Odiana (Pouliot) L.; e. Ecole supérieure Notre-Dame-de-Grâces, Qué. 1946-47; Acad. Commerciale de Qué. 1948; Univ. Laval R.I.A. 1956, C.G.A. 1961; m. Denise d. Henri Simard, Québec City, Qué. Oct. 1960; children: Louis, Danielle; VICE PRES. ADM. AND FINANCE, UNIV. DU QUEBEC since 1974, mem. Bd. Govs., Pres. of Comn. Administrative Affairs and Budget Comte., mem. Planning Comte.; Pres. Perm. Comte. of Vice Rectors, Conf. of Rectors and Principals Qué. Univs.; joined Machineries Provinciales Inc. as Controller and Offr. in affiliated co's: Eugène Falardeau Ltée, Armand Guay Inc., Compagnie de Marbre de Qué., Prefin Inc., 1963-69; Asst. Gen. Mgr., Que. Health Ins. Bd. 1969-74; author various articles cost mang.; Fellow, Soc. Mang. Accts. Can. (Hon. Treas. and mem. Extve. Comte. 1974-75, Vice Pres. 1977-78, Nat. Pres. 1978-79); mem. Cert. Gen. Accts. Assn. Que. (Dir. Quebec City Chapter 1966-67); Soc. Indust. Accts. Que. (Chrmn. Quebec City Chapter 1962-63, Pres. Prov. of Quebec 1967-68); R. Catholic; recreations: golf, skiing; Clubs: Quebec Garrison; Cercle Universitaire; Office: 2875 boul. Laurier, Ste-Foy, Qué. G1V 2M3.

LEFRANCOIS, Roland Gérard, Q.C.; transportation executive; b. Montreal, Que., 8 May 1919; s. Hon. Joseph Eugène (dec'd) and Rosina (Bélair) L.; e. St. Stanislas Primary and High Schs., Montreal, 1925-35; Jean-de-Brébeuf Coll. (Univ. of Montreal), B.A. 1939; Univ. of Montreal,

LL.L. 1942, Sch. of Comm., 1942-43; Columbia Univ., Sch. of Comm., 1943-44; m. Thérèse (dec'd), d. Hon. Joseph Jean, P.C., Q.C., Montreal 26 Feb. 1949; one child, Johane; C.O.B., Nordair Ltd.; Prudential Growth Fund Canada Ltd.; Prudential Income Fund of Can.; read law with Hyde & Ahern, Montreal; called to Bar of Que. 1942; cr. Q.C. 1961; Pres., Montreal Dist. Young Lib. Assn., 1948-49; Prov. Que. Young Lib. Fed., 1949-50; former Pres. and Chmn., Air Transport Assn. Can.; mem., Can. Bar Assn.; Chambre de Comm. du Dist. Montréal; Montreal Bd. Trade; rec'd Mérite Universitaire (Univ. of Montreal) 1943; Liberal; R. Catholic; Clubs: Mount Royal; Forest & Stream; Home: 3982 Côte des Neiges, Apt 1A, Montreal, Que. H3H 1W2; Office: Nordair Ltd., 100 Alexis Nihon Blvd., Saint Laurent, Que.

LEFSRUD, Erik Sigurd, Q.C., B.A., LL.B.; b. Viking, Alta., 25 Aug. 1933; s. late Sigurd, Q.C. and Jennie (Ness) L.; e. Univ. of Alta. B.A. 1955, LL.B. 1956; m. Helen Hazel d. Melvin Carlson, 2 June 1956; children: Erik Gregory, Kristin Lee, Karin Marie; SR. PARTNER, LEFSRUD, CUNNINGHAM, PATRICK; Lutheran; recreations: curling, golf; Club: Derrick Golf & Winter; Home: 68 Westbrook Dr., Edmonton, Alta. T6J 2E1; Office: 10232 — 112th St. Edmonton, Alta.

LEGARE, Most Rev. Henri Francis, O.M.I., LL.D., B.A., M.A., D.Sc.Soc. (R.C.) bishop; b. Willow Bunch, Sask., 20 Feb. 1918; s. Philippe and Amanda (Douville) Légaré; e. Coll. Cath. de Gravelbourg, Sask.; Sacred Heart Scholasticate (Philos. and Theol.) Lebret, Sask.; Social, Econ. and Pol. Sciences at: Laval, Cath. Univ. of America, St. Francis Xavier Univ., Catholic Univ. of Lille, France, Fribourg Univ., Switzerland; LL.D. Carleton 1959, Assumption 1960, Queen's 1961, Sask. 1963, Waterloo Lutheran 1965; ARCHBISHOP OF GROUARD-McLENNAN since 1972; Bishop of Labrador-Schefferville 1967-72; Nat. Chaplain and Executive Director, Catholic Hospital Assn. of Can.; o. Priest, June 1943; Prof. of Sociology, Laval Univ., Quebec, 1946; Treas, and Prof. at Grand Semy., St. Norbert, Manitoba, 1947-48; Prof. of Sociology, Grand Semy., St. Boniface, Man., 1950-52; Prof. of Sociology (fall term 1951), Univ. of Ottawa; Prof. of Med. Ethics, Faculty of Med., Univ. of Ottawa, 1955-58; Dean of the Faculty of Social, Econ. & Pol. Science, 1954-58, second Vice-Rector, 1955-58; Rector, 1958-64; Dir. of Studies, Oblate Prov. of Manitoba, 1966 and Prov. Superior there same year; consecrated 9 Sept. 1967; Asst. Editor of French Weekly "La Liberte et le Patriote", Winnipeg, Man., 1950-52; Editor, "L'Ami du Foyer" (mag.), 1950-52; Dir., Sch. of Social Action, St. Boniface, Man., 1951-52; mem., Internat. Acad. of Pol. Science; Candn. Welfare Council (French Comn.); mem., Ont. Cancer Treatment & Research Foundation; Pres. (1960-62), Nat. Conf. of Candn. Univs. & Colls.; Chrmn. (1960-62), Candn. Univs. Foundation; Pres., Western Catholic Conference of Bishops, 1974-80; Pres., Candn. Catholic Conference of Bishops, 1981-83; Vice-Pres., World Univ. Service of Can.; Hon. mem., "Le conseil de la vie française en Am."; Hon. Prof. of Ottawa, 1967; Address: Box 388, McLennan, Alta. T0H 2L0

LEGARE, Jacques; éducateur; né Montréal, Qué. 11 mai 1938; f. Arthur et Louisa (Laporte) L.; é. Univ. de Montréal B.Sc. 1960; Univ. de Paris Diplôme d'expert démographe 1963, Doctorat-Démographie 1969; ép. Gisèle Graton 12 décembre 1970; PROFESSEUR ET DIRECTEUR DU DEPARTEMENT DE DEMOGRAPHIE, UNIV. DE MONTREAL depuis 1973; Professeur à l'Université de Montréal depuis 1965, Directeur du Departement de démographie depuis 1973, Professeur titulaire depuis 1974; auteur "Démométrie et planification des ressources humaines" 1972; en collaboration "Evolution démographique du Québec et de ses régions 1966-86" 1969; "Repertoire des actes de baptême mariage, sépulture et des recensements du Québec ancien", 1980; mem. Société Royale du Can.; Union internationale pour l'étude scientifique de la population; Population Assn. Am.; Candn. Population Soc.; Assn. des démographes du Qué.; Adresse: 5637 Plantagenet, Montréal, Qué. H3T 1S3; Bureau: Montréal, Qué. H3C 3J7.

LEGAULT, Albert, M.A., (Hon.) Dr. de l'U. (Paris); educator; b. Montreal, Que. 7 June 1938; s. Fortunat and Félécilda (Geoffrion) L.; e. Coll. St-Laurent B.A. 1959; Univ. of Chicago M.A. 1961; Grad. Inst. Internat. Studies Geneva, Docteur ès sciences politiques 1964; Univ. de Paris-Sud, Dr. de l'U. (Paris) 1976; m. Cosima d. Max Dittus 27 July 1964; one d. Cornelia; PROF. OF POL. SCIENCE, LAVAL UNIV. since 1969; Dir. Gen., Centre québécois de relations internationales since 1973; Lectr., Grad. Inst. Internat. Affairs, Geneva 1964-66; Asst. Dir. Internat. Information Centre on Peace-Keeping Operations, Paris 1966-68; Visiting Prof. Chair of Strategic Studies, Queen's Univ. 1968-69; co-author "The Dynamics of Nuclear Balance" 1974, French and German transls.; over 40 articles scient. journs. and newspapers; mem. Internat. Inst. Strategic Studies; Internat. Studies Assn; Internat. Peace Acad.; Atlantic Inst.; Candn. Inst. Internat. Affairs (Assoc. Extve. Dir. since 1975); Task Force to Review Unification of the Armed Forces, 1979; Can. Expert, U.N. Study Group on Nuclear Weapons, 1979; Special Adv., Dept. of Nat. Defence, Ottawa, Sept 1980- ; R. Catholic; Home: 2038 blvd. Laurier, Sillery, Qué. G1T 1B6; Office: Pavillon de Koninck, Laval Univ., Québec, Qué. G1K 7P4.

LEGAULT, Hon. Fernand; judge; b. Lachute, Que., 27 June 1912; s. Louis Lorenzo, Q.C., and Georgiana (Paiement) L.; e. Montreal Coll.; Loyola Coll.; Univ. of Montreal; m. Beverley d. Arthur W. DeWolf, 30 April 1949; children: Pierre, Anne, Marie-Claire; JUSTICE, SUPERIOR COURT OF QUE., since 1963; called to the Bar of Que. 1936; cr. Q.C. Jan. 1951; Crown Atty. for many yrs.; prior to appt. to the Bench was Sr. mem. of law firm of Legault & Legault; formerly Pres. of Liberal Assn. of Co. Argenteuil, Pres. of Cath. Sch. Comn. of Lachute and Mayor of Town of Lachute, Past Pres., Rural Bar of Que., Bâtonnier (Pres.) of Laurentians Bar and Offr. of Que. Sec. of Candn. Bar Assn.; K. of C.; Roman Catholic; recreations: golf, skiing, swimming; Clubs: Lachute Golf & Country; Seigniory; M.A.A.A.; Home: 656 Sydney St. Lachute, Que. J8H 1L8; Office: 10 St. Antoine East, Montreal, Que. H2Y 1A2

LEGAULT, Ivan A., L.és Sc.; Fed. Public Servant; b. Ste-Adèle, Que., 4 March 1923; s. J. Albert and Marie-Rose (Gauvreau) L.; e. Ste-Agathe-des-Monts, Que.; L'Ecole Moyenne d'Agriculture de Mont-Laurier, Dipl. 1939; Univ. de Montréal, Dipl. Indust. Relations 1948, L.ès Sc. Soc. (Public Admin. 1950; m. Marthe, d. Rodrique Nadon, 8 Oct. 1949; children: Marie France, Pierre, Céline; DIR., CONSULTATIVE SER., CAN. EMPLOYMENT FOR QUE. REGION; served with Confédération des Travailleurs Catholiques du Can. as Tech. advisor with Fédération des travailleurs de l'industrie chimique, 1948-57; Extve. Dir., Que. Fed. of Labour, 1958-66; joined pregent Fed. as Extve. Secy. 1957; Sec., Enquiry Comm. on St. LawrencePorts 1966-68; joined present Fed. as Extve. Secy. 1957; founding co-secretary N.D.P.; ex-mem., Regional Comte., Placement de la Prov. Que.; N.D.P.; R. Catholic; recreations: gardening, reading, fishing, hunting, camping, beekeeping; Office: 550 Sherbrooke W., Montreal, Que.

LEGAULT, Maurice J., D.B.A.; b. Montreal, Que., 31 May 1926; s. Adolphe and Georgette (Trudel) L.; e. Elem. Sch., Champagnat, Montreal, Que. 1940; Fortin Bus. Coll., Montreal 1941; Sir Geo. Williams Univ. 1943; Univ. of W. Ont. (Marketing and Mang. Courses); D.B.A., Adm., Sherbrooke Univ.; m. Françoise, d. late Arthur Bastien, 1 June 1946; children: Monique, Robert, Normand; SR. VICE PRES., JOHN LABATT LTD., since 1977; Pres., Les Placements NOROMO Inc.; Dir., The Ogilvie Flour Mills Co.; with Quebec Liquor Commission, Accountant, Accounting Department and Inventory Control 1945; Mgr., Columbia Pure Spring Bottling Co., L'Epiphanie, Que. 1952; Rep.-Supv., Labatt Brewery Ltd. 1954, Chief Supv. 1956, Montreal Sales Mgr. 1957, Terr. Sales Mgr. 1959, Gen. Sales Mgr. 1964, Dir. of Marketing 1966, Vice-Pres. and Dir. of Marketing 1968, Vice-Pres. and Gen. Mgr. 1970, Pres. 1975; served in 2nd World War, R.C.A.F. 1943-44, AC2; Dir., La Cie d'Ass. Urgel Bourgie Ltée.; Théâtre de Marjolaine; Candn. Cancer Soc.; Life Gov., Notre Dame Hosp.; Fondation des Diplômés H.E.C.; Investissements Noromo Inc.; Travelling Salesmen Association Canada; Montreal Chamber Commerce; Assoc. des Diplômes H.E.C.; Canadian Chamber Comm.; K. of C.; R. Catholic; recreations: golf, fishing, hunting, skiing, photography, reading; Clubs: St-Denis; Laval-sur-le-Lac; St-Laurent Kiwanis; Lac d'Argent Fishing & Hunting; Longchamp Golf; Home: 120 François, Ile des Soeurs, Verdun, Qué. H3E 1E2; Office: P.O. Box 597, Place Bonaventure, Montreal, Que. H5C 1C5

LEGER, Rev. Hector, retired, B.A., S.Th.L., Ph.D. (R.C.) b. St. Anthony, N.B., 18 Jan. 1911; s. Ferdinand and Marie-Blanche (Allain) L.; e. St. Joseph's Univ., B.A. 1930, Ph.D. 1949; entered Holy Cross Order 1930; Grand Semy., Montreal, 1931-35; S.Th.L. 1935; Prov. Superior of Holy Cross Order, Acadian Province 1945-68; Prof. of Philos., St. Laurent Coll., Montreal, 1935-36; St. Joseph's Univ. 1936-41; Prof. of Theol., Holy Cross Semy., St. Genevieve, Que., 1941-44; Dir. there 1942-44; Pres., St. Joseph's Univ., 1944-48; Extve. Secy. of CRC-A (Atlantic Provs.) 1970-72; Chaplain, N.D.S.C. Motherhouse, Moncton 1969-79; Address: 24 Kendra St., Apt. 4, Moncton, N.B. E1C 4J8

LEGER, Joseph Claudius Ignace de Loyola, Q.C., B.C.L.; b. Saint John, N.B. 9 Sept. 1920; s. Jean Edmond and Léona Béatrice Marie (Johnson) L.; e. Moncton High Sch. 1940; St-Joseph Univ.; St-Thomas Univ.; Univ. of N.B. B.C.L. 1946; m. Lorraine Catherine d. late Adolphe L. Comeau 4 Sept. 1950; called to Bar of N.B. 1946; cr. Q.C. 1962; M.L.A. 1948-52; JUSTICE, SUPREME COURT OF N.B. mem. Candn. Bar Assn.; R. Catholic; recreation: golf; Club: Moncton City; Home: 224 MacBeath Ave., Moncton, N.B. E1C 7A3.

LÉGER, Hon. Marcel, M.N.A., B.A.; politician; b. Montréal, Qué. 8 June 1930; s. Arthur and Juliette (Doherty) L.; e. Ste-Marie Coll.; Univ. of Montréal; m. Jeanne D'Arc d. Edouard Lamontagne, Montréal 13 Sept. 1952; children: Francine, Nicole, Françoise, Hélène, Jean Marc; MIN. OF THE ENVIRONMENT, QUE. 1976 and 1981; Party Whip; Pres. Lumen Inc.; SIFAR Inc.; el. M.N.A. for Lafontaine prov. g.e. 1970, re-el. since; mem. St. Jean Baptiste Soc.; K. of C.; Parti Quebecois; R. Catholic; Office: 2360, Chemin Ste-Foy, Ste-Foy, Qué. G1V 4H2.

LEGER, Cardinal, His Eminence, Paul-Emile, C.C. (1968), L.Th., J.C.L., S.T.D., D.C.L., LL.D., D.Hum.Litt., K.H.S. (1950), Kt Grand Cross of Legion of Hon. (France 1958); b. Valleyfield, Que.; s. Ernest Leger and Alda (Beauvais); ; e. Montreal and Paris; o. 1929 (Sulpician Order); D.Litt., Assumption Coll. 1954; LL.D. McGill 1960, St. Francis Xavier 1961, Toronto 1965, Alberta 1967, D.C.L. Bishop's 1965; S.T.D. Laval 1951, Ottawa 1961; D.Hum.Litt. Waterloo 1969; Doctor Honoris Causa, Univ. of Montreal 1974; Doctor Honoris Causa, Univ. of Sherbrooke 1974; Doctor Honoris Causa, Univ. of Kingston, 1979; taught Philos. at Sulpician Semy., Fukuoka, Japan (which he founded), 1933-39; taught Sulpician Semy., Montreal, Que., 1939-40; Vicar Gen., Diocese of Valleyfield, 1940-47; Rector of Pontifical Candn. College, Rome, 1947-50; Archbishop of Montreal, 1950-53; cr. a Cardinal (6th in Can.) by Pope Pius XII, 12 Jan. 1953; resigned as Archbishop of Montreal to undertake missionary work, 9 Nov. 1967; left Can. for Africa 11 Dec. 1967; D. Th., Laval, 1951; D.ésL. l'Assomption, Mass., 1954; Sovereign Order of Malta, 1954; Papal Legate at closing

of Marian Year, Lourdes, 1954, Papal Legate for crowning of Statue of St. Joseph, 1955; to Ste. Anne de Beaupré, Tercentenary of the Sanctuary, 1958; Nomination as Parish Priest St. Madelaine Sophie Barat's Parish, 1974; Resignation as Parish Priest, 1975; Return to Africa, 1976; Return to Canada 1979; Sept. '79-Feb. 80 Co-Pres. Can. Foundation for Refugees; mem., Central Comn. preparatory to Council Vatican II, 1961; Council Comn. on Sacred Theol., 1962; Council Vatican Comn. on Canon Law, 1963; Council of Propagation of the Faith (Roma) 1972; Pontifical Commission for the Pastoral of Tourism (Roma) 1972; named a mem. of the Vatican Consistorial Cong., Apl. 1963; awarded Grand Cross de Benemerencia Republic of Portugal 1965; mem. Del. of Candn. Bishops, Synod of Bishops, Rome 1967; Royal Bank of Canada award for service to humanity 1969; Commdr. de l'ordre de la valeur et du mérite de la République du Cameroun 1972; rec'd. (2nd) Loyola Medal, 1967; Humanitarian Awd. of Variety Clubs Internat'l, 1976; Pearson Medal for Peace, 1979; Golden Jubilee of Priesthood; rec'd. "The Annual Man of the year Award", 1980; Address: c/o Cardinal Leger and His Endeavours, 130 Ave. de L'Epré, Montreal, Que. H2V 3T2 and C.P. 1500, Stn. A. Montreal, Que. H3L 2Z9

LEGERE, Martin J., O.C. (1974), M.Sc.Com., D.Sc.Soc., D.Sc.Adm., LL.D.; banker; b. Caraquet, N.B., 17 November 1916; s. Jean J. and Beatrice (Godin) L.; e. Caraquet (N.B.) Sch.; St-Francis-Xavier Univ.; Laval Univ.; Hon. M.Sc.Com., St. Joseph 1950; D.Sc.Soc., Sacred Heart Univ. 1953; D.Sc.Adm., Moncton 1971; LL.D. St. Francis Xavier 1974; m. Anita Godin, 5 June 1950; children: Louise, Louis, René, Claude; GENERAL MANAGER, LA FEDERATION DES CAISSES POPULAIRES ACADIENNE LTEE since 1946; Pres., of newspaper L'Evangeline, 1980. General Manager, La Société d'Assurance des Caisses Populaires Acadienne; L'Institute de Coopération Acadien (1978); Secretary, L'Union Coopérative Acadienne; Director, La Caisse Populaire de Caraquet, 1938-72; Co-Operative Fire and Casualty Insurance, 1964-77; Co-operative Life Insurance, 1964-77; Co-operative Insurance Services, 1964-77; La Compagnie de Gestion Atlantique Ltée; started career as Fieldman, Co-op. Movement, St-Francis-Xavier Univ., Antigonish, N.S. 1938; Auditor of Credit Unions, Prov. of N.B. 1940; Pres., Le Conseil Candn. de la Co-op; La Co-op. de Caraquet; N.B. (1947-78) Finance Bd., 1960-76; Secy., Chambre de Comm. de Caraquet; Treas., La Ville Beauséjour of Caraquet; Dir., La Société des Artisans; Le Conseil de Vie Française; Caraquet Hosp., 1960-75; Prés., Les Deuvres de Presse Acadienne, 1977; mem. Adv. Bd., Bathurst Coll., 1970-73; mem. Central Comte., Internat. Co-op. Alliance; Mun. Councillor 1950-55; Treas., Children's Aid Soc., Gloucester Co. 1948-66; Pres., Catholic Youth Assn. 1940-50; Dir., Atlantic Provs. Econ. Council 1956-62; mem. A8. Comte., Community Devel. Corp. (N.B.) 1965-66; awarded "Bene Merentis" medal by His Holiness Pope Pius XII, 1950; mem. Order of La Pleiade, 1980; Knight of Order of St. Lazarus of Jerusalem 1981; mem. Club des Cent Associes, 1980; mem. Internat. Platform Assn.; Club: Richelieu; Home: 312 W., Blvd. St. Pierre, Caraquet, N.B. E0B 1K0; Office: Caraquet, N.B. E0B 1K0

LEGG, Hon. Hugh P., B.A., LL.B.; judge; b. Whitley Bay, Eng. 13 Feb. 1922; s. Percival and Kate (Phillips) L.; e. Whitley Bay (Eng.) Grammer Sch. 1938; Univ. of B.C. B.A., LL.B. 1951; m. Marie Margaret d. late John J. Conway 24 June 1944; children: Elizabeth Straysky, Marie Tambellini, Hugh Conway, Phillip, Sarah; JUSTICE, SUPREME COURT OF B.C. since 1976; read law with Guild Yule & Co.; called to Bar of B.C. 1951; cr. Q.C. 1972; joined firm Lawson Lundell & Co. Vancouver 1956, Partner 1959 and subsequently Sr. Counsel until present appt.; served with RAF 1941-46, Pilot S.E. Asia Command, rank Sqdn. Leader; Bencher Law Soc. B.C. 1968-76 (Treas. 1975-76); mem. B.C. Council Candn. Bar Assn.

1961-64; Extve. Vancouver Bar Assn. 1960-61; recreation: golf; Clubs: University; Shaughnessy Golf; Home: 1826 Blanca St., Vancouver, B.C. V6R 4E5; Office: 800 Smithe St., Vancouver, B.C. V6Z 2E1

LEGGE, Laura, Q.C., B.A., R.N.; b. Delhi, Ont., 27 Jan. 1923; d. James and Lucy (Pratt) Down; e. Univ. of W. Ont. B.A. 1944; Toronto Gen. Hosp. Sch. of Nursing, R.N. 1945; Osgoode Hall Law Sch. 1948; m. Bruce Jarvis Legge, 21 July 1950; children: Elizabeth (Mrs. George Meanwell), John Bruce Jarvis, Bruce Richard Warren; PARTNER, LEGGE & LEGGE, with husband, Maj. Gen. B.J. Legge, CMM, CS&J, ED, CD, QC; called to Bar of Ont. 1948; cr. Q.C. 1966; Solr., Ont. Dept. of Health 1948-54; el. Bencher Law Soc. Upper Can. 1975 and 1979; Dir., Home Care Program of Metro Toronto; Dir. and Vice Pres. Ont. Safety League; mem. Candn. Bar Assn. (Council 1964-66); Soroptimist Club Toronto (Pres. 1974-1976); Women's Law Assn. Ont. (Pres. 1964-66); appointed mem. Council of Ont. Coll. of Art., 1980; Anglican; Home: 301 Lonsdale Rd., Toronto, Ont. M4V 1X3; Office: 60 St. Clair Ave. E., Toronto, Ont. M4T 1N5

LEGGET, Robert Ferguson, O.C. (1967), M.E., D.Eng., D.G.Sc., LL.D., D.Sc., F.R.S.C. (1956),; b. Liverpool, Eng., 29 Sept. 1904; s. Donald and Mercy (Thomson) L.; e. Merchant Taylor's Sch., Great Crosby, Eng.; Univ. of Liverpool, B.E. (Hons.) 1925, M.E. 1927; LL.D. McMaster, 1961, Queen's 1966, New Brunswick 1969, Toronto 1969, Glasgow 1971; D.Sc. Waterloo, 1963, Western 1969; D.G.Sc., Charles (Prague) 1969; D.Eng. Liverpool 1971; Nova Scotia Tech. Coll., 1972; D.Sc. Clarkson Coll. of Technol. 1972; Sir George Williams Univ. 1972; D.Eng. Carleton 1974; m. Lillian S., d. S. A. Free, Stratford, England, 28 February 1931; has one s., David; Assistant Engineer, C. S. Meik and Buchanan, Westminster, England, 1925-29; Resident Engr., Power Corporation of Canada Ltd., engaged on water power projects 1929-32; Engr., Candn. Sheet Piling Co. Ltd., Montreal, 1932-36; Lectr. in Civil Engn., Queen's Univ., 1936-38; Asst. Prof. of Civil Engn., Univ. of Toronto, 1938-43; Assoc. Prof. 1943-47; Dir., Div. Building Research, Nat. Research Council 1947-69; 1st recipient, Medaille d'or, Candn. Council Prof. Engrs. 1972; Julian C. Smith Medal 1971, Sir John Kennedy Medal 1978, Engn. Inst. Can.; Logan Gold Medal, Geol. Assn. Can. 1972; Leo B. Moore Gold Medal, Standards Engrs. Soc. 1974; Dumont Gold Medal, Geol. Soc. of Belgium 1976; 1st recipient, Wm. Smith Medal, Geol. Soc. of London 1977; Hon. Fellow, Inst. of Civil Engineers (London) 1980; Hon. M. ASCE, American Society of Civil Engineers (1977); Hon. Fellow, Royal Arch. Inst. Can.; Assn. Prof. Engrs. of Ont.; Pres., Am. Soc. for Testing and Materials, 1965-66; Pres., Geol. Soc. Am. 1966; Pres., Internat. Council on Building Research 1966-69; author of "Geology and Engineering", 1939, 2nd ed. 1962; "Rideau Waterway", 1955; "Standards in Canada", 1970; "Railways of Canada", 1973; "Cities and Geology", 1973; "Ottawa Waterway", 1975; "Canals of Canada", 1976; "Cdn. Railways in Pictures", 1977; "The Seaway", 1979; joint author (with C. P. Disney), "Modern Railroad Structure", 1949; Editor, "Soils in Canada", 1961 and "Reviews in Engineering Geology" Vol. 1 (with T. W. Fluhr), 1962; ed., "Glacial Till", 1976; has contributed numerous papers on engn. and research in field of soil mechanics; Home: 531 Echo Dr., Ottawa, Ont. K1S 1N7

LEHMANN, Carla (Hillerns); actress; b. Winnipeg, Man., 26 Feb. 1917; d. Dr. Julius Edouard and Elsa Louisa (Hillerns) L.; e. Grosvenor Sch.; Gordon Bell Jr. High Sch.; Riverbend Girls' Sch.; Rupert's Land Ladies' Coll. (Grad. 1934), all of Winnipeg, Man.; Royal Acad. of Dramatic Art, London, 1935-36; m. George Anderson McDowell Elliott, s. Brig. Gen. Gilbert Elliott, 5 May 1941; made first appearance on stage at Repertory Theatre, Croydon, Eng., Sept. 1936, as Lydia Kent in "Dusty Ermine"; first appearance in London at Apollo Theatre as Nora Stockton in "People at Sea"; subsequently acted

parts in "Mary Goes to See", 1938; "Banana Bridge", 1938; "Spotted Dick", 1939; "The Nutmeg Tree", 1941; "The Young and Lovely", 1943; "Appointment With Death", 1945; first appeared in motion pictures in "So This Is London", 1938; Conservative; Protestant; recreations: riding, reading, walking, talking; Address: c/o Playhouse Country Club, Cove Rd., Fleet, Hants, Eng.

LEHMANN, Heinz E., O.C., M.D., F.R.S.C.; psychiatrist; b. Berlin, Germany 17 July 1911; s. Richard R. and Emmy (Grönke) L.; e. Mommsen Gymnasium, Berlin 1920-1929; Univ. of Freiburg 1929, 1930-31; Univ. of Marburg 1929-30; Univ. of Vienna 1932-33; Univ. of Berin 1934 M.D. 1935; m. Annette d. late Urbain Joyal 28 July 1940; one s. François; EMERITUS PROF. OF PSYCHIATRY, McGILL UNIV. 1981; Prof. of Psychiatry 1965-81; Visiting Prof. Univ. of Cincinnati; mem. Research Adv. Comte. Dept. Mental Health State of N.Y.; Hon. Consultant Royal Victoria Hosp.; Douglas Hosp. (Verdun); Lakeshore Gen. Hosp. (Pointe Claire); Montreal Gen. Hosp.; Reddy Mem. Hosp. (Montreal); St. Mary's Hosp. (Montreal); Psychiatrist, Verdun Prot. Hosp. 1935-47; Clin. Dir. Douglas Hosp. Verdun 1947, Dir. of Research 1966-76; Chrmn. Dept. Psychiatry McGill Univ. 1971-74, Dir. Div. Psychopharmacol. 1976-77; Dir. of Research Operations, Dept. of Research for Mental Health, State of N.Y., 1979-80; Deputy Commissioner of Research, Office of Mental Health, State of New York, U.S.A., 1981-; rec'd Albert Lasker Award 1957; Fellow, The Royal Society of Canada (1970); Officer of the Order of Canada, (1976).; The Taylor Manor Hospital Psychiatric Award, 1978; The Psychiatric Outpatient Centres of America Award, 1980; L.L.D.(Hon.c.) Univ. of Calgary, 1980; co-author "Handbook of Psychiatric Treatment in Medical Practice" 1962; "Pharmacotherapy of Tension and Anxiety" 1970; "Experimental Approaches to Psychiatric Diagnosis" 1971; author book chapters and over 300 prof. publs. on psychiatry and psychopharmacol.; mem. Am. Coll. Neuropsychopharmacol. (Past Pres.); Collegium Internat. Neuro-Psychopharmacologium (Past Pres.); Candn. Psych. Assn.; Am. Psych. Assn.; Liberal; recreations: skiing, scuba diving, astronomy, gem collecting, lapidary; Home: 1212 Pine Ave. W., Apt. 908, Montreal, Que. H3G 1A9; Office: 1033 Pine Ave. W., Montreal, Que. H3A 1A1.

LEIGHTON, David, B.A., M.B.A., D.B.A., LL.D.; writer; educator; b. Regina, Sask., 20 Feb. 1928; s. Gordon Ernest and Mary Haskins (Robertson) L.; e. Glebe Coll. Inst., Ottawa, Ont., 1941-46; Queen's Univ., B.A. 1950 (Tricolour Soc.); Univ. of Toronto, 1950-51; Harvard Univ. (George F. Baker Scholar), M.B.A. 1953, D.B.A. 1956; m. Margaret Helen, d. John Albert House, St. Catharines, Ont., 25 Aug. 1951; children: Douglas, Bruce, Katharine, Jennifer, Andrew; Dir., Banff Sch. of Fine Arts and Centre for Continuing Educ.; formerly Prof., Univ. of W. Ont.; Dir., Scott's Hospitality Inc.; Gulf Canada Ltd.; Canadian Appliance Manufacturing Co. Ltd.; GSW Ltd.; Rio Algom Ltd.; Lornex Mining Corp.; John Wiley and Sons Ltd.; Standard Brands Ltd.; Dir. and Past Chrmn. (1st) Candn. Consumer Council; Gov., Glenbow-Alberta Inst.; Council on Bus. & the Arts; Resources for the Future Inc.; New Western Film & Television Foundation; Marketing Science Inst.; co-author: "Problems in Marketing" (2nd ed.), 1957, "Canadian Problems in Marketing", 1959 (rev. ed. 1965); "How Industry Buys", 1959 (won Media-Scope Award 1960); "The Distribution of Packaged Consumer Goods: An Annotated Bibliography", 1963; co-ed., "Marketing in Canada", 1958; author: "International Marketing", 1965; "Candn. Marketing: Problems and Prospects", 1973; "Case Problems in Marketing", 1973; mem., Am. Marketing Assn. (Founding Pres., London Chapter, 1958-61; Nat. Dir. 1964-66; Vice-Pres. 1969-70; Nat. Pres. 1971-72; Internat. Marketing Fed. Pres. 1972-73); recreations: tennis, skiing, music,; Home: 101 St. Julien Rd., Banff, Alta. T0L 0C0

LEIR, Rear Admiral Richard Hugh, C.D.; naval officer; b. Penticton, B.C., 19 Nov. 1921; s. Hugh Carlton Musgrove and Joyce Lillias Nita (Hassell) L.; e. Penticton (B.C.) Pub. Sch.; Shawnigan Lake Sch., 1939; Royal Naval Staff Coll., 1955-56; Nat. Defence Coll., 1968-69; m. Valerie Constance, d. late Alexander Hayward-Hawkins, 19 June 1948; children: Michael R., Andrew A., Vivian V.; served on HMS Prince of Wales 1940-41 (sunk); HMS Exeter 1942 (sunk); Japanese P.O.W., Dutch E. Indies, 1942-45; Gunnery Offr., E. Mediterranean, HMS Chevron, 1946-48; Operations Offr., Korean War, HMCS Athabaskan, 1949-51; 2nd-in-Command, HMCS Sioux, 1952-53; C.O. HMCS Crusader, 1953-55; Commandant, Fleet Sch., Halifax, 1957-58; 2nd-in-Command, HMCS Bonaventure, 1958-60; C.O. HMCS Skeena, 1961-62; HMCS Venture, 1962-63; Commandant, Naval Coll. First Candn. Escort Sqdn., Halifax, 1964-65; Candn. Commdr. Afloat, Halifax, 1966-68; Chief of Recruiting and Training, 1969-70; Commdr. Maritime Forces Pacific 1970; promoted Commdr. 1955; Capt. 1962; Commodore 1966; Rear Adm. 1970; Anglican; recreations: tennis, squash, sailing; Club: Union

LEISHMAN, John David, M.D., F.R.C.S.(C); consultant; director; b. Shoal Lake, Man. 2 Apr. 1911; s. Arnot G. V. and Ethel (Murray) L.; e. Univ. of Man. M.D. 1935; L.M.C.C. 1935; m. Gertrude E. d. late Clyde Lake, June 1942; children: David, Susan, Trudy Ann; Dir. Highland Crow Resources; Dir. Teck Corp.; Mutual Life Assurance Co. of Canada; med. Practice Iroquois Falls, Ont. 1937-39; Fort Francis, Ont. 1939-40; Urol., Regina Sask. 1946-65; Pres. and Chrmn. Canadian Devonian Petroleums 1951-61; served with R.C.A.M.C. 1940-45, rank Maj., Eng. Sicily, Italy; Past Pres. P. Cons. Assn. Sask.; Past Chrmn. Regina Un. Appeal; mem. Candn. Med. Assn.; Sask. Med. Assn.; B.C. Med. Assn.; Delta Upsilon; Freemason; P. Conservative; United Church; recreations: golf, fishing; Club: Arbutus; Home: 635 Glenmaroon, West Vancouver, B.C. V7S 1P5;

LEISS, William, M.A., Ph.D.; educator; b. New York City, N.Y. 28 Dec. 1939; s. William and Ethel (Walter) L.; e. Fairleigh Dickinson Univ. B.A. 1960; Brandeis Univ. M.A. 1963; Univ. of Cal. San Diego Ph.D. 1969; m. Marilyn Lawrence 20 Sept. 1973; PROF. AND CHRMN. OF COMMUNICATION SIMON FRASER UNIV. 1980- ; Asst and Assoc. Prof. of Pol. Science Univ. of Regina 1968-73; Assoc. Prof. of Environmental Studies York Univ. 1973-75, Prof. of Pol. Science & Environmental Studies 1976-79; Assoc. Prof. of Sociol. Univ. of Toronto 1975-76; author "The Domination of Nature" 1972; "The Limits To Satisfaction" 1976, Revised ed. 1979; Ed. "Ecology Versus Politics in Canada" 1979; various journ. articles technol., social theory, human needs and environment; mem. Candn. Pol. Science Assn.; Candn. Communications Assn.; recreations: cooking, sports, wine, old furniture; Office: Dept. of Communication, Simon Fraser Univ., Burnaby, B.C. V5A 1S6.

LEITCH, Hon. Clarence Mervin, Q.C., LL.B.; politician; lawyer; b. Creelman, Sask. 13 Jan. 1926; s. Peter Harold and Martha (Walker) L.; e. Sask. and Alta.; Univ. of Alta. LL.B. 1952 (Gold Medal); m. Margaret Joyce (d.) d. William Morris, Calgary, Alta. 17 Apl. 1954; children: Hugh Campbell, Margaret Jan, Catherine Anne, James Harold; m. Ardine Brissette, 23 Feb. 1980; MIN. OF ENERGY AND NATURAL RESOURCES, ALTA. since 1979; called to Bar of Alta. 1953; cr. Q.C. 1967; practiced law Macleod, Dixon, Calgary 1952-71; mem Extve. P. Cons. Party Alta. 1965-69; el. M.L.A. 1971, re-el. since; apptd. Atty. Gen. and Prov. Secretary 1971; Prov. Treas. 1975; served with R.C.N 1943-45; mem. Police Comn. City of Calgary 1966-69; mem. Council, Candn. Bar Assn.; Past Pres. Calgary Bar Assn.; Bencher, Law Soc. Alta.; P. Conservative; Anglican; recreations: golf, skiing; Clubs: Calgary Golf & Country; Mayfair Golf & Country (Edmonton); Home:

7907 Buena Vista Rd., Edmonton, Alta. T5R 5R3; Office 407 Legislature Bldg., Edmonton, Alta. T5K 2B6.

LEITCH, John Daniel; company president; b. Winnipeg Man., 11 Jan. 1921; s. late Gordon Clifford and Hilda (Bawden) L.; e. Appleby Coll., Oakville, Ont.; Trinity Coll., Univ. of Toronto; m. Margaret Beatrice, (d. 8 Nov 1979) d. Hon. Mr. Justice J. R. Cartwright, Ottawa, Ont. 14 June 1941; two d.; PRESIDENT, UPPER LAKES SHIPPING LTD.; Vice-Pres. and Dir., Canadian Imperial Bank of Commerce; Dir., Dom. Foundries & Steel Ltd.; Massey-Ferguson Ltd.; American Airlines Inc.; Home: 61 St Clair Ave. West, Apt. 509 Toronto, Ont. M4V 2Y8; Office 49 Jackes Ave., Toronto, Ont. M4T 1E2

LEITCH, Lorne Campbell, LL.B., M.B.A.; university administrator; b. Kerrobert, Sask., 6 Sept. 1925; s. Peter and Margaret Elizabeth (McLeod) L.; e. Pub. Schs., Winnipeg, Man. 1943; Univ. of Manitoba, LL.B. 1949; Univ. of Chicago, M.B.A. 1951; m. Kathleen Claire, d. R. B. McIntosh, 6 Sept. 1958; children: Christopher Lorne, Andrew Scott, Paul Robert; VICE-PRESIDENT (FINANCE AND ADM.) UNIV. OF ALBERTA, since 1972; read law with Parker, Parker, Hunter and Hamlin, Winnipeg, Man. called to Bar of Man. 1952; with Great-West Life Assurance Co. as Mortgage Analyst 1951, Asst. Treas. 1957 joined present Univ. as Assoc. Prof., Faculty of Comm 1961, Acting Chrmn., Div. Business Operations 1963 Acting Dean, Faculty Business Adm. and Comm. 1969 Assoc. Vice-Pres. (Finance and Adm.) 1970; Dir., Edmonton Opera Assoc.; Cdn. Assoc. of University Business Officers; Glenrose Hospital; Edmonton Research Park Authority; mem. Law Soc. of Man.; Candn. Assn. Univ Teachers; United Church; recreations: swimming, skiing Clubs: Royal Glenora; University; Home: 14008-76 Ave. Edmonton, Alta. T5R 2Z5; Office: 114 St. and 89 Ave. Edmonton, Alta.

LEITH, James Andrews, M.A., Ph.D. F.R.S.C.; university professor; b. Toronto, Ont., 26 Oct. 1931; s. Matthew Andrews and Harriette Emily (Ball) L.; e. E. York Coll Inst., Toronto, 1949; B.A. (Modern Hist.), Univ. of Toronto, 1953; M.A. (Hist.), Duke Univ., 1955; Ph.D (Hist.), Univ. of Toronto, 1960; m. Carole May, d. late Marshall Peter Lang Wood, 16 June 1956; children: Margot, Marc; PROF., DEPT. OF HIST., QUEEN'S UNIV., since 1968 (Chrmn. 1968-73); Lectr. in Hist., Univ. o Sask., 1958-61; joined present Univ. as Lectr., 1961-62 Asst. Prof., 1962-64; Assoc. Prof., 1964-68; Visiting Prof., Cornell Univ., spring semester 1964 and St. Antony's Coll. Oxford 1970-71; Australian Nat. Univ. 1974-75; R H. McLaughlin Research Professorship, 1965-66; has held maj. research grants from Royal Soc. of Can., Social Sci ences and Humanities Research Council, Can. Counci and the French Government; el. to Royal Soc. of Can. 1980; author of "The Idea of Art as Propaganda in France 1750-1799: A Study in the History of Ideas", 1965, "Media and Revolution: Moulding a New Citizenry in France during the Terror", 1968, "Facets of Education in the Eighteenth Century" 1977, "Images of the Commune/Im ages de la Commune", 1978, and numerous articles and reviews in scholarly journs.; mem. Soc. Française d'Etude du XVIIIe Siècle and Soc. Internat. d'Etude du XVIIIe Siècle; mem., Candn. Hist. Assn.; Am. Hist Assn.; Soc. for French Hist. Studies; Soc. d'Histoire Moderne; Candn. Soc. for Eighteenth Century Studies; recre ation: oil painting; field naturalism; photography; Home 1098 Johnson St., Kingston, Ont. K7M 2N5

LEITHEAD, William Grier, B.Arch., F.R.A.I.C., R.C.A F.A.I.A. (Hon.); architect; b. Northallerton, Yorks, Eng. 16 Oct. 1920; s. Matthew Grier and Lillian Holmes (Bateman) L.; e. primary educ. in Eng.; secondary educ. in Man.; Univ. of Man.; B.Arch. 1948; m. Kathleen Lillian Hannah Williams, 14 Feb. 1945; children: William Ballan tyne, Joanne Bowsfield; MEM., McCARTER, NAIRNE ARCHITECTS (gen. arch. practice); served with R.C.E. in

Can., U.K. and France, 1942-46; rank Capt.; Past Chrmn., Vancouver Downtown Redevel. Adv. Bd.; W. Vancouver Planning Comn.; Past Dir., Pacific Nat. Exhn.; Past Pres., Vancouver Bd. Trade; Past Pres. (1970), Royal Arch. Inst. Can.; Past Pres., Arch. Inst. B.C.; Hon. Fellow, Am. Inst. Archs.; Hon. mem., La Sociedad de Arquitectos Mexicanos; Chancellor, Coll. of Fellows, R.A.I.C.; Past mem. Science Council of Canada and B.C. Research Council; Pres., Greater Vancouver Convention and Tourist Bureau; recreations: golf, photography; Clubs: Vancouver; Capilano Golf & Country; Home: 3348 Radcliffe Ave., West Vancouver, B.C. V7V 1G6; Office: 1000-850 W. Hastings, Vancouver, B.C. V6C 1E3

LEITHWOOD, Kenneth Arthur, M.P.E., Ph.D.; educator; b. Toronto, Ont. 22 Feb. 1942; e. Univ. of Toronto B.A. 1964, Ph.D. 1969; McMaster Univ. B.P.E. 1966; Univ. of B.C. M.P.E. 1967; CHRMN. AND ASSOC. PROF. OF CURRICULUM, THE ONTARIO INST. FOR STUDIES IN EDUCATION 1976-; Secondary Sch. Teacher 1964-65; Grad. Asst. (part-time) Curriculum Dept. present Inst. 1967-69, Asst. Prof. of Curriculum 1970-72, Assoc. Prof. 1972, Devel. Offr. Trent Valley Centre OISE 1970-72, Head of Centre 1972-76; Asst. Prof. of Phys. & Health Educ. Univ. of Toronto 1969-70, Research Consultant 1970-72; Visiting Prof. of Psychol. Trent Univ. 1972-76; sr. investigator various research and devel. projects Ministry of Educ. Ont. and OISE; author "The Peterborough Project: A Case Study of Educational Change and Innovation" 1973; "The Individualized System: Courses and Patterns of Student Choice" 1974; "Effecting Curriculum Change: Experiences with the Conceptual Skills Program" 1974; "Planned Curriculum Change: A Model and Case Study" 1976; "Helping Schools Change" 1978; numerous journ. articles, reports, reviews, educ. personnel publs.; audio visual training packages and tapes; various conf. papers; ed. and co-author "Studies in Curriculum Decision-Making" (being reviewed for publ.); mem. Candn. Assn. Curriculum Studies (2nd Vice Pres. 1978-79, Publs. Ed. and Assoc. Ed. "Canadian Journal of Education" 1979-80, Pres. 1980-81); Candn. Soc. Studies in Educ.; Am. Educ. Research Assn.; Ont. Assn. Curriculum Devel.; Home: 156 Fitzgerald Ave., Unionville, Ont. K9J 7G5; Office: 252 Bloor St. W., Toronto, Ont. M5S 1V6.

Le LACHEUR, Rex A. de Putron; musician; baritone; b. Guernsey, Channel Islands, 5 Jan. 1910; s. Francis Martin and Clarice Maria (Mariette) Le L.; e. Guernsey (Channel Islands) Grammar Sch.; private instr. in music, Toronto and N.Y.; m. Marjorie Lucile, d. A. G. Penman, Neptune Forest, Fla., 23 Sept. 1933; one d.: Rivè Reine; A.O.C.A. art dir. Birks Jewllers, Montreal. apptd. Special Music Consultant to jt. Senate H. of C. Comte. on Nat. and Royal Anthems, 1967; Dir. and Founder, The Rex Le Lacheur Singers (1956) — 50 voice mixed choir in Ottawa; apptd Chorus master, 1958 Ottawa Philharmonic, Thos Meyer Conducting; apptd. Musical Advisor to Festival of the Performing Arts, 1963; has written 120 compositions incl. "Forever England", sung by Toronto Mendelssohn Choir, 1941; "Ave Maria" written for Lawrence Tibbett, 1942; "All Suddenly the Wind" written for John Charles Thomas, 1942; "Chant de Samson" written for Ezio Pinza, 1945; "Centennial Hymm" (topped secular and sacred music sales in U.S. and Can.), 1967; "Sonata da Chiesa for Carillon"; "She Walks in Beauty" (chosen by Eisteddfod Comte., Llangfollen, Wales for incl. in Festival Concert); "Cantata: The Resurrection and Ascension of our Lord"; "Missa Brevis" (used by CBC as background for "The Basilica" in Historic Ottawa series); "Seagulls" (comnd. for U.S. bicentennial, performed by Jacksonville Concert Chorale, Fla.); "Magnificat for Jr. Choir" (featured on prog. by Jr. Choir of St. Paul's-by-the-Sea, Fla., at the White House, Washington, D.C.); "Ah'se Not Afeared of Jesus" (featured by famous Negro Choir of Edward Waters Coll., Fla., on internat. tour);

Tetralogy on "Christus"; words by W. B. Shute; World Premier; Nat'l Arts Centre, Ottawa, with Rex Le Lacheur Singers, and woodwind section of N.A.C., orchestra, 1979, (director); Composed Centennial Anthem, "God of Life" for Wold Baptist Federation; Centennial Anthem for Salvation Army; Baritone Soloist with Centennial Choir; Metrop. Opera Auditions of the Air Finalist, Feb. 1944; N.Y. Stage Door Canteen; served as Lt.-Commdr. with RCSC during 2nd World War; Music Dir., HMCS Carleton, 1942-45; O.C., RCSC Falkland, 1944-51; Fed. Cons. cand. for Ottawa E in g.e. 1963, 1965 and 1968; named "Citizen of the Week," Ottawa, Apl. 1967; P. Conservative; United Church; recreation: tennis; Clubs: Canadian; Ottawa Tennis; Internat. Civitan; Ponte Vedra Golf & Country (Fla.); Roy. St. Lawrence Yacht Montreal; Arts and Letters (Toronto); Home: 2044 Woodglen Cres., Ottawa, Ont. K1J 6G4; Studio: 64 Fifth Ave., Ottawa, Ont. K1S 2M6

LELAND, Vernon J.; farmer, co-operative executive; b. Weldon, Sask. 23 Sept. 1936; m. Sylvia 24 August 1957; children: Gregory Dean, Kim Stuart, Lori Dawn; Tami Joanne; PRESIDENT AND DIR., FEDERATED CO-OPERATIVES LTD.: Chrmn., Co-operative Energy Corp.; Dir., Co-operative Union of Canada; Dir., Western Co-operative Fertilizers Ltd.; self-employed farmer; recreation: outdoor sports; Home: 630 Trent Cres., Saskatoon, Sask. S7H 4T6; Office: 401-22nd Street E., Saskatoon, Sask. S7K 3M9

LEMAN, Paul H., O.C. (1974), B.A., LL.L.; industrialist; b. Montreal, Que., 6 Aug. 1915; s. Beaudry & Caroline (Beique) L.; e. St-Mary's Coll., Montreal, B.A. 1934; Univ. of Montreal, LL.L. 1937; Harvard Bus. Sch. 1938; m. Jeannine, d. J. Alex Prud'Homme, Montreal, Que., 19 May 1939; children: Denise, Jacques, Nicole, Marc, Claire; DIRECTOR., ALCAN ALUMINUM LTD., since 1968; Pres., Alcan Aluminium Ltd.; 1972-77; Vice-Chrmn 1977-79; called to the Bar of Que., 1937, but did not enter practice; joined present firm in 1938; after holding various posts was appointed Treas. in 1949 and Vice-Pres. in 1952; el. a Dir. 1963; Extve. Vice Pres. 1964; Chrmn., Aluminum Co. of Can. Ltd., 1975-77; member, Royal Comn. on Banking & Finance (1962-64); Dir., Credit Foncier Franco-Canadien; Bell Canada; Canadian International Paper Company; Trustee, Nat. Museum of Can., 1979- ; Roman Catholic; recreations: golf, skiing, bridge; Clubs: University; Mount Royal; Mt. Bruno Golf; Home: 445 Ouest, Blvd. St-Joseph, Apt. 93, Outremont, Que. H2V 2P8

LE MARIER, Jean-Guy, B.A., L.Ph., S.T.D.; educateur; né Cap-de-la-Madeleine, Que. 29 mars 1929; fils Paul et Beatrice (Fugère) LE M.; é. Univ. d'Ottawa, B.A. 1950, L.Ph. 1951; Univ. du Latran (Acad. Alphonsienne) Rome, S.T.D. 1968; FACULTE DE THEOLOGIE, UNIV. ST. PAUL (Univ. d'Ottawa) et Prof. de Théol. depuis 1960; Prof., Faculté de Philos. Univ. d'Ottawa 1955; membre Soc. Candn. de Théol. Candn. Theol. Soc.; Amer. Theological Soc.; Assoc. de Theologiens pour l'étude de la Morale; Corp. pour la Publication d'Etudes Scient. en Religion au Can. articles dans différentes revues: Eglise et Théologie, Kerygma, Donum Dei, Hôpital Catholique etc.; Catholique Romaine (oblats de Marie Immaculée); résidence: 175 Main, Ottawa, Ont. K1S 1C3; bureau: 223 Main, Ottawa, Ont. K1S 1C4

Le MAY, His Hon. Gérard, LL.D.; retired judge; b. Quebec City, 27 June 1908; s. Charles Auguste and Laetitia (Alain) L.; e. Sacred Heart Coll., Bathurst, N.B.; Que. Semy., B.A. 1930; Laval Univ. LL.L. 1933; Univ. of Toronto, 1934; LL.D. Sacred Heart Coll., Bathurst, 1959; m. Jacqueline, d. Geo. I. Lachance, Quebec, Que., 31 Jan. 1939; children: Jacques, Michele, Yves, Cecile, Pierre A.; Lect. in Civil Procedure Faculty of Law, Laval Univ.; practised law with Hon. Lucien Moraud, K.C., Richard R. Alleyn, K.C. and Joachim Grenier, K.C., 1935-49;

Chairman, Transportation Bd., Que., 1949-55; Prov. Court Judge, P.Q. 1955-77; Pres., Highway Safety Bd. 1967; called to Bar of Que. 1933; cr. K.C. 1945; Pres., Que. Jr. Bar Assn. 1942; Nat. Pres., Saint-Vincent-de-Paul Soc. Can. 1969; Roman Catholic; Home: 800 - 380 Ch St.-Louis, Que.; G1S 4M1

LeMAY, Jacques, B.A., LL.L., D.E.S.; lawyer; b. Quebec City, Que. 10 July 1940; s. Gerard and Jacqueline (Lachance) LeM.; e. Seminaire de Que. B.A. 1959; Laval Univ. LL.L. 1962, D.E.S. 1965; Univ. of Toronto Law Sch. 1964; m. Paule d. Edmour J. Proulx, Quebec City, Que. 17 March 1972; two d. Chantal, Diane; PARTNER, FLYNN, RIVARD & PARTNERS 1980- ; called to Bar of Que. 1963; law practice Prevost, Gagne, Flynn, Chouinard & Jacques 1963-66; Prevost, Gagne, Flynn, Gobeil, Rivard, Jacques, Cimon, Lessard & LeMay 1966-69; Flynn, Rivard, Jacques, Cimon, Lessard & LeMay 1969-79; mem. Assn. du Barreau Canadien (Secy. Div. de Que. 1981-82); Soc. des Ajusteurs d'Assurances; R. Catholic; recreations: skiing, swimming, sailing; Club: Cercle Universitaire de Quebec; Home: 2760 Silencieuse, Ste-Foy, Que. G1W 2E7; Office: 2 ave. Chauveau, Quebec City, Que. G1R 4S6.

LEMELIN, Roger, C.C. (1980), F.R.S.C. (1949); writer, publisher; b. Quebec, Que., 7 Apl. 1919; s. Joseph and Florida (Dumontier) L.; eldest in a family of 10 boys; e. Que. Sch. (leaving sch. at age of 15); m. Valeda, d. Victor Lavigueur, Quebec, Que. 27 Oct. 1945; children: Pierre, Jacques, Diane and André (twins), Sylvie; PRES. & PUBLISHER, LA PRESSE since 1972; Rockefeller Fellowship 1947; Journalist Time, Life, Fortune magazines. 1948-52- mem. Roy. Soc. of Canada 1949; Foreign Member Acadamic Concourt 1974; Hon. degree in Lit. Laurentian U., Sudbury 1976; Canadian News Hall of Fame 1978; Companion, Order of Canada, 1980 Publications: Novels "Au Pied de la Pente Douce", (won successively, Prix David (Quebec), Prix de la Langue Française (France), and two Guggenheim Fellowships); "Les Plouffe", 1948 "Fantaisies sur les Péchés Capitaux", (short stories) 1949; "Pierre le Magnifique", (novel) 1952, ("In Quest of Splendour"); Essays: Les voies de l'esperance 1979; memoirs: "La Culotte en or", 1980; author of C.B.C. T.V. bilingual, "The Plouffe Family", weekly coast to coast 1953-59; in progress, film & TV mini-series based on The Plouffe Family; awarded Liberty Trophy, for best T.V. Dramatist in 1955; awarded Prix de Paris (for novel, "Pierre le Magnifique"); mem. Candn. Authors' Assn.; awarded French Lang. Medal by French Acad. 1965; el. Candn. mem. l'Académie Goncourt 1974; Roman Catholic; recreation: golf, fishing, reading, travel, chess; Address: 4754, St-Félix, Cap Rouge, Que. G0A 1K0 Office La Presse, 7 St. James St., Montreal, Quebec. H2Y 1K9

LEMESSURIER, Hon. Mary J., M.L.A.; politician; b. Montreal, Que. 12 June 1929; e. McGill Univ.; Royal Victoria Hosp.; m. Ernest Dawes; children: Willa, Jill, Tim, Andrew; MIN. OF CULTURE, ALTA. 1979- ; Vice Pres. and Pres. Miles for Millions 1973-77; served Alta. Ladies Golf Assn. local and prov. levels; Prov. Chrmn. Jr. Girls" Golf in Alta.; Candn. Save the Children Fund (Nat. Pres., Past Prov. Pres.); mem. Organizing Comte. 1980 Lassie (Candn. Ladies Curling Championship); el. M.L.A. for Edmonton Centre prov. g.e. 1979; P. Conservative; Office: 402 Legislative Bldg., Edmonton, Alta. T5K 2B6.

LEMIEUX, Rév. Germain, M.A., Ph.D., LL.D. (R.C.); éducateur; né Cap-Chat, Que. 5 jan. 1914; f. Norbert et Augustine (Pelletier) L.; é. Ecole élémentaire Cap-Chat 1927; Séminaire de Gaspé 1935; Univ. Laval B.A. 1935, M.A. 1956, Ph.D. 1961; York Univ. LL.D. 1977; Univ. Ottawa Litt.D. 1978; Prof. de folklore Centre franco-ontarien de folklore Univ. de Sudbury depuis 1970; Prof. d'Humanités classiques Coll. Sacré-Coeur, Sudbury, Ont. 1941-44 et 1956-59, Prof. d'hist. et de français 1949-

50; même emploi 1951-53; Prof. d'hist. médiévale et ancienne Univ. Laurentienne, Sudbury 1961-65; Prof. auxiliare de Folklore Univ. Laval 1966-69; auteur "Les Vieux M'Ont Conté" 16 vols. depuis 1974, "Chansonnier franco-ontarien" 2 vol. 1974 et 1976; divers articles; Ed. "Les jongleurs du billochet" 1972; a reçu Prix Champlain du Conseil de la vie française en Amérique 1973; Medaille Luc-Lacourcière, 1980; mem. de la Compagnie de Jésus depuis 1935; Bureau: Place Sainte-Joseph, 20, Chemin Saint-Anne, Sudbury, Ont. P3C 5N4

LEMIEUX, Hubert Edmond, B.Com., M.B.A.; executive; b. Ottawa, Ont. 17 March 1925; s. H. Edmond and Ida (Laframboise) L.; e. Ecole Garneau Ottawa; Univ. of Ottawa; Laval Univ. B.Com., M.B.A. (Internat. Marketing); Osgoode Hall Law Sch.; Nat. Defence Coll.; one s. Marc Philippe; DIR., INTERNAT. AND GOVT. AFFAIRS, TIW INDUSTRIES LTD.; Comm. Secy. Candn. Embassy Buenos Aires 1949; Consul and Trade Commr. Manila 1953, New York City 1956; Chargé d'affaires Guatemala City 1960; Extve. Asst. Dept. Industry Trade & Comm. 1965; Comm. Counsellor Madrid 1969; Dir. CANESCO Madrid; R. Catholic; recreations: fishing, golf; Clubs: Jockey; Candn. Businessmen's Madrid; Outaouais Golf; Home: Apt. 1205, 150 Maclaren St., Ottawa, Ont. K2P 0L2; Office: Suite 1100, 90 Sparks St., Ottawa, Ont. K1P 5B4.

LEMIEUX, Jacques, B.A., D.Sc.A.; consulting engineer; b. Weedon, Que., 24 Nov. 1919; s. Joseph Pierre Cyrinus and Orpha (Deveau) L.; e. Coll. St-Charles, B.A. 1939; Ecole Polytech., Univ. of Montreal, B.Sc.A. 1944; Univ. of Sherbrooke, D.Sc.A. 1964; m. Jacqueline, d. late Héctor Lanctôt, 5 May 1945; children: Raymond, Guy, Nicole, Chantal; PARTNER, LEMIEUX, ROYER, DONALDSON, FIELDS & ASSOC. since 1970; Co-founder, Univ. of Sherbrooke and Dean of Science there 1954-64 (mem. Corp.); Engr., Pub. Works Depts. on Bridge Constr. 1944; Consulting Engr., Crepeau, Cote, Lemieux 1945; Cote, Lemieux, Carignan & Bourque 1952; Lemieux, Carignan, Royer & Assoc. 1963; Commdr., Order of St-Gregoire; mem. Council Univs. Prov. of Que.; Adm., Sherbrooke Trust; La Laurentienne; Television St.-François (CKSH 9); mem. Office Engrs. Qué; Assn. Engrs. Can.; Prés. Télévision St-François (CKSH 9); Adm. Télévision St-Maurice (CKTM 13); R. Catholic; recreations: golf, skiing; Clubs: Social; Home: 120 Vimy, Sherbrooke, Que. J1J 3M7; Office: 144 Vimy, Sherbrooke, Que. J1J 3M7

LEMIEUX, Jean-Paul; artist; illustrator; b. Que. 1904; e. Coll. Loyola, Montreal; Colarossi and Grand Chaumière Acads., Paris; Ecole des Beaux-Arts, Montreal; taught at Ecole du Meuble, Montreal 1935-36; Ecole des Beaux-Arts, Que. 1937-64; one-man exhns. incl. Palais Montcalm, Quebec 1953; Roberts Gallery, Toronto 1963; Montreal Museum of Fine Arts 1967; 70 paintings toured Moscow, Leningrad and Paris 1974; group exhns. incl.: Musée d'art Moderne, Paris 1946, Sao Paulo Biennial, Brazil 1957, Brussels Internat. Exhn. 1958, Venice Biennial 1960, Musée Galliera Paris 1960; awards incl.: Prix Brymner 1934; Prix Philippe Hébert, St.-Jean Baptiste Soc. 1971; Molson Prize, Can. Council 1973. 2008 Dickson, Sillery, Que. G1T 1C5

LEMIEUX, Raymond U., O.C. (1968), B.Sc., Ph.D., D.Sc., F.R.S. (1967); chemist, university professor; b. Lac La Biche, Alberta; e. Univ. of Alta., B.Sc. (Chem); McGill Univ., Ph.D. 1946; D.Sc., Univ. of N.B. 1967; D.Sc., Laval Univ., 1970; D.Sc., Univ. de Provence, Marseille, France, 1972; Univ. of Ottawa, D.Sc. 1975; L.L.D., Univ. of Calgary, 1979; D.Sc.(Hon.c.) Univ. of Waterloo, 1980; hon. D.Sc., Memorial Univ., Nfld. 1981; Univ. Professor, 1980; after holding several posts in Candn. and U.S. universities, joined Univ. of Alberta in 1961; has made numerous important contrib. to study of general organic and carbohydrate chem. (main research related to methods for synthesis of complex carbohydrate structures); author of more than 175 publications; mem., Nat. Research Council of Can., 1976-79; Award of Achievement, Gov't of Alta., 1979; Issac J. Walton Killam Prize 1981; Home: 7602 119 St., Edmonton, Alta. T6G 1W3; Office: University of Alberta, Edmonton, Alta. T6G 2G2

LEMON, Kenneth William, F.C.A. (Ont.); b. Orillia, Ont., 1 Oct. 1916; s. late Thomas Henry and Blanche Eva (Snoulten); e. Humberside Coll. Inst., Toronto, Ont. 1936; C.A. 1942; F.C.A. (Ont.) 1956; m. Honor Florence Eileen, d. late Reginald Shribbs, 4 July 1942; children: Richard Henry, Peter William Reginald, Patricia Ann; PARTNER, CLARKSON GORDON since 1949; joined the Co. as a Student in Accounts, Toronto 1936, Resident Mgr., London Br. 1948; past Chrmn. Extve. Bd., Huron Coll.; mem. Executive Committe, Synod of Diocese of Huron; Pres., Un. Appeal, Greater London 1955-57; YMCA-YWCA, London 1958; London Little Theatre 1961-63; mem. Inst. Chart. Accts. Ont. (mem. Council 1965-72, Pres. 1971-72); Chart. Accts. Assn. of W. Ont. (Pres. 1949-50); Adm. Mang. Soc. (Pres. 1952-53); mem. Vocational Adv. Comte., London Bd. of Educ. 1952-70 (Chrmn. 1961-70); Treas., St. James (Westminster) Church; Chairman Mang. Avd. Bd. London Psychiatric Hosp. since 1973; Freemason; Anglican; recreations: golf, fishing; Clubs: London Hunt & Country (Pres. 1972); London; Caughnawana Fishing & Hunting; National (Toronto); Home: 154 Commissioners Rd. E., London, Ont. N6C 2T1; Office: Suite 1900, 380 Wellington St., London, Ont. N6A 5B5

LEON, John Joseph; food service executive; b. Toronto, Ont., 10 April 1921; s. Peter and Catharine (Thus) L.; e. St. Michael's Coll., Toronto, Ont. 1934-39; two s. John, Brian, one d. Peggy; PRESIDENT PRES., COL. SAUNDERS KENTUCKY FRIED CHICKEN LTD., AND DIR., SCOTT'S RESTAURANTS CO. LTD. (Pres. Jan. 1981-); commenced career with Swift Canadian Ltd. 1939-41; Chief Acct., Canadian Food Products Ltd. 1945-51; apptd. Dir., Scott's Restaurants Ltd. 1951, Gen. Mgr. 1957, Pres. 1965-1980; served in 2nd World War, R.C.A. 1941-43; R.C.A.F. 1943-45; mem. Candn. Restaurant Assn.; Bd. Trade Metrop. Toronto; Dir., Col. Sanders Charitable Foundation; recreations: golf, bridge, swimming; Club: Lambton Golf; Home: 55 Edenbrooke Hill, Toronto, Ont. M9A 4A1; Office: 2000 Jane St., Weston, Ont. M9N 2V2

LEONARD, Hon. Jacques, M.N.A., M.Sc., C.A.; politician; b. St-Jovite, Qué. 2 Dec. 1936; s. Odilon and Simone (Desjardins) L.; e. St-Jovite schs.; St-Joseph Semy.; Laval Univ.; m. Martine d. Olivier Maisani, France 17 July 1965; children: Christophe, Sophie, Emmanuelle; MIN. OF MUNICIPAL AFFAIRS 1980- ; Cand. prov. g.e. 1970, 1973, def.; el. M.N.A. for Laurentides-Labelle prov. g.e. 1976, re-el. M.N.A. for Labelle 1981; Min. of State for Land Use and Planning 1976-80; Vice Pres. Treasury Bd. 1978-79; Parti Quebecois; Office: Edifice G, 1039 de la Chevrotiére, Québec, Qué. G1R 4Z3.

LEONARD, John Charles, R.C.A.; artist; b. Oxted, Surrey, Eng. 5 May 1944; s. John Albert and Joan Violet (Barrow) L.; came to Can. 1946; e. Victoria (B.C.) High Sch. 1962; Ont. Coll. of Art A.O.C.A. 1969; m. Marilyn Doreen d. Robert Charles Hayes 13 Oct. 1968; two s. Jonathon Albert, Jamie Daniel; Dir., A.C.T. Gallery Toronto; rep. in over 120 exhns. pub. galleries and insts. Can., USA and overseas; rep. Can. Internat. exhns. incl. Festival of Can. N.Y. 1971; Candn. exhns. incl. Survey '70 Art Gallery Ont.; Montreal Museum of Fine Arts 1970; rep. in pub., corporate and private colls. incl. Nat. Gallery Can., Ont. Arts Council Toronto; teaching experience incls. courses, seminars, adjudications many univs., colls. and art schs. inc. Univ. of Toronto, York Univ., Ont. Coll. Art, Univ. of Guelph, Canador Coll. North Bay, Sheridan Coll. Oakville and Brampton, Mohawk Coll. Hamilton, Georgian Coll. Barrie, Arts Sake Inc. Toronto, Ont. Arts

Council; served with Candn. Scot. Regt. (Victoria, B.C.); recipient numerous competition awards target rifle shooting; Anglican; recreations: collecting World War I memorabilia, philately, canoe racing; Address: 207A Cowan Ave., Toronto, Ont. M6K 2N7.

LEONARDI, C. W., F.C.A. (Eng. and Wales), C.A.; b. Sfax, Tunisia, 27 May 1925; s. William and Beatrice May (Frost) L.; e. Finchley Grammar Sch., Eng.; Durham Univ.; EXTVE. VICE-PRES. FINANCE, JANNOCK LTD. since 1973; Supvr., Geo. A. Touche & Co., London, Eng., 1951-54; Secy.-Treas., Maple Leaf Services, Ottawa, 1955-59; Gen. Mgr., H. K. Porter (Can.) Ltd., Acton, Ont., 1959-60; Treas., Trafalgar Investment Ltd., 1960-64; subsequently Vice-Pres. and Treas. The Glengair Group; Financial Executive Inst.; Financial Council Conference Board of Canada; served with RAF as Flying Offr., 1943-47; rec'd. comn. RAF Coll., Cranwell; mem., Bd. Trade Metrop. Toronto; R. Catholic; recreations: fishing, tennis, golf; Home: 2323 Confederation Pkwy., Apt. 608, Mississauga, Ont. L5B 1R6; Office: (P.O. Box 43) Toronto-Dominion Centre, Toronto, Ont. M5K 1B7

LePAN, Douglas V., D. Litt., LL.D., F.R.S.C. (1968); b. Toronto, Ont. 1914; s. Lieut.-Col. Arthur D'Orr and Dorothy Lucinda (Edge) LeP.; e. Univ. of Toronto Schs.; Univ. of Toronto (Grad.); Oxford Univ. (Grad.); Univ. of Man., D.Litt. 1964; LL.D. Queen's 1969; York, 1977; D.Litt. Ottawa 1972, Waterloo 1973; L.L.D., Dalhousie, 1980 m., two s., Nicholas, Donald; UNIVERSITY PROFESSOR EMERITUS, UNIV. OF TORONTO since 1979; Lectr., Univ. of Toronto, 1937-38 and at Harvard Univ., 1938-41; served in 2nd World War; Educ. Adviser to Gen. A.G. McNaughton 1942-43; enlisted in C.F.A. as a Gunner and saw service in Italian Campaign; discharged in 1945; joined Dept. of External Affairs and served on staff of High Commr. in London for three yrs.; attended Paris Reparations Conf. 1945, Paris Peace Conference, 1946; studied writing under a Guggenheim Schol. (on leave of absence) 1948; Special Assistant to Min. of External Affairs, 1950-51; attended Colombo Conf. and Sydney and London Confs. on aid for S.-E. Asia; Minister Counsellor at Canadian Embassy, Washington, 1951-55; attended Commonwealth Economic Conf., 1952i, Commonwealth Trade & Econ. Conf., 1958; Secy. and Dir. of Research, Royal Comn. on Canada's Econ. Prospects, 1955-58; Asst. Under Secy. of State for External Affairs, 1958-59; Prof. of Eng. Lang. and Lit., Queen's Univ., 1959-64; Principal, Univ. College, Univ. of Toronto, 1964-70; University Professor, U. of Toronto, 1970-79; Sr. Fellow of Massey Coll., 1970; author of "The Wounded Prince" and "The Net and the Sword" (poems) "The Deserter" (fiction); "Bright Glass of Memory" (memoirs); rec'd. Gov. Gen. Lit. Award (poetry) 1954, (fiction) 1964; Lorne Pierce Medal, Roy. Soc. of Can., 1976; mem. Canada Council 1964-70; Pres., Academy of the Humanities and Social Sciences, Royal. Soc. of Can., 1978-79; Address: Massey College, 4 Devonshire Place, Toronto, Ont. M5S 2E1

LE PETIT, Jean-Michel; banker; b. Marrakech, Morocco 24 Aug. 1939; s. Eugene and Yvonne (Le Guevel) Le P.; came to Can. 1980; m. Eliane d. Paul Lescouarch 16 July 1963; children: Christel, Guillzume, Claire; PRES., SOCIÉTÉ GÉNÉRALE S.A. (CANADA) INC. 1980- ; (became a charter bank under the name Societe Generale Canada, 1981); joined Société Générale, France 1965, Inspr.; Vice Pres. 1972, First Vice Pres. 1979; recreations: tennis, jogging; Club: Rockland; Office: 630 Dorchester Blvd. W., Montreal, Que. H3B 1S6.

le RICHE, William Harding, M.D., M.P.H., F.S.S., F.R.C.P.(C), F.A.C.P.; professor; b. Dewetsdorp, South Africa, 21 March 1916; s. Josef Daniel and Georgina Henrietta Guest (Harding) le R.; e. University of Witwatersrand, B.Sc. 1936, M.B., Ch.B. 1943, M.D. 1949; Harvard Univ. (Rockefeller Fellowship), M.P.H. (cum laude) 1950;

m. Margaret Cardross, d. late Rev. Arthur Cardross Grant, 11 Dec. 1943; children: Jenny Harding, Robert Harding, Nicole Georgina Harding, Giles Harding, Claire Alison Harding; PROF. OF EPIDEMIOL., DEPT. OF PREVENTIVE MED. AND BIOSTATICS, UNIV. OF TORONTO, since 1975; Interne, Zulu McCord Hosp., Durban, 1944; apptd. by Union Health Dept. to Health Centre Service, firstly at Pholela, Natal, and later (1945) estbd. first Health Centre for White and Eurafricans at Knysna, 1945-49; Epidemiologist, Union (Fed.) Health Dept., 1950-52; Consultant in Epidemiology, Dept. of Nat. Health & Welfare, Ottawa (worked on background report of Candn. Sickness Survey), 1952-54; Research Med. Offr., Physicians Services Inc., Toronto, Ont., 1954-57; apptd. to Staff of Dept. of Public Health, Sch. of Hygiene, Toronto, Ont., 1957; apptd. Prof. of Pub. Health, Univ. of Toronto, 1959; Prof. and Head, Dept. of Epidemiol., Univ. of Toronto, 1962-75; Publications: (with J. Milner) "Epidemiology as Medical Ecology", 1971; "A Complete Family Guide to Nutrition and Meal Planning", 1976; over 130 articles; Assoc., Staff, Sunnybrook Hosp., Extended Care Clinic; Delta Omega; Anglican; recreations: riding, photography, medical practice; Office: 4th Floor, McMurrich Bldg., 12 Queen's Park Cres. W., Toronto, Ont. M5S 1A8

LERNER, Samuel, C.D., Q.C., B.A.; barrister; b. London, Ont. 27 Jan. 1916; s. Max and Minnie (Rosenthal) L.; e. Central Coll. Inst. London 1933; Univ. of W. Ont. B.A. 1936; Osgoode Hall Law Sch. 1939; m. Frances d. Aaron Weinstein 20 Aug. 1944; children: Michael, Patricia Ann Roditzky, Susan; SR. MEMBER, LERNER & ASSOCIATES; called to Bar of Ont. 1939; cr. Q.C. 1967; commenced law practice Lerner & Lerner 1939; Depy. Judge Small Claims Court Co. of Middlesex; Referee, Employment Standards Act Ont.; Arbitrator Labour Relations Ont.; Hon. Counsel: London Br. St. John's Ambulance; London Poppy Fund, Royal Candn. Legion (Hon. Pres. of Legion and of Duchess of Kent Br.); Cong. Or Shalom; Royal Candn. Regt. Assn. (Hon. Pres., Chrmn. Trust Fund); Past Pres., B'nai B'rith; N. London Kiwanis; Past Chrmn. London Pub. Lib. Bd. and Art Museum; Gov., Univ. of W. Ont. (Chrmn. Health Sciences Comte.); Candn. Corps Commissionaires; Past Pres. Extve. Comte. London Dist. Council Boy Scouts; mem. London Chamber Comm.; London Un. Service Inst.; served with Royal Candn. Regt. 1940-46 Can., UK, Mediterranean, N.W. Europe, rank Maj.; Candn. Army Militia 1953-63, rank Lt. Col.; rec'd Queen's Silver Jubilee Medal; Commdr. Bro. Order St. John; Fellow, Foundation for Legal Research in Can.; Bencher, Law Soc. Upper Can.; Past Pres. Middlesex Law Assn.; mem. Candn. Bar Assn. (Ont. Council); Candn. Tax Foundation; Freemason; Sigma Alpha Mu (Prior); Liberal; Jewish; recreation: boating; Clubs: Royal Candn. Mil. Inst.; Canadian; Baconian; Great Lakes Cruising (Rear Commodore Georgian Bay.); Home: 1004, 520 Wellington St., London, Ont. N6A 3R2; Office: (P.O. Box 2335 Stn. A) London, Ont. N6A 4G4.

LeROUX, Edgar Joseph, B.A., M.Sc., Ph.D.; ecologist; Canadian public servant; b. Ottawa, Ont. 24 Jan. 1922; s. Dieudonné and Amanada (Beauchêsne) LeR.; e. Carleton Univ., B.A. 1950; McGill Univ., M.Sc. 1952, Ph.D. 1954, Honorary D.Sc., McGill Univ. 1973; Ont. Inst. Prof. Agrologists, P.Ag. 1969; m. Ardis Myriam Andrew, Halifax, N.S., 30 June 1944; children: Estelle, Pierre, Elyzabeth; ASST. DEPUTY MIN., RESEARCH, AGRICULTURE CANADA; Assoc. Prof. of Entom., Macdonald Coll., McGill Univ. 1962-65; mem. and Vice-Chrmn. (1977) Agriculture Stabilization Board and Agricultural Products Board (1975-79); mem. Canadian Agric. Services Coordinating Comte (CASCC), (1975-);Vice-Chrmn. Can. Agric. Research Council (CARC), (1977-); Co-chrmn. Canada/Russia Agrobusiness Working Group (1978-); Chrmn., OECD Com. on Agric. (1978-80); Chrmn. Federal Interdepartmental Comte on Pesticides (FICP), (1978-); mem. Bd. of Dir. of Public Works Land Co. Ltd. (to

manage the mirable Peripheral Lands), (1978-79); Can. Egg Marketing Agency Research Comte, 1980-; Adv. Comte. on Inmate Employment (ACIE) of the Correctional Services of Canada (CSC), 1980-; Nat. Research Council of Canada, 1981-; mem., Task Force on Sci. and Prof. Category Interdepartmental Adv. Comm. 1981-: joined present Dept. as Research Co-ordinator, Research Br. 1965, Asst. Dir. Gen. (Insts.) 1968-72; Asst. Dir. Gen. (Planning) 1972-75; Asst. Dir. Gen. (Ops.) 1975-78; Grace Griswold Lectr., Cornell Univ. 1971; served as Writer, RCN, 1941-46; service on high seas; Pres., Comité des Paroissiens, Paroisse St-Gérard Magella, St-Jean, Que., 1959-62; Pres., Que. Div., Navy League of Can. 1961-64 (Vice Pres., Nat. Council, 1964-65; awarded Cert. of Merit); author, "Population Dynamics of Agricultural and Forest Insect Pests", 1963; "Recherces sur la Biologie et la Dynamique des Population Naturelles d'Archips argyrospilus dans le sud-ouest de Québec", 1965; "Population Dynamics and Biology of the Apple Leaf miner, Lithocolletis blancardella in Quebec", 1970; other writings incl. over 75 research publs. on subject of insect ecol. and physiol.; Chrmn., Insect Ecol. Panel, Study of Basic Biol. in Can., Biolog. Council of Can. 1969-70; mem. panel of experts, Integrated Pest Control, Food and Agric. Organ. of U.N.; official corr. in entom. for Commonwealth Inst. of Biol. Control; Candn. rep. for Plant Protection, Internat. Soc. for Hortic. Science; mem. Can. Dept. Indust., Trade and Comm., Tech. Apple Mission to Japan, Australia, New Zealand and S. Africa 1971; mem., Biol. Council Can. (Pres. 1970-71); Entom. Soc. Can. (Pres. 1969-70); Entom. Soc. Que. (Pres. 1965-66); Candn. Soc. Zools. (Dir. 1968-70); Que. Soc. Protection Plants (Dir. 1964-65); Agric. Inst. Can.; Prof. Inst. Can. (Pres. St-Jean Br., 1960-61); SCITEC (Hon. Treas. and mem. Extve. Council 1970); mem. Negotiated Grants Comte., N.R.C.; Publications Comte., Agric. Can.; Comte. for Internat. Plant Protection Congresses; Roman Catholic; recreations: fishing, golf, swimming, sailing; Home: 27 Keppler Cres., Nepean, Ont. K2H 5Y1; Office: Sir John Carling Bldg., Central Experimental Farm, Ottawa, Ont.

LeROY, Donald James, M.A., Ph.D., LL.D., D.Sc., F.C.I.C., F.R.S.C.; research scientist and science admin.; b. Detroit, Michigan, 5 March 1913; s. Charles Lafayette and Emma Frances (McCoubrey) L.; e. Univ. of Toronto, B.A. 1935, M.A. 1936, Ph.D. 1939; LL.D. Trent 1971; D.Sc. Laurentian 1973, McMaster 1982; D. ès Sc. Laval, 1976; D. Sc. Waterloo, Toronto, 1978; m. Lillice Marie Eyer, d. later Alexander P. Read of Toronto, Ont., 12 June 1940; children: Rodney Lash, Robert James, Alexander Charles, John Donald; SENIOR ADVISOR Science Council of Can. since 1981; mem. National Research Council of Canada, 1964-74; Chemist, Ont. Research Foundation, 1939-40; Chemist, National Research Council, 1940-44; Assistant Professor of Chem., Univ. of Toronto, 1944-47, Assoc. Prof. 1947-50; Prof. 1950-75, Chrmn. of Dept. 1960-71; Vice-Pres., Scientific, Nat. Research Council 1969-74; Princ. Research Offr., Nat. Research Coun., 1975-77; Sci. Adv., Sci. Council of Can.; mem., Am. Chem. Soc.; Royal Soc. of Chem.; Chem. Inst. of Can. (Dir. 1949-52); Royal Soc. of Can.; Candn. Assn. of Physicists; Candn. Soc. for Chem. Eng.; Am. Phys. Soc., contrib. of numerous papers to scient. journs. on research in field of physical chem.; Centennial Medal 1967; Chem. Inst. of Can Medal 1970; Queen's Jubilee Medal, 1977; Anglican; recreation: reforestation; Home: 111 Wurtemburg St., Ottawa, Ont. K1N 8M1;

LeROY, Hugh Alexander Côté, R.C.A.; sculptor; b. Montreal, Que. 6 Oct. 1939; s. Max Reekie Patrick and Marie Rose (Côté) L.; e. Montreal Museum of Fine Arts Sch. of Art & Design under Arthur Lismer; Sir George Williams Univ. Art Sch. grad. 1960; solo exhns. incl. Waddington Galleries 1963, 1972; McGill Univ. 1964; Gallerie du Siecle Montreal 1966; Galerie Godard-Lefort Montreal 1969; Anna Leonowen, Galley, Halifax 1981; rep. in numerous group exhns. incl. Montreal Museum of Fine Arts 1965; Nat. Gallery Can. 1966; Sculpture '67 and Survey '68 Toronto; Candn. Pavilion Expo '67; Ont. Centennial Art Comn. Art Gallery Ont. 1967; Antwerp Biennial 1971; Panorama de la sculpture au Que. 1945-70 Quebec and Paris; rep. in various pub. and private colls. incl. Musée d'Art Contemporain de Montréal; Can. Council Art Bank; Nat. Gallery Can.; Ont. Art Council; Montreal Museum of Fine Arts; rec'd Can. Council Bursaries 1966-68, Sr. Award 1969; First Prize-Sculpture, Perspective '67 Centennial Comn. 1967; UNESCO Fellowship 1968; teacher, Drummondville Art Assn. 1960-62; Sir George Williams Univ. 1966-67; Montreal Museum Sch. of Art & Design 1966-67, Dean of Sch. 1967-70; Chrmn. Sculpture Dept. Ont. Coll. Art 1970-71; Assoc. Prof. York Univ. Toronto 1974, 1977-78; N.S. Coll of Art and Design 1981; York Univ. 1981-82; taught and installed sculpture piece Banff Centre summer 1979; cited numerous bibliogs.; United Church; recreation: running; Address: 80 Grandravine Dr., Apt. 409, Downsview, Ont. M3J 1B2.

LESINS, Karlis Adolfs, D.Sc.; professor emeritus; geneticist; agronomist; b. Madona, Latvia, 30 July 1906; s. Janis and Anna (Lacis) L.; e. High Sch., Cesvaine, Latvia, 1924; Univ. of Latvia, grad. in Agric. 1928; Univ. of Kiel, postgrad. studies 1929; Royal Agric. Coll., Sweden, grad. Agric. 1950; Univ. of Álta., D.Sc. 1957; m. Irma Kaminskis (d. 1966); Dist. Agron., Bukaisi, Latvia, 1931; Headmaster, Sch. of Agric., Bebrene, Latvia, 1931; Supt. Agric. Research Stn., Osupe, Latvia, 1941; Agron., Swedish Seed Assn., Ultuna, Sweden, 1945-51; Research Assoc., Univ. of Alta., 1957-61, Assoc. Prof. 1962-65, Prof. of Genetics 1966 and Prof. Emeritus there since 1971; coauthor, "Alfalfa Science and Technology", 1972; "Evolution of Crop Plants," 1976; "Genus Medicago" 1979; also over 50 scient. papers; mem., Agric. Inst. Can.; Genetics Soc. Can.; Crop Science Soc. Am.; Am. Genetic Assn.; Am. Assn. Advanc. Science; Home: 9727 — 65 Ave., Edmonton, Alta. T6E 0K5

LESSARD, Hon. Lucien, M.N.A., B.Sc.; politician; b. Bergeronnes, Qué. 22 Feb. 1938; s. Léon and Marie (Morin) L.; e. Bergeronnes schs.; Coll. Sacré-Coeur Victoriaville; Coll. St-Laurent Montréal; Laval Univ.; m. Adrienne Brisson, Bergeronnes, Qué. 28 July 1962; children: Katia, François, Michel; MIN. OF YOUTH, RECREATION, FISH, GAME & SPORTS and VICE PRES. TREASURY BD., QUE. 1979-; Cand. prov. g.e. 1966, def.; el. M.N.A. for Saguenay prov. g.e. 1970, re-el. since; Min. of Transport 1976; Min. of Pub. Works & Supply 1976-77; professor, Parti Quebecois; R. Catholic; Office: 150 est, boul. St-Cyrille, Québec, Qué. G1R 4Y3

LESSARD, Pierre H., B.A., M.Sc., M.B.A., C.A.; executive; b. Quebec City, Que. 13 Feb. 1942; s. Maurice and Jacqueline (Lacasse) L.; e. Laval Univ. B.A. 1961, M.Sc.C., L.Sc.C. 1964; Harvard Univ. M.B.A. 1967; m. Andrée D. d. Philippe Dupuis, Quebec City, Que. 11 June 1966; children: Pierre Philippe, Stéphanie; PRESIDENT, CEO AND DIR. PROVIGO INC. since 1976; Dir. Provigo (Montreal) Inc.; Provigo (Sherbrooke) Inc.; Provigo (Saguenay) Ltée; Provifruit Inc.; Provi-Viande Inc.; Le Marché à Go-Go Inc.; Provi-Soir Inc.; Marché Aux Vraies Aubaines Inc.; Aubaines Alimentaires Ltée; Denault Investments Inc.; AVA Warehouse Market Ltd.; Provigo (Québec) Inc.; Jato Inc.; M. Loeb, Ltd.; Horne & Pitfield Foods Ltd.; Nat. Drug & Chem. Co. of Can. Ltd.; Market Wholesale Grocery Co.; Market Mgmt. Inc.; Auditor, Touche-Ross & Partners, Montreal 1964-65; Asst. to Pres., Treas. and Controller Denault Ltée, Sherbrooke 1967-68; Treas. and Controller present Co. 1970, Vice Pres. Finance and Adm. 1972; mem. Que. Inst. C.A.'s; Montreal Bd. Trade; St. Denis Club; R. Catholic; recreations: tennis, skiing; Home: 371 Lethbridge Ave., Town of Mount Royal, Que. H3P 1E6; Office: 800 Dorchester Blvd. W. Suite 400, Montreal, Que. H3B 1X9

LESTER, Alexander George; executive engineer; b. Montreal, Que., 6 May 1905; s. Geo. William and Harriet (Good) L.; e. High Sch. of Montreal, grad. June 1922; m. Alice, d. late William Ritchie, 20 Sept. 1930; children: (late) Roslyn Roy (Mrs. A. H. Pytel), Beverley Ruth (Mrs. A. D. Johnston); Dir. Unican Security Systems; joined Engn. Dept., Bell Can., 1922; aptd. co-ordinator local plant additions, 1941; after war service apptd. Special Studies Engr., Montreal, 1945; loaned to Fed. Govt. as Indust. Rep., Nat. Defence Coll., Kingston, 1949-50; loaned to Dept. of Defence Prod. as Assoc. Dir. of Electronics Div., 1952; named Asst. Gen. Mgr., Special Contract Dept., Bell Can., responsible for major defence projects incl. Mid-Can. Line, 1953; apptd. Gen. Mgr., Special Contract Dept., 1955; Asst. Vice-Pres., Engn., 1957, Vice-Pres., 1958; Extve. V. Pres. Planning & Research 1965, Corp. Studies 1969-70 when retired; joined Candn. Army (R) as Lieut., 1940; served with Royal Candn. Signals, 1942-45, East Coast (Atlantic Command) and Ottawa; released as Tech. Staff Offr. with rank of Maj.; life mem. Engn. Inst. Can.; Order of Engrs. Que.; Home: 115 Braemar Crs., Stratford, Ont. N5A 7C2

LESTER, Richard E.M., LL.B.; b. Toronto, Ontario 22 March 1928; s. Egerton H. H. and Letitia (Matheson) L.; e. Toronto Public School, 1934-46; Univ. of Toronto, 1946-47; Univ. of B.C., LL.B. 1952; m. Lois Audrey, d. late Erle F. Jensen, Bremerton, Wash.; children: Douglas, Reid, Mark, Gillian; read law with J. B. Clearihue, G. F. T. Gregory, Victoria; called to Bar of B.C. 1953; Pres., Pulp and Paper Industrial Relations Bureau; President, B.C. School Trustees Assn., 1961-63; Past Pres. W. Candn. Univs. Marine Biol. Soc.; Dir. of Canadian School Trustees Assn., 1961-63; Chairman, Bd. of Govs., Simon Fraser Univ. 1968-71; mem., Acad. Bd. of B.C., 1963-66; mem., Candn. Bar Assn.; Vancouver Bar Assn.; Anglican; recreations: sailing; travel; Home: 1065 Eyremount Dr., West Vancouver, B.C. V7S 2B6

LETARTE, Hon. René, B.A., LL.B.; juge; né Montréal, Que. 4 sept. 1931; f. Louis-Philippe et Henriette (Asselin) L.; e. Séminaire St-Hyacinthe; Externat Classique St-Jean Eudes, Que.; Séminaire de Que. B. ès A. 1951; Faculté de Droit de l'Univ. Laval 1951-55; ép. Claire f. Leo Gilbert 25 mai 1957; enfants: Michel, Danièle; JUGE, COUR SUPERIEUR DE QUE.; admission au Barreau de Que. 1955; nommé c.r. 1973; Associé senior de l'étude Letarte, Caron, Reinhardt; Dir. de la Comm. des Débats Interuniversitaires à Laval; chargé de l'enseignement du droit criminel à la Licence à l'Universitè Laval 1963-70, mem. du Conseil de la Faculté de Droit; chargé de cours de droit criminel à l'Extension de l'Enseignement de l'Académie de Que.; conférencier invité pour traiter des aspects juridiques de la drogue, aux cours annuels de l'OPTAT; divers Clubs sociaux de Que.; Barreau de Port-au-Prince, Haiti; dir. du Jeune Barreau de Que. 1957-58; conseiller du Barreau de Que. 1964-66 (prés. du Service d'Information 1970-72, Bâtonnier 1972-73); mem. du Conseil Général du Barreau de la Prov. 1965-66 et 1972-3, mem. du Comité Exécutif; conseiller spécial du Comité Interministériel du Que. sur l'étude du Rapport LeDain, invité comme témoin expert par la Comn. Prévost chargée de l'enquête sur l'Adm. de la Justice Pénale et Criminelle; Vice Prés. Nat. de la Société Canadienne pour l'Abolition de la Peine de Mort; Administrateur de la Soc. de Qué. de la Croix-Rouge Canadienne; R. Catholique; récréation: chasse, pêche; Club: Garnison; Résidence: 2180, Brûlart, Sillery, Que.; Palais de Justice, Québec, Qué.

LETENDRE, Rita, R.C.A.; painter; b. Drummondville, Que. 1 Nov. 1928; d. Héliodore Letendre; e. Ecole des Beaux-Arts Montreal and with Paul-Emile Borduas Montreal; over 37 solo exhns. Can., N.Y., Los Angeles, Europe and Israel incl. Montreal Museum of Fine Arts 1961, Travel Exhn. 1977; Gallery Moos Toronto 1972, 1974, 1977, Calgary 1979; Musée d'Art Contemporain Montreal

1972; Arras Gallery N.Y. 1974, 1976; Palm Springs (Cal.) Museum 1974; Galerie Gilles Corbeil Montreal 1975, 1978; Algoma Festival of Arts Sault Ste. Marie 1976; Equinox Gallery Vancouver 1976; West End Gallery Edmonton 1978; The Art Package Chicago 1979; Arwin Galleries Detroit 1979; rep. in over 43 group exhns. Can., USA, Europe, Japan; rep. in perm. colls. maj. Candn. museums and galleries, USA, various corporate and private colls.; comns. incl. "Sunforce" (outdoor mural) Cal. State Univ. Long Beach 1965; "Now" (acrylic on canvas) Berkshire House, Toronto 1971; "Sunrise" (Outdoor mural) Ryerson Polytech. Inst. Toronto 1971; 2 paintings Exxon Bldg. N.Y. 1971; "Tecumseh II" (indoor mural) Sheridan Mall, Pickering, Ont. 1972; "Urta" (outdoor mural) Toronto 1972; 2 murals J.C. Penney H.O., N.Y. 1972; "Summer Solstice" Dallas 1973; 2 murals Mountainville, N.Y. 1972; "Irowakan" (acrylic on canvas) Royal Bank Plaza, Toronto 1977; "Joy" skylight dome mural Glencairn Subway Stn. Toronto 1977; awards: Le Prix de la jeune Peinture Montreal 1959; Le Prix Rodolphe de Repentigny Montreal 1960; Le Prix de Peinture Concours Artistique du Qué. 1961; Can. Council Travel Grant 1962-63, Sr. Grant 1971, 1975; Bourse de Recherche Prov. Qué. 1967; Candn. Nat. Exhn. 1st Prize Painting 1968; Ont. Soc. Artists 1st Price Painting 1970; II Festival Internat. de Peinture Cagnes sur Mer (Prix Nat.) 1970; Address: 288 Sherbourne St., Toronto, Ont. M5A 2S1.

LETOURNEAU, Jean-Paul, C.R.I., Cert. Assoc. Mgmt.; assoc. exec.; b. St-Hyacinthe, Que. 4 May 1930; s. late Joseph Eugene and Annette (Deslandes) L.; e. Univ. of Montreal C.R.I. 1953; Syracuse Univ., N.Y. Cert. Assoc. Mgmt. 1962; m. Claire d. late Napoleon Paquin 24 Sept. 1956; EXEC. V.P. LA CHAMBRE DE COMM. DE LA P.Q. 1971- ; Sec.-Tres. Munic. of Mont St-Hilaire 1950-53; Personnel Dir. Dupuis Freres Mail Order House 1953; Ed. weekly newsp. of Fed. Des Chambres de Comm. des jeunes du Qué. 1953-54; Exec. sec. La Chambre de Comm. des Jeunes du dist. Montréal 1954-56; Asst. Gen. Mgr. La Chambre De Comm. De La P.Q. 1956-59, Gen. Mgr. 1959-71; author "Quebec, The Cost of Independence" 1969; Dir. The Children's Broadcast Inst. Toronto; La Fondation Crudem Canada-Haiti Inc.; Pres. elec. Chamber of Comm. Extves. of Can.; mem. La Corporation Prof. des Conseillers en Rel. Indust. Qué.; Amer. Chmbr. Comm. Extves; Club: St-Denis; Roman Catholic; recreations: reading, traveling; Office: 500 St-Francois-Xavier, Montreal, Qué.H2Y 2T6

LETSON, Maj.-Gen. Harry Farnham Germain, C.B., C.B.E., M.C., E.D., C.D., Ph.D., LL.D.; b. Vancouver, B.C., 26 Sept. 1896; s. James Moore Kelly and Mary Barbara (McIntosh) L.; Univ. of Brit. Columbia, B.Sc. 1919; London Univ., Ph.D. 1923; awarded Bernard T. Hall Prize of the Inst. of Mech. Engrs., England; Univ. of Brit. Columbia, LL.D. 1945; m. Sally McKee, d. Norman Lang, 10 May 1928; one stepson, John Lang Nichol; mem. of Advisory Bd., Royal Trust Co., Ottawa; Advisor on Militia, Candn. Army, 1954-58; Assoc. Prof. of Mech. Engn., U. of B.C., 1923-35; served in Candn. Militia 1910-58; commanded B.C. Regt. 1927-30; Univ. of B.C. C.O.T.C. 1930-36; Vancouver defences 1936-40; served in World War 1914-19; World War 1940-45 as Mil. Attaché, Washington, D.C., 1940-42; Adj. Gen. 1942-44; Chrmn., Candn. Joint Staff Mission, Washington, D.C., 1944-45; Secy. to Gov.-Gen. of Canada, 1946-52; Hon. Col., B.C. Regt. (D.C.O.) since 1963; awarded M.C.; U.S. Legion of Merit (two awards); Belgian Mil. Cross; Past Pres. and Hon. Life Pres., B.C. Rifle Assn.; Past Pres. and Life Gov., Dom. of Can. Rifle Assn.; commanded Candn. Bisley Team 1934; Fellow, Inst. of Engrs.; Life mem. Engn. Inst. of Can. and Assn. of Prof. Engrs. of B.C. (Past Pres.); Alpha Delta Phi; United Church; recreation: fishing; Clubs: Rideau; Vancouver; Home: 474 Lansdowne Rd., Ottawa, Ont. K1M 0X9

LEUNG, S. Wah, D.D.S., B.Sc., Ph.D., F.A.C.D., F.I.C.D., F.R.C.D.(C); educator; b. China 2 Nov. 1918; s. Chuk Ping and Sue (Gom) L.; e. Univ. of B.C. 1937-39; McGill Univ. D.D.S. 1943, B.Sc. 1945; Univ. of Rochester Ph.D. 1950; m. Sophia Ming Ren Chen 17 Aug. 1957; one s. Kenneth Walter; PROF. OF ORAL BIOL., UNIV. OF BRIT. COLUMBIA since 1962; Dean, Fac. of Dentistry, 1962-77; Coordinator, Chinese Scholars Exchange Progr., 1980- ; Assoc. Prof. of Physiol. Univ. of Pittsburgh Sch. of Dentistry 1950, Prof. and Chrmn. of Physiol. 1952-61, Prof. of Dental Research 1957-61, Dir. of Grad. Educ. 1956-61; Prof. of Oral Biol. Univ. of Cal. Los Angeles and Lectr. in Physiol. 1961-62; Test Constructor Nat. Bd. Dental Examiners (USA) 1960-66; Assoc. Comte. on Dental Research, Nat. Research Council 1965-68; Chrmn. Comte. of Examiners Nat. Bd. Dental Examiners 1967-71; Scientific consultant, Johnson & Johnson, 1950-58; Colgate Palmolive 1958-62; Lever Bros., 1963-65; Dir. Charles Chan Kent Scholarship and Charitable Foundation; Chrmn. of Bd. Vancouver Chinese Cultural Centre; rec'd. Montreal Dental Club Gold Medal 1943; Centennial Medal 1967; author over 40 articles scient. and prof. journs. and books; mem. Ed. Comte. "Journal of Dental Research"; Fellow, Am. Assn. Advanc. Science; Amer. Coll. Dentists; Intern. Coll. Dentists; Internat. Assn. Dental Research; Candn. Assn. Dental Research; Candn. Dental Assn.; Assn. Candn. Faculties Dentistry (Pres. 1970-72); Bd. of Dir., Vietramese Refugee Assistance Assn., 1979- ; Best Teacher Awards 1956 and 1958; Hon. mem. Vancouver & Dist. Dental Soc.; B.C. Dental Assn.; Coll. Dental Surgs. B.C.; Omicron Kappa Upsilon; Sigma Xi; Outstanding Citizen Award, Chinese Benevolent Assn. of Vancouver, 1980; Club: University; Home: 4883 College Highroad, Vancouver, B.C. V6T 1G6

LEVASSEUR, Pierre J., B.A., M.Com., M.B.A.; broadcasting executive; b. Québec City, Que. 26 Nov. 1938; s. Louis H. and Enid (Hart) L.; e. St. Dunstan's Univ., B.A. 1960; Laval Univ., B.Com. 1961, M.Com. 1962; Univ. Western Ont., M.B.A. 1966; m. Pauline, d. Guy Hamel, Cap Rouge, Que. 13 June 1964; children: Mimi, Mélanie; PRESIDENT, NATIONAL CABLEVISION LTD.; Chrmn. Bd., Video Service Inc.; Enterprises Consystel; Studios Marko; President, TéléCâble de Québec Inc.; Cablevision du Nord de Québec Inc.; Dir., Delta-Benco-Cascade Ltd.; Publico Inc.; Broadband Communications Networks Ltd.; Ballets Jazz de Montréal; began as Executive Assistant, Québec Min. of Education 1966; Secretary-General, Directorate Coll. Studies 1967; Director Gen., Federal Liberal Party (Que.) Montreal 1967; Dir. Operations, Trudeau Leadership Campaign, Ottawa 1968; Reg. Advisor, P.M. of Can. 1968; Dir., Airport Support Programmes, New Montreal Internat. Airport Project 1970-72; Teacher in Adm., Univs. Laval, Ottawa and Québec and Inst. of Urbanism Univ. of Montréal since 1966; currently Lectr. Centre de Perfectionnement en Adm. de l'Ecole des Hautes Etudes Comm.; mem. R.C.N.V.R.; last responsibility C.O., Univ. Training Div., HMCS Montcalm, Québec, Que.; Dir., Vanier Inst. Family; mem. Candn. Cable Television Association (Chairman Board Dirs.); Chambre de Comm. de Montréal; recreations: skiing, squash, swimming; Club: M.A.A.A.; Home: 365 Kitchener, Westmount, Que. H3Z 2G1

LEVER, Alfred Beverley Philip, B.Sc., Ph.D.; educator; research scientist; b. London, Eng., 21 Feb. 1936; s. Reginald Walter and Rose (Verber) L.; e. Imp. Coll., London Univ., B.Sc., A.R.C.S. 1957, Ph.D., D.I.C. 1960; m. Bernice Ann, d. Albert Roth, Kelowna, B.C., 19 July 1963; children: Gordon Joseph, Melanie Signe Anne, Janet Corinne; PROF. OF CHEMISTRY, YORK UNIV. since 1972; Dir. of Grad. Programme in Chem. there 1969-76; Postdoctoral Fellow, Univ. Coll. London, 1960-62; Visiting Research Assoc., Univ. of B.C., summer 1962; Lectr. Univ. of Manchester Inst. of Science & Technol., 1962-66; Visiting Research Assoc., Ohio State Univ., 1967;joined present Univ. as Assoc. Prof. 1967-72; Visiting Prof.,

Univ. of B.C. summer 1963, 1965; Univ. of Florence, summer 1973; Calif. Inst. of Technology, Pasadena, 1976-77; Univ. of Sydney, June-Aug. 1978; Plenary Lecturer, "XIV European Congress on Molecular Spectroscopy," Frankfurt, 1979; Sec. Lectr. — XV Internat. Conf. on Coordination Chem., Moscow, 1973; XIX, Prague, 1978; author, "Inorganic Electronic Spectroscopy", 1968; Ed., "Coordination Chemistry Reviews"; other writings incl. over 150 research publs.; mem. Chem. Soc. London; Am. Chem. Soc.; Chem. Inst. Can. (Chrmn. Inorganic Div. 1971-72); Amer. Assoc. for Advancem. of Science; Phi Lambda Upsilon; recreations: chess, music, swimming; Home: 79 Denham Dr., Thornhill, Ont. L4J 1P2; Office: 4700 Keele St., Downsview, Ont M3J 1P3

LEVESQUE, Albert, B.A., B.Bibl., M.L.S.; librarian; b. Campbellton, N.B., 3 June 1933; s. John and Laura (Parent) L.; two s., Pierre-Emmanuel, Jean-Sébastien; e. Univ. of Montreal, B.A. 1959, B.Bibl. 1962; Catholic Univ. of Am., M.L.S. 1970; m. Paulette, d. Roger T. Trudeau, Montreal, Qué. 17 Oct. 1970; LIBRARIAN, UNIV. OF MONCTON since 1973; Asst. Lib., Sém. St. Hyacinthe, Que. 1962; Founding Dir. of Lib., Nat. Univ. of Rwanda, Africa 1964-69 and Founding Dir., Rwandan Bibliographic Centre there 1970-72; Pub'l Contrib. to the Nat'l Bibliography of Rwanda 1965-1970; Pres., Council of Head Libraries of New Brunswick 1980; Liberal; Roman Catholic; Office: Moncton, N.B.

LEVESQUE, Hon. Denis, B.A., Ph.B., LL.L.; judge; b. Shawinigan, Que., 8 Sept. 1930; s. Georges and Antoinette (Lord) L.; e. Semy. Trois-Rivières, Que.; Univ. of Ottawa B.A., Ph.B.; Laval Univ. LL.L.; m. Françoise Dominique, d. François Guillaume Lahaise, 31 Aug. 1957; children: Martin, Rémy, Etienne, Agnès; JUSTICE, SUPERIOR COURT (QUE.); called to Bar of Que. 1956; R. Catholic; recreations: skiing, swimming, fishing; Home: 3830 Northcliffe, Montréal, Qué. H4A 3L1; Office: Court House, Montreal, Que.

LEVESQUE, Mt. Rev. Georges-Henri, O.C. (1967), LL.D., F.R.S.C. (R.C.); b. Roberval, Que., 16 Feb. 1903; s. Georges and Laura (Richard) L.; e. Coll. de Chicoutimi, B.A. 1923; Dominican Theol. and Philos. Coll., Lector in Sacred Theol., 1930; Univ. cath. de Lille (France), diplôme supérieur en Sciences sociales 1932; Univ. of B.C., LL.D. 1948; Hon. Doctorates Manitoba 1950; St. Francis Xavier 1951; Toronto 1952; Western 1953; St. Joseph 1954; Saskatchewan 1961; Ottawa 1961; Laval 1963; Sherbrooke 1967; McGill 1974; o. a Priest (Dominican) 15 April 1928; Predicator generalis of the Dominican Order; Professor of Social Philosophy, Dominican Theol. and Philos. Coll., Ottawa, Ont., 1933-38; Prof. Social Philos., Montreal Univ., 1935-39, and at Faculty of Philos., Laval Univ., 1935-38; organized a sch. of social sciences at Laval Univ. and was apptd. Dir. and Prof. of Econ. Philos., 1938; on elevation of this sch. to rank of faculty, apptd. Dean, 1943; Founder and First Pres. Univ. Nat. du Rwanda, Africa 1963-71, and Hon. Pres. and Advisor since 1971; Superior of Dominican Coll. (Montmorency House) 1955-63; in 1939 organ. "Le Conseil supérieur de la Coopération de la Que." of which he was first Pres. until 1944; Founder and First Dir., Les Cahiers de la Faculté des Sciences sociales; Foundateur de la revue "Ensemble!"; mem., Conseil supérieur du Travail de la P.Q.; Conseil d'orientation économique de la Que.; Canadian Youth Commission; Canadian Association for Adult Educ., Candn. Pol. Science Assn.; Am. Acad. of Pol. & Social Sciences; de la royal d'enquête sur les arts, les sciences et les lettres (1949); Roy. Soc. of Can. (1st Vice-Pres. 1962-63); mem. and Vice Chairman, The Canada Council; awarded Cross de Chevalier de la Legion d'Hon. (France) 1950; recreation: music 2715 Côre Ste-Catherine, Montreal, Que. H3T 1B6

LEVESQUE, Gerald; company executive; b. Woonsocket, R.I., 24 Feb. 1926; s. Georges-Etienne and Yvonne

(Lambert) L.; e. m. Anita, d. Ernest Lajoie, 29 May 1950; four s. Daniel, André, Pierre, Robert; PRES., MEAGHER'S DISTILLERY LTD. AND GILLESPIES AND CO. LIMITED; Coca Cola Ltd., 1949-52; Canadian Breweries Ltd., 1952-64; Vice-Pres., Marketing, Dow Brewery (Que.) Ltd., 1964-66; Vice-Pres., Marketing, Pepsi-Cola Canada Ltd., 1966-68; mem., Chambre de Comm. de Montréal; Ad and Sales Extve. Club of Montreal; Quebec Distillers Assoc.; Assn. of Candn. Distillers; R. Catholic; recreations: golf, sailing, skiing, cooking, painting; Home: 12 Woodridge Cres., Beaconsfield, Que. H9W 4G7; Office: 950 Chemin des Moulins, Montreal, Que. H3C 3W5

LEVESQUE, Hon. Gerard D., Q.C., M.N.A., LL.L.; b. Port Daniel, Bonaventure County, Que., 2 May 1926; e. Gaspe Semy.; Brebeuf Coll., Montreal; Univ. of Montreal, B.A. 1946; McGill Univ., LL.L. 1949; m. Denyse Lefort 24 Sept. 1949; children: Robert, Andre, Bertrand, Suzanne, Marie; partner, Sheehan and Levesque 1949-60; Levesque & Arsenault 1966-70; Levesque and Landry 1971-75; principal shareholder, Levesque Auto Ltd. Since 1951 and Carleton Auto Ltd. since 1957; 1st el. to Quebec Legislature for Bonaventure in 1956, re-el. 1960, 1962, 1966, 1970, 1973, 1976, 81; Minister of Game and Fisheries, 1960-62; Minister of Industry and Commerce, 1962-66; re-el. in Que. g.e. 1966 but Gov. def.; re-el. Apr. 1970 and apptd. Min. Industry and Commerce, 1970-72; apptd. Minister of Intergovtl. Affairs 1970-71 and 1972-75; Gov't House Leader 1971-76; minister responsible for Quebec Planning Office 1972-76; Minister of Justice 1975-76; Leader of Que. Lib. Party 1976-78; Leader of Official Opposition, Qué. Nat. Assembly 1976-79; HOUSE LEADER, OFFICIAL OPPOSITION, NATIONAL ASSEMBLY, QUE., 1979-; Dir., Que. Assn. of Auto Dealers 1955-57; Past Regional Pres. (1953), Gaspe Peninsula Chamber of Comm. (onetime Pub. Relations Dir. in E. sec. of Prov.); mem., Extve. Bd., prov. of Qué. Chamber of Commerce, 1955; chrmn., Baie des Chaleurs Automobiles Dealers Assn. 1952-55; called to the Bar of P.Q. 1949; K. of C. (4th degree); Liberal, Catholic; Clubs: Cercle Universitaire (Que.); Reform (Que.); Garrison (Que.); Homes: Paspebiac, Que. G0C 2K0 and 2550 de la Falaise, Sillery, Que. G1T 1W3; Office: New Carlisle, Co. Bonaventure, Que. G0C 1Z0 and Parliament Bldgs., Quebec, Que.

LEVESQUE, J.-Louis, C.M., D.C.Sc., D.P.Ec., L.L.D., D.Soc.Sc.; corporate executive; b. Nouvell, Bonaventure Co., Que., 13 April 1911; s. Jean and Mary (Greene) L.; e. Gaspé Coll.; St. Dunstan's Univ., D.C.Sc., St. Joseph Univ.; Laval Univ.; D.P.Ec., Sacred Heart Univ.; Univ. of Montreal; LL.D., St. Dunstan's Univ.; D.Soc.Sc., Univ. of Moncton; m. Jeanne Brisson, May 1938; two d., one s.; CHAIRMAN, LEVESQUE, BEAUBIEN INC.; Industrial Life Insurance Co.; Pres., Le Credit Interprov. Inc.; Dir., Librarie Beauchemin Ltée; Hilton Can. Ltd.; L'Equitable Co. d'Assurances Générales; Windsor Raceway Holdings Ltd.; J. Louis Levesque Investments Inc.; Montreal Heart Instit. Research Fund; Miami Heart Inst.; Indian Creek Country; Tropical Park Inc.; Trust., mem., Jockey Club of Can.; Ont. Jockey Club; Commdr. of Order of St. Gregory the Great; Kt. of Magistral Grace, Sovereign & Mil. Order of Malta; Order of Canada; Cdn. Business Hall of Fame; Roman Catholic; Clubs: Indian Creek Country (Miami); Home: 3465 Redpath St., Montreal, Que. H3G 2G8;

LEVESQUE, Most Rev. Louis, (R.C.); retired archbishop; b. Amqui (Matapédia), Que., 27 May 1908; s. Philippe and Catherine (Beaulieu) L.; e. Laval Univ., B.A. 1928, Ph.L. 1930, Th.L. 1931, Th.D. 1932; Biblical Insts., Rome and Jerusalem, S.S.L. 1935; Inst. catholique, P.P.C. 1936; taught Holy Scripture, Rimouski, 1936-52; Bishop of Hearst, Ont. 1952-64; Archbishop of Rimouski, 1964-73 Pres., Candn. Cath. Conf. 1965-67; mem., Cath. Biblical Assn. of Am.; Assn. Cath. Etudes Bibliques au Can.;

mem., Congregation of Bishops (Rome) 1968-73; Address: 57 Ave. Hôtel-de-Ville, Mont. Joli, Que G5H 1W9.

LEVESQUE, René; politician; b. 24 Aug. 1922, New Carlisle, Qué. s. late Dominique and Diane (Dionne) e. began studies in Gaspé, completed his classical course in Québec; m. Corinne Coté; (2 s., Pierre, Claude, Id. Suzanne, from previous marriage.) PREMIER OF QUEBEC since 1976; el. to Que. Leg. for Lib. Party for Montréal-Laurier, g.e. 1960; Min. of Public Works and Min. of Hydraulic Resources, July 1960-March 1961; Min. of Natural Resources, Apl. 1961-June 1966 Min. Family & Social Welfare 1966; def. in Que. g.e. Apl. 1970 and returned to journalism with "Journal de Montréal" and "Le Jour"; Co-founder, Mouvement Souveraineté Assn., 1968; Co-founder and Pres., Parti Québecois and led party to victory in 1976 and 1981 elections (rep. riding of Taillon); first worked as radio announcer; became a War Corr. for Amer. military forces, 1943-45, and for CBC in Korea 1952; Head of C.B.C. Raio & Television reporting, 1952-56; 1956-59, host of Radio Canada publ. affairs program "Point de Mire"; afterwards was freelance radio and TV commentator in Montréal; author: "An Option for Québec", 1968; "La Passion du Québec", 1978; "OUI" 1980; Grand Officer, Legion d'Honour, 1977; Medal of the City of Paris, 1977; Hon. Doctorate, Univ. Sorbonne (Paris) 1980; Office: Parliament Bldgs., Quebec, Que.

LEVESQUE, René Jules Albert, B.Sc., Ph.D.; physicist; educator; b. St. Alexis, Qué. 30 Oct. 1926; s. Albert and Elmina Louisa (Veuilleux); e. Sir George Williams Univ. B.Sc. 1952; Northwestern Univ. Ph.D. 1957; m. 6 Apl. 1956 (divorced); children: Marc, Michel, André; VICE PRES. (RESEARCH) UNIV. DE MONTRÉAL 1978- and Prof. of Physics 1967- ; Research Assoc. Univ. of Md. 1957-59; Asst. Prof. Univ. de Montréal 1959, Assoc. Prof. 1964-67, Dir. Nuclear Physics Lab. 1965-69, Chrm. of Physics 1968-73, Vice Dean Faculty of Arts & Science 1973-75, Dean 1975-78; mem. Comn. on Higher Educ. Qué. Ministry of Educ. 1972-78, Vice Pres. 1977-78; Vice Pres. Canada-France-Hawaii Telescope Corp. 1979, Pres. 1980; Vice Pres. Assn. Scient. Engn. & Technol. Community Can. 1979, Pres. 1980; Vice Pres. Interciencia Assn. 1979-80; Vice Pres. Natural Sciences & Engn. Research Council Can. 1981; mem. Bd. Hôpital du Sacré-Coeur Montréal; mem. Candn. Assn. Physicists (Pres. 1976-77); author numerous publs. nuclear structure field; rec'd Queen Elizabeth Silver Jubilee Medal; recreations: cycling, skiing; Home: 190 Willowdale, PH #1, Outremont, Qué. H3T 1G2; Office: (P.O. Box 6128 Stn. A) Montréal, Qué. H3C 3J7.

LEVINE, Les; artist; b. Ireland, 6 Oct. 1935; s. Charles Solomon and Murial (McMahon) L.; e. Central Sch. of Arts & Crafts, London, Eng.; came to Can. 1957; m. Catherine Kazuko, d. Alton Kanai, Honolulu, Hawaii, 26 Aug. 1973; Artist-in-Residence, N.S. Coll. of Art & Design, 1973; Assoc. Prof., N.Y. Univ. 1971, 1972; showings: "Etchings & Videotapes", Isaac's Gal., Toronto, 1980; "Ads", Marian Goodman Gal., N.Y., 1980; "Deep Gossip" and "I Am Not Blind", Ronald Feldman Gal., N.Y., 1980; "Peggy's Cove", Isaacs Gallery, Toronto, 1973; "Position", Fischbach Gallery, N.Y., 1972; photomedia exhn. "The Troubles", Finch Coll., N.Y., 1973; collections incl. Museum Modern Art, N.Y.; Whitney Museum, N.Y.; Philadelphia Museum; N.Y. Cultural Center; Nat. Gallery of Can. (Ottawa); Art Gallery of Ont. (Toronto); Vancouver Art Gallery; Assoc. Ed., "Arts Magazine" 1973-74; author, "House", 1971; other writings incl. ed's and articles in various journs.; mem., Arch. League N.Y. (Vice Pres. 1969-71); rec'd. 1st Prize, Candn. Sculpture Biennale, 1967; rec'd Nat. Endowment for the Arts Fellowship Award 1974 & 1980; N.Y. State Council of Arts Video Award 1980; Address: Museum of Mott Art, Inc., 20 East 20th., New York, N.Y.10003.

LEVINE, Norman, M.A.; writer; b. Ottawa, Ont., 22 Oct. 1924; s. Moses Mordecai and Annie (Gurevich) L.; e. York St. Sch. and High Sch. of Comm., Ottawa; Carleton Coll., 1945; McGill Univ., B.A. 1948, M.A. 1949; m. (late) Margaret, d. late Sydney Robert Payne, London, Eng., 2 Jan. 1952; children: Cass, Kate, Rachel; Head of Eng. Dept., Boys Grammar Sch., Barnstaple, N. Devon, 1953-54; first resident writer at Univ. of N.B., 1965-66; served Overseas with RCAF 1942-45; rank Flying Offr.; CBC film "Norman Levine Lived Here" made in 1970; BBC film "Norman Levine's St. Ives" 1972; author: "The Tightrope Walker"; "The Angled Road"; "Canada Made Me"; "One Way Ticket"; "From a Seaside Town"; "I Don't Want to Know Anyone Too Well and other stories" 1971; "Selected Stories" 1975; "I Walk by the Harbour" 1976; "In Lower Town" (story with photographs) 1977; "Thin Ice" 1979 (reviewed by Bernard Levin in Sunday Times); "Eein Kleines Stuckchen Blau" (selected stories — transl. by H. Boll) 1971; "Der Mann mit Dem Notizbuch" (stories) 1975; enlarged ed. 1979; Editor, "Canadian Winter's Tales"; writings incl. in various anthologies, Oxford Book of Canadian Verse, Penguin Book of Canadian Verse; The Puffin Book of Salt-Sea Verse; Major Canadian Writers; Contemporary Voices; The Best Modern Canadian Short Stories; Canadian Short Stories; Vogue's Gallery; Winter's Tales; Saturday Night; Sunday Times; Tamarak Reviw; B.B.C.; C.B.C. Anthology; subject to TV Ontario film in St. James Park, London, 1980; Interviewed by Philip Oakes in Sunday Times, July 1970; has contributed to various journs., magazines and newspapers; Address: 45 Bedford Rd., St. Ives, Cornwall, Eng.

LEVINSON, Charles, B.B.A., M.A., Ph.D.; trade unionist and writer; b. Ottawa, Ont., 19 Oct. 1920; s. Abraham and Gertrude (Isrealite) L.; e. St. John's Univ., N.Y. City, B.B.A. 1943; Univ. of Toronto, M.A. 1947; Univ. of Paris, Ph.D. 1949; m. Marie Rose, d. Baroness Theodore De Gunzburg of N.Y. City, May 1965; children: Catherine Gertrude, Alexandra Wilhelmina, Marrisa; SECY. GEN., INTERNATIONAL FED. OF CHEM. ENERGY & GEN. WORKERS' UNION since 1964; Dir. Gen., International Technical Assistance & Training Services (ITS); Asst. Ed., Labor Gazette, Dom. Dept. of Lab., 1945; Lectr. in Econ., Univs. of Paris and Toronto, 1947-49; Consultant on contractual basis with Am. Internat. Assistance Dept., 1950-57; Depy. Secy. Gen., Internat. Metalworkers' Fed. (IMF), Geneva, 1958-63; Dir. Tech. Assistance Dept. Organ. for Rehab. through Training (ORT), 1961-68; has surveyed and advised on vocational training and tech. educ. needs to 12 African govts., created and directed Vocational Training Schs. and Projects in numerous countries; served in 2nd World War, Pilot, R.C.A.F.; Flying Offr., Coastal Command Sqdn. 423; completed tour of operations in European theatre; mem. Extve. Council of Suisse-African Coll., (Univ. of Geneva); Council, Geneva-African Inst., Geneva, Switzerland; Swiss Socialist Party; N.D.P.; recreations: skiing, skating, golf, music, theatre; Home: 27 Ave. de Budé, Geneva, Switzerland; Office: 58 rue Moillebeau, Geneva, Switzerland.

LEVINTER, Benjamin V., Q.C., B.S.A., b. Toronto, Ont., 16 Dec. 1925; s. Isadore and Adeline (Miller) L.; e. Ont. Agric. Coll., Univ. of Toronto, B.S.A. 1947; Osgoode Hall Law Sch., 1952; m. Marion Elizabeth, d. Frederick J. Fischer, 1 March 1949; children: Dara Rebecca, Jan Fredericka, Shaun (Shoshana) Judith, Loretta Noreen Samuel Lyon; PAST CHRMN. OF BD., UNITY BANK OF CANADA (charter granted 1972) and Co-founder of Bank; Partner law firm Levinter and Levinter; read law with Isadore Levinter, Q.C.; called to Bar of Ont. 1952; cr. Q.C. 1964; Dir., York Finch Gen. Hosp.; Dir., Shareii Tefillah Congreg.; mem., Candn. Bar Assn.; Internat. Acad. Trial Lawyers; Co. York Law Assn.; Advocates Soc.; Agric. Inst. Can.; B'nai B'rith Hebrew; recreations: farming, horses fishing, boating; Clubs: Albany; Primrose; Home: R.R. 2, Woodbridge, Ont. L4L 1A6; Office: 111 Richmond St. W., Toronto, Ont. M5H 3R5

LEWIS, Clifford Wesley, Q.C., B.A.; b. Campbellton, N.B. 15 April 1922; s. Ernest Harold and Gladys Winnifred (MacArthur) L.; e. St. George's Sch. and Commissioner's High Sch. (Quebec, Que.); Univ. of Toronto, B.A. (Hons. Philos.) 1949; Osgoode Hall Law Sch. 1953; m. Nelda Jean, d. late Kenneth G. Brown 5 Sept. 1950; children: Barbara Jean, Katherine Ann; PARTNER, MILLER, THOMSON, SEDGEWICK, LEWIS & HEALY; called to Bar of Ont. 1953; cr. Q.C. 1965; R.C.A.F., Air Crew Offr. 1940-45; mem. Candn. Bar Assn.; Anglican; recreations: golf, skiing, sailing; Clubs: Toronto Golf; Caledon Ski; Home: 39 Ravensbourne Cres., Islington, Ont. M9A 2A9; Office: P.O. Box 27, 20 Queen St. W., Toronto, Ont. M5H 3S1

LEWIS, David Andrew, B.Com., S.M.; banker; b. Toronto, Ont. 26 Feb. 1937; s. George Dimmick and Kathleen Emma (Nettelfield) L.; e. Univ. of Toronto Schs. 1955; Univ. of Toronto B.Com. 1959; Mass. Inst. of Technol. S.M. 1967; m. Penelope Anne d. Robert Christopher Dobson, Toronto, Ont. 12 June 1959; children: David Nettelfield, Jennifer Robinson, Christopher Dobson; EXECUTIVE VICE PRES. AND CHIEF OPERATING OFFICER, CONTINENTAL BANK OF CANADA 1981- ; joined Imperial Bank of Canada, Toronto 1959, Regional Gen. Mgr. Alta. and N.W.T., Calgary 1967, Toronto 1969, Vice Pres. 1971, Sr. Vice Pres. Deposit Business, Marketing and Customer Services 1973; Sr. Vice Pres., Offc. of the Chrmn., 1979; Sr. Vice-Pres. Domestic Regions, 1980; dir., United Way of Greater Toronto, Pres. 1979-80, Chrmn. of Bd. 1980-82; dir., Continental Bank of Canada; Vice-Pres. and dir., United Way of Canada; mem. Adv. Council, Salvation Army; Anglican; recreations: skiing, golf, sailing; Clubs: Toronto; Toronto Golf; Badminton & Racquet; Office: 130 Adelaide St. W., Toronto, Ont. M5H 3R2.

LEWIS, Herbert, M.A., Ph.D.; educator; b. Montreal, Que., 12 Jan. 1929; s. Adolphe and Anne (Goldstein) L.; e. McGill Univ., B.A. 1953, M.A. 1954, Sch. of Social Work 1955-56; Johns Hopkins Univ. 1955; Univ. de Montréal, Ph.D. 1968; m. Sara Lee, d. Germain G. Levitan, 28 Apl. 1972; children: Monika, Adrian, Ira Gesser, Gina Gesser, Margo Gesser; PROF., DEPT. OF PHILOSOPHY, ACADIA UNIV. 1959-81; mem. Nat. Comte. W.U.S.C., 1961-67; Extve. Comte. C.U.S.O. 1965-67; mem., Candn. Philos. Assn.; Am. Assn. Advanc. Science; Candn. Soc. 18th Century Studies (Extve. 1971); Hebrew; recreations: philately, classical music; Home: 4 Fairfield St., Wolfville, N.S. B0P 1X0; Office: Wolfville, N.S. B0P 1X0

LEWIS, John Monk, B.A.; investment executive; b. Montreal 28 June 1924; e. McGill Univ. B.A. 1949; Khaki Coll. 1945-46; m. Joan Kalfeissen Hart 7 Oct. 1978; children: Eve, Suzanne, Catherine, Duncan, Michelle, Nicole, Christopher, Lisa; PRESIDENT, FRASER, DINGMAN & CO. LTD.: Clubs: Strollers; Badminton & Racquet; Home: 28 Metcalfe St., Toronto, Ont. M4X 1R6; Office: 199 Bay St., Toronto, Ont. M5J 1L4

LEWIS, Stephen (Henry), lecturer; b. Ottawa, Ont., 11 Nov. 1937; s. David, Q.C. (former Fed. Leader of New Democratic Party) and Sophie (Carson) L.; m. Michele Landsberg 30 May 1963; children: Ilana, Avram, Jenny; 1st el. to Ont. Leg., 25 Sept. 1963; Leader of Ont. N.D.P. 1970-78; became Leader of the official opposition in the Leg. 18 Sept. 1975; resigned seat 10 Nov. 1978; Home: 6 Montclair Ave, Toronto, Ont.

LEWIS, Victor Stanley George, P.Eng.; Hon. Maj. executive; b. Birmingham, Eng. 10 June 1919; s. Mark George and Nellie (Webster) L.; e. Coll. Sch. Saltley 1924; Birmingham Tech. Coll. Higher Nat. Cert. 1933, Mech. Engn. with Endorsements; m. Lucille Joan d. Nicholas Karlicki, Winnipeg, Man. 4 Feb. 1971; children: Mark Victor, Andrea Jodi; by previous marriage, Peter Noel, Simon Andrew, Julia Susan; PRES., GENSTAR DEVELOP-MENT CO. 1966- ; joined Brit. Army 1939, served as Engr. with Armd. Divisions, N. Africa 1941-47, rank Maj., War Office 1947-50, Germany 1950-53, NATO Exchange Offr. Can. 1953-55, Depy. Asst. Dir. Mech. Engn. War Office 1955-57; resigned comn. and emigrated to Can. 1957; Partner, Wilmac Construction 1957-58; Gen. Mgr., Calgary Suburban Developments 1958-59; Extve. Vice Pres., Engineered Homes 1959-66; Pres., Urban Devel. Inst. Alta. 1960-62; Candn. Home Mfrs. Assn. 1967-69; Urban Devel. Inst. Can. and Urban Devel. Inst. Man. 1967-69; Urban Devel. Inst. B.C. 1973-75; presented papers Candn. Trade Mission France, Germany and U.K. 1964; Head, Candn. Trade Mission to Spain, France, Germany and U.K. 1965; honoured by City of Calgary for indust. expansion 1966 and by Prov. Man. for contrib. to planning econ. devel. of prov. 1969; rec'd Queen's Silver Jubilee Medal 1978; mem. Inst. Mech. Engrs.; Assn. Prof. Engrs. B.C.; Anglican; recreations: music, gardening, swimming; Home: 14636 - 55A Avenue, Surrey, B.C. V3S 1B1; Office: Suite 400, 15225 104 Avenue, Surrey, B.C. V3R 6Y8.

LEWIS, W. James D., C.D., B.A., M.A., F.S.A., F.C.I.A.; insurance executive; b. Toronto, Ont. 1922; e. Public Sch. and Riverdale Coll. Inst., Toronto; Univ. of Toronto, B.A. 1947, M.A. 1948; m. Gertrude Ruth Ingram, Toronto, Ont.; three d., one s.; PRESIDENT, CANDN. OPERATIONS, PRUDENTIAL INSURANCE CO. OF AMERICA since 1972; Pres. and Dir., Prudential Growth Fund Canada Ltd.; Pres. and Trust. Prudential Income Fund of Can.; Dir., Prudential Fund Management Ltd.; PIC Realty Canada Ltd.; joined Confederation Life Insurance Co. 1948, Asst. Actuary 1949, Assoc. Actuary 1957, Actuary 1961,; c. computer operations 1961-64, Vice-Pres. Individual Ins. 1966; joined present Co. as Extve. Vice-Pres. Candn. Operations 1971; served in 2nd World War, R.C.A., rank on discharge Capt.; Pres. Candn. Inst. of Actuaries, 1977-78; Past Chrmn., Can. Life Ins. Ass'n.; Clubs: Royal Canadian Military Institute; Toronto; Faculty, Univ. of Toronto; Office: 4 King St. W., Toronto, Ont. M5H 1B7

LEWIS, Wilfrid Bennett, C.C. (1967), C.B.E. (1946), M.A., Ph.D., D.Sc., LL.D., F.R.S. (1945), F.R.S.C. (1952), F.Phys.S. (Lond.) F.A.P.S.; retired public servant; father and g. father both distinguished civil engineers; b. 24 June 1908; s. Arthur Wilfrid and Isoline Maud (Steavenson) L.; e. Clare House Prep. Sch., Beckenham, Kent, Eng., 1916-22; Haileybury Coll., Hertford, Eng., 1922-26; Gonville and Caius Coll., Cambridge Univ., B.A. 1930, M.A. 1934, Ph.D. 1934; Hon. Fellow 1971; D.Sc. Queen's 1960; Sask. 1964, Dartmouth 1967, McMaster 1965, McGill 1969; Roy. Mil. Coll. 1974; D. Sc., Laurentian Univ., Sudbury 1977; D. Sc. Univ. of Birmingham, England, 1977; LL.D. Dalhousie 1960; Carleton 1962, Trent 1968; Univ. of Toronto 1972; Univ. of Victoria 1975; with Research Lab., Chance Bros. Company Ltd., Smethwick, Birmingham, Eng., 1927; research at Cavendish Lab., Cambridge, under Sir Ernest (later Lord) Rutherford on accurate analysis of alpha particle groups from radioactive substances, 1930-34; Research Fellowship at Gonville and Caius Coll., 1934-40; Demonst. in Physics, Cambridge Univ., 1935-37; research on artificial disintegration in High Tension Lab., Cavendish Lab., Cambridge, with Dr. J.D. Cockcroft, 1935-37; Lect. in Physics, Cambridge Univ., 1937-39; design construction and operation of cyclotron at Cambridge, 1937-39; radar research, Bawdsey Research Station (which later became Telecommunications Research Estab.), 1939-46; Chief Supt., Telecommunications Research Estab. 1945-46; Dir., Atomic Energy Division, N.R.C., 1946-52; Vice-Pres., Research & Devel., Atomic Energy of Canada Limited, 1952-63, Sr. Vice Pres., Science, 1963-73; Candn. Rep. on U.N. Scient. Adv. Comte. since 1955; mem., 12 Nation Comte. of Experts, U.N. Secy. Gen. on Implications of Atomic Weapons; mem. Scient. Adv. Comte. to Dir.-Gen. of Internat. Atomic Energy Agency, 1958-78; Cambridge Univ.,

O.T.C., Signal Unit, 1927-30, as O.C., Capt. (T.A.), 1938-39; Fellow, Am. Nuclear Soc. (Pres. 1961-62); rec'd. (1st) "outstanding achievement award" introduced by Govt. to honour exceptional accomplishment in the nat. interest. Nov. 1966; Atoms for Peace Award 1967; 25th Anniversary Gold Medal, Candn. Assn. Physicists 1971; Royal Medal, Royal Soc.(London, Eng.) 1972; W.B. Lewis Medal, Candn. Nuclear Assn. 1973; Distinguished Prof. of Sc., Physics Dept., Queen's Univ., Kingston, 1973; Hon. Fellow, Inst. Elect. Engrs. 1974; Honorary Fellow, Manchester Institute Science and Technol. 1974; McNaughton Gold Medal 1981; Publications: "Electrical Counting", 1942; "Storing Radioactive Wastes in Cooled Pebbles", 1977; "Antiproliferation Fuel Cycles: The Low Cost Thorium Fuel Cycle", 1977; "Nuclear Energy Alternatives" Ballinger, 1980; "International Arrangements for nuclear Fuel Reprocessing" Ballinger 1977; 'New Ideas in Human Evolution", Trans. Roy. Soc. Canada Vo XVI; 1978; papers since 1929 in "Wireless Engineer", "Proceedings", Roy. Soc., "Proceedings", Cambridge Philosophical Soc., "Philosophical Magazine", "Journal" of Inst. of Elect. Engrs., "Proceedings" of Physical Soc. incl. I.E.E. Centenary Lecture Toronto, 1971; papers in Procs. of U.N. Confs. on Peaceful Uses of Atomic Energy, 1955, 1958, 1964, 1971; biographical memoirs on assocs.; Anglican; Home: 13 Beach Ave., Deep River, Ont. K0J 1P0

LEYRAC, Monique, C.C.; chanteuse; b. Montreal, Que. 26 Feb. 1928; trained in elocution and studied theatre with Jeanne Maubourg, Montreal; made debut as actress (Le Chant de Bernadette) on Radio 1944; toured France, Switzerland, Belgium, 1950-1; joined Théâtre du Nouveau Monde 1955-66; performed in "Three-Penny Opera", "Le Malade Imaginaire" and "Bérénice" among others; rec'd 1st Prize Internat. Song Festival, Sopot, Poland 1965 and Ostend, Belgium; major role Paul Almond's "Act of the Heart", 1970; proclaimed "best singer of year" twice, and "woman of the year" twice in the Canadian Press' annual survey of women's editors; named an officer of the Order of Canada in 1968; received the 1978 Prix de musique Calixa-Lavallée; has made numerous radio and TV appearances and recorded for Columbia Records.

L'HEUREUX-DUBÉ, Hon. Claire, B.A., LL.L.; judge; b. Québec, Qué. 7 Sept. 1927; d. Col. Paul H. and Marguerite (Dion) L'Heureux; e. Monastère des Ursulines, Rimouski; Coll. Notre-Dame de Bellevue, Qué. B.A.; Univ. Laval LL.L.; m. Prof. Arthur Dubé 30 Nov. 1957; children: Louise, Pierre; JUDGE, COURT OF APPEAL, QUE. 1979- ; Pres., Internat. Comm. of Jurists (Can. Sect.) 1981- ;called to Bar of Qué. 1952; cr. Q.C. 1969; mem. law firm Bard, l'Heureux & Philippon 1952-69; Sr. mem. L'Heureux, Philippon, Garneau, Tourigny & St-Arnaud 1969-73; Lectr. in Family Law, Cours de formation professionnelle du Barreau de Qué. 1968-73; Puisné Judge, Superior Court of Qué. 1973; Commr. to investigate and report on certain matters relating to Dept. Manpower & Immigration Montreal 1973; mem. Conseil consultatif de l'adm. de la justice de la Prov. de Qué. 1967-73, Vice Prés. 1973; Vice Pres., Can. Consumer Council 1970-73; The Vanier Inst. of the Family 1972-73; Chrmn. Human Rights & Family Law Comte. and Family Court Comte., Que. Civil Code Revision Office 1972-76; author various articles, book chapters; mem. Extve. Council, Barreau de Qué. 1968-70; Internat. Soc. Family Law (Extve. Council 1977-); R. Catholic; Home: 1014 Mont Saint-Denis, Sillery, Qué. G1S 1B3; Office: Palais de Justice (227), 12, rue Saint-Louis, Québec, Qué. G1R 4P6.

L'HEUREUX, Leon Joseph, B.A., B.Sc., M.A., D.Eng.; scientist; direct descendent of Louis Hébert, first settler in Canada who came with Champlain in 1608; b. Gravelbourg, Sask., 2 March, 1919; s. late Napoleon Joseph and Marie Anne (Morissette) L.; e. Public and High Schs., Gravelbourg, Sask.; Univ. of Ottawa (Mathieu Coll. Gravelbourg), B.A. 1940; Univ. of Sask., B.Sc. 1944;

Johns Hopkins Univ., M.A. (Elect. Engn.) 1948, D.Eng. 1949; m. Yvette Marie d. late Murdock McKenzie, 25 May, 1946; seven sons, one daughter; Chrmn., Defence Research Bd., 1969-77; joined Candn. Armament Research & Devel. Estab. as Research Scientist, 1947; Project Engr. on Devel. of air-to-air guided missile project at C.A.R.D.E., 1949-52, Supt., Guided Missile Wing, 1952-55; Depy. Chief Supt. 1956-60; attended Nat. Defence Coll., Kingston, 1960-61; Scient. Advisor to Chief of Gen. Staff, 1961-63; Chief Supt., Candn. Armament Research & Devel. Estab., 1963-67; Vice Chrmn. Defence Research Bd. 1967; Offr. R.C.C.S., 1943-47; Sigma Xi; Roman Catholic; recreations: camping, baseball; Home: 717 Portage Ave., Ottawa, Ont. K1G1T2; Office: 101 Colonel By Dr., Ottawa, Ont.

LIEBERMAN, Hon. Samuel Sereth, C.D., B.A., LL.B.; judge; b. Edmonton, Alta. 14 Apl. 1922; s. Moses Isaac Lieberman; e. Garneau High Sch. Edmonton 1939; Univ. of Alta. B.A. 1947, LL.B. 1948; m. Nancy d. late H. M. Berman, Chicago, Ill. 15 July 1950; children: David J., Jo Ann Wood, Audrey G.; JUSTICE OF APPEAL OF THE COURT OF APPEAL OF ALBERTA and Judge, Court of Appeal, N.W.T. since 1976; called to Bar of Alta. 1949; cr. Q.C. 1962; apptd. to Dist. Court of Alta. 1966; Trial Div. Supreme Court of Alta. 1970; Sessional Lectr. in Law, Univ. of Alta.; Past Chrmn. (1969-78) Alta. Adv. Bd. of Review; Alta. Legal Aid Soc.; mem. W. Bd., Candn. Council Christians & Jews; Hon. Dir. Can.'s Aviation Hall of Fame; Hon. Life mem. Bd. Govs., Technion-Israel Inst. of Technol. Haifa; served with RCAF 1940-45, pilot, rank Sqdn. Leader, RCAF Auxiliary 1949-56; RCAF Aide-de-Camp to Lt. Gov. of Alta. 1953-56; Jewish; recreations: fishing, skiing; Club: Mayfair Golf & Country; Home: Apt. 1206 Grosvenor House, 10045-118 St., Edmonton, Alta. T5K 2K2; Office: The Law Courts, Edmonton, Alta. T5J 0R2.

LIEFF, Hon. Abraham Herman; Q.C.; b. Poland, 5 March 1903; s. Bernard and Esther Malca (Pomerantz) L.; e. Elem. and Secondary Schs., Ottawa, Ont.; Osgoode Hall, Toronto, Ont.; m. Sadie, d. late Louis Lazarovitz, Quebec City, 22 Sept. 1929; two d., Miriam (Mrs. Horace B. Cohen), Lois (Mrs. Morton Bessner); Justice, Supreme Court, Ont. until 1975; called to the Bar of Ont. 18 Nov. 1926; cr. K.C. 1948; Asst. Crown Atty., 1935-37; relieved all Magistrates in E. Ont., 1937-43; Magistrate, Co. of Carleton, 1937-46; Solr., Agric. Devel. Bd., 1934 to el. of Drew Govt.; 1946 Counsel, H. of C. Comte., Industrial Relations; former Chrmn. of Vocational Adv. Comte., Ottawa Collegiate Inst. Bd. (mem. of Comte. for some yrs.); prepared Report of Special Comte. of Senate of Can. on Narcotic Drug Traffic, 1956; mem. Nat. Acad. for Adult Jewish Studies; Council of Un. Synagogue of Am.; Freemason (Royal Arch.); Sigma Alpha Mu; Hebrew; recreations: golf, books, gardening; Clubs: Primrose; Oakdale Golf & Country; Kiwanis (Hon.); Home: 400 Walmer Rd., Apt. 1023 ET, Toronto, Ont. M5P 2X7

LIETERMAN, Richard Mark, R.C.A.; cinematographer; b. Dome Mines, Ont. 7 Apl. 1935; s. Douglas McGregor and Moynette (Stone) L.; e. W. Vancouver Sr. High Sch., Univ. of B.C. 1 yr.; m. Margaret June d. Alfred Mansall, Edmonton, Alta. 10 Nov. 1960; children: Mark Julien, Rachel; DIR., WINDFORCE PRODUCTIONS LTD.; Newsreel and documentary cameraman London, Eng. and Toronto 1962-68; Cameraman and Co-dir. "Married Couple" 1969; Cinematographer "Goin' Down the Road" 1970 and eleven maj. Candn. feature films; Dir. various TV documentaries; rec'd Etrog Award "Best Cinematography" 1975; Address: 31 Kendal Ave., Toronto, Ont. M5A 1L5.

LIGERTWOOD, Douglas Alexander; publicist; executive; b. Winnipeg, Man., 20 July 1924; s. Frederick Boyce and Sarah Heather (Richardson) L.; e. Kelvin Tech. High Sch.; N. Vocational High Sch., Toronto; Univ. of Alta.,

Electronics Engn.; Internat. Correspondence Schs., Elect. Engn.; Royal Candn. Legion Correspondence Course, Elect. Engn.; Man. Inst. of Technol., Upgrade Electronics; m. Gwendolyn Ada, d. late Ambrose Spiece, 2 June 1945; children: Peter, Cheryl; formed own mfg. agency, Douglas A. Ligertwood Ltd. (inc. 1963), 1960; Dir., Selectrovac Heating; Micro-Com Electronics Ltd.; joined Canadian General Electric, Winnipeg, 1942; apptd. Indust. Products Dept. Rep. 1955; Lectr., Illuminating Engn. Soc. groups across w.; adviser control lighting Man. Theatre Center, Winnipeg Concert Hall, Royal Winnipeg Ballet, drama schs. and T.V.; served with RCNVR 1942-45; radio artificer; Pres., W. Can. Party since founding 1971; Owner Dals Westerners Hard Ball Team; served as an offr. and inst. Navy League Cadets and Sea Cadets for 20 yrs.; mem., Man. Elect. Assn.; Illuminating Engn. Soc. (Past Chrmn. Winnipeg Sec.); Ex Chiefs & Petty Offrs. Assn.; Freemason; Protestant; recreation: philately; Address: 103 Kingston Row, Winnipeg, Man. R2M 0S7

LIGHT, John Gideon, B.A.Sc.; retired executive; b. North Battleford, Sask., 5 May 1913; s. Gideon Seth and Minnie Emma (Short) L.; e. Univ. of B.C., B.A.Sc. (Chem. Engn.) 1938; m. Jean Frances Cully, 28 Dec. 1946; children: Mary, James, John; Vice Pres. (Refining), Texaco Canada Ltd., 1969-78; Vice Pres., Regent Refining Canada Ltd. (ret.); joined Bahrein Petroleum Co. (affiliated co.) as Jr. Engr., San Francisco, 1938; Shift Operator, Bahrein Island, 1938-40; transferred to present Co. as Refinery Supervisor, Montreal, 1940-44; Chief Process Engineer, 1950; Asst. to Mgr. Refining Dept., 1951; Mgr. of Dept., 1952 and Gen. Mgr. of Dept., 1963; Pres., Montreal Assn. for Mentally Retarded, 1967-69; Dir., Lauren Tide Chemical and Sulpher Ltd., Montreal; Hon. Life mem., Quebec Assns. for Mentally Retarded; Pres., Foundation for the Mentally Retarded (Que.) Inc., 1973; Dir. (1968-70) Candn. Assn. for Mentally Retarded; Assoc. Prof. Eng. Chem. (ret.); Life mem., Chem. Corp. Engrs. Que. (ret.); Protestant; recreation: fishing; Clubs: Mount Stephen (Montreal); Home: 15 Green Valley Rd., Willowdale, Ont. M2P 1A4;

LIGHT, Walter Frederick, B.Sc.; communications executive; b. Cobalt, Ont., 24 June 1923; s. Herbert and Rosetta Elizabeth (Hoffman) L.; e. Secondary Sch., Cobalt, Ont.; Queen's Univ., B.Sc. (Hons.) 1949; Hon. LL.D., Concordia Univ. 1980; Queen's Univ. 1981; Hon. D.Ap.Sci., Univ. of Ottawa 1981; m. Margaret Anne Wylie, d. Dr. J. R. Miller, Iroquois, Ont., 8 July 1950; children: Elizabeth Jean, Janice Catherine; PRES. (AUG. '74) AND C.E.O. (OCT. 1 '79) NORTHERN/Northern TELECOM LTD. Dir., Bell Canada; Genstar Ltd.; Hudson's Bay Oil and Gas Co. Ltd.; Inco Ltd.; Northern Telecom Ltd.; The Procter & Gamble Co.; Royal Bank of Can.; Canadian Executive Service Overseas; joined Bell Canada, Toronto, Ontario as Engn. Asst. 1949, variety managing posts Toronto and Montreal 1952-67; apptd. Vice-Pres. (Engn.) 1967; Vice-Pres. (Operations) 1969; Extve. Vice-Pres. (Operations) 1970; served with R.C.A.F. 1942-45; mem., Corp. of Engrs. of Que.; Assn. Prof. Engrs. (Ont.); C.D. Howe Research Inst.; Electrical manuf. Club; Fellow Engn. Inst. of Canada; Gov., Montreal Museum of Fine Arts and of Associates of Carlton U.; mem., Bd. of Trustees, Queen's Univ.; Clubs: Granite; York; Forest and Stream (Dorval); Mount Royal; Home: 16 Edmund Ave., Toronto Ont., M4V 1H3; Office: 33 City Centre Dr., Mississauga Ont. L5B 2N5

LIGHTFOOT, Gordon Meredith, O.C.; singer, songwriter; b. Orillia, Ont. 17 Nov. 1938; s. Gordon Meredith and Jessie Vick (Trill) M.; student Westlake Coll. Music, Los Angeles, 1958; divorced; children: Fred, Ingrid; singer, songwriter 1959- ; compositions incl. "Early Morning Rain", 1965, "Canadian Railroad Trilogy", 1967, "If You Could Read My Mind", 1970, "Sundown", 1974, "Carefree Highway", 1974, "The Wreck of the Edmund Fitzgerald", 1976, "Race Among the Ruins", 1976; decorated Order Canada, 1970; named Top Folksinger, Juno Gold Leaf Awards, 1965, 66, 68, 69, 73, 74, 75, 76, 77; Top Male Vocalist, 1967, 70, 71, 72, 74; Composer of Year, 1972, 76; recipient awards for songs ASCAP, 1971, 74, 76, 77; Pop record of Year Award Music Operators Am. 1974; Vanier award Canadian Jaycees, 1977; numerous Gold albums, Can., U.S., Australia; Platinum album for "Sundown", "Summertime Dream" and "Gord's Gold"; Gold record for "Sundown"; Address: 350 Davenport Rd., Toronto, Ont. M5R 1K8

LIGHTSTONE, Marilyn, B.A.; actress; b. Montreal, Que. 28 June 1940; d. Manuel and Dophie (Shulman) Lightstone; e. McGill Univ. B.A. 1962; Nat. Theatre Sch. grad. 1965; films incl.: "Lies My Father Told Me" (Candn. Film Best Actress Award) 1976; "In Praise of Older Women" (Candn. Film Award Best Supporting Actress) 1977; plays incl. "Miss Margarida" 1976; "The Dybbuk" Mark Taper Forum (Los Angeles Drama Critics Award) Los Angeles 1975; "Mary Queen of Scots" Charlottetown (P.E.I.) Festival 1974; "King Lear" Lincoln Center, New York 1972; "The Seagull" Stratford (Ont.) Festival 1968; "Electra" St. Lawrence Centre, Toronto, "Yard of the Sun" 1970; "Billy the Kid" Stratford (Ont.) Festival, "Mary and Joseph", "Lorimar" 1979; "Refugees" drama, opera 1979; numerous TV shows incl. "The Adventurers" "Man Alive", "Witness to Yesterday"; Home: 15 Olympus Ave., Toronto, Ont.; Office: c/o Moses Znaimer, 99 Queen St. E., Toronto, Ont. M5C 2M1.

LILLICO, Lloyd G.; industrialist; b. Ottawa, Ont., 4 April 1919; s. George Walter and Mary Anna (Haig) L.; e. Britannia Public Sch.; Woodroffe High Sch.; Ottawa Tech. High Sch.; m. Lenora Grace, d. Olaf Knudsen, 5 Aug. 1945; two s. David and Richard; PRESIDENT AND DIRECTOR, ERCO INDUSTRIES LIMITED since 1967; Pres., Dir., BBA Corp.; Toronto, Hamilton and Buffalo Railway; joined present Co. at Buckingham, Que. upon grad.; Plant Mgr. at Varennes, Que. 1957-59, N. Vancouver 1959; Gen. Mgr., Production, Toronto 1959-64; when Co. operations divisionalized in 1964 became Div. Mgr., Ind. Phosphates; Vice Pres., Ind. Chemicals 1965; mem. Sch. Bd., Buckingham High Sch. Que. 1950-53; Buckingham Golf Club, five times President, 1940-50; mem., Candn. Mfrs. Assn.; mem., Canadian Chemical Producers' Association; mem., Soap and Detergent Assn.; Chemical manufacturers Association; Chemical Institute of Canada; Soc. of Chem. Indust.; recreations: golf, sailing, curling; Home: 8 The Green Pines, Toronto, Ont. M9C 2K5; Office: 2 Gibbs Road, Toronto, Ont. M9B 1R1

LILLIOTT, William R.; company executive; b. Lyons, Ga. 10 Jan. 1919; s. Arthur Henry and Mary Rebekah (Smith) L.; m. Corinne Ada Lamb 6 May 1944; three s., two d.; CHRMN. OF THE BD., MERRILL LYNCH ROYAL SECURITIES LTD. since 1973; Dir. Merrill Lynch, Pierce, Fenner & Smith Inc.; joined Merrill Lynch, Pierce, Fenner & Smith Inc. 1945 becoming Account Extve. Miami Beach Office, Sales Liaison Staff Cleveland 1957, Mgr. Macon Office 1958 and Omaha Office 1959, rejoined Sales Liaison Staff 1962, Mgr. Cleveland Office 1964, Regional Vice Pres. for Midwest Region 1968,; Vice Pres. & Inst. Sales Div. Dir. 1969; Extve. Vice Pres. for present firm 1970, Pres. 1972; Club: Burlington Golf & Country; Home: 115 Appleby Pl., Burlington, Ont. L7L 2X2; Office: P.O. Box 31, Toronto Dominion Centre, Toronto, Ont. M5K 1C2

LIMERICK, Jack McKenzie, B.Sc., M.Sc., F.C.I.C. (1953); pulp, paper and container consultant; b. Fredericton, N.B.; s. Arthur Kerr and Lillian Ethel (McKenzie) L.; e. Fredericton, (N.B.) High Sch., 1924-27; Univ. of New Brunswick, B.Sc. (Hons. in Chem., Physics and Math.) 1931; Univ. of N.B. and McGill Univ., M.Sc. (Chem.) 1934; Queen's Univ., Sch. of Comm. and Adm. (Extve. Training Course) 1957; m. Elsie Anderson, d. James P.

Wetmore, Campbellton, N.B., 11 Sept. 1937; Research Chem., Fraser Cos., 1934-37; joined Bathurst Paper Co. Ltd. as Chief Chem., 1937; Supt. of Control Dept., 1941; Tech. and Research Dir., 1944-67; Assoc. Dir. Research and Devel., Consolidated-Bathurst 1967-71; set up own consulting practice 1971; consultant on estab. of pulp, paper & container indust. Iran, 1972-78; and in same capacity, Brazil, since 1973; built new bldgs. exclusively devoted to pulp & paper research (1944) & container research (1950); travelled extensively in Europe in interest of Pulp & Paper industry; lect. at Royal Tech. Inst., Stockholm, Sweden; Head, Tech. Del. of Pulp and Paper industry which made survey of mills and industry in Russia, 1959; mem.; Brit. Paper & Board Makers Assn.; Tech. Sec., Candn. Pulp and Paper Assn. (Chrmn. 1959); appointed to Adv. Panel, Pulp and Paper Research Inst. of Can., 1961; Tech. Assn. of Pulp & Paper Industry, Dir. 1962-65, Fellow 1968; mem. Alkaline Pulping Comte. (Chrmn.-1st Candn.-1958-59), and rec'd. award from Assn. 1959; mem., Chem. Instit. of Can. Fellow 1953; Cdn. Soc. for Chem. Engineering; Packaging Assn. of Can.; Bd. Govs., Univ. of N.B., 1947-52; Pres. Univ. of N.B. Alumni Assn., 1955-56; Past Pres., Bathurst Community Concert Assn.; Past Pres., Bathurst Rotary Club; Publications: numerous, mostly in field of pulp, paper and containers incl. portion of 1955 ed. "Pulp and Paper Manufacture"; Patents: a number on pulp, paper and container manufacture; Protestant; recreations: golf, fishing, hunting, music; Clubs: Bathurst (N.B.) Golf (Past Pres.); Royal Montreal Golf; Engineers; Oakville Golf; Address: 36 East St., PH 4, Oakville, Ont.

LIMERICK, Hon. Ralph Victor, B.A.; judge; b. Fredericton, N.B. 24 May 1910; s. Walter and Nellie (MacFarlane) L.; e. Charlotte St. Sch., Fredericton High Sch. 1927; Univ. of N.B. B.A. 1931; m. Martha Isabel d. late Alexander Fleming, Fredericton, N.B. 23 May 1938; children: John Alexander, Patricia Ann; JUDGE, COURT OF APPEAL, N.B. since 1964; called to Bar of N.B. 1933; cr. Q.C. 1952; Ald. City of Fredericton 1955-56; served with militia units 1929-31, Reserve of Offrs.; Freemason (P.M., P.S.G.W.); Past Commdr.-in-Chief, N.B. Consistory; Past Dir. Royal Order of Jesters; Prov. Grand Master Royal Order of Scot.; Presbyterian; recreations: golf, curling, hunting, fishing, travel; Clubs: Fredericton Garrison; Fredericton Golf; Fredericton Curling; Miramichi-Renous Fishing; Home: 723 George St., Fredericton, N.B. E3B 1K6; Office: (P.O. Box 6000) Supreme Court Chambers, Fredericton, N.B. E3B 5H1.

LIND, James Forest, M.D., C.M., F.R.C.S.(C), F.A.C.S.; surgeon; educator; b. Fillmore, Sask. 22 Nov. 1925; s. James Forest and Isabella (Pringle) L.; e. Queen's Univ. M.D., C.M. 1951 (David Edward Mundell Prize in Surg. Anat. and Medal in surg.); m. Dorothy Anne d. late Cecil Henry Berlette 23 Aug. 1950; children: Heather Anne, James Forest, David Scott, Robbie Stuart, Gregory Jon; PROF. AND CHRMN., DEPT. OF SURG., EASTERN VIRGINIA MEDICAL SCHOOL; Dir. of Surg., Norfolk Gen. Hosp.; Active Staff, Medical Center Hosp.; Children's Hosp. of King's Daughters; Consultant, De Paul Hosp.; U.S. Public Health Serv. Hosp.; Veterans Admin. Med. Center; Naval Regional Med. Center; internship Hamilton Gen. Hosp. 1951-52, Resident in Pathol. 1952-53; Teaching Fellow in Anat. Queen's Univ. 1953-54, Fellow in Med. Queen's and Kingston Gen. Hosp. 1954-55 and Fellow in Surg. 1955-56; Registrar in Surg. Clatterbridge Hosp. Eng. 1956-58; Dept. Physiol. Liverpool Univ. 1957-58; Fellow in Physiol. Mayo Foundation, Rochester 1958-60; Lectr. in Surg. Univ. of Man. 1960, Asst. Prof. 1962, Assoc. Prof. 1964, Prof. 1966-72, Head of Surg. 1969-72; former Surg.-in-Chief Winnipeg Gen. Hosp.; former Prof. and Chrmn. of Surg., McMaster Univ., Phys.-in-Chief (Surg.) McMaster Univ. Med. Centre; rec'd John S. McEachern Fellowship Candn. Cancer Soc. 1956-57; George Christian Hoffman Award in Surg. Queen's Univ. 1957-58; John and Mary Markle

Scholar in Acad. Med. 1960; Visiting Prof. (Surg.) various univs. and hosps. Can. UK USA; author or co-author numerous publs.; mem. Candn. Life Ins. Foundation (Chrmn. Med. Adv. Comte.); Ont. Cancer Foundation (Adv. Comte., Council); Nat. Cancer Foundation (Adv. Comte., Council); Nat. Cancer Inst. (Council, Nominating Comte.); served with RCAF 1943-45, Pilot Offr. Navig.; Surg. Lt. Commdr. RCN (R) since 1949; mem. Central Surg.; Candn. Med. Assn.; Candn. Assn. Clin. Surgs.; Candn. Assn. Gastroenterol. (Pres. 1972); Ont. Med. Assn.; Soc. Candn. Surg. Chrmn.; Soc. Surg. Chrmn.; Soc. Univ. Surgs.; Soc. Surg. Alimentary Tract; Southeastern Surgical Congress; Virginia Med. Soc.; Virginia Surg. Soc.; Am. Med. Assn.; United Church; Home: 4044 Sherwood Lane, Virginia Beach, Virginia 23455; Office: Norfolk, Virginia 23507.

LIND, Philip Bridgman, M.A.; executive; b. Toronto, Ont., 20 Aug. 1943; s. Walter Heming and Susan (Bridgman) L.; e. Upper Can. Coll. Toronto; Ridley Coll. St. Catharines, Ont.; McGill Univ.; Univ. of B.C., B.A. (Pol. Science); Univ. of Rochester M.A. (Pol. Sociol.); m. Anne d. Alex G. Rankin, Toronto, Ont., 19 Aug. 1967; one d. Sarah Gay, one s. Jed Alexander; SENIOR VICE PRES. ROGERS CABLESYSTEMS INC. since 1979; Dir. Ont. Hydro; Morguard Trust Co.; Blount Grp. of Cos.; Rogers Radio Broadcasting Ltd.; Premier Communications Ltd.; Rogers U.A. Cablesystems Inc.; Pres., U.S. Cablesystems Inc.; Asst. to Vice Pres. and Gen. Mgr. Taylor Pearson & Carson Ltd. (B.C.) 1966; Asst. to Nat. Dir. P. Cons. Party of Can. 1968; Dir. of Programming Rogers Cable TV 1970; Vice-Pres. and Secy. Rogers Cable Communications Ltd. 1973-79; Dir. Sierra Club of Ont. Foundation; former Dir. Conserv. Council Can.; Candn. Nature Federation; Dir. and former Chrmn. Candn. Cable Television Assn.; Zeta Psi; P. Conservative; Anglican; recreations: tennis, river tripping, travel and hiking in north, fishing; Clubs: Badminton & Racquet; Albany; Home: 183 Cottingham St., Toronto, Ont. M4V 1C4; Office: Ste. 2602, Commercial Union Tower, Box 249, T.D. Centre, Toronto, Ont. M5K 1J5

LINDEN, Allen Martin, Justice; b. Toronto, Ont., 7 Oct. 1934; e. Vaughan Rd. Coll. Inst., Toronto; Univ. of Toronto 1956; Osgoode Hall Law Sch., 1960; Univ. of Calif. at Berkeley, J.S.D. 1967; m. 27 June 1957; children: Wendy, Lisa, Robin; JUSTICE, SUPREME COURT OF ONT.;since 1978; read law with Levinter & Co.; Toronto; called to Bar of Ont. 1960; Prof. of Law, Osgoode Hall Law School, York Univ., 1961-78; mem. Candn. Bar Assn.; Publications: "Candn. Tort Law Cases, Notes and Materials" 7th ed. 1980; "Canadian Tort Law" 1977 2nd ed.; "Studies in Canadian Tort Law" (Ed.) 1968; The Canadian Judiciary (1976); also articles in Candn. Bar Review and other legal journs.; Home: 14 Steele Valley Rd., Thornhill, Ont. L3T 1M3; Office: Osgoode Hall, Toronto, Ont.

LINDGREN, Charlotte, B.Sc., R.C.A.; artist; b. Toronto, Ont. 1 Feb. 1931; e. Univ. of Mich. B.Sc. 1956; Haystack Sch. Me. (Scholarship) 1964; part-time design teacher Univ. of Man. 1957-63; leader 3-Dimensional Weaving session Haystack Sch. 1966; teacher, N.S. Coll. of Art & Design 1978, 1981-82; Banff Centre 1979; N.S. Rep. Candn. Artists Representation 1970; mem. Can Council Arts Adv. Panel 1971; Visiting Artist Pangnirtung, N.W.T. 1978-81, Consultant to Weaving Shop there 1978; Consultant "Sculpture Walk" Nat. Capital Comn. Ottawa 1978; rep. various exhns. incl. Confed. Centre Art Gallery Charlottetown 1965; Am. Fed. of Arts "Threads of History" travel exhn. maj. USA galleries 1966; Montreal Museum of Fine Arts 1966; Internat. Biennial of Tapestry Lausanne 1967, 1969; Nat. Gallery Can. 1967, Expo '67 Art Gallery, Winnipeg Art Gallery 1967; Expo '70 Osaka 1970; Art Gallery Ont. "Chairs" 1974; Internat. Women's Yr. Kingston, Jamaica 1975; Can. House London, Eng. 1976; Centre Culturel Canadien Paris 1977;

Harbourfront Toronto 1977; Candn. Tapestry travel exhn. Dept. External Affairs 1979; IV Triennale, Lodz, Poland 1981; Barbican Centre, London, Eng. 1982; rep. in various pub. colls. incl. Assn. Pierre Pauli, Lausanne; Can. Council Art Bank; Candn. High Comn. London; Dept. External Affairs Ottawa; recipient Can. Council Arts Award 1965; Candn. Centennial Comn. Perspective Exhn. maj. prize 1967; Vice Pres. R.C.A. 1978-; Address: 1557 Vernon St., Halifax, N.S. B3H 3M8.

LINDNER, Ernest, O.C., LL.D. R.C.A.; artist; b. Vienna, Austria 1 May 1897; s. Oswald and Louise Lindner L.; came to Canada 1926; e. Realschule, Vienna 1915; LL.D. Univ. of Sask. 1972; m. Bodil, d. Joseph Brostrom-von Degen 1935; one d. Degen; ex Instr. and Head Saskatoon Tech. Inst. Art Dept. 1936-62; exhns. incl. Nat. Gallery Can.; Ont. Soc. Artists; Candn. Soc. Painters in Watercolour; Candn. Soc. Graphic Art; Candn. Soc. Painters, Etchers & Engravers; Candn. Nat. Exhn.; W. Can. Art Circuit; Banfer Gallery, N.Y.; rep. in collections of: Sask. Arts Bd.; Saskatoon Gallery & Conserv. Corp.; Univ. of Sask. (Saskatoon); Sir George Williams Univ.; Hart House, Univ. of Toronto; Royal Ont. Museum; Art Museum, London, Ont.; Beaverbrook Gallery, Fredericton, N.B.; Winnipeg Art Gallery; Mt. Allison Univ.; Grand Central Galleries, N.Y.; Acad. Applied Art, Vienna; F.S. Mendel Collection; IBM Corp.; Vincent Massey Collection; Nat. Gallery Can.; Can. Council Art Bank; Art Gallery Ont.; Art Gallery of Greater Victoria, B.C.; Edmonton Art Gallery; Glenbow-Alberta Institute Calgary; Univ. of Calgary; and numerous private collections; work incl. in Paul Duval's "Canadian Drawings and Prints" 1952 and his "High Realism in Canada" 1974; C.P.E. Toronto Print of the Year 1944; received Canada Council study grant 1959; Glazedbrook Prize for Landscape Painting 1968; served in 1st World War, Austrian Army 1915-18; air force bombing sqdn., N. Italy 1918; mem. Fed. Candn. Artists; el. mem., Roy. Candn. Soc. of Artists; el. mem., Roy. Candn. Soc. of Artists; recreations: tennis, skiing, all sports; Home: 414-9th St. E., Saskatoon, Sask. S7N 0A8

LINDSAY, John R., M.D., C.M.; otolaryngologist; b. Renfrew, Ont., 23 Dec. 1898; s. John M. and Christena (Wright) L.; e. Elem. and High Schs., Renfrew, Ont.; McGill Univ., M.D., C.M., 1925; Univ. of Uppsala, M.D. (Hon.) 1963; post-grad. training in Bronchoesophagology, Chevalier Jackson Clinics, Philadelphia, 1930 and in Histopathol. of Inner Ear under Prof. Felix Nager, Zurich, 1931; m. Elisabeth Anne, d. Robert Wood, St. Paul, Minn., 6 Feb. 1937 (divorced 1955, remarried 1977); children: Christena Wright, Anne Swain, Elisabeth Wood; PROF. EMERITUS, DEPT. OF SURGERY, SECTION OF OTOLARYNGOLOGY UNIV. OF CHICAGO, since 1964; Internship, Ottawa Civic Hosp., 1925-26; Residency, Hosp. for Sick Children, Toronto, 1926-27 and Royal Victoria Hosp., Montreal, 1927-28; joined present Univ. as Asst. Prof. of Surg. (Otolaryngology), 1928-33; Assoc. Prof. 1933-40; Prof. of Surg. 1940-64 and Head, Otolaryngology Sec., 1940-66; rec'd George E. Shambaugh Prize in Otology, 1959; Citation of Honor, Am. Acad. of Opthalmol. and Otolaryngol., 1952; Award of Merit, Am. Otological Soc., Inc., 1961; author of over 150 contribs. to scient. lit. on histopathology of middle and inner ear disorders; contrib. Chapters in several text books on above diseases and to "Progress in Neurology and Psychiatry", 1955-68; Ed., "Ear, Nose and Throat Year Book", 1951-69; Hon. mem., Nat. Soc. Otorhinolaryngol. Japan; Internat. Coll. Surgeons; mem. Am. Bd. Otolaryngol. (Diplomate 1932; Dir. 1953-68; Sr. Counsellor 1968); Am. Coll. of Surgeons; Am. Med. Assn.; Chicago Med. Soc.; Chicago Laryngol. & Otological Soc. (Past Pres.); Inst. Med. Chicago; Am. Acad. Opthalmol. & Otolaryngol. (Past Pres.); Am. Laryngol., Rhinol. & Otological Soc. (Past Pres.); Am. Otological Soc., Inc. (Past Pres.); Am. Laryngol. Assn.; Am. Broncho-Espohagological Assn.; Am. Coll. Surgs.; Otosclerosis Study Group (Past Pres.); Collegium

Oto-Rhino-Laryngologicum Amicitae Sacrum (Past Pres.); Chicago Hearing Soc. (Dir. 1950-60); Beltone Inst. Hearing Research (Trustee); Trustee, Research Fund of Am. Otological Soc. Inc. 1953-68; Guest of Hon., Am. Acad. of Opthalmol. & Otolaryngol., 1963; Am. Otological Soc. Inc., 1970; Am. Soc. of Univ. Otolaryngologists; Sigma Xi; Nu Sigma Nu; Republican; Presbyterian; recreations: golf, fishing; Clubs: South Shore Country; Quandrangle; Home: 3217 Otto Lane, Evanston, Ill., USA 60201. Business: Univ. of Chicago, Dept. of Surgery, 950 East 59th St., Chicago, Ill.

LINDSAY, Malcolm Francis Aylesworth, B.A., LL.B.; R.C.M.P. (retired); b. Arkona, Ont., 4 Feb. 1909; s. Malcolm Francis Alexander and Mabel Emma Arloa (Aylesworth) L.; e. Univ. of Sask., B.A. 1930, LL.B. 1937; Candn. Police Coll., Regina, 1940; Nat. Defence Coll., Kingston, 1954; m. Diana June, d. late Alexander Alcorn Macdonald, 7 June 1941; three s., Malcolm Alexander Francis, Bruce Macdonald, Alan Douglas; joined RCMP 1934; in charge of various detachments in Sask.; served with Wartime Intelligence Service, Ottawa; in command Regina and Winnipeg subdivs.; Criminal Investigation Br. Offr., Regina, Winnipeg and Fredericton; Adj., Ottawa, 1955; Dir. of Personnel, 1960; Depy. Commr. (Adm.), 1963; Depy. Commr. (Operations), 1965; Commissioner 1967 — Oct. 1969; served with Saskatoon Light Inf., 1929-34; rec'd. Queen's Coronation Medal, 1953; Order of St. John of Jerusalem; R.C.M.P. Long Service & Good Conduct; Vice-Pres., Internal. Police Organ, 1967; mem., Internat. Assn. Chiefs of Police; Candn. Assn. Chiefs of Police; Anglican; recreations: gardening, fishing, boating; Home: 1695 Playfair Dr., Apt. 1127, Ottawa, Ont. K1H 8J6

LINDSAY, Thomas Alfred, B.Sc.; industrialist; b. Belfast, N. Ireland, 14 Oct. 1911; s. Thomas James and Edith (Ardis) L.; e. Belfast Royal Acad.; Kelvin Tech. High Sch., Winnipeg, Man.; Univ. of Manitoba, B.Sc. (Elect. Engn.); m. Florence Edith, d. Albert George Gibson, Toronto, Ont. 27 June 1942; children: Dr. Ardis Brian, Dr. Peter Alfred; Dir., Black & Decker Mfg. Co. Ltd.; Warnaco (Can.) Ltd.; R.H.P. Canada Ltd.; Pres. 1955-76; mem. Adv. Bd. Montreal Trust Co.; Gov., Candn. Export Assn.; Pres., Candn. Standards Assn., 1969-70; Pres. (1969-70) Candn. Elect. Mfrs. Assn.; mem., Engn. Inst. Can.; Assn. of Prof. Engrs. Ont.; United Church; Clubs: Grenadier Is.; Home: (Summer) 33 Riverview Dr., Brockville, Ont. K6V 2Y5; (Winter) 547 Parkwood Lane, Naples, Fla. 33940. Office: 33 Riverview Dr., Brockville, Ont. K6V 2Y5

LINDSEY, Casimir Charles, M.A., Ph.D., F.R.S.C.; educator; b. Toronto, Ont. 22 March 1923; s. Lt. Col. Charles Bethune, D.S.O. and Wanda Casimira (Gzowski) L.; e. Univ. of Toronto Schs. 1941; Univ. of Toronto B.A. 1948; Univ. of B.C. M.A. 1950; Cambridge Univ. Ph.D. 1952; m. Shelagh Pauline d. W. P. M. Kennedy, Toronto, Ont. 29 May 1948; DIR., INSTITUTE ANIMAL RESOURCE ECOLOGY, UNIV. OF B.C., 1980-; B.C. Game Dept. Div. Biol. 1952-57; Inst. of Fisheries and Dept. of Zool. Univ. of B.C. 1953-66; Prof. of Zool. Univ. of Man. 1966-79; Visiting Prof., Univ. of Singapore 1962-63 (organized Fisheries Training Unit); Fisheries Consultant to Univ. of S. Pacific for Candn. Internat. Devel. Agency 1972; Fisheries Adv. Reservoir Project, e. Pakistan 1964; Consultant on Fisheries Training to Papua-New Guinea inst. of Technol. 1972; External Assessor in Biol., Nanyang Univ., Singapore, 1979-80; External Assessor in Zool., Univ. of Singapore, 1980-81; Candn. Del. Pacific Science Congs. Thailand 1957, Japan 1966, Australia 1971, Vancouver 1975, Khabarovsk, U.S.S.R. 1979; Collecting Expdns. to Galapagos Islands 1953, S.E. Asia 1957, Malaysia 1962-63, Cocos Island, Costa Rica 1964, Bangladesh 1964, Revillagigedo Islands 1966, Hudson Bay 1967, Amazon Brazil 1976, N. Can. and Alaska 13 expdns. 1955-78; Wallace Mem. Lectr. Singapore 1963; rec'd Wildlife Soc. Publ.

Award 1972; Nuffield Foundation Travel Award to Cambridge 1973; Saunderson Award for Excellence in Teaching, Univ. Man. 1977; Rh. Instit. Awd. for Outstanding Contributions to Research, Univ. Man. 1979; Gov. Vancouver Pub. Aquarium 1956-66; served with Candn. Armoured Corps and Candn. Intelligence Corps 1943-45; author or co-author 3 books and over 60 papers principally biol. of fishes; mem. Candn. Soc. Zools. (Vice Pres., Pres. 1975-78); Candn. Soc. Environmental Biols. (Vice Pres. 1974-75); Am. Soc. Ichthyols. & Herpetols. (Gov.); Royal Soc. of Can. (Fellow 1974, Convenor of Animal Biol Subject Division, 1976-7); Home: 3757 W. 36th St., Vancouver, B.C.; Office: Vancouver, B.C.

LINDSEY, George Roy, M.A., Ph.D.; b. Toronto, Ont., 2 June 1920; s. Late Charles Bethune and Wanda Casimira (Gzowski) L.; e. Univ. of Toronto Schs., 1938; Univ. of Toronto, B.A. 1942; Queen's Univ., M.A. 1946; Cambridge Univ., Ph.D. 1950; Nat. Defence Coll., 1965-66; Candn. Govt. Bilingual & Bicultural Course, Quebec City, 1970-71; m. June Monica, d. late Frederick W. Broomhead, 20 Aug. 1950; children: Charles Robin, Jane Casimira; CHIEF, OPERATIONAL RESEARCH & ANALYSIS ESTABLISHMENT, since 1968; Military Operational Research, Defence Research Board, Ottawa, 1950-54; Senior Operational Research Officer, Air Defence Command, RCAF, 1954-59; Dir., Defence Systems Analysis Group, Ottawa, 1959-61; Head, Operational Research Group, SACLANT Antisubmarine Research Centre, Italy, 1961-64; Senior Operational Research Scientist, Defence Operational Research Establishment, Ottawa, 1964-67; served with RCA 1942-45; Brit. Army Operational Research Group 1944-45; rank Capt.; author of "The Dynamics of the Nuclear Balance" and "Le Feu Nucléaire" (with A. Legault) and of various scientific and military papers; mem., Canadian Operational Research Society (Past Pres.) International Inst. Strategic Studies; Candn. Inst. Internat. Affairs; Operations Research Soc. Am.; Candn. Assn. for the Club of Rome; Candn. Inst. of Strategic Studies; Zeta Psi; Home: 55 Westward Way, Ottawa, Ont. K1L 5A8; Office: Ottawa, Ont. K1A 0K2

LINEHAN, Brian Richard; television producer; journalist; host; b. Hamilton, Ont. 3 Sept. 1945; s. Leslie and Sally (Kotur) L.; e. Mem. Pub. and Delta Secondary Schs. Hamilton; Toronto French Sch. 2 yrs.; Ryerson Polytech. Inst. Pub. Relations Degree; PRODUCER, CITY TELEVISION, Host, City Lights series; owner Brian Linehan Associates Ltd.; producer/host radio series CFRB Ltd.; joined Rank Organization 1964-68 serving in advertising, publicity and pub. relations becoming Advertising Dir. for Can.; Gen. Mgr. Janus Films of Canada 1968-72; Dir. of Programming, City Television 1972; author numerous newspaper and mag. features arts and performing artists; continuing series personality profiles "Performance Magazine"; Anglican; recreations: reading, tennis, travel; Club: Arts & Letters; Office: 99 Queen St. E., Toronto, Ont. M5C 2M1.

LINELL, Eric Ambrose, M.D.; professor emeritus; neuropathologist; b. Preston, Lancs., Eng., 11 July 1891; s. William Henry and Letitia Tryphena Bayliss L.; e. King William's Coll., Isle of Man.; Univ. of Manchester, M.B., Ch. B. 1914, M.D. 1920; m. Frances Mary, d. Arthur Burwash, Arnprior, Ont., 10 Sept. 1926; children: Ruth Ann, Penelope Charlotte; Asst. Prof. of Anat., Univ. of Toronto, 1923-28; Assoc. Prof., 1928-31; Prof. of Neuropath, 1931-57; served in 1st World War as temporary Surg.-Lieut., Royal Navy, 1914-19; Hon. Life mem., Med. Alumni Assn., Univ. of Toronto; Ont. Psychiatric Assn.; Hon. Fellowship, Acad. of Med., Toronto; Candn. Neurological Soc.; Candn. Neurosurgical Soc.; Hosp. for Sick Children; Nu Sigma Nu; Alpha Omega Alpha; Liberal; Home: 253 Blythwood Rd., Toronto, Ont. M4N 1A7

LINTON, Rev. John A., D.D., M.A. (Bapt.); b. Saint John, N.B., 17 Feb. 1903; s. John Alfred and Avernia (Ra-

fuse) L.; e. Teacher's Coll., Fredericton, N.B. 1923; Acadia Univ., B.Th. 1930, M.A. 1931, D.D. 1958; Union Theol. Semy., N.Y., 1936; Yale Univ., Sch. of Alcohol Studies, 1945; Inst. of Scient. Studies, Cal. (summer) 1950; m. Mildred Frances, d. Murray McCutcheon, Saint John, N.B., 12 Aug. 1931; children: Gerald Cedric, Shirley Jean; Secy. for Can., The Intercoll. Assn. for the Study of the Alcohol Problem; Teacher & Lecturer on the Alcohol Problem; held pastorates in N.S. and N.B., 1929-46; Secy. of Social Service Bd., Bapt. Conv. of Atlantic Prov., 1936-46; Field Secy., Ont. Temperance Fed., Toronto, 1946-50; apptd. Gen. Secy., Candn. Fed. on Alcohol Problems, 1950; Research Assoc., Alcoholism & Drug Addiction Research Foundation, Ont., 1966-75; del. to World Conf. on Alcohol Problem, Istanbul, 1956, Frankfurt-on-the-Main, 1964, Stockholm (1960); recreations: reading, travel; Home: Apt. 903, 44 Charles St. W., Toronto, Ont. M4Y 1R7

LIPSEY, Richard G., M.A., Ph.D. F.R.S.C.; educator; b. Victoria, B.C., 28 Aug. 1928; s. Richard Andrew and Faith Thirell (Ledingham) L.; e. Oak Bay High Sch., Victoria, B.C., 1947; Univ. of B.C., B.A. (1st Class Hons.) 1951; Univ. of Toronto 1953; London Sch. of Econ., Ph.D. 1958; m. Diana Louise, d. J. A. Smart, London, Eng., 17 March 1960; children: Mark Alexander Daniels (step-s.), Mathew Richard, Joanna Louise, Claudia Amanda; SIR EDWARD PEACOCK PROF. OF ECON., QUEEN'S UNIV. since 1970; with B.C. Govt. as Research Asst. 1950-52; Asst. Lect., Lect., Reader and Prof., London Sch. of Econ., Eng. 1955-63; Visiting Prof. of Econ., Univ. of Calif. at Berkeley 1963-64; concurrently Prof. of Econ., Chrmn. Dept. Econ., Dean Sch. of Social Studies, Univ. of Essex, Eng. 1963-69; Visiting Prof., Univ. of B.C. 1969; Irving Fisher Visiting Prof., Yale Univ. 1979-80; Dir., Research into Obstacles to Growth in U.K., Nat. Econ. Devel. Council 1961-63; mem. Council, Brit. Social Sciences Research Council 1965-68; Governing Council and Adv. Council, Nat. Inst. for Econ. and Social Research (U.K.) 1964-70; Council, Royal Econ. Soc. (U.K.) 1967-70; Mang. Ed., Review of Econ. Studies 1961-65; Publications: "An Introduction to Positive Economics" 1963 (5th 1979, 4th 1975); "Economics" (with P. O. Steiner) 1966 (3rd 1972, 4th 1975, 5th 1980, 6th 1981); Candn. version with G. Sparks and P. O. Steiner (3rd 1979)); "An Introduction to a Mathematical Treatment of Economics" (with G. C. Archibald) 1967 (2nd ed. 1973, 3rd ed. 1977); "The Theory of Customs Unions: A General Equilibrium Analysis" 1971; other writings include numerous articles in prof. journs. on theoretical and applied aspects of econ.; Fellow, Econometric Soc.; Fellow, Royal Society of Can.; Pres., Cdn. Econ. Assoc. 1980-81; recreations: skiing, film-making; Home: Harbour Place, Suite 1603, 185 Ontario St., Kingston Ont., K7L 2Y7; Office: Dunning Hall, Kingston, Ont.

LIPSON, Samuel L., M.S.; retired university professor; b. Odessa, Russia, 30 July 1913; s. Morris and Annie (Wiser) L.; e. Univ. of B.C., B.A.Sc., 1936; Cal. Inst. of Tech., M.A. (Civil Engn.) 1937; m. late Dena Leah, d. late Samuel Lewis Pink, 26 Nov. 1944; children: Florence Faye, Morris David, Alisa Barbara; PROF. OF CIVIL ENGINEERING, UNIVERSITY OF B.C. 1949-79 and Department Head 1970-79; began as Designer, Consol. Steel Corp., Los Angeles, in 1937, and with Mark Falk, Consulting Engr. in Los Angeles, 1938; served Consol. Steel Corpn. as Estimator, 1941-43; and Chief Estimator, 1943-46; joined present Univ. as Assoc. Prof. of Civil Engn., 1946; has reading knowledge of Russian and Hebrew; author of numerous papers in structural engineering; mem., of Bd. and Extve. Comte., Vancouver Jewish Community Center; Chrmn. Un. Jewish Appeal of B.C. 1960; Pres. (1966-68) Pac. Region of Candn. Jewish Cong.; Pres., Vancouver Jewish Community Fund and Council 1973-74; Fellow, American Soc. of Civil Engineers; mem. Council, Association Professional Engineers B.C. 1967-72 (President 1971); mem. ; Cdn. Soc. of Civil

Engrs; Engn. Inst. Canada; Reg'd. Civil Engr. in State of Cal.; Reg'd. Structural Engr. B.C.; Hebrew; recreation: golf; Clubs: University; Richmond Country; Home: 1420 W. 45th Ave., Vancouver, B.C. V6M 2H1

LIST, Roland, Dr.sc.nat., F.R.S.C.; scientist and educator; b. Frauenfeld, Switzerland 21 Feb. 1929; s. August Joseph and Anna (Kaufmann) L.; e. Swiss Fed. Inst. of Technol. Dipl. Phys. ETH. 1952, Dr.sc.nat. 1960; m. Gertrud K. d. Jean Egli-Schatt, Switzerland 9 Apl. 1956; children: Beat Roland, Claudia Gertrud; PROF. OF PHYSICS (METEOROLOGY), UNIV. OF TORONTO since 1963, Assoc. Chrmn. of Physics 1969-73; Sec. Head, Atmospheric Ice Formation, Swiss Fed. Inst. for Snow and Avalanche Research 1952-63; Visiting Prof. Swiss Fed. Inst. of Technol. 1974; Adm. NCR Negotiated Devel. Grant Atmospheric Dynamics 1974-79; Chrmn. Panel of Experts on Weather Modification, Extve. Comte. World Meteorol. Organ. since 1972, Chrmn. Working Group on Cloud Physics and Weather Modification, Comn. for Atmospheric Sciences since 1970; mem. Internat. Cloud Physics, Comn. Internat. Assn. Meteorol. & Atmospheric Physics, Internat. Union Geodsy & Geophysics since 1971; Univ. of Toronto Scient. Rep. Univ. Corp. of Atmospheric Research, Colo. since 1971, Dir. 1974-77, mem. Scient. Program Evaluation Comte. 1974-75; mem. Subcomte. for Meteorol. & Atmospheric Physics, Assoc. Comte. Geodesy & Geophysics, Nat. Research Council 1971-74, Chrmn. 1972-74; mem. Candn. Nat. Comte. Nat. Research Council 1974-75; Adv. Comte. Cloud Physics & Weather Modification, Atmospheric Environment Service; Adv. Comte. Convective Storms Div. Nat. Center Atmospheric Research, Colo.; Scient. Council Atmospheric Cloud Physics Lab., Space Shuttle Program, Univ. Space Research Assn.; Certified Consulting Meteorologist; rec'd Sesquicentennial Medal Univ. of Leningrad; Patterson Medal in meteorology; author over 120 articles; Dir. Ont. Br. Kidney Foundation of Can. 1970-75; Fellow, Am. Meteorol. Soc., Royal Soc. of Can.; mem. Candn. Assn. Physicists; Candn. Meteorol. Soc.; Candn. Geophys. Union; Am. Geophys. Union; Royal Meteorol. Soc.; Swiss Phys. Soc.; Gesellschaft Ehemaliger Studierender der Eidgenössischen Technischen Hochschule Zurich; Ruppigusia Solodorensis Switzerland; Cdn. Academy of Sciences; R. Catholic; Home: 58 Olsen Dr., Don Mills, Ont. M3A 3J3; Office: Toronto, Ont. M5S 1A7.

LISWOOD, Sidney, B.A., M.B.A., M.P.H.; administrator; b. New York, N.Y., 21 June 1916; s. Isadore and Sylvia (Nadler) L.; e. Coll. of the City of New York, B.A. 1939; Univ. of Chicago, M.B.A. 1942; Harvard Univ., M.P.H. 1952; m. Natalie, d. late Joseph Springer, M.D., 4 April 1943; children: Joshua, Amy; PRES., MT. SINAI INST., since 1975; mem., Extve. Comte. and mem. Bd. of Dirs. and Extve. Dir. of Mt. Sinai Hosp., Toronto, since 1976; Prof. Emeritus, Department Health Adm., Div. of Community Health, Fac. of Med., Univ. of Toronto, since 1974; Adm. Resident, New Haven Hosp., New Haven, Conn., 1942-43; Asst. Dir., Beth Israel Hosp., Boston, Mass., 1946-53; Assoc. Adm., Beth Israel Hosp., Boston, Mass., 1953-54; Chief Extve. Offr., Mt. Sinai Hosp., 1954-76; served in 2nd World War; Capt., U.S. Army Med. Corps in four campaigns (Normandy, Ardennes, N. France and Central Europe); Bronze Star Medal; Vice-Pres. and Dir., Toronto Hospitals Steam Corp.; Founding mem. Bd. Govs., Toronto Inst. Med. Technol.; Dir., Ben Gurion Univ. of the Negev; Dir., Univ. of Haifa; Weizman Inst.; former Pres., Gen. Inst. Health Services; former Chrmn. Extve. Comte. and mem., Ont. Hosp. Assn.; mem. (Life) Am. Hosp. Assn.; Fellow, Am. Pub. Health Assn.; Am. Coll. of Hosp. Administrators; mem., Bd. of Govs., Queen Eliz. Hosp., Toronto; Bd. of Dirs., Sterisystems Ltd.; Pauline McGibbon Cultural Centre Comte. on Human Resources, Ont. Council of Health, Alternative Financial Resources Comte., Candn. Coll. of Health Service Extves.; Dir., Baycrest Geriatic Centres; awarded Civic Award of Merit, City of Toronto,

1975; Silver Jubilee Medal, 1978; Hon. Life mem., Candn. Coll. of Health Service Exec., 1980; Beta Gamma Sigma; Delta Omega; Hebrew; Home: 280 Simcoe St., Toronto, Ont. M5T 2Y5; Office: 600 University Ave., Toronto, Ont. M6G 1X5

LITHWICK, Sidney, B.Arch., A.R.I.B.A.; architect; b. Ottawa, Ont., 21 Aug. 1921; s. Abraham and Dora (Rosenberg) L.; e. Lisgar Coll. Inst., Ottawa, Ont.; McGill Univ. Sch. of Arch., B.Arch. 1943; m. Ida Irene, d. Sol Witchel, Sudbury, Ont., 21 Oct. 1945; children: Howard Alvin, Marilyn Elaine, Helene Ava; SR. PARTNER, LITHWICK, JOHNSTON AND MOY; Dir., Charles Ogilvy Limited; Dir., Ottawa Jewish Home for the Aged; mem., Central Can. Exhn. Assn.; Arch. Asst., Dept. of Works and Bldgs. of Naval Service of Can. 1943-44; joined predecessor of present firm in 1945 as Chief Draughtsman and entered into Partnership in 1946; architects for 18 million dollar new Childrens Hosp. for E. Ont. (1972); firm currently in joint venture with Zeidler Roberts Partnership as architects for 45 million dollar redevelopment of Ottawa Civic Hospital; mem., Royal Arch. Inst. of Can.; Ottawa Bd. Trade (Chapter of Arch.); Ottawa Extves. Assn.; Comm. & Indust. Devel. Corp. of Ottawa; mem., Assn. of Engrs. & Arch. in Israel; mem., Agudath Israel Cong.; Chrmn., Property and Ins. Comte., Boy Scouts of Can.; Jewish; Clubs: Kiwanis (Pres., Ottawa, 1967); B'nai Brith Lodge 885; Rideau View Golf; recreations: golf, reading; Home: 385 Island Park Dr., Ottawa, Ont. K1Y 0B1; Office: 880 Lady Ellen Place, Ottawa, Ont. K1Z 5L9

LITTLE, Arthur John, B.A., F.C.A. (1956); b. London, Ont., 17 Dec. 1913; s. late Arthur Thomas and late Lylian Edith (Hartson) L.; e. Public and High Schs., London, Ont.; Appleby Coll., Oakville, Ont. (1928-31): Univ. of Western Ont., B.A. 1935; m. Margaret Hunter, d. Dr. S. R. Moore, London, Ont., 28 Aug. 1939; children: Peter M., Elizabeth M.; Dir., Algoma Central Railway; T. Eaton Acceptance Co.; London Life Ins. Co.; Eaton's of Can. Ltd.; St. Mary's Cement Ltd.; Maclean-Hunter Ltd.; National Trust Co.; Pres., Canadian Chamber Commerce, 1964-65; Past President, Toronto Board Trade (1956-57); Toronto Community Chest (1954); Past Chrmn. of Candn. Tax Foundation; Past Pres., St. John Ambulance Ontario Council; past mem. of Board of Trustees, Toronto General Hospital; mem. of Board of Governors, Appleby College, Oakville, Ont.; joined Clarkson Gordon Co. (then Clarkson, Gordon, Dilworth, Guilfoyle & Nash) after grad. from Univ. in 1935; C.A. in 1939, and was admitted to Partnership in the firm in 1945, retired 1974; Anglican; recreation: fishing; Clubs: University; Toronto Hunt; The Toronto; The York; Nekabong Hunting & Fishing; Home: 70 Montclair Ave., Toronto, Ont. M5P 1P7

LITTLE, Dorington G.; executive; b. Los Angeles, Cal. 16 July 1927; s. Dorington G. and Marjorie Isabelle (Moore) L.; e. Colo. Sch. of Mines, Geol. Engr. 1950; m. Rosie d. K. L. Sim 18 Dec. 1976; children: Dorington G., Oliver J., Sandra L., Andrea D.; GEN. MGR., PRODUCING, MOBIL OIL CORP. 1981-; Vice Pres. and Dir. Rainbow Pipe Line Co. Ltd.; South Saskatchewan Pipe Line Co.; Les Peintures Mobil du Quebec Ltée.; Pres. and Dir. Mobil Chemical Canada Ltd.; Mobil Energy Minerals, Canada, Ltd.; Mobil Ventures Ltd.; The Island Development Co.; Transocean Oil Canada, Ltd.; Dir., Toronto-Dominion Bank; Mobil-TO Canada Inc.; Instrument Man, Sinclair Petroleum Co. Ethiopia 1949-50; Geol., Pure Oil Co. Fort Worth, Texas 1950; Honolulu Oil Co., Midland, Texas 1950-53; British American Oil Corp. Midland 1953-54; American Independent Oil Co. Kuwait 1954-56; Iranian Oil Exploration & Production Co. Iran 1956-64; Middle E. Exploration Adviser, Socony Mobil Oil Co. Inc. N.Y. 1964-65; Exploration Manager Abu Dhabi Petroleum Co., Abu Dhabi 1966; Exploration Mgr. Mobil Exploration Australia, Melbourne 1967-68; Exploration Mgr. and Vice Pres. Mobil Oil Libya Ltd. Tripoli 1968-71; Pres. and Gen. Mgr. Mobil Oil Indonesia Inc. Jakarta 1971-78; served as Radio Operator 1945-46; Distinguished Achievement Medal, Colorado Sch. of Mines 1980; Doctor of Eng.; Honoris Causa, Tech. Univ. of Nova Scotia, 1980; mem. Am. Assn. Petrol. Geols.; Geol. Soc. London; Canadian Society of Petroleum Geologists; recreations: tennis, swimming; Office: New York, N.Y.

LITTLE, J. Douglas, B.A.Sc.; consulting mining engineer; b. Francois Lake, B.C. 21 March 1920; e. Univ. of B.C., B.A.Sc. 1950; m. 1 May 1950; four d.; Mine Engr., Silver Standard Mine, Hazelton, B.C. 1950-51; Mine Engr., Mine Supt., Chief Engr. and Asst. Gen. Mgr., Canadian Exploration Ltd., Salmo, B.C. 1951-56, Asst. Gen. Mgr., Canadian Exploration Ltd., Vancouver 1956-64; joined Placer Development Ltd. as Vice Pres.-Operations 1964; Extve. Vice-Pres., 1970-77; employed as a consulting mining engineer 1978-; Pres. CEO, Brinco Mining Ltd. 1979-; served with Candn. Army Overseas 1940-45; mem. Assn. Prof. Engrs. B.C.; Candn. Inst. Mining & Metall.; Am. Inst. Mining & Metall.; Engn. Inst. Can.; Mining Assn. B.C. (Pres.); Clubs: Vancouver; Engineers; Royal Vancouver Yacht; Home: 4810 Puget Dr., Vancouver, B.C. V6L 2W3; Office: 2000 Guinness Tower 1055 West Hastings St., Vancouver, B.C. V6E 3V3

LITTLE, Richard (Rich) Caruthers; impressionist, actor; b. Ottawa, Ont. 26 Nov. 1938; s. Lawrence Peniston and Elizabeth Maud (Wilson) L.; e. Lisgar Collegiate, Ottawa 1953-57; student drama Ottawa Little Theatre, 1950-60; m. Jeanne E. Worden, 16 Oct. 1971; first TV appearance in U.S. on "Judy Garland Show," 1964; appearances films, TV, night clubs; host TV series "The Rich Little Show," 1975-76; Entertained at President Ronald Reagan's inauguration gala, 1981; Host, "You Asked For It," 1981-; winner Entertainer of Year award 1974

LITTLEJOHN, John Gordon, B.Eng. LL.B., P.Eng.; lawyer; mining executive; b. Montreal, Que. 25 June 1925; s. John Campbell and Florence Lillian (Morbey) L.; e. McGill Univ. B.Eng. (Mining) 1951; Osgoode Hall Law Sch. LL.B. 1960; m. Maureen Patricia d. late George Terrance 7 July 1956; children: Maureen Anne, Bruce Campbell; VICE PRES. AND GEN. COUNSEL, RIO ALGOM LTD. 1969- ; Dir. Mobrun Copper Ltd.; Nuclear Fuels of Canada Ltd.; Rio Algom Nuclear Products Ltd.; Rio Tinto Canadian Exploration Ltd.; called to Bar of Ont. 1962; Partner, Mills, Cochrane & Littlejohn 1962-66; Assoc., Robertson, Lane, Perrett, Frankish & Estey 1966-69; Dir. Centennial Nursery Sch.; served with R.C.N.V.R.; mem. Law Soc. Upper Can.; Assn. Prof. Engrs. Prov. Ont.; Candn. Bar Assn.; Assn. Candn. Gen. Counsel; United Church; recreation: skiing; Clubs: Engineers (Pres. 1980); Lawyers; Home: 117 Lytton Blvd., Toronto, Ont. M4R 1L5; Office: 120 Adelaide St. W., Suite 2600, Toronto, Ont. M5H 1W5.

LITTLER, William, B.A.; critic; educator; b. Vancouver, B.C. 12 July 1940; e. Univ. of B.C., B.A. 1963; also studied piano, theory, criticism; Conn. Coll. dance music, technique, composition and criticism 1971-72; freelance writer Vancouver Sun 1962 becoming Music and Dance Critic 1962-66; Music Critic Toronto Daily Star 1966 adding regular dance criticism 1971; reviews have been heard on various CBC radio series incl. "Critically Speaking", "The Arts in Review", "Arts National", "Stereo Morning"; writer and host CBC TV "Summer Concert" series Vancouver 1965; writer-host CBC TV specials on Nat. Arts Centre Orchestra and Toronto Symphony; began teaching courses in music and the theatre and in dance criticism York Univ. 1974; Guest Lectr. Univ. of Waterloo, Univ. of Calgary, McMaster Univ., Kent State Univ., Conn. Coll., Ohio State Univ., Peabody Conserv.; jury mem. CBC Talent Festival, Baldwin Nat. Piano and Organ Competition, Metropolitan Opera Auditions, Kennedy Center Friedheim Award for best US orchestral

composition 1979; writings incl. articles, reviews and liner notes various publs.; Vice Pres. Music Critics' Assn. 1969-77; Founding Chrmn. Dance Critics' Assn. N. Am. 1974; directed first Critics' Inst. in Candn. Music Toronto, Ottawa, Montreal 1975; consultant Urwick, Currie & Partners for study and report "An Assessment of the Impact of Selected Large Performing Companies upon the Canadian Economy" 1974; Address: c/o Toronto Star, 1 Yonge St., Toronto, Ont.

LITVAK, Isaiah A., B.Com., M.S., Ph.D.; educator; economist; b. Shanghai, China, 1 Oct. 1936; s. Matthew S. and Basia (Daitch) L.; e. McGill Univ., B.Com. 1957; Columbia Univ., M.S. 1959, Ph.D. 1964; m. Marilyn, d. Coleman Kenigsberg, 21 Sept. 1958; one s, Matthew Kenneth; PROF. OF BUSINESS AND PUBLIC POLICY, FAC. OF ADMIN. STUDIES, YORK UNIV., since 1978 Dir., Internat'l Business Programme there; Lectr. in Pol. Econ., McMaster Univ. 1961, Asst. Prof. 1962, Assoc. Prof., Faculty of Business, 1965, Prof. 1967-70; Prof. of Econ. and Internat. Affairs, Carleton Univ., 1970-77; Visiting Distinguished Prof., York Univ., 1973-74; Guest Lectr. univs. in Europe and Africa; Mang. Consultant to Fed. and Prov. Govts. and business; mem. McMaster Univ. Senate, Council Grad. Studies, Research Adv. Council and Extve. Council Sch. of Business; rec'd Research Grants from Can. Council 1962, 1969, 1971; McMaster Univ. 1963-69; Candn. Donner Foundation, 1968 & 1979; McLean Foundation, 1970 and 1974; Fed. Depts. Indust., Trade & Comm. and Energy, Mines & Resources, 1971-79; Ford Foundation Workshop Grant, 1964; publ. grant Social Science Research Council, 1971; author, "Marketing Management for the Middleman", 1967; co-author, "An Annotated Bibliography on Canadian Marketing", 1967; "Canadian Cases on Marketing", 1968; "Dual Loyalty: Canadian-U.S. Business Arrangements", 1971; Ed. and co-author, "Marketing: Canada", 1964, revised ed. 1968; "The Nation Keepers", 1967; "Foreign Investment: The Experience of Host Countries", 1970; "Cultural Sovereignty", 1974; "Corporate Dualism and the Candn. Steel Indus.", 1977; "Alcan Aluminum Ltd.: A Case Study", 1977; "Plant Efficiency and Competition Policy", 1979; "The Canadian Multinationals", 1981; other writings incl. booklets, articles and reviews in various learned and prof. journs.; mem., Candn. Econ. Assn.; Am. Econ. Assn.; Am. Marketing Assn.; Internat. Business Educ. Assn.; recreations: tennis, fencing; Clubs: Rockcliffe Lawn Tennis; Home: 193 Dunvegan Rd., Toronto, Ont. M5P 2P1; Office: Toronto, Ont.

LIVERGANT, Harold Leonard, B.Sc., F.A.C.H.A.; health services executive; b. Winnipeg, Man. 10 Nov. 1924; s. late Solomon and late Sarah (Friedman) L.; e. Univ. of Toronto B.Sc. 1945, Dipl. in Hosp. Adm. 1964; m. Lynda d. David Silverman 26 June 1972; children: Bradley, Susan, Elyssa; PRES. AND CHIEF OPERATING OFFR. EXTENDICARE LTD. 1980- ; Chrmn. and Dir. Caldonia Corp. Toronto; Dir. Crown Life Insurance Co.; Datacrown Inc.; The John G. Diefenbaker Mem. Fndn., Inc.; Sask. Mining Develop. Corp. (Regina) Medco Centers Inc. (Ind.); United Health Maintenance Inc. (Md.); Accounting Consultant Dept. Health Sask. 1954-58; Extve. Dir. Northwest Regional Hosp. Council North Battleford, Sask. 1958-62; Extve. Dir. Metrop. Toronto Hosp. Planning Council 1966-68; Chrmn. and Chief Extve. Offr. Extendicare Ltd. 1968-80; author various articles hosp. journs.; Fellow, Amer. Coll. of Hosp. Administrators; mem. Candn. Coll. Health Service Extves.; Candn. Chamber Comm. (Health & Welfare Comte.); Candn. Pub. Health Assn.; recreations: gardening, horse breeding; Club: Ontario; Home: 519 Spadina Rd., Toronto, Ont. M5P 2W6; Office: 700, One Yonge St., Toronto, Ont. M5E 1E5.

LIVESAY, Dorothy (Mrs. D. C. Macnair); poet; journalist; social worker, professor, b. Winnipeg, Man., 12 Oct. 1909; d. J. F. B. and Florence (Randal) Livesay; e. Glen Mawr., Toronto, Ont.; Trinity Coll., Toronto, B.A. 1931; Sorbonne, dipl. d'études supérieures 1932; Univ. of Toronto (Social Science) 1934; Univ. of B.C., M.Ed., 1966; D. Litt., Univ. of Waterloo (Ont.) 1974; m. Duncan Cameron Macnair, 14 Aug. 1937; children: Peter, Marcia Hay; winner of Gov. Gen's. Medal for Poetry, 1944 and 1947; Lorne Pierce Gold Medal, Roy. Soc. of Can., for Lit., 1946; author of "Green Pitcher", 1928; "Signpost", 1932; "Day and Night", 1944; "Poems for People", 1947; "Call My People Home", 1950; "Selected Poems, 1926-56", 1957; "The Unquiet Bed", 1967; "The Documentaries", 1968; "Plainsongs", 1970; "Two Seasons: Poems Collected and Uncollected", 1972; "A Winnipeg Childhood" (memoirs) 1973; "Ice Age" 1975; "Beginnings", 1975; ; "Right Hand Left Hand" (a collage of documents and writings from the 1930s), 1977; "The Woman I Am" (selection of feminist poems), 1977; "Room of One's Own", 1979; frequent contrib. to CBC programmes and talks; UNESCO Programme Asst. (Educ.) Paris, 1958-60, and in N. Rhodesia, 1960-63; Lectr. in Creative Writing, Univ. of B.C., 1965-66; Writer-in-Residence, University of N.B. 1966-68; Asst. Prof., Univ. of Alta., 1968-72; Univ. of Victoria, 1973-74;, Writer-in-Residence, Univ. of Manitoba 1975, Ottawa 1977 and Simon Fraser 1979; now retired but gives lectures and poetry readings across Can. and abroad; Address: R.R. #1, Galiano Island, B.C., V0N 1P0

LIVINGSTON, William Ross, B.Com.; insurance executive; b. Toronto, Ont. 8 Aug. 1922; s. Charles Wilmot and Gladys (Burton) L.; e. Univ. of Toronto Schs., 1935-40; Univ. of Toronto, 1940-42 and 1945-47; m. Joan, d. H. W. Vanstone, 25 Sept., 1948; children: Robert V., Brian W., Anne B.; PRESIDENT EATON BAY FINANCIAL SERVICES LTD; Eaton Bay Life Assur. Co.; Eaton Bay Insur. Co.; Eaton Bay Mutual Fund Co.; Eaton Bay Trust Co.; Commerce Capital Corp. Ltd.; since 1978; with Group Dept., Aetna Life 1947-50; New York Life at Toronto and New York as Regional Mgr., Dir. of Agencies and Asst. V-Pres., 1951-64; Vice. Pres., Pres., and Chmn., of Sovereign Life Assur. Co and Sovereign General Insur. Co., 1964-78; Family Life Assnce. Co.; United Invest. Life Ins. Co.; Westmount Life Ins. Co.; Dir., Barbecon Inc.; West Park Hospital; Chmn., Comm. on Internat. Affairs; of Exec. Comm., Candn. Red Cross Soc.; Deputy Chrmn., Can. Safety Council; Mem., Cdn. Life Ins. Assoc.; Trust Companies Assoc. of Can.; Investment Funds Instit. of Can.; United Church; recreations: golf, curling, cottage; Clubs: Rosedale Golf; University; Granite; Home: 142 Rochester Ave., Toronto, Ont. M4N 1P1; Office: 595 Bay St., Toronto, Ont. M5G 2C6

LIVINGSTONE, James George, P.Eng.; executive b. Toronto, Ont., 8 June 1920; s. late George Chesterfield, M.D. and Marione Lenore (Brown) L.; m. Audrey Louise, d. late Frederick Hunter, Edmonton, Alta., 25 June 1949; children: Virginia Louise, Donald James; PRES. AND DIR., IMPERIAL OIL LTD.; mem., Assn. Prof. Engrs. Ont.; Office: 111 St. Clair Ave. W., Toronto, Ont. M5W 1K3

LIZOTTE, André, B.Com.; CAAP; company executive; b. Montreal, Que., 20 January 1930; s. Maurice and Exilda (Frison) L.; e. Sir George Williams Univ. (evening) B.Comm. 1954; CAAP, Major Bus. Admin. 1971; two yrs. LaSalle Univ., Chicago; m. Denyse, d. René Moreau, 30 June 1960; children: Marc, Eric, Patrick, Carole; PRES., CEO AND DIR., NORDAIR LTD. since 1976; Chmn. of the Board, Treasure Tours (Can.) Ltd.; Les Voyages Treasure Tours Inc.; Dir., nternat. Fud, Ltd.; Sr. Vice Pres. and Gen. Mgr., Quebecair; Vice Pres. Oper. & Dir., Cadbury Schweppes Powell Ltd.; adv. agency experience with Young & Rubican Ltd., Toronto & Montreal; Cockfield Brown Ltd., Montreal; pharm. experience with Warner Lambert Ltd., Toronto; Dir. and 2nd Vice Chmn., Re-

gional Airline Group; qualified as Capt., C.S. of C.; Roman Catholic; recreations: golf, tennis; squash; fishing; Home: 13144 Aragon, Pierrefonds, Que.; Office: 100 Blvd. Alexis Nihon, St. Laurent, Quebec, Que.H4Y 1B8

LLOYD, Bernard (Ben) Hugh, B.A.Sc., P.Eng., F.M.C.; management consultant; b. Athabaska, Alta., 2 May 1921; s. Leonard R. and Kathleen (Sibbald) L.; e. High Sch. Woodstock, Ont.; Univ. of Toronto, B.A.Sc. (Mech. Engn.); m. Nancy R., d. William Bonnar 29 April 1954; children: John, Barbara, Kathleen; PARTNER PRICE WATERHOUSE ASSOCIATES since 1968; Staff Instr. Engn. Faculty, Univ. of Toronto 1944-45; Research Engr. Ontario Research Foundation 1945-47; Lect., Dept. Engn. and Business, Univ. of Toronto 1947-48; Systems Engr., Candn. Industries Ltd., Montreal, Que. 1948-54; Principal, Leetham Simpson Ltd., Management Consultants, Montreal, Que. 1954-58; joined present firm, Montreal, 1958; Dir., Management Consulting 1958-64; Partner, Price Waterhouse Associates 1968; Founding mem. and Fellow, Am. Soc. for Quality Control (Nat. Dir. 1954-56); Fellow, Inst. of Management Consultants of Ont. (Pres., 1974-75); mem., Assn. of Prof. Engrs. Provs. Ont. Candn. Pulp & Paper Assn.; Engn. Inst. of Can.; Anglican; recreations: golf, swimming, badminton (Past Pres. Que. Badminton Assn.); Clubs: Scarborough Golf; National; Home: 10 Lamport Ave. #306, Toronto, Ont. M4W 1S6; Office: First Canadian Place, Toronto, Ontario M5X 1H7

LLOYD, David Stevenson, O.C. (1971), B.A.Sc.; company executive; b. Winnipeg, Man., 5 Oct. 1903; s. Fred Norval and Edith Zilla (Stevenson) L.; e. Sault Ste. Marie (Ont.) High Sch.; Univ. of Toronto, B.A.Sc. (Applied Science); m. Elizabeth Helen Gibbs (d. 1980) d. John Jacob Drew of Guelph, Ont., 13 Oct. 1934; children: Ann Stevenson, Frederick Drew; Pres. and Dir., Pyrofax Gas Ltd. till Jan. 1967; formerly Pres., Linde Co., Division of Union Carbide Canada Limited; Past Chrmn. Adm. Board, Canadian Welding Bureau; Reg'd. Prof. Engr. (Ont.); prior to Oct. 1925 for short periods with Candn. Marconi Co., Robt. W. Hunt Co. Ltd. and Northern Devel. Br. of Ont. Gov.; Oct. 1925 to Nov. 1963 cont. employed by Candn. subsidiary Co's. of Union Carbide Corp., retired when Pyrofax Gas was sold to Texas Eastern; Past Chrmn., Candn. Sec., Compressed Gas Mfrs. Assn.; Life mem., Engn. Inst. Can.; Radio Soc. of Ont.; Past Chrmn., Adm. Bd., C.N.I.B. Amateur Radio Club; Delta Kappa Epsilon; Presbyterian; recreations: yachting, amateur radio (VE3AW); Clubs: University; Rotary; Home: 16 Hawthorne Ave., Toronto, Ont. M4W 2Z2

LLOYD, Gweneth, O.C. (1968), LL.D.; choreographer; teacher of ballet dancing; b. Eccles, Lancs., England, 15 Sept. 1901; d. Joseph Charles William and Winifred Mary (Stace) L.; e. Perse Sch., Cambridge, 1906-11; Woodrings, Sch., Hatch End, 1912-13; Northwood Coll., Middlesex, 1914-18; Liverpool Phys. Training Coll. (Grad.; 1st Class Hons.) 1919-20; Ginner-Mawer Sch. of Dance (1st Class Hons.) 1923-26; studied ballet under Margaret Craske (formerly of the Diaghilev Co.); Royal Acad. of Dancing Advanced Teachers Cert.; LL.D. Univ. of Calgary, 1968; came to Can. 1938; FOUNDER AND ARTISTIC DIRECTOR, ROYAL WINNIPEG BALLET OF CAN.; Choreographer and Founder, Canadian Sch. of Ballet, Toronto, Ont.; Instr. in Ballet, Banff Sch. of Fine Arts; her first Ballet was presented in a Civic Pageant, to celebrate the Candn. tour of King Geo. VI and Queen Elizabeth; has since created 34 original ballets incl. "Shadow on the Prairie" (premièred, 1952); Fellow, Acad. of Dancing; rec'd. Manitoba Hist. Soc. Centennial Medal 1971; now retired; recreations: reading, gardening; Address: R.R. 4, "Mellingey", Kelowna, B.C. V1Y 7R3

LLOYD, James Trevor, B.J.; b. Wawota, Sask., 26 Feb. 1925; s. late Rev. William and Frances Phyllis (Collins) L.; e. Carleton Univ., B.J., 1949; m. Yvonne Mae, d. A. C.

Shaw, Regina, Sask., 30 Nov. 1949; children: Wendy, David; PRES., PUBLIC & INDUSTRIAL RELATIONS LTD., Assoc. Ed., "Financial Post", 1952-55; joined present firm as Dir., 1955; Pres., Can. Scholarship Trust Foundation; mem., Bd. Govs., Carleton Univ.; mem. Nat. Council, Candn. Pub. Relations Soc.; United Church; recreations: curling, golf; Clubs: Canadian; Lambton Golf & Country; National; Home: 60 King George's Rd., Toronto, Ont. M8X 1L7; Office: 1 Yonge St., Toronto, Ont. M5E 1E5

LLOYD, Mostyn T.; financial executive; b. Rhayader, Radnorshire, Wales 23 June 1929; s. Thomas and Edith Jane (Hughes) L.; e. Llandrindod Wells Grammar Sch.; Grad., Inst. of Bankers; Stonier Grad. Sch. Banking; Rutgers Univ.; m. Susan Anne, d. late Samuel Huxley 15 Oct. 1957; children: Edward Griffith, Andrew Richard; came to Can. 2 June 1974; PRES. AND CHIEF EXTVE. OFFR., BARCLAYS BANK OF CANADA, since 1981; joined Barclays Bank Ltd., U.K. 1945-1956; held numerous mang. posts incl. Mgr. Avenue Central Br., Accra, Barclays Bank International, Ghana 1956-66; Barclays Bank of California, Secy.-Treas. 1966-68, Extve. Vice Pres. 1970, Sr. Extve. Vice Pres. 1971; Pres., Barclays Can. Ltd. 1974-81; mem. Inst. of Bankers; Conservative; Anglican; recreations: cross country skiing, swimming, reading; Home: 6 Peebles Ave., Don Mills, Ont. M3C 2N8; Office: Suite 3505, Commerce Court West, Toronto, Ont.

LLOYD, Roy E.; mining executive; b. Regina, Sask. 2 March 1941; s. late Timothy Ernest and Agnes (MacAlduff) L.; e. Fillmore (Sask.) Elem. and High Schs. 1959; Univ. of Sask. Coll. of Comm. 1963, grad. studies; m. Rose d. late George Dreher 7 Sept. 1963; children: Karen Louise, Leanne Rose; PRES., SASK. MINING DEVELOPMENT CORP.; Dir., Sask. Oil and Gas Corp.; Key Lake Mining Corp.; former Dir. of Fed.-Prov. Relations, Dept. of Finance, Sask., Dir. of Budget Bureau, Asst. Depy. Min. of Finance, Dir. of Energy Secretariat, Chief Planning Offr.-Extve. Council; mem. Uranium Inst.; Candn. Nuclear Assn.; R. Catholic; recreations: racquet sports, cross-country skiing, golf, reading; Club: Saskatoon; Home: 3910 Parkdale Rd., Saskatoon, Sask. S7H 5A7; Office: 122 - 3rd Ave. N., Saskatoon, Sask. S7K 2H6.

LLOYD, Trevor, B.Sc., Ph.D., D.Sc., Hon. LL.D., Hon. M.A., F.R.S.C.; univ. prof. and geographical consultant; b. London, Eng., 4 May 1906; s. Jonathan and Mary (Gordge) L.; e. Sidcot Sch., Somerset, Eng.; Univ. of Bristol, B.Sc. 1929, D.Sc. 1949; Clark Univ., Ph.D. 1940; Hon. M.A. Dartmouth Coll., 1944; LL.D. Windsor 1973; m. Joan, d. J. G. Glassco, 1936; divorced 1966; children: Mona Jean, Hugh Glassco; PROF. EMERITUS McGILL UNIV., since 1977; Chrmn., Department of Geography, 1962-66; Pres. U. of Bristol Students Union 1929-30; Schoolmaster, Ravenscourt School, Winnipeg, Man., 1931; Geography Specialist, Leader. Br. Universities Debating Team to Canada 1930; Pres. National Union of Students, U.K. 1930-31; Chrmn. Bd of Inquiry into studnet affairs, U. of Manitoba. 1932; Winnipeg Public Schools, 1936-42; Assistant Professor of Geography, Carleton Coll., Northfield, Minn., 1942; Asst. Prof. of Geog., Dartmouth Coll., 1942-44, Prof. 1944-59; Consul for Canada in Greenland, 1944-45; first Chief, Geographical Bureau, Ottawa, 1947-48; Prof. of Human Geography, McGill Univ., 1959-77; Dir., Centre of North. Studies and Research, McGill, 1973-77; Extve. Dir., Assn. of Candn. Univs. for North. Studies, 1977; Publications: "The Red River Valley", A religious Study 1940; "The Geography and Administration of Northern Canada, 1947; "Sky Highways", 1943; "Canada and Her Neighbours", 1947, 1957; "Southern Lands", 1956; "Lands of Europe and Asia", 1957, 1965; "A Geographer's World", 1968; many tech. papers in geog., internat. affairs, educ., etc.; Fellow, Gov., Chrmn. of Bd. 1967-68-69-70, Arctic Inst. N. Am.; Founding Ed. Journal "Arctic"; Am. Geog. Soc.;

Assn. of Am. Geog. (former mem. of Council); Am. Assn. for Advanc. of Science (Vice Pres. and Chrmn. Sec. Geol. & Geog. 1964); mem., Candn. Assn. of Geogs. (Past Pres.); Candn. Inst. Internat. Affairs; Greenland Soc., Copenhagen; Inst. of Current World Affairs (Gov. since 1959, Chrmn. Bd. 1976); Project Offr. Royal Comn. on Govt. Organ., 1961-62; Hon. Corres. Mem., Geographical Soc. of Finland; Gov. and Chrmn., Candn. Scandinavian Foundation; Geographic Fieldwork, Greenland, N. Scandinavia, N European Russia, Eastern Siberia, Peru, Bolivia, Togo, Mali. Soc. of Friends; awarded Centennial Medal, 1967; Silver Jubilee Medal, 1977; Candn. Assn. of Geographers Award for Service, 1977; Jens Munck Medal, Candn.-Danish Soc., Copenhagen, 1977; recreations: out-of-doors activities; Clubs: McGill Fac.; Address: 120 Wurtemburg, Apt. 2, Ottawa, Ont. K1N 8M3

LOCHHEAD, Douglas Grant, M.A., B.L.S., F.R.S.C.; author and professor; b. Guelph, Ontario, 25 March 1922; s. Allan Grant and Helen Louise (VanWart) L.; e. McGill Univ., B.A. 1943, B.L.S. 1951; Univ. of Toronto, M.A. (English) 1947; m. Jean St. Clair, d. John Harold Beckwith, Sydney, N.S., 17 Sept. 1949; children: Sara Louise, Mary Elizabeth; Edgar and Dorothy Davidson Prof. and Dir., Candn. Studies, Mt. Allison Univ., since 1975; Fellow Emeritus, Massey College; Librarian in Residence, Dalhousie Univ., 1981; engaged in Advertising and Information work, Toronto and Ottawa, 1947-50; Librarian, Victoria, (B.C.) Coll., 1951-52; Cataloguer, Cornell Univ. Lib., 1952-53; Univ. Lib., Dalhousie Univ., Halifax, N.S., 1953-60; Univ. Librarian, York Univ. and Asst. Prof. of Eng. there, 1960-63; Librarian & Fellow, Massey Coll. 1963-75; Professor of English, University of Toronto, 1965-75; served in the 2nd World War 1943-45 with Candn. Army, Inf. in Can. and Overseas, rank Lieut.; Publications: "Poems in Folio", 1959, 1963; "The Heart is Fire (poems), 1959; "It is all around" (poems), 1960; "Millwood Road Poems" 1970; "Prayers in a Field" (poems) 1974; "Collected Poems: The Full Furnace" 1975; "High Marsh Road" (poems) 1980; "Battle Sequence" (poems) 1980; "A & E" (poems) 1980; Joint Editor "Made in Canada" (poems) 1971; "100 Poems of Nineteenth Century Canada" 1974; Ed., "Bibliography of Canadian Bibliographies", 2nd ed. 1972; "Literature of Canada" series and Toronto Reprint Series; numerous articles in lib. prof. journs. and poems in many Canadian periodicals; mem., Bibliographical Society, London; Bibliographical Society of Canada (Pres. 1974-76); Bibliographical Society of America; Psi Upsilon; Presbyterian; Address: Centre for Candn. Studies, Mt. Allison Univ., Sackville, N.B. E0A 3C0

LOCKE, John Craig, B.Sc., M.D., C.M., Med.Sc.D., F.R.C.S. (C), F.A.C.S.; ophthalmologist; university professor; b. Winnipeg, Manitoba, 7 Dec. 1918; s. William Francis and Margaret (Spence) L.; e. Selwyn House Sch., Montreal, Que. (1928-33); Upper Canada Coll., Toronto, Ont. (1933-35); McGill Univ., B.Sc., M.D., C.M. (1935-42); Univ. of Toronto Jan.-June 1944; New York Univ. Postgrad. Sch., 1946-47; Columbia Univ., Med. Sc.D., 1951; m. Beatrice, d. late Dr. Charles Dillon, New York, 6 May 1950; children: James Edward Francis, Barbara Margaret Grace; PROF. DEPT. OF OPHTHALMOLOGY, McGILL UNIVERSITY; Sr. Ophthalmologist, Royal Victoria Hospital, Montreal, Quebec; Diplomate of American Board of Opthalmology; Chairman and member of Examining Boards, Royal College of Physicians and Surgeons Can., 1954-61; Schneider Foundation Mem. Lect., Interstate Postgrad. Med. Assn., Milwaukee, 1955; awarded Certs. of Merit for scient. exhibit on "Retrolental fibroplasia" by two Am. Assns. 1951 and 1952; annual Award in Med. of Royal Coll. of Phys. & Surgs. of Can. for essay "Contributions to Retrolental Fibroplasia", 1954; served in 2nd World War; Lieut., R.C.A.M.C., 1943-44, Capt., 1944-46, in Can.; author of a no. of original scient. publs. principally on opthal. subjects; mem.,

Candn. Med. Assn.; Assn. for Research in Opthal.; Candn. Opthal. Soc.; Am. Opthalmological Soc.; Jules Gonin Club; Soc. of Eye Surgeons (Ch. mem.); Fellow, Am. Acad. of Opthal. & Otolaryngol.; Hon. mem., Chilean Opthal. Soc. (1956); Delta Upsilon; Protestant; Clubs: Royal Montreal Golf; Montreal Badminton & Squash; Home: 1 Cressy, Montreal, Que. H3X 1R1; Office: 1414 Drummond St., Montreal, Que. H3G 1W1

LOCKHART, Very Rev. Wilfred Cornett, M.A., Ph.D., D.D., LL.D., D.C.L. (Un. Ch.); b. Dundalk, Ont., 17 Oct. 1906; s. Thos. Fraser and Harriet F. (Cornett) L.; e. Univ. of Toronto, Victoria Coll., B.A. 1929, M.A. 1932; Emmanuel Coll. 1933; Univ. of Edinburgh, Ph.D. 1936; m. Margaret Eileen, d. Albert Armstrong, 20 Sept. 1933; Asst. Toll Engr., Bell Telephone Co. Can., London and Hamilton 1929-30; Asst. Min., N. Leith Parish Ch. Edinburgh, Scot., 1934-35; Gen. Secy., Student Christian Movement, Univ. of Toronto, 1935-40; Min., Sherbourne Un. Ch., Toronto, 1940-42; Kingsway Lambton, Toronto, 1942-55; Principal, United Coll., 1955-67; Pres. and Vice-Chancellor, Univ. of Winnipeg 1967-71; Pres. Emeritus, Univ. of Winnipeg, 1971-; mem., Bd. of Regents, Victoria Univ., Toronto, 1950-55; Chrmn. of Bd., Coll. & Secondary Schs., Un. Ch. of Can., 1946-55; Chaplain, Univ. of Toronto C.O.T.C., 1939-46; first secy., Candn. Comte., World Council of Chs. 1937-40; Chrmn., Bd. of Govs., Balmoral Hall Sch. for Girls, 1957-58; Chrmn. of Winnipeg, Presbytery of Un. Ch. Can. 1962-63; mem., Man. Council on Higher Learning, 1965-67; Moderator, Un. Ch. of Can., 1966-68; mem., Prov. of Man. Local Boundaries Comn.; Publications: "John Fletcher-Evangelist", 1939; "In Such an Age", 1951; "Bethlehem", 1955; recreations: fishing, golf, gardening, curling; Club: Rotary (Pres. 1964-65); Home: Suite 2001, 2045 Lakeshore Blvd. W., Toronto, Ont. M8V 2Z6

LOCKWOOD, George Hepworth, M.A.; judge; b. Glasshoughton, Yorks., Eng. 18 Apl. 1923; s. George and Phoebe (Bradburn) L.; e. The King's School, Pontefract, Yorks, 1942; Univ. Coll. Oxford B.A. (Hons) 1950, M.A. 1956; Lincoln's Inn London, Barrister-at-Law 1958; m. Lissen Karen d. Ahlman and Ragnhild Eckhardt, Winnipeg, Man. 27 Jan. 1962; children: Mette Norma, Michael Hepworth, Martin Bradburn; by previous marriage, Jonathan Mauduit; JUDGE, CO. COURT OF EASTERN JUDICIAL DIST. and of The Surrogate Court of Man. 1978-; Local Judge, The Court of Queen's Bench of Man.; called to Bar of Man. 1958; cr. Q.C. 1975; Business Extve. and Mgr.; London and Kenya 1950-53; Colonial Service Offr. Kenya 1953-57; mem. law firm Guy, Chappell, Guy, Wilson & Coghlin 1958; Pitblado & Hoskin 1961-66; Partner and Sr. Partner, Fillmore & Riley 1966-78; sometime Pres., John Howard Soc. Can.; Bencher, Law Soc. Man.; mem. Nat. Council Candn. Bar Assn.; Dir. Legal Aid Man.; Part-time Judge of Prov. Judges Court (Criminal Div.); Dir. Forum Art Inst.; past Pres., Internat. Comn. of Jurists (Candn. Sec.); Past Pres. Amnesty Internat. Can.; Dir. Candn. Judges Conf.; Nat. Councillor Candn. Human Rights Foundation; Dir. Royal Winnipeg Ballet; Fellow, Foundation for Legal Research; served with RAF 1943-47, Flying Offr.-Navig.; recreations: sailing, tennis, golf, theatre, ballet, opera, reading; Home: 30 Roslyn Cres., Winnipeg, Man. R3L 0H7; Office: 132 Law Courts Bldg., Winnipeg, Man. R3C 0V8.

LOCKWOOD, John Crosby, B.A.; industrialist; b. Brentwood, Essex, Eng., 5 Jan. 1913; s. Crosby Marston and Kathleen (Reilly) L.; e. Ampleforth Coll., Yorkshire; Worcester Coll., Oxford (Grad. with Hons. in Classical Studies and Modern Hist.); m. children: Caroline, Marianne, Benedict, Sebastian, Francis, Stephen; DIR., CARLING O'KEEFE LTD.; joined Unilever organ. in Eng. in 1936; came to Can. 1946 as Advertising Mgr., Pepsodent Co. Canada; successively, Marketing Dir. to Pepsodent, Marketing Dir. for World Brands Ltd. (a Lever-owned subsidiary), Sales Dir. for Lever Bros., Marketing Dir. for Lever

Bros., Apptd. Mang. Dir. of Lever S.A. in Brussels, Belgium 1956; return to Can. Co. as Pres. and C.E.O. 1959; Chmn. Lever Brothers Ltd., 1974-75; Chmn., Carling O'Keefe Ltd. 1975-80; Co-Chmn., Candn. Council of Christians and Jews; Sen. of Stratford Festival Fdn.; Chmn., Medieval Studies Fdn.; Gov., Nat. Theatre Sch.; served in 2nd World War; enlisted Dec. 1939 as Driver in R.A.S.C.; commnd. in late 1940, landed in Normandy on D-Day plus 7 as Major, 43rd Inf. Div.; fought in France, Belgium, Holland and Germany; demob. 1946 with rank of Major; Mentioned in Despatches, 1944; commnd. in 1946 to R.C.A.S.C. and gaz. as Major on Reserve; Roman Catholic; recreations: books, theatre, pictures, sailing; Clubs: R.C.Y.C.; Toronto; Home: One Benvenuto Place, Apt. 501, Toronto, Ont. M4V 2L1

LODGE, Lorne Kenneth, B.Com., F.C.A.; co. executive; b. Toronto, Ont., 17 Sept. 1930; s. Louis W. and Hilda (Thomas) L.; e. Bowmore Road Pub. Sch. and Riverdale Coll. Inst., Toronto, 1935-48; Victoria Coll., Univ. of Toronto, B.Com. 1952; C.A. 1956; F.C.A. 1973; m. Imbi Sepa, 23 June 1978; children: Lee James, Linda Diane, Wendy Ruth, Susan Marie; CHMN. & PRES., IBM CANADA LTD., since 1976; Dir., Norwich Union Life Insurance Soc.; Norwich Union Fire Insurance Soc. Ltd.; Canada Security Assurance Co.; Toronto-Dominion Bank; Auditor, Price Waterhouse & Co., 1952-56; joined present Co. as Data Processing Salesman, 1956; Data Processing Marketing Mgr. 1962; Adm. Asst. to Pres. 1964; Mgr. of Budgets 1965; Assistant Controller 1966; Controller 1967; Extve. Vice Pres. 1968; Bd. of Dir., 1969; Pres. & C.E.O., 1972; Chmn. and Pres. 1976; Lieut. RCN(R); mem., Candn. Chamber Comm.; Candn. Inst. C.A.'s; Toronto Redevelopment Adv. Council; Candn. Mfrs. Assn.; Business Council on Nat. Issues; Business Comm. on Regulatory Reform; The Conf. Bd. in Can.; Candn.-Am. Comte.; Trustee, the Fraser Inst.; Inst. C.A.'s of Ont.; Theta Delta Chi; Anglican; recreations: golf, skiing; Clubs: Granite; Toronto; Rosedale Golf & Country; Mount Royal; Mailing Address: P.O. Box 392, Stn. "R", Toronto, Ont. M4G4C3; Office: 1150 Eglinton Ave. E., Don Mills, Ont. M3C 1H7

LOEWEN, Charles Barnard, B.A., M.B.A.; stockbroker; e. Winchester Coll. Univ. of B.C., B.A. 1954; Harvard Business Sch. M.B.A. 1956; PRESIDENT, LOEWEN, ONDAATJE, McCUTCHEON & CO. LTD., Founding mem. of firm 1970; Gov., Toronto Stock Exchange; joined W. C. Pitfield & Co. Montreal 1956; Pitfield, Mackay Co. Inc. New York 1959; Pitfield, Mackay & Co. Ltd. (subsequently Pitfield, Mackay, Ross & Co. Ltd.) Toronto 1962, Dir. 1966, Vice Pres. 1968; Clubs: Badminton & Racquet; Toronto Lawn Tennis; Tadenac; Devil's Glen Country; Home: 100 Park Rd., Toronto, Ont. M4W 2N7; Office: 20th Floor, 7 King St. E.; Toronto, Ont. M5C 1A2.

LOEWEN, General Sir Charles F., G.C.B., K.B.E., D.S.O., D.Sc., Commander, U.S. Legion of Merit; British army retired; b. Vancouver, B.C., 17 Sept. 1900; s. Charles Joseph and Edith (Warren) L.; e. University Sch., Victoria, B.C. till 1913; Haileybury Coll., Eng., 1913-16; Royal Mil. Coll., Kingston, Ont., 1916-18; D.Sc.Mil., R.M.C. (Can.), 1967; m. Kathleen Gordon, d. Maj.-Gen. J. M. Ross, London, Ont., 8 Oct. 1928; children: C. B., J. J. F.; Temp. Lieut., C.F.A., Mar. 1918; Commissioned into British R.H. & R.F.A., Sept. 1918; served in Middle East and in India, 1919-38; in 2nd World War, served in Norway, U.K. and Italy; in Italy Commanded successively 56th Div. Arty., 10th Corps Arty., and 1st Brit. Inf. Div.; since then successively, G.O.C., 6th Armoured Div.; G.O.C., 1st Armoured Div. (Palestine, Italy and Trieste); G.O.C., 50th (Northumbrian) Inf. Div. in U.K.; G.O.C.-in-C., Anti-Aircraft Command; G.O.C.-in-C., Western Command in U.K.; Commander-in-Chief, Brit. Far East Land Forces, 1953-56; Adj.-Gen. to the Forces, 1956-59; A.D.C. General to H.M. Queen 1956-59; Maj.-Gen. 1944; Lieut.-Gen. 1950; General 1954; Twice Mentioned in Despatches; Church of England; recreation: fishing; Address: Boyne Mills House, R.R. No. 3, Mansfield, Ont. L0N 1M0

LOEWENHEIM, Nandor Fernand; b. Vienna, Austria, 5 March 1905; s. late Leopold and late Ida (Procurator) L.; e. Academy of Commerce, Vienna, Austria; m. late Susie, d. late Leo Laszlo, 16 August 1936; one d. Juliet; BD. CHRMN., INTERCONTROL CANADA LTD.; Hon. Consul General of Austria; Grosses Ehrenzeichen of Austria; former member of the family concern of Sigmund Buchler & Co., Head Office, Budapest, Hungary (Co. formed by his grandfather in 1867) expropriated 1948; Roman Catholic; Home: 1 Bellevue Ave., Westmount, Que. H3Y 1G4; Office: 1350 Sherbrooke St. W., Montreal, Que. H3G 1J1

LOFQUIST, Jack Clifford; retired banker; b. Clarkson, Ont., 22 May 1912; s. J. Albin and Emma (Anderson) L.; e. Pub. Sch., Clarkson, Ont.; High Sch., Oakville, Ont.; m. Rita, d. John H. Gardner, 27 Sept. 1939; three s. John, Paul, Peter, two d. Mary, Anne; Chrmn. Bd. and Pres.; United Dominion Corp. (Canada) Ltd.; Chrmn. Bd., IBANCO Ltd.; Dir., United Dominions Investments Ltd.; United Dominions Finance Corp. Ltd.; Credit For Industry (Canada) Ltd.; Commerce Optimation Services Ltd.; Chargex Ltd., Chargex Ltée; with Imperial Bank of Commerce, Oakville, Ont., successively Br. Mgr., Toronto 1951, Supt. H.O., Toronto 1960, Asst. Gen. Mgr. 1965; vice-pres. 1971-77 (ret) Dir., Credit Counselling Service Metrop. Toronto; Catholic Family Services, Toronto; mem. Candn. Bankers Assn.; Bd. Trade Metrop. Toronto; R. Catholic; recreation: travel; Clubs: National; Empire; Home: 21 Ardrossan Place, Toronto, Ont. M4N 2X2

LOGAN, Frank Henderson; investment dealer; b. Montreal, Que., 19 May 1936; s. Frank Duncan and Mabel (Henderson) L.; e. Schs. of Westmount, (Que.); Princeton Univ.; m. Linda May, d. W. R. Hermitage, 26 Oct. 1962; two s.; VICE CANADIAN IMPERIAL BANK OF COMMERCE; 1981-; Dir., Trizec Corp. Ltd.; Dominion Foundries and Steel Ltd.; Chmn., Dominion Securities Ltd.; Ducks Unlimited (Can.); Leitch Transport Ltd.; Protestant; Clubs: Toronto; York; Princeton (N.Y.); Mount Royal Ivy (Princeton); Ranchmen's (Calgary); Granite (Toronto); Home: 165 Munro Blvd., Willowdale, Ont. M2P 1C9; Office; 309-8th Ave. S.W., Calgary, Alta. T2P 1C6

LOGAN, Hon. Rodman Emmason, C.D., Q.C., B.A., B.C.L., D.C.L.; politician; b. Saint John West, N.B. 7 Sept. 1922; s. Gilbert Earle, Q.C. and Emma Z. (Irwin) L.; e. Rothesay Coll. Sch. 1941; Univ. of N.B. B.A. 1949, B.C.L. 1951; St. Thomas Univ. D.C.L. 1974; m. Evelyn Pearl d. C. Ray DeWitt, Woodstock, N.B. 19 June 1948; children: Capt. John Bruce DeWitt, Ian David Alexander, Bruce Rodman Hans, Mary Jane Irwin; MIN. OF JUSTICE, N.B. since 1977; called to Bar of N.B. 1951, cr. Q.C. 1973; mem. Kings Co. Council 1952-54; el. to Leg. Assembly for Saint John Co. 1963, re-el. since for Saint John West; apptd. Min. of Labour and Prov. Secy. 1970, relinquished latter post 1972; re-apptd. Min. of Labour 1974 (subsequently Labour & Manpower 1975); Min. responsible for Housing 1974; served with Carleton and York Regt. 1943-45 UK N.Africa Italy N.W. Europe, twice wounded, rank Lt.; served with Militia 1946-60; Hon. Pres. 69 Br. Royal Candn. Legion (Hon. Solr. for Legion 1953-70), Carleton & York Regt'al Assn.; P. Conservative; Anglican; Home: 37 Buena Vista Ave., Saint John West, N.B.; Office: (P.O. Box 6000) Dept. of Justice, Fredericton, N.B. E3B 5H1.

LOGIE, David A., M.A., F.F.A., F.C.I.A., A.S.A.; b. Glasgow, Scot., 4 Nov. 1920; s. David and Margaret Paterson (Wood) L.; came to Can. Nov. 1949; e. St. Bees Sch., Cumberland, Eng.; Glasgow Univ., M.A. 1940; m. Roberta G., d. Robert O. Scholz, 1954; FINANCIAL VICE-PRES. AND SECY., ZURICH LIFE INS. CO. OF CANADA, 1971-80; Investment manager for Canada, Zurich Insurance Company and Alpina Insurance Company 1975-80; Investment Clerk, Scottish Amicable Life Assurance Society, Glasgow 1940-47; Fellow of the Faculty of Actuaries in Scot. 1947; Asst. Actuary for S. Africa, the Colonial Mutual Life Assnce. Soc. Ltd., Cape Town 1947-49; joined predecessor Co., The Continental Life Ins. Co. as Asst. Actuary 1949, Actuary 1952; Secy.-Treas. of present Co. 1969; Dir., Vice Pres. & Treas., The Robert O. Scholz Foundation; mem. St. Andrew's Soc.; Conservative; Presbyterian; Clubs: University; Albany; Granite; Home: 69 Donwoods Dr., Toronto, Ont. M4N 2G6

LOISELLE, Gérard, M.P.; insurance broker; b. Montreal, Que., 15 April 1921; s. Roméo and Lucienne (Laplante) L.; m. Claire, d. Pierre Dumouchel, 22 Feb. 1943; children: Huguette, René, Gérald, Diane, Nicole, Daniel, Sylvain; mem. of Municipal Council of Montreal 1950-70; 1st el. to H. of C. for Montreal-St. Ann, g.e. 1957; re-el. since for Montreal St-Henry; mem., Montreal Chamber Comm.; L.O.M.; K. of C.; Liberal; Roman Catholic; Home: 2160 rue Hall, Montreal 22, Que.;

LOMAS, Frederick Irvin, manufacturer; b. Toronto, Ont., 20 June 1910; s. Fred Henry and Lilian Pearl (Dicks) L.; m. Alice, d. William Macfarlane, Toronto, Ont., 29 June 1930; one s. William Fred; VICE CHMN., DACK CORP. LTD. (Shoe Mfrs., Estbd. 1834); VICE CHMN., Church & Co. (Canada) Ltd.; served with R.C.A. (Reserve); mem., Shoe Mfrs. Assn. Can.; Bd. of Trade Metrop. Toronto; Conservative; United Church; recreation: photography; Clubs: Boulevard; Markland Woods; Granite; Home: Palace Pier, Ste. 802, 2045 Lakeshore Blvd. W., Toronto, M8V 2Z6; Office: 2100 Golfshore Blvd. N., Naples, Florida, 33940, U.S.A.

LOMBARDI, John-Barbalinardo, O.C. broadcasting executive; b. Toronto, Ont., 4 Dec. 1915; s. late Leonard and late Theresa L.; e. Pub. and High Schs., Toronto; Toronto Central Tech. Sch.; m. Antonia Lena, 4 July 1949; children: Leonard, Theresa Maria, Donina Antonia; PRESIDENT AND MANG. DIR., RADIO 1540 and RADIO CHIN-FM LTD. Can. largest Multilingual Broadcasting operation (estab. 1966); Pres., Lombardi Italian Foods Ltd.; Bravo Records & Music Co. Ltd.; Carpejon Investments Ltd.; Italian Shows Ltd.; Originator of annual (Can.) Multicultural Songwriting Competition (est. 1974); also International Picnic, Canada's largest free annual festival of ethnocultural music, song, dance and amusements; Awards rec'd: Can. Family of Man Award, 1977; The Howard Caine Mem. Award (Broadcasting) 1976; Broadcaster of the year Award, 1980; co-winner AM station of the yr. Award 1980; mem. of various organizations: Canada Council; Variety Club; Toronto Musicians Assn.; Victorian Order of Nurses; Italian Chamber of Comm.; Pres. Can. Assn. Ethnic (Radio) Broadcasters; Dir.; Better Business Bureau, Toronto; Gov., Doctors Hospital; The Council for Candn. Unity; Nat. Council of Boy Scouts of Canada; Hon. Dir., Can.-Italian Am. Hockey League; Ont. Foundation for Visually Impaired Children; mem. Can Nat. Exhibition Assn.; Home: 127 Grace St., Toronto, Ont. M6J 2S6; Office: 637 College St., Toronto, Ont. M6G 1B6

LONDON, Byron Fraser; retired investment executive; b. Wickham, N.B. 11 July, 1922; s. Hilford M. and Mary (Smith) L.; e. Wickham Pub. and High Schs.; Business Adm., Modern Business Coll., Saint John, N.B. 1944; Extve. Adm. King's Coll., Halifax, N.S. 1960; m. Emma J., d. late Harry W. Somerville, 1 Sept. 1942; children: Blair, John; CHRMN., FINANCE COMTE., THE PROGRESSIVE CONSERVATIVE PARTY OF N.B.; Dir., Sussex Health Centre; Treas., Cole's Island Cemetery Inc.; mem., Adv. Bd., Central & Eastern Trust Co.; formerly Pres., Chief Extve. Offr. and Dir., Niagara Realty of Canada Ltd.; formerly Sr. Vice Pres., IAC Ltd; mem.,

Chancellor's Club., Univ. of N.B.; formerly Pres. Candn. Consumer Loan Assn. Chrmn. Bd. Mang., Codys United Baptist Church; Councillor, Albert Co., N.B., 1953-55; P. Conservative; Baptist; Clubs: Union (Saint John, N.B.), Chisholm Lake Fishing; Sussex (N.B.) Golf & Curling; M.A.A.A.; Home: Codys, Queens County, N.B. E0E 1E0

LONDON, Woodrow Parker, B.Sc.; engineer; consultant; b. Millinocket, Maine 28 Jan. 1914; s. Jepson F. and Alice Jane (Parker) L.; e. Univ of New Brunswick B.Sc., E.E., 1934; m. Joan Kennie 2 Oct. 1948; children: Susan Jane, John Christopher, Judith Anne; PRES. AND SR. EXTVE. OFFR., W.P. LONDON AND ASSOC. LTD. since 1960; Pres., London Nuclear Ltd., 1977- ; Pres., London Moneco Consultants Ltd., 1974-; Draftsman, The N.B. Electric Power Comn., 1935-36; Engn., Bathurst Power and Paper Co. Ltd., 1937-41; joined H.G. Acres and Co. Ltd. as Mech. Design Engr., 1941-42; Mech. Engn., 1942-57; Chief Engn., 1957-59; technical interests centre on the design of fossil fuel fired plants for the production of steam and electric power; mem., Assn. of Prof. Engn. of Prov. of N.B.; Assn. of Prof. Engn. of Prov. of Man.; Assn. of Prof. Engn. of the Prov. of Ont.; Life Fellow, Am. Soc. of Mech. Engn.; Am. Soc. for Testing and Materials; Candn. Elec. Assn.; Candn. Nuclear Assn.; Candn. Pulp and Paper Assn., Tech. Section; Candn. Standards Assn.; The Engn. Inst. of Can.; Home: 6050 Clare Cres., Niagara Falls, Ont. L2G 2C6; Office: 4056 Dorchester Rd., P.O. Box 1025, Niagara Falls, Ont. L2E 6V9.

LONERGAN, Rev. Bernard, C.C.(1970), S.T.D. (R.C.); b. Buckingham, Quebec, 17 December 1904; s. Gerald Joseph and Josephine Helen (Wood) L.; e. Loyola College, Montreal, P.Q.; Heythrop Coll., Chipping Norton, Oxon, England; University of London, B.A. (external) 1930; Pontifical Gregorian Univ., Rome, S.T.D. 1950; entered Soc. of Jesus, Guelph, Ont., 29 July 1922; Instructor, Loyola Coll., Montreal, Que., 1930-33; o. Priest 1936; Professor of Dogmatic Theol., L'Immaculee-Conception, Montreal 1940-47; Professor at Jesuit Seminary, Toronto, 1947-53; Professor Gregorian Univ., Rome, 1953-65; rec'd. Spellman Award for outstanding work in Sacred Theol.; 1949; Aquinas Medal for outstanding work in philosophy 1970; John Courtney Murray Award 1973; Publications: "Insight: A study of Human Understanding", 1957; "De constitutione Christi", 1956; "De Deo trino", 2 vols. 1964" "Collection, Papers by Bernard Lonergan", 1967; "Verbum: Word and Idea in Aquinas", 1967; "Grace and Freedom in Aquinas", 1971; "Method in Theology" 1972; "Philosophy of God and Theology" 1973; "A Second Collection" 1974; "The Way to Nicea", 1976; Stillman Prof. Harvard Divinity Sch. 1971-72; Visiting Disting. Prof. of Theology, Boston Coll., 1975-; holds Hon. degrees from St. Mary's (1964); Holy Cross and St. Michael's, Toronto (1969); Marquette and Boston Coll. (1970); Catholic Univ., Notre Dame, Fordham and Santa Clara (1971); St. Joseph's (Pa.) and St. Paul Univ. (1972); Wilfrid Laurier (1973); Chicago (1974); McMaster (1975); St. Anselm's (Manchester, N.H.) 1976; Concordia, 1977; Loyola (Chicago), 1978; Fairfield (CN) 1979; "Creativity and Method: In Honour of Bernard Lonergan" ed. by Matthew Lamb, 1981; recreations: walking, music; Address: St. Mary's Hall, Boston Coll., Chestnut Hill, Ma. 02167.

LONG, Rev. Ernest Edgar, B.A., M.Div., D.D., LL.D. (Un. Ch.); b. Brighton, Eng., 26 July 1901; s. Harry Oliver and Ellen Kate (Pierce) L.; e. Woodstock (Ont.) Bapt. Coll., 1916-18 (Gold Medallist and Gov.-Gen's. Medal); Univ. of Toronto (Victoria), B.A. 1924; Union Theol. Semy., N.Y., M.Div. (Magna Cum Laude) 1927; D.D. United Theol. Coll., Montreal, 1953, Emmanuel Coll., Toronto 1962; LL.D. Wilfrid Laurier Univ. 1964; m. Dorothy Elizabeth (Ph.D.), d. George Benjamin Toye, Toronto, 18 Aug. 1931; children: Peter, Elizabeth; SECY. OF GENERAL COUNCIL OF UNITED CH. OF CAN. (Chief

Exec. Staff Officer), 1955-72; ordained 1926; Dir. of Boys' Work, People's Settlement House, N.Y. City, 1924-26; Dir. of Religious Educ., West Side Ch., Ridgewood, N.J., 1926-27; Min., Avondale Un. Ch., Tilsonburg, Ont., 1927-33; Collier St., Barrie, Ont., 1933-40; Trinity, Kirkland Lake, Ont., 1940-43; Fairmount-St. Giles Ch., Montreal, 1943-53; Humbercrest Un. Ch., Toronto, 1953-55; Trinity Un. Ch. Peterborough, 1973-74; Metro. Un. Ch. Toronto, 1975-76; Westmoreland Un. Ch. Toronto, 1977-78; mem., Extve. and Sub-Extve., Un. Ch. of Can., 1938-40 and 1952-54; Chrmn., Montreal Presbytery 1952; Pres., Montreal and Ottawa Conf., Un. Ch. of Can., 1952-53; mem. Extve., World Meth. Council, and Internat. Cong. Council; mem. and Extv., World Presb. Alliance; Pres., North American and Caribbean Council, W.A.R.C., 1975-76; World Council of Chs. Central Comte. and mem. Div. of Inter-Ch. Aid 1961-72; recreation: gardening; furniture refinishing; Home: 17 Lytton Blvd., Toronto, Ont. M4R 1K9

LONG, John (Jack) W., B. Arch.; architect and urban planner; b. Johnstown, Pa., 12 Dec. 1925; s. J. W. and Esther T. L.; e. Penna. State Univ., B.Arch., 1950; C.M.H.C. Fellowship, McGill Univ. 1967; m.; PRINCIPAL, JACK LONG AND THE NEW STREET GROUP; with Vincent G. Kling, Philadelphia, then Resident Arch-Planner, Urban Devel. Project, Webb & Knapp, Washington, D.C. prior to estab. practice in Calgary, Alta. 1961; Special Planning Consultant, City of Calgary 1963; Partner, McMillan, Long and Assoc. 1964; mem. (Council) Alta. Assn. Archs.; Royal Arch. Inst. Can.; Nat. Council Arch. Registration Bds. (U.S.); Commonwealth of Penn. Registration; Town Planning Inst. Can.; Community Planning Assn. Can. (Past Chrmn.); Am. Soc. Planning Officials; Calgary Chamber of Comm. (Past Chrmn., Town Planning Comte.); Office: 26 New St. E., Calgary, Alta. T2G 3X9

LONG, Joseph, B.Sc.; electrical engineer; public administrator; b. Blackie, Alta. 5 July 1924; s. King Sing and Sze (Huey) L.; e. Univ. of Alta. B.Sc. 1950; Carleton Univ. D.P.A. 1971; m. Gloree Louise d. Lawrence Chen, Vancouver, B.C. 29 July 1961; children: Malcolm Jay, Adrienne Diane; GEN. MGR., NORTHERN CANADA POWER COMN. 1978- ; Constr. Engr. 1951-52, Elect. Engr. 1953-56, Mgr. of Hydro Plants 1957-67, Chief Engr. 1967-69, Asst. Gen. Mgr. 1969-78; served with RCAF Can. and Eng. 1943-45; mem. Assn. Prof. Engrs., Geols. & Geophysicists Alta.; Inst. Elect. & Electronic Engrs. (Past Chrmn. Ottawa Sec.); Assn. Prof. Engrs. Y.T.; Shriner; United Church; recreations: tennis, skiing; Clubs: Rotary; Derrick Golf & Winter; Home: P.O. Box 2, Site 1, R.R. 1, Edmonton, Alta. T6H 4N7; Office: P.O. BoX 5700, Stn. L, Edmonton, Alta. T6C 4J8.

LONGSTAFFE, John Ronald, B.A., LL.B.; executive; b. Toronto, Ont., 6 Apl. 1934; e. Upper Can. Coll., Toronto; Univ. of B.C., B.A. 1957, LL.B. 1958; one s., two d.; m. Jacqueline Slaughter 1978; EXTVE. VICE PRES. AND DIR., CANADIAN FOREST PRODUCTS LTD.; Extve. Vice Pres. and Dir. Canfor Investments Ltd.; Chrmn. and Dir., Balco Industries Ltd.; Yorkshire Trust Co.; Dir. Prince George Pulp and Paper Ltd.; Bank of Canada; Intercontinental Pulp Co. Ltd.; Takla Forest Products Holdings Ltd.; Westcoast Cellufibre Industries Ltd.; Versatile Corp.; Bralorne Resources Ltd.; Burrard Yarrows Corp.; Pirelli Can. Ltd.; 2nd Vice Chmn., Council of Forest Ind. of B.C.; mem., Can. Adv. Bd., Allendale Mutual Insurance Co.; articled with Lawson, Lundell, Lawson & McIntosh; joined present Co. as Solr. 1959 subsequently Secy.; leave of absence to serve Reed International Ltd., London, Eng. as Dir. of Corporate Planning 1969-72; rejoined present Co. as Vice Pres. 1972; Dir., Roy. Winnipeg Ballet; Candn. Council of Christians and Jews; Past Vice-Chmn. Nat. Museums of Can. 1968-69; mem., Vancouver Econ. Adv. Council; Vancouver Art Gallery (Pres. 1966-68); Law Soc. B.C.; Bd. of Trustees, St. Paul's Hospital, Vancouver (Chmn 1975-79); recreation: collector contemp. Candn. art and internat. graphics; Clubs: Vancouver, Vancouver Lawn Tennis & Badminton; Men's Canadian (Past Pres.); Office: 505 Burrard St., Vancouver, B.C.

LOOMIS, Brig.-Gen. Dan Gordon, M.C., O.M.M., C.D., B.Sc., M.A.; Canadian armed forces; b. Montreal, Que., 2 May 1929; s. Dan McKay and Marjorie Elizabeth (Ellis) L.; e. Lower Can. Coll., Montreal; Mount Royal (Que.) High Sch. 1942; Lisgar Coll. Inst., Ottawa 1947; Royal Roads, Victoria 1949; Royal Mil. Coll., B.Sc. (Chem. Engn.) 1952, M.A. 1969; Queen's Univ., B.Sc. 1954; Royal Mil. Coll. of Science 1959; Candn. Army Staff Coll. 1961; m. Diane Alexina, d. late Elmer Victor Finland, Victoria, B.C., 15 Aug. 1953; children: Daphne Pauline, Dan McKay; enlisted Candn. Army Reserve Force 1944, joining Active Force 1952; served in Korea with Royal Candn. Regt.; served with 1st Bn. in Can. and Europe 1954-56; posted to Jt. Atomic, Biol. and Chem. Warfare Sch., 1958; apptd. for 2 yr. tour 1st Brit. Corps HQ, Germany as exchange offr. 1964; served with Mobile Command 1966-67; apptd. C.O., 1 RCR, London, Ont., 1969 taking unit to Cyprus 1970 and serving as Nicosia Dist. Commdr.; returned to W. Que. during 1970 Oct. crises; assigned to CFHQ with Directorate of Strategic Planning, 1971; apptd. Dir. of Sovereignty Planning and subsequently joined ADM (Policy) staff when formed in 1972 as Dir. of Mil. Strategic Planning; apptd. Depy. Commdr. and Chief of Staff, Candn. Contingent, S. Vietnam, 1973; upon return to Can. named Special Policy Analyst with ADM (Policy) NDHQ; promoted to present rank and apptd. Chief of Staff, Operations, Mobile Command HQ, 1974; Anglican; recreations: physics, anthropology, writing, camping; Clubs: United Services Inst.; Royal Mil. Coll.; Office: St. Hubert, Que.

LORANGER, Fernand; brewing executive; b. Deschambault, Que., 10 June 1928; s. Laurent and Rachel (Paris) L.; m. Jose, d. Omer Vannieuwenhove, 26 July 1952; children: Ivan, Hughes, Andre; VICE-PRESIDENT OPERATIONS, LA BRASSERIE LABATT LTEE; joined Labatt Breweries of Canada Ltd. 1956; held various positions namely: Quality Control Supvr., Bottleshop Supvr., Plant Engr., Asst. Plant Mgr. and Dir. of Purchasing and Packaging and Vice-President Production; mem., Corp. Ingenieurs du Quebec; Liberal; R. Catholic; Home: 427 Montrose, Beaconsfield, Que. H9W 1H2; Office: 50 rue Labatt, La Salle, Que. H8R 3E7

LORCINI, Gino, R.C.A.; sculptor; b. Plymouth, Eng. 7 July 1923; s. Luigi and Marie (Stride) L.; e. Boroughmuir Secondary Sch. Edinburgh, Scot.; Montreal Museum Sch. of Art 1952; came to Can. 1948; m. Marie Iosch 30 May 1953; children: Barrie, Anna, Nina, Gregory; solo exhns. incl. Galerie Agnes Lefort Montreal 1963, 1966; Galerie Moos Toronto 1966, 1969; Galerie Godard Lefort 1968, 1970; Atlantic Provs. Museums (tour) 1971-72; Marlborough Godard Gallery Toronto 1973; 1974; London (Ont.) Art Gallery 1976; McIntosh Gallery Univ. W. Ont. 1977; Albert White Gallery Toronto 1979; Gallery Graphics Ottawa 1979; Thomas Gallery Winnipeg 1979; Art Expo N.Y. 1981; rep. in various group shows incl. Nat. Gallery Can. Candn. Sculpture 1964; Que. Prov. Competitions 1964-67; R.C.A. exhns. 1964-67; Art Gallery Ont. 1965 and Montreal Museum of Fine Arts; Univ. Vt. (Op from Montreal) 1965; Aspects Candn. Art Albright Gallery Buffalo 1974; rep. in various pub., corporate and private colls. Can., USA and Japan incl. Univ. Vt., Musée d'art contemporain Montréal, Nat. Gallery Can., Art. Gallery Ont.; recipient Jessie Dow Award Montreal Museum Fine Arts; Can. Council Arts Award; comns. incl. Montreal Forum mural; Nat. Arts Centre Ottawa; Court House London, Ont.; City Hall Kingston; Panasonic Eaton Centre Toronto; Asst. Prof. of Educ. McGill Univ. 1962-69; Resident Artist Univ. of W. Ont. 1969-72; served with R.A.M.C. 1942-46, Sgt./Instr. Educ.; recreations: exploring wilderness and ancient monuments; Address: 282 Ramsay Rd., London, Ont. N6G 1N6.

LORD, Arthur Edward, Q.C., LL.D.; b. Lulu Island, B.C., 22 February 1897; s. William Ross and Mary L.; e. King Edward High Sch., Vancouver, B.C.; Univ. of British Columbia, B.A., Hon. LL.D.; m. Myrtle Esther Kilpatrick, 20 September 1927; read law with Hunter & Davidson, Vancouver, B.C.; called to the Bar of B.C., 1923; cr. K.C. 1950; Asst. City Solr., Vancouver, B.C., 1924-35, and City Solr., 1935-47; Corp. Counsel, 1947-51; apptd. Co. Court Judge, Vancouver, 1951; Justice, Surpreme Court of B.C., 1955; Justice, Court of Appeal of B.C. 1963-68; mem. of Senate (1924-60) and mem. Bd. of Govs. (1939-60), University of B.C.; served in 1st World War with 46th Bn., 1916-17; invalided home, 1918; Freeman, City of Vancouver, 1968; Anglican; recreations: gardening, woodworking; Home: 4739 Drummond Dr., Vancouver, B.C. V6T 1B3

LORD, Clifford Symington, M.A.Sc., Ph.D., F.R.S.C.; geologist; b. New Westminster, B.C., 24 August 1908; s. John William Clifford and Jessie (Symington) L.; e. University of British Columbia, B.A.Sc., 1929, M.A.Sc. 1933; Massachusetts Institute of Technology, Ph.D. 1937; m. Beryl, d. William Arthur Sled, 1 May 1943; Geologist, Anglo-American Corp. of S. Africa, employed in N. Rhodesia, 1929-32; Asst. Geol., Geol. Survey of Can., 1938; Assoc. Geol. 1943; Geol. 1947; Chief Geol. 1954-73; assignments in Far East, India, E. Africa as adv. Candn. Internat. Development Agency 1963-71; work has included field work in Megantic area, Que.; Beresford Lake area, Man.; Snare River, Ingray Lake, Aylmer Lake, and Camsell River areas, N.W.T.; reconnaissance of S. Dist. of Keewatin, N.W.T.; McConnell Creek area, B.C.; Alaska Highway, B.C. and Yukon; gen. survey of mining and mineral indust. throughout N.W.T., 1939 and 1947; Fellow and past Chairman, Board of Governors, Arctic Institute of N. America; mem., Candn. Inst. Mining and Metall. (Distinguished Service Medal 1969); Fellow, Geological Association of Canada; attended 3rd course, Nat. Defence Coll., Kingston, Ont., 1949-50; Sigma Xi; Protestant; Home: 10-215 MacKay St., Ottawa Ont. K1M 2B6

LORD, G(eorge) Ross, B.A.Sc., S.M., Ph.D., D.Sc., F.E.I.C.; university professor; b. Peterborough, Ont., 2 Feb. 1906; s. Edward Everet and Katherine (Manser) L.; e. Univ. of Toronto, B.A.Sc. 1929; Mass. Inst. of Technol., S.M. 1932; Freeman Schol. to Europe; Am. Soc. Mech. Engrs., 1932-33; Univ. of Toronto Ph.D. 1939; D.Sc., York 1972; m. Catherine Nancy, d. Robert James Wilson, D.D., 10 Sept. 1932; children: Nancy, David, Robert, Douglas, John, Barbara, Patricia; PROF. EMERITUS OF MECHANICAL ENGN., UNIV. OF TORONTO; Comte., Faculty of Engn.; Chrmn., Metrop. Toronto & Region Conservation Authority, 1958-72; Consultant on Mine Ventilation, McIntyre, Lakeshore, Macassa, Falconbridge Mines, 1936-40; Water Power Engr., Hydro-Elect. Power Comn. of Ont., 1936-53; Consultant Flood Control, Gov't. of Ont., 1945-71; Chrmn., Bd. of Review, Oper. Engn. Act, Ont.; Life mem., Assn. of Prof. Engrs. of Ont. (Pres. 1946); Fellow, Engn. Inst. of Can.; Am. Soc. of Mech. Engrs.; mem., Bd. Trade of Metrop. Toronto; Pres., Royal Candn. Inst. 1972-73; Vice-Chrmn., North York Planning Bd.; Julian C. Smith Medal, Engn. Inst. of Can. 1971; Engn. Alumni Medal, Univ. of Toronto 1976; United Church; Clubs: Engineers; Empire; Home: 239 Dawlish Ave., Toronto, Ont. M4N 1J2

LORD, Ronald Daniel, P.Eng., LL.D.; b. England, 26 Dec. 1910; s. Daniel Henry & late Anne Mary (Chapman) L.; came to Can., 1912; e. Sydenham High Sch., Ont.; Queen's Univ., 1934-38, LL.D. 1972; m. Helen Dorothy, d. late Edwin Richards, 7 Oct. 1939; children: Ronald Graham, Norman William, Ian James; RESEARCH DIR., MINING INDUS. RESEARCH OF CAN.; employed by McIntyre-Porcupine Mines before and during univ. yrs.;

later Hardrock Gold Mines, and from 1938-1957, Preston East Dome Mines in capacities of Mill Supt., Plant Supt. and Mgr.; joined Rio Tinto Mining Co. of Canada in 1957 as Mang. Dir. of Mines, Pronto Uranium Mines, Milliken Lake Uranium Mines and Rix Athabaska Mines Ltd., Sask.; Chrmn. Adv. Council on Engineering, Queen's University 1969-70; mem., Canadian Institute Mining Metall. (mem. Council & Chairman, Executive Committee; Chairman Toronto Branch 1971-72; Pres. 1977-78; President (1968-69) Ont. Mining Assn.; Assn. Prof. Engrs. Ont.; Protestant; Home: 51 Heathcote Ave., Willowdale, Ont. M2L 1Y9; Office: Box 33 Commerce Court W., Toronto, Ont. M5L 1B3

LORENZ, Wayne, B.Sc., M.B.A.; executive; b. Osmond, Neb.; s. Walter and Beata (Schumacher) L.; e. Univ. of Neb. B.Sc. (Chem. Engn.) 1959; S. Ill, Univ. M.B.A.; m. Arlene d. Dave Johnson Sr. 29 Dec. 1957; two s. David, Steven; PRES., MONSANTO CANADA INC. since 1979; joined Monsanto Chemical holding various positions mfg. 1959-69, Mgr. Econ. Analysis 1969, Business Group Accounting Mgr. 1971, Mgr. Planning 1973, Mgr. Markets 1975, Dir. Planning & Coordination 1977-79; served with U.S. Army 1955-57; recreations: reading, canoeing; Office: 2000 Argentia Rd., Plaza Two, Mississauga, Ont. L5M 2G4.

LORIE, Lucille; b. New York City, N.Y. 6 Feb. 1904; d. Morris I. and Lenora (Steinberg) Ritterman; e. New York City elem. and high schs.; Ethical Culture Training Sch. for Teachers N.Y. 1923; m. Harold Lorie 15 Oct. 1925; children: Richard, Lenore; has served local, nat. and internat. welfare organs. for many yrs.; former Vice Pres., Internat. Council Jewish Women and Chrmn. Comte. on Community Services 6 yrs.; former Pres., Nat. Council Jewish Women of Can. 7 yrs., Pres. Toronto Sec. 1940-44, Hon. Nat. Pres., initiated Overseas program and served as Chrmn. 18 yrs.; active mem. W.P.T.B. during World War II; Charter mem. and mem. first Bd., Mt. Sinai Hosp. and Women's Auxiliary Baycrest Home for Aged; former Trustee, Holy Blossom Temple and Past Pres. of its Sisterhood (now Hon. Life mem.); Founding Pres., Fed. Jewish Women's Organ. 1959; first Chrmn. Women's Div. Un. Jewish Appeal; served Nat. Opera Guild; Art Gallery of Ont.; Toronto Symphony Orchestra; Nat. Ballet Guild of Can.; Candn. Women's Opera Comte.; teacher of gourmet cooking Central Tech. Sch.; rec'd Woman of Yr. Sigma Delta Tau Award 1952; Coronation Medal 1953; Centennial Medal 1967; Nat. Council Jewish Women Can. Community Service Award 1980; recreations: dramatics, cooking; Address: 613 Lonsdale Rd., Toronto, Ont. M5P 1R8.

LORIMER, James, Ph.D.; publisher; b. Regina, Sask. 27 July 1942; s. Wesley Crawford and Myrtle (Moore) L.; e. Univ. of Man. B.A. 1962; London Sch. of Econ. Ph.D. 1966; PUBLISHER, JAMES LORIMER & CO. LTD. 1969- ; Ed. Bd. mem. "City Magazine" 1974-79; Cultural Policy Columnist, "Quill and Quire" 1979-81; Asst. Prof. of Econ. York Univ. 1967-69; Founding Partner present Co. (then James Lewis & Samuel) 1969; Dir. Belford Book Distributing Co. Ltd. 1974-79; Trustee, Toronto Pub. Lib. 1974-79, Chrmn. 1976; Visiting Lectr., Osgoode Hall Law Sch.; Univ. of Toronto Sch. of Arch.; Dalhousie Univ. Law Sch. and Sch. of Lib. Services; author "The Real World of City Politics" 1970; "Working People" 1971; "A Citizen's Guide to City Politics" 1972; "The Ex: A Picture History of The Canadian National Exhibition" 1973; "The City Book" 1975; "The Second City Book" 1976; "The Developers", 1978; City Hall Pol. Columnist, "Globe and Mail" 1969-70; Founding mem. Assn. Candn. Publishers 1971, Pres. 1974; mem. Periodical Writers Assn. Can.; Home: 298 Sackville St., Toronto, Ont. M5A 3G2; Office: 35 Britain St., Toronto, Ont. M5A 1R7.

LORRAIN, Louis H.; labour union executive; b. Kenogami, Que., 23 March 1920; s. Joseph H. and Anna (Gin-

gras) L.; e. High Sch.; Business Coll.; m. Clara Grace, d. late Stephen Vatcher, 19 Jan. 1952; children: John Henry, Alice Louise, Carolyn; PRESIDENT, CANDN. PAPERWORKERS UNION since 1974; Gen. Vice President, Canadian Labour Congress; Bd. of Govs., Internat. Devel. Research Centre; Gov., Labour Coll. of Can.; mem., Candn.-Am. Comte.; joined pulp and paper indust. 1939; el. Pres., Gatineau Local of Internat. Brotherhood of Pulp, Sulphite & Paper Mill Workers, 1947; organizer and representative, 1950; el. Internat. Vice Pres. 1955, Vice Pres. and Candn. Dir. 1965; el. Extve. Vice Pres., United Paperworkers International Union 1972; mem. McGill Univ. Bd. Govs. & Senate; rec'd. Centennial Medal 1967; NDP; United Church; Home: 320 Main Rd., Hudson, Quebec J0P 1H0; Office: Suite 1501, 1155 Sherbrooke St. W., Montreal, Que. H3A 2N3

LORRAIN, Paul, M.Sc., Ph.D., F.R.S.C. (1967); physicist; b. Montreal, Que., 8 Sept. 1916; s. Dr. Joseph Alphonse and Marie Ange (LeBel) L.; e. Univ. of Ottawa B.A. 1937; McGill Univ., B.Sc. 1940, M.Sc. 1941, Ph.D. 1947; m. Dorothée, d. Arthur Sainte-Marie, Outremont, Que., 22 May 1944; children: François, Denis, Claire, Louis; Visiting Prof., Univ. of Grenoble (France), 1961-62; Univ. of B.C., summer 1965; Univ. of Madrid (Spain), 1968-69; Visiting Fellow, Oxford Univ., 1981; mem., Nat. Research Council, 1960-66; Dir., Dept. of Physics, Univ. de Montréal, 1957-66; mem., Candn. Assn. Physicists; Am. Physical Soc.; Publications: coauthor "Electromagnetic Fields and Waves" (2nd ed.), 1970; co-ed. "Nouvelles Tendances dans l'Enseignement de la Physique", UNESCO, 1972; Co-author, "Electromagnetism: Principles and Applications", 1979; many articles on ion sources, accelerators, nuclear physics, vibration isolators, electromagnetism; Home: 777 Chemin des Vieux Moulins, L'Acadie, Qué. J0J 1H0; Office: Université de Montréal, Montreal, Que. H3C 3J7

LORT, John Cecil Rolston, B.A., B.L.S.; librarian; b. Victoria, B.C., 18 May 1914; s. Ross Anthony and Cecilia Marion Frances (Rolston) L.; e. Collegiate school, Victoria; Magee High Sch., Vancouver, B.C.; Brentwood Coll., and Victoria Coll., B.C.; Univ. of Brit. Columbia, B.A. 1935; Univ. of Washington, B.L.S. 1938; m. Faith Elizabeth; d. late Charles Emmanuel Elm, 27 Dec. 1940; children: Marion Christine, Donald Cecil Rolston, Jennifer Elizabeth; Reference Asst., B.C. Prov. Lib., 1940-46; Lib., Ketchikan (Alaska) Public Lib., 1947-49; Oakalla Prison Farm, Burnaby, B.C., 1949-50; Vancouver Island Regional Lib., 1950-53; Asst. Lib., Victoria Public Library, 1953-54, Librarian, 1954-70; Bibliographer, Social Sciences Research Centre, University of Victoria 1971-1974; Rural Rep., Nanaimo Sch. Bd., 1952; served in 2nd World War, N.C.O., 1942-46; co-author "British Columbia Bibliography, Years of Growth, 1900-1950"; mem., B.C. Lib. Assn. (Pres.); Candn. Lib. Assn.; Pacific N.W. Lib. Assn.; Am. Lib. Assn.; Anglican; recreations: gardening, sketching, swimming; Club: Rotary; Home: 4932 Wesley Rd., Victoria B.C. V8Y 1Y7; Office: Victoria, B.C.

LORTIE, Leon, O.C. (1970), D.Sc., LL.D., F.R.S.C., F.C.I.C., F.R.S.A.; professor (retired); b. Montreal, Que., 31 Aug. 1902; s. J. Edouard and Léda (Tremblay) L.; e. Coll. Sainte-Marie, Montreal, Que., B.A. 1923; Univ. of Montreal, Lic. és Sciences chimiques 1927; Univ. of Paris, D.Sc. (Physics) 1930; Cornell Univ. (post-Grad.) 1931; D.Sc. Ottawa and Caen (France), Laval; LL.D. McGill, Mount Allison; m. Rhea Labrosse, 18 Feb. 1928; children: Monique, Gilles, Alain, Bernard, Hélène; mem., Can. Council 1968-71; Pres., Roy. Soc. of Can., 1968-69; mem., City Council of Montreal, 1944-60 and 1966-70; Pres., Greater Montreal Arts Council, 1957-73; Institut Scient. franco-canadien, 1962-68; Fellow, Rockefeller Foundation 1928-31; Asst. Prof. of Chem., Univ. of Montreal, 1926-35, Assoc. Prof. 1935-44 and apptd. Prof. of Inorganic Chem. and Hist. of Science 1944; Head of Dept. of Extension and Asst. to the Rector, 1952-62; Secy.-Gen., Univ.

of Montreal, 1962-68; Vice-Chrmn., Bd. of Govs., Nat. Film Bd. of Can., 1950-51; Pres., Candn. Inst. Chem. 1942-44; Pres., Soc. de Chimie de Montréal 1946-48; Pres., Assn. Candn.-française pour l'Avanc. des Sciences 1948-49; rec'd. Hon. D.Sc. Royal Mil. Coll.; D.l'Un. (Montreal); recreation: music; Montreal Medal, Chm. Inst. Can., 1958; Home: 5585 Gatineau, Apt. 1, Montreal, Que. H3T 1X6

LOSSING, Frederick P., M.A., Ph.D., F.R.S.C. (1956); chemist; b. Norwich, Ont., 4 Aug. 1915; s. Frank Edgar and Evelyn (Pettit) L.; e. Public and High Schs., Norwich, Ont.; Univ. of W. Ont., B.A. 1938, M.A. 1940; McGill Univ., Ph.D. (Chem.) 1942; m. Frances Isabella, d. Sydney J. N. Glazier, 11 June 1938, three d., Wilda Evelyn, Patricia May, Catherine Louise; Research Chemist with Shawinigan Chemicals Ltd., Shawinigan Falls, Que., 1942-46; employed by Nat. Research Council of Can. at McMaster Univ., Hamilton, Ont., 1946-47; since with N.R.C., Ottawa, and Univ. of Ottawa, doing research on reactions and properties of ions and free radicals by means of mass spectrometric techniques; Assoc. Dir., Div. of Chem., 1969-77; mem., Royal Astron. Soc. Can.; Protestant; recreations: music (cello), amateur astronomy; Home: 95 Dorothea Drive, Ottawa, Ont. K1V 7C6; Office: Dept. of Chem., Univ. of Ottawa, Ottawa, Ont. K1N 9B4

LOUCKS, Kenneth Edmun, B.A., M.B.A., Ph.D.; Professor; b. Chatsworth, Ont., 15 Aug. 1937; s. Cecil R. and Blanche J. (Lougheed) L.; e. Univ. of W. Ont., B.A. 1960, M.B.A. 1965, Ph.D. 1974; m. Mary J., d. Manual J. Watson, St. Catharines, Ont., 5 Dec. 1959; children: Carolyn, Christopher, John, Jeffrey; Professor since 1977; High Sch. Teacher 1960-64; Lectr., Sch. of Business Adm., Univ. of W. Ont. 1965-67; consultant; Dir. & Assoc. Prof., Sch. of Comm. & Adm., Laurentian Univ., 1970-77; rec'd Xerox Centennial Fellowship 1967-68; Ford Foundation Fellowship 1968-69, 1969-70; Vice Pres., Research Div., Internat. Council for Small Bus.; Chmn. Trillium Inst. of Mang., Inc.; Bd. of Dir., Sudbury Regional Devel. Corp.; Can. Pension Capital Corp.; mem. Ont. Econ. Council Research Mang. Team for N. Ont. 1974; recreation: private pilot; Home: SS1, Site 12, Box 22, Sudbury, Ont. P3E 4N3

LOUCKS, Wilfrid Artley, B.Sc.; natural resources executive; b. Invermay, Sask., 22 Apl. 1923; s. Harry Artley and Maude (Stephens) L.; e. Invermay (Sask.) High Sch. 1941; Univ. of Sask. B.Sc. (Geol. Engn.) 1949; m. Mary Anna Bernadette d. Thomas Daniel McNamee, Regina, Sask., 22 June 1946; children: Jacqueline Mollo, Maureen, Diane, Ellen, David, Gregory; PRESIDENT, COLEMAN COLLIERIES LTD. since 1975AND VICE-PRES., MINERAL & COAL FOR NORCEN ENERGY RESOURCES LTD.;since Jan. 1979; Dir. Prairie Oil Royalties Co. Ltd.; Oilfield Geol. and Engr. Edmunds, Coombes & Akehurst 1949-50; Operations Geol. and Reservoir Engr. Canadian Superior Oil Ltd. 1950-56; Sr. Geol. The Calgary and Edmonton Corp. 1956-62; Exploration Mgr. Medallion Petroleums Ltd. 1962-65; Vice Pres., Exploration Canadian Industrial Gas & Oil Ltd. 1965-73, Vice Pres. Finance 1974-75; served with RCAF 1942-46; mem. Candn. Soc. Petrol. Geols.; Assn. Prof. Engrs. Geols. & Geophysicists Alta.; recreations: golf, music, sailing; Clubs: Calgary Golf & Country; Earl Grey Golf; Calgary Petroleum; Glencoe; Home: 2609 — 10th St. S.W., Calgary, Alta. T2T 3H1; Office: 715 — 5th Ave. S.W., Calgary, Alta. T2P 2X7

LOUGHEED Hon. (Edgar) Peter, Q.C., M.L.A., LL.B., M.B.A.; politician; b. Calgary, Alta., 26 July 1928; s. late Edgar Donald and Edna Alexandria (Bauld) L.; e. Public and High Schs., Calgary, Alta.; Univ. Alta., B.A. 1950, LL.B. 1952; Harvard Univ. Grad. Sch. Business Adm., M.B.A. 1954; m. Jeanne Estelle, d. Dr. L. M. Rogers, Edmonton, Alta. 21 June 1952; children: Stephen, Andrea, Pamela, Joseph; PREMIER OF ALBERTA since 1971; read

law with Fenerty, Fenerty, McGillivray & Robertson, Calgary, Alta.; called to Bar of Alta. 1955 and practised law with same firm 1955-56; joined Mannix Co. Ltd. as Secy. 1956, named Gen. Counsel 1958, Vice-Pres. 1959, Dir. 1960; entered private legal practice 1962; el. to Alta. Leg. for Calgary W. and el. Leader Prov. P. Conservative Party 1967; re-el. since; recreations: skiing, golf, the symphony; Office: 307 Legislative Bldg., Edmonton, Alta.

LOUTHOOD, Lewis Alexander; retired publishing executive; b. Montreal, Que., 22 April 1917; s. Reginald William and Alice (Sweezey) L.; e. Westmount High Sch., Sr. Matric., 1934; McGill Univ., Arts, 2 yrs.; m. Anne, d. A. Guyon, Montreal, Que., 20 Sept. 1941; children: Donna, Laura, Katherine, Teresa, Margaret; Publishing Consultant; Past. Vice-Pres., Publishing, Montreal Standard Ltd., and Publisher, Weekend Magazine, 1976-79; past Dir., Perspectives, Inc., since 1967; Stenog., Beauharnois Power Corp., 1934-35; Dist. Circul. Mgr., Curtis Publishing Co., Montreal 1936-37; Paymaster, Lake Sulphite Pulp Co., Nipigon, Ont., 1937-38; Copywriter, T. Eaton Co., Montreal, 1938-41; joined Montreal Standard Ltd. as Promotion Mgr., 1941; Promotion and Circulation Dir., 1950, Dir., Newspaper Relations, 1951; mem., Am. Marketing Assn. (Past Pres., Montreal Chapter); Internat. Newspaper Promotion Assn. (Past Dir.); Internat. Newspaper Advertising Extves.; Internat. Circulation Mgrs. Assn.; Advertising & Sales Extves. Club of Montreal (Past Dir.); Theta Delta Chi; Anglican; recreation: fishing; Clubs: Cercle de la Place d'Armes; Ettezag Fish & Game; Trout Unlimited of Canada; Home: 6 High Park Blvd., Toronto Ont. M6R 1M4

LOVE, David Vaughan, M.F.; university professor; b. Saint John, N.B., 25 Aug. 1919; s. Robert Alan and Elizabeth Louise (Davies) L.; e. Univ. of New Brunswick, B.Sc.F. 1941; Univ. of Mich., M.F. 1946; m. Ruth Geraldine, d. late Guy Welch, 9 Jan. 1943; children: Patricia Elizabeth, Peter Alan, Nancy Katherine; PROFESSOR OF FORESTRY, UNIVERSITY OF TORONTO and Associate Dean, having joined Faculty of Forestry there as Lecturer, 1946; served in 2nd World War with R.C.N.V.R., 1942-45, Lieut.; mem., Candn. Inst. of Forestry (Pres., 1965-66); Pres. Conservation Council of Ont., 1975-76; Pres. Candn. Forestry Assn. 1975-76; United Church; recreation: skiing; Home: 16 Marchwood Drive, Downsview, Ont. M3H 1J8

LOVE, Gage Hayward, B.A.; manufacturer; b. Toronto, Ont., 17 Sept. 1917; s. Harry Hayward and Eva Burnside (Gage) L.; e. Univ. of Toronto Schs.; Univ. of Toronto, B.A. 1939; m. Clara Elizabeth, d. Sir Ellsworth Flavelle King, Ont., 20 Sept. 1941; children: Gage Ellsworth, David Hayward, Peter Flavelle, William Geoffrey; VICE-CHRMN. OF BD., BARBECON, INC.; Pres., W. J. Gage Ltd.; Dir., Bennett & Wright; Canplex Ltd.; Pres. Metrop. Toronto Bd. of Trade, 1967-68; served in 2nd World War, Lieut., R.C.N.V.R., 1942-45; Un. Church; Clubs: National; Home: "West Winds", R.R. 2, King, Ont.; Office: 2300 Yonge St. (Box 2406), Toronto, Ont. M4P 1E4

LOVE, Hugh Morrison, B.Sc., Ph.D.; educator; b. Downpatrick, N. Ireland, 21 Aug. 1926; s. Hugh and Anna (Martin) L.; came to Canada 1950; e. Down High Sch., N. Ireland; Queen's Univ. of Belfast, B.Sc. (Hons.) 1946, Ph.D. 1950; m. Jean Claudia, d. H. Willis Hawkins, Cobden, Ont. 1954; children: Maureen, Norah, Denise, Robin; VICE-PRINC. (SERVICES) QUEEN'S UNIV., since 1976; and Prof. of Physics; Lectr. in Physics, Univ. of Toronto 1950; joined present Univ. as Asst. Prof. 1952; research: Mass spectrometry, diffusion in solids and surface physics; mem. Candn. Assn. Phys.; Am. Phys. Soc.; Am. Vacuum Soc.; Am. Assn. Physics Teachers; Candn. Assn. Univ. Teachers; author of several scient. papers in learned and prof. journs.; Home: 119 Queen's Cres., Kingston, Ont. K7L 2S9; Office: Kingston, Ont.

LOVE, J. Douglas, M.A., Canadian public service; b. Toronto, Ont., 18 July 1926; s. late James and Eva (Perry) L.; e. Vaughan Road Coll. Inst., Toronto, Ont.; Univ. of Toronto, B.A. 1949, M.A. 1953; Nuffield Travelling Fellowship, U.K., 1964; DEPUTY MIN. EMPLOYMENT AND IMMIGRATION, AND CHRMN. CAN. EMPLOYMENT AND IMMIGRATION COMMISSION, Oct. 1979-; served in various brs. of Dept. of Labour, 1949-57; worked for Civil Service Comn. as Sr. Econ. and Asst. Dir. Pay Research Bureau and Special Asst. to Chrmn., 1957-63; attached part-time to Royal Comn. on Govt. Organization 1961-62; Secy. and Dir. of Studies, Preparatory Comte. on Collective Bargaining in the Public Service, 1963-65; also served as Dir. Bureau of Classification Revision, 1964-65; Asst. Secy. (Personnel), Treas. Bd., 1965-68; Depy. Min. of Labour and Rep. of Candn. Govt. on Gov. Body of I.L.O., 1969-71; Deputy Min. Regional Economic Expansion 1971-79; Chrmn., Comte. on the Concept of the Ombudsman, 1976-77; mem. Candn. Pol. Science Assn.; Candn. Inst. Public Adm.; Promenade du Portage, Hull, Québec; Office: Ottawa, Ont. K1A 0J9

LOVE, James Alexander, B.Com.; advertising and broadcasting executive; b. Moose Jaw, Sask., 22 Nov. 1920; s. Herbert Gordon and Mabel (Clarke) L.; Mary E., d. Norman Carmichael, Winnipeg, Man., 30 Sept. 1949; children: Tracey Mary, Susan Elizabeth, Alix Anne; VICE-PRES., ALBERTA BROADCASTING CORP. LTD. Dir., Cable West T.V. Ltd.; Central Interior Cablevision Ltd.; joined CFCN 1946; apptd. Program Dir., 1947; Vice Pres. 1949; Pres., 1959-66; served as Lt. with RCA during 2nd World War; N.W. Europe 2 yrs.; Past Pres., Calgary Y.M.C.A.; Better Business Bureau of Calgary; Dir., Calgary Foundation; Delta Upsilon; Freemason; Shriner; Anglican; recreation: travel; Clubs: Ranchmens; Calgary Golf & Country; Home: 403-318 26 Ave. S.W. Calgary, Alta. T2S 0M5

LOVESEY, Morris Roland Bazentin, B.Sc., M.Th., M.A., D.D.(Bapt.); educator; b. Watford, Eng., 8 Oct. 1916; s. late Roland and Winifred Hetty (Sparks) L.; e. Birmingham Univ., B.Sc. 1939; Univ. of London, Spurgeon's Bapt. Theol. Coll., B.D. 1948, M.Th. 1953; Oxford Univ., Mansfield Coll., B.A. (Theol.) 1950, M.A. 1954; McMaster Univ., D.D. 1970; m. Dorothy May, d. late Sidney Shone Surmon, Johannesburg, S. Africa, 4 Dec. 1943; children: Roland John Bazentin, Rosalind Edla May, Oliver Mark Bazentin; PROF. OF BIBLICAL STUDIES, ACADIA UNIV. and Acadia Divinity Coll., since 1968; Shift Boss, Robinson Deep Gold Mining Co., Johannesburg, S. Africa, 1939-44; Min., Kirby Muxloe Free Ch., Leicester, Eng., 1950-56; Assoc. Prof. of Biblical Lit., Sch. of Theol., Acadia Univ., 1956-58, Prof. 1958-68; served with 61st Tunnelling Co. (Mines Engrs. Bgde.), S. African Engr. Corps. Middle E., 1941-43; Wing Chaplain, Air Training Cadets, Eng., 1954-56; rec'd Am. Assn. Theological Schs. Theol. Faculty Fellowship for study in Britain 1966-67; Pres., Wolfville Inter-Ch. Council, 1972-74; (Treas. 1970-72); Atlantic Ecumenical Council, 1970-72 (Vice Pres. 1968-70); Secy. 1972-74 and 1976-78); author, "The Pastoral Epistles", 1956; "The Return from Exile" 1956; also numerous reports, articles and book reviews contrib. to various journs. and newspapers; mem. Humanities Assn. Can. (Past Pres. and Secy., Wolfville Br.); Soc. Biblical Lit.; Candn. Soc. Biblical Studies; Candn. Soc. of Patristic Studies; Candn. Theol. Soc.; Chaplain, Wolfville Br. No. 74, Royal Candn. Legion; Baptist; recreations: sight-seeing, walking, swimming, philately, reading; Home: 20 Westwood Ave., Wolfville, N.S. B0P 1X0; Office: Acadia Divinity Coll., Wolfville, N.S. B0P 1X0

LOVINK, Hon. Antonius Hermanus Johannes, D.C.L., LL.B.; b. The Hague, Holland, 12 July 1902; e. Christian High Sch., The Hague; Economic Univ., Rotterdam; LL.D. Queen's; Univ. of W. Ont. (1956); Univ. of Western Ont. (1964); Bishop's Univ. 1966; m. Clara Roeline Nagel, The Hague, 5 Sept. 1927; children: Hans, Marianne, Anton, Gijsbert; Asst. Vice Consul at Berlin, Frankfort and Paris, 1922-24; Netherlands Asst. to the Chinese Maritime Customs, 1924-28; joined Civil Service of Netherlands East Indies Govt. as an Adviser on Chinese and Japanese Affairs, 1928 and in 1934 rose to the function of Adviser on E. Asiatic Affairs to the Gov. Gen.; on invasion by Japanese in 1942 (wife and children taken captive 1942-45) reported to his Govt. in Exile in London becoming Under Secy. for Defence Coordination to the Prime Min. until Feb. 1943 when apptd. Ambassador to China at Chungking; Ambassador to U.S.S.R. at Moscow 1946-47; Under Secy. of State to the Dept. of Foreign Affairs, The Hague, 1947-49; in 1949 became the last High Rep. of the Crown in Indonesia, in which capacity he handed over sovereignty in Djacarta over Indonesia to the representative of Govt. of the United States of Indonesia on 28 Dec. 1949; Netherlands Ambassador to Canada, 1950-57, and to Australia, 1957-60 when reappt. to Can., serving in this office until retirement in 1968; Roy. Candn. Gographic Soc.; Offr., Order of Orange Nassau (Offr. 1937; Commdr. 1941; Grand Offr. 1949); Kt., Order of the Netherlands Lion (1941); Grand Cross of the Order of the Brilliant Star (China) 1948; recreations: fishing, polo, golf, canoeing, skiing, hunting; Address: 2194 Elder St., Ottawa, Ont. K2B 6N1

LOW, Douglas John, B.Com., C.A.; b. Toronto, Ont. 10 Feb. 1934; s. Douglas Andrew Graham and Florence Elizabeth (King) L.; e. Kent Pub. Sch. and Bloor Coll. Inst. Toronto 1951; Univ. of Toronto B. Comm. 1955; C.A. 1958; m. Jeanette Lynn d. Rev. Dr. William John MacDonald, Bracebridge, Ont. 10 Sept. 1960; children: Douglas Andrew Graham, Jacqueline Candace; MANAGING PARTNER, DELOITTE HASKINS & SELLS, MONTREAL since 1974 and mem. Policy Board, DH & S, Canada since 1975; joined present firm Toronto 1955, Audit Mgr. Montreal 1962, Partner and trans. to Toronto 1966, returned Montreal 1971; Past Pres. Tudor Singers of Montreal Inc.; mem. Candn. Inst. C.A.'s (Past Chrmn. Accounting Research Comte.); Ont. Inst. C.A.'s; Order C.A.'s Que.; Mem of the Bureau 1978-80; mem., Interpretations Comm. 1978- (Chrmn. 1978-80); mem. Adv. Comte to the Syndic, 1980- ; Past mem Education Committee; Past. mem. Profes. Inspection Comte.; Soc. Mang. Accts.; mem. Financial Statements/Financial Reporting task Force of the Financial Accounting Standards Board, U.S.A.; mem. Shareholders' Auditors' Adv. Comte. to the Inspector Gen. of Banks, 1980- ; Chrmn. Bd. of Trustees, First Baptist Church, Montreal, 1979- ; mem., Gen. Comte., St James's Club (Montreal) 1980-; Treas. 1981- ; Baptist; recreations: curling, tennis, bridge, philately, music; Clubs: St. James's; Royal Montreal Curling; Treasurer 1979-; Town of Mount Royal Country Club; Home: 280 Beverley Ave., Mount Royal, Que. H3P 1K9; Office: 1 Place Ville Marie, Montreal, Que. H3B 2W3

LOW, Orian Edgar Beverly, Q.C., B.A.; b. Ottawa, Ont., 17 Oct. 1911; s. Archie Edgar and Jane Eva (Slinn) L.; e. Glebe Coll. Inst., Ottawa, Ont.; Queen's Univ., B.A. 1934; Osgoode Hall, Toronto, Ont. 1937; m. Ethel, d. Thomas Addison Hand, Ottawa, Ont., 22 June 1940; children: Dr. Sandra Ann, Bonnie Lynn, Orian, Jr.; FORMER COUNSEL, LOW, MURCHISON, BURNS, THOMAS & McCAY; Vice-Pres., 161 Realty Ltd.; Dir., Hiram Walkers Resources Ltd.; Consumers Gas Co. Ltd.; C.O.B., Holo Investments Ltd.; Gen. Counsel and Secy. of Commodity Prices Stab. Corp. Ltd. (Crown Co.), 1942-46; served in N.P.A.M., 2nd Bn. Cameron Highlanders of Ottawa, 1941-46; Pres., Ottawa Jr. Bd. Trade, 1941-42; Ottawa Public Sch. Trustee, 1939-42 and 1945-52 (Chrmn. of Bd. 1942, Chrmn. of Property Comte. 1940-41, Chrmn. of Management Comte. 1949-51, Chrmn. of Finance 1946-47); former mem., Co. Carleton Bar Assn. (Past Trustee); Law Soc. Upper Can., called to the Bar of Ont., 1937; cr. K.C. 1951; Phi Delta Phi (Magister, 1936-37); Freemason (Scot. Rite; Consistory; Shrine); Anglican; recreations: photography, flying, travel, golf; Clubs: Laurentian

(Pres. 1958); Ottawa Hunt & Golf; Seigniory (Pres., Curling Club 1966-67); Kiwanis; Bird Key Yacht (Fla.); Longboat Key Golf (Fla.); Home: Apt. 2127, 200 Clearview Ave., Ottawa, Ont. K18 8M2; Office: 141 Laurier W., Ottawa, Ont. K1P 5J3

LOWDEN, James Arthur; real estate consultant b. Arden, Manitoba, 17 Feb. 1916; s. Stuart and Christina (Anderson) L.; e. Regina Central Collegiate (Sr. Matric. 1933); m. Cecilia Agnes. d. David Simpson, St. James, Man., 23 March 1940; children: James David, Donald Blake; PRES., T.I.W. INVESTMENT SERVICES LTD.; and CEJAB Holdings and Investment Ltd.; formerly vice Pres., Trizec Corp. Ltd.; Cummings Properties Limited; Pres., Canadian Interurban Properties Ltd., Montreal; Chrmn., Wilbr; & Devrin, N.Y.; joined the Mfrs. Life Ins. Co. at Regina, 1933; trans. to Winnipeg as Inspector, 1939; moved to Montreal, 1947; apptd. Br. Mgr., Mortgage Lending Dept., 1948; apptd. Pres., United Principal Properties Ltd., 1961; Past Pres., Candn. Assn. of Real Estate Bds.; Candn. Inst. of Realtors (Fellow); Past Pres., Am. Soc. of Real Estate Counselors; Soc. of Real Estate Appraisers, Montreal & Winnipeg Chapters; Past Vice-Pres., Appraisal Inst. of Can.; mem., Am. Inst. of Real Estate Appraisers (Governing Council); Nat. Assn. of Real Estate Bds.; mem. Urban Land Inst.; Conservative; Un. Church; recreations: reading, skating, sailing, skiing, swimming; Home: Apt. 1211, 10 The Driveway, Ottawa, Ont. K2P 1C7; Office: 90 Sparks St., Ottawa, Ont. K1P 5B4

LOWE, Donald C., B.A.Sc., M.Sc.; industrialist; b. Oshawa, Ont., 29 Jan. 1932; s. Samuel John and Corales Isobel (Cox) L.; e. Oshawa (Ont.) Coll. & Vocational Inst. 1950; Univ. of Toronto B.A.Sc. 1954; Univ. of Birmingham (Athlone Fellowship) M.Sc. 1957; Harvard Internat. Sr. Mgrs. Program Switzerland, grad. 1975; m. Susan Margaret Plunkett, 22 July 1955; children: Michelle, Jeffrey, Steven; CHMN. of BD., PRATT & WHITNEY AIRCRAFT (CANADA) LTD. Pres. & CEO Pratt & Whitney Aircraft (Canada) Ltd. 1975-81; joined General Motors of Canada Ltd. as Mgr. Forward Planning, Oshawa 1957, Mgr. Indust. Engn. 1962, Project Engr. Ste. Therese plant 1964, Plant Engr. St. Therese 1965 and Production Mgr. 1966, Plant Mgr. Body Assembly Oshawa 1967, Asst. Gen. Mgr. Ste. Therese 1969, Gen. Mgr. 1970, Dir. of Mfg. Vauxhall Motors Ltd. Luton, Eng. 1971-75; Dir., Allied Chem. of Can. Ltd.; Advisory Bd., Liberty Mutual Ins. Co. of Can.; Past Pres. Oshawa Jr. Chamber Comm.; Montreal Soc. Automotive Engrs.; mem. Phi Gamma Delta; Protestant; recreations: skiing, squash, tennis; Clubs: Les Ambassadeurs (London, Eng.); Mount Royal; Royal Montreal Golf; Montreal Badminton & Squash; Home: 5 Anwoth Rd., Westmount, Que. H3Y 2E5; Office: 1000 Marie Victorin Blvd., Longueuil, Que.

LOWER, Arthur Reginald Marsden, C.C. (1968), A.M., Ph.D., LL.D., D.Litt., D.C.L., F.R.S.C.; historian; b. Barrie, Ont., 12 Aug. 1889; s. Fredk. James and Sarah Anne L.; e. Univ. of Toronto, B.A. 1914, M.A. 1923; Harvard Univ., A.M. 1926, Ph.D. 1929; m. Evelyn Marion, d. George Smith, Folkestone, Eng., 1920; has one d. Louise; country sch. teacher for a short time; offr. to explore w. coast of James Bay in relation to its fisheries, 1914; Instructor in Lang. and Hist., Faculty of Educ., Univ. of Toronto 1914-16; Asst. to Chrmn., Bd. of Hist. Publs. Pub. Archives of Can., where engaged with editing, trans. and research in Candn. hist. 1919-25; Instr. in Hist., Tufts Coll., Mass., 1926-27; Instr. and Tutor in Hist., Harvard Univ., 1927-29; Prof. of Hist. and Head of Dept., United Coll., Univ. of Man., 1929-47; Douglas Prof. of Candn. History, Queen's Univ., Kingston, Ont., 1947-59; mem., Candn. Hist. Assn. (Pres. 1943); mem., Civil Liberties Assn., Winnipeg, Man. (Pres. 1940-47); Candn. Inst. of Internat. Affairs; President, Royal Society of Canada 1961-62; winner of Tyrrell Medal (Roy. Soc. of Can.) 1947; Gov. Gen's. Medal (Candn. Authors' Assn.) 1947 and

1955; I.O.D.E. Award 1947; Sr. Fellow, Canada Council 1959; Visiting Prof., Dalhousie, Wisconsin, Duke Univs.; Sir John A. Macdonald Visiting Prof., Univ. of Glasgow 1967; has travelled extensively; served in 1st World War 1916-19 with R.N.V.R.; service with Dover Patrol and in the North Sea; present at blockade of Ostende; Publications: "Documents Illustrative of Canadian Economic History", (with H. A. Innes) 1933; "Settlement and the Forest Frontier of Eastern Canada", 1936; "The North American Assault upon the Canadian Forest", 1938; "Canada and the Far East", 1940; "War and Reconstruction: Some Canadian Issues" (with J. F. Parkinson) 1942; "Colony to Nation: A History of Canada", 1946; "Canada, A Nation and How It Came To Be" (with J. W. Chafe) 1947; "Canada, Nation and Neighbour", 1952; "Unconventional Voyages", 1953; "This Most Famous Stream", 1954; "Canadians in the Making", 1958; "Evolving Canadian Federalism", 1958 (with others); "My First Seventy-Five Years", 1967; "Great Britain's Woodyard" 1973; "History and Myth" 1975; "A Pattern for History", 1978; Un. Church; recreations: sailing, canoeing, dogs; Home: "The Shipyard" Apartments, 33 Ontario St., Kingston, Ont.

LOWERY, Richard; consultant naval architect; b. Newcastle-on-Tyne, Eng., 26 Jan. 1910; s. James Beck and Mary (Ahern) L.; e. Heaton Tech. Sch., Rutherford Tech. Coll. and Armstrong Coll., Durham Univ.; Newcastle-on-Tyne; m. Dorothy, d. Thomas Heron, Eng., 22 Dec. 1936; children: Jane Margaret, Peter Richard; apprenticed to R. & W. Hawthorn Leslie & Co., Hebburn-on-Tyne, 1927-31; apptd. Asst. Naval Arch., 1931-36; Lectr. in Naval Arch. and Higher Math., Rutherford Tech. Coll., 1935-36; Asst. Naval Arch., Alfred Holt & Co., Liverpool, Eng., 1936-38; Naval Arch. and Asst. Gen. Mgr., Singapore Harbour Bd. Dockyards, 1938-42; Naval Arch. and Mgr., Melbourne Harbor Trust Shipyards and Advisor, Australian Commonwealth Salvage Bd., 1942-46; Naval Arch., Canadian Vickers Ltd., Montreal, becoming Vice-Pres., 1946-51; joined Canada Steamship Lines, 1951; as Vice Pres. & Pres. of Davie Shipbuilding Ltd., Kingston Shipyard, Candn. Shipbuilding Ltd., and Port Arthur Shipbuilding Ltd.; retired Jan. 1972; rec'd. "Jerry" Land Gold Medal for outstanding achievement in the Marine Field, Soc. Naval Archs. & Marine Engrs., 1964; Past Chrmn., Lloyd's Register of Shipping Candn. Comte.; Hon. Vice Pres. and Fellow, Soc. Naval Archs. and Marine Engrs. (1st Chrmn., E. Candn. Sec.); Past Pres., Canadian Shipbuilding and Ship Repairing Assn.; Fellow, Royal Inst. Naval Archs.; Anglican; recreations: golf, painting, reading; Homes: Apt 902 Ashby House, 114 Keith Rd. W., North Vancouver, B.C. V7M 3C9 and 2731 N.E. 8th Court, Pompano Beach, Fla. 33062

LOWY, Frederick Hans, B.A., M.D., C.M., FRCPS (c) FACP, FAC Psy.; psychiatrist; educator; b. Grosspetersdorf, Austria, 1 Jan. 1933; s. Eugen and Maria (Braun) L.; e. McGill Univ., B.A. 1955, M.D., C.M. 1959; m. firstly Anne Louise (d. 1973), d. late Alexander G. Cloudsley, 25 June 1965; three s., David A., Eric B., Adam H.; m. 2ndly Mary Kay, d. late Michael O.Neil 1 June 1975; 1 d., Sarah E.; DEAN, FAC. OF MEDICINE, UNIV. OF TORONTO July 1980- ; Dir., Psychiatrist-in-Chief, Clarke Inst. of Psychiatry 1974-80; prof. training Montreal and Cincinnati 1959-70; Demonst. Dept. Psychiatry McGill Univ. 1965, Lectr. 1966, Asst. Prof. 1968; Assoc. Prof. Univ. of Ottawa 1971, Prof. 1973; Clin. Asst. in Psychiatry, Royal Victoria Hosp., Allan Mem. Inst., Montreal, 1965; Asst. 1967 and Assoc. Psychiatrist, Royal Victoria Hosp. 1969; Psychiatrist-in-Chief, Ottawa Civic Hosp., 1971; Consultant, Ottawa Gen. Hosp., 1971; Ont. Cancer Inst. 1973; mem. Adv. Bd. Ont. Mental Health Foundation, 1972-78; author and co-author numerous articles in learned and prof. journs.; Ed. Canadian Psychiatric Association Journal, 1973-77 (Assoc. Ed. 1971-72); Ed. Emeritus, Cdn. Journal of Psychiatry; Fellow, Internat. Coll. Psychosomatic Med.; mem. Canadian Med. Assn.; Candn. Psychiatric Assn.; Ont. Psychiatric Assn.; Internat. Psychoanalytic Soc.; Am. Psychiatric Assn.; Am. Psychosomatic Soc.; Am. Assn. Advanc. Science; Candn. Psychosomatic Soc.; Alpha Omega Alpha; Home: 338 Inglewood Dr., Toronto, Ont. M4T 1J6

LUCAS, Alec, M.A., Ph.D.; university professor; b. Toronto, Ont., 20 June 1913; s. Bertie George and Emma (Crick) L.; e. Peterborough (Ont.) Normal Sch., 1935-36; Queen's Univ., B.A. (Hons. Eng. and Hist.) 1943, M.A. 1945; Harvard Univ., A.M. 1947, Ph.D. 1951; married; children: George Frederick, Suzanne Arbon, Roy Martin Ells; PROF., DEPT. OF ENGLISH, McGILL UNIV., since 1964; Teaching Fellow, Harvard Univ., 1947-50; Assoc. Prof., Univ. of New Brunswick, 1950-57; Asst. Prof. of Eng., McGill Univ., 1957-58; Assoc. Prof. 1958-64; Publications: Assoc. Editor, "Atlantic Anthology", 1961; Editor, Humanities Bulletin, 1958-62; Ed., "The Last Barrier and Other Stories by Charles G. D. Roberts", 1958; "the James Halliday Letters", 1966; Ed., "The Best of Peter McArthur", 1967; "Hugh MacLennan", 1970; "Great Canadian Short Stories", 1971; "Peter McArthur", 1975; "Farley Mowat", 1976; "The Otonabee School", 1977; many articles in popular and learned journs.; mem., Assn. Candn. Univ. Teachers of English; Home: 853 Sherbrooke St., West, Montreal, Que. H3A 2T6

LUCAS, Colin Cameron, M.A.Sc., Ph.D., D.Sc., F.R.S.C. (1959), F.C.I.C. (1947); professor emeritus; b. 15 Dec. 1903; Winnipeg, Man.; s. George Henry and Christina (Laing) L.; e. Univ. of Brit. Columbia, M.A.Sc. 1926; Univ. of Toronto, Ph.D. 1936; D.Sc. Acadia 1964; m. Mary McPhedran Elliot, 1942; one s.; former Prof., Banting and Best Dept. of Med. Research, Univ. of Toronto; Prof. emeritus (1969); Home: 19 Hillside Ave., Wolfville, N.S. B0P 1X0

LUCAS, Douglas M., M.Sc., forensic scientist; b. Windsor, Ont., 5 May 1929; s. Melvin and Gertrude (Fulcher) L.; e. Victoria Pub. Sch., 1942 and Kennedy Coll. Inst., 1948, Windsor, Ont.; Univ. of Toronto, B.Sc. 1953, M.Sc. 1957; m. Marie Michener, d. Marion M. Macdonald, Azusa, California, U.S.A.; children: Eric, Brian, Kristen, Kelley, Paul; DIR., CENTRE OF FORENSIC SCIENCES, PROV. OF ONT., since 1967; Chemist, Atty.-Gen.'s Lab., Ont. 1957; Sec. Head, 1960; author of no. of publs. in field of forensic science; rec'd Centennial Medal; Silver Jubilee Medal; Past Pres., Internat. Assn. Forensic Sciences; Past Pres., Candn. Soc. Forensic Sciences; Past Pres., Am. Acad. Forensic Sciences; Past Pres., Am. Soc. Crime Lab. Dirs.; Past Chrmn., Extve. Bd. Comte. on Alcohol & Drugs, Nat. Safety Council, U.S.A.; Psi Upilon; Protestant; recreations: golf, curling; Home: 36 Catherwood Court, Agincourt, Ont. M1W 1S1; Office: 25 Grosvenor St., Toronto, Ont. M7A 2G8

LUCKERT; Hans Joachim, Dr. Phil.; scientist; b. Germany, 26 Aug. 1905; s. Dr. Albert and Elisabeth (Wuenn) L.; e. Harvard Univ., A.M. 1929; Univ. of Berlin, Dr. Phil 1933; m. Ilse, d. late Robert Schwabedissen, Germany, 30 May 1953; one d. Doris Elizabeth: CONSULTANT TO POTTON TECHNICAL INDUSTRIES INC. 1980- ; Tutor, Tech. Univ. of Berlin, 1925-27; Asst. to Prof. of Math., Bergakademie of Freiberg, Germany, and Research Scientist, Consultant to Finance Min. of Saxony, 1929-34; Aerodynamics Research, Henschel Aircraft Co., Germany, 1935-37; Sr. Group Leader, Aerodynamics Dept., Arado Aircraft Co., Germany, 1937-45; Scientist, Br. Min. of Supply, Brunswick-Voelkenrode, 1945-47; Consultant, Control Comn. for Germany, 1947-51; joined Canadair Ltd., Montreal, 1952; Sec. Chief, Tech. Sec., 1957-63; Missiles and Space Research Sec., 1963-64; Staff Scientist, Research and Devel. 1964-65; Chief, Aerodynamics and Analysis Sec., Space Research Inst., McGill Univ., 1965; transf. to Space Research Inst. Inc. 1968; Space Research Corp., 1969-80; Fellow, Candn. Aero. and Space Inst.

(Nat. Vice Chrmn., Astronautics Sec. 1959-60; Nat. Chrmn. 1962-63; Chrmn., Montreal Group of Sec. 1959-64; Chrmn., Montreal Br. 1965-66); Assoc. Fellow, Am. Inst. Aero. & Astronautics; Chrmn., N.R.C. Research Co-ord. Group on Upper Atmosphere Research Vehicles, 1964-65; mem., Deutsche Gesellschaft fuer Luft-und Raumfahrt, Germany; N.R.C. Assoc. Comte. on Aerodynamics (1963-66) and on Space Research (1964-67); Hon. Research Assoc., McGill Univ., since 1967; has publ. numerous papers and reports on various math. and aerodynamics subjects; Protestant; Home: 197-58th Ave., Laval des Rapides, Que. H7V 2A5

LUCKYJ, George S. N., M.A., Ph.D.; university professor; b. Janchyn, Ukraine, 11 June 1919; s. Ostap and Irene Smal (Stocki) L.; e. Ukraine, 1929-37; Univ. of Berlin, 1937-39; Univ. of Birmingham, 1939-43, B.A., M.A.; Columbia Univ., Ph.D. 1952; m. Moira, d. J. J. McShane, J. P., 18 Feb. 1944; children: Natalie, Anna, Christina; ASSOC. DIR., CANDN. INST. OF UKRAINIAN STUDIES, UNIV. OF TORONTO, since 1976; Chrmn. of the Dept., 1954-61; Lectr., Univ. of Sask., 1947-49; Prof. of Slavic Studies, Univ. of Toronto, 1959 to present; served with Brit. Army of the Rhine, 1943-47; Publications: "Literary Politics in the Soviet Ukraine: 1917-34", 1956; "Between Gogol and Shevchenko", 1971; ed., "Sheuchenko and the Critics" 1980; co-author, "Modern Ukrainian Grammar", 1949; mem., Candn. Assn. of Slavists; Ukrainian Acad. of Sciences in U.S.; Greek Catholic; recreation: skiing; Home: 5 Kendal Ave., Toronto, Ont. M5R 1L5

LUDWIG, Jack, Ph.D.; author; b. Winnipeg, Man., 30 Aug. 1922; s. Misha and Fanny (Dolgin) L.; e. St. John's High Sch., Winnipeg, 1940; Univ. of Man., B.A. 1944; Univ. of Cal. Los Angeles, Ph.D. 1953; m. Leya Geraldine, d. Louis Lauer, Edmonton, Alta., 3 March 1946; children: Susan, Brina; Writer-in-Residence, Univ. Toronto, 1968-69; Assoc. of Stratford Shakespearean Festival, 1969-70; Jr. Stratford Co. Consultant, National Arts Centre 1970; CBC film on Joyceville minimum security facility 1970; Professor of Eng., Stony Brook Univ., N.Y., since 1961 ; Instr. and Lectr., Williams Coll., 1949-53; Asst. and Assoc. Prof., Bard Coll., 1953-58; Visiting Lectr., Univ. of Minn., 1958-61; Chrmn., Humanities Group, Harvard Univ. Internat. Seminar, 1963-66; Consultant, Comn. of Coll. Physics, 1965-66 and to mem. of Comn. on Automation, Tech. Econ. Progress; Visiting Prof. Contemp. Lit., Univ. of Cal., Los Angeles 1976; acting version "The Alchemist", Stratford Shakespearean Festival, 1969; author: "Confusions" (fiction), 1963; "Above Ground" (fiction), 1968; "A Woman of Her Age" (fiction) 1973; "Recent American Novelists" (criticism) 1962 ; "Hockey Night in Moscow" (non-fiction), 1972; "The Great Hockey Thaw" (non-fiction) 1974; "Games of Fear and Winning" (essays) 1976; "The Great American Spectaculars" (non-fiction) 1976; "Five Ring Circus" (non-fiction) 1970; "Soundings" (new Candn. poetry) 1970; co-ed., "Stories: British and American", 1953; "The Noble Savage", 1960-62; "Homage to Zolotova" (poetry) 1974; film script, "Hedda Gabler", CBC TV-Drama, 1978; and other writings incl. numerous short stories, part novels, essays and reviews in various Canadian and foreign publs. and anthologies; Principal Writer Banff Centre for Performing Arts 1974; received "Atlantic First" fiction award, 1960; Longview Foundation (fiction) Award 1960; Best Am. Short Stories, 1961,65; O. Henry Prize Stories award, 1961, 1965; Can. Council Sr. Fiction Award, 1967-68,1975-76; nominee Gov. Gen.'s Award in Lit. 1968; recreations: singing, swimming. Offices: P.O. Box "A", Setauket, N.Y., 11733; and in Can., c/o McClelland & Stewart, Toronto, Ont. M4B 3G2.

LUMBERS, Leonard George; industrialist; b. Toronto, Ont., 5 Feb. 1909; s. Leonard Oliver and Helen (Baker) L.; e. Rosedale Pub. Sch., Toronto, Ont.; St. Andrew's Coll., Toronto and Aurora, Ont.; m. Frances Gardiner

McNeillie; 26 June 1937; one s. and two d.; CHRMN. AND DIR., NORANDA MANUFACTURING LTD., and Noranda Aluminum Inc.; since 1970; Dir./Mines Ltd.; Noranda Metal Industries Ltd.; Norandex Inc.; Wire Rope Industries of Canada Ltd.; Leaworth Holdings Ltd.; Noranda Sales Corp. Ltd.; Budd Canada Inc.; Bundy of Canada Inc., Bundy Corp.; Royal Bank of Canada; Abitibi Paper Co. Ltd.; City National Leasing Co.; Vice-Chrmn. Bd. Governors, Ont. Research Foundation; Gov., York Univ.; St. Andrew's Coll.; Candn. Assn. for Latin Am.; mem. Adv. Comte., Tech Service Council; began career with Lake St. John Power & Paper Co. Ltd.; joined Can. Wire & Cable Co. Ltd., in Gen. Sales Dept., and Ont. Sales Dept., 1929; apptd. Toronto Dist. Mgr., 1945; Gen. Sales Mgr., 1948; Vice-Pres., 1951; el. a Dir. 1956; apptd. Vice-Pres. & Gen. Mgr., 1957; Pres. and Chief Extve. Offr., 1961; Chrmn. and Chief Extve. Offr., 1966; Pres. and Dir., present Co. 1967; Protestant; recreation: golf; Clubs: York; Rosedale Golf; Toronto: Country Club of Florida; Home: 37 Old Forest Hill Road, Toronto, Ont. M5P 2P8; Office: (P.O. Box 45) Commerce Court W., Toronto, Ont. M5L 1B6

LUMLEY, Hon. Edward C., M.P., P.C., B.Com.; politician; b. Windsor, Ont. 27 Oct. 1939; s. Chester and Norma (Roos) L.; e. Walkerville (Ont.) Coll. Inst.; Assumption Univ. Windsor; m. Patricia Arlene d. Robert Thomson, Windsor, Ont. 27 Jan. 1962; children: Robert Edward, Kelly Lynn, Dawn Marie, Cheryl Louise Christopher James; MIN. OF STATE FOR TRADE, CAN. 1980- ; Former businessman; Mayor, City of Cornwall 1972-74; Chrmn., Cornwall Bd. of Police Commrs. 1973-74; el. to H. of C. for Stormont-Dundas g.e. 1974, re-el. since; Chrmn., Standing Comte. on Reg. Devel. 1975; Parlty. Secy. to Min. of Regional Econ. Expansion 1976 and to Min. of Finance 1977; Liberal; United Church; Home: 302 Baldwin Ave., Cornwall, Ont. Office: House of Commons, Ottawa, Ont. K1A 0A6.

LUMSDEN, Hugh Everett, B.C.E., P.Eng.; company chairman; b. Hamilton, Ont., 18 April 1910; s. Charles and Gwylda (Peppiatt) L.; e. Pub. and High Schs., Hamilton, Ont.; Marquette Univ., B.C.E.; m. Gertrude, d. Joseph Wolf, 11 Nov. 1936; children: Neil J. Martha C. (Mrs. Ralph G. Douglas); CHRMN., LUMSDEN FINANCIAL ENTERPRISES LTD.; Dir., Gerling Global Life Insurance Co.; Gerling Global General Insurance Co.; Gerling Global Insurance Co.; Gerling Global Reinsurance Co.; Hurontario Investment Corp. Ltd.; after grad. entered life ins. business in Milwaukee, Wis. as Agent, assuming a succession of additional extve. responsibilities; joined Global Life Insurance Co., Toronto, Ont., as Vice-President in 1958; apptd. a Dir., 1958; Vice-Pres. and Mang. Dir., 1962, Pres. 1963; mem., Assn. Prof. Engrs. Ont.; Bd. of Trade Metrop. Toronto; Candn. Chamber Comm.; Social Planning Council of Metrop. Toronto; Anglican Church; Clubs: University; The London (Ont.); Scottish Rite; R.C.Y.C.; Toronto Golf; Home: 27 Blythdale Road, Toronto, Ont. M4N 3M3

LUNDRIGAN, Arthur Raymond; manufacturer; b. Blaketown, Trinity Bay, Nfld., 13 July 1922; s. William James and Naomi L.; e. Grade School, Corner Brook, Nfld.; m. Ida Amanda, d. late Olaf Gustaf Johnson, 17 Oct. 1946; four d., Ingrid, Astrid, Sigrid, Gudrid; PRESIDENT LUNDRIGANS LTD. (estbd. 1947); Chmn and Dir. Atlantic Gypsum Ltd; North Star Cement Ltd; Newfoundland Forest Products Ltd; Lundrigans Comstock Ltd.; Pres. and Dir., Lundrigan Holdings Ltd; Lundrigans Internat. Ltd.; Lundrigans Inc.; Atlantic Concrete Ltd; City Motors (Labrador) Ltd; City Motors (Nfld.) Ltd.; J.W. Randall Ltd; Newfoundland Mack Ltd; Halibuilding Ltd; E.H. Gullage Ltd; Vice-Pres. and Dir., Island Realty Ltd.; Dir., Newfoundland Telephone Co. Ltd.; Canadian Ultramar Ltd.; Comstock Internat. Ltd.; Sobeys Stores Ltd; Maritime Life Assurance Co.; Newfoundland Fibrply Ltd.; Chmn. of Adv. Bd., Corner Brook Br.; Central Trust

Co.; Home: 36 West Valley Rd., Corner Brook, Nfld. A2H 2X3; Office: P.O. Box 2002, Riverside Dr., Corner Brook, Nfld. A2H 6J5

LUNN, Alice Jean Elizabeth, M.A., Ph.D., B.L.S.; librarian; b. Montreal, Que.; d. Frederick William and Jean (Laughton) Lunn; e. McGill Univ., B.A. 1932, M.A. 1934, Ph.D. (History) 1942; McGill Univ. Library Sch., B.L.S. 1940; Royal Soc. of Can. Travelling Fellowship for Research in France, 1936-37; unm.; Cataloguer, McGill Univ., 1940-46; Librarian-in-Chief, Fraser Inst. Lib., Montreal, 1946-50; Dir. Cataloguing Br., Nat. Library of Can. and of nat. bibliog. "Canadiana" 1950-1973; Dir. Office of Lib. Standards Nat. Lib. of Can. 1973-75; Chrmn. Candn. Advisory Comte. on ISO/TC 46 1973-75, Canadian Committee on Cataloguing 1974-75; mem., Standards Council of Can., 1975-81, and of its Adv. Comte. on Standards Inform. Service, 1976-81; Canadian del. to Internat. Conf. on the improvement of Bibliographical Services, Paris, 1950 and to other internat. confs. on standards and bibliog.; reported for Can. to UNESCO annual publ. "Bibliographical Services Throughout The World"; dissertation, pub. on microfilm, "Economic Development in New France, 1713-1760"; has written articles on hist. and lib. journs.; in "Encyclopedia Canadiana", and in "Dictionary of Canadian Biography" also papers for various prof. confs.; mem., Candn. Lib. Assn.; Bibliog. Soc. of Can.; Anglican; Home: RR 3, Carp, Ont. K0A 1L0

LUSH, Sheldon H.; executive; b. Toronto, Ont., 9 March 1918; s. Harold V. and Ethel A. (Hatton) L.; m. Betty I. Allman, 27 Sept. 1941; children: Donald L., Joanne E., Gwendolyn, Mary L., David S.; CHRMN. AND CHIEF EXTVE. OFFR., SUPREME ALUMINUM INDUSTRIES LTD.; Chrmn., Supreme Industries Ltd. Barbados; Canadian China and Glass Ltd.; Spun Metals Ltd.; Dir., Profit Sharing Inst. Can.; Shepherd Products Ltd.; mem. Bd. Trade Metrop. Toronto; Protestant; recreations: golf, skiing; fishing; Clubs: Rotary; Scarborough Golf & Country; Home: 39 Hillcrest, Scarborough, Ont. M1M 1J3; Office: 3600 Danforth Ave., Scarborough, Ont. M1N 2E6

LUSSIER, Charles A.; avocat, haut fonctionnaire; né Montréal, Qué., 18 août, 1920; f. Joseph Irénée et Marie-Louise (Patenaude) L.; é. Coll. St.-Jean de Brébeuf; Univ. de Montréal; Univ. McGill; ép. Monique, f. Léon Lortie, 14 sept. 1953; 2 fils, 2 filles; DIR., CONSEIL DES ARTS DU CANADA 1976- ; reçu avocat (Montréal) 1945; avec spécialité en droit du travail, 1947-57; Dir. de la Maison des Etudiants canadiens à la Cité Univ. de Paris, 1957; Délégué général de la Prov. de Qué. en France, 1961; Sous-ministre adjoint (Citoyenneté) 1965; Détaché auprès du Ministère de l'Energie, des Mines et des Resources comme conseiller spécial au cours des négociations avec la France et les Etats-Unis sur le plateau continental, 1967; Sous-secrétaire d'Etat adjoint (Secrétariat d'Etat), 1968; Commissaire, Comm. de la Fonction publique du Canada, 1970-76; ancien Prés., Théâtre du Nouveau Monde, Montréal; Dir., Inst. canadien des Affaires Publiques; Conférencier invité à la Faculté de droit de l'Université de Paris et à l'Institut d'Etudes politiques de Paris sur le sujet du fédéralisme au Canada, 1957-64; Professeur à temps partiel à l'Université d'Ottawa Cours de maîtrise en droit civil: "La nature juridique de la convention collective dans la fonction publique", 1974-75 et 75-76; chef ou membre de délégations canadiennes de, 27ième Conférence internationale sur les Droits de l'homme à Genève, 1965; Mission minitérielle en Amérique latine (représentant le Secrétaire d'Etat), 1968; Mission canadienne à Niamey pour assister à la conférence sur la coopération multilatérale des pays de langue française, 1969; Conférence de l'Agence de coopération culturelle et technique à Lomé (Togo) sur "L'Analyse comparative des structures de la Fonction publique des Etats-Membres de l'ACCT", 1971; La Fédération du français universel à Liège (Belgique) en 1969, à Menton (France) en 1971, à Dakar (Sénégal) en 1973 et au Luxembourg en 1975; Membre de l'Institut d'administration publique du Canada; Directeur, Conseil canadien des Chrétiens et des Juifs; Membre de l'Institut scientifique franco-canadien (destiné à l'échange de professeurs subventionnés par le gouvernement); Directeur de l'Institut France-Canada; Membre et ancien vice-président, Alliance Française d'Ottawa; Directeur (à la fondation) du Centre de recherches en Relations humaines de l'Université de Montréal; Catholique; sports: tennis, natation; golf; Clubs: Larrimac Golf; Rockcliffe Lawn Tennis; Cercle Universitaire; résidence: 211 River Rd., Ottawa, Ont.;

LUSSIER, Gaétan, B.S.A., M.Sc., D.Sc.; Canadian public service; b. Marieville (Rouville), Qué., 24 May 1941; e. Acad. Crevier, Marieville, Qué.; Mont St-Louis, Montréal; Univ. Oka B.S.A. 1962 (Lt. Gov.'s Gold Medal); Macdonald Coll. M.Sc. 1964; S.Sc. (Hon.) McDonald Coll. McGill U., 1979; Univ. Laval Adult Educ. courses 1965; m. Nicole Fréchette 16 June 1962; children: François, Daniel, Geneviève; DEPY. MIN. OF AGRICULTURE CAN. 1977-; Teacher, Inst. de Technol. Agricole, St-Hyacinthe, Qué. 1964-66, Head of Extension and Research 1965; Tech. Adv. and Dir. of Promotions E. Can., Am. Potash Inst. 1966-68; Agric. Co-ordinator for Richelieu Region 1968-70; Asst. Depy. Min. of Qué. Ministry of Agric. 1970-71, Depy. Min. 1971-77; mem. Ont. Inst. Agrols.; Agric. Inst. Can.; Corp. des agronomes du Qué.; R. Catholic; recreations: reading, camping, skiing; Office: Sir John Carling Bldg., Ottawa, Ont.

LUUS, Rein, B.A.Sc., M.A.Sc., A.M., Ph.D.; university professor; b. Tartu, Estonia 8 March 1939; came to Can. 1949; s. late Edgar and Aili (Prakson) L.; e. Sault Ste. Marie Coll. Inst. 1952-57; Univ. of Toronto B.A.Sc. 1961, M.A.Sc. 1962; Princeton Univ. A.M. 1963, Ph.D. 1964; post-doctoral 1964-65; m. Hilkka d. late Fredi Jaakola 17 June 1973; children: Brian Markus; PROF. OF CHEMICAL ENGN., UNIV. OF TORONTO since 1974; Dir. Chem. Engn. Research Consultants Ltd.; came to the Univ. of Toronto as Asst. Prof. 1965-68; Assoc. Prof. 1968-74; consultant activities incl. Shell Can. 1966-70, 1979; Imperial Oil, 1974-77; Milltronics, 1967-71; Extve. Can. Society for Chem. Engn., Toronto, 1966-72 (Chrmn. 1969-70); co-author of "Optimal Control of Engineering Processes", 1967; articles in over fifty scientific publications; rec'd. E.W.R. Steaae Prize, 1976; ERCO Award, 1980; mem., Assn. of Prof. Engn. Ont.; Chem. Inst. of Can.; Candn. Society for Chem Engn.; Sigma Xi; Lutheran; Clubs: of Toronto Faculty; recreations; skiing, squash, swimming, teenis; Home: 3 Terrington Court, Don Mills, Ont. M3B 2J9;Office: Toronto, Ontario M5S 1A4.

LUZ, Virginia Erskine, R.C.A., O.S.A., C.S.P.W.C.; artist; b. Toronto, Ont. 15 Oct. 1911; d. G. John and Jessie (Minkler) L; e. Bloor Coll. Inst. Toronto Grad 1929; Central Tech. Sch. Toronto Special Art Course grad. dipl. 1932; McLane Art Inst. N.Y. City 1938; Ont. Training Coll. for Tech. Teachers Hamilton, Ont. grad. 1939; Ont. Coll. of Educ. Specialist Dipl. 1956; free-lance artist Toronto Studios 1932-38; Instr. of Illustration Art Dept. Central Tech. Sch. Toronto 1940-74, Asst. Dir. Art Dept. 1965-69, Dir. 1969-74; Exhns.: Royal Candn. Acad. 1952-57; Ont. Soc. Artists 1945-75; Candn. Soc. Painters in Water Colour 1947-75; Expo 1967; Candn. Group of Painters 1945-52; Candn. Women Artists Show New York 1947, Candn. Tour 1948-49; Montreal Museum of Fine Arts 1948-53; Candn. Nat. Exhn. Shows; one-man shows 1948, 1976, 1981; Two man shows 51, 53, Sisler Gallery Toronto "Tribute to 10 Women" 1975; "Artists' Choice" Etobicoke Civic Centre 1981; rep. various pub. and private colls. incl. Dept. External Affairs Ottawa, J.S. McLean Coll., London Art Gallery (Ont.), Robert McLaughlin Gallery Oshawa; mem. Roy. Con. Acad. of Arts; Ont. Soc. Artists (Extve. Council 1963-65); Candn. Soc. Painters in Water Colour; Fed. Candn. Artists

(Secy.-Treas. Ont. Region 1943-46); Address: 113 Delaware Ave., Toronto, Ont. M6H 2S9.

LYE, Brig.-Gen. William Kirby, M.B.E., C.D., B.Sc., P.Eng.; retired army officer; b. Ottawa, Ont., 14 July 1918; s. Ossian Gardiner and Florence Hilda (Kirby) L.; e. Guelph (Ont.) Coll. & Vocational Inst., 1936; Royal Mil. Coll., grad. dipl. 1939; N.S. Tech. Coll. 1939-40; Queen's Univ., B.Sc. (Civil Engn.) 1947; U.S. Marine Corps Schs., Quantico, Va., 1949-50; m. Beverly Julia, d. late Joseph Henry Winteringham Bower, 3 Nov. 1943; children: Maj. Joseph William Kirby, Beverley Joan Blackwell, R.N.; commissioned in RCE 1939; served in Can., N.W. Europe and U.K. 1939-45; Depy. Dir. of Engr. Devel. and Asst. Dir. of Works, HQ Ottawa, 1951; apptd. to Directing Staff. Candn. Army Staff Coll., 1954; Depy. Commdr., Candn. Base Units, Middle E., 1957; Asst. Adj. Gen., Directorate of Manning, 1958; Commandant, Royal Candn. Sch. of Mil. Eng., Vedder Crossing, B.C., 1961; Commdr., Candn. Base Units Europe, 1964; Commdr., N.S. and P.E.I. area, 1965; Chief of Staff Adm., Mobile Command HQ Montreal, 1966; Dir. Gen. Land Forces, CFHQ Ottawa 1967; Dir. Gen. Ordnance Systems, CFHQ, 1968; Dir. Gen. Operations (Land), CFHQ, 1970; Commandant Royal Mil. Coll. of Can. 1970-73; Dir. Physical Plant Dept., Univ. of Toronto 1974-81; Mentioned in Despatches; mem. Prof. Engrs. Prov. Ont.; Anglican; Club.: Royal Can. Military Int.; Home: 2327 Bennington Gate, Oakville Ont. L6J 5N7

LYLE, John Kennett Christopher, B.A., FRI.; real estate executive; b. Calgary, Alta., 4 March 1940; s. Kennett Irvin and Kathleen C. (Fewkes) L.; e. Pub. and High Schs., Calgary, Mt. Royal Jr. Coll., Univ. Western Ont., B.A. (Hons. Bus. Adm.) 1963; Univ. Alta., diploma, Advanced Real Estate Mang. 1969; m. Marilyn, d. Lawrence Hodgins, 21 May 1966; one s. Mark Lawrence Kennett; three d. Catharine Elizabeth, Mary Jane, Karen Penny; PRES., LYLE REAL ESTATE LTD. since 1976; DIR., ROKENHAN HOLDINGS LTD.; pres., Calmount Investment Mang. Ltd.; joined family business, Lyle Bros. Ltd., Real Estate Brokers, Calgary, in 1963 (Co. joined The Royal Trust Co. 1966); Residential Sales Mgr., Royal Trust Co. 1966; ALTA. Area MGR., Real Estate, The Royal Trust Co. 1974-76; mem., Real Estate Inst. of Can. (Chrmn. Calgary Chapter 1972, National Chrmn., FRI Div., 1974-75;) Pres., Real Estate Inst. of Alta. 1979; Canadian Real Estate Association; Calgary Real Estate Bd., (Dir. 1971-72 & 79-80). Alta. Real Estate Assn.; Pres., Calgary Jr. Football Assoc. 1979 and 1980; Assoc. Dir., Calgary Stampeder Football Club; Conservative; Anglican; recreations: skiing, water sports, hockey, photography; Clubs: Glencoe; Home: 3408 8A St. S.W., Calgary, Alta. T2T 3B2; Office: 8413 Elbow Dr. S.W., Calgary, Alta. T2V 1K8

LYNCH, Charles B., LL.D., O.C., journalist, radio and television commentator; b. Cambridge, Mass., 3 Dec. 1919; s. late Charles Victor and late Helen May (Burchill) L.; came to Canada 17 Dec. 1919; e. Saint John (N.B.) High Sch. 1932-35; Saint John Vocational Sch. 1935-36; m. Mary-Elizabeth, d. late Andrew D. Merkel, 16 Jan. 1941; children: Andrew B., C. Blake, Susan K., Daniel S., Lucinda E.; CHIEF, SOUTHAM NEWS, since 1960; began as Reporter, Saint John Citizen, 1936; Saint John Telegraph-Journal 1939; Candn. Press, Halifax, N.S. 1939; Bureau Chief, British United Press, Vancouver, B.C. 1940; trans. to Toronto 1941; Central Div. Mgr., Br. United Press, Toronto, 1942; joined Reuters and served in 2nd World War as War Corr.; Normandy, D-Day, 1944 to end of war; Chief of Team covering Nuremberg War Crimes Trial, 1945-46; Chief Corr. in S. Am. (Rio de Janeiro) 1946; in Canada 1947; Editor, Reuters N. Am. Service (N.Y.C.) 1950; Corr. at U.N. for CBC, 1956-57; Chief of Ottawa Bureau, present company, 1958; won Bowater Award for Journalism, 1961 for series of dispatches from Latin Am.; mem., Overseas Press Club, (N.Y.C.); Maganassippi Fish & Game; National Press Club (Ottawa); Past Pres., Candn. War Corr. Assn.; Past Pres., Parlty. Press Gallery (Ottawa); mem., Inst. of Internat. Affairs; won Nat. Newspaper Award for Staff Corr., 1965; Officer, Order of Canada, 1977; named to National Newspaper Hall of Fame, 1981; author of "China: One Fourth of the World"; Anglican; recreations: skiing, fishing, music; Clubs: Rideau; National Press; Overseas Press (New York); Home: 690 Island Park Drive, Ottawa, Ont. K1Y 0B7; Office: 151 Sparks St., Ottawa, Ont. K1P 5E3

LYNCH-STAUNTON, Hon. Frank C., B.A.Sc., LL.D.; b. Pincher Creek, Alta. 8 March 1905; e. North Fork Country Sch.; Western Can. Coll. Calgary 1922; Univ. of Alta. B.A.Sc. 1927, LL.D. 1980; m. Monica Adam (d. 1976) 21 Sept. 1929; children: Betty Lowe, Marina Field, Hugh; LT. GOV. OF ALTA. 1979- ; joined Imperial Oil for 2 yrs. before entering ranching partnership with father in 1929; sworn in as Lt. Gov. of Alta. 18 Oct. 1979; Past Councillor, Mun. Dist. Pincher Creek; Past Senator, Univ. of Lethbridge; Founding mem. and Dir. Community Auction Sales; Past mem. Claresholm Auxiliary Hosp.; mem. Can. Council 1959-65; Bd. of Glenbow Foundation 1974-79; Govt. House Bd. 1978-79; served with Militia and Army Reserves 1933-43, rank Maj.; Office: Legislative Bldg., Edmonton, Alta. T5K 2B6.

LYNDON, John L., B.A., LL.B.; insurance executive; b. 5 May 1934; e. Univ. of Alta. B.A., LL.B. 1961; m. Jane Mackie; children: Greg, Bruce, Charlene, Ian, Jacqueline & Jane Ayn; PRESIDENT, INSURANCE BUREAU OF CANADA; practiced law with Clement, Parlee 1961-64; Corporate Trust Offr. National Trust Co. Ltd. Toronto 1964; Vice Pres. Market Operations The Toronto Stock Exchange 1964; Dir. Cochran Murray Ltd. invest. dealers 1970; Depy. Min. of Consumer & Corporate Affairs, Alta. 1972; Sessional Lectr. in Law, Univ. of Alta. 1976-78; recreations: skiing, reading, music, theatre, horseback riding; Clubs: University; Boulevard; Home: 66 Donwoods Dr., Toronto, Ont. M4N 2G5; Office: 181 University Ave., Toronto, Ont. M5H 3M7.

LYNDON, Patrick Beresford, M.A., L.R.A.M.; publisher; b. England, 27 Jan. 1929; e. London Univ., L.R.A.M., 1946; Worcester Coll., Oxford Univ., B.A., M.A., 1949; m. Joan Geraldine Holland; children: Julia Muir, Natasha Rowe; Pres., P.B. Lyndon Internat. Inc. (internat. publg.); former Pres., Seccombe House Ltd.; Prof. and Chrmn., Centre for Communications and the Arts, Simon Fraser Univ. 1968-70; served with Royal Ulster Rifles, Brit. Army, Japan and Korea, 1949-51; rank Lieut.; Clubs: Metropolitan, New York; Canadian, New York; Home: 4559 West 3rd Ave., Vancouver, B.C. V6R 1N3

LYON, Peyton, M.A., D.Phil.; university professor; b. Winnipeg, Man., 2 Oct. 1921; s. Herbert Redmond and Frederica Iveagh (Lee) L.; e. Kelvin High Sch., Winnipeg, Man.; Univ. of Manitoba, B.A. 1949; Oxford Univ. (Rhodes Scholar), B.A. 1951, M.A., D.Phil. 1953; m. Francès Marion, d. Frank B. Hazleton, Winnipeg, Man., 26 June 1943; children: Russell Vaughan, Stephen Lee, Barbara Jane; PROF. OF POL. SCIENCE, CARLETON UNIV. (Chrmn. of Dept. 1965-68); joined Dept. of External Affairs, 1953-59; with Dept. of Pol. Science, Univ. of Western Ont., 1959-65; served with R.C.A.F. in U.K., Africa, 1940-45, rising to Flt. Lt.; author of "The Policy Question", 1963, "Canada in World Affairs, 1961-3", 1968, 'NATO as a Diplomatic Instrument', 1971, 'Canada — US Free Trade and Canadian Independence", 1975; co-author, "Canada and the Third World", 1975, "Canada as an Intewrnational Actor", 1979; and numerous articles in journs., newspapers, mags.; mem., Candn. Inst. Internat. Affairs; Candn. Pol. Science Assn.; Home: 17 Apache Cr., Ottawa, Ont. K2E 6H8

LYON, Sterling, Q.C., b. windsor, Ont., 30 Jan. 1927; s. David Rufus and Ella Mae (Cuthbert) L.; e. Central Public Sch. and Portage la Prairie (Man.) Coll. Inst. (rec'd Gov. Gen.'s Gold Medal); United Coll. (Univ. of Manitoba), B.A. 1948; Manitoba Law Sch., LL.B. 1953; m. Barbara Jean, d. late John Garnet Howard Mayers, 26 Sept. 1953; children: Nancy Jane, Andrea Elizabeth, Peter David Sterling, Jennifer Anne, Jonathan Miller; Premier of Manitoba, 1977-81; also Pres. of Extve. Council; Called to the Bar of Manitoba, 1953; cr. Q.C. 1960; with News Staff, Winnipeg Free Press, 1948-49; Crown Atty., Dept. of Atty.-Gen. 1953-57; Legal Consultant, The Man. Liquor Enquiry Comn., 1954-55; el. to Man. Leg. in g.e. June 1958; Atty.-Gen. 1958-63 & 1966-69; Acting Min. of Munic. Affairs, 1960-61; Min. of Publ. Utilities, 1961-63; Min. of Natural Resources, 1963-66; Min. of Tourism & Recreation, 1966-68; Comm. of Northern Affairs 1966-68; Gov't. House Leader, 1966-69; P. Cons. cand., Winnipeg S., g. el. 1974; re-el. to Man. Leg. 2 Nov. 1976; Leader of Opposition to Oct. 1977 and 1981-; M.L.A. for Charleswood; Recipient of 25th Anniv. Outstanding Grad. Award, Univ. of Winnipeg Alumni Assn., 1973; Former Vice Pres. & Dir. Ducks Unlimited (Can.); former mem. Man. & Candn. Bar Assns.; mem., Bd. of Regents, Univ. of Winnipeg; Trustee, the Wildlife Foundation of Manitoba; N. Am. Wildlife Foundation; Progressive Conservative; Un. Church; recreations: hunting, fishing; Home: 705 South Dr., Winnipeg, Man. R3T 0C2; Office: Legislative Bldg., Winnipeg, Man.

LYONS, G. Jarvis; real estate executive; b. Toronto, Ont., 13 Sept. 1922; s. Sigmund Elias and Fanny (Singer) L.; e. Univ. of Toronto Schs. (Grad. 1941); Univ. of Toronto, 1941-42; m. Elizabeth Ann, d. George Raymond Lehrer, Boston, Mass., 18 June 1955; children: Cynthia Lee, Gordon Raymond, Douglas Andrew; PRESIDENT, S. E. LYONS AND SON LTD. (Estbd. 1926), since 1959; joined the Co. in 1946 as a Salesman; subsequently apptd. Vice-Pres., served with R.C.N.V.R. retiring Jan. 1946 with rank of Lieut. R.C.N.(R); mem., Toronto Real Estate Bd. (Past Dir.); Jr. Bd. Trade, Toronto (Past Dir.); Soc. of Indust. Realtors (Past Pres., Central Candn. Chapter and V/P Dir., Internat.); Royal Candn. Mil. Inst.; Naval Offrs. Assn. Can. (Past Dir.); Conservative; Unitarian; recreations: photography, travel, gardening, writing, music; Clubs: Board of Trade; Kiwanis; Home: 1514 Kenneth Drive, Mississauga, Ont. L5E 2Y5; Office: 1515 Matheson Blvd., Ste 205, Mississauga Ont. L4W 2P5

LYONS, Joseph Chisholm, Q.C., B.A., M.B.A., LL.B.; barrister and solicitor; b. Halifax, N.S., 17 Oct. 1927; s. Dr. J. N. and Frances (Chisholm) L.; e. Pub. and High Sch., Halifax, N.S.; St. Francis Xavier Univ., B.A., 1948; Dalhousie Law Sch., LL.B.; Harvard Grad. Sch. of Business Adm., M.B.A.; m. Julianne, d. Mr. Justice W. D. Roach, 5 Oct. 1957; children: Julianne Frances; Catherine Ann, Patricia Gertrude, Joseph Chisholm, Elizabeth Chisholm, John Mark, Mathew; PARTNER, SMITH, LYONS, TORRANCE, STEVENSON & MAYER; read law with Stewart, McKeen & Covert, Halifax, N.S.; called to Bar of N.S., 1953; Bar of Ont., 1953; cr. Q.C. 1966; P. Conservative; R. Catholic; recreation: golf; Clubs: National; Toronto Golf; Home: 47 Edgevalley Dr., Islington, Ont. M9A 4P2; Office: Suite 3400, Exchange Tower, 2 First Canadian Place, Toronto, Ont.

LYSYK, Kenneth, Q.C., B.A., LL.B., B.C.L.; educator; b. Weyburn, Sask. 1 July 1934; s. Michael and Anna (Maradyn) L.; e. McGill Univ. B.A. 1954; Univ. of Sask. LL.B. 1957, Oxford Univ. B.C.L. 1960; m. Patricia Irene d. R.M. Kinnon, Lumsden, Sask. 2 Oct. 1959; three d. Joanne Rene, Karen Michele (d. Oct. 1979), Stephanie Patricia; DEAN OF LAW, UNIV. OF BRIT. COLUMBIA and Prof. of Law there since 1976; Chrmn. Alaska Highway Pipeline Inquiry 1977 (on leave from Univ. of B.C.); Dir. Potash Corp. of Sask., called to Bar of Sask. 1959, B.C. 1965, Yukon 1977; cr. Q.C. 1973; Lectr. Faculty of Law, Univ. of B.C. 1960, Asst. Prof. 1962, Assoc. Prof. 1965, Prof. 1968-70; Adviser, Privy Council Office (Constitutional Review Sec.) Ottawa 1969-70 (on leave from Univ. of B.C.); Prof. of Law, Univ. of Toronto 1970-72; Depy. Atty. Gen. Govt. of Sask. 1972-76; Legal Adviser and Dir. of Legal Research, Indian Claims Comn. 1970-72; Special Adviser to Dept. of Nat. Health & Welfare on constitutional matters 1970-71; mem. Law Foundation Sask. 1974-75; Commr. (Sask.) Conf. on Uniform Laws 1973-76; approved Arbitrator under Ont. Labour-Manag. Arbitration Comn. Act; Chrmn. various arbitration bds. B.C. and Ont. or sole arbitrator in labour matters; mem., Candn. Assn. Law Teachers; Chrmn., Comte of Candn. Law Deans, 1980-81; R. Catholic; recreation: sports; Home: 6950 Yew St., Vancouver, B.C. V6P 5W3

M

MABEE, Oliver Band, B.A.; retired; b. Toronto, Ont., 6 April 1918; s. Oliver and Maude (Band) M.; e. Upper Can. Coll., Toronto, Ont.; Univ. of Toronto, B.A. 1940; m. Barbara, d. Donald McK. McClelland, 8 Dec. 1945; children: Martha Virginia, Alexandra Catherine; Vice-Pres., Personnel and Pub. Relations, Simpsons Ltd., 1965-73; served with RN in Mediterranean, Europe, Atlantic, North Sea and Channel, 1940-45; retired with rank Lt. Commdr.: Past Pres., Navy League of Can. (Ont.); Metrop. Convention & Visitors Assn.; Gov., Corps of Commissionaires; Past Pres., Naval Offrs. Assn., Toronto; Kappa Alpha; Presbyterian; recreations: golf, swimming; Clubs: University; Toronto Golf; Home: 287 Lytton Blvd., Toronto, Ont. M5N 1R7

MacALLAN, Douglas Harry, B.A.; petroleum executive; b. St. Thomas, Ont. 26 March 1922; s. late Allan Harry and late Esther (Stewart) MacA.; e. Univ. of W. Ont., B.A.; m. Grace Allison; children: Richard, Janet; VICE PRES.-CORPORATE AFFAIRS AND GEN. SECY., IMPERIAL OIL LTD.; served with RCAF 1940-46; rank Flight Lt.-Pilot; Past Dir., Cdn. Chamber of Comm.; Better Business Bureau of Can.; Dir., Vanier Inst. of the Family; mem., C.D. Howe Research Inst.; Policy Analysis and Finance Comtes.; Chmn., Gov't. Operations Comte.-Can. Chamber of Commerce; mem. Bus. Comte. on Regulatory Reform; United Church; recreation: golf; Clubs: National; Granite; Donalda; Office: 111 St. Clair Ave. W., Toronto, Ont. M5W 1K3

MacASKILL, Maynard Clayton, B.Sc., M.D., M.H.S.A.; Health Care Administrator; b. Breton Cove, N.S. 17 Nov. 1938; s. Daniel and Christene (MacAskill) MacA.; e. Acadia Univ. B.Sc. 1962; Dalhousie Univ. M.D. 1967; Univ. of Alta. M.H.S.A. 1974; DIRECTOR, MEDICAL AFFAIRS, SQUIBB CANADA INC., since 1979 el. to N.S. Leg. 1974, Min. of Consumer Affairs 1975, Min. of Educ. 1975-76; Min. of Health, Nova Scotia, 1974-79; mem. N.S. Med. Soc.; Corp. Prof. des Medecins du Que. Candn. Med. Assn.; Cdn. Soc. for Clinical Pharmacology; Cdn. Cardiovascular Soc.; Medical Section, P.M.A.C.; Liberal; United Church; Club: Montreal Amateur Athletic Assn. Home and Office: 3940 Côte des Neiges, Apt. B-24, Montreal, Queb. H3H 1W2

MACAULAY, Hugh L., B.A.; executive; b. Toronto, Ont. 31 Jan. 1925; s. Leopold and Hazel Charlton (Haight) M.; e. Univ. of W. Ont. B.A. (Journalism) 1948; m. Dorothy Jean Taylor 11 Sept. 1946; children: Barbara (Mrs. F. W. Hacker), Robert James, Andrew Taylor; CHRMN., ONT. HYDRO 1979- ; joined Public and Industrial Relations Ltd. 1948-52; Ford Motor Co. 1952-54; Lawrence Motors Ltd. 1954-55; Owner, York Mills Pontiac Ltd. and York Mills Leasing Ltd. 1955-70; Vice Chrmn. Ont. Hydro 1979; Chrmn. Comte. on Organ. Ont. P. Cons. Party 1971-76; mem. and Chrmn. of Bd. Ryerson Polytech. Inst. 1964-71; mem. Comn. on Post-Secondary Educ. 1969-71; served with RCNVR 1943-45; recreations: boating, golf; Clubs: York-Downs Golf & Country; John's Is-

land (Vero Beach, Fla.); Home: 619 Avenue Rd., Toronto, Ont. M4V 2K6; Office: 700 University Ave., Toronto, Ont. M5G 1X6.

MacAULAY, John Blair, B.A., LL.B.; b. Winnipeg, Man., 13 March 1934; s. John Alexander and Phyllis Ardelle (McPherson) MacA.; e. Pub. Schs. and Ravenscourt Sch., Winnipeg; Univ. of Man., B.A.; Man. Law Sch., LL.B.; m. Margaret Mary Elizabeth (Libby), d. W. Archie Bell, Winnipeg, Man., 10 June 1960; children: Alix Elizabeth, Robin Carol, John Christopher, Lesley Barbara; PARTNER, FRASER & BEATTY; Dir., Bank of Montreal; The Great-West Life Assnce. Co.; Standard Aero Ltd.; Moffat Communications Ltd.; Fed. Industries Ltd.; Place Bonaventure Inc.; Canbridge Leasehold, Ltd.; read law with Mr. Justice R. G. B. Dickson; called to Bar of Man. 1960, Bar of Ont. 1977; mem., Canadian Bar Assn.; United Church; recreations: reading, sailing, electronics; Club: Manitoba; Home: 1126 Morrison Heights Dr., Oakville, Ont. L6J 4J1; Office: Box 100, First Canadian Place, Toronto, Ont. M5X 1B2

MACBETH, John Palmer, Q.C., B.A., M.P.P.; lawyer; b. Toronto, Ont., 19 Nov. 1921; s. John Charles McKay and Virginia Maria (Palmer) M.; e. Queen Victoria Pub. Sch. and Parkdale Coll. Inst. Toronto; Univ. of Toronto; Osgood Hall Law Sch.; m. Ruth, d. William Robert Stevens, Toronto, Ont. 16 June 1945; children: John S., Wendy, Nancy R.; M.P.P.; ONTARIO LEGISLATURE 1971-81; served RCN 1943-45, rank Petty Offr.; Depy. Reeve Twp. of Etobicoke 1961-62, Reeve 1963-66; mem. Metrop. Toronto Council 1963-66 (Extve. Comte. 1965-66); Pres. Ont. Div. Candn. Cancer Soc. 1969-71; mem. Bd. Educ. Twp. Etobicoke 1952-58 (Chrmn. 1955); Hydro-Electric Comn. Borough Etobicoke 1963-72; Etobicoke Br. Candn. Red Cross Soc.; el. M.P.P. for York W. prov. g.e. 1971, re-el. since for Humber; apptd. Min. of Labour 1974-75; Prov. Secy. for Justice and Solr. 1975-78; Gen. mem. Bd. Trade Metrop. Toronto; P. Conservative; United Church; Club: Kiwanis (Past Pres.); Home: 9 Palace Arch Dr., Islington, Ont. M9A 2R9;

MACBETH, Robert Alexander Leslie, B.A., M.D., M.Sc., F.R.C.S.(C), F.A.C.S.; association executive; b. Edmonton, Alta. 26 Aug. 1920; s. late Alfred William and late Agnes DeLena (Lewis) M.; e. Westmount and Victoria High Schs. Edmonton 1938; Univ. of Alta. B.A. 1942, M.D. 1944; McGill Univ. M.Sc. 1947, Dipl. in Surg. 1952; m. Monique Elizabeth d. late Philippe Filliol 10 Aug. 1949; children: Michèle Agnes Cliff, Nicole Elizabeth, Danielle Monique, Joanne Leslie (Cameron); EXTVE. VICE PRES., CANDN. CANCER SOC. AND NAT. CANCER INST. OF CAN. 1977- ; internship: Univ. of Alta. Hosp. and Royal Alexandra Hosp. Edmonton 1943-45; Fellow in Endocrinol. McGill Univ. 1946-47, Teaching Fellow in Anat. 1947-48; Surg. Residency: Montreal Gen. Hosp. and Royal Victoria Hosp. 1948-49, 1951-52; Children's Mem. Hosp. Montreal 1949-50; Postgrad. Med. Sch. Hosp. London, Eng. 1950-51; Instr. in Clin. Surg. 1953-54 and Clin. Lectr. in Surg. 1954-57 Univ. of Alta., Assoc. Prof. of Surg. 1957-60, Prof. and Chrmn. of Surg. Univ. of Alta., 1960-75; Dir. of Surg. Services Univ. of Alta. Hosp. 1960-75; Assoc. Dean and Prof. of Surg. Dalhousie Univ. 1975-77; Dir. of Postgrad. Med. Educ. N.B. 1975-77; mem. Active Staff Royal Alexandra Hosp. 1953-57; Univ. of Alta. Hosp. 1953-75; Saint John (N.B.) Gen Hosp. 1975-77; Consulting Staff, Edmonton Gen. Hosp., Miseracordia Hosp. and Royal Alexandra Hosp. Edmonton 1957-75; Surg. Consultant Dept. Veterans Affairs Col. Mewburn Hosp. Edmonton 1957-75; mem. Bd. Examiners Med. Council Can. (Surg.) 1958-60; Bd. Surg. Examiners 1960-65, mem. Council 1972-76, Royal Coll. Phys. & Surgs.; Examiner in Surg. Trinity Coll. Dublin 1968; Visiting Prof. Am. Sch. for Classical Studies Athens 1972; Prof. Étranger, Service de Pathologie Experimentale, Institut Pasteur, Paris 1972-73; Visiting Prof. Polish Acad. of Sciences Warsaw 1975; External Examiner and

Visiting Prof. of Surg. Univ. of W. Indies 1976; rec'd Mosher Mem. Medal and Harrison Prize Univ. of Alta. 1944; Nat. Research Council Can. Research Fellowship 1946-47; Nuffield Foundation Travelling Fellowship 1950-51; James IV Surg. Assn. Travelling Fellowship 1965; Dir. Nat. Cancer Inst. Can. 1972-77; Candn. Council on Hosp. Accreditation 1977- , Pres. 1980-81; served with Royal Candn. Army Med. Corps 1943-46, rank Capt.; author over 60 articles, book chapters various publs.; mem. Ed. Bd. "Canadian Journal of Surgery" 1960-80; Hon. mem. Flint Acad. of Surg. 1969; Corr. mem. Polish Acad. Surg. 1973; Pres. Edmonton Chapter 1968-69, mem. Bd. Govs. 1974-80, Chrmn. Alta. Adv. Bd. 1960-75 Am. Coll. Surgs.; mem. of Council, Int'l Union Against Cancer 1978- ; mem. Acad. Med. Toronto; Am. Assn. Hist. Med.; Am. Surg. Assn.; Candn. Assn. Gastroenterol.; Candn. Assn. Gen. Surgs.; Candn. Oncology Soc.; Candn. Soc. Clin. Investigation (Pres. 1971, mem. Council 1966-72); James IV Assn. Surgs.; Internat. Surg. Group; Soc. Univ. Surgs.; Surg. Biol. Club II; W. Surg. Assn. (U.S.A.); Phi Kappa Pi (Past Pres.); Alpha Omega Alpha; United Church; recreations: medical history, philately; Home7 Gordon Rd., Willowdale, Ont. M2P 1E2; Office: #1001, 130 Bloor St. W., Toronto, Ont. M5S 2V7.

MacCALLUM, Donald C., B.Eng.; mechanical engineer; b. Chicago, Ill. (of Candn. parentage), 12 Oct. 1916; s. Howard MacFarlane and Jean Baikie (Duncan) M.; e. Lower Can. Coll.; Westmount (P.Q.) High Sch.; McGill Univ., B.Eng. (Mech. Engn.) 1938; m. Marion Fenwick, d. Dr. F. L. Wilkinson, Montreal, P.Q., 6 March 1947; CHRMN., RACEY, MacCALLUM & ASSOCIATES LTD. (Consulting Engrs., estbd. 1952); Design Engr., Canadian Ingersoll-Rand Co. Ltd., 1938-40; Dir. of Rehab. & Employment, The Engn. Inst. of Can., 1945; Adm. Engr., Canadair Ltd., 1946 and Purchasing Buyer there 1947; Salary Consultant, Corp. of Prof. Engrs. of Que., 1948; Vice-Pres. and later Mang. Dir., Charles Warnock & Co. Ltd., 1949-52; Secy. and Dir., Construction Borings Ltd., 1949-52; served in 2nd World War in Can. and U.K. with Sherbrooke Fusilier Regt., 1940-43, then in N. Africa in 1943, then in Italy with Three Rivers Regt. as Major Commanding Tank Sqdn., 1943-44; Hon. Col., 3rd Field Eng. Regt.; Past Pres., Montreal Citizens Comte.; Mayor, City of Westmount; mem., Am. Soc. for Metals; Am. Soc. for Testing Materials; Fellow, Engn. Inst. Can. (Past Councillor); Assn. Prof. Engrs. Ont.; Order of Engrs. Que. (Past Councillor); Assn. Consulting Engrs. Can.; Montreal Bd. Trade; Past Chrmn., Montreal Port Council; Past Chrmn., Board of Governors, Lower Canada Coll.; Psi Upsilon (Past Pres., Montreal); Protestant; recreations: reading, fishing, golf; Clubs: University St. Maurice Fish & Game; Royal Montreal Golf; Home: 4300 de Maisonneuve Blvd. W., Westmount, Que. H3Z 1K8; Office: Westmount City Hall, 4333 Sherbrooke St. W., Westmount, Que. H3Z 1E2

MacCALLUM, Elizabeth Pauline, O.C. (1967), M.A., LL.D.; retired diplomat; b. Marash, Turkey, 20 June 1895; d. Rev. Frederick William, D.D. (Candn. missy.) and Henrietta Mima (Reid) MacC.; e. Kingston (Ont.) Coll. Inst. 1913; Calgary (Alta.) Normal Sch., 1st Class Teaching Cert. 1916; Queen's Univ., M.A. (Eng. & Hist.) 1919, LL.D. 1952; Columbia Univ., grad. studies in modern European hist. 1921-22, 1924-25; taught sch. in Sask. and Alta. before univ. grad. and in Dawson City, Y.T., 1919-21; Asst. Secy., Social Service Council of Can. and Asst. Ed., "Social Welfare", 1922-24; Near East expert, Research Dept., Foreign Policy Assn., New York, 1925-31; in charge of internat. affairs lit. service, League of Nations Soc. in Can., Ottawa 1936-40; Libs. Sec., Candn. Legion Educ. Services, Ottawa, 1940-42; Dept. of External Affairs, 1942-60, (Near and Middle E. affairs); Adviser to Candn. dels. San Francisco Conf. 1945, World Health Assembly, Geneva, 1951 and sessions of U.N. Gen. Assembly, 1947, 1951, 1952, 1957; temp. duty in Candn. Embassy, Athens, June-Oct. 1951; Chargé d'Affaires, Beirut,

1954-56 (first Candn. woman to carry official letter of appointment in such capacity to a foreign Govt.); historical division Ottawa 1958-60, 1964-67 and 1972-77 (on contract); worked on village devel. and afforestation and studied contemp. Turkish lit., Turkey. 1960-64: author: "The Nationalist Crusade in Syria", 1928; "Rivalries in Ethiopia", 1936; also 21 monographs on Near and Middle E., N. African and Balkan subjects in Foreign Policy Reports series; articles in "Foreign Policy Bulletin", 1925-31 and in Candn. and foreign journs.; recreations: walking, gardening, reading: Address: 145 Clarendon Ave., Ottawa, Ont. K1Y 0R4

MacCRIMMON, Kenneth Robert, B.S., M.B.A., Ph.D.; educator; b. Hamilton, Ont. 28 Dec. 1937; s. Archibald Robert and Dorothy Anna (Williams) MacC.; e. Univ. of Calif. Los Angeles B.S. 1959, M.B.A. 1960, Ph.D. 1965; m. Marilyn Louise d. Marion Francis Turner, Burbank, Calif. 3 Feb. 1962; children: Karyn Alene, Keith Stuart, Brian Cameron; EARLE DOUGLAS MacPHEE PROF. OF MANAGEMENT, UNIV. OF B.C. 1981- ; J. L. Kellogg Distinguished Prof. of Strategy & Decision, Grad. Sch. of Mang. Northwestern Univ. 1980- ; Asst. and Assoc. Prof. Grad. Sch. of Indust. Adm. Carnegie-Mellon Univ. 1964-70; Prof. of Comm. and Business Adm. present Univ. 1970- ; Can. Council Sabbatical Leave Fellow 1975-76; Fellow, Internat. Inst. of Mang., Berlin 1977; Consultant, The Rand Corp., Santa Monica 1962-70; rec'd McKinsey Foundation Research Design Award 1966; author numerous articles various publs.; mem. Candn. Assn. Univ. Teachers; Econometric Soc.; Inst. Mang. Sciences; Am. Econ. Assn.; Public Choice Soc.; Operations Research Soc.; Beta Gamma Sigma; Home: 4593 West Sixth Ave., Vancouver, B.C. V6R 1V4; Office: Vancouver, B.C. V6T 1Y8.

MACDONALD, A. Angus, artist; designer; b. Bristol, Eng., 22 July 1909; s. A. Angus and Leila (Hanson) M.; e. Upper Can. Coll., 1919-27; Trinity Coll., Univ of Toronto, 1927-31; m. Louise, d. E. J. Nicol of Edinburgh, Scot., 1959; children: John, Heather, Fiona Janette; with T. Eaton Co. Advertising Dept. 1929-30; Hunt Advertising Service, Toronto, Ont., 1930-32; J. M. Dent & Sons (Can.) Ltd., 1932-35; establ. his own art publ. business (Macdonald Galleries), Toronto, 1935-41; with Robt. Simpson Co. Ltd. as a Designer, 1941-46; following which he was engaged for three yrs. on large mural paintings at Sunnybrook Hosp., Toronto, Anaconda Copper & Brass Co., New Toronto, and Guaranty Trust Co., Windsor, Ont.; designed and decorated 11th floor of Royal York Hotel for C.P. Rly. Co.; designed (in new anodysing process) special doors for the Aluminum Co. of Can. Ltd. for new office at King & Bay Sts., Toronto, Ont.; founded Wilcam Fabrics (Inc.), Bronte, Ont.; latterly engaged in designing stained glass windows; made and designed 14 windows for St. Luke's Cath., Sault Ste. Marie, Ont., and one window for St. Jude's Ch. in Oakville, Ont. (for Lady Baillie); one-man show in Toronto, 1961; exhibited at Canada Council's Conf. of the Arts, 1961; also new process of using glass, and in this method, mural for Canada House, New York; recently executed windows for Hall of Fame, C.N.E.; Toronto; St. James Cath., Toronto; Bridge St. United Ch. and Albert Coll. Chapel, Belleville; Evel Bldg. Chapel, Hamilton Gen. Hosp.; St. George's Ch., Toronto; 5 complete walls in antique glass and reinforced concrete for Ch. of St. Charles of Borromeo, Toronto; murals and leaded windows for 3 pub. rooms in The King Edward Sheraton Hotel, Toronto; el. mem., Ont. Soc. of Artists, 1946 (resigned 1951); illustrated "I Married an Artist", by Billy Button (1951); created new kind of glass and steel sculpture, first exhibited at one-man show, Manchester (Mass.) Arts Assn., 1968; comn. to do 92 paintings for the oublic rooms and offices of the Credit Valley School of Nursing in Mississauga (1969-71); work on perm. exhn. Nancy Poole Studio, Toronto; Club: Pickering Yacht; chief hobby' collecting and making (then playing) drums; recreations: swimming, skiing, sailing, building; Address: 131 Northwood Dr., Willowdale, Ont. M2M 2K2

MacDONALD, Alan Hugh, B.A., B.L.S.; librarian; b. Ottawa, Ont. 3 March 1943; s. Vincent C. and Hilda (Durney) MacD.; e. Saint Patrick's High Sch. Halifax; Dalhousie Univ. B.A. 1963; Univ. of Toronto B.L.S. 1964; DIR. OF LIBRARIES, UNIV. OF CALGARY 1979- ; joined Dalhousie Univ. 1964-79 serving as Documents Librarian, Asst. to Dir., Law Librarian, Asst. Univ. Librarian, Health Sciences Librarian, Lectr. Sch. of Lib. Service 1969-79; Visiting Lectr. South Australian Inst. of Technol. 1975; Librarian, N.S. Barristers' Soc. 1969-74; mem. Nat. Lib. Adv. Bd. 1972-76; Min.'s Adv. Comte. on Univ. Affairs Alta. 1979-80; Pres. Teled Video Services 1972-74; mem. Univ. of Calgary Senate 1980- ; Fellow, Council on Lib. Resources 1975-76; author numerous papers, articles and addresses on libraries and information science; mem. Candn. Lib. Assn. (Treas. 1977-79, Vice Pres./Pres. 1979-81); Candn. Assn. Information Science (Pres. 1979-80); Atlantic Provs. Lib. Assn. (Pres. 1976-77); Candn. Health Libs. Assn. (Treas. 1976-79); Lib. Assn. Australia (Assoc.); N.Z. Lib. Assn.; Candn. Assn. Law Libs.; Candn. Civil Liberties Assn.; Home: 527 10th Avenue N.E., Calgary, Alta. T2E 0X7 Office: 2500 University Dr. N.W., Calgary, Alta. T2N 1N4

MacDONALD, Hon. Alexander Barrett, Q.C., M.L.A., B.A., LL.B.; b. Vancouver, B.C., 21 Oct. 1918; s. Malcolm Archibald and Ida (Williams) M.; e. Univ. of B.C., B.A.; Osgoode Hall Law Sch., LL.B.; m. Dorothy Anne, d. Collis Lewis Ottawa, Ont., 4 Nov. 1944; one d. Christina Anne; A.-G. for B.C. 1972-75 M. Industrial Trade and Commerce 1973; called to Bar of B.C.; cr. Q.C. 1972; former Parlty Secy. to Hon. M. J. Coldwell; el. to H. of C. for Vancouver-East; el. M.L.A. in prov. g.e. 1960; re-el. in gen. el. 1963, 1966, 1969, 1972, 1975 and 1979; NDP; Anglican; recreations: squash, tennis, badminton, fishing; Home: 3461 Pt. Grey Rd., Vancouver, B.C. V6R 1A6; Office: Parliament Bldgs., Victoria, B.C. V8V 1X4

MacDONALD, Maj.-Gen. Bruce F., D.S.O. C.D. Croix de Guerre (France); b. Edmonton, Alta., July 1917; e. Edmonton (Alta.) Schs.; Univ of Alta.; comnd. Calgary Highlanders, 1940; trans. to 2nd Armoured Regt. Lord Strathcona's Horse, 1941; served overseas with HQ, 5th Candn. Armoured Div. to 1943; served in France with 2nd Candn. Armoured Bgde. HQ and later with Fort Garry Horse in Belgium, Holland and Germany; served as Bgde. Maj., 4th Candn. Armoured Bgde. from 1945 until end of war; Commdr., Royal Candn. Armoured Corps Sch., Camp Borden, 1946; apptd. to directing staff, Candn. Army Staff Coll., Kingston, 1949; G.S.O.1, Central Command HQ, Oakville, Ont., 1952; Dir of Armour, Army HQ, 1955-57; apptd. Cdn. Staff Planner, N.A.T.O. Standing Group Staff, Washington, 1958; Joint Secy. and Extve. Staff Offr. to Chrmn., Candn. Joint Staff, Washington, 1959; Commdr., 1st Candn. Inf. Bgde. Group, 1962; Commdr., Nicosia zone, U.N. Forces in Cyprus, 1965; seconded to U.N. with rank of Under Secy. and apptd. Chief Officer, U.N. India-Pakistan Observation Mission 1965; Commandant, Candn. Army Staff Coll., Kingston, promoted Maj. Gen. and appt. Deputy Chief of Personel, 1966; apptd. Col. of the Regt., Fort Garry Horse, Sept. 1968; retired from Candn. Armed Forces Nov. 1968; Col. Commandant, Roy. Candn. Armoured Corps 1973-77; Pres., Candn. Chem. Producers Assn., 1968-79; Pres., Men's Candn. Club of Ottawa, 1975-76; mem. of. Bd., Reichold Ltd and Mallinckrot Can. Inc., 1980; Clubs: Rideau; Royal Ottawa Golf; Home: 1103 Ambleside Dr., Ottawa, Ont. K2B 8E2

MacDONALD, Donald, O.C. (1972), LL.D.; b. Halifax, N.S., 12 Sept. 1909; s. Daniel Joseph and Mary Elizabeth (Garnier) M.; e. Holy Redeemer Sch., Sydney, N.S., 1914-22; Sydney (N.S.) Acad. (Grad.) 1922-26; St. Francis Xavier Univ. (Extension courses, 1935, 1936, 1938), Hon.

LL.D. St. Francis Xavier University, 1957; Hon. LL.D. Univ. of Windsor, 1974; m. Mary Gertrude, d. late Peter Campbell, 16 Nov. 1937; one s., Donald Campbell; lived in Sydney, N.S., 1913-51; mem. of United Mine-workers of Am., 1927-55 (Pres. Local 4560, 1930-40); mem. of Internat. Woodworkers of America, since 1955; Secretary, Whitney Credit Union, 1935-50; President, McArthur Co-operative Housing Corporation Limited, 1940-51; Manager, Sydney Cooperative Society, Whitney Br., 1940-41; Gen. Rep., Candn. Cong. of Labour, 1942-45; Regional Dir., Candn. Cong. of Labour for Maritimes, 1945-51; Secy.-Treas., Candn. Cong. Labour, 1951-56 (moved to Ottawa, Ont. in 1951); Secy.-Treas., Candn. Labour Cong., 1956-67; Acting Pres. 1967, Pres. 1968-74; Pres. (1st non-European) Internat. Confed. Free Trade Unions 1972-75; mem. of Nova Scotia Legislature for Cape Breton South (Sydney) 1941-45; Leader of the C.C.F. in Nova Scotia, 1941-45; mem. of Executive Board of International Confederation of Free Trade Unions 1951-75; rec'd Award of Merit, Offr. Class, Fed. Republic of Germany, 1976; Commdr. of Order of Merit, Luxemburg, 1976; Hon. Life mem., Candn. Red Cross Soc.; N.D.P.; Roman Catholic; Clubs: Cercle Universitaire; Canadian; Home: 782 Lonsdale Road, Ottawa, Ont. K1K 0K1

MACDONALD, Hon. Donald Stovel, P.C., B.A., LL.M.; LL.D. (Hon.); D. Eng. (Hon.); b. Ottawa, Ont. 1 March 1932; s. Donald Angus and Marjorie Isabel (Stovel) M.; e. Ottawa Pub. Schs.; Ashbury College, Ottawa; Univ. of Toronto B.A. 1951; Osgoode Hall Law Sch.; Harvard Law Sch., LL.M., 1956; Trinity Hall, Cambridge Univ., Dipl. in Internat. Law, 1957; m. Ruth, d. Dr. George O. Hutchison, Ottawa, 4 March, 1961; four d., Leigh, Nikki, Althea,Sonja; PARTNER, McCARTHY & McCARTHY, TORONTO since 1977; el. to H. of C. for Toronto Rosedale in g.e. 1962; resigned Feb., 1978; former Parlty. Secy. to Min. of Justice; Parlty. Secy. to Min. of Finance 1965; to Secy. of State for External Affairs 1966; to Min. of Industry Jan. 1968; apptd. Min. without Portfolio Apl. 1968, performing duties of Acting Min. of Justice; Pres. of the Privy Council and Govt. House Leader, July 1968; Min. of Nat. Defence, Sept. 1970; Min of Energy, Mines & Resources, Jan. 1972; Min. of Finance Sept. 75-Sept. 77; read law with Gowling, MacTavish, Osborne & Henderson, Ottawa; called to Bar of Ont. 1955; practised law with McCarthy & McCarthy, Toronto, 1957-62; Chrmn. Internat. Development Research Centre of Canada.; Dir., Alta. Energy Co. Ltd.; Du Pont Can. Inc.; Boise Cascade Corp.; The Manufacturers Life Insurance Co.; The Bank of Nova Scotia; McDonnell Douglas Corp.; Gov. Massey Hall, Toronto; Nat. Theatre School; Mem.: Harold Innis Foundation; Howe Research Inst.; Cdn. Amer. Comte.; Corp., Trinity College, Toronto; Dir., Inst. Research on Public Policy; Chrmn., Ont. Liberal Leader's Foundation; Spec. Lecturer, Univ. of Toronto Law School; awarded Newton Wesley Rowell Fellowship of Candn. Inst. of Internat. Affairs, 1957; mem., Delta Kappa Epsilon (House Mgr. and Alumni Secy.); Liberal; Baptist; recreations: tennis, squash, fishing; Clubs: York; University; Jovial Fish and Game (Buckingham, P.Q.); Home: 29 Dunvegan Rd., Toronto M4V 2P5; Office: P.O.Box 48, Toronto Dominion Bank Tower, T-D Ctr., Toronto M5K 1E6

MACDONALD, Eva Waddell Mader, M.D., C.M., D.P.H.; educator; physician; b. Halifax, N.S. 7 Oct. 1902; d. Dr. Antony Ivan and Eva Anderson Waddell Mader e. Halifax Ladies Coll., Convent Sacred Heart, Halifax; Acadia Semy; Halifax Co. Acad. 1920; Dalhousie Univ. M.D., C.M. 1927; Univ. of Toronto, D.P.H. 1929; Hon. L.L.D Dalhousie Univ. 1976; Univ. of Toronto 1977; Hon. D. Hum. L. St. Vincent Univ. 1975; m. Charles Napier Macdonald, 25 Aug. 1931; two s., Donald Fraser, James Robert; Chancellor, Univ. of Toronto 1974-77; interned Children's Hosp., Halifax 1925-27; N.S. Sanatorium, Kentville 1927-28; Connaught Lab. Research Fellowship, Teaching Asst. Sch. of Hygiene, Univ. of Toronto 1929-33; Banting Fellowship 1933-36; Phys. Children's Aid Soc. 1930-39;

joined Women's Coll. Hosp. 1929, served as Chief Out-Patients Dept., Chief Med. Staff 1943, Dir. Labs. 1945-52; Dir. Hosp. Health 1953-68, Hosp. Bacteriol. 1939-45, Hon. mem. Staff since 1968; private med. practice 1952-62; has served in various capacities educ. and pub. insts. incl. YWCA (Nat. Bd.); Candn. Welfare Council; Un. Ch. of Can.; Dalhousie and Univ. of Toronto Alumni Assns.; Home & Sch. Assns. 1939-53; rec'd citation for work in Red Cross Blood Donor Clinics during World War II; Sr., Candn. Med. Assn.; Life mem. Coll. Phys. & Surgs. (Ont.); Pres. Fed. Med. Women Can. 1943, 1964; mem. Ont. Med. Assn.; United Church; recreation: travel; Clubs: Canadian; University Women's; English Speaking Union; Home: 83 Oriol Rd., Toronto, Ont. M4V 2G2

MACDONALD, Flora Isabel, M.P.; b. North Sydney, N.S. 3 June 1926; d. George Frederick and Mary Isabel (Royle) M.; e. N. Sydney High Sch.; Empire Business Coll.; Nat. Defence Coll.; unm.; Min of External Affairs, 1979-80; first el. to H. of C. g.e. 1972 (Kingston and the Islands) and since; Extve. Past Extve Dir., Comte. for an Independent Can.; Dir., Candn. Inst. Public Affairs; Past Pres., Elizabeth Fry Soc.; mem. Caandn. Inst. Internat. Affairs; mem. Caandn. Inst. Public Affairs; Candn. Pol. Science Assn.; Candn. Civil Liberties Assn.; P. Conservative; United Ch.; Home: c/o 324 Princess St. Kingston, Ont. K7L 1B6; Office: House of Commons, Ottawa, Ont. K1A 0A6

MacDONALD, George Crawford; b. Toronto, Ont., 9 Dec. 1914; s. George Harold Ross and Florence Helen (Crawford) M.; e. St. Andrew's Coll., Aurora, Ont.; Univ. of Toronto; m. Elizabeth Ann, d. late Mark Samuel and Mary Hastings Laing Hodgeman, 11 June 1938; children: Peter George, Susan Elizabeth; CHAIRMAN, PARIBA, BANK OF CANADA 1981- ; Former Chrmn., and Pres., McLeod Young Weir Ltd.; Dir., Fulcrum Invest. Ltd.; DSMA LTD.; joined McLeod Young Weir Ltd. 1933; served in Toronto, Ont., in various capacities, 1933-38, Peterborough, Ont., 1938-41, London, Ont., 1945-47, N.Y. City, 1947-61, Montreal, Que., 1961-68, Toronto, Ont. 1968-81; served during 2nd World War with R.C.N. 1941-45; retired with rank of Lt. Commdr.; Anglican; recreations: boating, fishing, golf; Clubs: The Toronto; Granite; Toronto Hunt; York, Toronto; Lambton Golf and Country; Belleview Biltmore Country, Belleair, Florida; Home: 70 Montclair Ave., P.H. 2, Toronto, Ont. M5P 1P7; Office: Box 433, Toronto-Dominion Centre, Toronto, Ont. M5K 1M2

MACDONALD, Grant Kenneth, LL.D., R.C.A.; painter; b. Montreal, Que., 27 June 1909; s. Rev. Kenneth Jonathan and Rilla Gertrude (McMahon) M.; e. Central Public Sch. and Coll. Inst., Galt, Ont. till 1928; Ont. Coll. of Art (part-time), 1929-30; Art Students League, 1931-32 and 1939-40 and several part-time terms studied; Heatherley's Art Sch., London, Eng., 1932-33; taught figure drawing, Summer Sch., Queen's Univ., 1948, 1952, 1953, 1964, 1965; executed series of paintings of their plant in Sarnia for Dow Chemical Co. of Can.; coll. of portrait drawings of players in Stratford Shakespearean Festival commissioned by "Globe & Mail", Toronto, and hung in Stratford Theatre, 1953-58 and 1961-62; his sketches of Celebrities, chiefly theatrical, have appeared in "Daily Telegraph", "The Sketch" (mag.), "The Bystander", "Play Pictorial", on theatre posters and programs in London, in "Herald Tribune" and "Theatre Arts Monthly" in N.Y., and in "The Gazette", Montreal, over the period 1932-50; series of armed-forces drawings in "The Gazette", Montreal, 1941-44; over 25 one-man exhibitions in Toronto since 1941 including Hart House and one at Victoria College; in University, Library and Comm. Galleries in Toronto, Montreal, Ottawa, Vancouver, Halifax, Oakville, Kingston, Hamilton, Windsor; also exhibited with R.C.A. and O.S.A.; theatre portrait collection, Art Gallery Windsor, Hamilton 1976; Art Centre, Univ. of N.B. 1979 followed by Maritime tour of uni-

versities and art galleries 1980; Retrospective Exhn., Agnes Etherington Art Centre, Kingston, Ont.; Tom Thomson Memorial Gallery, Owen Sound 1978; Illustrator of: "Sailors", 1945; "Sunshine Sketches of a Little Town", 1948; "Behind The Log", 1947; "First Nights and Noises Off", 1948; "Haida", 1946; "Eros At Breakfast", 1949; "A Sense of Urgency", 1952; "Renown at Stratford", 1953; "Twice Have The Trumpets Sounded", 1954, etc.; served in R.C.N.V.R., 1943-46 as Artist in the Directorate of Special Services; paintings are in colls. of: Hart House, Univ. of Toronto; Art Coll. Soc. of Kingston; Ontario Art Gallery; Redpath Lib. McGill Univ.; Art Gallery of Windsor; Arts Council Gt. Britain; Sarnia Public Lib. & Art Gallery; Chatham Public Lib.; K.C.V.I., Kingston; Whig-Standard, Kingston; many private colls. in Can., several in Eng. and U.S.; rec'd. Hon. LL.D. Queen's 1974; awards incl. Art Dirs. Club Medal 1952; J. W. L. Forster Award, O.S.A. Exhn. 1966; Price Fine Art Award 1970; Protestant; recreations: reading, music, walking; Studio: "Tarquin" 32 Lakeshore Road, Kingston, Ont. K7M 4J6

MACDONALD, Hugh Ian, O.C. (1977), K.L.J. B.Com., M.A., B.Phil., LL.D.; educator; economist; b. Toronto 1929; e. Univ. of Toronto, B.Com. 1952; Balliol Coll. Oxford Univ. (Rhodes Scholar) M.A. 1954, B.Phil. (Econ.) 1955; m. Dorothy M.; five children; PRESIDENT, YORK UNIV. since 1974 and Prof. Public Adm. and Econ. there; Dir., Candn. Gen. Electric Co. Ltd., Rockwell International of Canada Ltd. and the A.G.F. Companies; joined Teaching Staff, Univ. of Toronto 1955 becoming Dean of Men, Univ. Coll. and Asst. Prof. of Econ.; apptd. Chief Econ., Prov. Ont. 1965; Depy. Treasurer and Depy. Min. of Econ. 1967; Depy. Treas. and Depy. Min. Econ. and Intergovt'l Affairs 1972; Chrmn., Ont. Adv. Comte. on Confed.; Mem. Economic Council of Canada; Address: Downsview, Ont. M3J 1P3

MACDONALD, Innis Mary, M.B., F.R.C.S. (Edin.); ophthalmologist; b. Markham, Ont., 14 Nov. 1902; d. John Andrew and Mary Innis (Fleming) M.; e. Univ. of Toronto, B.A. 1924, M.B. 1927; Univ. of Pennsylvania, 1928-29; Oxford Univ., D.O. 1932; mem. Med. Alumnae, Univ. of Toronto (Pres. 1936); Acad. Med., Toronto, Address: (P.O. Box 4), Markham, Ont. L3P 3J5

MACDONALD, John, M.A., B.Ed., Ph.D.; educator; b. Bettyhill, Scot., 10 Oct. 1925; s. Donald and Dolina (Murray) M.; e. Edinburgh Univ., M.A. 1950, Dipl. Ed. 1951; Glasgow Univ., B.Ed. 1953, Ph.D. 1958; m. Catherine Shirley, d. late William Muir, July 1952; children: Nicholas, Caroline; DEAN, FACULTY OF EDUC., UNIV. OF CALGARY since 1971; Asst. Prof. of Educ. Psychol., Univ. of Alta. 1958, Assoc. Prof. 1962; Prof. of Educ., Sir George Williams University, 1966, Professor and Chairman, Department of Education 1968-71; served with British Intelligence Corps 1944-48; author, "Understanding Yourself and Your Society", 1964; "The Discernible Teacher", 1970; also various articles for educational journals; mem., British Psychol. Soc.; Candn. Soc. Study Educ.; NY Acad. Sciences; recreations: contract bridge, short-wave radio.

MacDONALD, John Allan, B.A.; public servant; b. Ottawa, Ont., 23 Aug. 1921; s. Donald Colin and Norah Agatha (O'Gorman) M.; e. McGill Univ., B.A. (Econ.) 1947; m. Nasrene A., d. M. S. A. Baig, 15 Sept. 1973; children: (by former m.) Ian Malcolm, David Michael, Kathy Ann; CHRMN. OF THE TARIFF BOARD since 1979; Dir. Emeritus, Panarctic Oils Limited; joined Industrial Develpment Bank 1947; Econ. Policy Div., Dept. of Finance, 1949; Nat. Defence Coll., Kingston, 1954; Treasury Bd. 1955; apptd. Dir., Defence Works and Contracts Div. of Bd., 1958; Asst. Secy. 1960; became Asst. Depy. Head, Bureau of Govt. Organ., 1963; joined Dept. of Northern Affairs & Nat. Resources as Asst. Depy. Min., 1964; Sr. Asst. Depy. Min. 1966, Depy. Min., March 1968; Depy.

Min. Public Works 1970; Chrmn. and Pres., Export Development Corp., 1975-79; served with Canadian Army in Canada and U.K., 1939-42; mem., Advisory Council School of Pub. Adm., York University; Adv. Council, Fed. Inst. of Mang.; Associate, Carleton Univ.; mem., Candn. Pol. Science Assn.; recreations: music, reading, swimming, walking; Clubs: Rideau; Country; Home: 2314 — 1375 Prince of Wales Dr., Ottawa, Ont. K2C 3L5; Office: 365 Laurier Ave. West, Ottawa, Ont. K1A 0G7

MACDONALD, Commdr. John Arthur, B.A.; retired civil servant; author; b. Toronto, Ont., 26 Sept. 1912; s. Duncan McGregor and Nellie Graham (Minns) M.; e. Upper Can. Coll.; Univ. of Toronto, B.A. 1935; m. Catherine Mary, d. late Albert Edward Hilder, 29 Nov. 1939; children: Catherine Muriel, Judith Ann, Margaret Duncan; Dir. Gen., Internat. & Emergency, Dept. Nat. Health & Welfare 1965-73; Spec. Rapporteur for UN; Candn. Rep., Extve. Bd. UNICEF, UN Social Devel. Comn. and other internat. bodies; consultant, Internat. Council on Social Welfare, 1973-74; served in World War 1939-45 with RCNVR; now Commdr. (S), R.C.N. (R); author of "Darkly the River Flows", 1945 (winner of $1,000 Fiction Award from Longmans Green Inc. and Coward McCann); Anglican; Address: 20 Kippewa Drive, Ottawa, Ont. K1S 3G4

MACDONALD, John Barfoot, D.D.S., M.S., Ph.D., LL.D., D.Sc., A.M.(Hon.) LL.D., Wilfred Laurier, Brock & West Ont. Univs; (Hon.) D.Sc. Univ. of Windsor; university professor; b. Toronto, Ont., 23 Feb. 1918; s. Arthur A. and Gladys L. (Barfoot) M.; e. Univ. of Toronto, D.D.S. (with Hons.) 1942; Univ. of Illinois M.S. (Bacteriol.) 1948; Columbia Univ., Ph.D. (Bacteriol.) 1953; Harvard Univ., A.M. (honorary) 1956; LL.D. Manitoba 1962, Simon Fraser 1965; D.Sc. Brit. Columbia 1967; m. Liba Kucera; children: Kaaren C., John G., Scott Arthur, Vivian Jane, Linda Rosemarie; CHMN., ADDICTION RESEARCH FOUNDATION 1981- ; President of Addiction Research Foundation 1976-81; Extve. Dir., Council of Ont. Univs. and Prof. of Higher Educ., Univ. of Toronto 1968-76; mem. Addiction Research Foundation of Ont.; Consultant, Nat. Insts. of Health; Lectr., Preventive Dentistry, University of Toronto, and private practice, 1942-44; after war service, Instructor in Bacteriol., Faculty of Dent., Univ. of Toronto, and private practice, 1946-47; Research Asst., Univ. of Illinois, 1947-48; Kellogg Fellow, and Candn. Dental Assn. Research Student, Columbia Univ., 1948-49; Asst. Prof. of Bacteriol., Univ. of Toronto (Faculty of Dent.), 1949-53, and Assoc. Prof., 1953-56; Chairman, Div. of Dental Research, Univ. of Toronto, 1953-56 and apptd. (full) Prof. of Bacteriol., 1956; Consultant in Dent. Educ., Univ. of B.C., 1955-56; Dir., Forsyth Dental Infirmary, Boston, Mass., 1956-62; Prof. of Microbiol., Harvard Sch. of Dent. Med., 1956-62, and Dir. of Postdoctoral Studies there, 1960-62; Assoc. Editor of "Journal of Dental Research" 1958-61; Regional Editor, "Archives of Oral Biology" 1958-62; Editor, "International Series on Oral Biology" 1958-63; Pres., Univ. of B.C., 1962-67; mem. Bd., Donwood Foundation, 1966-79, Chrmn. 1972-75; mem. Bd., Banff School for Advanced Mang. 1962-67 (Chrmn. 1966-67); mem. Bd. Dirs., Assn. of Univs. and Colls. of Can. 1964-67; mem., Visiting Comte., Harvard Med. Sch. & Sch. of Dental Med. 1967; Consultant, Science Council of Can. and Can. Council on Support of Research in Candn. Univs. 1967-69; Chrmn., Jt. Comte. of Candn. Dental Assn. and Candn. Med. Assn. on Fluoridation; mem., Candn. Nat. Research Council Comte. on Dental Research, 1950-60 (Chrmn. 1954-57); mem., Dental Study Sec., Nat. Insts. of Health; Chrmn., Comn. on Pharm. Services, Candn. Pharm. Assn., 1967; mem. Nat. Scient. Planning Council, Candn. Mental Health Assn. 1969; served in 2nd World War with Candn. Dental Corps, 1944-46; released with rank of Capt.; mem. Internat. Assn. for Dental Research (Pres. 1968); N.Y. Acad. of Sciences; Am. Assn. Advanc.

Science; Soc. of Am. Bacteriols.; New England Dental Soc.; Address: 33 Russell St., Toronto, Ont. M5S 2S1

MacDONALD, John James, B.Sc., M.A., Ph.D.; educator; b. New Glasgow, N.S. 30 Oct. 1925; s. John James and Margaret Jean MacD.; e. St. John's Acad. New Glasgow, N.S.; St. Francis Xavier Univ. B.Sc. 1945; Univ. of Toronto M.A. 1947, Ph.D. 1951; m. Mary Lou d. John E. C. MacIntyre, Moncton, N.B. 7 June 1952; children: John James, Nancy Patricia, Anne Louise, Joan Elizabeth, Ronald Joseph, Margaret Ethel, Alan Roderick; EXTVE. VICE PRES., ST. FRANCIS XAVIER UNIV. since 1978; Asst. Prof. of Chem. present Univ. 1949, Assoc. Prof. 1954, Dean of Science 1960, Prof. 1961, Acad. Vice Pres. 1970-78; Visiting Scient. Naval Research Estab. Dartmouth 1955; Research Study Leave, Univ. of Ottawa 1959-60; Study Leave, Higher Educ. Group, Univ. of Toronto and Visiting Prof. Ont. Inst. of Studies in Educ. 1976-77; rec'd Centennial Medal 1967; Dir. Maritime Telegraph & Telephone Co. Ltd. since 1973; Chrmn. Town Planning Bd. Antigonish 1962-68, War Supplies Agency E. N.S. Region; mem. Maritime Provs. Higher Educ. Comn. since 1974; Science Council of Can. since 1977; Chrmn., Sci. Council Transportation Study Comte. 1981; Mem., N.S. Task Forre on Research and Technological Innovation; NRC Advisory Comm., Atlantic Region; NSERC, Adv. Comm. on Regional Development; Mem.-at-Large, Candn. Nat. Comn. for UNESCO since 1968; served as Pilot Offr. 1956 before joining Sqdn. Leader and C.O. 294 Univ. Sqdn. 1968; mem. Assn. Univs. & Colls. Can. (Dir. since 1976); Chem. Inst. Can.; Comparative & Internat. Educ. Study; Candn. Soc. Study Higher Educ.; Brit. N. Am. Philatelic Soc.; Royal Candn. Philatelic Soc.; Candn. Philatelic Soc. Gt. Brit.; R. Catholic; recreations: fishing, golf, philately; Club: Antigonish Golf & Country; Home: 58 Hawthorne St., Antigonish, N.S. B2G 1A4; Office: Antigonish, N.S. B2G 1C0.

MacDONALD, John R., B.Sc.; executive; b. Charlottetown, P.E.I. 26 Aug. 1936; s. Allan J. and Mary (Pineau) MacD.; e. St. Dunstan's Univ. B.Sc. (Chem.); children: Paula, John; PRESIDENT AND CEO, STANDARD BRANDS LTD. since 1977; Dir., McGuinness Distillers Ltd.; Calona Wines Ltd.; Lowney Inc.; Chem. Acadian Distillers, Bridgetown, N.S. 1959-62, Distilling Supvr. 1962-65; Distilling Mgr. McGuinness Distillers, Toronto 1965, Vice Pres. Mfg. 1968-73; Pres. Wine & Spirits Div. present co. 1973, Area Vice Pres. International Standard Brands Inc. N.Y. 1977; served as Offr. RCNVR; mem. Bd. Trade Metrop. Toronto; Young Pres's Organ.; Harvard Business Sch. Club; Olympic Trust of Canada; recreations: tennis, golf; Clubs: Lambton Golf & Country; Cambridge; Canadian (N.Y.); Mount Royal (Montreal); Home: 18A Hazelton Ave. Apt. 305, Toronto, Ont. M5R 2E2; Office: 1 Dundas St. W. Suite 2800, Toronto, Ont. M5G 2A9.

MacDONALD, Keith Herbert; retired investment executive; b. Southampton, Ont., 24 March 1914; s. Duncan and Mary (Knechtel) M.; e. Stratford Normal Sch., grad. 1933; Waterloo Coll., 1934-35; m. Mary Tait, 19 Sept. 1939; children: Mary Jane, Tait; Ret. Chairman and Dir., IAC Ltd.; American Sterilizer Co. (US); Boiler Inspection and Insurance Co. of Canada; Ingram and Bell Ltd.; Uniroyal Inc.; Zellers Ltd.; Les Enterprises J.R. Ouimet Ltée; Past Pres., Can. Safety Council; Dir. and Past Chrmn. Extve. Comte., Roads & Transport. Assn. Can.; Past Dir. (1st Candn.) Internat. Road Fed., Washington & Geneva; School Teacher, 1934-35; with Owen Sound "Sun Times" & Kitchener "Record", 1935-37; Retail Credit Co., 1937-41; joined present Co., 1941; Br. Mgr., Peterborough, Sudbury, Calgary; Regional Sales Mgr., W. Provs., 1950, Ont., 1951-56; apptd. Asst. Vice-Pres. and Gen. Sales Mgr., 1956, subsequently Pres. and Dir.; served in 2nd World War with R.C.A.F. as Pilot Offr.; mem. Candn. Liver Found.; Chrmn. at. Program for the Mentally Retarded; recreations: golf, fishing, gardening; Clubs: Atlantis Golf; Toronto Golf; Rosedale Golf; Home: Apt. 901, 619 Avenue Rd., Toronto, Ont. M4V 2K6

MACDONALD, R. Ian, B.A., M.D., C.M., LL.D., F.R.C.P. (Lond.), F.R.C.P.(C), F.A.C.P.; physician;. Sydney, Nova Scotia, 23 May 1904; s. Donald John and Marion S. (Longworth) M.; e. Halifax Acad.; Dalhousie Univ., B.A. 1926; M.D., C.M. 1930; LL.D. 1968; post-grad e. Toronto Gen. Hosp., the London Hosp. and Nat. Hosp. for Nervous Diseases, London, Eng., M.R.C.P. Lond. 1933; F.R.C.P.(c) 1946; F.R.C.P. (London) 1954; F.A.C.P. m. Marjorie MacKinnon, Halifax, June 1932; children: Margaret, Isabel, Donald; practised Internal Med. in Halifax, 1934-36 and in Toronto, 1936-74; staff, Dept. & Med., Univ. of Toronto 1936-69; physician Tor. Gen. Hosp. 1936-74; associated appts.: Christie St. and Sunnybrook Hosp; D.V.A. 1945; Med. consultant 1947; Chief of Serv. Med. 1947-65; Advisor in Med. to D.G.T.S. (D.V.A.); dir. div. Post Grad. Med. U. of T. 1956-69; associate dean, faculty med. 1965-69; served in 2nd W.W. 1940-45 as med. spec. R.C.A.M.C Eng. and N.W.E.; Sr. mem. of Candn. and Ont. Med. Assoc.; post pres., Council of College of Phys. and Surgeons of Ont. and of Acod. Med., of Toronto; Charter mem., Ont. Council of Health; Home: P.O. Box 718, 89 Main St., Wolfville, N.S. B0P 1X0

MacDONALD, R. Neil, B.A., M.D., C.M., F.R.C.P. (C); b. Calgary, Alta., 6 Jan. 1935; s. Angus Neil and Florence (MacDonald) M.; e. St. Mary's Boy's High Sch., Calgary, 1952; Univ. of Toronto, B.A. 1955; McGill Univ., M.D., 1959; m. Mary Jane, d. James Frederick Whiting, Kingston, Jamaica, 30 June 1962; children: Cynthia, David, James, Gavin; PROF. AND DIR., DIV. OF ONCOLOGY, UNIV. OF ALBERTA; Dir., Cross Cancer Inst.; Interne (1959-60) and Resident in Med. (1960-62), Royal Victoria Hosp., Montreal, Fellow in Hematol. (1963-65), Fellow in Cancer Chemtherapy, Sloan-Kettering Inst., New York, 1962-63; joined McGill Univ., 1965, Assoc. Dean of Med. 1967-70; mem., Attending Staff; Royal Victoria Hospital, Montreal 1965-71; Dir., Cross Cancer Inst., Edmonton; and Prof., Dept. of Medicine, Univ. of Alta; awards: Joseph Morley Drake Prize (Path.) 1958; Mosby Book Prize, 1958; McGill Univ., James Eccles Schol., 1958; J. Francis Williams Med. Schol. 1959; Sir Edward Beatty Schol. (Post-Doctoral Studies) 1963; Queen's Jubilee Medal 1977; Albeta, Achievement Award 1980; author or co-author of many med. reports; mem., Candn. Med. Assn.; Alpha Omega Alpha; Nu Sigma Nu; Candn. Hematology, Soc.; Amer. Soc. of Clinical Oncology (Secy-Treas. 1979-82); Edmonton Academy of Med. (Past Pres.); Candn. Oncology Soc. (Past Pres.); Roman Catholic; recreations: squash; amateur historian; Home: 9330 118th St., Edmonton, Alta. T6G 1V1. Office: Edmonton, Alta. T6G 2E1

MacDONALD, Pierre, B.A., M.Com.; banker; b. Quebec City, 19 June 1936; e. Laval Univ. B.A. 1957, B.Com. 1959, M.Com. 1960; m. Magdeleine Godbout, June 1959; children: Jean, Claude, Ann, Julie; SR. VICE PRES. QUE. DIV., BANK OF MONTREAL; Chrmn. Canadian Arsenals Ltd.; Vice Pres. Johnson & Higgins, Willis Faber Inc. 1965-68; Extve. Vice Pres. & Gen. Mgr. Les Industries L'Islet Inc. 1970-74; Vice Pres. and Dir. La Société d'énergie de la Baie James; Dir. La Municipalité de la Baie James; La Société de développement de la Baie James; Sotel Inc.; service Candn. Armed Forces (Reserve), rank Col.; mem. Candn. Nuclear Assn.; Clubs: Cercle Universitaire Qué.; St-Denis; Laval-sur-le-Lac; Home: 39 White Pine Dr., Beaconsfield, Que. H9W 5E4; Office: 3100 CIL House, 630 Dorchester Blvd. W., Montreal, Que. H3B 1S6.

MacDONALD, Hon. Raymond Alexander, M.B.E., B.A., LL.B.; judge; b. Saskatoon, Sask. 14 March 1915; s. Bernard Donald and Marion (Egan) MacD.; e. elem. and high schs. Saskatoon; Univ. of Sask. B.A. 1936, LL.B. 1938; m. Helen Madeline J. d. late John A. Fraser, Q.C. 7

June 1947; children: J. Alexander, Roderick E., M. Susan Jane, R. Iain; JUDGE, COURT OF APPEAL SASK. 1981- ; read law with George Ferguson, Q.C.; called to Bar of Sask. 1939; cr. Q.C. 1964; Partner, Fraser & MacDonald, Regina 1939-56; MacDonald, Maclean, MacDonald 1956-60; Nicol, Keith, Armstrong, MacDonald & Cruickshank 1960-65; apptd. to Queen's Bench Court of Sask. 1965; Secy.-Treas. St. Olivier Separate Sch. 1947-60; served with Candn. Army 1940-45, Brit. and N.W. Europe, rank Maj.; Mentioned in Despatches; mem. Law Soc. Sask.; Candn. Bar Assn.; Candn. Inst. Adm. Justice; K. of C.; R. Catholic; recreations: golf, curling; Club: Wascana Country; Home: 272 Leopold Cres., Regina, Sask. S4T 6N9; Office: Court House, 2425 Victoria Ave., Regina, Sask. S4P 3E4.

MACDONALD, Ronald St. John, B.A., LL.M.; Judge; b. Montreal, P.Q., 20 Aug. 1928; s. Col. Ronald St. John and Elizabeth Marie (Smith) M.; e. St. Francis Xavier Univ., B.A. 1949; Dalhousie Univ., LL.B. 1952; Univ. of London (Eng.) LL.M. 1954; Harvard Law Sch., LL.M. 1955; Internat. Law Comn. Seminar, Geneva (Dipl.) 1952; PROFESSOR OF INTERNAT. LAW, DALHOUSIE UNIV. since 1979; Lectr. in Law, Osgoode Hall, 1955-57; Prof. there, 1957-59; Asst. Editor, Ont. Reports and Ont. Weekly Notes, 1956-57; Prof. of Law, Univ. of W. Ont., 1959-61; Prof. of Law, Univ. of Toronto, 1961-67, Dean of Law 1967-72; Dean of Law, Dalhousie Univ. 1972-79; Judge of the European Court of Human Rights, Strasborg, 1981- ; read law with McInnes, MacQuarrie & Cooper, Halifax, N.S.; called to the Bar of N.S. and of Ont., 1956; Consultant, Dept. of External Affairs, Prime Minister's Office (Ottawa) and Republic of Cyprus (1974-78); Candn. Rep. to U.N. Gen. Assembly 1965, 66, 68, 77; Advisor, American Law Institute; author of articles and essays in numerous prof. journs.; Sub-Lieut. R.C.N.V.R.(R), discharged 1946; mem., Inst. of Int. Law (Brussels); Candn. Bar Assn.; Candn. Inst. Internat. Affairs; Law Soc. Upper Can.; London Inst. World Affairs; Internat. Law Assn.; St. Andrew's Soc.; Zeta Psi; Liberal; R. Catholic; recreations: reading, walking, sailing, travelling; Home: 1173 Beaufort Ave., Halifax, N.S. B3H 3Y3; Office: Halifax, N.S.

MacDONALD, Stewart Ferguson, M.A., Dr.rer. nat., F.R.S.C.; retired chemist; b. Toronto, Ont., 17 Aug. 1913; s. Mervil and Margaret Stuart (MacGregor) M.; e. Univ. of Toronto Schs.; Univ. of Toronto, B.A., 1936; M.A., 1937; Technische Hochschule. Munich, Dr.rer.nat., 1939; m. Marian Katherine, d. late John Medley de Courcy O'Grady, 13 Oct. 1945; children: Peter, Lorna, Wanda, Constance, Sheila; Research Assoc., Banting and Best Dept. of Med. Research, Toronto, Ont., 1939-40; Chemist, Welland Chemical Works, Niagara Falls, Ont., 1940-42; Asst. Prof., Banting and Best Dept. Med. Research, and Research Assoc., Connaught Labs., Toronto, Ont., 1942-48; on leave at Imp. Coll., London and Cambridge Univ., 1946-47; Univ. Chemical Labs., Cambridge, Eng., 1948-52; with Nat. Research Council until 1952 (Div. of Pure Chem. 1952-68; Biol. Sciences since 1968); Gertrude Davis Exchange Fellowship, 1937, and Wellcome Fellowship, 1948-52; author of articles in tech. journs.; mem., Chem. Soc. (London); Am. Chem. Soc.; Chem. Inst. Can.; Protestant; Home: 2148 Beaumont Rd., Ottawa, Ont. K1H 5V3

MacDONALD, William Brien, B.A., M.D., F.R.C.P.(C); educator; b. Edmonton, Alta. 14 Dec. 1935; s. William Alexander and Margaret (O'Brien) MacD.; e. Luther Coll. Regina, Sask. 1953; Univ. of Sask. B.A. 1956, M.D. 1959; m. Mary Donna d. Michael Frederick Tomilin, Kamsack, Sask. 24 May 1958; children: William Charles, Catherine Mary; PROF. AND CHRMN. OF ANAESTHESIA, UNIV. OF SASK. since 1977, Asst. Dean of Medicine (Regina) 1977-79; Assoc. Dean, 1979- ; Asst. Prof. of Anaesthesia Univ. of Sask. 1964, Assoc. Prof. 1968-72, Prof. 1973; Assoc. Prof. of Anaesthesia Univ. of W. Ont. 1972-73; Pres.,

Sask. Div., Defence Medical Assn. of Can. 1973- , (Council mem., 1979- , Second Vice-Pres., 1981-); mem. Care-Medico (served in Malaysia 1966); served with Candn. Forces Med. Service Reserve, Commdr. Med. Co. Saskatoon, rank Lt. Col. on retirement 1971; mem. of Exec. of Council, Royal Coll. Physicians and Surgeons, Can., 1980- ; mem. Candn. Anaesthetists Soc. (Chrmn., Sask. Div., 1980-); Am. Soc. Anesthesiol.; Internat. Assn. Study Pain; P. Conservative; United Church; recreations: golf, boating, hunting; Clubs: Assiniboia; Wascana Country; Home: 73 Culliton Cres., Regina, Sask. S4S 4J5; Office: Plains Health Centre, 4500 Wascana Parkway, Regina, Sask. S4S 5W9.

MACDONELL, Harry Winsor, Q.C., B.Com.; b. Toronto, Ont., 19 July 1929; s. Charles Kenneth Sumner and Anita (Winsor) M.; e. Lakefield (Ont.) Prep. Sch., 1949; Carleton Univ., B.Com. (Medallist) 1952; Osgoode Hall Law Sch., 1956; m. Marie Martine Malevez, d. late Eugene Nestor Malevez, 20 Feb. 1960; children: Nicole Marie, Ian Kenneth, Winsor James; PARTNER, McCARTHY AND McCARTHY; Dir., Brinco Ltd.; Atomic Energy of Canada Limited; Wajax Ltd.; 3M Canada Inc.; Standard Life Assurance Co.; Woodbridge Foam Corp.; Can. Niagara Power Co. Ltd.; Paraplegic Assn.; read law with Fasken and Calvin; called to the Bar of Ontario 1956; cr. Q.C. 1969; Associate, Fasken and Calvin, Toronto, 1956; Partner 1962; mem., Canadian Bar Association; Co. York Law Assn.; Internat. Comn. Jurists (Candn. Sec.); Law Soc. Upper Can.; recreations: skiing, tennis; Clubs: Toronto; York (Toronto);University (Toronto); Toronto Lawn Tennis; Mount Royal (Montreal); Rideau (Ottawa); Home: 90 Dunvegan Rd., Toronto, Ont. M4V 2P7; Office: Toronto-Dominion Centre, Toronto, Ont. M5K 1E6

MACDONELL, Ian McLean, M.B.E., Q.C.; former judge; b. Toronto, Ont., 8 Aug. 1895; s. Alexander McLean, K.C., and Jane Marion (Powell) M.; U.E.L. ancestry on both sides; e. Upper Canada Coll., Toronto, Ont.; Univ. of Toronto, B.A.Sc. 1915; Osgoode Hall, Toronto; m. Maybelle Caird, d. Dr. Franklin Forrest, Port Hope, Ont., 29 Jan. 1936; children: Archibald McLean, Leta Catharine; ASSOC., WHITE, BRISTOL, BECK; called to Bar of Ont. 1920; cr. K.C. 1933; practised law with Bain, Bicknell, Macdonell & Gordon; Judge, Co. of York, 1933-70; former Vice-Chrmn., Ont. War Labour Bd.; Chrmn. Ont. Labour Relations Bd., and many times an Indust. Disputes Commr.; served in 1st World War, 1915-19; on Staff Candn. Arty. overseas; later Lieut.-Col. commanding Queen's Own Rifles of Can.; twice Mentioned in Despatches; Ald., Toronto, Ont., 1926-27; in charge of Civil Defence for Prov. of Ont., 1942-45; Past Pres., Co. Judges Assn. of Ont.; Alpha Delta Phi; Phi Delta Phi; L.O.L.; Anglican; recreations: golf, boating; Clubs: Toronto University; Toronto Golf; Royal Canadian Military Inst.; Home: 15 Ormsby Cres., Forest Hill, Toronto, Ont. M5P 2V2

MACDONELL, James Johnson, F.C.A.; b. Calgary, Alberta, 13 Sept. 1915; s. late Archibald Joseph and Lillian Catherine (Johnson) M.; e. Glengarry Co., Ont.; admitted C. A. (Que.) 1937; m. Audrey Mary, d. late Sydney G. Grafton, Hamilton, Ont., 15 May 1941; one d., Audrey Anne; CHRMN., CANADIAN COMPREHENSIVE AUDITING FOUNDATION 1980- ; P. S. Ross & Sons, Montreal, 1930-37; Candn. Industries Ltd., Montreal, 1937-45; in 1945 joined Price Waterhouse & Co. as Mgr. of newly-estbd. Systems & Methods Dept., apptd. Nat. Partner i/c Mang. Consult. Services Div., 1950; Sr. Partner of Price Waterhouse Assoc. 1968-73; Auditor Gen., Can. 1973-80; Pres. (1965-66) and Dir. (1963-73) Candn. Assn. Mang. Consultants; mem., Inst. of Chart. Accts. Que.; Inst. Chart. Accts. Ont. (Fellow 1956); Inst. Mang. Consultants Quebec (Fellow 1978); recreations: golf, photography, reading; Clubs: Rideau; Roy. Ottawa Golf; Metropolitan (N.Y.); Bruno Country; Mount Royal; Home: 195

Clearview Ave. Apt. 2110, Ottawa, Ont. K1Z 6S1; Office: Suite 1315, 112 Kent St., Ottawa, Ont., K1P 5P2

MacDONELL, Rev. Malcolm, M.A., LL.D. (R.C.); university president; b. Hillsdale, N.S., 15 Jan. 1919; s. William and Sarah (MacEachen) MacD.; e. St. Ninian, Judique, N.S.; Port Hood (N.S.) Acad.; St. Francis Xavier Univ., B.A. 1938; Queen's Univ.; Univ. of Toronto, M.A. 1945; Pontifical Inst. of Medieval Studies, Toronto; LL.D. St. Thomas University 1974, Memorial Univ. 1978; President, St. Francis Xavier University till June 1978; pt.-time mem., Candn. Human Rights Comm. since 1978; writings include various articles for hist. journs.; mem. Candn. Hist. Assn.; Candn. Cath. Hist. Assn.; recreations: golf, swimming, kayaking, music, art; Club: Kentigern; Home: 10 Glenville Terrace, Antigonish, N.S.B2G 1C0

MACDONNELL, Peter Logie Parkin, C.M., Q.C., M.A.; b. Toronto, Ont., 7 Oct. 1919; s. James MacKerras and Marjorie Randolph (Parkin) M.; e. Selwyn House Sch., Montreal, 1927-30; Upper Can. Coll., Toronto, 1930-37; Queen's Univ., B.A. (Pol. Science & Econ.) 1940; Cambridge Univ., M.A. (Law) 1946; Osgoode Hall Law Sch., 1946-47; m. Dorothea van Nostrand, d. late Brig. W. B. Wedd, 4 Aug. 1949; children: James Wedd, Martha Anne Grant, Christine Elizabeth; PARTNER, MILNER & STEER; Dir., The Royal Bank of Canada; CAE Industries Ltd.; Hiram Walker Resources Ltd.; Canadian Utilities Ltd.; Novacor Chemicals Ltd.; NOVA Corp. (Alta.); Alberta Energy Co.; Westn. Supplies Ltd.; Century Sales & Service Ltd.; IU Internat. Corp.; Associated Kellogg Ltd.; called to Bar, Middle Temple 1947, Ont. 1947, Alta. 1950; cr. Q.C. 1964; served with R.C.A.F. as Pilot 1941-45; seconded to RAF 1942-44 in N. Africa, Sicily and Italy; Mentioned in Despatches 1942; Past Pres., Alta. Div.; Candn. Arthritis Soc.; Past President, Edmonton Art Gallery; past Pres., Citadel Theatre; Chancellor, Anglican Diocese of Edmonton; mem., Middle Temple; Law Soc. Alta.; Law Soc. Upper Can.; Candn. Bar Assn.; P. Conservative; Anglican; recreations: golf, Clubs: Edmonton; Mayfair Golf & Country: Home: 10241 — 133rd St., Edmonton, Alta. T5N 1Z6; Office: 10040 — 104th St., Edmonton, Alta. T5J 0Z7

MacDOUGALL, Hartland M.; O.C.; banker; b. Montreal, Que., 28 Jan. 1931; s. Hartland Campbell and Dorothy (Molson) MacD.; e. Lower Can. Coll., Montreal, 1937-41; Bishop's Coll. Sch., Lennoxville, Que., 1941-47; LeRosey, Switzerland, 1947-48; McGill Univ., 1949-53; Harvard '74; AMP '76; m. Eve, d. late J. Keith Gordon. M.D., 29 Oct. 1954; children: Keith, Cynthia, Wendy, Willa, Tania; VICE-CHMN., BANKING, BANK OF MONTREAL, since 1981; served present Bank of Montreal, London (Ontario), Vancouver and Calgary; Sr. Vice President, Alberta Div., 1968-69, Ontario Div. 1969-70; Extve. Vice Pres. Toronto 1970-73; Dir., 1974; Extve. Vice Pres. 1973-74; Extve. Vice Pres. and Gen. Mgr., Central Operations 1975-76; Exec. Vice-Pres. and Gen. Mgr., Corp. Banking 1976-81; Founding Chrmn., Heritage Can.; Gov. and past Chrmn., Council for Cdn. Unity; Senator, Stratford Shakespearean Foundation; Gov., Olympic Trust; Dir., Cdn. Soc. for Weismann Inst. of Can.; Empire Club Found.; St. Michael's Hospital; Pres.; Duke of Edinburgh Awards; member, U.B.C. Faculty of Comn. Adv. Council; Trustee, Lester B. Pearson Coll. of the Pacific; winner, first Gabrielle Léger Medal; Awarded Order of Can. 1981; Anglican; recreations: skiing, tennis, farming; Clubs: Vancouver; Vancouver Lawn Tennis & Badminton; Ranchmen's, Calgary Petroleum; Montreal Racket; St. James's; Mt. Royal; Montreal Indoor; Badminton & Racquet; Toronto; York; Queen's; Home: Belfountain, Ont. L0N 1B0; Office: First Canadian Place, Toronto, Ont. M5X 1A1

MACDOUGALL, John William Graham, O.B.E., Q.C.; retired transportation executive; b. Sydney, N.S., 1914; s.

George D. Macdougall; e. Pub. and High Schs., Sydney and New Glasgow, N.S.; Dalhousie Univ., LL.B. 1940; Royal Mil. Coll., Candn. War Staff Course; m. Phyllis C. Stairs, Halifax, N.S., 1941; four s. Alan, Stuart, Drummond; Graham, Chrmn. and Pres', CANAC Consultants Ltd. 1974-77; called to the Bar of Nova Scotia 1941; cr. Q.C. 1958; joined Law Dept. of CN, Montreal, 1946; Regional Counsel, Atlantic Region, Moncton, 1948; Comn. Counsel, System H.Q., 1953; Gen. Solr. 1961; Gen. Counsel 1966; Vice Pres. (Atlantic Region) 1968-71, then Extve. Vice Pres., C.N. Railways 1971-77; Dir., TNT Can. Inc.; Montreal Refrigeration & Storage Ltd.; Gov., Dalhousie Univ.; served with Active Militia prior to War; Pictou Highlanders, rank Lt., 1940-42; apptd. Bgde. Intelligence Offr., 4 Candn. Armoured Bgde.; served in Eng., France, Belgium, Holland and Germany as Intelligence Staff Offr.; held appt. of Chief Counter Intelligence Staff Offr., H.Q. 1st Candn. Army with rank Lt. Col. at end of War; mem. Candn. Bar Assn.; N.S. Barristers' Soc.; Presbyterian; Clubs: University (Montreal); Royal Montreal Golf; Home: 1030 Churchill Rd., Town of Mount Royal, Que. H3R 3B6

MacEACHEN, Hon. Allan J., P.C. .(Can.), M.P., M.A., LL.D.; b. Inverness, N.S., 6 July 1921; s. Angus and Annie (Gillis) M.; e. St. Francis Xavier Univ., B.A. 1944; Univ. of Toronto, M.A. 1946 (Pol. Econ.); Univ. of Chicago (Econ.) 1948; Mass. Inst. Tech., Dept. Econ. and Social Science, 1951-1953; Hon. degrees; St. Francis Xavier, Acadia Univ., Loyola Coll. (Baltimore); LL.D. (Hon.), St. Marys Univ. 1973; Dalhousie Univ. 1974; Sir Wilfrid Laurier 1976; Deputy Leader of the Opposition and Opposition House Leader; 1979 DEPUTY PRIME MINISTER and MINISTER of FINANCE 1980- ; Prof. of Econ., St. Francis Xavier Univ., 1946-48 and subsequently Head, Dept. of Economics and Social Sciences; el. to H. of C. for Inverness-Richmond (now Cape Breton Highland,-Canso), g.e. 1953; re-el. g.e. 1957; def. g.e. 1958; apptd. Special Asst. and Consultant on Econ. Affairs to Hon. Lester Pearson, 1958; re-el. g.e. 1962 and since; Min. of Labour, 1963-65; Min. of Nat. Health & Welfare, 1965-68 (also Govt. House Leader 1967-68); Manpower and Immigration 1968-70; Pres. Privy Council and Govt. House Leader 1970-74; Secy. of State for Exteral Affairs 1974-76; Pres. Privy Council 1976-77; Deputy Prime Minister and Pres. Privy Council 1977-79; Depy. Leader of the Opposition and Opposition House Leader, 1979; Liberal; Roman Catholic; Home: R.R. 1, Whycocomagh, N.S.; Office: Parliament Bldgs., Ottawa, Ont.

MacEWAN, Douglas William, M.D., C.M.; radiologist; educator; b. Ottawa, Ont. 11 Nov. 1924; s. James Urquhart and Eleanor (Smith) MacE.; e. McGill Univ. B.Sc. 1948, M.D., C.M. 1952, Dipl. in Radiology 1958; m. Elizabeth d. Allan Turner Bone, Montreal, Que. 23 June 1951; children: Joanne, Elspeth, Eleanor, James; PROF. AND CHRMN. OF RADIOLOGY, UNIV. OF MAN. HEALTH SCIENCES CENTRE; served with RCAF 1943-45; Overseas Service in Coastal Command, rank Flying Offr.; rec'd Queen's Silver Jubilee Medal 1977; former Ed. 'Journal of the Canadian Association of Radiologists'; author over 40 scient. articles in field of Radiology; Chmn. of Bd., Radiol. Soc. N. Am.; Past Pres. Candn. Assn. Radiols.; Soc. Chrmn. Acad. Radiol. Depts.; United Church; recreations: sailing, skiing, curling; Club: Winnipeg Winter; Home: 30 Aldershot Blvd., Winnipeg, Man. R3P 0C8; Office: 700 William Ave., Winnipeg, Man. R3E 0Z3.

MacEWAN, Hon. John Walter Grant, B.S.A., M.Sc., LL.D. (Hon.); agriculturist; historian. Brandon, Man., 12 Aug. 1902; s. Alexander and Bertha (Grant) M.; e. Ont. Agric. Coll., B.S.A. 1926; Iowa State Coll., M.Sc. 1928; LL.D. (Hon.), Univ. of Alta. 1966; Calgary 1967; Brandon 1969; Guelph 1972; Sask. 1974; m. Phyllis, d. Vernon Cline, 1935; one d., Heather; Leader of Liberal Party in Alta., 1958-60; Mayor of Calgary, 1963-65; former M.L.A.

for Calgary; Lt. Governor of Alberta 1965-74; former Chairman, Calgary Community Foundation; former Dean, Faculty of Agric. & Home Econ., Univ. of Manitoba; co-author, "Candn. Animal Husbandry", 1936; "General Agriculture", 1939; author of "Breeds of Farm Livestock in Canada", 1941; "Feeding of Farm Animals", 1945; "Sodbusters", 1948; "Agriculture on Parade", "Between the Red and the Rockies", "Eye Opener Bob", 1957; "Fifty Mighty Men", 1958; "Calgary Cavalcade", 1958; "John Ware's Cow Country" 1960; "Blazing the Old Cattle Trails" 1962; "Entrusted to my Care" 1963; "Hoofprints & Hitchingposts" 1964; "Poking into Politics" 1965; "Tatanga Mani" 1966; "Harvest of Bread" 1967; "West to the Sea" 1968; "Portrait from the Plains" 1969; "Sitting Bull" 1973; "Power for Prairie Plows" 1972; "Battle for the Bay" 1975; "Mighty Women Too" 1975; "Memory Meadows" 1976; "Cornerstone Colony" 1977; "The Rhyming Horsemen of The Qu'Appelle" 1978; "Pat Burns, Cattle King" 1979; "Illustrated History of Western Canadian Agriculture" 1980; Métis Makers of History, 1981; recreation: equestrian activities; Home: 132 Hallbrook Dr. S.W., Calgary, Alta. T2V 3H6

MacEWEN, Gwendolyn; writer; b. Toronto, Ont., 1 Sept. 1941; d. Alick James and Elsie Doris (Mitchell) McE.; e. W. Tech. High Sch., Toronto, 1955-59; began writing career at age 18; engaged in temp. work in children's lib. until 1964; gave numerous pub. readings of her poetry at schs. and univs.; working knowledge of Greek and Arabic; travelled to Israel 1962, Egypt 1966, and Greece 1971 and 1976; author of numerous radio plays, verse drama, occasional pub. talk programs; rec'ord, CBC — OISE, 1969; LP record "Open Secrets", CBC; rec'd Can. Council Grants 1978 and 1981; CBC New Candn. Writing Contest, 1965; Gov. Gen.'s Lit. Award (poetry) for 1969 ("The Shadow Maker"): A. J. M. Smith Award 1973; author: "The Drunken Clock", 1961; "Julian the Magician" (novel), 1963; "The Rising Fire", (poetry) 1963; "A Breakfast for Barbarians", 1966; "The Shadow Maker". 1969; "King of Egypt, King of Dreams" (novel) 1971; "The Armies of the Moon" (poetry) 1972; "Noman" (short stories) 1972; "Magic Animals" (selected poems) 1974; "The Fire Eaters" (poetry) 1976; "Mermaid, and Ikons, A Greek Summer" (travel) 1978. "The Trojan Women" (play) 1978;

MacEWEN, Heber Ralph, Q.C., B.A.; b. P.E.I., 28 Feb. 1917; s' Bruce Walter and Eva (Webster) M.; e. Public Sch. and Prince of Wales Coll., P.E.I.; Mount Allison Acad., Sackville, N.B.; Mount Allison Univ., B.A. 1942; Osgoode Hall Law Sch., Toronto, Ont.; m. Leona, d. William Fleming, 7 Aug. 1960; one s. Bruce; SR. PARTNER, BORDEN & ELLIOT, since 1959; Dir., BESK Properties Ltd.; Pub. Sch. Teacher, 1935-36; read law witb present Co., 1945; called to Bar of Ont., 1945; cr. Q.C. 1964; mem., Candn. Bar Assn.; Co. York Law Assn.; Hon. mem., Big Brother Movement (Past Chrmn., Volunteer Comte.); Un. Church; recreations: curling, fishing, golf; Club: Scarborough Golf & Country; Home: 87 Parkview Hill Crescent, Toronto, Ont. M4B 1R3; Office: 250 University Ave., Toronto, Ont. M5H 3E5

MacFADYEN, Donald John, B.A., M.D., M.Sc., F.R.C.P.(C); neurologist; educator; b. Eden, Man. 27 March 1929; s. Donald Cecil and Margaret (Buck) M.; e. Kerrobert (Sask.) Pub. Sch. 1940; Maple Creek (Sask.) Pub. and High Sch. 1946; Univ. of Sask. B.A. 1949, M.Sc. (Neuropathol.) 1961; Univ. of Toronto M.D. 1953; Harvard Univ. Neurol. Service, Boston City Hosp. 1961-63; m. Frances Avery d. late J. W. Hagerman 3 Sept. 1951; children: Donald Roderick, Mary Katherine, Margot Jean, Mark Andrew; PROF. AND HEAD OF CLIN. NEUROL. SCIENCES UNIV. OF SASK. AND UNIV. HOSP. since 1977; Asst. Dean, Post Graduate Clinical Education, 1981- ; Asst. Prof. of Med. Univ. of Sask. 1963-65; Assoc. Prof. of Med. and Head, Div. of Neurol. Univ. of B.C.

and Vancouver Gen. Hosp. 1965-73, Prof. and Head of Div. 1973-77; Visiting Specialist, Care-Medico Program, Kabul, Afghanistan 1975; Chrmn. Med. Adv. Bd. Vancouver Gen. Hosp. 1972-74; Fellow, Am. Acad. Neurol.; Candn. Soc. EEG & Neurophysiol.; mem. Candn. Med. Assn.; Sask. Coll. Phys. & Surgs.; Sask. Med. Assn.; Candn. Neurol. Soc.; Freemason; Protestant; recreations: skiing, swimming, sailing; Home: 211 Poplar Cres., Saskatoon, Sask. S7M 0A8; Office: University Hospital, Saskatoon, Sask. S7N 0W8.

MACFARLANE, Hon. Alan Brock; judge; b. Victoria, B.C., 17 May 1924; s. late Justice Arthur Douglas and Myrtle Barnard (Sargison) M.; e. Oak Bay (B.C.) High Sch.; Victoria Coll.; Univ. of B.C., LL.B. 1949; m. Sheila Frances, d. late Frank Strachan, 22 Dec. 1945; JUSTICE, SUPREME COURT OF B.C., since 1968; called to Bar of B.C. 1949; Partner, Clay & Macfarlane, Victoria, 1949-51; Sr. Partner, Clay Macfarlane Ellis & Popham, 1951-68; served with RCAF 1943-45; rank Flying Offr. (Pilot); el. M.L.A. for Oak Bay in B.C. g.e. 1960, 1963 and 1966; resigned to accept present appt.; Dir. and Past Pres., YM-YWCA of Victoria; Past Pres., Victoria Bar Assn. (1965-66); mem., Candn. Bar Assn.; Anglican; recreations: boating, swimming, sailing, fishing, golf; Clubs: Union (Dir.); Victoria Golf (Dir.); Home: Apt. 301, 2148 W. 38th, Vancouver, B.C. V6M 1R9; Office: Law Courts, 800 W. Georgia St., Vancouver, B.C. V6C 1P6

MacFARLANE, Andrew, B.A., M.L.S., K.L.J.; b. Toronto, Ont., 18 Feb. 1928; s. late Joseph A., M.D. and late Marguerite (Walker) MacF.; e. Whitney Pub. Sch., Toronto; Univ. of Toronto Schs.; Univ. of Sask.; Univ. of Toronto, B.A. 1949; Univ. of Western Ont. M.L.S. 1977; m. Betty Doris Seldon; two d. by previous marriage, Jeanie Andreas, Catriona Flora; with Canadian Press, Toronto 1949; Reporter, "Halifax Mail-Star", 1950; City Ed., "Halifax Chronicle Herald", 1951; Reporter, "Scottish Daily Express", 1951-52; Sub-ed., "London Evening Standard", 1953-54; joined 'The Telegram" as Copy Ed., Toronto, 1955; subsequently held positions of Night Ed., Feature Ed., Gen. Reporter, Daily Columnist, Asst. to Publisher, Mang. Ed. and Extve. Ed.; joined Ont. govt. 1971; Dir., Citizens Inquiry Branch, Govt. Services until 1973, since when Prof. & Dean, Sch. of Journ., Faculty Grad. Studies, Univ. Western Ont. 1973-80; Prof. of Journalism, Univ. of Western Ont., 1981- ; rec'd National Newspaper Awards for Staff Corr. 1958 and Spot News Reporting 1959; Bowater Award, Commonwealth and Internat. Writing, 1960 Southam Fellowship 1961; Former Dir., Children's Aid Soc. Metrop. Toronto; Founder-Dir., Candn. Medic-Alert Foundation; mem. and former dir.,Candn. Mang. Eds.' Conf.; Founding Dir. and later Pres. and Trustee Candn. Nat. Magazine Awards; Chrmn., Advisory Council, Ont., Medal for Good Citizenship; recreations: horseback riding, baking, bagpipingphy, walking; Clubs: University (London); Toronto Press; London City Press; Royal Candn. Mil. Inst.; Home: 257 Bernard Ave., London, Ont.; Office: School of Journalism, Middlesex Coll., University of Western Ont., London, Ont.

MACFARLANE, Donald A., B.Comm., C.A.; executive; e. Univ. of Toronto B.Comm. 1945; C.A. 1949; PRES. AND TREAS., CONSOLIDATED RAMBLER MINES LTD.; prior to joining present co. Treas. Brunswick Mining & Smelting Corp. Ltd., becoming Secy. & Treas. Atlantic Coast Copper Corp. Ltd., First Maritime Mining Corp. Ltd., Key Anacon Mines Ltd. and Northern Canada Mines Ltd.; articled with Clarkson Gordon; Home: 114 Park Dr., Saint John, N.B. E2H 1A8; Office: (P.O. Box 937) Saint John, N.B. E2L 4E3

MacFARLANE, J. Douglas, M.B.E.; journalist; educator; b. Ottawa, Ont., 4 Oct. 1916; s. late Rev. James Phee and Annie Georgina (Nelson) M; e. Albert Coll., Belleville,

Ont. (Grad.); m. Kathleen Kendrick, Chatham, Ont., 1940; VICE-PRES. COMMUNICATIONS, A.E. LEPAGE LTD.; Dir., United Press Can.; entered newspaper work as a Reporter with the Windsor "Star" in 1934; Reporter, Toronto "Star", 1940-41; enlisted with Candn. Inf., Commissioned in Essex Scottish, 1942; Overseas 1943; Editor of Candn. Army newspaper "Maple Leaf", 1944-45; joined staff of Toronto "Globe & Mail", 1946 and apptd. City Ed. same yr.; apptd. City Ed. of 'The Telegram", 1 Jan. 1949, Asst. Mang. Ed., June 1951, Mang. Ed., Dec. 1952, Vice-Pres. and Extve. Ed. 1954, Vice-Pres. and Editor-in-Chief 1960-69; Chrmn., Dept. of Journalism, Ryerson Polytech. Inst., 1971-76; Ed. Dir., Toronto Sun 1976-81; Clubs: National; Mississaugua Golf; Home: 1945 Mississauga Rd., Mississauga, Ont. L5H 2K5; Office: 33rd floor, T-D Tower, King St. W., Toronto, Ont. M5K 1G8

MacGILLIVRAY, Cameron Knox, F.C.A., b. Chatham, Ont., 18 Mar. 1905; s. Rev. Angus Hector, M.A., and Lily Johanna (Cameron) M.; e. Hamilton (Ont.) Coll. Inst. (Grad. 1924); admitted mem., Inst. Chart. Accts. Ont., 1929 and el. a Fellow 1953 (for "distinguished service to the prof."); m. Marion Laura, d. late W. J. Lynn, Owen Sound, Ont. 14 Oct. 1933; children: Alan Lynn, Ann Marion, John Cameron; Extve. Dir., The Hamilton Foundation; formerly Sr. Partner, MacGillivray & Co.; former mem. Public Accts. Council of Ontario (Pres. 1961-62); former mem., Bd. of Govs., Candn. Tax Foundation; former mem., Council of Ont. Inst. C.A.'s; Past Pres., Men's Canadian Club, Hamilton, Ont.; United Nations Assn. (Hamilton Br.); Past Treas., Royal Hamilton Coll. Music; has contrib. a number of articles to acct. and financial mags.; Freemason; Presbyterian; recreations: travelling, writing, fishing, lawn bowling, photography, reading; Clubs: The Hamilton; Hamilton Thistle (Past Pres.); Hamilton Golf & Country; Home: 114 Mansfield Dr., Ancaster, Ont. L9G 1M7

MACGOWAN, Kenneth Owen, B.Com.; b. New Westminster, B.C., 11 Sept. 1921; s. Keith Campbell and Gertrude Augusta (Rand) M.; e. Herbert Spencer Pub. Sch., Duke of Connaught High Sch.; Univ. of B.C., B.Com. 1946; m. Audrey Marion d., Douglas Churchill, 31 May 1946; children: John D., Patricia E., Peter J., Colleen M.; PRES., KENNETH MACGOWAN HOLDINGS LTD.; since 1967; Dir., Seneca Investments Ltd.; Somac Developing Co. Ltd.; Cairn Investments Ltd.; The K. C. Macgowan Co. Ltd.; North Coast Enterprises Ltd.; Franklin Trout Farm Ltd.; Multiple Sclerosis Soc. of Can.; joined William M. Mercer Ltd., 1946; spent 3 months in Montreal office; returned to Vancouver transferring to Toronto as Asst. Mgr., 1948; Mgr., Vancouver office and apptd. a Dir., 1950; Vice-Pres. (supervising operations for Winnipeg, Calgary and Vancouver offices) 1955; apptd. Mang. Dir. 1966, Pres. 1969; Chrmn. Extve. Comte. of firm and Marsh & McLennan Ltd. 1972; Sr. Vice Pres. Admin., and Secty. (both firms) 1975; served with Coastal Command 1943-45; Past Chrmn., New Westminster Pub. Lib. Bd.; No. 513 Sqdn. Royal Candn. Air Cadets; Pres., New Westminster Chamber Comm. 1968-69; mem. Urban Redevel. Comte. for New Westminster 1965-68; Past Gov., Pacific Nat. Exhn.; Pres. Multiple Sclerosis Soc. of Can. 1977-79; mem. Bd. Trade Metrop. Toronto; Trustee, Franklin Fishing Club; Delta Upsilon; Anglican; recreations: golf, fishing; Clubs: Vancouver Golf; Terminal City; Vancouver (all B.C.); Toronto Hunt; National; Franklin; Home: 926-21 Dale Ave., Toronto, Ont. M4W 1K3; Office: 21 Dale Ave., Ste. 926, Toronto, Ont. M4W 1K3

MacGREGOR, Donald Chalmers, B.A., F.R.S.C. (1954); retired university professor; b. Toronto, Ont., 31 Aug. 1905; s. Alexander, Q.C., and Alice M.; e. Univ. Coll., Univ. of Toronto, B.A. 1928; Harvard Univ. 1929-30; m. Dorothy Rosebrugh, (died April, 1974) 19 Feb. 1938; one surviving s., Duncan Brec m. 2ndly Eleanor Margaret, d. late Rev. Gordon Jones, 16 June 1975; Prof. Of Economics, Univ. Of Toronto, 1953-72; Lect., Asst. and Assoc. Prof., 1931-53; Joint Editor, Bank of Nova Scotia Monthly Review, 1935-39; mem., Research Staff, Royal Comn. on Dom.-Prov. Relations, 1937-38; Guggenheim Fellow, 1943-44; Dir. and co-author of "National Income": A Study Prepared for Royal Comn. on Dom.-Prov. Relations (1939); Jt. Chairman, Ont. Govt. Comte. on Portable Pensions, 1960-62; Vice-Chrmn., Pensions Comn. of Ont. 1963-66; has contrib. many papers to prof. journs.; also submissions for pub. inquiries including studies in taxation (1970) and inflation (1974); collaborator in various works on Candn. econ. problems; Club: Faculty; Address: Univ. of Toronto, Toronto, Ont.

MacGREGOR, John; artist; b. Dorking, Eng., 12 Jan. 1944; s. Wallace Robert and Joan Pearl (Barter) MacG.; came to Can. 1949; e. York Mem. Coll Inst. and Central Tech. Sch., Toronto; m. Melanie Ann Furse; one d. Katherine Olivia; one-man exhns. Hart House, Univ. of Toronto, 1967; The Isaacs Gallery, Toronto, 1968, 70, 71, 72, 73, 74, 75, 77, 79, 81; Chatham Art Gallery 1972; Gallery III Montreal 1973; Gallery Graphics, Ottawa 1975; Time Tunnel Gallery, Windsor, Ont. 1981; other exhibitions including: The Isaacs Gallery, 1966 and (two man) 1967; Art Gallery of Ont. — Ont. Centennial Purchase Exhn. 1967, "The Collector Chooses" 1967 and Candn. Artists '68; McIntosh Gallery, Univ. of W. Ont., 1967; Erindale Coll., Univ. of Toronto, 1968; Winnipeg Show 1968, 70; Montreal Museum of Fine Arts 1968; "Art Sensual", Hart House, Univ. of Toronto 1970; Survey 70, Art Gallery, Ont., and Montreal Museum Fine Arts 1970; "Works on Paper", Inst. Contemp. Art, Boston 1970; 22nd Annual Exhn., Hamilton Art Gallery 1971; "Artario 72", CNE Art Gallery 1972; Musée d'Art Moderne, Yugoslavia 1972; Bienal Am. de Arts Graphica, Columbia 1973; Trajectory, Paris 1973; Art Gallery of Ont., "Contemporary Ontario Art" 1974, "Chairs" 1975; "Burnaby Print Biennial", B.C. 1975; "Six Artists", Art Gallery of Ont. 1978-79; "Twentieth Century Canadian Drawings", 1979; "Old Techniques in New Hands", Harbourfront Art Gallery 1981 and many others; rep. in coll. of Nat. Gallery of Can., Art Gallery of Ont. and in many public and private colls.; rec'd. Can. Council Awards 1967, 68, 69, 70, 71, 72; Sr. Arts Grant 1974, 76; Canada Council Short Ter Grants 1977-79; Ont. Arts Council Grants 1979-81; Winnipeg Biennial Purchase Award 1970; Teacher, Ont. Coll. of Art 1970-71; York Univ. 1971-72; New Sch. 1972-75 (Dir. 1977-78); Hart House, Univ. of Toronto, 1976, 77; Anglican; Studio: 346 Adelaide St. W., Toronto, Ont.; Office: c/o The Isaacs Gallery, 832 Yonge St., Toronto, Ont. M4W 2H1

MacGREGOR, Kenneth Robert, E.D., B.Sc., F.S.A., F.C.I.A.; executive; b. Ottawa, Ont., 21 July 1906; s. Robert and Margaret (Goundrey) M.; e. Lisgar Coll. Inst., Ottawa, Ont.; Queen's Univ., B.Sc. (Hons. Mech. Engn.) 1929; m. Charlotte Jessie, d. late Dr. T. F. Donnelly, 29 June 1935; children: Jayne Ennis, Kenneth Robert; CHRMN., THE MUTUAL LIFE ASSNCE. CO. OF CANADA, since 1973; Dir., Economical Mutual Insurance Company; Missisquoi and Rouville Insurance Co.; Hon. Dir., Canada Trustco Mortgage Co.; Canada Trust Co.; Lecturer, Queen's University, 1929-30; joined Federal Dept. of Ins., Ottawa, 1930; served in Actuarial & Examination Brs. and later in Adm. Br.; Supt. of Ins. (with rank Depy. Min.), 1953-64; Pres. Mutual Life Assurance Co. of Canada 1964; former Vice Pres. and mem. Bd. of Govs., Soc. of Actuaries; served as Major, Gov. Gen's. Foot Guards (1923-45); E. D. 1945; mem., Candn. Bisley Rifle Team. 1926-27-28 (Commandant, 1957); Life Gov., Dom. of Can. Rifle Assn.; Pres., Candn. Life and Health Ins. Assn., 1968-69; Hon. Life mem., Candn. Cancer Soc.; mem. Bd. Trustees, Queen's Univ.; Presbyterian; recreations: rifle shooting, skiing, golf; Clubs: Rideau; Royal Ottawa Golf; Westmount Golf & Country; National; York (Toronto); Balboa (Mexico); Home: 125 John Blvd.,

Waterloo, Ont. N2L 1C4; Office: 227 King St. S., Waterloo, Ont. N2J 4C5

MacGREGOR, Roderick A., B.Sc.; b. New Glasgow, N.S., 10 Aug. 1898; s. Peter A. and Minnie (MacKeen) M.; e. Pub. and High Schs., New Glasgow, N.S.; McGill Univ., B.Sc. 1922; m. Marian, d. George H. Webster, Montreal, P.Q., 1925; children: Mrs. K. Patricia Richardson, James Drummond; Pres. and Mang. Dir., MacGregor Properties Ltd.; Dir. and Past Pres. Nova Scotia Forest Products Assn. (Past Pres.); Past Chrmn. and a Dir., Maritime Lumber Bureau Assn.; Past President, E. Pictou Liberal Assn.; Hon. Prov. Commr., N.S. Boy Scouts Assn.; Pres., Bd. Trustees, New Glasgow Y.M.C.A.; served in 1st World War, enlisting with 2nd McGill Siege Arty. 1917, later 10th Candn. Siege Batty.; Phi Kappa Pi; Presbyterian; Clubs: Scotia; Bluenose Curling; Rotary; Abercrombie Golf; R.N.S.Y.S.; Chester Yacht; Chester Golf; Home: 191 George St., New Glasgow, N.S. B2H 2L1; Office: 114 Provost St., New Glasgow, N.S. B2H 2P4

MacGUIGAN, Hon. Mark R., M.P., M.A., Ph.D., LL.M., J.S.D., LL.D.; b. Charlottetown, P.E.I., 17 Feb. 1931; s. Hon. Mark R. (M.); e. Queen Square Sch.; Prince of Wales Coll., Charlottetown, 1946-49; St. Dunstan's Univ., B.A. 1951; Univ. of Toronto, M.A. 1953, Ph.D. 1957; Osgoode Hall Law Sch. 1954-58; Columbia Univ., LL.M. 1959, J.S.D. 1961; LL.D. Univ. of P.E.I. 1971; St. Thomas Univ., 1981; m. Maryellen, d. James H. Symons, 17 June 1961; children: Ellen, Mark, Thomas; SEC'Y OF STATE FOR EXTERNAL AFFAIRS 1980- ; read law with Hon. Mr. Justice Arthur Kelly, 1956-58; called to Bar of Ont., Sept. 1958; Asst. Prof. of Law, Univ. of Toronto, 1960-63, Assoc. Prof. 1963-66; Visiting Assoc. Prof. of Criminal Law, New York Univ., 1966; Prof. of Law Osgoode Hall Law Sch., 1966-67; Dean, Faculty of Law, Univ. of Windsor, 1967-68; author of "Jurisprudence: Readings and Cases" (2nd Ed. 1966); "Cases and Materials on Creditor's Rights" (2nd Ed. 1967), and many articles in learned journals & press; mem. of Fed. Govt. Special Comte. on Hate Propaganda 1965-66; Adv. to Fed. Govt. Special Counsel on the Constitution 1967-68; Const. Adv. to Gov. of P.E.I. 1968; el. to H. of C. for Windsor-Walkerville in g.e. June 1968; re-elected 1972, 74, 79, 80; Chrmn., Special Comte. on Statutory Instruments 1968-69; Joint Chrmn., Spec. Joint Comte. on Const. of Can. 1970-72; Parliamentary Secty. to Min. of Manpower and Immigration 1972-74; Parliamentary Secty. to Min. of Labour 1974-75; Chrmn., Standing Comte. on Justice and Legal Affairs 1975-79; Chrmn., Sub-Comte. on Penitentiary System in Can. 1976-77; Chrmn., Spec. Joint Comte. on Const. of Can. 1978; Opposition Critic for Sol.-Gen. 1979; recreations: running, skiiing, tennis, swimming; Liberal; Home: 2020 Willistead Cres., Windsor, Ont. N8Y 1K5

MacINNIS, Joseph B., C.M., M.D., F.R.C.G.S.; LL.D. (Hon.); underwater research consultant and scientist; b. Barrie, Ont., 2 March 1937; s. Allistair and Beverley (Saunders) MacI.; e. Univ. of Toronto, M.D. 1962; Univ. of Calgary, LL.D. (Hon.) 1981; PRESIDENT, UNDERSEA RESEARCH LTD.; holds or has held consulting contracts with U.S. Navy; Canadian Government; Smithsonian Institute; IBM; Nat. Geographic; Oceaneering Internat.; Intern, Toronto Gen. Hosp., 1963; Instr. in Pharmacol., Univ. of Pa. (Link Foundation Fellowship), 1964; licensed to practice med. in State of N.Y., 1965; actively engaged in undersea research and diving med. since 1960; life support physician for Man-In-Sea project Phase II sponsored by Edwin A. Link, Nat. Geog. Soc. and Smithsonian Inst., 1964 directed over 75 exper. dives at Ocean Systems' pressure facility, Linde Research Lab., 1965; cert. by U.S. Navy as a Man-In-Sea Aquanaut for Sealab III program; observer at Sealab I and II projects and apptd. Consultant to Sealab III, 1967; Scient. Dir. of 700 ft. dive made from world's 1st lock-out submarine, 1968; has travelled extensively for present Co. carrying out diving research in N.Sea, Grand Banks, Gulf of Mexico, Pacific, Bahamas, Gulf Stream and Caribbean; part of search team for nuclear submarine "U.S.S. Scorpion", 1968; took part in search and salvage of flight wreckage, Caracas, 1969; conceived and constr. "Sublimnos" (Can.'s 1st underwater habitat) to be placed in Georgian Bay for 2 yr. scient. study, 1969; formed James Allister MacInnis Foundation for underwater research and educ. in Can. 1970; led ten scient. diving expeditions to Resolute Bay 600 miles N. of Arctic Circle 1970-74, establishing first ever polar dive stn. "Sub-Igloo" under ice and leading first team diving scientists ever to N. Pole; discovered HMS BREADALBAME, a British barque sunic in 1853 off Beachey Island 1980; guest lectr. at 10 univs. incl. Univs. of Toronto, Pa., Ind. and Calif., Los Angeles; author of "Underwater Images" 1971; "Underwater Man" 1974; "Considerations for a National Ocean Policy" (Candn. govt. report); articles for "Scientific American" and "National Geographic"; over 30 papers on diving med.; contrib. to tech. and popular books incl. "The Ocean Realm" (Nat. Geog. Soc.); appointed Consultant, "Journal fo The American Medical Association". 1966; his underwater photographs have appeared in such publs. as "National Geographic" and "Sports Illustrated"; awarded Gold Medal of Excellence for film "Deep Androsia", Internat. Film Festival, Santa Monica, 1965; his motion pictures have been presented on Candn. and Am. networks; Host, "The New Wave", CBC television series, 1975-76; "The Newfoundlanders; Voices from the Sea", 1978; Fellow, Royal Candn. Geog. Soc.; mem. Order of Can. 1976; mem. Candn. Council on Fitness and Health; "Man-In-Sea Panel", Nat. Academy Engineering, Washington; Canadian Environmental Adv. Council; Candn. and Am. Med. Assns. and 15 other prof. socs.; Address: 178 Balmoral Ave., Toronto, Ont. M4V 1J6

MacINTOSH, Alexander John, Q.C., B.A., LL.B.; b. Stellarton, N.S. 10 July 1921; s. Hugh Ross and Katherine Elizabeth (Stewart) M.; e. Stellarton (N.S.) Pub. and High Schs.; Dalhousie Univ. B.A. 1942, LL.B. 1948 (Gold Medallist in Law); m. Elizabeth Agnes d. late Alexander Allen 5 Apl. 1944; one s. Donald Alexander; PARTNER, BLAKE, CASSELS & GRAYDON; Depy. Gov. Hudson's Bay Co.; Chrmn., Candn. Corporate Management Co.Ltd.; Dir. Canadian Imperial Bank of Commerce; Torstar Corp.; John Labatt Ltd.; Stelco Inc.; Fluor Canada Ltd.; Honeywell Inc.; George Wimpey Canada Ltd.; Simpsons Ltd.; Markborough Properties Ltd.; read law with T. D. MacDonald, Q.C., Depy. Atty.-Gen. of N.S. 1947-48; called to Bar of N.S. 1948, Ont. 1948; cr. Q.C. 1961; served with RCNVR 1942-45, rank Lt.; Trustee, Brock Univ.; Liberal; United Church; recreations: sailing, fishing; Clubs: Toronto; York; Home: 231 Strathallan Wood, Toronto, Ont. M5N 1T5; Office: (P.O. Box 25) Commerce Court West, Toronto, Ont. M5L 1A9.

MacINTOSH, Frank Campbell, Ph.D., LL.D., M.D. (hon.), D.Sc. (honory), F.R.S. (1954), F.R.S.C. (1956); b. Baddeck, N.S., 24 Dec. 1909; s. Rev. Charles Campbell D.D., and Beenie Annabel (Matheson) M.; e. Dalhousie Univ., B.A. 1930, M.A. 1932; McGill Univ., Ph.D. 1937, D. Sc. 1980; LL.D., Alta. 1964, Queen's 1965, Dalhousie 1976; Univ. of Ottawa, M.D. (Hon.) 1974; m. Mary MacLachlan, d. Rev. A. L. MacKay, Pictou, N.S., 14 Dec. 1938; children: Dr. Christine Lejtenyi, Mrs. Barbara Hardt, Dr. Andrew, Mrs. Janet Intscher, Roderick; Prof. Emeritus of Physiology, McGill Univ. since 1980; National Research Council Scholar, 1933-36, and Travelling Fellowship of Royal Soc. of Can., 1937-38; mem. of Scient. Staff, Med. Research Council of Gt. Brit., 1938-49; Joseph Morley Drake Prof. 1949-78; Chrmn., Dept of Physiol., McGill Univ., 1949-65; Treas., Internat. Union Physiol. Sciences 1962-68; mem., various scient. socs.; Ed., Candn. Journ. of Physiol and Pharmacol. 1968-72; Home: 145 Wolseley Ave., Montreal W., P.Q. H4X 1V8

MacINTOSH, Robert M., M.A., Ph.D. L.L.D.; banker, b. Stanstead, Que., 8 Jan. 1923; s. Gordon Leslie and Bernice Isobel (Mallory) McI.; e. McGill Univ., B.A. (Econ. and Pol. Science) 1947, M.A. 1949, Ph.D. 1952; Trinity Coll., Cambridge, post-grad. work, 1949-50; L.L.D., York Univ., 1976; m. Mary Louise, d. Theodore D. Crippen, Great Barrington, Mass., 17 May 1945; children Valerie, Jeffrey; 2ndly, Lynn Higgins Peers, 15 Sept. 1972; children: John, Justine; PRES., THE CANADIAN BANKERS' ASSN. Exec. Vice Pres., The Bank of Nova Scotia, 1972-80; Dir., The Quaker Oats Co. of Can. Ltd.; Chmn., Dominion & Anglo Investment Corp. Ltd.; C.D. Howe Inst.; Invest. Policy Comte., Ont. Mun. Employees Retirement Bd.; Asst. Prof. Econ., Bishop's Univ., Que., 1950-53; Econ., Research Dept., Bank of Nova Scotia, 1953, Investment Dept. 1957; apptd. Supervisor, Investments, 1957; Asst. Gen. Manager, Investments, 1962; Joint General Manager, 1966; Deputy Chief General Manager 1968; served in the 2nd World War with R.C.A., 1943-46; discharged with rank of Lieut.; author of numerous articles in prof. journs.; formerly, Chrmn., Bd. Govs., York Univ.; recreation: tennis, golf; Clubs: National; Queen's; Toronto Lawn Tennis; Office: P.O. Box 282, Toronto Dominion Centre, Toronto Ont., M5K 1K2

MacISAAC, Hon. John A., M.L.A.; politician; b. Inverness, N.S. 23 June 1939; s. John Archie and Dorothy (Kennedy) MacI.; e. New Victoria and Central High Schs. New Waterford; m. Evelyn d. William Chisholm 8 Apl. 1961; children: Heather, Ian, Ross; MIN. OF MUNICIPAL AFFAIRS, N.S. 1979- ; ins. agt.; served with Candn. Army 14 yrs (Militia), 1st and 2nd Btns. N.S. Highlanders, Sydney and New Glasgow; Pipe Maj. 1st Btn. 1965-69; el. M.L.A. for Pictou Centre prov. by-el. 1977, re-el. g.e. 1978; Min. Responsible for Adm. Civil Service Act 1978; Min. of Social Services 1978-79; mem. and Past Pres. New Glasgow Kinsmen; St. Andrew Soc. New Glasgow; Chrmn. Festival of Tartans Soc. 1972; Pres. N.S. Pipers & Pipe Band Assn. 1976; Instr. and Dir. New Glasgow Ceilidh Pipe Band; P. Conservative; R. Catholic; Office: (P.O. Box 216) Maritime Centre, 1505 Barrington St., Halifax, N.S. B3J 1A1.

MACK, Maurice Michael, B.E.; mechanical engineer; b. Montreal, Que., 30 Jan. 1931; s. Michael and Ann M.; e. Montreal High Sch.; McGill Univ., B.E. (Mech. Engn.) 1952; m. Shirley Mae, d. late John Bentley, Toronto, Ont., 18 May 1957; PRESIDENT, EMPIRE MAINTENANCE INC., since 1955; Engr., The Bell Telephone Co. of Can., 1952-53; joined present firm as Partner, 1953; mem., Young Presidents Organization; Corp. Prof. Engrs. Que.; Engn. Inst. Can.; Montreal Bd. Trade; Montreal Advertising & Sales Club; Phi Kappa Pi; Protestant; recreations: golf, squash, fishing, tennis, curling; Clubs: Canadian; Rotary; Boma; Empire, Toronto Bd. of Trade; Toronto Ad and Sales; Summerlea Golf and Country; Home: 17 Cambridge Dr., Baie D'Urfe, Que. H9X 2V5; Office: 180 Montée de Liesse, Montreal, Que. H4T 1N7

MACKASEY, Hon. Bryce, P.C. (1966), M.P., LL.D.; politician; b. Quebec City, Que., 25 Aug. 1927; s. Frank S. and Anne (Glover) M.; e. St. patrick's High Sch., Quebec, Que.; McGill Univ., Sir George Williams Univ., LL.D. 1970; m.; children: Bryan, Brenda, Michael, Susan; President, Air Canada, 1978-79; 1st elected to H. of C. for Verdun, Quebec in g.e. June 1962; apptd. Parlty. Secy. to Min. Nat. Health & Welfare, July 1965; Parlty. Secy. to Min. Labour, Jan. 1966; Min. without Portfolio, Feb. 1968; Min. of Labour, July 1968; Min. of Manpower and Immigration Jan. 1972; Min. of State Without Portfolio June 1974; Postmaster Gen. 1974-76; Min. of Consumer and Corp. Affairs 1976; resigned from Fed. cabinet in Sept. 1976 and resigned seat in H. of C., 27 Oct. 1976; el. to Que. Nat. Assembly for Notre Dame de Grace in g.e. 15 Nov. 1976; defeated in Federal by-election Oct. 1978; re-elected 1980; Delegate to U.N. 1963; Canadian Rep. on visit to the Republic of China 1965; Candn. Del., ILO, Geneva 1969, 1970; Gen. Chrmn., Nat. Tri-partite Conf. on Indust. Relations, Ottawa 1969; Past Chrmn., Nat. Lib. Caucus; Office: House of Commons, Ottawa, Ont.

MACKAY, Donald; journalist author; b. Portaupique, N.S.; 17 July 1925; s. William Glenthorne and Dorothy Agnes (MacRae) M.; e. Dalhousie Univ. (Lit., Pol. Science) 1946; m. Barbara Elizabeth, d. Gordon Fletcher: children: Marina, Karen: Author; "The Lumberjacks"; "Anticosti, The Untamed Island"; "Scotland Farewell, The People of the Hector", 1980; former Gen. Mgr., UPI of Canada Ltd.1970-76; Foreign Corr., London and Lisbon 1950-56, Munich 1957; Chief European Corr., RKO Radio Network (U.S.) 1959; European Mgr., Un. Press International Broadcast Div. 1962; recreations: sailing, skiing, hiking;

MACKAY, Douglas C., B.Com.; stockbroker; e. Dalhousie Univ. B.Com. 1953; VICE CHRMN., MEM. EXTVE. COMTE. AND DIR., PITFIELD MACKAY ROSS LTD.; Home: 29 Riverview Dr., Toronto, Ont. M4N 3C6; Office: (P.O. Box 54) Royal Bank Plaza, Toronto, Ont. M5J 2K5.

MacKAY, Hon. Elmer MacIntosh, M.P., Q.C., B.A., LL.B.; farmer; politician; lumberman; lawyer; b. Hopewell, N.S. 5 Aug. 1936; s. Gordon and Laura (MacIntosh) MacK.; e. Stellarton (N.S.) High Sch.; Acadia Univ. B.A. 1956; Dalhousie Univ. LL.B. 1959; m. 1stly 15 July 1961; children: Cethlyn Laura, Peter Gordon, Sheila Mary Louise, Andrew; m. 2ndly Laura d. Adrian MacAulay, Pictou, N.S. 17 July 1974; one d. Rebecca; Min. of Regional Econ. Expansion and Min. responsible for Central Mortgage & Housing Corp. 1979-80; called to Bar of N.S. 1960; prior to entering politics practiced law in Pictou Co., N.S.; founded law firm MacKay, White, Stroud & Langley, New Glasgow, N.S.; 1st. el. to H. of C. by-el. 1971, re-el. since; P. Conservative; Presbyterian; Home: R.R. 1, Hopewell, Pictou Co., N.S. B0K 1C0; Office: House of Commons, Ottawa, Ont. K1A 0A6.

MacKAY, Harold Hugh, Q.C., B.A., LL.B.; lawyer; b. Regina, Sask. 1 Aug. 1940; s. John Royden and Grace Madeleine (Irwin) MacK.; e. Weyburn (Sask.) High Sch. 1957; Univ. of Sask. B.A. 1960; Dalhousie Univ. LL.B. 1963; m. Jean Elizabeth d. James H. Hutchison, Sarnia, Ont. 27 Dec. 1963; children: Carol Anne, Donald Malcolm; PARTNER, MacPHERSON, LESLIE & TYERMAN 1976- ; Chrmn., Federal Business Development Bank; Secy., Interprovincial Steel and Pipe Corp. Ltd. (Vice Pres. 1975-76); Dir. Uranerz Exploration and Mining Ltd.; Ranch Ehrlo Soc. ; Gov., Donner Candn. Foundation; called to Bar of Sask. 1964; cr. Q.C. 1981; Assoc., MacPherson, Leslie & Tyerman 1963-69, Partner 1969-75, 1976- ; mem. Candn. Bar Assn.; Law Soc. Sask.; Phi Delta Theta; Liberal; United Church; Office: 2161 Scarth St., Regina, Sask. S4P 2V4.

MACKAY, Hugh Hazen; Company executive; b. Saint John, N.B., 6 Aug. 1915; s. late Hugh and Kate E. (Hazen) M.; e. Rothesay Coll. Sch., N.B.; Royal Mil. Coll., Kingston, Ont.; m. Geraldine, d. late C. S. Hanson, Montreal, P.Q., 1944; children: Sheila Charles, Frances; DIRECTOR DUCKS UNLIMITED (Can.); Vice Pres., Maritime Beverages; Dir., Can. Permanent Mortgage Co.; Can. Permanent Trust; 20 King St. Corp. Limited; McChip Resources Inc.; Maritime Beverages Limited; Great Pacific Industries Ltd.; Gold Circle Insurance Co. Ltd.; Jr. Clerk, Bank of Nova Scotia, Saint John, N.B., 1933-39; joined W. C. Pitfield & Co. Ltd. and Hugh Mackay & Co., 1945; admitted to Partnership of Hugh Mackay & Co., Saint John, N.B., and apptd. Resident Partner, 1947; subsequently trans. to Montreal, 1949 and to Toronto, 1951; P. Conservative; Anglican; Clubs: Union (Saint John); Parr Town (Saint John); The Toronto; Rosedale Golf; Home: (Box 280) Rothesay, N.B. E0G

2W0; Office: Suite 1200, One Brunswick Sq., Saint John, N.B. EZ2 4V1

MACKAY, John A. H.; Canadian public servant; b. Hankow, Hupeh, China, 27 Sept. 1928; s. John and Alys (Aiken) M.; e. Henley (Eng.) Tutorial Coll., 1947; Royal Tech. Coll., Manchester, Eng., Nat. Cert. Elect. Engn. 1952; McMaster Univ., (Cert. Indust. Mang.) 1957; m. Joan P., d. Lewis Hamer, 12 May 1951; children: Alyson, Anne; DEPY MINISTER OF PUBLIC WORKS CANADA since Jan. 1977; interned as civilian in Japanese camp 1942-45; Student, Elect. Engn., Metropolitan Vickers, Manchester, Eng., 1947-52; Candn. Westinghouse Co., Production Supt., Motor Div., 1952-60; Pres., ITT Canada Ltd. 1961-69; Deputy Post Master Gen., Can. 1970; mem., Am. Inst. Indust. Engrs.; Candn. Indust. Management Assn.; recreations: tennis, photography, curling; Home: 722 Echo Dr., Ottawa, Ont. K1S 1P3; Office: Sir Charles Tupper Bldg., Ottawa, Ont. K1A 0M2

MACKAY, (John) Ross, O.C., M.A., Ph.D., D.Geog., D.Env. Studies, F.R.S.C.; professor emeritus; b. Formosa, 31 Dec. 1915; s. Rev. George William, M.A., D.D., and Jean (Ross) M.; e. Clark Univ., B.A. 1939; Boston Univ., M.A. 1941; Univ. of Montreal, Ph.D. 1949; Univ. of Ottawa, D.Geog.; Univ. of Waterloo, D.Env. Studies; m. Violet Anne, d. J. C. Meekins, China Lake, Cal., 19 Feb. 1944; children: Margaret Anne, Leslie Isabel; Prof. Emeritus of Geography, Univ. of British Columbia; Asst. Prof., Dept. of Geog., McGill Univ., 1946-49; served in 2nd World War; Pte. to Major, Candn. Intelligence Corps, 1941-46; Publications: "The Anderson River Map-Area, N.W.T.", 1958; "The Mackenzie Delta Area, N.W.T.", 1963; numerous articles in scient. journs. on permafrost and cartography; rec'd. Massey Medal, Roy. Candn. Geog. Soc.; Miller Medal, Roy. Soc. Can.; Biely Faculty Research Prize, U.B.C.; Kirk Bryon Award, Geol. Soc. Amer.; Officer, Order of Can.; Hon. mem., Geog. Soc. U.S.S.R.; Fellow, Geol. Soc. of Am.; Fellow, Arctic Inst. N. Am. (Past Chrmn., Bd. of Govs., Outstanding Fellow Award); Past Pres., Candn. Assn. Geographers and Assn. Am. Geographers; Vice-Pres., Int'l. Geog. Union; Phi Beta Kappa; Presbyterian; recreations: camping, ornithology; Home: 4014 W. 37th Ave., Vancouver, B.C. V6N 2W7

MacKAY, John Stuart; broadcasting executive; b. Saskatoon, Sask., 26 May 1918; s. Edward Ewen and Margaret Winifred (Webb) M.; e. Pub. and High Schs., Lethbridge, Alta. and New Westminster, B.C.; m. Patricia Marilyn, d. G. T. Cunningham, Vancouver, B.C., 4 Sept. 1946; one s. Edward Stuart, twin d. Joanne Beverley, Barbara Joyce; PRESIDENT AND DIRECTOR, SELKIRK COMMUNICATIONS LTD. since 1965; Chrmn. and Dir, All-Canada Radio & Television Ltd.; Selkirk Communications Inc.; Fla.; Selkirk Films Ltd.; Dir. Niagara Television Ltd.; B.C. Broadcasting Co. Ltd.; Northern Broadcasting Co. Ltd.; Quality Records; Greater Winnipeg Cablevision Ltd.; Ottawa Cablevision Ltd.; Tocom Inc., U.S.A.; Tocom Can. Ltd.; Calgary Broadcasting Co. Ltd.; Island Broadcasting Co. Ltd.; Selkirk Communications Ltd., Eng.; Can. Satellite Communications Inc.; started in radio in 1937 as an Announcer at CJCA Edmonton; became Production Mgr. at CKRC Winnipeg; moved to Radio Stn. CKWX in Vancouver in 1940 as Chief Announcer, later Production Mgr., then Asst. Mgr.; in 1948 became Mgr. of CKRM Regina, 6 months later joined All-Canada Radio and Television Ltd. as Gen. Mgr.; Pres. 1959; Co. purchased by Selkirk Holdings Ltd. in 1965; mem., Candn. Assn. of Broadcasters; Metrop. Educ. Television Assn. of Toronto (Dir.); Pres. Canadian-Scottish Philharmonic Foundation; recreations: fishing, golf, swimming; Clubs: National; Granite; Canadian (N.Y.); Home: 17 Douglas Drive, Toronto, Ont. M4W 2B2; Office: 2 Bloor St. W., Toronto, Ont. M4W 3L7

MACKAY, Hon. Kenneth Charles, M.C.L.; judge; b. Montreal, Que., 29 Sept. 1920; s. Dr. Frederick H. and Marion Ferguson (Crowell) M.; e. St. Albans Sch., Brockville. Ont.; McGill Univ., B.C.L. 1950; M.C.L. 1951; two s., Charles, Iain; JUDGE OF SUPERIOR COURT, QUE., since 1969; read law with Hon. F. P. Brais, Q.C.; called to Bar of Que. 1950; cr. Q.C. 1965; Secy., Bar of Montreal, 1956-57; Dir., Legal Aid Bureau of Bar, 1956-61; Crown Atty., Dist. of Montreal, 1960-65; mem. Bar Examiners Comte., Bar of Que., 1964-67; Mun. Judge, Town of Hampstead, 1965-69; Lectr., Faculty of Law, McGill Univ., 1961-69; served as Comn. Counsel for numerous shipping casualty inquiries, 1965-69; formerly Partner, Paré, Mackay, Barbeau, Holden & Steinberg; Vice Pres., 1966-69, Que. Conf. Mun. Judges; mem. Council, Candn. Bar Assn., 1963-65, Chrmn., Maritime Law Sec. 1963-65; served with 1st Medium Batty., RCA, 1939-40; 1st Bn. Victoria Rifles of Can., 1940-42; No. 424 Sqdn., 6 Bomber Command RCAF (Overseas) 1942-45; rank Flight Sgt. Air Gunner; Hon. Col. 78th Fraser Highlanders; Compagnon, Fed. Nat. des Combattants Voluntaires Alliées; Lib. Cand. for N.D.G. Montreal in g.e. 1958; Vice Pres., Que. Lib. Fed. 1960-63; Dir., Reform Club. 1964-69; mem., Nat. Policy Comte., Lib. Party of Can., 1961; Gov., Candn. Corps of Commisioners (Que. Div.); Mackay Centre for Deaf and Crippled Children; Queen Elizabeth Hospital; Spera Foundation, Trafalgar Sch.; Dir., Knights Hospitaller Foundation, Montreal Military and Maritime Museum; mem., Jacques Viger Comn. for Old Montreal; Greater Montreal Arts Council; Past President, St. Andrews Society Montreal; N.D.G. Community Council Inc.; Past Vice-Pres., Montreal Parks and Playgrounds Assn.; Montreal Advocates Benevolent Assn.; Hon. mem. Candn. Maritime Law Assn.; Life mem. Caledonian Society of Montreal; Kt. of St. Lazarus of Jerusalem; mem., Internat. Comn. Jurists; Candn. Tax Foundation; Candn. Bar Assn.; Royal Canadian Legion (Pres. No. 1 Br.); Presb.; Clubs: University; Hillside Tennis; Homes: 3940 Côte des Neiges, Montreal, Que. and Glen Roy Farm, New London, P.E.I.; Office: Court House, Montreal, Que.

MacKAY, Robert deWolfe, Q.C., M.A., B.C.L.; b. Winnipeg, Man.; e. St. John's Coll., Winnipeg, Man.; Lower Can. Coll., Montreal, Que.; McGill Univ.; m. Mary Agnes de Lotbiniere, 1936 (deceased); children: Robert Alain, Peter Andrew, Margaret Diana, Mary Agnes; CHRMN., PHARMA-INVESTMENT LTD.; Past Chairman, Canadian Tax Foundation; Dir., TIW Industries Ltd.; called to the Bar of Que. 1932, cr. K.C. 1949; former Lectr. in Eng. Lit., McGill Univ.; Clubs: Mount Royal; St. James's; Mount Bruno Country; Rideau (Ottawa); Home: 3520 Ave du Musée, Montreal, Que. H3G 2C7; Office: Room 3411, 1 Place Ville Marie, Montreal, Que. H3B 3N7

MacKAY, Shane, B.A.; mining consultant; b. Ottawa, Ont., 21 May 1926; s. late Alice (Higgins) and the late Douglas D.; e. St. John's Ravenscourt Sch., Winnipeg, Man. (1933-42); Univ. of Manitoba, B.A. 1946; Harvard Univ. (Nieman Fellow, 1951-52); m. Shirley, d. Charles S. McDiarmid, Winnipeg, Man., 25 Sept. 1948; children: Douglas Charles, Sheila Athol (Brownscombe), Leslie Elizabeth (chalke); CONSULTANT, INCO LTD: 1980- ; Reporter, Winnipeg "Tribune" 1942; with The Canadian Press, Winnipeg and Ottawa Bureaux, 1946-47; joined Winnipeg "Free Press" as Leg. Corr. in 1948, and their Parlty. Corr.; Press Gallery, Ottawa, 1952-53, and Washington Corr., 1953-54; Mang. Ed., Reader's Digest Assn. (Can.) Ltd., Montreal, P.Q., 1954-59; Extve. Ed., Winnipeg Free Press, 1959-69 when apptd. Dir. of Public Affairs of present Co.; Vice Pres. 1972; Regional Vice Pres., 1976-80; first Candn. newspaperman to be awarded Nieman Foundation Fellowship, Harvard Univ.; Candn. Del., Commonwealth Press Union Conf., India-Pakistan, 1961; mem., Govt. Investigating Comte. on Hate Propaganda, 1965; with R.C.A.F. 1943-44; Liberal; Zeta Psi; Clubs: National (Toronto); Manitoba (Winnipeg); Homes:

700-245 Wellington Cresc., Winnipeg Man., R3M 0A1; 446 Pine Villa Dr., Atlantis, Fla. 33462; Office: 1705-155 Carlton St., Winnipeg R3C 3H8

MacKAY, William Andrew, Q.C. (1973), B.A., LL.M., LL.D.; university administrator; b. Halifax, N.S., 20 March 1929; s. Robert Alexander and Mary Kathleen (Junkin) M.; e. Public Schs., Halifax, N.S. and Ottawa, Ont.; Dalhousie Univ., B.A. 1950, LL.B. 1953, LL.M. 1954; Harvard Univ., Ford Foundation Fellowship for grad. study by law teachers 1960-61, LL.M. 1970, LL.D., Memorial Univ. 1976; m. Alexa Eaton, d. L. M. Wright, Riverside, N.S., 7 July 1954; one d. Margaret Kathleen; Vice-Pres., Dalhousie Univ., 1969, Pres. and Vice Chanc., 1980; Chrmn., N.S. Human Rights Comm. since 1968; Foreign Service Offr. 1, 2, Dept. of External Affairs, Ottawa, 1954-57; Asst. Secy., Royal Comn. on Canada's Econ. Prospects, Ottawa, 1955-57; joined staff of Dalhousie Law Sch. as Asst. Prof., 1957; Assoc. Prof. 1959-61, Prof. 1961; George Munro Prof. of Constit. Law, 1963; Dean and Weldon Prof. of Law 1964-69; served in C.O.T.C., Lieut. R.C.I.C. (Contingent Reserve); read law with Stewart, Smith & MacKeen, Halifax, N.S.; called to the Bar of N.S. 1954; mem., Soc. of Public Teachers of Law; Candn. Inst. Internat. Affairs; N.S. Barristers' Soc.; Candn. Bar Assn.; Assn. of Candn. Law Teachers (Pres. 1964-65); mem. Conf. of Gov. Bodies Legal Prof. in Can. (Pres. 1969-70); Dir., Halifax YMCA 1961-64; Bd. of Gov., Ambrae Academy, since 1976 (chrmn. 1977-80); Trustee, BM-RT Realty Investments; United Church; Clubs: Halifax; Saraguay; Rotary; Home: 1460 Oxford St., Halifax, N.S. B3H 3Y8

MacKEIGAN, Hon. Ian Malcolm, Q.C., M.A., LL.D.; b. Saint John, N.B., 11 April 1915; s. late Rev. John A. and Mabel (McAvity) M.; e. Moose Jaw, Sask. High Sch.; Univ. of Sask.; Dalhousie Univ. B.A. (Great Distinction) 1934, M.A. 1935, LL.B. 1938, LL.D. (Hon. Causa) 1975; Univ. of Toronto, M.A. (Public Adm.) 1939; m. Jean C., d. John D. Geddes, Halifax, N.S. 30 May 1942; children: John, Robert, Janet; CHIEF JUSTICE OF NOVA SCOTIA and Appeal Div. Supreme Court of N.S. since 1973; admitted to N.S. Bar 1939, to P.E.I. Bar 1970; practised law with Rutledge, MacKeigan, Cox & Downie (and predecessor firms) 1950-73; created Queen's Counsellor (N.S.), 1954; Depy, Enforcement Adm., W.T.P.B. and Depy, Comnr., Combines Investig. Comn. Ottawa 1940-50; Dir. John Labatt Ltd.; Gulf Oil Can. Ltd.; and other companies prior to 1974; Chrmn. Atlantic Devel. Bd. (Fed. Govt.) 1963-69; mem. Econ. Council of Can. 1965-71; Chrmn. Atlantic Research Centre for Mental Retardation 1968-73; Comnr. Victoria Gen. Hosp. 1970-73; Pres. N.S. Barristers Soc. 1960-61; Vice-Pres. Candn. Bar Assn. N.S. 1962-64; mem. Nat. Extve. Candn. Bar Assn. 1969-71; Pres., N.S. Div., Candn. Red Cross 1953-55; Gov. Candn. Tax Foundation 1963-64; Candn. Welfare Council 1961-64; Dir. N.S. Research Foundation 1970-73; Pres. Halifax-Dartmouth Welfare Council 1963; Lect. Dalhousie Law Sch. 1952-62; Trustee, Public Archives of N.S.; Fellow, Am. Coll. Trial Lawyers; Foundation for Legal Research in Can.; Hon. mem. & Hon. Vice-Pres. Candn. Red Cross Soc.; awarded Centennial Medal 1967; hQueen's Jubilee Medal 1977; Phi Kappa Pi; United Church; recreations: golf, fishing; Clubs: Halifax; Saraguay; Waegwoltic; Ashburn Golf; Home: 833 Marlborough Ave., Halifax, N.S. B3H 3G7; Office: P.O. Box 2314, Law Courts, Halifax, N.S. B3J 3C8

MacKENZIE, Bryce Robertson Parker, Q.C., B.A., B.Ed.; b. 6 April 1907; s. Kenneth Robertson and Isabelle (Parker) M.; e. Univ. of Saskatchewan, B.A. 1928, B.Ed. 1929; Osgoode Hall Law Sch., Toronto, Ont.; m. Florence Nowry, d. Joseph McKonald, Rothsay, Ont., 10 June 1933; two d., Jean Patricia, Marion Ann. COUNSEL, FASKEN AND CALVIN; called to the Bar of Ont., 1932; cr. K.C. 1950; mem., Candn. Bar Assn.; Presbyterian; Clubs: Ontario; Home: 73 Riverwood Parkway, Toronto,

Ont. M8Y 4E4; Office: (Box 30) Toronto-Dominion Centre, Toronto, Ont. M5K 1C1

MACKENZIE, Chalmers Jack, C.C. (1967), C.M.G., M.C., B.E., M.C.E., D.Sc., D.Eng., D.C.L., LL.D., F.R.S., F.R.S.C.; b. St. Stephen, N.B., 10 July 1888; s. James and Janet M.; e. Dalhousie Univ., B.E. 1909, LL.D. 1941; Harvard Univ., M.C.E. 1915; D.Sc. McGill 1941, Laval 1946, Cambridge 1946, Brit. Columbia 1947, Princeton 1949, McMaster 1951, Manitoba 1953, New Brunswick 1953, Montreal 1953, Ottawa 1958, Roy. Mil. Coll. 1964; LL.D., Western Ont. 1943, Queen's 1944, Algiers 1944, Saskatchewan 1944, Carleton 1968; Univ. of Toronto, D.Eng. 1944, N.S. Tech. Coll. 1950; Bishops Univ., D.C.L. 1952; m. 1st Claire Rees 1916; one s.; 2ndly Geraldine Gallon 1924; two d.; mem. of Council, Scient. & Indust. Research, 1935-64; practised as a Consulting Engr. in Alta., 1910-15; Prof. of Engn., Univ. of Sask., 1919-39, and Dean, Faculty of Engn. there, 1921-39; apptd. Acting Pres., Nat. Research Council of Can.; Oct. 1939 and Pres., 1939-52; pres., Atomic Energy of Can. Ltd., 1952-53; Chrmn., Atomic Energy Control Bd., 1947-61; formerly Chrmn., Invent. Bd. & War Tech. & Scient. Devel. Comtes.; served in 1st World War, 1916-18, with 54th Bn., C.E.F.; awarded M.C. 1918; Ald., City of Saskatoon, Sask., 1929-30, and formerly Chrmn. of Town Planning Comn. and mem. of Hosp. Bd. there; former mem., Council of Pub. Health, Sask.; cr. Chevalier de la Légion d'Hon. (France), 1947; awarded U.S. Medal for Merit, 1947; Royal Bank Centennial Award 1968; Hon. mem. Institution of Civil Engrs. 1968; mem., Engn. Inst. of Can. (Pres. and Past Chrmn., Sask. Br.); Sask. Assn. Prof. Engrs. (Past Chrmn.); mem. of The Canada Council, 1963-69; Chancellor, Carleton Univ. 1954-68; Home: 210 Buena Vista Road, Rockcliffe, Ottawa, Ont. K1M 0V7

MACKENZIE, Cortlandt John Gordon, M.D., C.M., D.P.H., F.R.C.P.(C); educator; b. Toronto, Ont. 6 Sept. 1920; s. John Gordon and Marjorie (Campbell) M.; e. Queen's Univ. M.D., C.M. 1951; Univ. of Toronto D.P.H. 1955; m. Jean d. late Col. William Barker, V.C., 6 Jan. 1945; children: Alexander J.G., Ian B. G., David W. G.; PROF. OF HEALTH CARE & EPIDEMIOL. UNIV. OF B.C. since 1972; mem. Pollution Control Bd. of B.C. 1967-82, Chrmn. 1977-82; mem., Environmental Appeal Bd. of B.C. 1982- ; mem. Health Offrs.' Council of B.C. since 1955; B.C. Inst. of Technol. Adv. Comte.; Pub. Health Insprs. Option 1965-75, Chrmn. 1965-75; Chrmn. Royal Comn. on Herbicides & Pesticides, Ministry of Environment B.C.; Chrmn. Adv. Comte. to Min. of Environment B.C. on Control of Eurasian Milfoil; Visiting Prof., Univ. of Papua, New Guinea, 1981; mem. and Chmn., C.P.H.A. Taskforce on Arsenic in Yellowknife, N.W.T. 1977; gen. med. practice Victoria 1952-54; Dir., Peace River Health B.C. 1954-55, West Kootenay Health Unit 1956-59, Selkirk Health Unit 1956-59, Central Vancouver Island Health 1959-63; Research Fellow, Dept. Health Care & Epidemiol. Univ. of B.C. 1961, Asst. Prof. 1963, Assoc. Prof. 1967, Acting Chrmn. 1969, Head of Dept. 1973-80; served with RCNVR 1941-45, Lt. Commdr.; author various reports, articles prof. journs.; Fellow, Royal Soc. Health; mem. Candn. Med. Assn.; Candn. Pub. Health Assn. (Extve. B.C. Br. 1960-62); Traffic Injury Research Foundation Can.; Candn. Assn. Teachers Social & Preventive Med. (Pres. 1976); Research Adv. Comte. B.C. Safety Council; Am. Pub. Health Assn.; Unitarian; Home: 3140 W. 55th Ave., Vancouver, B.C. Office: 2075 Wesbrook Mall, Vancouver, B.C. V6T 1W5.

MacKENZIE, Lt.-Gen. George Allan, C.M.M., C.D.; b. Kingston, Jamaica 15 Dec. 1931; s. George Adam and Annette Louise (Maduro) MacK.; e. Beckford and Smith's High Sch. Jamaica; Jamaica Coll. 1944-48; RCAF Staff Coll. Toronto 1965-66; m. Valerie Ann d. Louis Marchand, Sedley, Sask. 30 June 1971; children: Richard Michael, Barbara Wynne; EXEC. VICE PRES., GENERAL

DISTRIBUTORS OF CAN., LTD. 1980- ; Hon. mem. Bd. Govs., Candn. Corps Commissionaires; began flying career with British West Indian Airways; enlisted RCAF 1951 and comnd. as pilot Centralia, Ont. 1952; assigned to 412 Transport Sqdn. Rockcliffe, Ont.; following tour on staff of Directorate of Postings & Careers HQ Ottawa trans. to 437 Transport Sqdn. Trenton, Ont. 1962-65; flew numerous missions U.N. in Congo and Cyprus; completed first around-the-world flight in a Yukon; posted to HN Ottawa 1966 as staff mem. Dir. of Operations and Directorate of Equipment Requirements Air; promoted Col. and apptd. Base Commdr. CFB Greenwood, N.S. 1968; Depy. Chief of Staff, Operations, Maritime Command HQ Halifax 1971; promoted Brig.-Gen. and apptd. Chief of Staff Operations Maritime Command HQ 1974; apptd. Chief of Air Doctrine & Operations 1975, Maj.-Gen. 1976; Depy. Commdr., Air Command HQ Winnipeg 1977; Commdr., Candn. Armed Forces Air Command, 1978-80 (resigned 1 Apr. 1980); Hon. Vice Pres., Un. Services Inst. Can.; mem. Candn. Aeronautics & Space Inst.; Presbyterian; recreations: sailing, cycling, reading; Clubs: Rotary; Carleton (Winnipeg); Home: 383 Christie Rd., Winnipeg, Man. R0G 2A0; Office: 1370 Sony Place, Winnipeg, Man. R3C 3C3.

MacKENZIE, Gisèle (Marie Marguerite Louise Gisèle LaFleche); singer; violinist; dramatic actress; b. Winnipeg, Manitoba, Jan. 1927; d. Dr. George MacKenzie LaFleche, and Gabrielle Celine Oliva Marietta LaF.; began playing piano at an early age and violin at age seven; at age twelve made first appearance as a Violinist in recital at Royal Alexandra Hotel, Winnipeg, Man.; at age thirteen appeared as Concert Violinist with Que. Symphony Orchestra over C.B.C. network; studied violin under Kathleen Parlow at Royal Conservatory of Music of Toronto (won a no. of scholarships); while a student in 1946, contracted with C.B.C. for 15 min. show "Meet Gisele" which ran for four yrs.; established her reputation in "Gisele in Canada" with C.B.C.; chosen "most popular female singer in Canada" by radio critics in Ottawa, Vancouver, Toronto, 1949; appeared on Bob Crosby's "Club 15" (at this time changed surname from LaFleche to MacKenzie), 1951; sang on Mario Lanza Show, 1951; toured with Jack Benny playing violin duet, summers 1952-53; with "Your Hit Parade", weekly N.Y. TV show, 1953-57; appeared on 1st broadcast, "The Woolworth Hour", June 1955, and 100th broadcast, Apl. 1957; leading role in Dallas State Fair's production of "South Pacific", June 1955; Guest artist, Denver Symphony, July 1955; appeared at Flamingo Hotel, Las Vegas, Aug. 1955; has appeared at Las Vegas' Sahara Club with Bob Crosby and The Modernaires; voted "top Candn. artist" in 2nd annual B.U.P. poll of Disk jockeys, 1955; star of "Annie Get Your Gun", Kansas Starlight Theatre, July 1956; presented with silver tray by Candn. Nat. Sportsman's Show for "outstanding achievements in the TV and radio fields and for contrib. to the devel. of goodwill between Can. and U.S.", 1954; Hon. Mayor, Encino, Cal. 1962-63; m. Bob Shuttleworth 24 Feb. 1958; two children, Mac and Gigi; m. Robt. Francis Klein; hobby: cooking

MACKENZIE, Hugh Sinclair, Q.C.; b. Toronto, Ont., 2 Aug. 1911; s. Kenneth Ferns and Aileen (Sinclair) M.; e. Rosedale Public School and Upper Can. Coll., Toronto, Ont.; Univ. of Toronto (Trinity Coll.), B.A. 1932; Osgoode Hall Law Sch., Toronto, Ont.; m. Eleanor Smyth, d. William John Blair of Woodstock, Ont. and Provost, Alta., 20 Oct. 1934; one d., Jean Blair (Mrs. R.B. Dalton); COUNSEL, MACKENZIE, WOOD, & MAGILL partner in this, and predecessor firms 1935-77; Dir., Gascoigne Indust. Products Ltd.; Lockwood Geophysics Ltd.; and other Co's.; Osgoode Hall C.O.T.C. (R) 1939-42; served in World War 1942-47 as 2nd Lieut Candn. Inf. 1942, Lieut 1943 and Capt. (retired list) 1945; served in Can. 1942-44; with 8th Roy. Scots (15th Scot. Divn.) 1944 in England and Normandy; wounded Aug. 1944; rejoined firm on discharge from hosp. 1947; read law with Mackenzie & Saunderson; called to the Bar of Ont. 1935; cr. K.C. 1952; mem., Imp. Offrs. Assn. of Can. (Pres. 1958-59); Canloan Assn. (Pres., 1951-52); Delta Chi; Independent Conservative; Presbyterian; recreations: fishing, horses, bridge; Clubs: Caledon Mountain Trout; Royal Candn. Mil, Inst.; Royal Scots (Edinburgh); Home: 5 Summerhill Gardens, Toronto Ont. M4T 1B3 and RR 1, Terra Cotta Ont. L0P 1M0; Office: 85 Richmond St. W., Toronto, Ont. M5H 2C9

MACKENZIE, John Price Sinclair, B.Comm.; investment consultant; b. Montreal, P.Q., 28 Dec. 1923; s. late Helen Margaret MacMillan (Price) and John Sinclair M.; e. Westmount (P.Q.) High Sch., Jr. Matric., 1941; McGill Univ., B.Com., 1947; m. Lois Kernaghan, d. late Roy H. Parkhill, 3 Oct. 1970; Annette, d. late Harold A. Stevenson, 31 May 1947; children: John S.S., Alastair P. S., Carolyn M. S.; PARTNER, MACKENZIE & SARLOS LTD.; Chrmn., HCI Holdings Ltd.; MS2 Resources Ltd.; Elliot & Page Ltd.; Trustee, Canada Permanent Income Investments; Dir., Acct., Bank of Montreal, 1947-49; with Barclays Bank group 1949-55; London, 1949-50, Barclays Bank D.C.O., London, 1950-51; Banque de Comm., Antwerp and Brussels, 1952, Barclays Bank (France), Paris, 1952, Barclays Bank D.C.O., West Indies, 1952-53, Barclays Bank (Can.), Toronto, 1953-55; Partner, Mgr. Inst. Sales and Mgr. Money Market Operations, Greenshields Inc., 1955-62; Vice Pres., Fullerton Mackenzie & Assocs. Ltd., 1962-67, business and assets acquired by International Trust Co. in Jan. (1967); apptd. Pres., International Trust Co. 1967; Vice Pres., Can. Permanent Corp. 1969-77; served in war as Lieut., R.C.N.V.R., 1942-45; H.M.C.S. Brantford 1943, H.M.C.S. Thetford Mines (2nd in Command) 1944-45; Trustee, Nature Conservancy Can.; Dir., Shaw Festival; Gov. and Vice Chrmn., Heritage Can. Foundation; mem., Toronto Arts Council; Dir., Owl Magazine, Young Naturalists Found.; Toronto Free Theatre; Anglican; recreations: sailing, fishing, shooting, skiing, tennis; Home: 27 Rosedale Rd., Toronto, Ont. M4W 2P5; Office: Suite 1120, Richmond-Adelaide Centre, 120 Adelaide St. W., Toronto, Ont., M5H 1V1

MacKENZIE, Kenneth George; company executive; b. Mimico, Ont., 1 May 1931; s. John Percy and Petronella (Lammerse) MacK.; m. June Elizabeth, d. Frederick H. Laverty, 9 Feb. 1952; children: David S., Shawn B., Kirk A., Sharon D.; joined Goodyear Tire & Rubber Co. Ltd., as Time Clk., 1948; Factory Accounting 1949; Sales Accounting 1950; Gen. Accounting 1951; Office Mgr., Winnipeg, 1952-57; Credit Mgr., Edmonton, 1957-60; Office Mgr., Calgary 1961, Regina 1961, Toronto 1962; Nat. Credit Mgr. Retail, 1963; Asst. Gen. Credit Mgr. 1964; joined Seiberling Rubber Co. of Can. Ltd. as Secy.-Treas., 1964, Pres. 1967; Gen. Mgr., Retail Stores Div., Goodyear Can. Inc. 1977-79; mem., Candn. Credit Inst.; Freemason; P. Conservative; Protestant; recreations: youth work; curling;

MACKENZIE, Maxwell Weir, O.C. (1972), C.M.G., B. Com.; b. Victoria, B.C., 30 June 1907; s. Hugh Blair and Maude Marion (Weir) M.; e. Lakefield Prep. Sch., Ont.; Trinity Coll. Sch., Port Hope, Ont.; McGill Univ., B.Com. 1928; m. Jean Roger, d. J. M. R. Fairbairn, Montreal, 12 Sept. 1931; children: Marion, Alison, Hugh, Blair; Hon. Dir., Canron Ltd.; Dir. Emeritus, The Candn. Imperial Bank of Com.; Dir., Edifice Dorchester-Commerce Inc.; joined firm of McDonald, Currie & Co. (Chart Accts.) 1929 and Partner there 1935-45; called to Foreign Exchange Control Bd., Ottawa, 1939 and later Chrmn. of Management Comte.; trans. to W.P.T.B., 1942; apptd. Depy. Chrmn., 1943; returned to McDonald, Currie & Co., 1944; Depy. Minister, Dept. of Trade & Comm., 1945-51; Dept. of Defence Production, 1951-52; Extve. Vice-Pres., 1952-54, Canadian Chemical & Cellulose Co. Ltd., and apptd. Pres. in 1954; Chrmn. of Bd., Chemcell Ltd., 1964-66; mem., Roy. Comn. on Taxn. of Annuities

& Family Corps. 1944; Alternate Candn. Del. to U.N. 1946; Chrmn. Candn. Council, Nat. Indust. Conf. Bd., 1962-63; mem., Econ. Council of Can., 1963-71; Chrmn., Royal Comn. on Security 1966; Chrmn. Fed. Comn. Inquiry into Beef Marketing 1975; life mem.; Ordre de Comptables Agréés du Que.; Hon. LL.D. McGill 1973; Kappa Alpha; Anglican; Clubs: Rideau (Ottawa); Mount Royal; Home: 383 Maple Lane, Rockcliffe Park, Ottawa, Ont. K1M 1H7

MacKENZIE, Hon. Norman Archibald MacRae, C.C. (1969), C.M.G. (1946), M.M. and Bar (1918), Q.C., D.C.L., B.A., LL.B., LL.M., D.C.L., LL.D., Litt.D., D.Sc.Soc., F.R.S.C. (1943); president emeritus; b. Pugwash, N.S., 5 Jan. 1894; s. Rev. James A. and Elizabeth (MacRae) M.; e. Pictou Acad., N.S.; Dalhousie Univ., B.A. 1921, LL.B. 1923; Harvard Univ., LL.M. 1924; St. John's Coll., Cambridge, Post-grad. Dipl. 1925; Gray's Inn, London, 1924-27; LL.D., Mount Allison 1941; LL.D., Univ. of N.B. 1941; Toronto 1945; Ottawa 1947; Bristol 1948; Alberta 1950; Glasgow 1951; St. Francis Xavier 1953; Dalhousie 1953; McGill 1954; Sydney, Australia 1955, Rochester 1956, Alaska 1957, California 1958; Brit. Columbia 1962, Royal Mil. Coll. 1963; Cambridge 1965; D.C.L., Whitman 1946; Sask. 1960; D.Sc.Soc., Laval 1952; Litt.D., Memorial 1962; m. Margaret, d. A. W. Thomas, Toronto, Ont., 19 Dec. 1928; children: Susan Elizabeth, Patrick Thomas, Sheila Janet MacRae; Pres. Emeritus, Hon. Prof. of Internat. Law Univ. of Brit. Columbia; Chrmn., Consultative Comte. on Doukhobor Problems; Chrmn. and Hon. Pres., Candn. Save the Children Fund; mem., Univ. Advisory Bd., Dept. of Labour; Advisory Comte. on Univ. Training for Veterans, Dept. of Veterans Affairs; Legal Survey Comte. (survey of legal prof. in Can.); Trustee, Teacher's Ins. & Annuities Assn. of Am., since 1948; Carnegie Foundation for Advanc. of Teaching, since 1951; Dir. Bank of Nova Scotia; mem. Vancouver Adv. Bd., Canada Permanent Trust Co.; read law with McInnes, Jenks & Lovitt; called to the Bar of N.S. 1926; cr. K.C. 1942; Legal Adviser, Internat. Labour Office, Geneva 1925-27; Assoc. Prof. of Law, Univ. of Toronto 1927-33; Prof. of Internat. Law and Candn. Constitutional Law there 1933-40; Pres., Univ. of New Brunswick 1940-44; Pres., Univ. of British Columbia, 1944-62; Pres., Nat. Conf. of Candn. Univs. 1946-48; Candn. Club of Toronto 1939-40; Chrmn., Wartime Information Bd. of Can. 1943-45; Chrmn., Reconstr. Comn., Prov. of N.B.; Conciliatory Bds. in Labour Disputes, 1937-42; Victory Loan Extve. Comte., Fredericton & York, N.B. 1941-44; Pres., Toronto Br., League of Nations Soc. 1932-36; Del. to Inst. of Pac. Relations Confs., Shanghai 1931, Banff 1933, Yosemite 1936, Virginia Beach 1939, Mont Tremblant 1942; Del. Brit. Commonwealth Confs., Toronto 1933, Sydney 1938; Del. to 7th Cong. on Laws of Aviation, Lyons 1925; mem., Royal Comn. on Nat. Devel. in the Arts. Letters & Sciences 1949-51; mem. E. Africa Comn. on Univ. Educ., 1962; served in World War 1914-19 with Candn. Inf., 6th C.M.R.'s, 85th Bn., N.S. Highlanders; awarded M.M. and Bar; summoned to the Senate, Feb. 1966, retiring 1969; Chrmn., Univ. Grants Comte., Prov. of N.S. since 1963; mem. Royal Comn. on Higher Educ. P.E.I., 1964; Indust. Adv. Council, N.B. since 1965; Dir., Candn. Centennial Comn. since 1963; Chrmn., Candn. Centennial Council since 1963; Mediator, St. Lawrence Seaway wage dispute, 1966; author of "Legal Status of Aliens in Pacific Countries", 1937; "Canada and the Law of Nations" (with L. H. Laing) 1938; "Canada in World Affairs" (with others), 1941; a contrib. to Am. and Candn. law journs.; mem., Candn. Inst. Internat. Affairs (Chrmn. Research Comte. 1929-40; Chrmn., Nat. Council); Am. Soc. Internat. Law; Candn. Bar Assn.; Candn. Pol. Science Assn.; Y.M.C.A. (Nat. Council); Candn. Hist. Assn.; Vancouver Bd. Trade; Fellow, Roy. Soc. for Encouragement of Arts, Mfrs. & Comm.; Chrmn., Bd. of Trustees, Carnegie Foundation for Advanc. of Teaching, 1959; mem., The Canada Council (1957); Pres., Candn. Inst. on Pub. Affairs, 1963-64; awarded John E. Read Medal for Contribs.

to Internat. Law, 1975; United Church; recreations: fishing, hunting, golf, tennis, badminton, skiing; Club: Vancouver; Address: 4509 W. 4th Ave., Vancouver, B.C. V6R 1R4

MacKENZIE, Norman Hugh, M.A., Ph.D., F.R.S.C.; educator; b. Salisbury, Rhodesia 8 March 1915; s. Thomas Hugh and Ruth Blanche (Huskisson) MacK.; e. Rhodes Univ. S. Africa B.A. 1934, M.A. 1935, Ed. Dip. 1936; Univ. of London Ph.D. 1940; m. Rita Mavis Hofmann 14 Aug. 1948; children: Catherine Lynette, Ronald Philip; PROF. EMERITUS, QUEEN'S UNIV. 1980- ; Lectr. in Eng. Rhodes Univ. 1937; Univ. of Hong Kong 1940-41; Univ. of Melbourne 1946-48, Dir. Bd. Studies Journalism 1948; Sr. Lectr. in charge Dept. Eng. Univ. of Natal 1949-55, Dean of Men's Residence 1949-54; Prof. and Head of Eng. Univ. Coll. Rhodesia 1955-65, Dean of Arts 1957-60, 1963-64; Prof. and Head of Eng. Laurentian Univ. 1965-66; Prof. of Eng. present Univ. 1966-80, Dir. Grad. Studies in Eng. 1967-73, Chrmn. Bd. Grad. Studies & Research 1971-73; served with Hong Kong Volunteers Coastal Defence 1940-46, P.O.W. Hong Kong and Japan 1941-45; author "South African Travel; 1955; "The Outlook for English in Central Africa" 1960; "Hopkins" 1968; "Poems by Hopkins" 1974; "Reader's Guide to Gerard Manley Hopkins" 1981; co-ed. "The Poems of Gerard Manley Hopkins" 1967; various book chapters, articles; mem. Internat. Hopkins Assn. (Bd. of Scholars); Candn. Assn. Irish Studies (Treas. 1972-73); Hopkins Soc. (London, Pres. 1972-); Modern Lang. Assn.; Yeats Soc. (Life mem.); recreations: book collecting, listening to music, ornithology; United Church; Home: 416 Windward Pl., Kingston, Ont. K7M 4E4; Office: Kingston, Ont. K7L 3N6.

MacKENZIE, Walter C., O.C. (1970), B.Sc., M.D., C.M., M.S., F.A.C.S., F.R.C.S.(C), Hon. F.R.C.S. (Edin.), Hon. F.R.C.S. (Ireland), LL.D., McGill; b. Glace Bay, N.S., 17 Aug. 1909; s. late John Kenneth and Anna (Macaulay) M.; e. Ashby Sch., Sydney, N.S.; Sydney (N.S.) Acad.; Baddeck (N.S.) Acad.; Dalhousie Univ., B.Sc. 1929, M.D., C.M. 1933; L.M.C.C. 1933; Univ. of Minnesota, M.S. 1937; McGill Univ., Hon. LL.D. 1965; m. Dorothy Martin, d. late Richard C. Rosier, 25 June 1938; children: Kenneth Claude, Richard Bruce, Sally Ann; mem. of Surg. staff, Univ. Alta. Hosp. since 1946 (Dir. Surg. Services 1950-60); Sr. Surg. Consultant, Dept. of Veterans Affairs for N. Alta. 1948-66; Rotating Intership, Halifax (N.S.) Infirmary, 1932-33; Surg. Res. Royal Victoria Hosp., Montreal, July-Dec. 1933; Fellow in Surg., Mayo Foundation, Rochester, Minn., Jan. 1934-Sept. 1936; Surg. First Asst., Mayo Clinic, Rochester, Minn., Oct. 1936-Dec. 1937; Surg., Baker Clinic, Edmonton, Alta., 1938-40; Surg. Instr., Univ. of Alta Med. Sch. Alta., 1938-40; Surg. Instr., Univ. of Alta. Med. Sch. 1939-48; Clin. Prof. of Surg., 1948-50, Prof. 1950, Chrmn., Dept. of Surg., 1950-60; Dean of Med. 1959 till retired; now Emeritus Prof. of Surg.; served as Surg. Consult., RCN, 1940-46, with rank Surg. Commdr.; awarded Malcolm Hon. Soc. Medal (Dalhousie Univ.) 1933; Outstanding Achievement Award (Univ. of Minn.) 1964; Sir Arthur Sims Commonwealth Travelling Prof., 1962 (W. Indies, Africa, Gt. Brit.); Hon. Surg. to H.M. The Queen, Sept. 1966-68; author of 61 papers dealing with surg. and med. educ.; mem., Traffic Injury Foundation Can.; Edmonton Acad. Med. (Pres. 1951); Candn. Med. Assn., Alta. Div.; Royal Coll. Phys. & Surgs. Can. (Pres. 1964-66); Am. Coll. Surgs. (Pres. 1966-67); Candn. Assn. Clin. Surgs. (W. Div., Pres. 1956); Western Surg. Assn.; Alumni Assn. Mayo Found. (Pres. 1954); Defence Med. Research Can. (Pres. 1953); Am. Surg. Assn.; Surgeons' Travel Club (Pres. 1962); Candn. Soc. Clin. Investigation; Internat. Soc. Surg.; James IV Assn. Surgs., Inc.; Assn. Candn. Med. Colls. (Pres. 1968-69); Assn. Am. Med. Colls.; Candn. Assn. Gastroenterology (Pres. 1963-64); Internat. Surg. Group; Hon. F.R.C.S. Eng. and Glasgow; Hon. LL.D. Winnipeg; F.C.S. (S. Africa); rec'd. F.N.G.

Starr Award, Candn. Med. Assn.; Protestant; recreations: golf, fishing; Clubs: Mayfair Golf & Country; Edmonton Burns; Home: 10131 Clifton Pl., Edmonton, Alta. T5N 3H9

MACKENZIE, William Donald Cossar, B.Sc.; oil and gas consultant; b. Fort McLeod, Alta., 1 Sept. 1913; s. late Donald Gladston, K.C. and Charlotte (Sturrock) M.; e. Univ. of Alberta, B.Sc. (Mining Engn.) 1935; m. Elizabeth Jean d. Vance B. Graveley, Calgary, Alta., 31 Mar. 1939; children: Vance, Alexander; PRESIDENT, W. D. C. MACKENZIE CONSULTANTS LTD. since 1970; Dir.; Hudson's Bay Co.; Roxy Petroleum Ltd.; Easton United Securities Ltd.; various training positions, 1934-39 with Imperial Oil Ltd.; Petrol. Engr., Turner Valley, 1939; Norman Wells, NWT 1941; Chief Petrol. Engr., Toronto 1946; Asst. Mgr., W. Producing Dept. 1948; Gen. Mgr., 1951; a Dir. of the Co., 1955-58; W. Regional Mgr., Producing Dept., until apptd. Vice-Pres., Esso Europe Inc. 1968; Pres., Candn. Petroleum Assn., 1954-55; mem., Alberta Univs. Comn.; Am. Assn. Petroleum Geol.; Am. Inst. Mining & Metal Engrs. (apptd. Distinguished Lectr. Panel S.P.E., 1964-65); Candn. Inst. Mining & Metall.; Anglican; recreation: golf; Clubs: Calgary Golf & Country; Ranchmen's; Calgary Petroleum; Home: 728 Earl Grey Cres. S.W., Calgary, Alta. T2S 0N7; Office: 2nd Floor, 409 — 8 Ave. S.W., Calgary, Alta. T2P 1E3

MacKIMMIE, Ross Anderson, Q.C., LL.B., LL.D.; b. Sydney, N.S., 24 Aug. 1916; s. John Ross and Cassie (MacDonald) M.; e. Sydney (N.S.) Acad.; Acadia Univ. (pre-law); Dalhousie Univ., LL.B.; LL.D., Univ. of Alta.; m. Dorothy Isabella, d. late Cyril W. Stairs, Halifax, N.S., 6 Nov. 1943; children: Janet Anne, Donald Stairs, Christine Katherine, Patricia Elizabeth; PARTNER, MacKIMMIE, MATTHEWS; Chrmn., Alberta Natural Gas Co. Ltd.; Dir., North Canadian Oils Ltd.; Cominco Ltd.; Can-Del Oil Ltd.; Alberta and Southern Gas Company Ltd.; Pacific Gas Transmission Co.; member Advisory Committee, National Trust Company; Chairman Board Governors Univ. of Calgary; Pres., Calgary Bar Assn., 1958-59; Hon. Secretary and mem. Nat. Extve., Candn. Bar Assn.; Lieut.-Commdr. (Special Br.), R.C.N.V.R., 1942-45; mem., Law Soc. of Alta.; Candn. Bar Assn. (Vice Pres., 1961-62, Pres. 1962-63); read law with John MacNeill, Q.C., Sydney, N.S.; called to the Bar of N.S., 1941, Alta. 1950; cr. Q.C. 1955; United Church; recreations: golf, hunting; Clubs; Ranchmen's; Calgary Golf & Country; Glencoe; Calgary Petroleum; Home: 2211 Carleton St., Calgary, Alta. T2T 3K4; Office: 401 — 9th Ave. S.W., Calgary, Alta. T2P 2M2

MacKINNON, Hon. Angus Gordon, LL.B.; judge; b. Regina, Sask. 12 Sept. 1921; s. Andrew G. MacK.; e. Univ. of Sask.; Univ. of B.C. LL.B.; m. d. M.T. O'Neil, Edmonton, Alta. 29 Dec. 1951; children: Anna Mary, Theresa, Graeme, David, Maureen, Cameron, Marguerite (Peggy); JUDGE, SUPREME COURT OF B.C. since 1978; called to Bar of B.C. 1949; cr. Q.C. 1971; served with RCAF 1940-45; R. Catholic; recreations: golf, bridge; Clubs: Vancouver Golf; Canadian; Lawyers' Inn; Home: 233-2nd St., New Westminster, B.C.; Office: Court House, Vancouver, B.C.

MacKINNON, Hon. B. J.; judge; b. St. Eugene, Ont., 22 June 1921; s. John Archibald and Edna May (Campbell) M.; e. Vankleek Hill (Ont.) Coll. Inst.; McMaster Univ., B.A. Hons. (History) 1943, Oxford Univ. (Rhodes Scholar), B.A. Hons. (Juris.) 1948, B.C.L. 1949, M.A. (Juris.) 1952 LL.D., McMaster Univ. 1977; m. Joan Patricia Elaine, d. V. E. Ives, Peterborough, Ont., 9 Aug. 1952; children: Susan Joan, James Alastair, Robert Bruce, Iain Andrew, Blair Jonathan; ASSOC. CHIEF JUSTICE OF ONT., since 1978; formerly Counsel, MacKinnon, McTaggart; read law with Alex Stark, Q.C.; called to the Bar of Ontario 1949; cr. Q.C. 1959; Bencher, Law Soc. of Upper Canada and Chairman, Legal Educ. Committee

1965-74; Justice, Court of Appeal, Supreme Court of Ont., 1974-78; Assoc. Chief Justice, Ontario 1978- ; served with the R.C.N.V.R. 1942-44; seconded to R.N. Fleet Air Arm. 1944-45; discharged as Lt. (Observer); mem. Candn. Bar Assn. (Past Nat. Chrmn., Civil Liberties Sec., Legal Educ. Sec.; Chrmn. Special Comte. on Supreme Court of Can. Procedures); Queen's Jubilee Medal; Baptist; recreations: numismatics, beekeeping; Clubs: Ontario; Lawyers'; Home: 261 Rosedale Heights Dr., Toronto, Ont. M4T 1C7; Office: Osgoode Hall, Toronto, Ont. M5H 2N5

MacKINNON, Frank, O.C. (1969), M.A., Ph.D., LL.D.; university professor; author; b. Charlottetown, P.E.I., 24 Apl. 1919; s. Hon. Murdoch (former Min. of Agric. and later Lieut.-Gov., P.E.I.) and Perle Beecher (Taylor) M.; e. Prince of Wales Coll., Charlottetown, P.E.I.; McGill Univ., B.A. (Hons. in Econ. and Pol. Science) 1941; Univ. of Toronto, M.A. (Pub. Adm.) 1942 and Ph.D. (Pol. Science) 1950; Univ. of New Brunswick, LL.D. 1950, Dalhousie 1964; m. Margaret Daphne, d. Prof. C. P. Martin, 27 Apl. 1943; children: Philip Murdoch, David Cameron, Robert Peter, Pamela Martin; Prof., Pol. Science, Univ. of Calgary since 1968, and Head of Department there in 1971; Indust. Relations Offr. with Dept. of Labour, Ottawa 1942-45; Lectr. in Pol. Science, Univ. of Toronto 1945-46; Head of the Dept. of Pol. Science, Carleton Univ., Ottawa 1946-49; Principal, Prince of Wales Coll., Charlottetown, P.E.I. 1949-68; mem. of The Canada Council, 1957-63; Pres., Atlantic Provs. Econ. Council, 1958-59; Pres., Inst . Pub. Adm. of Can. 1964-65; Pres., Fathers of Confed. Mem. Foundation; author of: "The Government of Prince Edward Island", 1951 (rec'd the Gov. Gen. Lit. Award for Non-Fiction, 1951); "The Politics of Education", 1960; "Responsibility and Relevance in Education" 1968; "Postures and Politics" 1973; "The Crown in Canada" 1976, and numerous articles; mem., Royal Comn. on Electoral Reform (P.E.I.) 1961-62; mem. Comte. of Enquiry into Post-Secondary Educ. (Alta.) 1970-72; winner, Stratford Medal for Civic Design, 1964; Address: Dept. of Pol. Science, Univ. of Calgary, Alta. T2N 1N4

MacKINNON, Rev. Gregory A., B.A., S.T.L., S.T.D., Ph.D.; university president; b. Antigonish, N.S. 16 June 1925; s. William Francis, M.D. and Mary Patricia (Chisholm) MacK.; e. elem. and high schs. Antigonish, N.S.; St. Francis Xavier Univ. B.A. 1946; Holy Heart Semy. Halifax 1950; Univ. of Ottawa S.T.L. 1961, S.T.D., Ph.D. 1964; PRES AND VICE CHANCELLOR, ST. FRANCIS XAVIER UNIV. 1978- ; Asst. Pastor Mount Carmel Parish New Watford, N.S. 1950-54; Spiritual Dir. St. Francis Xavier Univ. 1954, Prof. and Chrmn. of Theol. 1963-73; Assoc. Dean of Arts and Dir. Summer Sch. 1970-78; mem. Acad. Council, Atlantic Inst. of Educ. 1975-78; Pres. Atlantic Ecumenical Comn. 1974-76; mem. Extve. Comte. and Extve. Council, Assn. Atlantic Univs.; mem. Council of Pres.'s, Assn. Univs. & Colls. Can.; mem. Adv. Comte. to Internat. Devel. Office Can.; mem. Soc. Scient. Study Religion; Coll. Theol. Soc.; R. Catholic; recreations: sailing, swimming, gardening, woodworking; Address: Antigonish, N.S. B2G 1C0.

MacKINNON, Kenneth J., M.D., C.M., F.R.C.S.(C); surgeon; b. Antigonish, N.S., 12 Apl. 1921; s. Dr. William F. and Mary Patricia (Chisholm) M.; e. St. Francis Xavier Univ., B.Sc. 1941; Dalhousie Univ., M.D., C.M. 1945; m. Ann Frances, d. Dr. Lloyd Meech, North Sydney, N.S., 8 Sept. 1945; children; Sheilagh Mary, W. Lloyd, Joann N., David Garth, Mairi, Susan, Kenneth J.C., Laurie Elizabeth, Kathryn; Prof. of Surgery, McGill Univ. since 1969; Surgeon, Royal Victoria Hosp.; on leave of absence from McGill and Roy Vic. Hosp. since 1979, acting as Extve. Dir., Aga Khan Hospital, Nairobi since 1979; apptd. to staff in Urol. at present Hosp., Jan. 1953; became Urol. in Chief, 1959; Assoc. Prof. of Surg., McGill Univ. 1961; served with R.C.A.M.C., 1943-46; discharged with rank

Capt.; mem., Candn. Med. Assn.; Candn. Urol. Assn. (Pres. 1973-74); Am. Assn. Genito-urinary Surgs.; Urols.; Urol. Investigators Forum; N.E. Sec. Am. Urol. Assn.; Am. Urol. Assn.; Clinical Soc. of Genito-Urinary Surgeons; R. Catholic; recreations: gardening, fishing; Address: Aga Khan Hospital, P.O. Box 30270, Nairobi, Kenya

MACKIW, Vladimir Nicolaus, D.Sc., FCIC; mining executive; b. Stanislawiw, W. Ukraine, 4 Sept. 1923; came to Canada 1948, naturalized 1953; e. Univs. of Breslau and Erlangen, Dipl. Chem. 1946; Univ. of Louvain, Post grad. studies 1948; Univ. Alta., D.Sc. (Hon.) 1976; m. Bohdanna Irene Kebuz; EXTVE. VICE-PRES., SHERRITT GORDON MINES LTD. since 1972; Chem., Lingman Lake Gold Mines, Winnipeg 1948; Man. Prov. Bureau of Mines 1949; joined Sherritt Gordon Mines Ltd. as Research Chem. 1949, Dir. of Research 1952, Dir. Research & Devel. Div. 1955-68, el. a Dir. 1964, Vice-Pres. 1967, Vice-Pres. Technol. & Corp. Devel. 1968; mem., Nat. Adv. Comte. on Mining & Metall. Research, Min. Energy, Mines & Resources, Ottawa, since 1972; Co-Chrmn. 1975; Past mem., Nat. Research Council of Can., 1971-77; Fellow, Chem. Inst. Can.; Am. Inst. Mining & Metall. Engrs.; Hon. mem. Shevchenco Scientific Soc.; American Powder Metall. Inst.; Assn. Prof. Engrs. Alta.; Candn. Inst. Mining & Metall.; Awards and Hons. incl.: Inco Platinum Medal, Candn. Inst. Mining & Metall. 1966; Jules Garnier Prize, Metall. Society France (co-recipient) 1966; R. S. Jane Mem. Award, Chem. Inst. Can. 1967; Airey Award (Noranda) Metall. Soc. of Candn. Inst. Mining & Metall. 1972; Gold Medal, Inst. of Mining & Metall., London, U.K. 1977; author or co-author over 50 publs. in numerous chem. and metall. journs. in field of extractive metall., hydrometall. and powder metall.; holder of over 45 patents; Ukrainian Catholic; Clubs: Engineers; Bd. of Trade Metrop. Toronto; Home: 9 Blair Athol Cres., Islington, Ont. M9A 1X6; Office: (Box 28) Commerce Court W., Toronto, Ont. M5L 1B1

MacLACHLAN, Graham Martin, B.A.; company official; b. Winnipeg, Manitoba, 4 June 1914; s. Daniel Campbell and Jean Agnes (Martin) M.; e. Ridley Coll., St. Catharines, Ont.; Univ. of Toronto, B.A.; Osgoode Hall Law Sch., Toronto, Ont.; m. Mary Howard, d. late Dr. Douglas McIlwraith, 12 Sept. 1957; two step-s.: C. K. Doolittle, J. D. Doolittle; Dir., United Funds Group Ltd.; Associates Capital Corp; United Funds Group; Gov., Ridley College, St. Catharines, Ont.; called to the Bar of Ont., 1940; joined Maple Leaf Mills Ltd. in 1945 as Extve. Asst.; promoted to Asst. Gen. Mgr., 1947; Vice-Pres. 1954; Extve. Vice-Pres. 1956, Pres., 1963; Chief Extve. Offr., 1966; Depy. Chrmn. Bd. 1969 till retirement 1971; served in 2nd World War with Candn. Army, 1940-45; Lieut.-Col., Royal Regt. of Can. and Royal Hamilton Light Inf.; mem., Bd. Trade Metrop. Toronto (Council 1967-70); Roy. Candn. Legion; Convocation Trinity Coll., Univ. of Toronto; Business Adv. Bd., York Univ.; Chrmn., Stroke Unit, Sunnybrook Medical Centre; Alpha Delta Phi; Anglican; recreations: music, photography, painting; Clubs: University (Pres. 1960); Toronto Golf; Home: 6 Wilket Rd., Willowdale, Ont. M2L 1N6

MacLAREN, Alethea (Lee), M.A.; educational executive; b. Memphis, Tenn.; d. Col. Americus and Charlotte Wardlaw Jackson Mitchell; e. Lausanne Sch. for Girls, Memphis; Vassar Coll. B.A.; Columbia Univ. M.A.; Carleton Univ. Candn. Pub. Admin. Course 1962-63; Univ. of Toronto Urban Studies; m. Roy MacLaren 25 June 1959; children: Ian, Vanessa, Malcolm; Dir. of Funding, Univ. of Toronto since 1975; Consultant, Llewellyn-Davies Weeks Canada 1973-77; Foreign Service Offr. Dept. of State US 1954-59 serving in Cairo (Vice Consul), Khartoum (1954-55), Saigon Consul 1956, Second Secy. (Econ.) 1957; mem. US Del. to Colombo Plan Conf. 1957; reassigned to Dept. of State Washington evaluating econ. reporting from missions abroad 1958; Economist Candn.

Govt. 1961-62; served Women's Comte. Nat. Gellery of Can.; Ang. Ch. groups, sch. comtes., fund-raising Candn. Cancer Soc., Candn. Red. Cross, and Lib. Party Ont.; mem. Extve. Comte. Un. Way Toronto; Dir., Toronto Arts Productions; Anglican; Liberal; Home: 425 Russell Hill Rd., Toronto, Ont. M5P 2S4

MACLAREN, Alexander Barnet; company officer; b. Buckingham, P.Q., 7 Mar. 1898; s. Alexander and Annie F. (Reid) M.; e. Upper Can. and Lower Can. Colls.; McGill Univ.; m. Mary, d. W. J. Gibbs, 12 Dec. 1923; children: Alexander Barnet, Margaret H., A. Carol; former Chrmn., Maclaren Power & Paper Co. Ltd.; Dir., The James Maclaren Co. Ltd.; Maclaren-Que. Power Co. Ltd.; served in 1st World War 1917-19, with 4th C.D.A.C.; Kappa Alpha; Presbyterian; recreations: golf. tennis; Clubs: Rideau; Royal Ottawa Golf; Home: 270 Buchan Rd., Ottawa, Ont. K1M 0W5

MACLAREN, Gordon F., M.B.E. (1945), Q.C.; b. Brockville, Ont., 30 Jan. 1902; g.g. son of David M., who settled Maclaren Landing on Upper Ottawa; s. John and Emma (Forin) M.; e. Brockville (Ont.) Coll. Inst.; Royal Mil. Coll. of Can. (Grad. 1922); Univ. of Toronto (Honour Physics 1923); Osgoode Hall Law Sch., Toronto, Ont.; m. Margaret Dow, d. Hon. Mr. Justice A. K. Maclean of Ottawa and Halifax, 18 May 1929; children: Alexander Kenneth, Margot Jean; Assoc. Counsel, MacLAREN, COR-IETT, TANNER & GREEWOOD Elder of St. Andrews Ch., Ottawa; called to the Bar of Ont. 1927; cr. K. C. 1948; served in N.P.A.M., 1st Field Bgde., Ottawa; 2nd World War, in Arty; overseas 1942; served on Beaches of Normandy to Germany 1944-45 as O.C. 1st L.A.A. Batty.; summer and fall of 1945, O.C., No. 1 Candn. Army Rehab. Sch. at Zeist, Holland; awarded M.B.E.; mem., Candn. Bar Assn.; Kappa Alpha; Presbyterian; recreations : gardening, fishing; Clubs: Rideau; Royal Ottawa Golf; Maganassippi Fish & Game; Candian; Home: 177 Howick St., Rockcliffe Park, Ont., K1M 0G9; Office: 30 Metcalfe St., Ottawa, Ont. K1P 5L4

MacLAREN, James Wade, B.A.Sc., S.M., P.Eng.; b. Toronto, Ont., 18 Oct. 1921; s. James Ferris and Dorothy (Wade) M.; e. Univ. of Toronto Schs., 1940; Univ. of Toronto, B.A.Sc. 1946; Mass. Inst. of Tech., S.M. 1947; m. Jessie Marie, d. Dr. Roy W. Simpson, 25 Sept. 1946; children: James, Ian, Andrew, Thomas; CHIEF EXECUTIVE OFFICER, MacLAREN ENGINEERS, PLANNERS & SCIENTISTS, INC. since 1962; served as Jr. Project Engr. on Mun. Works, Gore & Storrie Ltd., 1947-50; joined father's firm, James F. MacLaren Associates in similar capacity, 1950; apptd. Jr. Partner 1956; served with Candn. Armoured Corps, 1942-46; rank 2nd Lt.; Pres. Assn. Consulting Engrs. Can. 1974-75; mem., Bd. of Govs., Ont. Research Found.; Assn. Prof. Engrs. Ont., Man., B.C., N.B.; Soc. Am. Mil. Engrs.; Am. Acad. Environ. Engrs.; Am. Soc. Civil Engrs.; Engn. Inst. Can.; Bd. Trade Metrop. Toronto; Zeta Psi; Protestant; recreation: golf; Clubs: Granite; Bayview; Home: Apt. 214, 4005 Bayview Ave., Willowdale Ont., M2M 3Z9; Office: 1220 Sheppard Ave. E., Ste 100, Willowdale, Ont. M2K 2T8

MacLAREN, Roy, M.A.; executive, member of Parliament; b. Vancouver, B.C., 26 Oct. 1934; s. Wilbur and Anne (Graham) MacL.; e. Univ. of B.C., B.A. 1955; Cambridge Univ., M.A. 1957; Harvard Univ., Grad. Sch. of Business Adm. Advanced Mang. Program, 1973; m. Althea, d. Col. Americus Mitchell, 25 June 1959; children: Ian, Vanessa, Malcolm; PUBLISHER, CANADIAN BUSINESS MAGAZINE AND CHRMN., CB MEDIA LTD., since 1977; mem. of Fed. Parliament since 1979; joined Dept. of External Affairs, Ottawa, as Foreign Service Offr., serving with Internat. Supervision and Control Comn. in N. and S. Vietnam 1958-59; Second Secy., Prague, 1959-60; First Secy., Perm. Mission of Can. to UN, N.Y., 1964-68 and also served as mem. of Candn. del's to econ. conf's in Geneva, Vienna and New Delhi;

Depy. Head, Aid and Devel. Div., Dept. of External Affairs, Ottawa, 1968-69; apptd. Dir. of Pub. Affairs, Massey-Ferguson Ltd., 1969; Chrmn. and Chief Extve. Offr., Ogilvy and Mather (Can.) Ltd. 1975-77; Chrmn., Fed. Task Force on Business Govt. Relations 1977; elected M.P. for Etobicoke North, g.e. 1979, re-el g.e. 1980; Parlty Secy. to Min. of Energy, Mines & Resources, 1980- ; Dir., Candn. Inst. Internat. Affairs; Cdn. Inst. of Pub. Affairs; Council, Niagara Inst.; Gov., Etobicoke Gen. Hosp.; author "Canadians in Russia, 1918-19" 1976; "Canadians on the Nile, 1882-1898" 1978; "Canadians Behind Enemy Lines, 1939-45", 1981; various articles in mags., newspapers, journs.; Liberal; Anglican; recreations: tennis, cross-country skiing; Clubs: University; R.C.Y.C.; Rideau (Ottawa); Home: 425 Russell Hill Rd., Toronto, Ont.; M5P 2S4; and 40 Boteler St., Ottawa, Ont. K1N 9C8; Office: 70 The Esplanade, Toronto, Ont. M5E 1R5 and Room 531-S, House of Commons, Ottawa, Ont. K1A 0A5

MacLEAN, Guy Robertson, M.A., Ph.D.; educator; b. Sydney, N.S. 21 Dec. 1929; s. (Charles) Whitmore and Mary Melinda (Nicholson) MacL.; e. Sydney (N.S.) Acad. 1948; Dalhousie Univ. B.A. 1951, M.A. 1953; Oxford Univ. (Rhodes Scholar N.S.) B.A. 1955, M.A. 1960; Duke Univ. Ph.D. 1958; m. (Mary) Judith d. late H. Murray Hunter 1963; children: Colin, Jocelyn; PRES., MOUNT ALLISON UNIV. July 1980- ; Vice Pres. (Acad.), Dalhousie Univ., 1974-80; and Prof. of Hist. since 1965; Asst. Prof. of Hist. Dalhousie Univ. 1957, Assoc. Prof. 1961, Dean of Residence 1960-64, Asst. Dean of Grad. Studies 1965-66, Dean of Arts & Science 1969-75; Lectr., N.S. Tech. Coll. 1960-61, Univ. of Alta. 1962; Dean of Men, King's Coll. 1958-60; served with C.O.T.C. 1949-51; Dir. and Chrmn. Opera East; Dir. Sport N.S.; Dir. and Past Pres. Soccer N.S.; Br. Chrmn. Candn. Inst. Internat. Affairs; Dir., Donner Candn. Foundation; Gov., Coll. of Cape Breton; Commr., Maritime Provs. Higher Educ. Comn.; mem. Extve. Comte. Social Sciences & Humanities Research Council Can.; Dir. Dalhousie Alumni Assn.; mem. Nat. Extve. Council, Candn. Hist. Assn.; rec'd Centennial Medal; Jubilee Medal; Malcolm Honour Award; Graeme Fraser Award; edited with introduction "Life of A. T. Galt" 1966; author various articles Candn. and European hist.; United Church; recreation: gardening; Club: Waegwoltic; Home: Cranewood, Sackville, N.B. E0A 3C0 Office: Centennial Hall, Mount Allison University, Sackville, N.B. E0A 3C0

MacLEAN, Hon. Hugh Alan; retired judge; b. Victoria, B.C., 26 Sept. 1903; s. Hugh Archibald, K.C., and Charlotte Grace (Barrett) M.; e. Victoria Coll., Victoria, B.C. (1922); McGill Univ., B.A., 1924; m. Margaret Jean, d. late C. J. Wilson, Kamloops, B.C., 5 Aug. 1931; children: Hugh, Ann,; called to the Bar of B.C. 1927; cr. K.C. 1950; in private practice at Kamloops, B.C., and Vancouver, 1927-34; Asst. Deputy Atty.-Gen., 1954-57; apptd. Justice, Supreme Court of B.C. 1957; Justice, Court of Appeal BC. 1965-78 (ret.); Anglican; recreations: golf, fishing; Clubs: Union (Victoria); Vancouver; Home: 4971 College Highroad, Vancouver, B.C. V6T 1G7;

MacLEAN, James Alexander, O.B.E. (1978), B.Sc., P.Eng.; executive; b. Beauly, Scot., 3 Feb. 1913; s. John and Joanne (Cameron) M.; e. Dingwall Acad., Scot.; Univ. of Glasgow, B.Sc. (Elect. Engn.) 1936; Manchester Coll. of Tech., Dipl. in Indust. Adm.; m. Mary, d. late Sidney Furniss, 4 April 1941; children: Katherine Alison, Ian Michael; CHRMN. AND DIR., GEC CANADA LTD. and AEI Canada Ltd., since 1978; GEC Diesels Inc.; with Metropolitan-Vickers Elec. Co. Ltd. 1937-59 (employed in Manchester, London, Nairobi and Toronto); Vice-Pres. and Dir., Associated Electrical Industries (Canada) Ltd. 1959-69; Pres. and Chief Extve. Offr., English Electric-AEI Can. Ltd., 1969; Assn. Prof. Engrs. Ont.; Engn. Inst. Can.; Freemason; Presbyterian; Home: 54 Princess Anne Cres., Islington, Ont., M9A 2P5; Office: 5112 Timberlea Blvd., Mississauga, Ont., L6W 2S5

MacLEAN, Hon. John Angus, P.C., D.F.C., C.D., M.L.A., B.Sc., LL.D.; farmer; of Scottish ancestry; b. Lewes, P.E.I., 15 May 1914; s. George Allan and Sarah (MacLean) M.; e. Mount Allison Acad.; Summerside High Sch.; Univ. of B.C.; Mount Allison Univ., B.Sc. 1939, LL.D. 1958; m. Gwendolyn Esther, d. late Dr. Byron Burwash, Saskatoon, Sask., 29 Oct. 1952; children: Sarah Jean, Allan Duart, Mary Esther, Robert Angus; Premier of P.E.I. 1979-81; mem., Bd. of Regents, Mount Allison Univ.; served in 2nd World War as Flying Instr., Bomber Pilot and Test Pilot, 1939-1947, obtaining rank of Wing Commdr.; served Overseas, Jan. 1942-May 1943 and Oct. 1945-Aug. 1947; D.F.C.; D.C.; Mentioned in Despatches; 1st el. to H. of C. in by-el. for Queens, 25 June 1951; served 25 yrs. and then resigned Oct. 19, 1976; Minister of Fisheries, 1957-63; el. leader P. Cons. Party of P.E.I., Sept. 25, 1976; 1st el. to. P.E.I. Legis. 1977; revel. 1978, 1979; Del. NATO Parlty. Conf., Paris, 1956; led Candn. del., Colombo Plan Conf., Tokyo, 1960; led F.A.O. Cont., Rome, 1961; mem., Candn.-Japanese Ministerial del., Tokyo, 1963; Del., Commonwealth Parlty. Conf., Wellington, N.Z., 1965; 18th Parlty. Course Westminster, Eng., 1969; Inter-Parlty. Confs. on European Co-operation and Security, Helsinki 1973 and Belgrade 1975; Rep. of P.E.I. Legislature to Commonwealth Parliamentary Conference in Suva, Fiji, 1981; mem., Bd. of Dir., R.C.A.F. Memorial Fund; Past Pres., R.A.F. Escaping Soc.; mem., R.C.A.F. Assn.; Masonic Lodge A.F. 4 A.M.; Royal Can. Legion; Charlottetown C. of C. United Services Offrs. Club; Canadian of P.E.I.; Freemason (P.M.); P. Conservative; Presbyterian; recreations: country sports, hunting, fishing; Home: Lewes, Belle River R.R. 3, P.E.I. C0A 1B0

MacLEAN, Lloyd Douglas, B.Sc., Ph.D., M.D., F.A.C.S., F.R.C.S.(C), F.R.S.C.; surgeon; b. Calgary, Alta., 15 June 1924; s. Fred Hugh and Azilda (Trudell) M.; e. Univ. of Alberta, B.Sc., 1946, M.D., 1949; Univ. of Minnesota, Ph.D., 1957; m. Eleanor d. Alfred Colle, Minneapolis, Minn., 30 June 1954; 5 children: CHRMN., DEPT. OF SURGERY, McGILL UNIV.; Surgeon-in - Chief, Royal Victoria Hosp.; Internship, 1949-50, Univ. of Alberta; Straight Internship in Surgery (1950-51), Residency (training surg.), Univ. of Minn., 1951-56; Instr., Dept. of Surgery there, 1956-58; Asst. Prof., 1958-59, Assoc. Prof., 1959-62; Surgeon-in-Chief, Ancker Hosp., St. Paul, Minn., 1957-62; apptd. Prof. of Surg., McGill Univ. 1962; 2nd Lieut., R.C.A.M.C. (Reserve); mem., Soc. Univ. Surg.; Am. Assn. for Thoracic Surg.; Soc. for Exper. Biol. & Med.; Am. Physiol. Soc.; Am. Surg. Assn.; Central Surg. Assn.; Baptist; Home: 5 Renfrew, Westmount, P.Q. H3Y 2X3

MacLEAN, Robert Duncan, B.E., P.Eng.; b. Watrous, Sask. 5 July 1920; s. late Alexander Cameron and Amy (Tyler) MacL.; e. Nutana Collegiate, Saskatoon, Sask.; Univ. of Sask., B.E. (Chem. Engn.); Univ. of W. Ont. Dipl. Business Adm.; m. Iva Mae, d. late William Meyer Houghton, 26 June 1943; children: James Robert, Heather Ann; PRES. AND C.E.O., INLAND CEMENT INDUSTRIES LTD., since Oct. 1979 Production Engr., Aluminum Co. of Can., Arvida, P.Q., 1943; Sales Mgr., Castings Div., Toronto, Ont. 1959; apptd. Vice-Pres., Saskatchewan Cement Co. (Div. of Inland Cement Co. Ltd.), Regina, Sask., 1959; apptd. Vice-Pres., Marketing, Inland Cement Co. Ltd., Edmonton, Alta. 1961; Extve. Vice-Pres. & Gen. Mgr., Lake Ontario Portland Cement Co. Ltd. (predecessor Co.), 1962; Pres. and Dir., Lake Ontario Cement Co. Ltd. 1965-71; Pres. and Bd. mem., Portland Cement Assn., 1971-79; mem., Assn. Prof. Engrs. Ont.; United Ch.; recreations: golf, swimming, skiing; Clubs: Mayfair Golf and Country; Edmonton Petroleum; Home: 5603-Whitemud Rd., Edmonton Alta. T6H 4X3; Office: 8215-112th St., 11th Floor, Edmonton, Alta. T6G 2C8

MACLELLAN, David Kirkpatrick Stewart; editor; association executive; b. Liphook, Hants, Eng. 16 Feb. 1918; s. late Edward Kirkpatrick, M.D., C.M. and late Helen Stewart (Mackay) M.; e. Halifax Acad. and Dalhousie Univ.; m. Ruby Irene d. late Maurice Davis 28 June 1958; one d. by previous marriage, Elizabeth Ann James; ED. 'CANADIAN GEOGRAPHIC' since 1973; Gen. Mgr. and Extve. Secy. The Royal Candn. Geog. soc. since 1973; newspaperman, pub. relations, magazine ed. and publisher in Halifax, Ottawa, Toronto from 1934 to 1960 excepting 1940-45; Ed. and Mgr., Cdn. Printer and Publisher, 1954-60; managed Graphic Arts Industries Assn. 1960-72; organized Candn. Business Forms Assn. 1972; K. R. Wilson Mem. Award for Ed. Excellence 1958; 'Man of the Year' Candn. printing indust. 1963; Centennial Medal; Queen's Jubilee Metal; enlisted Princess Louise Fusiliers 1940; 1st Candn. Div. Sicily; O.C. Candn. Army Pub. Relations field unit Italy, rank Maj. 1944; Past Chrmn. Ottawa Chapter Inst. Assn. Extves. (Past Nat. Dir.); Phi Kappa Pi; recreations: reading, walking, swimming; Clubs: Rideau; Canadian. Home: 14 Jeffrey Ave., Ottawa, Ont. K1K 0E2; Office: 488 Wilbrod St., Ottawa, Ont. K1N 6M8.

MacLELLAN, Keith William, M.A.; diplomat; b. Aylmer East, Que., 30 Nov. 1920; S. William David and Edith (Olmsted) MacL.; e. Montreal Schools, McGill Univ. 1939-42; New Coll. Oxford Univ. M.A. 1947; m. Marie Antoinette d. late Count Adelin Le Grelle, 12 Sept. 1946; children: Keith, Anne Marie, Janet, Andrew; Indust. Relations Imperial Oil H.O. 1948-52; joined Dept. of External Affairs 1952; posted to Berne, Los Angeles, Rome, London, and Brussels, Commr. ICSC Laos. 1965-66; Ambassador to Pakistan and Afghanistan, 1974-77; Amb. to Yugoslavia and Bulgaria 1977-79; Delegate to various internat. meetings and confs. incl. ICAO, FAO, Atomic Energy, Vatican Ecumenical Council, Colombo Plan, World Bank Consortia, etc.; P.C. candidate, Ville La Salle, Que. 1979; served with Royal Montreal Regt. 1940-42, Parachutist 1st Special Air Service Regt/ 1943-45, N.W. European campaign; mem. CIIA; Candn. Pol. Sci. Assn; Sigma Chi; Cdn. Comprehensive Auditing Fdn.; Anglican; recreations: squash, shooting; Clubs: Ottawa Country; Carleton (London Eng.); Sind(Karachi); Circle Gaulois (Brussels): 331 Island Park Dr., Ottawa, Ont., K1Y 0A6

MacLELLAN, Rt. Rev. Malcolm, O.C. (1970), M.A., Ph.D., D.P., LL.D. (R.C.); b. Glenville, Inverness Co. N.S. 10 Mar. 1906; s. Archibald and Margaret (Kennedy) M.; e. St. Francis Xavier Coll., B.A., 1926; St. Augustine's Semy.; Toronto; Cath. Univ. of America; M.A. 1933, Ph.D. 1935; LL.D. Western Ontario 1970; former Professor of Education and Dean of Studies, St. Francis Xavier University then Principal, Xavier Coll., Sydney, N.S. (1951-63); Pres., St. Francis Xavier Univ. 1964-70; Chrmn., Mun. Sch. Bd., Antigonish, N.S.; mem., Advisory Council of Educ'., N.S.; author of "Catholic Church and Adult Education"; Address: St. Francis Xavier University, Antigonish, N.S.

MacLELLAN, Robert Simpson, Q.C., B.A., LL.B.; b. Sydney, N.S., 2 July 1925; s. Robert Simpson and Sarah (Ferguson) MacL.; e. St. Francis Xavier Univ., B.A. 1945; Dalhousie Univ., LL.B. 1948; m. Mary Margaret, d. Frank H. MacDonald, Sydney, N.S. 15 Aug. 1953; children: Robert Francis, Kathryn Michelle, Ian Donald, Gordon Kenneth, Nancy Marie, Peter Gerard, Hugh Douglas; formerly Partner, MacLellan, Burchell, Sullivan & Matheson; read law with Donald M. Nicholson, Q.C.; called to Bar of N.S., 1948; cr. Q.C. (Fed.) Dec. 1968; called to Bar of Ont. 1969; Del. to Atlantic Cong., NATO, London, Eng., 1959; Chrmn., Special Comte. of H. of C. Revision of Civil Service Superannuation Act, 1960, Revision of Civil Service Act, 1961; Del., NATO Parlty. Conf., Paris, 1960; Vice Chrmn., Candn. Del. to NATO Parlty. Conf., Paris, 1961; Chrmn., Candn. NATO Parlty. Assn., 1962;

def. cand. to H. of C. for Inverness-Richmond, g.e. 1957; el. 1958; def. 1962; Chrmn., Restrictive Trade Practices Comn., 1963 till resigned June 1970; assoc. in law practice with Burke-Robertson, Urie, Weller & Chadwick; appt. mem., Restrictive Trade Practices Xomm., 1974; K. of C.; R. Catholic; recreations: sailing, skiing, fishing; Clubs: Laurentian; Gatineau Fish and Game; Home: 2060 Cabot St., Ottawa, Ont., K1H 6J9; Office: P.O. Box 336, Station "A", Ottawa Ont. K1M 8V3

MACLELLAN, Stewart, C.A.; manufacturer; b. Toronto, Ont. 26 Apl. 1928; s. late Angus and Alexandria M.; m. Joan Edith d. Arthur Larlham 5 June 1954; children: Colin Angus, Janet, Karen; PRES., ELECTROHOME LTD, 1980- ; Chrmn., Ceo and Dir., Canadian Gypsum Co. Ltd. 1974-80; Dir. Peeters Carpets Ltd.; Constellation Carpet Ltd.; Peace Wood Products Ltd.; A. P. Green Refractories (Canada) Ltd.; Asst. Comptroller—Factories, Simpson-Sears Toronto 1957-67; Vice Pres.-Treas. Ontario Steel Products Co. Ltd. Toronto 1967-69; Mang. Consultant Ernst & Ernst Toronto 1969-71; Vice Pres.-Finance present Co. 1971, Extve. Vice Pres. 1973; mem. Inst. C.A.'s Ont; recreations: golf, skiing; Clubs: Thornhill Country; Granite; Home: 140 Dunbar Rd. S., Waterloo, Ont. N2L 2E9; Office: 809 Wellington St. N., (Box 2003) Kitchener, Ont. N2G 4J6

MacLENNAN, David H., B.S.A., M.S., Ph.D.; educator; b. Swan River, Man. 3 July 1937; s. Douglas Henry and Sigridur (Sigurdson) MacL.; e. Swan River (Man.) Coll. Inst. (Gov. Gen.'s Medal 1954); Univ. of Man., B.S.A. 1959 (Lt. Gov.'s Gold Medal); Purdue Univ. M.S. 1961, Ph.D. 1963; m. Linda Carol, d. Laurence C. Vass, Sydney, Australia, 18 Aug. 1965; two s: Jeremy Douglas, Jonathan David; PROF. BANTING AND BEST DEPT. OF MED. RESEARCH, UNIV. OF TORONTO since 1974; Acting Chrmn. 1978, Chrmn. 1980; Asst. Prof. Univ. of Wis. 1964; Assoc. Prof. present Univ. 1969; rec'd Ayerst Award in Biochem. 1974; Isaac Walton Killam Mem. Scholar 1977-78; author or co-author over 90 scient. research papers; Assoc. Ed. "Canadian Journal of Biochemistry" 1972-76; mem. Ed. Bd. "Journal of Biological Chemistry" 1975-80, 1982- ; mem., Medical Adv. Bd., Muscular Dystrophy Assn. Can., since 1976; Am. Soc. Biol. Chems.; Candn. Biochem. Soc.; Home: 293 Lytton Blvd., Toronto, Ont., M5N 1R7; Office: 112 College St., Toronto, Ont. M5G 1L6

MacLENNAN, Hugh, C.C. (1967), M.A., Ph.D., D.Litt., D.C.L., LL.D., F.R.S.L. (1956); novelist; university professor; b. Glace Bay, N.S., 20 Mar. 1907; s. Dr. Samuel J. (Surg.) and Katherine (McQuarrie) M.; e. Halifax Acad.; Dalhousie Univ., B.A. 1928 (winner of Gov.-Gen's. Gold Medal), Rhodes Scholar. rep. Can.-at-Large 1928; Oxford Univ. (Oriel Coll.), B.A., M.A., 1932; Guggenheim Fellow, 1943-44; Princeton Univ., M.A., Ph.D. 1935; LL.D., Dalhousie 1955, Sask. 1959, Toronto 1965, Laurentian 1966, Carleton 1967; D. Litt., W. Ont. 1952, Manitoba 1953, Waterloo Lutheran 1961, McMaster 1965, Sherbrooke 1967, B.C. 1968; Bishop's D.C.L. 1965; Hon. degrees St. Mary's Univ. 1970; Mt. Alison 1970, Laval 1973; P.E.I. 1974; Windsor 1976; Waterloo 1977; m. 1st Dorothy (d. 1957), d. Edwin L. Duncan, California, 22 June 1936; 2nd, Frances Aline, d. Frank Walker, Montreal, P.Q., 1959; Prof. Emeritus, Dept. of English, McGill Univ., 1979; winner of Gov.-Gen's. Award for Fiction, 1945, 1948, 1959, and for Non-Fiction, 1949, 1954, author of "Oxyrhynchus", 1935; "Barometer Rising", 1941; "Two Solitudes", 1945; "The Precipice", 1948; "Each Man's Son", 1951; "Cross Country", "Thirty and Three", 1954; "The Watch That Ends the Night", 1959 (Gov. Gen. Award for Eng. fiction, 1959); "Scotchman's Return and Other Essays", 1960; "Seven Rivers of Canada" 1961; "The Colour of Canada" 1967; Return of the Sphinx" 1967; "Rivers of Canada" 1974; "Voices in Time", 1980; has contrib. articles to "Sat. Review of Lit."; "Vogue"; Montreal "Standard"; "Maclean's", and "Saturday

NIGHT", etc.; awarded Lorne Pierce Gold Medal for Lit. by Royal Soc. Can., 1952; Assoc. Fellow, Royal Soc. Can. (1953); Clubs: Montreal Amateur Athletic Assn.; North Hatley; McGill Faculty; Address: McGill University, Montreal, P.Q.

MACLENNAN, James Dougald, C.A., B.Com.; executive; b. Regina, Sask., 22 March 1926; s. Joseph and Jeannette Constance (Wood) M.; e. Univ. of Sask. B.Com. 1948; C.A. 1951; m. Kathleen Mary d. John Clifford Wright, 26 Dec. 1947; children: Lorraine, Ian, Joan, Bruce; DIR., INTERPROVINCIAL STEEL AND PIPE CORP. LTD.; Dir. Royal Bank of Canada; Western Construction & Engineering Research Ltd.; Canadian Dredge & Dock Co. Ltd.; Marwell Dredging Ltd.; joined Marwell Construction Co. Ltd. Vancouver and assoc. Co's 1952-57; joined present Co. as Controller 1957 subsequently serving as Vice Pres. Finance; served with Candn. Army 1943-45; mem. Inst. C.A.'s Sask.; recreations: golf, skiing; Home: (69 Academy Park Rd., Regina, Sask. S4S 4T8; Office: (Box 1670) Regina, Sask., S4P 3C7

MacLEOD, Allen Joseph, Q.C. (Dom. 1955); Canadian pub. service (ret.); b. Revelstoke, B.C., 5 Nov. 1918; s. James William and Amanda May (Tossell) M.; e. Sydney (N.S.) Acad., Grad. 1936; Mount Allison Univ., B.A. 1939; Dalhousie Univ., LL.B. 1942; m. Margaret Eileen, d. W. R. Shaw, Charlottetown, P.E.I., 3 Sept. 1946; children: Nancy Jean, Lindsay Anne, Robert Allen; sometime Chrmn., Correctional Planning Comte., Dept. of Justice; Dir. of Criminal Law Sec., Dept. of Justice; Chrmn., Dept. of Justice Comte. on Juvenile Delinquency (1962); read law with Donald McInnes, Q.C., Halifax, N.S.; called to the Bar of N.S., 1945; joined the Dept. in 1946; apptd. Supt. of Bankruptcy, 1950; Commr. of Penitentiaries 1960-70;Special Adv. on Correctional Policy, Dept. of Solr.-Gen. 1970-74; served as Lieut. with West Nova Scotia Regt. in Italy, 1943; Secy., Criminal Law Sec., Conf. of Commrs. on Uniformity of Leg. in Can.; Secy. of Adm. of Criminal Justice Sec., Candn. Bar Assn. (1952-59); United Church;

MacLEOD, Donald G., M.B.A.; manufacturer; b. Montreal, Que., 17 Sept. 1928; s. Edward Russell and Mary G. (Goulding) M.; e. Cambridge (Ont.) High Sch. 1946; Extension Dept., McMaster Univ. Cert. in Indust. Engn. 1952; Extension Dept., Waterloo Coll., Cert. in Indust. Mang. 1956; Harvard Business Sch., M.B.A. 1958; m. Beth A., d. A. Carman Anderson, 22 March 1951; children: John A., Janet E., Mary K.; PRESIDENT AND MGR., SAVAGE SHOES LTD. since 1971; Dir. Offr., Savage Shoes Ltd.; joined Savage Shoes Limited, Industrial Engineering Department 1951, Mgr. Data Processing 1958. Comptroller 1964, Vice-Pres. and Treas. 1966, Extve. Vice-Pres. 1968; served in Candn. Army Militia, Capt. and Adjt. H.L.I. 1948-58; Past Pres., Waterloo P. Cons. Assn.; Pres., Shoe Mfrs. Assn. Can. 1976-79, Chrmn. 1980-81; Gov., Univ. of Waterloo; Bd. Govs., Stratford Festival Found.; Dir. Conference Bd. of Can.; Life mem., Candn. Inst. Mang.; Conservative; Anglican; recreations: curling, swimming; Clubs: National (Toronto); The London (Ont.); Home: 133 Blair Rd., Cambridge, Ont. N1S 2J2; Office: 1008 Queenston Rd., Cambridge, Ont. N3H 4S1

MacLEOD, Donald L., B.Com.; insurance executive; b. 15 Dec. 1924; e. Mount Allison Univ. B.Com.; PRESIDENT, THE EQUITABLE LIFE INSURANCE CO. OF CANADA 1981- , Dir. 1980- ; joined H.O. present co. as Asst. Supt. Agencies 1958 following Sales and Br. Mang. N.B. and Nfld., Supt. of Agencies 1962, Dir. of Agencies 1964, Vice Pres. Marketing 1967, Extve. Vice Pres. 1978; Office: One Westmount Rd. N., Waterloo, Ont. N2J 4C7.

MacLEOD, Duncan Rae, D.F.C., B.A., F.C.I.A., F.S.A.; insurance executive; b. Chesterville, Ont., 24 Jan. 1921; s.

Donald Alexander and Blanche Louise (Baldrey) M.; e. Glen Nevis (Glengarry Co., Ont.) Pub. and High Sch.; Kingston (Ont.) Coll. 1937; Queen's Univ., B.A. (Hons. Math. and Econ.) 1941; m. late Velma E. Martin, 19 Sept. 1951; children: John, Douglas, Elizabeth; VICE-PRESIDENT, MANUFACTURERS LIFE INSURANCE COMPANY since 1970; joined the Company in 1941; successively Asst. Actuary, Associate Actuary, Actuary, Sr. Actuary 1966, Group Vice-President 1967; served in the 2nd World War, R.C.A.F. 1941-45; Navig. Bomber Command; rank Flight Lieutenant; awarded D.F.C.; mem., Soc. of Actuaries; American Academy Actuaries; Ed., Canadian Inst. Actuaries 1969-70; Anglican; recreations: jogging, reading, swimming, Clubs: Board of Trade; Home: 21 Donna Mae Cres., Thornhill, Ont., L4J 1Z9; Office: 200 Bloor St. E., Toronto, Ont. M4W 1E5

MacLEOD, Innis G., O.C. (1971), Q.C., B.A., LL.B.; LL.D.; retired public servant; b. Sydney, N.S., 13 Feb. 1911; s. Alexander George and Christene Rebecca (Morrison) MacL.; e. Mount Allison Univ., B.A. 1934; Dalhousie Univ., LL.B. 1937, LL.D. 1977; m. Gladys Enid, M.D., C.M., d. William H. Johnson, 10 Sept. 1942; children: Gerard, Martha; read law with George Morrison; called to the Bar of Nova Scotia 1938; cr. Q.C. 1957; practiced law in Sydney, N.S., 1938-48; entered Public Service of N.S. as Solicitor, Dept. of Mines, 1948; served in following positions: Civil Service Commr.; Sr. Solr., Dept. of Atty. Gen.; Deputy Superintendent of Insurance; Administrative Asst. to Premier; Depy. Atty. Gen., 1969-72; Secty. of Extve. Council 1972-76; acted as Advisor to Prov. of N.S. on Fed.-Prov. fiscal and constitutional questions incl. Constitutional Confs. of 1950, 1960-61, 1967-71; 1978-79; mem., Candn. Bar Assn.; N.S. Barristers Soc.; N. Brit. Soc.; United Church; recreation: fishing; Home: 8 Glenwood Ave., Dartmouth, N.S. B2Y 3G7

MacLEOD, John Morrison, B.E.; corporate executive; b. Baddeck Bay, N.S. 13 Sept. 1931; s. late Norman Donald and Helen Marion (Morrison) MacL.; e. Baddeck Bay (N.S.) Sch. 1944; Baddeck (N.S.) Acad. 1948; Acadia Univ. 1949-52; Technical Univ. of N.S., B.E. (Metall. Engn.) 1954; m. Beverley Ann d. late Delbert Lorne Thurston 30 Sept. 1955; children: Heather Louise, Carol Jean, Sandra Joy, Alan Thurston; SR. VICE PRESIDENT AND DIRECTOR, SHELL CANADA LTD. since 1977; Pres. and Dir. Shell Canada Resources Ltd.; joined present Co. as Petroleum Engr. 1954, Chief Petroleum Engr. 1968, Production Dept, Mgr. 1969, Gen. Mgr. Frontier Div. 1971, Gen. Mgr. Production 1972, Supply & Logistics 1973, Vice Pres. (Corporate Planning & Pub. Affairs) 1975; Vice Pres. (Exploration & Production) 1977; Dir., Crows Nest Resources Ltd. 1978; Gov. and Past Chrmn., Candn. Petrol. Assn.; 1st Vice Chrmn Candn. Gas Assn.; mem. Calgary Chamber Comm.; Assn. Prof. Engrs. Geols. & Geophysicists Alta.; Candn. Inst. Mining & Metall.; Protestant; recreations: skiing, camping; Clubs: Calgary Petroleum; Calgary Golf & Country; Mississauga Gold and Country; Office: 505 University Ave., Toronto, Ont., M5G 1X4 and 400-4th Ave. S.W., Calgary, Alta. T2P 0J4

MacLEOD, Hon. Malcolm Noble, M.L.A.; politician; b. Moncton, N.B. 8 Feb. 1928; s. Noble Angus and Mary Celeste (McAleese) MacL.; e. Moncton, N.B.; m. Hazel Edith d. Harold M. Freeze, Penobsquis, N.B. 28 Dec. 1949; children: Gregory Harold, Robert Noble, Jane Elizabeth; MIN. OF AGRIC. AND RURAL DEVEL., N.B. 1974-; el. M.L.A. for Albert prov. g.e 1970, re-el. since 1974; Freemason; mem. Lions; Pythias; P. Conservative; Baptist; Office: (P.O. Box 6000) Fredericton, N.B. E3B 5H1.

MacLEOD, Robert Angus, M.A., Ph.D., F.R.S.C.; marine bacteriologist and professor; b. Athabasca, Alberta, 13 July 1921; s. Norman John and Eleonora Pauline Bertha (Westerhoff) M.; e. Douglas Road School, Burnaby,

B.C. 1927-35; Burnaby South High Sch. 1935-39; Univ. of B.C. B.A. 1943, M.A. 1945; Univ. of Wisc. Ph.D. 1949; m. Patricia Rosemarie, d. Edgar A. Robertson, Calgary, Alta. 1 Sept. 1948; children: Douglas J., Alexander R., Kathleen M., David J., Michael N., Susan J.; PROF., DEPARTMENT OF MICROBIOLOGY, MACDONALD COLLEGE OF McGILL UNIVERSITY; Instructor, Dept. of Chem., Univ. of B.C., 1945-46; Asst. Prof., Dept., of Biochem., Queen's Univ. 1949-52; Head. Biochem. Sec., Technol. Stn., Fisheries Research Bd. of Can., Vancouver, B.C. 1952-60; Assoc. Prof., Dept. of Microbiology, Macdonald Coll. 1960-64 and subsequently Prof., Chrm. 1968, 1974-79; mem., Marine Sc. Centre, McGill Univ. since organ. 1963; Fellow, Royal Soc. of Canada; mem., Am. Soc. Biol. Chem.; Am. Soc. Microbiol.; Candn. Soc. Microbiol.(Pres. 1976-77), C.S.M. award for research 1973; Que. Soc. of Microbiol.; author or co-author of over 100 scient. papers; recreations: camping, fishing; Home: 448 Greenwood Dr., Beaconsfield, Que., H9W 4Z9

MacMAHON, Harold Edward, B.A., M.D., D.Sc. (Hon.); pathologist; b. Aylmer, Ont., 30 March 1901; s. Hugh Percival and Ethel Clive (Holmes) MacM.; e. St. John's Coll., Winnipeg, 1910-12; Ridley Coll., St. Catharines, Ont., 1912-18; Univ. of W. Ont., B.A. 1922, M.D. 1925, D.Sc. 1944; m. Marian, d. George Edward Ross, 19 June 1934; children: Elizabeth, Hugh, D'Arcy, James; Pathol.-in-Chief, Hosps. of New Eng. Med. Center; Consultant to Hosps. of Bingham Fund; Consultant in Pathol. to Mt. Auburn Hosp., Carney Hosp., Malden Hosp., Lynn Hosp., Cape Cod Hosp., Providence Hosp. and others; also to Army, USPHS, V.A., Armed Forces Inst. of Pathol.; Intern. Montreal Gen. Hosp., 1925-26; Resident, Boston City Hosp., 1926-29; Asst., Univ. of Hamburg, 1929-30; Visiting Prof., Univ. of Berlin 1931-32; joined Tufts Univ. as Prof. of Pathol. and Bacteriol., 1930; Prof. and Chrmn., Dept. of Pathol., 1930-70; Prof. Emeritus 1971; Visiting Prof. of Pathol., University of Mass. 1971-82; co-author "Die Maligne Nephrosklerose", 1933; other writings include over 125 publications in American, German and Brazilian journals; also numerous original publ. observations in anatomic and histol. pathol.; mem. Royal College Physicians (London); Hon. Fellow, Royal College Physicians and Surgeons (Can.) 1979; rec'd. Tufts University Alumni Award, 1960; Sigma Xi; Alpha Omega Alpha; Republican; Episcopal.; recreations: gardening, cricket, tennis; Club: St. Botolph; Home: 19 Hubbard Park, Cambridge, Mass. 02138; Office: Univ. of Mass. Medical School, 55 Lake Ave. N., Worcester, Mass. 01605

MacMASTER, Hon. Ken. M.L.A.; politician; b. Peterborough, Ont. 12 May 1934; m. Lucille Rita; 2 children; MIN. OF LABOUR AND MANPOWER, MAN. 1979- and Min. Responsible for Civil Service Comn. and for Women's Bureau; el. M.L.A. for Thompson; Min. of Renewable Resources and Transportation Services and Min. of Northern Affairs 1977-79; mem. Treasury Bd.; Chrmn. Jt. Council Comte. of Cabinet; mem. Fed./Prov. Financial Arrangements Comte., Indian Land Claims and Polar Gas Comtes.; former Ald. and Depy. Mayor City of Thompson; served as Chrmn. every standing comte. Thompson City Council; former Chief Negotiator of City and past mem. Planning and Recreation Comns.; served as Personnel Supvr. Inco Ltd.; Past Vice Pres. Man. Fed. of Labour; Past Pres. Local 6166 U.S.W.A.; former sole arbitrator Thompson Hosp. Bd. and Retail Clks. Union; former Dir. Alcoholism Foundation Man.; former Thompson and Alcohol & Drug Educ. Service, Winnipeg; P. Conservative; Home: 43 Westwood Dr., Thompson, Man. R8N 0E3; Office: 227 Legislative Bldg., Winnipeg, Man. R3C 0V8.

MacMILLAN, Rev. Donald Neil, M.A., B.D., Ph.D.; educator; b. Finch, Ont. 19 Dec. 1909; s. Neil and Sarah MacM.; e. McGill Univ. B.A., M.A.; Presb. Coll. Montreal B.D.; Edinburgh Univ. Ph.D.; Hon. D.D., Presb. Coll., Montreal 1979; m. Jean d. A. K. Maclean 14 Oct.

1936; two s. Donald K., Robert N.; PROF. OF THEOL. PRESBYTERIAN COLL. 1959-78 and Acting Princ. there 1973-78; served with RCAF as Chaplain 1940-45; Home: R.R. 2., Finch, Ont. K0C 1K0

MacMILLAN, Keith Campbell, M.A.; music executive; b. Toronto, Ont., 23 Sept. 1920; s. Sir Ernest Campbell and Lady Laura Elsie (Keith) MacM.; e. Upper Can. Coll., Toronto, 1930-38; Central Tech. Sch., Toronto, 1938-39; (served with R.C.A.F. in Can., 1940-41, U.K., 1941-44 and N. Africa, summer 1943); Univ. of Toronto, B.A. (Biol.) 1949, M.A. (Biol.) 1952; m. Helen Patricia Dustan, 17 May 1949; children: Ian Keith, Donald Ross, Elizabeth Helen, Kevin Ernest; CHRMN., DEPT. OF MUSIC, UNIVERSITY OF OTTAWA, since 1977; Extve. Secy., Canadian Music Centre, since 1964; Dir., Toronto Mendelssohn Choir; Encyc. Music in Can.; Candn. Conf. of the Arts; joined CBC as Music Producer (Radio), 1952; Co-founder and 1st Pres. (1952), Hallmark Recordings Ltd.; pioneer in stereo recording and broadcasting in Can.; Ed., "Musicanada" (nat. bilingual music mag.); Co-Ed. (with John Beckwith), "Contemporary Canadian Composers" 1975; co-author, "Thee Canadian Limerick Book"; author of numerous articles on music in Can.; Pres., Internat. Assn. Music Information Centres 1976-77; Pres., Canadian Assn. Music Libs. 1973-75; Vice-Pres., Candn. Conf. of the Arts, since 1976; Cdn. Music Council Medal 1978; mem., Candn. Assn. of Univ. Schs. of Music, since 1967; Candn. Music Educators' Assn.; Toronto Symphony; Cdn. Music Council; recreations: electronics, computer programming, wine making, reprehensible verse; Home: 1948 Norway Cresc., Ottawa, Ont. K1H 5N7; Office: 1 Stewart St., Ottawa, Ont. K1N 6N5

MacMURCHY, Hon. Gordon, M.L.A.; politician; farmer; b. Semans, Sask., 4 July 1926; s. Edward and Laura (Geiger) MacM.; m. Jean, d. Garnet Neff, 7 Sept. 1949; children: Gordon Jr., Mark, Joyce; MINISTER OF AGRICULTURE, since 1979; Min. of Educ. 1971-75; Min. of Continuing Educ. 1973-75; MIN: OF MUN: AFFAIRS Past Pres., Sask. NDP; Past Chrmn., Bd. of Govan Sch. Unit No. 29; Mem., Sask. Wheat Pool; United Church; Home: Semans, Sask., S0A 3S0; Office: Room 328, Legislative Bldg., Regina, Sask. S4S 0B3

MacMURRAY, James A.; company president; b. Saint John, N.B., 1925; s. James and Ann Ogilvie (Peebles) M.; e. Pub. Schs. and Saint John High Sch.; Mount Allison Univ.; m. Jean F., d. Frank T. Palfrey, Vancouver, B.C., 19 May 1951; children: Ann F., Barbara J.; CHRMN., MARITIME BEVERAGES LTD.; Pres., M.R.A. Holdings Ltd.; Chrmn., Fundy Cablevision Ltd.; Edmundston Cablevision Ltd.; Vice Pres., Brunswick Square Ltd.; Fundy Broadcasting Co. Ltd.; Dir., N.B. Telephone Co. Ltd.; Wandlyn Motels Ltd.; Brunswick Mining & Smelting Corp. Ltd.; Miramichi Cable Ltd.; mem. St. John Adv. Bd. Montreal Trust Co.; joined Eastern Securities Co. Ltd. in 1945; el. Vice-Pres. in 1947, Pres. 1950 till July 1968; served in 2nd World War with R.C.A.F., 1944-45; United Church; recreations: golf, curling; Clubs: Union; Riverside Golf & Country; Home: Pelton Rd., R.R. 1, Saint John, N.B. E2L 3W2; Office: Box 6100, Stn. A, Saint John, N.B., E2L 4L7

MacMURRAY, William Brock, B.A., B.Paed.; retired headmaster; b. Ingersoll, Ont., 26 Sept. 1906; s. William John and Mary Ethel M.; e. Univ. of Toronto Schs.; Univ. of Toronto, 1927-31; Ont. Coll. Educ., 1932-33; m. Margaret Elizabeth, d. George H. Christilaw, Toronto, Ont., 30 July 1938; one s. Dr. Stuart Brock; Headmaster, Univ. of Toronto Schools, 1944-72; with Can. Life Assurance Co. 1924-27; Master, Ridley Coll., 1931-32; Teacher, Weston Coll. Inst. and Vocational Sch., 1933-39; Parkdale Coll. Inst., 1939-42; Master, Univ. of Toronto Schs., 1942-44; had broadcast weekly over C.F.R.B., "Great Canadians" 1946-47, 1951-52; Beta Theta Pi; Anglican; Clubs: Granite; recreations: golf, curling, swimming, motoring

MacNABB, Gordon Murray, B.Sc.; Canadian public servant; b. Almonte, Ont., 13 July 1931; s. Keith Charles and Grace Marshall (Stevenson) MacN.; e. Carleton Place (Ont.) Pub. and High Schs.; Carleton Univ., Engn. Dipl. 1952; Queen's Univ. B.Sc. (Civil Engn.) 1954; UD.Sc. (Hon.) Memorial Univ. 1979; Windsor 1980; LL.D. (Hon.) Concordia Univ. 1981; m. Lorna Amelia, d. W. P. Clayton, Osbornville, N.J., 24 Apl. 1954; children: Charles Kevin, Stewart Clayton, Steven Andrew, James Duncan, Linda Gail, Barbara Heather; PRES., NATURAL SCIENCES AND ENGN. RESEARCH COUNCIL; Pres., Uranium Can. Ltd.; Dir., AECL; Chrmn., Candn. Sec., Columbia River Treaty Perm. Engn. Bd.; Hon. Vice Chrmn., World Energy Conf.; Hydraulic Engr., Columbia River Hydro-Elect. Investigations, 1954-57; Tech. Asst. to Columbia River Treaty Negotiators, 1958-62; Sr. Engn. Adviser to Candn. Treaty Negotiators, 1962-64; Asst. Depy. Minister (Energy Devel.), Dept. of Energy, Mines and Resources; 1967; Sr. Asst. Depy. Min. 1973; Depy. Min. 1975-78; mem., Assn. Prof. Engrs. Ont.; United Church; recreations: sports, gardening; Home: 1799 Rhodes Cres., Ottawa, Ont., K1H 5T1; Office: Montreal Rd., Ottawa, Ont.

MACNAIR, Mrs. D. C. — see: Livesay, Dorothy.

MACNAMARA, John, M.Sc., Ph.D.; executive; b. Hamilton, Ont., 22 March 1925; s. John Edward and Rachel (Watt) M.; e. McMaster Univ., B.Sc. 1947, M.Sc. 1949, Ph.D. 1951; m. Maryjane Anne, d. Orville Walsh, 15 Oct. 1949; four s. John Alexander, Dean Stafford, Peter MacEvery, Stephen Walsh; CHMN. & CHIEF EXTVE. OFFR., THE ALGOMA STEEL CORP. LTD.; Dir., Cannelton Industries, Inc., W. Va.; Candn. Pacific Enterprises Ltd.; Am. Iron & Steel Inst.; Internat. Iron & Steel Inst.; started as Jr. Research Offr., Nat. Research Council, 1947; joined present Co. as Asst. Chief Chem.-Metall. 1951, Research Metall. 1955, Asst. to Supt. Bar & Strip and Cold Mill 1957, Jurisdiction over Cold Mill operation 1958, Asst. Supt. Cold Mill and Jurisdiction over Bar & Strip Finishing 1958, Asst. to Div. Supt. Coke Ovens and Docks 1960, Asst. Div. Supt. Primary Production 1963 and Div. Supt. 1968, Vice-Pres. and Works Mgr., Steelworks Div., 1971, Vice-Pres. operations 1973; Dir., Plummer Mem. Hosp.; mem. Nat. Open Hearth & Basic Oxygen Soc. (Past Chrmn.); Metall. Soc. N.Y. (Dir.); Protestant; recreation: golf; Club: Sault Ste. Marie Golf; Home: 6 Summit Ave., Sault Ste. Marie, Ont. P6B 2S1; Office: 503 Queen E., Sault Ste. Marie, Ont. P6A 5P2

MACNAUGHTON, Hon. Alan, P.C., Q.C., LL.D.; senator; b. Napanee, Ont., 30 July 1903; s. Donald Carmichael and Mabel Louise (Aylesworth) M.; e. Upper Can. Coll.; McGill Univ.; Univ. of London Grad Sch. of Econ. and Pol. Science (P.Q., I.O.D.E. Overseas Scholar.), B.A., B.C.L.; m. Mary Caroline, d. Fred Rollin White, 1 Aug. 1942; children: Elizabeth White, Alan Aylesworth, Jr., Laurence Robert Norton; COUNSEL, MARTINEAU, WALKER; Chrmn., Olivetti Can. Ltd., Milfoy Ltd.; Dir., Aviation Electric Ltd.; Boise Cascade Can. Ltd.; Saelectric Transmission Inc.; Vice Chrmn., Brown Boveri (Can.) Ltd.; Albion Ins. Co. of Can.; Federation Ins. Co. of Canada; read law with Brown, Montgomery & McMichael, Montreal, P.Q.; called to the Bar of Que. 1930; Crown Prosecutor, 1939-44; cr. K.C. 1944; Gov., Montreal General Hosp.; mem., H. of C. for Montreal-Mt. Royal, 1949-66; Speaker, H. of C. 1963-66 (Chrmn. Pub. Accts. Comte. First Opposition 1958-63 and Chrmn. Special Comte. on Procedure of Organ. 1963-65); Candn. Alternate Del. to 8th Session of U.N., New York, Sept. 1953; summoned to Senate of Can., 8 July 1966; Depy. Chrmn. Candn. Del. to U.N. Conf. on Environment, Stockholm 1973; Past Pres., Jr. Board of Trade, Montreal; Past Vice-Pres., Nat. Candn. Jr. Chamber of Comm.; Hon. Life mem., Assemblée Nat. de la France; Hon. Chrmn., World Wildlife Fund (Can.); mem. 1001 "Nature Trust"; Internat. Trustee, World Wildlife Fund; Past Pres., Roosevelt Campobello Internat. Park Comn.; Liberal; Anglican; Clubs: Reform (Past Chrmn.); University; Montreal; Rideau (Ottawa); Canadian (N.Y.); Royal Montreal Golf; St. James's; Mount Royal (Montreal); Buck's (London, Eng.); Mill Reef (Antigua, W.I.); Home: 7 Redpath Row, Montreal H3G 1E6; Office: 3400Stock Exchange Tower, Place Victoria, Montreal, Que. H4Z 1E9

MacNAUGHTON, Angus Athole, C.A.; b. Montreal, Que., 15 July 1931; s. Athole Austin and Emily Kidder (MacLean) MacN.; e. Lakefield (Ont.) Coll. Sch., 1941-47; Lower Can. Coll., Montreal, 1947-48; McGill Univ., Sch. of Comm.; Que. Inst. C.A.'s; m. Penelope Bower, d. (late) John Bower Lewis, Montreal, Que., 2 March 1957; children: Gillian Heather, Angus Andrew; CHRMN. AND C.E.O., GENSTAR CORP.; Dir. since 1976; Dir., Canadian Pacific Enterprises Limited; Sun Life Assurance Co. of Can.; Dart Containerline Inc.; Cdn. Commercial Corp.; joined Coopers & Lybrand as auditor 1949-55; joined present Co. as Acct. 1955, Asst. Treas. 1956; Treas. 1961; Vice Pres. 1964, Extve. Vice Pres. 1970; Pres., 1973-76; Vice Chrmn. & C.E.O., 1976- ; Chmn. and C.E.O., 1981; mem., Past Pres., Montreal Chapter, Tax Extves. Inst.; mem. Bd. Govs., Lakefield Coll. Sch.; recreations: skiing, tennis, water skiing; Clubs: Pacific Union; World Trade; Mount Royal; St. James's; Montreal Badminton & Squash; Canadian (Montreal); Office: Suite 3800, Four Embaradero Centre, San Francisco, California, 94111.

MacNAUGHTON, Charles Steel, LL.D.; b. Strasbourg, Sask., 8 May 1911; s. Alex M. and Elizabeth (Steele) M.; Public and High Schs., Brandon, Man.; m. Adeline, d. Samuel Fulcher, 22 Oct. 1938; children: Heather (Mrs. William T. Howitt), John; Dir., Bank of Montreal; Canadian Canners Ltd.; 1st el. to Ont. Leg. by-el. May 1958; re-el. g.e. 1959, 63, 67, 71; Commr., Ont. Water Resources Comn., Jan. 1960-Nov. 1961; apptd. Min. without Portfolio, 8 Nov. 1961; Min. of Highways, 25 Oct. 1962; Treas. of Ont., 24 Nov. 1966; Min. of Econ., 6 Oct. 1968; Min. of Highways and Min. of Transport, 1 March 1971; Min. of Transportation and Communications, 1 June 1971; Chrmn. Mang. Bd. of Cabinet 1972; former Mang. Dir. of Jones, MacNaughton Seeds Ltd.; for 9 yrs. mem. and 2 yrs. Chrmn. of S. Huron Dist. High Sch. Bd.; one of the Founders of S. Huron Hosp. in Exeter, Ont. and mem. of Hosp. Bd. of Management; Hon. Life mem., Candn. Seed Trade Assn.; Freemason; P. Conservative; United Church; Club: Albany; Home: 300 Huron St., Exeter, Ont., N0M 1S0; Office: P.O. Box 39, Toronto-Dominion Centre, Toronto, Ont., M5K 1B7

MACNEE, Walter Q., B.Sc., P.Eng.; civil servant; b. Kingston, Ont., 4 Aug. 1922; s. Barbara Gatehouse (Quirk) and the late Walter Kent M.; e. Kingston (Ont.) Coll. & Vocational Inst. (Sr. Matric.) 1940; Queen's Univ., B.Sc. (Civil Engn.) 1950; Yale Univ. (Cert. in Traffic Engn.) 1953; m. Mary Elizabeth Minnes, d. late Arnott James Minnes, Kingston, Ont., 7 May 1949; children: Walter Minnes, Nora Elizabeth, Peter Gordon; Coordinator Land Adm., Min. of Govt. Services Ont. until retired; began career with Ont. Dept. Highways, May 1950; became Traffic Engr. i/c (new) Traffic Sec., 1953, Traffic and Planning Studies Engr., 1962; Deputy Minister, Dept. of Transport Dec. 1966 to May 1971; Depy. Min., Lands & Forests May 1971-Apl. 1972, Dept. Natural Resources, Apl. 1972-May 1974; rep. of Province of Ontario on Jt. Comte. on Uniform Traffic Control Devices for Can. (Chrmn. of Jt. Comte. May 1954-69); Tech. Adv. to Select Comte. on Toll Roads and Highway Financing (Ont. Leg.) 1956-57; Vice Chrmn. of Tech. Adv. Comte. of Metrop. Toronto & Region Transp. Study from inception 1960 till Nov. 1966; served with R.C.O.C. Aug. 1942-May 1943; Perth Regt.-5th Candn. Armoured Div., May 1943-Feb. 1946; mem., Assn. Prof. Engrs. Ont.; Inst. Traffic Engrs. (Past Dir. for Canada); Presbyterian; Club: Kingston (Ont.) Yacht; Home: 114 St. Leonards Ave., Toronto, Ont., M4N 1K5

MacNEIL, Most Rev. Joseph Neil, B.A., J.C.D. (R.C.); archbishop; b. Sydney, N.S., 15 Apl. 1924; s. John Martin and Kate Alice (MacLean) MacN.; e. St. Joseph's Sch. and Sydney (N.S.) Acad.; St. Francis Xavier Univ., B.A. 1944; Holy Heart Semy., Halifax, o. 1948; Univ. of St. Thomas Aquinas, Rome, J.C.D. 1958; Univ. of Perugia, Inst. Catholique (Paris) and Univ. of Chicago, summers 1956, 1957, and 1964; ARCHBISHOP OF EDMONTON since 1973; Bishop of St. John, N.B. 1969-74; Chancellor, Univ. of St. Thomas 1969-73; mem. of Extve., Candn. Council on Rural Devel. 1965-75; Dir. of Program & Planning Agency, N.S. Govt., 1969; Exec. Comte., Atlantic Provinces Economic Council, 1968-73; Vice Chrm, N.S. Voluntary Econ. Planning Bd. 1965-79; mem. Bd. Dirs., Candn. Assn. for Adult Educ. (Past Pres., N.S. Div.); Past Pres., Candn. Assn. Dirs., Univ. Extension & Summer Schs.; Vice-Pres. for Adult Educ. and Dir., Extension Dept., St. Francis Xavier Univ., 1961-69; honoured by Pope Paul for work in field of social action by being named Domestic Prelate with title of Msgr., 1964; founding mem., Inst. for Research on Public Policy 1968-80; mem., Nat. Comm. for Cdn. Participation in Habitat 1976; mem. Bd. and Exec., Cdn. Conf. of Catholic Bishops 1975- ; Past Pres., Can. Conference of Catholic Bishops; Address: 10044-113th St., Edmonton, Alta. T5K 1N8

MacNEIL, Robert Breckenridge Ware; broadcast journalist; b. Montreal, Que. 19 Jan. 1931; s. Robert A.S. and Margaret Virginia (Oxner) M.; e. Dalhousie Univ. 1949-51; B.A. Carleton Univ. 1955; L.H.D. (hon.) William Patterson Coll., 1977, Beaver Coll., 1978, Bates Coll. 1979, Lawrence Univ., 1980; m. Rosemarie Anne Copland, 1956 (Div. 1964); children: Catherine Anne, Ian B.; m. 2ndly Jane J. Doherty, 29 May 1965; children: Alison N., William H.; EDITOR, CO-ANCHOR, MacNEIL/LEHRER REPORT, Sta. WNET-TV, N.Y.C., 1975- ; Recipient awards, incl. George Foster Peabody award U. Ga, 1977; Dupont award Columbia Sch. Journalism, 1977; Emmy award, 1974; mem. AFTRA, Assn. Radio and TV News Analysts, Writers Guild Am.; Clubs: American Yacht (Rye, N.Y.); Century, N.Y.C.; author: "The People Machine: The Influence of Television on American Politics", 1968; "The Right Place at the Right Time", 1982; Address: WNET/13 356 W. 58th St., New York, N.Y. 10019

MacNEILL, Hugh Gordon, B.A., manufacturer; b. Sydney, N.S., 13 July 1925; s. late Hugh Archibald & Jean Campbell (Murray) MacN.; e. Sydney (N.S.) Acad.; Acadia Univ., B.A. (Écon.) 1948; m. Barbara, d. Capt. R. L. McLellan, Sarasota, Fla., 22 July 1950; children: Glenn Gordon, Janice Ellen, Scott Leston, Jesslyn Jean; PRESIDENT AND CHIEF EXTVE. OFFICER, JÁNNOCK CORP. LTD. since 1976; Pres. & Dir., Kelly-Springfield Tire Co. of Canada Ltd.; Dir. Seilberling Rubber Co. of Can. Ltd.; Hallmark Automotive Centres Ltd.; Toronto-Dominion Bank; mem. Board of Governors, Acadia University; joined Goodyear Can. Ltd. Company in Toronto, 1948; transferred to Quebec City plant 1949; Devel. Mgr. 1956; Que. Plant Mgr. 1958; Plant Mgr., Bowmanville, Ont., 1960; Gen. Mgr., Indust. Products Div., 1963; Vice Pres. and Gen. Mgr., Gen Products Div., 1966; Extve. Vice Pres., Sales, Feb. 1969; Pres. and CEO 1970; served as sch. trustee and as a Dir., YMCA; also involved in community coll. work; mem., Candn. Inst. Mining & Metall.; Dir., Rubber Assn. Can.; mem., Bd. Trade Metrop. Toronto; P. Conservative; Presbyterian; recreations: golf, reading, music; Clubs: Mississauga Golf; The Toronto; Home: 1532 Point-O-Woods Road, Mississauga, Ont., L5G 2X7; Office: (P.O. Box 43) Toronto Dominion Centre, M5K 1B7

MacNICOL, Nicol, M.B.A.; executive; b. Toronto, Ont. 18 Apl. 1930; s. Nicol and Edith E. (MacIntyre) MacN.; e. Univ. of W. Ont. B.A. 1952; Univ. of Toronto M.B.A. 1956; m. Carol Gregory 10 Oct. 1953; children: Nicol, Heather; PRES. & C.E.O., CAMPBELL SOUP CO. LTD; Clubs: Toronto Golf; Badminton & Racquet; Home: 306

Vesta Dr., Toronto, Ont. M5P 3A3; Office: 60 Birmingham St., Toronto, Ont. M8V 2B8.

MacOWAN, William, M.B.E.; manufacturer; b. Glasgow, Scotland, 7 Jan. 1919; s. William and Elizabeth Williamson (Niven) M.; e. Queens Park High Sch., Glasgow, Scot. (1930-36); M. Heather Alyson, d. Geoffrey and Marguerite Atkinson, 1978; one s. Brian Henderson; VICE CHRMN, CORP. DEV. HOWDEN GROUP CAN. LTD.; Dir., Brown, Boveri, Howden; Howden Applied Research; Dir., Candn. Nuclear Assn.; joined James Howden and Company in Glasgow as Apprentice Engineer, 1936; after war service rejoined as Sales Engr., London, Eng., Apl. 1946; promoted to Depy. Export Sales Mgr., Oct. 1949; Depy. to Gen. Sales Mgr., Jan. 1951 and Gen. Sales Mgr., June 1955; Extve. Vice Pres. and Mang. Dir., James Howden & Co. of Canada Ltd., 1957-66; Pres., Howden Parsons Ltd. 1966-76; served in 2nd World War; Sgt., Cameronians, 1939-40; O.C.T.U. 1940-41; Major, 1941-46, Royal Corps of Signals and G.S.O. 11; action Middle East, Italy; M.B.E.; Mentioned in Despatches; Anglican; recreations: gardening, skiing; Clubs: Granite; R.C.M.I.; Home: 64 Balmoral Heights, Queensville Ont., L0G 1R0; Office: 1510 Birchmount Rd., Scarborough, Ont., M1P 2G6

MACPHAIL, M(oray) S(t. John), M.A., D.Phil., D.Sc., F.R.S.C.; university professor; b. Kingston, Ont.; 27 May 1912; s. James Alexander and Agnes Mary (Macmorine) M.; e. Kingston Collegiate; Upper Can. Coll., Toronto, Ont.; Queen's Univ., B.A. 1933; McGill Univ., M.A. 1934; Oxford Univ., D.Phil. 1936; Carleton Univ., D.Sc. (Hon.) 1978; m. Frances Marian, d. Dr. F. W. Patterson, Wolfville, N.S., 17 Aug. 1939; one s. James Alexander; PROF. EMERITUS OF MATH., CARLETON UNIV. (former Dean of Grad. Studies 1963-69); Instr., Acadia Univ., 1937-39, Asst. Prof. 1939-41; Instr., Princeton Univ., 1941-42; Assoc. Prof., Acadia Univ., 1942-44, Prof. 1944-47; Visiting Lectr., Queen's Univ., 1947-48; Assoc. Prof. Carleton Univ., 1948-53, and Prof. 1953-77; Assoc. Dean, Faculty of Arts & Science, 1956-63; Dir., Sch. of Grad. Studies, 1960-63; Visiting Prof., Univ. of Toronto, 1967-68; mem., Candn. Math. Cong.; Am. Math. Soc.; Math. Assn. of Am.; United Church; Home: 165 Powell Ave., Ottawa, Ont., K1S 2A2

MacPHAIL, Hon. Robert Lloyd George, M.L.A.; politician; b. New Haven, P.E.I. 22 March 1920; s. Robert Archibald and Catherine C. (MacLean) MacP.; e. New Haven Pub. Sch.; Prince of Wales Coll. Charlottetown; m. Helen Mae d. John W. MacDougall, Argyle Shore, P.E.I. 8 Jan. 1955; children: Judith Anne, Lynn, Ferne, Robert; MIN. OF FINANCE, P.E.I.1979- ; Min. of Devel. 1979-80; owner R.A. MacPhail & Son, Gen. Merchants; el. M.L.A. for 2nd Queens prov. by-el. 1961, re-el. since prov. g.e. 1962; Min. of Industry & Natural Resources and of Tourist Devel. 1965-66; P. Conservative; Office: (P.O. Box 2000) Shaw Bldg., Charlottetown, P.E.I. C1A 7N8.

MacPHEE, Earle Douglas, M.M., M.A., M.Ed., LL.D., D.C.L., F.C.I., F.A.S. (Scot.), C.A. (Hon.), C.G.A. (Hon.); educator; management consultant; b. Lower Millstream, King's Co., N.B., 19 July 1894; s. Henry Alfred and Ella Elizabeth (Leard) M.; e. Public and High Schools, Millstream, N.B.; Prov. Normal School, Fredericton, N.B. (1912); Acadia Univ.; Univ. of Edinburgh, M.A., M.Educ. 1920; LL.D., Alta., Brit. Columbia, York, Calgary; D.C.L. Acadia; m. Jennie Minerva, d. Guilford W. Steeves, 28 Dec. 1920; children: Dr. Douglas M., Dr. Kenneth E., Ralph L. E.; Dir. and Dean Comm. and Business Adm. and Dean of Adm. and Finance Univ. of British Columbia, 1950-63, and Banff School of Advanced Mang., 1955-65; Princ., High Schs. 1912-15; Instr. in Psychol., Acadia Univ., 1920-21; Asst. Prof., Univ. of Alta., 1921-24; Assoc. Prof., Univ. of Toronto, 1924-29; Visiting Prof., Univ. of Iowa and Univ. of Chicago, 1926-29; Re-

search Investigator in Mental Hygiene, Toronto, 1924-29; Comptroller, York Knitting Mills, Toronto, 1929-37; Mang. Dir., J. D. Woods & Co. Ltd., Toronto, 1932-37; Mang. Dir. and Depy. Chrmn. of Dent Allcroft & Co. Ltd., London, Eng., 1937-50; Supv., Short Bros. (Aircraft), 1941-43; Dir., Production Engineering Ltd.; 1934-50; Mang. Dir., Alginate Industries Ltd., London, 1943-50; apptd. Dean, Faculty of Comm. and Bus. Admn., Univ. of B.C., 1950 (now Dean Emeritus); Chrmn., Bd. of Mang., Carey Hall; served in 1st World War with 219th and 85th Bns. (Pte. to Co. Sgt. Major); Mil. Medal, 1918; Sole Roy. Comn. B.C. Tree Fruits 1957-58; Chrmn. Comn. B.C. Pharm. Soc.; Comn. B.C. Tugboats Enquiry; awarded Coat of Arms by Lord Lyon, King of Arms of Scot.; appointed Commander Macfie Van 1981; Publications: "Modern Language Methodology" (with J. Buchanan), 1928; Report of Royal Commission, Tree Fruit Industry of B.C. 1958; Manning of Tugboats 1966; Pharm. Planning Comn. B.C. 1967; "History of Clan MacDhubhshith" (5 vols.) 1970-74; "History of the Faculty of Commerce and Business Administration Univ. of B.C." 1976; "Autobiography of Earle Douglas MacPhee" 1978; "Pioneers of Our Clan in Prince Edward Island" 1978; articles on psychol., mental hygiene, management; Freemason; Liberal; Baptist; Home: 121—4875 Valley Dr., Vancouver, B.C., V6J 4B8

MACPHERSON, Crawford Brough, O.C., B.A., M.Sc., D.Sc., LL.D., D.Litt., F.R.S.C., F.R.Hist.S.; educator; b. Toronto, Ont., 18 Nov. 1911; s. Walter Ernest and Elsie Margaret (Adams) M.; e. Univ. of Toronto Schs.; Univ. of Toronto, B.A. 1933; Univ. of London, M.Sc. (Econ.) 1935, D.Sc. (Econ.) 1955; LL.D. Queen's 1970, Western Ont. 1973; Guelph 1980; D.Litt. Memorial 1970; m. Kathleen Margaret, d. Frederick Edward Walker, M.D., Bedford, Eng., 25 Sept. 1943; children: Susan Margaret, Stephen Denis, Sheila Jane; PROF. OF POLITICAL SCIENCE, UNIVERSITY OF TORONTO, since 1956; Lecturer in Pol. Econ., University of Toronto, 1935-42, 1944-45; Acting Professor of Economics and Political Science, University of New Brunswick, 1942-43; Extve. Offr., Wartime Information Bd., Ottawa, 1943-44; Asst. Prof. of Pol. Econ., Univ. of Toronto, 1945-51, Assoc. Prof., 1951-56; Fellow, Nuffield Foundation, 1952-53; Sr. Fellow, Can. Council, 1959-60; Fellow, Churchill Coll. Cambridge 1967-68; Visiting Prof. Hebrew Univ. Jerusalem 1972; Aarhus Univ. Inst. of Philos., Denmark 1975; Arizona State Univ., 1979; Visiting Research Fellow, Inst. Advanced Studies, Australian Nat. University 1973; apptd. (seventh) University Professor, University of Toronto 1975; Offr. Order of Can. 1976; author of "Democracy in Alberta", 1953, 2nd ed. 1962; "The Political Theory of Possessive Individualism", 1962, 2nd ed. 1964; "The Real World of Democracy", 1965; "Democratic Theory: Essays in Retrieval" 1973; "The Life and Times of Liberal Democracy" 1977; "Burke", 1980; numerous articles in journals; President, Canadian Association of Univ. Teachers, 1968-69; mem., Candn. Pol. Science Assn. (Pres. 1963-64); Internat. Pol. Science Assn.; Institut Internat. de Philos. Pol.; Am. Soc. for Pol. & Legal Philosophy; Conf. for the Study of Pol. Thought (Vice Pres. and Pres. 1973-77); Address: Toronto, Ont., M5S 1A1

MACPHERSON, Duncan Ian; cartoonist; b. Toronto, Ont., 20 Sept. 1924; s. Alexander and Margaret (Matheson) M.; e. Boston Museum Sch. Fine Art; Ont. Coll. Art, Toronto; m. Dorothy Blackhall; 1 s., Ian; free lance editorial and advt. illustrator, 1949-59; pol. cartoonist, Toronto Daily Star since 1959; served with RCAF 1942-46; recipient Nat. Press Club Award 1973; Molson Award Can. Council 1971; Nat. Newspaper Awards for ed. cartooning 1959, 60, 62, 65, 70, 72; Roy. Acad. Arts Medal 1966; named to Candn. News Hall of Fame 1976; Fellow Ont. Coll. Art; mem., Am. Assn. Ed. Cartoonists; Roy. Candn. Acad. Arts; author: "Reportage and Political Review" 1966; "Macpherson's Canada" 1969; also numerous cartoon annuals; patentee illus. for TV; research on history Upper Can.; Address: c/o Toronto Star, 1 Yonge St., Toronto, Ont.

MacPHERSON, Eric D., M.A., Ph.D.; educator; b. Hawkeye, Sask. 8 Apl. 1931; s. Duncan and Anna M. (Ohrn) MacP.; e. Univ. of B.C. B.A. 1952, M.A. 1960; Wash. State Univ. Ph.D. 1966; m. Fern d. Albert Bolger; 27 Dec. 1957; three s. James, Glen, Bruce; DEAN OF EDUCATION, UNIV. OF MANITOBA, since 1974; Prof. of Ed. and Math, Univ. of B.C. 1959-73, Dept. Head 1964-72, Assoc. Dean 1972-74; has engaged in minor athletic coaching; author "Contemporary Mathematics" 1964; "Ginn Elementary Arithmetic" 1972; "Mathematics in Modules" 1977; other writings incl. over 40 television programs and articles; mem. Nat. Council Teachers Math.; Phi Delta Kappa; recreation: chess; Home: 30 MacAlester Bay, Winnipeg, Man., R3T 2X5

MACPHERSON, Lawrence Gladwyn, B.A., LL.D., F.C.A.; b. Ottawa, Ont., 3 July 1906; s. John Angus and Elizabeth Robina (Gray) M.; e. Brandon Coll., B.A. 1927; C.A., Man., 1931; Ont. F.C.A. 1956; LL.D., Brandon Univ. 1975; Queen's 1977; m. Doris Lillian, d. Robert Riddell Dowling, Brandon, Man., 4 Oct. 1930; children: Diane (Mrs. Barry Hercus), Janet (Nrs. Gary Mooney); Dir., Bushnell Communications Ltd., Ottawa; mem. Kingston Adv. Bd., Royal Trust Co.; Life Gov., Kingston Gen. Hosp.; Dir. of Research, Candn. Inst. of Chart Accts., 1954-58; apptd. to staff, Sch. of Comm. and Adm., Queen's Univ., 1933; Dean, Sch. of Business 1958-65; Vice Principal, Finance (1965-71) ; mem. Bd. Mang. andHon. Treas., Queen's Theol. Coll.; mem., Inst. of Chart Accts. of Ont.; Home: 185 Ontario St., Kingston, Ont., K7L 2Y7

MACPHERSON,Marion Adams, M.A.; diplomat; b. Moose Jaw, Sask. 16 May 1924; d. John Archibald and Anne Penelope (Adams) M.; e. Moosomin (Sask.) Pub. Sch. and Coll. Inst.; Univ. of Sask. B.A. 1946; Univ. of Toronto M.A. 1947; AMBASSADOR TO DENMARK, 1979- ; joined Dept. of External Affairs 1948; Third Secy. Washington 1950, Second Secy. 1953; Adviser Internat. Truce Comn. Indo-China 1957; Second Secy. Accra 1957, First Secy. 1958; Counsellor Candn. Perm. Mission to UN, N.Y. 1963-68; High Commr. to Sri Lanka 1973-76; Consul Gen. Boston 1977; Inspr. Gen. External Affairs 1977-79; Presbyterian; Home: Dag Hammarskjolds Allé 26, 2100 Copenhagen, Denmark; Office: KR. Bernikows Gade 1, 1105 Copenhagen K, Denmark.

MacPHERSON, Hon. Murdoch Alexander. Jr., B.A., LL.B.; counsel; b. Swift Current, Sask. 15 Nov. 1916; s. Murdoch Alexander and Iowa (Briggs) MacP.; e. Regina, Sask.; Dalhousie Univ. B.A. 1936; Univ. of Sask. LL.B. 1938; m. Dorothy Pearl d. Romano Borutti, France, 2 Apl. 1945; children: Ian, Rosemary Christie, Alexandra Young; Judge, Court of Queen's Bench, Sask. 1961-81; called to Bar of Sask. 1939; Partner, MacPherson Leslie & Tyerman, Regina 1945-55; MacPherson Neuman & Pierce, Regina 1955-61; mem. Regina Pub. Sch. Bd. 1956-61; served with Candn. Army 1940-45 Overseas, rank Capt.; Mentioned in Despatches; Presbyterian; recreation: photography; Clubs: Assiniboia; Regina; Home: 2720 Assiniboine Ave., Regina, Sask. S4S 1C6.

MACQUARRIE, Heath Nelson, M.A., LL.D.; political scientist., senator; b. Victoria, P.E.I., 18 Sept. 1919; s. late Wilfred and Mary (Mallard) M.; e. Prince of Wales Coll., Charlottetown, P.E.I.; P.E.I. Normal Sch. (1st Class Teachers Lic.) 1936; Univ. of Manitoba, B.A. 1947; Univ. of New Brunswick M.A. 1949; McGill Univ.; Univ. P.E.I. LL.D. (Hon.) 1978; m. Jean Isabel, d. late George Neil Stewart, 27 De. 1949; children: Heather Jean, Flora Nary, Iain Heath; Teacher in Public and High Schs., P.E.I. 1936-43; Secy., P.E.I. Teachers Fed., 1943; Asst. Boys Work Secy., Y.M.C.A., Winnipeg, Man., 1943-47; Asst. Prof. of Econ. and Pol. Science, Univ. of N.B., 1947-49,

Lectr. in Pol. Science, McGill Univ., 1949-51; Instr., Asst. Prof. and later Prof. of Pol. Science and Internat. Relations, Brandon Coll., Man., 1951-55; Visiting Lect., Acadia Univ. Summer Sch., 1949 and 1952; Univ. of Man. Summer Sch., 1954; Mt. Allison Univ. Summer Sch., 1948 and 1955; News Analyst and Commentator, CKX, Brandon, Man., 1952-55; Research Assoc. in Pol. Science, Univ. of Toronto, 1957 (research grants); Instr. Internat. Relations, Carleton Univ. 1963-64; Assoc. Prof. Pol. Science, Mt. Allison Univ., 1978-79; Pres., Brandon P. Cons. Assn., 1955; Secy., Brandon-Souris Cons. Assn., 1954-55; 3rd Vice-Pres., P. Cons. Party of Can., 1955-58; mem., Bd. of Sch. Trustees, City of Brandon, 1955; el. to H. of C. for Queens in g.e. 1957, and re-el. since; summoned to Senate of Can. Oct. 1979; Parlty. Secy. to Secy. of State for External Affairs, 1962-63; mem., Candn. Del. to U.N. Gen. Assembly, 1957, '58, '59, '62, '71; Candn. Observer del. to Inter-Am. Conf., Punta del Este, Uruguay, 1961; Chrmn., Can. branch, Commonwealth Parlty. Assn., 1961-62; Chrmn., H. of C. Comte. on Privileges and Elections, 1957-61; author "The Conservative Party" 1965 and of numerous articles on national and international politics; co-author "Canada and the Third World"; a contrib. of articles to the press and learned journs.; Ed. (Carleton Library Edition) "Robert Laird Borden, His Memoirs" 1969; mem., Canadian Political Science Assn.; Nat. Council Canadian Human Rights Foundation; Patron, Un. Nations Assn. Can.; Candn. Inst. Internat. Affairs; Chmn., Comte. on Internat. Affairs, Presbyterian Church in Canada; Hon. mem. Oxfam Can., UNICEF; Freemason; Conservative; Presbyterian; recreations: swimming, skating, play-reading, reading; Home: Victoria, P.E.I. C0A 2G0

MacQUEEN, Very Rev. Angus James, D.D., LL.D., B.A., L.Th., B.D. (Un. Ch.); retired minister; b. Port Morien, N.S.; 3 JulY 1912; s. Duncan Archibald and Lillian Jane (Wadden) M.; e. Mount Allison Univ., B.A. 1933; Pine Hill Divinity Hall, L.Th. 1935, B.D. 1938, D.D. 1958; D.D., Victoria 1960; LL.D., Mount Allison 1959, W. Ont. 1959; m. Minetta Mae d. Calvin A. and Mary Ann MacFadyen, Sydney, N.S., 28 Oct. 1936; children: Marian (McNairn), Joan (Warren), Barbara, Heather (Niven); Min., Zion Robertson, Port Hawkesbury, N.S., 1936-39; St. James', Antigonish, N.S., 1939-42; Centenary-Queen Sq., Saint John, N.B., 1942-46; Robertson Ch., Edmonton, Alta., 1946-51; First-St. Andrew's Ch., London, Ont., 1951-64; St. George's Ch., Toronto, 1964-80; Chrmn. Bd. of Evangelism & Social Services, Un. Ch. of Can., 1954-58; el. Moderator, Un. Ch. of Can., 17 Sept. 1958; Chrmn., Bd. of Dirs. of "United Church Observer" 1973-80; mem. Comte. on Ch. and Internat. Affairs; apptd. Chancellor, Mt. Allison Univ. 1977; author: "Superman Is An Idiot" 1977; "The Ten Commandments: New Light From Old Lamps" 1978; has written for publs. in Can., Br., U.S. and has contrib. chaps. for 6 bks.; recreations: curling, swimming, golf, reading; Home: 326 Douglas Ave., Toronto, Ont., M5M 1H1

MacRAE, Donald Alexander, A.M., Ph.D., F.R.S.C.; astronomer; b. Halifax, N.S., 19 Feb. 1916; s. Donald Alexander and Laura (Barnstead) MacR.; e. Univ. of Toronto, B.A., 1937; Harvard Univ., A.M., 1940, Ph.D. 1943; m. Margaret Elizabeth, d. C. A. Malcolm, Port Stanley, Ont., 25 Aug. 1939; children: David M., Charles D., Andrew R.; PROFESSOR, DEPT. OF ASTRONOMY, UNIVERSITY OF TORONTO; Dir., David Dunlap Observatory 1965-78; mem., Am. Astron. Soc.; Candn. Astron. Soc.; mem. Bd. Trustees, Universities Space Research Assn. (operating Lunar Science Inst., Houston, Texas) 1969-76; mem., Bd. Dir., Can.-Fr.-Hawaii Telescope Corp. 1973-79; mem., Bd. of Trustees, Cdn. Corp. for Univ. Space Sci. 1978; author of numerous scient. articles; Address: David Dunlap Observatory, Box 360, Richmond Hill, Ont. L4C 4Y6

MACRAE, Herbert Farquhar, B.Sc., M.Sc., Ph.D.; educational administrator; b. Middle River, N.S. 30 March 1926; s Murdoch John and Jessie Matheson (MacLellan) M.; e. N.S. Normal Coll., Teacher's license 1948; N.S. Agri. Coll. Diploma 1952; McGill Univ. B.Sc. 1954, M.Sc. 1956, Ph.D. 1960; m. Mary Ruth d. late Roderick K. Finlayson 24 Sept. 1955; children: Roderick John, Elizabeth Anne, Christy Margaret, Mary Jean; PRINCIPAL, N.S. AGRI. COLL.; mem., Candn. Soc. of Animal Science; N.S. Inst. of Agrologists; Agri. Inst. of Can.; Sigma Xi; Protestant; Club: Rotary, Truro; Home: 7 Hickman Dr., Truro, N.S. B2N 2Z2; Office: Truro, N.S. B2N 5E3.

MACRAE, Marion Bell, architectural and design historian; b. Apple Hill, Ont. 30 April 1921; d. John Donald and Hazel Ross (Carlyle) M.; e. Apple Hill Pub. Sch. 1932; Maxville H.S. 1939; Ont. Coll. of Art, A.O.C.A. 1947; Postgrad., Univ. of Illinois, 1951-54; LECTR. HIST. OF DESIGN, ONT. COLL. OF ART since 1969; Instr., Design and Museum Studies, Ont. Coll. of Art, 1949-69; Mem., Adv. Cmte. on Design, U.C. Village Restoration, 1957-61; Special Asst. to Design Consultant, Dundurn Castle Restoration, 1963-67; Lectr. (Part-time), Hist. of Candn. Arch., Univ. of Toronto, 1973-78; author of "Settlement of the Old Eastern District", R.A.I.C., 1959; "The Ancestral Roof", 1963; "MacNab of Dundurn", 1971; co-author "Hallowed Walls", 1975; rec'd. Gov.-Gen. Literary Award (non-fiction), 1975; mem., Soc. of Architectural Historians (USA), 1954-79; Soc. for the Study of Arch. in Can.; Associate Mem., Interior Designers of Ont.; Natl. Trust. (U.K.); Natl. Trust for Scotland; Natl. Trust for Historical Preservation (USA); Victorian Soc. (U.K.); Arch. Conservation of Ont.; Ont. Hist. Soc.; Liberal; Christian; recreations: travel; Home: 80 Lawton Blvd., Apt. 19, Toronto, Ont. M4V 2A2; Office: 100 McCaul St., Toronto, Ont. M5T 1W1.

MacSKIMMING, Roy Alexander; government agency executive; b. Ottawa, Ont. 3 Jan. 1944; s. William Thomson and Dorothy Isobel (Batty) MacS.; e. Lisgar Coll. Inst. and Ridgemont High Sch. Ottawa 1962; Univ. of Toronto 1962-64; m. Suzette Louisa DeLey 19 Dec. 1965; two s. Graham William, Andrew Herbert; WRITING AND PUBL. OFFR., FEDERAL CULTURAL POLICY REVIEW COMTE. 1981- ; Ed., Clarke Irwin & Co. Toronto 1964-68; Partner and Publisher New Press Toronto 1969-74; Lit. Columnist & Book Page Ed. Toronto "Star" 1974-76; Writing and Publ. Offr., Canada Council, 1977-81; author "Formentera" (novel) 1972, French transl. 1976; various mag. articles and book reviews; Founding Secy. Independent Publishers' Assn. (now Assn. Candn. Publishers) 1971; Office365 Laurier Ave W., Ottawa, Ont. K1A 0C8.

MacSWEEN, Donald John Alexander, B.A., B.C.L.; b. Montreal, Que. 16 Jan. 1935; s. Sydney Alexander and Martha Gunhild (Christoffersen) MacS.; e. Willingdon Sch. and West Hill High Sch. Montreal 1951; McGill Univ. B.A. 1956, B.C.L. 1961; Univ. of Grenoble summer 1954; Laval Univ. 1958-59; m. Anne Sarah Douglas (divorced) d. Monteath Douglas, Magog, Que. 11 Nov. 1962; children: Alexander, Rebecca, Michal, Jared; m. Andrée Moro, 6 Sept. 1980; DIR. GEN. NATIONAL ARTS CENTRE since 1977; read law with Mr. Justice G. Miller Hyde; called to Bar of Que. 1962; law practice Howard, Cate, Ogilvy, Bishop, Cope, Porteous & Hansard (now Ogilvy, Renault) 1962-73, Partner 1971-73; Dir. Gen. Nat. Theatre Sch. of Can. 1973-77; mem., Bd. of Gov., McGill Univ., 1980- ; Gov. Fraser-Hickson Inst. Montreal 1969-75, Vice Pres. 1972-77; Dir. Centaur Foundation for Performing Arts Montreal 1971-74; mem. Que. Prov. Council Boy Scouts of Can. 1974-76; Corp. mem. Bishop's Univ. since 1975; mem. du conseil d'adm. Internat. Music Inst. of Can. since 1977; Co-creator (writer) "My Fur Lady" (Partner Quince Productions); performed role "Dylan Laydek" Candn. poet on Nat. tour 1957-58; Tutor Faculty Law McGill Univ. 1963-66; mem. and extve. Que. Bar Assn. 1962-76 and Candn. Bar Assn.

1962-76; mem. Bd. of Bar Examiners (Quebec) 1969-73; Secy. McGill Law Grads' Assn. 1966-67, Treas. 1967-68; Clubs: Montreal Canadian (Pres. 1973-74); Office: Confederation Square, Ottawa, Ont.

MacTAVISH, Raymond; executive; b. Charlottetown, P.E.I., 22 April 1928; s. Duncan Thomas and Annie-May (Murphy) MacT.; e. Pub. and High Schs. P.E.I.; Prince of Wales Coll., Charlottetown, P.E.I.; m. Jean, d. Roy Kehoe, 13 Aug. 1952; children: Deborah, Ian, Craig, Rory; Pres. and Dir., Kesmark Lt., and Other Subsidiaries; Pres. and Dir., Twentieth Century Finance Corp. Ltd. since 1973; with Foundation Co. of Canada Ltd. as Accountant 1948, Chief Interal Auditor 1957, Controller 1965; Controller, McNamara Corp. Ltd., Toronto 1965, Vice-Pres. Finance and Dir., 1969; mem. Candn. Constr. Assn. (Past Chrmn. Leg. Comte. on Taxation); United Church; recreations: swimming, fishing; Club: Toronto Cricket, Skating & Curling; Home: 1 Caronridge Crescent, Agincourt, Ont., M1W 1L1; Office: 243 Consumer Rd., Willowdale, Ont. M2J 4W8

MAGAGNA, Lino, M.A.Sc., Ph.D., P.Eng.; b. Revo, Trento, Italy, 23 Jan. 1933; s. Giuseppe and Meri (Bertoldi) M.; e. Shurpass Pacific Coll., Vancouver, 1956; Vancouver Tech. Coll., Diesel Mech. Course 1954; Univ. of B.C., B.A.SC. 1962; Univ. of Toronto, M.A.Sc. 1963, Ph.D. 1965; m. Rosemary Alice, d. Murdoch MacLean, N. Vancouver, 27 Aug. 1960; children: Mark Laurier, Marina Alice; joined Finning Tractor of Vancouver 1954-56; D.C.F. Systems Ltd. 1965-71 served as Consulting Engr., Partner and Mgr. of Indust. Systems; joined Ontario Hydro 1971; Pres. Bd., COSTI; 1970-1980; Vice Chrmn., Candn. Consultative Coundil on Multiculturalism 1973-78; Founder and First Vice-Pres., Nat. Congress Italian-Candns.; mem. Bd. Govs and Senate, York Univ.; mem. Bd. Trustees United Way Metro Toronto; twice rec'd Ford Foundation Fellowship; mem., Assn. Prof. Engrs. Ont.; Candn. Amateur Musicians; Home: 1650 Lincolnshire Blvd., Mississauga, Ont., L5E 2S7; Office: Ontario Hydro, 700 University Ave., Toronto, Ont.

MAGEE, Allan Gordon, B.A., M.B.E.; b. Montreal, Quebec, 12 December 1920; s. Allan Angus and Madeline (Smith) M.; e Selwyn House Sch., Montreal, Que.; Trinity Coll. Sch., Port Hope, Ont.; Bishop's Univ., B.A.; diploma in Indust. Relations, Queen's Univ.; m. Phoebe Ann Freeman, Montreal, Que., 12 Aug. 1944; children: Brian Eric (deceased), Willa Leslie, Margot; Pres. Sea Capt.'s Loft Ltd.; Gen. Mgr., Dow Brewery Ltd., Kitchener, Ont., 1954, Extve. Vice-Pres., Montreal, Que., 1959; Pres., Meagher's Distillery Ltd., 1962-67; served in 2nd World War in all European theatres, with R.C.R.; discharged with rank of Major; Anglican; recreations: golf, swimming; Home: 68 Queen St., St. Andrews, N.B., E0G 2X0; Office: 211 Water St., St. Andrews, N.B., E0G 2X0

MAGEE, Brian R. B., F.R.I., S.I.R., C.R.E.; b. Toronto, Ont., 4 May 1918; s. Col. R. H. Boyd and Evelyn Sarah (Cox) M.; e. Radley Coll., England; Trinity Coll. Sch., Port Hope, Ont.; Royal Mil. Coll., Kingston, Ont.; Univ. of Toronto; m. Elaine S. Leger, Montreal, P.Q., 1942; Dir., Hon. Chrmn., A.E. LePage Ltd.; Dir., AMCA Internat. Ltd.; AMCA Internat. Corp. (U.S.); AMCA BV (Holland); Rawson Trust Co. Ltd. (Nassau); Span Holdings Ltd. (Nassau); Span Internt. Ltd. (Nassau); Delta Hotels Ltd.; Past Dir., Candn. Nat. Sportsmen Show; Past Pres., Toronto Real Estate Bd.; Bd. of Trade of Metrop. Toronto; Candn. Real Estate Assn.; hon. life mem., Candn. Real Estate Assn.; Toronto Real Estate Brd; Anglican; recreations: flying, golf, shooting; Clubs: National; Toronto Racquet; Granite; Ristigouche Salmon; Lost Tree (Palm Beach Fla.); Hendon Gold (Eng.); Rosedale Golf; Lyford Cay (Nassau); M.C.C. (London, Eng.); Home: Flat 4, 1/3 Princes Gate, London SW7 England

MAGNA, Michael D.; manufacturer; b. Montreal, Que. 16 Aug. 1931; s. Domenic Michael and Kathleen (Morrissey) M.; e. Sir George Williams Univ.; Cornell Univ. Extve. Devel. Program grad. 1975; m. Eileen d. Edward J. McAllindon, Montreal, Que. 9 May 1953; children: Jo-Anne, Michael, Barry, Patricia, Kevin; PRESIDENT AND GENERAL MANAGER, CANADA SAND PAPERS, LTD.; served Candn. Carborundum Co. as Field Salesman, Sales Mgr., Gen. Sales Mgr., Marketing Mgr., and Pres. and Gen. Mgr.; mem. Soc. Mech. Engrs.; Sales & Marketing Assn.; Conference Bd. of Can.; R. Catholic; recreation: golf; Clubs: Niagara Falls (Can.) Ltd.; St. Catharines Golf; Home: 3777 Potter Heights, Niagara Falls, Ont., L2J 3E1

MAGNUSSEN, Karen Diane, O.C. (1973); world figure skating champion; b. Vancouver, B.C., 4 Apl. 1952; d. Alf John and Gloria (Johansson) M.; e Delbrook High Sch., N. Vancouver, 1968; Carson Graham Secondary High Sch., N. Vancouver, 1970; Simon Fraser Univ., 1971-72; m. Anthony R. Cella, 23 July 1977; one son, Eric John; Hon. Coach, Figure Skating, Special Olympic Winter Games, Vermont, U.S.A. 1981; Adv. Bd. mem., Calgary Devel. Comte. for the 1988 Winter Olympics; coaches figure skating, North Rinks, Danvers, Mass.; private instructor, Burlington Ice Palace; founder, Karen Magnussen Foundation, 1973; estbd. Karen Magnussen Enterprises Ltd. 1973; past star skater with Ice Capades; named B.C. Jr. Athlete of Yr. 1967, Sr. 1971, 1972; B.C. Sports Special Merit Award 1970; N. Shore Jr. Athlete of Yr. and Hall of Fame, 1971; Can.'s Female Amateur Athlete of Yr. 1971, 1972; B.C. Overall Athlete of Yr. 1972; Vanier Award Can.'s Outstanding Young Candn. 1972; Special Achievement Award, Sons of Norway of Am.; 1972; Award of Merit Candn. Figure Skating Assn. 1973; First Freeman Dist. of N. Vancouver 1973; Karen Magnussen Arena. Lynn Valley. N. Vancouver, named 1973; rec'd All Event Gold Pass Can. Summer Games 1973; Hon. Citizen Thunder Bay, Ont., 1973; Hon. Life mem. Pacific Nat. Exhn., 1973; Life mem. Vancouver Parks Bd. & Pub. Recreation, 1973; Internat. Hon. mem. Beta Sigma Phi; mem. B.C. and Candn. Sports Hall of Fame, 1973; named top female athlete of Can. of yr., Dec. 1973; biog. "Karen" publd. 1973; Lutheran; recreations: figure skating, golf, tennis, swimming; Clubs: Life mem.; N. Shore Winter (Gold Pass); Swedish Candn.; Nordlandslaget; New Westminster Skating; B.C. Jockey; Vancouver; Home: 2852 Thorncliffe Dr., N. Vancouver, B.C., V7R 2S8; Office: c/o Sports Mgmt. Ltd., #1000 , 65 Queen St. W., Toronto, Ont., M5H 2M5

MAGWOOD, John McLean, Q.C., B.A., M.A., LL.B., Dr. Jur.; lawyer; author; b. Toronto, Ont. 26 Aug. 1912; s. Samuel John Newton and Susannah Maud (McLean) M.; e. Univ. of Toronto Schs. 1922-29; Univ. of Toronto B.A. 1933, M.A. 1937, LL.B. 1938, Dr. Jur. 1981; Osgoode Hall Law Sch. 1933-36; m. Doris Rose d. O.P. Johnston 18 June 1938; children: Beverley Dawn (Jamieson), Charles Johnston; CHRMN., CANDN. EXTVE. SERVICES OVERSEAS; Dir. City of Toronto Non-Profit Housing Corp.; Dir. Toronto Symphony; called to Bar of Ont. 1936; cr. Q.C. 1956; practiced law in Toronto since 1936- ; Snr. Partner Magwood, Frith, Pocock (and successor firms) 1950-80; served with Candn. and British army, SHAEF, 1942-45; Retired, Maj. GSO II, 1945; mentioned in dispatches; awarded Can. Centennial Medal 1967, Queen Eliz. II Jubilee Medal 1977; Past Pres. Natl. Council YMCA's of Can.; Past Pres. Candn. Council for Intl. Cooperation; Past Pres. York County Law Assn.; Former Prov. Candidate and Vice Pres Ont. Liberal Assn.; author of "Competition Law of Canada", 1981; mem., Candn. Bar Assn.; York County Law Assn.; Psi Upsilon; Liberal; United Church; Clubs: Lawyers, Toronto; University; Strollers; Badminton and Racquet; Rosedale Golf; Osler Bluff Ski; recreations: riding, harness driving, skiing, sailing, golf, tennis; Home: 10 Avoca Ave., Toronto, Ont.

M4T 2B7; Office: 1 St. Clair Ave. W., Ste. 1201, Toronto, Ont. M4V 1K6.

MAHEUX-FORCIER, Louise; écrivain, née Montréal, Qué., 9 juin 1929; f. Louis-Alfred et Cécile (Giguère) Maheux; é. Diplôme cours Lettres-Sciences, Ecole Supérieure Sainte-Croix et Conservatoire de Musique et d'Art Dramatique de la P.Q. et Académie de Musique de Québec; Bourse du Gouvernement de la P.Q. pour séjour de deux ans au Conservatoire de Paris, époux Marcel Forcier, 8 Oct. 1955; auteur "Amadou" (roman) 1963; "L'Ile joyeuse" (roman) 1965; "Triptyque" (nouvelle) 1965; "Une forêt pour Zoé" (roman) 1969; "Paroles et Musiques" (roman) 1973; "Neige et Palmiers" et "Le Violoncelle" (pièces en un acte) 1974; articles: La Presse, Le Devoir; Prix du Cercle du Livre de France, 1963; radio-diffusions: "Neige et Palmiers" août 1970; "Le Violoncelle" août 1973; "Un ecrivain et son pays: Louise Maheux-Forcier et Huberdeau" 1975; "Du monde entier au coeur du monde: La Grèce" 1975; "Le papier d'Arménie", 1979; "Comme un oiseau", 1980; "Un Parc en Automne", 1981; téléthéâtre: "Un arbre chargé d'oiseaux" mai 1975; "Arioso", 1980; "Lepiano rouge", 1981; théâtre: "Le Coeur Étoilé" 1977; Roman: "Appassionata" 1978; attaché au CRCCF (Univ. d'Ottawa) 1972-73; écrivain résident l'Univ. d'Ottawa 1974; Prix du Cercle du Livre de France; Prix du Gouverneur Général, Canada, 1970; Bourse de travail libre du Conseil des Arts du Can. 1971; Capac, Soc. des Ecrivains; Membre du jury du Prix "Jean Béraud" (Cercle du Livre de France); mem. du jury Canado-Belge; mem. du jury au Concours d'Oeuvres dramatiques de Radio-Canada; Adresse: 4904 boul. Parkinson, Pierrefonds, Qué. H8Y 2Z4

MAHONEY, Hon. Patrick Morgan, P.C., Q.C., B.A., LL.B.; b. Winnipeg, Man., 20 Jan. 1929; s. Paul Morgan and Joan Ethel Tracy (Patrick) M.; e. Pub. and High Schs., Alta.; Mount Royal Coll., Calgary; Univ. of Alta., B.A. 1950, LL.B. 1951; m. Mary Alma, d. late George Homer Sneath, 28 June 1958; children: Michael George, Patrick Murray, Sheila Mary, D'Arcy Carole; called to Bar of Alta. 1952; cr. Q.C. 1972; JUDGE, TRIAL DIV., FEDERAL COURT OF CANADA since 1973; el. to H. of C. for Calgary S. in g.e. 1968; apptd. Parlty. Secy. to Min. of Finance 1970; Min. State 1972; Past Pres., Stampeder Football Club. Ltd.; Western Football Conf.; Candn. Football League; Senator, Univ. of Calgary (1966-72); Address: 3 Coltrin Place, Ottawa, Ont. K1M 0A5

MAHONEY, Richard A., B.A., M.B.A.; business consultant; b. Calgary, Alta., 14 Sept. 1916; s. Richard Marion and Pearl (Simpson) M.; e. Univ. of Manitoba, B.A. 1938; Harvard Sch. of Business Adm., M.B.A. 1940; m. Kathleen Marion, d. late Cedric A. Gallagher, 17 Nov. 1944; children: Shelagh, Richard, Susan; Past Pres., Mgmt. Research Consulting Ltd.; prior to 2nd World War worked in mail-order business in Chicago; joined Dept. of Comm., Univ. of B.C., 1946 and promoted to Assoc. Prof. 1947-50; Instr., Banff Sch. of Advanced Management, 1952-78 and former Assoc. Dean and Dir.; Delta Kappa Epsilon; Anglican; recreations: hunting, fishing, golf, gardening; Club: Shaughnessy Golf & Country; Home: 5930 Macdonald, Vancouver, B.C. V6N 1E4; Office: #508 - 1200 W. 73rd Ave., Vancouver, B.C. V6P 6G5

MAHONEY, Robert W., B.Sc., M.B.A.; executive; b. New York, N.Y. 10 Sept. 1936; s. Frank and Margaret M.; e. Villanova Univ. B.Sc. (Indust. Engn.) 1958; Roosevelt Univ. M.B.A. 1961; m. Joan Sheridan 3 Oct. 1959; children: Linda, Stephen, Brian; PRES., NCR CANADA LTD. 1980 ; Accounting Machine Sales, NCR Corp. Philadelphia 1961, Account Mgr. 1963, Mgr. Bank Div. 1967, Territory Mgr. Allentown, Pa. 1970, Dir. EDP Sales Atlanta Region 1973, Regional Dir. Financial Systems Atlanta 1974; Asst. Vice Pres. Financial Systems Div. U.S. Data Processing, Dayton, Ohio 1977; above position Far

E./Australasia, International Data Processing, Dayton 1979; served with U.S. Navy 1958-61, Naval Reserve until 1968, rank Lt. Commdr.; mem. Bd. Trade Metrop. Toronto; Business Adv. Council; Chamber Comm.; recreations: golf, tennis; Clubs: Granite; Rotary; Home: 486 Russell Hill Rd., Toronto, Ont. M5P 2S7; Office: 6865 Century Ave., Mississauga, Ont. L5N 2E2.

MAHONEY, William; retired labour union executive; b. Cardiff, Wales, 31 March 1917; s. Thomas J. and Annie C. (Mahoney) M.; came to Canada, 1918; e. Holy Angel Sch., Sault Ste. Marie, Ont.; Sault Ste. Marie Coll. Inst.; Sault Ste. Marie Tech. & Comm. Sch.; m. Annie Bernice, d. late William J. Currie, 18 Sept. 1936; children: Terance, Dennis, Michael, Sharon, Stephen, Susan, Kevin, Deborah, Kathleen; Nat. Dir. for Can., United Steel Workers of Amer., 1956-77; Vice-Pres., Canadian Labour Congress; mem. Economic Council of Can.; joined staff of United Steel Workers of Am. in Sault Ste. Marie, Ont., 1941; Western Dir., Candn. Cong. of Labour, 1947-49; Asst. to Nat. Dir., Un. Steel Workers of Am., 1949-56; N.D.P.; Catholic.

MAIER, Gerald James, B.Sc., P.Eng.; petroleum executive; b. Regina, Sask. 22 Sept. 1928; s. John Joseph and Mary (Passler) M.; e. Notre Dame Coll, (Wilcox); Univ. of Man.; Univ. of Alta. B.Sc. (Petroleum Engn.) 1951; Univ. of W. Ont. Mang. Training 1969; m. Mary Isobel d. late Donald Byron Grant, 14 Aug. 1952; Children: Dianne, Brad, Pat; CHAIRMAN OF THE BOARD, C.E.O. AND DIR. HUDSON'S BAY OIL & GAS CO. LTD. 1980- ; Chmn. of Bd. and Dir., Cyprus Anvil Mining Corp.; Petroleum Engr. Sun Oil Co. 1951-52 and Cactus Engineering Ltd. 1952-53; joined present Co. 1953 as Petroleum Engr., Sr. Vice Pres. 1975; Exec. Vice Pres. 1977-80; Hon. Life Dir. Calgary Booster Club (Past Pres.); Past Dir. YMCA; Past Vice Pres. Heart Foundation; Hon. life mem., Assn. Petrol. Engrs., Geols. & Geophysicists Alta. (Pres. 1978-79); mem., Am. Inst. Mining Engrs.-Soc. Petrol. Engrs.; Candn. Inst. Mining & Metall. (Past Dist. Chrmn.; rec'd Past Pres. Medal); P. Conservative; R. Catholic; recreations: skiing, golf, shooting, tennis, fishing, riding, hiking; Clubs: Calgary Golf & Country; Canyon Meadows Golf & Country; Calgary Petroleum; Ranchmen's; Home: 6843 Livingstone Dr. S. W., Calgary, Alta. T3E 6J4; Office: 700 — 2nd S.W., Calgary, Alta.

MAILLARD, Keith Lee; author; b. Wheeling, W. Va. 28 Feb. 1942; s. Eugene Charles and Aileen (Sharp) M.; e. Linsly Mil. Inst. Wheeling, W. Va. 1960; W. Va. Univ. 1961-63; Vancouver (B.C.) Community Coll. Dept. Music 1975-77; author novels "Two Strand River" 1976; "Alex Driving South" 1980; "The Knife in My Hands" 1981; "Cutting Through" 1982; "Motet" scheduled 1983; contrib. to "Instead of Revolution" 1971 (essays) and other publs.; Asst. Copy Ed. Porter Sargent Publisher, Boston 1968-69; writer and producer (pub. affairs) WBUR Boston 1969-70; free-lance writer CBC Radio (This Country in the Morning, Our Native Land, Five Nights) 1973-75; Teacher novel writing The Literary Storefront 1979-80; and lyric writing Dept. Creative Writing Univ. of B.C. 1980-82; Recorder teacher Continuing Educ. Services Vancouver Community Coll. and Vancouver Sch. Bd. 1976-82; guest lectr. on publishing and copyright Capilano Coll. and Univ. of B.C.; rec'd Can. Council Grant 1974, 2 grants 1977-78; recreations: long distance running, Irish traditional music; mem. Writers' Union Can. (Rep. B.C. and Y.T. Nat. Council) 1979-80, 2nd Vice Chrmn. 1980-81); Fed. B.C.; Comhaltas Ceoltóirí Éireann; Address: c/o The Writers' Union of Canada, 24 Ryerson Ave., Toronto, Ont. M5T 2P3.

MAILLOUX, Rev. Noel, O.C. (1967), B.A., Ph.D., S,Th.L., F.R.S.C. (R.C.); psychologist; b. Napierville, P.Q., 25 Dec. 1909; e. Coll. Sainte-Marie, Montreal, P.Q., B.A. 1930; Angelicum, Rome, Ph.D. (Philos. and Psychol.) 1934 and S.Th.L. 1938; o. Priest 1937; Research Fel-

low, Univ. of Cincinnati, 1939; Prof. of Psychol. of Personality, l'Ecole Normale Secondaire, and mem. of the Council of the Sch. 1941-75; Dir., Centre of Research on Human Relations, Montreal; Director-Founder of Inst. de Psychol. and Prof. of Exper. Psychol., Univ. of Montreal, 1942-75; Prof. Emeritus 1975; Prof. of Psychol., Coll. of Philos. and Theol., Dominican Order, Ottawa, 1938-41; author of "Scientific Methods in Education" (4 vols.); numerous contrib. on psychol. and educ. subjects to journs.; Chief Ed., "Contributions à l'Etude des Sciences de l'Homme"; Pres., Candn. Soc. of Criminology; Pres., Candn. Psychol. Assn., 1954-55; mem. of Extve. Internat. Union of Scient. Psychology; mem. Am. Assn. for Advanc. of Science; Am. Assn. on Mental Deficiency; Am. Psychol. Assn.; Psychol. Assn. of Que. (Pres. 1945-46); Assoc. mem., La Soc. française de psychol.; Address: 2715, côte Sainte-Catherine, Montreal, Que. H3T 1B6

MAIN, James Hamilton Prentice, B.D.S., Ph.D., F.D.S.R.C.S. Edin., F.R.C.D.C., F.R.C. Path.; denist; b. Biggar, Scot. 7 June 1933; s. George Prentice and Helen Hamilton (Stark) M.; e. Biggar (Scot.) High Sch., 1938-50; Univ. of Edinburgh, B.D.S. 1955, Ph.D. 1964 (Carnegie Research Fellow 1960-61); Northwestern Univ., 1955-56 (King George VI Mem. Fellow); m. Patricia Ann, d. Robert Logan Robertson, London, Eng., 28 July 1961; children: Fiona Gillian, George Iian Prentice; HEAD, DEPARTMENT OF DENTISTRY, SUNNYBROOK MEDICAL CENTRE, 1971-, and Professor of Oral Pathol., University of Toronto 1969- ; Pres., Roy. Coll. of Denists (Can.) 1981- ; House Surg., Edinburgh Dental Hosp. 1956-57; Lectr. in Dental Surg. and Pathol., Univ. of Edinburgh, 1961-64; Internat. Research Fellow, Nat. Insts. of Health, Bethesda, Md. 1964-65; Sr. Lectr. and Consultant to S.E. Scot. Hosps. in Dental Surg. and Pathol. 1966-69; served with RAF, NATO HQ, Fontainebleau, France, 1957-60; rank Flight Lt.; rec'd Colgate Prize for Dental Research, 1966; Clark Prize for Cancer Research, 1968; co-author, "Developmental Aspects of Oral Biology" 1972; "Applied Surgical Pathology" 1974; also numerous scient. and prof. articles in various journs.; mem. Candn. Dental Assn.; Candn. Acad. Oral Pathol. (Pres. 1974-75); Am. Acad. Oral Pathol.; Un. Church; recreations: golf, reading; Club: Sleepy Hollow Golf & Country; Home: 85 Dawlish Ave., Toronto, Ont. M4N 1H2; Office: 124 Edward St., Toronto, Ont. M5G 1G6

MAIN, John E., retired company executive; b. Hamilton, Ont., 19 July 1913; s. late George Edwin and Mary L. (Garnett) M.; m. Claudia V., d. late Dale M. Cahill, 28 June 1941; children: Mrs. David Hodges, Mrs. Michael Pollard; with Midland Securities Corp. Ltd., 1935-39; London & Western Trust Co., 1939-42; Dom. Government, i.c. foreign estates 1942-50; joined Montreal Trust 1950; Vice-Pres. 1965; Sr. Vice Pres., 1971; Dir., Beaverbrook Candn. Foundation; Anglican; Clubs: Thistle Curling; Engineers; Home: Apt. 81, 607 Cranbrook Rd., London, Ont. N6K 2Y4

MAIN, Lorne Gordon, B.A.; industrial executive; b. Smiths Falls, Ont., 4 April 1918; s. Halmer Judson and May Belle (Peachey) M.; e. Univ. of Man., B.A. 1941; m. Margaret Ruth, d. late Frank Wallar, 14 October 1944; three d.; DIR., EXPORT SALES AND DEVELOPMENT AND VICE PRESIDENT, MARKETING AND SALES, URBAN TRANSPORT DEVELOPMENT CORP.; Sales Rep., Canadian Industries Ltd., 1946-47; Vice President, Northern Shirt Co., Winnipeg, 1948-51; Gen. Sales Mgr.; Candn. Cottons Ltd., Montreal, 1952-57; Joined Hawker Siddeley Canada Ltd. as Coordinator of Merchandising, 1957-60; apptd. Product Devel. Mgr. 1960-63; Asst. Gen. Sales Mgr., Rly. Equipment, 1963-64; Gen. Sales Mgr., 1964-66; Vice-Pres., Exports, Dominion Steel & Coal Corp., 1966; Dir. of Marketing, Hawker-Siddeley Can. Ltd. 1969-74; Dir., Candn. Export Assn.; Sunbelt Investment Ltd.; served with R.C.N., Active Service, 1941-45; with R.C.N. Reserve to 1952; retired with rank Commdr.;

mem., Bd. Trade Metrop. Toronto; Phi Kappa Pi; Conservative; Un. Church; recreation: golf; Home: 76 Quail Valley Lane, Thornhill, Ont. L3T 4R3; Office: 2 St. Clair Ave. W., Toronto, Ont. M4V 1L7

MAIN, Oscar Warren, M.A., Ph.D.; university professor; b. Hamilton, Ont., 10 Aug. 1916; s. Oscar and Rose Alberta M.; e. Delta Coll. Inst., Hamilton, Ont.; McMaster Univ., B.A. 1938; Univ. of Toronto, M.A. 1943, Ph.D. 1953; m. Marion, d. C. M. McConkey, Sudbury, Ont., 29 Dec. 1948; PROF., FAC. MANG. STUDIES, UNIV. OF TORONTO since 1960 (Dean of Fac. 1960-71); Instr., Dept. of Pol. Econ., Univ. of Toronto, 1941-43, Lectr., 1945-48; Asst. Prof. of Commerce, Univ. of Sask., 1948-52, Assoc. Prof. 1952-53; Asst. Prof., Inst. of Business Adm., Univ. of Toronto, 1953-56; Assoc. Prof. 1956-59; Prof. since 1959; served in 2nd World War with R.C.A.F. as Meteorologist, 1943-45; Publications: "The Canadian Nickel Industry", 1955; articles on econ. and adm. in various learned journs.; mem., Candn. Econs. Assn.; Candn. Assn. Adm. Science; Am. Econ. Assn.; United Church; Home: 350 Lonsdale Rd., Toronto, Ont. M5P 1R6; Office: 246 Bloor St. W., Toronto, Ont. M5S 1V4

MAIN, Peter Thomas, B.A.; food company executive; b. Kitchener, Ont. 15 Aug. 1941; s. Howard William and Shirley Evelyn (Hankins) M.; e. Sheppard Pub. Sch. and Eastwood Coll. Inst. Kitchener 1960; Univ. of W. Ont. B.A. (Business Adm.) 1964; m. Ayleene Alice d. Walter Aram, Waterloo, Ont. 18 Sept. 1965; children: Kimberly Allison, Peter Cameron Ryan; PRES. AND DIR., CONTROLLED FOODS INTERNATIONAL LTD. since 1978; Pres. and Dir. Controlled Foods Corp. Ltd.; The Corckscrew Restaurant Ltd.; Hickory House Ltd.; Burnaby Foods Ltd.; Group Product Mgr. Colgate Palmolive, Toronto 1964-69; Corporate New Business Planning Mgr., General Foods Ltd. Toronto 1969-71, Pres. Canterbury Foods Ltd. 1971-73 and White Spot Ltd. Vancouver 1973-78; Group Chrmn. Un. Way Greater Vancouver 1974-75; mem. W. Vancouver Study on Youth 1975; W. Vancouver Family Court 1976; Delta Upsilon; P. Conservative; United Church; recreations: tennis, squash, fishing, jogging; Clubs: Terminal City; Hollyburn Country; Blue Mountain Racquet; Home: 615 Fairmile Rd., West Vancouver, B.C. V7S 1R1; Office: 226-4664 Lougheed Highway, Burnaby, B.C. V5C 4A4.

MAIR, Ian Douglas, F.C.I.I.; insurance executive; b. Dunblane, Scot. 15 June 1920; s. James Douglas and Agnes Jane M.; e. Clayesmore Sch., Dorset, Eng.; m. Margaret d. Dr. George Hunter Feb. 1962; children: Nancy, Douglas; PRES., PRUDENTIAL ASSURANCE CO. LTD. 1976- ; Chmn. Constellation Assurance Co. 1978- ; Dir., Prudential Assnce. Co., (Candn. Bd.); Pres. and Dir., Can. Life and Health Ins. Assn. Inc.; served with 7th Bn. Royal Marines and 48th Royal Marine Commando during World War II; Past Chmn. Facility Governing Comn. 1970-73, I.B.C. 1974-76; Ins. Inst. Can. 1980; voted "Insurance Man of the Year" 1971; recreations: squash, skiing, golf, tennis; Clubs: St. James's; M.A.A.A.; Kanawaki Golf; Caledonian (London); Office: 635 Dorchester Blvd. W., Montreal, Que. H3B 1R7.

MAIR, John; executive; b. Peterhead, Scot. 26 Aug. 1933; e. Univ. of Aberdeen; VICE PRESIDENT COCA-COLA LTD. 1980- ; joined Peat, Marwick, Mitchell & Co. London, Eng. 1959-63; The Coca-Cola Export Corp. New York 1963, Coca-Cola Argentina 1968, Coca-Cola Japan 1973-80; served with R.N.; mem. Inst. C.A.'s Scot.; Club: R.C.Y.C.; Home: 30 Glenn Elm Ave., Toronto, Ont. M4T 1T7; Office: 42 Overlea Blvd., Toronto, Ont. M4H 1B8.

MAIR, Kenneth Rafe, M.L.A., LL.B.; politician; b. Vancouver, B.C. 31 Dec. 1931; s. Kenneth Frederick Robert and Frances Tyne (Leigh) M.; e. Prince of Wales High Sch.; Univ. of B.C., LL.B.; m. Patricia Marie Ballard; children: Kenneth Rafe, Cindy, Shawn (d. 1976), Karen;

PUBLIC AFFAIRS BROADCASTER, C.J.O.R.Vancouver, 1981- ; Health, B.C. 1979-80; el. M.L.A. for Kamloops prov. g.e. 1975, re-el, 1979; Min. of Consumer Services 1975-76; Min. of Environment 1978; Social Credit; Anglican; Clubs; Vancouver; Union; Kamloops Racquet; Kamloops Gold & Country; Quilchena Golf & Country; Office: 840 Howe St., Vancouver, B.C. V6Z 1N6

MAIR, W. Winston, M.A.; personally employed; b. North Battleford, Sask., 26 July 1914; s. William Rufus and Mary Aveline (Stannard) M.; e. Univ. of British Columbia, B.A. (Hons. Zool.) 1949 and M.A. (Zool. with specialization in Wildlife Mang.) 1952; Nat. Defence Coll (N.D.C.) 1962; m. Jeanne Spurr, d. P.W. Farnsworth, Vancouver, B.C., 23 March 1940; children: Nancy Jeanne, Kenneth William; CONSULTANT, ENVIRONMENT, LAND USE AND INDIAN SOCIO-ECONOMIC DEVELOPMENT; farmed, trained with R.C.M.P. and other occupations, 1931-40; Supervisor of Predator Control, B.C. Game Dept. 1949-52; Chief, Candn. Wildlife Service, 1952-63; Chief, Nat. Parks Service, 1963-66; Depy-Min., Man. Dept. Mines, Resources and Environmental Mgmt. 1966-72; Policy Advisor West and Dir.-Gen. B.C., Dept. Regional Economic Expansion, 1972-75; served in 2nd World War with Candn. Army 1940-46; served Overseas over 5 yrs. in Eng., France, Netherlands, Italy, etc.; retired to Reserve with rank of Lt.-Col.; mem., The Wildlife Soc.; Candn. Nature Fed.; B.C. Wildlife Fed.; Fed. of B.C. Naturalists; Victorial Natural Hist. Soc.; Internat. Assn. of Fish and Wildlife Agencies; Nat. and Prov. Parks Assn. Can.; Arctic Inst. of N. Am.; Candn. Soc. of Environmental Biols.; Men's Candn. Club of Victoria; Royal United Services Inst. of Vancouver Island; United Church; recreations: hunting, reading; Home: 2250 Kinross Ave., Victoria, B.C. V8R 2N5

MAISLIN, Alan W.; transportation executive; e. Acad. Advanced Traffic, N.Y.; Rutgers Univ.; Sir George Williams Unit.; PRES. AND DIR., MAISLIN INDUSTRIES LTD.; Trainee Truck Driver, Maislin Transport 1965 becoming Terminal Mgr. Valleyfield, Que., Asst. to Regional Mgr. East Rutherford, N.J. Terminal, Dir. of Personnel, Dir. of Safety, Security & Indust. Relations, Vice Pres. of Safety, Indust. Relations and Cargo Claims, Vice Pres. Operations, Vice Pres. and Gen. Mgr. 1977-78; Lectr., Road Transport Mang. Course, McGill Univ.; Cert. Dir. of Safety; 1970 Que. Transport. "Man of the Year"; Dir. LaSalle-Verdun Br. YMCA (Past Dir. Metrop. YMCA Montreal); Past Pres. LaSalle Chamber Comm.; Gov., Regular Route Common Carrier Conf.; Dir. and Treas. Que. Safety League (Past Vice Pres.); Dir. Ont. Trucking Assns. (Past Vice Chrmn. Safety & Security Council); mem. Que. Trucking Assn. (Past Chrmn. Safety & Security Council); Am. Trucking Assns' Safety Council (Past Vice Chrmn. E. Region); Motor Transport Indust. Relations Bureau Ont. (Past Dir.); Motor Transport Indust. Relations Bureau Que. (Past Dir.); Past Chrmn. for Min. of Transport on Devel. Hazardous Materials Regulations for Surface Transport. Can.; Past Chrmn. Candn. Trucking Assns' Safety Council; Indust. Accident Prevention Assn. (Past Dir.); Montreal Bd. Trade (Past Council mem.); recreations: horseback riding, skiing, hockey, farming; Office: 7401 Newman Blvd., LaSalle, Que. H8N 1X4.

MAITLIS, Peter Michael, B.Sc., Ph.D., D.Sc., FCIC; university professor; b. 15 Jan. 1933; e. Univ. of Birmingham, (Eng.), B.Sc. 1953; Univ. of London, Ph.D., 1956, D.Sc. 1971; m. Marion Basco, 19 July 1959; 3 d.; PROF. OF INORGANIC CHEM., Univ. of Sheffield, England, 1972- ; researched in organometallic chem., catalysis and related subjects; author of "The Organic Chemistry of Palladium", (Vol. 1, Metal Complexes), (Vol. 2, Catalytic Reactions), 1971; over 160 research papers; awarded Steacie Prize in Natural Sciences, 1970 Fellow, Alfred P. Sloan Foundation, 1967-69; Tilden Lecturer of the Chemical Soc., London, 1979; mem. Chem. Soc. (London); Am.

Chem. Soc.; Address: Univ. of Sheffield, Sheffield, England.

MAJOR, André-Wilfrid; author; radio producer; b. Montréal, Qué. 22 Apl. 1942; s. Arthur and Anna (Sharp) M.; m. Ginette Lepage June 1970; children: Eric, Julie; author "Le Cabochon" roman 1964; "La Chair de poule" nouvelles 1965; "Le Vent du diable" roman 1968; "F.-A. Savard" essai 1968; "Poèmes pour durer" (1960-69) 1969; "Histoires de déserteurs" Vol. 1 "L'Epouvantail" 1974, Vol 2 "L'Epidémie" 1975, Vol. 3 "Les Rescapés" 1976 (Prix du Gouverneur général 1977); mem. CBC Radio-Canada; Union des écrivains québécois; Home: 10595 Tanguay, Montréal, Qué. H3L 3G9; Office: 1400 boul. Dorchester E., Montréal, Que. H3C 3A8.

MAJOR, Jean-Louis, L.Ph., M.A., Ph.D.; éducateur et essayiste littéraire; ne Cornwall, Ont. 16 juillet 1937; p. Joseph et Noëlla (Daoust) M.; é. Univ. d'Ottawa B.A., B.Ph. 1959, B.A. (Hon.), L.Ph. 1960, M.A. 1961, Ph.D. 1965; Ecole Pratique des Hautes Etudes, Paris 1968-69; ép. Bibiane p. Rodolphe Landry, St-Isidore-de-Prescott, Ont. 4 juin 1960; enfant: Marie-France; PROFESSEUR TITULAIRE DEPT. DE LETTRES FRANCAISES, UNIV. D'OTTAWA depuis 1971; Prof. de philosophie et de latin, Coll. Bruyère d'Ottawa 1960-61; Dépt. de philosophie, Univ. d'Ottawa (chargé de cours) 1961-65, prof. adjoint Dépt. de Lettres françaises 1965, prof. agrégé 1967; Visiting Prof. Univ. of Toronto 1970-71; auteur "Saint-Exupéry, l'écriture et la pensée" 1968; "Léone de Jean Cocteau" édition critique 1975; "Anne Hébert et le miracle de la parole" 1976; "Radiquet, Cocteau, Les Joues en feu" 1977; "La littérature française par les textes théoriques: XIX siécle" 1977; "Paul-Marie Lapointe: la nuit incendiée" 1978; "Le jeu en étoile" (essais) 1978; co-auteur 11 livres; Rédacteur de la chronique "Autobiographies" dans la revue "Lettres québècoises" depuis 1978; articles sur les littératures française et québécoise dans les revues en France et au Can.; critique littéraire "Le Droit" 1963-65; co-dir. "Cahiers d'Inédits"; mem. de la Société Royale du Can.; récreation: horticulture; Adresse: 1676 Boyer, Orléans, Ont. K1C 1R1; Bureau: Ottawa, Ont. K1N 6N5.

MAKIN, Andrew Julian, M.A.; b. London, Eng. 16 Apl. 1942; s. James and Mary (Morris) M.; e. Charterhouse 1959; Gonville & Caius Coll. Cambridge Univ. M.A. 1963; m. Maja Brigite Kucera 8 Feb. 1978; one d. Jessica Louise; EXTVÉ. VICE PRESIDENCE, B.C. AUTOMOBILE ASSOCIATION 1982- ; joined McCann-Erickson Advertising Ltd. London, Eng. 1963-67; Advertising and Promotions Mgr. Europe, British European Airlines 1967-72, Sales Mgr. USA 1972-74; Mgr. Scandinavia, British Airways 1974-78; Mgr. Can., Br. Airway, 1978-82; Councillor, Brit.-Candn. Trade Associates; recreations: books, music, skiing; Home: 110 Sunset Dr., Lions Bay, B.C.; Office: 999 W. Broadway, Vancouver, B.C. V5Z 1K5.

MALCOLM, Richard, C.D., M.Sc., Ph.D.; scientist; b. Ottawa, Ont. 20 July 1941; s. Peter Evelyn Reginald and Margot (Hamel) M.; e. Univ. of Ottawa B.Sc. 1964, M.Sc. 1966; McGill Univ. Ph.D. (Neurophysiol.) 1971; m. Claire Lise Gravel 31 Aug. 1963; two d. Tara, Tanya; Pres., Richard Malcolm Enterprises Inc.; Maltech Consultants Inc.; Scientist, Defence and Civil Inst. of Environmental Medicine 1970-79; RCAF Inst. of Aviation Medicine 1966-70; devel. Malcolm Horizon, a new level of aircraft instrumentation joined RCAF under ROTP 1959; author numerous papers in scient. journ. primarily in field of mech. of inner ear; mem. Baranay Soc.; recreations: canoeing, backpacking, skiing; Home: 432 Drummond Rd. Oakville, Ont. L6J 4L4; Office: 315 Lakeshore Rd. E., Oakville, Ont. L6J 1J3

MALHOTRA, Sudarshan K., M.Sc., M.A., Ph.D., D.Phil.; biologist; educator; b. India, 20 June 1933; s. Krishanlal and Vidyawati (Dhawan) M.; e. Panjab Univ.,

B.Sc. 1953, M.Sc. 1955, Ph.D. 1958; Oxford Univ., D.Phil. 1960, M.A. 1961; m. Kamini, d, late Bijai Krishan Dhaon, 30 Aug. 1963; two s. Shantanu, Atul; PROF. AND DIR., BIOL. SCIENCES ELECTRON MICROSCOPE LAB., UNIV. OF ALTA. since 1967 and Prof., Dept. of Zool. there; Research Fellow, New Coll., Oxford Univ., 1961-63; Research Fellow and Sr. Research Fellow, Div. of Biol., Calif. Inst. of Technol., 1963-67; Dean, Sch. of Life Sciences, Jawaharlal Nehru Univ. and Visiting Prof., All India Inst. of Med. Sciences, New Delhi, 1971-72; Hon. Prof., Dept. Pharmacol., Univ. of Alta. 1973-76; awarded Sr. Studentship, Royal Comn. for Exhn. of 1851, 1960-62; Del. E. Webb Visiting Assoc., Calif. Inst. Technol., 1980-81; author of various articles for learned journs.; Ed.; "Cytobios"; "Microbios"; "Microbios Letters"; mem., Candn. Soc. Cell Biol.; Soc. for Neurosci.; Am. Cell Biol. Soc.; N.Y. Acad. Science ; Microscopical Soc. of Can.; Hindu; recreations: photography, music; Home: 12916 - 63 Ave., Edmonton, Alta. T6H 1S1

MALLATRATT, William Alfred; exhibition administrator; b. Toronto, Ont., 26 March 1929; s. John William and Janet (Ball) M.; e. Toronto, Ont. Schs.; m. Gloria Marie, d. Harry Stanley Sainthill, 3 May 1958; three d. Amy, Susan, Lynn; GENERAL MGR., CANADIAN NATIONAL EXHIBITION since 1976; joined Lewis Brothers Hardware Ltd. 1948; engaged with Candian Retail Hardware Assn. in 1953 and shortly thereafter named Gen. Mgr.; apptd. Exhibits and Rentals Mgr. of Candn. Nat. Exhn. 1964-67; prior to present post was Gen. Mgr. of Grant Smedmor Ltd. a trade and consumer show-producing subsidiary of Southam Business Publications Ltd.; mem. Internat. Assn. of Fairs & Exhns.; Candn. Assn. of Exhns.; Showmen's League of America; United Church; recreations: golf, fishing; Clubs: Lagoon City Yacht; Rotary; Empire; Home: 32 Red Mapleway, Willowdale, Ont.; Office: Administrative Offices, Queen Elizabeth Bldg., Exhibition Place, Toronto, Ont.

MALLEN, Bruce, B.A., B.Comm., M.B.A., M.Sc., Ph.D.; educator, motion picture producer and mang. consultant; b. Montreal, Que., 4 Sept. 1937; s. Mitchell and Mary (Epstein) M.; e. Sir George Williams Univ., B.A. (Philos.) and B.Com. 1958; Columbia Univ., M.Sc. (Econ.) 1959; Univ. of Mich., M.B.A. 1960; N.Y. Univ., Ph.D. (Econ.) 1962 (Ford Foundation Fellow 1961-62; Founders Day Award 1963); m. Carol; two s. Howard Eliot, Jay Leslie; one d. Reesa Lynn; PRES. FILMCORP ENTÉRTAIN-MENT FINANCES INC.; Prof. of Marketing, COncordia Univ., 1967-81; Founding Chrmn., Grad. Studies (Comm.) 1968-73; Acting Dean, Faculty of Comm. and Adm. 1970-71; Pres., Bruce Mallen & Associates Inc. 1964-80; Sr. Consultant, P. S. Ross & Partners, 1961-64; joined present Univ. as Assoc. Prof. and Chrmn., Dept. of Marketing, 1964-71; Visiting Prof. of Marketing, Laval Univ., 1968-70; Visiting Scholar, Grad. Sch. Mang., Univ. of Calif., Los Angeles 1978-79; Visiting Prof., Univ. of Southern Calif. 1979-81; Founder and 1st Ed.-in-Chief, "The Candn. Marketer"; mem. Ed. Review Bd., "The Journal of Marketing"; mem. Ed. Bd., "Internat. Journ. of Physical Distribution" (U.K.); completed world fact finding and speaking tour sponsored by Ford Foundation, 1968; World Bank econ. devel. assignment, Togo, Africa, summer 1969; author: "The Marketing Channel", 1967; "The Costs & Benefits of Evening Shopping to the Canadian Economy", 1969; "Principles of Marketing Channel Management", 1977; co-author: "Marketing: Canada", 1968 (2nd ed.); "Marketing in the Canadian Environment", 1973; "Principles of Marketing In Canada" 1979; "Distribution of Canadian Feature Films in the U.S. Market" 1979; co-annotator, "Bibliography on Marketing in Canada", 1967; other writings incl. numer. monographs and articles for prof. journs.; Producer of feature film "The High Country", "Heartaches", "Paradise"; U.S. distributor of films "Blood Relatives", "Tomorrow Never Comes", "The Honour Guard"; Past Pres., Indust. Marketers and Assn. of Indust. Advertisers (Montreal); mem., Am. Marketing Assn. (Past Internat. Dir.; Past Pres., Montreal Chapter); Acad. of Cdn. Cinema; Cdn. Assn. of Motion Picture Producers; Producers Guild of Amer.; Am. Film Inst.; associate, Motion Picture Hall of Fame; recreations: reading philos. & hist., travel; Office: Filmcorp Entertainment Finances Inc., 1115 Sherbrooke St. W., Montreal, Que. H3A 1H3

MALLESON, Andrew Graeme, M.B., B.S., F.R.C.P.(C); psychiatrist; b. London, Eng., 3 Jan. 1931; s. Miles and Dr. Joan Graeme (Billson) M.; e. Leighton Park Sch., Reading, Eng.; Guy's Hosp. Med. Sch.; LRCP, MRCS 1954; M.B., B.S. 1954; MRCP (Eng.) 1960; DPM (Eng.) 1964; LMCC 1970; MRCPsych. (Eng.) 1972; came to Can. 1969; M. Dr. Donna Stuart; Asst. Prof., Depts. of Psychiatry & of Preventive Medicine, Univ. of Toronto; Staff Psychiatrist, Toronto Western Hosp.; Asst. Surg., SS Oronsay and Surg., SS Orsova, 1960; Scient. Offr., Med. Research Council Gt. Brit. 1963-65; Sr. Registrar in Biochem. and Psychiatry, Area Lab., West Park, Eng. 1965-66; author "Need Your Doctor Be So Useless" 1973; "The Medical Runaround" 1974; also assorted articles in various scient. journs. on biochem. of mental illness and on psychiatric subjects; served with RAMC 1955-56; rank Capt.; past Secy., Ont. Psychiatry Hosp. Assn. 1974; past mem., City of Toronto Bd. of Health; past Bd. mem., Planned Parenthood; past Pres., Med. Staff, Toronto Western Hosp.; Office: 25 Léonard Ave., Suite 303, Toronto, Ont. M5T 2R2

MALLETT, Jane (Mrs. Frederick John Mallett); actress (stage, radio, television, film); b. London, Ont.; d. Clifford Benjamin and Emily Isabel (Daly) Keenleyside; e. Public Sch. and Collegiate Inst., Regina, Sask.; Victoria Coll., Univ. of Toronto, B.A.; m. Frederick John, s. Thomas J. Mallett, 14 April 1925; one s. John Christopher Aldworth; began first prof. engagement of 40 weeks with an American Stock Co. which played in the old Empire Theatre in Toronto, Ont., playing everything from grande dames to ingenues; best known as a Comedienne began the revue roles in which she gained fame in 1934 with her own two-man show "Town Tonics" which lasted over a decade, followed by eight seasons with "Spring Thaw" and successively "The Crest Revue", "Fine Frenzy" and others; has written much of her material especially the solo pieces for her many personal appearances; has had many roles of great variety in various theatrical co's. in Toronto and Montreal incl. summer stock in Ont. and Que.; electronically has taken part in four memorable "first occasions"; has worked over television and radio, incl. C.B.C. "Stage Series" and "Wednesday Night" and many series and serials; has been engaged in film work for Nat. Film Bd., Crawley Films, Commonwealth Films; feature films, "Nothing Personal"; "Proper Channels", "Utilities"; co-produced and acted in Donald Harron's mini-musical "Here Lies Sarah Binks", which ran 8 weeks at Central Lib. Theatre, Toronto; rec'd. Order of Can. 1975; John Drainie Award for Distinguished Contrib. to Broadcasting 1976; Brenda Donohue Award 1980; Life mem., Assn. Candn. Television & Radio Artists; Candn. Actors Equity Assn.; Pres., Actors' Fund Can.; recreations: reading, swimming, boating, entertaining; Clubs: Toronto Heliconian; Celebrity; Address: 26 Chestnut Park Road, Toronto, Ont. M4W 1W6

MALLINSON, Thomas J., M.A., Ph.D.; educator; b. Calgary, Alta., 27 May 1919; s. Arthur and Mabel (Quimby) M.; e. Univ. of B.C, B.A. 1947; Columbia Univ., M.A. 1948; Univ. of Toronto, Ph.D. 1954; m. Anna Jean Thomson, 11 Sept. 1948; children: Arthur, Anthea, David, Miranda; PROF. AND CHRMN., DEPT. OF COMMUNICATION STUDIES, SIMON FRASER UNIV. since 1965; Special Lectr., Faculty of Med., Univ. of B.C.; with Goodrich Rubber Co. and Canadian Liquid Air Ltd., 1939-45; Univ. of Toronto, Dept. of Psychiatry, 1954-65; author numerous prof. articles; mem. Am. Psychol. Assn.; Inter-

nat. Communications Assn.; Soc. Study Social Issues; recreation: swimming; Home: 2770 Bellevue Ave., W. Vancouver, B.C.; Office: Burnaby, B.C. V7V 1E6

MALLORY, James Russell, M.A., LL.B., LL.D., F.R.S.C., (1964); university professor; b. St. Andrews, N.B., 5 Feb. 1916; s. late Charles Wesley and Eva Consuella (Outhouse) M.; e. Univ. of New Brunswick, B.A. (hons.) 1937, LL.D. 1968; Univ. of Edinburgh, LL.B. 1940; Dalhousie Univ., M.A. 1941; LL.D., Queen's Univ. 1977; m. Frances Daniel, d. late Daniel S. Keller, Lancaster, Penn., 24 June 1940; two s. James Russell, Charles Daniel; R.B. ANGUS PROF. OF POL. SCIENCE, McGILL UNIV., since 1977; Chrmn., Dept. of Econ. and Pol. Science there 1959-69; Chrmn., Social Science Research Council of Can. 1964-67; with Univ. of Sask. as Instr. in Pol. Science, 1941-43; Univ. of Toronto, Lectr. in Pol. Econ., 1943-44; Asst. Prof. of Pol. Econ, Brandon Coll., 1944-46; apptd. Asst. Prof. Pol. Science, McGill Univ. 1946; Assoc. Prof. 1948; Nuffield Foundation Travelling Fellow, 1953-54; Prof., McGill Univ. 1959-77; Can. Council Leave Fellowship 1969-70; Hon. Fellow, Faculty of Law, Univ. of Edinburgh, 1969-70; Can. Council Leave Fellowship 1977-78; Visiting Fellow, Australian National Univ., 1977-78; Distinguished Visiting Prof., Univ. of Guelph, 1980; author: "Social Credit and the Federal Power in Canada", 1954; "The Structure of Canadian Government", 1970; mem., Candn. Pol. Science Assn. (Vice Pres. 1964-66); Inst. Pub. Adm. of Can.; Pres. (1973-74) Sec. II Roy. Soc. Can.; Presbyterian; Home: 632 Grosvenor Ave., Westmount, Que. H3Y 2S8

MALLORY, Malcolm Ross; manufacturer; b. Sask., 16 Jan. 1922; s. Platt Robin and Margaret M. (Cruikshank) M.; e. Cobourg (Ont.) Coll. Inst.; Univ. of Toronto, Comm. & Finance; m. Lillian Bernice, d. late Howard J. Boothe, 23 Dec. 1943; children: Michael Boothe, Stephen John, Virginia Anne; PRESIDENT AND GEN. MGR., RUBBERMAID (CANADA) INC., since 1969; Gen. Mgr. Foam Rubber Div., Sporting Goods Div., Dunlop Canada Ltd., Toronto, 1954; Mgr. Marketing & Distribution, American Optical Co. Ltd., Toronto, 1960; Pres., Winchester Western (Canada) Ltd., Cobourg, 1962; Pres. Winchester Europe SA, Paris, France, 1966; served Overseas with RCA 1940-45; rank Lt.; Home: 73 Princess Margaret Blvd., Islington, Ont. M9A 2A3; Office: 2562 Stanfield Rd., Mississauga, Ont. L4Y 1S5

MALLORY, William Lloyd, B.S.; manufacturer; b. Petoskey , Mich., 27 Jan. 1938; s. O. K. and Mabel A (Chellis) M.; e. Pellston High Sch. 1956; Mich. Technol. Univ. B.S. (Mech. Engn.) 1961; Extve. Devel. Inst. 1972; Mahler Advanced Management Course, 1981; m. Elaine Marie d. Lester Shorter, Pellston, Mich., 28 June 1958; children: Sheree Lee, Brian, William, Leslie Kay; PRESIDENT AND CEO, INGERSOLL-RAND CANADA INC. since 1976; joined Ingersoll-Rand 1961, trans. to Montreal as Sales Engr. 1962, Sales Mgr. E. Can.-Pulp & Paper Div. 1969, Product Div. Mgr. 1971, Gen. Mgr. Pulp & Paper Div. 1971 and Mining & Constr. Div. 1972, Vice Pres. Marketing 1976, Sr. Vice Pres. Marketing 1976; served 8 yrs. with Mich. Nat. Guard; mem. Candn. Pulp & Paper Assn.; Candn. Inst. Mining; Machinery & Equipment Mfrs. Assn.; Candn. Soc. Mech. Engrs.; Protestant; recreation: golf; Club: Whitlock Golf; Home: 2944 Bugle Call Rd., Hudson, Que. J0P 1H0; Office: 630 Dorchester Blvd. W., Montreal, Que. H3B 1S6

MALMO, Robert Beverley, M.A., Ph.D., LL.D.; university professor; psychologist; b. Canal Zone, Panama, 24 Oct. 1912; s. Robert H. and Mary Welby (Beverley) M.; e. Univ. of Missouri, B.A. (with distinction) 1935; M.A. 1937; Yale Univ., Ph.D. 1940; LL.D. Manitoba, 1970; m. Mary Rose Helen Pitts, d. Marjorie Louise Ensminger, 12 Aug. 1966; PROF. OF PSYCHOLOGY, McGILL UNIVERSITY; Medical Scientist, Royal Victoria Hosp.; mem., Scient. Adv. Council DISCUS; Psychologist, Norwich State Hospital, Conn., 1941-42; apptd. Psychophysiologist, 1942; Public Health Officer, National Inst. of Health, USPHS, Bethesda, Md., 1944-45; joined staff McGill Univ., 1945, as Dir., Lab. of Psychol., Allan Mem. Inst. of Psychiatry, Sch. of Med.; Hon. Life Fellow, Candn. Psychol. Assn. (Pres. and Hon. Pres.); Fellow, Am. Psychol. Assn.; Pres., Interam. Soc. of Psychol.; mem., Exper. Psychol. Study Sec., Nat. Insts. of Health., U.S. Pub. Health Service; mem., Assoc. Comte. on Exper. Psychol., Nat. Research Council; rec'd. Centennial Medal; Citation of Merit, Univ. of Missouri; Lambda Chi Alpha; Phi Eta Sigma; Phi Beta Kappa; Sigma Xi; Protestant; recreations: photography, squash; Home: 814 Graham Blvd., Town of Mount Royal, Que. H3P 2E6; Office: 1033 Pine Ave. W., Montreal, Que. H3A 1A1

MALONE, Clifford S., B.A., B.C.L.; company chairman; b. Quebec City, Que., 4 Sept. 1925; s. Clifford James and Benedicta (Swindell) M.; e. Loyola High Sch., Montreal, 1938-42; Loyola Coll., Montreal, B.A., 1947; McGill Univ., B.C.L. (1948-50, 1954-56); m. Patricia Agnes McVey, 17 June 1950; one s., Kevin John; CHMN., CHIEF EXTVE. OFFR. AND DIR., CANRON INC.; 1981- ; Dir., Bralorne Resources Ltd.; Royal Bank of Can.; Allied Chemical Can. Ltd.; United Corps. Ltd.; Northern Telecom Ltd.; Kamyr Inc.; served as Pilot Offr., R.C.A.F., 1943-45; Vice Pres., Montreal Stock Exchange 1957; Secy., Candn. Chemical Co. Ltd. 1960; Vice Pres., Candn. Chemical Co. Ltd. 1962; Pres., C.E.O., and Dir. Chemcell Ltd. (later Celanese Can.) 1966-72; Pres. Chief Operating Offr. and Dir., Canron Ltd., 1972; Pres., C.E.O. and Dir., Canron Ltd., 1977; Canron Inc., 1978; mem., C.D. Howe Research Inst.; mem., Candn. Council, Conference Bd. of Can.; Roman Catholic; Clubs: Mount Royal (Montreal); Toronto; Recreation: golf, tennis, skiing; Home: 276 Forest Hill Rd., Toronto, Ont. M5P 2N6; Office: First Cdn. Place, Ste. 6300, P.O. Box 134, Toronto, Ont. M5X 1A4

MALONE, Rev. Patrick G., S.J., M.A., Ph.L., LL.D., S.T.L., F.R.S.A.; born Belfast, Northern Ireland, 28 June 1918; s. Hugh Patrick and Elizabeth (Malone) M.; e. St. Michael's Coll. Sch., Toronto, Ont.; Ignatius Coll., Guelph., Ont., B.A. 1942; Regis Coll., Toronto, Ont.; Lic. Phil. 1943; Univ. of Toronto, M.A. (Econ.) 1945; Regis Coll., S.T.L. 1950; o. Priest, 27 June 1949; Executive Secretary, Jesuit Educ. Consortium International since 1975; Dean of Studies, Prof. in Econ. Saint Mary's Univ., Halifax, N.S., 1951-56, Pres. there 1956-59; mem., Bd. of Govs., N.S. Tech. Coll., 1956-59; Bd. of Trustees, Maritime Sch. of Social Work, 1955-59 (Extve. Comte. 1958-59); Pres. Loyola Coll. (Montreal) 1959; Vice Rector Concordia Univ. 1974; LL.D. 1975; mem., Jesuit Educ. Assn.; Candn. Cath. Hist. Assn.; Candn. Assn. Econ. & Pol. Science; Candn. Assn. Adult Educ.; John Howard Soc.; K. of C.; Roman Catholic; Address: Borgo S. Spirito 5, 00100 Roma, Italy

MALONE, Richard Cook, B.A., LL.B.; publisher; b. Toronto, Ont. 4 March 1941; s. Brig. Richard Sankey, O.B.E., E.D. and Helen Mary (Cook) M.; e. Ridley Coll. St. Catharines, Ont. 1960; Univ. of B.C., B.A. 1964; Univ. of Man. LL.B. 1967, Candn. Securities Course 1968; former Publisher, Winnipeg Free Press; Publisher Free Press, Report on Farming since 1974; Dir. Ottawa Journal; Man. Medical Research Fndtn.; read law with Aikins MacAulay & Co.; called to Bar of Man. 1967; Asst. to Gen. Mgr. Ottawa Journal 1969; Globe and Mail, Toronto 1971; Asst. to Publisher Winnipeg Free Press 1973; served with COTC (Inf. Belt 1962), Q.O.R. (Germany 1963), Seaforth Highlanders of Can. 1964, Royal Winnipeg Rifles 1964-67; Dir. Royal Winnipeg Ballet; Dafoe Foundation; Bd. of Govs., Ridley Coll., St. Catharines, Ont.; comm. and instrument pilot's licence; Candn. mem. Crossroads Africa 1964; Candn. publishers Del. to China 1975; mem. Candn. Press; Candn. Bar Assn.; Candn. Daily Newspaper Assn.; Alpha Delta Phi; Anglican; recreations: run-

ning, outdoor activity, flying, sailing; Clubs: Manitoba; St. Charles Country; Winnipeg Squash & Racquet.

MALONE, Brig. Richard Sankey, O.B.E., E.D,; journalist publisher; b. Owen Sound, Ont., 18 Sept. 1909; s. the late Liet.-Col. Willard Park and Mildred Villiers (Sankey) M.; Univ. of Toronto Schs.; Bishop Ridley Coll., St. Catharines, Ont.; also various pub. schs. in Can.; m. 1st Helen Mary, d. Robert H. Cook of Toronto, Ont., 6 Aug. 1936; children: Robert Nesbit, Richard Cook, Deirdre; m. 2nd Ioana Soutzo; CHRMN., F. P. PUBLICATIONS LTD. 1975-79; Dir., Monarch Life Assnce. Co.; Past Pres., Winnipeg Chamber of Comm.; Hon. Mgr. for Imp. Press Conf., 1950; engaged in newsp. work with Toronto "Daily Star" 1927-28; Regina "Leader-Post" 1929-33; Saskatoon "Star-Phoenix" 1943; mem., Parlty. Press Gallery, Ottawa, 1934-35; Winnipeg "Free Press", 1936-64 (Publisher 1961-74); "The Globe and Mail" (Publisher 1974-78); apptd. Hon. A.D.C. to Governor-General of Canada 1946; served in 2nd World War, 1939-46; enlisted with P.P.C.L.I. 1939; Staff Secretary to Minister of Defence 1940; Grad. from Staff Coll.; Staff Capt., 5 Armoured Civ., and subsequently Bgde. Maj., 1st Div.; wounded and Mentioned in Despatches, Sicily Invasion; Personal Liaison Offr. to Field Marshal Montgomery in Italy; Asst. Dir. Pub. Relations, 21st Army Group, and in charge Candn. Pub. Relations of Normandy campaign; headed Candn. Mission to Gen. MacArthur's H.Q., Pacific; among first to enter Paris, Brussels, and Tokyo; present at peace signing on U.S.S. Missouri; founder of Candn. Army Newspaper "Maple Leaf" in Italy, France and Belgium, etc.; author of "Missing From the Record", 1946; Hon. Col. Royal Winnipeg Rifles; mem., Candn. Mil. Inst.; Ridley Old Boys' Assn.; Liberal; Anglican; recreation: painting; Clubs: Manitoba; St. Charles Country; York; Toronto; Home: Granite Place, 63 St. Clair Ave. W., Toronto, Ont.; Office: Thompson Newspapers, 65 Queen St. W., Toronto, Ont.

MALONE, Thomas Paul, B.A.; retired diplomat; b. Edmonton, Alta., 8 Feb. 1915; s. Thomas Peter and Sarah (MacMillan) M.; e. Univ. of Alta., B.A. 1936; m. Deirdre Lavallette, d. Sefton Ingram, Sydney, Aust., 9 July 1940; children: Anthony, Mark, Christopher, Patricia, David; Journalist, Edmonton Journ., 1936-38; Commonwealth Press Union Exchange Journalist, Eng. and Aust., 1938-40; Candn. Rep., Wartime Information Bd., Aust., 1942-46; joined Dept. of External Affairs, 1946; 2nd Secy., Canberra, 1946-48; 1st Secy., Washington, 1948-53; Dept. of External Affairs, Ottawa, 1953-58; Counsellor, The Hague, 1958-62; Ambassador to Iran 1962-67 (then concurrently to Iraq and Kuwait); High Commr. to Nigeria 1967-70; Depy. Commandant, Nat. Defence Coll. Can. 1970-72; Ambassador to Israel and concurrently to Cyprus 1972-75; apptd. Ambassador to Finland 1975; retired from Foreign Service, 31 Dec. 1979; mem. International Inst. of Strategic Studies; Delta Upsilon; Roman Catholic; recreation: golf; Clubs: Rideau; Home: Suite 1204, 20 Driveway, Ottawa, Ont. K2P 1C8 and Apt. 601, "Arcadia", 33 Stasinos St., Acropolis Nicosia, Cyprus.

MALONE, William James, B.A.Sc.; consulting engineer; b. Toronto, Ont., 23 Sept. 1924; s. Charles Stuart and Charlotte Lamont (Davidson) M.; e. Davisville Public and Northern Secondary Schs., Toronto; Univ. of Toronto, B.A.Sc. 1949; m. Heidemarie, d. Wilhelm Wilmschen, Moers, Germany, 4 July 1968; four children (two by former m.); Chrmn. Mascon Internat.; began as Jr. Research Engr., HEPC, Toronto 1949; Resident Engr., De Leuw Cather & Brill, N.Y. 1952; joined De Leuw Cather & Co. of Can., Toronto 1954 as Design Engr.; Br. Mgr. Ottawa 1957; Pres. 1960; Chrmn. 1967-79 (ret.); served in R.C.A.F., pilot Offr. 1942-44; with Fleet Air Arm, R.N.V.R., Sub-Lt. 1944-45; mem. Assn. Prof. Engrs. of Ont., Nfld. and N.S.; Engn. Inst. Can.; Am. Soc. Civil Engrs.; Am. Concrete Inst.; Inst. Traffic Engrs.; Consulting Engrs. Council; Road & Transport. Assn. Can. (Past

Chrmn., Tech. Council); Past Chrmn., Tech. Comte., Internat. Road Fed. Conf.; rec'd Distinguished Service Award, Candn. Good Roads Assn.; Centennial Medal 1967; author of numerous tech. papers dealing with transport.; recreations: golf, curling; Home: Jevington House, Knotty Green, Beaconsfield, Bucks., England; Office: 133 Wynford Dr., Don Mills, Ont. M3C 1K1

MALONEY, Aidan; executive; b. Kings Cove, Nfld., 12 Aug. 1920; s. Michael Edward and Alice Rose (Murphy) M.; e. R.C. High Sch., Kings Cove Nfld.; m. Eva M., d. William L. Wyse, 12 Aug. 1947; one d.; Maureen; CHRMN., FISHERIES PRICES SUPPORT BOARD OF CAN. since 1979; mem., Bd. of Dir., Fisheries Development Corp of Nfld.; Cdn. Saltfish Corp.; mem. Bd. of Regents, Memorial Univ. of Nfld.; Bd. of Govs., Coll. of Fisheries of Nfld.; Royal Comm. on Inshore Fisheries of Nfld. & Labradore; joined Royal Bank of Canada, 1938-44; apptd. Chief Acct., John Penny & Sons Ltd. (fish processors) Ramea, Nfld., 1944; Mgr. 1946; Mang. Dir. 1949-57; served with Dept. of Fisheries, Nfld. as Asst. Depy. Min., 1957-66; el. M.H.A. for Dist. of Ferryland in Prov. g.e. 1966; apptd. Min. of Fisheries and Min. of Community & Social Devel., retired from Pol. Apl. 1970; Pres. and Gen. Mgr., Cdn. Saltfish Corp. 1970-79; Vice Chrmn., Nfld. and Labrador Arts Council, 1979; mem. Executive, K. of C.; Vice Chrmn., Bd. of Govs. St. Clares Mercy Hospital; mem., N.W. Rotary Club, St. John's; mem. St. John's Bd. of Trade; Roman Catholic; recreation: painting; Home: 2 Laughlin Cres., St. John's, Nfld. A1A 2G2; Office: Dept. of Fisheries and Oceans, Pleasantville, St. John's, Nfld. A1C 5X1

MALONEY, Hon. Anthony William; b. Saskatoon, Sask. 12 May 1928; s. Leo and Katherine Jane (Shields) M.; e. St. Paul's Coll., Univ. of Man. B.A. 1949; Osgoode Hall Law Sch. grad. 1953; m. Marian Lucille Auringer 25 Nov. 1954; children: Patrick W., Michael L., James V.; JUSTICE, SUPREME COURT OF ONT.; read law with Weiler, Maloney, Nelson; called to the Bar of Ont. 1953; cr. Q.C. 1964; practised law in N. Ont. for 23 years; mem. Council Candn. Bar Assn.; Former Trustee, Ft. William Bd. of Educ.; Past Dir., Advocates Soc.; Ont. Legal Aid Plan; R. Catholic; Delta Upsilon; recreations: skiing, swimming, hunting; Club: Toronto University; Home: 96 The Kingsway, Toronto, Ont.; Office: Osgoode Hall, Toronto, Ont. M5H 2N5

MALONEY, Arthur, Q.C., LL.D.; b. Eganville, Ont., 26 Nov. 1919; s. Martin James and Margaret Mary (Bonfield) M.; e. Cont. Sch., Eganville, Ont. (1925-36); Lisgar Coll. Inst., Ottawa, Ont. (1936-37); St. Michael's Coll., Univ. of Toronto, 1937-40; Osgoode Hall, Toronto, Ont., 1940-43; LL.D., St. Dunstan's Univ., 1961; m. Lillian, d. Gilbert A. LaBine, Toronto, Ont., 11 Sept. 1948; children: Mary Martha, Matthew Joseph; read law with Smith, Rae, Greer and Cartwright, Toronto, Ont.; called to the Bar of Ontario, October 1943; cr. Q.C. December 1953; first el. to H. of C. for Toronto-Parkdale, g.e. June 1957; named Parlty. Asst. to the Min. of Labour 7 Aug. 1957; re-el. in g.e. March 1958; def. g.e. 1962; Bencher Law Soc. of Upper Can. since 1956; Ombudsman, Ont. 1975-78; mem., Candn. Bar Assn. (former Chrmn. of Criminal Justice Comte.); Dir., Candn. Soc. for Abolition of Death Penalty; The Advocate's Society of Ont.; Crim. Lawyers Assn. K. of C. (3rd degree); Conservative; Roman Catholic; recreations: swimming, reading; Clubs: Toronto Lawyers; Newman; Albany; Cercle Universitaire (Ottawa); Home: 40 Oaklands Ave. Ste 103, Toronto, Ont. M4V 2Z3; Office: Suite 400, 120 Adelaide St. W., Toronto Ont. M5H 1T1

MALONEY, Douglas W., B.Comm.; banker; b. Salmon Arm, B.C., 8 July 1920; s. James W. and Maude E. (Holliday) M.; e. Univ. of B.C., B.Comm. 1942; m. Alix, d. late Robert McPhail, 23 Dec. 1942; two d. Dianne (Mrs. Richard Hand), Sharon; CHRMN. OF THE BOARD AND DIR., CONTINENTAL BANK OF CAN. 1980- ; Dir., Ni-

agara Finance Co. Ltd.; joined IAC as Sales Rep., 1948, and Asst. Mgr. Vancouver 1950; Mgr. Winnipeg 1952; Regional Sales Mgr. Toronto 1956; Ont. Mgr. Business Devel., Toronto 1960; Assistant Vice President, Montreal 1961; Vice Pres. Business Devel. 1964; Depy. Gen. Mgr. 1966; Sr. Vice Pres. 1968; Sr. Vice Pres. & Gen. Mgr. Ont., W. and Indust. Div., Toronto 1970; Sr. Vice-President and Sr. General Mgr. 1973; Extve. Vice Pres. & Sr. Gen. Mgr. 1974; Pres. 1976; Vice Chmn. 1979; Chmn. 1980; served in Eng., Italy and N.W. Europe during World War II; recreations: golf, fishing; Home: 701 The Lonsdale, 619 Avenue Rd., Toronto, Ont. M4V 2K6; Office: 130 Adelaide St. W., Toronto, Ont. M5H 3R2

MALOUF, Hon. Albert-H., B.A., B.C.L.; judge; b. Montreal, Que., 17 Dec. 1916; s. Joseph H. and Emily (Kuzma) M.; e. McGill Univ., B.A. 1938, B.C.L. 1941; m. Mary, d. Elias N. Tabah, 23 Dec. 1961; two s. Paul, Marc; JUSTICE, COURT OF APPEAL, QUE. 1981- ; read law with Sullivan & Johnson; called to Bar of Que. 1942; cr. Q.C. 1959; Sr. Partner, Malouf & Shorteno and in 1959 Malouf, Pateras & Macerola; named Judge, Court of Sessions of the Peace, Que., 1968; Justice, Superior Court Que. 1972; served with RCA in Can., Italy and N.W. Europe 1942-46; rank Lt.; presently Hon. Col. 2nd Field Arty Regt.; Cmdr. Equestrian Order, Holy Cross of Jerusalem; mem. d'hon., Foundation de l'Université du Québec à Montreal; mem., Nat. Council, Candn. Human Rights Foundation; Gov., Cedars Home for Elderly; Lebanese Syrian Candn. Assn.; Dir., Arty. Offrs. Assn. Montreal; R. Catholic; recreations: skiing, swimming, tennis, golf, bridge; Club: Beaconsfield Golf & Country; Home: 240 Appin Ave., Town of Mount Royal, Que. H3P 1V8; Office: Court House, Montreal, Que. H2Y 1B6

MALTAIS, Armand, C.R.; né à Montrél, Qué., 22 août 1913; f. Guillaume et Suzanne (Alain) M.; é. coll. Jean de Brébœuf, Montréal, B.A.; Univ. Laval, Québec, LL.D., 1951; ép. Rosa-Rita, f. Georges Duchesne, St-Tite des Caps, Qué., 10 juil. 1943; enfant: Marie-Thérèse; admis au Barreau du Qué. en 1952; nommé C.R., 1966; Député, ancien comté de Quebec-est, 1956-62; Délégué du gouv. du Qué. aux fêtes commémoratives de la mort de Jacques Cartier à St-Malo, France, 1957; Président, comité des Bills privés de l'Assemblée législative et adj. parlement. du premier ministre Maurice Duplessis, 1958-59; Ministre d'Etat, gouv. Barrette, 1960; Premier reprs. du nouveau comté de Limoilou, 1966; Ministre d'Etat délégué au Justice, cabinet de l'hon. Daniel Johnson, 1966; Solliciteur Gén. du Qué. 1968-70; participation aux oeuvres du Conseil de vie fr. en Amérique; Présid. gén.; Soc. St-Jean Baptiste de Qué., 1952-56; Membre: Assoc. des Anciens du Séminaire de Gaspé; Assoc. des Anciens de l'Univ. Laval; Club Renaissance de Québec; Assoc. du Barreau can.; Soc. hist. et culturelle de citoyens d'ascendance fr.; Union commerciale de Qué.; Assoc. des Gaspésiens et des Madelinots de Qué.; Assoc. des Parlementaires du Commonwealth; Assoc. des Consommateurs du Canada; membre hon., Club de Golf de Lorette; Gouverneur hon. du Club Renaissance de Montréal; Residence: 2219 Monseigneur-Gosselin, Québec, Qué.

MALTAIS, Msgr. Roger, L.Ph., D.C.L. (R.C.); educator; b. Sherbrooke, Que., 24 July 1914; s. Henri and Elodia (Rouillard) M.; e. Séminaire de Sherbrooke, (high sch. 1925-29), training for priesthood (1933-37); o. Priest 1937; Univ. of Montréal, B.A. 1933; Pontifical Inst. of Philos. Rome, Italy, L.Ph. 1940;; D.C.L. Bishop's 1970; Prof. of Philos., St. Charles Semy., Sherbrooke, Que., 1940-49 and Dean of Studies there, 1949-54; Dean of Faculty of Arts, Univ. of Sherbrooke, 1954-64; Acad. Vice Rector, 1964-65, Rector 1965-75; Canon of Arch-diocese of Sherbrooke, 1958; Roman Prelate, 1963; Fellow, Royal Cdn. Coll. of Phys. and Surg. (honoris causa), 1976; Address: University of Sherbrooke, Sherbrooke, Que.

MANDEL, Eli, M.A., Ph.D.; educator; writer; b. Estevan, Sask. 3 Dec. 1922; e. Univ. of Sask. B.A. 1949, M.A. 1950; Univ. of Toronto Ph.D. 1957; m. Ann 18 Sept. 1967; 3 children; PROF. OF HUMANITIES AND ENG., YORK UNIV. 1980- ; Instr. Univ. of Toronto 1952-53; Asst. Prof. Coll. Militaire Royal de Saint Jean 1953, Assoc. Prof. 1955-57; Asst. Prof. Univ. of Alta. 1957, Assoc. Prof. 1959-63. Prof. 1964-65; Assoc. Prof. York Univ. 1963-64, Prof. 1967, mem. Bd. Govs. 1970-71; Visiting Prof. Univ. of Victoria 1979-80; Writer-in-Residence Regina 1978-79; mem. Humanities Research Council 3 yrs.; Johnson Soc. (Secy.-Treas. 1966-67); various comtes, Can. Council; Extve. Comte. ACUTE 1962-64; Centennial Comn. Poetry Awards Comte. 1967; Gov. Gen.'s Lit. Awards Comte. on Poetry 1973 and on Fiction 1973; Extve., Assn. Candn. Ethnic Studies 1975- ; Ministry of Educ. Curriculum Comte. 1975; author "Minotaur Poems" 1954; "Fuseli Poems" 1960; "Black and Secret Man" 1964; "An Idiot Joy" 1967; "Crusoe: Poems New and Selected" 1973; "Stony Plain" 1973; "Criticism: Silent-Speaking Words" 1967; "Canadian Writers and Critics: Irving Layton" 1969; "Out of Place" 1977; "Another Time" 1977; "Mary Midnight" 1979; "Life Sentence: Poems and Journals 1976-80" 1981; "Collected Poems" fall 1981; co-author "Teaching Poetry" 1979; Ed. "Five Modern Canadian Poets" 1969; "Poets of Contemporary Canada" 1972; "Contexts of Canadian Criticism" 1971; "The Poetry of Irving Layton" 1977; co-ed. "Poetry 62" 1962; "Eight More Canadian Poets" 1972; "English Poems of the Twentieth Century" 1971; numerous articles, papers, poetry readings and workshops; 2 poetry tapes; work incl. various anthols. and colls.; participant numerous radio and TV programs; rec'd IODE Scholarship 1950; Sir Joseph Flavelle Fellowship 1951; Can. Foundation Fellowship in Writing 1959-60; Univ. of W. Ont. Pres.' Medal in Poetry 1963; Gov. Gen.'s Award in Poetry 1967; Centennial Medal 1967; Can. Council Sr. Arts Award 1971-72; Ont. Arts Council Awards 1973, 1976, 1977, 1979, 1980; Queen's Silver Jubilee Medal 1977; served with R.C.A.M.C. Can. and Europe 1943-46; Home: 264 Glenview Ave., Toronto, Ont. M4R 1R3; Office: Downsview, Ont. M3J 1P3.

MANDRY, Wilfred John, B.S.c., P.Eng.; executive; b. London, Eng. 3 Apl. 1922; e. St. Dunstan's Coll. London, Eng.; Univ. of London B.Sc. (Engn.); m. Kathleen Rains 19 Dec. 1944; children: Michael, David, Rosemary, Angela; PRESIDENT, CEO AND DIR. C-I-L Inc. since 1976; joined present Co. as Maintenance Engr. Textile Fibres Div. 1955, held various production and engn. positions in Textile Fibres and in Paints until 1964 when apptd. Asst. Co. Secy., Distribution Mgr. 1966, Works Mgr. Polyester Fibres Plant Millhaven, Ont. 1967, Gen. Mgr. Agric. Chems. Div. 1968, Extve. Vice Pres. and Director of CIL 1970, trans. to ICI Americas Inc. Wilmington, Del. as Vice Pres. 1973, rtn'd to CIL Montreal as Pres. & Chief Operating Offr. and Dir. 1975; served with RAF 1940-46, rank Flight Lt. Bomber & Transport Command, RAFVR 1948-53; Fellow, Inst. Mech. Engrs. (UK); recreations: photography, carpentry, swimming; Clubs: St. James's; Canadian; Mount Royal; Forest & Stream; Office: 630 Dorchester Blvd. W., Montreal, Que. H3B 1S6

MANG, Henry Philip; farmer; b. Edenwold, Sask., 11 Dec. 1897; s. Karl and Regina (Schmidt) M.; e. Winnetka (Sask.) Pub. Sch.; Regina Coll. Inst. and Normal Sch.; Royal Coll. of Dental Surg. , Toronto, Ont.; Univ. of Toronto (Philos., Eng. and Hist.); Student Del. to Internat. Conv. of Student Vol. Movement Y.M.C.A. at Des Moines, Iowa (1920) and Indianapolis (1924); unm.; Pres., Farmers Mutual Petroleums Ltd.; Dir., Co-op. Hall Insurance Co.; began career by teaching sch. in Sask.; Princ. at Edenwool, Sask. 1927-28; with Sask. Wheat Pool Field Service organ. dept. 1928-31; engaged in Dairy and Grain farming 1931-35; practised Dentistry, 1935-41 and has been farming 960 acres since 1941; mem., Sask. Leg. Assembly 1934-38; el. to H. of C. for Qu'Appelle, g.e.

1953; def. g.e. 1957; mem., Agric. Comm. of Regina Chambre of Comm. since 1970; mem., Qu'Appelle Reg. Appeal Bd. of Sask. since 1968; Secy., Edenwold Agric. Soc. 1926-28; Edenwold Co-op. Assn. (inc. 1919); Pres., Francis Inspectorate of Sch. Teachers, 1925; Candn. Del. to World Fed. of Teachers Assn., Edin., Sept. 1925 (67 Nations rep.); attended Internat. Teachers Inst. at Heidelberg and Berlin 1925; served in 1st World War with R.F.C.; has travelled extensively in Can., U.S., Gt. Brit. and Europe; Hon. Indian Chief "Waakitosh" (smiling face or the cheerful one) Cree Tribe of Great Plains; Xi Psi Phi; Freemason; I.O.O.F.; Liberal; Lutheran; recreations: curling, soccer, football (Pres., Dale Rugby Club of Regina, Candn. Jr. Champions 1938); Address: Edenwold, Sask. S0G 1K0

MANN, Cedric Robert, M.Sc., Ph.D., D.Eng., FRSC; oceanographer; b. Auckland, N.Z. 14 Feb. 1926; s. late Duncan and Winifred Mary (Hood) M.; came to Canada 1949; e. Univ. of N. Z., B.Sc. 1948; M.Sc. 1950; Univ. of Brit. Columbia, Ph.D. (Physics) 1953; N.S. Tech. Coll., D.Eng. (hon. causa) 1972; m. Muriel Frances, d. late John May, Nanton, Alta. 18 Dec. 1950; one s. Robin Carl; DIR. GEN., OCEAN AND AQUATIC SCIENCES, PACIFIC REGION since 1975; Dir. Gen Ocean and Aquatic Sciences, Atlantic Region 1978-79; Dir., Atlantic Oceanographic Laboratory, 1975-78; Head, Ocean Circulation Div. 1965-75; Oceanographer, Bedford Inst. Oceanog. since 1961; Assoc. Prof., Dept. Physics, Dalhousie Univ.1961-75; Del., Internat. Council for Exploration of Sea1978-79; Chmn., Scientific Advisory Bd., Integovernmental Oceanographic Comn., 1978-81; Chmn., Sea Use Council U.S./Can. 1981- ; Physicist, Naval Research Estab., Defense Research Bd. 1953-61; Regional Research Oceanographer, Bedford Inst. Oceanog. 1962-65; organized and dir. "Hudson 70" Expdn.; mem. Candn. Meteorol. and Oceanog. Soc.; N.S. Inst. Science; author of numerous papers publ. in various journs.; elected Fellow of the Royal Soc. of Canada, 1979; Anglican; recreation: golf; Office: Inst. of Ocean Sciences, Box 6000, Sidney, B.C. V8L 4B2

MANN, Geoffrey Thomas, B.A., LL.B., M.D., F.R.S.T.M. & H., F.R.C. Path.; forensic pathologist; b. Regina, Sask., 28 May 1914; s. Geoffrey John and Kathleen (Elliott) M.; e. Univ. of Sask.; Univ. of Man., B.A. 1946, LL.B. 1941 and M.D. 1948; Lic. of Med. Council of Can.; m. Ann Elizabeth, d. John Charles Nixon, Regina, Sask., 28 Dec. 1936; one s. two d.; Chief Med. Examiner, Broward Co., Fla., since 1972; Chief Med. Examiner, State of Va. 1949-72; Professor and Head of Dept. of Legal Medicine, Medical College of Virginia; Prof. of Forensic Path., Dept. of Path., Med. Coll. of Virginia; Lectr. in Legal Med., Univ. of Virginia; Dir., Div. of Law, in Hosp. Adm., MCV (all 1949-1972); Medico-Legal Consultant to Saskatchewan Insurance Co.; Consultant to Fed. Aviation Agency; Armed Forces Inst. Path.; Visiting Prof., Univ. of S. Carolina; Fellow Coll. of Am. Paths.; Am. Soc. Clinical Paths.; mem., Am. Soc. of Paths. and Bacteriols.; mem., Coll. of Phys. & Surg., Sask.; Am. Med. Assn.; Fla. Med. Assn.; Nat. Assn. Med. Examiners; S. Fla. Soc. Pathols.; Broward Co. Medical Assn.; Richmond Acad. of Med.; Va. State Med. Soc.; Va. Soc. of Pathols.; Am. Acad. of Forensic Sciences; Sask. Law Soc.; Phi Rho Sigma; Anglican; recreations: hunting, fishing; Home: 227 Codrington Dr., Lauderdale-by-the-Sea, Fla.; Office: 5301 S. W. 31st Ave., Ft. Lauderdale, Fla. 33312

MANN, George Stanley; company president; b. Toronto, Ont., 23 Dec. 1932; s. David Philip and Elizabeth (Green) M.; e. Deer Park Public Sch., Toronto; N. Toronto Coll.; m. Saundra, d. Richard Sair of Montreal, 2 Jan. 1955; children: Michael, Tracy; PRESIDENT, UNICORP FINANCIAL CORP.; Dir., National Bank of Can.; Consumers Distrib. Co. Ltd.; Great Northern Financial Corp.; Pratt and Lambert Inc.; Chmn., Unicorp American Corp.; Trustee, San Francisco Real Estate Investors; with City

Mortgage Exchange & Mortgage Investors Corp. (Toronto) as Mortgage Broker, 1952; joined Mann & Martel Co. Ltd., 1958; Partner 1959; Vice-Pres., Commonwealth Savings & Loan Corp., 1963; Commonwealth Insurance Co., 1964; Extve. Vice-Pres. and Dir., Canada Health & Accident Assurance Corp., 1965; Pres., Rideau Trust Co. (Ottawa), 1969 (becoming United Trust Co., 1970); Pres., York Region Real Estate Bd. 1973; Douglas Leaseholds Ltd. 1974; Chrmn. Auto Electric Service Co. Ltd. 1974; Chrmn., Unity Bank 1974; Pres., Great Northern Financial Corp. 1974; Chrmn. 1975; Home: 18 Old Forest Hill Rd., Toronto, Ont. M5P 2P7; Office: 21 St. Clair Ave. E., Toronto, Ont. M4T 2T7

MANN, Kenneth Clifford, O.B.E. (1946), B.Sc., B.Ed., M.A., Ph.D.; physicist; university professor; b. Swift Current, Sask., 10 Apr. 1910; s. William Beecher and Gertrude Amy (Mathews) M.; e. Univ. of Sask., B.Sc. 1931, B.Ed. 1933; Univ. of Toronto, M.A. 1936, Ph.D. 1938; m. Iva Viola, d. Alex MacKenzie, Renfrew, Ont., 9 Sept. 1944; children: Shelley Anne; Assistant to Pewa., Univ. of B.C. 1977-81; Lectr. in Physics, Univ. of B.C., 1938-39; Asst. Prof. 1939-41; on leave of absence 1941-45, with Radio Br., Nat. Research Council, as Research Physicist on radar problems; Project Engr. on radar sets for Candn. Navy and Brit. Admiralty; sent to Eng. to test type "268" radar set, 1943; loaned to Research Enterprises Ltd., Leaside, Ont., as Engr. in Charge of Production of this set; apptd. Brit. Admiralty Tech. Mission rep. there 1945; Assoc. Prof. of Physics, Univ. of B.C. 1945-46; Prof., 1946-76; joined staff of Chalk River Lab. of Nat. Research Council on Atomic Energy 1946; mem., Can. Assn. of Physicists; Am. Phys. Soc.; Kappa Sigma; Liberal; Anglican; recreations: golf, curling, swimming; Home: 1808 Acadia Rd., Vancouver, B.C. V6T 1R3

MANN, Larry D.; actor & writer; b. Toronto, Ont., 18 Dec. 1922; s. Charles and Rose (Steinback) Libman; e. Rawlinson Pub. Sch. and Vaughan Rd. Coll. Inst., Toronto, 1940; Brit. Inst. of Technol.; Oxford Univ., extension courses; m. Gloria, d. late David and Freda (Kasman) Kochberg, 1 Sept. 1946; four s. Dan, Ron, Rick, Jeff; has appeared in over 2.000 TV shows and 20 maj. motion pictures in Can. and U.S.A. (2 films were nominated for Acad. Awards); also stage plays across Can. and U.S.; former radio newscaster, Can. and U.S. (covered Noronic fire disaster and subsequently was awarded Phi Beta Key by Variety, 1949); rec'd. Liberty Award 1959, 1960 and 1961 as best Candn. character actor on TV; served with RCAF in Can., Eng. and N.W. Europe; Mentioned in Despatches; mem., Screen Actors Guild; Assn. Motion Picture Arts & Sciences; Assn. Candn. Radio & TV Artists; Actors Equity; Am. Fed. Radio & TV Artists; recreations: hockey, swimming, camping; Club: Variety; Address: Larry Mann Enterprises, 5005 Bilmoor, Tarzana, Cal.

MANN, William Henry; executive; b. Chicago, Ill., 16 Apl. 1918; came to Can. 1952; became Candn. citizen 1969; s. William Henry and Lillian (Christy) M.; e. Univ. of Chicago 1936-38; m. Patricia Leighton, d. late Hugh Leighton, 28 Nov. 1980; four s.; PRES., D. A. STUART OIL INC. since 1952; joined D. A. Stuart Oil Co. Ltd., Chicago, 1947; served with U.S. Army 1941-46; rank Maj.; has served as Chrmn., Bd. of Stewards and as Secy., Royal York Rd. Un. Ch.; mem., Am. Soc. Lubrication Engrs. (Vice-Pres.-at-large 1973-74, Pres. 1974-75); Phi Delta Theta; United Church; recreation: golf; Clubs: Islington Golf (Pres. 1971-73, Dir. 6 yrs.); Toronto Golf; American; Home: 1400 Dixie Rd. #1109, Mississauga, Ont. L5E 3E1; Office: 43 Upton Rd., Scarborough, Ont. M1L 2C1

MANNING, C(harles) Terrill, Q.C., B.A., B.C.L.; b. Empress, Alta. 27 March 1925; s. N. Folsom and Mary Ethel (Terrill) M.; e. Huntingdon Acad. 1942; Bishop's Univ. B.A. 1946; McGill Univ. B.C.L. 1949; m. Hazel

Joyce, d. late Andrew Stuart Johnson, 1946; children: A. Terrill, Timothy F., Heather J., Annabelle H.; VICE PRES. AND SECRETARY, ROYAL TRUSTCO LTD. since 1978; read law with F. Winfield Hackett, K.C.; called to Bar of Que. 1949; cr. Q.C. 1968; law practice Hackett, Mulvena, Hackett 1949-56, Partner 1955; assoc. with Brinco 1956-69 serving latterly as Vice Pres. and Gen. Counsel; Vice Pres.-Legal, Churchill Falls Labrador Corp. Ltd.; Vice Pres. and Dir. Twin Falls Power Corp. Ltd. and British Newfoundland Exploration Ltd.; joined The Royal Trust Co. as Gen. Counsel 1970; Vice Pres. 1975; served with RCNVR 1944-45; Chrmn. Special Corp's Div. Combined Appeal 1971; Pres. Nat. Comte. Bishop's Univ. Alumni Assn. 1965-67; active Montreal W. Boy Scouts 1955-65; Dir. Weston Sch. Inc. 1973-76; mem. Candn. Bar Assn.; Que. Bar Assn.; Liberal; Anglican; recreations: boating, fishing, golf, skiing; Clubs: Donalda (Toronto), St. James' (Montreal); Home: 67 Pinnacle Rd., Willowdale, Ont. M2L 2V6; Office: TD Bank Tower, P.O. Box 7500 Station A, Toronto, Ont. M5W 1P9

MANNING, Hon. Ernest Charles, P.C. (1967), C.C. (1969), LL.D.; senator; ex premier; b. Carnduff, Sask., 20 Sept. 1908; George Henry and Elisabeth Mara (Dickson) M., both Eng.; e. Local Schs., Rosetown, Sask.; Calgary Prophetic Bible Inst. (1st Grad.); LL.D. McGill 1967; m. Muriel, d. William Preston, Calgary, Alta., 14 Apl. 1936; 1st el. to Alta. Leg. for Calgary, g.e. 1935; apptd. Prov. Secy. in Aberhart Cabinet, 3 Sept. 1935; Min. of Trade and Indust., 19 Oct. 1935; Premier, 31 May 1943 and Prov. Treas. 1944-54; resigned seat in Leg. Jan. 1969; summoned to the Senate of Can. 7 Oct. 1970; Chrmn., Manning Consultants Ltd.; Dir., The Steel Co. of Canada Ltd.; Manufacturers Life Insurance Co.; McIntyre Mines Ltd.; Burns Foods Ltd.; Canada West Found.; Coal Valley Invest. Corp.; Fluor Can. Ltd.; Melcor Devels. Ltd.; OPI Ltd.; Social Credit; Baptist; Home: (P.O. Box 2317), Edmonton, Alta. T5J 2P4

MANNING, Jo (Joan Elizabeth), R.C.A.; artist; b. Sidney, B.C. 11 Dec. 923; d. Frederick William and Elizabeth (Willcox) Manning; e. Gen Amherst Secondary Sch. 1941, Amherstburg, Ont.; Ont. Coll. of Art 1945; children: Paul, Peter, Ann and Mary Rothfels; solo exhns. incl. Pollock Gallery Toronto 1965, 1968; Gallery Pascal Toronto 1974, 1977, 1980; Univ. of Waterloo 1968; Mira Goddard Gallery Montreal 1976; Earlscourt Gallery Hamilton 1979; rep. numerous nat. and internat. (USA, Australia, Europe, S. Am.) group exhns. since 1966; rep. various pub., corporate and private colls. incl. Nat. Gallery Can.; Montreal Museum of Fine Art; Can. Council Art Bank; Dept. External Affairs; Nat. Lib. Can.; awards incl. Nat. Gallery Can. 1964; London Spring Show 1965; Nicholas Hornyansky Award CPE 1967; Northwest Printmakers Seattle 1970; Santiago, Chile 4th Am. Print Biennale First Prize 1970; Florence, Italy 2nd Print Biennale Gold Medal 1970; Graphex II Brantford 1974; Heinz Jordan Award CSGA 1974; Graphex III Brantford 1975; Kenneth Siddal Award "On View" Visual Arts Ont. 1976; Norwegian Print Biennale Hon. Mention 1976; OSA "Collectors Choice" Can. Perm. Trust 1978; mem. Print & Drawing Council Can.; Ont. Soc. Artists; Candn. Artists Representation; Visual Arts Ont.; recreation: photography with large format camera; Address: 61 Balmoral Ave., Toronto, Ont. M4V 1J5.

MANNING, Randolph William, F.C.A.; chartered accountant; b. Falmouth, N.S., 1 Aug. 1915; s. late Charles Randolph and late Mabel Vernon (Wilson) M.; e. Falmouth (N.S.) Sch., 1928; Windsor (N.S.) Acad., 1931; Kings Coll. Sch., Windsor, N.S., 1932; Maritime Business Coll., Halifax, 1936; C.A. 1942; m. Mary Kathleen, d. late W. G. Bauchman, 11 Sept. 1939; children: Terry Randolph, Mrs. Carolyn Celeste Allworth; CONSULTANT, H. R. DOANE AND COMPANY; Sessional Lectr., Univ. P.E.I.; Teacher, Maritime Business Coll., 1937; Student Acct., H. R. Doane and Co., 1938; became Partner 1942;

opened firm's 1st br. office, Charlottetown, P.E.I., 1944; joined mang. comte. on formation of present firm, 1959; el. Pres., Candn. Inst. of C.A.'s, 1967 (Chrmn., Adv. Comte. on Uniform Regulatory Leg. 1951; mem. Comte on Accounting & Auditing Research 1953; mem. Exrve. Comte. 1954-56 and 1965); mem., Inst. of C.A.'s of P.E.I. (Pres. 1948); United Church; recreations: golf, gardening, woodcarving; Club: Rotary; Home: 191 North River Rd., Charlottetown, P.E.I. C1A 3L4; Office: 199 Grafton St., Charlottetown, P.E.I. C1A 7K4

MANNING, Travis Warren, M.Sc., Ph.D.; educator; b. Okla., 17 June 1921; s. John and Ida (Young) M.; e. Univ. of Oklahoma 1947; Oklahoma State Univ., B.Sc. 1949; M.Sc. 1950; Univ. of Minn., Ph.D. 1954; m. Bobbie Jean, d. Robert Fulton, Hugo, Okla, 26 Jan. 1943; children: Barbara, Mary, Patricia, Nancy, John, Linda; PROF. OF AGRICULTURAL ECON., UNIV. OF ALBERTA since 1962; Instr., Univ. of Minn., 1950; Asst. Prof. to Prof., S.D. State Univ., 1953; Agric. Econ., Fed. Reserve Bank of Kansas City, 1959-62 ; Visiting Prof., Univ. of Cal. Berkeley, 1967-68; served with U.S. Army 1941-45; author of articles for various prof. journs.; mem., Agric. Inst. Can.; Alta. Inst. Agrol.; Am. Agric. Econ. Assn.; Am. Econ. Assn.; Candn. Agric. Econ. Soc.; W. Agric. Econ. Assn.; Internat. Assn. Agric. Econs.; Phi Kappa Phi; Pi Gamma Mu; Home: 10430-31A Ave., Edmonton, Alta. T6J 3B4; Office: Dept. of Rural Economy, Univ. of Alberta, Edmonton, Alta. T6G 2H1

MANNION, Edward James; publisher; b. Preston, Ont. 21 Sept. 1927; s. John and Elizabeth M.; e. St. Clements Sch. and Preston (Ont.) High Sch. 1943; Galt (Ont.) Coll. Inst. 1945; m. Marie Helene d. Oscar Messier, Montreal, Que. 22 Apl. 1950; children: James, Mary, Theresa, Kathleen; CHRMN. AND C.E.O., SOUTHAM COMMUNICATIONS LTD. since 1978; Chrmn. Trans Ad Ltd.; Dir. Southam Inc.; Panex Show Services Ltd.; Avcor Audio/-Visual Corp.; Coles Book Stores Ltd.; Journal of Commerce Ltd.; Southtimes Publishing Ltd.; Advertising Salesman, Galt Evening Reporter 1948-50, Advertising Mgr. 1952-53; Advertising Mgr. Timmins Daily Press 1950-52; Dir. Retail Advertising, Thomson Newspapers Ltd. 1953-57, Dir. of Sales 1957-66; Gen. Mgr. Thomson Newspapers Inc. (U.S.) 1966-68; Pres. and Publisher, Southstar Publishers Ltd. 1968-1978; R. Catholic; recreations: golf, tennis; Clubs: National; Donalda; Canadian (N.Y.); Home: 17 Dempsey Cres., Willowdale, Ont. M2L 1Y4; Office: 1450 Don Mills Rd., Don Mills, Ont. M3B 2X7.

MANNIX, Frederick Charles; b. Edmonton, Alta., 21 Oct. 1913; s. Frederick Stephen and Byrryid M.; m. late Margaret Ruth, d. Frederick Herbert Boughton, Ottawa, Ont., 25 Nov. 1939; two s. and one d.; m. Janice Christine, d. D. G. Florendine, Calgary, Alta., 3 Jan. 1981; Dir., Royal Bank of Canada; Steel Co. of Canada Limited; Partner, F. Mannix and Co., Calgary, Alberta, 1935; Vice-Pres., Fred Mannix & Co. Ltd., Calgary, Alta., 1943, and Pres., 1944; pioneered Coal Stripping in Canada; builder of numerous hydro-electric power projects, railroads, pipelines and highways in Canada, incl. the Northwest Terr. and Yukon Terr.; rec'd Hon. Doctorate, University of Alberta 1970; hon. mem., Assn. Prof. Engrs., Geologists and Geophysicists of Alta.; Laureate, First Cdn. Business Hall of Fame; Clubs: Calgary Petroleum; Calgary Golf and Country; Ranchmen's; Vancouver (B.C.); Home and Office: P.O. Box 2660, Calgary, Alta. T2P 2M7

MANSAGER, Felix Norman, LL.D., D.Hum.Litt.; retired executive; b. Dell Rapids, S.D., 30 Jan. 1911; s. Hoff and Alice (Qualseth) M.; e. Colton High Sch., 1928; Capital Univ., LL.S. 1967; Strathclyde Univ. (Scot.), LL.D. 1970; Walsh Coll., Ph.D. 1974; Malone Coll., D.Hum.Litt. 1972; Vaasa Univ. (Finland), Medal of Honor 1972; C.B.E. 1973; Univ. Coll. (Wales), Fellow 1973; Wartbury Coll.,

H.H.D. 1976; K.B.E. 1976; m. Geraldine, d. late S. E. Larson, 5 July 1931; children: Donna (Mrs. Harlan Hogsven), Eva Kay (Mrs. Walter Seiverts), Douglas Norman; joined Hoover Co. as Salesman, Green Bay, Wis., 1929; held various positions incl. Dist. Mgr., Sioux Falls 1940 and Milwaukee 1950; Br. Mgr., Minneapolis, 1952; Div. Mgr., Chicago, 1953; Field Sales Mgr., N. Canton, 1955; Gen. Sales Mgr. 1959; Vice Pres.-Sales 1959; Extve. Vice Pres. and Dir., Hoover Co., 1961; Hoover Group, 1963; Pres. and Dir. Gen., S.A. Hoover-France, 1966; Pres. and Chrmn. 1966-75 (ret.); Hon. Dir., Hoover; Prof., Sch. of Business, Univ. of Akron (Ohio) 1978-82; rec'd Chevalier Order of Leopold (Belgium) 1969; Order St. Olav (Norway) 1971; Trustee at Large, Ind. Coll. Funds Am.; Trustee Ohio Foundation Ind. Colls.; Augustana Coll., Graduate Theological Union, H.H.D.; rec'd Marketing Award 1971, Brit. Inst. Marketing; mem. of various assns. incl. Council on Foreign Relations; Nat. Foreign Trade Council; Ditchley Foundation (Gov.); Hon. mem., World League Norsemen; Torske Klubben; Freemason; Lutheran; recreations: golf, reading; Clubs: Metropolitan (N.Y.); Rotary Internat.; Home: 3421 Lindel Court N.W., Canton, Ohio 44718

MANSUR, David B., C.B.E. (1946), B.A.; b. Rock Island, P.Q., 27 Aug. 1905; s. Charles Henry and Mary Pomeroy (Ball) M.; e. St. John's Coll., Univ. of Manitoba, B.A. 1924; m. Mary Kathryn, d. Albert T. Spencer, 3 June 1933; children: Michael, Judith; with Sun Life Assurance Co. of Canada 1924-39; General Superintendent, Central Mortgage Bank, 1939; Asst. Chrmn. Foreign Exchange Control Bd., 1939-41 Asst. Chrmn., Nat. War Finance Comte., 1941-45; Pres., Central Mortgage & Housing Corpn., 1946-54; Pres., Consol. Toronto Devel. Corpn. Ltd., 1954-60; Consultant 1960-65; President Kinross Mortgage Corp. 1965-73; Assoc., Actuarial Soc. of Am.; Anglican; recreation: golf; Clubs: National; Royal Ottawa (Ottawa); St. George's Golf; Home: Apt. 500, 2645 Bloor St. W. Toronto, Ont. M8X 1A3

MANUGE, Robert W. M.; b. N.S., 31 July 1921; s. Fenwick William and Mable Ella (Dench) M.; e. St. Charles Comm., Amherst, N.S.; m. Elizabeth Starr (Goudey), 8 Oct. 1955; children: Timothy William, Marianne; EXTVE. CHRMN., MANUGE GALLERIES, since 1975; Dir., Empire Co. Ltd.; Industrial Estates Ltd; Chrmn., Cultural Foundation of Nova Scotia; joined Canadian National Rlys. 1940; Air Canada 1947; Henry Gatehouse and Son, Inc., Montreal (subsidiary of National Sea Products Ltd.) 1949; Div. Mgr. E. Can., Hussmann Refrigerator Co. Ltd. Brantford, Ont. 1952; Sr. Vice-Pres., Development Industrial Estates Ltd. 1961-73; Extve. Vice-Pres. & Gen. Mgr., Anil Can. Ltd. 1973-75; rec'd Centennial Medal 1967; collector of Candn. art; Anglican; Clubs: Halifax; RNSYS; Saraguay; Home: 764 Tower Rd., Halifax, N.S. B3H 2X8; Office: 1674 Hollis St., Halifax, N.S. B3J 1V7

MARCEAU, Hon. Louis, LL.D.; judge; b. Quebec City, Que. 6 Feb. 1927; s. Paul-V. and Marie-Laure (Picard) M.; m. Suzanne d. Robert Duquette, Quebec City, Que. 5 Jan. 1971; children: Danièle, Marie-Odile, Patrice, Nathalie; JUDGE, FEDERAL COURT OF CAN.; called to Bar of Que. 1949; R. Catholic; Home: 600 Besserer St., Ottawa, Ont. K1N 6C9; Office: Supreme Court Bldg., Wellington St., Ottawa, Ont. K1A 0H9.

MARCH, Beryl Elizabeth, B.A., M.S.A., F.R.S.C.; educator; b. Port Hammond, B.C. 30 Aug. 1920; d. James Roy and Sarah Catherine (Wilson) Warrack; e. Univ. of B.C. B.A. 1942, M.S.A. 1962; m. John Algot 31 March 1946; one child, Laurel Allison; PROF. OF POULTRY SCIENCE, UNIV. OF B.C.; mem. Nat. Research Council Can. 1977-80; Nat. Acad. Sci., Nat. Research Council Comm. on Animal Nutrition since 1980; Fellow, Agric. Inst. Can.; Poultry Science Assn.; author over 130 scient. papers on nutrition & physiol. with particular reference to poultry; rec'd Poultry Science Assn.'s Am. Feed Mfrs.

Assn. Nutrition Research Award 1969; Queen's Silver Jubilee Medal 1977; mem. Can. Soc. for Nutrition Sci.; mem. B.C. Agrols; World's Poultry Science Assn.; Am. Soc. Exper. Biol. & Med.; Am. Assn. Advanc. Science; Am. Inst. Nutrition; Candn. Soc. Animal Science; Home: 5808 Wallace St., Vancouver, B.C. V6N 2A4; Office: Vancouver, B.C. V6T 1W5.

MARCH, Ray M.; transport commissioner; b. Glasgow, Scot., 28 Jan. 1918; s. Percival Raymond and Alice Winifred (Macdonald) M.; e. Glasgow (Scot.) Acad.; HMS "Conway", Liverpool, Eng.; m. Evelyn Forbes, d. Hugh Inglis, Rutherglen, Scot., 12 May 1940; children: Raymond, Alice, Peter, Sarah-Maria, Richard, John, Sarah-Jane; COMMR., CANDN. TRANSPORT COMMISSION, since 1970; Asst. to Pres., Trovati & Co., Milan, 1946; Extve. Secy., Brit. Chamber Comm. for Italy, Milan, 1948; Stn. Mgr., British European Airways, Milan, 1953; Advertising Salesman, Halifax Herald Ltd., Halifax, N.S., 1955; Sales Mgr., Industrial Shipping Ltd., Mahone Bay, N.S., 1957; Extve. Secy., Port of Halifax Comn., 1960; served with RA 1938-46; service in Near E.; rank T/Maj. on discharge; Club: Halifax (N.S.); Home: 459 Billings Ave., Ottawa, Ont. K1H 5L5; Office: Candn. Transport Comm., Ottawa, Ont. K1A 0N9

MARCHAND, Clement, B.A., F.R.S.C.; journalist; poet; b. Ste-Geneviève de Batiscan (Champlain), P.Q., 12 Sept. 1912; s. Pierre and Pamela (Dessureault) M.; e. St. Joseph's Semy., Trois Rivières, P.Q., B.A. 1932; m. Georgette, d. Georges Huppé, 14 Sept. 1935; ls. Pierre; Directeur litteraire des Editions du Bien Public; winner of Prix David de poésie, 1939 and Prix David de litt. 1942; Dir., Pub. Library, Trois Rivières, P.Q.; mem. Soc. des Ecrivains; author of "La Geste de la Croix" (sonnets) 1931; "Courriers des Villages" (short stories), 1939: "Les Soirs Rouges" (poems), 1947; "Nerée Beauchemin" (criticism), 1957; Prix Benjamin-Sulte de journalisme 1974; prix. Ludger-Duvernay de litt. 1981; has also contributed to numerous literary journals and radio broadcasts; Roman Catholic; recreations: fishing; Home: 1637 Blvd. des Forges, Trois Rivières, Que. G8Z 1T7

MARCHAND, Hon. Jean, P.C. (1965), Senator, LL.S., D.Sc.Soc.; b. Champlain, Champlain Co., Que. 20 Dec. 1918; s. Gustave and Laura (Cousineau) M.; e. Commercial Acad. of Que.; Sch. of Social Sciences, Laval Univ.; Hon. Dr. of Indust. Relations, Univ. of Montreal; D.Sc.Soc., Laval Univ.; m. Georgette Guertin, 15 June 1946; one d. Marie-Eve; since 1942 has been a central figure in the labour movement in Quebec when he became an organizer of the National Fed. of Pulp and Paper Workers (apptd. Secretary of the Federation in 1943); named an organizer for the Confederation of Catholic Workers of Canada (CTCC), 1944 and assigned to the reorgan. of the Union of Asbestos Miners; apptd. Tech. Adviser of the Confed. for the Montreal region, 1945, apptd. Gen. Secy. of the CTCC, 1947-61 when el. to the Gen. Presidency of the newly-created Confed. of Nat. Trade Unions, which superseded the CTCC; following his decision to enter politics, resigned as a Member of the Royal Comn. of Enquiry on Bilingualism and Biculturalism (1963-65); also retired from the Econ. Council of Quebec, the Nat. Employment Advisory Comte. of the Unemployment Ins. Comn., the Jt. Candn.-Am. Comte. of the Nat. Planning Assn. of N. Am. and the Internat. Bureau of Christian Trade Unionists; first el. to H. of C. for Quebec-West in g.e. 8 Nov. 1965; apptd. Min. of Citizenship & Immigration; Min. of Manpower & Immigration, 1966-68, Min. of Forestry & Rural Devel. 1968-69; Min. of Regional Ex. Expansion, 1969-72; el. to H. of C. for Langelier June 1968; Min. Regional Econ. Expansion, 1969; re-el. g.e. Oct. 1972 and 1974; Min. of Trans. 1972-75; rec'd Hon. LL.D. St. Thomas & Memorial 1974; Summoned to Senate, 1976; nominated Speaker of the Senate, Mar. 1980; Liberal; Catholic; recreations: golfing, swimming; yachting; Home: 3 Park Samuel, Holland, Que. G1S 4M6; Office: The Senate, Ottawa, Ont. K1A 0A4

MARCHAND, Jean, B.A., M.Sc.C.; insurance executive; e. Académie de Qué. B.A. 1958; Laval Univ. B.Sc.C. 1960, M.Sc.C. 1961; C.L.U. 1963; I.D.A. 1964; PRESIDENT, L'UNIQUE ASSURANCE; Pres., Unigesco Inc.; Ins. Broker, Halle & Couture Ltée 1959, Mgr. 1961; Founder and Gen. Mgr. L'Unique Life Insurance 1967, Pres. and Gen. Mgr. 1972; Extve. Vice Pres. and Gen. Mgr. Unigesco Inc. Group 1972; Pres. and Gen. Mgr. L'Unique General Insurance Co. and Pres. Unigesco Inc.; mem. Chamber Comm.; recreations: boating, sailing, skiing, waterskiing, swimming; Clubs: Garrison; Nautique Fossambalut sur-le-Lac; Home: 1310 Firzpatrick, Sillery, Qué. G1T 2H7; Office: 2050 boul. St-Cyrille ouest, Québec, Qué. G1V 2K8.

MARCHAND, Hon. Jean-Louis, B.A., LL.L.; judge; b. St-Theophile du Lac, P.Q., 2 Dec. 1906; s. Louis-Philippe and Marie-Louise (Nobert) M.; e. Semy. des Trois-Rivieres, B.A. 1926; Laval Univ., LL.L. 1929; m. Eloise, d. J.-Olivier Lacoursierre, 7 Oct. 1933; one d. Louise; JUSTICE, SUPERIOR COURT OF P.Q., since Oct. 1956; called to the Bar of P.Q., July 1929; for many years mem. of the Three Rivers Bar (Batonnier 1953-54); before elevation to the Bench was for ten years Sr. mem. of the legal firm of Marchand & Lacoursierre, Three Rivers, P.Q.; Municipal Judge, 1940-45; Roman Catholic; recreation: golf; Club: Ki-8-EB Country; Home: 467 St-Francois-Xavier, Three Rivers, Que. G9A 1R1; Office: Court House, Three Rivers, Que.

MARCHAND, Lieut.-Col. Sarto, E.D., K.L.J.; industrialist; b. Montreal, P.Q., 17 Sept. 1913; s. Hon. Victor, M.L.A., and Yvonne (Desroches) M.; e. Coll. Notre Dame, Montreal; St-Laurent (P.Q.) Coll.; Montreal Tech. Sch.; Notre Dame Univ.; m. Gabrielle, d. Olympe Goyet, Joliette, P.Q., 19 Dec. 1945; CHMN. OF BD., MELCHERS DISTILLERIES LTD. (Estbd. 1898) since 1975; Chrmn., Les Distilleries Marchand Ltée.; Pres., Canada's Manitoba Distillery Ltd.; Dir., La Solidarite Compagnie d'assurance sur la vie, Inc.; Dupuis Freres Ltee.; Dir., Candn. Red Cross Soc.; Boy Scouts Assn.; Alumni Assn. of Coll. Notre Dame; Pres., Nat. Council of Candn. Prisoners of War; Past Pres., Conseil d'Expansion Economique Inc.; Pres., Que. Dietetic Assn.; Hon. Pres., Mission catholique chinoise de Montréal; Honorary Director, Soc. Amicale des Aveugles; Bro. Offr., St. John's Ambulance; joined Melchers Distilleries Ltd. in 1937 as Asst. Plant Mgr. at Berthierville, Que.; Dir. and Secy., 1945-58; Extve. Vice-Pres., 1958-60; el. Pres. Nov. 1960 and apptd. Mang. Dir., Nov. 1961; commissioned in N.P.A.M. in 1933 with Les Fusiliers Mont-Royal till 1939; served in 2nd World War with same Regt. leaving for Iceland with first group of 1st Bn., July 1940; stationed on Eng. coast, 1942; engaged in raid on Dieppe in command of "A" Co. of the Regt.; captured and Prisoner of War till 30 Apl. 1945; during confinement promoted to rank of Major (for services rendered in Dieppe raid); with Supplementary Reserve, Canada, 1945-50; attached to 11th Bgds. Hdqrs., 1950-52; returned to Les Fusiliers Mont-Royal as 2nd in command, 1952, and gaz. Lieut. Col. and C.O., May 1955; invested in the Priory of Can., Ven. Order of the Hosp. of St. John of Jerusalem, 1958; Kt. Mil. Order Hosp. St. Lazarus of Jerusalem; Grande Croix des Combattants d'Europe; mem., Montreal Bd. Trade; Chambre de Comm. des Jeunes de Dist. de Montréal (Pres. du Conseil des Gouverneurs); Assn. Candn. Distillers (Vice-Pres.); Candn. Mfrs. Assn.; K. of C. (3rd degree); Liberal; Roman Catholic; recreations: golf, tennis, fishing, curling; Clubs: Laval-sur-de-Lac Golf; St. Denis; Reforme; Canadian; Outremont Curling; Club Richelieu-Montréal

MARCHANT, Edward D., C.A.; b. Winnipeg, Man. 6 Sept. 1927; s. late Cecil William Stanley and late Florence Maud M.; e. Winnipeg, Man. C.A. 1958; m. Irene Elliott

d. late Robert Burton 18 June 1975; children: Diane, Joanne, Gregory, Ian, Daryl; PRES. AND C.E.O., EXCHEQUER FINANCIAL CORP. LTD. 1979- ; Pres. and CEO Marchant and Co. Ltd. 1972- ; Marchant Investments Ltd. 1972- ; operated own C.A. practice 1958-62, 1966-67 Winnipeg; Tax Partner Deloitte, Haskins & Sells 1962-66 Winnipeg; Coopers & Lybrand, Toronto 1967-69; Vice Pres. Finance Bramalea Consolidated Developments Ltd. Toronto 1969-70; Great Northern Capital Corp. 1970-72; Pres. M. M. Builders Funds Ltd. (Marine Midland Bank in Can.) 1972-76; Exchequer Trust Co. 1976-79; Dir. and Chmn., Audit Comm., Nat. Bank of Detroit, Can.; mem. Man. Inst. Tax Comte. and Pub. Relations 1958-66; Life Underwriters Educ. Comte. 1962-66; Chrmn. Urban Devel. Inst. Tax & Accounting Comte. 1969-72, Financing of Real Estate Comte. 1974-76, mem. Fed. Comte. 1976; Dir., Urban Development Inst. of Can., mem. Can. Inst. C.A.'s; Freemason; United Church; recreation: golf; Clubs: Mississauga Country; National; Home: 1425 Elaine Trail,, Mississauga, Ont. L5G 3W9; Office: 120 Adelaide St. W., Toronto, Ont. M5H 1T1.

MARCHMENT, Alan Roy B.A., F.C.A., C.T.C.I.; b. Toronto, Ont. 29 May 1927; s. William Roy and Alice C. M.; e. Univ. of Toronto, B.A. (Hons. Philos.); Ont. Inst. C.A.'s (F.C.A.); m. Patricia Anne, d. Frank S. Vanstone, 19 Jan. 1949; one s., one d.; CHAIRMAN, CHIEF EXECUTIVE OFFICER, AND DIR., TRADERS GROUP LTD. since 1979, and Chmn., Pres., C.E.O. and Dir., Guaranty Trust Co. of Can.; Auditor, Clarkson Gordon & Co. 1950; Secy.-Treas. Pacific Finance Corp. of Canada Ltd. and Chief Agent Olympic Insurance Co. 1955; Asst. Treas. and Asst. Secy. Pacific Finance Corp., L.A. 1960; Pres. and Dir. Transamerica International S.A. Paris, France 1963; Asst. Treas. The T. Eaton Co. Ltd. 1965, Treas. 1966, Vice-Pres. 1969; Pres. and Dir., Guaranty Trust Co. of Can. 1973; C.E.O. 1975; Chmn. 1979; Dir., Traders Group Ltd. 1977; Vice-Chmn. 1978; Chmn. and C.E.O. 1979; Dir., Cdn. General Securities Ltd.; Cdn. General Ins. Co.; Toronto General Ins. Co.; Traders General Ins. Co.; Cdn. General Life Ins. Co.; Chrmn. Bd. Govs. Univ. of Guelph; Pres. & Dir., Toronto Symphony; Trustee, Toronto Symphony Foundation; Past Pres., National Club; Gage Research Inst.; C.M. Hincks Treatment Centre; past Trustee, Toronto Western Hospital; past Gov., Cdn. Inst. of C.A.'s; Hon. Life Mem., Cdn. Wildlife Fed.; Hon. Mem., Nat. Council, Boy Scouts of Can.; Knight of Order of St. Lazarem of Jerusalem; Anglican; Clubs: National (Past Pres.); Toronto; York; Goodwood; Toronto Golf; Cambridge; Home: 18 Clarendon Ave., Toronto, Ont. M4V 1H9; Office: 625 Church St., Toronto, Ont. M4Y 2G1

MARCIL, André, O.C. (1971); retired banker; b. Montreal, P.Q., 3 Nov. 1910; s. Georges and Marie (Perrin) M.; e. Loyola High Sch. (Sr. Matric.); Loyola Coll.; m. Thérèse, d. late Léon Beauchamp, 8 Oct. 1938; children: Nicole (Mrs. Robert Gratton), André, Josette (Mrs. Marc Prevost); Past Chairman & Chief Executive Officer of Montreal City and District Savings Bank, and Mtl. C. & D. Trustees, 1976-81; Past Vice-Chrmn., Credit Foncier; Dpt. Chrmn. and Dir., The Mercantile and General Reins. Co. of Can. Ltd.; Dir., Schering Corp. Ltd.; Plough (Can.) Ltd.; Trustee, MTL. C&D Savings Bank; Credit Foncier; James T. Stanger and Co. (became Guardian Trust Co.), 1929-32; opened his own office (disposing of ins. sec. thereof, 1948), 1932; apptd. Mortgage Corr. for P.Q. and Maritimes, N. Am. Life Assce. Co., 1945; Standard Life Assce. Co., 1950, Dominion Life Assnce. Co., 1952, Northern Life Assnce. Co. of Can., 1962; Pres., Marcil Mortgage Corp., 1956-76; served overseas during 2nd World War with R.C.N.V.R., 1939-45, on loan to Royal Navy 1940-42 where served as Liaison Offr. with Gen. de Gaulle on Dakar expedition, B.A.R.M. at Washington; H.M.S. Liverpool, cruiser (CS10), on Murmansk and Malta Convoys; torpedoed June 1942 Malta Convoy; 1st Lt. H.M.C.S. Dunver, frigate (C5), N. Atlantic Convoys; Commdg. Offr. H.M.C.S. Jonquière, frigate

(EG26), from which retired with rank of Lt. Commdr.; Pres., Que. Div. Red Cross Trustees; Past Pres., Hdqrs. Candn. Corps of Commissionaires; Candn. Red Cross Soc.; past mem., Candn. Housing Design Council; Gov., Hopital Marie-Enfant; Montreal Children's Hosp.; Montreal Gen. Hosp.; Past Chrmn., Montreal Un. Services Inst.; Montreal Chapter, Soc. of Real Estate Appraisers; Past Chrmn., St. James's Club (Montreal); Past Vice Pres., Nat. Ballet Guild of Can.; R. Catholic; awarded Can. Centennial Medal 1967; Offr. of Merit, Sov. and Mil. Order of Malta 1967; Queen's Jubilee Medal; recreation: sailing; Clubs: St. Denis; St. James's; Royal St. Lawrence Yacht; Mount Royal; Toronto; Home: 87 McCulloch Ave., Outremont, Que. H2V 3L8;

MARCOLIN, Albert Victor, B.Sc.; b. Bellevue, Alta., 24 March 1919; s. Virginio and Marie (Bossano) M.; e. Pub. and High Schs., Bellevue, Alta.; Univ. of Alta., B.Sc. (Chem.) 1941; m. Grace Leiper, d. late Estay Chalmers Folkins, 19 Aug. 1944; children: Kenneth Victor, James Richard, Carol Jean Erk, Ronald George; GROUP VICE PRESIDENT, AT TRAIL, COMINCO LTD.; joined Cominco 1941; Research & Operating positions, Ammonia & Ammonium Nitrate Production, Calgary, 1941-46; Operation Hydrogen & P-9 Plants, Warfield, B.C., 1946-47; Ammonia Production 1947-48; Maintenance Engr. & Supt., Phosphate Plant, 1948-51; Special Assignments, Civil Defence, 1951; Asst. Group Supt. Fertilizer Dept. 1951-52; Supvr., Labor Dept., Personnel, Tradanac, 1952-58; Asst. Mgr. C & F Sales, Montreal, 1958-61; Asst. to Mgr. Metal Sales, Montreal, 1961; Mgr. Metal Sales 1961-64; Mgr., Research & Corp. Devel. 1966-67; Dir. Research 1967-69; Vice Pres., Cominco American Inc., Spokane, Wash., 1969-71; Sr. Vice Pres., Cominco American, 1971-72; Asst. to Pres., Vancouver, 1972; Vice-President Corp. Services, Cominco Ltd. 1972; mem., Candn. Inst. Chem.; Candn. Inst. Mining & Metall.; Inst. Mining & Metall., London; Lambda Chi Alpha; Protestant; recreations: golf, fishing, skiing; Clubs: Trail-Rossland Golf; Red Mountain Ski; Union - Victoria; Canadian (Vancouver); Home: 410 Ritchie Ave., Trail, B.C.; V1R 1H2; Office: Trail, B.C.

MARGESON, John Malcolm Russell, M.A., Ph.D.; educator; b. Trail, B.C. 21 May 1920; s. Karl Andrew and Jessie Gordon (MacPhail) M.; e. Univ. of B.C., B.A. 1942; Univ. of Toronto M.A. 1947, Ph.D. 1952; m. Sarah Muriel Nicol d. late James Killips 16 July 1947; children: Susan Mairi, Deirdre Jane Boothroyd, John Michael Breon; PROF. OF ENGLISH, SCARBOROUGH COLL. UNIV. OF TORONTO 1968- ; joined Acadia Univ. 1948, Prof. of Eng. 1953-56; Dir. of Studies in Eng., Gonville and Caius Coll. and mem. Faculty of Eng. Cambridge Univ. 1956-59; Visiting Prof. Univ. of Oslo 1960-61; Lectr. in Eng. Univ. of Hull 1961-64; Assoc. Prof. Univ. of Toronto 1964-68; Asst. Rep. for Brit. Council, Norway 1959-61; author "The Origins of English Tragedy" 1967; co-ed. "Shakespeare 1971" 1972; contrib. various publ. series, articles; served with RCAF 1942-46; mem. Internat. Assn. Univ. Profs. Eng.; Baptist; recreations: music, fishing, walking, skiing; Home: 8 Milepost Pl., #204, Toronto, Ont. M4H 1E1; Office: 1265 Military Trail, West Hill, Ont. M1C 1A4.

MARGISON, Arthur Donald, B.Eng.; P.Eng.; consulting engineer; b. Toronto, Ont., 18 May 1918; s. Oswald and Ida (MacDonald) M.; e. St. Michaels Coll., Toronto (Matric.); Univ. of Toronto (1939-40); McGill Univ., B.Eng. 1945; m. Helen Lavina, d. E. P. MacDonald, Toronto, Ont., 1 March 1940; children; Douglas Arthur, Edward Donald, Sharon Helen; PRESIDENT AND GEN. MGR., A. D. MARGISON & ASSOCIATES LTD., Consulting Engrs.; Pres., Barber Hydraulic Turbine Ltd.; Can. Frontier Water and Power Ltd.; Miner (underground) and as a Labourer in different trades of constr. industry, 1938-39; in constr. planning, design, etc., on several wartime projects, 1940-45; spent one year with a consulting firm in Montreal, 1945-46; in 1946, joined Margison & Babcock, and in 1948 became a Jr. Partner in charge of Mech. and Elect. Dept.; at formation of Margison, Babcock & Associates, 1950, apptd. Vice-Pres. and Gen. Mgr. to direct a major defence program; with dissolution of the partnership in 1954, firm name was altered to the present style; since 1950 the firm has designed many large projects, incl. Pinetree installations, Canada's largest aircraft hangars for R.C.A.F. and T.C.A.; Underground NORAD, North Bay, Gardiner Expressway; and bridges, indust. plants, etc,; mem. Bd. Govs., Univ. of Guelph 1964-70; Frontier Coll., 1958-63; Dir., Tech. Service Council, 1961-62; chrmn., Extve. Comte. Candn. Good Roads Assn., 1962-65; mem., Assn. of Prof. Engrs. Ont., Man. and Alta.; Corp. of Prof. Engrs. Que.; Am. Soc. Mech. Engrs.; Engn. Inst. Can.; mem. Bd. Trade Metrop. Toronto; recreations: flying; swimming; reading; Clubs: National; RCYC; Rideau (Ottawa); Caughnawana Fishing & Hunting;

MARGOLIS, Leo, M.Sc., Ph.D., F.R.S.C.; research scientist; b. Montreal, Que. 18 Dec. 1927; e. McGill Univ. B.Sc. 1948, M.Sc. 1950, Ph.D. 1952; m. Ruth Anne Lall; Children: Rhonda Lee, Robert Allan, Murray Howard, Conrad Anton; HEAD FISH HEALTH AND PARASITOLOGY SECTION, PACIFIC BIOL. STN., DEPT. OF FISHERIES & OCEANS CAN. 1981- ; Research Scient. (Assoc. to Princ.) Pacific Biol. Stn. 1952-67, head various Research Divs. and Section 1967- ; Adv., Fed.-Prov. (B.C.) Fisheries Comm. 1969, 70, 72; Co-Chrmn. Candn. Comte. on Fish Disease 1970-73; mem. Comte. on biol. and Research, Internat. N. Pacific Fisheries Comn. 1971- ; Sr.Can. Sci. mem. 1976- ; Adv., Can. Section Internat. N. Pacific Fisheries Comm. 1956-, Sr. Adv. 1976- ; Dept. of Fisheries and Oceans Can. Sci. Subvention since 1978; Adv. Bd., Sci. Infor. and Pub., Dept. of Fisheries and Oceans Can. since 1979; Science Council of B.C. Research Evaluation Comte. since 1979; author catalogue and synopsis of "Caligus" 1975 and Synopsis of the parasites of fishes of Canada 1979; over 80 articles on parasites and diseases of fish and marine mammals; Assoc. Ed. "Canadian Journal of Zoology" since 1971; mem., Ed. Referees Comm., Bulletin Internat. N. Pacific Fisheries Comm. 1976- ; Ed. Board "Journal of Parasitology" since 1977; Pres. B.C. Amateur Hockey Assn. 1963-66, Hon. Vice Pres. since 1966; mem. Candn. Soc. Zools. (Chrmn. Parasitol. Sec. 1977-78); Am. Soc. Parasitols. (Chrmn. Transl. Comte. 1977-78); Wildlife Disease Assn.; Am. Fisheries Soc.; Home: 200 Arrow Way, Nanaimo, B.C. V9T 1L1; Office: Nanaimo, B.C. V9R 5K6.

MARION, Séraphin, O.C., M.A., D.Litt., D.U.P., LL.D., F.R.S.C.; b. Ottawa, Ont., 25 Nov. 1896; s. Ernest and Floriane (Comtois) M.; e. Univ. of Ottawa, M.A. 1920; Univ. of Montreal, D. Litt., 1933; La Sorbonne, D.U.P. 1923; LL.D. Roy. Mil. Coll. 1966; m. Monique, d. E. Roy, 24 July 1924; children: Gilles, Colette, Jean, Claude; Assistant Prof. of French, Royal Mil. Coll., Kingston, Ont., 1920-25; Hon. Secy., Royal Soc. of Can., 1945-52; French Secy., Candn. Cath. Hist. Assn.; author "Relations des Voyageurs Francais en Nouvelle France au XVII siècle", 1923; "Pierre Boucher pionnier canadien", 1927; "Les Heures litteraires", 1929; "En feuilletant nos écrivains", 1931; "Sur les pas de nos littérateurs", 1933 and "La querelle des classiques et des romantiques dans le Can. français au XIX siècle"; "Les Lettres canadiennes d'autrefois", (9 vols.) from 1939 to 1958; "The Quebec Tradition" with the collab. of Dr. Watson Kirkconnell, 1946; "Hauts Faits du Canada français" 1972; awarded Tyrrell Medal by Royal Soc. of Can., 1953; O.C. 1976; officer, Internat. Assn. of Parliamentarians of Fr. Language 1980; bronze medal, Académie canadienne-française, 1980; Hon. Pres., L'Institut Canadien-Français d'Ottawa 1977; Roman Catholic; Home: 131 Sunnyside Ave., Ottawa, Ont. K1S 0R2

MARKLE, Fletcher; film and television writer-director-producer; b. Winnipeg, Man., 27 March 1921; s. George

Wilson and Meta Gertrude (Clarke) M.; m. Dorothy Conradt, 22 July 1962; one s. Stephen; Writer, Director, Actor in series "Imagine, Please", Vancouver, B.C., 1940-41; Author and Star of original dramatic series, "Baker's Dozen", C.B.C. 1942; Contrib. Writer, Actor, Director and Producer of many programs, C.B.C., 1942-45; Writer, Director and Commentator for B.B.C., London, Eng., 1943-44; Writer-Editor-Narrator of documentary film "V-1, Story of the Robot Bomb" (named picture of the month, Nov. 1944 by War Activities Comte.); featured player in film, "Journey Together", 1945; contract scenarist with Orson Welles and Sir Alexander Korda, 1946; Writer-Director-Producer of "Studio One" program, C.B.S., 1947-48 (winner of George Foster Peabody Award); Producer-Director of "Ford Theatre", C.B.S., 1948-49; "Sometime Every Summertime", original radio drama, incl. in "Radio's Best Plays" collection, 1947; Dir. of M.G.M. films, "Night into Morning" and "The Man with a Cloak", 1951; Producer, C.B.S.-TV series, "Studio One", 1952-53 (Christopher Award winner); Producer-Director, C.B.S.-TV series, "Life With Father", 1953-55; C.B.S.-TV series "Front Row Center", 1955; contributing Dir. and/or Producer, various TV film series, incl. "The Ford Theatre", "Panic", "M Squad", "Colgate Theatre", "Buckskin", "Tales of The Vikings", "Rendezvous", "Thriller", "Startime", "Hong Kong", "Father of the Bride", for C.B.S., N.B.C. or A.B.C. in U.S., 1956-61; Dir., Walt Disney feature film "The Incredible Journey" (filmed in Can.), 1962; Host, Contributing Writer and Dir., then Producer of C.B.C.-TV film series "Telescope", 1963-69; Contributing Writer, C.B.C.-TV "Festival" series, 1963-69; Head, TV Drama, C.B.C. 1970-72; Extve. Producer, "The Play's the Thing", CBC-TV 1973-74; Writer-in-res. Univ. of Toronto 1974-75; Producer, "The Olympics: A Television History of the Golden Games", CBC-TV 1976; contributing writer-producer, "That's Hollywood", ABC-TV, 1977-78; Sr. producer-dir., "Sears Radio Theatre", CBS 1979-80; "Mutual Radio Theatre", MBS, 1980-81; served in 2nd World War with R.C.A.F., 1942-45; mem., Directors Guild of Am.; Directors Guild of Can.; Producers Guild of Am.; Writers Guild of Am.; A.C.T.T. (Eng.); Acad. of Motion Picture Arts & Sciences; Acad. of Television Arts & Sciences; Home: 351 Congress Place, Pasadena, Calif. 91105

MARKLE, Gower H., B.A.; b. Hamilton, Ont., 26 Nov. 1915; s. Hugh C. and Martha M. (Woelke) M.; e. Univ. of W. Ont. B.A. 1945 (Gold Medal-Econ.); Inst. of World Affairs 1946; m. Beatrice E. d. Frank Green, Hamilton, Ont., 8 Sept. 1942; three s. Glen H., Paul E., Ross A., DIR., EMPLOYMENT RELATIONS & CONDITIONS OF WORK, LABOUR CAN. 1980- ; since 1977; formerly Dir. of Education and Welfare, United Steel Workers of America; participant and lectr. internat. labour seminars Internat. Confed. of Free Trade Unions (Brussels) Calcutta 1954, Accra 1955, Banff 1957, Petropolis 1960; conducted survey and study labour educ. needs of W. Indies 1959 (sponsored by Fed. Gov. of W. Indies, Univ. of W. Indies, Candn. Assn. Adult Educ., Ford Foundation); Tech. Advisor to Internat. Labour Organ. Geneva 1972; Co-ord., Labour Educ., Labour Can. 1977-80; mem. Educ. and Welfare Comtes. Candn. Labour Congress; served with RCNVR during World War II; Former Gov. McMaster Univ.; Labour Coll. of Can.; Trustee Toronto Gen. Hosp.; Nat. Museums of Can.; Former mem. Can. Manpower & Immigration Council; Past Pres. Ont. Welfare Council; former Dir. Ont. Mental Health Foundation; Past Gov. Can. Council for Social Devel.; Past Gov. and Vice Chrmn. George Brown Coll. of Applied Arts & Technol.; Past Chrmn. Educ. Comte. Ont. Fed. of Labour; Trustee Internat. Council for Adult Educ., mem. Candn. Assn. for Adult Educ. (Past Vice Pres.); NDP; recreations: sports, music, reading; Home: 17 Bay Hill Ridge, Stittsville, Ont.; Office: Labour Canada, Ottawa, Ont. K1A 0U2

MARKS, Gerald Samuel, M.Sc., D.Phil.; educator; b. Cape Town, S. Africa 13 Feb. 1930; s. late Simon and Annie (Goodman) M.; e. Univ. of Cape Town B.Sc. 1950, M.Sc. 1951; Oxford Univ. D.Phil. (Organic Chem.) 1954; m. Marion Zoe d. late George Lewis Tobias 6 March 1955; children: Lynne Sorrel, Saul Ian; PROF. AND HEAD OF PHARMACOL. QUEEN'S UNIV.; mem. Med. Adv. Bd. Muscular Dystrophy Assn. Can. 1971-79; Med. Research Council Grants Comte. for Metabolism, 1980- ; Pharmaceutical Sciences 1972-75, Studentship Comte. 1969-70; rec'd Aesculapian Soc. Lectureship Award Queen's Univ. 1973; M.R.C. Visiting Prof. of Pharm. Dalhousie Univ. 1974, Univ. of Alta. 1976; author "Heme and Chlorophyll, Chemical, Biochemical and Medical Aspects" 1969; book chapters and numerous publs. on biosynthesis of heme and porphyrins, adrenergic receptors, glycoproteins, tuberculolipids, pharmacology of organic nitrates; Assoc. Ed. "Canadian Journal of Physiology and Pharmacology" 1970-75, co-editor since 1981; mem. Council, Pharmacol. Soc. Can. 1969-71; Chrmn. Educ. Policy Comte., Candn. Pharmacol. Soc. since 1978; mem. Chem. Soc. (London); Am. Soc. Pharmacol. & Exper. Therapeutics; NPD; Jewish; recreations: swimming, squash, tennis, curling; Home: 15 Dickens Dr., Kingston, Ont.; Office: Kingston, Ont. K7L 3N6.

MARKS, Lawrence, Q.C., B.A., B.C.L.; b. Montreal, Que., 9 May 1908; s. Raphael and Bella (Horowitz) M.; e. Montreal (Que.) High Sch., 1916-25; McGill Univ., B.A. 1929; Sorbonne, summer 1929; Univ. de Montréal, B.C.L. 1933; m. Irene, d. David Marston, Montreal, Que., 26 May 1940; children: Isobel Carol, Karin Sheila; Sr. Partner, (ret.) Marks, Shapiro & Worsoff; Secy. and Dir., Financial Collection Agencies; Dir., Morbern Industries Ltd.; read law with Peter Bercovitch, M.L.A. Que.; called to Bar of Que. 1934; cr. Q.C. 1961; served with Candn. Officers Training Corp; Hon. Pres., Temple Emanuel, Montreal; Vice-Pres., Candn. Friends of Hebrew Univ.; Hon. Pres., Candn. Council of Reform Congs.; Nat. Chrmn., Labour Relations Sec., Candn. Bar Assn.; mem., Reading Soc.; Montreal Bar Assn.; Pi Lamba Phi; Liberal; Jewish; recreations: golf, swimming, reading, discussion clubs; Clubs: Reform; Montefiore; Lorraine Golf; Home: 400 Kensington, Westmount, Que. H3Y 3A2

MARKSON, Jerome, B.Arch., F.R.A.I.C., A.R.C.A.; architect; b. Toronto, Ont.; s. Charles and Etta (Levine) M.; e. Oakwood Coll, Inst., Toronto 1948; Cranbrook Acad. of Art 1952; Univ. of Toronto Sch. of Arch., B. Arch. 1953; m. Mayta Silver, Winnipeg, potter; children: Anna Fredda, Nancy Dara; commenced private arch. practice 1955; Pres., J.O.C. Consultants; mem. numerous juries; winner of many arch. awards incl. Massey Medal for Arch., O.A.A. Design Awards, C.M.H.C. Design Awards, Ont. Masons Relations Council Awards, Can. Arch. magazine Design Awards, Stelco and Wood Design Awards; Guest Lectr., Univ. of Toronto; mem. Assn. of Archs.; Royal Arch Inst. Can. (mem. Council 1964); Chrmn., RAIC Housing Comm.; mem., Visual Arts Ont.; mem. of Bd.; Nat. Tap Dance Co. of Can.; Koffler Art Gallery; mem. various govt. apptd. comtes.; Ont. Assn. Archs. (Pres., Toronto Chapter 1970-71); Arch. Conservancy (Vice Chrmn. Toronto Chapter 1978-79); Co-ed. "Exploring Toronto"; publication, "25 Years of Work" 1981; work widely publ. in arch press; Hebrew; recreations: sailing and cruising, travel, music; Home: 15 Poplar Plains Cres., Toronto, Ont. M4V 1E9; Office: 161 Davenport Rd., Toronto, Ont. M5R 1J1

MARLER, John de Montmollin, M.B.E., Q.C.; b. Montreal, Que.; e. Selwyn House Sch., Montreal; Lower Can. Coll., Montreal; McGill Univ., B.A. (Eng. & Hist.) 1929, B.C.L. 1932; m.; three children; COUNSEL TO OGILVY, RENAULT; called to Bar of Que. 1932; cr. Q.C. 1951; served with R.C.A. and Candn. Army staff for 6 yrs. during 2nd World War; Gov.; Montreal Museum of Fine Arts; Anglican; recreation: bridge; Clubs: Royal Montreal

Golf (Past Pres.); Mt. Bruno Country (Past. Pres.); St. James; Home: 638 Clarke Ave., Montreal, Que. H3Y 3E4; Office: 1981 McGill College Ave., Montreal, Que.

MARLIN, Kenneth N.; financier; b. Wolseley, Sask. 13 June 1923; s. late George Edwin and Gladys Nora (Seal) M.; e. Wolseley (Sask.) Pub. and High Schs. 1941; Am. Mang. Assn. Mang. Courses; Dartnell Inst. Mang. Course; Univ. of Alta. various extension courses; m. Helen Mary d. Andrew James Draper 8 Oct. 1944; children: Beverly Grant, Rodney Frank, Byron James Draper, Judith Lynn; PRESIDENT, CEO AND DIR., PRINCIPAL CONSULTANTS LTD. since 1971; Chrmn. of Bd. Marlin Management International Ltd.; Pres. and Dir. First Investors Corp. Ltd.; Associated Investors of Canada; Secy.-Treas., Principal Savings and Trust Co.; Vice Pres. and Dir. Principal Group Ltd.; Principal Life Insurance Co. of Canada; Collective Mutual Fund Ltd.; Principal Venture Fund Ltd.; Dir. Collective Securities Ltd.; estbd. Marlin Travel Service; Great Escape Vacations Ltd.; Rly. Telegrapher, CPR 1941, Train Dispatcher 1948-54; Regional Sales Mgr. First Investors 1954, Gen. Sales Mgr. 1956; Vice Pres. Sales, Principal Group Ltd. 1964-68; Gen. Mgr. Principal Savings & Trust Co. 1964-68; Chrmn. of Bd. Edmonton International Industries Ltd. 1969-75; Dir. Terra Mining and Exploration Ltd. 1967-68; mem. Town Council 1946-48; Chrmn. Order Rr. Telegraphers 1949-51; Del. to various nominating conventions, active fund raising campaigns (pol. and community); mem. Am. Mang. Assn.; Pres., Council Inst. Mang.; Sir Winston Churchill Soc.; Freemason; Shriner; P. Conservative; Protestant; recreations: travel, theatre, dancing, fishing, gardening; Clubs: Royal Glenora; Hillcrest (Pres. 1964-65); Edmonton; Home: 15525 RioPark Rd., Edmonton, Alta. T5R 5M3; Office: 2900 Principal Plaza, 10303 Jasper Ave., Edmonton, Alta. T5J 3M6

MARMET, Paul; O.C., D.Sc.; physicien; éducateur; né Lévis, Qué. 20 mai 1932; f. Albert et Corinne (Filteau) M.; é. Univ. Laval B.Sc. 1956, D.Sc. 1960; CSIRO Melbourne, Australia Postdoctoral 1960-61; ép. Jacqueline f. Albert Côté (dé.) 6 juin 1959; enfants: Louis, Marie, Nicolas, Frédéric; PROFESSÉUR DE PHYSIQUE, UNIV. LAVAL depuis 1970; Dir. du Lab. de Physique Atomique et Moléculaire depuis 1967; enseignement en Physique, Coll. Univ. Laval depuis 1958; Asst. de recherche CSIRO, Melbourne, Australia 1960-61; prof. auxiliaire, Univ. Laval 1961, prof. agrégé 1966, prof. chercheur 1974-77; année sabbatique au service de Chimie, Univ. de Liège, Belgique 1967; mem. co-fondateur de Centre de Recherche sur les Atomes et les Molécules, bureau de direction 1967-69; mem. du Comité de subventions du Gouvernement du Qué. 1975; Comité des Subventions-Physique du C.N.R.C. 1971-74, Comité de Consultation en Physique 1970-73, Comité de Consultation en Astro-physique 1972-75, délégué à Paris pour négocier l'Observatoire Can.-France-Hawaii 1973, Comité Conjoint CNRC et CCEA sur les priorités en Physique Nucléaire au Can. 1975-76; mem. du Comité Lawrence de l'Assn. Canadienne des Physiciens 1970-71; Vice prés. 1979-81; Pres. 1981-82; représentant Canadien, Union Internationale de Physique pure et appliquée 1976-79, Comité d'Organisation des IC-PEAC Paris 1977 et Tokyo 1979 (organisateur du IV Congrès Internationale de la Physique des Collisions Atomiques et Ioniques, Qué. 1965); Médaille Herzberg de l'Assn. Canadienne des Physiciens 1971; Prix Rutherford de la Société Royal de Can. 1960; Médaille Pariseau (ACFAS) 1976; Service Award Soc. Roy. d'Astronomie du Can.; Prix Concours Scientifique de la Prov. de Qué. 1962; Bourse de Professeur du Conseil Nat. de Recherche du Can. Belgique 1967, Bourse Post-doctorale Melbourne 1960, 3 bourses graduées 1957-59; co-auteur "High Resolution Electron Beams and their Applications" 1969; articles nombreux; mem. Conseil de Direction de la Commis. de Control de l'Energie Atomique du Can., 1979- ; mem. Société Royale du Canada Assn. Canadienne des Physiciens; Assn. Canadienne Française pour l'Avancement des Sciences; Am. Phys. Soc.; Inst. de Chimie du Can.; Soc. Royale d'Astronomie du Can.; Catholique; Adresse: 1001 De Grenoble, Ste-Foy, Qué. G1V 2Z8; Bureau: Québec, Qué. G1K 7P4.

MAROIS, Hon. Pierre, M.N.A.; politician; MIN. OF LABOUR AND INCOME SECURITY MANPOWER, QUE. 1976- ; lawyer; el. M.N.A. for Laporte prov. g.e. 1976, re-el. M.N.A. for Marie-Victorin 1981; Parti Quebecois; Office: 425, St-Amable, 4e étage, Quebec, Que. G1R 4Z1

MARON, Harvey Hirsh; real estate and construction executive; b. Montreal, Que. 28 Nov. 1928; s. Lionel Mortemer and Regina (Weiner) M.; e. Strathcona Acad. 1945; Univ. of Denver (major bldg. constr. and real estate); m. Rhoda, d. Harry Herlich, 7 March 1954; children: Mark, Cathy, Marlene, Michele; PRESIDENT, MARON PROPERTIES LTD.; areas of constr. incl. Apt. Housing Complexes 1949-51 and St. Therese-en-Haut Community Ville d'Anjou Industrial Park 1960-66; shopping centres built incl. Les Galeries La Grande Place, Rimouski, Que.; Loch Lomond, Saint John, N.B.; Bathurst Shopping Mall, N.B.; Plaze Ste-Therese-en-Haut, Que.; Les Galeries Val d'Or, Que.; Newcastle (N.B.) Shopping Mall; Grey Co. Mall, Owen Sound, Ont.; Moncton (N.B.) Shopping Mall; mem. Bd. Govs. YMHA; mem. Urban Land Inst.; Internat. Council Shopping Centers (Vice-Chrmn. Candn. Affairs Comte.) Jewish; recreations: horseback riding, golf, music, swimming; Clubs: Elmridge; Montefiore; Home: 618 Sydenham, Westmount, Que. H3Y 2Z4; Office: 4141 Sherbrooke St. W., Montreal, Que. H3Z 1B8

MAROTTA, Joseph Thomas, M.D., F.R.C.P.(C); physician; educator; b. Niagara Falls, N.Y. 28 May 1926; s. Alfred and Mary (Montemurro) M.; e. Univ. of Toronto M.D. 1949; Columbia Presb. Med. Centre, Neurological Inst. post-grad. training 1952-55; Univ. of London 1955-56; m. Margaret Elizabeth Hughes 31 Aug. 1953; children: Maureen, Patricia Ann, Margaret, Frederick, Thomas, Jo Anne, Michael, Martha, John, Virginia; ASSOC. DEAN OF CLINICAL & INSTITUTIONAL AFFAIRS, FACULTY OF MED., UNIV. OF TORONTO 1981- , Prof. 1969- ; Lectr. in Med. present Univ. and St. Michael's Hosp. 1957, Prof. and Phys.-in-Chief 1969-79; Prof. and Head Neurol Div. Wellesley Hosp. 1979-81; rec'd Queen's Silver Jubilee Medal; mem. Am. Acad. Neurol.; Toronto Acad. Med.; Ont. Med. Assn.; Candn. Med. Assn.; R. Catholic; Recreations: golf, gardening, furniture refinishing, reading, music, walking; Home: 8 Peebles Ave., Don Mills, Ont. M3C 2N8; Office: 2113 Medical Sciences Bldg., Toronto, Ont. M5S 1A8.

MARQUIS, Charles E., P.Eng.; b. Québec, Qué., 10 June 1925; s. Francois and Yvonne (LeFrancois) M.; e. Jesuit's Coll. 1945; Laval Univ. 1948; Univ. de Montréal 1950; m. Fernande, d. Francois Jobin, 30 May 1930; children: Andrée, Louise; PARTNER, BEAUDET-MARQUIS; Dir.; Fercal Inc.; Arteco Mortgage Invest. Corp.; Beaudeta Marquis Inc., Corp des Frères Mineurs (Franciscains); François Marquis Ltée.; Le Soleil Ltée; S.L.M. Inc.; La Banque Canadienne Nationale; Les Equipments St. Paul Inc.; Les Industries Valcartier Inc.; St. Lawrence Manufacuring Inc.; Thirco Construction Ltée; mem. Bd. Trustees, Hotel Dieu Hosp.; mem. Corp. Engrs. P.Q.; R. Catholic; recreations: golf, fishing, hunting; Clubs: Garnison, Quebec Royal Golf Club; Home: 1350 Patenaude, Sillery, Qué. G1T 2J6; Office: 615 Blvd. Pierre Bertrand, Ville Vanier, Qué.

MARQUIS, Hon. Eugene; retired judge; b. St. Alexandre, Kamouraska, P.Q., 11 Sept. 1901; s. Joseph and Eveline (Michaud) M.; e. St. Anne de Beaupré and Ste. Anne de la Pocatiere Colls.; Quebec Semy., B.A.; Laval Univ. LL.L.; LL.D., 1973; m. Veronique, d. Dr. J. A. N. Chabot, Ste. Claire de Dorchester, 14 Jan. 1931; children: Monique, Louise, Yves, Michel, Jean; Justice Superior Court, P.Q., 1949-73; Sr. Assoc. Chief Justice 1973-76; Crown

Atty. for Dist. of Que., 1931-36 and 1939-44; Hon. mem. Candn. Bar Assn., 1979; el. to H. of C. for Kamouraska, g.e. 1945; re-el. g.e. 1949; K. of C.; rec. Maltese Cross; Roman Catholic; Home: 939 Chanoine Scott S., Ste. Foy, Que. G1V 3N5

MARRIOTT, Joyce Anne (Mrs. Gerald Jerome McLellan); writer; b. Victoria, B.C., 5 Nov. 1913; d. Edward Guy and Catherine Eleanor (Heley) M.; e. The Poplars & Norfolk House, Victoria, B.C., Matric. 1932; journalism course, night sch., Victoria; London Sch. of Journalism (corr.) 1933; Univ. of B.C. (radio script writing course) 1942; m. Gerald Jerome, s. late Roland Hill McLellan, Amherst, N.S., 16 Dec. 1947; has won many local and nat. contests for verse and story writing; won (in collab.) Women's Candn. Club Lit. Award, 1944; Gov. Gen. Award for Poetry, 1941; has written many radio scripts for CBC, BBC and Aust. B.C., including "My Canada" series of Nat. Sch. Broadcasts, 1943; author of (poetry) "Calling Adventurers", 1941; (chapbooks) "The Wind Our Enemy", 1939; "Salt Marsh", 1942 (poetry) "Sandstone and Other Poems", 1945, has written reviews, commentaries, stories and poems for more than 50 Candn., U.S., and Eng. journals; writer for Nat. Film Bd., 1945-49; Women's Ed., Prince George "Citizen", B.C., 1950-52; mem., original business comte. (Founders) of "Contemporary Verse"; Asst. Ed., "Canadian Poetry Magazine" 1946-48; Ed. of verse column, "Victoria Times", 1940-43; stories broadcast on "Canadian Short Stories" and CBC "Anthology"; recreations: travelling, reading

MARROCCO, Alfred J., C.L.U.; insurance executive; b. New York, N.Y., 7 Oct. 1915; s. Frank and Clara (Brisotti) M.; came to Can. 1915; e. Toronto Pub. and High Schs.; m. Emeline, d. Stephen M. Mensour, 16 Sept. 1939; one s., Frank Neal Stephen; SR. VICE PRES. & CHIEF OPERATING OFFICER, GERLING GLOBAL LIFE INS. CO., 1980- ; Sales Dept., Prudential Ins. Co. of Am., 1936; Mgr., Northern Life Insurance Co. of Can., Windsor Ont., 1949-59; joined Global Life Insurance Co., Windsor as Mgr. 1959-64; Dir. of Brokerage Services, Toronto, 1964-69; Vice Pres. 1969; Vice Pres., Marketing 1970; Sr. Vice Pres., 1977; mem. Candn. Life Underwriters Assn.; Roman Catholic; recreations: golf, curling, bridge; Clubs: Weston Golf & Country; Essex Golf & Country; Windsor (Ont.); Home: 400 Walmer Rd., Toronto, Ont. M5P 2X7; Office: Global House, 480 University Ave., Toronto, Ont. M5G 1W8

MARRS, Douglas Charles; company executive; b. Hamilton, Ont., 27 Sept. 1913; s. late Mina Grace (Longhurst) and late Charles Hawkins M.; e. Public Sch. and Delta Coll. Inst., Hamilton, Ont.; m. Hilda Elaine, d. late Robert W. Witherspoon, 8 June 1946; children: Robert Douglas, Pamela Anne; CHRMN., BOARD OF DIRECTORS, WESTINGHOUSE CANADA INC. since 1978; Dir.; Toronto-Dominion Bank; Slater Steel Industries Ltd.; mem. Bd. Govs., McMaster Univ.; joined the Co. as a Clerk, 1936; National Operations Mgr., Canadian Westinghouse Supply Company, 1952-55; Assistant Comptroller, Canadian Westinghouse Co. Ltd., 1955-58; Manager Appliance-TV-Radio Division, 1958-60; Vice President, Consumer Products, 1960-66; Vice President, Planning 1966; Vice Pres., Adm., 1966-67; Executive Vice-President Adm. and Finance 1968-74; Pres., C.E.O., and Dir., Westinghouse Can. Ltd. 1974-78; served in 2nd World War with R.C.A.F. 1942-45; service in Far East, rank Flight Lieut.; P. Conservative; United Church; recreations: golf, boating; Clubs: Hamilton Golf & Country; Hamilton; Toronto; Tamahaac; John's Island (Florida); Home: 386 Bluebird Court, Burlington, Ont. L7T 2P7; Office: P.O. Box 28, First Canadian Place, suite 5840, Toronto, Ont. M5X 1A9

MARS, Patrick J., B.Com., M.B.A.; stockbroker; b. Waterlooville, Hants, Eng. 19 April 1940; e. McGill Univ.

B.Com. 1962, M.B.A. 1965; Chart. Financial Analyst 1971; m. Robin 5, Nov. 1966; children: Anthea, Euan; PRESIDENT AND DIR., ALFRED BUNTING & CO. LTD.; recreations: sailing, squash, skiing; Clubs: National; Royal St. Lawrence Yacht; Toronto Ski Club Home: 258 St. Leonard's Ave., Toronto, Ont. M4N 1L2; Office: 155 University Ave., 18th Floor, Toronto, Ont. M5H 3M3.

MARSH, Rt. Rev. Henry H., M.A. (Ang.); b. Lindsay, Ont., 6 Oct. 1898; s. Rev. Canon Charles H., D.D., and Emily Carew (Wilgress) M.; e. Univ. Coll., Univ. of Toronto, B.A. 1921, M.A. 1925; Wycliffe Coll, there; D.D., Wycliffe Coll., 1962; m. Margaret D. Heakes, 14 Aug. 1934; two children: Peter Timothy, Mary Marsh; o. Deacon 1924; Priest 1925; Asst. Curate, St. Anne's Ch., 1924-25; St. Paul's Ch., 1925-30; aptd. to establish the parish of St. Timothy, Toronto, in 1930 and was its only Rector for 32 yrs.; apptd. Canon of St. James Cath., Toronto, 1956; consecrated Bishop, Christ Ch. Cath., Victoria, March 1962; Bishop of Yukon, 1962-67; Address: "Hedgerows", R.R. 6, Cobourg, Ont. K9A 4J9

MARSH, Leonard Charles, B.Sc., M.A. Ph.D., LL.D.; social scientist; educator; b. Eng. 24 Sept. 1906; s. William James Anderson and Anne (Underwood) M.; e. Henry Thornton Secondary Sch. London; London Sch. of Econ. B.Sc. 1928 (Sir Edward Gonner Prize); McGill Univ. M.A. 1933, Ph.D. 1940; York Univ. LL.D. 1977; McMaster Univ. LL.D. 1978; m. Beatrice Mounsteven d. Sidney Bristow Wright 1 July 1945; Prof. Emeritus of Educ. Univ. of B.C. 1972- ; Dir. of Social Research McGill Univ. 1930-41, Lectr. in Pol. Econ. and in Sociol.; Hon. Lectr. Montreal Sch. of Social Work; mem. Bd. of Govs. and Del. to Montreal Council of Social Agencies 1934-38; Vice-Pres. Montreal Personnel Assn. 1935-36; Research Advisor Comte. on Post-War Reconstruction Ottawa 1941-44; Welfare Advisor, Sr. Ed. Offr. UN Relief & Rehabilitation Adm. Washington, London, Geneva 1944-46; Dir. of Research Sch. of Social Work Univ. of B.C. 1948-64, Prof. of Educ. Sociol. Faculty of Educ. 1964-72; Hon. Lectr. Sch. of Arch., Sch. of Community & Regional Planning, Dept. of Hist. of Science & Med. Faculty of Educ.; mem. Comte. on Higher Educ. Faculty of Educ. 4 yrs., Acting Chrmn. Dept. of Educ. Foundations 2 yrs.; Vice Pres. B.C. Div. Community Planning Assn. Can. 1947-48; Bd. mem. Community Arts Council Vancouver 1956-58; organizer and participant B.C. Arts Resources Confs. 1957, 1958; Founding Vice Pres. Friends of Chamber Music Vancouver 1948-52; W. Can. mem. Adv. Council, Amateur Chamber Music Players 1975-81; author "Employment Research" 1935; "Canadians In and Out of Work" 1940 (being prepared for re-pub. 1981); "Social Planning for Canada" (co-author) 1935, new ed. 1975; "Social Security for Canada" 1943, new ed. 1975; "Rebuilding A Neighbourhood" 1950; "A Regional College for Vancouver Island" 1966; "Communities in Canada" 1970, 2nd printing 1974; "At Home With Music; The Reflections and Recollections of an Unabashed Amateur" 1972; "Cats We Have Known: The Tales of a Cat-Lover" 1973; "Education in Action: Proposals for a Social Planetarium" 1973; "The Quality of Life: Can the Social Sciences Help?" 1980; Unitarian; recreations: music (amateur cellist), travel, country walking; Address: 3405 W. 18th Ave., Vancouver, B.C. V6S 1A8

MARSHALL, Col. the Hon. Jack.C.D.; senator; b. Glace Bay, N.S. 26 Nov. 1919; s. Louis and Rose (Moraff) M.; e. Glace Bay High Sch.; Mt. Allison Comm. Coll. 1938-39; m. Sylvia (d. 1975) d. late Harry Rothman, London, Eng. 27 Jan. 1946; children: Thomas Wendell, Beverlee Ann, Arlaine Fleury; served with N. Shore (N.B.) Regt. during World War II rank Capt., post-war 1950-68, Lt. Col. C.O. Royal Nfld. Regt. (M), Col. Commdr. Nfld. Dist. Militia 1967-68; el. to H. of C. g.e. 1968, re-el. 1972, 1974; summoned to Senate 1978; Past Pres. Candn. Inf. Assn.; Br. 13 Royal Candn. Legion Corner Brook; mem. Army Cadet League Can.; Hon. mem. War Amputations Can.;

Hong Kong Veterans Assn.; Nat. POW Assn. Can.; Hon. Commdr. Jewish Veterans Can.; Hon. Pres. Fed. Brit. Candn. Veterans; P. Conservative; Jewish; recreation: golf; Home: 33 Bayhill Ridge, Amberwood Village, Stittsville, Ont. K0A 3G0; Office: Rm 204, East Bock, Parliament of Canada, Ottawa, Ont.

MARSHALL, John Stewart, M.A., Ph.D., F.R.S.C. (1953); university professor; b. Welland, Ont., 18 July 1911; s. John Wells and Catherine Amelia (Stewart) M.; e. Queen's Univ., B.A. 1931, M.A. 1933; Cambridge Univ. (St. John's Coll.), Ph.D. 1940; m. Helen Elizabeth Réburn, d. late John Livingstone Scott, 19 Dec. 1940; two d., Claire, Heather; 1851 Exhn. Scholar, 1935-38; Research Fellow, Roy. Soc. Can. (nuclear physics) Cavendish Lab., Cambridge Univ. 1938-39; Jr. Research Physicist, Nat. Research Council, Ottawa, 1939-43; with Candn. Army Operational Research Group, 1944-45; apptd. Asst. Prof. of Physics, McGill Univ., 1945; Assoc. Prof., 1947; Prof., 1954, Macdonald Prof. of Physics and Meteorol., 1959; Dir., Observatory McGill Univ. 1960; Radar Weather Observatory 1972; Prof. Emeritus, McGill Univ. 1979; mem., Candn. Assn. of Physicists (Pres. 1950); Fellow, Am. Meteorol. Soc.; Pres. (1966) Science Sec. Roy. Soc. Can.; mem., Candn. Metorol. Soc.; Awards: Hugh Robert Mill Medal (Roy. Meteorol. Soc.) 1962; John Patterson Medal (Candn. Meteorol. Service) 1961; Sigma Xi; Presbyterian; Home: 604 Lakeshore Rd., Beaconsfield, Que. H9W 4K4

MARSHALL, Kenneth; insurance executive; b. Toronto, Ont., 14 Oct. 1910; s. William James and Alberta (Foote) M.; e. Toronto Pub. and High Schs.; m. Gertrude Lorraine, d. Samuel Trebar, 3 March 1933; two d., Diane Pryce, Donna Graham; PRESIDENT AND CHIEF EXECUTIVE OFFICER, MARSHALL & PRYCE INSURANCE BROKERS LTD, 1978- ; joined Dale Ross Holdings Ltd. as a trainee 1929; trans. to Sales Dept. 1936; Agency Supt. 1945-53; Mgr. Marketing 1953-63; apptd. a Dir. 1963; Mgr. for Prov. of Ont. 1965; Vice Pres. 1969; President and Chief Extve. Offr. 1970-75; Dir. Emeritus 1977-78; Dir. Albion Ins. Co. of Can.; member, Honorary Order Blue Goose International; Candn. Chamber Comm., Un. Ch.; recreations: golf, skating, curling; Clubs: Granite; Scarborough Golf & Country; Home: 537 Blythwood Rd., Toronto, Ont. M4N 1B4; Office: 1662A Avenue Rd., Toronto M5M 3Y1

MARSHALL, Lois, C.C. (1967), LL.D.,; soprano; b. Toronto, Ont., 1924; e. Wellesley Sch., Toronto; Royal Conservatory of Music, Toronto, where she studied under Weldon Kilburn (now her accompanist); won notice as a singer at age 12; won Eaton Graduate Award of $1,000, 1950; Singing Stars of Tomorrow Grand Prize, 1950; Walter W. Naumburg Musical Foundation Award, Dec. 1952; made debut in New York Town Hall, 1952; chosen by Toscanini to sing with N.B.C. Symphony, Carnegie Hall, N.Y., 1953; first sang with Toronto Symphony in 1947; made Toronto debut in 1950; began (1954) under 3 year contract to Columbia Artists Management Inc., under whom she has appeared in N.Y. with the Mendelssohn Glee Club, at the Ann Arbor May Festival with the Philadelphia Orchestra, with the Cincinnati Symphony at the Cincinnati Festival and two performances at the Bach Festival in Berea, Ohio; made London debut with Sir Thomas Beecham and the Royal Philharmonic Orchestra at Festival Hall (singing Mozart's Exultate Jubilate) May 1956; fall of 1956 two mth. concert tour, W. Can., Mid-W. Un. States, London and Amsterdam; 1957, Bach's St. Matthew Passion, Massey Hall, Toronto, recital at Edinburgh Festival and solo recital (first) at Royal Festival Hall, London; made Italian debut in Milan, Sept. 1958, and in Oct. was third Candn. artist to perform in U.S.S.R. in Leningrad, Moscow, Riga and Kiev; later performed in Amsterdam, Rotterdam, The Hague, Utrecht, London; took part in C.B.C. opera "Peter Grimes" Dec. 1958; held concert in Eaton Auditorium, Toronto, March 1959, and took part in all Bach program at Stratford Festival, Ont., Aug. 1959; made world tour, Jan.-March 1960, U.S.S.R., Netherlands, Australia, New Zealand; Hon. LL.D., Univ. of Toronto 1965; Award of Excellence, Candn. Music Council 1973; Address; 32 Golfhaven Dr., Scarborough, Ont. M1G 2C9

MARSHALL, Mortimer Villiers, B.A., B.Sc., Ed.D., D.Litt.; educator; b. Chebogue, Yarmouth Co., N.S., 26 May 1898; s. Frederick Lakeland Villiers and Mary Eliza (Knollin) M.; e. Acadia Univ., B.Sc. 1921, B.A. 1922, D.Litt. 1967; Harvard Univ., Ed.M. 1927, Ed.D. 1930; m. Vera Gould, d. John Goreham, Shelburne, N.S., 29 June 1927; children: Mary Bernice, Lydia Jane; Dean, Sch. of Educ., Acadia Univ., 1943-67; served in World War, 1916-19, with C.E.F. Corps Signals; World War 1943-45, with R.C.A.F., as Flight Lieut.; Life mem., Candn. Red Cross Soc.; Nova Scotia Teachers' Union; author of "Education as a Social Force", 1931; "An Introduction to Tests and Testing", 1944; "The Organization of Elementary Education in Canada", 1961; "Communities and their School Teachers", 1962; many articles, booklets and tests; recreations: oil painting, writing; Home: Windsor Elms, Windsor, N.S., B0N 2T0

MARSHALL, Paul Macklin, B.C.L.; company executive; b. Toronto, Ont., 21 Sept. 1923; s. Griffith Macklin and Josephine Angela (Hodgson) M.; e. St. Leo's Acad., Westmount, P.Q.; St. Michael's Coll., Toronto, Ont.; McGill Univ., B.C.L. 1949; m. Carol Ann, d. Wm. H. Dickie, Toronto, Ont.; four s., Blake, Gregory, Jonathan, Kirk; PRES. AND C.E.O., WESTMIN RESOURCES LIMITED 1978- ; Dir. Westmills Carpets Ltd.; Larcana Mining Corp., Brascade Resources Inc.; Noranda Mines Ltd.; Legal Asst., Sun Life Assnce. Co., Montreal, P.Q., 1949-52 (on loan to Govt. as Extve. Asst. to Min. Nat. Defence, 1952-54); joined Canadian Chemical & Cellulose Co. Ltd. as Asst. Secy., 1954, Secy. 1957, Secy.-Treas. 1958, Vice-Pres. 1959; Vice-Pres. and Secy.-Treas., Chemcell Ltd. and Vice-Pres. and Treas., Canadian Chemical Co., Ltd., Columbia Cellulose Co. Ltd. and Celgar Ltd., 1959; Pres. and Chief Extve. Offr., Columbia Cellulose Co., Ltd., 1962; Chrmn. of the Bd., Chemcell Ltd. 1967-69; Pres., Hamilton Brothers Exploration Co., Vice-Pres. Hamilton Brothers Petroleum Corp., Extve. Vice-Pres. Hamilton Brothers Oil Co. June 1969-June 1972; Pres., Cdn. Hydrocarbons Ltd. 1972-76; Pres. Brascan Resources Ltd., 1978-80; Vice Chrmn. & Dir., Western Mines Ltd., 1978-80; served in 2nd World War with R.C.A. 1943-45; discharged with rank of Lieut.; called to the Bar of Que. 1949; Clubs: Mount Royal (Montreal, Que.); The Vancouver (B.C.); Ranchman's; Glencoe; Petroleum (Calgary); Home: 805 Prospect Ave., Calgary, Alta. T2T 0W6; Office: 1800, 225 Fifth Ave. S.W., Calgary, Alta. T2P 3G6

MARSHALL, Tom, M.A.; poet; novelist; educator; b. Niagara Falls, Ont. 9 April 1938; s. Douglas Woodworth and Helen Steele (Kennedy) M.; e. Public Sch., Niagara Falls 1952; Niagara Falls Coll. 1957; Queen's Univ., B.A. 1961, M.A. 1965; Birkbeck Coll., Univ. of London 1966-68; Assoc. Prof. Dept. of Eng., Queen's Univ. since 1973; Sr. Tutor in Eng. 1964, Instr. 1965, Lectr. 1966, Asst. Prof. 1969; author of "The Beast with Three Backs" 1965; "The Silences of Fire" 1969; "The Psychic Mariner" 1970; "A.M. Klein" 1970; "Magic Water" 1971; "The Earth Book" 1974; "The White City" 1976; "Rosemary Goal" (novel) 1978; "Harsh and Lovely Land" 1979; "The Elements" 1980; co-ed., "Fourteen Stories High" 1971; "Four Kingston Poets" (record) 1972; has published several articles and reviews in numerous literary journals; Chief Ed. "Quarry" (lit. mag.) 1965-66, 1968-70; Ed. Quarry Press since 1965; Poetry Ed. "Canadian Forum" 1973-78; mem., Writers Union Can.; League Candn. Poets; Home: 451 Victoria St., Kingston, Ont. K7L 3Z8; Office: Dept. of English, Queen's University, Kingston, Ont.

MARSHALL, William Hext, M.B., B.Chir., M.D., Ph.D.; educator; b. London, Eng. 10 Apl. 1933; s. Leslie Phillips and Catherine Mary (Hext) M.; e. Marlborough Coll. Eng.; Cambridge Univ. M.B., B.Chir. 1957, M.D. 1965; London Hosp. Med. Coll. M.R.C.S., L.R.C.P. 1957; Melbourne Univ. Ph.D. 1967; M.R.C.P. 1961; F.R.C.P. (Lond.) 1981; m. Ingeborg Constanze Luise d. Alfred Ristow, E. Germany 16 Sept. 1961; children: Alfred, Christopher, Mary-Anne; PROF. OF IMMUNOLOGY, MEMORIAL UNIV. OF NFLD. since 1970; House Offr. and Sr. House Offr. The London Hosp. 1957-61; Jr. Lectr. in Physiol. The London Hosp. Med. Coll. 1961-63; Research Fellow and Asst. Phys. The Walter & Eliza Hall Inst. and The Royal Melbourne Hosp. 1963-66; Research Fellow N.Y. Univ. Med. Centre 1966-68; Assoc. prof. of Immunol. present Univ. 1968-70; author or co-author over 45 scient. papers on cellular immunology, clin. immunology and immunogenetics; mem. Candn., Australian and U.S. Socs. for Immunols.; Transplantation Soc.; Genetical soc.; Anglican; recreations: cinema and theatre, gardening, outdoor sports; Home: (P.O. Box 23) Site 76, Logy Bay Rd., St. John's, Nfld.; Office: Prince Philip Parkway, St. John's , Nfld. A1B 3V6.

MARSHALL, Hon. William W., M.H.A.; politician; PRES. OF EXTVE. COUNCIL AND GOVT. HOUSE LEADER, NFLD. 1979- ; el. M.H.A. for St. John's East prov. by-el. 1970, re-el. since g.e. 1971; Min. without Portfolio 1972; P. Conservative; Office: Confederation Bldg., St. John's, Nfld. A1C 5T7.

MARTEL, Hon. Edouard, B.A., LL.B.; judge; b. Sorel, P.Q., 24 Apr. 1915; s. J. Wilfrid and Louise (Labelle) M.; e. Coll. de Berthier; Coll. de Montreal, B.A. 1934; Seminaire de Philosophie, B.A. 1936; Univ. de Montreal, LL.B. 1939; m. Pierrette, d. J. Oscar Ducharme, 21 Apr, 1946; one d. Jocelyne; JUSTICE, SUPERIOR COURT, QUEBEC; Trustee, Thomas Aquinas Foundation of Can. (Philos.); read law with Charbonneau, Charbonneau and Charlebois, Montreal, Que., called to Bar of Que. 1939; cr. Q.C., 1960; Pte. Secy. to Prov. Secy., Min. of Health & Social Welfare, P.Q., 1939-44; Legal Counsel to City of Outremont, 1950-63; special French-speaking legal Counsel to Fed. Royal Comn. on Defence of Insanity and on Criminal Sexual Psychopaths, 1953; mem. Am. Judicature Soc.; Roman Catholic; recreations: travel, golf, fishing; Club: Cercle de la Place D'Armes (Montreal); Home: 36 Beverley, Town of Mount Royal, Que. H3P 1K4; Office: Court House, 1 Notre-Dame St. E., Montreal, Que. H2Y 1B6

MARTEL, Jean Jacques: consultant in business administration; agent; ancestors came to Can. around 1680, first settlers of Ville Marie; b. Baieville, Que., 3 Jan. 1927; s. Gérard and Irène (Simoneau) M.; e. Baieville Coll., Que.; Coll. of St. Frédéric, Amos Seminary; St-Simon Sch., Ellis Business Coll., Drummondville, Que.; m. Rolande Blais, Ste. Foy, Que., 10 Oct 1959; two s. Jean Claude, François, one d., Lucie; Vice-Pres. and Dir., Northern Que. Explorers Ltd.; started with Canadian International Paper Co. as Clerk 1943; then Clerk, Amos Bureau of Mines 1944-46; Amos Woolen Mills Inc. 1947-48; Prov. Asst. Mines, 1948-49; estbd. J. J. Martel Inc., 1954 for gen. ins. business, operating as business consultant private and co. since 1973; def. cand. to H of C. 1957; el. to H. of C. for Chapleau, 1958; def. in g.e. 1962 and 79 for Abitibi; Extve. Secy. to Candn. Min. of Mines, 1962-63; apptd. Extve. Secy. to Min. of Agric. and Colonization, Jan. 1967; Indust. Del., Que. Dept. Industry, Comm. & Tourism for N.W. Que. since 1971; Pres., Jr. Chamber of Comm., Amos, P.Q., 1953-54; Regional Pres., N.W. Que. Fed. 1955; Secy., Amos Br., N.W. Que. Prospectors Assn. Inc., 1946-57, Vice-Pres., 1957; K. of C.; Conservative; Roman Catholic; recreations: fishing, part time prospecting; Club: Richelieu; Office: (Box 276) 741 First St. W., Amos, Que. J9T 3A7

MARTIN, Mt. Rev. Albert, Th.L. (R.C.) bishop; b. Southbridge, Mass., 4 Oct. 1913; s. Arthur and Parmelia (Beaudoin) M.; e. Nicolet Acad., Nicolet Semy. (Classics and Philos.); Laval Univ., Faculty of Theol., Laval Univ., B.A. 1935, Th.L. 1939; BISHOP OF NICOLET since 1950; o. Priest, 1939; Prof. at Nicolet Semy. and Rector there 1946; Vicar-General of Nicolet Diocese, 1949, Address: Evêché de Nicolet, Nicolet, Que. J0G 1E0

MARTIN, D'Arcy Argue Counsell, Q.C., LL.D.; b. Hamilton, Ont., 23 Oct. 1898; s. D'Arcy Richard Charles, K.C. & Margaret Elizabeth (Stinson) M.; e. Highfield Sch., Hamilton, Ont., Trinity Coll. Sch., Pt. Hope, Ont.; Trinity Coll., Toronto, B.A. 1920; Upper Can. Law Soc. 1923; m. Margaret Ellen Howard (d. 1965), d. Hercule John Craig, Midland, Ont., 15 Sept. 1934; children: Frances Margaret Richardson, Catherine Howard Eaton; MEMBER, MARTIN AND MARTIN; former Chancellor of McMaster University; read law with Watson, Smoke, Smith and Sinclair, Toronto, Ontario; called to the Bar of Ontario, 1923; cr. K.C. 1934; served in 1st World War 1918, with Machine Gun Bn.; Alderman, City of Hamilton, 1927-31; mem. of Ontario Leg. for Hamilton W. 1931-34; mem. of Gov. Body, Trinity Coll. Sch.; Alpha Delta Phi; Freemason; Conservative; Anglican; Clubs: Hamilton; Tamahaac; Home: Apt. 2, Aberdeen Ave., Hamilton, Ont. L8P 2P6; Office: 15 King St. W., Hamilton, Ont. L8N 3P9

MARTIN, Fernand, M.A., Ph.D.; b. St. Hyacinthe, Que., 6 Dec. 1925; s. Victor and Adeline (Leblanc) M.; e. Laval Univ., Sch. of Soc. Science, 1948-49; McGill Univ., B.A. (Econ. & Pol. Science) 1952, M.A. (Econ.) 1958, Ph.D. (Econ.) 1962; London Sch. of Econ., Research Student, 1958-59; m. Solange, d. Ovide Pincince, 5 Dec. 1949; one s.; Assoc. Prof., Univ. de Montréal and Asst. Prof., McGill Univ., since 1965; in business 1952-56; apptd. Asst. Prof., Univ. of Man., 1959-60; Visiting Asst. Prof., Univ. of Sask., 1960-62; Asst. Prof., Univ. de Montréal, 1962-65; past Principal, Labour Coll. of Can.; awarded Can. Council Pre-Doctoral Fellowship 1958-59; has written articles for several learned journs.; Home: 150 La Broquerie, St. Bruno, Que.

MARTIN, Frederic S.; investment dealer; b. New Perth, P.E.I., 16 July 1922; s. George and Jennie (Shaw) M.; e. Prince of Wales Coll., Charlottetown, P.E.I.; Dalhousie Univ. (grad. Law); m. Ogden Frances, d. late Robert Lennox Blackburn, 8 Nov. 1956; children: Peter Charles Balckburn, Jane Lennox, Sarah Lennox, Caroline Mellish, Alexandra Mary; SENIOR VICE-PRESIDENT AND DIRECTOR, GREENSHIELDS INC.; Pres., Stanley Lands Ltd.; R. L. and R. Backburn Limited; Blackburn Bros. Limited; Culloden Investments Limited; Dir., C.E. Pickering Invests. Ltd.; Kilmuir Holdings Ltd.; Michaels Equipment Limited; Cochrane-Dunlop Hardware Limited; Norpak Ltd.; read law with McLeod and Bentley, Charlottetown, P.E.I.; called to the Bar of P.E.I. 1947; Extve. Asst. to Solr. Gen. and Leader of Govt. in Senate 1952-57; Legal Counsel to Central Mortgage and Housing Corp.; mem., Finance Comte., V.O.N.; Bd. Govs., Ashbury Coll.; Bd. Trustees, Confed. Centre of the Arts, Charlottetown; Children's Hosp. E. Ont.; Trustee, Foundation for Legal Research in Can., Forum for Young Cans.; mem. Adv. Bd., Ottawa, Salvation Army; Anglican; recreations: skiing, golfing, fishing; Clubs: Rideau; Royal Ottawa Golf; Ottawa Country; Maganassippi; Fish and Game; Lyford Cay, Bahamas; Home: Aylmer Rd., R.R. 2, Aylmer E., Que. J9H 5E1; Office: 151 Sparks St., Ottawa, Ont. K1P 5E3

MARTIN, Rev. George William, B.Th. (R.C.), LL.D.; university president; b. Chatham. N.B. 21 Sept. 1924; s. John Stephen and Mary Florence (Cassidy) M.; e. St. Michael's Acad. Chatham 1937; St. Thomas Coll. Prep. 1939 and High Sch. 1941; St. Thomas Coll. B.A. 1945; Holy Heart Semy. Halifax B.Th. 1949; Fordham Univ.

Grad. Studies 1953-55; PRESIDENT, ST. THOMAS UNIV. since 1975; Registrar present Univ. 1958, Extve. Vice Pres. 1971; served Senate of Priests Diocese of Saint John, Pres. 7 terms; mem. Nat. Bd. Distribution Clergy 1971; Nat. Fed. Senates of Priests, Regional Vice Pres. 2 Yrs., Pres. 1974-75; apptd. Vicar Gen. Diocese of Saint John 1975; Pres. Town Credit Union Ltd. Chatham, N.B. 2 terms; Address: College Hill, Fredericton, N.B.

MARTIN, H. George; insurance executive; b. London, Eng., 20 May 1921; s. Frank and Anne M.; e. High Sch., Eng., Brit. Sch. of Radio Technol.; came to Can. 1951; m. Mary, d. late Harry Snell, 23 Dec. 1951; children: Donald, Paul, Derek, Pamela, Kendra; CHIEF OPERATING OFFICER, VICE-PRES. & GEN. MGR. FOR CAN., AETNA CASUALTY AND SURETY CO. OF CANADA since 1972; Vice President, Excelsior Life Insurance Co.; mem. Bd. Dirs., PMS Co. of Canada; Pres., Ins. Crime Prevention Bureau; Dir. Ins. Bur. of Can.; Facility Assoc.; Insurors Advisory Organization; joined present Co., Rochester, N.Y. 1952; Claim Supt. Toronto 1961; Claim Mgr. Toronto 1963; Claims Mgr. for Can. 1966; served with RN and Merchant Navy 1937-50; Chief Offr., Communications Offr., served Dunkirk, Atlantic and Pacific areas: Dir., Ajax/Pickering Social Planning Council; Past Dpty. Reeve Village of Pickering, since 1968; Chrmn., Greenwood Ratepayers Assn.; mem., Community Centre Bd., Planning Bd., mem., Internat. Claim Assn.; Liberal; Protestant; recreations: hiking, painting; Clubs: Rotary (Past Pres.); Engineers; Home: Greenwood, Ont. L0H 1H0; Office: 20 Toronto St., Toronto, Ont. M5C 2C4

MARTIN, Hugh A.; company president; b. Los Angeles, Cal., 3 Feb. 1914; s. George Allen and Ruth (McDermid) M.; e. Public and High Schs., Vancouver, B.C.; Shawnigan Lake Sch., Vancouver Island, B.C.; m. Danae Maria, 15 June 1960; children: Melinda Jane, Hugh Gordon, Mrs. Carol Ruth Bartolic; PRESIDENT, WESTERN CONSTRUCTION & ENGINEERING RESEARCH LTD.: Chrmn., Cdn. Dredge and Dock Co. Ltd.;Dir., Candn. Pacific Airlines; PanCanadian Petroleum Ltd.; PeBen Oilfield Services Ltd.; Western International Hotels; Pres., Road Builders & Heavy Constr. Assn. of B.C., 1953; formed Marwell Construction Co. Ltd. in partnership with R. D. Welch in 1936, acting as Extve. Vice-Pres.; el. Pres. in 1957; Patron, Lester B. Pearson Coll. of Pacific and United World Colleges (Can.) Inc.; Hon. Patron, Vancouver Oral Centre for Deaf Children Inc. former Campaign Chrmn., Fed. Liberal Campaign; Liberal; Protestant; recreations: golf, swimming, music; Clubs: The Vancouver and Terminal City; Capilano Golf & Country; Shaughnessy Golf & Country; Home: 1870 S.W. Marine Dr., Vancouver, B.C. V6P 6B2; Office: 8th Floor, 1455 W. Georgia St., Vancouver, B.C. V6G 2T3

MARTIN, Jean-Claude, B.Pharm., M.H.A.; association executive; b. Montreal, Que. 21 Dec. 1929; s. Lorenzo and Alice May (Baillargeon) M; e. Coll. Mont Saint-Louis 1950; Univ. de Montréal B.Pharm. 1956, M.H.A. 1962; Candn. Army Offr. Courses; m. Yvette d. Roméo Leclerc, Portneuf, Qué. 30 June 1956; children: Denis, Diane, Benoit, Vincent; PRES., CANDN. HOSP. ASSN. 1977-; Pharm., Dorval Shopping Centre, Qué. 1956; Pharm. Lt. Candn. Forces Med. Services, Camp Borden, Petawawa, Toronto and Ottawa 1957-60; Resident in Hosp. Adm. Montreal Children's Hosp. 1961, Adm. Asst. 1962, Asst. Extve. Dir. 1963-65, Adm. (Services) 1969-71; Sr. Lectr. Inst. Hosp. Adm. Univ. of Montreal 1965-69; in charge of Hosp. Adm. Course, Dept. Continuing Educ. 1965-69, Lectr. in Pharm., Continuing Educ. in Hosp. Adm. and Dept. Health Adm. 1969-74; Asst. Prof. of Epidemiol. and Health McGill Univ. 1971-75; Extve. Dir. Montreal Jt. Hosp. Inst. 1971-75; Extve. Dir. Hôpital du Sacré-Coeur, Montreal 1975-77; mem. core comte. Nat. Health Grants and Sub-comte. on Analysis & Organ. Health Services 1971-75; Pres. Study Comte. on Out-patients Services & Emergency Services Montreal Region 1971; Adm. Centre

St-Vallier 1971-73, Dir. 1973-74; mem. Sub-comte. on Health & Welfare Montreal Urban Community 1972-73; Study Comte. on Emergency Services Metrop. Montreal Regional Council on Health & Social Services 1973-74, Dir. on Council 1975-77; mem. Que. Research Council 1976-77; Chrmn. Health Computer Information Bureau 1977-80; Dir. Cndn. Council Hosp. Accreditation 1977- ; Nursing Unit Adm. Program 1977- ; mem. Ottawa Gen. Hosp. Corp.; author various med. publs.; Ed. "Magazine Dimension in Health Services" 1977- ; Fellow, Am. Coll. Hosp. Adms.; mem., Bd. of Dir., Trans-Can. Job Exchange; Internat. Hosp. Fed.; mem. Candn. Coll. Health Service Extves.; Candn. Hosp. Assn.; Candn. Pub. Health Assn.; La Corp. des Administrateurs Agréés; Am. Hosp. Assn. (Del.); Ottawa Bd. Trade; R. Catholic; recreations: tennis, sailing, cross-country skiing; Home: 1449 Palen Ave., Ottawa, Ont. K1H 7E6; Office: 410 Laurier Ave. W., Ottawa, Ont. K1R 7T6.

MARTIN, John Rupert, B.A., M.F.A., Ph.D., D.Litt. (Hon.); professor; b. Hamilton, Ont., 27 Sept. 1916; s. John Smith and Elizabeth (Hutchinson) M.; e. Central Coll. Inst., Hamilton, Ont.; McMaster Univ., B.A. 1938; Princeton Univ., M.F.A. 1941, Ph.D. 1947; McMaster Univ., D.Litt. (Hon.) 1976; m. Barbara Janet, d. Duncan Malcolm, Hamilton, Ont., 23 Aug. 1941; one d., Hilary Jane; MARQUAND PROF. OF ART AND ARCHEOL., PRINCETON UNIV., since 1970; Prof. since 1961; Chrmn. Dept. 1973-79; Instr., Univ. Iowa 1941-42; joined present Univ. 1947; Bicentennial Preceptor 1952-55; McCosh Faculty Fellow 1964-65; Fellow, Am. Council of Learned Socs., 1965-66; Charles Rufus Morey Book Award, Coll. Art. Assn. Am. 1972; served with Candn. Army in Eng. & N.W. Europe 1942-46; rank Maj. on discharge; Mentioned in Despatches; author: "The Illustration of the Heavenly Ladder of John Climacus", 1954, "The Portrait of John Milton at Princeton and its Place in Milton Iconography", 1961; "The Farnese Gallery", 1965; "The Ceiling Paintings By Rubens for the Jesuit Church in Antwerp", 1968; "Rubens: the Antwerp Altarpieces", 1969; "Rubens' Decorations for the Pompa Introitus Ferdinandi", 1972; "Rubens before 1620" 1972; "Baroque", 1977; "Van Dyck as Religious Artist", 1979; also numerous articles; Editor-in-Chief "The Art Bulletin", 1971-74; mem., International Committee for History of Art; College Art Association Am.; Renaissance Soc. Am.; Democrat; Home: 3 Westfield Ct., Princeton, N.J. 08540

MARTIN, Joseph E., B.A. (Hons.), C.M.C.; certified management consultant; b. Kelvington, Sask., 13 Jan. 1937; s. late George Herbert and Jakobeina Sigurlaug (Einarsson) M.; e. Un. Coll. (Sr. Stick 1957-58), B.A. (Hons.) 1959; m. Sally Ann, d. late W. Noble Dagg, 16 July 1960; children: Marian Michelle, Jon Noble George, Michael Reid, Meredith Ann; PARTNER, TOUCHE ROSS & PARTNERS, since 1972; Invest. Analyst, The Monarch Life Assurance Co., 1959-61; served with Govt. of Man. 1961-66, Extve. Asst. to Prov. Treas. 1961, Extve. Secy. to Man. Royal Comn. on Local Govt. Organ. & Finance 1963, Extve. Dir., Man. Centennial Corp. 1964; joined present Firm, as Consultant, Winnipeg Office, 1966; transferred to Toronto 1968; served with COTC, Univ. of Man.; Prairie Command Personnel Selection Unit; retired with rank Capt. 1962; Past Pres., Man. Hist. Soc.; Manitoba YPC; author of various articles for magazines and journals; Pres., Institute Mang. Consultants Ontario; mem. Bd., Inst. Mang. Consultants Can.; Coach, NTHA; P. Conservative; Anglican; Clubs: Albany; Toronto Cricket Skating & Curling; Cambridge; Home: 215 Glencairn Ave., Toronto, Ont.; Office: P.O. Box 12, First Canadian Place, Toronto, Ont.

MARTIN, Rear-Admiral Michael Arthur, C.D.; Canadian armed forces; b. Calgary, Alta. 25 July 1927; e. Kingston, Ont. schs.; Royal Roads Naval Coll. grad. 1946; Royal Naval Staff Coll. 1959-60; Nat. Defence Coll. King-

ston 1973-74; m. Patricia Greer, Victoria, B.C.; 3 children; COMMDR. MARITIME FORCES PACIFIC AND COMMDR. PACIFIC REGION 1977- ; joined RCN as Midshipman 1946; served in HMCS Athabaskan followed by 2 tours in Korea in HMCS Cayuga; took command minesweeper HMCS Chaleur followed by service in HMCS Magnificent and Skeena; assigned to Naval HQ Ottawa 1958; RCN Liaison Offr. U.S. Navy Commdr. Hunter-Killer Forces Atlantic 1960; took command HMCS Ste-Therese 1962 and HMCS Skeena 1963; Extve. Offr. and Training Commdr. HMCS Cornwallis 1964; syndicate dir. Candn. Forces Staff Coll. Kingston 1966 followed by 3 yr. tour Maritime Command HQ as Depy. Chief of Staff for Combat Readiness; took command Second Candn. Destroyer Sqdn. Esquimalt 1970; promoted Commodore and apptd. Sr. Maritime Liaison Offr. Candn. Defence Liaison Staff, Washington, D.C. 1974; promoted to present rank 1977; Office: FMO Victoria, B.C. V0S 1B0.

MARTIN, Paul E., B.A., LL.B., b. Windsor, Ont., 28 Aut. 1938; s. Paul Joseph James and Eleanor Alice M.; e. Univ. of Ottawa; Univ. of Toronto, B.A. (Philos. & Hist., St. Michael's Coll.) 1960, LL.B. 1963; m. Sheila Ann, d. William A. Cowan, Windsor, Ont., 11 Sept. 1965; three s., Paul William James, Robert James Edward, David Patrick Anthony; PRES., CHIEF EXTVE. OFFR. & DIR., THE CSL GROUP INC.; Chrmn. Bd. Dirs. and Chief Extve. Offr., Can. Steamship Lines Inc.; Candn. Shipbldg. and Engn. Ltd.; Kingsway Transports Ltd.; Voyageur Enterprises Ltd.; Dir., Domglas Ltd.; Provinces Utilities, Canada Devel. Crp.; read law with Osler, Hoskin & Harcourt, Toronto; called to the Bar of Ont. 1966; former Vice Pres., Power Corp. of Can.; Consolidated Bathurst Ltd.; prior to Bar admission worked as a merchant seaman on various salvage operations in Arctic; also served in Legal Dept., European Coal and Steel Community, Luxembourg and worked as a roustabout in Alta. gas fields; mem., Law Soc. Upper Can.; Candn. Comte. of Lloyd's Register of Shipping; North-South Inst.; Candn. Econ. Policy Comte.; Gt. Lakes Waterways Assn.; Dominion Marine Assn.; Governor of Concordia Univ.; R. Catholic; recreations: sports, reading; Clubs: University (Montreal); St. James's; Mount Bruno Country; Home: 939 Moncrieff Rd., Town of Mount Royal, Que. H3R 3A3; Office: 759 Victoria Square, Montreal, Que. H2Y 2K3

MARTIN, Hon. Paul Joseph James, P.C., C.C., Q.C., M.A., LL.M.; diplomat; b. Ottawa, Ont., 23 June 1903; s. Philip Ernest and Lumina (Chouinard) M.; e. Pembroke Separate Sch.; St. Alexander's Coll., Ironside, Que.; St. Michael's Coll., Univ. of Toronto, B.A., M.A.; Osgoode Hall, Toronto, 1928; Harvard Univ., LL.M. 1929; Trinity Coll., Cambridge; Geneva Sch. of Internat. Studies, Switzerland, 1930 (Alfred Zimmern Scholarship, 1930); LL.D. (Hon.), Michigan, 1947; Dalhousie, 1950; Laval, 1952; Ottawa, 1952; Toronto, 1952; Assumption, 1954; Queen's 1954; Univ. de Montréal, Dartmouth, John Carroll Univ. 1956; St. Thomas Univ., 1961; Loyola of Los Angeles 1964; Univ. of B.C. 1966; Waterloo 1967; Univ. of N.B. 1967; Hanyang Univ., Korea 1973; D.C.L. (Hon.), Western Ont. 1954; Bishop's 1956; D.Humanities (Hon.), Wayne State Univ. 1964; Doctor of Law, LL.D., Cambridge Univ., Eng. 1980; D.L.H.S.; m. Alice Eleanor Adams, Windsor, Ont., 1937; has one s. and one d.; Govt. Leader in the Senate, 1968-1974; cr. K.C. 1937; Q.C. (Fed.) 1975; formerly a sr. partner, Martin, Laird, Easton and Cowan, Windsor, Ont. 1934-63; Assumption College, University of W. Ontario, 1931-34; def. cand. to Ont. Leg. for N. Renfrew, by-el. 1928; 1st el. to H. of C. for Essex E., g.e. 1935; M.P. 1935-68; Candn. Govt. Del. to 19th Assembly of League of Nations, Geneva, 1938; Parlty. Asst. to Min. of Labour 1943; Secy. of State and sworn mem. of P.C. 1945; Min. of Nat. Health & Welfare, 1946-57; Secy. of State for External Affairs, 1963-68; summoned to Senate Apl. 1968 and apptd. Senate Govt. Leader; resigned 1974; Candn. High Commr., London,

Eng. 1974-79; mem., Candn. del. to U.N. Gen. Assembly 1946 and 1949; Acting Chrmn. of del. 1952-53 and 1954; Chrmn. 1955; headed meetings to NATO, U.N., etc. and Can.-U.S. and Can.-Japan Ministerial Comtes.; proposed U.N. Peacekeeping Force in Cyprus, for which awarded Order of Ahepa 1968; el. Pres. NATO 1965; mem., Parlty. Del. to Czechoslovakia May 1968, and of various Candn. dels. in 1972 and 73; Chancellor, Waterloo Lutheran Univ. (now Wilfrid Laurier) 1972-78; Guest Lecturer, McGill Uni. 1980 and 1981; B'nai B'rith Humanitarian Award 1969; Grande Medaille d'Or de l'Ordre Internat. du Bien Public, Paris 1971; Hon. mem., Acad. Pol. Sci., N.Y.; Hon. Col. Windsor Regt.; Hon. life mem., Roy. Candn. Legion; Nat. Bd. mem., Candn. Council of Christians and Jews; C.C. 1976; Freedom of the City of London 1977; R. Catholic; Address: 2021 Ontario St., Windsor, Ont. N8Y 1N3

MARTIN, Robert William, B.A.Sc., P.Eng.; utility executive; b. Toronto, Ont. 7 June 1936; s. William George and Evelyn Irene (Philips) M.; e. Leaside High Sch. Toronto 1954, Vaughan Rd. Coll. Inst. 1953; Univ. of Toronto B.A.Sc. (Civil Engn.) 1958; m. Patricia Lorraine d. Albert George Norris, Leaside, Ont. 27 June 1959; children: Stephen Gregory, Robert Scott, Adrienne Christine; PRES. AND DIR., THE CONSUMERS GAS COMPANY LTD. 1981- ; Dir., St. Lawrence Gas Co.; St. Lawrence Gas Co. Service & Merchandising Corp.; Ottawa Gas; La Societe Gazifere de Hull; Underwater Gas Developers Ltd.; Staff Engr. Provincial Gas, St. Catharines 1958, Asst. Supt. Operations 1959, Gen. Supt. Operations 1964-69; Asst. to Vice Pres. Finance, Consumers' Gas, Toronto 1969, Mgr. Non-Utility Operations 1971, Mgr. Metrop. Toronto 1973, Vice Pres. Operations 1973, Sr. Vice Pres. Operations 1978; Exec. Vice Pres., 1981; mem. Assn. Prof. Engrs. Prov. Ont.; Candn. Gas Assn. (2nd Vice Chmn. and Dir.); Ont. Natural Gas Assn. (Past Pres.); Bd. Trade Metrop. Toronto; Protestant; recreations: racquet sports, fitness, bridge, golf; Clubs: Mississauga Golf & Country; Ontario Racquets; Engineers'; Cambridge; Home: 1411 Birchwood Dr., Mississauga, Ont. L5J 1T2; Office: (P.O. Box 90) 4200, 1 First Canadian Pl., Toronto, Ont. M5X 1C5.

MARTIN, Rochfort Kirwan, B.A.; investment counsel; b. Victoria, B.C., 3 Nov. 1908; s. Alexis Francis Ramsay and Emilie Alice Innocent (Mason) M.; e. Univ. Sch., Victoria, B.C. (1922-26); McGill Univ. (Hons. in Econ.) 1930; m. Laura Helen, d. Dr. A. A. Fletcher, Toronto, Ont., 20 June 1953; children: Stephen Richard, Caroline Mary (Mrs. R. Duncanson); CHRMN., MARTIN, LUCAS & SEAGRAM LTD., establ. 1952; Dir. Cox Systems Ltd.; Reporter, Victoria Daily Times, 1928-30; Invest. Dept. Sun Life Assurance Co. of Canada, Montreal, 1930-35; Secy. Newsprint Assn. of Canada, Montreal, 1935-41; Economist, Jt. Econ. Comte. of Can. and U.S., 1941-42; Special Consultant, Dept. of Trade & Commerce, Ottawa, 1945; Vice Pres., Canadian Management Co. and Canadian Corporate Management Co., Toronto, 1945-52; served in 2nd World War, Candn. Inf. Corps, rank of Capt., 1942-45; Dir., Toronto Mendelssohn Choir: mem. Adv. Bd. Nat. Ballet Guild Can.; Vice-Chrmn. St. George's Coll., Toronto; Kappa Alpha; Anglican; recreations: fishing, shooting, golf; Clubs: Toronto; York; Toronto Golf; Badminton & Racquet; Beaver Fishing; Home: 31 Dunloe Rd., Toronto, Ont. M4V 2W4; Office: 48 Yonge St., Toronto, Ont. M5E 1G9

MARTINEAU, Jean, C.C. (1969), Q.C., LL.L, D.C.L., LL.D.; b. Montreal, Que., 6 Oct. 1895; s. Hon. P.G. and Emma (Charbonneau) M.; e. Univ. of Montreal, B.A., B.C.L., D.C.L.; LL.D. Montreal, Dalhousie, Laval; COUNSEL, MARTINEAU WALKERHon. Dir., Royal Trust Co., Dir., The Readers Digest Assn. (Can.) Ltd.; called to Bar P.Q. 1919; cr. Q.C. 1929; Bâtonnier of Bar of Montreal and Bar of Que. 1953-54; Chrmn., Can. Council 1964-69; Chrmn. Adv. Council, Adm. Justice of P.Q.

1965-68; mem., Extve. Comte., Montreal Museum of Fine Arts; Vice Pres., Italian Chamber Comm. in Montreal; Pres., Club Gastronomic Prosper Montagné; Liberal; Clubs: Mount Royal; Garrison (Quebec); Rideau (Ottawa); Home: Apt. 5, 2156 Sherbrooke St. W., Montreal, Que. H3H 1G7; Office: Suite 3400, Stock Exchange Tower, Place Victoria, Montreal, Que.

MARTINEAU, Mr. Justice Paul, P.C. (Can.), J.C.S., Q.C., B.A., LL.L., K.C.S.G.; advocate; b. Bryson, Que., 10 April 1921; s. Aphonse and Lucienne (Lemieux) M.; e. St. John's Sch., Campbell's Bay; Ottawa Univ., B.A. 1941; Univ. of Montreal, LL.L. 1949; m. Hélène, d. Richard Neclaw, Poland, 3 Jan. 1946; two d. Alice, Gabrielle; JUSTICE, QUE. SUPERIOR COURT 1980- ; former Dir., Morrison Lamothe Bakery Ltd.; Télécable Laurentian Inc.; Pres., Astra Research Centre Inc.; read law with Hon. Edouard Asselin, Q.C., and the late John Crankshaw, Q.C., called to the Bar of Que. 1949; cr. Q.C. 1966; practised for one year in Montreal with late John Crankshaw, Q.C.; private practice, Campbell's Bay 1950-66; Hull, Que. 1966-80; apptd. Crown Attorney for Pontiac District in 1950-58; Past Pres. and Founder of Campbell's Bay Chamber of Comm.; Past Pres., Candn. Legion No. 162; Pontiac Br.; served in 2nd World War with R.C.A.F. 1942-46; 1st el. to H.C. for Pontiac-Témiscamique, g.e. March 1958; re-el. 1962, 1963; def. cand. g.e. 1965; apptd. Parlty. Secy. to the Prime Minister, 1959; Depy. Speaker of the H. of C., Jan. 1962; Min. of Mines and Tech. Surveys, Aug. 1962-Apl. 1963; mem., Que. Royal Comn. of Inquiry on Adm. of Justice 1967-69; mem., Candn. Bar Assn.; Commonwealth Parlty. Assn.; Inter Parlty. Union; K. of C. (4th degree); P. Conservative; Roman Catholic; recreations: painting, travelling, prospecting; Home: 1204 Mountain Road, Lucerne port, Alymer, Quebec. Office: Palais de Justice, 1, Notre Dame St. E., Montreal, Que.

MARTINO, Rocco Leonard, M.Sc., Ph.D., P.Eng.; management consultant; b. Toronto, Ont., 25 June 1929; s. Domenic and late Josephine (DiGuilio) M.; e. Univ. of Toronto, B.Sc. (Math & Physics) 1951, M.Sc. (Applied Math) 1952, Ph.D. (Inst. of Aerophysics) 1955; m. Barbara Italia, d. Alfred and Esther (Tucci) D'Iorio, Philadelphia. Pa., 2 Sept. 1961; four s. Peter Domenic, Joseph Alfred, Paul Gerard, John Francis; PRESIDENT, R. L. MARTINO & CO. LTD. since 1964; Pres. XRT Inc., Philadelphia; Chrmn. XRT Ltd., Toronto; Prof. of Math., New York Univ., Govt. Research Fellow and Consultant, 1951-56; Dir., Univac Computing Centers, Toronto, 1956-59; Prof. of Math., Univ. of Waterloo, 1959-62, and Prof. of Engn. & Dir., Systems Engn. there 1964-65; Pres., Mauchly Assoc., Can. Ltd., Toronto and Vice Pres., Mauchly Assoc., Can. Ltd., Toronto and Vice Pres., Mauchly Assoc., Inc., Ft. Washington, Pa., 1959-62; N.Y. Mgr.-Advanced Systems, Olin Mathieson Chem. Corp., 1962-65; Pres. and Chrmn. Bd., Information Industries 1967-70; Chrmn., Information Science Industries, Canada, Ltd. 1968-70; Consultant, State of Ill., five-year computer-use plan 1970-71; Chrmn., Task Force on Computer Use in Higher Educ.; Bd. of Higher Educ., Ill., Lectr, on computers and mang. topics. Can., U.S., Europe and Mexico; awarded a no. of scholarships and fellowships; author of "Finding the Critical Path," "Applied Operational Planning", "Allocating and Scheduling Resources", "Critical Path Networks", "Critical Path Network Analysis", "Resources Management", "Dynamic Costing", "Project Management", "MIS-Management Information Systems", "Decision Patterns", "Information Management: The Dynamics of MIS", "Methodology of MIS", "Personnel Information Systems", "Integrated Manufacturing Systems", "Impact-'70's", with John Gentile; numerous papers on mang. and planning; Dir., Computing Soc. Can. 1958-60; mem., Soc. Prof. Engrs.; Operation Research Soc. Am.; Assn. Computing Machines; Trustee, Yacht Club of Sea Isle City, 1980- ; (Commodore 1973-74); Commodore, S. Jersey Racing Assn., 1979-80; K. of C.; R. Catholic; recreations: reading, music, writing, sailing;

Clubs: Overbrook Golf and Country; Yacht Club of Sea Isle City; Commodore; S. Jersey Racing Assn.;

MARTITSCH, Karl; company executive; b. Ratnitz, Austria, 19 Nov. 1917; s. late Josef and late Martha (Schaunig) M.; e. Univs. of Vienna and Graz, Dipl. Engr.-Master Civil Engn.; came to Can. 1951; m. Beverly, d. Dr. G. E. Westman, Sault Ste. Marie, Ont., 12 Sept. 1953; Children: Karl Nicholas, Franchesca; SR. VICE PRES. & GEN. MGR. — SPECIAL PROJECTS, STONE & WEBSTER CANADA LTD. 1981- ; with Foundation Co. of Canada 1951-63; served as Field Engr., Resident Engr., Supt., Project Mgr. and Constr. Mgr.; joined present Co. 1963 as Vice-Pres. and Constr. Mgr.; Vice Pres. and Gen. Mgr. 1972; Dir., Nat. Constr. Indust. Devel. Foundation 1972-80; Candn. Construction Assn., 1972-76; Construction Labour Relations Assn., Ont., 1972-79; Toronto French School, 1973-78; mem. Construction Sector Comte., Economic Council of Can., 1973; ; mem., Assn. Prof. Engrs. Prov. Ont. (Citizenship Award 1973); Dir., mem. of Extve. Council and Mgmt. Comte., Constr. Safety Assn. Ont.; Indust. Contractors' Assn. Can. (Past Pres. & Dir.); mem., World Ski Council; Candn. rep. ski jumping & ski jump design; Olympic & F.I.S. ski jumping judge; recreations: skiing, tennis; Club: RCYC; Home: 55 Donwoods Dr., Toronto, Ont. M4N 2G3

MARTLAND, Hon. Ronald, LL.D.; judge; b. Liverpool, Eng., 10 Feb. 1907; s. John and Ada (Wild) M.; e. Univ. of Alta., B.A. 1926; LL.B. 1928, LL.D. 1964; Oxford Univ., B.A. 1930, B.C.L. 1931, M.A. 1935; m. Iris Euphemia Bury, 30 Mar. 1935; children: Patricia, John Gordon, Brigid Elizabeth; JUSTICE SUPREME COURT OF CANADA, since 1958; practised law at Edmonton, 1932 to 1958; Maj., 2nd Bn., Roy. Edmonton Regt. (Res.); read law with H. R. Milner, K.C., of Edmonton, Alta.; called to the Bar of Alta. 1932; cr. K.C. 1943; Hon. Prof., Faculty of Law, Univ. of Alberta and Univ. of Calgary; Bencher, Alta. Law Soc., 1948-58; Hon. Fellow, Hertford College, Oxford; mem., Canadian Bar Association; Freemason; Anglican; recreations: curling, golf; Clubs: Edmonton; Kiwanis; Rideau; Royal Ottawa Golf; Home: 55 Placel Road, Rockcliffe Park, Ont. K1L 5B9; Office: Supreme Court of Canada Bldg., Ottawa, Ont. K1A 0J1

MARTYN, Howe, M.A.; b. Bowmanville, Ont., 4 Aug. 1906; s. Dr. H. G. and Mabel (Rickard) M.; e. Victoria Coll., Univ. of Toronto, B.A. 1930; Christ Ch., Oxford, M.A. 1932; m. Marjorie, d. J. C. B. Horwood, Toronto, Ont., 24 June 1933; children: Nancy (Chadwick), Sylvia (Hubbard), Peter; Prof. Emeritus Internat. Business, American Univ., Washington, D.C.; sometime Ed. "Canadian Bookman" and contributor to "New York Times" Book Review; Guest Lecturer, Mass, Inst. of Tech.; author "Multinational Business Management"; "International Business Principles & Problems"; "Economie Sardonique"; Clubs: University; Travellers (London); Homes 4640 Tilden St. N.W., Washington, D.C. 20016 and Palgrave, Ont. L0N 1P0

MARTYN, Maxwell Pearson, C.D., B.A.; retired air force officer; b. Calgary, Alta., 29 June 1913; s. Angus Donald and Bernice Evelyn (Pearson) M.; e. Stanley Jones Pub. and Crescent Heights High Schs., Calgary, Alta.; Westmount and Victoria High Schs., Edmonton, Alta.; Univ. of Alta., B.A. (Hons.) 1936; m. 1stly, late Eva Macpherson, d. late J. H. Johnson, Edmonton, Alta., 8 June 1940; m. 2ndly, Virginia Helen Hopkirk, Montreal, Que., 25 Nov. 1967; children: Donald Macpherson, Heather Elizabeth; served with Candn. Mil., 1932-38; R.C.A.F. (Regular), 1938-65; posted to Planning Staff of R.A.F. Transport Command 1944 and later apptd. Sr. Air Staff Offr. of R.C.A.F. Transport Wing; served on staff of former N.W. Air Command H.Q., Ottawa, Ont. 1946; attended Jt. Services Staff Coll. in Eng., 1949; assigned to Edmonton, Alta., 1950 and held appt. of Sr. Air Staff Offr., N.W. Air Command until the organ. was replaced

by Tactical Air Command, at which time assigned the post of Chief Staff Offr.; assumed command of R.C.A.F. Stn., Penhold, Alta., 1954; trans. overseas as Chief Staff Offr., at the Candn. Jt. Staff, London, Eng., 1955; became Chief Staff Offr., at Training Command, H.Q., Winnipeg, Man., 1959; Chief of Training & Personnel Policy, Air Force H.Q., Dec. 1961; promoted Air Vice-Marshal, and named Depy. Chief Personnel, Candn. Forces, 1 Aug. 1964; apptd. Pres., Transair Ltd., July 1965, Chrmn. of Bd. and Pres., May 1967; Special Rep., New Business Devel., Richardson Securities of Can. 1968 until retirement 1970; Home: Dalbeth Farm, Merrickville, Ont. K0G 1N0

MASON, R. Larry, B.A.; banker; b. Winnipeg, Man. 12 June 1938; e. Univ. of Man. B.A. 1960; m. Diana 27 May 1967; children: Kelly, Stephen; VICE PRES. AND GEN. MGR. B.C. & YUKON REGION, THE BANK OF NOVA SCOTIA; Supvr. Invests. present Bank 1967, Asst. Gen. Mgr. Invests. 1973, Gen. Mgr. Invests. 1977, Gen. Mgr. Comm. Banking 1978, Vice Pres. and Gen. Mgr. Man. and N.W. Ont. Region 1978; mem. Candn. Council Christians & Jews, Un. Way; Vancouver Bd. Trade; Clubs: Shaughnessy Golf & Country; Vancouver; Arbutus; Canadian; Home: 4261 Musqueam Drive, Vancouver, B.C. V6N 3R8; Office: 11501 W. Georgia St., Vancouver, B.C. V6B 4N7.

MASON, Stanley George, B.Eng., Ph.D., F.C.I.C., F.R.S.C.; b. Montreal, P.Q., 20 March 1914; s. David MacCallum and Margaret (Fraser) M.; e. McGill Univ., B.Eng. (Chem.) 1936, Ph.D. 1939; m. Renata Vincenzi, 24 June 1969; two d. Cheryl, Andrea; Director, Applied Chemical Div., Pulp and Paper Inst. of Canada, and Head, Physical Chemistry Research Section, 1946-79; Prof., Chem. Dept., McGill Univ., since 1966; Lectr. in Chem., Trinity Coll., Hartford, Conn., 1939-41; Research Engr., Suffield Exper. Stn., Ralston, Alta. (Dept. of Nat. Defence) 1941-45; Scient., Atomic Energy Div., Nat. Research Council, 1945-46; Past Chrmn., Colloid and Surface Chem. Div., Am. Chem. Soc.; Fellow, Tech. Assn. Pulp and Paper Indust.; mem., Brit. and U.S. Socs. Rheology; written over 260 scient. and tech. papers based on his research; rec'd. Kendall Co. Award in Colloid Chem. 1967; Bingham Medal, Soc. of Rheology 1968; Anselme Payen Award, Am. Chem. Soc. 1969; Chem. Inst. Can. Medal 1973; Dunlop Award, Chem. Inst. Can. 1975; Foreign Assoc., Nat'l Academy of Eng. of the U.S.A. 1980; Howard N. Potts Medal, The Franklin Instit. 1980; Home: 12 Springfield Ave., Westmount, Que. H3Y 2L1; Office: McGill University, Montreal, Que. H3A 2A7

MASON, Vere K., B.Sc., B.Eng., P.Eng.; construction executive; b. N.S., 9 Dec. 1916; s. Reginald Holmes and Ella (Longley) M.; e. Mt. Allison Univ., B.Sc. 1939; McGill Univ., B.Eng. 1942 (awarded Brit. Assn. Medal); m. June, d. Harold Moses, 14 Feb. 1948; children: Elizabeth June, Linda Anne, David Vere, James Edward; PRESIDENT, GEN. MGR. AND DIR., V. K. MASON CONSTRUCTION LTD.; prior to gradn. worked on highway and bridge constr. then with Shawinigan Engineering Co. Ltd., Montreal; after gradn. joined Aluminum Company of Canada, Montreal, on structural design in connection with wartime expansion program; Constr. Mgr., George Hardy Ltd., Gen. Contractors, Toronto 1946; Chief Engr., Perini Ltd. 1953; Vice-Pres. 1959; served with R.C.N. 1942-46; rank at discharge Lt. (E) R.C.N.V.R.; mem. Engn. Inst. Can.; Assn. Prof. Engrs. Ont.; Bd. Trade Metrop. Toronto; Naval Offrs. Assn. of Can.; Phi Delta Theta; Anglican; Club: Donalda; Home: 27 Plymbridge Crescent, Willowdale, Ont. M2P 1P3; Office: 20 Eglinton Ave. W., Toronto, Ont. M4R 1K8

MASON, William Clifford, R.C.A.; film maker; artist; author; b. Winnipeg, Man. 21 Apl. 1929; s. late William Thomas Mason; e. Kelvin High Sch. 1947; Univ. of Man. Sch. of Art Dipl. in Fine Art 1951; m. Lorraine Joyce d.

late Duncan James Ferguson 16 May 1959; children: Paul, Becky; FILM DIR., NAT. FILM BD. 1975- ; Pres. Bill Mason Production Ltd.; Art Dir. Paul Phelan & Perry, Winnipeg 1961-66; film awards incl.: "Paddle to the Sea" 1st Prize Am. Film Festival (Children) N.Y. 1967; Salerno Internat. Festival 1st Prize (Information) 1967 (co-recipient); Children's Film Festival Tehran Golden Plaque 1967; Yorkton Internat. Film Festival Best Film 1967; Acad. Motion Picture Arts & Sciences Hollywood nominated Best Short Film 1968; Internat. Festival Films for Children La Plata Best Documentary 1968; Internat. Film Review Colombo Cert. Merit 1969; Internat. Festival Short Films Philadelphia Award 1971; Montreal Soc. Filmmakers Award 1966; "The Rise and Fall of the Great Lakes" SFTA London, Eng. 1971; Candn. Amateur Film Assn. Cert. Merit 1971; VII Fest. internacional de cine documental y experimental Montevideo 1st Prize 1971; 2nd Internat. Environmental Pollution Exhn. Best Film Winsted, Conn. 1975; 1st Internat. Film Festival Tel Aviv Cert. Merit 1969; 10th Internat. Yorkton Film Festival Prize 1969; 12th Am. Film Festival N.Y. 1970 Blue Ribbon; San Francisco Water Pollution Conf. Plaque 1970; 6th Internat. Scient., Educ. & Pedagogical Films Tehran 1st Prize 1969; "Blake" Candn. Film Awards Best Film under 30 mins. 1970; Melbourne Film Festival Grand Prix 1971; Yorkton Internat. Film Festival Golden Sheaf 1971; Acad. Motion Picture Arts & Sciences nominated Best Short Film 1970; "Cry of the Wild" 1st Internat. Film Festival Human Environment Montreal Dipl. Merit 1973; "Wolf Pack" Univ. of Mont. Film Festival Best Prof. Film 1978; "In Search of the Bowhead Whale" Am. Film Festival N.Y. Blue Ribbon 1975; Virgin Islands Internat. Film Festival Best TV Documentary 1975; Univ. of Mont. Film Festival Highest Merit 1978; Black Orchid Film Festival Seattle Best Film Exploration & Discovery 1978; "Face of the Earth" Am. Film Festival N.Y. Blue Ribbon 1977; "Death of a Legend" Candn. Film Awards Etrog 1971; Internat. Festival Short Films Philadelphia Award Merit 1971; Am. Film Festival N.Y. Red Ribbon 1972; II Jordadas Internacionales de cine cientifico y didactico Madrid Dipl. Honour 172; Yorkton Internat. Film Festival Awards (2) 1973; Internat. Festival Tourism & Folklore Films Brussels Gold Medal 1972; 22nd Internat. Festival Trento, Italy Award 1974; "Path of the Paddle" series, San Francisco Internat. Film Festival Special Jury Award 1977; Oberhausen Sports Film Festival W. Germany Grand Prix 1977; SFTA London, Eng. Best Specialized Film 1978; "Song of the Paddle" Candn. Film Awards 3 Etrogs 1978; author "Path of the Paddle" 1980; "When the Wolves Sang" 1980; Protestant; recreations: canoeing, hockey, skiing, broomball; Address: Meach Lake Rd., Old Chelsea, Que. J0X 2N0.

MASON, William L., M.Sc.; petroleum executive; b. Meridian, Miss. 29 Nov. 1926; s. Thomas Harrell and Elizabeth Lee (Suttle) M.; e. Univ. of Ala. B.Sc. (Petrol. Engn.) 1951, M.Sc. (Engn.) 1956; m. Jane Elizabeth Spann 23 Dec. 1951; children: William L., Jr., Elizabeth Mason Cummings; PRES. AND GEN. MGR. MOBIL OIL CANADA LTD. 1981- ; Dir. The Island Development Co.; Les Peintures Mobil du Quebec Ltee.; Mobil Chemical Canada Ltd.; Mobil Energy Minerals Canada Ltd.; Mobil Ventures Ltd.; Rainbow Pipe Line Co. Ltd.; Sovosco Petroleum Ltd.; TransOcean Oil Canada Ltd.; Instr. in Petroleum Engn. Univ. of Ala. 1953-56, Asst. and Assoc. Prof. 1958-61; Research Technol. Field Research Lab, Magnolia Petroleum Co. Dallas 1956-58 and Socony Mobil Oil Co. Inc. Dallas 1961-62; Engr. Mobil Oil Canada Ltd. 1962 Calgary, Production Supvr. Swift Current 1965, Chief Exploitation Engr. Calgary 1966, Evaluation Advisor and Production Coordinator 1967; Planning Analyst N. Am. Div. Mobil Oil Corp. New York 1968, Sr. Production Advisor Internat. Div. 1969-72, Production Mgr. 1975-76; Planning Mgr., Production Operations Mgr., Production Mgr. Mobil Oil Libya Ltd. Tripoli 1972-75; Prod. Mgr., Mobil Oil Corp. 75-76; Exploration and Producing Mgr. Mobil Oil A.G., Hamburg 1976-80; Gen. Mgr. Mobil Energy Minerals, Denver 1980; Gen. Mgr.

Mobil Uranium/Minerals 1980-81; mem. Soc. Petrol. Engrs.; Assoc. of Professional Engineers, Geologists & Geophysicists of Alberta; recreations: hiking, swimming, tennis; Office: 330 Fifth Ave. S.W., Calgary, Alta. T2P 2J7.

MASSE, J.-Paul; investment dealer; b. La Pocatière (Kamouraska), Qué., 8 Jan. 1929; e. Coll. Ste-Anne-de-la-Pocatière; Académie de Qué.; Univ. Laval; m. Louise Baribeau, 3 July 1954; children: Michel, Claude; PRESIDENT AND GEN. MGR., GRENIER, RUEL & CIE INC.; mem., Invest. Dealers' Assn. Can.; Montreal Stock Exchange; Dir., Textiles Dionne Inc.; David Lord Ltée; Bibby Foundry Ltd.; Geo-Air Ltée; Pres., Masseco Ltée, Québec 1934-1984; Treas., Aero Photo Inc.; Secy-Treas. Produits d'Architecture de Qué. (1979) Inc.; served with RCN (R); Past Chrmn., Invest. Dealers Assn. Can. (Que. Dist.); mem., Anciens de Laval; Chamber Comm.; Conseil du Patronat du Qué.; R. Catholic; recreations: skiing, yachting, tennis; Clubs: Garrison; Rotary; Yacht Club de Que. (Past Commodore); Home: 1324, des Gouverneurs, Sillery, Québec, Qué. G1T 2G5; Office: 1126 Chemin Saint-Louis, Sillery, Qué. G1T 2W2

MASSE, Lucien, C.A., LL.D.; b. Hull, Que., 6 June 1903; s. Gehusse and Elise (Fournier) M.; e. Univ. of Ottawa; Hon. LL.D.; FOUNDER, MASSE, VIEN, FLEURY, FORGET & COMPANY (Chartered Accts., estbd. 1926); Past Pres., La Société Gazifère de Hull Inc.; Past Dir., Candn. National Ins. Co.; The Commerce Gen. Ins. Co.; The Canadian Mercantile Assurance Co.; J. B. Harper Ltd.; M. Loeb Ltd.; Indst. Life Assnce. Co.; Alfred Lambert Inc.; Past Pres., Candn. Welfare Council; past mem., Montreal Board of Trade; Hull Chamber of Comm.; Institute of Chartered Accountants of Quebec and Ont.; French Canadian Institute; Commdr. and Superior Offr., Order of St. Gregory the Great; K. of C. (4th Degree); Roman Catholic; recreations: golf, fishing; Clubs: Rivermead Golf; La Gorce Golf, Miami Beach, Fla.; Matabi Fish and Game; University (Ottawa); Home: Apt. 801, 100 Bronson, Ottawa, Ont. K1R 6G8; Office: 112 Promenade de Portage, Hull, Que. J8X 2K1

MASSÉ, Marcel, B.A., LL.B., B.Phil.; Canadian public servant; b. Montreal, Que. 23 June 1940; e. Univ. of Montreal B.A. 1958; McGill Univ. LL.B. 1961; Univ. of Warsaw Dipl. in Internat. Law 1962; Oxford Univ. B.Phil. (Econ. 1966; Ecoles des Hautes Etudes Commerciales de Montréal Dipls. in Foreign Relations, Spanish, German, Italian & Econ. m. Josée M'Baye 17 July 1965; four children; PRES., CIDA, 1982- ; called to Bar of Que. 1963; served in Adm. and Econ., World Bank, Washington 1967-71; Econ. Advisor, Privy Council, Ottawa 1971-73; Depy. Min. of Finance, N.B. 1973-74, Chrmn. of Cabinet Secretariat N.B. 1974-77; Depy. Secy. to Cabinet for Fed.-Prov. Relations 1977-79; Depy. Secy. to Cabinet (Operations) 1979; Clerk of Privy Council and Secy. to Cabinet 1979-80; Pres., Can. Internat. Devel. Agency 1980-81; Home: 20 Chemin D'Amour, Aylmer, Que. Office: 200 Promenade du Portage, Hull, Que. K1A 0G4.

MASSEY, Arnold B., A.F.C.; b. Toronto, Ont., 26 July 1897; s. Arthur L. and Mary Ethel (Bonnell) M.; e. St. Andrews Coll. and Univ. of Toronto Schs., m. Dorothy, d. late Charles E. Dewey, 7 June 1924; children: Mrs. Charles H. Barrett, Arnold D.; former Vice President and Dir., Mills, Spence & Co. Ltd., Toronto, Ont. (Invest. Dealers); Gov., Invest. Bankers' Assn. of America, 1959-61; served in 1st World War in Candn. Army, R.N.A.S. and as Captain in R.A.F. overseas; Conservative; Anglican; recreations: golf, yachting, fishing; Clubs: R.C.Y.C.; Toronto Hunt; Home: Apt. No. 305, 581 Avenue Rd., Toronto, Ont. M4V 2K4

MASSEY, Geoffrey, B.A., M.Arch., F.R.A.I.C., A.B.C., R.C.A.; architect; b. London, Eng. 29 Oct. 1924; s. Raymond and Margery (Fremantle) M.; came to Can. 1942; e.

Harvard Coll. B.A. 1949; Harvard Graduate Sch. of Design M.Arch. 1952; m. Ruth Maud d. late Lawrence Killam 21 Sept. 1955; children: Raymond Hart, Vincent Lawrence, Nathaniel Killam, Eliza Ann; PARTNER, COAL HARBOUR ARCHITECTURAL GROUP 1975- ; Princ. private arch. practice 1956-63, 1972-75; Partner, Erickson/Massey 1963-72; Ald. City of Vancouver and mem. Greater Vancouver Regional Dist. Bd. 1973-75; Trustee, Vancouver Art Gallery 1973-80; Granville Island Trust Vancouver 1975- ; rec'd numerous arch. awards; served with Candn. Army 1943-45; mem. Arch. Inst. B.C.; recreations: skiing, sailing; Clubs: Vancouver; W. Vancouver Yacht; Home: 7290 Arbutus Pl., W. Vancouver, B.C. V7W 2L6; Office: 1661 Duranleau St., Vancouver, B.C. V6H 3S3.

MASSEY, Hart Parkin Vincent, M.A. (Oxon.), B.Arch., R.C.A., F.R.A.I.C.; b. Toronto, Ont. 30 March 1918; s. Charles Vincent and Alice Stuart (Parkin) M.; e. St. Alban's Sch. Washington, D.C. 1929; Upper Can. Coll. Toronto 1935; Balliol Coll. Oxford Univ. M.A. 1939; Univ. of Toronto B.Arch 1951 (Pilkington Scholarship 1951, R.A.I.C. Arch. Guild Gold Medal); m. Frances Melodie d. Henry Willis-O'Connor 4 Aug. 1947; children: Lillias Caroline, Jonathan Hart; arch. practice Ottawa 1953-70; recipient Massey Medals for Arch. 1958, 1964; Ministry of Pub. Works Design Award 1968; Ont. Assn. Archs. Ottawa Chapter Design Awards (3); Chrmn. Massey Foundation; Gov. Massey Hall Toronto; Sr. Fellow Massey Coll. Univ. of Toronto; craftsman (lost wax casting); co-author, "The Craftsman's Way"; served with RCAF Brit., France, Belgium, Holland 1939-45; rec'd Croix de Guerre (France); mem. Ont. Assn. Archs.; recreations: books, dogs, travel, canal cruising; Home: Durham House, R.R.1, Port Hope, Ont. L1A 3V5.

MASSEY, Raymond Hart, Litt.D., LL.D., D.F.A., D.Hum., D.Hum.Litt.; actor, producer and director, b. Toronto, Ont., 30 August 1896; s. late Chester Daniel and Anna (Vincent) M.; e. Upper Canada Coll.; Appleby Coll.; University of Toronto; Balliol Coll., Oxford; Lafayette Coll., Hon. Litt.D. 1939; LL.D. Queen's 1949; Litt.D. Hobart Coll., Smith Coll.; D.F.A. Ripon Coll. 1956, Northwestern 1959; D.Hum. Am. Internat. Coll. of Mass. 1960; D.Hum. Litt. Wooster Coll. 1966; m. Margery Fremantle 1921 (dissolved); 1 s. Geoffrey; m. Adrianne Allen 1929 (dissolved); 1 s. Daniel, 1 d. Anna; m. Dorothy Ludington, 1939; after short period in agric. machinery business made first prof. appearance in London 1922; has appeared in many plays incl. "At Mrs. Beam's", "Saint Joan", "The Man in Possession", "Spread Eagle", "Five Star Final", "Rats of Norway", "The Constant Nymph", "Idiot's Delight", "I Never Sang for my Father" (final London stage appearance) 1970; Dir. 28 stage productions in U.K. incl. "The Silver Tassie", "Grand Hotel", "Late Night Final", "The Sacred Flame" and in New York played "Hamlet", "The Shining Hour" (also in London), "Ethan Frome", "Abe Lincoln in Illinois", "Doctor's Dilemma", "Candida", "Lovers and Friends", "Pygmalion"; played in "Night of the Iguana", Los Angeles 1976; has appeared in over 70 films including "The Old Dark House", "The Scarlet Pimpernel", "Things to Come", "Hurricane", "The Prisoner of Zenda", "Drums", "Sante Fe Trail", "Action in the North Atlantic", "49th Parallel", "Possessed", "Mourning Becomes Electra", "East of Eden"; countless radio and TV performances incld. Dr. Gillespie in "Dr. Kildare" series; author of "The Hanging Judge", (play on the novel by Bruce Hamilton) produced London 1952 and on U.K. and U.S. TV; author of "When I was Young" 1976; "A Hundred Different Lives"; served in World War 1, 1915-19 as Lieut. C.F.A.; wounded in Belgium 1916; Instr. in Field Arty. to R.O.T.C. at Princeton and Yale Univ., 1917-18; with C.E.F., Siberia, 1918-19; World War II served as N.D.H.Q. in Adj. Gen's. br. 1942-43 with rank of Major; became citizen of U.S., Mar. 1944; Clubs: Century; Gar-

rick (London, Eng.); Address: 913 N. Beverly Drive, Beverly Hills, Calif.

MASSON, Claude, M.A.; university professor; economist; b. Quebec City, Que., 2 Oct. 1937; s. J. Maurice and Simonne (Laveau) M.; e. Laval. Univ,. B.A. 1956, M.A. (Econ.) 1960; Harvard Univ., 1960-63; m. Hélène, d. J. R. Proulx, 5 Sept. 1960; children: Bertrand, Benoît, Vincent, Valérie; Prof., Dept. of Economics, Laval Univ. mem.; Walter L. Gordon's Task Force on Structure of Canadian Industry and Foreign Ownership; mem., Candn. Econ. Assn.; Soc. Canadienne de Science Econ.; Assn. Économistes du Que.; R. Catholic; Home: 730 Claude Picher, Ste-Foy, Que. G1V 3J6

MASTERMAN, Jack Verner, B. Com.; insurance executive; b. Calgary, Alta. 8 Aug. 1930; s. late Lawrence Arthur and late Mary Francis Georgina (Robinson) M.; e. Kelvin H.S., Winn.; Univ. of Manitoba B. Com. 1953; m. Isabel Christine d. late Clarence Richard Kaitting 25 June 1953; children: Mary Christine (Murray), Lawrence Richard, Sheila Claire, Keith Charles; PRES. AND CHIEF OPERATING OFFR., THE MUTUAL LIFE ASSURANCE CO. OF CANADA since 1982; Chrmn., Extve. Financial Counselling Ltd.; Dir., Mu-Cana Investment Counselling Ltd.; Dir., R.D.C. Property Services Ltd.; Dir., M.L.C. Oil and Gas Ltd.; joined Mutual Life Assurance in 1953; Acturial Asst., 1958; Asst. Actuary, 1960; Assoc. Actuary, 1964; Actuary, 1966; Extve. Offr. (Individual Ins.), 1969; Vice Pres. Operations, 1971; Vice Pres. Individual Ins., 1975; Extve. Vice Pres. 1978; Dir of company, 1980; Chrmn., Consumer Relations Cmte. of Candn. Life and Health Insurance Assoc., Dir., Kitchener-Waterloo Art Gallery; Bd. of Management, Victorian Order of Nurses; Fellow, Candn. Inst. of Actuaries; Fellow, Soc. of Actuaries; Protestant; Club: National (Toronto); Home: 163 Tennyson Place, Waterloo, Ont. N2L 2T2; Office: 227 King St. S., Waterloo, Ont. N2J 4C5.

MASTERS, Donald Campbell Charles, M.A., Ph.D., D.C.L., F.R.S.C. (1953); university prof.; b. Shelburne, Ont., 8 Feb. 1908; s. Rev. Charles Keith, M.C., and Jean Campbell (Paterson) M.; e. Univ. of Toronto, B.A. 1930, M.A. 1931, MacKenzie Fellowship in Hist. 1931-32; Oxford Univ., Ph.D. 1935 (I.O.D.E. Overseas Scholarship); D.C.L. Bishop's Univ. 1975; m. Marjorie Winnifred, d. Frederick Harold Walker, 9 Sept. 1942; children: Margaret, Jane, Mary Ann, Lois, Charles; holder of post-doctorial Fellowship, Social Science Res. Council 1936- 37; Lectr. in Hist., Queen's Univ., 1938-39; Un. Coll., Winnipeg, 1939-41; Assoc. Prof. 1941-44; Prof. of Hist., Bishop's Univ., 1944-66; Prof. Candn. Hist. Univ. Guelph 1966-74; Visiting Prof. Simon Fraser Univ. 1974-75; Prof. Emeritus, Univ. of Guelph 1977; mem., Canadian History Association (mem. of Council 1956-59); Canadian Institute of Internat. Affairs (Chrmn., Sherbrooke-Lennoxville Br. 1947); author of "The Reciprocity Treaty of 1854", 1937; "The Rise of Toronto", 1947; "The Winnipeg General Strike", 1950; "Bishop's University: The First Hundred Years", 1950; "A Short History of Canada", 1958; "Canada in World Affairs", vol. VIII, 1953-1955, 1959; "Protestant Church Colleges in Canada", 1966; del. to Ang. Gen. Synod, 1965, 1969, 1971, 1975, 1977, 1980; Anglican; Address: 19 Monticello Crescent, Guelph, Ont. N1G 2M1

MATAS, Hon. Roy Joseph, LL.M.; judge; b. Winnipeg, Man. 10 July 1920; s. Simon and Anna (Rozler) M.; e. Norquay Elem., Aberdeen Jr. High, St. John's High Sch. 1937; Univ. of Man. B.A. 1941, LL.B. 1946 (Gold Medal 1946), LL.M. 1953; m. Ruth Gloria d. late Dr. Samuel Herbert Churchill 25 June 1946; children: Tannis Susan Dunn, Carol Rosaline Brask, Saul Jonathan; JUDGE, COURT OF APPEAL MAN. since 1973; called to Bar of Man. 1946; practiced law Winnipeg 1946-67; apptd. to Court of Queen's Bench Man. 1967; has held various extve. positions civic and pub. comtes.; Dir. Nat. Lib.

Fed. 1966, Pres. Man. Lib. Party 1966-67; Nat. Vice Pres. Candn. Technion Soc. since 1976; mem. Winnipeg Sch. Bd. 1957-61; Chrmn. 1960-61; Pres. Man. Sch. Trustees Assn. 1960-Nat. Dir. Candn. Sch. Trustees Assn. 1961; Pres. Royal Winnipeg Ballet 1968-70, mem. Adv. Council since 1970; mem. Internat. Bd. Govs. Israel Inst. of Technol. since 1974; Chrmn. Man. Univs. Grad. Courses Appraisals Comte. 1976-77; R. J. Matas Chair of Bio-Medical Engn. established at Israel Inst. of Technology, 1976; occasional lectr. Man. Law Sch., Bar and Bench seminars and confs.; served as Chrmn. various comtes. Man. Bar Assn., Candn. Bar Assn.; Bencher, Law Soc. Man.; Pres. Candn. Inst. for Adm. of Justice 1977-78; author various reports, articles; mem. B'Nai B'Rith; YMHA (Bd. Govs.); Hebrew; recreations: gardening, photography, reading, tennis; Home: 424 Bower Blvd., Winnipeg, Man. R3P 0L5.

MATCHETT, John Boyd, B.A.; b. Hamilton, Ont. 19 June 1923; e. Univ. of Toronto Schs.; Univ. of Toronto, B.A.; London (Eng.) Sch. of Econs.; m. Ottilie Rose, d. late George Meredith Huycke, Q.C., 13 March 1954; children: John, Robin, Rosalie; PRESIDENT AND DIR., CARA OPERATIONS LTD. (estbd. 1961), since 1969; Dir., Foodcorp Ltd.; Winco Restaurants Ltd.; Keg Restaurants Ltd.; Simpark Lands Ltd.; with Massey-Ferguson, Canada and U.S.A., 1948, Europe, Eng. and France, 1949-52; Gen. Mgr., one of their operating Divs., France 1955-59; with Urwick-Currie Ltd., Toronto, Ont., 1959-62; Gen. Mgr., Cara Operations Ltd., Toronto, June 1962; Vice-Pres., June 1963; Dir., Jan. 1964; Extve. Vice-Pres. 1965; served as Lieut. during 2nd World War with R.C.N.V.R., 1942-45; now holds retired rank, Lt. Commdr.; Kappa Alpha; Anglican; recreations: skiing, squash, tennis; Clubs: Badminton & Racquet; University (Pres. 1968-69); Osler Bluffs Ski (Dir.); Home: 43 Dunvegan Rd., Toronto, Ont. M4V 2P5; Office: 55 York St., Toronto, Ont. M5J 1S5

MATHERS, Andrew Sherlock, B.arch.; architect; b. Toronto, Ont., 16 Sept. 1934; s. Alvin Sherlock and the late Nesta Prudhomme (Verner) S.; e. Oriole Park Pub. Sch.; Upper Can. Coll.; Univ. of Toronto, B.Arch., 1959; m. Suzanne Freemont, d. the late Freemont Whitfield Doan, 16 Sept. 1961; one s. Andrew Freemont; two d., Mary Verner; Jane Freemont; PARTNER, MATHERS & HALDENBY, since 1961; became Jr. Partner with present Co., 1961; York Univ. Residence (Glendon Campus), 1962; design and constr., Queen's Univ. Library Wing, 1963; in charge design and constr., Can. Permanent Trust Co. Office Bldg., Ottawa, Ont., 1963; and Toronto-Dominion Bank Bldg., Sparks St., Ottawa, Ont., 1964; Faculty Club Bldg., Univ. of Waterloo; Athletic Complex, Wilfred Laurier Univ.; Royal Mil. Coll., Massey Library; Geology Bldg. and Mining Bldg., Queen's Univ.; Seneca Coll.; Humanities & Soc. Sc. Research Library, Laidlaw Library, Balmer Neilly Library, Wycliff Coll., Univ. of Toronto; North York Bd. of Educ. Bldg.; mem., Ont. Assn. of Arch.; Fellow, Royal Arch. Inst. of Can.; Arch. Div. Metrop. Toronto, Un. Appeal; Anglican; Delta Upsilon; recreations: skiing, tennis; Clubs: Toronto Hunt; Badminton & Racquet; University; Home: 53 RiverView Dr., Toronto, Ont. M4N 3C8; Office: 10 St. Mary St., Toronto, Ont. M4Y 1P9

MATHERS, John H., B.A.Sc., M.S.; executive; b. Penticton, B.C., 18 July 1923; s. Fred D. and Gladys C. (Robinson) M.; e. Pub. and High Schs., Vancouver; Univ. of B.C.; Univ. of Toronto, B.A.Sc.; Ore. State Univ., M.S.; m. Annamarie, d. A. S. Fumerton, Lethbridge, A.ta., 22 June 1949; children: three; PRESIDENT, ROYAL CITY FOODS LTD., since 1972; has served since 1949 in food processing indust. (buyer, production, production engr., sales and subsequently Vice Pres. Marketing); served with Candn. Army during World War II, rank Lt.; Past Pres., YM-YWCA and Kinsmen Club, New Westminster, B.C.; Anglican; recreations: golf, skiing, hunting; Clubs:

University; Vancouver Golf; Home: 119 E. 8th Ave., New Westminster, B.C. V3L 4J6; Office: 3376 Bainbridge, Burnaby, B.C. V5A 2T4

MATHESON, Edward Clay, B.A.; publisher; b. Toronto, Ont., 24 Aug. 1931; s. William Bell and Anna (Pasika) M.; e. Queen's Univ. B.A. 1957; Indust. Relations Dipl. 1958; m. Eunice A., d. Frederick A. Thorne, 23 April 1975; s. David Edward; EXEC. VICE PRES. AND DIR., AMPERSAND PUBLISHING SERVICES INC. 1973- ; McGraw-Hill Co. of Canada Ltd., Toronto, College Div., 1962; Gen. Mgr., Methuen Publications, 1964-71; former Pres., Collier-Macmillan Canada, 1971-73; served with R.C.A.F., 1948-50, rank Flying Offr.; Chrmn., Extve. Comte., Candn. Book Publishers' Council; recreation: golf; Home: R.R. 1, Caledon, Ont. L0N 1C0

MATHESON, Hon. Joel Rand, Q.C., M.L.A., B.Com., LL.B.; politician; b. 1930; e. Dalhousie Univ. B.Com. 1952, LL.B. 1954; m.; 3 children; MIN. OF FINANCE, N.S.; read law with Barss & Hatfield; called to Bar of N.S. 1954; cr. Q.C. 1980; Pres., Hillis Oil Sales Ltd. 1955-79; el. M.L.A. for Halifax-Bedford Basin 1978; Pres. Bd. Govs. Izaak Walton Killam Hosp. for Children 1974-77, mem. Bd. 17 yrs.; Past Pres. Halifax Dartmouth Constr. Assn.; mem. Halifax Bd. Trade; Anglican; Home: 30 Robert Allen Dr., Halifax, N.S. B3M 3G8; Office: Provincial Bldg., Hollis St., Halifax, N.S. B3J 2N3.

MATHESON, Col. His Hon. John Ross, C.D., M.A., LL.M., F.S.A. Scot.; judge; b. Arundel, Que. 14 Nov. 1917; s. Rev. Dr. Alexander Dawson and Gertrude (McCuaig) M.; e. Queen's Univ. B.A., Distinguished Service Award 1977; Osgoode Hall Law Sch.; Mount Allison Univ. M.A.; Univ. of W. Ont. LL.M.; m. Edith May Bickley 4 Aug. 1945; children: Duncan, Wendy (Mrs. Michael Simpson), Jill (Mrs. Brent Perry), Donald, Roderick, Murdoch; JUDGE CO. COURT OF LANARK 1978- ; Judge Judicial District of Ottawa-Carleton, 1968-78; called to Bar of Ont. 1948; cr. Q.C. 1967; former law practice Matheson, Henderson & Hart, Brockville, Ont.; served Overseas with 1st Regt. R.C.H.A., wounded, and retired 1944; Hon. Col. RCA; Genealogist Priory of Can. Most Venerable Order St. John of Jerusalem; el. to H. of C. for Leeds by-el. 1961, re-el. g.e. 1962, 1963, 1965, def. 1968; attended 16th Session UN Gen. Assembly; Chrmn. Commons Standing Comte. on External Affairs 1963-65; Parlty. Secy. to Prime Min. 1966-68; named Brockville Citizen of the yr. 1967; Hons. incl. Kt. of Justice Order of St. John; Kt. Commdr. of Merit Order of St. Lazarus; Armigerous by Lyon Court and Coll. of Arms; Companion of Most Hon. Order of Meritorious Heritage; Hon. Vice Pres. Un. Empire Loyalists' Assn. Can.; Hon. Secy. Candn. Amateur Boxing Assn.; Life Fellow, Royal Econ. Soc.; Fellow, Heraldry Soc. Can.; Life mem. Candn. Bar Assn.; Nat. Trust for Scotland; Roy. Cdn. Arty. Assn; Life Gov. Candn. Bible Soc.; mem. Candn. Olympic Assn.; Freemason, Scottish Rite 33°; author, "Canada's Flag: a Search for a Country", 1980; awarded Commonwealth Heraldry Bd. Essay Prize, 1980, for Beley Mem. Lecture (Heraldry Soc. Can.); Montreal Medal 1981; Phi Delta Phi; United Church; Home: Rideau Ferry, Ont. K0G 1W0 Office: Judge's Chambers, Court House, Perth, Ont. K7H 1G1

MATHESON, Wallace A., B.A.; publisher; b. Montreal, Que., 29 July 1931; s. Alexander G. and Grace de F. (Wallace) M.; e. St. Lambert (Que.) Public and High Schs., 1937-47; Acadia Univ., B.A. 1953; m. Martha Ann, d. Fred Driscoll, Montreal, Que., 25 May 1957; children: Heather Ann, Alexander James, Martha Jean; DIRECTOR, PRENTICE-HALL INC., U.S.A., since 1976; joined Prentice-Hall Inc. as Candn. Field Rep., Coll. Div., 1953 becoming Candn. Dist. Mgr. 1958; Vice Pres., 1961; Pres., 1965; mem. Aurora Centennial Adv. Comte., 1962-63; Pres., Candn. Univ. Press, 1952-53; Candn. Book Publishers' Council (Pres. 1972); Pres. (1966-67 and 1967-

68) and Dir. (1968-69), Candn. Lib. Exhibitors' Assn.; Gov., Candn. Copyright Inst. 1973-74; Chrmn., Candn. Bk. Design Comte. 1973-74, Dir. 1975-76; Dir., Assn. for Export Candn. Bks. 1973; Montreal Internat. Bk. Fair 1974-75; Freemason; Protestant; recreations: golf, reading; farming; Home: 8 Palomino Cr., Willowdale, Ont. M2K 1W1; Office: 1870 Birchmount Rd., Scarborough, Ont. M1P 2J7

MATHEWSON, Francis Alexander Lavens, C.M., B.Sc., M.D., M.A.C.P.; cardiologist; b. New Westminster, B.C., 1 Feb. 1905; s. Walter Hall and Marguerite Alexandra M.; e. St. Michaels Sch., Victoria, B.C. and Victoria Coll. there; Univ. of Manitoba, M.D. 1931 and B.Sc. (Med.) 1933; m. Elizabeth Roos, d. Robert Greer Baird, 25 Apl. 1936; children: Elizabeth Jane, Frances Diana; Director, Univ. of Manitoba Follow-Up Study; Assoc. Prof. of Med., Faculty of Med., Univ. of Man.; Physician Winnipeg Gen. Hosp. (retired); served in 2nd World War, 1940-45 with R.C.A.F. as Deputy Dir. of Med. Services; Past Pres., Defence Med. Assn. of Can.; Candn. Cardiovascular Soc.; Assn. Life Ins. Med. Dirs. of Am.; past Pres. Man. Museum of Man and Nature; Diplomate of Am. Bd. of Public Health, Aviation Med.; Fellow, Aerospace Med. Assn. of Am.; former Regional Gov., Am. Coll. of Phys.; former Trustee, Am. Coll. Cardiology; Zeta Psi; Clubs: Manitoba; St. Charles Country; Home: 283 Yale Ave., Winnipeg, Man. R3M 0L4; Office: 711 Medical Arts Bldg., 233 Kennedy St., Winnipeg, Man. R3C 3J5

MATHIEU, Hon. Guy, B.A., LL.B.; judge; b. Montreal, Que., 10 Dec. 1924; s. Joseph and Rose-Alma (Senécal) M.; e. Le Coll. de Montréal, B.A. 1946; Univ. of Montreal, LL.B. 1951; m. Lucie, d. P. D. Cossette, Town of Mount Royal, Que., 30 July 1960; children: Michel, Anik; JUSTICE, SUPERIOR COURT OF QUE., since 1969; called to Bar of Que. 1951; as lawyer, mem. Bd. Examiners, Bar of Que.; Depy-Trustee, Dist. of Terrebonne; Legal Advisor, Chamber Comm. St. Jerome; Past Dir., Victory Conveyor & Machine Ltd.; Chrmn., Bd. of Dirs., Hôtel Dieu of St. Jerome; R. Catholic; recreations: fishing, golf, skiing; Clubs: Rotary; Kinsmen; Home: 451 Madeleine St., St. Jerome, Que. J7Z 3S4; Office: Court House, Montreal, Que.

MATHIEU, Jean, M.D., F.R.C.P.(C); physician; educator; b. Montreal, Que. 7 Aug. 1926; s. Dr. Emile and Marie Berthe (Larivière) M.; e. Coll. Stanislas Montreal B.A. 1944; Univ. de Montréal M.D. 1950; Univ. of Toronto postgrad. course Internal Med. 1951-54; m. Anne-Marie d. M. Marius Mouren, Tangiers, Morocco 16 Aug. 1956; children: Bernard, Yves, Nicolas; PROF. AND CHRMN. OF MED. UNIV. DE MONTREAL since 1977; Physician, Dept. of Med. Hôpital Maisonneuve-Rosemont since 1956; Assoc. Dean, Faculté de médicine, Univ. de Montréal 1968-77; Gov. Que. Coll. of Physicians and Surgs. 1966-74; Adresse: 11 ave. Béloeil, Outremont, Qué. H2V 2Z1; Bureau: 1150 Boul St. Joseph est, Montréal, Qué. H2J 1L5

MATTE, Bernard William, B.Com., M.B.A.; manufacturer; b. Sherbrooke, Que. 31 March 1940; s. Joseph Osmond and Bertha (Lacoste) M.; e. Univ. of Ottawa B.Com. 1964; Univ. of W. Ont. M.B.A. 1966; m. Barbara Ida d. Dr. Harold E. Armstrong, Ottawa, Ont. 23 June 1962; children: John Cameron, Shelley Louise: VICE PRES., IMASCO LTD. since 1978; Dir. Can. Northwest Lands Ltd.; Hardee's Food Systems; Vice Pres. Greenshields Inc. 1966-74; Vice Pres. and Dir., G & H Steel Industries Ltd. 1974-77; R. Catholic; recreations: flying, golf, skiing, squash; Clubs: University; Lambton Golf & Country; Royal Montreal Golf; Home: 635 Carleton Ave., Westmount, Qué. H3Y 2Y3; Office: 4 Westmount Sq., Montreal, Que. H3Z 2S8.

MATTE, Pierre; librarian; b. Shawinigan, Que. 31 July 1918; s. late Auguste and late Josephine (Gaillardetz) M.;

e. Shawinigan-South Comm. Sch. 1935; St. Joseph Coll. Trois-Rivières 1942; Laval Univ. Faculty of Philos. 1942-43; Univ. of Montreal Faculty of Pharm. 1944-45, Statistics 1945-46, Sch. of Lib. Science 1947-48; m. Clothide d. late Victor Lessard 20 Oct. 1951; children: Johanne, Louise, Michelle; DIR., QUE. LIBRARY SERVICE AND SECY. QUE. PUB. LIB. COMN. 1975- ; Prof., St. Mary's Coll. Shawinigan 1943-44; Shawinigan Chemicals Ltd. classification of plans 1950; Maison Bellarmin Montreal 1950-51; Shawinigan Chemicals Ed. plant organ 1951-58; Service des bibliothèques publiques du Qué. and mem. of Comn. 1960; mem. Candn. Lib. Research and Devel. Council 1962-67; recipient Strathcona Medal; served with COTC 1942-45; author various papers; Pres. l'Assn. canadienne des bibliothécaires de langue française 1959-60; 2nd Vice Pres. Candn. Lib. Assn. 1966-67, Vice Pres. Candn. Lib. Week; mem. Am. Lib. Assn. 1966-71; R. Catholic; recreations: home work, handicrafts, skiing, skating, music; Home: 1228, De Repentigny St., Québec, Qué. G1S 1Y3; Office: 225 Grand-Allée E., Québec, Qué. G1R 5G5

MATTHEWS, Maj. Gen. Albert Bruce, C.B.E. (1944), D.S.O. (1943), E.D.; company executive; b. Ottawa, Ont., 12 Aug. 1909; s. Hon. Albert and Maud (Whiteside) M.; e. Upper Can. Coll.; Univ. of Geneva; m. the late Victoria Corse, d. Dr. Victor C. Thorne, N.Y., 25 Sept. 1937; two s. and one d.; PRES., MATTHEWS AND CO. INC.; Dir., Massey-Ferguson Ltd.; Dir. Economic Investment Trust Ltd.; Canada Permanent Trust Co.; Can. Permanent Mortgage Corp.; Dome Petroleum Ltd.; Third Candn. Gen. Investment Trust Ltd.; Canadian General Investments Ltd.; Chrmn. of Bd., Dome Mines Ltd.; with Matthews & Co., 1931; Partner 1932; Chrmn. Bd., Excelsior Life Insurance Co. 1963-74; served with Canadian Mil. 7th Toronto Regiment Roy. Candn. Arty., 1928-39; World War, 1939-45; proceeded overseas 1940 in Command of 15th Field Batty.; 2nd in Command 1st Medium Regt.; raised and Commanded 5th Medium Regt.; apptd. Counter Batty. Offr., 1st Candn. Corps, 1942; promoted Brig. 1943; C.R.A., 1st Candn. Divn. in Sicily and Italy; C.C.R.A., 2nd Candn. Corps in N.W. Europe; promoted Maj.-Gen. 1944; Commanded 2nd Candn. Divn., 1944-45; twice Mentioned in Despatches; Grand Offr., Order of Orange Nassau with Crossed Swords; Legion of Hon.; Croix de Guerre with Palm; apptd. Col. Commandant, Royal Regt. of Candn. Arty., 1964; Pres., Candn. Life Ins. Offrs. Assn., 1954-55; Past Pres., Nat. Liberal Fed. of Can.; recreations: golf, sailing; Clubs: Toronto; Toronto Golf; Royal Canadian Military Institute; Granite; York; Mount Royal (Montreal); Home: 19 Riverview Dr., Toronto, Ont. M4N 3C6; Office: 700, 320 Bay St., Toronto, Ont. M5H 2P6

MATTHEWS, Brig. Beverley, C.B.E., Q.C., B.A.; barrister; b. Toronto, Ont., 23 Feb. 1905; s. Frederick William and Elizabeth Mary (Leslie) M.; e. Univ. of Toronto Schs.; Univ. of Toronto, B.A.; Osgoode Hall Law Sch. (Gold Medal); m. late Pauline Ritchie, 29 April 1938; three s. and one d.; m. Phyllis McKinnon (Cowie) 7 Sept. 1978; SR. PARTNER, McCARTHY & McCARTHY; Chrmn. Bd., Candn. Niagara Power; Dir., Candn. Gypsum Co. Ltd.; Past Pres., Toronto Bd. of Trade; served in 2nd World War; joined 48th Highlanders of Can., 1939; served Overseas, 1940-45, retired with rank of Brig.; O.B.E. and Mentioned in Despatches (Italy); C.B.E. and Mentioned in Despatches (Continent); Commdr. of Order of Orange Nassau (Netherlands); called to the Bar of Ont., 1930 cr. K.C., 1945; Conservative; Anglican; recreations: shooting, fishing; Clubs: Toronto; York; University; White's (London); Home: 45 Ardmore Rd., Toronto, Ont. M5P 1V9; Office: (Box 48) Toronto-Dominion Tower, Toronto, Ont. M5K 1E6

MATTHEWS, Burton Clare, B.S.A., A.M., Ph.D., D.U.; university president; b. Kerwood, Ont., 16 Dec. 1926; s. Clarence D. and Meryl (Freer) M.; e. Univ. of Toronto,

B.S.A. 1947; Univ. of Missouri, A.M. 1948; Cornell Univ., Ph.D. 1952; Nuffield Foundation Post-Doctorate Fellow, Oxford Univ., 1961-62; Univ. of Sherbrooke, D.U., 1979; m. Lois Verna, d. Archibald Lewis, Ottawa, Ont., 23 June 1951; two s. David, Thomas; Chmn., Ont. Council of Univ. Affairs 1982- ; Dir., Campbell Soup Co.; Pres., Kitchener Waterloo YMCA; Dir., Ont. Educ. Communications Authority 1972-78; Assn. Univs. and Colls. Can. 1977-78; Extve., Council of Ont. Univ. 1972-74 and since 1979; Asst. Prof. of Soil Science, Ont. Agric. Coll., 1952-56; Assoc. Prof., 1956-58; Prof. 1958-62; Head, Dept. of Soil Science, 1962-66; V. Pres. (Acad.) Univ. of Guelph 1966-70; Pres. and Vice Chancellor, Univ. of Waterloo 1970-81 mem., Agric. Inst. Can.; Ont. Inst. Agrologists; Can. Soc. of Soil Sci.(Past Pres.); Soil Conserv. Soc. Am.; Am. Soc. Agron.; Sigma Xi; Freemason; Anglican; Home: 12 Westgate Walk, Kitchener, Ont. N2M 2T8

MATTHEWS, Donald Charles, M.Sc.; agrologist; company executive; b. Calgary, Alta., 24 Sept. 1918; s. Charles Curtice and Grace Miriam (Cathro) M.; e. Univ. of Alberta, 1937-39, 1945-47; B.Sc. (Agric.) with Distinction, 1947; Iowa State Coll., M.Sc. (Animal Breeding) 1948; m. Jean Lyndsay Lamaison, 1 Mar. 1941; children: Lyndsay Catherine, Robert Charles; PRESIDENT, HIGHLAND STOCK FARMS LTD., since 1967; previously Farm. Mgr. and Vice-Pres., 1948-67; Dir., Cdn. Pacific Ltd.; Chrmn., Adv. Comte. (Calgary), Guaranty Trust Co.; Hon. Pres. (1980) and past Pres., Alta. Aberdeen Angus Assn.; Past Pres., Candn. Jt. Beef Breeds Assn.; Found. mem., Dir. and Pres., Candn. Limousin Assn.; Dir. Candn. Cattlemen's Assn.; Charter Trustee and past Pres., Cdn. 4-H Foundation; mem., Agric. Inst. Can. (Pres. Calgary Br. 1952-53); Am. Genetics Assn.; Alta. Cattle Breeders Assn. (Past Pres. and Dir.); Candn. & Am. Soc. Animal Production; Past Pres. & Charter Dir., Candn. Agric. Hall of Fame; Past Pres., Calgary Exhibition & Stampede Co. Ltd., 1964-65 (Life Dir.); Past mem. Council and Past Chrmn., Agric. Bureau, Calgary Chamber of Comm.; Dir., Candn. Aberdeen Angus Assn., 1963-71, Extve. mem. 1967-68, Vice-Pres. 1968, Pres. 1969; Bd. Govs. 1977-80, and Senate, 1974-80, Univ. of Calgary; served in World War 1939-45 (Overseas 5 yrs.); discharged from 14th Candn. Armour. Regt. (K.O.R.) with rank Capt.; Centennial Medal 1967; Delta Kappa Epsilon; Anglican; recreation: riding; Club: Ranchmens'; Address: Highland Stock Farm, R.R. 1, Calgary, Alta. T2P 2G4

MATTHEWS, Francis Richard, Q.C., B.Com., LL.B.; b. Calgary, Alta., 19 Aug. 1920; s. Charles Curtice and Grace Miriam (Cathro) M.; e. W. Can. High Sch.; Univ. of Alta., B.Com. 1941, LL.B. 1948; m. Joyce Winter, d. J. Arthur Jarvis, Toronto, 10 Nov. 1944; children: James Richard, Michael John, Frances Elizabeth; PARTNER, MacKIMMIE MATTHEWS, since 1954; Dir., The Petrol Oil & Gas Co. Ltd.; Ranger Oil Ltd.; United Westburne Ind. Ltd.; Westburne Internat. Industries Ltd.; Dir. and Secy., Murphy Oil Co. Ltd.; Asst. Secy., Panarctic Oils Ltd.; read law with M. M. Porter, Q.C.; called to Bar Alta. 1949; cr. Q.C. 1963; assoc. with present firm until 1954; served with RCNVR 1941-45; rank Lt. (S) on discharge; Gov., Calgary Philharmonic Orchestra Soc. (Pres. 1954-55, 1961-62); mem., Alta. Bar Assn.; Candn. Bar Assn.; Calgary Chamber Comm.; Delta Kappa Epsilon; Anglican; recreations: skiing, sailing, flying, badminton, photography; Clubs: Glencoe; Calgary Petroleum; Cu-Nim Soaring; Home: 4612-5th St. S.W., Calgary, Alta. T2S 2E6; Office: Gulf Oil Building, P.O. Box 2010, Calgary, Alta. T2P 2M2

MATTHEWS, John Hugh; trust company executive; b. Viking, Alta. 14 Sept. 1935; s. Rt. Rev. Timothy John Matthews; e. Upper Can. Coll. Toronto, Ont.; Bishop's Univ. B.A. 1957; Univ. of W. Ont. M.B.A. 1960; m. Nancy Marilyn, d. Raymond Pond 10 May 1958; children: Timothy, Andrew, Lisa; EXTVE. VICE PRES., CANADIAN OPER-

ATIONS, AND DIR. ROYAL TRUSTCO LTD. 1981- ; Dir. Royal Trust Corp. of Can.; The Royal Trust Co.; Dustbane Enterprises Ltd.; Computel Systems Ltd.; Royal Trust Energy Corp.; Royal Trust Mortgage Corp.; Roy. Can. Geographical Soc.; Clk. Estates Dept. Royal Trust Montreal 1960, Mgr. Personal Trust Dept. Vancouver 1965, Asst. Br. Mgr. Winnipeg 1968 and Montreal 1971, Asst. Vice Pres. Pacific Region and Mgr. Vancouver Br. 1974, Vice Pres. W. Region Calgary 1976, Extve. Vice Pres. Regional Operations Calgary 1978, Extve. Vice Pres. Operations Toronto 1979; Sr. Extve. Vice Pres. and Chief Operating Officer 1980; Fellow, Trust Companies Inst.; Anglican; recreations: golf, tennis, curling, skiing; Clubs: Granite; Lambton Golf and Country; Office: (P.O. Box 7500 Stn. A) Toronto-Dominion Centre, Toronto, Ont. M5W 1P9.

MATTHEWS, John Pengwerne, B.A., LL.B., Ph.D.; educator; b. Sydney, Australia 22 Oct. 1927; s. George Pengwerne and Rosalie Crossland (Pulsford) M.; e. The Scots Coll. Sydney 1945; Univ. of Melbourne B.A. 1951, Dipl. in Educ. 1952; Univ. of London LL.B. 1954; Univ. of Toronto Ph.D. 1957; n. Flora Jean Cameron d. James Gilchrist 11 June 1955; children: Peter Edmund Vashdye Pengwerne, Rosalie Elizabeth Jane Pengwerne, Christopher John Charles Pengwerne; PROF. OF ENG., QUEEN'S UNIV. 1962- ; Princ. Investigator and Sr. Ed., The Disraeli Project 1974- ; Asst. Prof. St. John's Coll. Univ. of Man. 1956, Prof. and Head of Eng. 1957, Dean of Arts & Science 1957-62; joined Queen's Univ. 1962, Dir. Inst. of Commonwealth & Comparative Studies 1962-67, Assoc. Dean of Grad. Studies & Research, Dir. of Research Adm. 1974-75; Hon. Fellow St. John's Coll. 1963; Visiting Fellow Oriel Coll. Oxford 1972-73; Nuffield Fellow 1972-73; served with RAAF 1950-53, Pilot Offr.; RCAF Auxiliary Flying Offr. 1953-56, Flight Lt. 1956-59; author ''Tradition in Exile'' 1962; various book chapters, articles; Vice Pres. Kingston Symphony Assn.; Pres. Kingston Youth Orchestra 1968-74; Nat. Pres. Humanities Assn. Can. 1971-72 (Extve. 1973-); mem. Acad. Panel, Social Sciences & Humanities Research Council 1978-81; Anglican; recreations: chess, sailing; Home: 55 Watts Cres., Kingston, Ont. K7M 2P4; Office: Kingston, Ont. K7L 3N6

MATTHEWS, Rt. Rev. Timothy John, B.A., L.S.T., S.T.L., D.C.L. (Ang.); b. London, Eng., 8 July 1907; s. John Colmworth & Ethel May (Burns) M.; came to Can., 1913; e. Bishop's Univ., L.S.T. 1932, B.A. 1944, D.C.L. 1975; Gen. Synod. S.Th. 1942; m. Mary Eileen, d. Dr. T. E. Montgomery, Phillipsburg, Que., 27 July 1933; children: Timothy Peter, John Hugh, Philip Richard, Thomas Robert, Margaret Evelyn; o. Deacon 1932, Priest 1933 (Diocese of Edmonton); Vicar of Viking, Alta., 1933-36; Rector of Edson, Alta., 1936-40, Coaticook, Que., 1940-44, Lake St. John (and Rural Dean of Que.) 1944-52; Archdeacon of Gaspé, 1952-57; Rector, St. George's, Lennoxville, and Archdeacon of St. Francis Dist. 1957-71; Bishop Coadjutor elect May 1971; Bishop of Que. 1971-77; Lon. visitor, Bishop's Univ.; Corp. of B.C.S. King's Hall, Lennoxville, Que.; Candn. Gen. and Prov. Councils of The Boy Scouts; Freemason (W.M.); D.D.G.C.); Episcopal visitor, S.S.J.E. (Can.); recreations: golf, fishing, curling; Address: 23 High St., Lennoxville, Que. J1M 1E6

MATTHEWS, Vincent Leon, M.D., D.P.H., F.R.C.P.(C); educator; b. Kincaid, Sask. 6 Feb. 1922; s. Martin B. and Florence E. (McRoberts) M.; e. Univ. of Sask. B.A. 1943; Univ. of Toronto M.D. 1945, D.P.H. 1947; m. A. Patricia d. Herbert e. Keddy, Melfort, Sask. 2 Sept. 1946; children: Maureen Anne, Douglas M., David R.; PROF. AND HEAD OF SOCIAL & PREVENTIVE MED., UNIV. OF SASK. since 1964; Chief Examiner (Community Health), Roy. Coll. Phys. & Surg. 1981- ; Hon. Consultant, Univ. Hosp. Saskatoon; Acting Med. Offr. of Health, City of Saskatoon; Regional Med. Health Offr. Swift Current 1948-57; gen. practice Maple Creek, mem.

Maple Creek Clinic 1949-51; Dir. Med. & Hosp. Services Br., Sask. Dept. Pub. Health 1957-62, Acting Depy. Min. of Dept. 1962-63, Assoc. Depy. Min. 1963-64; Visiting Prof. Univ. of W. Indies 1977; rec'd World Health Organ. Travel Fellowship in Community Health 1975; mem. Bd., Candn. Council on Children & Youth; Adv. Comte. to Nat. Health Research & Devel. Program; served with RCAMC 1943-46; mem. Coordinating Comte., Ed. Bd. and co-author "Health Care An International Study" 1976; author or co-author various articles, reports; Fellow, Am. Pub. Health Assn. (Vice Pres. 1972); mem. Candn. Pub. Health Assn. (Pres. 1971); Club: Saskatoon Nutana Rotary; Home: 220 11th St. E., Saskatoon, Sask. S7N 0E6; Office: College of Medicine, Univ. of Saskatchewan, Saskatoon, Sask. S7N 0W0.

MAURER, Armand, M.A., M.S.L., Ph.D., F.R.S.C.; university professor; b. Rochester, N.Y., 21 Jan., 1915; s. Armand Augustine and Louise (Ribson) M.; e. Univ. of Toronto, B.A. 1938, M.A. 1943, M.S.L. (Pontifical Inst. of Mediaeval Studies) 1945, Ph.D. 1947; Post-doctoral studies, Univ. of Paris, 1948-49; Harvard Univ. and Italy (Guggenheim Fellowship), 1954-55; PROF. OF PHILOS., PONTIFICAL INST. OF MEDIAEVAL STUDIES AND UNIV. OF TORONTO; Roman Catholic Priest of Congr. of St. Basil; author of "Medieval Philosophy", 1962; co-author, "Recent Philosophy", 1966; mem., Am. Cath. Philos. Assn.; Candn. Philos. Assn.; Metaphysical Soc. Am.; Société internat. pour l'étude de la philosophie médiévale; recreations: golf, swimming, tennis; Address: 59 Queen's Park Cres., Toronto, Ont. M5S 2C4

MAURER, Pierre; insurance executive, b. Montreal, Que., 10 June 1924; s. Alexis Antoine and Jeanne (Marcotte) M.; e. St. Ignatius Jesuit Coll.; m. Armande, d. Armand Crete, 15 Feb. 1947; one s., Michel; EXEC. VICE-PRES. METROPOLITAN LIFE INS. CO. since 1978; Dir. Royal Bank of Canada; TIW Industries Ltd.; Warnock Hersey Internat. Ltd.; Chmn., Metropolitan Property and Liability Ins. Co.; Metropolitan Ins. and Annuity Co. 1981; joined present co. as Agt., Que., 1950; Group Supvr. Que. 1952; Assoc. Regional Mgr., E. Can., 1962, Regional Mgr. 1964, Regional Vice Pres., 1967; Vice Pres.-Group-Can. 1969; Vice Pres. Agency Operations-Can. 1970; Vice Pres. Operations-Can. 1972; Pres., Can. Operations, 1974-78; Exec. Vice-Pres., Corp. Exec. Office since Nov. 1978 mem., Extve. Office: One Madison Ave., New York, N.Y. 10010

MAURO, Arthur V., Q.C., B.A., LL.M.; financial executive; b. Port Arthur, Ont., 15 Feb. 1927; s. Arthur George and Maria (Fortes) M.; e. St. Andrews and Port Arthur (Ont.) Coll. Inst.; St. Patricks High Sch., Fort William, Ont.; St. Paul's Coll., Winnipeg, B.A. 1949; Univ. of Man., LL.B. 1953, LL.M. 1956; m. Nancie June, d. late H. Tooley, 1 Sept. 1951; children: Barbara, Christine, Jennifer, Gregory; PRES., THE INVESTORS GROUP, 1981- ; formerly Pres., Transair Ltd.; Dir., Investors Group; Investors Syndicate Ltd.; Pacific Western Airlines; Fed. Industries Ltd.; CP Hotels Ltd.; Great-West Life Assnce. Co.; Montreal Trust Co.; read law with Andrews, Andrews, Thorvaldson & Co.; called to Bar of Man. 1953; cr. Q.C. 1964; Special Counsel to Prov. of Man. 1958-69; Chrmn., Royal Comn. on N. Transport., 1967-69; Lectr. in Transport. and Communication Law, Univ. of Man. Law Sch., 1967-69; Chrmn. of Bd., St. Paul's Coll.; Past Pres., Winnipeg Art Gallery; named Kt. of St. Gregory 1967; mem., Man. Bar Assn.; P. Conservative; R. Catholic; Home: 1034 Wellington Cres., Winnipeg, Man. R3M 0E1; Office: 280 Broadway, Winnipeg, Man. R3C 3B6

MAWHINNEY, J. Donald, LL.B.; financial executive; e. Univ. of B.C. LL.B. 1954; PRESIDENT, BANCORP FINANCIAL LTD. 1979- ; Partner law firm Ladner Downs, Vancouver 1954-78, Mang. Partner 1977-78; Clubs: Vancouver; Rotary; Men's Canadian; Home: 4371 Arbutus

St., Vancouver, B.C. V6J 4S4; Office: (P.O. Box 11509) Vancouver Centre, Vancouver, B.C. V6B 4N7.

MAXWELL, Desmond Ernest Stewart, B.A., Ph.D.; educator; writer; b. Derry, N. Ireland, 6 July 1925; s. Ernest Victor and Mary Rose (Stewart) M.; e. Foyle Coll., Derry; Trinity Coll., Univ. of Dublin, B.A. 1947, Ph.D. 1950; m. Myra Joyce, d. John Eakin, Coleraine, N. Ireland, 1955; one d.; PROF. OF ENGLISH, YORK UNIV. since 1967 and Master of Winters Coll. there 1969-79; Lectr., Univ. of Ghana, 1956; Asst. Dir. of Exams., Civil Service Comn. (Eng.), 1961; Head, Dept. of Eng., Univ. of Ibadan, 1963; Dir. Grad. Programme in Eng. present Univ. 1967-70; author, "The Poetry of T. S. Eliot", 1952; "American Fiction", 1963; "Cozzens", 1964; "Melville", 1966; "Poets of the Thirties", 1969; "Brian Friel" 1973; "Androches and the Lion" A Commentary", 1980; co-author, "Yeats Centenary Essays", 1965; "English Poems of the Twentieth Century", 1970; mem. Modern Humanities Research Assn.; Internat. Assn. Univ. Profs. Eng.; Clubs: National Liberal; University (Dublin); Office: 4700 Keele St., Downsview, Ont. M3J 2R4

MAXWELL, Donald Spencer, Q.C., B.A.; transportation executive; b. Ottawa, Ont., 15 Dec. 1925; s. George Hartley and Harriet E. (Smith) M.; e. Lisgar Coll. Inst., Ottawa, Ont.; Queen's Univ., B.A. (Hon.) 1948; Osgoode Hall Law Sch. 1951; m. Christina Caroline, d. John Caldwell, Almonte, Ont., 12 Aug. 1950; three d. Deborah Carol, Joan Elaine, Frances Lynn; VICE PRES. LAW AND GEN. COUNSEL, CANADIAN PACIFIC LTD. since 1973; Dir. Soo Line Railroad Co.; Chateau Ins. Co.; called to the Bar of Ont. 1951; cr. Q.C., 1962; joined Fed. Dept. of Justice, 1951; Adv. Counsel 2 1952, Adv. Counsel 3 1953, Sr. Adv. Counsel and Dir. Civil Litigation 1955; First Assoc. Depy. Min. of Justice 1960, Depy. Min. of Justice and Depy. Atty. Gen. of Can. 1967; mem. Law Soc. Upper Can.; Candn. Bar Assn.; United Church; recreations: music, swimming; Clubs: Royal Ottawa; Le Cercle Universitaire; Rideau; M.A.A.A.; Office: Windsor Station, Montreal, Que. H3C 3E4

MAXWELL, John Alfred, M.Sc., Ph.D., F.R.S.C. F.C.I.C.; s. John Harold and Florence Lillian (Miller) M.; e. McMaster Univ., B.Sc. 1949, M.Sc. 1950; Univ. of Minn., Ph.D. (Geol. and Analytical Chem.) 1953; m. Helen Catharine, d. late Rev. S. H. Moyer, 20 Nov. 1953; DIR. CENTRAL LABS. & TECH. SERVICES, GEOLOGICAL SURVEY OF CANADA, since 1974; Research Fellow, Rock Analysis Laboratory, University of Minn., 1951-53; joined present organization as Geol., 1953; Head, Analytical Chem. Sec., 1957-67; rec'd Ont. Research Foundation, Scholarship, 1949 and 1950; author, "Rock and Mineral Analysis", 1968, 2nd ed. (with W. M. Johnson) 1981; other writings incl. scient. papers on analysis of rocks and minerals, mercury cathode and its applications, laser microprobe, lunar sample analysis; Fellow, Geol. Assn. Can.; mem. Mineralogical Assn. Can.; Protestant; Home: 672 Denbury Ave., Ottawa, Ont. K2A 2P3; Office: 601 Booth St., Ottawa, Ont. K1A 0E8

MAXWELL, John Spencer, B.Com., M.B.A.; company executive; b. Red Deer, Alta., 31 Mar. 1919; s. Albert Seymour and Mabel Harriet (Spencer) M.; e. Queen's Univ., B.Com. 1941; Harvard Business Sch., M.B.A. 1947; m. Mary Agnes, d. late Edward P. O'Toole, B.C.L., 6 June 1959; EXTVE. VICE-PRES., FINANCE AND DIR., CIP INC. 1971- ; Dir., Anglo-American Paper Co. Ltd.; CIP Pulp Ltd.; CIP Research Ltd.; CIP Daxion Inc.; Facelle Co. Ltd.; Hygrade Corrugated Containers Ltd.; Masonite Can. Ltd.; Miramichi Lumber Co. (Ltd.); New Brunswick Internat. Paper Co.; Tahsis Co. Ltd.; Ucona Holdings Ltd.; Chrmn. and Dir., CIP Inc. (Paper Products Div.); joined present Co. as Financial Trainee, 1947; apptd. Asst. Treas. 1953 and Dir. of Econ. Planning and Market Research, 1954; Asst. to Treas., Internat. Paper Co., N.Y. 1955 and Asst. Treas., 1960-64; Vice-Pres., Finance 1964;

mem. R.C.N.V.R., 1941-45, retired as Lt. Commdr. (S) RCN (R); Home: 1227 Sherbrooke St. W., Apt. 115, Montreal, Que. H3G 1G1; Office: Sun Life Bldg., Dominion Square, Montreal, Que. H3B 2X1

MAYBEE, Arthur Ryerson, B.A.; institutional and public affairs director b. Calgary, Alta. 15 April 23; s. late Arthur and Isabel (Ryerson) M; e. Strathcona School, Calgary; Upper Canada College, Toronto; Univ. of Toronto 1948; m. Helen Patricia, d. C.J. McDermott, Oakville, Ont. 7 July 51; three d. Kim (Twohig), Jill, Sarah; DIR. OFFICE OF UNIVERSITY ADVANCEMENT, LAKEHEAD UNIVERSITY, 1981; Asst. to Pres. Carleton College, Ottawa 1950-51; joined John Price Jones (Canada) Ltd. (later G.A. Brakeley & Co. Ltd. 1955, and The Ryerson Group Ltd, 1972) Toronto, in 1951 as Acct. Exec, becoming Vice Pres. & Dir, 1954; Exec. V.P., Montreal 1960; Pres. 1961 to 1975 when co. ceased operations; Senior Consultant, Management Services, Research & Productivity Council, Fredericton, N.B. 1976-80; served in 2nd World War in Belgium, Holland & Germany with R.C. Signals, rank of Lieut.; Dir., Jr. Achievement, Thunder Bay; Mem. Cdn. Ski Patrol System; recreations: golf, skiing, canoeing; Clubs: Royal Montreal Golf; University (Toronto); Ft. William Country; Home: Kelly's Creek. R.R. #6, Fredericton, N.B., E3B 4X7; Office: Oliver Road, Thunder Bay, Ontario P7B 5E1.

MAYBIN, John Edwin, M.Sc.; public utilities executive; b. Regina, Sask., 14 Feb. 1925; s. John and Gertrude (Hinton) M.; e. Calgary (Alta.) Pub. and High Schs.; Univ. of Alta.; Princeton Univ., B.Sc., M.Sc.; m. Ella Joy Louise, d. Dr. R. Parsons, Red Deer, Alta., 21 Dec. 1964; Dir., Alta. Energy Co.; Majestic Wiley Contractors Ltd.; joined Cdn. Western and Northwestern as prof. engr. 1949; Pres., Cdn. Western Natural Gas Co. and Northwestern Utilities Ltd. 1968-69; Chrmn. and C.E.O., Cdn. Utilities Ltd. 1969-72; Group Vice Pres., Utilities, IU International Corp. 1972-74; Chrmn. and C.E.O., Cdn. Utilities Ltd. 1974-81 (ret.); served with RN 1944-46; Pres., Candn. Gas Assn. 1971-72; recreations: golf, skiing; Clubs: The Edmonton; Ranchmen's (Calgary); The Toronto; Home: 88 Valleyview Cr., Edmonton, Alta. T5R 5T1

MAYHEW, Elza Lovitt, B.A., M.F.A., R.C.A.; sculptor; b. Victoria, B.C. 19 Jan. 1916; d. George and Alice (Bordman) Lovitt; e. Univ. of B.C., B.A.; studied with Jan Zach Victoria 1955-58; Univ. of Ore. M.F.A. 1963; m. Charles Alan Mayhew (d. 1943) 10 Sept. 1938; children: Anne Lovitt, Garth Alan; solo exhns. incl. The Point Gallery Victoria 1960, 1962; Art Gallery of Greater Victoria 1961, 1964, 1971 (Retrospective); Fine Arts Gallery Univ. of B.C. 1961; Lucien Campbell Plaza Univ. of Ore. 1963; Venice Biennale Candn. Pavilion 1964; Dorothy Cameron Gallery Toronto 1965; The Backroom Gallery Victoria 1978; Burnaby (B.C.) Art Gallery 1979; Equinox Gallery Vancouver 1980; Albert White Gallery Toronto 1980; Wallack Gallery, Ottawa 1981; rep. in nat. and internat. group exhns.; rep in various perm. colls. incl. Nat. Gallery Can., Nat. Capital Comn. "Meditation Piece" Rideau Canal Ottawa; comns. incl. B.C. Archives and Museum Victoria 1967; Expo '67 2 sculptures 1967; Bank of Can. Vancouver bronze mural 1968; Confed. Centre Charlottetown "Column of the Sea" Centennial Project 1973; rec'd Sir Otto Beit Medal Royal Soc. Brit. Sculptors 1962; B.C. Centennial Sculpture Exhn. Purchase Award 1967; Dir. Internat. Sculpture Center Kansas 1968-79; Consultant, B.C. Comte on Art 1974-76; work subject of film "Making of the Column of the Sea" 1973; cited various bibliogs.; Address: 330 St. Lawrence St., Victoria, B.C. V8V 1Y4.

MAYNARD, Edward, b. Green Island Brook, Nfld. 22 Feb. 1939; s. William Henry and Jane (Mitchelmore) M.; e. Green Island Brook, Nfld.; St. Bonaventure's Coll. and Prince of Wales Coll. St. John's Nfld.; RCAF Electronics Course Clinton, Ont.; m. Marlene Angela d. Reginald Offrey 10 May 1963; three d. Amanda, Colleen, Monique;

CHAIRMAN, WORKERS COMPENSATION BOARD; Mun. Councillor Hawke's Bay, Nfld. 1962-71; M.H.A. 1972-79; served with RCAF; Airborne Radar Tech. 1958-63; P. Conservative; Anglican; Home: 3 Dunlea St., St. John's Nfld. A1A 3B2; Office: W.C.B. Bldg., 146-148 Forest Rd., St. John's Nfld.

MAYNARD, John C., B.Sc., F.S.A., F.C.I.A.; financial consultant; actuary; b. Toronto, Ont., 30 July 1919; s. late Dr. John C. and Anne Marjorie (Wilson) M.; e. Univ. of Toronto Schs.; Lakefield Coll. Sch.; Trinity Coll., Univ. of Toronto, B.Sc. 1940; m. Margaret, d. late Dr. James C. McClelland, 1948; children: John, Jennifer, Judith; Sr. Vice Pres. and Chief Actuary, The Canada Life Assurance Co., 1977-81; joined Actuarial Div. 1945; apptd. Extve. Asst. 1951; Actuary 1961; Actuarial Vice Pres. 1968; Vice Pres. and Chief Actuary 1971; served with RCN 1940-45; on loan to RN for duties in naval radar, serving as radar offr. on HMS Revenge, HMS Victorious, HMS Implacable; rank Lt. Commdr. on discharge; mem., Soc. of Actuaries (Fellow 1949, Bd. Govs. 1972-76, Dir. 1972-73, Vice Pres. 1974-76); Candn. Inst. Actuaries (Pres. 1972-73); Bd. Dir., Candn. Corps. of Commissionaires; Dir., Canada Life Insur. Co.; Chmn Univ. of Waterloo Adv. Bd. on Actuarial Science; recreations: tennis, squash, fishing; Clubs: Toronto Badminton & Racquet; Anglican; Home: 115 Glenayr Road, Toronto, Ont. M5P 3C1;

MAYRAND, Hon. Albert, LL.D.; juge; né Longueuil, Qué. 19 février 1911; f. Oswald et Orphise (Gadbois) M.; é. Univ. d'Ottawa LL.D. 1965; Univ. de Montréal LL.D. 1978; ép. Lucienne f. Louis A. Boyer 30 juin 1940; enfants: Cécile, Nicole, Lise, Yves, Louis, Chantal; JUGE, COUR D'APPEL DU QUE. depuis 1974; admis au barreau 1934; Q.C. 1955; avocat 1934-48, étude Mayrand, Deslauriers et Trépanier; prof. Faculté des sciences sociales Univ. de Montréal 1940-48, Faculté de froit 1948-65, prof. émérite 1965; dir. Revue du Barreau prov. de Qué. 1955-65; juge, Cour supérieure 1965; prés. du Comité du droit de la famille et du Comité du droit des obligations, Office de révision du Code civil 1969-74; auteur "Les successions ab intestat" 1971; "Dictionnaire de maximes latines" 1972; "L'inviolabilité de la personne humaine" 1975; co-auteur "Quelques aspects du droit de la prov. de Québec" 1963; "Mélanges B. Bissonnette" 1963; "Mélanges R. Savatier" 1965; "Mélanges M.-L. Beaulieu" 1967-68; "Lois nouvelles" 1965 et 1970; catholique; Club: Cercle de la Place d'Armes; Adresse: 21 ave. Péronne, Outremont, Qué. H3S 1X7; Bureau: Palais de Justice, 1 rue Notre-Dame est, Montréal, Qué. H2Y 1B6.

MAYSE, Arthur; writer; journalist; b. Peguis, Man., 23 Oct. 1912; s. Amos William and Elizabeth Earle (Caswell) M.; e. Elem. Schs., Boissevain, Man.; High Sch., Nanaimo and Vancouver, B.C.; Univ. of B.C. (Arts, nongrad.); m. Winifred, Anne, d. Ernest N. Davey, Long Branch, Ont., 10 Sept. 1940; children: Ronald William, Susan Winifred; Reporter, Copy Reader and Sub-Editor, Vancouver "Daily Province", 1935-41; Reporter and Outdoors Columnist, "Vancouver Sun" 1941-44; Assoc. Ed. of trade mags., Maclean-Hunter Publ. Co., Toronto, Ont., 1944-45; Fiction Ed., "Maclean's Magazine", 1945-47; Columnist for "The Victoria Times", (1963); author of "Perilous Passage" (novel) 1949, serial pub. by "Saturday Evening Post"; "The Desperate Search" (novel), 1952; "Morgan's Mountain" (novel), 1960; has written and publ. numerous serials and short stories in general mags. in Can., U.S. and Eng., Scandinavian countries and Aust.; Liberal; United Church; Address: 2228 Arbutus Rd., Victoria, B.C. V8N 1V3

MAZANKOWSKI, Hon. Donald Frank, M.P.; politician; b. Viking, Alta. 27 July 1935; s. late Frank and late Dora (Lonowski) M.; e. Pub. and High Schs. Viking, Alta.; m. Lorraine Effie d. late Lawrence James Poleschuk 6 Sept. 1958; three s. Gregory, Roger, Donald; Min. of Transport,

Can. and Min. responsible for Candn. Wheat Bd. 1979-80; Past Pres. Vegreville P. Cons. Assn.; N. Vice Pres. and N. Chrmn. for Organ. of Alta. P. Cons. Assn., H. of C. since 1968; mem. Commonwealth Parlty. Assn.; Vegreville Chamber Comm.; K. of C.; Hon. mem. Indian Assn. Alta.; R. Catholic; Club: Rotary; Home: (P.O. Box 1350) Vegreville, Alta. T0B 4L0; Office: House of Commons, Ottawa, Ont. K1A 0A6.

McAFEE, Jerry, B.S., Sc.D.; oil company executive (retired); b. Port Arthur, Texas, 3 Nov. 1916; s. Almer McDuffie and Marguerite (Calfee) McA.; e. Univ. Texas, B.S. (Chem. Engn.) 1937; Mass. Inst. Tech., Sc.D. (Chem. Engn.) 1940; Univ. Pittsburgh, Student Mang. Problems for Extves., 1952; m. Geraldine, d. William H. Smith, 21 June 1940; children: Joe R., William M., Loretta M., Thomas R.; Chairman of the Board and Chief Extve. Offr., Gulf Oil Corp., 1976-81; Dir., Am. Petrol. Inst.; M.I.T. Corp.; Mellon Bank; Greater Pittsburgh Chamber of Comm.; Pittsburgh Symphony Soc.; World Affairs Council of Pittsburgh; Regional Indust. Devel. Corp. of S.W. Pa.; Aspen Inst. of Humanistic Studies; joined Universal Oil Products Co., Chicago as Research Chem. Engr., 1940-43; apptd. Operating Engr., 1944-45; Tech. Specialist, Gulf Oil Corp., Port Arthur, Texas, 1945-50; successively Dir. Chem., Asst. Dir. Research, Vice-Pres., Assoc. Dir., Gulf Research & Development Co., Harmarville, Pa., 1950-55; Vice-Pres. Engn. Mfg., Gulf Oil Corp., 1955-60; Vice-Pres. Extve. Tech. Advisor, 1960 and Dir. of Planning and Econ., 1962-64; Sr. Vice-Pres. of Corp. and Coordinator of Gulf Eastern Co., 1964-67; Dir., Extve. Vice Pres., Gulf Oil Can. Ltd. 1967-69; Pres. and C.E.O. 1969-76; Chrmn., Gulf Oil Corp. 1976-81; mem., Am. Inst. Chem. Engn. (Vice-Pres. 1959, Pres. 1960); Nat. Petrol. Council; Nat. Acad. Engn.; Am. Chem. Soc.; Pres-byterian; recreations: tennis, golf, music; Clubs: The Toronto; York; Duquesne (Pittsburgh); Links (N.Y.); Fox Chapel Golf; Laurel Valley Golf; Rolling Rock; Office: 435 Seventh Ave., Pittsburgh, Pa. 15230

McALPINE, Lt. Gen. Duncan Alastair; C.M.M., O.St.J., C.D., M.A.; company vice president; b. Montreal, 23 July 1922; s. Angus and Sarah (Cooper) McA.; e. Sir George Williams Univ., B.A. 1952; Univ. of Ottawa, M.A. 1961; L'Institut des Etudes Politiques, Univ. de Paris, 1962; Univ. of N.B., doctoral studies 1966; 2 Lt. to Lt. Col., Black Watch (RHR) of Can.; Nat. Defence Coll., 1967; m. Barnelle Alice, d. late Stanley Maurice Chatham; children: Lynn Carole, Bruce Duncan, Keith Andrew, Craig Alastair; VICE PRES., CORP. AFFAIRS, BRASCAN LTD.; since 1977; C.O. 2nd Bn. Black Watch of Can. in Germany, Can. and Cyprus 1963-66; Commdr., Combat Training Centre, 1970; Dir. Gen. Postings and Careers 1971; Assoc. Asst. Depy. Min. (Personnel) Dept. Nat. Defence 1972; Commdr. Candn. Mil. Component ICCS Vietnam 1973; Chief Personnel Devel. 1974; Commdr. Candn. Forces Europe 1975-76; mem. St. John Ambulance, Ont. Council; Metro Toronto Adv. Bd., Salvation Army; Bd. of Trustees, Toronto Grace Hospital; Vice-Pres., Can. Inst. of Strategic Studies; United Church; recreations: tennis, skiing; Home: 20 Fairground Lane, Woodbridge, Ont. L4L 3B6 Office: Box 48, Commerce Court P.O., Toronto, Ont. M5L 1B7

McARTHUR, Hon. Douglas Francis, M.L.A., B.S.A., M.A.; politician; b. Watrous, Sask. 21 June 1943; s. Neil and Marjorie McA.; e. Univ. of Sask.; Univ. of Toronto; Oxford Univ.; m. Wenda Jean Berglind 7 Sept. 1967; children: Neil, Kera; MIN. OF EDUC., MIN. OF CONTINUING EDUC., MIN. IN CHARGE OF SASK. POWER CORP., SASK. 1979-; el. M.L.A. for Regina Lakeview prov. g.e. 1978; economist; NDP; Office: Room 361 Legislative Bldg., Regina, Sask. S4S 0B3.

McARTHUR, Duncan Robert Baly, M.B.E., B.A.Sc., M.B.A., F.C.I.S., P. Eng.; industrialist; b. Yonkers, N.Y. (Candn. citizen by birth), 23 July 1918; s. late Alexander

Stanley and Dorothy Tertia (Rainbow) McA.; e. Univ. of Toronto (Ont.) Schs.; Univ. of Toronto, B.A.Sc. (Elect. Engn.); Harvard Univ., M.B.A.; m. late Nancy Mary, d. late John Smith, 12 March 1943; children: Peter David, late John Alexander, Robert Cameron, Christie Ann; CHRMN., CAN. DIAMOND BOART LTD.; UNITED DIAMOND DRILLING SERVICES LTD. AND SIBINTER LTD.; Dir., Canadian Utilities Ltd.; Alberta Industrial Holdings Ltd.; Mang. Consultant, Stevenson and Kellogg Ltd., 1947-52; Vice Pres., Western Minerals Ltd. to 1960; served successively as Secy.-Treas., Vice Pres., Extve. Vice Pres., Pres. & Chrmn. with Inland Cement Industries Ltd. (retired 1979); served with R.C.E.M.E. in Eng. and N.W. Europe 1940-45; Chrmn., Metric Comm. Can.; mem., Senate of Univ. of Alta.; Assn. Prof. Engrs. Alta.; Alpha Delta Phi; Anglican; recreations: golf, fishing, amateur radio; Clubs: Mayfair Golf & Country; Edmonton Petroleum; Edmonton; Home: 8907 Saskatchewan Dr., Edmonton, Alta; T6G 2B1

McARTHUR, (George) Arnold, C.M., O.S.M., F.C.C.T., M.A., D.C.L.; education consultant; b. Howick, Que. 21 June 1909; s. Peter Daniel and Marion Wilhelmina (Wright) McA.; e. Bishop's Univ. B.A. 1930, M.A. 1931, D.C.L. 1980; 1st Class High Sch. Dipl. (C.B.) 1931; Que. Educ. Dept. 1st Class Inspr.'s Cert. 1938, 1st Class Superior High Sch. Dipl. 1962; m. Audrey Jean d. Lt. Col. Norman C. MacKay, N.B. 19 Aug. 1933; two s. Donald Norman Wright, Peter Arnold; Asst. Princ. and Athletic Dir. Laurentide High Sch. Grand'Mere, Que. 1931-33; Math. and Science Specialist, Westmount High Sch. 1933-34; Princ. Arvida (Que.) High Sch. 1934-38; Inspr. of Schs. Que. 1938-40; Supt. and Princ. of Consolidated Paper Co. Schs. 1940-49, Shawinigan Falls High Sch. 1949-63, Rosemere High Sch. 1963-65; Dir. Gen. N. Island Regional Sch. Bd. 1965-68; Educ. Consultant to Gaspe Regional Sch. Bd., Dawson Coll., John Abbott Coll., Jewish Peoples' Schs., Manitou Coll. (Native N. Am. Culture Center), Vanier Coll.; Charter Pres./Chrm. Bd. Govs. Vanier Coll. 1970-73, Socio-Econ. mem. Bd. Govs., Vanier College 1973-77); mem. Prof. Staff, McGill Univ. 1970-73; Candn. Teachers Fed. Rep. to Kellogg Leadership Course, Univ. Alta. 1955; mem. Bd. Educ. Consultant Services since 1970; Dir.; Jr. Red Cross Leadership Training Center for E. Can. 1957; mem. Adv. Comte. to Grand'Mere City Council 1946-49; Dir., Les Loisirs de Shawinigan 1958-63; Gov., Internat. Rotary 779, 1959-60, Candn. Rep. Rotary Internat. Consultative Comte. 1962-63, and 1975-76; Chrmn. Foundation Comte. Dist. 779, 1977-78, Paul Harris Fellow since 1977; Charter mem. Que. Superior Council Educ. 1964-68; Pres. and mem. of Bd. PAPT Credit Union since 1968; rec'd Queen's Coronation Medal 1953; Order Scholastic Merit Que. 1957; Distinguished Service Award Que. Assn. Sch. Adms. 1979; Order of Canada, 1979; Fellow, Candn. Coll. Teachers; Doctor of Civil Law, Honoris Causa, Bishop's Univ. 1980; Past Pres., Prov. Assn. Prot. Teachers; Que. High Sch. Princ's Assn.; Past Dir., Candn. Teachers' Fed.; Assn. Candn. Community Colls.; Fed. des CEGEPS de la Prov. de Que.; mem. St. James Lit. Soc.; McGill Univ. Faculty Club; past Gov., Laurentide Men's Club; recreations: curling, golf, tennis, badminton, theatre, music; Presbyterian; Clubs: Town of Mount Royal Country; Town of Mount Royal Curling; Rosemere Curling Club; Oka Golf; Adress: Blainville Gardens, 20 Ravine Rd., Ste-Therese, Que. J7E 2T6.

McATEER, Ernerst Henry; stock broker; b. Kenora, Ont., 18 Dec. 1909; s. Samuel Henry and Mildred (Walkinshaw) M.; e. Public Schs., Kenora, Ont.; Assoc. and Fellow, Inst. Candn. Bankers; m. 1stly Alice Muriel, d. James Kirkpatrick, 5 Oct. 1940 (d.); d. Maureen Sarah; 2ndly Denise Martha, d. Yves Lagueux, 22 Dec. 1971; Pres.; Oswald Drinkwater & Graham Ltd.; Graham Armstrong Securities; Dir. Lévesque Beaubien Inc.; Partner, Graham & Co. 1951-63; Chrmn., Montreal Stock Exchange (1959), Past Chrmn. of Bd. of Mang.; Gov., Montreal General Hospital; Freemason; Protestant; recreation: golf; Clubs: Engineers; Royal Office: 360 St. James St. W., Montreal, Que.

MCAULAY, James Boyd; Hospital Administrator; b. N. Cobalt, Ont. 29 June 1927; s. Angus and Margaret (McKee); e. Runnymede Coll. Inst., Toronto; m. Jeanne d. Hubert Woolfrey 10 Apr. 1953; children: Nancy Kim (Low), Kathryn Irene, Carol Jeanne, Sharon June, James Boyd; EXTVE. DIR., TORONTO WESTERN HOSP. 1969- ; G.H. Woods Co. Ltd. 1946; Shanahan Cartage 1949; joined present hosp. 1950 and served in various positions, inc. Assoc. Extve. Dir. 1965-69; Trustee, Toronto Western Hosp.; Gage Research Inst.; Assoc. Prof. (Honorary), Fac. of Med., Univ. of Toronto; Past Pres., Assn. of Candn. Teaching Hospitals; Pres., Ont. Council of Administrators of Teaching Hospitals; mem., Amer. Assoc. of Hosp. Admnrs.; Candn. Coll. of Health Service Extves.; Conservative; Anglican; Clubs: York Downs Golf & Country; Bd. of Trade of Metro. Toronto; recreations: golf, curling; Home: 18 Aquila Ct., Rexdale, Ont. M9J 5W2; Office: 399 Bathurst St., Toronto, Ont. M5T 2S8

McAVITY, Lieut.-Col. James Malcolm, D.S.O., M.B.E.; retired executive; b. Westmount, Que., 20 Nov. 1909; s. late Allan Getchell and Amy Fellows (Adams) M.; e. Ridley Coll., St. Catharines, Ont. (1920-27, Sr. Matric.); Royal Mil. Coll., Kingston, Ont., 1927-31 (Dipl.); m. Margaret Audrey, d. Trevor H. Temple, Toronto, Ont., 30 Jan. 1937; children: Virginia Temple, Ian Malcolm; sales Rep., Toronto office Consumers Glass Co. Ltd., 1932-40; Asst. to the Gen. Sales Mgr., Jan.-Nov. 1946; apptd. Gen. Sales Mgr. of Jos. E. Seagram & Sons Ltd. 1946 and Vice-Pres., 1951; el. Pres. and Dir., The House of Seagram Ltd., 1956, and el. Chrmn. 1958; Pres., Candn. Export Assn. 1963-77; Founding Pres., Candn. South African Soc., 1979; joined Candn. Armoured Corps Jan. 1940, posted to Lord Strathcona's Horse (R.C.) in 1943, with rank of Major, promoted to Lt.-Col. in command 1944; brought Regt. back to Winnipeg, Jan. 1946; awarded D.S.O., M.B.E.; Pres., Candn. Lawn Tennis Assn., 1949-53; Gen. Chrmn., Welfare Fed. of Montreal (Red Feather) fund campaign, 1959; Past Pres., Sir Arthur Currie Br., (Que. No. 1), Royal Candn. Legion; Pres. (1960-61) Assn. of Candn. Distillers; Pres., Candn. Tourist Assn., 1958; Anglican; recreations: golf, fishing, curling; Clubs: St. James's; Mt. Bruno; Thistle Curling; Toronto Golf; Home: Apt. 1101, 3468 Drummond St., Montreal, Que. H3G 1Y4

McBEAN, John C., B.Sc., M.B.A., P.Eng.; executive; b. Kirkland Lake, Ont., 23 Nov. 1940; s. John W. and Doris (Chisholm) McB.; e. Swastika Public School; Kirkland Lake Coll. and Vocational Inst.; Queens Univ. B.Sc. (Geol.) 1962; Harvard Grad. Sch. of Business Adm., M.B.A. 1967; m. Barbara Daugherty, 14 May 1962; children: John C., Catherine Ann, Elizabeth Anne, Scott C., Marianne; PRES., GEN MGR., DIR AND CONTROLLING SHAREHOLDER OMNI DRILLING, 1980- ; Pres., John C. McBean Consulting Ltd., 1977- ; Shareholder and Dir., Joffre Resources Ltd.; 1977- ; Geol. Ont. Dept. Mines 1962; Mine Geol. Upper Canada Mines Ltd. 1962-64; Plant Engineer and Tech. Sales Rep. Cyanamid of Canada Ltd. 1964-65; Vice-Pres. and Dir. Heath & Sherwood Drilling Ltd. 1967-70; Exec. Vice Pres., Vice-Pres. Drilling Operations and Dir. Upper Canada Mines Ltd. 1970-72; Extve. Vice-Pres. Upper Canada Resources Ltd. 1972-73, Pres. 1974-75, Chrmn. 1976-77; Exec. Vice Pres., Bankeno Mines Ltd., 1970-73, Pres. and Dir., 1974-77; Pres., LeGrand Industries Ltd., 1977-79; Vice Pres., Dir. and Controlling Shareholder, Lakeshore Mtrs. of Kirkland Lake, 1977-79; Treas., Candn. Geol. Foundation, 1974-77; mem. Candn. Inst. Mining and Metall.; Engn. Inst. Can.; Am. Inst. Mining Metallurgical & Petroleum Engrs.; Adv. Bd. Northern Coll of Applied Arts & Technol. (Kirkland Lake Campus); Bd. Trade Metrop. Toronto; Assn. Prof. Engrs. Ont.; Past Chrmn. Kirkland Lake Devel. Comn.; Past Pres. Kirkland Lake Chamber of

Comm.; Canadian Diamond Drilling Assn.; recreations: skiing, golf; Clubs: Glencoe, Calgary; Pinebrooke Gold and Winter, Calgary; 400, Calgary; Calgary Petroleum; Home: 28 Medford Place S.W., Calgary, Alta. Office: Suite 3800, 708-11th Ave. S.W., Calgary, Alta.

McBRYDE, William Arthur Evelyn, M.A., Ph.D.; university professor; b. Ottawa, Ont., 20 Oct. 1917; s. Edwin Brooks and Evelyn Agnes (Riddick) M.; e. Univ. of Toronto Schs.; Univ. of Toronto, B.A. (Chem.) 1939, M.A. (Chem.) 1940; Univ. of Virginia, Ph.D. (Chem.) 1947; m. Marion Eleanor, d. John Robertson, Toronto, Ont., 28 May 1949; children: Ian Douglas, Sheila Kathleen; Teaching Asst., Univ. of Toronto, 1939-42; Chemist, Welland Chemical Works, Niagara Falls, 1942-44; Asst. Prof., Univ. of Toronto 1948-57; Travelling Fellowship, The Nuffield Foundation, Oxford Univ., 1954-55; Assoc. Prof., Univ. of Toronto, 1957-60; Prof., Univ. of Waterloo since 1960; Chrmn., Dept. of Chem., 1960-64, 1971-77; Dean, Faculty of Science 1961-69; Visiting Fellow, Aust. Nat. Univ. 1969-70; served in 2nd World War, 1944-45, R.C.N.V.R., Sub-Lieut. (Special Br.) 1945; Publications: "Elementary Experimental Chemistry" (with M. W. Lister), 1950, 4th ed. 1959; "The Outlines of Chemistry" (with R. P. Graham) 1966, 2nd ed. 1978; articles and papers to scient. journs.; mem., Chem. Inst. Can. (Councillor, 1958-61, Dir. 1960-63); Chem. Soc. (London); Presbyterian; recreations: golf, gardening, curling; Address: 101 John Boulevard, Waterloo, Ont. N2L 1C2

McBURNEY, Margot B., B.A., M.Sc.; librarian; b. Lethbridge, Alta.; d. Ronald L. M. and R. Blanche (Lott) Hart; e. Principia Coll. Elsah, Ill. B.A.; Univ. of Ill. M.Sc.; m. 4 Sept. 1954 (divorced); children: Margot Elisabeth (Lisa) (Mrs. Walter Critchett Lane), James Ronald Gordon; CHIEF LIBRARIAN, QUEEN'S UNIV. since 1977; Reference Librarian, Principia Coll. 1969; Systems Analyst, Univ. of Alta. 1970-71, Undergrad. Reference Librarian 1971-72, Ed., Periodicals Holdings List 1972-73, Serials Cataloguer 1973-74, Head of Acquisitions 1974-77; mem. Am. Soc. Information Science (Councillor 1976-79); Assn. Research Libs. (Dir. 1978-81); Candn. Assn. Research Libs.; Candn. Lib. Assn.; Am. Lib. Assn.; Ont. Council Univ. Libs.; P. Conservative; Christian Scientist; recreations: tennis, sailing, swimming, skiing; Home: Landmark #508, 165 Ontario St., Kingston Ont.; K7L 5C4; Office: Douglas Library, Queen's University, Kingston, Ont. K7L 5C4

McBURNEY, Air Vice Marshal Ralph Edward, C.B.E., C.D.; b. Montreal, P.Q., 1906; s. Irvile Albert M.; e. Univ. of Sask.; Univ. of Man.; m. Gertrude Elizabeth, d. William Bate, Saskatoon, Sask.; children: Peter, Kay, David; Cadet, R.C.A.F., 1924; Govt. flying operations Northern Canada 1927-31; Sch. of Army Co-operation, Old Sarum, 1931; Staff Pilot, Winnipeg Air Station, 1932; Instructor, R.C.A.F. School of Army Co-operation, Camp Borden, 1933-34; R.A.F. Wireless Sch., Cranwell, 1935, and R.A.F. StaffColl., 1939; Dir. of Signals, R.C.A.F. Hdqrs., Ottawa, 1935-39 and 1939-43; commanded R.C.A.F. Station, Trention, Ont., 1943; Overseas 1943-45 as Station and Base Commander, No. 6 R.C.A.F. Bomber Group, and as S.A.S.O., No. 6 Group Hdqrs.; apptd. A.O.C. Maintenance Command, R.C.A.F., 1945, and Chrmn., Candn. Joint Liaison Office, London, Eng., 1946-48; apptd. A.O.C., Air Materiel Command, 1948 before retiring from the forces in 1952; Mgr., Defence Equipment Div., Philips Industries Ltd., 1952-59; Indust. Consult. 1959-60; Chief, Tech. Information Svce. of Nat. Research Council Can. 1960-72 and Secy., Indust. Research Assistance Program 1962-72; Chrmn. Comte. for Information for Indust., Internat. Fed. for Documentation (F.I.D.), 1960-68; Pres., F.I.D. 1968-72; recreations: curling, square dancing; Home: 2022 Sharon Avenue, Ottawa, Ont. K2A 1L8

McCABE, St. Clair Landerkin; publishing executive; b. Toronto, Ont. 13 July 1915; s. Herbert St. Clair and Myrtle (Landerkin) M.; m. Margaret Letitia, d. late Norman Hamilton, Galt, Ont. 1981;; children: Mrs. J. Beatson, John Timothy St. Clair; DIRECTOR: THOMSON NEWSPAPERS LIMITED; Pres. and Dir., Thomas Newspapers Inc.; Douglas Dispatch, Inc.; Greenville Newspapers Inc.; Humboldt Newspapers Inc.; Chew Newspapers of Ohio Inc.; Key West Newspaper Corporation; Lock Haven Express Printing Company; Oxnard Publishing Company; Phenix Citizen Inc.; Punta Gorda Herald Inc.; Rocky Mount Publishing Company; San Gabriel Valley Tribune, Inc.; Thomson Newspapers (Alabama) Inc.; Thomson Newspapers (Florida) Inc.; Thomson Newspapers (Illinois) Inc.; Thomson Newspapers (Kentucky) Inc.; Thomson Newspapers (Michigan) Inc.; Thomson Newspapers (Minnesota) Inc.; Thomson Newspapers (New Hampshire) Inc.; Thomson Newspapers (Ohio) Inc.; Thomson Newspapers (Pennsylvania) Inc.; Thomson Newspapers (Wisconsin) Inc.; Thomson Publications of New York Inc.; Thomson Newsprint Inc., Dir., Central Canada Insurance Service Limited; The Guarantee Insurance Company; Replacement Sales Co. Ltd.; Scottish & York Holdings Limited; Scottish & York Insurance Co. Limited; Thomson Newspapers Ltd.; Victoria Insurance Company of Canada; Formerly Gen. Mgr. Galt "Evening Reporter" to 1949; Past Pres., Thomson Newspapers Ltd., Toronto; Member: Inter-American Press Association; International Press Institute; Freemason (Scot. Rite); recreation: Fishing; Home: 146 Harborage Crt., Clearwater, Florida, 33611; Office: Thomson Newspapers Inc., Ste. 401, 1111 N. Westshore Blvd., Tampa, Florida, and Thomson Newspapers Inc., 3150 Des Plaines Avenue, Des Plaines, Illinois, 60018.

McCAGUE, Hon. George Raymond, M.P.P.; politician; b. Alliston, Ont. 5 Dec. 1929; s. John Joseph Edward and Lillian Mae (Meek) McC.; e. Burns Pub. Sch. and Banting Mem. High Sch. Alliston, Ont.; Ont. Agric. Coll. 1952; m. Elizabeth Elaine d. Elwood Corbett 29 June 1955; children: Heather, Raymond, Barry, Ross; CHAIRMAN OF CABINET since 1979, and Chmn., Mgmt. Bd. since 1978; operated family farm to 1953; Owner McCague General Insurance 1953-56; Owner and Broker McCague Real Estate 1953-62; Secy. Glenafton Farms Ltd. 1960-69; Pres. McCague Merion Sod Ltd. since 1962; Chrmn. Niagara Escarpment Comn. 1973-75; Dir. Farmers' Central Mutual Fire Ins. Co. 1968; Chrmn. Allied Hortic. Trades Cong. 1972; Councillor Town of Alliston 1960, 1961, Depy. Reeve 1962, 1964, Co. Councillor 1962, 1964-66, Reeve 1965-66, Warden Simcoe Co. 1966, mem. Alliston Pub. Sch. Bd. 1967-68, Mayor 1969-73, mem. Pub. Utilities Comn. 1969-73; Chrmn. Bd. Govs. Georgian Coll. 1967-74; mem. Extve. Assn. Muns. Ont. 1970-73; Nottawasaga Valley Conserv. Authority 1970-73; Alliston Planning Bd. 1972-73; el. to Ont. Leg. 1975, re-el. 1977; Parlty. Asst. to Min. of Treasury, Econ. and Intergovt'al Affairs 1977; Min. of Govt. Services 1977; Minister of the Environment, 1978; Pres. Beeton Agric. Soc. 1959-60; Nursery Sod Growers Assn. Ont. 1969; mem. Ont. Nursery Trades Assn.; Ont. Landscape Contractors Assn.; Ont. Garden Maintenance & Landscape Assn.; Alliston Chamber Comm.; Royal Candn. Legion (Hon. mem.); Grey & Simcoe Foresters (Hon. mem.); P. Conservative; United Church; Clubs: Lions (Secy. 1974-75); Kinsmen (Hon. mem.); Alliston Curling (Secy. 1956-68); Home: 191 Albert St. W., Alliston, Ont. L0M 1A0; Office: 7th Fl. Frost Building South, Queen's Park, Toronto, Ont. M7A 1Z6.

McCAGUE, James Ashford, B.S.A.; dairy farmer; b. Gormley, Ont. 13 March 1918; s. George Arthur and Margaret Agnes (Gee) McC.; e. N. Toronto Coll. Inst.; Univ. of Toronto, B.S.A. (Ont. Agric. Coll.) 1940; m. Janet Barbara, d. Bert James, Brantford, Ont. 25 May 1946; children: Peter, Scott, Carol, Jamie; Pres., Dairy Farmers of Can.; Lodestar Farms Ltd.; Dir., Candn. Fed. Agric.; V.I.D.O.; mem. Agric. Research Inst. Ont.; Ont. Milk

Marketing Board; Candn. Agric. Hall of Fame; winner of numerous awards in dairy farming and agric. fields incl. Master Breeder Shield 1968, Centennial Medal (Ont. Agric. Coll.) 1974; owner Lodestar Farm; judged Holstein-Friesian Cattle, Sao Paulo, Brazil 1972; featured as "Man in the News", Globe & Mail, Feb. 1975; served with RCAF 1940-45; Pilot 412 Sqdn. Spitfires; P.O.W. 1942-45; Past Treas. Peel Dufferin Simcoe P. Cons. Assn.; Chrmn. Essa Twp. Planning Bd.; former mem. and Past Chrmn. Banting Mem. High Sch. Bd.; mem. Holstein-Friesian Assn. Can. (Dir. and Past Pres.); Alliston Agric. Soc. (Past Pres.); Agric. Inst. Can.; Ont. Agric. Coll. Alumni Assn.; Freemason; P. Conservative; United Church; recreations: bridge, fishing, curling; Clubs: Lions (Past Pres.); Curling (Past Pres.).

McCAIG, John Robert; transportation executive; b. Moose Jaw, Sask., 14 June 1929; s. John Waters and Stella May (Cook) McC.; e. Moose Jaw (Sask.) Tech. High Sch., 1946; m. Anne Shorrocks Glass, 11 March 1950; children: Jeffrey James, Joann, Melanie; CHRMN. & CHIEF EXECUTIVE OFFR., TRIMAC LTD. since 1972 and Dir. of all Trimac subsidiaries; NOVA, an Albertan Corp.; Pan-Alberta Gas Ltd.; Alberta Gas Ethylene Co. Ltd.; Urban Transportation Development Corp.; Kenting Ltd.; Royal Bank of Can.; Royfund (Equity) Ltd.; Trustee, Royfund Income Trust; Dir. Jr. Achievements S. Alta.; Candn. Vice-Pres., W. Highway Inst.; Dispatch/Operations, Maccam Transport Ltd., Moose Jaw, 1947-52; Gen. Mgr. 1952-60; Pres., HM Trimble & Sons, Calgary, 1961-68; Pres., Westburne International Industries Ltd., 1969-70; Pres. and Chief Extve. Offr. Trimac Ltd. 1970-72; Protestant; recreations: golf, skiing; Clubs: Glencoe; Calgary Golf & Country; Petroleum; Home: #2, 3315 Rideau Pl. S.W., Calgary, Alta. T2S 2T1; Office: 736-8th Ave. S.W., Calgary, Alta. T2P 1H4

McCAIG, John W.; transportation executive; b. Dumfriesshire, Scotland; e. Ayrshire, Scot.; CHAIRMAN BD., TRIMAC TRANSPORTATION SYSTEM LTD.; Pres., Maccam Transport Ltd.; Maccam Construction Ltd.; Redi-Mix Ltd.; Dir., Stothert Holdings Ltd.; Pres., Candn. Automotive Transportation Assn., 1952-53 and Pres., Sask. Motor Transport Assn., 1938-53; emigrated to Can. with his parents at age 14; became successively Farm Hand, Lumber-Jack, Miner, Construction Worker and Truck Driver; estbd. his own truck line in 1930, and after slowly building it up sold it in 1941 and joined Candn. Army as a Pte.; Commissioned in 1942 and served as an Inf. Transport Offr.; Chrmn., Sask. Diamond Jubilee & Centennial Comte.; Dir., Sask. Econ. Devel. Corp.; Carling Breweries (Sask.) Ltd.; Office: Junction No. 1 and 2 Highways N., Moose Jaw, Sask.

McCAIN, Andrew Henderson; executive; b. Florenceville, N.B., 12 Sept. 1921; s. Andrew Davis and Laura Blanche (Perley) McC.; e. Univ. of New Brunswick 1939-40; Acadia Univ. 1942-43; m. Marjorie Luella, d. of Joseph Pearson, Hartland, N.B., 26 July 1947; children: Allison, Kathy, Linda, Margaret, Stephen, Nancy; PRESIDENT AND C.E.O. McCAIN PRODUCE CO. LTD., since 1974 (Potato Exporters); Dir., N.B. Telephone Co. Ltd.; McCain Foods Ltd.; McCain Fertilisers Ltd.; Carleton Cold Storage Ltd.; chrmn. of Bd., Junipur Lumber Co.; joined present Co. 1940, Manager 1953; Freemason (Scot. Rite); Elks; Liberal; Anglican; recreation: golf; Club: Union (Saint John); Home: Florenceville, N.B. E0J 1K0; Office: Florenceville, N.B. E0J 1K0

McCAIN, G. Wallace F.; manufacturer; b. Florenceville, N.B., 9 April 1930; s. A. D. and Laura B. (Perley) McC.; m. Margaret L. A., d. J. P. Norrie; children: Scott, Michael, Martha, Eleanor; PRESIDENT, McCAIN FOODS LTD.; Chrmn. Bd., McCain Australia Pty. Ltd.; McCain Foods Inc. (U.S.); Thomas Equipment Ltd.; Pres., McCain Fertilizers; Valley Farms Ltd. Dir., McCain International Ltd. (Eng.); McCain Espana S.A.; McCain Europa S.A.; Day & Ross Ltd.; McCain Produce Co. Ltd.; Bilopage Inc.; Prudential Assurance Co. Ltd.; Anglican; recreations: skiing, swimming, tennis, hunting; Home: Florenceville, N.B. E0J 1K0; Office: Florenceville, N.B. E0J 1K0

McCAIN, H. Harrison, B.A.; board chairman; b. Florenceville, N.B., 3 Nov. 1927; s. A. D. and Laura B. (Perley) McC.; e. Florenceville (N.B.) Pub. and High Schs.; Acadia Univ., B.A.; m. Marion M., d. late J. B. McNair, 4 Oct. 1952; children: Mark, Peter, Ann, Laura, Gillian; CHRMN. OF THE BD., McCAIN FOODS LTD.; Chrmn., McCain International Ltd., McCain Alimentaire SARL, McCain Europa, B.V.; Eng.; McCain Espana S.A., Spain; Dir., Bank of Nova Scotia; McCain Australia Pty. Ltd.; McCain Foods Inc., U.S.; McCain Produce Co. Ltd.; Thomas Equipment Ltd.; M & D Transfer Ltd.; Day & Ross Ltd.; Petro Canada; Presbyterian; recreations: skiing; Home: Florenceville, N.B. E0J 1K0; Office: Florenceville, N.B. E0J 1K0

McCALL, Hon. Meg Sutherland, M.L.A.; politician; b. Mayo, Y.T. 24 May 1931; d. Hugh Cormack and Jessie Margaret (MacKay) Sutherland; e. Yukon, Calif., Vancouver, France, Germany; m. Dr. W. J. Ian McCall 1952; children: Ian Matthew (d.), Samuel Alexander, Hugh Sutherland, Lael Margaret Rosemary; MIN. OF HEALTH & HUMAN RESOURCES, Education, Recreation, Libraries and Information Resources, Y.T. 1979- ; freelance writer; playwright; producer; director; actress; columnist; antiquary; potter; Yukon historian; student of Fine Arts and Graphic Arts; el. M.L.A. for Klondike g.e. 1978; P. Conservative; Protestant; Office: (P.O. Box 2703) Whitehorse, Y.T. Y1A 2C6.

McCALLA, Arthur G., M.Sc., Ph.D., D.Sc. (Hon.), F.R.S.C., F.A.I.C.; professor emeritus; b. St. Catharines, Ont., 22 Mar. 1906; s. William Copeland and Margaret Adam (Ratcliffe) M.; e. Univ. of Alta., B.Sc. 1929; M.Sc. 1931; D.Sc. (Hon.) 1981; Univ. of Cal., Ph.D., 1933; Inst. of Phys. Chem., Uppsala, Sweden, 1939-40; m. Enid Frances, d. Rev. H. G. Rice, Edmonton, 5 Aug. 1931; children: Dennis, Donna, Kenneth; Research Asst., Dept. of Field Crops, Univ. of Alta., 1932-41; Prof. of Field Crops, 1941-44; Prof. of Plant Science, 1944-51; Dean, Faculty of Agric., 1951-59; Faculty of Graduate Studies, 1957-71; Pres., Edmonton Home and Sch. Council, 1945-47; mem., Nat. Research Council of Can. (1950-56); Agric. Inst. of Can.; Alta. Inst. of Agrol.; Candn. Commonwealth Scholarship Fellowship Comte. 1959-72; Candn. Bio-chem. Soc.; Sigma Zi; Un. Church; recreations: gardening, photography, woodworking; Home: 11455 University Ave., Edmonton, Alta. T6G 1Y9

McCALLA, Peter Douglas Whitby, M.A., D.Phil.; historian; educator; b. Edmonton, Alta. 4 Sept. 1942; s. Peter Douglas Ralston and Lois (Whitby) McC.; e. Strathcona Composite High Sch. Edmonton 1960; Queen's Univ. B.A. 1964; Univ. of Toronto M.A. 1965 (Woodrow Wilson Fellowship); Oriel Coll. Oxford Univ. (Rhodes Scholar) D.Phil. 1972; m. Anna Maria d. W. B. Skorski, Peterborough, Ont. 25 July 1970; PROF. OF HISTORY, LADY EATON COLL., TRENT UNIV. 1981- , Assoc. Prof. of Hist. 1973-81; Principal 1976-81; Asst. Prof. of Hist. Trent Univ. 1968-73; author "The Upper Canada Trade 1834-1872: A Study of the Buchanans' Business" 1979; various articles 19th century Candn. business, social and econ. hist.; Ed., Ont. Series, Champlain Soc.; mem. Ed. Adv. Bd. "Canadian Historical Review"; mem. Candn. Hist. Assn.; Econ. Hist. Assn.; Ont. Hist. Soc.; Am. Hist. Assn.; Econ. Hist. Soc.; Address: Peterborough, Ont. K9J 7B8.

McCALLION, David John, M.A., Ph.D., M.R.E.; university professor; b. Toronto, Ont. 25 Sept. 1916; s. John and Elizabeth (Service) M.; e. York Mem. Coll. Inst. (1938); McMaster Univ., B.A. 1942, M.A. 1947; Brown Univ.,

Ph.D. 1949; m. Norah Jean, d. late James Moore, 1 Sept. 1944; children: Kathryn, Sharon, Janet, James, Thomas, Margaret; PROF. OF ANATOMY, McMASTER UNIV.; Lectr. in Zool., McMaster Univ., 1945-47; Teaching Fellow, Brown Univ., 1947-49; Asst. Prof. Acadia Univ., 1949-51, and Prof. there 1951-55; Asst. Prof., Univ. of Toronto, 1955-58, Assoc. Prof. 1958-62; Prof. 1962-68; Prof. Anat., McMaster Univ., 1968-82; Prof. Emeritus, 1982; ordained Anglican Deacon, May, 1978; Priest, Dec. 1979; Assoc. Priest, Grace Church, Waterdown, Ont.; mem. Internat. Inst. for Embryology; Teratology Soc.; N.Y. Acad. of Sciences; Candn. Assoc. Anat.; Am. Assn. of Anat.; Sigma Xi; P. Conservative; Anglican; recreations: golf, cooking; Home: 722 Hiawata Blvd., Ancaster, Ont. L9G 3A7

McCALLUM, Donald R.; banker; b. Montreal, Ailsa Craig, Ont., 24 Nov. 1912; s. Charles Herbert and Laura May (Robinson) M.; e. Pub. and High Schs., Ailsa Craig, Ont.; m. Margaret Louise, d. B. W. Hoeschen, Saskatoon, Sask., 3 Nov. 1942; one s. John S.; Dir., Lloyds Bank Int'l Canada, since 1977; joined the Bank of Montreal in Ailsa Craig Ont., 1929; served in various capacities in several Ont. offices; apptd. Mgr., Toronto Yonge & St. Clair Br., 1955, Asst. Supt., International Div., H.O., Montreal, 1957, Supt., 1959; apptd. Manager, Main Br. London, England, 1963, Asst. General Mgr. for the United Kingdom and London, Eng., Manager, 1966; apptd. Vice-President for the U.K. and London Manager, 1967; apptd. Sr. Vice Pres., Internat. Banking 1968; apptd. Sr. Vice Pres. and Chief Agt., Bank of Montreal, N.Y. 1972 and retired 1976; served as Hon. Treas. Canadian Chamber of Commerce in Great Britain 1965-67; Dir., Candn. Export Assn.; R. Catholic; recreation: golf; Clubs: St. James's (Montreal); Kanawaki, (Montreal); Sunningdale (London, Ont.); Overseas Bankers (London, Eng.); Royal Mid-Surrey (London, Eng.); Apawamis (New York); National; Toronto; Mississauga Golf and Country; Home: 966 Cresthampton Lane, Mississauga, Ont. L5H 2X1

McCALLUM, Kenneth James, M.Sc., Ph.D., F.C.I.C., F.R.S.C.; university dean; b. Scott, Sask., 25 April 1918; s. James Alexander and Alice (Fines) M.; e. Univ. of Sask., B.Sc. 1936, M.Sc. 1939; Columbia Univ., Ph.D. 1942; m. Erika Connell, 16 Aug. 1974; children (by prev. m.); Patricia, Douglas; DEAN OF GRAD. STUDIES, UNIV. OF SASK., since 1970; Prof. of Chem. there 1953- present and Assoc. Dean of Grad. Studies, 1967-70; Jr. Research Offr., N.R.C. of Can., 1942-43; Asst. Prof. Chem., Univ. of Sask., 1943, Assoc. Prof. 1946; Pres., Chem. Inst. Can. 1968-69; Liberal; United Church; recreation: curling; Home: 1622 Park Ave., Saskatoon, Sask. S7H 2P3

McCAMMON, Morgan, Q.C., B.C.L.; executive; b. Montreal, Que., 20 Sept. 1922; s. John Whyte and Nora Banfield (Morgan) M.; e. Westmount (Que.) Public Schs.; McGill Univ. (1940-41 and 1945-49), B.C.L. 1949; EXEC. VICE-PRES., BREWING GROUP, THE MOLSON COS. LTD. since 1975; Chrmn. of Bd., Molson Breweries of Canada Limited; Dir., City & Dist. Savings Bank called to the Bar of Quebec, 1949; practised law Montreal, 1949-53; joined Steinberg's Limited, Montreal, in Real Estate Department in 1953, and apptd. Secy. and Gen. Counsel in 1957; joined Molson Breweries Ltd. (now The Molson Companies Ltd.) in 1958 as Secy. and Gen. Counsel; Vice-Pres. 1962; Vice-Pres., Corporate Devel., 1967; Sr. Vice-President Corporate Services 1968; served in the 2nd World War with Candn. Army Active, 1942-45; cr. Q.C. 1966; mem., Montreal and Que. Bar Assns.; Clubs: St. Denis; St. James's (Montreal); Office: 1555 Notre Dame St. E., Montreal, Que. H26 2R5

McCARDLE, James Joachim, B.A.; diplomat; b. Stratford, Ont. 27 Apl. 1922; s. John Patrick and Mary (Keegan) McC.; e. Univ. of Toronto, B.A. 1943; m. Lannie

Roth, d. Benjamin Harrison, Weyburn, Sask., 27 Nov. 1948; one d., Bennett; joined Candn. Foreign Service 1946; Candn. Liaison Mission, Tokyo, 1947-49, Ottawa 1949-53, 1956-59, 1962-69; Secy. to Candn. Del. to Peace Conf. with Japan, San Francisco, 1951, Washington, D.C. 1953-56; Secy. to Canadian Sec., Canada-U.S.A. Permanent Joint Board on Defence 1956-59; Delegate to North Atlantic Council, Paris 1959-62; Ambassador to Ireland 1969-72; High Commissioner to Australia and Fiji 1972-77; Dir. Gen. of Defense and Arm, Control Bureau, Dept. of Ext. Affairs 1977-80; Special Negotiator (Nuclear Safeguards) 1980-81; Consul Gen. of Can. in San Francisco, 1981; served with Candn. Army 1943-46; rank Lt.; R. Catholic; recreations: golf, bridge; Clubs: Rideau; Commonwealth (California); Home: 2500 Divisadero St., San Francisco, CA 94115 Office: Cdn. Consulate Gen., One Maritime Plaza, San Francisco, CA 94111-3468

McCARTER, John Alexander, M.A., Ph.D., F.R.S.C.; research chemist; educator; b. Wareham, Eng., 25 Jan. 1918; s. Alexander and Helen T. (McKellar) McC.; e. Dawson (Y.T.) Pub. Sch.; King Edward High Sch., Vancouver, B.C.; Univ. of B.C., B.A. 1939, M.A. 1941; Univ. of Toronto, Ph.D. 1945; m. Patricia Jocelyn d. late Oliver B. St. John, 27 Dec. 1941; children: David G., Robert M., Patricia L., William A.; PROF. OF BIOCHEM., UNIV. OF WESTERN ONT. 1965-, and Dir. of Cancer Research Lab. there 1965-80; Adjunct Prof. of Biochem., Univ. Victoria 1980-; Jr. and subsequently Asst. Research Off., Nat. Research Council, Atomic Energy Project, Chalk River, Ont. 1945; Assoc. Prof. of Biochem., Dalhousie Univ., 1948, Prof. and Head of Dept. 1950-65; awarded Exchange Fellowship, Brit. Empire Cancer Campaign, 1959-60; Queen's Jubilee Medal; author of over 50 scient. publs. in biochem., carcinogenesis and tumour virology; mem., Candn. Biochem. Soc. (Pres. 1967); Unitarian; recreations: ornithology, painting; Home: 3171 Henderson Rd., Victoria, B.C. V8P 5A3; Office: Univ. of Victoria, Victoria, B.C.

McCARTHY, Doris, R.C.A. (1951), O.S.A. (1945), CSPWC (1952); artist; teacher; b. Calgary, Alta., 7 July 1910; d. George Arnold and Mary Jane Colson Moffatt M.; e. Malvern C.I.; Ont. Coll. of Art; Central Sch. of Arts and Crafts, London, Eng.; Teacher and Administrator, Art Dept., Central Tech. Sch. Toronto 1932-72; regular exhibitor with Ont. Soc. Artists since 1931; Roy. Cdn. Acad. since 1934; Can. Soc. Ptrs. Water Colour since 1938; usually landscape from Haliburton Ont., Gaspé Dist. Que., Georgian Bay, Rocky Mtns, High Arctic and Nfld.; also liturgical art in wood sculpture, fabric wallhangings and banners, calligraphy, illuminating of memorial books; one man shows regularly since 1932 in Ont. and Que., esp. Toronto, Calgary and Ottawa; study trips around world 1951 and 62; Pres. OSA 1964-67; CSPWC 1956-58; rep. by Aggregation Gallery Toronto, Wells Gallery, Ottawa, Kensington Gallery, Calgary; work in perm. coll., A.G. Ont., Hamilton A.G., London A.G., DOFASCO, Imperial Oil, BA Oil, and many others; Anglican; Home: 1 Meadowcliff Drive, Scarborough, Ont. M1M 2X8

McCARTHY, Hon. Grace Mary, M.L.A.; politician; b. Vancouver, B.C. 14 Oct. 1927; d. George and Allrietta (McCloy) Winterbottom; e. Vancouver Grade 12 Cert.; m. Raymond McCarthy 23 June 1948; children: Mary Grace, Calvin G.R.; DEPY. PREMIER AND MIN. OF HUMAN RESOURCES, B.C. 1978-; Pres., Social Credit Party 1973-75; el. M.L.A. 1966, re-el. since; Min. Without Portfolio 1966-72; Prov. Secy., Depy. Premier and Min. of Recreation & Travel 1975-76; Prov. Secy., Depy. Premier and Min. of Travel 1976-78; Commr. Parks Bd. 1961-66; Vice Chrmn. 1966 City of Vancouver; Dir. Candn. Assn. Christians & Jews; mem. Adv. Bd. Salvation Army; Past Pres. FTD; Social Credit; Anglican; recreations: swimming, interior decorating; Club: Native Daughters;

Home: 4610 Beverly Cres., Vancouver, B.C. V6J 4E6; Office: Parliament Bldgs., Victoria, B.C. V8V 1X4.

McCARTHY, Walter J., B.Com.; insurance executive; b. Albany, N.Y., 20 Feb. 1923; s. J. Earle (dec.) and Katherine (Maxwell) McC.; e. St. Mary's Acad. (N.Y.) 1941; McGill Univ. B.Com 1950; Harvard Univ. Grad. Sch. Business Adm.-Advanced Mang. Program 1968; m. Margaret Leahy 1946; children: Sheila Anne (Mrs. H. Haddad), James, Susan (Mrs. D. Ternlund), John, David; SR. VICE PRES., INVESTMENTS, SUN LIFE ASSURANCE CO. OF CANADA 1979-; Vice Chmn. of Bd. and Dir., Can. Enterprise Development Corp. Ltd.; Pres. and Dir. Sun Life of Canada Investment Management Ltd.; Dir. Suncan Equity Services Co.; Trans Alta Utilities Corp.; Trans Alta Resources Corp.; served with R.C.A.F. 1941-46, rank Flight Lt.; recreation: flying; Home: 33 Harbour Sq., Toronto, Ont. M5J 2G2; Office: P.O. Box 4150, Station A, Toronto, Ont. M5W 2C9

McCAUGHEY, Andrew Gilmour, B.Com., C.A.; insurance executive; b. Montreal, Que. 8 Dec. 1922; s. Andrew Gilmour and Mary Doris (Sheldon) McC.; e. McGill Univ. B.Com. 1949; C.A. Inst. 1950; m. Lorraine Baltera; children: Jennifer H. (Mrs. Kirk Rott), Andrew John, Matthew James; PRES., CHIEF EXTVE. OFFR. AND DIR., NORTH AMERICAN LIFE ASSURANCE CO.; Dir. The Molson Companies Ltd.; Canadian Foundation Co.; served with RCAF as Pilot 1941-45 attached to RAF Europe and Mediterranean Theatres; mem. Inst. C.A.'s Que. and Ont.; Financial Extves. Inst. Toronto (Past Pres. Montreal Chapter); Anglican; Clubs: University; RCYC; Royal Candn. Mil. Inst.; Royal Air Force (London, Eng.); Lambton Golf & Country; Home: 87 Valecrest Dr., Islington, Ont. M9A 4P5; Office: 105 Adelaide St. W., Toronto, Ont. M5H 1R1.

McCAULEY, William Alexander, A.T.C.M., Mus.B., M.M., A.M.D., composer; conductor; performer (music); b. Tofield, Alta., 14 Feb. 1917; s. Alexander James Henry and Barbara Ann (Sinclair) McC.; e. Tofield (Alta.) Pub. and High Schs.; Royal Conserv. of Music of Toronto, A.T.C.M. (Piano); Univ. of Toronto, Mus.B.; Ont. Coll. of Educ., High Sch. Teachers Specialist and Amy. Cert. (Music); Eastman Sch. of Music, M.M., A.M.D.; m. Elaine Patricia, d. late C. Leslie McFarlane, Whitby, Ont., 2 Dec. 1950; children: Brian Matthew, Timothy John, Julie Megan; Dir. of Music, O'Keefe Centre, Toronto, since 1960; Dir. of Music, York Univ., 1961-69; formed McCauley Music Ltd. 1966; apptd. Dir. of Music, Ottawa Tech. High Sch., 1947 and played 1st Trombone in Ottawa Philharmonic and Nat. Film Bd. Orchestras; Dir. of Music for Crawley Films, Ottawa, 1949-60; wrote scores for over 125 films incl. winners of over 60 nat. and internat. awards; compositions incl.: "Concerto for Horn" (Alta. Centennial Comn. Award, 1967); "Newfoundland Scene"; "Saskatchewan Suite"; "Quebec Lumber Camp"; "Theme and Variations for Orchestra"; "Five Miniatures for Flute, Strings and Harp"; "Five Miniatures for Bass Trombone, Strings and Harp"; "Five Miniatures for Six Percussionists"; "Five Miniatures for Ten Winds"; "Contrasts for Orchestra"; "Metropolis" for Concert Band; "Fantasy on Canadian Folk Songs" (performed on Parlt. Hill, May, 1967); "Centennial Suite" for Concert Band; "Plus One" for C.P.R. Cominco Bldg. at Expo; "International Anthem" (words by Wilson McDonald); has conducted over 200 recording sessions for film, T.V. and records (incl. Columbia Records, Capitol Records and Mercury); Children's Concert with Toronto Symphony Orchestra; Variety Series for Screen Gems; Concert Series at York Univ.; Irish Radio Orchestra; Dublin (programme of own music); under his direction York Univ. Choir won Lincoln Trophy (highest honour for choral groups competing across Can.); composed music for Christopher Chapman film "Festivals" 1970 for Osaka World's Fair; for C.B.C. film series "Whiteoaks of Jalna"; arranged and conducted music from "Jalna" for Capital records; composed music for C.B.C.'s "Louis Riel"; Dir. Music, Seneca Coll, 1970-78; Conductor, North York Symphony 1973 to present; conducted series of Children's Concerts with North York Philharmonic 1978-79; recent works: "The Flute Family"; "Miniature Overture for Brass Quintet" (recorded by Candn. Brass); "Five Miniatures for Brass Quintet" (comnd. & recorded by C.B.C.); "Kaleidescope Québecoise" (comnd. by Canada Council); "Concerto Grosso" (comnd. by Can. Council, recorded by Canadian Brass); "Piano Concerto #1" and "String Quartet #2" (comnd. by Ont. Arts Council); "Five Miniatures for Four Trombones"; film score "Sunday in the Country"; "It Seemed like a Good Idea at the Time"; "City on Fire" (co-composer); mem., Toronto Musicians Assn.; Ottawa Mus. Assn.; Candn. Assn. Publ. & Composers; Canadian League Composers (mem. Bd.); recreations: golf, tennis, skating, reading; Address: 60 Castle Frank Rd., Toronto, Ont. M4W 2Z8

McCAW, Hon. Leland Watson, M.L.A.; politician; b. Oak Hill, Charlotte Co., N.B. 27 July 1927; s. Walter Watson and Margaret (McMorran) McG.; e. Oak Hill Sch.; m. Eileen Isabel d. late Karl F. Dick, Moore's Mills, N.B. 1 July 1947; one s. Richard Leland; MIN. OF TOURISM, N.B. 1978- ; former partner men's clothing store St. Stephen, N.B.; mgr. own woodlands producing sawlogs, pulpwood and Christmas trees; el. M.L.A. for Charlotte Co. 1967, re-el. 1970; re-el. for Charlotte West 1974, 1978; Depy. Speaker 1973; former Chrmn. Natural Resources Comte. and Select Comte. on Renewable Resources, N.B.; mem. Independent Order Oddfellows; Charlotte Co. Woodlot Owners Assn.; Freemason; Shriner; P. Conservative; United Church; recreations: fishing, hunting, snowmobiling, music; Home: Oak Hill, R.R.1, Moore's Mills, N.B. E0G 2L0; Office: (P.O. Box 12345) Fredericton, N.B. E3B 5C3.

McCHESNEY, Roy Kenneth; b. Toronto, Ont. 8 July 1917; s. Maitland Edison and May Florence (Walker) McC.; e. Timmins (Ont.) High & Vocational Sch. 1937; Hon. Chrmn. of Bd. Rudolph-McChesney Lumber Co. Ltd.; Pres. Owen Sound Transportation Co. Ltd.; Northern Canada Transportation Ltd.; Nipissing Central Railway Co.; Star Transfer Ltd.; Chrmn. Ont. Northland Transport. Comn. (apptd. Commr. 1974, Acting Chrmn. 1975); P. Conservative; Anglican; recreation: boating; Home: 166 Hemlock St., Timmins, Ont. P4N 6S6; Office: Box 1398, Timmins, Ont. P4N 7N2

McCLEAVE, Robert Jardine, Q.C., B.A., LL.B., D.C.L.; judge; b. Moncton, N.B., 19 Dec. 1922; s. Robert David and Marjorie Doherty (Jardine) M.; e. Dalhousie Univ., B.A. 1943, LL.B. 1946; D.C.L. University King's Coll. 1973; m. Ruth Loughead James, 31 August 1946; children: Christine Mary, Nicola Ruth, Melissa Hope, Robert James, Sarah Yuill; read law with J. McG. Stewart, Q.C.; called to Bar of Nova Scotia 1950; cr. Q.C. Jan. 1968; with British United Press as Radio News Editor 1946; Maritime Mgr. 1947, W. Mgr. 1948, Ottawa Mgr. 1949; assoc. with Messrs. Stewart, Smith, MacKeen, Covert, Rogers, Sperry & Cowan, Halifax, 1950-53; first Chief News Editor, Stn. CJCH, Halifax, 1954-57; Dean, Maritime Sch. of Journalism 1955-64; first Pres., Halifax Broadcasting Club, 1963-64; el. to H. of C. for Halifax, 1957; Parlty. Secy. to Min. of Public Works, 1962-63; def. in g.e. Apl. 1963, re-el. 1972 and 1974; Depy. Speaker 1973-74; Co-Chrmn. Comte. on Statutory Instruments 1974-77; resigned 8 Dec. 1977 and apptd. a judge of the Prov. Court; apptd. Chrmn., N.S. Labour Relations Bd. 1980; Presbyterian; recreations: cryptic crosswords; golf; Home: 1652 Robie St., Halifax, N.S. B3H 3E7

McCLELLAN, George Brinton; b. Moose Jaw. Sask., 13 Aug. 1908; s. George Brinton and Elizabeth (Cunnington) M.; e. Royal Mil. Coll., Kingston, Ont. (1926-29); Candn. Police Coll. (1938); Nat. Defence Coll. (1949-50); hon. LLD Royal Military College, Univ. of Alberta; m. Bertha Elizabeth Austin, 15 Feb. 1941; children: Barbara, Margaret, Miriam; joined R.C.M.P., 1932; Constable, Inspector, 1939, Supt. 1947, Asst. Commr. 1953, Deputy Commr. 1959; subsequently Commr. till retired 1967; Ombudsman, Prov. of Alta. 1967-74; chrmn., Alta. Rent Regulation Appeal Bd., 1967-78 retired; served in Sask., Alta., N.S., Ont. and B.C.; awarded King Haakon 7 Cross of Liberation (Norway); Freemason; Anglican; recreations: travel, cycling, writing, west. Candn. historical research; Home: 14011-101 Ave. Edmonton, Alta. T5N 0K2

McCLELLAN, His Hon. William Arthur, B.Com.; judge; b. Moose Jaw. Sask., 1 Sept. 1912; s. George Brinton and Elizabeth Anne (Cunnington) McC.; e. Elem. Schs. and High Sch., N. Vancouver, B.C.; Ridley Coll., St. Catharines, Ont.; Univ. of B.C., B.Com. 1934; Vancouver and B.C. Law Schs., 1943-46; m. Mildred Marie, d. Frank Pollock, 27 May 1939; children Jane Leslie, Michael; JUDGE, CO. COURT OF VANCOUVER, since Nov. 1967; read law with Lawrence and Shaw, Vancouver; called to Bar of B.C. 1946; began practice of law in Dawson Creek, 1946; formed firm of McClellan, Lundeen and Clancy, 1958; practiced in Peace River area till 1967; prior to legal career served 9 yrs. with Canada Packers in Toronto and Vancouver; mem. Dawson Creek, B.C., Village Council, 1954-57 (Chrmn. 1955); def. Lib. cand. for South Peace in Prov. g.e. 1964 and for Cariboo in Fed. g.e. 1965; former Gov., Ang. Theol. Coll., Univ. of B.C.; former Chancellor, Ang. Diocese of Caledonia; mem., Candn. Bar Assn.; Freemason; Psi Upsilon; Anglican; recreations: fishing, gardening; Home: 48 - 8111 Saunders Rd., Richmond, B.C. V7A 4L9; Office: Court House, 800 Smithe St., Vancouver, B.C. V6Z 2E1

McCLELLAND, Jack; O.C. (1976); publisher; b. Toronto 1922; s. Jack McC.; e. St. Andrew's Coll.; Trinity Coll. Univ of Toronto, grad. 1946; m.; four d. and one s.; PRESIDENT, McCLELLAND AND STEWART LTD. since 1951; joined the Co. (co-founded by father 1906) 1946; served in 2nd World War, R.C.N. 1945, skipper of motor torpedo boat; Office: 25 Hollinger Rd., Toronto, Ont. M4B 3G2

McCLELLAND, John Alexander, B.Com., F.C.A.; b. Toronto, Ont. 27 March 1928; s. D. McK. and Irene (Leishman) McC.; e. Upper Can. Coll. Toronto; Univ. of Toronto B.Com.; m. Anita d. late W. C. T. Cran 15 June 1956; two d. Heather, Sandra; F.C.A., COOPERS & LYBRAND; mem. Inst. C.A.'s Ont. and Bermuda; Presbyterian; recreations: golf, tennis, skiing; Home: 256 Forest Hill Rd., Toronto, Ont. M5P 2N5; Office: P.O. Box 49330, Bentall Postal Stn., Vancouver, B.C. V7X 1P1

McCLELLAND, Hon. Robert Howard; politician; b. Calgary, Alta. 2 Nov. 1933; s. Howard Everett and Isabel Irving (Gardner) McC; e. Calgary, Alta.; m. Christine Denise Mallinson 22 Nov. 1980; one child (by previous marriage); MIN. OF ENERGY, MINES & PETROLEUM RESOURCES, B.C.; Min. responsible for B.C. Hydro & Power Authority; B.C. Utilities Comn.; B.C. Petroleum Corp.; Chrmn. Cabinet Comte. on Econ. Devel.; mem. Environment & Land Use Comte.; Treasury Bd.; Alcan Pipeline Comte.; Maritime Boundaries Comte.; Planning & Priorities Cabinet Comte.; Social Credit; Office: Room 310, Parliament Bldgs., Victoria, B.C. V8V 1X4.

McCLELLAND, Thomas H., B.Sc., P.Eng.; mining executive; b. New York, N.Y., 28 Aug. 1909; s. late Thomas A. and Catherine (McGee) McC.; e. New York Univ., B.Sc. (Math.) 1930; Univ. of Cal., Berkeley, B.Sc. (Mining Engn.) 1932; m. Marjorie, d. late James Lea, 28 July 1941; children: Catherine (Mrs. John Crosby), Elizabeth Ann, Thomas Campbell; CHRMN., PLACER DEVELOPMENT LTD. since May 1975 to present; Chrmn. and Dir., Placer Amex Inc.; Marcopper Mining Corp.; Dir., Gibraltar Mines Ltd.; Noranda Mines Ltd.; Dir., New Perspective Fund Inc.; from 1931-37 employed with several mining co.'s in California, Colorado and Oregon; Asst. Chief Engr., Placer Management Ltd., San Francisco, 1937-40; Sr. and Chief Engr., Pato Consolidated Gold Dredging Ltd., Columbia, 1940-42; Asst. Field Mgr. 1946; Asst. Gen. Mgr. 1951-52; Div. Engr., Bd. of Econ. Warfare, U.S. Govt., Brazil, 1943-45; Field Mgr., Asnazu Gold Dredging Ltd., Columbia, 1947-50; Asst. Gen. Mgr. 1951-52; Asst. Gen. Mgr., Nechi Consolidated Dredging Ltd., Columbia, 1951-52; San Francisco 1952-55; Vice Pres., American Exploration & Mining Co. Ltd., 1954 (now Placer Amex Inc.); Vice Pres. of present Co. 1956-64; Pres., Chief Extve. Offr. 1964-75; Master mem. Employers' Council of B.C.; mem. Mining Association of B.C.; Mining Association Canada; Canadian Institute Mining and Metallurgy; American Inst. Mining & Metall. and Petroleum Engrs.; Fellow, Inst. Mining & Metall., London, Eng.; Founding mem., Canada-Philippines Council; Protestant; recreations: astronomy; Clubs: Vancouver; Prof. Engineers; Engineers (San Francisco); Home: 4450 Salish Dr., Vancouver, B.C. V6N 3M8; Office: 700 Burrard Bldg., 1030 W. Georgia St., Vancouver, B.C. V6E 3A8

McCLENAGHAN,, Herbert Edward; banker; b. Swift Current, Sask. 12 Aug. 1920; s. Thomas Edward and Caroline Ethel (Beaman) McC.; e. Elmwood Pub. Sch. and Swift Current (Sask.) Coll. Inst. Sr. Matric. 1937; SR. VICE PRES. GLOBAL ENERGY AND MINERALS GROUP since 1980; joined present Bank Swift Current 1937 serving in various Sask. brs. trans. to H.O. Montreal 1949, Asst. Mgr. Calgary Main Br. 1951, Mgr. 8th and Centre Br. Calgary 1955, opened Rep. Office Dallas, Texas 1958, Asst. Supvr. CID Montreal 1961, Chief Inspr. 1963, Asst. Gen. Mgr. Toronto 1964, Dist. Gen. Mgr. (Alta.) Calgary 1969, Gen. Mgr. Alta. 1974; Vice-Pres., Ont. 1975; Sr. Vice Pres., Ont. 1978; served with Candn. Army Overseas 1941-45; Protestant; recreations: golf, hunting, skiing; Clubs: Toronto; Granite; National; Lambton Golf; Ranchmen's (Calgary); Glencoe (Calgary); Home: #509, 3204 Rideau Place, S.W., Calgary, Alta. T2S 1Z2; Office: Royal Bank of Canada, P.O. Box 2534, Calgary, Alta. T2P 2N5

McCLUNG, Hon. John Wesley, B.A., LL.B.; judge; b. Edmonton, Alta. 15 July 1935; s. John Wesley and Lillian Mae (Johnstone) McC.; e. Univ. of Alta. B.A. 1957, LL.B. 1958; m. Eda d. Waldermar Matiisen 26 Oct. 1973; JUDGE, SUPREME COURT OF ALTA. (TRIAL DIV.) since 1977; called to Bar of Alta. 1959; cr. Q.C. 1973; Sr. Partner, McClung Frohlich & Rand, Edmonton until apptd. Judge, Dist. Court of Alta. 1976; United Church; recreations: golf, hunting waterfowl; Club: Edmonton Country; Home: 14631 Mackenzie Dr., Edmonton, Alta.; Office: Law Courts, Edmonton, Alta. T5J 0R2.

McCLURE, Robert Baird, M.B., D.Lit.S., LL.D., D.D., F.R.C.S. (Edin. 1931); missionary-surgeon; b. Portland, Ore., 23 Nov. 1900; s. William and Margaret (Baird) McC.; e. Mission Schs. in China to 1915; Harbord Coll. Inst., Toronto, 1915-17; Univ. of Toronto Med. Coll., M.B. 1922; post-grad. Surg. Edinborough, 1930-31; Victoria Univ., Toronto, D.Lit.S.; Univs. of Windsor, Waterloo, Toronto, LL.D.; Univs. of Sask., B.C., Dalhousie; D.D., Univ. Alta.; m. Amy Louise, d. John Hislop, 5 Oct. 1926; children: Norah Busby, Douglas B., Patricia Edds, Josephine Taylor; Mission Dr., Candn. Presb. Mission to Honan Prov., N. China, 1923-27 and to Taiwan, 1927-30; Surg., Honan Prov., 1930-37; private surg. practice in Toronto 1949; Ch. Missy. Soc. (Ang.) on Gaza strip working for Palestine refugees, 1950-54; in charge Ratlam Mission Hosp., Central India, 1954-67; Moderator, Un. Ch. of Can., 1968-71; missy. surg. Christ Hosp., Sarawak, Malaysia 1971-74; Peru 1975-76; Zaire 1977; served as Field Dir. for Internat. Red Cross in Central China during Sino-Japanese War 1937-41; served with Commandant of Friends Ambulance Unit on Burma Road, comnd. to Candn. Red Cross, 1941-48; Vice Pres., Christian Med. Assn. India, 1962-65 and Madhya Pradesh Med. Assn.

India, 1962-67; C.C. 1971; recreations: sailing, swimming; Club: Rotary (Past Pres. Rotary Ratlam); Address: Apt. 1910, 71 Thorncliffe Park Drive, Toronto, Ont. M4H 1L3

McCLYMONT, Hamilton, B.A.; association executive; b. Montreal, Que. 20 March 1944; s. Hamilton and Zoe A. (Cook) McC.; e. John Rennie High Sch. Pointe Claire, Que. 1960; Lower Can. Coll. Montreal 1961; Dalhousie Univ. B.A. 1970; m. Christine Anton 27 Dec. 1980; one s. Alexander Hamilton, GEN. MGR., VANCOUVER OPERA ASSN. 1978- ; Pres., Prof. Opera Co's of Can.; Chrmn., Candn. Comte. Opera Am.; Past Chrmn. Vancouver Music Alliance; mem. Candn. Conf. Arts; Candn. Music Council; Vancouver City Council Comte. on Arts; Sales Adm., Drummond McCall & Co. Ltd. Montreal, Halifax, Toronto 1963-69; Adm. Dir. Toronto Arts Productions 1969-74; Adm., Neptune Theatre Foundation, Halifax 1974-76; Music Offr. Finance, Can. Council 1976-78; served with UNTD 1961-63; HMCS Scotian, HMCS Cornwallis, HMCS Buckingham; mem. Assn. Cultural Extves.; ACTRA; Owners & Pilots Assn.; B.C. Aviation Council; Exper. Aircraft Assn.; Phi Delta Theta; recreation: flying; Home: 189 - 3031 Williams Rd., Richmond, B.C. V7E 4G1; Office: 111 Dunsmuir St., Vancouver, B.C. V6B 1W8.

McCOLOUGH, Charles Peter, LL.B., M.B.A.; industrialist; b. Halifax, N.S., 1 Aug. 1922; s. Reginald Walker and Barbara Theresa (Martin) McC.; e. Osgoode Hall Law Sch., Toronto, 1945-46; Dalhousie Univ., LL.B. 1947, LL.D. (Hon.) 1970; Harvard Univ., M.B.A. 1949; m. Mary Virginia, d. late James J. White, Jr., 25 Apl. 1953; CHRMN. AND CHIEF EXTVE. OFFR., XEROX CORP., since 1971; mem. Bd. Dirs., Fuji Xerox Co., Ltd., Tokyo; U.S./U.S.S.R. Trade and Econ. Council; Jt. Pres. Bd. Dirs., Rank Xerox Ltd., London, Eng.; Dir., Citibank N.A.; Citicorp and Overseas Devel. Council; Chrmn., Extve. Comte., Internat. Extve. Svce. Corps.; Union Carb Corp.; N.Y. Stock Exchange; read law with Borden, Elliott, Palmer & Sankey, Toronto and with McDonald, McInnes, Halifax; called to Bar of N.S. 1947; prior to joining present firm was Vice Pres., Sales, Lehigh Coal and Navigation Co., Philadelphia; joined Xerox as Gen. Mgr. of firm's 1st reproduction service centre, Chicago, 1954; Asst. to Vice Pres., Sales, Rochester, 1956; Mgr. of Marketing 1957; Gen. Sales Mgr. 1959; Vice Pres., Sales, 1960; Dir. and mem. Extve. Comte. 1961; Extve. Vice Pres. of Operations 1963; Pres. 1966; Pres. and Chief Extve. Offr. 1968; Chrmn. Extve. Comte. 1971; during World War II served as an Airman with RN in Eng.; Trustee, Univ. of Rochester; U.S. Council of Internat. Chamber of Comm. and Comte. for Econ. Devel.; Dir., Council on Foreign Relations; Chrmn., President; Comm. on Pension Policy; mem., Bus. Council; Bus. Roundtable; Econ. Club N.Y.; Council on Foreign Relations; Roman Catholic; recreation: sailing; Clubs: Harvard, River (N.Y.); Country, Genesee (Rochester); Stanwich, Belle Haven, Greenwich Country (Conn.); Office: Xerox Corp., Stanford, Conn. 06904

McCONICA, James K., M.A., D.Phil., F.R.H.S.; university professor; b. Sask., 24 Apl. 1930; s. Thomas Henry and Edith Wilma (Crates) McC.; e. Univ. of Sask., B.A. 1951; Oxford Univ. (Rhodes Scholar), B.A. 1954, M.A. 1957, D.Phil. 1963; Univ. of Toronto, M.A. 1964; PROF. OF HIST., PONTIFICAL INST. OF MEDIAEVAL STUDIES AND CENTRE FOR MEDIEVAL STUDIES, UNIV. OF TORONTO; Fellow, All Souls Coll., Oxford; Priest, Cong. of St. Basil; Fellow, John Simon Guggenheim Foundation, 1969-70; Visiting Fellow: All Souls Coll. 1969-71, 1977 and Corpus Christi Coll. 1972, James Ford Special Lecturer, Oxford Univ. 1977; author, "English Humanists and Reformation Politics", 1965 and Thomas More: "A Short Biography" 1977; also articles for various journs.; Ed., Vol. 3, official Hist. of Univ. of Oxford; Chrmn. of Ed. Bd., "Collected Works of Erasmus", annotator vols. 3 and 4; mem., Am. Hist. Assn.; Am. Soc. for

Reformation Research; Oxfordshire Architectural and Historical Soc.; Br. Records Assn.; Renaissance Soc. Am.; Candn. Assn. Rhodes Scholars; Candn. rep. to Internat. Comn. for History of Universities; Exeter Coll. (Oxford) Assn.; Oxford Soc.; Clubs: Athenaeum; Princeton (New York); R. Catholic; Address: 59 Queen's Park Cres., Toronto Ont. M5S 2C4 and All Soul's College, Oxford, Eng. 0X1 4A7

McCONKEY, Edward Bruce, C.A.; b. Barrie, Ont. 9 April 1924; s. Robert and Rita (Webb) M.; e. Private and High Schs., Barrie, Ont.; Inst. Chart. Accts., C.A.; m. Eileen, d. Charles Foote, 10 April 1949; children: David Bruce, Gregory Michael, Paul Andre, Brian James, Mary Diane, Janet Marie, Angela; VICE CHAIRMAN, DENISON MINES LTD., 1981- ; Dir., Lake Ontario Cement Ltd.; Standard Trust Co.; with Peat, Marwick, Mitchell & Co., Chart. Accts., 1943; J. Arthur Rank Organisation of Canada, 1951; joined present Co. as Asst. Treas., 1955; Comptroller, 1958, Treas. and Comptroller, 1964; Vice-Pres., Finance, and Treas., 1966; Vice Pres., Finance and Dir. 1967; mem., Inst. Chart Accts. Ont.; Bd. Trade Metrop. Toronto; Home: 11 Paddock Crt., Willowdale, Ont. M2L 2A7 Office: P.O. Box 40, Royal Bank Plaza, Toronto, Ont. M5J 2K2

McCONNELL, Edward J.; investment counsellor; b. Belfast, N. Ireland, 3 June 1931; s. late Edward and late Sarah (Maguire) McC.; e. St. Mary's Belfast; Queen's Univ. Belfast, Law grad.; m. Pauline B. Murphy, 31 May 1958; children: Eamonn, Stephen, Michael, David, Eileen; PRESIDENT, E.J. McCONNELL & ASSOC. LTD. since 1975; Dir.; Bow Rio Resources Ltd.; Internat. Fndtn. of Employee Benefits; INA Life Ins. Co. of Can.; joined Crown Trust Co. Montreal 1959; Asst. to Pres. Guardian Trust Co. Montreal 1962, Vice Pres. 1964; Gen. Mgr. Internat. Trust Co. Montreal 1965, Vice Pres. Toronto 1967, Extve. Vice Pres. 1969, Dir. 1970, Pres. and C.E.O. 1971; mem., Bd. of Govs. St. Michael's Coll. Univ. of Toronto; Catholic; recreations: golf, tennis, squash; Clubs: RCYC; Candn.; Ontario; Cambridge; St. George's Golf & Country; Waterville Golf Links; Home: 65 Highland Ave., Toronto, Ont. M4W 2A2; Office: 34 Adelaide St. W., Toronto, Ont. M5H 1L6

McCONNELL, Frank E., B.S.E., M.B.A.; executive; e. Princeton Univ. B.S.E. 1962; Harvard Business Sch. M.B.A. 1964; PRESIDENT, McCONNELL & CO. LTD.; Dir. Albany Oil & Gas Ltd.; Alberta Petroleum Investment Corp.; Barymin Explorations Ltd.; Carvern International Industries Ltd.; Conference Travel Inc.; Guy Chart Tools Ltd.; H. O. Financial Ltd.; Mountain Spring Vineyards Inc.; Novaro Industries Ltd.; The Opimian California Vineyards Corp.; Para II Leasing Ltd.; Clubs: University; Granite; Princeton (N.Y.); Office: 1910, 8 King St. E., Toronto, Ont. M5C 1B5.

McCONNELL, James Edward, Jr., B.A.; b. London, Ont., 25 July 1912; s. Edith Maude (Halliday) and the late James Edward M.; e. Ridley Coll., St. Catharines, Ont.; Univ. of Western Ont., B.A. (Business Adm.) 1936; m. Mary Priscilla, d. King Douglas Hazen, Saint John, N.B., 24 Apl. 1943; children: Malcolm Hazen, Mary C., John Hazen; Pres., McConnell Leaseholds Ltd.; Dir., Great Northern Capital Corp. Ltd.; Canerina Petroleum Corp.; Carib. Island Properties Ltd.; Great Northern Capital Co. Ltd.; Bureau of Mun. Research, Toronto, Ont.; mem. Bd. of Govs., Ridley Coll.; formerly Pres. and Mang. Dir., McConnell, Eastman & Co. Ltd., adv. agents having joined the Co. in 1936; served in 2nd World War with rank of Capt.; Pres. (1962-63), Candn. Assn. Adv. Agencies; Delta Upsilon; Conservative; Anglican; recreations: golf, fishing, hunting; Clubs: University; National; Granite; Rosedale Golf; St. James's (Montreal); Caledon Fishing; Richelieu Fish & Game of Que.; R.C.Y.C.; Royal Montreal Golf; Trembec Fish & Game, Que.; Georgian Peaks Ski; Mount Royal (Montreal); Ochtwan Sporting;

Hillside Tennis (Montreal); London (Ont.); Home: 97 Ardwold Gate, Toronto 178, Ont. M5R 2W1; Office: 234 Eglinton Ave. E., Toronto, Ont. M4P 1K5

McCONNELL, Rob, (Robert Murray Gordon); musician; b. London, Ont. 14 Feb. 1935; began career with Don Thompson's band, Edmonton 1954; continued as a pianist with Rhythm Rockets and as a trombonist with Bobby Gimby, Toronto; formed own rehearsal band; performed with Maynard Ferguson's big band, New York 1964; returned to Toronto becoming leading studio player, also an arranger and composer; mem. Nimmons 'N' Nine Plus Six 1965-69; formed Boss Brass 1968; performs in clubs and on CBC Radio with smaller groups incl. quintets with Rick Wilson and Ian McDougall; has recorded with Guido Basso, Ferguson, Moe Koffman, Nimmons and others; Boss Brass has recorded his compositions "My Man Bill", "It's Hard to Find One", "That's Right", "Tribute to Art Fern", "Runaway Hormones", "4,389,165th Blues in B Flat"; 4 Grammy nominations, 3 for best performance by Big Band; Winner 2 Juno Awards; arranger music sung by Singers Unlimited and Hi-Lo's; mem. CAPAC; Address: R.R. 3, Bancroft, Ont. K0L 1C0

McCOOL, John W.; banker; b. Liverpool, England 1935; e. St. Francois Xavier College; Children: Sean, Paul, Angela; SR. VICE PRES. REAL ESTATE, BANK OF MONTREAL; PRES. BANK OF MONTREAL REALTY INC.; Home: 21 Dale Ave., #918, Toronto, Ont. M4W 1K3; Office: 1 First Canadian Place, Toronto, Ont. M5X 1A1

McCORDICK, John Alexander, B.A.; consultant, former diplomat; b. Toronto, Ont., 11 Oct. 1915; s. late Arthur Stanley and late Enid Lillian (Alexander) M.; e. Upper Canada Coll., Toronto, Ont. (1927-33); Univ. of Toronto, B.A. 1938; Univ. of Vienna (summer 1934); Univ. of Heidelberg, 1936-37; Univ. of Paris, 1938-39; m. Clair, d. late Irvine Perley-Robertson, Ottawa, Ont.; 31 May 1952; children: Joan Alexandra, Brian Stanley, Evan Robertson; PRESIDENT, INTERSONDE CONSULTANTS LTD. since 1975; mem. Lloyd's of London; joined Dept. of External Affairs, 1943; Candn. Legation, Kuibyshev and Moscow, 1943-44; Candn. Mil. Mission, Berlin, Germany, 1946-47; Candn. Legation, Prague, 1947-48, Belgrade, 1948-49; attended Imp. Defence Coll., London, 1953; Candn. Embassy. Madrid, 1953-56; Adviser Canadian delegation to United Nations General Assembly, 1957; Chief of Protocol, Ottawa, 1958; Alternate Candn. Rep. at 10 Power Conf. on Prevention of Surprise Attack, Geneva, 1958; Head of U.N. Div., 1959-60; Adviser to Govt. of Fed. of Rhodesia and Nyasaland, Feb.-Apl. 1960; Min. to Czechoslovakia, 1960-62, Ambassador, 1962-64; Ambassador to Austria and concurrently Gov. for Can. of Internat. Atomic Energy Agency, Vienna, and Candn. Rep. to U.N. Indust. Devel. Organ. Vienna 1966-70; Ambassador to Poland, 1971-75; served as an Offr. in 48th Highlanders of Can. in U.K., Egypt and Iran, 1940-42; Zeta Psi; Anglican; Homes: 3-174 Dufferin Road, Ottawa, Ont. K1M 2A6; "Frangallem," 627 Avenue des Alpes, F-06250 Mougins, France

McCORMACK, William Charles, M.A., Ph.D., F.R.A.I.; educator; b. Sutherland, Iowa, 31 March 1929; s. late Dan Bicknell and Wilna (Plager) McC.; e. Univ. of Chicago B.A. 1948, Ph.D. (Anthrop.) 1956; Stanford Univ. B.A. 1949, M.A. 1950; Univ. of Calif. Berkeley 1950-51; Univ. of Mich. Summer Inst. Linguistics 1956; Univ. of Toronto Internat. Summer Inst. Semiotic & Structural Studies 1980 and 1982; m. Anna Mary d. late John Charles Pikelis 9 June 1962; PROF. OF ANTHROP. & LINGUISTICS, UNIV. OF CALGARY 1969- , Head of Linguistics 1972-73; Assoc. Research Anthrop. Modern India Project Univ. of Calif. Berkeley 1958-59; Visiting Lectr. in Indian Anthrop. Sch. of Oriental & African Studies Univ. of London 1959-60; Asst. Prof. Univ. of Wisc. 1960-64; Assoc. Prof. Duke

Univ. 1964-69; ed. consultant various univ. presses; mem. and chrmn. numerous grants evaluation comtes.; consultant on Kannada lit. Univ. Texas 1958, Univ. of Wisc. Lib. 1960-64; univ. external consultant; various pub. service lectures on India; participant numerous confs./congs.; recipient many scholarships, fellowships, grants incl. Ford Foundation, Rockefeller Foundation, Am. Council Learned Socs., U.S. Office of Education, Duke Univ., Can. Council, Univ. of Calgary; author "Kannada: A Cultural Introduction to the Spoken Styles of the Language" 1966; co-editor "Language and Man" 1976; "Language and Thought" 1977; "Approaches to Language" 1978; "Language and Society" 1979; "The Sixth LACUS Forum 1979" 1980; author various book chapters, articles prof. journs.; Fellow, Am. Anthrop. Assn.; Current Anthrop.; Life mem. Folklore Fellows India; Mythic Soc.; mem. various Candn. and foreign anthrop. and linguistic assns.; Scient. Research Soc.; Sigma Xi; Beta Theta Pi; recreation: travel; Club: Explorers (N.Y. City), Fellow; Home: 340-40 Ave. S.W., Calgary, Alta. T2S 0X4; Office: Dept. of Anthropology, University of Calgary, Calgary, Alta. T2N 1N4.

McCORRISTON, James R., B.A., M.D., C.M., M.Sc., F.R.C.S.(C), F.A.C.S.; surgeon; b. Ridgedale, Sask., 27 July 1919; s. Tolbert James and Grace (Peter) M.; e. Ridgedale (Sask.) High Sch. (1936); Univ. of Sask., B.A., 1939; Queen's Univ., M.D., C.M., 1943; McGill Univ., M.Sc., 1948, Dipl. in Surg., 1951; widower; children: Colin, Pamela, Janet; Prof. Surgery, Queen's Univ. (Head Dept. 1963-73); Surgeon, Kingston Gen. Hospital; Surg. Consultant, D.V.A. Kingston area; Clinical Asst. in Surgery, 1951, Assoc. Surgeon, 1959, Royal Victoria Hospital, Montreal, Que.; Lecturer in Surgery, McGill University, 1951, Associate Professor 1959; Publications: numerous articles and chapters in several medical books and journs.; United Church; Home: 234 Alwington Place, Kingston, Ont. K7L 4P8

McCRACKEN, Archie Ross, M.A., F.S.A. (1948) F.C.I.A.; retired insurance executive; b. Melbourne, Ont., 14 Feb. 1917; s. late Ross and Laura Belle (Sutherland); e. Univ. of Western Ont. (Hon. Math. and Physics), B.A. 1938, Gold Medalist; Univ. of Toronto M.A. (Meteorol.) 1944; m. Jocelyn Marie, d. late Arthur Jones, Belleville, Ont., 21 Dec. 1942; one s. Douglas R.: Sr. Vice Pres., North American Life Assurance Co., 1975-80; Asst. Actuary, 1950, Assoc. 1958; Vice Pres. and Actuary 1964; Vice Pres. and Chief Actuary 1969; mem., Soc. of Actuaries; Candn. Inst. Actuaries (Pres. 1967-68); Internat. Actuarial Assn. (Vice Pres. for Can. 1973-76); Protestant; recreations: golf, bridge; Clubs: St. George's Golf & Country; Home: 30 Bemersyde Drive, Islington, Ont. M9A 2S8; Office: 105 Adelaide St. W., Toronto, Ont. M5H 1R1

MCCREADY, Warren Thomas, M.A., Ph.D.; university professor; b. New York, N.Y. 8 Feb. 1915; came to Canada 1946; s. Thomas Burns and Louise Harriet (Rudolph) M.; e. Univ. of Chicago M.A. 1949, Ph.D. 1961; PROF., DEPT. OF SPANISH AND PORTUGUESE, UNIV. OF TORONTO, since 1969; Instr. Univ. of Indiana, 1950-53; Lectr. Queen's Univ., Kingston, 1954-56; came to Univ. of Toronto as Lectr. 1956-60; Asst. Prof. 1960-64; Assoc. Prof. 1964-69; merchant seaman 1933-40; served with U.S. Air Force, 1940-45, rank Sgt.; author of "La heráldica en las obras de Lope de Vega y sus contemporáneos", 1962; "Bibliografia temática de estudios sobre el teatro español antiguo", 1966; "El mejor mozo de España by Lope de Vega", 1967; other writings incl. bibliographical supplement to J.P.W. Crawford: "Spanish Drama Before Lope de Vega", 1967; articles on Spanish Golden Age Lit., cryptography; Ed., Bulletin of the Comediantes, 1967-72; mem., Intl. Assn. of Hispanists; Candn. Assn. of Hispanists; Am. Assn. of Teachers of Span. and Port.; recreations: reading, painting, traveling, cryptogram solv-

ing; Home: Greenbank, Ont. L0C 1B0; Office: Toronto, Ont. M5S 1A1.

McCREATH, Ross A.; company president; b. Toronto, Ont., 23 Jan. 1924; s. Bert H. and Margaret (MacKinnon) McC.; e. Whitney and Blythwood Public Schs.; Lawrence Park Coll. (all Toronto, Ont.); m. Marion (Dol) Parker, 14 Oct. 1949; children: David, Richard, Lynne, Brian; PRESIDENT, ALL-CANADA RADIO & TELEVISION LTD. since 1971; joined Ed. Dept., Toronto Star 1939; R.C.A. Army Show 1941; Media Dept., Spitzer & Mills Advertising Agency 1946; joined present Co., Radio Sales Divn. 1949, TV Sales Divn. 1953, Mgr. Toronto TV Divn. 1955, Nat. Sales Mgr. TV Divn. 1959, Vice Pres. T.V. 1964, Vice Pres. and Gen. Mgr. 1966; Pres., N. Toronto Amalg. Ratepayers Assn. 1967-72; Dir., Bur. of Broadcast Measurement since 1972, and Chrmn. of Bd. 1979-80; Dir., Radio Bureau of Can. 1980-81; Television Bureau of Can. 1966-73 (Chrmn. 1970-73); United Church; Home: 16 Lytton Blvd., Toronto, Ont. M4R 1L1; Office: 1000 Yonge St., Toronto, Ont. M4W 2K2

McCRIMMON, Hon. Donald James, M.L.A.; politician; optometrist; b. Red Deer, Alta. 1 March 1918; s. Farquhar Duncan and Lily Catherine (Dingwall) McC.; e. Sylvan Lake, Alta. Sr. Matric. 1936; Coll. of Optometry Ont., Toronto, Dr. of Optometry 1949; m. Lois Isabel d. late Frank Cunningham 29 Aug. 1947; children: Donald Frank, James Duncan, Leslie Alexander; MIN. OF NATIVE AFFAIRS, ALTA. since 1979; Optometrist, Ponoka, Alta. 1949-79; mem. Council, Ponoka, Alta. 1954-59, Mayor 1959-61; el. P. Cons. M.L.A. for Ponoka 1971, re-el. since; Depy. Speaker 1975-79; served with RCAF 1940-45, 412 and 402 Sqdns., Spitfire Pilot, shot down 1943, P.O.W. Germany 2 yrs., rank Flight Lt.; Freemason; P. Conservative; United Church; recreations: golf, fishing; Club: K-40; Home: P.O. Box 879, Ponoka, Alta.; Office: 229 Legislative Bldg., Edmonton, Alta.

McCUAIG, Robert Bruce, B.Sc.; executive; b. Montreal, Que. 19 Apl. 1923; s. John Naughton and Mary Lorenda (Lewthwaite) McC.; e. Strathcona Acad. Outremont, Que. 1940; McGill Univ. B.Sc. 1950; m. Marion Lesley d. late Leslie Kinch 23 Dec. 1948; children: Robert Leslie, Donald John, Janet Marion, Barbara Jean, Andrew Bruce: VICE PRES. BREWING OPERATIONS, LABATT BREWING CO. LTD. 1978- ; Brewing Training, National Breweries Ltd. Montreal 1949-51; joined Labatt Breweries of Canada 1954 as Asst. Brewmaster London, Dir. of Purchasing London 1958, Product Devel. Mgr. London 1959, Dir. of Production Que. Div. 1961-78; served with RCAF 1942-45, Pilot, rank Flying Offr.; mem. Master Brewers Assn. Am.; Brewing & Malting Barley Research Inst. (Dir.); United Church; recreations: golf, skiing, farming, scuba, amateur radio; Clubs: Sunningdale Golf & Country; Home: 453 Oak Park Pl., London, Ont. N6H 3N8; Office: 150 Simcoe St., London, Ont. N6A 4M3.

McCULLOCH, Ernest Armstrong, M.D., F.R.C.P.(C) F.R.S.C.; b. Toronto, Ont. 27 Apl. 1926; s. Dr. Albert Ernest McCulloch; e. Univ. of Toronto M.D. 1948; m. Ona Mary Morganty 21 July 1953; children: James A., Michael E., Robert E., Cecelia E., Paul A.; ASST. DEAN, SCHOOL OF GRADUATE STUDIES, UNIV. OF TORONTO since 1979; Phys. Ont. Cancer Inst.; Phys. Toronto Gen. Hosp. 1960-67; Prof. of Med. Biophysics, Univ. of Toronto 1966, Prof. of Med. 1970; Dir. Inst. of Med. Science 1975; Trustee, Banting Research Foundation; mem. Standing Comte. on Health Research & Development, Ont. Council of Health; numerous univ. nat. and internat. adv. comtes. on med. research; rec'd Starr Medal in Anat. 1957; William Goldie Prize in Med. 1964; Annual Gairdner Award 1969; Queen's Silver Jubilee Medal 1977; author over 150 scient. articles in fields of cancer research and hematology; Ed. 'Journal of Cellular Physiology'; mem. several ed. bds.; mem. Am. Assn. Cancer Research; Am. Soc. Exper. Pathol.; Candn. Soc.

Cell Biol.; Candn. Soc. Clin. Investigation; Internat. Soc. Hematology; Internat. Soc. Exper. Hematol.; Soc. Exper. Biol. & Med.; Royal Soc. Can.; Am. Soc. Hematol.; Candn. Hematol. Soc.; recreations: sailing, golf; Club: Badminton & Racquet; Home: 480 Summerhill Ave., Toronto, Ont. M4W 2E4; Office: 65 St. George St., Toronto, Ont. M5S 1A8 and 500 Sherbourne St., Toronto, Ont. M4X 1K9.

McCULLOCH, J. Clement, M.D., F.R.C.S. (C); physician; b. Belleville, Ont., 27 Dec. 1914; s. Robert John Percival and Ethel May (Jones) M.; e. Upper Canada Coll., Toronto, Ont.; Univ. of Toronto, M.D. 1939; Residency Ophthal., New York 1940-43; Cert. in Ophthal. 1945; m. Nancy, d. Percy Roberts, N.Y.C., 12 Dec. 1943; children: Barbara, John, Kenneth, Christina; PROF. AND HEAD, DEPT. OF OPHTHAMOL., UNIV. OF TORONTO; served in 2nd World War with R.C.A.F; Flight-Lieut. 1943, Sqdn. Leader on discharge March 1945; mem., Candn. Ophthal. Soc.; United Church; Home: 165 Teddington Park Ave., Toronto, Ont. M4N 2C7

McCULLOCH, Robert George, B.A.; investment dealer; b. Souris, Manitoba, 23 Sept. 1913; s. Richard James and Gladys Hardwick (McLelland) M.; e. Souris, Man., Pub. Schs.; Univ. of Manitoba; Brandon Col.; B.A. 1935, McMaster Univ.; m. Lois Aurice, d. George Wright, Winnipeg, Man., 4 Nov. 1939; children: William Robert, Carolyn Jane, R.N.; VICE CHAIRMAN AND DIRECTOR, MIDLAND DOHERTY LIMITED since 1973; President, Adanac Investment Corp. Limited; mem., Winnipeg Stock Exchange (Past mem. of Bd. of Govs. and Pres., 1958-60); mem., Winnipeg Chamber of Comm. (Extve. Comte. and Council); Gov., Durham Coll., Oshawa; joined staff of Wood, Gundy & Co. Ltd., Investment Dealers, in Winnipeg, 1935; Osler Hammond & Nanton Ltd. 1946, on discharge from the Navy, as Mgr. of Bond Dept.; apptd. Gen. Mgr., Invest. Securities Div., Oct. 1954 and el. a Dir., 1956; Partner, Osler Hammond & Nanton (Stock Brokers), 1958-63; Vice-Pres. & Dir., 1960-63; served in 2nd World War with R.C. Navy, 1941-46; discharged with rank of Lieut.-Commdr.; Pres., United Services Club of Manitoba, 1949-50; Vice-Pres., Investment Dealers Assn. of Can., 1953; Dir., Metrop. Winnipeg Better Business Bureau; mem., Extve. Bd., Comte. on Manitoba's Econ. Devel., 1962-63; Pres. Navy League of Can., Man. Div., 1959-60; mem. Royal Candn. Mil. Inst.; Phi Delta Theta; Un. Ch.; Clubs: Manitoba; Toronto; Cherry Downs Golf & Country; Home: R.R.2, Claremont, Ont. L0H 1E0; Office: Commercial Union Tower, Toronto, Ont.

McCULLOUGH, William Stewart, M.A., B.D., Ph.D., D.D. (Hon.); professor emeritus; b. Toronto, Ont., 12 May 1902; s. William and Margaret (Graham) M.; e. Univ. of Toronto (Univ. Coll.) B.A. 1924, M.A. 1925 and Ph.D. 1949; Harvard Univ. 1929-30; Knox Coll., Toronto, 1924-27; Emmanuel Coll., Toronto, B.D. 1945; Victoria Univ., D.D. (Hon.) 1976; m. Eleanor Slater (d. 1953), Toronto, Ont., 2 Sept. 1931; children: Sheila, Roger, Nora; 2ndly, Dorothy Madgett, Toronto, Ont., 25 Feb. 1956; o. to Un. Ch. ministry, 1927; taught at Univ. Coll., Univ. of Toronto finally as Prof. of Near Eastern Studies 1930-70; mem., Am. Oriental Soc.; Soc. of Biblical Lit.; author: "Jewish and Mandean Incantation Bowls in the Royal Ontario Museum", 1967; "The History & Literature of the Palestinian Jews from Cyrus to Herod, 550 to 4 B.C." 1975; co-author, "The Psalms" in Volume IV of the "Interpreter's Bible", 1955; contrib. "Interpreter's Dictionary of the Bible" (4 vols.) 1962; Home: 131 Heath St. E., Toronto, Ont. M4T 1S6

McCURDY, Howard Douglas Jr., M.Sc., Ph.D.; university professor; b. London, Ont., 10 Dec. 1932; s. Howard Douglas and Marion Bernice (Logan) McC.; e. St. George Pub. Sch., London, Ont., 1937-42; Amherstburg (Ont.) Pub. Sch., 1942-45; Gen. Amherst High Sch., Amherst-

burg, 1945-50; Assumption Coll., Univ. of W. Ont., B.A. 1953; Assumption Univ. of Windsor, B.Sc. 1954; Mich. State Univ., M.Sc. 1955, Ph.D. 1959; m. Patricia Lorraine, d. Howard Neely, 25 March 1956 (separated); children: Leslie Lorraine, Linda Louise, Cheryl Lauralyn, Brian Douglas Howard; HEAD OF BIOL., UNIV. OF WINDSOR, since 1974; joined present Univ. as Lectr. 1959, Asst. Prof. 1962, Assoc. Prof. 1965; Chrmn., Conf. Univ. Bros. Nat. Assn. Advanc. Coloured People (Mich.) 1958-59; Vice Pres. Essex W., N.D.P., 1962-63; Vice Chrmn., Windsor and Dist. Human Rights Inst., 1963-64; mem. Windsor Adv. Comte. on Employment Opportunity, 1968-69; Pres., The Guardians (Civil Rights), 1961-69; Nat. Chrmn., Nat. Black Coalition, 1969; Bd. of Dirs., Civil Liberties Assn. of Windsor; mem., Senate, Univ. of Windsor, 1969-70; Bd. of Govs., St. Clair Coll. of Applied Arts and Technol. (Chrmn. Curriculum and Extve. Comtes.) since 1967; rec'd. Centennial Medal 1967; author, "Myxobacterales" (Bergey's Manual of Determinative Bacteriology); also various articles in scient. journs.; Chrmn. Bd. of Govs. St. Clair Coll. 1973, 1974; mem. Bd. of Govs., Univ. of Windsor 1973-75; Pres. Assoc. Colls. of Applied Arts & Technol. 1974; mem. American Society of Microbiols.; Candn. Assn. Univ. Teachers (Vice Pres. 1966-67; Nat. Pres. 1967-68); Univ. of Windsor Faculty Assn. (Vice Pres., Pres. 1965-67); Sigma Xi; Phi Kappa Phi; Kappa Alpha Psi; New Democrat; Unitarian; recreations: golf, basketball, softball, hi fi, dancing; Clubs: University; Home: 3910 Mt. Carmel, Windsor, Ont. N9G 2C7

McCURDY, Sherburne G., M.A., Ph.D.; educator; b. Old Barns, Colchester Co., N.S. 30 March 1924; s. Raymond and Margaret Agnes (Crowe) McC.; e. Elem. and High Schs. Colchester Co. N.S.; Dalhousie Univ. B.A. 1949, M.A. 1950; Mem. Univ. of Nfld. undergrad. teacher training; Univ. of Alta. Ph.D. 1964; m. Elizabeth Blois d. late William Evans Jefferson and Ernabelle Clarke, Halifax, N.S. 8 Dec. 1943; children: Margaret Mackey, Earle, David (d), Bruce, Janet; PRESIDENT, ALBERTA COLL. since 1971; Princ. Prince of Wales Coll. St. John's, Nfld. 1950-62; Supvr. of Instr. St. John's Un. Ch. Sch. Bd. 1964-67; Extve. Secy. Nfld. Teachers Assn. 1967-71; served with RCAF Can. and Europe 1942-45; Pres. St. John's W. Dist. Lib. Assn. 1967-69; Del. to Fed. Lib. Leadership Convention 1968; Past Chrmn. and mem. Edmonton Assn. for Continuing Educ. and Recreation: Past Pres. Educ. Soc. Edmonton; Leader Candn. Del. Annual Meeting of World Confed. Organs. Teaching Prof. Stockholm 1962; Del. Third Internat. Curriculum Symposium Oxford 1967; rec'd Centennial Medal 1967; Pres. St. John's Br. Nfld. Teachers' Assn. 1955-57 (Pres. Assn. 1957-59); Pres. Candn. Teachers' Fed. 1961-62; Dir. Candn. Educ. Assn. 1961-63; mem. Nat. Comte. Candn. Conf. on Educ. 1961-63; Founder, Pres. and Exec. Dir., Bach Terecentenary Festival Fdn. 1985; Fellow, Candn. Coll. Teachers; mem. of Senate, Univ. of Alta., Chrmn. Senate Second Languages Task Force; author "The Legal Status of the Canadian Teacher", 1968; Phi Delta Kappa; Liberal; United Church; recreations: square dancing, classical music, spectator sport, family antiques; Club: Edmonton; Home: 4807-122 A St. Edmonton, Alta. T6H 3S8; Office: 10041-101 St., Edmonton, Alta. T5J 0S3

McCUTCHEON, Frederic York, B.A.; stockbroker; b. Toronto, Ont. 19 Sept. 1940; s. late Malcolm Wallace and Eva Trow (Borland) McC.; e. Univ. of Toronto Schs. 1957; Univ. of Toronto B.A. 1962; m. Margaret Lorna d. late James Smith 20 Oct. 1961; children: Lorna Kristine, Ian Alexander York, Kathleen Mary Alice, Patricia Colleen; PRESIDENT, ARACHNAE MANAGEMENT LTD. since 1976; Pres. Arachnae Securities Ltd. since 1980; Dir. North Canadian Oils Ltd.; Foodex Inc.; Brascan Ltd.; Kesmark Construction Ltd.; Lada Cars of Can. Inc.; Traders Group Ltd.; Hatleigh Corp.; Gov. Toronto Stock Exchange 1973-77, Chrmn. 1976-77; Group Actuarial Supvr. North American Life Assurance Co. Toronto 1962-65; Research Analyst, Underwriter, Institutional Salesman Pitfield, Mackay, Ross & Co. Ltd. Toronto and Montreal 1965-69; Prop. McCutcheon Securities Co. Toronto 1969-70; Vice Pres. and Secy. Loewen, Ondaatje, McCutcheon & Co. Ltd. Toronto 1970-77; Vice Pres., Martonmere Securities Ltd. 1977-80 served with Univ. Naval Training Divs. 1957-60, S/Lt. RCN(R) 1960; Pres. Westmount Young P. Cons. 1965-67; Chrmn. Ont. Waterfowl Research Foundation 1971-73; Chrmn. Bd. Trustees IODE Children's Hosp. since 1974; mem. Naval Offrs.' Assn. Can.; P. Conservative; United Church; recreations: flying, skiing, tennis; Clubs: Albany; Granite; Strollers; Chinguacousy Golf & Country (Inglewood, Ont.); Home: 58 Lympstone Ave., Toronto, Ont. M4N 1M7; Office: Buttonville Airport, Markham, Ont. L3P 3J9.

McDANIEL, Roderick Rogers, B.Sc.; P.Eng.; b. High River, Alta., 18 March 1926; s. Dorsey Patton and Daisy (Rogers) McD.; e. Central High Sch. Calgary, Alta.; Univ. of Alta. Engn. Sch.; Univ. of Okla. B.Sc. (Petroleum Engn.); m. Marilyn d. late Dr. Charles Bouck, 16 Oct. 1948; children: Nancy, Leslie; PRESIDENT, McDANIEL AND ASSOCIATES CONSULTANTS LTD. since 1955; Chrmn. of Bd. Pacific Western Airlines; Pres., Penny Lane Market Ltd.; City Savings & Trust Co.; Prudential Steel Ltd.; Calgary Exhibition and Stampede Bd; Petroleum Reservoir Engr. Creole Petroleum Corp. Venezuela 1947; Imperial Oil Ltd. 1948, Chief Reservoir Engr. 1952; Chrmn. Parking Authority City of Calgary 1968-74; mem. Heritage Park Soc. Calgary; Past Vice Chrmn. Strathcona Tweedsmuir Private Sch.; Pres. Calgary Chamber Comm. 1973-74; Calgary Petroleum Club 1973-79; Candn. Chamber Comm. 1974-75; mem. Assn. Prof. Engrs. Alta.; Candn. Inst. Mining & Metall.; P. Conservative; Protestant; recreations: golf, skiing, fishing, horse racing; Clubs: Calgary Petroleum; Ranchman's; Calgary Golf & Country; Home: 11-3231 Rideau Place, Calgary, Alta. T2J T2S; Office: 400 - 800 - 6th Ave., Calgary, Alta. T2P 0T8

McDERMOTT, Dennis; trade union leader; b. Portsmouth, Eng. 3 Nov. 1922; s. John and Beatrice (Sutton) McD; m. Mary Claire Elizabeth d. Adelard Caza 22 Oct. 1976; children: Michael, Mark, Patrick, William, Maureen; PRES., CANDN. LABOUR CONGRESS 1978- ; mem. Extve. Bd., Inter-American Regional Organ. of Workers; Internat. Confed. Free Trade Unions; Assembler and Welder, Massey-Ferguson 1948-54; Internat. Rep., Un. Automobile Workers Am. 1954-68, Candn. Dir. 1968-78; served with RN 1939-46; rec'd Candn. Centennial Medal 1967; Queen's Silver Jubilee Medal; mem. Prov. and Fed. Extves. New Democratic Party; Ont. Labour Relations Bd.; Chrmn. Bd. Govs. Labour Coll. Can.; Chrmn. Bd. Dirs. CLC Labour Educ. & Studies Centre; NDP; recreations: golf, gardening, oil and acrylic painting; Office: 2841 Riverside Dr., Ottawa, Ont. K1V 8X7.

McDIARMID, Ian Bertrand, M.A., Ph.D.; scientist; b. Carleton Place, Ont. 1 Oct. 1928; s. John and Lillian (Campbell) McD.; e. Queen's Univ. B.A. 1950, M.A. 1951; Univ. of Manchester Ph.D. 1954; m. Dorothy May Folger 16 Aug. 1951; children: John, Leslie; ASSOC. DIR. HERZBERG INST. OF ASTROPHYSICS, NAT. RESEARCH COUNCIL since 1975; Dir., Can. Centre for Space Sci. since 1980 Research Offr. Nat. Research Council 1955-64, Head Cosmic Ray Sec. 1964-69, Asst. Dir. Div. of Physics 1969-75; author over 100 scient. papers; mem. Royal Soc. Can.; Am. Geophys. Union; Candn. Assn. Physicists; Home: 901 - 60 McLeod St., Ottawa, Ont. K2P 2G1; Office: Ottawa, Ont. K1A 0R6.

McDIARMID, Orville John, Ph.D.; economist; b. Ottawa, Ont., 19 Oct. 1909; s. Fergus Archibald and Mabel (Martin) McD.; e. Univ. of Toronto, B.Com. 1932, M.A. 1933; Harvard Univ., Ph.D. 1936; m. Alice, d. John Morrissey, Livonia, N.Y., 17 May 1939; children: Marjorie Anne, John Fergus; Consultant, World Bank since 1974; Economist, U.S. Dept. of State, 1946-49; Chief, Monetary

Affairs Div., 1949-51; Asst. Dir., U.S. Aid Mission in Philippines, 1952-54; joined Internat. Bank for Reconstruction and Devel. as Econ. Adviser, 1955-68; apptd. Chief Economist 1968; Chief, World Bank Mission, India 1970-74; served with the U.S. Army 1942-46; rank Lieutenant Colonel on discharge; Maurice Cody Fellow, 1933-34; Royal Soc. of Can. Fellow, 1935-36; author: "Commercial Policy in the Canadian Economy", 1946; "Economic Development of Kuwait", 1964; "Unskilled Labor for Development — Its Economic Cost"; also numerous articles in prof. journs.; mem., Am. Econ. Assn.; Democrat; Protestant; recreation: golf; Address: 304 Lawton St., Falls Church, Va.

McDONALD, Donald John, B.Com.; b. Boissevain, Manitoba, 7 Jan. 1918; s. George William and Jane Myrtle (Taylor) M.; e. Public and High Schs., Boissevain, Man.; Univ. of Manitoba, B.Com. 1949; m. Alice Jean, d. E. C. Schoals, Fort William, Ont., 27 Aug. 1942; children: David George, Elizabeth Jane; Vice-Pres. & Dir., Nabors Drilling Ltd.; Dir., M. Loeb Ltd.; National Drug & Chemical Co. of Can. Ltd.; C. F. Haughton Ltd.; A. Pitts Engineering Construction Ltd.; Canval Ltd.; Can. Permanent Trust Co.; Canada Permanent Mortgage Corp.; Indal Canada Ltd.; with Dominion Bank in W. Can. and Lakehead, 1935-40; joined Osler, Hammond and Nanton Ltd., Winnipeg, Man., 1949-64; el. Dir. 1957; Vice-Pres. 1963; subsequently Extve. Vice-Pres. and Dir., Unas Investments Ltd., then Pres., Midland-Osler Securities Ltd. until resignation Jan. 1971; Extve. Vice Pres., Investors Group 1971-78 (retired); served with R.C.N. 1940-46; discharged with rank Commdr.; mem., Candn. Chamber Comm.; Bd. Trade Metrop. Toronto; United Church; recreations: golf, hunting, curling; Clubs: Manitoba; Lambton Golf & Country.

McDONALD, Douglas Peter, Q.C., B.A.; b. Rossland, B.C., 6 July 1905; s. Peter Ronald and Christina (Boyd) M.; e. Univ. of Alberta, B.A. 1926, LL.B. 1928; m. Kathleen Elizabeth, d. late Hugh Murray Shaw, 15 Oct. 1932; children: Wendy Kathleen, Douglas Murray; Dir., Saratoga Processing Co. Ltd.; Pacific Northern Pipelines Ltd.; called to the Bar of Alta., 1929; cr. K.C. 1947; P. Conservative; Anglican; recreation: golf; Clubs: Calgary Golf & Country; Ranchmens; Calgary Petroleum; Glencoe; Home: 3620 — 13th St. S.W., Calgary, Alta. T2T 3R1; Office: 420-44- 5 Ave. S.W., Calgary, Alta. T2P 2T8

McDONALD, Hugh Joseph, D.Sc.; university professor; b. Glen Nevis, Ont., 27 July 1913; s. Roderick J. and Annie Sarah (McDonell) McD.; e. Queen's Univ., 1930-32; McGill Univ., B.Sc. (1st Class Hons., Chem.) 1935; Carnegie-Mellon Univ., M.S. (Phys. Chem.) 1936, D.Sc. (Phys. Chem.) 1939; m. 1stly Margaret Taylor (d. 1963), 14 Feb. 1942; children: George Gordon, Jean Margaret, Gail Margaret; m. 2ndly Avis Eugenia Nieman, 8 Aug. 1964; PROF. EMERITUS, DEPT. OF BIOCHEM. AND BIOPHYSICS, STRITCH SCH. OF MEDICINE, LOYOLA UNIV. OF CHICAGO, since 1979; Chrmn. of. 1948-79; Teaching Asst. and part-time Instr., Carnegie-Mellon Univ., 1936-39; Instr. in Chem., Ill. Inst. of Technol., Chicago, 1939-41; Asst. Prof. 1941-43; Assoc. Prof. 1943-46; Prof. 1946-48; Consultant, Argonne Nat. Lab.; Prof. (Chem.) Engn., State of Ill.; Diplomate, Am. Bd. Clin. Chem.; Am. Bd. Bioanalysis; apptd. by Gov. of Ill. to serve on State Bd. of Health, Div. of Labs., 1968; mem., Postdoctoral Fellowship Comte., Nat. Science Foundation; served on Manhattan Project, Columbia Univ., during World War II; named Hon. Grad. Universidade Catolica do Rio de Janeiro, 1962; Fac. Mem. of the Yr. Award, Loyola Univ. Chicago, 1976; author "Ionography", "Electrophoresis in Stabilized Media", 1955; mem. Ed. Bd., "Clinical Chemistry", 1955-60; "Analytical Biochemistry" 1960-65; other writings incl. over 180 scient. papers; Fellow, Am. Assn. Advanc. Science; Am. Assn. Clin. Chem. (Chrmn., Comte. on Educ.; 1949-53); Nat. Pres. 1953-54; Nat. Award for Outstanding Efforts in

Educ. and Training 1976); Founder (1972) and Program Co-ord. (1972-75), Diabetes Discussion Group Chicago; Charter mem., Biophys. Soc.; Nat. Acad. Clin. Biochem. (Chrmn., Comte. on Educ. and Publ., 1977-78, and Bd. of Dir., 1978-80); mem., Am. Chem. Soc.; Am. Soc. Biol. Chems.; Soc. Exper. Biol. & Med.; Sigma Xi; Phi Lambda Upsilon; Alpha Chi Sigma; R. Catholic; recreations: pseudoscience; philately, numismatics; Club: Chaos; Home: 5344 Cleveland St., Skokie, Ill. 60077; Office: 2160 S. First Ave., Maywood, Ill. 60153.

McDONALD, J. Hugh, B.A., LL.B.; barrister; b. Winnipeg, Man., 16 Sept. 1927; s. John Hamilton and Marion (Drury) M.; e. Public Sch., Winnipeg, Man.; Ridley Coll., St. Catherine, Ont.; Royal Candn. Naval Coll., Royal Roads, B.C. (1944-46); Univ. of Manitoba, B.A. 1949; Manitoba Law Sch., LL.B. 1952; m. Diane, d. Arthur E. Holden, 11 Oct. 1958; VICE-PRESIDENT AND GENERAL MANAGER, MCDONALD GRAIN CO. LTD. (estbd. 1927); Barrister J. Hugh McDonald & Company; Corp. Counsel and Secy., Park Lane Ltd. and Northern Union Ins. Co. Ltd.; served in 2nd World War with R.C.N. 1944-46 with rank of Lieut.; read law with C. D. Shepard, Q.C.; called to the Bar of Man., 1952; Zeta Psi; Conservative; Anglican; recreations: squash, sailing, shooting; Clubs: Winnipeg Squash Racquet; Royal Lake of the Woods Yacht; Office: 1014-363 Broadway Ave., Winnipeg, Man. R3C 3N9

McDONALD, James Albert, B.A., B.Phil.; transportation executive; b. Winnipeg, Manitoba, 6 Nov. 1919; s. James Duncan and May Jean (MacDonald) M.; e. Saskatoon Tech. Collegiate Inst. (1936), Univ. of Sask., B.A. (magna cum laude) 1946, B.A. (high hons. in econ.) 1947; Rhodes Scholar (Sask.) 1947; Oxford Univ., B.Phil. (Econ.) 1949; m. Cedulia, d. Amadee Gagnon, Victoria, B.C., 27 Feb. 1943; children: Linda, Duncan, Ian, Janet; VICE-PRESIDENT INDUSTRY RELATIONS, CANADIAN PACIFIC since 1981; Dir., CanPac Terminals Ltd.; CHEP Canada Inc.; Bus. Linguistic Centre; Central Terminal Railway Co.; CP Ships; Toronto, Hamilton & Buffalo Railway Co.; CanPac International Freight Services Ltd.; Chrmn. Bd. CP Consulting Services Ltd.; Servicios de Consultoria Pacifico Can., S.A., Candn. Chamber of Comm.; mem., Can.-U.S. Adv. Comte., Corp. Affairs Comte., and Ottawa Liaison Comte.; began service with C.N.R. as Telegraph Operator 1937; trans. to Research and Devel. Dept. 1946; subsequently served in Personnel, Operating Depts. & President's Office; loaned to Royal Comn. on Transportation (Turgeon Comn.) in 1949-50; apptd. Special Asst. to Pres., 1950; Extve. Trainee, Central Region, 1954; Asst. Vice-Pres., Research Devel. Dept., 1956; Gen. Supt., N. Ont. Dist., 1959; Gen. Mgr., St. Lawrence Region, 1960; Vice-Pres. 1961; Vice-Pres., Production 1968; joined Penn Central Transportation Co., as Vice-Pres. and Extve. Asst. to President 1969; Extve. Vice-Pres. 1970; Vice-Pres., Corp. Devel., Canadian Pacific Ltd. 1974-81; served in 2nd World War: on active service with R.C.N.V.R. as Telegraphist, Sept. 1939; Commissioned Feb. 1942, serving as Extve. and Staff Offr. on corvettes, destroyers, N. Atlantic, N. Sea with Royal Navy; mem., Inst. of Adm. (Chrmn. 1962-63, mem. Council); Counc. of Corporate Planning Executives, Conference Bd. in Can.; Business Comm. on Regulatory Reform; mem., Exec. Comte., Adv. Bd., Concordia Univ., School of Community & Public Affairs; United Church; recreations: tennis, skiing, hunting, fishing; Office: Room 349, Windsor Station, Montreal, Que. H3C 3E4

McDONALD, John Angus; insurance executive (retired); b. Montreal, 23 June 1917; s. John and Jemima (Macdonell) McD.; e. Cath. High Sch., m. Hilda A., d. Charles Blickstead, 1944; children: John R., Barbara; with Northern Assurance Co. Ltd., 1936-41; Vice-Pres. and Dir., Redmond & Shaughnessy Ltd., 1946-56; Vice-Pres. and Dir., Willis Faber Redmond & Shaughnessy Ltd. 1956-67; Extve. Vice Pres., Johnson & Higgin Willis Faber Ltd.

1967-79 (ret.); served as Flying Offr., R.C.A.F, 1941-45; Trustee, Royal Candn. Legion; Past Pres., Chamber of Comm., Town of Mt. Royal; Prov. of Que. Blue Goose Ins. Soc.; mem., Montreal Bd. of Trade; Roman Catholic; recreations: curling, skiing, golf: Clubs: Mount Stephen; Kanawaki; Home: 183 Devon Ave., Town of Mount Royal, Que. H3R 1B6

McDONALD, John G., Q.C., LL.M.; b. Los Angeles, Cal., 28 June 1922; s. William Nish and Florence (Kinsella) M.; e. Public and High Schs., W. Vancouver, B.C.; Cal. Inst. Tech.; Univ. of Mich. (pre-law); Law Sch., Univ. of Brit. Columbia; LL.M. Columbia Univ.; m. 1stly, Aletta Jensen, 1 May 1944; children: David Ian, Patricia Maureen, Katherine Ann, William Nish; m. 2ndly, Dorothy Eleanor Lawrence, 28 June 1967; PARTNER, McDONALD & HAYDEN since 1970; Chrm. and Dir., Candn. Oil & Gas Fund Ltd.; Ranchmen's; Resources (1976) Ltd.; Special Lecturer, Osgoode Hall Law Sch., Toronto, 1957-69; read law with Sturdy & Anderson, Vancouver, B.C.; called to the Bar of B.C. 1949, to Bar of Ont. 1955, to Alta. Bar 1969; cr. Q.C. 1960; served in 2nd World War with R.C.A.F 1941-43, and with U.S.A.A.F. as Pilot, 1943-45; Publications: "Canadian Income Tax", 1955; "McDonald's Current Taxation Reports" 1960-70 (weekly pub.); mem., Law Soc. Upper Can.; Candn. Bar Assn.; Candn. Tax Foundation; Protestant; recreations: tennis, golf; Home: Calgary, Alta.; Offices: 1900 - 155 University Ave., Toronto, Ont. M5H 3B7; 5th Floor, Chevron Plaza, 500-5th Avenue S.W., Calgary, Alta. T2P 3L5

McDONALD, Norman Geddes, B.A.Sc., P.Eng.; retired consulting engineer; b. Victoria County, Oct., 4 Aug. 1893; s. Hugh and Mary (McLean) M.; e. Beaverton (Ont.) Pub. and High Sch.; Univ. of Toronto, B.A.Sc., m. Faith Frances, d. Richard Jones, 26 Aug. 1926; one d. Rosemary (Mrs. Dignam); Original mem. (1958), since retired as Chrmn. Bd., Eng. Consultants, Subway Constr., Toronto Transit Comn.; commenced with Hydro Electric Power Commission of Ont., as mem., Engn. Dept., 1919; apptd City Engr., City of Oshawa, Ont., 1921; joined Gore, Nasmith & Storrie (predecessor Co.) as Asst. Engr., 1922; became Partner, 1934; el. Vice-Pres., 1954 and Pres., 1956; resigned as Pres., Gore and Storrie Ltd. 1964; designed waterworks and pollution control projects in 175 municipalities and industries while with Gore and Storrie Ltd.; rec'd George Fuller Award 1962; Bedell Award, 1963; mem., Assn. Prof. Engrs. Ont.; Life mem., Engn. Inst. of Can.; Amer. Water Pollution Control Fed.; Am. Waterworks Assn.; Am. Soc. of Civil Engrs.; Eng. Inst. of Can.; Un. Church; mem; Senate, Univ. of Toronto 1964-68; recreations: fishing, golf; Homes: Summer: MacTier, Ont. P.0C 1H0 Winter: 2280 S.E. 8th St., Pompana Beach, Fla.

McDONALD, Norman J.; communications executive; b. North Bay, Ont., 29 Sept. 1919; s. John James and Mary Ida (Cullen) McD.; e. Scollard Hall, North Bay, Ont., 1936; Inst. of C.A.'s; m. Anne Isobel, d. late I. E. Godin, 22 Nov. 1947; one d., Elizabeth Anne (Mrs. Brian Curley); PARTNER AND CHRMN. EXTVE. COMTE., PUBLIC & INDUSTRIAL RELATIONS LTD., since 1965; private business, North Bay, 1946-52; served in various adm. appts. with RCN, Naval HQ, Ottawa, 1952-57; joined present firm as Sr. Account Extve., Montreal, 1957-61; held various extve. positions, Cyanamid of Canada Ltd., Montreal, incl. Extve. Asst. to Pres. and Secy. and mem. Mang. Comte., 1961-65; served with RCN, in N. Atlantic during World War II; rank Commdr.; Gov., St. Mary's Hosp., Montreal; mem. Extve. Council Candn. Chamber Comm.; mem., Candn. Pub. Relations Soc.; R. Catholic; recreations: golf, skiing; Clubs: Royal Montreal Golf; Mount Royal; Home: 239 Kensington Ave., Apt. 804, Westmount, Montreal, Que. H3Z 2H1; Office: 1808 Sherbrooke St. W., Montreal, Que. H3H 1E5

McDONALD,Russell James, D.V.M.; veterinarian; b. Woodstock, Ont. 25 Sept. 1922; s. William James and Sarah Jean (McMillan) McD.; e. Woodstock Coll. Inst. 1941; Ont. Veterinary Coll. Univ. of Guelph D.V.M. 1945; m. Margot Helen Whyte 7 Apl. 1945; children: Margot Jean, Catherine Anne, John Lachlan; GEN. MGR., WESTERN ONT. BREEDERS INC. 1969- ; Chrmn. Bd. Dirs., Semex Canada; gen. veterinary practice Waterloo, Ont. 1945-46; Mgr., Oxford Holstein Breeders Assn., Woodstock 1946-52; Gen. Mgr., Oxford & Dist. Cattle Breeding Assn. 1952-69; served with COTC Univ. Guelph 1941-45; Dir. and Pres., Oxford Lib. Assn.; mem. Agric. Research Inst. Ont. 1962-74 (Chrmn. 1966-74); rec'd Ont. Agric. Coll. Centennial Medal 1974; Univ. of Guelph Alumnus Honour Award 1979; author "Reproduction in the Cow" 1957; various articles; mem. Ont. Veterinary Assn. (Pres. 1959); Ont. Inst. Prof. Agrols.; Candn. Veterinary Med. Assn.; Am. Dairy Science Assn.; Woodstock Agric. Soc. (Pres.); Ont. Agric. Hall of Fame Assn. (Chrmn.); Woodstock YMCA (Pres.); Omega Tau Sigma; Liberal; United Church; recreations: golf, skiing, curling; Clubs: Oxford Golf & Country; Woodstock Curling; Woodstock Ski; Farmers' (London, Eng.); Home: R.R. 3, Woodstock, Ont. N4S 7V7; Office: P.O. Box 457, Woodstock, Ont. N4S 7Y7.

McDONALD, W. Scott, B.Com., M.B.A.; banker; b. Toronto, Ont., 9 June 1936; e. Univ. of Toronto, B.Com. 1959; Harvard Univ., M.B.A. 1961; m. Lois Wood, Gloversville, N.Y., July 1961; children: Lachlan, Lindsay, Susan, Neil; SR. EXTVE. VICE-PRESIDENT, THE BANK OF NOVA SCOTIA, since 1980; Deputy Chrmn., Bank of Nova Scotia Internat. Ltd.; Treasurer Nova Scotia Corp.; Export Finance Corp. of Can., Ltd.; Bd. mem., Canada-China Trade Council; The Bank of N.T. Butterfield & Son Ltd.; mem., Bd. of Govs., Candn. Assn. for Latin Am.; Dir., Maduro & Curiel's Bank N.V., Curacao, Netherlands Antilles; Caribbean Mercantile Bank, Curacao, Netherlands Antilles; West India Co. of Merchant Bankers Ltd.; Nat. Underwriters (Reinsur.) Ltd.; Trustee, Spencer Hall Fdn.; joined present Bank. Gen. Office, Toronto, 1961; Extve. Asst. to Pres. 1966; Depy. Chief Gen. Mgr. 1970; Etve. Vice Pres. 1972; Clubs: Badminton and Racquet; Toronto; York; Overseas Bankers; Toronto; Home: 174 Dunvegan Rd., Toronto, Ont. M5P 2P2; Office: Executive Offices, 44 King St. W., Toronto, Ont. M5H 1E2

McDONALD, William H.; banker; b. Ottawa, Ont. 8 . Sept. 1924; s. late Joseph and late Constance Mary (Gordon) McD.; e. Lord Selkirk High Sch. Winnipeg, Man. 1942; m. Dorothy Gwen d. late John Lorne Selkirk 8 July 1950; one d. Barbara Elaine Irwin; CHRMN. OF THE EXEC COMTE. CANADIAN COMMERCIAL BANK 1981- ; Chrmn. of the Bd., 1976-81; Dir. CCB Bancorp Inc.; Los Angeles; Boyd Stott & McDonald Technologies Ltd.; Pres., Marlcourt Properties Ltd. 1980- ; Administrative Offr. Dept. Finance Ottawa 1949-55; Asst. Gen. Mgr. Bank of Nova Scotia Toronto 1955-56; Dir. and Offr., Boyd Stott & McDonald Ltd. Toronto 1956-80; Dir. and Extve. Offr. Morguard Trust Co. 1966-76; Dir. and mem. Extve. Comte. Mortgage Insurance Co. of Canada, Central Covenants Ltd. and Markborough Properties Ltd. 1963-66; Chrmn. Bd. Govs. J. Douglas Ferguson Hist. Research Foundation; Past Pres., Candn. Paper Money Soc.; Internat. Bank Note Soc.; served with RCNVR 1943-45; P. Conservative; Anglican; recreations: bank note collecting, books, photographs; Club: Ontario; Home: 26 Meadowglade Cres., Willowdale, Ont. M2J 1C7; Office: (P.O. Box 46) 4900 - 1 First Canadian Place, Toronto, Ont. M5X 1A9.

McDONOUGH, James Maurice; Canadian public servant; b. Moose Jaw, Sask., 21 Aug. 1933; s. James and Winnifred (Lowe) McD.; m. Anna Marie, d. late Basil Hersche, Regina, Sask., 25 July 1953; three d., Debra, Jean, Joan; SR. COMMISSIONER, CANDN. TRANS-

PORT COMM., WESTERN DIV. 1979- ; Chrmn., Internat. Transport Policy Comte., C.T.C.; mem., Rail Transport Comte., Air Transport Comte., Motor Vehicle Transport Comte., Water Transport Comte., Commodity Pipeline Comte.; mem. of Bd., Candn. Livestock Feed Bd. (Ottawa) 1967-78; Dir., Grain Handling & Transportation Can. Grains Council (Winnipeg) 1973-75; appoint. Commisr., Candn. Transport Comm. (Ottawa) 1977; Home: 519 Sturgeon River Drive, Saskatoon, Sask.; Offices: (Western Headquarters) 350-3rd Ave., N., Saskatoon, Sask.; (Ottawa Headquarters) 1913-15 Eddy St., Hull, Qué.

McDORMAND, Rev. Thomas Bruce, B.A., B.D., Th.D., D.D., LL.D., L.H.D. (Bapt.); b. Bear River, N.S., 15 Mar. 1904; s. Charles Freeman and Maud May (Purdy) M.; e. Acadia Univ., B.A. 1929; St. Stephens Coll., Edmonton, Alta., B.D. 1935; Emmanuel Coll., Toronto, Th.D., 1952; D.D., McMaster Univ., 1952; Eastern Bapt. Semy. 1972; Acadia 1976; Judson Coll., LL.D. 1964; m. Irene Hickman, d. David Hibbert Webb, 26 Oct. 1931; Gen. Secy.-Treas., Baptist Convention of Ont. and Que., 1948-55; Gen. Secy.-Treas., Baptist Fed. of Can., 1955-59; Vice-Pres., Acadia Univ., Wolfville, N.S., 1959-61; Pres., Eastern Baptist Semy. and Eastern Baptist Coll., Philadelphia, Pa., 1961-67; Gen. Secy., Atlantic Bapt. Convention 1967-70; author of: "The Art of Building Worship Services"; "Studies in the Gospel of John"; "The Christian Must Have an Answer"; "Concordance to Hymns", 1965; "Unforgettable Encounters", 1975; "Understanding the Bible Today", 1976; Pres. (1970-73) Bapt. Fed. of Can.; Vice-Pres. (1970-75) Bapt. World Alliance 1970-75; rec. Queen's Jubilee Medal, 1978; recreations: golf, curling; Club: Rotary; Address: 50 Elmwood Dr., Amherst, N.S. B4H 2H3

McDOUGALL, Colin Malcolm, D.S.O., B.A., F.R.S.A.; b. Montreal, Que., 13 July 1917; s. late Hon. Mr. Justice Errol M., and Mary Wynifred (Rankin) M.; e. Lower Can. Coll. (1929-36); McGill Univ., B.A. 1940; m. Diana, d. Lionel A. Ekers, Montreal, Que., 4 Jan. 1941; one s. and three d.; SECY. GEN., McGILL UNIVERSITY, since 1973; Student Counsellor there, 1946-47, and Dir. of Placement Service, 1947-57; Registrar 1957-73; served in 2nd World War; Regt. duty with P.P.C.L.I. 1940-45 rank Major; D.S.O.; Mentioned in Despatches; Publications: short stories published in various magazines, one of these, "The Firing Squad" won first prize in MacLean's fiction contest, and was awarded The President's Medal (University of Western Ontario) as the best short story of the year by a Canadian; "Execution" (novel) 1958 (received Gov. General's Award for Fiction, 1959); Que. Literary Prize; 1st Pres. (1966-68); McGill Graduates Soc. Award of Merit (1975); Service for Admission to Coll. and Univ.; former mem. Coll. Entrance Exam. Bd. Comte. on Internat. Educ.; Anglican; Home: Apt. 41A, 1321 Sherbrooke St. W., Montreal, Que. H3G 1J4

McDOUGALL, Donald Blake, B.A., B.Ed., B.L.S.; librarian; b. Moose Jaw, Sask. 6 March 1938; s. Daniel Albert and Donella (McRae) McD.; e. Regina Central Coll. Inst. 1956; Univ. of Sask. B.A. 1966, B.Ed. 1966; Univ. of Toronto B.L.S. 1969; m. Norma Rose d. John Wesley Peacock 19 May 1962; LEGISLATURE LIBRARIAN, PROV. OF ALTA. 1974- ; Teacher and Vice Princ. Regina Bd. Educ. 1960-68; Chief Librarian, Stratford Pub. Lib. 1969-72; Head of Pub. Services, Edmonton Pub. Lib. 1972-74; C.O., Rosetown Legion Cadet Corps (Master Cadet, Nat. Award Camp); comnd. R.C.A.; Chairperson, Alta. Govt. Lib.'s Council; rec'd Queen's Silver Jubilee Medal 1977; Ed., "A History of the Legislature Library", 1979; mem. Bd. Mang. St. Andrew's Presb. Ch. Stratford and Elder, First Presb. Ch. Edmonton; mem. Edmonton Art Gal.; Edmonton Opera Soc.; Edmonton Symphony Soc.; Cracker Barrel (Debating Club) Stratford (Pres.); Friends of the Univ. of Alta.; Merril Wolfe Club Edmonton; mem. Assn. Parlty. Librarians Can. (Pres.); Edmonton Lib.

Assn.; Lib. Assn. Alta.; Candn. Lib. Assn.; Candn. Assn. Information Science; Hist. Soc. Alta.; Nat. Ballet of Can.; Candn. Air Hist. Assn.; Inst. Pub. Adm. Can.; Heritage Can.; Overseas Book Centre; Brit. Museum Soc.; Nat. Trust for Scot.; Presbyterian; recreation: vintage motor cars; Clubs: Edmonton Scottish Soc.; Edmonton Antique Car; Home: Apt. 1704, 9939 - 115 St., Edmonton, Alta. T5K 1S6; Office: 216 Legislature Bldg., Edmonton, Alta. T5K 2B6.

McDOUGALL, John Frederick, M.Sc., P.Eng.; b. Edmonton, Alta., 16 Nov. 1907; s. John Charles and Sophie Bernice (Tait) M.; e. Univ. of Alta. (Civil Engn.), B.Sc. 1930; McGill Univ. (Civil Engn.) M.Sc. 1931; m. Phyllis Eirene, d. Roland Sladden, Edmonton, Alta., 10 Sept. 1940; children: John Roland, Lori Jane, Eirene Bernice, Eleanor Phyllis Anne; PRESIDENT, McDOUGALL & SECORD, LTD. (Real Estate Devel. & Mang.) since 1952; Dir., Royal Trustco Ltd.; Sec. Treas., Dalcor Engineering Ltd.; mem. Friends of the Univ. of Alberta; with Highways Dept., Prov. of Alta., in various engn. positions, 1931-37; joined present firm in 1937 as Asst. Mgr. becoming Mgr. in 1951 and Vice-Pres. 1948-52; on leave of absence to work with Poole Construction Co. Ltd. on wartime constr. projects in W. Can. in 1943-45; mem., Bd. of Examiners in Prof. Engn. for Alta., 1953-59; mem., Interim Devel. Appeal Bd. (Town Planning), Edmonton, for 11 yrs. (Chrmn. final yr.); Pres Candn. Council Prof. Engrs. 1964-65; mem., Engn. Inst. Can.; Edmonton Chamber Comm.; Alta. & Northwest Chamber Mines & Resources; Assn. Prof. Engrs. Alta. (Registrar for 12 yrs., Councillor for 3 yrs.); Edmonton Chamber Music Soc.; Hist. Soc. Alta.; Fellow, Royal Commonwealth Soc.; Conservative; Presbyterian; recreations: music, photography; Clubs: Edmonton; Royal Glenora; Mayfair Golf & Country; Home: 8915 Saskatchewan Dr. W., Edmonton, Alta. T6G 2B1; Office: 1101 — 10080 Jasper Ave., Edmonton, Alta. T5J 1V9

McDOWELL, Charles Alexander, D.Sc., M.Sc., F.R.S.C.; university, professor; b. Belfast, Ireland, 29 Aug. 1918; s. Charles and Mabel (McGregor) McD.; e. Municipal High Sch., Belfast, Ireland; Queen's Univ. of Belfast; Univ. of Liverpool, B.Sc. (1st class Hons.), 1941, M.Sc. 1942, D.Sc. 1955; m. Christine Joan, d. W. C. Stoddart, London, Eng., 10 Aug. 1945; children: Karen Mary Anne, Christina Anne, Avril Jeanne; PROF. AND HEAD, DEPT. OF CHEM., UNIV. OF B.C.; Asst. Lectr., Queen's Univ. of Belfast, Ireland, 1941-42; Scient. Offr. U.K. Min. of Supply, 1942-45; Lectr. in Inorganic & Physical Chem., Univ. of Liverpool, 1945-55; awarded Letts Gold Medal in Theoretical Chem., Queen's Univ. of Belfast, 1941; Special Science Medal, Univ. de Liège, 1955; Chem. Inst. Can. Medallist 1969; Killam Sr. Research Fellow 1969-70; Centennial Medal 1967; Queen's Jubilee Medal 1978; Chem. Inst. Can. Montreal Medal, 1982; Gov. and Mgr., Sefton Park Modern Secondary Sch., Liverpool, 1949-55; Fellow, Royal Soc. of Can., 1962; mem. Churchill Coll., Cambridge, 1963-64; Nat. Research Council Sr. Research Fellow and Visiting Prof., Univ. of Cambridge, 1963-64; Visiting Prof., Kyoto Univ. 1965, 1969; Distinguished Visiting Prof., Univ. of Fla., Gainesville 1974; Distinguished Visiting Prof., Univ. of Cape Town 1975; Frontiers of Chemistry Lecturer, Wayne State Univ 1978; Pres. Chem. Inst. of Can. 1978-79; appointed Univ. Prof., Univ. B.C., 1981; Chmn., Int. Union Pure and Applied Chem., Vancouver, 1981; served in the 2nd World War in U.K. Civil Defence as Gas and Bomb Identification Officer; Publications: numerous scient. publ. on chem. kinetics, mass spectrometry, molecular structure, electron and nuclear magnetic resonance spectroscopy, heterogeneous catalysis; mem. Faraday Soc.; Chem. Soc. of London; Am. Chem. Soc.; Am. Physical Soc.; Mass Spectrometry Soc. of Japan; Combustion Inst.; Chem. Soc. of Can.; Royal Inst. Chem. of G.B.; Anglican; recreations: gardening, walking; Home: 5612 McMaster Rd., Vancouver, B.C. V6T 1J8

McEACHERN, Hon. Allan, B.A., LL.B.; judge; b. Vancouver, B.C. 20 May 1926; e. Vancouver and Penticton Pub. Schs.; Kitsilano Jr. High Sch.; Lord Byng Sr. High Sch.; Univ. of B.C. B.A. 1949, LL.B. 1950; m. Gloria 17 July 1953; two d. Jean, Joanne; CHIEF JUSTICE SUPREME COURT OF B.C. since 1979; law practice Russell & DuMoulin 1950-78; Pres., Kats Rugby Club 1953-64; B.C. Lions Football Club 1967-69; W. Football Conf. 1964; Candn. Football League 1967 (Commr. 1967-68); Dir. Vancouver Bar Assn.; Council, Candn. Bar Assn.; Pres., Legal Aid Society of B.C. 1977-78; Bencher 1971-79; recreations: sailing, skiing, walking, cottage; Office: Law Courts, 800 Smithe Street, Vancouver, B.C. V6Z 2E1.

McELHERAN, Brock, B.A., Mus.B.; conductor and music professor; b. Winnipeg, Man., 6 Jan. 1918; s. The Rev. Principal Robert B. and Irene B. (Brock) B.; e. Winnipeg, Man. Pub. Schs.; Univ. of Toronto Schs.; Univ. of Toronto, B.A. 1939, Mus.B. 1947; Royal Conservatory of Music of Toronto, 1934-47, Berkshire Music Centre, Lenox, Mass. 1947; PROF. OF MUSIC, POTSDAM COLLEGE OF ARTS AND SCIENCE, and Co-ordin. of Choral Activities; Conductor, Collegiate Singers (40 mixed voices); Montreal Elgar Choir 1972-79; Dir., Saratoga-Potsdam Choral Institute (assoc. with The Philadelphia Orchestra); Conductor, Crane Chorus (mixed voices); has collaborated with Stockhausen, Kagel and Foss in premieres of their vocal works; author of text book on conducting; composer of works for chorus, all in new notations; Meteorol. with the Canadian Dept. of Transport, 1940-42; R.C.N. (R), 1942-45; retired from the service with rank of Lieut; Anglican; recreations: camping; Address: State University College, Potsdam, N.Y. 13676

McELMAN, Hon. Charles Robert; senator; b. South Devon, N.B., 18 June 1920; s. late Frank E. and Amanda G. (Dunphy) M.; e. Fredericton (N.B.) High Sch. 1937; m. Jessie Faye Douglass, 22 Nov. 1941; children: James D., Barbara Jean (Mrs. Jock Jardine), Frederick C., Mary Faye (Mrs. Donald Smith); with Candn. Bank of Commerce, 1937-40; Secy., N.B. Liquor Control Bd., 1946-51; Private Secy. to Premier John B. McNair, 1951-52; with Dept. of Nat. Defence, 1953-54; Extve. Secy., N.B. Lib. Assn. 1954-60; Extve. Asst. to Premier Louis J. Robichaud, 1960-66; served with R.C.A.F., 1941-46; discharged with rank Sgt.; mem., Royal Candn. Legion; St. Andrews Soc.; Freemason; Liberal; Anglican; Home: 324 King's College Rd., Fredericton, N.B. E3B 2E9

McENTYRE, John Gear, Q.C., B.A., B.C.L.; executive; b. Montreal, Que., 17 Dec. 1912; s. John and May (Gear) M.; e. Bishop's Coll. Sch., Lennoxville, Que.; McGill Univ., B.A. 1934 and B.C.L. 1938; m. Lucienne, d. late Dr. Arthur Robichon, 24 May 1939; children: John, Louise (Mrs. Robert West), Lynn (Mrs. Thomas Camerford); DIR. OPERATIONS (EASTERN HEMISPHERE), CANDN. EXECUTIVE SVCES. OVERSEAS; called to Bar of Que. 1938, cr. Q.C. 1954; practised law with Audette & McEntyre, Montreal, 1938-42; Dept. of National Revenue, Ottawa, 1942; Depy. Min. (Taxation) 1954-66; Consul Gen. Los Angeles 1966-73; mem. Candn. Del. to U.N. Gen. Assembly 1972; Chrmn., Candn. Trade & Tariffs Comte., 1974-75; Anglican; recreations: golf, curling; Clubs: Royal Ottawa Golf; Saint James's (Montreal); Cercle Universitaire d'Ottawa; Home: 815 - 4555 Bonavista Ave., Montreal, Que. H3W 2C7; Office: 1130 Sherbrooke St. W., Suite 350, Montreal, Que. H3A 2M8

McENTYRE, Peter M., B.Com., C.A., C.F.A.; executive; b. Westmount, Que., 15 Aug. 1917; s. late May (Gear) and John M.; e. Argyle Pub. Sch., Westmount, 1923-28; Bishop's Coll. Sch.; McGill Univ., B.Com. 1939; m. Katharine, d. late Col. J. J. Creelman, 15 Mar. 1941; children: David, Mrs. Nancy Wright; PRESIDENT AND DIR., COMPTRUST HOLDINGS INC.; Chrmn. of Bd., Canada Cement Lafarge Ltd.; Dir., Lafarge Coppée S.A.; General Portland Inc.; Internat. Atlant. Ins. Ltd.; Standard Industries Ltd.; Starlaw Investments Ltd. Belding Corticelli Limited; served with R.C.N.V.R., 1941-46 (Mentioned in Despatches); Acct. with Creak, Cushing & Hodgson, Montreal, 1939-48 (Partner 1947); with St. Lawrence Sugar Refineries Ltd. 1948-63; Comm. Trust Co. Ltd. 1963-79; present Co. since 1979; Ald., City of Westmount and Commr. of Finance, 1962-68; Mayor, City of Westmount 1969-71; mem. Bd. of Dirs. Concordia Univ.; Chrmn. Boys Club of Canada Endowment Fund Inc.; Anglican; Clubs: University; St. James's; Mount Royal Clubs; Royal Montreal Curling; Montreal Badminton and Squash; Home: 444 Clarke Ave., Westmount, Que. H3Y 3C6; Office: Suite 508, 606 Cathcart St., Montreal, Que. H3B 1L7

McEWAN, Thomas Arthur, B.Com.; manufacturer; b. Townsend Twp., Ont., 5 Apl. 1925; s. Frederick Stanley and Ecclesia May (Campbell) McE.; e. Delta Coll. Inst., Hamilton, 1943; Veterans' Rehabilitation Sch., Hamilton, 1945-46; Queen's Univ., B.Com. 1949; m. Bessie Jane, d. Benjamin Stanley Sutton, 4 June 1955; children: Ian Angus Campbell, Melanie Anne; PRESIDENT AND DIR., BECTON, DICKINSON & CO., CANADA, LTD. since 1970; Dir., Invers-Lee Co. (Canada) Ltd.; Sales Rep., Union Carbide Canada Ltd., Toronto, 1949; Sales Mgr. to Pres., Sterling Rubber Co., Ltd. 1954; Vice Pres. and Gen. Mgr., Howmet of Canada, Ltd. 1962; joined present Co. as Extve. Vice Pres. 1968; served with RCAF 1943-45 as Pilot (GR); rank Flying Offr.; Pres., Ont. Soc. for Crippled Children and Chrmn., Bd. of Regents, Fed. Colls., Guelph, 1964-65; Chrmn., Bd. of Govs., Univ. of Guelph, 1964-68 (named Fellow of Univ. 1969); mem. Bd. of Educ., City of Guelph, 1960-63 (Chrmn. 1962-63); Chrmn., Comte. on Costs of Educ. for Ont., 1971-74; Presbyterian; recreations: golf, music; Club: Mississauga Golf; Home: 1036 Wenleigh Court, Mississauga, Ont. L5H 1M8; Office: 2464 S. Sheridan Way, Mississauga, Ont. L5J 2M8

McEWEN, Alexander Campbell, LL.M., Ph.D., F.R.G.S.; commissioner; b. Eng. 22 Aug. 1926; e. Univ. of London; Univ. of E. Africa; m. Patricia Stuart Richards; three d. Ann, Sheila, Laura; CANDN. COMMR., INTERNAT. BOUNDARY COMN.; Canada Lands Surveyor; mem. Council, Candn. Inst. of Surveying; former Dir., Policy & Planning, Dept. Forestry & Agric. Nfld.; Chrmn. Nfld. Land Use Task Force; Nfld. Rep., Fed. Prov. Comte. on Foreign Ownership of Land; posted Sabah, Malaysia (Colombo Plan); Seychelles (UN); Tanzania (CIDA); Jamaica (CESO); mem. Bd. Examiners, Assn. Nfld. Land Surveyors; Secy.-Treas. Assn. Ont. Land Surveyors; recreations: legal and historical research, writing; Home: 707 Mooney's Bay Place, Ottawa, Ont. K1V 8W4; Office: 615 Booth St., Ottawa, Ont. K1A 0E9.

McEWEN, Jean Albert, R.C.A.; artist (painter); b. Montreal, Que., 14 Dec. 1923; s. William and Eliane (Renaud) M.; e. Univ. of Montréal (Grad.); m. Louise, d. Paul Lebeau, 21 June 1947; children: Isabelle, Dominique; worked in Paris till 1953 (travelled to Spain, Italy, Holland); first one-man show in Montréal at Galerie Angès Lefort, since when has had more than ten, chiefly at Montréal, Ottawa, Toronto, New York and Paris; since 1961 a continuous exhibitor at Spring Exhn., Museum of Fine Arts, Montréal; among other exhibits incl. 3rd Candn. Biennial, Ottawa (1959), Candn. Coll. Musée de Bordeaux, France (1962), 25 Painters from Qué., Stratford Festival, Ont. (1962), Candn. Artists, Albright-Knox Gallery, Buffalo, N.Y. (1962), Commonwealth Art, Commonwealth Inst., London (1962), Contemp. Candn. Painting, Johannesburg, S.A. (1962), Dunn Internat. Exhn., Fredericton, N.B. and London, Eng., (1963), Five Candn. Painters, Musée Galliera, Paris (1963), Fifteen Candn. Artists, travelling exhn. organ. by Museum of Modern Art, N.Y. (1963), Sao Paulo Biennial, Brazil (1963), A quarter of a century of Candn. Painting, Tate Gallery, London (1964); awarded a Can. Council Grant,

1961; completed mural for Toronto Internat. Airport, 1963; designed stained glass window mural for Sir George Williams Univ. 1966; completed mural for Place des Arts Montreal 1967; awarded First Prize, Que., 1961, Jessie Dow Award, 1964, both at Spring Exhn., Montréal Museum of Fine Arts; work is in numerous public colls. incl. Nat. Gallery, Ottawa, Winnipeg, Edmonton, Toronto Art Galleries; Museum of Modern Art, N.Y. and other Am. galleries; Pres., Assn. of Non-Figurative Artists of Montréal, 1959-62; Vice Pres., Roy. Acad. of Arts since 1970; R. Catholic; recreation: music.

McFARLANE, Leslie, author; b. Carleton Place, Ontario, 25 October 1902; s. John Henry and Rebecca (Barnett) M.; e. Pub. and High Schs., Haileybury; m. Amy Ashmore, (d. 1955), d. Stephen Arnold, New Liskeard, Ont., 3 May 1928; children: Patricia, Brian, Norah: m. 2ndly Beatrice Greenaway Kenney (widow), d. late James J. Greenaway, Hamilton, Ont., 1957; has been writing fiction prof. since 1926; author of some 30 books for boys and girls, under various pseudonymns, together with a number of short stories, novelettes and serials appearing in mags.; on staff of National Film Bd. as Producer 1943-57; Chief Editor, CBC television drama 1959-60; has written and directed numerous films, including "The Boy Who Stopped Niagara", 1947; "A Friend at the Door", 1950; script, "Royal Journey", 1952; since 1956 has written 70 TV plays incl. "The Eyeopener Man", "Pilgrim, Why Do You Come?"; author of: "Streets of Shadow", 1930; "The Murder Tree", 1931; "The Last of the Great Picnics" and "McGonigle Scores!" 1965; "The Ghost of the Hardy Boys" 1975; "A Kid in Haileybury" 1975.

McGARRY, John Francis, Q.C.; b. Toronto, Ont., 23 July 1904; s. John Francis and Ethel May (Laxton) M.; e. Queen's Univ.; Univ. of Toronto, B.A. 1928; Osgoode Hall, Toronto, Ont., Grad. 1931; m. Marie Sinclair, d. Patrick J. Wilson, 30 July 1930; children: Jeanne-Marie, Margaret Ethel; Partner, McGarry & McKeon till retirement in 1977; read law with Hughes, Agar & Thompson, Toronto, Ont.; called to Bar of Ont., 1931; cr. K.C. 1946; has specialized in court work on civil side, particularly in br. of ins. and negligence law; Roman Catholic; recreation: racing; Clubs: Woodbine Turf; Home 640 Sheppard Ave., Willowdale, Ont. M2K 1B8

McGAUGHEY, Charles E., M.A.; former diplomat; b. North Bay, Ont., 26 Nov. 1917; s. late Charles Samuel and Beatrice Mary (Piercy) M.; e. Queen's Univ., B.A. 1938, M.A. 1939; Student's Internat. Union (summer) 1939; (Dipl. in Internat. Relations) Univ. of Chicago, 1940-41; m. Jessie Porter, 25 Oct. 1941; two s. Daniel Brien, Terrence Porter; with "Sudbury Star" and "North Bay Nugget", 1939; joined Dept. of External Affairs, Jan.-Aug. 1949; Vice-Consul, Chicago, Sept. 1949; Third Secy. Candn. Embassy, Tokyo, Sept. 1949; Second Secy., Apl. 1951; Ottawa, June 1952; First Secy., Candn. High Comn., New Delhi, May 1955; First Secy., Candn. High Comn., Wellington, N.Z., and Acting High Commr. there, May 1957; Ottawa, Aug. 1958; High Commr. to Malaya and also accredited Ambassador to Burma and Thailand, 1962-65; to Pakistan, 1966-69; High Commr. to Ghana 1965-66; Ambassador to Israel 1969 and concurrently High. Commr. to Cyprus 1970; Depy. Commandant and mem. Directing Staff, Nat. Defence Coll. 1972; served in 2nd World War; Pte., Canadian Army, 1941; Canadian Army Japanese Language School, Vancouver, B.C. 1944-45; served in the U.K., India, Malaya, Thailand, Nfld., discharged 1947 with honours; Office: National Defence College, Kingston, Ont.

McGAVIN, Allan Morton; manufacturer; b. Darvel, Scotland, 15 Jan. 1911; S. James and Annie Syme (Ferguson), M.; came to Canada, 1913; e. Upper Canada Coll., Toronto, Ont.; Army & Navy Acad., San Diego, Cal.; Ont. Agric. Coll., Guelph, Ont.; m. Beatrice W., d. Robert Norman Bell, Toronto, Ont., 1 June 1935; two s. Gerald Allan, Brian Norman; CHRMN. OF BD., McGAVIN FOODS LTD., since March 1961; Dir., British Columbia Forest Products Ltd.; John Labatt Ltd.; Trans Mountain Oil Pipe Line Co.; Hudson's Bay Oil & Gas Co. Ltd.; British Columbia Telephone Co.; Bank of Nova Scotia; Dir. and mem. Candn. Comte. of Bd., Hudson's Bay Co.; mem., Adv. Bd., Royal Trust Co.; Chancellor Emeritus, Univ. of Brit. Columbia; Vice-Pres., Nat. Counc. of the Baking Indust.; V.P., Candn. Olympics Comn.; began with McGavin Bakeries (estbd. by his father and g-father) in Edmonton, Alta., 1928 and worked in Los Angeles, Pasadena, Lethbridge and Vancouver; el. Pres. in 1948; present firm is an amal. of the McGavin Co's. and Canadian Bakers Ltd. plus the Canada Bread Co. Ltd. plants in Fort William and Winnipeg; Lieut.-Col. R.C.A. (Reserve); Protestant; recreations: golf, fishing; Home: 2180-W. 43rd., Vancouver, B.C. V6M 2E1;

McGAVIN, Gerald Allan Bell, B.Com., M.B.A., C.A.; trust company executive; b. Vancouver, B.C., 29 July 1937; s. Allan Morton and Beatrice W. (Bell) McG.; e. Shawnigan Lake (B.C.) Schs.; Univ. of B.C., B.Com. 1960; C.A. 1963; Univ. of Calif. M.B.A. 1965; m. Sheahan Beale, d. late Elmer Stephen Glaspie, 8 Sept. 1962; children: Catharine Sheahan, Alexia Russell; PRESIDENT AND C.E.O., DIR., YORKSHIRE TRUST CO. since 1975; Dir. The Resource Service Group Ltd.; Yorkshire Insurance Managers Ltd.; Br. Pacific Properties Ltd.; Fidelity Life Assur.; Audit Clk. Peat Marwick Mitchell, Vancouver 1960; Wood Supply Comptroller B.C. Forest Products Ltd. Vancouver 1965; Secy.-Treas. Ancore International Ltd. Vancouver 1969; joined present co. as Vice Pres. and Gen. Mgr. 1972; served with RCNVR 1955-60, rank Sub. Lt.; Dir. and Past Pres., Vancouver Symphony Soc.; Gov. and Chrmn., York House School; Trustee, Vancouver Art Gallery; B.C. Sports Hall of Fame mem. Inst. C.A.'s B.C.; Dir., Vancouver Bd. Trade; Trust Co's Assn. Can. (Council); Protestant; recreations: squash, tennis; Clubs: Vancouver; Vancouver Lawn Tennis & Badminton; Home: 1675 Laurier Ave., Vancouver, B.C. V6J 2V5; Office: 1100 Melville St., Vancouver, B.C. V6E 4B6

McGAW, Hon. Leland Watson, M.L.A.; politician; b. Oak Hill, N.B. 27 July 1927; s. Walter Watson and Margaret (McMorran) McG.; e. Oak Hill Elem. Sch.; m. Eileen Isabel d. Karl F. Dick, Moore's Mills, N.B. 1 July 1947; one s. Richard L.; MIN. OF TOURISM, N.B. 1977- ; el. M.L.A. for Charlotte West prov. g.e. 1967, re-el. since; Depy. Speaker 1972; lumberman; mem. I.O.O.F.; Charlotte Co. Woodlot Owners Assn.; Freemason; P. Conservative; United Church; Office: (P.O. Box 2345) Fredericton, N.B. E3B 5C3.

McGEACHY, Duncan Donald Cameron, B.Sc., P.Eng.; executive; b. Hazelton, B.C., 12 Dec. 1918; s. Edwin C. and Clara (Cameron) M.; e. Queen's Univ., B.Sc. (Mech. Engn.); Univ. of Western Ont. (Post Grad. course in Business Adm.); m. Donalda M., d. Milton N. Campbell, Hamilton, Ont., 1 May 1943; children: Edithe Lynn, Joan Margaret, Neil Wallace, Ruth Ann; Dir., Northern Life Assurance Co.; U.O.P. Ltd.; Eaton-Yale Ltd.; Ronyx Ltd.; Royal Trust Adv. Bd.; Timberjack Inc.; Gore Mutual Insurance Co.; Kenting Ltd.; Sheldons Engineering Co. Ltd.; Trimac Ltd.; Unit Drop Forge Inc. (Milwaukee); Photochemical Research Assoc. Inc.; Past Pres., Stratford Shakespearean Festival Foundation; Gov., Westminster Inst. for Ethics and Human Values; Dir., Huntec (70) Ltd.; served with British Admiralty and R.C.N.V.R.; mem., Assn. of Prof. Engrs. of Ont.; Un. Church; recreation: golf; Clubs: London Hunt & Country; London; London Flying (Past Pres.); Home: 1607 Gloucester Road, London, Ont. N6G 2S5; Office: 660 Richmond St., London, Ont. N6A 3G8

McGEE, Hon. Frank C., P.C. (Can.) 1963; b. Ottawa, Ont., 3 Mar. 1926; s. late Walter Robert and Frances (McCool) M.; e. Carleton Coll., 1946-50; St. Patricks Coll.,

High Sch., Ottawa, 1940-43 and 1945; m. Moira, d. Late Senator M. Grattan O'Leary, Ottawa, Ont., 16 June 1951; children: Maureen, Sheilagh, Owen; Vice-Pres., Public & Industrial Relations Ltd.; served in R.C.A.F. 1943-45; 1st el. to H. of C. for York-Scarborough, g.e. 1957; re-el. 1958, 1962; apptd. Minister without Portfolio in Diefenbaker Cabinet, 11 March 1963; def. g.e. 1963 1965 and 1972; P. Conservative; Roman Catholic; recreations: golf, fishing, swimming; Clubs: Albany; The Toronto Hunt; Home: 6 Waxwing Place, Don Mills, Ont. M3C 1N6

McGEER, Dudley M., B.Com.; petroleum executive; b. 24 July 1926; e. Univ. of B.C. B.Com. 1947; m. Mabel 6 Nov. 1954; children: Eric, James, Janet, Heather; SR. VICE PRES. ADM., CHIEF FINANCIAL OFFR. AND DIR., SUNCOR INC.; Controller, Sun Oil Co. Ltd. 1974; Vice Pres. Adm. Great Canadian Oil Sands Ltd. and Sun Oil Co. Ltd. (merged to become present co.) 1979; mem. Ont. Assn. Children Learning Disabilities; Financial Extves. Inst.; recreations: golf, bridge, gardening; Clubs: National; Islington Golf; Office: 16th floor 20 Eglinton Ave. W., Toronto, Ont. M4R 1K8.

McGEER, Hon. Patrick L., M.L.A., Ph.D., M.D.; politician; medical neuroscientist; b. Vancouver, B.C. 29 June 1927; s. James Arthur McG.; e. Princeton Univ. Ph.D. 1951; Univ. of B.C., M.D. 1958; m. Edith d. Charles Graef, New York City 15 Apl. 1954; children: Patrick Charles, Tad, Victoria L.; MIN. OF UNIVS., SCIENCE & COMMUNICATIONS, B.C. 1979- ; Dir. B.C. Hydro and Power Authority; British Columbia Petro Corp.; British Columbia Research Council; Discovery Foundation; Discovery Parks Inc.; Prof. Faculty of Med. Univ. of B.C. 1960- (leave-of-absence 1975-); el. M.L.A. 1962, re-el. since; Min. of Educ. 1976-79; Min. of Educ., Science & Technol. 1979; Nat. lectureships for Research Soc. of Am. and Soc. of Neuroscience; author ''Politics in Paradise'' 1972; ''Molecular Neurobiology of the Mammalian Brain'' 1978; over 200 articles scient. journs.; Protestant; recreation: tennis; Clubs: Vancouver Lawn Tennis; Union; Home: 4727 W. 2nd Ave., Vancouver, B.C. V6T 1C1; Office: Parliament Bldgs., Victoria, B.C. V8V 1X4.

McGIBBON, (James) Ian, B.Eng.; executive; b. Montreal, Qué. 15 Jan. 1927; s. late Roy H., M.D., and late Alice (Armitage) McG.; e. Royal Candn. Naval Coll., Royal Roads, B.C. 1946; McGill Univ., B.E. 1951; Univ. of W. Ont. Grad. Sch. of Business Adm. 1953-54; Harvard Business Sch. Advanced Mang. Program 1976; m. Catherine d. late George S. Veith, D.D.S. 13 Sept. 1957; children: Catherine, Jamie, Alexandra, Nicolas; GROUP VICE-PRES., FINANCE, ABITIBI-PRICE INC. 1980- ; Vice-Pres. Finance, the Price Co. Ltd.; Dir., Abitibi-Price Corp.; Mattabi Mines Ltd.; Gen. Mgr. Bldg. Materials present Co. 1963, Dir. of Planning 1969, Vice-Pres. Corp. Devel. 1974, Vice-Pres. (Finance), 1978- ; served with RCN and RCN(R) 1944-53, rank Lt.; Chmn. Bd. of Gov., St. Margaret's School (Elora) Ont.; mem. Ont. Forestry Assn.; Anglican; recreations: tree farming, tennis, cross-country skiing; Club: University; Home: R.R. 2, Erin, Ont. N0B 1T0; Office: Toronto-Dominion Centre, Toronto, Ont. M5K 1B3

McGIBBON, Hon. Pauline M., O.C. (1967), C.C. (1980), B.A., LL.D., D.U., D. Hum. L., D. Litt. S., B.A.A. (Theatre), Hon. F.R.C.P.S.(C.); b. Sarnia, Ontario, 20 October 1910; d. Alfred William and Ethel Selina (French) Mills; e. Pub. and High Schools, Sarnia, Ontario; University of Toronto (Victoria Coll.), B.A. (Modern Hist.) 1933; LL.D., Alta. 1967, Western 1974, Queen's 1974, Toronto 1975; D.U. Ottawa 1972; Laval 1976; D. Hum. L. St. Lawrence Univ., Canton N.Y. 1977; D. Litt. S. Univ. of Victoria, Toronto 1979; B.A.A. (Theatre) Ryerson Polytech. Inst. 1974; Hon. F.R.C.P.S. 1977; LL.D. McMaster Univ., 1981; LL.D. Carleton Univ., 1981; m. Donald Walker, s. late Donald McGibbon, 26 Jan. 1935; Lieut.-Governor of Ont. April 1974-Sept. 1980; (former Chancellor, 1st woman,

Univ. of Toronto 1971-74); first Woman Chancellor Univ. of Guelph 1977; first woman Gov. of Upper Canada College, 1971-74; Chrmn. du Maurier Council for Performing Arts; Mem. Bd. of Govs., Nat. Theatre Sch. (Chairman Bd. Govs. 1966-69); Hon. Vice-Pres., National Chapter, I.O.D.E. (Nat. Pres. 1963-65); Hon. Pres., Provincial Chapter; Hon. Vice-Pres. of the Municipal Chapter of Toronto; Past Pres., Dom. Drama Festival; 1st woman Pres., Candn. Conf. of the Arts 1972-73; Hon. Secy., Women's Adv. Comte. to Expo '67; Past Pres. (1st woman) Univ. of Toronto Alumni Assn.; Past Pres. Victoria Coll. Alumnae Assn.; Hon. Colonel (1st Can. Woman), 25 Toronto Service Battalion 1975-82; Hon. Colonel, 7 Cadet Corps of St Thomas; 1st Pres., Children's Film Lib. of Can. 1948-50; Vice-Pres., Candn. Assn. for Adult Educ. 1958-63; Past Chrmn., Ont. Theatre Study; past chrmn. Bd. Govs. Women's Coll. Hosp.; First Woman Director, IBM Canada (ret'd 1974); First Woman Dir., George Weston Ltd. 1981; First Woman to be Director, Imasco Limited (ret'd 1974); mem. Volunteer Comte., Art Gallery of Ont.; Hon. mem., Toronto Symphony Women's Comte; Senate. Univ. of Toronto 1952-61; 1st woman Chrmn. of Bd. of Trustees, Nat. Arts Centre (Ottawa) Oct. 1980; Dir., Massey Hall, Oct. 1980; mem. Extve., Candn. Scene 1951-59; Can. Council 1968-71; mem. Bd. Elliot Lake Centre for Continuing Educ. 1965-71; a Governor Candn. Centenary Council 1963-67; Hon. fellow, Heraldry Soc. of Can.; Hon. mem: Royal Candn. Yacht., National (first woman mem.), Granite, Toronto Ladies Golf, Boulevard clubs University Women's Club of Toronto, Toronto Ladies', The Bd. of Trade of Metro Toronto; rec'd. Canadian Drama Award 1957; Centennial Medal; Civic Award of Merit, City of Toronto 1967; Award of Merit, Candn. Public Relations Society, 1972; Queen's Jubilee Medal 1977; Paul Harris Fellowship Award, Rotary Club of Toronto-Forest Hill, 1977; Eleanor Roosevelt Humanities Award, State of Israel Bonds, 1978; Human Relations Award, The Can. Council of Christians and Jews, 1978; Ont. Teachers' Federation Fellowship, 1979; Humanitarian Award, B'nai Brith 1980; Dame, Order of St. Lazarus of Jerusalem 1972; Dame of Grace of the Order of St. John of Jerusalem, 1974; Grand Prior of the Order of St. Lazarus, 1982; Protestant; Clubs: University Women's; Toronto Ladies; Canadian; Empire; Heliconian; Home: Twenty Avoca Ave., Apt. 2004, Toronto, Ont. M4T 2B8

McGILL, Beverly John; b. Ice Lake, Manitoulin Island, Ont. 5 Oct. 1918; s. James Roger Beverly and Elizabeth Marguerite (Wright) McG.; e. Gore Bay (Ont.) Pub. Sch., Continuation and High Schs. 1936; m. Jessie d. late Edward Guthrie Coulthurst 10 Nov. 1951; one d. Helen Elizabeth; CHRMN. AND DIR., CANADIAN PACIFIC HOTELS LTD. since 1979; joined The Royal Bank of Canada, Sault Ste. Marie, Ont. 1938, Geraldton, Ont. 1940-41, Aylmer, Ont. 1946, Brs. and H.O. Montreal 1946-48, Staff Offr. and Credit Offr. Vancouver 1948-51, Credit Offr. H.O. Montreal 1951 — 54, Special Rep. Port of Spain, Trinidad 1954-55, Inspr., Asst. Supvr. and Supvr. H.O. Montreal 1955-64 (Internat. Div.), Chief Agt. N.Y. 1964-65, Asst. Gen. Mgr. and Chief Agt. N.Y. 1965-67, Depy. Gen. Mgr. Internat. Div. H.O. 1967-69 and Gen. Mgr. 1969-71, Vice Pres. and Gen. Mgr. of Div. 1971-74 and Sr. Vice Pres. and Gen. Mgr. 1974-77, Extve. Vice Pres. H.O. 1977-78; served with Royal Candn. Inf. Corps 1941-46, Overseas 1943-46, rank Capt.; Dir., Old Brewery Mission Inc. Montreal; Freemason; Shriner; United Church; Clubs: The Little Club; Delray Beach; Home: Apt. 4401, 44 Charles St. W., Toronto, Ont. M4Y 1R8; Office: 100 Front St. W., Toronto, Ont. M5J 1E3.

McGILL, Donald Gordon, B.A.; b. Toronto, Ont., 30 March 1918; s. Harold Linton and Lillian (Ireland) M.; e. Malvern Coll. Inst., Toronto, Ont.; Univ. of Western Ont., B.A., and Mang. Training course (1948); m. Margaret Naomi, d. Kenneth C. Greene, London, Ont., 21 Nov. 1942; children: Donald Gordon, Jr., Patricia Anne, Robert Bruce; PRESIDENT, DONMAR INVESTMENTS

LTD.; Chrmn., Labatt's British Columbia Adv. Bd.; joined John Labatt Ltd., 1940; Asst. Bottling Supt. 1945-49, & Bottling Supt. 1949-54; Dir. of Purchasing, 1954-56, Dir. of Indust. Relations, 1957; Vice Pres., Gen. Mgr., Man. Div., 1959; Vice-Pres., Western Can. Reg. 1965-78; served in 2nd World War with R.C.N.V.R., 1940-45; Pres. (1975) Vancouver Board Trade; mem., Adv. Bd., Fraser Inst.; Freemason; Anglican; recreations: golf, fishing; Clubs: Vancouver; Capilano Golf & Country; Home: 1410 Sandhurst Place, West Vancouver, B.C. V7S 2P3

McGILL, Hon. Edward Robert, M.L.A., B. Com.; politician; b. Vancouver, B.C. 21 Sept. 1912; s. Herbert Lionel and Ethel C. (Adams) McG.; e. Brandon, Man. schs.; Queen's Univ. B.Com.; m. Marguerite Eve d. Frederick Shaw, Saskatoon, Sask. 30 May 1942; children: Marguerite Eve, Douglas Crawford, Patricia Ellen, Frances Elizabeth; MIN. WITHOUT PORTFOLIO, MAN. 1979- ; el. M.L.A. for Brandon West prov. g.e. 1969, re-el. since; Min. of Consumer, Corporate & Internal Services, Min. of Co-operative Devel., Min. Responsible for Man. Telephone System & Communications and Min. Responsible for Adm. of Man. Lotteries Act 1977; Min. reporting for Man. Telephone System, Man. Forestry Resources Ltd. and Man. Pub. Insurance Corp. 1978; Mgr. Brandon Flying Club; served with RCAF 1940-45; rank Sqdn. Leader; Dir. Brandon Gen. Hosp.; mem. Brandon Police Comn.; Kinsmen; P. Conservative; United Church; Office: Legislative Bldg., Winnipeg, Man. R3C 0V8.

McGILL, John W., B. Com.; executive; b. Montreal, Que. 17 March 1932; s. Air Vice Marshal Frank S. and Margaret (Williamson) M.; e. Trinity Coll. Sch., Port Hope, Ont.; McGill Univ. B.Com. 1954; Centre d'Etudes Indust. Geneva 1959; m. Terrie Noelle Wilks 28 June 1968; children: Jennifer, Colleen, Sandra; EXTVE. VICE PRES. & CHIEF OF GROUP ENTERPRISES, AIR CANADA; Sales Mgr., Canadair Ltd. 1960-63; Gen. Sales Mgr., Air Canada 1963-68; Founding Pres. and Mang. Dir., Air Jamaica 1968-71; Chrmn., Air Transit 1973; Vice Pres. Marketing, Air Canada 1975-78; Sr. Vice-Pres., Sales & Services, 1978-80; served in R.C.A.F. 1951-54; Phi Delta Theta; Upsilan; recreations: skiing, fishing, shooting, golf; Clubs: Mt. Royal; Mount Bruno; Office: Place Ville Marie, Montreal, Que.

McGILLIVRAY, Hon. George Argo E.D., Q.C., B.A.; judge; b. Whitby, Ont., 9 Sept. 1900; s. Dr. Charles F. and Caroline (Argo) M.; e. Univ. of Toronto, B.A. 1927; Osgoode Hall, Toronto, Ont.; m. Sheila Playfair, d. Charles E. Lee, 2 June 1934; children: Sheila Lee, Donald Charles, Carolyn Ann, Ian George; Justice, Ont. Court of Appeal, 1957-74; read law with Gordon McMillan, Q.C., Toronto, Ont. called to the Bar of Ont. 1930; cr. K.C. Nov. 1945; Partner, McLeod & McGillivray, Toronto 1930-34; joined Legal Dept., Toronto Transit Comn., 1934; apptd. Gen Counsel, 1954; Past Vice-Pres., Candn. Bar Assn.; Past Pres., Lawyer's Club of Toronto; Co. of York Law Assn.; St. Andrew's Soc., Toronto; Toronto Hunt Club; served in 1st and 2nd World Wars; Phi Gamma Delta; Freemason; Presbyterian; Clubs: University; Arts & Letters; Toronto Hunt; Home: 191 Dunvegan Rd., Toronto, Ont. M5P 2P1

McGIVERIN, Donald S., B.Com., M.B.A.; merchant; b. Calgary, Alta., 4 April 1924; s. Alfred Chester & late Ella (Scott) McG.; e. Toronto. Ont. Schs.; Kelvin High Sch., Winnipeg, Man.; Univ. of Manitoba, B.Com.; Ohio State Univ., M.B.A.; m. Margaret Ann (d), d. late Harold Falconar Weld, 9 Sept. 1950; one d. Mary Edith; PRESIDENT, C.E.O. AND DIR., HUDSON'S BAY CO. since 1972; Deputy Chrmn. and Dir., Markborough Properties Ltd.; Dir. and Chrmn., Simpsons Ltd.; Dir., Dupont of Can. Ltd.; Manufacturers Life Ins. Co.; Noranda Mines Ltd.; Zellers Ltd.; mem. Internat. Adv. Bd., R.J. Reynolds Ind.; joined The T. Eaton Co. Ltd. 1946; joined present Co. as Mang. Dir. Retail Stores 1969; mem. Bd.

Govs. Olympic Trust of Can.; Candn. Council Christians & Jews; Dir., Council for Candn. Unity; mem., Can. Industrial Renewal Bd.; Phi Kappa Phi; recreation: golf; Clubs: Lambton Golf & Country; Rosedale Golf; The Toronto; York; Granite; St. Charles Country (Winnipeg); Mt. Royal (Montreal); Lyford Cay (Bahamas); Home: Apt. 4802, 44 Charles St. W., Toronto, Ont. M4Y 1R8; Office: 2 Bloor St. E., Toronto, Ont. M4W 3H7

McGIVERN, Rev. James S., S.J., M.B.E., C.D., Ph.D., F.R.G.S., F.S.A. (Scot.), G.C.K.H., E.C.L.J., O.C.M., O.S.L.; (R.C.), O.S.L.; b. Edmonton, Alta., 27 July 1908, of U.E.L. & Mayflower descent; s. Richard James & Mary Ellen (MacDonald) McG.; e. Vancouver Coll., (High Sch.) 1925; (Clerical Studies) Montreal, Toronto, Valkenburg (Holland), B.A., Ph.D., 1932; (Hist. Studies) Univ. Toronto, M.A., 1949; also Germany, Austria, Ireland, England, Wales; Ed. "Our Heritage", 1967; "Martyrs' Shrine Message"; Archivist, Canadian English Jesuits 1965-74 and R.C. Archdiocese of Toronto 1971- ; Assoc. Lect., Toronto School of Theol.; Nat. Chaplain Un. Empire Loyalist Assn. of Can.; Staff mem., Martyrs' Shrine, Midland, Ont.; o. Priest, 15 Aug. 1937; Guest Lectr. & Preacher Ireland, 1939; taught Campion Coll., Regina, 4 yrs.; Loyola Coll., Montreal, 1 yr.; Regis Coll., Toronto, 1 yr.; Chaplain in Active, Res. & Reg. Army, 1940-64; wartime service in Can., Eng., Sicily, Italy, France, Belgium, Holland; peacetime service in Can., Germany; retd. with rank of Maj.; awarded Premier of Ontario Placque; Assistant Chaplain, Christie St. Hosp., Red Chevron and Sunnybrook Hosp., Toronto 1947-49; Columnist, Toronto Telegram 1968-70; Founder, R.C.E. Mil. Museum, Chilliwack, B.C.; Co-founder, Brit. Mil. Hist. Soc., London Br. (now B.M.H.S. of Can.); Founding Secy., B.C. Museums Assn.; Founder, and 1st Gov., Candn. Br., Soc. of Mayflower Descendants; Ecclesiastical Commander, Order of St. Lazarus of Jerusalem (ECLJ); Pres., Toronto Br., United Empire Loyalists; mem. of Most Excellent Order of Br. Empire; Chev., Order of Constantine the Great (O.C.M.); Chev., Order of St. Lazlo (O.S.L.); life mem., Clan MacDonald Soc. (Can.); Queen's Jubilee Medal; Publications: "History of Royal Engineers in B.C.", "Shadow over Huronia" 1965, 3rd ed. 1966; "Your Name and Coat of Arms"; "In the Early Dawn": "Brebeuf in Song and Verse"; "Some Hidden Glories"; "A Saga of the Church in Canada"; other writings in "Martyrs' Shrine Message", "Our Heritage", "Canadian Register", "Jesuit Missions", Candn. "Messenger of the Sacred Heart", "Am. Eccl. Review", "The Canadian Sapper", "Candn. Cath. Hist. Report"; Ed., "Canadian Pilgrim", 1981; "Fidelity", Newsletter (Toronto Br. U.E.L.); Past Extve. Dir. Ont. Div., Multiple Sclerosis Soc.; mem. Candn. Ch. Hist. Soc.; Life mem. 3 Clandonald Soc. (1967); Heraldry Soc. of Can.; mem. Candn. Cath Hist. Soc. (Secy. 1947-50); Mayflower Descendants (life mem.); Clan McNeil Soc.; Clan Munro (Clan Chaplain) ; Life mem., New Eng. Geneal. & Hist. Soc.; U.E.L.; etc.; Conservative; recreations: reading; Address: Holy Name Parish, 71 Gough Ave., Toronto, Ont. M4K 3N9

McGOEY, Gerald Thomas, B.A., C.A.; executive; b. Toronto, Ont. 7 Apl. 1948; s. Gerald J. and Gertrude (Heenan) McG.; Univ. of Waterloo B.A.; Candn. Inst. C.A.'s, C.A.; m. Linda Jane Seccombe 11 June 1970; children: Andrew, Jordan, Linsey; SR. VICE PRES. AND CHIEF FINANCIAL OFFICER, CANADA DEVELOPMENT CORP. 1979- ; joined Thorne Riddell 1969, apptd. Audit Partner 1977; mem. Candn. Inst. C.A.'s; Inst. C.A.'s Ont.; Financial Extves. Inst.; recreations: ice hockey, tennis, squash, golf; Clubs: Granite, National, Cambridge, Muskoka Lakes Golf & Country; Home: 158 Alexandra Blvd., Toronto, Ont. M4R 1M4; Office: 444 Yonge St., Suite 200, Toronto, Ont. M5B 2H4.

McGORAN, Joseph; diplomat; b. Lochwinnoch, Scot. 15 Apl. 1941; s. Joseph and Isabella (McLeish) McG.; e. Holyrood Sch. Glasgow 1959; m. Mary d. late Alexander Ross McKay, Aberdeen, Scot. 30 July 1966; one s. Ross Joseph Alexander; VICE CONSUL, BRIT. CONSULATE-GEN. MONTREAL since 1978; served in London 1960-62, Ankara 1962-64, Peking 1965-66, Bahrain Persian Gulf 1966-69, U.K. Del. to European Econ. Community Brussels 1970-72, London 1969-70 and 1972-74, Rangoon 1974-78; mem. Soc. Civil & Pub. Servants; R. Catholic; recreations: swimming, music, bridge, travel; Clubs: Montreal Bd. Trade; Mount Stephen; Home: 1100 Doctor Penfield, Montreal, Que. H3A 1A8; Office: 635 Dorchester Blvd. W., Montreal, Que. H3B 1R6.

McGOWAN, George, B.A.; b. Winnipeg. Man.; e. Pickering Coll., Newmarket, Ont.; Univ. of Toronto, B.A. (Philos. & Eng.) 1952; m.; one s. Evan; taught at Pickering Coll.; first acted Hart House Theatre, Univ. of Toronto and later became mem. Candn. Repertory Theatre, Ottawa; turned from acting to directing with Crest Theatre and the Candn. Players; has directed stage plays in Toronto, Halifax, Winnipeg, Montreal and Stratford, Ont.; currently working out of Hollywood; has produced plays for such CBC-TV programmes as "Festival", "Playdate" and "Quest"; filmed a series of episodes for "The Forest Rangers" (children's programmes); some of his prods. incl. "The Feast of Lupercal", "Summer of the Seventeenth Doll", "Inherit the Wind", "Louis Riel", "Evelyn" (musical comedy); recreation: golf;

McGOWAN, J. William, D.Sc. F.A.P.S.; F.A.A.S. physicist; educator; b. Pittsburgh, Pa., 5 July 1931; s. James William and Margaret Eleanor (Campion) McG.; e. St. Francis Xavier Univ., B.Sc. 1953; Carnegie-Mellon Univ., M.S. 1958; Univ. Laval, D.Sc. 1961; m. Judy Diane, d. Ray Owen Kennedy, 21 Sept. 1957; children: Maura, Liam, Laurie, Colin, John, Michelle; PROF. OF PHYSICS, UNIV. OF WESTERN ONT. and Founding Chrmn., Centre for Interdisciplinary Studies in Chem. Physics there 1972-76; Instr., St. Francis Univ. 1955-56; Research Assoc., Westinghouse Research 1957; Instr., St. Lawrence Coll., Univ. Laval 1958-59; Staff mem. General Atomic, San Diego 1962-69; Visiting Fellowship, Jt. Inst. for Lab. Astrophysics, Univ. of Colo. 1966; joined present Univ. as Prof. and Chrmn., Dept. of Physics 1969; visiting prof., Centro Atomico, Bariloche, Argentina 1973; Facultés Universitaires, Namur Belgium 1976-77; Libera Universita di Trento, Trento, Italy 1976-77; Université de Louvain, Louvain la Neuve, Belgium 1978 to present; N.R.C. Exchange Fellowship USSR 1975; Lecturer for COSTED, India, 1977-79; Research Associate Lawrence Berkley Labs, Univ. of Calif. Berkley 1978 to present; has served as Advisor to Advanced Research Projects Agency; Nat. Science Foundation; Defence Research Bd.; Nat. Bureau Standards; Atomic Energy Comn.; Past Chrmn. Div. of Atomic and Molecular Physics, Canada Assn. Physics 1972-73; Past mem. Organ. Comte., Gaseous Electronics Conf. for Internat. Conf. on Physics of Electron & Atomic Collisions; Past Secy., Gaseous Electronics Conf.; Council mem., Electron & Atomic Physics Div., Am. Physical Soc. 1970-73; mem., Am. Phys. Soc. Panel on Pub. Affairs 1978 to present; Founding Chrmn. POPA Subcomte. on Internat. Scientific Affairs (S.I.S.A.); Organizing Chrmn., A.P.S. Workshop on Focus of Physics on Sci. & Technol. for Development (Baddeck, Oct. 1980); Secy. IUPAP Internat. Comm. on Physics for Devel.; 1980- ; Rapporteur for Global Seminar of Scientific and Eng. Socs. for Devel., (New Delhi, Dec. 1980); Chrmn., Council Ont. Physics Depts. 1972-73; founding Chrmn., V.L.S.I. Study Group (Univ. of Western Ont.) since 1980; Sr. Research Fellow, Bell Northern Research Labs 1981; Co-organizer of V.L.S.I. Implementation Workshop (Ottawa) 1980; holds patent for "Method and Apparatus for Sensing Gases", USA 1968; rec'd Bart Griffen Mem. Award, St. Francis Xavier Univ.; mem. Organ. Committee, University of Trento, Italy; Ed., "Gaseous Electronics — Some Applications", 1974; "The Excited State in Chemical Physics" Vol. 1 (1976), Vol 11 (1981); author of over 100 published papers on Physics of Collisions of Atoms, Electrons, Ions, Positrons, Photons with Atoms, Ions, and Molecules and Solids and Science for Development Studies in Can.; Development of VLSI microcircuits; Synchrotron Radiation Studies of Cells; Light Interaction with the Retina; mem., Amer. Physical Soc. (Fellow); Candn. Assn. Physicists; Am. Assn. Physics Teachers; Am. Assn. Advanc. Science (Fellow); Chem. Inst. of Can.; Amer. Vacuum Soc.; mem. of Pugwash Group; mem. of Can. Comte. of Concerned Scientists & Scholars, 1980- ; Founding Chrmn., Sci. Tech. and You (STAY) London; Dir., London Symphony Orch.; London Regional Children's Museum; Ont. Science Centre; K. of C.; R. Catholic; recreations: sailing, skiing; Home: 784 Riverside Dr., London, Ont. N6H 2S4; Office: London, Ont.

McGRAIL, John Simon, M.D., M.S., D.L.O., F.R.C.S. (C); physician-surgeon; educator; b. Wakefield, Yorkshire, U.K. 28 May 1931; s. William Anthony and Dorothy (John) M.; e. Univ. of Manchester M.D. 1955; Univ. of Mich. M.S. 1964; D.L.O. (London, U.K.) 1957; F.R.C.S.(C.) 1964; m. Terry d. Aidan Jenkins 4 Apr. 1959; children: Susan, Mark, Christopher, Justin; PROFESSOR OF OTOLARYNGOLOGY, UNIV. OF TORONTO: Chief, Dept. of Otolaryn., Wellesley Hosp.; Consultant in Otolaryn. to Ont. Cancer Inst. and Princess Margaret Hosp.; Consultant Throat Specialist to Toronto theatres; Physician, Toronto Maple Leafs and Team Canada; Capt., R.A.M.C. 1956-58; came to Can. 1960; author various articles on head-and-neck and reconstructive surgery; Dir., Candn. Inst. of Facial Plastic Surgery; mem. Candn. Acad. of Sports Med.; Royal Soc. of Med. (London, U.K.); Candn. Med. Assn.; Acad. of Med.; Amer. Acad. of Facial Plastic and Reconstructive Surgery; Conservative; Roman Catholic; recreations: tennis, soccer, theatre; Home: 111 Harrison Rd., Willowdale, Ont. M2L 1W3; Office: 160 Wellesley St. E., Toronto, Ont. M4Y 1J3

McGREGOR, Malcolm Francis, B.A., M.A., Ph.D., D.Litt., D.C.L., F.R.S.C.; univ. professor; b. London, Eng., 19 May 1910; s. Walter Malcolm and Alice Mary (Francklin) M.; e. Beckenham (Kent, Eng.) Sch.; came to Can., 1924; King George High Sch., Vancouver, B.C.; Univ. of British Columbia, B.A. 1930, M.A. 1931; Univ. of Mich.; Univ. of Cincinnati, Ph.D. 1937; D.C.L. Bishop's 1970; D.Litt. Acadia 1971; m. Marguerite Blanche, d. Fred P. Guinn, Princeton, N.J., 8 June 1938; children: Heather Mary, Malcolm Rob Roy; PROF. OF CLASSICS EMERITUS, UNIV. OF BRIT. COLUMBIA; Head of the Dept. 1954-75; Instr. in History, Vancouver Community Coll., Langara Campus since 1977; Hon. Prof. of Humanities, Univ. of Calgary since 1978; mem. of Mang. Comte., Am. Sch. of Classical Studies at Athens; from Acting Instr. to Prof. of Classics and Ancient Hist., Univ. of Cincinnati 1936-54 (Acting Dean, Grad Sch. of Arts & Sciences, 1941-42); Asst. to the Dean, Faculty of Arts and Science, Univ. of B.C., 1956-64; Dir. of Ceremonies, Univ. of B.C., 1968-77; mem. of Inst. for Advanced Study, Princeton, 1937-38, 1948; Award of Merit, Am. Philol. Assn., 1954; John Simon Guggenheim Mem. Fellow, 1948; Master Teacher 1974; Queen's Jubilee Medal; Order of the Phoenix (Commander) 1979; Publications: "The Athenian Tribute Lists", Vol. I, 1939, II-IV 1949-1950-1953 (in collab.); "Studies in Fifth Century Attic Epigraphy" 1974 (in collab.); articles and reviews; mem., Hellenic Soc.; Classical Assn. Can. (Pres. 1968-70; Hon. Pres. since 1977); Archaeol. Inst. Am.; Am. Philological Assn. (Pres. 1969-70); Ohio Classical Conf.; Classical Assn. Pacific Northwest (Pres. 1961-62, 73-74); Classical Assn. Cdn. West.; Visiting Prof., Am. Sch. of Classical Studies at Athens, 1967-68; Sr. Fellow, Can. Council 1967-68; Anglican; recreation: cricket; Home: 4495 W. 7th Ave., Vancouver, B.C. V6R 1X1

McGREGOR, William Cooper Young; labour leader; b. Winnipeg, Man., 22 June 1918; s. Thomas and Anne Ferguson (Young) McG.; e. Lord Selkirk and St. John Tech.

High Sch., Winnipeg; m. Margaret MacKie, d. John Russel Masterton, 17 May 1941; four d., Mrs. D. Grevstad, Barbara Bowles, Catherine Leigh, Margaret Robyn; Nat. Pres., Brotherhood Rly. & Airline Clks.; Gen. Vice Pres., Candn. Labour Congress (Chrmn. Human Rights Comte.); Chrmn., Candn. Rly. Labour Assn.; Extve. mem., Internat. Transport Workers' Fed.; Dir., Can. Devel. Corp.; A.E.S. Ltd.; served with Royal Winnipeg Rifles (Reserve 1939-40) and RCAF 1942-45; Home: 337 Preston Dr., Beaconsfield, Que. H9W 1Z2; Office: 2085 Union Ave., Suite 690, Montreal, Que. H3A 2C3

McGREGOR, William Stewart, company president; b. Saskatoon, Sask., 1 March 1916; s. James and Agnes (McKay) McG.; m. Verona Rowles, 15 May 1940; two children; PRESIDENT AND MANG. DIR., NUMAC OIL & GAS LTD., (Estbd. 1963); Dir., Union Gas Ltd., Candn. Utilities Ltd.; Bank of Nova Scotia; Felmont Oil Corp.; mem. Advisory Board, The Royal Trust Co., Edmonton; Gov., Independent Petrol. Assn. Can.; mem. Candn. and Edmonton Chamber Comm.; recreations: golf; Clubs: Edmonton Petroleum; Mayfair Golf & Country; Office: 9915 - 108 St., Edmonton, Alta. T5K 2G8

McHAFFIE, Hugh Gordon, B.Sc.; P.Eng.; b. 1904; e. George Watson's Coll., Edinburgh, Scotland; Edinburgh Univ., B.Sc. 1924; m. Elsa Samuelson, 18 Aug. 1932; children: Ian, Fiona; former Chrmn., Associated Electrical Industries (Can.) Ltd.; recreations: yachting, skiing; Clubs: R.C.Y.C.; Home: R.R. #1, Nottawa L0M 1P0

McHUGH, John Laurence, M.A., Ph.D.; oceanographer (fisheries); university professor; b. Vancouver, B.C., 24 Nov. 1911; s. John and Annie Margaret (Woodward) McH.; e. Pub. and High Schs., New Westminster and Vancouver, B.C., 1928; Univ. of B.C., B.A. 1936, M.A. 1938; Univ. of Cal. (Los Angeles) and Scripps Inst. of Oceanography, Ph.D. 1950; m. Sophie Kleban, 30 March 1979; children (by former marriage): Peter Chadwick, Heather, Jan Margaret; PROF. OF MARINE RESOURCES, MARINE SCIENCES RESEARCH CENTER, STATE UNIV. OF N.Y. since Sept. 1970; Scient. Asst., Fisheries Research Bd. of Can. 1938-41 and 1945-46; Research Asst., Scripps Inst. of Oceanography, 1946-48; Research Assoc. 1948-51; Dir. Va. Fisheries Lab. and Prof. of Marine Biol., Coll. of William and Mary, 1951-59; Chief, Div. of Biol. Research, U.S. Dept. of Interior, Bureau of Comm. Fisheries 1959-63; Asst. Dir for Biol. Research, 1963-66; Depy. Dir. of Bureau, 1966-68; Acting Director, Office of Marine Resources, Dept. of Interior, 1968-70; Head Office for Internat. Decade of Ocean Exploration, Nat. Science Foundation 1970; Consultant, Nat. Council on Marine Resources & Engn. Devel. 1970-71; served with Candn. Scot. Regt., 1940-44; Queen's Own Cameron Highlanders of Winnipeg, 1944-45; rank Capt. on discharge; U.S. Commr., Inter-Am. Tropical Tuna Comn. 1960-70; Chrmn., Internat. Whaling Comn. (Vice-Chrmn. 1968-71, Chmn. 1971-72 and Commr. 1961-72); mem. Adv. Comte. on Marine Resources Research to Dir.-Gen., Food and Agric. Organ. of U.N. 1965-69; mem. Nat Research Council (USA) 1965-70 and U.S. Nat. Comte. Internat. Biol. Program, 1967-69; mem. Comte. on Internat. Marine Science Affairs Policy of Ocean Bd., Nat. Acad. Sciences; Mid-Atlantic Fishery Mgmt. Council 1976-79; Fellow, Woodrow Wilson Internat. Centre for Scholars, 1971; M.S.R.C. Distinguished Teaching Award 1977; Head or mem. of U.S. dels. to numerous internat. fishery meetings; mem. Bd. of Trustees, Internat. Oceanographic Foundation, Coral Gables, Fla.; author of 150 scient. papers and tech. articles in various nat. and foreign scient. journs. and trade mags.; mem., Am. Inst. Fishery Research Biols.; Am. Inst. Biol. Sciences; Am. Fisheries Soc.; Nat. Shellfisheries Assn.; Va. Acad. Science (Past Chrmn., Biol. Sec.); Atlantic Estuarine Research Soc. (Past. Pres., Hon mem.); Beta Theta Pi (Past Secy.); Sigma Xi; Home: 150

Strathmore Gate Dr., Stony Brook, N.Y. 11790; Office: Stony Brook, N.Y.

McILHONE, John T., M.A. Ph.D.; educator; b. Montreal, Que., 26 Jan. 1911; s. Robert Emmett and Ellen Eva (O'Rourke) M.; e. Lajoie Elem. Sch., Outremont, Que., 1918-24; Acad. Commerciale, Loretteville, Que., 1924-26; Loyola Coll. High Sch., Montreal, Que., 1926-29; Loyola Coll., B.A. (Law); Univ. of Montreal, M.A. (Letters), 1939; B.Ed., 1940, Ph.D. (Educ.) 1942; Grad. Dipl. Extve. Devel. Inst. Adv. Mgmnt., 1970; m. Dorothy Agnes, d. Earl Henry Quinn, 20 June 1942; children: Quinn, Anne Marie; Director (Founding), Thomas More Inst. for Adult Education (Prof. of Eng. 1946-61); Trustee, Loyola Coll.; Gov., Concordia Univ.; mem. Que. Sch. Restructuration Council for Island of Montreal, since 1967; mem., Que. Royal Comn. of Inquiry on Educ., since 1961; mem., Comn. Pre-Univ. Prof. Éduc.; Dir., Candn. Cath. Trustees Assn.; with Montreal (Que.) Cath Sch. Comn. since 1934 in various teaching posts becoming Assoc. Gen. Dir. of Studies, 1952; Dir. of Eng. Schs. and Assoc. Dir. Gen. 1967; served with RCAF as Flying Offr. Instr., 1940.41; Flight Lt., Chief Instr., 1941-42; No. 4 Manning Depot, Que. City, Que., 1942-44; O.C. Sch. of English, Toronto, Ont., 1944-45; Depy. Dir. Gen. Montreal Catholic Sch. Comn. 1970-73, since when Dir. Gen. of Mt. Saint Patrick; Trustee, Montreal St. Patrick Orphan Asylum, 1973; has written various prof. papers in the educ. field ("The Classical College"; "The Gifted Child", etc.); mem., Candn. Educ. Assn.; Nat. Cath. Educ. Assn.; Candn. Coll of Teachers; life mem., Cdn. Educ. Assn.; awarded Coronation Medal; Centennial Medal; Commdr., Order of Sch. Merit, P.Q. (1956) Commdr. Order of Merit, Kts. of Malta; R. Catholic; recreations: skiing, golf, bowling; Club: Mt. Stephen; Home: 1440 Laird Blvd., Town of Mt. Royal, Que. H3P 2T4; Office: 6100 Deacon Rd., Montreal, Que. H3S 2P3

McILRAITH, Hon. George James, P.C. Q.C.; senator; b. Lanark, Ont., 29 July 1908; s. James and Kate (MacLeod) M.; m Margaret, d. Dr. A. V. Summers, Ottawa, Ont.; children: Janet Elizabeth, Mary Margaret, Catherine Ann, George Edward; formerly Partner, McIlraith & McIlraith; 1st el. to H. of C. for Ottawa West, g.e. 1940 and re-el. since; Parlty. Asst. to Minister of Reconstruction, 1945, to Min. of Trade & Comm., 1948, and to Min. of Defence Production, 1951; Minister of Transport, Apl. 1963, Min. of Public Works, July 1965-July 1968; Solr. Gen. of Can. 1968-70; summoned to Senate of Can. April 1972; one of four M.P.'s chosen to rep. Can. at Conf. of Empire Parlty. Assn., Bermuda, 1943; Candn. Del. to U.N. Gen. assembly, N.Y., 1946; Cand. Rep. at Commonwealth Ministers' Meetings on Econ. & Trade Matters, London, 1950; rep. Can. on Commonwealth Consultative Comte on S. and S.E. Asia (Colombo Plan), London, 1950 and at Karachi, 1952; Headed Candn. Del. to 17th C.P.A. Conf., Kuala Lumpur, Malaysia, Sept. 1971, and 18th C.P.A. Conf., Blantyre, Malawi, Africa, Oct. 1972; mem. Candn. Del., 20th Meeting, Can.-U.S. Inter-Parlty. Group to Alaska, Yukon & Alta., Aug. 1979; Counsel to law firm, MacDonald Affleck, Ottawa; Liberal; Presbyterian; Clubs: Rideau; Royal Ottawa Golf; Canadian; Office: The Senate, Ottawa, Ont. K1A 0A4

McINNES, David Leslie, B.S.F.; lumber executive; b. Nelson, B.C., 19 May 1928; s. Malcolm Leslie and Grace (MacPherson) McI.; e. Univ. of B.C., B.S.F. 1953; m. Winifred Marie, d. J. Archie Millar, 2 May 1953; 4 children; PRESIDENT CHIEF EXTVE. OFFICER AND DIR., WEYERHAEUSER CANADA LTD.; served with RCN Reserve 1953; rank Sub.-Lt.; Dir., Council of Forest Ind., Candn. Pulp & Paper Assn.; Forest Engineering Research Inst.; Candn. Forestry Assn.; recreations: boating, fishing,; Clubs: Vancouver; Home: 1378 Chartwell Dr., W. Vancouver, B.C. V7S 2R5; Office: 3010, 700 W. Georgia St., Box 10027,Vancouver, B.C.V7Y 1C8

McINNES, Donald, O.C., Q.C., LL.D., D.C.L.; b. Halifax, N.S., 4 Apl. 1904; s. Hector and Charlotte (MacNeill) M.; e. Ashbury Coll., Ottawa; Dalhousie Univ.; m. Constance, d. E. L. Rowan-Legg, 18 June 1932; children: Hector, Stewart, Roderick, Ann; SR. PARTNER, McINNES, COOPER AND ROBERTSON, since 1946; Hon. Director, The Bank of Nova Scotia; read law with Hector McInnes, K.C.; called to the Bar of N.S. 1926; cr. K.C. 1941; Pres., Candn. Bar Assn., 1960-61; Conservative; Un. Church; Clubs: Ashburn; Saraguay; Halifax; Office: 1673 Bedford Row, Halifax, N.S. B3J 1T1

McINNIS, Hon. Thomas Johnson, M.L.A., LL.B.; politician; b. Sheet Harbour, N.S. 9 Apl. 1945; s. Michael and Anne NcI.; e. Sheet Harbour schs.; St. Mary's Univ.; Dalhousie Law Sch. LL.B.; m. Bernadette Monk 1968; two s. Richard, Ryan; MIN. OF MUNICIPAL AFFAIRS, N.S., Min. of Transportation, and Min. Responsible for Office of Communications Policy 1981- ; mem. N.S. Wildlife Assn.; Block Parent Assn.; Prov. Extve. P. Cons. Party of N.S.; mem. E. Shore P. Cons. Assn.; el. M.L.A. for Halifax-Eastern Shore prov. g.e. 1978; P. Conservative; R. Catholic; Office: 9th Fl., Maritime Hall, 1505 Barrington St., Halifax, N.S. B3J 3K5

McINTOSH, Alexander McCombie, B.Sc.; petroleum executive; b. Blackburn, Scot., 11 March 1926; s. late George William and late Clementine (Hutchison) McI.; e. Univ. of Alta., B.Sc. (Petroleum Engn.) 1951; m. Irene Isabelle, d. late Archibald Leckie, 18 - Sept. 1947; children: Sandra Anne, Leslie Gail, Laurie Gene; PRES. & CEO, HOME OIL CO. LTD. 1979- ; Exec: Vice-Pres., Operations, Pacific Petroleums Ltd., 1975-79; joined present Co. as Field Engr., 1951-52; apptd. Prod. Supt. 1952-54; Chief Engr., Calgary, 1954-56; Dist. Mgr., Fort St. John, B.C., 1956-61; Operations Supt., Calgary, 1961-63; Mgr. of Prod. 1963-67; Vice Pres., Exploration & Production 1967-71; Vice Pres., Operations 1971-74; Sr. Vice Pres, Dir. 1974; served with RCAFC March-Aug. 1944 and with RCAC Aug. 1944-Oct. 1945; mem., Assn. Prof. Engrs. Alta.; past chrmn. Bd of Govs., Candn Petroleum Assoc.; recreations: golf, Club: Earl Grey Golfand Country; Calgary, Golf and country; The Ranchman's; Home: 2629 Linden Dr., Calgary, Alta. T3E 6C8; Office: 2300 Home Oil Tower, 324 8 Ave. S.W., Calgary, Alta. T2P 3Z5

McINTOSH, Alexander R., C.D.; executive; b. Aberdeen, Scot. 12 Sept. 1921; s. Alexander and Isabella McI.; e. Univ. of Toronto Schs.; Univ. of W. Ont.; Mil. Staff Coll.; m. Alice Elizabeth d. Frank Hugh Cotterll Sefton 4 May 1946; children: Elizabeth Anne (Mrs. Paul Crellin), Hugh, David, Ross, Heather; PRESIDENT AND CEO. ARVAK MANAGEMENT INC . (Controlling Co. Beaver Foods Ltd.); mem. W. Ont. Adv. Bd. Crown Trust Co.; served with Canadian Food Products 15 yrs. becoming Gen. Mgr. 1959; formed own co. Beaver Foods Ltd. 1960; served with Candn. Army during World War II, discharged as Maj.; Candn. Reserve Army, Past Area Commdr. Central Militia Area, retired as Brig. Gen. 1975; currently Hon. Lt. Col. 4th Bn. Royal Candn. Regt.; mem., Royal Cdn. Regt. Senate; Mentioned in Despatches; rec'd Centennial Medal 1967; Dir. YM-YWCA London; Past. Pres. and mem. Extve. Comm., Easter Seal Soc.; mem., Bd. of Dir., Ont. Safety League; mem. Human Nutrition Research Council of Ont.; Univ. of Guelph Policy Adv. Bd.; London Chamber Comm.; Candn. Restaurant Assn.; Diocese of Huron Finance Comm.; Adv. Bd., London Woman's Christian Assn.; Adv. Bd., London Symphony Orchestra; Adv. Bd, London Salvation Army; Nat'l. Adv. Bd., Salvation Army; London Bd. of Govs.; Cand'n Corps of Commissionners; Past Pres., London Club; Anglican; recreations: boating, photography, carpentry; Clubs: Rotary, Royal Candn. Mil. Inst.; London; London Hunt and Country; Empire; Home: 39 Hampton Cres., London, Ont. N6H 2N7; Office: 1925 Dundas St. East, London, Ont. N5V 1P7

McINTOSH, Cameron Irwin; editor, publisher; b. North Battleford, Sask., 1 July 1926; s. Cameron Ross and Pearl Susan (Irwin) M.; e. N. Battleford Coll. Inst.; Univ. of Saskatchewan; m. Barbara Lee, d. Wm. Aylesworth, Watford, Ont., 9 Oct. 1954; children: Irwin William Aylesworth, Rebecca Lee Aylesworth, Jean Ann Aylesworth; apptd.LT. GOVERNOR OF SASKATCHEWAN Feb 22, 1978 Publisher, McIntosh Publishing Co. Ltd.; Publisher Western Canada Outdoors; Pres. (1968-69) Candn. Community Newspapers Assn.; Trustee, N. Battleford Public Sch. Bd.; 1962-78, past pres., N. Battleford Br., Sask. Motor Club; former Chrmn., N. Battleford Planning Comn.; Pres. (1962), N. Battleford Chamber of Comm.; Past Pres. (1958), Sask. Weekly Newspapers Assn.; Sask. Jr. Chamber Comm. (1952); Nat. Vice-Pres. (1954) Jr. Chamber of Comm. of Can.; Pres., Sask. Travel Assn., 1963-64; apptd. Editor, N. Battleford News, 1951 and named Mgr. in 1952; Mang. Ed. and Secy.-Treas. of McIntosh Publishing Co. Ltd. upon merger of News and Optimist in May 1953; Past Chrmn., Table Mt. Regional Park; mem. Outdoor Writers Can.; Outdoor Writers Am.; Zone 2 Chrmn., Sask. Homecoming 1971; Freemason; Royal Candn. Legion; B.O.P. Elks; Liberal; Presbyterian; K-40; recreations: hunting, angling, skiing; Home: 9007 - 16th Ave. W., North Battleford, Sask. S9A 2T6; Office: Suite 511, Hotel Saskatchewan, Regina, Sask:

McINTOSH, Donald Alexander, Q.C.; b. Toronto, Ont., 13 Aug. 1912; s. Alexander Nelson and Mildred Edith (Winters) M.; e. Upper Can. Coll.; Univ. of Toronto, B.A. 1933; Osgoode Hall, Toronto, Ont.; m. Frances Isabel, d. C. Marlow Adams of Toronto, Ont., 9 Oct. 1937; children: Annabelle (Mrs. J. P. Garrow), Alexander C., John M.; PARTNER, FRASER & BEATTY; Vice Pres., and Dir., Confederation Life Insurance Co.; Dir., Canadian Reinsurance Co.; Canadian Reassurance Co.; Bank of Montreal; Argus Corpn. Ltd.; Hollinger Argus Ltd.; Kenting Ltd.; Charterhouse Development Canada Ltd.; Field Aviation Co. Limited; Canadian-Dominion Leasing Corp. Ltd.; Finlayson Enterprises Ltd.; A. C. Nielsen Co. of Can. Ltd.; Trimac Ltd.; Assoc. Biscuits of Can. Ltd.; Trustee, Ont. Jockey Club; read law with Fraser & Beatty; called to Bar of Ontario 1936; cr. K.C. 1952; Sigma Chi; Freemason; Anglican; recreation: golf; Clubs: Toronto; University; Rosedale Golf; Home: 95 Dinnick Crescent, Toronto, Ont. M4N 1L9; Office: (Box 100) First Canadian Place, Toronto, Ont. M5X 1B2

McINTOSH, Hilton Alexander, Q.C., LL.M.; b. Saskatoon, Sask., 8 Sept. 1930; s. Ranzo and Mary (Rennie) McI.; e. Caswell Hill Pub. Sch. and Bedford Rd. Coll. Inst., Saskatoon, 1948; Univ. of Sask., B.A. 1951, LL.B. 1953; Dalhousie Univ. (Sir James Dunn Scholar), LL.M. 1955; ASST. DEPY. MIN. (LEG. PROGRAMMING), DEPT. OF JUSTICE, since 1975; Chrmn., Statute Revision Comm. of Can. since 1976; read law with W. B. Francis, Q.C.; called to Bar of Sask. 1954; cr. Q.C. 1971; Lectr. in Leg., Univ. of Ottawa (Common Law), 1961-75; Secretary, Nat. Council on Adm. of Justice in Can., 1967-76; mem. Leg. Sec., Dept. of Justice, 1956-70; Jr. Adv. Counsel 1956; Sr. Adv. Counsel 1959; Dir., Dept. of Justice, Privy Council Sec., 1970-75; mem. Conf. of Commrs. on Uniformity of Leg. 1959-66; served with COTC, Univ. of Sask., 1948-53; rank Lt.; Gov. Gen.'s Foot Guards, 1956-58; rank Capt.; mem., Law Soc. Sask.; Candn. Bar Assn.; Fed. Lawyers' Club; Internat. Comn. Jurists; Protestant; recreations: reading, travel, tennis; Club: Larrimac Golf; Home: 111 Wurtemburg St., Apt. 1103, Ottawa, Ont. K1N 8M1; Office: Room 2022, West Memorial Bldg., 344 Wellington St., Ottawa, Ont. K1A 0H8.

McINTOSH, Lawrie Gandier, B.A.Sc., M.S.; product design consultant; b. Clinton, Ont. 24 June 1924; s. Rev. William Donald and Margaret Almina (Nicholson) McI.; e. Univ. of Toronto B.A.Sc. (Mech. Engn.) 1946; Ill. Inst. of Technol. M.S. (Product Design) 1951; Mass. Inst. Technol. various summer courses; m. Helen Kathleen d. Frederick William Cameron 17 Sept. 1949; children: Cameron Lawrie, Wanda Lee; PROP., LAWRIE McINTOSH DESIGN LTD. 1951- ; completed projects incl. products in indust., agric., comm. and inst., consumer fields; Dir., Cameron Enterprises Ltd.; winner various competitions and awards incl. N.D.C. Chair Competition 1952; Dipl. Di Medaglia D'oro Milan 1956; Stainless Steel Competition 1961; Candn. Souvenir Competition 1966; Consulting Tech. Ed. "Product Design and Engineering" 6 yrs.; occasional lectr. various univs. and community colls. Can.; mem. Adv. Panel to Candn. Gen. Standards Bd.; mem. Assn. Prof. Engrs. Prov. Ont.; Assn. Candn. Indust. Designers; Human Factors Assn. Can.; Soc. Plastics Engrs.; United Church; recreations: fishing, cross-country skiing; Home: 9 Sapling Court, Etobicoke, Ont. M9C 1K9; Office: 169 The West Mall, Etobicoke, Ont. M9C 1C2.

McINTOSH, Robert Lloyd, M.B.E., B.A., Ph.D., D.Sc., F.R.S.C., F.C.I.C.; educator; b. Montreal, Que. 16 Feb. 1915; s. Alexander Douglas and Bella (Marcuse) McI.; e. Halifax (N.S.) Pub. Schs. and Halifax Co. Acad. (Harris Gold Medallist); Dalhousie Univ., B.A. 1935, M.Sc. 1936; McGill Univ., Ph.D. 1939, D.Sc. (Hon. Causa) 1972; m. Margaret Jean, d. late Harcourt V. Callaghan 31 March 1966; children: Sharon (Mrs. J. T. Lamb), Janet (Mrs. P. T. Truant), Alec; EMERITUS PROFESSOR OF CHEMISTRY, QUEEN'S UNIV. since 1979; Offr. i/c Extramural Research, Directorate Chem. Warfare & Smoke 1940-45; Assoc. Prof. and Prof., Univ. of Toronto 1948-54; Prof. and Head Dept. of Chem. present Univ. 1961, Assoc. Dean (Sciences) Faculty of Arts & Science 1969; Dean, Sch. of Grad. Studies, Queen's Univ. 1970-79; mem. Scient. Adv. Comte., Candn. Soc. for Weizmann Inst. Science; awards incl. Royal Exhn. of 1851 Scholar. 1939; Chem. Educ. Award, Chem. Inst. Can. 1972; author of "Dielectric Behavior of Physically Adsorbed Gases" N.Y. 1966 and over 60 articles in scient. journs. in field of physical chem.; recreation: sailing; Clubs: Kingston (Ont.) Yacht; Home: 185 Ontario St., Unit 607, Kingston, Ont. K7L 2Y7; Office: Kingston, Ont. 3M6

McINTOSH, Walter L., M.C.S.; Certified Public Accountant; b. Kans., U.S.A. 2 June 1916; s. James and Opal B. (May) McI.; e. Benjamin Franklin Univ. Washington B.C.S. 1947, M.C.S. 1948; m. Constance M. d. late Louis Z. Fauteux 21 Aug. 1943; children: Diane L., James L., Patrice M., Mark D.; VICE PRES.-FINANCE, CELANESE CANADA INC. since 1978; Asst. Plant Acct. Celanese, Cumberland, Md. 1953, Mgr. Gen. Accounting Charlotte, N.C. 1957, Controller, Celanese Chemical Co. N.Y. 1958, Vice Pres. Adm. Celanese Plastics Co. Newark, N.J. 1963, Vice Pres. Chemical Group Co. N.Y. 1967, Vice Pres. and Controller, Celanese Coatings Co. Louisville, Ky. 1968-78; served with U.S. Navy 1942-45; mem. Am. Inst. Cert. Pub. Accts.; D.C. Inst. C.P.A.; Am. Inst. Accts.; Civitan Club (Pres., Secy. & Lt. Gov.); R. Catholic; Club: St. James's; Home: Apt. 504, 519 de Gaspe, Nuns Island, Montreal, Que. H3E 1E9; Office: 800 Dorchester Blvd. W., Montreal, Que. H3C 3K8.

McINTOSH, William G., D.D.S., M.Sc.D., LL.D., (Sask.), D.Sc. (McGill), F.R.C.D.(C), F.A.C.D.,.F.I.C.D.; dentist (ret.); b. Hanley, Sask., 1 December 1915; s. Charles Hamilton and Mable V. (Kneale) M.; e. Prince Albert (Sask.) Coll. Inst.; Univ. of Sask., 1932-33; Univ. of Toronto, D.D.S. 1937; m. Marion Louise, d. M. J. Patton, Toronto, Ont., 17 Aug. 1940; children: Marion Gail, William Chad, Charlotte Ann; Extve. Dir., Candn. Dental Assn., 1964-76; Assoc. Prof. of Periodontology, Univ. of Toronto, and a mem. of staff of Faculty of Dent., 1938-64; former Consultant in Periodontol., Sunnybrook Hosp. and Hosp. for Sick Children, Toronto; in gen. practice of his prof. 1937-42; served in 2nd World War with R.C.D.C., 1942-46; assigned to Med.-Dent. Unit, R.C.A.F., Trenton, Ont., for research and teaching duties; mem., Candn. Dental Assn. (Pres. 1959-60); Pres.

Candn. Acad. of Periodontol. (1958); mem., Am. Acad. of Periodontol.; Hon. mem., Am. Dental Assn.; Brit. Dental Assn.; Alpha Omega Internat. Frat.; Vice Pres., Fed. Dentaire Internationale 1972-77; mem. List of Honour, Fed. Dentaire Internat.; 1980 recipient of Pierre Fauchard Acad. Elmer S. Best Award; co-author of (articles) "The Relation of Ascorbic Acid Intake to Gingivitis", 1946; "The Nutrition & Health of the James Bay Indian", "Dental Studies & Nutritional Findings in the James Bay Indian", 1949; Xi Psi Phi; United Church; Home: 61 St. Clair Ave. W., Apt. 802, Toronto Ont. M4V 2Y8

McINTYRE, John George Wallace, B.Com., M.B.A.; executive; b. Toronto, Ont., 26 July 1920; s. late Dr. George Crerar and late Gwendolyn Alberta (Wallace) McI.; e. Univ. of Toronto Schs., 1937; Univ. of Toronto, B.Com. 1941; Harvard Grad. Sch. of Business Adm., M.B.A. 1947; m. Ruth Elizabeth, d. Percy A. Wilson, Weston, Ont., 26 July 1945; children: Angus, Heather, Robert, Anne; CORPORATE VICE PRES., REAL ESTATE AND DEVEL., HUDSON'S BAY CO., since 1974; Pres., Hudson's Bay Co. Developments Ltd.; Dir., Markborough Properties Ltd.; Budget Acct., Abitibi Paper Co., 1947; Budget Mgr., Ford Motor Co. of Canada Ltd., 1951 subsequently becoming Asst. Controller and Extve. Asst. to Vice Pres. Overseas Operations; Asst. Gen. Mgr., Windsor Mfg. Operations, 1958, Gen. Mgr. 1963; Asst. Mang. Dir., Ford Australia 1958, Mang. Dir., 1959-63; Extve. Vice Pres., Columbia Cellulose Ltd., Vancouver 1965, Pres. 1966; joined present Co. as Pres., Ruperts Land Trading Co. and Gen. Mgr. Retail Devel. 1967; served with Royal Candn. Ordnance Corps in Can. and overseas during World War II; rank Capt.; has served as Dir., CNIB; Un. Appeal; Jr. Achievement; Australian Productivity Council; Australian Indust. Adv. Bd. (mem.); Gov., Univ. of Windsor; Balmoral Hall, Winnipeg; United Church; recreations: swimming, chess, reading, restoration of old heritage bldgs.; Home: R.R. 1, King, Ont. L0G 1K0; Office: 2 Bloor St. E., Toronto, Ont. M4W 1A8

McINTYRE, Paul, D.Mus., A.R.C.T.; musician; university professor; b. Peterborough, Ont., 1 Oct. 1931; s. (John) Vincent and Mary H. (Poirier) M.; e. Royal Conservatory of Toronto, A.R.C.T. (Piano; Gold Medal for highest mark in Can.) 1950; Univ. of Toronto, B.Mus. 1951; Artist Dipl. of Royal Cons. (1st Class Hons. in Comp. and Piano) 1952; Univ. of Toronto, D.Mus. (1st Class Hons.) 1958; studied under Dr. Arnold Walter for Comp., Béla Böszörmènyi-Nagy and Alexander Uninsky for Piano, and others; Nicholas Goldschmidt for Conducting; awarded a Canada Foundation Scholarship for study in Europe, 1953; studied Comp. with Tony Aubin and Olivier Messiaen at Cons. Nat. in Paris; Conducting with Igor Markewitch and Wolfgang Sawallisch at Mozarteum in Salzburg and with Pierre Monteux, Hancock, Maine 1960-61; m. Phyllis Runge, 26 Dec. 1959; children: John Francis; Stephen Paul, Moira Clare, Lenore Therese, Judith Eva; Carnegie Visiting Assoc. Prof., and Head, Music Dept., Univ. of Alaska 1961-64; Asst. Prof., Music Dept., Univ. of Minnesota, 1964-67; Assoc. Prof. and Head, Music Dept., College of St. Catherine, St. Paul, Minn. 1967-70; PROFESSOR OF MUSIC, UNIVERSITY OF WINDSOR since 1970; Head of the Department and Dir. of Sch. of Music 1970-80; Compositions: "Trio in E minor", 1949; "Sonatina for Piano", 1950; song cycle "Four Poems of Walter de la Mare", 1950; "String Quartet", 1951; "Concerto for Piano and Orchestra", 1952; song cycle "Three Poems of Arthur Symons", 1953; "Song of Autumn" a poem for string orchestra, 1953; "Deux Etudes Poetiques" for piano, 1954; "Judith", a melodrama-cantata, 1957; "Symphonia Sacra" for Voices and Orchestra 1956; "Death of the Hired Man" (opera) 1960; "Jean de Brebeuf" (symphony) 1963; "Out of the Cradle Endlessly Rocking" (Chamber cantata) 1966; Permutations on a Paginini Caprice" (string quartet) 1967; "This Is Not True" (opera) 1967; "Encounters" for violin

and piano 1970; "The Little Red Hen" (Cantata for voices & orchestra) 1976; "Fantasy for Organ" 1977; "Song of Renewal" 1977; "Five Sonnets of Archebald Lampman", for Voice and Piano, 1978; "Commedia", for orchestra, 1978; "Three Preludes" for organ; comp. performed over CBC, Eaton Auditorium, Massey Hall, National Arts Centre, Orheum Theatre (Vancouver), Art Gallery of Windsor etc.; piano soloist on many occasions; Asst. Conductor Opera Festival Co. of Toronto, 1953 and 1955, and at Opera Summer Sch., Univ. of B.C. 1955; mem. Candn. League of Composers (Council 1956-57, and Vice Pres., 1980-81); Past Pres., Alumni Assn., Univ. of Toronto Faculty of Music; Roman Catholic; recreations: bridge, swimming; Home: 4285 Mitchell St., Windsor, Ont. N9G 2G1

McINTYRE, Hon. William Rogers, B.A., LL.B.; judge; b. Lachine, Que. 15 March 1918; s. Charles Sidney and Pauline May (Sifton) McI.; e. Univ. of Sask. B.A., LL.B. 1941; m. Hermione Elizabeth d. late Alexander Reeves, Newmarket, Eng. 12 Dec. 1944; children: Elizabeth Pauline, John Stuart; JUDGE, SUPREME COURT OF CAN. since 1979; called to Bar of Sask. 1947, B.C. 1947; apptd. Judge, Supreme Court of B.C. 1967 and Court of Appeal B.C. 1973; Bencher, Law Soc. B.C. 1965-66; served with Candn. Army 1941-46, UK, Sicily, Italy and NW Europe; Clubs: Union (Victoria, B.C.); Rideau; Home: 40 Boteler St., Ottawa, Ont. K1N 9C8; Office: Supreme Court of Can. Bldg., Ottawa, Ont. K1A 0J1.

McISAAC, Roderick Hugh; company president; b. Sudbury, Ont., 4 Sept. 1927; s. Roderick M. and Ellen (Bouzani) M.; e. Public Sch., Flin Flon, Man.; St. Paul's Coll., Winnipeg, Man.; m. Elizabeth Mary, d. John H. A. Wilmot, 3 Aug. 1950; children: Roderick Andrew, Michael John, Mary Catherine, Joan Maureen, Judith Ann, Susan Elizabeth, Peter Joseph; PRESIDENT, GREAT NORTHERN CAPITAL CORP.; Pres., Home Smith Ltd.; Home Smith Properties Ltd.; Humbria Ltd.; Home Smith International Ltd.; The Old Mill Ltd.; Canarma Western Ltd.; Sherwood Properties Co. Ltd.; Diamond Clay Products Inc.; Rodell Corp. (1967) Ltd.; Delro Industries; Midwest Diesel & Equipment; Midwest Drilling Co.; Columbia Forest Products Ltd.; Dir., Transair Ltd.; joined Midwest Diamond Drilling Ltd. in 1947; apptd. Gen. Mgr., 1952; Dir. R. C. Archiepiscopal Corp. of Winnipeg; St. Boniface Gen. Hosp.; mem., Canadian Diamond Drilling Assn.; Candn. Inst. Mining & Metall.; Candn. Mfrs. Assn.; former Bd. of mem., Man. Centennial Corp.; Catholic; Liberal; recreations: boating, flying, hunting; Clubs: The Manitoba; St. Charles Country; Winnipeg Winter; Engineers' (Toronto); Canadian (Winnipeg); Home: 14 Wilket Rd., Willowdale 430, Ont. M2L 1N6

McIVOR, D. K., (Don), B.Sc.; petroleum executive; b. Winnipeg, Man. 12 April 1928; e. Univ. of Man. B.Sc. (Geol.) 1950; Nat. Defence Coll. 1972-73; m. Avonia Isabel Forbes 1953; children: Gordon, Donald, Duncan, Deborah, Daniel; CHRMN. OF THE BD. AND CHIEF EXTVE. OFFR., IMPERIAL OIL LTD. 1982- ; joined Imperial Oil as geophysical trainee seismic crew Alta. 1950, held various operational and research positions in exploration 1950-58; held various positions incl. Asst. to Exploration Mgr., Supvr. Exploration Planning, Mgr. Exploration Research, Calgary 1958-68, also held assignments Angola, France and Tulsa, Okla. (Jersey Production Research Co.); Asst. Mgr. and Mgr. Corporate Planning, Toronto H.O. 1968-69, Exploration Mgr. 1970-72, Sr. Vice Pres. and Dir. 1973, Extve. Vice Pres. 1975, Vice Pres. Oil & Gas Exploration & Production, Exxon Corp. 1977-81; Depy. Chrmn. and Dir. Imperial Oil Ltd. 1981-82; mem. Candn. Soc. Petrol. Geols.; Office: 111 St. Clair Ave. W., Toronto, Ont.

McIVOR, George H., C.M.G.; executive; b. Portage la Prairie, Man., 1894; e. Pub. Sch. and Coll. Inst., Winnipeg. Man.; Chrmn., Calgary Adv. Comte. Crown Trust

Co.; engaged by Canadian Pacific Railway Telegraphs 1909-11; Clerk, McLaughlin Grain Company in charge of one of the country elevators; Br. Mgr., James Richardson & Sons, Calgary, Alta., 1921-24; Western Sales Mgr., Candn. Wheat Pools, 1924-27 and Gen. Sales Mgr., with offices at Winnipeg. Man., 1921-1930; Sales Mgr. assoc. with John I. McFarland in connection with Gov. Stabilization Operations 1931-35; Asst. Chief Commr., Candn. Wheat Bd., 1935-37; Chrmn., Cereals Comte., Internat. Food Council, Wash., D.C. 1942-47; Chief Commr., Candn. Wheat Bd., 1937-58 when resigned from govt. service; Chrmn., Robin Hood Flour Mills 1958-69; Dir., Candn. Imp. Bank of Commerce, 1959-66; Chairman, Canadian Hunger Foundation 1961-65; Roy. Comm., Fed. Inquiry on Freshwater Fish Marketing, 1955; Dir. Emeritus, Can. Imperial Bank of Commerce 1972- ; Home: 703-104-26th Ave. S.W., Calgary, Alta. T2S O54

McIVOR, R. Craig, M.A., Ph.D., F.R.S.C. (1963); university professor; b. Chatham, Ont., 4 Oct. 1915; s. William Russell and Mabel (Craig) McI.; e. Central Pub. Sch. and Chatham (Ont.) Coll. Inst.; Univ. of W. Ont., B.A. 1937; Univ. of Chicago, M.A. 1939, Ph.D.: 1947; m. Marion Louise Larson, 1943; children: Richard, Roderic, Marilyn, Sharon; CHRMN., DEPT. OF ECON., McMASTER UNIV.; Dean, Faculty of Soc. Sci.; Commr., Ont. Comte. on Taxation (Smith Comte.); mem., Ont. Adv. Comte. on Confed.; Asst. Prof. of Econ., Univ. of W. Ont., 1940-46; McMaster Univ., 1946; Assoc. Prof. 1948, Prof. 1951; mem., Research Staff, Royal Comn. on Banking and Finance, 1963-64; author of "Canadian Monetary, Banking and Fiscal Development," 1958; "The Postwar Taxation of Canadian Cooperatives," 1959; "The Recent Growth of Cooperative Enterprise in Canada," 1962; Commonwealth Banking Systems, 1965 (Candn. author); "Postwar Trends in the Financing of Canadian Economic Activity" 1973; numerous articles and reviews in learned and popular journs; Pres., Ont.-Que. Athletic Assn.; mem., Candn. Econ. Assn.; Am. Econ. Assn.; Candn. Tax Foundation; United Church; Home: 111 Arnold St., Hamilton, Ont. L8S 1R5

McKAGUE, Lieut.-Col. E. Victor, M.C., V.D., C.D., Q.C.; b. Toronto, Ont., 26 Aug. 1893; s. Hugh H. M.; e. Parkdale Coll. Inst., Toronto; Univ. of Toronto (S.P.S.), B.A.Sc. 1915; Osgoode Hall, Toronto, 1920; m. Muriel, (deceased 28 Aug. 1967) d. N. Jory, 6 Sept. 1922; children: Mrs. Joan Kitchen, James V.; PARTNER, TAYLOR, JOY & McKAGUE (semi-retired); called to Bar of Ont. 1920; cr. K.C. 1941; served in World War 1915-19; awarded M.C. 1917; World War 1942-45 as Lieut.-Col. and Offr. Adm. Niagara Camp, Ont.; mem., Law Soc. of Upper Can.; Candn. Legion; P. Conservative; Anglican; recreations: golf, fishing; Clubs: Rosedale Golf; National; Toronto Hunt; Lawyers; Home: Apt. 1610, 77 St. Clair E., Toronto, Ont. M4T 1M5; Office: 145 King St. West, Toronto, Ont. M5H 1J8

McKAY, Alexander Gordon, M.A., Ph.D., F.R.S.C.; educator; b. Toronto, Ont. 24 Dec. 1924; s. Alexander Lynn and Marjory Maud Redfern (Nicoll) McK.; e. Upper Can. Coll. Toronto 1942; Trinity Coll. Univ. of Toronto B.A. 1946; Yale Univ. M.A. (Classics) 1947; Princeton Univ. A.M. (1948), Ph.D. 1950; m. Helen Jean d. Gustav Walter Zulauf 24 Dec. 1946; step-children: Julie Anne Stephanie Fraser Brott, Danae Helen Fraser; PROF. OF CLASSICS, McMASTER UNIV. 1961- ; Vice Pres. Peers-McKay Productions; Dir. Classical Summer Sch. Italy, Vergilian Soc. Am. 1955- ; Instr. Princeton Univ. 1947-50; Univ. of Pa. 1950-51; Univ. of Man. 1951-52; Asst. Prof. Mount Allison Univ. 1952-53; Waterloo Coll. 1953-55; Univ. of Man. 1955-57; McMaster Univ. 1957-59, Assoc. Prof. 1959-61, Chrmn. of Classics 1962-68, 1976-79, Dean of Humanities 1968-73; Visiting mem. Inst. Advanced Study Princeton, N.J. 1979, 1981; Prof.-in-Charge Intercollegiate Center Classical Studies in Italy 1975; Extve. Dir. McMaster Univ. Archaeol. Survey Team Sacco-Liri Valleys, Italy 1977-79; Princ. Lectr. Royal Ont. Museum Cruises Mediterranean 1981, 1982; Historian, Christ's Ch. Cath. Hamilton; Dir. Hamilton Foundation 1970-73; Pres. Hamilton Philharmonic Orchestra, Hamilton Chamber Music Soc.; Chrmn. Candn. Comte. Lexicon Iconographicum Mythologiae Classicae; Acad. Adv. Comte. Candn. Archaeol. Inst. Athens; Candn. Acad. Centre Italy; recipient Queen's Silver Jubilee Medal 1977; Woodrow Wilson Fellowship; Award of Merit Classical Assn. Middle W. and S.; Killam Research Fellowship; author "Naples and Campania" 1962; "Vergil's Italy" U.S. 1970, Eng. 1971; "Ancient Camapnia" Vols. I and II 1972; "Houses, Villas and Palaces in the Roman World" 1975; "Vitruvius, Architect and Engineer" 1978; "Victorian Architecture in Hamilton" 1967; co-author "Roman Lyric Poetry; Catullus and Horace" 1969; "Roman Satire: Horace, Juvenal, Persius et al" 1976; various articles, reports; Councillor, Royal Soc. Can. 1967- , Hon. Ed. 1970- , Councillor Acad. Humanities & Social Sciences; Pres., Classical Assn. Can. 1978-80; Classical Assn. Middle W. & S. 1972-73; Vergilian Soc. Inc. 1972-73; Dir. Internat. Acad. Union 1982-84; recreations: pianoforte, travel, surface archaeological surveys; Liberal; Anglican; Clubs: Arts & Letters; Tamahaac; Princeton (New York); Canadian (Pres. Hamilton 1972-73); Home: One Turner Ave., Hamilton, Ont. L8P 3K4; Office: Dept. of Classics, McMaster University, Hamilton, Ont. L8S 4M2.

McKAY, Donald Douglas, F.I.I.C.; executive; b. Kildonan, Man., 20 Apr. 1920; s. Douglas and Isabel (MacDonald) M.; e. St. John's and United Coll. (1939), Winnipeg, Man.; m. Thelma M., d. Walter G. Draper, 20 June 1947; children: Donald Douglas, Jr., Ross George, Nancy Jane; PRESIDENT, CHIEF EXTVE. OFFR. AND DIR., THE GORE MUTUAL INSURANCE CO. since 1974; Past Chrmn., Can. Safety Council; Dir. Assn. Independent Insurers; Insurance Bureau of Can.; South Waterloo Vocational Centre; Cambridge United Way; Cambridge Chamber of Commerce; Pres., Heritage Cambridge; Chrmn., Facility Assn.; Underwriters Adjustment Bureau; joined W. Can. Insurance Underwriters Assn. 1938; Underwriting Mgr., Federated Mutual Insurance 1948-59; Br. Mgr., Prudential of England 1960-63; Auto. and Property Mgr., Canadian Surety Co. 1964, Pres. and Gen. Mgr. 1969, Chrmn. 1974; served as Lieutenant RCNR 1940-45; United Church; Home: 50 Brant Rd. N., Cambridge, Ont. N1S 2W2; Office: 252 Dundas St., Cambridge, Ont. N1R 5T3

McKAY, Donald G., B.Sc., P.Eng.; industrial executive; b. Regina, Sask., 3 Jan. 1926; s. Eric B. and Lydia (Gibson) McK.; e. Univ. of Sask., B.Sc. (Mech. Engn.) 1949; m. Patricia M. Girard, 30 July 1949; children: Eric, Adele; PRES., C.E.O. & DIR., KEEPRITE INC.; joined Phillips Cables Ltd., Brockville, Ont. 1949; Cables Conduits & Fittings Ltd., Saint-Jean, Que., 1949; joined Pirelli Cables Ltd. 1953; joined Keeprite Inc. 1980; mem., Corp. Prof. Engrs. Electrical and electronic Mfrs Assn. (Council of Execs.); mem. Cdn. Manuf. Assn.; HRAI; Protestant; recreations: music, skiing, golf; Clubs: Brantford; Brantford Golf & Country; Home: 3 Belholme Ave., Brantford, Ont. N3T 1R9; Office: 44 Elgin St., P.O. Box 460, Brantford, Ont. N3T 5P4

McKAY, Verne Gordon, B.Com., M.B.A.; financial executive; b. Calgary, Alta., 4 Oct. 1942; s. Gordon James and Edna Redman (Winters) McK.; e. Univ. of Alta. B.Com. 1964; Univ. of Toronto M.B.A. 1966; Queen's Univ. (Candn. Bankers' Assn. Fellowship) 1967; m. Patricia Mary, d. late David Nicol 21 Dec. 1963; children: Kathleen Mary, Margaret Anne, Susan Ellen; EXTVE. VICE PRES. AND C. OPER. OFFR. EXPORT DEVELOPMENT CORP. 1980- ; Vice-Pres. Operations, 1977-80; Vice-Pres. Finance, 1975-77; Reg. Loan Mgr. 1972-75; Toronto Dominion Bank-Int. Credit 1972; Agent, New York Agency 1969-72; Supervisor, Profit Planning 1968-69; Financial Analyst 1967-68; Sen. Credit Offr. 1966-67; Chrm. and

Dir., Coaching Assn. of Can.; present Co. 1972; Protestant; recreation: athletics; Home: 11 Calais Court, Nepean, Ont. K2E 7E1; Office: 110 O'Connor St., Ottawa, Ont. K1P 5T9

McKEAG, T. B. Oliver, Q.C., LL.B., B.L.; barrister and solicitor; b. Belfast, N. Ireland 21 March 1928; s. Thomas and Margaret (McCaffrey) McK.; e. St. Malachys Coll. Belfast; Queen's Univ. Belfast LL.B. 1948; Inn of Court N. Ireland B.L. 1950; m. Marie Cooper 8 Dec. 1956; children: Maura, Ellen, Siobhan, Kevin; COUNSEL, CAMPBELL GODFREY & LEWTAS 1980- ; Solr. Law Dept. Shell Canada 1956, Gen. Solr. 1969, Gen. Counsel 1973-80; called to Bar of Ont. 1956; cr. Q.C. 1971; Chrmn. of Bd. St. Joseph's Health Centre; Pres. St. Joseph's Research Foundation; Pres. Armour Heights Ratepayers Assn. 1970-71; mem. Candn. Bar Assn. (Pres. Ont. Br. 1973-74, mem. Nat. Extve. 1979-81); Lawyers Club; Co. York Law Assn.; Law Soc. Upper Can.; Dir. Candn. Mfrs. Assn. 1978-80; P. Conservative; R. Catholic; recreations: skiing, sailing; Club: R.C.Y.C.; Home: 49 Sandringham Dr., Toronto, Ont. M5M 3G4; Office: (P.O. Box 36) Toronto-Dominion Centre, Toronto, Ont. M5K 1C5.

McKEAG, Col. The Hon. William John, B.Com., LL.D., K.G.ST.J.; b. Winnipeg, Man. 17 March 1928; s. George Hammill and Elizabeth (Biggar) McK.; e. Univ. of Man. B.Com. 1949, LL.D. 1977; Univ. of Winnipeg LL.D. 1976; m. Dawn Rue-Ann d. Hon. D. L. Campbell 28 Dec. 1950; children: Janis, Darcy, Kelly, Douglas; PRES., McKEAG REALTY LTD. since 1960; Dir., Canadian Motorways Ltd.; The Investors Group; Johnson & Higgins Willis Faber Ltd.; Greater Winnipeg Cablevision Ltd.; Dominion Stores Ltd.; Greater Winnipeg Gas Co.; joined family firm Security Storage Co. Ltd. 1949, Pres. 1952-60; Lt. Gov. of Man. 1970-76; Chrmn. of Bd., Greater Winnipeg Gas Co., 1980- ; Dir., Norcen Energy Resources Ltd., 1980- ; Dir., Bd. of Mang., Grace Gen. Hosp.; Man. Museum of Man & Nature; Ducks Unltd. (Can.); Hon. Counsellor, Winnipeg Chamber Comm. 1976; Dist. Gov. W. Can. Kiwanis 1967; mem. The 1001 (Nature Trust); rec'd Univ. of Man. Alumni Jubilee Award 1973; apptd. Hon. Col. Fort Garry Horse 1973; Hon. Life mem. Winnipeg Rotary; Man. Curling Assn.; rec'd Queen's Silver Jubilee Medal 1978; Knight of Justice, Order of St. John, 1980; Zeta Psi; United Church; recreations: golf, curling, skiing, hunting; Clubs: Manitoba; Winnipeg Winter; St. Charles Country; Home: 560 Park Blvd. W., Winnipeg, Man. R3P 0H4; Office: 400-717 Portage Ave., Winnipeg, Man. R3G 0M8.

McKEEN, George Beverly, B.Com.; company officer; b. Vancouver, B.C., 26 Feb. 1924; s. Hon. Stanley S. and Roxie Mae (York) M.; e. Prince of Wales Sch.; Brentwood Coll.; Univ. of British Columbia, B.Com. 1947; m. Joan Louise, d. late Thomas C. Clarke, 4 June 1947; children: Clarke Stanley, Stephanie Joan, George Craig; CHRMN., CHM BURRARD YARROWS CORP Chrmn. & Dir.; McKeen Investments Ltd.; Waterfront Terminals Ltd.; Pres. and Dir., McKeen & Wilson Ltd.; Dir., Dir., Versatile Corp.; Dawson Construction Ltd.; Bralorne Resources Ltd.; Xerox Canada Inc.; Mark Products Inc.; Daon Development Corp.; Canada Tungsten Mining Corp.; Q. Broadcasting Ltd.; served in 2nd World War with R.C.A.F., Pilot Offr., Navigator, 1943-45, mem., Crown Trust Advisory Board (Vancouver); Protestant; recreations: fishing, golf, boating; Clubs: Vancouver; Shaughnessy Golf; Home: 5376 Angus Drive, Vancouver, B.C. V6M 3N2; Office: #1066—999 W. Hastings St., Vancouver, B.C. V6C 2W2

McKELVIE, Donald; public utilities executive; b. New Liskeard, Ont., 14 Apr. 1913; s. Angus Alexander and Jessie Marjorie (Dowzer) M.; e. Queen's Univ.; m. Aileen Laura, d. late R. H. Wright, Apl. 1941; children: Peter, Julie; DIR., NORTHERN TELEPHONE LTD. (Estb. 1905); Vice-Pres., The Hudson Bay Mines Ltd.; served in 2nd

World War as Pilot Offr., R.C.A.F., in Can. & U.K., 1942-44; Liberal; Un. Church; recreations: golf; Club: National (Toronto); Home: 91 Niven St., New Liskeard, Ont. P0J 1P0; Office: Paget St., New Liskeard, Ont. P0J 1P0

McKENNA, Kenneth J., florist; b. Montreal, Que., 31 Aug. 1931; s. Edward Philip and Kathleen Clare (McGrory) M.; e. Loyola Coll., Montreal (1950) and Macdonald Coll. (1951); m. Margaret Anne, d. late Robert Berry, 29 May 1954; children: Kathleen Jean, Kenneth Robert, Mary Martha, Josephine Anne, Brigid Rose; PRESIDENT AND GEN. MGR., McKENNA LIMITED, since 1957; entered the employ of the firm in 1951 in Greenhouse Department, working successively in various depts.; served in R.C.A.F. (Reserve) 1948-52; el. to Montreal City Council, 1960, re-el. 1962 (Pro-Mayor 1961); mem., Montreal Mil. and Maritime Museum; Founding mem., Glenfinnan Assn.; mem. Glengarry Hist. Society; Highland Society of Montreal; Caledonian Society of Montreal (Life); Past President, St. Patrick's Society, Montreal; mem., St. Andrew's Society; Canada Celtic Cong.; Hon. mem., Pipes and Drums, Black Watch (R.H.R.); recreations: music, literature; Clubs: University; Windsor (Pres.); Home: 359 Simcoe, Mount Royal, Que. H3P 1X3; Office: 4509 Côte des Neiges, Montreal, Que. H3V 1E8

McKENZIE, Dan, M.P.; politician; b. Winnipeg, Man. 25 March 1924; s. Daniel and Nancy (Brown) McK.; e. Winnipeg, Man.; m. Marion Krawetz 10 Oct. 1960; children: John, Karen; Winnipeg City Councillor 1971-72; el. to H. of C. g.e. 1972, re-el. since; served as Veterans' Affairs critic, Parlty. Secy. to Min. of Nat. Defence & Veterans Affairs, Vice Chrmn. Caucus Comte. on Nat. Defence, Rly. Pension Critic; prior to el. served Manitoba Telephone System; Vice Chrmn. Mun. Hosp. Comn. Winnipeg; served with RCN during World War II; mem. Army, Navy & Air Force Veterans' Assn.; Royal Candn. Legion; P. Cons. Club Greater Winnipeg; P. Conservative; United Church; Homes: 103 - 2629 Portage Ave., Winnipeg, Man. R3J 0P7; Office: House of Commons, Ottawa, Ont. K1A 0A6.

McKENZIE, Kenneth Albert, Q.C., B.A., LL.B.; b. Calgary, Alta., 29 March 1917; s. John Aldrid and Aveline Irene (Laws) McK.; e. Univ. of Alta., B.A. 1938, LL.B. 1939; m. Doris Vivian, d. Walter Grierson, 30 May 1942; children: Donald G., Mrs. Heather Nilsen, Gordon, Keltie; PARTNER, BISHOP & McKENZIE since 1950; Chrmn. Bd. Life Insurance Co. of Alberta; Dir., Toronto Mutual Life Ins. Co.; Coronet Leaseholds Ltd.; Campbelltown Sewer Services Ltd.; Conjuring Estates Ltd.; Counsel, Judge Comn. on Prov. and Mun. Taxation; Counsel, McNally Royal Comn.; Chrmn., Gasoline Marketing Enquiry, Alta. Govt.; called to Bar of Alta. 1940; cr. Q.C. 1955; Solr., Atty.-Gen's Dept., Alta. 1940-42; Crown Prosecutor, Edmonton 1946; Sessional Lect., Univ. of Alta. Law Sch. 1946; Leg. Counsel, Govt. of Alta. 1946-50; served in 2nd World War, R.C.A. 1942-46; Capt., Calgary Highlanders; Governor of Alberta and Terr. Br., Royal Life Saving Soc. Can.; Secy. Bd., St. Stephens Coll.; Secy. and Dir., Rundle's Mission Inc.; mem. Edmonton Bar Assn.; Law Soc. Alta.; Candn. Bar Assn.; Phi Kappa Pi; United Church; recreations: sailing, skiing, mountaineering; Clubs: The Edmonton; Itaska Yacht; Kiwanis; Home: 8726 — 120 St., Edmonton, Alta. T6G 1X3; Office: 2200 Royal Trust Tower, Edmonton, Alta.

McKENZIE, Hon. Lloyd George, B.A., LL.B., LL.D. (Hon.); judge; b. Penticton, B.C. 20 Aug. 1918; s. William Alexander McK.; e. Monterey Sch., Oak Bay High, Victoria High and Victoria Coll. B.C.; Univ. of B.C. B.A., LL.B.; Univ. of Victoria LL.D.; m. Dorothy Elizabeth d. late Andrew Amos Meharey 6 Jan. 1943; JUDGE, SUPREME COURT OF B.C. also Judge, Court Martial Appeal Court; called to Bar of B.C. 1948; cr. Q.C. 1960; practiced primarily in civil and criminal litigation; served 19 yrs. as mem. Bd. Govs. and Chrmn. Univ. of Victoria;

Pres. Victoria Bar Assn.; Bencher, Law Soc. B.C.; mem. Am. Coll. Trial Lawyers; served with Candn. Army 1942-45, UK, Italy and NW Europe, rank Capt.; Clubs: Union; Lawyers' Inn; Home: 755 Fairmile Rd., West Vancouver, B.C. V7S 1R1; Office: The Law Courts, 800 Smithe St., Vancouver, B.C. V6C 1P6.

McKENZIE, William Andrew, B.A.; executive; b. Sarnia, Ont. 7 Sept. 1923; s. Andrew Dominion and Alice May (Sharpe) McK.; e. St. Andrews Coll., Aurora, Ont.; Univ. of W. Ont.; m. Catherine Anne, d. Dr. J. F. M. Kennedy, Nassau, Bahamas 17 June 1950; children: Jane (Mrs. G.M. Armstrong), Julie (Mrs. David R. Gilbert), Martha, Andrea; PRESIDENT, ADMAC HOLDINGS LTD.; Pres., Allcraft Products Ltd.; Dir., Northern Life Assnce. Co. Ltd.; Toromont Industries Ltd.; Boness Investments Ltd.; Muskoka-Parry Sound Broadcasting System Ltd.; served in R.C.A. 1943-44; Vice-Chrmn. Adv. Bd., St. Joseph's Hosp. & Chrmn., Finance Comte., St. Joseph's Hosp. Foundn.; mem., Adv. Bd., St. Mary's Hosp.; United Church; Freemason; Kappa Alpha; recreations: hunting, fishing; Clubs: The London; London Hunt & Country; Home: 1394 Corley Drive, London, Ont. N6G 2K4; Office: Suite 1702, Northern Life Tower, 380 Wellington St., London, Ont. N6A 5B5

McKEOUGH, William Darcy, B.A., LL.D.; utility executive; b. Chatham, Ont., 31 Jan. 1933; s. Florence Sewell (Woodward) and late George Grant McK.; e. Cedar Springs (Ont.) Pub. Sch.; Ridley Coll., St. Catharines, Ont.; Univ. of W. Ont., B.A., 1954; LL.D., Univ. of Western Ont., 1979 (Hon. Causa) LL.D., Wilfrid Laurier Univ., 1980 (Hon. Causa); m. Margaret Joyce, d. Senator the Hon. D. J. Walker, P.C., Q.C., LL.D.; 18 June 1965; two s., Walker Stewart, James Grant; Pres. and C.E.O., Union Gas Ltd. since 1979; Dir., Algoma Central Railway; Cdn. Imperial Bank of Commerce; Consumers Glass Co. Ltd.; McKeough Sons Co. Ltd.; Noranda Mines Ltd.; Numac Oil and Gas Ltd.; Redpath Ind. Ltd.; Precambrian Shields Resources; member, Chatham City Council, 1960-61 and 1962-63 1st el. to Ont. Leg. for Kent West, 1963; re-el., 1967, 71, 75 and 77; apptd. Min. without Portfolio, Nov. 1966; Min. Municipal Affairs, Nov. 1967; Treas., Min. of Econ. and Chrmn. Treasury Bd. 1971; re-apptd. Min. of Municipal Affairs 1972; resigned as Treas. & Min., 1972; Parlty. Assistant to Premier 1973; Minister of Energy 1973-75; Treasurer and Min of Econ. and Intergovernmental Affairs 1975-78; resigned from Cabinet and as M.P.P. 1978; mem. Bd. of Gov., Ridley Coll.; Stratford Shakesperian Festival; mem. Cdn. group, Trilateral Comm.; Hon. Chmn., Chatham Jaycees, 1980- ; P. Conservative; Anglican; recreations: tennis swimming, gardening; Clubs: Kent; Toronto; Albany (Toronto); Badminton and Racquet (Toronto); Home: Bally McKeough, Cedar Springs Ont. N0P 1E0

McKILLOP, John Harvey, M.Sc.; geologist; civil servant; b. Detroit, Mich., 21 Sept. 1927; s. Angus Hugh and Helen (Harvey) M.; came to Canada 1930; e. High Sch. Judique, N.S.; St. Francis Xavier Univ., B.Sc. 1951; Memorial Univ., M.Sc. 1961; m. Teresa, d. James Penney, Holyrood, Nfld., 26 Dec. 1954; one d. Sheri Elizabeth Helen; one s. Andrew Robert Joseph; DEPY. MIN. MINES & ENERGY, NFLD., since 1973; with Geol. Survey of Can., 1951; joined Nfld. civil service as Asst. Govt. Geol. 1951 and later became Chief Staff Geol.; apptd. Dir. Mineral Resources 1964; Fellow, Geol. Assn. Can. (former Chrmn. Nfld. sec.); mem., Candn. Inst. Mining & Metall. (former dist. Vice Pres.); Roman Catholic; recreations: distance running, antique automobiles, lapidary art; Home: 17 Dublin Rd., St. John's, Nfld. A1B 2E7; Office: Eastern Canada Bldg., St. John's, Nfld.

McKIM, Anson C., O.B.E. (1946), B.A., B.Com. M.B.A.; company director; b. Montreal, Que., 24 Jan. 1905; s. John Nelson and C. (Burdette) M.; e. Roslyn Sch. and Westmount High Sch., Westmount, Que.; McGill

Univ., B.Com. 1924, B.A. 1927; Harvard Univ., M.B.A. 1929; Bishops Univ., Hon. D.C.L. 1979; m. Joan M., d. R. H. McMaster, Montreal, 8 June 1933; children: Anson R., Anne E.; mem., Adv. Bd. and Dir., National Trust Co. Ltd.; formerly Vice-President (Traffic), Trans-Can. Air Lines Ltd. 1945-51; joined Merck & Co. Ltd. as Vice-Pres. and Dir., 1951; Pres., 1952-60; with P. S. Ross & Sons, 1925-26; Canadian Industries Ltd., 1929-40, holding various positions in Chem. Group, becoming Asst. Gen. Mgr., Cellulose Products Group; Asst. to Hon. Arthur B. Purvis, Dir. Gen., Brit. Purchasing Comn. in Wash. 1940-42; Depy. U.K. Rep., Candn. Dept. of Mun. & Supply, 1942-45; Candn. Rep., Council of Internat. Civil Aviation Organ. 1946-47; Gov. Emeritus, McGill Univ.; Hon. Pres., Montreal Children's Hospital; mem., Board of Trustees, Quebec Arts Council; mem., Candn. Inst. Internat. Affairs; has contrib. articles on comm. rights in aviation to tech. journs.; Protestant; Clubs: University; Mt. Bruno Country; Montreal Racket; Mount Royal; Montreal Indoor Tennis; Home: 3057 Trafalgar Ave., Montreal, Que. H3Y 1H5

McKINLEY, Donald William Robert, O.B.E., M.A., Ph.D., F.R.S.C. (1952), F.A.P.S., F.I.E.E.E., F.E.I.C.; retired physicist; b. Shanghai, China, 22 Sept. 1912; s. David Fuller, M.D., and Susan Mabel (Burns) M.; e. Univ. of Toronto, B.A. 1934, M.A. 1935, Ph.D. 1938; m. 1st, late Norah Wilson, Dr. de l'U. (Paris), d. M. M. Stevenson, London, Eng., 11 Jan. 1941; children: Alan Duncan, Kathryn Jean; 2ndly, Barbara Mabel, M.Sc., Ph.D., d. A. R. Girdwood, Barrie, Ont., 25 Mar. 1950; former Vice. Pres., Nat. Research Council; retired 1974; joined Nat. Research Council 1938, engaged in radio and radar engn., research on meteors; served with R.C.A.F., 1942-43, on leave at Nat. Research Council; author: "Meteor Science and Engineering", 1961; mem., Am. Astron. Soc.; Assn. of Prof. Engrs. of Ont.; Candn. Assn. Physicists; Home: 1889 Fairmeadow Cres., Ottawa, Ont. K1H 7B8

McKINNA, Alfred John, M.D., C.M.; educator; b. Alida, Sask. 16 Apl. 1921; s. John and Maude Alice (Farr) McK.; e. Oxbow (Sask.) High Sch. 1940; Univ. of Sask. B.A. (Biol.) 1948; McGill Univ. M.D., C.M. 1952; m. Lois Patricia d. late Ernest George Saunders 3 Sept. 1955; children: John Saunders, Patricia Jane, Andrew James; PROF. AND CHRMN. OF OPHTHALMOL. UNIV. OF W. ONT. since 1975; Dir. Dept. Ophthalmol. Univ. Hosp.; Intern, Montreal Gen. Hosp. 1952-53, Resident Ophthalmol. 1957-59, Staff Ophthalmol. 1962; Resident Med. & Surg. Montreal Children's Hosp. 1953-54, Fellow 1961-62, Dir. of Ophthalmol. 1964; Fellow in Ophthalmol. Univ. of Cal. San Francisco 1959-60; Fellow of Wilmer Inst. Johns Hopkins Hosp. Baltimore 1960-61; Asst. Prof. of Ophthalmol. McGill Univ. 1964, Assoc. Prof. 1968; Assoc. Prof. Ophthalmol. Univ. of W. Ont. and Dir. Ophthalmol. Univ. Hosp. 1972; mem. Adv. Bd. Que. Assn. for Partially Sighted; mem. Candn. Med. Assn.; Ont. Med. Assn.; Candn. Ophthalmol. Soc.; Am. Acad. Ophthalmol.; Wilmer Residents Soc.; F. C. Cordes Residents Soc.; McGill Alumnae Assn.; Univ. of Sask. Alumnae Assn.; served with RCAF 1942-45; United Church; recreations: sport, travel; Club: M.A.A.A.; Home: 69 Green Acres Dr., London, Ont. N6G 2S4; Office: Univ. Hosp., London, Ont. N6G 5A5.

McKINNEY, James Russell, B.Com.; diplomat; b. Summer Hill, N.B., 28 June 1925; s. George Melbourne and Margaret Jane (Russell) McK.; e. Saint John (N.B.) High Sch., 1940; Dalhousie Univ., B.Com. 1949; Nat. Defence Coll., 1956-57; m. Chloe Constance, d. Col. George W. MacLeod, D.S.O. and Bar, Edmonton, Alta., June 1955; children: Jane, Mark, Nicholas; joined Dept. of External Affairs, 1949; Second Secy., Candn. Embassy, Belgrade, Yugoslavia, 1951-53; Ottawa and Nat. Defence Coll., 1954-57; First Secy., Djakarta, Indonesia, 1957-59; First Secy. and later Counsellor, Copenhagen, Denmark, 1959-

62; Depy. Head, Econ. Div., Dept. of External Affairs, Ottawa, 1962-66; High Commr. for Can. in Trinidad and Tobago and in Barbados, Candn. Commr. to W. Indies Assoc. States, 1966-69; Perm. Rep. and Ambassador to O.E.C.D. 1969-72; Minister, Candn. Embassy, Washington 1972-77; Dir. Gen., Bureau of U.S. Affairs and subsequently Asst. Under Secty. Dept. of External Affairs, Ottawa since 1977; served with RCAF 1943-45; rank Flying Offr.; Phi Kappa Pi; Anglican; recreations: yachting, skiing, fishing; Clubs: White Pine Fishing; Address: 762 Eastbourne Ave., Ottawa, Ont. K1K 0H7

MCKINNON, Alastair Thomas, B.A., M.A., Ph.D., B.D., F.R.S.C.; university professor; b. Hillsburgh, Ont. 25 May 1925; e. late Arnold Thomson and late Mary Ella M.; e. sec. sch. Erin, Ont. 1942; Guelph Coll. 1943; Vict. Coll. Univ. of Toronto B.A. 1947; Univ. of Toronto M.A. 1948; Univ. of Edinburgh Ph.D. 1950; McGill Univ. B.D. 1953; m. Mildred Mae d. late Wilson Bousfield Sutton 13 Sept. 1947; children: Mary Catherine (Pfaff), Frances Christine, Angus Thomson; PROF. OF PHILOSOPHY, MCGILL UNIV.; apptd. Prof. 1969; Macdonald Prof. of Moral Phil. 1971; Chrmn. of Dept. 1975; served with RCNVR, 1944-45; rec'd Rockefeller Travelling Fellowship 1961-62; author of "Falsification and Belief", 1970, 1978; "Kierkegaard in Translation/en Traduction/in Übersetzung", 1970; "Fundamental Polyglot Konkordans til Kierkegaards Samlede Vaerker", 1975; "Index Verborum til Kierkegaards Samlede Vaerker", 1973; "Computational Analysis of Kierkegaard's Samlede Vaerker", 1975; "Concordance to Wittgenstein's Philosophische Untersuchungen", 1975; Co-ed. "revue CIRPHO review", 1973-76; Ed., "The Kierkegaard Monograph Series",; "The Kierkegaard-Malantschuk Collection"; other writings incl. Kierkegaard, Wittgenstein, Philosophy of religion, moral phil., the use of computers and statistics as aids in the interpretation of philosophical and literary texts; bd. Dir. Candn. Fed. for the Humanities, 1979-; named charter mem. Kierkegaard Akademiet; 1977; mem., Candn. Theol. Soc. (Pres. 1959-60); Søren Kierkegaard Selskabet, 1968-; CIRPHO International (Pres. 1973-); Candn. Phil. Assn. (Pres. 1979-80); Assn. for Lit. and Ling. Computing; Chrmn. Specialist Group for Phil.; Assn. for Computers and the Humanities; United Church; Club: McGill Univ. Faculty; recreations: carpentry, sailing; Home: 3005 Barat Rd., Montreal, Que. H3Y 2H4. Office: 1001 Sherbrooke St. W., Montreal, Que. H3A 1G5.

McKINNON, Hon. Allan Bruce, P.C., M.C., C.D., M.P.; politician; b. Canora, Sask. 11 Jan. 1917; s. Peter MacDonald and Belle (Stewart) McK.; e. primary and secondary educ. Rokeby and Kincaid, Sask.; Candn. Army Staff Coll.; Univ. of Victoria; m. Elizabeth d. late Bertram Menzies, Kincaid, Sask. 2 Oct. 1947; two s. Ian Bruce, Peter Menzies; Min. of Nat. Defence and Veterans Affairs May 1979-Feb. 1980; el. to H. of C. 1972, re-el. since; served with Candn. Army during World War II, awarded Military Cross for action in Italy, remained in Perm. Force until retirement 1965, rank Maj.; served as Chrmn. and Trustee, Greater Victoria Sch. Bd.; P. Conservative; United Church; recreations: reading, brass-rubbing, bridge, walking, salmon fishing; Home: 504-1420 Beach Dr., Victoria, B.C. V8R 2N8 and 1604-20 Driveway, Ottawa, Ont. Office: House of Commons, Ottawa, Ont. K1A 0A7.

McKNIGHT,(Joseph) Charles (Robert): publisher; b. Wainfleet, Ont. 6 Dec. 1929; s. Robert James and Mary Agnes (Ramage) McK.; e. Wainfleet Pub. Sch. 1943; Welland (Ont.) High Sch. 1948; m. Patricia Marie d. Alfred Deyne, Vanessa, Ont. 13 Aug. 1976; children by previous marriage: Cameron, Carol (Mrs. D. Dunlop), Ann (Mrs. Walter Kleer), Lisa, Ashley, Louise, Rene: PUBLISHER, OTTER PUBLISHING LTD. 1974-; Pres. and Publisher, "Tillsonburg News" 1971-; joined above paper as Sports Reporter 1948, Advertising Mgr. 1957, Gen. Mgr. 1959,

Vice Pres. 1963; Ed. assoc. mag. "The Canadian Sportsman" 1951-57; purchased "Ingersoll Times" 1971, "Norwich Gazette" 1973, "The Port Colborne News" 1975; started "The Consumer News" Welland 1979; mem. Journalism Adv. Bd. Niagara Coll. Welland; Chrmn. of Bd., Candn. Community Newspaper Assn. 1979-80; Dir. Ont. Journalism Educators Assn.; Past Pres., Southwestern Ont. Newspaper Assn.; Ont. Weekly Newspaper Assn. 1972; Class "A" Community Newspapers Can. 1962; mem. Tillsonburg Chamber Comm.; Tillsonburg Business Assn.; Parking Authority; Past Pres. Tillsonburg Minor Hockey; served as Warden and mem. Bd. of Mang. St. John's Ang. Ch.; Freemason; P. Conservative; Anglican; Club: Kinsmen; Home: 3 Parkside Dr., Tillsonburg, Ont. N4G 4A1; Office: 25 Townline Rd., Tillsonburg, Ont. N4G 4H6.

McKNIGHT, Robert G., F.L.M.I.; insurance executive; b. Barrie, Ont. 19 Mar, 1938; s. Ernest and Norma Guthrie e. U of Tor., B.A. (1959); F.L.M.I. - LOMA (Data Processing); m. Leslie, d. Allan Scott, 1959; children: Timothy, Patricia; VICE PRES. - GROUP, METROPOLITAN LIFE INSURANCE CO. 1982-; joined Mutual Life Assurance Co. of Canada 1959-82: 1959-60 Claims Assessor; 1960-63 Programmer; 1963-66 Programming Asst.; 1966-67 Planning Asst.; 1967-69 Supvr. Computer Ops.; 1969-72 Computer Systems Development Officer; 1973-78 Executive Officer & Administration Executive (Group Life & Health Ops.); 1978-82 Executive Officer Group Marketing; Recreation: hockey, squash, skiing; Home: 326 Roger Rd., Ottawa, Ont. K1H 5C4; Office: 99 Bank St., Ottawa, Ont., K1P 5A3.

McKOWN, Roberta Ellen, M.A., Ph.D.; educator; b. Endicott, N.Y. 26 March 1932; d. Robert Edward and Rubina (Cunningham) McK.; e. Univ. of Ore. B.A. 1953, M.A. 1965, Ph.D. (Pol. Science) 1968; m. 1stly Harry Thomas Koplin 13 June 1953; children: Bruce Nicholas, Kathleen Mara Everett, Therese Elizabeth; m. 2ndly Thomas William Mapp 22 Dec. 1969, 9 June 1973; PROF. OF POL. SCIENCE, UNIV. OF ALTA. 1977-, Asst. Prof. 1968, Assoc. Prof. 1972, Chrmn. of Pol. Science 1975-82; Instr. Univ. of Ore. 1967-68; recipient Nat. Science Foundation (USA) Dissertation Grant 1966-67; Can. Council Research Fellowship 1971-72; SSHRCC Leave Fellowship 1978-79; author various articles comparative pol. studies; mem. Candn. Pol. Science Assn.; Can. African Studies Assn.; Internat. Studies Assn.; African Studies Assn. (USA); recreations: skiing, riding; Home: 9110 - 116 St., Edmonton, Alta. T6G 1P9; Office: Edmonton, Alta. T6G 2H4.

McLACHLAN, Lt. Gen. (Ret'd) Hugh, C.M.M., D.F.C., C.D.; company director; b. Gourock, Scot., 19 Sept. 1922; s. Hugh and Margaret (Campbell) McL.; e. Coalhurst, Alta., Sr. Matric. 1940; RCAF Staff Coll. 1953-54; Nat. Defence Coll. 1967-68; m. Sybil Ellen, d. late William George Naylor, 17 Aug. 1946; two d. Rhonda Ellen, Patricia May; DIR., ROLLS-ROYCE HOLDINGS NORTH AMERICA LTD. since 1977, Dir., Bristol Aerospace Ltd.; Rolls-Royce (Can.) Ltd.; comnd. as Pilot in RCAF. 1941; served in Middle E. and Greece with R.A.F. fighter sqdns. 1941-45; attained rank Sqdn. Leader; Customs & Excise Div., Lethbridge, Alta., 1945-46; re-enlisted in RCAF 1947; various staff and flying assignments 1947-53; various staff positions, Ottawa, 1954-57; C.O. 441 Fighter Sqdn. 1958-61, Marville, France; Directing Staff, RCAF Staff Coll., 1961-64; Staff, CFHQ, 1964-67; Commdr., 36 NORAD Div., Brunswick, Maine, 1968-69; Staff CFHQ 1969-71; promoted Maj. Gen. and mem., Min. of Nat. Defence Mang. Review Group, 1971; Commdr., Air Transport Command, Trenton 1972-74; Chief of Air Operations, NDHQ 1974; promoted Lt. Gen. and Depy. Chief of Defence Staff, 1975-77; Hon. Nat. Pres., RCAF Assn.; Anglican; recreations: golf, skiing, farming; Clubs: Royal Ottawa Golf; Royal Air Force; Home: R.R.1, Alcove, Que. J0X 1A0; Office: Suite 912, 130 Albert St., Ottawa, Ont. K1P 5G4

McLACHLAN, Malcolm Holland; insurance executive; b. Swansea, UK 5 Jan. 1930; s. George Blackstock and Violet Helen Palmer (Holland) McL.; e. Cardiff High Sch. 1947; London Univ. matric.; Oxford Univ. Sch. Cert.; m. Sandra Gail Ashley, 29 July, 1977; PRESIDENT AND DIR. THE GREAT LAKES REINSURANCE CO.; Dir. and Extve. Vice Pres. Munich Reinsurance Co. of Canada; Vice Pres., Munich Holdings Ltd.; Exec. Vice Pres. & Dir., Munich-Canada Management Corp. Ltd.; joined Prudential Assurance Co. Ltd. UK 1953; Inspr. Law Union & Rock Insurance Co. Ltd. 1956; Ins. Mgr. Harrison and Crosfield, Colombo, 1959-63; Agency Supt. New Zealand Insurance Co. Ltd., Johannesburg, S. Africa 1963-64; Gen. Mgr. Kenya National Assurance Co. Ltd. 1964-73 Nairobi Kenya; joined Munich Reinsurance Co., Munich 1973, trans. Toronto 1974; served with Royal Corps of Signals 1947-53 UK Sudan Egypt Cyprus; served as mem. Fire Ins. and Extve. Comtes. Ins. Assn. Sri Lanka; Motor Ins. and Extve. Comtes. Ins. Assn. E. Africa; Pres. Ins. Inst. Kenya; Ins. Golfing Soc. Kenya; Assoc., Chart. Ins. Inst. (London, Eng.); recreations: curling, home improvements, golf; Clubs: Commonwealth; Nairobi; Ontario; Home: 867 Sunningdale Bend, Mississauga, Ont. L5J 1G1; Office: Suite 606, 55 Yonge St., Toronto, Ont. M5E 1J4

McLACHLAN, William Ian, M.A.; author; educator; b. London, Eng. 20 Oct. 1938; s. William Nicol and Oonagh (McMartin) M.; e. Ryde Sch., Isle of Wight, 1956; Oxford, Eng. M.A. 1960; m. Dominique Francoise d. Marc Isabelle 20 Sept. 1960; children: Stephane Marc, Jerome Neil, Gavin Matthew; came to Can. 1970; CHRMN., CULTURAL STUDIES PROGRAM, TRENT UNIV. 1981- ; Prof. of English & Cultural Studies, 1976- ; Lecturer in English, Univ. of Hong Kong 1960-66, Sr. Lectr. and Chrmn., Dept. of Comparative Lit. 1967-70; Assoc. Prof. of English, Trent Univ. 1970-76, Chrmn., Comparative Lit. Program, 1971-75, Master, Peter Robinson College 1977-82; author "The Seventh Hexagram" 1976; "Helen in Exile" 1980; various articles and book chapters; mem., Writer's Union of Can.; Nat. Steering Comte. Cultural Workers Alliance; Bd. of Dir. Peterborough Artists, Inc.; Bd. of Dir. Candn. Images Film Festival; Bd. of Dir. Magic Circus Theatre Co.; winner of Books in Canada Best 1st Candn. Novel Award 1977; was curator "Arts Against Repression" exhibition, Artspace, Peterborough 1982; Marxist; recreations: work, cars, politics, travel; Home: R.R. 1, Ennismore, Ont. K0L 1T0; Office: Peterborough, Ont. K9J 7B8

McLAREN, Digby Johns, M.A., Ph.D., F.R.S., F.R.S.C.; geologist; b. Carrickfergus, N. Ireland 11 Dec. 1919; s. James and Louie (Kinsey) McL.; e. Sedbergh Sch. Eng. 1933-37; Univ. de Poitiers 1937-38; Queens Coll. Cambridge B.A. 1940, M.A. 1948 (Foundation Scholar 1948, Harkness Scholarship 1949); Univ. of Mich. Ph.D. 1951; Univ. of Ottawa, D.Sc. (H.C.) 1980; m. Phyllis Mary d. Charles Matkin, Lavenham, Eng. 25 March 1942; children: Ian Johns, Patrick, Alison Mary; SEN. ADVISOR, DEPT. ENERGY, MINNES & RECOURCES, 1981- ; Visiting Professor, Univ. of Ottawa, 1980- ; joined Geol. Survey of Can. as Scient. 1948, Head of Paleontol. 1959-67; Dir. Inst. Sedimentary & Petroleum Geol. 1967-73; Chrmn., Comn. on Stratigraphy, Internat. Union of Geol. Sciences 1972-76; Chmn. of Bd., Internat. Geol. Correlation Prog (IUGS-UNESCO) 1976-80; Dir. Gen., Geol. Survey of Can. 1973-80; Gold Medalist (Pure of Applied Science), Prof. Inst. of the Public Service of Canada; served with RA 1940-46, Iraq, Iran, Palestine, Syria, Egypt, Italy, rank Capt.; author over 70 publs.; mem. Am. Paleontol. Soc. (Pres. 1969); Candn. Soc. Petrol. Geols. (Pres. 1971); Fellow, Geol. Soc. of America; Foreign Assoc., Geol. Soc. France; Foreign Assoc., Nat. Acad. Sci. U.S.A.; recreations: gardening, orchid culture, cross-country skiing, flute; Home: 248 Marilyn Ave., Ottawa, Ont. K1V 7E5; Office: Dept. of Geology, Univ. of Ottawa, Ont. K1N 6N5.

McLAREN, Norman, C.C. (1973), D.Litt.; film producer; b. Stirling, Scotland, 11 Apl. 1914; s. William and Jean (Wilson) M.; e. Glasgow Sch. of Art. Scot.; D.Litt., Glendon Coll., York Univ. 1972; became interested in film at age 18, particularly its use for cinematic abstraction; while an art student, spare time was mostly taken up with film making, and organ, film showings within the art school of the early Russian classics; made first actuality film at art school, "Seven Till Five", a silent 16 mm, a formalized documentation of a day's activity at the school; success of two films sponsored by art school authorities attracted the attention of John Grierson, then Chief of Brit. Gen. P.O. Film Unit, and the result was an offer to join GPO Film Unit, and from 1937-39 he received apprenticeship and directed four films, two documentaries and two fantasies making first serious attempt in one of these to use cameraless technique of animation; about this time experimented in synthetic sound, and devel. a considerable range of semi-music sound effects, mostly percussive; in 1939, directed for Film Centre, London, Eng. "The Obedient Flame", a partly animated, partly straight-photography film on gas cooking; in 1939 moved to New York City and made a short "movie Christmas Card" for N.B.C. Television; then produced independently, and for Guggenheim Museum of Non-Objective Art, several abstract color films, "Stars and Stripes", "Boogie Doodle", "Scherzo", "Allegro", and "Loops" (all cameraless animation); joined Nat. Film Bd. of Canada in 1941; produced five short 35 mm color films, whose animations were all made by the cameraless, direct-drawing-on-film method, 1941-43; engaged in training and building up an animation unit, 1943-45; produced "C'est L'Aviron", "Keep Your Mouth Shut", "Hoppity-Pop", 1945; "La Haut sur ces Montagues", "A Little Phantasy of a 19th Century Painting", 1946; "Poulette Grise", a French folk-song in color using a further devel. of pastel-technique, and a serious attempt to bridge the gap between Painting, and the Animated Film; "Fiddle-de-Dee", 1947; "Begone Dull Care", 1949; "Around is Around", 1950-51; and "Now is the Time", 1951, in both of which sterographic animation was used; "Neighbours" (awarded "Oscar" Mar. 1953, for best documentary short of 1952, by Acad. of Motion Picture Arts & Sciences, Hollywood, 1952); "Two Bagatelles"; "Blinkety-Blank", the brawl of two chicken, etched directly on black film and hand-colored, 1954; "Rythmetic", 1955; "Chairy Tale" 1957; "Le Merle", 1958 (paper cutout method); "Short and Suite", 1959 (abstract engraved image to jazz tune); "Serenal", 1959 (abstract engraving on 16 mm film to folk tune); "Norman McLaren's Opening Speech", (a filmed welcome to the audience at Montreal Internat. Film Festival) 1960; "Lines-Vertical" and "Lines-Horizontal" (pure design, animation of straight lines, etched directly on the film and moved to music of Maurice Blackburn (Vertical) and Pete Seegar (Horizontal); "New York Lightboard" (animated drawings designed for showing on an electric sign board in Times Square, N.Y.C. to invite tourists to visit Canada); "Canon". (as illustration of principles behind a musical Canon) 1964; "Mosaic (pure design, animation of dots; sound track engraved on film), 1965; Pas de Deux (employing a multiple image technique) 1968 (named best animated film by Brit. Film Acad.); "Spheres" (abstraction to Bach music) 1969; "Synchromy" (synthetic animated music and visuals) 1971; "Ballet Adagio" (classical ballet in slow motion) 1972; "Animated Motion Parts 1, 2 and 3" 1977, parts 4 and 5, 1978; "Narcissus" (based on Greek legend) 1982; completed two assignments for UNESCO, one spent in China, 1949-50 and one in India, 1952-53; (awarded first Medal of Royal Candn. Acad. of Arts (Jan. 1963) as Internat. Best-Known Canadian Artist; Winner of 1971 Molson Prize; named Offr. Order of Can. 1968 (elevated to C.C. 1973); Home: P.O. Box 730, Hudson, Que. J0P 1H0; Office: National Film Board of Canada (P.O. Box 6100), Montreal, Que. H3C 3H5

McLAREN, Robert Wallace, B.A.; civil servant b. Hamburg, Germany 22 Jan. 1927; s. late Robert Wallace and Marjorie (Brunton) M.; came to Canada 1932; e. Assumption Coll., Windsor, B.A. 1948; Univ. of W. Ont. B.A. (Hons. Hist.) 1950; Postgrad. studies in Econs., St. Johns Coll., Cambridge 1972-73; m. Marion J., d. late Angus Urquhart Meikle, 30 June 1951; children: Margot (Mrs. D. Moore), (Andrea Mrs. C. McWhinney), Robert; with Nat. Research Council, Ottawa 1950-56; Attaché, Candn. Embassy, Washington, D.C. 1956-69; Nat. Research Council, Ottawa 1959-62; with Min. Transport, Ottawa 1962-65; Sr. Planner (Asia Program), Dir., Advisers Div., Dir. Educ. Div., Dir. Asia Div. with External Aid Office (later Candn. Internat. Devel. Agency) 1965-72; former Candn. High Commr. to Peoples' Republic of Bangladesh; Candn. High Commr. to Tanzania Seychelles, and Mauritius, Candn. Ambassador to Somalia, Madagascar and Comoro Islands; currently Candn. High Commr. to Zimbabwe; served as Pte., Candn. Army (AF) 6th Div. 1945; Hon. Secy., Holothurian Soc.; Un. Church; recreations: swimming, underwater photography boating; Candn. Home: 300 The Driveway, P.O. Box 1430, Ottawa, Ont. and 17 Bowoo Dr., Salisbury, Zimbabwe; Office: 45 Baines St., Salisbury, Zimbabwe

McLAUCHLAN, Murray Edward; musician; b. Paisley, Scot. 30 June 1948; came to Can. at 5; began career Toronto's Yorkville coffeehouses at 17; first maj. appearance Mariposa Folk Festival 1966; toured Can. and USA with Neil Young 1973 and solo 1974; toured Japan with Bruce Cockburn 1977; 1976 Candn. tour incl. concerts in over 50 cities as well as CBC TV appearances Gordon Lightfoot's Olympic Benefit and own special "On the Boulevard"; toured with The Silver Tractors 1976-77; songs incl. "Child's Song" and "Old Man's Song" both recorded by U.S. singer Tom Rush, "Farmer's Song (rec'd gold record 1973, Juno Awards best folk single, best country single and composer of the yr. 1973), "Down by the Henry Moore", "Hurricane of Change", "Honky Red", "Linda Wontcha Take Me In?", "Little Dreamer", "Getting Harder to Get Along"; songs recorded by various performers and used in films "Rip-Off" 1971, "Partners" 1976, BBC-TV Ont. co-production "Reflections of Toronto" 1975; numerous LPs; cited various bibliogs.; rec'd Juno Awards 1976, 1977 and 1979 for best male country singer; mem. CAPAC.

McLAUGHLIN, Edward T., B.S.A.; association executive; b. Iroquois, Ont., 9 April 1916; s. Harvey Peter and Annie Margaret (Colquhoun) M.; e. Morrisburg. (Ont.) Coll. Inst.; Ont. Agric. Coll., B.S.A. (Agron.); m. Margaret Ruth, d. Alfred Earl Merkley, 14 July 1938; two s. Ian Edward, Peter Ross; SENIOR ADVISOR, CANADIAN SEED GROWERS ASSN.; Mgr., A. E. McKenzie Ltd., Toronto, Ont., 1950-62; Vice-Pres., Rudy-Patrick Seed Co., Kansas City, Mo., 1963-64; Past Pres., Assn. of Official Seed Certifying Agencies 1977-79; The Candn. Seed Trade Assn.; Anglican; recreations: boating, fishing; Home: 2 Nanaimo Dr., Ottawa, Ont. K2H 6X5; Office: 237 Argyle, Nepean, Ont. K2P 1B8

McLAUGHLIN, Isabel; artist; b. Oshawa, Ont., d. Col. Robert S. and Adelaide Louise (Mowbray) M.; e. Ont. Coll. of Art; Art Students League, Toronto; Scandinavian Acad., and Sorbonne, Paris, France; studied in New Mexico under Bistram; has worked in Paris, Vienna and other parts of Europe; painted considerably in Northern Ont., Dawson, Yukon, West Indies and Bermuda; invited to contrib. to the important "Group of Seven" exhibit, the Roerich, N.Y.; rep. in numerous important exhns. abroad, includ. that which toured the Brit. Commonwealth; rep. in the Nat. Gallery, Ottawa and other public galleries; awarded Fellow of O.C.A. 1977; work is characterized by a bold and individual interpretation of nature; Pres., Candn. Group of Painters (1939); pictures include "Grey Ghosts of Algonquin", Chestnut Branch", "Tree", "Frogpond", "Prelude to Winter"

McLAUGHLIN, Leonard; trade unionist; b. Dunedin-Otago, N.Z., 8 May, 1925; s. Leonard John and Margaret B (Anderson) McL.; e. Public and High Schs., Otago and Dunedin, N.Z.; Extension Courses, Mass. Inst. Tech.; Ryerson Polytech. Inst.; McGill Univ.; came to Can. 1947; m. Mireille G., d. late Robert Boivin 1964; children: Allan James, Eric John; PRESIDENT, SEAFARERS' INTERNATIONAL UNION since 1964; Pres., Seafarers' Bldg. Corp.; Del. and E. Rep., Maritime Trades Dept.; A.F.L.C.I.O. Comnr., Jt. Maritime Comn., I.L.O. (U.N.); became union offr. after sea service 1950; apptd. Business Agent, Halifax, N.S. 1950, Thorold, Ont. 1951, Fort William, Ont. 1952, Vice-Pres. Thorold 1953; Secy.-Treas. Montreal 1954, Extve. Vice-Pres. 1960; active in water safety leg. and asstd. in formulation of St. Lawrence Traffic Control; el. by I.L.O. to Jt. Maritime Comn., Geneva 1970; el. Internat. Transport Workers, Fair Practices Comte., Vienna Congress 1971; an active proponent of toll free water highways; served in 2nd World War, Allied Merchant Services 1942-45 on all ocean fronts; Trustee, Candn. Seafarers' Welfare and Pension Plans; mem. C.L.C. Maritime Comte.; Internat. Assn. for Pollution Control; Otago Old Boys' Assn.; St. Lawrence Waterways Assn.; Candn. Rly. Labour Assn.; Presbyterian; recreations: bridge, tennis, golf; Club: Lorraine Tennis

McLAUGHLIN, S. Bruce, B.A., LL.B.; b. Toronto, Ont., 1926; s. Stuart Wilson and Florence Beatrice (Hamilton); e. W. Tech. Comm. Sch.; Univ. of Toronto, B.A. 1957, LL.B. 1960; m. Patricia Elaine Morrison, Parkhill, Ont., 1951; five children: CHRMN. OF THE McLAUGHLIN Group of Companies; Dir., Council for Candn. Unity; Candn. Equestrian Fed. (lifetime); Candn. Equestrian Team; Hon. Dir., Cyclos Theatre Co.; called to Bar of Ont., 1962; began business career with Bell Telephone Co. of Canada; operated and devel. a resort in Haliburton Highlands after War; sold resort holdings 1949; founded S. B. McLaughlin & Co. Ltd. 1949 and present Co. 1957; served with RCAF during World War II; mem., Peel Region Law Soc.; Urban Devel. Inst.; Bd. Govs., Appleby Coll.; recreations: riding, golf, skiing, tennis; Clubs: Eglinton Hunt; Mississauga Country; Chinguacousy Country; Griffith Island; Caledon Trout; Home: 1993 Mississauga Road, Mississauga, Ont. L5H 2K5; Office: 77 City Centre Drive, Mississauga, Ont. L5B 1M6

McLAUGHLIN, W. Earle, O.C., B.A., LL.D., K.G.St.J. banker; b. Oshawa, Ont., 16 Sept. 1915; s. late Frank and Frankie L. (Houlden) M.; e. Queen's Univ. (Econ. and Hist.) B.A. 1936; Bishop's Univ., LL.D. 1964; Queen's Univ., LL.D. 1976; Mt. Allison, LL.D.; m. Ethel, d. A. T. Wattie, 20 July 1940; one s. and one d.; FORMER CHRMN. OF THE BOARD THE ROYAL BANK OF CANADA; Dir., Royal Bank of Can.; Nabisco Brands, Inc., N.Y.; Ralston — Purina Canada Inc.; Metropolitan Life Insurance Company; Chrmn., Sun Alliance Insurance Co.; Trustee, Sun Alliance and London Insurance Group, Canadian Staff Pension Plan; Dir. Canadian Pacific Limited; Candn. Pacific Enterprises; Allied Chemical (Can.) Ltd.; Textran Canada Ltd.; The Algoma Steel Corpn. Limited; General Motors Corp., Detroit; Genstar Corp.; mem., Board of Governors, Royal Victoria Hosp.; Officer, Order of Canada; Chancellor, Concordia Univ.; joined the Bank, Toronto, 1936; 2nd Asst. Acct., Guelph, 1937; Acct., Toronto, College & Bathurst, Dec. 1937; Supt. Dept.,Toronto, 1938; Asst. Mgr., London, Ont. 1942; Candn. Creditors, H.O. 1945; 1st Asst. Mgr., Montreal Br., 1946, Mgr. 1951; Asst. Gen. Mgr., H.O., 1953; Asst. to the Pres. 1959; Gen. Mgr., 1960; Pres. 1960; Chrmn. and C.E.O. 1977; Chrmn. of Bd. 1979-80; 27th Winner, Queen's Univ. Alumni Assn. Montreal Medal, May 1967; Clubs: Seigniory; Mount Bruno; York (Toronto); Toronto; Mount Royal; Forest & Stream; St. James's; Canadian (N.Y.); The Mid — Ocean (Bermuda); Home: 67 Sunnyside Ave., Westmount, Montreal 6, Que. H3Y 1C3; Office: 1 Place Ville Marie, Montreal, P.Q.

McLEAN, Bruce, C.A.; utilities executive; b. 19 Feb. 1943; e. C.A. 1966; VICE PRES. & CONTROLLER, ICG UTILITIES LTD.; assoc. with Inter-City Group of Companies since 1967; Home: 49 Mager Dr. W., Winnipeg, Man. R2M 0S1; Office: 444 St. Mary Ave., Winnipeg, Man. R3C 3T7.

McLEAN, Donald Millis, B.Sc., M.D., F.R.C.P.(C); educator; m. Melbourne, Australia 26 July 1926; s. late Donald and Nellie Victoria (Millis) McL.; e. Univ. of Melbourne, B.Sc. 1947, M.B., B.S. 1950, M.D. 1954; m. Margaret Joyce d. late Charles Hicks 29 Dec. 1976; PROF. OF MED. MICROBIOL. UNIV. OF B.C.; Consultant Microbiol. to UBC health Sciences Centre Hosps. and Children's Hosp. Vancouver since 1967; Assoc. Prof. of Microbiol. Sch. of Hygiene Univ. of Toronto and Virologist Hosp. for Sick Children 1958-67; author "Virology in Health Care" 1980; various articles in Candn. and U.S. prof. journs.; mem. Candn. Med. Assn.; Candn. Pub. Health Assn.; Candn. Soc. Microbiols. and other prof. socs. Can., USA and UK; Presbyterian; Home: 2832 West 43rd Ave., Vancouver, B.C. V6N 3J1; Office: 6174 University Blvd., Vancouver, B.C. V6T 1W5.

McLEAN, Eric Donald, O.C. (1975); music critic. b. Montreal West, Que., 25 Sept. 1919; s. William Ernest and Emma Alice (Keillor) Mcl.; e. Montreal West (Que.) High Sch.; McGill Univ. Arts and Music 1945; studied composition privately with Claude Champagne; MUSIC CRITIC, THE MONTREAL GAZETTE 1979- ; joined The Standard (Montreal), first as entertainment critic (1945-47), then as editor of Standard magazine (1947-49); Music Critic, The Montreal Star, 1949-79; consultant restoration and conserv., City of Montreal, 1963-64; Gov. McGill Univ. 1970-80; mem. Arts Council of Greater Montreal, 1965-79 (Vice pres. 1977); mem. Can. Council 1965-79; Jacques Viger Comn.; appt. to Bd. of Trustees, Montreal Mus. of Fine Arts, 1977; served as Wireless Operator RAF Transport Command during World War II; rec'd Canada Music Council Award 1973; author "The Living Past of Montreal" 1964; Eng. Transl. Jean Palardy's "The Early Furniture of French Canada" 1963; mem. Internat. P.E.N.; Royal Soc. Arts; Music Critics' Assn. (Pres. 1964); Liberal; Protestant; recreation: restoration historic bldgs.; Club: McGill Faculty; Home: 440 rue Du Bon-Secours, Montreal, Que. H2Y 3C4

McLEAN, Grant; film producer; b. Saskatoon, Sask., 1921; e. Univ. of Toronto; PRES., McLEAN-WILDER ASSOC. LTD. (feature and documentary film prod.); formerly Pres., Visual Educ. Centre (production-distribution centre for educ. and documentary films and other visual materials); with Nat. Film Bd. 1941-67; successively Cameraman, Dir. of Photography, Producer-Writer-Dir., Extve. Producer; latterly Asst. Govt. Film Commr. and Dir. of Production; Address: 420 St. Andrew St. E., Fergus, Ont.

McLEAN, Col. Herbert Knox: retired manufacturer; b. Montreal, Que., 6 Jan. 1911; s. Charles Herbert and Mary Gertrude (Knox) M.; e. Selwyn House Sch.; Lower Can. Coll.; m. Lois Sigourney, d. Wm. M. Birks, Montreal, 22 June 1934; children: Phyllis L. (Mrs. D. R. Firth), Margot K. (Mrs. A. R. Aird), Wilson B.; PRESIDENT, BELMONT OILS LTD.;Vice Pres., Norpet Oil & Gas Ltd.; Past Chrmn., Canadian Textiles Inst.; Pres., Montreal Gen. Hospital Centre; served in World War, 1940-45, first with Black Watch; trans. to R.C.O.C. 1941; 2nd in Command, Longue Pointe Ord. Depot; discharged with rank of Col.; Presbyterian; recreations: skiing, fishing, tennis, golf; Clubs: Mount Bruno; St. James; Eagle Salmon; Hillside Tennis; Home: 8 Richelieu Place, Montreal, Que. H3G 1E7; Office: Ste. 600, 4060 St. Catharine St. W, Montreal, Que.

McLEAN, Hugh John, Mus.B. (Cantab), M.A. F.R.C.O. (1953), F.R.C.C.O. (1957), F.R.S.C. (1977); musician; edu-

cator; b. Winnipeg, Man., 5 Jan 1930; s. Robert and Olive May (Smallwood) McL.; e. Pub. and High Schs., Winnipeg; studied music privately Winnipeg and Vancouver 1937-49; Univ. of Man., Assoc. of Music 1947; Assoc. Bd., Royal Schs. of Music, Lic. 1948; Royal Coll. of Music, Assoc. 1951; Univ. of Cambridge, B.A. 1954; Mus.B. 1956, M.A. 1958; m. Gunlaug Julie Gaberg, 8 Jan. 1951, d. 1978; children: Robert Andreas, John Stuart, Hugh Dundas; m. Florence Anne Stillman, 18 Aug. 1979; PROF. FACULTY OF MUSIC, UNIV. OF WESTERN ONT. Dean, Fac. of Music, 1973-80; Founder (1958) and Music Dir., Hugh McLean Consort; CBC Vancouver Singers, since 1963; Music Consultant, Ang. Ch. and Un. Ch. of Can. Jt. Comte. on Preparation of Hymn Book, since 1964; Organist, St. Luke's Ang. Ch., Winnipeg, 1945-47; Candn. Mem. Ch., Vancouver, 1947-49; Organ Scholar, King's Coll., Univ. of Cambridge, 1951-55; Organist and Choirmaster, Ryerson Un. Ch., Vancouver, B.C. 1957-73; St. John's Angl. Ch., London, Ont., 1977- ; toured Switzerland as organist 1952, 1955, 1972; Finland 1975; Japan 1976, Germany 1980; England 1980-81; organ performances with Vancouver and Toronto Symphonies and Nat. Arts Centre Orch. (OH.); various CBC and BBC broadcasts; solo recitals in major Cdn. and Amer. cities; Founder and Music Dir., Vancouver Cantata Soc. 1958-67; toured W. Europe for CBC recording music on famous pipe organs, 1963; Asst. Prof. of Music, Univ. of Victoria, 1967-69; Assoc. Prof. of Music, Univ. of B.C., 1969-73; rec'd various scholarships, prizes and awards incl. Arnold Bax Commonwealth Medal 1954; Harriet Cohen Bach Medal 1955; Can. Council Grants 1960, 1965, 1972, 1980; compositions incl. incidental music for CBC radio dramas "Much Ado About Nothing", 1962; "Antony & Cleopatra", 1964; transcribed & ed. for CBC Festival of Music, 1966, 1973; Ed., "Organ Works" by Henry Purcell, 1957 (2nd ed. 1967); "Andante in F for Mechanical Organ" by W. A. Mozart, 1957; "Concerto in B Flat for Organ and Orchestra" by William Felton, 1957; "Two Voluntaries for Organ from the Nanki Manuscript" by John Blow, 1971; "Collected Works for Solo Instrument and Organ" by J. L. Krebs, 1981; "Suite in D for violin and harpsichord (Anon. Eng., 18th cent.)" 1981; "Ascensiontide cantata: Gott faehret auf" by J.L. Krebs, 1981; author various articles, incl. 19 for New Grove Dictionary of Music (1980), reviews and papers; mem., AF-MUSC Vancouver local; Am. Musicol. Soc.; Royal Musical Assn.; recreation: collecting antiquarian music and books; Clubs: University; Racquet (Victoria, B.C.); Home: 1020 Maitland St., London, Ont. N5Y 2X9; Office London, Ont.

McLEAN, Very Rev. James Lewis Walter, C.D., M.A., D.D. (Presby.); b. Peterborough, Ont., 19 May 1905; s. Thomas Walter and Winnifred (Messmore) M.; e. Port Perry, Ont. Pub. and High Schs.; Univ. of Toronto, B.A. 1927, M.A. 1929; Knox Theol. Coll., Toronto, 1930; Hon. D.D. 1952; m. Frances, d. Edward Blair, Mimico, Ont. 26 July 1933; children: Walter, Blair, David; MINISTER, GALE PRESBY. CH., since 1972; Min., St. Andrew's Ch., Victoria, B.C. 1938-72; Gale Presby Ch., Elmira, Ont. 1972-75; Moderator, 80th Gen. Assembly of the Presby. Ch. in Can. (mem., Bd. of Missions); Comnd. Capt., Candn. Army Chaplains Corps 1939; attached to the Candn. Scottish Regt. (Princess Mary's); Maj. (ret.); Candn-Presby. rep. on World Alliance of Reformed Chs. 1964; N.Z. and Australian Presby. Ch., 1967; Pres. Victoria Council of Chs. 1965; el. Alderman, Victoria N.Z. (first clergyman) 1959 and re-el. 1961; author of "Man's Chief End", and booklet "The Church-Presbyterian"; recreations: golf, fishing, motoring; Club: Kiwanis (Past Dir.)

McLEAN, John Ross, M.A., B.Litt.; retired broadcasting executive; b. Ethelbert, Man., 19 July 1905; s. John and Mary M.; e. Brandon Coll., Man.; Univ. of Man., B.A. 1926, M.A. 1927; Rhodes Schol., Man. 1927; Balliol Coll., Oxford, B.A. 1929, B.Litt., M.A. 1931; Belt Sr. Research

Scholarship in Colonial Hist., 1930-31; rec'd Coronation Medal, 1937; Confederation Medal, Canada Centennial, 1967; m. Beverley Cosh, 29 Dec. 1944; children: Digby Ross, Yolande Rosemary T.; Nat. Secty., Assn. of Cdn. Clubs 1932-34; Publisher, Ottawa Weekly Times 1934; Ed. Publications, Nat. Lib. Fed. 1935; Private Secty, High Commr. (Hon. Vincent Massey) for Can., London, Eng.; 1935-38; joined Nat. Film Bd. on its inception, 1939; Asst. Film Commr., 1941-43; Depy. Commr., 1943-45; Commr. 1945-50; 1945, mem. of Secretariate U.N. Preparatory Conf., San Francisco; Head, Films and Visual Information Div. at Unesco in Paris, and lived in Paris as a Sr. Extve. of Unesco 1950-1957 (among duties were the direction of internat. seminars and confs. at Paris, Messina (1953) and Tangier (1955), advisory missions to Latin Am. especially Mexico (1954), to Lebanon, Pakistan and India, and participation in one or other form of internat. conf. of meeting in many other countries); Writer and Broadcaster, Ottawa, 1957-60; Research Dir., Programmes, Bd. of Broadcast Govs., 1960-68; Spec. Adviser, Policy, C.R.T.C. 1968-73; mem., Candn. Pol. Sci. Assn.; Candn. Econ. Assn.; Candn. Inst. Internat. Affairs; Candn. Nat. Comn. for Unesco; Pacific Sci. Assn., Honolulu; Home: 33 First Ave., Ottawa, Ont. K1S 2G1

McLEAN, Ross Patterson, M.B.E.; company president; b. Ailsa Craig, Ont., 6 May 1919; s. Alexander and Edith (McGeary) McL.; e. Pub and High Schs., Ailsa Craig, Ont.; m. Geraldine, d. Sir Arthur Stonhouse, 28 May 1941; children: Dennis Jay, Bonnie Dee (twins), Lin Feron, Norma Lee (twins); PRESIDENT AND OWNER, CROYDEN FURNITURE SYSTEMS INC., (purchased from InterRoyal Corp. N.Y. in July 1977); joined Interroyal Corp. Ltd., in Sales Dept., 1946; Gen. Sales Manager 1947; Vice-President and Director 1954; served with R.C.A.F. as Flight Lieut.; awarded M.B.E.; Protestant; recreations: golf, swimming; Club: Waterloo County Golf & Country; Home: 67 Murray Rd., Cambridge, Ont. N1S 3T4; Office: #1 Hespler Rd., Cambridge, Ont. N1R 3G6

McLEAN, William Flavelle; company chairman; b. Toronto, Ont., 1916; s. late James Stanley and Edith (Flavelle) M.; e. Univ. of Toronto Schs.; Univ. of Toronto, B.Sc. (Hons. in Chem. Engn.), 1938; m. June McClure, Toronto, Ont.; two s. and one d.; CHRM., CANADA PACKERS INC., since 1968; Vice-Pres. and Dir., Canadian Imperial Bank of Commerce; Dir., Canadian General Electric Co. Limited; Steel Co. of Can. Ltd.; a year of post-grad. work in the U.S.; served with R.C.A.F., from 1942-46, on east coast of Can. and in Eng. on radar work; on discharge held rank of Flt. Lieut.; after the war directed Canada Packers' Research program; el. a Dir., 1950, Vice-Pres., and mem. of Extve. Comte., 1952, Pres. 1954, Chrm. 1968; Home: 32 Whitney Avenue, Toronto, Ont. M4W 2A8; Office: 95 St. Clair Ave. W., Toronto, Ont. M4V 1P2

McLELLAND, Rev. Joseph Cumming, M.A., B.D., Ph.D., D.D.; educator; b. Port-Glasgow, Scot. 10 Sept. 1925; s. David and Jessie (Cumming) McL.; e. Wentworth St. Pub. Sch. & Central Coll. Inst. Hamilton, Ont.; McMaster Univ. B.A. 1946; Knox Coll. Toronto B.D. 1951, D.D. 1976; Univ. of Toronto M.A. 1949; New Coll. Edinburgh Ph.D. 1953; Montreal Diocesan Theol. Coll. D.D. 1973; m. Audrey Mary d. Alexander Brunton 23 Aug. 1947; children: Jonathan Paul, Peter Joseph, Andrew David, Margaret Dorothy; DEAN OF RELIGIOUS STUDIES, McGILL UNIV. 1975- and McConnell Prof. Philos. of Religion 1964- ; o. 1949; Prof. of Hist. & Philos. of Religion & Christian Ethics, The Presb. Coll. Montreal 1957-64; Assoc. Prof. Philos. of Religion present Univ. 1959-64; mem. Reformed-Lutheran Consultation (N. Am.) 1963-67; Co-Chrmn. Reformed-Orthodox Consultation (N.Am.) 1968- ; mem. Orthodox-Reformed Consultation (Internat.) 1979- ; sometime mem. Faith & Order Comn. (Candn. Council Chs.) and dialogue groups; author "The Visible Words of God" 1957; "The Other Six

Days" 1959; "The Reformation and its Significance Today" 1962; "Toward a Radical Church" 1967; "The Clown and the Crocodile" 1970; "God the Anonymous" 1976; "Peter Martyr Vermigli and Italian Reform" ed. 1980; over 60 articles philos. religion and hist. theol.; former Book Review Ed. and Ed. "Studies in Religion/Sciences Religieuses"; mem. Candn. Theol. Soc. (Past Pres.); Candn. Soc. Study Religion; Presbyterian; recreation: Scottish country dancing; Home: 121 Alston Rd., Pointe Claire, Que. H9R 3E2; Office: 3520 University St., Montreal, Que. H3A 2A7.

McLEOD, Alex(ander) N(orman), Ph.D.; university professor; economist; b. Arcola, Sask., 6 May 1911; s. Norman Roderick and F. Mable (Baragar) McL.; e. Queen's Univ., B.A. (Math.) 1933, B.A. (Hons., Econ.) 1940; Harvard Univ., Master in Pub. Adm., 1946, Ph.D. (Econ.) 1949; m. Rosalind, d. late Rev. Robert A. Biggerstaff, 29 Sept. 1941; children: Norman Robert, Donald Bruce, Duncan Keith, Ronald Allan; PROF. EMERITUS, YORK UNIV.; prior to Second World War with Office of Auditor Gen., Ottawa, and subsequently with Dept. of Finance; joined staff of Internat. Monetary Fund, 1947; seconded to U.N. Mission to Haiti, 1948; subsequent missions to Honduras and Costa Rica (1949), Libya (1950-51), Nicaragua (1952), Saudi Arabia (1952-54) and Guatemala (1954-55) dealing with monetary and central-banking problems; apptd. Chief Econ., The Toronto-Dominion Bank, 1955 and also served as Chrmn. of Econs. Comte., Candn. Bankers' Assn.; Gov., Central Bank of Trinidad and Tobago 1966-69; Monetary Consultant to Govt. of Botswana (on leave 1973-74); rec'd several scholarships & Littauer Fellowship, Harvard Univ., 1945-47; author of numerous tech. articles for learned journs.; mem., Am. Econ. Assn.; United Church; recreations: sailing, photography; Home: 8111 Yonge St. #607, Thornhill, Ont. L3T 4V9;

McLEOD, Donald E., M.A.; transportation executive (ret); b. St. Leonards-on-Sea, Sussex, Eng., 15 May 1917; s. George Brown and Ruby Maud (Stephenson) McL.; e. Univ. of Alta. B.A. 1939, M.A. 1942; m. Margaret Mary d. George Spreull, Q.C., 3 Sept. 1943; two s. Ian George, Angus Spreull; Vice Pres. Public Affairs, Air Canada and mem. Extve. Comte. 1976-78; joined trans-Canada Airlines Winnipeg 1943 serving in various mang. positions incl. Dir. of Pub. Relations prior to present appt.; mem. Internat. Air Transport Assn. (Chrmn. Pub. Relations Adv. Comte.); Unitarian; recreations: reading, photography, gardening, fishing; Home: 61 Mount Pleasant, Valois, Pointe Claire, Que. H9R 2T3;

McLEOD, Donald J., B.Sc., M.S.; executive; b. Calgary, Alta 8 April 1931; e. Univ. of Alta. B.Sc. 1956; Univ. of Toronto Extension course in Business 1961; Univ. of Calif. M.S. 1955; m. Brenda M. 14 June 1958; children: David Bruce, Carol Ann, James; PRESIDENT & CHIEF OPERATING OFFR., REICHHOLD LTD.; joined Union Carbide Canada Ltd. 1955-69; recreations: tennis, skiing, golf; Club: Donalda (Dir.); Home: 3 Brushwood Court, Don Mills, Ont. M3A 1V9; Office: 600 The East Mall, Islington, Ont. M9B 4B1.

McLEOD, Very Rev. Hugh Alexander, M.A., D.D., LL.D., (Un. Ch.); b. Owen Sound, Ont., 15 Apl. 1894; s. Alexander Gilchrist and Alexina (Reid) M.; e. Queen's Univ., M.A. 1920; D.D. 1943; Knox Coll., Toronto, Ont., Grad. 1921; Man. Coll., B.D. 1922; LL.D. Memorial 1961; D.D. Victoria 1961; St. John's Coll., Univ. of Man. 1962; m. Doreene Taggart, 1 Sept. 1921; children: Donald, Hugh, Charles; Moderator, United Church of Canada, 1960-62, then retired; held charges at Luseland, Wolseley and Saskatoon, Sask., and Medicine Hat and Edmonton, Alta., Victoria, B.C. and Winnipeg, Man. (Knox); Pres., Conf. of B.C., Un. Ch. of Can. 1948, and of Man., 1954; recreations: walking, fishing; Home: 907 Bickerton Court, 250 Douglas St., Victoria, B.C. V8V 2P4

McLEOD, Ian Hadley, B.A., M.B.A.; executive; b. Bronxville, N.Y., 17 Jan. 1929; s. Ronald Norman and Dorothy (Buchanan) McL.; e. Culver (Ind.) Mil. Acad.; Wesleyan Univ., B.A.; Harvard Grad. Sch. of Business Adm., M.B.A.; m. Jane Anne, d. Lou B. Jordan, 2 Aug. 1952; children: Kim F., Laurie W., Jeffrey A.; PRES. AND CHIEF EXECUTIVE OFFICER, ALLPAK LTD. since 1978; Dir., Livingston Ind. Ltd.; Alcor Investments Ltd.; Chippewa-Camcor, Inc.; Allpak Ltd.; Dashwood Ind. Ltd.; Liquipak Internat. Inc.; Liquid Packaging (Holdings) Ltd.; Asst. to Vice Pres., Finance, Carling Brewing Co., Inc., Cleveland, Ohio, 1955, Asst. to Pres. 1956; Financial Coordinator, Blackhawk Manufacturing Co., Inc., Milwaukee, Wisc. 1958, Controller 1959; joined McKinsey & Co., Inc. as Assoc. Chicago and Cleveland 1961, Princ. Cleveland and Toronto 1967; Managing Dir. 1974-78; served with U.S. Marine Corps 1951-53 (Korea); rank Capt.; Dir., London Regional Art Gallery; Unitarian; recreations: tennis, furniture refinishing; Clubs: London Hunt and Country; The London (Ont.); Granite; Toronto Cricket Skating & Curling; Home: 236 Hyman St., London, Ont. N6A 1N5 Office: 380 Wellington St., London, Ont. N6A 5C3

McLEOD, John T., B.Com., C.A.; b. Vancouver, B.C., 26 Jan. 1934; s. Donald B. and Marion (Taylor) McL.; e. Univ. of B.C., B.Com. 1956; m. Joyce, d. Harold Gordon Douglas Lee, 5 Oct. 1956; children: Patricia, Janet, John Jr.; VICE PRES. AND GEN. MGR., BEROL CORP. OF CANADA LTD., since 1970; articled with Winspear, Hamilton, Anderson, Chart. Accts., 1956-60; joined Canadian Westinghouse Co. Ltd., Hamilton, Ont. as Product Mgr., Home Entertainment, 1960-63; Singer Co. of Canada Ltd., Product Diversification and Retail Store Devel., 1963-65; Singer Co. of New York, Regional Mgr., N. Europe, Brussels and Copenhagen, 1965-67; Mang. Consultant, P. S. Ross & Partners, Montreal, 1967-70; mem., Am. Marketing Assn.; Sales & Marketing Extves. Club; Montreal Chamber Comm.; Alpha Delta Phi; United Church; recreations: sailing, tennis; Clubs: Royal Vancouver Yacht; Royal St. Lawrence Yacht; Address 105 Rene Phillipe, Ville Le Mayne, Montreal, Que.

McLEOD, Lionel E., M.D., M.Sc., F.R.C.P. & S.(C), F.A.C.P.; physician; educator; b. Wainwright, Alta. 9 Aug. 1927; s. Frank E. and Anne (Withnell) McL.; e. Wainwright Pub. and High Schs.; Univ. of Alta. B.Sc. 1949, M.D. 1951; Univ. of Minn. Specialty Training; McGill Univ. M.Sc. 1957; m. Barbara Ann d. Clarence Lipsey 18 Oct. 1952; children: Laura Jane, Bruce E., Judy Ann, Nancy Joan; PRESIDENT, ALTA. HERITAGE FOUNDATION FOR MEDICAL RESEARCH 1981- ; mem. med. staff Univ. of Alta. Hosp. and Prof. of Med. Univ. of Alta. 1957-68; Prof. and Head of Med. Univ. of Calgary 1968-73, Dean of Med. 1973-81; Dir. of Med. Foothills Hosp. Calgary 1968-73, Trustee of Hosp.; rec'd Markle Scholarship in Med. Science 1958-62; Distinguished Med. Alumni Univ. Alta. 1976; Dir. Alta. Div. Candn. Cancer Soc.; Dir. Alta. Heart Foundation; Vice Pres. Calgary Un. Way; Pres. Elect, Royal Coll. Phys. & Surgs. Can.; Past Pres., Assn. Candn. Med. Colls.; Candn. Soc. Nephrology; Past Chrmn. Candn. Council Hosp. Accreditation; mem. Candn. Soc. Clin. Investigation; recreations: skiing, running, hiking, sailing; Club: Century; Home: 11220 - 99 Ave., Edmonton, Alta.; Office: 1200 Oxford Tower, Edmonton Centre, 10235 - 101 St., Edmonton, Alta. T5J 3G1.

McLEOD, Norman Bruce; financier; b. Winnipeg, Man. 7 Oct. 1938; s. John Martin and Dolly Emily Florence (Davey) McL.; e. Cecil Rhodes Elem. Sch. 1953; Daniel McIntyre Coll. Inst. 1957; m. Beverley Mavis d. Alexander Nicholson Nairn 1 Sept. 1962; children: Pamela, Deborah, Allison; PRESIDENT, SETTLERS SAVINGS AND MORTGAGE CORP.; Pres. Settlers Holdings Ltd.; The Settlers Fund Ltd.; NBMcLeod Consulting Services Ltd.; Unicity Mortgage Corp. Ltd.; Salesman, Manulife 1959; estbd.

NBMcLeod Consulting Services 1972; breeds and races thoroughbred horses under "Dunvegan Farm"; attempted prof. baseball career 1958; mem. Candn. Tax Foundation; Candn. Pension Conf.; P. Conservative; Protestant; recreations: curling, hunting, flying, horse racing; Clubs: Winnipeg Winter; Deer Lodge Curling; Home: 27 Prairie View Rd., Winnipeg, Man. R2J 1H1; Office: 877 Portage Ave., Winnipeg, Man. R3G 0N8

McLEOD, Norman William, Sc.D., D. Eng., F.R.S.C.; engineering consultant; b. Elora, Ont. 26 Nov. 1904; s. William and Elizabeth Helen (Ewen) McL.; e. Univ. of Alta. B.Sc. (Chem. Engn.) 1930; Univ. of Sask. M.Sc. 1936; Univ. of Mich. Sc.D. (Civil Engn.) 1938; D. Eng. (Hon.) Univ. of Waterloo; m. Irene Marguerite d. Thomas Arthur Briggs. Killarney, Man. 10 Feb. 1931; children: Norman Barrie, Muriel Irene, Ruth Marilyn, Murray Graeme, Susan Eileen; VICE PRES. AND ASPHALT CONSULTANT, McASPHALT ENGINEERING SERVICES since 1970; Adjunct Prof. of Civil Engn. Univ. of Waterloo since 1970; in charge of asphalt constr. and maintenance Dept. Hwys. Sask. 1930-38; Asphalt Consultant, Imperial Oil Ltd. 1938-69; Engn. Consultant on Pavements for Airports (part-time), Dept. Transport Can. since 1945; Official Guest, 5th and 6th Congreso Argentino de Vialidad y Transito 1964, 1968; rec'd U.S.A. Hwy. Research Bd. Award 1946; Charles B. Dudley Medal Am. Soc. Testing Materials 1952; Assn. Asphalt Paving Technols. Annual Award 1952; Univ. of Mich. Citation as Distinguished Alumnus 1953; Stevenson Travel Award (N.Z.) 1967; Candn. Centennial Medal 1967; R. F. Legget Award Candn. Geotech. Soc. 1972; Fellow, Roy. Soc. of Canada (Academy of Science) 1977; Prevost Hubbard Award Committee DO4 Am. Soc. Testing Materials 1978; The Engineering Medal, Assn. of Professional Eng. of Ont., 1979; Recognition of Achievement Award, Asphalt Emulsion Manuf. Assn. 1981; el. to Asphalt Inst. Roll of Honour 1971; Hon. mem. ASTM D18 on Soils & Rock for Engn. Purposes 1972; Hon. mem. ASTM DO4 on Road, Paving, Bituminous Materials 1979; author over 100 tech. papers and discussions soil mechanics, asphalt pavement structural design, design & constr. asphalt surfaces; Fellow, Am. Assn. Advanc. Science; mem. Ont. Assn. Prof. Engrs. Prov. Ont.; Roads & Transport. Assn. Can. (Past Chrmn. Tech. Council & Comte. on Vehicle Weights & Dimensions); Candn. Tech. Asphalt Assn.; Fellow Am. Soc. Testing & Materials, and Award of Merit, 1980; Transportation Research Bd.; Assn. Asphalt Paving Technols. (Past Pres.); Sigma Xi; United Church; recreations: photography, gardening; Home: 41 Glenrose Ave., Toronto, Ont. M4T 1K3; Office: (P.O. Box 247) West Hill, Ont. M1E 4RT.

McLOUGHLIN-GUEST, Michele Ida-Jane, R.C.A.; interior designer; b. Calgary, Alta. 18 Jan. 1944; d. Norman Ridley and Jenni (Apponen) Shaw; e. Univ. of Man. Bachelor of Interior Design 1965; m. Gowan Thomas Guest 6 May 1978; children: Marni Michele McLoughlin, Douglas Gowan Guest; PROP., SPECIALIZED PLANNING & CREATIVE ENVIRONMENT LTD. 1972- ; Instr. and Co-ordinator Interior Design Program Douglas Coll. 1979-80; interior designer with comm. firms 1965-72; mem. Interior Designers Can. (Past Pres.); Interior Designers Inst. B.C. (Past Pres.); Anglican; Address: 1390 W. King Edward, Vancouver, B.C. V6H 1Z9.

McMAHON, Andrew Maurice, B.Sc.; telecommunications executive; b. Renfrew, Ont., 24 July 1935; e. Renfrew, Ont.; Queen's Univ. B.Sc. 1959; VICE PRES., ENGINEERING, BELL CANADA since 1980; Dir., B.N.R. Inc.; Bell Communications Sytems Inc.; joined Bell Canada, North Bay holding various line and staff mang. positions Sudbury, Toronto, London and Montreal 1959-72; Gen. Mgr.-Computer Communications, Toronto 1972; Vice Pres., Computer Communications; Div. Chrmn., Ottawa-Carleton United Way 1979; Ottawa Unit Bd. f Dir., Cdn. Cancer Soc.; mem. Bd. of Trustees, Queen's

Univ.; mem. Queens Univ. Council; mem. Assn. Prof. Engrs. Ont.; Order Engrs. Que.; Past Pres. Toronto Br. Queen's Univ. Alumni Assn.; Office: 160 Elgin St., Ottawa, Ont. K2P 2C4

McMAHON, Hon. George Rudolph, Q.C., M.L.A., LL.B.; politician; b. Kensington, P.E.I. 30 May 1929; s. Peter Andrew and Emma Ruth (MacKay) McM.; e. Kensington High Sch.; King Edward High Sch. Vancouver; St. Dunstan's Univ.; Dalhousie Univ.; m. Gertrude Marie d. John Ferguson, Liverpool, N.S. 20 Sept. 1957; children: Lorraine, Marie, Marshall, Patrick; MIN. OF JUSTICE AND ATTORNEY GENERAL OF P.E.I. 1980- ; Min. of Public Works, P.E.I. 1980-81; Min of Highways P.E.I. 1980-81; Min. of Industry & Comm. 1979-80; Cand. prov. g.e. 1974, def.; el. M.L.A. for 5th Prince prov. by-el. 1976, re-el. since; P. Conservative; R. Catholic; Office: (P.O. Box 2000) Jones Bldg., 11 Kent St., Charlottetown, P.E.I. C1A 7N8.

McMAHON, Howard Oldford, M.A., Ph.D.; management consultant; b. Killam, Alta., 16 Sept. 1914; s. Thomas Alexander and Tryphina (Oldford) McM.; e. Univ. of B.C., B.A. 1935, M.A. 1937; Mass. Inst. of Technol., Ph.D. 1941; m. Edna Lucile, d. late Rufus Nelson, 2 July 1941; children: Thomas Arthur, Elizabeth Jean Humez, Nancy Lucile Swanborn CONSULTANT ARTHUR D. LITTLE INC., since 1977; Dir., and Chrmn. of Bd.Helix Technology Corp., formerly Arthur D. Little Inc. Cryogenic Technology Inc., Waltham, Mass; Research Assoc., Mass. Inst. of Technol., 1941-43; joined present Co. 1943; Science Dir. 1952; Vice Pres., Head of Advanced Research Div., 1956: Sr. Vice Pres. 1960; Head of Research and Devel. Div. 1962; el. a Dir., Extve. Comte., Extve. Vice Pres., 1963; Pres. and Dir. 1964-77; rec'd Edward Longstreth Medal, Franklin Inst., 1951; Frank Forrest Award, Am. Ceramic Soc., 1952; Samuel C. Collins Award, Cryogenic Engineering Conf. 1979; author many papers and articles on low temperature physics; mem., Am. Assn. Advanc. Science; Am. Acad. Arts & Sciences; Am. Chem. Soc.; Am. Phys. Soc.; N.Y. Acad. Sciences; Dirs. Indust. Research; Am. Soc. Testing & Materials (Dir.); Sigma Xi; Protestant; recreation: fishing; Home: Huckleberry Hill, Lincoln, Mass. 01773; Office: 25 Acorn Park, Cambridge, Mass.

McMARTIN, W. Finlay, B.A., M.D., C.M., F.R.C.P.; physician; cardiologist; b. Westmount, Que., 1 May 1908; s. Ernest William and Catherine Weir (Rough) M.; e. Westmount High Sch., 1922-26; McGill Univ., B.A. 1930, M.D., C.M. 1935; Cert. Specialist by R.C.P. & S. and Que. Coll. of Phys. & Surgs. in Internal Med.; m. Ethel Fraser, d. late W. H. D. Murray, 16 Nov. 1935; children: William Peter, James Murray, Lesley Weir; pt.-time consult. in Internal Med. and Cardiology, Hudson Med. Centre; mem. Hon. Staff, Queen Elizabeth Hosp.; formerly Sr. Physician and Cardiologist, and earlier, Physician-in-Chief and Chrmn. Med. Bd. there; Delta Sigma Phi; Freemason; Conservative; United Church; recreations: curling, golf; Clubs: Whitlock Golf and Country; Heather Curling (Past Pres.); Home: 84 Maple Ave., Hudson Heights, Que.

McMASTER, Juliet Sylvia, M.A., Ph.D., F.R.S.C.; educator; b. Kisumu, Kenya 2 Aug. 1937; children: Sydney Herbert and Sylvia (Hook) Fazan; e. Kenya Girls' High Sch. Nairobi Higher Sch. Cert. 1955; St. Anne's Coll. Oxford Univ. B.A. 1959, M.A. 1962; Mt. Holyoke Coll. Mass. 1959-60; Univ. of Alta. M.A. 1963, Ph.D. 1965; m. Rowland Douglas McMaster 10 May 1968; children: Rawdon Joseph, Lindsey Sylvia; PROF. OF ENG., UNIV. OF ALTA. 1976- , Asst. Prof. 1965, Assoc. Prof. 1970; author "Thackeray: The Major Novels" 1971; "Trollope's Palliser Novels: Theme and Pattern" 1978; "Jane Austen on Love" 1978; co-author "The Novel from Sterne to James"; various articles on Eng. novel learned journs.; ed. "Jane Austen's Achievement" 1976; rec'd Can. Council Post-

doctoral Fellowship 1969-70; Guggenheim Fellowship 1976-77; recreations: fencing, hiking, ceramic sculpture, teaching art to children; Home: 7815 - 119 St., Edmonton, Alta. T6G 1W5; Office: Edmonton, Alta. T6G 2E5.

McMICHAEL, Robert, C.M. (1974), D.Litt.; art director; b. Toronto, 27 July 1921; s. Norman & Evelyn May (Kennedy) McM.; e. Runnymede Pub. Sch. and Humberside Coll. Inst., Toronto, 1941; York Univ., D.Litt. 1970; Order of Canada (C.M.) 1974; Fellow, ont. Coll. of Art, 1979; m. Signe Kirstien, d. late Soren Christian Sorensen, 9 Feb. 1949; Co-founder "Canadian High News", 1940; Founder, "Robert McMichael Studios", 1946; Founder and Pres., "Travel Pak Ltd." 1952 and "Robert McMichael Inc." New York, 1959; assumed full-time direction of The McMichael Canadian Collection, Kleinburg, Ont., 1964; mem. B. McMichael Candn. Collection; served with RCN during World War 11; mem. Bd. of Trade Metrop. Toronto; recipient, Connie Award from Soc. of Amer. Travel Writers 1978; Anglican; Club: Arts & Letters; Address: Kleinburg, Ont. L0J 1C0

McMILLAN, John Clark; banker; b. Glasgow, Scot., 4 Jan. 1920; s. Thomas Paton and Lily (Clark) McM.; m. Orma Margaret, d. late Charles Lacheur, 17 Apl. 1946; EXTVE. VICE PRES. NAT. ACCOUNTS, ROYAL BANK OF CAN. 1980- ; Dir., RoyNat. Inc.; J. & P. Coats (Can.) Inc.; joined the Bank 1937, Sr. Asst. Mgr. Vancouver Br. 1956, Supvr., Que., N.B. and E. Ont. Brs. 1964, Dist. Gen. Mgr. Halifax, 1966, Depy. Gen. Mgr., Personnel 1970; Vice Pres. and Gen. Mgr., Adm. Jan.-Nov. 1974; Sr. Vice Pres. & Gen. Mgr., Corp. Banking (Can.) Dec. 1974; Exec. Vice Pres. & Gen. Mgr., Nat. Accounts Div., 1978-80; served with RCAF 400 City of Toronto Sqdn. during World War II; rank Flight Lt.; Past Pres., Candn. Heart Foundation; Dir., Dellcrest Children's Centre; Presbyterian; recreations: hunting, fishing, golf; Clubs: Canadian; Toronto; St. James's; Royal Montreal Golf; Lambton Golf & Country; Home: 57 Widdicombe Hill Blvd., 1803W, Weston, Ont. M9R 1Y4; Office: Royal Bank Plaza, Toronto, Ont. M5J 2J5

McMILLAN, Very Rev. Kenneth George, B.A., M.Div., D.D. (Presb.); b. Mount Forest, Ont., 28 Mar. 1916; s. George Henry and Gertrude Elizabeth (Watson) M.; e. Palmerston and Listowel, Ont. High Schs.; Univ. Coll., Univ. of Toronto, B.A. 1939; Knox Theol. Coll., Toronto, Grad. 1942, M.Div. 1946, D.D. 1964, Wycliffe Coll. 1974; Acadia Univ., D.D. 1978; m. Isobel Islay, d. Alexander McCannell, Port Elgin, Ont., 3 Aug. 1942; two d., Catherine Isobel, Barbara Jean; GEN. SECY., CANDN. BIBLE SOCIETY, since Jan. 1957; el. Chrmn. Gen. Comte. of Un. Bible Socs. of the World, 1976; Minister, Burgoyne and Dunblane, 1942-43; Drummond Hill Church, Niagara Falls, Ont., 1944-50; St. Andrew's Church, Guelph, Ont., 1950-57; Beguin Mem. Lectr., Australia 1974; Reserve Chaplain, R.C.N.; Canadian Representative on the United Bible Socs.; mem. of Comn. on Canadian Affairs, Candn. Council of Churches (mem. Personnel Comte.); Past Moderator, Presby. Synod of Toronto and Kingston; Moderator, Presb. Church in Can. 1979-80; author: "What But Thy Grace"; Freemason; recreations: camping, woodwork; Home: 69 St. Leonards Ave., Toronto, Ont. M4N 1K4; Office: Ste. 100, 10 Carnforth Rd., Toronto, Ont. M4A 2S4

McMORRAN, His Hon. Allen Stewart, B.A.; b. Vancouver, B.C., 12 Aug. 1919; s. Oscar Stewart and Sarah Louisa Parfitt (Mullett) McM.; e. Florence Nightingale and Cecil Rhodes Pub. Schs., King Edward High Sch., Vancouver, 1937; Univ. of B.C., B.A. 1941; Vancouver Law Sch., grad. 1946; m. Mary Adele, d. late Francis Augustus Whitfield, 31 Aug. 1951; children: Vanessa Lee, Lisa Anne, William Eric, Allen Steven; JUDGE, COUNTY COURT OF WESTMINSTER, B.C. since 1975; City Prosecutor, Vancouver, since 1953; read law with Tiffin Russell Dumoulin and Brown; called to Bar of B.C. 1946; cr. Q.C.

1964; joined Office of City Prosecutor as Asst. City Prosecutor, 1947; apptd. County Court Judge, Co. of Cariboo, B.C. 1974; served with 1st Bn. Irish Fusiliers 1942-44; rank Lt.; Adj. Capt. No. 11 Vocational Training Sch. Pacific Command, 1944-45; Past mem., Special Comte., Detoxification Soc. of B.C.; Vancouver Traffic & Safety Council 1947-73; Vancouver Official Traffic Commission 1953-74; Dir., Alcoholism Foundation of British Columbia 1958; Narcotic Addiction Foundation of B.C., 1956-74 (Pres., Chrmn. & mem. Extve. Comte 1963-65); Past Dir. Legal Aid Soc.1970-74; Dir. Candn. Council Christians & Jews; trustee, 1st Bn. Irish Fusiliers; mem. Shaughnessy Hts. Property Owners Assn.; mem., Vancouver Bar Assn. (Extve. 1965-67); Past mem. Law Soc. B.C. (Head of Criminal Law Tutorials 1956-74); Candn. Bar Assn. (Council B.C. Sec. 1961-65; Council 1961-65; Chrmn. B.C. Criminal Justice Sec. 1961-63, Nat. Chrmn. of Sec. 1963-65); Bencher, Law Soc. B.C. 1969, 1971, 1973; Commr. (Legal Adviser), Vancouver Basketball Comn.; Past Dir., Shaughnessy Little League Baseball; Past Chrmn. Archbishop's Comte. Diocese of New Westminster Eccl. Matrimonial Comn.; mem. Vancouver Mil. Inst.; Sir Winston Churchill Soc. (Vancouver); Kappa Sigma (Grand Master 1941; Alumnus Advisor); Anglican; recreation: fishing; Clubs: Point Grey Golf & Country; Arbutus; Westminster; B.C. Regt. Offrs.' Mess; Home: 1072 Matthews Ave., Vancouver, B.C.V6H 1W3; Office: Law Courts, Begbie Squ., New Westminster, B.C.

McMULLEN, Alvin L., B.Sc.; retired company executive; b. Akron, Ohio, 29 May 1917; s. Roma F. and Elsie May (Smith) McM.; e. Univ. of Akron, B.Sc. (Chem.) 1939; m. Phyllis May, d. late Willard Van Zandt, 25 Dec. 1939; two s., one d.; Dir. MDG Co. Ltd.; Devel. Chem., Seiberling Rubber Co., Barberton, Ohio 1939; Production Mang. 1949; Vice Pres.-Production and Dir. Seiberling Rubber Co. of Canada Ltd., Toronto 1957, Vice Pres. and Gen. Mgr. 1961, Pres. and Gen. Mgr. 1964-65; Pres. and Gen. Mgr., Mansfield-Denman General o. Ltd. 1969-79 (ret.); Account Extve. Private Brand Sales, Goodyear Tire & Rubber Co. of Canada Ltd. 1963-64, Gen. Mgr. Private Brand Sales Div. 1965-69; mem. Am. Chem. Soc. (Rubber Div.); Soc. Automotive Engrs.; Rubber Assn. Can. (Chrmn. 1975); Freemason; Protestant; recreations: fishing, skeet, golf, instrumental music; Clubs: Barrie Gun; Home: R.R.1, Kilworthy, Ont. P0E 1G0 (perm res.); 4025 Voorne St., Sarasota, Fla. 33580 (winter).

McMURRAY, Bruce J.; manufacturer; b. Toronto, Ont. 11 May 1930; s. William Edward and Beatrice (Gilmore) McM.; e. Malvern Coll. Inst. Toronto 1949; Univ. of W. Ont. Marketing Mang. Cert. 1964, Gen. Mang. Cert. 1974; m. Beverley d. Cyril Lewis 18 June 1955; three d. Donna Lynn, Kelly Ann, Susan Beverley; PRES. AND CHIEF EXTVE. OFFR., DIR., THE CANADIAN SALT CO. LTD. 1976- ; Dir. Canadian Rock Salt Co. Ltd.; Essex Terminal Railway Co.; Morton Terminal Ltd.; Morton Windsor Ltd.; Canadian Brine Ltd.; Sales Rep. present Co. 1953, Product Mgr. 1963, Regional Sales Mgr. Ont. 1967, Gen. Sales Mgr. 1969, Marketing Mgr. 1971, Vice Pres. Marketing 1973, Extve. Vice Pres. 1975; mem. Grocery Products Mfrs. Assn. Dir. and Treas.; Salt Inst.; Liberal; Anglican; recreations: golf, jogging, skiing; Clubs: St. James's; Summerlea Golf; Rotary; Home: 20-15th St., Roxboro, Que. H8Y 1N5; Office: 606 Cathcart St., Montreal, Que. H3B 1L6.

McMURRAY, MacKenzie, B.A.Sc., M.Com., P.Eng.; retired manufacturer; b. Toronto, Ont., 7 Apl. 1915; s. Samuel and Helen (MacKenzie) McM.; e. Harbord Coll. Inst., Toronto; Univ. of Toronto, B.A.Sc. 1939, M.Com. 1954; m. Helen Bernice, d. Samuel Wilson, 24 May 1951; Candn. Gen. Electric Co. Ltd.; Burns Foods Ltd.; Montreal Trust Co.; Allendale Mutual Ins. Co.; Detroit Marine Terminals, Detroit; Penobscot Bldg., Detroit; Imperial Trust, Montreal; joined Dominion Bridge Co. Ltd. 1940; apptd. Asst. to Vice Pres. and Mang. Dir., Montreal,

1956; Vice Pres., Finance, Montreal, 1957; Vice Pres., Ont. Region, Montreal, 1959-62; Vice Pres., Finance and Dir., 1962; Pres. and Chief Extve. Offr. 1963; Chrmn. Bd. 1974-77; Past Chrmn., Welding Inst. of Can.; mem., Engn. Inst. Can. (Toronto Br. Chrmn. 1954; Councillor 1954-57); Assn. Prof. Engrs. Ont.; Corp. Engrs. Que.; Presbyterian; recreations: golf, curling; Clubs: University; Montreal Thistle Curling: Engineers (Toronto); Toronto Cricket Skating & Curling; Forest & Stream; Kanawaki Golf; Mount Royal; Home: 4066 Gage Rd., Montreal, Que. H3Y 1R5; Office: Suite 2912, 1155 Dorchester Blvd. W., Montreal, Que.

McMURRICH, Arthur R., B.Com.; company executive; b. Toronto, Ont. 21 May 1917; s. Arthur R. and Muriel Logie (Smellie) McM.; e. Brown Public Sch., Toronto, Ont.; Upper Can. Coll.; McGill Univ., B.Com. 1939; m. 1stly, Carol Jean Roy, 14 June 1941 (d. 1967); children: Mrs. Margot Anne List, A. R., R.D.R., A.L.; m. 2ndly, Bridget Wendy Crutchlow, d. Burrell Page, Norfolk, Eng. Dec. 1969; VICE-PRES.-MARKETING & CORPORATE PLANNING, STELCO INC. 1978- ; Dir., Shaw Industries Ltd.; Guardian Ins. Co.; Montreal Life Ins.- Co.; joined the Co., Cost and Time Study Depts., Notre Dame Works, Montreal 1940-41; Export Div., Montreal 1946; Domestic Sales, Pipe Div. 1947; Sales Rep., Toronto 1948; Asst. to Sales Mgr., Bar Products, Hamilton, Ont. 1949; Toronto Dist. Sales Mgr. 1950; Sales Mgr., Sheet & Strip Div., Hamilton 1956; Gen. Mgr., Field Sales 1958; Gen. Mgr., E. Region, Montreal 1962; apptd. Vice-Pres. Sales, Finishing Mill & Tubular Products, Hamilton 1964; Vice Pres., Marketing, 1967; served in 2nd World War, Royal Highland Regt. Can. Black Watch (N.P.A.M.) Montreal; Royal Rifles Can., Quebec City; H.Q. 1st Candn. Army, Eng. 1943; H.Q. 4th Candn. Armd. Div. — GSO III, Eng., France, Belgium, Holland 1943-44; Vice Pres. and Dir., Toronto Symphony Orchestra; Past Pres., Bd. of Trade of metro. Toronto, 1976-77; Alpha Delta Phi; Anglican; recreations: golf, tennis; Clubs: National; St. James's (Montreal); The Hamilton; Badminton & Racquet, Toronto; Toronto Golf; Home: 21 Lonsdale Rd., Toronto, Ont. M4V 1W4; Office: Box 205, Toronto-Dominion-Centre, Toronto, Ont. M5K 1J4

McMURRICH, Norman Hay, B.Arch.; b. Toronto, Ont., 2 June 1920; s. Arthur Redpath and Muriel Logie (Smellie) M.; e. Upper Canada Coll.; Univ. of Toronto (Sch. of Arch.), B.Arch. 1946; m. (late) Mary, d. late Robert G. Armour, M.D., 1 June 1947; children: Marilyn, Sheila, Edward (Ted), Donald (deceased): PARTNER, McMURRICH & OXLEY: ARCHITECTS; joined firm as an Assoc. in 1946; main large projects which have been under his personal guidance are: Pembroke Gen. Hosp., additions to Candn. approach Plaza at the Peace Bridge; York Co. Hosp., and St. Mary's Hosp., Kitchener, Ont.; Acad. and Residence Bldgs., George Ignatief Theatre, Trinity Coll.; Toronto; Medical Sciences Bldg., Univ. of Toronto; Extensions to Havergal College; Restoration of St. Andrews Presbyterian Church, Toronto; Huronia District Hosp. (Midland); the firm has designed and supervised many important bldgs. in field of health and educ.; served in 2nd World War; Lieut., 48th Highlanders (R) 1941; on active service Overseas with 48th Highlanders in Eng., 1943, Italy, 1943-45 and Holland and Belgium, 1945; Pres., Arts & Letters Club (until May, 1982); Vice-Chmn., Planning & Development, Can. Cancer Soc.; mem. Bd. of Dirs., Young Peoples Theatre; Royal Arch. Inst. Can. 1968; Past Treas., Ont. Assn. of Archs. Council, and Past Chrmn., Toronto Chapter; el. Hon. Fellow, Am. Inst. of Arch. 1969; Hon. mem. Mexican Assn. of Arch.; Kappa Alpha; Presbyterian; recreations: squash, dramatics, sketching; Clubs: University; Arts & Letters; Home: 1 Knightswood Road, Toronto, Ont. M4N 2G9

McMURTRY, Hon. Roland Roy, Q.C., M.P.P.; politician; b. Toronto, Ont. 31 May 1932; s. Roland Roy and Doris Elizabeth (Belcher) McM.; e. St. Andrew's Coll.

Aurora, Ont.; Trinity Coll. Univ. of Toronto; Osgoode Hall Law Sch.; m. Ria Jean d. Dr. Harry Macrae, Toronto, Ont. 18 Apl. 1957; children: Janet, Jimmy, Harry, Jeanie, Erin, Michael; ATTY. GEN. FOR ONT. 1975- ; Sol. Gen. for Ont. 1978-82; called to Bar of Ont. 1958; cr. Q.C. 1970; Partner, Benson, McMurtry, Percival & Brown 1958-75; el. to Ont. Leg. 1975, re-el. 1977 and 1981; Gov. Frontier Coll.; Hon. Chrmn. Big Brothers of Metro Toronto; Nat. Dir. St. Leonards Soc. Can.; mem. Advocates Soc.; Candn. Bar Assn.; Zeta Psi; Phi Delta Phi; P. Conservative; United Church; recreations: painting, skiing, tennis; Clubs: Albany; Cambridge; Badminton & Racquet; Office: 18 King St. E., Toronto, Ont. M5C 1C5.

McNALLY, William James, B.A., M.D., C.M., M.Sc., LL.D., F.R.C.S.(C.); otolaryngologist; b. Bryson, Que., 27 Dec. 1897; s. Richard and Elizabeth (Ryan) M.; e. Dalhousie Univ., B.A. 1921 and M.D., C.M. 1922; McGill Univ., M.Sc. 1925, D.Sc. 1934; St. Francis Xavier Univ., Hon. LL.D. 1951; m. late Harriet (d. 1970), d. James Purcell, Antigonish, N.S., 27 Sept. 1927; children: Herbert Birkett, Ann Elizabeth; m. 2ndly, Andrea Hingston Dolan, widow of Dr. H. S. Dolan, d. Dr. Donald Hingston, Montreal; Hon. Consultant in Otolaryngol. Royal Victoria Hosp.; former Chrmn. and Prof., Dept. of Otolaryngol, McGill Univ.; Chairman of Panel on Auditory Problems, Defence Research Bd., Dept. of National Defence 1950-64; Nu Sigma Nu; Roman Catholic; Home: 25 Redpath Place, Montreal, Que. H3G 1E2

McNAMARA, Hon. William Craig; senator; grain expert; b. Winnipeg, Man., 8 Aug. 1904; s. James Richard and Margaret Hall (Craig) M.; e. Regina Schs., Sask.; m. Margaret Llewellyn, d. David Spencer Rowand, 4 Aug. 1928; children: Gail, Sandra, Sharon, Craig; with Standard Bank of Can., 1922-24; Sask. Co-operative Wheat Producers Ltd. and Sask. Pool Elevator Ltd., 1924-42; Mgr., Coarse Grain Sales Dept., 1942; joined Candn. Wheat Bd. as Supv. of Car Supply; apptd. Rep. of Candn. Wheat Bd. Washington, D.C., 1944; also served as alternative mem. for Candn. Govt. on Cereals Comte. of Combined Food Bd., 1944; apptd. Commr., Candn. Wheat Bd., 1945; Asst. Chief Commr., 1947-58; Chief Commr. 1958-70; summoned to Senate of Can. 7 Oct. 1970; United Church; Home 220 Carpathia Rd., Winnipeg, Man. R3N 1S9

McNAUGHT, Kenneth, M.A., Ph.D.; university professor; b. Toronto, Ont., 10 Nov. 1918; s. William Carlton and Eleanor Mildred (Sanderson) McN.; e. Upper Can. Coll., Toronto, Univ. of Toronto, B.A. 1941, M.A. 1946, Ph.D. 1950; m. Beverley Eileen, d. late S. W. Argue, 13 June 1942; children: Christopher, Allison, Andrew; PROF. OF HISTORY, UNIV. OF TORONTO, since 1959; Prof. of Hist., Un. Coll., Winnipeg, 1947-59; served with Candn. Army (RCOC) 1942-45; Contrib. Ed., "Saturday Night", 1959-69; Ed., "Canadian Studies in History and Government", 1959-66; mem. Ed. Bd., "Christian Outlook", Montreal, 1961-66, "Canadian Welfare", 1961-65; "Canadian Forum", 1968-78; Chrmn., CBC TV panel "Round Table", 1953-57; rec'd Can. Council Sr. Fellowships, 1963, 1969; Killam Award 1975; author, "A Prophet in Politics", 1959; "Manifest Destiny", 1981; "The Pelican History of Canada", 1981; "The Winnipeg Strike: 1919", 1974; co-author, "A Source-Book in Canadian History", 1959; "Canada & the United States", 1963; other writings include numerous articles in various journals; mem., Canadian Hist. Association; Organ. Am. Historians; Labor Historians (U.S.), Extve. Bd. 1970-76; NDP; Anglican; recreations: sailing, golf, sketching; Clubs: Kingston Yacht; Arts and Letters; Home: 121 Crescent Rd., Toronto, Ont. M4W 1T8

McNAUGHTON, Donald William; industrialist; b. Montreal, Que., 18 July 1926; s. Edmund Moore and Mildred Agnes (Caven) McN.; e. Loyola Coll., Montreal; Sir George Williams Univ.; m. Barbara Ann, d. late William

J. Little, 24 April 1954; children: John, Tim, Susan, Ann; PRESIDENT AND CHIEF EXTVE. OFFR., SCHENLEY CANADA INC., since 1972; Chrmn. and Pres., Park & Tilford Can. Inc.; Pres., Canadian Gibson Ltd.; John McNaughton Co. Ltd.; Dir., J.H. Henkes of Rotterdam (Can.) Ltd.; Canadian Gibson Distilleries Ltd.; Account Extve., McKim Advertising Ltd., Montreal, 1947-50; Adv. Asst., Canadian Liquid Air, Montreal, 1951-53; Gen. Supv., Display Adv., Air Canada, 1953-57; Que. Adv. Mgr., Carling Breweries, Montreal, 1957, Que. Pub. Relations Mgr., 1958, Que. Br. Mgr., 1960, Que. Marketing Mgr., 1962; Dir. of Adv. and Co-ordinator of Schenley Awards, 1963-66; Gen. Mgr., Canadian Park & Tilford Distilleries Ltd., 1966 (a Schenley subsidiary); Pres. 1967-69; joined present Co. as Pres. and C.E.O. 1969; Vice Chrmn., Montreal Alouette Football Council; Bd. of Dir., Que. Soc. for Crippled Children; Vice-Chmn. Finance, Canada Safety Council; Hon. Treas. and mem. St. Mary's Hosp. (Montreal); Dir., St. Patrick's Soc. of Montreal (Hon. life mem.); Loyola Found.; Life Gov., Montreal Gen. Hosp.; Chmn., Bd. of Gov., Concordia University; Dir. Loyola Coll. Alumni Assn. (Pres. 1965-67); Bd. of Admin., Notre Dame de la Garde Parish, St. Donat, Que.; Vice Chrmn., Concordia Development Fund Campaign; Vice Chrmn. Finance, Can. Safety Council; Hon. Vice Pres., Que. Prov. Council, Pres., Boy Scouts of Can.; Mem., Order of Lazarus of Jerusalem; Roman Catholic; recreations: boating, winter sports; Clubs: Mt. Royal; Saint James's; Montreal Badminton and Squash; The Vancouver (B.C.); Capilano Golf & Country (Vancouver); Toronto Home: 157 Ballantyne Ave. N., Montreal, Que. H4X 2B9; Office: 550 Sherbrooke St. W., Montreal, Que. H3A 1B9

McNEIL, Frederick Harold, A.F.C.; banker; b. Saskatoon, Sask., 17 Nov. 1916; s. Harold and Jean (Swan) McN.; e. Univ of Manitoba; Univ. of Sask.; m. Marian Doreen, d. Arthur Williams, Toronto, Ont., 16 Jan. 1943; children: Ronald F., Marie, Bruce H.; CHRMN. EXTVE. COMTE. BANK OF MONTREAL Jan. 1979; Dir. Bank of Montreal (Calif.); Internat. Resources and Finance Bank, S.A., Luxembourg; Seagram Co. Ltd.; Canadian Canners Ltd.; Dominion Life Assurance Co.; with Victoria Colonist and Vancouver Province as Reporter, City Ed. & Parlty. Corr. 1945-54; Mang. Consultant, Braun & Co., Vancouver, B.C. 1954; Dir. Mang. Services, Powell River Co., Vancouver 1956; joined Ford Motor Co. of Can. 1960, becoming Dir. Organ., Personnel & Adm. Planning; joined present Bank as Gen. Mgr., Personnel Planning and subsequently Gen. Mgr., Organ. & Personnel 1966, Vice-Pres., Organ. & Personnel 1967, Extve. Vice-Pres., Adm. 1968, Extve. Vice-Pres. and Gen. Mgr. 1970, Pres. 1973; Depy. Chrmn. and Chief Extve. Offr. Jan. 1975; Chrmn., 1975-81; Life Gov., Montreal Gen. Hosp.; mem. Adv. Bd. Univ. of Western Ont.; mem. Bus. Council on Nat. Issues; mem. Bd., Candn. Council of Christians and Jews; Hon. Vice Chrmn., St. John Ambulance Que. Council; Hon. Vice-President Quebec Prov. Council, Boy Scouts of Canada; served in 2nd World War, R.C.A.F. as Sqdn. Leader; Protestant; recreations: riding, ranching, golf; Clubs: Mount Royal; Toronto; Ranhmen's; Calgary Petroleum; Home: M Bar Ranch, P.O. Box 335, Granum, Alta. T0L 1A0; Office: Suite 300, 300 5th Ave. S.W., Calgary, Alta. T2P 3C4.

McNEILL, N. John, Q.C., LL.B.; b. Macleod, Alberta, 17 Dec. 1912; s. late His Hon. Edward Peele and Ellen Lydia (Ives) M.; e. Earl Grey Public Sch., Calgary, Alta.; Central Coll. Inst., Calgary, Alta.; Univ. of Alberta, LL.B., 1936; m. Mary Caroline, d. late Alec Addington Ballachey, K.C., High River, Alta, 21 Aug. 1940; children: Edward Alec, Gary Ballachey, William John, Margaret Ellen; Past Pres. Great Lakes Gas Trans. CO.retired ; read law with Frank L. Burnet, Q.C. Calgary Alta.; called to the Bar of Alberta, 15 June 1937; cr. Q.C., Dec. 1953; in gen. practice of law with firms successively known as Ballachey, Burnet & Heseltine, Ballachey, Burnet, Heseltine &

McNeill, Burnet, Heseltine & McNeill and Burnet, McNeill & Duckworth, Calgary, Alta., 1937-54; Partner, Milner, Steer, Martland & McNeill, Calgary, Alta. (specialized in public utility practice), Jan. 1955-Mar. 1957; apptd. Gen Counsel and Asst. Secy., Trans-Canada Pipe Lines Ltd. in June 1956; Vice Pres., Gen. Counsel, Secy. 1957-66; Sr. Vice Pres., Gen. Counsel, 1966-67; served in 2nd World War with Canadian Army (Armoured Corps), 1942-46; Lieut., 31st (Alta., Reconnaissance Regt., and subsequently Capt. and Adjutant; 10th War Staff course, R.M.C., Kingston; Staff Capt. (A), E Group, Canadian Army Overseas; mem., Law Soc. Alta. (Secy.-Treas. and Solr. 1952-57); Calgary Bar Assn. (Pres. 1953); Candn. Bar Assn.; Toronto Bd. Trade; Candn. Gas Assn.; Phi Delta Theta; Anglican; recreation: golf; Clubs: Country Club of Detroit; Detroit Economic; Ontario; Canadian (N.Y.); Calgary Golf & Country; York Downs Golf & Country (Toronto)

McNIE, John Duncan, B.A.; advertising executive; b. Toronto, Ont., 24 July 1920; s. John and Ann (Duncan) M.; e. Pub. Schs. and York Mem. Coll. Inst., Toronto, Ont.; Western Tech. School, Toronto, Ont.; B.A. McMaster Univ.; M.ed.; Univ. of Toronto; m. late Mary Kathleen, d. Alfred John Skeans, Q.C., Toronto, Ont., 8 Dec. 1951; children: Frances Ann, Heather Kathleen, Duncan Scott, John Thorp, Mary Alice; CHRMN., R. T. KELLEY INC. (Advertising Agency, Estbd. 1913); joined Salada Tea Co. Ltd., Toronto, Ont. in 1938-43; joined present firm in 1946 as Account Extve.; served in 2nd World War with R.C.A.F. 1943-45; el. to Ont. Leg. for Hamilton W., Oct. 1971; apptd. to Cabinet Oct. 1972-75; United Church; Clubs: Hamilton; Rotary; Home: 66 Forsyth North, Hamilton, Ont. L8S 4E3; Office: 627 Main St. E., Hamilton, Ont. L8M 1S5

McNUTT, James Wesley, B.Sc.F.; lumber manufacturer; forester; b. Westmount, Que., 26 Feb. 1909; s. James Watson Kirby and Dora Gertrude (Agnew) M.; e. Rosly Public Sch., Westmount, Que.; Ste.-Anne de Bellevue, Macdonald High Sch., Grad. 1926; McGill Univ., Faculty of Arts, 1926-27; Faculty of Forestry, B.Sc.F. 1932; m. Edith Gibbs, d. Fred Milne, North Bay, Ont., 27 Oct. 1934; children: Mrs. (Shirley Edith) Priolo, Frederick James; CHAIRMAN OF THE BOARD, WM. MILNE & SONS LTD. (Estbd. 1871); Vice-Chrmn.,Algonquin Authority since 1975; Ind. Forestry Consultant for Candn. Internat. Dev. Agency since 1972; Anglo Canadian Pulp & Paper Mills, Limoilou, Que., 1932-36; engaged with Kimberly-Clark Co. and subsidiaries, 1936-46in forest operations in Can. & U.S. Pres., Ont. Prof. Foresters Assn., 1961-62; P. Pres. Candn. Lumbermen's Assn.; Ont. Forest Industries Assn.; Forest Products Accident Prevention Assn.; mem. Candn. Inst. of Forestry; Phi Kappa Pi; Freemason; United Church; recreations: sailing, flying, fishing, skiing, photography; Club: Engineers (Toronto); Home: Corbeil, Ont.; Office: 214 Ninth St., North Bay, Ont. P1B 8H2

McOUAT, John Frederick, B.A.Sc., P. Eng.; executive; b. Toronto, Ont., 4 May 1933; s. James Harold and Muriel Gertrude (Benn) McO.; e. Univ. of Toronto Schs. 1952; Univ. of Toronto, B.A.Sc. (Geol. Engn.) 1956; m. Vodrie Jo-Anne, d. late Charles Miller, 12 Dec. 1959: children: Leslie Jo-Anne, Lindsey Dianne, Morrie Cathryn; John Gavin; PRES., WATTS, GRIFFIS AND McOUAT LTD. since 1962; Vice-Pres., Watts, Griffis and McOuat, Inc.; with Technical Mine Consultants Ltd. then Oceanic Iron Ore of Canada Ltd. 1956-57; Riocanex Ltd. (Rio Tinto Mining Co. of Canada) 1958; British Ungava Explorations Ltd. as Dir. and Chief Engr.; Chief Engr., Murray Mining Corp. and Raglan Nickel Mines Ltd. 1959; one of inc. of present Co.; mem. Candn. Inst. Mining & Metall.; Australian Inst. Mining & Metall.; Assn. Prof. Engrs. Ont.; author of numerous articles publd. in leading prof. journs.; P. Conservative; Protestant; recreations: hockey, children, reading; Club: Granite; Home: 24 Danville

Drive, Willowdale, Ont. M2P 1J1; Office: 159 Bay St., Suite 911, Toronto, Ont. M5J 1J7

McPHAIL, Donald Murdo, M.A.; company president; b. Edmonton, Alta., 29 Feb. 1936; s. Lachlin and Irene (Winterly) M.; e. Univ. of Alberta, B.Sc. 1958: Univ. of Toronto, M.A. 1959; m. Diane, d. Leo Bourbonnais, 1966; children: Cameron Douglas, Andrew Fraiser, Paula Chantal, Donald Charles, Elissa Noreen: PRESIDENT, COMTECH GROUP INTERNATIONAL LTD. since 1969; Pres., Comtech Ontario, Comtech Group Ltd.; Comtech Ltée.; Comtech New England Inc.; Claremore Systems, Investments Ltd.; Dir., British International Finance; started with Shell Oil, Calgary, Exploration Prod. Div., 1960; in charge of Scient. Programming, Toronto, 1961; Mang. Consultant, Urwick, Currie & Partners, Toronto, 1962; apptd. Dir. Research Devel., 1963; joined present Co., Vice-Pres. (Ont.), 1965; mem. Candn. Assn. Data Processing Service Organs. (Dir.); Am. Assn. Data Processing Service Organs.; recreations: skiing, gardening; Home: 4 Kilchurn Castle Drive, Agincourt, Ont. M1T 2W2;

McPHAIL, Donald Sutherland, M.A.; diplomat; b. Halifax, N.S., 26 May 1931; s. Donald and late Ruby (Sutherland) McP.; e. Univ. of N.B., B.A. 1952, M.A. 1953; Univ. of the Netherlands, summer session 1952; London Sch. of Econ. 1953-54; m. Ruth Elizabeth, d. late Herbert Tracy, Sackville, N.B., 27 May 1953; children: Kim Tracy, Jocelyn Nan, Donald Alexander; Econ., DuPont Co. of Canada Ltd., 1955; joined Dept. of External Affairs 1956; Third Secy., Paris, 1957; Second Secy. 1959; Econ. Divs., Africa and Middle E., Ottawa, 1961; First Secy., Candn. Del. to 1964-65 GATT Negotiating Conf., Geneva; Counsellor, CPMUN, Geneva, 1966; Head, Comn. Policy Div. Econ. Div., 1967; Ambassador to Venezuela and to Dominican Republic, 1970; Dir. Gen. Bureau of Econ. and Sci. Affairs, Ottawa 1972; Asst. Depy Min., Dept. of Regional Econ. Expansion (Atlantic Region) Moncton 1973; Asst. Under Sec. of State for External Affairs, Ottawa 1976; Ambassador and Permanent Representative to the Office of the United Nations of Geneva, to Gatt and to the Committee on Disarmament, Geneva 1979; recreations: gardening, golf, bridge; Home: 6 East Adams, Ottawa, Ont. K2G 0H9; Office: Canadian Permanent, Mission to the U.N., 10A Ave. De Bude, Geneva 1202, Switerland

McPHEE, Albert Roy, D.C.M.; executive; b. New Glasgow, N.S., 8 Jan. 1919; s. Duncan Roy and Mary-Anne (Brimage) McP.; e. Pub. Schs., Windsor, N.S.; High Sch., New Liskeard, Ont.; m. Betty Doreen, d. Alexander Brereton, V.C., 6 May 1951; children: Gordon Ronald, Mary-Jane; PRESIDENT AND DIR., REGENT DRILLING LTD.; Pres. and Dir., Fleetway Trucking Ltd.; served in 2nd World War with Algonquin Regt. 1940-46; awarded D.C.M.; Past Pres., Candn. Assn. of Oilwell Drilling Contractors (1973); Freemason; United Church; recreations: golf; cross country skiing; jogging; Clubs: Edmonton Petroleum (Dir.); Edmonton Golf & Country; Home: Deepwood Acre, R.R. #5, Edmonton, Alta.; Office: 12912 — Yellowhead Trail, Edmonton, Alta. T5L 3C1

McPHERSON, Hugo, M.A., Ph.D., LL.D.; university professor; b. Sioux Lookout, Ont., 28 Aug. 1921; s. late Rev. Peter Gordon and Nettie Louella (Perrin) McP.; e. Pub. Schs. in Ont., Alta. and Sask.; Prov. Normal Sch., Edmonton, Dipl. with First Class Hons. 1939; Univ. of Man., B.A. 1949, LL.D. 1970; Univ. of W. Ont., M.A. (First Class Hons.) 1950; Univ. of Toronto, Ph.D. (First Class Hon.) 1956; m. Louise, d. late Philippe Guertin, Winnipeg, 12 June 1951; GRIERSON PROF. OF COMMUNICATIONS since 1977; Prof. of English, McGill Univ. since 1970; taught McGill Univ. 1952-53; moved to Univ. of Man. for 2 yrs., Univ. of B.C. for one yr. and Univ. of Toronto for 9 yrs.: became Commonwealth Fellow, Yale Univ. for 2 terms; accepted sr. appt. in Candn.

and Am. Studies, Univ. of W. Ont., 1966; Govt. Film Commr. and Chrmn. of Nat. Film Bd. of Can. 1967-70; served with Candn. Army attached to RCAF 1942-45; rec'd Centennial Medal 1967; mem. Bd. Govs., Nat. Arts Centre 1967-70; Candn. Film Devel. Corp. 1968-70; Chrmn., Art Comte. of Hart House, Univ. of Toronto, 1963-66; author "Hawthorne as Myth-Maker", 1969; other writings incl. many articles, book chapters and essays; rec'd 3 research awards from Can. Council; mem., Soc. for Art Publs. (Chrmn. 1969; Vice Chrmn. 1970); Assn. Candn. Univ. Teachers Eng. (Secy. 1957-58); Candn. Assn. Am. Studies; Humanities Assn. Can.; membre du conseil d'adm. Théâtre du nouveau monde; mem. Bd. Candn. Broadcasting League; recreations: film, theatre, ballet, music, swimming, walking; Home: 4300 de Maisonneuve W., Montreal, Que. H3Z 1K8

McPHERSON, Ian Edward, D.F.C., Q.C., B.A., LL.M.; b. Victoria, B.C., 8 June 1920; s. late Thomas and Maude (Hyatt) McP.; e. Victoria (B.C.) Coll. 1941; Univ. of Brit. Columbia, B.A. 1948, LL.B. 1949; Inst. Internat. Air Law, McGill Univ., LL.M. 1955; m. Mary Alexa, d. Gordon McLeod Pitts, 21 Feb. 1959; children: Mary Margot Ann, Ian Andrew, Thomas Alexander Gordon; VICE PRES., LAW, AIR CANADA 1979- ; read law with late Mr. Justice George Gregory; called to Bar of B.C. 1949, of Que. 1968; practised law in Victoria, B.C. 1949-51; Solr., Canadian National Railways, Montreal 1952; Gen. Atty., Air Canada 1961; Gen. Counsel Air Canada, 1966; served in 2nd World War, R.C.A.F. 1941-45; Pilot R.A.F. Bomber Command; awarded D.F.C.: R.C.A.F. Auxiliary 1952-60; mem. Law Soc. B.C.; Candn. Bar Assn.; Que. Bar Assn.; Assn. Candn. Gen. Counsel (Pres. 1979-80); Internat. Air Transport Assn. Legal Comte. (Past Chrmn.); Inst. Air and Space Law Assn. (Past Pres.); Can. Bar Assn. (Past Chrm., Air law Section); Air Transport Assn. Law Council; Protestant; recreations: golf, swimming, travel; Home: 609 Clarke Ave., Westmount, Que. H3Y 3E5; Office: Place Ville Marie, Montreal, Que. H3B 3P7

McPHERSON, J.L., C.A.; mining executive; e. C.A. 1950 (articled with David Cooper & Co. Winnipeg); SR. VICE PRES. AND CHIEF FINANCIAL OFFR., CRAIGMONT MINES LTD., PLACER DEVELOPMENT LTD., GIBRALTAR MINES LTD.; Dir. Gibraltar Mines Ltd.; Craigmont Mines Ltd.; Placer Exploration Ltd. (Australia); Placer CEGO Petroleum Ltd.; Equity Silver Mines Ltd.; joined Placer Development Ltd. 1957, Secy. 1961, Vice Pres. Finance & Adm. 1969-77; mem. Adv. Bd. Div. Finance Univ. of B.C.; Past Pres. and mem. Inst. C.A.'s B.C.; Candn. Inst. C.A.'s; Dir. Mining Assn. Can.; Club: Capilano Golf & Country; Home: 3809 Bayridge Ave., West Vancouver, B.C. V7V 3J3; Office: 1600 - 1055 Dunsmuir St., Vancouver, B.C. V7X 1P1.

McQUAID, Hon. Melvin J., B.A., LL.B.; retired judge; b. Souris, P.E.I., 6 Sept. 1911; s. John and Annie (Mullally) McQ.; e. Souris High Sch.; St. Dunstans Univ. B.A. 1934; St. Francis Xavier Univ. B.A. 1936; Dalhousie Univ. LL.B. 1939; m. Catherine E. d. Austine Handrahan, Tignish, P.E.I., 16 Sept. 1947; children: John, Mary-Jo, Peter; Justice, Supreme Court of P.E.I. 1976-81; called to Bar of P.E.I. 1940; cr. Q.C. 1953; Town Clk. Souris 1940-58; mem. Leg. Assembly P.E.I. 1959-62 holding portfolios Min. of Finance and Min. of Justice, Leader of Official Opposition 1973-76; mem. H. of C. for Cardigan 1965-72; mem. Bd. of Govs. Souris Hosp. (Secy. 1950-58); mem. Atlantic Devel. Bd. 1963-65; Pres. P.E.I. Cons. Assn. 1956-59; Past Pres. Eastern King's Bd. Trade; mem. Eastern King's Chamber Comm.; K. of C.; mem. Law Soc. P.E.I. (Past Pres.); Candn. Bar Assn.; R. Catholic; recreations: baseball, swimming; Home: Souris, P.E.I. C0A 2B0

McQUEEN, David Lisle, M.A., Ph.D.; educator; b. Saskatoon, Sask. 25 Dec. 1926; s. late Robert and Monica (Lisle) McQ.; e. Univ. of Man. B.Com. 1947; Queen's Univ. M.A. (Econ.) 1948; London Sch. of Econ. Ph.D. (Econ.)

1952 (IODE Overseas Scholarship 1948-50); m. Janet Mary (divorced), d. late Maj. Arthur Gorham, 6 Sept. 1952; two s., Robert John, Martin Alexander; m. 2ndly Nancy Ker, d. Bruce and Molly Lawrence, 15 Dec. 1978; PRINCIPAL, GLENDON COLL., YORK UNIV. since 1975; Asst. en anglais, Coll. St-Cricq, Pau, Basses-Pyrénées, France 1950-51; Econ. and subsequently Research Offr., Asst. Chief, Research Dept. Bank of Can. 1952-65; Econ. subsequently Dir., Vice Chrmn. Econ. Council Can. 1965-69; Chrmn. Dept. Econ. present Coll. 1969; Senate rep. Bd. Govs. York Univ. 1973-75; Sch. Trustee Gloucester Twp. 1959-61; rec'd. Univ of Man. Alumni Assn. Jubilee Award 1947; co-author "Housing and Social Capital", 1956; author various book chapters, articles, conf. papers; contrib. Fed. Govt. econ. publs.; mem. Candn. Econ. Assn.; Soc. Canadienne de Science Economique; Amer. Econ. Assn.; Consumers' Assn. Can.; Ont. Hist. Assn.; recreations: photography, hiking, swimming, Office: 2275 Bayview Ave., Toronto, Ont. M4N 3M6

McRAE, Donald Lane, M.D.; physician; radiologist; b. Toronto, Ont., 23 July 1912; s. Walter James and Genevieve May (Lane) M.; e. Oakwood Coll. Inst., Toronto, Ont., 1925-29; St. Marys (Ont.) Coll. Inst.; Univ. of W. Ont., M.D. 1938; m. 1stly Beatrice Anne Graham (d.), 2ndly Patricia M. J. Murray; has two d., Mary Anna, Elizabeth Adelaide; Lectr. in Anatomy, Prof. Emeritus (Radiology), Univ. of Toronto; previously Prof. of Radiology, Univ. of Toronto and Radiologist-in-Chief, Sunnybrook Hospital, Toronto; previously Radiologist-in-Chief, Montreal Neurol. Institute and Assoc. Prof. of Neuroradiology, McGill Univ.; served in 2nd World War as Surg. Lieut. Commandr., R.C.N.V.R., 1941-45; F.R.C.P. (Can.); Fellow, Am. Coll. of Radiology; Pres., Internat. Symposium Neuroradiologicum 1957; Hon. mem., Radiological Soc. of North Amer.; mem., Candn. Med. Assn.; Candn. Assn. of Radiol. (Past Pres.); Am. Soc. of Neuroradiology (Past Pres.); Protestant; recreations: fishing, hunting; Address: 45 Wynford Hgts. Cres., Don Mills, Ont. M3C 1L3

McRAE, Robert Forbes, M.A., Ph.D.; university professor (emeritus); b. Winnipeg, Man., 27 June 1914; s. Duncan and Susan Helena (Rodgers) M.; e. Univ. of Toronto, B.A. 1936, M.A. 1938; Johns Hopkins Univ., Ph.D. 1946; m. Nora Frances. d. V. A. Beacock, Toronto, Ont., 1 Sept. 1950; children: Kiloran, Alison, Ellen; Prof. of Philos., Univ. of Toronto, 1960-79 (retired); Instr., Lectr., Asst. Prof., Assoc. Prof., there, 1945-1960: Nuffield Fellow, 1951-52; served in 2nd World War; Ordinary Seaman and Lieut. in R.C.N.V.R. 1940-45 on loan to Royal Navy; taken prisoner at Dieppe, 1942: Commndg. Offr., U.N.T.D., Univ. of Toronto, 1947-54, rank Lieut-Commdr.; author: "The Problem of the Unity of the Sciences: Bacon to Kant", 1961; "Leibniz: Perception, Apperception, and Thought", 1976; Home: 29 Dunbar Rd., Toronto, Ont. M4W 2X5

McROBIE, Commander Donald Robertson, O.B.E., B.Com.; advertising executive; b. Montreal, Que., 6 May 1911; s. late Col. Frederick MacKenzie and Susan Elizabeth (Robertson) M.; e. Westmount Que., Sch.; Lower Canada Coll., Montreal, Que.; McGill Univ., B.Com. 1934; m. Jean Audrey, d. late H. L. Doble, 30 Dec. 1936; children: Blair, Fred, Ann, David; CHAIRMAN AND DIR., COCKFIELD, BROWN & CO. LTD., since 1972; Gov. McGill Univ.; mem. of Corp., Lower Canada Coll.; early business training with Canada Steamship Lines in Montreal, Toronto, Detroit and Cleveland; joined present firm in 1934; el. a Dir., 1947; Extve. Vice-Pres. and Mgr. of Montreal Office, 1956; Pres. and Dir. 1958; served in 2nd World War; R.C.N.(R) 1940-45; O.B.E.; mem. Adv. Bd. Children's Hospital; Pres. (1961-62) Candn. Assn. of Adv. Agencies; Dir. and Past Pres., Inst. of Candn. Adv.; Zeta Psi; Protestant; recreations: tennis, skiing; Clubs: University; Hillside Tennis; Montreal Indoor Tennis;

Mount Bruno Golf: Canadian: Home: 3228 The Boulevard, Westmount, Que. H3Y 1S3; Office: Canada Cement Bldg., Montreal, Que.

McRUER, Hon. James Chalmers, O.C. (1968), LL.D., D.C.L.; b. Oxford Co., Ont., 23 Aug. 1890: s. John and Mary (Chalmers) M.; e. Univ. of Toronto; Osgoode Hall; LL.D., Laval Univ., 1947, Toronto 1964, Osgoode 1965, Trent 1968, Queen's 1971; D.C.L. Windsor 1970; m. the late Mary, d. Dr. James Dow of Toronto, Ont., Sept. 1919; children: Mrs. J. R. Gaby, Mrs. Katherine McIntyre, Lt. Commdr. John D.; m. 2ndly, Robena Mary Dow, 1969; read law with Proudfoot, Duncan, Grant & Skeans: called to the Bar of Ont. 1914, B.C. 1926, Alberta 1942; cr. K.C. 1929; Asst. Crown Atty., City of Toronto and Co. of York, 1921-25; resumed practice 1925; Lect. Law Sch., Osgoode Hall, 1930-35; mem., Roy. Comn., investigating the Penal System of Can.; Chrmn. of Royal Comn. to report on insanity as a defence to crime, and Chrmn. of Royal Comn. to report on amendments to the law respecting sexual offenders, 1955; apptd. a Royal Commr. on Inquiry into Civil Rights, Ont. 1964; Chairman of Ontario Law Reform Comn. 1964-66. Vice Chairman 1967-77; el. Bencher, Law Society of Upper Canada, 1936; apptd. to the Court of Appeal of Ontario, 1944; Chief Justice of the High Court of Justice for Ontario, 1945 till resignation 1 July 1964; served in 1st World War with C.F.A. and Anti-Aircraft Batty. with rank of Lieut.; wounded; Pres., Candn. Bar Assn. 1946-47; Hon. mem., Am. Bar Assn.; Hon. Consul for Netherlands 1941-44; Pres. Candn. Save the Children Fund 1946-57; Hon. Pres. Internat. Union Child Welfare; Chrmn. Candn. Corrections Assn. 1956-57; author of "The Evolution of the Judicial Process"; "The Trial of Jesus"; rec'd. John Howard Soc. Medal 1963; Offic., Order of Can. 1968; Civic Award of Merit, Corp. City of Toronto 1973; United Ch.; Home: 1005-9 Deer Park Crescent, Toronto, Ont. M4V 2C4

McTAGGART, Douglas G., B.A., L.I.M.I., C.L.U.; b. Toronto, Ont., 30 Sept. 1931; s. Donald H., Q.C. and Hazel G. (Defoe) McT.; e. Rawlinson Pub. Sch. and Forest Hill Coll. Inst., Toronto, 1950; Univ. of Toronto, Victoria Coll., B.A. 1954; Inst. of Ins. Marketing, Business Sch. of Adm., Southern Methodist Univ., Dallas, 1956; m. Audry, d. Charles Alfred John Spence-Jones, 4 June 1955; children: Pamela, Kimberly, Douglas Gregory; PRESIDENT AND DIR., PLANNED INSURANCE PORTFOLIOS CO. LTD., since 1969; Dir., Estate and Corporate Funding Programmes Co. Ltd.; Sales Agt., Canada Life Assurance Co., 1956; Mgr., Field Training Research, 1957-58; Agency Mgr., Toronto, 1958-63; conducted own Agency for Crown Life Insurance Co., Toronto, 1963-69; Past Chrmn., Ins. Sec.; Un. Appeal; fellow, Royal Ont. Museum; mem., Art Gallery of Ont.; Candn. Tax Foundation; mem., Edinburgh Language Foundation; Roy.Candn. Ins.; Life Ins. Mang. Assn.; Life Underwriters Assn. (Past Dir. and Offr.); Bd. Trade Metrop. Toronto; Million Dollar Round Table; Freemason; United Church; recreations: golf, hunting, boating, skiing, curling: Club: Granite; Empire; Boca Raton (Florida); Home: 34 York Valley Cres., Willowdale, Ont. M2P 1A7, Burnt Island Bay, Lake of Bays, Ont.and 1091 Bel Lido Dr., Highland Beach Office: 797 Don Mills Rd., Don Mills, Ont. M3C 1V2

McTAGGART-COWAN, Patrick Duncan, O.C., M.B.E., LL.D., D.Sc., F.R.Met.S.; b. Edinburgh, Scotland 31 May 1912; s. G. and Laura Alice (MacKenzie) M-C; e. Univ. of B.C. (Grad. with 1st Class Hons. in Math. and Physics) 1929-33. D.Sc. 1961: LL.D. St. Francis-Xavier 1970; Simon Fraser 1972; Lakehead 1974; D.Sc. McGill 1974; Univ. of N.B. 1976; Univ. of Guelph, 1981; Corpus Christi, Oxford (B.C. Rhodes Schol.), Grad. with Hons. deg. in Natural Sciences; Atlantic Training School, British Meteorol. Office, Croydon, Eng.; m. Margaret Lawson, d. late J. T. E. Palmer, 17 Oct. 1939; children: Gillian Hope, James Duncan; Offr. in charge, Meteorol. Office at Botwood and

then Gander, Nfld., 1937-42; Chief Meteorol. Offr., R.A.F. Ferry Command, 1942-45 (mem. of Jt. Control Bd. for delivery of aircraft across the N. Atlantic 1943-45); loaned to the Candn. Preparatory Comte. for the Provisional I.C.A.O. as Tech. Secy., 1945; awarded M.B.E. 1944; Coronation Medal 1953; Patterson Medal 1965; Centennial Medal 1967; Officer of Order of Can. 1979; Asst. Dir., Meteorol. Div., Dept. of Transport, 1946-57; Assoc. Dir., 1958-59: Dir., 1959-64: Pres., Simon Fraser Univ. 1963-68; Head Task Force, Operation Oil 1970-73; Gov. Arctic Inst. of N. Am. 1963-65 and 1968-74; Extve. Dir., Science Council of Can. 1968-75; non-viable farmer and consult. since retirement; mem., Bd. of Dirs., John Wiley and Sons, Can. Ltd.; rec'd. Robert M. Losey Award, 1959; Past Pres., Candn. Br., Royal Meteorol. Society; Fellow, American Meteorol. Soc. 1967, Hon. Life mem. 1978, Charles Franklin Brooks Award 1965, Cleveland Abbe Award 1976; Fellow, Am. Geophys. Union; mem., Candn. Assn. of Physicists (Charter mem.); Oxford Soc. (Life); Am. Assn. Advanc. Science; Fellow Arctic Inst. N. Am.; Dir., Bracebridge Agric. Soc., 1979- ; Anglican; recreations: skiing, golf, gardening; Club: Raleigh; Home: High Falls Rd., R.R. 2, Bracebridge, Ont. P0B 1C0

McVITTY, E. Hugh, Q.C., B.A.; insurance extve.; b. Toronto, Ont., 6 July 1920; s. Charles E. & Maud (Houghton) McV.; e. N. Toronto Coll. Inst., 1938; Univ. of Toronto, Trinity Coll., B.A. 1942; Osgoode Hall Law Sch.; 1949; m. Diana M., d. late F. R. B. DeGuerre, 12 Sept. 1952; children: Brian, Patricia, Susan, Catherine; LEGAL VICE-PRES. AND SECY, MANUFACTURERS LIFE INSURANCE CO. since 1972; read law with R. N. Starr, Q.C.; called to Bar of.Ont. 1949; joined Law Dept. of present Co. 1949,. Assoc. Legal Offr. 1957, Gen. Counsel 1966, Legal Vice-Pres 1970; served with RAF and RCAF Overseas 1942-45; Vice Pres. & Dir., Ont. Safety League; Dir., Can. Special Olympics; Arbitrators Inst. of Can.; mem. Candn. Bar Assn.; Assn. Life Ins. Counsel; Internat. Claim Assn. (Past Pres.); Internat. Assn. Ins. Law; Toronto Bd. Trade; P. Conservative; Anglican; recreations: sailing, skiing, golf; Club: Toronto Lawyers; Home: 18 Foursome Cres., Willowdale, Ont.M2P 1W2; Office: 200 Bloor St. E., Toronto, Ont. M4W 1E4

McWHINNEY, Edward, Q.C., LL.M., Sc.Jur.D.; professor; lecturer; writer; b. Sydney, Australia, 19 May 1924; s. Matthew Andrew and Evelyn Annie (Watson) M.; e. Yale Univ., LL.M. 1951, Sc.Jur.D. 1953; Acad. de Droit Internat., The Hague, Dipl. 1951: m. Emily Ingalore, d. late Hugo Sabatzky, Berlin, Germany, 27 June 1951; PROF. OF INTERNAT. LAW AND JURIS., SIMON FRASER UNIV. since 1974, also Chrmn. Dept. of Govt. there; Bursar, Carnegie Corp.; Fellow, Rockefeller Foundation (Div. of Social Sciences); mem., Prime Min. of Ont.'s Adv. Comte. on Confederation 1965-71; Lecturer in Constitutional Law, Yale University Law Sch., 1951-53; Asst. Prof. of Pol. Science, Yale Grad. Sch., 1953-55; Fellow of Silliman Coll., Yale Univ., 1953-55: Prof. of Internat. and Comparative Law, Univ. of Toronto, 1955-66; Prof. of Law and Dir., Inst. of Air and Space Law, McGill Univ. 1966-71; Prof. of Law and Dir. Internat. and Comparative Legal Studies, Univ. of Indiana 1971-74; Legal Consultant, United Nations, 1953-54; Visiting Prof., New York Univ., 1954, Ecole Libre des Hautes Études, 1952, Inst. Univ. du Luxembourg 1959-60, 1972, 74, 76, Max Planck-Inst. and Univ. of Heidelberg, 1960-61; Consultant (Internat. Law), U.S. Navy, 1961-68; Royal Commr., Comn. of Enquiry on the French Language and Language Rights in Quebec 1968-72; Special Counsel, Government of Quebec 1969-70, 1974-75; served in 2nd World War with Air Force, enlisting in 1943 as Flying Trainee; service from 1943-45; discharged with rank of Flying Offr.; Publications: "Judicial Review", 1956 (2nd ed. 1960, 3rd ed. 1965, 4th ed. 1969); "Canadian Jurisprudence. The Civil Law and Common Law in Canada", 1958; "Föderalismus und Bundesverfassungsrecht", 1961: "Constitutionalism in Germany", 1962; "Comparative Federalism, States'

Rights and National Power", 1962, 2nd ed. 1965; "Peaceful Co-existence and Soviet-Western International Law", 1964; "Law, Foreign Policy, and the East-West détente", 1964; "Federal Constitution-Making for a Multi-National World", 1966; "International Law and World Revolution", 1967; "Conflit idéologique et ordre public mondial", 1970; "The Freedom of the Air" (with M.A. Bradley), 1968: "New Frontiers in Space Law" (with M. A. Bradley) 1969: "The International Law of Communications", 1970; "Aerial Piracy and International Law", 1971; "Federalism and Supreme Courts and the Integration of Legal Systems" (with Pierre Pescatore) 1973; "The Illegal Diversion of Aircraft and Internat. Law" 1975; "The International Law of Détente" 1978; "The World Court and the Contemporary International Law-Making Process" 1979; "Quebec and the Constitution" 1979; "Municipal Government in a new Canadian Federal System", 1980; "Conflict and Compromise, International Law and World Order in a Revolutionary Age" 1981; "Constitution Making Principles, Power, Practice" 1981; "Mécanismes pour une nouvelle Constitution" (with E. Orban et al.) 1981; Special Commr. of Inquiry, Leg. of B.C. 1974-75; Chrmn., Research Task Force on Constitution, Fed. of Cdn. Municipalities since 1977; Chief Adv., Pépin-Robarts Comm. 1978; Commr. of Enquiry, Gov't. Structure in City of Vancouver 1979; Constitutional Advisor, Indian Assn. (Treaty Indians) of Alta., 1980; Special Advisor to Cdn. Delegation, 36th Annual Session, United Nations Gen. Assembly, 1981; articles, essays, etc., in Am., German, Spanish, French, etc., journs. and learned soc. pubs.; contrib. to "Encyclo. Britannica"; "International Encyclopaedia of the Social Sciences"; cr. Q.C. 1967; Visiting Prof., Univ. Laval, 1967; Univ. de Paris, 1968; Univ. da Madrid. 1968; Univ. d'Aix-Marseilles, 1969; Acad. Internat. Law, The Hague 1973; Aristotelian Univ. Thessaloniki 1974 & 78; Université de Nice 1976-77; Jaqeellonean University of Cracow 1976; el. an Associate of Institut de Droit International (1st lawyer from Canada), September 1967; elected Membre titulaire (Inst. de Droit Internat.) 1975; Dir., Instituto Interamericano de Estudios Juridicos Internacionales; President, Toronto and Montreal Brs., Internat. Law Assn. (Chrmn. Extve. Comte. Candn. Br. 1972-75); Yale Law School Association Canada; mem., Nat. Research Comte., Candn. Inst. Internat. Affairs: Un. Nations Assn., Toronto Br. (Extve.); Candn. Bar Assn. (former mem. Council, Ont. Sec.); Fellow Am. Soc. of Internat. Law. (mem. Council); recreations: tennis, swimming, walking, golf; Home: 1949 Beach Ave., Vancouver V6G 1Z2; Office: Burnaby, B.C.

McWHIRTER, George, M.A.; author; educator; b. Belfast, N. Ireland, 26 Sept. 1939; s. James and Margaret (McConnell) McW.; e. Grosvenor High Sch., Belfast; Queen's Univ. Belfast, B.A. Dipl. in Educ.; Univ. of B.C., M.A.; m. Angela Mairead, d. late William Coid, 1963; children: James Liam Yates, Grania Gema Louise; PROF., CREATIVE WRITING DEPT., UNIV. OF B.C.; Eng. Teacher, Kilkeel Secondary Sch. and Bangor Grammar Sch., N. Ireland; Escuella de Idiomas, Univ. of Barcelona; Alberni Dist. Secondary Sch., Vancouver Island, B.C.; author, "Catalan Poems" (awarded Commonwealth Inst. and Nat. Book League Jt. 1st Prize); "Bodyworks" (short stories), 1974; "Columbuscade" (poetry), 1974; "Queen of the Sea" (poetry), 1976; "Twenty-five" (poetry), 1978; "Ties" (pamphlet, League of Candn. Poets), 1980; "The Island Man" (poetry), 1981; "God's Eye" 1981; "Coming to Grips With Lucy" (Stones); anthologized in "Penguin Book of Canadian Verse" and "Stories of Pacific and Arctic Canada"; Assoc. Ed., "Contemporary Poetry of British Columbia", 1970; Ed., "Words from Inside" (Prison Arts Mag.), 1974, 75; Adv. Ed., "Prism International", since 1978); recreations: swimming, waterpolo, sailing; Home: 4637 West 13th Ave., Vancouver, B.C. V6R 2V6

MEAGHER, Blanche Margaret, O.C. (1974), M.A.; diplomat (ret.) b. Halifax, N.S., 27 Jan. 1911; d. John Nicholas and Blanche (Seals) M.; e. St. Patrick's High Sch., and

Mount St. Vincent Coll., Halifax, N.S.; Dalhousie Univ., B.A. 1932, M.A. 1935; Post-grad. studies in Political Science, 1937-38; D.C.L. (H.c.) Dalhousie Univ., 1970; St. Francis Xavier 1974; St. Mary's Univ. 1975; Governor for Can., Bd. Govs., Internat. Atomic Energy Agency, 1962 (el. Chairman of Policy-making Board 1964); Junior High Sch. Teacher, Halifax, N.S., 1932-42; joined Dept. of External Affairs, 1942; Third Secy., Candn. Embassy, Mexico, 1945-47 and Second Secy. there 1947-49; First Secy., Canada House, London, 1953-55, and Counsellor there, 1955-56: Chargé d'Affaires, Israel, 1957 and Ambassador there, 1958-61; High Commr. to Cyprus, 1961, concurrently with Israel assignments; Ambassador to Austria, 1962-66: subsequently High Commr. to Kenya and Uganda; Ambassador to Sweden 1969-73; Diplomat in Residence, Dalhousie Univ., 1973-74; mem Bd. of Trustees, Nat. Museums of Can. 1975-78; Bd. of Govs., Atlantic Sch. of Theology; Roman Catholic.; Address: 6899 Armview Ave., Halifax, N.S.

MEARNS, William Clark, B.A.; company president; b. Victoria, B.C., 19 Aug. 1909; s. William Hunter and Mildred (Baker) M.; e. Stanford Univ., B.A. (Elect. Engn.) 1932; Univ. of Washington, post-graduate work in Engn. and Business Adm., 1933; Harvard Business Sch., Advanced Management Program, 1954; m. Loula Cary, d. D. O. Cameron, 27 Jan. 1940; children: Craig Cameron, Dale Donnelly, Marily Ann, Lindsay J.; Pres., Rockcliffe Estates Ltd.; Dir., Bank of B.C.; former Chrmn. B.C. Harbours Bd.; began as Meterman, B.C. Electric Co. Ltd., 1934; Sales Engr., 1946; Operations Mgr., 1948; Acting Dir. of Research, Vancouver, 1955; special assignments, Western Devel. and Power Ltd., Vancouver, 1957; Vice-Pres., V.I. Div., B.C. Electric Vice-Pres. Devel., 1961-62; Extve. Dir., B.C. Hydro and Power Authority 1962-69; mem. of Adv. Bd., Y.M. and Y.W.C.A., Victoria; Hon. Gov., Candn. Assn. for Retarded Children; Dir. of Armed Services Centre, Victoria; Past Pres., B.C. Natural Resources Conf.; Past Vice-Pres. and Dir., Victoria Rotary Club; Past Dir., Queen Alexandra Solarium, Community Chest YMCA, Victoria; mem. Assn. of Prof. Engrs. B.C.; Inst. Elect. & Electronics Engrs.; Victoria Electric Club (Past Pres.); Pacific Northwest Trade Assn. (Past Vice-Pres. and Dir.); mem., Vancouver Bd. of Trade; Victoria Chamber of Commerce (Past Vice-Pres. and Dir.); Protestant; recreation: golf; Clubs: Union; Victoria Golf; Royal Colwood Golf & Country; Capilano Golf & Country; Home: 303 - 1211 Beach Dr., Victoria, B.C.; Office: 1239 Beach Dr., Victoria, B.C.

MEDJUCK, Ralph Marven, LL.B.; barrister; realtor; b. Halifax, N.S., 26 Sept. 1932; s. Irving and Blanche (Pascal) M.; e. Pub. Schs., Halifax, N.S.; Dalhousie Univ., LL.B. 1954; m. Shirlee Arron, 4 Jan. 1955; one s. Brian; three d. Pamela, Lynda, Beth; PRES., THE CENTENNIAL GROUP OF COMPANIES LTD.; C.E.O., Scotia Resources Ltd.; Scotia Liquicoal Ltd.; Pres., Commercial Developments (Maritimes) Ltd.; founding Gov., Candn. Internat. Devel. Research Centre; Dir., Central Co.; Dir., Oland's Breweries (1971) Ltd.; read law with G. B. Robertson, Q.C.; called to Bar of N.S., Nov. 1954; since 1959 has been responsible for major real estate devels. in Atlantic Provs.; Dir., Boys' Club Can.; Gen. Campaign Chrmn., Un. Appeal 1970; mem. Council, Bd. Trade; Vice-Chrmn., Zionist Organ. of Can. Charitable Fund Inc.; Regional Chrmn., Candn. Jewish Congress; Tau Epsilon Phi; Clubs: Royal Nova Scotia Yacht Squadron; The Halifax; Saraguay; Home: 5956 Emscote Dr., Halifax, N.S. B3H 1B3; Office: One Sackville Place, Halifax, N.S. B3J 2X1

MEDLAND, Charles Edward, B.A.; investment dealer; b. Toronto, Ont., 6 July 1928; s. Robert Charles and Winnifred (Parker) M.; e. St. Andrew's Coll., Aurora, Ont.; Univ. of Toronto, B.A. 1950; m. Julia Winsor Eby, 1 Feb. 1973; two d. Virginia, Zoe; two step s. Brian, Stephen; CHAIRMAN, PRESIDENT & CHIEF EXTVE. OFFR.,

WOOD GUNDY LTD. since 1978; Chrmn., Clover Meadow Creamery Ltd.; Dir., Irwin Toy Ltd.; Internat. Thomson Organisation Ltd.; The Seagram Co. Ltd.; Interprovincial Pipe Line Ltd.; Abitibi-Price Inc.; mem., B.C.N.I.; with Wood Gundy Ltd. since grad. 1950; el. a Dir. 1966; apptd. Vice-Pres. 1968; mem. Bd. Govs., Wellesley Hospital; Donwood Inst.; Alpha Delta Phi; Anglican; recreations: golf, tennis, skiing, bridge; Clubs: Toronto Golf; The Toronto; Badminton & Racquet; Craigleith Ski; Rosedale Golf; Mount Royal; York; Home: #1 Doncliffe Place, Toronto, Ont.; Office: Royal Trust Tower, Toronto-Dominion Centre, Toronto, Ont.

MEDLAND, John Aubrey, B.Com., C.A.; company president; b. Toronto, Ont., 17 July 1910; s. John and Mabel Millinet (Van Horne) M.; e. Howard Park Pub. Sch. and Univ. of Toronto Schs., Toronto, Ont.; Univ. of Toronto, B.Com., 1933; Cambridge Univ., Eng. (Econ.) 1933-34; C.A. 1937; m. Helen Marie d. Howard E. Smart, Los Angeles, Cal., Sept. 1936; has four children; PRESIDENT, AUBREY MEDLAND INVESTMENTS LTD; Vice-Pres. and Dir., Fidelity Insurance Co. of Canada; Dir., Paul Pogue Co's. Ltd.; CounselorTust Co. Ltd.; with Price, Waterhouse and Co. (Chartered Accountants), 1934-37, when he joined Culver House Canning Ltd., Pres. 1945-77; Candn. Food Processors Assn.; Inst. of Chart. Accts. of Ont.; Phi Delta Theta; United Church; recreations: golf, curling; Clubs: Granite; National; Rotary; Strollers; Rosedale Golf; Home: 12 Old Forest Hill Road, Toronto, Ontario M5P 2P7; Office: 141 Adelaide St. W., Toronto, Ont. M5H 3B8

MEECH, Richard C., Q.C., B.A., LL.M.; b. Portsmouth, Hampshire, Eng., 16 Sept. 1921; s. Richard George and Elizabeth (Campbell) M.; e. Ridley Coll., St. Catharine's, Ont.; Univ. of Toronto, B.A. 1946; Osgoode Hall Law Sch., Toronto, Ont.; Harvard Law Sch., LL.M. 1951; m. Carol, d. late Charles Crockett, 6 Oct. 1951; children: Richard George, Peter Campbell, Susan Crockett, Sarah Elizabeth, Nancy Bingham; PARTNER, BORDEN & ELLIOT since 1957; Dir., Vice-Pres & Secretary, Textron Can. Ltd.; Dir. & Vice Chrmn., Howden Group Canada Ltd.; Brown Bover; Howden Inc.; Dir. and mem. Extve. Comte.; Great Lake Forest Products Ltd.; Slater Steel Industries Ltd.; Hon. Consul of Thailand at Toronto 1967; Director, R. C. Cola Canada Ltd.; Barclays Canada Ltd.; Budd Canada Inc.; Howden Group Ltd.; Howden Group America Inc.; Personal Insurance Co. of Canada; Great Lakes Forest Products Ltd.; Secy., Candn. Securities Inst.; Nat. Contingency Fund; Dir. and Secy., Canabam Ltd.; Vice Chrmn., Business Section, Internat'l Bar Assoc.; Chrmn. Bd. of Trustees, Havergal Coll. Fdn. (1974-74); President, Harvard Law School Association of Ontario 1971-75; Trustee, Sunnybrook Medical Centre, Toronto, Ontario; Cadn. Hemophilia Soc.; Queen's Univ.; joined Borden, Elliot, Kelley, Palmer & Sankey (predecessor firm), 1951; read law with Daly, Thistle, Judson & McTaggart, Toronto, Ont.; called to Bar of Ont., 1950; cr. Q.C. 1960; served as Pilot during 2nd World War with R.C.A.F., 1942-46; discharged with rank of Flying Offr.; mem. Adv. Council, Ridley Coll., (gov. 1971-77); Havergal Coll; Gov. and Nat. Chrmn., Queen's Univ. Parents' Assoc.; mem. Advisory Bd., Salvation Army; mem., Candn. Bar Assn.; Can. Tax Foundation; Co. York Law Assn.; Kappa Alpha; Anglican; recreations: fishing, golf, skiing, tennis; Clubs: Badminton & Racquet; National (Pres.); York; Toronto Golf; Canadian; (Pres. 1974-75); Glenmajor Angling; Harvard (N.Y.); Coral Beach & Tennis (Bermuda); Garden of the Gods (Colo.); Home: 40 Stratheden Road, Toronto, Ont. M4N 1E4; Office: 250 University Ave., Toronto, Ont. M5H 3E5

MEEN, Arthur K., Q.C., P.Eng.; b. Toronto, Ont., 17 Mar. 1924; s. Benjamin and Mary Gertrude (Tidy) M.; e. Univ. of Toronto, Faculty of Applied Science & Engn., grad. 1946; Osgoode Hall Law Sch., grad. 1949; m. Shirley Anne, d. Dr. Leslie Code, 2 June 1951; three d., Marilyn, Elizabeth, Jennifer; LAWYER, FRASER, MEEN AND STRATTON since 1977; cr. Q.C. 1965; with Legal Dept., British American Oil Co. Ltd. 1949-55; private law practice 1955-63; Partner, Fraser & Meen, 1964-74; served with UNTD 1943-46; Hydro Commr. N. York 1961-69 (Chrmn. 1962, 1964, 1966 and 1967); el. MPP for York E. prov. g.e. 1967; re-el. 1971 and 1975; Parlty. Asst. to Treas. of Ont. 1972-74; Min. of Revenue, Ont. 1974-77; mem. Assn. Prof. Engrs. Ont.; Law Soc. Upper Can.; P. Conservative; Anglican; recreations: boating, fishing; Clubs: Albany; Granite; Home: 95 Lord Seaton Rd., Willowdale, Ont. M2P 1K7; Office: Suite 1450, 25 King St. W., Toronto, Ont.

MEEROVITCH, Eugene, B.Sc., M.Sc., Ph.D.; university professor; biologist; b. Vladivostok, Russia 11 July 1919; came to Can. 1953; s. late Boris and late Zoreva M.; e. St. John's Univ., Shanghai, China, B.Sc. 1947; McGill Univ. M.Sc. 1955; Ph.D. 1957; m. d. late Francisco Pedroso 16 May 1961; children: Karen Ray, Sandra Fay; PROF. AND DIRECTOR OF INSTITUTE OF PARASITOLOGY, MCGILL UNIV. since 1978; joined McGill Univ. as Asst. Prof. of Parasitology 1961; Assoc. Prof. 1965; Prof. 1971; author of chapts. in several books on technical subj. and of about 100 scientific papers; held and holding positions on exctve. boards of prof. societies; Jewish; Home: 5587 Ave. Côte St. Luc, Montreal, Que. H4V 2L8; Office: Macdonald Campus, Ste. Anne de Bellevue, Que. H9X 1C0.

MEGARRY, A. Roy; executive; b. Belfast, N. Ireland 10 Feb. 1937; s. Andrew Blain and Barbara (Bennett) M.; e. Annadale Grammar Sch. N. Ireland; R.I.A. degree; Princeton Univ. Mang. Devel. Course; m. Barbara Todd Bird d. Charles C. Bird, 31 May 1959; children: Andrew Roy, Kevin Charles, Lianne Jean; PUBLISHER AND CHIEF EXTVE. OFICER, THE GLOBE AND MAIL since 1978; Controller, Honeywell Controls, Toronto 1957-64; Daystrom (Heathkit) Ltd. Toronto 1964-66; Sr. Consultant Urwick Currie & Partners Ltd. Toronto 1966-69; Vice Pres. Finance International Syscoms Ltd. Toronto 1969-71; Vice Pres., Corp. Development, Torstar 1974-78; R. Catholic; recreations: sailing, skiing, tennis; Club: National; Granite; Home: 28 Flaremore Cres., Willowdale, Ont. M2K 1V1; Office: 444 Front St. W., Toronto, Ont. M5V 2S9

MEHLENBACHER, Lawson Bruce; b. Cayuga, Ont., m. Orpha McDonald, Cayuga, Ont.; one s.; two d.; PRESIDENT, L. B. MEHLENBACHER & SON LTD. (seeds); 3rd generation Ont. farmer, seedsman, cattleman and owner of natural gas wells; Past Pres., Candn. Seed Trade Assn.; Address: R.R. 3, Cayuga, Ontario N0A 1E0

MEIGHEN, Col. Maxwell Charles Gordon, O.B.E., B.A.Sc.; company executive; b. Portage la Prairie, Man., 5 June 1908; s. late Rt. Hon. Arthur, P.C., and Jessie Isobel (Cox) M.; e. Ottawa Lisgar Collegiate; Roy. Mil. Coll.; Univ. of Toronto, B.A.Sc.; m. Catherine Jane, d. late A. R. McWhinnie, Hamilton, Ont., 15 Sept. 1934; CHAIRMAN AND DIR., CANADIAN GENERAL INVESTMENTS LTD.; Vice-Pres. and Dir., The Canada Trust Co.; Canada Trustco Mortgage Co.; Metrop. Toronto Adv. Bd., Salvation Army; mem., Bd. of Mang., Grace Hosp.; engaged in various engn. projects until he joined present group of Co's., 1939; served in World War, 1939-45; 2nd Candn. Corps Hdqrs. as Depy. Dir. of Mech. Engn. (Col.), 1943-45; Delta Upsilon; Conservative; United Church; Club: Toronto; Home: 102 Binscarth Rd., Toronto, Ont. M4W 1Y4; Office: 110 Yonge St., Suite 1702, Toronto, Ont. M5C 1T4

MEINCKE, Peter Paul Max, B.Sc., M.A., Ph.D.; educator; b. Winnipeg, Man. 21 Jan. 1936; s. Paul Henry and Marie (Winther) M.; e. Royal Mil. Coll. 1958 (Sword of Honour); Queen's Univ. B.Sc. 1959; Univ. of Toronto M.A. 1960; Ph.D. 1963; m. Donna Pauline d. Albert Mallinson, Brampton, Ont. 28 June 1958; children: Thomas, Carolyn; PRESIDENT, UNIV. OF P.E.I. since 1978; RCAF Offr. teaching at Royal Mil. Coll. 1962-65; mem. Tech. Staff Bell Telephone Labs. Murray Hill, N.J. 1965-67; Asst. Prof. Erindale Coll. Univ. of Toronto 1967, Assoc. Prof. 1969, Assoc. Dean of Coll. 1970-72, Vice Provost of Univ. 1972-76; Prof. of Physics, 1977; Trustee, Educom; Gov. Ryerson Polytech. Inst.; Pres. and Chrmn. of Bd., Inst. Of Man and Res.; Chrmn., Assn. of Atlantic Univ. 1979-81; mem., Nat. Library Adv. Bd.; Can. Environmental Adv. Council;Min.; Adv. Bd. on Can. Military Coll.; Bd. of Intermediate Technology Devel. Group of N. America; author over 40 papers in Physics, Information Science Computing and Computer Assisted Learning, also conf. papers; Protestant; recreations: swimming, skiing; Home: 181 Fitzroy St., Charlottetown, P.E.I.

MEINIG, Walter Paul; banker; b. 25 August 25/32 - Davidson, Saskatchewan; e. Shellbrook, Saskatchewan High School; m. Jessie Eddleston 21 May 1956; children: Elaine, John, Dianne, Sandra; SR. VICE PRES. AND GEN. MGR. ONT. DIV., THE BANK OF NOVA SCOTIA 1980- ; Gen. Mgr. Adm. present Bank 1974, Gen. Mgr. W. & N. Ont. Region 1976, Vice Pres. & Gen. Mgr. Candn. Regions 1977, Sr. Vice Pres. Candn. Regions 1979; Clubs: St. George's Golf & Country; Toronto Squash; National; Home: 18 Butterfield Drive, Don Mills, Ontario M3A 2L8; Office: 44 King St. W., Toronto, Ont. M5H 1H1.

MEISEL, John, M.A., Ph.D., F.R.S.C.; educator; commission chairman; b. Vienna, Austria 23 Oct. 1923; s. Fryda S. and Anne (Heller) M.; e. Elem. and Secondary Schs. Czechoslovakia, Gt. Brit., Haiti, Pickering Coll. Newmarket, Ont.; Univ. of Toronto Victoria Coll. B.A. 1948, M.A. 1950; London Sch. of Pol. Science & Econ. Ph.D. 1959; m. Murie Augusta Kelly 6 Aug. 1949; CHRMN., CANDN. RADIO-TELEVISION & TELECOM-MUNICATIONS COMN. 1980- ; former Head of Pol. Studies, Queen's Univ. and Hardy Prof. of Pol. Science; Past Pres. Social Science Research Council Can.; Data Clearing House; joined Queen's Univ. 1949; Visiting Prof. Yale Univ. 1976-77; Commonwealth Distinguished Visiting Prof. Gt. Brit. 1978; served various Royal Comns., Task Forces and Inquiries incl. Biculturalism & Bilingualism, Nat. Unity, Status of Women, bias in newscasting; sometime adviser to Candn. and Ont. govts.; mem. Premier Robart's Adv. Comte. on Confederation; expert witness Que. govt.'s comte. on electoral reform; participated in inquiries conducted on behalf of La conf. des recteurs et des principaux des univs. du Qué.; frequent commentator and panelist CBC particularly French radio and TV; guest lectr. Can., U.S.A. and Europe; past mem. Inter-Univ. Consortium for Pol. Research; rec'd Can. Council Killam Award 5 yrs.; author "The Canadian General Election of 1957" 1962; "Papers on the 1962 Election" 1964, ed.; "L'évolution des partis politiques canadiens" 1966; "Working Papers on Canadian Politics" 1972, 1973, 1975; "Cleavages, Parties and Values in Canada" 1974; numerous articles; Ed. "International Political Science Review" 1979- ; mem. adv. bds. several pol. science journs. N. Am. and Europe; Gen. Ed. "Canadian Studies in the Structure of Power"; former Co-Ed. "The Canadian Journal of Political Science"; mem. Internat. Pol. Science Assn.; Candn. Pol. Science Assn. (Past Pres.); recreations: music, skiing, swimming, literature, nature; Home: Colimaison, R.R. 1, Tichborne, Ont. K0H 2V0; Office: Les Terrasses de la Chaudière, 1 Promenade du Portage, Hull, Que. K1A 0N2.

MELCHER, Antony Henry, B.D.S., H.D.D., M.D.S., Ph.D.; educator; b. Johannesburg, S. Africa, 1 July 1927; e. A. Robert and Anne (Lewis) M.; e. King Edward VII Sch., Johannesburg, 1934-45; Univ. of the Witwatersrand, B.D.S. 1949, H.D.D. 1958, M.D.S. 1960; Univ. of London, Ph.D. 1964; m. Marcia Ruth, d. Max Marcus, Pietersburg, S. Africa, 15 Nov. 1953; children: Rowena,

Lindsay; DIR., MED. RESEARCH COUNCIL GROUP IN PERIODONTAL PHYSIOL., UNIV. OF TORONTO since 1974 and Prof. of Dentistry there since 1969; private dental practice 1950-61; Demonst., Faculty of Dent., Univ. of Witwatersrand 1952-61 and mem. Jt. Dental Research Unit of Univ. and of C.S.I.R. 1956-61; Research Fellow, Inst. of Dent. Surg., Univ. of London 1961-62; Leverhulme Research Fellow, Royal Coll. of Surgs. Eng., 1963-69; author, "Biology of the Periodontium" 1969; also numerous publs. in scient. journs.; Ed., "Oral Science Reviews", Copenhagen; mem. Candn. Dental Assn.; Royal Soc. Med.; Bone & Tooth Soc.; Orthopaedic Research Soc.; Internat. Assn. Dental Research (Pres. 1982-83); Tissue Culture Soc.; Am. Assn. Advanc. Science; Am. Soc. Cell Biol.; recreations: music, theatre, sailing; Club: Island Yacht; Home: 101 Banstock Dr., Willowdale, Ont. M2K 2H7

MELDRUM, Wendell Wynn, Q.C.; b. Simpson's Corner, Lunenburg Co., N.S., 27 June 1924; s. Hazen Hibbert and Bernice Beatrice (Simpson) M.; e. Bridgewater (N.S.) Elem. and 2ndary Schs., 1930-42; Dalhousie Law Sch., LL.B. 1948; Univ. N.B., D.C.L. (Hon.) 1969; m. Dorothy Ferne, d. Sterling L. Downey, R.R. 3, Moncton, N.B., 4 Nov. 1944; children: Wynn Wendell, Kirk Walter; read law with George D. Harris, Halifax, N.S.; called to Bar of N.S. and N.B. 1948; cr. Q.C. 1965; Master of Supreme Court, N.B., Clerk of the Peace, Circuit and County Court, Registrar of Probate Albert Co., 1949-52; Lectr. in Comm. Law, Mount Allison Univ., 1956-65; Town Solr., Sackville, N.B., 1952-65; Attorney-Gen. N.B. 1965-66, 1970-77; Judge of the Co. Court 1977-79; presently Judge of Court of Queen's Bench; el. M.L.A. for Westmorland Co. in by-el. 1965; Min. of Educ. 1966 until Govt. def. 1970; served with R.C.A.F. as Flying Offr., 1942-45; Pilot with R.A.F. Ferry Command Dorval; served in U.K., N. Africa, India; Freemason; Liberal; United Church; recreations: golf, reading; Clubs: Sackville Golf (Past Pres.); Rotary (Past Pres.); Home: P.O. Box 38, Sackville, N.B. E0A 3C0; Office: 770 Main St., Moncton, N.B. E1C 8R3

MELLOY, Stanley Frank, D.F.C., B.A.; executive; b. Nfld., 12 July 1921; e. Univ.; Univ. of Toronto, B.A. 1948; m. Ellen E., d. Capt. Alex Smith, 11 Sept. 1948; children: David, Joanne; PRES., C.E.O. AND DIRECTOR, CONTINENTAL BANK OF CAN. 1982- joined I.A.C. 1948; Mgr., St. John's, Nfld., 1949-55; Reg. Mgr., Atlantic Provs., Ont. 1956-63; Vice-Pres. & Gen. Mgr., 1964-71; Chief Financial Officer 1972-74; Vice-Pres. Finance 1972; Sr. Vice Pres. 1973; Exec. Vice Pres. 1974; Extve. Vice Pres. & Dir. 1976; Pres. Continental Bank and IAC 1979; Pres. and C.E.O. 1980; Pres. and C.E.O., Continental Bank 1981; served with RAF 1941-45; rank Flight Lt.; Clubs: Toronto Golf; National; Metropolitan (N.Y.); Canadian (N.Y.); St. James's; Office: Continental Place, 130 Adelaide St. W., Toronto, Ont. M5H 3R2

MELNIK, David, Q.C., B.A., LL.B.; trust company executive; b. 26 Oct. 1931; e. McMaster Univ. B.A. 1954; Fac. of Law, Univ. of Toronto LL.B. 1957; Osgoode Hall Law School 1959; Harvard Business School 1982; m. June Ann Grant, 1970; children: Andrew Grant, Christy Elizabeth; Pres. & Chief Exec. Officer, Vanguard Trust of Canada Ltd.; Counsel, Melnik & Saunders; lectured extensively on real estate law and law of finance for Cdn. Institute of Bankers; special lectr. Osgoode Hall Law School, York Univ.; Dir. Metro Toronto & Region Conserv. Foundation; Dir. Singer Steel, Inc., Tulsa Oklahoma; Dir. Vanguard Trust; mem. Policy Comte. of Treas., Prov. Ont.; Dir. Ont. Energy Corp.; Dir. Cdn. Nat. Sportmen's Shows; Dir. The Holson Company, Wilton Conn.; Dir. Infosearch Inc., Albany, N.Y.; Home: 350 Lonsdale Road, Toronto, Ont. M5P 1R6; Office: P.O. Box 128, Suite 5240, 1 First Canadian Place, Toronto, Ontario M5X 1A4.

MELOCHE, Pierre; chartered insurance broker; b. Montreal, Que. 15 Jan. 1940; s. Jean and Marcelle (Pelland) M.; e. Coll. Jean de Brébeuf Montreal 1958; Ecole des Hautes Etudes Commerciales 1960; Sir George Williams Univ. 1961; m. Danielle d. Camille Archambault 15 Sept. 1962; children: Eric, Nathalie; PRESIDENT, CEO AND DIR. J. MELOCHE INC. since 1973; Pres., C.E.O., and Dir., Reed Stenhouse Personal Insurance Ltd.; Monnex Insurance Brokers Ltd.; Pres. and Dir. Sonef Insurance Management Ltd.; J. E. Smith & Co. Inc.; Laurin Beaudry Filion Dansereau Ltée.; Denmel Investments Ltd.; Dir. Reed Shaw Stenhouse Ltd.; Vice Chrmn., Soc. de Courtage Meloche Ltée.; mem. conseil de surveillance, Soc. Générale de Courtage d'Assurances, Paris; joined present Co. 1960, Vice Pres. and Dir. 1961, Extve. Vice Pres. 1969; Managing Dir. for Europe, Stenhouse Reed Shaw Management Serv. Ltd., Glasgow, 1976-78; Mem. of the Directoire, 1977-78 and Mem. Conseil de Surveillance, 1978-80, soc. Générale de Courtages d'Assurances, Paris; Lectr. on Ins. Coll. Maisonneuve, Montreal 1968-70; Past Pres. Research & Orientation Comte. paste mem. Ins. Brokers Assn. Prov. Que., Past Dir. and Secy. N. Sector Montreal Regional Comte. 1967-69; mem. Montreal Bd. Trade; R. Catholic; recreations: riding; golf; skiing; Clubs: St-Denis; Estérel; Home: 75 Dunrae Ave., Town of Mount-Royal, Que.; Offices: 50 Pl. Cremazie, Montreal, Que.

MELVILLE, Kenneth Ivan, M.Sc., M.D., C.M.; emeritus professor; b. Jamaica, B.W.I., 5 July 1902; s. Nathan Josiah and Rosamund (Smith) M.; e. McGill Univ., B.Sc. 1926, M.D., C.M. 1926 (Holmes Gold Medal), Research Fellow in Pharmacol. 1926-28, M.Sc. 1931; Nat. Research Council Med. Fellow, Faculty of Med., Paris, France, and Pasteur Inst. there 1928-30; m. Gladys Vivian, d. late David Brodber, 14 April 1933; children: Enid Lorraine, David Louis; apptd. Lectr. in Pharmacol., McGill Univ. 1930, Asst. Prof. 1933, Assoc. Prof. 1944, Prof. 1953-70, since when prof. emeritus; awarded Medal for Research in Anesthesia by Internat. Coll. of Anesthetists, 1948; apptd. mem. of Internat. Pharmacol. Comte. 1952; has contrib. some 60 articles in various med. journs. and Chapter 31 on "The Nitrites, Nitrates and Miscellaneous Drugs", in textbook of pharmacol. 2nd Ed. 1957; gen. scient. interests: cardiovascular pharmacol. and drugs affecting the autonomic nervous system; publications concern: actions of mercury compounds, effects of pituitary extracts, effects of chem. agents in exper. tuberculosis; new method for investigation of drugs affecting coronary circulation, mechanism of action of digitalis and other drugs on heart and blood pressure; Lic., Med. Council of Can.; mem., Am. Soc. of Pharmacol. & Exper. Therapeutics; Am. Assn. of Univ. Profs.; Am. Coll. of Cardiology; Candn. Physiol. Soc.; Candn. Heart Assn.; N.Y. Acad. of Science; Swiss Physiol. & Pharmacol. Soc.; Alpha Omega Alpha; Sigma Xi; Protestant; recreations: golf, gardening; Home: 4937 Circle Road, Montreal, Que. H3W 1Z8

MELVILLE, Robert D., B.S.M.E., M.B.A.; manufacturer; b. Montreal, Que., 28 Sept. 1937; s. Douglas Reid and Millicent (Hudson) M.; e. Sir George Williams Univ., Cert. in Engn. 1959; McGill Univ., B.S.M.E. 1962, M.B.A. 1969; m. Joyce Marie, d. Douglas Gunn, Grafton, Ont., 16 Sept. 1961; children: Douglas William, Susan Lynn, David Hudson, John Ramsey; PRESIDENT AND DIR., FLAKT CANADA LTD. since 1973; joined present Co. as Project Engr. 1962, apptd. Project Mgr. 1964, Sales Mgr. 1966, Vice-Pres. 1969; mem., Corp. Engrs. Que.; Assn. Prof. Eng. of Ont.; Assn. Prof. Eng. Geol. & Geophys., Alta.; recreations: skiing, squash, handball; Clubs: St. James's; The Country; Office: 1400 Merivale Rd., Ottawa, Ont.

MELVILL-JONES, Geoffrey, M.A., M.B., B.Ch., F.R.S.C.; university professor; b. Cambridge, Eng. 14 Jan. 1923; came to Can. 1961; s. Benett and Dorothy Laxton (Jotham) MJ.; e. King's Choir SCh., Cambridge, 1930-35; Dauntsey's Sch., Witshire, 1935-40; Cambridge Univ. B.A. 1944, MA. 1947, M.B., B.Ch. 1949; Middlesex Hosp., London 1945-49; Addenbrooke's Hosp., Cambridge 1949-51; m. Jenny Marigold Burnaby 21 June 1953; children: Katharine F., Francis H., Andrew J., Dorothy H.; PROF. OF PHYSIOLOGY, MCGILL UNIV.; first incumbent of the Hosmer Research Professorship in applied physiology, McGill Univ.; Dir., Aviation Medical Research Unit; Consultant in Neurosciences to NASA Skylab and Spacelab programs; served with RAF, 1951-55, rank sqdn. leader, Flying Personnel Med. Offr.; rec'd. Harry G. Armstrong Lectureship Award, Aerospace Medical Assn. 1968; Arnold D. Tuttle award for outstanding research in aerospace medicine, 1971; Skylab Achievement Award, 1974; author of "Mammalian Vestibular Physiology", 1979; articles in over 100 scientific publs.; el. Fellow, Royal Soc. of London, 1979; el. Fellow, Royal Soc. of Can., 1979; Fellow, Candn. Aeronautics and Space Inst.; Fellow, Aerospace Med. Assn.; Fellow, Royal Aeronautical Soc.; Fellow, Royal Soc. of Med.; mem., UK Physiol. Soc.; Candn. Physiol. Soc.; Candn. Soc. of Aviation Med.; Mtl. Physiol. Soc.; Society for Neuroscience; Intl. Collegium of Otolaryngology; Bàràny Soc.; Anglican Protestant; recreations: outdoor activities, music, reading; Home: 3265 Glencoe Ave., Montreal, Que. H3R 2C5; Office: Aviation Medical Research Unit, Dept. of Physiol., McGill Univ., 3655 Drummond St., Montreal, Que. H3G 1Y6.

MELVIN, William James Spencer, B.A., M.D., C.M., F.R.C.S. (Lond.); retired orthopaedic surgeon; b. Kingston, Ont., 20 Nov. 1920; s. late Dr. George Spencer and Isabella Luke (Stewart) M.; e. Victoria Pub. Sch., Kingston, 1926-32; Upper Can. Coll., Toronto, 1932-36; Queen's Univ., B.A. 1940, M.D., C.M. 1943; m. Kathleen, d. late Alex Marling, Victoria, B.C., 7 Aug. 1945; children: Alexander Spencer, Susan Diane; entered private practice of orthopaedics, Scarborough, Ont., 1967; Attending Staff, Scarborough Gen. Hosp.; post-grad. training, Vancouver Gen. Hosp., 1945; Queen's Univ. 1946; Eng. Hosps., 1946-50; Mass. Gen. Hosp. 1951; Assoc. Prof. of Surg. (Orthopaedics), Queen's Univ., 1952-65; in private practice Kingston, Ont., 1965-67; served with RCNVR as Surg. Lt., 1944-45; Trustee, Queen's Univ.; Chrmn., Frontenac and Dist. Rehab. Center, 1958-67; Athletic Bd. Control, Queen's Univ., 1957-67; Pres.; Ont. Med. Assn., 1967-68; mem. Med. Adv. Comte.; soc. Prof. of Surg. (Orthopaedics), Queen's Univ., 1952-65; Ont. Soc. For Crippled Children; Rehab. Foundation for the Disabled; Candn. Olympic Assn.; Candn. Occupational & Physiotherapy Assn.; mem., Toronto Medicolegal Soc.; Kingston Medicolegal Soc. (Pres.); Candn. Med. Assn.; Candn. Orthopaedic Assn.; Candn. Athletic Trainers' Assn.; Brit. Orthopaedic Assn.; Am. Coll. Sports Med.; Presbyterian; recreations: golf, boating, photography; Club: Cataraqui Golf & Country; Home: R.R. 1, Kingston, Ont. K7L 4V1

MEMBERY, Robert Edward, B.Com., C.A.; company executive; b. Toronto, Ont., 6 Feb. 1925; s. late Morris Howard and Late Ruth (Clarke) M.; e. McGill Univ., B.Com., 1948; Que. Inst. of C.A.'s, C.A. 1950; m. Isabel, d. late M. K. Hashim, 23 Feb. 1957; one d. Jennifer; VICE-PRES., FINANCE, PETROSAR LTD since 1977; Boise Cascade Canada Ltd.; served with RCAF 1943-46; rank Pilot Offr.; Delta Sigma Phi; Clubs: Garrison; St. James's Club (Montreal) Home: 1312 Maynard Rd., Sarnia, Ont.; Office: P.O. Bpox 7000, Corunna, Ont. M0M 1G0

MENDELSOHN, Nathan S., M.A., Ph.D., F.R.S.C.; university professor; b. Brooklyn, N.Y., 14 Apl. 1917; s. Samuel and Sylvia (Kirschenbaum) M.; came to Canada, 1917; e. Univ. of Toronto, B.A. 1939, M.A. 1940, Ph.D. 1942; m. Helen, d. Abraham Brontman, Toronto, 26 Oct. 1940; two s. Eric, Alan; PROF. OF MATH., UNIV. OF MANITOBA, since 1946, and Head of Dept. since 1963; Research Scient., Nat. Research Council and Inspection

Bd. of U.K. and Can., 1942-45; Lectr. in Math., Queen's Univ., 1945-46; Candn. Del. to Internat. Math. Union, Saltjobaden, Sweden, 1962; Del. to Univ. of Man. to Internat. Cong. of Math., Stockholm, 1962; mem., Assoc. Comte. of Pure and Applied Maths., Nat. Research Council, since 1963; Candn. rep. to Internat. Math. Union, Dubna, U.S.S.R., Aug. 1966; author of over 100 papers in prof. journs.; winner, Roy. Soc. of Can. "Henry Marshall Tory Gold Medal" 1979; named distinguished Prof. 1981; Dir., Computing and Data Processing Soc. Can.; mem., Candn. Math. Cong. (Pres. 1970-71); Am. Math. Soc.; Math. Assn. Am.; Soc. Indust. and Applied Math.; Jewish; recreations: chess, bridge, music; Home: 364 Enniskillen Ave., Winnipeg, Man. R2V 0J3

MENDES da COSTA, Derek, Q.C., LL.B.(Hons.) LL.M., S.J.D., LL.D.; lawyer; b. London, Eng. 7 March 1929; s. Judah and Esther (Ellis) M.; e. King's Coll. Univ. of London LL.B. 1955; Univ. of Melbourne LL.M. 1965; Harvard Univ. S.J.D. 1972; Univ. of London LL.D. 1980; m. Barbara Helen d. David Prevost, Stanmore, Eng. 26 June 1950; children: Virginia Sara (Murdoch), Philip Charles; CHRMN. ONT. LAW REFORM COMMISSION since 1977; Special Lectr. Univ. of Toronto since 1977; Chrmn. Bd. Dirs. Ont. Prov. Court (Family Div.) Conciliation Project 1976-81; Chrmn. Atty. Gen.'s Comte. on Representation of Children; mem. Statutory Powers Procedure Rules Comte.; Commr. for Ont. Uniform Law Conf. of Can.; Chrmn., Comte. on Sale of Goods of the Uniform Law Conf. of Canada, 1979-81; Asst. Lectr. in Law, King's Coll. Univ. of London 1955-58; Sr. Lectr in Law, Univ. of Melbourne 1958-65; Prof. Osgoode Hall Law Sch. 1965-68; Prof. of Law Univ. of Toronto 1968-77, mem. Council Sch. Grad. Studies 1971, 1975-77, Chrmn. of Council of School of Continuing Studies 1977-80; Fellow Victoria Coll. 1975-78; Visiting Prof. Ariz. State Univ. 1972; Univ. of Texas 1972; mem., Candn. Inst. Advanced Legal Studies since 1978 (Bd. of Gov. 1978-81); mem. Senate York Univ. 1966-68, Vice Chrmn, 1967-68; Internat. Faculty of Comparative Law (Strasbourg) since 1966; Special Comte. on Legal Educ. Law Soc. Upper Can. 1970-72; Solr. Supreme Court Judicature Eng. (Hons.) 1955; Barrister & Solr. Supreme Court Victoria, Australia 1963, Solicitor of Supreme Court Ont. 1966; cr. Q.C. 1972 (Ont.); Intermediate Laws Scholarship, 1952; John Mackrell Prizeman and City of London Solrs.' Co.'s Grotius Prizeman 1955; served with R.A.M.C. 1948-49; Research Assoc. Ont. Law Reform Comn. Family Law Project 1965-68; Law of Property Project 1968-71, 1973-76; co-author "Matrimonial Causes Jurisdiction" 1961; author various articles Candn. Commonwealth, and foreign law journs.; ed. and contrib., "Studies in Canadian Family Law"; ed., "The Cambridge Lectures"; mem. Law Soc. Upper Can.; Nat. Council & Ont. Council of the Candn. Bar Assn.; Law Soc. (Eng.); Selden Soc.; Soc. Pub. Teachers Law; Candn. Assn. Law Teachers; Medico-Legal Soc. Toronto; American Foreign Law Assn. Inc.; Internat. Soc. Family Law; Harvard Law Sch. Assn.; The British Inst. of International and Comparative Law; Club: Empire; Faculty, Univ. of Toronto; Phi Delta Phi (Hon. mem.); Jewish; Recreation: Walking my Old English Sheepdog; Home: 159 Shelborne Ave., Toronto, Ont. M6B 2M9; Office: 18 King St. E., Toronto, Ont. M5C 1C5.

MENELEY, Robert A., M.A., P.Eng.; petroleum executive; e. Univ. of Sask. B.A. (Geol. Engn.) M.A. (Geol.); GROUP VICE PRES. EXPLORATION, PETRO-CANADA; Dir. Panarctic Oils Ltd.; 15 yrs. experience exploration field maj. Candn. oil co., consulting practice specializing in frontier geol. and exploration planning; Vice Pres. Exploration, Panarctic Oils Ltd. 1973; and Petro-Canada Exploration Inc. 1976; mem. Candn. Soc. Petroleum Geols.; Am. Soc. Petrol. Geols.; Office: 407 Second St. S.W (P.O. Box 2844), Calgary, Alta. T2P 3E3.

MENKES, René, A.R.I.B.A.; architect; b. Paris, France, 10 Feb. 1932; e. Lower Can. Coll., 1944-49; McGill Univ., 1949-55; m. Ann Wallace Sullivan; PARTNER, WEBB, ZERAFA, MENKES, HOUSDEN; Partner, Webb, Zerafa, Menkès, Toronto and Kitchener, Ont.; firm won Massey Medal, Nat. Design and Nat. Steel Design Awards in 1964; designed and supv. constr. of most major type bldgs. incl. schs. and univs., hotels, commercial offices, shopping, indust. and residential centres and Govt. projects; also projects in Toronto, Montreal, Calgary, Lancaster, N.B., etc.; mem., Prov. Que. Assn. Archs.; Royal Arch. Inst. Can.; Home: 38 Belvedere Rd. Westmount, Mtl., Que. Office: 2075 University St., Montreal, Que.

MENSES, Jan, R.C.A.; painter; draughtsman; printmaker; b. Rotterdam, Netherlands 28 Apl. 1933; s. Jan and Elisabeth Wilhelmina (Schwarz) M.; e. Willem de Zwijger H.B.S. Rotterdam 1951; Degrees in Eng. lang. and Dutch lang. Rotterdam 1952, 1956; Royal Air Force Offrs.' Acad. Breda, Holland grad. 1954; Rotterdam Art Acad. Etching & Lithography 1959; study trips Europe, N. Africa 1956-58, Israel 1971; m. Rachel Régine d. late Rabbi Shlomo Kadoch, Morocco, 7 Dec. 1958; children: Solomon, Hnina Sarah, Nechama Elisabeth Halo; solo exhns. France, Holland, Spain, Morocco to 1960; Jewish Pub. Lib. Montreal 1960; McGill Univ. 1961; Penthouse Gallery Montreal 1962; Tifereth Jerusalem Cong. Montreal 1963; Isaacs Gallery Toronto 1964; Delta Gallery Rotterdam 1965; Galerie Godard Lefort Montreal 1966; Gallery Moos Toronto 1967; Galerie Martal Montreal 1971, 1972; Rotterdamse Kunststichting 1974; Galerie Mira Godard Toronto 1977, Montreal 1978; Montreal Museum of Fine Arts 1976 (retrospective); Studio Gravure G Ottawa 1979; Elca London Gallery Montreal 1979; Seasons Galleries The Hague 1980; Univ. of B.C. Fine Arts Gallery 1981; two-man shows Montreal Museum of Fine Arts 1961, 1965, Philadelphia Art Alliance 1969; rep. numerous group exhns. Can., USA, Europe; rep. maj. perm. colls. incl. Museum of Modern Art New York, Philadelphia Museum of Art, Solomon R. Guggenheim Museum New York, Brooklyn Museum, N.Y.; Art Inst. of Chicago; Cleveland Museum of Art, Detroit Inst. of Arts, Yale Univ., New Haven; Nat. Gallery Can., Can. Council Art Bank, Montreal Museum of Fine Arts, Rijksmuseum Amsterdam, Museo Ciani di Villa Caccia Lugano; Yad Vashem Holocaust Mem. Jerusalem, Victoria and Albert London as well as private colls. Can., USA, Europe, N. Africa, Australia & New Zealand, Japan, USSR; recipient 5 First Prizes Nat. Art Exhn. Que. 1960-64; Concours Artistiques de la Prov. de Qué. Grand Prize 1965; 10th and 11th Winnipeg Shows 1966, 1968; IX Internat. Exhn. Drawings & Engravings Lugano 1966; Official Centennial Art Competition Toronto "Perspective" Prize 1967; Hadassah Prizes Montreal 1967, 1969, 1970, 1971; Reeves of Can. Award Ont. Soc. Artists Toronto 1969, Tigert Award 1970, Loomis & Toles Award 1972; Lauréat Concours Artistiques Prov. Qué. 1971; J.I. Segal Arts Award Montreal 1975; Accademia Italia delle Arte e del Lavoro Italy Gold Medal 1980; Hon. degree, Universita Delle Arti, Italy 1981; Image 81 Award, Ont. Soc. Artists, 1981; various Can. Council grants and Sr. Arts Fellowships 1969-70, 1971-72, 1981-82; purchase awards; Lectr. in Fine Arts Concordia Univ. 1973-76; Visiting Artist Mount Allison Univ. 1978; maj. cycles of work: "Diabolica Series" 1961-62, "Victors Series" 1963, "Kaddish Series" 1965-80, "Klippoth Series" 1963-80, "Tikkun Series" 1978- ; illustrated vol. of poetry based on Exodus 1960; "Staub un Ebigkeit" 1981; served with Royal Dutch Air Force 1953-55; mem. Accademia Italia delle Arte e del Lavoro; Soc. des Artistes en Arts Visuels du Qué.; Royal Canadian Academy of Arts (R.C.A.); Address: 5571 Woodbury Ave., Montreal, Que. H3T 1S6.

MENZIES, Arthur Redpath, M.A.; diplomat; b. Changte-Ho, Honan, China, 29 Nov. 1916; e. Univ. of Toronto, B.A.; Harvard Univ., M.A.; m.; has two children; AMBASSADOR FOR DISARMAMENT, 1980- ;

joined Dept. of External Affairs in 1940; Second Secy., Havana, 1945-46; apptd. Head of the Candn. Liaison Mission in Tokyo, Nov. 1950, and following the conclusion of the Peace Treaty with Japan, became Chargé d'Affaires a. i. at Canadian Embassy, Tokyo in Apl. 1952; on return to Ottawa in June 1953, apptd. Head of the Far Eastern Divn. of the Dept.; High Commissioner to Fed. of Malaya and concurrently Ambassador to Burma, 1958-61; Head of Defence Liaison (1) Div., Ottawa, 1962-65; High Commr. to Australia 1965-72 (High Commr. concurrently to Fiji 1970-72); Permanent Rep. and Ambassador to North Atlantic Council 1972-76); Ambassador to People's Republic of China, 1976-80 concurrently, to socialist Republic of Vietnam accredited July, 1976-79; Address: 445 Maple Lane, Rockcliffe, Ottawa, Ont. K1M 1H8

MERCALDO, Edward L., B.Sc.; banker; b. Maryland 19 August 1941; e. Georgetown Univ., Washington, DC B.Sc. (Foreign Service) 1963; m. Bonnie June 1961; children: Edward, Karen, Michelle; SR. VICE PRES. AND DEPY. GEN. MGR., WORLD CORPORATE BANKING, BANK OF MONTREAL, 1981- ; Mgr. Internat. Operations, Wachovia Bank & Trust Co., Winston-Salem, NC 1963-65; Export Devel. Coordinator State of NC 1966-67; Vice Pres. Internat. Banking Wachovia Bank & Trust Co. 1968-70; served as Vice Pres. Internat. Banking, Sr. Vice Pres. Internat. Banking, Extve. Vice Pres. Funds Mang., Equibank N.A. 1970-76; Vice Pres. Loan Syndication present Bank 1976-80; Sr. Vice Pres. Internat. Banking, Can. Div., Bank of Montreal 1980-81; former lectr. Univ. of Pittsburgh; author various articles prof. subjects; Home: Birch Hill R.R. 1, King City, Ont. L0G 1K0; Office: First Canadian Place, Toronto, Ont. M5X 1A1.

MERCER, Ronald Leon, B.B.A.; executive; b. Dewey Co., Okla. 19 Oct. 1934; s. Joseph William and Lura Elizabeth (Dewald) M.; e. Bethany (Okla.) Nazarene Coll. B.B.A. 1955; Harvard Univ. Grad. Sch. of Business Adm. P.M.D. 1973; m. D. Yvonne d. Thomas F. Edwards 23 July 1954; children: Gary Dean, Marla Kay, Lisa Renee, Michael David; PRES., XEROX CANADA INC. 1979- ; Br. Mgr. Xerox Corp. Oklahoma City 1965, Product Group Mgr. Rochester, N.Y. 1970, Region Sales Mgr. Midwest Region, Chicago 1971, Vice Pres. and Gen. Mgr. Northeast Region, Greenwich, Conn. 1975-79; Trustee, Bethany Nazarene Coll.; Trustee, Nazarene Theological Seminary, Kansas City, Mo.; Visiting Fellow, Woodrow Wilson Fellowship Foundation; Protestant; recreations: golf, tennis; Club: Harvard (N.Y. City); Home: 11 Sagewood Dr., Don Mills, Ont. M3B 1T5; Office: 703 Don Mills Rd., Don Mills, Ont. M3C 1S2.

MERCIER, François, O.C. Q.C.; b. Paris, France, 13 April 1923; s. Dr. Oscar and Jeanne (Bruneau) M.; e. (came to Canada in 1927) Loyola Coll., B.A. 1942; Univ. of Montreal, LL.L. 1945; called to the Bar of Que., July 1945; C.R. Q.C. 3 Jan. 1961; m. Lucile, d. Avila Rouleau, Town of Mount Royal, Que., 25 May 1946; children: Genevieve, Jean-Francois, Madeleine, Hélène; MEMBER STIKEMAN TAMAKI MERCIER & ROBB ELLIOTT; Pres., La Libraire Fernand Nathan, Can. Ltée.; Vice Pres., Meridien Can. Ltée.; Dir.; Campeau Corp.; Popular Industries Ltd.; Mercanmor Ltd.; Peugeot Can. Ltée.; Deputy Chrmn. of The General Accident Group; Chrmn. Bd.Trustees, Place des Arts, Montreal1964-68; National Art Centre, Ottawa, Nov. 1969-77; Chrmn. Bd., Hôtel-Dieu Hospital, Montreal; actively engaged in trial law since 1945 (Fleury Hosp. Royal Enquiry, 1963; Regina vs. Reader's Digest, 1961; Regina vs. Hal C. Banks, 1964; Asbestos Corp. vs. Att. Gen. of Que., 1979; Sun Life Ass. Co. of Can. vs. Domglas Inc. 1980; Lectr. in Ins. Law, Univ. of Montreal, 1950-63; read law with Patenaude & Co., Montreal; mem., Montreal Bar Assn. (Secy. 1954, Dir. 1963-64); Candn. Bar Assn.; Liberal; Catholic; recreations: skiing, gardening; Club: Mount Royal; Home: 1 Spring Grove Crescent, Outremont, Montreal, Que. H2V 3H8; Office: 1155 Dorchester Blvd. W., Montreal, Que.

MERCIER, Hon. Gerald Wayne Joseph, Q.C., M.L.A., B.A., LL.B.; politician; b. Claresholm, Alta. 9 Nov. 1942; s. Gerard and Marjorie M.; e. St. Paul's High Sch. and Coll. B.A.; Univ. of Man. Law Sch. LL.B.; m. Merryl-Lee d. Fred M. Wood, Winnipeg, Man. 21 May. 1966; children: Guy Mathew, Mark Geoffrey, Leigh-Anne, Melissa-Lee, Cherie-Lynne, Michael Corey; MIN. OF URBAN AFFAIRS, MAN. 1979- ; Councillor City of Winnipeg 1971-77; el. M.L.A. for Osborne prov. g.e. 1977; Atty.-Gen., Keeper of the Great Seal, Min. of Mun. Affairs, Min. for Urban Affairs and Min. Responsible for Adm. Liquor Control Act 1977; Attorney-Gen., Min. of Mun. & Urban Affairs and Min. Responsible for Adm. Liquor Control Act 1977; Attorney-Gen., Min. of Mun. & Urban Affairs and Min. Responsible for Adm. Liquor Control Act 1978- ; Govt. House Leader, 1980- ; Kinsmen; P. Conservative; R. Catholic; Office: 104 Legislative Bldg., Winnipeg, Man. R3C 0V8.

MERCIER, Jean-Jacques; b. Joliette, Que., 4 Sept. 1918; s. J-Honoré & Atala (Gibeault) M.; e. Jardin de l'Enfance, Montreal; Coll. de l'Assomption, Cours classique; m. Lillian, d. late John Newby, 29 Aug. 1941; children: Claude, Pierre, Louise, Jean-Honoré, Louis; FOUNDER, PRESIDENT AND PUBLISHER, LA VOIX POPULAIRE, since 1946; Reporter for La Presse, Montreal, 1941-42; Reporter, Le Devoir, Montreal, 1942-44; Head of French Sec., Information Service, Nat. Film Bd., Ottawa, 1944; Pub. Relations Offr. for Que., 1945; Life Gov., Foyer Saint Henri; Pres., 1966-67, Hebdos de langue française du Can.; Cand. for St. Henry Riding, Que. g.e. 1962 and for La Prairie-Napierville Riding, Que. g.e. 1966, 1970; mem., Assoc. montréalaise d'action récréative et culturelle; Union Canadienne des Journ. de Lang. Français; Soc. Hist. de Montréal; Soc. Hist. de Saint-Heuri; Conseil Expansion Econ.; Fed. Candn. Advertising & Sales Club; Assoc. mem., Internat. Conf. of Weekly Newspaper Eds.; mem., Conseil l'administration, Soc. Can. du Cancer; Conseil l'administration, Soc pour les Enfants Infirmes du Que.; Assist. to Pres. (communications), City of Montreal Exec. Comte.; Chevalier de l'Ordre de Cein Clou; K. of C.; Roman Catholic; Clubs: Médaille d'Or, Optimiste St. Paul; Canadien; Canadian; Home: 1820 ave. de l'Eglise, Montreal, Que. H4E 1G8; Office: 275 est Notre-Dame, Suite 1202, Montréal, Qué. H2Y 1C6

MERCURE, Gilles, B.A., LL.L., M.B.A.; banker; b. Montreal, Que., 22 Feb. 1926; s. Joseph and Anita (Maheu) M.; e. Coll. Ste-Marie, B.A.; Univ. of Montreal, L.Sc.P and LL.L; Harvard Univ., M.B.A.; m. Huguette Jolicoeur, 25 Sept. 1954; children: Hélène, Louise, Luc; EXEC. VICE PRES. AND CHIEF OPERATING OFFICER, NATIONAL BANK OF CANADA 1981; extve. Vice Pres. 1979-81; Vice Pres. & Gen. Mgr. Provincial Bank of Can., 1977-79; Vice-pres.-internat. 1974-77; Asst. Gen. Mgr.1966-74; Jt. Secy., Royal Comm. on Banking and Finance, 1961-64; Pres., Soc. Nationale de Gestion, 1959-60; Asst. Treas., Soc. des Artisans; R. Catholic; recreations: golf; Home: 60 de Brésoles, Montreal, Que. H2Y 1V5; Office: 500 Pl. d'Armes, Montreal, Que. H2Y 2W3

MEREDITH, Harry A., B.A.; management consultant; b. Toronto, Ont., 26 March 1931; s. late Allen Osler and Jean Grahame (Wright) M.; e. Univ. of Toronto, B.A. 1952; m. Marie (Mimi), d. late Charles-Auguste Drouin; 5 children: PARTNER TOUCHE ROSS; mem. of Bd., Dir. and Nat. Dir., Human Resources, Touche Ross; served Dept. Citzenship and Immigration Winnipeg and Ottawa; became Partner present firm 1969; on loan to fed. govt. through Extve. Interchange Program (Treas. Bd., Ministry of Solr. Gen.) 1972-74; participated in Royal Comm. Govt. Org. (Glassco), Royal Comm. Gov't Admin (Sask.), Operation Productivity (Man.), Etude des rouages administratifs (Que.), Comte. on Govt. Productivity (Ont.), Royal Comm. on Financial Mgmt. & Accountability; mem. Inst. Mgmt. Consultants (Que.); Candn. Inst. Pub. Adm.; Pub. Personnel Assn.; Clubs:

Toronto; Rideau; Montreal Badminton & Squash; Home: 140 Howick, Rockcliffe Park, Ottawa, Ont. K1M 0G8; Office: 90 Sparks St., 9th Floor, Ottawa, Ont. K1P 5B4

MEREDITH, John, R.C.A.; artist; b. Fergus, Ont. 24 July 1933; s. Stanley Smith and Lilian (Plant) M.; e. Brampton (Ont.) High Sch.; Ont. Coll. of Art 1950-53; m. Kyoko d. M. Hyashi, Japan, July 1975; solo exhns.: The Isaacs Gallery Toronto 1961, 1963, 1965, 1967, 1973, 1977, 1980; Blue Barn Gallery Ottawa 1965; Gallery of Contemporary Art Toronto 1958, 1959; "John Meredith: Fifteen Years" Art Gallery of Ont. (travelling) 1974-75; "John Meredith: Drawings 1957-1980" Art Gallery of Greater Victoria 1980; rep. numerous group exhns. incl. Montreal Museum of Fine Arts, Nat. Gallery Can., musée Nat. d'Art Moderne Paris, Expo '67, Inst. Contemporary Art Boston, Edinburgh Festival 1968, Art Gallery of Ont., Lugano (Switzerland), Tel Aviv Museum; rep. pub., corporate and private colls. incl. Art Gallery of Ont., Nat. Gallery Can., Montreal Museum of Fine Arts, Can. Council Art Bank, Museum of Modern Art New York, Philadelphia Museum of Art, Dept. External Affairs, Govt. of Samoa; Address: c/o The Isaacs Gallery, 832 Yonge St., Toronto, Ont. M4W 2H1.

MEREDITH, John Roger, M.Ed., LL.D.; b. Kingston, Ont. 13 Sept. 1918; s. John Francis and Gertrude Mary (Bidwell) M.; e. elem. and high schs. Oak Bay, Victoria, B.C. 1937; Victoria (B.C.) Coll. 1939 (Pres. AMS); Univ. of B.C. B.A. 1941, B.Ed. 1955; Univ. of Alta. M.Ed. 1962; Simon Fraser Univ. LL.D. 1980; m. Jacqueline Helen Tweed 26 Dec. 1942; one d. Joan Evelyn; Teacher and Elem./Secondary Sch. Princ. 1942-47; Sr. Research Asst., B.C. Ministry of Educ. 1947, Asst. Dir., Dir. of Curriculum 1952-65, Consultant, C.E.A. Supts. Short Course 1960, 1963; Asst. Supt. of Educ. 1964-71 Supt. of Educ. 1971-77, Sr. Supt. of Pub. Instruction 1978-79; Chrmn., Soldiers Dependent Children's Act Comn. 1969-71; Chrmn., Tech. Adv. Comte. to Cabinet on Drugs, Alcohol & Tobacco 1968-70; mem. Candn. Del. to UNESCO 1968; mem. Regional Adv. Comte. to Candn. Educ. Study by Organ. for Econ. & Coop. Devel. 1974-75; mem. Candn. Educ. Del. to USSR 1973; Rep. to OECD Conf. on Secondary Educ. Bristol 1976; mem. Senate, Univ. of B.C. 1967-69; author "Manual of Reference for Alcohol Education" 1949; numerous curriculum guides, addresses and papers; mem. Victoria Symphony Soc. (Dir.); Pres. 1966-67); Hon. Life mem. B.C. Teachers' Fed.; Candn. Educ. Assn.; Psi Upsilon; Phi Delta Kappa; recreations: camping, hiking, fishing, bridge, music; Clubs: Camosun Gyro (Pres. 1961-62); Gyro Internat.; Home: 2452 Esplanade, Victoria, B.C. V8R 2W2.

MERIFIELD, Russell Roy, Q.C., B.A., B.C.L., A.C.I.S., F.T.C.I.; trust company executive; b. Chatham, Ont. 11 June 1916; s. Russell Stanley and Alice (Stevens) M.; e. N. Toronto Coll.; McGill Univ., B.A. 1938, B.C.L. 1941; Univ. of W. Ont. (Mang. Training Course) 1954; Univ. of Montreal (Business Adm.-French); m. Helen Margaret, d. George Kydd of Ottawa, 1943; children: Russell, Elizabeth, Thomas; VICE-PRES., GEN. COUNSEL AND SECY., VICTORIA AND GREY TRUST CO. since 1967; Dir., Internat. Savings and Loan Corp.; Cdn. First Mortgage Corp.; Secty., VGM Trustco Ltd.; mem., Bd. of Gov., Sir George Williams Univ., 1959-67; read law with Montgomery, McMichael, Common & Howard, Montreal; called to the Bar, Que., 1941; cr. Q.C., 1961; practised law in Montreal 1946-48; joined Patent Dept., Shawinigan Chemicals Ltd., 1948; trans. as Asst. Secy. and in charge of Legal Dept. to Shawinigan Power & Water Co.; apptd. Secy., 1954; also offr. and dir. of several cos. in Shawinigan organ.; joined Royal Trust Co., as Extve. Asst. and apptd. Secretary 1964; in 1966 apptd. General Supervisor, Corporate Trust; served with Candn. Navy, 1942-46; author of "Canadian Secretarial Practice"; Fellow, Trust Cos. Inst.; mem., McGill Grad Soc. (Hon. Secy., 1966-68); Chart. Inst. Secys. (Chrmn., Que. Br.

1961-63, Can. Div. 1965-67); mem. Extve. Comte. and Chrmn. Ins. Comte., Candn. Mfrs. Assn. 1960-63; Chrmn., Ins. Comte., Candn. Elect. Assn. 1960-63; mem. Bd. Trade Metrop. Toronto; Offrs. Comte., Trust Cos. Assn. Can. (Chrmn., Ont. Sec. 1971-72); Treas., Presb. Church in Canada; Pres., McGill Soc. of Toronto 1973-75; Pres. McGill Univ. Students' Soc. 1939-40; Presbyterian; recreations: curling, reading, music, golf; Clubs: Hermitage Country; National; Donalda; Home: 6 Stratheden Rd., Toronto, Ont. M4N 1E3; Office: 353 Bay St., Toronto, Ont. M5H 2T8 and Lindsay Ont.

MERKLEY, C. Lawrence, B.Com., M.B.A.; financial executive; e. Univ. of Alta. B.Com. 1967; Brigham Young Univ. M.B.A. 1969; PRESIDENT AND DIR., CANAVEST INC.; Sr. Analyst, Aetna Life & Casualty 1969; Asst. Dir. Business Research, Brigham Young Univ. 1971; Regional Mgr. New York, Data Resources Inc. 1972, Gen. Mgr. Can. 1974; Asst. Vice Pres. Portfolio Mang. Canada Permanent Trust Co. 1977; Pres., Toronto Stake, Ch. Latter Day Saints; Home: 2 The Outlook, Islington, Ont. M9B 2X6.

MEROLA, Mario, R.C.A.; sculptor; educator; b. Montreal, Que. 31 March 1931; s. Nicola and Octavie (Fitteau) M.; e. Ecole des Beaux-Arts Montréal 1946-52; Ecole Supérieure des Arts Décoratifs Paris 1952-52; m. Nicole Goyette 5 Aug. 1961; children: Caroline, Colette, Eleonora, Domenica, Nicola; PROF D'ART, UNIV. DU QUE. 1969- ; Prof., Ecole des Beaux Arts Montréal 1960-69; Founding Dir. Le Module Arts d'Environnement Univ. du Qué. 1969-70, Dir. Module Arts Plastiques 1973-74; has created over 60 sculptures and murals integrated to arch. environment since 1951; rep. in over 100 solo and group exhns. Montreal, Ottawa, New York, Paris, Brussels, Brest, Osaka, Vancouver, Milan; rep. in pub., corporate and private colls. incl. Nat. Gallery Can., Montreal Museum of Fine Arts, Musée du Qué., Musée D'Art Contemporain Can. Council Art Bank, Musée de Brest (France); recipient First Prize mural Hôtel de LaSalle Montreal 1951; French Govt. Grant 1952; First Prize mural Candn. Pavillion Brussels Internat. Exhn. 1957; Can. Council Grant 1963, 1968; 3 Hon. Mentions Montreal "Monuments-Fontaine Contest" 1965; Ministère des Affaires Culturelles du Qué. Grant 1972; First Prize several murals Institut d'Hôtellerie 1973, mural CEGEP du vieux Montréal 1975; Pierrefonds mural exhibited Milan Biennal 1968; Pres., Soc. des Artistes Prof. du Qué. 1967-68; Assn. des Sculpteurs du Qué. 1971-72; R. Catholic; Home: 216 rue Somerville, Montréal, Qué. H3L 1A3; Office: Univ. Du Qué. Dept. Art Plastique, C.P. 8888, Succ. A, Montreal, Que. H3C 3P8

MERRILL, Geoffrey H., M.A.; educator; b. Montreal, Que., 29 March 1925; s. Geoffrey Oliver and Margaret Manson (Hunter) M.; e. Roslyn Elem. Sch. Westmount (Que.) 1940; Westmount (Que.) High Sch. 1944; McGill Univ. B.A. 1949, M.A. 1966; m. Beatrice Taylor, d. Trevelyan Taylor, 13 April 1957; HEADMASTER, LOWER CANADA COLL. since 1968; Asst. Princ. Roslyn Sch. 1951-55; Dir. of Jr. Sch. present Coll. 1955-67; Programme Dir. Camp Nomininque 1950-66; served with RCN 1944-45; Pres. Westmount Mun. Assn. 1960; Life Dir. Montreal Gen. Hosp.; mem. Candn. Headmasters' Assn. (Pres. 1974); Que. Assn. Independent Schs. (Pres. 1975); Queen's Jubilee Medal 1978; Phi Delta Theta (Pres. 1949); Anglican; Clubs: University; Montreal Badminton & Squash; Home: 4655 Bonavista Ave., Montreal, Que. H3W 2C6; Office: 4090 Royal Ave., Montreal, Que. H4A 2M5

MERRITHEW, Hon. Gerald S., M.L.A., B.A., B.Ed.; politician; educator; b. Saint John, N.B. 23 Sept. 1931; e. Rothesay Consol. Sch., Grad., Teacher's Coll., Fredericton; B.A., B.Ed. Univ. of N.B.; m. Gloria McLean; six children; GOV'T HOUSE LEADER IN LEGISLATIVE ASSEMBLY since 1978; el. to Saint John City Council

1971; resigned following el. to Leg. Dec. 1972; Min. of Education 1974-76; Min. of Comm. and Development 1976; a sch. teacher and principal for over 25 years in Saint John area; former Pres., Saint John Teachers' Assn.; el to Candn. Coll. of Teachers 1962; served in Candn. Army Mil. 16 yrs. attaining rank Lt.-Col.; former C.O., Royal N.B. Regt.; hon. Lt. Col. First Battalion, Royal N.B. Regt. since 1977; Nat. Pres. (Past Pres. N.B. Br.) Candn. Inf. Assn.; Dir. Army Cadet League N.B.; mem. Red Cross Youth Adv. Bd.; Bd. Dirs. United Fund; Council, Saint John Art Club; Charter mem. Social Services Council of Saint John; Hon. Vice Pres., N.B. Rifle Assn.; Hon. Patron, Black Powder Assoc.; Home: 3 Kennington St., E. Saint John, N.B. E2J 2Z1; Office: Centennial Bldg., Fredericton, N.B.

MERTENS, Erwin M., Text. Eng.; executive; b. Radevormwald, W. Germany 25 Feb. 1931; s. Otto Albert and Philomene (Sevenich) M.; e. Techische Hochschule Aachen, Text. Eng. 1958; m. Dorothee, d. Karl Roebbecke, 19 Dec. 1959; children: Jan-Christoph, Mark-Oliver, Stefanie; PRES. & CHIEF EXTVE. OFFR., GWG INC. 1977- ; Gen. Mgr. & Treas., Clinton Hosiery Co. Ltd., 1959-60; Gen. Mgr. Mgr., Monarch Apparel Ltd. & Monarch Knitting Co. Ltd., 1960-65; with GWG since 1965, Extve. Vice Pres. 1976-77; mem., Bd. of Governors, Univ. of Alta.; Roman Catholic; Home: 10248 Connaught Dr., Edmonton, Alta. T5N 3J2; Office: 600 - 5240 Calgary Trail, Edmonton, Alta. T2J 2K6

METCALF, Frederick Thomas, C.D.; communications executive; b. Toronto, Ont. 17 March 1921; s. Charles and Mable (Atkinson) M.; e. N. Toronto Coll. Inst.; m. Kathleen May d. Arthur C. Adams 3 Oct. 1940; children: Douglas, David, Charles, Diane, Cheryl; PRES. AND CHIEF OPERATING OFFR., MACLEAN HUNTER LTD. 1977- ; Chrmn. and Dir. Maclean Hunter Cable TV Inc.; Suburban Cablevision (N.J.); Pres. and Dir. Peterborough Cable Television Ltd.; Chmn., Key Radio Ltd.; Data Business Form Ltd.; Dir. Transkrit Corp. (N.Y.); Canada Trust; Sales Rep. Dunn Sales Toronto 1946-47; Vice Pres. and Gen. Mgr. CJOY Ltd. Guelph 1947 Pres. Neighbourhood Television Ltd. 1952; Mang. Dir. Maclean-Hunter Cable TV Ltd. Toronto 1967, Pres. 1968; served with Candn. Army 1942-46, N.W. Europe; joined Militia 1948 retiring as C.O. 11th Field Regt., Royal Regt. Candn. Arty. 1961; apptd. Hon. Lt. Col. 1972, promoted Col. and apptd. Hon. Col. 1974; Founding Pres. Candn. Cable Television Assn.; mem. Candn. Assn. Broadcasters; recreations: swimming, hiking, reading, travel; Clubs: Guelph Country; Cutten; Royal Candn. Mil. Inst.; University (Toronto); Home: Wyndridge Acres, Box 78, Puslinch, Ont. N0B 2J0; Office: 481 University Ave., Toronto, Ont. M5W 1A7

MEWETT, Alan W., B.C.L., LL.M., S.J.D.; educator; b. Southampton, Eng., 25 Sept. 1930; s. Stanley Arthur and Kathleen (Mew) M.; e. King Edwards Sch., Eng., 1949; Birmingham Univ., LL.B. 1952; Hertford Coll., Oxford Univ., B.C.L. 1954; Univ. of Mich., LL.M. 1956, S.J.D. 1959, PROF. OF LAW UNIV. OF TORONTO, since 1967 and mem. Extve. Council, Centre of Criminology there since 1968; formerly taught at Chicago Univ., Univ. of Sask., Queen's Univ.; Acting Dean and Assoc. Dean, Osgoode Hall Law Sch., 1966-67; called to Bar of Ont. 1961; co-author, "Philosophy of Sentencing", 1970; "Criminal Law", 1978; Ed., "Criminal Law Quarterly" since 1966; "Martin's Criminal Code of Canada", 1965-68; "Butterworth's Canadian Criminal Law Series"; other writings incl. numerous periodical articles; mem., Assn. Candn. Law Teachers; York Co. Law Assn.; Medico-Legal Soc. Toronto; Hertford Soc. Oxford; Phi Delta Phi; recreations: bridge, backgammon, crosswords; Home: 179 Madison Ave., Toronto, Ont. M5R 2S6

MEYBOOM, Peter, M.Sc., Ph.D.; geologist; Canadian public servant; b. Barneveld, The Netherlands, 26 Apl.

1934; s. Petrus and Maria Catherina Jacoba (v. Wel) M.; e. State Univ. Utrecht, B.Sc. 1956, M.Sc. (Geol.) 1958, Ph.D. (Geol) 1960; m. Elisabeth, d. J. P. Janssen, 19 Dec. 1957; children: Jan Peter, Joost, Alexander; DEPY. SECY. ADM. POLICY, CAN. TREASURY BD. SECRETARIAT, since 1977; Research Scient., Alta. Research Council, Edmonton, 1958-61; Geol. Survey of Can. 1961-66; Head, Groundwater Subdiv., Inland Waters Br., Dept. Energy Mines & Resources, 1967-69; Science Advisor, Can. Dept. of Finance, 1970-72; Dir., Science Policy, Can. Dept. Environment, 1972-73; Dir. Gen., Science Procurement Sec., Can. Dept. of Supply & Services, 1973-75; Asst. Secy. (Indust.), Can. Min. of State Sci. and Technol., 1975-77; rec'd Candn. Centennial Medal 1967; mem., Prof. Engrs. Alta.; Home: 4 Cedarcrest Ave., Ottawa, Ont. K2E 5P8; Office: Ottawa, Ont. K1A 0S5

MEYER, Perry, Hon. Mr. Justice; b. Montreal, Que., 6 May 1928; s. Philip, Q.C., and Queenie (Klineberg) Meyerovitch; e. High Sch. of Montreal; McGill Univ., B.A. 1949 (1st Class Hons. Math.; Univ. Scholar); B.C.L. 1952 (1st Class Hons.; Eliz. Torrance Gold Medal; MacDonald Travelling Scholar); post-grad work at Univ. of Grenoble (France) 1952-53; m. Joy, d. David Ballon, M.D., Westmount, Que., 25 June 1952; children: Vicki Anne, Linda Ruth, Sarah Jane; PUISNE JUDGE, SUPERIOR COURT OF QUE., since 1975; Prof. of Law, McGill Univ., 1968-75; mem. Bd. Govs., McGill till 1975; former Prof. Faculté Internat. pour l'Enseignement du Droit Comparé (Strasbourg); Chrmn., Nat. Extve., Candn. Jewish Congress 1974-77; Adjudicator for Federal public service 1970-75; mem., Superior Council of Education of P.Q. 1964-71; Chairman (1967-70) Comn. of Higher Education of P.Q.; President, later Honorary President, Cercle Juif de Langue Française; Pres., Hampstead Mun. Assn. 1964-66; read law with Meyerovitch & Levy, Montreal; called to the Bar of Que. 1954 (awarded gold medal of Paris Bar for highest standing civil law in Que. Bar exams); practised law actively in partnership with father, Philip Meyerovitch, Q.C. till 1963; Lectr., Faculty of Law, McGill Univ., 1960-63; Assoc. Prof. 1963-68; cr. Q.C. 1973; Publications: Editor for Quebec, Canadian Bankruptcy Reports, 1962-65; shared $30,000 grand prize in 1967 Canadian Centennial writing competition "Canada-2000 A.D." for work on future of Canadian legal system; articles and book reviews in various publs.; mem., Internat. Law Assn.; Candn. Assn. of Comparative Law; l'Assn. internat. du droit comparé; Que. Council of Univs. 1972-75; Que. Human Rights Comn. 1975; Nat. Acad. Arbitrators; Hebrew; Home: 9 Thurlow Rd., Hampstead, Montreal, Que. H3X 3G4; Office: 1 Notre Dame East, Montreal, Que. H2Y 1B6

MEYERHOF, George Geoffrey, B.Sc., M.Sc., Ph.D., D.Sc., Dr. Ing., D.ès Sc., F.R.S.C. (1969); college professor; b. Kiel, Germany, 29 May 1916; s. late Prof. Otto, M.D., LL.D., F.R.S., and late Hedwig (Schallenberg) M.; e. Gymnasium, Berlin and Heidelberg; University Coll., London Univ., B.Sc. (1st Class Hon.) 1938 and Dipl. in Civil and Mun. Engn. with Distinction, also Vernon Harcourt Civil Engn. Prize; London Univ., M.Sc. 1944, Ph.D. 1950; D.Sc. 1954 (Eng.; for contrib. to soil mech. and study of foundations and structures); m. Elisabeth, d. late Hans Meyerhof, 22 Feb. 1947; two s., Thomas Paul, Peter George; PROF. CIVIL ENGN., TECH. UNIV. OF N.S. 1981; Dir., Sch. Grad. Studies 1962-64; Engr. with consultants for design of rein. concrete, steel bldgs., bridges, indust. structures and pub. works in Britain, 1938-43; supervised design of various civil engn. works in connection with 2nd World War, and in charge of soil mech. lab. for design of earthworks, earth retaining structures, foundations and aerodromes, 1943-46; Sr. Scient. Offr. at Brit. Govt. Bldg. Research Station, Garston, 1946-50; Principal Scient. Offr. and Head of Foundation Sec. at Bldg. Research Station, 1950-53; mem. of Staff of Foundation Co. of Canada and Supervising Engr. in Foundation of Canada Engineering Corp., 1953-55; Prof. and Head, Dept. Civil Eng. 1955-81 (Dean of Coll.

1964-70); awarded Research Medal of Inst. of Structural Engrs. (Eng.) 1953; Duggan Medal of Engn. Inst. Canada, 1958 and 1963; mem., Soils and Materials Comte., Candn. Good Roads Assn.; Civil Engineering and Earth Sciences Grants Comte. and Soil Mechanics Comte., Nat. Research Council Can.; former mem. of Foundation Research Comte., Inst. of Structural Engrs. (Eng.); Fellow, Engn. Inst. Can. (Vice-Pres. 1972-74); Am. Soc. Civil Engrs.; Inst. of Civil Engrs. (England); Inst. of Structural Engrs. (Eng.); Overseas Rep. for E. Can.); mem., Am. Concrete Inst.; Council for Can. of Institution of Civil Engrs. (Eng.); Internat. Assn. Bridge and Structural Engn.; Internat. Soc. Soil Mech. & Foundation Engn.; Assn. Prof. Engrs. N.S.; Hon. mem. N.S. Constr. Engn. Assn.; Pres. (1972-74) Candn. Geotech. Soc. (R. F. Legget Award 1974); Terzaghi Lecturer, American Society of Civil Engineers 1975; mem., Advisory Council, American Soc. for Hist. of Tech.; mem. Ed. Board, Pergamon Press, Oxford; Fellow, N.Y. Acad. of Sciences; mem., Bd. of Govs., N.S. Tech. Coll. 1964-77; Candn. Accreditation Bd., Can. Council of Prof. Engrs.; rec'd Can. Centennial Medal, 1967; Hon. Dr. Ing. Aachen 1973; Hon. D.èsSc. Ghent 1975; Queen's Silver Jubilee Medal 1978; Engineering Award, Assn. Prof. Engrs., N.S., 1977; life mem., Am. Soc. Civ. Engrs.; author of numerous papers on structural engn. and soil mech. subjects; Protestant; recreations: travelling, photography, music; Home: 889 Beaufort Ave., Halifax, N.S. B3H 3X7; Office: Spring Garden Road, Halifax, N.S. B3J 2X4

MHUN, Henri, economist; b. Romain, France, 16 March 1914; s. Henri and Lea (Bruno) M.; e. Coll. Jean de la Fontaine, Chateau-Thierry; Univ. de Paris Docteur en droit; Univ. de Montréal Docteur ès Sciences sociales et economiques; m. Francine Lacroix, 27 Jan. 1954; children: Catherine, Françoise, Sophie; PRESIDENT, MHUN & ASSOC. LTD.; Teacher Pub. Elem. Sch. 1932-35; Indo-China Bank 1937-39; Econ. Ministry of Indust. Production, Paris 1945; Pres. Mhun & Associates Ltd. 1968-71; corr. and collab. production several European and Cdn. publs. incl. Action Canada-France Le Monde 1951-61, Journal de Geneve 1948-70, L'Agence Economique et Financière 1953-68; commentator on Candn. radio (Service Internat. Radio Can.); mem. de la Comn. d'étude des problèmes intermun. Montreal 1966-67; Dir. de la Recherche Comn. Gendron sur la langue française Que. 1970-71; served in Algeria 1936-37, P.O.W. Germany during WW II; rec'd Chevalier de l'Ordre du Mérite France; mem. Chambre de Comm. Française au Can.; author "Le Commerce Imperial" 1946; "Inventaire economique du Canada" 1950; "L'Economie sans douleur" 1968; Assn. Canadienne d'Economique; Inst. Canadien des Affaires Internationales; R. Catholic; recreations: travelling; Home: 4954 Ponsard Ave., Montreal, Que. H3W 2A5; Office: 1110 Sherbrooke Ave. W., Ste. 1204, Montreal, Que. H3A 1G8

MIANO, Donald J., B.A.; financial executive; b. Boston Mass. 5 Aug. 1930; s. late Gordon Daniel and Mildred Donaldson (Hawes) M.; e. Tufts Univ. B.A.; m. Joyce Louise d. late Glynguard R. Burge 1964; VICE PRES. & DIR., E-L FINANCIAL CORP. LTD. 1975- ; Dir. Empire Life Insurance Co.; Dominion of Canada General Insurance Co.; Casualty Co. of Canada; Canadian and Foreign Securities Co. Ltd.; Economic Investment Trust Ltd.; Canadian Northern Prairie Lands Co. Ltd.; United Corp. Ltd.; Pres., G. Tower Fergusson Ltd.; came to Can. 1957; Founding Partner, Toronto Jones Heward Ltd. 1963-69; mem. Toronto Stock Exchange 1969-75; mem. Toronto Financial Analysts Soc.; recreation: sailing; Clubs: National; R.C.Y.C.; Beach (Palm Beach); Everglades (Palm Beach); Home: 113 Dunvegan Rd., Toronto, Ont. M4V 2P9; Office: 165 University Ave., Toronto, Ont. M5H 3B8.

MICHAEL, T. H. Glynn, B.A., F.C.I.C.; b. Toronto, Ont., 20 May 1918; s. John Hugh and Hilda (Clarke) M.; e. Upper Canada Coll.; Victoria Coll., Univ. of Toronto, B.A. (Chem.) 1940; m. Ruth Vivien Dexter, 1942; chil-

dren: Margaret Vivian (Dr. M.V. Tait), Barbara Elizabeth (Mrs. B.E. Drew), John Hugh; EXTVE. DIR. AND SECY., CHEMICAL INST. OF CAN., since 1958; also Extve. Dir., Candn. Soc. for Chem. Engn.; with Nat. Research Council, Ottawa, 1941-46; Chief Chemist, Woburn Chemicals Ltd., Toronto, Ont., 1946-53; Dir. of Research, Howards & Sons (Can.) Ltd., Cornwall, Ont., 1953-58; Treas., Youth Science Foundation, 1961-71; mem., Chem. Inst. of Can. (Chrmn. of Toronto Sec. 1951; Chrmn. of Protective Coatings Divn., 1950-51; Dir. and Treas. 1953-56); Am. Chem. Soc.; Inst. of Assn. Extves. (Pres. 1971-72); Council of Engn. & Scient. Soc. Extves. (Pres. 1969-70); United Church; Home: 295 Clemow Ave., Ottawa, Ont. K1S 2B7; Office: 151 Slater St., Ottawa, Ont. K1P 5H3

MICHAELS, Joel Bialys; motion picture producer; b. Buffalo, N.Y. 24 Oct. 1938; s. Alexander Bialys and Doris (Prais) M.; e. Buffalo Bennett High Sch. 1956; m. Diana Maddox 24 Aug. 1964; one child: Carey Drusilla; came to Can. 1962; Producer, Michaels[Drabinsky Productions; mem. Screen Actors Guild; Actors Equity Assn.; ACTRA; AFTRA; MPPA; Jewish; Home: 1614 Thayer Ave., Los Angeles, Cal. 90024; Office: 272 S. Lasky Dr., Suite 104, Beverly Hills, Cal. 90212.

MICHAELS, Lorne; television producer and writer; b. Toronto, Ont. 17 Nov.; writer, producer comedy spls. and dramas CBC, 1969-72; contbg. writer TV shows: Rowan and Martin "Laugh-In", 1968-69; producer, writer, "Saturday Night Live", NBC, 1975-80; writer, producer 4 Lily Tomlin Spls, 1972, 73, 74, 75; producer, writer TV spls: "Rutles" All You Need is Cash", 1978; "Paul Simon", 1977; "Beach Boys", 1976; "Flip Wilson", 1974; "Perry Como", 1974; Recipient Emmy awards as writer and producer for Sat. Night Live, 1976; 1 Emmy award as writer, 1977; Emmy award for Paul Simon Spl, 1978; San Francisco Film award, 1976; 4 awards Writers Guild; Winner award Nat. Acad. TV Arts and Scis (2); Address: c/o NBC Press, Dept 30, Rockefeller Plaza, New York, N.Y. 10020

MICHALS, George Francis, B.Com., C.A.; executive; b. Hungary 14 Sept. 1935; s. Todor and Ilona (Sinkovich) Mihalcsics; e. Sir George Williams Univ. B.Com. 1961; McGill Univ. C.A. 1963; came to Can. 1956; m. Patricia Elizabeth d. George Henry Hoffman, Daytona Beach, Fla. 18 June 1971; children: Kathrine, Julie, Elizabeth, Georgina; EXTVE. VICE PRES., GENSTAR LTD. since 1979; C.A. with Coopers & Lybrand, Montreal 1963-68; Treas., Dominion Textile Co. Ltd. 1968, Vice Pres. Subsidiaries 1970, Extve. Vice Pres. Knit Div. 1971; Vice Pres. Finance Genstar Ltd. 1974, Sr. Vice Pres. 1976; mem. Council Financial Extves. (Conf. Bd.); Financial Extves. Assn.; R. Catholic; recreations: tennis, squash; Clubs: St. James's; Home: 215 Round Hill Rd., Tiburon, Cal. 94920; Office: 4 Embarcadero Center Suite 4000, San Francisco, California 94111.

MICHAUD, Paul-André, C.A.; b. St. Juste du Lac, Temiscouata, Que., 9 Apl. 1935; s. Louis-Philippe and Simone (Dubé) M.; e. Ecole de Commerce, Rimouski, Que.; Laval Univ.; m. Liliane, d. Henri Buisson, 24 Sept. 1960; children: Suzanne, Helene, Eric; PARTNER, SAMSON, BELAIR & ASSOCIES. since 1969; employed with Iron Ore Co. of Canada as Sr. Internal Auditor 1959-63; tenure in the present firm 1954-59 and 1963-66 when apptd. Jr. Partner; apptd. Auditor of Bank of Canada 1975; Pres. Loto Quebec 1976-77; mem. of Prof. Assns.; comté. consultatif, Banque Fed. de developpement pour Que.; Catholic; recreations: squash, skiing, sailing; Clubs: Quebec Yacht Club; Cercle Universitaire de Que.; Mess des Officiers de la Citadelle de Que.; Tennis Montcalm; Home: 1340 Nelles, Ste-Foy, Que.; Office: 1 Parc Samuel-Holland, Quebec City, Que.

MICHENER, Rt. Hon. (Daniel) Roland, P.C. (1962), C.C., C.M.M., K.St.J., C.D., Q.C., M.A., D.C.L., LL.D.,

b. Lacombe, Alberta, 19 April 1900; s. Senator Edward and Mary Edith (Roland) M.; e. Univ. of Alta., B.A. 1920 (Rhodes Scholar Alta. 1919); Oxford University, B.A. 1922, B.C.L. 1923, M.A. 1929; LL.D. Ottawa 1948, Queen's 1958, Laval 1960, Alta. 1967, Toronto 1968, St. Mary's 1968, Mount Allison 1969, Brock 1969, Royal Mil. Coll. Can. 1969, McGill 1970, Manitoba 1970, York 1970, Brit. Columbia 1971, Jewish Theol. Semy. of America 1972, N.B. 1972, Dalhousie 1974, Law Soc. of Upper Can.; D.C.L. Bishop's 1968, Windsor 1969, Oxford 1970; m. Norah Evangeline, d. late Robert and Sarah Jane (Duffield) Willis, Vancouver, B.C., 26 February 1927; children: Joan (Mrs. Donald Rohr), Diana (Mrs. Roy Edward Schatz); Assoc. Counsel, Lang, Michener, Cranston, Farquharson & Wright; Hon. Chrmn. Bd., Victoria & Grey Trust; Hon. Chmn., Teck Corp. Ltd.; Hon. Dir., E.L. Financial Corp.; Dir., Pamour Porcupine Mines Ltd.; Chancellor, Queen's Univ. 1974-1980; past Pres. and mem. of council, Candn. Inst. Internat. Affairs; Chrmn., Candn. Council of H.R.H. The Duke of Edinburgh's Fifth Commonwealth Study Conf. — Can. 1980; Co-Chrmn., Can. Foundation for Refugees 1979-81; Prior for Canada and Kt. Justice, Most Ven. Order Hosp. St. John of Jerusalem, 9 June 1967; Hon. Fellow, Hertford Coll., Oxford (1961); Toronto Academy Medicine (1967); Roy. Coll. Phys. & Surg. Can. (1968); Roy. Arch. Institute of Canada (1968); Trinity College, Toronto (1968); Royal Society of Canada (1975); Hon. mem., Candn. Med. Assn. (1968); Hon. Bencher, Law Soc. Upper Can. (1968); called to Bar at the Middle Temple (Eng.) 1923, of Ont. 1924; cr. K.C. 1943; practising lawyer with firm of Lang, Michener etc., Toronto, Ont. 1924-57; served with R.A.F. 1918; comnd. Lt., R.C.A. (Res.) 1943; mem. Ont. Leg. for St. David, Toronto 1945-48; Prov. Secy. and Registrar, Ont. 1946-48; el. to H. of C. for Toronto-St. Paul's, g.e. 1953; re-el. 1957, '58; el Speaker, H. of C., 14 Oct. 1957 and 12 May 1958; mem. Council, Commonwealth Parlty. Assn. 1959-61; Chrmn., Manitoba Roy. Comn. on Local Govt. and Finance 1962-64; High Comnr. to India 1964-67; Gov. Gen. & Commdr.-in-Chief of Can. & Chancellor & Princ. Companion Order of Can. 1967-74; Gen. Secy. for Can., Rhodes Scholarships 1936-64; Hon. Patron, U.N. Assn. in Can.; former Hon. Pres., Katimavik; United Empire Loyalists Assn. of Can., Hon. Chrmn., Cdn. Assn. for Club of Rome; former Gov., Toronto W. Hosp. and Univ. of Toronto; former Pres., Lawyers Club, Empire Club (Toronto), Metrop. Toronto Bd. Trade; Past Hon. Counsel, Red Cross Ont. Div.; Past Chrmn. Extve., Candn. Assn. Adult Educ.; Past Offr. and Dir. of various mining and financial cos.; recipient, Royal Victoria Chain 1973; Home: 24 Thornwood Rd., Toronto, Ont. M4W 2S1; Office: (Box 10) First Canadian Place, Toronto, Ont.

MICHENER, Mrs. Roland (Norah Evangeline Willis), C.C. (1971), Ph.D., D.Litt., LL.D.; b. Manitoba; d. late Robert and Sarah Jane (Duffield) Willis; e. Univ. of British Columbia, grad. in Hist. & Econ.; Toronto Conserv. of Music; Univ. of Toronto, M.A., Ph.D., Pontifical Inst. of Mediaeval Studies; St. Mary's Univ., D.Litt.; Waterloo Lutheran, Queen's; LL.D.; York Univ., D.Litt.; Mt. St. Vincent Univ., D. Humane Letters; m. The Rt. Hon. Daniel Roland Michener; three d., Joan Rohr, Diana Schatz, Wendy Lawrence (dec'd.); Chrmn., Mothers' Placement Comte., Comte. for Brit. Overseas Children, Univ. of Toronto during World War II; Pres., Delhi (India) Commonwealth Women's Assn. and worked for relief in stricken areas during husband's tenure as High Commr.; Dame of Grace Most Venerable Order of Hosp. of St. John of Jerusalem; Dame Grand Cross, Order of St. Lazarus of Jerusalem; Centennial Medal 1967; Hon. Sgt. of the Gov. Gen.'s Horse Guards; Queen's Jubilee Medal 1977; author, "Maritain on the Nature of Man in a Christian Democracy", 1955; Address: 24 Thornwood Rd., Toronto, Ont. M4W 2S1

MICHIE, Ian Gordon, F.F.A., F.I.A., F.C.I.A., A.S.A.; insurance executive; b. London, Eng., 11 Aug. 1924; s.

John and Lilias Brebner (MacGregor) M.; e. Minchenden Sch., London, Eng., 1935-41; m. Molly, d. late Arthur J. Powell, 15 Nov. 1947; two d., Katharine Jean, Fiona Margaret; CHIEF AGT., PRESIDENT, N.A.L. OPERATIONS, THE MERCANTILE AND GENERAL REINSURANCE CO. LIMITED, since 1975; President and Chrmn., M & G Computer Systems Ltd.; since 1979; Dir., Atlas Assurance Co. Ltd., London, Eng., 1941-50; Bacon & Woodrow, Consulting Actuaries, London, Eng., 1950-57 — Partner 1954-57; joined present Co. 1957; Asst. Actuary, London, Eng., Feb.-Nov. 1957; Actuary for Can. (Toronto), 1957-64; Chief Agent (Life Br.) and Actuary for Can., 1965-68; Chief Agt., Extve. Vice-Pres. and Actuary 1969-74; served with RN Mediterranean Fleet, 1942-46 and Home Fleet 1951-52; mem. Pension Bd., Presb. Ch. of Can.; Treas., Candn. Inst. Actuaries, 1966-67, Vice Pres. 1977-78; Liberal; Presbyterian; recreations: gardening, travelling; Club: Ontario; Home: 256 Upper Highland Cres., Willowdale, Ont. M2P 1V3; Office: 141 Adelaide St. West, Toronto, Ont. M5H 3N2

MICKELSON, Norma I., B.Ed., M.A., Ph.D.; educator; b. Victoria, B.C. 5 Nov. 1926; d. Ambrose Seymour and Iva Matthews; e. Univ. of B.C. B.Ed. 1963; Univ. of Victoria M.A. 1968; Univ. of Wash. Ph.D. 1972; m. 12 Aug. 1946; children: Richard Paul, Irene Ann; Prof. and Dean, Univ. of Victoria; Teacher 1945-60; Supvr. 1960-66; Prof. since 1967; mem. P.E.O.; Internat. Reading Assn.; Phi Delta Kappa; recreation: bridge; Home: 2010 Ferndale Rd., Victoria, B.C. V8N 2Y7

MIDDLETON, Gerard Viner, B.Sc., Ph.D., D.I.C., F.R.S.C.; geologist; educator; b. Capetown, S. Africa 13 May 1931; s. Reginald Viner Cecil and Doris May (Hutchinson) M.; e. Mt. St. Mary's Coll. Spinkhill, Eng. 1949; Imp. Coll. Univ. London B.Sc., A.R.C.S. 1952, Ph.D., D.I.C. 1954; m. Muriel Anne d. William Zinkewich, Brantford, Ont. 4 Apl. 1959; children: Laurence, Teresa, Margaret; PROF. AND CHRMN. OF GEOL. McMASTER UNIV. since 1978; Geol. California Standard Oil Co. Calgary and Regina 1954-55; Dept. of Geol. McMaster Univ. 1955, Chrmn. 1959-62, Prof. since 1967; co-author "Origin of Sedimentary Rocks" 1972; author over 50 scient. articles various aspects geol. (sedimentol.); mem. Geol. Assn. Can. (Ed. 1972-74); Internat. Assn. Sedimentols. (Vice Pres. since 1978); Candn. Soc. Petrol, Geols.; Am. Assn. Petrol. Geols.; Soc. Econ. Paleontols. & Minerals.; Candn. Assn. Univ. Teachers; R. Catholic; Home: 90 St. Margaret's Rd., Ancaster, Ont. L9G 2K9; Office: Hamilton, Ont. L8S 4M1.

MIDDLETON, Robert M., B.A.; diplomat; b. Truro, N.S., 24 Feb. 1931; s. William Alexander and Jessie Marie (Smith) M.; e. Univ. of B.C. B.A. 1953; Ambassador to South Africa, 1979 with accred. as High Commr. to Botswana, Lesotho and Swaziland; joined Dept. External Affairs 1955; Third Secy. Djakarta 1957, First Secy. Rio de Janeiro 1962 and Chargé d'Affaires a.i. 1963-64, Advisor to Candn. Del. I.L.O. UN Econ. and Social Council and UN Gen. Assembly 1964-67, Counsellor Washington 1967-71, Dir. N.W. Europe Div. 1971-72 and Security & Intelligence Div. 1972-75 Ottawa, Bicultural Programme Quebec City 1975-76, High Commr. To Ghana 1976 with accreditations as Ambassador to Benin, Liberia and Togo; Anglican; recreations: tennis, riding, golf.

MIDDLETON, William Edgar Knowles, D.Sc., F.R.S.C.; b. Walsall Eng., 23 June 1902; s. Richard Edgar and Margaret Jane (Knowles) M.; e. Purdue Univ.; Univ. of Sask., B.Sc. 1927, M.Sc. 1929; D.Sc., Boston Univ. 1950; D.Sc., McGill Univ., 1976; m. Dorothy, d. Rev. D. C. Day, Saskatoon, Sask., 1 Feb. 1930; children: John, Diana; Hon. Lect., Dept. of Physics, Univ. of Toronto, 1933-39; with Meteorol. Service of Can., 1930-46; Sr. Research Offr., Nat. Research Labs., Instrumental Optics Sec., 1946 till retirement; Pres., Sub-Comn. on Atmospheric Optics 1947; Fellow, Optical Soc. of Am. (Ives Medal 1959); Roy.

Meteorol. Soc. (Pres., Candn. Br. 1944-46); Hon. mem., Amer. Meteorol. Soc.; Secy. Sec. III. Roy. Soc. of Can., 1945-48; Hon. Lectr., Dept. of Hist. of Med. & Science, Univ. of B.C. 1967-78; author of "Visibility in Meteorology", 1935, 2nd ed. 1941; "Meteorological Instruments", 1941, 2nd ed. 1943; "Vision Through the Atmosphere", 1952; "The History of the Barometer", 1964; "A History of the Theories of Rain", 1965; "A History of the Thermometer", 1966; "Invention of the Meteorological Instruments", 1969; "The Experimenters: a Study of the Accademia del Cimento", 1971; "Physics of the National Research Council of Canada, 1929-1952", 1979; "Lorenzo Magalotti at the Court of Charles II", 1980; "Radar Development in Can." 1981; has written about 100 scient. papers in fields of meteorol., optics, history of science and articles for "Encycl. Brit."; recreation: music; Address: Apt. 2406, 2020 Haro St., Vancouver, B.C. V6G 1J3

MIGICOVSKY, Bert Baruch, B.S.A., M.S., Ph.D., D.Sc., F.C.I.C., F.R.S.C.; b. Winnipeg, Manitoba, 14 March 1915; s. Samuel and Brocha (Winestock) M.; e. Univ. of Man., B.S.A. 1935; Univ. of Minn., M.S. 1937; Ph.D. 1939; post-doctorate study, Univ. of Cal., 1954; Hon. D.Sc. Carleton 1970; m. Geraldine, d. Jack Shnier, 15 Mar. 1943; children: John, Janet; Asst. Depy. Min., Research Br., Agric. Can. 1975-77 (ret.); Special Lectr., Dept. of Histol. and Embryol., Faculty of Med., Univ. of Ottawa; Research Asst., Univ. of Minn., 1937-40; joined Can. Dept. Agric. 1940; apptd. Chief of Biochem., Animal Research Inst., 1959; subsequently Asst. Dir. Gen. (Insts.), Research Br.; served overseas in 2nd World War with R.C.A.M.C., discharged with rank of Major; chapters in several books on isotopes, radioisotopes, control of cholesterol metabolism, calcium metabolism & Vit. D, etc.; F.A.O. report to U.N. on radioactive fallout in food and agric., 1959-60; Publications: numerous contrib. to scient. journs.; Pres., Ottawa Biol. & Biochem. Soc., 1960-61; Fellow, Agric. Inst. Can.; mem., Am. Biochem. Soc.; Candn. Biochem. Soc.; Candn. Physiol. Soc.; Nutrition Soc. Can.; Prof. Inst. Public Service; Fellow Royal Soc. of Can.; Chrmn., Gordon Research Conf. (on bones and teeth), 1959-60; rec'd. Hon. D.Sc. Manitoba 1973; Montreal Medal, Chem. Inst. of Can. 1975; Ottawa Biol. and Biochem. Award 1978; mem. Bd. of Dirs., Protein Oil Starch Pilot Plan Corp., 1973-78 Hebrew; recreation: golf; Club: Rideau View Golf & Country; Home: 185 Patricia St., Ottawa, Ont. K1Y 0C5

MIGUÉ, Jean-Luc, M.A., Ph.D., F.R.S.C.; economist; educator; b. St-Jacques, Qué. 13 Apl. 1933; s. Joseph Alfred and Laurence (Venne) M.; e. Univ. de Montréal B.A. 1953, M.A. 1956; London Sch. of Econ. 1958-60; Am. Univ. Ph.D. 1968; m. Renée d. Gaston Caron 13 Sept. 1958; children: Elizabeth Paule, Philippe Pascal, Sébastien Nicolas; PROF. OF ECON., NAT. SCH. OF PUB. ADM. since 1970; Research Offr., Bank of Canada 1957-58, Dept. of Educ. Qué. 1961-62; Prof. of Econ. Laval Univ. 1962-70; staff mem. Econ. Council of Can. 1973-74; author "Nationalistic Policies in Canada" 1979; "L'Economiste et la Chose Publique" 1979; co-author "The Price of Health" 1974; "Le Prix du Transport" 1978; Ed. "Le Québec D'Aujourd'hui" 1971; various articles; mem. Candn. Econ. Assn. (Extve. Council 1975-78); Am. Econ. Assn.; Pub. Choice Soc.; R. Catholic; recreation: greenhouse gardening; Home: 3181 de Galais, Québec City, Qué. G1W 2Z7; Office: 945 Wolfe, Québec City, Qué. G1V 3J9

MILAVSKY, Harold P., B. Comm.; executive; b. Limerick, Sask. 25 Jan. 1931; s. Jack and Clara (Levitsky) M.; e. Univ. of Sask. B.Com. 1953; m. Miriam R. d. Samuel Shugarman 5 Sept. 1954; children: Charlene, Roxanne, Gregory, Abbie, Carrie; PRESIDENT AND CEO, TRIZEC CORP. LTD. Dir., Brascan Ltd. (Toronto); Carena Bancorp-Inc. (Toronto); North Canadian Oils Ltd. (Calgary); Foodex Inc. (Toronto); Hatleigh Corp. (Toronto); Trizec

Equities Ltd. (Calgary); Trizec Western Inc. (Los Angeles); Central Park Lodges of Can. (Toronto); Mobile Home Communities Inc. (Denver); Pres. & Dir. Candn. Inst. Pub. Real Estate Co's. (Toronto); served as Treas. and Controller, Loram Internat. Ltd. 1956-64; Power Corp. Developments Ltd. and North American Recreation Ltd. 1965-69; joined Great West International Equities and present Co. 1969; Fellow, Chart. Inst. Secys.; mem. Inst. C.A.'s; Dir., Calgary Chamber of Comm.; recreations: skiing, tennis; Clubs: Calgary Petroleum; Glenmore Racquet; Univ. of Calgary Chancellor's; Home: 228 Pumphill Rise, S.W., Calgary, Alta. T2V 4C8; Office: 5 #3000, 700-2nd Street S.W., Calgary, Alta. T2P 2W2

MILES, Edgar Stuart, B.Com.; investment dealer; b. Quebec, Que., 23 Feb. 1919; s. Edgar Stuart and Janet Sandfield (McIntyre) M.; e. Runnymede Coll. Inst. Toronto 1938; Univ. of Toronto B.Com. 1942; m. Sylvia Margaret Devine, 6 Jan. 1971; children: Janet Elizabeth, Paul Radford, Stephen Michael, Mary Carol (all by previous marriage); former Chrmn. Extve. Comte. and Dir., Burns Bros. and Denton Ltd.; Chrmn. Bd. Govs. Toronto Stock Exchange; Dir. The Becker Milk Co. Ltd.; joined present Firm to initiate Research Dept. 1945, Dir. 1950, Vice Pres. 1960; served with RCAF as Navig. 1941-45; rank Sqdn. Leader; Mentioned in Despatches; Dir. Harold Innis Foundation; Past Dir. & Vice Pres. Jr. Invest. Dealers' Assn.; Past Chrmn. Educ. Comte. (Ont.) Invest. Dealers' Assn.; Past Pres., Secy. Analysts' Assn. Toronto; Gov. Toronto Stock Exchange 1962-65, 1974-75; recreation: golf; Clubs: National; Toronto Hunt; Home: 78 Chestnut Park Rd., Apt. 1, Toronto, Ont. M4W 1W9

MILL, William Arthur; retired company executive; b. Kensington, P.E.I., 2 May 1924; s. W. Roy and B. Irene (Semple) M.; e. Kensington (P.E.I.) High Sch.; Northwestern Univ., Marketing Course (2) 1963; Univ. of W. Ont., Mang. Course, 1970; m. Hazel L., d. Gordon Elliott, 27 Sept. 1952; Dir., Swift Eastern Limited; served in various Maritime Brs., Bank of Nova Scotia, 1941-44; joined Swift Cdn. Co. Ltd. Accounting & Provision Depts., Moncton, 1945-58; Asst., Gen. Provision Dept., Toronto, 1958-59; Provision Mgr., Calgary, 1959-61; Gen. Provision Mgr., Toronto, 1961-64; Asst. to Pres., Toronto, 1961-64; Business Planning Div., Swift & Co., Chicago, 1965-66; Plant Mgr., St. Joseph, Mo., 1966-68; Gen. Mgr., Presswood Bros. Ltd., 1968-69; Executive Vice President of present Co. 1969-73; Pres. and Dir. 1973-78; Chrmn. Bd. and Dir. 1978; Pres., Meat Packers Council Can.; Freemason; Shriner; Protestant; recreation: golf; Club: Credit Valley Golf & Country; Address: 44 Centennial Dr., Moncton, N.B.

MILLAR, Charles Gordon, B.Sc., P.Eng.; Executive; b. Montreal, Que. 28 Sept. 1926; s. Gordon Eric and Jennie Kathleen (Mitchinson) M.; e. Montreal W. High Sch. 1943; McGill Univ. B.Sc. 1947; P.Eng. (Chem.) 1963; m. Leonora Mary DeMers; children: Jennifer Gail; Andrea Mary; Executive V.P.-Operations Northern Telecom Inc.; Dir. Bell-Northern Research; Northern Telecom Ltd.; Northern Telecom Internat. Ltd.; Northern Telecom Can. Ltd.; Intersil Inc.; mem. Candn. Mfrs.' Assn.; Elect. & Electronic Mfrs. Assn. Can. (Chrmn.); Assn. Prof. Engrs. Prov. Ont.; Corp. Prof. Engrs. Que.; Home: 39 Old Mill Rd. Ph4, Toronto, Ont. M8X 1G6; Office: 33 City Centre Drive, Mississauga, Ont. L5B 2N5.

MILLAR, Margaret Ellis (Mrs. Kenneth); novelist; nature writer; b. Kitchener, Ont., 5 Feb. 1915; d. Henry William and Lavinia (Ferrier) Sturm; e. Kitchener-Waterloo (Ont.) Coll. Inst., 1933; Univ. of Toronto, 1933-36; m. 2 June 1938; one d., Linda Jane Pagnusat; author of following novels: "The Invisible Worm", 1941; "The Weak-Eyed Bat", 1942; "The Devil Loves Me", 1942; "Wall of Eyes", 1943; "Fire Will Freeze", 1944; "The Iron Gates", 1945; "Experiment in Springtime", 1947; "It's All in the Family", 1948; "The Cannibal Heart", 1949; "Do Evil in

Return", 1950; "Vanish In An Instant", 1952; "Rose's Last Summer", 1952; "Wives and Lovers", 1954; "Beast in View", 1955; "An Air That Kills", 1957; "The Listening Walls", 1959; "A Stranger In My Grave", 1960; "How Like An Angel", 1962; "The Fiend", 1964; nature book, "The Birds and the Beasts Were There", 1968; "Beyond This Point Are Monsters", 1970; "Ask For Me Tomorrow" 1976; "The Murder of Miranda" 1980; "Mermaid" 1982; rec'd Edgar Allan Poe Award, Mystery Writers of Am.; mem., Mystery Writers Am. (Pres. 1957); Nat. Audubon Soc.; Texas Ornithol. Soc.; Democrat; recreations: ornithology, gardening, swimming; Clubs: Coral Casino; Sierra; Home: 4420 Via Esperanza, Santa Barbara, Cal. 93110

MILLER, (Charles) George, M.Sc., D.Phil., F.C.I.C., P.Eng.; b. Winnipeg, Man. 1 Nov. 1932; s. Rossel Lorne and Mary Christine (Cornelius) M.; e. West Ward Pub. Sch. and Napanee (Ont.) Coll. Inst. 1950; Queen's Univ. B.Sc. (Engn. Chem.) 1954, M.Sc. (Phys. Chem.) 1955; Balliol Coll. Oxford Univ. D.Phil. (Phys. Chem.) 1957; m. Heather Sally, d. George Laing Howitt, Napanee, Ont. 21 Aug. 1954; children: Peter George, Patricia Margaret, David Lorne, Stephen James; ASST. DEPUTY MINISTER, MINERAL POLICY, ENERGY MINES & RESOURCES, CANADA 1981- ; Post Doctorate Fellow Nat. Research Council 1957; Research Group Leader Imperial Tobacco Co. Ltd. Montreal 1958; served with Celanese Canada Ltd. (formerly Chemcell Ltd.) successively as Devel. Sec. Head Edmonton, Supt. Chem. Devel., Supt. Process Systems, Dir. Manpower Planning Montreal, Mang. Dir. Chemcell S.A. Switzerland, Plant Mgr. Edmonton, Gen. Mgr. Chem. Div. 1960-72; Vice Pres. Operations, Stanley Associates Engineering Ltd. Edmonton 1972; Extve. Dir., Centre for Resource Studies, Queen's Univ. 1974-81; Past mem. Adv. Council on Engn. Queen's Univ.; Past Dir., Orphans Home and Widows Friend Soc. of Kingston; Past Dir. and Treas. Child Devel. Centre Edmonton; Past mem. Alta. Bd. Engn. Educ.; Past Chrmn. Science Adv. Comte. Alta. Environment Conserv. Authority; author or co-author various scient. papers; Gen. Ed. of series of monographs on mineral policy; CIMM distinguished lecturer, 1979/80; Fellow, Candn. Soc. Chem. Engn.; mem., Prof. Engrs. Assn. Ont.; Candn. Inst. Mining and Metall.; recreations: choral music, athletics; Home: 530 Laurier Ave., #603, Ottawa, Ont.; Office: Ottawa, Ont.

MILLER, Donald William, B.A., B.L.S.; librarian; b. Cornwall, Ont. 19 July 1933; s. William Laurence and Jessie Munro (MacDermid) M.; e. North Toronto Coll. Inst. 1954; Univ. of Toronto B.A. 1957; Univ. of B.C. B.L.S. 1964; m. Patricia Marie d. Nazem Kirk, Lethbridge, Alta. 27 March 1965; children: Michael Hugh, Alison Mary; DIR., GREATER VICTORIA PUBLIC LIBRARY 1971- ; Head Reference Dept. Calgary Pub. Lib. 1964-66; Asst. Dir. London (Ont.) Pub. Lib. and Art Museum 1966-71; mem. Art Gallery of Greater Victoria, Pres. 1976-78; mem. Candn. Lib. Assn.; B.C. Lib. Assn.; Inst. Victoria Librarians; recreations: skiing, bicycling; Home: 339 Foul Bay Rd., Victoria, B.C. V8S 4G6; Office: 735 Broughton St., Victoria, B.C. V8W 3H2.

MILLER, Douglas Wilfred, B.A.; executive; b. Vancouver, B.C. 13 July 1928; s. Jenny Josephine (Stifler) Spicer and late Wilfred Earle M.; e. Univ. of B.C., B.A. 1950; m. Margery Elaine d. late Archdeacon S. Williams 21 May 1954; children: D.Scott, Nancy J., Laura J.; Dir. and mem. Extve. Comte. Westmin Resources Ltd.; Dir., Private Energy Research Assn.; mem. Econ. Soc. Alta.; Phi Gamma Delta; Anglican; recreations: swimming, golf; Clubs: Calgary Petroleum; Ranchmen's; Home: 1702-24 A St. S.W., Calgary, Alta. T3C 1J4; Office: 1800, 255-Fifth Ave. S.W., Calgary, Alta. T2P 3G6

MILLER, Hon. Frank, M.P.P., P.Eng.; b. Toronto, Ont., 14 May 1927; s. Percy Frank and Margaret Stuart (McKe-

an) M.; e. Regal Road Public School and Oakwood Coll. Inst., Toronto, 1942; Gravenhurst (Ont.) High Sch., 1945; McGill Univ., 1945-49; m. Ann McArthur, d. William M. Norman, Montreal, 13 May 1950; children: Lawrence, Ross, Norman, Mary; TREASURER OF ONT. since 1978; Owner Patterson-Kaye Lodge, Bracebridge; Research Engr., Rubberset Co. Ltd., Gravenhurst 1949; Production Engr., Alcan, Arvida, Que. 1951; Chem. Teacher, St. Andrew's Coll., Aurora, Ont. 1953; Sales Engr. and Br. Mgr. Scarfe & Co., Brantford and Montreal 1956-60; Pres., Gordon Motor Sales Muskoka Ltd., 1962-69; Pres. Pinelands Lodge, Port Carling, Ont., 1970-73; Councillor, Bracebridge, 1967-70; el. MPP for Muskoka prov. g.e. 1971; Parliamentary Asst. to Min. of Health for Ont. 1972-74; Min. of Health for Ont. 1974-77; Min. of Nat. Resources 1977-78; mem., Assn. Prof. Engrs. Ont.; P. Conservative; United Church; recreations: skiing, flying, golf; Club: Rotary; Home: 355 Wellington, Bracebridge, Ont. P0B 1C0; Office: Parliament Bldgs., Queen's Park, Toronto, Ont. M7A 1W3

MILLER, Frank Patrick, B.A.; b. Victoria, B.C., 17 Aug. 1911; s. Rev. John Wesley, M.A., B.D., and Cynda Victoria (Patrick) M.; e. University of British Columbia, B.A. 1935; m. Ruth Helen, d. A. Gordon Gilroy, Ottawa, Ont., 15 Aug. 1942; children: Cynda Jane, Ruth Weslyn, Gordon Craig; Consultant, Internat. Criminal Justice since 1976 Candn. Coordinator, Fifth U.N. Congress On Prevention of Crime and Treatment of Offenders 1972-76 (Hon. vice pres. 1975); with Northern Electric Company, 1937-46; Branch Service Manager, 1946-47; part-time, John Howard Soc. of Ont., 1946-47; Sr. Classification Offr., Kingston Penitentiary, 1947-52; Remission Service Offr., Ottawa, 1952-53; Asst. Dir., Remission Service, Dept. of Justice, Ottawa, 1953-59; mem. Nat. Parole Bd. 1959-65; Extve. Dir., Nat. Parole Service, Nat. Parole Bd. 1965-72; served in 2nd World War; enlisted in R.C.O.C., 1941; Commd. 1944, Capt. 1945; mem., Assn. for Prevention of Crime; Royal Commonwealth Soc.; U.N. Assn of Can.; John Howard Award, Distinguished Humanitarian Service, 1973; J. Alex Edmison Award, Outstanding Contribution to Corrections & Criminology, 1980; United Church; Home: 552 Highcroft, Ottawa, Ont. K1Z 5J5

MILLER, Col. George W., M.D., D.P.H., F.R.C.P. (C); b. Newmarket, Ont., 23 Apl. 1904; s. John Wesley & Avelena Elizabeth (Martin) M.; e. Markham (Ont.) High Sch.; Univ. of Toronto (Victoria), B.A. with Hons. 1927; University of Toronto, M.D. 1930, and D.P.H., 1936; m. Elva Muriel, d. Charles W. Hastings, 27 Sept. 1930; children: Marilyn Elizabeth Hastings, Robin George Hastings, Timothy John Hastings; Civil Surg., Chindwara Dist., Centl. India, 1938; Health Offr. of Port of Bombay (Govt. of India) 1939; M.O.H., New Delhi, India, 1940; Depy. Pub. Health Commr. for India 1941; served with Indian Med. Service, Lieut. 1931, Capt. 1934 and Maj. 1939; served in 2nd World War with Roy. Indian Navy, Surg. Capt. 1941; retired 1945 with rank of Col.; Northumberland - Durham Health Unit (Ont.) 1945-49; Dir. Pub. Health Services, WHO, 1949-51; Asst. Dir., Dept. of Pub. Health, Prov. Ont., 1951-54; Nat. Dir., Candn. Red Cross Blood Transfusion Service, 1954-74; consultant, Connaught Labs., Toronto, 1974; Depy. Dist. Gov., Lions Internat. 1949; Fellow, Am. Pub. Health Assn.; Anglican; recreations: philately; Club: Thornhill Golf & Country; Home: Stouffville, R.R. 4, Ont. L0H 1L0

MILLER, Jack David Raoul, B.Sc., M.B., B.Ch.; neuroradiologist; b. Johannesburg, S. Africa 15 Apl. 1930; s. Harold and Inez Gwynneth (Behrman) M.; e. Parktown Boys' High Sch. Johannesburg 1946; Univ. of Witwatersrand B.Sc. (Mech. Engn.) 1950, M.B., B.Ch. 1956; m. Ruth Amalia d. late Harry Blumann 11 Apl. 1954; children: Richard Keir, Nina Kathleen, Gavin Keith; CLIN. PROF. AND CHRMN. OF RADIOLOGY, UNIV. OF ALTA. since 1971; Chrmn. Dept. Radiology, Univ. of Alta. Hosp.; interned Cornation Hosp. Johannesburg; residency Northwestern Univ. Med. Sch. Chicago 1961-63; Clin. Instr. Univ. of Alta. 1963, Clin. Lectr. 1967, Asst. Clin. Prof. 1968, Assoc. Clin. Prof. and Acting Chrmn. of Radiology 1969-70; author or co-author numerous articles diagnostic radiology; mem. Candn. Med. Assn.; Brit. Med. Assn.; Am. Coll. Radiol.; Am. Neuroradiol. Soc.; Assn. Univ. Radiols.; Candn. Assn. Radiols.; Hebrew; recreations: reading, squash, swimming; Clubs: Royal Glenora; Edmonton Flying; Nucleus Ambiguous; Home: 8608 137 St., Edmonton, Alta.; Office: 112 St. & 83 Ave., Edmonton, Alta. T6G 2B7.

MILLER, Hon. James Edgard M.L.A., B.Sc.; politician; farmer; rancher; b. Kitscoty, Alta. 31 March 1923; s. Charles Kerr and Cornelia (Bootsman) M.; e. Kitscoty, Alta.; Univ. of Sask. B.Sc. 1949; m. Margaret Mary d. Charles Joseph Quinn, Lloydminster, Alta. 5 July 1947; children: Kenneth, William, Sandra, Joseph, Daniel; ASSOC. MIN. OF PUBLIC LANDS AND WILDLIFE, ALTA.; el. M.L.A. for Lloydminster 1971, re-el. since; Trustee, Vermilion Sch. Div.; served with RCAF 2 yrs.; Protestant; recreation: sports; Home: Kitscoty, Alta. T0B 2P0; Office: Legislative Bldg., Edmonton, Alta.

MILLER, Hon. Tevie Harold, B.A., LL.B.; judge; b. Edmonton, Alta. 1 Jan. 1928; s. Abe William and Rebecca (Griesdorf) M.; e. Univ. of Alta. B.A. 1949, LL.B. 1950; m. Arliss June d. late Louis Toban, Vancouver, B.C. 24 June 1951; children: Catherine Dolgoy, Joshua, Lisa; JUDGE, COURT OF QUEEN'S BENCH ALTA. since 1979; called to Bar of Alta. 1951; cr. Q.C. 1968; joined in partnership with father 1951; Sr. Partner, Miller, Miller, Witten 1964; Chrmn. Jt. Law Soc. Alta. and Candn. Bar Assn. Comte. Kirby Comn. Prov. Court System; apptd. Judge, Dist. Court Alta. 1974; Depy. Judge N.W.T. 1976; apptd. to Trial Div. Supreme Court Alta. 1976; Depy. Judge Y.T. 1978; service as mem. Senate and Bd. Govs., Univ. of Alta., Trustee of Foundation, Sessional Lectr. in Law, Pres. of Gen. Alumni Assn.; Chrmn. Prof. Div., Three Alta. Univs. Fund Raising Campaigns; Bd. Govs. Alta. Coll.; Dir. Banff Sch. Advanced Mang., Lectr. in Business Law; Pres. Un. Way of Edmonton, Campaign Chrmn. Prof. Div.; Chrmn. City of Edmonton Community Foundation; Pres., Edmonton Symphony Soc.; mem. Bd. Edmonton Assn. Retarded Children; mem., Bd. of Gov., Universiade '83; Past Pres. Edmonton Jewish Community Council; Chrmn. Edmonton Un. Jewish Appeal; Pres., N.W. Candn. Council B'Nai Brith; Honeree, Edmonton Jewish Community Negev Dinner 1972; Pres. Edmonton Lib. Assn.; Convention Chrmn. Alta. Lib. Assn.; Lib. Cand. for Edmonton W. Fed. g.e. 1968; Dir. Edmonton Eskimo Football Club; Vice Pres. Bd. Dirs. Eleventh Commonwealth Games (1978) Foundation; Dir. YMCA; Sub-Lt. R.C.N. (R) retired; Past Pres. Edmonton Bar Assn.; mem. Council, Candn. Bar Assn. Alta. Div.; Hebrew; recreations: sailing, travel; Club: Univ. of Alta. Faculty; Home: 15 Riverside Cres., Edmonton, Alta. T5N 3M4; Office: Law Courts Bldg., Edmonton, Alta. T5J 0R2.

MILLER, W. Lockwood, B.Sc., J.D.; insurance executive; b. Winnipeg, Man., 11 March 1910; s. James Wilson and Berthe Emma (Lockwood) M.; e. Univ. of S. Cal., B.Sc. (Bus. Adm.) 1931, J.D. 1933; m. June, d. Ralph Arnold, Cal., 10 July 1938; children: James L., Virginia E.; GENERAL AGENT, OCCIDENTAL LIFE INSURANCE CO.; called to the Bar of Cal. 1933; Pres., Westminster Inst.; Delta Sigma Rho; Freemason (Commandery, Shrine); Liberal; United Church; recreation: travel; Home: 512 Colborne, London, Ont. N6B 2T5; Office: 433 Wellington St., London, Ont. N6A 3P7

MILLIGAN, Andrew Frank Barnett, M.B.E. (mil.), M.A.; b. Glasgow, Scot., 5 Dec. 1924; s. Francis Marshall and Elise Adrienne (Barnett) M.; e. Ayr. (Scot.) Acad., 1929-38; Fettes Coll. 1938-41; Univ. of Glasgow, 1941-42 and 1947-51; m. Linda Culter, 14 Feb. 1975; children: Bruce, Clive, Michele, Katie; PRES., GLENCOE MAN-

AGEMENT LTD. since 1975; Pres., TRV Minerals Corp.; Brace Resources Ltd.; Admiral Energy Corp.; Iona Industries Inc.; Dir., Host Ventures Ltd.; Goldstack Resources Ltd.; joined Bristol Aeroplane Company as Economist, 1951; appointed Assistant Overseas Contracts Mgr., 1954; Asst. Secretary, Bristol Aero Engines Limited, Montreal, 1956. Secy. 1958; Secy., The Bristol Aeroplane Co. of Can. Ltd. and Bristol Aero-Industries Ltd., 1958; Vice-Pres. and Dir., Bristol Aero-Industries Ltd. 1961; Vice-Pres. and Gen. Mgr., Power Machinery Div., 1964; established own mang. counselling business 1967; served with Royal Scots Fusiliers 1942-47; seconded to Somaliland Scouts 1944-47; served in U.K. and E. Africa; discharged with rank Maj.; recreations: swimming, scuba diving, racquetball, marathon running, reading; Home: 5811 Marguerite St., Vancouver, B.C. V6M 3K7; Office: 2380-1055 West Hastings St., Vancouver, B.C. V6E 2E9

MILLIGAN, Frank Archibald, M.A., LL.D.; b. Halifax, N.S., 4 May 1921; s. Rev. Francis Millidge and Josephine (MacDonald) M.; e. Univ. of Winnipeg (Un.Coll.) B.A. 1940, LL.D. 1976; Univ. of Man. M.A. 1948; Man. Law Sch. 1940-41; London Sch. of Econ. and Pol. Science 1949-51; Imp. Defence Coll. 1965; Memorial Univ. of Nfld. LL.D. 1976; Univ. of Guelph LL.D. 1979; m. Bernice d. George Pidcock, Courtenay, B.C., 18 Apl. 1944; children: Barbara (Mrs. W.C. McCallum), Janet, David, Douglas; Lectr. in Govt. Univ. of Man. 1947-49; Assoc. Prof. of Pol. Science Univ. of N.B. 1951-54; Dept. of Defence Production 1954-60 (Extve. Asst. to Depy. Min. 1957-60); Dir. of Research Royal Comn. on Govt. Organ. 1960-63; Assoc. Dir. for Univ. Affairs, Can. Council 1966-78; Extve. Dir., Soc. Sci. and Humanities Research Council 1978; Skelton-Clark Fellow, Queen's Univ. 1978-79; presently Consultant and Writer; Asst. Secy. to Cabinet 1963-66; Assoc. mem. Nat. Research Council 1970-78; served with Candn. Army Pacific Command, Italy, N.W. Europe 1941-45; Home: 69 Herchmer Cres., Kingston, Ont. K7M 2W1; Office: Dept. of Political Studies, Queen's Univ., Kingston, Ont. K7L 3N6

MILLIKEN, John A., M.D., C.M., F.R.C.P.(C); physician; b. Saskatoon, Sask, 15 May 1923; s. Robert Handside and Ethel May (McIntosh) M.; e. Queen's Univ., M.D., C.M. 1946; F.R.C.P.(C) 1954; m. Catherine Margaret, d. Dr. C. H. McCuaig, Kingston, Ont., 9 Feb. 1946; seven children; Prof. of Medicine Queen's Univ.; Deputy Chief of Med., Hotel Dieu Hosp., Kingston, Ont.; Fellow, Am. Coll. Cardiol.; Am. Coll. Phys. Am. Coll. Chest Phys.; mem., Candn. Cardiovascular Soc.; Candn. Med. Assn.; Ont. Med. Assn.; Kingston Acad. of Med.; United Church; recreation: golf; Clubs: Cataraqui Golf & Country; Royal Ottawa; Imperial Golf (Naples, Fla.); Home: R.R. #2, Kingston, Ont.; Office: Hotel Dieu Hospital, Kingston, Ont. K7L 3H6

MILLMAN, Peter MacKenzie, A.M., Ph.D., F.R.S.C. (1959); astronomer; b. Toronto, Ont., 10 Aug. 1906; s. Rev. Robert Malcolm, M.A., D.D., and Edith Ethelwyn (Middleton) M.; e. Candn. Acad., Kobe, Japan; Univ. of Toronto, B.A. 1929 (Gold Medal of Roy. Astron. Soc. of Can.); Harvard Univ., A.M. 1931, Ph.D. 1932; m. Margaret Bowness, d. Will Gray, Westville, N.S., 10 July 1931; children: Barry Mackenzie, Cynthia Gray (Mrs. Rowland Floyd); Assoc., Harvard Coll. Observatory 1955-75; Asst. in Astron., Univ. of Toronto, 1927-29; Harvard Univ., 1929-31; Demonst., Dept. of Astron., Univ. of Toronto (Dunlap Observatory), 1933-34; Lectr. there 1934-45; Astrophysicist, Dom. Observatory, 1946-51; Chief, Stellar Physics Div. there 1951-55; Head, Sec. Upper Atmosphere Research, Radio & Elect. Engn. Div., Nat. Research Council 1955-71 since when Guest Scientist; Navigation and Operational Research Offr. on active service, R.C.A.F., 1941-46; rank on transfer to Reserve. Sqdn. Leader; awarded J. Lawrence Smith Medal (in recognition of his distinguished work in the study of meteor spectra) by Nat. Acad. of Sciences, Wash., D.C., 1954;

awarded Gold Medal (for merit in advancement of physical sciences) by Presidium, Acad. of Sciences, Prague Czechoslavakia, 1980; Centennial Medal of Can., 1967; Queen's Silver Jubilee Medal, 1977; Life mem. Am. Assn. of Variable Star Observers (Council 1947-49, 1958-62); Life mem., Royal Astron. Soc. Can. (Pres. 1960-62) Hon. Pres., 1981-85; Counsellor, Smithsonian Institution, Washington, D.C. 1966-72; mem., Am. Astron. Soc. (Councillor 1947-50); Candn. Assn. of Physicists; Am. Inst. Aeronautics & Astronautics; Internat. Astron. Union (Pres. Comn. 22, 1964-67, Pres., Working Group or Planetary System Nomenclature, 1973-82); Candn. Astron. Soc. (Secy. 1971-77); Fellow, Candn. Aeronautics and Space Inst.; Meteoritical Soc. (Pres. 1962-66); Am. Assn. Advanc. Science; author: "This Universe of Space", 1961; Editor "Meteorite Research"; has been princ. concerned with work in meteoric astron., airborne solar eclipse observations, comparative planetology and radial velocities; Gamma Alpha (Harvard); Anglican; recreations: mountaineering, photography, philately; Home: 4 Windsor Ave., Ottawa, Ont. K1S 0W4; Office: Herzberg Institute of Astrophysics, National Research Council of Canada, Ottawa, Ont. K1A 0R6

MILLMAN, Thomas Reagh, Ph.D., D.D., D.C.L.; b. Kensington, P.E.I., 14 June 1905; s. James Borthwick and Lottie Everett (Smith) M.; e. Prince of Wales Coll., P.E.I.; Univ. Coll., Toronto, B.A. 1931, M.A. 1933; Wycliffe Coll., L.Th. 1933, B.D. 1938; McGill Univ., Ph.D., 1943; Univ. of W. Ont., D.D. 1953; Wycliffe Coll. 1974; Trinity Coll. 1977; D.C.L. Univ. King's Coll. 1974; m. Colena Margaret, d. J.A. McLeod, Lennoxville, Que., 1 August 1944; o. Deacon 1933, Priest 1934; Tutor and Dean of Residence, Montreal Diocesan Theol. College, 1935-41; Rector of Dunham and St. Armand East, Que., 1941-49; Prof. of Ch. Hist., Huron Coll., London, Ont., 1950-54; Archivist of Gen. Synod of Anglican Church of Can., 1956-75; Prof. Church Hist., Wycliffe Coll., 1954-74; Canon, St. James' Cathedral, Toronto 1969- ; Publications: "Jacob Mountain, First Lord Bishop of Quebec", 1943; "The Life of the Hon. the Rt. Rev. Charles James Stewart" 1953; "A History of the Parish of New London, Prince Edward Island", 1959; contribs. Dict. Candn. Biog.; Home: 27 Brookdale Ave., Toronto, Ont. M5M 1P2

MILLS, John Vernor, O.C., Q.C.; association executive; b. Windsor, Ont., 13 Feb. 1924; s. Dr. Cecil V. and Rose-Ann (Johnston) M.; e. Pub. and High Schs., Windsor; Western Univ., B.A., 1949; Osgoode Hall Law Sch., 1953; m. Helen Elliot, 20 July 1946; children: Coulson V., Douglas A., Karen J., Elizabeth J.; GEN. MGR., COMPOSERS, AUTHORS AND PUBLISHERS ASSOC. OF CANADA LTD. since 1968; read law with Gordon Ford, Q.C., Toronto, Ont.; called to Bar of Ont., 1953; cr. Q.C., 1963; practised law with Rowland & Mills, Toronto, 1953; joined present interest 1957 as Extve. Asst. to Gen. Mgr. and Gen. Counsel until apptd. Asst. Gen. Mgr. 1966; served in 2nd World War with R.C.A.F., 1942-46, Flt. Sgt.; mem. Co. of York Law Assn.; Candn. Bar Assn.; Law Soc. of Upper Can.; Anglican; recreations: golf, fishing, boating; Clubs: Lawyers; Rideau (Ottawa); Metrop. Bd. of Trade; Lambton Golf; Home: 6 Cherry Post Crescent, Etobicoke, Ont. M9C 2K1; Office: 1240 Bay St., Toronto, Ont. M5R 2A7

MILLS, Pauline — see: McGibbon, Hon. Mrs. Donald Walker

MILLS, Ralph Shaw, Q.C., D.Litt.S.; b. Toronto, 23 Oct. 1903; s. Alexander (K.C.) and Minnie L. (Shaw) M.; e. Rosedale Pub. Sch., Toronto; Univ. of Toronto Schs. (Sch. Capt. 1921); Victoria Coll., Univ. of Toronto, B.A. 1925; Osgoode Hall Law Sch., Toronto, Ont., 1928; D.Litt.S. Victoria Univ. 1974; m. Thora Rosalind, d. late Rev. W.A. McIlroy, 11 May 1929; five s., Alex, Donald, Howard, James, Paul; COUNSEL, MILLS AND MILLS; President and Director, Anson Securities Corporation

Ltd.; Secy. and Dir., Maplex Management & Holdings Ltd.; Abstainers' Insurance Co.; R. F. Heal Associates Ltd.; former President Toronto United Church Council, Toronto; mem., of Judicial Comte., Un. Ch. of Can.; former Chrmn., Board of Regents, Victoria Univ., Toronto, Ont.; former Pres., and life mem., Roy. Can. Inst.; Silver Jubilee Medal 1977; read law with Sir Wm. Hearst, K.C.; called to the Bar of Ont., 1928; cr. K.C. 1950; since entering upon the practice of law, has had extensive corp. and litigation experience, incl. Supreme Court of Can. and one appearance before the P.C. (1948); Lieut., Q.O.R. of Can., 1926-29; C.O.T.C. of Osgoode Hall, Toronto, 1940-41; sports career incl. Quarterback and Captain, Victoria Coll. Interfaculty football, 1921-23, Quarterback, Univ. of Toronto Intercoll. football, 1924; played hockey successively with Univ. of Toronto Schs., Victoria Coll., Varsity Jrs., Varsity Intermediates and Osgoode Hall Intermediates; played baseball with Toronto Fastball League, etc.; United Church; recreation: golf; Clubs: Lawyers of Toronto; York Downs Golf; Muskoka Lakes Golf; Home: 14 Meredith Crescent, Toronto, Ont. M4W 3B6; Office: 401 Bay St., Toronto, Ont. M5H 2Y4

MILNE, Eleanor Rose; sculptor; b. Saint John, N.B., 14 May 1925; d. William Harold and Irene Eleanor Mary (Gilhooly) M.; e. Saint Pauls Acad., Montreal; Sacred Heart Convent, Athunsic; Montreal Museum Sch. of Fine Art and McGill Lab. of Anatomy 1944-45; Central Coll. Arts & Crafts, London, Eng., 1945-46; L'Ecole des Beaux Arts, Montreal, 1946-48; Syracuse Univ., 1950-52; OFFICIAL SCULPTOR, CANADA, since 1961; formerly free-lance sculptor, stained glass window builder, engraver in wood, painter in water colors; makes her own bronze castings; has designed and built statues in wood, bronze and stone for both outdoor and indoor uses; many low relief panels in wood, stone and bronze; designed and carved (with assists.) high relief frieze "History of Canada" in Lobby, H. of C., Ottawa; designed and built (with assists.) 12 stained glass windows for Chamber of H. of C.; designed and built (with assists.) 12 stones for Chamber of H. of C. in theme of North Amer. Act; designed and made carvings and mosaic for 1st Speaker's chair for Yellowknife, N.W.T.; designed 1st Speaker's table and carved bronze mace cradle for Leg., Whitehorse, Yukon; Visiting Lecturer, Carleton Univ. Ottawa; lecturer to various groups in Can. & England; work has been seen in Montreal, Vancouver, Ottawa, N.Y.C., London, etc.; metal work sculpture in private collection, China; bronze and watercolours in Eng.; wood carvings in private collections, Montreal, Ottawa; awarded Centennial Medal; founding mem., IDEA; mem., Comte. of Judges to decide final design for Centennial Coins, Centennial Medal and Can. Medal; mem., Bd. Judges, Fine Arts, City of Ottawa; Am. Craftsmen's Council; Que. Sculptors Assn.; Smithsonian Inst.; Candn. Wildlife; Past mem., Platform Internat. Assn.; Zonta Internat.; Roman Catholic; recreations: modern history, landscape-gardening; Home: 229 Powell Ave., Ottawa, Que. K1S 2A4; Office: Box 162, House of Commons, Ottawa, Ont. K1N 8U2

MILNE, Jack N., B.Sc.; Semi-retired; association executive; b. South Porcupine, Ont., 9 Oct. 1912; s. late Charles Norman and late Edith (Patterson) M.; e. Woodford Coll., S. Woodford, Essex, Eng., 1921-25; Haileybury (Ont.) High Sch., 1925-29; Queen's Univ., B.Sc. (Elect. Engn.) 1935; m. Hilda Elizabeth, d. Canon D. Russell Smith, Oakville, Ont., 9 Sept. 1939; children: Virginia Elizabeth, John Charles Stuart, Peter Donald; joined Canadian General Electric Co., Toronto, 1935; became Mgr. Marketing Research (Corporate), 1952; joined MacLaren Advertising Co. Ltd., Toronto, as Asst. Mgr., Research, 1955 becoming Vice-Pres. and Dir. of Research; Mang. Dir. Inst. of Cdn. Advertising 1967-79 (ret.); Pres. Jamil Assoc.'s. 1979- ; mem. Council, Town of Oakville, 1946-48; Chrmn., Oakville-Trafalgar Planning Bd., 1948; Gov., Oakville-Trafalgar Mem. Hosp. since 1950 (Chrmn. 1957-

64); Chrmn., 1965-68, BBM Bur. Measurement; Dir., Candn. Advertising Research Foundation 1958-79 (Chrmn. 1962-65); mem., Toronto Bd. of Trade; Assn. Prof. Engrs. Ont.; Am. Econ. Assn.; Am. Marketing Assn. (Chrmn., Toronto Chapter 1957-58); Prof. Marketing Research Soc. (Pres. 1965-66); St. Andrews Soc.; Anglican; recreation: golf; Club: Oakville Golf; Home: 141 Gloucester Ave., Oakville, Ont. L6J 3W3

MILNE, Lorus Johnson, M.A., Ph.D.; naturalist; university professor; author; b. Toronto, Ont., 12 Sept. 1912; s. Charles Stanley and Edna Shepard (Johnson) M.; e. Humberside Coll. Inst., Toronto; Univ. of Toronto, B.A. (Biol.; Gold Medal) 1933; Harvard Univ., M.A. 1934, Ph.D. 1936; m. Margery Joan, Ph.D., d. S. Harrison Greene; PROF. OF ZOOLOGY, UNIV. OF NEW HAMPSHIRE; author and co-author (chiefly with wife) of over 40 books incl. many in several foreign eds., 2 selected for perm. White House Lib., 2 for "Books Across the Sea" program whereby Am. ambassadors provide books to rep. USA in foreign countries and 4 on long-play records for blind; other writings incl. over 200 pub. articles and reports and numerous book reviews in natural hist. field in Am. and foreign journs.; served with Office of Naval Research and Office of Scient. Research Devel., Univ. of Pa. Hosp., on night vision problems of armed services, 1942-47; exchangée on U.S.-S. Africa Leader Exchange Program for 3 months; Consultant-Leader for U.N. Educ. and Scient. Organ., in N.Z. for 3 months; Fellow, Am. Assn. Advanc. Science; mem., Am. Behaviour. Soc.; Am. Soc. Zools.; Conserv. Foundation; Explorers Club; N.H. Audubon Soc.; Sigma Xi; Republican; United Church; recreations: exploring, photography, natural history; Home: 1 Garden Lane, Durham, N.H. 03824; Office: 241A Spaulding Bldg. Durham, N.H. 03824

MILNER, Peter, M.Sc., Ph.D.; neuroscientist; Prof. and Chmn., Dept. of Psychology, McGill Univ.; b. Silkstone Common, Eng., 13 June 1919; s. David William M.; m. Susan Walker; one s. David Elliot; came to Can., 1944; Address: 1205 Dr. Penfield Ave., Montreal, Que. H3A 1B1

MILNER, Roy Wilfred; b. Brampton, Ont., 23 Mar. 1892; s. W.E. and Charlotte (Roberts) M.; e. Schs. of Brampton, Ont., and Winnipeg, Man.; two s. and three d.; retired Dir., Can. Steamship Lines Ltd.; Crown Trust Co.; Sovereign Life Assurance Co.; President, Winnipeg Grain Exchange 1936; with Zenith Grain Company 1909-11; then in transport work; mem. of staff, Alberta Pac. Grain Co. 1919; Assistant General Manager there, 1927-29; apptd. Vice-Pres. and Mgr., Jackson Bros. Grain Co. Ltd., Winnipeg, Man., 1931; later Gen. Mgr. and Dir., Alberta Pacific Grain Co. Ltd.; Transport Controller for Can., 1951-56; Chrmn., Bd. of Grain Commrs., Can., 1956-61; served in World War, 1914-19, with Motor Transport Corps; awarded Meritorious Medal 1917; United Church; recreations: golf, fishing, shooting; Clubs: The Ranchmen's (Calgary); Manitoba; Home: 51 Balmoral St., Winnipeg, Man. R3C 1X5

MILROY, Lt.-Gen. William Alexander, D.S.O.C.D.; Candn. Army retd.; b. Brownlee, Sask., 25 June 1920; s. William and Lillian Pearl (Webster) M.; e. High Sch., Westmount & Victoria High Sch., Edmonton, Alta.; Univ. Alta., Sch. of Com. (2 yrs.); m. Ann de Koven, d. Brig.-Gen. R.L. Tilton, Hampton, Va., 19 Oct. 1950; children: Elizabeth LaMotte Cates, Ann Alexandra, Rollin Larabee Tilton; Sqdn. Commander Lord Strathcona's Horse 1941-45; Staff Coll., Kingston, 1946-47; Liaison Offr., U.S. Army, 1948-51; Candn. Instructor, Staff Coll. Camberley, Eng., 1952-53; Joint Services Staff Coll. 1954; G.S.O.1, E. Command, 1955-57; Dir. Pub. Relations, Army, 1958-60; Commandant, Armoured Sch., 1960-61; Dir. Mil. Training 1962-65; Commdr., 3 Inf. Bgde. Group, 1965-66; apptd. Commandant, Candn. Army Staff Coll.,

1966; Candn. mem. of Observer Team to Nigeria, Sept. 1968-Jan. 1969; Chrmn., Candn. Defence Educ. Centre Planning Group, March 1969; apptd. Commdr., (new) H.Q., Candn. Defence Educ. Establishments 1970; Commdr., Training Command, Westwin, Man. 1971; promoted Lt. Gen. and apptd. Commdr., Mobile Command 1972; ADM (Pers) Dept. Nat. Defence 1973 till retired 1975; currently Vice-Pres. and Gen. Mgr., EAC Amy & Sons Ltd.; Delta Upsilon; Protestant;

MILTON, (John Charles) Douglas, B.Sc., M.A., Ph.D., F.A.P.S., F.R.S.C.; physicist; b. Regina, Sask. 1 June 1924; s. William and Frances Craigie (McDowall) M.; e. Greenway Elem. Sch., Gen. Wolfe Jr. High and Daniel McIntyre Coll. Inst. Winnipeg 1944; Univ. of Man. A.M.M. (Piano) 1944, B.Sc. 1947; Princeton Univ. M.A. 1949, Ph.D. 1951; m. Gwendolyn Margaret d. late Forrest Linden Shaw, O.B.E., Victoria, B.C. 10 Oct. 1953; children: Bruce Forrest, Leslie Jean Frances, Neil William Douglas, Theresa Marie; HEAD OF NUCLEAR PHYSICS, CHALK RIVER NUCLEAR LABS., ATOMIC ENERGY OF CAN. LTD. since 1967; joined present Labs. as Asst. becoming Sr. Research Offr. Physics 1951-67; Visiting Physicist, Lawrence Berkeley Labs. (Cal.) 1960-62, Bruyères-le-Châtel (France) 1975-76; Directeur de Recherche, CRNS Strasbourg, France 1975; Chrmn. Nuclear Physics grant Selection Comte. of Nat. Sci. & Eng. Research Council (NSERC) 1978- , (& 3 other grant selection comtes.); author over 40 scient. papers and reviews; mem. Candn. Assn. Physicists; Phi Kappa Pi; Sigma Xi; recreations: gardening, piano, boating; Club: Deep River Yacht & Tennis; Home: 3 Alexander Pl., Deep River, Ont. K0J 1P0; Office: Chalk River, Ont. K0J 1J0.

MILVAIN, Hon. James Valentine Hogarth, LL.D., Q.C.; retired judge; b. Livingstone, N.W.T., 14 Feb. 1904; s. James and Winifred Helen (MacKintosh) M.; e. Lee Sch. and Pincher Creek High Sch.; Univ. of Alta., LL.B. 1926; m. Edwina Belle, d. Edward C. Scheer, Los Angeles, 9 July 1932; one s. Robert Eliot Hogarth; CONSULTANT, ATKINSON-McMAHON; practised law in Calgary with Milvain & MacDonald; read law with A. G. Virtue; K.C., 1926; J. F. Scott, K.C., 1927; called to Bar of Alta. 1927; cr. K.C. 1944; formed partnership Scott & Milvain 1930 and continued until 1945; def. cand. to Alta Leg. for Calgary, g.e. 1935; Chief Justice, Trial Div., Supreme Court of Alta. 1968-79; mem., Law Soc. of Alta.; Candn. Bar Assn.; Calgary Bar Assn.; named Chrmn. of Fed. Conciliation Bd., Rlys. and Non-operating Unions, 1960; Anglican; recreations: shooting, fishing, ranching; Home: 505-3204 Rideau Pl. S.W., Calgary, Alta. T2S 1Z2; Office: 505 IBM Bldg., Calgary, Alta. T2P 1T1

MINAKER, Hon. George Clement, M.L.A., B.Sc.; politician; b. Morris, Man. 17 Sept. 1937; s. George David and Elizabeth Sarah (Muirhead) M.; e. Britannia Sch. and Linwood Sch. St. James, Man.; St. James Coll. Inst.; Univ. of Man. B.Sc. (Elect. Engn.); m. Olwen Rae d. Leslie Ramsden, Winnipeg, Man. 25 May 1957; children: Catherine Elaine, Donald Leslie, Russell Scott; MIN. OF COMMUNITY SERVICES & CORRECTIONS, MAN. 1979- ; Ald. City of St. James 1966-71; Councillor City of Winnipeg 1971-73; el. M.L.A. for St. James prov. g.e. 1973, re-el. 1977; mem. Assn. Prof. Engrs. Man.; P. Conservative; Protestant; Office: 314 Legislative Bldg., Winnipeg, Man. R3C 0V8.

MINARD, Guy McRae, M.B.E., B.Sc., LL.D.; P.Eng.; b. Ottawa, Ont., 19 Dec. 1906; s. Duncan McRae and Stella Lee (Allan) M.; e. Pub. Sch. and Lisgar Collegiate, Ottawa, Ont.; Queen's Univ., B.Sc. 1928, LL.D. 1971; m. Anne Marie, d. late R. D. Slingerland, 19 April 1933; children: Mrs. (Dr.) John D. M. Murray, Anthony; Dir., Kimberly-Clark Corp. 1964-78; joined Spruce Falls Power and Paper Co. Ltd., Kapuskasing, Ont.; as Groundwood Labourer, Aug. 1928; promoted to Chemist, Nov. 1928; Tech. Dir., 1930-40; returned (after war) as Asst. to

Mang. Dir., 1945; apptd. Mill Mgr., 1948; Vice-Pres., Dec. 1951; Vice-Pres., Mills, Kimberly-Clark Canada Ltd. and assoc. Co's., remaining as Vice-Pres. of Spruce Falls Power & Paper Co. Ltd., May 1957; apptd. Sr. Vice-Pres., Industrial Products Div., i/c Woodlands, Mfg. and Sales 1959; Pres., Spruce Falls Power & Paper and Kimberly-Clark Can. 1962-64; Chrmn. Spruce Falls 1964-70; Extve. Vice Pres. Kimberly-Clark Corp. 1964-67; Pres. 1967-70; Chrmn. 1970; retired 1972; served in 2nd World War with R.C.A.F., 1940-45; enlisted as Pilot Offr., Aero. Engn. Branch; served in Can. and S.E. Asia; retired with rank of Wing Commdr., 1945; awarded M.B.E., 1943; mem. Council, Town of Kapuskasing, Ont., 1947-52; Chrmn. of the Bd., Sensenbrenner Hosp., Kapuskasing, 1948-60; mem., Assn. Prof. Engrs. Ont.; Tech. Sec., Candn. Pulp & Paper Assn. (former Councillor and mem. Extve. Bd.); former sr. mem., The Conference Bd., Anglican; recreations: golf, curling, fishing, hunting; Clubs: Kapuskasing Golf; Augusta National Golf; Midland Valley Country; Home: 204 Laurel Circle, Graniteville, S.C. 29829

MINGAY, Arthur Hammond; trust company executive; b. Windsor, Ont. 26 Nov. 1919; s. John and Esther (Rodgers) M.; e. Windsor (Ont.) Pub. Schs.; Walkerville (Ont.) Coll. Inst.; m. Florence d. Henry Carmichael 15 Feb. 1947; children: Cameron, Mary Jane, Margo; CHRMN. OF BD. AND EXTVE. COMTE., DIR., THE CANADA TRUST CO. 1979- ; Dir. Canada Trustco Mortgage Co.; The Algoma Steel Corp. Ltd.; The Mutual Life Assurance Co. of Canada; Royal Insurance Co. of Canada; The Western Assurance Co.; Roins Holding Ltd.; Simpsons-Sears Ltd.; Simpsons-Sears Acceptance Corp.; T.I. Industries Ltd.; Inglis Ltd.; Loblaw Co. Ltd.; joined present Co. Windsor, Ont. 1938, Estates Offr. London, Ont. 1945, Trust Offr. Chatham, Ont. 1948, Mgr. Pension Trust Div. 1954, Asst. Gen. Mgr. Toronto Area 1959, Dir. 1964, Vice Pres. and Gen. Mgr. 1968, Pres. and Gen. Mgr. 1973, Pres. and Chief Extve. Offr. 1973, Chrmn. and Chief Extve. Offr. 1978; served with RCAF 1941-45, rank Flight Lt.; mem. Adv. Comte. Sch. of Business Adm. Univ. of W. Ont. Bd. of Gov., Massey Hall; Trustee, Art Gallery of Ont. Foundation; Dir., Council for Business & the Arts in Can.; Ont. Arthritis Soc.; United Church; recreations: golf, swimming; Clubs: Toronto; Granite; Rosedale Golf; London; London Hunt & Country; Canadian; Home: 35 Daneswood Rd., Toronto, Ont. M4N 3J7; Office: 110 Yonge St., Toronto, Ont. M5C 1T4.

MINGAY, Lieut.-Col. J. Donald, D.S.O., M.B.E.; mgmt. consultant; b. Barrie, Ont. 2 Feb. 1915; s. John and Esther (Rodgers) M.; e. Public and High Schs., Windsor, Ont.; m. Mary, d. late Walter L. McGregor, 4 Nov. 1939; children: John, Jill, Esther, Robert; Dir., Rous and Mann Brigdens Ltd.; Harding Carpets Ltd.; Excelsior Life Ins. Co.; Aetna Casualty Co. Can. Ltd.; served with Candn. Army, with rank of Lt.-Col., 1934-46; Un. Church; recreations: gardening, skiing; Clubs: Toronto; Badminton & Racquet; Home: Box 299, Creemore, Ont. L0M 1G0; Office: 20 Avoca Cres., Toronto, Ont. M4T 2B8

MINGO, J. William E., Q.C., B.A., B.A., LL.B., LL.M., LL.D. (Hon); b. Halifax, N.S., 25 Nov. 1926; s. late Edgar Willard and late Lila Theresa (McManus) M.; e. Dalhousie Univ., B.A. 1947, LL.B. 1949; Columbia Univ., LL.M. 1950; St. Mary's Univ., LL.D. (Hon) 1981; m. Edith Peppard, d. late Hon. C. G. Hawkins, Milford, N.S., 6 July 1953; children: James, Charles, Sally, Johanna, Nancy; mem., Stewart, MacKeen & Covert; Chrmn. of Bd., Halterm Ltd.; Dir., Bank of Canada; Montreal Trust Co. (ch., Halifax Adv. Bd.); Canada Devel. Corp.; CDC Ventures Inc.; Maritime Life Assurance Co.; RoyFund Equity Ltd.; Minas Basin Pulp and Power Co. Ltd.; Bowater Mersey Paper Co. Ltd.; National Sea Products Ltd. (Chrmn. Exec. Comte.); Maritime Telegraph & Telephone Co. Ltd.; Eastern Telephone & Telegraph Co.; Deuterium of Can. Ltd.; Canning Investment Corp. Ltd.; The Great Eastern Corp. Ltd.; Ben's Ltd.; ABCO Ltd.; Riversdale Lumber Ltd.; V.M. Automotive Warehousing Ltd.; Avon Foods Limited; Halifax International Containers Limited; Trustee, RoyFund Income Trust; read law with Stewart, Smith, MacKeen, Covert and Rogers; called to the Bar of Nova Scotia 1950; cr. Q.C. 1966; Chrmn., Halifax-Dartmouth Port Comn., since 1960 (mem. 1955-59); mem., Halifax Port Authority; N.S. Barristers' Soc. (Pres., 1975-76); Candn. Bar Assn.; (mem., Nat. Extve. Comm. 1973-76); Chrmn., Nat. Treasury Comm. of Lib. Party of Can.; Dir., Roy. Cdn. Geographical Soc.; N.S. Legal Aid Comm. 1977-80; Gov., Law Foundation of N.S.; Trustee, Foundation for Legal Research; Forum for Young Cdns.; Chrmn. of Bd., Halifax Grammar Sch. 1971-73; mem., CBA Spec. Comm. on Legal Ethics 1969-75; MRC Working Group on Human Experimentation 1977-78; Liberal; United Church; recreations: sailing, skiing; Clubs: Halifax; Faraguay; 1977-78 RNSYS; Home: 5860 Chain Rock Dr., Halifax, N.S.; Office: 1583 Hollis St., Halifax, N.S. B3J 2X2

MINOR, Arvil Dane; corporation executive; b. Bates, Ark., 11 Jan. 1919; s. William Henry and Mattie Mae (Travis) M.; e. Bethany (Okla.) Grammar and High Sch.; Bethany Peniel Coll.; m. Gladys Louise, d. Calvin C. Lucan, 7 Oct. 1939; one s. Arvil Dane, Jr.; CHRMN. AND PRESIDENT, RILEY'S DATASHARE INTERNATIONAL LTD.; Asst. Mgr., Circulation, Shreveport, (La.) Journ., 1938; joined Retail Credit Co., Shreveport, 1939; Sales Dept.; Coca-Cola Bottling Co., 1941; business on own account 1947; became assoc. with Riley's Reproductions Ltd., Wichita Falls, Texas, 1949; purchased controlling interest in that Co., Calgary (Alta.), 1950; served in 2nd World War with U.S.A.F. for 3½ yrs., discharged Lieut.; mem., Candn. Petroleum Assn.; Alberta Soc. Petrol. Geols.; Calgary Chamber Comm.; (Pres. Council), Am. Inst. Mang.; Soc. Reproduction Engrs.; Internat. Assn. Blue Printers; Calgary Football Club, (Past Dir.); Nat. Assn. Microfilm Industries; Pres., Alta. Chapter, Young Pres.'s Organ., Inc., 1965-66; Republican; Baptist; recreations: golf, hunting, fishing, photography; Clubs: Calgary Petroleum; Calgary Golf & Country; Cherry Hills Country (Denver, Colo.); Denver Athletic; Cactus (Denver, Colo.);

MINSHALL, William Harold, B.S.A., M.Sc., Ph.D.; research scientist; b. Brantford, Ont., 6 Dec. 1911; s. David William and Mary Etta (Kirpatrick) M.; e. Ont. Agric. Coll., B.S.A. 1933; McGill Univ., M.Sc. 1938; Ph.D. 1941; m. Reta Elizabeth, d. George J. McBride, Ottawa, 17 June 1939; children: Gaye Carol (Mrs. M. R. Sinclair), Bruce William; Sr. Plant Physiologist, Research Inst., Agric. Can., London, 1951-75; Hon. Research Assoc. since 1975; Hon. Lectr., Dept. of Plant Science, Univ. of W. Ont., 1952-76; joined Dept. of Agric., 1933 as Grad. Asst., Div. of Botany, Ottawa; Jr. Botanist there, 1941-45, Assoc. Botanist, 1945-48, Botanist, 1948-51; mem. Senate, Univ. of Guelph 1969-72; mem. Ont. Geneal. Soc. (Pres. 1971-72); Ont. Agric. Coll. Alumni Assn. (Pres. 1969-70); Prof. Inst. Pub. Service of Can. (Chrmn., London Br. 1957-58); Ont. Inst. Prof. Agrol. (Pres. 1963-64); Agric. Inst. Can. (mem. Extve. Council 1950-51; Fellow); Can. Weed Comte. (Pres. E. Sec. 1969); Candn. Soc. Plant Physiologists; McIlwraith Field Naturalists (Pres. 1968-69); Am. Soc. Plant Physiols.; Bot. Soc. Am.; Fellow (1980) Candn. Pest Mgmt. Soc. (Secretary-Treasurer 1955-72); English-Speaking Union of the Commonwealth in Can. (Pres. London Br. 1977-78); Fellow, Am. Assn. Advanc. Science; Fellow, Weed Science Soc. of Am. (mem. extve. comte. 1960-66); rec'd Centennial Plaque, Ont. Agric. Coll. 1974; Alumnus of Hon., Univ. Guelph 1977; Publications: numerous articles in scient. journs.; United Church; recreations: genealogy, phenology, stamps; Home: 91 Huron St., London, Ont. N6A 2H9

MIQUELON, Jean, Q.C., B.A.; Canadian public service; b. Danville, Que., 18 April 1910; s. Arsène Cyr and Eveline (Picard) M.; e. St. Hyacinthe (Que.) Semy.; Semy. of Quebec, B.A. 1930; Laval Univ., LL.L., Dec. 1933; m.

Francine, d. G. W. Lecrinier, Brussels, 9 Nov. 1946; children: Danièle, Bernard; MEMBER, PENSION REVIEW BOARD since 1973; mem., Copyright Appeal Board; read law with (now) Mr. Justice Paul Miquelon, Quebec, Que.; called to the Bar of Quebec, Jan. 1934; practised law in Val d'Or, Que., 1935-41; Prosecutor, 1936-39; after war service, Gen. Secy. of P. Conservative Party for Que. in Montreal Office, 1947-48; resumed legal practice in 1948 in Montreal till 1962; Part-time Rental Adm., City of Montreal, 1951-61; Special Fed. Prosecutor, 1957-62; Under Secy. of State and Depy. Registrar Gen. Can. 1962-64, Depy. Registrar 1964-67; President Crown Assets Disposal Corp. 1967-73; joined Candn. Active Army, 1941, commissioned in Artillery; Inst. in Anti-Aircraft, 1941-43; joined Office of Judge Advocate Gen., Ottawa, June 1943, serving overseas both in London and Continent, 1943-47; Deputy Judge Advocate Gen., Candn. Army Occupation Force in Germany, 1945-56; discharged with rank of Major, 1947; mem., Royal Candn. Legion (Vice-Chrmn. of Dom. Command, 1960-62); Roman Catholic; recreations: golf, tennis, skiing, reading; Home: 140 Minto Place, Rockcliffe Park, Ottawa, Ont. K1M 0B7; Office: Ottawa, Ont. K1A 0P4

MIRVISH, Edwin, O.C., C.M., LL.D.; entrepreneur; b. Colonial Beach, Va. 24 July 1914; s. David and Annie (Kornhauser) M.; came to Can. 1923; e. King Edward Pub. Sch. and Central Tech. Sch. Toronto; Trent Univ. LL.D. 1967; Univ. of Waterloo LL.D. 1969; m. Anne d. Jack Maklin, Columbia, Md. 29 June 1940; one s. David; Owner, Honest Ed's Ltd.; Ed Mirvish Enterprises; Royal Alexandra Theatre; operates three large restaurants, Ed's Warehouse, Old Ed's and Ed's Seafood; rec'd Telegram Theatre Award; Award of Merit City of Toronto; Jewish; recreation: ballroom dancing; Clubs: Arts & Letters; Variety; Canadian; Office: 581 Bloor St. W., Toronto, Ont. M6G 1K3 and 260 King St. W., Toronto, Ont. M5V 1H9.

MIRVISH, Robert Franklin; writer; ship's radio officer; b. Washington, D.C., 17 July 1921; s. David and Anna (Kornhauser) M.; e. Pub. Sch. and Central Tech. Sch., Toronto, Ont.; Univ. of Toronto, 1946-47; U.S. Merchant Service Radio Offrs. Cadet Sch., Gallups Island, Boston, Mass.; m. Lucille Angela Roccioppi de Giglio of N.Y., 1 June, 1963; children: Anthony David, John Richard; author of "A House of Her Own", 1953 (Dutch ed., "Nederlandsche Keurboekerij Lairessest"); "The Eternal Voyagers" (novel), 1953; "Texana" 1954; "A House of Her Own", 1954; "Red Sky at Midnight", 1956; "The Long Watch", 1955; "Woman in a Room", 1959; "Dust On The Sea", 1960; "Two Women, Two Worlds", 1960; "Point of Impact", 1961; "Cleared Narvick 2,000", 1962; "The Last Capitalist", 1962, all novels: "Business Is People", 1963; "There You Are, But Where Are You?", 1964; "Holy Loch", 1964; radio plays and short stories on CBC; mem., Am. Radio Ass.; served with U.S. Merchant Marine, June 1941 to end of War, and cont. service thereafter; Hebrew; Address: 32 Salonica Rd., Don Mills, Ont. M3C 2L9

MISENER, Austin Donald, M.A., Ph.D., F.R.S.C., F.Phys.S.; b. Toronto, Ont., 19 Jan. 1911; s. late Prof. Austin Perley and Ethel Wanita (Gould) M.; e. Candn. Acad., Kobe, Japan, 1919-29; Univ. of Toronto, B.A. (Math. and Physics) 1933 and M.A. 1934; Cambridge Univ., Ph.D. 1938; Univ. of Bristol, Research Fellow, 1939; m. Agnes Adelaide, d. late M. T. Crutcher, 15 Aug. 1936; children: Agnes Corinna, Donald James, Robert Leslie; m. 2ndly Eleanor Christina, d. late Scott Fairley, 21 Aug. 1971; Lecturer in Physics, University of Toronto, 1939-42; Jr. Research Physicist, National Research Council, Ottawa, 1942-43; Asst. Chief Engr., Armstrong Woods & Co., Toronto, Ont., 1943-44; Meadows Critoph & Misener, Toronto, 1944-49; Asst. Prof. of Physics, Univ. of Toronto, 1945-49; Prof. of Physics and Head of the Dept., Univ. of W. Ont., 1949-60; Mgr.-Dir., Ont. Research Foundation 1960-64; Dir., Inst. for Environmental

Studies and Prof. of Physics, Univ. of Toronto (ret. 1976); Prof. Emeritus, Assoc. Inst. for Environmental Studies 1976- ; Pres., Candn. Assn. of Physicists, 1950-51 (Registrar); mem., Research Council Can. (apptd. 1959); mem., Am. Assn. Advance Science; Am. Geophys. Union; Assn. Prof. Engrs. Ont.; Engn. Inst. Can.; has written numerous articles on low-temperature physics, geophysics and environment; recreations: boating, reading, travel; P.O. Box 2469, Picton, Ont. K0K 2T0

MISENER, Ralph Scott; transportation executive; b. 5 Dec. 1908; s. Robert Scott and Olive Elizabeth (Glass) M.; e. Sarnia (Ont.) Coll. Inst. and Tech. Sch.; Univ. of W. Ont.; m. Eleanor Gene, d. late Angus MacDougall, 12 April 1934; children: Scott Angus, Paul, Ralph Peter, Mrs. Heather Logan; CHAIRMAN BD., MISENER HOLDINGS; Past Pres. Ont. Div., Multiple Sclerosis Soc. of Can.; Dir., Council for Candn. Unity; C.N.I.B.; Freemason; recreations: boating, spectator sports; Clubs: Manitoba; Canadian (Winnipeg); Winnipeg Winter; Lions (Winnipeg); St. Catharines; Buffalo (Buffalo, N.Y.); Home: 24 Woodmount Dr., St. Catharines, Ont. L2T 2X9; Office: (P.O. Box 100) 63 Church St., St. Catharines, Ont. L2R 6S1

MISKA, John P., B.A., B.L.Sc.; librarian; author; translator; editor; bibliographer; b. Nyirbéltek, Hungary 20 Jan. 1932; s. Mihály and Teréz (Kovacs) M.; e. Bocskay Gymnasium; Univ. of Budapest; McMaster Univ.; Univ. of Toronto B.A., B.L.Sc.; m. Maria von Brockhausen; HEAD LIBRARIAN AGRIC. CAN. LETHBRIDGE RESEARCH STN. and Area Coordinator for Alta. since 1972; Head Engn. Lib. Univ. of Man. 1962-66; Head Acquisitions, Agric. Can. Ottawa 1969-72; author "Best Short Stories from English" 1965; "A Mug of Milk: Short Stories" (Hungarian) 1968; "Mending Our Fences: Selected Essays 1963-73" 1974 (Hungarian), rec'd Silver Medal Arpad Acad. Cleveland; Ed. "Antologia: Canadian-Hungarian Authors 1969-72" 3 vols. (Hungarian); "The Sound of Time: Anthology of Canadian-Hungarian Authors" 1974; bibliogs. incl.; "Agriculture: A Bibliography of Research" 1973 5 vols.; "Solonetz Soils of the World: A Bibliography" 1975; "Potato Seed Piece Decay 1920-1975: A Bibliography"; "Irrigation of the World: An Annotated Bibliography" 1977 4 vols.; "Hungarian-Canadian Literature: A Preliminary List of Creative Works"; "Bibliography of the Pea Aphid" "Ethnic & Native Canadian Literature, 1850-1979; A Bibliography of Primary & Secondary Materials, 1980 (2,960 references on microfiche);" 'Canadian Prose Written in English, 1833-1980', 1980 (3,360 citations on microfiche);" Cold Hardiness & Winter Survival of Plants: An Annotated Bibliography', 1980 (4,000 references); 1978; author more than 200 review articles in lit. and prof. journs.; Queen's Jubilee Medal, 1977; Alta. Achievement Award for Literature 1978; Home: 3206 South Parkside Dr., Lethbridge, Alta. T1K 0E2; Office: Library, Agriculture Canada, Research Station, Lethbridge, Alta. T1J 4B1

MISSEN, Ronald William, M.Sc., Ph.D., F.C.I.C.; educator; b. St. Catharines, Ont. 26 Feb. 1928; s. Edward Lionel and Helen Harrison (Miller) M.; e. Alexandra Pub. Sch. St. Catharines, Ont. 1940; Ryerson Sr. Pub. Sch. and Westdale Secondary Sch. Hamilton, Ont. 1946; Queen's Univ. B.Sc. 1950, M.Sc. 1951; Cambridge Univ. Ph.D. 1956 (Athlone Fellow 1953-55); m. (Elizabeth) Barbara d. late Norman E. Ward 28 July 1951; four d. Nancy Elizabeth, Kathryn Margaret, Brenda Carol, Lynne Patricia; Vice Provost (Prof. Faculties), Univ. of Toronto 1977-81 and Prof. of Chem. Engn. since 1968; Dir., Chemical Engineering Research Consultants Ltd.; Chem. Engr. Polysar, Sarnia, Ont. 1951-53; Asst. Prof. of Chem. Engn. Univ. of Toronto 1956, Assoc. Prof. 1961-68, Pres. Faculty Assn. 1970-71; mem. Gov. Council 1975-77, Assoc. Dean (Phys. Sciences) Sch. of Grad. Studies 1976-77; rec'd Plummer Medal Engn. Inst. Can. 1962; author over 30 articles mainly in Applied Chem. Thermodynamics various scient. and engn. journs.; mem. Candn. Soc. Chem. Engn.; Assn. Prof. Engrs. Prov. Ont.; Anglican; recreations: philately, reading; Home: 19 Didrickson Dr., Willowdale, Ont. M2P 1J7; Office: Toronto, Ont. M5S 1A4.

MITCHELL, Arthur Hoadley, S.B.; consulting petroleum engr.; b. New York, N.Y., 11 March 1919; s. Arthur Knox and Eunice (Bowser) M.; naturalized Candn.; e. Bronxville (N.Y.) Pub. Sch.; St. Michael's Sch., Victoria, B.C., 1930-34; Brentwood Coll., 1934-37; Mass. Inst. Tech., S.B. 1941; m. Ruth, d. Russell Brewster Horton, Victoria, B.C., 1 Oct. 1941; four s. David Hoadley, Bruce Horton, John Bowser, Mark Wattles; PRESIDENT, MITCHELL & ASSOC. LTD., Oil and Gas Consultants, formed 1949; Pres., Corvair Oils Ltd.; Vice Pres., Bank of B.C.; Dir., Interprovincial Steel and Pipe Corp. Ltd.; Bank of British Columbia; Northwestern Utilities Limited; Century Sales & Service Limited; Ajax Precision Mfg. Ltd.; mem., Edmonton Adv. Bd., National Trust Co.; prior to forming present Co., was ind. producer and served as Secy., Lloydminster Petroleum Assn.; served in 2nd World War with U.S.A.F., 1941-46; discharg. with rank of Major; mem., Assns. Prof. Engrs. B.C., Alta., Sask.; Engn. Inst. Can.; Candn. Inst. Mining & Metall.; Independent Petroleum Assn. Can.; Phi Delta Theta; Protestant; recreations: golf, skiing; Clubs: The Edmonton; Petroleum (Past Pres.); Mayfair Golf; Home: 13814 Ravine Drive, Edmonton, Alta. T5N 3M1; Office: 11030 St. Albert Trail, Edmonton, Alta. T5M 3K7

MITCHELL, Charles Stuart; farmer; b. Preeceville, Sask. 5 Apl. 1909; s. Harold and Susan (Smith) M.; e. pub. and high schs. Preeceville, Sask. 1927; m. Beda Annette d. late Peter Abramson 20 Apl. 1935; children: Robert, Derek, Donna, Sandra, Judith; Reeve of Rural Mun. of Preeceville #334 since 1957; el. Dir. Sask. Assn. Rural Muncs. 1959, Vice Pres. 1972, Pres. 1974-77; served 25 yrs. Preeceville Hosp. Bd.; Chrmn. Sturgis Sch. Unit Bd. 2 yrs.; served many yrs. as Dir. Sask. Fed. Agric., 7 yrs. as Vice Pres.; several yrs. as Bd. mem. and Extve. mem. Candn. Fed. Agric.; mem. Adv. Council on Transport.; Bd. Sask. Power Corp.; Sask. Farm Ownership Bd.; NDP; United Church; recreations: reading, curling, golf; Address: Sturgis, Sask. S0A 4A0.

MITCHELL, Claude Leslie; retired executive; b. Southampton, Eng., 6 July 1914; s. Charles Archibald and Edith Lucy (Newman) M.; came to Can. 1 Dec. 1914; e. Bloomfield High Sch., Halifax, N.S., grad. 1930; m. Ruth Margaret, d. late Harold Willard Tingley, 14 Oct. 1938; one d. Mrs. Corinne Andrea Walsh; with Bank of N.S., 1930-37; apptd. Salesman of H. J. Heinz Co. of Can., 1937-49; Dist. Supv., N.B. Sales, 1949-53; Sales Br. Mgr., Saint John, N.B., 1953-56; Mgr., Atlantic Region, 1956-61, Ont. Region, 1961-62; Mang. Dir., Netherlands 1962-64; Vice Pres. Sales, 1964-79 (ret.); mem., Maritime Comm. Travellers' Assn.; I.O.O.F.; Conservative; Protestant; recreation: spectator sports; Home: 16 Lyon Ave., Leamington, Ont. N8H 3Z4

MITCHELL, Howard Theodore; publisher; b. Ship Harbor, Nova Scotia, 12 Jan. 1902; s. Capt. Howard Gilford and Luella (Lynch) M.; e. Public Schs. and King Edward High Sch., Vancouver, B.C.; m. Janet Ruth, d. Hector MacDonald, Vancouver, B.C., 14 July 1932; two s. Donald H., Howard G.; CHRMN., MITCHELL PRESS LIMITED (Estbd. 1928, commercial printers & publishers); Pres., Mitchell, Shave & Associates Ltd., Northern Sentinel Press Ltd., (Kitimat); Pres., Candn. Chamber of Comm., 1963-64; Business Editor, "Vancouver Sun", 1924-28; during 2nd World War on loan to Dept. of Mun. & Supply, 1940-44; Past Pres. (1948), Vancouver Bd. Trade; United Church; recreations: gardening, woodworking; Club: Vancouver; Home: 1626 Drummond Drive, Vancouver, B.C. V6T 1B6; Office: 1706 W. 1st Ave., Vancouver, B.C. V6J 1G3

MITCHELL, Janet, R.C.A.; artist; b. Medicine Hat, Alta. 24 Nov. 1912; d. John and Janet (McLellan) Mitchell; e. Pub., High and Business Schs. Calgary; Calgary and London, Eng. art schs.; paintings exhibited across Can., Brit., Japan and USA since 1946; recipient several awards in maj. shows; rep. in many private colls.; mem. Adv. Purchasing Comte. Alta Art Foundation; 1975-77; Calgary Regional Foundation of Arts 1976-1978; subject of documentary on CBC TV; mem. Council R.C.A.; mem. Candn. Soc. Painters in Watercolour; Alta. Soc. Artists; Address: 85 Capri Ave. N.W., Calgary, Alta. T2L 0G9.

MITCHELL, Joni(Roberta Joan Anderson); singer; songwriter; b. Ft. Macleod, Alta. 7 Nov. 1943; d. William A. and Myrtle M. (McKee) A.; student Alta. Coll.; m. Chuck Mitchell, 1965, (div.); albums incl. "Song to a Seagull", "Clouds", "Ladies of the Canyon", "Blue", "For the Roses", "Court and Spark", "Miles of Ailes", "Hissing of Summer Lawns", "Hejira, Don Juan's Reckless Daughter", "Mingus", (Jazz Album of Year and Rock-Blues Album of Year, Downbeat mag. 1979), "Shadows and Light"; compositions incl. "Both Sides Now", "Michael from Mountains", "Urge for Going", "Circle Game"; Juno award for special achievement, 1981; Address: c/o Elliot Roberts Lookout Mgmt., 9120 Sunset Blvd., Los Angeles, CA 90069

MITCHELL, Maurice Stephen, B.Sc.; civil engineer; b. Cardiff, Alta., 10 May 1919; s. Hugh John and Agatha (Lillijord) M.; e. Garneau (Alta.) High Sch.; Univ. of Alta., B.Sc. (C.E.) 1942; m. Molly, d. W. D. Browning, 6 July 1946; children: Marda, Kurt Davison, Hugh Scott; with Aluminum Co. of Can., 1942-43; Hamilton Bridge Co. (Western) 1944; Univ. of Alta., Civil Engn. Staff, 1943-46; served C.O.T.C., Lieut., Reserve Signals, 1938-42; Cub Master, 1959-69, Boy Scouts of Can. and Pres. of S. Alta. Region 1971 (rec'd 15 yr medal 1975); Councillor, Lethbridge Chamber of Comm.; Senator, Univ. Lethbridge 1973-79; Budget Dir., United Way of Lethbridge 1975-81, Campaign Chrmn. 1978-79; Lethbridge Housing Authority 1977-81; Pres., United Way of Alta., 1979-80; Hon. Life mem. Assn. Prof. Engrs. Alta.; mem., Engn. Inst. Can. (Extve. Lethbridge Br.); Am. Concrete Inst.; Kappa Sigma (Alumnus Advisor 1945-46); Freemason; Liberal; Anglican; recreations: tennis, curling, golf; Clubs: Country; Tennis; Kiwanis (Vice Pres. 1955-56, Pres. 1958, Lt. Gov. 1964); Home: 1814-13 Ave. S., Lethbridge, Alta. T1K 0S2; Office: 1814 - 13 Ave. S., Lethbridge, Alta.

MITCHELL, Michael Frederick, B.A.; executive; b. Los Angeles, Cal., 1 Dec. 1946; s. Cameron and Johanna (Mendel) M.; e. pub. and high schs. Los Angeles; Univ. of Ariz. B.A. (Econ.) 1969; PRESIDENT, INTERCONTINENTAL PACKERS LTD. since 1976; joined Intercontinental Packers part-time 1965, full-time as Mang. Trainee 1969, subsequently serving as Salesman, Asst. to Pork and Beef Dept. Heads, Marketing Coordinator, Vice Pres. Marketing 1973; mem., Young President; Organization; Chrmn., Mendel Art Gallery; Meat Packers Coiuncil of Can.; Beta Theta Pi; recreations: golf, tennis, fishing, skiing, art, music; Clubs: Saskatoon; Riverside Golf & Country; Home: 21 Qu'Appelle Court, Saskatoon, Sask. S7K 1C2; Office: 3003 — 11th Street W., Saskatoon, Sask. S7M 1J9

MITCHELL, Hon. William, B.A.; B.C.L.; D.C.L.; judge; b. Montreal, Que. 7 Sept. 1907; s. Hon. W. G. and Antonia (Pelletier) M.; e. Bishop's College Sch., Lennoxville, Que. 1925; Bishop's Univ. B.A.; 1931; McGill Univ. B.C.L. 1934; m. Margaret Alice d. late Dr. F. H. Bradley 4 Aug. 1934; children: W. Bradley, Antonia Griffin, Jane Molson, William, Andrew; JUSTICE, SUPERIOR COURT QUE. since 1949; practiced law Montreal 1934-49; acted as Counsel and Secy. to Wartime Shipping Ltd. during World War II; Chrmn. of Bd., Bishop's Univ. since 1978 (Chrmn. Extve. Comte. 1963; Vice Pres. of Corp. 1970;

Pres. of Corp. 1971 Chancellor 1974); Dir. Bishop's Coll. Sch.; Wales Home, Richmond, Que.; Chrmn. Kings Hall, Compton, Que.; Past Dist. Commr. Boy Scouts Assn.; Anglican; recreations: fishing, skiing, hiking; Clubs: Mount Royal; Triton Fish & Game; Home: Massawippi, Que.; Office: Court House, Sherbrooke, Que.

MITCHELL, William Ormond, O.C. (1972), B.A.; author; b. Weyburn, Sask., 13 Mar. 1914; s. Ormond S. & Margaret Letitia (MacMurray) M.; e. St. Petersburg High Sch., Fla.; Univ. of Man., 1932-34; Univ. of Alta., B.A. 1942; m. Merna Lynne, d. Spurgeon M. Hirtle, Vancouver, B.C., 15 Aug. 1942; children: Ormond Skinner, Hugh Hirtle, Willa Lynne; Hon. mem., Eugene Field Soc.; author of "Who Has Seen the Wind", 1947; "The Kite"; "The Devil's Instrument" 1973; "Jake and the Kid" 1974; "The Vanishing Point" 1973; "The Black Bonpiel of Wullie MacCrimmon" 1974; "Back to Beulah" 1978; "How I Spent My Summer Holidays", 1981; contrib. to "Maclean's", "Liberty", "Atlantic Monthly", "Queen's Quarterly", "Canadian Forum", "Ladies' Home Journal."; incl. "Best American Short Stories", 1946; author of a number of radio scripts for CBC since 1947; awarded Leacock Medal for Humour (collected ed. of "Jake and the Kid"), 1962; former writer in residence. Massey College, U. of Calgary, U. of Alta., U. of Windsor; Delta Kappa Epsilon; Liberal; Presbyterian; recreations: angling, orchid culture, dramatics; Address: Calgary, Alta.

MITTON, Rev. Harold Logan, B.A., B.D., D.D. (Bapt.); b. Moncton, N.B. 20 Dec. 1919; s. Clifford John and Eva Isabelle (Logan) M.; e. Acadia Univ. B.A. 1944, B.D. 1946, D.D. 1966; special study and reading Princeton Theol. Semy., Fuller Theol. Semy. and Inst. for Advanced Pastoral Study 1970; m. Marguerite McKay d. late Burtt Rideout 9 Aug. 1944; children: Ronald Burtt, Ruth Christine; PRINCIPAL AND DEAN, ACADIA DIVINITY COLL. since 1975, mem. Bd. of Trustees and Senate there; Bd. of Govs. and Senate Acadia Univ.; held pastorates Aylesford and Windsor, N.S., Charlottetown, Brunswick St. Un. Bapt. Ch. Fredericton, First Bapt. Ch. Calgary; mem. of Faculty Acadia Univ. 1975; Pres. Atlantic Un. Bapt. Convention 1962; 1st Vice Pres. Bapt. Fed. of Can. 1968; Atlantic Bapt. rep. Candn. Council Chs.; apptd. to Candn. Bapt. Overseas Mission Bd. 1971; numerous speaking engagements; Field Assoc. "Faith at Work" and frequent leader Ch. Renewal Confs.; served as Chaplain with Candn. Army (Reserve) 1952-62, rank Maj.; author "Facing Today's World"; contrib. to various denominational journs.; syllabus and cassette lectures "The Psalms and Modern Man"; mem., Acad. of Homiletics of U.S. and Can.; recreation: swimming; Address: 18 Grandview Dr., Wolfville, N.S. B0P 1X0

MOCKLER, Hubert Joseph, B.A.Sc.; mining executive; b. Grand Falls, N.B., 13 June 1933; s. Lawrence Michael and Blanche Marie (Cyr) M.; e. Univ. of N.B., B.A.Sc. (Geol.) 1955; m. Kathleen Mary, d. Allan Hall, Newcastle, N.B., 11 Aug. 1956; two s., Terrance Allan, Howard Thomas; CHAIRMAN BD., CANADIAN MERRILL LTD.; Pres. and Dir. Bulora Corp. Ltd.; Dir. Quebec Uranium Ltd.; CHIB Kayrand Mines Ltd.; Chibex Ltd.; Midas Resources; Exploration Geol., Rio Canadian Exploration, 1955; Nama Greek Mines 1956; Canadian Johns Manville 1956-57; Canadian Javelin Limited, 1957-58; Financial Analyst, Greenshields Inc., 1958-62; Executive Assistant to President, Power Corp. of Canada, 1962-63; Dir. of Research, Mead & Co. Ltd., 1963; Pres., Merrill Island Mining Corp. Ltd. 1969; mem., Candn. Inst. Mining; R. Catholic; recreations: golf, squash, swimming, skiing; Clubs: Royal Montreal Golf; Montreal Badminton and Squash; Toronto Golf; Engineers; Cambridge; Laurentian Lodge; Home: 40 Scholfield Ave., Toronto, Ont. M4W 2Y3

MOCKRIDGE, Harold C. F., Q.C.; MEMBER, OSLER, HOSKIN & HARCOURT; Dir., Hudson Bay Mining & Smelt. Co. Ltd.; Home: Apt. 904, 500 Avenue Rd., Toronto, Ont. M4V 2V6; Office: P.O. Box 50, First Canadian Place, Toronto, Ont. M5X 1B8

MOENS, H. Peter B., B.Sc.F., M.A., Ph.D., F.R.S.C.; b. Sukabumie, Indonesia 15 May 1931; s. H. Peter B. and A. D. M. Ritsema van Eck M.; e. Univ. of Toronto B.Sc.F. 1959, M.A. 1961, Ph.D. 1963; m. Marja d. Jakob Schröder 8 May 1953; children: Richard, Theodore, Vivian, Cecilia, Francis; PROF. AND CHMN. DEPT. OF BIOL. YORK UNIV.; author over 50 articles cytogenetics; mem. Genetics Soc. Can. (Pres. 1978-79); Candn. Soc. Cell Biol.; Am. Soc. Cell. Biol.; recreations: sailing, tennis; Home: 217 Northwood Dr., Willowdale, Ont. M2M 2K5 ;Office: Dept. of Biology, York University, Downsview, Ont. M3J 1P3.

MOESER, William Alan, B.A.Sc.; industrialist; b. Toronto, Ont., 8 Feb. 1921; s. Frederick William and Estelle (Stanger) M.; e. Oakwood Coll. Inst. (Toronto); Univ. of Toronto, B.A.Sc. 1943, Business Adm. Dipl., 1950; m. May, d. W. W. Lindsay, 8 Feb. 1944; children: Mrs. Sheila Jean Roy, Douglas William, Lindsay Ann; CHRMN., PRES. & DIR., LEAR SIEGLER INDUSTRIES LTD.; Div.; Dir., Electrohome Ltd.; Canada Alloy Castings Ltd.; with Massey-Harris Co. in various mfg. capacities in Toronto 1945-52; trans. to Lille, France with Cie Massey-Harris S.A. as Works Mgr., 1952-55; became Mfg. Mgr., H. V. McKay-Massey-Harris Prop. Ltd., Melbourne, Australia, 1955-61; el. Dir., Massey-Ferguson (Australia) Ltd., 1958; returned to Can. in 1961 as Asst. Gen. Factory Mgr., Massey-Ferguson Ltd. until Apl. 1962; joined Studebaker of Can. Ltd. as Production Mgr., May 1962; apptd. Dir.-Mfg., Oct. 1963; Vice-Pres., Mfg., July 1964; apptd. Vice-President, Operations and Dir., General Spring Products Ltd. 1966 (predecessor to Lear Siegler Ltd.); appt. Pres. 1969; served in 2nd World War with R.C.N.V.R. as Lieut. (E), 1943-45; Adv. Extve. Council, Candn. Mfrs. Assn.; Rotary Club of Kitchener; member, Assn. Prof. Engrs. Ont.; Soc. Auto. Engrs.; Engn. Inst. Can.; Delta Upsilon; United Church; recreations: golf, photography; Clubs: Hamilton Golf; Royal Candn. Mil. Inst. (Toronto); Albany (Toronto); Fairlane (Dearborn); Westmount Golf; K-W Granite; Home: 657 Dunbar Rd., Kitchener, Ont. N2M 2X5; Office: 530 Manitou Dr., P.O. Box 758, Kitchener, Ont. N2G 4C2

MOFFAT, John William, Ph.D.; educator; artist; b. Copenhagen, Denmark 24 May 1932; s. George William McKay and Esther (Winther) M.; e. Trinity Coll. Cambridge Ph.D. 1958; two d. Sandra, Christina; PROF. OF PHYSICS, UNIV. OF TORONTO 1967- ; came to Can. 1964; paintings exhibited Realités Nouvelles, Paris 1949; Illums Bolighus, Copenhagen 1950; Victoria Coll. Univ. of Toronto 1982 (solo exhn.); author over 110 publs. theoretical physics internat. journs.; mem. Am. Phys. Soc.; Cambridge Philos. Soc.; recreations: jogging, travel; Home: 38 Albany Ave., Toronto, Ont. M5R 3C2; Office: 60 St. George St., Toronto, Ont. M5S 1A7.

MOFFAT, Donald Ormond, B. Arch.; architect; b. Hamilton, Ont. 11 Nov. 1933; s. Ormond George and Anne Mitchell (Souter) M.; e. Central and Ryerson Pub. Schs., Westdale Secondary Sch. Hamilton; Univ. of Toronto B.Arch.; m. Jane Ann d. Harold Freeburne 9 Sept. 1961; one d. Mary Elizabeth; PARTNER, MOFFAT KINOSHITA PARTNERSHIP; present firm estbd. mid-sixties with offices Hamilton and Toronto; projects incl. Sir Frederick Banting Research Centre; Royal Ont. Museum; firm recipient over dozen design awards; Pres., Hamilton Dist. Chamber Comm. 1979-80; Dir. 1974-81, Chrmn., Fed. Prov. Affairs Comte. 1975-76; Mun. Regional Affairs Comte. 1975-76; mem. Ont. Assn. Archs. (Vice Chrmn. Registration Bd. 1973-75, Chrmn. Prof. Educ. Comte. 1970-72); Pres., Delta Upsilon 1957; recreations: tennis, platform tennis, skiing, reading, gardening; Club: Badminton & Racquet; Home: 104 The Kingsway, Toronto, Ont. M8X 2T8; Office: Suite 200, 90 Eglinton Ave. E., Toronto, Ont. M4P 2Y3.

MOFFATT, Garfield Macleod, C.M., B.A., M.D., C.M., F.R.C.P. (C); physician; b. Sydney, N.S. 25 March 1921; s. John and Etta (Macfadygen) M.; e. Sydney Acad. 1939; Mount Allison Univ. B.A. 1942; Dalhousie Univ. M.D., C.M. 1947; m. Olive Arlene d. Arthur Fraser, Springhill, N.S. 4 June 1949; children: Neil, Ann, Blair, Scott, Bethany; Staff mem. Dept. Med., Dr. Everett Chalmers Hosp. Fredericton; Consultant in Internal Med., Hotel Dieu Hosp., Perth, N.B.; internship Victoria Gen. Hosp. Halifax 1947-49; Sunnybrook Hosp. Toronto 1949-53; Past Pres. and Past Hon. Pres., Un. Way Fredericton; N.B. Med. Soc. Rep. to Dept. Continuing Educ. Dalhousie Univ.; mem. St. Andrew's Soc.; N.B. Med. Soc.; P. Conservative; Anglican; recreations: swimming, sailing, salmon fishing, skating, skiing; Club: Fredericton Garrison; Home: 838 Regent St., Fredericton, N.B. E3B 3Y4;Office: 206 Rookwood Ave., Fredericton, N.B. E3B 2M3.

MOFFATT, Harding Pyle, C.M. (1975), M.Ed., D.C.L.; retd. public servant; educator; b. Canso, N.S., 24 Jan. 1905; s. Theodore Harding Porter and Lila Emma (Bigelow) M.; e. Acadia Univ., B.A. (summa cum laude), 1925; Harvard Grad. Sch. of Educ., M.Ed., 1927 (further study, 1929-30); Acadia Univ., Hon. D.C.L., 1950; m. Harriet Hammond, d. late Otis J. Carlton, Haverhill, Mass., 1931; Research Assoc., Inst. Public Affairs, Dalhousie Univ. since 1968; former mem. of Senate and Bd. Govs., Acadia Univ.; mem., Bd. Govs., N.S. Museum; Teacher of Eng. and Latin, Sydney Acad., N.S., 1925-26; New Rochelle (N.Y.) Jr. High Sch., 1927-29; Research Asst., Dept. of Educ. of N.S., 1930-46; Supv. of Attendance, 1933-38 and Registrar of N.S. Summer Sch.; Asst. Supt. of Educ., 1938-50; Depy. Min. of Educ. 1950-68; Past Pres., Candn. Educ. Assn., 1951-52 (mem. of Research Council; Rep., Candn. Education Assn. at Confs., Internat. Bureau of Educ., Geneva, 1955, 1959; Past Chrmn., Nat. Adv. Comte. on Sch. Broadcasting; has served on a no. of other important comtes.); Quance Lectr. in Educ., 1957; ("Educational Finance in Canada", 1958); co-author, "New Goals, New Paths" 1973; Past President, Canadian Council for Research in Educ.; sometime Vice-President, Dir. and Gov., N.S. Fish & Game Assn. (Past Pres. and Secy., Halifax Br.); mem., Halifax Bd. of Trade; Hon. mem., Candn. Red Cross Soc.; C.C.R.E. Whitworth Award for Service to Educ. Research 1968; Baptist; recreations: fishing, gardening, curling, golf; Clubs: Halifax Curling; Ashburn Golf; Home: 6095 Inglis St., Halifax, N.S. B3H 1L4; Office: Institute of Public Affairs, Dalhousie Univ., Halifax, N.S.

MOFFETT, Gillies Bramwell, B.A., M.B.A., M.E.D.; management consultant; b. Kingston, Jamaica 5 May 1932; s. Albert Edward and Lillian (Lyon) M.; e. Harrison Coll. Barbados; Queen's Univ. B.A., 1955; Univ. of W. Ont. M.B.A. 1960; Univ. of Toronto M.E.D. 1974; m. Lillian May d. B. H. Tippins 7 Feb. 1959; children: Michael, Jennifer; CHRMN. AND PARTNER, HAY ASSOCIATES CANADA LTD. since 1981; Free Lance Mang. Consultant 1960-65; Associate present firm Toronto 1965, Princ. 1967, Sr. Princ. 1971, Partner and Regional Mgr. 1974; Partner and Pres. 1976; served with RCAF Trenton, Ont. 1956-61, rank Flying Offr.; Anglican; Home: 2504 Homelands Dr., Mississauga, Ont. L5K 1H4; Office: 55 University Ave., Suite 1800, Toronto, Ont.

MOFFITT, Emerson Amos, M.D., C.M., M.Sc., F.R.C.P.(C); educator; anaesthetist; b. McAdam, N.B. 9 Sept. 1924; s. Amos Alexander and Ellen Selena (Wilson) M.; e. High Sch. McAdam, N.B. 1942; Univ. of N.B. 1942-44, 1945-46; Dalhousie Univ. M.D., C.M. 1951; Mayo Foundation, Specialist Training 1954-57; Univ. of Minn.

M.Sc. (Anesthesiol.) 1958; m. 1stly Helen Gertrude MacDonald (d. 1971) 19 May 1951; children: Eric Emerson, Mary Celene, Laurie Anne; m. 2ndly Phyllis Isabel d. Phillip Redden, Upper Stewiacke, N.S. 25 April 1973; ASSOCIATE DEAN OF MEDICINE, DALHOUSIE UNIV. since 1980; gen. practice North Sydney, N.S. 1951-54; Consultant in Anesthesiol. Mayo Clinic, Rochester 1957-72, Instr. to Assoc. Prof. Mayo Grad. Sch. 1959-72; Research Prof. of Anaesthesia present Univ. 1972-73; Prof. and Head of Anaesthesia 1973-80; served with RN Fleet Air Arm 1944-45; rec'd U.S. Nat. Inst. of Health Grant 1966-72; Dir. Maritime Heart Centre; Consultant in Anaesthesia, Defence Med. Bd. Ottawa, Dept. of Health N.S.; Assoc. Ed. 'Survey of Anesthesiology' since 1970; 'Anesthesia and Analgesia' 1973-77; mem. Ed. Bd. 'Canadian Anaesthetists' Society Journal'; author or co-author numerous publs.; Bd. Trustees, Internat. Anesthesia Research Soc. (Chrmn. 1977-79); Assn. Candn. Univ. Depts. Anaesthesia [Chrmn. 1977-78]; Acad. Anesthesiol. (Pres. 1978-79); Candn. Med. Assn.; N.S. Med. Soc.; Candn. Anaesthetists' Soc.; Am. Soc. Anesthesiol.; Am. Heart Assn.; Candn. Cardiovascular Soc.; N.Y. Acad. Sciences; Sigma Xi; Alpha Omega Alpha; Protestant; recreations: golf, skiing, photography; Club: Ashburn Golf; Home: 33 Wyndrock Dr., Halifax, N.S. B3P 1R8; Office: Sir Charles Tupper Medical Bldg., University Ave., Halifax, N.S. B3H 4H7.

MOHIDE, Thomas Patrick, LL.B., J.D.; b. Bristol, Eng., 22 July 1921; s. Patrick Joseph Thomas and Christina May (Lloyd) M.; e. St. Brendan's Coll., Clifton, Eng., 1936; Merchant Venturers' Tech. Coll., Bristol, grad. 1948; Blackstone Sch. of Law, Chicago, LL.B. 1970, J.D. 1972; m. Jean Dorothy, (Pres. Womens Aux., Hosp. Sick Children, Toronto) d. late William Joseph Dudbridge, 2 Sept. 1942; children: Patrick Thomas, M.D., F.R.C.S.(C), Deirdre Siobhan, B.Sc.; Dir., Mineral Resources, Govt. of Ont.; Sr. Asst. for Continental Sales, Internat. Nickel Co. of Can., London, Eng., 1950; Mgr. Overseas Sales, Falconbridge Nickel Mines Ltd., Toronto, Ont., 1956-66; Mgr. Gold and Silver Bullion Sales, Purchases and Inventory Control, Engelhard Industries U.S.A., 1967-72; Pres. Winnipeg Commodity Exchange 1972-73; has travelled widely throughout world in marketing & purchasing Candn. & other metals & commodities; rec'd. "Million Miler" Award in recognition of world business travel beyond that figure 1967; served with Irish Guards Regt., Household Brigade of Guards (Buckingham Palace) 1939-46; rank Capt.; el. Town Councillor, Merton and Morden, Eng., 1949-51; Vice-President Grenadier Guards Assn.; Past Dir., Rapeseed Assn. Can.; author, "Platinum Group Metals - Ontario and the World" 1979; "Gold" 1981; co-author of "Towards a Nickel Policy for Ontario" 1978; "The Future of Nickel and the Law of the Sea" 1980; "Report of the Interministerial Committee on Commodity Futures Trading"; recreation: golf; Clubs: Royal Candn. Mil. Inst.; Florham Park Country; Home: 44 Jackes Ave., Toronto, Ont. M4T 1E5; Office: Whitney Block, Queen's Park, Toronto, Ont.

MOHR, Lionel Charles, A.B., M.B.A.; management consultant; b. New York City, N.Y. 18 Dec. 1927; s. Lionel Charles and Emma Anne (Stohldrier) M.; e. Mayflower Pub. Sch. 1941; New Rochelle (N.Y.) High Sch. 1946; Wesleyan Univ. A.B. 1950; Harvard Univ. M.B.A. 1959; m. Anne Crosby Tredwell 1955, died 1965; m. Patricia Margaret d. late Clive Martin Sinclair 24 Aug. 1968; children: Lionel Thomas, Deborah Susan, Sharon Patricia, Deborah Anne, Douglas Tredwell, John David Edward; PRES. L. MOHR & ASSOC.,1979- ; Dir., Comac Communications Ltd. [Chrmn. 1954-79]; Retail Salesman, Scott Paper Co. New York 1950, Retail Dist. Sales Mgr. Binghamton, N.Y. 1954, Advertising Staff Asst. Philadelphia 1959, Asst. Merchandising Mgr. 1960; Mgr. Consumer Products Div. E. B. Eddy Co. Ottawa 1961; Product Mgr. General Foods Ltd. Toronto 1962, Sales Promotion Mgr.

1963, Product Planning Mgr. Birds Eye & Inst. Products Div. 1964, Sr. Product Mgr. 1965; Consultant, Stevenson & Kellogg, Toronto 1966, Princ. 1967, Princ.-in-Charge Marketing Function 1969; Dir. of Marketing and Corp. Planning, Toronto Star Ltd. 1971, Dir. of Marketing 1971, Vice Pres. Marketing 1974, Dir. 1974-76; Vice Pres. Toronto Star Newspapers Ltd. 1976, Dir. 1976-77; Vice Pres. Marketing and Dir., Torstar Corp. 1977-79; Adjunct Prof., Bus. Admin., Niagara Univ. 1981- ; Past chrmn. Div. Cong. Life & Work and Dept. Planning Assistance, Un. Ch. of Can.; Elder, First Presbyterian Church, Lewiston, N.Y.; mem. Confed. Ch. & Business People; Cdn. Diabetes Assn. Pub. Rel. Comm.; Founding Dir. Peel Family Services 1970; past Pres., mem. Bd. Govs. Candn. Opera Co.; Dir. Shaw Festival Theatre Foundation; Candn. Daily Newspaper Publishers Assn. 1975-79; mem. Newspaper Readership Council (N.Am.) 1978-79; Chrmn. Canadian Plans Bd. Newspaper Advertising Bureau 1978-79; Chrmn. Marketing Comte. Internat. Newspaper Advertising Extves. 1977-79; mem. Internat. Circulation Mgrs. Assn. 1971-79; Am. Marketing Assn. (Dir. Toronto Chapter 1965-69); Beta Theta Pi; Tau Pi; Free Mason served with U.S. Army Transport. Corps 1950-52; Presbyterian; recreations: golf, tennis, squash, cross-country skiing; Clubs: National; Mississauga Golf & Country; Niagara Falls (N.Y.) Country; Rotary; Canadian; Empire; Harvard Business (Past Chrmn., Past Pres.); Home: 460 Mountain View Dr., Lewiston, N.Y. 14092 Office: 105 Davenport Rd., Toronto, Ont.M5H 1H6

MOLLER, Dr. George, Dr. Juris; F.C.A., R.I.A., C.A., F.S.M.A.C., business consultant b. Prague, Czechoslovakia, 19 Oct. 1903; s. Ernest and Laura (Klepetar) M.; e. Univ. of Vienna (Dipl. in Comm. 1921); Univ. of Prague (Law and Pol. Science), Dr. Juris 1925; C.A. (Ont.) 1946, F.C.A. 1965; R.I.A. (Ont.) 1952 (Life mem. 1971); F.S.M.A.C. 1979; m. Edith R., d. late Rudolph Berger, 5 Oct. 1931; one s. Wayne Brian; Consultant and Dir., Robertson Building Systems Ltd.; Pres. Hansada Ltd.; Consultant, Dom. Auto Accessories Ltd.; Buck Bros. Ltd.; with Bohemian Union Bank, Prague (H.O.), 1928-39; came to Canada, 1939; Office Manager, Tru-Lite Ltd., and Armco Ltd., Toronto and Acton, Ont., 1939-42; articled with George A. Touche & Co., C.A.'s, Toronto, Ont., 1942 (Supervisor of Taxation Dept. 1946); joined Robertson-Irwin Ltd., Hamilton, Ont., 1949 as Asst. Controller; Controller, 1950, Treas. 1951, Dir. and Treas. 1955; Vice-Pres. 1958-70; Lectr. at McMaster University, 1949-56 and 1961-68; Lectr. University of Toronto 1973-74; served in Queen's York Rangers (Reserve), 1940-46; mem., Society Mgmt. Accts. Can.; Fellow, Soc. Mgmt. Accts. Can.; Inst. Chart. Accts. Ont. (Life); Fin. Extves. Inst. (Life); Adv. Council Internat. Assn. Fin. Extves. Institute; Gov. Hamilton Philharmonic; Unitarian; recreations: tennis, swimming; Clubs: Hamilton; Canadian (Burlington) (Dir.); Roseland Park Country; Home: 3164 Princess Blvd., Burlington, Ont. L7N 1G4; Office: 420 Keele St., Toronto, Ont. M6P 2L2

MOLLISON, Richard Devol, B.S., P.Eng.; executive; b. Faribault, Minn., 7 June 1916; s. Allan E. and Edna (Devol) M.; e. Univ. Minnesota, B.S. (Mining Engn.) 1941; m. Elizabeth, d. Harry B. Cobb, 7 June 1941; children: Steven, Ann, Mark; CHAIRMAN and C.E.O. , TEXASGULF INC. since 1981; Chrmn. and Dir., Texasgulf Canada Limited; joined Cerro de Pasco Copper Corporation, Peru, 1941; Mining Engineer with Newmont Mining Corporation, 1945; Phelps Dodge Corporation, New York, N.Y., 1947; joined Texas Gulf Sulphur Co. Inc. as Mining Engr., 1947; Mgr. Exploration 1958-62; Vice-Pres. and Mgr. Exploration, 1962-64; Vice-Pres., Metals Div., Texas Gulf Sulphur Co. 1964-71; Sr. Vice-Pres. 1972-73; Pres., 1973-79; Vice Chrmn. 1979-81; Dir., M&T Co. mem. Mining and Metall. Society of America; Candn. Inst. Mining and Metall.; Am. Inst. Mining & Metall. Engrs.; recreations: sailing, golf, hunting, woodworking; Clubs: Royal Canadian Yacht; Riverside Yacht; Mining (New York);

Landmark Club, Stamford Ct. 06870; Greenwich County (Ct.); Sky Club, NYC; Home: 13 Hendrie Dr., Old Greenwich, Conn.; Office: High Ridge Park, Stamford, Conn. 06904

MOLLOY, His Hon. William Austin, B.A., LL.B.; Retired Judge; b. Morris, Manitoba, 31 March 1917; s. Senator John Patrick and Helen Frances (Keeley) M.; e. Public and High Schs., Manitoba; Univ. of Manitoba, B.A. 1937; Manitoba Law Sch., LL.B. 1941; m. Ann Tompkins, 1963; three d.; called to the Bar of Man., 1941; practised law, 1941-56 Judge, County and Surrogate Courts of Man. 1956-78 (ret.); Liberal cand. for Winnipeg N. Center in Fed. el. 1949; K. of C.; Roman Catholic; Home: 2660 Shady Lane, Victoria, B.C. V8R 1R6

MOLNAR, George Dempster, B.Sc., M.D., Ph.D.; educator; b. Szekesfehervar, Hungary 30 July 1922; s. Eugene Frank and Clara Bertha (Becker) M.; e. Westdale Coll. Inst. Hamilton, Ont. 1940; Mount Royal Coll. Calgary, Alta. 1941; Univ. of Alta. B.Sc. 1949, M.D. 1951; Univ. of Minn. Ph.D. 1956; m. Gwendoline Esther McGregor; children: Gwendoline Jane, Charles McGregor; PROF. AND CHRMN. OF MEDICINE, UNIV. OF ALTA. since 1975; Dir., Muttart Diabetes Research and Training Centre, Univ. of Alta.; Consultant in Endocrinol. and Internal Med. Mayo Clinic 1956-75; Instr. in Med. Mayo Grad. Sch. 1956, Asst. Prof. 1963, Assoc. Prof. 1966, Prof. 1971; Prof. of Med. Mayo Med. Sch. 1973; served with Candn. Army 1942-45, rank Capt.; named Kt. Offr. of Netherlands Order of Orange-Nassau (with swords); mentioned in despatches; mem. Candn. Soc. Clin. Invest.; Royal Coll. Phys. & Surgs. Can.; W. Assn. Phys.; Am. Coll. Phys.; Am. Diabetes Assn.; Am. Fed. Clin. Research; Candn. Diabetic Assn.; Candn. and Alta. Med. Assn.; Endocrine Soc.; United Church; Home: 7216-114 A St., Edmonton, Alta. T6G 1N2; Office: 8-121 Clinical Sciences Bldg., Edmonton, Alta. T6G 2G3.

MOLSON, Eric H., A.B.; brewery executive; b. Montreal, Que. 16 Sept. 1937; s. Thomas Henry Pentland and Celia Frances (Cantlie) M.; e. Selwyn House Sch. Montreal 1948; Bishop's Coll. Sch. Lennoxville 1954; Le Rosey Switzerland 1955; Princeton Univ. A.B. 1959; McGill Univ. 1962-63; U.S. Brewers Acad. N.Y. 1960; m. Jane d. Hon. William Mitchell 16 Apl. 1966; 3 children; PRES., MOLSON BREWERIES OF CANADA LTD.; served as Apprentice Brewer, Chem., Asst. Brewmaster, Asst. to Pres., Market Research Analyst. Brewmaster, Vice Pres. Operations, Tech. Dir., Vice Pres. Corporate Devel., Pres. Molson's Ontario, Extve. Vice Pres. present Co.; Dir. Bishop's Coll. Sch.; Bishop's Univ.; Montreal Gen. Hosp. Foundation; Candn. Arctic Resources Comte., Toronto French Sch., Que. Easter Seals, Les Grands Ballets Canadiens, La Vie des Arts, Canadian, Princeton Alumni Fund, Selwyn House Endowment Fund; Anglican; Clubs: Mt. Royal; North Hatley Sailing; University; Office: 1555 Notre Dame E., Montreal, Que. H2L 2R5.

MOLSON, Hon. Hartland de Montarville, O.B.E., C.A., F.C.I.S., D.Sc.C. (Montreal), D. Univ. (Calgary), D.C.L. (Bishop's), LL.D. (R.M.C.); senator; b. Montreal, Quebec, 29 May 1907; s. Lieutenant-Colonel Herbert, C.M.G., M.C., and Elizabeth Zoe (Pentland) M.; e. Bishop's Coll. Sch., Lennoxville, Que.; Charterhouse, Eng.; Royal Mil. Coll., Dipl. 1928; C.A. 1933 m. Magda Posner, 29 Sept. 1939; one d. Zoe Anne; HON. CHRMN. & DIR., MOLSON COMPANIES LTD.; served in Militia as Lt., 27th Field Batty., 1928-33; joined the R.C.A.F. in 1939; served Overseas with No. 1 Fighter Sqdn., 1940; retired 1945 with rank of Group Capt., O.B.E. 1946; apptd. Senator, Dom. of Canada, July 1955; mem., Canadian Club of Montreal (Past Pres.); Soc. of Chart. Accts. of Que.; Inst. of Ch. Secretaries and Administrators; Anglican; Clubs: Mount Royal; St. James's; University (Montreal); Montreal Racket; Forest and Stream; Mount Bruno; Racquet and Tennis (N.Y.); Toronto; Rideau Country

(Ottawa); Home: 21 Rosemount Ave., Westmount, Que. H3Y 3G6; Office: 1555 Notre Dame St. E., Montreal, Que. H2L 2R5

MOLYNEUX, Thomas Emmet, B.Sc., P.Eng.; b. Gravelbourg, Sask., 9 Aug. 1918; s. John J. and Mary Ellen (Legree) M.; e. Yorkton High Sch., Sask., Grad. 1936; Univ. of Sask., B.Sc. (Civil Engn.) 1942; m. Reta Louise, d. Percy Witney, Stouffville, Ont., 10 Sept. 1949; has five children; Chrmn. and Dir., Kappele, Wright & MacLeod Ltd.; Pres., KWM Constructors Ltd.; began as Blasting Engr. with Hudson Bay Mining & Smelting Co. at Flin Flon, Man., 1938-41; City Asst. Engr., Yorkton, Sask.; Dept. of Highways, Yorkton, 1938; Resident Engr., U.S. Public Roads (Alaska Highway, Roads and Bridges) 1942-44; Design and Field Engr., C. D. Howe & Co., Consulting Engrs., Port Arthur, Ont., 1944-46; Sr. Design Engr., Abitibi Power & Paper Co. Ltd., Port Arthur, Iroquois Falls and Toronto Office, 1946-55; on loan to Defence Construction Ltd. as Asst. to Vice-Pres. (for one dollar), 1952, 1953; Vice-Pres., R. A. Hanright Co. Ltd., Consulting Engrs., St. Catharines, Ont., 1955-57; Chief Engr., St. Lawrence Const. Ltd. 1957-62; joined Domtar Pulp & Paper Ltd., 1962-64; mem., Engn. Inst. Can.; Assn. of Prof. Engrs. Ont. (mem. Pub. Relations Comte.); Corp. Prof. Engrs. Que.; Candn. Pulp & Paper Assn. (Tech. Sec.); K. of C.; Roman Catholic; Liberal; recreations: golf, tennis, reading; Home: 31 Grasspoint Cres., Etobicoke, Ont. M9C 2T9

MONAGHAN, James H.; publishing executive; b. Quebec, Que., 16 Feb. 1917; s. Joseph Edward and Bridget (McLaughlin) M.; e. St. Patrick's High Sch., Quebec, Que. (Grad. 1933); m. Mildred, d. Thomas Albert Crotty, 18 May 1940; children: Herbert Raymond, Barbara Ann, Nancy Joan; GEN. MGR. AND SECY.-TREAS., QUEBEC NEWSPAPERS LTD., since 1953; entered employ of present firm in Jan. 1935 as Asst. Accountant; promoted to Accountant, 1937; Controller and Secy.-Treas.; 1947; mem., Royal Rifles of Canada (R); Past-Trustee, St. Patrick's Church; Past Pres., St. Patrick's Old Boys' Assn.; Charter mem., Inst. of Newspaper Controllers & Finance Offrs. of N. Am.; mem.; Candn. Daily Newspaper Publishers Assn.; Conservative; Roman Catholic; recreation: golf; Clubs: Kiwanis; Quebec Winter; Quebec Garrison; Home: 868 Ave. Rochette, St. Foy, Que. G1C 1C2; Office: 255 Blvd. St. Sacrement, Quebec, Que. G1N 3X9

MONAGHAN, Patrick Anthony, C.M., B.E., M.Sc., M.B.A., O.L.S., P.Eng., F.E.I.C.; consulting engr.; b. Foam Lake, Sask., 15 Oct. 1926; s. Michael Joseph and the late Margaret Esther (McMurray) M.; e. Univ. of Sask., B.E., 1947, M.Sc., 1948; Univ. of Toronto, M.B.A., 1956; m. Margaret Catherine Melnick, 30 April 1954; children: Brian Michael, Patrick James, Morgan David; PRES., MARSHALL MACKLIN MONAGHAN LIMITED, 1974 (founding Partner 1952); Dir., and Chmn., Extve. Comte., Cansult. Ltd.; mem., Gov. Council, Assn. Prof. Engrs. Ont. (Pres. 1969); Fellow, Engn. Inst. Can.; mem. Assn. of Consulting Engrs. of Can.; Assn. Ont. Land Surveyors; former mem., Senate, Univ. of Toronto; former mem., Bd. of Gov., Ryerson Polytech. Inst.; N. York Gen. Hosp.; former Chmn., Ont. Housing Adv. Comm.; Bd. of Govs., North York Gen. Hospital; Roman Catholic; recreations: skiing, golf; Clubs: Donalda (Past Pres.); Osler Bluff Ski; Home: 102 Laurentide Drive, Don Mills, Ont. M3A 3E5; Office: 275 Duncan Mill Rd., Don Mills, Ont. M3B 2Y1

MONAST, André, Q.C., B.A., LL.L.; b. Québec, Que., 14 Dec. 1924; s. Medric and Lydie (LaPierre) M.; e. Garnier Coll., Québec City, B.A. 1945; Laval Univ. LL.L. 1948; m. Magdaleine Garneau, 24 Jan. 1953; children: André Jr., Michèle, Dominique; SR. PARTNER, LETOURNEAU & STEIN; Pres., Armaco Inc.; Vice-President and Dir., Canadian Imperial Bank of Commerce;

Secy. Valcartier Industries Inc.; Dir., Canada Wire & Cable Co. Ltd.; Canada Cement Lafarge Ltd.; Confederation Life Insurance Co.; Noranda Mines Ltd.; Noranda Metal Industries Ltd.; IBM Canada Ltd.; Dominion Realty Co.; Imbank Realty Co.; St. Lawrence Manufacturing Co. Ltd.; Brunswick Mining & Smelting Corp. Ltd.; Dominion Stores Ltd.; La Prévoyance Cie d'Assurances; called to Bar of Que. 1948; cr. Q.C. 1963; R. Catholic; Clubs: Qué. Garrison; Royal Qué. Golf; Home: 1270 Place de Mérici, Qué. G1S 3H7; Office: Suite 400, 65 Ste. Anne St., Québec, Qué. G1R 3X5

MONCEL, Lt.-Gen. Robert William, O.C. (1967), O.B.E. (1944), D.S.O. (1945), C.D., LL.D.; Canadian Army (retired); b. Montreal, Que.; 9 Apl. 1917; s. Rene Edward and Edith (Brady) M.; e. Selwyn House Sch., Montreal; Bishop's Coll. Sch., Lennoxville, Que.; McGill Univ., 1934-35; Staff Coll., 1940; Mt. Allison Univ., LL.D. 1968; m. Nancy Allison, d. Ralph P. Bell, N.S., 11 Nov. 1939; one d., Renée; served in World War, 1939-45, with Roy. Candn. Regt., 1st Armoured Bdge., 5th Armoured Divn.; 4th Armoured Divn.; Hdqrs., 2nd Candn. Corps; Commanded 18th Candn. Armoured Car Regt., 4th Candn. Armoured Bgde., 1945; promoted Capt., 1941, Maj. 1942, G.S.O.1 and Ltd.-Col. 1943, Brig. 1945; Mentioned in Despatches; Chevalier, Legion d'Honneur; Croix de Guerre avec Palme; Dir., Roy. Candn. Armoured Corps, 1946; Dir. of Mil. Training, Army Hdqrs., Ottawa, 1947-49; attended Nat. War Coll., Wash., D.C. 1949-50; Sr. Candn. Army Liaison Offr., England, 1951-53; Depy. Chief of Gen. Staff, 1954-56; Sr. Candn. Mil. Offr., Internat. Truce Comn., Indo China, 1957-58; Commdr., 3 Candn. Inf. Bgde., Gagetown, N.B., 1958-59; Quarter Master Gen., 1959-62; G.O.C. Eastern Command, 1962-64; Vice Chief of the Defence Staff, 1965-66; retired 1966; Co-ordinator for Visits of Heads of State, 1967; Chrmn. of Bd., The Fisermen's Memorial Hosp., Lunenburg, N.S. 1980; mem., Roy. Astronomical Soc. of Can.; Delta Upsilon; Anglican; recreations: golf, sailing, fishing; Clubs: Royal St. Lawrence Yacht; Royal Ottawa Golf; Royal N.S. Yacht Sqdn.; Home: "High Head", Murder Point, Mahone Bay, N.S. B0J 2E0

MONCUR, Robert H., B.Com., M.A.,; utilities executive; b. 7 March 1944; e. Univ. of Sask. B.Com. 1965; Oxford Univ. (Rhodes Scholar) M.A. (jurisprudence) 1968; Stanford Univ. 1973; m. Regina Louise Dishaw 1970; PRES., SASK. POWER CORP. 1981- ; mem. Adv. Council Centre for Resource Studies Queen's Univ. Kingston 1978- ; Dir. Candn. Inst. of Resources Law, Calgary 1979- ; Niagara Inst. Niagara-on-the-Lake 1981- ; Instr. in Business Adm. Univ. of Sask. 1968-69, summer 1970; Asst. Prof. of Business Adm. Queen's Univ. 1973-76; Policy Planning & Research Adm. Ministry of Solr. Gen. Can., Ottawa 1975-77; Depy. Min. of Mineral Resources, Sask. 1977-81; Chrmn. Interprov. Adv. Council on Energy 1978-80; recipient 4 Can. Council Doctoral Fellowships 1969-73; Stanford Univ. Tuition Fellowship 1969-73; named Outstanding Grad. Coll. of Comm. Univ. of Sask. 1965; co-author "Some Effects of Participative Budgeting Systems on Managerial Behavior" 1971; various articles, reviews; recreations: curling, badminton, wine collecting, gourmet cooking, philately; Home: 3312 Albert St., Regina, Sask. S4P 3P1; Office: 2025 Victoria Ave., Regina, Sask. S4P 0S1.

MONDOUX, Leon, B.Sc., F.S.A., F.C.I.A.; insurance executive; b. Hawkesbury, Ont., 30 April 1926; s. Jules and Alice (Bernard) M.; e. Univ. of Ottawa, B.Sc., 1946; m. Andrée, d. Napoleon de Villers, 1948; six children; VICE-PRES. AND ACTUARY, ALLIANCE MUTUAL LIFE, 1963- ; apptd. Actuary present Co. 1956; mem. Que. Health Board; past President Canadian Institute Actuaries; R. Catholic; recreations: swimming, reading; Club: M.A.A.A.; Home: 6280 Goncourt, Montreal Que. H1K 3X5; Office: 680 Sherbrooke St. W., Montreal, Que. H3A 2M7

MONET, Jacques, s.j., Ph.L., Th.L., M.A., Ph.D.,; educateur; né Saint-Jean, Qué. 26 jan. 1930; f. Fabio et Anita (Deland) M.; é. Univ. de Montréal, B.A. 1955; Immaculée Conception, Ph.L. 1956, Th.L. 1967; Univ. de Toronto, M.A. 1961, Ph.D. 1964; PRES., REGIS COLLEGE, TORONTO; Dir., Dept. d'Histoire 1972-77; o. prêtre Montréal, 9 juin 1966; derniers voeux dans la Cie de Jesus (Jésuites) Montmartre, 15 août 1971; Prof. (hist.) Saint Mary's Univ. High Sch. 1956; Loyola Coll. 1964-67; Asst. Prof. Univ. Toronto 1968; Prof. Agrége, Univ. d'Ottawa 1969-80; Titulaire, 1980-82; prés. (1975-76), Soc. hist. du Can.; mem. comité internat. des. hists. et des géogs. de langue française; comité de la politique de la Féd. candnne des sciences sociales 1976-78; Dir. de Recherche en histoire auprès du Gouv. gén. du Can. 1976-78; Conseiller spécial en politique culturelle, Sécretariat d'État 1978-79; Conseiller, Centre d'études du Qué., Sir George Williams Univ. 1966-70; mem. Counseil, Soc. hist. du Can. 1969-72 (Sec. 1969-75); Bureau de dir. French Can. Studies Programme 1965-70; comité consultatif d'Hist., gouvernement du Qué. 1964-67; mem. du Bureau des Gouverneurs, Univ. d'Ottawa 1974-77; élu à la Soc. royale du Can. 1978; mem. du Comité consultatif du design des Timbres-postes, Ministère des Postes, 1978- ; mem. du conseil Nat. de l'évaluation des Archives depuis 1979; mem., Queen Elizabeth Scholarship Comm.; auteur "The Last Cannon Shot: A Study of French Canadian Nationalism" 1969; "The Canadian Crown" 1979; "La Monarchie au Canada" 1979; "La Première Révolution Tranquille" 1981; aussi plusieuers articles de revue spécialisée et chapitres des volumes; Catholique r.; bureau: Ottawa, Ont.

MONEY, Maj. Kenneth, C.D., M.A., Ph.D.; physiologist; b. Toronto, Ont. 4 Jan. 1935; s. late Walter John and June Bladnee (Bate) M.; e. Whitney Pub. Sch. Toronto 1947; Noranda (Que.) High Sch. 1953; Univ. of Toronto B.A. 1958, M.A. 1959, Ph.D. 1961; Nat. Defence Coll. 1971-72; m. Sheila Mary d. Wildred Donnelly, Kirkland Lake, Ont. June 1958; one d. Laura Ann; Physiol., Dept. of Nat. Defence (defence and med. research); Assoc. Prof. Dept. of Physiol. Univ. of Toronto; discovered physiol. action of alcohol in inner ear 1974; rec'd. NASA contract for experiments on motion sickness and inner ear 1977; published impt. finding of evidence that sexual deprivation in young females causes physical damage in sensory receptor system for sexual stimuli, 1978; Air Reserve (pilot) 400 Sqdn. since 1956; Olympic Athlete 1956 (high jump); author over 50 scient. publs.; Fellow, Royal Soc. Health; mem. Candn. Physiol Soc.; Barany Soc.; Aerospace Med. Assn.; recreations: badminton, skiing, fishing; Home: 12 Audubon Court, Willowdale, Ont. M2N 1T9; Office: 1133 Sheppard Ave., Downsview, Ont.

MONEY, Peter Lawrence, M.Sc., Ph.D., P.Eng.; economic geologist; mining executive; b. Montreal, Que. 8 Feb. 1935; s. late Lawrence Charles and Phyllis Freeman (Bullock) M.; e. McGill Univ. B.Sc. 1956; Univ. of B.C. M.Sc. 1959; Univ. of Alta. Ph.D. 1967; Queen Mary Coll. London (UK), NRC Post-doctoral Fellow 1968-69; m. Frances Margaret d. late Edward Albert Munro 8 Sept. 1962; children: David, Katherine; VICE PRES., EXPLORATION, KIDD CREEK MINES LTD. 1982- ; joined Sask. Dept. of Mineral Resources as Regional Mapping Geol. and from 1965 as Resident Geol. Uranium City, 1960-68; Asst. Prof. Carleton Univ. Ottawa 1969-70; Sr. Staff Geol. Texasgulf Inc. 1970; Chief Geol. Can. Exploration 1975; Regional Mgr., Can. Exploration 1979; author or co-author various reports and papers; Fellow, Geol. Assn. Can.; mem. Candn. Inst. Mining & Metall.; Soc. Econ. Geols.; Assn. Prof. Engrs. Provs. Sask., Man. & Ont.; Club: Engineers; Home: 195 Stibbard Ave., Toronto, Ont. M4P 2C4; Office: Third Floor, 357 Bay St., Toronto, Ont. M5L 1E7.

MONK, Lorraine Althea Constance, C.M. (1973), M.A.; Canada public servant; author; b. Montreal, Que.; d. Edwin and Eileen Marion (Nurse) Spurrell; e. McGill Univ., B.A. 1944, M.A. 1946; m. John McCaughan Monk; children: Leslie Ann, Karyn Elizabeth, John Spurrell, David Chapman; currently Extve. Dir., Canadian Museum of Can.; rec'd. Centennial Medal 1967; Excellence of Service Award, Fed. internat. de l'art photographique; Nat. Assn. Photographic Art Gold Medal for "outstanding contribution to photography"; author, "Canada: A Year of the Land" 1967; "Ces Visages qui sont en pays" 1967; "Stones of History" 1967; "Call Them Canadians" 1968; "A Time to Dream — Reveries en Couleurs" 1971; "Canada" 1973; won Silver Medal at Leipzig Book Fair, 1975 in "Most Beautiful Book in the world" cometition; "The Female Eye" 1975; "Between Friends/Entre Amis" 1976 won many awards, including "best printed book" award at Int. Gallery of Superb Printing (U.S.A.) and first recipient of the Gold Medal, awarded in 1977 at the International Book Fair in Leipzig, Germany," in honour of her extraordinary achievement in the art of book creating"; other writings incl. 10 books in "Image" series; 3 books in "Signature" series; "The Robert Boudreau Monograph" 1980; Home: 176 Balmoral Ave., Toronto, Ont.; Office: Tunney's Pasture, Ottawa, Ont.

MONNIN, Hon. Alfred Maurice, B.A., LL.B., judge; b. Winnipeg, Manitoba, 6 March 1920; s. Alphonse Louis and Adele (Sperisen) M.; e. Provencher Coll. Inst., St. Boniface, Man.; St. Boniface Coll., B.A. (Latin Philos.) 1939; Univ. of Manitoba Law Sch., LL.B. 1946; m. Denise, d. late J. D. Pelletier, 30 Jan. 1943; children: Michel, Pierre, Bernard, Marc, Jean; JUSTICE, COURT OF APPEAL, MAN., since 1962; Chrmn., Man. Sch. Div. Boudaries Comn., since 1958; read law with F. T. Taylor, Q.C., T. M. Long and H. G. H. Smith, Q.C.; called to the Bar of Man., June 1946; cr. Q.C., Jan. 1957; practised law 1946-48 with J. T. Beaubien (later judge); Partner, Monnin, Grafton & Deniset, 1948-57; apptd. a Justice, Court of Queen's Bench, Man. 1957; Chrmn., St. Boniface Sch. Bd., 1953-57; Chrmn., Assn. d'Educ. des Canadiens Francais du Manitoba, 1956-57; served in 2nd World War, 1942-45; served in Canada (1942-43), U.K., France, Holland, Belgium, Germany (1943-45), Capt., Royal Regt. of Can.; mem., Candn. Centennial Conf.; Man. Centennial Corp.; Vice-Pres., Vanier Inst. of the Family; Past Pres., Winnipeg Symphony Orchestra Ltd.; final Festival Chrmn., Dom. Drama Festival, Winnipeg, 1962; mem., Candn. Bar Assn.; Man. Bar Assn.; recreation: drama; Clubs: Manitoba, Canadian; Home: 608 Aulneau St., St. Boniface, Man. R2H 2V4; Office: Law Courts, Winnipeg, Man.

MONSAROFF, Adolph, B.A.Sc., F.C.I.C.; company executive; b. Russia, 21 Feb. 1912; s. Boris and Sonya (Green) M.; e. Univ. of Toronto, B.A.Sc. (Chem. Engn. with Hons.) 1934; m. Marion Mink, 15 Jan. 1937; DIR., OFFICE OF INDUST. RESEARCH, McGILL UNIVERSITY, since 1977; after grad. from Univ. joined Mallinckrodt Chemical Works Ltd., Toronto, Ont., as Chem. Engr.; Plant Supt., 1936-44; joined Monsanto Can. Ltd., 1945; Vice-Pres., 1951-59; Extve. Vice-Pres., 1959-62; el. Dir. 1960; Vice-Pres., Marketing & Devel., Domtar Chemicals Ltd., 1963; Vice-Pres. and Mang. Dir., 1964-68; Pres. 1968-76; served with C.O.T.C. 1940; Fellow, Chem. Inst. of Can. (Chrmn., Bd. of Dirs., 1954-55, Vice Pres. 1973-74, Pres. 1974-75); mem., Soc. of Plastics Industry (Can.) Inc. (Pres. 1960-62); Bd. Dirs., Mfg. Chemists' Assn. (U.S.) 1974-77; Soc. of Chem. Industry; Am. Inst. Chem. Engrs.; Order Engrs. Que.; Am. Assn. Advanc. Science; recreations: literature, squash, golf, fishing; Clubs: University (Montreal); Montreal Badminton and Squash; Kanawaki Golf; Home: 4 Merton Cres., Hampstead, Que. H3X 1L5; Office: 408 - Dawson Hall, McGill Univ., 853 Sherbrooke St. W., Montreal, Que. H3A 2T6

MONTAMBAULT, Léonce, B.A., B.Sc.; telecommunications executive; b. Quebec, Que., 27 May 1932; e. Laval Univ. B.A. 1953, B.Sc. (Civil Engn.) 1957; EXTVE. VICE

PRES. QUEBEC REGION, BELL CANADA since 1979; Dir., Télébec Ltée; Sotel Inc.; Bell-Northern Research Ltd.; Ronalds-Federated Ltd.; Dir. 6 mem. Exec Comte. La Chambre de Commerce, P.Q.; mem. Consultative Comte. CIDEM; École de Tech. Supérieure (Univ. du Que.); joined Bell Canada, Quebec City 1957 serving in various mang. positions Engn., Plant, Commercial, Traffic and Personnel Depts.; Gen. Plant Mgr. — Que. 1968, Gen. Mgr. — Operations 1970; Vice Pres. (Prov. Area) 1971; Vice Pres. (Montreal Area) 1976; Vice Prs. (Customer Serv.) 1979; mem. of Bd. & Chrmn. (1982) Annual Financial Campaign, P.Q. Diabetes Assn.; mem. Order of Engrs. of Que.; Chamber of Comm. Can.; L'Orchestre Symphonique de Montreal; L'Association des Anciens de Laval; Centre des dirigeants d'entreprises; Clubs: St. Denis (Montreal); Montreal Chamber of Comm.; Office: 800 Victoria Sg., Room 4402, Montreal, Que. H4Z 1A2

MONTCALM, Ronald, B.A., LL.L.; lawyer; b. Trois Rivières, Que. 26 Dec. 1939; s. Aimé and Alida (Filion) M.; e. St. Sacrement Sch. Trois Rivières; Loyola High Sch. 1958; Loyola Coll. B.A. 1962; Univ. de Montréal LL.L. 1966; mem. law firm LAFLEUR, BROWN, de GRANDPRE; Dir. Teleglobe; Lectr., Order Prof. Engrs. Que.; called to Bar of Que. 1967; served with Univ. Naval Training Div. 1959-66, rank Capt.; mem. Montreal Bar Assn.; Que. Bar Assn.; Candn. Bar Assn.; R. Catholic; recreations: jogging, squash, tennis, skiing; Clubs: M.A.A.A.; Mount Royal Tennis; Home: 245 Kindersley Ave., Town of Mount Royal, Que. H3R 1R6; Office: Stock Exchange Tower (P.Ó. Box 214), Montreal, Que. H4Z 1E4.

MONTGOMERY, Donald, trade unionist; b. Canora, Sask., 8 June 1920; s. Milton Templeton and Margaret Geneva (Culbert) M.; e. elem. and high schs. Hamilton, Ont.; Turner Business Coll.; m. Lu Eirene d. Thomas Huggard, 20 May 1954; children: Charmiene, Donald Kirk; SECY.-TREAS. CAN. LABOUR CONGRESS since 1974 and Exec. Offr.; joined Steelworkers' Organ. Comte. (predecessor to United Steelworkers of Am.) at age 20; toured E. Ont. on variety of organ. drives for 10 yrs. from 1943; trans. to Toronto 1953 and apptd. Steelworkers Area Supvr. for Toronto-Barrie Area until present apptd.; el. Secy.-Treas. Toronto and Lakeshore Labour Council 1953 and re-el. to same position on merged Labour Council of Metrop. Toronto, el. Pres. 1964-74; Founding mem. Labour Council Devel. Foundation and served as Dir., Nat. Inst. for Social Assistance; former Dir. Social Planning Council Metro Toronto; served gov. bd. Un. Appeal; Adv. Vocational Comte. Borough York Bd. Educ.; John Howard Soc.; Riverdale Hosp. (Dir.); mem., founding Zool. Soc.; mem. Export Development Bd.; Aeronautics Adv. Bd.; Can. Inst. Internat. Affairs; serves on AFL-CIO-CLC Liaison Comte. and Can. Labour Congress Internat. Affairs Comte.; Maritime Comte.; Organ. and Pub. Relations Adv. Comtes.; Council for Performing Arts; White Collar Comte.; mem. NDP; recreation: woodwork; Home: 19 Baby Point Rd., Toronto, Ont. M6S 2E8; Office: 2841 Riverside Dr., Ottawa, Ont. K1V 8N4

MONTGOMERY, Hon. H(ugh) Edward, C.D., B.A., B.C.L.; judge; b. Woodstock, N.B. 19 Oct. 1929; s. Gage Workman and Queenie Victoria (Britton) M.; e. Woodstock High Sch. 1946; Mount Allison Univ.; Univ. of N.B. B.A. 1951, B.C.L. 1953; m. Mary Louise d. Wendell Kingston Hay, Fredericton, N.B. 24 Oct. 1953; children: Janice Elaine, (Gage) Bruce (Edward), Jennifer Leigh; JUDGE, COURT OF QUEEN'S BENCH N.B. FAMILY DIV. since 1979; called to Bar of N.B. 1953; private law practice Woodstock, N.B. 1953-58; Partner, Crocco & Montgomery 1958-71; Judge, Prov. Court N.B. 1971-79; served with Candn. Army (Reserve) 1948-70; former Councillor and Depy. Mayor, Town of Woodstock; Past Pres. and Dir. Carleton Manor Inc. Woodstock; Past Dir. L. P. Fisher Lib. Woodstock; Past Pres. Woodstock Rotary; Wood-

stock Jaycees; Protestant; recreations: fly fishing, bird hunting, flying; Home: 101 Deerwood Rd., R.R.6, Fredericton, N.B. E3B 5X7; Office: (P.O. Box 6000) Justice Bldg., Fredericton, N.B. E3B 5H1.

MONTGOMERY, William Harp, LL.M.; diplomat; b. Vancouver B.C. 11 Oct. 1933; s. William and Hazel (Hutcherson) M.; e. Univ. of B.C., B.A. 1956, LL.B. 1959; London Sch. of Econ. and Pol. Science LL.M. 1961; m. Julia, d. of late E. J. Meilicke 16 Dec. 1960; children: Andrea Claire, Ian Donald AMBASSADOR TO INDONESIA 1979- ; joined Dept. of External Affairs 1961; Extve. Asst. to Secy. of State for External Affairs 1962-63; New Delhi 1963-66; Bangkok 1968-70; Geneva 1973-77; Dir. Legal Adv. Div. Ottawa 1977-79; mem. Candn. Inst. Internat. Affairs; Candn. Council Internat. Law; Home: P.O. Box 52/JKT, Jakarta, Indonesia; Office: 125 Sussex Dr., Ottawa, Ont. K1A 0G2

MONTPETIT, Hon. Andre; b. Paris, France, 8 Dec. 1910; s. Edouard and Hortense (Varin) M.; e. St. Leo's Acad., Westmount, Que.; Montreal Coll., B.A. 1930; Univ. of Montreal, LL.L. 1933; m. Madeleine, d. Hon. Jean Prévost, 14 June 1934; two s. and two d.; JUSTICE, SUPERIOR COURT OF QUE., since 1951; Prof. at Faculty of Law, Univ. of Montreal, since 1955; mem. of Bd. of Govs., Univ. of Montreal, since 1961; read law with Beaulieu, Gouin, Mercier & Tellier; Advocate 1933; cr. K.C. 1943; rep. for Que., Youth Employment Comte.; Nat. Employment Comn., 1936; formerly Vice-Pres., Young Libs. Assn.; mem., Montreal Bar Assn.; Roman Catholic; recreations: golf, tennis, swimming; Home: 419 Mount Stephen, Westmount, Que. H3Y 2X7

MONTREUIL, Robert Clément; Canadian public servant; b. Ottawa, Ont. 19 Jan. 1937; s. Antonio and Mariette (Tissot) M.; e. Univ. of Ottawa Grad. in Pol., Socioecon. Sciences; m. Michelle Cécile d. late Joseph Albert St-Georges 30 Sept. 1961; one s. Stephane; DEPY. MIN., REGIONAL ECON. EXPANSION (DREE) 1979- ; Auditor, Office of Auditor Gen. Ottawa 1958-61; various mang. positions Dept. Industry, Trade & Comm. Ottawa and Montreal 1962-68, Chief Trade Missions 1968-69; various mang. and extve. positions DREE, Ottawa and Montreal, 1969-72, Asst. Dept. Min. DREE Que. Region, Montreal 1973-79; Dir., Can. Ind. Renewal Bd.; Fed. Bus. Devel. Bank; mem. R. Catholic; recreation: tennis; Home: 17 Place Garand, Ottawa, Ont. K1H 8M1; Office: 200 Promenade du Portage, Ottawa, Ont. K1A 0M4.

MONTY, Guy, B.A.Sc.; b. Montreal, Que., 17 March 1920; e. Jean-de-Brébeuf Coll.; Ecole Polytechnique de Montréal B.A.Sc. 1946; m. Béatrice Larose; one d. Marie-Claude; PRESIDENT AND CHIEF EXECUTIVE OFFICER, HYDRO-QUEBEC INTERNAT. since 1978; joined Hydro-Québec as Engr. in Substns. Service Montreal 1946, Engr. Projects Sec. Transmission Div. 1948, Constr. Engr. 1950, Asst. Transmission Engr. 1957, Transmission Engr. 1962, Asst. Chief Engr. Overhead and Underground Transmission 1964, Dir. Transmission Line Projects 1965, Gen. Mgr. Constr. 1969; Commissioner 1976; Dir. of the Corp. de l'Ecole Polytechnique; mem. Order Engrs. Que.; Engn. Inst. Can.; Can.-China Trade Council; Candn. Standards Assn.; Inst. Elect. & Electronics Engrs.; Internat. Conf. on Large High Voltage Elect. Systems (CIGRE); Russo-Candn. Comte. on Tech. & Scient. Coop.; Chambre de Comm. de Montréal; recreations: golf, cross-country skiing, reading; Club: St-Denis; Office: 870 de Maisonneuve Blvd. E., Montreal, Qué. H2L 4S8

MONZINGO, Bascom Harold, B.Sc.; petroleum executive; b. Minden, La., 25 Dec. 1926; s. Bascom H. and Carrie Mae (Swanner) M.; e. La. Tech. Univ., B.Sc. 1949, postgrad. studies in Business 1961-62; m. Betty Jean, d. Carl D. Elmore, Longview, Texas, 19 May 1951; children: Stephen Carl, Cynthia Ann; PRESIDENT, C.E.O. AND

DIRECTOR, MURPHY OIL CO. LTD. since 1973; Dir., Wascana Pipe Line Ltd.; Chrmn. of Bd. and C.E.O., Spur Oil Ltd.; joined Murphy Oil Corp. as Acct., El Dorado, Ark., 1949, Chief Acct. 1953, Asst. Controller 1964, Sr. Controller 1967; trans. to present Co. as Vice Pres. of Finance & Adm., Calgary 1968, Extve. Vice Pres. 1969; served with U.S. Army Ordnance 1944-46; Europe 1945-46; Gov., Cdn. Petroleum Assn. 1977; Comte'man, Boy Scouts of Can.; Deacon, First Bapt. Ch., Calgary 1970-73; Deacon and Chrmn. of Bd. First Bapt. Ch., El Dorado, Ark., 1959-68; Trustee, Ark. Bapt. Gen. Hosp., 1965-68; mem. Calgary Chamber Comm.; Pi Kappa Alpha (Pres. & Treas.); Sigma Iota Epsilon (Pres.); Phi Kappa Phi; Omicron Delta Kappa; Delta Sigma Pi; Freemason; P. Conservative; Baptist; recreations: golf, fishing, hunting; Clubs: Calgary Petroleum; Ranchmen's; Calgary Golf & Country; Home: 100 Colleen Cres. S.W., Calgary, Alta. T2V 2R3; Office: (P.O. Box 2721) Calgary, Alta. T2P 2M7

MOODY, Norman F.; B.E.F.I.E.E., F.I.E.E.E., F.C.M.B.E.S., F.R.S.C.; b. England; Hon. Prof. of Physics, Univ. of Victoria; Prof. Emeritus, Univ. of Toronto since 1977; former Prof. of Elect. Engn. & Biomed. Eng. and Dir. Inst. Biomed. Engineering, Univ. of Toronto; during war was research worker at Telecommunications Research Estab.; came to Canada 1948 to head Electronics Division, Atomic Energy of Canada Limited, Chalk River; became Senior Principal Scient. Offr. with a High Explosive Research Estab. in Eng., 1951; Head Basic Circuit Research, Defence Research Bd., Govt. of Can., to 1959; subsequently apptd. Head, Dept. Elect. Engn., Univ. of Sask.; Address: 1965 Saltair Cres., Victoria, B.C. V8N 2X6

MOOGK, Brig. Gen. Willis John, O.B.E., C.D.; b. Waterloo, Ont., 18 Aug. 1910; e. Royal Mil. Coll., Kingston, Ont. (Grad. 1934); Staff Coll., Camberley, Eng., p.s.c. 1942; Nat. Defence Coll., Kingston, Ont., n.d.c. 1954; m. Grace Elizabeth, Shuttleworth, London, Ont., 7 Sept. 1938; children: Christopher Anthony, Leslie Elizabeth, Peter Nicholas, Cynthia Ann, Mary Rosalind, Juliana Victoria; Lieut., Royal Candn. Regt., 1934; joined HQ 2 Candn. Div. on their arrival overseas summer 1940; promoted Lieut.-Col. and to Command Royal Winnipeg Rifles, July 1942; G.S.O. Combined Operations Training at HQ 21 Army Group; on return to Can. in 1945 apptd. Sr. Staff Offr., Dist. Hdqrs., London, Ont.; Depy. Dir. of Army Personnel Ottawa, 1950-52; promoted Col. in 1952 in charge Adm. Candn. Army Far East, also commanded Candn. Troops in Japan and was Candn. Advisor to C.-in-C. Brit. Commonwealth Forces (Korea); Naval, mil. and Air Attaché at Candn. Embassy to The Netherlands at The Hague, 1954-57; Commander Sask. Area, 1959-62; promoted Brig. 1961; Commander, Camp Borden, 1963-65; retired from Candn. Army 1965; Mang. Dir. Hamilton Hist. Bd. 1967-78; mem. Niagara Hist. Soc.; Royal Candn. Mil. Inst., Toronto; R.M.C. Club; Hon. Life mem., Regina Un. Services Inst.; Anglican; recreations: collecting art objects, Can. Social history; Home: "Storrington", Gage & Simcoe Sts., Niagara-on-the-Lake, Ont. L0S 1J0

MOON, Jack Mayhew; insurance broker; b. Victoria, B.C. 25 Oct. 1918; s. Charles Edward and Ethel Medwin (Gardner) M.; e. N. Vancouver High Sch. (Sr. Matric); Banking and Ins. Inst. courses; m. Marion Jean, d. Grant McNeil, 6 Dec. 1938; children: David R., Joanne E., John R., Kathleen M.; DIRECTOR, DRUMMOND HOLDINGS LTD.; Dir., Reed Stenhouse Companies Ltd.; with Royal Bank of Canada, 1937-40; Marsh & McLennan Limited, Insurance Brokers, Vancouver, B.C., 1946-47; B. L. Johnson Walton Co. Limited, Insurance Brokers (Mgr. of Fire and Inland Marine Department) 1947-50; opened and managed Calgary Office of B. L. Johnson Walton Co. Ltd., 1950-51; started the firm of R. M. Abernethy (Alberta) Ltd. as shareholder and Mang. Dir. expanding rapidly, 1951-59; merged with B. L. Johnson Walton Ltd. in 1959 which firm merged with Reed Shaw McNaught in Oct. 1959; past Pres. and CEO, Reed Shaw Stenhouse

and Partners Ltd.; served in 2nd World War, 1940-46; retired as Capt., R.C.A.P.C.; served Overseas with 6th Candn. Anti-Tank R.C.A., Camerons of Winnipeg and Fort Garry Horse; Conservative; United Church; recreations: skiing, golf, curling; Clubs: Ranchmen's; Calgary Golf & Country; Home: P.O. Box 25, Site 5, R.R. 8, Calgary, Alta. T2J 2T9; Office: 2700 One Palliser Sq., Calgary, Alta.

MOONEY, John James; horse racing executive; b. Toronto, Ont., 7 Sept. 1924; s. John James and Marjorie (Heffering) M., e. De La Salle Coll., Toronto; m. Bernice Gabriel Frezell, 8 Nov. 1947; children: John Edward, Paul, Michael, Patrick, Daniel, Maureen, Norah; PRES., LAUREL RACE COURSE; Dir.,Rexwood Publications Limited; (formerly Pres.); Dir. Emeritus Thoroughbred Racing Assn.; Founding Dir., Nat. Assn. Candn. Race Tracks; served with RCAF 1943-45; Roman Catholic; recreation: golf; Clubs: Metropolitan; Rosedale Golf, Cherry Hill Golf; Home: 10719 Willowgreen Dr., S.E., Calgary, Alta. T2J 1P7

MOONEY, Joseph Fraser, M.L.A.; pharmacist; politician; b. Glace Bay, N.S. 24 Feb. 1927; s. John Leo and Bridget (Fraser) M.; m. Barbara Ann d. James Freeman Harding, Yarmouth, N.S.; Pharm., City Drug Store; M.L.A. (Lib.) for Yarmouth Co.; former Min. of Hwys. N.S.; also held portfolios of Mun. Affairs, Tourism, Communications, Purchasing, Liquor Comn., Civil Service; former Pres., Roads & Transport. Assn. Can.; Office: 369 Main St., Yarmouth, N.S. and Province House, Halifax, N.S.

MOONEY, William John; B.Sc.; geologist; petroleum executive; b. Regina, Sask., 27 Feb. 1929; s. William Joseph and Esther Ellen (Murphy) M.; e. Notre Dame of Can. Wilcox, Sask., 1952; Colo. Coll. B.Sc. (Geol.) 1957; Banff Sch. Advanced Mang. 1971; m. Lois Carol d. Louis Marvin Larson, Los Angeles, Cal., 7 Nov. 1953; children: William Joseph, Michael Marvin, Timothy Stephen, Melissa Anne, Barbara Ellen; PRES. HARVARD RESOURCES LTD. 1980- ; Centipede Energy Ltd. 1980- ; Dir. Syncrude Can. Ltd., 1973-78; Pres. and Dir.; Canada-Cities Service Ltd. 1975-78; Pres. and Dir., 1975-78; Pres. Cities Service Europe-Africa-Middle East Petroleum Corp. 1978-80; mem. Bd. of Govs. Candn. Petroleum Assn. 1975-78; Dir., Candn. Petroleum Assn. (Alta., Sask.) 1975-78; Bd. of Govs. Oilmans 1975-78; Vice Chrmn. Alta. Enviromental Research Trust 1976-78; Co-Chrmn. Energy Zoo Fund; Bd. of Govs. & Bd. of Regents Athol Murray Coll. of Notre Dame; Bd. of Regents Candn. Oldtimers Hockey Assn.; Hon. Adv. Bd., Internat. Candn. Petroleum Exhib. & Conf.; Camp Cadicasu Bd. of Dir. & Chrmn. 1962-68; Am. Assn. Petrol. Geols.; Candn. Soc. of Petrol. Geols.; Am. Petrol. Inst.; Royal Candn. Legion 102; R. Catholic; recreation: golf; Clubs: Calgary Press; National Press; Wellington (London) 21 Club (London); Canyon Meadows Golf & Country; Calgary Petroleum; Home: 1110 Crescent Rd. N.W., Calgary Alta. T2M 4A8; Office: 1510 Canada Trust Bldg., 505-3rd St. S.W., Calgary, Alta. T2P 3E6

MOORADIAN, Ara John, M.Sc., Ph.D., D.Sc., F.C.I.C., F.R.S.C.; engineer; scientist; b. Hamilton, Ont., 21 May 1922; s. John Hogop and Nazen (Papertzian) M.; e. Univ. of Sask., B.Sc. (Chem. Engn.) 1945, M.Sc. (Phys. Chem.) 1948; Univ. of Mo., Ph.D. 1950; Univ. of Man., D.Sc.; m. Alice C., d. late Charles C. Clerkson, 19 May 1945; children: Jo-Anne, Carol, Peggy, Diana; CORPORATE VICE PRES. RESEARCH & DEVEL., ATOMIC ENERGY OF CAN. LTD., since 1978; Assoc. mem., Science Council of Can., 1972-73; Plant Tester, Alta. Nitrogen Div., Consol. Mining & Smelting Co., 1945-46; Asst. Research Offr., Chalk River Nuclear Labs., Nat. Research Council, 1950; Br. Head, Devel. Engn. of present labs., 1955, Fuel Devel., 1959; Dir., Devel. Eng. Div., 1964; Mang. Dir., Whiteshell Nuclear Research Lab., Pinawa, Man., 1966; Vice

Pres.-in-charge of WNRE — Atomic Energy of Canada Ltd., 1969; Vice Pres. i/c Chalk River Nuclear Labs. 1971; Extve. Vice Pres., Research and Devel. 1977; maj. contrib. to devel. of low cost nuclear fuel of CANDU nuclear power generating stns.; Trustee, Improvement Dist. Deep River; First Mayor, Town of Deep River; rec'd Can. Medal; rec'd. W.B. Lewis Award; author of over 40 papers and publs.; mem., CHEM: INST: OF CAN: (PRES: 1980-81); Am. Nuclear Soc.; Anglican; recreations: furniture design, golf, skiing; Home: (Box 1542) Deep River, Ont. K0J 1P0; Office: 275 Slater St., Ottawa, Ont. K1A 0S4

MOORE, Rev. Arthur Bruce Barbour, B.A., B.D., D.D., LL.D. (Un. Ch.); b. Keswick Ridge, N.B., 4 Feb. 1906; s. Churchill and Mary (MacDonald) M.; e. Ayers Cliff (Que.) Pub. and High Sch.; superior Sch., Keswick Ridge, N.B.; McGill Univ., B.A. 1927; United Theol. Coll., B.D. 1930 and D.D. 1947; Oxford Univ., 1931; Univ. of Sask., LL.D. 1952, McMaster 1960; Trinity Coll., Toronto, D.D. 1952, St. Andrew's Coll., Saskatoon 1961, Wycliffe Coll., Toronto 1970; Mount Allison, LL.D. 1963; m. Florence Margaret, d. Ernest S. Price, 22 April 1933; Moderator of Un. Church of Can. since 1971; Min., Un. Ch. of Can., 1931-36; Presb. Ch., U.S.A. 1936-40; Un. Ch. of Can., 1940-46; Principal and Prof. of Systematic Theology, St. Andrew's College, Saskatoon, Sask. 1946-50; Pres., Victoria Univ., Toronto 1950 till resigned 1970; Chancellor, Univ. of Toronto 1977; mem., Bd. of World Mission, Ch. Union Comn.; Publications: "Growth and Understanding" (both an Editor and Contrib.); "Jesus Christ and the Christian Life"; Clubs: Canadian; York; Address: Room 100, Simcoe Hall, University of Toronto, Toronto, Ont.

MOORE, Blythe Ernest; insurance executive; b. Wakefield, Que., 28 Aug. 1927; s. William E. and Ethel (Nelson) M.; e. Aylmer (Que.) High Sch.; Willis Business Coll., 1945; L.I.A.M.A. Agency Mang. Sch., 1955 and Offrs. Sch. 1959; McGill Univ., Adm. & Mang. Problems 1957; Univ. of W. Ont., Mang. Problems 1957; Univ. of W. Ont., Mang. Training 1963; Sir George Williams Univ., Behavioral Science and Communication 1968; m. Lois, d. Isaac Stokes, 30 Oct. 1948; children: Gary, Debra, Rhonda; GEN. MGR. AND CHIEF EXTVE. OFFR., HOLLAND LIFE INSURANCE SOC. LTD.; Dir. Stanstead & Sherbrooke Ins. Co.; Sterling Ins. Co. of Canada; Hessel Investments Ltd.; B. F. Goodrich Rubber Co., Ottawa, 1947-49; joined Sun Life Assurance Co. of Canada as Agt., Ottawa, 1950; Unit Suprvr. 1953; Inspr. of Agencies, H.O., Montreal, 1954; Asst. Supt. of Agencies, 1955; Supt. of Agencies 1957; Past Pres., Y's Men's Club; Life Underwriters Assn. Ottawa; mem., Candn. Life Ins. Assn.; Life Ins. Agency Mang. Assn.; Bd. Trade Metrop. Toronto; Candn. Chamber Comm.; United Church; recreations: curling, hunting, fishing, golf, reading, bridge, renovating 100 yr. old farm; Clubs: Rotary; Leaside Curling; Cedarbrae Golf; Home: 8 Sandpiper Court, Don Mills, Ont. M3A 3G8

MOORE, Brian; author; b. Belfast, N. Ireland, 25 Aug. 1921; s. late James Bernard and late Eileen (McFadden) M.; e. Ireland; m. Jacqueline, d. late Frank J. Scully, 28 Feb. 1951; one s. Michael; served with Brit. Ministry of War Transport (Civilian Overseas), 1943-45, N. Africa, Italy, France; author of: (novel) "The Lonely Passion of Judith Hearne", 1956 (Author's Club, Gt. Brit. Best First Novel Award, 1956; Que. Lit. Award, 1956; Beta Sigma Phi First Novel Award, 1956); "The Feast of Lupercal" (novel) 1957; "The Luck of Ginger Coffey", 1960 (Gov.-General's Lit. Award for Fiction, 1960); "An Answer From Limbo", 1962; "Judith Hearne" 1964; "The Emperor of Ice-Cream", 1965; "I am Mary Dune" 1968; "Fergus" 1970; "The Revolution Script" 1971; "Catholics" 1972; "The Great Victorian Collection", 1975; "The Doctor's Wife" (novel) 1976; "The Mangan Inheritance," 1979; "The Temptation of Eileen Hughes," 1981; Recip.

Quebec Prize, 1958; U.S. Nat. Arts & Remers Award; Governor General's Award, 1975; W.H. Smith Award, 1973; James Tait Black Mem. Award, 1975; Guggenheim Fellow, 1959; Can. Council Sen. Fellow, 1962, 76; Writer-in-Residence, Univ. of Toronto, 1982-: short stories in the "Atlantic Monthly", "The Cornhill", "Northern Review", "Tamarack Review", etc.; Address: 33958 Pacific Coast Hwy., Malibu, Calif. 90265 U.S.A.

MOORE, James Doran; manufacturing executive; b. Winnipeg, Man., 20 Feb. 1917; s. Patrick Joseph and Virginia Agnes (Rice) M.; e. St. Mary's Coll. (High Sch.) Calgary, grad. 1935; m. Patricia Anne, d. Rupert Henry A. Lacey, 17 May 1955; children: Marcia Jane, James Patrick, Margaret Suellen, Barbara Lynne, Nancy Ann, Michael Doran, Sarah Marie; Dir., Rubber Assn. of Can. 1969-81 (Chrmn. 1969-70 and 1977); on grad. began in jr. positions with Searle Grain Co., Calgary; three yrs. in sales with Heintzmann & Co. Ltd.; after war service joined Firestone Can. Inc. at Calgary as Wholesale Terr. Salesman, 1945; Mgr., Truck Tire Sales for Alta. Dist., 1946; Alta. Dist. Mgr., 1949, W. Ont. Dist. 1951; W. Can. Div. Mgr., 1954; Candn. Trade Sales Mgr., 1963; Candn. Gen. Sales Mgr., 1964; Vice-Pres., 1966; el. a Dir., 1967; Pres., Jan. 1969; chrmn. of Bd. 1978-81 (ret.) served with R.C.N., July 1941 to Oct. 1945; loaned to R.N. (motor torpedo boats) for 1 yr., after which saw service in Atlantic theatre (commanded Corvette 1944-45); mem., Toronto Bd. of Trade; Dir., Opera Hamilton; Dir. & Treas., Hamilton Foundation; R. Catholic; recreation: golf; Clubs: Hamilton; Hamilton Golf & Country; Home: 5087 Ashland Dr., Burlington, Ont. L7L 3H3; Office: #308-89 Queensway W., Mississauga, Ont. L5B 2V2

MOORE, (James) Mavor, O.C. (1973), B.A., D.Litt.; playwright, actor, producer, critic, university professor; b. Toronto Toronto, Ont., 8 March 1919; s. Francis John and Dora (Mavor) M.; e. Univ. of Toronto Schs.; Univ. of Toronto, B.A. (1st Class Hons. in Philos. and English) 1941; D.Litt. (Hon.) York 1969; m. 1stly, Darwina, d. Charles Faessler, Toronto, Ont., 14 Oct. 1943; four d., Dorothea, Rosalind, Marieli, Charlotte; 2ndly, Phyllis (Langstaff) Grosskurth, Toronto, Ont. 1969; CHAIRMAN, CANADA COUNCIL; Gov., Nat. Theatre Sch.; Pres., Mavor Moore Productions, Ltd.; C.B.C. Feature Producer, 1941-42; C.B.C. Internat. Service, 1944-45; C.B.C. Pacific Region, Sr. Producer, 1946; Chief Producer, Television 1950-54; U.N. Information Divn., 1947 and 1949 (New York); Chrmn., Radio Sec. UNESCO World Seminar on Educ., New York, 1948; Producer-Dir. of over 50 stage plays incl. several first performances, some Candn.; served in 2nd World War as Capt., Candn. Army Intelligence, Psychol. Warfare Offr.; author of verse ("And What Do You Do!"), articles (Maclean's, The Arts in Canada) etc., together with numerous radio scripts and plays; winner of three Peabody Awards; author and composer of many plays for stage, radio and TV incl. "Who's Who", 1949; the musical comedies "Sunshine Town", 1954, "The Best of All Possible Worlds" 1956, "The Ottawa Man" 1958, "Johnny Belinda" (John Fenwick composer) 1966; "Louis Riel" opera (Harry Somers composer) 1967; Producer-Dir. record breaking annual revue "Spring Thaw" 1948-57, 1961-65; "The Roncarelli Affair" 1973; mem. (1st) Bd. of Govs., Stratford Shakespearean Festival; Drama Critic and Columnist, Toronto "Telegram", 1959-60; Chrmn., Cultural Comte., Nat. Centennial Conf. 1966-67; Gen. Dir., St. Lawrence Centre, Toronto 1965-69; apptd. mem. of Can. Council 1974; awarded Centennial Medal; mem. Candn. Actors Equity; Assn. Candn. Radio & TV Artists; recreation: music; Club: Arts and Letters; Address Can. Council, Box 1047, Ottawa, Ont. K1P 5V8;

MOORE, John Henderson, LL.D., F.C.A.; retired executive; b. London, Ont., 27 Dec. 1915; s. late John McClary and late Phyllis E. Moore; e. Public Sch., London, Ont.; Ridley Coll., St. Catharines, Ont.; Royal Mil. Coll., Kingston, Ont. (four yrs.); m. S. Elizabeth, d. late S. F. Wood, London, Ont., 11 Dec. 1939; two s. and three d.; Dir., Bell Canada; Cadillac Fairview Corp. Limited; Canadian Corporate Management Co. Limited; Hudson's Bay Co.; Canadian Pacific Limited; London Life Ins. Co.; Northern Telecom Ltd.; Morgan Bank of Can.; Northern Telecom Canada Ltd.; mem., International Council, Morgan Guaranty Trust, New York; Partner, Clarkson, Gordon & Company, London, Ontario, 1950; Director of Finance and Treas., John Labatt Ltd., 1953; apptd. Extve. Vice-Pres. and Mang. Dir., 1957; Pres., 1958; Chrmn. Bd. and Pres. 1967; retired 1981; apptd. Pres., Brascan Ltd., 1969; Chmn., 1976; retired 1979; served in 2nd World War; 2nd in Command, 15th Field Regt., R.C.A., N.W. Europe; attended Staff Col., Camberley, 1944; Anglican; Clubs: London Hunt & Country; The London (Ont.); University; York; Toronto; Home: Creek Cottage, R.R. 2, Lambeth, Ont. N0L 1S0; P.O. Box 758, London, Ont. N6A 4Y8

MOORE, Keith Leon, B.A., M.Sc., Ph.D.; educator and medical author; b. Brantford, Ont., 5 Oct. 1925; s. late Rev. James Henry and Gertrude Myrtle (McCombe) M.; e. Elem. Sch., Wallacetown, Ont.; High Sch., Stratford, Ont.; Univ. of W. Ont., B.A. 1949, M.Sc. 1951, Ph.D. 1954; m. Marion Edith, d. late William McDermid, 20 Aug. 1949; children: Warren, Pamela, Karen, Laurel, Joyce; PROF. AND CHRMN. OF ANATOMY, UNIV. OF TORONTO since 1976; Consultant in Anat., Health Sciences Centre, Winnipeg 1965-76; Lectr. in Anat., Univ. of W. Ont. 1954-56; joined Univ. of Man. as Asst. Prof. of Anat. 1956, Assoc. Prof. 1959, Prof. and Head of Anatomy 1965-76, and mem. Senate 1958-76; served with RCNVR 1944-46; author, "The Sex Chromatin" 1966; "The Developing Human" 1973, 2nd ed. 1977, 3rd ed. 1982; "Before We Are Born" 1974, revised ed. 1975; "Study Guide and Review Manual of": "Human Embryology" 1975, 2nd ed. 1982; "Human Anatomy" 1976, revised ed. 1980; "Human Nervous System" 1978; "Clinically Oriented Anatomy" 1980; "Highlights of Prenatal Development" (16 mm. movie) 1978; "Formation of Sex Cells and Chromosol Abnormalities" part I & II (16 mm. movie) 1980; "Reproductive Cycles in the Human Female", part I & II 1981; also book chapters and over 60 publs. in scient. journs.; Fellow, Internat. Acad. Cytol.; Roy. Soc. of Med.; mem. Candn. Assn. Anats. (Pres. 1969-70); Candn. Fed. Biol. Socs. (Chrmn. 1970-71); Amer. Assn. Anats; Panamer Assn. Anats.; Teratology Soc.; Scient. Club Winnipeg (Secy. 1970-73); United Church; recreations: curling, swimming; Clubs: Mississauga Golf & Country; Home: 91 Winchester St., Toronto Ont. M4X 1B1; Office: Med. Sciences Bldg., 1 King's College Circle, Univ. of Toronto, Toronto, Ont. M5S 1A8

MOORE, Hon. Marvin Everard; politician; b. Grande Prairie, Alta. 31 Aug. 1938; s. Charlie Sydney and Winnifred (DeBolt) M.; e. elem. sch. DeBolt, Alta.; high sch. Grande Prairie, Alta.; m. Frances d. Graham Bodeker 20 Feb. 1959; children: Kerry, Lonny, Bernice; MIN. OF MUNICIPAL AFFAIRS, ALTA. 1979- ; el. to Leg. Assembly Alta. 1971, re-el. 1975 & 1979; former Min. of Agric.; mem. Toastmasters' Internat.; P. Conservative; United Church; recreations: curling, golf; Home: P.O. Box 447, DeBolt, Alta.; Office: 423 Legislative Bldg., Edmonton, Alta.

MOORE, His Excellency Robert, M.A., D.Phil.; diplomat; b. Guyana, 22 Nov. 1931; s. Edwin Shields and Muriel Ismey (Shanks) M.; e. Central High Sch., Georgetown, Guyana; Univ. of the W. Indies, B.A., Dipl. in Educ. 1955; Univ. of Cambridge, M.A.; Univ. of Sussex, D.Phil.; m. Alyma, d. M. K. Khan, 15 Jan. 1957; children: Fauzya Alyma, Lilah Audrey, Rayad Robert; High Commr. of Guyana to Can. 1974-80; Sr. Hist. Master, Queen's Coll., Georgetown, Guyana, 1957; Head, Div. of Caribbean Studies, Univ. of Guyana 1964-73, Head, Dept. of Hist., 1972-74; Ford Foundation Fellow, 1965-68;

Lectr. numerous socs. with Commonwealth interest in Eng. 1960-74; regular contrib. to BBC, Caribbean and World Services 1968-73; TV appearances on Thames Television, London, 1972; Acad. Visitor to Germany 1970; conducted research The Hague 1970-74; State Dept. visitor to USA 1972; Lectr. Am. univs. 1972; mem. Youth Adv. Comn., Nat. Sports Council; Depy. Chrmn., Nat. Hist. and Arts Council; Univ. of Guyana Appeal Fund; Adviser to Educ. Ministry on teaching of hist.; Gov., "Caribbean Contact"; Trustee, Univ. of Guyana Appeal Fund in Can.; co-author, "Troubling the Waters" 1973; author film script "World of the Caribbean"; also numerous newspaper and journ. articles, reviews in field of theol. and W.I. hist.; has lectured extensively in Can. to Univs.; Learned Socs. and Svce. Clubs; spoke at Couchiching Conf. 1975, Learned Soc. Conf. 1976; key note speaker, Ang. Synod of Ottawa 1975, Caribbean Univs. Conf., Curacao, 1977, Caribbean Council of Chs. Assembly 1977; Hon. mem. Royal Commonwealth Soc.; mem. Caribbean Assn. Hists.; Anglican; recreations: travel, public speaking, swimming, walking; Home: 160 Howick St., Rockcliffe Park, Ottawa, Ont.

MOORE, Sean, M.B., B.Ch., B.A.O., F.R.C.P.(C); pathologist; educator; b. Belfast, N. Ireland 24 Nov. 1926; s. James Bernard and Eileen (McFadden) M.; e. elem. sch. Belfast 1940; St. Malachy's Coll. Belfast 1944; Belfast Tech. Coll. 1944-45; Queen's Univ. of Belfast M.B., B.Ch., B.A.O. 1950 (Hutchison Stewart Scholarship, Adami Medal in Pathol.); m. Cynthia d. Reginald Ernest Balch, Fredericton, N.B. 19 Oct. 1957; children: John Brian, Martha Ailish, Patrick Balch; DIR. OF LABS. McMASTER UNIV. MED. CENTRE since 1972; internship Mater Infirmorum Hosp. Belfast, Royal Victoria Hosp. Montreal, Montreal Gen. Hosp. and St. Mary's Hosp; Asst. Prosector, Autopsy Service, Pathol. Inst. McGill Univ. 1953-54, Prosector 1956-57, Demonst. in Pathol. McGill 1955-56, Asst. Pathol. Montreal Gen. Hosp. and McGill 1958-61, Demonst. in Cytol. 1958, Lectr. 1959, Asst. Prof. 1964, Assoc. Prof. 1969-71, Assoc. Pathol. Montreal Gen. Hosp. 1961-69; Pathol.-in-Chief Jewish Gen. Hosp. Montreal 1969-71; Co-ord. Anatomic Pathol. and Prof. of Pathol. present Univ. 1972, Chrmn. of Pathol. and Dir. of Labs. 1972-78; McEachern Fellow Candn. Cancer Soc., Mem. Center for Cancer & Allied Diseases, Strang-Depew Clinic, New York 1957-58; mem. Prov. Lab. Adv. Comte. to Ministry of Health Ont.; Fellow, Council on Arteriosclerosis, Am. Heart Assn.; mem. Candn. and Ont. Med. Assns.; Ont. Assn. Pathols. (Council); Assn. Pathol. Chrmn. Can. (Secy.-Treas. 1974-77); Am. Assn. Pathols. & Bacteriols.; Fed. Am. Socs. Exper. Biol.; Internat. Acad. Pathol.; Candn. Cytology Council; Candn. Assn. Pathols. and other Candn. and Am. med. assns.; author numerous publs., presentations; recreations: reading, skiing; Home: 302 Bay St. S., Hamilton, Ont. L8P 3J8; Office: 1200 Main St. W., Hamilton, Ont. L8S 4J9.

MOORE, Trevor Frank, C.M., B.A.; retired executive; b. Watford, Eng., 26 Jan. 1905; e. Univ. of Toronto Schs.; Univ. of Toronto, B.A. 1928; m. Kathleen; Dir. Emeritus, Canadian Imperial Bank of Commerce; Dir., Budd Canada Inc.; Eaton Bay Financial Services; Gerling Global Insurance Group; Can. Southern Ry.; The Budd Co. U.S.; Toronto Western Hosp.; Gov. Massey Hall; Hon. Pres., Toronto Symphony; recreations: golf, music; Clubs: York; National; Toronto Hunt; Home: Apt. 1604, 20 Avoca Ave., Toronto, Ont. M4T 2B8

MOORE, Victor Campbell, B.A.; diplomat; b. Victoria, B.C., 25 Jan. 1918; s. Lt. Col. Frederick William Louis and Ruby Ermine (Jackson) M.; e. Cloverdale Pub. Sch. and Mount View High Sch., Saanich, B.C.; Victoria (B.C.) Coll.; Univ. of B.C., B.A. 1940; Georgia Augusta Univ., Germany, 1947-48; m. Kerstin Margaret, d. Ing. Cyrus Odemar, Sweden; children: Yan Paul, Catherine Anne Victoria; joined Dept. of External Affairs, Ottawa, as Foreign Service Officer 1948; 3rd Secy. Candn., Embassy, Bonn, 1951; 2nd Secy. 1952; Chargé d'affaires, a.i., Vienna, 1954; Advisor, ECOSOC Session, N.Y., 1956; 2nd Secy., Moscow, 1956; 1st Secy. 1958; Acting High Commr., Karachi 1958; Acting High Commr., Karachi 1960-62; Canadian Rep. Indus Waters Agreement, Karachi 1960; charge d'affaires Counsellor, The Hague 1962-65; World Politics Conf., Holland, 1965; Ambassador, Head of Candn. Del. to Internat. Comn. for Supervision and Control in Viet Nam, (saigon and Hanoi) 1965-67; Depy. Head, Office of Econ. Affairs, Ottawa, 1967-68; Advisor to Candn. Dels. to Commonwealth Finance Mins. Mtgs. 1967, 1971, 1974; Heads of Gov't Mtgs. 1973, 1975 and 1979; Sr. Officials Mtgs. 1972, 1974, 1976, and to World Bank/IMF Conf. 1967, to Carribean Devpt. Bank 1970 and 1971; Chrm., Interdepartmental Comte. on Commonwealth Caribbean - Canada Relations, 1967-68; Candn. Rep. to 5th Session of UNDP Governing Council, N.Y., Jan. 1968; Cdn. Del. to Maputo Conf. on Zimbabwe and Namibia 1977; Advisor to organizing comte. of Conf. on Comwel and NG bodies, Dalhousie Univ. 1976; High Commr. to Jamaica 1968-72 and Commissioner to Belize and to Bahamas; Dir., Commonwealth Div., Ext. Affairs, Ottawa, 1972-76; 1976-79, High Commr. to Zambia and Malawi and Amb. to Mozambique; Bd. of Gov., Commonwealth Africa Youth Devel. Centre; Cdn. rep. to Conference of NATO Defence Coll. Commandants, Rome, 1981; Depy. Commandant & Dir. of Studies, Nat. Defence Coll., Kingston. Ont. 1979- ; served with The Candn. Scottish Regt. (Princess Royals) NPAM 1938-39; C.O.T.C., Univ. of B.C.; Candn. Scottish Regt. (AF), Can., Eng., 1940-43; Seaforth Highlanders of Can., Italy 1943-44; Candn. Scottish (RF) Mentioned in Despatches; mem., Nat. Gallery Assn.; Commonwealth Society; Arch. Soc. of Jamaica; Zambia Wildlife Conservation Society; Malawi Fauna Preservation Society; Anglican; recreations: swimming, literature, music, art; Clubs: Cataraqui Golf & Country; Men's Canadian; Home: 70 Lundy's Lane, Fort henry Heights, Kingston; Office: Fort Frontenac, Kingston, Ont.

MOORES, Hon. Frank Duff, M.H.A.; b. Carbonear, Conception Bay, Nfld., 18 Feb. 1933; s. Silas Wilmot and Dorothy (Duff) M.; e. Un. Ch. Acad., Carbonear, Nfld.; St. Andrews Coll., Aurora, Ont.; m. 2ndly, Janis, d. Dr. Geo. Johnson, Winnipeg, Man., Aug. 1973; children (by 1st m.): Susan Joyce, Deborah Joan, Michele Jan, Elizabeth Jill, Nicole Jane, Stuart William Duff, Andrea Dorothy; (by 2nd m.) Tomas Stefan; Premier of Newfoundland, 1972-78; former Pres., North Eastern Fish Industries, Harbour Grace, Nfld.; el. to H. of C. for Bonavista-Trinity-Conception in g.e. 1968; el. Pres., Progressive Conservative Party of Canada, 1969; became Leader of P. Cons. Party of Newfoundland 1970 and el. to H. of A. for Humber West in g.e. 1971, 1972; Past Dir.: Avalon Telephone Co. of Nfld.; The Fisheries Council of Can.; Atlantic Provs. Econ. Council; Frozen Fish Trades Assn.; Past Gov., Coll. of Fisheries; mem. Royal Comn. on Nfld.'s Econ. Prospects; Freemason; United Church; recreations: golf, tennis, hunting, fishing; Clubs: Rideau (Ottawa); City; Kiwanis (Past Pres.); Home: Mt. Scio House, St. John's, Nfld.; Office: Confederation Bldg., St. John's, Nfld.

MOORHEAD, Ernest John, F.S.A.; retd. actuary; b. Winnipeg, Man., 23 Jan. 1910; s. Ernest S., M.B. & Elizabeth Maude (Ruckley) M.; e. Univ. of Liverpool, grad. 1929; m. Iris Gertrude, d. Jacobus P. de Wet, Winnipeg, 2 June 1938; children: Patricia E. (Mrs. Richard A. MacKinnon), Anthony J., Sheila I. (Mrs. K.T. Kelley); Ed. "The Actuary", newsletter of Soc. of Actuaries joined Great-West Life Assnce. Co., Winnipeg, 1929; Asst. Actuary 1938-45; Life Ins. Agency Mang. Assn., Hartford, Conn., 1945; Actuary 1947-48; Extve. Vice Pres., U.S. Life Insurance Co. New York, 1948-52; Assoc. Actuary, New England Mutual Life Insurance Co., Boston, 1952-53; Actuary 1954-60 Vice Pres. and Actuary 1961-64; Vice Pres. and Sr. Actuary 1964-67; Vice Pres., Integon Corp. & Chrmn.,

Special Comte. on Life Ins. Costs, 1969-72; mem. panel recommending changes in U.S. social security system to U.S. Cong.; Consultant, U.S. Senate Anti-Trust & Monopoly Subcomte. on Life Ins. Cost Comparisons; Nat. Assn. Ins. Commrs. on Life Ins. Cost Comparisons; Advisor to Fed. Trade Comn. on life insurance; Past Pres., Winnipeg Jr. Chamber Comm.; Pres., Triad N.C. Branch, Eng.-speaking union; Pres. Am. Acad. Actuaries 1973-74; Pres. (1969-70) Soc. Actuaries; Dir. (1966-70) Life Office Mang. Assn. (Chrmn. Educ. Council 1969-70); Corr., Candn. Inst. Actuaries; Episcopalian; Address: Bermuda Run, Box 780, Advance N.C. 27006

MORAN, Lord (Richard John McMoran Wilson), K.C.M.G.; diplomat; b. London, Eng. 22 Sept. 1924; s. late Lord Moran (Charles McMoran Wilson); e. Eton Coll. Windsor, Eng.; King's Coll. Cambridge; m. Shirley Rowntree d. late G. J. Harris 1948; children: Juliet (Mrs. Jeffrey Evans), James Wilson, William Wilson; BRITISH HIGH COMMR. TO CAN. 1981- ; Third Secy. Ankara 1948; Tel-Aviv 1950; Second Secy. Rio de Janeiro 1953; First Secy. FO 1956; Washington 1959; FO 1961; Counsellor S. Africa 1965; Head W. African Dept. FCO 1968-73; Ambassador to Chad 1970-73, Hungary 1973-76, Portugal 1976-81; served with RNVR 1943-45, HMS Belfast, Motor Torpedo Boats, HM Destroyer Oribi, rank Sub-Lt.; C.M.G. 1970; K.C.M.G. 1981; Grand Cross Order of Infante (Portugal) 1978; author "CB: A Life of Sir Henry Campbell-Bannerman" 1973 (Whitbread Award 1973); contrib. to "The Prime Ministers"; recreations: fly fishing, fly tying, ornithology; Clubs: Beefsteak (London); Flyfishers (London); Home: Earnscliffe, Sussex Dr., Ottawa, Ont. K1N 5A2; Office: 80 Elgin St., Ottawa, Ont. K1P 5K7.

MORAND, Hon. Donald Raymond; b. Windsor, Ont., 17 Jan. 1918; s. Hon. Raymond Ducharme, M.D., P.C. and Blanche (Moore) M.; e. Assumption High Sch., Windsor, 1935; Univ. of W. Ont., B.A. 1938; Osgoode Hall, Toronto, 1941; LL.D, Univ. of Windsor 1979; m. Agnes Angela, d. late Samuel Henderson, 28 June 1941; children: John, Raymond, Margaret, Catherine, Paula; OMBUDSMAN, ONT.; apptd. 1979; called to Ont. Bar 1941; cr. Q.C. 1955; former Justice, Supreme Ct. of Ont. Trial Division (ret. 1978); Head, Roy. Comm., Metropolitan Toronto Police Practices 1974-76; Roman Catholic; Home: 25 Sheffley Cres., Weston, Ont. M9R 2W5; Office: Office of the Ombudsman, 125 Queen's Park, Cres. Toronto, Ont. M5S 2C7

MORAWETZ, Oskar, D. Mus.; composer; university professor; b. Czechoslovakia, 17 Jan. 1917; s. Richard and Frieda (Glaser) M.; e. High Sch., Prague (1927-35); Univ. of Prague, 1935-37; came to Canada, June 1940; Univ. of Toronto, B.Mus. 1944, D.Mus. 1953; m. Ruth Spafford, d. N. C. Shipman, London, Ont., 7 June 1958; PROF. OF MUSIC, UNIV. OF TORONTO; his works soon came into prominence after winning awards in nation-wide competition held by Candn. Composers Assn. in 1945 and 1946; has since been heard frequently on trans-Can. concerts of CBC, as with many well-known conductors abroad; his orchestral compositions not only in the repertoire of all Candn. orchestras, but also by nearly 150 orchestras in Europe, N. & S. America, Australia and Asia; his "Divertimento for Strings" was conducted by Dr. Boyd Neel at Brussels World Fair (1958), "Overture to a Fairy Tale" conducted by Walter Susskind and his "Fantasy for Piano", played by Glenn Gould have been premiered at Stratford Music Festival; his choral comp. "Keep Us Free" chosen to precede the Queen's speech at state dinner in Ottawa; "Memorial to Martin Luther King" commissioned by M. Rostropovich and recorded by Zara Nelsova; first composer to receive a Can. Council comn. for a work premiered by Toronto Symphony Orchestra; has written works for full orchestra, string, orchestra, piano, voice, violin and string quartet, flute, oboe, clarinet & french horn; also music for several motion pictures; many recordings on Columbia, Capitol and RCA records, and C.B.C.; awards incl. Canada Council Fellowships 1961, 1967, 1974; CAPAC Award (String Quartet No. 1) 1944, (Sonata Tragica) 1945; Zubin Mehta Award (Piano Concerto No. 1) 1961; Critics Award, Internat. Competition Contemporary Music, Cava di Tirreni, Italy (Sinfonietta for winds and percussion) 1966; Segal Foundation Special Award (From the Diary of Anne Frank) 1971; mem., Candn. League of Composers; Composers, Authors & Publ. Assn. Can.; Home: 59 Duncannon Dr., Toronto, Ont. M5P 2M3

MORDEN, Ven. John Grant, D.D., D.Th. (Ang.); college principal; b. London, Eng., 17 Aug. 1925; s. Lt. Col. Walter Grant, J.P., M.P. and Doris (Henshaw) M.; e. Royal Masonic Schs., Bushy, Herts., Eng., 1940; Univ. of Toronto, B.A. 1949; Wycliffe Coll., Toronto, L.Th. 1952, B.D. 1953, D.D. 1963; Union Theol. Semy., New York, S.T.M. 1953; Gen. Theol. Semy., New York, D.Th. 1961; m. Elizabeth Grace, d. James A. Tannahill, 7 Sept. 1949; children: Ann, Margaret, James (deceased), Mary, Peter; PRINCIPAL, HURON COLL., since 1962; Archdeacon of Huron since 1968; mem. Corp. and Extve. Bd., Huron Coll. since 1961; mem. Senate, Univ. of W. Ont. since 1961; mem. Extve. of Diocese of Huron; mem. Gen. Synod of Ang. Ch. of Can.; with Cassidy's Ltd. as Clerk, 1940-43; Asst. Curate, Annunciation and All Soul's Parish, Toronto, 1951-53; St. Bartholomew's, White Plains, N.Y., 1953-56; Rector of St. Matthews, Toronto, 1956-57; Registrar and Asst. Prof. of Theol., Huron Coll., 1957; Prof. of Theol. and Vice Prin., 1961; served with R.C.A.F. 1943-46; Conservative; Address: Huron College, London, Ont. N6G 1H3

MORDEN, Hon. John W., B.A., LL.B.; judge; b. Toronto, Ont., 26 July 1934; s. Hon. Kenneth Gibson and Elizabeth Helen (Marquis) M.; e. Upper Can. Coll. Toronto 1952; Univ. of Toronto, Trinity Coll. B.A. 1956, Faculty of Law LL.B. 1959; m. Joyce Gillies, d. late Hon. G. Peter Campbell 6 Sept. 1958; two d., Mary Catherine, Martha Elizabeth; JUSTICE, COURT OF APPEAL, SUPREME COURT OF ONT. since 1978; called to Bar of Ont. 1961; practiced law Day, Wilson, Campbell 1961-73; Counsel Royal Comn. Inquiry Civil Rights 1964-71; Asst. Counsel H. of C. Special Comte. on Statutory Instruments 1969; Consultant, Law Reform Comn. B.C. 1971; Ont. Law Reform Comn. 1971-72; Law Reform Comn. Can. 1972-73; mem. Faculty Council Faculty of Law Univ. of Toronto since 1971; Bencher Law Soc. Upper Can. 1971-73; Justice, High Court of Justice, Supreme Court of Ont. 1973-78; mem. Statutory Powers Procedure Rules Comte (Ont.) 1975- ; Bd. of Knox Coll. 1980- ; Kappa Alpha; Presbyterian; Clubs: University; Toronto Hunt; Home: 12 Garfield Ave., Toronto, Ont. M4T 1E7; Office: Osgoode Hall, Toronto, Ont. M5H 2N6

MORDEN, Wilson Dorland Samuel, Q.C., B.A.; b. Toronto, Ont. 4 Feb. 1912; s. Wilson Saunders and Caroline Hope (Gibson) M.; e. Upper Can. Coll. 1921-30; Univ. of Toronto, B.A. 1934; Osgoode Hall, Toronto, Ont.; m. Margaret Logan Douglas, d. late John Hannay, Derbyshire, Eng. 10 March 1945; children: Nicholas Clark, Gillian Hope, Margaret Elizabeth: PARTNER, McLAUGHLIN, SOWARD, MARKLE (Estbd. 1900); Dir., The Boiler Inspection and Insurance Company of Canada; G.N. Johnston Equipment Co. Ltd.; Schenker of Can. Ltd.; called to the Bar of Ontario 1937; cr. Q.C. 1956; served in 2nd World War with 4th Anti-Tank Regt., R.C.A., in Italy and N.W. Europe, 1941-45; Kappa Alpha; Conservative; Presbyterian; recreations: golf, sailing, Clubs: University; Rosedale Golf; Home: 10 Rathnelly Ave., Toronto 5, Ont. M4V 2M3; Office: 200 University Ave., Toronto, Ont. M5H 3E1

MORE, Robert Hall, M.Sc., M.D., F.R.C.P.; retired professor; b. Kitchener, Ont., 16 Dec. 1912; s. Nellie Edna (Lackner) M.; e. Pub. and High Schs., Kitchener, Ont.;

Univ. of Toronto, M.D. 1939; McGill Univ., M.Sc. (Pathology) 1942; Certified as Specialist in Path. by Royal Coll. of Phys. & Surg. of Can. 1946; m. Dorothy Charlotte, d. John T. McOrmond, 29 July 1943; children: David, Patricia, Christopher; Jr. Interne, Toronto Gen. Hosp., 1939-40; Douglas Fellow in Path., McGill Univ., 1940-42; Sr. Interne in Surg., Toronto Gen. Hosp. and Fellow in Surg., Univ. of Toronto, 1942-43; Lectr. in Path., McGill Univ. and Prosecutor to the Royal Victoria Hosp., Montreal, 1943-46; Path., Women's Gen. Hosp., Montreal, 1945-46; Assoc. in Research, Dept. of Path., Cornell Univ. Med. Coll., 1946-47 and Asst. Path., New York Hosp.; Miranda Fraser Asst. Prof. of Comparative Path., McGill Univ., 1947-49 and Prof., 1950-51; Prof. of Path., and Chmn. of Dept. Queen's Univ., 1951-67; Prof. of Pathol., McGill Univ. 1978-81 (ret.) (Chmn. 1967-78); mem., Am. Assn. of Paths. & Bacterols.; Que. Assn. of Pathols.; Am. Soc. of Exper. Pathols.; Path. Soc. of Gt. Brit. & Ireland; Candn. Assn. of Pathols.; Ont. Assn. of Pathols.; Pres. Internat. Acad. Pathol. 1967-68; Publications: a number of articles in path. and other journs. on researches in atherosclerosis and other subjects; United Church; recreations: gardening, music; Address: RR#1, Martintown, Ont. K0C 1S0

MOREAU, Bernard L., B.Sc., P.Eng.; engineering consultant; b. Edmonton, Alta., 1 March 1928; s. Charles B. and Annette B. (Tellier) M.; e. Univ. of Alta., B.Sc. (Petrol. Engn.) 1951; m. Joan M., d. late Louis D. Belland, Edmonton, Alta., 10 Sept. 1953; two s., Charles, Paul; Engr. in Training, Schlumberger Well Surveying Corp., Calgary, 1951; Engr., Rotary Engineer Ltd., Calgary, 1952; Production Engr., Pacific Petroleums Ltd., Redwater, 1953; Reservoir Engr., Calgary, 1955; Engn. Asst. to Vice Pres., Westcoast Transmission Co. Ltd., Calgary, 1957; Chief Design Engr., Pacific Petroleums Ltd., 1958; joined Williams Bros. (Canada) as Project Mgr. 1959; Chief Engr. 1964, Vice Pres. 1969; Pres. & dir., William Brothers Can. Ltd. 1972-75; Vice President, Williams Bros. Eng., Tulsa and London, Eng. 1975-78; Am. and Eng. 1978-81; Private Practice London, Eng. 1981- ; (ret.); mem., Assn. Prof. Engrs. Geols. & Geophysicists Alta.; Assn. Prof. Engrs. B.C. and Sask.; Candn. Soc. Mech. Engn.; R. Catholic; recreations: sailing, hunting; Club: Calgary Petroleum; Home: 312 Shakespeare Tower, Barbican, London EC2 England

MOREAU, Jean R., Ph.D., F.R.S.A.; educator; b. Village des Aulnaies, Qué. 27 June 1924; s. Arthur and Hermance (Chouinard) M.; e. Coll. de Ste-Anne de la Pocatière B.A. 1944; Laval Univ. B.Sc. 19480 (Lt. Gov.'s Medal), Business Adm. Course 1952; Mass Inst. Technol. Ph.D. 1957 (Food Science); m. Jeannine d. Eugene Berube 22 June 1950; children; Andre J., Michel J., Mireille, Claude; PROF. OF FOOD SCIENCE AND OF BIOCHEM. ENGN., LAVAL UNIV. 1965- ; Pres., Biomassan Inc.; Vice Pres., Etabel Inc.; consultant to Candn. and Que. govts. food science, chem.; Sr. Research Scient. Canada Packers Ltd. Toronto 1957-64; Prof. of Food Chem. Univ. of Toronto 1964-65; holder or co-holder 15 patents; author or co-author various scient. papers; recipient Achievement Award Un. Inventors & Scients. Am. 19..; named Man of Yr. Coll. de Ste-Anne de la Pocatière Alumni 19..; Fellow, Internat. Biog. Assn.; mem. Internat. Platform Assn.; Candn. Inst. Food Science & Technol.; Order Chems. Qué.; Nutrition Today Soc.; Meat Scients. Can. (Chrmn. 2 yrs.); Soc. Am. Inventors; Phi Tau Sigma; Kt. Mark Twain (contrib. to modern educ.); R. Catholic; recreations: cross-country skiing, gardening, boating; Home: 2998 La Promenade, Ste-Foy, Qué. G1W 2J7; Office: Ste-Foy, Qué. G1K 7P4.

MORETON, A. G., M.Sc.; P.Eng.; executive; b. Windsor, Ont., 6 Sept. 1921; s. Ruby Irene (Kilty) and late Alfred M.; e. Queen's Univ., B.Sc. (Hons. Chem. Engn.) 1943, M.Sc. (Hons. Chem. Engn.) 1947; m. Marguerite (Peggy) Constance, d. late Walter Knight, 7 Feb. 1948;

children: Anne, Deborah, Barry, Elizabeth; VICE-PRES., IMPERIAL OIL LTD. and Pres., Esso Chemical Canada; commenced with Co.'s Mfg. Dept. Sarnia, Toronto, Edmonton in various positions involving engn. and plant mang. and prof. duties 1947-63; Mang. Asst., Mfg. Dept. 1963, New Ventures Coordinator 1964; Asst. Mgr., Chem. Products Dept., Imperial Oil Ltd. 1965, Gen. Mgr. 1967; Gen. Mgr., Esso Chemical Canada 1970, President, 1974; served in R.C.A.F., Navig. Instr. 1943-46; mem. Assn. Prof. Engrs. Ont.; Chem. Inst. Can., Fellow 1974; Soc. of Chem. Ind. (Extve. Comm.); Candn. Soc. for Chem. Engrn.; Dir. Candn. Chem. Producers' Assn. (Chrmn. 1972); Dir. Soc. Plastics Industry [Chrmn. 1977-79]; Anglican; recreations: sailing, swimming, skiing, bridge; Club: R.C.Y.C.; Home: 18 Heathview Ave., Willowdale, Ont. M2K 2C1; Office: 2300 Yonge St., Toronto, Ont. M5W 1K3

MORGAN, Alan Vivian, B.Sc., M.Sc., Ph.D.; educator; b. Barry, Glamorgan, Wales 29 Jan. 1943; s. Nicholas Gregory and Sylvia Nesta (Atkinson) M.; came to Can. 1970; e. Univ. of Leicester, Eng. B.Sc. 1964; Univ. of Alta. M.Sc. 1966; Univ. of Birmingham, Eng. Ph.D. 1970; Univ. of W. Ont. and Univ. of Waterloo Post-Doctoral Fellow 1970-71; m. Marion Anne d. Henry James Medhurst 14 June 1966; children: Sian Kristina, Alexis John; ASSOC. PROF., DEPT. OF EARTH SCIENCES & DEPT. OF MAN-ENVT. STUDIES, UNIV. OF WATERLOO, 1978- ; Asst. Prof. 1971-78; Visiting Prof., Univ. of Seattle 1978; Visiting Scientist, U.S. Geol. Survey 1979; Visiting Prof., Univ. of Kiel, Germany 1982; author over 30 scientific papers and book chapters on quaternary geol.; dir. and producer "The Heimaey Eruption: Iceland, 1973" (short documentary film); mem., Geol. Assn. of Can. (Secy-Treas., Councillor, mem. Extve. Comte.) 1975- ; Candn. Geoscience Council 1977- ; Sigma Xi; Brit. Quaternary Assn.; Amer. Quat. Assn.; Candn. Quat. Assn.; Club: Rotary Internat. (Waterloo); recreations: travel, natural hist., photography; Office: Waterloo, Ont. N2L 3G1

MORGAN, Hon. H. B., M.A.; judge; b. Harbour Deep, Nfld., 11 June 1919; s. late Jacob and Florence S. (Osborne) M.; e. Bishop Feild 1935; Mem. Univ. Coll. 1937; Dalhousie Univ. B.A. 1939; Pembroke Coll. Oxford Univ. (Rhodes Scholar) B.A. 1949, M.A. 1953; m. Betty Gradidge d. late Harold and Mary Maude Smith, 18 Oct. 1950; children: Christina, Christopher, Timothy; JUSTICE, COURT OF APPEAL, NFLD. since 1975; Chrmn. Nfld. Crimes Compensation Bd. 1972-75; Dist. Pensions' Advocate (Part time) Bureau of Pension Advocates 1963-75; Hon. Solr. Prov. Command Royal Candn. Legion 1963-75; Gov. Candn. Corps of Commissionaires; called to Bar of Eng. and Wales 1950; Bar of Nfld. 1950; cr. Q.C. 1972; served with RAF 1940-46, rank Flight Lt. (Pilot); rec'd Coronation Medal 1953; Confederation Medal; Past Pres. RCAF Assn.; former Bencher Law Soc. Nfld.; mem. Nfld. Game Fish Protection Soc. Ltd.; Anglican; recreation: fishing, Club: Officers' (Crows' Nest); Home: 6 Rendell Place, St. John's, Nfld. A1B 1L3; Office: Court House, St. John's, Nfld.

MORGAN, Rev. Ivan Clifford, B.A., B.D., Thm.M., D.D. (Bapt.); b. Paris, Ont., 14 Aug. 1912; s. Henry Thomas and Sarah Elizabeth (Benedict) M.; e. Pub. Sch. and Sir Adam Beck Coll. Inst., London, Ont.; McMaster Univ., B.A. 1938 and The Divinity Sch. there, B.D. 1942; Union Theol. Semy., Virginia, Th.M. 1963; D.D. Acadia 1968; m. Ruth Eleanor, d. Rev. Wm. Raithby, Strathroy, Ont., 30 Aug. 1939; children: Franklin William, Mary Ruth; Prof. Emeritus and Princ. Emeritus, McMaster Divinity Coll. since 1978; Prof. 1960-78; Princ. 1966-78; Pres., Bapt. Convention of Ont. and Que., 1953-54; o. 1939; Min., MacNeill Mem. Ch., Hamilton, Ont. 1938-46; Murray St. Ch., Peterborough, Ont., 1946-56; Temple Ch., Windsor, Ont. 1956-60; Dir., Children's Aid Soc., Hamilton, 1941-46, Peterborough, 1948-56; mem., Bapt. Convention of Ont. & Que. (mem., Bd. of Religious

Educ., 1930-33, 1940-43; Bd. of Evangelism & Social Service, 1939-45 and Chrmn. 1942-45; Candn. Bapt. Foreign Mission Bd., (Pres., 1953-54); recreations: golf, fishing. McMaster Divinity College, McMaster Univ. Hamilton, Ont. L8S 4L8

MORGAN, J. Graham, M.A., D.Phil.; retired college president; b. Barrow-in-Furness, England, 11 Aug. 1940; s. Stanley and Winifred (Richie) M.; e. St. Pauls Sch., Barrow-in-Furness, Eng., 1945-50; Sebright Sch., Worcestershire, Eng., 1950-59; Univ. of Nottingham, B.A. 1962; McMaster Univ., M.A. 1963; Balliol Coll., Oxford Univ., D.Phil. 1966; m. Marilyn Revell, d. Charles Ward, Merrick, N.Y., 21 June 1968; three children; ASSOC. PROF. OF SOCIOL., DALHOUSIE UNIV., 1970- ; Tutor in Sociol., Oxford Univ., 1965-66; Asst. Prof. of Sociol., Dalhousie, 1966-70; Pres., Univ. of King's Coll. 1970-77; Pres., Univ. of King's Coll. (ret.) writings incl. many journ. articles, book reviews and tech. reports; mem., Soc. Scient. Study Religion; Internat. Sociol. Assn.; Internat. Soc. for History of Soc. Sci.; Candn. Sociol. & Anthrop. Assn.; Anglican; recreation: music. Halifax, N.S. B3H 3J5

MORGAN, James Bartlett, retired company executive; b. Montreal, Que., 1911; s. Frederick Cleveland and Elizabeth Marcia (Shaw) M.; e. Schs. in Can. and France; Cambridge Univ.; Munich Univ.; Dir., Bank of Montreal; Candn. International Paper Co.; Clubs: St. James's; Montreal Racket; Mount Royal; Mount Bruno Country; Forest & Stream; Home: 264 Senneville Rd., Senneville, Que. H3B 2B2; Office: Suite 1440, 1 Place Ville Marie, Montreal, Que.

MORGAN, Hon. James C., M.H.A.; politician; b. Flat Islands, Nfld. 31 Oct. 1939; s. Samuel Robert and Helan M.; e. St. Nicholas High Sch.; Mem. Univ. of Nfld.; Sir George Williams Univ.; De Vry Tech. Coll. Toronto; m. Denise d. Emile Philippe, Luskville, Que. 14 Jan. 1967; one d. Kimberly Denise; MIN. OF FISHERIES, NFLD. 1980- ; teacher, ins. underwriter; Cand. prov. g.e. 1971, def.; el. M.H.A. for Bonavista South prov. g.e. 1972, reel. since; Min. of Transport. & Communications 1975; Min. of Tourism & Recreation 1978; Min. of Forestry & Agric. 1979; P. Conservative; Anglican; Office: 5th Floor, Atlantic Place, Water St., St. John's, Nfld. A1C 5T7.

MORGAN, James Evans; retired banker; b. Ottawa, Ont., 23 July 1916; s. Arthur Llewellyn and Ella Victoria (Evans) M.; e. Montreal West (Que.) High Sch.; McGill Univ. (Econ. & Pol. Science), B.A. (Hons.) 1937; m. Barbara Anne, d. late William A. Newman, 21 Dec. 1940; children: David James, Beverly Anne; Depy. Gen. Mgr., The Royal Bank of Canada and Corporate Planning Offr. (ret.); Dir., Youth Horizons Foundation, Mtl.; served in 2nd World War with 5 Candn. Armoured Div. Signals (1943-46); discharged with rank of Capt.; Sigma Chi; Anglican; recreations: gardening, travel, reading; Club: University; Home: R.R. #2, Brome, Que. J0E 1K0

MORGAN, Moses Osborne, C.C. (1973), C.D., D.C.L., LL.D.; b. Blaketown, Trinity Bay, Nfld., 28 Aug. 1917; s. Jacob and Flora Susannah (Osborne) M.; e. Bishop Feild Coll., St. John's, Nfld.; Memorial Univ. Coll.; Dalhousie Univ., B.A. 1939, M.A. 1946; Oxford Univ., B.A. 1948, M.A. 1951; LL.D. Mount Allison Univ., Univ. of N.B., St. Francis Xavier and Dalhousie Univ.; D.C.L. Univ. of King's College; m. Margaret Grace, d. William John Weymark, 6 July 1968; PRES. AND VICE CHANCELLOR, MEMORIAL UNIV. OF NFLD.; served with Candn. Army 1942-45; N. N.S. Highlanders European Theatre; served as Commdr. #1 Militia Group; present rank Brig. (Retired); Pres., Assn. of Univs. and Colleges of Can., 1977-78; served as Chrmn., Adv. Bd. Candn. Services Coll.; Chrmn., Mil. Studes Comte., A.U.C.C. (Dir.); Chrmn. many arbitration and conciliation bds.; writings incl. numerous articles; Anglican; recreations: fishing, hunting; Home: 117 Nagles Hill, St. John's, Nfld. A1B 2Z2; Office: St. John's, Nfld.

MORGENSTERN, Norbert Rubin, B.A.Sc., D.I.C., Ph.D., F.R.S.C.; educator; consulting engineer; b. Toronto, Ont. 25 May 1935; s. Joel and Bella (Skornik) M.; e. Harbord Coll. Inst. Toronto 1952; Univ. of Toronto B.A.Sc. 1956; Imp. Coll. of Science and Technol. D.I.C. in Soil Mechanics 1964; Univ. of London Ph.D. 1964; m. Patricia Elizabeth d. Ronald M. Gooderham, Terra Cotta, Ont. 29 Dec. 1960; children: Sarah Alexandra, Katherine Victoria, David Michael Gooderham; PROF. OF CIVIL ENGN. UNIV. OF ALTA. since 1968; Pres., Norbert R. Morgenstern Consultants Ltd.; Consulting Engr. to various private and pub. agencies on problems in engn. earth sciences since 1961; Engr., Geocon Ltd. Toronto 1956; grad. student and research asst. Imp. Coll. of Science & Technol. 1957-60, Lectr. in Civil Engn. 1960-68; rec'd Athlone Fellowship 1956; Brit. Geotech. Soc. Prize 1961, 1966; Huber Research Prize, Am. Soc. Civil Engrs. 1971; Cdn. Geotech. Soc. Prize 1977; Legget Award, Cdn. Geotech. Soc. 1979; Rankine Lecture, Br. Geotech. Soc 1981; Boase Lecture, Univ. of Colorado 1981; Engr. Alumni Award, Univ. of Toronto, 1981; Dir. Young Naturalists Foundation since 1975; Edmonton Symphony Soc. since 1978; author over 100 articles; mem. ed. bd. various scient. Journs.; mem. Assn. Prof. Engrs. Alta.; Engn. Inst. Can.; Candn. Geotech. Soc.; Candn. Soc. Civil Engrs.; Candn. Inst. Mining & Metall.; Am. Soc. Civil Engrs.; Geol. Soc. London; Brit. Geotech. Soc.; Assn. Engn. Geols.; mem., Extve., Can. Geosci. Council; recreations: tennis, skiing; Club: Royal Glenora; Home: 106 Laurier Dr., Edmonton, Alta. T5R 5P6; Office: Edmonton, Alta. T6G 2E1.

MORIN, Hon. Claude, B.Sc.Soc., M.A., M.S.W.; politician; b. Montmorency, Que. 1929; e. Séminaire de Québec; Laval Univ. B.Sc.Soc. 1952, M.A. (Econ.) 1954; Columbia Univ. M.S.W. 1956; m. Mary Lynch; 5 children; MIN. OF INTERGOVERNMENTAL AFFAIRS QUE. since 1976 and mem. Priorities Comte. Qué. Council of Mins.; Prof. Faculty of Social Sciences Laval Univ. 1956-63, also consultant to various private and social-econ. organs. and from 1960 to Econ. Orientation Council and Depts. of Finance, Family & Social Welfare Qué.; mem. Govt.'s Comte. on Pub. Welfare 1962-63; Econ. Advisor to Cabinet Qué. 1961-63; Depy. Min. Dept. Fed.-Prov. Affairs 1963 (subsequently Intergovernmental Affairs 1967); Prof. Nat. Sch. of Pub. Adm. Univ. du Qué. 1971; mem. Nat. Extve. Parti Québécois 1973-76; el. mem. for Louis-Hébert prov. g.e. 1976; Author "Le Pouvoir Québécois" 1972; "Le Combat québécois" 1973; Office: Parliament Bldgs., Quebec City, Que.

MORIN, Hon. Jacques-Yvan, M.N.A.; politician; b. Québec, Qué. 1931; s. Arsène M.; e. Univ. of Montréal; McGill Univ.; Harvard Univ.; Cambridge Univ.; m. Elisabeth Gallat; children: 2; VICE-PREMIER ET MIN. D'ETAT AU DEVELOPPEMENT CULTUREL ET SCIENTIFIQUE, 1981- ; Vice-premier et min. de l'Education, 1976-80; lawyer; professor; el. M.N.A. for Sauvé prov. g.e. 1973, re-el. since; Pres. Montreal Sec. Internat. Law Assn.; Parti Québécois; Office: 875, Grande-Allée est, Quebec, Que. G1R 4Y8

MORIN, Jean-Marie, né Rivière-Ouelle, Qué., 19 fév. 1929; f. François et Emilia (Lafrance) M.; é. La Pocatière (coll. classique) et pédagogie et psychol., litt. française, initiation à l'enseignement dans les labs. de langues aux univs.; ép. Pauline Turcotte, 15 juin 1959; SOUS-COMMISSAIRE AUX LANGUES OFFICIELLES, GOUV. DU CANADA depuis mars 1972; Prof. de langues, Coll. de Lévis, Que. 1948-66 (Dir. du Lab. de Langue 1962-66, Trésorier prov. des profs. de l'enseignement classique 1962-63); Député du comté de Lévis à la Législature prov. (Qué.) 1966-70; Secrétaire parlementaire au P.M. 1966-68; Ministre délégué au Haut-Commissariat à la Jeunesse,

aux Loisirs et aux Sports 1968; Min. d'Etat à l'Educ., Min. d'Etat aux Affaires intergouvernementales, Min. responsable de l'Office franco-qué, pour la Jeunesse 1968-70; Rep. le Qué. aux Jeux panam., Winnipeg 1967, aux Jeux olympiques de Grenoble 1968, de Mexico 1968; Dirige la Mission de la Jeunesse en France 1967; la Délég. candn. à la Conf. des mins. de l'Educ. des Etats d'Afrique et de Madagascar au Congo-Kinshasa, et à Paris 1969, Nouakchott en Mauritanie 1970; Min. délég. du Qué. à la Conf. des mins. candn. siégeant sur la Comité des langues officielles 1969-70; nommé Sous-Commissaire au bureau du Commissaire aux langues officielles, Ottawa, juin 1970 - août 1980; nommé Conseiller spécial en relations internat. et Chargé de mission de l'Agence de cooperation culturelle et technique près des Nations-Unies, sept. 1980; se mérite une bourse donnée par la Fondation Nuffield de Londres, mars 1971; Chev. de Colomb; Club: Lions du Lauzon (membre-fondateur); résidence: 20 rue Parmentier, 92200 Neuilly-sur-Seine, France

MORIN, Yves, B.A., M.D., F.R.C.P.(C); educator; b. Québec, Qué., 28 Nov. 1929; s. Lucien and Marcelle (Samson) M.; e. Univ. Laval, B.A. 1948, M.D. 1953; Nat. Inst. of Cardiology, London, Eng. (Rotary Internat. Foundation Fellow), 1954-55; m. Marie, d. Jean Sénécal, Québec, Qué., 15 Aug. 1959; children: Suzanne, François, Philippe, Frédéric; DOYEN DE LA FACULTE DE MEDECINE, UNIV. LAVAL depuis 1975; Chef, Service de Cardiologie, Hotel Dieu de Quebec, 1980- ; Vice-Doyen 1971, Dir. Dept. de Méd. 1970, Prof. titulaire 1970, agrégé 1966, adjoint 1961; Internship, L'Hôtel-Dieu de Québec, Sunnybrook Hosp. Toronto, Toronto Gen. Hosp., 1952-58; Asst. Service de Méd., Hôtel-Dieu de Qué. 1960, Dir. Lab. de Cardiol. 1961; Dir. Inst. de Cardiol. de Qué. 1966; Dir. Dépt. de Méd., C.H.U.L. 1971; author or co-author of over 47 publs.; mem., Soc. canadienne de cardiol. (Vice-Prés.); N.Y. Acad. Sciences; Soc. de cardiol. du Qué.; Soc. de cardiol. de Montréal; Club de recherches clinqiues du Québec (secy. général 1971); Soc. candnne. de recherches cliniques; Candn. Heart Foundation; Coll. Royal des méds. et chirurgiens du Can.; mem. Internat. Study Group for Research in Cardiac Metabolism (Am. Sec.); Council on Cardiomyopathies, Internat. Soc. of Cardiol.; Fellow, Am. Coll. Cardiol.; Candn. Founding Fellow, Am. Heart Assn.; Home: 1280 Pelletier, Sillery, Québec City, Qué. G1T 2H4; Office: 11 Cote du Palais, Québec, Qué. G1R 2J6

MORISON, David William, D.F.C.; B. Com.; financial consultant; b. Otterville, Ont. 29 Nov. 1915; s. David Howard and Gertrude Isabel (Holmes) M.; e. Univ. of Toronto B. Com. 1939; m. Elizabeth Enid d. Harry Westlake Angus 15 Dec. 1945; children: David Angus, Susan Elizabeth; CHMN., ROYMARK FINANCIAL SERVICES LTD. 1976- ; Chrmn., Reed Inc.; Dir.; Columbian Chemicals Canada Ltd.; Nu-West Florida Inc.; Mack Canada Inc.; Mediavision Inc.; Taylor-Forge Canada Ltd.; Yonge-Bloor Development Ltd.; joined Supvrs. Dept. Royal Bank of Canada 1939, Asst. Mgr. Toronto Br. 1952, Mgr. Toronto Yonge & Bloor Br. 1959, Mgr. Toronto Br. 1961, Asst. Gen. Mgr. Toronto 1964, Dist. Gen. Mgr. Winnipeg 1967, Dist. Gen. Mgr. Toronto 1970, Vice Pres. Ont. 1972-76; served with RCAF 1941-45, Navig. Offr. rank Flight Lt.; Presbyterian; recreations: golf, curling, fishing, hunting; freemason; Clubs: Granite; National; Toronto Golf; Home: 71 Arjay Cres., Willowdale, Ont. M2L 1C6; Office: 11 King St. W., Toronto, Ont. M5H 1A3.

MORISSET, Rev. Auguste-M(arie), O.M.I., C.M. (1976) B.S. (L.S.), M.S. (L.S.), L.J.C.; emeritus professor; b. Fall River, Mass., 27 Oct. 1900; s. Eugène and Rose (Roy) M.; e. Univ. of Ottawa, 1919-21; O.M.I. 1922; studied for priesthood 1921-28; (part time) L.J.C. 1930; B.A., University of Ottawa, 1935; School of Lib. Service, Columbia University, summers 1936-39; B.S. in L.S. 1938; M.S. in L.S. 1948; Founding Dir., Library Sch., Univ. of Ottawa

1938-71, since when Emeritus Prof. there; mem., Nat. Lib. Adv. Comte., 1949-52; Nat. Lib. Adv. Council, 1953-59; Chrmn., Lib. Bd., Univ. of Ottawa, 1959-65; Bursar and Curate, St. Pierre Apotre Parish, Montreal, 1928-29; Prof. of French and Latin Juniorat du Sacré-Coeur, Ottawa, 1929-30; Curate, Sacré-Coeur Parish, Ottawa, 1930-34; Librarian, Univ. of Ottawa, 1934-58; Lectr., Ecole de Bibliothècaires, Univ. de Montréal, 1937-62; Dir., "Academie" (French lit. soc.) Juniorat du Sacré Coeur, Ottawa, 1929-32; Can. delegate to Internat. Cong. of Libraries & Documentation centres, Brussels 1955; mem., Am. Lib. Assn. (Councillor, 1954-55); Cath. Lib. Assn.; Lib. Assn. of Ottawa (Pres., 1943-44, Hon. Life mem. 1971); Ont. Regional Group of Cataloguers (Pres. 1948-49); Special Lib. Assn.; Bibliographical Soc. of Can. (Founding mem.; Pres., 1950-52, hon. mem. 1979); Ont. Lib. Assn.; Candn. Lib. Assn.; Assn. Canadienne des Bibliothéaires de Langue Française (Pres. 1960-61, Hon. Life mem. 1968]; Candn. Music Lib. Assn. (Chrmn. 1961-62); mem., Liaison Comn., C.L.A.-A.L.A. Assns., 1951-55 (Chrmn. 1953-54); Adv. Comte., Bibliothéque Reg. du Nord de l'Outaouais, Hull, Que., 1961-64; Chrmn., French Sec., Candn. Lib. Week, 1966-67; mem., Que. Lib. Assn.; Assn. pour l'av, des sc. et des techn. de la doc. hon. mem. 1976; Alliance Française d'Ottawa; Candn. Writers' Foundation (Hon. Secy. 1960-66, Pres. 1966-68); Can. Assoc. Inf. Sc.-Assoc. Can. Sc. Inf., Founding mem. 1971, hon. life mem. 1981; contrib. articles on most rel. orders in Can., and on Univ. of Ottawa and affiliated Colleges to "Encyclopedia Canadiana"; contrib. to Encyc. Internat., Encyc. de Orientation Bibliografica, and various prof. journs.; awarded Centennial Medal 1976; mem. of Order of Can. (C.M.) 1976; Silver Jubilee Medal 1977; Home: Maison de L'Assomption, 305 Nelson St., Ottawa, Ont. K1N 7S5

MORIYAMA, Raymond, B.Arch., M.Arch., LL.D., D. Eng., F.R.A.I.C., M.C.I.P., R.C.A., F.R.S.A.; architect and planner; b. Vancouver, B.C., 11 Oct. 1929; e. Pub. and High Schools, Vancouver, B.C., Hamilton, Ontario and one year Public School, Tokyo, Japan; Univ. of Toronto, B.Arch.; McGill University, M.Arch.; LL.D. Brock University, York University, Trent University; Fellowship, Ryerson Polytech. Inst.; D. Eng. Tech. Univ. of N.S.; m. Sachi Miyauchi, 17 September 1954; children: Mark-Michi, Murina-Lei, Selena-Midori, Jason-Jun, Adrian-Keiju; commenced practice in May 1958; has wide range of experience ranging from Vancouver, U.S.A., Nassau, Bahamas, Germany to Pakistan; operates under firm name of Moriyama and Teshima, — Architects; Awards incl. Ont. Assn. Arch (Arch. Design); Toronto Guilds (Medal for Arch. Design); Presb. Ch. of Can. (First Prize, Ch. Design, Competition); Nat. Indust. Design Council (Hon. Award. Silver Tea Set Design); Massey Medal (Arch., 1961 and 76); Can. Archs. Award of Excellence for Centennial Baptist Ch. 1968 and Meewasin Valley Project, a 100 yr. conceptual Master Plan, 1979; Pre-Stressed Concrete Inst. Award for Ont. Science Centre 1969; Ont. Masons' Relation Council Award, Minota Hagey Residence, Univ. of Waterloo 1969; Burnhamthorpe District Library 1977; Malton Community Centre & District Library 1978; Whitby Municipal Bldg. 1979; Civic Award of Merit, Toronto, & other civic award and citizen's awards; has lect. in universities and to organizations in Can., Japan, and U.S.A.; mem., Ont. Assn. Arch.; Cdn. Inst. of Planners; Royal Arch. Inst. Can.; mem. of Bd., M.T.V; Roman Catholic; recreations: fishing, painting; Home: 196 Roxborough Drive; Toronto, Ontario M4W 1X8; Office: 32 Davenport Road, Toronto, Ont. M5R 1H3

MORLEY, H. Keith, B.Sc.; executive; b. Derby, Eng., 28 Dec. 1920; s. Harold Stephen and Elsie May M.; e. Derby (Eng.) Sch.; Manchester Univ. B.Sc. (Technol.); m. Rachel Marion d. late Conrad Howard Aug. 1949; children: James, Stephen, Nicholas, Alexander, Sara; CHRMN. OF BOARD, COSTAIN LIMITED. since 1981; Dir., Excelsior

Life Ins. Co.; Aetna Casualty Co. of Can.; Costain Holdings Inc.; Carswell Co. Ltd.; Con-Force Costain Concrete Tie Co. Ltd.; Can. Construction Mgmt. Development Inst.; mem.; Can.-U.S. Comm. of Cham. of Comm.; Chrmn., Construction Industry Devel. Council (Dept. of Ind. Trade and Commerce) 1976-79; Pres., Housing and Urban Devel. Assn. of Can. 1973; Dir. Toronto Symphony; Surveyor Morleys (Builders) Ltd. Derby, Eng. 1949, Dir. 1951; Vice Pres. and Gen. mgr. present Co. 1956; Pres. 1967-77; Chrmn. and C.E.O. 1977-81; served with RAF Coastal Command 1940-46, rank Flight Lt.; Club: Ontario; Home: 6 Burkston Pl., Islington, Ont. M9B 3E4; Office: Suite 2200, P.O. Box 248, 2 First Canadian Place, Toronto, Ont. M5X 1H9

MORLEY, Lawrence Whitaker, Ph.D., D.Sc., F.R.S.C., F.C.A.S.I. (1966); Candn. public servant; geophysicist; b. Toronto, Ont., 19 Feb. 1920; s. George Whitaker and Mary Olive (Boyd) M.; e. Brown Sch., Toronto; Victoria Sch., Collingwood, Ont.; Owen Sound (Ontario) Collegiate Institute; Lakefield (Ont.) Prep Sch., 1938; Univ. of Toronto, Ph.D. 1952; children: Lawrence, Patricia, Christopher, David; COUNSELLOR (SCIENTIFIC), CAN. HIGH COMMISSION, LONDON ENG. 1980-; Party Chief on world's first comm. airborne magnetometer project, Columbia and Venezuela, 1946-48; Chief, Exploration Geophysics Div., Geol. Survey of Can., 1957-69; propounded theory of magnetic imprinting of ocean floors by earth's reversing magnetic field, 1963; instigated Fed./Prov. Aeromagnetic Survey Plan for Can., 1962; instigated plans for Resource Satellite Planning for Can., 1970, then Dir. Gen. Can. Centre for Remote Sensing, Dept. Energy Mines & Resources; served as radar officer with RCNVR 1941-45; Ed. "Mining Geophysics" 1967; "Economic Geology Series"; many papers on geophys. exploration; Hon. D.Sc. York Univ. 1974; past Pres., Can. Aeronautics & Space Inst. (McCurdy Medal 1974); Gov., Imperial Coll. of Sci.; Soc. Exploration Geophysicists; Anglican; recreations: skiing, travel; Home: 40 Hanover House, St. John's Wood High St., London NW870Y ENG; Office: Canadian High Commission, Grosvenor Sq., London Eng.

MORNEAU, William Francis; executive; b. Detroit, Mich., 27 Feb. 1940; s. late William John and Eleanor (Payne) M.; e. Detroit, Mich. and Toronto, Ont. Schs.; m. Helen T., d. late Edward Lynch, 21 Oct. 1961; children: William Francis Jr., Teresa Jo-Anne, Margaret Anne, Mary Catherine, Michelle Christine; PRESIDENT, W. F. MORNEAU AND ASSOCIATES, since founding 1966; Pres., W. F. Morneau & Assoc.in Can. and U.S.; Chmn. of Bd., Supplementary Services Inc., U.S.; 415670 Ont. Ltd; Hornberger Music Ltd.; B&J Ltd.; Dir., Landholme Holdings Ltd.; Mentec Ltd.; Chrmn., 415670 Ont. Ltd.; Rep., Physicians & Surgeons Services Inc., 1957; Consultant, Wm. M. Mercer Ltd., 1959; mem. Candn. Conf. Bd.; Canadian Pension Conf.; Bd. of Trade Metrop. Toronto; R. Catholic; recreations: skiing, boating, badminton; Clubs: Granite; Craigleigh Woodlands Golf & Country (Dir.); R.C.Y.C.; The Halifax (N.S.); Empire; Home: 40 Butterfield Dr., Don Mills, Ont. M3A 2L8; Office: 199 Bay St., Toronto, Ont. M5J 1L4

MORRELL, Clarence Allison, M.A., Ph.D., F.R.S.C. (1947); b. Rochester, N.Y., 15 Mar. 1899; s. Richard and Jessie Della (Howes) M.; came to Can. 1905; e. Univ. of Toronto, B.A. 1924, M.A. 1925; Harvard Univ., Ph.D. (Med. Sciences) 1929; Yale Univ., 1929; Univ. Coll. London, Eng., 1932-33 (Travelling Fellow., Roy. Soc. of Can.); m. Jessie Brown, d. Thomas William Gibson, Toronto, 28 June 1930; one d., Sheila; Dir., Ciba Co. Ltd.; Consultant, Pan-Am. Health Organ. and World Health Organ., 1965-67; joined Dept. of Nat. Health as Chem. and Pharm., Lab. of Hygiene, 1930-37; Sr. Pharm., 1937-45; Asst. Chief, Food and Drug Divn., 1945-46; Chief Dom. Analyst and Dir., Food and Drug. Divs., 1947-65; mem. of W. Africa Yellow Fever Comn. of the Rockefeler

Foundation, 1928-29; mem., Expert Panel on Biol. Standardization of WHO; Gold Medalist, Prof. Inst. Pub. Service of Can., 1962; mem. and consultant, Consumers Assn. Can. (Past Vice-Pres.); mem.; Am. Soc. for Pharm. and Exper. Therapeutics; Candn. Physiol. Soc.; Am. Pharm. Assn.; Brit. Chem. Soc.; Phi Kappa Sigma; Anglican; recreations: motoring, reading, landscape painting; Home: 2625 Regina St., Apt. 1201, Ottawa, Ont. K2B 5W8

MORRIS, Carl R., B.Sc.; executive; b. Presque Isle, Me., 2 Dec. 1933; s. Alphy Leroy and Evelyn Fern (Knight) M.; e. Maine Maritime Acad. B.Sc. 1954; Northeastern Univ. Mang. Devel. Dipl. 1970; m. Shirley Irene d. Elwood Rusmussen, Fort Fairfield, Me., 2 Aug. 1954; four s. Carl Steven, Alan Dale, Eric Paul, John Elwood; VICE PRES. MFG. McCAIN FOODS LTD. since 1969; Dir. McCain Foods Inc.; Pres. Canadian Food Processors Ltd.; Plant Engr. Bird's Eye Div. General Food Corp. Caribou, Me. 1957, Plant Supt. 1959; Plant Mgr. present Co. 1963, Dir. of Mfg. 1967; served with US Naval Reserve 1954-60, rank Lt.; Dir. McCain Scholarship Comte.; Candn. Food Processors Assn.; R. Catholic; recreations: skiing, tennis; Clubs: Travelling Tennis; Home: Riverview Dr., Florenceville, N.B. E0J 1K0; Office: Florenceville, N.B. E0J 1K0

MORRIS, Hon. Edmund Leverett, M.L.A., B.A.; politician; b. Halifax, N.S. 4 Feb. 1923; s. Leverett De Vere and Catherine (Larsen) M.; e. St. Patrick's Sch.; St. Mary's Coll.; Dalhousie Univ.; m. Lorraine Elizabeth d. late William Ware 11 Feb. 1956; children: Christopher, Peter, Mary, John, Sarah, Paul;MIN. OF FISHERIES AND MIN. OF INTERGOVERNMENTAL AFFAIRS, N.S. 1980- ; journalist; Mayor City of Halifax 1974-80; el. to H. of C. g.e. 1957-63; el. M.L.A. for Halifax Needham prov. by-el. 1980; P. Conservative; R. Catholic; Office: (P.O. Box 2223), Maritime Centre, Halifax, N.S. B3J 3C4.

MORRIS, Joe; O.C.; labour executive; b. Lancashire, England, 1913; s. of a British Trade Unionist; m.; has four children; Pres., Canadian Labour Congress, 1974-78; began career as a logger in forest products industry & cont. till 1948; joined Lumber & Sawmill Workers' Union in 1934; on organ. of I.W.A. on Vancouver Is. in 1936, became an active member, later becoming Chairman of the Unions Plant Comte. within the operations of the Comox Logging & Rly. Co. Ltd. with hdqrs. at Ladysmith, B.C.; on the frustration of a secessionist movement in 1948, his leadership in the struggle brought about his el. as Pres. of the re-organ. local Union (1-80, I.W.A. Duncan), and a mem. of the Staff of the Internat. Union as Field Rep.; el. Vice-Pres. of the I.W.A. Dist. Council in 1949, 1st Vice-Pres. in 1951, Pres. 1953-62; Extve. Vice-President, Candn. Labour Congress 1962-74; Regional Vice-Pres., C.L.C., 1956-62; elected worker/member of I.L.O. Gov. Body 1966, 69, 72, 75, 78; chrmn. of worker's group and vice chrmn. Gov. Body I.L.O. in 1970 and 1977; chrmn. of I.L.O. Gov. body 1977-78; mem. Bd. Trustees, Queen's Univ.; mem. Nat. Sci. and Egn. Research Council; Independant Comn. on Internat. Development Concerns; awarded Oficer of the Order of Canada, 1979; recreations: music, sports; Address: 4257 Thornhill Cres., Bictoria, B.C. V8N 3G6

MORRISH, Allan Henry, B.Sc., M.A., Ph.D., FRSC, F.Inst.P., FAPS; educator; b. Winnipeg, Man., 18 Apl. 1924; s. Stanley and Agnes (Payne) M.; e. Univ. of Man., B.Sc. 1943; Univ. of Toronto, M.A. 1946; Univ. of Chicago, Ph.D. 1949; N.R.C. Postdoctoral Fellow, Bristol Univ., 1950; Guggenheim Fellow, Oxford Univ., 1957; m. Hilda Gertrude, d. late E. R. Fiske, Sept. 1952; two s., John Stanley, Allan Richard; PROF. AND HEAD, DEPT. OF PHYSICS, UNIV. OF MANITOBA since 1966; Prof. of Elect. Engn., Univ. of Minn. 1953; joined present Univ. 1964 as Prof. of Physics; has served on comtes. of Nat. Research Council and Defence Research Bd., Ottawa; served as Meteorol., RCAF, 1943-44; RCNVR 1944-45;

rank Lt.; convenor several confs. in physics 1972-74; contrib. new knowledge in magnetic materials; author, "The Physical Principles of Magnetism" 1965 (transl. Polish); article on Ferromagnetism in "Encyclopaedia Britannica" 1974; book chapter "Crystals" in "Problems in Solid State Physics" Vol. 2; author or co-author of over 100 papers in prof. physics journs'; Co-ed. 'Magnetic Materials Digest' 1964; mem. Candn. Assn. Physics (Pres. 1974-75); Cadn. Assn. Physicists; Gold Medal for Achievement in Physics 1977; Queen's Jubilee Medal; Sigma Xi; United Church; recreations; travel, swimming, hiking; Home: 71 Agassiz Dr., Winnipeg, Man. R3T 2K9; Office: Winnipeg, Man.

MORRISH, John Herbert, B.A.Sc., P.Eng.; b. Cherrywood, Ont., 6 Aug. 1930; s. late Albert Roy and late Mary Ella (Milroy) M.; e. Cherrywood (Ont.) Pub. Sch., 1943; Scarborough (Ont.) High Sch., 1948; Univ. of Toronto, B.A.Sc. 1952, Degree in Civil Engn. 1953; m. Elizabeth Anne; d. late Ernest Lunn, Bowmanville, Ont. 7 March 1953; children: Catherine, David; PRES. AND C.E.O., FORDING COAL LTD. since 1977; Dir., Fording Coal Ltd.; joined Engineering Department, Canadian Pacific Rly. Co. 1949, Asst. Engr. Toronto 1953, Asst. Div. Engr. Montreal 1957, Div. Engr. Schreiber, Ont. 1959, Moose Jaw, Sask. 1963, Winnipeg, Man. 1964, Mgr. Freight Devel. Vancouver 1966, Freight Sales and Devel. 1968, System Mgr.-Planning, Montreal 1969, Mgr. Market Devel. 1970; Vice Pres., Marketing and Sale, C.P. Rail 1974-77; Chmn., Coal Assn. of Can. 1981; mem. Internat. Energy Agency; Coal Ind. Adv. Bd; Assn. Prof. Engrs. Prov. Ont.; Univ. of Toronto Alumni Assn.; Office: 205 Ninth Ave. S.E., Calgary, Alta.

MORRISON, Rev. George Matthew, B.Com., B.D., D.D., F.C.A. (Un. Ch.); b. Toronto, Ont., 7 June 1913; s. George William and Hattie Euphemia (McCrimmon) M.; e. Univ. of Toronto Schs. 1931; Univ. of Toronto B.Com. 1936, Emmanuel Coll. B.D. 1956; Inst. C.A.'s, C.A. 1939; D.D. Victoria Univ., St. Andrew's (Scot.); m. Robina Douglas, d. late Andrew B. Taylor 2 Sept. 1940; children: Ian George, Janet Robina Carey; Acct. Fur Trade, Hudson's Bay Co. 1939-40, Partner Henry Barber Mapp & Mapp 1944-49; Controller IBM World Trade Corp. 1949-53; Secy. Div. Finance Un. Ch. Can. H.Q. 1958; Min. Ryerson Un. Ch. Vancouver 1966, Secy. Gen. Council 1971-75; Sr. Min., Timothy Eaton Mem. Ch., Toronto, 1975-78 (ret.); served with RCAF 1941-44, civilian observer; author various articles; Inst. C.A.'s Ont. and Can.; recreations: golf, curling; Home: Mayne Island, B.C. V0N 2J0

MORRISON, Harold Lavell, B.Sc.; consulting engineer; b. Edmonton, Alta., 2 Jan. 1928; s. Ibrahim F. and Kathleen B. (Lavell) M.; e. Univ. High Sch., Edmonton; Univ. of Alta., B.Sc. (Civil Engn.) 1950; m. Norma, d. Edward S. Forsyth, Regina, Sask., 5 March 1955; children: Nancy Gail, Ian Forsyth; PRES., EXTVE. OFFR. AND DIR., HARDY ASSOCIATES LTD., 1978- ; Pres. and Dir., Materials Testing Laboratories Ltd.; Non-Destructive Inspection Ltd.; Papaschase Developmets Ltd.; Dir., PDL2 Developments Ltd.; Aero-Hardy Mapping Ltd.; Maritime Testing Ltd.; Sessional Demonst., Univ. of Alta., 1950-51; Staff Engr., Brown & Root Ltd., Edmonton, 1951-58; Chief Engr. 1958-63; joined present Co. 1963 as Gen. Mgr.; mem., Assn. Prof. Engrs. Alta. (Council 1961-63; Vice Pres. 1963-64); Engn. Inst. Can.; Cdn. Soc. for Civil Eng.; Am. Soc. Civil Engrs.; Candn. Council Prof. Engrs. (Dir. 1965-71; Pres. 1971-72); Treas., Consulting Engineers of Alta., 1978-80; Dir., Assn. of Consulting Engrs of Can., 1980- ; Technical Serv. Council 1981- ; United Church, recreation: curling; Clubs: Rotary, Edmonton; Home: 14004 — 88 Ave., Edmonton, Alta. T5R 4J3; Office: 1350 Weber Centre, 5555 Calgary Trail, Edmonton, Alta. T6H 4J9

MORRISON, Roy Alexander; aviation executive; b. Hamilton, Ont., 10 Dec. 1940; s. Roy Buckley and Rosemary (Tulk) M.; e. Lisgar Coll. Inst., Ottawa, Ont.; Univ. of W. Ont.; m. (2nd) Donna Justine, d. Joseph Snow, 31 May 1973; children: Bruce John, Deborah Lynn; EXTVE. VICE-PRES., TRANSAIR LTD. since 1973; Dir. Airtransit Canada; Reporter, CFRA, Ottawa, 1960; Parlty. Corr., United Press Internat., Press Gallery, Parlt. Hill, Ottawa, 1963; Nat. Ed., CTV Nat. News, 1965; Extve. Asst., Min. of Transport, Ottawa, 1966; joined present Co. as Vice-Pres. Sales & Marketing 1969; rec'd Centennial Medal 1967; mem., Air Transport Assn. Can. (Chrmn.); Winnipeg Extves. Assn.; Liberal; Protestant; recreations: golf, fishing, Clubs: Southwood Golf & Country; Skal; Home: 202 Vernon Rd., Winnipeg, Man. R3J 2V9; Office: Winnipeg, Internat. Airport, Winnipeg, Man.

MORRISSETTE, Gaëtan C.; company executive; b. Quebec, Que., 9 May 1910; s. Achille and Augusta (Kerstius) M.; e. Mount St. Bernard Coll.; m. Lillian, (deceased) d. late J. A. Bilodeau, 18 Feb. 1933; children: Lise, Paul, John, Peter; m. Françoise Stringer, 7 March 1975; CHRMN. OF THE BD. STANDARD BRANDS LIMITED, since 1961; joined Standard Brands Limited as Acct., 1930; Comptroller and Asst. Secy., 1943; el. a Dir., 1944; Secy.-Treas., 1945; Vice-Pres., 1954; Vice-Pres.-Adm., 1958; R. Catholic; recreations: fishing; Clubs: St. Denis; The Mount Royal; Canadian (N.Y.); Kataska F&G; Mount Royal; Home: 37 Upper Trafalgar Place, Montreal H3H 1T2; Office: R. 230, 4 Westmount Sq., Montreal, Que. H3Z 2S6

MORROW, (Andrew) Keith, B.S.A.; broadcasting executive; b. Mermaid, P.E.I., 21 Dec. 1915; s. Fraser Thompson and Blanche Eleanor (Hyde) M.; e. Prince of Wales Coll., Charlottetown, P.E.I.; Ont. Agric. Coll., B.S.A., 1940; m. Marianne Grantham, d. late Lieut.-Col. K. S. Rogers, 9 Jan. 1942; two s. Andrew Keith, David Rogers; joined C.B.C. in 1945 as Farm Commentator at Halifax, N.S.; Asst. Supervisor of Farm & Fisheries Broadcast Dept., Toronto, Ont., 1950-51, and Supervisor, 1951-55; Co-ordinator of Radio, 1955-57; Asst. Controller of Operations, Ottawa, 1957-59; appt. Dir. of English Networks and the Toronto area, 1959, then Special Asst., Management Studies, Ottawa Hdqrs.; C.B.C. Dir. for Nfld., 1967-73; CBC Dir. for Maritimes 1973- ; mem. of Bd., Nat. Farm Radio Forum, 1950-55; served in 2nd World War; 2nd Lieut., R.C.C.S. (R.), Sub-Lieut., R.C.N.V.R., 1942; Lieut. 1943, Lieut.-Commdr. 1944-45; Dir., United Church; recreations: walking, swimming, reading; Clubs: Halifax; United Services Officers'; 1047 Tower Rd., Halifax, N.S. B3G 2Y6 Home: 1840 Bell Rd., Halifax, N.S.; Office: 95 University Ave., St. John's, Nfld. A1B 1Z4

MORROW, Graham, O.B.E., E.D., B.A.; lawyer; b. Toronto, Ont., 7 June 1908; s. George Andrew and Phoebe C. (Graham) M.; e. Upper Can. Coll., Toronto, Ont. (Grad. 1925); Univ. of Toronto, B.A. 1929; Osgoode Hall Law Sch., 1929-32; m. Doris C., d. Col. F. J. James, Regina, Sask., 29 Dec. 1931; children: Ann Elizabeth, Judith Christine; Dir., The National Trust Co. Ltd.; Royal Insurance Group; Western British America Group; mem., Candn. Adv. Bd., Royal/Globe Insurance Group; Trustee, Hosp. for Sick Children; read law with Long and Daly, Toronto, Ont.; called to the Bar of Ont. 1932; practised law with Long & Daly, Toronto, Ont., 1932-40; First Secy., Candn. Embassy, Washington, D.C., 1945-46; served in N.P.A.M. as Capt., Queen's Own Rifles of Can., 1927-38; served in 2nd World War, 1940-45, joining R.C.A.F. as Flying Offr. and promoted Group Capt. 1944; awarded O.B.E.; Kappa Alpha (Treas. 1928-29); Anglican; Clubs: Toronto; Toronto Golf; York; Home: 625 Avenue Rd., Apt. 2001, Toronto, Ont. M4U 2K7; Office: 34 King St. E., Suite 1200, Toronto, Ont. M5C 1E6

MORROW, Robert Ellis, D.F.C., Q.C., B.C.L.; b. Crossfield, Alberta, 20 Jan. 1916; s. Ellis Henry and Mary Christina (McMichael) M.; e. Univ. of Toronto Law Sch., B.A. 1938; McGill Law Sch., B.C.L., 1947; m. Constance

Louise, d. Hon. Charles L. Bishop, 12 Sept. 1942; five children; Counsel, Ogilvy and Renault; Dir., Consolidated Bathurst Inc.; Bathurst Paper Limited; Boeing of Can. Ltd.; Meaghers Distillery Limited; Chmn., Bouverie Investments Ltd.; Harmsworth Holdings Ltd.; Gov., Motreal Gen. Hosp.; Justine Hosp.; called to the Bar of Que., 1947; cr. Q.C. 1958; served in 2nd World War with R.C.A.F., rank Wing Commdr.; awarded D.F.C.; Anglican Church; Clubs: Mount Royal, St. James's; Mount Bruno Country; Home: 200 Habitat, Cité du Havre, Montreal, Que.

MORROW, William Owen, B.Com.; fishery executive; b. Lunenburg, N.S., 31 Dec. 1927; s. Clarence Joseph and Jean (Smith) M.; e. Lunenburg (N.S.) Acad.; Rothesay (N.B.) Coll. Sch.; Dalhousie Univ., B. Com. 1949; m. Ida Marita, d. George M. Hope, 7 June 1952; children: David William, Gillian Hope, Christopher James; PRESIDENT, CHIEF EXTVE. OFFICER AND DIRECTOR, NATIONAL SEA PRODUCTS LIMITED since 1969; Dir., Dover Mills Limited; Chrysler Canada Limited; mem., Halifax Adv. Bd., Montreal Trust Co.; joined present Co. 1949, Div. Asst. Sales Mgr. 1951, Div. Sales Mgr. 1953, Co. Gen. Sales Mgr. 1960, Vice-Pres.-Sales 1965; Pres., Fisheries Council of Can. 1969; Anglican; recreations: curling, sailing, fishing, skiing; Clubs: Royal Nova Scotia Yacht Squadron; Halifax Curling; Ashburn Golf; Halifax; Lunenburg Yacht; Bluenose Golf; Home: 360 Crowsnest Dr., Halifax, N.S. B3H 3X5; Office: Suite 1400, Duke Tower, Scotia Sq. P.O. Box 2130, Halifax, N.S. B3J 3B7

MORSE, Barry; actor; director; writer; b. London, Eng., 10 June 1918; s. Charles Hayward and Mary Florence (Hollis) M.; e. London, Eng. Schs.; Royal Acad. of Dramatic Art, London, Eng. (scholarship) 1935-37; m. Sydney, d. late Archibald Richard Sturgess, 26 March 1939; children: Melanie Virginia Sydney, Hayward Barry; first prof. appearance in London, Eng., Dec. 1936; first radio, BBC, London, 1936; first film, England, 1940; first television, Eng., BBC 1938; came to Canada, 1951 since when has appeared on radio and television for CBC in Can., BBC and ITV in England, and CBS, NBC and ABC in U.S. as well as many film and stage productions in all three countries as actor and director; to date has played over 2,000 roles on various media; five times winner of award for Best Actor in Candn. television (1954, 1956, 1959, 1960, 1961); starred in title role of "Hadrian VII" on Broadway and in Australia 1969; television series include "The Fugitive" 1963-67; "The Adventurer" 1973; "The Zoo Gang" 1974; "Space 1999" 1975-76;; "The Winds of War" 1981; "Whoops Apocalypse" 1981-82; feature films include "Power Play" 1977; "The Changeling" 1978; "The Shape of Things to Come" 1978; "Klondike Fever" 1979; "Cries in the Night" 1979; "The Hounds of Notre Dame" 1980; "A Tale of Two Cities" 1980; "Bells" 1980; "The Legacy of Mark Rothko" 1981; Artistic Dir.-Shaw Festival Niagara-on-the-Lake, Ont. 1966; Adjunct Prof. (1968) Drama Dept., Yale Univ.; Vice Pres. Shaw Soc. of U.K., 1970; Founding Artistic Dir., Globe Playhouse, Victoria B.C., 1980; Pres. Planet Productions Ltd., Ont.; Address: c/o 59 Lawrence Ave. W., Toronto, Ont. M5M 1A3

MORSE, Eric Wilton, C.M. (1975), M.A., LL.D., F.R.G.S.; consultant and writer; b. Naini Tal, India, 27 Dec. 1904; s. Wilton Henry and Florence M. (Griffin) M.; e. Trinity Coll. Sch., Port Hope, Ont.; Queen's Univ., M.A. (Modern Hist.) 1936, LL.D., (Hon.) 1980; Sch. of Internat. Studies, Geneva, Switzerland, 1935; m. 1st Mary Tena, d. Albert Robinson, 5 Sept. 1931; one s., Peter Wilton; one. d., Wendy Diana; 2nd, Pamela Mary, d. E. R. Clarke, Oct. 1959; served with R.C.A.F. 1942-45; demobilized as Sqdn. Ldr.; Nat. Secy., United Nations Assn. in Can., 1945-48; Nat. Dir., Assn. of Candn. Clubs 1949-71; Publication: "Fur Trade Canoe Routes of Canada — Then and Now", 1969; "Fresh Water Northwest Passage"; "Summer Travel on the Canadian Barren Lands"; also various articles in mags. and journs.; mem. Bd. Govs.,

Trinity Coll. Sch., 1968-71; Pres. Men's Canadian Club, Ottawa 1972-74; Protestant; recreations: skiing, canoeing; Club: Rideau; Home: "Wildwood", R.R. 3 Wakefield, P.Q. J0X 3G0

MORSE, Hon. Peter Scott, B.A., LL.B.; b. Winnipeg, Man., 29 May 1927; s. Harry Dodge and Tena Bell (Scott) M.; e. Ravenscourt Sch., Fort Garry, Man., 1944; Royal Candn. Naval Coll., Royal Roads, B.C., 1944-46; Univ. of Man., B.A. 1948, LL.B. 1952; m. Marjorie Jane, d. Wilford Edward Bull, Winnipeg, Manitoba, 19 September 1954; children: David Scott, Stephen Flanders, Ruth Elizabeth; JUSTICE, COURT OF QUEEN'S BENCH, MAN. since 1975; read law with D. A. Thompson, Q.C.; called to the Bar of Manitoba 1952; practised law with Aikins, MacAulay & Thorvaldson 1952-75; Anglican; Clubs: Manitoba; Home: 874 Wellington Cres., Winnipeg, Man. R3M 0C5; Office: Law Courts, Winnipeg, Man.

MORT, C.L., B.Sc.; executive; b. Toronto, Ont. e. Univ. of Toronto B.Sc. (Chem. Eng.) CHRMN. OF BD. DIRS., DOW CHEMICAL OF CANADA LTD. 1980- ; joined Dow Chemical as Process Engr. 1951, Solvents Plant Mgr. 1952, Sales Engr. Toronto, Gen. Sales Mgr. 1969, Business Devel. Mgr. and Dir. Dow Canada 1971, Vice Pres. Business Devel. 1972, Vice Pres. New Business Ventures, Services & Govt. Affairs 1976; Office: Sarnia, Ont.

MORTIMER, Alan John, B.Sc., M.Sc.; research scientist; b. Kingston, Ont. 7 Jan. 1950; s. Donald Charles and Mary Katherine (Robertson) M.; e. Carleton Univ. B.Sc. 1972, M.Sc. 1974; m. Patricia Adelaide d. late Sanford Stratton Burley 1 May 1976; children: Sandra Irene; RESEARCH OFFICER, NAT. RESEARCH COUNCIL OF CAN. 1975- ; Avionics Engr., Computing Devices of Can. 1974-75; invented Echo-Oculometer 1977; ongoing studies of therapeutic uses of ultrasound for heart disease; author "Characteristics of Ultrasound" 1982; sci. publications on ultrasound safety and instruments; mem., Candn. Med. and Biol. Eng. Soc.; Amer. Inst. of Ultrasound in Med. and Biol.; Alpine Club of Can.; Nat. Capital Runners Assn.; Ottawa River Runners; recreations: running, whitewater canoeing, mountaineering, music performance; Home: 3055 Huntindon Ct., Ottawa, Ont. K1T 1R1; Office: Ottawa, Ont. K1A 0R8

MORTON, Desmond Dillon Paul, M.A., Ph.D.; educator; author; b. Calgary, Alta. 10 Sept. 1937; s. Brig. Ronald Edward Alfred and Sylvia Cuyler (Frink) M.; e. Rothesay (N.B.) Consolidated Sch. 1946; Herchmer Sch. Regina 1949; Ravenscourt Sch. Winnipeg 1951; Kingston (Ont.) Coll. & Vocational Inst.; Candn. Acad. Kobe, Japan 1954; Coll. Militaire Royal de St-Jean 1957; Royal Mil. Coll. Can. B.A. 1959; Keble Coll. Oxford Univ. (Rhodes Scholar) B.A. 1961, M.A. 1966; London Sch. of Econ. Univ. of London Ph.D. 1968; m. Janet Lillian d. late William Henry Smith, North Bay, Ont. 7 July 1967; children: David William Edward, Marion Catherine; PROF. OF HIST. ERINDALE COLL. UNIV. OF TORONTO 1975- ; Asst. Prof. of Hist. Univ. of Ottawa 1968-69; Univ. of Toronto 1969, Assoc. Prof. 1971; Visiting Asst. Prof. Univ. of W. Ont. 1970-71; Visiting Assoc. Prof. Mich. State Univ. 1975; Assoc. Dean Erindale Coll. 1975-79, Vice Princ. (Acad.) 1976-79; joined Candn. Army 1954, comnd. Lt. 1959, Capt. 1962, trans. to Supplementary Reserve 1964; Asst. Prov. Secy. NDP Ont. 1964-68 , Fed. Council 1968-72, Cand. Mississauga N. (fed.) 1978, resigned 1979; Jt. Winner City of Toronto Book Prize 1873; Pres. and Dir. Canada Hamble Ltd.; mem. Ed. Bd. "History and Social Science Teacher"; author "Ministers and Generals: Politics and the Canadian Militia" 1970; "The Last War Drum: The North-West Campaign of 1885" 1972; "Mayor Howland: The Citizens' Candidate" 1973; "The Canadian General: Sir William Otter" 1974; "NDP: The Dream of Power" 1974; "Rebellions in Canada" 1979; "Working People: An Illustrated History

of Canadian Labour" 1980; "Canada and War" 1981; co-ed. "Telegrams of the North-West Campaign of 1885" 1972; various articles scholarly journs., newspapers, mags.; mem. Candn. Hist. Assn. (Pres. 1978-79); Candn. Comn. Mil. Hist. (Chrmn. 1976-); NDP; Anglican; Home: 362 Queen St. S., Streetsville, Ont. L5M 1M2; Office: Toronto, Ont. M5S 1A1 and Mississauga, Ont. L5L 1C6.

MORTON, Douglas Gibb, R.C.A. (1968) university professor; artist; b. Winnipeg, Man., 26 Nov. 1926; s. James Marshall and Mary Murdoch (Dickie) M.; e. Kelvin High Sch. and Un. Coll., Winnipeg, 1946; Univ. of S. Cal. Art Centre Sch., 1947-48; Ecole des Beaux Arts, Acad. Julian and Studio of André L'Hote, Paris, 1949; Camberwell Sch. and Studio of Martin Bloch, London, 1950; m. Edna Eileen, d. late William Henry Morgan, 23 April 1949; children: Mary Ruth, Nadene, Jocelyn, Cynthia, Taron, Douglas William; PROF. & DEAN OF FINE ARTS, VICTORIA UNIV. 1980- ; Prof. & Chrmn. of Visual Arts, Fac. of Fine Arts, York Univ., 1978-79; Assoc. Dean, 1972-75; Can. Council Sen. Arts Grant 1975-76; Curator, Calgary Allied Arts Centre, 1951-53; Mgr. Sask. Br. and Vice Pres., MacKay-Morton Ltd. (mfrs. agts.), 1954-67; Dir., Sch. of Art, Univ. of Sask., Regina, 1967-69; created mural Regina Pub. Lib.; rep. in colls. of Nat. Gallery of Can., Vancouver Art Gallery, Mendel Gallery (Saskatoon), Norman Mackenzie Gallery (Regina); Beaverbrook Gallery (Fredericton), Univs. of Alta. & York Toronto; served with Candn. Army 1945; mem., Candn. Conf. of Arts; Univ. Art Assn. Can. (Dir. 1967-69); Liberal; United Church; Home: 4903 Cordova Bay Rd., Victoria, B.C. V8Y 2K1

MORTON, Harry Stafford, O.B.E., C.D., B.A., M.Sc., M.B., B.S., F.R.C.S.(Eng.), F.R.C.S.(C), F.A.C.S., F.R.C.O.G.; consultant surgeon; b. Port Greville, N.S., 18 Aug. 1905; s. Charles S., M.D. and Maie Howard (Stafford) M.; e. St. Andrews Coll. Toronto 1918-21; Dalhousie Univ., B.A. 1925, M.Sc. 1927; Univ. of London, M.B., B.S., M.R.C.S., L.R.C.P. 1927-32; Hon LL.D., Mount Allison; m. Rachel Perot, d. late Gregor Wainwright, July 1937; Pres.; Haramo Investments Ltd.; Dir., Equitable Life Insurance Co. of Canada; mem., Bd. Regents, Mt. Allison Univ.; Hon. Attending Surg., Royal Victoria Hosp., Montreal, Que.; Hon. Consultant in Surg., Queen Mary Veterans' Hosp., Montreal; Consultant in Surg., Fishermans Mem. Hosp., Lunenberg, N.S.; Chrmn. and Examiner in Surg., Royal Coll. Surgs. Can.; Examiner in Surg., Med. Council Can. and McGill Univ.; Past Pres. and Founder, Quebec Tumour Registry, Nat. Cancer Registry, Ottawa; Hunterian Prof. a Surgery, Royal College of Surgeons, Eng. 1954; Founder of Tumour Registries, Royal Victoria and Queen Mary Veterans' Hosps.; Chrmn. Cancer Comte., Que. Med. Soc.; Sr. mem., Past Dir., Candn. Med. Assn.; mem Titular Internat. Surg. Soc. (Sr. mem. Central Surg. Soc.); mem. Candn. Assn. of Clinical Surgeons; Past Pres. Bd. of Governors, Pan-Canada Foundation 1976-78 (Past Pres. Bd. of Trustees, 1974-76); sometime Extve. Cancer Comn. and Chrmn. Local Programme Comte.; Am. Coll. Surgs.; mem. Comte. of Assessment, Nat. Cancer Inst. Can.; Past Treas., Montreal Medico-Chirurgical Soc.; mem. A.Y.R.S. (Britain); mem. Naval Officers Assn. of Nova Scotia; former Candn. Med. Assn. Rep., D.M.D. S.A.B.; served in R.C.N.V.R. 1938-51; 2nd World War 1939-45; O.B.E., C.D.; promoted Surg. Capt., R.C.N.(R) 1949; Phi Rho Sigma; United Church; recreations: sailing, farming, photography; Clubs: University; Rotary (Past Service mem.); Power Squadron; Fellow, Roy. Soc. Med. (Eng.); Life mem., Lunenberg Yacht (N.S.); London Hospital Medical (U.K.); Homes: 580 Claremont Ave., Montreal, Que. H3Y 2P1 and R.R. #1, Lunenberg, N.S. B0J 2C0

MORTON, John; construction executive; b. Newcastle, Eng. 9 Jan. 1927; s. Thomas Milton and Mary (Gourley) M.; e. Heaton Grammar Sch. Newcastle; m. Elizabeth H. M. d. late W. A. Edgeworth 1940; children: Bruce Milton,

Mark John; PRESIDENT, BCM CAPE LTD. 1980- ; Vice Pres. Robertson Yates Corp. Ltd. 1966-70; Mgr. Dir. Intercon Ltd. Bermuda 1970-74; joined present Co. 1974; served with R.E. then Glider Pilot A.A.C.; Pres. Ont. Gen. Contractors Assn. 1980-81; mem. Bd. Trade Metrop. Toronto; recreations: tennis, sailing; Club: Toronto Cricket Skating & Curling; P. Conservative; Anglican; Home: 2610, 95 Thorncliffe Park Dr., Toronto, Ont.; Office: 180 Duncan Mill Rd., Don Mills, Ont. M3B 3K2.

MORTON, John Kenneth, Ph.D., F.L.S.; educator; b. Tamworth, U.K. 3 Jan. 1928; s. Ernest and Evelyn Hodgson (Brewer) M.; e. Bede Coll. Grammar Sch. for Boys Sunderland, U.K. 1946; King's Coll. Univ. of Durham B.Sc. 1949, Ph.D. 1953; m. Doreen d. William Ernest Freeman 16 June 1951; children: David John, Eileen Heather; PROF. OF BIOL., UNIV. OF WATERLOO 1968- ; Lectr. Univ. Coll. of Ghana 1951-58, Sr. Lectr. 1958-61, Curator Ghana Herbarium 1951-61; Lectr. Birkbeck Coll. Univ. of London 1961-63; Prof. and Head of Botany, Fourah Bay Coll. Univ. of Sierra Leone 1963-67, mem. Bd. Govs. 1965-67, Dir. Botanic Garden & Arboretum 1963-67, Assoc. Dir. Inst. Marine Biol. & Oceanography 1963-67; Acting Princ. of Univ. 1967; Chrmn. of Biol. present Univ. 1974-80; rec'd Candn. Bot. Assn. Mary E. Elliot Award 1978; author "The Flora of Islay and Jura" 1959; "West African Lilies and Orchids" 1961; "The Flora of Manitoulin Island" 1977; co-author "An Atlas of Pollen of Trees and Shrubs of Eastern Canada and the Adjacent United States" Parts 1-4 1972-79; over 85 publs. Brit., W. Africa and N. Am. Bot.; mem. Candn. Bot. Assn. (Pres. 1974-75, Extve. Comte. 1970-80); Bot. Soc. Brit. Isles; Am. Soc. Plant Taxonomists; Bot. Soc. Edinburgh; Assn. Tropical Biol.; Internat. Assn. Plant Taxonomists; recreations: natural history, outdoors; Home: 501 Cedarcliffe Waterloo, Ont. N2K 2J2; Office: Waterloo, Ont. N2L 3G1.

MORTON, Paul Gustav, LL.B.; television executive; b. Winnipeg, Man. 29 May 1938; s. Henry A. and Eva Rebecca (Ginsberg) M.; e. Kelvin High Sch. Winnipeg; Univ. of Man. B.A., LL.B. 1962; m. Karen Marilyn d. Sidney J. Oreck, Vancouver, B.C. 1 June 1961; children: Henry, Elisa, Julie; PRES., GLOBAL COMMUNICATIONS LTD. since 1977; Pres. and Dir. Global Ventures Western Ltd.; Dir. and Chmn. Extve. Comte. Canwest Broadcasting Ltd.; Dir. Canwest Capital Ltd.; Crown Trust Ltd.; called to Bar of Man. 1964; Pres., Odeon Morton Theatres 1963-80; co-founder Canwest Broadcasting Ltd. Winnipeg 1974 and Global Ventures Western Ltd.; Pres., Winnipeg Blue Bombers Football Club 1974-75; mem. Candn. Football League Extve. Comte. 1974-75, Dir. since 1967; Div. Chrmn. Un. Way of Greater Winnipeg 1970; Chrmn. Variety Village Sports Training & Fitness Centre; Pres., Motion Picture Theatres Assn. Can. 1975-76; Dir. Royal Winnipeg Ballet; mem. Man. Motion Picture Theatres Assn.; Man. Bar Assn.; Candn. Bar Assn.; Sigma Alpha Mu (Regional Gov.); Jewish; recreations: squash, tennis, jogging, reading; Club: Winnipeg Squash; Home: 26 Alderbrook Rd., Don Mills, Ont. M3B 2B5; Office: 81 Barber Greene Rd., Don Mills, Ont. M3C 2A2.

MOSER, William Oscar Jules, B.Sc., M.A., Ph.D.; educator; b. Winnipeg, Man. 5 Sept. 1927; s. Robert and Laura (Fenson) M.; e. Univ. of Man. B.Sc. 1949; Univ. of Minn. M.A. 1951; Univ. of Toronto Ph.D. 1957; m. Beryl Rita d. Sidney Pearlman 2 Sept. 1953; children: Marla, Lionel, Paula; PROF. OF MATH., McGILL UNIV. 1966- ; Teaching Asst. Univ. of Minn. 1949-51; Teaching Fellow Univ. of Toronto 1953-55; Instr. Univ. of Sask. 1955, Asst. Prof. 1957-59; Assoc. Prof. Univ. of Man. 1959-64; Assoc. Prof. present Univ. 1964; mem. Senate 1970-72; recipient Isbister Scholarships 1946-48; Nat. Research Council Fellowships 1951-53; Univ. of Toronto Fellowship 1954-55; Can. Council Leave Fellowship 1971-72; invited lectr. numerous Candn., Am. and UK univs.; co-author "Generators and Relations for Discrete Groups" 1957, 4th

ed. 1980; Ed.-in-Chief Candn. Math. Bulletin 1961-70; Assoc. Ed. Candn. Journ. Math. 1981- ; mem. Candn. Math. Soc. (Pres. 1975-77); Am. Math. Soc.; Math. Assn. Am.; Soc. Indust. & Applied Math.; Fibonacci Assn.; London Math. Soc.; Sigma Xi; Hebrew; recreations: chess, billiards; Home: 1520 Dr. Penfield Ave., Apt. 82, Montreal, Que. H3G 1B9; Office: 805 Sherbrooke St. W., Montreal, Que. H3A 2K6.

MOSS, Edward John, Q.C., LL.B.; b. Sussex, Eng., 26 Apl. 1917; s. Henry John and Alice (Turner) M.; e. Brighton Grammar Sch. Eng.; London Univ. LL.B.-1939; m. Anne d. George Hodkinson, 21 Sept. 1946; one d. Sally Anne; PARTNER, BALFOUR, MOSS, MILLIKEN, LASCHUK, KYLE & VANCISE; admitted solicitor Eng. 1939, Bar of Sask. 1954, Bar of Alta. 1966; cr. Q.C. 1967; law practice London, Eng. after war; emigrated to Sask. 1954; former Lectr. in Oil and Gas Univ. of Sask. (part-time) and Bar Admission Course for Sask.; joined Sussex Yeomanry (Territorials) 1939, Active War Service 1939-46, comnd. RA 1944; Past Dir. Candn. Law Petroleum Foundation; Past Pres. Roy. Un. Services Inst. Regina; Fellow Am. Coll. Trial Lawyers (1976); Past Pres. Regina Bar Assn.; Regina Men's Candn. Club; mem. Law Soc. Sask. (Past Pres. and Bencher); Candn. Bar Assn.; Law Soc. Eng.; Law Soc. Alta.; Anglican; P. Conservative; recreations: natural history, gardening, motoring; Club: Assiniboia; Home: 3024 Rae St., Regina, Sask. S4S 1R7; Office: 1850 Cornwall, Regina, Sask. S4P 2K3

MOTT, Harold Edgar, B.Sc.; P.Eng.; b. Winnipeg, Man., 4 Dec. 1897; s. Ezra A. and Martha E. (Harold) M.; e. McGill Univ., B.Sc. 1922; m. Marion F., d. Rev. W. B. Caswell, Oakville, Ont.; children: Mary Frances, John Edgar, Elizabeth Anne, Margaret Jean, Ruth Helen; Supt. of Works and Works Engr., Candn. Marconi Co., Montreal, Que., 1922-27; Chief Engr., DeForest Crosley Radio Co., Toronto, Ont., 1927-28; Factory Mgr. and Chief Engr., Rogers Majestic Corp., Toronto, 1928-32; in a private practice as Consulting Engr., 1932-34; formed H. E. Mott Co., Ltd., mfr. of general industrial equipment and consumer durables in 1934, becoming Pres. and Gen. Mgr. and subsequently Chrmn. of Bd.; retired upon sale of Co. 1963; served in World War 1914-48; with C.E.F. (Cavalry); trans. to R.N.A.S. and served in France; retired with rank of Capt. R.A.F.; mem.; Engn. Inst. Can.; Delta Upsilon; Home: Apt. 101, 67 North Park St., Brantford, Ont. M3R 6N9

MOTT, John E., B.A.Sc.; manufacturer; b. Montreal, Que., 7 July 1924; s. Harold Edgar and Marian Frances (Caswell) M.; e. Univ. of Toronto, B.A.Sc. (Mech. Engn.) 1946; m. Diana Beverly Hitchon, 28 Oct. 1950; children: Howard Ian, Barbara Gay, Virginia; PRESIDENT, RAYMOND INDUSTRIAL EQUIPMENT LTD.; joined present Co. in 1965; Delta Upsilon; United Church; recreations: gardening, fishing, hunting; Home: 25 Riverview Dr., Brantford, Ont. N3T 5A8; Office: 406 Elgin St., Brantford, Ont.

MOTZ, Paul J., B.A.; publisher; b. Kitchener, Ont. 25 Jan. 1950; s. John E. and Mary (Stoody) M.; e. Univ. of W. Ont.; Univ. of Waterloo; Wilfrid Laurier Univ. B.A. 1971; two d. Mary Helen, Jane Ann; PRESIDENT AND GEN. MGR. KITCHENER-WATERLOO RECORD 1980- ; Co-ordinating Supvr. present newspaper 1971, Asst. to Pres. 1973, Vice Pres. 1975, Pres. 1978; mem. Candn. Press; Candn. Daily Newspaper Publishers Assn.; Am. Press Inst.; Am. Newspaper Publishers Assn.; Inland Daily Press Assn.; R. Catholic; recreations: music, reading, sports, consulting (business & trades); Home: 260 Sheldon Ave. N., Kitchener, Ont. N2H 6P2; Office: 225 Fairway Rd., Kitchener, Ont. N2G 4E5.

MOUNFIELD, William K., B.Com., M.B.A.; retired. industrialist; b. Toronto, Ont., 30 March 1924; s. William Mark and Emily Caryl (Jaques) M.; e. Queen Victoria

Public Sch., Toronto 1937; Univ. of Toronto Schs. 1942; Univ of Toronto, B.Com. 1948, M.B.A. 1960; m. Marion Helen, d. John Beaton Macmillan, 15 Nov. 1968; retired Vice Pres. Administration, Massey-Ferguson Ltd. since 1977; Chrmn. & Dir. Massey-Ferguson Ind. Ltd.; President and Dir. Massey-Ferguson Finance Co. of Canada Ltd.; Dir. Perkins Engines Canada Ltd.; chrmn. of Bd., Sunar Ltd. joined the Co. 1948, Sales and Adm. positions France and U.K. incl. Secy. MF U.K. and Br. Mgr. France 1952-59; Asst. to Mang. Dir. MF Italy 1960; Asst. Secy. Massey-Ferguson Ltd. 1960, Secy. and Dir. Legal Services 1972; Pres. Massey Ferguson Ind. Ltd. 1973; served in 2nd World War R.C.A. 1943-45, rank Lt.; Bd. of Govs., Univ. of Guelph; mem. of Council; Bd. Trade Metrop. Toronto; Presbyterian; recreations: golf, tennis, skiing; Clubs: University; Granite; Caledon Ski; Rosedale Golf; Toronto Lawn Tennis; Rotary; Home: 15 Glengowan Rd., Toronto, Ont. M4N 1E9;

MOUNTAIN, Sir Denis Mortimer, Bart.; insurance executive; b. London, Eng. 2 June 1929; s. Sir Brian Edward Stanley, Bart. and Doris Elsie (Lamb) M.; e. Eton, Eng. 1946; m. Helene Fleur Mary d. John William Kirwan-Taylor, Switzerland 18 Feb. 1958; children: Georgina Lily Fleur, Edward Brian Stanford, William Denis Charles; Chrmn. and Mang. Dir., Eagle Star Insurance Co. Ltd. (U.K.) and Eagle Star Holdings PLC 1974- ; joined ESI Co. Ltd.; 1959; Chrmn. or Dir. numerous firms U.K., S. Africa, Belgium, Australia, W. Indies, France, USA; Dir. Bank of Nova Scotia; Bank of Nova Scotia Trust Co. (Bahamas) Ltd.; Bank of Nova Scotia Trust Co. (Cayman) Ltd.; Bank of Nova Scotia Trust Co. (Caribbean) Ltd.; Bank of Nova Scotia International Ltd. (Bahamas); served with Royal Horse Guards, rank Lt.; mem. Winchester Div. Cons. Assn.; Inst. Dirs.; Conservative; Anglican; recreations: shooting, fishing; Clubs: Derby; National Sporting; Blues & Royals; Home: 12 Queens Elm Sq., London S.W. 3, Eng.;Office: 1 Threadneedle St., London, Eng. EC2R 8BE.

MOVAT, Henry Zoltan, M.D., M.Sc., Ph.D., F.R.C.P.(C); university professor; b. Romania, 11 Aug. 1923; s. Erwin Karl and Piroska (Kubitschka) M.; e. Univ. of Vienna; Univ. of Innsbruck, Austria, M.D. 1948; Queen's Univ., M.Sc. 1954, Ph.D. 1956; m. Ilse Adeline, d. Franz Hirselandt, Germany, 29 Dec. 1956; three s., Ronald, Kenneth, Douglas; PROF. OF PATHOL., UNIV. OF TORONTO, and Head Div. of Exper. Path., since 1967; Fellow in Pathol., Univ. of Innsbruck, 1948-50; Interne, Ottawa Civic Hosp., 1950-51, and Res. in Pathol. there, 1951-53; Fellow in Pathol., Queen's Univ., 1953-56; Mem. Centre for Cancer, New York, 1956-57; Asst. Prof. of Pathol., Univ. of Toronto, 1957-60; Assoc. Prof. 1960-66; mem., Am. Assn. Pathols.; Internat. Acad. Pathol.; Am. Assn. Immunol.; Candn. Assn. Immunol.; Soc. Exper. Biol. Med.; main interest: research in field of inflamation and immunopath.; Protestant; recreation: oenology, gardening; Home: 17 Truxford Rd., Parkway Woods, Don Mills, Ont. M3A 2S5

MOWAT, Farley, O.C., B.A., D.Litt.; author; b. Belleville, Ont., 12 May 1921; s. Angus McGill and Helen E. (Thomson) M.; e. Pub. Schs., Trenton, Windsor, Ont., and Saskatoon, Sask.; High Schs., Saskatoon, Sask., Toronto and Richmond Hill, Ont.; Univ. of Toronto, B.A. 1949; D.Litt. (Hon.) Laurentian 1970; D. Lows. Lethbridge, P.E.I. 1979 Toronto (both 1973);m. 1st, Frances Elizabeth, d. H. R. Thornhill, Toronto, 20 Dec. 1947; children: Robert Alexander, David Peter; 2ndly, Claire Angel Wheeler; began writing as Free-Lance author after return from two yrs. in Arctic (1947-48) at Palgrave, Ont.; has written for "Atlantic Monthly", "Saturday Evening Post" (regular contrib.), "Reader's Digest", "Maclean's Mag." etc.; author of: "People of the Deer", 1951; rec'd. Pres. Medal, Univ. of W. Ont. for best short story publ. by a Candn. in 1950; "The Regiment" (story of a Candn. Inf. Regt. in World War II), 1955; "Lost in the Barrens", 1956

(Gov. Gen. Award for Juvenile Lit.); "The Dog Who Wouldn't Be", 1957; "The Grey Seas Under", 1958; "Coppermine Journey", 1958; "The Desperate People", 1959; "Ordeal by Ice", 1960; "Owls in the Family", 1961; "The Serpents Coil", 1961; "The Black Joke", 1962; "Never Cry Wolf", 1963; "Westviking", 1965; "Curse of the Viking Grave", 1966; "The Polar Passion", 1967; "Canada North", 1967; "The Rock Within the Sea" (with John de Visser), 1968; "Sibir", 1969; "The Boat Who Wouldn't Float", 1970 (winner 1970 Stephen Leacock Mem. Medal for Humour); "A Whale for the Killing" 1972; "Wake of the Great Sealers" (with David Blackwood) 1973; "The Snow Walker", 1975; "Canada North Now", 1976; "And No Birds Sing", 1979; "The World of Farley Mowat", 1980; served in 2nd World War, 1940-46 mostly with Hastings and Prince Edward Regiment (Infantry) as Platoon Commander and Intelligence Officer through Sicily, North West Europe; received Anisfield-Wolf Award 1953 for outstanding work in field of race relations; Address: Port Hope, Ont.

MOWLING, J. Keith; executive; b. Montreal, Que., 25 Apl. 1944; s. Robert Jack and Helen Lilias (Chalmers) M.; e. Lorne Park (Ont.) Pub. and High Schs., 1964; Waterloo Univ. Coll., 1964-65; m. Ruth Anne, d. late Walter Grierson, Waterloo, Ont., 11 Nov. 1967; children: Robert H. Stephen, Christine Anne; PRESIDENT, JOSIAH WEDGWOOD CANADA LTD. since 1973; joined Border Brokers Ltd. as Customs Rater, Halifax, 1965; joined father's co. Jacksons Chinaware Ltd. 1965, served in Sales, E. Can. (co. subsequently amalgamated with present cos.), served as Mgr. Toronto Sales, Montreal Sales and Atlantic Regional Mgr. 1968-73; Nat. Marketing and Sales Mgr., Wedgwood Ltd., March-Oct. 1973; Dir., Candn. Gift and Tableware Assn.; mem. Brit. Candn. Trade Associates; United Church; recreations: golf, hockey, home decorating, philately; Club: York Downs Golf; Home: 192 Church St. Markham, Ont. L3P 2M7; Office: 271 Yorkland Blvd., Willowdale, Ont. M2J 1S5

MOYLS, Benjamin Nelson, B.A., M.A., A.M., Ph.D.;educator; b. Vancouver, B.C. 1 May 1919; s. Benjamin James and Jessie Catherine (Walker) M.; e. Univ. of B.C. B.A. 1940, M.A. 1941; Harvard Univ. A.M. 1942, Ph.D. 1947; m. 1stly Ina Elizabeth Barbour (dec.); children: Gregory Nelson, Peter William; m. 2ndly Toby Claire d. Nathan Buller 7 May 1976; HEAD OF MATH. DEPT., UNIV. OF B.C. 1978- ; Professor of Math., 1959- ; joined Univ. as Lectr. 1947, Asst. Prof. 1948, Assoc. Prof. 1954, Asst. Dean of Grad. Studies 1967-76; R.C.N.V.R. 1943-45 (retired as Elect. Lt.; author various research papers in linear and multilinear algebra; mem. Candn. Math. Soc.; Amer. Math. Soc.; Math. Assn. of Amer.; Soc. for Industrial and Applied Math; Amer. Assn for the Advancement of Sci.; Anglican; recreations: music, swimming; Home: 2016 Western Parkway, Vancouver, B.C. V6T 1V5; Office: 1984 Mathematics Rd., Univ. of B.C., Vancouver, B.C. V6T 1Y4.

MOYSE, Robert Joseph, M.A.; industrial executive; b. Winnipeg, Man., 24 Jan. 1920; s. Joseph and Mae (Miles) M.; e. Univ. of Man., B.A.; Univ. of Toronto; Baillol Coll., Oxford Univ., B.A., M.A.; m. Caryl Joyce Ray, 10 March 1972; children: David, Stephen, Sarah; VICE-PRES., ALCAN ASIA AND SOUTH PACIFIC since 1976; with Dept. of Finance, Ottawa, 1948-51; Aluminium Securities 1951-58; Secy.-Treas., Indian Aluminium Co., 1958-60; Financial Dir. and Chief Financial Offr., Alcan Industries Ltd., London, Eng., 1960-63; Vice-Pres. and Treas., Aluminum Co. of Canada 1964-65; Vice-Pres. Finance, Domtar Ltd. 1966-74; Vice Pres. Alcan Internat. 1974-76; served as Lieut. with R.C.N.V.R. 1940-45; Anglican; Clubs: Bengal; St. James's; Home: 169 Chartwell Cres., Beaconsfield, Que. H9W 1C2; Office: 1 Place Ville Marie, Montreal, Que.

MROZEWSKI, Andrzej Henryk, M.A., M.L.S.; librarian; b. Paris, France, 25 Feb. 1930; s. Stefan and Irena (Blizinska) M.; e. High Sch. and Coll., Poland and France; Univ. de Montréal; M.A. (Slavic Studies) 1954; Univ. of Ottawa, B.L.S. 1960; McGill Univ., M.L.S. 1972; Ecole du Louvre, Paris; m. Janina, d. late Maj. Witold Karolewski, Poland, 21 Aug. 1954; children: Monika-Marta, André Witold Jr., Jan Stefan; CHIEF LIBRARIAN, LAURENTIAN UNIV. OF SUDBURY since 1972; Chief Librarian, Coll. de Rouyn, 1960-64; Med. Librarian (part-time), Hôpital Youville, Noranda, 1962-64; Head of Acquisitions, Univ. de Sherbrooke, 1964, Head, Tech. Services 1965-68, Asst. Chief Librarian 1965-71, Acting Chief Librarian 1970-71; mem. Comité de coordination de la documentation dans les univs. du Qué., 1966-71; Comité de coordination des bibliothèques univs. du Qué., 1967-71; Ont. Council Univ. Libraries since 1972 (Chrmn. 1974); Lectr. Lib. Sch. summers 1962-64 and in Polish Lit. summers 1961-62, Univ. of Ottawa; Commemorative Cross for service in Polish Underground W.W. II; Médaille d'argent de l'Univ. du Sherbrooke; publ. articles and notes in field of librarianship and papers on comparative lit., bibliog.and graphic art; Candn. Lib. Assn.; Candn. Assn. Coll. & Univ. Libs.; Assn. pour l'avancement des sciences et des techniques de la documentation (Pres., Sec. des bibliothéques univis., gouvernementales et spécialisées, 1967); Assn. des bibliothécaires du Qué. (Pres. 1967-68, Ed. Newsletter 1967-71); Corp. des bibliothécaires professionnels du Qué. (Dir. 1969-70); Polish Candn. Librairies Assn.; mem. Polish Combattants Assn. (S.P.K.); mem Adv. Comte., Library Technician Program, Cambrian College; Sec. Sudbury and District Minor Soccer. Assn.; R. Catholic; recreations: nature, photography, collecting prints and books; Home: 2107 Josephine, Sudbury, Ont. P3A 2N1

MUIR, Robert, banker; b. Co. Durham, Eng. 8 Feb. 1925; s. Robert and Margaret Miller (Ferguson) M.; e. Consett (Co. Durham, Eng.) Grammar Sch.; Univ. of Glasgow 1942-43; m. Stella Margaret d. Prof. E. A. Allcut, Beaconsfield, Que. 10 June 1950; children: Margaret, David, Peter, Alexander, Douglas, Stanley, Andrew; VICE PRES. AND SECY. BANK OF MONTREAL since 1973; joined present Bank 1948 serving Brs. Toronto, Vancouver, Saskatoon; Montreal and H.O., Secy. 1972; served with RNVR 1943-46, rank Sub-Lt.; Fellow, Inst. Bankers (London, Eng.); Fellow, Inst. Candn. Bankers; Affiliate, Inst. of Chartered Secretaries and Administrators, Cdn. Div.; mem. Amer. Soc. of Corp. Secretaries Inc.; Presbyterian; Club: Cercle de la Place d'Armes; Home: 57 Beaconsfield Court, Beaconsfield, Que. H9W 5G5; Office: 129 St. James St., Montreal; Que.

MUIR, Hon. Robert; senator; b. Edinburgh, Scot. 10 Nov. 1919; s. James and Helen (Clark) M.; e. Sydney Mines, N.S.; m. Mary Melina d. Angus King, Sydney Mines, N.S. 22 Feb. 1944; children: Robert Munro, Gary Stuart, Ruth Lenora; came to Can. 1921; served in coal mines at early age and seriously injured 1940; held numerous positions local union of Un. Mine Workers of Am. and el. as del. to 3 dist. conventions and 3 internat. conventions; joined London Life Insurance Co. as salesman 1949; Sales and Credit Mgr. Moores Electric, Sydney Mines 1953; Town Councillor Sydney Mines 1948-58; Dir. Harbour View Hosp. 1944-58, Pres. of Bd. 1951-57; Chrmn. Cape Breton Regional Hosp. Assn. 2 terms; el. to H. of C. g.e. 1957 (M.P. for Cape Breton N. and Victoria), re-el. to 1974 (constituency changed to Cape Breton The Sydneys 1967); Parlty. Observer to UN Gen. Assembly 1960 and mem. Candn. Del. 1979; Head Del. N. Atlantic Treaty Organ. Cong. Washington 1962; Candn. Del. to Internat. Labour Cong. Geneva 1966; Del. Inter-Parlty. Conf. New Delhi 1969, Bonn 1978, E. Berlin 1980; organized and headed del. 3 Mems. and Sens. to Vatican 1969; Del. Commonwealth Parlty. Assn. Assembly Sri Lanka 1974; Del. N. Atlantic Assembly Brussels 1976; named Hon. Grand Chief MicMac Tribe 1977; mem. All Party del. to Repub. of China (Taiwan) 1977 and People's Repub. of China 1978; former Vice Chrmn. P. Cons. Party Caucus Comte. on Labour; summoned to the Senate 1979; Hon. mem. B'nai Brith Confed. Lodge Ottawa; Dir. Candn. Council Christians & Jews; Hon. mem. Royal Candn. Legion; Sydney Mines Fire Dept.; mem. Nat. Press Club Can.; Candn. NATO Parlty. Assn.; Commonwealth Parlty. Assn. (Candn. Br.); Candn. Group Inter-Parlty. Union; Can.-U.S. Inter-Parlty. Group; Can.-Japan Friendship Assn.; Hon. Pres., Royal Cdn. Legion, Br. #8, Sydney Mines, N.S.; Mem., Can.-Korea Parliamentary Group; Can.-Israel Parliamentary Friendship Group; Can.-German Friendship Assn.; Can.-Europe Parliamentary Group; Dir., John G. Diefenbaker Memorial Fdn., Inc.; P. Conservative; Presbyterian; Club: Northern Yacht (Hon. mem.); Home: 107 Shore Rd., Sydney Mines, N.S. B1V 1A4: Office: The Senate, Ottawa, Ont. K1A 0A4.

MUIR, W. Wallace, B.A.; Canadian public servant; b. London, Ont., 28 Feb. 1916; s. Tena Ellen (Wallace) and late Harry Basil M.; e. Queen's Univ., B.A. 1938, postgrad. course in Indust. Relations; m. Isabel Bryson, d. late James Campbell Hope, Ottawa, Ont., 12 Aug. 1939; children: Sally (Mrs. C. H. Rannells), Gordon, Barbara (Mrs. S. van Schaik), Andrew; FED. DEPY. AUDITOR GENERAL since Aug. 1977; on grad. joined Kingston "Whig Standard" as Reporter: apptd. News Ed. 1939; following the War joined Ford of Can. Ltd.; apptd. Exec. Asst. to the Vice-Pres., Indust. Relations, 1948; trans. to Overseas Operations Div. as Gen. Organ. Planning Mgr. 1952; joined H. H. Popham & Co. Ltd., Ottawa, as Gen. Mgr., 1953; estbd. mgmt. consulting firm, 1955; became Dir., Personnel Services (Mgmt. Consulting Services Div.), Price Waterhouse & Co., 1962; Vice-Pres., Personnel & Indust. Relations, Hawker Siddeley Can. Ltd. 1964-69; joined fed public service as Asst. Depy Min., Mgmt Services, Dept of Supply and Services 1969-76; apptd Asst. Aud. Gen. 1976; served in 2nd World War; enlisted as Seaman, R.C.N.V.R. 1940; comsnd. overseas; served as Aircraft Direction Offr. on loan to R.N. with Home and Eastern Fleets; retired with rank of Lt. Commdr., Oct. 1945; mem. Bd. of Trustees, Queen's Univ.; served as Consultant, Royal Comm. on Govt. Organ.; former mem. Comte on Labour-Mgmt. Relations, Econ. Council of Can; former mem. Indust. Relations Comte., Can. Manufacturers Assn. Home: 201 Grandview Rd., Nepean, Ont. K2H 8B9; Office: 240 Sparks St., Ottawa, Ont. K1A 0G6

MULCAHY, Sean, B.A.; director; actor; b. Bantry, Republic of Ireland, 5 Sept. 1930; s. John and Mary (Barry) M.; e. The North Monastery, Cork; The Sch. of Art Cork; Univ. of Bristol, B.A.; Dir. and Teacher, Drama Div., Banff Sch. of Fine Arts (Sr. Drama Instr. & Dir. 1969-70); Former Dir. Citadel Theatre; Drama Dir. and Lectr. at Univs. of Toronto, N.B., Alta., W. Ont., McMaster and Ryerson Coll.; Artistic Advisor, Sudbury Theatre, Sudbury, Ont.; mem. Bd. Dirs., Theatre Canada; TV panelist on CBC and CTV; has performed on most maj. CBC TV and radio series since 1957 and for Nat. Film Bd. since 1958; Assoc. Dir., The Shaw Festival, 1963-65; Artistic Dir., Instant Theatre, Montreal, 1964-66; Dir., Beaverbrook Playhouse, Fredericton, 1966-67; Artistic Dir., Georgian Foundation for Performing Arts, Barrie, Ont. and The Press Theatre, St. Catharines, Ont. 1974-76; narrated and starred in "Horseman Pass By" (documentary film in Ireland for CBC's "Camera Canada"), 1965; Dir. "The Picture of Dorian Gray" (Columbia Pictures TV) 1974; served with RAF 1948-52; rank Flight Lt.; Silver Jubilee Medal 1977; mem., Assn. Candn. Television & Radio Artists (Vice-Pres. 1960-61); mem. of Bd., Assn. of Cdn. TV and Radio Artists 1978; Chrmn., ACTRA 1978; mem. Council, Cdn. Actors' Equity Assn. 1978; Edmonton Chamber of Comm.; Liberal; R. Catholic; recreations: rowing, travel, talking; Club: Arts and Letters; Variety; Celebrity (Toronto); Home: 140 Carlton St., Suite 401 Toronto, M5A 3W7; Office: C/O Canadian Actors Equity Assn., 64 Shuter St., Toronto, Ont.

MULHALL, Kenneth Stephen C.; financial consultant; b. Winnipeg, Man. 26 Oct. 1916; s. Stephen Clements and Blanche Ada (Miller) M.; e. Queen's Univ. 1938; Banff Sch. Advanced Mang. 1956; m. Jeanne Lorraine d. late Dr. B. Funk 31 Oct. 1942; two s. Stephen, Douglas; self-employed consultant since 1976; Dir. and mem. Audit Comte., Halifax Ind. Ltd.; Dir. and mem. and Vice Chrmn. HALCO Inc.; joined Royal Bank of Canada 1934-54; Secy.-Treas. Royalite Oil Co. Ltd. 1954-58; Sr. Vice Pres. and Treas. Petrofina Canada Ltd. 1958-76; served with RCAF 1942-46 overseas; P. Conservative; Protestant; recreations: golf, skiing; Clubs: Massawippi Country (Pres.); Ranchmen's (Calgary); Address: (P.O. Box 450), North Hatley Que. J0B 2C0

MULHERIN, James Kenneth Conrad, B.Sc. professional engineer; b. Grand Falls, N.B., 8 Feb. 1925; s. Herbert Louis and Gladys (Estey) M.; e. Univ. of New Brunswick B.Sc. (Civil Engn.) 1945; m. Shelagh Bâ by d. Leo Doheny; children: Jeffrey, Jennifer, Stephen, Cynthia, Andrea; PRESIDENT, C.E.O. AND DIRECTOR, MONENCO LTD.; Pres., Gen. Mgr. and Dir., Montreal Engineering Co. Ltd.; Chrmn. & Dir. SBR Offshore Ltd.; Pres. and Dir. Monenco Holdings Ltd.; Monenco Inc.; Monenco Ont. Ltd.; Vice Pres. and Dir. La Société d'Ingénerie Cartier Ltée.; Dir. Baymont Engineering Co.; Canamont Construction Inc.; Kaiser Engineers Power Corp.; London Monenco Consultants Ltd.; MHG International Ltd.; Monenco Consultants Ltd.; Saskmont Engineering Co. Ltd.; Canatom Inc.; Shawmont Newfoundland Ltd.; Chrmn. and Dir., Monenco Ireland Ltd.; Monenco Pipe Line Consultants Ltd.; R. Catholic; recreation: golf, gardening; Club: Rosemere Golf; Mount Stephen; Home: 184 Oriole St., Rosemere, Que. J7A 1B5; Office 2045 Stanley St., P.O. Box 6088 Station "A", Montreal P.Q. H3C 3Z8

MULHOLLAND, Robert David (Peter), D.C.L.; extve.; b. Peterborough, Ont., 28 Sept. 1904; s. late T. David and late Dora M. (Pack) M.; e. Schs. in Peterborough, Ont.; Trinity Coll. Sch., Port Hope, Ont.; Hon. D.C.L. Bishop's 1968; m. Jean Somerset Aikins, Winnipeg, Man., 1935; two s. and one d.; joined Bank of Montreal at Peterborough, Ont., 1923; Asst. Mgr., Main Br., Vancouver, B.C., 1946; Mgr. Main Br., Victoria, B.C., 1948, Ottawa, Ont., 1951, Montreal, Que., 1953; Asst. Gen. Mgr., Ont. Div., Toronto, 1955; Gen. Mgr., 1959; el. a Dir. and Vice Pres., 1960; Chief Gen. Mgr., 1964, Extve. Vice-Pres. and Chief General Manager, 1966; President 1967; Vice Chairman 1968-74; served with Cdn. Army 1941-45; D.A.Q.M.G. at Staff Coll., R.M.C. Kingston, Ont., May 1943-May 1944 when proceeded overseas; Pres., Candn. Bankers Assn., 1961-63; life mem., Bd. of Gov., Trinity Coll. Sch., Port Hope; Anglican; recreation: gardening, golf; Clubs: Mt. Royal; St. James's; York (Toronto); Home: 2352 Carrington Pl. Oakville, Ont. L6J 5P4

MULHOLLAND, William David, A.B., M.B.A., LL.D. (Hon.); banker; b. Albany, N.Y., 16 June 1926; s. William David and Helen (Flack) M.; e. Christian Brothers Academy, Albany, N.Y.; Harvard Coll.; Harvard Graduate School of Business Administration; m. Nancy Louise Booth, New Scotland, N.Y.; five s. and four d.; CHAIRMAN AND C.E.O., BANK OF MONTREAL since 1981, also Dir., Vice Chrmn. Extve. Comte.; Chrmn. Pension Adv. Comm.; and mem. Extve., Mang. Resources and Pension Adv. Comtes.; Vice Chrmn., Allgemeine Deutsche Credit-Anstalt (Frankfurt); Dir. & mem. Finance Comte., Kimberly-Clark Corp.; Dir. Standard Life Assurance Co. (Edinburg); Dir. & Chrmn. Incentive and Compensation Comte. and mem., Audit Comte., The Upjohn Co.; Dir., Bank of Montreal Internat. Ltd.; Bank of Montreal (Bahamas & Caribbean) Ltd.; Dir., Montreal Symphony Orchestra; joined investment banking firm of

Morgan Stanley & Co., New York, 1952, becoming a Partner in 1962; Pres. and Chief Extve. Offr. Brinco Ltd. and Chrmn. and Chief Extve. Offr., Churchill Falls (Labrador) Corp. Ltd. 1969; Pres., Chrmn. and C.E.O., Bank of Montreal 1974-81; served in 2nd World War 1944-46 in Philippine Islands as a Company Commander, 342nd Infantry; mem., Council on Foreign Relations; Candn. Econ. Policy Comte.; Candn. Comte. Pacific Basin Econ. Council; recreations: fishing, shooting, riding, hunting; Clubs: Mount Royal; Forest and Stream; Canadian; Lake of Two Mountains Hunt; Knowlton Golf; Toronto; Metropolitan (N.Y.); St. Denis; Home: 1296 Redpath Cres., Montreal, Que. H3G 2K1; Office: 129 St. James St., Montreal, Que. H2Y 1L6

MULLIE, Joseph Robert, B.A., M.B.A.; company extve.; b. Arborfield, Saskatchewan, 4 March 1931; s. Julien Alphonse and Marie-Louise (Duthoit) M.; e. Univ. of Ottawa, B.A. 1953; Univ. of W. Ont., M.B.A. 1957; m. Tillie Catherine, d. B. J. Klotz, Vibank, Sask., 25 Aug. 1956; children: Stephen, Adele, Christine, Jennifer, Paul; SR. VICE-PRES. AND GEN. MGR., VICKERS & BENSON LTD. since 1973; with the Southam Newspapers, Toronto, 1957-59; with Sptzer, Mills & Bates, Toronto and Montreal, 1959-72; Charter mem., Candn. Marketing Research Soc.; Am. Marketing Assn. (Past Dir.); R. Catholic; recreations: restoring antiques, vending; Home: 5 Breton Woods, Beaconsfield, Que. H9W 5A6; Office: 2055 Peel St., Montreal, Que. H3A 1V4

MULLINS, Stanley George, C.D., M.A.; educator; b. Bristol, Eng., 29 Aug. 1920; s. Frederick Albert and Daisy (Lewis) M.; e. Riverdale Coll. Inst., Toronto, 1933-38; Univ. of Toronto, Trinity Coll. B.A. 1943, M.A. 1947; Laval Univ., grad. studies 1948-51; , Carleton and Univ. of Ottawa, 1970-73; m. Leatha Elizabeth, d. Robert Young, Sault Ste. Marie, Ont., 18 Sept. 1943; children: Naomi, Mary-Elizabeth, Robert, John (d.); former Pres., Laurentian Univ. (1963-70), and Prof. of Eng. and Candn. Studies, there; current Dir. Theatre Arts Programme, Thorneloe Univ.; Lectr., Faculté des Lettres, Laval Univ. 1951; Head of Dept. of Eng., 1958; served with Irish Regt. of Can. in Can., Eng., Italy and N.W. Europe, 1942-46; Candn. Army Militia 1952-62; retired with rank Lt. Col.; apptd. Hon. Lt. Col. of 2nd Bn., Irish Regt. of Can., 1966; has lectured on Candn. lit. and culture in many European Univs.; Chrmn., Comte. on Adoptions and Foster Child Care (Ont. Govt.), 1968-70; Anglican; recreations: music, reading; Clubs: Royal Candn. Mil. Inst. (Toronto); Home: 628 Pleasant Pk. Rd., Ottawa, Ont. K1H 5N5

MULRONEY, M. Brian, B.A., LL.L., LL.D.; executive; b. Baie Comeau, Que. 20 March 1939; s. Benedict and Irene (O'Shea) M.; e. St. Francis Xavier Univ. B.A.; Univ. Laval LL.L.; L.L.D. (Hons) Memorial Univ.; St. Francis Xavier Univ.; m. Mila d. Dr. D. Pivnicki, Montreal, Que. 26 May 1973; children: Caroline Ann, Benedict Martin, Robert Mark; PRESIDENT AND DIR. IRON ORE CO. OF CANADA since 1977; Pres. & Dir. Quebec North Shore & Labradore Railway; Dir. United Provinces Insurance Co.; Qué. Telephone; Hollinger North Shore Exploration Ltd.; Can. Imp. Bank of Comm.; Provigo Inc.; Labrador Mining and Exploration Co. Ltd.; Hanna Mining Co.; Standard Broadcasting Corp.; CJAD Ltd.; T.I.W. Industries Ltd.; Ritz-Carlton Hotel Co. of Montreal Ltd.; called to Bar of Que. 1965; joined Ogilvy, Cope, Porteous, Montgomery, Renault, Clarke & Kirkpatrick remaining as Partner until 1976; apptd. to Cliche Royal Comn. 1974; joined present Co. as Extve. Vice Pres. Corporate Affairs 1976; Cand. for Nat. Leader P. Cons. Party Can. 1976; mem. Bd. of Gov., Concordia Univ. (Montreal); mem. Bd. of Govs. & Internat. Chrmn. Univ. Fund Raising Campaign, St. Francis Xavier Univ.; Chrmn. 1977 Centraide Campaign Greater Montreal; mem. Bar Prov. Que.; Candn. Bar Assn.; Conf. Bd. Can.; Conseil du Patronat; Mining Assn. Can.; Que. Metal Mining Assn.; mem. Extve. Comm., Cdn. Club; Trustee, Schenley Awards;

Conservative; R. Catholic; recreation: tennis; Clubs: Mount Royal; University; Garrison; Mount Royal Tennis; Albany; Home: 68 Belvedere Rd., Westmount, Que. H3Y 1P8; Office: 1245 Sherbrooke St. W.; Montreal, Que. H3G 1G8

MUMFORD,Ira Kidd; corporate executive; b. Mortlach, Sask. 6 Jan. 1920; e. Mortlach, Sask. Pub. and High Schs. 1937; Normal Sch. Moose Jaw 1937-38; Banff Sch. of Advanced Mang. 1961; m. Marjorie Louise Barron; four s. John Thrasher, David, Brian, Larry; SR. ADVISOR TO BOARD, SASK. WHEAT POOL 1981- ; Chmn., Western Co-operative Fertilizers Ltd.; 1st Vice Pres., CSP Foods Ltd.; Vice Chmn., Co-op. Energy Corp., mem. Operations Review Comte., Central Canada Potash; Crop Reporting and Grain Variety Testing, Sask. Wheat Pool 1938-40, Secu. Asst. 1945, Asst. Secy. 1958, Corporate Secy. 1964, Gen. Mgr. 1967-79, C.E.O. 1979-81; Dir., Banff Sch. Advanced Mang. 1965-71; Past Pres. Regina Br. Agric. Inst. Can. and Sask. Inst. Agrols.; mem. Un. Services Inst.; served with RCAF 1940-45, Pilot-Navig., Can.-U.K.-N. Africa-Italy, coastal and transport commands; Protestant; recreations: golf, skiing; Clubs: Regina Rotary; Wascana Golf & Country; Home: 20 Dunning Cres., Regina, Sask. S4S 3W1; Office: 2625 Victoria Ave., Regina, Sask. S4P 2Y6.

MUNCASTER, J. Dean, B.A., M.B.A., LL.D.; wholesaler; b. Sudbury, Ont., 23 Oct. 1933; s. W. Walter and Beatrice M. (Vance) M.; e. Sudbury (Ont.) High School; Univ. of W. Ont., B.A. (Business Adm.) 1956; Northwestern University, M.B.A. 1957; Laurentian Univ., LL.D. 1976; m. Evelyn; children: Robert Dean, Bernard Walter; PRESIDENT, C.E.O. AND DIR., CANADIAN TIRE CORPORATION LTD. (Estbd. 1927) since 1966; Vice-Pres. and Dir., Canadian Tire Acceptance Ltd.; Dir., National Trust Co. Ltd.; Black & Decker Mfg. Co. (U.S.); Royal Ins. Group; Consolidated Foods Corp., Chicago, Ill.; Bell Canada; joined present Corp. as Financial Analyst, Toronto, Ont., 1957; Retail Store Mgr., Sudbury, Ont., 1960; Vice-Pres., Toronto, 1963; Dir. and mem. Extve. Comte., Retail Council of Canada; mem., Adv. Bd., Univ. Western Ont. Bus. Sch.; Young Presidents Organ.; Un. Church; recreations: skiing, sailing; Clubs: York; Granite; Caledon Ski; Home: 338 Douglas Dr., Toronto, Ont. M4W 2C4; Office: 2180 Yonge St., Toronto, Ont. M4P 2V8

MUNDELL, David Walter, Q.C., B.A., LL.B., B.C.L.; b. Moosomin, Sask., 2 July 1914; s. David and Stella Mildred (Reany) M.; e. Public Sch., Moosomin, Sask.; Univ. of Sask., B.A., LL.B.; Oxford Univ., B.C.L.; called to Bar of Sask. 1939, and of Ont. 1953; cr K.C. 1949; mem. of legal staff, Dept. Justice, in litigation, legislative drafting and adv. divns., Ottawa 1939-53; seconded as Solr. to the Treasury, Dept. Finance, 1947-49; Sr. Counsel, Dept. Justice, 1950; mem. firm of Manning, Mortimer, Mundell & Reid, Toronto, Ont., 1953; Prof. Osgoode Hall Law School, 1959-69, teaching constit. law, adm. law and leg.; Asst. to Commr. Hon. J. C. McRuer on Royal Comn. "Inquiry into Civil Rights" 1964-69; joined staff of Min. of Atty.-Gen., Ont., 1969; Counsel, Constit. Law, Civil Br., until retirement 1980; author of various legal articles relating to constit. and adm. law, and Crown problems; Presbyterian; Home: 18 Boulton Dr., Toronto, Ont. M4V 2V4

MUNDY, David Beatty, B.Com.; executive; b. Edmonton, Alta., 20 Aug. 1919; s. Christopher Gordon and Irene (Tardrew) M.; e. Public and High Sch., Edmonton, Alta.; Univ. of Alberta, B.Com. 1940; m. Denise Michell Shirley, d. late Capt. Desmond FitzHarry Dolphin, R.N., 29 May 1943; children: Roderick David, Louise Anne, John Michell, Georgina Denise; joined Trade Commr. Ser., Dept. of Trade & Comm., 1945; Asst. Trade Commr., Liverpool, Eng., 1946-48; Comm. Secy., Candn. Leg., Stockholm, 1948-49; on loan to Dept. of Fisheries as

Chief Statistician, Vancouver, B.C., 1949-50; on loan to Dept. of Defence Production as Special Asst. to Co-ordinator of Production, 1951-53; Production Adviser to Candn. Del. to N.A.T.O., Paris, 1954-55; joined Dept. of Defence Production as Dir., Ammunition Br., Nov. 1955; apptd. Assoc. Dir., Electronics Br., Apl. 1956; Dir., Aug. 1956; Asst. Depy. Min. 1962; Asst. Depy. Min., Depts. Defence Production & Industry 1963; Asst. Depy. Min (External Services) Dept. Industry, Trade & Comm. 1968; Pres. Air Industries Assn. of Can. 1970-79; served in 2nd World War; enlisted as 2nd Lieut., 5 July 1940 with Loyal Edmonton Regt.; served Overseas in U.K., France, Belgium, Holland and Germany, 1941-45; retired to Reserve with rank of Capt.; Kappa Sigma; Anglican; recreations: skiing, canoeing, sailing; Club: Rideau; Home: Oakley Farm, R.R. #3, Carp. Ont. K0J 1L0;

MUNRO, Alice; writer; b. Wingham, Ont., 10 July 1931; d. Robert Eric and Anne Clarke (Chamney) Laidlaw; e. Wingham (Ont.) Pub. and High Schs.; Univ. of W. Ont.; m. James Armstrong Munro, 29 Dec. 1951, divorced 1976; children: Sheila, Jenny, Andrea; m. 2ndly, Gerald Fremlin, 1976; author, "Dance of the Happy Shades", 1968 (winner Gov.-Gen.'s Award for Lit., 1968); "A Place For Everything", 1970; "Lives of Girls and Women", 1971; (Candn. Booksellers Award 1971); "Something I've Been Meaning to Tell You", 1974.; Winner, Canada-Australia Literary Prize. c/o Writers' Union of Canada, 24 Ryerson St., Toronto, Ont.

MUNRO, Charles Graham; retired farmer; b. Embro, Ont., 13 Jan. 1916; s. John William and Lillian Mabel (McKay) M.; e. Embro Public Sch., Cont. Secondary Sch.; m. Janet Grace, d. William L. Sutherland, 9 June 1943; children: Mary Elizabeth, John William, Fred Sutherland; Pres., Ornum Farms Ltd.; Bd. Trustees, Ont. Sci. Centre; mem. Adv. Comm., Can. Livestock Feed Bd.; Pres., Candn. Fed. of Agric., 1969-77; Past Pres., Co-Operators Ins. Assn., Guelph, Ont.; Pres. & Dir., S. Easthope Mutual Ins. Co., Tavistock, Ont.; Past Dir., Co-Operator (Nat.); Past Pres., Internat. Fed. of Agric. Producers, Paris, France; past Dir., Can. Grain Council, Winnipeg; Dir. Adv. Comte., Can. Farm Credit Corp.; Past Pres., Ont. Fed. of Agric.; Oxford Co. Soil & Crop. Assn.; Oxford Co. Holstein Breeders' Club; West Zorra & Embro Agric. Soc.; Past mem. Ont. Economic Council; Can. Science Council; Brit.-N.Am. Comte., Washington; C.S.M., Oxford Rifles; Laymen., Law Soc. Council of Ont.; Freemason (P.M.); Presbyterian; Address: R.R. 1, Embro, Ont. N0J 1J0

MUNRO, Charles James; manufacturer; b. Hamilton, Ont. 20 Dec. 1925; s. Alexander Lindsay and Isabella Miller (McInnes) M.; e. Westdale Coll. Inst. Hamilton 1944; McMaster Univ. 1945-47; m. Margaret Frances d. Roderick Ashley 7 Feb. 1948; four d. Gail, Mary, Cathy, Jean; PRES., INTERNATIONAL HARVESTER CANADA LMITED since 1979; Dir. Pacific Truck & Trailer Ltd.; International Harvester Credit Corporation of Canada Limited; Salesman present co. 1948, Asst. Dist. Mgr. Agric. Ottawa 1954, Edmonton 1956, Hamilton 1958, Dist. Mgr. Hamilton 1959, Mgr. Tractor Sales (Can.) 1962, Agric. & Indust. Sales 1965, Mgr. Agric. Marketing Burlington 1973; served with RCAF 1944-45; Dir., Motor Vehicle Mfrs. Assn.; Candn. Farm & Indust. Equipment Inst.; 4-H Council of Canada; Junior Achievement of Hamilton; Ryerson (Elder)United Church; recreations: golf, curling; Clubs: Dundas Valley Golf & Curling; Rotary Ancaster; Hamilton Golf & Country; Hamilton; Home: 9 Postans Path, Ancaster, Ont. L9G 3P8; Office: 208 Hillyard St., Hamilton, Ont. L8N 3S5.

MUNRO, Donald Wallace, M.A., M.P.; b. Regina, Saskatchewan, 8 April 1916; s. Fenton and Nellie (Ellis) M.; e. Model Sch., Regina; Lord Byng High Sch., Vancouver; Univ. of B.C., B.A. (Hons. French) 1938; Teaching Cert. 1939; awarded French Govt. Scholarship for study at Sorbonne, 1939; Univ. of Toronto, M.A. 1946; m. Evelyn May, d. late Capt. Arthur and Louise Secombe, Cape Town, S. Africa, 7 Sept. 1944; High Sch. Teacher, Coquitlam, B.C. 1939-40; joined Dept. of Ext. Affairs, 1946; served in Paris 1947-49; Ankara 1949-51; Dublin 1954-55; Brussels 1955-57; Beirut 1960-63; Head of Candn. Del., Internat. Supervisory Comn., Vientiane, Laos, 1964-65; Nat. Defence Coll., Kingston, 1965-66; Advisor to Candn. Del., XIVth Session, Gen. Assembly UNESCO 1966; Acting Head, Cultural Affairs Div., Ottawa, 1967; Head, Commonwealth Div., 1967-68; Ambassador to Costa Rica, Nicaragua, Honduras, El Salvador and Panama, 1968-71; Foreign Service Visitor, Centre for Pol. Studies, Dalhousie Univ. 1971-72; el. M.P. for Esquimalt-Saanich Oct. 1972; re-el. since; served in 2nd World War, RCAF (F'Lt.) Nav. 1940-45; N., E. and S. Africa — Coastal Command and Instr.; mem., Candn. Inst. Internat. Affairs; Monarchist League; Roy. Commonwealth Soc.; R.U.S.I.; P. Conservative; recreations: reading, history, philosophy, philately, cartography; Club: University; Home: 5035 Lochside Dr., Victoria, B.C.; Office: House of Commons, Ottawa, Ont. K1A 0A6

MUNRO, Hon. John, P.C., M.P.; b. Hamilton, Ont., 16 March 1931; s. late Katherine Alexander (Carr) and late John Anderson M.; e. Westdale Composite, Hamilton, Ont.; Univ. W. Ont.; Osgoode Hall, Toronto, Ont.; m. Dr. Lily, Oddie, Hamilton; three children, Susan, Ann, John Jr.; read law with J. Bowlby; called to the Bar of Ontario 1956; entered law practice under the name of Munro and Munro, 1956; joined in partnership, John Pelech, 1958; Alderman, Hamilton City Council, 1955; el. to H. of C. in g.e.1962; re-el. since; former Parlty. Secretary to Minister of Citizenship & Immigration (1963); served in similar capacity with Mins. of Nat. Health & Welfare, Trade & Comm., and Manpower & Immigration; apptd. Min. Without Portfolio, 1968; Min. of Health and Welfare, 1968; Min. of Labour 1972-78; Min. of Indian Affairs and Northern Development 1980; Past Chairman, Hamilton Transport, Traffic Committee; Hamilton Beach Committee; mem., Canadian Institute of Internat. Affairs; Liberal; Anglican; Clubs: Lawyers' (Hamilton); Glendale Golf & Country (Hamilton); Home: Hamilton, Ont.; Office: 407 Confederation Block, Ottawa, Ont. K1A 0Z2

MUNRO, John McCulloch, B.A.; insurance executive; b. Toronto, Ont., 27 Sept. 1913; s. late Archibald and late Margaret (McCulloch) M.; e. Jarvis Coll. Inst., Toronto; Queen's Univ., B.A. (Jenkins Trophy); Univ. of Toronto, Post-grad. studies; m. Bette M., d. C. R. Gilmour, 24 May 1941; children: Michael John, Brian, Elizabeth Ann (Mrs. J. M. Piggott III); SR. VICE-PRES. AND DIR. OF AGENCIES, THE CANADA LIFE ASSURANCE CO., since 1976; joined present Co. as Salesman, 1946; Mgr., Field Training and Research, 1951; Mgr., Toronto Bayview Br., 1953; Asst. Supt. of Agencies H.O., April 1957 and of Ont. Brs., Dec. 1957; Agency Supt. 1960; Supt. of Agencies 1962; Dir. of Agencies, Canada, 1965; Vice-Pres. and Assoc. Dir. of Agencies, 1968; apptd. mem., Mang. Comte., Canada Life 1968; Vice Pres. and Dir. of Agencies 1969; served with Candn. Grenadier Guards during World War II; rank Maj.; Past Trustee, Candn. Schenley Football Awards; former Candn. Prof. Football League player with Toronto Argonauts; former Sr. Field Official, Candn., Football League; Chrmn. Bd., Life Ins. Marketing and Research Assn. 1975-76; Chrmn., Agency Offrs. Round Table, L.I.M.R.A., 1974-75; Candn. Comte., L.I.M.R.A.; Past Chrmn., Extve. Comte., Sr. Marketing Offrs. Sec., Candn. Life Ins. Assn.; mem., Pedlars; Life Underwriters Assn. Can.; Bd. Trade Metrop. Toronto; Clubs: Rosedale Golf; Granite; Empire; Argonaut "A"; Pedlars (N.Y.); Home: 30 Glengrove Ave. W., Toronto, Ont. M4R 1N6; Office: 330 University Ave., Toronto, Ont. M5G 1R8

MUNRO, June E., B.J., M.L.S.; librarian; b. Echo Bay, Ont. 20 June 1921; d. late Neil and late Agnes (MacLeod)

M.; e. Sault Ste. Marie (Ont.) Coll. Inst. 1939; Carleton Univ. B.J. 1961; Univ. of Toronto B.L.S. 1962, M.L.S. 1972; DIR. OF LIB. SERVICES, ST. CATHARINES PUB. LIB. 1973- ; Head, Children's Lib. Services Sault Ste. Marie Pub. Lib. 1941-51; Children's Librarian;, London Pub. Lib. 1951-53; Head Children's Lib. Services Leaside Pub. Lib. 1953-56; Asst. to Extve. Dir. and Publs. Production Ed. Candn. Lib. Assn. 1956-61; Supvr. Extension Service and Ed. "Ontario Library Review", Ont. Prov. Lib. Service 1961-70; Book Acquisition Adv., Coll. Bibliocentre, Toronto 1970-72; Chief, Pub. Relations Div. Nat. Lib. of Can. 1972-73; mem. Bd. Trustees, Carousel Players St. Catharines; rec'd Librarian of Yr. Award Ont. Lib. Trustee Assn. 1971; author various publs.; mem. Am. Lib. Assn.; Candn. Lib. Assn.; Ont. Lib. Assn.; Council Adms. Large Urban Pub. Libs.; Chief Extves. Large Pub. Libs, Ont.; Protestant; recreations: dance, theatre; Clubs: St. Catharines Golf & Country; University Women's; Home: Apt. 710, 35 Towering Hts., St. Catharines, Ont. L2T 3G8; Office: 54 Church St., St. Catharines, Ont. L2R 7K2

MUNRO, Lloyd Alexander, M.A., Ph.D., F.R.S.C., F.C.I.C.; emeritus prof.; b. Toney Mills, N.S., 10 Jan. 1899; s. Henry Dan and Jessie Ann (MacKenzie) M.; e. Dalhousie Univ., 1921, M.A. 1922; McGill Univ., Ph.D. 1925 (Nat. Research Council Bursary Scholar. and Fellowship 1922-25); m. Della May, d. Rev. J. R. Douglas, 27 Dec. 1930; one s., Douglas; Asst. Prof. of Chem., Univ. of Man., 1925-29; Queen's Univ., 1929-38; Assoc. Prof., 1938-45; Prof. 1945-67; served in World War, 1917-19, with Candn. Engrs. (Signals); 2nd World War with P.W.O.R. (M.G.) in Reserve Army with rank of Capt.; Chem. research for Dept. Nat. Defence 1940-45; mem. Adv. Bd., former journ. "Candn. Chem. and Process Industries"; Hon. Ed., "Chem. Inst. News"; mem. Ed. Bd., "Chemistry In Can." 1959-64; author of chemical research papers "Chemistry in Engineering" (10th printing 1973); "Quimica en Ingenieria (5th printing 1981); "Hemija U Tehnici" (3rd reprint 1974); awarded Centennial Medal; Freemason; 32° AASR; United Church; Home: 93 Beverley St., Kingston, Ont. K7L 3Y7

MUNRO, (Robert) Ross, O.C. (1975), O.B.E., LiH.D; newspaperman; 3rd generation of the family in Candn. newspaper work; b. Ottawa, Ont., 6 Sept. 1913; s. James Ross and Ann (Cobean) M.; e. Humberside Collegiate Institute, Toronto; University of Toronto, Hons. in Political Science and Economics, 1936; m. Helen-Marie, d. late Cecil L. Stevens, Dunnville, Ont., 8 May 1943; one d., Ann; PRES., THE CANADIAN PRESS, 1974-76 and 1978-79; Dir., Dominion Life Ins. Co.; Reporter and editor with CP Toronto, Ottawa, Winnipeg, Montreal, N.Y. and Wash.; European Corr. of Candn. Press, 1945-47; joined Southam Newspapers 1948, and assigned to Ottawa Bureau of Southam News Services; joined Vancouver Province, 1951, as Asst. to Publisher; apptd. Ed.-in-Chief, 1955; Asst. Publisher and Ed.-in-Chief, 1957; Publisher, "Winnipeg Tribune", 1959-65; Publisher, "The Canadian Magazine", Toronto, 1965-68; Publisher, Edmonton Journal, 1968-76; Publisher, Gazette, Montreal, 1976-79 (retired); served with Canadian Militia as 2nd Lieut., 1939-40; Hon. Col. 20th Field Regt. RCA, Edmonton 1971-74; with Canadian Army overseas as War Corr. 1940-45; accompanied Canadian troops on landings in Spitzbergen, Dieppe, Sicily, Italy and Normandy; author of "Gauntlet to Overlord", 1945; Home: R.R. 1, Loretto, Ont. L0G 1L0

MUNRO, William G., B.Com.; insurance executive; b. Toronto, Ont. 9 July 1926; s. late H. Elmer and late Hazel (Gourlay) M.; e. Univ. of Toronto B.Com. 1949; m. Mary Patricia d. late George D. Fleming, Owen Sound, Ont. 25 June 1949; one s., two d.; PRESIDENT AND DIR. THE IMPERIAL LIFE ASSURANCE CO. OF CANADA since 1977; Dir. Victoria & Grey TRUSTCO Ltd.; Victoria & Grey Trust Co.; Laurentiann Mutual Ins.; Northern Life Assurance Co. Can.; joined H.O. Imperial Life 1949,

Asst. Treas. 1959, Assoc. Treas. 1964, Asst. to Adm. Vice Pres. 1967, Extve. Offr.-Adm. 1969, Adm. Vice Pres. 1971, Extve. Vice Pres. 1974; Fellow, Life Office Mang. Inst.; Dir., Can. Life and Health Ins. Assn. Inc.; mem. Bd. of Govs. St. Andrew's Coll,. (Aurora, Ont.); Vice Pres., Greater Toronto Region, Boy Scouts of Can.; Dir., Multiple Sclerosis Soc. of Can.; United Church; recreations: Tennis, squash; Club: Badminton & Racquet; Home: 27 Oriole Rd., Toronto, Ont.; Office: 95 St. Clair Ave. W., Toronto, Ont. M4V 1N7

MUNROE, Eugene G., M.Sc., Ph.D., F.E.S.C., F.R.E.S., F.R.S.C. (1966); Self-emp. consultant and research scientist; b. Detroit, Michigan, 8 Sept. 1919; s. Donald Gordon and Helen Grace (Carroll) M.; e. Westmount (Que.) High Sch.; McGill Univ., B.Sc. 1940, M.Sc. 1941; Cornell Univ., Ph.D. 1947; m. Isobel Margaret, d. David Douglas, Toronto, Ont., 1944; children: Janet Gordon (Wilson), Donald Douglas (deceased), Susan Margaret, Elizabeth Anne; Research Assoc. Biosystematics Research Inst., Canada Dept. of Agric.; Research Commr., Internat. Comn. on Zool. Nomenclature, 1963-75; Lecturer and Research Assistant, Institute of Parasitology, Macdonald College, Quebec, 1946-50; Research Scientist, Canada Dept. of Agric., 1950-65, 1968-79; Taxonomy Sec., Entom. Research Inst. 1962-65; Science Adviser, Science Secreatriat, Privy Council Office, 1965-67; Princ. Scient. Adv. and Head of Studies, 1967-68; Visiting Prof., Univ. of Cal., Berkeley, 1960-61; Hon. Lectr., Carleton Univ., Ottawa, 1966; served with R.C.A.F. 1942-45, rank Flying Offr.; Dir. Wedge Entomol. Research Foundation since 1974; Vice pres. & Mang. Dir., 1979- ; Chrmn. Bd. of Eds. "The Moths of America North of Mexico"; Ed., "The Canadian Entomologist", 1957-60; author of some 250 scient. papers and books; mem., Entom. Soc. Am.; Entom. Soc. Can. (Past Pres.); Entom. Soc. Ont.; Entom. Soc. Que.; Lepidopterists' Soc. (Past Pres. and Hon. mem.); Assn. Tropical Biol.; Soc. Hosp. Lus Am. de Lepidopterol. (Socio de Hon.); Prof. Inst. Pub. Service Can. (Past Dir.); Am. Assn. Advanc. Science; Candn. mem., Standing Comte. on Pacific Entom., Pacific Science Assn.1947-65; Sigma Xi; Anglican; Home: Granite Hill, R. R. #2 Dunrobin, Ont. K0A 1T0; Office: Biosystematics Research Institute, Agriculture Canada, Central Experimental Farm, Ottawa, Ont. K1A 0C6

MURASUGI, Kunio, D. Sc., F.R.S.C.; educator; b. Tokyo, Japan 25 March 1929; s. Kiyoshi and Torae (Nakatani) M.; e. Tokyo Higher Normal Sch. 1949; Tokyo Univ. of Educ. B.Sc. 1952, D.Sc. 1961; Univ. of Toronto M.Sc. 1961; m. Yasue d. late Jisuke Kuwahara 30 Oct. 1955; children: Chieko Wright, Kumiko, Sachiho; PROF. OF MATH. UNIV. OF TORONTO 1969- ; Research Assoc. Princeton Univ. 1962-64; Asst. Prof. Univ. of Toronto 1964, Assoc. Prof. 1966; Visiting mem. Inst. Advanced Study Princeton 1974; Visiting Prof. Univ. of Southwestern La. 1978; Tsukuba Univ. Japan 1979; author "On Closed 3-Braids" 1974; various articles learned journs.; Ed. "Canadian Journal of Mathematics" 1969-71; mem. Candn. Math. Soc.; Am. Math. Soc.; Japanese Math. Soc.; Anglican; recreation: go (Japanese game); Home: 611 Cummer Ave., Willowdale, Ont. M2K 2M5; Office: 100 St. George St., Toronto, Ont. M5S 1A1.

MURCHIE, William Thomson, company executive; b. Ayr, Scotland, 9 July 1916; s. William Thomson and Ruby Lilburn (Martin) M.; e. (came to Canada 1920) N. Toronto Coll. Inst.; War Staff Coll., Royal Mil. Coll., Kingston, Ont.; Harvard Grad., Sch. of Business Adm., AMP 1964; m. Merle Irene, d. George A. McGregor, 15 March 1941; two d., Margaret, Marion; Dir., Magic Pantry Foods Ltd.; Pet Milk Canada Ltd.; Corp. Foods Ltd.; Chrmn. Bd., United Biscuits (Can.) Ltd.; Mgr., London & Western Trusts, Windsor, Ont. 1938-40; Secy. Treas., Marshalls Co. Ltd., Toronto, 1945-48, Gen. Mgr., 1948-56, Vice-Pres. and G.M. 1956-59; apptd. Vice-Pres. and Gen. Mgr. of Pet Milk Co. Ltd., 1959; Pres. and Dir., 1961-68; served

in 2nd World War; Staff Capt. R.C.A. 2nd Candn. Div.; Past Dir., Nat. Dairy Council; Past Chrmn., Candn. Produce Council; Dairy Poultry Br., Toronto Bd. Trade; Poultry Products Inst.; Past President, Eglinton Riding, Progressive Conservative Association; Gov., Canadian Corp. Commrs.; Pres., Travellers Aid Soc.; mem., Royal Candn. Mil. Inst.; Freemason; P. Conservative; recreations: golf, swimming, skiing; Clubs: Roy. Candn. Military Inst.; Board of Trade; Home: 477 Oriole Pkwy., Toronto, Ont. M5P 2H9

MURPHY, Arthur Lister, B.A., M.D., C.M., LL.D., F.A.C.S. (1937); surgeon; author; b. Dominion, N.S., 8 Feb. 1906; s. George Henry and Helena (Macneil) M.; e. Dalhousie Univ., B.A. 1926, M.D., C.M. 1930; Post-Grad., Montreal Gen. Hosp.; m. Mary Sylvia, d. H. B. Shore, Halifax, N.S., 1932; children: Joanne, Arthur L., Paul M.; m. Barbara McIver, 1978; PROF. DEPT OF THEATHRE, DALHOUSIE UNIV. 1977- ; Consultant Surgeon, Victoria Gen. Hosp., and Halifax Infirmary, Halifax, N.S.; Chrmn., N.S. Univ. Grants Comte. till 1974; Adv. in Higher Educ. to N.S. Govt. 1974-77; Fellow, Am. Assn. for the Surg. of Trauma; Past Pres., Halifax Med. Soc.; N.S. Med. Soc.; mem., Candn. Med. Assn.; Phi Rho Sigma; author: "The Story of Medicine", and various scient. papers, essays, plays and other fiction; Founding Pres., Neptune Theatre Foundation; rec'd. Malcolm Honor Award; Can. Drama Award; Conservative; Roman Catholic; Club: St. Margaret Sailing; Dalhousie Faculty; Royal N.S. Yacht Squadron; Home: Whynacht, Point, Tantallon, N.S. B0J 3J0, and Apt. 1, 1991 Prince Arthur St., Halifax, N.S. B3H 4H2

MURPHY, Charles Terrence, Q.C., M.P., B.A.; judge; b. Sault Ste. Marie, Ont., 19 Oct. 1926; s. Charles Joseph and Monica (Walsh) M.; e. Sault Ste. Marie (Ont.) Coll. Inst., 1943; Assumption Coll.; Univ. of W. Ont. B.A. 1946; Osgoode Hall Law Sch.; m. Dorothy Anne, d. Lloyd Jenkins, 30 Aug. 1952; children: Sean Terrence, Karen Anne, Mary Lynn, Michaela Marie, Timothy Robert; DIST. COURT JUDGE, DIST. OF MANITOULIN 10 July 1980- ; called to Bar of Ont. 1949; cr. Q.C. 1960; Ald., Ward One, Sault Ste. Marie City Council, 1965-66; el. M.P. for Sault Ste. Marie in g.e. 1968; Past Pres., N. Atlantic Assembly; mem. Bd. Trustees, Un. Appeal (Campaign Chrmn. 1967); mem., Candn. Bar Assn.; R. Catholic; recreations: golf, swimming, curling; Club: Kiwanis (Hon. mem.); Home: 159 Pointe Louise Dr., Sault Ste. Marie, Ont.; Office: Judge's Chambers, Court House, 155 Elm St. W., Sudbury, Ont. P3C 1T9

MURPHY, David Knox; manufacturer; b. Winnipeg, Man. 26 Jan. 1917; s. William Wallace and Edith (Simpson) M.; e. Public Sch. Winnipeg; St. Johns Coll.; Univ. of Man.; m. Margaret McCracken 14 June 1941; children: Kenneth W., David R., Margaret E.; VICE CHRMN. AND DIR., BARBECON INC. since 1978; joined Barber-Ellis as Clerk, Winnipeg 1934, Sales Regina, Sask. 1938, Ottawa 1942, Br. Mgr. Winnipeg 1950, Vancouver 1955, Extve. Vice-Pres. 1972, Pres. 1974, Barbecon Inc. became the Corp. offices 1978; mem. Envelope Makers Inst. of Can.; Candn. Paper Trade Assn.; Bd. Trade Metrop. Toronto; United Ch.; recreations: golf, bridge; Clubs: Toronto Hunt; Granite; Home: 109 Cheltenham Ave., Toronto, Ont. M4N 1R1; Office: 2300 Yonge St., Ste 1900, Box 2406, Toronto, Ont. M4P 1E4

MURPHY, J. Elmer; retired newspaper publisher; b. Summerside, P.E.I., 27 Jan. 1914; s. late Patrick Alphonsus and Josephine Frances (Power) M.; e. Summerside High Sch. 1930; St. Dunstan's Univ. 1930-32; m. Mary Pearl, d. late Daniel F. McNeill, 7 Oct. 1947; children: Mary Maureen, John Michael; RETIRED PUBLISHER, THE JOURNAL-PIONEER; Summerside Citizen of the Year 1970; mem. Candn. Mang. Eds. Conf.; Candn. Daily Newspapers Assn.; R. Catholic; recreations: swimming, photography; Clubs: Rotary; Kinsmen (Life mem.); K. of

C. (Past Grand Kt.); Home: 186 Hanover St., Summerside, P.E.I. C1N 1E6; Office: Water at Queen Sts., Summerside, P.E.I.

MURPHY, Kenneth Wallace; director; b. Hamilton, Ont., 22 May 1906; s. William Wallace and Edith Helen (Simpson) M.; e. St. Johns Coll., Winnipeg, Man., 1924; m. Helen Edith, d. late George Shield, 8 June 1935; Dir. Barber-Ellis of Canada Ltd.; W. V. Dawson Ltd.; Gage Envelopes Ltd.; Munn Envelopes Co. Ltd.; Anglican; recreation: gardening; Clubs: Granite; National; Engineers (Montreal); Brantford (Ont.) Golf & Country; Rotary; Toronto Hunt; Home: 79 Highland Ave., Toronto, Ont. M4W 2A4

MURPHY, Sean Buller, S.B., M.D., C.M.; ophthalmologist; b. London, Eng., 25 Jan. 1924; s. late John Joseph Aloysius and late Cecil Tremaine (Buller) M.; e. Downside Sch., Stratton-on-the-Fosse, Eng.; Worcester (Mass.) Acad., 1940; Harvard Univ., S.B. 1943; McGill Univ., M.D., C.M. 1947; m. Elizabeth Anne, d. Hollis H. Blake, Westmount, Que., 8 Aug. 1950; children: Elizabeth Gaill, Brian Buller, Carolyn Anne; Intern, Royal Victoria Hosp. 1947-48; Attending staff 1955, Opthalmol. 1966, Opthalmologist-in-Chief 1970; research, Montreal Neurol. Inst., 1948-49; Asst. Resident 1950-52 and Resident 1952; Inst. of Ophthalmol., Presb. Hospital, New York; Asst. Prof., Dept. of Ophthalmol., McGill Univ., 1966; Assoc. Prof. 1970, Prof. and Chrmn. 1975; served with RCAF 1953-55; rank Wing Commander; Pres., The Montreal Museum of Fine Arts, 1968-79 (Councillor since 1959; Chairman Acquisition Committee since 1966; Vice President 1968-79; Hon. Pres. 1979); mem. Can. Council 1977-79, Extve Comte. 1978-79, Investment Comte. 1978-79, Council Rep. to Arts Panel 1978-79; Chrmn., Nat. Museums of Can. 1979; writings include several articles for prof. journals; mem., Candn. Med. Assn.; Que. Med. Assn.; Que. Fed. Specialists; Eye Study Club; Candn. Ophthalmol. Soc. (council mem. 1975-77; Pres. 1978); Que. Assn. Ophthalmol. (Extve. Comte. 1970-73; Pres. 1973-76); Montreal Ophthalmol. Soc.; Am. Acad. Ophthalmol. & Otolaryngol.; Candn. Museums Assn.; Am. Assn. Museums; mem. Order of Can. 1976; Queen's Jubilee Medal 1977; mem. Can. Council 1977-79; Zeta Psi; Alpha Kappa Kappa; Alpha Omega Alpha; R. Catholic; recreations: tennis, skiing, travel; Home: 578 Claremont Ave., Montreal, Que., H3Y 2P1; Office: 687 Pine W., Montreal, Que. H3A 1A1

MURRAY, Anne, O.C. (1974); singer; b. Springhill, Nova Scotia, 20 June 1945; d. James Carson, M.D. and Marion Margaret (Burke) M.; e. Springhill (N.S.) High Sch., 1962; Mount St. Vincent Coll., Halifax; Univ. of N.B., B.P.E. 1966; Univ. of N.B., D.Litt. (Hon.); taught phys. educ., Athena Regional High Sch., Summerside, P.E.I., 1966-67; entered full-time show business career 1967; named Top Candn. Female Vocalist of 1970 (R.P.M. Award); Top Candn. Female Entertainer of the Yr. 1970 (Candn. Press); Best Female Newcomer of the Yr. 1970-71 (Record World Mag., U.S.); Top Newcomer Female Vocalist of the Yr. 1970-80 (Cashbox Mag., U.S.); 1st Candn. female to win Gold Record in U.S., 1970; Juno Award (Canada's Top Female Vocalist) 1970-79; Grammy Award (U.S.) Best Female Vocal Performance (Country) 1974; incl. in Nashville's Country Music Hall of Fame "Walkway of Stars" 1974; Best Female Vocal Performance (Pop) 1978; Vanier Award, Outstanding Young Canadian; voted Cdn. Female Recording Artist of Decade by C.R.I.A. and C.A.R.A.S.; "own star" placed in Hollywood's "Walkway of Stars" June 1980; Grammy Award, Best Female Vocal Performance (country) 1980); Roman Catholic; first television special, "Anne Murray's Christmas Special" 1981; recreation: sports; Address: 2180 Yonge St., P.O. Box 18, Toronto, Ont. M4J 2B9

MURRAY, Charles Ivor, B.A.; investment executive; b. Charlottetown, P.E.I. 27 Jan. 1923; s. Frederick Carol and

Sara Eunice (Steeves)M.; e. Halifax public schools; Acadia Univ. B.A. (Economics & Maths.); m. Joan Elizabeth, of Robert W. Starr 25 June 1947; two s.: William and Colin; VICE-PRES., AND DIR. MIDLAND-DOHERTY LIMITED, Investment Dealers; Secretary, Cyrus Eaton, Otis & Co., Cleveland U.S.A., 1946-48; Research Asst., Invest. Dept., Sun Life Assurance Co. of Canada, Montreal 1948-50; Institutional salesman, Milis, Spence & Co., Montreal, Toronto and Kitchener, 1950-53; Nesbitt, Thomson & Co., Toronto, 1953-54, Asst. Mgr. 1954-57; Mgr. then successively Vice Pres. and Pres. New York 1957-64; V-Pres., Montreal, 1964-69; Pres., Canadian Depository for Securities, Toronto, 1969-71; Vice Pres., Midland-Doherty Ltd., since 1972; served with Candn. Army in Canada, North Atlantic Area and Overseas, 1942-45 with rank of Lieut.; mem., Toronto Soc. Financial Analysts, 1972; First Chrmn. of Bd., and one of Founders, Financial Research Institute; United Church; recreations: skiing, fishing, shooting; Home: 72 Prince George Dr., Islington, Ont. M9A 1Y6; Office: P.O. Box 25, Commercial Union Tower, Toronto-Dominion Centre, Toronto, Ont. M5K 1B5

MURRAY, John W., M.A., executive; b. London, Ont., Sept. 1920; s. K. D. and Mrs. H. S. (Simpson) M.; e. Public and High Schs., London, Ont.; Ridley Coll., St. Catharines, Ont.; Univ. of Western Ont., B.A., M.A.; m. Marion, d. D. F. Hassel, Oct. 1942; children: John, Kenneth, Anne; EXTVE. VICE PRES., INTERNATIONAL, LABATT BREWERIES CANADA LTD. since 1979; Dir., Labatt Breweries of Can. Ltd. Olands Breweries Ltd.; began with Hygrade Containers Limited, London, Ontario, 1946; Sales Manager, Hobbs Hardware Co., 1948; joined John Labatt Limited in Purchasing Department, 1956; Director of Purchasing, 1957, Export Sales Mgr., 1958; Vice-Pres. and Dir. of Marketing, Lucky Lager Breweries Ltd., Vancouver, B.C. 1958-61; Dir. of Marketing, John Labatt Limited, Ontario Div., Toronto, 1961-64; Pres., Labatt's Ontario Breweries Ltd., 1964-67; Vice-Pres., Planning & Devel., John Labatt Ltd., 1968-71; Vice President, Maritime Region, 1971-74; Vice Pres., Corp. Affairs, Labatt Breweries of Can., 1974-79; served in the 2nd World War with R.C.N. 1941-45; discharged with rank of Lieut.; Anglican; recreation: golf; Clubs: Lambton Golf; London Hunt & Country; The London (Ont.); Home: 1106 The Parkway, London, Ont. N6A 2X3; Office: 451 Ridout St., (P.O. Box 5050), London, Ontario, N6A 4M3

MURRAY, Kenneth Sherwood, B.A.; merchant; b. London; Ont., 3 June 1916; s. Kenneth Donald and Hazel Kirke (Simpson) M.; e. Pub. Schs., London, Ont.; Ridley Coll., St. Catharines, Ont.; Univ. of Western Ont., B.A. 1937, with Hons. in Business Adm.; m. Anne Elizabeth, d. Alexander Harvey of London, Ont., 1 June 1940; two d., Allison Ann, Martha Elizabeth; CHAIRMAN RUSE-TRAVEL AGENCY LTD.; since 1971 Pres. & Managing Dir., Hobbs Hardware Co. Ltd. 1960-71; mem. Extve. Comte., London Health Assn.; Past Pres. Boy Scouts Assn.; past mem., Bd. Govs. and Senate, Univ. of W. Ont.; Past Pres., Univ. of W. Ont. Great Artists Concerts; Past Pres., Can. Wholesale Hardware Assn.; Jr. Extve. with Murray Selby Shoe Co. London, Ont., 1937-42; served in World War, 1939-45, with C.O.T.C.; 1939-42, and Lieut., Roy. Candn. Navy, 1943-45; Freemason; Delta Upsilon; Conservative; Anglican; recreations: golf, hockey; Clubs: London Hunt and Country (Past Pres.); London; Home: 597 Cranbrook Rd., London, Ont.; Office: 463 Richmond St., London, Ont.

MURRAY, Sister M. Janet, B.A., LL.D.; health care executive; b. Toronto, Ont. 29 May 1915; d. Hugh Norman & Anne (Walke) Murray; e. Univ. of Toronto B.A. 1936, Post-grad. Dipl. in Hosp. Adm. 1955; Ont. Coll. of Educ. 1943; York Univ. LL.D. 1979; CHRMN. HEALTH SERVICES PLANNING COMTE., SISTERS OF ST. JOSEPH'S, TORONTO 1980- ; Admr., St. Michael's Hosp. Toronto 1956-63; Teacher, St. Joseph's High Sch. Islington 1963-

65, Vice Princ. 1965-67; Princ. St. Joseph's Morrow Park, Willowdale 1967-68; Exec. Dir., S. Joseph's Hosp. 1968-80; Chrmn. Bd. Dirs. Hosp. Purchasing Inc. 1978-80; Biomed. Engn. Shared Services 1976-80; Dir., St. Elizabeth Visiting Nurses' Assn. of Ont.; Catholic Health Conf. of Ont.; Home Care Program for Metro Toronto; mem. Sub-comte. on Bargaining, E.R.C.P. of the Ont. Hosp. Assn.; Consulting Assoc. Diversicare Corp., London Ont.; Life mem. St. Joseph's Health Centre Research Foundation; Charter (Founder) mem. Candn. Coll. of Health Service Execs.; Fellow Am. Coll. Hosp. Admin.; P. Conservative; R. Catholic; Address: 3377 Bayview Ave., Toronto, Ont. M2M 3S4.

MURRAY, Michael Joseph; executive; b. Renfrew, Ont., 6 Jan 1921; s. J. L. and Stella (O'Brien) M.; e. Separate and High Schs., Renfrew, Ont.; St. Michael's Coll., Toronto, Ont.; m. Joan, d. Richard Thomson, 23 June 1945; children: Brian, Virgina, Janet, Catherine, Mark, Robert; PRESIDENT AND DIR., M. J. O'BRIEN, LTD., since 1969; Pres. and Dir., Taiga Goose Resources Ltd.; Madawaska Investments Ltd.; Ottawa Uplands Ltd.; Chrmn., Dir., O'Brien Explorations Ltd.; Murvant Lottery Bond Ltd.; Dir., Carleton Tavern Ltd.; Air Canada; Horton Heights Developments Ltd.; R. Catholic; recreations: fishing, boating, antique and classic cars, music, sports; Clubs: Rideau; Royal Ottawa Golf; Britannia Yacht; Home: 24 Clemow Ave., Ottawa, Ont. K1S 2B2; Office: 803-90 Sparks St., Ottawa, Ont. K1P 5T6

MURRAY, Robert George Everitt, M.A., M.D., C.M., F.R.S.C. (1958); bacteriologist; university professor; b. Ruislip, Middlesex, Eng., 19 May 1919; s. Everitt George Dunne, O.B.E.; and Winifred Hardwick (Woods) M.; e. Summer Fields, Oxford, Eng., 1927-30; Lower Can. Coll., Montreal, Que., 1931-36; McGill Univ. (1936-38) and (1941-43), M.D., C.M.; Cambridge Univ., Eng., B.A. 1941 and M.A. 1945; m. Doris, d. late Richard Werner Marchand, 1944; two s. and one d.; PROFESSOR OF MICROBIOLOGY AND IMMUNOLOGY UNIV. OF W. ONT., since 1945; mem., Ed. Bd., "Microbiological Reviews" (formerly "Bacteriological Reviews") 1967-79 and Ed. 1969-79; mem., Gov. Bd. Biol. Council Can. 1966-72; Editor, "Canadian Journal of Microbiology", 1954-60; mem. of Ed. Bd., "Journal of Bacteriology", 1951-56; Lect., Dept. of Bacter. and Immunology, University of Western Ontario, 1945; Professor and Head of Dept. 1949-74; Acting Dean of Sci. 1973-74 Capt., R.C.A.M.C. 1944-45; mem., Candn. Pub. Health Assn. (Chrmn., Lab. Sec., 1951); Am. Soc. for Microbiol. (Vice-Pres. 1971-72, Pres. 1972-73); Candn. Soc. Microbiol. (Org. Chmn. 1951-52 and Pres. 1952-53); Soc. for Gen. Microbiol.; Cdn. and Amer. Socs. for Cell Biol.; Electron Microscope Soc. Am.; Pathol. Soc., Gt. Brit. and Ireland; rec'd Harrison Prize, Roy. Soc. Can., 1957; Fellow, Roy. Soc. Ca. 1958; Roy. Soc. Can. Travelling Award, 1961; Candn. Soc. Microbiols. Prize, 1963; Fellow, Am. Acad. of Microbiol. 1974; mem. Bd. of Govs. Am. Acad. of Microbiol. 1980-; mem., Bd. Trustees, Bergey's Manual Trust 1964, Chrmn. since 1976; recreation: fishing, flying; Address: London, Ont. N6A 5C1

MURRAY, Warren James, Ph.D.; educator; b. St. Paul, Minn. 3 Dec. 1936; s. James Bernard and Louise (Bilodeau-Robertson) M.; e. Wisc. State Univ. B.Sc. (Chem.) 1962; Univ. Laval B.Ph. 1964, B.Ph. 1965, Ph.D. 1966; m. Mary Ann McAulay 18 July 1959; children: Mark, Anne, Kathleen; PROF. OF PHILOS. OF SCIENCE, UNIV. LAVAL 1966- , Vice Dean 1979-81; Analytical Chem., 3M Co. 1967, Research Chem. 1961-63; Invited Prof. Univ. de Paris 1969, 1972, 1975, 1975, 1982; Foreign Exchange Teaching Grantee Prov. Que. 1969; author various publs.; mem. Soc. Aristotelian Studies (Pres.); Candn. Soc. Hist. & Philos. of Science; Am. Phys. Soc.; Am. Cath. Philos. Soc.; R. Catholic; Home: 716 Carré d'Anjou, Ste-Foy, Qué. G1X 2X7; Office: Cité Universitaire, Qué. G1K 7P4.

MURTON, Kenneth Gow, B.Com.; investor; b. Toronto, Ont., 6 Apl. 1930; s. Kenneth Sidney and Marion Lavinia (Gow) M.; e. Scarborough Coll. Inst., 1948; Univ. of Toronto, B.Com. 1952; m. Marilyn Julia, d. Roy Angus McLeod, Vancouver, B.C., 5 Oct. 1964; children: Dana Laurel, Dr. Andrew Grant, Christy Elizabeth (all from previous marriage), Kenneth John; joined A. E. Ames & Co. Ltd., Toronto, 1952; Rep. of firm in London, Ont., 1954-57; returned to Toronto 1958-61; joined A. E. Ames & Co. Inc. (New York City subsidiary) 1962, becoming Pres., Treas. and Dir. 1965; Sr. Extve. overseas operations, First Boston Corp. (London & Zurich) 1971-74; Extve. Vice-Pres. and Dir., Basic Resources Internat. S.A.1974-78; currently Chrmn. Petrotech, Inc.; rec'd Centennial Medal; Former Gov. Bd. (1st Candn.), Midwest Stock Exchange, Chicago; Dir. and Chrmn., Canuc Resources Inc.; Union Trust Co., San Juan, Puerto Rico; Ont. Consolidated Realty Invest. Ltd.; Office: 25 Burr Farms Rd., Westport, Conn. 06880

MUSSALLEM, Helen K., O.C., B.N., M.A., Ed.D., LL.D, D.Sc., F.R.C.N.; b. Prince Rupert, B.C.; d. late Annie (Bassette) and Solomon M.; e. Vancouver Gen. Hosp., Sch. of Nursing, Dipl.; Univ. of Washington., Dipl. - Teaching, Supvn. and Adm.; McGill Univ., B.N.; Teachers Coll., Columbia Univ., M.A.; Columbia Univ., Ed.D.; Memorial Univ., D.Sc.(Hon.); Univ. of N.B., LL.D.(Hon.); Extve. Dir., Candn. Nurses Assn., 1963-81; Active Service 1943-46, Lieut. (N/S), R.C.A.M.C., Can. and overseas; Staff Nurse, Head Nurse and Supv., Vancouver Gen Hosp.; Instr., Sr. Instr., Dir. Nursing Educ., Vancouver Gen. Hosp., Sch. of Nursing, 1947-57; Dir., Pilot Project for Evaluation of Schs. of Nursing in Can., Candn. Nurses Assn., 1957-60; Dir. of Special Studies, Candn. Nurses Assn. 1960-63; (Seconded to Roy. Comn. on Health Svces. for Study of Nursing Educ. in Can., 1962-63); Secy.-Treas., Candn. Nurses Found. since 1966; mem. of and/or adv. to many nat. and internat. organs. incl. Econ. Council of Can.; WHO; Pan Am. Health Organ.; Commonwealth Caribbean Regional Nursing Body; Commonwealth Nurses Fed.; Roy. Soc. of Health; Candn. Forces Med. Council, Bd. of Consults.; CIDA; Candn. Assn. of Univ. Schs. of Nursing; Candn. Assn. of Adult Educ.; Candn. Council on Internat. Coop.; Candn. Council on Social Devel.; Candn. Red Cross Soc.; St. John Ambulance; Victorian Order of Nurses; Candn. Lung Assn.; Health League of Can.; Nat. Comte., UNICEF; Candn. Pub. Health Assn.; CUSO Health Dept.; Candn. Nurses Found.; Law Reform Comn. of Can.; major publications: "Spotlight on Nursing Education" 1960; "Path to Quality" 1964; "Trends in Research in Nursing" 1963; "Social Change and Nursing Education" 1964; "Nursing Education in Canada" 1965; "Studies on Nursing in Canada" 1966; "Nursing Fifty Years Hence in 2020," 1970; "Changing Patterns in Nursing Practice", 1971; "A Glimse of Nursing in Cuba," 1973; "Nurses and Political Action", 1977; "Through the Eyes of Continuing Education in Canada, 1980; over 40 articles in prof. journs.; chaps. in bks. on nursing; Offr. Order of Can. 1969; Award for Distinguished Achievement in Nursing Research & Scholarship, Columbia Univ., N.Y. 1966; Centennial Medal 1967; Commdr., Order of St. John of Jerusalem; Hon. Mem., Assn. of Nurses of P.E.I.; Hon. mem. Assn. of Reg. Nurses in provinces of Sask., Alta., Man., N.B., honored by Candn. Nurses Assn.; Special Citation of Recognition, Candn. Red Cross Soc., 1974; Fellow, Roy. Coll. of Nurses of U.K. 1976; Awarded Florence Nightingale Medal, 1981; National Nursing Library named Helen K. Mussallem Library; Queen's Jubilee Medal 1977; Medal for Distinguished Service, Teacher's College, Columbia Univ., 1979; Office: Suite 1706, 20 The Driveway, Ottawa, Ont. K2P 1C8

MUSTARD, James Fraser, M.D., F.R.C.P.(C), F.R.S.(C.); b. Toronto, Ont. 16 Oct. 1927; s. Alan Alexander and Jean Ann (Oldham) M.; e. Whitney Pub. Sch., Toronto; Univ. of Toronto Schs., Sr. Matric 1946 (Nesbitt

Silver Medal); Univ. of Toronto, M.D. (Hons.) 1953 (Cody Silver Medal, Roy Simpson Scholar, in Paediatrics, Chapel Prize in Clin. Med.); Cambridge Univ. (Elmore Studentship, Dept. of Med.), Ph.D. 1956; m. Christine Elizabeth, d. Harry S. Sifton, London, Ont., 4 June 1952; children: Cameron Alexander, Anne Elizabeth, James Sifton, Duncan Mowbray, John Fraser, Christine MacFarlane; DEAN, FACULTY OF HEALTH SCIENCES, McMASTER UNIV., 1972-80; Vice Pres. Health Sciences, 1980-82; mem. Ont. Council on Univ. Affairs (1974-81); chrmn., Ont. Advisory Council on Occupational Health and Safety; Jr. Interne Toronto Gen. Hosp., 1953-54; Sr. Interne, Sunnybrook Hosp., 1956-57; Sr. Research Assoc., Dept. of Veterans Affairs, 1957-60; Fellow, Dept. of Med., Univ. of Toronto, 1957-61, Research Assoc., 1961-63; Asst. Prof., Dept. of Pathol., 1963-65; Assoc., Dept. of Med., 1963-65, Asst. Prof. 1965; Prof. and Chrmn., Dept. of Pathol., McMaster Univ.; 1966-72; Research Assoc., Nat. Heart Foundation of Can., 1960-61; Consultant to Dept. of Physiol. Sciences, Univ. of Guelph, 1957-66; Sr. Research Assoc., Candn. Heart Foundation, 1961-63; Research Assoc., Med. Research Council 1963-66; rec'd Medal in Med., Roy. Coll. Phys., Can., 1958; author of over 300 scient. articles; Pres., Internat. Soc. for Haemostasis and Thrombosis 1979-81; mem. Ont. Council Health 1966-71 (Chrmn. Health Research Comte. 1966-72); mem. Council on Arteriosclerosis; Am. Heart Foundation (Extve. Council 1964-65); mem., Am. Soc. for Clin. Investig.; Am. Assn. Physicians; Candn. Soc. for Clin. Investig. (Pres. 1965-66); Candn. Physiol. Soc.; Am. Soc. Hematology (mem. Council 1962-64, Secy. 1964-67, Pres. 1970); Soc. for Exper. Path.; Consultant to Internat. Comte. on Hemostasis and Thrombosis; mem. Royal Comn. on Asbestos, Govt. of Ont. 1980- ; Gairdner Foundation Internat. Award for Med. Research 1967; Alpha Delta Phi; Anglican; recreation: farming; Home: 31 Sydenham St., Dundas, Ont. L9H 2T6

MUSTARD, William Thornton, O.C., M.B.E., M.D., M.S., F.R.C.S. (C), F.A.C.S., F.A.C.C.; cardiac surgeon; b. Clinton, Ont. 8 Aug. 1914; s. late James Thornton and late Pearl (Macdonald) M.; e. Model Sch., and Univ. of Toronto Schs., Toronto, Ont.; Univ. of Toronto (1931-37); Toronto Gen. Hosp. (1937-38); Hosp. for Sick Children, Toronto (1938-39); New York Orthopedic Hosp. (1939-40); Toronto Gen. Hosp. (Gallie Course) 1940-41; M.S., Toronto, 1947; m. Elise, d. late Lyman P. Howe, 17 Oct. 1941; two s. and five d.; served in 2nd World War with Candn. Army, Sept. 1941-June 1945; O.C. No. 7 Field Surgical Unit; M.B.E.; Offr.; Order of Can. 1976; Protestant; Home: P.O. Box 164, Dorset, Ont.

MYERS, C. Roger, M.A., Ph.D., LL.D.; Professor Emeritus, Dept. of Psychology, Univ. of Toronto, since 1956 (Chrmn. of the Dept. 1956-68); b. Calgary, Alta.; e. Univ. of Toronto, B.A., M.A., Ph.D.; Univ. of Manitoba; joined Staff of the Univ. in 1927; Consultant Psychol. to Ont. Dept. of Health, 1930-64; Training Adviser to Air Min. in Eng., 1941-45; Past Pres., Ont. Psychol. Assn.; Past Pres., Candn. Psychol. Assn. (Extve. Offr. 1971-78); Diplomate in Clin. Psychol., Am. Bd. of Examiners in Prof. Psychol.; Home: 209 St. Leonards Ave., Toronto, Ont. M4N 1K8

MYERS, Donald W., B.Com.; retired communications executive; b. Halifax, N.S., 27 Apl. 1915; s. Alpin Grant and Isabel Alison (Collings) M.; e. Cumberland Co. Acad., Amherst, N.S., 1933; St. Mary's Univ., B.Com. 1958; m. Gertrude, d. late John McQuarrie, 12 Aug. 1941; children: John Grant, Janet Kathryn; CO-ORDINATOR, CASE — HALIFAX 1979 (joined Maritime Telegraph & Telephone Co. Ltd. as Surveyor's Helper, 1934; apptd. Pay Stn. Collector, Sydney, N.S. 1936; Chief Clerk 1939; Office Mgr., Halifax, 1941; Gen. Comm. Supvr. 1945; Gen. Comm. Mgr., 1958; Extve. Asst. 1962; Vice-Pres. Finance, and Dir. 1963; Vice-Pres. and Gen. Mgr. 1966; Extve. Vice Pres. 1969-76; Depy. Co-ordinator, Case-Hali-

fax 1976-81; United Church; recreation: golf; Club: Ashburn Golf & Country; Home: 1628 Cambridge St., Halifax, N.S. B3H 4A7Office: 2000 Barrington St., Ste. 710, Halifax, N.S.

MYERS, Martin, M.A.; author; b. Toronto, Ont. 7 Dec. 1927; s. Max and Esther (Friedman) M.; e. Harbord Coll. Inst. Toronto 1945; Univ. of Toronto B.A. 1951; Johns Hopkins Univ. M.A. 1969; m. Colleen Sue Croll 25 June 1955; children: Lori Sue, Marshall Bradley; author "The Assignment" 1971, Paperjacks 1975; "Frigate" 1975, Paperjacks 1976; "Izzy Manheim's Reunion" 1977; Writer-in-Residence and Visiting Assoc. Prof. Scarborough Coll. Univ. of Toronto 1972-74; Lectr. Writers Workshop, York Univ. 1971-73 and New Coll. Univ. Toronto 1974-75; mem. ACTRA; Candn. Authors Assn.; Authors Guild; Address: 59 MacPherson Ave., Toronto, Ont. M5R 1W7.

MYLYMOK, William James Jr., B.A.; financial executive; b. Wakaw, Sask. 10 Feb. 1939; s. William James M.; e. Univ. of Sask. B.A. 1961; m. Joyce Winnifred Maureen Wellman; 4 children; SR. VICE PRES. AVCO FINANCIAL SERVICES CANADA LTD.; Dir. Avco Financial Services U.K. Ltd.; London & Midland Insurance; has held various positions with Avco Can. UK and USA; Home: 230 Baseline Rd. E., London, Ont. Office: 201 Queens Ave. (P.O. Box 5875), London, Ont. N6A 1J1.

N

NABORS, Clair A., B.S.; Executive; B. Mart, Texas 30 Jan. 1912; s. Charles A. and Ella Virginia (Swaim) N.; e. Univ. of Texas B.S. (Mech. Engn.) 1935; m. Lillian Mae Demings 16 May 1964; CHRMN. OF THE BD., NABORS DRILLING LTD.; Dir. Western Rock Bit Co.; Anglo Energy Ltd.; served with US Navy 4½ yrs.; P. Conservative; Baptist; recreation: golf; Clubs: Calgary Golf & Country; Calgary Petroleum (Gov.); Home: 1909 90th Ave. S.W., Calgary, Alta. T2V 4R9; Office: 1107-324 8th Ave S. W., Calgary, Alta. T2P 2Z2

NADEAU, Bertin F., D.B.A.; executive; b. N.B. 26 May 1940; s. J.- D. and Irène (Daigle) N.; e. Coll. St-Louis, Edmunston, N.B. B.A. 1961; Ecole des Hautes Etudes Commerciales de Montréal L.ès Sc. 1964; Harvard Univ. Grad. Sch. of Business; Ind. Univ. Grad. Sch. of Business D.B.A. 1969; m. Juliette d. Warren M. Angell, Shawnee, Okla. 24 July 1971; children: Eric, Shahn, Stéphanie; CHMN. NADEAU CORP. LTD. Chrmn. and C.E.O., Unigesco Inc.; Chmn., Corp. de l'Ecole des Hautes Etudes Commerciales; Soc. d'Investissement Desjardins; Research Asst., Ecole des Hautes Etudes Commerciales de Montréal 1964-66, Asst. then Assoc. Prof. of Business Policy 1969-76; Dir. of Ph.D. Program in Adm. given jointly by McGill Univ., Concordia Univ., l'Univ. du Qué. à Montréal and l'Ecole des Hautes Etudes Commerciales 1975-76; co-author "Le Management, Textes et Cas" 1973; author various articles, papers; recreations: skiing, tennis; Clubs: Montreal Badminton & Squash; Cercle de la Place d'Armes; Home: 3118 Chemin Daulac, Montréal, Qué. H3Y 1Z9; Office: 206 rue St-Paul ouest, Montréal, Qué. H2Y 1Z9.

NADEAU, Claudette; née Montréal, Que. 18 février 1938; f. Joseph Rudolphe Bernard et Dorina Joséphine (Robitaille) Laliberté; é Coll. Basile Moreau 1953; Univ. McGill; ép André Nadeau 25 août 1955 (divorce 1977); enfants: France, Marc, José; ép Yvon Gariepy 14 fev. 1981; PRÉSIDENT ET DIRECTEUR GÉNÉRAL, CORP. DE DISPOSITION DES BIENS DE LA COURONNE depuis 1975; Asst. Travail de Verification Etats Financiers, McDonald Currie & Co., 1955; Comptable et gérant de bureau, Laurentian Landscape Ltée 1963-65; asst. au vice-prés. exécutif, Simard-Beaudry Inc. 1965-68; agent de vente et service à la clientèle Metrocan Leasing Ltée 1968-69;

consultant — confort au foyer, Shell Canada Ltée 1969-70; asst. au vice-prés. des ventes, Canagex Ltée — (Banque Canadienne Nationale) 1970-72; aviseur, plans de pension et fonds mutuels, Geoffrion, Robert & Gélinas Ltée 1972-74; Pres. Sortant, Institut de la gestion financière; Dir., la Fondation communantaire d'Ottawa et de la région; Pres. Campagne Centraide, Ottawa, Carleton, 1980; récréation: golf, ski; Club: Cercle universitaire; résidence: 37 Linden Terrace, Ottawa, Ont. K1S 1Z1; bureau: 450, rue Rideau, Ottawa, Ont. K1G 3J8

NADEAU, Leopold Maurice, B.A.Sc.; D.Eng. (Hon.); P.Eng.; F.E.I.C.; consulting engineer; b. Montreal, Que., 29 Nov. 1913; s. Joseph-Alphonse and Marie-Louise (Laroie) N.; e. Querbes Acad., Outremont, Que., 1919-28; St. Louis High Sch., Montreal, Que., 1929-30; Ecole Polytechnique of Montreal, B.A.Sc. 1936 (Civil Engn.); m. Huguette, d. late Joseph Emery Lavigne, 3 Dec. 1942; children: Jacques, Pierre, Louise, Gilles, Marie; began career as Asst. Plant Engr. at Port Alfred mill of Consolidated Paper Corp., then as Resident Engineer, Que. Dept. of Highways, subsequently joining Tech. Staff of Candn. Underwriters' Assn. as Fire Protection Engr.; joined staff of Corp. of Prof. Engrs. of Quebec in 1946 as Asst. Gen. Secy. and became Gen. Secy. in 1949; in 1955, joined Racey MacCallum and Associates Ltd., Consulting Engrs., where he held the position of Dir. and Extve. Engr. in charge of Montreal Div.; Gen. Mgr., Cdn. Council of Professional Engineers 1959-79; Vice-Pres., World Fed. of Engn. Organizations 1974-79; Dir. for Can., Pan Am. Union for Engn. Societies; Fellow, Engn. Inst. Can.; Nat. Soc. of Prof. Engrs., U.S.A.; Order Engrs. Ont.; Engrs. Que.; Cercle Universitaire, Ottawa; Rivermead Golf Club, Aylmer; Roman Catholic; recreations: fishing, golf, skiing; Home: 25 Acadie St., Aylmer, Que. J9J 1H7; Office: 25 Acadie St., Aylmer, Que. J9J 1H7

NADEAU, Paul S., paramedical executive; b. La Tuque, Que., 6 Sept. 1920; s. late Alfred, Q.C. and Joséphine (Lacroix) N.; e. St. Sacrement Sch. and Jesuits Coll., Quebec City, 1938; St. Patrick's Coll., Ottawa, 1938-40; Univ. of W. Ont., Marketing Grad.; m. Myrtle, d. late T. J. Kelly, 16 Feb. 1946; children: Helen Louise Weightman, Marc (d), Paul Jr.; DIR. GEN. FATHER DOWD MEMORIAL HOME 1980-; retired Vice Pres., Corporate Affairs, Schering Can. Inc. 1977-1979; served with RCAF 1940-45; Wireless Air Gunner; Past Pres. Bd. of Dirs., Grace Dart Hosp., Montreal; Pres., Que. Muscular Dystrophy Assn. of Can.; Founder, Drug Salesmen's Assn. (Pres. 1954); Past Councillor, Montreal Bd. of Trade; mem., Candn. Chamber Comm.; Comm. Travellers' Assn. Can.; Liberal; R. Catholic; recreations: skiing, swimming; Clubs: St. Denis; Montreal-Lakeshore Rotary (Pres. 1974-75); Home: 730 Montpelier Blvd. Apt. 203, Ville St. Laurent, Que. H4L 5B3; Office: 6565 Hudson Rd., Montreal, Que. 43S 2T7

NADEAU, Pierre; B.Comm.; company chairman; b. Quebec, Que., 22 Apr. 1925; s. P.A. and Claire (Raymond) N.; e. Laval Univ., B.Com. 1950; m. Claire, d. Henri Tesier, 17 May 1952; 1 s. Richard and 3 d. Lucie, Sylvie, Claire; CHRMN: OF BD., PRES. AND C.E.O. PETRO-FINA CANADA INC. 1977-; Chrmn. of Bd. & Pres. Finahem Can. Inc., 1976-; Dir. Am. Petrofina Inc.; The Royal Bank of Can.; The Conference Bd. of Can.; joined Indust. Acceptance Corp. Ltd. (I.A.C.) 1950; Vice Pres. Bus. Development, 1969; appointed Chrmn. & Pres. James Bay Devel. Corp. by Premier Robert Bourassa, 1971, resigned 1972; appointed Vice Chrmn. & Dir. Petrofina Can. Inc. 1972; Pres. & C.E.O. 1973; mem. Nat. Adv. Comte. on Petroleum (NACOP); Gen. Council of Indust. of Que.; Commr., Royal Commission on Corp. Concentration 1975-78; mem. Bd. of Govs., Conseil du Patronat du Que.; Nat. Co-Chrmn., Candn. Council of Christians & Jews; R. Catholic; recreations: skiing, fishing, tennis; Clubs: Mount Royal; St. Denis; Residence: Montreal, Que.

NADON, Maurice Jean; b. Mattawa, Ont., 8 July 1920; s. late Z. A. and Emma (Leblanc) N.; e. Ottawa Univ. High Sch., 1936; Ottawa Tech. High Sch., 1940; Candn. Police Coll., Regina Sask., Sr. Police Course 1957; m. Madeleine, d. late Joseph Desrosiers, Rimouski, Que., 25 Sept. 1948; children: Suzanne Shield, Robert; joined ranks RCMP 1941, comnd. 1958, responsible for Criminal Investig. Br., Vancouver 1958; Asst. CIB Offr., "C" Que. Div., Montreal HQ 1961; Offr. Commdg., Que. Sub/Div. 1962; Liaison Offr., HQ, Ottawa 1965; Crime Intelligence Offr. for E. Can. 1966; Offr. i/c, Criminal Investig. Br., HQ, Ottawa 1967; Asst. Dir., Criminal Investig., HQ 1968-69; C.O., "O" Div., Toronto 1970; Officer Brother, Order of St. John, 1973; Commander Brother, Order of St. John, 1976; Commander Companion, Order of St. Lazarus, 1978; Depy. Commr., Criminal Operations, HQ 1972-74; Commr., R.C.M.P., 1974-77; Member of Candn. Del. to ICPO Interpol, 1967-73; Head, Candn. Del. to ICPO 1974-77; — Interpol; mem. Extve. Comte., Internat. Assn. Chiefs Police, Washington, D.C. 1972-74; rec'd. Centennial Medal 1967; Offr. Br., Order St. John Jerusalem; Long Service Medal 1961; Bronze Clasp 1966; Silver Clasp 1971; Gold Clasp 1976; Jubilee Medal, Her Majesty the Queen, 1977; recreations: tennis, camping, canoeing, skiing, curling; Home: 1935 Tweed Ave., Ottawa, Ont. K1G 2L8

NAIRN, John Graham, B.Sc.Phm., Ph.D.; educator; b. Toronto, Ont., 23 Aug. 1928; s. Lawrence Graham and Aileen Euphemia (McAlpine) N.; e. Humewood Pub. Sch. and Vaughan Rd. Coll. Inst., Toronto 1946; Ont. Coll. of Pharm., Univ. of Toronto, B.Sc.Phm 1952; Univ. of Buffalo, Ph.D. 1959; m. Mary Kathleen F., d. late Robert Pollock, 2 Aug. 1954; children: Dawn Kathleen, David Graham, Diane Aileen, Debra Margaret; PROF OF PHARMACY, UNIV. OF TORONTO since 1973; joined present Univ. as Asst. Prof. 1958, Assoc. Prof. 1965-72; author various research and prof. publs.; mem., Pharm. Examining Bd. of Can.; Assn. Faculties Pharm. Can.; Candn. Pharm. Assn.; Candn. Foundation Advanc. Pharm.; Ont. Coll. Pharm.; Royal Candn. Geog. Soc.; Univ. of Toronto Faculty Association; United Church; recreations: camping, canoeing, skiing;

NAKAMURA, Kazuo; artist; b. Vancouver, B.C., 13 Oct. 1926; s. Toichi and Yoshiyo (Uyemoto) N.; e. Central Tech. Sch., Toronto, Ont. (Grad. 1951); m. Lillian Y. Kobayakawa, 1967; children: Elaine Y., Bryan K.; rep. in following public collections: Nat. Gallery Can.; Museum Modern Art, N.Y.; Art Gallery Toronto; Beaverbrook Art Gallery, Fredericton, N.B.; Hart House, Univ. of Toronto; Victoria Coll., Toronto; Univ. of W. Ont.; R. McLaughlin Gallery, Oshawa; Hamilton Art Gallery; Lugano Coll., Switzerland; Hallmark Collection, U.S.A.; Dept. of External Affairs, Can.; Winnipeg Art Gallery; has exhibited in Group Shows since 1952 in Canada and abroad, and in Candn. Paintings, Polish Tour 1962; Candn. Biennials, Nat. Gallery Can.; Contemp. Candn. Art, Central Africa, Candn. Paintings, London, Eng. (1963), World Show, N.Y. (1964), Canada '68 Exhbn., Toronto 1968; Painters Eleven in Retrospect, 1979-81; Home: 3 Langmuir Cres., Toronto, Ont. M6S 2A6

NAKONECHNY, Victor Peter, B.Sc., B.Ed., b. Boyle, Alta., 28 Aug. 1932; s. late Steve and Sally (Ryl) N.; e. Univ. of Alta. B.Ed. 1957, B.Sc. 1963; m. Geraldine Marie, d. late N. A. Melnyk 3 June 1960; two s. Lorne, Gregory; Princ., Londonderry School, 1981-; Edmonton Savings Bd., 1980-; Pres. Bd. of Dirs. Edmonton Savings & Credit Union 1972-80, Vice Pres. 1969-72; Princ. Hardisty Sch. 1974-81, Asst. Princ. 1967-69; Pres. NST Enterprises Ltd. since 1975; Teacher Highlands Sch. 1959-64; Asst. Princ. Westglen Sch. 1964-67; Princ. Rosslyn Sch. 1969-74; Pres. Nigon Investments Ltd. 1971-72, Dir. 1970-75; mem. Extended Practicum Comte. Univ. of Alta.; vice pres. Northmount Community League since 1977; served in various adm. positions teaching field since 1960; Vice-

Pres., Order of St. Andrew, 19181-; Treas., Sr. Citizens Home of St. John, 1981-; Vice Pres. St. John's Cath. Ch. Bd. 1967-72 (Chrmn. Finance 1968-72); mem. Alta. Teachers Assn. (held various extve. positions); Edmonton Pub. Sch. Adm. Assn.; Phi Delta Kappa; Ukrainian Orthodox; Home: 9528 — 142 Ave., Edmonton, Alta. T5E 6A5

NANKIVELL, Neville John, B.A., M.B.A.; editor; b. Cottesloe, W. Australia 8 Dec. 1934; s. John Penn and Ivy Savage (Smith) N.; e. Scotch Coll. Swanbourne, W. Australia 1951; Univ. of W. Australia B.A. (Econ.) 1955; Univ. of Toronto M.B.A. 1960; m. Joan d. late Clive B. Davidson 13 Sept. 1958; two s. William Penn, Jeffery John; EDITOR-IN-CHIEF, THE FINANCIAL POST DIV., MACLEAN HUNTER LTD. 1981-; joined The Financial Post 1960, Invest. Ed. 1964, Assoc. Ed. 1968, Mang. Ed. 1972, Ed. 1977; mem. Metrop. Toronto Dist. Health Council; Trustee, Candn. Outward Bound Wilderness Sch. 1980-81, mem. Adv. Bd. 1982; Pres. Univ. of Toronto Schs. Parents Assn. 1979-80, 1980-81; Dir. Toronto Free Theatre 1977-81; co-author "How to Make Your Money Grow" 1966; Fellow, Financial Analysts Fed.; mem. Toronto Soc. Financial Analysts; recreations: rugby, squash; Home: 290 Sheldrake Blvd., Toronto, Ont. M4P 2B6; Office: 481 University Ave., Toronto, Ont. M5W 1A7.

NARANG, Saran A., M.Sc., Ph.D., F.R.S.C.; research scientist; b. Agra, India 10 Sept. 1930; s. Sant Dass and Kirpal Devi N.; e. Panjab Univ. B.Sc. 1951, M.Sc. 1953; Calcutta Univ. Ph.D. 1960; m. Sandhya d. Babu Ram Dheer, New Delhi, India 7 Oct. 1959; one d. Vandna Agoo; SR. RESEARCH OFFR., NAT. RESEARCH COUNCIL OF CANADA 1973-; Adjunct Prof. of Chem., Carleton Univ., The Johns Hopkins Univ.; Research Assoc., The Johns Hopkins Univ. 1962-63; Project Assoc. Enzyme Research Inst. Univ. of Wis. 1963-66; Asst. Research Offr. present Council 1966, Assoc. Research Offr. 1967-73; rec'd Coochbihar Postgraduate Mem. Award 1973; Johns Hopkins Scholar Medal 1979; Ottawa Biol. & Biochem. Soc. Award 1979; author over 100 research papers; achieved the Synthesis and Cloning of Human Proinsulin Gene; mem. Fed. Am. Socs. Exper. Biol.; Hindu; recreations: Indian classical music, chess, sculpture, painting; Home: 30 Higgins Rd., Ottawa, Ont. K2G 0R5; Office: 100 Sussex Dr., Ottawa, Ont. K1A 0R6.

NARVESON, Jan, Ph.D.; educator; b. Erskine, Minn. 15 June 1936; s. Carl Robert and Sophie Helen (Krbechek) N.; e. Moorhead State Teachers Coll. Sch. and Moorhead High Sch. Minn.; Univ. of Chicago B.A. 1955, 1956; Harvard Univ. Ph.D. 1961; children: Kaja Lee, Jascha Wallace, Julia Amadea; PROF. OF PHILOSOPHY, UNIV. OF WATERLOO; 1963-; Dir., Kitchener-Waterloo Symphony Orchestra Assn.; Kitchener-Waterloo Philharmonic Choir; Kitchener-Waterloo Chamber Music Soc. (Pres.); author "Morality and Utility" 1967; various papers primarily on Ethics; weekly columnist (music) "University of Waterloo Gazette"; commentaries and musical selections weekly radio program (chamber music); mem. Candn. Philos. Assn.; Am. Philos. Assn.; Candn. Assn. Publishing in Philos.; recreation: music; Home: 57 Young St. W., Waterloo, Ont. N2L 2Z4; Office: Waterloo, Ont. N2L 3G1.

NASGAARD, Roald,M.A., Ph.D.; museum curator; art historian; b. Denmark 14 Oct. 1941; s. Jens Larsen and Petra (Guldbaek) N.; e. Univ. of B.C., B.A. 1965, M.A. 1967; Inst. of Fine Arts, N.Y. Univ. Ph.D. 1972; m. Susan Ursula d. Eric D. Watterson 8 Sept. 1967; CURATOR, ART GALLERY OF ONT.; exhns. Art Gallery of Ont. incl. Ron Martin; World Paintings 1976, Peter Kolisynk 1977, Structures for Behaviour 1977, Garry Neill Kennedy: Recent Work 1978, Yves Gaucher: A Fifteen Year Perspective 1978, 10 Candn. Artists in the 1970's 1980; author various articles; mem. Coll. Art Assn.; Univ. Art Assn. Can.; Internat. Art Critics Assn.; Office: 317 Dundas St. W., Toronto, Ont. M5T 1G4.

NASH, (Cyril) Knowlton; journalist; broadcasting executive; b. Toronto, Ont., 18 Nov. 1927; s. Cyril Knowlton and Alys (Worsley) N.; e. Forest Hill Village Pub. Sch. and Coll. Inst., Toronto; Univ. of Toronto, 1 yr.; one d. Anne; CHIEF CORRESPONDENT, C.B.C. TELEVISION NEWS Dir., Television News and Current affairs C.B.C.; sports writer, "Globe and Mail", Toronto, 1946; fiction mag. editing, Toronto, 1946; Ed. of weekly newspaper, Toronto, 1947; Bureau Mgr., Brit. United Press in Halifax, Vancouver and Toronto, 1947-51; Dir. of Information, Internat. Fed. of Agric. Producers, Washington and Paris, 1951-58; writer/broadcaster (CBC Washington Corr., Financial Post, various Candn. newspapers) 1958-69; apptd. Dir., News & Public Affairs, C.B.C. 1969; Rapporteur various U.N. Comtes., 1951-58; former Pres., CBC Corrs. Assn.; former Pres., Candn. Corrs. Assn. (Washington); and White House Correspondents Assn.; Overseas Writers Club; mem. Bd. of Dirs. Couchiching Inst. on Pub. Affairs; former chrmn, Toronto Branch, Candn. Mental Health Assn.; recreations: books, jogging; Clubs: National Press, Washington; Toronto Press; Home: 66 Collier Street, Toronto, Ont. M4W 1L9; Office: Box 500, Terminal "A", Toronto, Ont. M5W 1E4

NASH, Peter Hugh John, Sr., M.A., M.C.P., M.P.A., Ph.D.; educator; b. Frankfurt-on-Main, Germany, 18 Sept. 1921; s. John Hans Joseph and Alice (Heuman) N.; e. Lindisfarne Coll., Essex, Eng. 1937; Los Angeles City Coll., A.A. 1941; Univ. of Cal. (Los Angeles) B.A. 1942 (Gruen Fellow), M.A. 1946; Univ. of Grenoble, Cert. d'Etudes 1945; Harvard Grad. Sch. of Design (Holtzer Fellow) M. City Planning 1949. Pub. Adm. M.P.A. Harvard 1956; Architectural Sciences Ph.D. Harvard 1958; Univ. of Cincinnati Law Sch., 1961-63; m. Inez Mae, d. late Bertram Frost, 30 July 1955; children: Carina Frost, Peter Hugh Jr.; PROF. OF ENVIRONMENTAL STUDIES, ARCHITECTURE, GEOGRAPHY AND PLANNING, UNIV. OF WATERLOO since 1970; and Dean 1970-75; Princ. Planning Asst., Boston City Planning Bd. 1949; Sr. Planner, Planning Dept., City of Worcester, Mass. 1950; Asst. Chief. Urban Redevel. Div., Boston Housing Authority 1951; Dir., Planning Dept., City of Medford, Mass. 1952-'56; Visiting Critic, Harvard Grad. Sch. of Design and Asst. Prof. of Geog., Boston Univ. 1956; Assoc. Prof. of City & Regional Planning and Research Assoc., Inst. for Research in Social Science, Univ. of N.C. 1957-'59; Prof. and Head, Dept. of Geog. and Regional Planning, Univ. of Cincinnati 1959-63; Dean of Grad. Sch. and Prof. of Geog. & Regional Planning, Univ. of R.I. 1963-70; Visiting Prof., Inst. of Human Sciences, Boston Coll. 1969-70; Sr. Mang. Consultant, Battelle Mem. Inst., Columbus, Ohio, 1969-74; served with U.S. Army in N.W. and Central Europe 1942-45; rec'd Purple Heart with Oak Leaf Cluster; Bronze Star; Croix de Guerre; recipient numerous research and foreign travel grants, acad. and civic honours and awards in U.S. and other countries; including Univ. of Liège; Aligarh Muslim Univ., India, and City of Yokohama Japan; mem. various bds., comns. and councils; author of two books and over 140 articles, chapters and reviews in books and prof. or learned journs.; Bd. of Dir., K/W Philharmonic Choir (Chrmn. 1977-79); mem. Kitchener Rotary Internat.; Am. Assn. Geogs. (Life); Am. Planning Assn.; Am. Assn. Advanc. Science; Am. Soc. Pub. Adm.; Am. Geographical Society (Life); Assn. Coll. Schs. Planning (Treas. 1967-70); Candn. Assn. Geogs.; Harvard Grad. Sch. Design Assn. (Pres. 1966-70); Inst. Alpine Geog. (Hon.); Internat. Geog. Union Comm. Appl. Geog. (W. Hemisphere Rep.); Internat. City Mang. Assn.; Regional Science Assn.; Candn. Inst. Planners; World Soc. Ekistics (Delos Symposion: 1967, 1970, 1974); Alpha Mu Gamma; Kappa Delta Pi; Phi Kappa Phi (Hon.); Pi Gamma Mu; Sigma Nu; Sigma Xi; Freemason (K.T.); Unitarian; recreations: skiing, swimming; Home: 588 Sugarbush Dr., Waterloo, Ont. N2K 1Z8

NASTICH, Milan M., B.A., B.A.Sc.; utility executive; b. Vancouver, B.C. 27 Feb. 1926; s. Midzor and Rose (Snihur) N.; e. Drumheller High Sch. Alberta; Univ. of B.C. B.A. 1947, B.A.Sc. (Elect. Engn.) 1948; m. Mary Hudson 15 May 1954; one s. Jeffrey; PRES. AND DIR., ONTARIO HYDRO 1980- ; joined Ontario Hydro 1949, Comptroller 1964, Dir. of Computing Services 1967, Dir. of Property 1970, Asst. Gen. Mgr. Finance 1972, Vice Pres. Resources 1974, Extve. Vice Pres. Planning & Adm. 1978; Past Pres. Arthritis Soc.; Kennedy House for Boys 1971-73; Warden, Iron Ring Ceremony for Prof. Engrs.; Treas. Chevalier de Tastevin 1980; mem. Soc. Ont. Hydro Prof. Engrs. (Pres. 1956-57); Assn. Prof. Engrs. Prov. Ont.; Greek Orthodox; recreations: curling, cross-country skiing, target shooting, arms collecting, chess, farming, wine tasting; Clubs: Toronto; Kiwanis; Ticker (Past Pres.); Royal Candn. Mil. Inst.; Home: 259 Yonge Blvd., Toronto, Ont. M5M 3J1; Office: 700 University Ave., Toronto, Ont. M5G 1X6.

NAYAR, Baldev Raj, M.A., Ph.D.; educator; b. Gujrat, Punjab, India 26 Oct. 1931; s. Jamna Das and Durga Devi (Marwah) N.; e. Punjab Univ. B.A. 1953, M.A. 1956; Univ. of Chicago M.A. 1959, Ph.D. 1963; m. Nancy Ann d. Durward A. Skinner 27 Aug. 1961; children: Sheila Jane, Kamala Elizabeth, Sunita Marie; PROF. OF POL. SCIENCE, McGILL UNIV. 1971- ; Asst. Prof. of Pol. Science Calif. State Coll. Hayward 1963-64; Asst. Prof. present Univ. 1964, Assoc. Prof. 1966; author "Minority Politics in the Punjab" 1966; "National Communication and Language Policy in India" 1968; "The Modernization Imperative and Indian Planning" 1972; "Violence and Crime in India: A Quantitative Study" 1975; "American Geopolitics and India" 1976; mem. Internat. Pol. Science Assn.; Candn. Pol. Science Assn.; Candn. Asian Studies Assn.; Assn. Asian Studies; Home: 441 Lansdowne Ave., Westmount, Que. H3Y 2V4; Office: 855 Sherbrooke St. W., Montreal, Que. H3A 2T7.

NAYSMITH, Duncan, B.Sc.F., R.P.F.; executive; b. Toronto, Ont., 6 April 1921; s. Mary (Kennedy) and late Duncan N.; e. Univ. of Toronto, B.Sc.F. 1946; m. Edith, d. Edward Morgan Taylor, 23 April 1947; children: Duncan James, Alan Kennedy, Margaret Elizabeth; DIRECTOR OF FORESTRY, ABITIBI PAPER CO. LTD. since 1968; joined the Co. as Forester, Sault Ste. Marie, Ont. 1946, Field Chief 1948, Div. Forester, Pine Falls, Man. 1949, Sault Ste. Marie 1955, Asst. Chief Forester, Toronto 1964; mem. Ont. Prof. Foresters Assn.; Ont. Forestry Assn. (Pres. 1970); Candn. Forestry Assn. (Dir.); presented J. A. Bothwell Award "for Achievement in Forest Conservation" by Candn. Pulp & Paper Assn. 1950; P. Conservative; Presbyterian; recreation: summer property; Home: 25 Widdicombe Hill, Weston, Ont. M9R 1A9; Office: P.O. Box 21, Toronto-Dominion Centre, Toronto, Ont. M5K 1A1

NEALE, Ernest Richard Ward, B.Sc., Ph.D., LL.D.; geologist; b. Montreal, Que. 3 July 1923; s. Ernest John and Mabel Elizabeth (McNamee) N.; e. McGill Univ. B.Sc. 1949; Yale Univ. Ph.D. 1952; Univ. of Calgary LL.D. 1977; m. Roxie Eveline d. late Arthur Ernest Anderson 3 June 1950; children: Richard Ward, Owen Curtis; VICE-PRES. (ACADEMIC), MEMORIAL UNIVERSITY OF NEWFOUNDLAND Head of Geol. Information Subdiv. Inst. of Sedimentary And Petroleum Geol. since 1976; 1982-; Adjunct Prof. 1976-80; mem. of Senate, 1980-81); Univ. of Calgary; Asst. Prof. Univ. of Rochester 1952-54; Head of Appalachian Sec. Geol. Survey of Can. 1959-63, Head of Precambrian Sec. 1965-68; Commonwealth Geol. Liaison Offr. London, UK 1963-65; Prof. and Head of Geol. Mem. Univ. of Nfld. 1968-76; rec'd Bancroft Award, Royal Soc. Can. 1975; Queen's Silver Jubilee Medal 1977; served with RCN 1943-45; Dir. Candn. Geol. Foundation 1973-78; author "Some Guides to Mineral Exploration" 1965; "Geology of the Atlantic Area" 1967; "The Earth Sciences in Canada" 1968; "Geology and Geophysics in Canadian Universities", 1980; various articles geol., popular sci-

ence, geo-politics; editor, Can. Journal of Earth Sciences 197480; mem. Royal Soc. Can. (Councillor 1972-74); Geol. Assn. Can. (Pres. 1972-73); Candn. Geoscience Council (Pres. 1976); Geol. Soc. London; Geol. Soc. Am.; recreations: cross-country skiing, golf, hiking, canoeing; Home: 23 Belfast St., St John's Nfld.; Calgary, Alta. Office: Memorial University, St. John's Nfld. A1C 5S7

NEASE, Thomas S.; executive; b. Calgary, Alta., 29 Sept. 1927; s. Frederick George and Margaret (Jewitt) N.; e. Pub. and High Schs., Toronto; Univ. of Toronto; m. Irene, d. Richard Jane, 13 Feb. 1954; four s. Stephen, Bradley, Michael, David; PRESIDENT AND DIR., ADIDAS (CANADA) LTD. since 1971; Exec. Vice-Pres. & Dir., Adidas (U.S.) Inc. 1980; Dir., Powlesland Engineering Ltd.; Sales Rep., Canada Cycle and Motor Co. Ltd., 1947, Export Mgr. 1953, Extve. Vice Pres. 1959, Pres. 1962-70; Gov. and Dir. Participation House; Past. Chrmn., Young Pres.' Organ.; Anglican; recreations: golf, tennis; Club: Bd. of Trade Country; Home: 8299 Kipling Ave., Woodbridge, Ont. L4L 1A8; Office: 550 Oakdale Rd., Downsview, Ont. M3N 1W6

NEATBY, H. Blair, M.A., Ph.D.; educator; b. Renown, Sask. 11 Dec. 1924; s. Walter B. and Margaret (MacKay) N.; e. Univ. of Sask. B.A. 1950; Oxford Univ. M.A. 1955; Univ. of Toronto Ph.D. 1956; m. Jacqueline Côté 15 Apl. 1961; children: Nicole, Pierre, Jacques; PROF. OF HIST. CARLETON UNIV.; author "W.L. MacKenzie King" Vol. 1 1923-32, 1963, Vol. II 1932-39, 1976; "Laurier and a Liberal Quebec" 1972; "The Politics of Chaos" 1972; Home: 12 Allan Pl., Ottawa, Ont. K1S 3T1; Office: Ottawa, Ont.

NEDDEAU, Donald Frederick Price, A.O.C.A., O.S.A., F.I.A.L. (1960), R.C.A.; artist, painter, designer, teacher; b. Toronto, Ont., 28 Jan. 1913; s. Frederick Price and Pearl Franklin (Bland) N.; e. Ont. Coll. Art, A.O.C.A. (Hons.) 1936; post grad. work in fine art, 1937; Ont. Coll. Educ., Univ. of Toronto, grad. 1954; has exhibited with major art socs. and galleries in Can. and U.S.A.; one-man shows in Can.; U.S.A., New Zealand; Head of Art, Princ. of Art Summer School; Emeritus, 1978, Central Technical School, Toronto; served in 2nd World War with R.C.A.F. and Canadian Army, 1942-45; member, Canadian Guild Pottery; Canadian Society Painters in Water Colour (President, 1964-66); member, Am. Craftsmen's Council; Ont. Craft Foundation; Assoc., Candn. Craftsmen's Assn.; el. Roy. Candn. Acad. of Arts, 1976; Anglican; recreations: mountain climbing, swimming, golf, tennis; Club: Arts & Letters; Address: 21 Sherwood Ave., Toronto, Ont. M4P 2A6

NEELANDS, Donald Grant, Q.C.; retired trust company executive; b. Toronto, Ont., 21 March 1916; s. Ernest Victor and Jessie Margaret (Easson) N.; e. Cobalt (Ont.) Public and High Schs.; Upper Canada Coll., Toronto, Ont. (1934); Trinity Coll., Univ. of Toronto, B.A. 1938; Osgoode Hall Law Schs., Toronto, Ont.; m. Christine Martin, d. Arthur E. MacGregor, Toronto, Ont., 16 April 1942; three d., Nancy, Margaret, Patricia; mem. Bd. of Govs., Central Hosp.; Trustee, Nat. Sanitarium Assn.; called to the Bar of Ont. 1941; Legal Asst., Candn. Tax Foundation, 1946-49; joined Toronto Gen. Trusts Corp. (predecessor Co.), 1949 as Trust Offr.; Corp. Trust Offr., 1956, Estates Mgr. 1959; Asst. Gen. Mgr. 1960; Depy. Gen. Mgr. and Asst. to Pres., Can. Permanent Mortgage Co. and Can. Perm. Trust Co. 1968, Extve. Vice-President February 1969; President 1969; Chrmn., Canada Permanent Mortgage Corp. and Canada Permanent Trust Co. 1975-81; Captain, Canadian Intelligence Corps. 1941-45; Bd. of Dir., Empire Club Fdn.; Phi Kappa Pi; Presbyterian; Clubs: Toronto; Toronto Hunt; York; Empire; Home: 170 Inglewood Drive, Toronto, Ontario M4T 1H7

NEILL, D. Malcolm; radio broadcasting executive; merchant; b. Fredericton, N.B., 23 April 1915; s. James Stewart and Hannah Muriel (Logan) N.; e. Fredericton

Schs.; Bishop's Coll. Sch., Lennoxville, Que.; m. Norah Louise, d. Frank A. Hicks, Toronto, Ont., 28 Oct. 1939; children: Andrew, Eric, Deborah, Graham; PRESIDENT, RADIO STATION CFNB (Estbd. 1923), since 1945; Vice-Pres., James S. Neill & Sons Ltd. (Hardware Merchants, Estbd. 1838); Pres., Candn. Assn. of Broadcasters 1950, 1958 and 1959 (Chairman 1951 and 1952); Hoon. chrmn. Miramichi Salmon Assn.; Vice Pres., Miramichi, Fish and Game Club Ltd.; began with C.B.C., Ottawa, as an apprentice, May 1937; moved to Program Dept., Toronto, 1938 and became Asst. to Supervisor of Station Relations till 1945; United Church; recreations: fishing, gardening, photography; Clubs: Fredericton Golf; Union (Saint John); Miramichi Fish & Game; Sandy Lane Golf (Barbados); Rotary (Hon. mem.); Pres.); Home: 277 Woodstock Road, Fredericton, N.B. E3B 2H8; and High Point, Sandy Lane Estates, St. James, Barbados, W.I. Office: 125 Hanwell Rd., Fredericton, N.B. E3B 4Z4

NEILSON, John Warrington, B.A., M.Sc., D.D.S., F.I.C.D., F.A.C.D.; university dean; dentist; b. Saskatoon, Sask., 13 Feb. 1918; s. Hattie Laura (Warrington) and late James N.; e. Buena Vista Sch., Nutana Coll. Inst., Saskatoon, Sask.; Willard Jr. High Sch., Berkeley, Cal.; Univ. of Sask., B.A. 1939; Univ. of Alberta, D.D.S. 1941; Univ. of Mich., M.Sc. 1946; m. Elizabeth Verna, d. Rt. Rev. A. H. Sovereign, Vernon, B.C., 20 Aug. 1947; children: Kathryn Elizabeth, John Arthur, Barbara Ellen; DEAN, FACULTY OF DENT., UNIV. OF MANITOBA, since 1957; Consultant in Dent., Winnipeg Gen. Hosp.; mem. of Visiting Staff (Dent.), Sick Children's Hosp., Winnipeg; Asst. Prof. of Dent., Univ. of Alta., 1946-47, Assoc. Prof. 1947-52; Assoc. Prof. of Dent., Univ. of Wash., 1952-57; Diplomate, Am. Bd. of Periodontol.; mem. of Assoc. Comte. on Dental Research, N.C.R. of Can., since 1959; Comte. on Curricula, Am. Assn. of Dental Schs., since 1960; Dir., Winnipeg Children's Aid Soc.; Knowles Sch. for Boys, Winnipeg; served in 2nd World War with R.C.D.C., Can., U.K. and N.W. Europe, 1941-45; now Major, R.C.D.C. (inactive reserve); Examiner in Oral Med., Nat. Dental Examining Bd. of Can., 1958-60; mem., Winnipeg Dental Soc.; Man. Dental Assn.; Am. Acad. of Periodontol.; Candn. Acad. of Periodontol.; Am. Acad. of Oral Path.; Phi Kappa Pi; Omicron Kappa Upsilon; United Church; recreations: golf, curling, fishing, bridge, reading; Clubs: St. Charles Country; Winnipeg Winter; Rotary; Home: 196 Yale, Winnipeg, Man. R3M 0L8

NELSON, Arnold Luther Manfred, B.Com.; telecommunications executive; b. Percival, Sask. 29 June 1921; s. Ivan Florentine and Anna Sofia (Anderson) N.; e. elem. sch. Percival, Sask.; high sch. grade XI Correspondence 1937, grade XII Candn. Vocational Training Prince Albert 1947; Univ. of Sask. B.Com. 1950; m. Irene Margaret d. Walfred Carlson, Canwood, Sask. 31 Dec. 1950; children: Daryl Craig, Rodney Dale, Sandra Lee, Gregory Arnold, Susan Dee; PRES., SASK. TELECOMMUNICATIONS Dir., SASK COMP: Candn. Telecommunications Carriers Assn.; mem. Bd. Mang. TransCanada Telephone System; served with RCAF 1941-46, Europe 1944-46; Lutheran; recreations: golf, curling, skiing; Clubs: Rotary Internat.; Assiniboia; Wascana Country; Home: 136 Westfield Dr., Regina, Sask. S4S 2S7; Office: 2121Saskatchewan Dr., Regina, Sask. S4P 3Y2.

NELSON, James Gordon, M.A., Ph.D., educator; b. Hamilton, Ont. 3 Apl. 1932; e. McMaster Univ. B.A. 1955; Univ. of Colo. M.A. 1957; Johns Hopkins Univ. Ph.D. 1959; m. 3 children; DEAN OF ENVIRONMENTAL STUDIES, UNIV. OF WATERLOO and Prof. of Geog. there since 1975; Post Doctoral Fellow Johns Hopkins Univ. 1959-60; Asst. Assoc. and Prof. Univ. of Calgary 1960-71, also served as Head Dept. Geog., Assoc. Dean Planning, Asst. to Vice Pres. Special Projects; Prof. of Geog. Univ. of W. Ont. 1971-75; Consultant to Parks Can., Dept. of Environment, Econ. Council of Can.; Dir.

Renewable Resources Project, Inuit Tapirisat of Can. 1974-75; mem. non-govt. Candn. Adv. Comte. for Stockholm Conf. on Environment; Alaska Hwy. Pipeline Panel 1976-79; Trustee, Nat. & Prov. Parks Assn. Can. 1968-78 (Past Pres.); Pres., Assn. of Cndn. Univ. for Northern Studies; rec'd. Kitchener Police Citation 1976; Gilman Fellow; Bissing Post-Doctoral Fellow; Natural Heritage Award, 1978; author "The Last Refuge" 1973; "Man's Impact on the Western Canadian Landscape" 1976; Ed. "Canadian Parks in Perspective" 1971, various other books and journal articles; Past Pres. Candn. Assn. Geogs.; mem. Am. Assn. Geogs.; Am. Assn. Advanc. Science; Ecology Commn; Internat. Union for the Conservation of Nature and Natural Resources; Sigma Xi; Home: 296 Edgehill Dr., Kitchener, Ont.; Office: University Ave., Waterloo, Ont.

NELSON, Ronald Digby, C.A., R.I.A. executive; b. Sunderland, Co. Durham, Eng. 31 Dec 1935; s. Ronald D. Nelson; e. Queen's Univ. C.A. 1964; McMaster Univ. R.I.A. 1967; m. Renée C. d. of A. Sauvageau, Trois Rivieres, Que. 18 Apv. 1963; children: Ronald Digby, Tania Marie, CONTROLLER AND CHIEF FINANCIAL OFFICER, ANDEX OIL CO. LTD.;Lacombe Drilling Ltd.; Amisk Oil Co. Ltd.; Chrmn. and CEO, Pulsar Resources Ltd.; Student in Accounts, Butterfield & Steinhoff, Hamilton, Bermuda 1954-60; Acct., Reynolds International Inc. Bermuda 1960-63; Works Acct. Canadian Industries Ltd. Montreal, Shawinigan, Sarnia 1963-67; Aluminum Co. of Canada Toronto, Montreal, Vancouver 1967-70, Gen. Mgr. B.C. & N. Alta.; Vice-Pres. and Controller, Evans Products Co. Ltd. Vancouver 1971-74; Vice Pres. Finance and Administration, Weyerhaeuser Canada Ltd. Vancouver 1974-77; Vice Pres. Project Control and Acct., Foothill Pipelines (Yukon) Ltd. 1978-80; mem. Financial Extve. Inst.; Tax Extve. Inst.; R.I.A. of B.C. and Alta.,; Candn. Inst. C.A.'s Alta., Ont. and B.C.; Dir., and Past Pres., Project Management Inst. of Alta. (PMI); Petroleum Accts. Soc. of Western Canada (PASWC); First Vice-Pres., Assoc. of Chartered Accountants of Calgary; mem., 1980 and '81 Theme Comm., Calgary Ex. and Stampede; Calgary Professional Club, Y.M.C.A.; Chrmn., Spring bank Group Comm., Boy Scout, of Can.; P. Conservative; Anglican; recreations: canoeing, riding, gardening, back-packing, skiing; Home: R.R. 2, Calgary, Alta. T2P 2G5; Office: Ste. 1501-500-4 Ave. S.W. Calgary, Alta. T2P 2V6.

NEMETZ, Hon. Nathaniel Theodore, LL.D.; b. Winnipeg, Man., 8 Sept. 1913; s. late Samuel Abraham and late Rebecca (Birch) N.; e. Prince of Wales Sch., Vancouver, B.C.; Univ. of B.C., B.A. (1st Class Hons., Hist.) 1934; Vancouver Law Sch., 1937; m. Bel d. late Emanuel Newman, 10 Aug. 1935; one s. Pr. Peter Nemetz; CHIEF JUSTICE OF B.C., since January 1979; Chancellor, Univ. of B.C. 1972-75; read law with C. L. McAlpine, K.C.; called to Bar of B.C. 1937; cr. K.C. 1950; former Sr. Partner , Nemetz, Austin, Christie and Bruk, former Special Counsel (Labour Relations), City of Vancouver, City of New Westminster, Mun. of Burnaby, Elec. Assn. of B.C., B.C. Hosps. Assn.; Special Commr. apptd. by Govt of Can. & Prov. of B.C. to inquire into Fishing Industry Dispute, 1954; Special Counsel Pub. Utilities Comn. of B.C. Inquiry into Natural Gas Rates B.C. Electric, 1958 and Inland Natural Gas, 1959; Sr. Counsel, Royal Comn. on Expropriation, 1961; apptd. Judge, Supreme Court of B.C., 1963; Royal Commr. to investigate Election Irregularities, 1965;B.C. Indust. Enquiry Commr. to inquire into dispute of Forest Industry and Internat. Woodworkers, 1966; Special Commr. to Govt. of B.C. after Investigation on Swedish Labour Law and Practices, 1967; del., World Assembly of Judges, Geneva, 1967; Free Trade Conf., U.S., Can. and Gt. Brit., N.Y., 1968; Justice Appeal Court of B.C. 1968-75; mediator & arbitrator in labour disputes 1970, 1971; apptd. Chief Justice, Supreme Court of B.C. 1973; Publ. "Judicial Administration and Judicial Independence," 1976; Chrmn. Bd. of Govs., Univ. of

B.C., 1965-68 (mem. Senate 1957-66); del. 4th Gen. Conf. Internat. Assn. of Univs., Tokyo, 1965; Commonwealth Univs. Congress, Sydney, 1968; Head, official Candn. Educ. Del. to People's Rupub. of China 1974; Past Dir., Sick Children's Foundation; Past Chrmn., Univ. Dist. Sch. Bd.; Past Pres., Alumni Association of B.C.; mem., Bd. of Govs., Candn. Inst. for Advanced Legal Studies (Cambridge); Vancouver Lodge B'nai B'rith; Vancouver Inst.; Past Dir., Vancouver Festival; Playhouse Theatre; Vancouver Community Chest; Recipient Human Relations Award, Candn. Council of Christians and Jews, Vancouver 1958, and Beth Emeth Bais Yehuda Brotherhood Award, Toronto, 1968; Univ. of B.C. Students Great Trekker Award, 1969; mem., Candn. Bar Assn.; World Assembly of Judges; Internat. Law Assn.; Candn. Inst. Internat. Affairs; Convocation Fndg. mem., Simon Fraser Univ.; Hon. LL.D. Notre Dame of Nelson 1972; Simon Fraser 1975; U.B.C. 1975; Victoria 1976; Distinction Award U.B.C. Alumni, 1975; Red'd. Canada Medal 1967; Silver Jubilee Medal 1977; Hon. Fellow, Hebrew Univ., Jerusalem 1976; el. Sponsor Mayo Fdn., 1976; Special Grant, Amer. Chief Justices Conference, Anchorage, Alaska 1980; Zeta Beta Tau; Jewish; recreations: swimming, billiards; Club: University (Past Pres.); Fac. Club, Univ. of B.C.; Union Club, Victoria; Vancouver Club, Vancouver; Office: Law Courts, Vancouver, B.C.

NEPVEU, Paul A., B.A.; executive; b. Montreal, Que. 13 June 1916; e. Univ. of Montreal B.A. 1935; Ecole des Hautes Etudes Commerciales grad. work Math. 1937; Univ. of W. Ont. Dipl. in Mang. 1961; CHMN. OF BD. AND DIR. C.I.P. INC.; Dir., Canadian Pacific Enterprises Ltd.; Dir., Cominco Ltd.; PanCanadian Petroleum Ltd.; Canadian Pacific Securities Ltd.; Great Lakes Forest Products Ltd.; Marathon Realty Co. Ltd.; Chateau Insurance Co.; The Algoma Steel Corp. Ltd.; Canadian Pacific Hotels Ltd.; Syracuse China Corp.; Canadian Pacific Enterprises (U.S.) Inc.; Cost Analyst, Dufresne Engineering 1939-41; joined Canadian Pacific Cost Accounting Dept., Angus Shops 1942, Gen. Stat. 1953 Asst. Comptroller 1964, Vice Pres. Accounts & Data Systems 1969, Vice Pres. and Comptroller 1973, Vice Pres. Finance & Accounting Canadian Pacific Ltd. and Canadian Pacific Investments Ltd. 1973; Vice-Chmn., Canadian Pacific Enterprises 1979; mem. Chambre de Comm.; Montreal Bd. Trade; Clubs: St-Denis; Oka Golf; Office: 1155 Metcalf St., Montreal, Que. H3B 2X1.

NESBITT, Herbert Hugh John, Ph.D., D.Sc., F.L.S., F.R.E.S., F.E.S.C., F.Z.S.; retired university dean; b. Ottawa, Ont., 7 Feb. 1913; s. Herbert Hugh Wright and Anne Violet (Gould) N.; e. Queen's Univ., B.A. 1937; Univ. of Toronto, M.A. 1939; Ph.D. 1944; Univ. of Leiden, D.Sc. 1951; D.Sc. (hon) Carleton Univ., 1978; m. Mary Elizabeth, d. T. E. Clendinnen, Ottawa, Ont., 24 June 1944; children: Eleanor Anne, Thomas H. D., David A.C., Robert I. M.; CLERK OF SENATE CARLETON UNIV., since 1975; Agric. Scientist, Dept. of Agric., Ottawa, 1939-48; Asst. Prof. of Biol., Carleton Univ., 1948, Assoc. Prof. 1952; Prof. 1956; Prof. Emeritus, 1978; Dean, Faculty of Science 1963-75; Fellow Linnean Soc. of London; Entomol. Soc. Am.; Fellow, Entomological Society of Canada; Conservative; mem. Bd. of Governors, Algonquin College, Ottawa; United Church; Address: Carleton University, Ottawa, Ont.

NESMITH, M. Eugene; banker; b. 19 June 1928; e. Matriculation; m. Adele Patricia (Dunsmore) 1951; children: Wade, Alison, Karen; PRESIDENT AND CHIEF EXTVE. OFFR., HONGKONG BANK OF CANADA 1980- ; joined Bank of Montreal 1946-80 becoming Sr. Vice Pres. B.C. and Yukon Div.; Nat. Dir. Jr. Achievement Can.; Hon. Treas. & Gov. Vancouver Sch. Theol.; Sr. Vice Chrmn. and Vice Pres. Vancouver Bd. Trade; Fellow, Inst. Candn. Bankers; Clubs: Vancouver; Vancouver Lawn Tennis & Badminton; Shaughnessy Golf & Coun-

try; Home: 6345 Adera St., Vancouver, B.C. V6M 3J7; Office: 1818, 200 Granville St., Vancouver, B.C. V6C 1L3.

NETTEN, Edward William, B.Com., C.A., F.M.C.; management consultant; b. Corner Brook, Nfld. 17 Oct. 1930; e. McGill Univ., B.Com. (magna cum laude) 1951; C.A. Que. 1953, B.C. 1963, Ont. 1973; m. Sheila, d. Stanley Jackson 24 Nov. 1956; children: Linda, June, Cynthia, Shirley; MANAGING PARTNER FOR CANADA, AND IN CHARGE TORONTO OFFICE, PRICE WATERHOUSE ASSOCIATES since 1981; with McDonald Currie & Co. as Student and Supvr. Montreal 1951; Cooper Bros. & Co. (Staff exchange) London, Eng. 1955 = 56; joined present Co. as Consultant, Montreal 1957, Mgr. 1960, Partner 1965; i.c. Mang. Consulting Services W. Can. Vancouver 1963, Partner i.c. consulting services in mang. controls Montreal 1967, Partner i.c. Montreal office 1968, Partner i.c. client services in mang. planning, information and control 1971; trans. to Toronto 1973; Partner in charge, Toronto Office 1974; mem. Inst. Mang. Consultants Can. (Pres. 1974-76, Past Dir. & Secy.); author numerous articles on mang. policy, organ., mang. controls, accounting and operations research; Anglican; recreations: golf, tennis, skiing; Clubs: Toronto Club; Ontario Racquet; Terminal City (Vancouver); Montreal Country (Past Dir. and Treas.); Home: 1491 Watersedge Rd., Mississauga, Ont. L5J 1A5; Office: First Canadian Place,Toronto, Ont. M5X 1H7

NEVILLE, John, O.B.E.; actor; director; b. London Eng. 2 May 1925; s. Reginald Daniel and Mabel Lillian (Fry)N.; e. Grammar Sch. London, Eng.; Royal Acad. Dramatic Art London; m. Caroline Hooper 9 Dec. 1949; children: Rachel, Emma, Thomas, Sarah, Matthew, Stephen; joined Bristol Old Vic Company 1950-53; played numerous leading parts Old Vic Company, London 1953-61; made first New York appearance Winter Garden Theatre 1956 playing Romeo followed by Richard II, Macduff in "Macbeth" and Thersites in "Troilus and Cressida"; after touring US returned to London for 1957-58 season; toured US 1958-59 playing Hamlet and Sir Andrew Aguecheek; directed Henry V 1960; joined Nottingham Playhouse Co. 1961, Assoc. Producer 1961, Jt. Theatre Dir. 1963-67, played various leading roles incl. Macbeth and Sir Thomas More in "A Man for All Seasons" (appeared in both roles Malta 1961); appeared opening Chichester Festival 1962 as Don Frederick in "The Chances" and Orgilus in "The Broken Heart"; toured W. Africa with Co. for Brit. Council 1963; appeared Edinburgh Festival 1970 for Prospect Productions Garrick in "Boswell's Life of Johnson" and Benedick in "Much Ado About Nothing"; toured US 1970; films incl.: "Oscar Wilde" 1960, "Billy Budd" 1961, "Topaze" 1961; TV appearances incl.: "Henry V" 1957, "Romeo and Juliet" 1957 and "Hamlet" 1959 both New York; leading role in "Sherlock Holmes", Broadway, N.Y. summer 1975; came to Canada, 1972, dir. "The Rivals" and played Prospero in 'The Tempest," Ottawa, Judge Brack in 'Hedda Gabler," Manitoba Theatre Centre, Theatre Dir. at Citadel Theatre, Edmonton, Alta. 1972, dir. 'Romeo & Juliette", "The Master Builder". "Schweyk in the Second World War," and "Antigone," appeared in several plays; currently Theatre Div., Neptune Theatre, Halifax, May 1978, appeared in "Othello" and "Staircase," dir. "Les Canadiens" and "The Sea Gull"; served with RN 1942-46; rec'd Alta. Achievement Award; mem. Brit. Actors Equity; Candn. Actors Equity; ACTRA; Anglican; recreations: music, opera, ballet; Club: Savage (London, Eng.); Home: 6370 Pepperell St., Halifax, N.S. B3H 2P4

NEW, C. John; industrialist; b. Prince Albert, Sask., 8 March 1921; s. Charles George and Elizabeth H. (McDowell) N.; m. Una Rae Gillis, 25 Nov. 1944; children: Janet Leslie, Douglas Charles; VICE-PRES & DIR., HIRAM WALKER & SONS LIMITED, 1981-; Pres. and Chief Extve. Offr., Corby Distilleries Ltd. 1970-81; spent early yrs. in Man. and B.C.; with Lever Brothers Ltd. and several other cos. prior to joining Libby, McNeil & Libby of Canada Ltd., Chatham, Ont. 1962; Pres. and Mang. Dir. 1966; served with Canadian Army in 2nd World War; gaz. Capt. 1942; grad. Mil. Staff Coll. 1943; a Gov., Jr. Achievement of Canada and Founder, Jr. Achievement (Chatham, Ont.); mem. Associates of Sir George Williams Univ.; Assoc. mem., Candn. Conf. of the Arts; mem. Montreal Bd. of Trade; Clubs: National (Toronto); Granite (Toronto); Mount Royal; M.A.A.A.; Home: 1210, 65 Harbour Sq., Toronto, Ont. M5J 2L4

NEWALL, James Edward Malcolm, B.Com.; executive; b. Holden, Alta. 20 Aug. 1935; s. Robert Robertson Newall; e. elm. sch. Edmonton, Alta. and Prince Albert, Sask.; Prince Albert Coll. Inst.; Univ. of Sask. B.Com. 1958; m. Margaret Elizabeth Lick; CHRM. OF THE BOARD, PRES. DIR. DU PONT OF CANADA LTD. 1979-; Vice-Pres. Canadian Manufacturing Assoc; mem. Business Council on Nat'l Issues; Dir. Petrosar Ltd.; joined Du Pont as internal sales rep. Chem. Dept. Toronto 1958, Sales Promotion Rep. Fibres, Montreal 1959, Sales Rep. Nylon Toronto 1963, Merchandising Supvr. Knitwear Montreal 1964, Sales Mgr. Texturing 1965, Merchandising Services Mgr. Textile Fibres 1966, Marketing Mgr. Textile Div. 1968, Mgr. Strategic Planning Marketing 1970, Asst. Dir. Fibres Group 1971, Dir. Fibres Group 1972, Vice Pres. Corporate Devel. 1974, Vice Pres. Marketing 1975, Extve. Vice Pres. 1975, Dir. 1976; Chrmn. and Dir. Candn. Textiles Inst.; Dir. Candn. Chem. Producers Assn.; Candn. Export Assn.; recreations: golf, reading; Clubs: St. James's; Forest & Stream; Mount Royal; Rideau (Ottawa); Office: 555 Dorchester Blvd. W., P.O. Box 660, Stn. A., Montreal, Que. H3C 2V1

NEWBOLD, Brian T., D.Sc., C.Chem., F.R.S.C. (U.K.), F.C.I.C., F.R.S.A.; educator; b. Manchester, Eng. 21 June 1932; s. John Stanley and Florence (Wray) N.; e. schs. Eng. and Wales; Univ. of Manchester B.Sc. (Chem. & Physiol.) 1953; Laval Univ. D.Sc. (Organic Chem.) 1957, Post-Doctoral Fellow 1957-58; m. Mary Cecile Evelyn, d. late William Patrick LaRoche, 16 Aug. 1958; children: Linda, Trevor; VICE PRES. UNIV. OF MONCTON since 1979; Prof. Chem., U. of Moncton 1965-; Dir. of Research, Pres. Research Council (1969-75) and mem. Acad. Senate (1963-75, 1976-77, 1979-); Bd. of Govs. (1979-); Asst. Prof. of Chem. St. Joseph Univ. 1958, Assoc. Prof. 1960, Head Dept. of Chem. 1961; joined present Univ. as Assoc. Prof. and Head Dept. of Chem. 1963, Vice-Dean Faculty of Science 1963-69; Visiting Lectr. in biochem. Mount Allison Univ. 1962-63; Visiting Prof. Laval Univ. 1975-76; mem. N.B. Higher Educ. Comn. 1967-74; rec'd "Plaque de 10 ans" (Univ. Moncton) 1973; mem. and Pres. (1971-72) St. Henri Home & Sch. Assn. Moncton; Candn. nat. repres. Comte. on Teaching Chem., Internat. Union Pure & Applied Chem. 1969-; Cultural Exchange Comte. Can. Council, 1971-74; co-author "Chemical Canada" 1970; author or co-author over 90 research publs. incl. book chapters, papers, articles; columnist "Gliding" Quebec Chronicle Telegraph 1956-58; Sr. mem. Am. Chem. Soc.; Pres., New Brunswick Environ Council, (1975-79), Pres. 1974-75, Beauséjour Home and Sch. Assn., Moncton; mem. Royal Netherlands Chem. Soc.; Natural Science & Engn. Research Council of Can. 1978-80; Chem. Inst. Can. (Dir., 1968-71); Candn. Soc. Study Higher Educ. (Extve. Council), 1970-74, 1975-76; Assn. Canadienne française pour l'avancement des sciences (Dir., Prés. Comité des Publs.); Candn. Assn. Univ. Research Adms. (Extve. Council) 1972-74; Hon. Sec. SCITEC 1977-79; Ed. SCITEC Bulletin 1977-79; Ed. Can. Chem. Educ. (1965-75); Rec'd Union Carbide Award for Chem. Educ. 1977; mem. Nat. Council Candn. Fed. of Human Rights, 1980-; Sr. Univ. Admrs. Course, Univ. of W. Ont. 1980; Consultant to Maritime Provinces Higher Educ. Comn. 1976-80; mem. Comté consultatif, Sci. et tech., Soc. Radio Canada, 1978-; mem. Assn. for Educ. of Sci. Teachers, 1979-81; Inst. Candn. des affairs internat., 1979; Liason Officer,

Univ.Moncton for C.I.D.A., 1981-; mem., N.S. Art Gallery (1979-80); Bd. of Govs., Beaverbrook Art Gallery, 1981-; Consultant to Internat. Devel. Research Centre (1981); Citation Directory of World Researchers (1981); Rec'd Hon. Citizenship and Friendship Medal from Munic. of St. Pierre, French Territory of St. Pierre et Mignelon (1981); Anglican; recreations: gliding (pilot 1954-58); bridge, hockey, soccer (coach University Moncton 1970), reading, philately, numismatics, painting; Home: 167 Edgett Avenue, Moncton, N.B. E1A 7B4; Office: Sunny Brae Campus, Moncton, N.B.

NEWBOUND, Kenneth B., M.Sc., Ph.D.; physicist; educator; b. Winnipeg, Man., 12 March 1919; s. Albert Everard and Bertha Beatrice (Bateman) N.; e. Daniel McIntyre Coll. Inst., Winnipeg, 1935; Univ. of Man., B.Sc. 1940, M.Sc. 1941; Mass. Inst. of Technol., Ph.D. (Physics) 1948; m. Lyndell Hilda, d. late Russell St. George Edmonds, 15 July 1947; children: Beatrice Elizabeth, Kenneth Randolph, Lawrence Douglas, Peter Edmonds; PROF. OF PHYSICS, UNIV. OF ALBERTA since 1958 and Dean of Science 1976-81; Jr. Research Physicist, Div. of Physics & Elect. Engn., Nat. Research Council, 1941-43; joined present Univ. as Asst. Prof. of Physics 1948, Assoc. Prof. 1953; Asst. to Dean of Arts & Science 1954, Asst. Dean of Arts & Science 1961; Assoc. Dean of Science 1964; Defence Scient. Service Offr., Defence Research Bd., Naval Research Estab., Dartmouth, N.S., 1956-57; served with R.C.N.V.R., Naval Research Estab., Halifax, 1943-45; rank Lt. on discharge; author various papers reporting exper. work from 1940-63; mem., Triumf Bd. of Mang.; Candn. Assn. Physicists; Anglican; recreations: music, travel, philately; Home: 8910 Windsor Rd., Edmonton, Alta.; Office: Edmonton, Alta. T6G 2A2

NEWCOMBE, Howard Borden, B.Sc., Ph.D., D.Sc., F.R.S.C.; biologist; b. Kentville, N.S., 19 Sept. 1914; s. Edward Borden and Mabel Elsie (Outerbridge) N.; e. Acadia Univ., B.Sc. (Biol.) 1935; McGill Univ., Ph.D. 1939; Imp. Coll. of Tropical Agric., Trinidad, W.I., A.I.C.T.A. 1938; D.Sc. McGill Hon.; Acadia 1970; m. Beryl Honor, d. Capt. George W. Callaway, Plymouth, Eng., 14 Feb. 1942; children: Kenneth Donald, Charles Philip, Richard William; 1851 Science Research Scholar, John Innes Hort. Inst., 1939-40; Research Assoc., Carnegie Inst. of Wash., Dept. of Genetics, 1946-47; joined present Co. in 1947; Visiting Prof. of Genetics, Indiana Univ. (spring), 1963; Lieut., R.N.V.R., 1941-46; Head, Population Research Br., Atomic Energy of Canada Ltd, retired 1979; author: numerous scien. papers (mutations in microorganisms; effects of ionizing radiations; methods of study of human population genetics); mem., Internat. Comn. on Radiological Protection, 1965-77; Genetics Soc. Am. (Secy., 1956-58); Am. Soc. Human Genetics (Pres., 1965); Genetics Soc. of Can. (Pres. 1965); Home: 67 Hillcrest Ave., Deep River, Ont. K0J 1P0; 67 Hillcrest Ave., Deep River, Ont. K0J 1P0

NEWELL, Paul Scudder; manufacturer; b. Toronto, Ont. 10 July 1918; s. Edward N.; m. Betsy Lee, Toronto, Ont., 15 Jan. 1942; one d. Kristen; PRESIDENT, DOMINION ENVELOPE, since 1947; Chrmn. of Bd., Merry Packaging; Commercial Mailings Unlimited Inc.; Dir., Redpath Indus. Ltd.; Compro Ltd.; Capital Growth Fund Limited; joined present Company in 1937; Plant, 1940; Assistant Sales Mgr. 1941, Sales Mgr. and Dir., 1942; Pres., 1947; Pres., Envelope Makers Inst. Can. 1962-63; Pres. (1972-73) Envelope Inst. of Am.; Dir. (1970-72) Candn. Flexible Packaging Inst.; Clubs: Rosedale Golf; Lyford Cay (Nassau); Home: 65 Castle Frank Rd., Toronto, Ont. M4W 2Z9; Office: 39 Greenbelt Drive, Don Mills, Ont. M3C 1M2

NEWFELD, Frank; book designer; publishing consultant; b. Brno, Czechoslovakia 1 May 1928; s. Arnold and Rose (Deutsch) Neufeld; e. Central Sch. of Arts & Crafts, London, Eng. Hons. Dipl. 1952; m. Joan Barrie d. late William Hart 25 Aug. 1958; children: Philip Laurence, David Stefan; Pres., MacPherson Newfeld; Dir. McClelland and Stewart Ltd.; estbd. Frank Newfeld Studio 1954; Teacher, Central Tech. Sch. 1955-56, Ryerson Inst. of Technol. 1956-57, Ont. Coll. of Art 1958-65; joined McClelland and Stewart Ltd. 1963 as Art Dir., Dir. of Design & Production 1964, Creative Dir. 1965, Vice Pres. Publishing 1969, Dir. 1974, Consultant 1976-78; joined MacPherson Newfeld Ltd. 1970; Publishing Consultant, Nat. Gallery of Can. 1973-75; Lectr. and mem. Adv. Council, Sheridan Coll.; design and illustration for various publishing firms Can., USA and UK; design for museums and galleries incl. Art Gallery of Ont., Museum of Modern Art N.Y., Nat. Gallery of Can., Nat. Museums of Man, Royal Ont. Museum; design and illustration for various mags.; exhns. of work Can., Czechoslovakia, Germany, Holland, Isreal, Japan, Spain, UK, USA; rec'd numerous awards/certs. since 1955 incl. 6th Annual Book Jacket Competition Scot. 1960, Hans Christian Andersen Awards 1962, 1975, Annual Book Exhn. Leipzig 1963, Internat. Book Exhn. Leipzig 1965, 1977, Printing Industs. Am. 1968, 1971, Soc. of Illustrators 1968, Look of Books 1970, 1972, 1974, 1976, Ruth Schwartz/CBA Award for Best Children's Book 1978; Candn. Centennial Medal 1967; Queen's Silver Jubilee Medal 1977; author "The Princess of Tomboso" 1960; co-author "Great Canadian Painting" 1965; "Simon and the Golden Sword" 1976; mem. Royal Candn. Acad. (Council); Am. Inst. Graphic Arts; recreations: horses, theatre; Home: 34 Palmdale Dr., Agincourt, Ont. M1T 3M7; Office: 111 Queen St. E., Toronto, Ont. M5C 1S2.

NEWHOOK, Hon. Hazel, M.H.A.; politician; MIN. OF MUNICIPAL AFFAIRS 1981; el. M.H.A. for Gander prov. g.e. 1979; Min. of Consumer Affairs & The Environment, 1979-81; P. Conservative; Office: Confederation Bldg., St. John's, Nfld. A1C 5T7.

NEWLOVE, John Herbert; poet; b. Regina, Sask., 13 June 1938; s. Thomas Harold and Mary Constant (Monteith) N.; e. Senior Matriculation, Sask., 1956; m. Susan Mary, d. H. J. Phillips, Vernon, B.C., 9 Aug. 1966; stepchildren: Jeremy Charles, Tamsin Elizabeth; author: "Grave Sirs", 1962; "Elephants, Mothers & Others", 1964; "Moving In Alone", 1965, new ed., 1977; "Notebook Pages", 1966; "What They Say", 1967 and 1968; "Black Night Window", 1968; "The Cave", 1970; "Lies" 1972; "The Fat Man (Selected Poems)", 1977; ed., "Canadian Poety: The Modern Era", 1977; "Dreams Surround Us" (with John Metcalf). 1977; other writings inc. works in anthols.; received grants from Canada Council and Koerner Foundation of B.C.; Deep Springs (Cal.) Coll. Arts Award; Governor General's Award, Poetry, 1972; Poet-in-residence, Loyola Coll. 1974-75; Univ. Western Ont. 1975-76; Univ. of Toronto 1976-77; Regina Public Library, 1979-80; Address: c/o McClelland and Stewart, 25 Hollinger Road, Toronto, Ont. M4B 3G2

NEWMAN, Barry G., M.A., Ph.D.; university professor; b. Manchester, Eng., 23 May 1926; s. Frederick Challender and Dorothy Edna (George) N.; e. Manchester Grammar Sch., Eng.; Cambridge Univ., B.A. 1947, M.A. 1951 (Strathcona Open Major Scholar in Math., St. John's Coll.); Sydney Univ., Ph.D. 1952; m. Joan, d. Arthur Farmer, Arnprior, Ont., 10 Sept. 1955; one s., Duncan; two d. Joanna, Charlotte; CANADAIR PROF. OF AERODYNAMICS, McGILL UNIV., since 1959; Secy. Grad. Faculty there 1963-65 and Chrmn., Dept. of Mech. Engn. 1969-72; mem. Senate there, 1979-; mem. Nat. Research Council Assoc. Comte. on Aerodynamics 1962-64 and 1978-79; and Chrmn. 1968 and 1979; Consultant to Canadair Ltd.; Pratt & Whitney Canada; Pulp & Paper Research Inst. Can.; Vice-Chmn., Aeronautics Advisory Board, Dep't of Transport; Research Student & Jr. Res. Fellow, Sydney Univ., 1947-51; Scient. Offr. Royal Aust. Air Force (Flight Research on Aerodynamic Problems) 1951-53; Research Offr., Nat. Research Council, Ottawa,

1953-55; Univ. Lectr. in Aerodynamics, Cambridge Univ., 1955-58; Canadair Visiting Prof. in Fluid Mech., Laval Univ., 1958-59; Contrib. to: "Boundary and Flow Control", "Scale Effects in Animal Locomotion", and "Fluid Mechanics of Internal Flow"; Fellow, Candn. Aero. & Space Inst.; Royal Aero Soc. (Rec'd. (with C. Bourque) Edward Busk Mem. Prize 1961); recreations: squash, sailing; Home: 49 Nelson St., Montreal West, Que. H4X 1G5

NEWMAN, Christina McCall, B.A.; writer & editor; b. Toronto, Ont., 29 Jan. 1935; d. Christopher Warnock and Orlie Alma (Freeman) McCall; e. Jarvis Coll. Inst. Toronto, 1952; Victoria Coll., Univ. of Toronto, B.A. 1956; m. 1. Peter Charles Newman, divorced, 2. Stephen Hugh Elliott Clarkson; one d., Jennifer Ashley Newman; Ed. Asst., Maclean's 1956-58; Assoc. Ed., Chatelaine Mag., 1958-1963; freelance writer and broadcaster, 1963-67; Ottawa Ed., Saturday Night, 1967-70; Assoc. Ed., Maclean's 1971-74; National Reporter, The Globe & Mail (Newspaper) 1974-1976; Extve Ed., Saturday Night, 1976; received several Press Club Awards for Mag. writing; Pres.'s Medal of Univ. of Western Ont. for Best Mag. Article 1970; Southam Fellowship in Journalism at Univ. of Toronto 1977; Nat. Magazine Award Gold Medal 1981; has served on several Can. council juries and committees, and as jurist for the Toronto Book Award; Dir., Telecanada; author, "The Man from Oxbow" 1967; Home: 44 Rosedale Rd. Toronto, Ont. M4W 2P6; Office: 70 Bond St., Toronto, Ont. M5B 2J3

NEWMAN, John, R.C.A.; artist; b. Toronto, Ont. 6 Apl. 1933; s. John William and Pearl (Beatty) N.; e. Ont. Coll. of Art 1952-56; Art Acad. of Cincinnati 1956-57; various European museums 1966, 1971-72, 1976-78; m. Shirley Corrine d. Lennox Dow MacGregor 1 Sept. 1956; three s. John MacGregor, Peter George, Adam Errol; CHRMN., FINE ART DEPT., ONT. COLL. OF ART 1979 - full-time mem. Faculty 1963- , Acting Chrmn. Fine Art Dept. 1977-78; Exhibit Designer Royal Ont. Museum 1958-63; solo exhns.: Victoria Coll. Univ. of Toronto 1963, St. Michael's Coll. 1971, Erindale Coll. 1973, Scarborough Coll. 1974; Rodman Hall Arts Centre St. Catharines 1969; Laing Gallery Edmonton 1971; Althouse Coll. Univ. of W. Ont. 1973; Art Gallery Gander, Nfld. 1973, Corner Brook Arts & Culture Centre and Grand Falls Art & Culture Centre 1974, Mem. Univ. of Nfld. 1974; Galerie de l'Esprit Montreal 1975; Brock Univ. St. Catharines 1976; Art Gallery of Hamilton 1976; Palazzo Strozzi Florence, Italy 1977; Prince Arthur Galleries Toronto 1979; Hett Gallery Ltd. Edmonton 1981; rep. various group exhns. incl. Royal Acad. London 1972, Metrop. Gallery Tokyo, Le Salon 77 Paris, Nat. Gallery Can., Montreal Museum of Fine Arts, Art Gallery of Ont., Cincinnati Art Museum; rep. in perm. and private colls. Can., Eng., Italy, U.S.A.; recipient 1st Prize Internat. Painting Competition Candn. Nat. Exhn. 1956; Art Acad. Grad. Div. Scholarship 1956, Prize for Drawing 1957, Cincinnati; Can. Council Grant 1966; John Alfsen Award for Drawing Candn. Soc. Graphic Art 1973; Candn. Soc. Painters in Watercolour Honour Award 1973, A. E. Ames Purchase Award 1973, Curry Award 1976; Ont. Council for Arts Grant 1976; Sun Oil Canada Ltd. "On View" Award 1976; mem. Candn. Soc. Painters in Watercolour; Print & Drawing Council of Can.; Address: 170 Hammersmith Ave., Toronto, Ont. M4E 2W8.

NEWMAN, Murray Arthur, C.M., B.Sc., M.A., Ph.D.; aquarium director; b. Chicago, Ill. 6 March 1924; s. Paul Jones and Virginia (Murray) N.; e. Univ. of Chicago B.Sc. 1949; Univ. of Hawaii 1950; Univ. of Cal. Berkley M.A. 1951; Univ. of B.C. Ph.D. 1960; m. Katherine Lloyd Rose d. Godfrey Greene 8 Aug. 1952; one d. Susan; DIR. VANCOUVER PUBLIC AQUARIUM; Pres. Mana Aquarium Consultants; participated capture first live killer whale 1964; W. Candn. Exhibits and Beluga Pool 1967; New Guinea Expdn. 1969-70; Killer Whale Pool 1971; Narwhal

Expdn. 1971; Sea Otter Pool 1973; Seal Pool 1978; Amazon Expdn. 1979; Council mem. Westwater Research Centre, Univ. B.C.; served with U.S. Navy 1943-46; rec'd Harold J. Merilees Award 1976; Candn. Centennial Medal 1967; Man of Yr. City of Vancouver 1964; mem. Candn. Assn. Zool. Parks & Aquariums (Pres. 1978-79); Am. Assn. Zool. Parks & Aquariums (Bd. 1972-75); Internat. Union Dirs. Zool. Gdns.; Chrmn. Bamfield Marine Sta. Adv. Comte.; N.Y. Acad. Sciences; recreations: boating, fishing, travel; Clubs: Vancouver; University; Round Table; Home: 4915 Beacon Lane, West Vancouver, B.C. V7W 1K6; Office: (P.O. Box 3232) Vancouver Aquarium, Vancouver, B.C. V6B 3X8.

NEWMAN, Peter Charles, O.C. B.A., M.Com., D.Lit. (York), LL.D. (Brock), F.R.S.A.; editor; writer; b. Vienna, Austria, 10 May 1929; s. Oskar Charles and Wanda Maria (Newman) N.; came to Canada 1940; e. Upper Canada College, Toronto, Ontario; University of Toronto, B.A. 1950; University of Toronto Inst. Business Administration, M.Com. 1954; m. 1. Christina McCall, divorced, 2. Camilla Jane Turner, 5 Aug. 1978; EDITOR MACLEAN'S MAGAZINE since 1971 and Dir., Maclean-Hunter since 1972; joined the "Financial Post" as Asst. Editor 1951; apptd. Montreal Ed. 1954 and Production Ed. 1955; resigned 1956 to become Asst. Ed. "Maclean's Magazine"; appt. Ottawa Ed. 1960, Nat. Affairs Ed. 1963; Ottawa Ed., "Toronto Daily Star" and syndicated pol. columnist in 29 Candn. newspapers 1964-69; Editor-in-Chief 1969-71; served as Commander R.C.N.(R) 1950-54; has written extensively on Candn. business and pol. in many U.S., U.K. and Candn. mags. incl. "The Times" of London, "Queen's Quarterly", "Public Affairs" and "The New York Times"; toured Europe for the "Financial Post" 1954 ; Asia and Middle E. for Maclean's in 1961; author of "Flame of Power", intimate profiles of Can.'s greatest businessmen 1959 (became nat. best-seller, reprinted three times); "Renegade in Power: The Diefenbaker Years" 1963 (became Candn. pol. best-seller, reprinted six times); "The Distemper of Our Times", pol. hist. of Can. 1963-68, 1968 (Book of Month Club selection); "Home Country-People, Places and Power Politics" (Lit. Guild Selection) 1973; "The Canadian Establishment — Vol. 1 The Great Business Dynasties" (all-time Candn. best-seller); "The Canadian Establishment", 1975; "Bronfman Dynasty" The Rothschilds of the New World" (Book-of-the-Month Club Selection in Canada and U.S. Also published in U.S. as "King of the Castle"), 1978; "The acquisitors-The Canadian Establishment, Volume II" 1981; 1975; co-author of 90-minute television documentary awarded CBC's Wilderness Award for best production of year 1967; co-author CBC-TV series "The Tenth Decade" which won Michener Award for Journalism; author seven-part T.V. series on "The Canadian Establishment"; awarded Nat. Newspaper Award for Journalism 1971; Univ. of W. Ont. Pres. Medal for Best Mag. Article 1973; Achievement in Life Award by Encyclopedia Brit. Pubs., 1977; Quill Award for Excellence in Candn. Journalism, 1977; Installed Officer Order of Canada April 1979; Invested, Knight Order of Saint Lazarus, Apr. 1980; Invested Kn. of Lippe; North West Territories Royal Life Saving Soc. medal, Life Saving Soc. of Portugal, Silver Medal Japanese Red Cross Soc.; Depy. Gov. (Can.) Internat. Press Inst. 1969-71; mem. Bd. Govs., Univ. of Toronto 1972-74; Dir., Nat. Youth Orchestra of Can. 1968-72; Visiting Prof. of Pol. Science, McMaster Univ. 1969-71; visiting Prof., Political Sc., York U., 1979-80; recreations: sailing, skiing; Clubs: Rideau (Ottawa); R.C.Y.C.; Strollers; Home: 64 Admiral Rd., Toronto, Ont. M5R 2L5; Office: 481 University Ave., Toronto, Ont. M5W 1A7

NEWMAN, Sydney, O.C., F.R.S.A.; TV executive and producer; b. Toronto, Ont., 1 Apl. 1917; e. Central Tech. Sch., Toronto, in Comm. and Fine Arts Course; m. Margaret Elizabeth McRae; three d. Deirdre, Jennifer, Gillian; PRES., SYDNEY NEWMAN ENTERPRISES INCORP.,

since 1977; CHIEF CREATIVE CONSULTANT FOR CANADIAN FILM DEVEL. CORP., since 1978; painter; stage, indust. and interior designer; still and cinema photographer, 1935-41; joined Nat. Film Bd. of Canada, under John Grierson as splicer-boy, 1941; Editor and Dir. of Armed Forces training films and war information shorts, 1942; Producer, "Canada Carries On", 1945; Extve. Producer in charge of all films for cinemas, incl. short films, newsreels, films for children and travel, 1947-52; over 300 documentaries, incl. U.N. "Suffer Little Children"; "It's Fun to Sing" (Venice Award); "Ski Skill"; "After Prison, What?" (Canada Award); reported to NBC in New York on TV techniques for Nat. Film Bd. of Can., 1949-50; joined CBC as TV Dir. of Features and Outside Broadcasts, 1952; Supv. of Drama, and Producer, "Gen. Motors Theatre", "On Camera", "Ford Theatre", "Graphic", 1954; Producer first plays by Arthur Hailey, incl. "Flight into Danger", "Course for Collision"; Ohio State Award for Religious Drama; Liberty Award Best Drama Series; appt. Supv. of Drama and Producer of "Armchair Theatre", ABC TV, Eng, 1958; comnd. and produced first on-air plays of Alun Owen, Harold Pinter, Angus Wilson, Robert Muller, Hugh Leonard, Peter Luke; also plays by Clive Exton and David Perry; Head of Drama Group, BBC Television 1963-68, responsible for all drama and opera incl. "Z-Cars", "The Wednesday Play"; "The Forsythe Saga"; personally produced "Stephen D" by Hugh Leonard from James Joyce, "The Tea Party" by Harold Pinter and "The Rise and Fall of the City of Mahogany" by Kurt Weill and Berthold Brecht; created TV series "The Avengers", "Adam Adamant Lives!" and "Dr. Who"; Extve. Producer, Feature films, Associated British Picture Corp., Elstree, Eng. 1969; Dir. Programmes, C.R.T.C., Ottawa 1970; Dir., CBC, 1972-75; Candn. Film Devel. Corp., 1970-75; Trustee, Nat. Arts Centre, 1970-75; Gov't Film Commr. and Pres., Nat. Film Bd. of Can., 1970-75; Special Adv. on Film to Secy. of State, 1975-77; Gov't, Candn. Conf. of the Arts, 1978; mem., New Western Film and TV Fdn., 1978; rec'd. awards from Soc. of Film and Television Arts, and Writers Guild of Gt. Brit.; Special Recog. Award from Soc. of Motion Pictures and TV Engrs., 1975; Kt. of Mark Twain; Fellow Soc. Film & Television Arts; Officer, O of Canada 1981; recreations: sculpture, painting; Address: 3 Nesbitt Dr., Toronto Ont. M4W 2G2

NEWMARK, John H., O.C. (1974); D: Mus. (McGill Univ. 1975); musician; b. Bremen, W. Germany; came to Canada 1940; studied music in Leipzig, Germany; has played with over 80 internat. famed vocal and instrumental artists and over 160 Candn. musicians; perm. accompanist to Maureen Forrester; active in Jeunesses Musicales of Can. and is a regular performer on CBC Radio and TV; has participated in Edinburgh, Casals, Vancouver and Stratford Festivals; won Grand Prix du Disque (with late Kathleen Ferrier) for year's best recording 1952; has toured in Can., U.S., S. Am., Europe, Australia and N.Z. and recorded for RCA Victor, Decca, London, Pathé-Marconi, Westminster, Polydor, Folkways and Select; Address: 47 — 3261 Forest Hill Ave., Montreal, Que. H3V 1C4

NEWSON, Frank Jost, Q.C., B.A., LL.B.; of pre-U.E.L. descent; b. Charlottetown, P.E.I., 18 July 1904; s. Frederick Peter and Mary Allison (Jost) N.; e. Victoria High Sch., Edmonton, Alta.; Univ. of Alberta, B.A. 1924, LL.B. 1926; m. Affy Dorothea, d. Ernest Fosbery, R.C.A., 29 June 1931; children: Affy Joan Brumlik, Ernest Francis Peter; Partner, Newson Brumlik 1973-81; read law with W. Dixon Craig, K.C.; called to the Bar of Alta., 1927; cr. K.C. 1947; Partner with the late A. B. Harvey, 1927-29; Associate and Partner, Friedman, Lieberman & Newson, 1929-73; mem., Edmonton Bar Assn.; Alta. Law Soc.; P. Conservative; United Church; Clubs: Mayfair Golf and Country; Home: 303-11920-100th Ave., Edmonton, Alta. T5K 0K5; Office: 700 Chancery Hall, #3 Sir Winston Churchill Square, Edmonton, Alta. T5J 2C6

NEWTON, Elaine Merle Lister, M.A.; educator; b. Toronto, Ont. 10 March 1935; d. Lou and Faye (Gorvoy) Lister; e. Univ. of Toronto B.A., M.A. 1954; York Univ. M.A. 1968; children: Jack, Marla, Lori; ASSOC. PROF. OF HUMANITIES, YORK UNIV., former Co-ordinator of Individualized Studies, Dir. Faculty of Arts-Faculty of Educ. Insight Program, Past Sr. Tutor Calumet Coll., mem. Senate; Psychol. YMCA 1954-57; Book Critic Globe & Mail 1954-63; Psychometrist N. York Bd. Educ. 1963-68, Consultant 1971-74; Lectr. York Univ. 1968, Asst. Prof.; Visiting Prof. of Pol. Science Carleton Univ. 1979; papers given Can., U.K., USA and Switzerland; served Bds. Metrop. Social Planning Council, Nat. Council Jewish Women, Holy Blossom Temple, YM-YWHA; acad. consultant Metrop. Social Services Comte.; planned and conducted Adult Study Groups throughout Toronto; recipient Prov. Ont. OCUFA Teaching Award 1971; named Toronto's Foremost Prof. by "Toronto Life" 1981; NDP; Hebrew; recreations: theatre, tennis, jogging, bridge, music, travel; Club: Mayfair Tennis; Home: 88 Waterloo Ave., Downsview, Ont.; Office: 4700 Keele St., Downsview, Ont. M3J 1P3.

NEWTON, Robert, M.C., B.S.A., M.Sc., Ph.D., D.Sc., L.L.D., F.R.S.C.; university president (emeritus); biochemist; b. Montreal, P.Q., 7 Feb. 1889; s. John and Elizabeth (Brown) N.; e. McGill Univ., B.S.A. 1912; Univ. of Minnesota (Shevlin Research Fellow), M.Sc. 1921, Ph.D. 1923; Univ. of Alta., D.Sc., 1933; D.Sc., Cambridge Univ.; Univ. of Manitoba; Univ. of Minnesota; LL.D., Univ. of Alta.; Univ. of Sask.; m. Emma Florence, d. Rev. Francis Winter Read, 31 July 1914; Prof. of Plant Biochem. and Head of Dept. of Field Crops, Univ. of Alberta, 1924-32; Acting Dir., Divn. of Biol. and Agric., Nat. Research Council, 1928-32; Dir. 1932-40; Dean of Agric., Univ. of Alberta, 1940-41; Pres., Univ. of Alberta, 1941-50; apptd. by Internat. Educ. Bd. to make survey and report on post-grad. instr. and research in agric. in Can., 1928; by Nat. Research Council to make survey and report on tech. aspects of wheat marketing in U.S.A. and Europe, 1929; by Memorial Univ., Nfld., to prepare plan for its long-range devel., 1951; by Agric. Inst. of Can. to direct survey and edit report on agric. research in Can., 1951-52; one of Founders & 1st Gov., Arctic Inst. of North Am., 1944; served in World War 1915-19 as Capt., C.F.A.; wounded 1916; awarded M.C. 1917; Centennial Medal, 1967; Fellow, Agric. Inst. of Can.; Alpha Zeta; Sigma Xi; Phi Lambda Upsilon; Gamma Sigma Delta; Gamma Alpha; recreations: walking, gardening, reading; Home: 23871 Willows Dr., Blg. W-25, Apt. 254, Laguna Hills, Ca. 92653

NEWTON, Theodore Francis Moorhouse, M.A.; retired diplomat; b. Sarnia, Ont., 15 July 1903; s. Rev. Frank Gibson and Mary Agnes (Robinson) N.; e. Sarnia (Ont.) Coll. Inst.; McGill Univ., B.A. 1925 and M.A. (English) 1927; M.A. (Harvard); Travelling Fellowships (Harvard) 1931 and 1935 for research work in London, Oxford and Cambridge; m. Margaret Edythe, d. late Alexander Bruce, 9 Sept. 1943; one stepson, John Fraser Cameron; mem., Eng. Dept., Harvard Univ., 1928-37; Assoc. Prof. of Eng. and Asst. Warden of Douglas Hall, McGill Univ., 1937-43; joined Wartime Information Bd., Ottawa (on loan) 1943; trans. to N.Y. and apptd. Dir. of N.Y. Information Office 1945; Supv. of Candn. Information Service in U.S. 1946; Information Offr., with rank of 1st Secy., Candn. Embassy, Washington, 1946-48; Candn. Counsul. for New Eng. (First) with hdqrs. at Boston, 1948-50; Dir. of Information, North Atlantic Council (on loan to N.A.T.O.), London, England, and Paris, France, 1950-53; Min.-Counsellor, Candn. Embassy, Tokyo, 1954-57; Ambassador to Indonesia, 1958-60, to Colombia and Ecuador, 1961-64; returned to Dept., Ottawa, 1964; Official Canadian Rep. to UNIO, 1943-45 (two terms as Chrmn.); Consultant to Candn. Del., U.N. Conf., San Francisco, 1945; mem. of Candn. Del. to U.N. Assembly, N.Y., Oct.-Dec. 1946; Corr. for Montreal "Star" and Montreal

"Standard" 1926-28; has pub. various studies on the reign of Queen Anne and the early hist. of Eng. journ.; Phi Delta Theta; Club: Rideau; Home: 149 Manor Ave., Rockcliffe Pk., Ottawa, Ont. K1M 0H1

NICHOL, B. P.; writer; b. Vancouver, B.C., 30 Sept. 1944; s. Glen Fuller and Avis Aileen (Workman) N.; employed by Therafields Environmental Centre; rec'd Gov. Gen.'s Award for Poetry 1970; author: "Journeying and the Returns", 1967; "Two Novels", 1969; "Still Water", 1970; "The Martyrology" (Books I & II) 1971; "ABC" 1971; "Monotones", 1971; "Love: a book of remembrances" 1974; "Horse d'Oeuvres" 1975, (Four Horsemen); "The Martyrology" (Books III & IV) 1976; "Journal" 1978; "Craft Dinner" 1978; "Translating translating Appolinaire" 1979; "In England Now That Spring" 1979, with Steve McCaffery; "As Elected" 1980; "Extreme Positions" 1981; "Moosequakes and Other Disasters" 1981; numerous pamphlets incl.: "Konfessions of an Elizabethan Fan Dancer", 1967; "The True Eventual Story of Billy the Kid", 1970; "Beach Head", 1970; "The Captain Poetry Poems", 1971; ed. "The Cosmic Chef: An Evening of Concrete", 1970; "Story so four" 1976; (with Steve McCaffery), "Sound Poetry, A Catalogue," 1978 (with Steve McCaffery); "Canadian" Pataphysics 1981 (Toronto Research Group); cut records "Borders" 1966; "Motherlove", 1968; "Canadada" 1973; (Four Horsemen); 'Live in the West" 1977, (Four Horsemen); "Appendix" 1978; mem., Four Horsemen; Toronto Research Group; Address: 310 Dupont Street, Toronto, Ont. M5R 2L7

NICHOL, John, B.Com.; b. Vancouver, B.C., 7 Jan. 1924; s. John M. and Sally (Lang) N.; e. Royal Canadian Naval College 1942-43; University of B.C., B.Com. 1948; m. Elizabeth, d. Kenyon Fellowes, Ottawa, Ont., 1951; three d., Marjorie, Barbara, Sarah; served with R.C.N.V.R. in N. Atlantic and Eng. Channel, 1943-45; retired as Lieut.; Dir., Crown Zellerbach (Canada) Ltd.; Alcan Aluminium Ltd.; Alumnium Co. of Canada Ltd.; Advance Mining and Exporation Ltd.; mem. Senate of Can. 1966-73; Chrmn. Lester B. Pearson Coll. Pacific; mem., Adv. Bd., Salvation Army; Anglican; Home: 5450 Marguerite, Vancouver, B.C. V6M 3K6

NICHOL, Lyndon Elvert; director; b. Lennoxville, P.Q., 8 Aug. 1914; e. Bishop's Univ., 1934; McGill Univ., 1935-36; m. Louise Nelson Cann, 24 Sept. 1938; children: Peter Nelson, Nancy (Mrs. M. F. Moriarty); joined IAC Ltd. (formerly Industrial Acceptance Corp. Ltd.) Acct. Dept. Montreal 1938, later in Windsor and Ottawa, Mgr. Halifax Br. 1939-48, Regional Sales Mgr. W. Can. 1949, Br. Mgr. Toronto 1949, Asst. Vice-Pres. 1952, Vice-Pres. and Asst. Dir. Operations 1948, Gen. Mgr. 1963, Sr. Gen. Mgr. 1964, Extve. Vice-Pres. 1965, Pres. and Vice-Chrmn. Extve. Comte. 1967, Chrmn. Bd. 1971 till retired 1974; Clubs: Rancho Santa Fe Golf; Pauma Valley Country; Home: (P.O. Box 1505) Rancho Santa Fe, Calif. 92067.

NICHOLL, Christopher Iltyd Hubert, D.F.C., B.Sc., M.A.Sc., Ph.D.; professor; b. Winnipeg, Man. 22 May 1922; s. Henry Iltyd and Louise Dent (Bell) N.; e. Ridley Coll. St. Catharines, Ont.; Queen's Univ. B.Sc. 1947; Univ. of Toronto M.A.Sc. 1949, Ph.D. 1951; Cambridge Univ. Ph.D. 1960; m. Margaret Fenwick d. William Duffield Harding, Baltimore, Ont. 19 May 1951; children: John, Katherine, Christina, Sarah, Lucy; PRINCIPAL AND VICE-CHANCELLOR, BISHOP'S UNIV. since 1976; Jr. Research Offr. 1947-49, Asst. Research Offr. 1954-56 Div. Mech. Engn. Nat. Research Council, Ottawa; Prof. Agrégé 1956-60, Prof. Titulaire 1960-76 Dépt. Génie Mécanique Univ. Laval, Dir. du Dépt. 1968-71, mem. du Conseil de L'Univ. 1973-76; served with RCAF 1942-45, Pilot and Capt. Lancaster Aircraft; Sch. Commr. Greater Que. Sch. Bd. 1963-65, E. Que. Regional Sch. Bd. 1973-76; author various research papers in fluid mech.; Fellow, Candn. Aeronautics & Space Inst.; mem. Order

Engrs. Que.; Am. Soc. Mech. Engrs.; Candn. Pulp & Paper Assn. (Tech. Sec.); Anglican; recreations: walking, sailing; Club: University (Montreal); Home: 5 Harrold Dr., Lennoxville, Que. J1M 1Z7.

NICHOLLS, Lavinia Grace; company director; b. Toronto, Ont., 10 July 1902; d. late Herbert Samuel and Grace L. M. (Gardner) N.; e. Toronto Pub. and Secondary Schs.; Univ. of Toronto Extension Courses; studied Journalism under J. Wellington Jeffers; private tuition with Jessie Alexander Roberts and teachers affiliated with Conservatory School of Expression; m. F. E. Wellwood, May 1972; DIRECTOR, TORONTO MUTUAL LIFE INSURANCE CO. 1969-80; commenced career as Secy.-Acct., Ins. Dept., Ancient Order of Foresters, Toronto, 1917 (Co. was later mutualized as Toronto Mutual Life Ins. Co.); Sr. Acct., Asst. to Actuary, 1923-30, High Court Secy., 1931-34; apptd. Mang. Dir. of Toronto Mutual Life Ins. Co. 1935, Vice-Pres. and Managing Director, 1954-69; President, Sunshine Club, Toronto; has extensive library featuring poetry and drama; is an ardent canoeist having travelled by canoe through numerous Ont. rivers and lakes in her study of natural life; is particularly interested in colour in outdoors, photography, flower arrangements and fabrics; P. Conservative; Anglican; Clubs: Soroptimist (President, Soroptimist Federation of the Americas, 1950-52); Granite; Alpine; Home: Apt. 101, 2135 Avenue Road, Toronto, Ont. M5M 4B3

NICHOLLS, Ralph William, A.R.C.S., Ph.D., D.Sc., F.A.P.S.; F.Inst.P., F.R.A.S., F.R.S.C., F.O.S.A., F.C.A.S.I.; educator; research physicist; b. Richmond, Surrey, Eng. 3 May 1926; s. late William James and late Evelyn Mabel (Jones) N.; e. Co. Sch. for Boys, Hove, Eng. 1943; Imp. Coll. of Science and Technol., Univ. of London, Assoc. Royal Coll. of Science 1945, B.Sc. (Physics) 1946, Ph.D. (Physics) 1951, D.Sc. (Spectroscopy) 1961; m. Doris Margaret, M.D., Ph.D., d. late Frederick McEwen, 28 June 1952; PROF. OF PHYSICS AND DIR., CENTRE FOR RESEARCH IN EXPER. SPACE SCIENCE, YORK UNIV. since 1965 Sr. Astrophysics Demonst., Imp. Coll., Univ. of London, 1945-48; joined Univ. of W. Ont. as Instr. 1948, Lectr. 1950, Asst. Prof. 1952, Assoc. Prof. 1956, Prof. 1958, Sr.Prof. of Physics 1963; Prof. and Chrmn., Dept. of Physics, York Univ. 1965-69; Consultant, Heat Div., US Nat. Bureau of Standards, 1959-60; Visiting Prof. of Aerophysics and Astrophysics, Stanford Univ., 1964, 1968, 1973; mem., NRC Assoc. Comte. on Space Research; Sensors Working Group, Interdept'al Agency on Satelite and Remote Airborne Sensing; Consultant numerous US and Candn. Aerospace and Govt. Research Labs.; research activities incl. Exper. and Theoretical Lab. Astrophysics, Molecular Spectroscopy and Aeronomy, Shockwave Phenomena, Rocket Spectroscopy of Aurora, Sun and Moon, Remote Sensing of Earth Resources; co-author, "Emission, Absorption and Transfer of Radiation in Heated Atmospheres", 1972; Assoc. Ed., "Journal of Quantitative Spectroscopy and Radiative Transfer"; other writings incl. book chapters and over 200 scient. papers in various prof. journs.; Fellow, Candn. Aeronautics & Space Inst.; Assoc. Fellow Am. Inst. Aeronautics & Astronautics; mem., Internat. Astron. Union; Internat. Union Geodesy & Geophysics; Candn. Assn. Physicists and other prof. assns.; Anglican; recreations: writing, music, travel; Home: 9 Pinevale Rd., Thornhill, Ont. L3T 1J5; Office: Downsview, Ont. M3J 1P3

NICHOLLS, Robert Van Vliet, B.Sc., M.Sc., Ph.D., F.R.S.A., F.C.I.C.; emeritus professor; chem. consultant; b. Montreal, Que., 18 Feb. 1913; s. Albert George and Lucia Pomeroy (Van Vliet) N.; e. McGill Univ., B.Sc. (Hons. in Chem.) 1933, M.Sc. 1935 and Ph.D. 1936; Cornell Univ.; Polytech. Inst. of Brooklyn; Cambridge Univ.; m. Mabel Eleanor Miner, 1945; two d.; joined the staff of the Dept. of Chem. McGill Univ. 1936; subsequently Assoc. Prof. of Chem. and Assoc. Dean of Grad. Studies and Re-

search till retired, since when emeritus prof.; served 1940-45 with Candn. Reserve Army as Offr. Instr., McGill C.O.T.C., attaining rank of Major; author of a number of scientific and historical papers and books; Pres. Canadian Soc. for Hist. and Philos. of Sc.; Hon. Pres. Candn. Railroad Hist.Assn.; mem., Soc. of Chem. Indust. Soc. of the Plastics Indust.; Inst. Textile Sc.; Received Confederation Medal and Jubilee medal; Sigma Xi (Past Secy., McGill Chapter); Anglican; recreations: travel, photography, railway history; Clubs: University; McGill Faculty;

NICHOLS, Lawrence Malcolm, B.A., C.A.; communications executive; b. St. Catharines, Ont. 24 July 1929; s. John N.; e. Univ. of Toronto B.A. 1952; C.A. 1957; Ruth Marion d. Harold J. Russell 20 Sept. 1952; children: Graham, Gordon, Robert; PRESIDENT, BUSHNELL COMMUNICATIONS LTD. since 1975; Dir. Standard Broadcasting Corp.; CTV Television Network Ltd. Télécâble Laurentian Inc.; Skyline Cablevision; Yorkville Studio Centre Ltd.; VTR Productions; Video House Ltd.; Intermedia Electronic Services Ltd.; Staff Sr. Clarkson, Gordon & Co. 1956, Staff Mgr. 1958; Comptroller, CFTO-TV Ltd. 1961, Vice Pres. Finance 1964; Vice Pres., Treas. Baton Broadcasting Inc. 1971; Anglican; recreations golf, travel; Clubs: Rideau; Royal Ottawa Golf; Home: 36 Old English Lane, Thornhill, Ont. Office: 2 St. Clair Ave. West., Toronto, Ont.

NICHOLS, Hon. Marcel, B.A., LL.B.; b. St. Hyacinthe, Que., 16 Dec. 1927; s. J. Ernest and Henriette (Peloquin) N.; e. Univ. of Ottawa, B.A. 1949; Univ. of Montreal, LL.B. 1953; m. Madeleine, d. Dr. René Millet, Drummondville, Que., 4 July 1953; children: François, Marie, Renée; JUSTICE OF SUPERIOR COURT OF QUE., since 1968; called to Bar of Que. 1953; Mayor, Drummondville West, 1960-66; K. of C.; R. Catholic; recreations: fish and game, golf; Clubs: Club Santiago, Manzanillo, Mexico; Home: 2 Des Lilas Ave., Drummondville, Que. J2C 3K6; Office: Court House, Montreal, Que. H2Y 1A2

NICHOLS, Thomas E., B.A.; retired publisher; journalist; b. Winnipeg, Man., 26 April 1907; s. Mark Edgar and Dora Beatrice (Wood) N.; e. Trinity Coll. Sch., Port Hope, Ont.; Mount Allison Univ., B.A. 1927; London Sch. of Economics (Post-Grad. studies); m. Sheila Margaret, d. Dr. J. G. FitzGerald, St. Catharines, Ont., 8 Sept. 1939; children: Christopher Graham, Hester Patricia; mem. Hamilton Adv. Bd., The Royal Trust Co.; Vice Pres. and Publisher, The Hamilton Spectator 1955-71; winner of Nat. Newspaper Award for Editorial Writing, 1954; Citation for Staff Corresponding, 1953; with R.C.N.V.R., 1939-45 (Lieut.-Commdr.); Church of England; recreations; golf, boating; Clubs: Tamahaac; Hamilton; Hamilton Golf; Home: 12 Old Ancaster Rd., Dundas, Ont. L9H 3P9

NICHOLSON, John Greer, Ph.D.; educator; association executive; b. Peacehaven, Sussex Eng. 8 May 1929; s. late Arthur and late Margaret Maud (Jones) N.; e. Waterloo-With-Seaforth Grammar Sch. 1947; Cambridge Univ. Queens' Coll. B.A. 1952, M.A. 1958; Univ. de Montréal Ph.D. 1963; m. Monique Marguerite Constance Marie d. late Calixte Forthomme 6 Sept. 1952; children: Greer Calixte, Geoffrey William Greer, Giles Timothy Greer; EXTVE. DIR., SOCIAL SCIENCES AND HUMANITIES RESEARCH COUNCIL OF CAN. 1978- ; Lectr. in Slavonic Studies, Univ. of London 1952-54; Researcher and Dept. Head, Am. Comte., Munich 1954-57; Ed. and Head, Russian Sec. CBC Internat. Service, Montreal 1957-61; Asst. Prof. McMaster Univ. 1961-62; Assoc. Prof. McGill Univ. 1962, Prof. 1965-79, Chrmn. and Prof. of Russian & Slavic Studies 1962-77, Chrmn. of French Lang. & Lit. 1973-74; Visiting Prof. of Russian, Oxford Univ. 1972; mem. Nat. Publ. Comte. Humanities Research Council of Can. 1972-78; served with Brit. Army 1947-49, Intelligence Corps; author "Russian Normative Stress Notation" 1968; various articles Russian domestic and foreign policy, modern Russian lang. and lit.; numerous reviews and articles on East-West tensions; Pres., Candn. Assn. Slavists 1970-71; Montreal Br. Secy., Candn. Inst. Internat. Affairs 1973-75; mem. Candn. Inter-Univ. Council on Acad. Exchanges with USSR & E. Europe, Chrmn. 1976-78; Philol. Assn. Gt. Brit.; Anglican; recreation: swimming; Home: 364 Stewart St., Ottawa, Ont. K1N 6L1; Office: 255 Albert St. (P.O. Box 1610), Ottawa, Ont. K1P 6G4

NICHOLSON, Hon. John Robert, P.C.(1963), O.B.E., Q.C., LL.D., K.St.J.; b. Newcastle, N.B., 1 Dec. 1901; s. Robert and Margaret Isabel (Russell) N.; e. Pub. Schs. and Harkins Acad., Newcastle, N.B.; Dalhousie Univ., B.A. 1921, LL.B. 1923, LL.D. 1967; m. Jean, d. Frederick William Annand, Halifax, N.S., 22 Aug. 1924; one. s. John Robert Jr., mem. Law Firm Lawrence & Shaw; Dir. Crestbrook Forest Industries Ltd.; read law with A. A. Davidson, K.C., Newcastle, N.B.; called to the N.S. Bar 1923, B.C. 1924; assoc. with J. A. Russell, K.C., Vancouver, B.C., 1924-26; Partner Russell, Nicholson & Co., Vancouver, B.C., 1927-33; Partner, Locke, Lane & Nicholson (later Locke, Lane, Nicholson & Shephard) there, 1933-41; Deputy Controller of Supplies, Department of Munitions & Supply, Ottawa, 1941-42; General Manager and Secretary, Polymer Corpn. Ltd., Sarnia, Ont., 1942-43; Mang. Dir., 1943-47 and Extve. Vice-Pres. 1947-51; Extve. Vice-Pres., Cobast, also Vice-Pres. and Mang. Dir. of operating subsidiaries of Brazilian Traction, Light & Power Co. Ltd. in Brazil, 1952-56; Partner, Guild, Nicholson, Yule, Schmitt, Lane & Collier, 1957-60; Pres. of the Council of the Forest Industries of B.C., 1960-61; Min. of Forestry, Can., April 1963-64; Postmaster Gen., 1964-65; Min. of Citizenship & Immigration, Feb. '65 Dec. '65, Min. of Labour, 1965-10 Apl. 1968 when resigned; served as Capt., 2nd Bn., B.C. Regt., D.C.O.R.; M.P. for Vancouver Centre, 1962-68; Lieut. Gov. of B.C. 1968-73; mem., Chem. Inst. of Can.; Candn. Bar Assn.; Freemason (P.M.); Liberal; United Church; recreations: riding, fishing; Home: 5, 2002 Robson St., Vancouver, B.C. V6G 1E9; Office: 2500, 595 Burrard St., Vancouver, B.C.

NICHOLSON, Leonard Hanson, O.C. (1967), M.B.E. (1944), LL.D., G.C.St.J. (1971); b. Mount Middleton, N.B., 8 June 1904; s. Richard and Margaret Jane (Porter) N.; e. N.B. Schs.; Univ. of New Brunswick, LL.D. 1955; m. Mary Olive, d. F. W. Copeland, Moncton, N.B., 20 Sept. 1930; children: Mary Anne, Mrs. I. M. Galbraith; Constable, R.C.M.P., 1923-26; Constable, Sgt., Inspr., N.B. Prov. Police, 1928-30; Inspr. and Supt., N.S. Police, 1930-32; with R.C.M.P. as Inspr., Supt. and Asst. Commr., 1932-51; apptd. Commr. 1951; resigning 1959; i.c. Criminal Investigation Br., N.S. 1932-37; Sask., 1938-41; Dir. Criminal Investigation 1946-51; awarded Jubilee Medal 1935; Coronation Medal 1937; RCMP Long Service Medal; served in World War, 1941-46, in Eng., Italy and N.W. Europe; held rank of Col. on demobilzation; Mentioned in Despatches; Commandant, Candn. Bisley Team, 1954; Col. Commandant Candn. Provost Corps 1960-70; apptd. to U.N. mission to investig. Internat. Drug Smuggling in Middle East, 1959; Life Gov., Dom. of Can. Rifle Assn.; mem., Council of N.W.T. 1951-60; Hon. Chief Blackfoot Confederacy 1955; Hon Chief Blood Tribe (The Kainai) 1957; Deputy Chief Scout 1960-65, Internat. Commr. Boy Scouts of Can. 1965-71 (Hon. Pres. 1975); Chief Commr., St. John Ambulance Bgde., 1960-65, Long Service Medal 1972; Chancellor Priory of Can., Order of St. John of Jerusalem 1969-72; Dir., Candn. Wildlife Fed. 1975; awarded Vanier Medal by L'Assn., des Scouts du Can., 1964; Silver Wolf by Boy Scouts Can. 1970 and Bronze Wolf by Boy Scout World Conf. 1971; awarded Coronation Medal, 1953; Centennial Medal, 1967; Jubilee Medal, 1977; Winchester Can., CWF and Outdoor Writers "Sportsman of the Year" Award for 1976; United Church; recreations: golf, badminton, swimming, rifle shooting; Address: R.R. 1, Woodlawn, Ont. K0A 3M0

NICHOLSON, Martin P. D., manufacturer; b. Dodworth, Eng., 30 July 1907; s. Trevor George and Mae Ellis (Hurley) N.; e. Private Schools, Dodworth, Eng.; High Sch. of Comm., Bradston; m. Margaret Lewiss, d. late Henry F. Naylor, 22 May 1958; two s. Peter Roger, Henry Arthur; PRES. AND CHIEF OPERATING OFFR., ROUL LTD. since 1969; Pres., P. D. Lewiss Ltd.; Yawl Containers Ltd.; joined present Co. as Jr. Clerk 1924, Sales Offr. (Can.) 1928, Sales Mgr. 1931; apptd. County Br. Mgr. 1942, Gen. Mgr. 1949 and subsequently Vice-Pres.; Special Rep., Can., Extve. Goods & Service 1965; mem. C.Y.E.A.G.; Freemason; Anglican; recreations: golf, music, sports; Clubs: Harford Mear Golf; Millers Pond Trout; Rotary; Address: 625 Cosburn Ave. Toronto, Ont. M4C 2V1

NICHOLSON, Norman Leon, B:A:, M.Sc., M.Ed., Ph.D., Ed. D., F.R.G.S.; geographer; b. Barking, Essex, England, 14 Oct. 1919; s. Albert Leon and Dorothy N.; e. Univ. of London, B.Sc. (Inter.) 1939; Univ. of W. Ont., B.A. 1943, M.Sc., 1947; McGill Univ. Carnegie Foundation Fellow, 1948-1950; Univ. of Ottawa, Ph.D. 1951; Univ. of Toronto M.Ed. 1973, Ed.D. 1975; m. Helen Emily, d. Nathan Smith, Stratford, Ont., Oct. 1947; SR. PROF. OF GEOG., UNIV. OF WESTERN ONT., since 1964 and Dept. Chrmn. since 1979; Meteorol., Brit. Air Ministry, 1939-43; Lect. in Geog., Univ. of W.Ont., 1946-49; Dir., Geog. Br., Dept. Mines & Tech. Surveys, Ottawa, 1949-64; Dean. Univ. Coll., Univ. of W. Ont. 1967-69; Coordinator of Grad. Studies in Educ., Univ. of W. Ont. 1970-77; served in 2nd World War with R.A.F. (Meteorol. Br.) in Can., U.K., Belgium and Norway, 1943-46; sometime Lect. in Geo., Univ. of Ottawa and Carleton Univ.; Visiting Prof. of Geog., Univ. of Edinburgh, Univ. of B.C.; Chrmn. Candn. Perm. Comte. on Geog. Names, 1959-64; mem. Bd. of Dirs., Royal Candn. Geog. Soc. 1963-65; mem. Int. Ed. Board "Geoforum" 1969-77; "Geo Journal" since 1977; Publications: "The Boundaries of Canada, Its Provinces and Territories", 1954; "Canada in the American Community", 1963 Ed., "Atlas of Canada" 3rd ed. 1958; "Breve Geografia Regional de Canada", 1967; "The Boundaries of the Canadian Confederation", 1979; "The Maps of Canada", 1981; many articles and book reviews in Candn. Brit. and Am. publs.; mem., Candn. Assn. of Geogs.; Anglican; Club: University, London, Ont.; Home: 66 Wychwood Park London, Ont. N6G 1R6

NICKERSON, Frederick Albert, Ph.C.; b. Dartmouth, N.S., 7 Nov. 1907; s. Joseph Albert and Margaret Clarice (Dunbrack) N.; e. Dartmouth (N.S.) High Sch.; Dalhousie College (Grad. in Pharm.) 1929; m. Margaret Annjanette, d. William Bentley, Middle Musquodoboit, N.S., 16 Sept. 1934; children: Joan Margaret, Mary Elizabeth; Vice-Pres., Ross Drug Co. Ltd.; Past Pres., N.S. Pharm. Soc.; Past Pres., Yarmouth Bd. Trade; Treas. and Past Pres., Yarmouth Y.M.C.A.; Treas., Beacon United Ch.; Treas. Yarmouth Hist. Soc.; Pharmacy Examiner for Prov. of N.S., 1944-53; mem. of Council, Can. Pharm. Assn. for seven yrs.; mem. of Yarmouth Town Council for four yrs.; Director, C.N.I.B., Yarmouth Branch; Freemason (P.M.); Protestant; recreations: golf, curling; Clubs: Yarmouth Golf (Treas.); Yarmouth Curling (Treas.); Rotary (Treas.and Past Pres.); Home: 36 Chestnut St., Yarmouth, N.S. B5A 2N6

NICKERSON, Jerry Edgar Alan, B.Com.; executive; b. North Sydney, N.S. 28 Apl. 1936; s. Jeremiah Beldon and Jean Frances (Inness) N.; e. Rothesay (N.B.) Coll. Sch. 1953; Dalhousie Univ. B.Com. 1958; m. Jean Frances d. Willoughby Ross Ritcey 20 Sept. 1958; two s. Mark Alan, Jerry Ross; CHAIRMAN H.B. NICKERSON & SONS LTD. and its related companies; Dir. National Sea Products Ltd.; Sydney Steel Corp.; Industrial Estates Ltd.; W. H. Schwartz & Sons Ltd.; Export Development Corp.; Canada Cement Lafarge Ltd.; Great West Life Assur. Co.; Bank of Montreal; mem. Young Pres's Organ.; Zeta

Psi; Baptist; recreations: golf, tennis; Clubs: Halifax; Seaview Golf & Country; Home: 59 Meech Ave., North Sydney, N.S.; Office: (P.O. Box 130) North Sydney, N.S.

NICKERSON, Mark, A.B., D.Sc., Ph.D., M.D., F.R.S.C.; educator; physician; b. Montevideo, Minn., 22 Oct. 1916; s. Mark and Ada May (Honey) N.; e. Linfield Coll. (Ore.), A.B. 1939; Brown Univ., ScM. 1941; Johns Hopkins Univ., Ph.D. 1944; Univ. of Utah, M.D. 1950; m. Elizabeth Eileen, d. C. T. Smith, Dallas, PROF. PHARMACOL. AND THERAPEUTICS, McGILL UNIV., since 1967; Chrmn. 1967-75; Consultant Royal Victoria Hosp.; Research Biochem., Nat. Defence Research Comte., 1943-44; Instr. in Pharmacol., Univ. of Utah, 1944-47; Asst. Prof. 1947-49; Assoc. Prof. 1949-51; Assoc. Prof., Univ. of Mich., 1951-54; Prof. and Chrmn., Pharmacol. and Therapeutics, Univ.of Man., 1954-67; mem., Candn. Drug Adv. Comte., 1960-62; Drug Efficacy Study, U.S. Nat. Acad. of Sciences, 1966-68; mem., Ed. Bds., "Canadian Journal of Biochemistry and Physiology", 1956-62; "Circulation Research", 1954-59; "Pharmacological Reviews", 1953-60; "Proceedings Society for Experimental Biological and Medicine", 1952-57; "Annual Review of Pharmacology" 1972-77; co-author, "Pharmacological Basis of Therapeutics", 1955-77; author of over 200 scientific papers published in various professional journs.; discoverer of haloalkylamine adrenergic blocking agents (patents); rec'd John J. Abel Prize for Pharmacol. Research, 1949; Upjohn Award for Pharmasol. Res. in Can. 1978; Fellow, Deutsche Akademie der Naturforscher Leopoldina (Halle) 1974; rec'd Hon. D.Sc. Med. Coll. of Wisc. 1974; Hon. mem., Czechoslovak Med. Soc., 1965; mem., Candn. Physiol. Soc.; Candn. Fed. Biol. Socs. (Chrmn. 1971-72); Nat. Bd. Med. Examiners (Pharmacol. Comte. 1970-74); Pharmacol Soc. Can. (Council 1956-59); Pres. 1960-61); Soc. Exper. Biol. & Med.; Candn. Soc. Clin. Investigation; Am. Chem. Soc.; Am. Physiol. Soc.; Am. Soc. Pharmacol. & Exper. Therapeutics (Council 1969-72, Pres. 1975-76); Brit. Pharmacol. Soc.; Candn. Med. Assn. (Chrmn., Pharm. Comte., 1960-62); Internat. Union Pharmacol. (Council, Treas. 1966-72); Sigma Xi; recreations: bonsai culture, fishing; Home: Laboratory, 845 Sherbrooke St. W., Montreal, Que. H3G 1Y6

NICKLE, Carl O.; industrialist; b. Winnipeg, Man., 12 July 1914; s. Samuel Clarence and Olga (Simonson) N.; e. Pub. and High Schs., Calgary, Alta.; Mount Royal Coll., Calgary; m. Diana Smith, 25 May 1960; children: Carl Terrance, Sheri Diane; PRESIDENT, CONVENTURES LTD.; Pres., Conventures, Inc.; Dir., Alberta Natural Gas Co. Ltd.; Alberta & Southern Gas Co. Ltd.; Calgary Inn Ltd.; Canada Trust Co.; Pacific Gas Transmission Co.; Candn. Montana Pipe Line Ltd.; Candn. Montana Gas Co. Ltd.; Roan Resources Ltd.; Dillingham Corp. Can. Ltd.; General Distributors Ltd.; mem., Bd. of Govs., Candn. Petroleum Assn.; worked in News Room, Radio Stn. CFCN, Calgary, 1936; commenced publ. of "Daily Oil Bulletin". 1937, presently Ed. Emeritus; served with Calgary Highlanders Militia and Reserve, 1930-49; el. to H. of C. for Calgary S., in g.e. 1951; re-el. 1953; Chrmn., Bd. of Govs., Univ. of Calgary; Pres., Nickle Family Foundation; Gov., Glenbow-Alba. Inst.; Candian Petroleum Assocition; Calgary Philharmonic Soc. (Past Pres.); Hon. Pres., Calgary Dist., Boy Scouts of Can.; Dir., Calgary Community Foundation; Assoc. Dir., Calgary Exhn. & Stampede; Past Pres., Calgary Allied Arts Foundation; Calgary Chamber Comm.; Independent Petroleum Assn. Can.; mem., Newcomen Soc.; Assn. Petroleum Writers; Freemason; P. Conservative; Anglican; recreations: numismatics; Clubs: Calgary Petroleum (Past Pres.); Glencoe; Ranchmen's; Kiwanis; Home: 1132 Prospect Ave., Calgary, Alta. T2T 0W9; Office: Suite 402 The Bradie Building, 630-6th Ave. S.W., Calgary, Alta. T2P 0S8

NICOL, Eric P., M.A.; writer; b. Kingston, Ont., 28 Dec. 1919; s. William and Amelia Camille (Mannock) N.; e. Lord Byng High Sch., Vancouver, B.C.; Univ. of Brit. Co-

lumbia, B.A. 1941, M.A. 1948; Univ. of Paris (Sorbonne) 1949-50 (French Govt. Scholar); m. Myrl Heselton, Sept. 1955; Columnist "Vancouver News-Herald" and "Vancouver Daily Province"; Radio Writer, C.B.C. (plays); B.B.C. (comedy series and special broadcasts) 1950-51; served in 2nd World War with R.C.A.F., 1942-45; author of "Sense and Nonsense", 1947; "The Roving I", 1950 (Stephen Leacock Medal for Humour, 1950); "Twice Over Lightly", 1953; "Shall We Join the Ladies°", 1955 (awarded Leacock Medal for Humour); "Girdle Me A Globe", 1957 (Leacock Medal); "An Uninhibited History of Canada", 1960; "Say, Uncle", 1961; "A Herd of Yaks," 1962; "Russia, Anyone°" 1963, "Space Age, Go Home"! 1964; "Like Father, Like Fun" (comedy), 1966; "A Scar Is Born", 1968; "The Fourth Monkey" (stage comedy), 1968; "Vancouver", 1970; "Don't Move!", 1971; (stage plays-children) "Beware the Quickly Who", 1967, "The Clam Made a Face", 1968; "Still A Nicol", 1972; "One Man's Media", 1973; "Pillar of Sand" (play), 1973; "Letters To My Son" 1974; "The Citizens of Calais" (play), 1974; "There's A Lot of it Going Around", 1975; "Canada Cancelled Because of Lack of Interest" (with Peter Whalley illust.), 1977; "The Joy of Hockey" (with Dave More illust.), 1978; "Free At Last" (stage comedy) 1979; "The Joy of Football", (with Dave More, illust.), 1980; "Ma" (stage comedy) 1981; has contrib. articles to "Macleans", "Saturday Night", etc.; Agnostic; recreations: sports, tennis, badminton; Address: 3993 W. 36th Ave., Vancouver, B.C. V6N 2S7

NICOLET, Roger Richard, M.Sc., consulting engineer; b. Brussels, Belgium, 19 Dec. 1931; s. David and Madeleine (Borel) N.; e. Elem. Schs., Brussels, Belgium and Uzwil, Switzerland, 1937-43; High Schs., Brussels, Belgium and "Aetenaeum", Zurich, Switzerland 1944-50, leading to Maturity Cert.; Federal Inst. of Tech. (ETH), Zurich, Switzerland, 1950-54 (Engn. Dipl., 1954); Ecole Polytech., Montreal, Que. (M.Sc. 1956); children: Marc Viviane, Jannick, Eric; PRINCIPAL, NICOLET CHARTRAND KNOLL & ASSOC., since 1964, associated with such projects as C.N. Tower, Toronto; Royal Bank Building, Toronto; Terminal Building at Mirabel; Place Bonaventure, Montréal; New Campus for UQAM, Montréal; engaged in research work, Dept. of Strength of Materials, Ecole Polytechnique, Montreal, Que., 1955-56; in charge of design analysis of some lift bridge work, the St. Lawrence Seaway Authority, Structural Steel Dept., 1957-58; Project Mgr., Royal Bank of Can. Bldg., Place Ville Marie, Brett, Ouellette, Blauer & Assoc., Consulting Engrs.; Project Mgr. for study of Boucherville crossing of St. Lawrence by Trans-Can. Highway, Brett & Ouellette, Consulting Engrs., 1958-62; Project Co-ordinator, planning and construction commencement, Boucherville Tunnel, (Tunnel Louis-Hyppolite Lafontaine), Société d'Ingénieurs-Conseils de Boucherville, 1963; mem., Corp. Engrs. Quebec; Engn. Inst. of Can.; Internat. Assn. for Bridge and Structural Engn.; Am. Concrete Inst.; State of Vermont Prof. Engrs.; Assn. Prof. Engrs. Alta.; Protestant; Home: R.R. 1, Austin (Brome County), Que.; Office: 620 Dorchester St. W., Montreal, Que. H3B 1N7

NICOLL, Marion Florence, R.C.A.; painter, designer; printer; b. Calgary, Alta. 11 Apl. 1909; d. Robert Alexander and Florence (Gingras) Mackay; e. Ont. Coll. of Art 1927-28; Prov. Coll. of Art Calgary 1928-31 (student-Instr.); London, Eng. 1 yr.; m. 20 Sept. 1940; rep. in 12 exhns. in 10 yrs., mostly solo exhns.; 2 accepted works in Survey, Montreal; 2 films available Calgary Pub. Lib.; author small booklet "Batik" 1945; large retrospective by Brooks Joyner 1979; sometime teacher Univ. of Alta. Extension; Alta. Coll. of Art, past mem. of Coll. Bd. and Univ. Extension Bd.; Head, Bd. of Art for opening of Auditoriums in Calgary; Life mem. Alta. Soc. Artists (former mem. Bd.); Protestant; Address: 7007 Bow Cres. N.W., Calgary, Alta. T3B 2C9.

NIELSEN, Arne Rudolf, M.A.; geologist; petroleum executive; b. Standard, Alta. 7 July 1925; s. Aksel Harald N.; e. elem. and high schs. Standard, Alta.; Univ. of Alta. Honours Degree in Geol. 1949, M.A. 1950; children: Allan, Brian, Robin, Garry, Paul, Kent, Dianne; PRES., CHIEF EXTVE. OFFR. AND DIR., CANADIAN SUPERIOR OIL LTD. 1977- ; Dir. Toronto-Dominion Bank; Rockwell International of Canada; McIntyre Mines Ltd.; Excelsior Life Insurance Co.; Ingersoll-Rand Canada Inc.; Phillips Cables Ltd.; Costain Ltd.; joined Socony-Vacuum Exploration (now Mobil Oil Canada) 1950; held various geol. positions Calgary, Edmonton, Regina becoming Chief Geol.; trans. to U.S.A. 1959 serving in sr. exploration and mang. positions New York, Denver, Houston; Vice Pres. Exploration 1966, Calgary; Pres. 1967-77; mem. Candn. Petrol. Assn.; Alta. Soc. Petrol. Geols.; Assn. Prof. Engrs. Alta.; Houston Geol. Soc.; Assn. Petrol. Geols.; served with Candn. Armoured Corps 1943-45; Lutheran; Clubs: Calgary Petroleum; Glencoe; Calgary Golf & Country; Ranchmen's; Home: 4404 Britannia Dr. S.W., Calgary, Alta. T2S 1J5; Office: 3 Calgary Pl., 355 Fourth Ave. S.W., Calgary, Alta. T2P 0J1.

NIELSEN, Hon. Erik, P.C. D.F.C., Q.C., M.P., LL.B., barrister; b. Regina, Sask., 24 Feb. 1924; s. Ingvard Evesen and Mabel Elizabeth (Davies) N.; e. Dalhousie Univ., LL.B. 1950; m. late Pamela June, d. Jack Hall, Louth, Lincs., Eng., 3 May 1945; children: Lee Scott, Erik Rolf, Roxanne; read law with N.D. Murray, Q.C., Halifax, N.S., and Gordon L. S. Hart, Dartmouth, N.S.; called to the Bar of N.S. 1952 and Yukon 1952; cr. Q.C., 1962; served in 2nd World War with R.C.A.F., Feb. 1942-Oct. 1951; awarded D.F.C.; 1st el. to H. of C. for Yukon in by-el. 16 Dec. 1957; re-el. since; mem., Candn. Bar Assn.; N.S. Bar Assn.; Yukon Bar Assn.; Minister, Public Works, Canada, June 4, 1979-February 29, 1980; appointed Depy. Opposition House Leader 1980; appointed Opposition House Leader 1981; Conservative; Anglican; recreations: fishing, hunting, flying; Office: Room 103, 107 Main St., Whitehorse, Yukon. Y1A 2A5

NIELSEN, Hon. James Arthur, M.L.A.; politician; b. Moose Jaw, Sask. 6 Aug. 1938; s. Erling Oscar and Lillian (Douglas) N.; e. Moose Jaw, Sask,; Richmond, B.C.; m. Edith Jean d. Rev. Robert Fred Filer 10 March 1961; children: Robert, Brent, Richard, Darin, Raymond, Christopher, Debra, Julia, Michael; MIN. OF HEALTH, B.C.; fed. P. Cons. Cand. for Burnaby-Seymour g.e. 1974; el. M.L.A. for Richmond Prov. g.e. 1975; B.C. Social Credit; recreations: reading, writing, trap-shooting, golf; Home: 4271 Waller Dr., Richmond, B.C. V7E 5J4; Office: 346 Parliament Bldgs., Victoria, B.C. V8V 1X4.

NIELSEN, Kenneth F., B.Sc., Ph.D., b. Cardston, Alta. 3 July 1927; s. Oliver Frederick and Erma Belle (Peterson) N.; e. High Sch. Barnwell, Alta.; Brigham Young Univ. B.Sc. 1949; Ohio State Univ. Ph.D. (Soil Science) 1952; m. Beatrice d. Henry Folsom, Hillspring, Alta. 30 Dec. 1947; children: Deborah Rowley, Mark, Thomas, Gregory, Elizabeth; PRES. AND CEO, WESTERN CO/OPERATIVE FERTILIZERS LTD. since 1979; Gen. Mgr. and Ceo, Western Cooperative Fertilizers Ltd. 1972-79; Chrmn. Canadian Fertilizers Ltd.; Pres., W.C.F.L. (U.S.) 1978; Asst. Prof. Univ. of Maine 1952; Head, Soil Fertility Unit, Can. Dept. Agric. Ottawa 1955, Head Soil Sec. Exper. Farm Swift Current, Sask. 1959-65; joined present Co. 1965; Candn. del. 8th Internat. Grassland Conf. Eng. 1960; 9th Internat. Cong. Soil Science and Technol. mission to Japan 1972; Consultant to Gov't Can., 1980, re. participation in building world scale fertilizer complex in Bangladesh; Chrmn. Candn. Centennial Wheat Symposium Saskatoon 1967; Candn. Forage Crop Symposium Edmonton 1969 (Ed. publs. of these Symposia); post-doctorate trans. Rothamsted Exper. Stn. Eng. 1962-63; has studied agric. practices and lectured in USSR, Israel, India, Central Am. and Caribbean; Trustee, Pub. Sch. Bd. Swift Current, Sask. 1960-62; Dir. Alta. Agric. Research Trust

1974-76; Science Ed. "Canadian Journal of Soil Science" (Rutgers); author over 30 scient. papers soil science and plant science Candn. and internat. journs. research; Dir. Agric. Inst. Can. 1970-72; Secy. Nat. Soil Fertility Comte. 1957-59 (Chrmn. W. Sec. 1960-62); Fellow, Candn. Soc. Soil Science (Pres. 1970-71); Pres. W. Can. Fertilizer Assn. 1970-72; Chrmn. Candn. Fertilizer Inst. 1977-78; Pres. Calgary Br. Alta. Inst. Agrols. 1977-78; mem. Am. Soc. Soil Science; Internat. Soc. Soil Science; Sigma Xi; Phi Lambda Upsilon; P. Conservative; Mormon; Home: 2020 Bayshore Rd. S.W. Calgary, Alta. T2V 3M1; Office: (P.O. Box 2500) Calgary, Alta. T2P 2N1

NIELSON, Glenn E., B.S.; independent oil & gas operator & investor; b. Aetna, Alta., 26 May 1903; s. James E. and Margaret Melinda (Pilling) N.; e. Raymond Agric. Coll., 1921; Univ. of Alta., B.S. (Agric. & Econ.) 1933; m. Olive W., d. late Edward James Wood, 25 Dec. 1928; children: Margaret Ruth Bullock, Joanne Livingston, James E., Anne Marie Hales, G. William; former Chrmn. and/or Pres., Husky Oil Ltd.; Chrmn. Nielson Enterprises Inc.; Dir., First Security Corp.; Univ. of Utah Hsop.; mem. Trustee Buffalo Bill Mem. Assn., Cody, Wyo.; Past Pres., 25 yr. Club of Am. Petrol. Inst.; mem. Nat. Petrol. Council; Ch. of Jesus Christ of Later-day Saints; recreations: fishing, riding; Clubs: Alta-Salt Lake City; Olive-Glenn Country (Cody Wyoming); Home: 625 Skyline Drive, Cody, Wyo. 82414; Office: (P.O. Box 730) Cody, Wyo. 82414 Alta. T2P 1Y1

NIKIFORUK, Gordon, M.S., D.D.S., F.R.C.D.(C); university dean; b. Redfield, Sask., 2 Nov. 1922; s. Andrew and V. (Lazorko) N.; e. Univ. of Sask., pre-dental training 1940-42; Univ. of Toronto, D.D.S. 1947; Univ. of Illinois, M.S. 1950; m. Margaret Jordis Nockleberg, 23 Dec. 1950; two s., Andrew, Christian; DEAN, FACULTY OF DENTISTRY, UNIV. OF TORONTO, 1970-77; Chrmn. Research Comte. Candn. Assn. of Faculties of Dent., 1980-82; mem. staff Hosp. for Sick Children, Toronto; apptd. mem. Med. Research Council 1972-73; joined present Univ. as Instr., Dept. of Paedodontics, 1947-48; Assoc. Prof. of Preventive Dent. 1950-56; Prof. 1956-64; Prof. and Dir., Div. of Biol. Sciences, 1970; mem. Div. of Dental Research 1952-64 (Chrmn. 1954-64); Asst. Dir., Dept. of Dent., Hosp. for Sick Children, 1952-64; joined Univ. of Cal., Los Angeles as Prof. and Chrmn., Div. of Pediatric Dent., 1964-66; Prof. of Pediatrics, Sch. of Med. and of Pediatric Dent., 1964-69; mem. Dental Study Sec., Div. of Research Grants, Nat. Insts. Health, 1966-68 (Chrmn. of Sec. 1967-68); Chrmn., Div. of Oral Biol. 1966-69 (Dir. Grad Training Program 1966-69); Dir., Dental Research Inst., UCLA Center for Health Sciences, 1968-69; Acting Dean, Sch. of Dent., 1968-69; Regional Ed., Archives of Oral Biology, 1966-68; mem. Review Comte., Sr. Coordinating Comte., Govt. of Ont.; served with ROTC 1941-44; mem., Internat. Assn. Dental Research; Candn. Dental Assn.; Acad. Dent.; Am. Assn. Advanc. Science; Council Dental Therapeutics in field Fluoride Metabolism Studies; United Church; Home: 55 Leonards Ave., Toronto, Ont. M4N 1K1

NIKIFORUK, Peter N., Ph.D., D.Sc., F.R.S.A. F.Inst.P., F.I.E.E., F.E.I.C. P.Eng.; educator; b. St. Paul, Alta., 11 Feb. 1930; s. DeMetro N. and Mary (Dowhaniuk) N.; e. Queen's Univ., B.Sc. (Engn. Physics) 1952; Manchester Univ., Ph.D. (Elect. Engn.) 1955, D.Sc. 1970; m. Eugenie F., d. late William Dyson, 21 Dec. 1957; two d. Elizabeth Mary, Adrienne Eugenie; DEAN OF ENGINEERING, UNIV. OF SASK., since 1973; Chrmn., Sask. Sci. Council; chrmn., Bd. of examiners, Assn. of Professional Engs. of Sask.; Mem. Sask. Res. Coucil; Defence Scient. Offr., Defence Research Bd., Que., 1956-57; Systems Engr., Canadair Ltd., Montreal, 1957-59; joined present Univ. as Asst. Prof., Dept. of Mech. Engn. 1959-61, Assoc. Prof. 1961-65; Prof. since 1965; Head of Dept. 1966-73; Chrmn., Div. of Control Engn., 1964-69; author or co-author of over 150 scient. papers; mem., Candn. Soc. Mech. Engn.;

Engn. Inst. Can.; Assn. Prof. Engrs. Can.; Inst. P.; Inst. Elect. Engrs.; Bd. Trade Saskatoon, Sask,; Anglican; Home: 31 Bell Crescent, Saskatoon, Sask. S7J 2W2; Office: Saskatoon, Sask.

NILES, William Isaac Campbell, C.A.; financial executive; b. Calgary, Alta., 28 Dec. 1929; s. Donald Campbell and Viva (Niven) N.; m. Sheila Lee, d. A. C. Talbott, Lethbridge,Alta.; children: Laurie, Christopher, Alicia, Sara; EXTVE. VICE PRES., FINANCE, CANRON INC.; Articled Clk., Geo. A. Young & Co., Lethbridge, Alta. 1946-51; C.A. 1951-53; Sr. Acct., Price Waterhouse & Co., Caracas, Venezuela, 1953-56; Asst. Controller, Schlumberger Surenco, Caracas 1956-63; Treas., Schlumberger Ltd., New York, 1963-71; service with RCA (Supplementary Reserve); rank Capt.; mem., Insts. C.A.'s Alta. & Ont.; Financial Extves. Inst.; Anglican; Clubs: National; Home: 40 Hillcrest Dr., Toronto, Ont. M6G 2E3; Office: 1 First Canadian Place, Suite 6300, Toronto, Ont. M5X 1A4

NIMMONS, Phillip Rista, B.A.; composer; educator; conductor; clarinetist; b. Kamloops, B.C. 3 June 1923; s. George Rista and Hilda Louise (McCrum) N.; e. Univ. of B.C., B.A. 1944; Scholar, Juilliard Sch. of Music 1945-47; Royal Conserv. Music Toronto 1948-50; m. Noreen Liese Spencer 5 July 1950; children: Holly Jayne, Carey Jocelyn, Phillip Rista; composer numerous jazz works incl. "The Atlantic Suite" 1974, "Transformations" 1975, "Invocation" 1976; recording artist; performances incl.; CBC Radio and TV Specials 1948-79, CBC Drama, Musical Comedy, Variety Shows and own jazz program 1953- ; appearances incl.: Royal Alexandra Theatre and Crest Theatre (Toronto), Toronto Symphony Orchestra, Expo 67, 1976 Olympics; co-founder Advanced Sch. Contemporary Music 1960, Dir. 1961-66; toured Candn. bases with CBC 1965-72, Atlantic Provs. 1974, 1977; Dir. Jazz Program, Prof. of Music Univ. of Toronto 1970- , Univ. of N.B. summers 1967- , Banff Sch. Fine Arts 1972, Univ. W. Ont. 1968- ; Leader Nimmons 'n Nine Plus Six jazz ensemble 1953- ; Pres. Nimmons 'N Music Ltd. 1975- ; lectr. schs., colls. & community groups; adjudicator numerous festivals; mem. Adv. Bd. Humber Coll., Banff Sch. Fine Arts; Trustee and Chrmn. York Educ. Clinic 1968-74; mem. Parents Adv. Bd. Thornlea Secondary Sch. 1967-72; rec'd Govt. Can. Cert. Music Contrib. Expo 67 1967; BMI (Can.) Cert. Honour 1968; City of Fredericton Cert. of Recognition 1975; Candn. Soc. Recording Arts & Sciences Juno Award 1976; mem. Am. Fed. Musicians; PRO Can.; Candn. League Composers (Charter); Candn. Music Centre; Club: Celebrity; Address: 114 Babcombe Dr., Thornhill, Ont. L3T 1N1.

NIND, Thomas Eagleton Westwood, M.A.; educator; b. London. Eng. 16 June 1926; s. John Warwick and Amy Mary (Greatbatch) N.; e. Windsor Co. Boys' Sch. Eng. 1943; St. Catharine's Coll. Cambridge Univ. B.A. 1946, M.A. 1949; Royal Sch. of Mines 1950-51; m. Jean Helen d. late Frank F. Marriott 22 May 1954; children: Christopher John Marriott, Sarah Catharine, Andrew Thomas; PRES. AND VICE CHANCELLOR, TRENT UNIV. 1972-79; Prof. of Math.; Dir. Quaker Oats Co. of Canada Ltd.; Asst. Assoc. and Prof. of Geol. Sciences Univ. of Sask. 1958-66; mem. Oil & Gas Conserv. Bd. Sask. 1959-66, mem. Hydrology Subcomte. Nat. Research Council 1964-68; Chrmn. Hydrology Symposium Sask. 1968; Dean of Arts & Science Trent Univ. 1966-71, Vice Pres. (Acad.) 1971-72; Visiting Prof. Universidad Nacional Autonomia de Mexico 1972, Univ. of W. Indies Trinidad 1978; author 'Principles of Oil Well Production' 1964, 2nd ed. 1918l; several papers on oil well production and ground water hydrology; Gov. Sir Sandford Fleming Coll. of Applied Arts & Technol. Peterborough 1969-77; mem. Candn. Math. Cong.; Assn. Prof. Engrs. Prov. Ont.; Am. Inst. Mining Engrs.; Fellow, Cambridge Philos. Soc.; Anglican; recreations: reading, walking; Clubs: University (Toronto); Peterborough; Home: 29 Merino Rd., Peterborough, Ont. K9J 6M8; Office: Peterborough, Ont. K9J 7B8.

NISSENSON, Abraham; manufacturer; b. Montreal, Que., 13 Dec. 1891; s. Louis and Beila (Rother) N.; e. Pub. and High Schs. and Business Coll., Montreal, Que.; unm.; PRESIDENT, SOCIETY BRAND CLOTHES LTD., since 1945; mfr. of Thos. Heath Clothes; Pres., Anjar Realty Corp.; Jr., office of Mr. Samuel Hart, who later inc. present Co., 1909; Secy. Treas., Society Brand Clothes Ltd., 1915, Dir. 1918, Vice-Pres. and Mang. Dir. 1935; Dir., Family and Child Welfare Bur., Montreal, Que.; Treas., Baron de Hirsch Inst.; Gov., Montreal Gen. Hosp., Verdun Prot. Hosp., Jewish Gen. Hosp. and Children's Mem. Hosp.; mem., Montreal Bd. of Trade; Candn. Clothing Mfrs. Assn.; Freemason; Hebrew; recreations: golf, fishing; Clubs: Montefiore; Elmridge Golf; Home: 281 Dufferin, Hamppstead, Que.

NITESCU, Trajan, M.E.; petroleum consultant; b. Craiova, Roumania, 11 Oct. 1902; s. Ioan and Elena (Becheru) N.; e. Polytechnical Sch. of Bucharest Grad. (Mining Engn); m. Florica Nitescu-Constantineanu; Dir., Canadian Petrofina Ltd.; formerly Chrmn. and Chief Extve. Offr., Canadian Fina Oil Ltd.; engaged in the oil industry in Roumania since grad. in 1924 till 1948 when forced to escape Communist regime; served as flying Offr.; former Offr. of Roumanian Coll. of Engrs.; Roumanian Economic Inst.; former Pres. of the Assn. of Engrs. & Technicians of the Roumanian Mining & Petroleum Industry; Orthodox; Clubs: The Ranchmen's; Calgary Golf & Country; Address: 409 Rutland House, 3316 Rideau Place S.W., Calgary, Alta. T2S 1Z4

NIXON, Peter M., steel company executive; b. Sault Ste. Marie, Ont. 25 Dec. 1929; s. George E. and Isobel (Young) N.; e. elem. and high schs. Sault Ste. Marie; Queen's Univ. B.Sc. (Mining Engn.) 1953; m. Dorothy Herbst 1953; children: Carol Ann, Ian James; PRES., CHIEF OPERATING OFFR. AND DIR., THE ALGOMA STEEL CORP. LTD. 1981- ; Dir. AMCA International; CIP Inc.; Steep Rock Iron Mines; Ingersoll-Rand Canada Inc.; Mine Supt., Dominion Steel and Coal Corp. 1955-59; Algoma Ore Div. present Co. 1959-68; Asst. to Vice Pres.; Asst. Vice Pres., Vice Pres., Group Vice Pres. 1968-81; mem. Assn. Prof. Engrs. Prov. Ont.; Candn. Inst. Mining & Metall.; Am. Iron & Steel Inst.; Mining Assn. Can. (Dir.); Protestant; recreations: sailing, skiing, hunting, fishing; Home: 49 Alworth Pl., Sault Ste. Marie, Ont. P6B 5W5; Office: 503 Queen St. E., Sault Ste. Marie, Ont. P6A 5P2.

NIXON, Robert Fletcher, M.P.P., B.Sc.; farmer; politician; b. St. George, Ont., 17 July 1928; s. Harry Corwin and Alice Anne (Jackson) N.; e. McMaster Univ., B.Sc.; Ont. Coll. of Educ.; rec. Hon. LL.D. 1976; m. Dorothy Christine, d. T. Owen Loveless, St. George, Ont., 16 Aug. 1952; children: John Corwin, Jane Elizabeth, Harry Owen, Sara Margaret; Son of former Ont. Premier, 1943; el. to Ont. Leg. for Brant in by-el., 1962; re-el. since; leader, 1967-76; Freemason; Liberal; Protestant; Home: St. George, Ont.; Office: Parliament Bldgs., Toronto, Ont.

NIXON, Stanley Elkin; financial consultant; company director; b. Saint John, N.B., 13 Mar. 1912; s. Clarence Pengilly and Nellie Keillor (Thorne) N.; e. Pub. and High Schs., Saint John, N.B., and Westmount, Que., Grad. 1928; m. Marie Elizabeth d. Harold Brooks Wilson, Port Hope, Ont., 12 July 1941; children: Martha Elizabeth, David Brooks; Dir., Canadian Pacific (Bermuda) Ltd.; Continental Illinois Canada Ltd.; Rolls Royce Holdings North America Ltd.; Trizec Corp. Ltd.; Arion Insurance Co. Ltd.; entered Dom. Securities Corp. Limited, Montreal, 1928; undertook additional work as Specialist in Public Finance with Royal Commission on Dominion-Provincial Relations, 1938-39; served Nat. War Finance Committee, Ottawa first with Bank of Canada, then Dept. of Finance, 1940-45, returning to Dominion Securities in 1946; el. a Dir. 1950; Vice-Pres. 1953 and Extve. Vice-Pres., 1962, Vice Chrmn. 1969-70, retired 1972; Pres.

(1968-69) Invest. Dealers Assn. Can.; Anglican; recreation: golf; Clubs: Riddell's Bay Golf & Country; Coral Beach & Tennis (Bermuda); Mt. Royal; Hermitage (Magog. Que.); Address: 3468 Drummond Street, Apt. 606, Montreal, Que. H3G 1Y4

NOBLE, Hon. George Edward, LL.B.; judge; b. Biggar, Sask. 13 June 1927; s. George Smith and Jessie Chisholm (MacKay) N.; e. Biggar (Sask.) High Sch. 1945; Univ. of Sask. LL.B. 1950; m. Edna Marion d. late Fred S. McKay 15 Aug. 1953; children: Richard D., Janet Lynn, Nancy Ann; JUSTICE, COURT OF QUEEN'S BENCH, SASK. since 1976; read law with E. W. Van Blaricom, Tisdale, Sask.; called to Bar of Sask. 1952; cr. Q.C. 1965; law practice McMillan & Noble, Wadena, Sask. 1953-59; Sallows, Osborn & Noble, Battleford, Sask. 1959-76; Mayor, Town of Wadena, Sask. 1958-59; Chrmn. N. Battleford, Sask. Community Planning Comn. 1962-77; Trustee, N. Battleford Pub. Sch. Bd. 1970-76, Chrmn. 2 yrs.; Lib. Can. for Humboldt-Melfort fed. g.e. 1957; Bencher, Law Soc. Sask. 1974-76, Vice Pres. at time of elevation to Bench; mem. K-40 Clubs of Can.; Protestant; recreations: golf, curling, skiing, tennis, jogging; Home: 226 Trent Place, Saskatoon, Sask. S7H 4S6; Office: Court House, Saskatoon, Sask. S7K 3G7.

NOBLE, Robert Laing, M.D., Ph.D., D.Sc., F.R.S.C. (1950); D. Sc. (Hon., Univ. of W. Ont. 1973); professor emeritus; b. Toronto, Ont., 3 Feb. 1910; s. Robert Thomas and Susanah Harriett (Hodgetts) N.; e. Univ. of Toronto Schs.; Univ. of Aberdeen, Scot., 1929-31; Univ. of Toronto, M.D. (Hons.) 1934, (winner of Ellen Mickle Fellow. and David Dunlap Prize in Psychiatry); Leverhulme Fellow, Roy. Coll. of Phys., Eng., 1934-39 Univ. of London, Ph.D. 1937, D.Sc. 1946; m. Mary Aimee Eileen, d. L. C. Dillon, Aug. 1935; children: Robert, John, Richard, Michael; EMERITUS PROF. OF PHYSIOLOGY, U.B.C.; Sr. Research Scientist, Dept. Cancer Endocrinology, Cancer Control Agency of B.C., 1979-; engaged in research at Courtauld Inst. of Biochem., Middlesex Hosp., London, Eng., 1934-39; McGill Univ., 1939-47; Univ. of Western Ont., 1948-60; Dir. Cancer Research Centre, U.B.C., 1960-75; mem., Candn. Physiol. Soc. (Past Pres.); Physiol. Soc. (Eng.); Am. Physiol. Soc.; has contrib. various papers on med. research (cancer) and problems relating to war med. to scient. journs.; Discovery: Vinca alkaloids (cancer); Developped No strain of Inbred rats and unique tumor models; Kappa Alpha; Alpha Omega Alpha; Sigma Xi; United Church; Office: Dept Cancer Endocrinology, Cancer Control Agency, Vancouver, B.C.

NOCK, Rt. Rev. Frank, B.A., D.D. (Ang.); b. Toronto, Ontario, 27 Feb. 1916; s. David and Beatrice Esther (Hambidge) N.; e. Trinity College, University of Toronto, B.A. 1938; Trinity College, B.D. 1946, D.D. 1957; S.T.D. Thorneloe Univ. 1980; m. Elizabeth Hope Adams, 30 May 1942; children: Nora Esther, David Allan; BISHOP OF ALGOMA since 1975 (formerly Dean of St. Luke's Cath.); Chancellor Thorneloe Univ., Sudbury, Ont.; Dir., Sault Ste. Marie & Dist. Group Health Assn.; mem., Bd. of Dirs., Community Concerts Assn., Sudbury and Sault Ste. Marie; Conservative; recreations: golf, skiing, music, Home: Bishophurst, 134 Simpson St., Sault Ste. Marie, Ont. P6A 3V4

NODE-LANGLOIS, Patrick, D. ès Sc.(Econ.); exécutif; né Marseille, France, 10 mai 1936; fils Robert et Nelly (Daher) N-L.; é Ecole de Provence (Jésuits) Marseille; Univ. de Paris, Faculté de Droit et de Sc. Econ., Lic. en droit et dipl. de l'Inst. d'adm. des entreprises, D. ès Sc. écon.; ép. Monique, f. Jacques Dalbanne, Neuilly/Seine, France, 11 oct. 1961; enfants: Charles-Eric, Stéphanie, Alexandre, Sonia; VICE-PRES, EXECUTIF, LAFARGE COPPÉE; Pres., Ciment Fondu Lafarge Corp.; Administrateur et mem. du Comité Exécutif, Ciments Can. Lafarge et Citadel Cement Corp.; Admin., Lafarge Fondu Internat; Lafarge Conseils et Etudes; Lafarge Consultants

Ltée; Lone Star Lafarge Inc.; Com. Coppée de Dével Ind.; ORSAN; Pres. de la Fondation Nationale pour l'enseignement de la gestion des entreprises; Prés du Comité Can. du C.N.P.F.; Vice-Prés., Chambre de Comm. France-Can.; ancien Prés. (1975), Chambre de Comm. Française au Canada; Catholique; recreations: natation, ski, golf, montagne; Clubs: Mont Royal (Montreal); Union Interalliée; Cercle du Bois de Boulogne à Paris; residence: 110 avenue du Roule, 92200 Meuilly-sur-Seine, France; bureaux: 28 rue Emile Menier, 75166 Paris, France606 Cathcart, Suite 800, Montréal, Qué H3B 1L7.

NOEL, Hon. C.; judge; b. Sandy Lake, Man., 23 Sept. 1912; s. Eugene and Annie (Cayouette) N.; m. Blanche, d. Noël Belleau, 12 Sept. 1942; children: Marie, Jacques Simon, Marc, Dominique; ASSOCIATE CHIEF JUSTICE, FEDERAL COURT OF CANADA; called to Bar of Que., 1938; cr. Q.C. 1950; practised law with St. Laurent, Tashereau, Letourneau, Johnston, Noël & Pratte, 1945-53; with Noël Alleyn, Rioux & Deblois, 1953-62; served as Capt., Candn. Army, 1935-45; Catholic; recreations: tennis, fishing, hunting; Clubs: Rideau; Country; Garrison (Quebec); Home: 185 Acacia, Rockcliffe Park, Ont. K1M 0R5; Office: Supreme & Federal Court Bldg., Ottawa, Ont. K1A 0H9 or K1A O51

NOEL, Msgr. Laurent, B.A., Lic. Phil., D. Théol.; n. St-Just de Bretenières, P.Q., 19 Mars 1920; f. J. Rémi et Albertine (Nadeau) N.; é Coll. de Lévis, B.A. 1940; Grand Sém. de Québec; Faculté de Phil., Univ. Laval, Lic. Phil. 1950; Univ. Angelicum (Rome), D. Théol. 1951; EVEQUE AUXILIAIRE, QUEBEC; Prof., Faculté de Théol., Univ. Laval, 1951-63; Faculté de Méd., 1952-63; Faculté de Méd., Univ. de Montréal, 1962; et dans plusieurs écoles d'infirmières; Aumonier prov.; Assoc. cath. des infirmières, 1957-63; Syndicat professionel des infirmières caths., 1957-63; Administrateur apostolique du diocèse de Hauterine 1974; évêque de Trois-Rivières 1975; Publications: "De natura gratiae actualis openantis", 1952; "Précis de Morale Médicale", 1962; Collab. à "La Semaine religieuse de Québec" et "Le Bulletin dea Infirmières catholiques"; Résidence: évêche de Trois-Rivières, 362 Bonaventure, Trois Rivières, Qué. G9A 5J9

NOEL, Hon. Nathaniel Stewart, LL.B.; b. St. John's, Nfld., 29 Nov. 1920; s. Thomas Corbin and Flora May (Winsor) N.; e. Springdale St. Sch. and Bishop Feild Coll., St. John's, Nfld.; Memorial Univ. of Nfld.; Dalhousie Univ., LL.B. 1949; m. Dorothea Olga, d. David R. Thistle, St. John's, Nfld., 26 Apl. 1945; children: Natalie Parsons, Phillip, Carolyn, Neil; called to Bars of N.S. and Nfld. 1949; served with 59th (Nfld.) Heavy Regt. 1940-46; rank Lt.; M.H.A. 1966-71 (Depy. Speaker and Chrmn. of Debates); JUSTICE, SUPREME COURT OF NFLD., mem. Royal Candn. Legion; Anglican; recreation: sailing; Home: St. Phillip's, Nfld. A1B 3N4

NOLAN, Frank J., executive; b. St. John's Nfld. 1935; e. St. John's, Nfld.; m. Regina 1957; children: Janet, Christopher, Lesley; CHRMN. AND PRESIDENT, NEWFOUNDLAND & LABRADOR DEVELOPMENT CORP. 1977-; Acct., Royal Bank of Canada 1952-56; Br. Mgr. IAC/Continental Bank 1957-72; Vice Pres. present co. 1973-76; mem. St. John's Bd. Trade; recreations: curling, skiing, fishing; Clubs: St. John's Curling; Rotary; Home: 26 Eastview Cres., St. John's, Nfld.; Office: 44 Torbay Rd., St. John's, Nfld. A1A 2Y4.

NOORDHOEK, Harry Cecil, R.C.A.; artist; b. Moers, Germany 10 Feb. 1909; s. Charles and Anna Maria Elisabeth Christina (Zur Linde) N.; came to Can. 1914; e. Alta.; Gemaelde Gallerie Kassel, W. Germany 3 yrs.; m. Lorraine Mary Grace d. late Jackson Adams 23 Apl. 1960; exhns. various Candn. galleries 1934-74; London, Eng. and St. Ives 1968; Zurich 1969; Boca di Magra, Florence 1970; Milan 1971; Biennale Internazonale Carrara, Italy

1969; Mostranationale del Marmo-Sezione Internazionale di Scultura Carrara 1972; Estate Valsesiana Lago Maggiore, Italy 1972; Homburg-Saar, W. Germany 1974; Meschede, Cologne, Baden-Baden, W. Germany 1975; Dortmund, W. Germany and Dallas, Texas 1976; Eutin, W. Germany and Paris, France 1977; Eutin and Brilon, W. Germany, Prince Albert and Edmonton, Can. 1978; Norderstedt Hamburg 1980 and Saarbrucken, W. Germany; Soest 1981; rep. Can. various internat. open-air symposiums sculpture incl. Alma, Que. (10 ton calcite sculpture) 1965; Hamburg-Saar (1½ ton marble sculpture) 1974; Liberty Hill (Austin) Texas (3 ton cordova limestone sculpture) 1976; Eutin, W. Germany (1½ ton carrara marble sculpture acquired by Dist. Lib. Comn.) 1977; Norderstedt, W. Germany (2 ton carrara marble sculpture acquired by City) 1980; recipient Sir Otto Beit Medal for Sculpture 1965; Acquisition Prize Concours Artistique Qué. 1966; Can. Council Awards 1967, 1968; Renato Colombo Gold Medal for Sculpture 1972; The Pres. of the Repub. of Italy Gold Medal for Sculpture in Bronze 1972; Accademia Italia Delle Arti e Del Lavoro Gold Medal 1980; comn. for cast aluminum sculpture perm. coll. Musée d'Art Contemporain Montréal, 1974; served with Candn. Army 1942-46; mem. Accademia Italia Delle Arti e Del Lavoro; Royal Candn. Acd.; recreations: golf, violin and viola, country fiddle music, h-fidelity recording, walking, gardening; Home: Via Roccatagliata C. No. 62, Fossone Alto, Carrara 54033, Italia; Office: C.P. 263, Carrara 54033, Italia.

NORDHEIMER, Victor Roy Boulton; banker; b. Toronto, Ont. 1 Apl. 1920; s. Roy Boulton and Edna Caroline (Reid) N.; e. Brown Pub. Sch. Toronto; Univ. of Toronto Schs.; m. Nellie d. Herbert Blackburn, Toronto, Ont. 4 July 1942; children: Ian Victor, Mrs. Caroline Flewwelling; SENIOR VICE-PRES. AND REG. GEN. MGR. CALGARY, CANADIAN IMPERIAL BANK OF COMMERCE since 1981; joined present Bank 1936 holding Br. Mang. positions Calgary Main Office, Ont. and Que., Asst. Gen. Mgr. European Operations Office 1973; Vice-Pres. European Operations office 1976; Pres. and CEO, Internat. Energy Bank Ltd. (London, Eng.); Vice-Pres. and Reg. Mgr. Calgary 1978; served with Candn. Army Can. 1940-45, Overseas 1946-48; Anglican; recreation: golf; Clubs: Ranchmen's; Calgary Petroleum; Home: 1011 Prospect Ave. S.W., Calgary, Alta, T2T 0W8; Office: 309-8th Ave. S.W., Box 2585, Calgary, Alta. T2P 2P2

NORDIN, Vidar John, Ph.D.; educator; consultant; b. Sweden, 28 June 1924; s. John Herman and Beda Catherina (Wahlen) N.; e. Univ. of B.C., B.A. 1946, B.Sc.F. 1947; Univ. of Toronto, Ph.D. 1951; m. Julianne Leona, d. Anton Zerr, 11 Oct. 1947; children: Christopher Eric, M.D., Katrin Anne; DEAN AND PROF., FACULTY OF FORESTRY, UNIV. OF TORONTO, since 1971; Offr. in Charge, Forest Pathol. Lab., Fredericton, N.B., 1949-51; Calgary, 1952-57; Assoc. Dir., Forestry Biol. Div., Fed. Agric. Dept., 1958-65; Research Mgr., Fed. Environment Dept., Ottawa, 1965-71; Dean and Prof., Fac. of Forestry and Landscape Architecture Univ. of Toronto, 1975-78; Co-Chrmn., Univ. of Toronto Un. Way Campaign, 1973-74; Bd. Chrmn., Algonquin Forestry Authority Corp. since 1974; mem. Prov. Parks Adv. Council 1974-77; Board mem., Forest Engineering Research Institute of Canada; Ed., "European Journal of Forest Pathology" since 1970; author of over 60 papers in fields of forest protection, mang. and educ. for various research and trade journs.; mem., Candn. Inst. Forestry (Pres. 1967-68); Internat. Union Forestry Research Organs. (Past Subject Group Chrmn.); Ont. Forestry Assn. (Dir. 1972-73); Ont. Prof. Foresters Assn.; Soc. Am. Foresters; Candn. Owners and Pilots Assn.; recreations: music, photography, skiing, flying; Home: 50 Clarendon Ave., Toronto, Ont. M4V 1J1

NORMANDEAU, André, Ph.D.; criminologist; educator; b. Verdun, Que. 4 May 1942; s. Gabriel and Laurette

(Sauve) N.; e. Univ. de Montréal B.A. 1962, B.Sc. 1964, Univ. of Pa. M.A. (Criminol.) 1965, Ph.D. (Sociol.) 1968 m. Pierrette d. Romeo Lapointe, Montreal, Que. 14 Aug 1965; children: Alain, Louis, Jean; PROF. OF CRIMINOL OGY, UNIV. DE MONTREAL 1968- , Chrmn. of Crim nology 1970-80; mem. Bd., Internat. Center for Compara tive Criminology, Paris, France and Montreal, Que 1970- ; Chrmn. Research Council Ministry of Educ. Que and mem. Adv. Comte. Ministry of Justice Ottawa 1975 80; Montreal City Counselor 1974-78; Parti Quebecoi Cand. Dist. of Mount Royal prov. g.e. 1970, 1973, 1976 1981; author "Public Opinion and Crime" 1970 "Deviance and Crime" 1975; "Armed Robbery is Quebec" 1980; over 300 articles violence, adm. justice prevention of crime various nat. and internat. publs. rec'd Lt. Gov. Que. Award 1980; mem. Candn. Assn Prevention Crime (Pres.); Am. Soc. Criminology (Dir.) Internat. Soc. Criminology (Vice Pres.); R. Catholic; re creations: tennis, cinema, skiing, theatre; Home: 315 Kent, Montreal, Que. H3S 1N1; Office: Montreal, Que H3C 3J7.

NORRIS, Leonard Matheson, M.B.E., LL.D., R.C.A. cartoonist; illustrator; b. London, Eng. 1 Dec. 1913; s Thomas Mathew and Ellen (Brown) N.; e. Eng.; Port Ar thur (Ont.) High Sch. 1929; Univ. of Windsor LL.D. (Hon. Causa) 1973; m. Marguerite Dunn 1 Oct. 1938; tw s. Stephen Lee, John Gordon; EDITORIAL CARTOON IST, VANCOUVER SUN 1950- ; Arch. and Civil Engr Draftsman Port Arthur 1929-33; Art Dir. Advertising Agency Toronto 1942; Art Dir. Automotive Journs. Ma clean Hunter 1946; Canadian Homes & Gardens mag. freelance illustration 1950; illustrator various children' books incl. "Johan's Gift to Christmas" 1974- ; author 2 annual colls. of cartoons 1951-78; rec'd Nat. Newspaper Award (cartooning) 1961; el. to News Hall of Fame; 197 served with Royal Candn. Elect. & Mech. Engrs. 1942-45 Ed. and Illustrator Cam (Candn. Army Maintenance Mag. Ottawa 1943-45, motorcycle testing and crash he met design Nat. Research Council, rank Capt.; mem Assn. Am. Ed. Cartoonists; Art Dirs. Assn.; recreation golf; Club: Capilano Golf & Country; Home: 4227 Almon del Rd., W. Vancouver, B.C. V7V 3L8; Office: 2250 Gran ville St., Vancouver, B.C. V6H 3G2.

NORRIS, Mackenzie Charles, B.A.Sc.; transportatio executive; b. Silverton, B.C., 2 June 1925; s. Charles an Genevieve (Johnston) N.; e. Univ. of B.C., B.A.Sc.; m Patricia Anne Wastell, 23 Sept. 1950; one s., Mark Mack enzie; PRES. AND C.E.O., BRITISH COLUMBIA RAILWAY since 1978; Dir., B.C. Harbours Board; Dir Public Employers 1978-; joined Canadian Pacific Railroa 1952; held various positions incl. Rail Terminal Supvr. Asst. Supt. and Transport Engr.; joined present Co. a Regional Mgr., Vancouver, 1970, Gen. Mgr. 1972, Vic Pres.-Operations 1973, Vice Pres. and Gen. Mgr. 1977 served as Pilot with RCAF and RNVR Fleet Air Arm dur ing World War II; mem. Terminal City Club; Vancouve Board of Trade; recreations: skating, hiking, camping Home: 2584 Ottawa Ave., West Vancouver, B.C. V7 2T4; Office: 1095 W. Pender, Vancouver, B.C. V6E 2N6

NORTH, John Andrew, B.A., A.L.A.; librarian; b. St. Al bans, Herts., Eng. 13 March 1942; s. Henry Joseph an Eileen (Harvey) N.; e. St. Albans Sch. 1959; North Wes London Polytechnic A.L.A. 1963; Univ. of Toronto 196 children: Andrew Peter, Gavin Craig; DIR., LEARNING RESOURCES CENTRE, RYERSON POLYTECH. INST 1974- ; Asst. Lib. Natural Rubber Producers' Researc Assn. U.K. 1959-61; Lib., Morgan Bros. (Publishers) Ltd. London, Eng. 1961-64; Mang. Ed., Co-operative Boo Centre Toronto 1964-67; Coll. Lib., Centennial Coll. Scar borough 1967-72 and Mount Royal Coll. Calgary 1972-74 Gov., Ryerson Polytech. Inst. 1978-82; Book Reviewe (Crime & Mystery), "Quill & Quire", Library Journa Candn. Book Review Annual; author various articles lib journs.; mem. Candn. Lib. Assn. (Councillor 1974-76) andn. Assn. Coll. & Univ. Libs. (Secy. 1972-73); Ont. ib. Assn.; Am. Lib. Assn.; Lib. Assn. (U.K.); recreaons: crime fiction, gardening, golf; Home: 4 Plaxton res., Toronto, Ont. M4B 1L1; Office: 50 Gould St., Tonto, Ont. M5B 1E8.

IORTHORP, Supt. Bruce Lionel, C.M.; retired RCMP fficer; b. Vancouver, B.C. 26 March 1927; s. late George Vashington and Annie Beatrice (King) N.; e. Sir Alexaner McKenzie Pub. and John Oliver High Schs. Vancouer; Candn. Police Coll. Regina 1965; m. Mabel Louisa d. te John Fancy Kerr 26 June 1954; two s. Robert Bruce, urray Ronald; has served as police offr. over 32 yrs. oth uniformed and plainclothes duties; over 23 yrs. serice related to plainclothes work involving investig. crimal offences; has directed and participated in many inestigs. murders, armed robberies, kidnapping and rture, also activities related to outlaw motorcycle gangs nd organized crime; as Police Operations Commdr. and legotiator has successfully handled many hostage incients, 2 internat. hijacking incidents and 2 maj. riot/hosge incidents B.C. Penitentiary; Past Chrmn. ad-hoc Poce Comte. dealing with problems that develop during bour dispute/strikes; served with Candn. Army (RCE) 945, rec'd war medal; Reserve 1947-49; rec'd RCMP ommr.'s Commendation for Bravery; 2 RCMP C.O.'s ommendations for Outstanding Police Work and letter f recognition from Dir. of FBI; RCMP Long Service ledal with Clasp and Star; Queen's Silver Jubilee Medal; ife mem. Kings Co. Hist. Soc. (Sussex Corner, N.B.); aptist; Home: 4692 Clinton St., Burnaby, B.C. V5J 2K7;

IORTHWAY, Mary L(ouise), M.A., Ph.D., D.Litt.; psyhologist; b. Toronto, Ont. 28 May 1909; d. Arthur Garfild and Lucy (McKellar) Northway; e. Bishop Strachan ch. Toronto 1927; Univ. of Toronto B.A. 1933, M.A. 934, Ph.D. 1938; Cambridge Univ. one yr. grad. study 935-36; Trent Univ. D.Litt.; Reader to Assoc. Prof. of 'sychol. Univ. of Toronto 1934-68, Supvr. of Research 1st. of Child Study 1953-68, Co-ordinator Brora Centre 969-78; Founder and Chrmn. Adv. Bd. Neathern Trust ince 1963; Pres. and Dir. The Northway Co. Ltd. 1950-3; Program Dir. Glen Bernard Camp 1930-39; Co-dir. Vindy Pine Point 1941-50; author "Primer of ociometric Testing" 1957; "Sociometric Testing" 1952; "Laughter n the Front Hall"; "The Camp Counselor's Book" 1966; ome 120 articles on camping, psychol., educ.; Fellow, Candn. Psychol. Assn.; Ont. Psychol. Assn. (mem.); Int. Camping Assn. (Hon. Life mem.); Kappa Kappa Jamma; P. Conservative; Baptist.

IORTON, Hon. Keith Calder, Q.C., M.P.P., B.A., L.B.; politician; b. Claremont, Ont. 26 Jan. 1941; s. John Andrew and Ina Merinda (Redshaw) N.; e. Claremont 'ub. Sch.; Pickering Dist. High Sch.; Queen's Univ. .A., LL.B.; MIN. OF THE ENVIRONMENT, ONT. 981- ; Ald. and Depy. Mayor Kingston 1972, 1974; el. M.P.P. for Kingston and The Islands prov. g.e. 1975, rel. since; Parlty. Asst. to Treas. of Ont.; Min. of Econ. & ntergovernmental Affairs; Min. of Community & Social ervices 1977; P. Conservative; United Church; Office: 35 St. Clair Ave. W., Toronto, Ont. M4V 1P5.

NOURSE, L. W.; manufacturer; b. Grahamsville, Ont. 7 May 1912; s. Rev. Fred Arthur and Nettie May (Undervood) N.; e. Williamson Rd. Pub. Sch. and Malvern Coll. nst., Toronto; m. Merilyn, d. late Robert Niven, 30 Sept. 969; one d., Wendie Anne; CHRMN., WIX CORP. LTD., since 1942; Pres. and Dir., Wix International Corp., Gastonia, N.C.; Dir., Canadian Strut Manufacturing Co.; UK); Eco-Tec.; Clk., Thomson McKinnon, stockbrokers, N.Y., 1933-37; Mgr., Fyfe Oil Filter Ltd., 1937-42; Past Chrmn., Can. Section SAE; recreations: flying, cottage; Clubs: Toronto Hunt; Rotary; Home: 1 Fallingbrook Dr., Scarborough, Ont.; M1N 1B3; Office: 25 Curity Ave., Tonto, Ont. M4B 1X9

NOVOTNY, George Milos, CD, M.D., F.R.C.S.(C), F.A.C.S.; otolaryngologist; educator; b. Prague, Czechoslovakia 7 March 1929; s. late Joseph V. and Maria (Cermak) N.; e. Sr. Matric. Prague X 1948; Charles' Univ. Prague 1st yr. med. 1948-49; Univ. of Toronto M.D. 1958; Queen's Univ. Surg. 1962-63; McGill Univ. Otolaryngol. 1964-67; m. Elfriede Anna d. late Karl Gruber, Austria 20 Dec. 1952; children: Susan Anna, Tina Marie; PROF. AND HEAD OF OTOLARYNGOL. DALHOUSIE UNIV. since 1974, Assoc. Prof. Sch. of Human Communication Disorders, Research Assoc. Dept. Psychol. (Grad. Studies), mem. Senate; Dir. N.S. Hearing and Speech Clinic; Head of Otolaryngol. Halifax Infirmary, Victoria Gen. Hosp.; Sr. Consultant, Candn. Forces Hosp., Halifax; Active Sr. Consultant, The Izaak Walton Killam Hosp. for Children; Consultant, Camp Hill Hosp.; Dartmouth Med. Centre; N.S. Rehabilitation Centre, Grace Maternity Hosp.; joined Candn. Forces Med. Service 1957, "Air" Element, rank Lt. Col. 1972, Consultant in Otolaryngol. since 1967; rec'd CD (Canada Decoration) 1969, Queen's Silver Jubilee Medal 1977; mem. Claims Evaluation Comte. N.S. Med. Services Ins.; Hearing Aid Adv. Bd. N.S. Dept. Consumer Affairs; author or co-author various publs. and papers; mem. Candn. Forces Med. Service Offrs. Assn.; Am. Council Otolaryngol.; Candn. Otolaryngol. Soc. (Educ. Comte. & Council); N.S. Soc. Ophthalmol. & Otolaryngol.; Dartmouth Med. Soc.; Candn. Soc. Aviation Med.; Soc. Acad. Chrmn. Otolaryngol.; Royal Soc. Med.; Candn. Med. Assn.; N.S. Med. Soc.; Halifax Med. Soc.; E. Can. Otolaryngol. Soc. (Secy.-Treas. 1976-78, Pres. 1978-79); Fellow in Otolaryngol. Dalhousie Univ. 1967, Lectr. 1970, Asst. Prof. 1974, Acting Head 1973; recreations: skiing, sailing, gardening, painting, art; Clubs: Waegwoltic; Wentworth Valley Ski; Home: 40 Clayton Park Dr., Halifax, N.S. B3M 1L6; Office: Halifax Infirmary, Halifax, N.S. B3J 2H6

NOWACZYNSKI, Wojciech Jerzy, D.Sc.; endocrinologist; educator; b. Nisko, Poland 27 March 1925; s. Jan and Irena (Listowska) N.; e. Prince Poniatowski Coll. Warsaw, Poland 1939; Cyprian Norvid Polish Coll. Paris, France B.Sc. 1942; Polish Coll. Zurich, Switzerland B.Sc. 1944; Univ. of Fribourg Doctorandum 1950, D.Sc. 1952; children: Maria, Barbara, Mark, Francis, Paula, Peter; PROF. OF MEDICINE, UNIV. OF B.C. 1979- ; mem. Div. Endocrinol. St. Paul's Hosp. Vancouver, Dir. Steroid Research Lab. 1979- ; Research Assoc. Med. Research Council Can. 1962-65, . Research Assoc. 1965, Princ. Investigator, Research Group on Hypertension 1972-79, Career Investigator 1979- ; Asst. Prof. of Med. Univ. de Montréal 1962-65, Assoc. Prof. 1965, Prof. 1970; Lectr. in Investigative Med. McGill Univ. 1964, Asst. Prof. of Exper. Med. 1965, Assoc. Prof. 1966, Prof. 1970; Dir. Steroid Research Dept. Clin. Research Inst. Montreal 1967; First recipient Marcel Piche Award for Excellence in Research 1976; author numerous publs. hypertension, book chapters, presentations; Fellow, Council for High Blood Pressure Research; mem. Internat. Soc. Hypertension; Candn. Soc. Clin. Investigation; Am. Endocrine Soc.; Inter-Am. Soc. Hypertension (Council); Candn. Soc. Hypertension; Home: 4356 Quinton Pl., Vancouver, B.C. V7R 4A7; Office: St. Paul's Hospital, Vancouver, B.C. V6Z 1Y6.

NOWELL-SMITH, Patrick Horace, A.M.; educator; b. Polzeath, Cornwall, Eng., 17 Aug. 1914; s. Nowell Charles and Cecil (Vernon-Harcourt) Smith; e. Winchester Coll., 1933; New Coll., Oxford Univ. B.A. 1937, M.A. 1946; Harvard Univ., A.M. 1938; m. 1stly Perilla Thyme, d. Sir Richard Southwell, F.R.S., 1946; children: Richard Wingate, Viola Margaret, Robert Vernon, Timothy David; m. 2ndly Felicity Margret, d. Dr. R. L. Ward, Blackburn, Eng., 17 Aug. 1968; children: Harriet Flora, Kate Prudence; PROF. OF PHILOSOPHY, YORK UNIV. since 1969; Fellow, Trinity Coll., Oxford Univ. 1945-56; Prof. of Philos., Leicester Univ. 1956-64; Univ. of Kent, Canterbury, 1964-69; Visiting Prof., Univ. of Texas, 1965; Univ. of Calif., 1968; served in Egypt, Sudan and India

1940-45; author, "Ethics", 1954; also numerous philos. articles; Home: (P.O. Box 63) King City, Ont. L0G 1K0; Office: 4700 Keele St., Downsview, Ont. M3J 1P3

NOWLAN, Alden, D.Litt., LL.D.; writer, journalist; b. Windsor, N.S., 25 Jan. 1933; s. Freeman and Grace (Reese) N.; Hon. D.Litt., Univ. New Brunswick 1971, Hon. research assoc.; m. Claudine, d. Claude Orser of Hartland, N.B.; one s.; joined staff, The Observer, Hartland, N.B., 1952; later News Ed.; Can. Council Arts Schol., 1961; joined the Telegraph-Journal, Saint John, N.B. 1963; News Ed., 1965-68; since then Writer-in-Residence, Univ. New Brunswick; Can. Council Special Award, 1966; Guggenheim Mem. Foundation Schol., 1967; President's Medal, Univ. W. Ont., 1970, 1972; Hon. LL.D., Dalhousie, 1976; Can. Authors' Association Silver Medal for Poetry, 1977; Silver Jubilee Medal, 1978; Evelyn Richardson Prize for Non-Fiction, 1978; Nat. Magazine Assn. Award, 1980; Publications: "The Rose and The Puritan", 1958; "A Darkness in the Earth" 1959; "Wind In a Rocky Country" 1961; "Under the Ice" 1961; "The Things Which Are", 1962; "Bread, Wine and Salt", 1967; "Miracle at Indian River" 1968; "Playing the Jesus Game" 1970; "The Mysterious Naked Man" 1969; "Between Tears and Laughter" 1971; "Various Persons Named Kevin O'Brien" 1973; "Shaped by this Land" (with Tom Forrestall) 1974"; "I'm a Stranger Here Myself" 1974; "Frankenstein: The Man Who Became God" (play, with Walter Learning) 1974; "Campobello; The Outer Island" 1975; "Smoked Glass", 1977; "Double Exposure", 1978; Plays (with Walter Learning): "The Dollar Woman", 1977; "The Incredible Murder of Cardinal Tosca", 1978; "Might Not Tell Everybody This" 1982; Home: 676 Windsor St., Fredericton, N.B. E3B 4G4

NOWLAN, James P., B.Sc., M.A., Ph.D.; geologist; consultant; b. Port Hilford, N.S., 26 March 1910; s. Rev. Peter DeLong and Bertha (Parker) N.; e. Acadia Univ., B.Sc. (cum laude), 1928; Univ. of Toronto, M.A. 1930, Ph.D. 1935; m. late Bernice, d. late John H. Nance, 3 Feb. 1933; two s. David Michael, John Graeme; Beatrice Cluett, 1975; mem. Candn. Environmental Adv. Council, 1974-1978; engaged in general geological field work in Can., Rhodesia, Brazil, 1928-39; Mgr., Yama Gold Mines Ltd., 1939-42; Supervisor, Canadian Industries Ltd., Brownsburg, 1942-45; Chief Geol., Cochenour Willans Mines Ltd., 1945-48; Chief Geol., Dominion Gulf Co., 1948-53; Extve. Vice-Pres., McPhar Geophysics Ltd., and Geol. Consultant, 1953-58; Depy. Min. Mines, N.S., 1958-73; mem. Geol. Assn. Can. (Pres. 1964-65); Soc. of Econ. Geols.; Candn. Inst. Mining & Metall. (Pres. 1973-74); Mining Soc. N.S. (Pres. 1968-69); Assn. Prof. Engrs. Ont. and N.S.; Clubs: City; Dartmouth Curling; Address: 6525 Waegwoltic Ave., Halifax, N.S. B3H 2B5

NUGENT, Terence James, B.A., LL.B.; b. Taber, Alberta, 9 Dec. 1920; s. late Patrick Bernard abd Bridget (Duke) N.; e. Univ. of Alberta (1946-51), B.A., LL.B.; m. Irene Glugowski, 7 Aug. 1946; one s., Rory Michael; since 1971; Pres., Construction Alberta News Ltd.; read law with Wm. J. Haddad; called to the Bar of Alta., 1952; served in 2nd World War; enlisted February 1942 with R.C.O.C.; Overseas, Dec. 1942-Feb. 1946; discharged with rank of Cpl.; def. cand. to H. of C. for Edmonton-Strathcona, g.e. 1957; el. for same constit. in g.e. 1958 till def. 1968; member, Alberta Law Society; Candn. Bar Assn.; Conservative; Unitarian; recreations: golf, curling; Club: Lions; Home: 9715 - 72 Ave., Edmonton, Alta. T6E 0Y9; Office: 220-#11 Fairway Dr., Edmonton Alta. T6J 2W4

NUTT, Jim Sutcliffe, B.A.; foreign service officer; b. Calgary, Alta., 20 June 1919; s. Fred and Jennie (Sutcliffe) N.; e. Crescent Heights High Sch., Calgary, 1937; Mount Royal Coll., Calgary, 1938; Trinity Coll., Univ. of Toronto, B.A. 1946; Osgoode Hall Law Sch. grad. 1949; m. Grace Ethelwyn, d. late Clarence Niddery, 7 Sept. 1940; children: Carol, Ronald; called to Bar of Ont. 1949; joined Dept. of External Affairs 1947; Second Secy. and Vice

Consul, Rio de Janeiro, 1951-54; First Secy. and subsequently Counsellor, Washington, 1958-62; Depy. Head, Defence Liaison Div., Ottawa and Secy., Candn. Sec., U.S.-Can. Perm Jt. Bd. on Defence, 1962-63; Head of Legal Div. 1963-65; Head of Defence Liaison Div. and mem. Can.-U.S. Perm. Jt. Bd. on Defence, 1965-68; Acting Chrmn., Candn. Sec. of Jt. Bd. 1966-67; Dir. Gen., Politico-Mil. Affairs, Ottawa, 1968-69; Consul Gen., San Francisco and for N. Cal., Hawaii, Wyo., Colo., Utah and Nev., 1969-73; Dir. Gen., Bureau of W. Hemisphere Affairs, Dept. External Affairs, 1973-77; Deputy Under Secy. of State for External Affairs 1977-79; Consul General, New York, and for N.J. and Conn., concurrently Comm. for Can. to Bermuda 1979-80; apptd. to Candn. Del. to 35th Session of U.N. General Assembly with rank of Special Ambassador; now Consul Gen., Los Angeles & for Clarke County, Nevada, Arizona & New Mexico; served with RCAF 1939-45; mem., Law Soc. Upper Can.; recreation: fishing, photography; Clubs: Chimo; Whitepine; Metropolitan Canadian, N.Y.; Home: 165 South Muirfield Rd., Los Angeles, Calif. 90014; Office: Canadian Consulate-General, 510 West Sixth St., Los Angeles, Calif. 90014

NUTTER, Most Rev. Harold L., M.A., M.S.Litt., LL.D., D.D. (Ang.); b. Welsford, N.B., 29 Dec. 1923; s. William Lawton and Lillian Agnes (Joyce) N.; e. Welsford (N.B.) High Sch., 1940; Mount Allison Univ., B.A. 1944, LL.D. 1972; Dalhousie Univ., M.A. 1947; Univ. of Kings Coll., M.S.Litt. 1947, D.D. 1960; m. Edith Maud, d. late Rev. B. E. Carew, 21 Sept. 1946; children: (Mrs.) Patricia Ann Hunsley, William Bruce; ARCH BISHOP OF FREDERICTON AND METROPOLITAN OF THE ECCLESIASTICAL PROVINCE OF CANADA. 1980, since 1971; Rector: Parish of Simonds & Upham, 1947-51; Woodstock 1951-57; St. Mark, Saint John, 1957-60; Dean of Fredericton, 1960-71; Vice Chrmn., Bd. of Govs., Univ. of King's Coll.; Bd. Regents, Mt. Allison Univ.; Bd. St. Thomas Univ.; Bd. of Rothesay Coll. Sch.; Co. Chrmn. and Co-author Report of N.B. Task Force on Social Devel., 1970-71; Vice Pres., Can. Bible Society, 1979; Address: 791 Brunswick St., Fredericton, N.B. E3B 1H8

NYBURG, Stanley Cecil, B.Sc., Ph.D., D.Sc.; professor; b. London, Eng., 15 Dec. 1924; s. Cecil Charles and Nina Belle (Dellow) N.; e. King's Coll., London Univ., B.Sc. 1945; D.Sc. 1973; Leeds Univ., Ph.D. 1949; m. Josephine Melville Tuke, 20 Aug. 1949; two d. Anna, Elizabeth Helen; PROF. OF CHEMISTRY, UNIV. OF TORONTO; prev. Sr. Lectr. in Chem., Univ. of Keele, Eng., Pubs.: "X Ray Analysis of Organic Structures", 1961; numerous scient. papers; mem. Am. Crystallographic Assn.; London Chem. Soc.; Inst. of Physics; recreations: all the arts, tennis, piano; Home: 133 Belsize Drive, Toronto, Ont. M4S 1L3

O

OANCIA, David; writer; b. Stonehenge, Sask., 6 Dec. 1929; e. Twelve Mile Lake Sch., Stonehenge; Central Coll., Moose Jaw; Sir George Williams Univ.; m. Maria Asuncion Prieto-Cereceda, 1963; two s. David Stephen, Patrick John; began journalism with Moose Jaw Times Herald, 1952; subsequently joined The Leader-Post then while with Canadian Press worked in most parts of Can.; on 3 yr. tour in London travelled extensively through Europe, N. Africa and Middle East; opened Montreal bureau for Globe & Mail, Toronto, 1963; posted to China, 1965, where main task was reporting on Great Proletarian Cultural Revolution; left China 1968; with Montreal Star 1971-74; Dir. Journalism Program, Sir George Williams Campus, Concordia Univ. 1974-78; Dir. Schl Journalism, Univ. of King's College, Halifax 1978-79; Dir. Television News, C.B.C. 1979; rec'd. Nat. Newspaper Award, 1967; Southam Fellow, Univ. of Toronto 1974-75; recreations: fishing, camping, travel; Address: 218 Crichton Ave., Dartmouth, N.S.

O'BRIEN, Allan R. B., LL.B., M.B.A.; barrister; b. Windsor, N.S., 10 Apl. 1932; s. late Robert Bell and Josephine Marie (Bremner) O'B.; e. King's Coll. Sch., Windsor, N.S.; Univ. of King's Coll.; Dalhousie Univ. Law Sch., LL.B.; Univ. of W. Ont., M.B.A.; m. lstly Helen Mary Louise (d.), d. late Harold Roscoe, 4 Aug. 1957; children: Timothy Harold DeB., Katherine Louise, Robert Andrew; m. 2ndly Robyn Hortie, Jul. 22, 1978; PARTNER, GOWLING & HENDERSON; read law with Burchill, Smith & Co., Halifax, N.S.; called to Bar of N.S. 1960, Bar of Alta. 1961 and Bar of Ont. 1970; Solr., Interprovincial Pipe Line Co., 1960-64; Asst. to Gen. Counsel, 1964-66; former Nat. Organizer, Liberal Party of Can.; mem., Law Soc. Alta., Law Soc. of Upper Canada and Candn. Bar Assn.; Phi Kappa Pi; Liberal; Anglican; recreations: skiing, fishing; Home: 426 Cloverdale, Rockcliffe Park, Ottawa, Ont. K1N 0Y4; Office: 160 Elgin St., Ottawa, Ont. K1N 8S3

O'BRIEN, David, B.A., B.C.L.; petroleum executive; b. Montreal, Que. 9 Sept. 1941; e. Loyola Coll., B.A. Honors Economics 1962; McGill Univ. B.C.L. 1965; appointed Queen's Counsel Dec. 1980; m. Gail Corneil 1 June 1968; children: Tara, Matthew, and Shaun; SR. VICE PRES. AND GEN. COUNSEL, PETRO-CANADA; law practice 1967-77; Lectr. in Law of Banking, McGill Univ. 1970-74; Home: 2922 Montcalm Cr., Calgary, Alberta, T2T 3M6; Office: P.O. Box 2844, Calgary, Alberta, T2P 3E3

O'BRIEN, Vice-Admiral John Charles, O.C. (1970), C.D.; b. Montreal, Que., 16 Dec. 1918; e. Royal Mil. Coll. of Can., 1937; joined Royal Can. Navy 1937; joined destroyer Saguenay for N. Atlantic escort duties, 1940; served for 2 yrs. as Flotilla Signals Offr., 4th Destroyer Flotilla, 1942, followed by signal duties in Can.; served on R. N. Signal Book Comte., 1946 then took command destroyer Crescent; later became Offr.-in-Charge, Communications Sch., Halifax; served for yr. on staff of Supreme Allied Commdr. Atlantic, Norfolk, Va.; became Extve. Offr., HMCS Stadacona, Halifax, 1953; later Extve. Offr. of Aircraft Carrier Magnificent; apptd. Dir., Naval Training, Naval H.Q., 1955 and Dir., Naval Communications there 1957; Co-ordinator, Personnel Structure Comte., 1958-59; took command Bonaventure, 1959; Naval mem., Candn. Joint Staff, Washington, 1961; apptd. Sr. Candn. Offr. afloat Atlantic, 1964; Commdr., Maritime Command 1966-70; Commandant NATO Defence College 1970-73; apptd. Dir. Gen., Revenue Dir., Organizing Comte. for XXIst Olympiade Nov. 1974; awarded Grande Ufficiale del ordine di Merito della Rep. (Italy) 1973; rec'd. Hon. D. Sc. Mil., Roy. Mil. Coll. 1974; Address: Box 62, Georgeville, Qué. J0B 1T0

O'BRIEN, John J., B.Com.; marketing executive; b. U.K. 20 June 1942; s. John Joseph O'B.; e. Melbourne Univ. B.Com. 1970; Hemmingway Robertson A.S.A. 1971; m. Helen Joan d. late George Hendrickson Antcliffe 19 Dec. 1964; children: Lewis John, Jay Andrew, Aran Thomas, Kerby Ruth; VICE PRES.-MARKETING, BENSON & HEDGES (CANADA) INC. since 1978; joined J. Walter Thompson as Mgr. Business Operations, Acct. Service Supvr.; Mang. Dir. P. T. Philip Morris, Indonesia 1975-77, Finance Mgr. 1973-74; Dir. of Planning present Co. 1977-78; mem. Australian Soc. Accts.; Liberal; R. Catholic; recreations: swimming, running, badminton, water skiing; Home: 276 Kenaston Ave., Town of Mount Royal, Que. H3R 1M5; Office: Suite 400 Place du Canada, Montreal, Que. H3B 2P4.

O'BRIEN, John Wilfrid, M.A., Ph.D., D.C.L., LL.D; univ. pres.; b. Toronto, Ont., 4 Aug. 1931; s. Wilfred Edmond and Audrey (Swain) O.; e. Owen Sound Coll. & Voc. Inst.; McGill Univ. B.A., 1953; Inst. of Pol. Studies, Paris, France 1954; McGill Univ. M.A. 1955, Ph.D. 1962, L.L.D. 1976; Bishop's Univ. D.C.L. 1976; m. Joyce Helen d. Joseph Bennett, 4 Aug. 1956; children: Margaret Anne, Catherine Audrey; RECTOR AND VICE CHANCELLOR, PRES., CONCORDIA UNIVERSITY since 1974; mem. Council of Univs. (Que.) since 1969-76; joined Sir George Williams Univ. as Lect. in Econ., 1954-57, Asst. Prof., 1957-61; Assoc. Prof. 1961-65; Asst. Dean of Univ. 1961-63; Prof. 1965; Dean of Arts 1963-68, Vice Princ., Academic 1968-69; Princ. Vice Chancellor & Pres., 1969-74; mem. Prov. Educ. TV Comte., Dept. Educ. Que., 1962-66 (Dept. Chrmn. 1965-66, mem. Teacher Training Planning Comte. 1964-66); mem. Gauthier Ad Hoc Comte., Univ. Operating Budgets, 1965-68; Council of Univs. 1969-76; Pres., Conf. of Rectors & Prins. of Que. Univs. 1974-77; Council of Assn. of Commonwealth Univ., 1975-78; Bd. of Dirs., Assn. of Univs. & Colls., Can., 1977-79; Conseil consultatif sur L'Immigration, Govt. of Que., 1977-79; Bd. of Govs. YMCA 1969-; Vanier Coll. 1975-79; Fraser-Hickson Inst. 1975-; Que. Div., Candn. Mental Health Assn. 1977-79; Hon. Vice Pres., Que. Prov. Council, Boy Scouts of Can. 1974-; Hon. Councillor, Montreal Mus. Fine Arts, 1969-; author "Canadian Money and Banking", 1964 (2nd ed. with G. Lermer 1969); mem. Candn. Econ. Assn.; Am. Econ. Assn.; Am. Assn. Higher Educ.; Home: 38 Holton Ave., Westmount, Que. H3Y 2E8; Office: 1455 de Maisonneuve Blvd. W., Montreal, Que. H3G 1M8

O'BRIEN, Michael John, M.A., Ph.D.; educator; b. New York City, N.Y. 27 Apl. 1930; s. Michael J. and Mary E. (Collins) O'B.; e. Regis High Sch. New York 1947; Fordham Univ. B.A. 1951; Princeton Univ. M.A. 1953, Ph.D. 1956; m. Anne Jordan d. Dr. Joseph P. Webb, Kalamazoo, Mich. 25 July 1959; children: David, Emily; PROF. OF CLASSICS, UNIV. OF TORONTO 1969- ; Instr. in Classics Wesleyan Univ., Conn. 1955-56; Instr. to Assoc. Prof. of Classics Yale Univ. 1956-66; Assoc. Prof. of Classics present Univ. 1966-69, Chrmn. of Classics 1973-75, 1975-81; Morse Research Fellow 1963-64; Guggenheim Research Fellow 1972-73; author "The Socratic Paradoxes and the Greek Mind" 1967; Ed. "Twentieth-Century Interpretations of Oedipus Rex (essays) 1968; various articles Greek philos. and tragedy; mem. Classical Assn. Can.; Ont. Classical Assn.; Am. Philol. Assn.; Classical Assn. (Brit.); Soc. Ancient Greek Philos.; R. Catholic; Home: 67 Paperbirch Dr., Don Mills, Ont. M3C 2E6; Office: Toronto, Ont. M5S 1A1.

O'BRIEN, Robert Neville, M.A.Sc., Ph.D., F.R.S.A., F.C.I.C.; educator; technology executive; b. Nanaimo, B.C. 14 June 1921; s. Robert Emmette and Mary-Ann (Crossan) O'B.; e. Univ. of B.C. B.A.Sc. (Chem. Engn.) 1951, M.A.Sc. (Metall. Engn.) 1952; Nanchester Univ. Ph.D. 1955; m. Helen T. Bryan 28 June 1952; children: Daniel Bryan, Martha Elizabeth, Robert Douglas Young, Timothy Ian Hal, William Patrick Thomas; PROF. OF CHEMISTRY, UNIV. OF VICTORIA 1968- ; Pres. and Chief Consultant, ReTech-Capital Applied Research & Technology Ltd.; Pres., O.E.L. Oxygen Engineering; J & R Research; Secy. and Dir. H & R Electromines Ltd.; served with RCA 1942-43; RCAF 1943-46 (Pilot), Burma, rank Capt.; co-author "A Laboratory Manual of Modern Chemistry" 1964; author over 100 artlices prof. journs., book chapter; mem. Chamber Comm.; Am. Chem. Soc.; Eletrochem. Soc.; Am. Assn. Advanc. Science; Internat. Electrochem. Soc.; recreations: boating, caoneing, sailing, squash, badminton, gardening; Home: 2614 Queenswood Dr., Victoria, B.C. V8N 1X5; Office: (P.O. Box 1700) Victoria, B.C. V8W 2Y2.

O'BRIEN, Robert Stephen, B.A., B.C.L., Q.C.; lawyer; b. Montreal, Que. 21 Oct. 1929; s. John Lewis, Q.C. and Ethel (Cox) O'B.; e. McGill Univ. B.A. 1951, B.C.L. 1953; m. Julian E. d. late Charles H. A. Armstrong, Q.C., Toronto, Ont. 22 June 1957; children: Charles, Claire, Jane; PARTNER, LAVERY, O'BRIEN; called to Bar of Que. 1954; cr. Q.C. 1972; mem. Candn. Bar Assn.; Bar of Que.; Bar of Montreal (Treas. 1976-77); Fed. Ins. Counsel; Zeta Psi; Liberal; R. Catholic; recreations: reading, gardening, swimming; Club: University; Home: 310 Roslyn Ave.,

Westmount, Que. H3Z 2L6; Office: 3100, 2 Complexe Desjardins, Montreal, Que. H5B 1G4.

O'BRIEN, William L. S., B.Com.; investment dealer; b. Montreal, Que., 1 Nov. 1914; s. William Patrick and Marie Yvonne (Beaubien) O.; e. Selwyn House, Montreal; Portsmouth Priory Sch., Rhode Island; McGill Univ., B.Com.; divorced;; children: Shaun Maureen, William Stuart, Stuart Patrick; DIR., VICE-PRES., BRAULT, GUY, O'BRIEN INC.; former Sr. Partner, O'Brien & Williams Ltd.; Dir.; Palermo Holdings Ltd.; Ile Bizard Realties Ltd.; Secfin Co. Ltd.; Canafund Co. Ltd.; Precision Instruments Inc.; Lewis, Keefer Penfield Ltd.; mem. Adv. Bd., Crown Trust Co.; Dir., Canada World Youth, Chrmn., Finance Comte.; Dir., Que. Soc. for Crippled Children; Dir. and mem. Extve. Comte. (Que. Div.), The Candn. Mental Health Assn.; mem. Adv. Bd., St. Mary's Hosp.; served in 2nd World War; Pilot, R.C.A.F., 405 Sqdn.; Roman Catholic; Club: The St-Denis (Former Pres.); Mt. Royal; Hillside Tennis; Mt. Royal Tennis; Home: 4300 Blvd. de Maisonneuve, Montreal, Que. H3Z 1K8; Office: 635 Dorchester Blvd. W., Suite 1000, Montreal, Que. H3B 1R8

O'CALLAGHAN, Jeremiah Patrick; journalist; publisher; b. Mallow, County Cork, Ireland 8 Oct. 1925; came to Can. 1959; s. Michael Joseph and Marguerita (Hayes) O'C.; e. Christian Brother's Sch., Limerick, Ireland; St. Joseph's Elem. Sch., Worcestershire, Eng.; Worcester Jr. Commercial Sch.; Cotton Coll., N. Staffordshire; m. Lorna Elizabeth d. Thomas Francis Nattriss 28 June 1947; children: Patrick, Michael, Sean, Brendan, Fiona; PUBLISHER, EDMONTON JOURNAL since 1976; Vice Pres., Southam Inc.; Vice Pres. Candn. Daily Newspaper Publishers' Assn.; Dir. and Extve. Mem., The Candn. Press; Dir. Am. Press Inst.; Reporter, Malvern Gazette Worcestershire, Eng., 1941-43; Sub-ed., The Northern Echo, Darlington, 1947; Sub-ed., Yorkshire Eve. Press, York, 1947-48; Sports Sub-ed., Yorkshire Eve. Post, 1948-53; Sub-ed., Liverpool Daily Post and Asst. Ed. Liverpool Echo, 1953-59; Man. Ed., Asst. Publ., Red Deer Advocate, Alta. 1959-68; Asst. to Publ., Edmonton Jnl., 1968-69; Extve. Ed., Southam News Service, Ottawa, 1969-71; Extve. Asst. Southam Press, 1971-72; Publ., Windsor Star, 1972-76; served with RAF, 1943-47, wireless operator/air gunner; mem., Intl. Press Inst. and Commonwealth Press Union; non-partisan; R. Catholic; Clubs: Edmonton; Mayfair Golf and Country; The Centre; recreations: golf, reading; Home: 11 Riverside Cresc., Edmonton, Alta. T5N 3M4; Office: 10006 - 101 St., Edmonton, Alta. T5J 2S6.

OCKENDEN, Maj. Gen. Gordon Frederick, D.F.C., C.D.; retired air force officer; b. Vermilion, Alta., 20 July 1923; s. Frederick Clarence and Ruby Elizabeth (Cooper) O.; e. Oliver Pub. and Eastwood High Schs., Edmonton, 1941; 8 Service Flying Training Sch., Moncton, N.B., grad. Fighter Pilot; U.S.N. Ground Controlled Intercept Course, Glenview, Ill. 1948; RCAF Staff Coll. 1959-60; Nat. Defence Coll. 1966-67; m. Mary Patricia, d. R. Slessor, Penticton, B.C., 2 June 1948; 5 sons, Timothy, Gary, Monty, James, Edward; DIR., INTL. MARKETING, DEFENCE PRODUCTS BRISTOL AEROSPACE LTD., since 1978; joined RCAF 1941; served in Nfld. and N.S. before joining 443 Fighter Sqdn. in Europe; left service 1945 and rejoined as a transport pilot, Edmonton 1946; C.O., 1 Aircraft Control & Warning Unit, St. Hubert, Que.; Chief Controller, 1 Air Defence Group HQ, 1951; served on exchange duties with USAF, Stewart Air Force Base, N.Y., 1953-55; trans. to 61 Aircraft Control & Warning Sqdn., Metz, France as Chief Operations Offr.; served on exchange duties with USAF, Stewart Air Force Base, N.Y., change duties with USAF, Stewart Air Force Base, N.Y., 1953-55; trans. to 61 Aircraft Control & Warning Sqdn., Metz, France as Chief Operations Offr.; C.O. of Sqdn. 1957; Direction Center Chief, Detroit NORAD Sector, 1960; Depy. Dir. of Operations 1962; C.O., RCAF Stn. St. Margarets, N.B. 1964; promoted Col. and apptd. C.O., RCAF Stn. Centralia, 1965; Commdr., Candn. Forces Base, Borden, 1967; Command Dir., NORAD's Command Post, Cheyenne Mt. 1970; pro-

moted Brig. Gen. and apptd. Depy. Asst. Depy. Chief of Staff for Combat Operations, NORAD Command, HQ, Colo. Springs, 1971; awarded USAF Air Weapons Controller Wing 1978; Dir. Gen. Mang. Information Services, NDHQ, Ottawa, 1975; promoted Major General, 1976; Candn. Def. Attaché and Commander, Candn. Def. Liasion Staff, Washington, D.C., 1976-78; retired RCAF and CF, 1978; Anglican; recreations: camping, badminton, curling, skiing; Homes: 1119 Ambleside Dr., Ottawa, Ont. K2B 8E2 and 3217 Topham Rd., Kelowna, B.C. V1Z 2J7; Office: Suite 912, 130 Albert St., Ottawa, Ont. K1P 5G4.

O'CONNELL, Hon. Martin, O.C. (1971), M.P., Ph.D.; former univ. prof. & investment dealer; business & financial consultant; b. Victoria, B.C., 1 Aug. 1916; s. James and Mary (Kyle) O'C.; e. Queen's Univ., B.A. 1942; Univ. of Toronto, M.A., Ph.D. 1954; m. Helen Alice, d. late Clement Dionne; children: Caryn Elizabeth Margaret, John Martin; MIN. OF LABOUR, 1978-79; Parlty. Secy. to Min. Regional Econ. Expansion 1969-70; Min. of State 1971; apptd. Min. of Labour 28 Jan. 1972; def. in g.e. Oct. 1972 and apptd. Princ. Secy. to Prime Min. Nov. 1972; re-el. to H. of C. in g.e. July 1974; def. in gen. el. May 1979 & Feb. 1980; served with C.A.S.C. and Candn. Inf. Corps 1942-45; rank Capt. on discharge; Co-Chrmn., Special Joint Comte. of Parlt. on Immigration Policy; Past Co-Chrmn., Canada-U.S. Interpavlty group; Past Pres., Candn. Parlty Helsinki Monitoring Group; Past Pres., Bd. Indian-Eskimo Assn. Can.; mem. Inter-Parlty. Union; Liberal; Roman Catholic; Office: Ste. 719, 2 Carleton St., Toronto, Ont. M5B 1J3

O'CONNOR, Arthur J., B.Sc. Eng.; utilities executive; b. Harvey, N.B., 26 Oct. 1924; s. Frederick James and Mary (Long) O'C.; e. Univ. of N.B., B.Sc. Eng. (Elect.) 1945; m. Mary Kathleen, d. late John Whalen, 21 Sept. 1950; six s. and two d.; GEN. MGR., N.B. ELECTRIC POWER COMN. since 1967; joined the Comn. as Engr. (Distribution) 1949; also served as Resident Engr. Tobique Narrows Hydro Project, System Operating Engr., Asst. Chief Engr., Mgr. of Engrn., Asst. Gen. Mgr. and Chief Engr.; mem. Fredericton Bd. Trade; Candn. Nuclear Assn. (Pres. 1973-74); Candn. Elect. Assn. (Past-Pres.); Assn. Prof. Engrs. N.B.; Candn. World Energy Conf.; Candn. Comte. on Large Dams; Chmn., Eastern Council of Inst. Elect. & Electronic Engrs.; mem. Science Council of Canada; K. of C.; R. Catholic; recreations: tennis, skiing; Home: 467 Squire St., Fredericton, N.B. E3B 1E7; Office: 527 King St., Fredericton, N.B. E3B 4X1

O'CONNOR, Thomas Patrick, Q.C.; B.A.; b. Toronto, Ont., 25 Apl. 1911; s. Charles Arthur and Mary Agnes (Heydon) O.; e. De La Salle Coll., Toronto, Ont.; St. Michael's Coll., and Univ. of Toronto, B.A. 1932; Osgoode Hall, Toronto, Ont., Grad. 1935; m. Agnes Christine, d. Goodwin M. Bernard, Niagara-on-the-Lake, Ont., 6 Aug. 1938; children: Terrance Patrick, Dennis Rory, Shelagh Louise; ASSISTANT DIR., LEGAL SERVICES, OFFICE OF THE OMBUDSMAN; Partner, O'Connor, Coutts, Crane, Ingram; read law with MacMurchy and Spence, C.P.R. Solicitors, Toronto, Ont.; called to the Bar of Ontario, 1935; cr. Q.C. 1955; Sr. Solr.; Ont. Securities Comn., 1946-49; served in 2nd World War; Lieut.-Col., R.C.A.S.C., 1940-45; served in Claims Br., C.M.H.Q., London, 1941-44; Asst. Dir., Claims & Hirings Hdqrs., First Candn. Army in European campaign 1944-45; mem., Candn. Bar Assn.; County of York Law Assn.; Roman Catholic; recreation: golf; Clubs: Rosedale Golf; Royal Canadian Military Inst.; Canadian; Lawyers; Home: 10 Hi Mount Drive, Willowdale, Ont. M2K 1X4; Office: 65 Queen St. W., Suite 600, Toronto, Ont. M5H 2M5

O'DEA, Hon. Fabian, Q.C., LL.D.; b. St. John's Nfld., 20 Jan 1918; s. Hon. John V., K.S.G. and May (Coady), M.B.E., O'Dea; e. St. Bonaventure's Coll., 1923-34; Memorial Univ. of Nfld., 1934-36; St. Michael's Coll., Univ. of Toronto, B.A. 1939; Dalhousie Univ., 1939-40; Christ Church, Oxford Univ., B.C.L. 1948; LL.D. Memorial Univ. 1969; m. Constance Margaret, d. Edgar G. Ewing, St. John's, 9 Aug. 1951; children: Deborah, Victoria, Stephen, Jane; PARTNER, O'DEA, GREENE, NEARY & PUDDESTER; Lt.-Gov. Nfld. 1963-69; called to Bar of Eng. at the Inner Temple, 1948, Nfld. 1949; cr. Q.C. 1963; practised law in London, Eng., 1948 and in St. John's since 1949; Rhodes Scholar for Nfld. 1939; Hon. A.D.C. to Gov.-Gen. of Can., 1949-52; Hon. A.D.C. to Lieut.-Govs. of Nfld., 1949-61; Consular Agent for France in Nfld., 1957-62; Hon. Solicitor for Nfld. Prov. Command of Roy. Candn. Legion, 1950-63; Hon. Life mem. of Nfld. Prov. Command of Roy. Candn. Legion 1963; Dir., Nfld. Telephone Co. Ltd.; Browning harvey Ltd.; mem. St. John's Adv. Bd.; Can. Permanent Trust Co.; Chrmn. Outport Arts Fndtn.; mem., Bd. of Regents, Memorial Univ. of Newfoundland, 1959-63; Vice-Pres. for Nfld. of Candn. Bar Assn., 1961-63; Secy. Rhodes Scholar Selection Comte. for Nfld. 1951-62, Chrmn. 1963-69; Kt., Order of St. John of Jerusalem (1963); served in 2nd World War with R.C.N.V.R., 1940-45; on loan to Roy. Navy, 1943-44; C.O., H.M.C.S. Cabot, 1952-55; Commander, R.C.N.R. (retired); Roman Catholic; Office: 263 Duckworth St., St. John's, Nfld.

ODETTE, Edmond George; B.Sc., Ph.D.; contractor; b. Tilbury, Ont. 1 Jan. 1926; s. Louis L. and E. (Ritter) O.; e. St. Michael's Coll. High Sch. Toronto; Univ. of Toronto B.Sc. 1948; Univ. of Assumption Ph.D. 1970; m. Gloria A. d. Frederick McEwan, Windsor, Ont. 8 Sept. 1951; children: Edmond George, Curtis M., Mary, Anne, Andrea; PRES., EASTERN CONSTRUCTION CO. LTD. 1951- ; Pres. Sun Construction Co. Ltd.; Associated Leaseholds Ltd.; Dir. I.A.C. Ltd. - Continental Bank; Hiram Walker-Consumers Home Ltd.; Dir., Uniroyal Ltd.; mem. Assn. Prof. Engrs. Prov. Ont.; R. Catholic; recreations: golf, tennis; Clubs: Rosedale Golf; Granite; Lost Tree; Jupiter Hills Golf; Essex Golf; Detroit Athletic; Home: 21 High Point Rd., Don Mills, Ont. M3B 2A3; Office: (P.O. Box 440 Stn. Q) Toronto, Ont. M4T 2R8.

O'DETTE, John Herbert, C.M., M.Sc.; metallurgical engineer; conservationist; b. Brockville, Ont. 17 Feb. 1920; s. Charles Herbert and Gertrude (Brady) O'D.; e. St. Francis Separate Sch. and Brockville Coll. Inst. 1939; Queen's Univ. B.Sc. 1944, M.Sc. 1946; m. Irene Pearl d. late Ross Paul, Napanee, Ont. 14 Sept. 1946; children: Cheri (Mrs. S. Lipin), Leanne, Brian, Craig; SR. RESEARCH ENGINEER, KINGSTON RESEARCH & DEVELOPMENT CENTRE, ALUMINUM CO. OF CANADA; mem. Research Div. Consolidated Mining & Smelting Co. (Cominco) Trail, B.C., also postgrad. teaching Queen's Univ. 1944-46; Alcan Research & Devel. Kingston, Ont. 1946-79; Kingston City appointee to Cataraqui Region Conserv. Authority 1970-75, 1978-81; mem. Adv. Comte. to Min. of Lands & Forests Ont. 1968-72; Dir., Ont. Fed. Anglers & Hunters 1952-79 (Past Pres.); Candn. Wildlife Fed. 1965-79 (Past Pres.); Sportsmen's Conserv. Workshops in Ont. 1960-79; rec'd Carling Conserv. Award 1968; White Owl Conserv. Award 1974; Winchester Outdoorsman of Yr. 1978; Am. Motors Conserv. Award 1979; served with C.O.T.C. Queen's Univ., also Special Weapons Training Offr., rank Capt.; author numerous articles fish and wildlife, resource mang.; lectr.; Columnist "Ontario Angler and Hunter"; prepared many briefs resource mang. Ont. and Fed. Govts.; mem. Soc. Explosives Engrs.; Candn. Inst. Mining & Metall.; R. Catholic; recreations: hunting, fishing, golf, tennis, target shooting; Clubs: Kingston & Dist. Rod & Gun (Past Pres. and Dir.); Frontenac Rifle and Pistol (Pres. & Dir. 1956-79); Home: 377 Bath Rd., Kingston, Ont. K7M 2Y1; Office: (P.O. Box 8400) Kingston, Ont. K7L 4Z4.

O'DONNELL, Rev. James Reginald, M.A., Ph.D., D.Litt. (Hon. C.), F.R.S.C., (R.C.); retired university pro-

fessor; b. Jarvis, Ont., 19 Aug. 1907; s. John Myles and Mary Elizabeth (Hunks) O.; e. Univ. of Toronto, B.A. 1931, M.A. 1936, Ph.D. 1946; D. Litt. (honoris causa); post-grad. studies in Poland, Germany, France; retired Prof., Dept. of Classics, Sch of Grad. Studies, Univ. of Toronto, and at Pontifical Inst. of Mediaeval Studies; (Canada Council Sr. Fellowship 1960-61 spent in Florence and Rome); Editor of "Mediaeval Studies" 1970-74; mem., Inst. for Advanced Study, Princeton, N.J., 1968-69; Publications: many articles on mediaeval subjects, critical reviews, articles in encyclopedias; Address: 59 Queens Park Cres. East, Toronto, Ont. M5S 2C4

O'DONNELL, John W., B.A.; manufacturer; b. Hamilton, Ont., 26 Feb. 1934; s. Frederick W. and Jean M. (Hossack) O.; e. Univ. of Toronto, B.A. 1954; Harvard Business School, 79th AMP; m. Helen Ann, d. late Lorne Innes, 27 Aug. 1955; children: Megan, Victoria, John, Charles, Joseph, Melissa; PRESIDENT, MONARCH FINE FOODS CO. LTD. since 1970; Dir., Riviera Foods Ltd.; joined Lever Bros. (Canada) Ltd. 1954 and following a variety of marketing positions apptd. Marketing Dir., Lever Detergents Ltd. 1969; Past Pres., Inst. Edible Oil Foods; mem. Grocery Products Mfrs. Assn. Can.; Bd. Trade Metrop. Toronto; Clubs: Mississauga Golf and Country Club; R. Catholic; Home: 223 Trelawn Ave., Oakville, Ont. L6J 4R3; Office: 6700 Finch Ave. W., Humber Tower Bldg., 8th floor, Rexdale, Ont. M9W 1G9

O'DONNELL, Patrick Joseph, Ph.D.; physicist; educator; b. Port Glasgow, Scot. 16 Oct. 1938; s. Daniel and Mary (Blaney) O'D.; e. Univ. of Glasgow B.Sc. 1960, Ph.D. 1963; m. Mary Agnes d. George Reynolds, Baillieston, Scot. Aug. 1964; three s. Daniel Paul, George Ciaran, Quentin Patrick; PROF. OF PHYSICS, UNIV. OF TORONTO 1977- ; Research Asst. Univ. of Durham 1963-65; Acting Chrmn. Div. Physical Science, Scarborough Coll. present Univ; Asst. Prof. of Physics present Univ. 1966-70, Assoc. Prof. 1970-77; SRC (UK) Sr. Research Fellow, Southampton Univ. 1976; Sr. Research Fellow Univ. of Glasgow 1979; author numerous articles particle physics prof. journs.; mem. Candn. Assn. Physicists (Chrmn. Div. Particle Physics 1981-82); Am. Phys. Soc.; N.Y. Acad. Sciences; Inst. Particle Physics (Can., Council mem.); recreations: skiing, squash; Club: Skyloft Ski (Candn. Ski Patrol Leader); Home: 36 Sandrift Sq., West Hill, Ont. M1E 4N6; Office: Toronto, Ont. M5S 1A7.

O'DONOGHUE, Paul Henry, B.A., B.Th.; insurance broker; b. Toronto, Ont., 24 May 1931; s. Henry Dillon and Stella Mary (Lynch) O'D.; e. St. Michael's Coll., Univ. of Toronto, B.A. 1952, B.Th. 1955; m. Denyse Mercier, 29 March 1969; PRES. & CHIEF EXTVE. OFFICER AND DIR., MARSH & McLENNAN LTD., Dir., Marsh & McLennan International; Marsh & McLennan World Services; William M. Mercer Ltd.; Pratte-Morrissette Inc. (Quebec City); Turner Ins. Agency Inc. (Saskatoon); BNP Canada Inc.; Dir. and Past Pres., Ont. Sec. French Chamber of Comm.; Vice-Pres. & Trustee Toronto French School Foundation; mem. Bus. Council on Nat. Issues; former mem. Extve Council, Candn. Chamber of Comm., Past Chrmn. Ont. Reg. Comte.; Liberal; Catholic; recreations: tennis, skiing; Clubs: Rosedale Golf; Toronto; Caledon Ski (Dir.); University; Badminton and Racquet; Boulevard C.; Toronto Board of Trade; Home: 181 Warren Rd., Toronto, Ont. M4V 2S4; Office: P.O. Box 58, 1 First Canadian Place, Toronto, Ont. M5X 1G2

O'DONOHUE, Melville J. B., Q.C., B.Com.; b. Toronto, Ont. 3 Jan. 1923; s. Eugene Joseph and Mary Josephine (Sweeney) O'D.; e. De La Salle College, Oaklands; Univ. of Toronto, B.Com. 1946; Osgoode Hall; read law with late Hon. Frank Hughes, Q.C., 1949-51; called to the Bar of Ont., 1951; cr. Q.C. 1963; m. Gloria, d. of late Albert Knox, K.C.; children: Stephen, Gregory, Mary-Jo and Melanie; PARTNER, O'DONOHUE, WHITE & CHRISTO since 1979; Dir., A.P. Green Refractories (Canada) Ltd.; Jamger Investments Ltd.; Ohio Nut and Bolt (Canada) Ltd.; Pony Express Residential Security Inc.; Pyrotronics Canada Ltd.; Supreme Aluminium Industries Ltd.; Tamcon Engineering Ltd.; Wells Fargo Armcar Inc. Wells Fargo Alarm Services of Can. Ltd.; Pres., Canexpo Marketing Ltd., Beirut, Lebanon; Partner, Melville O'Donohue, Toronto, 1951-53; O'Donohue and Hague, 1954-62; O'Donohue and White, 1962-63; Gardiner, Roberts, 1963-79; O'Donohue, White & Christo, 1979-; mem. Examining Bd. and Bd. of Review, Law Soc. of Upper Canada; mem. Candn. Tax Foundation; Co. of York Law Assn.; P-Pres. Thos. More Lawyers' Guild; Liberal; Roman Catholic; recreations: hunting, farming; Clubs: Eglinton Equestrian; Granite; National; Toronto Lawyers; Home: 35 St. Edmunds Dr., Toronto, Ont. M4N 2P7; Office: Suite 2010, 401 Bay St., Toronto, Ont. M5H 2Y4

O'DRISCOLL, Hon. John Gerald Joseph, B.A.; judge; b. Sault Ste. Marie, Ont., 3 March 1931; s. Michael Joseph and Gertrude (Mulligan) O'D.; e. Sacred Heart Sch., Sault Ste. Marie, Ont.; Sault Coll. Inst. St. Michael's Coll. Sch., and St. Michael's Coll., Univ. of Toronto, B.A. 1951; Osgoode Hall Law Sch.; m. Patricia Marie, d. H. J. Slattery, Toronto, Ont., 17 May 1958; three s. John Joseph, Michael Sean, Patrick Francis; JUSTICE, SUPREME COURT OF ONT. since 1971; read law with Arthur Maloney, Q.C.; called to Bar of Ont. 1955; cr. Q.C. 1967; R. Catholic; Home: Toronto, Ont.; Office: 130 Queen St. W., Toronto, Ont. M5H 2N5

O'DRISCOLL, Robert, M.A., Ph.D.; university professor; author; b. Conception Harbour, Nfld., 3 May 1938; s. William Joseph and Annie May (Conners) O'D.; e. Conception Harbour (Nfld.) and St. Bonaventure's Coll. St. John's, Nfld. 1954; Memorial Univ. of Nfld. B.A. (Educ.) 1958, B.A. 1959, M.A. 1960; Univ. of London Ph.D. 1963; m. singer Treasa Ni Argadain d. Brian Hardiman, Ireland, 18 July 1966; children: Brian William Butler, Michael Robert, Declan Patrick, Emer Anne; PROF. ST. MICHAEL'S COLL. UNIV. OF TORONTO since 1975; Research Fellow Univ. of Reading 1963-64; Visiting Prof. Univ. Coll. Dublin 1964-66; joined present Univ. as Asst. Prof. 1966, Assoc. Prof. 1969; service with RCN (Reserve), rank Capt.; author: "Intruder: A Poem" 1972; "Symbolism and Some Implications of the Symbolic Approach: W. B. Yeats During the Eighteen-Nineties" 1975; "An Ascendancy of the Heart: Ferguson and the Beginnings of Modern Irish Literature in English" 1976; Ed.-in-Chief, with Lorna Reynolds, "Yeats Studies" series of which five volumes have appeared: "Yeats during the 1890's" (1971), "Jack Yeats and John Synge" (1972), "Yeats and the Theatre" (1975), "Yeats and the Occult" (1975), "The Speckled Bird" (1977); Ed. "Theatre and Nationalism in 20th Century Ireland" 1971; "A Quest Through Europe, or, The Long Way Round to the Edinburgh Festival," 1980; "The Celtic Consciousness", 1981; author various articles; Founder and first Chrmn. Candn. Assn. for Irish Studies 1968-72; Founder and Artistic Dir. Irish Theatre Soc. and Irish Arts Can. 1967-74; Artistic Dir., Celtic Arts (1977-present); Extve. Comte. Internat. Assn. Studies Anglo-Irish Lit. since 1969; mem. Nat. Lib. of Ireland Comte.; recreations: book collecting, theatre, talk, traditional music; Home: 50 Summerhill Gardens, Toronto, Ont. M4T 1B4; Office: 81 St. Mary St., Toronto, Ont. M5S 1J4

OESTERLE, Leonhard F., R.C.A.; sculptor; b. Bietigheim, Germany 3 March 1915; s. Wilhelm and Sophie (Seher) O.; e. elem. sch. Bietigheim, Germany; Tech. Sch. Stuttgart-Feuerbach, apprenticeship as Fine Mech.; Art Coll. Zurich 1 yr.; studies with Fritz Wotruba, Zug and with Otto Müller, Zurich; INSTR. AND HEAD OF SCULPTURE, ONT. COLL. OF ART; Fellow, Stong Coll. York Univ.; rep. various exhns. Can., USA and Europe; sculpture work subject of 2 CBC films; pol. prisoner Germany 8 yrs.; came to Can. 1956; Past Vice Pres. Sculptors' Soc. Can.; mem. Royal Can. Academy of Arts; Ont. Soc.

Artists; Lutheran; Home: 27 Alcina Ave., Toronto, Ont. M6G 2E7; Office: 100 McCaul St., Toronto, Ont. M5T 1W1.

OGILVIE, Will A., C.M., M.B.E., R.C.A.; artist; b. Cape Province, S. Africa; e. Art Students League, N.Y.; came to Can. 1925; Dir., Art Assn. Sch., Montreal; Instr., Queen's Univ. of Fine Art (summer), 1947; Instr., Ont. Coll. of Art; exhibited with Carl Schaefer, Kingston, Ont., 1947, sketches of the Trun-Chambois area of Normandy after break-through at Falaise 1944; rep. at Candn. exhibit, Phila. Water Colour Club show; executed mural in chapel, Hart House, 1936 and Massey Mem. stained glass windows 1969; rep. in National Gallery of Canada, Ottawa; served in World War 1941-45, Overseas with Candn. Army 1941; Official War Artist 1942; served with 1st Div. in Sicily and Italy, and with the 4th. Candn. Armd. Divn. in N.W. Europe; promoted Capt. 1943; discharged with rank of Maj.; mem., Candn. Group of Painters; Candn. Soc. Painters in Water Colour; paintings include: "Bombed House and Church of Ste. Agathe"; "Disabled German Light Tank and Prisoners, Sicily", 1943; "Mule Train Above a River Bed", 1943; "Prisoner Type", 1943; "Swimming Parade" (Mediteranean), 1944; "Mule Train, Agira, Sicily", 1944; Special Lectr., Dept. Fine Art, Univ. of Toronto from 1960 to 1969; rep. in Galleries: National Can., Toronto, Hamilton, London. Winnipeg, Edmonton, Vancouver; exhibited: S. Doms. (1936), Tate (1938), World's Fair, N.Y. (1939), Gloucester (1939); War Art (Brussels 1944), Nat. Gallery (London 1944), Ottawa (1944); Rio (1946), UNESCO (1946), Johannesburg, Hart House, Toronto; Address: Apt. 212, 70 Heath St. W., Toronto, Ont. M4V 1T4

OIKONOMIDES, Nicolas, Dr.de 3e cycle; educator; b. Athens, Greece 17 Feb. 1934; s. Anthony and Iphigeneia (Peppa) O.; e. Univ. of Athens B.A. (Philos.) 1956; Univ. of Paris Dr.de 3e cycle. (Byzantine Hist.) 1961; m. Elizabeth Zachariadou 29 Oct. 1966; children: Catherine, Theodora; CHRMN. OF HISTORY, UNIV. DE MONTREAL 1981- , Prof. of Byzantine Hist. 1969- ; Advisor in Sigillography, Dumbarton Oaks, Trustees Harvard Univ. 1979- ; Chrmn. of Hist. present Univ. 1976-80; mil. service Greece 1956-58; author "Actes de Dionysiou" 1968; "Actes de Kastamonitou" 1978; "Les listes de Preseance Byzantines des IX et X Siècles" 1972; "Hommes d'Affaires Grecs et Latins à Constantinople" 1979; over 50 articles Byzantine hist., econ., inst., art; mem. Assn. Internat. des Etudes Byzantines (Treas.); Medieval Acad. Am.; Greek Orthodox; Home: 4801 Dornal, Montreal, Que. H3W 1V9; Office: (C.P. 6128, Succursale A) Montreal, Que. H3C 3J7.

OKA, Takeshi, Ph.D. F.R.S.C.; physicist; b. Tokyo, Japan 10 June 1932; s. Shumpei and Chiyoko (Ozaki) O.; e. Univ. of Tokyo B.Sc. 1955, M.Sc. 1957, Ph.D. 1960; m. Keiko d. Kozo Nukui, Saitama, Japan 24 Oct. 1960; children: Ritsuko, Noriko, Kentaro, Yujiro; PROFESSOR, UNIVERSITY OF CHICAGO, Dept. of Chem., Astronomy and Astrophysics since 1981; Sr. Research Offr., Hertzberg Inst. of Astrophysics, Nat. Research Council 1971-81; Asst., Univ. of Tokyo 1960-63; Postdoctorate Fellow, Nat. Research Council 1963, Asst. Research Offr. 1965, Assoc. Research Offr. 1968-71; rec'd Steacie Prize 1972; Earl K. Plyler Prize 1982; mem.; Am. Phys. Soc.; Internat. Astron. Union; Am. Astron. Soc.; Optical Soc. of America; recreation: running, judo; Home: 1463 East Park Place, Chicago, Illinois, 60637 Office: 5735 South Ellis Ave., Chicago Illinois, 60637

O'KELLY, Edward Ross, C.A.; retired company executive; b. Toronto, Ont., 3 Dec 1912; e. Univ. of Toronto (extra mural); Vice-Pres., Mfg., and Dir., GTE Automatic Electric (Canada) Ltd. 1937-1977; with Wm. Wrigley Jr. Co. Ltd., 1933-37; served in 2nd World War with R.C.N., 1940-45; Lt. Commdr., R.C.N.(R) retired; Dir., St. Vincent de Paul General Hospital; mem., Ontario and Canadian Institute of Chartered Accts.; Ontario Employers' Labour Relations Comte.; Naval Offrs.' Assn. Can.; Candn. Power Squadrons; recreations: boating, skiing, hunting, riding; Clubs: Brockville Country; Brockville Yacht; Home: 191 Hartley St., Brockville, Ont. K6V 3N4

OKULITCH, Vladimir Joseph, M.A.Sc., Ph.D., F.R.S.C., F.G.S.A., D.Sc. (Hon.) U.B.C. 1972; dean emeritus; b. St. Petersburg, Russia, 18 June 1906; e. Peabody Grammar Sch., Cambridge, Mass.; Russo-Serbian Lyceum, Belgrade, Yugoslavia; Univ. of Brit. Columbia, M.A.Sc. (Geol. Engn.) 1932; McGill Univ., Ph.D. (Geol.) 1934; Harvard Univ., Research Fellow 1934-36; m. Suzanne, d. Peter V. Kouhar, 19 Jan. 1934; children: Andrew, Peter; Mine Geol., Atlin Silver-Lead Mines, 1930-32; Lectr. and Asst. Prof., Univ. of Toronto, 1936-44; Assoc. Prof. of Geol., Univ. of B.C., 1944-49; subsequently Prof. of Palaeontol. and Stratigraphy and Head Dept. of Geol. there; retired as Dean Emeritus of Science Sept. 1971; Fellow, Palaeontol. Soc.; Geol. Society of America; Royal Astron. Society of Canada; Royal Society of Canada; author of "North American Pleospongia", 1943 (monograph on Cambrian organisms); has contributed over sixty scientific papers to technical journals; Greek Orthodox; recreations: photography, astronomy, camping, mountain climbing; Club: University; Home: 1843 Knox Rd., University Hill, Vancouver, B.C. V6T 1S4

OLAND, Bruce S. C.; masterbrewer; b. Guildford, Eng., 31 March 1918; s. Col. Sidney Culverwell and Herlinda (deBedia) O.; e. King's Coll. Sch., Windsor, N.S.; Beaumont Coll., Old Windsor, Eng. (3 years); Un. Brewers' Acad., U.S.A., 1 yr.; m. Ruth, d. James Edward Hurley, Westfield, N.J., 17 Nov. 1956; children: Richard Hurley, Deborah Ruth; DIR., OLAND BREWERIES LIMITED, Halifax; President, Culverwell Holdings Limited; Lindwood Holdings Limited; served with 1st Halifax Coast Regt., R.C.A., 1939-45; rank Maj. on discharge; Reserve Army 1946-51; joined R.C.N. Reserve 1951; Sr. Reserve Naval Advisor to Depy. Gen. Reserves; rank Commodore; Dir., R.C.N. Benevolent Fund; Chrmn. of Bd., Hon. Govs., N.S. Div., Candn. Assn. Mentally Retarded; Dir. and Past Pres., Halifax Sch. for Blind; Dir., Un. Services Inst.; mem., Naval Offrs.' Assn; Nat. Council, Duke of Edinburgh's Award in Can.; R. Catholic; recreations: squash, sailing, numismatics, philately; Home: "The Anchor", Marlborough Woods, Halifax, N.S. B3H 1H9; Office: 1475 Hollis St., Halifax, N.S. B3J 1V1

OLAND, Don James; b. Havana, Cuba, 18 Feb. 1922; s. Col. Sidney C. and Herlinda (deBedia) O.; e. Beaumont Coll., Old Windsor, Eng.; Dalhousie Univ.; m. Elizabeth Marjorie, d. George Shuter, Montreal, Que., 10 May 1947; children: James Shuter, Mrs. Jennifer Paterson, Brenda Marjorie; Sr. Vice-President and Dir., Lindwood Holdings Limited; Dir., Atlantic Trust; Dir. and Past Pres., Atlantic Winter Fair; Phi Delta Theta; R. Catholic; recreations: yachting, farming, hand gun shooting; Clubs: Royal N.S. Yacht Squadron; Home: 6300 Oakland Rd., Halifax, N.S. B3H 1P2; Office: 1475 Hollis St., Halifax, N.S. B3J 1V1 Farm: Hosmer Farms, Kinsmans Corner, Woodville, (King's County) N.S.

OLAND, Philip W., O.C. (1970), C.D., B.Sc., LL.D., D.Litt.; brewery executive; b. Halifax, N.S., 1910; m. Mary H. Frink, Rothesay, N.B., 1936; children: Derek, Richard, Jane (Mrs. T. Winton Toward); PRESIDENT, DIR. AND MANG. DIR., MOOSEHEAD BREWERIES LTD.; Dir., M.R.A. Holdings Ltd.; Moosehead Holdings Ltd.; Alpine Holdings Ltd.; C.N. Marine; mem. Advisory Board, Royal Trust Company; served with Candn. Army in N.W. Europe; Commdr., 6 Militia Group until 1961; rank Brig. Gen.; Bd. of Govs., St. Thomas Univ. Nat. Youth Orchestra; Hon. Pres. N.B. Youth Orch.; Pres., Saint John Foundation Inc.; Office: Saint John, N.B. E2M 3H2

OLAND, the Hon. Victor deBedia, O.C., E.D., C.D., D.C.L., LL.D., D. Litt., K.G. St. J.; b. Halifax, N.S., 9 Aug. 1913; s. late Col. Sidney C. and Herlinda (deBedia) O.; m. Nancy Jane, d. late William B. Medcalfe, 17 April 1939; children: Sidney, Susan, Peter, Victoria; CHAIRMAN OF BD., LINDWOOD HOLDINGS LTD.; Dir., Texaco Can. Ltd.; Bank of Montreal; VS Services Ltd.; Trustee of The Fraser Inst.; Lieut. Gov. of N.S. 1968-73; Past Pres., Candn. Chamber of Commerce and Candn. Tourist Assocn.; Dir., World Wildlife Fund (Canada); National Council, Candn. Human Rights Foundation; Gov., Canada's Sports Hall of Fame; Kt. Malta; R. Catholic; Clubs: Halifax; York (Toronto); Mt. Royal (Montreal); Home: 788 Young Ave., Halifax, N.S. B3H 2V7; Office: "Keith Hall", P.O. Box 2066, Halifax, N.S. B3J 2Z1

OLDHAM, Ronald, D.F.C., M.A., Dr. de l'U(Paris); educator; b. Calgary, Alta. 11 June 1914; s. John Niven and Elizabeth Bryce (Buchan) O.; e. Mount Royal Coll. Calgary; Victoria (B.C.) High Sch.; Univ. of B.C.B.A. 1938, M.A. 1947; Dr. de l'U(Paris) 1951; m. Dorothy d. late William Smith 15 Oct. 1954; one d. Nesta Reymond; Dean of Arts, Royal Roads Military Coll., 1971-79; Head of French Dept., 1965-79; Prof. of French, 1963-79; joined present Coll. as Asst. Prof. of French 1952, Assoc. Prof. 1953; served with RCAF, RAF and Free French (Forces Françaises Libres) 1940-45; awarded Croix de Guerre et Palme; Centennial Medal 1967; mem. Humanities Assn. Can.; Air Force Offrs. Assn.; Royal Un. Services Inst.; Liberal; United Church; recreations: golf, gardening; Club: R.A.F., London, England; Home: 101-1150 Rockland Ave., Victoria, B.C. V8V 3H7

O'LEARY, Hon. Dennis F., B.A.; judge; b. Downeyville, Ont., 7 Nov. 1926; s. Dennis Michael and Kathleen (O'Brien) O'L.; e. St. Michael's Coll., Univ. of Toronto, B.A. 1949; Osgoode Hall Law Sch.; m. Betty Aileen, d. George Graham, Lindsay, Ont. 22 June 1957; children: Dennis, Lisanne, Bridget, Sean; JUSTICE, SUPREME COURT OF ONT. since 1973; called to Bar of Ont. 1953; cr. Q.C. 1966; law practice in Hamilton, Ont. 1953-73; def. Lib. cand. for Hamilton Center Ont. ge. 1959; former Council mem., Candn. Bar Assn.; Past Pres., St. Thomas More Lawyer's Guild; Hamilton Mt. Lib. Assn.; R. Catholic; recreations: golf, tennis; Club: Hamilton Lawyers' (Past Pres.); Office: Osgoode Hall, Toronto, Ont. M5H 2N6

OLIPHANT, Betty, O.C. (1975), LL.D. (hon.) Queen's Univ. and Brock Univ. 1978, Univ. of Toronto, 1980; artistic dir. & ballet principal; b. London, Eng., 5 Aug. 1918; d. Stuart and Yvonne (Mansfield) O.; e. Queen's Coll. Sch. and St. Mary's Coll. Sch., London, Eng.; rec'd classical ballet training from Tamara Karsavina and Laurent Novikoff; two d.; ARTISTIC DIR. AND BALLET PRINCIPAL, THE NATIONAL BALLET SCHOOL; estbd. own sch. for prof. dancers in London, Eng. and created and directed dance sequences in W. End theatres prior to coming to Can. in 1947; estbd. Betty Oliphant School of Ballet 1948-59; Ballet Mistress, Nat. Ballet of Can., 1951-62; Founder, Dir. & Principal, Nat. Ballet Sch., 1959; Assoc. Artistic Dir., Nat. Ballet of Can. 1969-75; as lectr., examiner and auditioner has travelled across Can., U.S., and abroad; 1967 reorganized the Royal Swedish Opera Ballet Sch.; 1978 reorganized Ballet Sch. of the Royal Danish Theatre, and has visited Moscow and Leningrad as guest of Bolshoi and Kirov Ballet Schs.; attended First Internat. Ballet Competition in Moscow as a guest of honour of Soviet Union, 1969; mem. of jury, Third International Ballet Competition, Moscow, 1977; rec'd. Centennial Medal 1967; created Officer, Order of Can. 1975; Molson Prize, 1978; Fellow and Examiner, Imp. Soc. Teachers Dancing; Charter mem. and a Past Pres., Candn. Dance Teachers Assn.; Founding mem., Can. Assn. of Professional Dance Organizations, Liberal; Anglican; recreations: reading, swimming, theatre, concerts;

Club: 21 McGill; Home: 137 Amelia Street, Toronto, Ont. M4X 1E6

OLIVER, Michael Kelway, M.A., Ph.D., LL.D., D.U.; educator; b.; North Bay, Ont., 2 Feb. 1925; s. Canon Gilbert Salt and late Winifred Maud (Kelway) O.; e. Westmount (Que.) High Sch.; McGill Univ., B.A. 1948, M.A. 1950, Ph.D. 1957; Inst. des Etudes Politiques (Paris), 1949; m. Joan Alexander, d. late Warren D. Nelson, 18 Dec. 1948; children: David N., James K., Victoria J., Geoffrey M., Cynthia J.; DIR., INTERNATIONAL DEVELOPMENT OFFICE, ASSN. OF UNIVERSITIES AND COLLEGES OF CAN. since 1979 (formerly Pres., Carleton University, 1972-78; Vice Princ. (Acad.) 1967-72, and Prof. Dept. of Pol. Science, McGill Univ.); sometime Research Dir., Royal Comn. on Biling & Bicult.; Past Pres., (Fed.) New Democratic Party; served in 2nd World War, 1943-45; Can. Brit. and N. Europe with 18th Batty., 2nd Candn. Anti-Tank Regt., R.C.A.; discharged with rank of Bombardier; mem., Candn. Pol. Science Assn.; Internat. Pol. Science Assn.; Anglican Church; recreation: golf; Address: International Development Office, 151 Slater Street, Ottawa, Ont. K1P 5N1

OLIVER, William Murray, R.C.A.; interior designer; b. Aurora, Ont. 16 June 1929; s. Thomas Howard and Leta Pearl (Sproxton) O.; e. Ont. Coll. of Art A.O.C.A. 1952; Ecole de Beaux-Arts Fontainebleau, France; m. Barbara Grace d. Charles Alexander Sharp 30 Aug. 1956; three s. Christopher David, Jeremy Andrew, Charles Adrian; PROP., W. MURRAY OLIVER LTD. 1978- ; Part-time Instr. Ont. Coll. of Art 1963-70, 1974- ; Interior Designer T. Eaton Co. Ltd. Studio of Interior Design 1952-64, Design Dir. Eaton Design Group 1964-73; Design Dir./Design Consultant Skyline Hotels Ltd. 1973-78; rec'd William Blair Bruce Foundation Grant 1966; mem. Interior Designers Ont.; Interior Designers Can.; United Church; Club: Arts & Letters; Address: 19 Edgewood Cres., Toronto, Ont. M4W 3A8.

OLIVIER, William George Marcel; former diplomat; b. Sherbrooke, Quebec, 6 April 1915; e. St. Francis Xavier Univ. (Science and Engn.); McGill Univ. (Law); m. has two children; enlisted in Candn. Army, 1940; trans to R.C.A.F. 1941; served Overseas and was a prisoner of war, 1943-45; discharged with rank of Flt. Lieut., 1945; called to the Bar of Que., 1948, and joined Dept. of External Affairs same year; assigned to Candn. Permanent Del. to U.N., New York, 1951 as Adviser; served with the Candn. Embassy in Wash., D.C., as First Secy., 1953-55; Candn. Commr. to Internat. Supervisory Comn. for Laos, 1957-58; Counsellor, Candn. Embassy, Madrid, 1959-62; Ambassador to Costa Rica, Panama, Nicaragua, El Salvador and Honduras, 1964-66; to Indonesia, 1966-68; High Commr. to Kenya and Uganda 1972-75; Depy. Commandant, National Defence Coll. 1975-1976; Address: 121 Range Road, Ottawa, Ont. K1N 8J7

OLSEN, John Leroy, , P. Eng.; business executive; b. Trondheim, Norway, 22 Dec. 1920; s. Lind and Lena (Bjerkan) O.; e. Sunlight Sch. Sedgewick, Alta. 1927-35; Seaview Sch. Vancouver, B.C. 1945-46; Univ. of B.C. grad. Mech. Engn. 1950; m. Randi d. Kristen Haakensen, Burnaby, B.C., 2 Sept. 1947; children: Greg John, Brenda Ann Pelletier; PRES. DIR. AND CHIEF EXTVE. OFFR. PHILLIPS CABLES LTD. since 1976; Pres. and Dir., Phillips Cables Inc., 1981-; 1976; Dir. Phillips CBA Conductors Ltd.; BICC International Ltd.; BICC Research and Engineering Ltd; mem. Atomic Energy Control Bd.; joined Canadian General Electric Co. 1950, C.G.E. Test Course followed by Jet Engine Repair assignment and Plant Engn. Indust. Products Div. 1950-55, Nuclear Power Dept. 1955-67 (2 yrs. Chalk River, 10 yrs. Marketing and Sales and finally Gen. Mgr. until Nuclear Power Plant Project terminated), Dist. Mgr. Que. and Maritime Apparatus Sales 1967-69; Sr. Vice Pres. Associated Tube Industries 1969-70; joined present Co. as Vice Pres. Mag-

net Wire 1970 and Power & Magnetic Wire (Brockville) 1972, Dir. 1973, Extve. Vice Pres. Power, Communications and Constr. 1975, Pres. and Chief Operating Offr. 1975; served with RCAF 1941-45; Vice-Chmn., Elect. & Electronic Mfrs. Assn. Can.; mem., Candn. Elect. Assn.; Candn. Mfrs. Assn.; Assn. Prof. Engrs. Prov. Ont.; Engn. Inst. Can.; Candn. Soc. Mech. Engn.; Candn. Chamber Comm.; Montreal Bd. Trade; United Church; recreations: sailing, cross-country skiing; Clubs: St. James's (Montreal); Forest and Stream; Brockville Country; Brockville; Home: 14 Rockcliffe Rd., Brockville, Ont. K6V 2Z6; Office: King St. W., Brockville, Ont. K6V 5W4

OLSON, Hon. Horace Andrew (Bud), P.C.; farmer; merchant; b. Iddlesleigh, Alta., 6 Oct. 1925; s. Carl M. and Alta I. (Perry) O.; e. Iddlesleigh and Medicine Hat; m. Marion Lucille, d. John W. McLachlan, 26 Jan. 1947; children: Sharon Lee Andrea Lucille, Juanita Carol, Horace Andrew; MIN. OF STATE FOR ECONOMIC DEVELOPMENT 1980-; Min. Responsible for the Northern Pipeline Agency 1980-; M.P. for Medicine Hat 1957-58, 1962, 1963, 1965, 1968; Min. of Agriculture, Can. 1968-72; Chmn., Sub-Comte. for revising rules of procedure H. of C. 1963-64; Citation for Distinguished Citizenship, Medicine Hat College 1968; mem., Econ. Council of Can. 1975-79; Candn. Parlty. delegation to U.S.S.R. and Czechoslovakia 1965; Commonwealth Parlty. delegation to Nigeria 1962; Inter-Parlty. Union delegation to Bulgaria 1977; Attended U.N. Gen. Assembly October-November 1966; Chmn., Alta. Liberal Caucus 1973-74; Appointed to Senate 1977; Chmn., Special Comte. of the Senate on a Northern Gas Pipeline 1978; Centennial Medal 1967; Queen's Silver Jubilee Medal 1977; Hon. Col. South Alta. Light Horse Regt. 1970; Liberal; Lutheran; recreations: hunting, fishing; Home: Iddlesleigh, Alta. T0J 1T0; Office: The Senate, Ottawa, Ont. K1A 0A4

OLSON, Stanley Granville, B.S.; retired petroleum executive; b. Watford City, N.D. 10 Oct. 1918; s. Oscar Thorolf and Hilda Marie (Swanson) O.; e. Dawson Co. Jr. Coll. Glendive, Mont./ Mont. Sch. of Mines B.S. (Geol. Engn.) 1948, Hon. Degree in Petroleum Engn.; Stanford Univ. Extve. Program 1968; m. Lillian June d. William E. Ralph 6 March 1944; children: Michael Eric, Thora Lynn; Chrmn. of Bd. Sultran Ltd.; Dir. of The Sulphur Inst.; Geol. Engr. Continental Oil Co. Ponca City 1948-50, Houston 1950-52; Petrol. Engr. Hudson's Bay Oil & Gas Co. 1952, Dist. Supt. 1954, Asst. Mgr. Production 1960, Mgr. Production 1965, Vice Pres. 1970, Extve. Vice Pres. 1974; Pres. & C.E.O. 1977-80; served with USAAF during World War II, awarded D.F.C. Air Medal with 5 clusters; mem. Candn. Petrol. Assn. (Gov.); Association of Professional Engineers, Geologists and Geophysicists of Alberta; Am. Inst. Mining, Metall. & Petrol. Engrs.; Candn. Inst. Mining & Metall.; Theta Tau; recreations: golf, fishing; Clubs: Calgary Petroleum; Willow Park Golf; Ranchmen's;

O'MALLEY, Brian Richard, B.A., B.Com.; trust company executive; b. Toronto, Ont. 16 Aug. 1937; s. Andrew Mangan O'M.; e. De La Salle Coll. 'Oaklands' and N. Toronto Coll. Inst.; Univ. of Windsor B.A., B.Com.; m. Anneliese d. Anton Wex 3 July 1965; children: Andrew Sean, Nadine Anne; PRES. AND CEO, STANDARD TRUSTCO LTD.; Chrmn. Providence Hosp; Providence; Villa; Dir., St. Michael Coll. Foundation; Gov., Univ. of Windsor; recreations: squash, skiing, travel; Clubs: Ontario; Cambridge; Home: 7 Garfield Avenue, Toronto, Ontario M4T 1E6 Office: 69 Yonge St., Suite 200, Toronto, Ont. M5E 1K3

ONDAATJE, Michael, writer; film maker; b. Colombo, Ceylon, 12 Sept. 1943; s. Philip Mervyn and Enid Doris (Gratiaen) O.; e. St. Thomas Coll., Colombo, Ceylon; Dulwich Coll., London, Eng.; Bishop's Univ. 1962-64; Univ. Coll., Univ. of Toronto, B.A. 1965; Queen's Univ., M.A. 1967; m. Kim (Betty Jane), d. Frank Maston Kimbark, Toronto, Ont., 1963; children: Zillah Quintin, Philip Christopher Griffin; films made incl. "Sons of Captain Poetry", "Great Canadian Hounds", "The Clinton Special" — a film about Theatre Passe Muraille's *The Farm Show*; author "The Dainty Monsters" (poetry) 1967; "The Man with Seven Toes" (poetry) 1968; "Leonard Cohen" (criticism) 1968; "The Collected Works of Billy the Kid" (poetry and prose) 1970; Ed., "The Broken Ark", 1971; "How To Train A Bassett", 1971; "Rat Jelly" 1973; "Coming Through Slaughter" (prose) 1976; "The Long Poem Anthology" (ed.) 1979; "There's a Trick with a Knife I'm learning to Do" (poetry) 1979; Stage Adaptation of The Collected Works of Billy the Kid performed at the Stratford Festival and Toronto Free Theatre and in theatres in Canada and the U.S.; rec'd. Gov. Gen.'s Award 1970 and 1980; Books in Canada First Novel Award, 1977; has developed and bred new strain of spaniel "The Sydenham Spaniel", Candn. Kennel Club 1970, with Livingstone Animal Foundation Kennels; mem. staff, Eng. Dept., Glendon Coll., York Univ.; recreations: tennis, films; Home: 2275 Bayview Ave., Toronto, Ont.

O'NEIL, Mt. Rev. Alexander Henry, B.D., M.A., D.C.L., LL.D., D.D. (Ang.); archbishop (retired); b. McGillivray Twp., Clandeboye, Ont., 23 July 1907; s. Alexander and Anna (Henry) O.; e. Univ. of W. Ont., B.A. 1928, B.D. 1936, M.A. 1943, D.D. 1945; Huron Coll., L.Th. 1929; Wycliffe Coll., Toronto, D.D. 1954; King's College, Halifax, D.D., 1958; LL.D. Western Univ. 1962; St. Thomas Univ. 1970; m. Marguerite Isabelle, d. John A. Roe, Atwood, Ont., 16 July 1931; one s. Terence; Life mem., Huron Coll. Corp. 1971; Hon. Life Gov., Brit. & Foreign Bible Soc. in Eng., since 1947; Rector of Atwood, 1929-35; Gorrie, 1935-39; Clinton 1939-41; Principal and Prof. of Divinity, Huron Coll., London, Ont., 1941-52; Prof. of Hebrew, Univ. of W. Ont., 1944-52; Gen. Secy., Brit. & Foreign Bible Soc. in Can., 1952-56; Bishop of Fredericton, 1957-63 and Archbishop there 1963-71; Secy., Bd. of Examiners for Divinity Degrees of Ch. of Eng. in Can., 1946-52; mem. of Senate, Univ. of W. Ont., 1941-52; Del. to Gen. Synod of Ch. of Eng. in Can., 1943-52; Dom. Chaplain, Ang. Young People's Assn., 1940-42; D.C.L. Bishop's Univ. 1964; Home: 1 Grosvenor St., Apt. 807, London, Ont. N6A 1Y2

O'NEIL, Donald F., B.A.; manufacturer; b. London, Ont., 19 Sept. 1923; e. London (Ont.) Central Coll. Inst., 1941; Univ. of W. Ont., B.A. (Business Adm.) 1949; m. Shirley Mae Morgan; children: John, Patricia; PRESIDENT, AMERICAN-STANDARD (Div. of Wabco-Standard Inc.); served with RCAF 1942-45; Past Chrmn., Mfrs. Council, Housing & Urban Devel. Assn. Can.; Past Pres., Candn. Inst. Plumbing & Heating; recreations: golf, reading; Home: 70 Princess Margaret Blvd., Islington, Ont. M9A 2A4; Office: 80 Ward St., Toronto, Ont. M6H 4A7

O'NEIL, William Andrew, B.A.Sc.; transportation executive; b. Ottawa, Ont. 6 June 1927; s. Thomas Wilson and Margaret (Swan) O'N.; e. Ottawa Tech. High Sch. 1945; Carleton Univ. 1945-46; Univ. of Toronto B.A.Sc. (Civil Engn.) 1949; m. Dorothy d. Ivan Adrian Muir 21 Apl. 1950; children: Janice, Kathy, Jeffrey; PRES., THE ST. LAWRENCE SEAWAY AUTHORITY 1980- ; Pres., The Seaway International Bridge Corp.; Dir. Thousand Islands Bridge Authority; The Jacques Cartier and Champlain Bridges Inc.; Canarctic Shipping Co. Ltd.; joined Dept. Transport Ottawa 1949 serving in engn. capacity Lachine and Welland Canals, Resident Engr. with Special Projects Br. 1954; Div. Engr. Welland Canal, St. Lawrence Seaway Authority 1955, Dir. of W. Region 1960, Dir. of Constr. 1964-71; Depy. Adm. Marine Services, Candn. Marine Transport. Adm. 1971-75; Commr. Candn. Coast Guard and Depy. Adm. Marine Transport 1975-80; el. Chrmn. Council Intergovt'al Maritime Consultative Organ. 1979, re-el. 1981; apptd. Hon. Commo-

dore Candn. Coast Guard 1981; rec'd Engn. Medal Assn. Prof. Engrs. Prov. Ont. 1972; Distinguished Pub. Service Award U.S. Dept. of Transport. 1980; mem. Assn. Prof. Engrs. Prov. Ont.; Am. Soc. Civil Engrs.; Freemason; Anglican; recreations: reading, swimming, golf; Home: 21 Aleutian Rd., Nepean, Ont. K2H 7C7; Office: Tower A, Place de Ville, 320 Queen St., Ottawa, Ont. K1R 5A3.

O'NEILL, James Patrick, B.Sc., M.B.A.; investment executive; b. Milwaukee, Wis. 10 May 1935; s. Edward John and Helen Ann (White) O'N.; e. Marquette Univ. B.Sc., M.B.A. 1961; Harvard Univ. Grad. Sch. of Business Advanced Mang. Program 1975; m. Mary Gretchen d. Maurice W. Fieweger 7 June 1958; children: Kevin, Patrick, Sean, Matthew, Kathleen, Margaret, Amy; PRES., GEN. MGR. AND DIR., FIRST CHICAGO INVESTMENTS CANADA LTD. since 1975; Trust Offr. Marine National Exchange Bank, Milwaukee 1959-62; Sr. Consultant Peat, Marwick, Mitchell, Chicago 1962-65; Mgr. Profit Planning and National Bank of Detroit 1965-68; Depy. Comptroller First National Bank of Chicago 1968-73; Dir. of Corporate Planning First Chicago Corp. 1973-74; Vice Pres. Adm. and Finance First Chicago Leasing Co. 1974-75; Lectr. in Profit Planning Bank Adm. Inst. Univ. of Wis., mem. Toronto, Chicago Detroit Chapters Planning Extves. Inst.; R. Catholic; recreations: curling, sailing; Clubs: Ontario; Whitehall (Chicago); Home: 37 Roxborough St. E., Toronto, Ont. M4W 1V5; Office: (P.O. Box 275) Suite 2200 Commerce Court North, Toronto, Ont. M5L 1E9

O'NEILL, Mt. Rev. Michael C., O.B.E. (1945), LL.D. (R.C.); b. Kemptville, Ont., 15 Feb. 1898; s. Peter J. and Maude E. (Vroom) O.; e. Vankleek Hill (Ont.) Coll. Inst.; St. Michael's Coll., Univ. of Toronto, B.A. 1924, LL.D. 1952, D.D. (Hon.) 1977; St. Augustine's Semy., Toronto (Theol.) 1924-27; LL.D. Sask. (Regina Campus) 1974; o. Priest 1927; with Candn. Explosives Ltd., Vaudreuil, Quebec 1915-16; Soldiers' Settlement Bd., Ottawa, 1919-21; Prof., St. Joseph's Semy., Edmonton, Alta., 1928-30; Rector, 1930-39; apptd. Archbishop-elect of Regina, 4 Dec. 1947; subsequently Archbishop till retired 1973; served in World War, 1916-19; awarded Mil. Medal; overseas as Driver and Signaller, 27th Batty., C.F.A.; World War, 1939-46, with Candn. Chaplain Service; National Luther Merit Award, 1974; Hon. LL.O. Univ. of Saskatchewan (Regina Campus) 1974; Hon. D.D., Univ. of St. Michael's Coll., 1977; Chaplain, 2nd Inf. Bgde., Edmonton Regt.; Sr. Chaplain, 1st Divn., 1st Candn. Corps.; Princ. Chaplain (R.C.), Candn. Mil. Hdqrs.; K. of C.; Address: 67 Hudson Dr., Regina, Sask. S4S 2W1

O'NEILL, W. Paul, B.A., C.A.; executive; b. Toronto 1938; e. Univ. of Toronto B.A. 1960; C.A. (Ont.) 1964; m. Marilyn; children: Michael, Lori; CORP. EXEC. VICE PRES. & CHIEF FINANCIAL OFFICER, ATOMIC ENERGY OF CANADA LTD.; Coopers & Lybrand 1960-65; Accounting Mgr. ESB Canada Ltd. 1965-69; Controller & Asst. Treas. General Tire & Rubber Co. of Canada Ltd. 1969-72; Controller, ITT Grinell Ltd. 1972-74; Vice Pres. Finance, Control Data Canada Ltd. 1974-78; Director, Control Data Canada Ltd. 1977-78; Vice Pres. Finance, Atomic Energy of Canada Ltd. 1978-82; Club: The Country Club; Home: 3 Okanagan Dr., Ottawa, Ont. K2H 7E7; Office: 275 Slater St., Ottawa, Ont. K1A 0S4

ONLEY, Toni, R.C.A.; artist; b. Douglas, Isle of Man. 20 Nov. 1928; s. James Anthony and Florence (Lord) O.; e. St. Mary's Primary Sch. and Ingleby Secondary Sch. Isle of Man; Douglas Sch. of Fine Arts 1942-46; Doon Sch. of Fine Art 1951; Inst. Allende Mexico 1957 (scholarship); London, Eng. 1963; m. 1stly Mary Burrows (d.) 1950; two d. Jennifer, Lynn; m. 2ndly Gloria Knight 1961; one s. James Anthony; m. 3rdly Yukiko Kageyama 23 Aug. 1979; former teacher Dept. of Fine Arts Univ. of B.C.; solo exhns. incl.: Okanagan Regional Lib. Kelowna 1957; Coste House Gallery Alta. 1958; Vancouver Art Gallery 1958; New Design Gallery Vancouver 1959, 1962, 1964,

1966, 1968; Dorothy Cameron Gallery Toronto 1960, 1961, 1962, 1964; Blue Barn Gallery Ottawa 1961, 1967; Point Gallery Victoria 1961; Otto Seligman Gallery Seattle 1962; Galerie Camille Heýbert Montreýal 1963; Pandora's Box Gallery Victoria 1966; Topham Brown Art Gallery Vernon 1967; W. Circuit B.C. & Alta. 1966-67; Douglas Gallery Vancouver 1967; Owens Gallery Sackville 1967; Dalhousie Univ. 1967; Confed. Centre Art Gallery Charlottetown 1968; Agnes Etherington Art Centre Kingston 1968; Albert White Gallery Toronto 1968; Gallery Pascal Toronto 1968, 1970; Art Gallery Greater Victoria 1968; Griffith Galleries Vancouver 1968; Bau-Xi Gallery Vancouver 1968, 1969, 1971; Simon Fraser UniV. 1969; Fleet Gallery Winnipeg 1969, 1971; Prince Albert (Sask.) Lib. 1969; Graphic Gallery San Francisco 1969; New Westminster Pub. Lib. 1970; Allied Art Centre Brandon 1970; Alta. Coll. Art 1971; Godart-Lefort Galerie Montréal 1971; rep. in numerous maj. nat. and internat. group shows; rep. in various pub. and private colls. incl. Art Gallery Ont., Montreal Museum of Fine Arts Musée d'Art Contemporain Montréal, Vancouver Art Gallery, Seattle Museum of Fine Arts, Museum of Modern Art N.Y., Tate Gallery London, Eng.; recipient Can. Council Grant 1961, 1963; Jessie Dow Award 1960; Spring Purchase Award Montreal Museum Fine Arts 1962; Sam & Ayola Zacks Award 1963 (Polar #1); Can. Council Sr. Fellowship 1964; rep. in Paris Biennial 1961; Canadn. Biennials 1959, 1961, 1963, 1965, 1968; Trustee, Emily Carr Coll. of Art Vancouver; cited numerous bibliogs.; flying (since 1968 has used his own aircraft to search out his subjects from Mexico to Baffin Island); Address: 4279 Yuculta Cres., Vancouver, B.C. V6N 4A9.

ONSTAD, Duane M., life insurance executive; b. Moose Jaw, Sask. 20 July 1917; e. Univ. of B.C.; m. Lorraine 8 Jan. 1948; children: Tierney, Melissa, Leslie, Michael, Anthony, Sunny; PRESIDENT CANDN. DIV., OCCIDENTAL LIFE INSURANCE CO. 1979- ; joined Monarch Life Insurance, Vancouver 1945-53; Br. Mgr. Western Life Insurance, Vancouver 1953-55; Br. Mgr. present co. Vancouver 1955-78; mem. Candn. Life Underwriters (Past Pres. Group for B.C. Mainland); Home: 26 Rachel St., Toronto, Ont. M4W 1M5; Office: 2180 Yonge St., Toronto, Ont. M4P 2G4.

ONYSZCHUK, Mario, M.Sc., Ph.D., F.C.I.C., F.C.S.; educator; b. Wolkow, Poland 21 July 1930; s. Andrew Onyszchuk; e. High Sch. of Montreal 1948; McGill Univ. B.Sc. 1951, Ph.D. 1954; Univ. of W. Ont. M.Sc. 1952; Cambridge Univ. Ph.D. 1956; m. Anastasia Anna Kushnir 24 June 1959; three s. Ivan Matthew, Gregory Andrew, Timothy Stephen; PROF. AND CHRMN. OF CHEM., McGILL UNIV. 1979- , Lectr. in Chem. 1956, Asst. Prof. 1957, Assoc. Prof. 1963, Prof. 1968- ; Visiting Prof., Univ. of Southampton 1968-69, Univ. of Sussex 1977-78; author or co-author various research articles; mem. Am. Chem. Soc.; Sigma Xi; Protestant; recreations: photography, philately, swimming, tennis, cross-country skiing, skating; Home: 60 Balfour Ave., Town of Mount Royal, Que. H3P 1L6; Office: 801 Sherbrooke St. W., Montreal, Que. H3A 2K6.

ORCHARD, Hon. Donald Warder, M.L.A., B.S.A.; politician; b. Miami, Man. 11 Apl. 1946; s. Warder Franklin John and Muriel Bernice (King) O.; e. Miami Elem. Sch.; Midland Coll. Inst. Miami; Univ. of Man. B.S.A.; m. Edna Jane d. James A. Simpson, Winnipeg, Man. 19 July 1969; children: Eric Donald, Arlene Eden, Onalee Jill; MIN. OF HIGHWAYS & TRANSPORTATION, MAN. 1979- ; Min. responsible for the Manitoba Telephone System and Manitoba Data Services; Min. responsible for Communications; Chrmn., Prov. Land Use Comn. 1980- ; Roads and Transp. Assn. of Canada; Council of Ministers" Responsible for Transportation and Highway Safety; farmer; el. M.L.A. for Pembina prov. g.e. 1977; P. Conservative; United Church; Office: 203 Legislative Bldg., Winnipeg, Man. R3C 0V8.

OREFFICE, Paul F., B.S.; executive; b. Venice, Italy, 29 Nov. 1927; s. Max and Elena (Friedenberg) O.; e. Quito (Ecuador) High Sch., 1944; Purdue Univ., B.S., C.E. 1949; m. Franca Giuseppinna, d. Angelo Ruffini, 26 May 1956; children: Laura E., Andrew T., DIR., THE DOW CHEMICAL CO., mem. of Extve. Comte. since 1970; Pres., Dow Chemical Co. 1978; Pres., Dow Chemical U.S.A. 1975-78; Financial Vice-Pres. 1970-75; Chmn., Extve. Comte., Dow Chemical Co.; Chmn. of Bd., Chem. Manufacturers Assoc.; Dir., National Board of Junior Achievement, Inc.; First Bank Corpn. of Midland; Dow Corning Corpn.; Conneticut General Ins. Co.; Bd. of Trustees, Amer. Enterprise Inst.; Midland Community Centre; Bd. of Govs., Purdue Univ. Fdn.; Policy Comte., Business Roundtable; joined present co. as Supervisor, Latin America, Midland, Mich., 1953; Mediterranean Area Sales Mgr., Milan, Italy, 1955; Mang. Dir., Dow Quimica do Brasil, 1956; Comm. Dir., Dow-Unquinesa, Bilbao, Spain and Gen. Mgr., Dow Iberian operations, 1963; Gen. Mgr., Latin Am. Area, 1965; Dir., Financial Services, Midland Mich., 1969; el. Dir. 1971; served with U.S. Army 1951-53; rec'd. Encomienda del Merito Civil, Govt. of Spain, 1966; Republican; recreations: golf, tennis, swimming, bridge; Office: 2030 Dow Center, Midland, Mich.

O'REILLY, James Meredith, B.Com., C.A.; financial executive; b. Winnipeg, Man. 8 Feb. 1926; s. James and Marion (Meredith) O'R.; e. Upper Can. Coll. Toronto 1943; McGill Univ. B.Com. 1947; C.A. 1950; m. Louisa Laurie d. Evan W. T. Gill, St. Andrews, N.B. 23 July 1955; children: Gillian Ann, James, Sheila Margaret, Diana Catherine; VICE PRES. AND TREAS., CANADA DEVELOPMENT CORP. since 1976; Student-in-Accounts and C.A., McDonald Currie & Co. Montreal 1947-51; Secy.-Treas., Controller, Dir., Rolph-Clark Stone-Benallack Ltd. Montreal 1951-60; Budget Dir., Rolph-Clark-Stone Ltd. Toronto 1960-63; Dir.-Finance, Dominion Forge Co. Windsor, Ont. 1963-68; Controller-Liquifuels Div., Canadian Fuel Marketers Ltd. Toronto 1969-73; Controller, Canada Development Corp. 1973-75; served with RCA 1944-45, Reserve 1951-57, rank Lt.; Gov., Havergal Coll. Toronto since 1978; mem. Inst. C.A.'s Ont.; Financial Extves. Inst.; University Club of Toronto; R. Catholic; Home: 97 Strathallan Blvd., Toronto, Ont. M5N 1S8; Office: 444 Yonge St., Toronto, Ont. M5B 2A4

OREOPOULOS, Dimitrios G., M.D., Ph.D., F.A.C.P., F.R.C.P. & S.(C); physician; educator; b. 24 May 1936; s. George and Antigoni (Antoniadou) O.; e. Evangeliki School, L Petroyannopoulos, Athens, Greece 1954; Univ. of Athens M.D. 1960; Queen's Univ. Belfast Ph.D. 1966; m. Nancy C. I. d. Edwin R. K. Hooker, Islington, Ont. 19 Sept. 1971; children: George, Philip, Antigoni; John; DIR., PERITONEAL DIALYSIS UNIT AND KIDNEY STONE CLINIC, TORONTO WESTERN HOSP. and mem. of Staff Div. of Nephrology there since 1970; Prof. of Med. Univ. of Toronto 1979- , Charles Mickle Fellow 1981; Intern, Resident, Sr. Resident and mem. Staff Dept. Med. Hippokratean Hosp. Greece 1960-64; Specialist in Internal Med. Greece 1963; Sr. Registrar Dept. of Med. Queen's Univ. Belfast 1966-69; served with Greek Army Med. Corps 1960-62; co-author "Strategy In Renal Failure" 1978; "An Introduction to Continous Ambulatory Peritoneal Dialysis" 1980; "Peritoneal Dialysis" 1981; Ed. "Peritoneal Dialysis Bulletin"; mem. Greek Soc. Nephrol.; Candn. Soc. Nephrol.; Am. Soc. Nephrol.; Greek Orthodox; Home: 10 Ladywood Dr., Rexdale, Ont. M9V 1K9; Office: 399 Bathurst St., Toronto, Ont. M5T 2S8.

ORR, James Cameron, B.Sc., Ph.D.; educator; b. Paisley, Scot. 10 Aug. 1930; s. James and Jean Stark (Ketchen) O.; e. Paisley Grammar Sch. 1935; Shawland's Acad. 1944; Cheshunt Grammar Sch. Herts. 1947; Royal Coll. of Science (Imp. Coll.) A.R.C.S., B.Sc. 1954; Birkbeck Coll. London grad. study; Glasgow Univ. Ph.D. 1960; Iowa State Univ. (Rockefeller Foundation Fellowship); m. Robin Denise Moore 22 Nov. 1958; children: Andrew

Cameron, Fiona Kathleen; PROF. OF BIOCHEM. AND CHEMISTRY, MEM. UNIV. OF NFLD. since 1976; Research Chem. Syntex S.A., Mexico City, 1959-63; Research Assoc. to Assoc. Prof. Harvard Med. Sch. 1963-75; mem. Med. Research Council Biochem. Comte.; served with RAF 1949-51, Leading Aircraftsman, Air Sea Rescue; contributing author 'Biochemical Mass Spectrometry' 1972; research and publishing on organic and enzymic reaction mechanisms; Exec. and mem. of Senate, Memorial Univ.; mem. Am. Assn. Advanc. Science; Am. Chem. Soc.; Am. Soc. Biol. Chems.; Candn. Biochem. Soc.; Candn. Soc. Endocrinol. & Metabolism; Chem. Soc. (Brit.); Endocrine Soc.; Internat. Soc. Magnetic Resonance; Paleopathol. Assn.; Sigma Xi; Royal Scot. Dance Soc.; Teachers' Assn. Can.; Independent; recreations: sailing, swimming, chemistry, glass blowing; Home: 360 Hamilton Ave., St. John's, Nfld. A1C 1K2; Office: Memorial University Medical School, Prince Philip Dr., St. John's, Nfld. A1B 3V6.

ORR, John Alexander, F.C.A.; b. Toronto, Ont., 14 Oct. 1920; s. Dr. James W. Ross and Gladys Alvera (Johnston) O.; e. Lake Lodge Naval Sch., Grimsby, Ont. (1927-33); Upper Canada Coll., Toronto, Ont. (1933-39); Univ. of Toronto, 1939-40; m. Anne Isabel, d. Dr. E. J. Trow, Toronto, Ont., 23 May 1942; children: Judith Anne, Katherine Ross, Robert Alexander, James Trow; PARTNER, TOUCHE, ROSS & CO.; mem., Inst. of Chartered Accountants; Fellow, Inst. of Chartered Accountants, Ont. 1959; served in 2nd World War with Canadian Armoured Corps; Bgde. Major, 4 Candn. Armoured Bgde.; subsequently discharged with rank of Major, S. Alta. Regt.; Zeta Psi; Anglican; recreations: golf, fishing, hunting; Clubs: University; Toronto Hunt; Toronto Club; Home: Divilabit Farms, R.R. #2, Blackstock, Ont., L0B 1B0; Office: First Canadian Place, Toronto, Ont. M5X 1B3

ORR, Robert (Bobby) Gordon; hockey player (retired), business executive; b. Parry Sound, Ont., 20 Mar. 1948; m. Peggy; children: Darren Brent; shortstop MacTier, Ont. provincial champion jr. baseball team 1963; from hometown minor hockey ranks to Oshawa Generals OHA junior A club at 14; led team to OHA title 1966; with help of Alan Eagleson signed reported $70,000 pro contract Boston Bruins Sept. 1966; deal considered cornerstone for NHL Players' Association; 1966-76 played 651 regular season games scoring 268 goals, 643 assists for 911 points, 949 penalty minutes, plus 74 playoff games, 26 goals, 66 assists for 92 points, 107 penalty minutes; NHL regular season assist record of 102 in 1970-71; record point total for defenceman of 139 same season; playoff assist record with 19, 1971-72; playoff point record for defenceman same season with 24; regular season goals record for defenceman with 46, 1974-75; helped bruins win two Stanley Cups; played out option, signed by Chicago Black Hawks 1976; six knee operations make future play impossible; assistant coach Chicago 1976-77; Calder Memorial Trophy as NHL rookie of year 1967; Art Ross scoring title 1970, 1975; Hart MVP Trophy 1970, 1971, 1972; twice Conn Smythe Trophy; eight times James Norris Memorial Trophy, 1968-75; MVP Canada Cup 1976; Lou Marsh Trophy 1970; Canadian CP poll male athlete of year 1970; Sports Magazine, Sports Illustrated athlete of year awards.

ORSER, Earl Herbert, B.Com., C.A.; executive; b. Toronto, Ont., 5 July 1928; s. late Frank Herbert and late Ethel Marjorie (Cox) O.; e. Danforth Tech. High Sch., Toronto, Ont.; Univ. of Toronto, B.Com. 1950; Chart. Acct. 1953; m. Marion Queenie, d. Robert Frank Ellis, 4 Aug. 1951; children: Darlene, Barbara, Beverley, Nancy; PRES. AND CEO, LONDON LIFE INS. CO.; former Pres. & Chief Extve. Offr., The T. Eaton Co. Ltd.; Director of London Life Ins. Co. and SPAR Aerospace Ltd.; Canada Trust; Museum of Indian Archology, Bd. of Govs., Univ. of Western Ont.; mem. Inst. Chart. Accts., Ontario; Financial Extves. Inst.; Delta Chi; Howe Inst. Policy Analy-

sis Comte.; Queen's Business Sch. Adv. Council; Presidents Assoc.; United Church; Liberal; recreations: skiing, tennis; Clubs: National (Toronto); St. James's; Granite, London, London Hunt; Office: London Life Ins. Co., 255 Dufferin Ave., London, N6A 4K1

ORTIZ-PATINO, Jaime; executive; b. Paris, France 20 June 1930; s. Jorge and Graziella (Patino) Ortiz-Linares; m. Uta Krebber 28 March 1970; children: Carlos, Felipe (by previous marriage); CHRMN., PATINO, N.V.; Vice Chrmn. Brascan Ltd.; Dir. John Labatt Ltd.; Wheelock Marden & Co. Ltd. (Hong Kong); Consul Gen. of Costa Rica in Geneva; Pres. World Bridge Fed.; Trustee, Fondation S. I. Patino, Geneva; recreations: bridge, golf, tennis; Home: 54, route de Vandoeuvres, 1253 Vandoeuvres, Geneva, Switzerland; Office: c/o Brascan Ltd., Commerce Court West, Box 48, Commerce Court Postal Stn., Toronto, Ont. M5L 1B7.

OSBALDESTON, Gordon Francis Joseph, B.Com., M.B.A.; civil servant; b. Hamilton, Ont., 29 Apl. 1930; s. John Edward and Margaret (Hanley) O.; e. St. Jeromes Coll., Kitchener, Ont., 1947; Univ. of Toronto, B.Com. 1952; Univ. of W. Ont., M.B.A. 1953; m. Geraldine, d. Eugene Keller, Kitchener, Ont., 1 Oct. 1953; children: Stephen, David, Robert, Catherine; under-SECRETARY OF STATE, MIN. OF EXTERNAL AFFAIRS, 1982-; Secy., Treasury Bd. of Can. 1973-82; joined Dept. Trade & Comm., Can. as Foreign Service Offr., Trade Commr. Service 1953; Vice Consul & Asst. Trade Commr., Sao Paulo, Brazil 1954 & Chicago, Ill., 1957; Consul and Trade Commr., Los Angeles, Cal., 1960; apptd. Asst. Dir., Personnel, Trade Commr. Service, 1964 and Asst. Dir., Operations, 1966; Extve. Dir. of Service 1967; Asst. Depy. Min. Consumer Affairs, Dept. of Consumer & Corp. Affairs 1968; Depy. Secy. of the Treasury Bd. 1970; Depy. Min. Dept. Consumer & Corp. Affairs Can. 1972; apptd. Depy Min. Dept. Industry, Trade & Comm. Dec. 1976; apptd. mem. Nat. Film Bd. 1976-77; mem. Bd. of Dirs. of Export Development Corpn.; Canada Development Corpn. (ex officio); de Havilland Aircraft of Canada, Ltd.; Federal Business Development Bank; Niagara Inst.; Psi Upsilon; Roman Catholic; Home: 42 Foothills Dr., Ottawa, Ont. K2H 6K3; Office: Place Bell Canada, Ottawa, Ont.

OSBERG, Gunder, B.Sc.; communications executive; b. Galahad, Alta., 5 Oct. 1920; s. Lars and Gunhild (Guttormson) O.; e. Alta. Pub. Schs.; Strathcona High Sch., Edmonton, Alta.; Univ. of Alta., B.Sc. (Elect. Engn.) 1942; m. Nancy Eileen, d. Walter Walton, Calgary, Alta., 25 March 1945; children: Linda, Kari, Gunder, Keith; ASST. VICE-PRES., REAL ESTATE & ADMIN. SERVICES, BELL, CANADA; joined The Bell Telephone Company of Canada, Engn. Dept.-Outside Plant, Ottawa, 1946; trans. to Transmission Engn. 1946 and returned to Outside Plant Engn. 1952; apptd. Supervising Engr., Belleville Sec. Kingston, 1953; Vehicles Supt., W. Region, Toronto, 1956; Bldgs. Vehicles & Supplies Supt., N. Div., W. Area, 1959; Constr. Supt., N. Ont., North Bay, 1961; Dist. Comm. Mgr., Fort William, 1961; Outside Plant and Constr. Mgr., N. Div., W. Area, Toronto, 1963; joined Avalon Telephone Co. as Vice-Pres. of Operations 1965, Pres. & Mang. Dir. 1965; returned to Bell Can. as Gen. Mgr. S. Div., W. Area 1970-71; Gen. Traffic Mgr., W. Area 1972-75; Asst. Vice-Pres. (Mat. & Automotive Equipment) 1976-78, and Asst. (Real Estate & Admin. Services), 1979-80; served as Lt. RCNVR 1942-45; attended Royal Roads, 1942; on loan to R.N. Home Fleet, Murmansk Run, 1942; HMCS Prince David, 1943-45; Pres. (1969-70) Telephone Assn. Can.; mem. Assn. Prof. Engrs. Ont.; Pres. Jr. Achievement of Canada 1974-75; Liberal; Protestant; recreations: golf, curling, skating; Home: 14 Kingsway Cres., Toronto, Ont. M8X 2R2; Office: 393 University Ave., Toronto, Ont. M5G 1W9

OSBORN, Stella Brunt (Mrs. Chase S.), A.M., Litt.D. (U. of MICHIGAN); author; editor; organization executive; b. Hamilton, Ont., 31 July 1894; d. Edward and Rosa (Lee) Brunt; e. Pub. and High Schs., Hamilton, Ont.; Scott High Sch., Toledo, Ohio, 1917-18 (gold medalist); Univ. of Mich., A.B. (magna cum laude) 1922, A.M. 1930, Outstanding Achievement Award 1967, Litt.D. 1978; m. Chase Salmon Osborn (Gov. of Mich. 1911-12), 9 Apl. 1949; Vice Pres., Internat. Movement for Atlantic Union, since 1965; Hon. Vice-Pres., Internat. Assn. for the Union of Democracies since 1972; secretarial work Hamilton, Ont. and Toledo, Ohio, 1911-18 and Univ. of Mich., 1918-22; Teacher, Mo. Ozarks, 1922-23; Staff Ed., New Internat. Yearbook, 1923; Contrib. Ed. in Sociol. and Econ., New Internat. Encyclopedia Supplement, 1924; Co-founder, Meiji Univ. Lib. Comte. 1924; Asst. Ed., Good Health Magazine, 1925; Ed., Univ. of Mich. Official Publ., 1925-30; Secy. and Co-author with former Gov. C. S. Osborn, 1931-49; joined Atlantic Union Comte. 1949; served on various comtes. and bds. 1949-61; Extve. Dir., Mich. Br., 1951-52; publisher-ed., Atlantic Union Herald, Sault Ste. Marie, Mich. and Ont. 1950-52; Chrmn. 1952-61; Extve. Vice Pres., Ga. Br., 1953-61; Hon. mem., Union Atlantischer Foederalisten, Munich 1955; a Founder IMAU 1958, Secy. for N. Am. 1958-65; a vice-pres., official observer and rep. to various confs. in Europe, Can. and U.S. 1959-77; Bd. mem. Fed. Union, Inc.; holds various positions with other affiliated Atlantic groups; mem., Poulan, Ga. Community Council; Mich. State-wide Comte. for Mackinac Straits Bridge, 1938; named Council mem. of Yr., Atlantic Union Comte., 1950 (Special Citation 1961); nominee, Atlantic Union Pioneer Award 1970 (Richard Nixon Awardee); nominee, Second and Third Triennial Estes Kefauver Union of the Free Award 1971, 1974 (Edward Heath and Paul Findley Awardees); received First Frank Cyril James Award of the Internat. Assocn. for the Union of Democracies 1977; mem. Organizing Comte., Free Nation Fed. Assn. 1970-72; a founder, hon. vice-pres., Internat. Assocn. for the Union of Democracies 1972; author: "Eighty and On", 1941; "A Tale of Possum Poke in Possum Lane", 1946; "Balsam Boughs", 1949; "Jasmine Springs", 1953; "Polly Cadotte", 1955; "Beside the Cabin", 1957; "Iron and Arbutus", 1962; Co-author: "The Conquest of a Continent", 1939; "Schoolcraft-Longfellow-Hiawatha", 1942; "Hiawatha with Its Original Indian Legends", 1944; "Errors in Official U.S. Area Figures", 1945; Ed., "An Accolade for Chase S. Osborn", 1940; "Northwoods Sketches", 1949; Contrib. Ed. "Freedom & Union" (mag.), 1965-72; mem., Mich. Acad. Science, Arts & Letters; Wilderness Soc.; Nat. Audubon Soc.; Assn. Am. Indian Affairs; Adult Educ. Assn. U.S.A.; Soc. for Citizen Educ. in World Affairs; Friends of Mich. Hist. Colls., Univ. of Mich. (mem. extve. comte.); Am. Assn. of Univ. Women; League Women Voters of U.S.; Nat. Council Women U.S.; Am. Acad. Pol. and Social Science; Candn. Inst. Pub. Affairs; Eng.-Speaking Union; London Inst. World Affairs; Grotius Foundation (Munich); Ga. Authors Assn.; Poetry Soc. Mich.; Poetry Soc., Inc. (London, Eng.) and various hist. and other assns.; Phi Beta Kappa (life mem. Assoc.); mem., Adv. Council Youth for Internat. Fed. Union; mem. The European-Am. Movement (TEAM); sponsor Atlantic Council of U.S.; Distinguished Prof. Humanities and mem. Pres. Club, Abraham Baldwin Agric. Coll. of Ga.; Capital Club's Woman of the Year 1973; Flint River Girl Scout Council (life mem.); Chehaw Council of the Boy Scouts of America (benefactor mem.); Republican; Presbyterian; recreations: poetry, drama, reading; Clubs: Mich. League; Presidents (Ann Arbor, Mich.); Business & Prof. Women (D.C.); Trustee (1970-72) YMCA Internat. Crossroads; Homes: Possum Poke in Possum Lane, Box 245 Poulan, Ga. 31781 and Sault Ste. Marie, Mich. (summer) 49783.

OSEASOHN, Robert Oscar, B.S., M.D., F.A.C.P., F.A.C.E.; epidemiologist; educator; b. New York, N.Y. 23 Jan. 1924; s. William Oseasohn; e. Stuyvesant High Sch. New York 1940; Tufts Univ. B.S. 1943 (Olmstead Fellowship in Biol. 1943); Long Island Coll. of Med. M.D. 1947; m. Celia d. late Morris Silverman 16 June 1948; children: Michael, Sara, Nancy; PROF. AND CHRMN. OF EPIDEMIOL. & HEALTH, McGILL UNIV. and Prof. of Med. since 1974; Assoc. Phys. Royal Victoria Hosp.; Review Comte. Nat. Health Research and Devel. Program, Health & Welfare Can.; Consulting Specialist Epidemiol. Montreal Gen. Hosp.; internship and residency Harlem Hosp. and Mount Sinai Hosp. New York, Michael Reese Hosp. Chicago, Cushing V.A. Hosp. Framingham; Demonst. in Preventive Med. and Med. Western Reserve Univ. 1951-52, Sr. Instr. Preventive Med. 1957-60, Sr. Instr. Med. 1957-61, Asst. Prof. Preventive Med. 1960-64 and of Med. 1961-67, Assoc. Prof. Preventive Med. 1964-67 and Acting Chrmn. 1965-66; med. practice Hopkinton, Mass. 1954-57; Chief, Epidemiol. Sec. and Depy. Dir. Pak-SEATO Cholera Research Lab. Dacca, E. Pakistan 1963-65; Cholera Panel mem. US-Japan Coop. Med. Science Program 1965-66; Consultant, World Health Organ. 1967 and 1980; Prof. and Chrmn. of Epidemiol. and Community Med. Univ. of New Mexico 1967-72, Prof. of Med. 1968-72; Assoc. mem. Comn. on Immunization, Armed Forced Epidemiol. Bd. 1964-69, mem. 1969-71; mem. Nat. Bd. Med. Examiners Preventive Med. and Pub. Health Comte. 1970-73; Consultant, Nat. Aeronautics & Space Adm. 1972-73; Prof. of Epidemiol. and Assoc. Dean for Student Affairs, Univ. of Texas Health Science Center 1972-74, Prof. of Med. 1972-74; author or co-author numerous publs.; served with U.S. Army 1943-46, 1952-54, rank Capt., Med. Corps; mem. Am. Assn. Advanc. Science; Mass. Med. Soc.; Internat. Epidemiol. Assn.; Am. Epidemiol. Soc.; Central Soc. Clin. Research; W. Soc. Clin. Research; Alpha Omega Alpha; Sigma Xi; Jewish; recreations: swimming, jogging, cross-country skiing; Home: 4800 Demaisonneuve W., Westmount, Que. Office: 3775 University St., Montreal, Que. H3A 2B4.

OSLER, Britton Bath, Q.C.; b. Ottawa, Ont., 17 Dec. 1904; s. Glyn and Florence K. (Scarth) O.; e. Crescent Sch., Toronto, 1913-15; The Grove, Lakefield, Ont., 1915-16; Ridley Coll., St. Catherines, Ont., 1916-21; Roy. Mil. Coll., Grad. 1925; Osgoode Hall, Toronto, 1929; m. Barbara E., d. Godfrey B. Greene, Ottawa, Ont., 23 Apl. 1930; children: Glyn W., Derek B., Pamela G., G. Featherston; PARTNER, BLAKE, CASSELS & GRAYDON, since 1933; Dir., Kiwi Polish Co. Canada Ltd.; Dir., Selco Inc.; read law with Blake, Lash, Anglin and Cassels (now Blake, Cassels & Graydon) 1926-29; called to the Bar of Ontario, 1929; joined Blake, Lash, Anglin and Cassels 1929-; served with Canadian Mil., as Lieut., Gov.-Gen. Bodyguard, 1926-29; served in World War, 1939-46, with Reserve Army, R.C.A., 1940-42, and as C.O., 2 Light A.A. Regt., R.C.A., C.A.(A.), in Can., 1942-43; at Candn. Mil. Hdqrs., London, 1943-44; C.O., 32 Field Regt., R.C.A. (Reserve), 1945-46; Zeta Psi; Anglican; recreations: fishing, duck-shooting, golf; Clubs: Toronto; Toronto Golf; York; Home: 62A Glen Rd., Toronto, Ont. M4W 2V4; Office: Commerce Court West, Toronto, Ont.

OSLER, Campbell, Revere Q.C.; b. Toronto, Ont., 21 June 1918; s. Britton and Marion (Glyn) O.; e. Upper Canada Coll., Toronto, Ont.; Trinity Coll. School, Port Hope, Ont.; Trinity Coll., Univ. of Toronto; Osgoode Hall Law Sch., Toronto, Ont.; m. Dorothy, d. Lawton Ridout 12 Jan. 1940; children: Lawton Britton Campbell, Richard Ridout, Campbell Charles William, Elizabeth Victoria; PARTNER, OSLER, HOSKIN & HARCOURT, since 1950; read law with Osler Hoskin & Harcourt, Toronto, Ont., 1945-48 joining the firm as an Assoc., 1948; called to Bar of Ont., 1948; cr. Q.C. 1961; served with Royal Candn. Artillery in Eng., Italy and France during 2nd World War, 1939-45; discharged to Reserve with rank of Major; Reserve to 1950, retired with rank of Lt. Col.; mem., Candn. Bar Assn.; Co. York Law Assn.; Law Soc. Upper Canada; Phi Kappa Pi; Anglican; recreations: golf, fishing, cruising, shooting; Clubs: The Toronto; Toronto

Golf; Goodwood; Badminton & Racquet; Home: 350 Lonsdale Rd., Toronto, Ont. M5P 1R6; Office: Box 50, First Canadian Place, Toronto, Ont. M5X 1B8

OSLER, Gordon Peter; executive; b. Winnipeg, Man. 19 June 1922; s. Hugh Farquarson and Kathleen (Harty) O.; e. Ravenscourt Sch. Winnipeg; Queen's Univ.; m. Nancy Adina d. Conrad S. Riley 20 Aug. 1948; children: Sanford L., Susan H. (Mrs. R. B. Matthews), Gillian G.; CHRMN. AND DIR., STANTON PIPES LTD. 1975- ; Chrmn. Slater Steel Industries Ltd.; Canadian Surety Co.; Dir. Toronto-Dominion Bank; North American Life Assurance Co.; Inter-City Gas Ltd.; Interprovincial Steel & Pipe Corp.; Trans-Canada Pipelines Ltd.; Lehndorff Corp.; Maclean Hunter Ltd.; Uniroyal Ltd.; Household Internat. Inc.; British Steel Corp. Inc.; British Steel Canada (1979) Inc.; Trustee, Canada Permanent Investment Income; joined Osler, Hammond & Nanton Ltd. Winnipeg becoming Pres. and Chief Extve. Offr. 1952; Chrmn., Pres. and Chief Extve. Offr. Unas Investments, Toronto 1964; Chrmn. Slater Steel Industries Ltd. 1972; Vice Chrmn. and Chief Extve. Offr. British Steel (Canada) Ltd. 1972; served with Royal Candn. Armoured Corps 1942-46, rank Lt.; recreations: tennis, golf; Clubs: Toronto; Toronto Golf; York; Lost Tree Village; Home: 112 Dunvegan Rd., Toronto, Ont. M4V 2R1; Office: (P.O. Box 346) Toronto-Dominion Centre, Toronto, Ont. M5K 1K7.

OSLER, Hon. John Harty, B.A.; judge; b. Winnipeg, Manitoba, 28 Feb. 1915; s. Hugh F. and Kathleen (Harty) O.; e. Appleby Coll., Oakville, Ont.; Trinity Coll., Univ. of Toronto, B.A. 1937; Osgoode Hall Law Sch., Toronto, Ont.; m. Elizabeth, d. J.S.H. Guest, Oakville, Ont., 5 June 1937; children: Ann Harty (Malcolmson), Janet Kathleen (MacDonald), Hugh John; JUSTICE, SUPREME COURT OF ONT. since Nov. 1968; read law with Cassels, Brock & Kelley, Toronto, Ont.; called to the Bar of Ont., June 1940; cr. Q.C. 1954; engaged in the practice of law since grad. except for war service, limiting practice mainly to labour relations and trade union law; Partner, Jolliffe, Lewis and Osler, prior to present appointment; mem., Candn. Bar Assn. (Vice-Pres. for Ont. 1961-62, Nat. Extve. 1963-64); served in 2nd World War; Lieut. R.C.N.V.R., 1942-45; Phi Kappa Pi (Pres. 1936); recreation: sailing; Clubs: University; Home: 48 Old Forest Hill Rd., Toronto, Ont.; M5P 2P9; Office: Osgoode Hall, Toronto, Ont. M5H 2N5

OSLER, Peter Scarth, Q.C.; b. Toronto, Ont., 31 May 1916; s. Glyn and Florence (Scarth) O.; e. Trinity Coll. Sch., Port Hope, Ont.; Royal Mil. Coll., Kingston, Ont.; Osgoode Hall, Toronto, Ont.; m. Cecily Taylor, 23 Jan. 1943; children: Christopher, Deborah, Ian, Martha; PARTNER, BLAKE, CASSELS & GRAYDON; Dir., V.O.N., Toronto Br.; read law with Blake, Cassels & Graydon; called to the Bar of Ont., June 1940; cr. Q.C. 1956; mem., Candn. Bar Assn.; Champlain Soc.; Conservative; Anglican; recreations: fishing, golf, skiing; Club: The Toronto; Home: 198 Warren Rd., Toronto, Ont. M4V 2S5; Office: (Box 25) Commerce Court W., Toronto, Ont. M5L 1A9

OSMOND, Dennis Gordon, M.B., Ch.B., D.Sc.; educator; b. New York, N.Y. 31 Jan. 1930; s. Ernest Gordon and Marjorie Bertha (Milton) O.; e. City of Bath (Eng.) Boys' Sch.; The Grammar Sch. Chipping Sodbury, Eng.; Univ. of Bristol BB.Sc. 1951, M.B., Ch.B. 1954, D.Sc. 1975; m. Anne Welsh 30 July 1955; three s. Roger Gordon, Martin Henry, David Richard; ROBERT REFORD PROF. OF ANATOMY, McGILL UNIV. 1974- , Assoc. Prof. of Anatomy 1965-67, Prof. of Anatomy 1967-74; House Surg. Royal Gwent Hosp. Newport, Eng. 1954; House Phys. Bristol Royal Infirmary, Eng. 1955; Demonst. in Anatomy Univ. of Bristol 1957, Lectr. 1959-64; Instr. in Anat. Univ. of Wash. 1960-61; Med. Research Council Visiting Scient. Walter & Eliza Hall Inst. Med. Research Melbourne, Australia 1972-73; Visiting Hon. Re-

search Fellow Univ. of Birmingham 1979; Visiting Scient. Basel Inst. for Immunology, Switzerland 1980; served with R.A.M.C. Eng. 1955-57, rank Capt.; co-ed. "Stem Cells of Renewing Cell Populations" 1976; numerous articles cellular immunology & haematology prof. journs.; mem. Candn. Assn. Anats. (Vice Pres.); Am. Assn. Anats. (Extve. Comte.); Anat. Assn. Gt. Brit. & Ireland (Overseas Council mem. 1975-78); Internat. Soc. Exper. Hematol. (Bd. Dirs. 1976-79); Candn. Soc. Immunology; Am. Assn. Immunols.; Reticuloendothelial Soc.; recreations: travel, theatre, reading, skiing, squash, domestic hobbies; Home: 116 rue de Touraine, St. Lambert, Que. J4S 1H4; Office: 3640 University St., Montreal, Que. H3A 2B2.

OSTASHEWSKY, Roman J., C.M., B.Phil., B.Th., B.L.S.; museum director; b. Western Ukraine 19 Apl. 1924; s. Joseph and Theophilia (Lysko) O.; e. pub. and high schs. Lviv, W. Ukraine 1942; Agric. Coll. Tchernytsia, W. Ukraine 1943; Univ. of Rome B.Phil. 1947, B.Th. 1950; McGill Univ. B.L.S. 1963; Univ. of Denver Dipl. in Archives Adm. 1967; m. Lillian d. late George Makuch 20 Sept. 1952; children: Taras A., Theresa C., Sonia M.; DIR., UKRAINIAN CULTURAL HERITAGE VILLAGE since 1975; came to Can. Edmonton 1951, Autobody Painter 1952-58, Postal Clk. 1958-59; Lib., Edmonton Pub. Lib. 1959-66; Sr. Archivist, Prov. Archives Alta. 1966-75; Pres. Edmonton Lib. Assn. and Dir. Alta. Lib. Assn. 1964-65; Chrmn., Ukrainian Art & Lit. Club Edmonton 1966-68; Comte. for Ukrainian Patriarchate 1972-75; Ukrainian Drama Club 1968-72; Cultural Devel. Comte., U.C.C. since 1966; Heritage Series of Concerts since 1977; Secy. Ukrainian Cath. Council Alta. 1964-67; Pres.; Ukrainian Candn. Comte. 1969-71; Ukrainian Prof. & Business Club 1974; Ukrainian Nat. Fed. 1972 — 73, 1975-76; Dir. Nat. Extve. of U.N.F. Toronto since 1978; Council mem. Ukrainian Culture in Can. Winnipeg 1974-77; mem. Taras Shevenko Scient. soc. since 1971; Program Chrmn. Ukrainian Symphony Concerts Edmonton 1974, 1978; Producer weekly Ukrainian Radio Program Edmonton 1955-77; Host and Producer weekly Ukrainian TV Program "Kontakt" since 1973; Narrator Ukrainian short stories and poetry and organizer many concerts and festivals; rec'd Achievement Award Prov. Alta. 1976; Shevchenko Gold Medal 1977; Queen's Silver Jubilee Medal 1977; Life mem. Ukrainian Prof. & Business Club Edmonton; Order of Canada, 1979; Ukrainian Catholic; Home: 8011-145 Avenue, Edmonton, Alta. T5C 2S8; Office: 14th fl., C.N. Tower, Edmonton, Alta. T5J 0K5.Location, 50 km. Hwy 16 East of Edmonton.

OSTIGUY, Jean Paul Wilson, O.C. (1978), LL.D.; investment dealer; b. Montreal, Que., 4 March 1922; s. Paul E. and Marguerite (Wilson) O.; e. Coll. Jean de Brebeuf; Ecole des Hautes Etudes Comm. (Faculty of Comm., Univ. of Montreal); Royal Mil. Coll. of Can., Kingston, Grad. 1942, LL.D. (Hon.) 1978; m. Michelle, d. Achille Bienvenu, 5 Oct. 1946; children: Marc, Claude, Danielle, Denise, Suzanne; CHRMN. OF THE BD., GREEN-SHIELDS INC. since 1977; Pres. & Chief Extve. Offr., Crang & Ostiguy Inc. 1972-77; Dir., Biologicals, Inc.; Canadian Imperial Bank of Commerce (Extve. Comte.); Canadian Pacific Airlines, Limited; The General Accident Assurance Co. of Canada; Sintra Ltd.; Kerr Addison Mines Ltd. (Extve. Comte.); Ford Motor Co. of Canada Ltd.; Dominion Life Assurance Co. of Can.; Ciba-Geigy Can. Ltd.; Canadian Canners Ltd.; Procor Ltd.; Green-shields Inc.; with Stevenson & Kellogg Ltd., 1945-47; Vice-Pres. and Dir., Casgrain & Co. Ltd., 1948-56; with Morgan, Ostiguy & Hudson Inc. 1956-72; National Pres.; Invest. Dealers' Assn. of Can., 1965-66; Pres., Montreal Chamber Comm. 1966-67; Pres., La Maison des Etudiants Canadiens à Paris; President, Royal Mil. College Club of Canada, 1967-68; Chrmn., Bd. of Trustees for Nat. Museums of Can., 1968-73; Kt. of Magistral Order of Malta; Order of St. Lazarus; served overseas during 2nd World War with 4th Princess Louise Dragoon Guards; wounded

Sept. 1, 1944 in Italy and discharged with rank of Capt., Oct. 1945; Roman Catholic; Clubs: St. James's; Mount Royal; Toronto; Home: 318 Geneva Cres., Town of Mount Royal, Que. H3R 2A9; Office: 4 Place Ville Marie, Montreal, Que. H3B 2E8

OSTIGUY, Jean René, B.A.; art Critic and historian; Canadian public service; b. Marieville, Que., 14 Aug. 1925; s. Joseph and Jeanne (Dussault) O.; e. Séminaire de Valleyfield; Univ. of Montreal, B.A. 1947; Ecole des Beaux-Arts de Montréal, 1947-50; Sch. of Art & Design, 1950-52 (Dipl.); m. Denise Aurella, d. Joseph Coté, Valleyfield, Que., 8 July 1953; children: Monique, Christine, David; RESEARCH CURATOR (CANDN. ART), NATIONAL GALLERY OF CANADA; Art Critic for (newspaper) "Le Devoir", Montreal, Que.; Lectr. in Hist. of Candn. Art, Univ. of Ottawa 1966-71; Prof. in Basic Design and Hist. of Art, Ecole des Beaux-Arts, Montreal, 1952-55; Prof. of Art Appreciation at Semy. de Valleyfield, Que., and at Valleyfield Sch. Comm., 1952-55; author; "Un siècle de peinture canadienne (1870-1970)", 1971; Roman Catholic; recreations: painting, canoeing; Home: 21 Rue Thibeault, Hull, Qué. J9A 1H4; Office: National Gallery, Elgin St., Ottawa, Ont.

OSTLER, John William Langton; b. Hamilton, Ont.; m.; one s. one d.; President and Gen. Manager, Canadian Meter Co., 1957-76 (retired); Dir., Darnell Corp.; joined Candn. Bank of Commerce, Hamilton, 1929; joined present Co. 1937; apptd. Gen. Mgr. 1950; Vice Pres. 1955; Past Pres., Candn. Gas Assn.; Ont. Natural Gas Assoc.; Past Pres., Indust. Instrument Mfrs. Assn.; Past Pres., Milton Chamber Comm.; Rotary Club of Milton; Past President Ontario Hospital Association; Past Chairman, Provincial Advisory Committee on Nursing Education; Past Chairman and Member of Board Milton District Hospital; Past Vice-Chrmn. and Founding Bd. Mem., Sheridan Coll. and Credit Valley Sch. of Nursing (now part of Sheridan); Past President of Hamilton Philharmonic Society which operates the Philharmonic Orchestra; Past President Halton Lung Association; Address: 99 Mill St., Milton, Ont., L9T 1R8

OSTRY, Bernard, B.A.; Canadian public servant; b. Wadena, Sask., 10 June 1927; s. Abraham and Tobie (Goldman) O.; e. Primary Schs., Flin Flon, and Winnipeg, Man.; Pub. Schs., St. John's Coll. and St. John's Tech. High Sch., Winnipeg, Man.; Univ. of Manitoba 1943-48; post-grad. work in field of Diplomatic Hist. at Univ. of London (L.S.E.) under the late Sir Charles K. Webster and Prof. W. N. Medicott 1948-52; m. Dr. Sylvia; two s., Adam, Jonathan David; DEPY - MIN. OF INDUSTRY AND TOURISM. GOV'T OF ONTARIO, 1981-; Special Advisor, Communications, Canadian Embassy, Paris, 1980-81; Depy. Minister of Communications 1974-78; Research Assoc., University of Birmingham, England, 1951-55; Special Assist. and Advisor to Leader of Indian Delegation to United Nations, 1951-52; David Davies Fellow in International Hist., University of London, London School of Economics & Political Science, 1956-58; Executive Secretary-Treasurer, Commonwealth Inst. of Social Research, 1959-61; Secretary-Treasurer, Social Science Research Council of Canada, 1961-63; Moderator, Nightline, Canadian Broadcasting Corporation, 1960.63; Supervisor, Department of Public Affairs (Radio & T.V.) CBC, 1963-68. Winner of several awards for public affairs broadcasting, including the Ohio State Award and Special Wilderness Award. Regular moderator and commentator on CBC, private radio and TV Public affairs programmes. Director, Regulations Policy, Canadian Radio Television Commission, 1968-69; Commissioner, Prime Minister's Task Force on government Information, 1968-70; Assistant Under Secretary of State (Citizenship), 1970-73; Secretary-General, National Museums of Canada, 1973-1978; Gov. Heritage Canada; life mem., Candn. Historical Assocn.; mem., Bd. of Govs., Candn. Conference of the Arts; Candn. Museums Assocn.; Administrative Council

of the Internat. Fund for the Promotion of Culture, U.N.E.S.C.O.; Author, "Research in the Humanities and Social Sciences in Canada", 1962; "The Cultural Connection", 1978; articles on Canadian labour and international hist. and politics in "Canadian Historical Review", "Canadian Journal of Economics and Political Science", & other learned journs., newspapers, mags., etc.; co-author, "The Age of Mackenzie King", 1955; "To Know and Be Known", 1969; regular moderator and commentator on CBC, private radio and TV Pub. Affairs Programs; recreations: reading, travelling; Office: 900 Bay St., Hearst Block, Queen's Park, Toronto, Ont. M7A 2E2

OSTRY, Sylvia (Mrs. Bernard), Ph.D., LL.D.; civil servant; economist; b. Winnipeg, Man., 3 June 1927; d. Morris J. and B. (Stoller) Knelman; e. Winnipeg (Man.) Pub. and High Schs.; McGill Univ., B.A. (Econ.) 1948, M.A. 1950, Ph.D. 1954; Cambridge University Ph.D. (residence) 1950-51; 1954; LL.D. York and New Brunswick 1971, McGill 1972, Western Ont., McMaster, B.C. 1973, Queen's, Brock, Mount Allison 1975, Laurentian 1977; D.M.Sc. Ottawa Univ. 1976; m. Bernard Ostry; children: Adam, Jonathan; APPOINTED HEAD OF THE ECON. & STATS. DEPT., ORGANIZATION OF EC. COOPERATION & DEVELOPMENT, PARIS, 1980; Chrmn., Economic Council of Can. 1978-80; Lectr. and Asst. Prof., McGill Univ., 1948-54; Research Offr., Inst. of Stat., Univ. of Oxford, 1955-57; Asst. Prof., Univ. of Montreal, 1962-64; Dir., Special Manpower Studies, Dom. Bureau of Stat., 1964-69; Dir., Economic Council of Canada 1969-72; Chief Stat., Statistics Can. 1972-75; Deputy Min. of Consumer and Corp. Affairs, Can. 1975-78; co-author, "Labour Economics in Canada", 3rd edition 1979; other writings incl. publs. in fields of labour economics, demography, productivity, competition policy; mem., Candn. Econ. Assn.; Am. Econ. Assn.; Editorial Board Can. Public Policy 1976; Ontario Selection Committee, Rhodes Scholarship Trust, 1976; Econ. Visiting Comte. Bd. of Overseers Harvard Coll. 1973; Bd. Govs. Carleton Univ. 1970-79; Mang. Adv. Council, Faculty Mang. Studies University of Toronto 1974; Adv. Council Faculty Adm. Studies, York Univ. 1975; mem. Comte. on Univ. Affairs, Prov. Ont. 1971-72; Fellow Am. Stat. Assn.; recreations: films, theatre, contemporary reading; Club: Cercle Universitaire; Address: 94 rue CHARDON-LA-GACHE 75016, Paris France

O'SULLIVAN, Hon. Joseph F., M.A., LL.B.; judge; b. Brandon, Man., 25 Feb. 1927; s. Patrick and Marie Louise (Poirier) O'S.; e. St. Augustine's Parochial Sch. 1940, Earl Haig 1941 and Brandon (Man.) Coll. Inst. 1943; Univ. of Man. St. Paul's Coll. B.A. 1947; Man. Law Sch. LL.B. 1953; Univ. of Toronto M.A. 1949; JUSTICE, COURT OF APPEAL FOR MAN. since 1975; read law with E.J. McMurray; called to Bar of Man. 1953; cr. Q.C. 1969; private law practice 1953-75; Past Pres. Man. Lib. Party and mem. campaign comtes. 1956-75; Secy. Bd. Dirs. St. Boniface Gen. Hosp.; Past Pres. Man. Med. Legal Soc.; K. of C.; R. Catholic; Home: 403 Percy St., Brandon, Man. R7A 5R9; and 1050 Grosvenor Ave., Winnipeg, Man. R3M 0N7; Office: Law Courts, Winnipeg, Man.

OSWELL, Kenneth Rupert, F.C.A., F.I.M.C.; chartered accountant; b. Toronto, Ont., 18 May 1922; s. late Rupert Stanley and Beatrice (Humphreys) O.; e. Eastern High Sch. of Comm.; children: Kenneth Randall, Susan Kathleen; SR. PARTNER, TOUCHE ROSS & CO.; former Regional Partner, Middle East and Africa, Touche Ross International, 1974-78; former Dir. Internat. Mang. Consulting, Touche Ross & Partners; former mem. Adv. Council, Min. of Industry, Trade and Comm., Ottawa, Ont.; admit. Inst. of Chart. Accts. of Ont. 1947; Fellow 1965; Jr. Acct., Chas. Greer & Co., Toronto, 1939-42; joined P. S. Ross & Sons 1945, admit. to Partnership 1953; Partner, Touche, Ross & Co., Toronto since 1953; Partner, Touche Ross & Partners, Mang. Consultants, since 1958; served during 2nd World War in R.C.N., discharged as Lt.; Campaign Chrmn., Toronto Humane Soc. 1981; Past Pres. North York Br. Metrop. Toronto Y.M.C.A.; Past Pres., Candn. Assn. Mang. Consultants; Charter mem. and Past Pres., Inst. of Mang. Consultants of Ontario Fellow 1970; mem., Society for Advanc. Mang.; Inst. Management Consultants Inc. New York; former mem. Council, Inst. Mang. Consultants Can.; Fellow, British Inst. of Mang.; Freemason; Anglican; recreations: travel, photography; Clubs: Ontario; Granite; Canadian (N.Y.); Canadian Society of N.Y.; Travellers' Century, Los Angelos; Home: Granite Place, Ste. 1204, 63 St. Clair Ave. W., Toronto, Ont. M4V 2Y9 Office: Box 12, First Canadian Place, Toronto, Ont. M5X 1B3

OTLEY, G. Roger, B.Sc.; executive; b. Huddersfield, Yorks., 22 May 1934; s. late Gerald William and Phillis Mary (Greenwood) O.; e. Bryanston Sch. Dorset, Eng. 1951; McGill Univ. B.Sc. (Agric. Econ.) 1959; m. Carolyn Anne d. late Carl Reeves, Mulgrave, N.S., 8 June 1957; children: Gerald, Kathryn, Tony, John; EXEC. VICE PRES. FUNCTIONAL OPERATIONS, THE ROYAL TRUST since 1982; joined present Co. as Invest. Analyst 1959, Mgr. Invest. Research 1966, Mgr. Invests. 1968, Gen. Supvr. Invest. Research 1969, Asst. Vice Pres. Pensions 1971, Vice Pres. Pensions 1973; Extve. Vice-Pres., and C.O.O., Computel Systems Ltd., Ottawa, 1974; Group Vice-Pres., Investments, 1975; Group Vice-Pres., Trust and Investment Services, 1979; Dir., Computel Systems Ltd., Ottawa; The Canadian Depository for Securities Ltd., Toronto; Royal Trust Energy Corp., Calgary; Town Councillor Baie d'Urfe, Que. 1974; mem. Toronto Soc. Financial Analysts; Anglican; recreations: tennis, golf; Clubs: The Oakville; The National; Oakville Golf; Home: 1243 Lakeshore Rd. East, Oakville, Ont. L6J 1L5; Office: Toronto Dominion Tower, P.O. Box 7500, Station A, Toronto, M5W 1P9

OTTENHEIMER, Hon. Gerald, M.H.A., M.A.; politician; b. St. John's, Nfld. 4 June 1934; s. Frederick and Marguerite (Ryan) O.; e. St. Bonaventure's Coll.; Fordham Univ. N.Y.; Mem. Univ. of Nfld.; Univ. of Paris; Univ. of Rome; Univ. of Ottawa; Cambridge Univ.; m. Alma d. John Cullimore, Trinity, Nfld. 20 Aug. 1957; children: Geraldine, Susanne, Bernadette, Annmarie; MIN. OF JUSTICE & ATTORNEY GENERAL, NFLD. 1979- ; educator, former Leader of the Opposition and Leader of Nfld. P. Cons. Party 3 yrs.; Cand. Fed. g.e. 1965, def.; el. M.H.A. for Waterford-Kenmount prov. g.e. 1966, resigned 1970, re-el. since prov. g.e. 1971; Min. of Intergovernmental Affairs 1972; Min. of Educ. 1972; Speaker 1975; P. Conservative; R. Catholic; Office: Confederation Bldg., St. John's, Nfld. A1C 5T7.

OUELLET, L'Hon. André, P.C.(1972), M.P., B.ès A.; avocat; né à St. Pascal, comté Kamouraska, Québec, 6 avril 1939; f. Albert et Rita (Turgeon) O.; é. Univ. d'Ottawa, B.ès A. 1960; Univ. de Sherbrooke, Diplôme en-Droit 1963; Membre Qué. Barreau 1964; ép. Edith, fille de Jean-Marie Pagé, 17 juillet 1965; enfants: Sonia, Jean, Olga, Pierre; MIN. CONSOMMATION & CORPORATIONS & MIN. RESPONSABLE DE LA SOCIETE CANADIENNE DES POSTES élu Député Montréal-Papineau élection partielle 1967 et ré-élu aux élections générales de 1968, 1972 et 1974, 1979 et 1980; Président du Caucus Liberal Fédéral du Québec 1968; Secrétaire Parlementaire du Secrétaire d'Etat aux Affaires Extérieures 1970; Secrétaire Parlementaire du Ministre de la Santé Nationale et du Bien-Etre Social 1971; Min. Postes nov. 1972; Min. Consommation et Corps oct. 1974; Min. d'Etat chargé des Affaires Urbaines nov. 1976; Min. des Travaux publics nov. 1978; membre; Barreau de la Province de Québec; Libéral; Catholique; Résidence: 17 Chase Court, Ottawa, Ont. K1V 9Y6; Bureau: Pièce 509-S, Chambre des Communes, Ottawa, Ont. K1A OA6

OUELLET, Cyrias (Joseph Lucien), B.A., B.Sc.A., D.Sc., F.R.S.C., F.C.I.C.; university professor; b. Quebec,

Que., 19 Jan. 1906; s. Joseph Pierre and Marie (Chapleau) O.; e. Que. Semy.; Laval Univ., B.A. 1926, B.Sc.A. (Chem.) 1930; Federal Polytech., Zurich, Switzerland, D.Sc. 1932; Cambridge Univ. (Research), 1932-35; Univ. of California (Guggenheim Fellow), 1949; joined the staff of Laval Univ., Dept. of Phys. Chem. 1935-73; mem. of Nat. Research Council; Assn. canadienne-française pour l'Avanc. des sciences (Pres.); author of a number of scient. papers mainly on research on adsorption, chem. kinetics and photosynthesis; Home: #405, 2276 Ch. Ste-Foy, Ste-Foy, Que., G1V 1S7

OUELLET, Msgr. Gilles, (R.C.); né Bromptonville, Qué. 14 août 1922; f. Joseph Adélard et Armande (Biron) O.; é. Séminaire de Sherbrooke, B.A.; Grand Séminaire des Missions Etrangères, (Théologie), Pont-Viau, Qué.; o. prêtre, 30 juin 1946; Université Grégorienne, Rome, Italie, D. Droit Canonique, 1947-50; Diplôme, admin. ecclésiastique, Phillippines 1955; ARCHEVEQUE DE RIMOUSKI, QUE. depuis 14 juin 1973; Mission de Davao, Phillippines, secrétaire, Chancelier, dir. de l'Action Catholique diocésaine, Vicare Général 1950-57; Supérieur Missions Etrangères, 1958-67; Oeuvre de la Propagation de la Foi, Oeuvre Pontif. de St. Pierre Apôtre, 1968-77; Evêque de Gaspé, Que. 1968-73; Club: Chevaliers de Colomb; Résidence: 34 Ouest, rue de l'Evêché, C.P. 370, Rimouski, Que. G5L 7C7

OUELLET, Hon. Jean-Pierre, M.L.A., B.Ed.; politician; b. St-Eleuthère, Qué. 21 Aug. 1946; s. Zéphirin and Bertha (Chamberland) O.; e. Baker-Brook (N.B.) Elem. Sch.; Trois-Rivières (Que.) Semy.; Coll. St-Louis, Edmundston B.A. 1967; Univ. of Moncton B.Ed. 1969; m. Nicole d. Joël Lang, Lac Gerry, Qué. 16 Aug. 1969; children: Dominique, Pierre Luc, Stephanie;MIN. OF YOUTH, RECREATION & CULTURAL RESOURCES, N.B.1978- ; el. M.L.A. 1974, re-el. 1978; Min. of Youth 1975; P. Conservative; R. Catholic; Home: Bakerbrook, N.B.; Office: (C.P. 6000) King's Pl., Fredericton, N.B.

OUGHTRED, William Wallace, B.Eng.; retired industrialist; b. Ainsworth, B.C. 19 Sept. 1917; s. late Lawrence William and Jean (McKinnon) O.; e. Hume Sch. and Nelson Jr. High Sch., Nelson, B.C.; St. Lambert (Que.) High Sch.; McGill Univ. B. Eng. (Mining) 1946; m. June Archibald, d. late Frank A. D. Bourne, St. Lambert, Que., 3 April 1941; children: Angus Winn, Frances Jill (Mrs. N. E. Quick), John William, Kathryn Mary, Christopher Wayne; summer employment in mining, 1935-40; joined present Co. as Superintendent of exploration project in Newfoundland 1946; appointed Exploration Manager, Thetford Mines, Que., 1949; also Cost Control Manager, 1952; apptd. Asst. Gen. Mgr. Asbestos Corp. Ltd. and Mgr. Asbestos Corp. (Explorations) Ltd. 1954; Vice Pres. and Gen. Mgr. 1964; Extve. Vice-Pres., 1964-67; Pres. and C.E.O., Asbestos Corp. Ltd. 1967-76; through sales and exploration activity has made numerous trips around the world visiting nearly all countries; served in 2nd World War as Pilot, R.C.A.F. 1940-45; Candn. Inst. Mining & Metall.; Gardening; Protestant; recreations: gardening, fishing, hunting, golfing, curling; Home: 29 Upper Canada Dr., Niagara-on-the-Lake, Ont. L0S 1J0

OUIMET, J. Alphonse, C.C. (1968), D.A.Sc., LL.D., D.C.L., D.S.Soc., D.Adm., D.ès Arts P.Eng., F.I.R.E.; b. Montreal, Que., 12 June 1908; s. late J. Alphonse and late Marie-Blanche (Geoffrion) O.; e. St. Mary's Coll., Montreal, B.A. 1928; McGill Univ., B. Eng. (Elec.) 1932, LL.D. 1963; Univ. of Montreal, D.A.Sc. 1957; D.C.L. Acadia Univ., 1962; LL.D., Univ. of Sask., 1962; D.S.Soc., Univ. d'Ottawa, 1968; D.Adm., Univ. de Sherbrooke, 1968; LL.D., Royal Mil. Coll. of Can., 1974; D. ès Arts, Univ. Laval, 1978; m. Jeanne, d. late J. E. Prévost, 24 May 1935; one d. Denise; Research Engr., Candn. Television Ltd., 1932-33; Research Engr. and Dir., Candn. Electronics Co. 1933-34; Research Engr., Canadian-Radio Broadcasting Comn. and C.B.C., Ottawa, 1934-37; Operations Engr.,

C.B.C., Montreal, 1937-39; Gen. Supv. Engr., 1939-40; Asst. Chief Engr., 1941-49, Chief Engr. and Co-ordinator of TV, 1949-51; Asst. Gen. Mgr., 1951-52; apptd. Gen. Mgr., 1953; Pres., 1958; subsequently Pres. and Chrmn. of Bd. of Dirs. until resignation, Dec. 1967; Chrmn. of Bd., Telesat Canada, 1969-80; Dir., 1980-; Chrmn. CBC Corporate Olympics Comte., 1973-76; Chrmn., Communications Res. Ad.Bd., 1975-80; Archambault Medal, la Société Canadienne-française pour l'avancement des sciences, 1958; awarded Ross Medal, 1948 and Julian C. Smith Medal, 1959 by Engn. Inst. of Can.; Fellow Inst. of Radio Engrs.; rec'd. Emmy Directorate Award of Internat. Council of Acad. of Television Arts & Sciences, N.Y. 1977; Sir John Kennedy Medal, 1969; McNaughton Medal, 1972; Spec. Award, Soc. of Motion Picture and T.V. Engrs., 1974; The Gold Medal of the Cdn. Council of Prof. Engrs., 1975; Great Montrealer Award, 1978; Walter Gordon Lecturer, 1980; mem., Engn. Inst. of Can.; Corp. Engrs. of Que.; Comité Internat. de Télévision; Roman Catholic; 227 Lakeview Ave., Pointe Claire, Que. H9S 4C8

OUIMET, J. Robert, M.Com., M.B.A., M.Pol. & Soc. Science; industrialist; b. Montreal, Que., 9 Apl. 1934; s. J-René and Thérèse (Drouin) O.; e. Ecole des Hautes Etudes Commerciales, Montreal, M.Com. 1956; Internat. Univ. of Fribourg, M. Pol. & Soc. Science 1959; Columbia Univ., M.B.A. 1960 (Magna Cum Laude); m. Myriam, d. Lionel Maes, Belgium, 3 July 1965; children: Joanne, Marie-Diane, J. René II, J. Robert II; PRESIDENT, CHIEF EXTVE. OFFR. AND DIR., J. RENE OUIMET ENTERPRISES LTD.; Pres., Chief Extve. Offr. and Dir., Cordon Bleu International Ltd.; Cordon Bleu Ltd.; J. René Ouimet Ltd.; Freddy Inc.; Candn. Food Processors Assoc.; Grocery Product Manufacturers of Can.; Buffet Food Corpn. Ltd.; Dir., Petro Canada; National Bank of Canada; Zeller's Ltd.; Industrial Life Insurance Co.; Chrmn. of Bd., Pabi Inc. (Poyeye Burger); Conserverie Notre Dame Ltd.; Dir. of Marketing, Cordon Bleu Ltd.; J. René Ouimet Ltd., 1960; apptd. Extve. Vice-Pres., Cordon Bleu Ltd., J. René Ouimet Ltd., and J. René Ouimet Enterprises Ltd. 1960; Extve. Vice-Pres. Cordon Bleu International Ltd. 1971-74; Pres. Buffet Foods Corp. Ltd. 1971-74; mem. Que. Gen. Council on Industry; Min. Adv. Council, Min. of Industry, Trade and Comm.; Clubs: Saint-Denis; Mount Royal; Hermitage (Magog); Coral Beach & Tennis (Bermuda); Toronto Club; Office: 8585 Jeanne-Mance, Montreal, Que. H2P 2S8

OUIMET, Marcel, O.B.E. (1946); former broadcasting executive; b. Montreal, Que., 9 Jan. 1915; s. Paul and Marguerite (Desmarteau) O.; e. Univ. of Ottawa, B.A. 1934; Post Grad., Ecole des Hautes Etudes Sociales, Paris; Nat. Defence Coll., Kingston; m. Jacqueline, d. Albert Tétrault, Montreal, 20 Sept. 1941; children: Paule (Mrs. Hugh M. Scott), Lise (Mrs. John C. Ouimet-McPherson), Mrs. A.A.T. Ouimet-Storrs; Vice-Pres., Special Services Div., C.B.C., 1972-75; mem., Ed. Staff "Le Droit", Ottawa, 1934-37; joined C.B.C. as Bilingual Announcer, 1939; Sr. Ed., Montreal newsroom, 1941-43; Supv. of Talks and Pub. Affairs, C.B.C., Montreal, 1945; Special Corr. at Peace Conf. in Paris and Un. Nations Assembly, 1946; Dir. of the French Network 1947-53; Asst. Dir. of Programmes, 1953; Asst. Controller of Broadcasting, 1957 and Depy. Controller, 1958; Vice-Pres. and Gen. Mgr., Network Broadcasting (French), 1959-68; Vice-Pres. of Programmes 1968-72; mem., Candn. del. to UNESCO Gen. Conf., Paris, 1958; served in World War, 1943-45, as War Corr. in Sicily, Italy, France, Belgium, Holland and Germany; trustee, Montfart Hospital, Ottawa, Past Pres.; Royal Candn. Legion (Press-Radio Br.); Past Pres., Nat. Gallery Assn. of Ottawa; Past Pres. of L'Alliance française d'Ottawa; Roman Catholic; recreations: reading, golf, swimming; Clubs: Life Member National Press; Past Pres., Larrimac Golf (Kirk's Ferry, Que.); Home: "Dufferin House", 18 - 174 Dufferin Rd., Ottawa, Ont. K1M 2A6

OUIMET, Hon. Roger, LL.D.; judge; b. Montreal, 1908; s. Paul Gédéon and Marguerite (Desmarteau) O.; e. University of Ottawa, B.A., Ph.L. 1926; Laval University, 1928-30; LL.D. (honoris causa) University New Brunswick 1971; m. Odette, d. Right Hon. Ernest Lapointe, 25 Sept. 1937; children: Hugues, Elisabeth (Mrs. Ross Goodwin), André (d. 1976); eight grandchildren; JUSTICE, SUPERIOR COURT OF QUEBEC, since 1955; read law with the Rt. Hon. Louis St. Laurent, P.C.; called to the Bar of Que., 1930; cr. K.C. 1944; Crown Attorney, Dist. of Montreal, 1940-44; Fed. Prosecutor and Counsel, Dept. of Justice and of Nat. Health & Welfare; general law practice before trial and appeal courts; cand. for Action Libérale Nationale in Prov. gen. el., 1935 (Verchères); official cand. for Liberal Party, Prov. el. 1948 (Montréal-St. Jacques); served in Reserve Army, Les Fusiliers Mont-Royal, 1942-45 with rank of Lieut.; Chrmn., Canadian Comte. on Corrections, Ottawa 1965-69; Roman Catholic; recreations: reading, travelling; Home: 3 Westmount Sq., Westmount, Que. H3Z 2S5; Office: Palais de Justice, Montreal, Que. H2Y 1A2

OUTERBRIDGE, Col. the Hon. Sir. Leonard Cecil, Kt. (1946), C.C. (1967), C.B.E. (1926), D.S.O. (1919), C.D., K.St.J., B.A., LL.B., LL.D.; merchant; b. Asheville, N.C., 6 May 1888; s. Sir Joseph, Kt. and Maria Harvey (Tucker) O.; e. Bishop Feild Coll., St. John's Nfld.; Marlborough Coll., England; Univ. of Toronto, B.A. 1911. LL.B. 1915; Osgoode Hall, Toronto; LL.D., Toronto 1950; Laval 1952; Memorial 1961; m. Dorothy W., d. John A. Strathy, Barrie, Ont., 23 Jan. 1915; one d., Nancy D.; former Lieut.-Gov. of Newfoundland, 1949-57; Chrmn. and Dir., Harvey & Co. Ltd. (estbd. 1767), steamship and airline agents, importers, etc., and director of other Co.'s; served in 1st World War, 1914-19, with 35th and 75th Bns., C.E.F.; Staff Capt., 1st Candn. Inf. Bgde.; twice Mentioned in Despatches; D.S.O.; Hon. Pte. Secy. to successive Govs. of Nfld., 1930-44; Pres., Nfld. Bd. of Trade 1925; Dir., Civil Defence, 1942-45; Hon. Col., Royal Nfld. Regt., 1950-75; Anglican; Address: 3 Pringle Place, St. John's, Nfld.

OUVRARD, Pierre, R.C.A.; bookbinder; b. Québec City, Qué. 8 Feb. 1929; s. Jean de la Salle and Bernadette (Boily) O.; e. Coll. Jean de Brébeuf and Ecole des Beaux-Arts, Montréal; Ecole des Arts Graphiques Dipl. in Graphics specialization Art Bookbinding; m. Marie-Thérèse d. Joseph Xavier Guitard 27 Nov. 1973; 4 children (2 by previous marriage); PROP., PIERRE OUVRARD, RELIEUR; Teacher in Hist. of Art and Bookbinding, Cegep Ahuntsic 11 yrs.; Dir. Papeterie St-Gilles (hand-made paper); rep. in numerous exhns. nat. and internat.; author "La Reliure" 1974; mem. Chambre Syndicale Nationale de la Reliure Dorure (France); Hand Bookbinders of Calif.; Graphic Arts Internat. Union; R. Catholic; Address: 355, rue Principale, St-Paul-de-L'Ile-Aux-Noix, Qué. J0J 1G0.

OVEREND, Neil, M.A.; financial executive; b. Vancouver, B.C. 12 Sept. 1929; s. Albert O.; e. Carleton Univ. B.A. 1964; Univ. of Cal. Berkeley M.A. 1965; m. Francesca Peschl 29 March 1970; children: Marcus, Alissa; Pres., SASK. ECON. DEVEL. CORP. (SEDCO) since 1978; held various positions Candn. Internat. Devel. Agency, Ottawa 1966-73, Vice Pres. Bilateral Programs 1973-76; Asst. Deputy Minister for Intergovt'al Affairs, Ministry of State for Urban Affairs, Ottawa 1976-78; served with Candn. Army (Regular) 1952-60, rank Lt.; mem. Regina Offrs. Mess; recreations: golf, camping; Home: 447 Habkirk Drive, Regina, Sask. S4S 6B3 Office: 1106 Winnipeg St., Box 5024, Regina, Sask. S4P 3M2.

OWEN, Rev. Derwyn Randulph Grier, L.Th., M.A., Ph.D., D.D., D.C.L.; (Ang.); retired university professor; b. Toronto, Ont., 16 May 1914; s. the late Mt. Rev. Derwyn Trevor and Nora Grier (Jellett) O.; e. Ridley Coll.; Trinity Coll., Univ. of Toronto, B.A. 1936 and L.Th 1940; Corpus Christi Coll., Oxford, B.A. 1938; M.A. 1942;

Union Theol. Semy., 1940-41; Univ. of Toronto Ph.D. 1942; D.D., Wycliffe; St. John's Coll.; King's Coll., Emmanuel Coll., Saskatoon; D.C.L., Bishop's Univ.; m. Anne Kathleen, d. late Dr. R. G. Armour, Toronto, 30 May 1942; children: David, Timothy; Asst. at St. Cuthbert's Ch., Leaside, Ont., 1941-57 Lect., Dept. of Ethics and Philos., Trinity Coll., 1941-42; Assoc. Prof. in Ethics & Philos. of Religion, 1946-54; subsequently Prof. of Religious Knowledge 1954-57, Provost and Vice Chancellor 1957-72; Professor of Religious Studies 1972-79; served in World War 1942-46, with Candn. Chaplain Services; Hon. Capt., No. 2 District Depot, Toronto, 1942-43; Westminster Regt., 5th Candn. Armoured Divn. in Eng., Italy, N.W. Europe, 1943-45; Khaki Univ. of Can. Eng., 1945; Publications: "Scientism, Man and Religion", 1952; "Body and Soul", 1956; Alpha Delta Phi; Home: 26 Eastbourne Ave., Toronto, Ont. M5P 2E9

OWEN, Hon. George Robert Whitley, M.A., B.C.L.; judge; b. Malta 29 Apl. 1912; s. Frank Whitley and Annie (Birchall) O.; came to Can. 1913; e. McGill Univ. B.A. 1933, M.A. 1934, B.C.L. 1937; Ecole Libre des Sciences Politiques and Sorbonne, Paris; m. Jean Christy d. late James Penrose Anglin 22 May 1940; two d. Jane Christy (Aikman), M. Sherrill (Edwards); JUDGE, QUE. COURT OF APPEAL since 1955; called to Bar of Que. 1937; cr. Q.C. 1952; law practice Meredith Holden Heward & Holden 1937-55; Lectr. in Law McGill Univ. 1942-69; Anglican; recreations: golf, curling; Clubs: Royal Montreal Golf; Kanawaki Golf; Cercle de la Place d'Armes; Mid Ocean (Bermuda); Hon. Co. of Edinburgh Golfers; R. & A.G.C. St. Andrews; Home: 973 Dunsmuir Rd., Montreal, Que. H3R 3A1; Office: 1 Notre Dame E., Rm. 1793, Montreal, Que. H2Y 1B6.

OWEN, Robert Derwyn; retired newspaperman; b. Toronto, Ont., 13 Aug. 1908; s. late Mt. Rev. Derwyn Trevor (late Archbishop of Toronto and Anglican Primate of All Canada) and the late Nora Grier (Jellett) O.; e. Trinity Coll. Sch., Port Hope, Ont. (1919-25); m. 1st, Katharine Nicholson (died 7 Oct. 1948) 16 Sept. 1935; 2ndly, Phyllis Dorothy; d. C. M. K. Woods, Kingston, Ont., 12 Sept. 1953; children: Peter B. Pennington, Robert D. Myles, Nancy N. Kathleen, Dorothy J. Grier; Reporter, Hamilton "Spectator", Hamilton, Ont., 1930-34; Ont. Mgr., British United Press, Toronto, Ont., 1934-40; Parlty. Press Corr., Press Gallery, Ottawa, 1940: with Montreal "Daily Star", 1940-41; Mang. Ed., Kingston "Whig-Standard", Kingston, Ont., 1941-56; Extve. Ed. 1957-67; Editor-in-Chief, Kingston Whig-Standard, 1968-74; Past Pres., Candn. Mang. Editors' Conf.; Anglican; recreation: fishing; Clubs: Frontenac Officers' Mess, Nat. Defence Coll. (Associate); Home: 25 Dickens Drive., Woodlands, Kingston, Ont. K7M 2M5

OWEN, Warwick Jack Burgoyne, M.A., Ph.D., F.R.S.C.; educator; b. Auckland, N.Z. 12 May 1916; s. Walter Graham and Elizabeth Frances (Williams) O.; e. Auckland Grammar Sch. 1933; Univ. of Auckland B.A. 1937, M.A. 1938; St. Catherines' Coll. Oxford B.A. 1941, M.A. 1946; Univ. of Wales Ph.D. 1955; m. Betty Isabel d. James Drummond 20 Dec. 1945; children: Lynette Isabel, Graham Warwick; PROF. EMERITUS OF ENGLISH, McMASTER UNIV. 1981- ; Asst. Lectr. in Eng. Univ. of Auckland 1938-39; Asst. Lectr., Lectr., Sr. Lectr. in Eng. Univ. Coll. of North Wales 1946-65; Prof. of Eng. McMaster Univ. 1965-81; Assoc. Trustee, Dove Cottage Trust, Grasmere, Eng.; Ed. Adviser "The Wordsworth Circle"; author "Wordsworth as Critic" 1969; ed., "Wordsworth's Preface to Lyrical Ballads" 1957; "Wordsworth & Coleridge, Lyrical Ballads 1798" 1967; "Wordsworth's Literary Criticism" 1974; co-ed. 'The Prose Works of William Wordsworth" 1974; numerous articles annotes William Wordsworth and Edmund Spenser; Can. Council Leave Fellow and Fellow, Inst. Advanced Studies in Humanities Univ. of Edinburgh 1973-74; SSHRCC Leave Fellow and John Simon Guggenheim Mem. Fellow 1980-81;

served with Brit. Army 1942-46, U.K., N. Africa, Italy, rank Capt.; mem. ACUTE; MLA; MHRA; Internat. Assn. Univ. Profs. Eng.; Victorian Studies Assn.; recreation: music; Home: 340 Elizabeth Place, Ancaster, Ont. L9C 3G3; Office: Hamilton, Ont. L8S 4L9.

OWENS, Rev. Joseph, C.Ss.R., M.S.D., F.R.S.C., (R.C.); b. Saint John, N.B., 17 Apl. 1908; s. Louis Michael and Josephine (Quinn) O.; e. St. Peter's Sch., Saint John, N.B., 1914-22; St. Mary's Coll., Brockville, Ont., 1922-27; St. Anne's, Montreal, Que., 1928-30; St. Alphonsus Semy., Woodstock, Ont., 1930-34; Pontifical Inst. of Mediaeval Studies, Toronto, Ont., 1944-48, M.S.D. (Mediaeval Studies) 1951; PROF. SCH. OF GRAD. STUDIES, UNIV. OF TORONTO since 1961; Staff mem., Pontifical Inst. of Mediaeval Studies, Toronto, since 1954; Mem., Edit. Bd. of "The Monist"; Parish Asst., St. Joseph's, Moose Jaw, Sask., 1934-35; St. Patrick's, Toronto, Ont., 1935-36; Lect. in Philos., St. Alphonsus Semy., Woodstock, Ont., 1936-40, 1948-51, 1953; Missionary, Dawson Creek, B.C., 1940-44; Lect., Accademia Alfonsiana, Rome, Italy, 1952-53; Visiting Lect., Assumption Univ., Windsor, Jan.-June, 1954; Asst. Prof., Univ. of Toronto, Assoc. Prof. 1954-61; Publications: "The Doctrine of Being in the Aristotelian Metaphysics", 3rd ed. 1978; "St. Thomas and the Future of Metaphysics", 1957; "A History of Ancient Western Philosophy", 1959; "An Elementary Christian Metaphysics", 1963; "An Interpretation of Existence", 1968; "The Wisdom and Ideas of St. Thomas Aquinas" (with E. Freeman), 1968; "The Philosophical Tradition of St. Michael's College, Toronto", 1979; "St. Thomas Aquinas on the Existence of God" 1980; critical reviews in various learned journs.; mem., Metaphys. Soc. of Am. (Pres. 1971-72); Am. Cath. Philos. Assn. (Pres. 1965-66); Candn. Philos. Assn.; Soc. for Ancient Greek Philos (Pres. 1971-73); Am. Philos. Assn.; rec'd. Hon. D.Litt. Mt. Allison 1975; recreations: swimming, tennis, hockey; Address: St. Patrick's Rectory, 141 McCaul St., Toronto, Ont. M5T 1W3

OXLEY, Loren Arthur, B.Arch., F.R.A.I.C.; b. Ottawa, Ont., 1917; s. late James Morrow and Elizabeth Harriet (May) O.; e. Upper Canada Coll.; Univ. of Toronto, Sch. of Arch., B.Arch. 1947; Columbia Univ.; m. Elizabeth Ruth, d. late Stanley B. Craig, Midlothian, Scot., 1944; children: Elizabeth Susan, Janet Barbara, James Craig; PARTNER McMURRICH & OXLEY; comns. for pub. and inst. bldgs. incl. chs., hosps. and univ. bldgs., in Toronto, Hamilton, Kitchener, Brantford, Barrie, Newmarket and other centres; served in 2nd World War, Lieut., R.C.E. in Canada, the Aleutians, Eng. and the Netherlands; Past Chrmn. Toronto Chapter, Ont. Assn. Arch.; Toronto Area Bldg. Code Comte.; City of Toronto Planning Bd.; Anglican; Clubs: Arts and Letters; recreation: tree farming; Home: 73 South Drive, Toronto, Ont. M4W 1R4; Office: 70 The Esplanade, Toronto, Ont. M5E 1R2

OZMON, Kenneth Lawrence, M.A., Ph.D.; educator; b. Portsmouth, Va. 4 Sept. 1931; s. Howard Augustine and Annie Josephine (Lynch) O.; e. St. Joseph's High Sch. (Portsmouth, Va.); St. Bernard Coll. (Ala.) B.A. 1955; Cath. Univ. of Am. M.A. 1963; Univ. of Me. Ph.D. 1968; m. Elizabeth Ann d. Raymond Morrison, Bangor, Me. 6 July 1968; two d. Angela Francene, Kendi Elizabeth; PRESIDENT, SAINT MARY'S UNIVERSITY, HALIFAX, since 1979; Dean of Arts, University of P.E.I. Assoc. Prof. and Chrmn. Dept. of Psychol. there since 1969; Teacher St. Bernard High Sch. 1955-57; Instr. St. Bernard Coll. 1960-62; Visiting Lectr. Marianopolis Coll. 1963-65; Lectr. St. Joseph's Teachers Coll. 1964-65; Discussion Leader Thomas More Inst. 1963-65; Asst. Prof. Cal. State Univ. Chico 1968-69; Gov. Univ. of P.E.I. 1974-76; Dir. Atlantic Inst. of Educ. 1976-79; Atlantic Research Centre on Mental Retardation 1977-79; mem. Nat. Council Canada. Human Rights Foundation; United Way of Halifax - Dartmouth (Bd. of Dirs.); United Way Community Volunteer Steering Comte. (Chmn.); AAU/MPHEC Finance Comte.;

author various articles prof. journs. and other publs.; mem. Candn. Assn. Mentally Retarded (Dir.); Candn. Psychol. Assn.; Candn. Assn. Deans Arts & Science (Secy.-Treas. 1973-76); Candn. Assn. Univ. Teachers (Vice Pres. 1970-72); Candn. Assn. Gerontol.; recreations: fishing, golf, running; Home: 5895 Gorsebrook Ave., Halifax, N.S., B3H 1G3

P

PACE, Hon. Leonard, Q.C., B.A., LL.B., M.L.A.; b. Glen Margaret, N.S., 27 Apl. 1928; s. Bruce H. and Eva (Graves) P.; e. Glen Margaret (N.S.) Elem. Sch.; Horton Acad., Wolfville, N.S.; Acadia Univ.; B.A. Dalhousie Univ., LL.B.; m. Jean Shirley, d. Lloyd W. McFadgen, 1951; children: Beverley Ann, Robert Leonard, David Bruce; JUSTICE OF THE SUPREME COURT OF NOVA SCOTIA, APPEAL DIVISION since 1978; Min. Highways (1972), Mines & i/c Communications (1973) N.S.; called to Bar of N.S. 1954; cr. Q.C. 1970; el. M.L.A. and apptd. Atty. Gen. & Min. Labour 1970; mem., Nova Scotia Barristers' Society; Candian Bar Association; Fed. Ins. Counsels; Freemason; Liberal; United Church; recreations: fishing, hunting, gardening; Club: Halifax; Home: Seabright, R.R. 1, Tantallon, Halifax Co., N.S. B0J 3J0; Office: Law Courts, Halifax, N.S.

PADDON, Hon. William Anthony, C.M., M.D., Dip.P.H., D.Sc.; b. Indian Harbour, Labrador 10 July 1914; s. Harry L., M.D. and Mina (Gilchrist) P.; e. The Lenox (Mass.) Sch.; Trinity Coll. Hartford, Conn. B.Sc. 1936, D.Sc. 1975; N.Y. State Med. Sch. (Dowstate) M.D.; Univ. of London Dip.P.H. 1957; Memorial Univ. Hon. Degree D.Sc. 1977; m. Sheila Mary d. Frank Fortescue, Loughton D2 Essex, Eng. 20 Sept. 1952; children: David F., Michael A. C., Thomas F., Elizabeth M.; LIEUTENANT GOVERNOR OF NFLD. AND LABRADOR since 1981; Dir., Northern Medical Services, Internat. Grenfell Assn., 1960-78, internship St. Luke's Hosp. N.Y. City 1940-42; Resident D2 Med. and Surg., Internat. Grenfell Assn. St. Anthony, Nfld. 1945; Med. Offr. in Charge, North West River, Labrador, Nfld.; served on various sch. bds. as mem. or chrmn. 32 yrs.; mem. Bd. Regents, Mem. Univ. Nfld. 1972-74; co-winner Royal Bank of Can. Award 1977; served with R.C.N. 1942-45, Surg. Lt. becoming Surg. Lt. Commdr.; author various prof. articles, papers; mem. Candn. Med. Assn.; Nfld. Med. Assn.; Coll. of Family Practice; Am. Thoracic Soc.; Liberal; Anglican; recreations: horticulture, carpentry, writing, marine zoology; Home: North West River, Labrador, Nfld. Government House, Military Rd., St. John's, Nfld.

PAGE, Donald Herman, F.C.G.A.; investment dealer; b. St. Thomas, Ont., 2 May 1933; s. late James Herman and Gertrude Georgina (Campbell) P.; e. Tyrconnell Pub. Sch., W. Elgin High Sch., St. Thomas, Ont., 1951; Westervelt Business Col., 1952; C.G.A. 1962; Univ. of W. Ont. Mang. Training Course, 1972; m. Marion Gertrude, d. late John Clarence Patterson, 22 Nov. 1952; children: Donald James, Gerald Richard, Paul Douglas, Andrew Patterson, Marion Elaine; EXTVE. VICE PRES. FINANCE AND ADM. & DIR., MIDLAND DOHERTY LIMITED; Dir., Midland Doherty Inc., N.Y.; joined Midland Securities Corp. Ltd. as Clk., London, Ont., 1952; Br. and H.O. Accounting, Money Market Desk, Stock Order Clk. 1954-62; apptd. Comptroller (on merger) 1963, Asst. Secy. 1965, Dir. 1969, Vice Pres. Finance and Adm., Compliance Offr. and Secy. 1971; merger of present firm 1974; mem. Boy Scout Assn. 1961-67; Treas., Kiwanis Music Festival Metrop. Toronto, 1966-67; N. York Baseball Assn. 1968-69 (Pres. 1970); Chrmn., Parkwoods Un. Ch. Central Bd., 1972; Toronto Stock Exchange Mem. Seat Holder 1971; elected to Bd. of Gov., Toronto Stock Exchange, 1981; mem., Cert. Gen. Acct's Assn. (Bd. of

Govs. Ont. 1970; Ont. mem. Nat. Educ. Council 1971-74 and Pres. 1976); Nat. Pres., Candn. Cert. Gen. Acct's 1979-80 (Life mem. 1976); apptd. to Commodities Futures Bd. of Ont. Securities Comn. 1979; apptd. to Bd. of Trustees, Doctors' Hospital, 1980; Invest. Dealers' Assn. Can. (Financial Adm. Sec. 1966, Chrmn. 1971-72, Ont. Dist. Extve. 1971-72); Queen's Jubilee Medal 1978; Freemason; P. Conservative; United Church; recreations: tennis, golf, curling, farming; Clubs: Donalda; Empire; Kiwanis; Home: 26 Beveridge Dr., Don Mills, Ont. M3A 1N9; Office: Toronto Dominion Centre, Toronto, Ont. M5K 1B5

PAGE, Francis Hilton, M.A., D.D.; educator; b. Toronto Ont., 11 Apl. 1905; s. Francis Harold and Charlotte Louisa Maria (Shepherd) P.; e. Univ. of Toronto, B.A. 1925, M.A. 1927; Harvard Univ.; Univ. Coll., London, Eng.; D.D. Pine Hill Divinity Hall, 1966; m. Lilian Ashmere, d. Arthur Stanley Barnstead, Halifax, N.S., 6 Nov. 1931; Vice-Pres., Univ. of King's Coll. 1959-69; Acting Pres. and Vice Chancellor 1969-70; Prof. of Philosophy; formerly Chrmn., Dept. of Psychol. 1948-62; Chrmn. Dept. of Philos. 1962-71; Bd. of Govrs., Dartmouth Academy 1962-75; Inst. of Human Values, St. Mary's Univ., Halifax; Hon. Life Fellow, Candn. Psychol. Assn.; Home: 1135 Rockcliffe St., Halifax, N.S. B3H 3Y7

PAGE, Garnet Thomas, B.A., F.C.I.C.; association executive; b. Halifax, N.S., 28 Oct. 1920; s. William Thomas and Mabel Lauretta (Coolin) P.; e. Univ. of Sask., B.A. (Chem.) 1940; PRES., COAL COAL MINING RESEARCH CENTRE since 1978; part-time Instr., Chem. Dept., Univ. of Sask., 1938-40; Instr. at N.P.A.M. Camps in Chem. Warfare (summers) 1937-40; served in 2nd World War with Candn. Army Active Force, 1940-46; retired with rank of Lieut.-Col.; Gen. Mgr. and Secy., The Chem. Inst. of Canada, 1946-57; Gen. Secy., Engn. Inst. Can., 1958-68; Visiting Prof., Hist. of Science, Univ. of Ottawa, 1954-56; Candn. Del. to UNESCO Confs., 1946, '48, '49, '50, '52, '54, '56; mem., U.S. Nat. Comn. for UNESCO, 1948-55; Consultant on UNESCO and Canada Council, since 1951; mem., Candn. Comte. on Brussels World Fair (1958), since 1955; mem., Advisory Council on Prof. Manpower, Dept. of Labour, since 1956; Chrmn., Nat. Adv. Comte. on Technol. Educ. 1961-65; Nat. Tech. & Vocational Training Adv. Council, 1965; Consultant to OECD 1964-65; named Dir., Pilot Projects Br., Dept. Manpower, Can. 1966; Dir. Gen. Tech. Services & Special Projects Div., Dept. Regional Econ. Expansion, Can. 1968; Pres., Coal Assn. of Canada, 1974-78; has served in the Dept. of Trade and Comm. on various comtes. and in various advisory capacities; Mem., Intern. Comte. for Coal Research; Candn. Extve. Comtes. of World Energy Conference and World Mining Congress; Can.-Japan Business Cooperation Comte.; Canada-Korea Business Council; Candn. Comte. for UNESCO "Man and the Biosphere" project; Publications: numerous papers, reports on U.N. and UNESCO affairs, chem. indust., educ., etc.; mem., Am. Chem. Soc.; Am. Soc. of Civil Engrs.; Am. Soc. of Mech. Engrs.; Assn. of Tech. Writers & Editors; Business Newspapers Assn.; Candn. Council for Reconstr. through UNESCO (Treas. 1948-52); Candn. Educ. Assn.; Candn. Film Inst. (Dir., 1954-55; mem. of Council since 1946); Candn. Inst. Chem.; Inst. of Trade Assn. Extves.; La Société Chimique de France (Paris); Soc. of Chem. Industry (U.K.), The Wine & Food Soc. (U.K.); awarded Silver Medal, Univ. of Turin, 1950; Coronation Medals, 1937, 1953; Medal from Pope Pius XII 1950; Medal of Greek Red Cross, 1953; Queen Elizabeth II 25th Anniv. Medal; Pasteur Medal Inst. Pasteur, Paris, 1948; Hon. Vice-Consul of France in Calgary; recreations: painting, travel, people; Clubs: The Ranchmen's, Calgary; Office: Suite 210, 505 - 5th Ave. S.W., Calgary, Alta. T2P 0N8

PAGE, Patricia Kathleen (Mrs. William Arthur Irwin); writer, painter; b. Eng., 23 Nov. 1916; d. late Maj. Gen. Lionel F. and Rose Laura (Whitehouse) P.; came to Can.

1919; e. St. Hilda's Sch. for Girls, Calgary, Alta.; m. Wm. Arthur Irwin, 1950; author of "The Sun and the Moon", 1944; "As Ten As Twenty", 1946; "The Metal and the Flower", 1954; "Cry Ararat! — Poems New and Selected", 1967; "The Sun and the Moon and Other Fictions" 1973; "Poems-Selected and New" 1974; also poems, short stories in various magazines and anthologies; ed. "To Say the Least" (anthology of short poems) 1979; "Evening Dance of the Grey Flies" (poems and short story), 1981; winner of Oscar Blumenthal Award (Poetry: Chicago) 1944; Governor-General Award for Poetry, 1954; as P. K. Irwin has held one-man shows in Mexico and Canada, been represented in various group shows and has work in the National Gallery of Canada, the Art Gallery of Ontario and many others; Offr. Order of Can., 1977; Address: 3260 Exeter Road, Victoria, B.C. V8R 6H6

PAIKIN; Marnie Marina Suzanne, B.A., LL.D.; b. Toronto, Ont. 13 Apl. 1936; d. Jack George and Shirley Ruth (Sutin) Sibulash; e. John R. Wilcox Pub. Sch. and Vaughan Rd. Coll. Inst. Toronto 1954; Univ. of W. Ont. B.A. 1958; Univ. of Toronto LL.D. 1981; m. Lawrence Sidney Paikin, Hamilton, Ont. 18 Dec. 1956; children: Steven Hillel, Jeffrey Shalom; Pres. Paikin Steel Products Ltd.; Dir. Southam Inc.; mem., Ont. Council on University Affairs 1981-84; Ont. Council of Health 1980-83; Bd. of Trustees, Toronto General Hospital 1980-84; Governing Council Univ. of Toronto 1972-80 (Chrmn. 1976-80); Trustee, Royal Ont. Museum 1976-80; McMaster Univ. Med. Centre 1970-78; Dir. Hamilton Foundation (Vice-Pres. 1979-80, Pres. 1980-81); McMaster Univ. Med. Centre Foundation 1976-78; Hamilton Performing Arts Corp. 1972-77, Chrmn. 1973-75; Temple Anshe Sholom 1970-74; Ont. Fed. Symphony Orchestras 1972-75; Lynwood Hall 1969-73; Hamilton & Region Arts Council 1971-73; Hamilton Philharmonic Orchestra Soc. 1968-73, Pres. 1969-71; Chrmn. Un. Jewish Welfare Fund Hamilton, Women's Div. 1976; Vice Chrmn. Hospitality Comte. Grey Cup Festival 1972; Pres. Deborah Sisterhood Temple Anshe Sholom 1970-72; Secy. Philharmonic Children Hamilton 1967; Social Chrmn. Hillfield Strathallan Parents' Assn. 1967; Life mem. Hamilton Hadassah Organ.; mem. Steering Comte. Hamilton-Wentworth Dist. Health Council 1977-78; Celebrations Comte. City of Hamilton 1972-76 (125 Anniversary Comte. 1971); Mgr. Training Dept. Simpson's London Ltd. 1958-59; rec'd 'Outstanding Woman' Award Prov. Ont. 1975; Queen's Silver Jubilee Medal 1978; regular columnist restaurant reviews 'The Entertainer Newspaper' Hamilton 1974-76; Jewish; recreations: tennis, music, sports; Club: Hillside Racquet; Home: 868 Danforth Place, Burlington, Ont. L7T 1S2

PAINE, Paul Britton, Q.C., B.A.; trust company executive; b. 1917; e. Univ. of B.C., B.A. 1938; CHRMN. AND PRES., MONTREAL TRUST CO.; Vice Chrmn. & Dir. Montreal Assur. Co.; Laurentide Financial Corp. Ltd.; Dir., Power Corp. of Can. Ltd.; Shawinigan Industries Ltd.; Trans-Can. Corp. Fund; Laurentide Acceptance Corp.; Commonwealth Indust. Bank Ltd., Bahamas; Warnaco of Can. Ltd.; Candn. Overseas Packaging (GB) Ltd.; called to Bar of B.C. 1941; cr. Q.C. 1960; Pres. and C.E.O. Montreal Trust Co. 1973; former Bencher, Law Soc. B.C.; Clubs: St. James's; Mount Royal; Toronto; Manitoba; Vancouver; Mount Bruno Golf & Country; Shaughessy Golf & Country; Country Club of Florida; Office: 1 Place Ville Marie, Montreal, Que. H3B 3L6

PALLET, John, Q.C., B.A.; barrister and solicitor; b. Dixie, Ont., 15 Feb. 1921; s. Leslie Howard and Gladys Grace (Lesley) P.; e. Dixie (Ont.) Pub. Sch.; Port Credit (Ont.) High Sch.; Univ. of Toronto, B.A., June 1941; Osgoode Hall Law Sch., Toronto, Ont.; m. Mary Virginia, d. J. H. S. Leuty, Cooksville, Ont., 20 Dec. 1947; children: James McCormack, Megan Jane, Bruce Cameron, Drew Malcolm, Wesley Newman; PARTNER, PALLETT VALO, BARSKY & HUTCHESON called to the Bar of Ont., 1948;

appointed Queen's Council, 1959; served in 2nd World War with Candn. Army Hdqrs., and with Gov.-Gen. Horse Guards in Italy and N.W. Europe, 1942-46; Mentioned in Despatches; 1st el. to H. of C. in by-el. for Peel, 22 Mar. 1954; re-el. g.e. 1957, 1958; def. g.e. 1962; Parlty. Observer to U.N., 1956-57; Chrmn. of Candn. Del. to NATO Parlty. Confs. in Paris, 1957 and 1958; Chrmn. of Banking & Comm. Comte., H. of C., 22nd Parl.; apptd. Chief Govt. Whip, Jan. 1959; Parlty. Secy. to Min. of Trade & Comm., Nov. 1959; apptd. a 2nd Parlty. Secy. to Prime Minister (cont. as Chief Whip in H. of C.), Nov. 1960; mem., Candn. Bar Assn.; Bencher of Law Soc. of Upper Canada 1972-79; P. Conservative; C. of E.; Home: 5 Mississauga Rd., Mississauga, Ont.; Office: Mississauga Exec. Centre, Mississauga, Ont. L4Z 1H8

PALLIE, Wazir, M.B., B.S., D.Phil., (Prim.) F.R.C.S.; educator; b. Colombo, Ceylon 12 March 1922; s. Arifin Ekin and Hamida (Rahim) P.; e. St. Clare's Coll. and Royal Coll. Colombo; Univ. of Ceylon M.B., B.S. 1945; Oriel Coll. Oxford Univ. D. Phil. 1955; m. Wenche Elisabeth d. Erling Kare Michelsen, Bergen, Norway 24 Nov. 1953; children: Kare, Sven, Olaf; PROF. AND CHRMN. OF ANAT. McMASTER UNIV. since 1975; Residency, Gen. Hosp. Colombo 1945-47; Dist. Med. Offr./Med. Offr. of Health Ceylon 1948-51; Tutor and Demonst. Oxford Univ. 1951-55; Foundation Head, Dept. Anat. Faculty of Med. Peradeniya 1961-62; Foundation Chrmn. and Prof. of Med. Kuala Lumpur 1962-68; Prof. of Anat. McMaster Univ. since 1969; research positions Oxford Univ. 1951-55, Univ. Bonn 1955, Univ. Cal. Los Angeles 1957-58, Karolinska Inst. Stockholm 1965, Kumamoto, Japan 1966, Ceylon, Malaysia and Can.; rec'd Smith-Mundt and Fulbright Scholarship-Research Fellowship 1957-58; Research Grantee Nat. Inst. Health USA since 1977; co-author "The Artery" 1978; author over 40 publs. med. and scient. journs.; Past Pres. Ceylon Assn. Advanc. Science; Life mem. Ceylon Med. Assn.; mem. Candn. Assn. Anats.; Am. Assn. Anats.; Royal Soc. Med. (Affiliate); World Fed. Neurol. (Commr. Comparative Neuroanat.); Health Sci. Communications Assn.; Can. Amateur Music Assn.; Liberal; recreations: golf, tennis, music (violin playing); Clubs: Burlington Tennis; Royal Selangor Golf; Home: 3112 Woodward Ave., Burlington, Ont. L7N 2M4; Office: 1200 Main St. W., Hamilton, Ont. L8S 4J9.

PALLISTER, A. E.; B.Sc.; geophysicist; b. Edmonton, Alta., 28 Oct. 1927; s. Ernest Henry and Beatrice Amelia (Shore) P.; e. Univ. of Alta., B.Sc. 1948; m. LaVonne Eunice, d. late Maynard S. Larsen, 28 Sept. 1953; children: Jeffrey, Cynthia, Kent; PRES., PALLISTER RESOURCE MANGMT. LTD. since 1973; Assoc., Devonian Gp. of Charitable Foundations, Calgary since 1974; mem. & Past Chrmn., Veterinary Infectious Disease Organ., Univ. Sask., Saskatoon; mem. & Past Chrmn., Centre for Cold Ocean Resources Engn., Memorial Univ., St. John's, Nfld.; Chrmn., CanOCean Resources Ltd.; mem. Bd. Dirs., NOVA an Alta. Corp. (formerly Alta. Gas Trunk Line Co. Ltd.); Algas Resources Ltd.; Chrmn., Alta. and NWT Regions of Enterprise Devel. Bd., Indust., Trade and Commerce; mem. Bd. of Dirs. Husky Oil Ltd.; Chrmn. Bd. of Adv., Water Resources Project; Vice-Pres., Science and Devel., Kenting Ltd., 1967 to present; with United Geophysical Co., Calif. and Persian Gulf 1948; Party Chief, Century Geophysical Corp., Canada 1950; Party Chief, Sub-Surface Exploration Ltd. 1952; Asst. Chief Geophysicist, Canadian Seaboard Oil Co. 1954; Tech. Operations Mgr., Accurate Exploration Ltd. 1958; Pres., A. E. Pallister Consultants Ltd. (now Ken-Quest Exploration) 1962; served in R.C.N.(R), Sub-Lt.; mem. (Vice-Chrmn.) Science Council of Can.; Alta. Soc. Petroleum Geols. (Past Pres.); Am. Assn. Petroleum Geols., Assn. Prof. Engrs., Geols. and Geophysicists Alta.; Candn. Soc. Exploration Geophysicists; European Assn. Exploration Geophysicists; Naval Offrs. Assn.; mem., Bd. Dirs., Calgary Philharmonic Soc., Bd. Trustees, Candn. Veterinary Research Trust Funds; Past Dir.,

Univ. of Calgary Alumni Assn.; 1980 D.Sc. (Hon. c.) Memorial Univ. of Nfld.; Sr. Vice-Chrmn. Campaign Co-ordinator, United Fund 1971 Campaign; named "Oilman of the Year" by Oilweek Mag. 1970; has organized multidiscliplne "Quest" mineral and petroleum exploration programs in Candn. Arctic; author and co-author of numerous scient. papers; Anglican; recreations: tennis, sailing; Clubs: Calgary Petroleum; Glencoe; Postmasters International (Past Internat. Dir.); Home: 4407 Britannia Dr., S.W., Calgary, Alta. T2S 1J4; Office: 700 — 6 Ave. S.W., Calgary, Alta. T2P 0T8

PALMAS, Mt. Rev. Angelo, L.Ph., D.Th., D.C.L., D.Cn.L.; archbiship (R.C.); b. Villanova Monteleone, Italy 21 Dec. 1914; e. Primary Sch. Villanova Monteleone, Sardinia; Minor Semy. of Alghero; Pontifical Semy. Cuglieri D.Th.; Gregorian Univ. Rome L. Ph.; Lateran Pontifical Univ. Rome D.C.L., D.Cn.L.; APOSTOLIC PRO-NUNCIO IN CAN. since 1975; o. 1938; Secretariat of State 1946; Secy. Apostolic Nunciature in Belgium 1947, Auditor Switzerland 1952, Auditor and Counsellor Lebanon 1954; Secretariat of State 1960; o. Archbishop 1964 and apptd. Apostolic Del. in Vietnam; Apostolic Nuncio in Colombia, S.A. 1969; Address: Apostolic Nunciature, 724 Manor Ave., Ottawa, Ont. K1M 0E3.

PALMER, Keith E.; banker; b. Ottawa, Ont. 17 Dec. 1927; SR. VICE PRES. AND DEPY. GEN. MGR. WORLD CORPORATE BANKING, BANK OF MONTREAL, 1981- ; Mgr. Credit Man./Sask. Div. present Bank 1971, Mgr. Corporate Credit 1973, Sr. Mgr. Credit Que. Div. 1974, Vice Pres. & Mgr. Toronto Br. 1975, Vice Pres. Corporate Banking 1977, Sr. Vice Pres. 1978, Sr. Vice Pres. & Depy. Gen. Mgr. Corporate Banking 1980; Office: (P.O. Box 1) 1 First Canadian Place, Toronto, Ont. M5X 1A1

PALMER, Rev. Roland Ford, B.A., L.Th., D.D. (Ang.); b. London, Eng., 12 Dec. 1891; s. Edw. and Anne (Andrewes-Ford) P.; e. Trinity Coll., Univ. of Toronto, B.A. 1916, L.Th. 1914, D.D.; o. Deacon 1916; Priest 1917; Rector at Englehart, Ont., and St. George's Ch., Port Arthur, Ont.; entered Novitiate, Soc. of St. John the Evangelist, at Cambridge, Mass., 1919; professed vows, 1921; served as Novice Master in U.S. for two yrs.; Superior of the Order, San Francisco, Cal., 1926-28; Provincial Superior, Soc. of St. John the Evangelist in Can., 1928-49; at the invitation of Bishop Rocksborough Smith of Algoma, came with two others to organize a community life for men in the Ch. of Eng. in Can. at Emsdale, Ont., removed seat of the order to Bracebridge, Ont., 1929; took lead in building western house of Soc., 1947; Diocesan Missioner of Algoma, (1952); apptd. Canon, St. Luke's Cath., Sault Ste. Marie, 1955; mem. of Gen. Synod of Ch. of Eng. in Can. (active on Comtes. on Re-union & Prayer Book Revision); apptd. Hon. Arch-priest of the continuing Anglican Ch. 1979; helped clergy and people of Coptic Orthodox Ch. who came from Egypt to Can. and U.S.; assisted in transl. of Coptic liturgy into English; Publications: "Good News"; "Our Mother's Song"; "Come and Worship"; "At One"; "His Worthy Praise", 1960; "Readiness and Decency", 1961; "The Catechist's Handbook", 1962; and a number of articles and booklets; Address: Apt. 303, 845 Burdett Ave., Victoria, B.C. V8W 1B3

PANABAKER, Frank Shirley, R.C.A.; artist; landscape painter; b. Hespeler, Ont., 16 Aug. 1904; s. David Norman and Sarah Elizabeth (Anderson) P.; e. Hespeler Pub. Sch.; Coll. Inst., Galt; Valparaiso Univ.; studied art with F. McGillivray Knowles, R.C.A. at Ont. Coll. of Art, Grand Central Sch. of Art, New York, and Art Students' League there; m. Katherine Marks, d. W. S. Connolly, Morrisburg, Ont. 1927; awarded Dow Prize of Montreal Art Assn., 1930; has exhibited at Nat. Acad. Design; Allied Artists' of Am.; Roy. Candn. Acad., and other Candn. socs.; is rep. in public galleries and many private collections; author of "Reflected Lights", 1957, Trustee,

Nat. Gallery of Can., 1959-66; Address: 375 Wilson, Ancaster, Ont. L9G 3L3

PANABAKER, John Harry, M.A.; insurance executive; b. Preston, Ont., 31 July 1928; s. John Russel and Violet (Steel) P.; e. High Sch., Preston, Ont.; McMaster Univ., B.A. 1950, M.A. 1954, LL.O. 1981; m. Janet Mary, d. late David G. Dickson, 24 April 1954; children: David, James, Leslie, Debra, Ian; PRES. & C.E.O. MUTUAL LIFE ASSURANCE CO. OF CANADA since 1973 and a Dir. since 1971; Chrmn., R.D.C. Property Services Ltd.; Mu-Cana Investment Counselling Ltd.; Extve. Financial Counselling Ltd.; Dir., mem. Extve. Comte., Chmn., Compensation and Human Resources Comte., Canada Trustco Mortgage Co.; Canada Trust Co.; and mem. Exec. and Audit Comtes., Dir. Maple Leaf Mills, Toronto; joined Securities Dept. of present Co. 1950; apptd. Asst. Treas. 1954, Extve. Asst. 1960, Asst. to Pres. 1962, Treas. Jan 1964, Vice-Pres. and Treas. Dec. 1964, Vice-Pres. Investments and Corp. Services 1968, Executive Vice President, 1969, Co-Chmn., Long Range Planning Comte.; Life Office Mang. Assn. (Dir. 1971-74, 1976-79, Chrmn. 1977-78); Vice-Pres., Bd. of Dir., Chrmn. Comte. on the Future of the Pension System, and Past Chrmn., Public Relations Comte., Canadian Life Insurance Assn.; Past President, Freeport Hosp. Kitchener, Ont.; Past Chrmn. & current mem. Bd. Govs. McMaster Univ.; Presbyterian; Clubs: Westmount Golf & Country, Kitchener; National, Toronto; Toronto; Home: 36 Buttonwood Dr., Kitchener, Ont. N2M 4R1; Office: 227 King St. S., Waterloo, Ont. N2J 4C5

PANET-RAYMOND, Bernard, B.A., B.Eng.; company executive; b. Montreal, Que., 1 Feb. 1917; s. late Boisdoré and Lizette (Painchaud) P-R.; e. St. Leo's Acad., Westmount, Que. 1927; Coll. Jean de Brébeuf, B.A. 1937; McGill Univ., B.Eng. 1947; m. Hélène, d. late Hon. Pierre F. Casgrain and late Sen. Thérèse Casgrain, 1 May 1943; one s. Pierre; PRES., O.R.C. CANADA INC. since 1981; Chairman and Dir. Manicouagan Power Co.; Phillips Cables Ltd.; Dir., Q.N.S. Paper Co. Ltd.; Québec-Téléphone; Organization Resources Counselors Inc., Liquid carbonic Can. Ltd.; Trust Général du Canada; served with R.C.A. and R.C.E. 1942-45; rank Capt.; Past Pres., Candn. Chamber Commerce; Past Chrmn., Indust. Relations Sec., Candn. Pulp & Paper Assn.; mem. Corp. Engrs. Que.; Engn. Inst. Can.; R. Catholic; recreation: golf; Clubs: Mont Royal C.C.; Mount Bruno; Home: 3524 Avenue de Musée, Montreal, Que. H3G 2C7; Office: 3 Place Ville Marie, Montreal, Que. H3B 2E3

PANITCH, Leo Victor, M.Sc., Ph.D.; educator; b. Winnipeg, Man. 3 May 1945; s. Max and Sarah (Hoffman) P.; e. St. John's High Sch. Winnipeg 1962 (Valedictorian); Univ. of Man. B.A. (Hons.) 1967; London Sch. of Econ. & Pol. Science M.Sc. (Econ.) 1968, Ph.D. (Govt.) 1974; m. Melanie Risë d. David Pollock, Winnipeg, Man. 24 Aug. 1967; children: Maxim Serge, Vida Mira; ASSOC. PROF. OF POL. SCIENCE, CARLETON UNIV. 1977- ; Lectr. present Univ. 1972, Asst. Prof. 1974; Gen. Co-Ed. "State and Economic Life" series; Co-Founder and Extve. Bd. mem. "Studies in Political Economy"; contrib. Ed. "Canadian Dimension"; author "Social Democracy and Industrial Militancy" 1976; ed. and co-author "The Canadian State" 1977; various articles pol. science; mem. Movement for an Independent & Socialist Can. 1973-75; mem. Extve. Ottawa Comte. for Labour Action 1975- ; mem. Candn. Pol. Science Assn.; Comte. on Socialist Studies; Home: 180 Belmont Ave., Ottawa, Ont. K1S 0V8; Office: Colonel By Dr., Ottawa, Ont. K1S 5B6.

PAPE, Gordon Kendrew, B.A.; publisher; author; b. San Francisco, Cal. 16 March 1936; s. late Clifford Baume and late Lethe Mary (Chenevert) P.; came to Can. 1950; e. Three Rivers High Scho., Trois Rivieres, Que. 1954; Carleton Univ. B.A. 1959; Univ. of Toulouse 1960-61 (Rotary Foundation Fellowship); m. Shirley Ann d. late Joseph Peter Cloutier 5 May 1962; children: Kimberley Anne, Kendrew Gordon, Deborah Margaret; PRESIDENT AND PUBLISHER, "TODAY MAGAZINE" since 1980; Dir. Today Magazine Inc.; Educ. Writer "The Gazette" Montreal 1961-63, Que. Bureau Chief 1963-66, Partly. Corr. Ottawa 1966-70, Assoc. Ed. Montreal 1973-74; Bureau Chief, Southam News Service, London, Eng. 1970-73; Asst. to Publisher, "Financial Times of Canada" 1974-76; Publisher, "The Canadian" mag. 1976-79; Publisher, "Canadian Weekend" Magazine 1979-80; Host CBC Radio "Capital Report" 1968-70; rec'd Heritage Can. Communications Award 1976; Candn. Wine Taster Yr. 1975 Opimian Soc.; co-author "Montreal at the Crossroads" 1975; "Chain Reaction" 1978; "The Scorpion Sanction", 1980; "The Music Wars", 1982; numerous newspaper and mag. articles nat. and internat. topics; mem. Mag. Assn. Can. (Vice-Chmn., Dir. & Chrmn. Educ. and Exec. Comte.); Nat. Mag Awards Foundation (Pres. & Dir.); Internat. Wine & Food Soc.; Opimian Soc.; Protestant; recreations: fishing, golf, reading, skin diving, oenology; Clubs: Donalda; Rockingham Fish & Game; Wig & Pen (London); Home: 372 Woodsworth Rd., Willowdale, Ont. M2L 2T6; Office: 2180 Yonge St., Suite 1702, Toronto, Ont. M4S 3A2.

PAPINEAU-COUTURE, Jean, O.C. (1968), B.A., B.Mus.; musician; b. Outremont, Que., 12 Nov. 1916; (grandson of Guillaume C., one of the first Candn. composers and conductors); s. Armand and Marie-Anne (Dostaler) P-C.; e. Coll. St. Ignace; Coll. Jean de Brébeuf, B.A. 1938; New England Conservatory of Music, B.Mus. 1943; m. Isabelle, d. Dr. Joseph Baudouin, 15 June 1944; children: Nadia, Ghilaine, Francois; Prof. of Theoretical Subjects at Conservatoire de Musique d'Art Dramatique de la P.Q., 1946-64; Prof., Faculty of Music, Univ. of Montreal since 1953, Dean of the Faculty of Music, 1968-73; mem. of Bd. of Dirs., Canadian Music Center and of The Candn. Music Council; Past Pres., Montreal Br. of Les Jeunesses Musicales du Canada; Candn. League of Composers; Pres. Humanities Research Council, 1977-78; Prix Denise-Pelletier 1981; since 1942 has written and publ. many musical works; Roman Catholic; Home: 912 Dunlop Ave., Outremont, Que. H2V 2W8

PAQUET, Gilles, B. Phil., M.A., F.R.S.C.; economist; b. Québec City, Qué. 19 July 1936; s. Charles Noel and Rosette (Marois) P.; e. Laval Univ. B.A. 1956, B. Phil. 1956, M.A. 1960; Queen's Univ. Doctoral studies 1960-62; m. Muriel Moisan 21 Oct. 1958; children: Pascale, Valérie; DEAN, FACULTY OF ADMINISTRATION, UNIV. OF OTTAWA since 1981; Dean of Grad. Studies and Research, Carleton Univ. 1973-79; Chrmn. of Econ. Carleton Univ. 1969-72; Research Dir. Special Senate Comte. on Science Policy 1968-70; Chrmn. Consumer Research Council 1974-75; Consultant to O.E.C.D. 1974-76; Sec.-Treas., Cdn. Econ. Assoc. 1967-81; rec'd O.C.U.F.A. Teaching Award 1973; co-author "Patronage et pouvoir dans le Bas Canada au tournant du XIX siècle" 1973; Ed. "The Multinational Firm and the Nation State" 1972; co-ed. "Urban Studies: A Canadian Perspective" 1968; author various articles regional devel., econ. hist., regulation of socio-econ. systems; recreations: reading, biking, hiking; Club: Cercle Universitaire d'Ottawa; Home: 18 Woodlawn Ave., Ottawa, Ont. K1S 2S9; Office: 115 Wilbrod St., Ottawa, Ont. K1N 9B5.

PAQUET, Jean-Guy, B.A.Sc., M.Sc., Ph.D., F.R.S.C.; educator; b. Montmagny, Qué. 5 Jan. 1938; s. Laurent W. and Louisianne (Coulombe) P.; e. Laval Univ. B.A.Sc. 1959, Ph.D. 1963; Ecole nationale supérieure de l'aéronautique Paris M.Sc. 1960; RECTOR, LAVAL UNIV. since 1977; Assoc. Prof. of Elect. Engn. Laval Univ. 1967, Prof. 1971, Head of Dept. 1967-69, Vice Dean (Research) Faculty of Science & Engn. 1969-72; Vice Rector (Acad.) 1972-77; Special Asst. to Vice Pres. (Scient.) Nat. Research Council of Can. 1971-72; Pres. Conf. of Rectors and Princs. Que. Univs. 1979-81; Bd. of Associa-

tion des universités partiellement ou entièrement de langue française 1981- ; Inst. of Cdn. Bankers 1980- ; Interamer. Org. for Higher Educ. 1980- ; Hockey Canada 1979- ; Pres., Corp. of Centre hospitalier de l'Univ. Laval 1976- ; Bd. of Observatoire astronomique du Quebec 1975-77; Dir., Innovation Mgmt. Inst. of Can. 1974-79; mem. Bd. Assn. Univs. & Colls. Can.; Assn. Canadienne-Française pour l'Avancement des Sciences 1969-71; mem. Council Qué. Univs. 1973-77; Pres. Assn. Scient., Engn. & Technol. Community Can. 1975-76; Special Task on Research & Devel. Science Council Can. since 1976; Extve., Candn. Assn. Univ. Research Adms. since 1974; Fellowships: French Govt. 1959, Nat. Research Council Can. 1961, 1964-77, Nat. Science Foundation 1964, Que. Govt. 1975, Defence Research Bd. Can. 1965-76; Fellow, Royal Soc. of Canada 1978; Amer. Assn. for Advancement of Science 1981; author 2 books and over 50 publs. scient. journs.; mem. Order Que. Engrs.; Inst. Elect. & Electronic Engrs.; Am. Soc. Engn. Educ.; Candn. Research Mang. Assn.; Am. Assn. Advanc. Science; Innovation Mang. Inst. Can.; Soc. Research Adms.; Inst. d'admin. publique du Canada; Assn. Canadienne des Administrateurs de Recherche Universitaire; New York Academy of Science; Amer. Mangt. Assn.; Assn. of the Scientific, Engineering, and Tech. Community of Can.; Assn. canadienne-française pour l'avancement des sciences; R. Catholic; recreations: jogging, tennis, golf, skiing; Clubs: Cercle universitaire de Qué.; Club de golf de Cap-Rouge; Confrérie de la Chaine des Rotisseurs; Home: 1517 rue Commerciale, St-Romuald d'Etchemin, Qué. G6W 1Z6; Office: Laval Univ., Québec, Qué. G1K 7P4.

PAQUIN, Roger; transportation executive and administrator; b. Trois-Rivières, Que., 3 Aug. 1927; s. Lucien and Marguerite (Lord) P.; e. Elementary Sch., Trois-Rivières; Loyola Coll., Montreal; Laval Univ.; Sch. Business Adm.; m. Lucille, d. Mrs. Rose Soublière; 8 Aug. 1960; three d., Suzanne, Madeleine, Nicole; PRESIDENT, LOGISTEC CORPORATION since 1969; Chrmn. of the Bd.: Bulkmar Canada Inc.; Ramsey Greig & Co. Ltd.; Les Industries A.C. Davie Inc.; J. C. Malone & Co. Ltd.; Termino Corp.; Malone Marine Agency Ltd.; International Terminal Operators Ltd.; Cullen Stevedoring Co. Ltd.; Logistec Navigation Inc.; March Shipping Corp.; March Shipping Ltd.; Sun Fly/Cruise Inc.; Technitransport International Inc.; Aquatrans Ltd.; Cullen Terminals Ltd.; Logistec International Ltd.; Logistec Investments Inc.; March Chartering Limited; March Shipping Passenger Services Limited; March Terminals Ltd.; Maritime terminals Inc.; Moorings (Trois Riviéres) Ltd.; SABB (Montreal) Inc. Services Terrokon Inc.; Mercator Travel Inc.; commenced as Wharf Supt., Three Rivers Shipping Co. Ltd., Trois-Rivières 1950; Pres. and Gen. Mgr., Quebec Terminals Ltd. 1952-68; Past Pres., Que. Traffic Club Inc.; R. Catholic; Clubs: Garrison (Quebec); St. James (Montreal); Whitlock Golf & Country; Lake of Two Mountains Hunt; Quebec Traffic; Home: 3501 Redpath St., McGregor Place, Montreal, Que. H3G 2G7; Office: 360 St. Jacques St., 15th Fl., Montreal, Que. H2Y 1P5

PARADIS, François Pierre, B.A.; executive; b. Montreal, Que. 29 Aug. 1919; e. Elem. and Secondary Schs. Montreal; Brébeuf Coll., B.A.; m. Raymonde Hebert 18 Oct. 1947; children: Raymond, Louise, Robert, Francine; SR. VICE PRES. AND GEN. MGR. (QUE.), THE ROYAL BANK OF CANADA, QUE. since 1978; previously Sr. Vice Pres., IAC Ltd., Toronto; Dir., Cdn. Council for Christians and Jews; Quebec Industrial Innovation Centre; Cdn. Bankers Assn., Quebec Comte.; CIREM; C.D. Howe Inst., Regional Comte.; Treas., La Chambre de Commerce de la Prov. de Québec; Clubs: St.-Denis (Secy.-Treas.); Home: 38 Ile Roussin, Laval sur le Lac, Quebec, H7R 1E7; Office: P.O. Box 6001, Montreal, Que. H3C 3A9

PARADIS, Lieut.-Gen. Jean-Jacques, C.M.M., O.St.J., C.D., B.A.; army officer (retired); b. Montreal, Que. 7 Nov. 1928; s. Louis A. and Marie Anne (Déry) P.; e. Private Sch. Val-Dombre, Chambly Canton, Que.; Coll. de Montréal; Coll. Jean de Brebeuf, B.A. 1948; m. Margaret, d. Albert Gosselin 26 May 1956; children: Dominique, Marguerite; DIR., INTERNAT. MARKETING, LES INDUSTRIES VALCARTIER INC.; Offr. Cadet 1948, enrolling as Lieut. in Vandoos (R22eR) 1950; posted 2nd Bn R22eR Aug. 1950, Korea 1951-52; Winter Warfare and Airborne Training 1952; Staff Capt. A&Q Valcartier 1953; Airborne 2 Bn R22eR 1956; Staff Capt. HQ 4 Candn. Inf. Brigade Germany 1957; Second in Command Co. 3 Bn R22eR, Europe 1958-59; Capt. Adj. 3 Bn 1960; Maj. Co. Commdr. 2 Bn R22eR 1961; Staff Coll. Kingston, Ont. 1963-65; apptd. Brigade Maj. HQ 3rd Candn. Inf. Brigade Gp Gagetown, N.B. 1965; Lieut.-Col. C.O. 3 Bn R22eR 1966-68; Directing Staff and Depy. Commandant Staff Coll. and promoted Col. 1969-70; Imp. Defence Coll., U.K. 1971; promoted Brig.-Gen. and apptd. Commdr. 5 Combat Group Valcartier 1972; promoted Maj.-Gen. and apptd. Depy. Commdr. Mobile Command 1973-75; Chief Personnel Devel. NDHQ 1975-77; apptd. Commdr. Mobile Command and promoted Lieut.-Gen., 1977; Relinquished Command, 1981; R. Catholic; recreations: golf, music, reading; Clubs: Garnison; USI Home: 8405 Av. Sorel, Brossard, Que.; Office: 1010 Sherbrooke W., Montreal, Que.

PARDEE, Charles Henry; company Chrmn. of Board; b. Edmonton, Alta., 6 Jan. 1919; s. Edwin Charles and Marjorie (Mowat) P.; e. Westward Ho, Westmount and Garneau High Schs., Edmonton, 1937; Banff Sch. of Advanced Mang., 1967; m. Thelma Rawlings, 6 April 1973; stepsons: John Sutton, Jeffrey Rawlings; children: Peter, Marjorie, Timothy, Mark, Frances, Blaire; PRESIDENT, PARDEE EQUIPMENT LTD., since 1951; with Bank of Montreal, 1936-38; Engrs. Dept., City of Edmonton, 1938-40; Salesman, Wilkinson & McClean Ltd., 1945-51; served as Lieut. Commdr., R.C.N., 1939-45; Naval A.D.C. to Lieut. Gov. Alta. 1946-48; Dir., Harbour View Housing Soc., Chemainus, B.C.; Treas. & Dir., Pacific Wax Museum Ltd., Victoria, B.C.; Past mem., Regional & Prov. Councils, Boy Scouts of Canada (rec'd "Silver Acorn" 1964); mem., Alta. and N.W. Chamber of Mines & Resources (Pres., 1967-68); Candn. Assn. Equipment Distributors (Pres. 1969-70); Past Pres., Edmonton Regional Council, Boy Scouts of Can., 1961-63; Liberal; Protestant; Clubs: Rotary; Edmonton Petroleum; Home: Thetis Island, B.C. V0R 2Y0; Office: 16815 — 106 Ave., Edmonton, Alta. T5P 4G1

PARE, Fernand, F.S.A., F.C.I.A.; insurance executive; b. Quebec City, Que. 11 Nov. 1931; s. Paul and Maria (Jinchereau) P.; e. Laval Univ.; m. Rose d. John D'Amboise 22 Aug. 1959; children: Hélène; DIR. AND PRESIDENT, LA SOLIDARITE, COMPAGNIE D'ASSURANCE VIE (Head Office, Paris); also Dir. of Caisse de dépôt et placement du Québec; Société Générale de Financement; Noranda Mines; Société Québecoise d'Assainissement des Eaux; L'Unique, compagnie d'assurances générales; Home: 1416 Gaspard Fauteux, Sillery, Que. G1T 2T6; Office: 925 St-Louis Road, Québec, Que. G1S 1C1.

PARE, Lorenzo; journalist; b. Québec, P.Q. 22 Aug. 1913; s. Ulric and Laurenza (Gagnon) P.; e. Qué. Seminary; Laval Univ. (Philos.); m. Vianuna, d. Magloire Théorêet, 10 April 1944; children: Marie-Line, Laurent-Jacques; EDITOR-IN-CHIEF, EXTVE. VICE-PRES., "L'ACTION" (Estbd. 1907), since 1963; Dir., Nat. Centennial Comn.; started in journalism with "L'Evénement", Québec, P.Q., 1936; Parlty. Corr., Que. Leg., 1936-38; Press Gallery, Ottawa, 1939-52; served in 2nd World War as War Corr., Pacific, 1943; at Quebec, Washington, London Confs.; Del. of Can., Geneva Conf. on Freedom of Information, 1948; Secy., Atty.-Gen's. Comte. of Fed.-Prov. Conf. on Constitution, 1951; War Corr., Korea, 1952; Editorialist and Assoc. Ed., "Le Soleil" Quebec, 1952; Parlty. Corr. in Ottawa for "L'Action" 1953-62; world travel with Hon. L. B. Pearson, 1959; visits to Gt. Brit. and Israel on govt. invitations; 1959; R. Catholic; recreations: travelling, reading, golf, gardening; Clubs: Richelieu; Royal Quebec Golf; Home: 950 Louis-Fréchette, Québec, P.Q. G1S 3N5; Office: Place Jean-Talon, Québec, P.Q.

PARE, Most Rev. Marius; bishop (R.C.); b. Montmagny, Que., 22 May 1903; s. Joseph and Lucie (Boulet) P.; Bishop of Chicoutimi, 1961-79; o. Priest 3 July 1927; el. Titulary Bishop d'Ege and Auxiliary to Bishop of Chicoutimi 7 Feb. 1956 (consecrated 1 May 1956); nominated Coadjutor to the See of Chicoutimi, 6 Feb. 1960; Consultor Sacred Congregation for Catholic Teaching, Roma, May 1968-May 1978; Bishop-del. to Nat. Centre of Vocations, Conf. of Bishops of Can. 1961-67 and to Episcopal Comn. of Clergy Seminaries and Vocations (Pres. 1967-74); mem., Extve. (1972-76), Comité du Clergé (1956-79; Pres. 1965-74), Assemblée des Evêques du Qué.; Kt. Grand Cross, Order E. St. Sepulcre; Knight of Columbus, 4th degree; retired 5 Apr. 1979; Address: 927 Jacques-Cartier East, Chicoutimi Que. G7H 2A3

PARE, Paul, B.C.L.; executive; b. Montreal, Que., 30 May 1922; s. Arthur Alphonse and Lucy Victoria (Griffiths) P.; e. St. Leo's Academy; Loyola Coll., B.A.; McGill Univ., B.C.L.; m. Mary Audrey, d. James Drury, 24 July 1948; children: Victor, Ronald, Jane, Cathy; CHMN & CEO; IMASCO LTD., since 1979; DIR., Royal Bank of Can. 1970; C.I.P. Inc. 1975; Candn. Pacific Enterprises Ltd., 1974; Candn. Pacific Ltd. 1973; Canron Ltd. 1973; Liquid Carbonic Can. Ltd. 1975; Candn. Investment Fund Ltd. 1978; Candn. Fund Inc. 1978; I.B.M. Can. Ltd. 1979; The SNC Group 1980; read law with Slattery, Belanger & Paré; called to Bar of Que.; began in Law Dept., Imperial Tobacco Co., Montreal, 1949; Extve. Asst. to Hon. Brooke Claxton, Department of National Defence, Ottawa, 1950-52; rejoined Law Dept., Imperial Tobacco, 1952-55; President and General Manager, Canadian Tobacofina, Montreal, 1955-62; Vice-President, Imperial Tobacco Sales Company, Montreal, 1962-64; Vice-Pres. and Dir. Imperial Tobacco Co. of Canada Ltd., 1964-66; Extve. Vice-Pres., 1966-69; Gov., St. Mary's Hosp., Montreal, 1970; The Portage Program for Drug Dependencies Inc.; Olympic Trust of Canada, 1972; Douglas Hosp. Corp.; mem. Montreal Children's Hosp. Foundation; Bd. of Trustees, The Fraser Inst.; Hon. Vice Pres., St. John Ambulance Council for Quebec; mem., General Council of Industry; served as Lieut. Commdr., R.C.N., 1941-45; R. Catholic; Clubs: Mount Royal; Royal Montreal Golf; The Forest & Stream Clubs; Augusta National; Muirfield Village Golf; Montreal Indoor Tennis; Toronto; Queen's; Home: 3004 Breslay Rd., Montreal, Que. H3Y 2G7; Office: 4 Westmount Square, Montreal, Qué. H3Z 2S8

PARENT, (Joseph Albert) Oswald, B.Com., C.A.; né Hull, Qué. 30 Sept. 1925; f. Alfred et Hélène (Massé) P.; é. Ecole supérieure de Hull; Queen's Univ. B.Com. 19..; ép. Claudette Jean 19..; enfants: 4; ASSOCIE DE PARENT, PREFONTAINE & ASSOCIES; Prés. de Conseillers Professionnels (Hull) Inc.; Prés. de Immeubles Carmen Inc.; Administrateur de Informatek F. M. H. Ltée; Trésorier, Parti Libéral du Qué. 1955-57; elu membre de l'Assemblée Législative du Qué. pour la circonscription électorale de Hull 1956, réélu 1960, 1962, 1966, 1970, 1973, défait 1976; Adjoint parlementaire du ministre du Tourisme, de la Chasse et de la Pêche 1960-66; Ministre d'Etat au ministère des Finances 1970-76; Ministre d'etat au ministère des Affaires Intergouvernementales et responsable des négociations avec la Comn. de la Capitale Nationale 1970-76; Vice-prés. Conseil du Trésor 1971-76; Ministre d'Etat au ministère de la Fonction publique 1972-73; Ministre de la Fonction publique et ministre responsable des négociations collectives avec les employés des secteurs publics et parapublics de Qué. 1973-76; Prés. Fédération des Jeunes Chambres de Comm. du Qué. 1952-53; Vice Prés. Jeune Chambre de Comm. du Can. 1953-55; Sénateur, le Sénat J.C.I. du Can. 1953- ; Prés. régional, La Chambre de Comm. de l'Ouest du Qué. 1955-57; Comptable public et vérificateur sous la raison sociale Oswald Parent & Cie 1946-65; mem. Institut canadien des comptables agréés; Institut des comptables agréés de l'Ont.; Pub. Accts. Council Prov. Ont.; Ordre des comptables agréés du Qué.; corp. professionnelle des administrateurs agréés du Qué; Catholique; récréations: golf, natation, voyages; Clubs: Rivermead; Golf; Kingsway Park Golf & Country; Residence: 110 Chemin du Château, app. 2301, Hull, Qué. J9A 1T4; Bureau: 112 Promenade du Portage, Hull, Qué. J8X 2X1.

PARENT, Omer, O.C. (1971); peintre, éducateur; né Québec, P.Q., 7 avril, 1907; f. Omer et Rachel (Gauvin) P.; é. Ecole des beaux-arts de Qué.; Ecole nat. des arts décoratifs de Paris; ép. Evangeline; f. Charles Bélanger, Qué., le 5 août, 1943; prof., Ecole des beaux-arts de Qué., 1936-70, Dir. des études 1949-54; Prés., Comité des Arts et de l'Educ., Exposition prov., 1951-68; Dir.-fondateur, Ecole des Arts visuels. Univ. Laval 1970-72; 1972 peinture, enseignement temps partiel, Univ. Laval; depuis 1974 peinture et artivités connexes surtout; Professeur émérite de l'Université Laval, 1975; secretaire de la Conf. candn. des arts, 1958; murales, peintures dans de nombreuses collections; Catholique; récréations: voyages, photographie; résidence; 1227, ave. des Pins, Sillery, Que. G1S 4J3

PARENT, Simon G., Q.C. (1959), B.A., LL.M., LL.D.; b. Quebec, Que., 16 Aug. 1913; s. Hon. Senator George, K.C. and Kathleen (Grenier) P.; e. Quebec Semy.; St. Dunstan's Univ.; Laval Univ., B.A. 1934, LL.M. 1937, Docteur en Droit, 1951; m. Louise, d. Hon. Mr. Justice Noel Belleau, 2 March 1943; children: Georges N., Louis B.; Director and Officer of several corporations; Counsel, McNicoll & Parent, Advocates; Ambassador Extraordinary and Plenipotentiary to Haiti of Sov. Mil. Hosp., Order of St. John of Jerusalem, Rhodes, and Malta, 1976-80; Pres., Assn. of Cdn. Knights of the Sovereign Military Order of Malta, 1981; author of "Le Nom Patronymique dans le Droit québécois" (1951), "The Quebec Garrison Club, 1879-1979", and of articles in French legal periodicals; Gov., Vice-Pres., St. Dunstan's Univ. Alumni Assn., 1952-55; Kt. of Grace of Sovereign Order of Malta (1955), Kt. Grand Cross (1961); read law with Taschereau, Parent, Taschereau & Cannon; called to the Bar of Que. 1938; Prof. of Engn. Law, Laval Univ.; served World War, 1939-45; proceeded Overseas 1940; served in field with Royal 22nd Regt. till 1941; trans. to Candn. Mil. Hdqrs., London, in Judge Advocate's Br.; Co. Commdr., Les Voltigeurs de Québec (Motor) 1946-49; O.C. Laval Univ. Contingent, C.O.T.C., 1949-53; mem., Heraldry Soc. of Can.; Royal Candn. Legion, (Ex-Chrmn. of Que. City & Dist. Council); United Services Inst. of Que. (Past Pres.); Life mem., Soc. Généalogique C.-France (1956); Pres., L'Amicale du 22c Inc. (1955-56); Vice-Pres., Candn. Assn., S.M. Order of Malta 1968-69; Roman Catholic; recreations: swimming, skiing; Clubs: Quebec Garrison (Pres., 1964-65); Cercle Universitaire; Home: 1144 Turnbull Ave., Quebec, P.Q. G1R 2X8; Office: 1170 ave. de Salaberry, Quebec. G1R 2V9

PARENTEAU, Roland, B.A., L.Sc. Com.; éducateur; né Montréal, Qué. 13 decembre 1921; f. Arsène et Emerentienne (Bureau) P.; é. Coll. André-Grasset, Univ. de Montréal B.A. 1942; Ecole des Hautes Etudes commerciales L.Sc.Com. 1945; Faculté de Droit. Univ. de Paris; Institut d'Etudes politiques Paris, Dipl. 1949; ép. Jeanne d'Arc f. Leandre Julien (décédé) 28 juin 1947; enfants: Danielle, Michel, Claude, Jean-Luc, Dominique, Eric, PROFESSEUR D'ADM. ET ORGAN. DES RESOURCES HUMAINES, ECOLE DES HAUTES ETUDES COMMERCIALES; professeur, Ecole des Hautes Etudes Commerciales 1949-64; directeur, Conseil d'Orientation

économique du Qué. 1964-68; Office de Planification du Qué. 1968; Ecole Nationale d'Adm. Publique 1969-74, professeur 1974-78; mem. Conseil Supérieur du Travail 1963-65; agent de recherches à la Comn. royale d'Enquête sur les écarts de prix des denrées alimentaires 1958; mem. Exécutif, Inst. Canadien d'Educ. des Adultes 1961-63; Conseil d'adm. de la Caisse des Dépôts et Placements 1966-69; Conseil scientifique de l'Ecole internationale de Bordeaux 1970-72, 1974-78; missions d'évaluation pour l'ACDI en Algérie 1976-78, au Rwanda 1977, 79, au Bénin 1978, au Sénégal 1981; auteur, chaps. dans "Developpement Urbain et Analyse Economique" 1968; "Le Canada Français d'Aujourd'hui" 1970; "Regional Economic Development" 1974; articles nombreux; mem. Assn. canadienne des Economistes (Prés. 1961-62); Société royale du Can.; Académie des Sciences morales et politiques; Conseil de Recherches en Sciences Humaines du Can.; Comm. de l'Ensei prement supérieur du Conseil Supérieur de l'Education du Québec; catholique; Adresse: 1685 Lajoie, Outremont, Qué. H2V 1R8; Bureau: 5255 Decelles, Montréal, Qué. H3T 1V6.

PARIZEAU, Jacques, Ph.D.; né Montréal, P.Q., 9 août 1930; f. Gérard et Germaine (Biron) P.; é. Collège Stanislas, Montréal; licencié Ecole des Hautes Etudes Commerciales, Montréal; études supérieures sciences économiques (Paris); Institut d'Etudes Politiques (Paris); London School of Economics (Londres) Ph.D. (Econ.); ép. Alicja Poznanska, 2 avril 1956; enfants: Bernard, Isabelle; MINISTRE DES FINANCES ET DU REVENU, CONSEIL DU TRÉSOR DE LA P.Q.; membre conseil, Univ. Montréal; sec. gén., Actualité Economique, 1955-61; consultant gouvernement du Québec, 1961-65; conseiller écon. & financier du Conseil des Ministres du Québec, 1965-67; membre des conseils d'adm., Société générale de financement, caisse de dépôt et placement, soc. québecoise exploration minière et régie de l'assurdépôts du Québec jusqu'en 1969; chargé de recherche, Comn. royale d'enquête sur le Système bancaire et financière (1963); Prés. du Comité d'étude sur l'inst. financières (1966 à 1969); membre du Conseil exécutif du Parti Québecois (Nov. 1969); élu député aux élections de Novembre, 1976; dans la circonscription de l'Assomption, Montréal; auteur des: "The Terms of Trade of Canada", 1966; Rapport du Comité d'Etude sur les inst. fin. publié par le gouvernement du Québec, juin 1969; nombreux articles publiés dans divers journaux de langue française et anglaise; Catholique R.; récréations: lecture, musique, ski; Club: cercle universitaire de Montréal; Résidence: 40 avenue Robert, Outremont P.Q. H3S 2P2; Bureau: Parliament Bldg., Quebec, Que.

PARK, Maurice W., B.A., F.R.I.; real estate executive; b. Barrie, Ont., 12 Nov. 1914; s. William and Emma Jane (Wilson) P.; e. Pub. and High Schs., Barrie, Ont.; Toronto (Ont.) Normal Sch., grad. 1936; Queen's Univ., B.A. 1942; m. Marion (Terry), d. Dr. E. G. Berry, Feb. 1946; children: Ian Gregory, Deborah Jane; PRESIDENT AND DIR., MAURICE W. PARK REALTOR since 1971; taught sch. Brentwood and Barrie, Ont. 1936-40; life ins. sales and mang. 1946-55; Sales, Ken Wiles Ltd., 1955; A. E. Le Page Realtor 1958; founded present firm 1960; served with Candn. Army and RCAF 1942-46; rank Flying Offr.; mem. Toronto Real Estate Bd.; (Dir. 1966-73, Pres. 1974); Ont. Real Estate Bd.; United Church; recreations: sailing, curling; Clubs: Candn. Real Estate Bd.; Candn. Real Estate Assn.; Donalda; Port Credit Yacht; Homes: 25 Leith Hill Rd., Willowdale, Ont. M2J 1Z1 and R.R. 1, Coboconk, Ont.; Office: 801 York Mills Rd., Toronto, Ont. M3B 1X7

PARKER, Benjamin Stuart, B.A., LL.B.; b. Winnipeg, Man., 26 Feb. 1914; s. Benjamin Cronyn, K.C. and Jessie C. (Alward) P.; e. Winnipeg Pub. Schs.; Univ. of Manitoba, LL.B., 1936 and B.A., 1938; m. Margaret Mary, d. late Prof. Henry E. Bletcher, Winnipeg, Man., 6 Sept. 1936; one son: Robert Stuart; PARTNER, PARKER & WERIER;

Pres., Pigeon Lake Farm Lands Ltd.; Vice-Pres., Hammarstrand & Greeniaus Limited; National Construction Ltd.; Secy., Wilson-Gregory Lumber Co. Ltd.; Chief Agent for Can. of Lutheran Brotherhood; Chief Agent for Man. of Standard Life Assnce. Co.; mem. of Bd. of Regents, United Coll., Winnipeg; Bd. of Trustees of The MacKinnon Foundation; Central Western Div., C.N.I.B.; read law with Benjamin C. Parker, K.C.; called to the Bar of Man. 1937; mem., Man. Law Soc.; Man. Bar Assn.; Candn. Bar Assn.; Zeta Psi; Freemason (D.G.M.), Offr. Prudential Chapter Sask. and Man. Royal Order of Scotland Past Presiding Offr. Scottish Rite of Freemasonry, mem. Kartoum Temple, A.A.O.N.M.S.; Liberal; Protestant; recreations: hunting, fishing, gardening, reading; Clubs: Kiwanis International (Past Pres.); Empire; Canadian; Home 380 Elm, Winnipeg, Man. R3M 3P3; Office: 1708 — 1 Lombard Place, Winnipeg, Man. R3B 0X3

PARKER, Dale G., banker; b. N.S. 16 April 1936; e. Harvard AMP; m. Joan Mary 1962; children: 1 s. Shane; EXEC. VICE-PRES. AND GEN. MGR. DOMESTIC BANKING, BANK OF MONTREAL 1982- ; Vice-Pres. & Asst. Gen. Mgr. Domestic Banking, Toronto, 1980; Sen. Vice-Pres. B.C. Div., Sen. Vice-Pres. and Dep. Gen. Mgr. Domestic Banking; Gov., Inst. Candn. Bankers; Clubs: Ont. Club and Mississauga Golf & Country Club; Office: 1 First Canadian Place, Toronto, Ont. M5X 1A1

PARKER, Edward, B.A., B.Ed.; public relations executive b. Winnipeg, Man., 1 Jan. 1918; s. Harry and Rose (Perlmutter) P.; e. United Coll., Univ. of Man., B.A. 1939; Univ. of Toronto, B.Ed. 1955; m. Ilene Theresa, d. John Vlahov, Long Island, N.Y., 13 Aug. 1955; children: Joshua, Ivor, Tia, Ara; FOUNDER (1963) AND PRESIDENT, EDWARD PARKER PUBLIC RELATIONS LTD.; Ed.-in-Chief, "The Manitoban", Univ. of Man., 1939; Stage and Screen Ed., "The Winnipeg Tribune", 1940; Staff Writer, Photo Ed., "The Montreal Star", 1941; Publ. Offr., Dept. of Munitions & Supply, Ottawa, 1941-43; Dir. and Organizer of Recreation Program, Ottawa Civil Service Recreation Assn., 1943-44; Publ. Offr., Govt. Sask. and Depy, Dir., Adult Educ., 1944-46; Freelance Corr. in Europe and Staff Writer "Ottawa Journal", 1947; Founder and 1st Dir., Sch. of Journalism and Graphic Arts, Ryerson Polytech. Inst., 1948-55; Dir., Pub. Relations, Rio Tinto Group in Can., 1955-61; conducted pub. relations projects in Chile, Ireland and Japan, 1962-63; Instr., Creative Writing, Extension Dept., Univ. of Waterloo, 1963-65, York Univ., since 1966; Guest Instructor, Univ. of Nevada (Las Vegas) Spring program, 1979, 1981; Exec. Ed., Issues Report, Royal Comn. on the Northern Environment, Ont. Govt., 1978; Past mem. Bd., Candn., Mental Health Assn.; Script Writer, "Front Page Challenge", C.B.C., 1962-63; Past mem. Bd., Candn. Crest Players Foundation; Patrons of Canadian Art; mem., Candn. Pub. Relations Soc.; Bd. Trade Metrop. Toronto; Commonwealth Soc.; Dir. (Candn. mem.) Public Relations Internat. Organ., London, Eng.; recreations: reading, walking, theatre; Club: Empire; Home: 214 Vesta Dr., Toronto, Ont.;

PARKER, Jack Horace, M.A., Ph.D., F.R.S.C.; educator; b. Parkersville, Ont. 4 Apl. 1914; s. Ernest Frank and Jessie Blanche (Bain) P.; e. Bracebridge (Ont.) High Sch. 1931; Univ. of Toronto B.A. 1935, M.A. 1936, Ph.D. 1941; m. Marjorie Beatrice (d.) d. late William H. Minnes 11 June 1946; children: John Geoffrey Minnes, Ceciley Margaret; SPECIAL LECTR. IN SPANISH, UNIV. OF TORONTO 1979- , Instr. in Spanish 1936-41, Asst. Prof. of Spanish & Portuguese 1946-53, Assoc. Prof. 1953-57, Prof. 1957-79, Chrmn. of Italian & Hispanic Studies 1966-69, Assoc. Dean (Div. I Humanities) Sch. Grad. Studies 1969-73; Instr. in Spanish Columbia Univ. 1941-42, Ind. Univ. 1942-43; Asst. Prof. of Spanish Univ. of B.C. 1945-46; named Kt. Order Civil Merit Spain 1977; served as Research Offr. Nat. Research Council Ottawa 1943-45; author "Breve historia del teatro espanol" 1957; "Gil Vicente" 1967; "Juan Pérez de Montalvan" 1975; articles

Spanish & Portuguese drama of 16th and 17th centurie Life mem. Ont. Modern Lang. Teachers Assn.; mem Candn. Assn. Hispanists (Pres. 1968-70); Am. Assr Teachers Spanish & Portuguese (Pres. 1975); Moder Lang. Assn. Am.; Internat. Assn. Hispanists; Libera Protestant; recreations: gardening, walking, trave Home: 100 Wychwood Park, Toronto, Ont. M6G 2V5; O fice: Toronto, Ont. M5S 1A1.

PARKER, James William, B.Sc.; company executive; b St. John's Nfld., 22 May 1923; s. John Joseph and Flor (Frew) P.; e. Ampleforth Coll., Yorkshire, Eng., 1933-3 Loyola Coll., Montreal, P.Q., 1940-41; Macdonald Col (McGill Univ.), B.Sc. (Agric.) 1947; m. Geraldine Mary, c Dr. E. Leo Sharpe, St. John's, Nfld., 20 June 1951; chi dren: James Francis, Joan Elizabeth, Janet Mary, Brend Mary, Barbara, Elizabeth, Louise; PRESIDENT, PARKE & MONROE LTD. (Wholesale, Retail, Jobbers in Foo wear); mem. Nfld. Adv. Bd., Royal Trust Co.; Pres Nfld. Bd. Trade 1970-71; mem. Adv. Comte., Real Prop erty of the Nat. Capital Comn.; joined the present firr in Sept. 1947; served in 2nd World War with R.C.A.F 1943-45, Pilot Offr. (Air Bomber); Roman Catholic; recrea tion: working on and enjoying country property at Man uels, Nfld.; Clubs: Rotary (Past Pres.); Bally Haly Golf & Country; Home: #39 Topsail Road, St. John's, Nfld. A1 2A6; Office: Water St., St. John's, Nfld.

PARKER, John Havelock, B.Sc.; commissioner; b. Dids bury, Alta. 2 Feb. 1929; s. Bruce T. and Rose (Husband P.; e. Didsbury High Sch.; Univ. of Alta. B.Sc. (Engr Geol.) 1951; m. Helen A. d. Harold E. Panabaker 195! children: Sharon, Gordon; COMMR. OF THE N.W.T Depy. Commissioner 1967 — 79; Pres.; Precambrian Mir ing Services Ltd. 1964 — 67; Councillor, Town of Yellow knife 1959 — 63, Mayor 1964 — 67; mem. N.W.T. Counc 1967 — 74; Past Pres. & Patron, N.W.T. Boy Scout Coun cil; Fellow, Arctic Inst. N. Am.; mem. Candn. Inst. Min ing & Metall.; Assn. Prof. Engrs. Alta.; recreations: gar dening, boating, cross-country skiing, collectin, northern art and sculpture; Home: (P.O. Box 878) Yellow knife, N.W.T. X0E 1H0; Office: Yellowknife, N.W.T. X1/ 2L9.

PARKER, John Paul; company executive; b. Toronto Ont., 31 Oct. 1916; s. Hugh Radclyffe and Emily Jan (Clark) P.; e. Public Schs. and Danforth Tech. Sch., To ronto; m. Lois Harriet, d. Charles R. Vint, Toronto : Sept. 1940; VICE-PRES. AND DIR., CANADIAN COR PORATE MANAGEMENT CO. LTD.; Pres. & C.E.O. Regal Greetings & Gifts; Cashway Building Centres Pres., Regal Stationary Co.; Vice-Pres. and Dir., Richard son, Bond & Wright Milltronics Peterborough; Dir. Tender Tootsies Ltd.; Fine Art Developments, England Australian Greetings, Melbourne, Australia; mem. Candn. Mfrs. Assn.; Christian Scientist; Clubs: Granite Bd. Trade Metrop. Toronto; Home: 66 Collier St., Toron to, Ont. M4W 1L9; Office: Box 131, Commerce Cour Postal Stn., Toronto, Ont. M5L 1E2

PARKER, Ralph Douglas, B.Sc., LL.D.; industrialist; b Lockeford, Cal., 27 Apl. 1898; s. Joseph Douglas and late Minerva (Hartley) P.; e. Elem. and High Schs., Cal. Univ. of Cal. (Berkeley), B.Sc. (Mining); LL.D., Lauren tian Univ., 1961; Univ. Calif. 1965; m. Mina Bayne (d.), d Charles Clark Todhunter, 1 Jan. 1930; m. 2ndly, Mar guerite A., d. Leo Gauthier, May 1979; began with Place Mining in Butte Co., Cal.; then to Cherry Creek Mining Co., Vernon, B.C., 1920-21; Asst. Mine Supt., McIntyr Porcupine Mines, Schumacher, Ont., 1921-28; The Inter nat. Nickel Co. of Can., Ltd., Copper Cliff, Ont., Supt. Creighton Mine, 1928-29; Supt., Frood Mine, 1929-31 Supt. of Mines, 1931-35; Gen. Supt., Mining and Smelt ing Div., 1935-47; Asst. Vice-Pres., 1947-54; Asst. Vice Pres. and Gen. Mgr. of Candn. Operations, 1955-57; el. a Dir. 1957; Vice-Pres. i/c Candn. Operations, 1958-60; Sr Vice-Pres. and Dir., 1960-63; served in U.S. Army, 1917-

8, Machine Gun Corps and O.T.C.; mem., Candn. Inst. Mining & Metall. (Pres. 1964-65); Am. Inst. Mining Metall. & Petroleum Engrs.; Protestant; recreations: golf, hunting, fishing; Clubs: Toronto; Rosedale Golf; Toronto Hunt; York; Idylwylde Golf and Country (Sudbury); Address: Apt. #503, 235 St. Clair Ave. W., Toronto, Ont. M4V 1R4

ARKER, Hon. William Dickens; judge; b. Hamilton, Ont. 25 Aug. 1914; s. Robert and Minnie (Dickens) P.; e. Hamilton (Ont.) Central Collegiate; Osgoode Hall Law Sch., Toronto, Ont. (1939); m. Inez Eleanor, d. George Hill, Hamilton, Ont., 28 Aug. 1938; children: Deborah, Patricia, John: ASSOC. CHIEF JUSTICE OF THE HIGH COURT of Ont.; read law with Mr. Justice C. W. R. Bowlby; called to the Bar of Ont., 1939; cr. Q.C. 1953; served in 2nd World War with Candn. Army, 1942-45; Capt., Royal Hamilton Light Inf.; Past mem. of Council, Candn. Bar Assn.; Past Pres., Hamilton Lawyers Club; Phi Delta Phi; Anglican Church; recreation: golf; Office: Osgoode Hall, Toronto, Ont. M5H 2N6

ARKHILL, Douglas Freeman, B.A.Sc.; D.Eng.; Canadian public servant; b. Toronto, Ont., 19 Dec. 1923; s. Clarence Freeman and Catharine Beverley (Murphy) P.; e. Univ. of Toronto, B.A.Sc. (Elect. Engn.) 1949; D.Eng. Univ. of Ottawa 1971; m. Gudbjorg Unnur Kristjansson, 29 Jan. 1955; children: Douglas Fridrik, Patricia Bjorg; ASST. DEPY. MIN. (RESEARCH), DEPT. OF COMMUNICATIONS; Engr., Canadian Comstock Frequency Standardization Div., St. Catharines, Ont., 1949-51; Head, Systems Planning Dept., Computing Devices of Canada Ltd., Ottawa, 1951-55; Supvr. of Engn., Crosley Defence and Electronics Div., AVCO of Canada, Weston, Ont., 1955-56; Depy. Mgr. Computer and Electronics Systems Dept., AVCO R & D Div., Wilmington, Mass. 1956-58; Chief Engr., Advanced Devel. Dept., General Dynamics Information Technol. Div., Rochester, N.Y., 1958-61; Head, Communications Satellite Systems Dept., Mitre Corp., Bedford, Mass., 1961-69; served with RCAF 1942-45; author, "Challenge of the Computer Utility", 1966; Co-ed., "Gutenberg II", 1979; winner McKinsey Award for "Distinguished Contribution to Management Literature", 1966; Pres. Internat. Council for Computer Commun. 1981-84 term; mem., Assn. Prof. Engrs. Ont.; Inst. Elect. & Electronic Engrs.; Am. Assn. Advanc. Science; Scient. Research Soc. Am.; Unitarian; recreations: skiing, swimming, golf, writing; Home: 204 Sandridge Rd., Rockcliffe Park, Ottawa, Ont. K1L 5A2; Office: 300 Slater St., Ottawa, Ont. K1P 6A6

PARKIN, John Cresswell, C.C. (1972), K.C.L.J., O.M.L.J., C.M., M.Arch., F.R.I.B.A., F.R.A.I.C. (1960), P.P.R.C.A. (1964), F.S.I.A.D., F.R.S.A., D.Sc. (Hon.) McGill, D. Eng. (Hon.) N.S.; b. Sheffield, Eng. of Canadian parentage, 24 Mar. 1922; s. Thomas Cresswell II, F.C.A., and Marie Louise Parkin; e. Univ. of Manitoba, B.Arch. (Hons.), 1944; Harvard Univ., M.Arch., 1947; children: John Cresswell Jr., Geoffrey Cresswell, Jennifer Ann Cresswell; SENIOR PARTNER, PARKIN PARTNERSHIP ARCHITECTS; Chrmn., Parkin Engineers Limited; Pres., Parkin Arpac Limited; Dir., Transo Corp. Ltd.; Eastern Utilities Ltd.; Trans-Canada Freezers Ltd.; American Consumers Industries; former Visiting Prof., Univs. of Toronto, McGill, Manitoba, North Carolina, etc., prior to forming present firm worked with various Winnipeg, Toronto and N.Y. design firms; Partnerships responsible for (among others): Hdqrs. Bldg. of Ont. Assn. of Architects, Toronto (competition); Consultants, Confederation Sq. Redevel. Ottawa, Nat. Capital Comn.; Toronto Internat. Airport Terminal I; Bata Internat. Centre, Don Mills; Ottawa Union Station; Imperial Oil Ltd. Ont. Regional Hdqrs. Bldg.; International Business Machines Hdqrs. Bldg. Don Mills; International Nickel Co. of Can. Ltd. Research Lab.; Etobicoke Gen. Hosp.; St. John's (Nfld.) City Hall; in joint venture, Robt. Simpson Co. Ltd. Office Tower; Assoc. Arch. (with late Viljo Re-

vell), new Toronto City Hall; Toronto Dominion Centre; York Univ.; Brock Univ.; Safeco Ins. Co. of America; 1500 Don Mills Rd.; T. Eaton Co. Ltd. executive offices, Toronto; Bank of Montreal Central Computer Complex No. 2; Health Sciences Complex, St. John's, Nfld.; winner nat. competition, proposed Nat. Gallery of Can.; rec'd. 14 Massey Medals in Arch., incl. Gold Medal, 1950; Massey Silver Medals for Hosp., Indust., Comm. and Church Arch., 1950; Massey Silver Medals for Indust. Comm. & Special Award, 1955; Massey Silver Medal for Indust. Arch., 1958, and seven special mentions; five Massey Special Mentions, 1961; three Massey Silver Medals for Indust., Telecommunications and Comm. Arch. 1964; Premier Candn. Arch. Award, Olympics Art Exhn., Helsinki, 1952; Hon. Mention, Vancouver Civic Auditorium Competition, 1954; Pres., Roy. Candn. Acad. of Arts 1970- ; mem., Adv. Council, Sch. of Adm. Studies, York Univ.; former Gov., Nat. Film Bd. 1964-67; Pres., 1955-57, Candn. Conf. of The Arts; Past Chrmn., Bd. Govs., Ryerson Polytech. Inst.; Chrmn., Arch. Adv. Bd., Expo '67, Montreal; former Chrmn. Bd. Trustees, John A. MacLaren Newspaper Awards 1972; mem. Bd. Trustees, Art Gallery of Ont.; mem., Internat. Council, Museum of Modern Art, N.Y.; mem., Soc. Arch. Historians of Gr. Brit.; mem. Energy Task Force, R.A.I.C.; former mem., Bd. of Dirs. and Planning Comte., Toronto Symphony Orchestra; Fellow, Roy. Soc. Arts. U.K.; Fellow, Soc. Indust. Artists and Designers, London; mem., Corp. of Professional Urbanists of Que.; Am. Planning Assn.; Former mem., Young Pres. Organ.; mem., Bd. of Trade of Metrop. Toronto; former mem. of Adm. Comte. and Nat. Extve. Assn. of Candn. Clubs; mem., UNESCO Nat. Comn., Govt. of Can.; Candn. del., Ninth Gen. Conf., UNESCO, New Delhi, 1956; apptd. by Royal Arch. Inst. of Can. a mem. of (3-man) Comte. to make full scale inquiry into design of residential areas in Can., 1959; mem. of Jury, Govt. of U.K. Commonwealth Competition for the Addition to the Houses of Parlt., Westminster, 1968-72; Oscar Cahen Mem. Award of Art Directors Club for continuous service to Canadian Art, 1960; Chrmn., Nat. Design Council, Govt. of Can. 1961-70; Life mem., Assn. of Candn. Indust. Designers; Royal Arch. Inst. Can.; Citation, Bd. of Dirs., Candn. Corp. for the 1967 World Exhn., 1968; Centennial Medal 1967; Alumni Jubilee Award Univ. of Man. 1968; Companion of the Order of Canada 1972; Hon. mem., National Academy of Design (U.S.A.) 1972; Queen's Jubilee Medal 1977; R.A.I.C. Gold Medal 1979; Hon. mem., Royal Scottish Academy, 1980; Zeta Psi; Clubs: York; Toronto; Granite; Rideau (Ottawa); Mount Royal (Montreal); Principal Office: 55 University Ave., Toronto, Ont. M5J 2H7

PARKIN, Margaret Lillian, B.A., B.L.S.; librarian; b. Toronto, Ont., 31 Mar. 1921; d. John Hamilton and Margaret Gertrude (Locke) P.; e. Elmwood Girls Sch., Rockcliffe Pk., Ont., Sr. Matric., 1938; Univ. of Toronto, B.A. 1942; Ottawa Univ., B.L.S., 1960; INDEXER, CANADIAN PERIODICAL INDEX, since 1979; with Nat. Research Council of Can., 1946-50; Head Report Sec., Div. Mech. Engn.; Dept. of Labour, Econ. and Research Br., Library, 1961-62; Unemployment Ins. Comn., Library, 1962-63; Carleton Univ., Catalogue Dept., 1963-64; Librarian, Candn. Nurses' Assn., 1964-79; served in 2nd World War as Flight Offr., RCAF (WD) 1942-46; Flight Lieut., RCAF, 1951-58; mem., Can. Library Assn.; Ont. Library Assn.; Library Assn. of Ottawa; Canadian Health Library Assn.; Indexing and Abstracting Assn. of Can.; Anglican; recreations: handicrafts; Club: Women's Canadian; Home: Apt. 301 — 10 Driveway, Ottawa, Ont. K2P 1C7;

PARKINSON, Derek Henry, F.C.A.; executive; b. Bolton, Lancs., Eng. 8 Aug. 1925; s. Frederick Henry and Laura (Heenan) P.; e. Bolton Sch. Eng.; C.A. (U.K.) 1951; m. Marlene Anne d. Robert Busby 8 Oct. 1981; two d. by previous marriage Janet, Maureen; SR. VICE PRES. FINANCE & PLANNING, MacMILLAN BLOEDEL LTD. 1977- ; Dir. Canada Trust Co.; Chrmn. Council Financial

Extves. Conf. Bd. Can.; private C.A. practice U.K. after W.W.2; joined Price Waterhouse & Co. Vancouver 1951, Partner 1965; Dir. Financial Services MacMillan Bloedel Ltd. 1970, Vice Pres. Finance 1973; author various articles prof. journs.; served with R.A.F. 1944-47; Fellow, Inst. C.A.'s B.C.; mem. Financial Extves. Inst.; P. Conservative; Anglican; recreations: tennis, hiking; Clubs: Vancouver; Hollyburn Golf & Country; Home: 1002, 2075 Comox St., Vancouver, B.C. V6G 1S2; Office: 1075 W. Georgia St., Vancouver, B.C. V6E 3R9.

PARKINSON, Joseph Frederick, B.Com.; economic consultant; civil servant (retired); b. Wallasey, Eng., 5 June 1904; P.; e. Liverpool Coll. Sch., Eng.; London Sch. of Econ., Univ. of London, B.Com. 1928; m. Dorothy, d. Henry Hudson, Liverpool, Eng., 10 Oct. 1928; children: J. Patricia, Joyce; Asst. Prof. and Assoc. Prof., Dept. of Political Econ., Univ. of Toronto 1929-46; Founding mem. League for Social Reconstruction, 1932; Econ., Candn.-Am. Joint Econ. Comtes., Dept. of External Affairs, Ottawa, 1941-42; Econ. Advisor, W.P.T.B., Ottawa, 1943-46; Govt. of Can. Dept of Finance, 1946-49; Alternate Dir. (for Can.) on Internat. Bank for Reconstr. & Devel. and Internat. Monetary Fund, 1947-51; Financial Counsellor, Candn. Embassy, Wash., 1947-51; Head of Candn. Del. to O.E.E.C., Paris and rep. Can. on the Econ. and Financial Bd. of N.A.T.O., Paris. 1951-52; Financial Counsellor, Canada House, London, Eng., 1952-53; Dir., Economic Policy Divn., Dept. of Finance, Ottawa, 1954-56; Econ. Adv., Dept. of Finance 1956-69; Dir., Central Mortgage & Housing Corp., Ottawa, 1954-69; Secy., Royal Comn. on Energy, 1957-59; Chrmn., Municipal Devel. & Loan Bd., Ottawa, 1964-69; mem. Buffalo & Fort Erie Public Bridge Authority since 1969; Dir., Northern Can. Power Comm. 1960-78; Consultant, governments of Botswana, Swaziland, Lesotho, on Monetary & Currency Questions, 1970-71; Advisor, Govt. of Bahamas, 1974; author: "The Bases of Canadian Commercial Policy, 1926-39", 1939; part author, L. S. R. Research Comte., "Social Planning for Canada", 1935; Ed. "Canadian Investment & Foreign Exchange Problems", 1941; "Canadian War Economics", 1942; Address: 1503-211 Wurtemburg St., Ottawa, Ont. K1N 8R4

PARR, James Gordon, Ph.D., F.R.S.C.; F.R.S.A., F.E.I.C.; b. Peterborough, England, 26 May 1927; s. Reuben Scotney and Edith Grace (Rollings) P.; e. Deacon's School, Peterborough, England; Univ. of Leeds, B.Sc. (Metall.) 1947; Univ. of Liverpool, Ph.D. 1953; children: Mark Anthony, Katharine Elizabeth, Daniel John; CHRMN. & CHIEF EXTVE. OFFR., TVONTARIO; formerly Depy. Min. Colls. & Univs. Govt. Ont.; formerly Professor and Dean, Faculty of Applied Science, University of Windsor and President, Indust. Research Inst. there; author: "Man, Metals and Modern Magic", 1958; co-author; "The Engineer's Guide to Steel", 1965; co-author: "An Introduction to Stainless Steel", 1965; "Any Other Business: How To Be A Good Committee Person", 1977; "Is There Anybody There?", 1979; other writings incl. tech. publs. and articles in prof. and popular press; also frequent contrib. to CBC radio; awarded Centennial Medal; Jubilee Medal; Fellow, Am. Soc. for Metals; Ryerson Polytech Inst.; Bd. of Gov., Ont. Inst. for Studies in Education; mem. Soc. for the Hist. of Technol.; Assn. Prof. Engrs., Ont.; Candn. Inst. Mining & Metall.; recreation: writing; Club: Arts & Letters (Toronto); Home: 10 Governor's Rd., Toronto, Ont. M4W 2G1

PARRISH, William Bruce; grain merchant; b. Winnipeg, Manitoba, 8 May 1926; s. Frederick William and Vera E. (Cadle) P.; e. Public Schs. and Kelvin Tech. and High Sch.; Univ. of Manitoba; m. Donna Marie, d. Dr. J. S. McInnes, Winipeg, Man., 14 July 1954; children: William S., David L., Elizabeth D.; VICE PRES. AND DIR., PARRISH & HEIMBECKER LTD.; Pres., Parkdale Farms Ltd.; Vice Pres. and Dir., Great Lakes Elevator Co. Ltd.; Dir., New Life Mills; Traders Building Assn.; mem., Winnipeg

Adv. Bd., Gov., Winnipeg Commodity Exchange (Chrmn. 1967); Chrmn. of the Bd., Grain Insurance & Guarantee Co. Ltd.; Winnipeg Health Sciences Centre; Past Pres., Candn. Cancer Soc.; Freemason (Scot. Rite); United Church; Club: Winnipeg Winter; Home; 4701 Roblin Blvd., Winnipeg, Man. R3R 0G2; Office: 700-360 Main Street., Winnipeg, Man. R3C 3Z3

PARROTT, Hon. Harry, D.D.S.; orthodontist; politician; b. Mitchell, Ont., 30 Nov. 1925; s. William C. and Laura Ethel (Horn) P.; e. Mitchell, Ont.; Univ. of Toronto D.D.S. 1947, Dipl. in Orthodontics 1965; m. Isobel Walker, d. John Walker Mitchell Sept. 1947; children: Craig, Nancy, Lori; Min. of The Environment, 1978-81; Min. of Colleges and Universities, Ont. 1975-78; Lectr. Univ. of Toronto Grad. Clinic and Studies 1965-69; Lectr. Univ. of W. Ont. 1969-71; served Woodstock Bd. of Educ. 1954-56; Woodstock City Council 1961-63, 1966-67; Woodstock Pub. Utilities Comn. 1968-71; el. M.P.P. 1971, re-el. until he resigned seat prior to 1981 election; Parlty. Asst. to Min. of Colls. and Univs. 1974; Past Pres. Oxford Co. Red Cross; Past Campaign Chrmn. Woodstock Un. Appeal; P. Conservative; Protestant; recreations: golf, standardbred horse farming; Home: 350 Vincent St., Woodstock, Ont. N4S 5M4; Office: 22 Wellington St. N., Woodstock, Ont. N4S 6P2

PARSONS, G. G.; company executive; b. Goderich, Ont., 19 Dec. 1921; s. late Lionel G. and Hattie Jacquetta (Saults) P.,; e. Upper Canada College, Toronto; divorced; children: Mrs. S. Davidchuk, Mrs. F. Gardiner, Mrs. B. MacDonald, Elizabeth, Paul, John, David; PRESIDENT AND C.E.O., GODERICH ELEVATORS LTD.; served with R.C.A.F. 1942-46; joined present Co. 1946; Past Chrmn., Bd. of Govs., Goderich Hosp.; mem., Candn. Owners & Pilots Assn.; Chrmn. Eastern Elevator Assn. Can.; United Church; recreation: active private pilot; Club: Lions; Home: R.R. 4, Goderich, Ont. N7A 4C6; Office: Wharf, Goderich, Ont. N7A 3Y5

PARSONS, Sydney J., C.A.; executive; b. Winnipeg, Man., 23 March 1925; s. late Sidney and Katherine (Derry) P.; e. Earl Grey Sch. and Kelvin High Sch., Winnipeg; Univ. of Manitoba, C.A. 1950; m. Elizabeth Josephine, d. Arthur Torrens, 4 Nov. 1950; children: Carol, Shelley, Nancy, John, Susan; CHRMN. AND GEN. MGR., MANITOBA DEVEL. CORP. since 1972; Chrmn., Flyer Industries Ltd.; Pres., Huggard Equipment Co. Ltd.; Ace Motor Machine Co. Ltd.; Vice Pres., Canadian Quetico Outfitters Ltd.; Dir., Manitoba Forestry Resources Ltd.; A. E. McKenzie Co. Ltd.; ; Tantalum Mining Corp. of Canada; served in R.C.A.F. 1944, in R.C.C.S. 1945; joined Huggard Equipment Co. Ltd. as Secy.-Treas. 1950, Pres. 1963; Past Pres., Treas. and Dir., Fort Garry Community Club; mem. Manitoba Institute Chart. Accts.; Candn. Assn. Equipment Distrubutors; Winnipeg Chamber Comm.; Freemason (Shriner, Scot. Rite); United Church; recreations: curling, golf, fishing; Clubs: Granite Curling (Past Pres.); Ft. Garry Community (Past Pres.); Winnipeg Flying; Duke of Kent Legion; Home: 448 Lamont Blvd., Winnipeg, Man. R3P 0G3; Office: 600 — 428 Portage, Winnipeg, Man. R3C 0E4

PARTRIDGE, Bruce J., A.B., LL.B., J.D., LL.B.; b. Syracuse, N.Y., 4 June 1926; s. Bert J. and Marion L. (Rice) P.; e. Cazenovia (N.Y.) Central Sch., 1942; Oberlin Coll., A.B. (cum laude) 1946; Blackstone Coll. of Law, LL.B. (U.S.) 1950, J.D. 1952; Univ. of B.C., LL.B. (Candn.) 1975; m. Mary Janice, d. Bernard F. Smith, Winter Haven, Fla., 13 June 1948; children: Heather Leigh, Eric James, Brian Lloyd, Bonnie Joyce; Research Physicist, American Gas Assn., 1946-47; Business Mgr., Cazenovia Coll., 1948-51; Asst. Treas., Baldwin-Wallace Coll., 1951-53; Asst. Comptroller, Rochester Inst. of Technol., 1953-58; Vice Pres. for Business and Mang. and Lectr. in Business Law, Univ. of Del., 1958-64; Vice Pres. for Adm. and Treas., The Johns Hopkins Univ., 1964-69; Pres. of Univ. of Victoria, B.C., 1969-72; law student, Univ. of B.C., 1972-74; solicitor, Clark Wilson & Co., Vancouver, 1974-78; solicitor, Cominco Ltd., Vancouver, 1978-79; Managing Solicitor, Cominco Ltd. 1980- ; co-author, "College and University Business Administration", 1968; mem., Nat. Bd. of Advisors, Nat. Assn. for Retarded Children; Trustee, Assoc. Univs., Inc.; mem., Am. Council on Educ. (Chrmn., Comn. on Adm. Affairs, 1965-69); Anglican; mem. Acad. Council of B.C., 1979- ; mem. Adv. Comte., Centre for Resource Studies, Queen's Univ., 1980- ; recreations: sailing, travel, theatre; Home: 3939 Arbutus St., Vancouver, B.C. V6J 4T2

PARTRIDGE, David Gerry, B.A., R.C.A., F.R.S.A.; artist; b. Akron, Ohio 5 Oct. 1919; s. Albert Gerry and Edith (Harpham) P.; e. Mostyn House Sch. and Radley Coll., Eng. 1935; Trinity Coll. Sch. Port Hope, Ont. 1938; Trinity Coll. Univ. of Toronto B.A. 1941; Art Students League New York 1948; Slade Sch. London, Eng. 1950-51; Atelier 17 Paris 1958; m. Helen Rosemary d. Capt. John S. Annesley, R.N., 14 June 1943; children: Katharine Annesley, John David Harpham; Dealer, Gallery Quan, Toronto; Art Teacher, Appleby Coll. 1946; Ridley Coll. 1946-50, 1951-56; St. Catharines Coll. Inst. 1952-56; Queen's Univ. Summer Sch. 1958-60; Curator, St. Catharines Pub. Lib. & Art Gallery 1954-56; Teacher, Ottawa Civic Art Centre 1958-61; Trustee, Art Gallery of Ont. 1977-82; nail sculptures incl. Tate Gallery London, Eng.; Nat. Gallery Can.; Art Gallery Ont.; Westminster Cathedral, London, Eng.; Montreal Museum Fine Arts; Gallery New S. Wales Sidney, Australia; Lib. of Cong.; Victoria & Albert Museum (graphics latter 2 colls.); maj. comns. York Univ. Toronto; Toronto City Hall mural; Windsor Art Gallery mural; rep. in numerous pub., univ. and private colls.; rec'd Brit. Council Scholarship 1950-51; Sculpture Prize Montreal Museum Fine Arts 1962; R.C.A. Sculpture Competition 1977; served with RCAF 1942-45, Flying Instr., rank Flight Lt.; mem. London (Eng.) Group of Painters; recreations: tennis, sailing, carpentry; Home: 77 Seaton St., Toronto, Ont. M5A 2T2; Studio: 1112 Queen St. E., Toronto, Ont.

PASHLER, Peter Edward, M.A.Sc., Ph.D.; physicist; executive; b. Toronto, Ont. 4 Dec. 1919; s. Lawrence John and Georgina Mary (Hutton) P.; e. Parkdale Coll. Inst. Toronto 1937; Univ. of Toronto B.A.Sc. (Engn. Physics) 1941, M.A.Sc. 1945, Ph.D. 1947; VanderWaals Lab. Univ. of Amsterdam Post-Doctorate Fellow 1947; m. Margaret Marianne d. late John Car Moreland, Hamilton, Ont. 8 June 1943; children: Josephine E. Briggs, M.D., rev Lawrence John, Harold Edward; VICE PRES.- CORPORATE TECHNOL., CANADIAN GENERAL ELECTRIC CO. LTD., joined Dept. of Physics, Univ. of Toronto 1946 becoming Asst. Prof.; joined General Electric Corp. Research 1950; held various tech. and mgr. positions incl. Research Assoc., Liaison Scient., Branch and Lab. Mgr. and latterly Mgr. Technol. Evaluation Operation in Electronics; contributor to dev. of CAT Scanner and other electronic imaging means; Engaged in war research (devel. of radio proximity fuses artillery shells) Defence Research Bd. Can. 1941-46; author various tech. papers and articles; mem. Am. Phys. Soc.; IEEE (active in tech. comtes.); Soc. Motion Picture & TV Engrs.; Candn. Assn. Physicists (Treas. 1949); Chmn., R. & D. Comte.; Cdn. Manufacturers Assn.; Exec. Comte., Cdn. Research Management Assn.; recreations: photography, skiing, hiking, canoeing; Home: 7 Green Valley Rd., Willowdale, Ont. M2P 1A4; Office: (P.O. Box 417) Commerce Court North, Toronto, Ont. M5L 1J2.

PATERSON, A. K., Q.C., B.A., D.C.L.; b Montreal, Que. 7 March 1932; s. Hartland MacDougall and Jean (Kennedy) P.; e. Trinity Coll. Sch. Port Hope, Ont. 1948; Bishop's Univ. B.A. 1952, D.C.L.; McGill Univ. B.C.L. 1956; m. Joan d. Philip Robb 3 Sept. 1955; children: Robb, Timothy, Angela, Alex; PARTNER, McMASTER, MINNION & ASSOCIATES since 1969; read law with He-

ward, Holden & Associates; called to Bar of Que. 1957, Bar of Alta. 1971; cr. Q.C. 1973; joined Heward Holden Hutchison Cliff McMaster Meighen 1957; Asst. Prof. of Med. Jurisprudence McGill Univ. 1973; Mun. Judge Senneville, Que.; Commr. for Sch. Disputes; Co-Chrmn. Positive Action Comte.; Pres. Bishop's Univ.; MacKay Centre for Deaf and Crippled Children; mem. Candn. Bar Assn.; Candn. Medical-Bar Assn. Comte.(Chrmn. 1976); Candn. Bar Council; Vice Pres., Que.-Can. Pre-referendum Comte.; Liberal; Anglican; recreations: golf, tennis, squash, skiing; Clubs: University; Le Cercle; Montreal Badminton & Squash; Home: 14 Elmwood Ave., Senneville, Que. H9X 1T4; Office: 630 Dorchester Boulevard West, Montreal, Que. H3B 4H7

PATERSON, Christopher Blaikie, C.M., C.A.; b. London, Eng. 11 Nov. 1927; s. Donald Hugh and Dorothy Reed (Blaikie) P.; e. Trinity Coll. Sch. Port Hope, Ont. 1943; Harrow Sch. London, Eng. 1946; McGill Univ. 1946 — 47; m. Lorraine d. Abraham Gotlib, Toronto, Ont. 19 Apl. 1975; children (by first marriage): Susan, Douglas, Claire; PARTNER, PRICE WATERHOUSE & CO. since 1967; joined Price Waterhouse Vancouver 1947, C.A. 1953, trans. Toronto 1955; mem. Candn. Red Cross Soc. (Pres. Toronto Br. 1971-72, Pres. Ont. Div. 1978-80, Hon. Treas. Nat. Soc. 1981); Past Dir. Candn. Yachting Assn.; Past Treas. Ont. Sailing Assn.; Past Pres. Candn. Albacore Assn.; Past Dir. Sport Ont.; author various articles; Anglican; recreations: golf, skiing, sailing; Clubs: Toronto Golf; R.C.Y.C.; Devils Glen Country; Home: 238 Forest Hill Rd., Toronto, Ont. M5P 2N5; Office: (P.O. Box 51) Toronto-Dominion Centre, Toronto, Ont. M5K 1G1.

PATERSON, Donald Savigny, D.F.C., B.A.; company executive; b. Fort William, Ont., 22 Apr. 1918; s. Senator Norman McLeod and Eleanor Margaret (Macdonald) P.; e. Ashbury Coll., Ottawa. Ont.; Bishop's Univ., B.A.; McGill Univ.; m. Jane Bernadette d. John Lynch, Galway, Ireland, 2 Aug. 1947; children: Norman Macdonald, Charles Lynch, John James, Andrew Bartholomew, Ellen Margaret; PRES. AND DIR., N.M. PATERSON & SONS LTD.; Pres. and Dir., Stall Lake Mines Ltd.; Traders Building Assoc. Ltd.; Dir., Grain Insurance & Guarantee Co. Ltd.; Grain Insurance Brokers Ltd.; Voyager Explorations Ltd.; served with R.C.A.F. in Can. and Eng. 1940-45; retired with rank Flt. Lt.; Freemason; Zeta Psi; Presbyterian; recreations: golf, fishing, sailing, flying, hunting; Clubs: St. Charles Golf & Country; Royal Lake of the Woods Yacht; Manitoba; Home: 131 Ridgedale Cr., Winnipeg, Man. R3R 0B4; Office: 609 — 167 Lombard Ave., Winnipeg, Man. R3B 0V5

PATERSON, Garnet Russell, Phm.B., B.S.P., M.Sc., Ph.D.; educator; b. Hamilton, Ont., 31 July 1919; s. Peter and Ethel Minnie May (Barrett) P.; e. Ont. Coll. of Pharm., Univ. of Toronto, Phm.B 1942; Univ. of Sask., B.S.P. 1947, M.Sc. 1948; Univ. of Wis., Ph.D. 1954; m. (Jessie) Ida (Bernice), d. James Griffith, New Toronto, Ont., 7 Sept. 1946; two s. Andrew James, (Lorne Kenneth) Charles; EXTVE. DIR., HANNAH INST. FOR THE HISTORY OF MEDICINE since 1975; Prof., Faculty of Pharmacy, Univ. of Toronto, since 1961; Asst. Prof., Ont. Coll. of Pharm., 1951; Faculty of Pharm. of present Univ. 1953; Assoc. Prof. 1954; served with RCA and RCAMC 1943-46; rec'd Centennial Medal 1967; Can. Council Leave Fellowship 1971-72; writings incl. over 40 research papers in pharm. chem. and hist. of pharm.; Affiliate, Inst. for Hist. and Philos. of Science and Technol.; Assoc. Fellow, Acad. Med.; mem. L'Acad. Internat. d'Histoire de la Pharm.; Candn. Conf. Pharm. Faculties (Secy.-Treas. 1959-62, Vice Chrmn. 1964-65, Chrmn. 1965-66); Candn. Acad. Hist. Pharm. (Dir. 1955-68, Secy.-Treas. 1968-75, Hon. Pres. 1980-); Panam. Fed. Pharm. & Biochem. (Dir. 1963-75, Candn. Del. 1963, 1966, 1969, 1972); Candn. Soc. Hist. & Phil. Science (mem., 1972-78; Pres., 1978-); Candn. Soc. Hist. Med. (Vice Pres. Ont. 1975-79, Sr. Vice-Pres. 1979-80; Pres. 1980-); recreation: music;

Home: 50 Prince Arthur Ave., Apt. #1504, Toronto, Ont. M5R 1B5

PATERSON, Hon. Norman McLeod, D.C.L., LL.D., K.G.St.J.; senator; b. Portage La Prairie, Manitoba, 3 August 1883; s. Hugh S. and Ella (Snider) P.; e. Pub.. Schs., Portage La Prairie and Toronto, Ont.; LL.D., Carleton University; D.C.L. Lakehead Univ.; m. late Eleanor Margaret, d. J.M. Maccdonald, Winnipeg, Manitoba, 2 June 1915; children: Donald, John, Mary (Mrs. A. Norton Francis), Nancy (Mrs. Paul A. McFarlane Jr.), Joan (Mrs. Ayton G. Keyes), late Elizabeth (Mrs. E. Webster); PRES. & DIR., N. M. PATERSON & SONS LTD., which controls and operates 109 elevators between Thunder Bay and Sask., and a four million bushel terminal elevator at Thunder Bay and operates 35 lake freighters; Pres. and Dir., Western Engineering Service; Chrmn. of Bd., Royal Edward Hotel; summoned to the Senate of Can., 9 Feb. 1940; invested by the King at Coronation with Offr. Brother of St. John Ambulance Assn. and raised to the rank of Commdr. in 1943; apptd. Knight of the Order of St. John by the King in Nov. 1945; Freemason; Protestant; recreations: golf, motoring, shooting, fishing, skiing, yachting; Clubs: Rideau; Manitoba; Fort William Country; Royal Lake of the Woods Yacht; Maganassippi Fish & Game; Home: 500 Wilbrod St., Ottawa, Ont. K1N 6N2; Office: The Senate, Ottawa, Ont. K1A 0A4

PATERSON, Sheena; editor; b. Bridge of Allan, Scot. 8 May 1942; d. James and Jean (Kelly) Michie; e. Clydebank High Sch.; London Coll. of Music and Speech, Teaching Associateship A.L.C.M. (Elocution) 1958; m. Robert McLeish Paterson 19 Aug. 1961; children: Karen, Paul; SATURDAY ED., TORONTO STAR; reporter, columnist, Clydebank Standard 1958; Scottish Daily Record and Scottish Sunday Mail 1959-66; joined Weekend Magazine as Asst. to Toronto Ed. 1969, Toronto Ed. 1970, Mang. Ed. 1973, Acting Ed. 1974, Chief Ed. 1975-76; Insight Ed., Toronto Star 1977-78; Home: 66 Balmoral Ave., Toronto, Ont.

PATON, Samuel Todd; banker; b. Stonehouse, Lanarkshire, Scotland, 12 Oct. 1910; e. Allan Glen's Sch., Scotland; former Depy. Chmn., Toronto Dominion Bank; Dir., Toronto-Dominion Realty Co. Ltd.; Canvil Ltd.; A. E. LePage Ltd.; Hayes-Dana Inc.; Dana Corp.; AGF Group of Cos.; Kellogg-Salada Canada Ltd.; Bird Construction Co. Ltd.; Canadian Motorways Ltd.; Outboard Marine Corp. of Can. Ltd.; A.E. LePage (Ont.) Ltd.; Shipp Corp.; entered service with Bank at Kipling, Sask., 24 Aug. 1928; subsequently served at Welwyn, Sask., Edmonton, Montreal, Toronto; First Asst. Mgr., St. James and McGill, Montreal, 1949; Credit Supervisor, Toronto, June 1950; Asst. Chief Supervisor, Western Dept., Toronto, Oct. 1950; Asst. Gen. Mgr., Dec. 1953; Deputy Gen. Mgr., Dec. 1960; Gen. Mgr., Dec. 1962; Vice-Pres., Dec. 1963; Vice Pres., Chief General Manager & Director 1965; Executive Vice-President 1968; Depy. Chrmn. 1972-75; Mem. Emeritus, City of Toronto Redevelopment Adv. Council; Past Pres., Candn. Bankers' Assn.; mem. St. Andrews Soc.; United Church; recreations: curling, golf; Clubs: Granite; National; Canadian; Office: (P.O. Box 1) Toronto-Dominion Centre, Toronto, Ont. M5K 1A2

PATON, William John Ross, B.Sc., LL.D.; industrialist; b. Fort William, Ont., 17 July 1915; s. James Martin and Mary A. (Ross) P.; e. Central Sch. Coll. Inst., Fort William, Ont.; Business Coll., Ft. William, Ont.; Tri-State Coll., Angola, Ind., B.Sc. (Mech. Engn.) 1940 m. Margaret, d. Wilmington A. Cross, 1940; children: William, Mary, Anne, Susan; CHAIRMAN, JANNOCK CORP. LTD. since 1973; Chrmn., Lyman Tube Ltd.; Sonco Steel Tube Ltd.; Allanson Mfg. Co. Ltd.; Atlantic Consolidated Foods Co. Ltd.; Canada Brick Co. Ltd.; Jannock Industries Ltd.; Ocean Maid Foods Ltd.; Pres. and Chief Extve. Offr., Northern Engineering and Supply Co. Ltd.; Atlantic Fish Processors Company Limited; Life Gov., Mont-

real Gen. Hosp.; began with Northern Engineering & Supply Co. Ltd., Fort William, Ont., 1932-37; Canadian Car & Foundry Co. Ltd., Aircraft Div., Fort William, Ont., 1939-40; Dept. of Munitions & Supply, Ammunition Production Div., Toronto, Ont., 1940-41; The Weatherhead Co. of Can., St. Thomas, Ont., 1942-49; joined Robin Hood Flour Mills Limited 1949, became Vice-President; joined Atlantic Sugar Refineries Company Limited as Executive Vice-President and General Manager, 1957, President and Chief Executive Officer 1961; mem., International Sugar Research Assn. (Extve. Comte.); Sugar Assn. Inc.; Trustee, Public Sch. Bd., St. Thomas, Ont. (Chrmn. 1945-49); Vice-Pres., Port Colborne Chamber of Comm., 1953; Dir. (Class XIII) Indust. Accident Prevention Assn., 1950-53; Freemason; Protestant; Clubs: St. James's; Union (Saint John, N.B.); Beaconsfield Golf; Home: 4603, 44 Charles St. W., Toronto, Ont. M4Y 1R8; Office: (Box 43) Toronto Dominion Centre, Toronto, Ont. M5K 1B7

PATRY, Marcel, M.A., Ph.D., D.P.H., o.m.i. (R.C.); educator; b. Beaumont, Qué. 31 Jan. 1923; s. Armand and Yvonne (Marcoux) P.; e. Univ. of Ottawa, B.A.-B.P.H. 1945, M.A.(PH) 1947, Ph.D. (PH) 1949, D.P.H. 1955; DIR., INST. OF SOCIAL COMMUNICATIONS, ST. PAUL'S UNIV., 1980- ; Prof. in Communication Studies, St. Paul's Univ., 1978-80; Pres. and Rector, St. Paul's Univ., 1968-77; Prof. of Philos., Univ. of Ottawa 1950-68; mem. Senate Univ. of Ottawa; Bd. of Adm. Le Droit Ltée; mem. Assn. Candn. Française pour l'avancement des sciences; Assn. Candn. de Philos.; Assn. Candn. de Communication; author of "Delienatio Cursus Logicae" 1955; "L'Object et les Limites de la Logique" 1955; "Reflexions sur les lois de l'intelligence" 1965; also various briefs and articles in numerous learned and prof. journs.; recreations: skiing, fishing; Home: 305 Nelson, Ottawa, Ont. K1N 7S5; Office: 223 Main St., Ottawa, Ont. K1S 1C4

PATTERSON, Clyde Rodier, B.A.; retired government administrator; b. Portage la Prairie, Man., 14 June 1918; s. Margaret S. (Rodier) and the late Walter P.; e. Calgary Pub. Schs.; Univ. of Alta., B.A. 1940, High Sch. Teaching Cert. 1941; Laval Univ., Bicultural-Bilingual Devel. Program, 1967; Cert. in Visual Arts, Ottawa Univ. 1974; m. Frances Lillian, d. (late) Samuel Hunter Adams, Q.C., Ganges, B.C., 25 Dec. 1941; children: Sydney Margaret (Bright), Douglas Ross; Dir. Gen., Emergency Planning Can.(ret.) High Sch. Vice-Princ. and Princ., 1940-42; Occupational Counsellor, Dept. of Veterans Affairs, 1945-46; Regional Dir., Civil Service Comn. of Can. (Edmonton), 1946-52; Asst. Dir., Personnel Selection, Ottawa, 1952-58, Dir., 1958-62, Dir., Operations 1962-65; Nat. Coordinator, Civil Emergency Measures, 1965; Volunteer Consultant (Performance Measurement) with Candn. Extve. Svce. Overseas to Treasury of Malaysia 1978-79; Reg'd. Consultant, E.A.C. Amy & Sons, Ottawa; served with R.C.A.C. in Can. and U.K.; retired as Lieut. 1944; mem., Personnel Comte., Boy Scouts Assn. of Canada; Inst. Civil Defence (Fellow honoris causa); Anglican; recreations: photography, pottery, gardening, painting, primitive hand tools; writing; Club: Metcalfe; Home: Oxford Mills, Ont.;

PATTERSON, Freeman Wilford, B.A., M.Div., D.Litt., R.C.A.; photographer; writer; educator; b. Long Reach, N.B. 25 Sept. 1937; s. G. Gordon and Ethel Winnifred (Crawford) P.; e. Greys Mills (N.B.) Sch. 1944; Long Reach (N.B.) Sch. 1951; Macdonald Consolidated Sch. Kingston, N.B. grad. 1955; Acadia Univ. B.A. 1959; Union Theol. Semy. New York M.Div. 1962; Univ. of N.B. D.Litt. 1980; Dean of Religious Educ. Albert Coll. Edmonton 1962-65; Photographer Stills Div. Berkeley Studios, Un. Ch. of Can. Toronto 1965-66; freelance photographer 1966- ; Co-Partner Summer Photography Sch. Shamper's Bluff, N.B. 1973-77; seminar lectr. across Can., USA and S. Africa (Cong. of Photographic Soc. S. Africa 1976, 1980) 1972-80; judge nat. and internat. salons; photographs incl. many books incl. "Canada, A Year of the Land"; "Canada"; "Between Friends- Entre Amis" and Reader's Digest Candn. nature series (4 books); rep. in over 1000 competitive internat. exhns.; colour prints many exhns. incl. Metrop. Museum New York; Nat. Film Bd.'s Can., A Yr. of the Land, Can.'s Colour Photographers, The Magic World of Children, Freeman Patterson Monograph; recipient Nat. Film Bd. Can. Gold Medal 1967; Sch. Trustee Dist. 19 N.B. 1974- ; author "Photography For the Joy of It" 1977; "Photography And The Art Of Seeing" 1979; various articles; Ed. "Foto Flash" 1964-68; "Camera Canada" 1968-78; Hon. EFIAP, Fed. Internationale de l'Art Photographique, Berne; Fellow, Photographic Soc. Am.; Fellow, Photographic Soc. S. Africa; Hon. Life mem. Toronto Guild for Colour Photography (Dir., Vice Pres., Pres.); mem. Nat. Assn. Photographic Art (Pres.); N.B. Fed. Naturalists; Candn. Nature Fed. (Comte.); Ont. Fed. Nature; Audubon Soc.; Address: Shampers Bluff, Clifton Royal, N.B. E0G 1N0.

PATTERSON, Gordon Neil, M.A., Ph.D., LL.D., D.Sc., F.R.Ae.S. (1950), F.C.A.S.I. (1955), F.A.I.I.A., (1956), Hon.F.C.A.S.I. (1981); educator; b. Medicine Hat, Alta., 16 July 1908; s. Thomas Ernest and Lyra Mabel (O'Neil) P.; e. Univ. of Alta., B.Sc. 1931, LL.D. 1958; Univ. of Toronto, M.A. 1933, Ph.D. 1935, D. Sc. 1977 (Sesquicentennial Convocation), (winner of Open Fellowship, Univ. of Toronto and Bursary and Studentship from Nat. Research Council, Ottawa), D.Sc (Waterloo) 1962; D.Sc. (McGill) 1965; m. Myrtle Alberta, d. Frank J. Weber, Kimberley, Ont., 4 Nov. 1935; one d. Dona; Founding Dir. Institute for Aerospace Studies, Univ. of Toronto, 1949-1974; Prof. of Aerodynamics, 1947-1974; mem., Science Council of Can., 1966-1973; Gas and Plasma Dynamics Research Panel, Defence Research Bd., Ottawa, 1950-66; Member of Advisory Ballistics Panel, U.S. Naval Ordnance Lab., Silver Springs, Md., 1949-55; Scient. Offr., Aerodynamics Dept., Royal Aircraft Estab., Farnborough, Eng., engaged in wind tunnel research leading to improvements on aircraft, 1935-39; Offr. in Charge, Aerodynamics Sec., Divn. of Aeronautics, Council for Scient. & Indust. Research, Melbourne, Aust., 1939-44; engaged in advanced studies in U.S.A., 1944-46; Chrmn. Adv. Aeroballistics Panel, U.S. Naval Ordnance Lab. 1956-59; Pres., Candn. Aero & Space Inst. 1957 (W. Rupert Turnbull Lectr. 1957); McCurdy Trophy, 1962; C. D. Howe Award, 1972; Assoc. Ed., Physics of Fluids, Am. Inst. of Physics, 1958-61; apptd. mem. Tech. Adv. Panel of (Candn.) Nat. Aero. Research Council, 1961; mem., Research Adv. Comte. on Fluid Mech., U.S. Nat. Aeronautics and Space Adm., 1962-65; Chrmn., Fourth Internat. Sympos. on Rarified Gas Dynamics, 1964; selected to present 28th Wright Bros. Lecture to Am. Inst. of Aero. & Astronautics, Jan. 1965; author: "Molecular Flow of Gases", 1956; "Introduction to the Kinetic Theory of Gas Flows", 1971; "Pathway to Excellence" (UTIAS the First Twenty-Five Years), 1977; "The Race for Unlimited Energy", 1979; "Molecular Nature of Aerodynamics", 1981; recreation: golf; Home: P.O. Box 47, Thornbury, Ont. N0H 2P0

PATTERSON, Harry Thomas, O.C. (1968), B.A., theatrical director; b. Stratford, Ont., 11 June 1920; s. Harry and Lucinda (Whyte) P.; e. Avon Sch. and Collegiate Vocational Sch., Stratford, Ont.; Trinity Coll., Univ. of Toronto, B.A. 1948; twice m.; children: Robert, Penelope Margot, Timothy John Cecil, Lucy Ann, Lyle Scott; VICE PRES., LOCKWOOD PATTERSON ASSOCIATES LTD., CONSULTANTS. Permanent Consultant to Sarnia, Ont. Arts Foundation (presently involved in formation of Sarnia Light Opera Festival with Artistic Dir., Dr. Boyd Neel); Consultant, Dawson City Festival Foundation, Dawson City, Yukon Terr.; mem. Bd. of Govs., Nat. Theatre Sch. of Canada; after grad. from univ. joined Maclean-Hunter Publishing Co. Ltd., Toronto, Ont., as Assoc. Editor of Civic Administration Magazine; Founder and Dir., Stratford Shakesperean Festival Foundation;

since age of 14 had been working on the idea of creating an internat. theatre in Stratford; after an initial failure in 1946, obtained the backing of the Stratford City Council in Jan. 1952, and after a trip to New York in search of talent was authorized to call Tyrone Guthrie at his home in Ireland; after various negotiations the Festival idea was consummated by obtaining Alec Guinness as star, Tanya Moiseiwitsch as designer, Cecil Clarke as Asst. Dir. and Tyrone Guthrie as Dir.; apptd. Gen. Mgr. of the Festival, which was officially chartered in Nov. 1952; formed the Canadian Players Ltd., a touring prof. company in 1954; awarded 2nd Annual Award of Canada Arts Council; also President's Award, Canadian Council of Authors and Artists, 1955; served in 2nd World War with Candn. Dental Corps as Sgt., 1939-45; Overseas in Eng., France, Belgium, Holland and Germany, 1940-45; Presbyterian; recreation: gardening. 40 Madison Ave., Toronto, Ont. M5R 2S1

PATTERSON, Hon. Henry Stuart, C.D., LL.B.; judge; b. Calgary, Alta. 9 Oct. 1913; s. Henry Stuart and Margaret Cogswell (Chase) P.; e. Western Can. High Sch. 1930; Comm. High Sch. Calgary 1931; Univ. of Alta. B.A. 1936, LL.B. 1937; m. Laura Stuart d. late Thomas A. Lydiard 5 Dec. 1940; children: Luana Alice (Waldron), Catherine Anne (Ainsworth). John Thomas, Sylvia Stuart (Polachuk); JUDGE, COURT OF QUEEN'S BENCH, ALTA. 1979- ; called to Bar of Alta. 1938; cr. Q.C. 1960; Judge, Dist. Court of S. Alta. 1960; mem. Calgary Police Comn. 1956-66; Chrmn. Comte. on Adoptions in Alta. 1964-65; served with 1st and 3rd Candn. Div. Signals 1940-45, rank Maj.; presently Hon. Lt. Col. 746 Communications & Electronics Sqdn.; mem. Candn. Signals Assn. (Pres. 1956, 1976); Calgary Bar Assn.; Law Soc. Alta.; Candn. Bar Assn.; P. Conservative; United Church; recreation: woodworking; Home: 816-32 Ave. S.W., Calgary, Alta. T2T 1V2; Office: Court House, Calgary, Alta. T2P 1T5.

PATTERSON, Howard L., B.S.A., M.A., Ph.D.; agriculturist; b. Boissevain, Manitoba, 20 May 1904; s. James Alexander and Anne Elizabeth (Linklater) P.; e. Univ. of Manitoba, B.S.A. 1930, M.A. 1933; Cornell Univ., Ph.D. 1946; m. Ellen Alexandra, d. Oswald Hibbert, Boissevain, Man., 4 Aug. 1934; children: David H., Alice Diana, Dorothy Anne, Carolyn Ellen; joined Manitoba Dept. of Agric. in 1934, and Fed. Dept. of Agric. in 1937 (Econ. Div.) stationed successively at Ottawa, Edmonton, Winnipeg; served in O.T.C., Univ. of Alta., 1941-42; Dir., Farm Econ. & Stat. Br., Dept. of Agric. Ont. 1948 till retired; Publications: five booklets and numerous articles on farming and farm econ.; prepared briefs on "Ont. Agriculture" for Royal Comn. on Candn. Econ. Prospects, 1955, "The Small Farm Problem" for Senate Investig. Comte. 1959 and "Farm Management in Ont." for Agric. Marketing Enquiry Comte. reviewing farm management work in Ont., 1960; mem., Agric. Inst. Can. (Pres. 1962-63; Candn. Agric. Econ. Soc. (Past Dir.); Candn. Soc. Agron.; Am. Farm Econ. Assn.; United Church; recreations: bowling, curling; Club: Wells Hill Bowling; Home: 108 Hilton Ave., Toronto, Ont. M5R 3E7

PATTERSON, John Breden, B.A., F.S.A., F.C.I.A.; actuary; b. Windsor, Ont. 19 Sept. 1927; e. Univ. of Toronto B.A. 1949; m. Beryl Norma 1951; children: Kimberly, Chris; PRESIDENT, ACTUARIAL CONSULTANTS OF CANADA LTD.; Asst. Actuary Crown Life Insurance Co. 1949-57; Vice Pres. and Actuary Gerling Global Life Insurance Co. 1957-65; Freemason; Club: Donalda; Home: 54 Beveridge Dr., Don Mills, Ont. M3A 1P3; Office: (P.O. Box 38) 1505, 401 Bay St., Toronto, Ont. M5H 2Y4.

PATTERSON, William Edwin, M.B.E. (1945); E.D., B.A.; real estate executive; b. Toronto, Ont., 24 Nov. 1902; s. George Emmanuel and Elizabeth (Lodge) P.; e. Jarvis Coll. Inst. and Univ. of Toronto Schs.; Univ. of Toronto, B.A. 1925; m. Kathleen Grace, d. Dr. Albert E. McCordick, Ottawa, 7 Mar. 1932; one d. Jane (Mrs. James

Domm); CHAIRMAN, WOOD, FLEMING & CO. LTD. since 1972; Dir., Lewis Craft Supplies Ltd.; Hon. Pres., C.N.I.B.; became assoc. with present Co. over thirty years ago; served with Candn. Mil. 1923-35 with Queen's York Rangers (1st Am. Regt.); held rank of Lieut. and Capt.; served in World War 1940-46 with Candn. Army (Active) in Can., U.K., Central Mediterranean area and Continental Europe; R.O. since 1946; Mentioned in Despatches; apptd. Hon. Lieut.-Col., Queen's York Rangers, 1955-65; mem., Central Council, Brit. Sailors' Soc. (Can.); Psi Upsilon; Conservative; Anglican; recreations: fishing, reading; Clubs: National; Toronto Hunt; Naval & Military Club (London, Eng.); Home: 19 Whitehall Rd., Toronto, Ont. M4W 2C5; Office: 7 King St. E., Toronto, Ont. M5C 1A2

PATTISON, James A.; executive; b. Sask. 1 Oct. 1928; s. Chandos P.; e. John Oliver High Sch., Vancouver; Univ. of B.C.; m. Mary Ella, d. George Hudson, Moose Jaw, Sask. 30 June 1951; children: James Allen Jr., Mary Ann, Cynthia; CHAIRMAN, PRES. AND CHIEF EXTVE. JIM PATTISON INDUSTRIES LTD.; Jim Pattison Enterprises Ltd.; AirBC Ltd.; Great Pacific Industries Ltd.; Pres. and Dir., Jim Pattison Sports Ltd.; formerly Gen. Mgr., Bowell McLean, Vancouver; estbd. own automobile dealership 1961 and acquired radio stns. in Vancouver and Winnipeg in addition to Muzak franchise for B.C.; purchased control of Neon Products Ltd. 1967; mem. General Motors Pres.'s Adv. Council, 1965-66; mem. Young Pres.'s Organ.; Alpha Tau Omega; Home: 855 Eyremount Dr., West Vancouver, B.C. V7S 2B2; Office: 1055 W. Hastings St., Vancouver, B.C. V6E 2H2

PAUL, Rémi, CR.; LL.L.; avocat; né Louiseville (Maskinongé) Qué. 10 juin 1921; f. Edmond Paul et Maria (Descheneaux) P.; é. Collège Saint-Louis de Gonzague, Louiseville, Qué.; Séminaire Saint-Joseph de Trois-Rivières, Qué.; Univ. Laval, licence en droit; ép Rita Caron, sept. 1948; enfants: René, Denis, Francine; reçu au Barreau du Qué. 1948; nommé conseil de la Reine 1966; élu député dans Berthier-Maskinongé de la Naudière à la Chambre des communes le 31 mars 1958; réélu aux élections générales de 1962 et 1963; se retire de la politique fédérale en sept. 1965; fut candidat de l'Union Nationale et élu à l'assemblée législative du Québec pour la comté de Maskinongé et élu orateur 1966; assermenté comme Secrétaire de l'Etat du Québec 1968 et ministre responsable de la Protection civile 1969; ministre de la Justice et procureur général de Qué. 1969; réélu député Union Nationale 1970; assermenté juge de la Cour Provinciale pour le district de Québec, 1974; catholique romain; Résidence: 392 Saint-Augustin, Louiseville, Qué. J5U 1B7; Bureau: Palais de justice, 12, rue St-Louis, Québec, Qué.

PAUL, Robert Henry, B.A.Sc.; P.Eng.; executive; b. Edmonds, B.C. 31 Jan. 1920; s. William and Ruth Jane (Bates) P.; e. Univ. of B.C. B.A.Sc. 1952; m. Phyllis Elizabeth d. late Roy E. Lapp 22 March 1951; children: Mrs. Louise Alice McCann, Wendy Ruth, Margaret Ann, James Robert; PRES. AND DIR., BECHTEL CANADA LTD. 1973- ; Pres. and Dir. Bechtel Quebec Ltée; Vice Pres. and Dir. Bechtel Petroleum, Inc.; Dir. Bechtel Power Corp., Bechtel Civil & Minerals, Inc.; joined Canadian Bechtel Ltd. 1952, apptd. Vice Pres. 1967; Mgr. Div. Business Devel., Refinery & Chem. Div., Bechtel Corp. San Francisco 1969; Vice Pres. Bechtel Corp. and Bechtel Inc. 1971; Chrmn. Business Devel. Comte., The Bechtel Group, San Francisco 1972-73 and 1980- ; Vice Pres. and Mgr. Marketing, Petroleum Group, Bechtel Petroleum, Inc. 1980; mem., Planning Comte., Bechtel Group Inc. 1981; served with Royal Candn. Corps of Signals 1941-46; mem. Assn. Prof. Engrs. Prov. Ont.; Assn. Prof. Engrs. Geols. & Geophysicists Alta.; Candn. Soc. Civil Engrs.; Engn. Inst. Can.; Candn. Inst. Mining & Metall.; Am. Petroleum Inst.; Presbyterian; recreations: golf, fishing, woodworking; Clubs: Granite; Sarnia Golf & Curling; Shaughnessy Golf & Country (Vancouver); Carmell Val-

ley Ranch Golf; Home: 3011 Point Grey Rd., Vancouver, B.C. V6K 1A7; Office: Suite 3090, 650 W. Georgia St., VAncouver, B.C. V6B 4N7

PAULIN, Kenneth Burnside; construction executive; b. Hamilton, Ont., 17 July 1915; s. Frederick W. and Winonah M. (St. John) P.; e. Pub. and High Schs., Hamilton, Ont.; McMaster Univ.; m. Jeanne, d. J. Russell Laidman, 8 Feb. 1946; children: James F., Elizabeth Anne; PRESIDENT, GEN. MGR. AND DIR., CANADIAN ENGINEERING AND CONTRACTING CO. LTD., since 1957; mem., Adv. Bd., Canada Permanent Trust Co.; joined Great Lakes Concrete Pipe Ltd., District Improvement Corp. as Dir. of Sales, 1938-45; Sales Dept., American Tobacco Co., 1942 and McQuay Norris Manufacturing Co. Ltd., 1946-50; el. Dir. of present Co. 1950; apptd. Gen. Mgr. and Dir. 1956; Pres., Gen. Mgr. and Dir. 1957; served with U.S.A.F. 1942-45; rank Staff Sgt. on discharge; Past Pres., Metrop. Bd. Hamilton Y.M.C.A.; mem., Hamilton Art Gallery; Past Pres., Ont. Fed. Constr. Assn.; Hamilton Constr. Assn.; Ontario Gen. Contractors Assn.; mem. Hamilton Chamber Comm.; Presbyterian; recreations: golf, curling, fishing; Clubs: Hamilton Golf & Country (Past President); The Hamilton; Hamilton Thistle; Canadian; Seigniory (Montebello); Kiwanis (Past Pres.); Home: 180 Concession Street, Hamilton, Ont. L9A 1A8; Office: 121 Shaw St., Hamilton, Ont. L8L 3P6

PAVILANIS, Vytautas, M.D.; b. Kaunas, Lithuania 7 June 1920; s. Kazys and Antonina (Eimontas) P.; e. Univ. of Kaunas M.D. 1942; Institut Pasteur, Paris Dipl. in Microbiol. 1947; Dipl. in Serology & Hematol. 1948; m. Irene, Ph.D. d. late Col. Bruno Stencelis 8 March 1947; children: Alain, M.D., Christine D.V.M., Marina Branigan, Ingrid; ASST. DIR. TEACHING AND RESEARCH, INSTITUT ARMAND-FRAPPIER since 1978, Dir. Quality Control since 1976; Hon. Consultant in Virol. Queen Elizabeth Hosp.; Consultant in Bacteriol. Brome-Missisquoi-Perkins Hosp. Cowansville, Que.; Assoc. Prof. Univ. de Montréal since 1956, Asst. Prof. 1948-56; Prof. Univ. du Qué. since 1974; Asst. Prof. of Pathol. Univ. of Kaunas 1942-44; Resident Physician in Siegbourg, Germany 1944-45; Asst. Institut Pasteur, Paris 1945-48; Head of Virus Dept. Institut Armand-Frappier 1948-75, Scient. Dir. 1970-75, Research Coordinator 1975-78, Teaching Coordinator 1977; Elected Fellow of the Royal Soc. of Canada, 1973 co-author "Manuel de techniques virologiques" 1978; over 137 publs. virol. mem. Coll. of Phys.; Candn. Soc. Microbiol. (2nd Vice Pres. 1966); Candn. Pub. Health Assn. (Chrmn. Lab. Sec. 1969); Virology Club Montreal (Pres. 1969); Candn. Med. Assn.; Candn. Assn. Med. Microbiol.; R. Catholic; recreations: skiing, riding; Club: Brome Lake Boating; Home: 4742 The Boulevard, Westmount, Que. H3Y 1V3; Office: (P.O. Box 100) Laval-des-Rapides, Que. H7N 4Z3.

PAWLEY, Howard Russell, Q.C.; LL.B.; b. Brampton, Ont., 21 Nov. 1934; s. Russell and Velma Leone (Madill); e. Brampton High Sch., Man Teachers Coll., United Coll., University of Winnipeg, Man. Law Sch.; m. Adeline, d. Joseph Schreyer 26 Nov. 1960; children: Christopher Scott, Charysse; PREMIER OF MANITOBA 1981- ; el. Man. Leg. g.e. 1969; re-el. 1973, 1977 and 1981; Min. of Public Works (Min. of Government Services) and Min. of Urban Development 1969-71; Min. of Municipal Affairs 1969-76; Attorney Gen. and Keeper of the Great Seal 1973; Min. responsible for the Liquor Control Act 1976; Min. responsible for the Man. Public Insur. Corp.; and Man. Housing and Renewal Corp.; Chosen Leader of Man. N.D.P. 13 Jan. 1979; Address: 97 Dorchester Ave. Selkirk, Man. R1A 0K1

PAWLING, John D., B.A.Sc.; management consultant; b. Toronto, Ont., 23 Oct. 1922; s. Charles Roy and Lottie Belle (Hildreth) P.; e. Bloor Coll. Inst., Toronto; Univ. of Toronto, B.A.Sc. 1948; m. Mary Eileen, d. late William B.

Clare; two d., Barbara Joan (Hejouk), Kathleen Anne; PRES. AND C.E.O., MOHAWK INDUSTRIES; Pres., J.D. Pawling and Assoc. Ltd., Management Consultants since 1980; Partner, Haskins and Sells Associates, 1974-79; Vice President Dir., Tecumseh Metal Products Ltd.; Steel Master Tool Co. Ltd.; Dir. Mfg. Services, Price Waterhouse & Co., 1957-59; from 1959-65 variously Mgr. Mfg. Services, Hinde & Dauch (Canada) Ltd., subsequently integrated with Domtar Ltd.; Gen. Mgr. Carton Specialties Div., Domtar Packaging Ltd., Toronto; Asst. to Vice Pres., Domtar Pulp & Paper Ltd.; Dir., Simpson Riddell Stead & Assoc., 1965; Extve. Vice Pres. and Dir., Samson Belair Riddell Stead Inc., Montreal, 1968-72; Pres. and Dir., Riddell Stead & Assocs. Ltd. 1972-74; served as Candn. Offr. on loan to Brit Army 1942-45; N.W. Europe with 1st Bn., Border Regt., 1st Airborne Div.; rank Lt.; Pres. (1973), Candn. Assn. Mang. Consultants (Dir. since 1969); mem., Montreal Bd. Trade; Chambre Comm. Montréal; Liberal; Protestant; recreation: tennis; Club: Downtown Tennis; Home: 60 High Park Ave., Toronto, Ont. M6P 2R9;

PAYNE, Robert Walter, B.A., Ph.D.; university professor; b. Calgary, Alta. 5 Nov. 1925; s. Reginald Wm. and Nora Winnifred (Cowdery) P.; e. Central Coll. Inst., Calgary 1943; Univ. of Alberta B.A. 1949; Univ. of London Ph.D. 1954; children: Raymond Wm., Barbara Joan, Margaret Jane, George Reginald Alexander, Robin Charles; PROF. OF PSYCHOLOGY, DEAN FACULTY OF HUMAN AND SOCIAL DEV., UNIV. OF VICTORIA since 1978; Consultant psychol. (part-time) W. Park Hosp. for Nervous and Mental Diseases, Surrey, Eng., 1950-52; Lectr. Psychol., Inst. of Psychiatry (Maudsley Hosp.) Univ. of London, 1952-59; Assoc. Prof., Prof. of Psychol., Queen's Univ. (Kingston, Ont.) 1959-65; Temple Univ. Sch. of Med., Phil, Pa., Prof. of Psychol. and Chrmn. Dept. of Behavioural Science, 1965-73, Prof. Psychiatry, 1973-78; Sr. Med. Research Scientist, East. Penna. Psychiatric Inst., Phil, Pa., 1965-78; served with Can. Army (active) 1943-45; Candn. volunteer medal (with clasp); war medal 1939-45; author of "Cognitive Abnormalities", 1973; "Cognitive Defects in Schizophrenia: Overinclusive Thinking", 1971; "Disorders of Thinking", 1970; "The Measurement and Significance of Overinclusive Thinking and Retardation in Schizophrenia", 1966; "Thought Disorder in Psychotic Patients", 1960; also chpts. in textbooks and articles in prof. jnls.; rec'd Stratton Research Award in Psychiatry, 1964; Fellow, Br. Psychol. Soc.; Fellow, Am. Psychol. Assoc.; Fellow, Candn. Psychol. Assoc.; mem., Am. Psychopathological Assn.; Club: Univ. of Victoria Faculty; recreations: tennis, reading; Home: 949 Pattullio Place, Victoria, B.C. V8S 5H6; Office: P.O. Box 1700, Victoria, B.C. V8W 2Y2.

PAYNTER, Kenneth Jack, D.D.S., Ph.D. F.R.C.D., F.I.C.D.; b. Kingston, Ont., 17 Feb. 1918; s. Frederick Thomas and Norma (Knapp) P.; e. Public and High Schs., Kingston, Ont.; Univ. of Toronto, D.D.S. 1944; Columbia Univ., Ph.D. 1953; m. Kathleen Evelyn, d. late J. Bawden, Kingston, Ont., 8 Sept. 1945; children: James Thomas, Susan Eileen, Terrence Jack; Dir., Med. Research Council Can.; former Prof. and Dean, Coll. Dentistry, University of Sask.; former Prof. Dentistry, Univ. of Toronto; in private dental practice in Ottawa, Ont., 1947-49; served in 2nd World War with Candn. Dental Corps, 1944-47; mem., Candn. Dental Assn.; Ont. Dental Assn.; Internat. Assn. for Dental Research; Candn. Assn. Anatomists; United Church; Home: #1811, 211 Wurtemburg St., Ottawa, Ont. K1N 8R4

PEACOCK, Rev. F. A. W., O.C. (1968), M.A., D.Litt.; b. Southville, Bristol, Eng., 14 Apl. 1907; s. Frederick Arthur and Nellie (Bryant) P.; e. Bristol Univ. (Workers' Educ. Assn.); Manchester Univ., C.B.K. 1935; Missy. Sch. of Med., 1940; Univ. of Montreal, M.A. 1948; D.Litt., Memorial 1971; m. Doris Marian, B.Sc., d. Victor Davis, 30 Dec. 1939; one d. Stephanie Mary, B.Sc., B.Ed.;

o. Deacon 1935; Visiting Fellow, Mem. Univ. Nfld.; o. Presbyter. 1939; apptd. Supt., Moravian Mission, 1941; Scout Master and Cub Master 1938-59; formed first Boy Scout Troop in N. Labrador, 1938, Makkovik and Nain 1940; mem. Prov. Libs. Bd. of Nfld. 1968-74; mem. Happy Valley Libs. Bd., mem. Nat. Council Boy Scouts' Assn.; Del. to Faith & Order Conf., World Council of Churches, Montreal, 1963; rep. Moravian Missions on Fraternal Visit to Greenland, 1964, Del. to Gen. Synod of Moravian Ch., Potstjen, Czechoslovakia, 1967; Chrmn., N. Labrador Community Schs.; Hamilton Amalgamated Sch. Bd. (later Labrador E. Integrated Sch. Bd.); rec'd Coronation Medal, 1953; author: "Some Psychological Aspects of the Impact of the White Man Upon the Labrador Eskimos", 1948; "The Cultural Changes Among the Labrador Eskimos Incident to the Coming of the Moravian Mission", 1964; "The Eskimos of Labrador" and "The Moravian Mission in Labrador", "Book of Newfoundland", Vol. 4, 1968; "Eskimo Grammar"; Book of Exercises in the Eskimo Lang.; "Graded Readers in the Eskimo Language"; "The Moravian Mission in Labrador (200 Years of Service)", English and Eskimo Eds.; published English-Eskimo Eskimo-English Dictionary; "Dictionary of Synonyms" 1974; "The Labrador Inuit Lore and Legend", 1981; other writings incl. articles on Eskimos and Moravian Mission for various journs.; Secy., Happy Valley Athletic Assn. 1962-65; mem., Bristol (Eng.) Greenland Club, 1978; Queen's Jubilee Medal, 1978; Protestant; Address: Apt. 143, Bldg. 804, Pleasantville , St. John's, Nfld. A1A 1R4

PEAKE, Rev. Frank Alexander, M.A., D.D., D.S.Litt., F.R.Hist.S.; b. Watford, Herts., UK, 16 Apl. 1913; s. Alexander Tod and Amy Grace (Clennett) P.; e. Mundella Secondary Sch. and Univ. Coll., Cert. in Textiles 1935, Nottingham; Emmanuel Coll., Saskatoon, L.Th. 1943; Univ. of Sask., B.A. 1947; Ch. Divinity Sch. of the Pacific, Berkeley, B.D. 1949; Univ. of Alta., M.A. 1952; Huron Coll., Univ. of W. Ont., D.D. 1965; Thorneloe Univ., D.S. Litt. (Jure Dignitatis), 1974; m. Constance Helen Tyndale, d. late Thomas Kilshaw, 28 Aug. 1945; children: John Maurice Clennett, Kenneth Richard Tyndale, Marjorie Grace (Mrs. Conlan); Associate Professor of History, Laurentian University since 1966, Prof. 1978-80; o. Deacon 1941, Priest 1942; Curate of Clandonald, Alberta 1941; Vicar of Onoway 1943, Ponoka 1946; W. Field Secretary, Gen. Bd. of Religious Education 1948; Prof. of Ch. Hist., Ang. Theol. Coll., Vancouver 1953-59; Hon. Lectr. in Hist., Univ. of B.C. 1955-59; Dir. of Religious Educ., Diocese of Huron, 1959-66; Hon. Asst. Priest, Church of the Epiphany, Sudbury, 1966- ; Pres. and Vice Chancellor, Thorneloe Univ. 1970-74 and 1981- ; author, "Seeing and Believing" 1950; "Towards a Living Faith" 1955; "The Anglican Church in British Columbia" 1959; "The Story of British Columbia" 1966; "The Bishop Who Ate His Boots" 1966; also numerous hist. articles; contributor, "Dictionary of Canadian Biography"; mem. Hist. Assn. Gt. Brit.; Candn. Hist. Assn.; Anglican; recreations: reading, travel, photography; Home: 234 Wilson St., Sudbury, Ont. P3E 2S2; Office: Sudbury, Ont.

PEARKES, Maj.-Gen. the Hon. George Randolph, V.C., P.C. (Can.), C.C. (1967), C.B., D.S.O., M.C., K.G.St.J. (1961); b. Watford, Eng., 1888; s. George and Louise (Blair) P.; e. Berkhamsted Sch., Eng.; Staff Coll., Camberley, Eng. (P.S.C.); m. Constance Blytha, d. W.F.U. Copeman, Victoria, B.C., 1925; one s. John André; Lieut.-Gov. of British Columbia, 12 Oct. 1960-1 July 1968; R.C.M.P., 1911-14; served in World War 1914-18; enlisted 2nd Bn., C.M.R., Victoria, B.C.; Temporary Lieut. in the field, 1916; promoted Capt., Maj. and Lieut.-Col., Commanding 116th Bn., C.E.F.; awarded V.C.; wounded in action 5 times; apptd. to Candn. Perm. Forces, 1919; Commanded 1st Candn. Divn., 1940-42; retired when G.O.C. in Chief, Pacific Command; 1st el. to H. of C. for Nanaimo, g.e. 1945; re-el. g.e. 1949; re-el. for Esquimalt-Saanich, g.e. 1953, 1957, 1958; Minister of Nat. Defence,

1957-60; P. Conservative; Anglican; Home: 1268 Tattersall Drive, Victoria, B.C. V8P 1Z3

PEARSE, Peter Hector, B.S.F., M.A., Ph.D.; educator; b. Vernon, B.C. 26 Nov. 1932; s. Frederick Robert and Eleanor Jane (Lea) P.; e. Vernon (B.C.) Elem. Sch. 1946; Kamloops (B.C.) High Sch. 1951; Univ. of B.C. B.S.F. 1956; Edinburgh Univ. M.A. 1959, Ph.D. 1962; m. Penelope Ann d. Richard B. Wilson, Victoria, B.C. 28 Apl. 1973; children: Grant Peter, Jane Elizabeth, Sarah Wilson Lea; PROF. OF ECON. & FORESTRY, UNIV. OF B.C. since 1962; Forester-in Training, B.C. Forest Products Ltd. 1957 — 57; Asst. Lectr. in Econ. Univ. of Edinburgh 1959 — 61; Econ., Organ. for Econ. Co-op. & Devel. Paris 1961 — 62; Commr., Royal Comm. on Forest Resources for B.C. 1975 — 76; Royal Comm. on Pacific Fisheries Policy 1981; rec'd Gold Medal Univ. B.C. 1956; various scholarships and research awards; Candn. Forestry Achievement Award 1977; Distinguished Forester Award 1980; author "Timber Rights and Forest Policy in British Columbia" 2 vols. 1976; Ed. and Co-author "The Mackenzie Pipeline: Arctic Gas and Canadian Energy Policy" 1974; numerous articles econ. problems in devel. and mang. natural resources; mem. Candn. Consumer Council 1970 — 72; Econ. Council Can. 1978-81; Bd. Govs. Univ. B.C. since 1978; mem. Candn. Econ. Assn.; Assn. B.C. Reg'd Foresters; Candn. Inst. Forestry; Past Pres. and Vice Pres. Univ. B.C. Faculty Assn.; Liberal; recreations: skiing, windsurfing; Club: University; Home: 6450 Elm St., Vancouver, B.C. V6N 1B3; Office: Faculty of Forestry, Univ. of B.C., Vancouver, B.C. V6T 1W5.

PEARSE, Ronald William; executive; b. Peterborough, Ont., 23 Nov. 1931; s. Robert Neale and Violet May Margery (Hallowell) P.; e. Univ. of Toronto, Sch. Business; Univ. of Waterloo, Marketing Extension; one d. Elizabeth, two s. Richard Clinton, Michael William; PRESIDENT, PEARSE SALES MARKETING INC.; Seaglobe Inc.; Foodworld Sales (Atlantic) Ltd.; commenced with Quaker Oats Co. of Canada Ltd., Peterborough, Ont. 1952, Sales Mgr., Toronto 1956; joined Kitchens of Sara Lee (Canada) Limited as Marketing Manager 1966, Vice-President, Marketing 1968, Extve. Vice-President and Gen. Mgr. 1969, Pres. and Chief Extve. Offr. 1971-74; extensive intl. travel — est. Sara Lee overseas; Pres., Chief Extve. Offr. and Dir. Pearse Sales Marketing Inc. 1974; Vice-Pres. and Gen. Mgr., Canadian Food Products Ltd., 1978; Mgmt. Consult. to Irving Group re Cavendish Farms, 1979-80; mem. Am. Inst. Mang.; Grocery Products Mfrs. of Can.; Bd. Trade Metropolitan Toronto and Halifax; Canadian Frozen Foods Industry Association; former Campaign Mgr., Ont. Heart Foundation; Conservative; Presbyterian; recreations: water skiing, curling, sailing, golf; Clubs: Variety; Canadian; Home: Stillwater Lake, R.R. 2, Tantallon, N.S. B0J 3J0.

PEARSON, Arthur MacDonald, M.Sc., Ph.D.; Canadian public service; b. Brandon, Man. 26 Feb. 1938; s. Arthur Cartwright and Norma Agnes (MacDonald) P.; e. High Sch. Brandon, Man.; Univ. of B.C. B.Sc. 1958, M.Sc. 1960; Univ. of Helsinki Ph.D. 1962; m. Sandra Jean d. Charles Mooney, Prince Albert, Sask. 26 Oct. 1959; children: David Warren Lars, Cynthia Rae, Howard Brent; PRES., RAMPART DEVELOPMENT CORP. since 1979; Pres., 210446 Holdings Ltd. since 1978; Dyea Developments Ltd. since 1971; Biol. and Research Scientist, Candn. Wildlife Service, Whitehorse 1962-71, Research Scientist Edmonton 1972-74, Acting Head Co-op. Research Program 1975-76; Commr. of Yukon Territory, Whitehorse 1976-8; mem. Whitehorse Bd. of Health 1970-71; Dir. Yukon Social Service Soc. 1967-71 (Pres. 1969-70); Dir. and Charter mem. Univ. of Can. N. 1970-71; Dir. Yukon Research & Devel. Inst. 1968-71; Instr. in Ecology Arctic Summer Sch. Univ. of Alta. 1972-75; Dir. Candn. Soc. Fisheries & Wildlife Biols. 1967-71; Arctic Internat. Wildlife Range Soc. 1970-76; mem. Council Bear Biol. Assn. (Internat.) 1977; mem. Extve. Council, Alaska Div.,

Am. Assn. for Advancement of Sci., 1980; Protestant; recreations: hockey, golf, skiing, hunting, fishing, philately, numismatics; Home: 124 Alsek Rd., Whitehorse, Yukon Y1A 3K6; Office: 209B Main St., Whitehorse, Yukon Y1A 2B2

PEARSON, Hon. Christopher William, M.L.A.; politician; b. Lethbridge, Alta. 29 Apl. 1931; s. Albert and Henrietta (Van Lohuizen) P.; e. Lethbridge, Alta.; m. Aliceanne d. Ford Scouten, Kingston, Ont. 29 Sept. 1961; children: Laura, Joyce, Danny; GOVT. LEADER AND MIN. OF FINANCE Y.T.; el. M.L.A. for Whitehorse Riverdale North g.e. 1978; Chrmn. Yukon Elect. Pub. Utilities Bd. 1973-78; mem. Yukon Small Business Loans Bd. 1974-78; Pres., Whitehorse Chamber Comm. 1976-77; Yukon Amateur Hockey Assn. 1976-78; Whitehorse Minor Hockey Assn. 1974-75; Whitehorse Fastball Assn. 1968; Bd. mem. Whitehorse Un. Ch., Pres., 1965; P. Conservative; United Church; Clubs: Rotary Whitehorse (Pres. 1977-78); Whitehorse Curling, Pres. 1961; Office: (P.O. Box 2703) Whitehorse, Y.T. Y1A 2C6.

PEARSON, Gerald E., B.Com.; chartered accountant; e. Edmonton Pub. Schs.; Trinity Coll. Sch., Port Hope, Ont.; Univ. of Alberta, B.Com.; m. four children; PARTNER, CLARKSON, GORDON, Chartered Accts.; long engaged in Edmonton vol. community service; Chrmn., Salvation Army Adv. Bd., etc.; former mem. of Senate, Univ. of Alta.; former Gov., Trinity Coll. Sch.; el. Pres. of Edmonton Chamber of Comm. 1972, later a Dir. of Alta. Chamber, Chrmn. of Regional Comte. of the Candn. Chamber and a Dir. thereof (two terms on Policy Comte.); el. Nat. Vice Pres. of Candn. Chamber 1974 and Pres. 1975-76; recreations: skiing, sailing, hunting water fowl; Office: 1700 — Continental Bank Bldg., 10250 — 101 St., Edmonton Centre, Edmonton, Alta. T5J 3P4

PEARSON, Hugh John Sanders; company president; b. Edmonton, Alberta, 9 Sept. 1921; s. late Hugh Edward and Constance Jukes (Sanders) P.; e. Trinity Coll. Sch., Port Hope, Ont. (1940); Royal Mil. Coll., Kingston, Ont. (1942); m. Kathleen Primrose, d. late William Hastie, 7 Dec. 1945; children: Kathleen Margaret, Ronald Hastie, Ian Sanders; CHRMN. & C.E.O., CENTURY SALES & SERVICE LIMITED; Chrmn. Alberta Gas Trunk Line Co. Ltd.; The Bishops Men, Edmonton; Chrmn. and Dir. Edmonton Broadcasting Co. Ltd.; Dir., Selkirk Communications Ltd.; Mutual Life Assnce. Co. of Can.; Enesco Chem. Ltd.; Alberta Gas Ethelene Ltd.; Novacor Chem. Ltd.; Northam Estates Ltd.; Rows Holdings Ltd.; Prudential Steel Ltd.; Chmn., Council for Cdn. Unity; joined the Taylor Pearson & Carson organization in 1946 and was employed in various capacities, became Manager of Taylor, Pearson & Carson (B.C.) Ltd., in 1956; el. Dir. of the Co., 1957, Pres. 1959; served in 2nd World War with The Calgary Highlanders, overseas 1942-45, rank Capt.; Mentioned in Despatches; Anglican; recreations: shooting, fishing, golf; Clubs: Edmonton; Mayfair Golf and Country; Office: 4940-93 Avenue, (P.O. Box 1218), Edmonton, Alta. T5J 2M6

PEARSON, Stanley Gordon Breckenridge, B.Sc.; geologist; retired petroleum extve.; b. Pincher Creek, Alta., 12 Dec. 1917; s. late Stanley and Agnes McVickers (Breckenridge))P.; e. Pub. and High Schs., Pincher Creek, Alta.; Univ. of Alta., B.Sc. (Geol.) 1941, post-grad. (Geol.) 1942; Univ. of W. Ont., Dipl. in Business Mang. 1959; m. Helen Beatrice, d. late H. J. Tracy, 30 June 1945; children: Gail Helen, Judith Anne, Patricia Elizabeth, Donald Stanley; Geol. Survey of Canada, Summer 1941; Geol. and Geophysicist, Canadian Gulf Oil Co., 1945-51; Geophysical Co-ordinator, 1951-53; Exploration Mgr., Candn. Gulf Oil Co. 1954-56; Exploration Mgr. B.A. Oil Co. Ltd. 1956-66; Gen. Mgr. Expl. and Prod. 1966-67, and apptd. Vice-Pres., Mineral Devel., 1968; Mgr. Exploration Gulf Oil Co., E. Hemisphere 1968-73; Vice Pres., Gulf Can. 1973; Sr. Vice Pres. 1977-78(ret.); served with R.C.A. in Sicily,

Italy and Holland, 1942-46; rank Lt.; mem., Assn. Prof. Engrs., Alta.; Am. Assn. of Petroleum Geols.; Soc. Exploration Geophysicists; Canadian. Society of Exploration Geophysicists; Candn. Soc. of Petroleum Geols.; Candn. Inst. Mining & Metall.; Freemason; United Church; recreations: tennis, horsemanship; Address: P.O. Box 280, Cremona, Alta. T0M 0R0

PEART, Arthur Francis Whittaker, M.B.E., M.D., C.M., D.P.H., F.R.S.H., F.R.C.P. (C); b. Freeman, Ont., 9 Feb. 1915; s. Grant Somerville and Bessie Pearl (Whittaker) P.; e. Ont. Agric. Coll., 1933-35; Queen's Univ., M.D., C.M. 1940; Univ. of Toronto, D.P.H. 1943; Harvard Sch. of Pub. Health, 1949-50; Roy. Coll. Phys. & Surgs. Can., Cert. in Pub. Health F.R.C.P.(C) 1953, Fellow in 1972; m. Gwendolyn, 20 Mar. 1943; children: Nancy, Frances, William, James; served in 2nd World War with R.C.A.M.C., 1940-46; held appointments on Staff, Lab. and Field Hygiene Section; awarded M.B.E.; M.O.H., Health Region No. 1, Swift Current, Sask., 1946; in gen. practice, 1947; apptd. Chief, Div. of Epidemiol., Dept. of Nat Health & Welfare, Ottawa, 1948; apptd. Asst. Secy., Candn. Med. Assn., 1954, Depy. Gen. Secy., 1960, and Gen. Secy. 1966-70; apptd. Med. Dir., Traffic Injury Research Foundation 1970-75; Pres., World Med. Assn. 1971; Pres., Medifacts Ltd.; Candn. Med. Assn.; Ont. Med. Assn.; Roy. Coll. of Phys. & Surgs. of Can.; Hon. mem., Am. Med. Assn. 1967; author of articles and reports in med. and pub. health journs.; awarded Queen's Jubilee Medal 1977; Freemason; United Church; Clubs: Rotary; Royal Ottawa Golf; Beaver Valley Ski; recreations: golf, skiing, carpentry; Home: 128 Noel St., Ottawa, Ont. K1M 2A5; Office: 471 Richmond Rd., Ottawa, Ont. K2A 0G3

PEASTON, Rev. Monroe, Ph.D.; b. Liverpool, Eng., 5 Sept. 1914; s. late Arthur and Lydia (Green) P.; e. Liverpool Inst. (Capt. of Soccer, Athletics and Head of Sch.) 1926-33; Brasenose Coll., Oxford Univ., B.A. 1936; M.A. 1943; Wycliffe Hall, Oxford Univ., 1936-38; Univ. of London B.D. 1948; Union Theol. Semy., N.Y., Ph.D. 1964; D.D. (Hon., Mont Dioc. Theol. Coll.), 1975; m. Phyllis Mary, d. Albert E. Gleave, Wallasey, Cheshire, England, 12 June 1940; one d. Ann Christine; o. Deacon 1938, Priest 1939; Assistant Curate, St. Helen's Parish Church, 1938-40; Claughton , Birkenhead, 1940-43; Organizing Secy., Ch. Missy. Soc., 1943-45; Chaplain, Wrekin Coll., Wellington, Salop, 1945-48; Vicar of Wadestown, Northland, Wellington, N.Z., 1948-52; Master of Coll. House, Christchurch, N.Z., 1952-59; Vice Princ., Christchurch Coll., N.Z., 1959-64; Assoc. Prof. of Pastoral Psychol., McGill Univ. since 1967; Hon. Canon, Christchurch Cath., N.Z., 1961-64; Hon. Canon, Christ Church Cathedral, Montreal, since 1966; Principal, Montreal Diocesan Theol. Coll. 1965-74; Clin. mem. Am. Assn. Marriage & Family Therapy 1974; author of "A Time to Keep", 1963; "Personal Living: An Introduction to Paul Tournier" 1972; Address: 3481 University St., Apt. 11, Montreal, Que. H3A 2A8

PECK, Brig.-Gen. Charles Arnold, O.B.E., C.D., B.Sc.; retired association executive; b. Hillsboro, N.B., 18 Jan. 1912; s. Charles Allison and Mary Romaine (Beatty) P.; e. Univ. of N.B., B.Sc. (EE) 1932; British Army Staff Coll., Surrey, Eng., grad. 1947; Candn. Nat. Defence Coll., 1961-62; m. Jean Doris, d. J. Stuart Grant, Rockcliffe Park, Ottawa, 18 November 1939; two d. Judith Doris, Susan Jean; PRES., MACHINERY AND EQUIPMENT MFRS. ASSN. OF CAN. 1968-78; served overseas in 2nd World War with Candn. Army in U.K., Italy, N.W. Europe, 1941-45; Army Hdqrs., 1946-50; C.O., Roy. Candn. Sch. of Signals, 1950-55; Dir. of Signals, Army Hdqrs., 1955-58; Depy. Army Mem., Candn. Jt. Staff, London, Eng., 1958-61; Sr. Mil. Adv., Candn. Del. to Internat. Supy. & Control Comn., Indo China, 1962-63; Depy. Adj.-Gen., 1963-64; apptd. Dir.-Gen. of Centennial Planning, Dec. 1964; retired from Candn. armed forces Jan. 1968; mem., Assn. Prof. Engrs., Ont.; Anglican; recreations: golf, ski-

ing; Clubs: Royal Ottawa Golf; Home: 300 Driveway, Ottawa, Ont. K1S 3M6;

PECKFORD, Hon. Alfred Brian, M.H.A., B.A. (Ed.); politician; b. Whitbourne, Nfld. 27 Aug. 1942; s. Ewart and Allison (Young) P.; e. Lewisporte High Sch.; Mem. Univ. of Nfld. B.A. (Ed.) 1966; m. Marina d. Raymond Dicks, South Brook, Nfld. 11 Oct. 1969; two d. SueAnn, Carolyn; PREMIER OF NFLD. AND LABRADOR and Leader of the P. Cons. Party of Nfld. 1979- ; Teacher, Lewisporte 1962-63; High Sch. Teacher, Grant Coll. Inst. Springdale 1966-72, Head of Eng. 1971; el. Pres. Green Bay Dist. P. Cons. Assn. 1971; el. M.H.A. for Green Bay Dist. Prov. g.e. 1972, re-el. since; Special Asst. to Premier 1973; Min. of Mun. Affairs & Housing 1974; Min. of Mines & Energy 1976 as well as Min. of Rural Devel. 1978; el. Leader P. Cons. Party Nfld. & Labrador 1979; sworn in as Premier 26 March 1979, re-el. Premier prov. g.e. June 1979; recreations: reading, sports, swimming; & skiing Office: Confederation Bldg., St. John's, Nfld.

PEDERSEN, Chris L., Q.C., LL.B.; b. Milestone, Sask., 19 Aug. 1908; s. William and S. Rebecca (Christensen) P.; e. Milestone (Sask.) High Sch.; Regina Coll.; Luther Coll.; Univ. of Sask. LL.B.; m. Margaret V. d. Jack Miller 14 Sept. 1938; PARTNER, PEDERSEN, NORMAN, McLEOD & TODD; served City of Regina in various pub. service extve. positions; called to Bar of Sask. 1941; cr. Q.C. 1964; mem. Sask. Bar Assn.; Freemason; Clubs: Assiniboia; Wascana; Home: 25 Academy Park Rd., Regina, Sask. S4S 4M8; Office: 1795 Rose, Regina, Sask. S4P 1Z4

PEDERSEN, Eigil Dalsgaard, M.A., Ed.D.; educator; b. Montreal, Que., 2 Nov. 1929; s. Arne Dalsgaard and Gudrun (Jorgensen) P.; e. Macdonald Coll., Montreal, Teaching Cert.; Sir George Williams Univ., B.A. 1956; McGill Univ., M.A. (Educ.) 1961; Harvard Univ., Ed.D. (Sociol.) 1966; m. Madge, d. George Abbott, 28 June 1952; children: John, Philip, David, Gordon, Thomas, Susan; Vice-Princ. (Acad.) McGill University 1972-81; Assoc., Harvard Grad. Sch. of Educ. 1981-82; Visiting Scholar, Centre for Multicultural Educ., Univ. of London Inst. of Educ.; and Professor of Educ.; began as Teacher, Public Schs., Montreal 1952; Lectr. in Educ., McGill Univ. 1958-62; Research Assoc., Harvard Univ. 1965-66; Prof. of Education, McGill University 1958-63 and since 1966; mem. Canadian Association Professors of Education (Pres. 1971-72); Candn. Educ. Researchers Assn.; Candn. Soc. for Study of Educ. (Vice-Pres. 1972-73); Phi Delta Kappa; recreation: music; Office: 845 Sherbrooke St. W., Montreal, Que. H3A 2T5

PEDERSEN, K. George, B.A., M.A., Ph.D., F.C.C.T.; educator; b. Three Creeks, Alta. 13 June 1931; s. Hjalmar Nielsen and Anna Marie (Jensen) P.; e. Chilliwack (B.C.) Jr. and Sr. High Sch. 1950; Vancouver Prov. Normal Sch. Teaching Dipl. 1952; Univ. of B.C., B.A. (Hist. and Geog.) 1959; Univ. of Washington M.A. (Geog. and Educ.) 1964; Univ. of Chicago, Ph.D. (Educ. and Econ.) 1969; m. Joan Elaine, d. James Earl Vanderwarker, 15 Aug. 1953; children: Gregory George, Lisa Marie; PRESIDENT AND VICE-CHANCELLOR, SIMON FRASER UNIV.. since 1979; began teaching in Elem. and Secondary Schs., N. Vancouver, B.C. 1952; Staff Assoc., Midwest Adm. Center, Univ. of Chicago 1965, Teaching Intern there 1966, Research Assoc. (Asst. Prof.) 1966; Lectr. and Asst. Prof., Dept. Educ. Adm., Ont. Inst. for Studies in Educ., Univ. of Toronto 1968; Asst. Prof. Dept. of Educ., Univ. of Chicago and Assoc. Dir., Midwest Adm. Center, Grad. Sch. of Educ. there 1970; Dean, Fac. of Ed., Univ. of Victoria 1975; Past Pres., N. Vancouver Teachers' Assn., N. Vancouver Principals' and Vice Principals' Assn.; mem. Am. Assn. Sch. Administrators; Am. Educ. Research Assn.; B.C. Teachers Fed.; Past Secy. Treas. of the Canadian Assn. of Deans and Directors of Education; Candn. Educ. Assn. Candn. Educ.

Researchers' Assn; Candn. Soc. for Study of Educ.; Internat. Council on Educ. for Teaching; Nat. Educ. Ass; Comparative & Internat. Educ. Soc.; Candn. Foundation for Econ. Education; National Society for the Study of Education; Candn. Tax Foundation; Cdn. Bureau for Internat. Educ.; Commonwealth Assn. of Universities; Inst. of Public Admin. of Can.; Internat. Assn. of Univ. Presidents; Member of Board of Trustees of Discovery Foundation (B.C.); Member of Board of Directors of Public Employers Council of B. C.; Mem., Bd. of Dir., Assn. of Universities and Coll. of Can.; Inter-American Org. for Higher Educ., Bd. of Gov., the Leon and Thea Koerner Fndn.; Fellow, Candn. Coll. of Teachers, elected 1977; author of "The Itinerant Schoolmaster: A Socio-Economic Analysis of Teacher Turnover" 1973; also book chapters, articles, reviews, critiques and research papers in numerous prof. journs.; Phi Delta Kappa; Protestant; recreations: sailing, golf, fishing; Home: President's Residence, Burnaby, B. C. V5A 1S6

PEDERSEN, Paul Richard, B.A., M.Mus., Ph.D.; educator; composer; b. Camrose, Alta. 28 Aug. 1935; s. Einer Richard and Anna (Rasmussen) P.; e. Camrose Lutheran Coll. 1953; Univ. of Sask. B.A. 1957; Univ. of Toronto M.Mus. (Composition) 1961, Ph.D. (Musicology) 1970; m. Jean Frances d. Albert Stollery, Armena, Alta. 6 Aug. 1956; children: Rebecca, David, Katherine, Andrew; DEAN OF MUSIC, McGILL UNIV. 1976- , Prof. of Music 1966- ; Extve. Producer McGill Univ. Records; Music Dir. Camrose Lutheran Coll. 1962-64; Chrmn. of Theory Faculty of Music present Univ. 1970-74, Dir. Electronic Music Studio 1970-74, Assoc. Dean of Music 1974-76; author various articles psychol. of music; music compositions various media; mem. Candn. League Composers; Candn. Univ. Music Soc.; Candn. Assn. Publishers, Authors & Composers; Lutheran; recreation: photography; Home: 125 Percival Ave., Montreal West, Que. H4X 1T7; Office: 555 Sherbrooke St. W., Montreal, Que. H3A 1E3.

PEEL, Bruce Braden, M.A., B.L.S.; librarian; b. Ferland, Sask., 11 Nov. 1916; s. late Alice Annie (Switzer) and William John P.; e. Normal Sch., Moose Jaw, Sask.; Univ. of Sask., B.A. 1944, M.A. 1946; Univ. of Toronto Lib. Sch., B.L.S. 1946; m. Margaret Christina, d. James Fullerton, Regina, Sask., 28 July 1950; children: Brian David, Alison Mary; CHIEF LIBRARIAN, UNIV. OF ALBERTA, since 1956; began teaching pub. sch. in Sask. for four yrs.; Canadian Lib. in charge of Adam Shortt Collection, Univ. of Sask. Lib., 1946-51; Chief Cataloguer Univ. of Alta. Lib. 1951-54; Asst. Chief Librarian, 1954-55, Acting Chief Librarian, 1955-56; mem. of study team on Resources of Canadian Academic Libraries, 1966-67; Publications: "The Saskatoon Story, 1882-1952" (with Eric Knowles), 1952; "A Bibliography of the Prairie Provinces to 1953", 1956; second enlarged ed., 1973; "Supplement", 1963; "Steamboats on the Saskatchewan", 1972; Editor, "Librarianship in Canada, 1946 to 1967", 1968; "Early Printing in Red River Settlement" 1974; "The Rossville Mission Press" 1974; various articles on bibliography and regional history; Tremaine Medal for outstanding service to bibliog. in Can.; Bibliog. Soc. of Can. 1975; mem. various library assns.; United Church; Home: 11047 - 83 Ave., Edmonton, Alta. T6G 0T8

PEERS, Frank Wayne, Ph.D.; educator; b. Alsask, Sask. 18 Jan. 1918; s. Warren Fountain and L. M. (McKim) P.; e. Mount Royal Coll. Calgary; Univ. of Alta. B.A. 1936, B.Ed. 1943; Univ. of Toronto M.A. 1948, Ph.D. 1966; PROF. OF POL. SCIENCE, UNIV. OF TORONTO; Asst. Dir. of Extension Univ. of Alta. 1943-47; Asst. Dir. Banff Sch. of Fine Arts 1945-47; Asst. Supvr. and Supvr. of CBC Pub. Affairs Toronto 1948-60, Dir. of Information Programming 1960-63; author "The Politics of Canadian Broadcasting 1920-51"; "The Public Eye: Television and the Politics of Canadian Broadcasting 1952-68"; articles various publs.; contrib. to radio and TV programs; former Ed., "Canadian Journal of Political Science"; mem.

Candn. Pol. Science Assn.; Candn. Hist. Assn.; Inst. Pub. Adm. Can.; Internat. Inst. Communications; recreations: travel, theatre; Home: Apt. 704; 190 St. George St., Toronto, Ont. M5R 2N4; Office: 100 St. George St., Toronto, Ont. M5S 1A1.

PEERS, Robert J., B.S.; petroleum executive; b. Selkirk, Man. 23 Sept. 1944; s. Gerald Warren and Anne (Hucula) P.; e. Selkirk (Man.) Pub. Grade Sch.; Univ. of Denver B.S. (Business Adm.) 1966; m. Joyce Elaine d. late Josef Hall 19 Aug. 1967; one s. Darren Thomas; one d. Diane Elaine; VICE PRES. LAND & ADM. AND DIR., PAN OCEAN OIL LTD. since 1976; Dir. Pan Ocean Oil (Canada) Ltd.; P.V. Container Systems Ltd.; Landman, Amoco Canada Petroleum Co. Ltd. 1967; Landman present Co. 1972, Chief Landman 1974; Dir. Candn. Assn. Petrol. Landmen; Am. Assn. Petrol. Landmen; Protestant; recreations: golf, squash, skiing; Clubs: Calgary Petroleum; 400; Home: 124 Lake Linnet Close S.E., Calgary, Alta. T2J 2J1; Office: 300-5th Ave. S.W., Calgary, Alta.

PEITCHINIS, Stephen Gabriel; M.A., Ph.D.; educator; b. Macedonia, Greece, 12 Oct. 1925; s. Gabriel K. and Afrodita (Sarbinoff) P.; e. (primary) Greece; (secondary) 7th Boys Gymnasium, Sofia, Bulgaria, 1945; Univ. of W. Ont., B.A. 1954, M.A. 1955; London Sch. of Econ., Ph.D. 1960; m. Jacquelyn A., d. J. C. Elliott, Sault Ste. Marie, Ont. 13 Sept. 1952; Prof. of Econ., Univ. of Calgary; DEAN AND PROF., FACULTY OF BUSINESS, UNIV. OF CALGARY 1973-76; Instr. in Econ. and Pol. Science, Univ. of W. Ont. 1955-58, Asst. Prof. 1960, Assoc. Prof. 1963; joined present Univ. as Prof. 1968; Research Assoc., Task Force on Labour Relations, Ottawa, 1968; Assoc. Dir., Human Resources Research Council of Alta., 1969-71; Chrmn. and Dir. of Research, Comm. Inquiry into Financing Post-Secondary Educ. in Can. 1970-71; author, "Employment and Wages in Canada", 1965; "Canadian Labour Economics", 1970; "Labour-Management Relations in the Railway Industry", 1971; "Financing Post-Secondary Education in Canada"; 1971; "The Employability of Welfare Recipients", 1972; "The Canadian Labour Market", 1975; "The Implications of Technological Change for Employment and Skills", 1977; "The Attitudes of Trade Unions Towards Technological changes, 1980'; "The Employment Implications of Computers and Telecommunications Technology", 1981; and a number of other studies in the general area of Technology and Employment; also articles in various prof. journs.; mem., Bd. of Gov., Cdn. Council on Social Development; Candn. Econ. Assn.; Am. Econ. Assn.; Indust. Relations Research Assn.; London Sch. Econ. Soc.; Phi Delta Theta; Anglican; recreation: golf; Home: 4155 Varsity Rd. N.W., Calgary, Alta.

PEKARSKY, Daniel U., LL.B.; executive; b. Edmonton, Alta. 24 Sept. 1937; s. Leo and Minnie (Dlin) P.; e. Univ. of Alta. B.A. 1959, LL.B. 1960; m. Trudy d. late Henry Singer, Edmonton, Alta. 5 March 1963; children: Lise, Josh, Adam; EXEC. VICE-PRES., BEL-FRAN INVESTMENTS LTD.: Dir. Bank of British Columbia; First City Properties Inc.; Dir. and Offr. numerous private Candn. corps.; called to Bar of Alta. 1961; practiced law Edmonton 1961-79; joined present firm 1979; mem. Law Soc. Alta.; Candn. Bar Assn.; Jewish; Home: 1598 Angus Dr., Vancouver, B.C. V6J 4H3; Office: 18th Floor, 777 Hornby St., Vancouver, B.C. V6Z 1S4.

PÉLADEAU, Pierre, L.Ph., M.A., B.C.L.; editor; publisher; b. Montreal, Que. 11 Apl. 1925; s. Henri and Elmire (Fortier) P.; e. Académie Querbes; Coll. Jean-de-Brébeuf; Coll. Ste-Marie; Univ. de Montréal L.Ph., M.A.; Univ. McGill B.C.L.; m. 1stly Raymonde Chopin 26 May 1954; m. 2ndly Line Parisien 1979; children: Eric, Isabelle, Pierre-Karl, Anne-Marie, Esther, Simon-Pierre; ED. AND PUBLISHER, QUEBECOR INC.; Dir. La Caisse de Dépôt et Placement du Québec; Club: St-Denis; Home: 1373

Chemin Ste-Marguerite, Ste-Adèle, Qué. J0T 2K0; Office: 225 Roy St. E., Montréal, Qué. M2W 2N6.

PELLAN, Alfred, C.C., LL.D., Dr. Fine Arts, Litt.D., A.R.C.A.; painter; artist; b. Quebec, Que. 16 May 1906; s. Alfred and Marie Regina (Damphousse) P.; e. École des Beaux-Arts Que. (rec'd First Prizes with Medals for Painting, Design, Sculpture, Sketching, Advertising, Anat.) 1920-25; École Supérieure Nationale des Beaux-Arts de Paris (Prov. of Que. Bursary 1926-30); Ottawa Univ. Dr. Fine Arts 1969, Laval Univ. 1971; Sir George Univ. LL.D. 1971; Univ. de Montréal Litt.D. 1974; m. Madeleine d. Savaria Poliseno, Montreal, Que. 23 July 1949; worked in Grand Chaumiére and Colarossi Acads. and alone in Paris until 1940; Teacher, Superior Course in Painting, Ecole des Beaux-Arts Montreal 1943-52; rtn'd to Paris on Royal Soc. Can. Bursary and remained 1952-55; Art Teacher (Painting) The Art Centre, St. Adele, Que. summer 1957; rep. in various museums and colls. incl.: Musée nat. d'Art moderne Paris; Musée de Grenoble France; Wellesly Coll. Museum Philadelphia; Musée du Qué.; Nat. Gallery Can.; National Museum of Fine Arts; Art Gallery of Ont.; Lord Beaverbrook Art Gallery N.B.; Art Gallery of Hamilton; Art Gallery of Edmonton; Kitchener-Waterloo Art Gallery; Norman Mackenzie Art Gallery Regina; Vancouver Art Gallery; Musée d'Art contemporain Montreal; Dalhousie Art Gallery; Willistead Art Gallery of Windsor; CIL Art Coll. Montreal; Agnes Etherington Art Centre Queen's Univ.; Art Bank Can. Council; Ont. Heritage Foundation Ottawa; Sir George Williams Art Galleries, Concordia Univ. Montreal; one-man exhns. incl.: Acad. Ranson Paris 1935; Galerie Jeanne Bûcher Paris 1939; Musée de la Prov. Que. 1940; Montreal Museum of Fine Arts 1940; 3714 Jeanne-Mance St. Montreal 1941; Galerie Bignou N.Y. 1942; Galerie municipale Que. 1942; Galerie l'Atelier Ottawa 1952; Coq Liban Paris 1954; Cercle Paul Valéry Paris 1954; Retrospective, Musée nat. d'Art moderne Paris 1955; Retrospective, Hall of Honour City Hall Montreal 1956; Laing Galleries Toronto 1957; Galery Denyse Delrue Montreal 1958; "Hommage à Pellan" 1960; Robertson Galleries Ottawa 1960; Retrospective, Nat. Gallery Can., Montreal Museum Fine Arts, Musée de la Prov. de Qué., Art Gallery of Toronto 1960-61; Roberts Gallery Toronto 1961; "Présence de Pellan" Galerie Libre Montreal 1963; Kitchener-Waterloo Art Gallery 1964; Sherbrooke-Art, Domaine Howard 1964; Rodman Hall St. Catharines & Dist. Arts Council 1964; Roberts Gallery Toronto 1964, 1971 (constumes & décors theatre); Winnipeg Art Gallery 1968; "Voir Pellan" Musée d'Art contemporain 1969; Centre culturel canadien, Costumes for Nuit des Rois, Paris 1971; Retrospective: Musée du Qué., Montreal Museum Fine Arts, Nat. Gallery Can. 1972-73; Ecole des Arts visuels Univ. Laval décors & costumes theatre 1972, Galerie de Montréal 1977; "Hommage à Pellan" Galerie Signal 1977; theatre designs incl.: "Madeleine et Pierre" Montreal 1944-45; "Twelfth Night" Montreal 1946; Montreal Theatre Ballet design of curtain 1957; murals: Candn. Embassy Rio de Janeiro (painting); Tétrault Shoe Ltd. Montreal (painting); Late Mr. Jean Désy Can. (fluorescent painting); City Center Bldg. Montreal (mosaic) 1957; Ecole Saint-Patrice Granby (mosaic) 1958; Ecole Secondaire Immaculée-Conception Granby (ceramic) 1960; 3 murals for the Mirons, Montreal (ceramic and mosaic) 1962; Winnipeg Airport (painting) 1963; Place des Arts Montreal (stained glass) 1963; Ch. St-Théophile de Laval-Ouest (stained glass) 1964; Nat. Lib. & Archives Ottawa (painting) 1967; Jardin d'Olivia (tapestry) Musée du Qué. 1970; monographs and films: Maurice Gagnon: Pellan et son oeuvre (microfilms); Germain Lefebvre: Pellan 1943; Conquante Dessins d'Alfred Pellan 1945; Georges Francon: Reportage Alfred Pellan (film) 1961; Nat. Gallery Can. film 1961; Donald W. Buchanan: Alfred Pellan 1962; Guy Robert: Pellan 1963; Louis Portugais: Voir Pellan (film) 1969; Les Editions Yvan Boulerice (slides with cat.) 1971; Bibliothéque nat. du Qué.: A. Pellan 1973; Claude Péloquin: Pellan Pellan (album) 1976; rep. numerous group exhns. Can., Europe, Australia, Ja-

pan; awards: First Prizes - Ecole des Beaux-Arts de Paris 1926, First Gt. Exhn. Mural Art in Paris 1935, 65th Annual Spring Exhn. Montreal Museum Fine Arts 1948, Candn. mural competition City Centre Bldg. Montreal 1957; Can. Council Sr. Fellowship 1958, Medal 1965, Molson's Prize 1972; Nat. Award in Painting & Related Arts Univ. Alta. 1959; mem. Internat. Jury Paris 4th Biennial Exhn. 1965; Candn. Centennial Medal 1967; Hon. Chrmn. Atelier libre de Recherches graphiques Montreal 1971; Prix Philippe-Hébert, Soc. St-Jean Baptiste Montréal 1972; Hon. mem. Vie des Arts 1976; Dipl. d'Honneur Candn. Conf. of Arts Vancouver 1977; Hon. Comte. Rencontre des Arts et des Arts et des Sciences de la Couleur, Centre québécois de la couleur Montréal 1978; nominated "most outstanding Montrealer in field of Fine Arts" 20th anniversary Queen Elizabeth Hotel 1978; recreation: gardening; Address: 649 Des Mille-Isles Blvd., Auteuil, Laval, Que. H7L 1K5.

PELLETIER, Andrée, B.A.; actress, sculptor and artist; b. Montreal, Qué. 24 Aug. 1951; d. Gérard and Alexandrine (Leduc) P.; e. Maternelle Leveillée, Montreal 1955; Ecole Ste. Catherine Sienne 1959; Coll. Marie de France 1963; Acad. Michèle Provost 1967; Coll. Ste. Marie 1968; Univ. du Québec, B.A. (Hons.) 1971; exhns. incl. Galerie Gadbois 1962; Pavillon Lafontaine (graphics and sculptures) 1968; Pavillon St Joseph (graphics) 1970; Galerie Luducu (graphics and sculptures) 1972; studied drama under Ghislain Fillion 1966-67; appeared in "Les Parascos Du Saint-Marie" 1968-69; "Le Chien Show" Univ. du Qué. 1970; "Le Show de la Mort" Pavillon St-Joseph 1971; "An Italian Straw Hat" Stratford, Ont. 1971; "Ni Professeur Ni Gorille " La Quenouille Bleue Que. Tour 1972; has appeared in TV, radio and film incl. "Le Sel De La Semaine" 1969; "A La Seconds" 1970; "Pierre, Jean, Jacques" 1970-71 (all TV); "Le Festin Des Morts" (Nat. Film Bd.) 1965; "Les Males" (feature film) 1970; "A Moving Experience" (Nat. Film Bd.) 1973; "The Man Who Ran Away" (CBC "To See Ourselves" Series) 1973; "The Execution of Private Slovik" 1974; "The Apprenticeship of Duddy Kravitz" 1974 (both feature films); author of "Manifeste de la Quenouille Bleue" 1972; "La vie magique de Java le Pou" (illustrator) 1974; recreations: dancing, tennis;

PELLETIER, Hon. Gérard, P.C., B.A.; politician; b. Victoriaville, Que., 21 June 1919; s. Achille and Leda (Dufresne) P.; e. Nicolet Semy.; Mont-Laurier Coll.; Univ. of Montreal, B.A.; m. Alexandrine, d. Joseph Leduc, Montreal, Que., 27 Feb. 1943; children: Anne-Marie, Louise, Jean, Andrée; appt. Ambassador and Can's Permanent Rep. to U.N. (New York) 1981; Secretary-Gen. Jeunesse étudiante catholique, 1939-43; Field Secy., World Student Relief, Geneva, 1945-47; Reporter, "Le Devoir" 1947-50; Dir., "Le Travail" (trade union organ) 1950-61; Editor of "La Presse", 1961-65; a Broadcaster and Columnist since 1950; 1st el. to H. of C. for Hochelaga in g.e. 1965; re-el. g.e. June 1968; apptd. Parlty. Asst. to Secy. of State for External Affairs, 20 Apl. 1967; Minister without Portfolio, 20 Apl. 1968; Secy. of State July 1968; Min. of Communications, Trudeau cabinet, 1972-75; Can. Ambassador to France 1975-81; author "La Crise d'Octobre" 1971; Liberal; Roman Catholic; Home: 550 Park Ave., New York, N.Y.; Office: 866 United Nations Plaza, Ste. 250, New York, N.Y. 10017

PELLETIER, Gerard Eugene, M.Sc., Ph.D.; university professor; b. Ottawa Ont., 18 June 1930; s. Romuald William and Laetitia (Lavigne) P.; e. Univ. of Ottawa, M.Sc. (Chem.) 1955; Laval Univ., Ph.D. (Chem.) 1960; m. Marcelle Thérèse, d. late Joseph Beaudoin, 30 Sept. 1961; children: Chantal, François; Director, Dept. of Chem., Faculty of Science, Univ. de Sherbrooke; joined OPW Paints Ltd., Ottawa, as Chemist, 1951-53; Research Chemist, Imperial Oil Ltd., Sarnia, Ont., 1960-62; R. Catholic; recreations: golf, boating, skiing; Home: 425 Meilleur, Sherbrooke, Que. J1J 2P4

PELLETIER, Wilfrid, C.C. (1967), C.M.G., Mus.D.; musical conductor; b. Montreal, Que., 20 June 1896; s. Elzear and Zelire P.; e. awarded Que. Govt. Scholarship for European Study (Prix d'Europe); studied piano in Paris under Isidore Philipp, harmony with Rousseau, composition with Widor, opera tradition with Bellaigue; Hon. degrees from Univ. of Montreal, McGill, Laval, Univ. of Que., Banff School of Fine Arts, Hobart and Wm. Smith Colleges, New York City College; m. Rose Bampton (Soprano), 24 May 1937; children: Camille, (late) François; Dir. Gen. of Music Teaching, Min. of Cultural Affairs, Que. 1961-70; Founder and Dir. Gen., Conservatory of Music and Dramatic Art, Montreal, 1943-61; Conductor, Montreal and Quebec Symphony Orchestras; made his debut as Accompanist with De Gogorza; was regular Conductor, Metropolitan Opera Assn. of New York 1917-50; Conductor, Metropolitan Opera Assn. Sunday Concerts 1917-50; Musical Dir., l'Assn. des Concerts Symphoniques de Montréal; Dir. of the New York Philharmonic Youth Concerts; Dir., The Quebec Symphony, Quebec City; Conductor, Ravinia Opera, Chicago, during 9 consecutive summers; also Los Angeles and San Francisco Opera Co's; joined Metropolitan Opera House 1917; directed orchestra when Lawrence Tibbett sang in the "Emperor Jones" on the Pacific Coast; also directed the premiere of "Marouf" and "Le Coq d'Or" on the Pac. Coast; writes music for opera and radio programs; has made a hobby of collecting penguins; awarded The Canada Council Medal, 1961-62; honoured by Govt. of Que. (naming of national park lake Wilfrid Pelletier) and City of Montreal (naming of W. Pelletier Grammar School, W. Pelletier Music School, Salle Wilfrid Pelleteir and Place Des Arts, Montreal); Home: 322 East 57th Street, New York 10022, U.S.A.

PENDERGAST, James F., E.M., C.D., D.Sc.; retired regular army and civil servant; archaeologist; b. Cornwall, Ont., 26 May 1921; s. Harold James and Mary Evelyn (Thompson) P.; e. St. Columbans Sch.; Cornwall (Ont.) Coll. Inst.; Arty. Staff Course 1950; Candn. Army Staff Coll. 1953; McGill Univ. D.Sc. (Hon. c.) 1976; m. Mary Margaret d. late John Strong Denton, 21 Oct. 1944; children: James Denton, Mary Margaret Isobel, Elizabeth Anne, Harold John; Asst. Dir. Operations, Nat. Museum of Man, Nat. Museums of Can. 1972-78; enlisted Stormont Dundas and Glengarry Highlanders NPAM 1936, CASF 1940; served UK Theatre 1941-43, seconded US Army Intelligence 1945, enrolled Candn. Regular Army (Intelligence) 1946, trans. RCA 1949, retired Lt. Col. 1973; Aide-de-Camp Lt. Gov. Sask. 1955-56; rec'd Commendation Medal US Army 1947; Bd. mem. Nat. Ski Museum 1973-74; largely responsible for archaeological definition of St. Lawrence Iroquoian tribe; co-author "Cartier's Hochelaga and the Dawson Site" 1972; author various articles, books, and papers in archaeol., ethnohistory and mil. fields; Vice Pres. Candn. Archaeol. Soc. 1971-72; Pres., Merrickville Hist. Soc. 1978-79; mem. Champlain Soc.; Ont. Archaeol. Soc. Ottawa Chapter; Pa. Archaeol. Soc.; N.Y. State Archaeol. Assn.; Candn. Archaeol. Assn.; Regional Chrmn., Eastern Ont., Heritage Can. 1979-81; mem. Candn. Archaeol. Council; Royal Candn. Arty. Assn.; Exec. Central Region, 150th Anniversary Rideau Canal, 1979-82; awarded Jubilee Medal, 1978; R. Catholic; recreations: skiing, philately, history, farming; Home: "The Willows", Merrickville, Ont. K0G 1N0

PENHALE, Alfred Lloyd, D.C.L., D.Sc.; retired executive; b. Sherbrooke, Que., 11 October 1901; s. Col. John J., D.S.O., and Alice (Somers) P.; e. Sherbrooke High Sch.; m. Edith, d. Cornelius McNaughton, Thetford Mines, Que.; children: Beverley Ann, John A., Bonnie, David Ian; Vice-Pres. and Gen. Sales Mgr., Wabasso Ltd.; joined Asbestos Corpn. Ltd., 1923; apptd. Gen. Sales Mgr., 1937, Secretary 1943, General Manager 1947, and Pres. and Managing Dir., 1948, Chrmn. 1967-69; Pres., Thetford Mines Branch, Canadian Red Cross; Pres., Candn. Inst. Mining & Metall., 1955-56; Anglican; recreations: fishing, golf, curling;

Clubs: Mount Royal (Montreal); Canadian (New York); St. George's (Sherbrooke); Address: (Box 150) North Hatley, Que. J0B 2C0

PENNER, David; construction executive; b. U.S.S.R. 16 May 1924; s. John J. and Helen (Weibe) P.; came to Canada 1926; e. Langham (Sask.) High Sch. 1942; Banff Sch. Advanced Mang. 1967; Univ. West. Ont.,m Internat Bus. Mang. 1978; m. Jean Elizabeth, d. Franklin Cavers 27 Dec. 1952; children: Tracy, Mark; VICE-PRES. WESTERN CAN., BG CECHO INTERNATIONAL LTD.; Protestant; Club: Cercle Universitaire d'Ottawa; Home: 1860 Henderson Hwy., Winnipeg, Man. R2G 1P2; Office: 5314-97th St., Edmonton, Alta. T6E 5W5

PENNY,Walter Frederick, B.A., C.A.; executive; b. Toronto, Ont. 16 May 1929; s. Leo Walter and Lillian (Morgan) P.; e. Regal Rd. Pub. Sch. and Oakwood Coll. Inst. Toronto 1946; Univ. of Toronto B.A. 1949; C.A. 1953; m. Jean d. Charles Graham, Val d'Or, Que. 5 July 1952; children: Brian, Kevin, Stephen, Janet, Lesley; PRES. AND C.O.O., ST. LAWRENCE CEMENT CO. 1981- ; articled J. Clare Wilcox & Co. 1949-52; Audit Supvr. Riddell, Stead, Graham & Hutchison 1952-55; joined present Co. 1955 serving as Chief, Acct., Treas. and Vice Pres. Finance; recreations: golf, tennis, reading; Clubs: Financial Extve. Inst.; Royal Oak Tennis; Hudson Yacht; Whitlock Golf & Country; St. James's; Home: (P.O. Box 654) Windcrest Ave., Hudson, Que. J0P 1H0; Office: 50 Place Cremazie, Nontreal, Que. H2P 2T7.

PENTLAND, William Thomas, B.Arch., A.R.I.B.A.; architect; b. Toronto, Ont., 30 Oct. 1919; s. late William James (former Pres. and Founder of Dominion Stores Ltd.) and Edith U-Raynor (Smith) P.; e. Forest Hill Public Sch., Toronto, Ont.; St. Andrews Coll., Aurora, Ont.; Univ. of Toronto, B.Arch. 1946; PARTNER, PENTLAND & BAKER; Gen. Arch. Designers, Estbd. 1952; with Constr. Design Dept., Ajax Div., Defence Construction Ltd., 1941; admitted a mem. of Royal Arch. Inst. of Can., 1948; began private practice of Arch., 1949; joined in Partnership in 1952 by L. G. Baker; comns. executed by the firm incl. design of new office, factory and warehouse of R. Laidlaw Lumber Co., Weston, Ont., chosen by Comte. of Ont. Assn. of Arch. as the "building of the year" 1956 for visit and study at their convention; served in 2nd World War; Lieut., 48th Highlanders (R). 1941; on active service Overseas with 48th Highlanders in Eng., 1943, Italy 1943-45 and Holland and Belgium, 1945; Chrmn. of Toronto Chapter, Ont. Assn. of Arch., 1957-58; Zeta Psi; Anglican; recreations: golf, hunting; Clubs: University; Toronto Golf; Home: 355 St. Clair Ave. W., Toronto Ont. M5P 1N; Office: 62 Charles St. E., Toronto, Ont. M4Y 1T1

PENTZ, Donald Robert, M.F.A., R.C.A.; artist; b. Bridgewater, N.S. 18 Sept. 1940; s. Cyril Robert and Marjorie Ione (Frank) P.; e. Davis Mem. High Sch. Bridgewater Sr. Matric. 1959; N.S. Coll. of Art one yr.; Mount Allison Univ. B.F.A. 1966; Univ. of Regina M.F.A. 1979; Banff Sch. of Fine Arts summer 1979; m. Mary Ann Louise d. John Edward Rudolph, Truro, N.S. 31 Aug. 1974; one s. Benjamin Christopher; Asst. Curator, Confed. Centre Art Gallery Charlottetown 1966; Zool. Illustrator Nat. Museum of Natural Science Ottawa 1968-70; instr. various painting workshops 1970-80; Teaching Asst. Visual Arts Univ. of Regina 1977-79; yearly solo exhns. paintings and drawings Halifax, Ottawa, Toronto; Regina, Calgary since 1967; rep. in various group exhns. incl. Expo '67, Montreal Olympics 1976, N.S. Art Bank 1980; rep. in pub., corporate and private colls. incl. Can. Council Art Bank, Art Gallery N.S.; awards rec'd N.S. Govt., N.S. Talent Trust, Sask. Arts Bd.; Centennial Award Best Painting 1967 (Maritime Art Assn.); Twining Scholarship Banff Sch. Fine Arts 1979; Can. Council Award 1980; author/illustrator "Risser's Beach Salt Marsh" 1975; "Some Common Shore and Ocean Birds of

Nova Scotia" 1975; "Risser's Beach-Some Common Beach Finds" 1975; weekly columnist ("The Packbasket") "Bridgewater Bulletin"; mem. Soc. Candn. Artists; recreations: canoeing, ornithology, outdoor sketching, photography, hiking, writing, archery; Address: R.R.1, Pleasantville, N.S. B0R 1G0.

PEPER, Dirk, B.A.; b. Zandvoort, Holland, 6 Jan. 1928; s. H. J. and H. C. (Driehuyzen) P.; e. Huygens Lyceum, Amsterdam, 1940-46; Queensland Univ., B.A. 1957; m. Tamara Laine Randmae, 12 Sept. 1952; children: Tiia, Derek, Heli; m. 2ndly, Rose Marie Patton 20 Dec. 1980; TREASURER, ONT: HYDRO; Asst. Acct., Commonwealth Pub. Service of Australasia, Dept. of Works, Port Moresby, New Guinea, 1951-57; Acct., Canada Metal Co. Ltd., Toronto, 1957-58; Div. Office Mgr., Canada Dry Ltd., Toronto/ Montreal, 1958-61; Comptroller and Dir., Klein Manufacturing Co., 1961-62; Assistant to Comptroller, United Shoe Machinery Corp.; Montreal, 1962-64; Consultant, Mang. Services, Peat, Marwick, Mitchell & Co., Montreal, 1964-68; Comptroller and Depy Min. of Finance, Gov't of Nfld. and Labrador 1970-74; Treasurer and Commissioner of Finance, Municipality of Peel 1974-78; served with Dutch Army Royal Blue Hussars in Indonesia, 1947-51; mem. Inst. Pub. Adm. Can. (Council);700 University Ave., Toronto, Ont. M5G 1X6

PEPIN, Hon. Jean-Luc, C.C., P.C., B.A., L.Ph., LL.L., D.E.S.D. (Diploma in Higher Studies of Law); b. Drummondville, Que., 1 Nov. 1924; s. Victor & Antoinette P.; e. Drummondville (Primary); St. Hyacinthe Semy.; Univ. of Ottawa; Univ. of Paris; m. Mary, d. Harding Brock-Smith, Winnipeg, Man., 12 Apl. 1952; two children; MIN. OF TRANSPORT 1980- ; former Pol. Science Prof. at Univ. Ottawa; rep. of Nat. Film Bd. in London, 1956-58; first el. to H. of C. for Drummond-Arthabaska, g.e. 1963; appt. Min. without Portfolio, July 1965; Min. of Mines & Tech. Surveys, Dec. 1965, Energy, Mines & Resources, 1966 (also Dept. of Labour); Min. of Industry, Trade & Comm. 1968 till def. in g.e. 1972; Pres., Interimco Ltd., 1973-75; Chrmn. of the Anti-Inflation Bd., 1975-1977; Co-chrmn., Task Force on Candn. Unity, 1977-79; re-el. to H. of C. for Ottawa-Carleton, g.e. 1979 and 1980; mem. Extve. Comte. Trilateral Comm. until 1975; doctorates from Univs. of Sherbrooke, Laval, Ottawa and Bishop; Liberal; Catholic; Home: 16 Rothwell Dr., Gloucester, Ont. K1J 7G4

PÉPIN, Lucie, R.N.; b. St-Jean d'Iberville, Que. 7 Sept. 1936; d. Jean and Thérèse (Bessette) P.; e. St-Jean d'Iberville Hospital, Qué. R.N. 1959; post-grad. studies Notre-Dame Hosp., Montreal 1959-60; Univ. of Montreal 1965; Montreal Sch. of Fine Arts 1966; McGill Univ. 1975; Univ. of Montreal 1977; children: Nathalie, Sophie; PRES., CANDN. ADVISORY COUNCIL ON THE STATUS OF WOMEN, 1981- ; Head Nurse, Gyn. Dept., Notre-Dame Hospital, 1960-61; Head Nurse, Family Planning Clinic, Fac. of Med., Univ. of Montreal 1966-70; Consultant, Family Planning Ed. Prog., Red Cross, 1970; Candn Rep., World Health Org. 1972-74; Instr., Contraception, Dept. of Nursing, Dept. of Med., Univ. of Montreal 1972-77; Nat. Coordinator, Candn. Comte. for Fertility Research 1972-79; Consultant, 'Femmes d'aujourd'hui' Radio-Canada (TV) 1974; Coordinator, Federal Badgley Report, Justice Canada 1975; Instr., Contraception & Sexuality, Fac. of Med., Univ. of Montreal 1976-78; Coordinator, Internat. Symposium (Canada/France/Gt. Brit.) on Family Planning 1979; Coordinator, Internat. Conference, Internat. Centre for Contraception Research, 1979; Coordinator, Nat. Symposium, Candn. Fertility Society, 1979; Vice-Pres., Candn. Adv. Counc. on the Status of Women; Dir., Niagara Inst. 1981; Vice-Pres., Women's Comte., United Appeal (Montreal) 1979-80; Vice-Pres., Extve. Comte., Rosemont Hosp., Montreal 1979-80; mem., Comte. on Sexual Offences Against Children, Justice Canada/Health & Welfare Canada 1981; Comte. for Gifted Children, Que. 1970-

71; Chamber of Comm., Que.; Fédération des Femmes du Qué.; Assn. des femmes diplômées des universités; Candn. Fed. of Univ. Women; Assn. des infirmières et infirmiers de la province de Qué.; Amer. Obstetrics & Gyn. Assn. of Nurses; Family Planning Assn. of Montreal; Ligue des femmes du Qué.; Nat. Action Comte. on the Status of Women; hon. mem., Pioneer Women; Roman Catholic; Clubs: Canadian (Montreal); Le Cercle Universitaire d'Ottawa; Le Musée de Beaux Arts (Montréal); Hillside Tennis; recreations: tennis, sailing, painting, horseback riding; Home: 5405 Place Grovehill, Montreal, Que. H4A 1J8; Office: P.O. Box 1541, Station B, Ottawa, Ont. K1P 5R5

PEPPER, John J., Q.C., B.A., B.C.L.; b. Montreal, Que., 17 Feb. 1928; s. late William and Blanche (Frigon) P.; e. Westmount (Que.) High Sch. 1945; Loyola Coll., B.A. 1949; McGill Univ., B.C.L. 1952; m. Anita Claire, d. Edward J. Turcotte, 19 Sept. 1953; children: John T., David T., Timothy T., Anthony T., Andrew T.; PARTNER, CAMPBELL, PEPPER, LAFFOLEY; Pres. and Dir., Soges Inc.; O.A. Travel Inc.; British Airways Holidays Ltd.; Dir., Canadian Ultramar Ltd.; Ultramar Canada Inc.; Marwest Hotel Co.; Broadcast Relay Service Canada Ltd.; W.I.H. Holdings Ltd.; Western International Hotels Ltd.; Rediffusion Inc.; Canadair Ltd.; Hulme Marketing Associates Limited; Odeon Cinemas Limited; Scaffold Fast Limited; Transvision (Eastern Townships) Limited; read law with Hon. F. Philippe Brais, Q.C. and A. J. Campbell, Q.C. 1949-53; called to Bar of Que. 1953; cr. Q.C. 1969; assoc. with law firm of Brais & Campbell 1953 and successor firms (now present name); mem. Adv. Bd. Crown Trust Co.; Dir. and Secy. St. Mary's Hospital Foundation; Dir. & Pres. St. Mary's Hospital Centre; Dir., of the Corp. of St. Mary's Hospital, Montreal; Dir. of Montreal Joint Hosp. Inst.; Loyola of Montreal (Pres. Alumni and mem. Bd. Govs. 1968-69); mem. Bd. Govs. Concordia Univ.; Montreal Bd. Trade; Montreal Children's Hosp. Foundation; Fellow Am. Coll. Trial Lawyers; mem. Bar of Que. (mem. Board Discipline 1968-, General Council & Extve. 1977-); Pub. Information Bureau, Bar of Que. (1971-);Bar of Montreal; Past Director, Legal Aid Bureau 1962-63, Secy. 1963-65, Batonnier 1978-79; Canadian Bar Assn., Chrm. Nat. Membership Comte.; mem. Nat Extve. (1975-1977) and Council; Secretary (1963) and President (1965) Insurance Section, Quebec Branch, Special Fed. Crown Prosecutor 1954-57; Judge, Ad Hoc Cdn. Citizenship Court (1957); Kt of Magistral Grace, Sovreign and Mil. Order of Malta; Kt. of Mil. & Hospitaller Order of St. Lazarus of Jerusalem; Liberal; R. Catholic; recreations: fishing, golf, skiing; Clubs: Mount Royal; Royal Montreal Golf; St. James's; Forest and Stream; Badminton & Squash; Mont Tremblant Golf & Country; Montreal Reform (Past Pres. and Dir.); Garrison (Quebec City); Romaine River Salmon; Delta Upsilon; Mount Bruno; Canadian; Home: 3637 The Boulevard, Westmount, Que. H3Y 1S6; Country residence: La Ferm Forestière, Lac Supérieur, Co. Laurentides-Labelle, Qué.; Office: One Place Ville Marie, Montreal, Que. H3B 2B3

PEPPER, Kathleen Daly, R.C.A.; O.S.A., A.O.C.A., artist; b. Napanee, 28 May 1898; d. Denis Henry Aldworth and Mary (Bennett) Daly; e. Havergal Coll. Toronto; Univ. of Toronto 1920; Ont. Coll. of Art grad. 1924, Etching 1925-26; Academie de la Grande Chaumière Paris 1924-25; Parsons Sch. of Design Paris; m. George Pepper 30 Sept. 1929; solo exhns. incl. Vancouver Art Gallery 1945; Hart House Univ. Toronto 1953; Banff Sch. Fine Arts 1958; La Jolla, Calif. 1958; Banff Lib. & Archives of Candn. Rockies 1969 (50 W. drawings); rep. in maj. exhns. across Can. and maj. travelling exhns. Nat. Gallery Can. 1930-57; reg. contrib. to annual exhns. various art societies and frequently in Candn. Nat. Exhn. Shows since 1925; rep. in maj. group exhns. incl. Buenos Aires; Group of Seven; Brit. Empire Exhn. (portrait "Rene, French Canadian Boy" reproduced on cover Coronation issue of "The Listener" 1936); S. Doms. Exhn.; Tate Gallery London, Eng.; Art Gallery Ont.; N.Y. World' Fair 1939; rep. in numerous pub. and private colls. incl. Nat. Gallery Can., Art Gallery Ont., McMichael Candn. Coll. Kleinburg; rec'd Dept. N. Affairs invitation to study and paint E. Arctic 1960; protrait comns. incl. Hon. Herbert Greenfield 1946; Dr. Thomas S. Cullen, Baltimore 1941; Abdeslam El Hach, Morocco 1955; author "Morrice" 1966; various articles painting in Morocco, Eskimo Art and studies of the Eskimo, Indians and coal miners of Alta.; co-illustrator "Kingdom of Saguenay" 1936; nominated as an Academic of Italy with Gold Medal; Alpha Gamma Delta; United Church; recreations: travel (n. areas), sketching outdoor activity; Clubs: Heliconian; Zonta Internat.; Address: 561 Avenue Rd., Apt. 1101, Toronto, Ont. M4V 2J8.

PEPPIATT, Frank; writer-producer; b. Toronto, Ont., 19 Mar. 1928; s. Frank Bernard and Sarah (Grant) P.; e. Pub. and High Schs. Toronto and Montreal; Univ. of Toronto; m. Marilyn Patricia Frederickson, 15 Oct. 1954; children: Robyn, Marney, Melissa; CBC Writer 1952-59; Steve Allen Show 1958; Andy Williams Show 1959; Perry Como Show 1960-63; Judy Garland Special 1962; Frank Sinatra Special; Herb Alpert Specials; "Hee Haw" Producer 1969-71; Osmond Bros. Special; John Wayne Special; rec'd Emmy Award for "Frank Sinatra - A Man and His Music"; served with COTC for 8 months; Psi Upsilon; Liberal; Anglican; recreations: golf, tennis; Clubs: Granite (Toronto); Riviera Country; Home: 1271 N. Doheny Dr., Los Angeles, Cal.; Office: Yongestreet Productions, 357 N. Canton Dr., Los Angeles, Cal.

PERCY, Herbert Roland (Bill), C.D.; author; b. Burham, Kent, Eng. 6 Aug. 1920; s. Herbert George Percy; e. Royal Naval Artificers' Training Estab. Chatham, Eng. 1936-40; RCN Prep. Sch. Esquimalt, B.C. 1954-55; RN Engn. Coll. Manadon, Devon 1955; m. Mary Davina d. late Arthur James 28 March 1942; children: Arthur Jonathan, Roger James, Pauline Elizabeth; Co-Prop. The Moorings Guest House, Granville Ferry, N.S.; Bd. Govs. Anapolis Royal Heritage Foundation; author "The Timeless Island and Other Stories" 1960; "Joseph Howe" 1976; "Thomas Chandler Haliburton" 1980; "Flotsam" novel 1978; "Gallery" novel 1982; short stories various periodicals; rep. Candn.; U.S. and U.K. anthols.; Ed. "The Canadian Author and Bookman" 1963-65; contrib. weekly column "A Critic at Large" Ottawa Journal 1963-65; joined Royal Navy 1936 as Engine Room Artificer Apprentice, Engine Room Artificer and Chief 1940-52, served in HM Ships King George V, Hawkins, Belfast and others; Chief Engine Room Artificer RCN 1952-54, Engn. Offr. 1955-71, served in HMC Ships Cape Breton, Quebec, Sioux, Swansea and CFHQ Ottawa, rank Lt. Commdr.; Fellow, Inst. Marine Engrs. (London); mem. Writers' Union Can. (Past Atlantic Regional Rep.); Writers' Fed. N.S. (Founding Chrmn.); Candn. Authors Assn.; N.S. Naval Offrs. Assn.; recreations: tennis, gardening, walking; Address: The Moorings, Granville Ferry, N.S. B0S 1K0.

PERHAM, J. Allan, B.Eng.; retired company executive; b. Montreal, Que., 23 Oct. 1916; s. late Lewis Phillips and Grace Marion (Corner) P.; e. Strathcona Acad. (1933); McGill Univ., B.Eng. 1938; m. Mary Josephine, d. late Joseph Eldridge, Sudbury, Ont., 13 June 1944; children: (Jean) Elizabeth, David (Eldridge), (Allan) Randolph; Chairman of the Board, Canadian Oxygen Limited, 1973-81; President, Edwards High Vacuum Canada Limited; Chrmn., Compair Canada Limited; Chrmn., Medishield Inc.; began as Jr. Engineer, Howey Gold Mines Ltd., Red Lake, Ont., 1938; joined Internat. Nickel Co., Sudbury, Ont., in 1939, and successively Shoveller, Driller, Timberman, Stopeboss, till 1941; Sr. Safety Engr., Levack Mine, 1942; Shift Boss, 1943-44; Head Efficiency Engr., Levack Mine, 1945; Mine Supt., Senator-Rouyn Ltd., Noranda, Que., 1946-49; joined Atlas COPCO as Gen. Sales Mgr. for Canada, 1949; Mang. Dir., England, 1952-55;

Vice-Pres.-Sales, Stockholm, 1955-58; Resident Dir., U.S.A. 1958; President Canadian Oxygen Ltd. 1959-73; life mem., Canadian Institute Mining & Metall.; Mem., Association Prof. Engrs. Ontario; President (1970-71) Compressed Gas Assn. Inc., N.Y.; Delta Sigma Phi (Treas.); Protestant; recreations: golf, skiing; Clubs: Craigleith Ski; Mississauga Golf & Country; Home: 1517 Camelford Road, Mississauga, Ont. L5J 3C8

PERKIN, James Russell Conway, M.A., D.Phil.; academic administrator; b. Northamptonshire, Eng. 19 Aug. 1928; came to Can. 1965; s. Wm. and Lily Maud (Drage) P.; e. gram. sch. Northamptonshire; Oxford Univ. (Eng.) B.A. 1952; M.A. 1955; D.Phil. 1955; Strasbourg Univ., France 1954-55; m. Dorothy Joan Louise d. John Ingraham Bentley 7 April 1953; children: James Russell, John, Anne Louise; PRES., ACADIA UNIV. since 1982; Min. of Altrincham Bapt. Ch., Cheshire, Eng. 1956-62; Lectr. New Test. Greek, New Coll., Edinburgh, Soct., 1963-65; Assoc. Prof. New Test. Interp., McMaster Divinity Coll, Hamilton, Ont. 1965-69; joined Acadia Univ. as Prof. Religious Studies and Dept. Head, 1969-77; Dean of Arts, 1977-80; Vice Pres. (Academic), 1980-81; served with RAF, 1946-49; author of ten books incl. "Handbook for Biblical Studies", 1973; "In Season", 1978; "With Mind and Heart", 1979; "Seedtime and Harvest", 1982; several articles on biblical, theological, and linguistic subj. in more than 20 jnls.; mem., Soc. for New Test. Studies; Candn. Soc. for the Study of Religion; Candn. Soc. for Biblical Studies; Phi Delta Kappa; recreations: reading, gardening, sailing, squash; Home: Box 355, Wolfville, N.S. B0P 1X0; Office: Wolfville, N.S. B0P 1X0.

PERLMUTTER, David Martin, B.Com., C.A.; executive; b. Toronto, Ont. 22 Sept. 1934; e. Univ. of Toronto B.Com. 1956; C.A. 1959; m. Renee 29 June 1961; children: Stacey, Dean; PRESIDENT, QUADRANT FILMS LTD. Founder 1971; Quadrant Group of Companies (including National Film Finance Corp.; Compass Film Sales Ltd.; Gaunt Films Ltd. & several others); Vice Pres. Duncan Mill Group; Secy.-Treas. Superior Crane & Hoist Rental; Partner, Perlmutter Orenstein Giddens, Newman & Kofman, C.A.'s; retired 1968 to form Claranton Management Ltd.; Dir. Jewish Community Centre Toronto; Candn. Soc. Weizmann Inst. Science; Club: York Raquets; Home: 47 Elgin Ave., Toronto, Ont. M5P 2R8; Office: 950 Yonge St., Toronto, Ont. M4W 2J4.

PEROWNE, Ronald Herbert, B.Com.; textile executive; b. Montreal, Que., 15 Jan. 1918; s. late Herbert and Anna (Hooks) P.; e. Town of Mount Royal (Que.) High Sch.; McGill Univ., B.Com.; m. Eunice, d. late John Frank Hellyer, 4 Oct. 1945; children: Barbara Jo Ann (Meade), Catherine Jean (Lymburner), Margaret Elaine (Metze), Ronald Grant, Ian Herbert; CHRMN. AND C.E.O. DOMINION TEXTILE INC., 1974; Dir., DHJ Industries Inc. N.Y.; Howard Cotton Co., Memphis; Swift Textiles Inc., Columbus, Ga.; Linn-Corriher, North Carolina; joined Industy. Relations Dept. of present Co. 1945; Mgr. 1948; Sales Mgr., Work Clothing, 1954; Gen. Sales Mgr. 1961; Vice Pres., Sales, 1963; Vice Pres., Marketing, 1966; Vice Pres. & Gen. Mgr., 1967; Pres. and C.E.O. 1969; Chmn. of Bd. 1977; served with RCNVR 1941-45; rank Lt.; mem., Martlet Soc.; Allendale Mutual Assur. Co., Cdn. Adv. Bd.; Protestant; recreations: golf, tennis; Clubs: University; Kanawaki Golf; Montreal Badminton & Squash; Mount Royal; Home: 58 Roselawn Cres., Montreal, Que. H3P 1H9; Office: 1950 Sherbrooke St. West, Montreal, Que. H3H 1E7

PERRAULT, Charles, M.Eng.; management consultant; b. Montreal, Que., 22 Sept. 1922; s. late Jean Julien and Laurette (Beaubien) P.; e. McGill University, B.Eng., 1943 (Metall.): M.Eng. (Metall.) 1946; PRESIDENT, PERCONSULT LTD., Dir., Avon Canada Inc.; B.P. Can. Inc. Beaubran Canagex Inc.; Canron Inc.; Gaz Métropolitain inc.; The Molson Companies Ltd.; North American Life As-

PERRAULT / PERRIER   835

urance Co.; Northern Telecom Ltd.; The Oshawa Group
.td.; Quaker Oats of Canada Ltd.; Taurus Fund Ltd.;
res. Casavant Frères Ltée 1958-71, Chrmn. 1971-76;
'res. Conseil du Patronat du Qué. 1969-76; mem. Con-
eil, d'orientation economique du Qué 1961-66; Conseil
onsultatif du travail et de la main d(oeuvre (Qué) 1969-
6; mem., Econ. Council Canada 1968-76; Bd. of Gov.,
McGill Univ.; Extve. Comte, Howe Research Inst.;
North-South Inst.; Candn-Am Comt-.; Inst. Donations
und Public Affairs Research; Mem. Howe Inst. Policy Advisory Comte.; served in 2nd World War; Lieut.,
R.C.E.M.E.; served Overseas (50 Candn. L.A.D.) Italy,
rance, Belgium, Holland, Germany, U.K.; Liberal; Ro-
nan Catholic; recreations: skiing, sailing, music, reading;
Club: Cercle Universitaire Laval; Home: Apt. 501, 1545
ve Docteur Penfield, Montreal, Qué. H3G 1C7; Office:
uite 910, 2050 Mansfield, Montréal, Qué. H3A1Y9

PERRAULT, Guy, M.Sc.A., Ph.D., F.R.S.C.; b. Amos,
5 Sept. 1927; s. C. R. and Laurenza (Maurice) P.; e. Ecole
Polytech., B.Sc.A. 1949; Univ. of Toronto M.Sc.A., 1951;
h.D., 1955; m. Hélène d. Pascal Lachapelle of Montreal,
4 June 1957; children: Marie, Sylvie, Isabelle; PROFES-
SOR OF MINERAL ENGN., ECOLE POLYTECHNIQUE;
arty Chief, Geol. Mapping, iron ranges, Labrador and
New Québec, Iron Ore Company of Canada (summers)
949-52; Mapping and Prospecting, Norancon Explora-
ion Company Ltd., 1953; apptd. Field Engr., Diamond
Drilling Programs, Moneta Porcupine Mines Ltd., 1954-
6; Asst. Prof. of Mineralogy, Ecole Polytech., 1956; Asoc. Prof. of Mineralogy and Crystallography, 1957; Prof.
of Crystallography, 1965; Chrmn., dépt. de génie géologique, Ecole Polytechnique, 1966-72; Chrmn., dépt.de
génie minéral, Ecole Polytechnique, 1974-75; Vice Pres.,
Research and Foreign Projects, SOQUEM 1975-77; Prof.,
dépt. de génie minéral, Ecole Polytechnique, since 1977;
Man. Dir., Mineral Exploration Research Inst. 1981-;
Ion. Pres., Montreal Gem & Mineral Club; Hon. mem.,
Walker Mineral. Club; Mérite honorofique, Assn. Etudi-
nts l'Ecole Polytechnic; Fellow, Mineralogical Soc. of
Am.; author of numerous scient. papers; mem., Mineral.
Assn. Can. (Pres. 1967-68); Geol. Assn. Can.; Ordre des
ngénieurs de la P.Q.; Fellow, Mineral. Soc. Am.; Geol.
oc. of Am.; Soc. of Economic Geologists; Can. Institute
of Mining and Metallurgy; awarded Prix Scientifique du
Québec (1971); Queen's Jubilee Medal 1977; Catholic;
Iome: 11811 Jean Massé, Montreal, Qué. H4J 1S2; Office:
.P. 6079, Succ. A., Montreal, Que. H3C 3A7

PERRAULT, Hon. Raymond, P.C., B.A.; senator; b.
Vancouver, B.C., 6 Feb. 1926; s. Ernest Alphonse and
lorence (Riebel) P.; e. Sir Guy Carleton Elem. and John
Oliver Secondary Schs. Vancouver; Univ. of B.C. B.A.
947; m. Barbara Joan d. late Albert Edward Walker, 10
Aug. 1963; children: Yvonne Marie, Mark Raymond,
Robert Ernest Albert; GOVERNMENT LEADER IN
SENATE since 1980; Leader of Opposition in the Senate,
979-80; summoned to Senate 1973 and Leader of Govt.
n Senate 1974-79; Candn. Sessional Del. and Spokesman
o Special Comte. UN, N.Y. 1969; mem. first Candn.
972; mem. Candn. Parlty. del. to Soviet Union 1975;
Candn. Cabinet rep. Coronation of King Juan Carlos of
pain 1975; Leader, Can. Del. to U.N. Water Conf., Mar
del Plata, Argentina, 1977. el. Leader of Lib. Party in B.C.
959; el. to B.C. Leg. 1960, 1963, 1966; el. to H. of C. g.e.
968; Parlty. Secy. to Min. of Labour 1970, Manpower &
mmigration 1971; Liberal; R. Catholic; recreations: pho-
ography, gardening, swimming; Club: University;
Iome: 437 Somerset St., North Vancouver, B.C. V7N
G4; Office: The Senate, Ottawa, Ont. K1A 0A4

PERREAULT, Germain; banker; b. Montréal, Qué., 23
May 1916; s. Lucien and Maria (Dufault) P.; CHRM. OF
THE BD., and CHRM. OF EXTVE. COMTE.,
NATIONAL BANK OF CANADA, Dir., Domco Indus-

tries Ltd.; Les Ensembles Urbains Ltée; Les Nouveaux
Ensembles Urbains Ltée; Régie de la Place des Arts; Vice
Pres., Canada Council; Vice Pres., La fondation des Di-
plômés HEC; Mem. of the Conseil Consultatif de la Com-
mission d'initiative et de développement économiques de
Montréal (CIDEM); Mem. Bd. of Dir., Montreal Heart
Inst. Research Fund; began with Montréal Stock Ex-
change 1936; Garneau, Ostiguy & Co. 1937-39; joined
B.C.N. Head Office 1939; appt. Asst. Mgr., Invest. Dept.
1947; Asst. Gen. Mgr. 1964; Gen. Mgr. 1968; Chief Gen.
Mgr. 1971, mem. Bd. and Extve. Comte. 1972, Vice-Pres.
and Chief Gen. Mgr. 1972, Extve. Vice-Pres. and Chief
Gen. Mgr. 1974; Pres., 1974; Pres. and C.E.O., 1976;
Chrmn. of the Bd., Pres., and C.E.O. 1978; Nov. 1st,
1979, Chrm. of Bd. and Chrm. of Extve. Comte., National
Bank of Canada; mem., La Chambre de Comm. du dist.
de Montréal; Les Diplômés HEC; Canadian Chamber of
Comm.; La Chambre de Comm. de la prov. de Québec;
Canadian Club of Montreal; Candn. Council of Christi-
ans and Jews (Quebec Reg. Bd. of Directors); Gov. and
mem. of the Bd. of Directors and Extve. Comte. of the
Quebec Hosp. Service Assn. (Blue Cross); Gov., Hôpital
Notre-Dame de Montréal; Douglas Hospital; recreation:
music; reading; golf; Clubs: St. Denis Laval-sur-le-Lac;
Mt. Royal; Office: 500 Place d'Armes, Montréal, Qué.
H2Y 2W3

PERRELLA, Guido, D.Eng.; mechanical consulting engineer; b. Italy, 1921 (naturalized Candn. Citizen); e. Univ.
of Genoa, D.Eng. (Mech.) 1946; m. Christine, d. Sabino
Gallo; s. Italo; PRESIDENT, DBM INDUSTRIES LTD.,
since 1968; has been engaged in engn. work in various
mfg. plants in Italy, Brazil before coming to Canada as
Consultant and Technical Manager respectively to two
plants; formerly co-owner, Dynacast Ltd., 1964-67; Publication: a tech. book on Cost Calculation (3rd ed.); holder
several patents for machines and products; speaks and
writes fluently in five lang.; mem., Corp. Engrs. Que.;
Royal Astron. Soc. Can.; Soc. Diecasting Engrs.; Candn.
Owners & Pilots Assn.; Internat. Aerobatic Club; Roman
Catholic; hobbies: astronomy, music, aerobatic flying;
Home: 28 Senneville Rd., Senneville, Que. H9X 1B6; Office: 10340 Côte de Liesse, Lachine, Que. H8T 1A3

PERRETT, John Felix, Q.C.; b. Simcoe, Ont., 2 Sept.
1912; s. John Kingcombe and Jeanne (DesBats) P.; e. Pub.
and High Schs., Simcoe, Ont.; Univ. of Toronto, B.A.
(Hons. Law) 1935; Osgoode Hall Law Sch., Toronto,
Ont.; m. Ruth M., d. late J. E. L. Stimson, 8 Jan. 1971;
PARTNER, ROBERTSON & PERRETT, since 1949; Dir.,
Canada Permanent Mortgage Corporation; Canada Permanent Trust Company; Chief Agent in Canada, Washington National Insurance Co.; Pacific Mutual Life Insurance Co.; Dir., Square D Canada Electrical Equipment
Inc.; read law with McMaster, Montgomery, Fleury and
Co., Toronto, Ont.; called to Bar of Ont., 1938; cr. Q.C.
1953; served with Royal Candn. Arty., 1940-45; discharged with rank of Capt., 1945; began career as Solr.
for Commr. of Agric. Loans of Ont., (Treas. Br.) 1938-39;
joined Robertson, Fleury, Lane, 1945-47; mem., York Co.
Law Assn.; Candn. Bar Assn.; Psi Upsilon; Anglican; recreations: fishing, boating, bridge; Clubs: National; Board
of Trade; Lawyers; Gyro; Home: Apt. 1603, 55 Erskine
Ave., Toronto, Ont. M4P 1Y7; Office: 180 Dundas St. W.,
Toronto, Ont. M5G 183

PERRIER, Andre J.; Canadian public servant; b. Ottawa,
Ont. 5 Feb. 1931; s. Emile and Yvonne (Hurtibise) P.; m.
Jeannine, d. Conrad Parent, Lucerne, Que. 11 April 1953;
children: Claude, Robert, Michel; ASST. DEPY. MIN.,
DEPT. OF PUBLIC WORKS, CAN.; directed devel. of
many large real estate projects incl. Place De Ville, Ottawa 1967-70 and Harbour Sq., Toronto since 1971; a former Pres., Blake Investment Ltd.; Past Vice-Pres., Campeau Corp. Ltd.; Kanata Development Co. Ltd.;
Canadian Interurban Properties Ltd.; Place Longueuil
Shopping Centre; Place de Saguenay Ltd.; served in

R.C.A.F., Flying Offr. 1952-58; recreations: golf, swimming, skiing; Home: 25 Castelbeau Rd., Lucerne, Que. J9J 1C9; Office: Sir Charles Tupper Bldg., Riverside Drive, Ottawa, Ont.

PERRON, Michel; industrialist; b. La Sarre, Qué. 27 Apl. 1932; s. Henri and Lucie (Vandal) P.; e. Mont St-Louis' Coll. Montréal; St-Jerome's Coll. Kitchener, Ont.; Forestry Sch. of Duchesnay (Qué.) m. Lise d. C. R. Perreault 14 Apl. 1956; children: Anne-Marie, Bertrand, Claude, Denise, Eric, François, Geneviève, Henri; PRES., NORMICK PERRON INC.; Chmn., Télé Capital Inc.; Dir. Corp. de Gestions La Vérendrye; Mercantile Bank of Can.; Forintek Canada Corp.; Donohue Normick Inc.; served with RCAF Ground Observer Corps, Air Defence Command; Dir. Sedbergh Sch.; mem. Adv. Council, Candn. Forest; Liberal; R. Catholic; recreations: tennis, skiing, fishing, flying; Clubs: St-Denis; Rotary; Home: 250, 9e Ave. E., La Sarre, Qué.; Office: (P.O. Box 2500) La Sarre, Qué. J9Z 2X6.

PERRY, Bob G., B.Sc.; industrial executive; b. Amarillo, Texas 1934; e. Univ. of Texas B.Sc. (Chem. Engn.) 1956; m. Gayle McClain; children: David, Debora, and Bruce; SR. VICE PRES., UNION CARBIDE CANADA LTD. 1981- ; Production Engr. Plastics & Chem. Union Carbide Corp., Seadrift, Texas 1956, Plant Mgr. Taft, La. 1973, Mgr. Operations Ethylene Oxide/Glycol New York 1976, Vice Pres. Mfg. Chems. & Plastics Operations Div. New York 1978, Vice Pres. Operations Ethylene Oxide/Glycol Div. 1979; mem. Am. Inst. Chem. Engrs.; Home: 1166 Bay, Toronto, Ont.; Office: 123 Eglinton Ave. E., Toronto, Ont. M4P 1J3.

PERRY, Frank, B.A., R.C.A.; sculptor; b. Vancouver, B.C. 15 Jan. 1923; s. Frank and Martha (Mack) P.; e. Univ. of B.C. B.A. 1949; Regent St. Polytechnic London, Eng. Art Sch. 1953-55; Central Sch. Arts & Crafts London, Eng. 1954-55; m. Joan Margaret Ramsay 30 Dec. 1977; exhns. Galleria Numero Florence, Italy 1958; Gimpel Fils Gallery London, Eng. 1959; Laing Gallery Toronto 1959-60; New Design Gallery Vancouver numerous shows 1958-67; Burnaby Art Gallery 1977, 1980; Vancouver Art Gallery 1977; Mira Godard Gallery Toronto 1978; Gallery Move 1979; outdoor sculpture exhns.: Univ. of B.C. 1956, 1958; B.C. Centennial Outdoor Show 1958; Que. Outdoor Nat. Sculpture Show 1960; Vancouver Outdoor Centennial Sculpture Show 1967; rep. in various pub. and private colls. Can. and Europe; recipient Jessie Dow Award Montreal Museum Spring Show 1958; First Prize Sculpture, Burnaby Centennial Outdoor Sculpture Show 1958; First Prize Centennial Outdoor Sculpture Show Vancouver 1967; Can. Council Fellowship 1958; mem. Adv. Design Panel Dist. N. Vancouver 1969-73; served with Royal Candn. Engrs. 1943-46; mem. Sculpture Soc. B.C.; Sculpture Soc. Can.; recreation: fishing; Home: 3526 Everglade Pl., North Vancouver, B.C. V7N 3T9; Office: Carson Graham Sr. Secondary School, 2145 Jones Ave., North Vancouver, B.C. V7M 2W7.

PERRY, (Gordon) Neil, B.A., M.P.A., A.M., Ph.D., LL.D.; educator; b. Victoria, B.C., 22 Nov., 1909; s. late John Oswald and late Agnes Mary (McLorie) P.; e. Victoria (B.C.) High Sch., 1923-26; Victoria Coll., 1929-31; Univ. of B.C., B.A. (Econ.) 1933, LL.D. 1966; Harvard Univ., M.P.A. 1943; A.M. and Ph.D. (Econ.) 1952; m. Helen McGregor Hunter, 29 June 1940; two d.: Margaret Elaine, Donna Louise; MEM., UNIVERSITIES COUNCIL OF B.C. since 1978; during depression apptd. Secretary to Econ. Council of B.C.; served Prov. of B.C. in various capacities until 1947 (1st Dir. of Bureau of Econ. and Stat.; Econ. Adviser, Dom. Prov. Relations, 1947); became Asst. Dir., Internat. Econ. Relations Div., Dept. of Finance, Ottawa, 1947; also served as Candn. Alternate Extve. Dir. on Bds. of Internat. Monetary Fund and Internat. Bank for Reconstr. and Devel. (World Bank) and as Financial Counsellor to Candn. Embassy, Washington;

invited to Ethiopia as Econ. Adviser to Min. of Financ 1954, and subsequently Gov. State Bank of Ethiopia; returned to World Bank as Asst. Dir. of Operations in Asia and Middle East, 1956; Asst. Dir. of Bank's oper tion in W. Hemisphere, 1958; appt. Dean of Comm Univ. of B.C., 1960, 1st Vice-Pres., 1963; loaned to U.N as Econ. Adviser of E. African Common Services Organ Apl.-Aug. 1963; Depy. Min. of Educ., B.C. 1965-70; Ass Depy. Min. Manpower & Immigration, Can. 1970-7 Prof. and Dir., School of Public Admin., Univ of Victor 1973-77; Consultant, Univ. of Sierra Leone 1977-78; Co sultant, OECD Manower and Social Affairs, 1976-78; h served as an Indust. Inquiry Commr. in difficult labou man. disputes mem. of Senate, Simon Fraser Univ Chrmn., Adv. Council, B.C. Inst. of Tech.; awarded C der of Star of Ethiopia, 1956; Centennial Medal, 1967; a thor "Report of the Advisory Committee on Inter-Unive sity Relations" (The Perry Report) 1972, also numerou articles for learned and prof. publs.; mem., Candn. Eco Assn.; Am. Econ. Assn.; Royal Econ. Soc.; Inst. Pu Adm.; apptd. Chrmn. of Comte. on Inter-Univ. Relatio by Min. of Educ., B.C. 1968; United Church; recreatio golf; Club: Victoria; Home: 3240 Beach Drive, Victori B.C. V8R 6L8

PERRY, J. Harvey, B.A.; consultant; b. Toronto, Ont., : Aug. 1912; s. N. Roy and late Marguerite Winnifred P.; Toronto Pub. Schs.; Univ. of Toronto, B.A. (Econ. an Pol. Science) 1935; m. Florence Ruth Downes; childre Peter Harvey, Sharron Ruth, Frances Lynn; CONSUI TANT, CANADIAN BANKER'S ASSN., 1975-80; Pres Candn. Foundation for Econ. Educ. 1977-80; mem Royal Comn. on Taxation (1962-66); Ontario Adv. Comt on Federation 1965-72; Pres. Candn. Council on Soci Devel. 1977-79; entered Dept. of Finance, Ottawa, 193 and for 16 yrs., among other duties, was one of the of cials who advised the Min. of Finance on taxation ma ters; joined staff of Candn. Tax Foundation in 1952 Dir. of Research; apptd. Dir. and Chief Extve. Offr., 195 carried out special mission for Colonial Office, Niger 1954; carried out special mission for U.N. Tech. Assi tance Adm. in Ghana, Jan.-Feb. 1958; Executive Direct Canadian Bankers' Assn. 1961-74; author of: "Taxation Canada", 1951, 2nd ed. 1953, 3rd ed. 1961; "Taxes, Tar iffs and Subsidies", 1955; co-author of "Financing Cana dian Federation"; recreations: golf, gardening; Club Ontario; Bayview Country; Home: Bayshore Village, R.I 3, Brechin, Ont. L0K 1B0; Office: (Box 282) Toronto-D minion Centre, Toronto, Ont. M5K 1K2

PERRYMAN, Eric Charles William, M.A., F.R.S.C.; m tallurgist; b. Stanwell, Eng. 7 Feb. 1922; s. Frederick an Violet (Plow) P.; e. Cambridge Univ. M.A. 1943; M. Gl dys Winifred Field d. late Ewart Taylor 21 May 1945; chi dren: Gavin, Marcia, Anthony, Roger; GEN. MANAG COMMERCIAL OPERATIONS, ATOMIC ENERGY O CANADA LTD. since 1979; joined Metall. Dept. Roy Aircraft Estab. Eng. 1943-46; Brit. Non-Ferrous Meta Research Assn. Eng. 1946-51; Aluminum Laboratorie Ltd. Kingston, Ont. 1951-54; on attachment to Atom Energy of Canada Ltd. 1954-57, joined AECL 1957 b coming Asst. Dir. Chem. & Metall. Div. 1958-60, 1963-6 Dir. of Div. 1965-67, Dir. Fuels & Materials Div. 1967-7 Dir. Applied Research & Devel. 1970-78; Depy. Head Reactor Materials Lab. UKAEA, Culcheth, Eng. 1960-6 Chmn. Deep River Youth Hostel (9 yr) SERVAS host; au thor over 45 tech. publs.; Corr. mem. Brit. Nuclear Er ergy Soc.; Can. Nuclear Soc.; Can. Nuclear Assn Candn. Inst. Mining & Metall.; Anglican; recreation tennis, sailing, table tennis, skiing, gardening; Club: Deep River Yacht & Tennis; Home: 17 Beach Ave Deep River, Ont. K0J 1PO; Office: Chalk River, On K0J 1JO.

PERSAD, Emmanuel, M.B., B.S., F.R.C.P.&S.(C); psy chiatrist; b. Trinidad, W.I. 25 Dec. 1935; s. Kali and Chris tiana (Baboolal) P.; Nariva Govt. Sch., Progressive Educ nst. Trinidad; Durham Univ. M.B., B.S. 1964; Univ. of Toronto Dipl. in Psychiatry 1969 (Gold Medal); L.M.C.C. 1972; m. Decima d. James W. Mignon 1967; children: Sheldon, Natalie; HEAD, AFFECTIVE DISORDER UNIT, CLARKE INST. OF PSYCHIATRY since 1976, Staff Psychiatrist and Chief of Service, Educ. Coordinator and mem. Extve. Comte.; Assoc. Prof. of Psychiatry, Univ. of Toronto since 1978, Lectr. in Psychiatry Dept. Rehabilitaive Med.; Intern. Gen. Hosp. Port of Spain, Trinidad 1964; House Offr. Ministry of Health, Trinidad 1965, St. Ann's Hosp. Trinidad 1965-66; Resident in Psychiatry Univ. of Toronto 1966-69; Registrar, Ministry of Health Trinidad 1970; joined Staff present Inst. 1971; Asst. Prof. of Psychiatry Univ. of Toronto 1974; mem. Task Force on Specialized Services Ont. Council of Mental Health; author various publs.; mem. Candn. Psychiatric Assn.; Candn. Med. Assn.; Ont. Med. Assn.; Anglican; recreation: reading; Home: 8 Foxwarren Dr., Willowdale, Ont.; Office: 250 College St., Toronto, Ont.

PERSAUD, Trivedi Vidhya Nandan, M.D., Ph.D., D.Sc., M.R.C. Path.(Lond.) F.A.C.O.G.; educator; b. Port Mourant, Brit. Guiana (Guyana) 19 Feb. 1940; s. Ram. Nandan and Deen (Raggy) P.; e. Rostock Univ. Germany M.D. 1965 (Brit. Guiana Scholar 1960-65), Outstanding Student of the Yr. Award 1964, Distinguished Young Scient. Award 1965, D.Sc. 1974; Univ. of the W. Indies Ph.D. (Anat.) 1970; m. Gisela Gerda Zehden; children: Indrani Uta, Sunita Heidi, Narendra Rainer; PROF. AND HEAD. OF ANAT. UNIV. OF MAN. since 1977; Assoc. Prof. of Obstetrics and Gynecology 1979- ; Consultant in Pathology and Teratology, Children's Centre, Winnipeg since 1973; Scient. Staff (Lab. Services) Health Sciences Centre Winnipeg since 1973; Intern. Kleinmachnow Hosp. Postdsam, Germany 1965-66; Govt. Med. Offr. Guyana 1966-67; Lectr. in Anat. Univ. of the W. Indies 1967-70, Sr. Lectr. 1970-72; Assoc. Prof. of Anat. Univ. of Man. 1972-75, Prof. of Anat. and Dir. Teratology Research Lab. 1975-77; named Hon. Citizen of New Orleans 1972; rec'd Carveth Jr. Scient. Award Candn. Assn. Pathols. 1974; Distinguished Services Award Pan Am. Assn. Anat. 1975; Rh-Inst. Award (Health Sciences) Univ. Man. 1975; Albert Einstein Centennial Medal, Academy of Sciences, GDR 1981; author "Study Guide and Review Manual of Human Anatomy", W.B. Saunders Co., Philadelphia, 1976; "Problems of Birth Defects", Univ. Park Press, Baltimore, 1977; "Prenatal Pathology: Fetal Medicine", Charles C. Thomas, Springfield, 1978; "Teratogenesis: Experimental Aspects and Clinical Implications", Gustav Fischer Verlag, Jena, 1978; "Advances in the Study of Birth Defects": Vol. 1. Teratogenic Mechanisms, vol. 2 Teratological Testing, vol. 3 Abnormal Embryogenesis: Cellular and Molecular Aspects, vol. 4 Neural and Behavioral Teratology, University Park Press. Baltimore, 1979; mem. Royal Soc. Med. London; Royal Coll. Pathols. London; Royal Microscopical Soc. London; Candn. Assn. Pathols.; Am. Assn. Anats.; Candn. Assn. Anats. (Vice-Pres. 1979-81; Pres. 1981-83); Midwest Anats. Assn. (Pres. 1979-80); Anatomische Gesellschaft; Pan Am. Assn. Anat.; Teratology Soc.; European Soc. Teratology; Soc. Study Reproduction; Assn. Anat. Chrmn.; Soc. Obstericians & Gynaeols. Can.; Ed. "West Indian Medical Journal" 1970-73; mem. ed. bds. several med. journs.; Home: 70 Folkeston Blvd., Winnipeg, Man. R3P 0S3; Office: 730 William Ave., Winnipeg, Man. R3E OW3.

ERSER, Alan W.; company president; b. Kingston, Ont., 13 Oct. 1910; s. Wesley and Maud (Gilmore) P.; e. Public and High Schs., Toronto, Ont.; m. Octavia, d. Martin Jossa, 1932; two s., Donald, Martin; PRESIDENT, ERHOLD LTD. (holding co.) and Publishing Div. Inexa Publications; assoc. with insurance, banking and advertising firms before establishing City-Wide Telehone Services in 1949; became Pres. on inc. of the Co. in 1951, until sold, 1964; estbd. Airtel Limited (radio communications) 1964, sold to Maclean Hunter Communica-

tions Ltd. 1971; estbd. Indexa Publications 1973; served in 2nd World War with R.C.A.F., 1940-45; Founder, Past Chrmn. Bd. and Hon. Chrmn., Radio Common Carriers Assn. of Can.; mem., Bd. of Trade Metrop. Toronto; Candn. Power Sgdn.; recreations: boating, photography, target shooting; Homes: 10 Woodmere Court, Islington, Ont. M9A 3J2 and 963 Hillsboro Mile, Hillsboro Beach, Fla., 33062; Office: 385 The West Mall, Suite 405, Etobicoke, Ont. M9C 1E7

PERSON, Clayton Oscar, M.A., Ph.D., F.R.S.C.; F.A.P.S.; educator; b. Regina, Sask. 16 May 1922; s. Oscar and Alma (Eriksson) P.; e. Univ. of Sask. B.A. 1949, M.A. 1951; Univ. of Alta. Ph.D. 1953; Univ. of Lund, Sweden and Univ. of Adelaide, Australia Postdoctoral study; m. Mary Millicent d. Robert Meyer 9 March 1946; children: Jan, Joan, Lisa; PROF. OF BOTANY, UNIV. OF B.C. since 1966; Research Offr. Dept. of Agric. Can. Research Lab. Winnipeg 1956-61; Prof. and Head of Genetics, Univ. of Alta. 1961-66; Consultant on Coffee Diseases, Ethiopia F.A.O. 1975; Designated a Fellow of the Am. Phytopathological Society, 1981; Awarded a British Columbia Science Council Gold Medal for contributions to scientific research; awarded U.B.C. Killam Fellowship for study and research; served with RCN during World War II, participated Dieppe raid (wounded), N. Africa and Sicily landings; author over 50 scient. papers, book chapters; mem. Candn. Genetics Soc. (Pres.); Am. Bot. Soc.; Am. Phytopathol. Soc.; recreation: music; Office: Vancouver; B.C. V6T 1W5.

PETCH, Howard E., M.Sc., Ph.D., D. Sc., F.R.S.C.; physicist; b. Agincourt, Ont., 12 May 1925; s. Thomas Earle and Edith May (Painter) P.; e. Sarnia (Ont.) Coll. Inst. & Tech. Sch.; Norwich (Ont.) High Sch.; McMaster Univ., B.Sc. (Hon. Chem. and Phys.) 1949, M.Sc. (Physics) 1950; Univ. of B.C., Ph.D. (Physics) 1952; McMaster Univ., D. Sc.; m. late Rosalind June, d. late Alfred E. Hulet, 1949; children: Stephen, Patricia; rem. Linda Schlechte, 1976; one s., Jeremy; PRESIDENT AND VICE-CHANCELLOR, UNIVERSITY OF VICTORIA and Professor of Physics there since 1975; Dir., TRIUMF; Canada/Fance/Hawaii Telescope Corp.; Discovery Fdn.; Postdoctorate Fellow, McMaster University, 1952-53; Rutherford Mem. Fellow, Cavendish Lab., Cambridge Univ., 1953-54; Asst. Prof. of Physics, McMaster Univ., 1954-57: Assoc. Prof., 1957-60; Prof. of Metall. and Metall. Engn., 1960-67; Principal, Hamilton Coll., McMaster Univ., 1963-67; Dir. of Research there 1961-67 and Chrmn. Interdisciplinary Materials Research Unit 1964-67; Prof. of Physics, Univ. of Waterloo 1967-74; Pres. (acting) 1969-70; Vice-President Acad., 1967-68, 1970-75; served with R.C.A.F. 1943-45; awarded Ont. Research Foundation Schols. 1949-52; Convocation Founder of Simon Fraser Univ. 1965; mem. Bd. Govs., McMaster Univ.; mem, Candn. Assn. Physicists (Pres. 1967-68); Am. Phys. Soc.; Internat. Union of Crystallography 1954; Am. Crystallographic Assn.; Candn. Research Mang. Assn.; and Inst. of Mining & Metall., Comte. for Research; rec'd. Centennial Medal; Alpha Sigma Mu; recreation: gardening, fishing; Home: 3775 Haro Rd., Victoria, B.C. V8P 5C3

PETER, Friedrich, R.C.A.; graphic designer; calligrapher; educator; b. Dresden, Germany 23 Feb. 1933; s. Karl and Lena (Brueckner) P.; e. apprenticeship in graphic design, 1947-50, Dresden; 1956, Hochschule für bildende Künste, Berlin, grad. in lettering and graphic design; Meisterschüler dipl. 1957; m. Christine d. Gotthold Rossbach, West Germany, 1 June 1957; children: Jan, Martin, Andrea; INSTR., EMILY CARR COLL. OF ART 1979- ; free-lance designer (graphic, lettering, typeface, stamp, book illustration) since 1957; came to Can. 1957; Instr. Vancouver Sch. of Art 1958-79; winner Internat. Typeface Design Competitions N.Y. and London 1966 "Vivaldi", 1973 "Magnificat"; designer "O Canada" 2 postage stamps commemorating Candn. Nat. Anthem

1980; Postage Stamp, commemorating Terry Fox and Marathon of Hope 1982-82; calligrapher "Im Aufwind" 1977, 4th printing 1981; "Searching for You", 1978; "Into your light", 1979; 12 llustrations "Der Turm", 1979; awarded Canada's commemorative Silver Dollar celebrating Centennial of Regina 1980; Participant in "Calligraphy Today", New York exhibition 1980; Exhibited at Royal Cdn. Acad. of Arts Centenniary Exhibition, Toronto 1981; author of various articles graphic design educ.; mem. Graphic Designers Can. (Founding mem. B.C. Chapter 1974; Regional Rep. Dist. of B.C.); Lutheran; recreations: hiking, painting, drawing; Home: 193 E. St. James Rd., North Vancouver, B.C. V7N 1L1; Office: ECCA, 1399 Johnston St., Vancouver, B.C. V6H 3R9.

PETER, John Desmond, B.A., LL.B., D.Litt.; educator; author; b. Queenstown, S. Africa 8 Oct. 1921; s. Edward Frederick and Leila Hedwig (Lehman) P.; e. Queen's Coll. Queenstown; Rhodes Univ. Coll., Univ. of S. Africa B.A. 1941, LL.B. 1944, D.Litt. 1957; Rhodes Univ. D.Litt., 1973; Gonville & Caius Coll. Cambridge B.A. 1947, M.A. 1951; m. Barbara Mary d. late Arthur Inglis Girdwood 6 Dec. 1946, divorced 1976; children: Jonathan William, Christopher Justin, Katherine Mary, Nicholas Michael, Stephanie Joan Louise; PROF. OF ENGLISH, UNIV. OF VICTORIA, B.C. 1961- ; Supvr. Eng. Studies Gonville & Caius Coll. Cambridge 1947-50; Assoc. Prof. of Eng. Univ. of Man. 1950, Prof. 1956-61; LeMay Fellow Rhodes Univ. and Sr. Fellow Humanities Research Council Can. 1957-58; Visiting Prof. Univ. of Wisc. 1964-65; Commonwealth Visiting Prof. Oxford Univ. 1966-67; Exchange Prof. Univ. of Mass. 1981; Sr. Arts Fellowship Can. Council 1973-74; served with S. African Arty. 1943; author "Complaint and Satire in Early English Literature" 1956; "A Critique of 'Paradise Lost'" 1960; "Along That Coast" 1964 (Doubleday Candn. Novel Prize 1964); "Take Hands At Winter" 1967; "Runaway" 1969; "Vallor" short stories 1978; essays, stories, poems numerous journs.; mem. Writers' Union Can. (B.C. Rep. 1976-77); recreations: golf, music; Home: 9594 Ardmore Dr., Sidney, B.C. V8L 3S1; Office: Victoria, B.C. V8W 2Y2.

PETERS, Arnold, M.P.; union organizer; b. Uno Park, Ont. 14 May 1922; s. William Robert and Margarette Sadie (Fennell) P.; e. New Liskeard High Sch.; Brockville Dept. of Veterans' Affairs Re-hab. School, Sr. Matric.; Carleton Univ. 2nd year journalism; m. Zelma Ethelyn, d. late William John Watson, 3 March 1940; children: William Ronald, Robert Arnold, Donald Tony; Northern Ontario Organizer, Internat. Woodworkers of Am. C.L.C.-C.I.O. since 1956; worked underground at the Delnite Gold Mines, Timmins (except for war service) for 15 years; joined Internat. Wood workers of Am. as Organizer; asst. in forming Local 100 of C.C.L., and later Steelworkers' unions in Timmins Area; active leader of Miners' Strike, 1953; moved to New Liskeard in 1956, and asst. in organ. several locals of Ontario Farmers' Union; served in 2nd World War in R.C.A.F. as Engine Mechanic with No. 124 Ferry Squadron for 3 yrs.; held various positions in C.C.F. Party; def. cand. in g.e. 1953; el. to H. of C. for Temiskaming in g.e. 1957; re-el. since; CCF-NP Whip 1958-62; in conjunction with Frank Howard was instrumental in obtaining new divorce laws for Canada; former Pres., Local 4460, U.S. of A.; Porcupine Matheson Labour Council; former Treas., N. Ont. Dist. Labour Council; former Pres., Porcupine Steelworkers Area Council C.L.C.-C.I.O.; N.D.P.; Protestant; Clubs: Royal Candn. Legion; Dale Carnegie (Internat.); Home: (P.O. Box 642), New Liskeard, Ont. P0J 1P0

PETERS, Douglas Dennison, B.Com., Ph.D.; economist; banker; b. Brandon, Man., 3 March 1930; s. Dr. Wilfrid Seymour and Mary Gladys (Dennison) P.; e. Brandon (Man.) Coll. Inst.; Queen's Univ., B.Com. 1963 (Medal in Comm.); Wharton Sch. of Finance & Comm., Univ. of Pa., Ph.D. 1966 (Ford Foundation Fellowship 1966); m. Audrey Catherine, d. F. E. Clark, Carnduff, Sask., 26

June 1954; children: David Wilfrid, Catherine Elaine, SENIOR VICE PRES. AND CHIEF ECON., TORONTO-DOMINION BANK, since 1981; joined Bank of Montreal 1950; held various appts. mainly in Winnipeg (1 Yr. Swift Current, Sask.) 1950-60; joined present bank as Chief Econ. and Head, Econ. Research Dept. 1966, Vice-Pres. 1972; co-author "The Monetarist Counterrevolution: A Critical Review of Post-1975 Monetary Policy in Canada" 1979; mem., Toronto Assn. Business Econ's. (Founding mem. and 1st Pres. 1970-71); Candn. Econ. Assn. (Extve Council 1969-72); Am. Econ. Assn.; Nat. Assn. Business Econ's; Am. Finance Assn.; Royal Econ. Soc.; Chrmn. Candn. Comte., Pacific Basin Econ. Council, 1980-82 Trustee, The Frazer Inst., Vancouver; recreation: tennis Home: No. 6, 28 Admiral Rd., Toronto, Ont. M5R 2L5 Office: (P.O. Box 1) Toronto-Dominion Centre, Toronto, Ont. M5K 1A2

PETERS, Norbert Melville, B.A.; counsel; executive; b Ottawa, Ont., 6 June 1926; s. Francis M. and Marie (Des roches) P.; e. St. Patrick's Coll., Ottawa, B.A. 1946; Osgoode Hall Law Sch. 1949; m. Cecilia Roy, Ottawa, Ont. 1950; children: Norbert J., Daniel L., Kenneth A., Eric F. Mary Anne, Claire C.; VICE PRES., GEN. COUNSEL & SECY., BRINCO LTD., since 1975; Vice-Pres., Secy., British Mining Limited; Abitibi Asbestos Mining Co. Ltd. Secy. Brinco Oil & Gas Ltd.; Secy. and Dir., Sharondale Corp.; Pres., Fernie Coal Mines Ltd.; Iskut Pulpower Ltd.; called to Bar of Ont. 1949; Partner, McHugh and Peters, Ottawa 1949-58; Gen. Solr., IAC Ltd. 1958-70; mem Law Soc. Upper Can.; Bar of Que.; Candn. Bar Assn. Club: St. James's; Home: 323 Chartwell Rd., Oakville, Ont. L6J 4A1 Office: 20 King St. W., Toronto, Ont. M5F 1C4

PETERSEN, Niels F., C.T.C.I.; company president; b Lytham-Ste Anne's, Lancs., Eng., 3 July 1912; s. Neils Gregers and Lillian Amelia (Ayriss) P.; e. St. Cuthbert's Sch.; Gasvaerksvet Kommune Skole Forkammersvejen Mellum og Real Skole; m. Margaret Bettina Bauckham, 7 Feb. 1942; children: Charles, Jane; CHRMN.OF BOARD STERLING TRUST CORP. since 1977; Pres., Investors Finance Corp. Ltd.; Vice-Pres., Western Stockyards Co Ltd.; Chrmn. of Bd. and Dir. Commercial Finance Corporation Limited; with Massey-Harris Co. Ltd., Toronto, Acct. and Engn. Depts., 1929-39; Acct. Procedure Div. Research Enterprises Ltd., 1939-42; Mgr., John Madsen Mfg. Co., Unionville, Ont., 1946-48; active in Real Estate Appraisal and Land Acquisition and Sub-Divn. in Toronto and vicinity, 1948-53; Extve. Asst. to Pres., Sterling Trust Corp., 1953, el. a Dir., 1953; Secy. 1956; Pres. and Dir. 1962; served in 2nd World War with Q.O.R., 1942-46; Chrmn. Finance & Adm., World Alliance, YMCA's Geneva, Switz.; Hon. Pres. Nat. Bd. of YMCA's; Pas Pres., Central Br., Y.M.C.A.; Offr., Trust Co.'s Assn. Can.; P. Conservative; United Church; recreations: sail ing, colour photography; Clubs: National; Royal Canadian Yacht; Granite; Home: Suite 10C, 66 Collier St., Toronto, Ont. M4W 1L9; Office: 220 Bay St., Toronto, Ont M5J 2K8

PETERSON, David Robert, Q.C., B.A., LL.B.; politician b. Toronto, Ont. 28 Dec. 1943; s. Clarence and Laura Marie (Scott) P.; e. Univ. of W. Ont. B.A. 1964; Univ. of Toronto, LL.B. 1967; Univ. of Caen, France; Osgoode Hal Law School; m. Shelley d. Donald Matthews 16 Jan. 1974 children: Benjamin David, Chloe Matthews, Adam Drake Scott; LEADER OF THE LIBERAL PARTY OF ONTARIO LEADER OF THE OFFICIAL OPPOSITION, 1982- called to the Bar of Ont. 1969; cr. Q.C. 1981; former Pres C.M. Peterson Co. Ltd.; first el. M.P.P. for London Centre, 1975; re-el. 1977, 1981; served with Frontier Coll.; Dir of Legal Services with a community youth organization Yorkville; mem., London Chamber of Commerce; Law Soc. of U.C.; United Church; Clubs: London Hunt Coun try; Young Presidents' Organiz.; London Racquets; Ca nadn. Club; YMCA; recreations: jogging, tennis, skiing

Office: Rm. 116, Legislative Bldg., Queen's Park, Toronto, Ont. M7A 1A2.

PETERSON, Edwin Arthur, M.Sc., Ph.D.; research scientist; b. Tugaske, Sask., 13 May 1921; s. John Emil and Anna Lilly (Bylund) P.; e. Bashaw (Alta.) High Sch., 1940; Univ. of Alta., B.Sc. 1950, M.Sc. 1952; Univ. of London, Ph.D. 1957; m. Margaret Muriel, d. George Skillen, Fairview, Alta., 22 Dec. 1946; one s. Barry Lynn; with Can. Dept. of Agric. since 1952 conducting research on agric. microbiology: participated in discovery and devel. of Myxin (antibiotic capable of inhibiting growth of variety of microorganisms); served with R.C.A.F. 1941-45; Radar Tech.-Overseas; has written over 28 research papers for various scient. journs.; mem., Prof. Inst. Pub. Service Can.: Brit. Mycological Soc.; Candn. Soc. Microbiol.; Candn. Phytopathol. Soc.; United Church; Home: 5 Majestic Drive, Apt. 1, Ottawa Ont. K2G 1C5; Office: Research Branch, Dept. of Agriculture, Ottawa, Ont. K1A 0C6

PETERSON, Hon. Leslie Raymond, Q.C., O.St.J., LL.D., Ed.D., LL.B., F.R.S.A.; b. Viking, Alberta, 6 October 1923; s. Herman S. and Margaret (Caren) P.; e. Vikinq High School, Alta.; Camrose Lutheran College, Alberta; McGill Univ.; London University (Eng.); Univ. of Brit. Columbia, LL.B. 1949; Simon Fraser Univ., LL.D. 1965; Notre Dame Univ. of Nelson, Ed.D. 1966; m. Agnes Rose, d. Harold Hine, Regina, Sask., 24 June 1950; children: Raymond Erik, Karen Isabelle; read law with late Howard C. Coulter; called to the Bar of British Columbia 1949; cr. Q.C. 1960; self-employed barrister, Vancouver, 1949-52; amalg. Peterson & Anderson, 1952, and later Boughton, Peterson, Anderson, McConnel, Dunfee, Jensen & Lorimer, 1956; el. to B.C. Leg. for Vancouver Centre Jan. 1956; re-el. 1956, 1960, 1963; el. for Vancouver-Little Mountain 1966; apptd. Min. Educ. Sept. 1956; Min. of Labour Nov. 1960; Atty.-Gen. 1968; served in 2nd World War; joined Candn. Army (R.C.A.) and served in Eng. and Continent, 1942-46; Past Dir., Westn. Soc. of Rehab.; Past Dir., Y.M.C.A., Victoria, B.C.; Past Pres., Twenty Club; Hon. mem., Vancouver Junior Chamber Comm.; former Vice-Pres., Normanna Old People's Home; mem., Vancouver Bar Assn.; Law Soc. of B.C.; Founding mem. of Convocation, Simon Fraser Univ. and Univ. of Victoria; Pres. (1964-65), Internat. Assn. of Govt. Labour Officials Chrmn., Standing Comte., Candn. Mins. of Educ, 1965-66; Hon. mem., French Chamber of Deputies, Paris, France; Hon. Commr. of Labor, State of Okla.; Dir., Calor Laterite Corp.; Chrmn., Vancouver Advisory Bd. and Dir., Guaranty Trust Co. of Canada, 1978; Pres, Adams Silver Resources Inc.; Dir., Morflot Freightliners Ltd.; Chrmn., Bd. of Governors, Univ. of B.C., 1979-81; Freemason (A.A.O.N.M.S.) Gizeh Temple Shrine; Social Credit; Protestant; recreations: skiing, golf, fishing, huntinq; Clubs: Scandinavian Business Men's (Past Pres.); Canadian; Hazelemere Golf & Tennis (Secy.); Seymour Golf & Country (Vancouver): Union (Victoria); Terminal City (Vancouver); Home: 814 Highland, W. Vancouver, B.C. V7S 2G5; Office: 1600-1100 Melville St., Vancouver, B.C. V6E 4B4

PETERSON, Oscar E., O.C. (1972); concert pianist; b. Montreal, Que., 15 Aug. 1925; s. Daniel William and Kathleen Olivia (John) P.; e. Royal Arthur Sch., Montreal; Montreal High Sch.; Montreal Conserv. Music; LL.D., Queen's Univ. 1976; m. Sandra Cythia, d. H. A. King, 23 April 1966; children (by previous m.); Lynn Cheryl, Sharon Vivian, Gay Carol, Oscar Emanuel Jr., Norman Raymond; has made world wide concert appearances since 1950; Pres., Regal Recordings Ltd.; Hon. Pres., Toronto Jazz Club; awards incl. Edison Award (Europe) for best jazz LP of year; Down Beat Award (12 times winner) for year's best jazz pianist; Play Boy Award (12 times silver medallist) for best musician's musician; Gold Rose Award, Montreux Jazz Festival 1968; Golden Disc Award (Japan); Achievement Award, Lakeshore Lions Club, Toronto 1966; Award of Appreciation, B'Nai Brith E. Regional Council, Montreal 1969; Toronto 1969; Toronto Civic Medal 1971; Testimony of Gratitude from public of Mexico 1969; Oscar Peterson Trio, award for best jazz combo of the year; nominated 5 times for recording best album of the year, Nat. Acad. Recording Arts and Sciences; Freemason; Anglican; recreations: photography, fishing;

PETT, Lionel Bradley, M.D., B.Sc.A., M.A., Ph.D., b. Winnipeg, Man., 13 Nov. 1909; s. Lionel Henry and Sadie Bradley (Saunders) P.; e. Ont. Agric. Coll., B.Sc.A. 1930; Univ. of Toronto, M.A. 1932; Ph.D. 1934; 1851 Exhn. Scholar. (Eng.); Univ. of Stockholm, 1934-35; Cambridge Univ., 1936; Univ. of Alta., M.D. 1942; m. Lois Eileen, d. H. M. McAfee, Edmonton, Alta., 9 May 1941; children: Hugh, Robert; Sr. Fellow in Biochem., Univ. of Toronto, 1933-34; Lect. in Biochem., Univ. of Alta., 1936-40; apptd. Chief, Nutrition Div., by Dom. Govt.; 1941; patented the "Vitometer", an instrument for measuring the recovery time from exposure to bright lights and its relation to Vitamin A; served as Nutritional Adviser to Bermuda Govt. 1942, India 1960, Jamaica 1962, and to UNRRA and Candn. dels. at several internat. conf. on health, food, agric., etc.; has contrib. about one hundred scient. papers to various technical journs.; Protestant; recreations: photography, woodworking; Home: 815-345 Quebec St., Victoria, B.C. V8V 1W4

PETTICK, Joseph, FRAIC; architect; b. Nyirparasznya, Hungary, 8 Oct. 1924; s. Leslie Petuk and Julian (Szepovitch) P.; e. pub. and high schs. Regina, Sask.; became Reg'd Arch. through Apprenticeship Program 1946-54; Univ. of Okla. Sch. of Arch. special student Aesthetic Design, Structure & Town Planning 1955; m. Jean Irene Margaret d. R. R. McKenzie, Regina, Sask., 1 June 1949; estbd. private practice Joseph Pettick, Architect, Regina 1956; projects incl. H.O. Bldg. for Sask. Power Corp. (Regina), new Regina City Hall and comm. residential inst. indust. and sports bldgs.; served with RCNVR during WW II; Chrmn. Regina Local Housing Authority 1960-64; Rep. RAIC to Internat. Union of Archs.; headed Candn. dels. to World Congs. London, Havana, Paris, Mexico City, Prague; Chrmn. Civic Comte. Regina Chamber Comm. 1961-65; mem. Structural Adv. Group Nat. Research Council formulating 1965 Nat. Bldg. Code; rec'd Massey Medal for Arch. 1961 (Moose Jaw Civic Centre); Life mem. Regina Soc. for Humane Care of Animals; Secy.-Treas. Sask. Assn. Archs. (Pres. 1965); past mem. Council RAIC; mem. Illuminating Engn. Soc.; Solar Energy Soc. Can.; Unitarian; Home: 2500 Garnet St., Regina, Sask. S4T 3A1; Office: 3034 Twelfth Ave., Regina, Sask. S4T 1J6

PETTY, George S., B.Com.; pulp and paper executive; b. Montreal, Que. 1 Aug. 1933; s. George Anson and Laura (White) P.; e. Montreal West High Sch.; McGill Univ. B.Com. 1954; m. Virginia Hale d. John Heaton 30 Dec. 1972; children: Geoffrey, Laura Jean; CHRMN. AND CHIEF EXTVE. OFFR., TEMBEC INC. 1973- ; Founder 1973; Chrmn. and Chief Extve. Offr., Midtec Paper Corp. (Kimberly, Wis.) 1976- , Founder 1976; Nitec Paper Corp. (Niagara Falls, N.Y.) 1974- , Founder 1974; Acadia Forest Products Ltd. 1980- , Repap Ent.; Sales Trainee, Canadian International Paper Co. 1954; Sales Mgr. International Pulp Sales, N.Y. 1966; Vice Pres. 1967; Vice Pres. Pulp Sales, Parsons & Whittemore Inc. 1968 and Pres. Prince Albert St. Anne Pulp Sales Co. 1969; Founder, Penntech Paper Inc. 1969, Extve. Vice Pres. 1970-72; served with RCAF-ROTC 1951-53, comnd. 1953; recreations: skiing, skating, golf, tennis; Clubs: Mount Royal; Royal Montreal Golf; Home: 2305 Bord du Lac, Ile Bizard, Que. H9C 1A7

PHILLIPS, Arthur, B.Com.; investment analyst; b. Montreal, Que., 12 Sept. 1930; s. Frederick William and Renée Josephine (Snackers) P.; e. Univ. of Br. Columbia,

B.Com. 1953 (divorced); m. Patricia Beaumont, d. Norman G. B. Burley, Sechelt, B.C., 8 May 1953; children: Susan, Norman, John Frederick, David Arthur, Liso Renée; rem. Carole Sandra Phillips, d. Clifford Goss, Toronto, Ont. 3 June 1977; Pres., Phillips Consulting Services Ltd. 1972-76; former Pres. Phillips, Hager and North Limited 1965; former Director, Grouse Mountain Resorts Limited; 1st el. Alderman, City of Vancouver 1968, re-el. 1970; 1st el. Mayor, City of Vancouver 1972, re-el. 1974; el. to lt. of C. (Liberal) for Vancouver Centre, g.e. 1979; joined Capital Management Corporation Limited as Dir. and Invest. Analyst (participated in formation of All-Candn. Funds), 1954; became Extve. Vice Pres., Capital Management Ltd. (successor firm) 1961; formed present firm 1965; Past Pres., TEAM (electors action movement of Greater Vancouver); former Chrmn, B.C. Police Comm.; Vancouver Soc. of Financial Analysts; Phi Delta Theta (Past Pres.); former Chrmn., Waterfront Theatre, Vancouver; recreations: curling, skiing, tennis, swimming; Home: 801 Ferry Row, Vancouver, B.C.V5Z 3Z5;

PHILLIPS, Charles Edward, B.A., D.Paed.; b. Toronto, Ont., 16 Sept. 1897; s. Robert Arthur and Elizabeth (Waugh) P.; e. Harbord Coll. Inst., Toronto, Ont. (Prince of Wales Scholarship); Univ. of Toronto (Trinity Coll.), B.A. 1921 and D.Paed. 1935; m. Clara Jane Gratton: children: Mrs. K. S. Treviranus (Jacqueline Ann), Edward Gratton; formerly Dir. of Grad. Studies, Ont. Coll. of Educ., Univ. of Toronto; Pres. (1959-60) and Life mem., Candn. Educ. Assn.; Hon. Life mem., Candn. Assn. for Adult Educ.; Teacher, Univ. of Toronto Schools, 1929-39; Editor, "The School", 1939-45; Extve. Secy., Candn. Educ. Assn., 1943-47; Quance Lect., Univ. of Sask., 1955; Pres. (1972), Planned Parenthood, Toronto; mem. Prov. Comte. on Aims under Min. of Educ. Ont.; author of "The Develpment of Education in Canada"; co-author of "A World History from Ancient Times to 1760" (New and Phillips); Home: 189 Grandview Ave., Thornhill, Ont. L3T 1J3

PHILLIPS, Donald John, B.Sc.; mining executive; b. Ebbw Vale, Wales 8 Jan. 1930; s. Archie Thomas Phillips; e. Univ. of Wales B.Sc. 1951; m. Wendy Leonora Billsborough 29 Oct. 1976; children: Janet Katherine, Simon Hugh; PRES., INCO LIMITED 1980- ; Dir. Mining Assn. of Canada; Toronto-Dominion Bank; Internat. Copper Research Assn. Inc.; Am. Standard Inc.; Tech. Offr. Inco Europe Ltd. 1956-67, Sales Dir. 1967-69, Gen. Marketing Mgr. 1969-70, Asst. Mang. Dir. 1970-71, Mang. Dir. 1971-72, Chrmn. and Chief Offr. 1972-77; Pres., Inco Metals Co., 1977; Pres. and Chief Executive Offr. Inco Metals Co. 1979-80; served with RAF 1952-54, rank Flying Offr.; Companion, Brit. Inst. Mang.; mem. Can.-Japan Bus. Cooperation Comte., Can.-U.S. Adv. Comte., Candn. Inst. of Mining & Metallurgy; Bd. Trade Metrop. Toronto; recreations: golf, tennis, squash; Clubs: National; Canadian (N.Y.); Hurlingham (London,Eng.); Home: 33 Harbour Sq., Apt. 404, Toronto, Ont. M5J 2G2; Office: (P.O. Box 44) 1 First Canadian Pl., Toronto, Ont. M5X 1C4.

PHILLIPS, Hon. Donald McGray, M.L.A.; politician; b. Woodstock, N.B. 29 Aug. 1929; s. Frank Porter and Charlotte B. (Gray) P.; e. Woodstock High Sch. and Alexander Hamilton Inst.; children: Dale Edward, John Robert, Mark Richard, Neal Kenneth:MIN. OF INDUSTRY AND SMALL BUSINESS DEVEL., B.C.1979-80; Dir. B.C. Railway; B.C. Development Corp.; Chrmn. B.C. Harbours Bd.; el. M.L.A. for South Peace River prov. g.e. 1966, not a Cand. 1969, re-el. since 1972; Min. of Agric. 1975-76; Min. of Econ. Devel. and Minister of Tourism 1975-79; Past Pres. Dawson Creek Chamber Comm.; Past Pres. and Life mem. Dawson Creek Centennial Band; Past Dir. Rotary; Freemason; Shriner; Office: Parliament Bldgs., Victoria, B.C. V8V 1X4.

PHILLIPS, Edwin C.; executive; b. Saskatoon, Sask., 19 Oct. 1917; s. late Dr. Charles Henry and Beatrice Grace (Johnson) P.; m. Elizabeth Winnifred, d. late Edward Westwood Johnston, 27 June 1942; children: Diane, Carol, Glen, Earl, Jane, Sue; CHRMN. and C.E.O., WEST-COAST TRANSMISSION CO. LTD., 1980- ; Pres. and Dir., Foothills Oil Pipe Line Ltd.; Vice Chrmn. and Dir., Foothill Pipe Lines (Yukon) Ltd.; Dir., Barclays Bank of Canada; Dynalectron Corp.; Pacific Northern Gas Ltd.; Emco Limited; Saratoga Processing Company Limited; Westcoast Petroleum Ltd.; British Columbia Resources Investment Corp.; Asst. Buyer, Loblaw Groceterias Co., Toronto, 1938; Advertising Mgr., Canada & Dominion Sugar Co., Chatham, 1945; Asst. to Gen. Mgr., Consumers' Gas Co., Toronto, 1947; Asst. Gen. Mgr., Trane Co. of Canada, Toronto, 1952; Vice Pres. and Gen. Mgr. 1957; Extve. Vice Pres. and Gen. Mgr. 1964; Pres. 1966; joined present Co. as Vice Pres., 1968; Group Vice Pres. 1969; Vice Pres.-Adm. and Dir. 1970; Extve. Vice Pres. 1971; Pres. 1972; Pres. & C.E.O. 1976-80; served with RCAF as Flying Instr. during World War II; Reg. mem. The Conference Bd.; mem. Bd. of Trustees, The Frazer Inst.; Bd. of Governors of the Employers' Council of B.C.; Conservative; Baptist; recreation: riding; Clubs: Shaughnessy Golf; Southlands Riding; The Vancouver; Home: 4458 W. 2nd Ave., Vancouver, B.C. V6R 1K5; Office: 1333 W. Georgia St., Vancouver, B.C. V6E 3K9

PHILLIPS, John Charles, Q.C.; petroleum executive; b. Metcalfe, Ont., 27 Apl. 1921; s. late Charles Cuthbert and Katherine Ann (Porter) P.; e. Ashbury Coll. Ottawa, Ont.; Univ. of Toronto Trinity Coll. B.A. 1940; Osgoode Hall Law Sch. grad 1949; m. Grace Ewart, d. late Archibald Purves, 31 Oct. 1947; children: John, Kathy, Barbara, Janet; CHRM. OF THE BOARD, GULF CANADA LTD. since 1979; called to Bar of Ont. 1949; cr. Q.C. 1967; private law practice Toronto 1949-56; Solr. Law Dept. present Co. 1956, Asst. Gen. Counsel 1960, Gen. Counsel 1964, Vice Pres. Gen. Counsel and Secy. 1971; Sr. Vice Pres. 1976; Extve. Vice Pres. 1977; served with RCAF 1940-46, Overseas 1941-45; Dir., Bank of Nova Scotia; Canada Life Assurance Co.; Cdn. Paraplegic Assn.; Emeritus mem., Assn. of Cdn. General Counsel; mem. Adv. Bd. Paterson Centre; Phi Delta Phi; Anglican; recreations: golf, curling; Clubs: Donalda; The National; The York; Canadian; Empire; Lawyers; Home: 6 Tetbury Cres., Don Mills, Ont. M3A 3G3; Office: 130 Adelaide St. West, Toronto, Ont. M5H 3R6

PHILLIPS, John Edward, M.Sc., Ph.D., F.R.S.C.; educator; b. Montreal, Que. 20 Dec. 1934; s. William Charles and Violet Mildred (Lewis) P.; e. Colchester Co. Acad. Truro, N.S. 1952; Dalhousie Univ. B.Sc. 1956 (Univ. Medal). M.Sc. 1957; Cambridge Univ. Ph.D. 1961 (Nat. Research Council Overseas Grad. Studentship 1957-60); m. Eleanor Mae d. Marston Richardson, Halifax, N.S. 8 Sept. 1956; children: Heather Anne, Jayne Elizabeth, Jonathan David, Catherine Melinda, Wendy Susannah; PROF. OF ZOOL. UNIV. OF B.C. since 1971; Asst. Prof. Dalhousie Univ. 1960-64; Assoc. Prof. Univ. of B.C. 1964-71; Visiting Researcher Dept. Zool. Cambridge Univ. 1972, 1976, 1980-81; Chrmn. Grant Selection Comte. on Animal Biol. Nat. Research Council of Can. 1969-71; author over 50 articles in scient. journs. on membrane transport processes, their control, and regulation of blood composition in Arthropods; mem. Candn. Soc. Zool. (Secy. 5 yrs., Vice Pres. 2 yrs., Pres. 1978-79); Am. Physiol. Soc. (Ed. Bd.); Am. Soc. Zools.; Soc. Exper. Biol. UK; Vancouver Bach Choir; recreation: music; Home: 2033 W. 58th Ave., Vancouver, B.C. V6P 1X3; Office: 2075 Wesbrook Pl., Vancouver, B.C. V6T 1W5.

PHILLIPS, Lazarus, O.B.E. (1946), Q.C., LL.D.; b. Montreal, Que. 10 Oct. 1895; s. Fischel and Deborah (Cohen) P.; e. Aberdeen Sch., Montreal; Montreal High Sch.; McGill Univ., B.C.L. 1918, LL.D. (Hon. c.) 1965; Hon. F.

of the Soc. of F's of The Jewish Theol. Semy. of Am., 1972; Hon. LL.D., Jewish Theol. Semy. of Am. 1978; Hon. LL.D., Yeshiva Univ. (N.Y.) 1979; Hon. Fellow & Hon. LL.D., Bar-Ilan Univ. 1979; m. Rosalie, d. Isidore Idelson, Johannesburg, S. Africa, 6 Mar. 1923; children: Neil, Ivan; SR. PARTNER, PHILLIPS & VINEBERG; Dir., C. W. Lindsay & Co. Limited; Associated Screen News Limited; Chairman Board, Inter-City Papers Ltd.; Trizec Corp. Ltd.; Steinberg's Ltd.; Great Universal Stores of Can. Ltd.; Chairman and Dir., Domco Ltd.; member of Council, Montreal Museum of Fine Arts: Royal Empire Society (Montreal Br.); read law with S. W. Jacobs, K.C., M.P.; called to the Bar of Que. 1920; cr. K.C. 1930; practised in Montreal as Partner of S. W. Jacobs, K.C., 1920-38; served in C.O.T.C., Laval Univ.; def. cand. to H. of C. for Cartier in by-el. 1943; summoned to Senate of Can. Feb. 1968 and retired Oct. 1970; former Pres., Jewish Parochial Schs., Montreal; Hon. Vice-Pres., Candn. Jewish Cong.; Treas., Un. Jewish War Relief; Hum. Relations Award, Can. Council of Christians and Jews, 1970; honored by creation of Senator Lazarus Phillips Chair in History, Fac. of Humanities, Bar-Ilan Univ., 1976; his portrait painted by Richard Jack, R.A.; Freemason; Liberal; Hebrew; Clubs: Mount Royal; Montefiore; Home: 48 Belvedere Place, Westmount, Que.; H3Y 1G6; Office: Suite 930, 1 Place Ville Marie, Montreal, Que. H3B 2A4

PHILLIPS, Neil F., Q.C., B.A., LL.B., B.C.L.; b. Montreal, Que., 1 Nov. 1924; s. Lazarus, Q.C., and Rosalie (Idelson) P.; e. Westmount (Que.) High Sch.; Williams Coll., B.A., Yale Univ. Law Sch., LL.B.; McGill Univ., B.C.L.; m. Sharon Whitely, d. James W. Greer, Southern Pines, N.C., 24 Sept. 1957; children: Greer Laurence, Melissa Rosemarie; PARTNER, PHILLIPS & VINEBERG; Dir., Aquitaine Co. of Canada Ltd.; Ritz-Carlton Hotel Co. Ltd.; Stewart Smith (Canada) Ltd.; Uranerz Canada Limited; Royal Bank of Canada; Canadian Pacific Enterprises Ltd.; Yale Alumni Assn. of Canada; read law with Phillips, Bloomfield, Vineberg & Goodman; called to the Bar of Quebec 1950 and subsequently Partner, Phillips & Vineberg; author of "United States Taxation of Foreign Entities" 1952; served in 2nd World War, R.C.N.V.R. (Lieut.) 1942-45; Phi Alpha Delta; Jewish; recreations: golf, skiing; Club: Mount Royal; Home: 634 Clarke Ave., Westmount, Que. H3Y 3E4; Office: 5 Place Ville Marie, Montreal, Que. H3B 2A5

PHILLIPS, Hon. Orville Howard, D.D.S.; senator; dental surgeon; b. O'Leary, P.E.I., 5 April 1924; s. J. S. and Maude (MacArthur) P.; e. Prince of Wales Coll., Charlottetown, P.E.I.; Dalhousie Univ., D.D.S. 1952; m. Marguerite, d. Robert Woodside, 21 Aug. 1945; children: Brian, Betty, Robert, Patricia; mem. H. of C. for Prince in 1957-62; summoned to Senate of Can. Feb. 1963; served in 2nd World War with R.C.A.F. 1942-45 in Can. and Overseas; mem., P.E.I. Dental Assn.; Royal Candn. Legion; Air Force Assn.; P. Conservative; United Church; recreations: curling, hunting; Address: Box 155, Alberton, P.E.I. C0B 1B0 (summer); 2317 Whitehaven Crescent, Ottawa, Ont. K2B 5H2

PHILLIPS, Robert Arthur John, B.A.; writer; b. Toronto, Ontario, 19 April 1922; s. Charles and Margaret (Waugh) P.; e. Univ. of Toronto, B.A. 1942; m. Mary Anne, d. Charles N. Cochrane, 15 June 1946; three d., Margaret W., Brigid A., Jennifer N.; Extve. Dir., Heritage Canada (retired 1980); ; joined Department of External Affairs 1945; Secy., Candn. Embassy, Moscow, 1947-49; Nat. Defence Coll., Kingston, 1949-59; Candn. Secy., Permanent Jt. Bd. on Defence, 1950-52; with Privy Council Office, 1952-54; joined Dept. Northern Affairs 1954; Dir., Northern Adm. Br., 1964-65; Asst. Secy. of the Cabinet, Privy Council Office 1965-69; Depy. Director Gen. Information Canada 1970-72; served in 2nd World War with Candn. Army in Can. and N.W. Europe; Anglican: Home: P.O. Box 319, Cantley, Que.

PHILLIPS, Robin; director, actor; b. Haslemere, Surrey, Eng. 28 Feb. 1942; s. James William and Ellen Ann (Barfoot) P.; e. Midhurst Grammar Sch., Sussex; trained for stage under Duncan Ross, Bristol Old Vic Theatre Sch.; unm.; came to Canada 1973; first prof. appearance Mr. Puff in "The Critic" 1959; Assoc. Dir., Bristol Old Vic 1960; acted in Sir Laurence Olivier's first Chichester season 1962; with Oxford Playhouse co. in "Six Characters in Search of an Author" 1964; Asst. Dir., Royal Shakespeare Co., Stratford-upon-Avon 1965; directed "The Ballad of the False Barman" Hampstead 1966; Assoc. Dir., Northcott Theatre 1967-68; directed "The Seagull", Thorndike, Leatherhead 1969; "Tiny Alice" for Royal Shakespeare Co., Greenwich 1970; "Abelard and Heloise" London and Broadway, N.Y. 1970; "Two Gentlemen of Verona" at Stratford (Eng.); "Caesar and Cleopatra" starring Sir John Gielgud and "Dear Antoine" starring Dame Edith Evans, Chichester 1971; "The Lady's Not for Burning" starring Richard Chamberlin 1972; instrumental in forming "Company Theatre"; apptd. Artistic Dir., Greenwich Theatre 1973; apptd. Artistic Dir. Stratford Festival Theatre (Can.) 1974-80; directed Stratford (Can.) Festival Theatre on nat. tour "Two Gentlemen of Verona" and "The Comedy of Errors"; and for festival season "Measure for Measure", "Trumpets and Drums", "The Importance of Being Earnest" 1975; dir. Antony and Cleopatra, A Midsummer Night's Dream, The Way of The World, 1976; Co-dir. Hamlet and The Tempest, restaged Measure for Measure, The Importance of Being Earnest, 1976; dir. Richard III, The Guardsman, A Midsummer Nights Dream, As You Like It, Hay Fever, 1977; dir. As You Like It, The Devils, Judgement, 1978; Co-dir. Macbeth, The Winter's Tale, Uncle Vanya, Private Lives, 1978; dir. King Lear, Importance of Being Earnest, co.-dir. Love's Labour's Lost, 1979; dir. Twelfth Night Virginia, Much Ado About Nothing, King Lear, Long Day's Journey Into Night. Co.-dir. The Seagull, Foxfire, The Beggar's Opera, 1980; films incl. "Miss Julie" (Dir.); "Decline and Fall" (actor); "David Copperfield" (title role); "Tales from the Crypt"; television appearances: Wilfred Desert in "The Forsyte Saga" B.B.C.; Constantin in "The Seagull" B.B.C.; recreation: painting; Address: P.O. Box 51, Stratford, Ont.

PHILLIPS, Roger, B.Sc.; executive; b. Ottawa, Ont. 17 Dec. 1939; s. Norman W. F. and Florence Elizabeth (Marshall) P.; e. McGill Univ. B.Sc. 1960; m. Katherine Ann, d. George Wilson, June 1962; one d. Andrée Claire; PRES. AND C.E.O., INTERPROVINCIAL STEEL AND PIPE CORP. LTD. 1982- ; Vice Pres., Research, Engineering, and Technology, Alcan Aluminum Ltd. 1980-81; Pres., Alcan International Ltd. 1980-81; joined Aluminum Co. of Canada 1960, Asst. to Treas. 1965, Gen. Mgr., Sheet and Plate 1967; Vice Pres., Mill Products, Alcan Canada Products Ltd. 1970, el. a Dir. 1972, Extve. Vice Pres. 1974; Pres. and Dir., Mel Williamson Foundation; Club: University; St. Denis; Home: 1 de Casson, Montreal, Que.; Office: Armour Siding, Regina, Sask.

PHILLIPS, Ross F., F.C.A.; corporate consultant; b. Winnipeg, Man., 21 Oct. 1926; s. Albert Sidney and Olive Ford (Hawkin) P.; e. Daniel McIntyre Coll. Inst., Winnipeg; Univ. of Man.; m. Mary Robinson, d. John Langan King, 28 July 1956; children: David Ferguson, Janet King; Dir.; Trans Alta Utilities Corp.; Air Canada; Vice-Chrmn. Comm. Life Assurance Co. of Can.; Halifax Ins. Co.; Morguard Investment Services Ltd.; Dover Park Devel. Corp. Ltd.; Barton Aschman Can. Ltd.; mem. Adv. Council, Calgary Club of Univ. W. Ont. Business Sch.; Calgary Adv. Board, Crown Trust Company; Chrmn., Pres. and Dir., Br. Can. Resources Ltd.; Student in Accountants, Millar Macdonald & Co., Winnipeg, 1943; Internal Auditor, Traders Finance Corporation, Toronto, 1949; joined Home Oil Co. as Chief Acct. 1953, Comptroller 1959, Vice Pres.-Adm. 1966, Sr. Vice Pres. Finance 1971, Pres. and Dir. 1973, Pres. and Chief Extve. Offr. Oct. 1973-80 (ret.); Mem. Bd., Calgary Foothills

Prov. General Hosp.; Dir. and Hon. Treasurer, Calgary Exhibition and Stampede Ltd; mem. Insts. C.A.'s Man. (Fellow mem. 1977) & Alta.; Clubs: Glencoe; Earl Grey Golf; Ranchman's; Calgary Petroleum; recreations: golf, swimming; Home: 6925 Lefroy Court S.W., Calgary, Alta. T3E 6H1; Office: Suite 770, 620-12th Ave. S.W., Calgary, Alta. T2R 1J3

PHILLIPS, Roy A., B.A.Sc.; association executive; b. Vancouver, B.C., 18 May 1918; s. Arthur and Jane Patricia (Little) P; e. Univ. of B.C., B.A.Sc. 1939; m. Barbara Lee, d. Cecil Everett Avis, 24 May 1941; children: Robert N., Gordon A., Catherine L., Nancy L.; PRES. AND EXTVE. DIR., CANDN. MANUFACTURERS' ASSN. since 1975; Engr., Switchgear Dept., Canadian General Electric Co., Peterborough, 1939-49; Chief Engr., Montreal Works, 1949-52; Mgr. Product Planning, Maj. Appliance Dept., 1952-57; Mgr. Marketing, Appliance Div., 1957-64; Pres., Taylor Pearson Carson Ltd. and Taylor Pearson Carson (BC) Ltd., 1964-66; Dir., Prairie Pacific Distributors Ltd., 1964 and Vice-Pres. and Dir., 1965-66; Pres., Prairie Pacific Distributors Western Ltd., Edmonton, 1965-66; Pres., Motor Car Supply Co. of Canada Ltd., Calgary, 1965-66; Vice-Pres., RCA Ltd. 1967-75; Dir. 1968-75; mem. Extve. Comte. of Bd. of Dirs. 1969-75; Corp. Planning 1967; Gen. Mgr. Consumer Electronics & Appliance Div. 1968-74; Consumer Relations 1975; served with 4th Field Batty. (Reserve) and 4th H.A.A. Batty. (Reserve) during 2nd World War; rank Maj.; Pres., Electronics Industs. Assn. Can. 1968-69, Chrmn. 1969-70; mem. Candn. Bus. and Indust. Internat. Adv. Comte.; Chrmn., Adv. Comte. on Inmate Employment Candn. Correction Service; mem. Assn. Comte., St. John Ambulance Brigade; mem. Adv. Comte., Candn. Commercial Corp.; mem., Engn. Inst. Can. (Vice-Pres. 1963-64; mem. Council 1960-64); Corp. Engrs. Que. (Vice-Pres. 1956; mem. Council 1952-56); United Church; Clubs: Edmonton; Forest & Stream; National; Rotary Club of Toronto; Home: 2149 Parker Dr., Mississauga, Ont. L5B 1W3; Office: One Yonge St., Toronto, Ont. M5E 1E5

PHILLIPS,Theodore Denton, B.B.A., M.A.; librarian; b. Kansas City, Mo. 13 June 1929; s. Theodore Denton and Helen Jean (Wofford) P.; e. Univ. of New Mexico B.B.A. 1956; Univ. of Denver M.A. 1957; m. Elinore Stanley Brown 13 Jan. 1973; two d. Julia Carol, Lisa Marie; UNIV. LIBRARIAN, MT. ALLISON UNIV. 1980- ; Lib. Asst., Peabody Inst. Lib. Baltimore 1944-45; Joslyn Mem. Art Lib. Omaha 1947-48; Univ. of New Mexico, Albuquerque 1953-56; Univ. of Denver 1956-57; Librarian, Fed. Reserve Bank of Kansas City 1957-63; Asst. Librarian, ASD Div. IBM Corp. Los Gatos, Cal. 1963-65, Lib. Mgr. SDD Div. San Jose, Cal. 1966; Asst. Chief Librarian, Queen's Univ. Kingston 1967-69, Assoc. Librarian 1969-74; Univ. Librarian, Memorial Univ. of Nfld., 1974-80; John Cotton Dana Lectr., Univ. of B.C., 1968; Pres., Kingston (Ont.) Choral Soc. 1972-74; Bd. of Dir., Nfld. Symphony Orchestra 1978-80; contrib. to prof. journs.; served with U.S. Navy 1948-52; mem. Candn. Lib. Assn.; Atlantic Provinces Lib. Assn.; Anglican; recreations: photography, walking, singing; Home: The Different Drummer, Sackville, N.B. E0A 3C0; Office: Sackville, N.B. E0A 3C0

PHILLIPS, Timothy Adair; artist; b. Toronto, Ont., 12 March 1929; s. William Eric and Doris Delano (Smith) P.; e. Upper Can. Coll., Toronto, Ont. (Sr. Matric. 1945), pre-med. course, Univ. Academy Simi, Italy and Academy Julien, Paris; also studied with Pietro Annigoni in Italy and Salvador Dali in Spain; m. Helen Gertrude, d. Clarence Lockwood, 11 June 1966; children: Melissa, Melinda; awarded prize, O'Keefe's Young Can. Competition, Art, 1950; one-man show, Upper Grosvenor Gallery, London, Eng., 1963 and then at Galerie Ror Volmar, Paris, 1964; Hon. Mention in the Paris Salon, 1963 and 67; one-man shows at Collectors' Gallery, London, Eng., 1964; Harrovian Gallery, London, Eng., 1974; Flair Gallery, Palm Beach, Fla., 1973, 1977; Ontario Place, Toron-

to, Ont.; R. M. Gallery, Toronto, 1972, 1973, 1974, 1975, 1976; KAR Gallery, 1978; Dir., Ont. Inst. of Painters; Conservative; New Apostolic; recreation: swimming; Club: Granite; Studio: 174 Teddington Pk., Toronto, Ont. M4N 2C8; Home: 476 Richmond St. W., Toronto, Ont. M5V 1Y2

PHILLIPS, William Gregory, M.A., Ph.D.; university professor; b. Brantford, Ont., 3 Dec. 1921; s. Wilfred Joseph and Josephine (Kew) P.; e. Brantford (Ont.) Coll. Inst. 1935-40; Univ. of Toronto B.A. 1944, M.A. 194 7, Ph.D. 1953; m. Helen Margaret, d. John Patrick Ryan, 26 Aug. 1950; children: Douglas, Gerard, Mary-Josephine, John; DEAN OF SOC. SCIENCE, UNIV. OF WINDSOR, since 1975; joined faculty as Asst. Prof. 1950; Assoc. Prof. 1952; Prof. 1954; Head, Dept. of Econ. 1953-70; Assoc. Dean, Arts and Sciences 1964; Dean of Arts and Science 1970-74; Pres., Greater Windsor Foundation 1964-66; Personal Econ. Adv. to Pres. K. D. Kaunda of Zambia full-time 1966-67 and part-time since 1968; mem. Ont. Comte. on Costs of Educ. 1971-76; author of "The Agricultural Implement Industry in Canada" 1956, (Japanese Lang. Ed. 1961); "Canadian Combines Policy: The Matter of Mergers" 1964; "Government Conciliation in Labour Disputes" 1956; mem., Candn. Economic Assn.; Am. Econ. Assn.; Home: 1186 Grand Marais Rd. W., Windsor, Ont. N9E 1C7

PHILLIS, John Whitfield, D.V.Sc., Ph.D., D.Sc.; educator; b. Trinidad, W.I. 1 Apl. 1936; s. Ernest and Sarah Ann (Glover) P.; e. Kings Sch. Canterbury, Eng. 1951; Canberra High Sch. Australia 1952; Univ. of Sydney B.V.Sc. 1957, D.V.Sc. 1976; Australian Nat. Univ. Ph.D. 1961; Monash Univ. Melbourne D.Sc. 1970; m. Shane Beverly d. Frederick Wright, Bedford, Eng. 24 Jan. 1969; PROF. AND CHMN. OF PHYSIOL. WAYNE STATE UNIV. since 1981; Lectr. and Sr. Lectr. Monash Univ. 1963-69; Visiting Prof. Ind. Univ. 1969; Assoc. Prof. and Prof. Univ. of Man. 1970-73, Assoc. Dean of Med. Univ. of Man. 1971-73; Prof. and Head of Physiology, Univ. of Sask., 1973-81; Asst. Dean Univ. of Sask. (Med.) 1973-75; author 'The Pharmacology of Synapses' 1970; Ed. 'Veterinary Physiology' 1976; Ed. 'Progress in Neurobiology'; mem. Ed. Bd. 'General Pharmacology'; 'Pain'; mem. Med. Research Council Scholarship Comte. 1973-74, Neurological Science Comte. 1974-79; served with Australian Nat. Service and Citizens Mil. Forces, rank Lt. 1955; mem. Candn. Physiol. Soc. (Pres. 1978-79); Brit. Physiol. & Pharmacol. Socs.; Soc. for Neuroscience; Internat. Brain Research Organ.; Am. Physiol. Soc.; Anglican; recreations: squash, cycling, fishing, reading, riding; Office: Wayne State Univ., School of Medicine, Detroit, Michigan

PHILPOTT, David G.; real estate executive; b. White Plains, N.Y., 10 Aug. 1927; s. Wilbur Morgan and Ruth (Goodwin) P.; came to Canada, 1931; e. Public Schs. and Jarvis Coll. Inst., Toronto, Ont.; Univ. of Toronto Sch. of Arch. (1945-47); m. Wanda Audrey, d. Ross W. Hutchings, Ottawa, Ont., 20 May, 1950; children: Stephen Ross, Wendy Ruth; EXEC. VICE-PRES., THE CADILLAC FAIRVIEW CORP. LTD. since 1981; after four yrs. as Draftsman with Molesworth, Secord & Savage, Architects, Toronto, Ont., spent one yr. as Gen. Supt. of T. J. Colborne Construction Ltd. of Toronto; joined Principal Investments Ltd. in 1952 and was in charge of Shopping Centre constr. in Ont. and W. Can.; apptd. to assume a similar role with Webb & Knapp (Canada) Ltd. in 1959; Pres.; Triton Centres Ltd.; Scarborough Shopping Centre Ltd.; Granite Holdings of Canada Ltd.; Vice Pres. and Dir., Trizec Corp. 1963-73; Pres., D.G. Philpott & Assoc. Ltd., 1973-81; Dir., Seel Mortgage Investment Corp.; Dir., "Odyssey Magazine Pub. Corp."; Presbyterian; recreations: sailing, cycling, skiing; Clubs: R.C.Y.C.; Caledon Ski; Home: 1470 Pinetree Crescent, Mississauga, Ont. L5G 2S8; Office: 1200 Sheppard Ave. E., Toronto, Ontario M2K 2R8

PHINNEY, R. Wendell; merchant; b. Kentville, N.S., 16 Feb. 1926; s. Lewis Wendell and Lillian May (Andrews) P.; e. Kings Co. Acad., 1943; Mount Allison Univ., Business Adm. Dipl. 1944; m. Georgie Emelyn, d. W. L. Palmeter, Kentville, N.S., 26 June 1947; children: Bruce Wendell, Joan Meredith; PRESIDENT R. W. PHINNEY HOLDINGS LTD.; Mayor, Town of Kentville, 1974-79; first Vice-Pres. Union of N.S. Mun's, 1978-79; Dir., Central and Eastern Trust Co.; Fed. of Candn. Mun.; served with RCNVR 1944-45; Past Prov. Comm. & Nat. Growth Coordinator, Nat. Council Boy Scouts of Can.; mem., Royal Candn. Legion Candn. Power Sqdn.; Retail Merchants Assn. (Past Pres.); Kentville Bd. Trade (Past Pres.); Maritime Provs. Bd. Trade (Past Dir.); Musical Dir. S.P.E.B.S.Q.S.A.; Dir. B.F.M. Hosp. Bd.; P. Conservative; United Church; Clubs: Lions (Past Pres.); Glooscap Curling (Past Pres.); Home: 98 Park St., Kentville, N.S. B4N 1M4; Office: 64 Webster, Kentville, N.S. B4N 1H7

PHIPPS, Norman Ernest, Q.C.; b. Revelstoke, B.C., 22 Feb. 1907; s. Albert Edmund and Sydney Florence (Boultbee) P.; e. Trinity Coll. Sch., Port Hope, Ont.; Trinity Coll., Univ. of Toronto, B.A. 1929; Osgoode Hall, Toronto, Ont.; m. Dorothy Lillian, d. Arthur Kendal-Quarry, 15 Aug. 1944; children: David, Penelope Ann; Dir., Gerling Global Gen. Ins. Co.; Gerling Global Reins. Co.; Gerling Global Life Insurance Co.; Pres., Hostmann-Steinberg (Can.) Ltd.; Secy. & Dir., Acrow-Richmond Ltd. and Acrow (Canada) Ltd.; Dir., Internat. Harvester Credit Corp. of Can. Ltd.; read law with Bain, Bicknell, White & Bristol; called to the Bar of Ont., 1932; cr. K.C. 1951; served in 2nd World War (Overseas) with Royal Candn. Arty., 1941-45; Gov., Trinity Coll. Sch., Port Hope, Ont.; Delta Kappa Epsilon; Conservative; Anglican; Clubs: Toronto Hunt; Home: Apt. 401, 717 Eglinton Ave. West, Toronto, Ontario M5N 1C9; Office: 330 University Ave., Toronto, Ont. M5G 1S1

PICARD, Laurent A., C.C. (1976), B.A., B.A.Sc., Ph.D., D.B.A.; b. Quebec City, Quebec, 27 Oct. 1927; s. Adel Edouard and Alice (Gingras) P.; e. Laval Univ., B.A. and B.Phil. 1947, B.A.Sc. (Physics) 1954; Harvard Univ., D.B.A. 1964; m. Thérèse Germain, Oct. 1954; 5 sons; DEAN, FACULTY OF MANAGEMENT STUD., McGILL UNIV., 1980- ; Prof., Faculty of Comm., Laval Univ., 1955-59; Research Assoc. and Asst., Harvard Business Sch., 1960-62; Prof. and Assoc. Dir., l'Ecole des Hautes Etudes Commerciales, Univ. of Montreal, 1962-68; Extve. Vice-Pres. C.B.C. 1968-72, Pres. & C.E.O., 1972-75; joined Marine Industries Ltd. in sr. extve. capacity 1975; Dean, Faculty of Management McGill Univ., 1978; first Pres. of Commonwealth Broadcasting Assn.; mem. Comte. for Higher Educ., Superior Council of Educ. Que.; Past Pres., Research Comn. on Shoe Industry of Prov. of Que.; former Commr., Indust. Inquiry Comn. on St. Lawrence Ports; has provided research and consultative services for several industs. incl. aluminum, printing, electronics, chem., rlwy., paper and wood products; mem. Bd. Dirs., Petrofina Can., Atomic Energy of Can.; Sidbec; Sidbec Dosco; Menasco (Can.); Via Rail; mem. Royal Commission on Concentration in the Newspaper Industry; Club: Mount Bruno Golf Club; Home: 591 St. Catherine Rd., Outremont, Que. H3A 1S5; Office: Faculty of Management, McGill University, 1001 Sherbrooke St. W., Montreal, Que. H3A 1G5

PICHE, André, M.S.C., B.Com.; company executive; b. Pont Rouge, Que., 1916; e. Sch. of Comm., Laval Univ., M.S.C., B.Com.; m. Claire Gignac; children: Jean, Yves, Louis, Denise; DIR., PRESIDENT, REYNOLDS ALUMINUM CO. OF CANADA LTD., since 1977; Pres., Reycan Research Ltd.; Reynolds Cable Co. Ltd.; Wabasso Limited; Reynolds Extrusion Co. Ltd.; Eskimo Pie Corporation of Canada Limited; Paragon Business Forms Ltd. started career with a firm of Chartered Accountants in Quebec City; later apptd. Chief Acct. of Que. Shipyards Ltd.;

joined present Co. as Treas. and Comptroller, 1945; el. a Dir., 1946 and Managing Dir., 1949; Executive Vice-President and Managing Dir., 1950-77; Pres., Fondation du C.E.U. de Trois Rivières; mem., Bd.Gov., Conseil du Patronat; Bus. Council on National Issues; Internat., Cdn., Que., Chamber of Comm.; past mem., Can. Council of Conference Bd. in Can.; mem., Can. Trade Mission to U.K. 1957; Clubs: Mount Royal; Ki-8-EB Golf; St. Maurice Fish & Game; Mount Bruno Country; Home: 240 Berlinguet Terrace, Trois-Rivières, Que. G8Z 1A6; Office: 290 St. Laurent Blvd., Cap-de-la Madeleine, Que. G8T 7W9

PICHE, Lucien, B.Sc., Ph.D., F.C.I.C. (1955); educateur; né Montréal, Que. 22 juillet 1915; f. Jean B. et Marie (Lagadec) P.; é. Univ. Montréal B.Sc. 1935, Ph.D. 1940; Mass. Inst. Tech. stage postdoctoral 1945-46; ép. Andrée L. Lespérance, 12 juin 1945; enfants: Nicole A. et Robert L.; PROFESSEUR TITULAIRE AU DEPARTEMENT DE CHIMIE, UNIVERSITE DE MONTREAL (Chimie de l'environnement) depuis 1969; chargé cours Faculté des Sciences, Univ. Montréal 1938-43; prof. chimie, Collège Jean de Brébeuf, 1940-42; Vice-prés. et Dir., Pharmed Cie Ltée. 1947-51; Prof. de chimie organique et dir. du Dépt. 1951-59; Vice-doyen et dir. des études, Faculté des sciences 1959-61; Vice-recteur, 1961-71; Dir. Presses de l'Univ. de Montréal 1963-67, président du conseil Adm. 1966-71; membre Conseil National des Recherches 1966-72; Président du Conseil d'adm. de l'Institut de chimie du Canada 1957-58; Prés. de l'Acfas 1961-62; Vice-prés. exécutif, Comité France-Amérique de Montréal 1964-67; Vice Président, Conseil consultatif de l'environnement, Que. 1973-78; Prés., Comté. assoc. pour les critères de qualité de l'environnement, Conseil nat. de recherches, 1973; Médaille du Can. (Centenaire) 1967; Officier de l'Ordre nat. de la Valeur du Cameroun, 1968; auteur d'un Manuel d'enseignement "Chimie organique: Travaux de laboratoire", 1956, ainsi que de nombreux articles depuis 1939 portant spécialement sur la chimie organique; Prix David (sec. sciences) 1942; Médaille Montréal de l'Inst. chimie du Can., 1980; Catholique; récréation: photographie; Résidence: 520 Habitat '67, Montréal, Qué. H3C 3R6

PICHE, Marcel, O.C. (1969), Q.C., B.A., LL.L.; b. Les Eboulements, Co. of Charlevoix, Que., 16 Feb. 1914; s. Odilon and Antonia (Cousineau) P.; e. St. Louis de Gonzaque, Que.; Semy. of Que.; Univ. of Ottawa, B.A. 1935; Laval Univ., LL.L. 1938; Superior Sch. of Comm., Quebec, Que. (Accounting); m. Béatrice, d. Arthur Foster, Quebec, Que., 28 Sept. 1940; one d. Hélène; SR. PARTNER, BLAIN, PICHE, EMERY & ASSOCIÉS; Chrmn. Corby Distilleries Ltd.; Hon. Pres. Régie de la Place des Arts; Chrmn., Institut de Recherches Cliniques de Montréal; Pres., Havre Champlain Inc.; Vice-Pres. and Dir., Trust Général Du Canada; Secy., Precision Instruments Inc.; Reynolds Aluminum Co. of Canada Ltd.; Dir., Dieter Hugo Stinnes, Inc.; Transocean Machine Co. Inc.; La Presse; ITT Industries of Can.; Chancellor and mem. Extve. Comte., Univ. of Montreal1967-77, hon. member since 1978; Clerk-in-Law, Chauveau, Rivard & Blais, Quebec, Que., 1935; Jr. Partner 1938; called to the Bar of Que. 1938; cr. K.C. 1949; Enforcement Counsel, W.P.T.B., Que., 1941-44; practised law in firm of Piché & Flynn, Montreal, Que., 1944; Dir., Jr. Bar Assn., Quebec, 1943-44; Prof., Practical Works in Comm. Law, Univ. of Montreal; winner of Médaille de Vermeille of French Govt., 1935; Gold Medal for Pub. Debating, Univ. of Ottawa 1935; Pres., Theatre Comn. of Student Assn., Laval Univ., 1937; mem., Que. Bar Assn.; Roman Catholic; recreations: reading, golf; Clubs: Mt. Stephen; Mt. Bruno Country; St. Denis; Home: 8 Springrove Crescent, Outremont, Que. H2V 3H9; Office: 1010 Sherbrooke St. W., 25th Fl., Montreal, Que. H3A 1S6

PICK, Alfred J., B.C.L., M.A.; retired diplomat; b. Montreal, Que., 28 April 1915; s. Francis Joseph Thomas and Maud (Taylor) P.; e. Westmount (Que.) High. Sch.;

McGill Univ., B.A. 1936, M.A. 1937, B.C. L. 1940; Ecole Libre Des Sciences Politiques, Paris 1936-37; m. Patricia, d. Albert Ross, Sydney, Aust. 25 Jan. 1946; children: Paula, Lawrence, Frances; former ambassador to Organization of Am. States; joined Dept. of External Affairs, 1940; served in Nfld., Australia, S. Africa, India, Italy; Ambassador to Peru, 1958-62; Tunisia and Libya 1966-69; The Netherlands 1969-72; Head of Latin Am. Div., Ottawa, 1962-66; read law with Chauvin, Walker; called to Bar of Que. 1940; United Church; recreations: tennis, canoeing, skiing; Home: 11 Ellesmere Pl., Rockcliffe Park, Ottawa, Ont. K1M 0P1

PICKARD, Franklin George Thomas, B.A., P.Eng.; mining executive; b. Sudbury, Ont. 10 Sept. 1933; s. Chester William P.; e. Queen's Univ. B.A. 1957; m. Audrey Elaine Bull 29 Apl. 1967; two d. Barbara Elaine, Beverly Joan; DIR. METALL. & ENGN., FALCONBRIDGE NICKEL MINES LTD. 1980- ; Vice Pres. and Dir. Lakefield Research of Canada Ltd.; Dir. Kiena Gold Mines Ltd.; joined present Co. 1957, Strathcona Project Metall. Engr. 1964, Strathcona Mill Supt. 1967, Sr. Asst. Smelter Supt. 1974, Chief Metall. Engr. 1975-80; mem. Assn. Prof. Engrs. Prov. Ont.; Am. Inst. Mining & Metall. Engrs.; P. Conservative; United Church; recreation: golf; Club: Engineers'; Home: 135 Grandview Ave., Thornhill, Ont. L3T 1H7; Office: (P.O. Box 40) Commerce Court W., Toronto, Ont. M5L 1B4.

PICKARD, George Lawson, M.B.E., M.A., D.Phil., F.R.S.C.; educator; b. Cardiff, Wales 5 July 1913; s. Harry Lawson and Phoebe (Crosier) P.; e. Manchester Grammar Sch. Eng. 1932; Hertford Coll. Oxford Univ. B.A. 1935, M.A. 1947, Clarendon Lab. D.Phil. 1937; m. Lilian May d. late Ernest Perry 26 Apl. 1938; 2 children; DIR. INST. OF OCEANOGRAPHY, UNIV. OF B.C. 1958-79; Prof. of Physics since 1954; Emeritus Professor since 1979; Scient. Offr. Royal Aircraft Estab. 1937-42; Scient. Offr. Operational Research Sec. Coastal Command R.A.F. 1942-47, Sr. Scient. Offr. 1944, Princ. Scient. Offr. 1947; Assoc. Prof. of Physics Univ. of B.C. 1947-54; mem. Nat. Research Council Comte. Geodesy & Geophys. 1955-67; Bd. Mang. B.C. Research Council 1960-67; Fisheries Research Bd. of Can. 1963-72; Vice Chrmn. Internat. Coord. Group for Tsunami Warning System for Pacific 1968-75; Visiting Scient. Sec. d'Océanographie, Orstom, Nouméa 1967, 1970, 1975-76; Australian Inst. Marine Science 1976; served on numerous curriculum comtes. for schs. and univs.; served with R.A.F.V.R. 1944-47, Hon. Sqdn. Leader; rec'd Queen's Centennial Medal 1967; Queen's Silver Jubilee Medal 1977; author "Descriptive Physical Oceanography" 1964, 2nd ed. 1974, 3rd ed. 1979; co-author "Introductory Dynamic Oceanography" 1978; numerous papers oceanography of fjord estuaries, equatorial oceanography; Fellow, Am. Assn. Advanc. Science; mem. Am. Geophys. Union; Am. Soc. Limnology & Oceanography (Vice Pres. 1962-63); B.C. Acad. Science (Pres. 1956); Candn. Oceanographic & Meteorol. Soc.; recreations: flying, scuba diving; Home: 4546 W. Fifth Ave., Vancouver, B.C. V6R 1S7;

PICKERING, Brig.-Gen. Alan, C.M.M., C.D., B.Sc.; Canadian forces; b. Wimbledon, Eng. 18 July 1929; s. late Robert Lawrence and Ethel (Hodgson) P.; came to Can. 1930; e. Sarnia (Ont.) Inst. & Tech. Sch. 1948; Royal Mil. Coll. Kingston 1953; Queen's Univ. B.Sc. (Mech. Engn.) 1954; R.C.A.F. Staff Coll. 1965-66; U.S. Navy War Coll. 1973-74; m. Margaret Anne d. late Thurlow Ward and Helen (Gill) Campaigne 12 Sept. 1953; children: Brian Charles, Catharine Anne, Lynda Gail, Ellen Christine; COMMDR., MARITIME AIR GROUP 1979- ; Air Cadet Sarnia (Optimist) Sqdn. 1943-48; R.C.A.F. (Supplementary Reserve) 1949-52. (Regular) 1952-68, Candn. Forces since 1968; Pilot, 435 (Transport) Sqdn. Edmonton 1954-56, 115 Air Transport Unit, UN Emergency Force, Naples 1956-57; Instr., 4 (Transport) Operational Training Unit, Trenton 1957-61, 437 (Transport) Sqdn. 1961-62; Chief,

Engn. Div., Gemini Target Vehicle, U.S. Air Force Space Systems Div. Los Angeles 1962-65; Dir. of Cadets & Mil. Training, Royal Mil. Coll. Kingston 1966-69; C.O., 404 Maritime Patrol Sqdn. Greenwood, N.S. 1969-72, Base Operations Offr. 1972-73, Base Commdr. 1974-76; Commdr., Aurora Program Detachment, Burbank, Cal. 1976-79; mem. Engn. Inst. Can.; R.C.A.F. Assn.; Royal United Services Inst.; United Church; recreations: golf, sailing, curling; Home: 830 Young Ave., Halifax, N.S. B3H 2V7; Office: Halifax, N.S. B3K 2X0.

PICKERING, Edward Abram, business consultant; b. Windsor, Ont., 20 June 1907; s. Abram James and Oliva (Charbonneau) P.; e. Windsor (Ont.) Coll. Inst.; McMaster Univ. B.A. 1928; m. Miriam Margaret Drew, 20 Oct. 1938; children: Janet Elizabeth Formanek, Alan Drew; Asst. Private Secy. to Prime Min. Mackenzie King 1929-38; Asst. to Gen. Mgr. C.B.C. 1938; joined the Simpsons organ. as Circulation Mgr. Mail Order Div., Toronto 1939; Gen. Mgr. Robert Simpson Western Ltd. Regina 1941; Gen. Supt. Employee & Public Relations, Robert Simpson Co. Ltd. Toronto 1950-52; Gen. Personnel Mgr. Simpsons-Sears 1953, Vice-Pres. Personnel 1958, Vice-Pres. Catalogue Order 1966-72; Chrmn. Council of Profit Sharing Industries 1958-66; Pres. Toronto Symphony 1964-67; Project Dir. Special Study Ont. Med. Assn. 1972-73; Chrmn. Ont. Health Disciplines Bd. since 1974; Pres. Massey Hall since 1972; Clubs: Toronto; York; Rosedale Golf; Home: 80 Highland Cres., Willowdale, Ont. M2L 1G9; Office: Suite 822, 40 University Ave. Toronto, Ont. M5J 1T1

PICKERSGILL, Hon. John W., P.C. (1953), C.C. (1970), M.A., M.Litt., LL.D., D.C.L.; b. Wyecombe, Ont., 23 June 1905; s. Frank Allan and Sara C. (Smith) P.; e. University of Manitoba, B.A. 1926 and M.A. 1927; Oxford University, 1927-29 (History); post-graduate studies at Oxford and Paris, summers, 1930-33, 1935 and 1937; m. Beatrice Landon (died 17 Jan. 1938), d. Dr. F. A. Young, Winnipeg, Man., 3 July 1936; 2ndly, M. Margaret, d. J. T. Beattie, Winnipeg, Man., 23 June 1939; children: Jane, Peter, Alan, Ruth; Lecturer in Hist., Wesley College, University of Manitoba, 1929-37; joined Dept. of External Affairs as Third Secy., 1937; served in various capacities in the Prime Minister's office, 1937 till appt. as Clerk of the Party Council and Secy. to the Cabinet, June 1952-June 1953; sworn of the P.C. and appt. Secy. of State, June 1953; mem. H. of C. for Bonavista-Twillingate, 1953-67; Min. of Citzenship & Immigration, 1954-57; Secy. of State, Apl. 1963-Feb. 1964; Min. of Transport, Feb. 1964-Sept. 1967 when resigned as M.P.; Pres., Canadian Transport Comn. 1967 till retired 1972; author "The Mackenzie King Record, 1939-44", Vol. I, 1960; Vols. II, III, and IV with D. F. Forster, 1968-70; "The Liberal Party of Canada", 1962; "Le Parti Liberal", 1963; "My Years With Louis St. Laurent", 1975; "Louis St. Laurent", 1981; United Church; Home: 550 Maple Lane E., Rockcliffe Park, Ottawa, Ont. K1M 0N6

PICKETT, William Stephen; industrialist; b. Toledo; Ohio, 1 Apl. 1920; s. Clarence C. and Myra (McMaken) P.; e. Univ. of Toledo, grad. 1942 (named "Outstanding Alumnus" 1966); Univ. of Texas, grad. 1943; m. Marian, d. Willard Cannan, Toledo, Ohio, 14 Aug. 1948; children: Stephen, Michael, Anna Leigh; PRESIDENT AND GEN. MGR., AMERICAN MOTORS (CANADA) LTD., since 1971; Pres. and Gen. Mgr., Jeep of Canada; Mang. Dir., American Motors Overseas Corp., N.V.; Vice Pres., American Motors Pan-American; Extve. Vice Pres., American Motors International; Dir. and Vice Pres., Development Credit Corp. (Northern Ltd.); joined Willys-Overland Motors, Inc. as Asst. to Pres. 1946; served as Dir. of Marketing, Dir., Defense Products, Vice Pres.-Export Sales (1955); joined American Motors as Director of Automotive Export, 1960; Vice Pres., Automotive Internat., 1966; Vice Pres. of Sales, U.S. sales operations, 1967; Vice Pres., Dealer & Distributor Relations, 1970;

part-time lectr., Univ. of Texas, 1946-53; served with USAF 1941-46; Dir., Traffic Injury Research Foundation Can.; mem. Highway Users Fed.; mem., Motor Vehicle Mfrs.' Assn. (Dir.); Candn. Mfrs.' Assn. (Extve. Council); Soc. Automotive Engrs.; Am. Econ. Soc.; Phi Kappa Psi; Tau Beta Pi; Episcopalian; recreation: golf; Clubs: Canadian; Hundred (Detroit); Brampton Golf; Forest Lake Country; Home: Applewood Landmark, 1300 Bloor St., Ste. 307, Mississauga, Ont. L4Y 3Z2; Office: Kennedy Rd. S., Brampton, Ont.

PICOT, Jules Jean Charles, B.E., M.Sc., Ph.D.; educator; b. Edmundston, N.B. 23 July 1932; s. Joseph Ernest and late Marie Blanche (Lebel) P.; e. St. Francis Xavier Univ. Eng. Cert. 1953; Tech. Univ. of N.S., B.E. 1955; Mass. Inst. of Technol. M.Sc. 1957; Ecole Nationale Supér. de Mecanique et d'Aérotechnique, Poitiers, France 1958-59; Univ. of Minn. Ph.D. (Chem. Engn.) 1966; m. Mary Carol d. late John Adams Creaghan 25 Aug. 1956; children: Mary Nicole, Joseph Andre; PROF. OF CHEM. ENGN. UNIV. OF N.B., Chrmn. of Chem. Engn. 1969-76; mem. Natural Sciences & Engn. Research Council Grants Comtes. (Chrmn., Chem. & Metall. Engn. Comte. 1974, 1967 Science Scholarship Comte. 1979); various Candn. Council Prof. Engrs. Accreditation Comtes.; various articles transport phenomena in polymers, technol. of aerial spraying insecticides; Fellow, Candn. Soc. Chem. Engn. (Past Dir.); mem. Assn. Prof. Engrs. N.B.; Am. Inst. Chem. Engn.; R. Catholic; recreations: cross-country skiing, golf; Home: 29 Simcoe Ct., Fredericton, N.B. E3B 2W9; Office: Fredericton, N.B. E3B 5A3.

PIDGEON, Lloyd Montgomery, M.B.E., B.Sc., Ph.D., F.R.S.C., LL.B., D.Sc.; b. Markham, Ont. 3 Dec. 1903; s. Edward Leslie and Edith (Gilker) P.; e. Univ. of Man., B.A. 1925 (Gold Medal); McGill Univ. B.Sc. (winner of Nat. Research Council Bursary 1926; Studentship 1927; Sir Wm. Ramsay Mem. Schol. 1929), Ph.D. 1929; Oxford Univ., B.Sc. 1932; Univ. of Toronto, LL.B. (Hon.) 1973; McGill Univ., D.Sc. (Hon.) 1972; m. Frances, d. W. Rundle, Winnipeg, 8 Sept. 1928; children: Ruth, Leslie; former Professor and Head, Dept. of Metallurgical, Engn., Univ. of Toronto; Dir. and Tech. Adv., Dom. Magnesium Co. Ltd.; awarded Platinum Medal (Candn. Inst. of Mining & Metall.); Medal (Prof. Assn. of Civil Service); mem., Candn. Inst. of Mining & Metall.; Inst. of Prof. Engrs. of Ont.; has contrib. numerous scient. papers on carbon black, magnesium production, titanium, etc. to scient. journs.; Delta Upsilon; United Church; recreation: music; Home: R.R. No. 1, Shanty Bay, Ont. L0L 2L0

PIELOU, Evelyn C., B.Sc., Ph.D., D.Sc.; research professor; b. Bognor Regis, Eng. 20 Feb. 1924; came to Can. 1947; d. J.B. Hancock and Dorothy Holmes; e. Royal Naval Sch., Twickenham, Eng.; Univ. of London B.Sc. 1951, Ph.D. 1962, D.Sc. 1975; m. D.P. Pielou 22 June 1944; children: Ruth (Shapka), Richard, Frank; OIL SANDS ENVIRONMENTAL RESEARCH PROF., UNIV. OF LETHBRIDGE since 1981; Research Scientist Candn. Dept. of Forestry, 1963-64; Research Scientist Candn. Dept. Agric., 1964-67; Visiting Prof., North Carolina State Univ., 1967; Visiting Prof. Yale Univ., 1968; Prof. of Biology, Queen's Univ., Kingston, 1968-71; Killam Research Prof., Dalhousie Univ., Halifax, 1971-74; Visiting Prof. Univ. of Sydney, Australia, 1974; Prof. of Biology, Dalhousie Univ., 1974-81; author of "Introduction to Mathematical Ecology", 1969; "Population and Community Ecology", 1974; "Ecological Diversity", 1975; "Mathematical Ecology", 1977; "Biogeography", 1979; other writings incl. over sixty research papers, review articles, book reviews, encyclopedia articles on mathematical ecology and evolutionary biogeography; Fellow of the Royal Soc. of Arts; mem., Biometric Society; Ecological Soc. of Am.; recreations: tennis, hiking, canoeing, sailing, skiing, natural hist.; gardening; Home: 33 Dalhousie Court, Lethbridge, Alta. T1K 4C8; Office: Lethbridge, Alta. T1K 3M4.

PIEPENBURG, Willard Warren, M.S., Ph.D.; educator; b. Reedsville, Wis., 6 Oct. 1922; s. Reynold A. and Esther (Otto) P.; e. Univ. of Wis., B.S. 1947, M.S. 1948; King's Coll., Cambridge Univ., Ph.D. (Hist.) 1951; PROF. OF HISTORY, YORK UNIV. since 1964; mem. Dept. of Hist., Univ. of Toronto, 1952-64; Assoc. Dean, Faculty of Arts at present Univ. 1964-71; Dir. Grad Programme in History 1971-80; Nuffield Fellow, U.K., 1961-62; Fullbright Fellow, Cambridge Univ., 1949-51; author, "Twin Heritages", 1967; also various articles and reviews in prof. journs.; mem. Am. Hist. Assn.; Candn. Hist. Assn.; Eng. Hist. Assn.; Liberal; Anglican; recreations: reading, travel; Home: 90 Heath St. W., Toronto, Ont. M4V 1T4; Office: 4700 Keele St., Downsview, Ont. M3J 1P3

PIERCE, John Edward, B.Com.; banker; b. Sarnia, Ont., 12 July 1943; s. Edward Orville and Louise Irene (Robertson) P.; e. Univ. of Brit. Columbia, B.Com. 1967; M. Dianne, d. late Thomas McClendon, 29 May 1976; children: Carol Elizabeth, Gary Michael, Kimberley Anne; SR. VICE-PRESIDENT, THE MERCANTILE BANK OF CANADA since 1974; joined Bank H.O. Montreal 1967; Official Asst. Vancouver Br. 1968, Asst. Acct. 1969, Asst. Mgr. 1970; Supv. H.O. Montreal, 1971, Mgr. Montreal Br. 1974, Vice-Pres. 1974, Sr. Vice-Pres. E. Div. 1974; Sr. Vice Pres. Central Div. 1976; Sr. Vice Pres. Western Div. 1980; recreations: tennis, squash; Home: 1136 West 7th Ave., Vancouver, B.C.; Office: 1177 West Hastings St., Vancouver, B.C.

PIERCEY, George Charles, C.M.M., E.D., C.D., Q.C.; b. Halifax, Nova Scotia, 22 February 1919; s. William Drysdale and Annie Margaret (Forbes) P.; e. Dalhousie Univ., B.Com. 1938, B.A. 1939, LL.B. 1941; m. Geraldine May, d. Walter K. Peart, 11 May 1946; children: William, Catherine, Randall, Charles; Chrmn. of the Bd., Nova Scotia Savings & Loan Co.; Pres. & Mang. Dir., Piercey Investors Ltd.; Dir., Maritime Telegraph & Telephone Co. Ltd.; called to Bar of N.S. 1941; cr. Q.C. 1967; served with RCA and Candn. Intelligence Corps in U.K., Italy and N.W. Europe, 1941-46; rank Capt.; served with Candn. Army Mil. 1948-72; Commdr., Mil. Area Atlantic 1970-72; rank Brig.-Gen.; Hon. A.D.C. to Gov. Gen. Can. 1965-73; Hon. Colonel 33 (Halifax) Service Bn. 1974- ; Past Pres., Halifax Jr. Chamber Comm.; John Howard Soc. of N.S.; N.S. Army Cadet League; Mem. N.S. Adv. Council on Heritage Property; Dir., World Vision of Canada; Halifax Protestant Youth Foundation; The Army Museum, Halifax Citadel; mem., N.S. Barristers Soc.; Candn. Bar Assn.; N. Brit. Soc. Halifax (Pres. 1971-72); Scot. Rite; P. Conservative; United Church; recreations: tennis, skiing, golf; Clubs: Halifax; Saraguay; Bd. of Trade; Home: 3098 Dutch Village Rd., Halifax, N.S. B3L 4G1; Office: P.O. Box 996, Armdale, N.S. B3L 4K9

PIERCEY, Reginald Matheson, B.Com.; real estate executive; b. Westmount, Sydney, N.S., 1 Oct. 1904; s. William Drysdale and Annie Margaret (Forbes) P.; e. Halifax (N.S.) Pub. Schs.; King's Coll. Sch., Windsor, N.S. (Grad. 1921); Dalhousie Univ., B.Com. 1925; m. Lilian Marguerite, d. Rev. A. D. MacKinnon, New Minas, N.S., 7 Sept. 1932; two d., Sheila, Barbara; CHRMN. OF BD., PIERCEY INVESTORS LTD., established 1933; began business career with Piercey Supplies Ltd., Halifax, N.S., Wholesale & Retail Lumber & Bldg. Supply Dealers, 1925; Shipper, 1925-28; Br. Mgr., 1928-30; Asst. Mgr., Head Office, 1931; Vice-Pres. and Dir., 1932-55 (when sold interest); with W. D. Piercey organ. Windsor Supply Co. Ltd., Windsor, N.S., 1933, and was Dir. and Secy. till 1956 when sold interest; appt. a Commr. of The Supreme Court of N.S. 1932; Past Pres., N.S. and P.E.I. Retail Lbr. Dealers Association; Past Vice-President, Canadian Builders Supply Association; Bd. mem., C.N.I.B. (Maritime Division); mem. Bd. of Govs., Gaelic Coll. of Celtic Folk Arts, St. Ann's, Cape Breton; mem., Halifax Bd. Trade; Past District Gov., Gyro Internat. (Past Pres., Halifax Gyro Club); mem., North British Soc. (Past Pres.); Conservative; United Church (Past Chrmn. Bd. Trustees, Bethany Ch.); recreations: curling, golf, fishing, hunting; Clubs: Mayflower Curling; Ashburn Golf; Halifax Gyro; Home: 3070 Dutch Villiage Road, Armdale, Halifax, N.S. B3L 4G1; Office: P.O. Box 996, Armdale, N.S. B3L 4K9

PIERS, Rear Admiral Desmond William, D.S.C., C.D., D.Mil. Sc., K.L.J. retired navy officer; b. Halifax, N.S., 12 June 1913; s. late William Harrington and late Dr. Florence Maud (O'Donnell) P., M.D.; e. Halifax Co. Acad.; Royal Mil. Coll. 1930-32; Royal Naval Staff Coll. 1949; Nat. Defence Coll. 1951-52; m. Janet Macneill, d. late Dr. Murray Macneill, LL.D., M.A., Halifax, N.S., 2 Sept. 1941; one step d., Mrs. Conyers Baker (Caroline Anne Christine Aitken); joined R.C.N. as Cadet 1932; C.O., HMC Destroyer Restigouche and Sr. Offr. Fourth Candn. Escort Group on N. Atlantic convoy routes 1941-43; awarded D.S.C. 1943; C.O., HMC Destroyer Algonquin with Brit. Home Fleet, Scapa Flow, and participated in invasion of Normandy and convoys to N. Russia, 1944-45; (Commdr.), 1945; Extve. Offr. HMC Aircraft Carrier Magnificent 1947-48; Dir., Naval Plans and Operations, Naval Hdqds., Ottawa (Capt.) 1949-50; Asst. Chief of Staff (Personnel and Adm.) to Supreme Allied Commdr. Atlantic, 1952-53; Naval Dir., Nat. Defence Coll. (Commodore) 1953-55 C.O., HMC Cruiser Quebec, 1955-56; Sr. Candn. Offr. Afloat (Atlantic) 1956-57; Commandant, Royal Mil. Coll. Can., and Hon. ADC to His Excellency the Governor General 1957-60; Asst. Chief of Naval Staff (Plans) Naval Hdqrs., 1960-62; Chrmn. Candn. Defence Liaison Staff, Washington, D.C., and Candn. Rep. on N.A.T.O. Mil. Comte., (Rear Admiral) 1962-66; retired 1967; Agent-Gen. of N.S. in U.K. and Europe 1977-79; Freeman of the City of London, 1978; Hon. Doctor of Mil. Science, Royal Mil. Coll. of Can., 1978; Gov., Candn. Corps of Commissioners; mem. Bd., South Shore Community Service Assn.; Candn. Human Rights Foundation; Order St. Lazarus of Jerusalem; mem., VII Pan Am. Wheelchair Games; Mermaid Theare (Wolfville, N.S.); Fellow, Roy. Commonwealth Soc.; mem., Roy. Candn. Legion; Candn. Inst. Internat. Affairs; Candn. Civil Liberties Assn.; Canadian Trauma Foundation; Navy League of Can.; Roy. United Services Inst. N.S.; Heritage Can.; Heritage N.S.; Naval Offrs. Assn. Can.; Royal Candn. Naval Assn.; United Church; recreations: golf, tennis, figure skating, skiing, sailing, photography; Clubs: Halifax; Rideau (Ottawa); Halifax Golf and Country; R.N.S.Y.S.; Chester Golf, Curling, Tennis & Figure Skating; Home: The Quarter Deck, Chester, N.S. B0J 1J0

PIGEON, Hon. Louis-Philippe, LL.D. c.c.; professor; b. Henryville, Que., 8 Feb. 1905; s. Arthur and Maria (Demers) P.; e. Petit Séminaire de Qué., B.A. 1925; Laval Univ., LL.L. 1928, LL.D.; Univ. of Ottawa, LL.D.; Bishop Univ., LL.D.; m. Madeleine, d. Marc Gaudry, 29 Aug. 1936; children; Jacques, Madeleine, Louise, François, Yves, Michel; PROFESSOR, UNIVERSITY OF OTTAWA, FACULTY OF LAW, CIVIL LAW SECTION, responsible for Post-Graduate Program of Legislative Drafting (French) since 1980; called to Bar of Que. 1928 cr. K.C. 1940; private practice with St.-Laurent, Gagné, Devlin & Taschereau, 1928-37; Hudon & Pigeon, 1938-40; Germain, Pigeon, Thibaudeau & Lesage, 1946-67; Law Clk. of Leg. of Que., 1940-44; Legal Adviser of Prime Min. of Que., 1960-66; Prof. of Constitutional Law Laval Univ., 1942-67; Bâtonnier of Dist. of Que., 1960-61; Chrmn., Nat. Council on Adm. of Justice, 1963-67; Vice Pres., Conf. of Commrs. for Uniformity of Leg. in Can., 1966-67; Chrmn., Nat. Prof. Conduct Comte., 1966-67; Vice Pres. for Prov. of Que., Candn. Bar Assn., 1965-66; Justice, Supreme Court of Canada 1967-80, R. Catholic; Club: Cercle Universitaire (Quebec); Home: 200 Rideau Terrace, Ottawa, Ont., K1M 0Z3; Office: Univ. of Ottawa, Faculty of Law, 57 Copernicus, Ottawa, Ont. K1N 6N5

PIGGOTT, William Douglas; retired transportation executive; b. Barrie, Ont. 21 Aug. 1912; m. Helen Marie Abraham; children: Lynn, Bill; joined the Co. as Extra Gang Timekeeper Stratford Div. 1929, Apprentice London, Stratford, Toronto and Sarnia 1933, Locomotive Foreman, Supvr.Equipment and Asst. Works Mgr. Montreal 1943, Asst. Gen. Supt. Motive Power Toronto 1955, Special Assignments 1958, Gen. Supt. Equipment Montreal 1960, Toronto 1961, Gen. Supt. Transport. 1962, Asst. Gen. Mgr. Edmonton 1964, Gen. Mgr. Mountain Region 1966; apptd. Vice-Pres. Grand Trunk Western 1969; Asst. Vice-Pres. Great Lakes Region 1970, Vice-Pres. Great Lakes Region 1972, System Vice Pres. 1974; retired as Corp. Vice Pres. 1977; recreations: gardening, reading; Home: 13708 - 90th Ave., Edmonton, Alta. T5S 4T4; Office: (Box 8100) Montreal, Que., H3C 3N4

PIGOTT, Jean; executive; politician; b. Ottawa, Ont. 20 May 1924; d. George Cecil and Margaret Jane Kelly (Cotter) Morrison; e. Ottawa Ladies Coll.; Albert Coll.; m. Arthur Campbell Pigott 8 Oct. 1955; children: John, David, Mary Jane; CHRMN. of BD., MORRISON LAMOTHE INC. 1980- ; Pres. & C.E.O., Morrison Lamothe Foods, 1967-76; former Dir. (first woman) & mem. Audit Comte., Ont. Hydro, to 1976; Dir. of Candn. Devel. Corp. & mem. Audit Comte., to 1976; Dir. Candn. Council of Christians & Jews to 1976; former Chrmn. MacDonald Cartier Library; Ottawa Regional Hosp. Planning Council; former Vice Pres. Local Council of Woman (Ottawa); el. by-election Oct. 1976 to House of Commons; Chrmn. Conservative Caucus as Sr. Adv. for Human Resources 1979; mem. Candn. Assn. of the Club of Rome; Publications: "Feeding the Nation and the World", (working papr, Policy Committee, Leader of the Opposition) 1979; "Special Interest Advocacy—a Right, a Necessity or a Danger?", Conference Bd. 1980; Diabetic Assn. 1980; Trustee, Ottawa Gen. Hosp.; Gov. Carleton Univ.; Gov. Elmwood Sch.; Hon. Chrmn. Ottawa Cancer Unit; Dir. the Kidney Foundation; Centennial Medal (for work for Expo) 1967; Distinguished Service to the Business Community Award, Ottawa Bd. of Trade 1975; Award by Assn. des Détaillants en Alimentation, 1975; Queen's Jubilee Medal 1977; Kiwanis Club of Ottawa Citation as Outstanding Citizen of Ottawa & the Prov. of Ont. (Internat. Women's Year); Knight of the Golden Pencil Award 1978; P. Conservative; Protestant; recreations: cooking, needlework, cross-country skiing; Clubs: Cercle Universitaire; Ottawa Women's Canadian; Rideau (first woman mem.); Albany; Home: 50 Fuller St., Ottawa, Ont., K1Y 3R8; Offices: Langevin Block, Ottawa, Ont. K1A 0A2; and Suite 1401, 275 Slater St., Ottawa, Ont. K1P 5H9

PIGOTT, Jean Jacques, B.A.Sc.; P. Eng.; construction executive; b. Detroit, Mich., 16 Dec. 1916; s. Joseph Michael and Yvonne (Prince) P.; e. St. Joseph's Separate Sch. and Cathedral High Sch., Hamilton, Ont.; Univ. of Toronto, B.A.Sc.; children: Susan Carol, Jean Jacques, Jr., Douglas D'Arcy, Christopher Sean; PRES., MARANJAC HOLDINGS LTD.,NSTRUCTION LTD., Dir., Pigott Investments Ltd.; Southam Inc.; Southam Communications Ltd.; Southam Printing Ltd.; North American Life Assnce. Co.; Victoria and Grey Trustco Ltd.; Victoria and Grey Trust Co.; Pres., Cdn. Paraplegic Assn.; Trustee, Lyndhurst Hosp.; served in 2nd World War, 1940-45, RCN, rank Lt.-Commdr.; mem., Assn. Prof. Engrs. Ont.; Clubs: York; Home: R.R. #1, Bolton, Ont. L0P 1A0; Office: 304 The East Mall, #609, Islington, Ont., M9B 6E2

PIGOTT, Marjorie, R.C.A.; artist; b. Yokohama, Japan 6 Jan. 1904; d. Harold Charles and Mitsu (Sakurai) Pigott; e. private Eng. governesses Japan and private Eng. schs. Yokohama; Nanga Sch. of Art Tokyo, Yokohama, Kobe and Osaka 12 yrs., rec'd Teacher's Dipl.; probably first to teach Nanga Art (Sumi-é) in Can. 1955-65; rep. in various exhns. incl. 4th Biennial Candn. Art, Nat. Gallery Can.; 50 Yrs. Retrospective, Art Gallery of Ont. 1975; Watercolour Japan-Can., Tokyo and Toronto 1976-78; Am. Watercolour Soc./Candn. Soc. Painters in Watercolour, N.Y. 1967; Sumi-é Soc. Am., N.Y. 1967; rep. various perm. colls. incl. Nat. Gallery Can.; limited ed. publ. 1978 containing 19 reproductions princ. paintings; mem. Candn. Soc. Painters in Watercolour; Ont. Soc. Artists; P. Conservative; Anglican; Address: 1503, 77 St. Clair Ave. E., Toronto, Ont. M4T 1M5.

PIGOTT, William Prince, B.A., B.A.Sc., P.Eng.; civil engineer; b. Prince Albert, Sask., 28 Sept. 1914 s. Joseph Michael, C.B.E., K.C.S.G., and Yvonne (Prince) P.; e. St. Joseph's Separate Sch., Hamilton, Ont. (1927); Cathedral High Sch., Hamilton, Ont. (1932); Univ. of Toronto, B.A. 1935 and Sch. of Practical Science, B.A.Sc. 1939; m. Edith Hope, d. Hon. Charles McCrea, Toronto, Ont., 9 May 1941; children: William McCrea, James Dent, Yvonne Hope, Anthony Prince, Charles Benjamin, Andrew David, Ann Louise; PRESIDENT, PIGOTT CONSTRUCTION LTD. (Engrs. and Contractors, Estbd. 1875), since 1956; Chrmn., Capital Construction Equipment Ltd.; Dir., Canada Permanent Mortgage Corp.; Canada Permanent Trust Co.; Silverwood Industries Ltd.; Westinghouse Canada Ltd.; Chrmn. Hamilton Adv. Bd., Canada Permanent Co's.; began career with present Co. as Field Engr. on various projects in Ont., 1939-43; Chief Engr., Hamilton Office, 1954-56; Trustee, Chedoke-McMaster Hospitals; Chmn. Bd. Govs McMaster Univ.; mem., Assn. Prof. Engrs. Ont.; Hamilton Chamber Comm. (Past Pres.); Hamilton Builders Exchange (Past Pres.); Delta Upsilon; R. Catholic; recreations: golf, tennis, music; Clubs: Hamilton City; Hamilton Thistle; Hamilton Golf & Country; Home: Ancaster, Ont.; Office: 4 Hughson St. S., P.O. Box 309, Hamilton, Ont., L8N 3G7

PILKEY, Clifford G.; labour executive; b. Pickering, Ont. 27 July 1922; s. William George and Jennie (Grosbeck) P.; e. Oshawa (Ont.) Coll. & Vocational Inst.; grad. no. labour courses; m. Viola Elizabeth M. d. S. C. Brooks, Oshawa, Ont. 25 Sept. 1942; children: Allan C., Jacqueline MacKay; PRESIDENT, ONT. FED. OF LABOUR; Vice Pres. Candn. Labour Congress; Secy.-Treas. Local 222 Un. Auto Workers, Oshawa 1954-57, Pres. 1957-59; Pres. Candn. Un. Auto Workers Council 1957-58; Pres. Oshawa & Dist. Labour Council 8 yrs,; Dir. Citizenship & Leg. Dept. for Un. Auto Workers Candn. Region; served with Candn. Army during World War II; Ald. City of Oshawa 8 yrs.; el. M.P.P. for Oshawa Riding 1967-71; mem. Bd. of Govs. Durham Coll. Oshawa; mem. Royal Candn. Legion; NDP; Protestant; recreation: golf; Home: 801 Regent Dr., Oshawa, Ont., L1G 1H8; Office: 15 Gervais Dr., Don Mills, Ont., M3C 1Y8

PILKINGTON, Harry, D.F.C., B.Sc.; public utilities executive; b. Darwen, Eng. 11 Sept. 1922; s. Henry and Emma (Oldham) P.; e. Darwen, Eng.; Sir George Williams Univ., B.Sc. 1953; m. Gwendoline, d. T. Evans, Medicine Hat, Alta., 13 Aug. 1945; children: Jocelyn Belden, Kendall Swales, Thomas Hugh Pilkington; VICE PRES. (MARKETING), BELL CANADA since 1974; joined present Co. Montreal 1947; held various mang. positions, Traffic Depts., Montreal, Kitchener and Toronto, 1947-61; Area Traffic Mgr., Montreal, 1961; Asst. Comptroller, Systems & Procedures, 1964; Asst. Vice Pres. 1965; Comptroller 1968; Vice Pres. (Operations Staff) 1969; Vice Pres. (Toronto) 1970; served with RAF 1942-46; rank Flight Lt.; Lectr., Sir George Williams Univ. 1961-68;United Way Campaign 1980; mem. Bd. Dirs., Traffic Injury Research Found. Can.; Chrmn., Conference Bd. Compensation Research Centre; Anglican; recreations: walking, swimming; Club: University (Toronto); Home: R.R. #1, Belleville, Ont.; Office: 393 University Ave., 21st Fl., Toronto, Ont. M5G 1W9

PILON, Jean-Guy, B.A., LL.L. M.S.R.C. (1968); auteur; né St-Polycarpe, 12 nov. 1930; fils Arthur et Alida (Besner) P.; é. Univ. Montréal, B.A. 1951; Univ. Montréal, LL.L. 1954; enfants: François, Daniel; CHEF DU SER-

VICE DES EMISSIONS CULTURELLES — RADIO CANADA; Revue Liberté (co-fondateur); Publications (poèmes): "La Fiancée du Matin", 1953; "Les Cloîtres de l'Eté"; 1955; "L'Homme et le Jour", 1957; "La Mouette et le Large", 1960; "Recours au pays", 1961; "Pour saluer une ville", 1963; "Comme eau retenue", 1969; "Saisons pour la Continuelle", 1969 (Prix van Lerberghe); "Silences pour une souveraine" 1972; Prix: David (poésie, 1957); Louise-Labé (1969); France-Canada (1969); Gouverneur Général du Canada (mai 1970); membre Soc. Royale du Canada et de l'Académie canadienne-française; Résidence: 5724 Côte St-Antoine, Montréal, Qué. H4A 1R9

PINARD, Bernard, M.N.A.; barrister; b. Drummondville, Que., 24 March 1923; s. Arthur and Yvonne (Lupien) P.; e. St. Frederic's Acad.; arts at Nicolet and Joliette Seminaries; Ottawa Univ. and Univ. of Montreal (law); special courses at the Internat. Univ. of Santander, Spain; Hon. Dr.'s degree, Faculty of Law, Sherbrooke Univ., 1966; called to the Bar of Que. 1950; m. Jacqueline, d. Leonidas Lamothe, Drummondville, Que., 18 Sept. 1954; children: Dominique, Elizabeth, Philippe; el. Pres., Young Liberals Assn. of Co. of Drummondville in 1951; el. to Que. Leg. for Drummond, 1952, def. 1956, re-el. 1960, 1962, 1966, 1970; Min. of Roads, Que., 1960-66 and Min. of Public Works and Transport 1970-73; apptd. Judge of Prov. Ct. and Prees. of Tribunal of Trans. 1973: formerly mem., Soc. of Concerts, Jeunesses, Musicales; Drummondville Chamber Comm.; hon. mem., Roy. Candn. Legion; Am. Right of Way Assn.; Commonwealth Parlty. Assn. (Que. Br.); Gov., Drummondville Recreation Centre; K. of C.; Liberal; Clubs: Richelieu; des Francs; Garrison (Quebec); Reform (Quebec); Home: 1380 Power Silery, P.Q.; Office: 930 Chemin Ste. Foy, P.Q.

PINARD, Gilbert, B.A., M.D., F.R.C.P.(C); psychiatrist; educator; b. Montreal, Que. 19 July 1940; s. Roland, Q.C. and Gaby (Laurendeau) P.; e. Loyola Coll. Montreal B.A. 1961; Univ. of Montreal M.D. 1965, Dipl. in Studies of Psychiatry 1970; m. Andrée d. Pierre Pouliot 17 Aug. 1963; children: Eric. Marc; PROF. AND HEAD OF PSYCHIATRY, UNIV. OF SHERBROOKE since 1976; Psychiatrist, Hôpital Louis-H. Lafontaine, Montreal 1970-76; mem. du Comité de Direction, Institut Nat. de Recherche Scientifique, Montreal 1974-76; Pres. Psychiatric Comm., Conseil Régional de la Santé des Services Sociaux des Cantons de l'Est; author numerous publs. Scient. Research (Psychopharmacol.-Psycholinguistics); mem. Assn. des Psychiatres du Can./Candn. Psychiatric Assn.; Candn. Coll. Neuropsychopharmacol. (Chrmn. Liaison Comte.); Chrmn., Candn. Assn. Profs. of Psychiatry; Sci. Program Comm., Can. Psych. Assn.; Fellow, Am. Psychiatric Assn.; mam., Accreditation Comm., R.C.P.; R. Catholic; recreations: sailing, skiing, tennis; Home: 420 Duvernat St., Sherbrooke, Quebec. J1L 1J1; Office: Centre Hospitalier Universitaire, Sherbrooke, Que. J1H 5N4.

PINARD, Msgr. Irénée, B.A., B.D.C., D.C.L., D. de L'Un.; prêtre; né St-Georges de Windsor, Qué. 28 fév. 1905; f. Alfred et Marie-Louise P.; é. Sem. de Sherbrooke 1923-30; Univ. de Montréal, B.A. 1930; Angelicum, Rome, B.D.C. 1939; Bishop's Univ., D.C.L. 1962; D. de L'Un., Sherbrooke 1969; Chancelier, Diocèse de Sherbrooke 1940-47; Curé de la Cathédrale 1947-55; Recteur, Univ. de Sherbrooke 1955-65; retraité depuis 1968; Chanoine du Diocèse de Sherbrooke 1944; Prélat de la Maison de S.S. Pie XII 1949; Protonotaire Apostolique 1959; Assn. Internat. des présidents d'Univs.; Résidence: 1370 rue Parent, Sherbrooke, Qué., J1K 2E1

PINARD, Maurice, LL.L. M.A., Ph.D.; sociologist; educator; b. Drummondville, Que. 25 Apl. 1929; s. J.-Ernest and Aline (Masson) P.; e. Univ. of Montreal B.A. 1951, LL.L. 1954, M.A. (Law) 1955; Johns Hopkins Univ. Ph.D. (Sociol.) 1967; m. Minola Saragea 10 June 1967; one s. Pierre; PROF. OF SOCIOL. McGILL UNIV.; author "The

Rise of A Third Party: A Study In Crisis Politics" 1971, enlarged ed. 1975; mem. Royal Soc. Can.; R.Catholic: Home: 3467 Vendome Ave., Montreal, Que. H4A 3M6; Office: 855 Sherbrooke St. W., Montreal. Que. H3A 2T7.

PINARD, Raymond R., B.A., B.E.; corporate executive; b. Trois-Rivières, Qué. 13 May 1930; s. Albert and Mariette (Dufresne) P.; e. Laval Univ. B.A. 1951; McGill Univ. B.E. 1955; m. Estelle d. Antonio Fréchette; one d., one s.; EXEC. VICE-PRES. DOMTAR INC. since 1981; Gen. Mgr. Kraft Paper & Bd. Div. Domtar 1970, Gen. Mgr. and Vice Pres. Pulp Div. 1973 and Newsprint Div. 1975, Extve. Vice Pres. Pulp & Paper Products Group 1978; Pres., Pulp and Paper Producs Group, 1979; mem. Tech. Sec., Candn. Pulp & Paper Assn.; TAPPI; Dir. & mem. Extve. Bd., Fondation de l'UQAM-SIDBEC; C.P.P.A.; C.D. Howe Research Inst.; Engn. Inst. Can.; Sigma Chi; recreations: tennis, skiing, sailing, hunting, fishing; Clubs: M.A.A.A.; St-Denis; Office: 395 de Maisonneuve Blvd. W., Montréal, Qué. H3A 1L6.

PINARD, Hon. Yvon, M.P., B.A., LL.L.; politician; b. Drummondville, Que. 10 Oct. 1940; s. Jean-Jacques and Cécile (Chassé) P.; e. Immaculate Conception Sch. Drummondville; Nicolet Semy. (Lt. Gov. Onésime Gagnon Medal for Acad. Merit); Univ. de Sherbrooke (Lt. Gov. Paul Comtois Medal for Acad. & Social Merit); m. Renée d. Marcel Chaput, Richmond, Que. 19 Dec. 1964; two d. Hélène, Andrée; PRES. OF PRIVY COUNCIL and Govt. House Leader 1980- ; Pres., Sherbrooke Univ. Law Faculty 1963; called to Bar of Que. 1964; Pres. and Founder, Drummond Caisse d'Entraide Economique; Pres., Drummond Co. Lib. Assn. 1968-70; Dir. and Founder Drummondville Rangers; Dir. Drummondville Royals; mem. Adm. Council Centre Communautaire d'Aide juridique Maurice-Bois-Francs region; Gov., Hockey Can.; mem. Commonwealth Parlty. Assn.; Candn. Del. Interparlty. Union; el. to H. of C. for Drummond g.e. 1974, re-el. since; Parlty. Secy. to Pres. of Privy Council 1977; Club: Drummondville Golf & Curling (Dir. 1973-74); Liberal; R. Catholic; Home: 10 Rogers Lane, Drummondville, Que. ; Office: House of Commons, Ottawa, Ont. K1A 0A6.

PINCOCK, J. Graham, M.D., L.M.C.C., F.R.C.P.(C), F.A.C.P.; b. Winnipeg, Man., 16 Nov. 1919; s. James Clayton and Olive Haviland (Stothart) P.; e. Univ. of Man., M.D. 1943; Med. Council Can., L.M.C.C. 1943; m. Shirley Jane, d. William Norman Gordon, 4 Sept. 1943; children: Margaret L. Kavanagh, Helen S. Dartnell, Mary O. Park, James Gordon, Donald Graham; gen. med. practice Oak River, Man. 1946; Resident, Deer Lodge Hosp. 1948; Consulting Practice, Internal Med., Winnipeg, 1950; Dir. of Assessment and Rehabilitation and Head of Phys. Med., 1957; Asst. to Pres., Planning and Devel., Univ. of Winnipeg, 1968-78; Fed. Rep., Disability Allowance Bd. of Man. 1955-73; served with RCAF as Med. Offr. 1943-46; Elder, Un. Church 1949-78; Chrmn. Bd. or Men, Un. Ch. of Can. 1962-68; mem. Bd. of Regents, Un. Coll., 1957-68; mem. Winnipeg Med. Soc.; Home: 501 Churchill Dr., Winnipeg, Man., R3L 1W3; Office: 515 Portage Ave., Winnipeg, Man. R3B 2E9

PINDER, Herbert Charles, B.A., M.B.A.; merchant; b. Saskatoon, Sask., 26 April 1923; s. Mary Helen Charlotte (Rose) and the late Robert Mitford P.; e. City Park Coll. Inst., Saskatoon, Sask.; Univ. of Sask., B.A. 1942; Harvard Grad. Sch. of Business Adm., M.B.A. 1947; m. Shirley Jean, d. late Allan P. Hughes, Regina, Sask., 25 Jan. 1946; children: Herbert C., Jr., Gerald, Richard, Thomas, Patricia; PRES., SASKATOON TRADING CO. LTD. since 1947 (operating Pinder's Drug Stores, Prairieland Drug Wholesale Ltd., Dir., The Royal Bank of Canada; John Labatt Ltd.; TransCanada PipeLines Limited; Western Shopping Centres Limited; Bird Machine Co. of Can. Ltd.; Ideal Basic Industries Inc; Lieutenant-Commander (retired), RCNVR; Prov. Liberal candidate Saskatoon (1960); apptd. Min. of Industry & Econ. Devel. Sask.; def.

in by-el. Dec. 1964; active in land and shopping centre devel. since 1956; Past Gov. and Bd. Chrmn., Univ. of Sask.; United Church; recreations: golf, hunting; Club: Kinsmen (Past Nat. Pres. 1953-54); Home: 214 Saskatchewan Crescent W., Saskatoon, Sask., S7M 0A4; Office: 102 Melville St. (Box 1648), Saskatoon, Sask. S7K 3R9

PINET, Edith B., C.M.; nurse; b. Burnsville, N.B. 4 June 1904; d. Angus John Stephen and Victoria (Cormier) Branch; e. rec'd Nursing Dipl. 1928; m. William Pinet 28 July 1928; children: Edith, Ethel, Kathleen, Betty, William, Denis, Winnifred, Jean, Patricia-Anne; began nursing career delivering babies 1929 and has nursed every ailment which could cope without a doctor; assisted her husband farming; presently owns small pantry store; named to Honour Roll of Can.; P. Conservative; R. Catholic; Club: Golden Age; Home: R.R.1, P.O. Box 6, Paquetville, N.B. E0B 2B0.

PINK, Irving C., Q.C.; b. Yarmouth, N.S., 10 May 1913; s. Joseph and Rose (Safier) P.; e. Dalhousie Univ. (Arts 1934, Law 1936); L.L.D. (St. Anne's), 1977; m. Ruth Marilyn, d. Solomon Goodman, 19 Oct. 1938; children: Steven, Joel, Ronald, Darrel; PARTNER, IRVING C. PINK & ASSOCIATES; Dir., Central & Eastern Trust Co.; Vice-Pres., Grand Hotel, Yarmouth, N.S.; called to Bar of N.S.; cr. Q.C. 1957; Chrmn. Bd. Trustees, The Yarmouth Regional Hosp.; mem. N.S. Bar Soc.; Candn. Bar Soc.; Liberal; Hebrew; Club: Rotary; Home: 9 Seminary St., Yarmouth, N.S., B5A 2B3; Office: 379-1/2 Main, Yarmouth, N.S., B5A 1G1

PINSENT, Gordon Edward, LL.D.; actor; writer; b. Grand Falls, Nfld., 12 July 1930; s. late Stephen Arthur and Flossie (Cooper) P.; e. Grand Falls (Nfld.) Acad.; LL.D. University P.E.I. 1975; m. Charmion, d. Charles W. King, Toronto, Ontario, 2 November 1962; one child, Leah King; stage performances include Winnipeg Repertory Theatre, Man. Theatre Centre 1954-60 and in Toronto, Straw-hat Players, New Play Soc., Crest Theatre 1960-69; Stratford (Ont.) Shakespearean Festival 1962, 75; other performances incl. radio, TV anthologies and series in Winnipeg, Toronto, Montreal and N.Y.; Features in Hollywood and Greece; played role of Quentin Durgens, M.P., CBC TV for 3 yrs.; served with Royal Candn. Regt. 1948-51; with wife recently honored by Grand Falls, Nfld.; author of screenplays & novels, "John and the Missus" 1968, "The Rowdyman" (also film) 1969; Anglican; recreations: painting, hiking, swimming; Address: 3779 Whitespeak Dr., Sherman Oaks, Cal. 91403.

PINTAR, Milan Mik, M.Sc., Ph.D.; educator; b. Celje, Yugoslavia 17 Jan. 1934; s. Rihard and Milena (Kovac) P.; e. High Sch. Ljubljana, Yugoslavia; Univ. of Ljubljana Dipl. in Engn. Physics 1958, M.Sc. (Physics) 1964, Ph.D. (Solid State Physics) 1966; came to Can. 1966; m. Sandra Dawn d. James A. Burt, Port Carling, Ont. 1974; children: Richard, Katarina, Andrej; PROF. OF PHYSICS, UNIV. OF WATERLOO 1975- ; Chrmn. Waterloo NMR Summer Sch. 1969- ; Research Fellow Inst. J. Stefan, Univ. of Ljubljana 1957-66; Postdoctoral Fellow, McMaster Univ. 1966-67; Asst. Prof. 1967-69, Assoc. Prof. 1969-75; Ed. and Co-author "Introductory Essays-NMR Basic Principles and Progress" 1976; mem. Ed. Bd. "Bulletin of Magnetic Resonance" 1981- ; author over 100 research papers; rec'd Nat. Award for Science "B. Kidric" Yugoslavia 1965; "F. Presern" Award Univ. of Ljubljana 1956; mem. Candn. Assn. Physicists; Am. Phys. Soc.; N.Y. Acad. Sciences; Internat. Soc. Magnetic Resonance (Secy. Gen.); recreations: skiing, sailing; Home: 134 Dunbar Rd. S., Waterloo, Ont. N2L 2E9; Office: Waterloo, Ont. N2L 3G1.

PIPPERT, Ralph Reinhard, B.A., M.S., Ph.D.; educator; b. Sheboygan, Wis. 23 March 1922; s. George Frederick and Louise Heartha (Berndt) P.; e. Mission House Coll., B.A. 1944; Univ. of Wis., M.S. 1950, Ph.D. 1959; m.

Theresa Ann, d. Frank Fydenkevez, Hadley, Mass., 24 June 1967; children: Mark, Rolf, Eric, Dianne, Christine; PROFESSOR, FACULTY OF EUDUCATION, BRANDON UNIV. since 1977; Teacher, pub. sch. Wis. 1944; Prof. of Educ., Lakeland Coll., Wis., 1954; Prof. and Asst. Dean, Univ. of Mass., 1959; Prof. and Head Educ. Psychol., Univ. of Man., 1967; Chrmn., Counsellor Educ. Dept., S. Ill. Univ., 1970-71; Dean, Faculty of Education, Brandon Univ., 1972-77; author of various articles in prof. journs.; mem.; Am. Psychol. Assn.; Candn. Personnel & Guidance Assn.; United Church; recreation: woodcarving; Home: 7 Grant Blvd., Brandon, Man., R7B 2L4

PIRLOT, Paul L., Ph.D., D.Sc., educator; b. Mettet, Belgium 17 March 1920; s. Léon and F. (Quinet) P.; e. Jury Central, Brussels Licence Phil. Let. (Hist. of Science) 1942; Univ. de Louvain Licence Sc. Zool. 1946, Agrégé de l'Enseignement 1949, D.Sc. 1959; Univ. of London Ph.D. (Zool.) 1949; children: Marie-Antoinette, Jean-Paul, Brigitte; PROF. OF BIOL. UNIV. DE MONTREAL 1963- ; Alumnus, Fondation universitaire de Belgique 1939-40, 1944-46; Scholar, Brit. Council, London 1946-48; Scholar (Beccario) Consejo Superior de Investigaciones Cientificas, Spain 1948; Part-time 1949-51 and Full-time 1951-57 Research Assoc. Inst. pour la recherche scientifique en Afrique centrale, Republic of Zaire; Special Advanced Fellow, Belgian-Am. Educ. Foundation USA and Visiting Prof. Carroll Coll. Helena, Mont. 1955-56; Post-doctoral Fellow, Nat. Research Council Can. 1958, yearly grantee since; Assoc. Prof. present Univ. 1958-63; Research Assoc. Max-Planch-Institut für Hirnforschung, Frankfurt/Main 1968, 1969, 1971 and invited lectr. NATO Advanced Study Inst. Istanbul 1969; Visiting Prof., Univ. of Tokyo, Monash Univ. Australia 1974; Fundação Oswaldo Cruz, Rio de Janeiro, invited lectr. Monash Univ. and Univ. of Tasmania, Visiting Scient. Hadassah Inst. Jerusalem 1978; Research Assoc., Visiting Scient. numerous insts. S. Am., Middle and Far E., Europe, Africa, Caribbean, Mexico; author "Morphologie Evolutive des Chordés" 1969; "Le Pays entre l'Eau et le Feu" 1969; co-author "L'Homme dans son Milieu" 1968; "Organe et Fonction" 1977; over 90 scient. papers morphology of brain and ecology; mem. Candn. Kennel Club; Can.-China Soc.; Assn. des Ecrivains de Langue Française; Soc. Study Evolution; Soc. Scientifique de Bruxelles; Candn. Soc. Zools. (Vice Pres. 1964, Pres. 1965); Candn. Soc. Hist. & Philos. Science; Am. Soc. Anatomists; N.Y. Acad. Sciences; Am. Soc. Naturalists; R. Catholic; recreations: photography, sculpture; Home: Abercorn, Que. J0E 1B0; Office: Montreal, Que. H3C 3J7.

PITERNICK, Anne Brearley, B.A., A.L.A.; librarian; educator; b. Blackburn, Eng. 13 Oct. 1926; d. Walter and Ellen (Harris) Clayton; e. Manchester Univ. B.A. 1948; A.L.A. 1955; came to Can. 1956; m. George Piternick 6 May 1971; PROF. OF LIBRARIANSHIP, UNIV. OF B.C. 1978- ; joined Univ. of B.C. Lib. 1956, Head, Science Div. 1960-61, Social Sciences Div. 1964-66, Asst. Prof. of Librarianship 1966-73, Assoc. Prof. 1973-78, mem. Senate 1969-72, Senate Lib. Comte. 1969- , Secy. Faculty Assn. 1967-69; Information Offr.; Candn. Uranium Research Foundation 1961-63; mem. Comte. on Bibliog. and Information Services for the Social Sciences and Humanities, 1975- , Chrmn. 1979- ; Nat. Lib. Adv. Bd. 1978- ; Social Sciences and Humanities Research Council of Can., Adv. Academic Panel, 1981- ; rec'd Queen's Silver Jubilee Medal 1977; Fellow, Council on Lib. Resources 1979-80; Ed., Proceedings, 1974 Nat. Conf. on State of Candn. Bibliog. (published 1977); author manuals and journ. articles; mem. Candn. Lib. Assn. (Pres. 1976-77); B.C. Lib. Assn.; Lib. Assn. (Gt. Brit.); Am. Soc. Information Science; Special Libs. Assn.; Bibliog. Soc. Can.; recreations: music, cuisine; Home: 1849 W. 63rd Ave., Vancouver, B.C. V6P 2H9; Office: School of Librarianship, Univ. of B.C.; Vancouver, B.C. V6T 1W5.

PITFIELD, Peter Michael, Q.C. (Fed.), B.A.Sc., B.C.L., D.E.S.D., D. Litt. (Hon.); Candn. civil servant; b. Montreal, 18 June 1937; s. Ward Chipman and Grace Edith (MacDougall) P.; e. Lower Can. Coll., Montreal and Sedbergh Sch., Montebello, 1951; St. Lawrence Univ., B.A.Sc. 1955, D. Litt. (Hon.) 1979; McGill Univ., B.C.L. 1958; Univ. of Ottawa, D.E.S.D. 1961; m. Nancy Snow, Toronto 1971; children: Caroline, Thomas, Katie; CLERK OF PRIVY COUNCIL AND SECY. TO CABINET 1975-79; reappointed 1980; read law with Mathewson, Lafleur & Brown, Montreal; called to the Bar of Quebec 1962; cr. Q.C. (Fed.) 1972; assoc. with Mathewson, Lafleur & Brown, Montreal, 1956-59; Adm. Asst. to Min. of Justice and Atty. Gen. of Can., Ottawa, 1959-61; Secy. and Extve. Dir., Royal Comn. on Publs., Ottawa, 1961-62; Attache to Gov. Gen. of Can. 1962-65; Secy. and Research Supvr. of Royal Comn. on Taxation 1963-66; joined Privy Council Office and Cabinet Secretariat Govt. of Can. 1965; Asst. Secy. to Cabinet 1967; Deputy Secretary to Cabinet (Plans) and Deputy Clerk Council 1969; Deputy Minister Consumer and Corporate Affairs 1973-74; Fellow Harvard Univ., 1974; MacKenzie King Professor of Can. Studies, Harvard univ., 1979-80; Lieutenant, R.C.N.R.; member, Canadian, Quebec and Montreal Bar Assns.; Candn. Institute of Public Adm.; Candn. Hist. Assn.; Candn. Pol. Science Assn.; Internat. Comn. Jurists; Am. Soc. Pol. & Social Science; Beta Theta Pi; Anglican; recreations: squash, skiing, reading; Clubs: University (Montreal); Home: 305 Thorold Road, Ottawa, Ont. K1M 0K1; Office: Langevin Block, Wellington Street, Ottawa, Ont. K1A 0K3

PITFIELD, Ward Chipman, B.Com.; b. Montreal, Que., 6 Sept. 1925; s. Ward Chipman and Grace (MacDougall) P.; e. Bishops Coll. Sch., Lennoxville, Que.; McGill Univ., B.Com. 1948; m. Diana, d. William Sutherland, 26 Sept. 1953; children: Chipman, Elizabeth, John, David, Sally; PRES. AND DIR., PITFIELD MACKAY ROSS LTD.; Dir., WCI Canada Limited; Ontario Jockey Club; CAE Industries Limited; White Consolidated Industries Ltd.; Candn. General Investments Ltd.; Hosp. for Sick Children Foundation; Toromont Industries Ltd.; served with the R.A.F. Transport Command during 2nd World War.; Alpha Delta Phi; Anglican; recreations: golf, riding, fishing; Home: 6 Highland Ave., Toronto, Ont., M4W 2A3; Office: P.O. Box 54, Royal Bank Plaza, Toronto, Ont., M5J 2K5

PITMAN, Walter George, M.A.; educator; journalist; b. Toronto, Ont., 18 May 1929; s. Ernest George and late Elsie (Kendrick) P.; e. Univ. of Toronto, B.A. 1952, M.A. 1954; McGill Univ., Doctor of Law (honoris causa) 1981; m. Florence Ida, d. late Frank Collinge, 4 Sept. 1952; children: Wade George, Cynthia Lynn, Mark Donald, Anne Lorraine; EXEC. DIR. ONT. ARTS COUNCIL 1980- ; former Pres., Ryerson Polytech. Institute 1975-80; Head, Hist. Dept., Kenner Collegiate Inst., Peterborough, Ont., 1956-60; Assoc. Registrar and Dir. Part-Time Studies, Trent Univ., 1965-67; M.P. for Peterborough 1960-62; M.P.P. for Peterborough 1967-71; Dean, Arts & Science, Trent University 1972-75; rec'd. Centennial Medal 1967; Centennial Medal of O.R.T. 1980; Grier Award (OEA) 1980; Fellow, OISE 1976; Columnist, Toronto Daily Star; Past Pres., Ont. Educ. Assn.; Chairman, Metro Toronto Comte on Hum. Rel's, 1977; Pres., Can. Assoc. for Adult Educ., 1978-82; Cdn. Civil Liberties Assn., 1981- ; NDP; United Church; recreations: music, sailing; Home: 79 Crimson Millway, Willowdale, Ont. M2L 1T8; Office: 151 Bloor St. W., Toronto, Ont. M5S 1S4

PITT, David George, M.A., Ph.D.; university professor; b. Musgravetown, Nfld., 12 Dec. 1921; s. Rev. Thomas J., D.D. and Edith Florrie (Way) P.; e. Pub. and High Schs. in Nfld.; Mount Allison Univ., B.A. 1946 (magna cum laude); Univ. of Toronto, M.A. 1948, Ph.D. 1960; m. Una Marion, d. Rev. Wilfred J. Woolfrey, 5 June 1946; children: Ruth Marion; Robert David; PROF. OF ENGLISH,

MEMORIAL UNIV. OF NFLD., since 1961, and Head of Dept. since 1970; apptd. Assoc. Prof. of Eng. at present Univ. 1949; mem. Senate, Memorial Univ. of Nfld.; Ed. of no. of sch. and univ. texts incl. Shakespeare and other Eng. classics and poet E. J. Pratt; mem., Humanities Assn. Can.; Assn. Univ. Teachers Eng.; Assn. for Can. and Que. Lit.; United Church; Home: 7 Chestnut Pl., St. John's Nfld., A1B 2T1

PITTS, John W., B.E., M.B.A.; transportation executive; b. Victoria, B.C., 13 Oct. 1926; s. Clarence H. and Doris L. (Wilson) P.; e. Brentwood Coll.; McGill Univ., B.E. 1949; Harvard Univ., M.B.A. 1951; m. Margaret B., d. K. E. Brunsdale, Minneapolis, 8 June 1951; children: Jennifer B., Cynthia M., Charles K.; CHRMN., PRESIDENT AND CHIEF EXTVE. OFFR., DIR., OKANAGAN HELICOPTERS LTD., since 1970; Dir.; British Columbia Telephone Co.; Paccar Inc.; British Columbia Sugar Refining Co.; Royfund Ltd.; British Columbia Resources Investment Corp.; joined Vancouver Iron & Engineering Works 1951-55; self-employed in own mfg. businesses: Spruce Specialties Ltd., Transco Mfg. Ltd. and S & V Manufacturing Ltd. 1955-70; served with Candn. Army 1945; Alpha Delta Phi; Anglican; recreations: tennis, skiing, sailing, shooting; Clubs: Vancouver; Shaughnessy Golf and Country; Vancouver Lawn Tennis & Badminton; Home: 1742 W. 40th Ave., Vancouver, B.C. V6M 1W3; Office: 4391 Agar Dr., Vancouver International Airport, Richmond, B.C. V7B 1A5

PLAA, Gabriel Leon, M.Sc., Ph.D.; educator; b. San Francisco, Cal. 15 May 1930; s. Jean and Lucienne (Chalopin) P.; e. Univ. of Cal. Berkeley B.Sc. 1952, San Francisco M.Sc. 1956, Ph.D. 1958; m. Colleen Neva d. Harold Brasefield, Oakland, Cal. 19 May 1951; children: Ernest (d.), Steven, Kenneth, Gregory, Andrew, John, Denise, David; Prof. de Pharmacologie, Univ. de Montréal since 1968, Chrmn., Dépt de Pharmacologie 1968-80, and Vice-Dean, Fac. des Études Supérieures since 1979; Asst. Prof. of Pharmacol. Tulane Univ. Med. Sch. New Orleans 1958-61; Assoc. Prof. of Pharmacol. Univ. of Iowa 1961-68; served with US Army Reserve 1952-60, active duty Korea 1953, rank Lt.; rec'd Achievement Award Soc. Toxicol. 1967; Claude Bernard Medal Univ. de Montréal 1971; Thienes Mem. Award Am. Acad. Clin. Toxicol. 1977; Lehman Award Soc. Toxicol. 1980; author or co-author numerous articles and abstracts; Ed. 'Toxicology and Applied Pharmacology'; mem. Ed. Bd. various scient. journs.; mem. Pharmacol. Soc. Can. (Past Pres.); Am. Soc. Pharmacol. & Exper. Therapeutics; Soc. Toxicol. (Vice-Pres.); Soc. Toxicol. Can. (Pres.); Soc. Exper. Biol. & Med. (Councillor); Am Acad. Forensic Sciences (Fellow); Phi Kappa Tau (Vice Pres., Secy.); R. Catholic; Home. 236 Meredith St., Dorval, Que. H9S 2Y7; Office: (C.P. 6128) Montréal, Qué. H3C 3T7.

PLAMONDON, Huguette; labour executive; b. Prov. of Que., 6 Jan. 1926, in a worker's family, her father being a mem. of the Brotherhood of Rly. Carmen of America; e. Madeleine-de-Verchères and Ste-Philomène-de-Rosemont Schs.; O'Sullivan Coll. (Business course); McGill Univ. (English); C.C.L. Labour Schs.; VICE-PRESIDENT AT LARGE, CANADIAN LABOUR CONGRESS; Pres., Montreal Labour Council (first woman to hold such an office in Canada) since Feb. 1955; mem., Que. Econ. Adv. Council; Adv. Council for Consumers, Dept. of Nat. Health & Welfare; Staff Rep. United Packinghouse Workers of America since 1954; began career as a Stenographer in a steel industry which was unorganized; after United Steelworkers of Am. started organ. the plant, lost her job because of her sympathies towards organ. labour, which induced her to start in the movement as Office Secy. of the United Packinghouse Workers of Am.; participated in a number of strikes and became prominent in various organizing drives, as well as negotiating and servicing of Labour agreements; served on several comtes. of the Que. Fed. of Indust. Unions, and takes an active interest

in the Labour Comte. against Racial Intolerance; a convinced Socialist, has been an active mem. of the Que. Fed. of Indust. Unions Pol. Action Comt.; Home: 1835 St. Joseph Blvd. East, Montreal, Que., H2H 1C8; Office: 4645 D'Iberville St., Montreal, Que., H2H 2L9

PLANCHE, Hon. Hugh Lakin, M.L.A., B.Com.; politician; b. Calgary, Alta. 3 Oct. 1931; s. Clifford C. and Ann Ruth (Easel) P.; e. Univ. of Alta. B. Com.; m. Elizabeth Jean d. Clare Barclay, Calgary, Alta. 5 Dec. 1952; three s. David, Donald, Bruce; MIN. OF ECON. DEVELOPMENT, ALTA. 1979- ; former businessman; el. M.L.A. for Calgary Glenmore prov. g.e. 1975, re-el. 1979; P. Conservative; Protestant; Clubs: Calgary Petroleum; Calgary Golf & Country; Office: 320 Legislative Bldg., Edmonton, Alta. T5K 2B6.

PLASKETT, Harry Hemley, M.A., LL.D., F.R.S. (1936); emeritus professor; astronomer; b. Toronto, Ontario, 5 July 1893; s. John Stanley, D.Sc.; astronomer, and Rebecca Hope (Hemley) P.; e. Ottawa Model Sch.; Ottawa Coll. Inst.; Univ. of Toronto, B.A. 1916; Oxford Univ., M.A.; St. Andrews Univ., LL.D. 1961; m. Edith Alice, d. J. J. Smith, Ottawa, Ont., 4 Jan. 1921; children: Barbara Rochester, John Stanley; Astronomer, Dom. Astrophys. Observatory, Victoria, B.C., 1919-27; Prof. of Astrophys., Harvard Univ., 1928-32; Savilian Prof. of Astronomy, Oxford Univ., 1932-60; Emeritus since; Emeritus Fellow, New Coll., Oxford; served in World War, 1917-1918, as Lieut., 3rd Bgde., 4th Divn., C.F.A.; World War, 1939-45, in 252 H.A.A. Batty. and engaged in navig. research for Min. of Aircraft Prod.; author of articles on observational astrophys. in various observatory publs. and in Monthly Notices, Roy. Astron. Soc.; (Gold Medal, 1963); mem., Roy. Astron. Soc.; Am. Astron. Soc.; Home: 48 Blenheim Drive, Oxford, Eng. OX2 8DQ

PLAUNT, William B.; company president; b. Renfrew, Ont., 2 Sept. 1915; s. William B. and Mildred (Hicks) P.; e. Pub. Schs., North Bay and Sudbury, Ont.; Sudbury (Ont.) High Sch.; St. Andrew's Coll. (Grad. 1935); m. Agnes, d. Leon Roy, 2 Sept. 1939; children: Sandra, Donald, Misty, Mary-Lee, Laurie; PRESIDENT AND DIR., W. B. PLAUNT & SON LIMITED, since 1947; Pres. and Dir., United Broadcasting Ltd.; Dir., General Leaseholds (Sudbury) Ltd.; Wm. Milne & Sons Ltd.; Ash Mount Holding Co. Ltd.; Gray Coach Lines Ltd.; began with present Co. as Gen. Supt.; apptd. Gen. Mgr.; 1940; mem. Sudbury Chamber Comm.; Candn. Assn. Broadcasters; Presbyterian; recreations: fishing, camping; Clubs: Albany (Toronto); Idylwylde Golf & Country; Granite; Copper Cliff; Home: 340 Laura Ave., Sudbury, Ont., P3E 3R9; Office: 336 Ash St., Sudbury, Ontario

PLAUT, Rabbi W. Gunther, O.C., J.S.D., D.D., LL.D., D.Hum.Litt.; author; lecturer; b. Munster, Germany 1 Nov. 1912; s. Jonas and Selma (Gumprich) P.; e. Univ. of Heidelberg; Univ. of Berlin LL.B. 1933, J.S.D., 1934; Hebrew Union Coll. Cincinnati M.H.L. 1939; D.D. 1964; Univ. of Toronto LL.D. 1978; General Coll. of Jewish Studies D.Hum.Litt. 1979; m. Elizabeth d. Harry Strauss 10 Nov. 1938; children: Rabbi Dr. Jonathan Victor, Judith, M.A.; pulpits: Chicago, Ill. 1939-48; St. Paul, Minn. 1948-61; Toronto, Ont. 1961-77; served with U.S. Army as Chaplain 1943-46, rec'd Bronze Star; Chrmn., Gov's. Comn. on Ethics in Govt. (Minn.) 1958-61; Pres., St. Paul Gallery & Sch. of Art 1953-59; World Federalists Can. 1966-68; Un. Jewish Appeal Campaign Toronto 1970; Co-Chrmn. Can.-Israel Comte. 1975-77; Nat. Pres. Candn. Jewish Cong. 1977-80; Vice Chrmn. Ont. Human Rights Comn.; Gov., World Union Progressive Judaism; Vice Pres. Central Conf. Am. Rabbis; Lectr. Haifa Univ. Israel; Fellow, York Univ. Toronto; Councillor, Sch. Continuing Studies Univ. of Toronto; contrib. various newspapers, mags.; editor "Affirmation" (human rights quarterly); frequent TV and radio appearances; Negev Dinner Honouree; rec'd Candn. Council Christians & Jews Humanitarian Award; Sadowski Medal Civic Service; author "The Torah" (commentary) 1981; "Unfinished Business" (autobiog.) 1981; "Numbers" (commentary) 1979; "Hanging Threads" (short stories) 1978, in U.S.A. "The Man in the Blue Vest" 1980; "Time to Think" 1977; "Genesis" (commentary) 1974; and others; recreations: tennis, golf, chess; Clubs: York Raquets; Oakdale Golf & Country; Primrose; Office: Holy Blossom Temple, 1950 Bathurst St., Toronto, Ont. M5P 3K9.

PLESHOYANO, Dan V.; company executive; b. Paris, France 9 June 1929; s. late Virgil V. and Manuela (Soutzo-Vlahoutzi) P.; e. Coll. Ste. Marie, Paris, 1948 Baccalauréat Philosophie-Lettres; Inst. d'Etudes Politiques Paris 1949-51; McGill Univ. post-grad. studies in Econ. 1954-55; Mass. Inst. of Technol. 1967; U.S. Brewers' Acad. 1969; children: Nicolas, Stefan, Alexandra; SR. VICE PRES., PLANNING & DEVELOPMENT, THE MOLSON COMPANIES LTD. 1980- ; joined Banque Canadienne Nationale 1951-52; Merck & Co. Ltd. 1952-54; Econ. Research Analyst, The Royal Bank 1954-55; Financial Analyst, Credit Suisse (Canada) Ltd. 1956-57; joined Que. Div. present Co. as Marketing Research Analyst 1957, Asst. Marketing Research Mgr. 1959, Marketing Research Mgr. 1960 and H.O. 1963, Dir. Marketing Research H.O. 1966, Extve. Asst. to Pres. 1969, Vice Pres. Marketing Que. Div. 1970; Pres. and Dir., Molson Brewery Quebec Ltd. 1975; Extve. Vice Pres. Molson Breweries of Can. Ltd. 1979; Dir., Adv. Comte., CIDEM; Past Pres. La Revue Commerce and Les Editions Commerce; Past Prof. Marketing College Ste-Marie (Montreal); Past Dir. and First Vice Pres., Chambre de Commerce du Distr. de Montréal; Past Dir., CEFECQ (MIC) and CHUDEC; Gov. CRUDEM, N.D. Hospital; mem.: Am. Marketing Assn.; Publicité Club de Montréal (founding member and past 1st Vice Pres.); R. Catholic; recreations: skiing, sailing, reading, travel; Clubs: St-Denis; Royal St. Lawrence Yatch; MAAA; Office: 2 International Blvd., Rexdale, Ont., M9W 1A2

PLETCHER James Henry, B.A.Sc.; public utility executive; b. Cranbrook, B.C., 4 Aug. 1931; s. Henry and Grace P.; e. Pub. and High Schs., South Burnaby, B.C.; Univ. of B.C., B.A.Sc. (Chem. Engn.); m. Engelina Catherina, d. Gerritt Grootenboer, 1955; children: Allan James, Gary Edward, Grace Margaret, Carolin Jo-Ann; SENIOR VICE-PRESIDENT, CANADIAN WESTERN NATURAL GAS CO. LTD. AND NORTHWESTERN UTILITIES, LTD., since 1973; Dir., Candn. Western Natural Gas Co. & Northwestern Utilities Ltd.; Engr., Oil & Gas Conserv. Bd., Alberta, 1955; Evaluation & Gas Engr., Canadian Industrial Gas & Oil Ltd., Calgary, 1963; joined present co.'s as Gas Supply Engr., 1966; Vice Pres. Gas Supply, 1968; mem., Assn. Prof. Engrs., Alta.; Candn. Gas Assn. (Dir.); Candn. Inst. Mining & Metall.; Am. Gas Assn.; Chamber Comm.; Alta. N.W. Chamber of Mines; Conservative; United Church; recreations: golf, hunting, fishing, skiing; Clubs: Earl Grey Golf; Glencoe; Edmonton Petroleum; Mayfair Golf; Royal Glenora; Rotary; Home: 14108 - 47 Ave., Edmonton, Alta., T6H 0B7 Office: 10040 - 104 St., Edmonton, Alta., T5J 0Z2

PLEWES, Lawrence William, C.B.E. (1965) M.A., M.D., F.R.C.S. (Edin.) 1935; orthopaedic surgeon; b. Hants Harbour, Nfld., 17 Nov. 1908; s. W. F. and Ethel (Burns) P.; e. Univ. of Toronto Schs., 1918-25; Univ. of Toronto, B.A. 1929, M.D. 1932, M.A. 1933; Rockefeller Foundation Scholar, 1933; Nuffield Research Scholar, 1938; m. Faith, d. W. F. Downing of London, Eng., 30 Dec. 1939; children: John Lawrence, Richard Franklin; Surgeon in charge of accident services, Luton and Dunstable Hosp., Luton, Beds., Eng.; Consulting Surg. to Luton and Hitchin Group of Hosp.; Chrmn., Bd. of Dirs., Ludun Sheltered Workshop for employment of severely disabled men; mem., Nat. Adv. Comte. to Min. of Labour, on employment of disabled persons; mem., Nuffield Prov. Trust casualty survey team; Treas., B.O.A., 1953-59; Con-

sultant in Rehabilitation, World Health Organ.; author of articles on osteo arthritis of hip, hand and finger infections, rehab. in industry and rehab. in hosp.; author of: "Sudeck's Atrophy", 1956; Progress in Fracture Surgery (British Surgical Practice); Chapter in rehab. in "Recent Advances in Trauma"; Editor of "Accident Service" 1965; Anglican; recreation: gardening; Address: Gate House, Kensworth, Bedfordshire, England LU6 3RH

PLOURDE, Gerard, B.A., M.Com.; business administrator; b. Joliette, Que. 12 Feb. 1916; s. Louis-Georges and Rose deLima (Jolicoeur) P.; e. Jean-de-Brebeuf Coll., Montreal, B.A. 1936; Univ. of Montreal, M.Com. 1939; m. Jeannine, d. R. Martineau, Outremont, Que., 1943; three children; Chrmn. of the Bd., UAP Inc. (formerly United Auto Parts Inc.), since 1970; Vice-Pres. and Dir., Alliance Cie Mutuelle d'Assurance-Vie, The Toronto Dominion Bank; Dir., Bell Canada; Gulf Canada Ltd.; Northern Telecom Ltd.; Rolland Inc.; Steinberg's Inc.; The Molson Companies Ltd.; after being employed by a soap company for one year in the office joined the present organ. as Acc.; in 1945 Co. acquired the interests of International Electric Co. Ltd., Montreal, a Co. specializing in elect. carburation and diesel injection and was placed in charge of and managed that operation, 1945-51; Pres. of the Co. 1951-70; del. from Univ. of Montreal to meeting of Candn. Univ. Students in Winnipeg, and to World's Assn. of Cath. Univ. Students in Wash. D.C., 1939; mem., Montreal Bd. Trade; Chambre de Comm. de Montréal; Soc. of Automotive Engrs.; Roman Catholic; recreations: skiing, golf; Clubs: St-Denis; Laval-sur-le-Lac; Canadian; Home: 6065 de Vimy, Montreal, Que., H3S 2R2; Office: 630 Dorchester Blvd., W., Suite 3210, Montreal, Que. H3B 1S6

PLOURDE, Mt. Rev. Joseph Aurele, D.D., K.H.S.; archbishop (R.C.); b. St. François. Madawaska Co., N.B., 12 Jan. 1915; s. Antoine and Suzanne (Albert) P.; e. Bathurst (N.B.) Coll.; Bourget Coll., Rigaud, Que.; St. Joseph Univ., B.A.; Holy Heart Semy., Halifax; Univ. of Ottawa, Lic. in Social Studies; Gregorian Univ., Rome; Univ. of Moncton, Ph.D. (Hon.) in Educ.; ARCHBISHOP, ARCHDIOCESE OF OTTAWA; Past Pres., Candn. Cath. Conf.; Chancellor, St. Paul's Univ., Ottawa; served with RCA Chaplain Corps during World War 11; Kt. of Malta; Address: 143 St. Patrick St., Ottawa, Ont. K1N 5K1

PLOW, Maj.-Gen. Hon. Edward Chester, C.B.E. (1945), D.S.O. (1944), C.D., D.C.L., D.M.S.; b. St. Albans, Vt., 28 Sept. 1904; s. late John & Hortense Harlow (Lynch) P.; e. Rossland Ave. Sch., Westmount, Que.; Lower Canada College, Montreal; Westmount (Que.) High School; Royal Military College, Kingston, Ont., 1921-25; m. Mary Nichols, d. late T. E. G. Lynch, Digby, Nova Scotia, 8 Sept. 1937; one d. Kathleen Mary Locklin; commnd. in R.C.H.A., 1925, and served in various appointments in Canada, and the U.K. until 1939; served overseas in U.K., Italy and N.W. Europe during World War, 1939-45, chiefly as Arty. Staff Offr. and Commdr.; during latter part of War was Sr. Arty. Offr. to Candn. Army; Twice Mentioned in Despatches; awarded Commdr., Order of Orange Nassau (Netherlands); after War served with Occupational troops in Germany and various appointments in Can. & U.K.; G.O.C. Eastern Command, Can., 1950-58; Lieut-Gov. of N.S., 15 Jan. 1958-March 1963; K.St.J.; Dir., Candn. Imperial Bank of Commerce 1963-74; mem. of the Bd. of Govs. of the Izaak Walton Killam Hosp. for Sick Children, Halifax; Bd. of Govs., Candn. Corps of Comms.; Patron, St. John Ambulance Assn.; Life Mem., Roy. Candn. Artillery Assn.; Anglican; Club: Brockville Country; Halifax; Address: "Locklands", R.R. 1, Brockville, Ont., K6V 5T1

PLUMMER, Christopher, C.C. (1968); actor; b. Toronto, Ont., of parents native of Montreal, 13 Dec. 1929; e. Montreal High Sch.; m. 1stly Tammy Lee Grimes (actress), 19 Aug. 1956; one d. Amanda Michael (marriage dissolved); 2ndly, Patricia Audrey Lewis (journalist), 4 May 1962, (marriage dissolved); spent most of his early youth in Senneville, Que.; began training for the stage under Doreen Lewis of the Montreal Repertory Theatre, and Rosanna Seaborn Todd of the Open Air Theatre Company; first professional appearance made at age 17 at Ottawa, Ont., and thereafter for the next two yrs. played in over 75 productions, incl. Shakespeare, Moliere and Shaw plays; also engaged in some radio work; made first Broadway appearance in "The Starcross Story", followed by "Home Is the Hero" and "The Dark Is Light Enough", and as 'Jason' in "Medea" at the International Festival in Paris, later winning considerable applause for his role in "The Lark" (1955); played Mark Antony opposite Raymond Massey's Brutus in Stratford, Conn. Shakespearean Festival; first played Stratford (Ont.) Shakespearean Festival in "Henry V", 1956, proceeding with it to the Edinburgh Festival; played Shakespeare Festival, Stratford, Ont., July 1957, title part in "Hamlet" and Sir Andrew Aguecheek in "Twelfth Night"; June 1958, played Benedick in "Much Ado About Nothing", Leontes in "The Winter's Tale" and Bardolph in "Henry IV" Part 1; A.N.T.A., N.Y., Dec. 1958; played Nickles in 1960, played The Bastard in "King John", Mercutio in "Romeo and Juliet"; made his debut at Shakespeare Mem. Theatre, Stratford-on-Avon in title role of "Richard III" and Benedick in "Much Ado About Nothing"; played Henry II in London production of "Becket" at Aldwych Theatre and later starred same role in West End; summer of 1962, returned to Stratford, Ont., to appear as Cyrano in "Cyrano de Bergerac", 11 Nov. 1963; starred on Broadway in title role of "Arturo Ui" by Brecht, Nov. 1963; last appeared on New York Stage in the role of 'Pizzarro' in "The Royal Hunt of the Sun" in 1965; made first film appearance 1957; starred in "Fall of The Roman Empire", "The Sound of Music" and "Inside Daisy Clover"; more film engagements were "The Man Who Would Be King", 1975; "Return of the Pink Panther", 1975; "Conduct Unbecoming", 1975; "The Silent Partner, 1979"; "Night of the Generals" - "Triple Cross" - "Oedipus Rex" (filmed in Greece) - "Nobody Runs Forever" - "Lock Up Your Daughters" - "Battle of Britain" and "The Royal Hunt of the Sun"; made first T.V. appearance in 1953; has been starred in "Oedipus Rex"; "The Lady's not for Burning", "The Doll's House", "The Prince and the Pauper", "Little Moon of Alba", "Captain Brassbound's Conversion", "Cyrano de Bergerac", "Prisoner of Zenda", "Time Remembered". "Macbeth" (Telstar) and "Hamlet"; recreations: skiing, piano, tennis; Club: Player's (N.Y.); Address: c/o Stanley Gorrie Whitson & Co., Cavendish Sq., London, England

PLUMMER, George Frederick, F.C.A.; company officer; b. Westmount, Que., 5 Nov. 1914; s. Cyril Percy and Violet May (Brown) P.; e. N. Toronto Coll. Inst., Toronto, Ont. (Sr. Matric. 1933); Inst. of Chart. Accts. of Ont. C.A. 1940; m. Adelene. d. late Albert Lewis Lipsett, 20 May 1944; children: Douglas George, Wendy Ann Elizabeth, Lynn Margot, David John; PRES. AND DIR., G.F. PLUMMER & ASSOCIATES LTD.; Chrmn. and Dir., Trent Rubber Services Ltd.; Dir., Grant Bros. Ltd.; joined Dunlop Canada Ltd. in 1940 as Br. Auditor; Mgr., Br. Clerical Operations, 1941; Cost Acct., 1945; Asst. Secy-Treas., 1947; Secy.-Treas., 1948; Asst. to Dir. of Production & Research, Dunlop Rubber Co. Ltd., England, 1952; Asst. Gen. Mgr., 1953; el. a Dir., 1954; Vice-Pres. (Auto Div.) 1955-59; Vice-Pres., Dir. and Gen. Mgr., 1959-61; Pres. 1961-68; Chrmn. 1968; Pres. (1968-69) Rubber Assn. Can.; Chrmn. United Way 1974-75; Chrmn. Ont. Congress Centre, Citizens' Comte. Anglican; Clubs: Granite; National; Canada (London, Eng.); Board of Trade; Home: 6 Brian Cliff Dr., Don Mills, Ont., M3B 2G2; Office: Suite 409, 120 Adelaide St. W., Toronto, Ont. M5H 1T1

PLUMPTRE, Beryl Alyce (Mrs. Arthur Fitzwalter Wynne), B.Com, D.C.L., LL.D. (Hon.); retired econo-

mist; b. Melbourne, Australia, 27 Dec. 1908; d. Edward Charles and Alyce Maud (Hughes) Rouch; e. Presb. Ladies' Coll., Melbourne; Univ. of Melbourne, B.Com. 1931; Cambridge Univ., post-grad. work; m. 21 May 1938; children: Mrs. Alexander Gillam Wedderspoon, Timothy Wynne; Chairman, Food Prices Review Board since 1973-75; Vice Chrmn. A.I.B. 1975-76; Dir., Canada Permanent Mortgage Corp.; The Canada Life Assce. Co.; Canada Permanent Trust Co.; Dominion Stores Ltd.; Pres., Vanier Institute of the Family, 1968-73; mem., Econ. Council of Can.; Ont. Econ. Council; Candn. Consumer Council; Research Offr., W.P.T.B., 1946-47; Econ. Consultant, Tariff Bd., 1954-55; Econ. Consultant, Royal Comn. on Coasting Trade; mem., Toronto Bd., Children's Aid Soc., 1947-48 and Ottawa Bd., 1950-51; Dir., Consumers' Assn. of Can. (Nat. Pres. 1961-66); mem. Bd, Family Service Agency, Ottawa, 1962-64; Dir., Candn. Welfare Council; Pres., Kidney Foundation (Ottawa Valley);Gov. Carleton Univ.; recreations: reading, ornithology, golf; Club: Royal Ottawa Golf; Address: 85 Lakeway Dr., Rockcliffe Park, Ottawa, Ont., K1L 5A9

POCKLINGTON, Peter H., executive; b. Regina, Sask. 18 Nov. 1941; s. Basil B. and Eileen (Dempsey) P.; e. Medway High Sch. London, Ont.; m. Eva d. Jack McAvoy 2 June 1974; two s., two d.; CHRMN., POCKLINGTON FINANCIAL CORP. LTD.; Pres., Westown Ford, Tilbury, Ont. 1967-69; Chatham, Ont. 1969-71; Edmonton, Alta. 1971- ; formed Patrician Land Corp. Ltd. 1973 (owner Edmonton Oiler NHL Hockey Club); acquired control Fidelity Trust 1979; Christian; recreations: boat racing, skiing; Clubs: London (Ont.) Hunt & Country; Primrose (Toronto); Mayfair Golf & Country (Edmonton); Office: 2500 Sun Life Place, 10123-99 Street, Edmonton, Alta. T5J 3H1.

POCOCK, Mt. Rev. Philip Francis, D.D., J.C.D., LL.D. (R.C.): retired archbishop; b. St. Thomas, Ont.; s. Stephen Bernard and Sarah-May (McCarthy) P.; e. London (Ont.) Coll. Inst.; Assumption Coll., Windsor, Ont.; St. Peter's Semy., London, Ont.; Windsor, Ont.; St. Peter's Semy., London, Ont.; Cath. Univ. of Am.; Angelico, Rome, J.C.D. 1934; LL.D. W. Ont. 1955, Ottawa, 1958, Man. 1958, Aussumption 1961; o. Priest 1930; Prof. of Moral Theol. and Canon Law, St. Peter's Semy., London, Ont., 1934-44; Bishop of Saskatoon, 1944-51; Coadjutor Archbishop of Winnipeg 1951-52, Archbishop, 1952-61; Coadjutor Archbishop of Toronto, Feb. 1961; Archbishop of Toronto, 1971-78; Address: 3 Woodbrook Dr., Brampton, Ont., L6W 3P2

PODLECKI, Anthony Joseph, M.A., Ph.D.; educator; b. Buffalo, N.Y. 25 Jan. 1936; s. Anthony Joseph and Eugenia Evelyn (Jendrasiak) P.; e. Canisius High Sch. Buffalo 1953; Coll. of Holy Cross Worcester, Mass. B.A. 1957; Lincoln Coll. Oxford Univ. B.A. 1960, M.A. 1962; Univ. of Toronto M.A. 1961, Ph.D. 1963; m. Jennifer Julia d. Prof. G.M.A. Grube, Toronto, Ont. 28 July 1962; children: Christopher, Julia, Antonia; PROF. AND HEAD OF CLASSICS, UNIV. OF B.C. 1975- ; Part-time Instr. in Classics Trinity Coll. Univ. of Toronto 1961-62; Instr. and Asst. Prof. of Classics Northwestern Univ. 1963-66; Assoc. Prof. and Head of Classics Pa. State Univ. 1966, Prof. and Head of Classics 1970-75; Visiting Fellow, Wolfson Coll. Oxford 1970; author "The Political Background of Aeschylean Tragedy" 1966; "Aeschylus 'The Persians'" verse transl. with commentary 1970; "The Life of Themistocles" 1975; "Age of Glory; Imperial Athens in the Age of Pericles" 1975; Ed. "Ancient Ships" 1964; co-ed. "Panathenaia: Studies in Athenian Life and Thought in the Classical Age" 1979; various articles Classical Greek hist. and lit.; mem. Am. Philol. Assn.; Classical Assn. Can.; Archaeol. Inst. Am.; Candn. Mediterranean Inst.; Cambridge Philol. Assn.; Classical Assn. Gt. Brit.; Jt. Assn. Classics Teachers; Classical Assn. Pacific Northwest (Pres. 1977-78); Classical Assn. Candn. W. (Extve. Comte.); NDP; R. Catholic; recreations: sailing, choral singing; Home: 4524 W. 7th Ave., Vancouver, B.C. V6R 1X3; Office: 1866 Main Mall, Vancouver, B.C. V6T 1W5.

POINTING, Arthur Derham; retired company director; b. Bath, Eng., 6 Dec. 1897; s. Henry Derham and Ada (Martin) P.; e. Portway Sch., Bath, Eng.; m. Mary Catherine Alberta Ahern, 1932; children: Philip James, John Derham, Dorothy Anne; Dir., Sir Isaac Pitman and Sons (Can.) Limited (formerly Chairman of Board) ret. 1980; joined Sir Isaac Pitman and Sons Ltd., Bath, Eng. 1913; Br. Mgr., Sir Isaac Pitman and Sons (Can.) Ltd., 1923-33, Mang. Dir. 1933-46, Pres., 1946-63; served in 1st World War N. Somerset Yeomanry, Somerset Light Inf. and R.A.F., 1915-19; Anglican; recreations: gardening, reading, photography; Home: 9 Forest Wood, Toronto, Ont., M5N 2V5

POIRIER, Rolland, B.A., B.A.S., M.S., Ph.D., Canadian public service; b. Montreal, Que., 20 July 1917; s. Samuel and Emma (Demers) P.; e. Coll. Brebeuf, B.A. 1938; Inst. Agric. d'Oka, B.A.S. 1949; Iowa State Univ., M.S. 1951, Ph.D. 1952; m. Mariette, d. late Eugene Lachapelle, 6 Sept. 1941; three s. Jacques, Jean-Guy, Claude; CHRMN., FARM CREDIT CORP., OTTAWA, since 1977; Sales Mgr. of Feeds Div. for Que., Maple Leaf Mills Ltd., 1956-59; Prof. of Animal Breeding, Macdonald Coll., 1959-62; Dean, Faculty of Agric. Laval Univ. 1962-67; Asst. Depy. Min. Agric. Can. 1967-75; Vice Pres., Candn. International Development Agency, 1975-77; served overseas in the 2nd World War with Royal Canadian Artillery 1942-45; discharged with Royal Canadian Artillery 1942-45; discharged with rank of Lieut.; mem., Corp des Agronomes; Agric. Inst. Can.; Candn. Agric. Economics Soc.; R. Catholic; recreations: skiing, fishing; Home: 1833 Riverside Dr., #807, Ottawa, Ont., K1G 0E8

POISSANT, Charles Albert, C.A.; b. Montreal, Que., 13 Sept. 1925; s. Adrien and A. (Courchesne) P.; e. L'Ecole des Hautes Etudes de Montréal, Diplome; m. Florence d. Georges Drouin, 23 June 1951; children: Louise, Marc André, Hélène, Isabelle, SR. PARTNER, THORNE, RIDDELL & CO.; Adv. to Senate Standing Comte. on Banking Trade & Commerce; Dir., Beaubrau Inc.; Verry Management; mem. Extve. Comte. and Past Pres., (Candn. Branch) Internat. Fiscal Assn.; mem. of the Bd. of Management, Université du Quebec à Montréal; Mem. of Bureau de l'Ordre des comptables agréés du Qué.; Pres., Legislative Committee of the Order; Roman Catholic; recreation: golf; Clubs: St. Denis; Laval-sur-le-Lac; Mount Royal; Home: 333 Somerville, Ahuntsie, Que., H3L 1A4; Office: 630 W. Dorchester, Suite 2500, Montreal, Que.

POITRAS, Jean-Marie, O.C.; insurance executive; b. Macamic, Québec 1918; e. Séminaire de Québec; Académie de Québec, Univ. Laval; m. Thérèse Michaud 29 July 1944; six children: Michel, Claude, Claire, Lise, Diane, Marie; CHRMN. OF THE BD. AND CHIEF EXEC. OFFICER, THE LAURENTIAN GROUP CORP.; Chrmn. of Bd, Pres. & Chief Extve Offr. The Laurentian Mutual Insur.; The Provident Assur. Co.; The Laurentien General Insur. Co.; The Laurentian Shield Insur. Co.; The Personal Insur. Co. of Canada; The Canadian Providentien General Insur.; Chrmn. of Bd. & Pres. Paragon Insur. Co. of Canada; Vice Chrmn. of Bd. The Imperial Life Assur. Co. of Canada; Loyal Amer. Life Insur. Co.; The Northern Life Assur. Co. of Canada; Vice Pres. The Laurentian Fund Inc; Dir. Imbrook Properties Ltd; Chrmn. F-I-C Fund Inc.; Vice Pres. La Cité Travel Inc.; Pres. The Laurentian Real Estate Investments Inc.; Chrmn. of Bd. Netcom Inc.; Vice Chrmn. of Bd. Montreal City and District Savings Bank; Dir. Alcan Aluminium Limited; Crédit Foncier Inc.; Novacap Inc.; Sodarcan Inc.; formerly owner J.E. Poitras Enr. 1940-59 and Pres. & Gen. Mgr. J.E. Poitras Inc. 1959-73; served with Royal Candn. Ordnance Corps, rank Lt.; Bd. mem. Candn. Chamber Comm; Chrmn. Bd. Govs. Chamber Comm. Prov. Que. (pres. 1977-78); Founding Pres., Ins. Inst. Que. Chapter

1954-56; Pres. Tourist & Convention Bureau Metrop. Que. 1969-70; Bd. Trade Dist. Que. 1969-70; Que. Symphony Orchestra 1970; La Régie du Grande Théâtre de Qué. 1970-76; Vice Pres. L'Opéra du Québec 1971-76; Commdr. Equestrian Order of The Holy Sepulchre of Jerusalem, 1972; recreations: fishing, hunting, philately, numismatics; Clubs: Garrison Club; Cercle Universitaire (Québec); Cercle de la Place d'Armes (Montréal); Home: 1155 Turnbull Ave, #903, Quebec, Que. G1R 5G3; Office: 500 Grande-Allée E., Québec, Qué. G1R 2J7.

POITRAS, Hon. Lawrence, B.A., LL.L.; judge; b. Montreal, Que., 3 Apl. 1931; s. late Harold Edward and Anne-Marie (Gendron) P.; e. Loyola High Sch. 1948; Loyola Coll. 1951; McGill Univ. B.A. 1953; Univ. de Montréal LL.L 1957; m. Marie-Thérèse, d. Arsène Boivin 10 May 1958; children: Thomas Harold, Anne-Marie, Marie-Claire; JUSTICE OF SUPERIOR COURT QUE. since 1975; read law with Duquet, MacKay, Weldon & Tetrault; called to Bar of Que., 1957; cr. Q.C. 1972; part-time newspaperman The Montreal Star 1948-57; mem. law firm Duquet, MacKay, Weldon & Tetrault 1957-70; Partner, Laing, Weldon, Courtois, Clarkson, Parsons, Gonthier & Tetrault 1970-75; Lectr. in Commercial. Law McGill Univ. 1964; Dir. Royal Edward Laurentian Foundation; mem. Extve. Comte. Que. Dir. & Vice Pres. Candn. Red Cross Soc.; Gov. Hôpital Marie-Enfant 1976-81; Dir. and Vice-Pres., Montreal Chest Hospital; rec'd Distinguished Service Award Town of Dollard des Ormeaux 1975; mem. Candn. Bar Assn. (served in various capacities incl. mem. Que. Council 1972-76 and Nat. Council 1973-76); mem., Qué. S.C. Judges General Comte., 1977-81; Dir., Vice-Chrmn. (1979-81), and Chmn. (1981-82), Candn. Judges Conference; Gov. and mem. of exec. comte. of Candn. Inst. for Advanced Legal Studies; R. Catholic; recreations: tennis, squash, skiing, golf; Clubs: Montreal Badminton & Squash (Dir. 1975-78); Shawbridge Golf & Country (Dir. 1976-81); Home: 46 Glamis St., Dollard des Ormeaux, Que., H9A 1M5; Office: Montreal Court House, 1 Notre Dame St. E., Montreal, Que., H2Y 1B6

POLANYI, John Charles, C.C., Ph.D., D.Sc., LL.D., F.R.S., F.R.S.C.; educator; b. 23 Jan. 1929; e. Manchester Grammar Sch. Eng; Manchester Univ. B.Sc. 1949, M.Sc. 1950, Ph.D. 1952, D.Sc. 1964; Hon. D.Sc.: Univ. Waterloo 1970, Mem. Univ. Nfld. 1976, McMaster Univ. 1977, Carleton Univ., 1981; Hon. LL.D. Trent Univ. 1977; m. Anne Ferrar Davidson 1958; one s., one d.; UNIV. PROF., UNIV. OF TORONTO since 1974 and Prof. of Chem. since 1962; Postdoctoral Fellow, Nat. Research Council Can. 1952-54; Research Assoc. Princeton Univ. 1954-56; Lectr. Univ. of Toronto 1956, Asst. Prof. 1957, Assoc. Prof. 1960; awards and lectureships: Sloan Foundation Fellow 1959-63; Marlow Medal Faraday Soc. 1962; Centenary Medal and Lectureship Chem. Soc. Gt. Brit. 1965; Steacie Prize Natural Science (co-recipient) 1965; Noranda Award & Lectureship Chem. Inst. Can. 1967; Mack Award & Lectureship Ohio State Univ. 1969; William D. Harkins Lectr. Univ. Chicago 1970; Reilly Lectr. Univ. Notre Dame 1970; Purves Lectr. McGill Univ. 1971; Brit. Chem. Soc. Award 1971; F. J. Toole Lectr. Univ. N.B. 1974; Philips Lectr. Haverford Coll. 1974; Kistiakowsky Lectr. Harvard Univ. 1975; Camille & Henry Dreyfus Lectr. Univ. Kansas 1975; J. W. T. Spinks Lectr. Univ. Sask. 1976; Laird Lectr. Univ. W. Ont. 1976; Chem. Inst. Can. Medal 1976; Hon. Foreign mem. Am. Acad. Arts & Science 1976; Henry Marshall Tory Medal Royal Soc. Can. 1977; CIL Distinguished Lectr. Simon Fraser Univ. 1977; Gucker Lectr. Ind. Univ. 1977; Remsen Award & Lectureship Am. Chem. Soc. 1978; Jacob Bronowski Memorial Lectr., Univ. of Toronto 1978; Hutchison Lectr., Univ. of Rochester 1979; Companion, Order of Can. 1979; Guggenheim Memorial Fellow 1979-80; Foreign Assoc. Nat. Acad. Sciences USA 1978; Priestly Lectr., Penn State Univ., 1980; publications: over 100 papers scient. journs., articles on science policy and control of armaments various journs., newspapers, mags.; film: "Concepts in Reaction Dynamics'' 1970; co-ed. ''The Dangers of Nuclear War'' 1979; Home: 3 Rosedale Rd., Toronto, Ont. M4W 2P1; Office: Toronto, Ont. M5S 1A1.

POLLACK, Isidore Constantine, B.A., LL.L.; lawyer; b. Quebec City, Qué., 30 Oct. 1913; s. Maurice and Rebecca (Tourantour) P.; e. Comnrs. High Sch., Que.; McGill Univ., B.A.; Laval Univ., LL.L.; m. Roselee d. late Edward A. Hart, Hartford, Conn., 24 July 1950; children: Adelle-Laudrey, Jon Hart; MEM., LETORNEAU AND ASSOCS.; Dir., Trizec Corporation Limited; Dir. and mem. Executive Committee, Trust Général du Canada; Chairman, Quebec Port Authority; Can. Employment and Immigration Advisory Council; practised law with Angers, Caisse & Pollack, Montreal, 1938-39; Department of External Affairs, Ottawa, 1947-51; Secy. Gen. Candn. Del. to U.N., 1950; Pres. and Mang. Dir. M. Pollack Ltée 1951-69; served as Lieut., R.C.N., 1939-46; retired with rank of Commdr.; Past Pres., Chamber Comm. & Indust. Metrop. Que.; Vice Pres., Can.-Israel Chamber Comm. & Indust.; mem., Senate & Conseil, Univ. Laval; Can. Manpower & Immigration Council; Extve. Comte. & Bd. Govs., Candn. Council on Social Devel.; Bd. Govs., Weizmann Inst. Science; Dir., Nat. Youth Orchestra; World Wildlife Fund (Can.); recreations: fishing, tennis, farming; Clubs: Quebec Winter; Montefiore (Montreal); Cap Rouge Golf; Home: Abel Skiver Farm, 3805 Ste. Foy Rd., St. Foy, Que., G1X 1T1; Office: 65 rue Ste. Anne, Suite 326, Quebec, Que., G1R 3X5

POLUNIN, Nicholas, M.A., M.S., D.Phil., D.Sc., C.B.E., F.R.G.S., F.R.Hort.S., F.L.S.; enviromentalist (formerly scientific explorer); author; editor; b. Checkendon, Oxfordshire, Eng., 26 June 1909; s. late Vladimir and Elizabeth Violet (Hart) P.; e. The Hall Sch., Weybridge, Surrey; Latymer Upper Sch., London, Eng.; Oxford Univ. (Christ Church, Open Scholar), B.A. (1st Class Hons., Bot. & Ecol.) 1932; Yale Univ. (Pierson Coll., Henry Fellow), M.S. 1934; Oxford Univ. (New Coll.), Sr. Research Scholar 1934-36; Oxford Univ., M.A. 1935, D.Phil. 1935, D.Sc. 1942; Harvard Univ. (Research Assoc.) 1936-37; m. Helen Eugenie d. late Douglas Argyle Campbell, Toronto, Ont. & Montreal, Que., and g.d. of Senator Hon. Archibald Campbell, Toronto, Ont., 3 Jan. 1948; children: April Xemia, Dr. Nicholas Vladimir Campbell, Douglas Harold Hart; Secy.-Gen. & Editor, Internat. Confs. on Environmental Future, since 1971; Founding ed., Environmental Conservation since 1974; Pres. Foundation for Environmental Conservation since 1975; Convener & Gen. Ed., Environmental Monographs & Symposia, since 1979; Member, Oxford Univ. Lapland Expdn, 1930; Hudson Strait (Labrador and Akpatok Island) Expdn 1931; explored Corsican Mountains 1932; conducted pte expdns across Lapland, winter and spring 1933, and across Spitsbergen (summer 1933); Fla and Rocky Mts (1934); Candn E. Arctic patrols around Hudson Bay and Strait and to Southampton, Baffin, Devon, and Ellsmere Islands, 1934 and 1936; higher Alps 1935; own expdns (sponsored by the British Museum) to S.W. Greenland in 1937 (where discovered plants introduced by Vikings from Am.) and N.W. Iceland in 1938; Candn. E. Arctic Airborne Expdn. 1946 (confirmed Spicer Islands in Foxe Basin, & discovered last large islands which were confirmed by R.C.A.F. in 1948 and in 1949 named Price Charles Is. & Air Fiorce Is. & finally put on world map(1); W. Arctic 1947, incl. north magnetic pole; visited Alaska and made flight over geog. north pole Sept. 1948 making first recorded observation of microbial life in atmosphere there, also winter flight over north pole Mar. 1949, making various scient. observations; field work in Candn E. Sub-Arctic and Arctic northwards to Cornwallis Island (summer) 1949; collections in Museum of Natural Sciences, Ottawa, U.S. Nat. Herbarium, Washington, D.C., Gray Herbarium of Harvard Univ., Br. Museum (Nat. Hist.) etc.; Fielding Curator and Keeper of the Univ. Herbaria, Univ. Demonst. and Lect. in Bot., Oxford Univ., 1939-47; Lect. of New Coll., Oxford from 1942, and sub-

sequently also Sr Research Fellow there; Visiting Prof. of Bot., McGill Univ. 1946-47; Macdonald Prof. of Botany, McGill Univ., 1947-52; Haley Lecturer at Acadia Univ. 1950; Lecturer in Plant Geography at Yale Univ. and in Biology at Brandeis Univ. 1953-55, while Director of U.S. Air Force Research Project; Professor of Plant Ecology and Taxonomy, Dir. of Univ. Herbarium, etc., and Head of Dept of Botany, Univ. College of Arts and Science, Baghdad, Iraq, 1956-59; while advising on establ. of Univ. of Bagdad; Guest Prof., Univ. of Geneva, 1959-61 & 1975-76; Prof. of Botany and Head of Dept. 1962-66 and Founding Dean of Faculty of Science, Univ. of Ife, Ibadan and Ile-Ife, Nigeria, where also Dir. of Biol. Garden & helped to plan main campus; Ed. of ''International Industry'', 1943-46; Founding Ed. of World Crops Books 1954-74 and of Plant Science Monographs 1954-78; Founding Ed. of ''Biological Conservation'' 1967-74; Founding Ed. of ''Enviromental Conservation'' 1974- ; awarded Goldsmith's Sr. Studentship at Christ Ch., Oxford, 1932; Henry Fellowship, Yale University 1933; Department of Scient. & Indust. Research (London), Sr. Research Award, 1935-38; Foreign Research Assoc., Harvard Univ., 1938; Rolleston Mem. Prize 1938; Leverhulme Research Award, 1941; Arctic Inst. of N. Am. Research Fellowship, 1946-47; Guggenheim Fellowship, 1950-52; Research Fellowship of Harvard Univ., 1950-53; Ford Foundation Award in Scandinavia and U.S.S.R., 1966-67; Medaille Marie-Victoria for services to Canadian Botany; U.S. Order of Polaris; Comndr. Br. Empire; served during 2nd World War as vol. mem. of Home Guard (Intelligence Offr., Oxford), 1942-45; author of ''Russian Water'', 1931; ''The Isle of Auks'', 1932; ''Arctic Unfolding'', 1949; ''Introduction to Plant Geography'', 1960; ''Eleménts de Géographie Botanique'', 1967; ''Circumpolar Arctic Flora'', 1959, reports and bulls. for Dept. of Mines & Resources; 3 Vols. on ''Botany of the Canadian Eastern Arctic'', 1940, 1947, 1948; ''The Environmental Future'' (Ed.), 1972; Ed. ''Growth without Ecodisasters?'' 1980; numerous research and review articles contrib. to various Brit., Candn., U.S., Scandinavian & Swiss journs., chiefly on arctic plant taxonomy, phytogeog. and ecology, also on aerobiology and, latterly, conservation; Fellow, A.A.A.S.; Arctic Inst. of N.Am.; first Hon. mem., Biological Soc. of Iraq; mem., Brit. Ecological Soc.; Systematics Assn.; Internat. Union for Conservation of Nature and Natural Resources; Bot. Soc. Am. (Life mem.); Bot. Soc. Br. Isles (Life mem.); Brit. Assn. Advanc. Science (Life); Am. Fern Soc. (Life); Sigma Xi; Christian; recreations: travel, walking, stock markets; Clubs: Life mem. Torrey Botanical; Life mem. Harvard (N.Y.C.); Life mem. Field-Naturalists' (Ottawa); Life mem. Reform (London); Address: Environmental Conservation, 15 ch. F.-Lehmann, 1218 Grand-Saconnex, Geneva, Switzerland.

POMERLEAU, René, O.C., D.Sc., LL.D.; forest pathologist; b. Saint-Ferdinand, Qué. 27 Apl. 1904; s. Pierre and Éxérile P.; e. Saint-Joseph Coll. Saint-Ferdinand 1920; Laval Univ. B.S.A. 1924; Macdonald Coll. McGill Univ. M.Sc. 1927; La Sorbonne, Univ. de Paris 1927-29; École Nationale des Eaux et Forêts, Nancy, France 1929-30; Univ. de Montréal D.Sc. 1937; Sir George Williams Univ. LL.D. 1970; m. Cécile d. Laurent Mesnard 12 Oct. 1932; Forest Pathol. Dept. Lands & Forests Qué. 1930-52; Dir. de recherches, Lab. of Forest Pathol. Candn. Dept. Forestry, Qué. 1952-70; teacher Faculty of Forestry Laval Univ. 1940-65, Faculty of Science 1942-65; rec'd prix David (Qué.) 1937; Médaille Pariseau (ACFAS) 1955; Médaille de la Fondation Marie-Victorin 1970; Maple Leaf Award 1969; Médaille du Centenaire de la Société de Géographie de Qué. 1977; Prix Marie-Victorin 1981; Prof. émérite de l'Univ. Laval 1981; author ''Champignons de l'Est au Canada et des Etats-Unis'' 1951 (Eng. version also); ''Flore des Champignons du Québec'' 1980; over 250 papers tree diseases, mycology, nature conserv.; Founder Mycol. Clubs Montréal 1950, Québec City 1951; Trustee, N. Am. Mycol. Assn.; mem. Royal Soc. Can. (Convener

Plant Biol. Sec. 1966); Société Linnéenne de Qué. (Prés. 1944); Assn. Canadienne-française pour l'Avancement des Sciences (Prés. 1951-52); Société de Géographie de Qué. (Prés. 1970-72); R. Catholic; recreation: field mycology; Address: 1395 parc Champoux, Québec 6, Qué. G1S 1L7.

PONTE, Vincent de Pasciuto, M.A.; city planning consultant; b. Boston, Mass., 27 Oct. 1919; s. Salvatore Raffaele and Marie (Mitrano) P.; e. Harvard Univ., B.A. 1943, M.A. (City Planning) 1949; Univ. of Rome (Fullbright Scholar) 1953-54; came to Can. 1967; HHFA-FHA Site Planning, Washington, D.C., 1950; N.Y. City Planning Dept., Asst. Planner in Transport., 1951-52; Webb & Knapp Inc., Urban Redevel. Dir., N.Y., 1956-58; I. M. Pei & Assocs., N.Y. 1959-63; established Vincent Ponte, Planning Consultant, Montreal, 1964; specialist in problems of downtown areas planning research for large-scale pub. and private projects in N. Am., European and Australian cities; proponent of "Multi-Level city"; prof. advisor to Selective Am. Realty Fund N.V.; master planning of pedestrian systems, office and retail projects across Can.; Consultant to Nat. Capital Comn.; Guest Lectr., Univs. of Montreal, State, Houston, York Univ. (Eng.), Rice Univ., Columbia Univ.; author or co-author: "The American Civil Engineering Practice", 1957; "To Everything There Is A Season", 1967; "Institute of Planning and Zoning", 1968; other writings incl. various articles related to arch.; mem., Candn. Inst. Planners; La Corp. Prof. des Urbanistes Que.; Am. Inst. Planners; Roman Catholic; recreations: books (history), sailing; Home: 3450 Drummond St., #921, Montreal, Que., H3G 1Y3

POOLE, James Winfield, B.A., B.Ed., M.A., S.T.D.; educator; b. St. Stephen, N.B. 16 July 1926; s. Victor Bliss and Florence Agnes (Osborne) P.; e. Milltown (N.B.) High Sch. 1943; St. Joseph's Univ. Memramcook, N.B. 1943-45; Univ. de Montréal B.A. 1947, S.T.B. 1950, S.T.L. 1951, S.T.D. 1952; St. Thomas Univ. B.Ed. 1953; Fordham Univ. M.A. 1962; Univ. of Toledo 1968-69; Univ. of Maryland 1980-81; VICE PRES. (ACAD.) ST. THOMAS UNIV. since 1977; Prof. of Math. present Univ. 1954-75, Acting Vice Pres. (Acad.) 1975-77, Pres. Faculty Assn. 1972-73; Pres. Fed. N.B. Faculty Assns. 1973-74; mem. Candn. Math. Cong.; Math. Assn. Am.; Humanities Assn. Can.; Candn. Inst. Internat. Affairs; Candn. Profs. for Peace in Middle E. (Secy.-Treas. Fredericton Chapter 1976-77); Sigma Xi; R. Catholic; recreations: theatre, classical music, travel; Address: St. Thomas Univ., Fredericton, N.B. E3B 5G3.

POOLE, William Robert, Q.C.; b. Neepawa, Man., 16 May 1918; s. John Silas and Mary Elizabeth (McFadden) P.; e. Univ. of Man. B.A. 1939; McGill Univ., Post Grad. Eng., 1945-46; Osgoode Hall Law Sch., 1946-49; m. Nancy Helen, d. late John Hardy Geddes, 15 Aug. 1952; one d. Andrea Mary; PARTNER, POOLE, BELL & PORTER; Prof.; Criminal Law, Univ. of Western Ont.; mem., Ont. Law Reform Comn.; Atty. Gen. Comte. on the Admin. of Justice for Ont.; called to Bar of Ont., 1949; Q.C., 1959; served during 2nd World War with R.C.N., 1939-45; retired with rank of Lt. Commdr.; Chrmn. (1967-68) London Public Lib.; mem., Candn. Bar. Assn.; Middlesex Law Assn.; Zeta Psi; recreations: reading, gardening; Clubs: London; London Hunt; Rideau (Ottawa); York (Toronto); University (Toronto); Canadian (Past Pres.); Home: R.R. No. 5, London, Ont., N6A 4B9; Office: 444 Waterloo St., London, Ont., N6B 2P3

POPE, Hon. Alan William, M.P.P., B.A., LL.B.; politician; b. Ayr, Scot. 2 Aug. 1945; s. Reginald Harry P.; e. Timmins High Sch.; Waterloo Lutheran Univ.; Osgoode Hall Law Sch.; m. Linda Marie d. Tony Fillion, Mattice, Ont. 18 Dec. 1976; MIN. OF NATURAL RESOURCES, ONT. 1981- ; Ald. City of Timmins 1973-74; Nat. Pres. Young P. Cons. 1969-71; Cand. prov. g.e. 1975, def.; el. M.P.P. for Cochrane South prov. g.e. 1977; Parlty. Asst.

to Min. of Culture & Recreation 1978 and to Min. of Consumer & Comm. Relations 1978-79; Min. without Portfolio 1979; P. Conservative; Anglican; Office: Queen's Park, Toronto, Ont. M7A 1A1.

PORTEOUS, Timothy, B.A., B.C.L.; Canadian public servant; b. Montreal, Que. 31 Aug. 1933; s. John Geoffrey and Cora Ann (Kennedy) P.; e. Selwyn House Sch. Montreal 1946; Bishops' Coll. Sch. Lennoxville, Que. 1950; McGill Univ. B.A. 1954, B.C.L. 1957; Univ. de Montréal 1957-58; Univ. de Paris Institut de Droit Comparé 1958-59; m. Wendy Elizabeth Farris 28 June 1968; one d. Vanessa Bell; DIR., CANADA COUNCIL 1982- ; Assoc. Dir., 1973-82; called to Bar of Que. 1958; practiced law with Bourgeois, Doheny, Day & MacKenzie, Montreal 1958-66; Extve. Asst. to Min. of Industry 1966-68; Special Asst. and Extve. Asst. to Prime Min. of Can. 1968-73; co-author and assoc. producer "My Fur Lady" (musical satire); recreations: skiing, tennis, scuba diving, wind surfing; Clubs: Rockcliffe Park Tennis; Ottawa Athletic; Home: 161 Mariposa Ave., Ottawa, Ont. K1M 0T8; Office: 255 Albert St., Ottawa, Ont. K1P 5V8.

PORTER, Arthur, M.Sc., Ph.D., F.I.E.E., F.R.S.A., F.R.S.C. (1970); university prof.; b. Ulverston, Lancs., England, 8 Dec. 1910; s. late Mary Anne (Harris) and John William P.; e. Univ. of Manchester, B.Sc. (1st Class Hons. Physics) 1933; M.Sc. 1934, Ph.D. 1936; Mass. Inst. Tech. (1937-39); m. Phyllis Patricia, d. late V. G. Dixon, London Eng., 26 July 1941; one s. John Arthur Harris; PROF. EMERITUS OF INDUSTRIAL ENGINEERING, UNIV. OF TORONTO, since 1976; Asst. Lectr., Univ. of Manchester, 1936-37; Commonwealth Fund Fellow, M.I.T., 1937-39; Scient. Offr., Admiralty, London, 1939-45; Princ. Scient. Offr., Nat. Physical Lab., 1946; Prof. of Instrument Tech., Royal Mil. Coll. of Science, 1946-49; Head of Research Div., Ferranti Electric Ltd., Toronto, Ont., 1949-55; Prof. of Light Elect. Engn., Imp. Coll. of Science & Tech., Univ. of London, 1955-58; Dean of Engn., Univ. of Sask., 1958-61; Acting Dir., Centre for Culture & Technol., Univ. Toronto 1967-68; Chmn. Adv. Comte. for Science and Med., Cdn. World Exhn. Corp. (Montreal, 1967); Acad. Commr., The Univ. of W. Ont. 1969-71; Chrmn. Candn. Environmental Adv. Council 1972-75; Chrmn. Ont. Royal Commission on Electric Power Planning 1975-80; Chmn. of Bd., Scientists and Engrs. for Energy and Environmental Security Inc. 1981- ; Centenary Lecturer, Institution of Electrical Engrs., London, Eng. 1971; Professor and Chrmn., Dept. of Industrial Engineering, Univ. of Toronto 1961-76; Pres., Arthur Porter Assoc. ltd., Ontario; Publications: "Introduction to Servomechanisms", 1950; "Cybernetics Simplified", 1969; "Towards a Community University", 1971; and various scient. research articles in learned journs.; Fellow. Inst. of Elect. Engrs. (London); mem., Soc. of Instrument Tech. (London); Assn. Prof. Engrs., Ont.; Operations Research Soc. Can.; Anglican; recreations: music, landscape gardening, travel; Clubs: Athenaeum (London); Arts and Letters (Toronto); Home: Belfountain, Ont., L0N 1B0

PORTER, Bruce T., M.B.A., M.P.A., C.A., C.M.C.; b. Toronto, Ont. 12 Nov. 1943; s. Walter Alvin and Doris Ellen (Jarvis) P.; e. York Univ. B.A. 1968, M.B.A. 1969, M.P.A. 1974; C.A. 1972; m. Mary Catherine d. Paul Graham 7 Aug. 1970; one son: David Bruce; joined Clarkson Gordon & Co. 1969-73; Woods Gordon & Co. 1973-78; manager, The Clarkson Co. Ltd., since 1978; Teaching Master Seneca Coll.; Chrmn. of Accounting, Finance Adv. Comte. to the Bd. of Govs., Seneca Coll., 1980-82; author various articles; mem. Inst. Pub. Adm.; Inst. C.A.'s Ont.; Candn. Inst. C.A.'s; Ont. Inst. of Management Consultants; P. Conservative; Anglican; recreations: flying, curling, golf; Club: Bayview Country; Home: 16 Paultiel Dr., Willowdale, Ont., M2M 3P3; Office: Royal Trust Tower, Toronto, Ont.

PORTER, Donald Arthur, C.D., B.A., M.S., Ph.D.; educator; b. Montreal, Que., 17 Aug. 1935; s. Arthur Robert and Ruth Crutchlow (Packard) P.; e. Westmount (Que.) High Sch. 1952; McGill Univ. 1954; University of Sask., B.A. 1958; University of North Dakota, M.S. 1963; University of Minnesota, Ph.D. 1967; m. Caroline Susan, d. Kenneth Graham Lynn, 10 June 1968; children: Hugh John William, Patrick James Edward, Andrew Kenneth Neil, Kathryn Susan Elizabeth; PRINCIPAL, RICHMOND CAMPUS, KWANTLEN COLL. since 1970; Alderman, Corp. Delta 1975-79; Chrmn. Delta Industrial Development Advisory Comte. 1975-79; Princ., Westbourne Collegiate, Man. 1964-66; Asst. Supt. (Personnel) Edmonton Pub. Schs. 1967-69; served in Saskatoon Light Inf. 1955-59; Candn. Intelligence Corps. 1959-64, R.C.A. 1965-74; author of "Factors Influencing Catholic High School Enrollment" 1967; Chrmn., Fraser Valley Reg. Library Bd. of Management 1978-79; Chrmn., Boundary Union Bd. of Health 1977-79; Chrmn. Associated Bds. of Health of B.C. 1978-79; B.C. Chamber Comm. Educ. Comte. 1974-80; mem. Library Adv. Council of B.C. 1980- ; Chrmn. Boundary Bay Airport Comte. 1980- ; Returning Offr., Electoral Dist. Richmond-South Delta 1979- ; mem., Am. Assn. of Community and Junior Colleges; Nat. Soc. for the Study of Education; B.C. Genealogical Soc.; Irish Genealogical Research Soc.; The Soc. of Genealogists (London); New Engl. Historic Genealogical Soc.; Bd. of Assts., The General Soc. of Mayflower Descendants; Anglican; Home: 4892 Dogwood Drive, Tsawwassen, Delta, B.C., V4M 1M5; Office: 5840 Cedarbridge Way, Richmond, B.C., V6X 2A7

PORTER, Gilbert Bailey; retired company executive; b. Thunder Bay, Ont. 8 Mar. 1920; s. George Herbert and Wilhelmina (Neve) P.; e. Sudbury and Mattawa, Ont. High Schs.; post-war course Business Admin., Toronto, Ont.; m. Ruth, d. the late Robert Bell, 26 Dec. 1946; children: Linda, Owen; Pres., G. T. Fulford Co. Ltd. 1979-81; Pres., Fulford Williams (International) Ltd. since 1970; Dir., Barret S.A., France; commenced with Ault & Wiborg Co., Toronto, Ont., Acct. 1948-50; McConnachie Sales Co. Ltd., Toronto, Controller 1950-60; Morse Jewellers Ltd., Toronto, Controller 1960-61; J. Lyons & Co. (Canada) Ltd., Controller 1961-62; G. T. Fulford Co. Ltd., Secy.-Treas. 1962-70; served with R.C.A.F. (Air Crew) 1940-45; Prisoner of War in Germany 1942-45; recreations: golf, swimming, skiing, music, dancing; Clubs: Celebrity; Bd. of Trade; Whitevale Golf; Home: 57 Dennett Dr., Agincourt, Ont., M1S 2E8; Office: 161 Alden Rd., Markham, Ont. L3R 3W7

PORTER, John McKenzie, M.C., T.D. F.R.S.A.; journalist; b. Accrington, Lancs., Eng. 21 Oct. 1911; s. John McKenzie and the late Amy Muriel (Smith) P.; e. Bolton Sch. Lancs., Eng. 1926; Baine's Grammar Sch. Poulton-le-Fylde, Eng. 1928; m. Kathleen d. William Gathercole, Bury, Lancs. 5 Sept. 1936; one s. Timothy McKenzie; SYNDICATED COLUMNIST AND DRAMA CRITIC, TORONTO SUN since 1971; Reporter, Manchester Evening Chronicle 1929 — 31; Feature Writer, Daily Express 1931 — 36; News Ed. Daily Mirror 1936 — 38; Film Critic, Evening Standard 1938 — 39; Night Ed. Daily Sketch 1939; Paris Corr. Kemsley Newspapers 1946 — 48; Writer, Maclean's Magazine 1948 — 62; Columnist, Toronto Telegram 1962 — 71; served as Rifleman, London Irish Rifles 1939 — 41; The Cameronians (Scot. Rifles) 1941 — 46, action in Egypt, Syria, Sicily, Italy 1942 — 44; wounded Battle for Cassino 1944, seconded to Pol. Warfare Extve. Rome, Athens, Vienna 1944 — 46, rank Maj.; Trustee Lib. Bd. East Gwillimbury, Ont. 1976 — 78; author "Overture to Victoria" a biography of Prince Edward, Duke of Kent 1962; 26 short stories under pseudonym William Bennett 1932 — 48; The President's Medal, Univ. of W. Ont. 1960 for best gen. article of the year (biogr. of Frederick Varley); City of Rome Gold Medal for best article by a foreigner on subj. of Italy, 1960; el. Fellow, Royal Soc. of Arts, 1971; P. Conservative; Anglican;

recreation: travel; Home: 235 Victoria St., Niagara-on-the-Lake, Ont. L0S 1J0; Office: 333 King St. E., Toronto, Ont. M5A 3X5.

PORTER, Julian, B.A., Q.C.; b. Toronto, Ont. 4 Dec. 1936; s. Dana Harris and Dorothy Ramsay (Parker) P.; e. Upper Can. Coll.; Univ. of Toronto Schs.; Univ. of Toronto B.A.; Osgoode Hall Law Sch.; m. Anna Marie Szigethy 8 Jan. 1972; children: Susan Eva, Jessica (from previous marriage), Catherine, Julia; PARTNER, PORTER & POSLUNS: called to Bar of Ont. 1964; cr. Q.C. 1975 mem. Candn. Del. to UNESCO Copyright Convention concerning U.C.C. and Berne Convention, Paris 1971; Past Pres., Candn. Nat. Exhn.; Chrmn., Toronto Transit Comn.; mem. Bd. Harborfront; mem. Bd. of Govs. The Stratford Shakespearean Festival Foundation of Can.; Ont. Cancer Research Foundation; Writer's Devel. Trust; Key Publishers Ltd.; mem. Advocates Soc.; Delta Kappa Epsilon; P. Conservative; Protestant; recreations reading, sailing, football, hockey, squash; Clubs: University; Albany; Badminton & Racquet; Home: 16 Rose Park Cres., Toronto, Ont. M4T 1P9; Office: (P.O. Box 365) Commerce Court, Toronto, Ont. M5L 1G2.

PORTER, Keith Roberts, Ph.D., D.Sc.; educator; biologist; b. Yarmouth, N.S., 11 June 1912; s. Aaron C. and Josephine (Roberts) P.; e. Acadia Univ., B.S. 1934, Harvard Univ., M.A. 1935, Ph.D. 1938; Acadia Univ., N.S., D.Sc. (Hon.) 1964; Queen's Univ., Kingston, hh.D. (Hon.) 1966; Medical coll. of Ohio, D. Sc. (Hon.) 1975; Rockefeller Univ., N.Y., D.Sc. (Hon.) 1976; Univ. of Toronto, D.Sc. (Hon.) 1978; Univ. Pierre et Marie Curie, (honoris causa); m. Elizabeth Lingley, 16 June 1938; PROF., MOLECULAR, CELLULLAR & DEVEL. BIOL., UNIV. OF COLORADO since 1968; Chairman Department 1968-75; Director, Marine Biological Laboratories 1975-77; Nat. Research Fellow, Princeton University, 1938-39; Research Asst., Rockefeller Institute, N.Y., 1939-45; Assoc. 1945-50; Assoc. mem. 1950-56; mem. and Prof. 1956-61; Chrmn., Dept. of Biol., Harvard Univ. 1965-67 and Prof. there 1961-70; co-recipient Warren Triennial Award 1962; co-recipient Passano Award 1964; Gairdner Foundation Award 1964; Fellow, Guggenheim Foundation, 1967-68; author, "An Introduction to the Fine Structure of Cells and Tissues", 1963, 2nd ed. 1964, 3rd ed. 1968 (German, Spanish, Italian and Japanese transls.); "Introduction to the Fine Structure of Plant Cells", 1970; other writings incl. over 200 articles for prof. journs.; contribs. to science incl. Porter-Blum microtome; Editor (1st), Journal of Cell Biol.; co-ed., "Protoplasma"; Ed. "Molecular & Cellular Biology"; Co-recipient, Louisa Gross Horwitz Prize 1970 and Paul-Ehrlich-Ludwig-Darmstaeder Prize 1971; Teaching Recognition Award, Univ. of Colorado, 1971; Co-recipient with George Palade, Dickson Prize, 1971; Robert L. Stearns Award, Univ. of Colorado, 1973; Council on Research and Creative Work lecturer, Univ. of Colorado, 1975; Recipient. The National Medal of Science, 1977; Distinguished Professorship, Univ. of Colorado, 1978; Waterford Bio-Medal Award, Scripps Clinic and Research Foundation, 1979; Chairman and Organizer, First International Congress on Cellular Biology, 1976; mem. National Academy of Sciences, 1964; (Advisory Committee on U.S.S.R. & E. Europe); Electron Microscope Am. (Pres. 1962-63); Am. Philosophical Soc., 1977; Am. Acad. Arts & Science 1957; Internat. Soc. Cell. Biol.; Am. Soc. Cell Biol., 1977-78, (1st Pres.); Pres., Tissue Cult. Assoc., 1978-80; Harvey Soc.; Am. Assn. Anat.; Sigma Xi; Home: 748 11th St., Boulder, Colo. 80302; Office: Dept. of Molecular, Cellular and Developmental Biology, Univ. of Colorado, Boulder, Colo. 80309

PORTER, Robert Keith, B.Com.; company chrmn.; b. Medicine Hat, Alta., 7 March 1918; s. Earl Richard Dundas and Clara May (Bumgardner) P.; e. Univ. of Brit. Columbia, B.Com. 1942; m. Agnes Merle, d. late Dr. H. L. W. Turnbull, Vancouver, B.C., 11 July 1942; children: Lawrence Keith, Robert Elgin, William David, Barbara

Merle Mills; CHRMN., C.E.O., and DIR. THOMAS J. LIPTON INC. & SUBSIDIARY COMPANIES; Dir., Lever Bros. Ltd.; Salesman, Lever Bros. Co., Vancouver, 1946, and Supervisor, Toronto, Ont., 1946-47; Sales and Ad. Mgr., Pepsodent Co. of Can. Ltd., Toronto, Ont., 1948; Gen. Mgr., Harriett Hubbard Ayer of Can. Ltd., Montreal, Que., 1948-50; Gen. Sales Mgr., Harriett Hubbard Ayer Inc., New York, 1950, and Pres. 1951-54; joined present Co. as Extve. Vice-Pres. and Gen. Mgr., 1954; Pres., 1964; Chrmn., 1978; served in 2nd World War in Eng. and N.W. Europe with R.C.A.S.C. with rank of Capt., 1942-46; Staff Offr., 7th Bdge. Hdqrs. at end of war; Past Pres. & Dir., Candn. Council, Internat. Chamber Comm.; Past Chrmn. Tea Council of Can.; Past Chrmn., Grocery Products Mfrs. of Can.; mem., Toronto Board of Trade; Beta Theta Pi (Pres.); Sigma Tau Chi; Protestant; recreations: golf, traveling; Clubs: Metropolitan (N.Y.); Rosedale Golf; Granite; Toronto Lyford Cay (Nassau); Home: 7 Valleyanna Dr., Toronto, Ont., M4N 1J7; Office: 2180 Yonge St., Toronto, Ont., M4S 2C4

POSER, Ernest George, M.A., Ph.D.; educator; b. Vienna, Austria 2 March 1921; s. Paul and Blanche (Furst) P.; e. Queen's Univ. B.A. 1946, M.A. (Psychol.) 1949; Univ. of London (Maudsley Hosp.) Ph.D. 1952; m. Maria Jutta d. late Heinz Cahn 3 July 1953; children: Yvonne Melanie, Carol Ann, Michael Paul; PROF. OF PSYCHOL. McGILL UNIV.1969- ; Dir. Behavior Therapy Unit, Douglas Hosp. Centre 1966- ; Asst. Prof. of Psychol. Univ. of N.B. 1946-48; Asst. Prof. of Psychol. McGill Univ. 1954, Assoc. Prof. 1957-69, Assoc. Prof. of Psychiatry 1963- ; Sr. Psychol. Mental Health Div. Dept. Health N.B. 1952-54; Chief Psychol. Montreal Rehabilitation Centre 1955-57; Dir. of Psychol. Dept. Douglas Hosp. Center 1957-66; Consultant Forensic Psychiatry Unit McGill Univ. 1966-67; Hon. Fellow, Middlesex Hosp. Med. Sch. London, Eng. 1964-65; mem. Que. Govt. Comte. Mental Health Services 1971-72; Visiting Prof. Univ. of Berne 1972-73; recipient numerous Candn. and U.S. research grants; author "Behavior Therapy in Clinical Practice: Decision-making, Procedure and Outcome" 1977; co-author "Behavior Modification with Children" 1973; author numerous articles prof. journs.; Fellow, Candn. psychol. Assn. (Dir. 1960-63); mem. Am. Psychol. Assn.; Que. Corp. Psychols. (Dir. 1967-68); Pres., Psychol. Assn. Prov. Que. 1961; recreations: tennis, skiing, swimming; Home: 3460 Simpson, Apt. 406, Montreal, Que. H3G 2B1; Office: 1205 Dr. Penfield Ave., Montreal, Que. H3A 1B1.

POST, George; Canadian public servant; b. Stirling, Ont. 28 June 1934; s. R. Elmer and Florence (Bailey) P.; e. Stirling (Ont.) High Sch. 1952; Queen's Univ. 1952-56; Northwestern Univ. 1956-59; m. Shirley, d. Luther Alyea, Belleville, Ont. 15 June 1957; children: Ellen, Christine, Richard; DEPT. MIN. OF CONSUMER AND CORP. AFFAIRS since 1978; Vice Chrmn., Economic Council of Canada, 1975-78; Lectr. Queens' Univ. 1959-62; Research Dept. Bank of Canada 1962, Chief Dept. Banking & Financial Analysis 1970-71; Asst. Secy. to Cabinet, Privy Council Office, Ottawa 1972-74; mem. Candn. Econ. Assn.; Am. Econ. Assn.; United Church; Home: 48 Powell Ave., Ottawa, Ont., K1S 2A1; Office: Place du Portage, Hull, Que., K1A 0C9

POTTER, H. Neville, B.A.Sc., F.C.I.C., P.Eng.; retired manufacturer; b. Toronto, Ont., 12 May 1914; s. Henry Ernest and Ada Ethel (Cole) P.; e. Alexander Muir Pub. Sch. and Central Tech. Sch., Toronto, Ont.; Univ. of Toronto, B.A.Sc. 1937; m. Eileen Marjory, d. George W. Elms, Toronto, Ont., 24 June 1939; children: Eileen Nancy, Catherine Jane; President, Dearborn Chemical Co. Ltd., 1971-79; joined Dearborn Chemical Co. as Chem. Engr. 1937, apptd. Tech. Dir. 1945 and el. a Dir. 1946; Extve. Vice-Pres., Dir. and Gen. Mgr. 1949; served in 2nd World War, 1940-45; Arty. Br., C.O.T.C., 1940; 30th Batty., 7th Toronto Regt., 1941; enlisted in R.C.A.F. as Navigation Offr. 1941; Flight Lieut. on instr. duties 1942-45;

Anglican; recreations: photography, travel; Club: Metrop. Toronto Board of Trade; Home: Apt 2116, 1333 Bloor St., Mississauga, Ont., L4Y 3T6

POTTER, Joseph Denton Rand, LL.B.; executive; b. Digby, N.S. 18 Dec. 1942; s. E. Keith and Ruberta (Rand) P.; e. Acadia Univ. 1962-65; Dalhousie Univ. LL.B. 1968; m. Edith B. d. George A. Evenden, Hamilton, Ont. 21 Aug. 1965; three d. Janet Lynn, Jennifer, Sarah; PRES. ATLANTIC TRUST CO. 1980- ; called to Bar of Ont. 1970; joined Algoma Steel Corp. as Legal Asst. 1968, Asst. Secy. 1970; Secy. 1971, Vice Pres.-Corporate Services 1976; Group Vice-Pres. (Finance & Corp. Services) 1977-80; mem. Law Soc. Upper Can.; Am. Iron & Steel Inst.; Financial Extves. Inst.; Protestant; Home: 1966Woodlawn Terrace, Halifax, N.S. B3J 2A4; Office: 1741 Barrington St., Halifax, N.S. B3J 2A4

POTTER, Norris Franklin, F.C.B.A.; banker; b. Tillsonburg, Ont. 20 July 1936; s. Franklin Smith and Anne Agatha (Corrigan) P.; m. Mary Jean d. Henry Borden, C.M.G., Q.C., Toronto, Ont. 9 Dec. 1961; children: Margot Jean, Ian Henry Franklin, Andrew Henry Borden; SR. VICE PRES. BANK OF MONTREAL since 1978; Dir. Pension Fund Soc. Bank of Montreal; Bank of Montreal (Bahamas & Caribbean) Ltd.; Bank of Montreal Internat. Ltd., Nassau; Canadian Dominion Leasing Corp. Ltd.; enrolled Candn. Offrs. Training Corps 1954; grad. 1957; comnd. Royal Candn. Dragoons; resigned 1962; joined Canadian Imperial Bank of Commerce as Mang. Trainee Toronto serving in various mang. positions Can., Switzerland and UK; Asst. Gen. Mgr. The Toronto-Dominion Bank 1970 becoming Vice Pres. and Gen. Mgr., service in Middle E., Europe and Can.; Gov. Candn. Opera Co.; Trustee, Havergal Foundation; Anglican; Clubs: Toronto; Overseas Bankers (London); Home: Kinkyle Farm, R.R.2 King, Ont. L0G 1K0; Office: First Canadian Place, Toronto, Ont. M5X 1A1.

POTTER, William W.; C.T.C.I.; association executive; b. Toronto, Ont. 20 July 1921; s. late Frederick and late Violet (Armstrong) P.; e. Bedford Park Pub. Sch. and Lawrence Park Coll. Inst. Toronto; m. Ruby Loretta Skidmore 23 Aug. 1947; children: William J., Susan L.; EXTVE. VICE PRES. TRUST COMPANIES ASSN. OF CAN. since 1974; Asst. Mgr. Beneficial Finance Co. of Canada, Toronto 1946, Asst. Vice Pres., 1954; Vice Pres. Beneficial Management Corp. Toronto 1964; also served in extve. capacity Eng. USA Beneficial Finance Group 1960-69; Pres. Beneficial Mangement Corp. Toronto 1969-73; served with RCAF 1940-45, attached RAF 1941-43, RCAF 1943-45, overseas 1941-45, Navig. rank Flight Lt.; Pres. Candn. Consumer Loan Assn. 1971-72; mem. Bd. Trade Metrop. Toronto; 32° Mason — Shriner — Tigris Temple; Freemason; Anglican; recreations: golf, swimming; Club: National (Toronto); Home: 143 Royal Orchard Blvd., Thornhill, Ont., L3T 3E1; Office: 11 Adelaide St. W., Toronto, Ont., M5H 1L9

POTTLE, Herbert Lench, M.A., Ph.D.; retired public servant; direct descendant of Thomas Pottle lay preacher who, under Rev. Lawrence Coughlan (sent to Nfld. by John Wesley), helped to establish the Meth. Ch. in early 19th century at Harbour Grace, once Nfld. capital, Carbonear and neighbouring settlements; b. Flatrock, Carbonear District, Nfld., 16 Feb. 1907; s. William Thomas and Patience Susannah (Evely) P.; e. Mount Allison Univ., B.A. 1932, (Gold Medalist); Univ. of Toronto, M.A. 1934, Ph.D. 1937; m. Muriel Ethel, d. Benjamin F. Moran, Trenton, Ont. 2 Aug. 1937; children: Helen Louise, Kathryn Elaine; served on staff, Dept. of Psychol., University of Toronto, 1934-37; Clinical Psychol., Infants Home, Toronto, 1937-38; Executive Officer United Church Schs. Newfoundland, 1938-44; Director of Child Welfare, and Judge of the Juvenile Court, St. John's, Newfoundland, 1944-47; appointed Commissioner for Home Affairs and Educ. in the Nfld. Comn. of Govt. until Confed., 1947-49;

1st el. to H. of A. for Dist. of Carbonear-Bay de Verde, in g.e. 1949 and re-el. g.e. 1951; Minister of Public Welfare, Nfld., 1949-55 when resigned; Secy., Bd. of Information & Stewardship, Un. Ch. of Can., 1955-63; Principal Research Offr. (Welfare), Dept. of Nat. Health & Welfare, 1963-68 (Internat. Welfare and Special Projects) 1968-72; former mem. of Board of Govs., Memorial Univ. Coll., St. John's, Nfld.; former Regent of Mount Allison Univ.; U.N. Social Welfare Adv. to Govt. of Libya (on leave) 1961-62; Rapporteur, Interregional Expert Meeting, U.N. on Social Welfare, Organ. & Adm., Geneva 1967; author of "Dawn Without Light: Politics, Power and the People in the Smallwood Era"; United Church; Home: Apt. 2202, Park Place, 1025 Richmond Rd., Ottawa, Ont., K2B 8G8

POTTS, Hon. Joseph Henry, C.D., Judge, B.A., LL.B., M.A.; b. Saskatoon, Sask. 17 July 1925; s. Maj. Gen. A. E. and Mary (Stewart) P.; e. Public and High Schs. Saskatoon, Sask.; Univ. of Brit. Columbia; Univ. Coll., Univ. of Toronto. B.A. (Hons. Pol. Sc. & Econ.) 1949; Trinity Coll., Cambridge Univ., B.A. 1951, LL.B. 1952, M.A. 1977; m. Dawn, d. Colin Rober, 3 March 1954; children: Joseph, Roberta, Arthur, Richard, Diana, Gordon, Bruce; JUSTICE OF THE HIGH COURT OF JUSTICE FOR ONT. 1982- ; former Partner, McTaggart, Potts, Stone, Winters & Herridge; called to Eng. Bar, Gray's Inn 1952, to Bar of Ont. 1953; with firm of Slaght McMurtry & Co. 1953, joining present firm (then Wright & McTaggart) 1956; cr. Q.C. 1969; served in 2nd World War, R.C.I.C. 1943-46; active service in Holland with Sask. Light Infy. (M.G.); in Can. with Princess Patricia's Candn. Light Infy.; rank on discharge Lt.; Capt. and Adj. Univ. of Toronto C.O.T.C. 1946-49; 48th Highlanders of Can. 1953-60; rank on discharge Maj.; Past Pres., Central Neighbourhood House; Past Chrmn. Organ. Comte., Cathedral Dist. Boy Scouts; Past Chrmn., Nat. Membership Comte. and Public Relations and Membership Comtes. (Ont. Br.) Candn. Bar Assn.; Pres., (Ont. Br.) Candn. Bar Assn.; Gov., Inst. for Advanced Legal Studies; Past Warden St. Paul's Anglican Church; Dir. and mem. Exec. Council, Inst. for Political Involvement; Dir., Epilepsy Ont.; Rep., Univ. Coll. Alumni Assoc. to College of Electors, Univ. of Toronto; Past Pres., Rosedale Lib. Assn., St. David's Lib. Assn., Toronto & Dist. Lib. Assn.; Past Chrmn., Liberal Union; Past Vice-Chrmn. Candn. Univ. Lib. Assn.; Prov. Lib. Cand., St. David's Riding 1963, 1967; mem., York Co. Law Assn.; Candn. Tax Foundation; Ft. York Br., The Royal Canadian Legion; Liberal; Anglican; recreations: politics, camping, swimming; Clubs: Empire (Past Pres.); Lawyers (Past Pres.); Canadian; Arts and Letters; Can. Inst. of International Affairs; Royal Candn. Mil. Inst.; Home: 40 Nanton Ave., Toronto, Ont., M4W 2Y9; Office: Osgoode Hall, 130 Queen St. W. Toronto, Ont., M5H 2N6

POTTS, J(oseph) Lyman, C.M.; broadcasting and recording consultant; b. Regina, Sask. 11 Nov. 1916; s. William Joseph and Eva dePearl (Warren) P.; e. Central Coll. Inst. Regina, Sask.; m. Michele d. late Albert C. Bole, Regina, Sask. 3 Oct. 1940; one s. Joel Lyman Albert; PRES., J. LYMAN POTTS AND ASSOC.; Announcer, Writer, Producer, Program Dir. Radio Stn. CKCK Regina 1935 — 40; Program Mgr., Asst. Mgr. Radio Stn. CKOC Hamilton, Ont. 1940 — 56; Gen. Mgr. Radio CKSL London, Ont. 1956 — 59; Production Mgr. Radio Stn. CJAD Montreal 1959 — 62; Gen. Mgr. Radio Stn. CJFM-FM Montreal 1962 — 63; transferred to Toronto in 1963 serving as Asst. to Pres., Standard Broadcasting Corp. and Mgr. FM Div., Pres. and Mgr. Dir. Stand. Broadcast Prod. Ltd. (incl Candn. Talent Lib., Standard Broadcast News, Deer Park Music, Conestoga Music, Syndication Serv.) 1965-81 (incl. Mgr. Dir. Standard Brdcst. Corp. (U.K.) Ltd. 1970-74); mem. Broadcast Extves. Soc.; Protestant; Home: 22 Thelma Ave., Toronto, Ont. M4V 1X9

POTTS, Nadia; ballerina; b. Eng. 1949, came to Can. 1953; e. Nat. Ballet Sch. Toronto; chosen to dance in "Bayaderka" during 1st season with Nat. Ballet Co. 1966; during 2nd season danced leading roles in "The Nutcracker" and "Cinderella"; promoted soloist 1968 and princ. 1969; with Clinton Rothwell won prize for best pas de deux, Internat. Ballet Competition, Varna 1970 and rec'd Bronze Medal for Solo Dance; danced with Baryshnikov 1975 and as Giselle with Nureyev 1976.c/o National Ballet of Canada, 157 King St. E., Toronto, Ont.

POULIN, Louis-Philippe; né St-Georges, Co. Beauce, Qué., 20 nov. 1921; é. Acad. du Sacré-Coeur, St.-Georges, Qué.; Coll. de Ste-Anne-de la Pocatière; Univ. Laval, Diplôme en agronomie 1941, Faculté des Sciences Sociales (sciences écon.) 1941-42; ép. Jacqueline Renaud 1945; enfants: Claude, Nicole, Jacques; DIRECTEUR GENERAL, COOPERATIVE FEDEREE DE QUEBEC depuis 1976; Recherchiste, Union Catholique des Cultivateurs (Union des Producteurs Agricoles du Qué.) 1942, Dir. Dépt. de l'Econ. Rurale 1944, Secrétaire gén. 1953; Secretaire général, Coopérative Fédérée de Québec 1963-1976; mem. de Conseil d'admin. du Conseil Candn. de la Coopération 1963-64; Pres. Conseil de la Coopération du Qué. 1970-72; mem. du Conseil de planification et de Dével. du Qué. 1971-77; mem. du Comité exéc. du Conseil de la Coopération du Qué. 1972-77; mem. du Conseil Econ. du Can. 1973-77; Administrateur de Culinar Inc. 1978; Administrateur de la Sauvegarde, Cie d'Assurance-Vie 1979; administrateur de la Soc. de Développement International Desjardins 1980; membre Ordre des Agronomes de la Prov. Qué.; Chambre de Commerce de la Province de Québec; Centre des Dirigeants d'Entreprise; Am. Mang. Assn.; décoré Commdr. de l'Ordre du Mérite Agricole 1966; décoré de l'Ordre du Mérite Coopératif, 1978; bureau: 1055 du Marché Central, Montréal, Qué. H4N 1K3

POULIOT, Jean A., C.M., B.A., B.A.Sc.; television exécutive; Quebec, Que., 6 June 1923; s. of Adrien and Laure (Clark) P.; e. Séminaire de Québec; Laval Univ., Science Faculty; m. Rachel, daughter of Flavius Lebel; children: Jean, Vincent, Louis, Adrien, Martin; PRESIDENT AND CHIEF EXTVE. OFFR. of CFCF INC, since 1979; President and Chief Extve. Offr., Télé-Capitale Ltée. 1971-78; Pres. Red Carpet Aero Services Inc.; Quebec Aviation Ltd.; Quebec Aviation Air Services Ltd.; Broadcast News; Northern Multicorp Ltd.; Unicom Broadcast Sales Ltd.; Broadcast News; Northern Multicorp Ltd.; Unicom Broadcast Sales Ltd.; Electromedia Sales Ltd.; Ciné-Capitale Ltée; Vice Pres. CHRC Ltée Ciné-Vidéo Inc.; Les Productions du Verseau; Radio Laval Inc.; Dir. Télé-Métropole Inc.; Cité-Jardin vantadour Québec Inc.; Télévision de la Baie des Chaleurs; mem. Consulting Comm., Royal Trust Co.; Electronic Research Engineer, Canadian Army, Ottawa 1945-49; Superintendent Canadian Navy Laboratories, Ottawa 1949-52; Executive Engineer, Television Department, Famous Players Company, Toronto 1952-57; Gen. Mgr. Télévision de Qué. (Canada) Ltd. 1957-62; Man. Dir. of this enterprise 1962-71; Pres. (1965-67), Canadian Assn. of Broadcasters; mem. Assn. Prof. Engrs.; Roman Catholic; Recreations: golf; chess; Clubs: The Garnison Club; Royal Quebec Golf; Home: 99 Gordon Crescent, Westmount, Montreal, Quebec H3Y 1N1 Office: 405 Ogilvy Avenue, Montreal, Quebec H3N 1M4.

POUND, Harold Delmar; public servant; b. Empress, Alta., 2 Jan. 1925; s. Edwin Delmar and Leone (Buxton) P.; e. high sch.; m. Phyllis Mary Sunstrum, 16 May 1948; two s.; CHIEF COMMR., CANDN. GRAIN COMN., since 1971; Farm Mgr., McCabe Grain Co., Brooks, Alta., Seed Plant Mgr. and Elevator Supt. 1953; Sales Co-ordinator, Oliver Industrial Supplies, Lethbridge, Alta., 1960; Extve. Vice Pres. and Gen. Mgr. Calgary, 1968; Commr., Bd. of Grain Commrs., Winnipeg, 1970; Pres., Alta. Jr. Chamber Comm., 1956-57; recreation: golf; Home: 45

Stillwater Rd., St. Boniface, Man. R2J 2R2; Office: 600 - 303 Main St., Winnipeg, Man. R3C 3G8

POUND, Richard William Duncan, B.Com., B.A., B.C.L.; lawyer; b. St. Catharines, Ont. 22 March 1942; s. William Thomas and Jessie Edith Duncan (Thom) P.; e. McGill Univ. B.Com. 1962, Licentiate in Accounting 1964, B.C.L. 1967; Sir George Williams Univ. B.A. 1963; m. Julie Houghton d. Donald Kennedy Keith 4 Nov. 1977; children: William Trevor Whitley, Duncan Robert Fraser, Megan Christy; mem. law firms Stikeman Elliott Tamaki Mercier & Robb, Montreal and Stikeman Elliott Robarts & Bowman, Toronto 1972- ; called to Bar of Que. 1968, Bar of Ont. 1980; joined Riddell Stead Graham & Hutchison 1965-71; Sessional Lectr. McGill Faculty of Law (Taxation) 1977-80; Lectr. McGill Center for Continuing Educ. 1968-76; Lectr. Que. Real Estate Assn. 1972-78; mem. Red Cross Water Safety Comte. Royal Life Savings Soc.; Secy., Candn. Olympic Assn. 1968-76, Pres. 1977-82; mem. Internat. Olympic Comte.; Double Olympic Finalist (swimming) Rome 1960; recipient 1 gold, 2 silver, 1 bronze medals Commonwealth Games (swimming) Perth, Australia 1962; Candn. Champion Freestyle 1958, 1960, 1961, 1962, Butterfly 1961; mem. Candn. Swimming Hall of Fame; Candn. Amateur Athletic Hall of Fame; Trustee, Martlet Foundation; Pres. Grad. Soc. McGill Univ. 1981-82; Director Allegro Foundation; mem. McGill Athletics Bd.; Coaching Assn. Can. 1976-82; Gen. Ed. "Doing Business in Canada" 1979; mem. ed. bd. "Canadian Tax Service" 1972-80; author "The Olympic Boycott 1980" in preparation; various book chapters, articles; mem. Candn. Bar Assn.; Candn. Tax Foundation; Internat. Fiscal Assn.; Assn. Québecoise de Planification Fiscale et Successorale; Que. Bureau du; Ont. Bar; Que. Order C.A.'s; Ont. Inst. C.A.'s; Kappa Alpha Society; Protestant; recreations: squash, tennis, raquets, swimming; Clubs: Montreal Racket; Montreal Badminton & Squash; M.A.A.A.; Hillside Tennis; R.C.Y.C.; Home: 87 Arlington Ave., Westmount, Que. H3Y 2W5; Office: 3900, 1155 Dorchester Blvd. W., Montreal, Que. H3B 3V2.

POUNDER, Elton R., A.F.C., Ph.D., F.R.S.C.; educator; b. Montreal, Que., 10 Jan. 1916; s. Rev. Roy M. and Norval (McLeese) P.; e. McGill Univ., B.Sc. 1934, Ph.D. 1937; m. Marion Crane, d. George S. Wry, 15 Feb. 1941; MACDONALD PROF. OF PHYSICS, McGILL UNIV., since 1976, Prof. of Physics there since 1958; Dir., Ice Research Project, since 1955; with Bell Telephone Co. as Engr., 1937-39; apptd. Asst. Prof. of Physics, McGill Univ. 1945, Assoc. Prof., 1948; served in 2nd World War 1939-45; Wing Commdr., R.C.A.F.; awarded Air Force Cross; Fellow Royal Soc. of Can. 1974; mem., Candn. Assn. of Physicists (Pres., 1961-62); Am. Physical Soc.; Am. Geophysical Union; Internat. Glaciological Soc.; recreations: music, golf, skiing; Home: 3468 Drummond Street, Montreal, Que. H3G 1Y4

POWELL, Brian, M.A. b. Montreal, Que., 25 May 1934; s. Clifford Baden and Doris Kathleen (Sharples) P.; e. St. George's Sch., Vancouver, B.C., 1942-46; Lower Can. Coll., Montreal, Que., grad. 1952; McGill Univ., B.A. 1956; M.A. 1967; Univ. of London, Dipl. in Business Adm. 1957; Oxford Univ., Dipl. in Educ. 1963; Consultant in English, Prot. Sch. Bd. of Montreal, since 1969; Dir., Powell Foods Ltd.; Teacher of Eng., Lower Can. Coll., Montreal, 1956-66; Asst. Headmaster 1964-66; Lectr., Sydney Univ. and Cranbrook Sch., Sydney, Australia, 1966-67; Instr. in Eng., Phillips Exeter (U.S.A.) Acad., 1967-68; Headmaster, Shawnigan Lake Sch., Quebec 1968-69; teaching and lecturing experience in Eng., Russia and S. Am.; mem., Candn. Nat. Ski Team 1958-64; Winner, Roberts of Kandahar Downhill Ski Race 1957; mem., Que Willingdon Cup Interprov. Golf Team, 1962-63; E. Candn. Six-Mile Road Running Champion 1966; author of "English Through Poetry Writing", 1967; Ed. "Jackrabbit: His First Hundred Years", 1975; mem., Bd.

of Mgrs., St. Andrew's Un. Ch., Westmount; Kappa Alpha; P. Conservative; United Church; recreations: travel, sports, reading, writing; Clubs: Mount Bruno Golf: Cascade Golf & Tennis (Dir.); Montreal Badminton & Squash; Address: 38 Church Hill, Montreal, Que. H3Y 2Z9

POWELL, Clarence W., B.Sc., L.L.D.; consulting engineer; b. Carbonear, Nfld., 6 June 1913; s. George Bertram and Susannah (Thistle) P.; e. U.C. Superior Sch., 1919-28; Prince of Wales Coll., St. John's, 1928-29; Memorial Univ. Coll., St. John's, 1929-32; N.S. Tech. Coll., B.Sc. (Elect. Engn.) 1934; m. Elsie Doris, d. late John Morgan, 30 Dec. 1936; has four children; former Chrmn., Nfld. Bd. of Commrs. of Public Utilities (retired); served as Stipendiary Magistrate, 1935-49; was apptd. under Comn. of Govt., and became Chief Adm. Offr. in dist., being responsible for the adm. of roads, health, welfare and various schemes of agric. assistance in addition to judicial duties; in 1944 trans. to office of Dept. of Justice, St. John's as Adm. Offr.; in 1947 trans. to Dept. of Health & Welfare as Dir. of Local Govt. (Mun.) Affairs; in 1949 Local Govt. Divn. was trans. to Dept. of Supply; Deputy Min. of Supply, 1949-52; Depy. Min. of Municipal Affairs, 1952-65; mem., Meth. Coll. Lit. Inst.; Freemason (Jr. Warden); Un. Church; recreations: gardening, driving; Home: 9 Stoneyhouse St., St. John's, Nfld. A1B 2T5;

POWELL, Clifford Baden; b. Westmount, Que., m. Doris Kathleen, d. William Sharples, Quebec, Que., 28 December 1931; children: Brian Sharples, Ann Murray, Timothy Clifford; CHRM., C.B. POWELL LIMITED; Pres., Powell Investments Ltd.; McIlhenny & Powell Limited; Dir., Candn. Olympic Assn.; Old Brewery Mission, Montreal; Pres., Metis Beach Community Assn.; Candn. Amateur Bobsleigh and Luge Assn.; Trustee, Metis Beach Un. Ch.; Clubs: Mount Bruno Country; St. James's; Montreal Badminton & Squash; Royal Wimbledon (U.K.); Vancouver (B.C.); Capilano (Vancouver); Home: 38 Church Hill, Westmount, Que. H3Y 2Z9

POWELL, Fred; sculptor; b. Toronto, Ont. 1924; e. Upper Can. Coll. Toronto; served with Candn. Army Overseas 1942-46; from 1952 lived and worked in S. Cal., N.Y. City and San Miguel de Allende, Mexico before returning to Can. 1975; one-man exhns. incl. Santa Barbara Museum of Art 1952, 1967; Rex Evans Gallery Los Angeles 1963; Charles Fiengarten Gallery Los Angeles 1964, 1967, 1969; Belles Artes Mexico City 1971; Roberts Gallery Toronto 1973; Galerie Dresdnere Toronto 1976; Gallery Moos Ltd. Toronto 1978; Hokin Gallery Chicago 1978; rep. in numerous group exhns. US and Can. 1952-79 incl. Hokin Gallery, Palm Beach, Fla. 1979; rep. in collections of Phoenix Art Museum; Museum of Modern Art Mexico City; Candn. Embassy Mexico City; Art Bank Ottawa and private collections in Can. US and Mexico

POWER, Hon. Charles Joseph, M.H.A., B.A., B.A. (Ed.); politician; b. Tors Cove, Nfld. 29 Feb. 1948; s. Michael and Margaret (O'Driscoll) P.; e. Sacred Heart Sch. Tors Cove; Holy Cross Sch. St. John's; Mem. Univ. of Nfld.; m. Dorothy d. Aloysius and Margaret Glynn, Bay Bulls, Nfld.; children: Brenda Lynn, Keegan, Rogan; MIN. OF FOREST RESOURCES & LANDS, NFLD. 1980- ; sch. teacher 5 yrs.; el. M.H.A. for Ferryland prov. g.e. 1975, results overturned by Supreme Court, re-el. prov. by-el. 1977, g.e. 1979; Min. of Tourism 1979; P. Conservative; R. Catholic; Office: P.O. Box 4750, St. John's, Nfld. A1C 5T7.

POWER, Noble Edward Charles, M.A.; diplomat and public servant; b. Montreal, Que., 17 Sept. 1931; s. Richard Michael Hugh, M.D. and Kay M. (Phelan) P.; e. Univ. of Montreal, B.A. 1953; Columbia Univ., New York, Latin Am. Studies, M.I.A. 1955; grad. studies Universidad de Mexico and Sorbonne, Paris, France 1955 and 1956; m. Sarah Kellogg, d. Morgan Goetchius, New

York, 23 Feb. 1956; children: Christopher Noble, Susannah Morgan, Alexandra Kay; Min.'s Staff, Dept. of Nat. Defence, Ottawa, 1956-62; External Aid Office, Ottawa, 1962-66; Dir., Commonwealth Africa Aid Programme, CIDA, Ottawa, 1966-70; served as Head, Candn. Del. to IMF and IBRD meetings and other aid groups, 1966-70; ICER Task Force (Interdepartmental Comte. on External Relations), Ottawa, 1970-71; High Commr. to Ghana and Ambassador to Benin and Togo, 1971-74; Dir.-Gen. (Asia) Canadian International Development Agency (C.I.D.A.) 1974-1977; Vice-Pres,, C.I.D.A., since 1977; Del. to Colombo Plan Conf., Singapore 1974 and Head Candn. Del. various IBRD Consortia, Paris 1974-81; Alt. Dir., Bd. of Dir., Export Devel. Corp., Ottawa, 1977-81; mem., Bd. of Gov., Elmwood, Ottawa, 1977-80; served with the Black Watch (RHC) of Can. 1950-53; rank Lieut.; recreations: riding, hunting, skiing, tennis; Clubs: Rideau; Country; Ottawa Valley Hunt (Pres. 1967-70); Home: Basswoodhill Farm, Dunrobin, Ont. K0A 1T0; Office: CIDA, Place du Centre, Ottawa/Hull.

POWER, Hon. Peter Charles Garneau, B.Com., LL.B.; judge; b. Montreal, Que. 16 Apl. 1930; s. Francis Xavier Power; e. Dalhousie Univ. B.Com. 1953, LL.B. 1956; m.; 8 children; JUDGE, COURT OF QUEEN'S BENCH; called to Bar of Alta. 1957, Alta. 19; cr. Q.C. 1976; Ald., City of Red Deer, Alta. 1961-66; Pub. Sch. Trustee Red Deer Sch. Bd. 1971-79; mem. Law Soc. Alta.; Candn. Bar Assn.; R. Catholic; recreations: golf, skiing, sailing; Home: 3360 Varna Cres., N.W., Calgary, Alta. T3A 0E6; Office: 611-4th St. S.W., Calgary, Alta. T2P 1T5.

POWER, Most Rev. William E., D.D., B.A. (R.C.); bishop; b. Montreal, Que., 27 Sept. 1915; s. Nicholas Walter and Bridget Elizabeth (Callaghan) P.; e. St. Patrick's Sch., Montreal, Que.; Montreal Coll., B.A. 1937; Grand Semy., 1937-41; BISHOP OF ANTIGONISH, since 1960 (named 12 May, consecrated 20 July, installed 10 Aug.); Chancellor, St. Francis Xavier Univ. since 1960; o. 7 June 1941; Asst. Priest, St. Thomas Aquinas, 1941-42; St. Willibrod's, 1942-47; Vice Chancellor, Diocese of Montreal, 1947-50; Diocesan Chaplain to Young Christian Workers, 1950-59, and Nat. Chaplain, 1955-59; mem. of Extve. of Internat. Young Christian Workers rep. North Am., 1957-59; Parish Priest, St. Barbara's Parish, Lasalle, Que., Apl. 1959-May 1960; served with R.C.N.(R) 1947-51, and inactive force, 1951-60; Pres. (1971-73), Candn. Conf. of Catholic Bishops, mem., Administrative Bd. of C.C.C.B.; Address: P.O. Box 1330, 149 Main St., Antigonish, N.S. B2G 2L7

POWIS, Alfred, B.Com.; mining executive; b. Montreal, Que., 16 Sept. 1930; s. Alfred and Sarah Champe (McCulloch) P.; e. Westmount (Que.) High Sch., 1947; McGill Univ., B.Com. 1951; m. Louise Margaret Finlayson, 1977; CHRMN. & PRES., NORANDA MINES LTD., since 1977; Dir., Tara Exploration & Development Co.; Dir., Canadian Imperial Bank of Commerce; Ford Motor Co. of Can. Ltd.; Gulf Oil Canada Ltd.; MacMillan Bloedel Ltd.; Placer Development Ltd.; Kerr Addison Mines Ltd.; Sun Life Assurance Co. Canada; Simpsons-Sears Limited; also no. of subsidiaries of Noranda; Invest. Dept., Sun Life Assurance Co. of Can., 1951-55; joined present firm 1956; Asst. Treas. 1958; Asst. to Pres. 1962; Extve. Asst. to Pres. 1961; Dir. 1964; Vice Pres. 1966; Extve. Vice Pres. 1967; Pres. and C.E.O., 1968; Chrm., The Conference Board in Cnada; Vice-Chmn., Bd. of Trustees, Toronto General Hospital; Dir. Stratford Festival (Can.); Anglican; Clubs: York; Mount Royal (Montreal); Home: 70 Woodlawn Ave., W. Toronto, Ont. M4V 1G7; Office: P.O. Box 45, Commerce Court West, Toronto, Ont. M5L 1B6

POYEN, John S., B.A., LL.B.; retired association executive; b. New York City, 7 Oct. 1915; s. John S. and Verna (Robbins) P.; came to Canada 1948; Candn. citizen since 1960; e. Univ. of Cal. at L.A. 1933; Univ. of Colo. B.A. (Econ. Geol.) 1937; LL.B. 1940; Harvard A.M.P. 1962; m.

Betty L. Boerstler, 7 Sept. 1939; one s. John S. Jr.; Chrmn., Total Leonard Inc.; Pres., Eastcan Exploration Ltd.; Dir., Alberta Natural Gas Co. Ltd.; Great Basins Petroleum Co. (U.S.A.); Bow Valley Ind. Ltd.; read law with Strachan & Horn, Colorado Springs, Colo. 1940; U.S. Commr. Colo. 1940; in law practice 1946; involved in petrol. drilling, negotiations, productions etc. 1947-51; with Imperial Oil Ltd. 1952-71, various mang. assignments in exploration and production becoming Gen. Mgr.-Producing Dept.; President and Chief Executive Officer, Total Petroleum (N.A.) Limited 1971-73; Pres. and C.E.O. Candn. Petroleum Assn. 1973-76(ret.; served in 2nd World War, U.S. Army Air Force with rank of Major; Dir. American Petroleum Institute; Canadian Petroleum Association (Alta. Br.); former mem. Am. Bar Assn.; Chi Psi; Sumalia Scimitar (Univ. of Colo.); Anglican; recreations: golf, hunting, fishing; Clubs: Calgary Petroleum; Calgary Golf & Country; Home: #4-68 Baycrest Pl. S.W. Calgary, Alta. T2V 0K6; Office #1520-335 8th Ave. S.W. Calgary, Alta. T2P 1C9

POYNTZ, A(rthur) Ross, B.A., F.C.I.A.; A.S.A.; company director; b. Toronto, Ont.; 8 Apl. 1909; s. Arthur and Lula Heath (Deadman) P.; e. Upper Can. Coll., Toronto; Univ. of Toronto, B.A. 1929; m. Katherine Jean, d. George Wood, Rochester, N.Y., 14 Oct. 1933; children: Judith, Ross, Katherine; Dir., Imperial Life Assnce. Co. since 1950; Dir., Hiram-Walker Resources Ltd.; joined present Co. in 1931; apptd. Asst. to Gen. Mgr. 1942; Asst. Gen. Mgr. 1944; Gen. Mgr. 1946; el. a Dir. and apptd. Mang. Dir., 1950; el. Pres., 1953; Chrmn. of the Bd., 1964-77; Dir. Inst. of Life Ins., 1961-62; Pres., Candn. Life Ins. Offrs. Assn., 1959-60; Phi Gamma Delta; United Church; Clubs: Granite; Rosedale Golf; York; Rotary; Home: 349 St. Clair Ave. W., Toronto, Ont. M5P 1N3; Office: 95 St. Clair Ave. W., Toronto, Ont. M4V 1N7

PRATLEY, Gerald; writer; broadcaster; b. London, Eng., 3 Sept. 1923; s. Arthur and Agnes (Norwood) P.; e. various Schs. and Colls. in Eng.; m. Margaret, d. John Kennedy, 26 April 1948; children: Orize, Denise, Jocelyn; Film Critic and commentator for CBC 1948-75; Dir. Ont. Film Inst.; Candn. Film Institute; Stratford Film Festival; Canadian Film Awards; author, "John Frankenheimer" 1970; "Cinema of Otto Preminger" 1972; "Cinema of David Lean" 1973; "Cinema of John Huston" 1975; film teacher, Univ. Toronto, York Univ., Seneca Coll., McMaster Univ.; Award of Merit, Min. of Culture, Poland, 1981; life-mem.; Ont. Film Assn.; mem. Soc for Cinema Studies; mem. Internat. Juries; Cracow, Chicago, Montreal (and other) Film Festivals; Protestant; Office: 770 Don Mills Rd., Don Mills, Ont. M3C 1T3

PRATT, Charles Edward, B.Arch., F.R.A.I.C., F.A.I.A., R.C.A.; architect; b Boston, Mass. 15 July 1911; s. Edward Porter and Francis Ellen (Sharpe) P.; came to Can. 1921; e. Brentwood Coll. 1930; Univ. of B.C. 1930-33; Univ. of Toronto B.Arch. 1938 (R.A.I.C. Gold Medal); m. Catherine Gordon d. late Arthur Gordon Lang July 1938; children: Peter Whitney, Antoinette Lang; Sr. Partner Thompson Berwick & Pratt 1946-76; designed and executed B.C. Hydro Bldg. 1957 (mentioned for Massey Medal); B.C. Hydro Dal Grauer Sub Stn. 1960; Thea Koerner Grad. Centre Univ. of B.C. (Massey Gold Medal 1970); Univ. of B.C. Mem. Gymnasium (mention for Massey Medal); Tilden-U-Drive Stn. (Massey Silver Medal); Housing Devel. Victoria (Massey Gold Medal); mem. R.A.I.C. Comte. of Inquiry on Residential Environment 1960; mem. Paul Hellyer's Task Force on Housing in Can.; rowed for Can. 1932 Olympic Games Los Angeles, Bronze Medal; served with RCAF 1942-45; Zeta Psi; Liberal; Anglican; recreation: rowing; Clubs: Vancouver; Vancouver Rowing; Home: 430 Stevens Dr., West Vancouver, B.C.Office: 1553 Robson St., Vancouver, B.C.

PRATT, Christopher, O.C.(1973), B.F.A., D.Litt., LL.D., R.C.A.; artist and printmaker; b. St. John's, Nfld.; e.

Prince of Wales Coll., St. John s Nfld. 1952; Glasgow (Scot.) Sch. of Art; Mt. Allison Univ. B.F.A. 1961; has exhibited throughout Can. and in U.K.; colls. incl. Nat. Gallery of Can.; has developed style known as "conceptual realism"; mem. Candn. Soc. Graphic Artists; Canada Council; Clubs: Commodore; Royal Nfld. Yacht; Address: P.O. Box 87, Mount Carmel, St. Mary's Bay, Nfld. A0B 2M0

PRATT, Ewart Arthur, B.Sc., company executive; b. St. John's, Nfld., 20 March 1919; s. late Hon. Sen. Calvert Coates and late Agnes Green (Horwood) P.; e. Holloway Sch. and Prince of Wales Coll., St. John's Nfld., Phillips Exeter Acad., Exeter, N.H., 1935-38; Univ. of Pennsylvania, B.Sc. (Econ.) 1942; m. Yvonne, d. late James Rorke, Carbonear, Nfld., 30 Oct. 1943; children: Kathleen Agnes, James Rorke; CHAIRMAN, STEERS LTD. (Merchants, estbd. 1924); Dir., Steers Insurance Agencies Ltd.; Pres., Pratt Representatives (Nfld.) Ltd.; Steers Exports Ltd.; Pres., Colonial Business Properties Ltd.; Standard Manufacturing Co. Ltd.; Dir., Terra Nova Telecommunications Ltd.; Newfoundland Light & Power Co. Ltd.; Pratt Investment Co. Ltd.; Dir., Candn. Imperial Bank of Commerce; C.N. Marine Corp.; Newfoundland Steamships (1964) Ltd.; Canadian National Railways; mem., St. John's Adv. Bd., Canada Permanent Trust Co.; Bd Govs., Coll. of Fisheries, St. John's, Nfld.; served in 2nd World War as Offr., R.C.N., 1942-45; mem., Nfld. Bd. Trade (Councillor, 1950-52, 1964-65; Pres. 1967); Extve council, Candn. Chamber Comm. (Dir. 1967, Nat. Dir. 1968-69, Vice Pres. for Nfld. 1971-72); Candn. Council, Internat. Chamber Comm. (Dir.); Pres. (1970-71) Candn. Mental Health Assn., Nfld. Div.; Royal Commonwealth Soc., London, Eng.; Un. Church; recreation: boating; Clubs: Rotary (Pres. 1974-75); Bally Haly Golf; Murray's Pond Fishing; R.N.S.Y.S.; Royal Newfoundland Yacht; Granite (Toronto); Mount Royal (Montreal); University (Montreal); Canadian (N.Y.); Metropolitan (N.Y.); Home: 140 Waterford Bridge Rd., St. John's Nfld. A1E 1C9; Office: Water St., St. John's, Nfld

PRATT, R. John, B.Arch.; b. London, Eng., 28 Feb. 1907; s. John and Norah (Kelly) P.; e. Private Tuition in Eng; McGill Univ., B.Arch. 1933; m. Dorothy Nesbitt, d. Fleetwood Ward, Montreal, Que., 19 Aug. 1935; two s. John Stuart, Robin Alan; 2ndly, Louise, d. Dr. A. Giguere, Montreal, Que., 23 Dec. 1958; mem., Bd. of Govs., Nat. Theatre Sch. of Can.; Bd. of Dirs., Lakeshore Gen. Hosp., Montreal; McGill Chamber Orchestra; Montreal Repertory Theatre; General Contractor, 1933-35; Owner-Builder, residential property, and Operator of Residential Realty, since 1935; pioneered in Candn. Motion Pictures, 1936-48; Theatrical production in Can. and U.S., 1948-59; pioneered in Candn. TV Films, 1950-52; engaged in Civic pol. and radio-TV films 1952-57 and in Civic and Fed. pol. since 1957; 1st Vice-Chrmn. of Metrop. Council of Arts of Greater Montreal; mem., Master Planning Comte., Metrop. Corp. of Montreal; served in McGill C.O.T.C. 1928-36; Commnd. in 6th Duke of Connaught's Royal Candn. Hussars in 1936; resigned rank of Major to join Navy in 1942; toured with Navy Show, 1943-46; Alderman of Dorval, 1952-55, and Mayor there 1955-64; el. to H. of C. for Jacques Cartier-La Salle, g.e. June 1957 and re-el. g.e. March 1958; def. g.e. Apl. 1963; apptd. Depy. Dir. of Operations and Producer of Entertainment Expo '67; mem., Order Archs. Que.; Royal Arch. Institute of Can.; Actors Equity; Am. Guild of Variety Artists; Assn. of Candn. Radio & Television Artists; Gov., Candn. Jr. Chamber Comm.; mem. Bd. Dirs., Bldg. Owners & Mgrs. Assn.; Destination Habitat Corp.; St. Patrick's Development Corp.; St. Patrick's Soc. Montreal; Les Ballets Jazz du Can.; The Montreal Museum of Fine Arts; The Canadian Club of Montreal; The Roy. Candn. Hussars Inst.; Naval Offrs. Assn. of Can.; Conservative; recreation: theatre; Clubs: Naval Officers; Bonaventure; Royal St. Lawrence Yacht; Home: 66 Allan Point, Dorval, Que. H9S 2Z2

PRATT, Robert Cranford, B.A., B.Phil., F.R.S.C.; educator; b. Montreal, Que. 8 Oct. 1926; s. Robert Goodwin and Henrietta (Freeman) P.; e. West Hill High Sch. Montreal 1943; McGill Univ. B.A. 1947; Inst. de Science Politique, Paris; Balliol Coll. Oxford Univ. (Rhodes Scholar) B.Phil. 1952; m. Renate d. Dr. Gerhard and Heidi Hecht, Germany 15 July 1956; children: Gerhard, Marcus, Anna; PROF. OF POL. SCIENCE, UNIV. OF TORONTO since 1966, Dir. Internat. Studies Programme 1967-72; Lectr. Makerere Univ. Coll. Uganda 1954-56; Asst. Prof. McGill Univ. 1952-54 and 1956-58; Research Offr. Inst. Commonwealth Studies, Oxford 1958-60; Princ., Univ. Coll. Dares-Salaam, Tanzania 1961-65; Consultant, Candn. Internat. Dev. Agency, Ford Foundation, Office of the Pres. Tanzania, United Nations Univ. Sout Tanzania: World Bank; rec'd Killam Award 1969; Research Fellowship, Internat. Devel. Research Centre 1978-79; Commonwealth Visiting Prof., Univ. of London, Eng. 1979-80; mem. Ecumenical Forum of Can., Chrmn. 1980-82; Chrmn. Ed. Bd. Centre for Devel. Area Studies, McGill 1969-75; Ed. Bd., The Political Economy of World Poverty Series, Univ. of toronto Press, 1981- ; author "The Critical Phase in Tanzania 1945-68"; Nyerere and the Emergence of a Socialist Strategy" 1976; co-author "Buganda and British Overrule" 1960; co-ed. "Towards Socialism in Tanzania" 1979; "A New Deal in Central Africa" 1960; acad. articles on African politics, devel. issues and Candn. foreign policy; mem. Candn. Assn. African Studies (Pres. 1976-77); Candn. Pol. Science Assn.; NDP; United Church; Home: 205 Cottingham St., Toronto, Ont. M4V 1C4; Office: Dept. of Political Economy, Univ. of Toronto, Toronto, Ont. M5S 1A1.

PRATTE, Claude, Q.C.; b. Quebec City, Que. 11 Jan. 1925; s. Gaston and late Jeannette (Verge) P.; e. Univ. of Montreal; Laval Univ.; B.A., LL.L.; m. France, d. His Excellency the late Hon. Onésime Gagnon, Quebec City 15 June 1957; PARTNER, LETOURNEAU & STEIN Pres., Lepra Inc.; Frontenac Broadcasting Co. Ltd.; Kawartha Broadcasting Co. Ltd.; Katenac Holdings Ltd.; Les Immeubles des Braves Ltée; Placements Verpra Inc.; Sopra Investments Ltd.; Vice Pres., Compagnie de Radiodiffusion de Shawinigan, Falls Ltée; Radio Saguenay Ltée; R. Couillard and Assoc. Inc.; Dir., Candn. Pacific Ltd.; Royal Bank of Canada; Candn. International Paper Co.; National Life Assurance Co. of Canada; Quebec-Telephone; Prades Inc.; Inter-Québec Publicité Inc.; Nordex 1978 Ltd.; Power Corp. of Canada Ltd.; Shawinigan Industries Limited; Trans-Canada Corp. Fund; Canadian Ultramar Limited; Ultramar Canada Inc.; mem., Bar Que.; Candn. Bar Assn.; R. Catholic; recreations: fishing, hunting; Clubs: The Mount Royal; Mount Stephen; Garrison; Canadian (Montreal); Home: 720 Chemin St. Louis, Quebec, Que. G1S 1C2; Office: 65 St. Anne., Quebec, Que. G1R 3X5

PRATTE, Yves, Q.C., B.A., LL.L.; lawyer; b. Quebec City, Que., 7 Mar. 1925; s. Garon and Georgine (Rivard) P.; e. Coll. Garnier, Quebec, B.A., 1944; Laval Univ., LL.L., 1947; Univ. of Toronto, post-grad. courses on taxation and corporate law, 1947-48; m. Paule, d. late Ernest Gauvreau, 1 Mar. 1963; children: Josette, Guy, André; PARTNER, COURTOIS, CLARKSON, PARSONS & TÉTRAULT, since 1979; called to the Bar of Quebec 1947 and to Bar of Ont. 1980; cr. Q.C. 1958; practised law with St. Laurent, Taschereau, Noel and Pratte, 1948-53; Sr. Partner, Pratte, Côté, Tremblay, Beauvais, Bouchard, Garneau & Truchon, 1954-68; Dean, Faculty of Law, Laval Univ., 1962-65; special Legal Counsel for Prime Ministers Jean Lesage and Daniel Johnson 1965-68; mem., Roy. Comn. on Security apptd. by Fed. Govt., Nov. 1966-68; Chrmn. of the Bd. and C.É.O., Air Canada, 1968-75; Mem. of the Bd., Candn. Nat. Railways, 1968-75; Senior partner, Desjardins, Ducharme, Desjardins, Bourque & Pratte, Montreal, 1976-77; Justice Supreme Court of Canada, 1977-79; mem. of Bd., Domtar, 1980; Power Corp. of Can. 1981; La Presse Limitée, 1981; National Bank of Canada, 1981; R. Cath.; Clubs: Mt. Royal; St. James; Quebec Garrison; Ocean Club of Florida; Mt. Bruno Country; Home: Château Apts., Apt. A-110, 1321 Sherbrooke, Montreal, Que.; Office: 630 Dorchester Blvd. W., Montreal, Que. H3B 1V7

PREECE, Norman Brian, M.A.; manufacturer; b. Eng. 20 Oct. 1931; e. Middlesbrough High Sch. 1950; Oxford Univ. M.A. 1955; Harvard Business Sch. AMP 1970; m. Rita Brown; 3 children; PRES., STANTON PIPES LTD. 1964- ; Vice Chrmn. Sidbec-Normines Inc.; Dir. Slater Steel Industries Ltd.; Ipsco; Gen. Mgr. Stanton Pipes (Canada) Ltd. 1958; Vice Pres. Sales, Stanton Pipes Ltd. 1961-64; served with The Green Howards 1950-52, rank Lt.; Pres. Hamilton/Burlington Y.M.C.A.; Chrmn. Hamilton & Dist. Br. Candn. Mfrs. Assn.; Home: Hillholm, Park Rd. S., R.R. 1 Grimsby, Ont.; Office: (P.O. Box 849) Hamilton; Ont. L8N 3N9.

PRENDERGAST, James B., D.F.C.; finance executive; b. Victoria, B.C., 23 Feb. 1920; s. Robert Bernard and Lucille (Halliday) P.; e various schs. in Victoria, m. Patricia Kate, d. Gerald D. Brophy, 23 Sept. 1950; children: Mary Kate, Megan Patricia, James Brian, Jane Diana; PRES., C.E.O. & DIR., WESTROC INDUSTRIES LTD. since 1975; Chrmn. of the Bd. and Dir., Vulcan Industrial Packaging Ltd.; Dir., Ivanhoe Insurance Managers Ltd.; Northumberland General Insurance Co.; United American Fund Ltd.; United Venture Fund Ltd.; United Accumulative Fund Ltd.; United Horizon Fund Ltd.; Trustee, United Accumulative Retirement Fund; United Venture Retirement Fund; United Security Fund; Lukis, Stewart and Co., Ins. Brokers, Montreal, 1946-52; on loan to Dept. Defence Production, Ottawa, 1952; Marsh & McLennan Ltd., Toronto, 1952-55; Pres., various subsids., Combined Enterprises Ltd., 1955-60; with Allied Chemical Corp., N.Y. in various extve. positions incl. Pres., Barrett Div., and Pres., Agric. Div., 1960-69; Depy. Dir., Resources Group, and Pres., Material Service Corp., General Dynamics Corp., Chicago, 1969-70; Pres., C.E.O. and Dir., United Financial Management Ltd., 1970-75; served in 2nd World War as Sqdn. Ldr., R.C.A.F., 1941-45; awarded D.F.C.; Protestant; recreations: golf, squash, skiing, photography; Clubs: Toronto Golf; National; Empire; Canadian; St. James's (Montreal); Royal and Ancient Golf of St. Andrews (Scotland); Home: 58 Old Forest Hill Rd., Toronto, Ont. M5P 2R2; Office: 2650 Lakeshore Highway, Mississauga, Ont. L5J 1K4

PRENT, Mark George, B.F.A.; sculptor; b. Montreal, Que 23 Dec. 1947; e. Sir George Williams Univ. B.F.A. 1970; solo exhns. incl. Sir George Williams Art Galleries Montreal 1971, 1978-79; The Isaacs Gallery Toronto 1972, 1974, 1978, 1981; Warren Benedek Gallery N.Y. 1972; York Univ. Toronto 1974; Akademie der Kunste Berlin 1975-76; Kunsthalle Nurnberg, W. Germany 1976; Stedelijk Museum Amsterdam 1978; Musée d'art contemporain Montreal 1979; Art Space Peterborough, Ont. 1979; Saw Gallery Ottawa 1979; rep. in various group exhns. incl. Survey '70 Montreal Museum of Fine Arts; R.C.A. Travel Exhn. 1971; 8— Biennale de Paris, Musée nat. d'art moderne, Musée d'art moderne de la ville de Paris 1973; 9 out of 10 travel exhn. Ont. 1974-75; Candn. Contemporary Sculpture, Centre Saidye Bronfman Montreal 1978; Birmingham (Ala.) Festival of the Arts 1979; 11th Internat. Sculpture Conf. Dupont Centre, Washington, D.C. 1980; Que. Sculpture 1970-80, Musée d'art contemporain Montreal and Chicoutimi 1980; Maison de la Culture Rennes, France 1980-81; "Sculpture 1980", Maryland Inst., Coll. of Art, Baltimore, Md.; "Prince, Prent, Whiten", The Agnes Etherington Art Centre, Kingston, Ont.; 1981; Univ. of Hawaii and Manoa, Hawaii, 1980; rep. various pub. colls. incl. Art Bank Can., Art Gallery of Ont., Sir George Williams Art Galleries, Musée d'art contemporain; documentary films; "If Brains Were Dynamite, You Wouldn't Have Enough to Blow Your Nose" 1976; "Mark

Prent: Overmood" 1980; recipient Can. Council Arts Awards 1971-78, Sr. Arts Grants 1978, 80, 81; Guggenheim Mem. Foundation Fellowship 1977; Victor M. Lynch-Staunton Award 1978; Guest of Deutsches Akademischer Austauschdienst Artist in Berlin Program 1975; Address: Suite 54, 1610 Sherbrooke West, Montreal, Que. H3H 1E1

PRENTICE, John Gerald, O.C., LL.D.; b. Vienna, Austria, 27 Feb. 1907; s. Otto and Katherine (Pollack-Parnau) Pick; e. Grad., Textile Engn. Sch., Reutlingen, Germany; LL.D. Univ. of Vienna; m. Eva Schlesinger-Acs, 24 May 1932; two d. Mrs. Joseph B. Jarvis, Mrs. John Hurst; CHAIRMAN, CANADIAN FOREST PRODUCTS LTD., since 1970 (Pres. 1950-70); Chrmn., Canfor Limited; Dir., Prince George Pulp & Paper Ltd.; Intercontinental Pulp Co. Ltd.; mem., Vancouver Adv. Board, Royal Trust Co.; Convocation Founder, Simon Fraser Univ.; mem., Candn. Council of Christians & Jews; Chess Fed. of Can. (F.I.D.E. rep.); Hon. Life President, Playhouse Theatre Co.; before coming to Can. in 1938, actively engaged in textile business in Austria and Czechoslovakia; entered plywood industry and in 1940 formed Pacific Veneer Co. Ltd.; acquired Canadian Forest Products Ltd. in 1944; Vice-Pres. until 1950; acquired Howe Sound Pulp Co. Ltd. (merged 1953); mem., Brit. N. Am. Comte.; Candn. Council of The Conference Bd. in Canada; Candn. Chamber Comm.; Vancouver Bd. Trade; New Westminster Chamber Comm.; Newcomen Soc. of N. Am.; B.C. Research Council; Inst. for Research on Public Policy, Ottawa; Extve. Bd., Candn. Pulp & Paper Assn.; Deputy Pres., Fed. Internat. des Echecs (F.I.D.E.); Anglican; Clubs: Men's Canadian; Southlands Riding & Polo; Vancouver Lawn Tennis & Badminton; Capilano Golf & Country; Manhattan Chess; Home: 1537 Matthews Ave., Vancouver, B.C. V6J 2T1; Office: 505 Burrard St., Vancouver, B.C. V7X 1B5

PREST, Victor Kent, M.Sc., Ph.D., F.R.S.C.; geologist; b. Edmonton, Alta. 2 Apl. 1913; s. late John and late Elizabeth (Buckley) P.; e. pub. schs. Edmonton, Toronto and London; high schs. London and Winnipeg; Univ. of Man. B.Sc. 1935, M.Sc. 1936; Univ. of Toronto Ph.D. 1941; m. E. S. Patricia d. late William Horder 24 Oct. 1942; children: Sherron Gail (Mrs. G. C. T. Armstrong), Wayne Horder; Party Chief, Ont. Dept. Mines 1937-40; Research Lab. International Nickel Co. Copper Cliff 1941; Perm. Staff Ont. Dept. Mines 1945-50 and Geol. Survey of Can. 1950-77; Consultant, Ont. Geol. Survey, Toronto 1978-81; served with RCNVR 1942-45, rank Lt.; author book chapters geol. of soils in Can., conserv. geol. features in Can., annd Quaternary geol. of Can.; numerous prof. reports, papers and maps on bedrock and surficial (glacial) geol.; mem. Geol. Assn. Can.; Assn. Québécois pour l'Etude du Quaternaire (Hon. mem.); Am. Quaternary Assn.; Christian Scientist; recreation: curling; Clubs: City View Curling (Pres. 1958); Hon. Gov. Gen.'s Curling (Pres. 1972); Candn. Br., Royal Caledonia Curling (Council of Mang. 1974-79); Home: Apt. 405, 1465 Baseline Rd., Ottawa, Ont. K2C 3L9.

PRESTHUS, Robert Granning, M.A., Ph.D.; educator; author; b. St. Paul, Minn. 25 Feb. 1917; s. Andrew Granning and Edna (Farmen) P.; e. Univ. of Minn. B.A. 1940, M.A. 1941; Univ. of Chicago Ph.D. 1948; Univ. of London Research Scholar 1948-49; m. Sarah d. Charles James Churchill 1 Sept. 1967; one s. Robert Churchill; PROF. OF POL. SCIENCE, YORK UNIV. 1968- ; joined Univ. of S. Calif. 1948-50; Mich. State Univ. 1951-56; Cornell Univ. 1955-67; Un. Nations, Dir. of Research Inst. Pub. Adm. Turkey & Middle E. 1954-55; served with U.S. Navy 1942-46, First Special Service Force Jt. Am.-Candn. Ranger Bgde. Aleutian Campaign, rec'd Commendation 1943; author "The Turkish Conseil d'Etat" 1956; "Public Administration" 6th ed. 1975; "Behavioral Approaches to Public Administration" 1960; "Men at the Top" 1964; "Elite Accommodation in Canadian Politics" 1973; "Elites in the Policy Process" 1974; "The Organizational Society" 2nd ed. 1978; "Cross-National Perspectives: U.S. and Canada" 1978; various articles; Ed. "Administrative Science Quarterly" 1957-67; mem. Ed. Bd. "Theory and Decision"; "Comparative Political Studies"; Research Consultant, Can. Council Social Science & Humanities Div. 1968- ; visiting lectr. numerous Candn. and foreign univs.; mem. Am. Pol. Science Assn.; Am. Sociol. Assn.; Am. Assn. Advanc. Science; Pi Sigma Alpha; Pi Lambda Phi; recreations: golf; Home: 14 Green Valley Rd., Willowdale, Ont. M2P 1A5; Office: 4700 Keele St., Downsview, Ont. M3J 1L2.

PRESTON, Melvin Alexander, C.D., M.A., Ph.D., F.A.A.A.S. (1980), F.R.S.C. (1961); educator; b. Toronto, Ont., 28 May 1921; s. Gardener Alexander and Libbie Hazel (Melvin) P.; e. Earl Haig Coll. Inst., Willowdale, Ont.; Univ. of Toronto, B.A. 1942, M.A. 1946; Univ. of Birmingham, Ph.D. 1949; m. Dorothy Mary Knowles, d. Randal Whittaker, Birmingham, Eng., 16 Aug., 1947; two s. Jonathan Melvin, Richard Franklyn; 2ndly. Eugene, d. F. Shearer, Simcoe, Ont., 25 June 1966; Asst. Lectr. in Math. Physics, Birmingham Univ., 1947-49; Asst. Prof. Physics, Univ. of Toronto, 1949-53; McMaster Univ. appointments 1953-77; Assoc. Prof. and Prof. of Physics; Prof. of Applied Mathematics; Chrmn. of Applied Mathematics, 1962-65 and 1975-77; Dean of Graduate Studies 1965-71; Extve. Vice Chrmn. of Adv. Comte. on Acad. Planning Council of Ont. Univs. 1971-75; Prof. of Physics (1977-) and Vice Pres. (Academic) (1977-82), Univ. of Saskatchewan; Visiting Scientist, Atomic Energy of Canada Ltd., Chalk River, Ont. (summers 1950, 1951, 1952, 1960); Nuffield Travel Grant for Research in Eng., Jan.-July 1957; National Research Council Senior Fellow, Copenhagen, 1963-64; research interests are theoretical and nuclear physics; Publication: "Physics of the Nucleus", 1962; "Structure of the Nucleus", 1975, and many scient. papers in field of physics; retired R.C.A. major; served in 2nd World War in Can. and U.K.; Trustee, Dundas Twp. Sch. Area Bd., 1954-57 (Chrmn. 1957-59); Pres. (1971) Candn. Assn. of Graduate Schs.; Chrmn. (1970-71) Ont. Council on Grad. Studies; mem., Bd. of Governors McMaster Univ. 1966-68, 1976-77; Fellow, Am. Physical Society; mem., Candn. Assn. Physicists (Councillor 1951-52, Treas. 1952-58); Pres., Saskatchewan Sailing Assoc.; Anglican; recreations: sailing, photography; Address: Univ. of Saskatchewan, Saskatoon, Sask. S7N 0W0

PRESTON, W. Jeffrey; manufacturer; b. Montreal, Que., 18 April 1916; s. James and Flroence (Campbell) P.; e. Public Sch. and Stratford (Ont.) Coll. Inst.; m. Isabel, d. Alexander Carstairs, 27 Jan. 1945; children: Jane, James, William; Chmn., Prestonia Stationery Mfg.; MacMillan Office Appliances Company Ltd.; President (1965) Stratford United Appeal; mem., Stratford Bd. Educ.; Chrmn. Stratford Parks Bd., Past Pres., Candn. Furniture Mfrs. Assn.; Stratford Rotary Club; Comte. of Stewards of St. Johns Ch.; served in 2nd World War, 1940-1945, Major, Cameron Highlanders of Ottawa; served in Britain, France; Mentioned in Despatches; mem., Candn. Office Products Association (Past President); United Church; recreations: golf, curling; Club: Stratford Country & Curling; Home: 133 Elizabeth St., Stratford, Ont. N5A 4Z4 Office: 163 King St., Stratford, Ont. N5A 4S2

PRETTY, David Walter, M.B.A.; retired insurance executive; b. Toronto, Ont., 23 Aug. 1925; s. Joseph Melville and Olive Francis (Page) P.; e. Blythwood Pub. Sch., 1938 and Earl Haig Coll. Inst., 1943; Univ. of Toronto, B.Com. 1947, M.B.A. 1955; unm.; PRES. PRETTY CONSULTANTS INC., 1980- ; Dir., General Accident Assnce. Co. of Can.; North Amer. Life Assur. Co. 1947; apptd. Mgr., Securities Dept., 1950; Asst. Treas. 1955; Assoc. Treas. 1959; Treasurer 1965; Vice President and Treasurer 1966; Vice-Pres., Finance 1968; Extve. Vice-Pres. 1971; Pres., 1972-80; rec'd. Centennial Medal; Gov., Ont. Br. and former Nat. Vice Pres., Royal Life Saving Soc. Can.;

Chrmn., Div. of Finance & former Chrmn., Investment Comte., United Church of Canada; Mem. and Past Pres., Bd. of Govs., The Queen Elizabeth Hosp.; Treas. and mem. of the Bd. of Regents, Victoria Univ.; Vice Pres., The Boy Scouts Assn. of Metro Toronto; Liberal; Un. Church; recreations: golf, gardening; Clubs: Toronto; Toronto Golf; Granite; Bd. of Trade Metrop. Toronto; Office: 206 St. Leonard's Ave., Toronto, Ont. M4N 1K7;

PREVOST, Hon. Claude; retired judge; b. St. Jerome, Que., March 1909; s. Hon. Jean and Gabrielle (Gagnon) P.; e. Coll. Ste-Marie, Montreal, B.A. 1928; Univ. of Montreal, LL.B. 1931; m. Marguerite, d. L. P. Pelletier, Apl. 1938; children: Jean, Marc, Alain, France (Mrs. Marc Bourgeois); Justice, Superior Court of Que. 1952-78; read law with Brown, Montgomery & McMichael and with Hyde, Ahern, Perron, Puddicombe and Smith; cr. K.C. (now Q.C.) 1944; practised law with latter firm prior to founding law firm of Prevost, Montpetit, Noel, Desjardins & Ducharme, 1945; Jr. Crown Prosecutor for Dist. of Montreal 1939, Sr. Crown Prosecutor 1942; Prof. of Law, Univ. of Montreal, 1947-56; Kt. Grand Cross Magistral Grace Sovereign and Mil. Order of Malta; former Dir., Montreal Council of Bar and of Bar Assn. Prov. Que., former Pres., Young Libs. Assn. Montreal; Vice Pres., Twentieth Century Lib. Assn. Can.; recreations: tennis, golf, music, reading, travel; Home: 620 Graham Blvd., Town of Mount Royal, Que. H3P 2E2;

PRÉVOST, (Joseph Gaston Charles) André; composer; educator; b. Hawkesbury, Ont. 30 July 1934; e. St-Jérôme, Qué.; Séminaire de St-Thérèse; Coll. de St-Laurent; studied harmony and counterpoint, composition CMM (Premier prix harmony, composition 1960); rec'd Sarah Fischer Concerts composition prize 1959; Chamber Music Award Amis de l'art foundation 1959; studied analysis with Olivier Messiaen, Paris Conserv. and worked with Henry Dutilleux, Ecole normale 1961 (Can. Council and Que. Govt. grants); studied electronic music with Michel Phillipot at ORTF, Paris 1964; teacher at Séminaire de Joliette and Coll. des Eudistes, Rosemont 1962; joined Faculty of Music, Univ. of Montreal 1964; attended Berkshire Music Center Tanglewood 1964; rec'd Prix d'Europe for composition 1963; symphonic work "Fantasmes" rec'd Amis de l'art foundation prize 1963 and Montreal Symphony Orchestra prize 1964; U.S.A. premiere Carnegie Hall 1977; rec'd comn. for musical work on "Man and His World" Expo 67; recording of his "Sonato" for violin and piano rec'd Festival du disque Prize, Montreal; "Suite for String Quartet" comnd. by Ten Centuries Concerts Toronto in collaboration with Candn. Music Centre and Candn. Confed. Centennial Comn. 1966, premiered by Orford String Quartet 1968; "Terre des Hommes" for large orchestra, 3 choirs and 2 narrators premiered Place des Arts 1967 at inauguration Expo 67 World Festival; by late 1970's had rec'd and completed over 20 comns. from orchestras and other organs. incl. "Paraphrase" for string quartet and orchestra premiered by Toronto Symphony Orchestra (also comnd. by TSO) and Orford String Quartet 1980; named Dir. Candn. Music Centre 1971; Pres. Groupe Nouvelle-Aire 1973; rec'd Candn. Music Council Medal 1977; St-Jérôme auditorium named after him; mem. Candn. League Composers; affiliate PRO Canada; Assoc., Candn. Music Centre; Address: 227 ave Querles, Outremont, Montreal, Que. H2V 3W1.

PRICE, Derek A., A.B.; executive; b. Quebec City, Que., 10 Aug. 1932; s. John H. and Lorna (MacDougall) P.; e. Bishop's Coll. Sch., Lennoxville, Que.; Princeton Univ., A.B. 1954; m. Jill McConnell, 29 June 1954; three d.; CHRMN. STARLAW INVESTMENTS LTD.; Trustee, Princeton Univ.; with Bank of Montreal, 1954-57; Vice-Pres., Willyn Industries Ltd., 1957-61; St. Lawrence Sugar Refineries, 1961-63; joined Montreal Standard Publishing Co., 1965, becoming Asst. to Mang. Dir., 1966; joined Montreal Star Co. Ltd. as Asst. Vice-Pres., 1966;

Dir., Vice-Pres. and Gen. Mgr. 1967-68; Chrmn. and Chief Extve. Offr. 1968-70; Publisher 1970; Anglican; Clubs: Montreal Racket; Home: 3999 Montrose Ave., Westmount, Que. H3Y 2A3;

PRICE, Fred W., M.A.; retired public service; b. Montreal, Que., 13 Dec. 1916; s. Frederick S. and Mary J. (Johnson) P.; e. High Sch. of Montreal; McGill Univ., B.A. 1937, M.A. 1942; m. Nan., d. late Percy Roycroft, 6 April 1942; one d. Holly; Public Relations Counsel, Ottawa; High Sch. Teacher, Montreal Prot. Sch. Bd., 1937-46; with Engn. and Comm. Depts., The Bell Telephone Co. of Canada, 1946-62; Mgr. of Information & Publications, Northern Electric Co. Ltd., Research & Devel. Labs., Ottawa, Ont. 1962-63; Extve. Dir., Candn. Conf. on Educ., 1959-62; Extve. Dir., Roy. Arch. Inst. of Can., 1963-67; Sr. Consultant and Dir. of Health Information Programs, Dept. of Nat. Health and Welfare, 1967-79; mem. of Ottawa Public Sch. Bd., 1963-69; Extve. mem., Candn. Comn. for Human Rights, 1967; accredited mem., Candn. Pub. Relations Soc.; mem., Social Planning Council of Ottawa-Carleton; Pres., Fraternity House 1974-76; served in 2nd World War Candn. Armoured Corps (17th Duke of York's Royal Candn. Hussars), Reserve 1940-42, Active Service in Can., U.K. and N.W. Europe 1942-46; United Church; recreations: skiing, golf; Clubs: Candn. Legion; Kiwanis; Home: 131 Mountbatten Ave., Ottawa, Ont. K1H 5V6

PRICE, Brig. Gen. John Herbert, O.C., O.B.E., M.C., E.D., D.C.L.; retired industrialist; b. Quebec, Que., 5 Aug. 1898; s. Sir William and Lady Amelia Blanche P.; e. Bishop's Coll. Sch., Lennoxville, Que.; Roy. Mil. Coll.; m. Katherine Lorna, d. H. B. MacDougall, Montreal, 23 Sept. 1924; Dir., Saguenay Power Co. Ltd.; J. H. Minet & Co. (1954) Canada Ltd.; Robert McAlpine Ltd.; Consol. Plant Airport Building Holdings Ltd. (and related co.'s); Dir. Bishops University Foundation; served in 1st World War with 70th and 147 Army Brigade, R.F.A., 15th Scottish Division; wounded; awarded Military Cross 1918; 2nd World War, with Royal Rifles of Canada at Hong Kong; Knight, St. Lazarus of Jerusalem; Hon. Pres., Candn. Human Rights Foundation; Freemason; Anglican; recreations: golf, skiing, fishing; Clubs: Mount Royal; Garrison (Quebec); The Brook (N.Y.); Canadian; Montreal Racket: Mount Bruno Golf & Country; Hermitage; Farmers of Montreal; Carleton (London, Eng.); Canadian (N.Y.); Home: 2 Westmount Square, Montreal, Que. H3Z 2S4

PRICE, Hon. Norma Lorraine, M.L.A.; politician; b. Winnipeg, Man. 19 Aug. 1920; d. Clement A. and Aurora (Martel) Killeen; e. Immaculate Conception Sch.; St. Mary's Acad.; m. James Edward Price 1 Feb. 1940; children: Linda, Randy, Donna; MIN. OF CULTURAL AFFAIRS & HISTORICAL RESOURCES, MAN. 1979- ; el. M.L.A. for Assiniboia prov. g.e. 1977; Min. Responsible for Civil Service Act, Civil Service Superannuation Act, Pub. Servants Ins. Act, Pensions Benefits Act 1977; Min. of Tourism & Cultural Affairs 1978; P. Conservative; R. Catholic; Office: 343 Legislative Bldg., Winnipeg, Man. R3C 0V8.

PRICE, Raymond Alexander, B.Sc., M.A., Ph.D., P. Eng., F.G.S.A., F.R.S.C.; b. Winnipeg, Man. 25 March 1933; s. Alexander Fredrick and Edith Olga (Arlt) P.; e. Univ. of Man. B.Sc. 1955; Princeton Univ. M.A. 1957, Ph.D. 1958; m. Wilhelmina Sofia d. Theodore John Geurds 15 Sept. 1956; children: Paul Raymond, Patricia Ann, Linda Marie; DIR.-GENERAL GEOL. SURVEY OF CANADA, Dept. of Energy, Mines and Resources Can. since 1981; Geol. and Research Scient. Geol. Survey of Can. Dept. Energy Mines & Resources Can. 1958-68; Assoc. Prof. Queen's Univ. 1968-70, Prof. of Geol. Sciences, 1970-81, Head of Geol. Sciences 1972-77; Fellow, Geol. Assn. Can; mem. Assn. Prof. Engrs. Prov. Ont; Pres. Internat. Council of Scientific Unions Interunion Comm. on

the Lithosphere; R. Catholic; Home: 1 Inuvik Cres., Kanata, Ont. K2L 1A1; Office: 601 Booth St., Ottawa, Ont. K1A 0E8.

PRICHARD, John Stobo, M.C., M.A., M.B., B.Chir., F.R.C.P. (London), F.R.C.P. (Can.), F.A.A.N.; b. Barry, Wales 16 May 1914; e. Private Schs. Eng.; Cambridge Univ. M.A., M.B., B. Chir. 1938; m. Joan Suzanne, M.B.E. d. Sir Robert Webber, Cardiff, Wales; Children: Dr. Jane Gaskell, Robert, LL.M., Dr. Sarah, F.R.C.P.; Retired Head Div. of Neurol. and Dept. of Electroencephalography, and now Consultant, Dept. of Paediatrics, and Dir. Child Development Clinic, Hosp. for Sick Children, Toronto; Prof. of Paediatrics, Univ. of Toronto; Consultant, Surrey Place Centre, Toronto; Ed. in Chief "International Review of Child Neurology"; Chrmn. Ont. Adv. Council for Special Educ.; Candn. Advisor in Neurol. to Thailand Govt. 1964, 1969; Chrmn. Candn. Cong. Neurol. Sciences 1968; Pres. Candn. Neurol. Sc. 1968; Pres., E. Electroencephalography Soc. 1968; Internat. Child Neurol. Assn. 1973-75; Founder mem. Research Group Dyslexia, World Fed. Neurol. 1968 and mem. Research Group Paediatric Neurol. 1971; Pres. First Internat. Cong. Child Neurol. 1975; served in 2nd WW 1939-45, Awarded Military Cross 1941; rec'd Brit. Postgrad. Travelling Fellowship 1949; Candn. Centennial Medal 1967; author or co-author book chapters, series; numerous journ. publs. on child neurol.; Pres. E. Electroencephalography Soc. 1968; Pres. Internat. Child Neurol. Assn. 1973-75; Hon. mem. Pediatric Soc. Peru 1969; Purkinje Soc. (Czeckoslovakia) 1975; Clubs: Rosedale Golf; Glen Major Angling; Home: 22 Old Yonge St., Willowdale, Ont. M2P 1P7 & Sand Lake, Kearney, Ont. P0A 1M0

PRIESTLEY, Francis Ethelbert Louis, M.A., Ph.D., D.Litt., F.R.S.C. (1953), F.R.S.L. (1958); university professor; b. Banbury, Eng., 12 Mar. 1905; s. George Ernest and Catherine Mary (Roberts) P.; e. Northampton Town & County Sch., Eng.; Lethbridge H.S.; Calgary Normal School; Univ. of Alta., B.A. 1930, M.A. 1932; Univ. of Toronto, Ph.D. 1940; D.Litt. Mount Allison 1964; Alberta 1973; Western Ontario 1973; Hon. Lifetime Fellow, Huron College, 1977; m. late Carman Dixon, d. W. Dixon Craig, K.C., Edmonton, Alberta, 2 August 1933; one s. Christopher Douglas Craig; PROF. EMERITUS OF ENGLISH, UNIV. OF TORONTO and Assoc., Inst. for Hist. and Philos. of Science and Technol.; mem., Humanities Research Council Can., 1961-64; Gen. Editor, "Collected Works of J. S. Mill", 1962-71; mem., Ed. Bd. of "Journal of the History of Ideas"; Instr., Univ. of Alta., 1931, 1934-36; Asst. Prof., Univ. of B.C., 1940-44; joined faculty of Univ. of Toronto, 1944; Publications: Godwin's "Political Justice" (critical ed.) 1946; part author of "Science and the Creative Spirit", 1958; special ed. "The Canadian Dictionary", 1962; author "The Humanities in Canada", 1964; "Language & Structure in Tennyson's Poetry" 1973; numerous articles & reviews in learned journs.; mem., Internat. Soc. for Hist. of Ideas (Dir.); Internat. Assn. Univ. Profs. of Eng. (Internat. Comte.); Humanities Assn. Can. (Pres. 1962-64); Open Fellowships, Univ. of Toronto, 1937-39; Travelling Fellowship, Royal Soc. of Canada, 1939; First Nuffield Commonwealth Fellow in the Humanities, 1949; Can. Council Fellowship, 1964-65; rec'd Queen's Jubilee Medal; Conservative; recreations: photography, music; Home: 269 Woburn Ave., Toronto, Ont. M5M 1L1

PRIESTMAN, Brian, B.Mus., M.A.; orchestral conductor; b. Birmingham, Eng., 10 Feb. 1927; s. Miles and Margaret Ellen (Messer) P.; e. Sidcot Sch., Eng., 1938-43; Univ. of Birmingham, B.Mus. 1950 (1st Class Hons.), M.A. 1952; Conservatoire Royal de Bruxelles, 1950-52 (Diplome Superieur de Direction); came to Canada in 1964; unm.; Conductor, Edmonton Symphony Soc. 1964-68; Conductor, Nat. Youth Orchestra, Can. 1967 and 1970; Musical Dir. of various organs, in U.K., incl. Royal

Shakespeare Theatre at Stratford-on-Avon, Eng., 1960-63 and U.S., incl. M.D. Denver Symphony 1970-78 Dir., South African Coll. of Music, Univ. of Cape Town and Dean of Fac. of Music; widely travelled as a conductor of orchestral concerts and opera, incl. many performances at Carnegie Hall and Philharmonic Hall, N.Y.; has executed records for RCA and Westminster; frequently Conductor for CBC radio and television; Home: 200 S.E. 15 Rd., Miami, Fla. 33129; Office: Univ. of Cape Town, South Africa

PRIMEAU, Raymond, B.A., B.Sc.A., LL.L., D.B.A., D.E.S.; educator; b. Howick, Que. 29 Jan. 1928; s. late Joseph Aimé and Félixine (Vincent) P.; Univ. of Montreal B.A. 1948 (Coll. of Valleyfield), B.Sc.A. 1953, LL.L. 1957, D.E.S. 1967; London Sch. of Econ. (Brit. Council Scholarship 1957-58) D.B.A. Dipl. 1958; m. Jeannine d. late Gédéon Bernard 30 Aug. 1955; children: François, Marie; PROF. OF FINANCE & ECON. ECOLE POLYTECHNIQUE, UNIV. OF MONTREAL since 1975; Dir. Crown Life Insurance Co. Ltd.; mem. Invest. Comte. Can. Council; Prof. of Law Univ. of Montreal 1959-60; The Provincial Bank of Canada 1961-74, Chief Operating Offr. 1967-74, Dir. and Vice Pres. Bd. Dirs. 1970-74; mem. Bd. Jr. Chamber Comm. 1958-60; Indust. Expansion Council Montreal 1967-69; Fonds Internat. de Coop. Universitaire 1968-69; Assoc. Hon. Treas. Candn. Chamber Comm. 1971-73; Fed. Adv. Comte. Northern Pipeline Financing 1973; mem. Bd. Hôpital St-Luc 1968-73 (Chrmn. Finanne Comte.); Corp. Ecole Polytechnique 1969-71; Gov. Conseil du Patronat du Qué. 1969-74; mem. Econ. Council of Can. 1973-79; Pres. Que. Foundation Econ. Educ. 1978-79; mem. Candn. Bankers' Assn. (Extve. Council 1967-74, Vice Pres. 1970-74); served with COTC, rank Lt.; author 'Problèmes de Financement' 1978; R. Catholic; recreations: skiing, golf, music; Home: 1844 Ave. Lajoie, Outremont, Qué. H2V 1S3; Office: (C.P. 6079) Montreal, Qué. H3C 3A7.

PRINCE, Alan T., M.A., Ph.D.; retired scientist; civil servant; b. 15 Feb. 1915; e. Univ. of Toronto, B.A. 1937, M.A. 1938; Univ. of Chicago, Ph.D. 1941; 2 children; Pres., Atomic Energy Control Board, 1975-78; Junior Research Chemist, Division of Chem., Nat. Research Council, 1940-43; Research Chem. and Petrographer, Canadian Refractories Ltd., Kilmar, Que., 1943-45; Lectr., Univ. of Man., 1945-46; joined Dept. of Mines & Tech. Surveys as Head, Ceramic Sec., Mines Br., Ottawa, 1946-50; Head, Phys. and Crystal Chem. Sec., 1950-55; Sr. Research Off., Mineral Dressing and Process Metall. Div., 1955-59; Chief, Mineral Sciences Div., 1959-65; Dir., Water Research Br., Dept. Energy Mines & Resources 1965-67; Dir. Gen., Inland Waters Br., Dept. Environment 1967-73; Asst. Depy. Min. (Planning & Evaluation) Dept. Energy, Mines & Resources 1973-75; Pres., Atomic Energy Control Bd., 1975; published articles and patents; Candn. Chrmn. (four Adv. Bds.). Internat. Jt. Comn., Great Lakes Water Quality Bd.; Fraser River Flood Control Bd.; Sask.-Nelson Basin Bd.; Okanagan Basin Bd.; Fellow Chem. Inst. Can.; Mineral. Soc. Am.; mem., Candn. Inst Mining & Metall.; Mineral Assn. Can.; Assn. Prof. Engrs. Ont.; Home: 20 Riverside Drive (P.O. Box 106), Manotick, Ont. K0A 2N0

PRINCE, Richard Edmund, B.A., R.C.A.; artist; educator; b. Comox, B.C. 6 Apl. 1949; s. Charles Robert and Patricia Rosalene (Stubbs) P.; e. Univ. of B.C. B.A. 1971, grad. studies 1972-73; m. Kathryn Diane Beaulieu 5 Sept. 1970; Asst. Prof. of Art Univ. of B.C. 1978- ; Pres. Bd. Dirs. Green Thumb Theatre for Young People 1979- ; Instr. in Sculpture Vancouver Sch. of Art (Night) 1973-74; Vancouver Community Coll. Langara 1974-75; Univ. of B.C. 1975-77, Visiting Lectr. in Sculpture 1977-78; Artist in Residence Queen Charlotte Island, Nat. Museums of Can. 1975; Juror City of Vancouver Art Purchase Award Program 1976; Dir. Vancouver Art Gallery 1977-80; solo exhns. incl. N.S. Coll. Art & Design 1974; Isaacs Gallery

Toronto 1976, 1978; Equinox Gallery Vancouver 1977; rep. in numerous group exhns. since 1970; rep. in pub., corporate and private colls. incl. Nat. Gallery Can., Can. Council Art Bank, Vancouver Art Gallery; rec'd Can. Council Arts Bursary 1972-73, Arts Grants 1974-75, 1977-78; Art Vancouver '74 Purchase Award 1973-74; cited various bibliogs.; mem. Univs. Art Assn. Can. (B.C. Rep. to Bd. Dirs.); Address: 285 W. 18th Ave., Vancouver, B.C. V5Y 2A8.

PRINGLE, Donald McKinnon, Q.C., B.A.; b. Toronto, Ont., 28 Dec. 1923; s. Kenneth McKinnon and Catherine Isobel (McEachern) P.; e. Upper Canada Coll. (1941); Univ. of Toronto, B.A. 1944; Osgoode Hall Law Sch.; m. Phyllis Katharine, d. A. L. Anderson, Toronto, Ont., 23 April 1949; children: Andrew McKinnon, Kenneth Anderson, John Gerald, Donald Anthony Geoffrey; PARTNER, LASH, JOHNSTON; Chrmn., Royal Ins. Group; Dir., Gananoque Electric Co. Ltd.; H. I. Thompson Co. of Canada Ltd.; Kimberly-Clark of Canada Ltd.; St. Lawrence Starch Co. Ltd.; Neosid (Can.) Ltd.; Inglis Ltd.; read law with Lash & Lash; called to the Bar of Ont. 1948; cr. Q.C. 1960; served in Candn. Army 1943-45, Lieut.; mem., Candn. Bar Assn.; York Co. Law Assn.; Delta Kappa Epsilon; Anglican; Clubs: The Toronto; Badminton & Racquet; Toronto Hunt; Home: 5 Dunloe Road, Toronto, Ont. M4V 2W4; Office: North Tower, P.O. Box 11, Royal Bank Plaza, Toronto, Ont. M5J 2J1

PRINGLE, John Alexander, E.D., C.D., B.Acc.; university administrator; b. Treherne, Man. 6 Aug. 1915; s. Eva Maude and late Ernest Hamilton P.; e. Elem. Schs. Winnipeg, Man. 1922 and Craik, Sask. 1928; High Sch. Craik, Sask. 1930 and Harris, Sask. 1932; Univ. of Sask., B.Acc. 1938; m. Marion Ethel, d. late Henry Thompson 29 April 1942; children: Robert John, Donald Alexander, Harry William; VICE-PRES., ADM., UNIV. OF SASKATCHEWAN since 1975; joined Sask. Govt., Prov. Auditor's Dept. 1939; Asst. Bursar, Univ. of Sask. 1947, Business Mgr. 1956, Controller and Treas. 1957; COTC Univ. of Sask. 1936; 2nd Lt.-Maj. 8Fd Regt R.C.A. 1939-45, Italy and N.W. Europe; Mil.-Maj. O/C 18 Batty RCA — and subsequently Lt. Col. and C.O. 17 LAA Regt. R.C.A., 10 Med. Regt. R.C.A. and Brig-Gen. Commdr. 21 Mil. Group 1946-63; Trustee, Army Benevolent Fund 1962-79; Chrmn. Saskatoon Poppy Fund; mem. Bd. Govs. Corps. Commissionaires Saskatoon; Adv. Bd. for Mil Colls. 1973-76; mem. Sask. Bd. CNIB (Vice-Chrmn. N. Sask. Adv. Bd.); Financial Extves. Inst.; Candn. Assn. Univ. Business Offrs. (Past Pres.); Past mem. Batten Comn. on Public Accounting 1966-67; Un. Church; recreations: hunting, golf; Clubs: Faculty; Saskatoon; USI (Regina); Joel; Rotary; Riverside Country; Home: 1124 Main St., Saskatoon, Sask. S7H 0K9; Office: Saskatoon, Sask.

PRINGLE, Robert W., O.B.E. (1967), B.Sc., Ph.D., F.Inst.P., F.R.S.E. (1964), F.R.S.C. (1955); physicist; b. Edinburgh, Scotland, 2 May 1920; s. late Robert and late Lillias Dalgeish (Hair) P.; e. George Heriot's Sch., Edin.; Univ. of Edinburgh, B.Sc. (1st Class Hons. in Physics) 1942 and Ph.D., 1944; m. Jean Clunas, Tweed, Ont; d. late John Foster Stokes, 21 Sept. 1948; children: Vivien Claire, Robert Shaun, David Moray, Andrew Roderick John; Lectr. in Physics., Edin. Univ., 1945-48; Assoc. Prof. of Physics, Univ. of Man., 1948-51; Prof. 1951-56; Chrmn. of Physics Dept., 1953-56; from 1949-56 was responsible for the devel. of a research group in nuclear physics at Univ. of Man., specializing in nuclear spectroscopy, and in the devel. of the "scintillation counter"; Managing Director, Nuclear Enterprises Ltd., Edinburgh 1956-76; Pres., Nuclear Enterprises Ltd., Winnipeg, Man., since 1950; mem., Astron., Space, and Radio Bd. of Science Research Council of U.K. 1970-72; mem., Science Research Council of U.K. (and Nuclear Physics Bd. there 1972-76); Scottish Econ. Council 1971-74; mem. of Court of Edinburgh Univ. 1967-75; Hon. Fellow, Royal

Scottish Soc. Arts 1972; Conservative; Presbyterian; Home: 27 Avenue Princess Grace, Monaco; Office: Nuclear Enterprises Ltd., 61 Cordova St., Winnipeg, Man.

PRISCO, Walter Alexander, B.A., M.B.A.; banker; b. Vermillion, Alta, 11 April 1934; s. late John Harry and Alexandra P.; e. North Bay (Ont.) Coll. Inst.; McMaster Univ.; Univ. of Western Ont., B.A., M.B.A.; PRES. AND C.E.O. NORLAND BANK; Pres., Sovereign Hotel Operating Co. Ltd.; Dir. American Hoist of Canada Ltd.; Candn. Superior Oil Ltd.; Machinery Investment Co. of Can. Ltd.; Calgary Stampede Football Club; joined The Industrial Development Bank as Credit Offr., Montreal 1962; Mgr., St. Regis Hotel, North Bay, Ont. 1964; Extve. Trainee, Mercantile Bank of Canada 1966, Asst. Mgr. Vancouver 1967, Mgr. Calgary 1969, Regional Gen. Mgr. E. Region 1970, Vice-Pres. E. Region 1972; Vice Pres., Ont. Div., & Sen. Vice Pres., Ont. Div., 1974; Extve. Vice Pres. & Chief Gen. Manager, Montreal, 1975; Extve. Vice Pres. & Chief Gen. Mgr., Merchant Banking Div., Toronto, 1979; Home: 512 Coach Grove Rd., N.W., Calgary, Alta. T3H 1J4 Office: 1200 Home Oil Tower, 324 - 8th Ave. S.W., Calgary, Alta. T2P 2Z2I1

PROCTOR, John Stewart; L.L.D.; retired banker; b. Vancouver, B.C., 14 July 1904; s. late William Frederick and Katherine Mary P.; e. Victoria (B.C.) High Sch.; Victoria Coll., Univ. of Brit. Columbia; m. Kathleen Allan, d. late Frank Colpman, 17 Apl, 1929; one d. Dianne Mary; Gen. Accident Assnce Co. of Canada; Chrmn., Dir. and mem. Extve. Comte., R. L. Crain Ltd.; Vice-Pres. and Dir. Mutual Life Assurance Co. of Can.; Dir., Princess Margaret Hosp., Toronto; Hon. Dir., Wellesley Hosp., Toronto; Hon. Dir., Bank of Nova Scotia; founding mem., Bd. of Govs., York Univ.; Chrmn. Bd. of Trustees, Ont. Crippled Children's Centre; Home: Granite Place, 63 St. Clair Ave. W., Suite 1701, Toronto, Ont. M4V 2Y9; Office: Box 14, First Canadian Place, Toronto, Ont. M5X 1A9

PROULX, Mt. Rev. Adolphe (R.C.); b. Hanmer, Ont., 12 Dec. 1927; s. Augustin and Marie-Louise (Tremblay) P.; e. Hanmer, Ont., Sudbury (Ont.) High Sch.; Sacred Heart Coll., Sudbury; Laval Univ., B.A.; St. Augustine's Semy., Toronto, Ont.; Angelicum, Rome, Lic. in Canon Law 1958; BISHOP OF HULL, since 1974; (former Auxiliary Bishop of Sault Ste. Marie); Titular Bishop of Missua; o. Priest 1954; appointed Assistant, St. Vincent de Paul Parish, North Bay, then Our Lady of Mercy Parish, Coniston, Ont., 1955; Chancellor of Diocese of Sault Ste. Marie, North Bay, 1958; Bishop of Alexandria 1967-74; served also on Matrimonial Tribunal as Defender of the Bond and Officials and appointed Director of Catholic Action for French-speaking sec. of Diocese and Asst.-Dir. of Vocations: named Papal Chamberlain by Pope John XXIII; has served as a Diocesan Consultor since 1963; mem. of the Social Affairs Commn. of the Candn. Conf. of Catholic Bishops; Pres., Human Rights Commn. for the same conference; mem. of the Episcopal Comte. for Social Affairs and for Theology for l'Assemblée des Eveques du Québec; Address: 115 Carillon St., Hull, Que. J8X 2P8

PRUS, Victor Marius, M.Arch., R.C.A., F.R.A.I.C., C.I.P., R.I.B.A., Hon. F.A.I.A.; architect; b. Poland 19 Apl. 1917; e. Chelmno 1930-35; Warsaw Tech. Univ. Dipl. Arch. 1939; Univ. of Liverpool 1945-46 Inq. Arch. (M. Arch.), m. Maria Fisz 22 Sept. 1948; came to Can. 1952; PRINC., VICTOR PRUS & ASSOCIATES, ARCHITECTS AND URBANISTS; Arch.: Montreal Convention Centre; New Internat. Airport, Barbados; Observatory Mauna Kea, Hawaii; Grand Théâtre de Québec; Conserv. of Music, Que.; Montreal Metro Stns.: Bonaventure, Mt. Royal, Langelier; Brudenell River Resort, P.E.I.; Place Longueuil Commercial Centre; Rockland Shopping Centre; Centaur Theatres, Montreal; Expo '67 Stadium; James Lyng Sch., Montreal; recipient Massey Medal for Arch.; Candn Arch. Award; 1st Prize Que, Performing Arts Centre; 1st

Prize RCAF Mem.; 1st Prize Montreal Congres Centre; visit. prof. McGill Univ., 1953, 1966, 1972; prof. Ecole d'arch. Quebec 1959; visit. prof. Washington Univ. St. Louis, Mo., 1978; served with 305 (P) Sqdn. RAF World War II, rank Flying Offr.; rec'd Polish Cross of Valour (twice); Fellow, Royal Arch. Inst. of Can.; Academician, Royal Can. Academy of Arts; Hon. Fellow, Am. Inst. Archs.; mem. Royal Inst. Brit. Archs.; Candn. Inst. Planners; Home: 108 Senneville Rd., Senneville, Que. H9X 1B9; Office: 1420 Sherbrooke St. W., Suite 301, Montreal, Que. H3G 1K5.

PRYCE, Melvin Clare, B.A., F.S.A., F.C.I.A.: retired insurance executive; b. Windsor, Ont., 12 March 1914; s. Chester Frederick and Lillie Clare P.; e. Lord Roberts Pub. Sch. and Central Coll., London, Ont.; Univ. of W. Ont., B.A. 1936, Mang. Training Course 1961; m. Ruth Fairfax, d. late Augustus Collyer, 24 May 1940; two d. Mary Jane, Barbara Ruth; joined London Life Insurance Co. 1936; Asst. Actuary 1950; Assoc. Actuary 1957; Actuary 1960; Vice-Pres. and Gen. Mgr. 1970; Extve. Vice Pres. 1971-79; served with RCAF 1940-45; rank Sqdn. Leader; mem., Vimy Br., Roy. Candn. Legion; Delta Upsilon; P. Conservative; Presbyterian; recreations: golf, bridge; Club: London Hunt & Country; The London; Home: 196 Bridport St., London, Ont. N6A 2A8

PUCCETTI, Roland Peter, B.A., M.A., D. de l'Univ.; educator; b. Oak Park, Ill. 11 Aug. 1924; s. George and Marie (McKone) P.; came to Can. 1971; e. Univ. of Ill. B.A. 1948; Univ. of Toronto M.A. 1950; Univ. of Paris, D. de l'Univ. 1952; m. Marie Rose Jeanne Maroun 7 Nov. 1959; children: Maïa Clara, Peter Harry; PROFESSOR, HEAD OF PHILOSOPHY, DALHOUSIE UNIV. 1976- ; Instr., Assoc. Prof. of Phil., Amer. Univ. of Beirut 1954-65; Prof. and Head of Phil. Dept., Univ. of Singapore 1965-71; Prof. and Chrmn., Dept. of Phil., Dalhousie Univ. 1971-76; U.S. Parachute Infantry (Cpl.) 1942-44; author "Persons" 1969; "The Death of the Fuhrer" 1972 (novel); "The Trial of John and Henry Norton" 1973 (novel); numerous articles in professional journals; mem., Candn. Assn. of Univ. Teachers; Dalhousie Faculty Assn. (Pres. 1976-77); Univ. of Singapore Academic Staff Assn. (Pres. 1970); Candn. Phil. Assn.; Amer. Phil. Assn.; listed in "Who's Who in America" since 1974; Can. Council Leave Fellowshp. 1977-78; Club: Dalhousie Univ. Faculty; Home: 14 Oceanview Dr., Purcell's Cove, Halifax, N.S. B3P 2H3; Office: Halifax, N.S. B3H 3J5

PUCKETT, Terence Charles, M.B.A.; accountant; executive; b. London, Eng. 4 Aug. 1940; s. George and Kathleen (Lehain) P.; e. Roan Grammar Sch. for Boys Blackheath, Eng. 1958; York Univ. Toronto M.B.A. 1975; m. Marion Frances d. Richard White 21 Nov. 1961; two s. Ian Charles, Kevin Richard; VICE PRES. FINANCE AND DIR. THE ONTARIO PAPER CO. LTD. 1981- ; Dir. Quebec and Ontario Transportation Co. Ltd.; Q.N.S. Paper Co. Ltd.; Manicouagan Power Co. Ltd.; Gen. Acct. Prudential Assurance, Eng. 1958-64; Financial Analyst Ford Motor Co., Eng. 1964-66; Co. Acct. Molins Machine Co., Eng. 1966-68; Asst. Controller American Motors, Can. 1968-75; Gen. Operations Mgr. Reed Paper, Can. 1975-68; Consultant Currie, Coopers & Lybrand 1969-81, Can.; Dir. Ont. Paper Foundation; Fellow, Assn. Cert. Accts.; P. Conservative; Anglican; recreations: chess, squash, reading; Club: St. Catharines; Home: 2745 Wessel Dr., R.R. 1, St. Catharines, Ont. Office: (P.O. Box 3026) 80 King St., St. Catharines, Ont. L2R 7G2.

PUDDINGTON, Ira Edwin; M.Sc., Ph.D., F.R.S.C., F.C.I.C.; retired from Canadian public service; b. Clifton, Royal, N.B., 8 Jan. 1911; s. Charles E. and Elizabeth (Currie) P.; e. Prov. Normal Sch., Fredericton, N.B.; Mount Allison Univ., B.Sc. 1933; McGill Univ., M.Sc. 1936 and Ph.D. 1938; m. Hazel Jean, d. James Duncan, Upper Blackville, N.B., 27 Aug. 1936; one s. James; former dir., Div. of Chem., National Research Council, 1952-1974;

currently consultant; Lectr., McGill Univ., 1936-37; Sir George Williams Coll., Montreal, Que., 1937-38; mem., N.R.C., Colloid Sec., Chem. Div., 1938-74; Pres., Chem. Inst. Can. 1967-68; recreation: gardening; Home: 2324 Alta Vista Drive, Ottawa, Ont. K1H 7M7; Office: Montreal Road, Ottawa, Ont. K1A 0R9

PUGSLEY, William Howard, B.Com., M.B.A., Ph.D., writer; executive; grands. of Hon. Wm. Pugsley, P.C., K.C., D.C.L. of N.B., Min. of Pub. Works in Laurier Cabinet of 1907, and Lt.-Gov. of N.B.; b. Montreal, Que., 10 Mar. 1912; s. William Gilbert, K.C., and Marion Howard (Ross) P.; e. Bishop's Coll. Sch., Lennoxville, Que.; Ashbury Coll., Ottawa; Sorbonne, Paris, 1930; McGill Univ., B.Com. (Hons.) 1934, and Ph.D. (Econs.) 1950; Harvard Univ., M.B.A. (multa cum laude) 1936; PROF. OF MANAGEMENT, McGILL UNIV., 1970-80, retired; Asst. Prof. 1954-60; Assoc. Prof. 1960-70; Prof. Emeritus, 1981; with R.C.N.V.R. as Lt.(S), 1939-42; Able Seaman 1943; Leading Seaman 1944; Lt.(S) 1945; Lt. Cdr.(S), R.C.N.(R.), Ret'd. 1954-60; with Anglo American Chemicals Ltd., Montreal, as Asst. to the Pres., 1946-48; Ciba Ltd., Basle, Switzerland, as Asst. Secretary, 1948-53; Phi Delta Theta; author "Saints, Devils and Ordinary Seamen" 1945; "Sailor Remember", 1948; "Return to Sea", 1960; "Canadian Business Organization and Management", 1965; Club: University (Montreal); Home: 151 Bay St., Apt. 507, Ottawa, Ont. K1R 7T2

PULLEN, Rear-Admiral Hugh Francis, O.B.E. (1944), C.D. (1951); R.C.N. (retired); b. Toronto, Ont., July 1905; s. Maj. Frank and Gladys Mary (Cummins) P.; e. Lakefield (Ont.) Prep. Sch.; m. Helen Magdalen, d. Wm. K. McKean, Halifax, N.S., 15 Oct. 1932; entered Royal Naval College of Canada in 1920, and later spent two yrs. at sea with Candn. Pacific Steamships; rejoined R.C.N. in 1924; served in the R.C.N. 1924-60, retiring with rank of Rear Admiral; last appt. as Flag Offr. Atlantic Coast, Maritime Commdr. Atlantic and Commdr. Atlantic Sub Area (NATO), 1957-60; Mentioned in Despatches 1943; Chrmn., World Refugee Campaign in N.S., 1960; Chrmn., Halifax-Dartmouth Un. Appeal, 1961; Depy. Commr. and Gen. Mgr., Atlantic Provinces Pavilion at Expo '67, 1965-67; mem. Royal Commonwealth Soc.; Champlain Soc.; Canadian Forces Sailing Assn.; Roy. N.S. Yacht Squadron; N.S. Schooner Assn.; Navy Records Soc.; Soc. for Nautical Research; recreations: sailing, fishing, gardening, naval history, nautical research, ship model bldg.; Address: "Big Hill", Chester Basin, N.S. B0J 1K0

PULLEYBLANK, Edwin George, Ph.D., F.R.S.C.; educator; b. Calgary, Alta, 7 Aug. 1922; s. late William George Edwin and Ruth Elizabeth (Willoughby) P.; e. Central High Sch. Calgary 1939; Univ. of Alta. B.A. 1942; Univ. of London Ph.D. (Chinese) 1951; m. Winona Ruth (d. 1978), d. late Douglas McCrum Relyea, Prescott, Ont. 17 July 1945; children: David Edwin, Barbara Jill, Marcia Ruth; PROF. OF ASIAN STUDIES, UNIV. OF B.C. 1966- ; Head of Asian Studies 1968-75; joined Nat. Research Council Ottawa 1943-46; Lectr. Sch. of Oriental and African Studies Univ. of London 1948-53; Prof. of Chinese Univ. of Cambridge 1953-66, Fellow of Downing Coll. 1954-66; author "The Background of the Rebellion of An Lu-shan" 1955; "Chinese History and World History" (inaugural lecture) 1955; co-ed. "Historians of China and Japan" 1961; numerous articles and reviews learned journs. and coll. publs. Chinese and Central Asian Hist., linguistics; mem. Philol. Soc.; Assn. Asian Studies; Am. Oriental Soc.; Linguistic Assn. Am.; Candn. Asian Studies (now Candn. Asian Studies Assn.), Pres. 1971-74; Candn. Linguistic Assn.; Home: 6216 Mackenzie St., Vancouver, B.C. V6N 1H5; Office: Vancouver, B.C. V6T 1W5.

PURCELL, Gerald L.; banker; e. Mem. Univ. of Nfld. Comm. Law; St. Mary's Univ. Halifax, Accounting; SR.

VICE PRES. DOMESTIC BANKING, BANK OF MONTREAL; Bank Premises Mgr. H.O. 1969-70, Vice Pres. W. Ont. 1970-76, Vice Pres. On-Line Installation, 1 yr., Vice Pres. Metro Region becoming Sr. Vice Pres. Central Ont.; Vice Pres. Un. Community Fund Toronto; Campaign Chrmn. Un. Way Metro Toronto 1978, Pres. 1980-81; mem. Extve. Council, Ont. Chamber Comm.; Jr. Achievement; Toronto Re-devel. Adv. Council; Clubs: National; Donalda; Granite; Home: 162 Burbank Dr., Willowdale, Ont. M2K 1P2; Office: 1 First Canadian Place, Toronto, Ont. M5X 1A1.

PURDIE, Kingsley Bernard; controller; b. Adelaide, Australia 7 Jan. 1940; s. Idris Cyril and the late Laurel Lucy (Lomas) P.; m. Glenda Mavis d. Benjamin Franklin Lawrance, Adelaide, Australia 27 March 1965; children: Justin Kingsley, Tara Glenda; VICE PRES.-CONTROLLER, ATCO LTD. since 1978; Dir., ATCO Ltd.; ATCO Drilling; ATCO Gas and Oil; ATCO Holdings; ATCO Industries (Australia); Inter ATCO; MISMAT; ATCO Industries (Australia) Pty. Ltd., Elizabeth West, S. Australia, Controller, Secy. and Finance Mgr. 1967 — 74, Gen. Mgr. 1974 — 77; Gen. Mgr. Sales & Service, ATCO Structures Ltd. (Calgary) 1977 — 78; mem. Australian Soc. Accts. (Assoc. 1965, Sr. Assoc. 1969); Inst. Chart. Secy's & Adms. (Assoc. 1965); Church of Christ; recreations: squash, skiing; Club: Calgary Winter; Home: 52 Bow Village Cres. N.W., Calgary, Alta. T3B 4X2; Office: 1243 McKnight Blvd. N.E., Calgary, Alta. T2E 5T2.

PURDIE, Kingsley Bernard; controller; b. Adelaide, Australia 7 Jan. 1940; s. Idris Cyril and Laurel Lucy (Lomas) P.; m. Glenda Mavis d. Benjamin Franklin Lawrance, Adelaide, Australia 27 March 1965; children: Justin Kingsley, Tara Glenda; VICE PRES.-CONTROLLER, ATCO LTD. since 1978; ATCO Industries (Australia) Pty. Ltd., Elizabeth West, S. Australia, Controller, Secy. and Finance Mgr. 1967 — 74, Gen. Mgr. 1974 — 77; Gen. Mgr. Sales & Service, ATCO Structures Ltd. (Calgary) 1977 — 78; mem. Australian Soc. Accts. (Assoc. 1965, Sr. Assoc. 1969); Inst. Chart. Secy's & Adms. (Assoc. 1965); Australian Inst. Mang.; Church of Christ; recreations: squash, skiing, basketball; Club: Calgary Winter; Home: 52 Bow Village Cres. N.W., Calgary, Alta. T3B 4X2; Office: 1243 McKnight Blvd. N.E., Calgary, Alta. T2E 5T2.

PURDY, Alfred; writer; b. Wooler, Ont., 30 Dec. 1918; s. Alfred and Eleanor Louise P.; e. Dufferin Pub. Sch., Trenton, Ont.; Albert Coll., Belleville, Ont.; Trenton (Ont.) Coll. Inst.; rec'd. Can Council Fellowships 1960 and 1965; m. Eurithe Mary Jane, d. James Parkhurst, Belleville, Ont., 1 Nov. 1941; one s. Alfred; served with RCAF during 2nd World War; author of "The Enchanted Echo", 1944; "Pressed on Sand", 1955; "Emu, Remember", 1957; "The Crafte So Longe To Lerne", 1956; "Poems For All The Annettes", 1962; "The Blur In Between", 1963; "The Cariboo Horses", 1965; "North of Summer", 1967 "Wild Grape Wine" 1968; "Love in a Burning Building" 1970; "Selected Poems" 1972; "Hiroshima Poems" 1972; "Sex and Death" 1973; "In Search of Owen Roblin" 1974; ed. "The New Romans" (anthol.) 1968; "Storm Warning" 1971; "On the Bearpaw Sea", 1973; "Sundance at Dusk", 1976; "The Poems of Al Purdy" (NCL), 1976; "At Marsport Drugstore", 1977; "No Other Country", 1977; "A Handful of Earth", 1977; "No Second Spring", 1978; "Moths in the Iron Curtain", 1978; "Being Alive, Poems 1958-78", 1978; "Storm Warning 2," 1976; Andrew Suknaski, "Wood & Mountain Poems", 1976, edited and introduced by Purdy; "The Stone Bird" 1981; edited and introduced "I've Tasted My Blood" by Milton Acorn 1969; has written radio and television plays, short stories, articles; rec'd. Governor Gen. Literary Award for Poetry, 1966; President's Medal of the Univ. of W. Ont. for best poem by a Candn. publ. in a mag., 1963; A.J.M. Smith Award, 1973; Acad. of Can. Writers, 1977; Jubilee Medal, 1978; Can. Council Fellowship, Greece, Italy, Eng. 1968-69; Hiroshima, Japan 1971;

Can. Council awards to South Africa, 1973; Peru, 1975; Galapagos Islands, 1980; presently Sen. Award receip.; Writer-in-res., Loyola (Mtll), 1973-74; Univ. of Man., 1975-76; Univ. of W. Ont., 1977-78; N.D.P.; recreation: travelling; Address: R.R. 1, Ameliasburg, Ont. K0K 1A0

PURDY, Henry Carl, R.C.A.; artist; educator; b. Wolfville, N.S. 11 Nov. 1937; s. Carl Augustus and Florence Margaret (Langille) P.; e. elem. and jr. high schs. Wolfville; Armdale (N.S.) High Sch. 1954; N.S. Coll. of Art Assoc. 1958 (Lt. Gov.'s Medal); N.B. Inst. of Technol. Vocational Teachers Cert. 1963; m. Gertrude Ann d. Herbert Hill, Halifax, N.S. 19 Apl. 1959; children: Henry Scott, Daniel Blair, Sharon Mary; DIR. SCH. OF VISUAL ARTS, HOLLAND COLL., mem. Bd. Govs. 1969-73; Graphic Artist, CFCY-TV Charlottetown 1958-63; designed, instituted and taught comm. art course Prov. Vocational Inst. 1963-69; designed and taught comm. design program Holland Coll. 1969-77, Chrmn. Applied Arts Div., designed formation Sch. Visual Arts 1977; comns. incl. 22 ft. sculpture Confed. Centre Charlottetown 1973; 12 ft. metal fountain Parkdale, P.E.I.; murals, 11 ft. sculpture Univ. P.E.I.; solo exhns. incl. N.B. Museum & Theatre N.B. 1974; St. Dunstans Univ. 1968; Isle St. Jean Gallery Charlottetown 1974; Gallery On Demand 1976; Confed. Centre 10 yr. retrospective 1978; Rothman Gallery Moncton 1980; four one man shows in 1981: Truro, N.S.; Moncton, N.B.; Summerside, P.E.I.; Sydney, N.S.; two two-man shows in 1981: Charlottetown, P.E.I.; St. Andrews, N.B.; rep. in various group shows, nat. and internat. pub. and private colls.; Chrmn. Design Comte. P.E.I. Centennial 1973 and 1981; mem. Senate Univ. of P.E.I. 1970-74; Founding mem. P.E.I. Council of Arts 1974, presently Chrmn.; mem. Extve. P.E.I. Handcraft Council; P.E.I. Extve. Comte. Task Force on Candn. Unity; mem. Bd. Atlantic Inst.; Bd. Govs. Candn. Conf. of Arts; Exec.; R.C.A.; C.C.A.; rec'd Painting and Sculpture Awards P.E.I. 1967; 4 published works drawings and poetry; pub., "Prince Edward Island Sketchbook" (a book of 113 drawings); Gold Medal Art P.E.I. 1973; received Royal Soc. of Arts (Manufacturers of Commerce) Atlantic Region Silver Medal for contribution to the Fine Arts in Atlantic Canada, 1981; mem. Maritime Art Assn. (P.E.I. Vice Pres.); Sand Patterns Publ. Assn.; R.C.A. Council; Assn. Candn. Studies; Candn. Vocational Assn.; Assn. Candn. Community Colls.; Chamber Comm. Greater Charlottetown; Friends Confed. Centres; Anglican; recreations: sports, cross-country skiing, reading, music, teaching night art classes & giving workshops; Home: 6 St. Peters Rd., Parkdale, P.E.I. C1A 5N2; Office: Burns Ave., West Royalty, P.E.I. C1A 7N9.

PURSE, Ross Charles; administrator; b. Roland, Man. 10 Sept. 1918; s. Charles Chester and Ethel Mary (Gilligan) P.; e. Roland (Man.) High Sch. 1937; Univ. of Sask. Regina Cert. Business Adm. 1962; m. Vivian Marie d. late Harry Austin and Clara Bell (Levins) Millman 5 Jan. 1946; three s. John, Robert, Steven; NAT. MANG. DIR. CNIB since 1973; Property Mgr.-Estate Old Harbour W. Indies 1946-47; joined Catering Services CNIB Man. 1948, Field Rep. Man. 1950, Dist. Adm. Sask. 1955, Div. Dir. Sask. 1961, B.C.-Yukon 1964, Ont. 1969-73; served with Winnipeg Grenadiers 1939-46, Atlantic-Pacific, 4 yrs. P.O.W. Japan; mem. Welfare Council Can.; Inst. Assn. Extves.; Hon. mem. Candn. Ophthalmol. Soc.; former Extve. and Past Secy. of Bd. Am. Assn. Workers for Blind; Past Chrmn. N.Am.-Oceania Region; mem. Extve. Bd. World Council for Welfare of Blind; Chrmn. N. Am. Region and Extve. Bd. mem. Internat. Agency for Prevention Blindness; Past Chrmn. Candn. Co-ordinating Comte. Blindness Prevention; rec'd Coronation Medal 1953; Queen's Silver Jubilee Medal 1977; Ambrose Shotwell D.S.M. 1979; Freemason; Protestant; recreations: golf, curling; Clubs: Rotary; Thornhill Country; Home: 2 Arnall Ave., Scarborough, Ont. M1W 3A6; Office: 1929 Bayview Ave., Toronto, Ont. M4G 3E8

PURVES, Robert P., B.Com.; merchant; b. Winnipeg, Manitoba, 15 August 1927; s. Robert Alexander and Helen K. (MacPherson) P.; e. Winnipeg (Man.) Pub. and High Schs., 1944; Univ. of Man., B.Com. 1948; m. Doreen M. Tynan, 16 Nov. 1957; children: John A., Peter D., Margaret J., Helen D.; PRESIDENT, INTER-OCEAN GRAIN CO. LTD., since 1962; Dir., Greater Winnipeg Gas Co.; Grain Insurance and Guarantee Co.; Vice Chrmn., Health Sciences Centre Research Foundation; Chrmn., Winnipeg Commodity Exchange, 1971-72; Gov. since 1965; joined present Co. 1948; Dir. or mem. Bd.; Winnipeg Foundation; Royal Canadian Flying Clubs Association; Freemason; Shriner; Protestant; recreations: boating, flying; Clubs: Manitoba; Home: 117 Grenfell Blvd., Winnipeg, Man. R3P 0B6; Office: 704-167 Lombard Ave., Winnipeg, Man. R3B 0V4

PURVIS, A. Blaikie, B.A., M.B.A.; executive; b. New York, N.Y., 20 Nov. 1924 (came to Can. Dec. 1924); s. Rt. Hon. Arthur Blaikie, P.C., and Margaret (Jones) P.; e. Eton Coll., Eng., 1938-43; Bishop's Coll. Sch., Lennoxville, Que., 1940-41; McGill Univ., B.A. 1949; Harvard Business Sch., M.B.A. 1951; m. Peggy M. Wright, B.Sc., 9 Sept. 1951; children: Michael, Christopher, Lois Mary, Andrew; PRESIDENT AND MANG. DIR., CALVIN BULLOCK, LTD., since 1972; Dir., Chrmn. of Bd., Acrofund Ltd.; Vice Pres. and Secy., Canadian Investment Fund; Dir.; Vice Pres. and Asst. Secy., Canadian Fund, Inc.; Chrmn. Bd. of Trustees, Banner Fund; Pres. C.I.F. Income Fund; joined present Co. 1951; Vice Pres. and Mang. Dir. 1968; Pres. 1972; served with Brit. Army 1943-46; commd. Lt. in Scots Guards 1944; served in N.W. Europe and occupation of Germany; served on various Montreal area Sch., Ch. and Clubs Bds. and Comtes.; Gov. and Past Chrmn., Investment Funds Inst. of Canada; Anglican; recreations: skiing, sailing, racquets; Clubs: University; Montreal Racket; Home: 1745 Cedar Ave., Apt. 902 Montreal, Que.; Office: CIL House, Montreal, Que.

PUSHIE, Gordon F.; industrial consultant; b. St. John's Nfld., 24 July 1915; e. Pub. and High Schs., St. John's, Nfld.; Memorial Univ., St. John's; m. Jean Bowden; has two d.; Dir., North Star Cement Ltd.; Brinco Ltd.; Consolidated Rambler Mines Ltd.; Atlantic Coast Copper Corpn. Ltd.; formerly in journalism having joined the staff of "Evening Telegram", St. John's, Nfld. where he rose from reporter to City Editor; Contrib. Ed., "Time" mag. New York 1945-50 and at the same period in charge of Toronto Bureau and later of Chicago Bureau; returned to Nfld. in 1950 and apptd. Chief of Research in Dept. of Econ. Devel.; 1951; Dir. Gen. Devel., Nfld., 1953-62; Presbyterian; recreations: fishing, shooting, photography; Clubs: Newfoundland Yacht; Murray's Pond Fishing; Canadian (N.Y.); Home: 2 Strawberry Marsh Rd., St. John's, Nfld. A1B 2U4;

PUTNAM, Rev. Max, D.D. (Presb.); minister; b. Smiths Falls, Ont., 12 Jan. 1920; s. Hope Chiles and Lucy Olivia (Robinson) P.; e. Smiths Falls (Ont.) Secondary Schs.; McGill Conservatory (vocal); Univ. of W. Ont.; Knox Theol. Coll., Hon. D.D.; Moderator, Presb. Church in Can. 1972-73; served in World War II, five years, R.C.E.M.E. in Can., Eng., N.W. Europe; P. Conservative; mem., Kingston Church Athletic League; Home: 146 Clergy St. E., Kingston, Ont.; K7K 3S3; Office: 50 Wynford Dr., Don Mills, Ont. M3C 1K1

PUTNAM, Robert Wayne, B.A., M.D.; b. Truro, N.S. 7 Feb. 1944; s. Robert Edmund and Phyllis (Barnhill) P.; e. Truro elem. and high schs. 1961; Mount Allison Univ. B.A. 1964; Dalhousie Univ. M.D. 1969; M. Joan Joyce Ervin 26 Dec. 1968; children: Kimberley, Lorian, Stefan; ASST. DEAN AND DIR. CONTINUING MED. EDUC. DALHOUSIE UNIV. since 1977; private practice Fredericton, N.B. 1969-75; Asst. Dir. Div. Continuing Med. Educ. Dalhousie 1975, Acting Dir. 1977; mem. Med. Soc. N.S.;

Coll. Family Phys. Can.; Standing Comte. on Continuing Med. Educ. Assn. Candn. Med. Colls.; United Church; recreations: racquetball, skiing, tennis; Clubs: Dalhousie Racquetball; Home: 6429 Norwood St., Halifax, N.S. B3H 2L4; Office: Sir Charles Tupper Med. Bldg., Halifax, N.S. B3H 4H7.

PUTON, Roland Roger; executive; b. Paris, France, 26 Jan. 1935; s. Georges and Constance (Cuenin) P.; e. Comm. Sch. of Switzerland, Degree in Business Adm.; post-grad. studies relating to watchmaking industry; m. Béatrice, d. Teunis Blakenstijn, 6 May 1961; children: Patrick Laurent, Véronique Florence, Lionel Robin; PRES., DIR. AND MEM. BD., ROLEX WATCH CO. OF CANADA LTD. since 1972; began as Sales Rep. for various Swiss watch cos., covering most European countries 1958; apptd. Sales Mgr. with responsibilities for Middle E. and later S. Am. markets 1961; joined Rolex Organ. as Mang. Dir., Candn. Sales and Service Office 1967; served with Swiss Army as Capt., discharged 1966; Dir., Candn. Jewellers Assn.; mem. Bd. Trade Metrop. Toronto; Swiss Candn. Business Assn.; R. Catholic; recreations: reading, skiing, cycling; Club: Rotary; Home: 708 Nautalex Court, Port Credit, Ont. L5H 1A7; Office: 80 Richmond St. W., Toronto, Ont. M5H 2A4

PUTTOCK, Nigel W., M.A., P.Eng.; manufacturer; b. Horsham, Eng., 27 Jan. 1927; s. late Eric C. and Mary W. P.; e. Oundle Sch., Northamptonshire, Eng.; Clare Coll., Cambridge Univ., M.A.; m. Barbara Ann, d. late A. J. C. Arley Bugler, Horsham, Eng., 1949; children: Roger Nigel Arley, Shirley Mary, Pamela Jane, Carol Ann; PRES., PUTTOCK INDUST. MANG. LTD.; Vice-Pres. and Assoc. Broker, W. H. Bosley & Co. (Ont.) Ltd.; Salesman, Transparent Paper Ltd., Eng., 1948; Gen. Mgr., Tubular Case & Carton Co. Ltd., 1949; Gen. Mgr., Flexible Packaging Ltd., 1950; Gen. Mgr., Flexible Packaging Div., Metal Box Co. Ltd., Eng., 1954; Production Mgr., Ont. Plant, Transparent Paper Products Ltd., Toronto, 1957; Extve. Vice Pres., Montreal, 1957; Gen. Mgr., Interstate Building Products Ltd., Hamilton, 1958; Asst. to Pres., Western Gypsum Products Ltd., Winnipeg, 1959; Extve. Vice Pres. 1960; Pres., Western Gypsum Products Ltd., Toronto, 1963; Pres., Westroc Ind. Ltd.; Chrmn. and Pres., Barringham Plastics Ltd.; Blue Diamond Transport Rentals Ltd.; Perlite Ind. Ltd.; Wesco Paints Ltd.; Western Gypsum Ltd.; Westroc Building Components Ltd.; served with RAF and RAF Vol. Reserve 1946-54; Fellow, Inst. Dirs. (U.K.); mem., Assn. Prof. Engrs. Ont.; Bd. Trade Metrop. Toronto; recreations: sailing, squash, tennis, music; Clubs: Oakville; Devonshire & Royal Automobile (London, Eng.); Home: 292 Burgundy Dr., Oakville, Ont. L6J 4G1; Office: 321 Lakeshore Hwy. E., Oakville, Ont. L5J 1J4

PUXLEY, Rev. Canon Herbert Lavallin, M.A., L.Th., D.D., D.C.L., D.Litt. (Ang.); retired univ. president b. Goring-on-Thames, England, 6 Nov. 1907; s. Herbert and Kate P.; e. Eton Coll. (Capt. of Oppidans, Chairman of Eton Soc., etc.); Brasenose Coll., Oxford (Heath Harrison Exhibitioner, Bible Clerk, etc.), B.A. (Hons.) 1929, M.A. 1934; Commonwealth Fund Fellow, Yale Univ. (1929-32), M.A. 1931; Trinity Coll., Toronto, Ont., L.Th. 1948, Hon. D.D. 1955; D.C.L. Acadia 1962; D.D. King's 1963; Wycliffe 1966; D.Litt St. Mary's (Halifax) 1965; m. Mary Robertson, d. Mr. Justice Geo. H. Sedgewick, Toronto, Ont., 22 June 1932; children: Mary, Peter, David; Canon, All Saints Cath., Halifax, N.S.; o. Deacon, Dec. 1947, and Priest, May 1948; Prof. of Econ., St. John's Coll., Agra, India, 1932-40; incumbent of Roches Point, Ont., 1947-49; Gen. Secy., Student Christian Movement of Can., 1949-53; Asst. Secy., Candn. Council of Churches (Dept. of Overseas Missions & Evangelism), 1953-4; Pres., Univ. of King's College, 1954-63; Dir., Canadian School of Missions and Ecumenical Institute 1963-73; retired 1973; Chairman Ecumenical Study Commission on Religion in Public Education; served in 2nd World War; Comnd. in

Indian Army, Nov. 1940; retired as Lieut.-Col., 1946; Publications: "Critique of the Gold Standard", 1933; "Agricultural Marketing in Agra District", 1935; "Christian Land Settlements", 1941; numerous articles in "Indian Economic Journal", "Asia", etc.; Chaplain, Order of St. Lazarus of Jerusalem 1967; Knight Commander, 1970; Religion in Public Education 1969-73; Home: R.R. 1, Claremont, Ont., L0H 1E0

PYKE, Stephen Thomas; b. Springhill, N.S., 11 May. 1916; s. Ebenzer and Millicent (Baggs) P.; e. Springhill (N.S.) Schs.; m. Eleanor Martin; children: Charles, David, Gerald, Jo-Anne, Stephen; Chrmn. of Workmen's Compensation Bd., N.S., since Sept. 1968; el. M.H.A. for Cumberland Centre in N.S. g.e. 1953; Min. of Labour and Min. of Pub. Works, 1956-68; Min. of Pub. Works and Min. of Lands & Forests, 1968, when resigned; served as Flying Offr. with RCAF during 2nd World War; Chrmn., Springhill Disaster Comte.; el. Pres., Candn. Goods Roads Assn. 1967; Dir., Can. Safety Council N.S. Rehabilitation Centre; Pres. Assn. Workmen's Compensation Bds. Can. (1974); Secy.-Treas., International Assn. Indust. Accident Bds. and Comns.; Officer Order of St. John; mem., K. of P.; Royal Canadian Legion; Progressive Conservative; United Ch.; recreations: hunting, fishing, photography; Home: 46 Newcastle St., Dartmouth, N.S. B2Y 3M5; Office: Workmen's Compensation Centre, Halifax, N.S.

Q

QUALTER, Terence Hall, Ph.D.; educator; b. Eltham, N.Z. 15 Apl. 1925; s. Michael Frederick and Kathleen Mary (Hall) Q.; e. Univ. of N.Z. B.A. 1951; London Sch. of Econ., Univ. of London Ph.D. 1956; m. Shirley Anne d. late John Alfred Card, Masterton, N.Z. 19 May 1951; children: Karen Anne, Matthew John, Paul Michael, Adam James; PROF. OF POL. SCIENCE, UNIV. OF WATERLOO 1967- ; Lectr. Un. Coll. Winnipeg 1957-58; Special Lectr. Univ. of Sask. 1958-60; Lectr. in Pol. Science present Univ. 1960, Asst. Prof. 1961, Assoc. Prof. 1964, Chrmn. of Pol. Science 1965-67, 1970-73; author "Propaganda and Psychological Warfare" 1962; "The Election Process in Canada" 1970; "Graham Wallas and the Great Society" 1980; numerous articles pol. science; served with Royal N.Z. Air Force 1944-46; mem. Candn. Pol. Science Assn.; NDP; R. Catholic; recreation: travel; Home: 249 Storybrook Dr., Kitchener, Ont. N2M 4L8; Office: Waterloo, Ont. N2L 3G1.

QUASTEL, Judah Hirsch, C.C. (1970), B.Sc., Ph.D., D.Sc., F.R.I.C. (1930), F.R.S. (1940), F.R.S.C. (1952); scientist; university professor; b. Sheffield, Eng., 2 Oct. 1899; s. late Jonas and late Flora (Itcovite) Q.; e. Central Secondary Sch., Sheffield, Eng., 1911-17; Univ. of London, Imp. Coll. of Sciences 1919, A.R.C.S. 1921, B.Sc. 1921, D.Sc. 1926; Cambridge Univ., Trinity Coll., Ph.D. 1924; McGill Univ., Hon. D.Sc. 1969; Hebrew Univ. (Hon.) Ph.D. 1970; m. late Henrietta Jungman 1931; 2ndly Shulamit Ricardo 14 July 1975; children: Michael, Ph.D., M.D., David, Ph.D., M.D., Barbara Glick, M.A.; PROF. OF NEUROCHEMISTRY, FACULTY OF MED., UNIV. OF B.C., since 1966; Lectr. in Biochem., Cambridge Univ., 1923-29; Dir. of Research, Cardiff City Mental Hosp., Wales, 1929-41; Dir., Unit of Soil Metabolism, Agric. Research Council U.K. (war appt.), 1941-47; Prof. of Biochem., McGill Univ. and Dir., McGill-Montreal Gen. Hosp. Research Inst., 1947-66; Leeuwenhoek Lectr. of Royal Soc., London, 1954; Kearney Foundation Lectr., Univ. of Cal., 1958; Royal Soc. Visiting Prof., India, 1966; Visiting Prof. National Hosp. (Neurology), London, U.K. 1976-77; served with Brit. Army 1917-19; co-discoverer of herbicidal activity of 2:4D, 1942; contrib. to devel. of synthetic soil conditioners (e.g. Krilium), 1951 and of sciences of neurochem., biochem. pharmacol. and enzymol.; discovered in 1928 inhibitory activities on enzymes of substrate analogues or antimetabolites important for the study of cell metabolism and in pharmacol.; initiated systematic studies of chem. of brain leading to practical devels. in field of psychiatry, 1931; initiated devels. in biochem. study of soil 1942; mem., Bd. of Govs., Hebrew Univ., Jerusalem, since 1950; former mem., Water Pollution Research Bd. and of various specialist comtes. of Med. Research Council, Agric. Research Council, Forestry Comn. all of U.K.; rec'd Meldola Medal, U.K., 1927; Candn. Microbiol. Soc. Award 1965; Flavelle Medal (Roy. Soc. Can.) 1974; Gairdner Internat. Award for Medical Research 1974; Seventh Jubilee Lecturer, Biochem. Soc. (U.K.); author: "Neurochemistry", 1955, 2nd ed. 1962; "Methods in Medical Research", volume 9, 1961; "Chemistry of Brain Metabolism", 1961 "Metabolic Inhibitors", vols. 1 and 2, 1963; vol. 3, 1972; vol. 4, 1973; also over 360 scient. publs. chiefly in field of biochem.; sometime mem., Ed. Bds. of various scient. journs.; el. Fellow of Trinity Coll., Cambridge Univ., 1924; Fellow, N.Y. Acad. Science (1954); Hon. Fellow, Japan Pharmacol. Soc. Candn. Soc. of Microbiol. (1966); Pres., Candn. Biochem. Soc., 1963; Hon. Pres., 11th Internat. Congress of Biochem., Toronto, 1979; Honorary mem. Biochem. Soc. (U.K.); mem. various Candn. and Am. Scient. Socs.; Home: 4585 Langara Ave., Vancouver, B.C. V6R 1C9

QUENNEVILLE, Hon. Robert, M.N.A., M.D.; né à Kénogami, Qué., 2 avril 1921; f. Ulric et Noella (Robert) Q.; é. l'Univ.de Montréal, B.A. 1941, M.D. (cum laude) 1947; ép. Claire, fille de Hormidas Mayer (décédé), 8 mai 1948; 5 garçons: Serge, Alain, Jean, Martin, Simon; Ministre d'Etat responsable de l'OPDQ (Est) 1972-76; Ministre d'Etat aux Affaires sociales, 1970, et Ministre responsable du placement étudiant et de l'intégration des assistés sociaux au marché du travail, février 1971; Min. responsable de l'ODEQ 1971; Ministre du Revenu du Quebec 1975-76; def. in Que. g.e. 1976; Chef Obstétrique, Hôpital St. Eusèbe de Joliette; directeur de Deka Inc.; Société Immoblière de Joliette; Président des Loisirs de Joliette; du Centre Civique de Joliette; Député du comté de Joliette depuis 5 mai 1970; militaire: RCAMC, 1944; A/Capt. Régiment de Joliette, 1941; Directeur de Chambre de Commerce; Chevalier de Colomb; Catholique Romaine; loisirs: golf, pêche, curling; Clubs: Richelieu; Vauvert Inc.; Club de Golf de Joliette (Directeur, 1967-68); Résidence: 365 Boul. Manseau, Joliette, Qué. J6E 3C9;

QUILICO, Louis, C.C. (1975); opera singer; b. Montreal, Que., 14 Jan. 1929; s. Louis and Geanne (Gravel) Q.; e. Maness Coll. of Music, New York City; Conservatoir de la Province de Qué. (Montreal); Conservatoir de Santa Cecilia, Rome, Italy; m. Lina, d. Nicola Pezzolongo, 29 Oct. 1949;P children: Donna Maria, John; Prof. of Music Univ. of Toronto; mem. Metrop. Opera Co. New York; Paris Opera Co. Paris, France; Covent Garden, London, Eng.; Candn. Opera Co., Toronto, Ont.; Bolshoi Opera, Moscow; Rome Opera, Italy; Colon Opera, Buenos Aires; Mexico Opera; New York City Opera; rec'd Centennial Medal 1967; R. Catholic; recreations: photography, model building; Address: 31 Claver Ave., Toronto, Ont. M6B 2V7

QUINLAN, John Joseph, Q.C.(Fed.); retired government administrator; b. Winnipeg, Man., 28 Oct. 1913; s. William Joseph and Mabel M. (Webster) Q.; e. St. Ignatius Sch. and Kelvin High Sch., Winnipeg; Univ. of Man., B.A. 1933, LL.B. 1937; m. Margaret Anne, d. Dr. J. I. Kelly, Calgary, Alta., 26 June 1943; children: Michael John, Mary Ellen; Chrmn., Restrictive Trade Practices Comn., 1974-77; Lectr., Competition Policy, Univ. Ottawa Faculty of Law (Common Law) 1973-78; read law with Parker, Richardson, Patterson & Drewry; called to Bar of Man., 1937; cr. Q.C. 1963 (Fed.); Asst. Dir., Casualty Dept., Brewster, Cross & McLaws, Winnipeg 1937-41; Asst. Enforcement Counsel, W.P.T.B., Toronto, 1944-45; Depy. Enforcement Counsel, 1945-46; Sr. Enforce-

ment Counsel, 1946; joined Combines Br., Ottawa, as Combines Investigation Offr. in 1946 becoming Sr. Combines Investigation Offr. 1956; Depy. Dir., Investigation and Research 1960-74; Acting Dir. 1973-74; Vice Chrmn., Can. Labour Relations Bd. 1966-73; served with Royal Canadian Army in Can., 1941-44; comnd. Lt., 1941; Instr. in Arty. Wing Offrs. Training Centre, Victoria, 1942-43; mem., Candn. Bar Assn.; Law Soc. Man.; R. Catholic; recreations: golf, bowling, reading; Club: Rivermead Golf (Lucerne. Que.); Home: 613 Mansfield Ave., Ottawa, Ont. K2A 2T3

R

RABINOWITCH, David George, B.A., R.C.A.; b. Toronto, Ont., 6 March 1943; s. Joseph and Ruth Elizabeth (Calverly) R.; e. Richmond Hill (Ont.) Pub. and High Schs., 1963; Univ. of W. Ont., B.A. (Eng.) 1966; m. Sheila Joy, d. Philip Harold Martin, 27 June 1965; one-man shows incl. Pollock Gallery, Toronto, 1968: 20/20 Gallery, London, Ont., 1968; Carmen Lamanna Gallery, 1969-82; Joseph Helman Gallery, St. Louis 1971; Gallery Rolfricke, Cologne 1971-74; Bykert Gallery, N.Y. 1973, 1975; Greenberg Gallery, St. Louis 1973; Stimson Gallery, Vancouver 1973; Daniel Weinberg Gallery, San Francisco 1974, 1978; Franco Toselli, Milan 1975; Museum Weisbaden, 1975; Clock tower, N.Y., 1976; Haus Lange Museum, Krefeld, 1978; Galerie M, Bochum, 1977-82; Richard Bellamy Gallery, N.Y., 1975-82; Art Museum Gent, Belgium, 1979; Group shows include: Can. Trust Show, Toronto, 1968; "New Visions", Pollock Gallery Toronto, 1968; Univ. of Waterloo (two-man show), 1968; "Heart of Londo", Nat. Gallery of Can., 1968; "Swinging London", 1968; Survey of London Artists 1968; "Canadian Artists '68" and "The Selective Eye", 1969, Art Gallery of Ont.; York Univ. (two-man show), 1969; Anne Marie Verna, Zurich, 1977, 1978; Hetzlert Keller, Stuttgart, 1975-78; Texas Gallery, Houston, 1975, 1978; Richard Bellamy Gallery, N.Y., 1978, 1981; "Options and Alternatives" Yale 1973; "Project 74" Kunsthalle, Cologne 1974; "Drawings" Leverkusen 1975; "PSI", N.Y., 1976; "Bruckner Festival," Linz, Austria, 1977, "Documents VI," Kassel 1977; "Biennial de Paris", Museum of Modern Art, Paris, 1977; "Structures for Behaviour", A.G.O. Toronto, 1978; "Recent Acquisitions", Museum of Modern Art, N.Y., 1977; Cologne Art Fair, 1977; Bologna Art Fair, 1977; "International Sculpture of the 20th Century", Basel, Switzerland, 1980; "Ten Canadian Artists", A.G.O., Toronto, 1980; "Construction in Process", Lodz, Poland, 1981; Guggenheim Fellow 1975; Lynd-Staunhton Award for Distinction, Canada Council, 1977; mem. Faculty, Yale Univ. 1974-75; Artist's statement published in: "Skira Art International", 1978; "Structures of Behaviour "Catalogue, 1978; "Ten Canadian Artists" Catalogue, 1980; "International Sculpture of the 20th Century" Catalogue; "David Rabinowich, Skulpturen", 1978; Address: 49 East 1st St., New York, N.Y. 10003.

RABORN, Smiley, Jr., B.S., executive; b. Robeline, Louisiana, U.S.A., 6 May 1915; s. Smiley Francis and Evie (Box) R.; e. Pleasant Hill (La.) High Sch. (1932); Louisiana State Univ., B.S. 1939; m. Bernice Louise, d. late John Renee Romero, 18 June 1940; children: Anita Francine, Smiley III, Suzanne Marie; CHRMN. OF THE BD. CANDEL OIL (Estbd. 1950), since 1977; mem., Adv. Bd. and Dir., National Trust Co. Ltd.; Dir., TransCanada PipeLines Ltd.; St. Joe Minerals Corp.; Calgary Inn Ltd.; with Magnolia Petroleum Co., 1939-42; Mayes-Bevan Co., 1946-50 when joined present Co.; served as Extve. Vice-Pres. and Gen. Mgr. until 1965, when made Pres. and C.E.O.; served in 2nd World War, Major, U.S. Army Engrs., 1942-46; Dir., Council for Business & the Arts in Can.; West. Div. Candn. Council of Christians and Jews; Dist. Pres., Calgary Philharmonic Soc.; Calgary Reg. Arts Fdn.; Clubs: Calgary Golf & Country; Ranchmen's; Calgary Petroleum; Home: 6128 Belvedere Road S.W., Calgary, Alta. T2V 2E1; Office: Suite 2840, Calgary Place 1, 330 5th Ave. S.W., Calgary, Alta. T2P 0L4

RADDALL, Thomas Head, O.C. (1970), LL.D., Litt.D., F.R.S.C.; author; b. Hythe, Kent, Eng., 13 Nov. 1903; s. Lt.-Col. Thomas Head, Sr., D.S.O. (Winnipeg Rifles, killed in action 1918) and Ellen (Gifford) R.; e. St. Leonard's Sch., Hythe, Eng.; Chebucto Sch., Halifax, N.S.; Halifax Acad.; Dalhousie Univ., LL.D. 1949; m. Edith Margaret, d. Frederick Freeman, Milton, N.S., 9 June 1927; children: Thomas, Frances; served as Bookkeeper for a N.S. pulp mill, 1923-27; Clerk, constr. co., 1928; Acct., newsprint paper mill, 1929-38; served as Wireless Offr. on various R.N. transport vessels and later Candn. Merchant Marine and E. Coast wireless stns., 1918-22; Lieut., Reserve Army, 1942-43; winner of Gov.-Gen's. Award for Candn. Lit., 1944, 48 and 57; awarded Lorne Pierce Medal by Roy. Soc. Can. for outstanding contrib. to Candn. Lit., 1956; Fellowship, Haliburton Soc., King's Coll., N.S., 1945; author of "Pied Piper of Dipper Creek", 1939; "His Majesty's Yankees', 1942; "Roger Sudden", 1944; "Tambour", 1945; "Pride's Fancy", 1946; "The Wedding Gift and Other Stories", 1947; "History of West Nova Scotia Regiment", 1948; "Halifax, Warden of the North", 1948; "The Nymph and The Lamp", 1950; "Tidefall", 1953; "A Muster of Arms", 1954; "The Wings of Night", 1956; "The Path of Destiny", 1957; "The Rover", 1958; "The Governor's Lady", 1959; "Hangman's Beach", 1966; "Footsteps On Old Floors", 1968; "In My Time" (autobiog.), 1976; mem., Queens Co. Hist. Soc.; N.S. Hist. Soc.; Candn. Hist. Assn.; Royal Candn. Legion (Past Pres. Queen's Br.); United Church; recreations: hunting, fishing, golf; Home: 44 Park St., Liverpool, N.S. B0T 1K0

RADFORD, Ralph David, M.Comm., F.L.M.I.; executive; b. Toronto, Ont. 15 Apl. 1930; s. R. M. and late I. D. (Lopez) R.; e. pub. Schs. Sudbury, Ottawa, Toronto; Malvern Coll. Inst., Toronto; Victoria Coll., Univ. of Toronto B. Comm. 1953, M.Comm. 1956; m. Jean Maxwell, d. H. M. McGoveran 10 Sept. 1955; children: Brian David, Kathryn Anne; VICE PRES. AND TREAS., THE CANADA LIFE ASSURANCE CO. and mem. Mang. Comte. since 1973; joined Canada Life, Toronto Invest. Div. 1953, Extve. Asst., Securities and Offr. of Co. 1960, Asst. Treas. 1963, Assoc. Treas. 1968, Financial Vice Pres. and Treas. 1971; mem., Toronto Soc. Financial Analysts (Pres. 1968-69); Financial Analysts Fed.(Dir. 1974-77); mem., Bd. of Gov., Ont. Research Foundation; Fellow Life Mgmt. Inst.; recreations: curling, bridge, reading; Home: 3 Allangrove Crescent, Agincourt, Ont. M1W 1S4; Office: 330 University Ave., Toronto, Ont. M5G 1R7

RADFORTH, Norman William, M.A., Ph.D., F.R.S.A. (1955), F.R.S.C. (1959); palaeobotanist; organic terrain consultant; b. Barrow-in-Furness, Lancs., Eng., 22 Sept. 1912; s. Walter Joseph and Kate Emma (Langley) R.; e. Primary Schs., Eng. and Can.; Univ. of Toronto, B.A. 1936, M.A. 1937; Glasgow Univ., Ph.D. 1939; m. Isobel, d. Dr. Milton H. Limbert, Parry Sound, Ont., 30 June 1939; children: John Robert, Janice Langley; CONSULTANT, RADFORTH & ASSOC., since 1977 and Hon. Research Assoc., Univ of N.B.; Prof. and Head, Dept. of Botany, McMaster Univ. 1946-51, Chrmn. Dept. Biology, 1960-66; Chrmn. Organic and Associated Terrain Research Unit there 1963-68; Prof. and Head Dept. of Biol. and Dir., Muskeg Research Inst., Univ. of N.B. 1968-77; Chrmn. Subcomte. on Muskeg, Assoc. Comte. on Geotech. Research, Nat. Research Council, 1948-75; Dir., Roy. Bot. Gardens, Hamilton, Ont., 1946-53; Demonst., Glasgow Univ., 1937-39; Roy. Soc. of Can. Research Fellow, 1938-39; Special Lect., McMaster Univ., 1939-40; Lect. Univ. of Toronto, 1940-41; Prof. and Dir. Muskeg Research Inst., Univ. of N.B., 1970-77; Ed.; Journal of Terramechanics; Past Pres., Internat. Soc. for Terrain Vehicle Systems; has written prof. papers on bot.

and palaeobot. topics and on terrain interpretation (muskeg); Protestant; recreation: oil painting; Address: Parry Sound, Ont. P2A 2W9

RADLER, Franklin David, B.Com., M.B.A.; publisher; b. Montreal, Que. 3 June 1942; s. Herbert A. Radler; e. McGill Univ. B.Com. 1963; Queen's Univ. M.B.A. 1967; m. Rona Beverley Lassner 26 March 1972; children: Melanie, Melissa; PRES. AND DIR., STERLING NEWSPAPERS LTD.; Chrm., Slumber Lodge Development Corp.; Empire Energy Inc.; Pres. and Dir. Dominion Malting Ltd.; Vice Pres. and Dir. Argus Corp. Ltd.; Dir. and Vice Chrmn. Extve. Comte. Massey-Ferguson Ltd.; Dir. Doman Industries Ltd.; British Columbia Development Corp.; The Ravelston Corp. Ltd.; Hollinger-Argus Limited; Crown Trust Co.; mem. Candn. Press; Candn. Daily Newspaper Publishers Assn.; Brewing & Malting Barley Research Inst.; Young Pres. Organ.; Adv. Bd., Sch. of Business, Queen's Univ.; Home: 2146 S.W. Marine Drive, Vancouver, B.C.; Office: 540 I.B.M. Tower, Pacific Centre, 701 W. Georgia St., Vancouver, B.C. V7Y 1B6.

RAE, Robert Keith, B.A., B.Phil., LL.B.; politician; b. Ottawa, Ont. 2 Aug. 1948; s. Saul Forbes and Lois Esther (George) R.; e. pub. schs. Ottawa and Washington, D.C.; Internat. Sch. of Geneva 1966; Univ. of Toronto, Univ. Coll. B.A. 1969, LL.B. 1977; Oxford Univ. Balliol Coll. (Rhodes Scholar) B.Phil. 1971; m. Arlene d. Al Perly, Toronto, Ont. 23 Feb. 1980; LEADER, NDP PARTY, ONT., 1982- ; called to Bar of Ont. 1980; mem. law firm Sack, Charney, Goldblatt & Mitchell, Toronto; Dir., Douglas-Coldwell Foundation; Couchiching Inst. of Pub. Affairs; el. M.P. for Broadview-Greenwood by-el. 1978, re-el. 79, 80; Financial Spokesman for NDP in H. of C. 1979-82; resigned federal seat, February 1982; mem. Comn. on Univ. Govt. Univ. of Toronto 1968-69; community worker London, Eng. 1973-74; extensive legal aid and community work Toronto since 1974; Asst. to Candn. Gen. Counsel, Un. Steelworkers of Am. 1975-77; Special Lectr. in Indust. Relations Univ. of Toronto 1976-77; author various articles on pol. theory, Candn. politics, indust. relations, constitutional and labour law; Vice Chrmn. Can.-U.S. Interparlty. Group. NDP; Anglican; recreations: tennis, skiing, music, reading; Home: 5 Withrow Ave., Toronto, Ont. M4K 1C8; Office: Parl. Bldgs., Queen's Park, Toronto, Ont.

RAGINSKY, Nina, B.A., R.C.A.; photographer; b. Montreal, Que. 14 Apl. 1941; d. Bernard Boris and Helen Raginsky; e. Rutgers Univ. B.A. 1962; one d. Sofya Katrina; Instr. in Photography, Vancouver Sch. of Art 1972- ; photographer since 1964; solo exhns. incl. Vancouver Art Gallery; Victoria Art Gallery; Edmonton Art Gallery; Art Gallery of Ont.; San Francisco Museum of Art; Acadia Univ.; photographs incl. various books such as "Call Them Canadians", "Canada Year of the Land", "Between Friends-Entre Amis" "BANF Purchase", and other Nat. Film Bd. publs.; work incl. various nat. and internat. mags.; recreations: walking, kite flying, gardening; Home: 102 S. Turner St., Victoria, B.C. V8V 2J8.

RAHILLY, Thomas Francis Jr., B.Sc., P.Eng.; industrialist; b. Sault Ste. Marie, Ont., 8 Apl. 1916; s. Thomas Francis and Violet Regina (Kennedy) R.; e. Pub. and High Schs., Sault Ste. Marie; Queen's Univ., B.Sc. 1939; m. Evelyn, d. Richard A. Brown, 4 July 1942; two s. Thomas Francis, Richard James, deceased; PRESIDENT, AND CHIEF EXTVE. OFFR., NATIONAL STEEL CAR LTD.; mem. Hamilton Adv. Bd., Can. Permanent Trust Co.; Asst. Master Mechanic, Algoma Steel Corp. Ltd., Sault Ste. Marie, 1939-41; Chief Engr. 1954; Asst. Gen. Mgr., Trafalgar Consultants Ltd., 1954-56; Gen. Mgr., Hamilton Bridge (Div. of Bridge and Tank Co. of Canada) 1956-58; Vice Pres. and Dir. 1958-62; joined present Co. as Vice Pres., Research and Devel., 1962-66; simultaneously Dir. Canadian Trailmobile Ltd.; Toronto, 1962, Vice-President and Director 1963-66; Pres., Gen. Mgr. and Dir. 1966;

Past Ald., Sault Ste. Marie, Ont.; Anglican; Clubs: Hamilton; Hamilton Golf & Country; Home: 713 Courtland Pl., Burlington, Ont. L7R 2M7; Office: Kennilworth Ave., Hamilton, Ont.

RAMSAY, Donald A., M.A., Ph.D., Sc.D., F.R.S., F.R.S.C., F.A.P.S., F.C.I.C.; research scientist; b. London, Eng., 11 July 1922; s. Norman and Thirza Elizabeth (Beckley) R.; e. Latymer Upper Sch., London, Eng., 1933-40; St. Catharine's Coll., Cambridge Univ., B.A. 1943, M.A. 1947 Ph.D. 1947; Sc.D. 1976; Doctoris honoris causa, Univ. de Reims, France 1969; m. Nancy d. Frederick and Mary Beatrice (Garside) Brayshaw 8 June 1946; children: Shirley Margaret, Wendy Kathleen, Catharine Jean, Linda Mary; PRINCIPAL RESEARCH OFFR., NAT. RESEARCH COUNCIL, since 1968; joined Council as Jr. Research Offr., 1947-49; apptd. Asst. Research Offr., 1949-54; Assoc. Research Offr., 1954-61; Sr. Research Offr., 1961-68; mem., Candn. Assn. Physicists; Chem. Inst. Can.; Vice Pres. Academy of Science, Royal Soc. of Canada, 1975-76; Hon. Treas. Royal Soc. of Canada 1976-79; Queen Elizabeth II Silver Jubilee Medal, 1977; Publications: Numerous articles on molecular spectroscopy and molecular structure, esp. free radicals; Un. Church; recreations: rowing, fishing; Club: Leander; Home: 1578 Drake Ave., Ottawa K1G 0L8, Ont.; Office: 100 Sussex Dr., Ottawa, Ont. K1A 0R6

RAND, Duncan Dawson, B.A., B.L.S.; librarian; b. Biggar, Sask. 28 Oct. 1940; s. Dawson Ellis and Elizabeth Edna (Gabie) R.; e. Univ. of Sask. B.A. 1965; McGill Univ. B.L.S. 1964; m. Nancy Jean Daugherty 7 Sept. 1963; children: Duncan, Thomas, Jennifer; John; CHIEF LIBRARIAN, LETHBRIDGE PUBLIC LIBRARY 1974- ; Lib. Coordinator Regina Separate Sch. Bd. 1966-69; Asst. Chief Lib. Regina Pub. Lib. 1969-71; Depy. Dir. London (Ont.) Pub. Lib. and Art Museum 1971-73, Acting Dir. 1973-74; Pres., Lethbridge Council Candn. Parents for French 1981- ; Dir. Lethbridge Symphony Assn. 1977; Pres., Lethbridge Lifelong Learning Assn. 1976; Trustee, S. Alta. Art Gallery Assn. 1975-77; Vice Pres. S. Alta. Region Scouts Can. 1976-77; recipient Regina Pub. Lib. Honeyman Scholarship 1963; co-author "Prairie Conference on Library Standards for Canadian Schools" 1968; various book chapters, articles; mem. Sask. Genealogical Soc. (Pres. 1970-71); Lib. Assn. Alta. (Vice Pres. 1980-81); Candn. Assn. Pub. Libs. (Pres. 1976-77); Candn. Lib. Assn. (Dir. 1976-77); Lethbridge Chamber Comm. (Dir. 1975-76); Elks; I.O.F.; YMCA Health Club; recreations: golf, hiking, running, reading, music, musical theatre; United Church; Office: 810 5 Ave. S., Lethbridge, Alta. T1J 4C4.

RANKIN, Alexander Gormaly, B.Com., F.C.A.; b. Toronto, Ont., 18 Sept. 1916; s. Robert Benson and Alice Mary (Rooney) R.; e. Univ. of Toronto Schs. (Sr. Matric.); Univ. of Toronto, B.Com. 1938; C.A. 1947; m. Norah Maureen, d. Judge Thomas Moore Costello, 19 Sept. 1942; two s. and six d.; Vice Pres. Business affairs, Univ. of Toronto, 1967-82; Dir., United Dominions Corp. (Can.) Ltd.; Weldwood of Can. Ltd.; Barbecon Inc. with Clarkson, Gordon & Co., Toronto, Ont., 1938-42 and 1945-47; acted as Special Asst. to Col. W. Eric Phillips, Toronto, 1947-51; Gen. Mgr. of Univ. of Toronto Press, 1949-53; Comptroller of Univ. of Toronto, 1951-55; Vice-Pres. (Finance) British Columbia Forest Products Ltd., 1955-67; served in 2nd World War, 2nd Lieut. to Capt. in R.C.O.C. (in Can.), 1942-45; Vice-Pres., B.C. Council of Boy Scouts; Past Pres., Vancouver Chapter, Financial Extves. Inst.; Trustee, Un. Community Fund of Greater Toronto 1968-73; mem. Council Bd. Trade of Metrop. Toronto 1969-74; mem., Ont. Inst. Chart. Accts.; Past Pres., Candn. Assn. of Univ. Business Offrs.; Delta Upsilon; Roman Catholic; recreation: golf; Clubs: Vancouver; Shaughnessy Heights Golf (Vancouver); Lambton Golf & Country; University; Home: 16 Ridgefield Road,, Toron-

to, Ont. M4W 3H8; Office: Simcoe Hall, Univ. of Toronto, Toronto, Ont.

RANKIN, Bruce I., B.Com.; diplomat (retired); b. Brandon, Man., 20 March 1918; s. John Howard and Janet Irving (Steel) R.; e. Univ. of Alta., B.Com. 1941; Nat. Defence Coll., 1953-54; Princeton Univ., Hon. mem. Class of 1938; m. Mona, d. Roy Miller, 14 Jan. 1948; three d., Janet, Marilyn, Susan; joined Candn. Foreign Service 1945; served in Sydney, Shanghai, Canberra, Bombay, Madrid, Berne; Depy. Consul Gen., New York, 1959-64; Ambassador to Venezuela and to Dominican Republic 1964; Consul Gen. New York since 1970; Candn. Ambassador, Econ. & Financial Comte. (2nd Comte.), UN Gen. Assembly, since 1967; Chrmn. of Comte. 1972; Pres., UN Devel. Program Pledging Conf., 1968; Ambassador to Japan since 1976-81; rep. Can. on Econ. & Social Council, 1966-67; served on no. of UN comte's Geneva and N.Y.; served with RCN 1941-45 in Pacific and Atlantic, Naval Service HQ Ottawa; rank Lt. Commdr. on discharge; awarded UN Medal of Excellence 1972; Phi Kappa Pi; Currently Consultant to INCO Ltd., Toronto, Mancal Ltd., Calgary; Mem. Bd. Industrial Bank of Japan (Canada) Ltd., Toronto Protestant; recreations: swimming, reading; Club: Canadian; Home: 10 Steeplechase Ave., R.R. 2, Aurora, Ont. L4G 3G8

RANKIN, Daniel Allan Stephen, B.A., M.B.A.; marketing executive; b. Inverness, N.S. 26 Dec. 1936; s. Michael and Agatha (MacLennan) R.; e. St. Francis Xavier Univ. B.A.; Queen's Univ. M.B.A.; m. Carol Ann d. Angus MacDonald Waye, Port Hawkesbury, N.S. 4 Aug. 1962; children: Sharon Cathy, Michael Waye, Stephen Joseph; PRES. AND CHIEF EXECUTIVE OFFICER, CAPE BRETON DEVELOPMENT CORP. since 1979; Dir. Adv. Bd. Central & Eastern Trust; Asst. Personnel Supvr. present Co. 1962-64, Sales Mgr. 1971-74; Vice Pres. Sales, N.S. Forest Industries; Sales Mgr. Stora Kopparberg Corp. 1964-71 (New York, N.Y.); mem. Econ. Council Can.; Chrmn. of the Bd., Cape Breton Devel. Corp.; mem. Bd. Govs. St. Francis Xavier Univ.; Depy. Mayor Town of Port Hawkesbury 1961-64; mem. Bd. Sch. Commrs. Port Hawkesbury; Chrmn. Annual Meeting N.S. Lib. Assn. 1977; Dir. N.S. Health Council; Strait of Canso Indus. Devel. Authority; mem. Candn. Pulp & Paper Assn.; Tech. Assn. Pulp & Paper Assn. US; Brit. Woodpulp Assn. London, Eng.; Liberal; R. Catholic; recreations: tennis, skiing, golf, skating, farming; Clubs: Port Hawkesbury Tennis; Ski; Home: Embree Island, Port Hawkesbury, N.S. B0E 2V0; Office: (P.O. Box 59) Port Hawkesbury, N.S. B0E 2V0

RANKIN, William Cunningham, B.Com., C.A.; executive; b. Toronto, Ont. 16 Oct. 1929; s. Robert Benson and Alice Mary (Rooney) R.; e. Univ. of Toronto Schs.; Univ. Coll. Univ. of Toronto B.Com. 1952; C.A. 1955; m. Nancy Elizabeth Owens 21 Nov. 1953; children: Heather F., Mary A., Andrew E., Rob C.; SR. VICE PRES. AND CONTROLLER, NOVA, AN ALBERTA CORP. (formerly The Alta. Gas Trunk Line Co. Ltd.) 1978- ; Dir. Algas Mineral Enterprises Ltd.; Alberta Gas Ethylene Co. Ltd.; CanOcean Resources Ltd.; Husky Oil Ltd.; joined Clarkson Gordon 1952-59, apptd. Mgr. 1957; Controller, Colonial Homes Ltd. 1959-60; Business Mgr. The Globe & Mail Ltd. 1960-66; Vice Pres. Finance & Adm. Torstar Corp. 1966-74; Sr. Vice Pres. Finance & Adm. T. Eaton Co. Ltd. 1974-78; served as Sub Ltd. (S), RCN(R), retired; former Dir. and Treas. Candn. Daily Nespaper Publishers Assn.; mem. Ont. Inst. C.A.'s; Delta Upsilon (Pres. 1952); recreations: bridge, sailing; Clubs: Ranchmen's; Petroleums; Home: 2612 Lindstrom Dr. S.W., Calgary, Alta. T3E 6E1; Office: (P.O. Box 2535) Calgary, Alta. T2P 2N6.

RANSOM, Hon. Alan Brian, M.L.A., B.Sc.A., M.Sc.; politician; b. Boissevain, Man. 6 June 1940; s. Sidney Edwin and Kathleen Mary (Ashworth) R.; e. Mountainside

Sch.; Brandon Coll., Univ. of Man. B.Sc.A.; Univ. of Alta. M.Sc.; m. Judith Anne d. J.W. McKenzie, Inglis, Man. 2 June 1962; children: Richard Jeffrey, Brett Jason, Daniel Grant, Christine Diana; MIN. OF FINANCE, MAN. and Chrmn. of Treasury Bd. 1979- ; resource mgr. and farmer; el. M.L.A. for Souris Killarney prov. g.e. 1977; Min. of Mines, Resources & Environmental Mang. 1977; Min. of Mines, Natural Resources & the Environment 1979; P. Conservative; Protestant; Office: 103 Legislative Bldg., Winnipeg, Man. R3C 0V8.

RANTA, Lawrence Edward, M.D., D.P.H., F.R.S.A., F.R.C.P. (C); administrator; b. Toronto, Ont., 30 Apl. 1910; s. John, one of the first Finnish immigrants to Toronto, who became active in Finnish colonization in Ont., and Matilda (Lindala) R.; e. Univ. of Toronto M.D. 1936; D.P.H. (Hastings Mem. Fellow) 1939; L.M.C.C. 1936; Specialty Cert. in Bacteriol. 1947 and in Public Health 1951 Roy. Coll. of Physicians and Surgs. of Can.; m. Pauline Katharine d. James Daniel McMartin Vancouver, B.C., 20 Aug. 1941; children: James Lawrence, Patricia Joan, Peter Alan John, Robert Paul, Susan Mary; AMBULATORY CARE COORDINATOR, GREATER VANCOUVER REGIONAL HOSPITAL DIST., & CONSULTANT, B.C. HEALTH ASSN. 1980- ; apptd. Research Asst., Connaught Medical Research Labs., 1939, and moved to W. Divn. at Univ. of B.C.; apptd. Asst. Prof. of Bacteriol. and Preventive Med., 1939, and Lectr. in Dept. of Nursing and Health; promoted Research Assoc. at Connaught Med. Research Labs., 1946; Assoc. Prof. of Bacteriol. and Preventive Med., 1947; and Assoc. Prof. of Nursing and Health, 1948, Univ. B.C.; resigned from Connaught Med. Research Labs., 1950; Asst. Dean, Faculty of Med., Univ. of B.C., 1950 and Prof. and Head, Dept. of Public Health, 1952; Asst. Dir., Medical, Vancouver Gen. Hosp., 1952-60; Assoc. Dir., Medical, 1960-66, Dir., Med. Services 1966-70; Med. Dir., 1970-75; Dir. of Health Care Services, B.C. Health Assn., 1975-80; has served on local comtes. on nutrition, incl. Red Cross Assn.; Trooper, Mississauga Horse Guards N.P.A.M., 1926-29; awarded C.D.; Lt. Col. R.C.A.M.C., C.O. Univ. B.C. Contingent, C.O.T.C. 1963-68; Fellow, Am. Pub. Health Assn.; A.A.A.S.; mem. of Senate, Univ. of B.C.; Life mem., Candn. Med. Assn.; Vancouver Med. Assn.; B.C. Med. Assn.; mem. Am. Soc. of Law & Medicine; Candn. Pub. Health Assn.; B.C. Acad. of Science (Pres.); Defence Med. Assn.; Greater Vancouver Health League (Pres.); Am. Coll. Hosp. Adms.; Am. Hosp. Assn.; Bd. of Dirs., B.C. Cancer Research Fdn.; Narcotic Addiction Foundation of B.C. (Pres.); Med. Advisory Council, G.F. Strong Rehabilitation Centre; B.C. Council of Psychiatric Nurses; Community Chest and Council of Greater Vancouver Area (Pres.); Vancouver Bd. of Trade; Royal Soc. of Health; Charter mem., Candn. Coll. Health Service Extves.; Hon. mem., Hosp. Adm. Assn. B.C.; Vancouver Gen. Hosp. Med. Staff; Hon. Lecturer, Dept. Health Care and Epidemiology, Fac. of Med., Univ. of B.C.; has written various scient. articles on nutrition, scarlet fever, cholera vaccine, salmonellosis, med. educ. and hospital adm. for tech. journs.; Kappa Sigma; Protestant; recreations; medical history, fine arts; Address: 4182 W. 8th Ave., Vancouver, B.C. V6R 1Z6

RAPOPORT, Anatol, S.M., Ph.D., D.Hum.Litt., F.A.A.S.; b. Lozovaya, Russia 22 May 1911; s. Boris and Adel R.; e. Vienna Huchschule fur Music Dipls. in Piano, Composition, conducting 1934; Univ. of Chicago S.B. 1938, S.M. 1940, Ph.D. (Math.) 1941; Univ. of W. Ont. D.Hum. Litt. 19..; m. Gwen Goodrich 29 Jan. 1949; children: Anya, Alexander, Charles Anthony; DIR., VIENNA INST. FOR ADVANCED STUDIES 1980- ; Instr. Math. Ill. Inst. Technol. 1946-47; Research Assoc., Asst. Prof. Comte. Math. Biol. Univ. of Chicago 1947-54; Fellow, Center Advanced Study Behavioral Sciences, Stanford, Calif. 1954-55; Prof. of Math. Biol. and Sr. Research Math., Mental Health Research Inst. Univ. of Mich. 1955-70; Prof. of Psychol. and Math. Univ. of Toronto 1970-80;

Guest Prof., Univ. of Warsaw 1961-62; Vienna Inst. Advanced Studies 1968, 1976, 1977; Tech. Univ. of Denmark 1968-69; Wissenschaftszentrum Berlin 1978; Univ. of Hiroshima 1978; Univ. of Louisville 1979; served with U.S. Air Force 1942-46, rank Capt.; author "Science and the Goals of Man" 1950; "Operational Philosophy" 1953; "Fights, Games and Debates" 1960; "Strategy and Conscience" 1964; "Two-Person Game Theory" 1966; "N-Person Game Theory" 1970; "The Big Two" 1971; "Conflict in Man-Made Environment" 1974; "Game Theory as a Theory of Conflict Resolution" 1974; "Mathematische Methuden in den Sozial Wissenschaften" 1980; co-author "Prisoner's Dilemma" 1965; "The 2X2 Game" 1976; Ed. "General Systems" 1956-77; Assoc. Ed. "Journal of Conflict Resolution"; "Behavioral Science"; over 300 articles; recipient Lenz Internat. Peace Research Prize 1976; mem. Am. Math. Soc.; Soc. Math. Biol.; Internat. Soc. Gen. Semantics (Pres. 1953-55); Soc. Gen. Systems Research (Pres. 1965-66); Candn. Peace Research & Educ. Assn. (Pres. 1972-75); Home: 38 Wychwood Park, Toronto, Ont. M6G 2V5; Office: A-1060 Stumpergasse 56, Vienna, Austria.

RAPPAPORT, Aron M., M.D., Ph.D.; surgeon; b. Sereth, Austria, 7 June 1904; s. Samuel Aba (descendant of an old family of writers, theologians and physicians); and Henrietta (Rabinowitz) R. e. High Sch., Austria; German Univ., Prague, M.D. 1929; Post-Grad. work in Surg. Berlin and Paris; Diploma Ass. Etranger à la Faculté de Médicine, Paris, 1934; Univ. of Toronto, Ph.D. (Physiol.) 1952; m. Rosa, M.D., d. late Naum Koslowsky, Latvia, 24 Dec. 1950; children: Henrietta Sophie, Norman Samuel; PROF. EMERITUS, DEPT. OF PHYSIOLOGY, FACULTY OF MED., UNIV. OF TORONTO, since 1973; Sr. Research Scientist, Dept. of Medicine, Div of Gastroenterol, Sunnybrook Hospital 1977; Research Assoc., Dept. of Surgery, Univ. of Toronto, 1962-66; Lectr. in Physiol., Univ. of Toronto, 1952-55; Research Assoc., Banting & Best Dept. of Med. Research, Toronto, 1948-55; Assoc. Prof. Physiol., Univ. of Toronto, 1955-62; Clinical Asst. in Surg., Toronto Gen. Hosp., 1952-61; pract. his prof. in Roumania, 1934-48, where he became interested in cardio-vascular surgery; main contrib. to research have been in exper. cardiac surg., vascular surg., structure microcirculation and pathology of the liver and the technic of selective catheterization and radiography of the hepatic (vessels) and abdominal vessels; since 1966 research on pancreas, quantitation and regulation of its insulin production; has contrib. over 90 articles to scient. journs. and monographs; mem., Candn. Physiol. Soc.; Am. Assn. for Study of Liver Disease; Am. Microcirculatory Soc.; Can. Microcirculatory Soc.; European Microcircul. Soc.; Toronto Diabetes Assn.; Ont. Assn. of Pathologists; Alpha Omega Alpha; Hebrew; recreations: philosophy, music, sculpture; Home: 160 Lytton Blvd. Toronto, Ont. M4R 1L4; Office: Medical Sciences Building, Taddle Creek Road, Toronto, Ont.M5S 12A and Sunnybrook Med. Centre, 2015 Bayview, Ave., Toronto M4N 3N58

RAPSEY, Hugh Albert, M.B.E., B.Com.; financial consultant; b. Port Arthur, Ontario, 12 June 1909; s. James Albert and Paulina (Younghusband) R.; e. Port Arthur Coll. Inst.; Ridley Coll., St. Catharines, Ont. (1927); Trinity Coll., Univ. of Toronto, B.Com. 1931; m. Dorothy Winnifred, d. Rudolph Carl Riedel, Toronto, Ont., 22 May 1943; children: Michael Douglas, Peter James, Terence Hugh, Paul Stuart, Timothy John; Dir. and Vice Pres., Candn. Anaesthetists Accumulating Fund Ltd.; Dir., Cdn. Reinsurance Co. Ltd.; Cdn. Reassurance Co. Ltd.; Swissre Management Ltd.; mem. Advisory Council, Ridley College mem., Corp. Trinity Coll.; mem. Endowment and Investment Comte.; YMCA Metrop. Toronto; joined Manufacturers Life Insurance Co. in 1931; Res. Invest. Offr., London, Eng.; 1948-55; Asst. Treas., 1955; Assoc. Treas., 1956-60 Financial Vice Pres. and i.c. investments outside Canada and U.S. 1961-74; served in 2nd World War with R.C.A.M.C. R.C.A.P.C. and R.C.O.C.;

seconded to R.C.E.M.E. to write report on "Workshop Procedure for Canadian Army in the Field"; awarded M.B.E.; Mentioned in Despatches; retired with rank of Major; Delta Kappa Epsilon; Anglican; recreation: bridge; Clubs: National (Toronto); Home: 40 South Drive, Toronto, Ont. M4W 1R1

RAPSEY, Keith H., B.A.Sc.; b. Port Arthur, Ont., 28 Oct. 1908; s. George H. and Eva V. (Woodside) R.; e. N. Toronto Coll. Inst., 1926; Univ. of Toronto, B.A.Sc., 1930; m. Amy Thompson, 24 May 1938; children: Karen (Widmeyer), Marilyn; former member Board Education, Weston and Galt, Ont.; former Chairman Galt and Suburban Planning Board; former Pres., Cdn. Mfrs. Assn. and Cdn. Electrical Mfrs. Assn.; Club: National (Toronto); Home: R.R. 3, Ayr, Ont. N0B 1E0; Office: 135 Dundas St., Cambridge, Ont. N1R 5X1

RAPSON, W(illiam) Howard, M.A.Sc., Ph.D., D.Eng., D.Sc., F.R.S.C. (1971), F.C.I.C., P.Eng.; Chemical Engineer; b. Toronto, Ont., 15 Sept. 1912; s. Alfred Ernest and Lillian Jane (Cannicott) R.; e. Riverdale Coll. Inst., Toronto, Ont., University of Toronto, B.A.Sc. 1934, M.A.Sc. 1935, Ph.D. 1941; D.Eng. (Hon. c.) Univ. of Waterloo, 1976; D.Sc. (Hon. c.) McGill Univ., 1980; m. Mary Margaret, d. late Martin Livingstone Campbell, 29 Jan. 1937; children: Margaret Lillian, Lorna Jean, Linda Mary, William Howard, Jr.; PROF. OF CHEMICAL ENGN., UNIV. OF TORONTO, 1953-76 and 1981-, Univ. Professor 1976-81; Univ. Professor Emeritus 1981; Bd. Chrmn., W.H. Rapson Ltd. 1977 (Pres. 1964-77); Pres., Chem. Engn. Research Consultants Ltd., 1970-81; Toronto; Consulting Chem. Engr., since 1953; Demonst. in Chem. Engn., Univ. Toronto, 1934-40 and Instr. 1940; Research Chemist., Candn. Internat. Paper Co., Hawkesbury, Ont., 1940-48; i/c of Pioneering Research, Indust. Cellulose Research Ltd., Hawkesbury, Ont., 1948-53; inventor of Candn. and foreign patents on chem. processes; Trustee, Hawkesbury Pub. Sch. Bd., 1947-53 (Chrmn. 1949-53); served in 2nd Bn. (Reserve) Stormont, Dundas & Glengary Highlanders 1942-45; mem., Tech. Sec., Candn. Pulp & Paper Assn. (Weldon Gold Medal, 1954; Chrmn. 1969-71; Hon. Life mem. 1973); Fellow, Chem. Inst. Can. (Palladium Medal 1980, Hon. fellow 1981); mem., Assn. Prof. Engrs. Ont. (Gold Medal, 1977); Tech. Assn. of Pulp & Paper Industry (U.S.A.) (Dir. 1973-76, Tappi Medal, Hon. Life mem. 1977); Candn. Soc. for Chem. Engn. (Dir. 1967-68; R. S. Jane Award 1966); mem. Bd. Govs. Ont. Inst. for Studies in Educ. 1970-77; mem., Am. Inst. of Chem. Engrs., (Forest Prod. Div. Award, 1977); Anselme Payen Award, Am. Chem. Soc. 1978; Foreign mem., Swedish Roy. Acad. of Engn. Sciences, 1978; Shalimar Gold Medal, Indian Pulp & Paper Assn., 1975; Medal of the Brazilian Pulp & Paper Tech. Assn., 1974; McCharles Prize, Bd. of Govs., Univ. of Toronto, 1966; Royal Society of Canada, James W. Eadie Medal 1981; Liberal; United Church; recreation: photography; water skiing; Home: 110 Bloor St. W., Toronto, Ont. M5S 2W7

RASKY, Harry, B.A.; film and TV producer, director, writer; b. Toronto, Ont. 9 May 1928; s. Louis and Pearl (Krazner) R.; e. Regal Rd. Pub. and Oakwood Coll. Inst. Toronto; Univ. of Toronto, B.A. 1949; m. Ruth Arlene Werkhoven, 21 March 1965; children: Holly Laura, Adam Louis; Reporter no. of daily Newspapers Kirkland Lake, Ont., 1949; News editor-producer, CHUM, Toronto, 1950; News editor-producer CKEY, Toronto, 1951-52; co-founder new documentary dept., CBC., 1952-55; Assoc. editor, Saturday Night, 1955; producer-dir.-writer, N.Y.C. 1960-61; Pres. Harry Rasky Productions Inc. since 1967; received world-wide acclaim for documentaries on Marc Chagall, Tennessee Williams, Arthur Miller and George Bernard Shaw; has produced, directed and written programs for maj. TV networks in Can., U.S. and Eng.; world leaders interviewed incl. Pres. and Mrs. Johnson, Mrs. Roosevelt, Fidel Castro, David Ben Gurion, King of Sweden, Martin Luther King, Emperor Haile Selassie, Queen Elizabeth, foreign ministers of most major nations, Lester Pearson; performers directed incl. Orson Welles, Sir Ralph Richardson, Dame Edith Evans, Dirk Bogarde, James Mason, Emlyn Williams, Lynn Redgrave, Siobhan McKenna, Bob Hope, Jack Benny, Benny Goodman, Mahalia Jackson, Christopher Plummer, Geneviève Bujold, John Colicos; stage dir. in Eng. and Can.; Lectr., New Sch. for Social Research, Columbia Univ., Iowa State Univ.; awards incl. Venice Film Festival 1970 ("Upon This Rock"); Emmy and Internat. Golden Eagle Awards ("Hall of Kings"); San Francisco Film Festival Participation Prize; Peabody Award, TV Guide Award; Sylvania Award; Freedom Foundation; Sch. Bell Award; Ohio State; Overseas Press Club; Am. Council for Better Broadcasts Award; Candn. Radio Award; books incl. "Lower than the Angels"; "Tales of Acapulco Ladies"; memoirs, "Nobody Swings on Sunday" 1980; "TV Bitch"; play, "No Big Deal"; contrib. to various newspapers and mags.; mem., Dirs. Guild Am.; Writers Guild Am. (Offr); Acad. TV Arts & Sciences (judge); recreation: swimming; Office: c/o CBC, Box 500, Stn. A., Toronto, Ont. M5W 1E6

RASMINSKY, Louis, C.C. (1968), C.B.E., B.A., D.C.L., LL.D., D.H.L., economist; banker; b. Montreal, Que., 1908; s. late David and Etta (R); e. Pub. Schs., Toronto, Ont. and Harbord Coll. Inst. there (winner of three scholarships); Univ. of Toronto, B.A. (Hons. Econ.) 1928, LL.D., 1953; London Sch. of Economics; D.H.L. Hebrew Union Coll. 1963; LL.D. Queen's 1967; D.C.L. Bishop's 1968; LL.D. McMaster 1969; Hon. Doctorate, Yeshiva University 1970; LL.D. Trent 1972, Concordia 1975; Univ. of W. Ont., 1978; Univ. of B.C.; m. Lyla, d. late Harry Rotenberg of Toronto, Ont.; children: Michael, Lola, GOV. BANK OF CANADA 1961-1973; joined staff of Econ. and Financial Sec. of League of Nations, 1930; joined staff of Bank of Canada, 1940; organ. Res. & Stat. Sec., Foreign Exchange Control Bd., 1940; Asst. to Chrmn., 1941; Chairman (Alternate), 1942; Extve. Asst. to Govs., 1943-54; Depy. Gov., 1955-61; Extve. Dir., Internat. Monetary Fund, 1946-62; Internat. Bank for Reconstruction & Devel., 1950-62; Alternate Gov. for Can., Internat. Monetary Fund, 1950-62; Chrmn., Bd. Govs., Internat. Devel. Resource Centre, 1973-78; Hon. Fellow, London Sch. of Econs. 1959; rec'd "Outstanding Public Service Award" 1968; Vanier Medal, Inst.-Public Adm. 1974; recreations: golf, fishing, Clubs: Cercle Universitaire (Ottawa); Rideau; Five Lakes Fishing (Wakefield, Que.); Home: 440 Roxborough Ave., Rockcliffe Park, Ottawa, Ont. K1M 0L2

RASMUSSEN, L. Merrill, B.Sc.; petroleum executive; b. Cardston, Alta., 17 Apl. 1920; s. Lyman Merrill and Annie (Woolf) R.; e. Elem. and High Sch., Cardston, Alta.; Normal Sch., Calgary; Mount Royal Coll., Calgary; Univ. of Okla., B.Sc. (Petroleum Engn.); m. Enid, d. Henry H. Atkins, 3 June 1943; children: Ronald, Karen; PRES. AND CEO. AND DIR., HUSKY OIL CO. since 1979; with Gulf Oil Corp. and Br. Am. Oil co., 1949-59; mgr production, Pacific Petroleums Ltd., 1959-64; Vice-Pres exploration and production, 1964-67; Sr. Vice-Pres., 1967-69; exec. Vice-Pres., 1969-70; pres., 1970; C.E.O. 1974-79; also Dir; Dir., Husky Oil Ltd.; Husky Oil Operations Ltd.; Foothills Pipe Lines (Yukon) Ltd.; Royal Bank of Can.; Westcoast Transmission Co. Ltd.; Energy Equipment Systems Inc., Grove Valve and Regulator Co., Oakland; WAGI Internat., Rome; served with Candn. Army for 3½ yrs. during World War II; rank Lieut.; mem. Prof. Engineers Assn. Alta.; Candn. Petroleum Assn. (Past Chrmn., Bd. of Gov.); Candn. Gas Assn. (Dir., past Chrmn.); recreations: golf, other sports; Clubs: Calgary Petroleum; Glencoe; Calgary Golf & Country; Ranchmen's; Desert Island Country (Rancho Mirage CA); Eldorado Country; Indian Wells, CA; Olive-Glen Country Club, Cody, Wyoming; The Alta. Club; SLC, UT; The Denver Petroleum, Denver, CO; Home: 9260 E. Crestline Ave., Denver, Colorado 80111: Office: 600 So. Cherry St., Denver, CO. 80222.

RASMUSSEN, Theodore, M.D., M.S., F.R.C.P. & S(C.); b. Provo, Utah, 28 April 1910; s. Andrew Theodore and Gertrude (Brown) R.; e. Univ. of Minn., 1927-30; Univ. of Minn. Med. Sch., 1930-34; Mayo Foundation, Rochester, Minn., 1936-39; Montreal Neurol. Inst. of McGill Univ., 1939-42; B.S. and M.B. 1934, M.D. 1935, M.S. 1939; M.D. (Hons.) Univ. of Edinburgh, 1980; m. Catherine Cora, d. R.McG. Archibald, 18 Dec. 1947; children: Donald, Ruth, Mary, Linda; PROF. OF NEUROL. & NEURO-SURG., McGILL UNIV., since 1954; Sr. Neurol. consultant, Montreal Neurol. Inst., since 1972; Lectr. and Res. Fellow, McGill Univ., 1946-47; Prof. of Neurol. Surg., Univ. of Chicago, 1947-54; Depy. Dir. and Neurosurgeon, Montreal Neurol. Inst. 1954-60; Dir., 1961-72; Dir., Neurol. & Neuro-surgeon-in-chief, Royal Victoria Hosp. 1961-72; served in 2nd World War; active duty U.S. Army Medical Corp, October 1942 (First Lt.) to March 1946 (Lt. Col.); Chief of Nerosurgical Section, 14th Evacuation Hosp., China-Burma-India Theatre; rec'd. "Outstanding Achievement-Award" Univ. Minn. (1958), Univ. of Chicago (1963); Ambassador Award, Epilepsy Internat. 1979; Emeritus Prof. Award, McGill Univ., 1980; Publications: "Cerebral Cortex of Man" (with Wilder Penfield), 1950; "Functional Neurosurgery" (with Raul Marino Jr.) 1979; over 100 contrib. to prof. journs. textbooks and monographs; Alpha Omega Alpha; Sigma Xi, etc.; Christian; Club: Canadian; Home: 29 Surrey Drive, Montreal, Que. H3P 1B2; Office: 3801 University St., Montreal, Que. H3A 2B4

RASTORP;Robert Harry, B.A.; industrial executive; b. Matheson, Ontario, 1 Sept. 1932; s. Robert C. Rastorp and Florence (Child); e. Univ. of Toronto B.A.; m. Gertrude Elizabeth Walsh, 30 May 1964; children: Robbie Alex Neil. SR. VICE PRES., UNION CARBIDE CANADA LTD.: mem. Bd. Trade Metrop. Toronto; Automotive Industries Assn.; Grocery Products Mfrs. Can.; Candn. Mfrs. Assn.; recreations: Member of the Magic Circle, London, Eng.; International Brotherhood of Magicians, fishing, gardening, art; Home: 29 Bellehaven Cresc., Scarborough. Office: 123 Eglinton Ave. E., Toronto, Ont. M4P 1J3

RATHGEB, Charles I.; construction executive; s. Charles C. R.; m. Rosemary, d. Desmond Clarke, Montreal, Que.; CHRMN. COMSTOCK INTERNATIONAL LTD.; Dir., Brights Wines; Canadair Ltd.; I.A.C.; Liquid Carbonic Canada Ltd.; The Royal Bank of Canada; Steep Roc ines Ltd.; Houston Natural Gas Corp.; Olympic Trust of Can.; Home: 180 Teddington Park, Toronto, Ont. M4N 2C8; Office: 2 St. Clair Avenue W., Toronto, Ont. M4V 1L5

RAWLINSON, E. A., C.A.; radio executive; b. Qu'Appelle, Sask. 2 June 1912; s. Arthur George and Marion (Henley) R.; e. High Sch., Qu'Appelle, Sask.; Univ. of Sask. (Accounting); m. Georgina Agnes, d. G. A. Lapp, Abbotsford, B.C., 15 Aug. 1936; children: Gordon Stanley, Douglas Edward; OWNER AND GENERAL MANAGER, RADIO STATION CKBI, since 1946 and CKBI-TV; Past Dir., Candn. Assn. of Broadcasters; Past Pres., Western Assn. of Broadcasters; practised his prof. of Chart. Accountancy until 1946; served in 2nd World War as Mgr., No. 6 E.F.T.S., Brit. Commonwealth Air Training Plan; Past Pres., Sask. Inst. of Chart. Accts.; Prince Albert Bd. of Trade; Young Men's Chamber of Comm., Prince Albert; Past Chrmn., Bd. of Gov., Victoria Hospital, Prince Albert; mem., of Extve. (Prince Albert), Candn. Red Cross Soc.; Freemason; Anglican; recreations: golf, curling; Clubs: Prince Albert; Kiwanis (Past Pres.); Edmonton (Alta.); Home: 345-11th St. E., Prince Albert, Sask. S6U 1A4; Office: CKBI Bldg., Prince Albert, Sask.

RAY, Gerald Joseph, B.A.Sc., F.C.I.C.; company president; b. Toronto, Ont., 26 June 1926; s. Isaac and Molly (Cornfield) R.; e. Harbord and Vaughan Rd. Coll. Inst., Toronto; Univ. of Toronto, B.A.Sc. 1949 (Hugh Gall Award 1947); m. Esther Magerman, 8 May 1948; three s., Keith Lawrence, Richard David, Howard Stephen; PRES. AND CHRMN., THE BORDEN CO., LTD., since 1971; joined The Dunlop Tire & Rubber Co., Toronto, 1949; Tech. Sales Rep., American Resinous Chemicals of Canada Ltd., 1953; West Hill (now Borden Chemical, The Borden Co. Ltd.) 1953-54; Chief Chem. 1954-55; Gen. Mgr. 1955-57; Pres. 1957; el. a Dir. of present Co. 1968; Past Chrmn., Grocery Products Mfrs. Can.; Dir., Vice Pres. and Dir., Baycrest Centre for Geriatric Care; member, Association Professional Engineers Province Ontario; Chemical Institute Canada; Candn. Chem. Prod. Assn.; B'nai B'rith; recreations: golf, woodworking; Club: Donalda Country; Home: 4 Chieftain Cres., Willowdale, Ont. M2L 2H4; Office: 1275 Lawrence Ave. E., Don Mills, Ont. M3A 1C5

RAYNAULD, André, F.s.r.c.; économiste; n. Ste-Anne-de-la-Pocatière, Que., 20 Oct. 1927; f. Ernest-Léopold et Blanche (Gauthier) R.; e. Univ. de Montréal, B.A. 1948, M.A. 1951; Univ. de Paris, Dr. de l'UN. (Science économique) 1954; m. Michelle f. Gaston Nolin, Outremont, 15 Oct. 1951; enfants: François, Olivier, Dominique, Isabelle; Asst.-Prof., Science Economique, 1954-58; Prof. agrégé 1958, et Dir., Dept., Science Economique, 1958-63 et 1965-67; Prof. titulaire 1966; Dir. et fondateur, Centre de recherche en développement Economique, Univ. of Montréal 1970-72; Prés. du Conseil Econom. du Can. 1972-76; élu M.N.A. (Qué.) 1976-80; Prof. titulaire Univ. de Montréal 1980- ; Publications: "Croissance et structure économiques de la Province de Québec", "Situation et perspectives de l'enseignement en Haute-Volta", "le Rôle de l'Etat", "Institutions economiques canadiennes" "The Canadian Economic System", 1967: "Le développement économique"; "Les orientations du développement économique régional dans la Province de Québec" 1971; "Le financement des caisses de retraite"; "La propriété des entreprises au Québec" 1974; "Le financement des exportations" 1979; et nombreaux autres travaux et articles; mem., Conseil de la Faculté, Science Sociale, Univ. de Montréal, 1958-67; exécutif, Association des Profs., Univ. de Montréal, 1960-61; Conseil Canadien en Rech. Sociales, 1959-61; Mem. Am. Econ. Assn.; Société Canadienne de Sc. economiques (Prés. 1967-68); mem. Conseil Econ. du Can. 1966-69; Conseiller, Econ. du Sous-Ministre des Finances, 1967-68; mem., Soc. Royale du Canada; Can. Pol. Sc. Assn.; Président, Inst. Canadien des affaires publiques 1961-62; Trés. Montréal Econ. Assn. 1957-58; Chef de mission, Haute-Volta, pour l'UNESCO, 1961; Arbitre dans différents conflits du travail, mem., Soc. Radio-Canada; 1964-67; Aviseur, Etudes Economiques, Commission Royale sur le Bilinguisme et le Biculturalisme 1964-70; mem. Bd. of Dir. Inst. for Research on Public Policy, 1980- ; Missions à l'étranger, Niger, Côte D'Ivoire, Zaire, Japon, Srilanka, Guatemala, Brésil, Mexique; mem. groupe consultant; D.Sc.Econ. hon., Univ. de Sherbrooke 1976; Univ. d'Ottawa 1976; Catholique; Résidence: 4820 rue Roslyn, Montréal, Qué. H3W 2L2; Bureau: Université de Montréal, Bureau 6041, Montréal.

RAYNER, Gerald Theodore, M.B.A., M.P.A.; Canadian public servant; b. Montreal, Que. 19 March 1929; s. William Eric and Dorothy Ann (Addyman) R.; e. Montreal High Sch. for Boys; Bishop's Univ. B.A. 1951; Harvard Univ. M.B.A. 1953, M.P.A. 1973; m. Barbara Marion d. late Austin Ralph Chadwick 26 Sept. 1970; one s. Michael Edward Chadwick; SR. ASST. UNDER SECY. OF STATE 1977- ; Contracts Mgr., Comm. Mgr., Co. Secy., ROLLS-ROYCE OF CANADA LTD., Montreal 1953-64, Dir. Rolls-Royce Inc., New York 1962-64; Depy. Dir., Dir. Aerospace Br. Dept. of Industry Ottawa 1964-68; Treasury Bd. Secretariat 1968-72; Asst. Under Secy. of State-Corporate Mang. Dept. Secy. of State 1973-77; Anglican;

recreations: skiing, sailing, Canadiana; Clubs: Rideau; Royal St. Lawrence Yacht (Montreal); Harvard (N.Y. City); Men's Canadian (Extve. Comte.); Home: 190 Dufferin Rd., Ottawa, Ont. K1M 2A6; Office: Dept. of Secretary of State, Ottawa, Ont. K1A 0M5.

RAYNER, Michael H., C.St.J., B.A., C.A.; Canadian civil servant; e. Carleton Univ. B.A. 1965; C.A. 1969; DEPY. AUDITOR GEN. OF CANADA 1981- ; Gov., Candn. Comprehensive Auditing Foundation; joined Touche Ross & Co. 1965-70; Educ. Co-ordinator, Audit Services Bureau, Dept. Supply & Services, Ottawa 1970-72; Sr. Project Offr. Treasury Bd. Secretariat, Ottawa 1972-75; Extve. Secy. Independent Review Comte. Office of Auditor Gen. Can. 1974-75, various positions 1975-80, Depy. Auditor Gen. Planning/Reports/Standards Br. prior to Acting Auditor Gen. Can. 1980-81; Treas. St. John Ambulance Priory Can. 1976-80; mem. Ed. Adv. Bd. Candn. Inst. C.A.'s; Boy Scouts Assn. (Group Comte, Chrmn.); Home: R.R.1, Alcove, Qué. J0X 1A0; Office: 240 Sparks St., Ottawa, Ont. K1A 0G6.

REA, W. Harold, C.M.F.C.A., LL.D.; b. Kincardine, Ont., 26 Sept. 1907; s. Mr. and Mrs. Joseph W. Rea; e. Kincardine Pub. and High Schs.; Port Colborne, Ont., High Sch.; Inst. Chart. Accts. Ont., C.A. 1931, F.C.A. 1953; m. Marion Josephine Currie, Woodstock, N.B.; two d. Marilyn, Barbara; Past Chrmn of Bd, Axel Johnson Ind. Ltd.; Vice Pres. and Dir., Mutual Life Assnce. Co. of Can.; Dir., The Bank of Nova Scotia, 1955-77; Interprov. Pipe Line Co., 1952-78; Moore Corp. Ltd.; Dominion Foundries and Steel Limited; Kerr Addison Mines Ltd.; Candn. and Foreign Securities Co. Ltd., Vice Pres. and Dir., Mutual Life Assnce. Co. of Can.; Life mem., Toronto Adv. Bd. Salvation Army; National Council of YM-CAs of Canada; entered the firm of Thorne, Mulholland, Howson & McPherson, Chart. Accts., Toronto, Ont., as jr. Feb. 1926; joined Candn. Oil Co.'s Ltd. Apr. 1933 as Internal. Aud.; trans. to Sales Dept., 1937; loaned by the Co. to Candn. Govt. to serve as Liaison Offr. between the Oil Controller and the Armed Services in Ottawa, 1942; apptd. Extve. Asst. to the Oil Controller, in charge of supply and transportation, and in this capacity spent much time in Washington and worked closely there with the Petroleum Adm. for War, 1944; returned to Canadian Oil Companies Ltd. in Sept. 1945 and apptd. Extve. Asst. to the Pres., el. Pres., April 1949; retired from the Co. Jan. 1963; Chrmn., Great Candn. Oil Sands, 1964-77; Hon. Chrmn. (1975), Canada's Sports Hall of Fame, Toronto; United Church; recreations: fishing, gardening, golf; Clubs: York; Granite; Toronto; Rosedale Golf; Canadian (Past Pres.); Home: 27 Blyth Hill Road, Toronto, Ont. M4N 3L6; Office: Suite 1505, 44 King St. W., Toronto, Ont. M5H 1E2

READ, Rt. Rev. Allan Alexander, B.A., D.D. b. Toronto, Ont., 19 Sept. 1923; s. Alec P. and Lillice (Matthews) R.; e. Forest Hill Village Schs., Toronto; Univ. of Toronto, B.A.; D.D. Trinity Coll., Wycliffe Coll.; m. Beverly, d. Frank E. Roberts, 28 Sept. 1949; children: John, Elizabeth, Peter Michael, Martha; Bishop of Ontario, Kingston Suffragan Bishop, Diocese of Toronto 1972-81; Parish of Mono 1947-54; Barrie 1954-71; Archdeacon of Simcoe 1960-71; mem. Barrie Sch. Bd. 1954-63; Citizen of the Year, City of Barrie, 1968; Home: 23 Riverside Dr., R.R. 1, Box 2234, Kingston, Ont.; Office: Anglican Diocesan Centre, 90 Johnson St., Kingston, Ont. K4L 1X7

READ, Wallace F., B.Sc., P.Eng.; executive; b. Fort William, Ont., 4 Oct. 1921; s. Samuel Charles and Fannie (Bennett) R.; e. Queen's Univ., B.Sc. (Chem. Engn.) 1943; Univ. of W. Ont., Business Mang. 1956; m. Grace Louise, d. William Kellough, 14 Dec. 1945; children: Charlotte Ann Reeve, Alan, Nancy, Paul, Tracy, Elizabeth, Mary, David; SR. VICE PRES. AND DIR., JOHN LABATT LTD. since 1973; Dir., Can. Malting Co. Ltd.; Asst. Brewmaster, Canadian Breweries Ltd. 1946-49;

Chief Chem., Edible Oils Ltd., 1949-50; joined present Co. as Research Engr. 1951, Quality Control Mgr. 1953; Production Mgr., Labatts Ont. Breweries, 1958; Dir. of Production, John Labatt Ltd., 1962; Vice Pres. Production, Labatt Breweries of Can. 1964, Pres. 1967; served with Royal Candn. Engrs. 1943-46; rank Ltd.; Depy. Chrmn., Un. Way Campaign, 1973, Gen. Chrmn. 1974; Past Pres. and Dir., Jr. Achievement, London; Dir., Un. Community Services, London; Depy. Chrmn., Brescia Coll. London; mem., Assn. Prof. Engrs. Ont.; Assn. Brewing Chems.; Master Brewers Assn. Am. (Past Pres. Candn. Group); Inst. Brewing (Eng.); Anglican; recreations: golf, fishing, boating; Clubs: London; London Hunt & Country; Home: 440 Wonderland Rd., London, Ont. N6K 1L4; Office: 451 Ridout St., London, Ont. N6A 4M3

READ, Wallace Stanley, B.Eng., P.Eng.; utilities executive; b. Corner Brook, Nfld., 18 Apl. 1930; s. James Alexander and Olive May (Rafuse) R.; e. Corner Brook Pub. Sch., 1946; Mt. Allison Univ., Engn. Cert. 1949; N.S. Tech. Coll., B.Eng. (Elect.) 1951; m. Ida Marjorie Laura, d. late Arthur Wellon, Deer Lake, Nfld., 15 Jan. 1960; four s., Wallace Arthur Javies, David Alexander, Christian William, Gregory Allister Frederick; SR. VICE-PRES., NEWFOUNDLAND AND LABRADOR HYDRO since 1975; Director, Churchill Falls (Labrador) Power Corp.; Elect. Engr. on Capital Expansion, Bowater's Newfoundland Pulp and Paper Mills Ltd. Corner Brook, 1951; Chief Engr., Bowater Power Co. Ltd. Deer Lake, 1955, Plant Supt. 1959, Asst. Gen. Mgr. 1962; joined Newfoundland and Labrador Power Comn. as Chief Engr. 1964, Depy. Chrmn. 1968, Chrmn. 1974; mem. Assn. Prof. Engrs. Nfld.; Institute Electrical and Electronic Engrs.; Freemason (P.M.); Anglican; recreations: hunting, fishing, curling; Home: 44 Thorburn Rd., St. John's, Nfld. A1B 3L9;; Office: Philip Pl., St. John's Nfld.

READY, Vernon Strang, B.A.; educator; b. Lanark, Ont., 2 March 1918; s. Robert Franklin and Rachel Ella (Babcock) R.; e. Perth (Ont.) Coll. Inst.; Ottawa Normal Sch.; Queen's Univ., B.A.; Ont. Coll. of Educ., Univ. of Toronto; Inst. of Educ., Univ. of London, (Assoc.); m. Eileen Stephens, d. Marinus Bonde Sorensen, 10 Sept. 1952; two s., Robert Brian, Eric Thomas; PROF. QUEEN'S UNIV. since 1966; Chrmn. Bd. of Govs., Ont. Inst. for Studies in Educ.; Teacher 1936-47; Head, Dept. of Hist., Kingston (Ont.) Coll. and Vocational Inst., 1947-52, Princ. 1954-64; Assoc. Dean, Faculty of Educ. (Althouse Coll.), Univ. of W. Ont. 1964-66; Dean of Educ., Queen's Univ. 1966-77; rec'd Centennial Medal 1967; mem., Candn. Assn. Profs. of Educ. (Pres.); Candn. Educ. Assn.; Candn. Humanities Assn.; Candn. Soc. Studies in Educ. (Extve.); United Church; Home: 249 Fairway Hills Cres., Kingston, Ont. K7M 2B5; Office: Kingston, Ont.

REANEY, James, M.A., O.C., F.R.S.C.; poet; playwright; university teacher; b. nr. Stratford, Ont., 1 Sept. 1926; s. James Nesbitt and Elizabeth (Crerar) R.; e. University of Toronto (Univ. Coll.), B.A. 1948, M.A. 1949, Ph.D. 1958; m. Colleen Thibaudeau, 29 Dec. 1951; two children; author of "The Red Heart" (poetry), 1949; "A Suit of Nettles", 1959, rec'd. Gov. General's Award for Poetry, 1949, 1959 and 1962; "The Killdeer", 1959, winner of award for best Candn. play performed at Dom. Drama Festival, Vancouver 1960; "The Boy with an R in his hand" (hist. fiction), 1965; in 1968 John Hirsch produced "Colours in the Dark" at Stratford Festival; recent plays incl. "Listen to the Wind", "Name & Nicknames", "The Easter Egg"; "The Donnellys: Sticks & Stones, St. Nicholas Hotel, Handcuffs" (trilogy); "Baldoon", "The Dismissal", "Wacousta", "King whistle", "Fourteen Barrels from Sea to Sea"; wrote and publ. with Alphabet Press "The Dance of Death at London, Ontario"; edited and published a literary review "Alphabet 1960-70"; contributor of various short stories published in Candn.

mags.; Cong.; recreation: croquet; Address: University of Western Ontario, London, Ont.

RECTOR, Luther Griffith; manufacturer; b. Sodus, Michigan, 6 Nov. 1909; s. Samuel James and Florence Etta (Griffith) R.; e. Pub. and High Schs., Dowagiac, Mich.; High Sch., Miami, Fla.; Gregg Business Coll., Chicago; Armour Inst. of Techol. (night sch. chem. courses), 1927-28; Cornell Coll., Mount Vernon, Iowa 1929-30; m. Eileen Margaret, d. the late Alexander C. Riddell, 28 June 1935; children: Donald James, Darcy Griffith, Sally Janet; CHRMN., THE GRIFFITH LABORATORIES LTD. (Manufacturing Food Chemists); Dir., Griffith Laboratories, Inc., Chicago, Illinois; Past President, Canadian Spice Association; Past President, Rotary Club of Leaside, Ontario; Past President, Employees' Welfare Service Fund, Toronto; former Campaign chrmn., United Appeal of Metro Toronto; Past Pres. and Chrmn., United Community Fund of Metro Toronto; on leaving sch., joined the Griffith Laboratories Inc., Chicago, 1927; on estbl. of present Co. in Can. May 1929, accepted a position with the Co.; Protestant; recreations: photography, golf; Clubs: Rotary (Leaside, Ont.); Granite; Empire; Rosedale Golf; Home: 1 Valleyana Drive, Toronto, Ont. M4N 1J7; Office: 757 Pharmacy Ave., Scarborough, Ont. M1L 3J8

RECTOR, Maurice; retired company executive; b. Sodus Mich., 12 Jan. 1908; s. Samuel James and Florence Etta (Griffith) R.; e. Pub. and High Sch., Dowagiac, Mich.; Univ. of Miami (two yrs.); American Sch. of Baking; m. Audrey Catherine, d. David Evans, Peterborough, Ont., 5 Oct. 1934; children: Alan David, Robert Maurice, Catherine Florence; Vice Chairman, the Griffith Laboratories Ltd., 1946-77 (ret.); joined the Griffith Laboratories, Incorporated in Chicago, Illinois in 1929; Freemason; Protestant; recreations: golf, photography, fishing; Clubs: Granite; Rosedale Golf; Rotary (Toronto-Leaside) Past Pres., Past Dist. Gov., Rotary Internat.: Home: 150 Heath St. W., Toronto, Ont. M4V 2Y4

REDFERN, Donald Blaine, B.A.Sc., P.Eng.; b. Toronto, Ont., 15 Nov. 1927; s. Wesley Blaine and Donella (Kinghorn) R.; e. Public and High Sch., Forest Hill Village, Ont.; Univ. of Toronto, B.A.Sc. 1948; m. Joan Phin, d. Burleigh P. Ballantyne, Toronto, Ont., 23 Sept. 1960; children: Andrew, Alan, Janet, Pamela; CHAIRMAN PROCTOR & REDFERN LIMITED, CONSULTING ENGINEERS AND PLANNERS; Pres., Proctor & Redfern International Ltd.; worked with present Co. during summers while attending univ., joining the firm immediately on grad.; became a partner in 1954 (incorp. in 1968); has worked in many Ont. and E. Candn. centres on municipal engn. projects, incl. Metrop. Toronto, Hamilton, St. Catharines, Sault Ste. Marie, Kitchener, Waterloo, Galt, Saint John, N.B.; mem., Candn. Council of Prof. Engrs. (Pres. 1968-69); The Candn. Inst. on Pollution Control; The Engineering Inst. of Can.; The Assn. of Consulting Engrs. of Can.; Assn. Prof. Engrs. Ont. (Pres. 1965-66); Am. Waterworks Assn.; Delta Kappa Epsilon; recreations: fishing, boating, reading, travel; Hobby: farming; Clubs: Engineers'; Badminton & Racquet; Home: 95 Roxborough St. E., Toronto, Ont. M4W 1V9; Office: 75 Eglinton Ave. East, Toronto, Ont. M4P 1H3

REDFERN, John D., B.Sc., P.Eng.; executive; b. Ottawa, Ont., 9 May 1935; s. Harry Clare and Mary Margaret Evelyn (MacLaurin) R; e. Carleton Univ.; Queen's Univ., B.Sc. (Civil Engn.) 1958; m. Ann Findlay, d. Alexander Watson, Ottawa, Ont. 29 June 1957; children: John Stephen, Bruce Douglas, David Scott, Christine Evelyn; PRESIDENT AND CHIEF EXECUTIVE OFFICER CANADA CEMENT LAFARGE LTD. since 1977; Project Mgr., Ont. Dept. of Highways, Kingston, ont. 1958; Tech. Sales Engr., Canada Cement Co. Ltd.; Ottawa 1958; Sales Mgr., Maritime Cement, Moncton, N.B. 1962; Dist. Sales Mgr., Canada Cement Ottawa 1965 and Toronto 1966, Vice Pres. Halifax 1969; Vice Pres. & Gen. Mgr. W. Re-

gion 1971; Vice-pres. Operations 1974; Extve. Vice-pres. and Gen. Mgr. 1976; Dir. Can. Cement Lafarge Ltd.; Chrmn. Citadel Cement Corp., Lafarge Consultants Ltd.; Lafarge Conseils et Etudes; Canterra Energy Ltd.; mem. Bd. of Dirs. CENTRAID; Chrmn. Candn. Portland Cement Assn.; served with RCN, Sub. Lt. (Ret.); member Assn. Prof. Engineers. Ont.; Candn. Mfrs. Assn.; Candn. Chamber Comm.; Candn. Constr. Assn.; Candn. Council of Conf. Bd. in Can.; Bd. of Gov., Le Conseil du Patronat du Qué.; United Church; recreations: skiing, golf, squash, swimming; Club: M.A.A.A.; Mount Royal; St. James; Royal Montreal Golf; Glencoe (Calgary); Home: 319 Pinetree Cres., Beaconsfield, Que. H9W 5E2; Office: 606 Cathcart St., Montreal, Que. H3B 1L7

REDFORD, Donald Bruce, M.A., Ph.D., F.R.S.C.; egyptologist; educator; b. Toronto, Ont. 2 Sept. 1934; s. Cyril and Kathleen (Coe) R.; e. Univ. of Toronto B.A. 1957, M.A. 1958, Ph.D. 1965; Brown Univ. 1959-60; m. Susan d. Frank Pirritano, Scranton, Pa. 30 Jan. 1982; children: Christopher, Philip (by previous marriage); PROF. OF NEAR EASTERN STUDIES, UNIV. OF TORONTO 1969-, Lectr. 1961, Asst. Prof. 1965, Assoc. Prof. 1967; Consultant Akhenaten Temple Project, Univ. Museum, Univ. of Pa. in Cairo 1971, Dir. 1972- ; Research Assoc. Univ. Museum Univ. of Pa. 1972- Royal Ont. Museum 1973- ; Assoc. Trustee, Am. Schs. Oriental Research 1977- ; co-organizer Internat. Cong. on Egyptology, Cairo 1975; guest lectr. and keynote speaker many univs. and museums; participated First Cong. on Hist. & Archaeol. of Jordan, Oxford 1980; recipient Reuben Wells Leonard Scholarship; Lyle Silver Medal for Hebrew; W. R. Taylor Mem. Scholarship; 2 Univ. of Toronto Open Fellowships; Teaching Fellowship Brown Univ.; 5 Can. Council Grants; 4 Killam Program Fellowships; 5 Smithsonian FCP Grants; mem. Soc. Study Egyptian Antiquities (Past Vice Pres.); Am. Research Center in Egypt; Candn. Mediterranean Inst.; Oriental Club of Toronto (Secy.); author numerous publs.; Anglican; Home: 22 Nesbitt Dr., Toronto, Ont. M4W 2G3; Office: 280 Huron St., Toronto, Ont. M5S 1A1.

REDHEAD, Paul Aveling, B.A., M.A., Ph.D., F.A.P.S., F.I.E.E.E., F.R.S.C.; physicist; b. Brighton, Eng. 25 May 1924; s. Daniel Albert and Gwedoline (Aveling) R.; e. Taunton Sch. 1942; Cambridge Univ. B.A. 1944, M.A. 1948, Ph.D. 1969; m. Doris Beatrice d. late A. J. Packman 1948; children: Janet Anne Randall, Patricia Joan; DIR. DIV. OF PHYSICS, NAT. RESEARCH COUNCIL OF CAN. since 1973, Group Dir. Phys./Chem. Science Labs. since 1974; Scient. Dept. Naval Ordnance 1944-45, Services Electronics Research Lab. (Brit. Admiralty) 1945-47; Research Offr. Nat. Research Council Can. 1947-54, Head of Electron Physics Sec. 1954-70, Head Program Planning and Analysis Group 1970-71, Dir. Gen. (Planning) 1972-73; rec'd Medard W. Welch Award Am. Vacuum Soc. 1975; Pres. Ottawa Chapter, Ont. Heart Foundation 1973-77; author "The Physical Basis of Ultra-High Vacuum" 1968; over 60 scient. papers electron, vacuum and surface physics; Hon. mem. and Past Pres. Am. Vacuum Soc.; mem. Candn. Assn. Physicists; Chem. Soc. (Faraday Div.); Home: 1958 Norway Cres., Ottawa, Ont. K1H 5N7; Office: Ottawa, Ont. K1A 0R6.

REDING, Most Rev. Paul F. (R.C.); b. Hamilton, Ont., 14 Feb. 1925; s. Thomas Augustine and Florence Ann (Fleming) R.; e. St. Ann's Separate Sch., 1931-39, Hamilton; Cathedral Boys' High Sch., 1939-43, Hamilton; St. Augustine's Semy., Toronto, 1943-50: BISHOP OF HAMILTON, since 1973; Chancellor, Diocese of Hamilton, 1955-66; Rector, Cath. of Christ the King, Hamilton, 1959; Auxiliary Bishop of Hamilton, Titular of Liberalia 1966-73; Home: 722 King St. W., Hamilton, Ont. L8P 1C7; Office: 700 King St. W., Hamilton, Ont. L8P 1C7

REDMOND, Donald Aitcheson, B.Sc., B.L.S., M.S.; librarian; b. Owosso, Mich., 19 May 1922; s. Athol Aitcheson and Hilton Edna (Rhind) R.; e. Mount Allison Univ., B.Sc. 1942; McGill Univ., B.L.S. 1947; Univ. of Ill., M.S. (Lib. Science) 1950; m. Ruth Marian, d. late Frank Clinton White 1948; children: Christopher, Derek, Margaret; PRINCIPAL LIBRARIAN, QUEEN'S UNIV. since 1977; Librarian, Candn. Book Center, Halifax, 1948-49; N.S. Tech. Coll., Halifax, 1949-60; Science and Engn. Librarian, Asst. Dir. of Libs. (Reader Services) Univ. of Kans., 1961-65; Tech. Lib. Advisor, Ceylon Inst. of Scient. and Indust. Research, Colombo, 1957-58; Dir. of Lib., Middle E. Tech. Univ., Ankara, 1959-60; Chief Librarian, Queen's Univ., 1966-77; author, "BSJ 1946-69" (a cumulated index to Baker St. Journ.), 1970; edit. checklist and index of Conan Doyle Coll., Metro. Toronto Central Library, 1972, 1974; also articles in prof. lib. and other journals; member Am., Candn. Lib. Assns.; Baker St. Irregulars; Sherlock Holmes Soc. of London; United Church; recreations: Sherlock Holmes, model railways; Home: 178 Barrie St., Kingston, Ont. K7L 3K1

REDNER, Alan Keith; manufacturer; b. Belleville, Ont., 29 Apl. 1934; s. Robert Keith and Marion Winnifred (Fox) R.; e. Ryerson Inst. of Technol., 1955; Univ. of W. Ont.; Am. Mang. Assn.; m. Nancy E., d. late Brig. I. H. Cumberland, 5 Oct. 1956; children: John David, Linda E., Michael Christopher Cumberland; VICE PRESIDENT MARKETING SERVICE SYSTEMS OF APPLIED POWER INC., MILWAUKEE; since 1977; Asst. Mgr., Hotel Leonard, St. Catharines, 1955; joined Bear Equipment Services Ltd. (predecessor co.) as Asst. Sales Mgr. 1956; Asst. to Pres. 1960; Pres., Applied Power Automotive (Can) Ltd.; Pres., Bear Mfg., Illinois U.S.A.; served with Gov. Gen.'s Horse Guards (Reserve); rank Capt.; Pres., Automotive Indust. Assn. Can. 1971-72; Past Dir., Automotive Service Mfrs. Assn.; P. Conservative; Anglican; recreations: sailing, skiing; Club: Toronto Cricket Skating & Curling; Home: 345 Lakeshore Rd., Port Hope, Ont.; Office: 305 Progress Ave., Scarborough, Ont. M1P 2Z8

REDPATH, James B., B.Sc.; mining engineer; b. Lethbridge, Alta., 1908; e. McGill Univ., B.Sc. (Mining Engn.) 1931; DIR., DOME MINES LTD., since 1959; Dir., Sigma Mines (Quebec) Ltd.; Chrmn. & Dir. Canada Tungsten Mining Corp. Ltd.; Dir. Pilot Insurance Co.; McIntyre Mines Ltd.; Clubs: National; Engineers; Home: 339 Riverview Dr., Toronto, Ont. M4N 3C9; Office: P.O. Box 270, 1 First Canadian Pl., Toronto, Ont. M5X 1H1

REECE, David Chalmer, B.A.; diplomat; b. Winnipeg, Man., 14 Feb. 1926; s. Rupert and Mary Gwendolen (Marples) R.; e. Ravenscourt Sch., Winnipeg, Man. 1943; Univ. of Manitoba 1943-46; Cambridge Univ., B.A. (Hons.) 1949; m. Nina Marjorie, d. E. L. Stone, 25 Jan. 1958; children: Mary Katherine, Michael Francis, Caroline Megan; called to the Bar, Inner Temple 1951; joined Dept. External Affairs as Foreign Service Offr. 1952; served in New Delhi 1954-57, Kuala Lumpur 1958, Bonn 1959, London 1960-62, New Delhi 1967; Min. and Depy. Permanent Rep. to U.N., New York 1969-71; High Commr. to Trinidad, Tobago, Barbados and Commr., Assoc. States B.W.I. 1972; High Commr. to Ghana and Ambassador to Dahomey, Togo and Liberia, 1974-76; Ambass. and Hd., Candn. Delegation to Mutual and Balanced Force Reduction Talks, Vienna, since 1978; served in R.C.N.V.R., active May 1944-Oct. 1945; entered as Ordinary Seaman, rank on discharge P/Sub. Lt.; Zeta Psi; Anglican; recreations: tennis, reading, theatre, swimming; Office: Luegerring 10, A-1010, Vienna, Austria

REECE, Everette A.; manufacturer; b. Greenwood, Neb. 27 July 1914; s. Henry Arthur and Mabel Ann (Weideman) R.; e. Univ. of Neb. Business Adm. 1932; Iowa State Univ. Business Adm. 1933; Washington Univ. Grad. Sch. Business Adm. 1964; m. Irene May d. Irvin Parrish 3 Dec. 1929; children: Darlene Louise LeClair, Ronald Arthur, Donald Ray: VICE PRES. AND GEN. MGR., CHRMN. BD. DIRS., McDONNELL DOUGLAS CANADA LTD.

1976- ; joined Douglas Aircraft Co. Long Beach, Cal., Oklahoma City and Santa Monica, Cal. 1938-48; McDonnell Aircraft Co. St. Louis, Mo. 1948-69; McDonnell Douglas Canada Ltd. VIce Pres. Mfg. 1969, Acting Pres. 1974-75; Dir., Air Industries Assn. Can.; Candn. Export Assn.; mem. Candn. Chamber Comm.; Bd. Trade Metrop. Toronto; Protestant; recreation: golf; Club: Canadian; Home: 25 Warrender Ave., Islington, Ont. M9B 5Z4; Office: (P.O. Box 6013) Toronto, Ont. L5P 1B7.

REED, Graham Frederick, M.A., M.Litt., Ph.D.; educator; b. Coventry, Eng. 13 March 1923; s. Fred and Winifred (Graham) R.; e. Blackpool (Eng.) Grammar Sch.; Cambridge Univ. B.A., M.A. 1950; Univ. of Durham M.Litt. 1964; Univ. of Manchester Ph.D. 1966; m. Jean d. late John Rutter 13 Dec. 1947; one d. Lindsey; VISITING PROF., CLARK INST. OF PSYCHIATRY, UNIV. OF TORONTO. 1981-82; Dean, Faculty of Grad. Studies, York Univ. 1973-81; Educ. Psychol. Kingston-on-Hull 1949, Sr. Educ. Psychol. 1955-59; Lectr. in Clin. Psychol. Univ. of Manchester 1959-66; Sr. Lectr. in Psychol. Univ. of Aberdeen 1966-69; Prof. of Psychol. present Univ. 1970, Chrmn. Atkinson Coll. Psychol. Dept. 1970-73; served with Royal Signals Egypt, Italy, India 1942-47, rank Capt.; author "Fisher's Creek" 1963; "How to Read Faster Under Water" 1967; "The Psychology of Anomalous Experience" 1972; also numerous articles and reviews in various learned journs.; mem. Brit. Psychol. Soc.; Royal Stat. Soc.; Royal Soc. Health (Comte. mem.); Candn. Psychol. Assn.; Anglican; recreations: writing, jazz music, walking, old prints; Home: 1357 Mount Pleasant, Toronto, Ont. M4N 2T6; Office: 4700 Keele St., Downsview, Ont. M3J 1P3

REEKIE, Charles Douglas, C.A.; industrialist; b. Montreal, Que. 20 Aug. 1924; e. Elizabeth Ballantyne Pub. Sch., Montreal W.; Montreal W. High Sch.; McGill Univ.; Chart. Acct., 1948; m. Lorna Elsie Bridge, Montreal; children: Jennifer Ann, John Douglas; PRES. AND CHIEF EXTVE. OFFR., CAE INDUSTRIES LTD., since 1967; Chrmn. of Bd. & Dir., CAE Electronics Ltd.; CAE Metals Ltd.; Candn. Bronze Co. Ltd.; Union Screen Plate Co. Ltd.; CAE Aircraft Ltd.; Webster Mfg. (London) Ltd.; CAE Fiberglass Products Div.; Accurcast Die Casting Ltd.; CAE Montupet DieCast Ltd.; Dir. CAE Machinery Ltd.; Northwest Ind. Ltd.; Cdn. Enterprise Development Corp. Ltd.; Can. Pacific Enterprises Ltd.; Colonial Life Ins. Co.; with Sharp Milne & Co., Chart. Accts., Montreal, 1941-47; Riddell Stead Graham & Hutchison, Chart. Accts., 1947-49; Secy.-Treas., Canadian Baker Perkins Ltd., 1950-55; joined present Co. (then Candn. Aviation Electronics Ltd.), 1955, Pres., Northwest Industries Ltd. (a subsidiary), Edmonton, Alta., 1963-67; mem., Order of Chart. Accts. Ont. recreations: golf, reading; Clubs: Royal Montreal Golf; Mount Royal; Montreal Badminton & Squash; Lyfords Cay; National, Lambton Golf & Country; Home: 18 Taylorwood Dr., Islington, Ont. M9Y 4R7 Office: Suite 3060, P.O. Box 30, Royal Bank Plaza, Toronto, Ont. M5J 2J1

REEKIE, J. Alistair, C.A.; b. Montreal, Que., 23 Dec. 1921; s. John and Mary Clark (Winter) R.; e. Montreal W. High Sch.; McGill Univ., C.A. 1944; m. Audrey Louise, d. R. A. Kirkpatrick, 25 June 1949; children: Marilyn Louise, Ian Bruce, Leslie Joan, Catherine Ann; VICE-PRESIDENT, FINANCE AND TREASURER, CANADIAN VICKERS LTD., since 1959; Director and Treasurer, Vickers-Krebs Ltd.; Montreal Dry Docks Ltd.; C.A. Apprentice, Rutherford Williamson & Co., 1938-39; Riddell, Stead, Graham & Hutchison, 1939-45, and auditing there, 1945-46; Audit. Peat, Marwick, Mitchell & Co. 1946-47; Price Waterhouse & Co., 1947; Canadian Industries Ltd., Accts. Dept., 1946; Chief Acct., then Div. Comptroller, Dominion Bridge Co. Ltd., 1947-58; Chief Travelling Acct., C.P.R., 1958-59; since when successively Comptroller and Comptroller and Treas. with present firm; Gov., Que. Hosp. Assn.; Finance Commr.,

Town of Montreal West since 1969; Pres., Inst. Chart Accts., Que. 1971-72; Protestant; recreations: golfing, skiing,; Clubs: St. James's; Kanawaki Golf; Home: 209 Westminster N., Montreal W., Que. H4X 1Z5; Office: 5000 Notre Dame St. E., Montreal, Que. H1V 2B4

REEVES, John, athlete, author, broadcaster, composer; b. Merritt, B.C., 1 Dec. 1926; s. Rev. A.G . and D. H. (Swinburn) R.; e. St. John's Coll., Cambridge Univ., B.A. (Classics) 1948; m. late Charlotte Pasinsky, 1962; children: Frances, Robert; m. Shirley Gow, 1977; EXTVE. PRODUCER OF RADIO FEATURES, ENG. NETWORK, CBC; athletic achievements include former holder Candn. veteran records for half-mile, mile, two miles, three miles, six miles, ten miles; founder Hart House Marathon; joined CBC as Radio Producer (Music and Drama), 1952; pioneered stereophonics broadcasts in Canada 1954; authored world's first quadriphonic radio play in 1970; introduced Kunstkopf recording N. Amer. 1975; received Italia Prize for Radio Drama 1959; Gabrielle Prize for Religious Broadcasting 1978; served with Brit. Itelligence Corp. 1948-49; author, "A Beach of Strangers", 1960; "Triptych" 1972; "The Arithmetic of Love", 1976; "Murder by Microphone", 1978; numerous radio plays, features and documentaries, and TV films; also a body of verse some of which issued in 1954 by Hallmark Recordings; composer, chamber and choral pieces, principal works include "Hallelujah Psalms", "For the Feast of All Hallows", "Two Fifteenth Century Lyrics", "Canons for String Orchestra", "The Deploration of Rachel", "Missa Brevis", "Compline Cantata", "Ecumenical Evening Service", "Twelve Haikuku", "Aphorisms", "Antiphons", "Commemorations", "advent Cantata", "Four Songs for Voice and Violin"; avocation: Czech politics; Clubs: Univ. Toronto Track; Home: 2 Wychwood Pk., Toronto, Ont. M6G 2V5; Office: CBC, Box 500, Station A, Toronto, Ont. M5W 1E6.

REEVES, John Alexander, R.C.A.; photojournalist; b. Burlington, Ont. 24 Apl. 1938; s Walter James and Jean (McCrimmon) R.; e. Burlington Central High Sch. 1956; Sir George Williams Art Sch. 1957; Ont. Coll. of Art A.O.C.A. Dipl. 1961; prof. gen. features photographer for maj. mags. Can. and USA; many assignments Nat. Film Bd. Still Photo Div. incl. numerous photo stories for Photomedia and N.F.B. Press Service; served as Consultant to Nat. Film Bd. in production of "Between Friends-Entre Amis" 1976; contrib. to numerous N.F.B. books and exhns. incl. "Call Them Canadians" (book & exhn.) 1967; "Image 5" (book and exhn.) 1968; "Many Happy Returns" N.W.T. Centennial (exhn.) 1969; coll. "Fifty Portraits of Canadian Women" exhibited as a monograph Nat. Conf. Centre Ottawa 1975; coll. "Thirty Portraits of Women" Deja Vue Gallery Toronto 1977; "The MAgic Word", Nat. Photog. Collection of Public Archives, 1981; "Photojournalism", NFC Gallery, Ottawa, 1981; "Inuit Art World", The Canadian Centre of Photography, 1982 (one-man show); began writing for mags. 1972 preparing several feature articles for "Toronto Life"; produced photographic and written essay on Jean Vanier's work with mentally handicapped in France for "Maclean's" 1973; travel feature E. Africa 1975; photo-essay ocean yachting for "Saturday Night" 1977; has produced word-and-picture packages on interesting people for maj. mags.; comns. rec'd from various business enterprises involving annual reports, recruiting and promotional material; co-author "John Fillion-Thoughts About My Sculpture" 1968 (selected for exhn. Am. Inst. Graphic Arts Book Show 1969); recipient various Graphic Arts Awards incl. acceptance Le Fed. Internationale de l'Art Photographique Exhn. 1968, 1969; rec'd Internat. Assn. Printing House Craftsmen Award 1977; Graphica Club Montreal and Toronto Art Dirs. Club Awards; Cdn. Nat. Magazine Award for Photo-journalism, 1980; commenced radio and TV broadcasting activities 1968 becoming Host of "Toronto in Review" CBC radio; many appearances on radio and TV shows; cited various bibliogs.; Council

mem. Royal Candn. Acad. 1980-81; Anglican; recreation: sailing;Address: 11 Yorkville Ave., Apt. 602, Toronto, Ont. M4W 1L3.

REEVES, Hon. Paul G.; judge; b. Ottawa, Ont., 27 June 1928; s. late J. Oscar and Marie-Jeanne (Lemieux) R.; e. Coll. de Saint-Laurent (Que.), B.A. 1948; Univ. de Montréal, LL.L. 1952; Goethe Inst., Montreal, degree in German lang. 1973; m. Agnès G., d. C.E. Millet, Longueuil, Que. 23 May 1955; children; Hélène, Jean Isabelle, Marie-Angès; JUSTICE, SUPERIOR COURT, QUE., since 1973; read law with Marcel Piché; called to Bar of Que. 1952; cr. Q.C. 1967; Prof. of Eng., Coll. de St. Laurent 1952; Part-time Prof. of Law 1953-62; Legal Advisor, Claims Dept., United Provinces Insurance Co. 1953; Jr. Partner, Pagé Beauregard Duchesne Renaud & Reeves 1957; Partner, Lalande Brière Reeves Paquette & Longtin 1963-67; Crown Atty. 1962-64; Mun. Judge, Ville Le Moyne 1962-73; Legal Advisor and Dir., Reeves Security Agency Ltd. 1955-73; Sr. Partner, Reeves Longtin Cantin & Villeneuve 1968-73; has served on various bar comtes.; responsible for post-grad. teaching ins. law, Prof. Law Sch. of Que. Bar 1970-71; author various articles in legal journs.; mem. Candn. Bar Assn.; R. Catholic; recreations: skiing, travel, photography, theatre, concerts; Home: 630 Victoria Ave., Longueuil, Que.; Office: Court House, Montreal, Que. H2Y 1B6

REEVES, Sidney A., B.E., P.Eng.; construction engineer; b. Sydney, N.S., 21 Jan. 1927; s. Sidney Ellison and Ella Marjorie (Fownes) R.; e. Sydney (N.S.) Acad. 1944; Acadia Univ.; N.S. Tech. Coll., B.E. (Civil Engn.) 1949; m. Mary Charlotte, d. Willard MacIntyre, 15 July 1950; children: Deborah Jane, David Alexander, Susan Marjorie; CHAIRMAN MARITIME BUILDERS LTD.; Canda. Dir.; Candn. Owners & Pilots Assn.; Pres., Reeves' Building Supplies Ltd.; Sidella Enterprises Ltd.; Fisher Electronics Ltd.; Shaw and MacDonald Ltd.; Seveer Realty Ltd.; Vice Pres., Mid-Town Management Ltd.; Dir., Oland's Breweries (1971) Ltd.; Maritime Telegraph & Telephone Co. Ltd.; Dominion Life Assce. Co.; joined Ont. Hydro Electric Co. as Jr. Engr. 1949; Head of Engn. Dept., Superline Oils Ltd. and Assoc. Co's 1950; Pres. and Gen. Mgr., Maritime Builders Ltd. 1952; mem. N.S. Voluntary Econ. Planning Bd.; Past Pres., Sydney YMCA; Past Gen. Chrmn., Sydney Centennial Comn.; Past Pres., Sydney Bd. Trade and Assn. Bds. Trade Cape Breton; Past N.S. Vice Pres., Candn. Constr. Assn.; Past Pres., Cape Breton Is. Constr. Assn.; mem. Assn. Prof. Engrs. N.S.; Engn. Inst. Can.; Baptist; recreations: curling, golf, skiing, flying; Club: Lingan Golf & Country (Past Pres.); Home: 68 St. Peters Rd., Sydney, N.S. B1P 4P4; Office: 335 Welton St., Sydney, N.S. B1P 5S6

REFORD, L. Eric; steamship executive; b. Montreal, Que., 12 Dec. 1900; s. Robert Wilson and Elsie Stephen (Meighen) R.; e. Rugby Sch., Eng.; Royal Mil. Coll., Kingston, Ont.; McGill Univ., B.A. 1921; Oxford Univ. (New Coll.), B.A. 1923; m. Katharina Nikolaivna Pletschikova, d. Nikolai Nicolaivitch Pletschikoff, 10 Sept. 1927; has two s. and one d.; CHRMN., ROBERT REFORD INVESTMENTS LTD.; Dir., Mount Royal Rice Mills Ltd.; entered Robert Reford Co., 1924; Vice-Pres., 1929; became Pres. The Robert Reford Co. Ltd. 1946; Councillor, City of Montreal, 1944-47, 1947-50 and 1950-54; mem. of Council, Montreal Bd. of Trade, 1937-38; Pres., Shipping Fed. of Can., 1943-45; Hon. Pres., Que. Divn., Navy League of Can.; Conservative; Anglican; Clubs: University; Mount Stephen; Home: 3627 Redpath St., Montreal, Que. H3G 2G9

REFORD, Robert W.; b. London, Eng. 1 May 1921; s. Robert Bruce Stephen and Evelyn Margaret Robinson (MacInnes) R.; came to Canada 1946; e. Winchester Coll., Eng. 1934-39; New Coll. Oxford Univ. 1940; m. Stephanie Lee McCandless 26 Nov. 1972; children: Lisa E., Sharon V. (by previous marriage); step-children: James A. and

Nancy B. Hudson; PRES., REFORD-McCANDLESS INTERNAT. CONSULTANTS CORP.; Reford-McCandless Internat Inst.; with British United Press 1946-52; Ottawa Liaison Offr., CBC Internat. Service 1953-65; Edit. Writer, Ottawa Citizen 1965-67; U.N. Correspondent 1968; Special Asst. to Dir. of Research, U.N. Inst. for Training & Research 1970; Extve. Dir., Candn. Inst. of Internat. Affairs, 1971-78; served in 2nd World War, Irish Guards 1940-46; active service in N.W. Europe and Malaya; Vice-Chrmn., Ottawa Br., Candn. Inst. Internat. Affairs 1966-67, Chrmn. N.Y. Br. 1969-70, mem. Nat. Educ. Comte. of Inst. 1962-71; author of numerous articles in Candn. newspapers and journs.; frequent commentator and interviewer on radio and TV; author of "Canada and Three Crises" 1968; Anglican; recreations: golf, skiing; Clubs: Rideau; Royal Ottawa Golf; Toronto Golf; Home: 12 Metcalfe St., Toronto, Ont. M4X 1R6

REGAN, Francis Vincent, Q.C.; b. Toronto, Ont., 13 Dec. 1922; s. James D. and Irene (Duggan) R.; e. Univ. of Toronto; Osgoode Hall Law Sch., Toronto, Ont.; m. Barbara Jane, d. John Callahan, Q.C., 26 April 1947; children: Paul, Michael, John, Rosemary, Deborah, Mary-Anne; Pres., London Broadcasters Ltd.; Cawthra Apartments Ltd.; Secy.-Treas. and Dir., Pleasant Valley Aggregates Ltd.; Rick-Rod Corp.; Levine Bros. Hides (Ont.) Ltd.; Internat. Systems Ltd., Dalfer Indus. Ltd.; Wallace-Davey Industries Ltd.; Secy. and Dir., C.F. Anderson Concrete Products Ltd.; Anjamin Mines Ltd.; Cayuga Materials & Construction Co. Ltd.; C.F.A. Operations Inc.; K & R Readi-Mix (1971) Ltd.; R. H. Nichols Co. Ltd.; Dir., Dominion-Consolidated Holdings Ltd.; Dominion-Consolidated Truck Lines Ltd.; Transport McCallum (Qué.) Inc.; Truck-Air Ltd.; read law with Reid, Allen, Hunter and Campbell, Toronto, Ont.; called to the Bar of Ont. 1949; cr. Q.C. 1965; mem., York Co. Law Assn.; Candn. Bar Assn.; Liberal; R. Catholic; Club: Ontario; Office: 65 Queen St. W., Toronto, Ont. M5H 2M5

REGAN, Hon. Gerald A., P.C., Q.C., M.P.; b. Windsor; N.S., 13 Feb. 1928; s. Walter Edward and Rose M. (Greene) R.; e. Windsor (N.S.) Acad.; St. Mary's Univ.; Dalhousie Univ.; Dalhousie Law Sch.; m. A. Carole, d. late John H. Harrison, 17 Nov. 1956; children: Gerald, Geoffrey, Miriam, Nancy, David, Laura; MINISTER OF LABOUR AND SPORTS. since 1980; called to the Bar of N.S. 1954; cr. Q.C. 1970; Lib. cand. in prov. g.e. 1956 and 1960 and in fed. g.e. 1962; el. to H. of C. in g.e. 1963; 1st Candn. to be named Chrmn. of Extve. Comte. of Commonwealth Parlty. Assn., served 1973-76; el. Leader, Lib. Party in N.S., 1965; el. M.L.A. in prov. g.e. 1967 for Halifax Needham; re-el. g.e. 1970; Premier of N.S. 1970-78; el. to H. of C. in g.e. 1980 in Halifax; mem., N.S. Barristers Soc.; Liberal; R. Catholic; recreation: tennis; skiing; Club: Halifax; Office: House of Commons, Ottawa, Ont.

REGAN, (Helen) Gail, Ph.D., M.B.A.; b. Toronto, Ont. 5 July 1944; d. Paul James and Helen Doris (Gardiner) Phelan; e. Univ. of Toronto B.A. 1965, Ph.D. 1973, M.B.A. 1978; m. 15 June 1963; children: Sean, Tim, Ellen, Honor; Tutor in Hist., Univ. of Toronto; Bd. mem., Cara operations; Cara Holdings; Langar; T.J.R. Holdings; Women's Coll. Hosp.; Toronto French Sch.; author various articles; recreations: sailing, skiing, tennis; Clubs: Badminton & Racquet; R.C.Y.C.; Ojibway; Osler; Home: 1 May Sq., Toronto, Ont. M4W 1S8; Office: 371 Bloor St. W., Toronto, Ont.

REGEHR, Rev. John, B.Ed., M.A., Th.D. (Mennonite); educator; minister; b. Mexico 29 Dec. 1925; s. Henry and Katherine (Siemens) R.; came to Canada 1926; e. Mennonite Coll. Inst., Gretna, Man. 1947; Univ. of Manitoba, B.A., B.Ed. 1950; Winona Lake Sch. of Theol. (summers) M.A.; Mennonite Brethren Bible Coll. 1950 (part-time 1960-65) B.D.; N. Am. Baptist Semy. (part-time) 1957-59; S. Baptist Theol. Semy., Th.D. 1970; m. Mary, d. late Jacob H. Unger, 27 Aug. 1949; children: Reynold John,

Sharon Lenore, James Mark, Jenny Marie; Instr., Mennonite Brethren Bible Coll., Winnipeg, Man. since 1968 and Acting Pres. there 1972-1974; o. 1957; began teaching in Jr. and Sr. High Sch., West Kildonan, Winnipeg 1950; Princ., H.C. Avery Elem. Sch., Winnipeg 1956; Pastor, Silver Lake Mennonite Brethren Ch., Marion, S. Dak. 1957; Instr., Mennonite Brethren Coll. Inst. 1959-66; Asst Pastor, Elmwood Mennonite Brethren Ch. 1962-66; Pastor, Georgetown (In.) E.U.B. Ch. 1966-68; mem. Bd. Interfaith Pastoral Ins. 1972-74; articles and sermons published in numerous theological magazines and journs.; Home: 275 Bredin Drive, Winnipeg, Man. R2K 1N7 Office: 77 Henderson, Winnipeg, Man. R2L 1L1

REGENSTREIF, S. Peter, Ph.D.; university professor; political consultant; b. Montreal, Que., 9 Sept. 1936; s. Albert Benjamin and Miriam Lillian (Issenman) R.; e. Strathcona Acad., Montreal, 1949-53; McGill Univ., B.A. (Pol. Science & Econ., 1st Class Hons.) 1957; Cornell Univ., Ph.D. (Govt.) 1963; m. Donna Lorraine, d. Charles Irony, Montreal, Que., 9 June 1959; children: Anne Erica, Mitchell Chester, Jeffrey Gerson, Gail Aviva; PROF. OF POL. SCIENCE AND CANDN. STUDIES, UNIV. OF ROCHESTER, since 1970; Research Assoc. there, 1961-63; Asst. Prof. 1964-66, Assoc. Prof. 1966-70; Pol. Columnist, Toronto Star since 1963 (Montreal Star 1962 and 1963); Editorial Consultant, Toronto Star, since 1968; political Consultant, Alfred Bunting & Co. Ltd., since 1973; Visiting Prof., Univ. of Montreal, 1965, Glendon Coll., 1968-69; with McGill COTC 1954-57; rank Lt. Suppl. Reserve; Consultant Royal Comn. on Bilingualism and Biculturalism; a Pol. broadcaster for C.B.C. and C.T.V.; author of "The Diefenbaker Interlude: Parties and Voting in Canada" 1965; numerous articles in various learned journs.; mem., Candn. Pol. Science Assn.; Am. Pol. Science Assn.; Assn. of Candn. Studies in the U.S.; Phi Beta Kappa; Hebrew; recreation: music (pianist); Home: 260 Ashley Dr., Rochester, N.Y. 14620

REICHERT, Donald Karl, .B.F.A., R.C.A.; artist; educator; b. Libau, Man. 11 Jan. 1932; s. George and Theresa (Riehl) R.; e. Libau, Man. 1947; St. John's Coll. Sch. and St. Paul's Coll. Winnipeg 1951; Univ. of Man. B.F.A. 1956; Instituto Allende Mexico 1957-58; m. Mary d. Ernest Thorpe 17 June 1957; children: Karl, Lisa, Jacob, Ernest; PROF. OF ART. UNIV. OF MAN. SCH. OF ART, Acting Dir. of Sch. 1973-74; solo exhns. incl. Winnipeg Art Gallery 1960, 1969, 1975; Yellow Door Gallery Winnipeg 1965; rep. in numerous group shows incl. Mexico City 1958; St. Ives Cornwall 1963; Travelling Exhns. W. Painting '67, Nat. Gallery 1968; Candn. Canvas Time/Life 1975-76; 150 Yrs. of Art in Man. 1970; W. Candn. Painting Bronfman Centre Montreal 1974; Montreal Olympics '76; Designer/Draughtsman, Disply Fixtures Ltd. Winnipeg 1959-61; Artist-in-Residence Univ. of N.B. 1961-62; joined Univ. of Man. Sch. of Art 1964; Teacher, Banff Sch. of Fine Arts summer 1974, Visiting Artist 1979; Visiting Artist Mt. Allison Univ. 1975; Instr. in Painting Emily Carr Coll. of Art 1979; Continuing mem. Man. Dept. Pub. Works Art Adv. Comte. 1978; rep. in Can. Council Art Bank and many pub. and private colls.; rec'd Can. Council Art Awards Jr. 1962-63, Sr. 1968-69, 1975-76; recreations: painting, drawing, teaching, flying (private pilot), canoeing, cross-country skiing, electronic music making, photography, reading; Home: 228 Glenwood Cres., Winnipeg, Man, R2L 1J9; Office:Winnipeg, Man.

REID, Hon. Daniel Spencer, M.D.; b. Middle Musquodoboit, N.S. 25 July 1944; s. Ralph Kenneth and Jenny (Harrison) R.; e. Musquodoboit Rural High Sch. 1962; Dalhousie Univ. M.D. 1970; m. Anne Marie d. William A. MacDonald, Pictou, N.S. 28 July 1973; children: Kenneth Alexander, Peter Anthony; Min. of Fisheries, N.S. 1976-80; el. to N.S. Leg. 1974; estbd. med. practice Pictou, N.S. 1970, opened Med. Center there as an original Partner 1970; mem. Med. Staff and Bd. Sutherland-Harris Mem. Hosp.; mem. Candn. Med. Assn.; N.S. Med. Soc.;

Candn. Acad. Sports Med.; Commonwealth Parlty. Assn.; Phi Rho; Liberal; United Church; recreations: gardening, golf, hockey, fishing; Clubs: Pictou Golf; Pictou Men's; Rotary; Home: 42 Haliburton Rd., Pictou, N.S. B0K 1H0; Office: 1690 Hollis St., Halifax, N.S. B3J 3T4.

REID, Dennis Richard, M.A.; curator; art historian; b. Hamilton, Ont., 3 Jan. 1943; s. Walter Alexander and Letitia Ethel (Johnson) R.; e. Univ. of Toronto, B.A. 1966, M.A. 1967; m. Alison Sheila, d. R. G. D. Anderson, Toronto, Ont., 1966; two d., Jessica Alison, Naomi Gloria; CURATOR OF CANADIAN HISTORICAL ART, ART GALLERY OF ONTARIO Since 1979; joined National Gallery of Can. as Asst. Curator 1967; Curator of Past-Confed. Art 1970; has organized numerous exhns. with accompanying catalogues at National Gallery; author, "The MacCallum-Jackman Bequest", 1969; "The Group of Seven", 1970; "A Bibliography of the Group of Seven", 1971; "Bertram Brooker", 1973; "A Concise History of Canadian Painting", 1973; "The Jack Pine", 1975; "Edwin Holgate", 1976; " 'Our Own Country Canada' . . .", 1979; also various articles for art journs.; Home: 79 Borden St., Toronto, Ont. M5S 2M8 Toronto, Ont.

REID, Donald James; insurance executive; b. Montreal, Que. 9 Dec. 1929; s. John and Myrtle Leona (Nosworthy) R.; e. Woodland Sch. Verdun, Que.; Verdun (Que.) High Sch.; McGill Univ. Mang. Devel. Course 1952; Seneca Coll. Mang. Devel. Course 1970; m. Noreen Janet d. late William C. Hickey, Montreal, Que. 16 Sept. 1950; children: David Michael, John Scott, Robin Dorothy; PRES. UNITED CANADA INSURANCE CO.; joined Guarantee Co. of North America serving as Bond Underwriter, Auto Underwriter and Casualty Mgr. 1949-60; Casualty Supt. Commercial Union Insurance Co. Montreal 1960, Br. Supt. Montreal 1962, Asst. Mgr. Maritimes Saint John 1965 and Toronto 1969-71; Extve. Vice Pres. and Gen. Mgr. 1972; Past Vice Pres. Montreal Jr. Bd. Trade; mem. Ins. Inst. Can.; Bd. Trade Metrop. Toronto and Montreal; recreations: golf, skiing, fishing; Club: Lions (Charter mem.); Past Vice Pres. Saint John and La Prairie); Home: 5358 Riverside Dr., Burlington, Ont. L7L 3X8; Office: 155 University Ave., Toronto, Ont. M5H 3B7

REID, E. A. Stewart, M.D., C.M., F.R.C.P., F.A.C.P.; cardiologist; b. Montreal, Que., 29 June 1917; s. Rev. Dr. William D. and Daisy F. (Stanford) R.; e. Westmount (Que.) High Sch., 1934; McGill Univ., B.A. 1938; M.D.C.M. 1942; Dipl. Internal Med. 1952; m. Barbara M., d. late Hugh Pibus, Magog, Que., 1952; children: Jane B., E. A. Stewart, Dugald A. S.; CARDIOLOGIST, COWANSVILLE HOSPITAL; Montreal Gen. Hospital; Assoc. Prof. Med., McGill Univ.; Consultant in Cardiology, Ormstown Hosp.; Huntingdon Co. Hosp.; Medical Resident, Montreal Gen. Hosp., 1942-43, 1946-47, 1949-50; Mass. Gen. Hosp., Cardiology, 1947-48; Hammersmith Hosp., London, Eng., 1948-49; served with R.C.A.M.C. 1942-46 in U.K. (1943), Italy (1943-44), N.W. Europe (1945); awarded Snyder (Econ.) 1937-38, Caverhill (Cardiology) 1947-49 and Life Assn., 1949-52, fellowships; has written sundry med. articles for prof. journs.; Fellow, Am. Coll. Cardiology (Gov. Quebec Br. 1967); Am. Coll. Chest Phys.; Past Pres., Montreal Soc. Cardiol.; Fellow, Am. Heart Assn.; member Candn. Cardiovascular Assn.; Presbyterian; recreations: farming, skiing; Home: Reidscroft RR #1, College Road, Dunham, P.Q. J0E 1M0 Office: 401 South St., Cownsville, P.Q. J2K 2X6

REID, Escott Meredith, C.C. (1971), M.A., b. Campbellford, Ont., 21 Jan. 1905; s. Rev. Alfred John and Morna (Meredith) R.; e. Trinity Coll., Toronto, B.A. (1st Class Hons. in Pol. Science) 1927; Rhodes Schol., Ont., 1927; Jr. George Webb Medley Schol. in econ. (Oxford) 1928; Gladstone Mem. Exhn. Schol. (Christ Ch.) 1929; Rockefeller Fellow, Soc. Sciences, 1930-32; Oxford Univ. (Christ Ch.) B.A. (1st Class Hons. in Modern Greats) 1929, M.A. 1935; (Hon.) Doctor of Laws, Mount Alison, York, Carle-

ton Univs.; m. Ruth Murray, d. William Herriot, Winnipeg, Man., 30 Aug. 1930; children: Patrick Murray, Morna Meredith, Timothy Escott Herriot; Skelton-Clark Fellow, Queen's Univ., 1972-73; Clk., Audit Department, Government of Ont., Toronto 1921-23; National Secy., Candn. Inst. Internat. Affairs 1932-38; Acting Prof., Govt. and Pol. Science, Dalhousie Univ. 1937-38; 2nd Secy., Candn. Leg. at Wash., D.C., 1939-41; Dept. of External Affairs 1941-44; 1st Secy., Wash., D.C. 1944-45; Counsellor, London 1945-46; Counsellor, Ottawa, 1946-47; ; Asst. Under-Secy. of State for External Affairs 1947-48; Acting Under-Secy., Depy. Under-Secy. 1948-52; High Comnr. for Canada to India, 1952-57; Ambassador to Germany, 1958-62; Dir. of Operations for S. Asia and Middle East, Internat. Bank for Reconstruction & Devel., 1962-65; First Principal, Glendon Coll., York Univ. 1965-69; Consultant to Pres., Candn. Internat. Devel. Agency 1970-72; attended the following unofficial international conferences 1933-38; Institute of Pacific Relations, Banff, 1933, and Yosemite 1936; British Commonwealth Relations, Toronto 1933; Internat. Studies, London, 1935; attended foll. official internat. confs. as Adviser or Alternate Rep. on Candn. del.: Internat. Civil Aviation, Chicago 1944; San Francisco 1945; Extve. Comte. of the Prep. Comn. of the U.N. and Prep. Comn., London 1945; 1st session of the Gen. Assembly, U.N., London and N.Y. 1946; 2nd session, N.Y. 1947; Commonwealth Foreign Ministers, Colombo, 1950; Chrmn., Gen. Assembly's Comte. on Procedures and Organ. 1947; 12th Session of the Gen. Assembly, 1957; Publications: "Strengthening the World Bank" 1973; "Time of Fear and Hope: The Making of the North Atlantic Treaty 1947-49", 1977; "Envoy to Nehru", 1981; Anglican; Home: R.R. 2, Ste. Cécile de Masham, Qué. J0X 2W0

REID, John M., M.P., M.A.; b. Fort Frances, Ont. 8 Feb. 1937; s. John M. and Marie Ena (Harrington) R.; e. Univ. of Man. B.A. 1959, M.A. (Hist.) 1961; Univ. of Toronto (Hist.) 1961-65; m. Marie Ellen, d. Edward O. Balcaen, 19 Feb. 1966; children: Katherine, John, Arianne, George; Min. Federal-Provincial Relations, 1978-79; elected Chrmn. H. of C. Comte on Procedure and Organization, 1978; el. to H. of C. g.e. 1965; re-el. since; Chrmn. H. of C. Standing Comte. on Broadcasting, Film and Assistance to the Arts 1969-72; Parlty. Secy. to Pres. of Privy Council 1972-75; Liberal; R. Catholic; Home: (P.O. Box 208) Kenora, Ont. P9N 3X3; Office: House of Commons, Ottawa, Ont. K1A 0A6

REID, Kate, O.C. (1974), Ph.D.; actress; b. England 1930; d. late Col. Walter C. and Helen Isabel (Moore) R.; e. Havergal College, Toronto; Royal Conserv. Music; Ph.D.; York 1970; m. 1stly Michael Sadlier; 2ndly Austin Willis; children: Reid, Robin; began acting career with Hart House Theatre; starred in "The Rainmaker" at Crest and Vineland Theatres & signed to star in W. End Lond. prod., 1956; played "The Three Sisters"; Crest Theatre, 1956 & "The Stepmother", W. End Lond., 1958; toured with Am. Co. of The Candn. Players in "The Cherry Orchard" and "The Taming of the Shrew", 1959; began assn. with Stratford Shakespearean Festival as Cecilia in "As You Like It" and Emilia in "Othello" 1959; played the nurse in "Romeo and Juliet" and Helena in "Midsummer Nights Dream", 1960; Queen Katherine in "Henry VIII" and Jaquenetta in "Loves Labour Lost", 1961; Lady Macbeth in "Macbeth", 1962; Adriana, "Comedy of Errors", Cassandra, "Troilus and Cressida" and played in "Taming of the Shrew" 1962; Cyrano De Bergerac", 1963; Portia, "Julius Caesar" and Mme. Ranevkaya, "Cherry Orchard", 1965; starred in "Who's Afraid of Virginia Woolf" as Martha in N.Y. matinee, 1962; played opposite Sir Alex Guinness as Caitlin in "Dylan", 1964; signed to do Hollywood movie "This Property is Condemned" with Natalie Wood, 1965; co-starred with Margaret Leighton and Zoe Caldwell in "Slapstick Tragedy" (Tony Award nomination 1967) on Broadway, 1965; played in "The Ottawa Man", Charlottetown Summer Festival, 1966; starred in "The Subject Was Roses", Ottawa, and Toronto, 1966; "The Price", New York and London 1970; "The Andromeda Strain" (film); "The Rainbow Boys" (film, with Donald Pleasance) 1972; co-starred (with Katherine Hepburn) in "A Delicate Balance" (Golden Globe nomination) 1973; Big Mama in "Cat on a Hot Tin Roof" 1974-75; Broadway: "Freedom of the City" 1974-75; has engaged in TV work in England and North America incl. C.B.C. serial "The White Oaks of Jalna"; rec'd Maurice Rosenfeld Award for most promising newcomer in radio, 1954; shared Bronze Medal for outstanding work 1955; voted best actress in Can. by newspaper and TV critics in Liberty mag. poll, 1956; nominated for Emmy Award for role as Queen Victoria in Hall of Fame's "Disraeli", 1963; nominated for Tony Award for role in "Dylan", 1965; rec'd Hon. D.Litt. York Univ. 1970; Address; c/o Reid Willis, 14 Binscarth Rd., Toronto, Ont. M4W 1Y1

REID, Morgan, B.A.; company executive; b. Trimley, Suffolk, England, 22 May 1916; s. Col. Richard and Alice Louise (Mulholland) R.; e. Arnold House, London, Eng.; Blue Ridge Acad., Hendersonville, N.C.; Trinity Coll., Univ. of Toronto, B.A. (Pol. Science and Econ.); m. Elsie Marguerite d. Frederick Leighton Abrey, Toronto, Ont., 30 May 1942; three s., Richard Morgan, Frederick Leighton, Robert Douglas; Dir., St. Laurent Shopping Centre Ltd.; Project 200 Properties Ltd.; Kelsey-Hayes Canada Ltd.; Regional Shopping Centres Ltd.; Surrey Place Ltd.; Kelfor Holdings Ltd.; Kerrybrooke Devel. Ltd.; Secy., Management Advisory Comte., The Robert Simpson Co. Ltd., 1945-52; Asst. Vice-Pres., Retail and Public Relations Offr., Simpsons-Sears Ltd., 1953-56; Gen. Mgr., Planning & Corporate Devel., 1957-64; Vice Pres., Planning & Development, Simpson-Sears Ltd. 1964-81; Dir. & Chrmn., Audit Comte., Fruehauf Inc.; Past Director, Canadian Chamber of Commerce mem. (Past member, Ottawa Liaison Comte.): Asst. Retail Trade Adm., W.P.T.B., 1942-45; Vice-Chrmn., Civilian Wool Requirements Comte., W.P.T.B., 1943-45; Vice Pres. (1972-74), Candn. Council, Internat. Chamber of Commerce; Nat. Bd. of Dirs., Canada-U.S. Comte. (Chrmn. 1962-63 (l) Chrmn. Extve. Council 1958-59; Chrmn. Ont. Regional Comte. 1957-58; Chrmn. Pub. Finance & Taxation Comte. 1954-55; mem., Conf. of Business Econs., U.S.A.; Candn. Business & Industry Adv. Comte. for O.E.C.D.; Adv. Invest. Comte. Gen. Synod. Ang. Ch. of Can., 1960-66; Extve. Comte., Corp. of Trinity Coll.; former mem., Adv. Council, Queen's Sch. of Business; Pres., Ticker Club of Toronto, 1952-53; mem., Candn. Inst. Internat. Affairs (Chrmn. Toronto Br. 1951-52; mem. of Extve. Comte. and Nat. Council); Trustee, Quetico Foundation; Anglican; recreations: golf, fishing, chess; Clubs: Toronto: Badminton & Racquet; University: Empire; Canadian (Pres. 1961-62); Home: 174 Forest Hill Road, Toronto, Ont. M5P 2N4;

REID, Richard Gavin, B.Sc.; petroleum executive; b. Edmonton, Alta., 11 Dec. 1922; s. Richard Gavin and Marion (Stuart) R.; e. Univ. of Alta., B.Sc. (Chem. Engn.) 1949; m. Shirley, d. Walter MacDonald, Victoria, B.C., 4 Sept. 1946; children: James, Shirley, Donald, Barbara, Cathy; PRESIDENT, ESSO EUROPE INC., London, Eng., since 1978; joined Imperial Oil Ltd., Edmonton, 1949; Supply & Transport. Dept., Esso International Inc., N.Y., 1967; Gen. Mgr., Logistics Dept., Imperial Oil Ltd., 1969; Extve. Vice Pres. and Dir. 1971; Pres. 1974; Extve. Vice Pres., Esso Europe 1975-78; served with RCAF 1943-45; mem., Assn. Prof. Engrs. Ont.; Presbyterian: recreations: swimming, golf, gardening, running; Office: 50 Stratton St., London W1X 6AU, England.

REID, Hon. Robert Franklin judge; b. Stratford, Ont., 21 June 1923; s. Robert Alexander and Edith (Robens) R.; e. Univ. of W. Ont. B.A. 1945; Osgoode Hall Law Sch. 1949; m. Elisabeth Denise Hall, d. Maj. A. Denison Pearce, 3 Sept. 1949; children: John Denison, Deborah Robens, Elisabeth Jane Rivers; JUSTICE, SUPREME COURT OF ONTARIO; read law with Hon. Leopold Macaulay, Q.C. and W.B. Common, Q.C.; called to Bar of Ont. 1949; cr. Q.C. 1961; practised law in Toronto; Lectr. in Adm. Law Osgoode Hall Law Sch. 1951-60; mem. Jt. Comte. on Legal Aid (report basis for present Ont. Legal Aid Plan); lectr. and mem. various confs. on adm. law and law relating to addictions Can. Mexico and USA; served as Pilot RCAF; Past Pres. Festival Singers; Save the Children Fund (Toronto Br.); Depy. Secy. Law Soc. Upper Can. 1955-58; former Trustee Co. York Law Assn.; former Chrmn. Publ. Comte. Candn. Bar Assn.; Past Pres. Advocate's Soc.; Trustee Sir William Campbell Foundation; author "Administrative Law and Practice" 1971 and numerous papers on legal topics; Delta Upsilon; Anglican; Chambers: Osgoode Hall, Toronto, Ont. M5H 2N5

REID, Stanley J., B.A.; company president; b. Listowel, Ont., 26 Oct. 1933; s. Warren Edward and Mabel (Hawthorne) R.; e. Pub. and High Schs., Listowel, Ont.; Pre-Teachers' Coll. 1952-53; McMaster Univ., B.A., 1967; m. Marion Joy, d. Wm. Mason, 7 July 1957; DIRECTOR ELEMENTARY DIVISION, SCIENCE RESEARCH ASSOCIATES INC., since 1979; taught elem. sch. for two years; with Jack Hood School Supply Co., Stratford, Ont. 1954-57, left as W. Can. Sales Mgr.; joined Thomas Nelson & Sons (Canada) Ltd., publishers, 1957 as Educ. Rep., Text Book Div. — last 2 yrs served as Science Research Associates Sales Supv., Candn. Sales; apptd. Vice-Pres., Sales. Science Research Associates (Canada) Ltd., 1965, Vice-Pres., Marketing, 1967; Pres. and C.E.D. 1969-79 (ret.); Bd. of Gov., Science Research Assoc. (Can.) Ltd.; Pres., Candn. Educ. Publishers' Group; Ont. Educ. Assn.; mem., Candn. Book Publ. Council (Past Comte. Chrmn.); Internat. Reading Assn.; Candn. Assn. of Publishers Educ. Reps. (Past Pres.); Ont. Assn. for Curriculum Devel.; Un. Ch.; 1126 Warrington Rd., Deerfield Ill. 60015; Office: 155 M. Wacker Dr., Chicago, Ill. 60606

REID, William J., B.Com.; industrial executive; b. Montreal, Que., 8 June 1925; s. George Orion and Janet Reid (Bell) R.; e. Strathcona Acad., Montreal, 1939-43; McGill Univ., B.Com. 1947; Centre d'Etudes Industrielles Geneva Cert. in Internat. Business Adm.; m. Joan Patricia, d. Donald Lloyd Witter, Montreal, Que., 14 June 1952; children: Andrea Janet, Heather Anne, Suzanne Patricia; VICE PRESIDENT, FINANCE, AIR CANADA; Vice-Pres., Finance, Air Canada; summer student, Aluminium Ltd. Arvida and Shawinigan Falls 1944-46; with Aluminum Securities Ltd. 1947-48 and 1945-55 becoming Vice President 1961-65; Assistant Treasurer, Southeast Asia Bauxites Ltd., 1955 (Director and Treasurer 1963-64); Chief Financial Officer in Brazil, 1955-61 (Secretary-Treasurer, Alumino do Brazil S.A., Sao Paulo; Treas., Alumino Minas Gerais, S.A., Minas Gerais); Vice Pres. Finance, Treas. and Dir., Aluminum Co. of Canada Ltd. 1966-73; Vice Pres. Finance and Dir., Alcan Internat. Ltd. 1973-77; member, Canadian Institute International Affairs; Sigma Chi; Liberal; Protestant; recreations: golf, photography, skiing; Clubs: Canadian; St. James; Royal Montreal Golf; Home: 45 Franklin Ave., Town of Mount Royal, Que. H3P 1B8; Office: Air Canada, Place Ville Marie, Montreal, Que. H3B 3P7

REID, Rev. William Stanford, M.A., Th.M., Ph.D., F.R.S.A., F.R.Hist.S. (Presb.); professor b. Montreal, Que., 13 Sept. 1913; s. late Rev. William Dunn and Daisy Fanny (Stanford) R.; e. McGill Univ., B.A. 1934 (Eng. and Hist.) and M.A. 1935 (Hist.); Westminster Theol. Semy., Phila., Pa. (1935-38), Th.B., Th.M.; Univ. of Penna. (Leib Harrison Grad. Fellow), Ph.D. (Hist.) 1941; D.D., Presbyterian Theological Coll., Montreal 1979; m. Priscilla, d. late Henry Stewart Lee, 24 Aug. 1940; PROF. EMERITUS UNIV. OF GUELPH; Trustee, Westminster Theol. Semy. since 1944; mem., Bd. of Mang. of Presby. Theol. Coll. of Montreal, 1943-45; Min., Fairmount Taylor Presb. Ch., Montreal 1941-45; Founder and Min. of the Presb. Church of the Town of Mount Royal, Que. 1945-51;

mem., Dept. of History, McGill Univ. 1941-65, Warden of Douglas Hall, there 1952-65; Univ. Marshal 1950-65, Dir. of Men's Residences 1962-65; rec'd. grants from Candn. Social Science Research Council (1944), and Am. Philos. Soc., Phila. (1947 and 1949); Candn. grant for research in Candn. Hist. and Am. grant for study in Scot. and Europe on Scot. hist.; Special Lectr., Oxford Univ., 1959, Univ. of the West Indies, 1962-64, Westminster Theological Seminary, Philadelphia, 1972, 75, 78, Fuller Theological Seminary, Auburn Univ. 1978; Trinity Evangelical School, Deerfield Ill. 1979; Ont. Theological Seminary 1979, Knox College, Toronto 1979; Union Theological Seminary, Tokyo, Japan; Reformed Theological Seminary, Kobe, Japan; Hop Tong Theological Seminar, Seoul, Korea; Presbyterian Church Conferences, Melbourne, Sydney & Brisbane, Australia; Knox College, Dunedin, N.Z., 1980; founder and first chrmn., Dept. of Hist., Univ. of Guelph, 1965-70; author of "The Church of Scotland in Lower Canada", 1936; "Economic History of Great Britain", 1954; "The Scottish Reformation", 1960; "Skipper from Leith: The Life of Robert Barton of Over Barnton", 1962; "The Protestant Reformation: Revival or Revolution'", 1968; "Trumpeter of God: A Biography of John Knox" 1974; "A Century and a Half of Witness 1828-1978: The Story of St. Andrews Presbyterian Church, Guelph, Ontario", 1980; ed. and contributor, "Called to Witness; Profiles of Canadian Presbyterians"; various articles on Scot. & Candn. hist. and on theol. in learned journs.; mem., Candn. Hist. Assn.; Ch. Hist. Soc. of Am.; Medieval Acad. of Am.; Scot. Hist. Soc.; Hist. Soc. of Montreal (Hon. Pres.); Am. Soc. of Ch. Hist. (Council); Pres., Conf. on Scottish Studies 1970-72; rec'd. Grant from Inst. for Advanc. Christian Studies 1970; Canada Council 1969, 1967, 1970, 1976, for research in Scot. hist. and 1973, for sabbatical; Gov't. of France 1966, 1968; Ed. and contrib., "The Scottish Tradition in Canada", 1976; Hon. L.H.D., Wheaton Coll., Ill. 1975; Independent Liberal; recreations: painting, camping, travel, photography, Club: Faculty (Univ. Guelph); Address: 320 Scottsdale Rd., Guelph Ont. N1G 2K8.

REIFEL, George H., B.S.A.; distiller; b. Vancouver, B.C., 22 July 1922; s. George Conrad and Alma Lucy (Barnes) R.; e. Univ. of British Columbia, B.S.A. 1944; m. Norma Eileen, d. Norman R. Williams, Calgary, Alta., 14 Oct. 1949; children: George Conrad, Peter Randy, Barney William, Tracy Eileen; CHRMN. OF BD. OF DIRS.; ALBERTA DISTILLERS LTD., since 1968; joined present Co. in 1946 and made Gen. Mgr. same year; el. a Dir. 1946 and Vice-Pres. and Gen. Mgr.; Pres., 1955-68; Phi Gamma Delta; Sigma Tau Upsilon; Anglican; Clubs: University (Vancouver); Desert Island Golf (Ca.); Ranchmens (Calgary); Calgary Golf and Country; Office: 2585 Point Grey Rd., Vancouver, B.C.

REIMER, Cornelius; labour executive; b. Kitchkas, Ukraine, 3 July 1921; s. Cornelius J. and Marie (Dyck) R.; e. Glidden, Sask. Public.; Univ. of Sask. (1939-42); m. Merry Elaine, d. Mark Spurko, 9 Mar. 1945; two children: Janice Rhea, Gregory Neil; VICE-PRESIDENT, CANADIAN LABOUR CONGRESS, since Apl. 1956; Exec. Comte., I.C.E.F.; Nat'l Dir., Energy and Chem. Workers Union; Candn. Dir., Oil, Chemical & Atomic Workers Internat. Union, since 1953 (youngest to hold this post); Rep. of Candn. Labour Cong. on I.C.F.T. Atomic Energy Comte.; employed by Consumers Co-Operative Refineries, Regina, Sask., 1943-51 in refinery; became Internat. Rep. of Oil Workers Internat. Union, July 1951; el. to Extve. Comte. of Candn. Cong. of Labour, Oct. 1954; rep. Can. as a Worker's Del. to last ILO Chem. Meeting; el. Prov. Leader of N.D.P. 1963 and re-el. 1964, 1965; served on Alta. Health and Safety Comm. to recommend legislation; recreations: golf, bowling, chess, fishing; Home: 8203-101 Ave., Edmonton, Alta. T6A 0K7; Office: 105-10319, 106 Ave., Edmonton, Alta. T5H 0P3

REIMER, Donald S.; transportation executive; b. Steinbach, Manitoba, 29 Jan. 1933; s. Frank F. and Margaret (Penner) R.; e. Pub. Sch. and Coll., Steinbach, Man.; m. Anne d. John Olfert, Sr., Winnipeg, Man., 25 June 1953; three sons: Douglas Miles Donald, James Stuart Gordon, Kelly Richard Craig; PRESIDENT AND GEN. MGR., REIMER EXPRESS LINES (Estbd. 1950); Dir., Reimer Express Lines (Western) Ltd.; Reimer Express (Pacific) Ltd.; Mid-Continental Leasing Corp. Ltd.; Universal Holdings Ltd.; Past Pres. and Dir. Manitoba Trucking Assn.; Dir., Pres., Cdn. Trucking Assn.; Inter-provincial Carriers Sec., Auto. Transport Assn. Ont.; mem., Winnipeg C.B.M. Canada; Bd. Dirs., Youth for Christ Can.; Transport Indemnity Co. of L.A.; West. Hwy. Inst. of San Francisco; Candn. Transport Tariff Bur.; Hon. Counsellor, Winnipeg Chamber Comm.; mem., Winnipeg Extves. Assn.; Protestant; recreations: flying, golfing, boating; Clubs: Manitoba; Winnipeg Flying; Rotary; Home: 300 Dunkirk Dr., Winnipeg R2M 3W9, Man.; Office: 1400 Inkster Blvd., Winnipeg, Man. R2X 1R1

REISMAN, Sol Simon, O.C. (1978) M.A.; financial executive; b. Montreal, Que., 19 June 1919; s. Kolman and Manya R.; e. McGill University, B.A. (Hons. Econ. and Pol. Science) 1941, M.A. (summa cum laude) 1942; London Sch. of Econs. (1945); m. Constance Augusta, d. W. N. Carin, Montreal, Que., 17 Oct. 1942; children: John Joseph, Anna Lisa, Harriet Frances; Chrmn., Reisman & Grandy Ltd.; Dir., George Weston Ltd.; B.C. Packers Ltd.; Bombardier Inc.; A.C. Blands Ltd.; Kelly Douglas Ltd.; E.B. Eddy Ltd.; joined Civil Service of Can. Dept. Labour 1946, trans. Dept. Finance same yr.; Dir. Internat. Econ. Relations Div., Dept. Finance 1956-61; Assistant Deputy Minister, Dept. Finance 1961-65; Depy. Min. Industry 1964-68; Secy. of Treas. Bd. 1968-70; Depy. Min. Finance 1970-74; Royal Commissioner to investigate Candn. Auto Ind.; Canadian Delegation to Geneva Trade and Tariff Conf., 1947; World Conf. on Trade and Employment, Havana, 1947-48; 1st Session, Gen. Agreement on Tariffs & Trade; all sessions of GATT, 1948-54; Econ. & Social Council, U.N., Geneva (1952) and N.Y. (1953); Commonwealth Finance Ministers Conf., London, 1950 and Mont Tremblant 1957; Commonwealth Trade & Econ. Conf., Montreal 1958; participated in negotiation of numerous trade agreements during this period; served as Asst. Director of Research on Royal Comn. on Canada's Econ. Prospects, 1955-57 (author of book prepared for the Comn. "Canada-United States Economic Relations", 1957, and two books entitled "Canada's Export Trade" and "Canadian Commercial Policy"); served in 2nd World War with R.C.A. as Regt. Offr. 1942-46; Overseas Nov. 1942-Jan. 1946 with 11th, 15th and 17th Field Arty. (Troop Commander); Outstanding Public Service Award Can. 1974; Bd. Govs. Carleton Univ.; Dir. & mem. Extve. Comte. C.D. Howe Research Foundation; member, Ottawa Chapter, Economical and Political Science Association (Director); Am. Econ. Assn.; Candn. Econ. Pol. Science Assn.; Hebrew; recreations: golf, skiing, fishing, reading; Clubs: Cercle Universitaire; Five Lakes Fishing; Rideau; Rideau View Golf & Country; Home: 146 Roger Road, Ottawa, Ont. K1H 5C8; Office: 350 Sparks St., Suite 1004, Ottawa, Ont. K1R 7S8

RELYEA, Thomas Arnold, B.Com.; investment executive; b. Prescott, Ont., 16 May 1907; s. Thomas George and Jeannette (Brownell) R.; e. Univ. of Toronto, B.Com. 1929; m. Margaret Eva, d. late Rev. R. W. Collins, 28 Oct. 1939; children: Brian, Diane; TRUSTEE, SECRETARY-TREASURER JACKMAN FOUNDATION; Dir., Canadian & Foreign Securities Co. Ltd.; Canadian Northern Prairie Lands Co. Ltd.; Vice-Pres., Debenture & Securities Corpn.; E-L Investment Management Ltd.; Dir., Dondale Investments Ltd.; P. Conservative; United Church; recreations: riding, skiing; Clubs: National; Granite; Board of Trade; Home: 14 Cranleigh Court, Islington, Ont. M9A 3Y4; Office: 165 University Ave., Toronto, Ont. M5H 3B8

REMPEL, Averno Milton, B.A., M.Ed., Ph.D.; college president; b. Saskatoon, Sask., 15 Feb. 1919; s. Gerhard Solomon and Lena (Schultz) R.; e. Univ. of Sask., B.A. (cum laude) 1940, B.Ed. 1949; Univ. of Omaha, M.Ed. 1951; Univ. of Iowa, Ph.D. 1954; m. Wendlyn Otti, d. late John Henry Wiebe Reimer, Steinbach, Man., 6 July 1944; children: Donna Lynn, Deborah Ann, Gerard Taves; ASST. VICE CHANCELLOR, ORE. STATE SYSTEM HIGHER EDUC. since 1974; School Principal and High School Teacher in Lipton, Saskatchewan and Steinbach, Man., 1941-49; Instr., Univ. of Omaha, 1950-51; Research Asst., Univ. of Iowa, 1951-54; Dean of Coll., Minot (N.D.) State Coll., 1954-57; Adm. Asst., Assoc. Prof., Dept. of Educ., Purdue Univ., 1957-60; Extve. Asst. 1960-62; Prof., Head of Dept. 1962-64; Pres., Eastern Oregon College 1964-74; Director, Union County Chamber Comm.; Union Co. Good Neighbors (Pres. 1969-70); St. Joseph Hosp.; Hon. mem., Nat. Council, Boy Scouts of Am.; writings incl. numerous publs. in field of educ.; mem., Am. Educ. Research Assn.; Assn. Supervision & Curriculum Devel.; Ore Educ. Assn.; Assn. State Coll. & Univs.; Nat. Comn. on Accrediting; Am. Assn. Colls. Teacher Educ.; Kappa Delta Pi; Phi Sigma Phi; Phi Delta Kappa; Mennonite; recreations: music, golf, skiing; Clubs: Kiwanis; Lions; Rotary; Elks; Home: 2405 Olive St., Eugene, Ore. 97405

RENISON, George Everett, D.S.O., U.E.L.; bookseller; b. Hamilton, Ont., 25 Aug. 1918; s. Mt. Rev. Robert John, D.D., and Elizabeth Maud (Bristol) R.; e. Trinity Coll. Sch., Port Hope, Ont.; Trinity Coll., Univ. of Toronto; m. Nancy E., d. John T. Stirrett, 15 Dec. 1945; children: Carol Ann, Katharine, Michael Barrie; CHRMN. AND CHIEF EXTVE. OFFICER, W. H. SMITH CANADA LTD.; W. H. Smith Ltd.; Pres., W. H. Smith Cassettes Ltd.; served in 2nd World War with 48th Highlanders Can.; commanded Hasting & Prince Edward Regiment; First Canadian Infantry Brigade; D.S.O.; Mentioned in Despatches; Staff College, Camberley (p.s.c. and Dagger); Dir., Retail Council of Can.; Barclays Can. Ltd.; Harvey Woods Ltd.; member, Canadian Retail Booksellers' Association; Brit. Candn. Trade Assoc.; Retail Council Can.; Am. Booksellers Assn.; Zeta Psi; Conservative; Anglican; recreations: squash, golf; Clubs: Toronto; Badminton & Racquet; Toronto Hunt; University; York; Home: 48 Russell Hill Road, Toronto, Ont. M4V 2T2; Office: 113 Merton St., Toronto, Ont. M4S 1A8

RENNIE, Donald A., B.S.A., Ph.D.; university professor; b. Medicine Hat, Alta., 21 Apl. 1922; s. Edward MacKenzie and Leila Nellie (Andrews) R.; e. High Sch., Gull Lake, Sask.; Univ. of Sask., B.S.A. 1949; Univ. of Wisconsin, Ph.D. 1952; m. Margaret June, d. late W. J. S. Hooper, 28 Aug. 1948; children: Robert John, Wendy Diane, Joan Darlene; PROF. AND HEAD, DEPT. OF SOIL SCIENCE, UNIV. OF SASKATCHEWAN, since 1964; Dir., Sask. Inst. of Pedology, since 1965; served with Bank of Nova Scotia, Swift Current, Sask., as Bank Clk., 1940-42; joined present Univ. as Asst. Prof., Dept. of Soil Science, 1952-57; Assoc. Prof. 1957-64; served as Head, Soils, Irrigation and Crop Production Section, Internat. Atomic Energy, Vienna, Austria, July, 1968-July 1970; served as Pilot, 407 Coastal Command Sqdn., Eng., 1942-45; rec'd Am. Chem. Soc. Award 1967; Centennial Medal 1967; author of over 60 research papers for scient. journs.; Fellow, (1978) Agric. Inst. Can. (Dir. 1958-60, Vice Pres., 1959-60); Fellow (1971) Candn. Soc. Soil Science (Secy.-Treas. 1957-59, Pres. 1976-77); Fellow, Am. Soc. Agron.; Fellow, Soil Science Soc. Am.; mem., Internat. Soc. Soil Science; Candn. Assn. Univ. Teachers; West Can. Agron. Award 1979; Past Master, Lodge Progress No. 92; P. Conservative; United Church; recreations: golf, curling; Home: 134 Highbury Pl., Saskatoon, Sask. S7H 4X7

RENOUF, Harold Augustus, O.C., B.Com., F.C.A., L.L.D.; Canadian civil servant; b. Sandy Point, Nfld. 15 June 1917; s. late Capt. John Robert and late Louisa Maud (LeRoux) R.; e. elem. and high schs. Halifax, N.S.; Dalhousie Univ. B.Com. 1938; C.A. 1942; R.I.A. 1950; m. Janet Dorothy d. late John T. Munro, Halifax 16 June 1942; children: Janet Dorothy, Ann Louise (Mrs. Evan Petley-Jones), John Robert, Susan Elizabeth (Mrs. Scott Thompson); CHRMN., PETROLEUM MONITORING AGENCY; Dir. The Imperial Life Assurance Co.; The Nova Scotia Municipal Finance Corp.; joined H. R. Doane and Co. 1938, Partner 1942, Partner-in-charge New Glasgow, N.S. 1947-62, Partner-in-charge Mang. Services Halifax 1963-67, Chrmn. of Partnership 1967-75; mem. Bd. Dirs. Associated Accounting Firms International, New York 1967-75; Commr., Anti-Inflation Bd., Atlantic Region 1975, Chrmn. of Bd. 1977; Consultant to N.S. Prov. Mun. Fact-Finding Comte. 1967-70; former Dir. Cape Breton Development Corp.; Past Chrmn. Budget Comte. Pictou Co. Un. Appeal; Trustee St. Andrew's Un. Ch. Halifax; (Chrmn.) Dalhousie Sch. Business Adm.; Candn. Inst. Child Health; author Royal Comn. Reports Milk Industry Inquiry Comte. 1966-67, Price Structure of Gasoline & Diesel Oil in N.S. 1968; rec'd Queen's Silver Jubilee Medal; received honorary LL.D. Dalhousie, 1981; mem. Inst. C.A.'s N.S. (Pres. 1948); Candn. Inst. C.A.'s (Pres. 1974-75); Soc. Mang. Accts. N.S.; Halifax Bd. Trade; Candn. Tax Foundation (Gov. 1969-71); Freemason; Liberal; United Church; recreations: boating, fishing; Clubs: Halifax; Saraguay (Treas. 1972-75); Waegwaltic; Royal William Yacht (New Glasgow; Treas. 1958-59); Home: 5929 Rogers Dr., Halifax, N.S. B3H 1E9; Office 580 Booth St., Ottawa, Ont. K1A 0E4.

RENWICK, James Alexander, Q.C., M.P.P., B.A.; b. Toronto, Ont., 29 Nov. 1917; s. late George Hamilton and late Margaret Wright (Pritchard) R.; e. Fern Ave. Pub. Sch. and Univ. of Toronto Schs., Toronto, Ont.; Univ. of Toronto, B.A. 1939; Osgoode Hall Law Sch.; children: Marilyn Margaret, Elizabeth Ann, Margaret Maureen; read law with Richard H. Sankey, Q.C.; called to the Bar of Ont., 1947; Partner, Borden, Elliot, Kelley, Palmer & Sankey, 1947-60; Lang, Michener, Cranston & Renwick, 1961-63; served in 2nd World War 1941-45 with Candn. Armoured Corps; with 28th Candn. Armoured Regt. (BCR) 1942-45; Capt. and Adjt., 1943-44; Mentioned in Despatches; mem. of Prov. Leg. Ont. for Riverdale since Sept. (by-el.) 1964; Pres., New Democratic Party 1967-69; N.D.P. Chairman of Caucus in Ontario Legislature 1967-75; member, Law Society of Upper Can.; Phi Delta Theta; N.D.P.; Anglican; Home: 5 Hurndale Ave., Toronto, Ont. M4K 1R4; Office: Parliament Bldgs., Queen's Park, Toronto, Ont. M7A 1A2

RENZONI, Louis S., M.Sc., D.Sc.; chemical engineer, b. Copper Cliff, Ont., 7 Feb. 1913; s. Secondo and Emma (Furlani) R.; e. St. Michael's Coll. Sch., Toronto, Ont. (Grad. 1931); Queen's Univ., B.Sc. 1935, M.Sc. 1936, D.Sc. 1969; m. Germaine, d. late Adelard DeGuire, 27 Dec. 1937; children: Carl L., Joanne R. Tomlinson, Peter D., Louis T.; PRES., CHEM. INST. OF CANADA, Chemist, G. F. Sterne & Sons, Brantford, Ontario, 1936; Research Chemist. Inco, Port Colborne, Ontario, and Superintendent of Research there, 1944; Asst. Supt. of Research, Inco, Copper Cliff, Ont., 1948 and Supt. 1956; Mgr. of Process Research (Canada), Toronto, Ont. 1960; apptd. Asst. Vice Pres., Toronto, 1964; Vice-Pres., 1967; Vice-Pres., Special Tech. and Environ. Projects, Inco, 1969-77; consultant to Inco, 1977; Dir., G. F. Sterne and Sons; McIntyre Research Fdn.; Toronto; mem., Am. Inst. of Mining Metall. & Petroleum Engrs.; Am. Chem. Soc.; Candn. Inst. Mining & Metall.; Chem. Inst. of Can.; Chrmn., Cdn. Nat. Comm., Internat Union of Pure and applied Chemistry; Fellow, Am. Assn. For Advanc. Science; Publications: many papers and articles on Metallurgy; holds patents on Extractive Processes in Nickel Metall.; rec'd. Gold Medal Award, Extractive Metall. Div. of Am. Inst. of Mining, Metall. & Petroleum Engrs., 1960 and 1963; H. T. Airey Mem. Lecture Award, Metall. Div.,

Candn. Inst. of Mining & Metall.; R. S. Jane Mem. Award, Chem. Inst. of Can., 1968; Roman Catholic; Clubs: Engineers; Mining (New York); Home: 44 Charles St. W., Apt. 4711, Toronto, Ont. M4Y 1R8; Office: P.O. Box 44, 1 Canadian Place, Toronto, Ont. M5X 1C4

REUBER, Grant L., B.A., A.M., Ph.D., F.R.S.C.; economist; b. Mildmay, Ont., 23 Nov. 1927; s. Jacob Daniel and Gertrude Catherine (Wahl) R.; e. Walkerton (Ont.) High Sch.; Univ. of Western Ont., B.A. (Hons. Econ.) 1950; Harvard Univ., A.M. (Econ.) 1954, Ph.D. (Econ.) 1957; research student Sidney Sussex Coll., Cambridge Univ., 1954-55; m. Margaret Louise Julia, d. Clifford J. Summerhayes, Springfield, Ont., 20 Oct. 1951; children: Allison Rebecca, Barbara Susanne, Mary Margaret; DEPUTY CHAIRMAN DEPUTY CHIEF EXECUTIVE AND DIR. BANK OF MONTREAL 1981- ; with Bank of Canada Research Dept., 1950-52; Dept. Finance (Econ. & Internat. Relations Div.) Ottawa, 1955-57; Univ. of W. Ont., Asst. Prof. Econ. 1957-59, Assoc. Prof. 1959-62, Prof. and Head of Dept. 1963-69; Dean Faculty of Social Science 1969-74; Vice-Pres. (Acad.) and Provost, mem. Bod. of Gov. 1974-78; Sr. Vice Pres. and Chief Economist, Bank of Montreal 1978-79; Depy. Min. for Finance, Ottawa, 1979-80; Extve. Vice Pres., Bank of Montreal 1980-81; member, Institute for Economic Research, Queen's University 1961; staff member, Royal Comn. on Banking and Finance, 1962-63; Consultant on Internat. Trade, Nat. Council of Applied Econ. Research, New Delhi, 1964; Consultant, OECD Paris 1969-72; Chrmn., Ont. Econ. Council, 1973-78; numerous contrib. in econ., univ. and banking publs.; Pres., Candn. Econ. Assn., 1967-68; Fellow, Roy. Soc. of Can.; mem., Am. Econ. Assn.; Royal Econ. Soc.; Econometric Soc. Cdn. Econ. Policy Comte., British-North Amer. Comte.; Dir., Cdn. Ditchley Fdn.; Anglican; recreation: tennis; Home: 1285 Redpath Cr., Montreal, Ont. H3G 1A1 Office: 129 St. James St., Montreal, Que. H3Y 1L6

REUCASSEL, William Ross; b. Toronto, Ont., 14 Jan. 1937; s. William and Dora (Kear) R.; e. William Burgess, Danforth Park and Selwyn St. Clair Sec. Schs., Toronto, Ont.; St. Andrew's Coll., Aurora, Ont.; Waterloo (Ont.) Coll.; Univ. of W. Ontario; m. Pamela Elizabeth; children: Kenneth William, Catherine Helen, John Ross; CHMN. AND C.E.O. INTERNATIONAL WAXES LTD. Chrmn. of Bd. Sports Administration Inc., Montreal; Boler Petroleum Co. U.S.A.; Malcolm Nicol & Co. U.S.A.; Pres., Baychem International Inc.; Dir., Jean Beliveau Inc., Montreal; mem., Packaging Assn. Can.; Candn. Mfrs. of Chem. Specialties Assn.; Adhesives Manufacturers Assn.; Rubber Div., Am. Chem. Soc.; Young President's Organization, Inc.; Church; recreations: tennis, golf, swimming; Clubs: Granite; Glen Abbey; Scarborough Golf & Country; Office: 50 Salome Dr., Agincourt, Ont. M1S 2A8

REVELL, Ernest John, M.A., Ph.D.; educator; botanical artist; b. Bangalore, India 15 Apl. 1934; s. Alfred John and Edith Mary Peckham (Sheppard) R.; e. The Dragon Sch. Oxford, Eng. 1946; Ridley Coll. St. Catharines, Ont. 1952; Univ. of Toronto, Trinity Coll. B.A. 1956, Ph.D. 1962; St. John's Coll. Cambridge B.A. 1958, M.A. 1962; m. Ann Margaret d. John Stuart Morgan, Philadelphia, Pa. 6 June 1959; children: Alfred John, Bridget Margaret; PROF. OF NEAR EASTERN STUDIES, VICTORIA COLL., UNIV. OF TORONTO; botanical art exhns. various galleries Toronto and Vancouver Univ. Bot. Garden "Cloud Flowers-Rhododendrons East and West" 1981; illustrator "And Some Brought Flowers" 1980; author "Hebrew Texts with Palestinian Vocalization" 1970; "Biblical Texts With Palestinian Pointing and Their Accents" 1977; transl. "Introduction to the Tiberian Masorah" 1980; various articles biblical Hebrew grammar and hist. of biblical text; mem. Am. Oriental Soc.; Assn. Jewish Studies; Soc. Old Testament Study; Brit. Sch. Archaeol. in Jerusalem; Royal Hortic. Soc.; Champlain Soc.; Anglican; recreation:

gardening; Home: 151 Blythwood Rd., Toronto, Ont. M4N 1A4; Office: Toronto, Ont. M5S 1A1.

REYDA, Jerome, Q.C. B.A., LL.B.; b. Alberta, 12 Nov. 1917; s. Joseph and Anna (Wolsyn) R.; m. Eith Olive, d. William Anderson, 6 Oct. 1944; two d., Joan Elaine, Carolyn Ann; PRESIDENT, CONSOLIDATED FIVE-STAR RESOURCES LTD.; Chrmn of Bd., Silver Chief Minerals Ltd.; Pres. North Empire Gas Co. Ltd.; former Dir. and Gen. Counsel, Canadian Bonanza Petroleums Ltd.; Pres. F. and R. Oil and Gas Co. Inc., (U.S.A. and Australia) read law with Roy E. Jackson, Q.C.; cr. Q.C. 1966; actively engaged in exploration of mining properties and internat. exploration for oil and gas; mem. Candn. Bar Assn.; Candn. Petroleum Law Foundation; Rocky Mountain Mineral Law Foundation; Law Soc. of Alta; Candn Bar Assn.; mem. Alta. Econ. Mission to Japan (Invest. & Finance Task Force 1972); Past Chief Ranger, I.O.F.; P. Conservative; Protestant; recreations: golf, hunting, fishing; Clubs: Edmonton Petroleum; Royal Glenora; Glendale Golf & Country; Home: 24 Riverside Cres., Edmonton, Alta. T5J 3P4; Office: 460 Continental Bank Bldg., 10250-110 St., Edmonton, Alta.

REYNO, Lt. Gen. Edwin Michael, A.F.C., C.D., B.A., D.C.L.; air force officer; b. Halifax, N.S., 1917; e. St. Mary's Univ., B.A. 1936, D.C.L. 1965; RCAF Staff Coll. Toronto, 1947; Imperial Defence Coll. Eng., 1960; joined RCAF 1938; served overseas with 1 Fighter Sqdn. which participated in Battle of Britain; returned to Can. 1941 and served at RCAF Stns. Rockcliffe, Ont. and Mossbank, Sask.; apptd. Chief Instr., Wartime Operational Training Unit, Bagotville, Que. 1942; Commdr., RCAF Stn. Greenwood, N.S. 1944; apptd. Sr. Personnel Offr., W. Air Command, Vancouver, B.C., 1946; Chief Instr., RCAF Staff Coll., 1949 and later Dir., Air Plans Strategy, Ottawa; Deputy Air Offr. Commanding, Air Def. Command, St. Hubert, Que. 1955; Depy. Vice Chief of Air Staff, 1960; Chief of Staff 4th Allied Tactical Air Force HQ, NATO Germany 1963; Depy. Chief Personnel, CFHQ, 1965, Chief 1966-69; Vice Chief of the Defence Staff, Jan.-Dec. 1969; Depy. Commdr., NORAD 1969-72; Vice-Pres. Internat. Operations, L.T.V. Corp. 1972-78; Univ. of Texas, Lect. Internat-Marketing (Eron.) 1979- ; joined LTV Aerospace Corp.; Home: 704 Castlewood Lane, Arlington, Texas 76012 Office: Dept. of Marketing, Coll. of Business, Univ. of Texas, Arlington Texas 76019.

REYNOLDS, C. Warren; advertising executive; b. Toronto, Ont., 4 Oct. 1914; s. Edward William and Mary Kathleen (McComb) R.; m. Ruth Garland, d. John B. Byers, Washington, D.C., 23 Oct. 1939; four s.; John W., Edward W., David W., Charles W.; Past. Pres., Candn. Assn. Advertising Agencies; Past Chrmn., Business Conference, Univ. of W. Ont.; Gov., The Frontier Coll.; Gov. Etobicoke General Hosp.; Past Chrmn., Audit Bureau of Circulations U.S.A. and Can.; Past Chairman Board of Mang. O'Keefe Centre for the Performing Arts; awarded Assn. of Candn. Advertisers Inc. Gold Medal, 1964; Fellow, Inst. Cdn. Advertising; Dir., Professional Artists Guild (Florida); Founder, John Milton Soc. for the Blind in Canada; member, Ruskin Soc.; Guild of Portrait Painters-Canada; Boca Raton Centre for the Arts (Florida); Protestant; recreations: fishing, golf, oil painting Clubs: Board of Trade (Toronto); Lambton Golf & Country; Canadian (Toronto); Boca Raton (Fla.); Hillsboro Mile Ocean (Fla.); Home: 10 Country Club Dr., Islington, Ont. M9A 3J4

REYNOLDS, J. Keith, M.Sc., Ph.D.; consultant; director b. London, Ont., 29 Sept. 1919; s. John William and Beatrice E. D. (Stewart) R.; e. Univ. of W. Ont., B.Sc. 1949, M.Sc. 1950, Ph.D. (Biology) 1952; m. Ida Maude, d. Byron McLaughlin, 29 Sept. 1945; children: Jane, Brian, John; PRES., J.K. REYNOLDS CONSULTANTS INC., 1982- ; Chrmn., Metropolitan Toronto and Region Conservation Authority 1981-82; Wildlife Biol., Ont. Dept. of

Lands & Forests, 1952-54; Assistant District Forester 1954-56; District Forester 1956-63; Fisheries Supervisor 1963-64; Chief Executive Officer, Dept. of Prime Minister, Ontario, 1964-69; Secretary to Cabinet and Deputy Min., Dept. of Prime Minister 1969-72; Deputy Provincial Secretary for Resources Devel. 1972-74; Dep. Min. of Nat. Res., Ont. 1974-80; served with RCAF 1940-45; rank sqdn. Leader; Mentioned in Despatches; Dir. Forintek Can. Corp.; Rio Algom Ltd., Dome Mines Ltd. Ont. Nat. Ballet of Canada; Historical Studies Series; mem., Fac. Adv. Bd., Forestry, Univ. of Toronto; Adv. Council, Fac. of Admin. Studies, York Univ.; Bd. of Trustees, Candn. Nat. Sportsmen's Fund; Cana Place; Anglican; recreations: fishing, hunting, photography; Home: 43 Bridlewood Blvd., Agincourt, Ont. M1T 1P6; Office: P.O. Box 309, Stn. D., Scarborough, Ont. M1R 5B8

REYNOLDS, (Mrs.) Margaret Norene, B.A., B.L.S.; librarian, retired; ancestors were U.E.L.; b. Moncton, N.B., 15 June 1914; d. William Lewis and Jane Laura (Barter) Allen; e. Avondale (N.B.) Grammar School; New Glasgow (N.S.) High School; Dalhousie Univ. B.A. 1935; McGill Univ. B.L.S. 1938; m. late Major Edward A. C. Reynolds, 2 Nov. 1941; one s. Charles Edward Allen; began as Clerk Head Office, Bank of Montreal, Montreal, Que. 1936-37; Asst. Librarian, Royal Bank of Can., Montreal, Que. 1939-42; Dir., Candn. Book Centre, Halifax, N.S. 1948-50; served in 2nd World War in Auxiliary Services as Chief Librarian, Candn. Legion Educ. Services, Ottawa, 1942-44; Overseas Librarian, London, Eng. 1944-46; Dir. of Libraries, Candn. Dep't. of Agric., 1950-1975; Anglican; recreations: travel; Home: 18 Marco Lane, Ottawa, Ont. K1S 5A2;

REYNOLDS, Ralph Edward, B.A.; diplomat; b. Sarnia, Ont., 27 March 1920; s. Joshua Edward and Hattie May (Hack) R.; e. Lisgar Coll. Inst. Ottawa 1939; Queen's Univ. B.A. 1949, post-grad. studies Hist. 1949-50 (Sir James Aikens Fellow in Canadian history); m. Katherine Louise (author "Agnes: The Biography of Lady MacDonald"); d. late John D. MacLeod, Kinross, P.E.I., 19 July 1941; children: Rennie, Carol (Mrs. Derek Godsmark), Gary, Jackie; Tutor in Hist. Royal Mil. Coll. Kingston 1948-50; Jr. Research Offr. Nat. Research Council of Can. Ottawa 1950; joined Dept. of External Affairs 1950, served in Commonwealth, Econ., Consular and European Divs., Second Secy. Prague 1953, Advisor Candn. Perm. Del. to UN Geneva 1954, Second Secy. Copenhagen 1956 (First Secy. 1958), Econ. Div. Ottawa 1959, Counsellor London (Eng.) 1962, Chargé d'Affaires a.i. Warsaw 1967, Dir. Transport, Communications and Energy Div. 1967 (Ottawa), Ambassador to Ethiopia with concurrent accreditation to Madagascar and Somalia 1971, Ambassador to Costa Rica with concurrent accreditation to Honduras, Nicaragua, Panama and El Salvador 1975; Special Adv. to Extv. Dir., Immigration & Demographic Policy, C.E.I.C. 1978; Co-ordinator, Internat. Appointments, Access to Information & Privacy Legislation, Dept. of External Affairs, 1980; headed Candn. Dels. to Internat. Confs. 1969-74 (INTELSAT Conf. Washington, Container Conf. and Code of Conduct for Liners Confs. Geneva); served with RCAF 1940-45, Territorial Patrol Pilot, rank Flight Lt.; mem. Prof. Assn. Foreign Service Offrs.; Anglican; recreations: riding, hiking, paddling, golf; Club: San José Country; Address: 26 Herschel Cres., Kanata, Ont. K2L 1Z6

RHIND, John A., M.Com., M.B.A.; life insurance executive; b. Toronto, Ont., 1 May 1920; s. John E. and Sybil (Gayford) R.; e. Univ. of Toronto Schs., 1933-38 (Matric.); Univ. of Toronto, B.Com. 1942 and M.Com. 1953; m. Katharine Elizabeth, d. G. E. D. Greene, Agincourt, Ont., 4 Sept. 1948; children: Susan, Ian, Alexander; PRESIDENT AND C.E.O., CONFEDERATION LIFE INSURANCE CO., since 1976; Dir., Economic Investment Trust Ltd.; Campbell Soup. Co. Ltd.; Continental Bank of Canada; Slough Estates (Canada) Ltd.; Imm. Past chrmn. Toronto

Western Hosp. and mem Bd of Trustees; with Invest. Dept. of Nat. Life Assnce. Co. of Can., 1945-47; Econ. & Statistician, Mills, Spence & Co., Stockbkrs., Toronto, Ont. 1947-48; Treas., Nat. Life Assnce. Co. of Can. 1948-55; apptd. Vice-Pres., 1955; Gen. Mgr., 1957; Pres. 1966; served in 2nd World War; Comnd. in 1942; served in Italy and N.W. Europe with RCA, 11th Field Regt.; Past Pres., Candn. Life Ins. Assn.; Anglican; recreations: golf, fishing; squash; Clubs: Toronto Golf; Badminton & Racquet; Osler Bluff Ski; University; York; Home: 38 Edgar Ave., Toronto, Ont. M4W 2A9; Office: 321 Bloor St. E., Toronto, Ont. M4W 1H1

RHIND, John Christopher, F.I.I.C., C.A.E.; insurance executive; b. Birmingham, Eng. 19 Feb. 1934; s. John James and Helen Florence (Walker) R.; e. Salesian Coll., Oxford, Eng.; York Univ. Mang. Educ. Program 1972-75; Certified Association Executive 1980; m. Rita D. d. John Evans, Ramsgate, Eng. 21 June 1958; children: Oonagh Catherine, Michael John, Christopher James, Sarah Caroline; PRES. AND CEO. THE INSURANCE INST. OF CAN. 1979- ; joined Car & General Insurance Co. U.K. prior 1958; Pearl Assurance Co. Toronto 1958-59; Guardian Insurance Co. of Canada 1959-75 becoming Adm. Mgr. and Claims Mgr. 1974; Asst. Gen. Mgr., The Ins. Inst. Can. 1975, Gen. Mgr. 1977; served with Royal Army Service Corps 1952-54, rank Sgt.; mem. Adv. Council, Sch. of Contin. Studies, Univ. of Toronto; Friend of Seneca Coll. (Adv. Group); mem. Business Adv. Comte. George Brown Coll.; author or co-author various book chapters, ins. articles; Gen. Mgr., Ins. Inst. Ont.; Dir. Gen., L'institut d'Assurance du Que.; mem. Inst. Assn. Extves.; Bd. Trade Metrop. Toronto; P. Conservative; R. Catholic; recreations: golf, coaching minor sports, reading; Home: 2400 Yolanda Dr., Oakville, Ont. L6L 2H8; Office: 55 University Ave., Toronto, Ont. M5J 2H7.

RHODES, Andrew James, M.D., F.R.C.P.(C). F.R.C.P. (Edin.), F.R.S.C., F.F.C.M.; medical microbiologist; b. Inverness, Scotland, 19 Sept. 1911; s. William Thomas and Maud (Innes) R.; e. Wellington Coll., Berkshire, Eng., 1924-29; Univ. of Edinburgh (1929-34) M.B., Ch.B. (Hons.), M.D. 1941, F.R.C.P. 1941; Chrmn. Rabies Adv. Comte., Ont. Ministry of Nat. Resources; Med. Dir., Public Health Labs., Ont., Min. of Health, Toronto, 1970-76; Lecturer in Bacteriology, University of Edinburgh, 1934-41; Pathologist Roy. Infirmary, Shrewsbury, England, 1941-45; Lecturer in Bacteriology, London (England) School of Hygiene and Tropical Medicine, 1945-47; Prof. Emeritus, Dep't. of Microbiology and Parasitology, Univ. of Toronto, 1977; Research Assoc., Connaught Medical Research Labs., Univ. of Toronto, 1947-53; Dir., Sch. of Hygiene, Univ. of Toronto and Head, Dept. Microbiol. there 1956-70; Head, Grad. Dept. Hygiene 1956-70; Prof., Sch. of Hygiene since 1947; Consultant in Virology, The Hosp. for Sick Children, Toronto, since 1951 (Dir., The Research Inst., 1953-56); Anglican; Home: 79 Rochester Ave., Toronto, Ont. M4N 1N7

RHUDE, Henry B., D.F.C., Q.C., LL.B.; b. Halifax, N.S., 11 Nov. 1923; s. Samuel Burton and Laura Gertrude (Latter) R.; e. Halifax Pub. and High Schs.; Dalhousie Univ., LL.B. 1950; m. Elsie Foster, 21 Dec. 1946; three s.: David Burton, John Peter, Michael Henry; Chrmn. and C.E.O., Central & Eastern Scotia Trust Co.; Pres., Sobey Leased Properties Ltd.; Chrmn., National Sea Products Ltd.; Dir., Sobeys Stores Ltd.; United Financial Management Ltd.; Atlantic Shopping Centres Ltd.; Empire Co. Ltd.; MICC Investments Ltd.; and other co.'s; called to Bar of N.S. 1951; cr. Q.C. 1966; served with RCAF 1941-45; Navig. in Bomber Command; rank Flying Offr.; Past Gov., Candn. Tax Foundation; Mt. St. Vincent Univ.; Past Chrmn., N.S. Rehabilitation Centre; Halifax Grammar Sch.; mem., N.S. Barristers Soc.; Candn. Bar Assn.; Liberal; United Church; recreations: skiing, sailing; Club:

The Halifax; Home: 6095 Coburg Rd., Halifax, N.S. B2N 1X5; Office: 5151 Terminal Rd., Halifax, N.S. B3J 1V4

RHYDWEN, David A.; librarian; b. Scarborough, Ont., 14 June 1918; s. Caradog and Jessie (Tiffin) R.; e. Scarborough Elem. Schs.; Scarborough Coll., 1932-37; CHIEF LIBRARIAN, THE GLOBE AND MAIL, since 1944; joined present Lib. 1938; Sales Mngr, Info Globe Div. of Globe and Mail, 1979-80; Editorial Administrator, 1980- ; rec'd Jack K. Burness Mem. Award for distinguished librarianship, 1966; Awarded Special Libraries Assoc. Newspaper Div. Award of Honour, 1979; mem., Comte. Adjustment, Town of Markham, since 1964; mem., Special Libs. Assn.; Protestant; Home: 260 Wellington St. W., Markham, Ont. L3P 1B9; Office: 444 Front St. W., Toronto, Ont. M5V 2S9

RIBENBOIM, Paulo, B.Sc., Ph.D., F.R.S.C.; educator; b. Recife, Brazil, 13 March 1928; s. Moysés and Anna (Drechsler) R.; e. Colegio Anglo Americano and Colegio Andrews, Rio de Janeiro, 1945; Univ. do Brasil, B.Sc. 1948; Univ. de Sao Paulo, Ph.D. 1957; m. Huguette, d. late Henri Demangelle, 19 Dec. 1951; two s.: Serge Charles, Eric Leonard; PROF. OF MATHEMATICS, QUEEN'S UNIV.; visiting lectr. univs. in Can., U.S.A., S.Am., Mexico, Europe and Japan; author, "Théorie des Groupes Ordonnés", 1963" "Functions, Limits and Continuity", 1964; "Rings and Modules", 1969; "Algebraic Numbers", 1972; "L'Arithmétique des Corps", 1972; "13 Lectures on Fermat's Last Theorem", 1979; also over 50 research papers and articles; Ed., "Queen's Papers in Pure and Applied Mathematics"; Mathematical Reports of the Acad. of Sciences, Roy. Soc. of Can.; rec'd hon. degree from Univ. de Caen, France; Assoc. Ed., Candn. Journal of Mathematics; mem. Am. Math. Soc.; Candn. Math. Soc.; Soc. Mathématique de France; Soc. Mathématique Suisse; Sociedad de Matematica Mexicana; Home: 4 Watts, Cres., Kingston, Ont. K7M 2P3; Office: Kingston, Ont. K7L 3N6

RIBNER, Herbert Spencer, M.S., Ph.D., F.R.S.C. (1976); physicist; b. Seattle, Wash., 9 Apr. 1913; s. Herman Joseph and Rose Esther (Goldberg) R.; e. Cal. Inst. Tech., B.S. 1935; Wash. Univ., St. Louis, M.S. 1937, Ph.D. 1939; m. Lelia Carolyn, d. Harvey R. Byrd, 29 Oct. 1949; children: Carol, David; PROF., INST. FOR AEROSPACE STUDIES, UNIV. OF TORONTO, since 1959; Distinguished Research Assoc., N.A.S.A. Langley Res. Ctr., 1978- ; with Brown Geophysical Co., Houston, 1939-40; Langley Lab N.A.C.A., 1940-49; Lewis Flight Propulsion Lab., Cleveland N.A.C.A., Division Consultant, later Section Head, 1949-54; Research Assoc., later Asst. and Assoc. Prof. of Aerophysics, Inst. of Aerophysics, Univ. of Toronto, 1955-59; Consultant to De Havilland Aircraft of Canada Ltd., Min. Transport, General Electric & others; Visiting Prof., Department of Aeronautics, University of Southampton, 1960-61; Staff Scientist, NASA Langley Res. Ctr. 1975-76; Publications: over 95 scient. papers and articles; Chrmn. Sonic Boom Panel, Internat. Civil Aviation Organ. 1969-70; mem. Candn. Acoustical Assn. (Chrmn. 1966-68); Fellow, Acoustical Soc. Am. (mem., Noise Comte.); Am. Physical Soc.; Candn. Aero. & Space Inst. (Chrmn. Astronautics Sec. 1958-59; Turnbull Lectr. 1968); Am. Institute Aero. & Astronautics (mem., Aero-Acoustics Comte. 1970-73, Aero-Acoustics Award 1976, Dryden Lectureship in Research 1981); Adv. Comte. Hearing, Bioacoustics & Biomechanics, U.S. Nat. Acad. Sciences; Home: 60 Inverlochy Blvd., Apt. 608, Thornhill, Ont. L3T 4T7

RICARD, L. Edmond; executive; b. Montreal, Qué., 26 Oct. 1921; e. L'Ecole Saint-Edouard, Montreal; St-Agnes Boys' Acad. (Matric.); post-grad. studies in Comm., Sir George Williams Univ.; m. Jacqueline René de Cotret; children: Paul Edmond, Denise, Madeleine, Carole; PRES. & CEO, IMASCO LTD., CHMN. OF BD., IMPERIAL TOBACCO LTD., IMASCO FOODS LTD. and IM-

ASCO ASSOCIATED PRODUCTS LTD., Dir., Pascar of Canada Ltd.; Wabasso Limited; Hardec's Food Systems, Inc.; The Continental Bank of Canada; CFCF Inc.; IAC Limited; Joined Imperial Tobacco in 1941; Sales Rep. District Sales Mgr; Publications Mgr; Mgr Radio-Television Advertising; Divisional Mgr, Advertising Dept; Product Mgr; Vice-Pres, Marketing, General Cigar Company, Montréal, 1963; Vice-Pres, B. Houde & Grothé Ltd., October 1964; Vice-Pres, Imperial Tobacco Sales, 1967; Vice-Pres, Imperial Tobacco Company of Canada Limited, 1968; Dir., Vice-Pres. and Gen. Mgr, Imperial Tobacco Products Limited, 1969; Dir. and Vice-Pres, Imasco Limited, 1970; Pres, General Cigar Company Limited, 1971; Pres., Imperial Tobacco Products Limited, 1972; Exec. Vice-Pres. Imasco Limited 1978; President and Chief Operating Officer, Imasco Limited, 1979. served in R.C.A.F., four and a half years; Gov., Conseil du Patronat du Qué.; mem. Council, Bd. Trade of Montreal; recreations: golf, bridge; Residence: 27 Holton Ave.,Westmount, Qué. H3Y 2E9

RICARD, Hon. Théogène, P.C. (1963), M.P.; b. St. Guillaume, Que., 29 Apr. 1909; s. Xavier and Délia (Taillon) R.; e. Collège St. Joseph, St. Guillaume, Que., 1916-25; Victoriaville Comm. Coll., Que. 1925-28; m. Mariette, d. Omer Bourret, St. Guillaume, Que., 7 Aug. 1937; children: Jan-Denis, Monique, Suzanne, Louise, Roger; Personnel Mgr, Goodyear Cotton Co. during 24 years; Adm., Social Service, St. Hyacinthe, Que.; el. to H. of C. for St. Hyacinthe-Bagot since 1957; apptd. Minister without Portfolio in Diefenbaker Cabinet, 18 March 1963; mem., St. Hyacinthe Sch. Bd.; K. of C.; Conservative; Roman Catholic; Home: 1325 Bourassa St., St. Hyacinthe, Que. J2S 1P9

RICE, George Richard Agar, LL.D. (Alta. 1965); - broadcasting extve.; b. Teddington, Eng., 24 Jan. 1901; s. George Alexander and late Susan R.; came to Can. 1920; OWNER, PRES., AND GEN. MGR., SUNWAPTA BROADCASTING CO. LTD. (CFRN & CFRN-TV); mem., Edmonton Adv. Bd., Royal Trust Co.; with Marconi Co., Chelmsford, Eng., 1915; opened Stn. CJCA, Edmonton, Alta., for the Edmonton "Journal", 1922; bought Stn. CFRN, Edmonton, then CFTP, in Partnership with H. F. Nielson, 1934; inaugurated Edmonton's 1st Radio Press Bur. with Brit. Un. Press teletype, 1939; served with Marconi-Admiralty Wireless Service, 1916-18; Commdr. Brother, Order of St. John of Jerusalem; mem., Edmonton Chamber of Comm.; Candn. Assn. of Broadcasters (Hon. Pres. 1947; Chrmn. 1948); Radio Pioneers Club; Candn. & U.S.A.; N.W. Chamber of Mines; 50-Year Club of Radiomen; Anglican; Clubs: Edmonton; Rotary; Edmonton Petroleum; Home: 4 Valleyview Point, Edmonton, Alta. T5R 5T4; Office: (Box 5030, Station "E"), Edmonton, Alta. T5P 4C2

RICE, Victor A.; manufacturer; b. Hitchin, Herts., Eng. 7 March 1941; m. Sharla Waitzman 25 June 1970; children: Jonathan, Kristin, Gregg; came to Can. 1975; CHRMN., PRES. AND CHIEF EXTVE. OFFR., MASSEY-FERGUSON LTD. 1980- ; served in various financial positions U.K., Ford 1957-64, Cummins Engines 1964-67, Chrysler 1968-70; joined Massey-Ferguson's Perkins Engines Group Ltd. Peterborough, Eng. as Comptroller N. European Operations subsequently serving as Dir. Finance, Dir. Sales & Market Devel.; Depy. Mang. Dir.-Operations Perkins Engines 1974; trans. to H.O. Massey-Ferguson Toronto as world-wide Comptroller 1975, Vice Pres. Staff Operations 1977, Pres. Mem. Bd. of Directors, 1978; Dir. Farm & Indust. Equipment Inst.; mem. Bd. Trade Metrop. Toronto; Financial Extves. Inst.; Pres.'s Assn. Am. Mang. Assn.; Brit. Inst. Marketing; Inst. Dirs.; recreations: golf, squash, music, reading; Clubs:Carlton (London, Eng.); RCYC; Toronto Golf; Home: 52 Old Forest Hill Rd., Toronto, Ont. M5P 2P9; Office: 200 University Ave., Toronto, Ont. M5H 3E4.

RICH, Colwyn George; executive; b. Cardiff, Wales 12 Nov. 1927; s. Robert George Rich; e. Manchester Coll. of Technol. Assoc. 1950; m. Jean d. Charles McRae; children: Peter John, Jane Elizabeth, David Michael; PRES. AND DIR., CHAMPLAIN INDUSTRIES LTD.; Dir. Brooke Bond Inc. Can.; Promil Foods Ltd. Can.; Champlain Protex Ltd. U.K.; came to Can. 1967; Office: Stanbridge Station, Que. J0J 2J0.

RICH, Patrick Jean Jacques, executive; b. Strasbourg, France 28 March 1931; s. Henri and Marianne Marguerite (Thull) R.; e. Univ. of Strasbourg; Harvard Univ.; holds degrees in Pol. Science, Econ. and Law; m. Louise Dionne 8 July 1961; children: Jean Luc, Eric, Nathalie; REG. EXEC. VICE PRES. ALCAN ALUMINIUM LTD. (CAN., U.S. & CARIBBEAN), PRES. & C.E.O. ALUMINUM CO. OF CAN. LTD. AND ALCAN SMELTERS & CHEMICALS LTD.; Dir. Alcan Aluminum Ltd. since 1976; el. to Bd. of Canada Cement Lafarge Ltd., 1979; el. to Bd. of N.V. Bekaert S.A. (Belgium), 1980; joined Alcan 1959; Treas. Bauxites du Midi 1961, Mang. Dir. Alcan Industries Ltd. (UK) 1963, Secy. and Treas., Vice Pres. Alcan Argentina S.A.I.C. 1965, Chief Financial Offr. Alcan Aluminio Iberico S.A. Madrid 1968, Mang. Dir. Angeletti & Ciucani Fonderia Laminatoio S.P.A. Italy 1969, Area Gen. Mgr. for Alcan's Latin Am. operations 1971, Regional Extve. Vice Pres. Europe, Near E., Africa and Latin Am. Alcan Vice pres. Alcan Ore Ltd. 1972; Reg. Exec. Vice Pres. Alcan Aluminium Ltd. (Europe, Africa & Latin Am.) 1975; of Alcan, U.S. & Caribbean, 1978- ; served with French Army 1956-69 Capt. (Res.) 5e Bureau 11e Demi-Bgde. Parachutistes; rec'd Croix valeur militaire à l'ordre du Corps d'Armée; Home: 765 Lexington Ave. Westmount, Que. H3Y 1K8; Office: (P.O. Box 6090) Montreal, Que. H3C 3H2

RICH, Raymond A., B.S.; company officer; b. Los Angeles, Calif., 11 Jan. 1916; s. Arthur Henry and Loretta (Baker) R.; e. Iowa State Coll., B.S. 1935; Drake Univ.; Univ. of Arizona; m. Virginia, d. L. Dayton Garberson, Sibley, Iowa, 27 June 1936; children: Susan Webb, John Dayton; CHAIRMAN AND DIR., CANADIAN HYDROCARBONS LTD.; Chairman and Dir., Alberta Underground Storage Ltd.; Chrmn. and Pres., Knox Glass Corpn.; Pres and Dir., Blackfoot Hills Pipe Line Ltd.; Chrmn. and Chief Extve. Offr., Great Northern Gas Utilities Ltd.; Dir., Bank of Great Western Arizona; Canadian Propane Ltd. (C.P.L., Ont., Man. and Sask.); Fort St. John Petroleum, Vancouver, B.C.; Chrmn. and Dir., McCall Corp., N.Y.C.; with General Elec. Co., 1939-46 as successively Engr., Sales Manager, Purchasing Manager, Superintendent, Supt. War Prod. Plant; Partner, Van Doren, Knowland & Schladermundt, Designers and Engrs., N.Y.C., 1945-46; with Philco Corp., 1946-56, successively Product Mgr., Vice-Pres. and Gen. Mgr.; Pres., Dir., and mem. of Extve. Comte., Avco Corp., 1956-58; Dir., Norton Simon Corp. 1968-70; Chmn. and C.E.O., Patagonia Corp. 1967-81; Chmn., Pres. and C.E.O., United States Filter Corp. 1971-81; and Chrmn. and Dir. of various companies in U.S. and Canada; formerly Advisor, Smaller War Plants Corp., Wash., D.C., and Regional Mgr. of Comte. for Econ. Devel. of 2nd and 3rd Fed. Reserve Areas; served in 2nd World War; Lieut., U.S. Navy Reserve (two yrs. Pacific Ocean areas — Japan); Clubs: Calgary Petroleum; University (N.Y.C.); Nantucket (Mass.) Yacht; Home: Rose Tree Rach, Elgin, Arizona 85611; Office: 200 Park Ave., Ste. 4410, New York, N.Y. 10166

RICHARD, Jean L., B.E., M.B.A.; banker; e. Coll. Militaire Royale de St-Jean; Royal Mil. Coll. Can.; Univ. of W. Ont. B.E. (Civil) 1962, M.B.A. 1969; SR. VICE PRES. CORPORATE BANKING, BANK OF MONTREAL; served as offr. RCN, H.M.C.S. St-Laurent, H.M.C.S. Skeena 1962-65; Canada Cement Co. Ltd. Montreal and Toronto 1965-67; Research & Econ. Dept. Greenshields Inc. Montreal 1969-70, Institutional Sales London, Eng.

1970-73, Corporate & Project Financing Montreal 1973-77, Corporate Finance Partner Alta. 1977-80; mem. Soc. Franco-Canadienne de Calgary; Calgary Chamber Comm.; Assn. Prof. Engrs. Prov. Ont.; Assn. Canadienne Française de l'Alta.; Office: 129 St. James St., Montreal, Que. H2Y 1L6.

RICHARD, Hon. Kenneth Peter, B. Com., LL.B.; judge; b. Dartmouth, N.S. 31 Jan. 1932; s. Harry Bernard and Jean Grace (Tobin) R.; e. St. Thomas Aquinas Sch. and Queen Elizabeth High Sch. Halifax 1948; St. Francis Xavier Univ. B.Com. 1952; Dalhousie Univ. LL.B. 1967; m. Elizabeth Bernadette d. David Fraser Sears 15 Aug. 1953; children: Debra Marie, Kenneth Peter, Stephen David, Gary Andrew, Michael Tobin; JUDGE, TRIAL DIV., SUPREME COURT OF N.S. 1978- ; called to Bar of N.S. 1967; part-time lectr. in Business Law, St. Francis Xavier Univ. 1970-76; Seminar Leader, Candn. Hosp. Assn. 1975-77; Vice Chrmn. N.S. Environmental Control Council 1973-76; Dir. Atlantic Trust Co. 1974-76; mem. Adv. Bd. Montreal Trust Co. 1970-74; Ald. City of Halifax 1963-66; Lib. Cand. Halifax Chebucto prov. g.e. 1967; Past Pres., Atlantic Provs. Chamber Comm.; St. Martha's Hosp. Antigonish; mem. Council, N.S. Barristers Soc. 1969, Candn. Bar Assn. 1972-74; mem. Candn. Judges Conf.; Am. Assn. Law & Medicine; R. Catholic; recreations: running, boating, fishing; Home: 110 Hazelholme Dr., Halifax, N.S. B3M 1N5; Office: (P.O. Box 2314) The Law Courts, Halifax, N.S. B3J 1S7.

RICHARD, Brig.-Gen. Marcel; Canadian armed forces; b. Quebec, Que., 19 March 1921; s. Louis Arthur and Simone (de Varennes) R.; e. Que. Semy., 1938; Royal Mil. Coll. 1939-41; Candn. Army Staff Coll., p.s.c. 1952; Jt. Services Staff Coll., j.s.s.c. 1959; Nat. Defence Coll., n.d.c. 1966; Laval Univ., Dipl. in Pub. Adm. 1969; m. France, d. late Lt.-Col. L. J. A. Amyot, 1 July 1948; two s., four d.; initial mil. training in N.P.A.M. 1937-39; served with R22eR in Can., U.K., Sicily, Italy and N.W. Europe during World War II as Inf. Offr.; Mentioned in Despatches; served also in Korea and in N. Can.; Staff Learner, Chief Instr. for Recruit Training, Staff Offr., Nat. Defence HQ, 1946-50; Sr. Candn. Instr. at Haramura Battle Sch., Commdr. of jr. NCOs' Sch. in Korea, 1951-52; G.S.O. 2, Que. Command HQ, Montreal, 1953-54; Head of Operations Br. of E. Que. Area HQ, Quebec, 1955-57; Exchange at War Office, London as G.S.O. 2; Second-in-Command of 2 Bn. R22eR, 1952-61; C.O. of 3 Bn. R22eR (Airborne), 1961-64; Sr. Staff Offr. for Inf. Equipment Requirements, Nat Defence HQ, 1964-65; Commdr., Base "Valcartier", 1966-68; Depy. Commdr., 5e Groupement de Combat, 1968-70; Chief of Staff for Adm. of Mobile Command, 1970; mem., Candn. Inst. Internat. Affairs (Chrmn., Que. Br., 1956-57), 1954-57; Inst. Pub. Adm. Can.; R. Catholic; recreations: skiing, fishing, hiking, running, books, music; Clubs: R.M.C.; Que. Garrison

RICHARDS, Earle Blake, B.A., C.A.; retired. newspaper executive; b. St. Thomas, Ont., 17 Aug. 1915; s. Emery A. and Frances Matilda (Erb) R.; e. Public and High Schs., St. Thomas, Ont.; Univ. of Western Ont., B.A. (Hon. Business Adm.); m. the late Anne Margaret Bowes, (dec. 18 Mar. 1980) d. Dr. Charles B. Taylor, 3 April 1943; children: Barbara, Gordon, Robert; Past Dir., Extve. Vice-President, The Globe & Mail, 1965-79; Past Pres., Candn. Daily Newspaper Publishers Assn.; with Clarkson, Gordon & Co. Chart. Accts., 1939-49; The Globe & Mail, 1949-79; served in 2nd World War with R.C.N., 1942-45; Lieut.; mem., Inst. Chart. Accts. Ont.; Delta Upsilon; United Church; recreations: curling, fishing; Clubs: Granite; Toronto Hunt Kiwanis; Home: 5 Pine Forest Rd., Toronto, Ont. M4N 3E6; Office: 444 Front St. W., Toronto, Ont. M5V 3S9

RICHARDS, James Paul, B.A.Sc., M.B.A.; executive; b. Toronto, Ont. 15 July 1934; s. James Stanley and Margaret Ellen (Newall) R.; e. Forest Hill Coll. Inst. 1952; Univ.

of Toronto B.A.Sc. (Indust. Engn.) 1956, M.B.A. 1962; m. Marjorie Joyce Garson, Ph.D. June 1978; children: James Timothy, Jennia Penelope, Jordan Chandler, Sara Gwyn Beam, Matthew Thomas Beam; PRES., O.H. JOHNS GLASS CO. LTD. (JOHNS SCIENTIFIC) 1979- ; Pres.; Sci-Can Scientific Ltd. 1972- ; Glass Pack Ltd. 1969- ; Foreign Service Offr. and Trade Commr. Govt. Can. 1962-66, Rio de Janeiro 1963-66; Pres., Candn. Red Cross (Ont. Div.) 1980-81, Vice Pres. 1976-80; mem. Assn. Prof. Engrs. Prov. Ont.; Mooredale Assn.; Art Gallery of Ont.; Candn. Wildlife Assn.; recreations: hiking, skiing, tennis, music, theatre; Clubs: Granite; Craigleith Ski; Downtown Tennis; Home: 1 Heathbridge Park Dr., Toronto, Ont. M4G 2Y6; Office: 219 Broadview Ave., Toronto, Ont. M4M 2G4.

RICHARDS, Linden J.; B.S., A.M.P.; oil and gas consultant; b. Arnett, Okla. 12 Sept. 1908; s. Otis H. and E. Bell (Carper) R.; e. Okla. State Univ., B.S. (Civil Engn.); Harvard Univ., A.M.P.; m. Irene Worten, 20 Aug. 1937; children: Irene Alley, Nancy Kate Ritchie; CHRMN. of BD. of DIRECTORS, TOTAL PETROLEUM (NORTH AMERICA) LTD.; Filtrol Corp.; Engineer, Oklahoma State Highway Dept., 1936; Geophysicist, Continental Oil Co. of Del., 1937-48; joined Hudson's Bay Oil & Gas Co. Ltd. as Chief Geophysicist, 1948-52; apptd. Asst. Gen. Mgr., 1952-54, Vice Pres.-Adm., 1953-58, Sr. Vice Pres., 1958-62, Extve. Vice Pres., 1962-65; Pres. and Dir. 1965-70; Chrmn. of Extve. Comte. Apl. 1970-Oct. 1971; Past Chrmn., Oil & Gas Comte., Calgary Chamber Comm.; Pres. (1968-69) Candn. Petroleum Assn.; mem., Soc. Exploration Geophysicists; Beta Theta Pi; Protestant; recreations: golf, hunting, fishing; Clubs: Petroleum; Calgary Golf & Country; Tucson Country; Home: 2561 N. Camino Valle, Verde, Tucson, Arizona; Office: 444-5th Ave. S.W., Calgary, Alta.

RICHARDS, Robert C., B.A.; executive; b. Ironton, Ohio, 15 Feb. 1930; s. William H. and Edna M.; e. Ironton High Sch.; Morehead Univ. B.A. 1956; m. Alwina A., 28 Aug. 1955; children: Craig, Judith, Margaret; PRES. A.M. INTERNATIONAL INC. OF CANADA ., since 1974; Salesman, Charleston, W. Va. 1958; Marketing Devel. Mgr., Cleveland, O. 1961; Asst. Br. Mgr., Washington, D.C. 1964; Br. Mgr., Buffalo, N.Y. 1966; Regional Mgr., Atlanta, Ga. 1969; served in U.S. Navy 1951-55; mem., Bd. Trade Metrop. Toronto; Candn. Business Equipment Mfrs. Assn.; Episcopalian; recreations: golf, hunting, fishing; Club: York Downs Golf & Country; Home: 18 Blencathra Hill, Cachet C.C. Gormley, Ont. L0H 1G0 Office: 165 Milner Ave., Scarborough, Ont. M1S 4G7

RICHARDS, Vincent Philip Haslewood, A.L.A., B.L.S.; librarian; b. Sutton Bonington, Notts., Eng. 1 Aug. 1933; s. Philip Haslewood and Alice Hilda (Moore) R.; e. Richmond & East Sheen Grammer Sch. London, Eng. 1949; Kingston Polytechnic Coll., Kingston-Upon-Thames, Surrey 1950; Army Sch. of Educ., Beaconsfield, Bucks., Teaching Cert. 1952; Ealing Coll. (Sch. of Librarianship) London, Eng. A.L.A. 1955; Univ. of Okla. B.L.S. 1966 (Bachelor of Lib. Studies); B.C. Cert. of Prof. Librarianship; m. Ann d. Frank Beardshall, Scarborough, Eng. 3 Apl. 1961; children: Mark, Christopher, Erika; DIR. OF LIBRARIES, EDMONTON PUB. LIBRARY 1977- ; Consultant, Manresa Coll. London, Eng.; St. Augustine's Abbey Lib., Ramsgate, Eng. and Westminster Abbey Lib., Mission, B.C. 1954-67; joined Brentford & Chiswick Pub. Libs., London, Eng holding various positions incl. Asst. Reference Librarian and Asst. Cataloguer 1949-56; Asst. Librarian, B.C. Pub. Lib. Comn, Peace River Br.; Dawson Creek, B.C. 1956-57; Asst. Dir. Fraser Valley Regional Lib. Abbotsford, B.C. 1957-67; Chief Librarian, Red Deer (Alta.) Coll. 1967-77, Bd of Govs. 1972-73, Pres. Faculty Assn. 1971-72; Dir. Red Deer Educ. TV Authority 1975-77; Vice Pres. Jeunesses Musicales; Adv. Bd. mem. Sch. Paperback Journ. N.Y. 1962-65; served with E. Surrey Regt. (Cadet Corps) 1948-49, Royal Sussex Regt. 1951,

Royal Army Educ. Corps 1952-53 Instr., Middle E. and Egypt 1952-53, R.A. (Territorial Reserve) London 1954-56; contrib. to prof. journs. librarianship in U.K., U.S. and Can.; Dir., Candn. Assn. Coll. & Univ. Libs. 1971-74; mem. Library Assn. (U.K.); Candn. Lib. Assn.: Lib. Assn. Alta.; Pacific Northwest Lib. Assn. (Secy. 1958); Council for Computerized Lib. Networks; Council of Adms. Large Urban Pub. Libs.; Fellowship of St. Alban & St. Sergius; Third Order of Mt. Carmel; P. Conservative; R. Catholic; recreations: reading, music, photography, travel, camping, cross-country skiing, sailing, kayaking; Club: Rotary; Home: 5103-109th Ave., Edmonton, Alta. T6A 1R9; Office: 7 Sir Winston Churchill Sq., Edmonton, Alta. T5J 2V4.

RICHARDSON, Arthur John Hampson, B.A.; b. Lennoxville, Que., 31 July 1916; s. Arthur Vernon, M.A., D.C.L., and Margaret Wynona (Thornton) R.; e. Bishop's Coll. Sch. 1924-32; Bishop's Univ., B.A. 1935; McGill Univ., 1935; m. Marie Gertrude, d. David Couture, Ste. Marie (Beauce), Que., 20 Dec. 1947; children: Marie Elizabeth Margaret, Peter David Arthur, John Andrew, Marie Suzanne; Preparing definitive study for Dept. of Environment (special assignment on arch. Quebec City); Chief, Map Div., Public Archives of Can., 1946-54; subsequently Chief, Nat. Hist. Sites Div., Secy. Hist. Sites & Monuments Bd. of Can. & Head, Arch. Hist. Sec., Dept. Indian & Northern Affairs; served in 2nd World War; Lieut. (S.B.), R.C.N.(R), 1942-46; Anglican; recreations: walking, swimming, reading; Home: Apt. 1908, 400 Stewart St., Ottawa, Ont. K1N 6L2

RICHARDSON, Cameron S., B.Com.; executive; b. Tuberose, Sask. 1932; e. Univ. of Alta. B.Com. 1953; SR. VICE PRES. FINANCE & DIR., ATCO LTD.; DIR. & DEPY CHRMN. CANADIAN UTILITIES LTD.; Assessor, Fed. Dept. Nat. Revenue 1953-59; joined ATCO Industries Ltd. 1959; Dir. Alberta Distillers Ltd.; Dir. Stampeder Football Club; mem. Council Financial Extves.; Chamber Comm.; Home: 2028 Uralta Rd. N.W., Calgary, Alta. T2N 4B4 Office: 1243 McKnight Blvd. N.E., Calgary, Alta. T2E 5T2.

RICHARDSON, George Taylor, B.Com., LL.D.; business executive; b. Winnipeg, Man., 1924; s. late Muriel (Sprague) and James Armstrong R.; e. Univ. of Man., B.Com. 1946; PRES. AND DIR., JAMES RICHARDSON & SONS LTD., since 1966; Gov., Hudson's Bay Co.; Sr. Partner, Richardson Securities of Canada; Chairman, James Richardson & Sons, Overseas Ltd.; Pioneer Grain Co. Ltd.; Richardson Terminals Ltd.; Richardson Securities Inc.; TopNotch Feeds Ltd.; Green Valley Fertilizer & Chemical Co. Ltd.; Buckerfield's Ltd.; Marine Pipeline Construction of Canada Ltd.; Pioneer Grain Terminal Ltd.; Vice-Pres. & mem. Extve. Comte., Candn. Imperial Bank of Commerce; Dir., Inco Ltd.; Hudson's Bay Oil and Gas Co. Ltd.; Home: Briarmeade, Lot 197, St. Mary's Road, St. Germain P.O., Manitoba R0G 2A0; Office: One Lombard Place, Winnipeg, Man. R3B 0Y1

RICHARDSON, Hon. James Armstrong, P.C., b. Winnipeg, Man., 1922; s. late James Armstrong and Muriel (Sprague) R.; e. St. John's-Ravenscourt Sch.; Queen's Univ., B.A.; m. Shirley Anne, d. John R. Rooper, Shamley Green, Surrey, Eng., 10 Sept. 1949; two s., three d.; NATIONAL CHAIRMAN, CANADIANS FOR ONE CANADA; Dir. James Richardson & Sons, Ltd.; Nat. Chrmn. Commonwealth Games Campaign; with James Richardsons & Sons, Ltd., 1945-68; Chrmn. and Chief Extve. Offr. 1966-68; el. to H. of C. for Winnipeg, S., g.e. June 1968; apptd. Min. without Portfolio, July 1968; Min. Supply & Services 1969-72; re-el. g.e. 1972; apptd. Min. of Nat. Defence 1972, resigned 1976 over constitutional language issue; crossed the floor of H. of C. to sit as Independent, 1978; served with R.C.A.F. as Pilot, 1943-45; Un. Church; recreations: sailing, golf; Home: 5209 Roblin Blvd., Winnipeg, Man. R3R 0G8

RICHARDSON, John Clifford, M.B.E. (1943), M.D., F.R.C.P.(C.) and (Lond.); physician; b. Owen Sound, Ont., 10 Jan. 1909; s. John Alfred and Blanche Evalorne (Hill) R.; e. Univ. of Toronto, M.D. 1932, B.Sc. 1935 (several undergrad. and one post scholar.); Post-Grad. Studies (Neurol.), London, Eng.; m. Winifred Frances Gertrude, d. Lieut.-Col. J. H. Murray, Brasted, Kent, Eng., 4 Aug. 1937; children: Peter, Timothy; Senior Phys., previous to 1938 held interne appts. and fellowships Toronto Gen. Hosp. and Dept. of Path., Univ. of Toronto; House Phys., Nat. Hosp. for Nervous Diseases, London, Eng., 1936-37; Toronto Gen. Hosp.; Prof. and Head, Dept. of Neurol., Univ. of Toronto, and Consultant in Neurol. to other hosps.; Emeritus Prof. of Neurology, Univ. of Toronto, 1976; Acad. of Med. (Chrmn. Neurol. and Psychiatry Sec., 1947-48); Assn. for Research in Nervous and Mental Diseases; Am. Neurol. Assn.; Past Pres., Candn. Neurol. Soc.; has contrib. several papers on neurol. subjects to med. journs.; Alpha Kappa Kappa; Alpha Omega Alpha; Protestant; recreations: golf, fishing; Clubs: Toronto Golf; York; Home: 19 Avondale Rd., Toronto, Ont. M4W 2R7; Office: 170 St. George St., Toronto, Ont. M5R 2R7

RICHARDSON, Robert J., B.A.Sc., Sc.D.; company director; b. North Bay, Ont. 17 Aug. 1928; s. Willard Richardson; e. North Bay Coll. Inst. & Vocational Sch. 1941-46; Univ. of Toronto, B.A.Sc. (Hons. Chem. Engn.) 1950; Mass. Inst. Tech., Sc.D. (Chem. Engn.) 1954; m.; two d., one s.; DIR. & SR. VICE PRESIDENT, E.I. duPONT de NEMOURS AND CO. 1980- ; Dir., Dupont Canada, Inc.; Toronto-Dominion Bank; Bell Canada Ltd.; Delaware Trust Co.; joined present Co. as Tech. Asst., Maitland Works, Ont. 1954; with Organic Chems. Dept., E.I. du Pont de Nemours & Co., Chamber Works, N.J. 1955; Research Supervisor, Du Pont of Canada Research Centre, Kingston, Ont. 1955; Tech. Mgr., Maitland Works 1957; Asst. Works Mgr., Kingston, Ont. 1962; Sales Mgr. for nylon indust. and tire yarn 1964 Montreal; Mgr., Research and Develop. Dept. 1965; Asst. Mgr., Textile Fibres Dept. 1965; Mgr., Textile Div. 1968; Dir., Chems. Group 1969; Operations and Strategic Planning Group 1970; Dir., Corp. Planning and el. mem. Co.'s Policy Comte. 1970; Extve. Vice-Pres. and Dir., 1971; Pres. and Chief Extve. Offr. 1972; Chrmn. of Bd. of Dirs. 1975; Vice-Pres. & Treas., E. I. du Pont de Nemours & Co. 1976; Vice-Pres. Finance 1977; Sr. Vice Pres. & Dir. 1980; mem., Candn.-Am. Comte; Chem. Inst. Can.; Am. Inst. Chem. Engrs.; Soc. Chem. Indust.; Recreations: sailing, curling, golf, canoeing, skiing; Home: Greenville, Delaware

RICHARDSON, Ross Frederick, B.A., F.S.A., A.I.A.; executive; b. Renfrew, Ont., 4 Feb. 1928; s. Garfield Newton and Mary Grace (MacLean) R.; e. Renfrew (Ont.) Dist. Coll. Inst., 1946; Queen's Univ., B.A. (Math. & Physics) 1950; m. Betty B.; children: Sheri Joan, Robert John, Paul Frederick; Sr. Vice-Pres & Dir. World-wide Life Insurance Operations, Hartford Insce. Group, 1980- ; Dir. Hartford-Europe, Abbey Life Group, and other Associated Cos., Empire Life Insurance Co. 1950-54; Maritime Life 1955-72, appts. as Sec., Supt. of Agencies, Asst. Gen. Mgr., Gen. Mgr., Pres. & C.E.O. (1969-72); has served various community projects; Fellow, Candn. Inst. Actuaries; Chart. Life Underwriters; recreations: golf, skiing; Clubs: Hendon Golf; Inst. of Dirs. (London); Home: 29 Western Ave., Branksom Park, Poole, Dorset, England; Office: 80 Holdenhurst Rd., Bournemouth, Eng.

RICHER, (François) Yvon, M.L.S.; librarian; b. Hull, Que. 2 July 1943; s. François and Yvette (Villeneuve) R.; e. Univ. of Ottawa B.A. 1964, B.L.S. 1965; Univ. of Toronto M.L.S. 1971; m. Suzanne d. Andre Naubert 4 Feb. 1967; one s. François-Yves; UNIV. LIBRARIAN, UNIV. OF OTTAWA 1978- ; Sr. Catloguer Laval Univ. Lib. 1965-68, Head Catalogue Dept. 1968-71, Head Processing Div.

1971-75; Asst. Dir. (Systems) Catalogue Br. Nat. Lib. Can. 1975-76; Assoc. Univ. Lib. Univ. of Ottawa 1976-78; mem. Candn. Lib. Assn.; Am. Lib. Assn.; CAIS; ASTED; Corp. Bibl. Profs. du Qué.; R. Catholic; Home: 40 Eastpark Dr., Ottawa, Ont. K1B 3Z9; Office: Morisset Library, 65 Hastey St., Ottawa, Ont. K1N 9A5.

RICHER, Jean H., B.A., B.Eng.; transportation executive; b. Montreal, Que., 24 March 1918; s. Georges and Alice (Blain) R.; e. Jean de Brébeuf Coll., Montreal; Univ. of Montreal, B.A.; McGill Univ., B.Eng.; m. Louise, d. late René Turcot, 1 June 1946; children: Claire, Suzanne, Hélène, Georges, Louis; CHRMN., CANAC CONSULTANTS LTD.; joined Quebec North Shore Paper Co., Baie Comeau, Que., 1946; with H.O., Montreal Tramways Co., 1946 becoming Extve. Asst. 1947, Supvr. of Timetables 1949 and Asst. Supt. of Transport, 1952; joined Brazilian Traction, Light and Power Co. Ltd., Rio de Janeiro, as Extve. Consultant on mass transport, 1955; apptd. Asst. to the Pres. and Gen. Mgr., Montreal Transport Comn., 1956; Dir. of Transport. Services, 1956; joined Candn. National Railways as Special Asst. to Vice Pres., St. Lawrence Region, 1962; Asst. Mgr., Montreal Area, 1963; Mgr., Champlain Area, 1963-64; Vice Pres., Passenger Sales & Services, 1965-67; Vice-Pres., St. Lawrence Region 1968-72; Extve. Vice Pres. System 1972-76; Sr. Vice-Pres., System 1976-77; served with RN and RCN 1943-46; Alderman, City Westmount since 1965-72; Pres., Westmount Mun. Assn. 1964; Centraide Montreal 1975-77; Pres., Montreal Symphony 1977-78; Pres., J.H. Richer Associés Ltée.; Dir., Imasco Ltd.; Guardian Ins. Co.; Montreal Life Ins.; Franki Can. Ltd.; Imasco Capital Mgmt. Inc. 2; Grand Trunk Corp.; Duluth Winnipeg and Pacific Railway; Central Vermont Railway; CN (France) Ltd.; Participaction Canada; Nat. Sports & Rec. Centre; Centraide, Montreal; Montreal Symphony; Mount Royal Ski Tows Inc.; mem., Bd. of Govs., McGill Univ.; mem. Corp. Engrs., Que.; R. Catholic; recreations: tennis, skiing, golf, reading, bridge, walking, sailing; Clubs: University; Montreal Indoor Tennis; Mount Royal Tennis; Mt. Bruno Country; Laurentian Golf and Country; Home: 1545 Docteur Penfield, Apt. 803, Montreal, Que. H3G 1C7; Office: P.O. Box 8100, Montreal, Que. H3C 3N4

RICHLER, Mordecai; writer; b. Montreal, Que., 27 Jan. 1931; s. Moses Isaac and Lily (Rosenberg) R.; m. Florence Wood, 27 July 1960; children: Daniel, Noah, Emma, Martha, Jacob; Awards and Hons. rec'd.: Can. Council Jr. Arts Fellowship, 1959-60 (renewed, 1960-61); Guggenheim Fellowship, creative writing, 1961-62; President's Medal, Univ. Western Ont. (Best Gen. Article publ. in Can., 1963); Can. Council Sr. Arts Fellowship, 1966-67; Paris Review Humour Prize for excerpt from "Cocksure," 1967; Publs.: (novels) "The Acrobats" 1954; "Son of a Smaller Hero" 1955; "Choice of Enemies" 1957; "The Apprenticeship of Duddy Kravitz" 1959; "The Incomparable Atuk" 1963; "Cocksure" 1968; "Hunting Tigers Under Glass" (essays and reports) 1968; "The Street Stories," 1969; "St. Urbain's Horseman" (novel) 1971 (Gov. Gen.'s Lit. Award 1972); "Jacob Two-Two Meets the Hooded Fang" (Ruth Schwartz children's book award) 1976; "Joshua Then and Now," 1980; Editor, "New Canadian Writing", 1969; (anthols.) Points of View, a "Spectator" Anthol.; Modern Occasions, "Best American Short Stories" 1963, Great Canadian Writing, Canadian Short Stories, A Book of Canadian Short Stories, Ten for Wednesday Night: "The First Five Years", a Tamarack Anthol.; (films) No Love for Johnnie, Life at the Top; Awarded for Screenplay of "The Apprenticeship of Duddy Kravitz": Amer. Screenwriter' Guild, Best Comedy; ACTRA, best Cddn. Screen play; Academy Award Nomination, best comedy screenplay; Golden Bear Award, Berlin Film Festival 1975; stories, essays, criticism regularly in English and Am. mags.; was Writer-in-Residence at Sir George Williams Univ., Montreal 1968-69 and apptd. same post at Carleton Univ. 1972; Appt. Editorial Bd., Book of the Month Club, N.V. 1977; Address: c/o McClelland & Stewart, 25 Hollinger Rd., Toronto, Ont. M4B 3G2

RICHMOND, Anthony Henry, B.Sc., M.A., Ph.D., F.R.S.C.; educator; b. Ilford, Essex, Eng. 8 June 1925; s. late Henry James and late Ellen Bertha (Hankin) R.; e. Co. High Sch. Ilford 1943; London Sch. of Econ. B.Sc. (Econ.) 1949); Univ. of Liverpool M.A. 1951; Univ. of London (external student) Ph.D. 1964; m. Freda d. late Owen John Williams 29 March 1952; child: Glenys Catriona; PROF. OF SOCIOL. YORK UNIV. 1965- , Dir. Inst. for Behavioural Research there; Prop., Anthony H. and F. Richmond, Social Research Consultants; Research Offr. Univ. of Liverpool 1949-52; Lectr. Univ. of Edinburgh 1952-63; Reader, Bristol Coll. of Science and Technol. 1963-65; came to Can. 1965; Visiting Prof. Univ. of B.C. 1960-61; Univ. of Sussex 1970; Australian Nat. Univ. 1971, 1977; Univ. of Wales 1978; rec'd various Can. Council and SSHRCC Fellowships and Awards; served with Friends Ambulance Unit 1943-46; author "Colour Prejudice in Britain" 1954, 2nd ed. 1971; "The Colour Problem" 1955, revised ed. 1961; "Post-War Immigrants in Canada" 1967, reprinted 1970; "Migration and Race Relations in an English City" 1973; co-author "Immigrant Integration and Urban Renewal in Toronto" 1973; "Factors in the Adjustment of Immigrants and their Descendants", 1980; ed. with Introduction "Readings in Race and Ethnic Relations" 1972; co-ed. "Internal Migration: The New World and the Third World" 1976; author or co-author book chapters, research monographs, papers in refereed journs.; mem. ed. bds. various journs.; mem. Candn. Sociol. & Anthrop. Assn.; Candn. Population Soc.; Internat. Union for Scient. Study Population Internat. Sociol. Assn.; Society of Friends; recreations: photography, walking, classical music; Home: 22 Almond Ave., Thornhill, Ont. L3T 1L1; Office: 4700 Keele St., Downsview, Ont. M3J 2R6.

RICHMOND, John Russell, R.C.A.; artist; writer; b. Toronto, Ont. 25 Oct. 1926; s. John Melville and Sylvia Elizabeth (Newberry) R.; e. Frankland Pub. Sch. Toronto 1939; Fergus (Ont.) High Sch. 1944; Ont. Coll. of Art 1947; m. Lorraine Joy Surcouf 21 Oct. 1949; children: Leigh Anne, Victoria Louise, Stephanie Marie, John Stuart Grant, Julius John Martin; mem. Faculty, Ont. Coll. of Art 1975- ; estbd. Upper Canada Scribble Works; Publisher "Gambit" 1958-63; author "Tearful Tour of Toronto's Riviera" 1961; "Around Toronto" 1969; "Sex Stuff" 1970; "Discover Ontario" 1974; "Discover Toronto" 1976; "Illustrated Enquiry into the RIGHT/LEFT Hemisphere" 1981; columnist "Discover Ontario" 1969-79; various articles, reviews mags.; rec'd Can. Council Grant 1966, 1968; Ont. Arts Council Grant 1978, 1980; Dir. Latcham Gallery, Stouffville, Ont. 1980-81; R. Catholic; mem. Ont. Soc. Artists; (retired) Candn. Soc. Painters in Watercolour (retired) (Treas., Vice Pres., Pres. 1962); Exec. Council, Royal Can. Academy 1980-81; recreations: skiing, swimming, farming, building; Address: R.R.1, Claremont, Ont. L0H 1E0.

RICKER, William Edwin, M.A., Ph.D., LL.D., D.Sc., F.R.S.C. (1956); biologist; ret. public servant; b. Waterdown, Ont., 11 Aug. 1908; s. Harry Edwin Benson and Rebecca Helena (Rouse) R.; e. Coll. Inst., North Bay, Ont.; Univ. of Toronto, B.A. 1930, M.A. 1931, Ph.D. 1936; D.Sc. Manitoba 1969; LL.D. Dalhousie University 1973; married Marion Torrance, daughter late John Cardwell, 30 March 1935; children: Karl Edwin, John Fraser, Eric William, Angus Clemens; Scient. Assistant, Biol. Bd. of Canada, 1931-37; Junior Scientist, International Pacific Salmon Fisheries Commission, New Westminster, B.C., 1938; Asst. Assoc. and Prof. of Zool., Indiana Univ., 1939-50; Editor, Fisheries Research Bd. of Canada, 1950-62; Acting Chairman, Fisheries Research Bd. of Can. 1963-64; Chief Scientist, 1965-73; received Wilflife Society Award for the "outstanding publication in aquatic wild-

life ecology and management", 1953-54 and 1959; Baldi Mem. Lectr., International Cong. of Limnology, Helsinki, 1956; Publications: (monographs) "Stoneflies of southwestern British Columbia", 1943; "Systematic Studies in Plecoptera" 1952; "Handbook of computations for Biological Statistics of Fish Populations", 1958; "Russian-Eng. Dictionary for Students of Fisheries and Aquatic Biology," 1973; "Computation and Interpretation of Biological Statistics of Fish Populations", 1975; numerous papers contrib. to scient. journs. and bulls.; mem., Am. Assn. Advanc. Science; Am. Fisheries Soc. (Award of Merit 1969); Am. Ornithol. Union; Candn. Soc. of Zool.; Candn. Soc. of Environmental Biol.; Am. Soc. of Ichthyols. & Herpetols.; Am. Soc. of Limnol. & Oceanography (Pres. 1959); Am. Soc. of Naturalists; Arctic Inst. N. Am.; Biometric Soc.; Ecological Soc. Am.; Entomol. Soc. of B.C.; Entomol. Soc. Can.; Internat. Assn. for Limnol.; Soc. for Systematic Zool.; Soc. for Study of Evolution; The Wildlife Soc.; Wilson Ornithol. Soc.; awarded Flavelle Medal of Royal Soc. Can. 1969; recreations: hiking, golf; Club: Explorers (N.Y.); Home: 3052 Hammond Bay Rd., Nanaimo, B.C. V9T 1E2

RICKERD, Donald, Q.C., B.A., M.A.; foundation executive; b. Smiths Falls, Ont. 8 Nov. 1931; s. Harry and E. Mildred (Sheridan) R.; e. Queen's Univ. B.A. 1953; St. Andrews Univ. Scot. 1951-52; Oxford Univ. B.A., 1955, M.A. 1963; grad. of Osgoode Hall Law Sch. 1959; m. Julie d. John Rekai 1968; one s. Christopher Robert John; PRESIDENT, DONNER CANADIAN FOUNDATION since 1968; Pres. W. H. Donner Foundation Inc. New York; read law with Fasken & Calvin; called to Bar of Ont. 1959; law practice Fasken & Calvin 1959-61; York Univ. 1961-68, Registrar and Secy. of Senate, Master-Winters Coll., Asst. Prof. Faculty of Adm. Studies; mem. Comn. inquiry RCMP 1977; Chrmn. Ont. Coll. of Art; mem. Bd. Central Hosp. Toronto; mem. Law Soc. Upper Can.; recreations: tennis, boating; Clubs: University; United Oxford & Cambridge Universities (London, Eng.); Home: 21 Elm Ave., Toronto, Ont. M4W 1M9; Office: (P.O. Box 122), Toronto-Dominion Centre, Toronto, Ont. M5K 1H1

RIDDELL, John Evans, B.Eng., M.Sc., Ph.D., F.R.S.C., F.G.A.C. F.G.S.A.; geologist; b. Montreal, Que., 21 May 1913; s. Clarence Percival and Mary Marguerite (Evans) R.; e. Westmount High Sch. (Sr. Matric. 1931); McGill Univ., B.Eng. (Mining) 1935, M.Sc. (Geol.) 1936, Ph.D. (Geol.) 1953; m. Helen Joan, d. late Dr. Edward Archibald, 8 Feb. 1939; children: John, Joanne, Michael, Edward, Christie; PRESIDENT, INTERNATIONAL GEOCHEMICAL ASSOCIATES LTD.; Surveyor, Union Corp., Johannesburg, S.A., 1936-38; Field Engr., Dome Mines Ltd., N.W.T., 1939; Special Lectr., Dept. of Geol., Univ. of Sask., 1947-49; Asst. Prof., Dept. of Geol. Sciences, McGill Univ., 1950-56; Assoc. Prof., 1956-58; Chrmn., Dept. of Geol., Carleton Univ., 1958-61; served in 2nd World War with R.C.A.F. 1940-45; F.O., Navig. Instr., 1940-43; Flight Lieut., Navig., Bomber Command, 1943-45; Mentioned in Despatches (1945); mem., Candn. Inst. Mining & Metall.; Assn. Expl. Geochem; Am. Inst. Min. and Met. Eng. Sigma Xi; Phi Kappa Pi; Anglican; recreations: skiing, sailing; Address: Box 220, Bridgetown, N.S. B0S 1C0

RIDDELL, William Andrew, O.C. (1974), M.Sc., Ph.D., L.L.D., F.C.I.C.; b. Hamiota, Man., 6 July 1905; s. Thomas and Jane Taylor (Rankin) R.; e. Univ. of Manitoba, B.A. 1925, B.Sc. 1926; Univ. of Sask., M.Sc. 1928; Research Fellow, Leland Stanford Jr. Univ., Ph.D. 1931; m. Beryl Evelyn, d. late Frederick James Oaten, 21 Aug. 1931; two d. Catherine Jane, Mary Margaret; Chrmn., Sask. Arts Bd., 1950-65; mem., Nat. Bd., Candn. Centenary Council; Councillor, Chem. Inst. of Can. (1953); joined staff of Univ. of Sask. as Instr., 1926; Lectr., 1928; Asst. Prof. of Chem., Regina Coll., 1931-36; Research Chemist, Fisheries Research Br. of Can., 1936-38; Prov.

Analyst, Sask., 1938-50; Dir., Divn. of Labs., Sask. Dept. of Pub. Health, 1942-50; Dean and Prof. Chem., Regina Coll., Univ. of Sask., 1950-62; apptd. Principal 1962 Regina Campus, Univ. of Sask. (ret. 1973); Chrmn., Bd. of Nursing Educ. since 1977; Treas., Wascana Centre Authority; mem., Chrmn. S. Sask. Hosp. Centre Bd. 1971-76; Extve. mem., Sask. Research Council; Fellow, Am. Assn. Advanc. Science; Chrmn., Health Sci. Library Council, Regina since 1977; United Church; recreations: music, cabinet work; Club: Gyro (Past Pres.); Address: 2124 Dufferin Rd., Regina, Sask.

RIDLEY, John B., O.C.; executive; b. Toronto, Ont., 20 May, 1898; s. late James S. M. and Isabella (Bryson) R.; e. Univ. of Toronto Schs. 1916; Univ. Coll., Univ. of Toronto 1920; secondly, Norma Livingston Hallman; Dir., Grafton Group Ltd.; Grafton's Ltd.; Grafton-Fraser Ltd.; Maher Shoes Ltd.; Chrmn., Quetico Foundation; joined A. E. Ames & Co. Ltd. 1920; Extve. Vice-Pres. and Dir. on retirement 1958; mem. Adv. Bd., Un. Community Fund, Toronto; Vice-Pres., Art Gallery of Ont.; Vice-Pres., Conservation Council of Ont. 1967; Pres., Investment Dealers' Assn. Can. 1949-50; Prov. Ont. Extve. Council, Boy Scouts Can. 1951-57, 1963; Founding Chrmn. Adv. Bd., Scarborough Gen. Hosp.; Vice Chrmn., Extve. Council (1960) and Chrmn., Educ. Comte. (1961-63), Candn. Chamber Comm.; Psi Upsilon; R. Catholic; recreations: golf, gardening; Clubs: National; University; Granite; Lambton Golf & Country; Homes: 21 Dale Ave., Apt. 544, Toronto, Ont. M4W 1K3

RIECKHOFF, Klaus Ekkehard, M.Sc., Ph.D.; educator; b. Weimar, Germany, 8 Feb. 1928; s. Herbert J. and Gertrud (Nagel) R.; e. High Sch., Abitur 1946, Weimar, Germany; Karlsruhe Univ., math. & physics 1947-49; Univ. of B.C., B.Sc. 1958, M.Sc. 1959, Ph.D. (Physics) 1962; m. Marianne Neder, 30 Dec. 1949; children: Bernhard A., Claudia A., Cornelia A.; PROF. OF PHYSICS, SIMON FRASER UNIV. since 1966 and Assoc. Dean of Grad. Studies there 1973-76; Research Staff mem., IBM-Research Lab., San Jose, Cal. 1962-65 (Research Consultant there 1967-69, Visiting Scientist 1976-77); joined present Univ. as Assoc. Prof. of Physics 1965, Acting Dean of Science 1966-67, mem. of Senate 1965-81; mem. Bd. of Govs. 1978-81; Visiting Professor, Inst. of Applied Physics, Karlsruhe Univ., Germany, 1969-70; author or co-author of over 40 research papers in areas of Solid State Physics, Molecular Physics and Nonlinear Optics published in various scient. journs. and conf. proceedings; mem. Candn. Assn. Physicists; Am. Phys. Soc.; N.Y. Acad. Science; Am. Assn. Advanc. Science; W. Spectroscopy Assn. (Extve. 1964-68); Candn. Assn. Univ. Teachers; Aircraft Owners & Pilots Assn. (U.S.A.) Home: 212 Newdale Court, N. Vancouver, B.C. V7N 3H1; Office: Burnaby, B.C. V5A 1S6

RIEDEL, Bernard E., C.D., B.Sc., M.Sc., Ph.D.; university dean; b. Provost, Alta., 25 Sept. 1919; s. Martin Ewald and Naomi Edna (Klingaman) R.; e. Fairview (Alta.) Rural High Sch., 1937; Univ. of Alta., B.Sc. (Pharm.) 1943, M.Sc. (Pharm.) 1949; Univ. of W. Ont., Ph.D. (Biochem.) 1953; Inst. of Nuclear Studies, Tenn., Course in Radioisotope Technol. 1956; m. Julia Constance, d. late Dr. William Clare McClurg, 5 March 1944; children: Gail Lynne (Mrs. W. Kinloch), Dwain Edward, Barry Robert; DEAN AND PROF., FACULTY OF PHARM. SCIENCES, UNIV. OF BRIT. COLUMBIA, since 1967; Coord. of Health Sciences, 1977; Asst. Prof. of Pharm., Univ. of Alta., 1946-50, Assoc. Prof. 1953-58, Prof. 1959; Extve. Asst. to Vice Pres. 1961; Dept. of Health Research Fellow, Atomic Energy of Can. Ltd., Chalk River, summer 1953; summer Research Scientist, Suffield Exper. Stn., Defence Research Bd., 1957; served with RCAF during World War II; Navig.-Bombardier with Coastal Command; rank Flying Offr. on discharge; Univ. of Alta. Sqdn. Support Offr. 1949-50; C.O. Univ. of Alta, Sqdn. with rank Wing Commdr. 1954-67; apptd. to

Med. Research Council 1969; Extve. Edmonton Region, Boy Scouts of Can.; mem. Bd. of Dirs., Assn. Univs. and Colls. of Can.; mem. Bd. of Dirs., Assn. Univs. and Colls. of Can.; rec'd. Gold Medal in Pharm. 1943; Lt. Gov.'s Gold Medal for Proficiency 1943; Centennial Medal 1967; contrib. over 28 articles to scient. journs.; mem., B.C. Coll. of Pharm. (Councillor); Alta. Pharm. Assn.; Candn. Pharm. Assn.; Assn. Faculties Pharm. Can. (Chrmn. 1959 and 1969); Candn. Biochem. Soc.; Pharmacol. Soc. Can.; Am. Assn. Advanc. Sci.; Am. Chem. Soc., Med. Chem.; Can. Assn. Univ. Teachers; Assn. Deans Pharm. Can.; Liberal; Protestant; recreations: golf, curling; Clubs: Vancouver Curling; University; Point Grey Golf & Country; Home: 8394 Angus Dr., Vancouver, B.C. V6P 5L2

RIEDL, W.R., B.Com., M.B.A.; stockbroker; e. Univ. of B.C. B.Com. 1963; York Univ. M.B.A. 1969; Chart. Financial Analyst; CHRMN. AND CHIEF EXTVE. OFFR., ALFRED BUNTING & CO. LTD.; Dir. Lighthouse Resources Inc.; Oil Analyst present co. 1967, Dir. 1968, Vice Pres. 1968, Extve. Vice Pres. 1970, Pres. 1977, Dir. and Chrmn. of Bd. 1978; Founding Pres. Candn. Assn. Petrol. Invest. Analysts; mem. Bd. Trade Metrop. Toronto; Full Gospel Business Fellowship Internat.; Elder, Lawrence Park Community Ch.; recreations: tennis, squash, skiing; Clubs: Adelaide; National; Home: 176 Golfdale Rd., Toronto, Ont. M4H 2B9.

RIEGER, Budd Huntington; industrialist; b. Wallace, S. Dakota, 2 Sept. 1908; e. Univ. of Man.; Univ. of Minn. (Chem. Engn.); m. Christine, d. late Dr. William Turnbull, Winnipeg, Man., 1936; children: William Arthur, John Charles, Martha Ann; Vice Chairman, Consumers Glass Co. Ltd.; Dir., Candn. Corporate Management Ltd.; Chrmn., Canadian Dominion Leasing Ltd.; United Church; recreations: fishing, hunting; Clubs: York; Rosedale Golf; Toronto Badminton & Racquet; Mount Royal (Montreal); Toronto Hunt; Home: 22 Brendan Road, Toronto, Ont. M4G 2X1; Office: Suite 2080, Commerce Court W., (P.O. Box 131) Toronto, Ont. M5L 1E6

RIEL, Maurice, C.R., B.A., LL.B.; avocat; n. St-Constant, Co. Laprairie, Que., 3 avril, 1922; f. Ubald et Robertine (Charron) R.; e. école paroissiale, St-Constant; Coll. Ste-Marie, Montréal, Que.; Coll. St-Jean, St-Jean, Que.; Coll. Ste-Croix, Montréal, B.A. 1940; Univ. de Montréal, LL.B. 1944; ép. Laurence f. Louis-Philippe Cloutier, St-Jean, 10 mars 1945; enfants: Louise, François, Hélène; CONSEIL ET PARTENAIRE, STIKEMAN, ELLIOTT, TAMAKI, MERCIER & ROBB; mem. du Senat du Canada en 1973; Admis au Barreau du Qué., 1945; nommé C.R. 1958; Admin. Candn. Liquid Air Ltd.; The Candn. Provident-General Ins.; The Candn. Provident-Life Ins.; Cegelec Can. Inc.; Cegelec Industries Inc.; Degrémont Infilco Ltée; Dumez (Can.) Ltée; Food Services Ltd. and subsidiaries; Laboratoire d'Hydraulique LaSalle Ltée.; Marcel Didier (Can.) Ltée; PPG Industries Can.; The Royal Trust Group; Saft Batteries Ltée.; Voyages-Missions Ltée.; William Houde Ltée.; Compagnie Européene d'Accumulateurs CEAC; mem. Soc. des Amis de Colette; Chambre de Comm. Française au Can.; Commanderie de Bordeaux; Union Internat. des Advocats; Libéral; Catholique; récreations: arts, vie de campagne; Clubs: Cercle Universitaire d'Ottawa; Mount Royal; Résidence: 2 Westmount Sq., Westmount, Québec; H3Z 2S4 Bureau: Suite 3900, 1155 Dorchester Blvd. West, Montréal, P.Q. H3B 3V2.

RIESE, Karl Theodore, M.D., F.R.C.S.(C); b. Selkirk, Man. 31 Jan. 1930; s. Henry B. and Helene (Schilling) R.; e. Univ. of Man., M.D. 1954, F.R.C.S. 1958; Dipl. Am. Bd. of Surg. 1963; m. Carmel M., d. Marc Regnier; Prof. Of Surgery, Univ. Of Manitoba and Vice Pres., Medical, St. Boniface Gen. Hosp.; Office: 409 Tache, Winnipeg, Man. R2H 2A6

RIESE, Laure E., M.A., Ph.D.; university professor; b. Neuchatel, Switzerland, 28 Feb. 1910; d. Frédéric and Laure (Vuilleumier) R.; e. Secondary Sch., Switzerland; Dipl. d'Etude Sup.; Dipl. de l'Inst. de Phonétique (La Sorbonne); came to Canada, 1928; Univ. of Toronto, B.A. 1933, M.A. 1935, Ph.D. 1946; PROF. OF FRENCH, VICTORIA UNIV.; and Assoc. Ed., Modern Drama and Prof. at the Grad. Centre for Study of Drama; Radio and TV Broadcaster for the French Sch.; Publications: "L'Ame de la Poesie Canadienne Francaise" (anthology); "Les Salons Littéraires féminins du Second Empire à nos jours" (awarded Broquette — Gonin Lit. Prize from L'Acad. Française, 1962); "Un peu de nouveau"; has written many articles and reviews for French Canadian and French American journals; Offr. d'Acad. Francaise, 1946; Chrmn., Cdn. Swiss Cultural Assn.; Gov., Fed. of Alliances française Can.; Ont. Modern Language Teacher's Assn.; mem., la Soc. des Gens de Lettres de France; Offr. d'Instruction Publique; Bd. of Theatre Plus; Chevalier de la Légion d'Honneur (France) 1971; Pres. d'Honneur, Alliance Française; Protestant; recreation: travelling; Home: 103 Avenue Rd., Apt. 912, Toronto, Ont. M5R 2G9

RIGAULT, André Albert L., L.ès L.; university professor; b. Chambourcy, France, 6 June 1922; s. Camille V. and Pierrette J. (Maison) R.; e. Faculty of Letters, Univ. of Paris (1944-49), L.ès L. 1947; Dipl. d'Etudes Supérieures (1948); Dipl. de Phonétique (1949); m. Odette S., d. Jean Bruet, Bandol, France, 1948; children: Elisabeth, Olivier, Geneviève, Véronique, Marie-Clotilde, Antoine; PROF., GEN. PHONOLOGY, McGILL UNIV. and Chrmn. Department Linguistics 1966-71; Dir., Phonetics Research Lab. there, since 1963, Lang. Lab., 1961-69; Asst. Prof., Inst. of Phonetics, Sorbonne, Paris, 1948-49; Asst. Prof., Dept. of Romance Lang., McGill Univ., 1949-61, Assoc. Prof. 1961-65, Prof. 1965; Dir., McGill French Summer Sch., 1954-61; Research Fellow, Canada Council, 1959-60, 1971-72, 1978-79; Visiting Lectr., Univs. Besançon, Rennes, Rabat, Prague, Bucharest, Michigan; Chevalier, Légion d'honneur (France); Officer, Ordre des Palmes Academiques (France); mem., Société de Linguistique de Paris; Canadian Linguistic Association (President 1970-72); Secy. Gen., 7th Internat. Cong. Phonetic Scs., Montreal 1972; Linguistic Society of Am.; Pres. Assn. Prof. Français au Can. 1969-75; mem. Hon. Comte., 8th Internat. Cong. Phonetic Scs. Leeds, Eng. 1975 Assn. Phonétique Internationale; Internat. Permanent Council of Phonetic Sciences; Internat. Linguistic Assn.; Hon. mem. Council Phonetic Soc. Japan 1972; Chrmn. Comité-Inter-union. Recherches Linguistiques sur le Français au Canada, 1964-69; Hon. Vice-Pres., Internat. Soc. of Phonetic Sci. 1979; engaged in research on the analysis synthesis of speech, Univ. of Lund (Sweden) and Univ. of Edin., 1959-60; Royal Inst. of Technol. (Stockholm) 1972, 1979; author of seven books and 40 papers on linguistics; Office: Dept. of Linguistics, 1001 Sherbrooke, W., Montreal, Que. H3A 1G5

RILEY, Anthony William, D.Phil., F.R.S.C.; educator; b. Radcliffe on Trent, Eng. 23 July 1929; s. late Cyril Frederick and late Winifred Mary (White) R.; e. West Bridgford Grammar Sch. Notts., Eng. 1947; Univ. of Manchester B.A. 1952; Univ. of Tübingen D.Phil. 1958; m. Maria Theresia d. late Karl Walter, Schwäbisch Gmünd, Germany 16 July 1955; children: Christopher Karl Cyril, Katherine Mary, Angela Theresia; PROF. OF GERMAN LANG. AND LIT., QUEEN'S UNIV. 1968- ; Lektor, Univ. of Tübingen 1957-59, 1960-62; Asst. Lectr. Queen Mary Coll. Univ. of London 1959-60; Asst. Prof. of German present Univ. 1962, Assoc. Prof. 1965, Head of German Lang. & Lit. 1967-76; Distinguished Visitor, Univ. of B.C. 1980; Lansdowne Visitor, Univ. of Victoria, B.C. 1981; served with Brit. Army (Intelligence Corps) 1947-49; author "Elisabeth Langgässer Bibliographie mit Nachlassbericht" 1970; co-ed. "The Master Mason's House" 1976; ed. "Der Oberst und der Dichter/Die Pilge-

rin Aetheria" 1978; "Der unsterbliche Mensch/Der Kampf mit dem Engel" 1980; "Jagende Rosse/Der schwarze Vorhang und andere frühe Erzählwerke" 1981; "Wadzeks Kampf mit der Dampfturbine" 1982; numerous articles learned journs.; mem. Candn. Assn. Univ. Teachers German (Vice Pres. 1973-75, Pres. 1975-76); Humanities Assn. Can.; Candn. Comparative Lit. Assn.; Modern Lang. Assn. Am.; Thomas Mann-Gesellschaft; Deutsche Schillergesellschaft; Internat. Vereinigung für Germanische Sprach- und Literaturwissenschaft; recreations: gardening, oenology; Home: 108 Queen Mary Rd., Kingston, Ont. K7M 2A5; Office: Kingston, Ont. K7L 3N6.

RILEY, Conrad Sanford, M.B.E.; executive; b. Winnipeg, Man., 19 Jan. 1916; s. Conrad Stephenson and Jean Isabel (Culver) R.; e. Gordon Bell High Sch., Winnipeg; Univ. of Man.; m. Mary Frances Myrtle, d. Gordon Harold Aikins, 4 May 1940; children: Conrad Sanford Jr., Dennis Albert; CHRMN. OF BD., CANADIAN INDEMNITY CO. since 1970; Pres. and Dir., United Canadian Shares Ltd.; Dir., Wickett and Craig Ltd.; Dir., Canadian Imperial Bank of Commerce; Pres., Insurance and General Agency Ltd., Winnipeg, 1946-52; served with RCA 1940-45, European Theatre; rank Capt.; recreations: flying, hunting, fishing; Clubs: Manitoba; St. Charles Country; Winnipeg Winter; Toronto; Home: 1001 Wellington Cres., Winnipeg, Man. R3M 0A7; Office: 1661 Portage Ave., Winnipeg, Man. R3J 3V8

RILEY, Norman; company executive; b. Toronto, Ont., 11 May 1916; s. George and Isabella (Brahm) R.; e. Oakwood Coll., 1928-33; Tor. Normal Sch., 1933-34; m. Lillian, d. William Marshall, Willowdale, Ont., 14 Oct. 1939; children: Richard, Douglas, Kathryn Ann; CHRMN OF THE BOARD AND C.E.O. NACAN PRODUCTS LTD., Nov. 1979- ; Past Pres. Nacan Prod. Ltd., 1966-79; Pres., LePages Ltd.; Lab. Tech. with Dr. F. A. J. Zeidler, Research and Analytical Lab., 1934-39; joined O'Cedar of Can. Ltd. as Chemist, 1939; promoted Plant Mgr., Sales Mgr., Vice-Pres. Sales, resigning as Vice-Pres. and Asst. Gen. Mgr., 1953; joined present firm as Mgr., Retail Sales, 1953; Mgr., Montreal Div., 1957; promoted to Vice-Pres., 1958; el. a Dir., 1960; Pres. (1968-69) Packaging Assn. Can.; Pres., Adhesives and Sealant, Mfrs. Assn. of Can. Conservative; Anglican; recreations: golf, music, spectator sports; Clubs: Toronto Bd. of Trade; St. George's Golf & Country; Sales Research; Home: RR#1, Inglewood, Ont. L0N 1K0; Office: 50 West Drive, Bramalea, Ont. L6T 2J4

RILEY, Ronald Thomas, B.E., M.B.A.; executive; b. Toronto, Ont., 28 Feb. 1935; s. Ronald T. and Margaret M. (Black) R.; e. Bishop's Coll. Sch., Lennoxville, Que.; McGill Univ., B.E. (Mech.) 1956; Univ. of Pa., M.B.A. 1959; m. Jessie M. Fulcher, 27 Sept. 1963; children: Ronald T. Jr., Michael G., Gillian M.; VICE PRES., ADMIN., CANADIAN PACIFIC LTD., since 1976; Chrmn. and Dir., Canadian Pacific Transport Co. Ltd.; Chrmn. and Dir., Chateau Insurance Co.; CanPac Internat. Freight Services Ltd.; Pres. and Dir., Cascade Pipe Line Limited; Director, CP Consulting Services; CP Securities; Provident Properties Limited; CanPac Terminals Ltd.; Chep Canada Inc.; Arion Ins. Co. Ltd.; Argus Corp. Ltd.; Hollinger Argus Ltd.; Dominion Stores Ltd.; joined Accounting Department present Company, Montreal, 1961; became Supervising Analyst; Supervisor Product Research, Traffic Research Dept., Montreal, 1964; Mgr., Freight Devel.; E. Region, CP Rail, Toronto 1965, Alta. 1966; Asst. Gen. Mgr., Pacific Region, Vancouver, 1968; Regional Mgr., Operation & Maintenance, Pacific Region, 1969; Dir. Corporate Planning, Montreal, 1971; Vice Pres., Transport & Telecommunications, 1972; Clubs: University; Mount Bruno Golf; Hillside Tennis; Office: Windsor Station, Montreal, Que. H3C 3E4

RIMROTT, Friedrich Paul Johannes, M.A.Sc., Ph.D., Dr.Ing. F.E.I.C.; engineer; b. Halle, Germany 4 Aug.

1927; s. Ernst Georg Johannes and Margarete (Hofmeister) R.; came to Canada 1952; e. Martin Luther Univ. 1946; Univ. Karlsruhe, Dipl.Ing. 1951; Univ. of Toronto M.A.Sc. 1955; Penn. State Univ., Ph.D. 1958; Ecole Polytech. Montreal 1960; Tech. Hochschule Darmstadt, Dr.Ing. 1961; m. Elsa Doreen, d. late Robert Henry McConnell 7 April 1955; children: Karla, Robert, Kira, Elizabeth-Ann; PROFESSOR OF MECH. ENGN., UNIV. OF TORONTO since 1967; Dir. of Schs., Deutsche Sprachschulen (Metro Toronto) Inc.; Asst. Prof. Penn. State Univ. 1958; Asst. Prof. Univ. of Toronto 1960, Assoc. Prof. 1962; Visiting Prof., Wien 1969, Hannover 1970, Bochum 1971, Wuppertal 1978; Consultant Univ. de la Habana 1972; Founding Chrmn. Candn. Congs. Applied Mechs.; Candn. Consultative Council on Multiculturalism; Candn. Soc. Mech. Engn. (Pres.); Candn. Metric Assn. (Pres.); Verein Deutscher Ingenieure; Gesellschaft für Angewandte Math. und Mech. (Dir.); Am. Acad. Mech.; German-Candn. Hist. Assn. (Vice-Pres.); author of over 50 scholarly papers in mech. and mech. engn., books "Was du ererbt" (with W. Eichenlaub); "Mechanics of Solid State" (with J. Schwaighafer); "Theoretical and Applied Mechanics" (with B. Tabarrok); Sigma Xi; Lutheran; Home: 6 Thurgate Cres., Thornhill, Ont. L3T 4G3; Office: 5 King's College Rd., Toronto, Ont.

RINFRET, Hon. Gabriel Edouard, P.C. (Can.) 1949; b. St. Jerome, Que., 12 May 1905; s. Rt. Hon. Thibaudeau and Georgine (Rolland) R.; e. Cote des Neiges Coll.; Petit Seminaire, Montreal; Ste.-Marie Coll.; McGill Univ.; Univ. of Montreal, LL.L.; LL.D. (U.B.C.) m. 12 Nov. 1929; children: Claude, Andre; COUNSEL, PEPIN, LETOURNEAU, ROY & ASSOC. since Aug. 1980; formerly practised with firm, Campbell, Weldon, McFadden and Rinfret, Montreal, Quebec; Vice Pres., Conservatoire Lassalle; Advocate 1928; cr. K.C. 1943; Treas., Jeune Barreau, Montreal, 1930; Pres., Jeunesse Liberale, Que., 1935; Secy., Comn. of Inquiry on Electricity Conditions in Que. 1936, and on Tax Problems in Que., 1936; Extve. Secy., Newsprint Adm. and Legal Advisor, Pulp and Paper Adm., W.P.T.B., during 2nd World War; 1st el. to H. of C. for Outremont in Lib. interest, g.e. 1945; re-el. 1949; Postmaster of Can. 1949; resigned Feb. 1952; Justice, Que. Court of Appeal 1952-77; Chief Justice of Que. 1978-80; Roman Catholic; Home: 121 Melbourne Ave., Town of Mount Royal, Que. H3P 1G3; Office: 500 Place D'Armes, Montreal, Que. H2Y 3S3

RINFRET, Pierre André, M.B.A., Dr. pol. economy, LL.D.; financial consultant; economist; b. Montreal, Que., 1 Feb. 1924; s. Alfred William and Laura (Chartrand) R.; e. Univ. of Maine, Cert. of E.E. 1943; N.Y. Univ., B.S. (Comm.) 1948; N.Y. Univ. Grad. Sch. Business Adm., M.B.A. 1949 (N.Y. Univ. School of Comm., Econ. Fellow 1947-48, Financial Fellow 1948); Fulbright Fellowship to France, 1949; University of Dijon, Dr. pol. economy 1950; Pepperdine University LL.D. 1973; on Fac. of New York Univ. Graduate School of Business Admin., 1952-59; Visiting Lecturer, The Colgate Darden Grad. School of Business Admin. of Univ. of Virginia, 1976- ; m. Aida Marie, d. late Giovanni Ceci, 18 September 1948; PRES., RINFRET — ASSOC. since 1967; Dir.; Brunswick Corp.; Genesco, Inc.; MacAndrews & Forbes Group Inc.; with Foster, Brown as Financial Analyst 1946-48; Staff Econ., Lionel Edie & Co. 1951, Dir. Econ. Research 1954, Dir., Econ. Services 1960, Chrmn. Bd. 1963-66; served in U.S. Army, Inf. 1943-45; Advisor to Pres. Kennedy, Pres. Johnson and Pres. Nixon; Chief Econ. Spokesman Nixon campaign 1972; sometime Advisor to Secys. Treas. Connally, Shultz, Simon and to Wilbur Mills, Edmund S. Muskie, and to Republican Pres. Cand. (R. M. Nixon) 1968, mem., Econ. Research Staff Candidate Nixon, 1968; rec'd. N.Y. Univ. School of Comm. Alumni Award, 1968; Educ. & Cultural Exchange program Grantee 1973 and 1980; mem., Am. Econ. Assn.; Roman Catholic; recreations: golf, sailing, skiing, scuba;

Clubs: University; New York Yacht; Office: 641 Lexington Ave., New York, N.Y.

RIOPELLE, Jean-Paul, C.C. (1969); painter; artist; b. Quebec, 1923; has been painting in Paris since 1947 where he has established a reputation for his unusual and original work; his painting "Toscin" (1953) chosen by Nat. Gallery to be sent abroad representing Candn. work; paintings selected for exhibit at 42nd Pittsburgh Internat. Exhn. (inaugurated by Andrew Carnegie "to show old masters of tomorrow") 1961; a 3-week exhn. of 82 paintings at Nat. Gallery, Ottawa, 1963; "Ficelles et Outres Yeux" Exhn., Musée d'Art Moderne, Paris 1971; book on Riopelle by Pierre Schneider pub. 1971; Address: 10 rue Frémincourt, Paris XV, France.

RIOUX, Hon. Claude, B.A., LL.L.; judge; b. Sayabec, Que. 20 May 1930; s. Albert and Aline (Mercier) R.; e. Jesuits Coll. Quebec City B.A. 1950; Laval Univ. LL.L. 1953; m. Marie-Jose. Marcel Garneau, Arthabaska, Que. 2 Dec. 1961; one d. Sophie; JUDGE, SUPERIOR COURT OF QUE. since 1979; called to Bar of Que. 1954; cr. Q.C. 1970; practiced law particuarly with Camil Noël, Q.C. and Jacques Alleyn, Q.C. 1954 — 66; Asoc. Depy. Min. of Justice Que. Govt. 1966 — 70, 1973 — 75 and Dep. and Assoc. Secy.-Gen. Extve. Council 1975 — 79; R. Catholic; Home: 403 — 5 Jardins Merici, Quebec City, Que. G1S 4N7; Office: 39 rue St-Louis, Quebec City, Que.

RIPLEY, T. Stewart; company executive; b. Toronto, Ont., 8 Aug. 1921; s. Thomas Sedgwick and Lilla (Dicks) R.; e. Pub. Schs., Toronto; Central Tech. Inst.; m. Dorothy Elizabeth, d. Edwin Dayman, Linden, Ont., 5 Oct. 1946; three s.: Douglas Stewart, Bruce Cornell, Stephen Ross; CHRMN. OF BD., CANADIAN INVESTORS AND CHAIRMAN & CHIEF EXTVE. OFFR., CANREIT ADV. CORP.; Dir., Canreit Investors; Dir. and mem. Extve. Comm., Crown Trust Co.; Chrmn., Canwest Trust Co.; Vice Chrmn., Canwest Financial Corp.; Chrmn. of the Bd., Candn. Realty Investors; began career with Co. of York Registry Office for Lands and Titles, 1938-40; Real Estate Rep., Wartime Housing Ltd., 1945-46; Assessor, Corpn. of Village of Swansea, 1946-47; H. M. Davy Co.; Property Manager, Real Estate Dept., National Trust Co., 1947-49, Chief Appraiser, Crown Life Ins. Co., 1949-53; Mgr., Mortgage and Real Estate Depts., Montreal Trust Co., Toronto, 1954-62; Extve. Vice-Pres., Gen. Mgr. and Dir. 1962; Pres. and C.E.O., Metropolitan Trust Co. 1971-78; Chrmn, 1978-79; Chrmn. & C.E.O., VGM Trustco Ltd. 1978-79; Internat. Vice-Pres. and Sr. Mem., Soc. Real Estate Appraisers 1963; Candn. Gov., Soc. Residential Appraisers 1960-62; mem., Roy. Regt. Can. Offrs. Assn.; Past Pres., Trust Co. Assoc. of Can.; Councillor, Trust Co. Inst.; served overseas in second World War with Candn. Army in U.K. and W. Europe; Protestant; Clubs: Albany; Donalda; Empire; Toronto Bd. of Trade; Home: 1092 Argyle Dr., Oakville, Ont. L6J 1A7; Office: 40 University Ave., Suite 1012, Toronto, Ont. M5J 1M4

RISI, Joseph, D.Sc., D.h.c.; b. Ennetburgen, Switzerland 13 March 1899; s. Aloîs and Marie (Rothenfluh) R.; e. St. Michael Coll. Zug, Switzerland B.A. 1918; Univ. of Fribourg D.Sc. 1925; Laval Univ. D.h.c. 1977; m. Alice (d. 1969) d. Casimir Neuhaus, Fribourg, Switzerland 23 June 1926; children: Hélène, Charlotte, André, Marcel; Prof. of Organic Chem. Laval Univ. 1925-54, Prof. of Wood Chem. 1954-60, Dean of Grad. Sch. 1960-71; author over 150 papers in. science, organic chem., oceanography, wood chem. and technol.; Hon. mem. Am. Chem. Soc.; mem. Assn. Canadienne Française pour l'Avancement des Sciences (former Pres.); R. Catholic; recreations: fishing, chess; Address: 1 Parc Samuel Holland, Apt. 1549, Québec, Qué. G1S 4P2

RIST, John Michael, M.A., F.R.S.C. (1976); educator; b. Romford, Eng. 6 July 1936; s. Robert Ward and Phoebe May (Mansfield) R.; e. Brentwood Sch. Eng. 1954; Cambridge Univ. B.A. 1959, M.A. 1963; m. Anna Thérèse d. Sidney Vogler, London, Eng. 30 July 1960; children: Peter, Alice, Thomas, Rebecca; REGIUS PROF. OF CLASSICS UNIV. OF ABERDEEN since 1980; Lectr. in Greek Univ. of Toronto 1959, Asst. Prof. 1963, Assoc. Prof. 1965, Prof. 1969-80; Chrmn. Grad. Dept. Classical Studies 1971-75; former Bd. mem. Oxfam Can.; Canairelief; Past Pres. Coalition for Life; author "Eros and Psyche" 1964; "Plotinus, the Road to Reality" 1967; "Stoic Philosophy" 1969; "Epicurus: An Introduction" 1972, Italian Transl. 1978; "On the Independence of Matthew and Mark" 1978; Ed. "The Stoics" 1978; over 40 articles mainly on ancient philos.; served with RAF 1954-56; mem. Class Assn. of Scotland Classical Assn. Can.; recreations: swimming, walking; Home: 107 High St., Old Aberdeen, Aberdeen AB2 3EM; Office: King's College, University of Aberdeen, Scotland.

RITCHIE, Albert Edgar, C.C. (1975), LL.D.; diplomat; b. Andover, N.B., 20 Dec. 1916; s. Stanley W. and Beatrice (Walker) R.; e. Mount Allison Univ., B.A. 1938, LL.D. 1966; Oxford Univ. (Rhodes Scholar), B.A. 1940; LL.D. St. Thomas Univ. 1968; m. Gwendolin, d. late John G. Perdue, Ottawa, Ont., 20 Dec. 1941; children: Gordon, Heather (Mrs. L. Zourdoumis), Donald, Holly; AMBASSADOR TO IRELAND, since 1976; with Brit. Purchasing Comn., 1941-42; Ministry of Econ. Warfare Mission (Brit. Embassy), Washington, 1942-44; joined Dept. of External Affairs as 3rd Secy., Washington, July 1944; 2nd Secy. 1946; resigned 1946 to become Special Asst. to Asst. Secy.-Gen., Econ. Affairs Dept., U.N., 1946-47; Special Asst. to Extve. Secy. of U.N. Prep. Comte. and Conf. on Trade and Employment, 1947-48; rejoined External Affairs as Foreign Service Offr., 1948; 1st Secy., London, Dec. 1948, Counsellor, 1952; Ottawa, May 1952; Candn. Embassy, Washington, D.C.; Min., 1957; Chargé d'Affaires a.i. 1958-59; Asst. Under-Secy. of State for External Affairs, Ottawa, 1959 and Depy. Under-Secy., 1964; Regent, Mount Allison Univ.; Ambassador to U.S.A. 1966-69; Under-Secy. of State for External Affairs, 1970; Outstanding Achievement Award, Public Service of Canada 1974; Un. Church; recreations: walking, fishing; Office: 65 St. Stephens Green, Dublin 2, Ireland.

RITCHIE, Cedric E.; banker; b. Upper Kent, N.B., 22 Aug. 1927; s. Thomas and Marion (Henderson) R.; e. Bath (N.B.) High Sch.; m. Barbara Binnington, Saskatoon, Sask., 20 Apl. 1956; CHAIRMAN, CHIEF EXTVE. OFFR., BANK OF NOVA SCOTIA since 1974; Chrmn., C.E.O. and Dir., Bank of Nova Scotia; Bank of Nova Scotia N.V.; Chrmn. and Dir., Bank of Nova Scotia Asia Ltd.; Bank of Nova Scotia Channel Islands Ltd.; Bank of Nova Scotia International, Ltd.; Bank of Nova Scotia Trust Co. (world wide affiliates); BNS Internat. (U.K.) Ltd.; Scotia Realty Ltd.; Depy. Chairman Scotia-Toronto Dominion Leasing Ltd.; Pres. and Dir., Nova Scotia Corp.; Spencer Hall Foundation; Dir., Bank of Nova Scotia Jamaica Ltd.; Bank of Nova Scotia Trust Co. of Jamaica Ltd.; BNS International N.V.; BNS International Hong Kong Ltd.; BNS International (Ireland) Ltd.; West India Co. of Merchant Bankers; The Bank of N.T. Butterfield & Son Ltd.; Beatrice Food Co.; Mercedes-Benz Can. Inc.; Candn. Council of Christians and Jews; Candn. Extive. Service Overseas; mem. Internat. Adv. Council, Centre for Inter-American Relations; Internat. Monetary Conference; Maduro Curiel's Bank N.V. Minerals and Resources Corp. Ltd.; Moore Corp. Ltd.; Schroder Darling and Company Holdings Ltd.; Canada Life Assurance Co.; Gov., Jr. Achievement of Can.; Olympic Trust of Can.; mem., Candn. Economic Policy Comte.; School of Business Admin. Advisory Comte., Univ. of Western Ont.; trustee, Queen's Univ.; joined present Bank, Bath, N.B., 1945; served at various Maritime brs. and in Montreal; trans. to Inspection staff; apptd. an Assistant Inspector, 1954; Accountant, Toronto Branch 1956; Inspector, Credit Dept., Gen. Office, 1959; Assistant Mgr.,

Toronto Br., 1959; Chief Acct., 1960; Asst. Gen. Mgr., Adm., 1963; Jt. Gen. Mgr., 1966; Chief. Gen. Mgr., International, 1968; Chief Gen. Mgr. 1970, el. a Dir. 1972, Pres. and Chief Extve. Offr. 1972; Chrmn., Pres. & C.E.O. 1974; Chrmn. & C.E.O. 1979; Office: 44 King St. W., Toronto, Ont. M5H 1H1

RITCHIE, Charles Stewart Almon, C.C. (1969), M.A., D.C.L.; diplomat; b. Halifax, Nova Scotia, 23 Sept. 1906; s. William Bruce Almon Ritchie, K.C., and Lillian Constance Harriette (Stewart) R.; e. Trinity Coll. Sch., Port Hope, Ont.; Univ. of King's Coll., Halifax, N.S.; Oxford Univ., B.A., M.A. 1929; Harvard Univ., M.A. 1930; Ecole Libre des Sciences Politiques, Paris (1931); D.C.L., Univ. of King's Coll., Trent Univ., McGill Univ., Acadia Univ.; m. Sylvia Catherine Beatrice, d. James Smellie, Ottawa, Ont., 16 Jan. 1948; joined Dept. of External Affairs as Third Secy., Aug. 1934; Third Secy., Washington, Oct. 1936; Second Secy., London, Jan. 1939, First Secy. Jan. 1943; First Secy., Ottawa, Jan. 1945; Counsellor, Paris, Jan. 1947; Asst. Under-Secy. of State for External Affairs, Jan. 1950, Deputy Under-Secy., Nov. 1952; Ambassador to Federal Republic of Germany, and Head of Military Mission, Berlin, May 1954; Ambassador and Permanent Rep. to the United Nations, Jan. 1958-62; Ambassador to the United States, Jan. 1962-66; Permanent Rep. and Ambassador to the N. Atlantic Council and to the Office of EEC, 1966-67; High Commr. to U.K. 1967; Special Advisor to Privy Council, Ottawa, 1971-73; Author, "The Siren Years" 1974; "An Appetite for Life" 1977; Hon. Fellow, Pembroke Coll., Oxford University, 1963; Anglican Church; Club: Brooks's (London); Rideau (Ottawa); Address: 216 Metcalfe St., Ottawa, Ont. K2P 1R1

RITCHIE, Christopher, B.Sc.; company executive; b. Edmonton, Alberta, 5 Jan. 1914; s. John Scobie and Katherine Ritchie; e. Strathchona High Sch., Edmonton, Alta.; Univ. of Alta., B.Sc. (Elect. Engn.) 1935, post-grad. studies in Radio Engn. and Math. (1936); m. Eileen Ethel, d. William Baker, Edmonton, Alta., 10 Nov. 1939; children: Carol, Gary; CHRMN. AND DIR., MONTREAL ENGINEERING CO. LTD., AND MONEN CO. LTD., since 1974; Chrmn. & Dir. Baymont Engineering co.; Monenco Inc.; Pres. & Dir., Monenco Consultants Ltd.; Monenco Consultants Pacific Ltd.; Montec Ltd.; Monenco Consulting Engineers Ltd.; Dir., E. & B. Cowan Ltd.; Saskmont Engineering Co. Ltd.; joined Calgary Power Ltd., 1936 and present Co. in May 1940 as Design Engr.; apptd. Engn. Mgr., 1953; Vice pres. and Gen. Mgr. 1961, Pres. 1964; el. a Dir. in 1956; Reg'd. Prof. Engr., Que., Alta. & Nfld.; mem. and Fellow, Engn. Inst. Can.; mer. Candn. Elect. Assn.; Hon. mem., Assn. Consulting Engrs. Can.; Candn. Nuclear Assn.; Protestant; recreations: golf, curling; Clubs: Beaconsfield Golf (Mtl.); Silver Springs (Calgary) Electrical; Home: 103 Roxboro House - 330-26 Ave. S.W. Calgary, Alta. T2S 2T3 Office: 900 One Palliser Sq., Calgary, Alta. T2G 0P6

RITCHIE, Gen. Sir Neil Methuen, G.B.E. (1951), K.C.B. (1947), K.B.E. (1945), C.B. (1944) C.B.E. (1940), D.S.O. (1917), M.C.; b. Georgetown, Brit. Guiana, 29 July 1897; s. Dugald MacDugald and Anna Catherine (Leggatt) R.; e. Lancing Coll. and R.M.C., Sandhurst, Eng.; m. Catherine Taylor, d. James A. Minnes, Kingston, Ont. 4 Dec. 1937; children: Arnott Dugald Neil, Isobel Anne; Dir. Emeritus, Mercantile and General Reinsurance Co. of Canada, Ltd.; Dir., Electra Investments (Can.) Ltd.; Tanqueray, Gordon & Co. (Can.) Ltd.; 2nd Lt. The Black Watch, 1914; Ltd. 1915; Capt. 1917; Bt. Major 1933; Major 1934; Bt. Lt.-Col. 1936; Lt.-Col. on trans. to Command 2nd Bn., King's Own Royal Regt. (Lancaster) 1938; Col. 1939; Brig. 1939; Maj.-Gen. 1943; Lt.-Gen. 1945; Gen. 1947; at Regt. duty 1914-18; awarded D.S.O. and M.C.; Staff Coll., 1929-30; Gen. Staff, India, 1932-36; B.G.S. 2nd Corps 1939; G.O.C. 51 (Highland) Div. 1940; Chief of Staff, Middle East 1941; Commdr., 8 Army 1941-42; Commdr., 52 (Lowland) Div. 1942-43; Commdr., 12

Corps 1943-45; G.O.C.-in-C. Scotland and Gov. of Edin. Castle 1945-47; Commdr.-in-Chief Far East Land Forces 1947-49; A.D.C. Gen. 1947-51; Brit. Jt. Chiefs of Staff, Washington, D.C., 1950-51; retired pay, 1951; succeeded the late Field Marshal Earl Wavell as Col. of The Black Watch 1950-52; succeeded the late Lord Derby as Hon. Col., 5 King's Own Roy. Regt. at Lancaster 1948-58; Hon. Lt.-Col. 59 Light Anti-Aircraft Regt. (Lanark & Renfrew Scottish) 1950-59; Queen's Bodyguard for Scotland (Roy. Co. of Archers) 1946; Vice-Pres., St. John Ambulance (Ont. Council), 1959, Pres. 1961, Hon. Pres. (1964); Life Hon. Chrmn., Toronto Br., Royal Commonwealth Soc., 1957; Conservative; Presbyterian; recreations: shooting, fishing, golf, riding; Clubs: York; Caledonian (London); Home: 355 St. Clair Ave. W., Toronto, Ont. M59 1N5

RITCHIE, Hon. Roland A., D.C.L.; judge; b. Halifax, N.S., 19 June 1910; s. William Bruce Almon and Lillian Constance (Stewart) R.; e. Trinity Coll. Sch., Port Hope, Ont.; Univ. of King's Coll., Halifax, N.S.; Pembroke Coll., Oxford; m. Mary Lippincot, d. late Harry McNab Wylde, 6 May 1936; one d. Elizabeth Stewart; PUISNE JUDGE, THE SUPREME COURT OF CANADA, since 1959; read law with J. Macg. Stewart, Q.C.; called to the Bar of N.S. 1934; cr. K.C. 1950; practised law with the firm of Stewart, Smith, MacKeen & Rogers, Halifax, N.S., 1934-40; on return from active war service, 1945, formed a partnership with A. McL. Daley, Q.C. and L. F. Daley in the firm of Daley, Phinney & Ritchie, which later became Daley, Ritchie, Black & Moriera; Chancellor, Univ. of King's College; Hon. Fellow, Pembroke Coll., Oxford; former Gov., Dalhousie Univ. and Univ. of King's Coll.; former 1st Vice-Pres., N.S. Barristers Soc.; mem., Candn. Bar Assn.; served in 2nd World War; Capt. R.C.A., West N.S. Regt., 1940-41; 4th Light Anti Aircraft Regt. (100th Batty.) 1941-44; Asst. Judge Advocate Gen., 3rd Candn. Div., 1941-43; Anglican; Clubs: Rideau; Halifax; R.N.Y.S. (Halifax); Royal Ottawa Golf (Aylmer, P.Q.) Home: 177 Coltrin Road, Rockcliffe, Ottawa, Ont. K1M 0A3; Office: Supreme Court Bldg., Ottawa, Ont. K1A 0J1

RITCHIE, Ronald Stuart, M.A.; consulting economist; b. Charing Cross, Kent Co., Ont., 4 July 1918; s. Thomas Duncan and Maggie (Sterritt) R.; e. Univ. of W. Ont., B.A. (Gold Medallist in Econ. and Pol. Science) 1938; Queen's Univ., M.A. (Econ.) 1960; m. Phyllis, d. Alfred Ernest Plaskett, Toronto, Ont. 4 Feb. 1950; children: Beverly Janet, Barbara Diane, Patricia Ann, Karen Heather, Margot Lynn; Life Underwriter, Standard Life Assurance, London, Ont., 1938-39; Lectr., Econ. Dept., Ont. Agric. Coll., Guelph, Ont., 1940-41; Extve. Asst. to Depy. Chrmn., Wartime Prices & Trade Bd., 1941-44; Mgr., Ottawa Civil Service Recreational Assn., 1944-45; Depy. Chief Prices Div., W.P.T.B., 1945-47; joined Imperial Oil Ltd. and posted to Standard Oil Co. (N.J.), 1947; Head Econ. & Stats. Group. Co-Ordination & Econ. Dept., Toronto, 1948-50; Asst. Div. Mgr., Ont. Marketing Div., 1950-52; Asst. Div. Mgr., B.C. Marketing Div., Vancouver, B.C., 1953-55; Mgr., B.C. Marketing Div., Vancouver, B.C., 1955-58; Asst. Gen. Mgr., Marketing Dept., Toronto, 1958; Employee Relations Mgr., 1959-60; Extve. Asst. to the Bd., Special Projects, 1962-63; on loan as Extve. Dir., Roy. Comm. on Gov't. Organ., Nov. 1960-Jan. 1962; Dir., Imperial Oil Ltd. 1963-74; Sr. Vice Pres. 1971-74; P. Conservative cand. Algoma, 1974 g.e.; Princ. Asst., Office, Ldr. of Opposition, Ottawa 1974-75; elected M.P., York East 1979; appld. Parliamentary Secty. to Min. of Finance 1979; Sr. Policy Advisor, Investment Dealers Assn. of Can., 1980- ; Pres., Canadian Ditchley Foundation; Gov., The Ditchley Foundation (U.K.); Dir. Candn. Council of Christians and Jews; Bd. Dirs. North-South Inst. 1975-79; Bd. Govs., Found. for Int. Tng. in Third World Countries; Chairman, Board of Governors, University of Guelph, 1966-71; mem., Club of Rome; mem., Canada-U.S. Comte., Canadian Chamber of Commerce, 1967-73; Chrmn. 1972-73; mem., Board of Governors, The Atlantic

Inst., Paris, since 1965; mem., Nat. Extve. Comte. Candn. Inst. Internat. Affairs 1960-75; Chrmn. Inst. for Research on Public Policy, 1972-74; Candn. Del., Commonwealth Conf., Lahore, Pakistan 1954; ILO, Geneva, 1960, and various internat. relations confs.; author of: "NATO: The Economics of an Alliance", 1956; "An Institute for Research on Public Policy" 1971; "Ritchie Report on Canada's Postal Service" 1978; Ed. and Publisher, "The Canadian Conservation"; also various articles on management, econ. policy and internat. affairs; mem., Candn. Econ. & Pol. Assn.; Candn. Hist. Assn.; United Ch.; recreations: golf, skiing, swimming, music, reading; Clubs: University (Toronto); Rideau (Ottawa); Home: 33 Harbour Square, Apt. 3501, Toronto, Ont. M5J 2G2; Office: 300-1235 Bay St., Toronto, Ont. M5R 3K4

RIVA, Walter Joseph, B.Sc.; mining executive; b. Canmore, Alta. 9 May 1922; s. Joseph and Dorothy Grace (Walker) R.; e. Univ. of Alta. B.Sc. (Mining Engn.) 1949; m. Lorraine Cormier; children: LeEllen, Raymond, Patrick, Don, Michael, Susan; CHRMN. AND CHIEF EXTVE. OFFR., B.C. COAL LTD. 1981- ; held various positions Western Canadian Collieries, Great West Coal Co., The Canmore Mines Ltd., Alta. 1947-72; Vice Pres. Denison Mines Ltd. 1972-73; Vice Pres. Coal Mining Operations B.C., Kaiser Resources Ltd. 1973-79, Pres. Coal Div. 1979-80; Pres. and Chief Extve. Offr. present Co. 1980-81; served with RCAF World War II, rank Flying Offr.; Candn. Employers' Del. Internat. Labour Organ. Conf. Geneva 1964; CIM Distinguished Lectr. 1971; Selwyn G. Blaylock Medal Distinguished Service Candn. Coal Industry 1973; inventor patented form-coke processing and co-inventor pelletizing process; author several tech. papers mining, form-coke process, pelletization, coal industry market econ.; Dir., Vancouver Bd. Trade; B.C. Resources Invest. Corp.; Fellow, Inst. Mining Engrs.; mem. Assn. Prof. Engrs. Alta., B.C.; Candn. Inst. Mining & Metall.; Coal Assn. Can. (Past Chrmn., Pres. 1968-70); recreation: golf; Club: Pt. Grey Golf; Home: 3522 S.W. Marine Dr., Vancouver, B.C. V6N 3Z2; Office: 1176 W. Georgia St., Vancouver, B.C. V6E 4B8.

RIVARD, Jean, Q.C., LL.L.; b. Quebec, Que., 22 Dec. 1926; s. Antoine and late Lucille (Garneau) R.; e. Jesuits' Coll., Quebec, Que.; Laval Univ., LL.L. 1950; m. Janine, d. late Hon. Jean Raymond, 7 Nov. 1955; children: Louise, Michèle, Line, Pierre, Guy; SR. PARTNER, FLYNN RIVARD AND ASSOC.; called to Bar of Que. 1950; cr. Q.C. 1964; R. Catholic; recreations: golf, skiing, squash, tennis, swimming; Clubs: Quebec Garrison; Royal Quebec Golf; Home: 1438 Des Gouverneurs, Sillery, Que.; Office: 2 Chauveau, Quebec, Que. G1R 4J3and 2020 University, Montreal, Que. H3A 2A5

RIVIERE, Paul; farmer; financier; b. Radville, Sask. 20 May 1920; s. Henri and Angele (Malet) R.; e. Lacadia Sch.; France 1934-36; Co-op. Coll. of Can.; m. Andrea d. Napoleon Fradette, Radville, Sask. 30 Jan. 1945; children: Maurice, Raymond, Roger, Jeannette, Marcelle; Pres., Chrmn. of Bd. and Dir. Co-operative Trust Co. of Canada Ltd. since 1975; Dir., Co-op. Union of Can. 1976- ; Sask. Oil and Gas Corp. 1979- ; Pres.; Conseil de la Co-operation (Sask.); Dir. Credit Union Central (Sask.); Vice Pres. Co-operative Trust Co. of Canada 1969; Commr. Sask. Hog Marketing Comn. 1974; Councillor Rural Mun. of the Gap 39 (Sask.) 1948-62; Administrateur Le Conseil Canadien de la Co-operation 1972-75; rec'd Master Farm Family Award for S. Sask. 1968; Gov. Gen. Candn. Silver Jubilee Medal 1978; Gov., Co-operative College of Can. 1978; mem. Sask. Wheat Pool; Nat. Farmers Union; served during World War II; Sch. Trustee 1945-55; R. Catholic; recreations: bowling, curling, dancing; Clubs: Lacadia Community; Elks; Address: 43 Rainy Court, Saskatoon, Sask. S7K 4G1

RIVINGTON, George Neville Campbell, B.Sc.; engineer; b. Huntley Twp., Ont. 10 May 1920; s. late Thomas

Ruggles and Myrtle (Campbell) R.; e. Queen's Univ. B.Sc. (Elect. Engn.) 1942; m. Halvarda Ruth d. late Herbert Edgar Chatham 24 Nov. 1945; children: Diana J., Dr. Robert N., Louise H. (Brownlee), T. David; GROUP VICE PRES. AND DIR., MONTREAL ENGINEERING CO. LTD.; Dir. Teshmont Consultants Inc.; Chmn. and Dir., Staff Corrosion Engineers Ltd.; Pres. and Dir. EHV Consultants Ltd.; Monenco Japan Inc.; Vice Pres.-Engn. & Mang. Services and Dir. Monenco Ltd.; Vice Pres. and Dir. Monenco Holdings Ltd.; Dir. Monenco Computing Services Ltd.; Monenco Consultants Pacific Ltd.; Monenco Ontario Ltd.; Maritime Electric Co. Ltd.; Newfoundland Light & Power Co. Ltd.; Petro-Metals Recovery Systems Ltd.; served with RCNVR 1942-46, rank Lt.; Sr. mem. Inst. Elect. & Electronics Engrs.; Candn. Elect. Assn.; Anglican; recreations: golf, gardening, skiing; Clubs: Mt. Stephen; Whitlock Golf & Country; Home: 54 Elmwood Ave., Senneville, Que. H9X 1T7; Office: (P.O. Box 6088 Stn. A) Montreal, Que. H3C 3Z8.

ROACH, Richard Joseph, B.A.Sc., P.Eng.; consulting engineer; b. Toronto, Ont. 20 March 1922; s. Richard Louis and Marie Veronica (Mullin) R.; e. N. Toronto Coll. Inst. 1940; Univ. of Toronto, B.A.Sc. 1950; Ont. Mining Assn. post-grad. course 1950-51; m. Hazel Winnifred Lee 20 Feb. 1946; children: Michael, Patricia; SR. EXEC: VICE PRES. AND DIR., KILBORN ENGINEERING LTD. since 1963; Dir. Kilborn Engineering (B.C.) Ltd.; Kilborn International; Kilborn Inc.; Kilborn (Sask.) Ltd.; Mill Engr. Lake Shore Gold Mines Ltd., Kirkland Lake, Ont. 1951-52; Metall. Normetal Mines Ltd., Normetal, Que. 1952-53; Asst. Mill Supt. Belleterre Gold Mines, Belleterre, Que. 1953-55; Metall. Gaspe Copper Mines Ltd., Murdochville, Que. 1955-56; Mill Supt. and Consulting Metall. Faraday Uranium Mines Ltd., Bancroft and Toronto, Ont. 1956-63; served with R.C.A.F. as Pilot 1940-45; active duty European theatre; mem. Assn. Prof. Engrs. Ont.; Assn. Prof. Engrs. Sask.; Candn. Inst. Mining & Metall.; Am. Inst. Mining Engrs.; Assn. Consulting Engrs. Can.; Bd. Trade Metrop. Toronto; Liberal; R. Catholic; recreations: golf, electronics, hunting; Club: Bd. of Trade Golf and Country; Home: 279 Donnelly Dr., Mississauga, Ont.

ROBARTS, Hon. John P., P.C., C.C. (1972), Q.C., B.A., D.C.L., LL.D.; b. Banff, Alberta, 11 Jan. 1917; s. Herbert and Florence May (Stacpoole) R.; e. Univ. Western Ont., B.A. (Hon. Business Adm.) 1939; Osgoode Hall Law Sch., Toronto, Ont. 1947; LL.D., W. Ont. 1960; Queen's 1961; Toronto 1962; Ottawa, 1962; Laurentian 1963; St. Dunstan's 1964; McMaster 1966; McGill 1967; also, P.E.I.; Law Soc. of Upper Can.; Ryerson Polytechnical Inst.; D.C.L., Univ. of N.B. 1966; m. Katherine Sickafuse; children: Robin Hollis, Kimberley Ann; Partner, Stikeman, Elliott, Robarts & Bowman; Dir., Canadian Imperial Bank of Commerce; Bell Canada; Metropolitan Life (N.Y.); Reed Stenhouse Companies Ltd.; Abitibi Paper Co. Ltd.; Power Corp. of Canada Ltd.; Burns Foods Ltd.; Candn. Realty Investors (Secretary); Toronto Blue Jays Baseball Club; Matthews Group; Dir., Mercedes-Benz Can. Inc.; Atlantic Energy & Development Corp.; Chrmn. of the Bd., Reed Stenhouse Ltd.; called to the Bar of Ont. 1947; cr. Q.C. 1954; mem., London, Ont. City Council, 1950; el. to Ont. Leg., g.e. 1951; Min. without Portfolio, Ont., 1958-59; Min. of Educ., 1959-61; el. Leader of Ont. Cons. Party, 25 Oct. 1961; Prime Minister, Ont. 1961-71; former mem., Water Resources Comn. Ont.; apptd. one-man Royal Comn. on Metro Toronto 1974 (2 yr. study); apptd. co-chrmn. of Task Force on Canadian Unity 1977; served in 2nd World War with R.C.N.V.R., 1940-45; Mentioned in Despatches; retired with rank of Lieut.; K.G. St. J. 1966; Chancellor, Univ. Western Ont. 1972-76; York Univ. since 1977; Delta Upsilon; P. Conservative; recreation: sailing, fishing; Clubs: Albany (Toronto); Ontario; York; Home: 64 St. Andrews Gdns., Toronto, Ont. M4W 2E1 Offices: Suite 4950, Commerce Court W. (P.O. Box 85), Toronto, Ont. M5L 1B9

ROBB, J. Preston, M.Sc., M.D., C.M., F.R.C.P.; neurologist; b. Montreal, Que., 4 April 1914; s. Joseph Doig and Janie McLeod (Preston) R.; e. Westmount High Sch.; McGill Univ., B.Sc., M.Sc. (Neurol.), M.D., C.M.; m. Mary Grierson, d. Stephen Waller, 19 Oct. 1940; children: William David, Christopher John, Mary Alison, James Bruce; Sr. Consultant, Montreal Neurological Hosp.; Prof. of Neurology and Neurosurg., McGill Univ.; Consultant, Montreal Children's Hosp.; served in 2nd World War with R.C.N.V.R., 1941-45, Surg. Lt. Cmdr.; mem., Candn. Med. Assn.; Candn. Neurol. Soc.; Montreal Neurol. Soc.; Fellow Am. Acad. of Neurol.; Am. Neurol. Assn.; United Church; recreations: fishing, farming; Club: University; Home: Box 43, Lyn, Ont. K0E 1M0; Office: Montreal Neurological Institute, 3801 University St., Montreal, Que. H3A 2B4

ROBB, James Alexander, Q.C., B.A., B.C.L.; lawyer; b. Huntingdon, Que. 3 May 1930; s. late Alexander George and late Irma Mary (Martin) R.; e. Huntingdon Acad.; McGill Univ. B.A. 1951, B.C.L. 1954; Univ. of Montreal postgrad. studies 1961-63; m. Katherine Ann d. Norman Teare 25 June 1960; children: John, Laura, Andrew; PARTNER, STIKEMAN, ELLIOTT, TAMAKI, MERCIER & ROBB; Dir. Robapharm (Canada) Ltd.; C. Itoh & Co. (Canada) Ltd.; YKK Canada Inc.; Hitachi (HSC) Canada Inc.; Champlain Industries Ltd.; Expasa Canada Ltd.; Hitachi Credit Canada Inc.; Japan-Alberta Oil Mill Co. Ltd.; called to Bar of Que. 1955; cr. Q.C. 1971; Pres. Westmount Lib. Assn. 1971-72; Vice Pres. Lib. Party Que. (Prov.) 1976-79; Chrmn. Martlet Foundation Bd. Trustees 1967-69; mem. Adv. Comte. McGill Univ. Centre for Regulated Industries 1981- ; mem. Westmount Sch. Bd. 1972-73; Prot. Sch. Bd. Greater Montreal 1972-74 (Vice Chrmn. Parents' Comte. 1973-74); Pres. McGill Student Soc. 1953-54; Chrmn. Consumers' Assn. Can. Regulated Industries Bd. 1976-79; mem. Que. Trade Del. to Japan 1974; Coll. Council, Marianopolis Coll. 1978-81; mem. Que. Bar Assn.; Candn. Bar Assn.; Am. Bar Assn.; Treas. Jr. Bar Assn. 1964 (Council 1960-64); Phi Kappa Pi (Pres. 1952); served with RCAF (Reserve) 1949-54, rank Flying Offr.; Liberal; Protestant; recreations: politics, skiing; Clubs: University; Kanawaki Golf; Gaughnawaga; Royal Montreal Curling; Home: 9 Renfrew Ave., Westmount, Que. H3Y 2X3; Office: 3800, 1155 Dorchester Blvd. W., Montreal, Que. H3B 3V2.

ROBB, Malcolm, D.F.C., Q.C.; b. Toronto, Ont., 15 July 1917; s. Charles Wesley and Nora Margaret (Hamilton) R.; e. Oakwood Coll. Inst., Toronto, Ont.; Univ. of Toronto; Osgoode Hall Law Sch.; m. Edith Muriel, d. Dr. Walter Phillips, F.R.C.S. (Eng.) 15 Jan. 1944 (divorced 1966); m. 2ndly Joan Constance; children: John Walter, Shelley Jane, John Howard, Lisa Anne, Julie Allison; formerly a Partner of Robb, Ross, Cass & Hurley, Belleville, Ont., and of Slaght, Robb & Hayes, Toronto, Ont. (1954-58); read law with J. C. M. MacBeth, K.C. and A. G. Slaght, K.C.; called to the Bar of Ont., 1939; cr. Q.C. 1953; practised his prof. with Slaght, Ferguson & Carrick, Toronto 1939-41; sometime Special Counsel for Min. of Justice in prosecution of income tax fraud cases and for R.C.M.P. in prosecuting throughout Ontario in cases of conspiracy to export diseased cattle into U.S.; Counsel in 1948 to Royal Comn. to investigate charges of corruption in Ont. Prov. Police made by John E. Keays; def. cand. for Cons. nomination (Fed.) for S. Hastings 1952; served in 2nd World War with R.C.A.F. joining as Aircraftsman in June 1941; gaz. P.O. Feb. 1942; served in Eng., France, Belgium and Holland and promoted Flight Lieut.; awarded D.F.C.; with Judge Advocate's Branch, R.C.A.F. Hdqrs., London, Eng. 1944-45; mem., Council of Profit Sharing Industries; Conservative; United Church; recreations: fishing, golf; Clubs: The Toronto; Summit Golf; Office: Suite 1150, Box 365, Commerce Court N., Toronto, Ont. M5L 1G2

ROBB, William D.; manufacturer, retired; b. Detroit, Mich. 29 July 1911; m. Frances Wilmington White, 11 Sept. 1937; children: Judith (Mrs. Ian Griffin), Joseph Doig, Jennifer (Mrs. Steven Dattels); Dir., Robco Inc.; Anchor Packing Co. Ltd.; Albion Asbestos Packings Co.; Vice Pres. and Dir., Ontario Rubber Co.; Dir., National Refractories Co.; A. C. Rubber Co.; Prestonia Stationery Manufacturing Co.; McMillan Office Appliances Co.; mem., Adv. Bd., Crown Trust Co.; Pres., Springdale Foundation; Vice Pres., Ont. Deafness Research Foundation; Can. Hearing Soc. Foundation; Past Pres., Montreal Boys' Home; Camp Weredale; Gov., Weredale Foundation; Past Dir., Roy. Victoria Hosp.; Chrmn. Bd. of Trustees, St. Andrew's Ch., Westmount; mem. Adv. Bd. Montreal YMCA; Clubs: Mount Royal; Forest & Stream; York; Kanawaki; Rosedale (Toronto); Rotary Toronto (Past Dir.); Rotary Montreal; Ojibway (Pointe au Baril, Ont.; Past Pres.); Home: 25 Cedarwood Ave., Willowdale, Ont M2L 2X6; Office: 5600 Philippe-Turcot St., Montreal, Que. H4C 1V7 also, 32 Colville Rd., Toronto, Ont., M6M 2Y4

ROBBINS, John Everett, LL.D., M.A., Ph.D., D.Sc.Soc., F.S.S.; retired diplomat; b. Hampton, Ont., 9 Oct. 1903; s. John and Gertrude May (Brown) R.; e. Univ. of Man., B.A. 1928, M.A. 1929; Research Fellow in Econ., McMaster Univ., 1929-30 Carnegie Travelling Fellow to Europe 1933; Univ. of Ottawa, Ph.D. 1935; LL.D., New Brunswick, 1959; British Columbia, 1959; Manitoba, 1967; Carleton, 1969; Brandon, 1974; D.Sc.Soc., Laval, 1967; m. Catherine, d. Honoré Saint-Denis, 11 June 1934; children: Bernard, Emmet; Dir., Wawanesa Mutual Insurance Co. 1961-79; Dir., Brandon Sun Publishing Co.; Ed.-in-Chief, Encyclopedia Canadiana, 1952-60; Pres., Brandon Univ. (Brandon Coll. prior to July 1967), 1960-69; Extve. mem., Un. Nations Assn. in Can.; 1945-60; mem. Bd. of Govs., Carleton Univ., Ottawa, 1942-61; mem. Extension Comte., National Council of Y.M.C.A. and Bd. of Dirs. of Ottawa Y.M.C.A., 1945-60; Fellow of Candn. Geog. Soc. and mem. of Edit. Bd. of "Canadian Geographic Journal", 1946-62; mem. of Candn. del to UNESCO Confs., London, 1945, Mexico, 1947, Beirut, 1948, Florence, 1950; taught sch. in Sask., 1922-25; apptd. Asst. Chief, Educ. Br., Dom. Bur. of Stat. 1930, Dir. of Educ. Div., 1936-52; on leave (one yr.) as Dir. of Educ. for Palestine Refugees in the Near East; Hon. Secy.-Treas., Candn. Social Science Research Council, 1940-61; Humanities Research Council, 1943-61; Treas., Canada Foundation, 1950-60; Dir., Canadian Writers' Foundation 1950-61, 1975, Pres., 1976-78; Pres., Canadian Citizenship Council, 1960-61; (Hon. Life mem. 1956), Candn. Assn. Adult Educ.; apptd. (1st) Candn. Ambassador to the Vatican, Oct. 1969; Amnesty International Can. (Extve. Chrmn. 1973-74, Treas. 1974-75); World Federalists of Canada, Pres. 1977-79 (Treas. 1976-77); Home: 336 Island Park Drive, Ottawa, Ont. K1Y 0A7

ROBBINS, Ray C.; company executive; b. Syracuse, New York, 15 Sept. 1920; children: Sandra, Ray Jr.; CHRMN. OF THE BD. LENNOX INDUS. INC.; Dir., Lennox Industries Inc.; Central National Bankshares, Inc.; Financial Security Co.; mem., Am. Soc. Heating & Air Conditioning Engrs.; Dir., Air Conditioning Refrigeration Inst.; Nat. Assn. Mfrs.; Past Dir., Big Brother of Metrop. Toronto 1964-69; Queensway Gen. Hosp. 1957-69; Bd. Trade Metrop. Toronto; Past Chrmn., Toronto Dist., Candn. Mfg. Assn.; Candn. Gas Assn.; Home: 16510 Fallkirk, Dallas, Texas, 75248: Office: Promenade Tower, Box 400450, Dallas, Texas, 75240

ROBBINS, Hon. Wesley Albert, M.L.A., B.A.; b. 14 Aug. 1916; s. Norman and Charlotte Jane R.; e. Univ. of Sask.; m. Marion Nicol 14 June 1946; children: Barbara Anne, James William, Janis Mary; MIN. OF REVENUE, SUPPLY AND SERVICES, SASK. 1979- ; el. M.L.A. for Saskatoon Nutana prov. g.e. 1964, def. 1967, re-el. since 1971; Del. Interprov. visit Commonwealth Parlty. Assn.

P.E.I. 1972; Min. of Finance 1973; Min. of Health 1975; Min. of Revenue 1977; Min. of Co-operation & Co-operative Devel. 1977; Min. of Consumer Affairs, 1979; Session mem. Grace Westminster Un. Ch. Invest. Comte.; mem. Saskatoon Credit Union and Co-op Superannuation Soc.; NDP; United Church; Office: Legislative Bldg., Regina, Sask. S4S 0B3.

ROBERGE, Fernand, M.Sc.A., Ph.D.; éducateur, ingénieur biomédical; né Pontbriand, Co. Megantic, Qué., 11 juin 1935; f. Lauréat et Léonilde (Paré) R.; é. Ecole Polytech. (génie), Univ. de Montréal, M.Sc.A., 1960; Univ. McGill, Ph.D., 1964; ép. Gladys, f. Charles Pagé, Montréal, 8 février 1958; enfants: Vivyane, Carolyne, Eric, Nicolas; DIR. INSTITUT DE GENIE BIOMED., ECOLE POLYTECHNIQUE ET UNIVERSITE DE MONTREAL; Prof. titulaire; Chef, dépt. génie bioméd., Hôpital du Sacré Coeur, Montréal; mem. Conseil de Recherches Méd. (Comité de génie bioméd.); Conseil des Arts du Can. (Comité du programme Killam); Fondation Candnne. des Maladies du Coeur (Comité scient.); mem. Candn. Med. and Biol. Engn. Soc.; Sr. mem., Inst. of Elect. and Electronics; mem. Biomed. Engn. Soc.; Soc. Canadienne de Physiol.; Am. Assn. Advancement Science; écrit une centaine d'articles scient., chapitres de livres, etc.; reçu D. W. Ambridge Award, Univ. McGill, 1964; Catholique; récréations: golf, natation; résidence: 216 Lazard, Ville Mont. Royal, P.Q. H3R 1N9

ROBERGE, Hon. Gabriel, B.A., B.Ph., LL.L.; judge; b. St. Ferdinand d'Halifax, Co. Megantic, Que., 30 March 1918; s. P. Allyre and Irene (Duchesneau) R.; e. Semy. de Quebec, B.A. 1938; Laval Univ., B.Ph. 1938, LL.L. 1941; m. Denyse, d. Jules E. Lemay, 29 Sept. 1956; one d. Suzanne; JUSTICE SUPERIOR COURT OF QUE., since 1963; read law with St.-Laurent, Gagné, Devlin & Taschereau; called to the Bar of Que. 1941; cr. Q.C. 1961; practised law alone, 1942-43 and 1946-48; Partner, Talbot & Roberge, 1948-56; alone 1956-58; Roberge & Gobeil, 1958-63, continuously in Thetford Mines, Que.; served in Candn. Army, Inf. and Law Br., 1943-46, Capt. Supplementary Reserve (retd.); M.P. for Megantic (Liberal) 1958-62; K.C.L.J.; R. Catholic; recreations: golf, skiing; Clubs: Cap Rouge Country; University (Quebec City); Home: 250 W. Grande-Allée, Québec, Que. G1R 2H4; Office: Court House, Quebec, Que. G1R 4P6

ROBERGE, Guy, Q.C., B.A., LL.L., D.C.L.; b. St. Ferdinand d'Halifax, Quebec, 26 Jan. 1915; s. P. Allyre and Irène (Duchesneau) R.; e. Laval Univ., B.A. 1934, LL.L. 1937, D.C.L. Bishop's 1967; m. Maxine Raymond, Q.C., Montreal, Que., 26 Aug. 1957; VICE-PRES., CANADIAN TRANSPORT COMMISSION since Aug. 1971; former Chrmn., Nat. Film Bd. of Can.; Agent Gen. for Que. in the U.K. 1966-71; mem. Restrictive Trade Practices Comn. 1955-57; mem., Bd. of Dirs. and Extve. Comte. of Candn. Corp. for 1967 World Exhn.; mem., Candn. Bar Assn.; called to the Bar of Que., 1937; cr. Q.C. 1957; Doctorate (Hon.) Laval Univ., 1975; Roman Catholic; Clubs: Rideau; Quebec Garrison (Quebec); Home: 415 Wood Ave., Rockcliffe, Ottawa, Ontario; K1M 1J8 Office: 15 Eddy, Hull; postal address: Ottawa, Ont. K1A 0N9

ROBERGE, Philippe, LL.L.; notary; b. Inverness, Que., 16 Oct. 1924; s. P. A. and Irène (Duchesneau) R.; e. Univ. of Montreal, B.A. 1945; Univ. of Laval, LL.L. 1948; m. Hélène, d. Louis Morin, 24 Sept. 1949; children: Louis, Paule, Jacques; PARTNER, MARLER, TEES, WATSON, POITEVIN, JAVET & ROBERGE; Dir., Montreal City & District Savings Bank; Credit Foncier Franco Canadian; Canadian Automobile Assn.; Beaubran Corp.; CBC; Bell, Rinfret & Company Limited; called to the Bar of Que. 1948; in law practice as Notary, Thetford Mines, Que. 1948-61, specialising in mining and corporate law with experience in mun. affairs; joined present firm (then McLean, Marler, Common & Tees) Montreal 1962; Lt.,

Les Voltigeurs de Qué.; City Councillor, Thetford Mines 1955; recreation: golf; Clubs: St. James's; Board of Trade; Winchester; Montreal Touring (Pres.); Home: 42 Claude Champagne Ave., Outremont, Que. H2V 2X1; Office: 620 Dorchester Blvd. W., Suite 1200, Montreal, Que. H3B 1P3

ROBERT, Gilles, R.C.A.; graphic designer; b. Montréal, Qué. 25 Apl. 1929; s. Rosaire H. and Thérèse (Bédard) R.; e. Institut des Arts Graphiques de la Prov. de Qué. Dipl. 1949; m. Céline d. Emile Pilon 31 July 1951; children: Dominique, Martin, Simon; PROP., GILLES ROBERT & ASSOCIÉS INC. 1968- ; Asst. to Art Dir., Rolph-Clark-Stone-Bennalack 1950-53; Free-lance artist and design instr. Qué. Inst. of G-A 1953-60; Ed. Art Dir. "La Presse" 1960-65; Prop. L & R inc. 1966-68; mem. Soc. des Graphistes du Qué. (Vice Pres.); Am. Inst. Graphic Arts; Liberal; R. Catholic; recreations: golf, cross-country skiing; Home: 1828 Van Horne, Outremont, Qué. H2V 1M5; Office: 306 Place Youville Pièce C.10, Montréal, Qué. H2Y 2B6.

ROBERTS, Charles Augustus, M.D.C.M., F.R.C.P.(C.), F.A.P.A.; physician; b. St. John's, Nfld., 31 March 1918; s. Job Henry and Effie Jane (Taylor) R.; e. Dalhousie Univ., B.Sc. 1939, M.D., C.M. 1942; m. Margaret Alice, d. Charles Manson, North Lochlaber, N.S., 7 Feb. 1942; one d., Ruby Avalon; PSYCHIATRIST, THE HOMEWOOD SANITARIUM Guelph, Ont. 1981- ; Prof., Psychiatry, Univ. Ottawa, (Chrmn. Dept. 1969-74); Supt., Hosp. for Mental and Nervous Diseases, St. John's, Nfld., 1945-50; Supt., Gen. Hosp., St. John's, Nfld., 1950-51; Chief, Mental Health Div., Dept. Nat. Health & Welfare, 1951-54 & Princ. M.O. in charge Mental Health & Health Ins. Studies, 1954-57; Med. Supt., Verdun Prof. Hosp. 1957-63; Asst. Prof., Dept. of Psychiatry, McGill Univ. 1957-64; Extve. Dir., Clarke Inst. of Psychiatry, Assoc. Prof., Dep't of Psychiatry, U. of Toronto, 1954-59; served in 2nd World War with C.A.M.C., 1942-45 in Can. and Overseas; Past Pres. Québec Psychiatric Assoc.; Candn. Psychiatric Assn. (Past Pres.); mem., Candn. Med. Assn.; Freemason; Address: 150 Delhi St., Guelph, Ont. N1E 6K9

ROBERTS, Edward Joseph, B.Com.; food processing executive; b. Chesterville, Ont. 31 Dec. 1925; s. Alfred Joseph and Margaret (MacMillan) R.; e. St. Malachy's Sch. Ottawa 1939; St. Patrick's Coll. Ottawa 1943; St. Patrick's Coll. Ottawa Univ. B.Com. 1950; m. Kathleen T. d. late A. E. Edwards, Ottawa, 23 July 1949; one d. Paula Karen; EXECUTIVE VICE PRES. CANADA PACKERS LTD.; Dir., P.H.H. Canada Services Inc.; Canadian Meat Council (Pres. 1976); Grocery Product Manufacturers of Can.; served with RCAF 1944-45; R. Catholic; recreations: skiing, golf, curling, swimming, fishing; Clubs: St. George's Golf & Country; Toronto Bd. of Trade; Home: 39 Eden Valley Dr., Islington, Ont. M9A 4Z5; Office: 95 St. Clair Ave., W., Toronto, Ont. M4V 1P2.

ROBERTS, Harry Duncan, C.M., M.D., F.R.C.S.(C.) L.L.D.; surgeon, retired; b. St. John's Nfld., 21 Nov. 1908; s. JOb Henry and Effie Jane (Taylor) R.; e. Meth. Coll.; Mem. Univ.; McGill Univ.; Dalhousie Univ., M.D. 1936; Memorial Univ., LL.D. (Hon.) 1980; m. Mary Katharine, d. Edward Gilmour Moxon, Truro, N.S., 21 June 1938; three s., Edward Moxon, Harry Douglas, Peter Job; Dir., Nfld. Steamships Ltd. 1974-80; Foundation Co. of Canada Ltd.; mem. Bd. of Regents, Mem. Univ., 1968-74; mem. Adv. Board, Canada Permanent Trust Co.; mem. Bd. of Finance (Nat.), Un. Ch. 1968-71; Royal Comn. on Econ. State and Prospects of Nfld. and Labrador, 1965-67; Chrmn., Gower St. Ch. Bd. of Stewards 1954-71; mem. Un. Ch. and Prot. Sch. Bds. 1940-68; Chrmn., Prince of Wales Coll. Bd., 1954-62; organ. Sea Cadets in Nfld. 1951; Pres., Guards Athletic Assoc., 1960-62; Nat. Pres., Navy League of Can., 1964-66; rec'd. Centennial Medal 1967; Jubilee medal, 1978; Order of Canada 1979; mem., Nfld.

Med. Assn. (Hon. Secy. 1939-47; Pres. 1950; Extve. 1962-65); Candn. Med. Assn. (Pres., 1971-72); Freemason; Liberal; United Church; Clubs: St. John's Fish & Game; Rotary; Home: Apt. 714, Elizabeth Towers, St. John's, Nfld. A1B 1S1; Office: 95 Le Marchant Rd., St. John's, Nfld. A1C 2H1

ROBERTS, Henry Reginald, B.A., LL.D., D.Hum. Lit., F.S.A.; b. Toronto, Ont., 2 June 1916; s. Alfred Reginald and Mary Margaret (Creighton) R.; e. Oakwood Collegiate Institute, Toronto, 1933; University of Toronto, B.A. 1937; Clarkson College of Technol., Dr. Humane Letters 1965; LL.D., Trinity College, 1970; Hartford 1971; m. Margaret Elizabeth, d. late Dr. Alexander Fisher, 23 May 1940; children: Michael Alfred, Barbara Elizabeth (Mrs. John Hegel), William Henry, Margaret Jane; CHRMN. OF BOARD, CONNECTICUT GENERAL INSURANCE CORP., since 1976; Dir. Gen., Foods Corp. & the Southern New England Telephone Co.; with Manufacturers Life Insurance Co., Toronto 1937-42; joined Group Pension Dept., Conn. Gen. Life Ins. Co., 1945; Asst. Secy. of Dept. 1948; Secy., Individual Accident and Health Ins. 1950; 2nd Vice Pres. 1958; Extve. Vice Pres. & el. a Dir., 1960; President Dir., Connecticut Gen. Life Ins. Co. 1961-76; Chrmn. of Bd., Aetna Ins. Co. (property & casualty affiliate of Conn. General) 1966; Pres., Conn. Gen. Ins. Co., on formation of the parent organization, 1967; served with RCAF 1942-45; rank Flight Ltd.; council mem. Internat. Extve. Service Corps; Chrmn of Bd of Trustees, Kingswood-OxfordSch.; Trustee-Hartford Graduate Center., Conn. Educational Telecommunications Corp., and YMCA of Metro Hartford; Corporator, Mt. Sinai, Hartford and St. Francis Hosps.; Conn. Inst. for Blind; Past Dir., Amer. Council of Life Ins.; former chrmn. Ins. Assn. of Conn.; Past Chrmn. Greater Hartford Chamber of Comm.; mem. Adv. Comte. on Business Programs, The Brookings Inst.; Home: 171 Bloomfield Ave., Hartford Conn.; Office: 900 Cottage Grove, Rd., Bloomfield, Conn.

ROBERTS, J. Frank; transportation executive; b. Quebec City, Que. 20 Oct. 1922; s. John and Ann (O'Doherty) R.; e. St. Patrick High Sch. Quebec City 1939; Staff Coll. 1954; m. Olga d. Anton Oniu 27 Apl. 1946; one s. Donald; CHRMN., PRESIDENT & C.E.O., VIA RAIL CANADA INC. since 1977 Chrmn 1978- ; joined CN as machinist-apprentice 1939, various positions incl. train-master and supt. of equipment 1945-61, Mgr. Champlain Area 1961, Montreal Area 1963, Gen. Mgr. St. Lawrence Region 1966, Gen. Mgr. Passenger Services 1969, Asst. Vice Pres. Freight Market Devel. 1970, Vice Pres. St. Lawrence Region 1972; served with RCAF 1942-45, Pilot Navig.; Offr. Order St. John Jerusalem; mem. Chambre de comm. du dist. de Montréal; Montreal Bd. of Trade Council; HRH The Duke of Edinburgh's, Fifth Commonwealth Study Conference, 1980; Conseil du Patronat du Qué.; Candn. Rlwy. Club; Cdn. Chamber of Comm.; Centres des dirigeants d'enterprises; Centraide Bd. of Dir., La fondation pour le Conseil de Presse du Qué.; R. Catholic; recreations: golf, fishing, photography; Clubs: St. Denis; Canadian; Kanawaki Golf; Traffic Club 50 Montreal; Canadian Railway Club; Home: 23 Westland Dr., Montreal West, Que. H4X 1L9; Office: (P.O. Box 8116), Montreal, Que. H3C 3N3

ROBERTS, Hon. John, P.C., M.P., B.A., B.Phil., D.Phil.; politician; b. Hamilton, Ont. 28 Nov. 1933; s. John Cecil and Jean Fitch (Batty) R.; e. Oakwood Coll. Inst. Toronto; Univ. of Toronto; Oxford Univ. Trinity Coll., St. Anthony's Coll.; Ecole Nationale d'adm., Paris; m. Beverly Hamm; MIN. OF SCIENCE AND TECHNOL., CAN. and Min. of the Environment 1980- ; Foreign Service Offr. Dept. of External Affairs 1963-66; Extve. Asst. to Min. of Forestry & Rural Devel. 1966-68; el. to H. of C. g.e. 1968; Parlty. Secy. to Min. of Regional & Econ. Expansion; def. g.e. 1972, re-el. 1974, def. 1979, re-el. 1980 (St. Paul's); Secy. of State and Sworn of Privy

Council 1976; Liberal; Home 27 Hillcrest Park, Toronto, Ont. Office: House of Commons, Ottawa, Ont. K1A 0A6.

ROBERTS, Kenneth Bryson, M.B., B.S., M.A., D.Phil.; educator; b. London, Eng. 7 Sept. 1923; s. William Charles Roberts, O.B.E.; e. Emanuel Sch. London; Univ. of London M.B., B.S. 1945; Oxford Univ. M.A., D.Phil. 1952; m. Ruth Mary d. E. St. John Catchpool, C.B.E. Apl. 1945; children: Daniel John, Peter Simon, Alason Clare, Benjamin Hugh; JOHN CLINCH PROF. HIST. OF MED. & PHYSIOL. MEMORIAL UNIV. OF NFLD. since 1978; Lectr. in Physiol. Exeter Coll. Oxford Univ. 1950-53; Assoc. Prof. of Physiol. Med. Sch. Baghdad 1954-56; Sr. Lectr. in Physiol. Med. Sch. Edinburgh Univ. 1956-61; Reader in Physiol. Univ. of London 1961-68; Prof. of Physiol. present Univ. 1968-78, Assoc. Dean of Med. 1968-75; co-author "General Pathology" 1954; "Introduction to Molecular Biology" 1964; "Companion to Medical Studies" 1968; various papers in scient. journs.; mem. Council, Med. Research Council 1968-73, mem. various comtes. since 1968; Past Chrmn. Scient. Adv. Subcomte. Candn. Heart Foundation; mem. various scient. and med. socs.; NDP; recreations: books, films, gardening, rowing; Office: Health Science Centre, St. John's, Nfld. A1B 3V6.

ROBERTS, Paul E(agon), B.A.; retired industrialist; b. Parkersburg, W. Va., 25 Jan. 1903; s. late Louis Rorer and late Lucy Lillian (Eagon) R.; e. "Kiski" Preparatory Sch., Saltsburg, Pa. (Grad. 1921); Lehigh Univ., B.A. 1925; Post-Grad. in Mining Engn. there; m. late Mary C., d. late Joseph Dailey; one d., Angela C. (Mrs. T. R. Pogue); 2ndly Betty C. Carlo, Dec. 1970; Dir. and mem. Extve. Comte., Abitibi Paper Co. Ltd.; Dir., Abitibi Corp.; began with U.S. Gypsum Co., Chicago, Ill., 1926, serving in various capacities in Operating, Sales and Engn. Depts.; ultimately became Eastern Operating Mgr. in charge of their Candn. & Eastern U.S. plants as well as Atlantic ships; joined Abitibi Power & Paper Co. Ltd. in 1949 as Manager of New Developments and Member of Management Comte.; in 1953, became Vice-Pres. and Gen. Mgr., Alaska Pine & Cellulose Ltd. (also a Dir.), and also a Dir. of Western Forest Industries Ltd. and Canadian Puget Sound Lumber & Timber Co.; apptd. Vice-Pres., Abitibi Paper Co., 1955; el. a Dir., October 1961; Executive Vice-President, 1961; President 1963; Chairman 1967-72; Director, Pulp & Paper Research Inst. Can., 1965; Trustee, Un. Appeal for Metrop. Toronto (1963); mem., Bd. Govs., Brock Univ. (1964); Chrmn., Finance Comte., Chrmn. (1967) Extve. Bd., Candn. Pulp & Paper Assn.; Trustee and Dir. (1963) The Quetico Foundation; Sigma Chi (Pres.); Omicron Delta Kappa (Hon.); became a Candn. citizen, 1959; Presbyterian; recreations: photography, golf, fishing; Clubs: York; Boca Raton (Florida); Royal Palm Golf & Country (Boca Raton, Fla.); Canadian; Rosedale Golf; Home: 1884 Thatch Palm Dr., Boca Raton, Fla.

ROBERTS, Richard James, Q.C.; barrister; b. Toronto, Ont., 17 March 1922; s. Charles Anthony and Eva Lloys (Lundy) R.; e. High Schs., Toronto and Wingham, Ont.; Osgoode Hall Law Sch.; called to the Bar of Ont. 1948; cr. Q.C. 1959; m. Lexie Andrena (Campbell); children by previous marriage: Mary Virginia, Catharine Elizabeth, Anne Victoria; PARTNER, ROBERTS & DRABINSKY; partner Roberts & Anderson, 1948; estbd. own practice 1968; partner Thomson, Rogers, 1971-78; Gunner with Royal Candn. Arty. 1941; rose through ranks to Capt.; landed in France on D-Day 6 June 1944; awarded Croix de Guerre and cr. Chevalier de l'Ordre de Leopold II de Belgique, avec palm; discharged 1946; former Lecturer, Osgoode Hall Law Sch.; Past Chrmn., Examining Bd. and Past Dir. Bar Admission Course, Law Soc. Upper Can.; Past mem., Bd. Dir., Law Soc. Foundation; mem. Co. York Law Assn.; recreations: music, reading, Candn. art; Clubs: University; Celebrity; Lawyers'; Bd. of Trade; Cambridge; Adelaide; Home: 73 Tranby Ave., Toronto,

Ont. M5R 1N4; Office: Suite 6965, First Canadian Pl., Toronto, Ont. M5X 1B1

ROBERTS, Thomas (Tom) Keith, R.C.A., O.S.A.; artist; b. Toronto, Ont., 22 Dec. 1908; s. Percy and Frieda (Humme) R.; e. N. Toronto (Ont.) Coll. Inst.; Central Tech. Sch., Toronto; Ont. Coll. of Art; m. Mary Regina, d. late James Quigley, 14 Sept. 1940; two d., Jane Grenville, Celia Mary; has exhibited with Royal Candn. Acad. since 1931, Ont. Soc. of Artists since 1929, Montreal Museum of Fine Arts since 1932 and Candn. Nat. Exhn. since 1931; exhibits in many travelling exhns.; a full-time painter, out-of-doors in 4 seasons, paints in Canada from coast to coast, experimentally in studio; solo exhibitions in Halifax, Montreal, Ottawa, Toronto, Winnipeg, Vancouver; rep. in many pub. and private colls. in Can., U.S.A. and Europe; winner of Rolph Clarke Stone Award 1949; served with RCE during World War II; me. (life), Ont. Soc. of Artists 1944- ; Roy. Candn. Acad. of Arts, 1945- ; Liberal; Protestant; recreations: hockey, music, reading, travel; Address: 1312 Stavebank Rd., Mississauga, Ont. L5G 2V2

ROBERTSON, Hon. Alexander Bruce, Q.C., B.A., b. Victoria, B.C. 23 Sept. 1904; s. Harold Bruce and Helen McGregor (Rogers) R.; e. Shawnigan Lake Sch. (B.C.) 1918; Trinity Coll. Sch. Port Hope, Ont. 1921; Univ. of Toronto B.A. 1925; Vancouver Law Sch.; m. Jean Keefer d. Dr. Neil Campbell, Thorold, Ont. 15 Feb. 1924; children: Joan Marjorie DeLong, Harold Barnard R.; called to Bar of B.C. 1928; cr. K.C. 1950; Assoc., Robertson, Douglas & Symes, Vancouver 1928 — 33, mem. 1933 — 46; successively Gen. Counsel, Vice Pres., Sr. Vice Pres., British Columbia Electric Co. Ltd. and its parent B.C. Power Corp. Ltd. 1946 — 61; Chrmn. and Pres., B.C. Power Corp. Ltd. 1961 — 63; Pres. Wilshire Oil Co. of Texas 1965; assoc. with Russell & Du Moulin, Vancouver 1964 — 67; Justice, Court of Appeal B.C. 1967 — 79; resumed association with Russell & Du Moulin October 1979; Alpha Delta Phi; Anglican; recreations: shooting, fishing; Home: 1329 Balfour Ave., Vancouver, B.C. V6H 1X8.

ROBERTSON, Alexander Campbell Macintosh, F.F.A., F.C.I.A.; insurance executive; b. Glasgow, Scot., 26 May 1923; s. Mr. and Mrs. A. S. Robertson; e. Robert Gordon's Coll., Aberdeen, 1936-40; St. Andrews Univ., 1941 and 1945-47; Faculty of Actuaries 1954; Fellow of Candn. Inst. of Actuaries, 1965; m. Joyce F. Bradford; children: Andrew Scott, Anna Marie; SR. VICE PRES. & CHIEF ACTUARY, SUN LIFE ASSURANCE OF CANADA, since 1973; joined present Co. in London, Eng., 1947; trans. to H.O. 1952; apptd. Actuarial Asst. 1952; Asst. Math. 1954; Math. 1955; Asst. Actuary 1956; Asst. Group Actuary 1958; Assoc. Group Actuary 1959; Group Actuary 1962; Extve. Offr., Group, 1965; Vice-Pres., Group Operations 1968, Vice Pres., Group 1970; served with R.A.F. as Flight Lieut., 1942-45; Clubs: M.A.A.A.; Dunany Country; Home: 4 Minorca Pl., Don Mills, Ont M3A 2Z6; Office: P.O. Box 4150, Station A, Toronto, Ont., M5W 2C9

ROBERTSON, Hon. Brenda Mary; b. Sussex, N.B., 23 May 1929; d. John James and Clara (Rothwell) Tubb; e. Sussex (N.B.) High Sch.; Mount Allison Univ.; m. Wilmot Waldon Robertson, 23 July 1955; children: Douglas John, C. Leslie Rae, Tracy Beth; MIN. OF HEALTH N.B. since 1976 engaged in management of W. W. Robertson Ltd.; 1st el. to N.B. Leg. in prof. g.e. 1967; re-el. 1970, 1974 and 1978; Min. of Youth and Social Serv. 1970-74; Past Prov. Pres., N.B. Home Econ. Assn. (1952-53); N.B. Women's P. Cons. Assn.; mem., Coverdale Women's P. Cons. Assn.(first pres.) ; United Church; Clubs: Moncton Golf & Country; Home: 108 Fairway Blvd., Riverview, N.B. E1B 1T3; Office: Centennial Bldg., P.O. Box 6000, Fredericton, N.B. E3B 5H1

ROBERTSON, David Struan, Ph.D.; consulting geologist; b. Winnipeg, Man., 3 Mar. 1924; e. Colin Archibald and Maud (Hocken) R.; e. Univ. of Man., B.Sc. (Hons., Phys. Chem. & Geol.), 1946; Columbia Univ., Ph.D. (Geol.), 1949; m. Wanda Lee, d. Lennon Spears, 24 Jan. 1951; children: Jennifer Lynne, Joanna Lee, Julia Merriam; PRESIDENT, DAVID S. ROBERTSON & ASSOC. LTD., since 1965; Chrmn., Pres., David S. Robertson & Assocs. Inc., Denver, Colorado; Party Chief, Geol. Survey of Can., 1946-49; Asst. Prof., Univ. of Va., 1949-51; Sr. Research Geol., International Nickel Co., 1951-53; Chief Geol. (Angola), E. J. Longvear Co., 1953-54; Chief Geol. and Vice-Pres., Stancan Uranium Corpn., 1955-58; Vice-Pres. and Dir., Dir., Stanrock Uranium Mines Ltd., 1956-67; Pres., GMX Corpn., 1958-60; Consulting Geol., 1960-65; Dir., S. W. Tyler Co. of Can. Ltd.; Combustion Engineering-Superheater Ltd.; mem., Assn. Prof. Engrs., Ont.; Candn. Inst. Mining & Metall.; Soc. Econ. Geols.; Geol. Assn. Can.; Geol. Soc. Am.; Geol. Soc. S. Africa; Delta Upsilon; United Church; recreation: curling; cross country skiing, fishing; Clubs: Granite; Engineers (Toronto); Caledon Mountain Trout; Home: 10 King Maple Place, Willowdale, Ont. M2K 1X6; Office: 65 Queen St. W., Toronto, Ont. M5H 2M7

ROBERTSON, Elizabeth Chant, M.D., M.A., Ph.D., C.M.; physician; b. Toronto, Ont., 17 Apl. 1899; d. Clarence Augustus Chant and Jean (Laidlaw) C.; e. Univ. Coll., Univ. of Toronto, B.A. 1921; M.B. 1924, M.A. 1928, Ph.D. 1937; Sch. of Hygiene, Johns Hopkins Univ., Fellow in Hygiene, 1925-26; m. Hartley Grant, s. J. C. Robertson, 30 June 1926; children: Mary Elizabeth, Helen Chant; Hon. Consultant and Research Assoc., Hosp. for Sick Children, Toronto, Ont.; House Phys., Toronto Gen. Hosp., 1924-25; engaged in med. research, Connaught Labs., Univ. of Toronto, 1926-28; mem., Am. Inst. Nutrition; Candn. Paediatric Soc.; Cdn. Nutrition Soc.; Toronto Acad. of Med.; author of "Fundamentals of Health", 1943 (Can.), 1948 (N.Y.); sr. author, "Health, Science and You" (books 1, 2, 3, 4, 1967 and 1969); "Today's Child", 1971 (Can.), 1972 (N.Y.); co-author "The Normal Child", 1958; "Nutrition for Today", 3rd ed. 1968; "Tomorrow is Now", 1971; "The Right Combination (A Guide to Food and Nutrition)", Eng. ed. 1975, Fr. ed. 1978; Metric Ed. 1979; Alpha Omega Alpha; Liberal; United Church; Home: 503 Davenport Rd., Toronto, Ont. M4V 1B8; Office: 555 University Ave., Toronto, Ont. M5G 1X8

ROBERTSON, Gardner Thomas, C.D., B.A., F.I.C.B.; banker; b. Toronto, Ont., 25 Apl. 1926; s. Thomas Preston and Sarah (Gardner) R.; e. Univ. of Toronto, Victoria Coll. B.A. 1949, Ont. Coll. of Educ. 1954; Sch. of Tank Technol. U.K., 1951-52; m. Jene Agnes, d. Edward McClung, 15 July 1950; children: Jane, Ian, Kathryn Ann; VICE PRES., TRAINING, BANK OF MONTREAL since 1981; Teacher, Collingwood (Ontario) Coll. Inst., 1954-57; Ford Motor Co. of Canada Ltd., Oakville, 1957-66; held various positions incl. Training & Safety Mgr.; joined Bank of Montreal 1966; served as Manpower Planning & Development Manager for four years; apptd. Asst. to President then Vice President (Marketing), 1970; Sr. Vice Pres., Personnel 1975; Vice-Pres., Personnel, Falconbridge Nickel Mines, 1978-81; Lecturer, Department of Continuing Education, McGill University, 1967-73; served with Royal Canadian Armoured Corps and Royal Candn. Dragoons during World War II and post-war; rank Maj.; mem. Oakville-Trafalgar Bd. of Educ. 1962-66; Fellow, Inst. of Canadian Bankers; mem., Univ. of Toronto Alumni Assn.; Inst. Candn. Bankers Past Chrmn., Bd. of Gov.; Am. Soc. Training & Devel. (Past Pres. Ont, Chapter); Sales & Marketing Extves.-Internat.; Presbyterian; recreations: reading, skiing, woodworking; Clubs: University; Home: 75 Ford Dr., Oakville, Ont. L6J 6E2; Office: Bank of Montreal Institute Wellington Square, 26 Wellington St. E., Toronto, Ont. M5E 1S2

ROBERTSON, George Burnley, C.M.M., E.D., C.D., Q.C., LL.M.; b. Bridgewater, N.S., 8 Aug. 1916; s. Robert Burnley Hume & Olive Mary (Stairs) R.; e. Bridgewater (N.S.) Pub. Schs., 1922-26; Halifax (N.S.), 1926-34; Dalhousie Univ., B.A. 1938, LL.B. 1940; Harvard Law Sch., LL.M. 1946; m. Shirley Elizabeth, d. Fred B. Barnstead, Halifax, N.S., 6 May 1950; children: Heather, Cynthia, Judith, Janet; PARTNER, McINNES, COOPER & ROBERTSON; Dir., Central Trust Co.; The Canadian Surety Co.; Ellis-Don Ltd.; Loblaw Co. Ltd. United Funds Management Ltd.; Enheat Inc.; Chrmn. of Bd., Maritime Life Assnce. Co.; Special Lecturer in Political Science, Dalhousie University, 1947-48; Lecturer in Corp. Law, Dalhousie Law School, 1949-54; read law with Arthur S. Pattilo, Q.C.; called to the Bar of Nova Scotia, 1941; cr. Q.C. 1957; served with 1st (Halifax) Coast Regt. RCA (NPAM), 1930-39; CASF (RCA), 1939-46 in Can.; U.K. and N.W. Europe; grad. RCAF Staff Coll. 1944; with Candn. Army Militia 1948-70; Brig. Gen. Sr. Militia Adv., Atlantic Region to Candn. Forces HQ 1966-70; Commr., Pub. Service Comn. of Halifax since 1957 and presently Vice Chrmn.; Fed. of Ins. Counsel; Pres., N.S. Barristers Soc., 1962-63; Vice Pres. for N.S. Candn. Bar Assn., 1964-66; Phi Delta Theta (Prov. Pres. 1961-63); Pres. (1969-70) Halifax Bd. of Trade; Liberal; United Church; recreations: philately; Clubs: R.N.S.Y.S.; Halifax; Waegwoltic; Royal Candn. Mil. Inst. (Toronto); Home: 1080 Ridgewood Dr., Halifax, N.S.; B3H 3Y4 Office: 1673 Bedford Row, P.O. Box 730, Halifax, N.S. B3J 2V1

ROBERTSON, George Hillyard; writer, broadcaster; b. Regina, Sask., 4 Nov. 1922; s. Thomas Hillyard and Ida (Voligny) R.; e. Victoria Pub. Sch., Campion Coll. and Central Coll., Regina, 1939; Wesley Un. Coll., Winnipeg, 1944-45; m. Phyllis May, d. Edmund Andrews, Sydney, N.S., 9 Oct. 1954; children: George Gavin, Athol Edmund, Morna Cairine; Announcer, CJRM Regina, 1939-40; Announcer-Actor, CBC Winnipeg, 1940-42, 1944-45; Producer, CBC Internat. Service, 1945-46; Free-lance Writer and Broadcaster, Montreal, 1946-49 and Toronto, since 1949; writings incls. over 100 dramas produced by CBC TV and radio, gen. articles for various mags. (Toronto Ed., "Canadian Art", 1952-54) and documentary films; 1st radio drama 1943 and 1st TV drama 1952, CBC; wrote 30 episodes "Moment of Truth" for NBC/CBC-TV; 50 episodes "Scarlett Hill" CBC/ATV TV; created "Quentin Durgens, M.P." and wrote all episodes CBC/TV; developed, princ. writer and script ed. "House of Pride", all episodes CBC/TV; princ. writer and assoc. producer "Snelgrove Snail" World synd. TV; acted in all princ. TV and radio drama series since 1949 incl. "CBC Stage", "Ford Theatre", "GM Presents", "Show of the Week"; commentary and criticism incl. CBC's "Critically Speaking", "CJBC Views the Shows"; wrote and broadcast "Worth Knowing" daily 1952-60; narrator National Film Board films; Co-founder Jupiter Theatre 1951; nominated for Canadian Film Awards "Best Screenplay" ("The Night Nothing Happened"), 1969; feature films include "The Road to Chaldaea", 1968; "Face-Off" 1970; "Party Games" 1970; co-author (with Scott Young), "Face-Off", novel 1971; served as Radar Tech. with RCAF 1942-44; mem., Assn. Candn. TV & Radio Artists (Pres., Montreal Br., 1946-48); Anglican; recreations: bridge, tennis, swimming, cooking, wine-making; Club: Toronto Lawn Tennis; Home: 158 Glen Rd.,Toronto, Ont. M4W 2W6

ROBERTSON, H. Rocke, C.C. (1969), B.Sc., M.D., C.M., D.Sc., LL.D., F.R. S. (C.) F.R.C.S.(C), F.A.C.S., F.R.C.S.(E); b. Victoria, B.C., 4 Aug. 1912; e. St. Michael's Sch.; Ecole Nouvelle, Coppet, Switzerland; Brentwood Coll.; McGill Univ., B.Sc. 1932, M.D. 1936; D.C.L. Bishops Univ. 1963; LL.D., Manitoba, Toronto, Victoria, (B.C.) 1964, Glasgow 1965, Michigan, Dartmouth 1967, McGill 1970, Sir George Williams 1971; D.Sc., Brit. Columbia 1964; Memorial 1968; Jefferson 1969; D. de l'Un. Montréal 1968; m. Beatrice Roslyn Arnold, Montreal, Que.; four children; Director, Bell Telephone Company of Canada; Ralston Purina Co. of Can.; Interne, Montreal General Hospital, 1936-38; Clinical Assistant in Surgery, Royal Infirmary, Edinburgh, 1938-39; Jr. Assistant in Surgery, Montreal General Hospital, 1939-40; Assistant Surgeon, 1940-44, Chief of Surg., Vancouver, (B.C.) Mil. Hosp., 1944-45; Head Surg., Shaughnessy Hosp., D.V.A., 1945-50; Prof. of Surg., Univ. B.C., 1950-59; Surgeon in chief (Protem) Peter Bert Brigham Hospital Boston 1956; Visiting Lectr., Harvard Univ. 1956; apptd. temp. Dir., Professional Unit, St. Bartholomew's Hsop., London Eng. 1958; Surg.-in-Chief, Montreal Gen. Hosp. Chrmn., Dept. of Surg., Faculty of Medicine of McGill Univ., 1959-62; Principal and Vice-Chancellor, McGill Univ. 1962-70; served overseas in second World War with R.C.A.M.C., 1940-45, discharged with rank of Lieut.-Col.; author of numerous articles in scient. journs; has lectured extensively in Can. and United States; Bd of Curators, Osler Library, McGill Univ.; Royal Coll. Physicians and Surgs. Can. (Vice-Pres., 1955); Hon. Archivist, 1977- ; Am. Coll. Surg. (Bd. of Regents, 1961); Sci. Council of Can.; Home: R.R. 2 Mountain, Ont. K0E 1S0

ROBERTSON, James Lovett, Q.C.; b. Chilliwack, B.C., 6 March 1920; s. James William and Mabel Elva (Bishop) R.; e. pub. and high schs. St. Walburg, Sask.; m. Kathleen d. Archer P. Richardson, 15 March 1944; children: Reynold A. J., Roberta A.; PARTNER, ROBERTSON, MUŻYKA, BELL, ROBERTSON & NIEMAN; read law with Moxon, Schmitt & Estey, Saskatoon; called to Bar of Sask. 1949; cr. Q.C. 1964; served with 2nd Div. Candn. Army Overseas WW II, rank Lt.; mem. Law Soc. Sask.; Candn. Bar Assn.; United Church; Clubs: Saskatoon; Riverside Golf & Country; Home: 27 Kirk Cres., Saskatoon, Sask. S7H 3B1; Office: i311 Twentieth St. East, Saskatoon, Sask.S7K 0A9

ROBERTSON, James MacPhie, C.L.U.; executive; b. N. Sydney, N.S., 27 April 1926; s. Margaret Jessie (MacPhie) and late George Browe R.; e. Sydney (N.S.) Acad.; Am. Coll. of Life Underwriters, Bryn Mawr, Pa.; m. Margaret Adeline, d. late George Mackley, 9 Aug. 1952; children: George Mackley, James Andrew, Catherine Lillian; EXTVE. VICE-PRES. AND DIRECTOR, MANUFACTURERS LIFE INSURANCE CO. since 1978; commenced as Reporter, then Editor, 4, 1947-50; Sydney Post Record 1943; with Candn. Press, Toronto, Ont. 1950; joined present Co. in H.O. 1950; trans. to Los Angeles Br. as Asst. Mgr. 1955; Mgr., Hartford Br. 1959; Mgr., Cleveland Br. 1963; Br. Mgr., Boston 1969; Agency Vice-Pres., Candn. Div., Toronto 1970; Vice-Pres., Candn. Operns., 1972; Vice Pres. Marketing Operns., 1973; Sr. Vice Pres., 1974; Exec. Vice Pres., 1976; Dir. 1978; served in Candn. Parachute Corps. 1945-46; mem., Bd. of Dir. Candn. Opera Assn.; Ont. Heart Fdn.; Am. Soc. Chart. Life Underwriters; Life Ins. Marketing & Research Assn.; Am. Council of Life Ins.; Candn. Chamber of Commerce; Conference Bd. of Can.; United Church; recreations: sailing, travel; Clubs: R.C.Y.C.; Toronto Cricket Skating and Curling; Office: 200 Bloor St. E., Toronto, Ont. M4W 1E5

ROBERTSON, John R., F.C.A.; Canadian civil servant; b. Toronto, 29 Aug. 1933; e. C.A. Ont. 1959, Fellow 1976; m. Lilliam Margaret, June 21, 1958; children: Melodie Colleen, Robbyn Lyn, Noreen Jacqueline; DIR. GEN. COMPLIANCE DIRECTORATE, NAT. REVENUE TAXATION, CAN. 1982- ; served as auditor Toronto and Calgary Dist. Offices Revenue Can., Taxation; Audit Review Div. Taxation Operations Br. 1970-73, Asst. Dir. Tech. Interpretations Div. 1973-75, Dir. Tax Avoidance Div. 1975-77; Dir. Gen. Corporate Rulings Directorate 1977-82; served various community assns.; Home: 1910 Oakdean Cres., Ottawa, Ont. K1J 6H3; Office: 875 Heron Rd., Ottawa, Ont. K1A 0L8.

ROBERTSON, Joseph H., M.A.; industrialist; b. Neepawa, Man., Sept. 1918; e. Brandon Coll. (Univ. of Manitoba); Univ. of Toronto, M.A. 1941; SR. VICE PRES., DOMTAR INC.; 1979- ; joined the Co. as Research Chem. Cornwall, Ont. 1941, subsequently Tech. Supt., Head Paper Research & Devel., Asst. to Dir. Research and Tech. Dir.; apptd. Asst. Gen. Mgr. Howard Smith Div. Domtar Pulp & Paper Ltd. 1961, Gen. Mgr. 1962, Vice Pres. and Gen. Mgr. 1966 (Div. name changed to Domtar Fine Papers Ltd. 1968); Pres. Domtar Pulp & Paper Products Ltd. 1974; Exec. Vice-Pres. Domtar Inc., 1979; Dir., Domtar Inc.; mem. Candn. Pulp & Paper Assn. (Past Chrmn. Tech. sec.); Tech. Assn. Pulp & Paper Industry U.S.; Vice-Pres. and Treas. Reddy Mem. Hosp. Montreal; Chrmn. Reddy Memorial Hosp. Foundn.; Corp., Rep. Internat. Mgmt. & Devel. Inst., Washington, D.C.; recreations: squash, golf, fishing, cross-country skiing; Royal Montreal Golf and Country; Clubs: Cornwall (Ont.) Golf & Country; St. James's; M.A.A.A.; Office: 395 de Maisonneuve Blvd. W., Montreal, Que. H3A 1L6

ROBERTSON, Commodore Owen Connor Struan, O.C. (1970), G.M., R.D., C.D., D.Sc., D.M.Sc.; master mariner; arctic consultant; b. Victoria, B.C., 16 March 1907; s. Capt. George Edward Livingstone and Mabel Johanna (Connor) R.; e. Univ. Sch., Victoria, B.C., 1915-16; Shawnigan Lake Prep. Sch., B.C., 1917-19; St. Albans Sch., Brockville, Ont., 1920-23; West Hill High Sch., Montreal, 1923-26; obtained Masters (Foreign Going) Cert. of Competency, 1932; RCAF Search and Rescue and Survival Sch., grad.; McGill Univ., D.Sc.; m. Marjorie Sylvia, d. late George Wise, 21 Aug. 1939; two d. Sandra Louise Wilson, Michele Straun LaCasse; began career with Candn. Govt. Merchant Marine (cargo ships); Third Offr. to First Offr., Candn. Nat. Steamships (passenger ships); Sub-Lt., RCN Reserve, 1931; served in RCN in various appts. (Lt. to Capt.) 1938-46; Extve. Offr. and C.O. Sail Training Ship and Auxillary Cruiser; C.O., Minesweeper and as Flotilla Commdr.; Offrs. Training Estab., Fleet Estab. and H.M.C. Dockyard, Halifax and as King's Harbour Master; C.O., Fleet Estab., H.M.C. Dockyard, Ships in Reserve and as King's Harbour Master, rank A Capt. 1946-52; also C.O., Destroyer and as Flotilla Commdr.; C.O., H.M.C.S. Niobe; served as Sr. Candn. Naval Offr. with RN; Naval mem., Candn. Jt. Staff (London); Candn. Naval. mem., Mil. Agency for Standardization; Naval. Adv. Comte. of W. Europe Regional Planning Staff; Commdr. (designate) Arctic Patrol and Research Vessel, service with U.S.N. forces in Arctic, 1952-54; Commanding H.M.C.S. Labrador, Arctic Research and Patrol Vessel (circumnavig. of N. Am.), 1954-57; also Commdr., U.S.N. Task Group 6.3; on loan to U.S.N. as Depy. Commdr. for Polar Operations; Mil. Sea Transport Service; Commdg. H.M.C.S. Niagara, Naval mem. Candn. Jt. Staff (Washington), 1957-62; during this period loaned to U.S.N. for various periods on Polar operations; retired from RCN 1962; Depy. Dir., Arctic Inst. of N. Am. (on loan to Expo '67 as Scient. Adviser), 1962; Co-Founder, Northern Associates Reg'd., 1967; conducted Panarctic Sea Lift to Melville Isl., environmental study for S.S. Manhattan, 1968-69; has served as Gov., Arctic Inst. of N. Am.; Hon. Lectr., McGill Univ.; mem., Geotech. Comte., Nat. Research Council; Dir., Last Post Fund; mem., Nat. Comte. on N. & Arctic Scouting; Arbitrator, Maritime Appeals Bd.; Chrmn., Comte. on Shipbldg. in Can.; Consultant; David Sarnoff Research Lab.; U.S. Office of Naval Research; USAF Geophys. Comte.; Comn. on N. Transport.; awarded Back Grant; Massey Medal; Centennial Medal; writings incl. articles for various tech. publs.; book chapters, TV and radio documentaries; Fellow, Arctic Inst. N. Am.; mem., Marine Techonol. Soc.; Anglican; recreations: swimming, golf, fishing; Club: University; Home: 108 King St., Oakville, Ont. L6B 1B1

ROBERTSON, (Robert) Gordon, C.C., LL.D., F.R.S.C.; b. Davidson, Sask., 19 May 1917; s. John Gordon and Lydia Adelia (Paulson) R.; e. Public and High Schs., Regina, Sask.; Univ. of Sask., B.A. 1938, LL.D. 1959; Oxford Univ., B.A. (Juris.) 1940; Univ. of Toronto, M.A. 1941, LL.D. 1973; LL.D. McGill University, 1963; Dalhousie, 1977; Laval, D.Univ. 1975; m. Beatrice Muriel, d. late Rev. Dr. and Mrs. C. B. Lawson, Toronto, Ont., 14 Aug. 1943; children: John Lawson, Karen Martha; PRES., INST. FOR RESEARCH ON PUBLIC POLICY since 1980; Chancellor, Carleton Univ. since 1980; Third Secy., Dept. of External Affairs, 1941; Asst. to Under-Secy. of State for External Affairs, 1943-45; Secy. to the Office of the Prime Minister, 1945-49; Member of Cabinet Secretariat (Privy Council Office), 1949-51; Asst. Secy. to the Cabinet, 1951-53; Depy. Min., Dept. of N. Affairs & Nat. Resources, 1953-63; Commr., N.W. Terr., 1953-63; Clerk of the Privy Council and Secy. to Cabinet 1963-75; Secy. to Cabinet for Prov.-Fed. Relations 1975-79 (ret.); awarded Vanier Medal by Inst. Pub. Adm. Can. 1970; United Church; recreations: reading, skiing; Club: Rideau; Home: 20 Westward Way, Rockcliffe Park, Ottawa, Ont. K1L 5A7; Office: Federal-Provincial Relations Office, Ottawa, Ont. K1P 5Y7

ROBERTSON, Ronald, Q.C., lawyer; b. Windsor, Ont., 14 April 1926; s. Peter Comrie and Agnes (Baillie) R.; e. Public Sch. and Patterson Coll. Inst., Windsor, Ont.; Univ. of Western Ont., B.A. 1948; Osgoode Hall Law Sch. (1956); m. Wanza Kate, d. Eric Buckley, 1 Sept. 1951; children: Holly Anne, Peter Norman, Heather Agnes (dec. 16 May 1980), and Elizabeth Kate; PARTNER, McCARTHY & McCARTHY; Dir., Canadian Tax Foundation, 1961-67; Extve. Asst. to the Dir., Canadian Tax Foundation, 1958-61; Reporter, The Windsor Daily Star, 1948-52; Past Pres., Ont. Leg. Press Gallery; called to the Bar of Ont.; 1956; cr. Q.C. 1969; practised law, Windsor, Ont., Messrs. Fraser & McPherson, and Messrs. Brown & Robertson, 1956-58; R.C.A.F., 1944-45; Presbyterian; Home: 1238 Wildfield Cres., Mississauga, Ontario L5H 3C2; Office: 48th Floor, Toronto-Dominion Bank Tower, Toronto, Ont. M5K 1E6

ROBERTSON, William James; air traffic controller; labour association executive; b. Toronto, Ont. 8 Jan. 1946; s. Bruce Alexander and Dorothy Margaret (Hemphill) R.; e. elem. and high schs. Ont.; m. Elizabeth Anne d. late Barry Bertrand Benness 30 Sept. 1978; one s. Ian Gregory; Pres., CANDN. AIR TRAFFIC CONTROL ASSN. 1979- ; licenced Air Traffic Controller 1967; Ont. Regional Dir. present Assn. 1973/1975, Nat. Vice Pres. 1975/1979; mem. Internat. Fed. Air Traffic Controllers Assn. (Regional Councillor N. and Central Am. 1977/1979); Soc. Air Safety Investigators; Home: 25 Beechmont Cres., Ottawa, Ont. K1B 4A7; Office: 604, 1 Nicholas St., Ottawa, Ont. K1N 7B7.

ROBERTSON, William Struan, Q.C.; b. Milton, Ont., 6 May 1921; s. Donald S. and Katherine M. (Dewar) R.; e. Pub. Sch., Milton, Ont.; Appleby Coll. (Oakville); Univ. of Toronto, B.A.; Osgoode Hall Law Sch.; m. Barbara Joan d. Alexander S. Elliott, 17 May 1944; children: Rebecca Ann, Mary Jane, Struan Elliott; PARTNER, BORDEN, & ELLIOT; Dir., Loblaw Cos. Ltd.; Ilford Photo (Canada) Ltd.; National Tea Co.; Canadian Hilti Ltd.; Paderno Canada Ltd.; Dir. & mem. Extve. Comte., Trans Canada Freezers Ltd.; American Consumer Industries Inc.; Secy., Dir. & mem. Extve Comte., Eastern Utilities Ltd.; read law with Borden, Elliot, Kelley & Palmer; called to Bar of Ont. 1948; Q.C. 1962; served in 2nd world war with R.C.A.F. as Flight Lieut.; awarded D.F.C.; mem. & Secy., Bd. Govs. Appleby Coll.; mem., Candn. Bar Assn.; York County Law Assn.; Psi Upsilon; Presbyterian; recreations: tennis, skiing, aviation; Clubs: York; Toronto; Toronto Lawn Tennis; Osler Bluff Ski (Hon. Pres.); Queen's; Home: 103 Crescent Rd., Toronto, Ont. M4W 1T7; Office: 250 University Ave., Toronto, Ont. M5H 3E9

ROBIC, Raymond Andre; patent attorney; b. St. Malo, France, 24 Mar. 1899; s. Victor and Celestine (Petit) R.; e. Jesuit Coll., Brest, France; Montreal Tech. (Grad. with Distinction); m. 1st, Beatrice Stanton (died); 2ndly, Irene, d. V. E. Beauchemin, Sorel, Que., 17 Sept. 1924; children: Mrs. Jean Marchand, Jean Marc, Mrs. J. Brunet; came to Can. 1910; DIR., PROP., MARION, ROBIC & ROBIC (patent attorneys); with Steel Company of Canada Ltd.; Montreal Locomotive Works, Canadian General Electric Company, Peterborough, Ontario, 1914-17; read patent law with Marion and Marion, Montreal, 1917-21; admitted to practice, Canada and U.S.A., 1921; Partner, Linton, Kellogg, Robic and Bastien, Washington, D.C., 1922; Marion and Marion, Montreal 1922; Prof. Faculty of Econ. and Political Science Laval Univ., 1945; Gen. Propagandist of Tech. Educ. of Que., 1936; war services 1941-46; successively Mgr. for Que. and Ottawa Valley, Indust. and Sub-Contract Co-ordination Br., Dept. of Mun. & Supply; Special Rep. of Co-ordinator of Production on Mobilization Br. at Montreal and Que.; Dir. of Personnel and Supt. of Manpower Training, Que. Shipyards Ltd.; Tech. Advisor on Econ. Advisory Bd. of Que.; Asst. Dir. Gen. Dept. of Mun. & Supply, Montreal; Asst., Co-ordinator of Pub. Projects, Dept. of Reconstr., Ottawa; Pres. and Gen. Mgr., Welcker Lyster Co. Ltd.; Founding mem. (1926) and past Pres. Patent and Trademark Inst. of Can. (1937); mem., Comn. of Studies, Montreal Tech. Sch. 1936; Candn. Group, Internat. Assn. for Protection of Indust. Property (Pres. 1964-66); Chart. Inst. of Patents Agents, London, Eng.; Soc. des Ingénieurs Civils de France, Paris; Am. Soc. for Metals; French Chamber of Comm.; Past Dir. Chamber of Comm. of Dist. of Montreal; mem., Am. Inst. of Mgmt., Ind. Commrs. Ass. of Que.; Gen. Secy., Corp. Prof. Tech's., Que.; Small Indust. Co-ordinator, Que. Dist., Dept. of Defence Production, 1951-52; Life Gov., Notre Dame Hosp., Montreal; hon. mem., Candn. Patent and Trademark Inst. 1977; recreations: travel, scientific experimenting; Club: Mount Stephen; Home: 49 Hazelwood Ave., Outremont, Que.; H3T 1R2 Office: 1514 Ave. Dr. Penfield, Montreal, Que. H3G 1X5

ROBICHAUD, Hon. Hédard-J., P.C. (Can.); b. Shippegan, N.B., 2 November 1911; s. John G. and Amanda (Boudreau) R.; e. Acad. Ste. Famille Tracadie; Sacred Heart Univ.; Saint-Joseph Univ.; m. Gertrude, d. Frederick Leger, 29 Oct. 1937; nine children; Lieutenant Governor, N.B., 1971-81; Inspector of Fisheries with Dominion Govt., 1938-46; Dir. of Fisheries for N.B., 1946-52; 1st el. to H. of C. for Gloucester, G.E. 1953; Minister of Fisheries, 22 Apl. 1963-68; summoned to the Senate of Can. July 1968; Director, National Sea Products Limited; mem. Roosevelt Campobello International Park Com. 1970- ; Liberal; Roman Catholic; recreation: fishing; Home: 238 Waterloo Row, Fredericton, N.B. E3B 1Z3; Office: Government House, Fredericton, N.B.

ROBICHAUD, Hon. Louis J., C.C. (1971), P.C. (1967), Q.C., B.A., D.C.L., LL.D., Dr. Pol. Sc.; senator; b. St. Anthony, New Brunswick, 21 October 1925; s. Amédée and Annie (Richard) R., both Acadians; e. Sacred Heart Univ., Bathurst, N.B., B.A. 1947, Dr. Pol. Sc. 1960; Laval Univ., 1946-49; admitted to the Bar of N.B. 1952; LL.D. New Brunswick 1960, Montreal, St. Joseph's, 1961; Ottawa 1962, St. Dunstan's 1964, St. Thomas 1965, McGill, Dalhousie 1969, D.C.L., Mount Allison 1961, Moncton 1973; m. Lorraine, d. P. B. Savoie, Neguac, N.B., 9 Aug. 1951; children: Jean-Claude, Paul, Louis-René, Monique; first el. to N.B. Leg., g.e. 1952; Leader of Opposition in the Leg., 1958-60; Premier 1960-70 and Attorney General, N.B. 1960-65; Min. of Youth 1968-70; Leader of Opposition 1970; Chrmn. Candn. Sec. Internat. Jt. Comn. 1971; summoned to Senate of Can., 21 Dec. 1973; read and articled in law with Albany Robichaud, Q.C.; cr. Q.C. July 1960; Liberal; Roman Catholic; Home: 2365 Georgina Dr., Ottawa, Ont. K2B 7M6; Office: Senate of Canada, Ottawa, Ont. K1A 0A4

ROBICHAUD, Michel; couturier; b. Montréal, Qué. 9 June 1939; s. Emile and Charlotte (Laberge) R.; e. Scholar, Chambre Syndicale de la couture parisienne 1960-61; Probationer, Nina Ricci's Workshop, Paris 1962; Designer, Guy Laroche House of Fashion, Paris 1962; m. Lucienne d. Léo Lafrenière, Shawinigan Sud, Qué. 7 March 1963; PROP., MICHEL ROBICHAUD INC.; mem. Chamber Comm. Montréal; R. Catholic; Club: Beaver; Home: 1321 ouest, rue Sherbrooke, Montréal, Qué. H3G 1J4; Office: 2195 Crescent St., Montréal, Qué. H3G 2C1.

ROBINETTE, John Josiah, C.C. (1973), Q.C., D.C.L., LL.D.; b. 1906; s. late Thomas Cowper R., K.C., noted lawyer; e. Univ. of Toronto Schs.; University of Toronto (Gold Medallist); Osgoode Hall Toronto (Gold Medallist); L.L.D., Toronto; D.C.L. Western Ontario; LL.D Queen's; married; three d., Joan, Wendy, Dale; PARTNER, McCARTHY & McCARTHY; Bencher, Law Soc. of Upper Can. (Past Treas.); has been mainly engaged in civil practice of his profession, but gained public renown for his role as defence counsel in a number of criminal cases, particularly that of the Crown vs. Evelyn Dick, charged with murder, in which he obtained an acquittal; after grad. joined the teaching staff of Osgoode Hall till 1943; Editor of "Ontario Law Reports", 1935-40; acted as Special Prosecutor for the Crown in several celebrated cases, ranging from a gold smuggling conspiracy trial to war-time draft evasion; in recent years has been counsel in the Supreme Court of Can. in several leading constitutional and civil cases; Liberal; recreations: swimming, golf; Home: 408 Glenayr Rd., Toronto, Ont. M5P 3C7; Office: Box 48, Toronto-Dominion Centre, Toronto, Ont. M5K 1E6

ROBINS, Sydney Lewis, B.A., LL.B., LL.M., LL.D.; b. Toronto, Ont., 24 May 1923; s. Samuel and Bessie (Kamarner) R.; e. Univ. of Toronto, B.A. 1944, LL.B. 1947; Osgoode Hall Law Sch., 1947; Harvard Law Sch., LL.M. 1948; m. Gloria, d. S. I. Robinson, Winnipeg, Man., 8 Aug. 1951; children: Erica, Gregg, Reid, Blair; JUSTICE, SUPREME COURT OF ONT. since 1976; formerly sr. partner Robins & Robins; called to Bar of Ont. 1947; cr. Q.C. 1962; Special Lectr., in Torts, Osgoode Hall Law Sch., 1948-61; Lectr., Law Soc. Special Lectures, 1960-62, 1976 and 1979; mem., Senate, York Univ. 1968-71; Dir., Baycrest Home for the Aged; Past Dir., New Mount Sinai Hosp.; Past Gov., Beth Tzedec Synagogue; Bencher, Law Society of Upper Canada, since 1961 (Treasurer 1971-73; Past Chrmn. Continuing and Legal Educ. Comtes.); mem., Candn. Bar Assn. (Council mem.; Past Chrmn. Civil Justice Sec. & Labour Relations Sec.); Chrmn., Law Foundation Ont. 1974-76; Hon. Counsel, United Jewish Welfare Fund of Toronto 1973-76; mem., Club: Oakdale Golf & Country (Dir.); Office: Osgoode Hall, Toronto, Ont.

ROBINSON, Gerald D.; food company executive b. Regina, Sask., 10 Dec. 1923; s. George McDougal and Violet (Copeland) R.; e. Scott Collegiate, Regina, Sask. (Grad. 1940); m. Violet, d. George Walter Guthrie, 26 Oct. 1946; children: Pamela Starr, Janis Claire, Carol Anne; PRES., KELLOGG INTERNATIONAL; Vice Pres., Kellogg Co. 1981- ; Joined Kellogg Co. of Canada Ltd. as Salesman, Regina, Nfld.; 1949-51; Sales Supvr., Winnipeg, Vancouver districts, 1954; Asst. Sales Mgr., London office, 1954; Sales Mgr. & Vice-Pres., 1958; Vice-Pres. & Asst. Gen. Mgr. 1959; Pres & Gen. Mgr.; 1960; Pres. & CEO 1962; Pres. & Chmn. of Bd., 1964; Dir. Salada Foods 1969; Chmn. of Bd. 1970; Pres., 1971; Dir. Kellogg Co. of Gt. Britain, 1976; Managing Dir., 1976; Chmn. & Managing Dir., 1976; Dir. of European Operations 1977; Vice-Pres. Kellogg Co. 1979; Pres. Kellogg International, 1981; served in Royal Canadian Navy, March 1942-Sept. 1947; United Church; recreations: hunting, fishing Office: 235 Porter St., Battle Creek, MI 49016

ROBINSON, Gilbert de Beauregard, M.B.E., Ph.D., F.R.S.C.; educator; b. Toronto, Ont. 3 June 1906; s. Percy James and Esther (de Beauregard) R.; e. Rosedale Pub. Sch. Toronto 1916; St. Andrew's Coll. Aurora, Ont. 1923; Univ. of Toronto B.A. 1927; St. John's Coll. Cambridge Univ. Ph.D. 1931; m. Joan d. John Howard 1 Sept. 1935; children: Gilbert John, Nancy Alice (Mrs. James Hill); Prof. of Math. Univ. of Toronto since 1931, part-time since 1974, Vice Pres. Research 1964-71, Chrmn. Plateau Comte., Adm. Inst. of Environment 1971-72, Research Offr. Faculty of Educ. 1972-74; Visiting Prof. Mich. State Univ. 1953, Australian Universities, 1963, Univ. of B.C. 1963, Christchurch, N.Z. 1968; served with Nat. Research Council Ottawa 1941-45; author "Foundations of Geometry" 1939; "Representation Theory of the Symmetric Group" 1961; "Vector Algebra" 1962; "Collected Papers of Alfred Young" 1977; "The Mathematics Dept., Univ. of Toronto" 1979; numerous papers math. journs.; mem. Candn. Math. Soc., Am. Math Assn., Amer. Math Soc.; Pres., Can. Math Soc. 1953-57; Pres., Can. soc. Hist. and Phil. Sc. since 1979; Liberal; United Church; recreations: sailing, carpentry, photography; Club: Madawaska; Home: 1 Neville Park Blvd., Toronto, Ont. M4E 3P5; Office: University College, Univ of Toronto, Ont. M5S 1A6.

ROBINSON, H. Basil, M.A.; Canadian public servant; b. Eastbourne, Sussex, Eng. 3 March 1919; s. late Basil O. and Charlotte Agnes (Graham) R.; e. N. Shore Coll. N. Vancouver, B.C. 1937; Univ. of B.C.B.A. 1940; Oxford Univ. (Rhodes Scholar) M.A. 1948; Hon. Fellow, Oriel College, Oxford, 1975; m. Elizabeth Ann d. late G. H. Gooderham 16 Dec. 1950; children: Katharine, David, Ann, Geoffrey; PRINCIPAL, MANAGEMENT STUDIES PROGRAM, PUBLIC SERVICE COMMISSION Touraine, Que. since 1981; joined Dept. External Affairs 1945, UN Div. 1949, Second Secy. London, Eng. 1951, First Secy. Paris 1955, Head Middle E. Div. Ottawa 1956, Special Asst. (External Affairs) Office of Prime Min. 1957, Min. Washington 1962, Asst. Under-Secy. of State for External Affairs, Ottawa 1964, Depy. Min. of Indian Affairs and N. Devel. 1970, Under-Secy. of State for External Affairs 1974; Commr., Northern Pipe Line 1977; Dept. of External Affairs, Special Advisor to Undersecretary; served with Candn. Army 1942-45 Can. UK and N.W. Europe; Protestant; Clubs: MCC (London, Eng.); Home: 17 Mariposa Ave., Ottawa, Ont. K1M 0T9; Office: Staff Development Centre, 646 Ave. Principale, Touraine, Que. K1A 0M5

ROBINSON, J. Lewis, M.A.; Ph.D.; b. Leamington, Ont., 9 July 1918; s. William John and Emily Laverne (Dunphy) R.; e. Kennedy Coll. Inst., Windsor, Ont.; Univ. of W. Ont., B.A. 1940; Syracuse Univ. M.A. 1942; Clark Univ., Ph.D. 1946; m. Mary Josephine, d. C. Herbert Rowan, Fredericton, N.B., 14 Oct. 1944; children: David Norman, Jo-Anne Marie, Patricia Louise; PROF., DEPT. of GEOGRAPHY, UNIV. OF B.C.; Geographer, N.W. Terr. Adm., Dept. of Mines & Resources, 1943-46; authorof 9 books and more than 100 professional articles, chapters and maps on aspects of the geog. of Can., including "Resources of the Canadian Shield", and "British Columbia: 100 Years of Geographical Change"; Pres., Candn. Assn. of Geographers, 1955-56; awarded Candn. Geog. Soc. Massey Medal 1971; Service to the Profession Award from Candn. Assn. of Geog. 1976; Address: Univ. of British Columbia, Vancouver, B.C. V6T 1W5

ROBINSON, Peter L., investment dealer; b. Toronto, Ont., 21 Jan. 1911; s. Herbert Arthur and Lydie (Scholes) R.; e. St. Andrew's Coll., Aurora, Ont.; m. Eallien Louise, d. Thomas Crawford-Brown, Toronto, Ont., 16 Dec. 1947; one d. Eallien Roberta; DIRECTOR, YORK-TOM SECURITIES; has been in the stock brokerage business over 30 yrs. having begun with the firm of Thomson, McKinnon & Co.; served in 2nd World War; Lieut. in Royal Candn. Navy (Extve. Br.); Anglican; recreation:

golf; Clubs: Toronto Golf; Badminton & Racquet; Pine Tree Golf (Florida); Board of Trade; Home: 45 Hillholm Road, Toronto, Ont. M4P 1M4; Office: 11 King St. W., Toronto, Ont. M5H 1A3

ROBINSON, Russell Alexander, B. Com.; petroleum executive; b. Toronto, Ont. 14 July 1927; s. Violet (Gooder) Robinson; e. Univ. of Toronto B.Com. 1948; m. Marilyn Joan Roszell 12 July 1952; children: Susan L., Judith D. Brooks, Joan C., Catherine G., Donald F.; SR. VICE PRES. (OPERATIONS) AND CONTROLLER, HUSKY OIL LTD. 1979- ; joined Western Decalta Petroleum Ltd. 1961-77 serving as Comptroller, Treas., Vice Pres. Finance; Vice Pres. Finance, Pembina Pipe Line Ltd. and Western Decalta Petroleum (1977) Ltd. 1977-79; mem. Candn. Inst. C.A.'s; Financial Extves. Inst.; Tax Extves. Inst.; P. Conservative; Protestant; recreations: golf, curling, bridge; Clubs: Calgary Petroleum; Earl Grey Golf; Glencoe; Home: 3404 - 58th Ave. S.W., Calgary, Alta. T3E 5H6; Office: (P.O. Box 6525) 505 Fifth Ave. S.W., Calgary, Alta. T2P 3G7.

ROBINSON, Thomas More, B.A., B.Litt.; educator; b. Houghton-Le-Spring, U.K. 4 Nov. 1936; s. Alban Bainbridge and Emily Evangeline (Tolmie) R.; e. Ushaw Coll. Durham, U.K. 1956; Univ. of Durham B.A. 1961; Oxford Univ. B.Litt. (Greek Philos.) 1965; Sorbonne 1962-63; PROF. OF PHILOS. AND CLASSICS, UNIV. OF TORONTO; Chrmn., Dept. of Philos.; came to Can. 1964; writer and host "The Greek Legacy" CBC FM Radio "Ideas" Series 1978; Ed. "Phoenix" 1971-76; co-ed. "The Phoenix Pre-Socratics Series"; author "Plato's Psychology" 1970; "Contrasting Arguments: An Edition of the Dissoi Logoi" 1979; "The Greek Legacy" 1979; various articles and reviews Greek philos.; mem. Candn. Philos. Assn.; Classical Assn. Can. (Council 1969-78); Am. Philol. Assn. (Nominating Comte. 1971-74); Am. Philosoph. Assn.; Manuscripts Review Comte., Univ. of Toronto Press; Editorial Comte., "Philosophers in Canada" Monograph Series; Adv. Comte. on Academic Planning, OCGS; Corresponding mem. (Univ. of Toronto), Gen. Assembly of the Candn. Federation for the Humanities; Home: 173 Strathearn Rd., Toronto, Ont. M6C 1S3; Office: Toronto, Ont. M5S 1A1.

ROBINSON, William A., D.S.O., B.A.Sc., M.B.A.; retired mining executive; b. Toronto, Ont., 5 June 1917; s. George Edward and Ella May (Crabbe) R.; e. Oakwood Coll. Inst., Toronto; Univ. of Toronto, B.A.Sc. 1941; Harvard Univ., M.B.A., 1951; m. Jean, d. A. Bell Mitchell, 11 Dec. 1952; children: William Arthur, Richard James, Kathleen-Jean; engaged in various mining operations in N. Ont. 1936-48; Dept. Mining Engn., Univ. of Toronto, 1948-49; Geol. with Dom. Gulf Co. (subsidiary of Golf Oil Corp.) 1949-55; Mining Engr., Partner and Dir., Gairdner & Co., 1959-64; Dir. and Secy., Candn. Gas & Energy Fund Ltd., 1960-64; Pres. and Chrmn., Newconex Holdings Ltd.; Newconex Exploration Ltd. 1965-79 (ret.); served with 1st Hussars, 2nd Cdn. Armoured Bgde. 1940-46, with rank Maj. (overseas 1941-46); Awarded Disting. Service Order, 1945; mem., Candn. Inst. Mining & Metall. Assn. Prof. Engrs. Ont.; Inst. of Mining & Metall. (London); Prospectors & Developers Assn.; Am. Inst. Mining Engrs.;Sigma Chi; Conservative; United Church; recreations: fishing, music; Clubs: Engineers' Toronto; Boisclair Fish & Game; Royal Candn. Mil. Inst.; Toronto Cricket Skating & Curling; Home: 37 Streathearn Rd., Toronto, Ont. M6C 1R2

ROBINSON, Col. William George MacKenzie, O.B.E. (1944), C.A.; b. Port Arthur, Ont., 28 Nov. 1914; s. William (Writer to H.M. Signet) and Jane Thompson (Doctor) R.; e. St. Clements Sch. and Upper Can. Coll., Toronto; C.A. 1947; m. Nora, d. Ernest G. West, Toronto, 6 Feb. 1940; children: Ian MacKenzie, Andrew MacKenzie, Gregor MacKenzie, Sheila West, Phyllis Mary, Nora Blair; Dir., Pigott Constr. Ltd.; Gov., Art Gallery of Ham-

ilton; Dir., Chedoke Health Corp.; with Dominion Bank, 1933-35; Clarkson Gordon & Co., 1935-48; with Gordon MacKay & Co. Ltd. Dir. and Vice-Pres. 1951-62; Pigott Group 1962-79; served in 2nd World War 1939-45; Capt., Toronto Scot. Regt. (M.G.) 1939; Maj. 1941; Lt.-Col. 1945; attended Cdn. War Staff Coll., Kingston, Ont., 1942; Hdqrs., 1 Cdn. Corps, 1943; Bde. Maj., 3rd Cdn. Inf. Bde., 1944 G.S.O.1, 4th Cdn. Armoured Div., 1945; apptd. Hon. Col. Toronto Scottish Reg't. 1977 and 1980; twice Mentioned in Despatches; awarded Golden Aristion Andrias (Greece); Presbyterian; Clubs: Badminton & Racquet (Toronto); The Hamilton; Tamahaac; Home: 51 Markland St., Hamilton, Ont. L8P 2J5;

ROBISON, James E., D.F.C., M.B.A., D.C.S., D.S.A.; executive; b. Alfred, N.D. 22 Nov. 1915; s. John J. and Myrtle (Klundt) R.; e. Univ. of Minn. B.B.A. 1938; Harvard Univ. M.B.A. 1940 (Baker Scholar), D.S.A. 1969; Suffolk Univ. D.C.S. 1968; m. Jeannette Hoffman 6 June 1942; one d. Martha Ann; CHRMN. OF THE BD., NARRAGANSETT CAPITAL CORP. retired 1980; Pres. Lonsdale Enterprises Inc.; Dominion Bridge Co. Ltd.; Houbigant Inc.; Founder, Retired Chrmn. and Chief Extve. Offr., Indian Head Inc. 1967 — 72, Chrmn. Finance Comte. 1972 — 75; Extve. Vice Pres. Textron Inc. 1950 — 53; Vice Pres. Nashua Mills Div. 1947 — 50; Nashua Mfg. Co. 1940 — 47; Past Dir., American Television & Communications Corp., INSILCO, Realty Income Trust; Trustee and mem. Finance Comte. Air Force Aid Soc.; Dir. Business Comte. for Arts; Trustee, Cal. Inst. Technol.; Comte. for Econ. Devel. 1965 — 74; Dir., Assoc. Harvard Grad. Sch. Business Adm.; Am. Textile Mfrs. Inst. 1961 — 64; Manhattan Eye, Ear & Throat Hosp. 1969 — 79; served with U.S. Army Air Crops 1941 — 46, rank Maj.; rec'd Air Medal with 3 Oak Leaf Clusters; Phi Delta Theta; Protestant; recreations: golf, soaring, skiing; Clubs: Bedford Golf & Tennis; Harvard Business Sch. Greater N.U. (Dir.); Harvard N.Y.; Lyford Cay (Bahamas); Racquet & Tennis (N.Y.); Soaring Soc. Am.; Stanwich (Greenwich, Conn.); Stowe (Vt.) Country (Dir.); Home: Windmill Farm, 12 Spruce Hill Rd., Armonk, N.Y. 10504; Office: 20 Haarlem Ave., White Plains, N.Y. 10603.

ROBITAILLE, Jean, F.I.I.C.; insurance executive; b. Montreal, Que. 23 Dec. 1926; s. Jacques and Marie (Delfausse) R.; e. Jardin de L'Enfance 1939 and Cath. High Sch. 1945 Montreal; Sir George Williams Coll. 1946-49; m. Lucie d. late Sarto Viau 23 Feb. 1951; children: Pierre, Andre, Louise, Julie; PRES., C.E.O. AND DIR. ROYAL INSURANCE CO. OF CANADA since 1979; Dir. Western Assurance Co.; Quebec Assurance Co.; Roins Holding Ltd.; Ins. Bureau of Can.; Insurers' Adv. Organ of Can.; Facility Assoc.; Pres., Centre for Study of Ins. Operation; joined present co. Montreal 1952, Br. Mgr. Quebec City 1956-74, Vice Pres. Marketing 1974-76, Sr. Vice Pres. Underwriting & Claims 1976-78; Extve. Vice Pres., Operations 1978; Dir. 1978; Gov. Royal Candn. Golf Assn.; R. Catholic; recreations: golf, fishing, skiing, music, reading, crafts; Clubs: Lambton Golf & Country; Toronto; The Boulevard; Cambridge; Caledon Mountain Trout; Home: 56 McGill St., Toronto, Ont. M5B H2; Office: 10 Wellington St., Toronto, Ont. M5E 1L5.

ROBLIN, Hon. Duff, P.C., C.C. (1970), LL.D.; b. Winnipeg, Manitoba, 17 June 1917; s. C. D. and Sophia May (Murdoch) R.; grand-son of Sir R. P. Roblin, Premier of Manitoba, 1900-15; e. Winnipeg Public Schs.; St. John's Coll. Sch., Winnipeg, Man.; Univ. of Manitoba; Univ. of Chicago; LL.D., McGill 1967; Man. 1967; Winnipeg 1968; m. Mary MacKay, 30 Aug. 1958; one s. Andrew, one d. Jennifer Mary; CHRMN., METROPOL SECURITY LTD.; former Premier of Manitoba until resigned Nov. 1967; Pres. and Dir., Canadian Pacific Investments Ltd. 1970-74; summoned to Senate of Can., 1978; served in 2nd World War; Wing Commdr., R.C.A.F., 1940-46; 1st el. to Manitoba Leg., g.e. Nov. 1949; chosen Leader of P. Conservative Party in Manitoba 17 June 1954; resigned as

M.L.A. May 1968; Anglican; Office: 103 Water Ave., Winnipeg, Man. R3C 0J2

ROBSON, Charles J., M.D., F.R.C.S.(C), F.A.C.S.; urologist; b. Ramsgate, England, 29 May 1917; s. Charles Harold, M.D., and Flora (Dalgleish) R.; e. Upper Canada Coll., Toronto, Ont. (Sr. Matric.); Univ. of Toronto, M.D.; m. Joan Sawyer, d. W. A. Woodcock, Toronto, Ont., 14 Apl. 1943; children: Charles John, Donald Arthur, Nancy-Elspeth; PROF. & CHRMN., DIV. UROL. SURG., UNIV. TORONTO; Head, Div. Urol. Surg., Toronto Gen. Hosp.; Sr. Consultant, Women's College Hosp. for Sick Children, and Sunnybrook Hosp; served in Royal Candn. Navy, 1943-45, Surg.-Lieut.; mem., Candn. Med. Assn.; Ont. Med. Assn.; Amer. Assoc. of G.U. Surgeons; Past Pres.; Am. Urol. Assn. Past Pres., Candn. Urol. Assn.; Past Pres. Can. Acad. Urological Surgeons; Past Pres. Northeastern Section, American Urological Assoc.; mem. Brit. Assn. of Urol. Surgeons; International Soc. of Urol.; Southeastern Section A.U.A.; North Central Section A.U.A.; Amer Soc. for Pediatric Urology; Bd. of Gov. Lyndhurst Hosp. Conservative; United Church; recreations: fishing, farming, hunting; Clubs: Badminton & Racquet; Celebrity; Home: 185 Roxborough Dr., Toronto, Ont. M4W 1X7; Office: 170 St. George St., Toronto, Ont. M5R 2M8

ROBSON, John M., M.A., Sc.D., F.R.S.C., F.A.P.S.; physicist; b. London, Eng., 26 March 1920; s. Stanley and Elsie Norah (Forster) R.; e. Clifton Coll., Bristol, Eng.; Kings Coll., Cambridge Univ., B.A. 1942, M.A. 1945, ScD. 1963; m. Helen Phyllis, d. Victor Summerhays, 17 June 1950; children: Michael, Elisabeth, Peter; PROF., DEPT. PHYSICS, McGILL UNIV. since 1968; mem., Nat. Research Council 1967-73; with Radar Research and Devel. Establishment, Eng., 1942-45; came to Can. 1945; joined Atomic Energy Research Establishment, 1945-50; Atomic Energy of Can. Ltd., 1950-60; Chrmn., Dept. of Physics, Ottawa Univ. 1960-68; Chrmn., Dept. Physics, McGill Univ., 1968-76; Hon. Secy., Royal Soc. Can. 1968-1970; author of over 30 scient. papers; has specialized in radioactivity of the neutron; mem., Candn. Assn. of Physicists; Anglican; recreations: fishing, hunting; Address: Physics Dept., McGill Univ., Montreal, Que.

ROBSON, John Mercel, M.A., Ph.D., F.R.S.C.; university professor; b. Toronto, Ont., 26 May 1927; s. William Renton Mercel and Christina Henderson (Sinclair) R.; e. Swansea Pub. Sch. and Runnymede Coll. Inst., Toronto; Univ. of Toronto, B.A. 1951, M.A. 1953, Ph.D. 1956; m. Ann Provost, d. Dr. Bertie Wilkinson, Toronto, 8 Aug. 1953; children: William, John, Ann; PROF. OF ENGLISH, VICTORIA COLL., UNIV. OF TORONTO, since 1967; Teaching Fellow, Dept. of Eng., Univ. Coll., Univ. of Toronto, 1952-54; Instr. in Eng., Univ. of B.C., 1956-57; Asst. Prof., Univ. of Alta., 1957-58; joined present Coll. as Asst. Prof. 1958-63; Assoc. Prof. 1963-67; Principal 1971-76; author: "The Improvement of Mankind: The Social and Political Thought of John Stuart Mill", 1968; "The Hmnnn Retort", 1970; Gen. Ed.; "Collected Works of J. S. Mill", also author of numerous articles and book chapters and ed. of various works; Vice Pres., Royal Soc. of Can., and Pres., Academy II, Roy Soc. of Can.; mem., Adv. Bd., Univ. of Toronto Quarterly; adv. ed., "Wellesley Index"; Chrmn., Disraeli Project, Queen's Univ.; mem., Adv. Ed. Bd., Bertrand Russell Papers, McMaster Univ.; Bentham Comte., Univ. Coll., London, Eng. and Tulane Univ., U.S.A.; Centre for Editing Early Candn. Texts, Carleton Univ.; Candn. Assn. Univ. Teachers; Assn. Candn. Univ. Teachers Eng.; Brit. Studies Assn.; Victorian Studies Assn.; recreation: reading, writing, running; Home: 28 McMaster Ave., Toronto, Ont. M4V 1A9

ROCH, Ernst.R.C.A., A.G.I.; graphic designer; b. Osijek, Yugoslavia 8 Dec. 1928; s. Hans Roch; e. Staatliche Meisterschule fur angewandte Kunst Graz, Austria,

M.F.A. 1953; came to Can. 1953; children: Ursula M.D., Uli, Barbara; PROP. ROCH DESIGN 1978- ; Asst., Prof. Hans Wagula Graz, Austria 1952-53; Designer, Y & M Studio Montreal 1954-59; Lectr. in Hist. and Devel. Lettering in Basic Typography Montreal Museum of Fine Arts Sch. Art & Design 1956-58; Design Dir. Montreal Office James Valkus Inc. N.Y. 1960; own office graphic design 1960-65; Princ. and Founding mem. Design Collaborative Ltd. Montreal and Toronto 1965-77; visiting lectr. graphic design Concordia Univ., McGill Univ., N.S. Coll. Art & Design, Ohio State Univ. 1980; Founding mem. Signum Press Ltd. 1973; mem. Postage Stamp Design Adv. Comte. Can. Post 1975-80; maj. projects incl. visual identity program Nat. Arts Centre Ottawa 1965; exhibition "Munich Olympic Games", Montreal Museum Fine Arts and Art Gallery Ont. 1972; official poster Montreal Olympic Games 1976; definitive issue postage stamp Queen Elizabeth II 1963, commemorative postage stamp Sir Oliver Mowat 1967; editor/designer "Arts of the Eskimo: Prints" 1974; author/designer "Paper Zoo" 1973; recipient numerous awards and prizes Can., USA and Europe incl. Am. Inst. Graphic Arts, Lahti (Finland) Poster Biennale, Leipzig Internat. Book Fair, Biennale of Graphic Design Brno, Czechosolovakia, Poster Biennale Warsaw; cited numerous bibliogs.; mem. Alliance Graphique Internationale; Assn. Graphic Designers Can.; Am. Inst. Graphic Arts; Internat. Centre Typographic Arts; Address:(P.O. Box 1056 Stn. B) Montreal, Que. H3B 3K5.

ROCHE, David Joseph, B.A.; corporation executive; b. Toronto, Ont. 4 April 1924; e. St. Michael's Coll., Toronto; Univ. of Toronto, B.A. and Business Adm.; Osgoode Hall Law Sch.; m. Mary Claire, d. Ernest and Clare Seitz 18 June 1947; children: David, Gregory, Brian, Dereck, Kevin, Paul, Beverley, Mary Catherine, Yvonne; DIRECTOR AND EXTVE. VICE-PRESIDENT, MARKETING, JOSEPH E. SEAGRAM AND SONS, LTD.; joined Candn. Breweries Ltd. 1949 and became Extve. Asst. to Vice-Pres. of Sales 1952; Asst. to President 1954; apptd. Vice-Pres., O'Keefe Brewing Co. 1957; Vice-Pres. of Adm. & Planning for O'Keefe and Dow Breweries across Canada 1965; Dir. of Operations for all Candn. Breweries Ltd. plants in Ont. 1967; Vice-Pres. and Gen Mgr., Candn. Breweries Ltd., E. Div., Pres. Dow Que. Ltd. and Pres. O'Keefe Brewing Co. Que. Ltd. 1968; joined present firm 1969; served for 3 yrs. in 2nd World War with 1st Candn. Parachute Bn. in Canada, Eng. and Europe; mem., Candn. Assn., Sovereign & Mil. Order of Malta; Law Soc. Upper Can.; Roman Catholic; recreations: sailing, fishing, hunting, cooking; Clubs: Caledon Mountain Trout; University (Toronto); Forest and Stream; Home: 20234 Lakeshore Rd., Baie d'Urfé, Que. H9X 1P7; Office: 1430 Peel St., Montreal, Que. H3A 1S9

ROCHE, Douglas James, M.P., B.A.; politician; b. Montreal, Que. 14 June 1929; s. James Joseph and Agnes (Douglas) R.; e. St. Patrick's High Sch. Ottawa 1947; St. Patrick's Coll. Univ. of Ottawa B.A. 1951; m. Eva Mary d. Michael Nolan. Ottawa, Ont. 28 Sept. 1953; children: Evita, Michaelene, Douglas F., Mary Anne, Patricia; Reporter, "Ottawa Journal" 1949-50; News Ed., "Ensign" Montreal 1951-52; Pol. Reporter, "Toronto Telegram" 1952-55; Reporter and Columnist, "Catholic Universe Bulletin;; 1956-57, Cleveland; Assoc. Ed., "Sign Magazine" 1958-65, Union City, N.J. (rec'd Cath. Press Assn. Award Best Mag. Article 1963); Founding Ed., "Western Catholic Reporter" 1965-72, Edmonton (Paper won 11 nat. awards Cath. PRESS Assn. and Assoc. Ch. Press, ed. cited for Best Ed. Writing 1971); el. to H. of C. for Edmonton Strathcona 1972, 1974, for Edmonton S. 1979, 1980; P. Cons. Spokesman on External Affairs 1977-79, Chrmn. P. Cons. Caucus Comte on External Affairs 1979, Parlty, Secy. to Secy. of State for External Affairs. Candn. Del. to 34th Gen. Assembly UN; Secy., Edmonton Council Chs. 1970-71; Pres., Candn. Ch. Press 1971; Unicef Chrmn.; UN Assn. Edmonton 1971; Bd. mem. and Vice Chrmn.

Finance Comte., World Conf. on Religion & Peace 1974-79; Vice Pres. Inter-Parlty. Union Can. 1977-79; mem. Nat. Council (Alta.), Candn. Human Rights Foundation 1978-80; Candn. mem., North-South Roundtable & Soc. for Internat. Devel. 1978-80; apptd. Vice Chrmn., Parlty. Task Force on North-South Relations, 1980; Internat. Chmn., Parliamentarians for World Order, 1980- ; author "The Catholic Revolution" 1968; "Man to Man" 1969; "It's A New World" 1970; "Justice Not Charity: A New Global Ethic for Canada" 1976; "The Human Side of Politics" 1976; "What Development Is All About: China, Indonesia, Bangladesh" 1979; various book chapters, articles; numerous Candn. and foreign lectures and study tours; P. Conservative; R. Catholic; recreations: skiing, swimming, reading; Home: 8923 Strathearn Dr., Edmonton, Alta. T6C 4C8; Office: House of Commons, Ottawa, Ont. K1A 0A6.

ROCHE, John Redmond, O.B.E., E.D., C.D., Q.C., F.R.S.A; retired judge; b Ottawa Ont., 18 June 1907; s. Henry George and Eve de Montigny (Gingras) R.; e. Univ. of Ottawa (elem. schooling); Bourget Coll., Rigaud, Que. (Arts Course) 1926; Univ. of Montreal, B.L., LL.B. 1930; m. Alice, d. H. Brunel, 17 Oct. 1934; children: Marie José, Christine, Anne, Sylvie; called to Bar of Que. 1930; called to Bar of Eng., Lincoln's Inn, 1941; cr. K.C. 1945; practised law with firm of Adam, Roche & Bock, Montreal 1930-39; with Roche, MacNaughton & Bruneau 1946-56; mem. Que. Leg. for Chambly (Nat. Union) 1948-56; Parlty. Asst. to Min. of Finance 1954-56; Judge, Court of Sessions, Montreal 1956-78; Commr., Nat. Parole Bd. 1978-79; served in Candn. Mil. 1930-39; R.C.A. (active) 1939-46; Overseas 1939, Off. in chg., Cdn. Sect. G.H.Q. 2rd Echelon 1940-41; Commanded 1st Bn., Rég. de Maisonneuve 1941-42; promoted to substantive rank of Col., Branch of Adjutant-General 1942; awarded O.B.E.; Pres., Last Post Fund (Can.); Chancellor, The Order of St. John, Priory of Can. 1972-75; Chrmn., Que. Comte., Army Benevolent Fund; Trustee and Vice-Chrmn., Bd. Trustees, Greater Montreal Poppy Fund; Nat. Pres., Royal Candn. Legion 1970-72; Kt. Justice, Ven. Order of St. John; Knight of Malta; Roman Catholic; Club: United Services; Home3445 Drummond St. (Apt. 706), Montreal, Que. H3G 1X9;

ROCHELEAU, Serge, B.A.; executive; b. Montreal, Que. 24 Apl. 1942; s. Honoré and Gertrude (Cadieux) R.; e. Coll. St-Viateur Montreal B.A.; m. Louise d. Dr. Georges Rousse 16 May 1964; children: Katerine, Jean-François, Luc; PRES. AND C.E.O. PRENOR GROUP LTD. since 1971; Pres. and Dir. North America Trust; Chrmn., C.E.O. Société de Courtage Immoblier du Trust Général Inc.; Pres. and Dir., NATC Investments Ltd.; Natinvest Ltd.; Vice Pres. and Dir., Canaprev Inc.; Dir. Prevest Management Co. Ltd.; Trust Général du Canada; Dir. and mem. Exec. Comte., Quebec Heart Foundation; Bolton, Tremblay & Co.; Val Royal LaSalle Ltd.; Taurus Fund; Canada Cumulative Fund; Planned Resources Fund Ltd.; Vice Chrmn. and Dir., Jr. Achievement of Que.; R. Catholic; Home: 7 Courcelette, Outremont, Que. H2V 3A5; Office: 801 Sherbrooke St. E., Montreal, Que. H2L 1K7

ROCHER, Guy, C.C. (1971), M.A., Ph.D.; professeur; né. Berthierville, Qué., 20 Avril 1924; fils Barthelemy et Jeanne (Magnan) R.; é. Univ. de Montreal, B.A. 1943; Univ. Laval, M.A. (Sociologie) 1950; Harvard Univ., Ph.D. (Sociol.) 1957; ép. Suzanne Cloutier, Montréal, 10 Oct. 1949; enfants: Genevieve, Anne-Marie, Isabelle, Claire; PROF. TITULAIRE, UNIV. DE MONTREAL, depuis 1960 et sous-ministre au développement culturel, Gouv. du Qué., 1976-79; depuis 1979 attaché au Centre de recherche en droit public, Faculté de Droit, Univ. de Montréal; Sous-Ministre au Développements Social, Gouvernemend du Québec, 1981- ; Pres. du Conseil d'administration de Radio-Quebec 1979-81; (Dir. Dept. Sociol. 1960-65; Vice-Doyen, Faculté des Sciences Sociales

1962-67); Asst. Prof., Univ. Laval. 1952-58. Prof. Agrégé, 1958-60; mem., Comn Royale d'enquête sur l'Enseignement (Québec) 1961-66; Prés. Comn. D'enquête sur la nouvelle Univ. Francaise à Montréal, 1965; Gouv. du Coll. Canadien des Travailleurs, 1963-66; du Bureau de la Radio Diffusion, 1966-68; mem. Comn. Scolaire d'Outrement, du Conseil d'adm. du conseil des Oeuvres de Montréal, 1966-68; Fellow, de l'Am. Sociol. Assn.; (Prés. 1961-62) de l'Assn. Canadienne de Sociol.; Prés. (1966-67) de l'Assn. Canadienne des Sociologues et Anthropologues de langue Francaise; Trésorier (1958-59) Assn. Internat. des Sociol. de langue Francaise; Prés.; Nat. de la Jeunesse Etudiante Catholique, 1945-48; Publ. "Famille et Habitation" (en collab.) 1960; Rapport de la Comn. Royale d'enquête sur l'Enseignement (en collab.) 5 vols. (1963-1966); "Introduction à la sociologie générale" (3 vols.), 1968; "Le Québec en mutation", 1973; "Talcott Parsons et la sociologié américaine", 1972; "Ecole et société au Québec" (en collaboration), 1971; plusieurs articles; Catholique; Résidence: 3650 Chemin St.-Louis, Ste-Foy, Qué. G1W 1S9

ROCHETTE, Louis, M.Com., C.A., R.I.A.; b. Quebec City, Que., 19 Feb. 1923; s. Evariste and Blanche (Gaudry) R.; e. St. Dominique, Que.; Coll. St. Charles Garnier, Que.; St. Joseph High Sch., Berthierville, Que.; Laval Univ., M.Com. 1948; m. Nicole, d. E. C. Barbeau, Verdun, Que., 12 Oct. 1968; children: Louise, Anne, Guy; PRES. DU CONSEIL ET CHEF DE LA DIRECTION, LES CHANTIERS DAVIES; Chrmn. & C.E.O. Davie Shipbuilding, lauzon P.Q. since 1976; Chief Auditor, Retail Sales Tax Service, Province of Quebec, 1953-55; Treas., Davie Shipbuilding Ltd., 1955-65; Financial Dir. and Treas., Sidbec, 1965-66; Extve. Vice Pres. Marine Ind. Ltd. 1966-76; served as Pilot with RCAF 1943-45; author, "Le Rêve Sépartiste", 1969; mem., Inst. C.A.'s; Soc. Indust. Accts.; Past Pres., Candn. Shipbuilding and Shiprepairing Assn.; Roman Catholic; recreations: fishing, skiing, flying; Clubs: Garnison; Cercle Universitaire; Mount Bruno Country; Home: 1155 Turnbull, Apt. 1002, Quebec, Que. G1R 5G3; Address: Case Postale 130, Levis, P.Q. G6V 6N7.

ROCKINGHAM, Maj.-Gen. John Meredith, C.B. (1952), C.B.E., D.S.O. and Bar, E.D., C.D.; Army Offr. (retired); b. Sydney, N.S.W., Australia, 24 Aug. 1911; s. Walter Edward and Ethel Vincent (Meredith) R.; e. Melbourne, Aust., Grammar Sch. (Jr. Matric. 1928); Halifax, N.S. Schs., 1922-24; Barbadoes, B.W.I., Schs., 1924-26; m. Mary Carlyle, d. the late Herbert R. Hammond, 11 Jan. 1936; Children: John Robert Meredith, Audrey Vincent; with Candn. Scottish Regt., N.P.A.M., 1933-39; served in 2nd World War, 1939-45; Lieut. and later Capt. with 1st Candn. Scot Regt., 1939-42; Maj. to Lieut.-Col. in U.K. and N.W. Europe with Royal Hamilton Light Inf., 1942-44; Brig., 9 Inf. Bgde., in U.K. and N.W. Europe, 1945; awarded C.B.E., D.S.O. and Bar; Offr. Order of Leopold I with Palme (Belgium); Croix de Guerre with Palm (Belgium); Personnel Supv., B.C. Electric Rly. Co., Victoria, B.C., 1945-48; Staff Asst. to Gen. Mgr. of Transportation, 1949; Asst. Gen. Supt. of Vancouver and Intercity Lines, Vancouver, B.C., 1949-50; Supt. Pac. Stage Lines, June-Aug. 1950; Commdr. (U.N.) 25th Bgde. (Can.) 1950-51; Commdr., Candn. Troops in Korea, 1951-52; awarded U.S. Legion of Merit; C.B. (Mil. Div.); attended Imp. Defence Coll., Eng., 1952-53; apptd. Commdr., Third Candn. Inf. Bgde., Dec. 1953; 1 Candn. Inf. Div., 1954; apptd. G.O.C., Quebec Command, Dec. 1957; Western Command, 1961-66; apptd. Hon. Co., Candn. Scottish Regt. (Princess Mary's) Victoria B.C., Aug. 1978; employed in Mannix Group, 1966-72; Councillor, Can. West Foundn., 1972; now fully retired; Anglican; Home: R.R. #1, Qualicum, B.C. V0R 2T0

RODGER, Maj.-Gen. Norman Elliot, C.B.E. (1944), C.D.; Canadian Army (retired); b. Amherst, N.S., 30 Nov. 1907; s. Norman Clarence and Harriet Thompson

(McLennan) R.; e. Amherst High Sch., N.S.; Roy. Mil. Coll. Grad. (Hons.) 1928; McGill Univ., B.Sc. 1930; m. Isabel, d. W. F. Wilson, Ottawa, 8 Sept. 1934; three s. Wilson, Nicholas, Elliot; joined Candn. Army, Royal Candn. Engineers, 1928; District Engn. Officer, Kingston, 1938-39; served in World War, 1940-45; attended War Staff Coll., Camberley, Eng., 1940; Personal Asst. to Gen. A. G. L. McNaughton, 1941-42; Brig. Gen. Staff, Candn. Mil. Hdqrs., London, 1942-43; commanded 10th Candn. Inf. Bgde., 1943-44; Chief of Staff, 2nd Candn. Corps, 1944-45; Candn. Army Staff, Wash., 1946; awarded Legion of Merit (U.S.); Commdr., Order Orange Nassau (Netherlands); Q.M.G., Candn. Army, Ottawa, 1946-51; attended Imp. Defence Coll., 1951; G.O.C. Prairie Command, 1952-55; Vice Chief of the Gen. Staff, Nov. 1955-Aug. 1956; Chrmn., Manitoba Liquor Control Comn., 1959-68; Anglican; recreations: canoe trips, golf, fishing; Address: 1402 — 323 Wellington Crescent, Winnipeg, Man. R3M 0A4

ROGERS, (Amos) Robert, M.A.; Ph.D.; university professor; b. Moncton, N.B., 9 Sept. 1927; s. Amos Rollen and Ethel Lena (Lutes) R.; e. Moncton (N.B.) High Sch., 1944; Univ. of N.B., B.A. 1948; Univ. of Toronto, M.A. 1950; Univ. of London, Acad. Post Grad. Dipl. in Librarianship 1953; Univ. of Mich., Ph.D. 1964; m. Rhoda Mae, d. late Frank Page, Lima, Ohio, 18 Dec. 1960; one s.: Mark Alan; DEAN, SCH. OF LIB. SCIENCE, KENT STATE UNIV., since 1978, and Prof. there since 1969; Asst. Librarian, Univ. of N.B., 1951-55; Head Librarian 1955-56; Adult Asst., Detroit Pub. Lib., 1957-59; Asst. to Dir., Bowling Green State Univ. Lib. 1959-61; Acting Dir. 1961-64, Dir. 1964-69; mem. Bd. Trustees, Ohio Coll. Lib. Center 1967-69; Un. Christian Fellowship, Bowling Green State Univ. 1966-69; Visiting Prof., Dept. of Library Science, Pahlavi Univ. Shiraz, Iran, 1976-77; Acting Dean, Sch. of Lib. Sci., Kent State Univ. 1977-78; author, "Books and Pamphlets by New Brunswick Writers, 1890-1950", 1953; "The White Monument", 1955; "American Recognition of Canadian Authors Writing in English, 1890-1960", 1965; "The Humanities: A Selective Guide to Information Sources" 2rd ed., 1979; also a number articles in various journs.; mem., Adv. Council Fed. Lib. Programs (Ohio) 1971-76, 1978; Am. Lib. Assn. (Council mem. 1972-76; Budget & Leg. Assemblies, 1974); Candn. Lib. Assn.; Bibliog. Society Canada; Library Association Great Britain; Ohio Library Association (Dir. 1968-76, 1979-81, Pres. 1979-80); Ohioana Lib. Association; chosen "Librarian of the Year" by Ohio Library Assn.; 1976; Democrat; Methodist; recreations: reading, walking, swimming; Home: 1965 Pine View Drive, Kent, Ohio 44240

ROGERS, Benjamin, B.A., M.Sc. (Econ.); diplomat; b. Vernon, B.C., 3 Aug. 1911; s. Reginald Heber and Anna Elizabeth (Fraser) R.; e. Prince of Wales Coll., Charlottetown, P.E.I. (1927-30); Dalhousie Univ., B.A. 1933; Univ. of London, M.Sc. (Econ.) 1935; m. Frances, d. Dr. M. D. Morrison, Halifax, N.S., 27 Nov. 1939; one s. David M.; prior to joining Dept. External Affairs 1938, employed briefly by Royal Inst. of Internat. Affairs, London, England, and Candn. Inst. of Internat. Affairs (as Acting Nat. Secy. 1937-38); served in Canberra, 1939-43, Washington 1943-44, Rio De Janeiro 1944-48, Ottawa 1948-50; Chargé d'Affaires, Prague, 1950-52; Ottawa 1952-55; Ambassador to Peru 1955-58, to Turkey, 1958-60; Deputy High Commr. to Brit., 1960-64; Ambassador to Spain and Morocco, 1964-69; Ambassador to Italy and concurrently High Commr. to Malta 1970-72; apptd. Chief of Protocol, Dept. of External Affairs 1972, retired 1975; co-author (with R. A. MacKay) "Canada Looks Abroad", 1938; mem., Internat. Peace Acad.; United Church; recreations: community activities, gardening, skiing; Address: 450 Piccadilly Ave., Ottawa, Ont. K1Y 0H6

ROGERS, Hon. Charles Stephen, M.L.A.; politician; b. Vancouver, B.C. 28 March 1942; s. Forrest and Gwynneth

(Thomas) R.; e. St. George's Sch.; Vancouver City Coll.; Central Offrs. Sch. RCAF Centralia, Ont.; m. Margaret d. C.G. Wallace, Montreal, Que. 22 Apl. 1967; two s. Mark Hayden, Ryan Wallace; MIN. OF ENVIRONMENT, 1979- ; air line pilot; el. M.L.A. for Vancouver South prov. g.e. 1975, re-el. 1979; Depy. Speaker 1979; Social Credit; Clubs: Vancouver; Royal Vancouver Yacht; Royal Flying; Office: Parliament Bldgs., Victoria, B.C. V8V 1X5.

ROGERS, Edward Samuel, B.A., LL.B.; communications executive; b. Toronto, Ont., 27 May 1933; s. Edward Samuel and Velma Melissa (Taylor) R.; e. Upper Can. Coll.; Toronto; Univ. of Toronto (Trinity Coll.), B.A. 1956; Osgoode Hall Law Sch., LL.B. 1961; m. Loretta Anne Robinson, d. Rt. Hon. Lord and Lady Martonmere of Bermuda and Nassau, 25 Sept. 1963; children: Lisa Anne, Edward Samuel, Melinda Mary, Martha Loretta; VICE CHAIRMAN AND C.E.O., ROGERS CABLESYSTEMS INC.; Pres. Rogers Telecommunications Ltd.; Dir., Rogers Radio Broadcasting Ltd.; Thomas I. Hull Insurance Ltd.; Josiah Wedgwood & Sons (Canada) Limited; Famous Players Ltd.; Gage Educational Publishing Ltd.; Talcorp Ltd.; Premier Communications Ltd.; read law with Tory, Tory, DesLauriers & Binnington; called to the Bar Ont. 1962; Gov., Lyfordcay Club Sigma Chi; P. Conservative; Anglican; Clubs: The Toronto; Royal Canadian Yacht; Muskoka Golf & Country; York; Albany; Granite; Rideau (Ottawa); Lyford Cay (Nassau); Home: 3 Frybrook Rd., Toronto, Ont. M4V 1Y7; Offices: 25 Adelaide St. E., Toronto, Ont. M5C 1Y2 and Ste. 2602, Commercial Union Tower, P.O. Box 249, TD. Centre, Toronto, Ont. M5K 1J5

ROGERS, Forrest L., B.Sc.; economist; b. Brantford, Ont. 1921; e. Univ. Coll. Univ. of Toronto B.Sc. 1944; m. Mary Robertson Oct. 1946; children: Janet, Nancy, Joanne; ECON. ADVISOR, THE BANK OF NOVA SOCTIA; joined present Bank 1945; mem. various organs. prof. econs. Can. and abroad; active in Candn. Inst. Internat. Affairs; Club: Ontario; Home: 110 Brentcliffe Rd., Toronto, Ont. M4G 3Y9; Office: 44 King St. W., Toronto, Ont. M5H 1H1.

ROGERS, George A., B.A., LL.B., LL.M.; b. Saint John, N.B. 3 Feb. 1929; s. George Herbert and Hazel Blanche (White) R.; e. Univ. of Kings Coll. B.A. 1950; Dalhousie Univ. LL.B. 1952; S. Meth. Univ. LL.M. 1953; VICE PRES. AND GEN. COUNSEL, IMPERIAL OIL LTD. since 1976; read law with Stewart, Smith, MacKeen; called to Bars of N.S. 1953, Alta. 1957, Ont. 1970; joined Dept. of Justice Ottawa Civil Litigation 1954-56; joined Calgary Law Dept. present Co. 1956, H.O. Law Dept. 1968, Regional Counsel Calgary Law Dept. 1974, Asst. Gen. Counsel Toronto Law Dept. 1975; Summer Air Training Course 1949-51, comnd. Pilot Offr. R.C.A.F., listed Supplementary Reserve; mem. N.S. Barristers Soc.; Assn. of Cdn. Gen. Counsel; Law Soc. Alta.; Law Soc. Upper Can.; Candn. Bar Assn.; P. Conservative; United Church; recreations: golf, curling; Club: Mississauga Golf & Country; University (Toronto); 111 St. Clair Ave. W., Toronto, Ont. M4V 1N5

ROGERS, Guy Warwick; company officer; b. Toronto, Ont., 10 June 1910; s. Alfred and Winifrede (Warwick) R.; e. Ridley College, St. Catharines, Ont.; Upper Canada Coll., Toronto; m. Mary, d. of George Booth, 1933; children; Marianne, Winifrede, Margaret Gay; Chrmn. of Bd., St. Marys Cement Ltd.; joined Elias Rogers Co. Ltd. in 1930 and since occupied posts of Sales Mgr., Vice Pres., Pres. and Chrmn.; served in R.C.A.F.; Flying Offr., 1940-45; Anglican; recreations: golf, fishing, curling; Clubs: Toronto; Toronto Hunt; National; Rosedale Golf; York; R.C.Y.C.; Cricket Skating & Curling; Home: 1 Benvenuto Place, Toronto, Ont. M4V 2L1; Office: 2200 Yonge St., Toronto, Ont. M4S 2C6

ROGERS, Harold Allin, O.C., O.B.E.; b. London, Ont. 3 Jan. 1899; s. Charles Frederick Arthur and Minnie (Dawe)

R.; e. Colborne St. Pub. Sch. and Westervelt Business Sch. London, Ont.; m. Elspeth A. E. d. Rev. William A. McIlroy 12 Sept. 1925; children: Harold Stewarton, Diane Patricia; Pres., Canadian Telephones Rentals Ltd.; T. R. Services Ltd.; Beaverton Boatel; former Publisher and Pres., H. A. Rogers & Co. Ltd. (business sold 1970); Chrmn., Telephone Comte., Ont. Hydro Electric Comn. 1953 — 56; Ont. Telephone Authority (now Comn.) 1956 — 58; Pres., Ont. Telephone Development Corp. (Crown Co.) 1956 — 58; Founder, Assn. of Kinsmen Clubs, Nat. Chrmn. Kinsmen War Services World War II, Fountain in Gore Park, Hamilton, Ont. honouring Founder (1920); Pres. Nat. Adv. Council of All Service Clubs of Can. (men and women) after World War II at request Candn. Govt.; Paul Harris Fellow-Rotary Internat.; mem. Bd. Educ. Village of Forest Hill (Chrmn. 1944 — 51, Vice Chrmn. 1939 — 43); joined 173rd Argyle & Sutherland Bn. 1916, served in France & Belgium with 54th Kootenay Battalion 1917 — 18, gassed at Paschendaele, wounded Amien Front 1918, invalided to Eng., discharged 1919; rec'd Centennial Medal 1967; Queen's Silver Jubilee Medal; Lamp of Learning Secondary Sch. Teachers Ont.; Hon. Citizen of Man. and City of Winnipeg; Freedom of the City given by numerous cities Can.; Freemason (Life mem.); P. Conservative; United Church; recreations: travel, golf, lawn bowling; Clubs: Empire; Kinsmen; Toronto Cricket Skating & Curling; The English Speaking Union; Address: 35 Wynford Htd. Cres., Apt. 2305, Don Mills, Ont. M3C 1K9.

ROGERS, Rix Gordon, B.A., M.Sc.; social agency administrator; b. Fort William (Thunder Bay), Ont., 5 June 1931; s. Albert Henry and Evelyn Sadie (Heard) R.; e. Univ. of Toronto, B.A. 1954; Springfied (Mass.) Coll., M.Sc. 1956; YMCA Cert. 1959; m. Barbara Ann, d. Carl Dawes, Franklyn, N.Y., 22 Dec. 1956; children: Mark, Scott, Susan, Deborah, Karen; GEN. SECY., NAT. COUNCIL OF YMCA OF CAN., since Apl. 1971; Extve. Secy., Lakeshore Br. YMCA 1956-63; Coordinator of Program and Staff Devel., Metrop. Office YMCA, 1963-65; Asst. Gen. Secy., Montreal YMCA, 1965-68; Gen. Secy. 1968-70; Asst. to Pres. 1970-71; has also served as Fellowship Student, Counsellor and Group Work Supr. at various YMCA Brs.; Lectr., Dept. of Applied Social Science, Sir George Williams Univ. & mem. Bd. of Govs.; Past Dir., LaKeshore Gen. Hosp. Foundation; mem., Extve. Comte., Montreal Council of Social Agencies; Bd. mem., Assn. of Leisure Time Services; Past Pres., Pointe Claire Chamber Comm.; Presbyterian; recreations: skiing, golf, boating, camping; Home: 28 Brookfield Rd., Oakville, Ont. L6K 2Y5; Office: 2160 Yonge St., Toronto, Ont. M4S 2A9

ROGERS, Robert G.; b. Montreal, Que.; e. Univ. of Toronto Schs.; R.M.C.; Univ. of Toronto, Civil Engn.; m. Elizabeth Jane Hargrave; children; two d., one s.; CHRMN. AND CHIEF EXTVE. OFFR., CROWN ZELLERBACH CANADA LTD., since 1976; Dir., Candn. Imperial Bank of Commerce; Crown Zellerbach Internat., Inc.; Genstar Ltd.; Gulf Can. Ltd.; Hilton Canada Ltd.; served in various extve. capacities with Domtar Ltd.; Brantford Roofing Co., Cooksville-Laprairie Brick Ltd.; Mgr., Philip Carey Ltd., Montreal, 1947-50; joined present Co. in 1960; el. Dir. 1962; Extve. Vice Pres. 1963; Pres. 1964-76; served with Candn. Armoured Corps during 2nd World War; took part in D-Day invasion of France; Dir., Candn. Council, Internat. Chamber of Comm.; Chrmn., Candn. Forestry Adv. Council; Trustee, Olympic Trust of Can.; mem., Candn. Pulp & Paper Assn. Extve. Comte.; Vice Chrmn. Lester B. Pearson College of the Pacific; Hon. Vice Pres., Nat. Council, Boy Scouts of Can.; Bd. of Govs., B.C. Lions; Dir., Nat. Council, Candn. Council of Christians and Jews; Home: 1691 W. 40th Ave., Vancouver, B.C. V6M 1W1; Office: 815 W Hastings St., Vancouver, B.C. V6C 1B4

ROGERS, Robert Louis, B.A.; diplomat; b. Toronto, Ont., 23 Nov. 1919; s. Gordon Sidney Fenton and Lillian Kathleen (Thompson) R.; e. Riverdale Coll. Inst., Toronto, 1938; Univ. Coll., Univ. of Toronto, B.A. 1942; m. Elizabeth June, d. late Humphrey Hume Wrong 17 June 1949; children: Christopher Hume, Peter Martin, Rebecca Joyce, Hume Alexander; joined Dept. of External Affairs, Apl. 1946; 3rd. Secy., Embassy Washington, 1946-49; 1st Secy., Embassy Tokyo, 1952-55; Counsellor, Canada House, London, 1958-60, and Candn. Del. to N.A.T.O., 1960-63; Ambassador to Israel, 1965-69; Depy. High Commr. to U.K. 1969-72; Ambassador to Yugoslavia and concurrently accredited to Bulgaria and Rumania 1972-74; Dir. Gen. Bureau of Asian and Pacific Affairs, Dept. of External Affairs 1977-77; High Commissioner to India and Nepal, 1977-79; Co-ordinator and Cdn. Ambassador at Large for the Conference on Security and Co-operation in Europe, 1979- ; served in 2nd World War with Lincoln and Welland Regt. in Newfoundland, United Kingdom, France, Belgium, Netherlands, Germany; retired with the rank of Major 1946; Mentioned in Despatches; author of "History of the Lincoln & Welland Regiment", 1954; Anglican; recreations: photography, reading; Home: 1404-71 Somerset St. W., Ottawa, Ont. K2P 2G2; Office:c/o External Affairs Dept., Lester Pearson Bldg., 725 Sussex Dr., Ottawa, Ont. K1A 0C2

ROGERS, William R., B.Ap.Sc., M.B.A., P.Eng.; executive; b. Regina, Sask. 6 July 1940; s. Roy and Grace (Furneaux) R.; e. Davin Sch. Regina; Oak Bay High and Victoria (B.C.) Coll.; Univ. of B.C.B.Ap.Sc. (M.E.) 1963; Stanford Univ. M.B.A. 1968; m. Ann Mary d. D.M. Mackenzie, Trail, B.C. 9 Oct. 1965; children: Janine Grace, Catharine Ann, William Mackenzie; EXTVE. VICE PRES. AND GEN. MGR. ROGERS CABLE TV since 1976; Dir. Cable 10 Mississauga Ltd.; joined United Aircraft of Canada Ltd. 1963-66 serving as Aerodynamics Engr. and Sales Engr.; American Standard (Div. of Wabco-Standard Ltd.) 1968-76 serving as Asst. to Vice Pres. Finance, Mgr. Systems and Data Processing, Mgr. Engn., Plant Mgr.; mem. Assn. Prof. Engrs. Prov. Ont.; Assn. Systems Mang.; Bd. Trade Metrop. Toronto; Liberal; Protestant; recreations: sailing, swimming, curling; Clubs: Boulevard; Toronto Sailing & Canoe; Home: 14 Wainwright Dr., Islington, Ont. M9A 2L7; Office: 855 York Mills Rd., Don Mills, Ont. M3B 1Y2

ROGERS, William Selby, M.A.; university professor; b. Toronto, Ont., 6 July 1918; s. William Henry and Lillian Maria Selby (Carter) R.; e. Univ. of Toronto (Trinity Coll.), B.A. (Modern Lang.) 1940; Columbia Univ., M.A. 1941; awarded French Govt. Scholarship for study in France at Sorbonne, 1946-47; m. Marjorie Anne Bryan Sims, 1950 (divorced 1970); children: Patricia Lilian, Cynthia Rae; m. Marjory Peters Seeley 1976; Prof. & Head French Dept., Trinity Coll., Univ. of Toronto, 1949-72;Dean of Arts and Programme Dir. 1973-78;served in 2nd World War, joining R.C.N.V.R. as Sub-Lieut. and serving in Intelligence Div., Naval Service Hdqrs., Ottawa; resigned with rank of Lieut. 1944; joined UNRRA 1944 and served with that organ. overseas till 1946; among other duties assisted in founding UNRRA D.P. Univ. in Munich; Can. Council Sr. Research Fellow in Paris, France, 1961-62 1971-72; Chrmn. of Humanities Research Council of Can., 1964-66; mem. Toronto Mendelssohn Choir 1947-72, Dir. since 1950; mem., Modern Lang. Assn. of Am.; Alliance Française of Toronto (Pres. 1949-52); mem., Candn. Del. to UNESCO Gen. Confs. 1968, 1970; Mem.-at-large, Candn. Nat. Comn. for UNESCO 1970-73; recreations: travel, arts, languages, music; Club: Arts & Letters; Home: 24 Bishop St., Toronto, Ont. M5R 1N2

ROHMER, Richard, Maj. Gen., retired C.M.M., D.F.C., C.D., Q.C., LL.D.; b. Hamilton, Ont. 24 Jan. 1924; s. Ernest and Marion (Wright) R.; e. High Sch. Fort Erie, Ont.; Assumption Coll., Univ. Western Ont., London, Ont.,

B.A. 1948; Osgoode Hall, Toronto, Ont.; m. Mary-O., d. Walker Whiteside; two d.; Catherine, Ann; COUNSEL, FROST AND REDWAY; (formerly Partner, Rohmer & Swayze); Chancellor, U. of Windsor; Chrmn., Royal Comn. on Publishing (Ont.)1970-72; ccounsel, Royal Comm. on Metro Toronto 1975-77; Chrmn. and Originator, Mid-Canada Devel. Corridor Concept and Conf.; Mediacom Ltd.; Candn Corps. of Commissionnaires; Patron, Metro Toronto St. John Ambulance; called to Bar of Ont. 1951, Bar of Northwest Territories 1970; read law with Phelan, O'Brien and Phelan; cr. Q.C. 1961; served with R.C.A.F. 1942-45 as Fighter Pilot; participated in D-Day invasion of Normandy and with Second Tactical Air Force, France, Belgium and Holland; awarded D.F.C. 1945; flew Vampire jet fighters with R.C.A.F., Toronto, Reserve 1950-53; commanded both 400 Sqdn. (City of Toronto) and 411 Sqdn. (Co. of York) 1952-53; retired 1953, rank Wing Commdr.; apptd. Hon. Lt. Col. and then Col. 411 Co. of York Squadron, Reserve 1971; apptd. Brig. Gen. and Sr. Air Reserve Advisor to chief of Defence Staff and Commander of Air Command, 1975; apptd. Commander of newly formed Air Reserve Group in Air Command 1976; promoted to Major Gen. & apptd. Chief of Reserves, Can. Armed Forced responsible to Chief of Defence Staff for Militia & àNaval, Air and Communications reserves 1978-81 (ret.); served on Council of Twp. North York 1958-59 (Chrmn., Works Comte. and Personnel Comte.); served on Bd. Govs. and Secy. North York Gen. Hosp.; Chrmn. Bd. Dirs., Univ. of Can. N.; Chrmn. and Pres., Ascension Charitable Foundation Inc., operating Thompson House, Home for Aged (138 beds), Don Mills, Ont. and Taylor Place; Bd.; joined Don Mills Civitan Club 1954; Pres. Don Mills Club 1961-62; Judge-Advocate Civitan International 1962-63, 1966-67 (Internat. Vice-Pres. Zone 4, 1963-64; International Treas. 1965-66; Candn. Dist. Honour Key 1965; Civitan Internat. Honour Key 1966); mem., Community Planning Assn. of Can.; Candn. Bar Assn.; Ont. Bar Assn.; Northwest Terr. Bar Assn.; Co. of York Law Assn.; awarded Centennial Medal 1967; Commissioner's Award for Public Service to N. W. Territories 1972; Apptd. Commander of the Order of Military Merit, 1975; LL.D. U. of Windsor 1975; author: "The Green North: Mid-Canada," 1970; "The Arctic Imperative" 1973; "Ultimatum" (novel) 1973; "Exxoneration" (novel) 1974; "Exodux/U.K." (novel) 1975; " Separation" (novel) 1976; "E.P. Taylor, 1978" (non-fiction) "Balls!" (novel) 1979; "Periscope Red" (novel) 1980; "Patton's Gap" 1981, (non-fiction); Delta Chi; Clubs: Albany; Home: 21 Dale Ave., Toronto, Ont. M4W 1K3; Office: 2180 Yonge St. Toronto, Ont. M4J 2B9

ROKEBY-THOMAS, Rev. Howard R., K.H., K.L.J., B.Sc., L.Th., M.A., Ph.D., F.R.G.S., F.R.S.A. (Ang.), F.H.S.C.; b. Eastcombe, Gloucestershire, Eng., 13 June 1907; s. Egbert Ivan and Ethel Ann (Bartlett) T.; e. Inst. Philotech, Bruxelles B.Sc. (Econ. Geog.) 1935; Wycliffe Coll., Toronto, L.Th. 1939; M.A. 1960; Ph.D. (Burton) 1961; m. Anna Elma, R.N., d. Frederick Edwin Roszell, Puslinch, Ont., 10 Aug. 1936; children: Emily (Mrs. Dr. J. W. McLean), David, Derwyn; Rector, Kirkton, Ont. 1969-72; Port Stanley Marina Limited Executive Vice President 1959-62 Director, 1959-71; o. Deacon and Priest, Toronto, 1934; Missy., Cambridge Bay, Victoria Land, 1934-39; 1st Missy. to visit King Wm. Land and Matty Isl., 1936; Rector Walter's Falls 1939-41; Port Stanley, 1948-60, Diocese of Huron; Advertising Mgr., "Canadian Churchman", 1958-69 and Huron "Church News", 1950-67; Hon. Asst., Christ Ch., Scarboro, Ont., 1960-62; Church of The Redeemer, Toronto, 1963-69; served in World War 1941-45 as H. Capt. with Candn. Chaplain Service in Can. and U.K. and with Roy. Candn. Regt. in Italy; Fellow Roy. Commonwealth Soc.; mem., Soc. of Genealogists; Hon Genealogical Soc.; Hon Soc. of Cymmrodorion; at one time interested in aviation and was one of original mem. of the London Aeroplane Club 1925; has lect. to Roy. Geog. Soc. on S.E. Victoria Island and the Queen Maud Gulf 1944; author of "Church in the Valley", 1949;

"Chronicle of the Rooks and Ravens", 1950; articles in learned and popular publ. since 1931; Hospitaller Order of St. John of Jerusalem, Knight 1972, Bailiff Grand Cross 1975, Grand Chancellor 1975-78; Grand Bailiff 1979- (Grand Priory of Can.); Military and Hospitaller Order of St. Lazarus of Jerusalem, Knight 1974; Freemason; recreation; travel; Club: Empire; Address: 74 Jackson Ave., Kitchener, Ont. N2H 3P1

ROLAND, Charles Gordon, M.D.; educator; b. Winnipeg, Man. 25 Jan. 1933; s. John Sandford and Ethel Leona (McLaughlin) R.; e. Kenora-Keewatin Dist. High Sch. 1951; Oakwood Coll. Inst. Toronto 1952; Univ. of Toronto premed. 1952-54; Univ. of Man. M.D., B.Sc. (Med.) 1958; m. Constance Lynn d. late Dr. Roy W. Rankin, Tillsonburg, Ont. 22 Sept. 1979; JASON A. HANNAH PROF. HISTORY OF MEDICINE, McMASTER UNIV. 1977- , Assoc. mem. Dept. Hist. 1978- ; private med. practice Tillsonburg, Ont. 1959-60, Grimsby, Ont. 1960-64; Sr. Ed. Journal of Am. Med. Assn. Chicago 1964-69; Lectr. Northwestern Univ. 1968-69; Assoc. Prof. Mayo Med. Sch. Rochester 1969, Prof. 1973-77; Curator, Osler Lib. McGill Univ.; co-author "An Annotated Bibliography of Canadian Medical Periodicals 1826-1975", 1979; "An Annotated Checklist of Osleriana" 1976; numerous scholarly publs. hist. med. Can. and hist. med. journalism; mem. Am. Osler Soc. (Secy.-Treas.); Candn. Soc. Hist. Med.; Am. Assn. Hist. Med. and other assns.; recreations: mountaineering, scuba diving; Clubs: Royal Candn. Mil. Inst. (Toronto); Literary (Chicago); Osler (London, Eng.); Toronto Hist. Med.; Theta Kappa Psi; Home: 1835 Heather Hills Dr., Burlington, Ont. L7P 2Z1; Office: 3N10-HSC, Hamilton, Ont. L8N 3Z5.

ROLFES, Hon. Herman Harold, M.L.A., B.A., B.Ed.; politician; b. Humboldt, Sask. 13 July 1936; s. Joseph and Josephine (Heckmann) R.; e. St. Peter's Coll. Muenster, Sask.; Teachers' Coll. Saskatoon 1955-56; Univ. of Sask. B.A. 1960, B.Ed. 1964, Masters Degree in Guidance & Counselling 1971; m. Myrna Josephine d. Robert Hopfner, Lake Lenore, Sask. 4 Apl. 1961; children: Debora Lynne, Brian Joseph; MIN. OF HEALTH, SASK. since 1979; mem., Treasury Bd. former Princ. St. Paul's N. Elem. Sch. Saskatoon, St. Charles Elem. Sch., Bishop Murray Elem. Sch., St. Philip's Elem. Sch.; former Dir. of Guidance, Holy Cross High Sch. Saskatoon; el. M.L.A. for Saskatoon Buena Vista 1971, re-el. 1975; Min. of Social Services, 5 Nov. 1975; addit. portfolio of Min. of Continuing Education, 21 Dec. 1978; Past Pres., Saskatoon Elem. Teachers' Assn.; St. Thomas More Alumni Assn.; K. of C.; NDP; R. Catholic; recreations: tennis, golf, curling; Home: 2802 Calder Ave., Saskatoon, Sask.; Office: 208 Legislative Bldg., Regina, Sask. S4S 0B3.

ROLLAND, Lucien Gilbert, D.C.S., B.A., B.A.Sc., C.E.; industrialist; b. St. Jerome, Que., 21 Dec. 1916; s. Olivier and Aline (Dorion) R.; e. Jean de Brebeuf Coll. and Loyola Coll., Montreal, Que.; Univ. of Montreal, B.A., B.A.Sc., C.E.; m. Marie, d. Louis-Raoul deLorimier, 30 May 1942; children: Nicolas, Natalie, Stanislas, Dominique, Christine, Etienne, David; PRESIDENT AND C.E.O., ROLLAND INC. (Estbd. 1882) Chairman and Director, ASEA Limited; ASEA Industries Limited; Dir., Bank of Montreal; Director, U.A.P. Inc.; Philips Can. Ltd.; Montreal Symphony Orchestra; Canadian Pacific Ltd.; Bell Canada; Canadian Investment Fund Ltd.; Canadian Fund Inc.; Donohue Inc.; Stelco Inc. Munich Reinsurance Co. of Can.; Great Lakes Reinsurance Co.; Inco Ltd.; Standard Life Assurance Co., Edinburgh; Atlas-Copco Canada Limited; Governor, Notre Dame Hospital; Hôpital Marie Enfant; Montreal Children's Hosp.; Montreal Gen. Hosp.; Hon. Vice Pres., Canadian Red Cross Soc.; began as Engr., Rolland Paper Co. Ltd., Mt. Rolland, Que., 1942; Mgr., St. Jerome Mill, 1947; Asst. Gen. Mgr., 1949; Vice-Pres. and Gen. Mgr., 1952; Pres. and Gen. Mgr. 1952-78; cr. Kt. Commdr. Order of St. Gregory 1958; mem., Candn. Mfrs. Assn.; Candn. Pulp

& Paper Assn. (Extve. Bd.); Corp. Prof. Engrs. Que.; Montreal Bd. of Trade; Candn. Chamber Comm.; Chambre de Comm. de la P.Q.; Engn. Inst. Can.; (Hon.) mem., Univ. of Montréal Bd. of Dirs.; Roman Catholic; recreations: hunting, fishing; Clubs: St. James's; St-Denis; Montreal Indoor Tennis; Mount Royal; Toronto Hunt; Home: 1321 Sherbrooke St. W. Apt. B-60, Montreal, Que. H3G 1J4; Office: Suite 3620, 800 Place Victoria, Montreal, Que.H4Z 1H3

ROLPH, Frank Mackenzie, company president; b. Toronto, Ont., 13 Aug. 1928; s. Frank and Margaret Yuille (King) R.; e. Upper Can. Coll. (Toronto); St. Andrew's Coll. (Aurora); Racine Lithographic Inst. (Wis.), grad. 1950; m. late Beverley d. Colin W. Webster, 21 June 1957; m. Kathy, 26 June 1976; children: Cynthia,Colin, Virginia, Mary, David; PRES. & C.E.O. RONALDS-FEDERATED LTD. 1980- ; Dir., North America Trust; Rolph McNally Ltd.; Lithographic Apprentice, Rolph-Clark-Stone Ltd. (Toronto) 1948-53; Sales Rep. 1953-56; Sales Mgr. 1956-59; Gen. Mgr. Rolph-Clark-Stone Benallock Ltd. (Montreal) 1960-63; Pres. 1963-65; Pres. & C.E.O., 1965-78; Pres. & C. Oper. Offr. Ronalds-Federated Ltd. (Montreal) 1978-80; served 3rd Batal. (Reserve) Queen's Own Rifles, 1949-54 (Lieutenant); Pres., Graphic Arts Industries Assn. 1971-72, Immed. Past Pres. 1972-73; Dir. & mem. Extve. Comte., Printing Industries of Am., 1968-73, Chrmn. of Bd. 1976-77; P. Conservative; United Church; recreations: golf, tennis, skiing, squash; Clubs: Toronto Hunt; Montreal Badminton & Squash; Montreal Racket; Mount Bruno Golf & Country; Home: 21 Shorncliffe Ave., Westmount, Montreal, Que. H3Y 1A8; Office: Suite 1470, 1801 McGill College Ave., Montreal, Que. H3A 2N4

ROMAINE, Henry Simmons, B.A.; insurance executive; b. New York, N.Y., 30 May 1933; s. Theodore Cole and Cornelia Neilson (Simmons) R.; e. St. Mark's Sch., Southboro, Mass., 1950; Harvard Coll., B.A. 1954; unmarried; children: Henry S. Jr., Hilary H.; EXEC. VICE-PRES., MUTUAL OF NEW YORK 1978- ; Chrmn. and Trustee, MONY Mortgage Investors; Pres. and Dir., The MONY Fund, Inc.; Dir. MONY Life of Can.; mem. Lower Manhattan Adv. Bd., Chemical Bank; joined present Co. as Invest. Analyst 1958; served as U.S. Naval Aviator 1954-57; rank Lt. on discharge; Episcopalian; Clubs: The Links; Bedford Golf & Tennis; Harvard; Home: 162 Croton Lake Rd., Mt. Kisco, N.Y. 10549; Office: 1740 Broadway, New York, N.Y. 10019

ROMAN, Stephen B., LL.D., K.C.S.G.; b. Slovakia, 17 April 1921; s. George and Helen (Kostura) R.; e. Pub. and High Schs. Slovakia; LL.D. Toronto 1967, St. Francis Xavier 1967; came to Can. June 1937; m. Betty d. John Gardon, 20 Oct. 1945; children; Stephen George, Paul Michael Adrian, John Peter, David Andrew, Helen Elizabeth, Angela Maria, Anne Catherine Ruth; CHRMN. OF BD. AND CHIEF EXTVE. OFFR, DENISON MINES LTD.; Chrmn., Roman Corp. Ltd.; Lake Ontario Cement Ltd.; Pres. and Dir., Romandale Farms; Dir., Crown Life Insurance Co.; Guaranty Trust Co. of Canada; Pacific Tin Consolidated Corp.; Pres., Slovak World Congress; served in 2nd World War with Candn. Army; Kt. Comdr. of the Order of St. Gregory the Great; Hon. Dir., Royal Agric. Winter Fair Assn. of Can.; mem., Bd. Trade Metrop. Toronto; Candn. Inst. Mining & Metall.; Catholic; Clubs: Engineers; Canadian Slovak League; Office: P.O. Box 40, Royal Bank Plaza, Toronto, Ont. M5J 2K2

ROMANOW, Hon. Roy John, Q.C., M.L.A., B.A., LL.B.; s. Michael and Tekla R.; e. Bedford Rd. Coll.; Univ. of Sask.; MIN. OF INTERGOVERNMENTAL AFFAIRS, SASK. 1979- ; Chrmn., Potash Corp. of Sask.; el. M.L.A. for Saskatoon Riversdale prov. g.e. 1967, re-el. since; Prov. Secy. 1971-72; Atty. Gen. 1971; NDP; Office: Legislative Bldg., Regina, Sask. S4S 0B3.

ROMPKEY, Hon. William H., M.P., M.A.; politician; b. Belleoram, Nfld. 13 May 1936; s. William Henry and Margaret Lillian Edith (Fudge) R.; e. Bishop Field Coll. St. John's, Nfld.; Mem. Univ. of Nfld.; Univ. of London; Univ. of Toronto; m. Carolyn Cicely d. Harvey Pike, St. John's, Nfld. 15 Apl. 1963; children: Hilary Nanda, Peter Jonathan; MIN. OF NAT. REVENUE, CAN. 1980; Supt. of Educ. Nfld. 1968-71; Pres., Labrador N. Chamber Comm. 1968-69; Vice Chrmn., Goose Bay Local Improvement Dist.; mem. Toastmasters Internat.; former Lt. RCN (R); el. to H. of C. for Grand Falls-White Bay-Labrador g.e. 1972, re-el. since; Parlty. Secy. to Min. of Environment 1972 and to Min. of Manpower & Immigration 1974; Liberal; Anglican; Home: 4 Costello Ave., Ottawa, Ont.; Office: House of Commons, Ottawa, Ont. K1A 0A6.

RONA, George, M.D., FRCP, FCAP; pathologist; university professor; b. Budapest, Hungary, 8 March 1924; s. late Dr. Adolf and Ilona (Steiner) R.; e. Med. Univ. of Budapest 1st Inst. of Pathol. and Cancer Research M.D. 1949 (Gold Medalist); m. Agnes Etelka d. late Dr. Jano Szilas, 13 Jan. 1950; children: Zoltan, Gabriel; PROF. OF PATHOL. McGILL UNIV. since 1971; Dir. of Labs. Lakeshore Gen. Hosp. Pointe Claire 1965-79; Dir. & Pres., Lakeshore Diagnostic Services, 1976- ; Consultant Pathol. Bio-Research Labs. Pointe Claire since 1967; Asst. Pathol. 1st Inst. of Pathol. and Cancer Research Med. Univ. of Budapest 1951-53, Assoc. Prof. 1953-54, Depy. Dir. 1954-56; Resident in Pathol. St. Mary's Hosp. Montreal 1957-59; Sr. Pathol. Ayerst Research Lab. Montreal 1957-61, Consultant Pathol. 1961-73; joined present Univ. as Demonst. Dept. Pathol. 1961, Lectr. 1962, Asst. Prof. 1964, Assoc. Prof. 1967; Visiting Prof. Inst. of Pathol. Univ. of Geneva 1973-74; awarded Arthur Weber Internat. Prize 1976; author over 90 papers in scient. journs.; Assoc. Ed. "The Journal of Molecular and Cellular Cardiology"; mem. Ed. Bd. "Basic Research in Cardiology"; Series Ed. "Recent Advances in Studies on Cardiac Structure and Metabolism" (12 vols.); "Myocardiology" (4 vols.); Fellow, Coll. Pathols. (London, Eng.); mem., Candn. Assn. Pathols.; Que. Assn. Pathols. & Lab. Physiol.; Am. Assn. Pathol. & Bacteriol.; Internat. Acad. Pathol.; Internat. Soc. Heart Research (Chrmn. Am. Sec.); Am. Soc. for Exper. Pathol.; Home: 80 Henley Ave., Town of Mount Royal, Que. H3P 1V3

RONALD, John F., B.Com.; executive; b. Toronto, Ont. 5 Oct. 1926; s. George F. and Ethel (Smith) R.; e. Lawrence Park Coll., Toronto; Victoria Coll., Univ. of Toronto, B.Com. 1949; Advanced Management Program, Harvard Business School 1978; m. Lillian I., d. W. B. Bray, 2 April 1955; children: John, David, Peter, Ann; PRESIDENT, CATELLI LTD. since 1968; Sr. Vice Pres., Ault Foods Ltd.; Pres., Candn. Pasta Mfrs. Assn.; Vice Pres., Ogilvie Mills Ltd.; Dir., Perkins Papers Ltd.; Chrmn. of the Board, Catelli-Habitant Inc. (Manchester, N.H.); Romi Foods (1966) Limited; mem. of Council of Montréal Bd. of Trade 1980-81; mem. Comm. & Admin. Consultative Comte., Concordia Univ.; Dir. & mem. Public Relations Comte., Grocery Products Manufacturers of Can.; commenced with Procter & Gamble Company of Canada Limited 1950; Advertising Manager, Procter & Gamble de Mexico, S.A. de C.V. 1958; with Company in Cincinnati, Ohio 1963-64; Dir., Marketing-Internat., Quaker Oats Co., Chicago, Ill. 1964; served in 2nd World War, R.C.N.V.R. 1944-46; Chrmn. Bd., Grocery Products Mfrs. of Can. 1972; mem., and Dir., Nat. Macaroni Mfrs. Assn.; Protestant; recreations: golf, skiing; Club: Royal Montreal Golf; Home: 20 Aberdeen Ave., Westmount, Que. H3Y 3A4; Office: Plaza Alexis Nihon, Suite 1200, 1500 Atwater St., Montreal, Que. H3Z 1X5

RONALD, William, R.C.A.; artist; broadcaster; b. Stratford, Ont., 13 Aug. 1926; s. William Stanley and Lilliam May (Plant) Smith; e. Ont. Coll. of Art 1951; m. Helen Marie d. Russell Higgins, 6 Sept. 1952; two d. Suzanne

Marie, Dianna Louise; Founding Mem. Painters Eleven; One-Man Shows: Hart House Univ. of Toronto 1954; Greenwich Gallery Toronto 1957; Kootz Gallery New York 1957, 1958, 1959, 1960, 1962, 1963; Laing Galleries Toronto 1960; Isaacs Gallery Toronto 1963; Douglas Coll. Rutgers Univ. 1963; David Mirvish Gallery Toronto 1965; Dunkelman Gallery Toronto 1965; Tom Thompson Mem. Gallery Owen Sound 1971: Brandon Univ. 1972; Robert McLaughlin Gallery Oshawa 1975; Morris Gallery Toronto 1975; Musee d'Art Contemporain Montreal 1975; Rodman Hall Arts Centre St. Catharines 1975; Beaverbrook Art Gallery Fredericton 1975; Confederation Centre Art Gallery & Museum Charlottetown 1975; Edmonton Art Gallery 1975; Burnaby Art Gallery 1976; Art Gallery of Windsor 1976; Gustafssen Gallery Brampton 1976; one man shows, Morris Gallery, Toronto 1977-x80 rep. in 65 museums and pub. colls. incl.: Art Gallery of Ont., Brooklyn Museum, Carnegie Inst., Solomon R. Guggenheim Museum, Museum of Modern Art N.Y., Nat. Gallery of Can., Montreal Museum of Fine Arts, Phoenix Art Museum, Baltimore Museum of Art, Gallery of Modern Art Washington, Newark Museum, N.J. State Museum; bibliog. "A Concise History of Canadian Painting", "Four Decades", "Great Canadian Painting", "On the Enjoyment of Modern Art", "Contemporary Canadian Painting", "300 Years of Canadian Art", "Catalogue, Toronto Painting 1953-65", art journs. and mags. incl. "Art International", "Macleans", "New Yorker", "Time" and "Saturday Night"; host CBC TV "The Umbrella" 1966-67, CBC FM Radio "Theme & Variations" 1968, CBC Radio "As it Happens" 1969-72, CITY-TV "Free For all" 1972-74; rec'd Hallmark Art Award 1952, Nat. Award-Candn. Sec. Internat. Guggenheim Awards 1956, Second Biennial Exhn. Candn. Painting Nat. Gallery Can. 1957; Can. Council Sr. Arts Award 1977; Address: 392 Brunswick Ave., Toronto, Ont. M5R 2Z4

ROOK, John William, B.A.Sc., M.B.A.; company director; b. Brooklyn, N.Y., 19 Nov. 1915; s. William Arthur and Frances Kathleen (Price) R.; came to Can., 1936; e. Upper Canada Coll., Toronto, Ont.; Univ.; Univ. of Toronto, B.A.Sc. (Chem. Engn.) 1946; Harvard Sch. of Business Adm., M.B.A. with distinction, 1949; mem., Bd. of Management, Queen Elizabeth Hosp., Montreal; Time & Motion Study Engr., Procter & Gamble Mfg. Co. Ltd., Hamilton, Ont., 1946-47; with Industrial Devel. Bank, Montreal and Vancouver 1949-52; Asst. to the Pres., Yorkshire Securities Ltd., Vancouver, B.C., Apl. 1952-Nov. 1953; Asst. to the Vice-Pres., Cochran, Murray & Co. Ltd., Toronto, Ont., Dec. 1953-Dec. 1955; joined Power Corp. of Can. Ltd. in Jan. 1956 as Asst. to the Pres.; Gen. Mgr. 1956-62; mem., Corp. of Prof. Engrs. Que.; Lambda Chi Alpha; Protestant; recreations: skiing, skin-diving, prospecting, reading; Home: R.R. 16, Ste. Adele, Que. J0R 1L0

ROONEY, Paul George, B.Sc., Ph.D., F.R.S.C. (1966); university professor; b. New York City, N.Y., 14 July 1925; s. Geoffrey Daniel and Doris Elizabeth (Reeve) R.; e. Univ. of Alberta, B.Sc. 1949; Cal. Inst. of Tech., Ph.D. 1952; m. Mary Elizabeth, d. Albert E. Carlisle, June 1950; children: Francis, Elizabeth, Kathleen, John, James; PROF. OF MATHS., UNIV. OF TORONTO, since 1962; Dir., Francis F. Reeve Foundation; Lecturer, University of Alta., 1952-54, Asst. Prof., 1954-55; Asst. Prof., Univ. of Toronto, 1955-60; Assoc. Prof., 1960-62; served in 2nd World War with Candn. Army, 1944-45; author of various tech. articles in math. journs.; mem., Candn. Math. Cong.; Am. Math. Soc.; Math. Assn. Am.; Liberal; Anglican; Home: 26 Alderbrook Dr., Don Mills, Ont. M3B 1E5

ROOT, Claude Milton, B.A.; executive; b. Montreal, Que. 20 June 1929; s. Claude Arlington and Kathleen (Gilloran) R.; e. Westmount (Que.) High Sch. 1948; Queen's Univ. B.A. 1955, post-grad. Indust. Relations 1956; m. Cynthia Mary Boyd Wickes 26 Dec. 1951; three s. Michael, Brian, Peter; VICE PRES. REAL ESTATE,

ROYAL TRUST CO. since 1976; joined Sun Life of Canada, Kingston, Ont. 1956, Inspr. of Agencies Montreal 1959, Supt. of Agencies 1968; joined present Co. as Asst. Vice Pres. Marketing 1972, Vice Pres. Sales and Marketing 1974; service with Reserve unit Black Watch — Royal Montreal Regt.; rec'd Hicks Mem. Fellowship 1955; Protestant; Dir. and mem., Mgmt. Bd., Cdn. Real Estate Assn.; recreations: golf, squash, skiing, reading, writing; Clubs: St. George's Golf & Country; Cambridge; Home: 8 Edenbrook Hill, Islington, Ont.; Office: Toronto-Dominion Centre, Toronto, Ont.

ROSCOE, Muriel Victoria, A.M., Ph.D., D.Sc., LL.D.; b. Centreville King's Co., Nova Scotia, 24 May 1897; d. Clarence Miner and Mary Amelia (Morton) R.; e. Acadia University, B.A. 1918; Radcliffe College, A.M. 1925, Ph.D. 1926; D.Sc. Acadia 1948; LL.D. Queen's 1952, McGill 1967; Teacher of Science Colchester Acad. Truro, N.S., 1920-23; Inst. in Biol., Acadia Univ., 1926-27, Asst. Prof. 1927-29, Prof. 1929-40; Asst. Prof. 1940-43; Assoc. Prof. 1943-48; Prof. 1948-55; Macdonald Prof. of Botany 1955-65; Chrmn. Dept., McGill Univ., 1945-62; Warden, Roy. Victoria Coll., there, 1940-62; Prof. of Biol., Acadia Univ. 1967-69 and concurrently Dean of Women there; mem., Am. Assn. Advanc. Science: Bot. Soc. Am.; author of a number of important cytol. studies; Baptist; Address: (Box 968) Wolfville, N.S. B0P 1X0

ROSE, Albert, Ph.D.; educator; b. Toronto, Ont. 17 Oct. 1917; s. Mark Edward and Frances (Spiegel) R.; e. Riverdale Coll. Inst. Toronto 1935; Univ. of Toronto B.A. 1939 (H.A.C. Breuls gold Medal); Univ. of Ill. M.A. 1940, Ph.D. 1942; m. Thelma Bernice d. Samuel Aaron Harris, Toronto, Ont. 7 June 1942; children: Jeffrey Raymond, Leslie Harris, Janis Margaret; PROF. OF SOCIAL WORK, UNIV. OF TORONTO since 1956; Dir. Ont. Housing Corp.1964-79; Ont. Council Health 1973-79; Beacon Hill Lodges Ltd. Winnipeg; Jewish Vocational Service; Home Care Program for Metrop. Toronto; mem. Adv. Comte. Laidlaw Foundation; Hosp. for Sick Children Foundation; Hon. mem. Inst. Housing Mang. Ont.; Chrmn., Metropolitan Toronto Housing Authority, 1980- ; Asst. Econ. J. D. Woods & Gordon 1942-43; Research Dir. Welfare Council Toronto 1946-48; Asst. Prof. present univ. 1948, Assoc. Prof. 1952, Dir. Sch. of Social Work 1969-72 and Dean 1972-76; awarded Sr. Fellowship, Central Mortgage & Housing Corp. 1962-63; Centennial Medal 1967; served with Candn. Army 1943-46, rank Lt.; author 'Local Housing Conditions and Needs' 1953; 'Regent Park: A Study in Slum Clearance' 1958; 'Governing Metropolitan Toronto' 1973; "Canadian Housing Policies, 1935-80"; 1980; Ed. 'A People and Its Faith' 1959; various book chapters, studies for gov't'al and voluntary organs., numerous articles in prof. journs.; mem. Candn. Inst. Pub. Adm.; Candn. Assn. Social Workers (Pres. 1971-73); Candn. Council Social Devel.; Internat. Fed. for Housing & Planning; Council on Social Work Educ. (US); Nat. Assn. Social Workers (US); Candn. Assn. Schs. Social Work; Community Planning Assn. Can. (Vice Pres. 1955); Jewish; recreations: philately, numismatics; Home: 225 Cortleigh Blvd., Toronto, Ont. M5N 1P6; Office: 246 Bloor St. W., Toronto, Ont. M5S 1A1.

ROSE, David John, B.A.Sc., Ph.D., F.A.P.S., F.A.A.S.; university professor; physicist; b. Victoria, B.C., 8 May 1922; s. David Angus and Nora (Birkett) R.; e. Victoria (B.C.) Coll., 1939-40; Univ. of B.C., B.A.Sc. (Engn. Physics) 1947; Mass. Inst. of Technol., Ph.D. (Physics) 1950; m. Renate Papke, 1973; children (by previous marriage to Constance Vivienne Fox): Elizabeth Constance, Victoria Ann (deceased), Hugh Alexander, Andrew David; PROF. OF NUCLEAR ENGN., MASS. INST. OF TECHNOLOGY, since 1960; Distinguished Scientist & Dir. Long Range Planning, Oak Ridge Nat. Lab., 1969-71 and Physicist, B.C. Research Council, 1950-51; mem. Tech. Staff, Bell Telephone Labs., 1951-58; joined present Inst. as Assoc. Prof., 1958-60; mem. Faculty, seminar in

Am. Studies, Salzburg, Austria 1973; served with R.C.A. 1942-45; rank Capt.; rec'd. Univ. of B.C. Convocation Prize; Arthur Holly Compton Award (American Nuclear Society) 1975; James R. Killian Jr. Faculty Achievement Award, 1979; co-author, "Plasmas and Controlled Fusion", 1961; other writings incl. over 150 articles in fields of controlled nuclear fusion, plasma physics, electron and atomic physics, science policy, environmental policy, energy policy; mem., American Nuclear Society; American Association Advancement of Science; World Council of Churches Adv. Comtes.; Sigma Xi; Episcopal; Office: Nuclear Engineering Dept. Mass. Inst. of Technology, Cambridge, Mass. 02139

ROSE, Donald Charles, O.B.E. (1946), M.Sc., Ph.D., F.R.S.C.; b. Prescott, Ont., 17 Apl. 1901; s. Robt. Chas. and Jennie Adina (Shellington) R.; e. Queen's Univ., B.Sc. 1923 (N.R. Council Bursary), M.Sc. 1924 (Nat. Research Council Studentship); Exhn. Overseas Schol., 1924-27; Cambridge Univ., Ph.D. 1927; 1851 Exhn. Sr. Studentship 1927-29; m. Winnifred Louise d. W. B. Stanford, Halifax, N.S., 17 June 1929; Lect., Dept. of Physics, Queen's Univ., 1929-30, when he joined Nat. Research Council; Scient. Adviser to Chief of Gen. Staff Dept. of Nat. Defence 1943-45; Chief Supt., Candn. Armament Research & Devel. Establishment, Valcartier, Que., 1945-47; Physicist, N.R.C., Can., 1947-61; Assoc. Dir. Div. of Pure Physics 1961-66; retired 1966; Consultant and Visiting Prof., Dept. of Physics, Carleton Univ. 1968; Fellow, Cambridge Philos. Soc.; mem., Am. Phys. Soc.; Pres.; Candn. Assn. of Physicists 1949-50; Chrmn. of U.N. Tech. Comte. on Outer Space, 1959; Protestant; recreations: golf, tennis; Home: 281 King St. E., Brockville, Ont. K6U 1E3

ROSE, Dyson, M.Sc., Ph.D.; retired research biochemist; b. Delia, Alta., 3 Dec. 1916; s. Roger and Elizabeth Esther (Dodwell) R.; e. Univ. of Alta., B.Sc. (Agric.) 1939, M.Sc. 1941; Univ. of Toronto, 1941-42, 1945-46, Ph.D., 1947; m. Jessie Violet d. late William H. Wilson, 1 Feb. 1947; children: Helen Frances, Doreen Elizabeth; joined staff of Nat. Research Council as Sr. Research Asst., 1942; Asst. Research Biol., 1946; Assoc. Research Offr., 1950; Sr. Research Offr., 1956; Princ. Research Offr., 1963-77 (retired); rec'd. Am. Chem. Soc. Borden Award in Dairy Chem., 1967; Publications: chapter on Can. in "Food Technology the World Over"; approx. 95 scient. papers; Pi Tau Sigma (Charter mem.); Conservative; United Church; Home: 21 Wolff St., Ottawa, Ont. K1K 1K6

ROSEBRUGH, F. Don, manufacturer; b. York Twp., Ont., 15 Oct. 1925; s. Fred Taylor and May Gertrude (Torgis) R.; e. Humewood Pub. Sch. 1939 and Vaughan Rd. Coll. Inst. 1944 Toronto; Univ. of Toronto 1946-48; m. Elaine Jean d. Allan W. Andrews, Toronto, Ont., 21 May 1958; children: Patricia Ann, Douglas Alan, James Donald, Catherine Elaine; PRESIDENT, DOVER CORP. (CANADA) LTD./INDUST. DIV. since 1967; Vice Pres. and Dir. Dover Corp. Canada Ltd. since 1966; Dir. Federal Business Development Bank, 1975-78; Dir. Grand Trunk Corp. (1980); Detroit, Toledo & Ironton Railway (1980); Salesman Kinzinger Rankin Agency Ltd. Toronto 1948-56; Sales Mgr. Rotory Lift Co. of Canada Ltd. 1956-58; Vice Pres. Sales Dover Products Corp. Canada Ltd. 1958-67; served with Candn. Army (Active) 1944-45; Dir. Lib. Party Ont. 1969, Secy. 1970-71; mem. Automotive Industs. Assn. Can. (Dir. 1970-71, Pres., 1977-78); Dir. Cdn. Nat. Rlys. July 77; Liberal; Anglican; recreations: boating, golf snowmobiling; Home: 8 Danville Dr., Willowdale, Ont. M2P 1H8; Office: 31 Progress Crt., Scarborough, Ont. M1G 3V5

ROSENBERG, Rabbi Stuart E., M.A., M.H.L., Ph.D., D.D.; b. New York City, N.Y., 5 July 1922; s. Hyman and Kate (Weissman) R.; e. Columbia Univ., M.A. 1948, Ph.D. 1953; Jewish Theol. Semy. of Am., Rabbi 1945, M.H.L. 1949, D.D. 1971; m. Hadassa Agassi, 20 Feb.

1944; three d.; Rachelle, Ronni, Elissa; came to Can. 1956; Lectr. in Religion, Univ. Sch., Univ. of Rochester, 1951-56; taught at Grad. Ecumenical Inst. of Can., 1967, Toronto; Visiting Lectr. (Extension), Univ. of Toronto; Nat. Pres., Candn. Foundation for Jewish Culture; Vice Pres., Nat. Foundation for Jewish Culture (U.S.); Chrmn. and Founder, Ont. Comte. for Govt. Aid to Jewish Day Schs.; Chrmn., Un. Jewish Appeal of Toronto, 1966-67; Extve., Candn. Red Cross; Nat. Exec. Vice-Pres., Cdn. Friends of Tel Aviv Univ., 1977-80; Chmn., Funeral Services Review Bd., Gov. of Ont. 1977- ; Visiting Lecturer, San Diego State Univ., 1981; mem., Bd. of Gov., Tel Aviv Univ., 1977- ; mem., Council of School of Continuing Studies, Univ. of Toronto 1980- ; toured USSR 1961 and E. Europe as official observer of refugee operations, 1967; rec'd Citation for Leadership, Candn. Mental Health Assn., 1963; professorship estbd. in his name, Jewish Theol. Semy. Am.; author of "The Jewish Community in Rochester", 1954; "Man Is Free", 1957; "A Time to Speak", 1960; "Bridge to Brotherhood — Judaism's Dialogue with Christianity", 1961; "The Bible Is For You", 1961 (Hebrew translation); "More Loves Than One — The Bible Confronts Psychiatry", 1965 (Hebrew translation); "Lines On Life", 1965; "America Is Different", 1964 (paperback ed. "The Search For Jewish Identity In America", 1965 (Hebrew translation); "The Road To Confidence", 1969; "To Understand Jews", 1970; "Judaism" (transl. French, Dutch, Spanish); "Great Religions of the Holy Land: An Historical Guide to Sacred Places and Sites", 1971; "The Jewish Community in Canada" (2 Volumes), 1971; co-author, "What Do We Believe: The Stance of America Religion", 1968; Ed., "A Humane Society", 1962; syndicated weekly columnist "Lines on Life"; Host, Metro Cable T.V. weekly "Cross Examination"; Ed. Canadiana Dept. "Encyclopedia Judaica".77 St. Clair Ave. E., Toronto, Ont. M4T 1M5

ROSENBLATT, Joe; poet; editor; b. Toronto, Ont. 26 Dec. 1933; s. Samuel and Bessie (Tee) R.; e. Toronto Central Tech. Sch.; George Brown Coll.; m. Faye, d. Howard Lorne Smith, 13 Oct. 1970; one s. Eliot Howard; author "Voyage of the Mood" 1960; "The L.S.D. Leacock" 1963; "The Winter of the Luna Moth" 1968; "Greenbaum" (drawings) 1970; "Bumblebee Dithyramb" 1972; "Blind Photographer" 1973; "Dream Craters" 1974; "Virgins & Vampires" 1975; "Top Soil" 1976; "Dr. Anaconda's Solar Fun Club" (drawings) 1978; "Loosely Tied Hands" 1979; "Tommy & the Ant Colony" 1979; "Sleeping Lady" 1980; artwork incl. limited edition (100 copies) of portfolio of 30 drawings, 1979; Editor, "Jewish Dialogue" (fiction, poetry, short stories) since 1969; poems included in numerous anthologies, notably Oxford Book of Canadian Verse (1968), Poets of the Sixties (Eli Mandel ed.) 1973, Penguin Anthology of Canadian Verse (R. Gustafson ed.) 1976, Poets of Canada (J.R. Colombo ed.) 1978, Literature in Canada (D. Daymond & L. Monkman ed.); contributed to numerous periodicals; appeared on many T.V. and radio networks, incl. readings & interviews; lectures and readings at Artists Workshops, high schools, colleges; Writer-in-Residence Univ. W. Ont., Sept. 1979-Apr. 1980; nom. for Gov. Gen.'s Short List, 1974; Gov. Gen's. Award for Poetry 1976; Can. Council Sr. Arts Award 1973 and 1976; Ont. Arts Council Poetry Award 1970; N.D.P.; Hebrew; recreations: basketball, hockey; cat fancier; Home: Office: #7—1498 Yonge St., Toronto, Ont.

ROSENBLUTH, Gideon, Ph.D.; educator; b. Berlin, Germany 23 Jan. 1921; e. London Sch. of Econ. 1938-40; Univ. of Toronto B.A. 1943; Columbia Univ. Ph.D. 1953; m. Annemarie Fischl 1944; two children; PROF. OF ECON. UNIV. OF B.C.; Research Training Fellowship, Social Science Research Council (U.S.) Nat. Bureau of Econ. Research, N.Y. 1950-51, Research Assoc. 1951-52; Asst. Prof of Econ. Stanford Univ. 1952-54; Assoc. Prof. of Econ. Queen's Univ. 1954-62; Visiting Assoc. Prof. Univ. of Wash. 1961; author "Concentration in Canadian Manufacturing Industries" 1957; "The Canadian Economy and Disarmament" 1967, new ed. 1978; co-author "Canadian Anti-Combines Administration 1952-60" 1963; various publs. prof. journs., book chapters, papers; mem. Candn. Econ. Assn. (Chrmn. Stat. Comte. 1958-60, Pres. 1978-79); Am. Econ. Assn.; Candn. Assn. Univ. Teachers (Pres. 1966-67); Royal Econ. Soc.; Royal Soc. Can.; Home: 4639 Simpson Ave., Vancouver, B.C.; Office: 2075 Wesbrook Pl., Vancouver, B.C. V6T 1W5.

ROSENTHAL, Joseph(Joe), R.C.A.; artist; b. Kishinev, Rumania 15 May 1921; s. Samuel Rosenthal; came to Can. 1927; e. Central Tech. Sch. 1940; Ont. Coll. of Art 1946; m. Margaret Joyce d. Walter Louis Dowson 14 Feb. 1948; children: Susan Mary, Ronald Lee; 20 solo exhns. since 1961 Toronto, Hamilton, Detroit, Winnipeg, Edmonton, Ottawa; rep. in many group exhns.; rec'd 1st Prize Art Gallery of Ont. War Poster Competition 1941; Can. Council Grant 1969; author "Old Markets, New World" 1964; "Indians, A Sketching Odyssey" 1971; "As the Artist Sees It" 1971; Exhn. Chrmn. 50th Anniversary Sculptors Soc. Can. 1978; served with Candn. Forces 1942-45; mem. Royal Canadian Academy; Ont. Soc. Artists; Candn. Artists Representation; Print & Drawing Council of Can.; recreations: swimming, skiing, camping, reading; Address: 49 Belvedere Blvd., Toronto, Ont. M8X 1K3.

ROSENTHALL, Edward, M.Sc., Ph.D.; university professor; b. Montreal, Que., 3 June 1916 s. Samuel and Eva (Cronenberg) R.; e. McGill Univ., B.Sc., 1937; M.Sc. 1938; Cal. Inst. of Tech., Ph.D., 1944; m. Sarah, d. Louis Segal, Montreal, Que., 30 Aug. 1942; children: Richard Alan, Rosalie Binnie, Gilda Donna; Chrmn., Dept. of Maths., McGill Univ., 1960-79; Teaching Fellow, Cal. Inst. of Tech., 1938-40; Lectr., McGill Univ., 1940-45; Fellow in Applied Math., Brown Univ., 1943; Asst. Prof., McGill Univ., 1945-47; mem., Inst. for Advanced Study, Princeton, 1947-48; Assoc. Prof., McGill Univ., 1948-54; Prof., 1954; Peter Redpath Prof. of Pure Math. 1977; member, Centre de Recherche, Université de Montréal 1979-80; Emeritus Prof. 1981; Hebrew; recreations: photography, gardening; Home: 3237 Appleton, Montreal, Que. H3Z 1L6

ROSEVEAR, Alfred Beatty, Q.C., B.A., LL.B.; b. of Candn. parentage, Detroit, Mich., 16 Feb. 1894; s. Alfred Ernest and Sara Jane (Beatty) R.; e. Westmount (Que.) Acad.; McGill Univ., B.A. 1916; Univ. of Manitoba, LL.B. 1920; m. Dorothy Eleanor Craig, d. Douglas G. Mathias, 16 Oct. 1929; two d.; practiced law in Winnipeg, Man., 1920-36; cr. K.C. 1934; Solr., Law Dept., Canadian Nat. Rlys., Winnipeg, 1936-45, Asst. Gen. Solr., Montreal, 1945-56; Gen. Atty., Air Canada 1949-59; Gen. Solr., C.N.R., 1956-59; Dir., Inst. of Air & Space Law, McGill Univ. 1959-62, Lectr. in Air Law there 1959-65; author of a number of articles and notes on air and space law in certain learned journals; served in 1st World War with R.F.C. and R.A.F. as Fighter Pilot, 1917-19; 2nd World War with R.C.A.F. as Adm. Offr. with rank of Sqdn. Leader, 1942-45; mem. and Chrmn. of Finance Comte., Winnipeg Public Sch. Bd., 1934-37; Legal Adviser to Candn. Del. to ICAO, 1948, 1949 and 1954; Hon. mem., Candian Inst. Internat. Affairs; Past Pres., Internat. Law Assn. (Candn. Br.); Freemason; Anglican; recreations: travel, lawn bowling; Address: 392 Pearl St., #313, Burlington, Ont. L7R 2M9

ROSEVEAR, Robert Allan, M.M., D.Mus.; professor emeritus of music education; b. East Orange, N.J. 9 July 1915; s. Morris Burt and Mabel Frances (Opie) R.; e. Bloomfield (N.J.) High Sch. 1933; Cornell Univ. A.B. 1937; Eastman Sch. of Music, Univ. of Rochester B.M. 1939, M.M. 1943; Julliard Sch. of Music N.Y. 1937; Ind. Univ. 1960 — 61; Univ. of W. Ont. D.Mus. (Hon.) 1979; came to Can. 1946; m. Clara Helen d. late Frederick Hoffman Rhodes, DeLand, Fla. and Ithaca, N.Y. 5 Aug. 1939; one s. Frederick Morris; Prof. of Music Educ. Univ. of To-

ronto 1946 — 78, Asst. to Dir. 1953 — 68, Chrmn. of Music Educ. 1968 — 72, mem. of Senate 1956 — 68; Specialist in teaching sch. instrumental music; Founder and Conductor, Univ. Toronto Concert Band 1962 — 74; Royal Conserv. Symphonic Band 1946 — 50; Conductor, Univ. Toronto Symphony Orchestra 1953 — 59; Guest Conductor in schs., music festivals (adjudicator), music camps; Examiner and Consultant in Wind and Percussion Instruments, Royal Conserv. Music; prof. performer on French Horn TV, Radio, Symphony, Opera, Ballet, Concert Band; taught instrumental music Music Summer Sch. Ont. Dept. Educ. 1947 — 50, 1952 — 54, 1956 — 58; music teacher St. Louis Co., Mo. Schs. 1939 — 46; Bd. of Dir. Univ. Settlement Music Sch. Toronto; mem. Session Glenview Presb. Ch. 1952 — 75, Clk. 1964 — 69; rec'd Sesquicentennial Long Service Honour Award Univ. of Toronto; author various articles; mem. Am. Bandmasters' Assn.; Music Educators Nat. Conf.; Ont. Music Educators' Assn. (Hon. Life mem., Pres. 1949 — 50); Toronto Musicians' Assn. (Life mem.); Presbyterian; recreations: photography, travel, camping; Club: Kiwanis Internat.; Home: 2714 Saratoga Rd. N., DeLand, Fla. 32720

ROSIER, Claude Harry, P.Eng.; executive; b. Brooklyn, N.S., 23 Dec. 1915; s. Richard C. and Lillian (Aston) R.; e. Dalhousie Univ. (Science) 1937; Technical Univ. of N.S. (Hons. Mech Engn.) 1939; Northwestern Univ. (Management) 1958; m. Edna Louise, d. Cassium M. Belden 1947; children: Wendy Alice, Linda Louise, Ross Cassius; DIR., ABITIBI-PRICE INC., since 1978; Business Consultant 1981 Dir., Abitibi-Price Corp.; Crum & Forster of Can. Ltd.; IAC Ltd.; Continental Bank of Can.; Internat. Minerals & Chem. Corp. (Can.) Ltd.; Mannesmann Demag AG; Oakville-Trafalgar Memorial Hospital; Mgr.-Engn., U.S. Gypsum Company, 1951, General Production Manager 1955, Operations Manager 1957-59; joined present Co. 1959; Vice-Pres. and Gen. Mgr., Abitibi Corp., 1959-61; Vice-Pres., Board Products, 1961-63; Vice-Pres., Devel., Research & Board Products, 1963-65; Sr. Vice-Pres., Board Products Group, 1965-66; Sr. Vice-Pres., Planning Devel., 1966-68, Dir. 1968; Extve vice pres. Corp. Affairs 1968-69; Extve. vice pres. 1969-72; Pres. and Chief Oper. Officer 1973-78; Vice Chrmn. of Bd. 1978-81; served in 2nd World War as Engr. Offr. with R.C.N., 1941-46; Dir., Oakville-Trafulgar Memorial Hospital; mem., Assn. Prof. Engrs. Ont.; Freemason; Conservative; Anglican; Clubs: Mississauga Golf & Country; Toronto; Oakville Golf; Home: 2260 Chancery Lane Oakville, Ont. L6J 6A3; Office: (Box 21) Toronto-Dominion Centre, Toronto, Ont. M5K 1B3

ROSS, Alastair Henry, M.B.A.; petroleum executive; b. Calgary, Alta., 29 March 1923; e. Univ. of Alta. (Civil Engn.); Harvard Univ., M.B.A.; m.; two s., four d.; PRESIDENT AND DIR., ALLARO RESOURCES LTD.; Dir., Acrofund Ltd.; R. Angus Alberta Ltd.; Nat. West Can. Ltd.; Commercial Union of Can. Holdings Ltd.; with Calgary Power after grad., then Montreal Engineering, Montreal and Newfoundland; mem., Calgary Adv. Comte., Royal Trust Corp. of Can.; Dir., Phillips Petroleum Canada Ltd.; past Pres. Ind Petroleum Assn. of Can.; Past Pres., Western Decalta Petroleum Ltd. Pembina Pipeline Ltd.; Mgr., Hawke Drilling Company; Candn. Amateur Ski Assn., Alta. Div. Past Finl Chrmn. 1971; Past pres., Calgary Chamber of Comm.; Past Dir., United Way of Calgary (past gen chrmn.); mem., Economic Council of Can; chrmn., Cndn Energy Research Inst.; Calgary Research and Development Authority; recreations: golf, skiing, reading; Club: Calgary Petroleum (Past Pres.); Ranchman's; Calgary Golf and Country; Home: 348 Scarboro Ave. S.W., Calgary, Alta. T3C 2H3; Office: 1610, 311 - 6th Ave. S.W., Calgary Alta. T2P 3H2

ROSS, Andrew Donald; diplomat; b. Moncton, N.B., 18 Sept. 1914; s. Rev. William Alister, M.A. and Dorothy (Donald) R.; e. Pub. and High Schs., N.B.; Mount Allison Univ., 1932-35; War Intelligence Course, Royal Mil. Coll.;

Nat. Defense Coll. 1958-59; m. Phyllis Joan, d. Charles C. Godding, Ottawa, Ont., 2 Sept. 1944; children: Gregory Laird, David Alastair, Virginia Joan Susan; Desk Clk., Candn. Pacific Hotels, Kentville and Digby, N.S., 1936-38; held various ed. positions in Toronto, Halifax and Ottawa Bureaus of The Candn. Press, 1939-43 and 1945-46; Candn. Information Service 1946-47; joined Dept. of External Affairs, Information and Commonwealth Divs., 1947; Second Secy., Canberra, 1947-51; Information Div., Ottawa, 1951-53; Consul and Information Offr., New York, 1953-56; Press Offr., Candn. Del. to U.N., 1954-56; Head of Press Office, Ottawa, 1956-58; First Secy. and Consul, Caracas, 1959-62; Defence Liaison Div., Ottawa, 1962-64; Counsellor, Rio de Janeiro, 1964-67; Chargé d'Affaires, Dominican Republic, 1967-70; Pierce Task Force Staff, Ottawa, 1970; Staff mem., Inter-dept'mental Comte. on External Relations, 1970-71; Ambassador to Chile, Feb. 1971-75; Secretary, Inter-Departmental Comte on Ext. Rels. & Dir. of Secretariat, Ottawa, 1975-77; Candn Consul General, Atlanta, Ga. 1977-79; served with Candn. Army 1943-45 in Can. and SHAEF London and Paris; comnd. Lt. 1943; United Church; recreations: tennis, gardening, lapidary hobbies; Club: Rideau Tennis and Squash; Ottawa Lapsmith (Ottawa); Address; 1343 Chattaway Ave., Ottawa Ont. K1H 7S2

ROSS, Charles Bruce, B.Sc., P.Eng.; mining executive; b. London, Ont. 15 July 1920; s. Robert Bruce and Helen Gertrude Richardson) R.; e. London (Ont.) Central Coll. Inst. 1938; Univ. of W. Ont. 2 yrs.; Queen's Univ. B.Sc. (Mining) 1947; m. Mary Isabel d. Dr. R.D. Dewar 11 Oct. 1947; children: Jennifer, Barbara, Catherine, John, Sarah; EXTVE. VICE PRES. AND GEN. MGR., HOLLINGER ARGUS LTD.: Pres. and Gen. Mgr. Labrador Mining and Exploration Co. Ltd.; Hollinger North Shore Exploration Co. Ltd.; Dir. Norcen Energy Resources Ltd.; held various supervisory positions Hollinger Mines Ltd. Timmins, Ont. 1947-61; Consultant, Urwick Currie Ltd. 1961-65; Gen. Mgr. since Co. 1965; served with R.C.E. 1940-45, rank Capt.; mem. Assn. Prof. Engrs. Prov. Ont. (Councillor 1978-); Candn. Inst. Mining & Metall. (Chrmn. Toronto Br. 1979-80); P. Conservative; Anglican; recreation: gardening; Club: Engineers; Home: 67 The Kingsway, Toronto, Ont. M8X 2T3; Office: (P.O. Box 221) 601 Commerce Court East, Toronto, Ont. M5L 1E8.

ROSS, Donald A.; company executive; b. Calgary, Alta., 17 Dec. 1925; s. David Alexander and Florence (Kearney) R.; e. Public and Central High Sch., Calgary; m. Vera, d. Clarence Johnston, 17 March 1951; two s: David Wilfred and Donald Alan; PRESIDENT, PARAMOUNT MANG. LTD.; Quesaida Invest. Ltd.; DAR Holdings Ltd.; Dir., Inns of the Park Ltd.; served with Candn. Infantry 1944-45; discharged with rank of 2nd Lt.; articled with Helliwell, Maclachlan, Vancouver, B.C., 1945-50; Partner, Wm. F. Reid & Co., 1951-52; Macintosh, Ross & Co., 1952-55; Ross, Newborn & Co., 1955-60; Gunn Roberts & Co., 1960-66; mem., Inst. of Chart. Accts., Alta. & B.C.; Conservative; Freemason (Shriner); Protestant; Clubs: Calgary Golf & Country; Glencoe; Home: 3207 3rd St. S.W., Calgary, Alta. T2S 1V4; Office: 460, 602-12 Ave. S.W., Calgary, Alta. T2R 0H5

ROSS, Donald A., B.E.E., M.Sc., Ph.D.; research physicist; b. Montreal, Que., 16 May 1922; s. John Donald and Esther Marshall (Read) R.; e. McGill Univ., B.E.E. 1947; Yale Univ., M.Sc. (Phys.) 1954, Ph.D. (Phys.) 1957; m. Cecily Mary, d. Archibald Campbell Galbraith, 25 Nov. 1951; one s. Donald Murray; GROUP HEAD, ELECTRONIC PRINTING, RCA LABS., since 1964; joined St. Lawrence Sugar Refinery 1947-48; General Electric X-ray Corp. Ltd. 1948-59; High Voltage Engn. Corp. 1948-53, 1957-58; RCA Labs., Indust. Reactor Lab., 1958-62; apptd. Mgr., Corp. Grad. Recruiting, 1962-64; served with Candn. Army Signal Corps 1940-43; mem., Am. Phys. Soc.; Am. Assn. for Advancement of Science; Republican; Protestant; recreations: riding, golf; Club: Ro-

tary Princeton; Home: 24 Nelson Ridge Rd., Princeton, N.J. 08540; Office: Princeton, N.J.

ROSS, Donald M., M.A., Ph.D., Sc.D., F.R.S.C.; educator; b. Sydney, N.S., 21 May 1914; s. Murdoch Willard and Jennie Ross (Fail) R.; e. Dalhousie Univ., B.A. 1934, M.A. 1936; Cambridge Univ., Ph.D. 1941, Sc.D. 1966; m. Ruth Emily, d. late Lewis B. Green, Ceylon, 31 May 1941; children: Mary Isabel, Andrew John; PROF. EMERITUS, UNIV. OF ALBERTA since 1979; Scient. Research Offr., Sch. of Agric., Cambridge Univ., 1941; Lectr. in Zool., Univ. Coll., Univ. of London, 1946-60; joined present Univ. as Prof. 1961-79 and Head, Dept. of Zool., 1961-64; Dean, Faculty of Sci. 1964-76; mem. Bd. of Govs. 1967-69 1974-77; rec'd Queen's Jubilee Medal, 1978; Bronze Bucranium, Internat. Science Film Festival, Univ. of Padua; Spec. Prize, 8[th]Festival of Sci. and Tech. Films, Budapest 1979; Fry Medal, 1980 (Cdn. Soc. Zool.); author of book chapters and scient. articles in various biol. journs.; Past Pres., Candn. Science Film Assn.; Past Pres., W. Candn. Univs. Marine Biol. Soc.; Fellow, Am. Assn. Advanc. Science; Zool. Soc. London; mem., Candn. Soc. Zools.; Am. Soc. Zools.; Physiol. Soc. (UK); NDP; recreations: hiking, ski touring; Home: 11603-77 Ave., Edmonton, Alta. T6G 0M4; Office: Dept. of Zoology, University of Alberta, Edmonton, Alta.

ROSS, Henry Raymond, govt. relations, business and communication consultant; b. Toronto, Ont. 9 Nov. 1919; s. Joseph Samuel and Mary (Rotenbury) R.; e. elem and sec. sch. Toronto; Art College of Ont. 1939; m. Ann Clarfield 5 Nov. 1944; children: Janice Carol, Ellen Louise; CONSULTANT, HENRY R. ROSS CONSULTANTS, INC.; Chrmn., ICA/ACS Joint Broadcast Cmte.; Dir., Candn. Advertising Research Found.; Trustee, Am. Fed. of Musicians; Pres., Ross Ferris, Motion Picture Theatres, 1946; Sr. Vice Pres., then Dir. F.H. Hayhurst Co., 1957-79; Research Advisor, Fed. and Prov. govts. in development of advertising, business practice laws; author of articles on advertising, communications, govt. relations; Fellow, Inst. of Candn. Advertising; mem., adv. Bd., Humber Coll.; Conservative; Clubs: Donalda; Art Directors; recreations: golf, bridge; Home: 127 Munro Blvd., Willowdale, Ont. M2P 1C7; Office: 55 Eglinton Ave. E., Ste. 505, Toronto, Ont. M4P 1G9.

ROSS, (James) Sinclair; writer; b. Wild Rose, Sask., 22 Jan. 1908; s. Peter and Catherine Foster Fraser R.; Grade 11 schooling, Country and small town schools; Joined Royal Bank of Canada in 1924, retired 1968; author "As For Me and My House" 1941; "The Well" 1957; "The Lamp at Noon and other stories" (stories) 1968; "Whir of Gold" 1970; "Sawbone's Memorial" 1974; Address: c/o Writers' Union of Canada, 24 Ryerson Ave., Toronto, Ont. M5T 2P3

ROSS, John H., B.Sc., P.Eng.; consulting engineer; b. Orillia, Ont., 11 June 1908; s. James Henry and Mary Adelaide (Laidley) R.; e. Coll. Inst., Orillia; Central Tech. Sch., Toronto; Queen's Univ., B.Sc. (Mech. Engn.) 1935; m. Edna May, d. Henry Howard Hawke, 10 Apl. 1937; with Candn. Nat. Carbon Co. Ltd., Toronto, 1936-37; apptd. Works Engr., Eveready S.A., Buenos Aires, Argentina, 1937-38, and John Inglis Co. Ltd., Ordnance Divn., Toronto, 1938-39; Asst. Mech, Engr., Hydro-Elec. Power Comn. of Ont., Toronto, 1939-40; in 1940 was Project Engr., Nobel Nitroglycerine Sec., Defense Indust. Ltd., Montreal; with Small Arms Ltd., Long Branch, Ont., as Works Engn. and Security Offr., 1940-44; Mech. Engr., with G. Lorne Wiggs, Consulting Engr., Montreal, 1944-45; began private practice as Consulting Engr. in Toronto, June 1945; incorp. 1957; Pres., John H. Ross & Assoc. Ltd. 1957-76; returned to private practice 1976; retired 1980; 2nd Lieut., 2nd Field Park Co., R.C.E., N.P.A.M.; Dec. 1938, and promoted Lieut., July 1939; discharged as med. unfit, Sept. 1939; mem., Assn. of Prof. Engrs. Ont. (Council 1954-56, 1964-70); Sons of

Martha Medal, 1965; Companion of the Order of the Sons of Martha, 1980; American Society of Heating, Refrigerating and Air Conditioning Engineers (President, Ontario Chapter 1952-53; National Council 1956-58, 1961-64 and 1966-67; National Treas. 1964-66, Distinguished Service Award 1968, Fellow 1972; Presidential Citation 1979; Pres. Rep. for Can., 1976-82; Pres., A.S.H.R.A.E. Research Can., 1978-80; Association of Consulting Engineers of Can. (Dir. 1953-56, 1959-62, President 1961); American Inst. Consulting Engrs. (Council 1967-69); Tau Beta Pi; Conservative; Protestant; recreations: photography, hunting, fishing, skeet-shooting; Clubs: Engineers (Toronto) Pres. 1972; Rotary; Home: 9 Cobble Hills, Islington, Ont. M9A 3H6;

ROSS, John Turner; company president; b. Quebec City, Que., 12 June 1930; s. J. Gordon and Kathleen (Turner) R.; e. Bishops Coll. Sch., Lennoxville, Que. (1947); Middlebury (Vt.) Coll. (1952); m. Rosemary, d. David W. MacKeen, 15 May 1954; children: John, Wendy, Alson, Shelagh; PRESIDENT AND DIRECTOR, ROBERT LAWRENCE PRODUCTIONS (CANADA) LTD., since 1958; commenced as school teacher, Montebello, Que., 1952-53; engaged as Radio and TV Producer, Cockfield, Brown & Co. Ltd., Montreal, Que., 1953-55; joined Robert Lawrence Productions (Canada) Ltd., as Gen. Mgr., 1955; apptd. Vice Pres., 1957; mem., Metrop. Toronto Bd. of Trade; Soc. Motion Picture & Television Engrs.; Past Pres. Assn. Motion Picture Producers & Labs. of Can.; United Church; recreations: squash, golf, reading, travel, music; Clubs: Oakville; Carleton; R.C.Y.C.; Empire; Canadian (N.Y.); Home: 1255 Lake Shore Rd. E., Oakville, Ont. L6J 1L5; Office: 38 Yorkville Ave., Toronto, Ont. M4W 1L5

ROSS, Malcolm, O.C., M.A., Ph.D., LL.D., F.R.S.C. (1955); university professor; b. Fredericton, N.B., 2 Jan. 1911; s. Charles Duff and Cora Elizabeth (Hewitson) R.; e. Univ. of New Brunswick, B.A., 1933, D.Litt., 1962, LL.D. St. Thomas Univ. 1976; Univ. of Toronto, M.A. 1934; Cornell Univ., Ph.D. 1941; m. Lois Natalie, d. A. V. Hall, Toronto, Ont., 4 June 1938; one d. Julie Martha; THOMAS McCULLOCH PROF., DALHOUSIE UNIVERSITY, since 1973; Editor of"Queen's Quarterly", 1953-56; Lecturer, Cornell University, 1939-41; Indiana University, 1941-42, attached to Distribution Div., National Film Board, Ottawa, 1942-45; joined English Dept. of Univ. of Manitoba, 1945, resigning in 1950; Guggenheim Fellow, 1949-50; apptd. Prof. of Eng., Queen's Univ., 1950; Prof. and Head, Dept. of Eng., 1957-60; James Cappon Prof. of Eng., 1960-62; Prof. of Eng. Lit., Trinity Coll., Univ. of Toronto 1962-68 and Dean of Arts there 1965-68; apptd. Prof. of English, Dalhousie University 1968; Chrmn., Nuffield Comte. on Humanities and Social Sciences, 1961-62; Publications: "Milton's Royalism", 1943; "Our Sense of Identity", 1954; "Poetry and Dogma", 1954; "The Arts in Canada", 1958; Ed. "Man and his World" (with John Stevens), 1961, ed., New Canadian Library; various articles in learned journs.; Apptd. to Adv. Bd. of Nat. Library of Can., 1977; mem. Arts Adv. Panel, Can. Council, 1980- ; mem., Nat. Extve., Humanities Assn. of Can.; Chrmn. of the NCCUC Comte. in Teaching and Research; mem.; Acad. Panel of the Can. Council, 1966-68; Pres. (1970-71) Sec. II, Royal Soc. Can.; Chrmn. (1969-72) Dalhousie Comte. on Cultural Activities; Anglican; recreations: music, gardening; Home: 1750 Connaught Ave., Halifax, N.S. B3H 4C8

ROSS, Murray George, O.C. M.A., Ed.D., D.C.L., D.Litt., D.Un., F.A.S.A., LL.D.; president emeritus; b. Sydney, N.S., 12 April 1910; s. George Robert and Catherine (MacKay) R.; e. Acadia Univ., B.A. (Econ. and Sociol.) 1936; Univ. of Toronto, M.A. (Sociol.), 1938, LL.D. 1971; Univ. of Chicago, post-grad. work (Sociol.) 1939; Columbia Univ., Ed.D. (Sociol Psychol.) 1949; Acadia Univ., D.C.L. 1960; Univ. of Toronto, LL.D. 1970; York Univ., D.Litt. 1971; Laurentian Univ., LL.D. 1976; m.

Janet Kennedy, M.D., F.C.F.D., d. Col. W. A. Lang, 10 May 1941; children: Susan Janet, Robert Bruce; Dir., Continental Group of Canada Ltd.; Associates Acceptance Co. Ltd.; Capital Growth Fund; Time Canada Ltd.; McGraw-Hill Ryerson; North Am. Adv. Bd., Volvo (Dir. Emeritus); Hon. Dir., Nat. Council of YMCA; Chrmn. Bd. of Trustees, Ont. Hist. Studies Series; Trustee, Sunnybrook Hosp.; Research Assoc., Candn. Youth Comn.; 1945-47; Extve. Secy., Candn. Inst. of Pub. Affairs, 1945-48; Assoc. of Social Work, Univ. of Toronto, 1951-55; Prof. 1955; Extve. Asst. to Pres., 1956-57; Vice-Pres. 1957-60; Pres., York Univ. 1960-70 and Professor of Social Sc. there 1970-72 since when President emeritus; Chrmn. Bd. Trustees, Ont. Hist. Studies Series; Fellow, Am. Sociol. Assn.; mem., Am. Acad. of Pol. and Social Science; Am. Assn. for Adv. of Science; Publications: "The New University", 1961; "Case Histories in Community Organization", 1958; "New Understandings in Leadership" (with C. E. Hendry), 1957; "Community Organization: Theory and Principles", 1955; "The Y.M.C.A. in Canada", 1951; "Religious Beliefs of Youth", 1950; "Towards Professional Maturity" (Ed.), 1948; "The Years Ahead: A Study of the Canadian Y.M.C.A.", 1945 (completed as Dir. of this study); "New Universities in the Modern World", 1965; "The University: The Anatomy of Academe", 1976; "Canadian Corporate Directors on the Firing Line", 1980; also numerous pamphlets incl. "Education in the U.S.S.R.", 1958; UNESCO Report, "Theory and Principles of Community Development", 1954; "Education in Candian Institutions", 1952; many articles in prof. mags. and journs. incl. "The Ethical Goals of Modern Education", 1962; "How to Fight Failure in High School", 1961; "Trends in Higher Education", 1961; Awarded Centennial Medal, 1967; Borden Medal (Book Award), 1976; Silver Jubilee Medal, 1978; Officer, Order of Canada, 1979; Protestant; recreations: bridge, tennis, music, reading; Clubs: Art and Letters; Queen's; Badminton & Racquet; Hillsboro; York; Home: 75 Highland Cres., Willowdale, Ont. M2L 1G7; Office: Glendon College, 2275 Bayview Ave., Toronto, Ont. M4N 3M6

ROSS, Robin, M.B.E., M.A.; university official; b. Tayport, Fife, Scotland, 25 Jan. 1917; s. Robert and Marjorie R.; e. Hamilton Acad., Scot.; St. Andrews Univ., M.A. (1st Class Hons. in Classics); Jesus Coll., Oxford; m. Elspeth Madge, d. Franklin Ritchie, Lake Port, Cal., 14 Aug. 1946; one s. Ian; VICE-PRINCIPAL AND REGISTRAR, ERINDALE CAMPUS, UNIVERSITY OF TORONTO, since July 1977; Dist. Magistrate and Collector, Indian Civil Service, 1940-47; Principal, Commonwealth Relations Office, 1947-57; Supervisor of Adm., Central Mortgage & Housing Corp., Ottawa, Ont., 1957-58; apptd. Assistant Registrar, University of Toronto, 1958; Registrar 1959; Vice-Pres. and Registrar 1967; Vice Provost 1972; 1966-67 Coordinator of Federal Govt. Activities in Higher Education in Department of Secretary of State; served in 2nd World War; 2nd Lieutenant, Queen's Own Cameron Highlanders; awarded M.B.E.; Presbyterian; recreations: golf, fishing, climbing; Home: Suite B-8, 296 Mill Rd., Etobicoke, Ont. M9C 4X8

ROSS, Romaine Kay, Q.C., LL.M.; b. Wellandport, Ont., 7 Oct. 1903; s. James Alway and Sarah Agnes (Kay) R.; e. Osgoode Hall Law Sch., grad. 1931; Univ. of Toronto, LL.B. 1937, LL.M. 1943; m. Mary Margaret, d. Dr. Stephen F. Millen, Woodslee, Ont., 31 Oct. 1939; three d. Jane Elizabeth, Mary Kay, Suzen Elaine; President, Kitchener-Waterloo Developments Ltd.; Dir., Halton Crushed Stone Ltd.; called to Bar of Ont., 1931; cr. K.C. 1947; has appeared as Counsel before Judicial Comte., H.M. Privy Council; submitted brief before Special Comte. of Senate of Can. on Human Rights and Fundamental Freedoms; pol. speaker (P.C.) in Ont. for candidates, 1926-1950; el. to Council, Village of Port Dalhousie, 1946, Reeve then Mayor, 1949; mem., St. Catharines City Council, 1951-60; def. cand. (Fed.) for Lincoln, 1953, 1963; author of: "Local Government in Ontario", 1949, 2nd ed. 1962; "Regional

Government in Ontario" 1970; former mem., Lincoln County Board of Education; Ontario Association Children's Aid Societies (past President); St. Catharines and District, Chamber of Comm. (past Pres.); mem., Canadian Bar Assn. (Past mem. Council); Candn. Authors Assn. (Past mem. Nat. Exec.); P. Conservative; United Church; recreations: travel, fishing, athletics; Clubs: St. Catharines Golf; Port Dalhousie Yacht; Home: 18 South Dr., St. Catharines, Ont. L2R 4T8

ROSS, Sam Foster, Q.C., B.A.; b. Hamilton, Ont., 30 June 1915; s. William Leaper, K.C. and Florence Alice (Griffith) R.; e. Public Schs., Hamilton, Ont.; McMaster Univ., B.A. 1936; Osgoode Hall Law Sch., Toronto, Ont.; m. Marjorie King, d. Septimus Stuart DuMoulin, Hamilton, Ont., 25 July 1942; children: Andrews Foster, Marjorie Alice, Judith Ann, Mary Rebecca; PARTNER, ROSS & McBride (Estbd. 1890); Pres., First Hamilton Corp.; Wenagara Corp. Ltd.; Dir., Hamilton Wire Products Ltd.; Philpco Investments Ltd.; Felton Brushes Ltd.; The Grafton Group Limited; called to the Bar of Ont., 1939; cr. Q.C., Dec. 1957; Commnd. Probationary Sub-Lieut., RCNVR, 1940; served in 2nd World War, RCNVR 1940-45; discharged with rank of Lieut.-Commdr.; apptd. C.O., HMCS "Star" (Hamilton) Reserve Naval Div., 1946; retired from active Reserve with rank of Commdr. RCN(R) 1950; mem. Bd. of Govs., The Art Gallery of Hamilton; Hamilton Philharmonic Orchestra; Bd. of Trustees, Hamilton Cerebral Palsy Centre Sch.; Kappa Alpha; P. Conservative; Anglican; recreation: golf; Clubs: The Hamilton; Tamahaac; Hamilton Golf & Country; Home: 50 South St. W., Dundas, Ont. L9H 4C6; Office: 1 James S., Hamilton, Ont. L8N 3PG

ROSS, T. Bruce, LL.D.; retired company officer; b. Winnipeg, Man., 29 Aug. 1904; s. Thomas and Mary (Sutton) R.; e. Winnipeg Schs., Man.; LL.D. Winnipeg 1970; m. late Beryl McIntosh, d. late William Armstrong, Winnipeg, Man., 21 Oct. 1933; children: Mary Jean (Connacher), Elizabeth Jane (Smith); 2ndly Edna May Scott, Toronto; past Chrmn., the Monarch Life Assurance Co. (Estbd. 1906); mem. Winnipeg Adv. Bd.; Can. Permanent Trust Co.; joined Canadian Indemnity Co. and Canadian Fire Insurance Co., Winnipeg 1921, Secy. 1946, Asst. Gen. Mgr. 1952, Gen. Mgr. 1954, Pres. 1963-70; Hon. Fellow, Ins. Inst. Can.; Chrmn. Bd., Univ. Winnipeg 1960-68; Past Dir. (one of original Dirs.) Ins. Bureau of Can.; Dir., YMCA, Past Vice Pres., Winnipeg YMCA 1947; Un. Church; recreations: golf, curling; Clubs: The Manitoba; St. Charles Country; Royal Lake of the Woods Yacht; Winnipeg Home: 1204 —200 Tuxedo Blvd., Winnipeg, Man. R3P 0R3;

ROSS, W(illiam) Grant, B.Com., F.C.A.; b. Toronto, Ont., 13 May 1912; s. David Waters and Helen Miller (Grant) R.; e. Upper Can. Coll.; Univ. of Toronto, B.Com. 1933; C.A. 1937; m. Margaret Kinnisten, d. John Walter Young, Toronto, Ont., 25 Mar. 1939; children: Walter Grant, Elizabeth Margaret, Jane Edith, Mary Helen; retired, Partner, Clarkson, Gordon, 1945-77; joined firm 1933; mem., Inst. of Chart. Accts. Ont.; Bd. mem. Women's College Hosp., Orthopaedic & Arthritis Hosp; United Church; recreations: fishing, gardening; Past Chrmn., Civic Garden Garden Centre; Clubs, Caledon Mountain Trout; National; Home: 17 Glenallan Rd., Toronto, Ont. M4N 1G6; Office: (Box 126) Toronto-Dominion Centre, Toronto, Ont. M5K 1H1

ROSSITER, Hon. Leo Francis, M.L.A.; politician; b. Morell, P.E.I. 13 Jan. 1923; s. J. Ernest and Catherine (Clarkin) R.; e. Morell Sch.; St. Dunstan's Univ.; m. Anna d. Elija Pierce, Elmira, P.E.I. 17 Oct. 1946; children: Jacqueline, Gerald, Eugene, Melvin; MIN. OF FISHERIES, P.E.I. 1979- and MIN. OF LABOUR, P.E.I. 1980- ; prov. Secy. 1979-80; merchant and farm machinery dealer; Gen. Mgr. Dingwell & Rossiter; el. M.L.A. for 2nd Kings prov. g.e. 1955, re-el. 1959, 1966, 1970, 1974, 1978, 1979;

Min. of Industry & Natural Resources and of Fisheries 1959-65; Min. of Fisheries and Municipal Affairs 1965-66; Assoc. mem. United Offrs. Service Club Charlottetown; K. of C.; Chmn., Morell Village Commn; P. Conservative; R. Catholic; Office: (P.O. Box 2000) Shaw Bldg., Charlottetown, P.E.I. C1A 7N8.

ROTENBERG, Kenneth, B.Com.; realestate executive; b. Cobourg, Ont., 1 Sept. 1922; s. Harry and Pearl (Greisman)R.; e. Univ. of Toronto Schs., 1940; Univ. of Toronto, B.Com. 1944; m. Doris J., d. late Charles Sommer, Montreal, Que., 22 June 1949; children: Arthur, Bettina, Deborah, Virginia, Rebecca: VICE CHRMN., CEO., AND DIR., ROSTLAND CORP., Pres. and Dir., Kenair Apartments Ltd.; Trustee, BM-RT Realty Investments: Dir., Dominion Life Assurance Co.; Mercantile Bank of Can.; Engineering Interface Ltd.; formed present co. 1976; Pres., Y & R Properties Ltd. 1968-76; joined that co., then Yolles & Rotenberg Ltd., 1946; served with R.C.A.F. 1943-46; Dir. C.K. Clark Psychiatric Research Foundn.; Bd. Govs., Lester B. Pearson Coll. of Pacific; Mount Sinai Hosp.; Jewish; recreations: skiing, tennis, reading; Clubs: Donalda; National; Craigleith Ski; Home: 14 Bridle Path, Willowdale, Ont. M2L 1C8; Office: 390 Bay St., Toronto, Ont. M5H 2Y2

ROTH, Frederick Burns, M.D.; b. Tavistock, Ont., 30 March 1913; s. Adam E. and Annie Reynolds (Anderson) R.; e. Woodstock (Ont.) Coll. Inst.; Univ. of W. Ont., M.D. 1936; Sch. of Hygiene, Univ. of Toronto, 1948-49; m. Edith Audrey, d. George Ryder, Whitehorse, Y.T., 7 Nov. 1945; children: Kenneth B., Randall G., Cynthia Ann; practised medicine at Atlin, B.C. 1937-39 and Whitehorse, Y.T. 1939-48; Adm. Asst., Winnipeg (Manitoba) Gen. Hosp., 1949-50; Dir., Hosp. Adm., Dept. of Pub. Health, Sask., 1950-51; Depy. Min. of Pub. Health Sask., 1952-62; Head, Dept. of Hosp. Admin., Sch. of Hygiene, Univ. of Toronto, 1962-67, Chrmn. Dept. Health Adm. 1967-73, Associate Director School Hygiene 1967-75; Prof., Health Admin., 1975-78; Prof. Emeritus since 1978; Pres., Home Care Program of Metrop. Toronto since 1970; Gov., Univ. Sask.; Hon. Fellow Am. Coll. of Hosp. Admrs.; mem., Candn. Med. Assn.; Delta Upsilon; United Church; Home: 95 The Kingsway, Toronto, Ont. M8X 2T6

ROTH, Hubert A., B.A.Sc.; telecommunications executive; b. Tavistock, Ont., 7 Aug. 1923; e. Univ. of Toronto B.A.Sc. 1950; VICE PRES. NETWORK SERVICES, BELL CANADA since 1979; joined Bell Canada, Stratford, Ont. 1946, Engn. Asst., Toronto 1950; held various line and staff mang. positions Engn. and Plant Depts. Montreal and Toronto; Area Plant Supvr. 1965 and Area Plant Mgr. 1966 Toronto Area, Asst. Vice Pres.-Engn. Montreal 1970; Vice Pres. Operational 1972; Vice Pres. N.E. Area 1976; Vice Chrmn. and C.E.O., Northern Telephone Ltd.; served with RCN 1942-45; rank Sub-Lt.; mem. Assn. Prof. Engrs. Ont.; Home: RR1, Ilderton, Ont.; Office: 100 Dundas St. W., London, Ont.

ROTH, Millard S., B.Mgt. Eng., M.Sc.; management and financial consultant; b. Toronto, Ont. 28 Oct. 1937; s. Manuel J. and Juanita (Axler) R.; e. Pub. and High Schs., Toronto; Rensselaer Polytechnic Inst., Troy, N.Y. B.Mgt.Eng. 1959; Purdue Univ., M.Sc. (Indust. Mang.) 1960; m. Sonia, d. Max Kaplan, 12 Apr. 1962; children: Andrew, Maxine; PRESIDENT AND DIR., BUSINESS VENTURECO INC. since 1979; Extve. Dir., Candn. Motion Picture Distrubutors Assn.; Dir., Lease-Rite Corp. Inc.; Inniskillin Wines Inc.; Conservatory of Cinematic Art, Montreal; mem., Adv. Grp., Candn. Film Dev. Corp.; Asst. to Gen. Mgr. of Production, Electric Reduction Co. of Canada Ltd., 1960-62; Consultant, VRSK Management Consultants, Toronto, 1962-63; Corporate Controller, Levy Industries Ltd., 1963-64; Partner, Hecker, Roth and Associates, 1964-65; Pres. and Dir., Corporate Growth Assistance Ltd. since 1965; mem., Engn.

Inst. Can.; Inst. of Mang. Consultants of Ont.; Assn. Prof. Engrs. Prov. Ont.; Dir., Baycrest Centre for Geriatric Care; recreation: golf; Club: Oakdale Golf & Country; Home: 14 Berkindale Dr., Willowdale, Ont. M2L 1Z5

ROTHMAN, Hon. Melvin L., B.A., B.C.L.; judge; b. Montreal, Que., 6 Apl. 1930; s. Charles and Nellie (Rosen) R.; e. Roslyn Sch. and Westmount (Que.) High Sch., 1946; McGill Univ., B.A. 1951, B.C.L. 1954; m. Joan Elizabeth, d. F. W. Presant, Toronto, Ont., 4 Aug. 1954; children: Ann Elizabeth, Claire Presant, Margot Sneyd; DEPUTY JUDGE, SUPREME COURT OF NORTHWEST TERRITORIES; since 1977; Dir., Cdn. Judges Conf.; read law with Phillips Vineberg Goodman Phillips & Rothman; called to Bar of Que. 1955; cr. Q.C. 1971; practised law with Phillips Vineberg Goodman Phillips & Rothman until 1971; Justice, Que. Superior Ct. since 1971; has served as Pres., McGill Students Soc.; Dir., Summerhill Homes Inc.; Dir. and Secy., Inst. Philippe Pinel; Secy., McGill Law Grads. Assn.; Trustee and Gov., Martlet Foundation; Pres., Jr. Bar Assn. Montreal; mem. Council, Bar of Montreal (Dir., Legal Aid Bureau); Jewish; recreations: skiing, sailing, photography; Clubs: Lord Reading Yacht; Home: 487 Argyle Ave., Westmount, Que.; Office: 10 Craig St. E., Montreal, Que.

ROTHNEY, Gordon Oliver, M.A., Ph.D., F.R. Hist. Soc.; historian; b. Town of Richmond, Que., 15 Mar. 1912; s. William Oliver, M.A., B.D., Ph.D. and Agnes Brodie (Linklater) R.; e. Sherbrooke, Que., High Sch.; Univ. of Bishop's Coll., B.A. (1st Class Hons. in Hist.; Gov.-Gen. Medal) 1932; Univ. of London (King's Coll.), M.A. (with Distinction) 1934, Ph.D. 1939; m. Alice Russell, B.A., d. Rev. Alex. R. Ross, 31 July 1943; children: William Oliver, Russell George, Jean Elizabeth; VISITING FELLOW, ST. JOHN'S COLLEGE, UNIV. OF MANITOBA, 1979-; taught sch. at Shekatika Bay, Que., Labrador Coast, 1932; at Bishop's Coll. Sch., Lennoxville, Que., 1939-41; Lect., Social Sciences Div., Sir Geo. Williams College Montreal, 1941; Prof. of History 1948-51; Prof. and Head., Dept. of Hist., Memorial Univ. of Nfld., 1952-63; first Dean of Arts, Lakehead Univ., Ont., 1963-68; Visiting Prof. of Hist., Univ. of W. Ont., 1969-70; Prof. of History, Univ. of Man., 1970-79; summer appts. Rural Adult Ed. Service, McGill Univ., 1940; Wartime Infor. Bd., Ottawa, 1943; Univ. of Sask., 1946, 1947, 1956, 1962; Laval, 1948; C.F.B., Baden, West Germany, 1978; Que. Govt. European Post-grad Scholarship 1932-34; Can. Council Sr. Research Fellow, New Delhi, India, 1959-60; Geneva, 1968-69; mem. Comité (Bureau) de Direction, Institut d'Hist. de l'Amerique française (Montreal), 1947-71; Council, Can. Hist. Assn., 1948-51; Corp., St. John's Coll., Man. 1972- ; rep. of Canada, Gen. Ass., Internat. Comte of Hist. Sciences, Sweden, 1960, Vienna, 1965; Chmn., Humanities Research Council of Canada, 1963-4; Fellow, Royal Hist. Soc., London, Eng., 1969; author of "Newfoundland A History" (Can. Hist. Assn.); "Canada in One World"; articles and reviews; contested Brome, P.Q. Prov. el., 1944 (Bloc populaire canadien) and Port Arthur, Fed. els., 1965, 1968 (N.D.P.); a Nfld. Dem. Party delegate at N.D.P. founding convention, Ottawa, 1961; rep. CCF at Praja Socialist Party Silver Jubilee, Bombay 1959, and NDP at Congress of Socialist International, Eng., 1969; United Church; Home: 121 Greendell Ave., Winnipeg, Man. R2M 2R2

ROTHSCHILD, Maj.-Gen. Robert P., M.B.E. (1944), C.D.; retired army officer; b. Cochrane, Ont., 22 Dec. 1914; s. Benjamin and Anne Frances (Silverstone) R.; e. Westmount (Que.) High Sch.; Royal Mil. Coll., Kingston, Ont., Grad. 1936; McGill Univ. B.Sc. (Mining Engn.) 1938; Nat. Defence Coll., 1951; m. Patricia Esmée, d. George Loranger Magann, 17 July 1950; children: Michael Robert, George Emmanuel, Jonathan Andrew, Esmée Ann, Alison Mary; joined Royal Candn. Horse Arty., 1938 as Lieut.; served with Candn. Army during the 2nd World War; Capt. and Adj., R.C.H.A. 1940; Candn. War

Staff Course, 1941; Bgde. Major support Group 5 Candn. Armoured Div., 1941-42; Major and Batty. Commdr., 110th Field Batty, R.C.A., 1942-43; Bgde. Major, 2nd Candn. Armoured Bgde., 1943-44; promoted Lieut.-Col. and apptd. G.S.O. 1, H.Q. 2nd Candn. Corps, 1944-45, G.S.O. 1, H.Q. 3 Can. Div. CAOF 1945-46, Dir. Candn. Army Staff Coll. 1946-47; Candn. Mil. Attaché, Athens, Greece, 1947-50; Candn. Army mem. of Dir. Staff, Nat. Defence Coll., Kingston, Ont., 1951-53; Deputy Co-ordinator, Jt. Staff, Nat. Defence Hdqs., 1953-54; Dir. Gen. Ops. and Plans, Army H.Q. 1954-55; Coord. Jt. Staff N.D.H.Q. 1955-57; Dir. Reg. Offr. Trg. Plan N.D.H.Q. 1957-60; Army Mem. Candn. Jt. Staff London, Eng. 1960-62; Q.M.G. Candn. Army, 1962-65; Commdr., Materiel Command 1965-68; Deputy Comptroller-General, Candn. Forces H.Q., 1968 till retirement in 1970; Mentioned in Despatches, 1945; Offr., Order of Orange-Nassau, 1945; Orthodox Jewish; recreations: sailing, skiing, philately, carpentry; Home: RR1, McDonald's Corners, Ont. K0G 1M0

ROTHSTEIN, Aser, B.A., Ph.D.; research scientist; b. Vancouver, B.C., 29 Apl. 1918; s. Samuel and Etta (Wiseman) R.; e. King Edward High Sch., Vancouver, 1934; Univ. of B.C., B.A. 1938; Univ. of Cal. (Berkeley), 1940; Univ. of Rochester, Ph.D. 1943; m. Evelyn, d. late Leo Paperny, 18 Aug. 1940; children: Sharon Liptzin, David Michael, Steven Jay; DIR., RESEARCH INST., THE HOSP. FOR SICK CHILDREN, from 1972 and Prof. Med. Biophysiol.; joined U.S. Atomic Energy Project as Asst. 1943-45; Assoc. 1945-47; Chief, Physiol. Sec., 1948-58; Assoc. Dir. 1961-65; Acting Head, Div. Radiation Chem. and Toxicology, 1963-64; Co-dir. 1965-72; Instr. in Pharmacol., Univ. of Rochester Sch. of Med. and Dent., 1946; Asst. Prof. 1948; Assoc. Prof. 1953; Assoc. Prof., Radiation Biol., 1958; Prof. 1960; Vice Chrmn., Dept. of Radiation Biol. and Biophys., 1961; Co-chrmn. 1965-72; author of over 200 tech. articles, reviews, book chapters; Ed., "Journal of General Physiology"; "Journal Membrane Biology"; "Journal of Cellular Physiology"; "Current Concepts in Membranes and Transport"; mem. Internat. Cell Research Organ. of UNESCO (Council); Biophys. Soc. (Council); Internat. Union Physiol. Sciences (Chrmn. Comte. Cell Physiol.); Internat. Union Pure & Applied Biophysics (Secy. Commission Membrane Biophys.); Society General Physiologists (President); Am. Physiol. Soc.; Am. Assn. Advanc. Science; recreations: concerts, theatre, travel, tennis, squash, skiing; Home: 33 Harbour Sq., Toronto, Ont.; Office: University Ave., Toronto, Ont.

ROTHSTEIN, Samuel, B.A., M.A., B.L.S., Ph.D., LL.D.: librarian; educator; b. Moscow, Russia 12 Jan. 1921; s. Louis Israel and Rose (Checov) R.; came to Can. 1922; e. Univ. of B.C., B.A. 1939, M.A. 1940; Univ. of Cal. grad. studies 1941-42, B.L.S. 1947; Univ. of Wash. grad. studies 1942-43; Univ. of Ill. Ph.D. (Lib. Science) 1954; York Univ. LL.D. 1971; m. Miriam Ruth d. late Max Teitelbaum 26 Aug. 1951; two d. Linda Rose, Sharon Lee; PROF. OF LIBRARIANSHIP, UNIV. OF B.C. 1970- ; Teaching Fellow Univ. of Wash. 1942-43; Princ. Lib. Asst. Univ. of Cal. Lib. 1946-47; Reference Librarian, Univ. of B.C. Lib. 1947, Head of Acquisitions Dept. 1948, Asst. and Assoc. Univ Librarian 1954, Acting Univ. Librarian and Dir. Sch. of Librarianship 1961, Dir. and Prof. of Librarianship 1961-70; Visiting Scholar Univ. of Hawaii 1969; Visiting Prof. Univ. of Toronto 1970, Hebrew Univ. Jerusalem 1973; Consultant, Science Secretariat Can. 1969, various univ. libs. 1970-77; Visiting Librarian Univ. of Toronto 1979; Dir. Vancouver Jewish Community Centre 1962- ; Past Pres.; served with Candn. Army, Intelligence Corps Can. and Europe 1943-36; rec'd Carnegie Corp. Fellowship 1951-54; Dr. Helen Gordon Stewart Award (BCLA) 1970; author "The Development of Reference Services" 1955; "Training Professional Librarians for Western Canada" 1957; co-author. "As We Remember It" 1970; "The University - The Library" 1972; mem. ed. bds.

several journs.; contrib. to several encyclopedias; various articles and reviews; mem. Assn. Am. Lib. Schs. (Past Pres.); Candn. Assn. Univ. Teachers; B.C. Lib. Assn. (Past Pres.); Pacific Northwest (Lib. (Past Pres.); Candn. Lib. Assn. (Past Councillor); Am. Lib. Assn. (Past Councillor); Jewish; recreations: reading, tennis, golf, bridge; Home: 1416 W. 40th Ave., Vancouvour, B.C. V6M 1V6; Office: 2075 Wesbrook Mall, Vancouver, B.C. V6T 1W5.

ROTHWELL, Donald Stuart, B.E., M.B.A., Ph.D.; transportation executive; b. Chicago, Ill. 25 Apl. 1929; s. Clifford and Gladys (Peterkin) R.; e. Ottawa (Ont.) Tech. High Sch.; McGill Univ. B.E. 1952, M.B.A. 1967, Ph.D. 1973; PRES. AND GEN. MGR., GREAT LAKES WATERWAYS DEVELOPMENT ASSN.; service as Br. Mgr. Peacock Brothers, Montreal; Dist. Mgr. De Laval Turbine, Montreal; Sr. Econ., Econ. Council Can., Ottawa; Econ. Advisor, Transport Can., Ottawa; author several articles transport. mang. and econ.; mem. Candn. Transport. Reserach Forum; Ottawa Assn. Applied Econ.; Assn. Prof. Engrs. Prov. Ont.; Protestant; recreations: cycling, swimming; Clubs: Men's Canadian; Rideau; Home: 17 McLeod St., Ottawa, Ont. K2P 0Z4; Office: 606 — 116 Albert St., Ottawa, Ont. K1P 5G3.

ROTSTEIN, Abraham, B.A., Ph.D.; educator; b. Montreal, Que. 10 Apl. 1929; s. Hyman and Fanny (Mosenson) R.; e. Bancroft Sch. and Baron Byng High Sch. Montreal 1945; McGill Univ. B.A. 1949 grad. work Univ. of Chicago 1949-50, Columbia Univ. 1950-51; Univ. of Toronto Ph.D. 1967; m. Diane Louise Whitman, Lansing Mich. 18 Feb. 1966; children: Daniel, Eve; Prof. of Econ. Univ. of Toronto, Sr. Fellow Massey Coll.; served as Indust. Econ. 1951-59; Founding mem. Univ. League for Social Reform 1962; Comte. for an Independent Can. 1970; Can. Inst. for Ecomonic Policy, 1979; mem. Fed. Task Force: Foreign Ownership and Structure of Candn. Indust. (Watkins Report) 1967-68; author "The Precarious Homestead, Essays in Economics, Technology and Nationalism" 1973; co-author "Dahomey and the Slave Trade" 1966; Mang. Ed. "The Canadian Forum" 1968-73; Ed. "The Prospect of Change, Proposals for Canada's Future" 1965; "Power Corrupted, The October Crisis and the Repression of Quebec" 1971; An Industrial Strategy for Canada" 1972; "Beyond Industrial Growth" 1976; co-Ed. "Independence, The Canadian Challenge" 1972; "Read Canadian, A Book About Canadian Books" 1972; "Nationalism or Local Control" 1972; "Getting it Back, A Program for Canadian Independence" 1974; "Beyond Industrial Growth", 1976; Jewish; recreation: music; Home: 102 Admiral Rd., Toronto, Ont. M5R 2L6; Office: 100 St. George St., University of Toronto, Toronto, Ont. M5S 1A1

ROUILLARD, Clarence Dana, A.B., A.M., Ph.D., Litt.D., F.R.S.C.; professor emeritus; b. Bath, Maine, 7 July 1904; s. George Frederic and Ellen Maria (Gooch) R.; e. Bowdoin Coll., A.B. 1924; Harvard Univ., A.M. 1925, Ph.D. 1936; m. Harriet Page, d. late Alfred Church Lane, 23 June 1928; Instructor in French Harvard University, 1925-27; Amherst Coll., 1927-37; Asst. Professor, Univ. Coll., Univ. of Toronto, 1937-45, Assoc. Prof., 1945-49, Prof. 1949, Head of Department 1959-69; Head of Grad. Department of Romance Languages, University of Toronto, 1956-63; emeritus professor 1972; Research Officer, National Research Council, and Instructor at Carleton Coll., Ottawa, 1942-45; C.R.B. Fellow (Belgium), 1930-31; Publications: "The Turk in French History, Thought and Literature, 1520-1660" (No. 13 in the series "Etudes de Littérature Etrangère et Comparée"), Paris, 1940; co-editor of Georges Duhamel, "Le Notaire du Havre", 1954; editor, "Souvenirs de jeunesse: an anthology", 1957; various articles in learned journs.; mem., Alliance Française de Toronto (Pres., 1945-49); Féd. de l'Alliance Française des Etats-Unis et du Canada (Dir. 1945-52); Union des Alliances Françaises au Can. (Councillor, 1951-63); mem., Modern Humanities Research Assn.; Modern Lang.

Association Am.; Internat. Comparative Lit. Assn.; Assn. Internat. des Etudes Françaises; cr. F.R.S.C. 1956; Officier d'Acad. (1949), Chevalier de la Légion d'honneur (1968); Hon. Litt.D. 1964; Alpha Delta Phi; Phi Beta Kappa; Protestant; recreations: music, gardening; Home: 209 Rosedale Heights Drive, Toronto, Ont. M4T 1C7

ROULEAU, Alfred, C.C. (1973), D.Sc.; executive; b. Sherbrooke, Qué., 19 Aug. 1915; Sen. consultant Mallette, Benoit, Boulanger, Rondeau & Associés, chartered accountants; Mem. of the Bd., Bank of Canada. Mem. of Bd., Caisse de dépôt et de placement du Québec; Pres., Institut National de Productivité; Past pres., Confédération des caisses populaires et d'économie Desjardins du Québec; Caisse Centrale Desjardins; Société d'Investissement Desjardins; Place Desjardins Inc.; La Sauvegarde: Founding Dir. Gen. and subsequent pres. assurance-Vie Desjardins; Past Pres. Conseil de la Coop. du Québec; Past Vice-Pres., Canadian Council of Social Development, past mem., Economic Council of Canada, Conseil de la vie française en Amérique and frequent panelist and lecturer to prof. and civic organs.; Home: 165 Chemin de la Côte Ste-Catharine, apt. 402 Outremont, H2V 2A7.

ROUNTHWAITE, C(yril) Frederic T(homas), E.D., B.Arch., F.R.A.I.C., A.R.I.B.A.; b. Sault Ste. Marie, Ont., e. Pub. Schs., Sault Ste. Marie; Univ. of Toronto, B.Arch. 1942; m. Shelagh Macdonnell; Toronto, Ont., 23 Dec. 1942; children: Frederic David, Katherine Elizabeth, Jane Shelagh, John Macdonnell; PARTNER, ROUNTHWAITE, DICK & HADLEY, formerly Marani, Rounthwaite & Dick; Reg'd 1946; Co-recipient, Massey Foundation Gold Medal for design for Stratford Festival Theatre 1958; work of the firm incl. Metrop. Toronto Court House; new Bank of Canada Bldgs.; Metropolitan Life Insurance Headquarters, Ottawa; new Alcoholism & Drug Addiction Research Foundation Bldg., Toronto; Women's Coll. Hosp. Extension; Exhibition Stadium Enlargement, Toronto; Toronto Trans. Terminal (Union Station) alterations for GO Transit; work in the High Arctic and the Caribbean; 1942-46: Major, Royal Candn. Engineers, served in Can., U.K., N.W. Europe; Pres., Commonwealth Assn. of Archs.; Fellow, R.A.I.C., (Past Pres. 1972-73) Hon. Fellow, Amer. Inst. of Archs; mem. Ont. Assn. Archs.(O.A.A.); Candn. Inst. Internat. Affairs; John Howard Soc. of Ont.; Past Chrmn., Mil. Engrs. Assn. (M.-E.A.C.) Past mem. Senate, Univ. of Toronto; Anglican; recreations: fishing, skiing, golf, sailing; Clubs: Royal Canadian Military Institute; The York; Royal Canadian Legion; Home: 7 St. Andrews Gardens, Toronto, Ont. M4W 2C9; Office: Suite 400, 112 Merton St. Toronto M4S 2Z9

ROUSSEAU, Alain P., M.D., F.R.C.S.(C); ophtalmologist; educator; b. Paris, France 10 March 1929; s. Paul and Marguerite (Alain) R.; e. Coll. Ste Anne de la Pocatière 1949; Coll. universitaire Laval B.A. 1951; Univ. Laval M.D. 1956; L.M.C.C. 1956; Ophthalmol. Specialization Harvard Univ. 1958, Univ. of Toronto 1958-61; certified 1962; Retina Fellowship, Retina Foundation, Boston, Mass., 1961-62; m Madeleine d. late Leon Leduc 29 Sept. 1958; children: Denis, Anne, Hélène; PROF. AND HEAD OF OPHTHALMOL. LAVAL UNIV. since 1968; Dir. of Ophthalmol. C.H.U.L. since 1970; mem. Examinatins Comte and Nucleus Comte., ophthalmol.; Roy. Coll. Phys. & Surg. Can., 1980-; Chrmn. Bd. Examiners in Ophthalmol., Que. Corp. Surgs. and Royal Call, 3 terms each; ; Asst. Prof. Laval Univ. 1966, Assoc. Prof. 1968, Prof. 1975; Hôpital de l'Enfant-Jésus 1963-70, Head of Ophthalmol. 1965-70; served with RCAMC (R) 1955-57, rank Capt., Consultatant Candn. Armed Forces 1969-72; Visiting Lectr. in France 1971; Visiting Prof. McGill Univ. 1976; mem. Nat. Defence Research Bd. Vision Sec.; Adv. Comte. Candn. Nat. Inst. Blind; author or co-author numerous articles, papers; mem. Club Jules Gonin; Retina Soc. (Founding mem.); Soc. Française d'Ophtalmologie;

Am. Acad. Ophthalmol.; Soc. Canadienne d' Ophtalmologie (Council); Soc. d'Ophtalmologie de Qué.; Candnn. Med. Assn.; Retina Service Alumni, Mass. Eye & Ear Infirmary Boston; R. Catholic; recreations: tennis, skiing; Home: 2790 Mont Royal, Quebec City, Que. G1W 2E2; Office: 2705 Boul. Laurier, Quebec City, Que. G1V 4G2.

ROUSSEAU, Charles Odilon Roger, C.C.B.Com., M.B.A.; diplomat; b. Trois-Pistoles, Que., 6 Feb. 1921; s. Joseph-Hervé and Corinne (Bélanger) R.; e. Sacred Heart Coll., Bathurst, N.B., 1940; Sir George Williams Univ., B.Com. 1948; New York Univ., M.B.A. 1950; m. Françoise, d. Gleason Belzile, Rimouski, Que., 15 June 1950; children: Denis Edouard, Hugues Real; HIGH COMMISSIONER TO NEW ZEALAND, FIJI, KERIBATI, TUVALU TONGA AND WESTERN SAMOA since 1981; Asst. to Dir. of Colombo Plan, Dept. of Trade & Comm., Ottawa, 1950; Vice Consul and Asst. Trade & Commr., New Orleans, 1952; Asst. Comm. Secy., Mexico D.F., 1954; Comm. Secy., Beirut, 1957; Comm. Counsellor, Buenos-Aires, 1961; Asst. Dir. (Personnel), Trade Commr. Service, Ottawa 1963, Extve. Dir. 1964; Min.-Counsellor (Comm.), Paris, 1967; Ambassador to Cameroun and concurrently for the Central African Republic, Chad and Gabon 1970-72; Pres. Organizing Comte., Pres. Olympic Lottery, & Commr.-Gen., 1976 Olympic Games, 1972-76; Ambassador to Venezuela and Dominican Republic 1977-81; mem. Candn. delegation to U.N. 1978; served with RCAF in Europe, 1940-45; P.O.W. 1942-45; rank Flying Offr.; mem., Prof. Assn. Foreign Service Offrs.; R. Catholic; recreations: golf, ski, fishing, music, reading; Clubs: Royal Ottawa Golf; Caracas Country; Wellington Golf; Heretaunga, N.Z.; Address: c/o Dept. of External Affairs, Ottawa, Ont. K1A 0G2

ROUSSEAU, Jeannine Marie, B.A., LL.L.: lawyer; executive; b. Montreal, Que. 29 Aug. 1941; d. Joseph Rodolphe and Mary Sara (MacIntosh) R.; e. Coll. Jesus-Marie d'Outremont (Univ. of Montreal) B.A. 1961; Univ. of Montreal LL.L. 1965; VICE PRES., SECY. AND GEN. COUNSEL, ASBESTOS CORP. LTD. 1979- ; called to Bar of Que. 1966; comm. law practice with various legal firms Montreal 1966-71; Asst. Secy. and Legal Counsel, Janin Foundation Group, Montreal and Toronto 1971-76; Asst. Secy. Northern Telecom Ltd. Montreal 1976-77; Secy. and Gen. Counsel present Co. 1977-79; mem. Candn. Bar Assn.; Le Barreau du Que.; Am. Soc. Corporate Secy.'s Inc.; Assn. des Secretaires et Chefs de Contenieux du Que.; Home: 573 Côte St. Catherine Rd., Outremont, Que. H2V 2C2; Office: 1940 Sun Life Bldg., 1155 Metcalfe St., Montreal, Que. H3B 2X6.

ROUSSEL, Claude; artist; b. Edmundston, N.B., 6 July 1930; s. Denis and Dorothée (Pelletier) R.; e. Edmundston High Sch.; Ecole des Beaux Arts, Montreal, teaching Dipl. in Art, 1955 Sculpture Dipl., 1956; m. Brigitte, d. Charles E. Belzile, 6 Aug. 1956; children: Denise, Francine, Claire, Suzanne, Huguette, Sylvie; Resident Artist and founder of Art Dept. and Art Gallery, Univ. de Moncton, since 1963; Art Instructor, Edmundston Public Sch., 1956-59; Asst. Curator, Beaverbrook Art Gallery, Fredericton, N.B., 1959-61; completed over 26 sculpture and mural projects in Atlantic Provs. and Maine; rep. in N.B. Museum; Mount Allison Univ.; Dalhousie Univ.; Univ. de Moncton; O'Keefe Centre, Toronto; Smithsonian Inst., Washington; Confed. Art Gallery; recent exhns, incl. Smithsonian Inst.; Terre des Hommes, Montreal; Centre Culturel de Chauvigny, France; Owens Art Gallery; 1 man shows: Univ. de Moncton; Confed. Art Gallery; N.B. Museum, Saint John, 1976; Art Gallery of N.S., Halifax, 1977; Univ. de Moncton, 1977; Galerie Colline, Edmunston 1978; Owens Art Gallery, 1979; granted a Sr. Fellowship by the Can. Council to study arch. decoration, 1961; awarded, Allied Arts Medal by Royal Arch. Inst. Can., 1964 and ten prizes in sculpture and painting in nat. competitions since 1951; First Prize, St. John City Hall Sculpture competition, 1972; winner of a comn. for a

sculpture at site of Sailing Olympics, Kingston, Ont., 1976; works presented in film "Painting a Province" and on television "Take 30", 1963; mem. Can. Council, 1972-75; Rep. Candn. Artist Representation; Catholic; recreations: camping, gardening; Home: 905 Amiraut, Dieppe, Moncton, N.B. E1A 1E1

ROUTHIER, Mt. Rev. Henri, O.M.I., Ph.D., D.D. (R.C.); g.s. of Chief Justice A. B. Routhier of Que., author of "O Canada"; b. Pincher Creek, Alta., 28 Feb. 1900; s. Jean-Chas. and Elodie (Pelletier) R.; e. Separate Sch., Pincher Creek, Alta.; St. John's Juniorate, Edmonton, Alta.; Gregorian Univ., Rome, Ph.D. 1922; Angelicum Univ., Rome, D.D.; first native bishop of Alta.; O.M.I. 1919; o. Priest 1924; consecrated Bishop by Cardinal Villeneuve, 1945, at St. Albert, Alta.; Archbishop Grouard McLennan until 1972; received medal "BeneMerenti" from Pope Pius XI, (for active part in missy. exhns.) in Rome; K. of C.; Address: 3 St. Vital Ave., St. Albert, Alta. T8N 1K1

ROUX, Jean-Louis, O.C. (1971), B.A.; directeur, comédien, auteur; né Montréal, 18 mai 1923; f. Louis et Berthe (Leclerc) R.; é. Coll. Ste.-Marie, Univ. de Montréal, cert. d'études chim., phys., et biol., 1943; é. en France, 1946-50, Boursier du gouvernement français en art dramatique, 1947-48; ép. Monique, f. Leo Oligny, 25 oct. 1950; un f. Stéphane; DIR. ARTISTIQUE, LE THÉATRE DU NOUVEAU MONDE, Montréal; rôles théâtrales: Louis Laine, dans "l'Echange", de Claudel; Jacques Hury, dans "l'Annonce faite à Marie", de Claudel; Louis, dans "le Pain dur" de Claudel; Hippolyte, dans "Phèdre" de Racine; Higgins dans "Pygmalion" de Shaw; Titus dans "Bérénice" de Racine; Martland dans "Témoignage Irrécevable" d'Osborne; Almaviva dans "Le Mariage de Figaro" de Beaumarchais; Cassius dans "Julius Caesar" de Shakespeare; Georges dans "L'Otage" de Claudel; Le Philosophe dans "Le Neveu de Rameau" de Diderot; Charles dans "L'Escalier" de Charles Dyer; Burgundy dans "Henry V" et "Henry VI" de Shakespeare etc.; rôles à la télévision: Ovide dans "La Famille Plouffe" de Roger Lemelin; La Comte dans "La Répétition" d'Anouilh; Lui dans "La Nuit de la Saint-Théodore" de Réal Benoît, etc.; divers rôles à la Comédie des Champs Elysées, Théâtre Gramont, Théâtre Sarah Bernhardt; nombreuses tournées comme acteur et metteur-en-scène en France, Belgique, la Suisse, l'Afrique du Nord, New York, et toutes les villes principales du Can.; rôle enregistré, dans "Le Philocète" avec Jean Gascon et André Gide; rôles téléthéatrales: Ovide, dans "la Famille Plouffe" pendant 7 ans; rôles dans "Pas d'Armour" d'Ugo Betti, "les Trois Soeurs" de Tschékhov, "l'éternel Mari" de Dostoievski, "Living Room" de Graham Greene, etc.; rôles cinémathiques dans "Docteur Louise", "The Pyx" et "The Thirteenth Letter", en 1949; fonde en 1950 le Théâtre d'Essai de Montréal, ou il mont "Un Fils a Tuer" d'Eloi de Gramont, et "Rose Latulippe" dont il est l'auteur; fonde avec Jean Gascon le Théâtre d'Essai de Montréal, ou il mont "Un Fils a Tuer" d'Elio de Gramont, et "Rose Latulippe" dont il est l'auteur; fonde avec Jean Gascon le Théâtre du Nouveau Monde, 1951; scripteur de plusieurs scénarios et adaptions de texte pour la télévision de Radio-Canada; auteur aussi de "En Greve", 1963, et "Bois Brulés" (réportage épique sur Louis Riel) en 1967, aussi bien que nombreuses articles de revues et de journaux; prés. de la Soc. des Auteurs, 1963-64; du Congrès du Spectacle, 1960; secrétaire adm. du Centre du Théâtre Candn. 1959-64; prés. de la Conf. Canadienne des Arts, 1967-69; du Centre du Théâtre Canadienne 1965-69; nommé mem. du Conseil d'adm. de l'ONF en 1968, devenu vice-prés.; mem. du Conseil d'adm. de l'Union des Artistes; mem. du Comté exécutif, Inst. internat. du Théâtre; médaille du Centenaire de la Confed., 1967; médaille du Soc. St.-Jean Baptiste; cert. (Kiwanis); meilleur Acteur, 1960, Congrès du Spectacle; mem. hon. des diplômés de l'Univ. de Montréal 1971; recréations: tennis, échecs, natation; résidence: 231 ave. Kensington, app. 30, Montréal, Qué. H3Z 2G9

ROW, William Stanley, B.Sc., P. Eng.; mining engineer; b. Curries, Ont., 1 Feb. 1904; s. Frederick and Clara Ann (Putnam) R.; e. Pub. Sch., Curries, Ont.; High Sch., Woodstock, Ont.; McGill Univ., B.Sc. (Mining) 1926; m. Helen Shirley, d. Hiram Rogers, 16 Feb. 1933; one s., one d.; DIRECTOR, NORANDA MINES LIMITED, since 1974; Canada Potash Company Limited; Belledune Fertilizer Limited; Brunswick Mining and Smelting Corporation Limited; East Coast Smelting and Chemical Co. Limited; Kerr Addison Mines Limited; President and Dir., Galinee Mattagami Mines Ltd.; Isle Dieu Mattagami Mines Ltd.; Mattabi Mines Ltd.; Mattagami Lake Mines Ltd.; Vice-Pres. and Dir., Aunor Gold Mines Ltd.; Empresa Fluorspar Mines Ltd.; Empresa Minefa de El Setentrion; Garon Lake Mines Ltd.; Gaspe Copper Mines Ltd.; Hallnor Mines Ltd.; Pamour Porcupine Mines Ltd.; Dir., Bell Allard Mines Ltd.; Brenda Mines Ltd.; Brynnor Mines Ltd.; Canada Wire & Cable Co. Ltd.; Canadian Copper Refiners Ltd.; Canadian Electrolytic Zinc Ltd.; Chile Canadian Mines, S.A.; Guaranty Trust Co. of Canada Ltd.; Joutel Copper Mines Ltd.; Noranda Australia Ltd.; Noranda Sales Corp. Ltd.; Orchan Mines Ltd.; Panarctic Oils Ltd.; Placer Development Ltd.; St. Lawrence Fertilizers Ltd.; Mining Engr., Cerro de Pascoe Copper Corp., Peru 1927-30; Frood Mine, International Nickel Co. Ltd. 1930; Asst. Chief Engr. and subsequently Shaft Capt. Lake Shore Gold Mines, 1931-37; Mgr., Kerr Addison Mines Ltd., 1937 Extve. Vice Pres. and Dir., 1955; Pres. 1958; Chrmn. 1967; Extve. Vice Pres. and Dir., Noranda Mines Ltd. 1965; Pres. and Dir., Brunswick Mining & Smelting Corp. and East Coast Smelting & Chemical Co., 1967; mem., Candn. Inst. Mining & Metall.; Am. Inst. Mining Engrs.; Assn. Prof. Engrs. Prov. Ont.; Mining Assn. Can. (Past Pres.); Ont. Mining Assn. (Past Pres.): United Church; recreations: fishing, hunting, curling, golf; Clubs: National; Granite; York Downs Golf; Goodwood; Home: 63 St. Clair Ave. W., Toronto, Ont. M4V 2Y9; Office: Box 45, Commerce St. W., Toronto, Ont. M5L IB6

ROWAT, Donald Cameron, M.A., Ph.D.; university professor; b. Somersetts, Man., 21 Jan. 1921; s. William Andrew and Bertha Elizabeth (Moore) R.; e. Univ. of Toronto, B.A. 1943; Columbia Univ. M.A. 1946, Ph.D. 1950; m. Frances Louise, d. John E. Coleman, Mart, Texas 1948; children: Linda, Steven; PROF. OF POLITICAL SCIENCE, CARLETON UNIV., since 1958; joined Dept. of Finance Ottawa, as Research Asst., 1943-44; apptd. Adm. Offr., Dept. Nat. Health & Welfare, 1944-45; Lectr. in Pol. Science, N. Texas State Teachers Coll., 1947; Dir. of Research, Inst. Pub. Affairs and Lectr. in Pol. Science, Dalhousie Univ., 1947-49; Lectr. in Pol. Science, Univ. of Brit. Columbia, 1949-50; Asst. Prof. Pol. Sci., Carleton Coll., 1950-53, Assoc. Prof. 1953-58; apptd. U.N. (TAA) Expert in Pub. Adm., Ethiopia, 1956-57; Acting Dir., Sch. of Pub. Adm. at present Univ., 1957-58; Chrmn., Dept of Pol. Science, 1960-65; Supv. of Grad. Studies in Pol. Science 1965-66; Awarded Can. Council Sr. Research Fellowship to study govts. of W. Europe 1960-61, and grant to study Ombudsman system in Scandinavia and Council of State in France, summer 1962; served as expert witness, Standing Comte. of H. of C. on Privileges & Elections respecting Bill c-7, Oct. 1964; presented brief to Ont. Royal Comn. on Civil Rights regarding Ombudsman, Jan. 1965; Can. Council Sr. Fellow to tour and study govts. of fed. capitals, 1967-68; Co-commr., Comn. on Relations between Univs. and Govts., 1968-69; Chrmn. Policy Comte. for Parlty. Internship Program 1971-76; Visiting Prof. Univ. of Calif., Berkeley 1972; Exchange Fellow Univ. Leningrad 1974; Canada Council Leave Fellow, Europe 1974-75; author or editor of, among others, "Your Local Government", 1955 (rev. ed. 1975); "Basic Issues in Public Administration", 1961; "The Ombudsman; Citizen's Defender", 1965; "The Canadian Municipal

System", 1969; "The Government of Federal Capitals", 1973; "The Ombudsman Plan: Essays on the Worldwide Spread of an Idea", 1973; "The Provincial Political Systems", 1976; "Political Corruption in Canada", 1976; "Administrative Secrecy in Developed Countries", 1979; "International Hankbook on Local Government Reorganization", 1980; has written no. of reports, etc. and more than 70 articles on pol., govt. and adm.; rec'd. no. of critical reviews incl. Sunday Times (London); mem., Council and Extve. Comte., Soc. Science Research Council of Can., 1974-77; Vice Pres., Soc. Science Fed. of Can., 1978-79; mem., Candn. Assn. Univ. Teachers; Candn. Pol. Science Assn. (Pres. 1975-76); Internat. Pol. Science Assn.; Inst. Pub. Adm. Can.; Appraisals Comm., Ont. Council on Grad. Studies 1977-80; Carleton Senate 1979-82; Address: Dept. of Political Science, Carleton Univ., Ottawa, Ont. K1S 5B6

ROWE, Hon. Frederick William, B.A., D.Paed.; senator; b. Lewisporte, Nfld., 28 Sept. 1912; s. Eli and Phoebe Ann (Freake) R.; e. Prince of Wales Coll., St. John's; Nfld. Normal Sch., Grad. 1930; Memorial Univ. Coll. Grad with 1st Class Hons., 1936; Mount Allison Univ., B.A. 1941; O. E. Smith Schol.; Univ. of Toronto, B.Paed. (Hons.) 1949, D.Paed., 1951; m. Edith Laura, d. G. C. Butt, Bonne Bay, Nfld., 25 Dec. 1936; children: Frederick Butt, Stanley Harold, William Neil, George Edward; Sch. Principal at Bonne Bay, 1931-33; Bishop's Falls 1934; Lewisporte 1934-35; Wesleyville 1936-40; Grand Bank 1941-42; Supervising Inspr. of Schs., 1942-43; first Princ. of Curtis Acad., St. John's, 1943-48; first Pres. St. John's Br., Nfld. Teachers' Assn. 1945; first Depy. Min. of Pub. Welfare 1949-52; el. (by accl.) for Dist. of Labrador Prov. Leg., 1952; Dist. of White Bay South 1956, Dist Grand Falls 1966; Min. Mines & Resources 1952-56, Public Welfare 1955-56, Education, 1956-59, Highways, 1959-64, Finance 1964-67, Community & Social Devel., 1966-67, Labrador Affairs Sept. 1967-July 1968; Min. of Educ. 1967-71; Min. of Finance and Pres. of the Council, July 1971; Depy. Premier (Nfld.) 1969-71; summoned to Senate of Can. Dec. 1971; while at Toronto, 1948-49, engaged in research for Central Y.M.C.A., "Factors Influencing Membership", gave series of talks over Trans-Canada Network for CBC on various aspects of Nfld. life and culture, at time of union of Nfld. and Canada; gave weekly talks on Social Welfare over CBC Station in Nfld., 1950-52; Secy., Lit. Assn., Nfld., 1935-36; mem., United Church Council of Educ. for Nfld. 1952-56, mem., first Bd. of Regents, Mem. Univ. of Nfld., Pres., Candn. Good Roads Assn. (1963); Vice-Chrmn., Candn. Comn. to UNESCO, Paris 1970; mem. Inter Parlty. confs. Rome 1972; Colombo, Sri Lanka 1975; Senate rep., Council of Europe Conference, Strasbourg, Fr. 1978; author of "History of Education in Newfoundland", 1952; "Blueprint for Education in Newfoundland", 1958; "The Development of Education in Newfoundland", 1964; "Education and Culture in Newfoundland", 1976; "Extinction: The Beothuks of Newfoundland", 1977; "History of Newfoundland and Labradore", 1980; contrib. articles on pol. hist. of Nfld. to "Encyclopaedia of Canada"; contrib. articles on Nfld. to "The World Book Encyclopaedia"; many articles for Nfld. newspapers and mags., dealing chiefly with Nfld. educ. and history; Liberal; United Church; recreations: swimming, bridge; Home: Elizabeth Towers, St. John's, Nfld. A1B 1S1; Office: The Senate, Ottawa, Ont. K1A 0A4

ROWE, Kevin S.; banker; b. Seldom come bye, Nfld. 14 Feb. 1938; e. Curtis Academy, St. John's, Nfld.; m. Valma Jean, R.N. 28 Aug. 1958; children: Todd, Michelle, Natalie, Scott; VICE PRES. & GEN. MGR., PACIFIC REGION, THE BANK OF NOVA SCOTIA, 1977- ; Dir. Private Development Finance Co. of Indonesia; Bank of Nova Scotia International (Hong Kong) Ltd.; Singapore Gold Clearing House; Agent present Bank New York 1970-73, Area Mgr. Puerto Rico, Brit. & U.S. Virgin Islands 1973-77; worked in many of the Bank's branches in Can. 1955-70; Home: 1384 Campanilla Street, Dasmarinas Village, Makati, Metro Manila, Phillipines; Office: (CCPO Box 2341) 108 Paseo de Roxas, Makati, Metro Manila, Phillipines

ROWE, Hon. William Earl, P.C. (Can.), 1935, LL.D., D.Sc.Soc.; b. Hull, Iowa, 13 May 1894; s. William and Isabella (Watson) R., both Candns.; e. Pub. and High Schs., Simcoe Co., Ont.; Business Coll., Toronto, Ont.; m. Treva, d. James Lennox; children: Jean, William, Lennox; engaged in farming and breeding of Standard Bred horses.; Reeve, Twp. of Gwillimbury, 1919-23; el. to Ont. Leg. for Simcoe Co. at g.e. 1923; resigned his seat to accept a nomination for H. of C. to H. of C. for Dufferin-Simcoe at g.e. 1925; re-el. at g.e. 1926, 1930 and 1935; apptd. Min. without Portfolio in the Bennett Adm., 30 Aug. 1935; resigned on the def. of Govt., Nov. 1935; apptd. Leader of the Cons. Party in Ont. at Gen. Conv., May 1936, and resigned 1937; re-el. to H. of C. for Dufferin-Simcoe at g.e. 1940, 1945, 1949, 1953, 1957, 1958, 1962; Lieut.-Gov. of Ont. 1963-68; Home: R.R. 2, Bradford, Ont. L0G 1C0

ROWLAND, Beryl, M.A., Ph.D., D.Lit.; professor; author; b. Scot.; came to Can. 1952; e. Univ. of Alta., M.A. 1958; Univ. of B.C., Ph.D. 1962; U. of London, D.Lit. 1980 m. Dr. Edward Murray Rowland, 3 Sept. 1948; PROF. OF ENGLISH, YORK UNIV. since 1962; author of "Blind Beasts: Chaucer's Animal World", 1971; "Animals with Human Faces: A Guide to Animal Symbolism", 1973; "Birds with Human Souls: A Guide to Bird Symbolism", 1978; "Medieval Woman's Guide to Health: The First Gynecological Handbook", 1981; "Chaucer and Middle English Studies in Honor of Rossell Hope Robbins" (ed.), 1974; "Companion to Chaucer Studies" (ed) 1968-rev. ed., 1979; "Cressida in Alberta" (winner of Alberta Golden Jubilee Drama Award 1955); CBC Drama "Behold a Pale Horse", 1956; Assoc. Ed. "The Variorum Chaucer", "Florilegium", and "The Chaucer Review"; numerous articles in various lit. journs.; mem., Assn. Candn. Univ. Teachers Eng.; Humanities Assn. Can.; Internat. Assn. Univ. Profs. Eng. (mem., Internat. Consult. Comte, 1974- ; Huntington Fellow, 1976); Eng. Assn.; Modern Langs. Assn. (Chrmn. Sec. III 1975); Medieval Acad. America; New Chaucer Soc. (internat. Secy. 1978-); Winner, Amer. Univ. Presses Book Award 1974; Club: Granite; Home: 32 Valentine Dr., Don Mills, Ont. M3A 3J8; Office: York University, Downsview, Ont.

ROWLES, Charles A., B.S.A., M.Sc., Ph.D.; university professor; b. Crandal, Man., 8 May 1915; s. Thomas and Gertrude Mary (Williamson) R.; e. Univ. of Sask. B.S.A. with distinction, 1935 (Sask. Research Scholarship) and M.Sc. 1937; Univ. of Minn., Ph.D. 1940; m. Janet M. Doyle, Feb. 13, 1976; children: Charles Garfield, Thomas Gordon; PROF. OF SOIL SCIENCE, UNIV. OF B.C., and Chrmn. of the Dept., since 1956; Soil Surveyor, Univ. of Sask., 1935-37 and Lectr., Dept. of Soils there 1940-41; Chief Chemist and Inspecting Offr. (Chem. and Explosives Divn.), Inspection Bd. of U.K. and Can., Winnipeg, 1941-42, Valleyfield, Que., 1942-43, and at Hdqrs. Ottawa, 1943-45; Assoc. Prof. of Soils, Ont. Agric. Coll., 1945-46; apptd. Assoc. Prof., Univ. of B.C., 1946; mem. Bd. of Mang. (1956-60) B.C. Research Council; Senate, Univ. of B.C. 1960-63; Tech. Adv. to Govt. of Venezuela, FAO of U.N. 1962-63; mem., Chem. Inst. Can.; Candn. Soc. of Soil Science (Sec. Past Pres.); Internat. Soc. of Soil Science; Agric. Inst. of Can.; B.C. Inst. of Agrol.; Sigma Xi; Protestant; Home: 4660 W. 10th Ave. Apt. 1404, Vancouver, B.C. V6R 2J6

ROWLEY, Major-Gen. Roger, D.S.O. and Bar, E.D., C.D., D. Mil. Sc., K.C.L.J.; Canadian Army (retired); b. Ottawa, Ont., 12 June 1914; s. William Horsley and Eliza Wildman (Ritchie) R.; e. Ashbury Coll., Dalhousie Univ.; m. a d. of late Frank J. Mitchell, 23 Apl. 1964; 2ndly Barbara Elizabeth Stephenson, widow of the late Air Commodore J. G. Stephenson, OBE, AFC, RCAF; children: Mrs. Charles Eric DeLotbiniere Panet, Roger Christian

Graves; commissioned in Cameron Highlanders of Ottawa, N.P.A.M. 1933 serving with that unit 1939-42 in Can., Iceland and Britain; promoted Capt., 1941, Major in June 1942 and in Feb. 1943 Lieut.-Col. and in command of Candn. Army Battle Sch. in Eng.; in Aug. 1944 apptd. C.O. of Stormont, Dundas & Glengarry Highlanders (D.S.O. for campaign N.W. Europe); after war and prior to return to Can., commanded 3rd Candn. Inf. Div. Battle Sch.; on return given command of 1st Pacific Inf. Training Bn.; served in Ottawa Dec. 1945-Jan. 1946 and during 1946 was Asst. Adjt. and Q.M. Gen. at Hdqrs. Northwest Highway System, Whitehorse, Y.T.; attended Brit. Army Staff Coll., Camberley, Eng., 1947 and later same yr. apptd. to Candn. Army Staff, Wash., D.C.; apptd. Dir. of Mil. Operations & Plans, Army Hdqrs., 1949, Dir. of Inf. 1950, and Dir. of Mil. Training in 1951; following attendance at Imp. Defence Coll., 1953-54, returned to Can. and promoted Brig. and apptd. to command 2nd Candn. Inf. Bgde. Group in Germany; returned to Can. 1957 and employed in Gen. Staff Br. at Army H.Q.; Commandant, Candn. Army Staff Coll., 1958-62; Vice Adjt. Gen., Jan. 1962; promoted Maj.-Gen. Sept. 1962; Commdr. of Army Tactics & Organ Bd. and subsequently Depy. Commdr. of Operations, Mobile Command hdqrs. Longueuil, Que.; before retirement 1968 apptd. Chrmn. of Offr. Devel. Bd.; Apptd. Col. Reg. of Candn. Guards, 1966; Hon. Col., Cameron Highlanders of Ottawa; Phi Kappa Pi; recreations: skiing, golf, hunting, fishing; Club: Rideau, Royal Ottawa Golf; Cavalry & Guards Club (London).

ROWZEE, (Edwin) Ralph, S.M., D.Sc., F.C.I.C.; chemical engineer; b. Washington, D.C., 17 May 1908; s. Edwin Styears and Henrietta (Carpenter) R.; e. Pub. and High Schs., Washington, D.C.; Mass. Inst. of Tech., S.B. (Chem. Engn.), 1930 and S.M. (Chem. Engn.) 1931; Laval Univ., D.SC. 1955; m. Mary Elizabeth, d. Mrs. S. J. Hudson of Detroit, Mich., 22 Apl. 1935; children: Susan Anne, Mary Elizabeth, Nancy Lee; Form. Hon. Chairman of Board, Polysar Ltd.; Chmn. of Bd., Urban Transportation Dev. Corp. 1973; mem., Bd. of Govs., Ont. Research Foundation; Chemical Engineer, Goodyear Tire & Rubber Co., Akron, Ohio, 1931-42; Mgr., Candn. Synthetic Rubber Ltd., 1942-44; Dir. of Research & Devel., Polymer Corp. Ltd., 1944-46; subsequently Dir. of Sales, Mgr., Vice-Pres. and apptd. Pres. 1957; Purvis Mem. Lectr. of Soc. of Chem. Industry, 1949; Eighteen Foundation Lectr., Inst. of Rubber Industry, England, 1963; rec'd R. S. Jane Mem. Lectr. Award of Chem. Inst. Can., 1960; mem., Chem. Inst. of Can. (Pres., 1954-55); Sarnia Chamber of Comm. (Pres., 1949-50; Dir. 1947-55); Candn. Chamber of Comm. (Dir. 1953); Am. Chem. Soc.; Soc. of Chem. Industry (Pres. 1969-70); Phi Sigma Kappa (Pres., Omicron Chapter, M.I.T., 1929-30); Anglican; Clubs: Detroit Athletic; The Toronto; Home: 580 Woodrow Ave., Sarnia, Ont. N7V 2W2

ROY, Adolphe J., Q.C., B.A., LL.B.; lawyer; business executive; b. Armagh, Bellechasse Co., Que. 6 Aug. 1930; s. J. J. Aimé and Marie-Louise R.; e. Semy. of Qué. B.A.; Laval Univ. LL.B. 1955; Coll. Civil Defence grad. 1962; Coll. Nat. Defence grad. 1974; m. Lucie d. Joseph Dussault, Quebec City, Que. 8 June 1955; children: Marie Elaine, François Allan, Julie June, Marie Shirley; PRESIDENT AND DIR. LE PRET HYPOTHECAIRE since 1977; Counsel law firm Amyot, Lesage, Bernard, Drolet 1974-79; called to Bar of Que. 1956; cr. Q.C. 1971; legal practice Beaupré, Choquette & Roy 1956-58; Denys Dionne 1958-60; City Clerk and Legal Adv. City of Charlesbourg 1960-65; City Clerk of Quebec City 1966-69; Special Adv. to Prime Min. of Que. 1969-77; Assoc. Secy. Gen. of Cabinet Que. 1970-75; Depy. Min. of Transport Que. 1971-72; Chrmn. and Gen. Mgr. Que. Deposit Ins. Bd. 1975-77; Lectr. Laval Univ. Faculty of Comm. & Adm. Sciences 1964-69, Faculty of Law 1965-69; Hon. mem. Offrs. Mess Royal 22nd Regt. since 1968; mem. Cercle Universitaire 1979- ; Knight of Malta; former mem. Candn. Progress

Club; Councelor, La Société Amour des Jeunes; Prière Secours; Services Myriam Beth'lehem; mem. Bd. Jr. Bar Assn. 1958; mem. Que. and Can. Bar Assn.; mem. Bd., Vice Pres. and Regional Pres., Prov. Vice Pres., mem. Nat. Extve., Vice Pres. and Nat. Pres. Inst. Pub. Adm. Can. 1965-73; Anciens de Laval; R. Catholic; recreations: jogging, bridge, tinkering, gardening; Home: 7175 Doucet Ave., Charlesbourg, Que. G1H 5M9; Office: 919 Mgr. Grandin, Ste-Foy, Que. and 7175 Doucet Ave, Charlesbourg, Que. G1H 5M9

ROY, Antoine, D. ès L., F.R.S.C.; archiviste conseil; b. Levis, Que., 24 Dec. 1905; s. Pierre-George and Eugenie (Marsan) R.; e. Coll. de Levis; Laval Univ.; Ecole des Chartes (Paris); Coll. de France and The Sorbonne, Paris; Univ. de Paris, Docteur ès lettres, 1930; m. Gilberte, d. Ferdinand Hudon, 6 July 1931; children: Denyse (Mrs. Jacques Charest), Nycole (Mrs. Jacques A. Bussieres); Chief Archivist, Prov. of Que., 1941-63; Prof. Laval Univ., Quebec, Que.; Dir. and Editor, "Bulletin des Recherches Hist."; Past Pres. Royal Soc. of Can. (Sec. 1); Dir. of the Libraries of L'Institut Canadien de Quebec; Dir., Soc., Canadienne de l'Histoire de L'Eglise Catholique; Inst. l'Histoire de l'Amerique Française; Soc. d'Histoire de la Médecine; Dir., Soc. of Am. Archivists; Assn. des Anciens du Coll. de Lévis; Dir., Comité. des Visiteurs, Citadelle de Québec; Past Fr. Secy., Candn. Hist. Assn.; mem. Soc. des Dix; Soc. Hist. de Montreal; Bibliog. Soc. of Can.; Soc. of Autograph Collectors; mem. de l'Inst. des Arts Polonais; Hon. mem., Mess des Offrs. Du Royal 22nd Regt.; mem. d'Honneur de la Soc. Gen. C. d'Etude du XVIIe s.; Dir., Table Ronde du Conseil Internat. des Archives; Kt. of Malta; author of "Les Lettres, Les Arts et les Sciences au Canada Sous Le Regime Français"; "L'Oeuvre Historique de Pierre-Georges Roy: Bibliographie Analytique"; Rapports de l'Archiviste de la Prov. de Québec, 1941-61; Inventaire des Greffes des Notaires du Regime Français (21 vols.); "Bibliographie des Généalogies et Histoires de Familles"; "Bibliographie des Histoires de Paroisses"; "Les Evenements de 1837-38 dans la Province de Quebec"; "Ce Qu'Ils Lisaient"; "Les Sauvagesses de Chateaubriand"; "Bibliographie des Voyageurs au Canada, 1534-1978", 1978; and many others; Roman Catholic; recreation: book collecting; Home: 3 Parc Samuel Holland, Apt. 1226, Quebec, Que. G1S 4M6

ROY, Gabrielle (Mrs. Marcel Carbotte), O.C. (1967), C.C., F.R.S.C. (1947); novelist; b. St. Boniface, Man.; e. St. Joseph Acad., St. Boniface, Man.; Teachers Training Sch., Winnipeg, Man.; m. Marcel Carbotte, St. Boniface, Man., 1947; during course of teaching career became interested in the theatre and became mem. of Cercle Molière appearing in cast winning French Trophy in Ottawa at dramatic festival upon two occasions; sailed for Europe to study drama 1937, staying in Paris, London and in region of Provence; began lit. career by publ. stories in St. Boniface; later some of her papers were accepted by a Parisian newspaper; on return to Can. 1939 settled in Montreal, collab. with "Le Jour" and "Revue Moderne"; did some reporting for the "Bulletin des Agricultures", includ. articles on ethnic groups of Can. and on different Candn. industs.; also wrote news articles for "Le Canada" covering the Alaska Highway; author of "Bonheur d'Occasion", July 1945 (Eng. transl. "The Tin Flute" made in Dec. 1945 and chosen book of the month selection by The Lit. Guild Am. May 1947); "La Petite Poule d'Eau" (novel) 1950; "Where Nests the Water Hen", 1951; "Alexandre Chenevert", 1954 ("The Cashier"); "Rue Deschambault", 1957 ("Street of Riches"); "La Montagne secrète" ("The Hidden Mountain") 1961; "La Route d'Altamont" ("The Road Past Altamont"), 1966; "La rivière sans repos" ("Windflower") 1970; "Cet été qui chantait" 1972 (Enchanted Summer", 1976); "Un jardin au bout du monde" 1975; ("Garden in the Wind", 1977); "Ma Vache Bossie" (conte pour enfants), 1976; "Fragiles Lumières de la Terre", 1978; "Ces Enfants de ma Vie" ("Children of my

Heart"), "Courte-Queue" (conte pour enfants) 1979; 1979; awarded Medal of French Acad. and prize by French-Canadian Acad.; Prix Femina (France) 1947; le Prix Duvernay, 1956; Governor General's Award three times, for "Bonheur d'Occasion", "Alexandre Chenevert", "Ces Enfants de Ma Vie"; awarded Can. Council Medal for "outstanding cultural achievement", 1968; presented with Prix David, 1971; Molson Award 1977;302 - 135 ouest, Grande Allée, Quebec, Que. G1R 2H1

ROY, Jean-Marie, B.A., M.A., D.Univ. (Grenoble); né a Levis, Que., 5 Sept. fils Lucien et Alice (Carrier) R.; ép. Jacqueline Begin, 1953; enfant: Jean-Pierre; é. Etudes primaries et secondaires a Lévis; B.A. Univ. Laval 1938; Scolarité de M.A., McGill Univ. 1947-49; Docteur de l'Univ. de Grenoble, France; PROF., FACULTE DES ARTS, UNIV. DE SHERBROOKE depuis 1957; Doyen de la Faculté 1964-67; (Dir., Dept. de Geog. 1963-65); Prof. au Coll. Saint Alexandre, Que., 1942-43; Séminaire de Remouski, Que. 1943-45; Tilton (N.H.) Prep. Sch. 1946-47; l'Univ. Laval, 1951-56; Catholique; Bureau: Univ. de Sherbrooke, Sherbrooke, Qué.

ROY, Katherine (Mrs. Philippe Roy); author; b. Sosua, Puerto Plata, San Domingo, W.I., 4 Dec. 1906; d. late Dr. William Augustine (born in Nfld. and Specialist in Tropical Diseases) and Rose Mary (Kennedy) Morris; e. Privately at home; Northwestern Univ. (Special student); Univ. of Berlin (one year); m. 1st. late Pio Ethier, Montreal, Que., 1 Sept. 1926; one d., Mrs. Brock F. Clarke; 2ndly, late Philippe Roy, 6 Nov. 1943; has engaged in Free-lance publicity campaigns at various times; Free-lance journalism; Editor of "Beau" mag., Montreal (now defunct), 1938-40; served as civilian Public Relations Offr. for C.W.A.C., 1942-45; author of: "Lise" (novel) 1954; "The Gentle Fraud" (novel), 1959; various short stories; mem., Authors Guild and Authors League of Am., Inc.; Pres. 1963-66, 1973-75, Candn. Centre of Internat. P.E.N.; Roman Catholic; recreations: music, theatre; Address: 3460 Simpson St., Apt. 604, Montreal, Que. H3G 2J4

ROY, His Eminence, Maurice, Cardinal, C.C. (1971), O.B.E. (1945), D.Ph., D.Th., D.D., LL.D. (R.C.); b. Quebec, Que., 25 Jan. 1905; s. Ferdinand and Mariette (Legendre) F.; e. Petit Seminaire, Québec, Que., B.A. 1923; Laval Univ., D.Th., D.D., 1927; Inst. Angelicum, Rome, D.Ph. 1929; Institut Cath. and Sorbonne, Paris (Philos and Lit.) 1930; LL.D., Univ. of Toronto, 1958; CARDINAL ARCHBISHOP OF QUEBEC since 1965; Chancellor of Laval Univ., since 1947; Pres., Council of the Laity and of Pontifical Comn. for Justice and Peace, Rome 1966; Primate of Canada (1956); o. Priest 1942; Secy., Faculty of Philos., Laval Univ., 1930-34; Rector, Grand Semy. of Que. 1945; Bishop of Three Rivers, Que., 1946; Archbishop of Quebec, 1947; cr. a Cardinal by Pope Paul VI, 25 Jan. 1965 and consecrated 22 Feb. 1965; served in World War, 1939-45; Army Chaplain 1939; Hon. Capt., attached to Roy. 22nd Regt., Eng., 1941; Hon. Lieut.-Col., Depy. Asst. Princ. Chaplain, R.C. Hdqrs., 1st Candn. Corps in Eng. and Italy, 1944; Hon. Col., Asst. Princ. Chaplain, Hdqrs., 1st Candn. Army, N.W. Front; Mentioned in Despatches; Bishop Ordinary to the Candn. Armed Forces (Mil. Vicar) 1946; Chaplain, Que. Cath. Rover Scouts 1934-35; Address: Archevêché de Québec, Québec, Que. G1R 4R6

ROY, Mrs. Philippe — see: Roy, Katherine.

ROY, Reginald H., C.D., M.A., Ph.D., F.R. Hist.S; educator; b. New Glasgow, N.S. 11 Dec. 1922; s. Charles Henry and Florence Hanna (Potkin) R.; e. Victoria Coll. 1948; Univ. Brit. Columbia, B.A., M.A. 1951; Univ. of Wash. Ph.D. 1963; m. Ardith Joan, d. Franklyn Christie 1945; one d. Franklyn Ann; PROF. OF HISTORY, UNIV. OF VICTORIA since 1959; Assoc. and Acting Dean of

Grad. Studies, 1973-75; with Army Hist. Sec., Candn. Army H.Q. 1951; Dom. Archives 1953; B.C. Prov. Archives 1954; Instr., Royal Roads Mil. Coll. 1958; served in Candn. Army 1939-45, Can. and Overseas; rank Inf. Lt.; mem. and Past Pres., Cdn. Inst. Internat. Affairs (Victoria Br); mem., International Institute of Strategic Studies; author of 5 books and over 20 articles; United Church; recreations: reading, gardening; Home: 2841 Tudor Ave., Victoria, B.C. V8N 1L6

ROYCE, Marion V., O.C. (1971), M.A., D.C.L.; b. St. Thomas, Ont.; e. McMaster Univ., Grad.; Ont. Coll. of Educ.; Univ. Toronto M.A.; Post-grad. studies in Social Sciences, Univ. of Chicago; taught at Moulton Coll., Toronto, and became its Principal; formerly for two yrs. was staff mem. of Montreal Y.W.C.A. and later for 10 yrs. Consultant for Social and Internat. Questions and Rep. at U.N. for The World Y.W.C.A., with Hdqrs. in Geneva; became first Dir., Women's Bureau, Dept. of Labour, Can., 1954; retired 1967; then research and writing in educ. of women in Candn. Women's Hist. Series at Ont. Inst. for Studies in Educ. 1967-81; Nat. Girls' Work Secy. of Religious Educ. Council of Can., 1928-32; mem. of ILO Panel of Consultants on Problems of Women Workers, 1963-68; Consultant to Royal Comn. on Status of Women in Can.; rec'd. D.C.L. Acadia Univ. 1975; Persons Award, 1979; Address: 30 Hillsboro Ave., Toronto, Ont. M5R 1S7

RUBES, Jan.; opera and concert singer; actor; director; b. Volyne, Czechoslovakia, 6 June 1920; s. Jan and Ruzena (Kellnerova) R.; e. Real-Gymnasium, Strakonice, Czechoslovakia, 1938; Med. Sch., Prague Univ.; Prague Conserv. of Music (won scholarship) m. Susan Douglas, 22 Sept. 1950; children: Christopher Jan, Jonathan Mark, Anthony Dean; prior to musical career won several championships in skiing and tennis; became youngest basso at Prague Opera House in 1945 singing over 30 leading operatic bass roles there and at the Opera House of Pilsen; selected to rep. Czechoslovakia at Internat. Music Festival in Geneva, 1948; came to Can. 1948; gained recognition through CBC radio show he authored and starred as singer narrator "Song of my People" 1953-63; TV dramas: "Catsplay" (1978); "The Harvest" (1980), T.V. Series: "Sidestreet"; "New Avengers" "Matt and Jenny" "Pheonix Team"; and many TV specials, operas etc., nominated for best performance on Can. T.V. 1977 in "The Day Grandad Died"; author and star of "Guess What", education T.V. children's program; film roles incl. "Forbidden Journey", "The Incredible Journey"; "Lions for Breakfast"; "House on Front St."; "Your Ticket is no longer Valid"; "Mr. Patman"; "Utilities", 1982; "The Amateur", 1982; musical comedy roles incl. "South Pacific", "The Sound of Music", "Man of La Mancha"'has sung some 97 leading bass roles in 6 langs. with such co's as Candn. Opera Co., New York City Centre, Pittsburgh, Washington, Chicago, New Orleans, Seattle, Havana, and in Mexico and Germany; has toured U.S. and Can. in concert with symphony orchestra; sang operas at Stratford Festival, Ont.; rejoined COC for "Lulu" 1980; tought at Royal Conserv. Opera Sch., York Univ.; Univ. of Saskatoon Artist in Residence, Wilfred Laurier Univ., Waterloo, 1981; Dir. Touring & Program Devel. Ont. for C.O.C. (Toronto) 1974-76; took part in opening of "Young People Theatre Centre", 1977, founded by wife Susan, in a multimedia show known as "Laterna Magica"; rec'd Centennial Medal 1967; Queen's Jubilee Medal; 1978; named Hon. Citizen of Winnipeg, Saskatoon, Sydney (N.S.); recreations: tennis, skiing, golf, scuba diving, Address: 131 Bloor St. W., The Colonnade, Toronto Ont. M5S 1S3

RUBESS, Bruno R.; automotive executive; b. Riga, Latvia, 21 Dec. 1926; s. Nikolajs and Milda (Lapins) R.; came to Canada 1953; e. High Sch. Augustdorf Germany; 60th Advanced Mang. Program, Harvard Business Sch.; m. Biruta, d. Peteris Broks, Toronto, Ont. 24 May 1953; chil-

dren: Baiba, Banuta, Balvis; PRESIDENT, VOLKSWAGEN CANADA INC. since 1972; Extve. Vice Pres., Latvian Foundation Inc., 1970-76; Dir. Metro Toronto Caravan, 1974-75; Chrmn., Automobile Importers of Can., 1974-75, Dir., 1981; Pres., Harvard Business Sch. Club of Toronto, 1977; Dir. 1977-81; Dir., Ont. Chamber of Commerce, 1978-80; mem. of Council, Univ. of Toronto Sch. of Continuing Studies 1979-80; Mem. Ont. Economic Council 1980; commenced as Journalist, Germany 1950; Life Ins. Underwriter, Toronto 1953; Salesman, Product Mgr., Sales Mgr., Mercedes Benz of Canada 1955-61; Sales Training Mgr., Volkswagen Canada Ltd. 1962; Vice Pres., Harbridge House Inc. and Dir. Harbridge House Europe, Frankfurt, Germany 1964; Vice Pres. Harbridge House Inc. and multi-Nat. Client Co-ord., Toronto 1970; Home: 162 Munro Blvd., Willowdale, Ont. M2P 1C8; Office: 1940 Eglinton Ave. E., Scarborough, Ont. M1L 2M2

RUBINOFF, Arnold Sidney, B.Com., M.A.; Canadian public servant; b. Toronto, Ont., 13 Feb. 1926; s. Meyer Philip and Sally (Spector) R.; e. Givens Pub. Sch. and Central High Sch. of Comm., Toronto, 1944; Univ. of Toronto, B.Com. 1948, M.A. (Econ.) 1949; m. Florence Alma, d. Frederick Pike, R.R. 4, Athens, Ont., 19 May 1954; children: Carolyn Beth, Philip Andrew, David Matthew; ASST. DEPUTY MIN., ECON. PROGRAMS & GOVT. FINANCE, since 1976; Acting Asst. Deputy Minister, Tax Policy, since 1980; joined Nat. Income Div., Dom. Bureau of Statistics, 1950-56; seconded to Econ. Sec., NATO Secretariat, Paris, 1956-59; joined Econ. Analysis and Financial Affairs Div. of Present Dept., 1959; Dir., Econ. Analysis Div., 1964-70, Dir., Fed.-Prov. Relations Div. 1970-73; Gen.-Dir., Tax Policy & Fed.-Prov. Relations, 1973-76; participated in Govt.'s Bilingual and Bicultural Devel. Programme, Quebec City, 1967-68; served as mem. and as Head, Candn. Dels. to various OECD meetings, Paris, 1961-69; mem., Fed. Govt. Del. to Fed.-Prov. meetings of Continuing Comte. of Officials on Ecom. and Fiscal Matters, 1964-75; Secy., Fed. Prov. Comte. on Econ. and Fiscal Matters, 1970; Bd. of Dir., Tesesat Can.; Uranium Cam.; Lower Churchill Devel. Corp.; served with RCASC (Militia) 1951-56; rank Lt.; Hebrew; recreations: skiing, fishing, reading; Club: YMCA Health; Home: 458 Halldon Pl., Ottawa, Ont. K2B 7B8; Office: Place Bell Canada, Ottawa, Ont. K1A 0G5

RUBINOFF, Robert A.; company executive; b. Toronto, Ont. 24 March 1939; s. David and Rachel (Rosenberg) R.; e. Masonville Pub. Sch., London, Ont. 1951; Medway High Sch., Arva, Ont. 1956; m. Anne Cressy Marcks, 3 July 1970; two s., Daniel, Matthew; Pres. and Dir. Daray Holdings Ltd.; Pres. and Dir., Rubicam Creative Prod. Ltd.; Dir., Can. Cham. of Comm.; Flame Oil & Gas Ltd.; Isolation Systems Ltd. Partner, The White Oaks Grp.; Dir., Landar Devel. Ltd.; Dir. and Pres., Ont. Chamber of Comm.; joined Leeds Sportswear Ltd. 1959; Pres. 1963; joined Commonwealth Holiday Inns of Can. Ltd., becoming Innkeeper, Holiday Inn, London S. 1966, Dir. of Operations 1967, Vice Pres.-Inn Operations 1967, opened London, Eng. Office as Dir. of European Operations 1968, Vice Pres. 1968, Sr. Vice Pres. 1972, Extve. Vice Pres. and Dir. 1975-79; mem. Candn. Chamber Comm.; York Racquets Club; Jewish; recreation: tennis; Home: 166 Warren Rd., Toronto, Ont. M4V 2S5; Office: Suite 2800, 55 Avenue Rd., Toronto, Ont. M5R 3L2

RUBY, Clayton Charles, LL.M.; barrister; b. Toronto, Ont. 6 Feb. 1942; s. Louis W. and Marie (Bochner) R.; e. Forest Hill Coll. Inst. Toronto; York Univ. B.A. 1965; Univ. of Toronto LL.B. 1968; Univ. of Cal. Berkeley LL.M. 1973; PARTNER, RUBY & EDWARDH; called to Bar of Ont. 1970; author "Law Law Law" 1971; "Sentencing" 1974; various legal articles; Bencher, Law Soc. Upper Can.; mem. Council Amnesty Internat.; Home: 80 Bedford Rd., Toronto, Ont. Office: 11 Prince Arthur Ave., Toronto, Ont. M5R 1B2.

RUDD, D'Alton Stafford (Bill), B.A., F.C.I.A., F.S.A.; actuary; company executive; b. Montreal, Que., 30 Nov. 1929; s. D'Alton Stafford and Ada Isabelle (LeRiche) R.; e. London (Ont.) Central Coll. Inst. 1942-44; Ridley Coll., St. Catharines, Ont., 1944-47; Univ. of W. Ont., B.A. 1951 (Gold Medal Actuarial Science); m. Ann Elizabeth, d. H. C. Cottrell, Vancouver, B.C., 8 March 1958; children: Sally, John; SR. VICE PRESIDENT LONDON LIFE INSURANCE CO. since 1978; joined present Co. 1951, Asst. Actuary 1957, Assoc. Actuary 1960, Dir. of Product Devel. 1969, Actuary 1970, Vice President & Chief Actuary 1971, Vice Pres. and Gen. Mgr. 1975, Sr. Vice Pres. 1978; apptd. to Pension Commission of Ontario 1963 and Vice Chrmn. since 1967; Trustee, London Bd. of Educ., 1967-69 (Chrmn. 1968); Pres., London P. Cons. Assn. 1969-72; Anglican: recreations: skiing, tennis; Clubs: London Hunt; Granite (Toronto); Albany (Toronto); Home: 149 Victoria St., London, Ont. N6A 2B6; Office: 255 Dufferin Ave., London, Ont. N6A 4K1

RUDERMAN, Armand Peter, B.S., M.B.A., M.A., Ph.D.; educator; b. New York, N.Y. 19 Nov. 1923; s. late Louis M. and Lillian G. (Prigohzy) R.; e. Harvard Univ. B.S. 1943, M.A. 1946, Ph.D. 1947; Univ. of Chicago M.B.A. 1944; m. Alice Helen d. Late Joseph Holton 17 June 1948; children: Ann (Mrs. William Keane), Mary (Mrs. Alan Cooke) William, John; PROF:; HEALTH ADMINISTRATION, DALHOUSIE UNIV. 1981-, and Prof., Preventive Med., 1975- ; taught econ. various Am. univs. 1946-50; Stat. Internat. Labour Office 1950-59; Stat. Pan American Health Organ. 1960-61, Head, Office of Evaluation & Reports 1962, Econ. Adv. 1963-67; Prof. of Health Adm. Sch. of Hygiene, Univ. of Toronto 1967-75; Dean of Admin. Studies; Dalhousie Univ. 1975-80; Special Ad., Medical Services Br., Dept. Nat. health & Welfare, 1980-81; served as Chrmn. Pub. Health Research Adv. Comte. Dom. Council Health; Coordinator Ont. Jt. Comte. on Phys's Compensation 1973-75; Chrmn., Soc. & Econ. Sci. Working Group of the World Health Org. (WHO) Tropical Disease Research Programme, 1979- ; consultant to health services adm. and health econ. to prov. and nat. govts., internat. agencies; author over 50 prof. articles, textbook chapters and monographs mainly in health econ.; mem. Candn. Pub. Health Assn (Past Chrmn. Med. Care Sec.); Candn. Assn. Teachers Social & Preventive Med. (Treas. 1970-71, Pres. 1977-78); Inst. Pub. Adm. Can.; recreations: amateur radio, reading, writing, walking; Clubs: Halifax Amateur Radio; Canadian; Home; 10 Glenmore Ave., Halifax, N.S. B3M 1W4 Office: Dalhousie University, Halifax, N.S. B3H 4H6

RUDGE, Charles W.; company executive; b. Birmingham, Eng., 19 July 1905; s. late Charles Noah and late Ada May (Jenkins) R.; e. Prince Albert, Sch. and Belmont High Sch., Montreal, Que.; Sir George Williams Univ.; m. Gabrielle, d. late Jean Louis Keuninckx, 1 Aug. 1940; one s., Peter C.; CHRMN. OF THE BD. AND DIR., JEFFREY MFG. CO. LTD., since 1968; Dir., Duras Forgings and Castings Ltd.; Apprentice-Engn., Darling Brothers Ltd., 1922-26;; Designer, Canada Sugar Refining Co. Ltd., 1926-28; joined present Co. as Designer and Sales Rep., 1928; apptd. Dist. Sales Mgr., Feb. 1946; Mgr. of Sales, Nov. 1946; Vice Pres. Sales and Dir., 1947; Pres. 1948; Pres. and Treas. 1949; Freemason (P.M.); Protestant; recreations: golf, swimming; Club: Kanawaki Golf; Home: 213 Hyman Drive, Dollard des Ormeaux, Quebec H9B 1L5; Office: 227 Braebrook Ave., Pointe Claire, Que. H9R 1V7

RUDNYCKYJ, Jaroslav Bohdan, M.A., Ph.D., F.I.A.A.(Paris); university professor and diplomat; b. Peremyshl-Zasannja, 28 Nov. 1910; s. Anthony and Juliana (de Shawala) R.; e. Univ. of Lviv, M.A. 1934, Ph.D. 1937; m. Marina d. Dmytro Antonovych, 1943; two children; Prof. Prague, 1940-45; Heidelberg and Munich, 1945-48; 1949 joined Univ. of Manitoba; founding head, Dept. of Slavic Studies, Univ. of Man.; Prof. Emeritus 1977; visiting lecturer, Universities of Adelaide, Sydney, Melbourne, Monash 1978-79; visiting prof., Univ. of Ottawa, 1979-80; mem., Roy. Comm. on Bilingualism & Biculturalism; numerous learned assns. and insts. incl. Ukrainian Free Acad. of Sciences; Acad. Internat. Sciences et Lettres (Paris); Centre Internat. Sciences Onomastiques (Louvain); Am. Name Soc. (Pres. 1959); Candn. Linguistic Assn. (Pres. 1958-60); Linguistic Circle, Man. & N. Dakota (Pres. 1971-72); Candn. Assn. of Slavists; Hist. & Scient. Soc. of Manitoba; Ukrainian Research Inst. of Volyn', etc.; author, lit. critic and translator; greatly contrib. to Slavic Candn. lit. criticism by his many reviews of poetry, prose, and drama; author of over 280 books incl. 6 vols. of travel diaries; numerous articles in learned journs.; awarded San Remo Medal, 1963, Margaret McWilliams Medal, 1971; founder of "Onomastica", since 1951; "Slavistica", since 1948: Vice Chrmn., Public Lib. Bd., Winnipeg, Man.; Candn. Hon. Life mem. Internat. Centre of Onomastics, Belgium; mem., Humanities Research Council, Ottawa, 1967-71; Chrmn. Human Rights Comte., Canadian Citizenship Fed. 1975-81; Vice Pres. Canada Press Club (Winnipeg) 1975-76; Vice-Pres., Candn. Citizenship Fed., 1977-79; Adv., Library of Congress, 1977-79; Adv. Nat. Library, Ottawa, 1980-81; Pres., Ukrainian World Acad. Comte., 1977-80; hon. mem., Cdn. Bibliographic Soc.; Pres., Ukrainian Mohylo-Mazepian Academy of Arts and Science, since 1978; Chrmn., Comte. Cdn. Const. of Cdn. Citizenship Federation 1979-81; mem., Gov't. (in exile), Ukrainian National Republic, 1978-80; Prof. Christian; recreation: travel; Club: University; Home: Cote St. Luc, Que. H4W 2V2

RUETER, William, R.C.A., M.G.D.C.; graphic designer; b. Kitchener, Ont. 4 Aug. 1940; s. Gustav and Gladys (Brubacher) R.; e. Bathurst Heights Secondary Sch. North York 1959; City Literary Inst. London, Engl. 1960-61; Ont. Coll. of Art 1962-65; m. Marilyn d. Eric Meister 28 June 1968; two s. Lucas, Simon; SR. DESIGNER, UNIV. OF TORONTO PRESS 1976- ; Prop. The Aliquando Press; Designer, Leslie Smart & Associates Toronto 1965-68; Designer, Univ. of Toronto Press 1969-; recipient The Look of Books, Toronto 3rd Prize 1974, 1976; Schönste Bücher aus Aller Welt, Leipzig Bronze Medal 1976; Internat. Buchkunst-Ausstellung, Leipzig Bronze Medal 1977; various awards Design Can., Am. Inst. Graphic Arts, Assn. Am. Univ. Presses; rep. in nat. and internat. book and design exhns.; Lectr. Faculty of Fine Arts York Univ. 1973-75; Seneca Coll. North York 1977; Georgian Coll. Barrie 1979; Massey Coll. Toronto 1980; Am. Typecasting Fellowship New Rochelle, N.Y. 1980; rec'd Can. Council Grant 1968; author "Order Touched with Delight" 1976; numerous articles aspects of printing and reviews; Ed. "The Devil's Artisan"; mem. Assn. Am. Univ. Presses Book Design & Production Comte. 1975; Juror, The Look of Books, Toronto 1975, mem. Jury Selection Comte. 1976; Ont. Assn. Art Galleries Annual Show 1980; Founding mem. Soc. Candn. Book Designers; mem. Royal Candn. Acad. 1976; Soc. Graphic Designers Can.; Assn. Typographique Internationale; Am. Printing Hist. Assn.; Typocrafters; Am. Typecasting Fellowship; Bibliog. Soc. Can.; recreations: private printing; binding, music, reading; Home: 236 Major St., Toronto, Ont. M5S 2L6; Office: Toronto, Ont. M5S 1A6.

RUFFO, John Joseph, B.A.; company executive; b. Montreal, Que, 15 Oct. 1937; s. Paul and Aurelle (Crocetti) R.; e. Public and High Schs. Toronto, Ont.; McGill Univ. B.A.(Econ.) 1959; m. Margaret, d. Michael Shore 8 July 1961; children: Andrea, Kenneth; EXEC VICE PRES. IMASCO ASSOCIATED PRODUCTS LTD. and Pres. Imasco retail div. since 1978; Chrmn, Pres. andDir. Imasco Associated Products Ltd. 1971; Vice Pres Imasco Ltd.; Chrmn. United Cigar Stores Ltd.; Collegiate Sports Ltd.; Top Drug Mart; President UnitedCigar Stores Ltd. 1969; joined Imperial Tobacco Co. Ltd. as Econ. Research Mgr. 1959, Co-ord. Acquisitions and Devel. 1965; R. Catholic;

recreations: tennis, skiing, swimming, football; Home: 22 Woodthrush Court, Willowdale, Ont. M2K 2B1; Office: Royal Bank Plaza, Toronto M5I 2J1

RUGGLES, Charles Mervyn, C.M., B.Sc.; art conservator; b. London, Eng. 25 June 1912; s. late Charles and late Ethel (Langford) R.; e. Lisgar Coll. Inst. Ottawa; St. Patrick's Coll. Univ. of Ottawa B.Sc. 1935; m. Winnifred d. late A. W. Hughes 4 Nov. 1944; children; William Peter, Janet Evelyn, Mary Anne; Chem. Asst., Chem. Lab. Canadian International Paper Co. Gatineau, Que. 1936 — 40; Art Conservator, Nat. Gallery of Can. 1945 — 48, Chief Conservator 1948 — 60, Chief Scient. Research Conservator 1960 — 70, Head of Restoration & Conserv. Lab. 1970 — 77; Prof., Master of Art Conserv. Program Sch. of Grad. Studies Queen's Univ. 1977 — 79; served with RCAF and RAF 1940 — 45 in Europe, Malta & Middle East rank Flight Lt.; rec'd Queen's Silver Jubilee Medal; study tour maj. art conserv. labs. six European countries 1969, art labs. and museums Japan 1970, conserv. labs. Moscow and Leningrad 1974; mem. Official Candn. Del. opening exhn. "Canadian Landscape Painting" in Peking followed by visits to several restoration labs. China 1975; consultant in art. conservation, Montréal Mus. of Fine Arts, 1980; consultant and lecturer, Nat. Laboratory for Conservation of Cultural Property, Lucknow, India, 1981; author numerous articles relating to art restoration and conserv.; Fellow, Internat. Inst. for Conserv. Historic & Artistic Works (London, Eng.); Fellow, Am. Inst. Conserv. Historic & Artistic Works (Washington, D.C.); mem. Chem. Inst. Can.; Founding mem. and first Chrmn. Candn. Assn. Prof. Art Conservators; First Hon. mem. and Councillor, Internat. Inst. for Conserv. (Candn. Group) 1978; mem. Candn. Owners & Pilots Assn.; Royal Candn. Flying Clubs Assn.; Ottawa Flying Club; Royal Candn. Legion; Candn. Museums Assn.; Anglican; recreation: flying light aircraft; Home: 15 Letchworth Rd., Ottawa, Ont. K1S 0J3.

RUGGLES, Edgar Lenfest, B.E.; retired civil engineer; company president; b. Regina, Sask., 12 Aug. 1913; s. late Emma (MacLachlan) and Edgar N. R.; e. Public and High Schools, Regina, Sask.; Univ. of Sask., B.E. (Civil Engn.) 1935; m. Jean F., d. late Robert G. Cooke, Fillmore, Sask., 4 May 1940; children: Donald, Allan, Robert; Past Pres. and Dir Dir., Perolin-Bird Archer Limited (Water treatment chemicals and equipment, and indust. chemicals, Estbd. 1929); with Geol. Survey of Canada, 1935-37; joined the present Co. in 1927 as Field Engineer in Western Canada; District Mgr., 1943-46; Assistant Gen. Mgr., 1946-51; Vice-Pres. and Gen. Mgr., 1951-58; el. a Dir., 1952; Pres. 1958-77; Chrmn. 1977-78; mem., Assn. of Prof. Engrs. Ont.; Engn. Inst. Can.; United Church; recreations: music, photography; Club: Rotary (Pres. 1955-56, Gov., Rotary Internat., Dist. 707, 1958-59); Home: 31 Glen Watford Road, Cobourg, Ont. K9A 2C7;

RULE, Jane Vance, B.A.; author; b. Plainfield, N.J. 28 March 1931; d. Arthur Richards and Carotta Jane (Hink) R.; e. Palo Alto (Cal.) High Sch. 1947; Mills Coll. Oakland, Cal. B.A. 1952; Univ. Coll. London, Eng. 1952-53; Stanford Univ. 1953; Teacher of Eng. Concord (Mass.) Acad. 1954-56; Asst. Dir. Internat. House Univ. of B.C. 1958-59, sometime lectr. in Eng. or Creative Writing 1959-73; rec'd Ardella Mills Award 1951; Can. Council Jr. Arts Scholarship 1969-70, 1970-71; Candn. Authors' Assn. Award Best Novel 1978; Benson & Hedges Award Best Short Stories 1978; Gay Acad. Union (U.S.A.) Lit. Award 1978; author novels "The Desert of the Heart" 1964; "This Is Not For You" 1970; "Against the Season" 1971; "The Young in One Another's Arms" 1977; "Contract With the World" 1980; "Lesbian Images" (Criticism and social comment) 1975; "Theme for Diverse Instruments" (short story collection) 1975; "Outlander" (stories & essays) 1981; numerous short stories mags. and anthols., articles; mem. Writers Union Can.; Phi Beta Kappa; NDP; recrea-

tions: walking, swimming, collecting paintings; Address: The Fork Route 1, Galiano, B.C. V0N 1P0.

RUMGAY, Donald Anderson, B.Com., C.A.; company president; b. Toronto, Ont., 25 Nov. 1924; s. James and Caroline (Caldwell) R.; e. Univ. of Toronto, B.Com. 1949; C.A. 1952; m. Joan, d. William Petri, Oct. 1969; children (by previous m.); James, Paul, Peter, Patricia; PRESIDENT, AEROQUIP CANADA LTD. since 1963; with Riddell Stead & Co. (Toronto) from 1949; C.A., 1952; joined present Co. as Controller, 1955; Vice-Pres. and Gen. Mgr., 1957; served in 2nd World War, R.C.N., 1944; recreation: sailing; Home: 21 Dorset St. E., Port Hope, Ont.; Office: 287 Bridgeland Ave., Toronto, Ont. M6A 1Z7

RUNCIMAN, Alexander McInnes, LL.D.; b. Invergordon, Ross-shire, Scot., 8 Oct. 1914; s. Alexander and Evelyn (Anderson) R.; e. High Schs. in Scot. and Can.; LL.D. Univ. Manitoba 1974; Univ. of Sask. 1977; m. Marjorie Evelyn, d. James Dick, Abernethy, Sask., 8 Oct. 1949; two d. Dorothy E., Catherine J.; PRESIDENT, UNITED GRAIN GROWERS LIMITED, since 1961; Dir.; Royal Bank of Can.; Great-West Life Assurance Co.; Canadian Pacific Ltd.; Massey-Ferguson Limited; Canada Grains Council; C.D. Howe Research Inst.; Great Lakes Waterways Devel. Assn.; lived on farm until emigrated to Canada in his teens and settled on farm nr. Balcarres, Sask.; after mil. service, returned to farm and operated grain and livestock projects 1945-61; became Secy. of Abernethy United Grain Growers Local Bd., Sask., when it was organized in 1953; el. to Bd. Dirs., present Co. 1955; served during 2nd World War with RCOC., Jan. 1940 to July 1945; in Gt. Brit., N. Africa, Sicily and Italy; discharged as W.O.I.; hon. Col., Queen's Own Cameron Highlanders of Can.; active in community affairs as Municipal Councillor, School Secretary, 4-H Club Leader and many other activities; member, Candn. Delegation to Internat. Wheat Agreement in Geneva, 1962 and 1978; mem. Candn. Govt. Oilseeds Trade Mission to Japan, 1964; mem. Candn. del. to GATT Cereals negotiations, Geneva, 1967; Del. to Internat. Fed. of Agric. Producers' Conf. (IFAP) in Dublin, Eire, 1963, New Zealand, 1964, England 1966, Austria 1974; mem. econ. Council Can. 1974-80; Trustee Victoria Gen. Hosp.; Dir. Man. Clinic Foundn. Inst.; rec'd. Centennial Medal; Queen's Silver Jubilee Medal; Life mem. Rapeseed. Assn. Can.; Univ. of Man. Alumni Assn.; Hon. Life mem. Candn. Seed Growers' Assn.; Hon. mem. Agric. Inst. Can.; Man. Inst. Agrols.; Candn. Seed Trade Assn.; mem. St. Andrew's Soc. Winnipeg (Pres. 1966-67); Protestant; recreations: curling, gardening; Clubs: Manitoba; Winnipeg Winter; Home: 225 Kingsway Ave., Winnipeg, Man. R3M 0G5; Office: (Box 6600), Winnipeg, Man. R3C 3A7

RUNNALLS, Oliver John Clyve, M.A.Sc., Ph.D., P.Eng.; university professor; b. Barrie Island, Ont. 26 June 1924; s. John Lawrence and Ethel Mae (Arnold) R.; e. Public and High Schs. North Bay, Ont.; C.A.U.C. (Univ. of Toronto) 1944; Univ. of Toronto, B.A.Sc. (ceramic engn.) 1948, M.A.Sc. (metall. engn.) 1949, Ph.D. (extractive metall.) 1951; Nat. Defence Coll. 1960; m. Vivian Constance, d. late George Stowe 13 Sept. 1947; children: David John, Catherine Ruth; Prof. of Energy Studies, Faculty of Applied Sci. and Eng., Univ. of Tor. since 1979; Bd. mem., Ont. Hydro; Uranium Can. Ltd.; Uranerz Exploration and Mining Ltd.; commenced with Atomic Energy of Canada Ltd. metall. research and devel. Chem. Br., Chalk River, Ont. 1951, Head Fuel Devel. Br. 1956-59, Head Research Metall. Br. 1961-67; Consultant (part-time) Eldorado Nuclear Ltd. 1962-67; Asst. Dir. Chem. and Materials Div. Atomic Energy of Canada Ltd. 1967-69; Chief Liaison Offr. Europe, Paris 1969-71; Sr. Adviser, Uranium and Nuclear Energy, Dept. of Energy, Mines and Resources, Ottawa, 1971-79; Extve. Vice Pres., Uranium Canada Ltd. 1974-79; mem of Bd., Cdn. Energy Research Inst. Calgary 1975-79; served in 2nd World War

R.C.C.S. 1944-45; mem. Assn. Prof. Engrs. Ont.; Candn. Inst. Mining and Metall.; Candn. Nuclear Assn.; Past Pres. Community Skiways Inc.; Deep River Home and Sch. Assn.; Past Chrmn. Deep River Mun. Recreation Comte.; Past Vice-Chrmn. Deep River Public Sch. Bd.; Renfrew Co. Public Sch. Bd.; author of some 90 scient. papers and reports primarily on ceramic and metall. research and devel., and on uranium, nuclear and energy policy; Protestant; recreations: skiing, woodworking; Home: 170 Lytton Blvd., Toronto, Ont. M4R 1L4; Office: Faculty of Applied Science and Engineering, Univ. of Toronto, Toronto, Ont. M5S 1A4

RUSH, Ian Cameron Macdonnell, M.Sc., FCIC; company president; b. Bexhill, Eng., 18 Nov. 1918; came to Can. 1920; e. Univ. of B.C., B.Sc. 1942; M.Sc. 1943; m. Joan Mary Thompson, 15 Jan. 1944; children: James Cameron, Janet Margaret; CHRMN. & CEO, POLYSAR LTD.; Chrmn., Petrosar Ltd.; Home: 1262 Green Acres Rd., Sarnia, Ont. N7S 2M7; Office: 201 Front St. N., Polysar Bldg., Sarnia, ont. N7T 7V1

RUSSEL, Archibald D.; industrialist b. Dorval, Que., 16 Aug. 1918; s. Archibald Montgomery and Georgina Nona (Dennistoun) R.; e. Upper Can. Coll., Toronto, Ont.; Montreal (Que.) High Sch.; Trinity Coll. Sch., Port Hope, Ont.; m. Elzina Grace Kennedy, d. late Mervin Kennedy Allen, Vancouver, B.C., 29 Dec. 1941; children: Philip, Suzanne, Hugh, Jeffrey, Guy; CHRMN. & PRES., STONEHENGE SYSTEMS INC. 1980- ; Retired Chrmn. Hugh Russel Inc. (Estbd. 1784; Industrial Distrubutors); Dir., Templeton Growth Fund; Gov., Lakefield Coll. Sch.; Past National Dir., Young Presidents' Organization, Inc.; formerly Vice-Pres. in 1962; served in 2nd World War with Candn. Active Army and R.C.A.F.; Anglican; recreations: music, sculpture, boating; Clubs: The National; Ocean Reef; Lyford Cay; Home: 82 Crescent Rd., Toronto, Ont. M4W 1T5; Office: 124 Merten St., Toronto, Ont.

RUSSELL, Hon. David John, M.L.A., B.Arch., M.L. Arch.; politician; architect; b. Calgary, Alta. 29 July 1931; s. David Hay Sutherland and Mary (Baron) R.; e. Univ. of Man. B.Arch.; Cornell Univ. M.L.Arch.; MIN. OF HOSPITALS & MEDICAL CARE, ALTA. 1979- ; Ald. City of Calgary 1960-61, 1963-67; Dir. Calgary Zool. Soc.; Heritage Park Soc.; Allied Arts Centre; Calgary Jeunesses Musicales; Calgary Philharmonic Soc.; Assoc. Dir. Calgary Exhn. & Stampede; mem. Bd. Calgary Pub. Lib.; Calgary Gen. Hosp.; el. M.L.A. for Calgary-Elbow prov. g.e. 1967, re-el. since; Min. of Mun. Affairs 1971-75; Min. of the Environment 1975; P. Conservative; Lutheran; Office: 420 Legislative Bldg., Edmonton, Alta. T5K 2B6.

RUSSELL, Frederick William, C.M., C.D., LL.D.; company president; b. St. John's Nfld., 10 Sept. 1923; s. Jean (Campbell) and late Herbert John Russell, C.B.E.; e. Holloway Sch. and Prince of Wales Coll., St. John's; Dalhousie Univ.; m. Margaret Miriam, d. late Ewart C. Cross, Port Credit, Ont., 15 June 1946; children: Douglas, Janice, James, Peter; PRESIDENT, TERRA NOVA MOTORS (1962) LTD.; Pres., General Industries Ltd.; Dir., National Sea Products Ltd.; Nfld. Liquor Corp.; served with R.C.A.F. as Pilot during 2nd World War; now Wing Commdr. (Ret.), R.C.A.F. (R); A.D.C. (Hon.), Gov. Gen. of Canada, 1949-60 and Lieut. Gov. of Nfld., 1954-62; mem., Nfld. Labour Relations Board since 1953; Royal Trust Adv. Comm. (St. John's); Chrmn., Bd. of Regents, Memorial Univ. of Nfld. since 1974; Vice-Chrmn., Nfld. Labour-Management Cooperation Comte.; Pres., Nfld. Bd. of Trade, 1960; United Church; recreations: fishing, boating; Clubs: Rotary; Eagle River Salmon; Crow's Nest Officers'; Royal Nfld. Yacht; Home: 100 Elizabeth Ave., St. John's, Nfld. A1B 1S1; Office: Fort William St., St. John's, Nfld. A1C 5V5

RUSSELL, Loris Shano, M.A., Ph.D., LL.D., F.R.S.C., F.G.S.A.; palaeontologist; b. Brooklyn, N.Y., 21 Apl. 1904; s. Milan Winslow and Matilda (Shano) R.; e. Pub. and High Schs., Calgary, Alta.; Univ. of Alta., B.Sc. 1927; Princeton Univ., M.A. 1929, Ph.D. 1930; m. Grace Evelyn LeFeuvre, 1938; Curator emeritus, Royal Ontario Museum and Prof. Emeritus, University of Toronto, since 1971; Field Geologist, Research Council of Alberta, 1928-29; Assistant Palaeontologist, Geol. Survey of Canada, Ottawa, 1930-37; Assistant Professor of Palaeontol. (1937-48) and Assoc. Prof., Univ. of Toronto, 1948-50; Ass. Dir. (1938-46) and Dir. (1946-50), Royal Ont. Museum of Palaeontology; Chief of Zoology Sec., Nat. Museum of Can., 1950-56; Dir., Nat. Museum of Canada, 1956-63; Chief Biologist, Royal Ontario Museum, and Prof., Dept. of Geol., Univ. of Toronto, 1963-71; served in 2nd World War in Candn. Active Army, 1942-45; in N.P.A.M. with R.C.C.S. (Reserve) for 3 yrs. after 2nd World War; author of over 100 papers on the geology and vertebrate or invertebrate palaeontol. of W. Can.; three books on 19th C. material culture; Fellow, Palaeontol. Soc.; Soc. Vertebrate Palaeontol.; Geol. Assn. Can.; Candn. Museums Assn.; Hon. mem., Royal Cdn. Inst.; Ottawa Field Naturalists Club; mem., Malacolog. Union; Am. Soc. of Mammalogists; awarded Willet G. Miller Medal by Royal Soc. Can., 1959; Silver Jubilee Medal, 1978; recreations: amateur radio, painting, antiquarian research; Home: 55 Erskine, Toronto, Ont. M4P 1Y7

RUSSELL, Peter Howard, M.A.: educator; b. Toronto, Ont. 16 Nov. 1932; s. Alexander William and Jean Port (Griffin) R.; e. Univ. of Toronto Schs.; Univ. of Toronto B.A. 1955; Oxford Univ. (Rhodes Scholar) M.A. 1957; m. Eleanor Sewell d. late Robert A. Jarvis 16 May 1958; children: Catherine, Mary, Barbara, Alexander; PROF. OF POL. SCIENCE, UNIV. OF TORONTO: Dir. of Research, Royal Comn. of Inquiry RCMP; mem. Legal Aid Comte. Ont.; Dir., Univ. Settlement; PMA Books; Visiting Prof. Harvard Univ. 1967; Prof., Makerere Univ. Uganda 1969-71; Princ. of Innis Coll. Univ. of Toronto 1971-76; rec'd C. D. Howe Fellowship 1967-68; author "Nationalism in Canada" 1967; "Leading Constitutional Decisions" 1966; "The Supreme Court as A Bilingual Bicultural Institution" 1969; "The Administration of Justice in Uganda" 1971; various articles constitutional law, Supreme Court judicial power, indian land claims; mem. Candn. Pol. Science Assn.; Law & Soc. Assn.; Candn. Assn. Adm. Justice; Anglican; Home: 14 Wychwood Park, Toronto, Ont. M6G 2V5.

RUSSELL, Richard Doncaster, M.A., Ph.D., F.R.S.C.; university professor; b. Toronto, Ont., 27 Feb. 1929; s. Ada Gwennola (Doncaster) and late Richard Douglas R.; e. N. Toronto Coll. Inst., 1942-47; Univ. of Toronto, B.A. (Physics and Chem.) 1951, M.A. (Physics) 1952, Ph.D. (Geophysics) 1954; post doctorate Univ. of Chicago and Oxford Univ.; m. Virginia Ann Reid, d. late Bernard Clippingdale, 11 Aug. 1951; children: Linda Jean, Morna Ann, Mary Joyce; PROF. OF GEOPHYSICS, UNIV. OF BRIT. COLUMBIA, since 1963 and Head of the Dept. of Geophysics & Astronomy 1968-79; mem. of Bd. of Govs. 1978-81; Lectr., Univ. of Toronto, 1954-56; Asst. Prof. of Physics, 1956-58; Prof. of Physics and mem. Inst. Earth Sciences, 1962-63; joined present Univ. as Assoc. Prof. of Physics and mem. Inst. Earth Sciences, 1958; Acting Dir., Inst. of Astronomy & Space Sciences, 1969-70; mem. Geol. Assn. of Can.; Candn. Geophys. Union; B.C. Geophys. Soc.; Candn. Soc. Expl. Geophys.; Am. Geophysical Union; Home: 2061 Allison Rd., Vancouver, B.C. V6T 1T2

RUSSELL, Hon. Ronald S., M.H.A.; politician; b. Auckland, N.Z. 22 July 1926; e. Ryerson Inst. of Technol. grad. in Indust. Math.; Queen's Univ. Psychol.; Candn. Forces Staff Sch. grad.; Sch. of Mang. Engn. grad.; m. Anna Isfeld, Winnipeg Beach, Man.; two s.; MIN. OF CONSUMER AFFAIRS, N.S. and Min. Responsible for Adm.

Residential Tenacies Act 1980- ; served with Royal N.Z. Air Force and Royal Australian Air Force World War II; came to Can. 1949; joined RCAF 1950 retiring with rank Sqdn Leader after 25 yrs. service; Duty Airport Mgr. Halifax Internat. Airport; mem. Council W. Hants Mun.; W. Hants Sch. Bd., Bd. Health and Bd. Hants Co. Sr. Citizens" Home; el. M.H.A. for Hants West prov. g.e. 1978; Speaker H. of A. 1978-80; P. Conservative; Office: (P.O. Box 998) 5151 Terminal Rd., Halifax, N.S. B3J 2X3.

RUSSELL, Sheila MacKay, R.N.; public health nurse; author; b. Airdrie, Alberta, 10 May 1920; d. William MacKay and Catherine (Reid) R.; e. Central High Sch., Calgary, Alta., Grad. 1937; Calgary Gen. Hosp. (Grad. in Nursing) 1942; Univ. of Alberta (Grad. in Pub. Health Nursing), 1944; m. 7 Mar. 1947; Staff Nurse, Red Deer Mun. Hosp., Alta., 1942-43; Prov. District Nurse, Alta., 1944-45; Asst. Dir. of Pub. Health Nursing and Asst. Dir. of Health Educ., Alta., 1945-47; author of "A Lamp Is Heavy", 1950; "The Living Earth", 1954; assorted short stories, prof. articles and health manuals; Protestant; Address: 9703-87 St., Edmonton, Alta. T6C 3H9

RUST, Thomas Grant, B.Sc.; pulp and paper executive; b. Stratford, Ont. 23 Sept. 1919; s. Stanley R.; e. Avon Sch., Stratford, Ont.; Stratford Coll. Inst.; Queen's Univ., B.Sc. (Chem. Engn.); m. Mary, d. Harry McLean 26 Jan. 1945; children: James T., Anne: PRES. AND CHIEF EXTVE. OFFR., CROWN ZELLERBACH CAN. LTD., since 1976; Dir., Inland Natural Gas Company Limited; Quadrant Development Limited; The Bank of Nova Scotia; Candn. Pacific Ltd.; began as Quality Control Engr., Dominion Rubber Co., Kitchener, Ont. 1946; Groundwood Control Engr., Ontario Paper Co., Thorold, Ont. 1947; Groundwood Supt., Quebec North Shore Paper Co., Baie Comeau, Que. 1951, Asst. Gen. Supt. 1959, Div. Mgr. 1961; Vice-Pres. Pulp & Paper, B.C. 1964, Extve. Vice-Pres. 1968; joined Weyerhaeuser Can. Ltd. (name then Kamloops Pulp & Paper Co. Ltd.) as Pres. and Chief Extve. Offr. 1970 (Co. name changed to present 1971); Chrmn. and Chief Extve. Offr., 1973; served in 2nd World War, R.C.O.C. 1942-46; mem., Engn. Inst. Can.; Candn. Pulp & Paper Assn.; Pulp & Paper Research Inst. Can.; recreation: golf; Clubs: The Vancouver; Shaughnessy Golf & Country; Office: 815 W. Hastings St., Vancouver, B.C. V6C 1B4

RUSTED, Nigel Francis Scarth, B.Sc., M.D., C.M., D.Sc., F.R.C.S.(C), F.A.C.S., F.I.C.S.; b. Salvage B.B., Newfoundland, 1 July 1907; s. late Rev. Canon Ernest Edward and Faith Amy Margaret (Hollands) R.; e. Bishop Field Coll. (1923-25) and Memorial Coll. (1925-27), St. John's, Nfld.; Dalhousie Univ., B.Sc. 1929 and M.D., C.M. 1933; m. Florence Haig, d. Thomas Anderson, M.D. 21 June 1944; children: Joan Margaret, Elaine E. W., Thomas Nigel; Hon. Surgeon, St. John's Gen. Hosp.; Sr. Consultant, Grace Gen. Hosp.; Consulting Surg., St. Clares Hospital; Janeway Children's Hospital; Clinical Prof. of Surg., Memorial Univ. of Newfoundland; Anglican; recreations: fishing, philately, amateur radio, photography; Address: 28 Monkstown Rd., St. John's, Nfld. A1C 3T3

RUSTON, Rudolf Steadman, M.B.E., F.R.S.A.; company executive; b. Wolverhampton, Eng., 27 June 1912; s. Rupert Samuel and Clara Elizabeth (Steadman) R.; e. St. Mary's Sch., Wolverhampton, Eng.; Staffordshire Tech. Coll. (Eng.); Royal Military College of Science; m. Muriel Liliam d. late Albert Horace Sadler, 2 July 1938; CHRMN., CHUBB HOLDINGS (N.A.) Ltd.; Engn. Apprentice, Chubb & Son, England, 1929; Works Director, 1947; came to Canada 23 April 1954; apptd. Pres., Chubb Safe Co. (Canada) Ltd. and organized Candn. operations of company, 1954; served in 2nd World War with Royal Artillery, 1939-45, Lt. Col.; Mentioned in Despatches; awarded M.B.E.; mem., Canadn. Mfrs. Assn.; Protestant; recreation: golf; Clubs: National; Mississauga Golf;

R.A.S.C. (Eng.); Home: Barringham Dr., Oakville, Ont.; Office: Queen St. E., Brampton, Ont.

RUTHERFORD, Lt. Col., The Hon. Mr. Justice Robert Campbell, M.B.E., C.D.; b. Owen Sound, Ont. 29 Nov., 1922; s. Brig. Gen. Thomas John Rutherford, C.B.E., E.D.; e. Dufferin Pub. Sch. and Owen Sound Coll. Inst.; Khaki Coll. of Can. London, Eng. 1946; Osgoode Hall Law Sch. 1950; m. The Late Elizabeth Ann Sutcliffe, Sept. 1949; children: Susan Elizabeth, Robert Sutcliffe; m. Donna Lee d. William Robert Lawrence Richards, Kitchener, Ont. Nov. 1975; HIGH COURT OF JUSTICE, THE SUPREME COURT OF ONT.; read law with Thomas N. Phelan, Q.C. and Brendan O'Brien, Q.C.; called to the Bar of Ont. 1950; cr. Q.C. 1960; specialized as Trial Counsel; Lectr. in Civil Procedure, Bar Admission Course Law Soc. Upper Can. for 17 yrs.; Part-time Lectr. in Trial Procedure Osgoode Hall, York Univ.; served as Tank Commdr. Royal Canadn. Armoured Corps Africa, Italy, N.W. Europe during World War II; C.O. Gov. Gen. Horse Guards 1956-60 (Hon. Lt. Col. 1976); Hon. Aide-de-Camp to Gov. Gen. Vincent Massey and Gov. Gen. Georges Vanier; rec'd Queen's Silver Jubilee Medal; Past Gov. Trinity Coll. Sch.; Gov. Corps of Commissionaires Ont.; Dir. Royal Commonwealth Soc.; Bencher Law Soc. Upper Can. 1975; mem. Council Medico-Legal Soc. Toronto; Candn. Bar Assn.; St. Andrew's Soc.; Delta Chi; mem. the Order of Saint Lazarus; United Church; recreation: riding; Clubs: Royal Candn. Mil. Inst. (Pres. 1972-77); Tor. North York Hunt Club; Lawyers'; Home: 106 Douglas Dr., Toronto, Ont. M4W 2B4; Office: Osgoode Hall, 130 Queen St. W., Toronto, Ont. M5H 2N5.

RUTHERFORD, Ronald M., B.Eng., B.Com.; executive; b. Revelstoke, B.C., 8 Nov. 1915; s. John and Jessie Ramsey (Ruickbie) R.; e. Revelstoke Pub. & High Schs.; McGill Univ., B.Eng. 1938; Sir Geo. Williams Univ., B.Com. 1951; m. Beatrice J., d. E. S. Feldsted, 1943; children: Janet, Carol, Murray, Sherrill; PRESIDENT, R.M. Rutherford Consultants LTD. since 1977; Vice-Pres., Westcoast Transmission Co. Ltd.; commenced as Engr., Shawinigan Water & Power Co., Montreal, 1938-52; Asst. Chief Engr., Public Utilities Comn. B.C., Victoria, 1952-54; apptd. Chief Engr., Inland Natural Gas Co. Ltd., Vancouver, 1954; Consulting Engr., Bechtel Corp., San Francisco, Calif., 1959-66; Extve. Vice-Pres., Inland Natural Gas Co. Ltd. 1966; Mgr., Gas Sales & Planning, Westcoast Transmission Co. Ltd. 1969-70; Pres., Pacific Northern Gas Ltd. and Vice Pres., Westcoast Transmission Co Ltd. 1970-75; Extve. Vice Pres., Foothills Pipe Lines Ltd. 1975-77; served RCNVR, retired Lieut. Commdr.; Protestant; Home: 1642 W. 37th Ave., Vancouver, B.C. V6M 1M7

RUTTAN, Hon. John Graham, M.A., B.C.L., LL.D.; judge; b. Winnipeg, Man. 11 Feb. 1913; s. Arthur Charles and Beatrice Wilson (Robertson) R.; e. Monterey Pub. Sch., Coll. Private Sch., Oak Bay High Sch. 1929, Victoria (B.C.) Coll. 1930; Univ. of B.C. B.A. 1933; Oxford Univ. B.A. (Hon. Sch. of Jurisprudence), M.A., B.C.L. 1936; Univ. of Victoria LL.D. (Hon. c.) 1978; m. Mary-Louise d. late Charles E. Harrison, Hamilton, Ont. 8 June 1946; children: Stephen Forsyth, Susan Elizabeth, Robert Graham, Deborah Jane; JUDGE, SUPREME COURT OF B.C. since 1956; called to Bar of B.C. 1937; practised law Victoria, B.C. 1937 — 39, 1946 — 56; served with RCNVR 1940 — 45, convoy duty N. Atlantic, anti-submarine specialist R.N., rank Lt. Commdr.; mem. Oak Bay Council 3 yrs.; Past Pres. Family & Children's Service; Hon. Dir. B.C. Automobile Assn.; Anglican; Clubs: Union; Victoria Golf; Arbutus; Home: 1039 Deal St., Oak Bay Victoria, B.C. V8S SG6; Office: Law Courts, 850 Burdett St., Victoria, B.C. V8W 1B4.

RYAN, Aylmer Arthur, M.A., LL.D.; educator; b. Can., 5 Aug. 1912; s. Robert Arthur and Mabel Agnes (Miller)

R.; e. Mount Royal Coll., Calgary, Alta.; Univ. of Alta., B.A. 1939, M.A. (Eng.) 1940; Univ. of Cal., Berkeley, 1941-42, 1948-49; Sir George Williams Univ., LL.D. 1972; m. Mona Margaret, d. late James Skead, 10 Nov. 1946; children: Cynthia Kathleen, Philip James, David Arthur; Prof. of Eng., Provost and Extve. Asst. to Pres., Univ. of Alta., now retired; served with COTC 1939; Candn. Army Can., Eng. and Italy, 1942-46; rank Maj.; Candn. Army Active Reserve 1950-60; rank Lt. Col.; mem. Candn. Assn. Univ. Teachers Eng.; Candn. Student Affairs Assn. (Past Pres., rec'd Award of Outstanding Merit 1967); Awarded Candn. Assn. of Coll. and Univ. Student Services Award of Merit, 1977; Univ. of Alberta Alumni Golden Jubilee Award, 1977; Phi Kappa Pi; Protestant; recreation: sports; Home: 11811-87 Ave., Edmonton, Alta. T6G 0Y5

RYAN, Claude; politician; b. Montreal, Que., 26 Jan. 1925; s. Henri-Albert and Blandine (Dorion) R.; e. Collège St-Croix, Montréal, 1937-44; Sch. of Social Service, Univ. of Montreal, 1944-46; Dept. of History, Pontifical Gregorian Univ., Rome, 1951-52; m. Madeleine, d. Jos.-L. Guay, 21 July 1958; children: Paul, Monique, Thérèse, Patrice, André; LEADER, LIBERAL PARTY, QUEBEC; Past Publisher, "Le Devoir" (daily newspaper estbd. 1910), and Mang. Dir., Imprimerie Populaire Ltée., May 1978; Gen. Secretary, L'Action Catholique Canadienne, 1945-62; joined "Le Devoir" as Editorial Writer, June 1962; Pres., Inst. canadien d'Educ. Adultes, 1955-61; rec'd Human Relations Award, Candn. Council of Christians & Jews, 1966; apptd. to Candn. News Hall of Fame, 1968; Independent; Roman Catholic; recreations: reading, walking; Home: 425 West St. Joseph Blvd., Montréal, Que. H2V 2P3; Office: 460 Gilford St. Montréal, Qué.

RYAN, Francis J., Q.C.; b. St. John's, Nfld., 28 March 1926; s. James V. and Edith (McGrath) R.; e. Holy Cross Sch., Nfld., St. Bonaventure's Coll., Nfld.; m. Sheila Anne, d. Hon. Mr. Justcie C. J. Fox, 21 April 1949; children: Dennis J., John N., Robert G.; PARTNER; STIRLING, RAYN, REID, HARRINGTON AND ANDREWS (est. 1963); Chrmn. Price (Nfld) Pulp & Paper Co. Ltd.; Dir., Abitibi Price Inc.; The Price Co. Ltd.; Bowring Brothers Ltd., and a number of other companies; Chrmn. Adv. Bd. Montreal Trust Co. in Nfld.; Past Gov., Candn. Tax Foundation; post commnt. of Conference on Uniformity of Legislation; called to Bar of Nfld. 1947; cr. Q.C. 1963; mem. Law Soc. Nfld.; Past Vice-Pres. for Nfld.; Candn. Bar Assn.; R. Catholic; recreation: fishing; Club: Bally Haly Golf & Country; Home: 9 Winter Ave., St. John's, Nfld.; Office: Royal Trust Building, Water Street, St. John's, Nfld. A1C 5V3

RYAN, Leo Edward, B.Sc.; b. Montreal, Que., 24 Oct. 1909; s. Leo George and Mary Bond (Doran) R.; e. McGill Univ. (Grad. Chem. Engn.); m.; has two s. and one d.; joined Mallinckrodt Company (fine chemicals) on leaving univ.; apptd. Vice-Pres. and Dir. of Monsanto Canada Ltd., 1945, Extve. Vice-Pres. in 1949, el. Pres., 1955; Chrmn. of the Bd., 1962, till resignation 31 Dec. 1964; Pres., Candn. Exporters' Assn., 1957-58; recreations: fishing, golf, gardening, philately; Clubs: Royal Montreal Golf; Union; Royal Colwood Golf; Victoria Golf; Home: 3821 Miramontes Dr., Victoria, B.C. V8N 4L1

RYAN, Noel, B.A., M.L.S.; librarian; b. St. John, N.B. 27 May 1925; s. late Fergus James and Evelyn Grace (Hayes) R.; e. Cath. High Sch. Montreal 1944; McGill Univ. 1947-49, M.L.S. 1967; Sir George Williams Univ. B.A. 1964; m. Doreen Lillian d. late William Webster and late Gladys L. (founder N. York Lib. System) Allison 19 Dec. 1950; children: Colin Allison, Karen Jennifer; CHIEF LIBRARIAN, MISSISSAUGA LIBRARY SYSTEM 1971- ; Vice Pres. Temco Electric Manufacturing Co. Montreal 1949-57; Owner, Local Photo, Montreal 1957-67; Chief Librarian, Dorval, Que. 1967-69, Brampton, Ont. 1969-71; served

with Victoria Rifles of Can. (Reserve) 1942-44, Candn. Inf. Corps 1944, Black Watch of Can. 1945, Cameron Highlanders of Ottawa 1945-46, France-Germany; co-author "Juxtaposised" 1974; mem. Ont. Lib. Assn.; Candn. Lib. Assn.; Am. Lib. Assn.; recreations: music, painting, writing; Home: #35, 55 Falconer Dr., Mississauga, Ont. L5N 1B3; Office: 1350 Burnhamthorpe Rd. E., Mississauga, Ont. L4Y 3V9.

RYAN (Sylvester) Perry, Q.C., B.A., LL.M.; lawyer; b. Toronto, Ontario, 12 January 1918; s. Ernest Anthony and Mary Marguerite R.; e. St. Mary's Separate Sch., Barrie, Ont.; Barrie Coll. Inst.; St. Michael's Coll., Univ. of Toronto, B.A., 1939; Osgoode Hall Grad, 1942; York Univ. LL.M., 1977; Univ. of the Air Grad. 1980; m. Dolores Margaret, d. late Arthur Pothier, Ft. William, Ontario, 2 April 1956; children: Anne Marie, Michael Anthony; PARTNER, RYAN AND HOGAN; Chairman, Health Services Appeal Bd. of Ontario; Dir., Ainsworth Elec. Co. Ltd.; Bard Pharmaceuticals Ltd.; Blair Pharmaceuticals, Ltd.; Canmark Services Ltd.; Gray Pharmaceutical Co. (Can.) Ltd.; The Purdue Frederick Co. (Can.) Ltd.; Those Magnificent Men & Their Flying Machines Inc.; Lawrence Ave. Medical Bldg. Ltd.; read law with Briggs, Frost & Birks; called to the Bar of Ontario 1942; served in the 2nd World War with C.O.T.C., Osgoode Hall; def. candidate for Greenwood (Toronto) in g.e. 1949; el. to H. of C. for Spadina (Toronto) in g.e. 1962; re-el. until def. Oct. 1972; Past Chrmn., NATO Parlty. Assn.; Past Vice Chrmn., Standing Comte. on External Affairs and Nat. Defence; Past mem., Standing Comte. NATO Parlty. Assembly; mem., Law Soc. of Upper Can.; Candn. Bar Assn.; Bd. of Trade; Monarch of Lions'; Pres., Anson Hunt Club; Pres. Kawartha Soaring Club Inc.; Catholic Big Brothers of Toronto (former Pres.); Conservative; Roman Catholic; recreations: golf, tennis, hunting, fishing, power flying, gliding, boating; Office: 1863 Danforth Ave., Toronto, Ont. M4C 1J3

RYNARD, Hugh Cameron, B.A.Sc., P.Eng.; consulting engineer; b. Zephyr, Ont., 3 March 1924; s. William M. and Sadie Isabel (McLellan) R.; e. Pub. Sch., Zephyr, Ont.; High Schs., Uxbridge and Newmarket, Ont.; Univ. of Toronto, B.A.Sc. 1951; PRESIDENT & DIR., ACRES CONSULTING SERVICES LIMITED since 1971; employed by Acres Consult. Services Ltd. and predecessor H. G. Acres & Co. Ltd., 1951 to present; mem., Assn. Prof. Engrs. Prov. Ont., Man., and Nfld.; Corp. Engrs. Prov. Que.; Engn. Inst. Can.; Assn. Consulting Engrs. Can.; recreations: golf, swimming; Club: Bayview Golf & Country; Office: 480 University Ave., Toronto, Ont. M5G 1V2

S

SABOURIN, Louis, F.R.S.C., Ph.D., LL.L.; educator; b. Quebec, Que., 1 December 1935; s. Rolland P. and Valeda (Caza) S.; e. Univ. of Ottawa, B.A. (Pol. Science), 1956, LL.L. 1961; Sorbonne, Dipl. de Litt, Française Cont. 1957; Inst. Etudes Pol. de Paris, Dipl. Internat. Relations 1958; Doctoral work, Columbia., 1962-64; research at Harvard Univ. and Stanford Univ.; Ph.D. Columbia Univ. 1971; D.Univ. nat. du Dahomey (Africa) 1973; m. Agathe, d. Dr. C. E. Lacerte, St. Eugene, Ont., 18 July 1959; children: Pierre, Nicole, Nathalie; PRES., OECD DEVELOPMENT CENTRE, PARIS, FRANCE since 1978; Past Dir., Inst. for Internat. Co-op., Univ. of Ottawa, and Prof. of Pol. Science; Past Dean, Faculty Social Sciences; regular commentator on pub. and internat. affairs on radio and TV; French Govt. Fellow, 1956; Ford Internat. Fellow, 1962-63; Can. Council Scholar 1963-64; Visiting Sr. Research Fellow, Jesus Coll., Oxford 1974-75; Visiting Prof. several Candn. and foreign univs. incl. Northwestern Univ., Chicago 1975-77; has written numerous books and articles on Canadian foreign policy and public law and international development; mem., Candn. Inst. Internat. Affairs; Candn. Assn. Pol. Science; Pres., Soc. Can. De Science Pol. (Past Pres.); Soc. Internat. Law (Ottawa Chapter); International Comte. Social Science Research Council Can.; Pres., Scient. Council "Ecole internat. de Bordeaux"; el. to Acad. Social Sciences, Roy. Soc. Can. 1977, to Club of Dakar, 1978; mem., Am. Soc. International Law; Candn. Inst. Internat. Law; Soc. Internat. Devel.; Past Pres. Candn. Assn. African Studies; Que. Bar Assn.; R. Catholic; recreation: travel; skiing; tennis;

SADDLEMYER, (Eleanor) Ann, LL.D., M.A., Ph.D., F.R.S.C.; educator; author; b. Prince Albert, Sask. 28 Nov. 1932; d. Orrin Angus and Elsie Sarah (Ellis) S.; e. Univ. of Sask. B.A. 1953 (Eng. & Psychol.), 1955 (Eng. Hons.); Queen's Univ. M.A. 1956, LL.D. 1977; Bedford Coll. Univ. of London Ph.D. 1961; PROF. OF ENGLISH, VICTORIA COLL., UNIV. OF TORONTO since 1971 and Prof. of Drama, Grad. Centre for Study of Drama; Lectr. Victoria (B.C.) Coll. 1956-57, Instr. 1960, Asst. Prof. 1962, Assoc. Prof. (Univ. of Victoria) 1965, Prof. 1968-71; Lectr. Univ. of Sask. summer 1957; Dir. Grad. Drama Centre, Univ. of Toronto 1972-77; Visiting Prof. Berg Chair N.Y. Univ. 1975; Sr. Fellow, Massey Coll.; mem. Univ. Council Queen's Univ. 1975-80; Vice Pres. Bd. Theatre Plus; mem., Bd. of Dir., Colin Smythe Publishers Ltd.; author "The World of W. B. Yeats" (with Robin Skelton & others) 1965; "In Defence of Lady Gregory, Playwright" 1966; "The Plays of J. M. Synge, Books One and Two" 1968; "Synge and Modern Comedy" 1968; "The Plays of Lady Gregory" 4 vols. 1970; "A Selection of Letters from J. M. Synge to W. B. Yeats and Lady Gregory" 1971; "Letters to Molly: J. M. Synge to Maire O'Neill" 1971; "Theatre Business, the correspondence of the first Abbey Theatre directors" 1981; "The Collected Lettersof J. M. Synge" 2 vols. (to be publ.); various articles and reviews; gen. ed. 2 vol. hist. theatre in Ont. (Ont. Hist. Studies Series); co-ed. of journal, "Theatre History in Canada/-Histoire du Théâtre au Canada"; mem. Ed. Bds. "Canadian Theatre Review"; "English Studies in Canada"; "Irish University Review"; "Journal of Irish Studies"; "Canadian Journal of Irish Studies"; "Modern Drama"; "Themes in Drama"; "Research in the Humanities"; "The Shaw Review"; mem. Internat. Assn. Study Anglo-Irish Lit. (Past Chrmn.); Assn. Candn. Theatre Hist. (Founding Pres.); Candn. Assn. Irish Studies; NDP; recreations: book collecting, music, theatre, travel; Home: 297 Watson Ave., Oakville, Ont. L6J 3V3

SADLEIR, Richard H., B.A., M.A.: b. Toronto, Ont., 23 April 1929; s. Harry Llewellyn and Mary Irene (Hay) E.; e. Univ. of Toronto, Trinity Coll., B.A. 1951; Ont. Coll. of Educ. 1953; Trinity Coll., Cambridge, M.A. 1956; m. Joan Walker, d. John J. Robinette, Toronto, Ont., 19 Dec. 1959; children: Thomas Robinette, Mary Walker, Catherine Hay; PRINCIPAL, UPPER CANADA COLL., since 1975; Exec. Comm. of Convocation, Trinity Coll., 1952-54; Eng. Master, Upper Canada Coll., 1956-63 also House Master of Scadding's House there; Dean of Men, Trent Univ. 1963 and Master, Peter Robinson Coll. there 1964-69; Dir., Peterborough Community Concert Assoc., 1965-71; Chmn., Peterborough Symphony Orchestra Bd; 1968-71; Ont. Fed. of Symphony Orchestras, 1970-71; Vice Pres. and Assoc. Prof. Eng. Trent Univ. 1969-70; Mem., Corp., Trinity Coll., Univ. of Toronto, 1969-80 (Exec. Comm., 1977-80), (Vice Chrmn 1980); Pres. Can. Headmasters Assoc. 1979-80; awarded Centennial Medal 1967; Home: Grant House, Upper Canada Coll., 200 Lonsdale Rd., Toronto, Ont. M4V 1W6

SADLER, James Arthur, B.Eng., mining executive retired; b. Montreal, P.Q., 26 Mar. 1915; s. James and Lavenia (McCollough) S.; e. Verdun (Que.) High Sch.; Westmount (Que.) High Sch.; McGill Univ., B.Eng. (Mining) 1944; m. Thelma Marion, d. Llewellyn Adams, Verdun, P.Q., 15 June 1940; children: Wayne, Heather, Barry, Sherry; former President, Rio Tinto Canadian Exploration

Ltd. (Estbd. 1953); worked in various mines in Canada before and after grad., incl. Siscoe Gold Mines, Hollinger Gold Mines, International Nickel Co. of Can., and Kerr-Addison Gold Mines; in 1946 accepted a post in Tanganyika, E. Africa as Mine Capt. and rose through Mine Supt., Gen. Supt., Asst. Mgr. to Gen. Mgr. of Geita Gold Mining Co. Ltd.; travelled through much of Central Africa incl. "Copper Belt" of N. Rhodesia; returned to Can., 1955 as Asst. Mgr. of Chibaugamau Explorers Ltd.; Chief Mining Engr., Mines Br., Prov. of Manitoba, 1955-56; joined Rio Algom Ltd. as Asst. Mgr. 1956; retired as Vice Pres. (Exploration) 1977; mem., Inst. of Mining & Metall. (London); Candn. Inst. Mining & Metall.; Conservative; Protestant; Home: RR 4, Grand Valley, Ont. L0N 1G0

SADLER, S. W. R., B.B.A.; company executive; b. Montreal, 24 Nov. 1938; s. Albert Corneil and Esther Isabel (Walsh) S.; e. Lower Canada Coll., 1951-57; Univ. of New Brunswick, B.B.A. 1962; m. Valerie Adele Miller; children: Grant S. A., Erika V.; PRESIDENT AND GEN. MGR., SADLER INC.; Protestant; recreation: snow and water skiing; Club: Rotary; Office: 1845 William St., Montreal, P.Q. H3J 1R6

SADOWSKA-SIWINSKI, Kzystyna, artist; b. Lublin, Poland, 2 June 1915; d. Wladystaw and Kazimiera Kopczynski; e. Sch. of Decorative Arts, Warsaw, Poland; Academy of Fine Arts, Warsaw, Poland; Free Sch. in Paris, France; Central Sch. of Art and Design, London, Eng.; m. Kopcrynska Sadowska, 2 July 1939; has participated in exhns. in Paris, Helsinki, New York, Edinburgh, Sao Paulo, Rio de Janeiro, Washington, Ottawa, Brussels and numerous other countries; awarded Gold Medal for Tapestry by French Govt., 1937; Silver Medal for Tapestry by Brazilian Govt., 1947; 2nd Prize for Tapestry at Internat. Exhn., Greensboro, N.C., 1949; Grand Award and 1st Prize for Tapestry, London Art Museum, London, Ont.; 1st Prize for Tapestry, 1961 and for Batik, 1962 by The Canadian Handicraft, Montreal, P.Q.; author of 'Thirteen Polish Legends", 1944; has been reviewed in such journals of art as "Craft Horizons", 1951, 1954; "Handweaver and Craftsman", 1953; "Vie des Arts", 1958; "The Studio", 1958; and numerous others; In recent years executed several commissions for large scale metal sculpture from Govt. of Ont., Univ. of Saskatoon, Univ. of Waterloo, Bd. of Educ. of Etobicoke, Royal Bank, Jesuit Coll. (Toronto), Rio Algom (Toronto Dominion Bank, Calgary House (Calgary); Roman Catholic; Address: 561 Spadina Road, Toronto, Ont. M5P 2W9

SAFARIAN, Albert Edward, B.A., Ph.D., F.R.S.C.; b. Hamilton, Ont., 19 Apl. 1924; s. Israel and Annie (Simonian) S.; e. Jarvis Coll. Inst., Toronto, 1937-42; Univ. of Toronto, B.A. (Pol. Econ.) 1946; Univ. of Cal. (Berkeley), Ph.D. (Econ.) 1956; m. Joan Elizabeth, d. C. H. Shivvers, Phoenix, Ariz., Jan. 1950; children: Mark, David, Laura, Paul; PROF. OF ECON., UNIV. OF TORONTO, since 1966; Dean, Sch. of Grad. Studies 1971-76; Stat., Balance of Payments, Dom. Bureau of Stat., Ottawa, 1950-55; research staff, Royal Comn. on Can.'s Econ. Prospects, Ottawa, 1956; Assoc. Prof., Prof. and Head, Dept. of Econ. and Pol. Science, Univ. of Sask., 1956-66; mem., Task Force on Structure of Indust., Ottawa, 1967; author: "The Canadian Economy in the Great Depression", 1958; "Foreign Ownership of Canadian Industry", 1966; "Canadian Federalism and Economic Integration", 1974; mem., Candn. Econ. Assn. (Pres. 1976-77); Ont. Econ. Council; Am. Econ. Association; Royal Econ. Soc.; Cdn.-Amer. Comn.; Home: 58 St. Andrews Gardens, Toronto, Ont. M4W 2E1

SAFDIE, Moshe, B.Arch.; architect, urban designer; b. Haifa, Israel, 14 July 1938; s. Leon and Rachel (Esses) S.; e. McGill Univ., B.Arch. 1961 (Lt.-Gov.'s Gold Medal); m. Nina, d. Henry Nusynowicz, 6 Sept. 1959; children: Taal, Oren; re-married Michel Ronnen. 1981; arch. of Habitat, Montreal, 1967; San Francisco State Coll. Union,

1968; Habitat Puerto Rico, 1968; Habitat Israel 1969; Yeshivat Porat Joseph and sephardic Synagogue, Old City of Jerusalem, 1970; Israeli Army training 1970; Coldspring New Town, Baltimore, Maryland; Keur Farah Pahlavi New Town, Senegal; Ivory Coast Blood Centres; author of "Beyond Habitat", 1970 "For Everyone a Garden", 1974; 'Form and Purpose', 1980; and various publs. relating to arch.; mem., Order of Archs. of Que; Royal Canadian Academy of Arts, Ont. Assn. of Archs.; Royal Arch. Inst. Can.; Assn. Engrs. & Archs. Israel; Dir., Urban Design Program, Harvard Grad. Sch. of Design since 1978; Chrmn., Internat. Design Conf. Aspen 1980; Offices: 3601 University St., Montreal, Que. H3A 2B3 2 Faneuil Hall Marketplace, Boston, M.A. 02109; 15 Manilla St., Jerusalem, Isreal.

ST. GERMAIN, Guy, LL.L., M.A.; executif; n. St-Hyacinthe, Qué. 8 mars 1933; f. Joseph Lucien et Angéline (Audet) St. G.; e. Coll. Jean-de-Brébeuf B.A. 1953; Univ. de Montréal LL.L. 1956; Barreau du Qué. 1957; Merton Coll. Oxford Univ. M.A. 1960 (Boursier Rhodes 1957); Inst. des Hautes Etudes Politiques Paris 1961; é Denise f. Dr. Rosaire Lauzer 25 juin 1958; enfants: Charles, Claire, Phillippe, Antoine; DIR., BUREAU D'ASSURANCE DU CANADA; MEMBRE DU CONSEIL: GROUPEMENT TECHNIQUE DES ASSUREURS; Dir. Dominion Electric Protection Ltd.; Imprimerie Populaire; Bureau d'Expertise des Assureurs Ltée; Banque Nationale du Canada; Mercona Limitée; Provigo Inc.; Téléglobe Canada; récréations: mem. du conseil d'admin., Banque Nationale du Canada; Le Groupe Commerce Co. d'assurances; Le Groupe Mercona Ltée.; ADT Security Systems — Systèmes Sécuritaires; Téléglobe Canada; Provigo Inc.; natation, pêche, tennis; Maison: 48 Robert, Outremont, Qué. H3S 2P2; Bureau: 2450 Girouard, St-Hyacinthe, Qué. J2S 3B3

SAINT-PIERRE, Guy, B.A.Sc., M.Sc., D.I.C.; né Windsor Mills, Qué. 3 août 1934; f. Armand et Alice (Perra) St-P.; é Acad. St.-Louis et Coll. du Sacré-Coeur, Victoriaville, 1946-53; Univ. Laval, B.Sc., 1957; Imp. Coll. Science and Technol., D.I.C., 1958; Univ. de Londres, M.Sc., 1957-59; ép. Francine, f. Marcel Garneau et Françoise Champoux; 4 mai 1957; enfants: Marc, Guylaine, Nathalie; VICE-PRES. AND PRINCIPAL, JOHN LABATT Ltée. 1977- ; Pres. & Chef de la Direction, Les Minoteries Ogilvie Ltée.; Admin., Suncor Inc.; Zymaize Inc.; Industries Popular; Miron Inc.; Groupe Commerce; Inst. de Recherches Cliniques de Montréal; Officier dans le Corps de Génie Royal Candn., Camp Gagetown, N.B., 1959-64; Régistraire, Corp. des Ingénieurs du Qué., 1964-66; Dir. techn., IRNES, 1966-67; Vice Prés. Acres Qué. Ltée, 1967-70; Min. de l'Education du Qué. 1970-72; Min. de l'Industrie et Comm. du Qué. 1972-76; Adjoint au Prés. de John Labatt Ltée., 1977; Prés, & Dir. Gen. Les Minoteries Ogilvie Ltée., 1978; Vice Prés. Conseil pour l'Unité canadienne, 1977- ; Prés., Campagne de Claude Ryan au leadership du Parti Libéral, 1978; mem. Chambre de Comm. de Montréal; l'Ordre des Ingénieurs du Qué.; l'Inst. Candn. des Ingénieurs; Ordre Militaire et Hospitalier de St.-Lazare de Jérusalem; Libéral; Catholique; récréations; natation, golf, ski; Clubs: Mount Bruno Golf; St.-Denis; Mount Royal; Forest and Stream; Résidence: 1227 ouest, rue Sherbrooke, app. 64, Montréal, Qué. H3G 1G1; Office: 1, Place Ville Marie, suite 2100, Montréal, Que. H3B 2X2

SAINT-PIERRE, Jacques, M.A., Ph.D.; statistician; b. Trois-Rivières, Qué. 30 Aug. 1920; s. Oscar and Lucie (Landreville) S-P; e. Univ. de Montréal, 1945 = 51, M.A. (Math.); Univ. of N. Carolina, Ph.D. (Math. Stat.) 1954; m. Marguerite Lachaine, 15 July 1947; children: Marc, Guy, André; Louis; François, Mireille; VICE PRES., PLANNING, UNIV. de MONTREAL since 1972; full professor since 1960; Vice-Dean and Dir. of Studies, Faculty of Sciences (1961-64); Dir. of Computing Centre (1964-71), of Computer Science Dept. (1966-69); has publ. numerous scient. papers in math. stat. and allied topics; mem. Inst. of Math. Stat.; Am. Stat. Assn.; Biometrics Soc. (N.E. Sec.); Candn. Operational Research Soc.; Soc. Math. du Canada; Assn. Math. du Qué.; Assn. for Computing Machinery; Pres. Candn. Assn. of Univ. Teachers, 1965-66; Home: 1795 Croissant-Daviault, Duvernay, P.Q. H7G 4E2; Office: C.P. 6128, Montréal, Qué.

ST. PIERRE, Leon E., Ph.D.; university professor;.b. Edmonton, Alta., 1 Sept. 1924; s. Joseph Leon and Adele St. P.; e. Univ. of Alta., B.Sc. (Hons. Chem.) 1951; Univ. of Notre Dame, Ph.D. (Chem.) 1954; m. Pauline E. A., d. Louis T. Oel, Calgary, Alta., 25 July 1949; children: Denise L.; Jerome P., Noel J., Louis C.; Claire G., Martin G., Michele A.; (PROFESSOR OF POLYMER CHEM. since 1976; Chemist, General Electric Research Laboratory, Schenectady, N.Y., 1954-61; Mgr. Polymer and Interface Studies Sec., 1962-65; Chrmn., Dept. of Chem., McGill Univ. 1972-76; co-author, "High Polymer Series" Vol. XIII ("Polyethers") 1964; has written over 60 papers and holds two patents; inventor of new family of aluminum lubricants now licensed world-wide by Gen. Electric; served with R.C.A.F. 1944-45 and Candn. Inf. Corp. 1945-46; mem., Chem. Inst. Can.; Am. Chem. Soc.; Faraday Soc.; Soc. Plastics Engrs.; Am. Assn. Advanc. Science; N.Y. Acad. Science; R. Catholic; recreations: skating, music; Home: Frelighsburg, Que.

SAINTE-MARIE, Guy, B.A., M.D., Ph.D.; educator; b. Montréal, Qué. 22 May 1928; s. Hubert and Hélène (Legault) S.; e. Coll. Ste-Marie Montréal B.A. 1950; Univ. de Montréal M.D. 1955; McGill Univ. Ph.D. 1962; m. Marielle d. benoit Leblanc 23 July 1955; children: Bernard, Marc, Luc; CHRMN. DEPT OF ANATOMY, UNIV. DE MONTREAL since 1976; Research Fellow Nat. Cancer Inst. Can., Dept. of Anat. McGill Univ. 1955-58, Centre National de Transfusion Sanguine, Paris 1958-59; Research Fellow Dept. Immunology Harvard Univ. 1959-61; Asst. Prof. and Sr. Researcher Nat. Cancer Inst. Can.; Cancer Research Lab. Univ. of W. Ont. 1961-64, Assoc. Prof. 1964-66; Prof. and Assoc. Med. Research Council Can., Dépt. d'Anatomie Univ. de Montréal 1966-76; author or co-author numerous publs.; recreations: farming, beekeeping; Home: 62 Boul. Deguire, Ville Saint-Laurent, Qué. H4N 1N4; Office: (C.P. 6128) Montréal, Qué. H3C 3J7.

SALBAING, Pierre Alcée; company executive; b. Lectoure, France, 8 May 1914; s. Jean and Sylvia (Laforgue) S.; e. Prytanée de la Flèche, Caen Univ., 1935; Ecole Polytech., Paris, grad. 1937; Ecole du Génie Maritime, Paris, grad. 1939; m. Geneviève Nehlil; four s.: Michel, Christian, François, Patrick; came to Canada 1946; PRES. & CHIEF EXTVE. OFFR., LIQUID AIR CORP. NORTH AMERICA (San Francisco); Vice-Chrmn & Gen. Mngr., L'Air Liquide, Paris, France; Vice Chmn. of Bd., Canadian Liquid Air Ltd., Montreal, Que.; Vice Chrmn., U.S. Divers Inc., Santa Anna, Cal.; Manager, Research Laboratory, North America Dept., L'Air Liquide, Montreal, Que., 1946-48; Mgr., Engn. and Constr. Div., 1948-57; Asst. Gen. Mgr. there and Extve. Vice-Pres. present Co., 1957; Gen. Mgr., N. Am. Dept., L'Air Liquide, 1960; served in French Navy, 1939-46; retired with rank of Lieut.-Commdr.; mem., Société des Ingénieurs Civils de France; Assn. des Eléves de l'Ecole Polytech. de Paris; Officer Order of French Legion of Honour; R. Catholic; Home: 16 Rue Barbet de Jouy, Paris, 75007 France; Offices: 75 Quai D'Orsay, Paris, France1 Embarcadero Cntre., San Francisco, Cal., 94111, U.S.A.

SALES, Michel, B.A., F.L.M.I.; life insurance executive; b. France, 8 March 1928; s. Clement A. and Agnes A. (Angot) S.; e. High Sch., Paris, France; Univ. of Paris, B.A. 1947; children: Dominique M., Andrée A., Michel J., A. Christina; PRESIDENT, DIR., AND CHIEF EXTVE. OFFR., CANADIAN REASSURANCE CO., 1968- ; Pres., Dir., C.E.O. Candn. Reinsurance Co., 1977- ; Mgr. (Life) in Can. for Swiss Reinsurance Co.; Gen. Mgr., SwissRe Mang. Ltd.; served with French Foreign Service in S.Am. as Asst. to Trade Commr., 1948-49; joined Confederation Life Assn., Toronto, 1950-51; Prudential Insurance Co. of America, Toronto, 1951; North American Reassurance Co., N.Y. City, 1959; helped organize present Co. in 1960; apptd. Secy. and Chief Underwriter; Vice-Pres. and Chief Underwriter 1963; Extve. Vice-Pres., 1966; Pres. and Dir. 1968; mem., Life Office Mang. Assn.; Bd. Trade Metrop. Toronto; Candn. Chamber of Comm.; Conservative; Anglican; recreations: swimming, sailing; Clubs: R.C.Y.C.; Granite; Home: 362 Russell Hill Rd., Toronto, Ont. M4V 2T9; Office: 95 St. Clair Ave. W., Toronto, Ont. M4V 1N9

SALHANY, Hon. Roger Elias, B.A., LL.B.; judge; b. Cornwall, Ont. 21 Oct. 1937; s. Nelson and Sadie S.; e. Bishop's Coll. Sch. Lennoxville, Que. 1954; McGill Univ. B.A. 1958; Osgoode Hall Law Sch. LL.B. 1961; Cambridge Univ. Dipl. Comparative Legal Studies 1962; m. Elizabeth d. A. Furnival Francis,Toronto, Ont. 11 May 1969; children: Ann, Karen Ruth, Roger Christopher; JUDGE, CO. COURT OF ONT.; called to Bar of Ont. 1964; cr. Q.C. 1976; served with Victoria Rifles 1956 — 1958, rank 2nd Lt.; Bencher of the Law Soc. of Upper Canada 1975-78; author "Canadian Criminal Procedure" 3rd ed. 1978; "The Police Manual of Arrest, Seizure and Interrogation", 1981; co-author "Studies in Canadian Criminal Evidence" 1972; numerous articles criminal law; Anglican; recreations: skiing, swimming, tennis, gardening; Home 135 Ross Ave., Kitchener, Ont.; Office: 20 Weber St., Kitchener, Ont.

SALISBURY, Richard Frank, Ph.D., F.R.A.I., F.R.S.C.; professor; b. London, England, 8 Dec. 1926; s. Thomas and Marjorie Beatrice S.; e. Univ. Coll. Sch., London, 1937-45; St. John's Coll., Cambridge Univ. (Open Scholar), B.A. 1949, M.A. 1956; Harvard Univ., M.A. 1955; Australian Nat. Univ., Ph.D. 1957; m. Mary Elizabeth, d. Henry Ernest Roseborough, Toronto, Ont., 28 Aug. 1954; children: Thomas Stephenson, John William, Catherine Elizabeth; PROF. OF ANTHROP., McGILL UNIV. since 1966 (Dept. Chairman 1966-70); Dir., Centre for Developing Area Studies, 1975-78; Arnold Fellow, Harvard Univ., 1951-52; Asst. & Research Assoc. 1954-56; research in New Guinea & Australia as Australian Nat. Univ. Research Scholar, 1952-54; Asst. Prof., Tufts Univ. 1956-57 and Univ. of Cal., Berkeley, 1957-62; joined present Univ. as Assoc. Prof. 1962-65; research in Guyana 1964-66; Visiting Prof., Univ. of Papua and New Guinea, 1967; served with Royal Marines 1945-48; final rank Lt.; apptd. mem., Social Science Research Council of Can., 1969; mem. Academic Panel, The Canada Council 1974-78; Sect., Acad. of Humanities and Social Sciences, 1977-80; Council mem., Inst. Qué. de Recherche sur la Culture, 1979- ; Bd. mem., Cdn. Human Rights Fdn. 1980- ; Consultant to Can. Dept. of Agric. (1970-72), to Adm. of Papua and New Guinea (1971), to James Bay Development Corp. (1971-72), to Indians of Que. (1972-74), Candn. Dept. of Communications (1974-78); Dept. of Indian Affairs (1975, 1979, 1981); Labrador Inuit Assn., 1980; mem. Comn. on the Future of Que. Univs., 1977-79; author: "From Stone to Steel", 1962; "Structures of Custodial Care", 1962; "Behavioral Science Research in New Guinea", 1967; "Vunamami: Economic Transformation in a Traditional Society", 1969; "Development & James Bay" 1972; "Not By Bread Alone: Subsistence Resource Use among James Bay Cree" 1972; "Development? Attitudes of Natives of the Mackenzie District" 1975; "The End of the Line: Communications in Paint Hills" 1976; "A House Divided?" 1978; writings incl. over 60 articles on New Guinea, Northern Can., etc. in various anthrop. journs.; mem. Anthrop. Assn.; Am. Ethnol. Soc. (Pres., 1980); Candn. Ethnol. Assn.; Candn. Sociol. & Anthrop. Assn. (Past Pres.); Polynesian Soc.; N. E. Anthrop. Assn. (Past Pres.); Soc. for Econ. Anthropology

(Pres.-Elect); Home: 451 Strathcona Ave., Westmount, Que. H3Y 2X2

SALMON, C. R. B., M.C., C.A.; b. England; e. England; Pres., Candn. Odeon Theatres Ltd.; served in the 2nd World War with British Army, 1939-46 and discharged with rank of Lieut.-Col.; joined Peat, Marwick, Mitchell & Co., Chart. Accts., London, Eng., following the war; apptd. Secy.-Treas. of the Rank Group of Canadian Co.'s in 1951 and el. a Dir., 1952; Home: 68 Hawkesbury Dr., Willowdale, Ont. M2K 1M5; Office: 225 Consumers Rd., Willowdale, Ont. M2J 4G9

SALMON, Edward Togo, M.A., Ph.D., D. Litt., LL.D., F.R.S.C. (1954), F.R.Hist. S. (1957), F.B.A. (Corr. 1971); historian; b. London, Eng., 29 May 1905; s. Edward Holmwood and Florence (Lowen) S.; e. Univ. of Sydney, B.A. 1925; Cambridge Univ., B.A. 1927, M.A. 1932, Ph.D. 1933; Brit. Sch. at Rome, 1927-29; D.Litt., Acadia Univ. 1964, Wilfrid Laurier Univ. 1973; McMaster Univ. 1975; LL.D. Univ. Windsor 1972; Univ. of Alta., 1980; m. Marina Teodora, d. Alexandru Popescu, 22 August 1930; Radio News Commentator, CKOC, Hamilton, 1939-55; Assistant Professor of Classics, Acadia University, 1929-30; Assistant Professor of Classics, McMaster Univ., 1930-34; Assoc. Prof. 1934-44; Prof. of Ancient History, 1944-54; Messecar Prof. of History and Head of Department, 1954-61, Princ. of University College 1961-66 and Vice President, Academic (Arts) 1967-68; University Orator 1972-74; Emeritus Messecar Professor of History 1973; Prof. in charge, Intercoll. Classics Centre, Rome, 1969-72; served with McMaster C.O.T.C. 1940-45; C.O. with rank of Major, 1946-54; Honorary member, Society for Promotion of Roman Studies (London); Australian Classical Soc.; mem., Classical Assn. of Can. (Past Pres.); Am. Philol. Assn. (Past Pres.); The Brit. Sch. at Rome; Candn. Hist. Assn.; Classical Assn. (U.K.); Assoc. of Ancient Historians (U.S.A.); Candn. Acad. of Humanities & Social Sciences (Past Pres.); author of "History of the Roman World, 30 B.C. to A.D. 138", 6th edition 1968 (8th reprint); "Samnium and the Samnites" 1967; "Roman Colonization under the Republic" 1969; "The Nemesis of Empire" 1974; "The Making of Roman Italy" 1982; honoured with Festschrift "Polis and Imperium" 1974; recreation: museum crawling; Home: Auchmar Road, Hamilton, Ont.

SALOMONE, Alphonse William; hotel executive; b. Winnipeg, Man., 17 June 1919; s. Alphonse William and Marie (Verschoot) S.; e. Catholic High Sch., Knoxville, Tenn.; Univ. of Tenn.; m. Bernadette Ann Villano, 23 Nov. 1946; children: Robert, Lourdes, Gregg; SENIOR VICE PRESIDENT, HILTON HOTELS CORP., & Mang. Dir.; New York Hilton, since 1970; Resident Mgr., Plaza Hotel, N.Y. City, 1947-56; Gen. Mgr., Caribe Hilton, San Juan, Puerto Rico and Vice Pres., Caribbean Area, Hilton Hotels Internat., 1956-63; Vice Pres. and Mang. Dir., Hotel Plaza, Hotel Corporation of America 1963-67; President, Realty Hotels Inc. 1967; served with United States Army in Europe during World War II; rank Maj. on discharge; awarded Bronze Star and five battle citations, Magistral Kt., Sovereign Mil. Order of Malta (U.S.A.); Consult., Office of Emergency Preparedness, Washington, D.C.; Dir.; N.Y. Convention & Visitors Bureau; N.Y. Bd. of Trade; Am. N.Y. State and N.Y. City Hotel Assn.; received N.Y. State Hotel/Motel Assn. Meritorious Service Award 1981; West Side Award of West Side Assn. of Commerce 1981; Republican; R. Catholic; recreations: gardening, fishing, boating; Club: Tavern; Home: Beach Ave., Bay Crest, Huntington Bay, Long Island, N.Y. 11743; Office: 1335 Ave. of the Americas, New York, N.Y. 10019.

SALSMAN, Dean W.; company executive; b. Waterville, N.S.; 11 July 1923; s. Richard D. Salsman; e. Waterville High Sch.; m. Evelyn M., d. Sidney Stc Jones, 8 Oct. 1948; children: Richard, Alan, Robert, Lyn; Chairman,

Parker Brothers (1972) Limited; PRESIDENT, SALSMAN INVESTMENTS LIMITED; served as Chrmn and CEO of Industrial Estates Ltd, 1971-1978; Dir., Nova Scotia Savings and Loan Company; Dir., ICG Scotia Gas Ltd; mem. Board of Governors, Pine Hill Divinity College; Chrmn., Halifax Industrial Comm.; mem. Bd. of Gov., Mt. St. Vincent Univ.; mem., World Business Council; served with R.C.N. 1942-47; Past Pres. Constr. Assn. of N.S.; Past Pres., Young President, Organization; Halifax Y.M.C.A.; Liberal; United Church; recreations: golf, curling; Clubs: Ashburn Golf; Halifax Curling; The Halifax (past Pres.); Saraguay; Home: 1760 Connaught Ave., Halifax, N.S. B3H 4C8; Office: 2635 Clifton St., P.O. Box 1571, Halifax, N.S. B3J 2Y3

SALTER, John Henry, B.A.Sc.; retired metallurgist; company executive; b. Woodstock, Ont., 12 Nov. 1912; s. Wesley John and Mary (Adams) S.; e. Univ. of Toronto, B.A.Sc. (Metall. Engn.); Harvard Univ., Advanced Mang. Course; m. Mary Lockhart, d. James Buchanan, 26 March 1937; two d.; Dir., Vestgron Mines Ltd.; Fording Coal Ltd.; Advisory Board, The Royal Trust Company; joined Cominco Ltd. 1934; served as Assayer, Lab. Supr., Plant Supt., Tech. Supvr. and Research Engr., Trail B.C.; 1934-44; Sr. Engr., Projects, 1944-46; Supt. Tech. Information Services, 1946; Asst. Mgr., Personnel Div., 1946-51; Adm. Asst. 1951-56; Gen. Supt. Chems. & Fertilizers Div.; 1954-63; Asst. Gen. Mgr. 1963; Vice Pres., W. Region, 1965; Vice Pres. Operations 1970; Extve. Vice Pres. and Chief-Operating Officer, 1975-77(ret.);Hon. Lieut.-Col., 44th Field Sqdn., RCE; Offr. Bro., Order of St. John; mem., Chem. Inst. Can.; Candn. Inst. Mining & Metall.; Assn. Prof. Engrs. B.C.; United Church; recreations: gardening, fishing; Clubs: Vancouver; Capilano Golf and Country; Home: 1001 - 2246 Bellevue Ave., W. Vancouver, B.C. V7V 1C6

SALTER, Robert Bruce, O.C. (1977), M.D., M.S., F.R.S.C., F.R.C.S.(C), F.A.C.S., Hon. F.R.C.S. (Glasg. 1970, Edin. 1973, Eng. 1976, Ire. 1978); Honorary F.C.S. (South Africa 1975), Hon. F.R.A.C.S (1977), Hon. M.C.F.P.C. (1977); b. Stratford, Ont., 15 Dec. 1924; s. Lewis Jack and Katherine G. (Cowie) S.; e. Lawrence Park Coll. Inst., Toronto; Univ. of Toronto, M.D. 1947, M.S. 1959; Post-grad. studies, Toronto and London, Eng.; m. Agnes Robina, d. Hector McGee, 3 July 1948; children: David, Nancy, Jane, Stephen, Luke; SR. ORTHOPAEDIC SURG., HOSP. FOR SICK CHILDREN; Research Assoc. there and Prof. and Head of Orthopaedic surgery, Univ. of Toronto; Chmn., Bd. of Trustees, Wycliffe Coll., Univ. of Toronto; Trustee, Internat. Grenfell Assn. (Grenfell Mission); apptd. to Med. Research Council Can. 1967; Council of Roy. Coll. of Phys. and Surgs. 1967 (Vice Pres. for Surg. 1970-71, Pres. 1976-78); Gairdner Foundation Internat. Award for Med. Science, 1969; Sims Commonwealth Prof. 1973; Nicholas Andry Award 1974; Charles Mickle Fellowship Award 1975; Offr., Order of Canada 1977; Offr., Order of St. John 1977; Commander, Order of St. John 1981; rec'd hon. degree from Univ. of Uppsala of Sweden (500th Anniv.) 1977; Fellow, Royal Soc. of Can. 1979; appointed Univ. Prof., Univ. of Toronto, 1981; author of numerous scient. articles and textbook related to orthopaedic surg.; Anglican; recreations: oil painting, Canadiana; Home: 79 Rosedale Height Dr., Toronto, Ont. M4T 1C4; Office: 555 University Ave., Toronto, Ont. M5G 1X8

SALTER, W. Ralph, Q.C.; of Candn. antecedents; b. Auburn, N.Y., 22 Jan. 1897; s. Theodore and Alice (Elizabeth (Rumney) S.; came to Canada 1903; e. Parkdale Coll. Inst., Toronto; Univ. of Toronto, B.A. 1918 (1st Class Hons. in Pol. Science and Law; two 1st Class Schols. and Gol Medal, LL.B.) 1921; Osgoode Hall (Schol. 1921); m. Hilda, d. Dr. Herbert H. Best, 13 September 1924; children: Elizabeth Joan, Charles, Ralph; Honorary Counsel SALTER, APPLE, COUSLAND AND KERDEL read law with Kerr, Davidson, Paterson and McFarland, Toronto,

Ont.; called to the Bar of Ontario (with Hons.) 1921; cr. K.C. 1937; mem. of Council, Royal Candn. Inst.; Past Chrmn., Toronto Board of Trade Club and of Toronto Extves. Assn.; Past Secy., Ont. Bar Assn.; Clubs: National; Granite; R.C.Y.C.; Home: 1 Overland Dr., Apt. 229, Don Mills, Ont. M3C 2C3

SALVATORE, Anthony Francis, B.E.; insurance broker; b. Montreal, Que., 5 May 1922; s. Francesco and Angelina (Maimone); e. Inst. Français, Montreal; McGill Univ. B.E. 1949; m. Josephine Elizabeth, d. late Joseph Dyson, 24 Sept. 1948; children: Paul Anthony, John David, Mark Dyson, Elizabeth Anne, Anthony Peter, MaryJo; DIR. REED STENHOUSE INC.; served with Candn. Army in Can., UK and Europe 1943-46; Sigma Chi; recreations: boating, golf, skiing; Clubs: University; Royal Montreal Golf; Canadian Club, NYC; Home: 1160 Park Ave., New York, N.Y. 10028

SAMIS, Bruce Clinton; retired investment dealer; b. Merryfield, Sask., 16 Nov. 1909; s. Harry Clinton and Emma Elizabeth (Walley) S.; e. Univ. of British Columbia (Arts); m. Gladys Helen, d. John Albert Riggall, 18 Oct. 1933; two s. Robert B. E., John D. W.; Pres., Samis and Co. Ltd., Investment Dealers, 1940-70; Dir., Dominion Securities Ltd., 1970-73; Rep. Dominion Securities Corp. Harris & Partners Limited till 1978; Chairman of Board, Pacific Western Airlines till 1975; President, Mr. and Mrs. P. A. Woodward's Foundation; Chairman of the Board of Governors, Vancouver Stock Exchange 1964-65; Dir., B.C. Youth Foundation; Protestant; recreation: fishing; Clubs: Terminal City; Vancouver; Home: Suite 1101, 5555 Yew St., Vancouver, B.C. V6M 3X9

SAMPLE, John T., M.A., Ph.D.; educator; b. Kerrobert, Sask., 4 May 1927; s. George Frederick and Catherine (Scheidt) S.; e. Univ. of B.C., B.A. 1948, M.A. 1950, Ph.D. 1955; m. Dorothy Gwendolyn Lambe, 2 May 1953; children: Catherine, Frederick, Irene, Michael, Patricia; PROF. OF PHYSICS, UNIV. OF ALBERTA since 1965 and Chrmn. of Dept. 1967-76; Exec. Dir., B.C. Secretariat on Research 1981- ; Dir., TRIUMF 1976-81; Scient. Offr., Defence Research Bd. of Can., 1955; joined present Univ. as Asst. Prof. 1958, Assoc. Prof. 1960; Visiting Scientist, Brookhaven Nat. Lab.; author of numerous research papers in physics journs.; mem., Candn. Assn. Physicists; Am. Phys. Soc.; Am. Inst. Physics; Am. Assn. Physics Teachers; Home: 6625 Balaclava St., Vancouver, B.C. V6N 1M1

SAMPLES, Reginald McCartney, C.M.G., D.S.O., O.B.E., . B.Com.; b. 11 Aug. 1918; s. William and Jessie S.; e. Rhyl Grammar Sch., Wales; Liverpool Univ., B.Com.; m. Elsie Roberts Hide, 1947; two s., 1 step-d.; ASSISTANT DIRECTOR, ROYAL ONTARIO MUSEUM since 1979; served with R.N.V.R. (Air Branch) 1940-46; torpedo action with 825 Squadron; Eng. Channel 1942 with Scharnhorst and Gneisenau; wounded; rank Lt. (A); Central Office of Information (Econ. Ed., Overseas Newspapers), 1947-48; Br. Diplomatic Serv. 1948-78; CRO (Brit. Inf. Services, India), 1948; Econ. Information Offr., Bombay, 1948-52; Ed.-in-Chief, BIS, New Delhi, 1952; Depy.-Dir., BIS, New Delhi, 1952-56; Dir., BIS, Pakistan (Karachi), 1956-59; Counsellor (Information) & Dir., BIS, Can. (Ottawa), 1959-65; Counsellor (Information) to Brit. High Commr. India and Dir. BIS India (New Delhi), 1965-68; Ass't Under Secy. of State, Commonwealth Office, 1968; British Consul-General, Toronto 1969-78; recreations: tennis, watching ballet; Clubs: York; Queens Arts and Letters (Toronto) The Naval (London); Address: Royal Ontario Museum, Queen's Park, Toronto, Ont.

SANDERSON, Ronald Eugene; real estate broker; b. Caledon E., Ont., 21 June 1914; s. Walter Murray and Edna Mae (Toye) S.; e. Runnymede Pub. Sch.; Humberside Coll., Toronto, Ont., grad. 1937; m. Jeannette J., d. Edmond Dugas, Nice, France, 11 Aug. 1976; children:

Wendy Mae, Peter Murray; SR. VICE-PRES., A. E. LeP-AGE LTD., (estbd. 1913); joined the Co. in 1950, Vice-Pres. 1953; Partner, with Erieau Ship Bldg. and Dry Dock Co., 1945-50; Dir., Nat. Assn. Real Estate Bds. (U.S.A.); Candn. Real Estate Bd. Foundation; Pres., Candn. Assn. Real Estate. Bds., 1967-68; Past-Pres., S. Peel Real Estate Bd.; Ont. Assn. Real Estate Bds.; Pres., Oakhall Developments; mem., Toronto, S. Peel, Oakville & Brampton Real Estate Bds.; served as Chief Petty Offr., R.C.N.; Conservative; Anglican; recreations: hunting, fishing; Clubs: Oakville; Gun and rods; Lotus Canada; Home: 1116 Balmoral Pl., Oakville, Ont. L6J 2C9;

SÁNDORFY, Camille, Ph.D., D.Sc., F.C.I.C., F.R.S.C.; educator; b. Budapest, Hungary 9 Dec. 1920; s. late Dr. Kamill and Paula (Fényes) S.; e. Cistercian Coll. Budapest 1939; Univ. of Szeged, Hungary B.Sc. 1943, Ph.D. 1946; Sorbonne D.Sc. 1949; m. Rolande d. late Etienne Cayla, Paris, France 24 Aug. 1971; PROF. DE CHIMIE, UNIV. DE MONTREAL since 1959; Asst. Tech. Univ. Budapest 1946; Attaché de Recherches, Centre Nat. de la Recherche Scientifique, France 1947-51; Postdoctorate Fellow, Nat. Research Council of Can. 1951-53; joined Univ. de Montréal 1954; Visiting Prof. Univ. of Paris 1968, 1974; rec'd 1er prix de live scientifique du Qué. 1967; Médaille Pariseau 1974; Killam Mem. Scholarship 1978; Herzberg Award 1980; author "Les Spectres Electroniques en Chimie Théorique" 1959; "Electronic Spectra and Quantum Chemistry" 1964; co-author "Semi-empirical Wave-Mechanical Calculations on Polyatomic Molecules" 1971; over 150 research publs. in chem; mem. Internat. Acad. Quantum-Molecular Science; Home: 4612 Stanley Weir, Montréal, Qué. H3W 2C9; Office: Montréal, Qué. H3C 3V1.

SANDWELL, Bernard Danton, B.A., LL.D.; book publisher; b. Boston, Mass., 24 Jan. 1915; s. Arnold Hugh and Helen (Bower) S.; e. Elem. Schs. in B.C.; Harris Acad., Dundee, Scotland; 2ndary Sch. Que.; Upper Can. Coll. Toronto; Univ. of Toronto, B.A. (Pol. Science & Econ.) 1938; LL.D., Trent Univ., 1980; m. Helen Mary, d. A. R. Kaufman, Kitchener, Ont., 10 June 1939; children: Joan Patricia, Douglas Bernard, Mary Helen; former Chrmn. of Bd. and Pres., Burns & MacEachern Limited, since 1964; Vice Pres. and Dir., House of Anansi Press Ltd., Toronto; upon graduation joined Educ. Dept., Macmillan Co. of Can. Ltd., Toronto; apptd. Asst. Mgr., Coll. and Med. Books Dept., 1946, Mgr. 1948; el. Mang. Dir., Collier-Macmillan Can. Ltd. of Galt and Toronto, 1961; Vice Pres., Superior Box Co., Ltd., Kitchener, 1960-66; during 2nd World War served with the Irish Regt. of Can. in Italy and Holland, rank Capt.; Hon. Bd. mem., Trent Univ. (Chrmn. Bd. Govs. 1971-75); Past Chrmn., Candn. Book Publishers Assn.; Past Trustee, Ont. Waterfowl Research Foundation; Hon. Fellow, Champlain Coll., Trent Univ.; rec'd Centennial medal, 1967; Anglican; recreations: duck shooting, fly fishing, wilderness travel; Home: Reffoli, R.R. 2, Caledon, Ont., L0N 1C0

SANKEY, Charles Alfred, B.A.Sc., M.Sc., Ph.D., D.Sc. (Hon.), F.R.S.A.; F.C.I.C., P.Eng.; b. Waskada, Man., 31 July 1905; s. Charles Arthur and Anna Josephine (Ponton) S.; e. Belleville (Ont.) High Sch.; Upper Can. Coll., Toronto; Univ. of Toronto, B.A.Sc. (Chem. Engn.) 1927 (medallist), (Hall of Distinction 1980); McGill Univ., M.Sc. (Chem.) 1928, Ph.D. (Chem.) 1930; Queens Univ., Hon. D. Sc. 1980; m. Alice Winifred, d. Archibald E. Wallace, 1 Oct. 1938; children: George H. King, John D., Mrs. P. L. Northcott (Grace W.), Janet E.; Chemist, Research Dept., Price Bros. & Co. Ltd., Quebec, Que., 1930-35; joined The Ontario Paper Co. Ltd. as Research Engr. 1935, Research Dir. 1943, Vice-Pres., Research 1965-70; publications and patents in pulp and paper technol., vanillin and other by-products, lignin and lignosulfonic acids; author of "PAPRICAN: The First Fifty Years" 1976; Fellow, American Association Advancement Science; mem., American Institute Chemical Engineers; Am.

Chem. Soc.; Assn. Prof. Engrs. Ont.; Citizenship Award, 1978; Assn. Chem. Prof. Ontario; Technical Section, Canadian Pulp and Paper Association (Honorary Life member, Past Councillor; Past Chairman Research Committee; Past Chrmn. Comte. on Phys. & Chem. Standards; Weldon Medallist; F. G. Robinson Service Award); Tech. Assn. Pulp & Paper Indust. (U.S.); Tech. Sec., Australia & New Zealand Pulp & Paper Indust.; Chancellor, Brock Univ. 1969-74; (Hon. Life mem. Faculty); Freemason; (Past Active mem. Supreme Council 33°; A. & A.S.R. P.D.D. G.M.); recreation: music; Club: Niagara Falls; Home: 46 South Dr., St. Catharines, Ont. L2R 4V2

SANSOM, Lieut.-Gen. Ernest William, C.B. (1943), D.S.O. (1919), K.St.J. (1978); army officer (retired); b. Stanley, N.B., 18 Dec. 1890; s. Maj. John and Minnie (Howe) S.; e. Stanley (N.B.) Pub. Schs.; Univ. of Toronto; m. 1st, Eileen Curzon-Smith (d. 1927); two d.; 2ndly, Lucy Aymor (d. 1974), d. John Waddell, D.Sc., 1 Feb. 1930; one d.; joined 71st York Regt., Candn. Militia, 1906; Lieut. 1907; served in 1st World War, 1914-19; Lieut.-Col. in command of 2nd Bn., and 1st Bn., Candn. Machine Gun Corps: apptd. to Candn. Permanent Forces 1920; organ. and commanded Roy. Candn. Machine Gun Bgde. until 1923; Staff Coll., Camberley, 1924-25; G.S.O.2, Halifax, N.S., 1926-27; Nat. Defence H.Q., Ottawa; 1928-30; A.A. and Q.M.G., M.D. No. 12, 1931-34; G.S.O.1 M.D. No. 4, Montreal, 1935-36; Dir. of Mil. Training for Can. 1937-39; proceeded overseas 1939 as A.A. and Q.M.G., 1st Candn. Div.; C.O., 2nd Inf. Bgde. and served as D.A.G., Candn. Mil. H.Q., London, July-Nov. 1940; promoted Maj.-Gen. and to command 3rd Candn. Div. Nov. 1940; 5th Armoured Div., March 1941-Jan. 1943; promoted Lieut.-Gen. and to command 2nd Candn. Corps on organization; invalided to Can. Feb. 1944; Inspector-Gen., Candn. Army Overseas, Jan. 1945; resigned from Candn. Army to contest riding of York-Sudbury in P. Cons. interest, June 1945 (def.) and again in el. Oct. 1947; el. Pres., Candn. Foundation for Poliomyelitis 1951; Past Pres., Royal Candn. Legion (Fredericton, N.B. Br.) and N.B. rep. on Dom. Command; Pres., York-Sunbury Hist. Soc.; Nat. Hist. Sites Bd. of Can.; Adm. Offr. N.B. Liquor Control Bd., 1954-60; P. Conservative; Anglican; recreations: shooting, fishing; Address: R.R. #2, Fredericton, N.B.

SAPP, Allen, R.C.A.; artist; b. Red Pheasant Reserve, Sask. 2 Jan. 1929; has related in oils and acrylics the life of Cree indians on the reservation; exhns. of his work incl. Alwin Gallery, London, Eng. and other galleries in maj. cities across Can. and USA incl. The McMichael Candn. Coll. Kleinberg, Ont.; subject of CBC TV 'Telescope' 1971 and "News Profile" 1973; chosen with other artists for Nat. Film Bd. Documentary 1973; subject of book chapter in "Portraits of the Plains" by Grant MacEwan 1971; rec'd Can. Council Arts Bursary 1969; UNICEF internat. chose painting "Christmas Evening" to highlight 1979 Children's Fund Christmas card selection; painting presented to Princess Margaret by Sask. Govt. 1980; Address: 7283 Cambie St., Vancouver, B.C. V6P 3H2.

SARGENT, B(ernice) Weldon, M.B.E. (1946), M.A., Ph.D., F.R.S.C.; university professor; b. Williamsburg, Ont., 24 Sept. 1906; s. Henry J. and Ella V. (Dillabogh) S.; e. Chesterville (Ont.) High Sch.; Morrisburg (Ont.) Coll. Inst.; Queen's Univ., B.A. (Hons.) 1926, M.A. 1927, Univ. Cambridge (1928-30), Ph.D. 1932; m. Dorothy Estelle, d. Otis E. and Mabel (Gordon) Gage, Kingston, Ont. 24 Aug. 1940; Emeritus Prof. of Physics, Queen's Univ., since 1972; Head of the Dept. there 1951-67; R. Samuel McLaughlin Research Prof. 1954-72; mem., Nat. Research Council of Can., 1956-62; joined Queen's Univ. as a Lectr., Dept. of Physics, 1930; Asst. Prof., 1936-43; Associate Research Physicist, 1943; Sr. Research Physicist, Principal Research Physicist, 1949-51, Head of Nuclear Physics Br., 1945-51, Asst. Dir. in charge of Physics Subdiv., 1951, Atomic Energy Project, Nat. Research

Council, Chalk River, Ont.; awarded Coronation Medal 1953; Candn. Assn. Physicists Medal 1959; publications: scient. papers on radioactivity, ranges of beta particles, diffusion of neutrons, neutron physics of heavy water reactors, photonuclear reactions, nuclear spectroscopy and the history of physics; mem., Candn. Assn. Physicists; Home: 4 - 115 Wright Cres., Kingston, Ont. K7L 4T8

SARLOS, Andrew, C.A.; b. Hungary, 24 Nov. 1931; s. Julius and Frederika (Szigeti) S.; e. Pub. Sch., Hungary; Univ. of Budapest, Faculty of Econ., grad. 1956; C.A., Toronto, 1962; m. Mary Fennes, Aug. 1958; one s., Peter; PRESIDENT MACKENZIE & SARLOS LTD.; Pres., HCI Holdings Ltd.; Chrmn. Policy Comte., Elliott & Page Ltd.; Dir., Cineplex Corp.; Dir., MSZ Resources Ltd.; Dir., GM Resources Ltd.; Mackenzie & Sarlos Ltd.; Chrmn. and Dir., Temagami Oil & Gas Ltd.; recreations: sailing; Clubs: Albany; Donalda; Home: 19 Barnwood Ct., Don Mills, Ont. M3A 3G2; Office: Ste. 1120, 120 Adelaide St. W., Toronto, Ont. M5H 1V1

SARWER-FONER, Gerald J., C.D., M.D., F.R.C.P.&S.(C), F.R.C. Psych. (Gt. Br.); psychiatrist; educator; b. Volkovsk, Poland 6 Dec. 1924; s. Michael and Ronia (Caplan) S-F.; e. Univ. of Montreal B.A. (Loyola Coll.) 1945, M.D. 1951; McGill Univ. D. Psychiatry 1955; Western Reserve Univ. Psychiatry 1952-53; Candn. Inst. of Psychoanalysis 1958-62; m. Ethel d. I. Sheinfeld, Montreal, Que. 28 May 1950; children: Michael, Gladys, Janice, Henry, Brian; PROF. AND CHRMN. OF PSYCHIATRY, UNIV. OF OTTAWA since 1974; Dir. Dept. of Psychiatry Ottawa Gen. Hosp; Consultant in Psychiatry, Royal Ottawa Hosp.; Nat. Defence Med. Centre Ottawa; Ottawa Civic Hosp.; Children's Hosp. of E. Ont.; Hôpital Pierre Janet, Hull; Chrmn. Scient. Program Comte. VI World Cong. of Psychiatry, Honolulu 1977; Chrmn. Comte. on Psychiatry and the Law 1974-77; Chrmn. Task Force on Model Commitment Code Am. Psychiatric Assn. 1975-77; mem. Panel on Psychiatry, Defence Research Bd. of Can. 1958-62; Adv. Comte. on Health City of Westmount, Que. 1969-74; Gov. Queen Elizabeth Hosp. Montreal (Dir. of Psychiatry 1966-71); Consultant to Prot. Sch. Bd. Westmount and N.D.G. 1966-71; Ottawa Bd. of Educ.; Consultant in Psychiatry and Dir. Psychiatric Research Queen Mary Veterans' Hosp./McGill Univ. 1955-61; Prof. of Psychiatry, Univ. of Ottawa since 1971; Visiting Prof. of Psychiatry Laval Univ. since 1964; Demonst., Lectr., Asst. and Assoc. Prof. of Psychiatry McGill Univ. 1955-71; Lectr. in Psychiatry Univ. of Montreal 1953-55; Visiting Prof. of Psychiatry Chicago Med. Sch. 1968-76; Hassan Azima Mem. Lectr. Soc. Biol. Psychiatry; First Samuel Bellet Mem. Lectr. Inst. of Law & Psychiatry Univ. of Pa. 1978; Sandoz Visiting Prof. of Psychiatry of Candn. Med. Schs. 1976-77; Karl Stern Mem. Lecture, U. Ottawa, Fac. Medecin, 1979; Simon Bolivar Lecturer, Am. Psychiatric Assn. Annual Meeting, (New Orleans) 1981; Asst. Psychiatrist and Dir. Psychiatric Clin. Investigation Unit, Jewish Gen. Hosp. Montreal 1955-66, Assoc. Psychiatrist 1961-71; service RCAMC (CA(M), rank Lt. Col.; author "The Dynamics of Psychiatric Drug Therapy" 1960; "Research Conference on the Depressive Group of Illnesses" 1965; "Psychiatric Cross-Roads — The Seventies" 1972; author or co-author over 120 scient. papers, teaching audio and video tapes; Ed-in-Chief "The Psychiatric Journal" Univ. of Ottawa since 1976; Assoc. Ed. "Bulletin Amer. Acad. Pychiat. Law" since 1974; Adv. Ed. "Psychosomatics" since 1978; mem. various ed. bds.; ed. reviewer and contrib. ed. various prof. journs.; Fellow and mem. Bd. Regents, Am. Coll. Psychiatrists; Fellow, mem. off Bd. and Pres., Am. Coll. Psychoanalysts; Foundation Fellow, Royal Coll. Psychiatry (UK); Charter Fellow, Am. Coll. Neuropsychopharmacol.; Fellow, Am. Psychiatric Assn.; Internat. Coll. Psychosomatic Med. (Sec. since 1979-81); Am. Assn. Advanc. Science; Am. Orthopsychiatric Assn.; Am. Acad. of Psycho Analysis; Diplomate, Am. Bd. Psychiatry and Neurology; Founder, Group-Without-A-Name Psychiat-

ric Research Soc.; mem. Candn. Assn. Profs. Psychiatry (Pres. 1975-76); Que. Psychiatric Assn. (Pres. 1966-68, Treas. 1959-66); Candn. Psychoanalytic Soc. (Pres. Nat. Soc. since 1978); Am. Acad. Psychiatry and the Law (Past Pres.); Candn. Psychiatric Assn. (Dir. 1958-62), Soc. for Biol. Psychiatry (Vice-Pres., 1981-) and mem. various other med. assns.; recreations: fishing, swimming, rowing; Clubs: Cosmos (Washington, D.C.); Le Cercle Universitaire; Home: 152 Kamloops Ave., Ottawa, Ont. K1V 7C9; Office: 501 Smyth Rd., Ottawa, Ont. K1H 8L6.

SATOK, David; company president; b. Toronto, Ont., 22 Aug. 1931; s. Max and Molly (Silverberg) S.; e. Oakwood Coll. Inst., Toronto; Univ. of Toronto; m. Lyla, d. late Percy Stern, 12 Dec. 1958; children: Paula, Mark, Maxine, Jonathan; Managing Director, Associated Development Group until 1981; Pres., La Scala Construction; Great Eastern Financial Management of Canada Ltd.; Camaro Resources; Marcana Resources; Asstok Construction Ltd.; Pres., Cedarvale Rate Payers Assn. 1968; Toronto Home Builders Assn. 1969; Past Chrmn. Extve. Comte., Ont. Adv. Comte. on Housing; Chrmn., Candn. Jewish Congress Central Region; Nat. Vice Pres., Candn. Jewish Congress; recreations: book collecting, tennis; Club: York Racquet; Home: 482 Russell Hill Rd., Toronto, Ont. M5P 2S7;

SATTERLY, Jack, M.A., Ph.D., F.R.S.C. (1954). F.G.A.C.; geologist; b. Cambridge, England, 28 Sept. 1906; s. John and May Mary Jane (Randall) S.; e. Univ. of Toronto Schs.; Toronto, Ont.; Univ. of Toronto, B.A. 1927 (Coleman Gold Medal in Geol.), M.A. 1928; Exhn. Overseas Scholar, 1929-30, 1930-31; Univ. of Cambridge, Ph.D. 1931; Princeton Univ., 1931-32; m. Eileen, d. Robert Sims, 2 March 1935; children: Peter Randall, Elizabeth Hamilton; Research Assoc. (hon.), Dept. of Mineralogy and Geol., Royal Ont. Museum since 1971; Student Asst. (summers) and Asst. (winter), Geol. Survey of Can., 1926-30; Asst. (winter) 1928-29; Asst. (summer), Princeton Summer Sch., Montana, 1932; Asst. (winter), Royal Ont. Museum of Mineralogy, Toronto, 1932-33; Geol., Loangwa Concessions (N.R.) Ltd., N. Rhodesia, 1933-34; Student Asst. (summer), Ont. Dept. of Mines, 1934; Geol. Guysborough Mines Ltd., N.S., 1934-35; Prospector (summer) for W. F. James, 1935; Instr. (1935-36), Lectr. (1936-39), Dept. of Geol., Univ. of Toronto; Asst. Dir., Royal Ont. Museum of Geol., Toronto, 1936-39; Geol., Ont. Dept. of Mines, 1939-60; Sr. Geologist 1961-67; Chief, Review & Resources Sec., Geol. Br., Ont. Dept. Mines and N. Affairs 1967-71; Jack Satterly Geochronology Lab., Roy. Ont. Museum named in his honour, 1977; Centennial Medal 1967; new mineral from Yukon named Satterlyite in his honour, 1978; Fellow, Geol. Assn. Can.; mem., Candn. Inst. Mining & Metall. since 1974, mem. since 1941; mem., Mineral. Assn. Can.; Toronto Ornithol. Club; recreation: bird-watching; Home: 15 Aldbury Gdns., Toronto, Ont. M4N 1B6; Office: Royal Ontario Museum, 100 Queen's Park, Toronto, Ont. M5S 2C6

SAUCIER, John James, Q.C.; b. Calgary, Alta., 15 May 1903; s. Xavier and Ann Josephine (Flanagan) S.; e. St. Mary's Sch. and Western Can. Coll., Calgary; Univ. of Alta., B.A. (cum laude) 1924; LL.B. (cum laude) 1926; m. Lillian, d. Dr. C. H. DuBois, San Rafael, Cal., 15 June 1933; children: Marie DuBois, Suzanne, Carolyn; Assoc., Bennett Jones, Honorary Bencher and Past President, Law Society of Alberta; read law with J. A. Weir, K.C., Edmonton, Alberta; called to the Bar of Alta. 1927; cr. K.C. 1946; Asst. Private Secy. to Prime Minister of Can. 1934-35; Pres., Calgary Bd. of Trade, 1947; mem., Calgary Bar Assn. (Past Pres.); mem., Law Soc. Alta. (Past Pres.); Pres. (1968-69), Candn. Bar Assn.; Past Pres., Calgary Chamber Comm.; Past Chrmn., Alta. Press Council; Conservative; United Church; recreations: swimming, walking, reading; Clubs: Ranchmen's (Past Pres.); Calgary Golf and Country; Home: 2725 Carleton St. S.W.,

Calgary, Alta. T2T 3L1; Office: 3200, 400 - 4th Ave. S.W., Calgary, Alta. T2P 0X9

SAULNIER, Lucien, C.C.(1971), Dr. de l'U. (Montréal); public administrator; b. Montreal, 25 July 1916; s. Exhimer and Régina (Gravel) S.; e. Comn. des Ecoles Catholiques de Montréal; Univ. de Montréal, Dr. de l'U. 1966; m. Juliette Beaulieu, 5 Sept. 1938; children: Jean-Pierre, André, Jean-Maurice, Louise, Monique, Hélène; CHRMN. OF BOARD, HYDRO QUEBEC AND JAMES BAY ENERGY CORP., since 1978; entered municipal politics in Montreal civic el. 1954; re-el. 1957, 1960, 1962 and 1966; Co-Founder Civic Party of Montreal 1960; mem. Bd. of Adm. and Extve. Comte. of Candn. Corp. for 1967 World Exhn. (Expo '67); Chrmn., Montreal Civic Extve. Comte. 1960-70; Chrmn. Extve. Comte., Montreal Urban Community 1970-72; Pres. and Gen. Mgr. Quebec Ind. Development Corp. 1972-75; Head, Que. Housing Corp and Consultant to Extve. Council P.Q. since 1975; Chrmn. of Bd., Hydro-Québec, 1978-80; Chrmn. of Bd., Regie des Installations Olympiques 1980; mem. Bd. of Adm. and Extve. Comte., Univ. of Montreal; Econ. Council of Can.; Blier Comn.; Montreal Bd. Trade; Chambre de Comm. du Dist. de Montréal; R. Catholic; recreations: gardening, music, reading, golf; Clubs: Mt. Stephen; Garrison; Home: 2159 Bord du Lac, Ile Bizard, Que.;

SAUNDERS, Bernard S., M.B.E.; Vice President and Mang. Dir., Wabasso Ltd.; Vice Pres., Gen. Mgr. and Dir., Woods Bag & Canvass Co. Ltd.; Vice Pres. and Dir., Treeford Ltd.; Dir., Hugh Francis & Co. Inc. (Memphis, Tenn.); left England in 1924 to come to Canada and spent pre-war years in the food industry; served in 2nd World War with R.C.A.; discharged with rank of Major; after the war engaged in the paper industry; joined Woods Bag interests in 1954 as Asst. Gen. Mgr. and named Vice Pres. in 1956; apptd. to present position (controlled by Woods) in 1958; Home: 2396 Graham Blvd., Town of Mount Royal, Que.; Office: 1825 Graham Blvd., Town of Mount Royal, Que. H3R 1H2

SAUNDERS, Doris B., M.A., M.Litt., LL.D.; b. Winnipeg, Man., 1901; d. W. J. Saunders; e. Univ. of Man., B.A. and M.A.; Oxford Univ., Diploma in Educ. 1923, and B. Litt. 1936; Univ. of B.C., LL.D. 1957; Prof. Emeritus, Univ. of Man., 1968; M.Litt. Oxford Univ., 1979; formerly Prof. of English and sometime Dean of Jr. Women there; awarded Travelling Scholar., Candn. Fed. of Univ. Women, 1925-26; Winifred Cullis Lecture Fellowship, Eng., 1966; Hon. Fellow, Univ. Coll., Univ. of Man., 1968; mem., Winnipeg Poetry Soc.; Pres., Univ. Women's Club of Winnipeg, 1943-45; Pres., Women's Br., Candn. Inst. Internat. Affairs, 1951; Pres. Candn. Fed. of Univ. Women, 1955-58; Pres. Winnipeg Br., Humanities Assn., 1967-68; Pres. Women's Candn. Club of Winnipeg, 1976-78; Pres., Twenty Club, 1980-82; awarded Centennial Medal (Canada), 1967; Delta Delta Delta; Home: 503, 245 Wellington Cres., Winnipeg, Man. R3M 0A1

SAUNDERS, Hon. Edward, B.A.; judge; b. Toronto, Ont. 17 June 1925; s. Robert Porteous and Annie Maude (West) S.; e. Crescent Sch. 1937 and Upper Can. Coll. 1943 Toronto; Trinity Coll. Univ. of Toronto B.A. 1949; Osgoode Hall Law Sch. 1953; m. Mary Louise d. late Ven. Archdeacon Julian Sale Smedley, Port Arthur, Ont. 16 Sept. 1950; children: Elizabeth Anne, Michael James, Catherine Mary; JUSTICE, SUPREME COURT OF ONT.; called to Bar of Ont. 1953; cr. Q.C. 1968; McMaster Montgomery & Co. 1953-54; Osler Hoskin & Harcourt 1954, Partner 1959; Warden Christ Ch. Deer Park 1974-76; Dir. Downtown Ch. Workers Assn. 1976-77; mem. Candn. Tax Foundation (Gov. 1966-69); Candn. Bar Assn.; served with Candn. Army 1943-46, UK and N.W. Europe 1944-45, Reserve Militia 1947-51; Anglican; recreations: tennis, golf; Clubs: Badminton & Racquet; Toronto Golf; Univer-

sity; Home: 153 Rosedale Hts. Dr., Toronto, Ont. M4T 1C7; Office: Osgoode Hall, Toronto, Ont. M5H 2N5.

SAUNDERS, Ernest Erle, Q.C., B.A., B.C.L.; lawyer; telecommunications executive; b. Bridgeport, Conn. 18 July 1925; s. Erle Freeman and Ora Mable (Jackson) S.; came to Can. 1929; e. Elizabeth Ballantyne Sch. and Montreal West (Que.) High Sch.; McGill Univ. B.A. 1947, B.C.L. 1950 (Gold Medal, MacDonald Travelling Scholarship); Ecole du Droit Univ. de Paris; m. Janine Marie d. Charles Rowe 2 Aug. 1952; two d. Mary Evelyn, Patricia Jan; VICE PRES. LAW AND CORPORATE AFFAIRS, BELL CANADA 1978- ; called to Bar of Que. 1950; cr. Q.C. 1968; law practice O'Brien, Hall, Saunders, Montreal 1951-78, Partner 1962-78; Lectr. in Law McGill Univ. 1964-68; Lectr. Prof. Training Sch. Bar of Que. 1969-70; served with RCAF 1943-45, rank Flying Offr. (Navig.); mem. Barreau de Montréal (Treas. 1967-68); Barreau du Qué.; Candn. Bar Assn.; Internat. Bar Assn.; Assn. Candn. Gen. Counsel; Candn. Chamber Comm.; Protestant; recreations: golf, curling, skiing, scuba diving; Clubs: St-James's; Royal Montreal Curling; Royal Montreal Golf; Laurentian Lodge Ski; Home: 605 Côte St-Antoine Rd., Westmount, Qué. H3Y 2K5; Office: 1050 Beaver Hall Hill, Montréal, Qué. H2Z 1S4.

SAUNDERS, Harry James, insurance executive; b. Eastleigh, Hampshire., Eng. 8 Sept. 1932; e. Peter Symonds, Winchester; m. Aileen Elizabeth McNamee 2 Aug. 1958; children: Anthony John, Michael Charles, Kathleen Allison; MGR. FOR CAN., ZURICH INSURANCE CO. 1974- ; Underwriter, Ocean Accident, Southampton, Eng. 1953; Underwriter present co. Toronto 1956, Alta. Br. Mgr. Edmonton 1960, Asst. Mgr. Toronto 1966, Automobile Mgr. Can. 1968, Asst. Mgr. Can. 1973; served with RAF 1951-52; Dir. Ins. Bureau Can.; past Pres. Ins. Inst. Ont.; recreations: golf, sailing, skiing, squash, bridge; Clubs: Ontario; Mississauga Golf & Country; Ontario; Home: 1048 Roper Ave., Mississauga, Ont. L5H 1B9; Office: 188 University Ave., Toronto, Ont. M5H 3C3.

SAUNDERS, Peter Paul, B.Com.; financier; b. Budapest, Hungary, 21 July 1928; s. Peter Paul, LL.D., and Elizabeth (Halom) Szende; came to Canada, 1941; e. Vancouver Coll. (1944); Univ. of British Columbia, B.Com. 1948; m. Nancy Louise, d. R. G. McDonald, New Westminster, B.C., 11 Feb. 1956; two d. Christine Elizabeth, Paula Marie; Chrmn. and Pres., Versatile Corp.; Dir., Bralorne Resources Ltd.; Dir., B.C. Broadcasting Co. Ltd.; Wajax Ltd.; Western Broadcasting Co. Ltd.; Bank of British Columbia; Northwest Sports Enterprises Ltd.; Canfor Invests. Ltd.; mem., Vancouver Adv. Bd., National Trust Co. Ltd.; Pres., Vancouver Art Gallery Assn.; Gov., Vancouver Opera Assoc.; after grad. from univ., employed by Candn. Pac. Rly. Co. as an Acct. in Vancouver, B.C., remaining with the Rly. for three years during which had several promotions; one of the Founders of Laurentide Financial Corp. Ltd. and its Pres. from inc. in 1950 to 1966; Dir., B.C. and Yukon Region, Candn. Cancer Soc.; Vancouver Symphony Soc.; mem. B.C. Regional Comte., Candn. Chamber Comm.; mem., Vancouver Bd. Trade; recreations: golf, skiing, hunting, boating; Clubs: University; Vancouver; Roy. Vancouver Yacht; Shaughnessy Golf and Country; Thunderbird Country (Rancho Mirage); Vancouver Lawn Tennis & Badminton; Home: 2186 S.W. Marine Dr., Vancouver, B.C. V6P 6B5; Office: P.O. Box 49153 — Bentall Centre, 595 Burrard St., Vancouver, B.C. V7X 1K3

SAUNDERS, Richard Lorraine de Chasteney Holbourne, M.D., F.R.M.S., F.R.S.E.; university professor; b. Grahamstown, S. Africa, 29 May 1908; s. Col. Frederick Anastasius (F.R.C.S.) and Lucy Anderson (Meiklejohn) S.; e. St. Andrews Coll., Grahamstown, S. Africa; Rhodes Univ. there; Edinburgh Univ., M.B., Ch.B., 1932, M.D. 1940; m. Sarah Cameron, M.B., Ch.B., d. Maj. Alexander Cameron Macintyre, M.C., 25 Mar.

1936; Research Prof. Inst. da Rocha Cabral, Lisbon, and Radcliffe Infirmary, Oxford, Eng.; served as Visiting Phys., Settler's Hosp., S. Africa, 1932-33; House Surg., Bradford Royal Infirmary, Eng., 1933; Lectr. and Demonst. in Anat., Univ. of Edinburgh, 1933-37; came to Can. 1937; Asst. Prof. of Anat., Dalhousie Univ., 1937-42; Assoc. Prof. 1942-48; Prof. of Path. Anat. and Dir., of Med. Museums there, 1948-50; Head of Anatomy Dept. 1950-73 when emeritus; author "X-ray Microscopy" in Encyc. Microscopy & Microtechnique; co-author, "X-ray Microscopy in Clinical and Experimental Medicine", "Microfocal Radiography" and numerous articles; mem., Anat. Soc. of Great Britain; American Assn. of Anat.; Fellow, Am. Assn. Advanc. Science; New York Acad. Science; Alpha Eta Chapter of Phi Rho Sigma (Hon. mem.); Alpha Omega Alpha; recreations: fishing, sketching; Home: "Summerhill", West Jeddore by Head of Jeddore, Halifax Co., N.S. B0J 1P0

SAUNDERS, Richard Merrill, M.A., Ph.D.; historian; b. Gloucester, Mass., 16 Nov. 1904; s. Lee and Grace Martha (Merrill) S.; e. Quincy High Sch., Mass.; Clark Univ., B.A. 1924, M.A. 1925; Cornell Univ., Ph.D. 1931; m. Anna Blythe, d. Robert Haldane West, 30 June 1929; one d., Sarah Jane; Instr. in Hist., Am. Univ. of Beirut, Lebanon, 1925-28; Teaching Asst. in Ancient Hist., Cornell Univ., 1928-30; Boldt Fellow in Hist. there, 1930-31; Lect. in Hist., Univ. of Toronto, 1931-38, Asst. Prof. 1938-43, Assoc. Prof. 1943-54, Prof. 1954-71; former Assoc. Ed., "Candn. Hist. Review"; mem., Fed. Ont. Naturalists (Past Dir.); Past Pres., Toronto Field Naturalists' Club; Pres. (1966-67), Candn. Hist. Assn.; Past Chrmn., Toronto Ornithological Club; author of "French Canada and Britain" (transl. of "Ton Histoire est une épopée", by Abbé Arthur Maheux), 1942; "Education for Tomorrow" (ed.) 1946; "Flashing Wings", 1947; "Carolina Quest", 1951; co-author of "Canadian Wildflowers", 1976; has contrib. to journs., articles on French Can., the Middle East, on birds and on historiography; United Church; recreations: ornithology, nature photography; Home: 9 McMaster Ave., Toronto, Ont. M4U 1A8

SAUNDERS, William Allison Baxter, M.Sc.; retired Alta. public service; b. Calgary, Alta., 11 Nov. 1914; s. Harry Percy and Eva Rosalie (McCain) S.; e. High Sch., Calgary; S. Alta. Inst. of Technol., Dipl. in Technol. for Geol. and Surveying, 1935; Univ. of N.B., B.Sc. (Civil Engn.) 1941, M.Sc. (Civil Engn.) 1950; Banff Sch. of Advanced Mang., grad.; m. Mary Constance, d. late James H. Conlon, 13 April 1942; children: Dr. William Murray, Dr. Harry Duston, Constance Janet Dutczak; Depy. Min., Dept. Housing And Pub. Works, Alta. (former Pres. N. Alta. Inst. Technol.); served with RCAF 1941-45; Past mem., Senate, Univ. of Alta.; Past Pres., Alta. Assn. Prof. Engrs.; mem., Engn. Inst. Can.; Club: Edmonton Rotary (past pres.); Home: 7306 - 154A St., Edmonton, Alta. T5R 1V1; Office: 10050 - 112 St., Edmonton, Alta.

SAUNDERSON, Hugh Hamilton, B.A', M.Sc. Ph.D., D.Sc., LL.D., F.C.I.C.; university president (emeritus); b. Winnipeg, Man., 23 Nov. 1904; s. Hugh Hamilton and Lina Dunham (DuVal) S.; e. Univ. of Manitoba, B.A. 1924, M.Sc. 1930; McGill Univ., Ph.D. 1932, D.Sc. 1962; m. Patricia Jean, d. late Dr. C. E. Coke, 15 June 1934; children: Carol Patricia, Hugh Lawrence; Pres. Emeritus, Univ. of Manitoba since 1970; Dir. Sanatorium Bd. Man.; Research Chemist with International Paper Co., 1933-34; Asst. Prof. of Chem., Univ. of Manitoba, 1934-42; Assoc. Prof., 1942-45; Prof. of Chem. and Dean of Arts & Science, 1945-47; Dir., Div. of Information Services, Nat. Research Council, Ottawa, 1947-54; Pres., Univ. of Manitoba 1954-70; Hon. Fellow, Internat. Coll. Dentists; Chem. Inst. Can.; Hon. mem. Pharmaceutical Assn.; United Church; Clubs: Manitoba; Canadian; Rotary; Home: 311 Kelvin, Tuxedo, Winnipeg, Manitoba. R3P 0J1

SAUVE, Hon. Jeanne, P.C.; b. Prud'Homme, Sask., 26 April 1922; d. Charles Albert and Anna (Vaillant) Benôit; e. Notre-Dame du Rosaire Convent, Univ. d'Ottawa; Univ. de Paris, Faculty des Lettres; Hon.Dr. (Science) Univ. of New Brunswick; m. Hon. Maurice, s. J. H. Sauvé, Montreal, Que., 24 Sept. 1948; SPEAKER OF HOUSE OF COMMONS 1980- ; one s. Jean-François; free-lance journalist; former Dir., CKAC; Bushnell Communications Ltd.; Assistant to Director of Youth Section of UNESCO Paris, 1950-51; Panel mem. interviewer and commentator CBC Radio-Can., CTV, and contrib. to NBC and CBS, 1952-72; edit. contrib. to Montreal Star, Toronto Star 1970; el. to H. of C. for Ahuntsic g.e. Oct. 1972, July 1974, May 1979 and Feb. 1980; sworn of the P.C. and appointed Minister of State for Science and Technology 1972; Min. of Environment 1974; Min. of Communications 1975-79 Advisor to the Sec. of State for External Affairs for relations with the French-speaking world, Nov. 1978; elected Speaker of the House of Commons, April, 1980; Director, Institute for Research on Public Policy; Pres., Candn. Inst. of Pub. Affairs 1964; mem. Centennial Comn. 1967; Secretary Gen. Fed. des Auteurs des Artistes du Can.; mem. Bd. Dir., Montreal Y.M.C.A.; Union des Artistes (mem. of Bd. 1961, Vice Pres., 1968-70); mem. ACTRA; R. Catholic; Office: Parl. Bldgs. Ottawa, Ont. K1A 0A6

SAUVE, Hon. Maurice, P.C.(Can.), B.A., LL.B., Ph.D.; b. Montreal, P.Q., 20 September 1923; s. Joseph Honoré and Mélanie (Duguay) S., both French Candns.; e. St. Mary's Coll., B.A. 1942; Univ. of Montreal, LL.B. 1948; London Sch. of Economics; Univ. Paris, Ph.D. (Econ.) 1952; m. Jeanne, d. Charles Albert Benoit, Ottawa, Ont.; one s. Jean-François; VICE PRES., ADM., CONSOLIDATED-BATHURST INC., since Sept. 1968; Dir., BP Canada; Benson & Hedges (Canada) Ltd.; The Halifax Insurance Co.; Commercial Life Assurance Company of Canada; Automobiles Renault Canada Ltée.; Andrès Wines Ltd.; Barclays Canada Ltd.; M.P. for Iles-de-la-Madeleine 1962-68; Min. of Forestry Feb. 1964-Oct. 1966; Min. of Forestry & Rural Devel. 1966-68; Present title, Exec. Vice-Pres., Admin. and Public Affairs; Liberal; R. Catholic; Home: 281 McDougall, Outremont, P.Q. H2V 3P3; Office: 800 Dorchester Blvd. W., Montreal, Que. H3B 1Y9

SAVAGE, George Alfred, C.A.; insurance executive; b. Waterford, Ont., 6 Sept. 1914; s. Thomas Charles and Martha Alice (Christie) S.; e. C.A. 1950; m. Dorothy Ruth, d. Dr. A. H. Fromow, 3 June 1944; children: Ruth Blair, Margaret Robertson, Stephen Harris, John Burgess; DIR., PRESIDENT AND CHIEF EXTVE. OFFR., GUARANTEE CO. OF NORTH AMERICA since 1971; Dir. and Vice-Pres., Frank Cowan Co. Ltd.; Dir., Princeton Holdings Ltd.; Secretary-Treasurer, Kitchens Ltd., Brantford, 1949-50; Sr. Partner, Waters, Savage, Horne & Ronson (C.A.'s), Brantford and Simcoe, 1950-65; Vice Pres. and Secy.-Treas., Duo-Matic of Canada Ltd., Waterford, 1965-68; Pres. and Mgr. 1968-70; Vice Pres. and Dir., Brant Beverages Ltd., Brantford, 1954-71; Secy.-Treas. and Dir., London Bottling Ltd., London, 1969-71; Pres. and Dir., Duo-Heet Distributors Ltd., Waterford, 1968-70; Dir., Beth Sar Shalom Mission Inc. (Hamilton) 1973-80; Am. Bd. Mission to the Jews (New York, N.Y.) 1975-80; mem., Indust. Commission Waterford 1965-71; Inst. C.A.'s Ont.; recreation: numismatics; Homes: 90 Temperance St. E., Waterford, Ont.; Office: Place du Canada, Montreal, Que.

SAVAGE, Hugh Baldwin, B.Com., C.A.; b. Montreal, P.Q., 10 May 1913; s. Edward Baldwin and Marion Douglas (Creelman) S.; e. Pub. and High Schs., Montreal; Trinity Coll. Sch. Port Hope, Ont.; McGill Univ., B.Com., L.I.A.(1936); Inst. of Chart. Accts., C.A.; m. Margaret Elizabeth, d. John B. How, Bronxville, N.Y.; one s. John Edward Clark; Dir., Marine & Power Equipment Ltd.; Sparta Consultants Ltd.; McDern Binding

Ltd.; Malabar Ltd.; Audit Clerk, Peat, Marwick, Mitchell & Co., 1936-38; Div. Acct., Canadian Industries Ltd., 1939; Group Acct., Defence Industries Ltd., 1940-41; Lectr. in Accountancy, McGill Univ. and Sir George Williams Univ., 1946-48; formed own firm of Chart. Accts., 1946 becoming Savage, Kendall, Trudell & Co., 1948 and presently H. B. Savage and Co.; served in 2nd World War with R.C.N.V.R., 1941-45; Lt. Commdr., R.C.N.(R); Mun. Councillor, City of Montreal, 1957-60; Dir., City Improvement League, City of Montreal; Pres., Jr. Chamber Comm., 1960; Chrmn., Prot. Bd. of Sch. Commrs., City of Montreal; Commr., Prot. Sch. Bd. of Greater Montreal; author of "Tax-Saving"; mem., Inst. of Chart. Accts. Que.; Chart. Inst. of Secys. (Assoc.); Am. Inst. of Mang.; Montreal Bd. Trade; Am. Marketing Assn.; Montreal Advertising & Sales Extves. Assn.; Chambre de Comm.; Protestant; Liberal; recreations: swimming, skiing, hunting, fishing; Clubs: University; Mount Bruno; Reform; M.A.A.A.; Naval Officers; Mount Royal Tennis; Home: 4044 Trafalgar Road, Montreal, P.Q. H3Y 1R2; Office: 1310 Greene, Montreal, P.Q. H3Z 2B2

SAVARD, F. G. Kenneth, D.Sc.; educator; b. Quebec City, Que. 26 Feb. 1918; s. Joseph D. and Isabel Jane (Davis) S.; e. Laval Univ. B.Sc. 1939, D.Sc. 1946; McGill Univ. M.Sc. 1943; m. 1stly 1945 Lorraine I. Kelly; children: Christopher James, Julia Ann Jane Mitchell; m. 2ndly Shirley E. FitzGerald 1973; PROF. OF BIOCHEM., UNIV. OF MONTREAL since 1977, Chrmn. of Biochem. since 1977; Scient. Med. Research 1947 — 73; Adm. Med. Research Programs 1973 — 77; affiliations: Univ. of Miami Sch. of Med.; Worcester Foundation Exper. Biol.; Cleveland Clinic Research Foundation; Sloan-Kettering Inst. N.Y.; Ayerst, McKenna & Harrison Ltd. Montreal; Consultant: Am. Cancer Soc. N.Y. Awards Program; Nat. Inst. Health-Center Population Research Washington; author over 150 med. and scient. publs.; Dir. Laurentian Hormone Conf.; mem. various prof. scient. socs.; recreation: sailing; Home: E1204 — 4870 Côte des Neiges, Montreal, Que. H3V 1H3; Office: (C.P. 6128) Montreal, Que. H3C 3J7.

SAVARD, Guy, M.B.E., D.Eng.; research director; b. Quebec, Que., 3 July 1915; s. late Justice Alfred and Kathleen (Logan) S.; e. High Sch. of Que., 1933; Royal Mil. Coll., 1937; Ecole Supérieure de Soudure, Paris, 1938; D.Eng. (hon.), R.M.C. 1976; m. Anne Marie, d. late Royal Le Sage, 24 May 1941; children: Mrs. William Bowen (Carolyn Anne), Logan; CONSULTANT, CANADIAN LIQUID AIR since 1981; Dir. Of Research, Liquid Air Corp., 1964-81; joined present Co. as Welding Engr., 1939-40; Mgr., Devel. & Engn., 1950-58; Mgr., Que., 1959-63; Mgr., Far East Oxygen Co., Singapore, 1946-49; served with Royal Candn. Dragoons overseas 1941-45, second-in-command; Ald., Vaudreuil, 1960-63; Dir. of Research, Can. Liquid Air Co. 1964-80; mem. Nat. Research Council of Can.; Pres., Que. Div., Candn. Arthritis Soc.; mem., Eng. Inst. Can.; Nat. Sci. and Eng. Research Council; Airey Award of Cdn. Inst. of Mining and Metallurgy 1974; R. Catholic; recreations: sailing, farming; Club: University; Home: 539 Grosvenor Ave., Westmount, Que.; Office: 1155 Sherbrooke St. W., Montreal, Que. H3A 1H8

SAVARD, Jean-Guy, éducateur et linguiste; né. St-Alban, Qué. 7 août 1931; f. Alfred et Angélina (Lahaye) S.; e. Univ. Laval B.A. 1955, B.Péd. 1956, L. en Péd. 1963, L.ès L. 1965, Dipl. d'études supérieures en linguistique 1966; ép. Réjeanne Marcotte 25 août 1956; enfants: Jacinthe, Raymond, Yolande, Vincent; Prof. Univ. Laval depuis 1966; Dir. intérimaire du Dépt. de linguistique 1970-71; Dir. du Centre internat. de recherche sur le bilinguisme 1972-78; Prés. de la Comm. de la recherche, Univ. Laval depuis 1978; gratification pour succès dans l'enseignement; Ministère de l'éduc. du Qué. 1961; Bourse d'études du Ministère de l'éduc. du Qué. 1963-66; subventions de recherche du Conseil des arts et du Se-

crétariat d'Etat (Ottawa) et du Ministère de l'éduc. du Qué.; auteur "La valence lexicale" 1970; "Les indices d'utilité du vocabulaire fondamental français" 1970; "Bibliographie analytique de tests de langue/Analytical Bibliography of Language Tests" 1969 et 1977; co-auteur "Le vocabulaire disponible du français" 1971, du Test Laval formules A, B, et C et de Minorités linguistiques et interventions: Essai de typologie 1978; mem. Ass. canadienne de linguistique appliquée (prés. 1977-79); Ass. canadienne de linguistique; Ass. des prof. de français des univ. canadiennes; Ass. canadienne française pour l'avancement des sciences; membre correspondant de la Fédération Cdn. des études humaines, 1971-81; mem. du comité des candidatures de la Fédération Candn. des études humaines, 1980- ; Del. de l'Assn. Candn. de ling. appliq. à la Comm. des tests de l'Assn. internat. de ling. appliq. 1980- ; responsable du Comite des Actes du Ve. congrès internat de ling. appliq. tenu à Montréal, 1978; mem. de l'Assn. Candn. d'admins. de recherche univ. 1980- ; R. Catholique; résidence: 3334 Radisson, Ste-Foy, Qué. G1X 2K3

SAVARD, Pierre, D.E.S., D.ès L.; historien; éducateur; né Québec, Qué. 10 juin 1936; f. Charles E. et Gilberte (Lavallée) S.; é. Petit Séminaire de Qué.; Univ. Laval B.A., B.Ph., L. ès L., Univ. de Lyon D.E.S. (histoire); D. ès L. Univ. Laval (histoire); ép. Susan Blue f. Rear Adm. Frederick B. Warder, Ocala, Fla. 6 Juin 1960; enfants: Marie, François, Michel; PROF. TITULAIRE D'HISTOIRE, UNIV. D'OTTAWA; Dir. du Centre de Recherche en Civilisation Canadienne-Française depuis 1973; Prof. Adjoint puis Agrégé d'Histoire, Univ. Laval 1961 — 72, Dir. Dép. d'Histoire 1970 — 71; Prof. Agrégé puis Titulaire d'Histoire, Univ. d'Ottawa depuis 1972; Président de la Société historique du Canada 1979-80; Dir; Dir., 'Revue de l'Université' d'Ottawa; Prés. du Groupe d'Etude des Arts chez les Franco-Ontariens (rapport 1977); Prés., Conseil canadien de recherches sur les humanités, 1975-76; auteur; "Jules Paul Tardivel, La France et les Etats-Unis 1851 — 1905" 1967; "Le Consulat Général de France à Québec et à Montréal 1859 — 1914" 1970; 'Aspects du catholicis canadien-français du XIXe siècle', 1980; manuels scolaires, articles et chapitres d'ouvrages sur l'histoire culturelle du Can. français; mem.; Conseil d'Admin.; Fondation d'études du Can.; Multicultural Hist. Soc. Ont. (mem. du Conseil); Soc. Royale du Can.; Soc. historique du Can. (Ancient Président); Inst. d'histoire de l'Amérique Française; Soc. des Dix; catholique; récréations: marche à pieds, voyages; Adresse: 3242 chemin Southgate, Ottawa, Ont. K1V 8W2; Bureau: CRCCF Université d'Ottawa, Ottawa, Ont. K1N 6N5.

SAVILE, Douglas B(arton) O(sborne), B.S.A., M.Sc., Ph.D., D.Sc., F.R.S.C.; mycologist; b. Dublin, Ireland, 19 July 1909; s. Hugh Osborne and Kathleen E. (Barton) S.; e. Braidlea Sch., Bristol, Eng.; Weymouth Coll., Weymouth, Eng.; McGill Univ., B.S.A. (Macdonald Coll.) 1933, M.Sc. 1934, D.Sc. (Hon.) 1978; Univ. of Mich., Ph.D. 1939; m. Constance Eleanor, d. late Walter B. Cole, 1939; children: Harold A., Elizabeth (Mrs. D. F. Rhodes); Research Assoc. Emeritus, Can. Dept. Agric. (formerly Princ. Mycologist there); has carried out Bot. and Mycological field work in Newfoundland, N.S., N.B., Quebec, Ontario, Manitoba, Alta., B.C., Keewatin and Franklin; worked in Arctic 1950, '58, '59, '60 and '62; served with R.C.A.F. (Aero-Engn. Br.), 1941-43; author of "Collection and Care of Botanical Specimens", "Arctic Adaptations in Plants", and some 125 research papers; Fellow, American Association Advanc. of Science (mem. Council 1962, '64, '65); Arctic Inst. N.Am.; mem., Am. Ornithols. Union; Am. Soc. Plant Taxonomists; Candn. Bot. Assn. (Lawson Medal 1976); Candn. Phytopathol. Soc.; Internat. Assn. Plant Taxonomists; Mycological Soc. Am.; Soc. for Study of Evolution (Ed. Bd. 1959-61); recreations: ornithology, gardening, hist. of science; Home: 357 Hinton Ave., Ottawa, Ont. K1Y 1A6; Office: Biosystematics

Research Inst., Central Experimental Farm, Ottawa, Ont. K1A 0C6

SAVILLE, Frederick Alan; executive; b. Launceston, Tasmania 30 Jan. 1922; s. Frederick and Kathleen (McKenzie) S.; e. Scotch Coll. Tasmania; m. Margaret Pauline d. William Gordon Allen March 1945; two s. James Michael, Jeffrey Stephen; PRESIDENT, CEO AND DIR. COMMERCIAL UNION ASSURANCE CO. OF CANADA and Commercial Union of Canada Holdings Ltd. since 1975; Chmn., Pres., and CEO, Canada Accident and Fire Assurance Co.; Pres., CEO and Dir., Stanstead & Sherbrooke Insurance Co.; Pres. and CEO for, Canada, Commercial Union Assurance Co. Ltd.; Dir., Insurance Bureau of Canada; Insurers Advisory Organization of Canada; joined Commercial Union, Launceston, Tasmania 1938, Br. Mgr. Hobart 1955; Mgr. Queensland Australian Mutual Fire Insurance Society Ltd. 1959; State Mgr. Commercial Union Western Australia 1964; Gen. Mgr. Commercial Union of Rhodesia and also Mgr. for Central Africa 1973; Gen. Mgr. Commercial Union of New Zealand 1974; served with Royal Australian Air Force 1941-46, Coastal Command RAF, European Theatre, rank Flight Lt.; Presbyterian; Clubs: Toronto, National, Ontario; Home: 210 Riverside Dr., Toronto, Ont. M6S 4A9; Office: Commercial Union Tower, Toronto-Dominion Centre, Toronto, Ont.

SAVOIE, Hon. Georges, B.A., LL.L.; judge; b. Roberval, Lake St. John, Qué. 29 Nov. 1927; s. Dr. Louis-Philippe and Thérèse (Bernier) S.; e. Jésuites Coll. St. Charles Garnier, Québec City B.A. 1948; Laval Univ. LL.L. 1951; m. Gisèle d. late Joliette P. Lemieux, Québec City, Qué. 15 Nov. 1952; children: Louis Philippe, Marc, Claire, Pierre; JUDGE, SUPERIOR COURT OF QUE. since 1978; called to Bar of Qué. 1952; C.R. Q.C. 1968; Jr. Partner, Desruisseaux, Fortin & Savoie 1954 — 58; private law practice Richmond, Qué. 1958 — 71; Sr. Partner, Leblanc Barnard & Associates 1971, Barnard, Fournier, Savoie 1972, Fournier, Savoie, Demers & Associates 1974 — 78; Mayor, Town of Richmond 1967 — 68; Campaign Mgr. and Legal Advisor Lib. cands. prov. and fed. els. 1963 — 66; Pres. R.C. Sch. Bd. and Commr. 1960 — 68; Pres., St. Francis Bar 1968, also served as counsellor and Secy.; R. Catholic; recreations: sailing, jogging, skiing; Home: 1570 Longchamp, Sherbrooke, Qué. J1J 1J1; Office: Court House, 191 Palais St., Sherbrooke, Qué. J1H 4R1.

SAVOIE, Leonard N., B.Sc., M.B.A.; transportation executive; b. Manchester, N.H., 8 Aug. 1928; came to Canada 1928; s. Joseph Peter and Angelina (Desmarais) S.; e. Queen's Univ., B.Sc. (Mech. Engn.) 1952; Univ. of Detroit, M.B.A. 1955; m. Elsie Anne, d. Albert Berscht, 9 June 1951; children: Deborah Anne, Judith Lynn, Andrew Peter; PRESIDENT AND CHIEF EXTVE. OFFR., ALGOMA CENTRAL RAILWAY since 1970; Pres., Algoma Steamships Ltd.; Algocen Mines Ltd.; Dir., Algoma Steel Corp.; All Candn.-Am. Investments Ltd.; Casualty Co. of Can.; Dominion of Canada General Insurance Co.; E-L Financial Corp. Ltd.; Empire Life Ins. Co.; Newaygo Forest Products Ltd.; Ontario Hydro; Thibodeau-Finch Express Ltd.; with Kelsey-Hayes Canada Ltd. as Indust. Engr., Windsor, Ont. 1952; Mang. Consultant, P.S. Ross & Partners, Toronto 1960; Pres. and Gen. Mgr., Kelsey Hayes Canada Ltd. 1964; mem. Bd. Trustees, Plummer Hospital; Dir., Windsor Indust. Comn. 1969-70; mem. Assn. Prof. Engrs. Ont.; Engn. Inst. Can.; Candn. Chamber Comm.; Young Presidents Organ. Inc.; recreations: golf, bridge, fishing, photography; Clubs: Toronto; Algo; Golf & Country; Railway (Toronto); Home: 19 Atlas St., Sault Ste. Marie, Ont. P6A 4Z2; Office: 289 Bay St., Sault Ste. Marie, Ont. P6A 5P6

SAVOIE, M. Adelard, O-C. (1976),Q.C., B.A., B.S.S., D.C.L., LL.D., F.R.S.A.; b. Neguac, New Brunswick, 21 Nov. 1922; s. Prudent B. and Genevieve (Basque) S.; e. Lower Neguac (N.B.) Elem. Sch., 1930-38; St. Joseph's Univ., B.A. 1945; Laval Univ., B.S.S. 1948; D.C.L., Mt. Allison 1969; LL.D., St. Thomas 1971; m. Jeannette, d. Edmund B. Rouselle, Sheila, N.B., 4 Sept. 1950; children: Michelle, Carole, Jacques; PARTNER, YEOMAN, SAVOIE, LEBLANK & DEWITT; former Pres., Univ. of Moncton; called to the Bar of N.B. 1950; practised law 1950-69, Moncton, N.B.; Gen. Organizer, Acadian Bicentenary Celebrations, 1954-55; Dir., Greater Moncton Community Chest, 1956-60; Dir., Dieppe Credit Union, 1956-66; Pres., L'Imprimerie Acadienne Ltée, 1956-65; Legal Advisor, Acadian Assn. of Educ. (Vice Pres., 1954-65); La Société Nationale des Acadiens since 1957; La Societé l'Assomption since 1955 (1st Gen. Vice Pres. since 1959); Past Dir., Comn. Permanente des Etats Génereaux du Can. Français; mem. N.B. Research and Productivity Council; Greater Moncton Water Comn.; Anti-Inflation Bd. (1977); Dir., Centennial Internat. Devel. Program; Extve. mem., Candn. Nat. Comn. for Unesco; Vanier Inst. of Family; Candn. Assn. Educ.; Pres., Assn. Canadienne des Éducateurs de Langue Française (1964-66); M.L.A. of N.B., 1948-52; Mayor of Town of Dieppe, 1952-54; mem. Mun. Council Westmorland Co., 1952-54; Dir., Young Lib. Fed. Can., 1950-52; mem., Moncton Barristers Soc.; Barristers Soc. N.B.; Candn. Bar Assn.; Internat. Comn. Jurists; Liberal; R. Catholic; recreations: reading, music, outdoor life; Clubs: Richelieu; Beauséjour Curling; Home: 375 Grand Pré St., Dieppe, N.B. E1A 1Y3

SAVORY, Roger Mervyn, Ph.D., F.R.S.C.; educator; b. Peterborough, Eng. 27 Jan. 1925; s. Henry Savory; e. Oxford Univ. B.A. (Oriental Studies) 1950; Univ. of London Ph.D. (Persian Studies) 1958; m. Kathleen Mary d. late Bertram Plummer 27 March 1951; children: Jill Elizabeth Hawken, Julian Roger; PROF. OF MIDDLE EAST AND ISLAMIC STUDIES, UNIV. OF TORONTO 1976- , mem. Gov. Council of Univ. 1982- ; Lectr. in Persian Sch. Oriental & African Studies Univ. of London 1950-60; Assoc. Prof. of Near E. Studies present Univ. 1960-61, Assoc. Prof. of Islamic Studies 1961-65, Prof. and Assoc. Chrmn. 1965-68, Prof. and Chrmn. 1968-73, Prof. 1973-76 (dept. change to present name); cross-apptd. to Trinity Coll. Middle E. & Islamic Studies, Religious Studies 1976; Ed. Asst. New Ed. "Encyclopaedia of Islam" 1954-56, Ed. Secy. Eng. Ed. 1956-60; author "Iran Under the Safavids" 1980; co-author "Persia in Islamic Times—A Practical Bibliography of its History, Culture and Language" 1981; Ed. "Introduction to Islamic Civilisation" 1976; transl.. "The History of Shah ʿAbbas the Great (Tārīk-e ʿAlamārā-ye ʿAbbāsī)" 2 vols. 1978; numerous book chapters, contribs. to encyclopaedias, articles, reviews; served with Brit. Army and Foreign Service in Iran (1945-47), 1943-47; mem. Middle E. Studies Assn. N. Am. (Dir. 1969-71, Vice Pres. 1973-74); Anglican; recreation: gardening; Home: 55 Mason Blvd., Toronto, Ont. M5M 3C6; Office: Trinity College, Toronto, Ont. M5S 1H8.

SAWYER, John Arthur, B.Com., M.A.; Ph.D.; economist; b. Toronto, Ont., 24 Aug. 1924; s. Arthur J. and Bessie S. (Livingstone) S.; e. Oakwood Coll. Inst., Toronto, 1943; Univ. of Toronto, B.Com. 1947, M.A. 1948; University of Chicago, Ph.D. 1966; m. Virginia Kivley, d. late George M. Peterson, 30 Dec. 1952; three s. Peter Douglas, Robert James, Alan Bruce; PROF., FACULTY MANG. STUDIES, UNIV. OF TORONTO, since 1965, Prof., Dept. Pol. Econ. since 1969; Dir., Inst. Policy Analysis 1975-80; Associate Dean, School of Graduate Studies 1970-72; Lectr., Dept. of Pol. Econ., Univ. of Alta., 1949-50; Asst. Prof., Dept. of Econ., Royal Mil. Coll. of Can., 1951-53; Econ., Dom. Bureau of Stat., Ottawa, 1953-60; joined present Univ. as Asst. Prof. 1960; apptd. Assoc. Prof. 1961; mem., Candn. Econ. Assn.; Am. Econ. Assn.; Econometric Soc.; mem. Bd. of Dir., Data Clearing House for Soc. Sciences in Canada, 1973-78; Harold Innis Fdn. 1977- ; recreations: photography, golf; Home: 118 Betty Ann Dr., Willowdale, Ont. M2N 1X4

SAXTON, Andrew E.; financial executive; b. Szeged, Hungary, 24 Sept. 1929; s. Francis and Rhoda (Schaffer) Szasz; e. The Holy Order of the Piarists Szeged, Hungary; Univ. of British Columbia; children: Richard Leslie Douglas, Shelley Susan, Anne Marie, Andrew E. Jr.; PRES. ANDREW SAXTON & SONS LTD.; Dir., Grouse Mountain Resourts Ltd.; British Columbia Television Broadcasting System Ltd.; CHAN T.V. Vancouver; CHEK T.V. Victoria; Kaiser, Saxton & Stiles, Inc.; Victoria Shipping Co. Inc.; co-founder Laurentide Financial Corp. Limited 1950; subsequently Extve. Vice-Pres., Gen. Mgr. and Dir. to 1966; Dir., Internat. Soc. & Fed. of Cardiology; Candn. heart Foundn.; Vancouver Bd. of Trade; Phi Kappa Pi; Presbyterian; Clubs: Vancouver Lawn Tennis & Badminton; Shaughnessey Golf & Country; Royal Vancouver Yacht; Home: 3637 Angus Dr., Vancouver, B.C. V6J 4H4.

SAYWELL, John Tupper, M.A., Ph.D.; writer and university professor; b. Weyburn, Sask. 3 April 1929; s. John Ferdinand Tupper and Vera Margaret S.; e. Victoria Coll., Univ. of B.C., B.A., M.A.; Harvard Univ. Ph.D.; divorced; children: Elizabeth Lynn, John Stephen Tupper, Graham Anthony Tupper; UNIVERSITY PROFESSOR and Professor of History and Environmental Studies, York University; General Editor, Clarke Irwin Collegiate Texts in Hist.; Lect., Univ. of Toronto, 1954; Asst. Prof. 1957; Editor, Candn. Hist. Review 1957-63; Assoc. Prof., 1962; Ed., Candn. Annual Review, 1960-79; Associate Prof. and Dean, York Univ., 1963-73; author of: "The Office of Lieut.-Gov." 1957; "The Candn. Journal of Lady Aberdeen" 1960: "How Are We Governed"; "Parliament and Politics" (column) Candn. Annual Review, 1960/79; numerous mag. and newspaper articles and book reviews; mem., Candn. Hist. Assn.; Candn. Pol. Sc. Assn.; recreation: tennis; Home: 158 Fulton Ave., Toronto, Ont. M4K 1Y3; Office: 4700 Keele St., Downsview, Ont. M3J 1P3

SCALES, Alan K., Q.C., LL.B.; lawyer; b. Summerside, P.E.I. 16 Oct. 1934; s. Austin Alexander and Lillian (Dobson) S.; e. Univ. of W. Ont. Honours Business Adm. 1958; Dalhousie Univ. LL.B. 1961; m. Patricia K. d. late Dr. Harold Shaw 6 July 1963; children: Brian Geoffrey, Gary Shaw, Caroline Patricia; SR. PARTNER, SCALES, GHIZ, JENKINS & McQUAID: Dir. The Island Telephone Co. Ltd.; mem. Adv. Bd. Olands Breweries Ltd.; Canada Permanent Companies; called to Bar of P.E.I. 1961; cr. Q.C. 1973; Gov. Dalhousie Univ.; Dir. Confed. Centre of Arts; P. Conservative; United Church; recreations: golf, tennis; Home: 99 Prince Charles Dr., Charlottetown, P.E.I. C1A 3B1; Office: 70 Kent St., Charlottetown, P.E.I. C1A 8B9.

SCALES, Austin Alexander, B.S.A., LL.D.; industrialist; b. St. Eleanors, P.E.I., 4 Jan. 1886; s. Henry and Gulielma (Lefurgey) S.; e. Coll. of Agric., Truro, N.S., Grad. 1911; Ont. Agric. Coll., Guelph, Ont. B.S.A. 1918; LL.D., U.P.E.I. 1972, m. Lillian Helen d. John Dobson, Summerside, P.E.I., 19 July 1928; children: Joan (Mrs. Raymond M. Stunden), David A; J. Henry, Alan K., Brian, Nora; PRESIDENT AND MGR., ISLAND FERTILIZERS LTD.; Dir., Bank of Canada 1958-60; Past Pres., Prince County Hosp. and Past Chrmn. of Bd. of Trustees, Summerside, P.E.I.; mem., Charlottetown Bd. of Trade; former mem. Summerside Bd. Trade; Charlottetown Br., Agricultural Institute of Canada; Past Pres., Industrial Enterprises Ltd.; Protestant; Clubs: Canadian; Rotary; Home: 78 Brighton Rd., Charlottetown, P.E.I., C1A 1T9; Office: Riverside Dr., (Box 334) Charlottetown, P.E.I. C1A 7K7.

SCARFE, Neville Vincent, M.A.; university dean; b. England, 8 March 1908; s. Albert and Emilie Laura (South) S.; e. King Edward VI Grammar Sch., Chelmsford, Eng.; Univ. of London, B.A. 1928 (1st Class Hons. in Geog. 1927); Teachers Dipl. 1928, M.A. 1932; m. Gladys Ellen, d. Rowland Hunt, England, 1 Aug. 1936; three s. Colin David, Brian Leslie, Alan John; Sr. Geog. Master; Bemrose Sch., Derby, Eng., 1928-30; Lectr., Geog., Univ. of Nottingham, 1931-35; Sr. Lectr. and Head of Dept., Inst. of Educ., Univ. of London, 1935-51; Visiting Prof. of Educ., Syracuse Univ., 1948-49; McGill Univ., 1951, Clark Univ., 1952; Dean of Educ., Univ. of Manitoba, 1951-56; Dir. of Press Censorship Min. of Information, London 1939-45; Co-ordinator, UNESCO Internat. Seminar, Montreal, 1951; Chrmn., International Comn. on the Teaching of Geog., 1952-56; Dean of Education, Univ. of B.C. 1956-73; Publications: 'Land of Britain', 1941; 'Handbook of Suggestions on Teaching Geography', 1951; Philosophy of Education', 1952; 'Conflicting Theories of Education', 1959; 'A New Geography of Canada', 1963; and numerous articles on educ. and geog. in learned journs.; Pres., National Council for Geog. Educ. of Am., 1965; mem., Candn. Assn. Univ. Profs.; Candn. Assn. of Profs. of Educ.; Candn. Assn. Geographers; Candn. Educ. Assn.; Philos. of Educ. Soc.; Liberal; Anglican; recreation: travel; Home: 2233 Allison Rd., Vancouver, B.C. V6T 1T7.

SCARGILL, Matthew Harry, Ph.D., F.R.S.C.; educator; b. Barnsley, Yorks. Eng. 19 Sept. 1916; s. late Matthew and Emma (Lister) S.; e. Wheelwright Grammar Sch. Eng.; Univ. of Leeds B.A. 1938, Ph.D. 1940; m. Eileen Mildred d. late Harry Tomlin, Summerland, B.C. 1948; PROF. OF LINGUISTICS, UNIV. OF VICTORIA since 1964, Dean of Grad. Studies 1968-70, Dir. Lexicographical Centre since 1964; rec'd Queen's Silver Jubilee Medal 1978; author "Modern Canadian English Usage" 1974; "Short History of Canadian English" 1977; "Dictionary of Canadianisms" 1967; Home: 2883 Sea Point Dr., Victoria, B.C. V8N 1S9; Office: Clearihue Building, University of Victoria, victoria, B.C. V8W 2Y2.

SCARTH, John C., B.Sc.; industrialist; b. Sherbrooke, Que., 5 July 1924; s. H. A. and Christine (MacIntosh) S.; e. Stanstead (Que.) Coll.; Bishop's Univ., B.Sc. 1945; m. Ellen Marion, d. late H. G. Frazer, Richmond, Que., 8 June 1948; children: Ian Campbell, Harriet Jane; PRESIDENT AND CHIEF EXTVE. OFFR., E. B. EDDY FOREST PRODUCTS LTD, since 1972; Chrmn. of Bd., Eastern Fine Paper Inc., Brewer; Maine; Dir.; George Weston Ltd.; Eddy Paper Co. Ltd.; Pineland Timber Co. Ltd.; Rudolph McChesney Lumber Co. Ltd.; joined the KVP Co., Kalamazoo, Mich., 1948; Pulp Mill Chem., Espanola, Ont., 1948-52; Sales Mgr. Toronto 1952-60; Asst. to Pres., Kalamazoo, 1960-62; Vice Pres., KVP Sutherland, Marketing, 1962-65; Vice Pres. Marketing, Brown Co., New York, 1965-66; Tech. Dir., Forest Products, Chase Manhattan Bank, New York, 1966-67; Pres., Deerfield Glassine Co.; Munro Bridge, Mass., 1968-69; joined present co. as Extve. Vice Pres. 1969; Gov., Ashbury Coll.; mem., Candn Pulp & Paper Assn.; Pulp & Paper Indust. USA; Protestant; recreations: swimming, golf; Clubs: Rideau; Royal Ottawa Golf; Home: 8 Qualicam St., Ottawa, Ont. K2H 7G8; Office: Eddy St., Hull, Que..

SCHACHTER, Albert, D.Phil.; educator; b. Winnipeg, Man. 22 Aug. 1932; s. Harry and Rebecca (Raskin) S.; e. McGill Univ. B.A. 1955; Oxford Univ. D.Phil. 1968; m. June d. late Charles Hoysapr 11 Aug. 1956; PROF. OF CLASSICS, McGILL UNIV. 1972- , Chrmn. of Classics 1970-74; Visiting Fellow, Wolfson Coll. Oxford 1982-83; author "Cults of Boiotia" Vols. 1 and 4 1981; co-author "Ancient Greek: A Structural Programme" 1973; Gen. Ed. "Teiresias" 1971- ; various articles ancient Boiotia and teaching of ancient Greek; mem. Classical Assn. Can. (Council); Hellenic Soc.; Am. Philol. Assn.; Archaeol. Inst. Am.; Home: 5559 Borden Ave., Côte St. Luc, Montreal, Que. H4V 2T7; Office: 855 Sherbrooke St. W., Montreal, Que. H3A 2T7.

SCHAEFER, Carl Fellman, R.C.A. (1964); artist; b. Hanover, Ont., 30 Apl. 1903; s. John D. S.; e. Pub. and High Schs, Hanover, Ont.; Ont. Coll. of Art, Toronto, Ont., under Arthur Lismer, J. E. H. MacDonald, C. M. Manley, George A. Reid, Robt. Holmes and J. W. Beatty; Central Sch. of Arts and Crafts, London, Eng.; Univ. of Waterloo, D. Lett. (Hon.) 1976; m. Lillian Marie Evers, N. Dakota, 17 Mar. 1927; children: Mark, Paul; Instr., Ont. Coll. of Art., Toronto, Ont., 1948; Head, Drawing & Painting Dept., 1956-68; Chrmn. Emeritus, Painting Dept. 1968-70; Free-Lance Artist and Designer until 1931; Instr. of Art, Central Tech. Sch., Toronto, Ont., 1931-47; Instr., Art Centre, Art Gal. of Toronto, 1935-37; Dir. of Art, Hart House, Univ. of Toronto 1934-56; Instr. Candn. Recreational Inst., Nat. Council, Y.M.C.A., Lake Couchiching Ont., 1934-36; Instr. in Art, Trinity Coll. Sch., Port Hope, Ont., 1936-39, 1946-48; awarded Fellowship in painting by Guggenheim Mem. Foundation, N.Y., 1940-41; Instr., Sch. Fine Arts (painting div.), Queen's Univ., 1946-50, Doon School of Fine Arts, Doon, Ont., 1952-64; Upper Can. Acad. 1965; Instr. Schneider Sch. F.A., Actinolite, 1967- ; Exhns. incl. Group of Seven, 1928 and 1931; 1st Internat. Expn. of Wood Engraving Poland, 1933; Century of Cdn. Art, Tate Gallery, London, 1938; 11th Internat. Exhn. Water Color, Brooklyn Museum 1941; 20th Int. Chicago Art Inst. 1940-41; New York World's Fair, 1939; Nat. Gal., London, Eng. 1944; Museum of Modern Art, Paris, 1946; 50 Years of Painting, Art Gallery of Toronto, 1949; first Candn. Exhn. to Asia (India, Ceylon, Pakistan), 1955; Australia, 1955-56; first Biennial, Sao Paulo, Brazil, 1951-52; Nat. Gallery, Washington, 1950; Internat. Exhn., Contemporary Candn. Art, Mexico City, 1960; Exhn. of Candn. Paintings to Bermuda 1962; Retrospective Exhn. 1969; 'Candn. Painting in The Thirties' (cross-Can.) 1975; 'Half a Century of Water Colour' Art Gallery of Ont. 1975; one-man show, Roberts Gallery, Toronto, 1963, 70; Commonwealth Arts Festival, England, 1965; '300 Years of Canadian Art', Nat. Gallery, Ottawa, 1967; Aviation Paintings, Candn. War Museum, Ottawa, 1972; Eposition of Candn. Paintings, China, 1975; "Carl Schaefer, Thirty-Five Years of Painting, 1932-67;, McLaughlin Gallery, Oshawa, touring 1976; Portrait Drawings, Jerrold Morris Gallery, Toronto, 1976; 100 Yrs., Evol. of the Ont. Coll. of Art; Art Gallery of Ont., 1976, Art Gallery of York Univ., Art Deco Tendencies, 1977; Cdn. Paintings in the Univ. of Toronto, Art Gallery of Ont., 1978; Univ. of Waterloo, 1976; Carl Schaefer Paintings 1931-67, Tom Thompson Memor. Gallery, Owen Sound, 1978; 20th Cent. Drawings, The Gallery Stratford, 1979; Carl Schaefer's Hanover Paintings in the Thirties, , 1980, Edmonton Art Gallery; Victoria Art Gallery, B.C.; Glenbow Museum, Calgary; Saskatoon Art Gallery; Dalhousie Art Gallery; Confederation Centre of the Arts 1981; Art Gallery of Ont. 1981; participated in 12 Centennial Exhns.; held over 16 one-man shows, rep. in several permanent coll. incl. Nat. Gallery Ottawa, Art Gallery of Ont., Hart House (Univ. of Toronto), Queen's Univ., Art Gallery of Hamilton, Dalhousie Univ., Vancouver Art Gallery, Royal Bank of Can.; Va. Museum Fine Arts Richmond, Art Bank Can., Univ. of Guelph, Winnipeg Art Gallery, Edmonton Art Gallery, Memorial Univ. of St. John's, Nfld., Confed. Art Gallery, Charlottetown, P.E.I., Hopkins Art Gallery, Dartmouth Coll., Hanover, N.H., Shell Resources, Calgary, Alta., A. E. Ames and Co., Toronto, Dartmouth Heritage Museum, Dartmouth, N.H., Rodman Hall Art Gallery, St. Catharines, Ont., Sarnia Art Gallery, Windsor A. Gal.; Read Paper Co.; Metropolitan Life; Sir George Williams Univ., Montreal; Tom Thomson Mem. Gal., Owen Sound; Glenhurst Gal., Brantford; 7 Annil Hill A. Gal, Burnaby B.C.; Candn. Imp. Bank of Comm., Toronto; Rothmans Limited and private collections in Canada, England and U.S.A.; served in 2nd World War, 1943-46; appointed Official War Artist R.C.A.F. 1943; wounded twice 1944; awarded Coronation Medal, 1953; Centennial Medal, 1967; Queen's Jubilee Medal 1978; Publications: "Watercolour as a Painting Medium", Maritime Art Magazine, 1943; "Atlantis on the Artic Circle", Canadian Art Magazine, 1946; "Northward Journal, 24 drawings with diaries, 1926-27; "Carl Schaefer, Twelve Northern Draw-

ings 1926-33" 1979; "Carl Schaeffer, Twelve Farm Drawings 1927-32", 1980; el. Life Fellow, International Institute Art and Letters, 1958; Fellow, Ont. Coll. of Art, Toronto, 1976; Fellow, Roy. Soc. of Arts, London, Eng. 1977; mem., Canadian Group of Painters 1936; Canadian Society of Graphic Art (1932); Canadian Soc. of Painters in Watercolour (1933); Ord. of Can., 1978; Royal Cdn. Academy of Arts (Assoc., 1949, Academician 1964); Home: 157 St. Clements Ave., Toronto, Ont. M4R 1H1.

SCHAEFER, Donald Elwood McKee; investment dealer; b. Fordwich, Ont., 1 Sept. 1923; s. Ira H. and Hazel (Sothern) S.; e. Fordwich (Ont.) Cont. Sch.; m. Elizabeth M., d. late Frank Allin, 5 July 1947; children: Judith Anne, John David; SENIOR VICE PRESIDENT & DIR., NESBITT THOMSON & CO. LTD., joined present firm as Mgr., Kitchener, Ont. Office, 1954-57; Mgr. Institutional Sales, Toronto, 1957-60; Mgr., Prov. of Que., 1960-65; Appointed Dir., 1962; Asst. Sales Manager, Montreal, 1965-66; Senior Vice President 1966; served with the R.C.A.F. during the 2nd World War; Conservative Protestant; recreations: curling, golf, boating; Clubs: Engineers; Beaconsfield (Que.) Golf; Thornhill (Ont.) Country; London Hunt; The London; Home: 389 Dundas St., Apt. N184, London, Ont.; Office: 171 Queens Ave., Ste. 701, London, Ont. N6A 5J7.

SCHAEFER, H. G., B.Com., C.A.; b. Calgary, Alta. 18 Oct. 1936; s. Ernest A. S.; e. Univ. of Alta. B.Com. 1957; Alta. C.A. Inst. C.A. 1959; m. Joanne M., d. Gustav Wiedenroth, Edmonton, Alta. 26 Sept. 1958; children: Katherine, Karen, Robert; SR. VICE PRES., FIN., AND CORP. PLANNING, TRANSALTA UTILITIES CORP.; Pres. and Dir., Transalta Resources Corp.; Vice Pres. Finance and Dir., AEC Power Ltd.; Canada Northwest Land Ltd.; Dir., Kanelk Transmission Co. Ltd.; Western Fly Ash Ltd.; Financial Executives Inst.; Alta. Children's Hosp.; Financial Extves. Inst. Can. (Chrmn. 1978-80; Pres. 1977-78); Protestant; recreations: badminton, squash, tennis; Clubs: Ranchmens; Winter; Home: 1239 - 18th St. N.W., Calgary, Alta. T2N 2G8; Office: 110-12th Ave. S.W., Calgary, Alta. T2P 2M1.

SCHAEFER, Theodore Peter, M.Sc., D.Phil., F.C.I.C., F.R.S.C.; educator; b. Gnadenthal, Man. 22 July 1933; s. Paul Jacob and Margareta (Wiebe) S.; e. Mennonite Coll. Inst. Gretna, Man. 1950; Univ. of Man B.Sc. 1954, M.Sc. 1955; Oxford Univ. D.Phil. 1958; m. Nicola Caroline d. late Hugh Sewell, Majorca, Spain 26 Dec. 1960; children: Catherine, Dominic Peter, Benjamin Richard; PROF. OF CHEM. UNIV. OF MAN.; joined Univ. Man. as Asst. Prof. 1958; Visiting Scient. Nat. Research Council Can. Ottawa 1959, 1962, Argonne Nat. Labs. USA 1967, 1968, Nat. Phys. Lab. UK 1960, 1964, Oxford Univ. 1964, 1971; Extve. Chem. Inst. Can. 1977-79; mem. Nat. Research Council Can. Grants Comtes. 1975-77; mem. Nat. Sci. & Eng. Research Council of Can., 1980-83; rec'd Noranda Award Chem. Inst. Can. 1973; Herzberg Award Spectroscopy Soc. Can. 1975; Teaching Award, Grad. Students Assn., Univ. of Manitoba, 1980; author 185 papers and reviews nuclear magnetic resonance; mem. Candn. Assn. Univ. Teachers; Protestant; recreations: walking, reading, music; Home: 210 Oak St., Winnipeg, Man. R3M 3R4; Office: 330 Parker Bldg., Winnipeg, Man. R3T 2N2.

SCHAFFTER, Henry John Pemell, M.A.; headmaster; b. Isfahan, Iran 12 Dec. 1925; s. Dr. Charles Merrill, O.B.E., F.R.C.S. (Edin.) and Grace (Brownrigg) S.; e. Trent Coll. Derbyshire, Eng. 1944; King's Coll. Cambridge Univ. B.A. 1950, M.A. 1955; m. Catherine Anne d. Frederick Joseph Overend 14 July 1952; children: Catherine, Timothy, Jann; joined Upper Can. Coll. Toronto 1950, Head of Hist. and Geog. Dept. Prep. Sch. 1954-68, Asst. to Headmaster Prep. Sch. 1967-69; Headmaster St. Johns Ravenscourt Sch. Winnipeg 1969-77; St. Michael's Univ. Sch. since 1977; served with RAF 1944-47; Bd. mem. Winnipeg Symphony Orchestra 1975-77; Hon. Fellowship St. John's Coll. Univ. of Man. 1973; co-author "The Winds of Change" 1961; "Modern Perspectives" 1969; mem. Candn. Independent Schs. Headmasters' Assn.; Pacific Northwest Independent Schs. Headmasters' Assn.; Lit. Soc. Cambridge; Kings Coll. Cambridge Rugby Football Club; Queen's Jubilee Medal; R. Catholic; recreations: antique firearms, Candn. hist.; Home: Gate House, St. Michael's Univ. Sch., 3400 Richmond Rd., Victoria, B.C. V8P 4P5.

SCHEIDEGGER, Jean-Pierre, B.Com.; banker; b. Neuchatel, Switzerland 21 May 1942; e. Zurich Coll. of Finance B.Com. 1966; m. Dolores 1964; children: Nathalie, Jean-Jacques; PRESIDENT AND CHIEF EXTVE. OFFR., UNION BANK OF SWITZERLAND; Rep. present Bank, Montreal 1973-78, First Vice Pres. Zurich 1978-81; mem. Swiss Candn. Chamber Comm.; Clubs: Royal Montreal Golf; National; Empire; Home: 18 Tudor Gate, Willowdale, Ont. M5L 1N4; Office: (P.O. Box 500) 1000, 2 First Canadian Place, Toronto, Ont. M5X 1E5.

SCHEIRER, Lloyd H., publisher; b. Fort Frances, Ont., 2 June 1938; s. Fred and Eleanore (Kitsch) S.; e. Fort Frances (Ont.) High Sch.; Ryerson Polytech. Inst. Toronto; PRESIDENT AND CHIEF EXTVE. OFFR. DIR. McGRAW-HILL RYERSON; served with present Co. 1961- ; Home: 23 Vernham Court, Willowdale, Ont. M2L 2B3; Office: 330 Progress Ave., Scarborough, Ont. M1P 2Z5.

SCHERK, Peter, Ph.D.; educator; b. Berlin, Germany 2 Sept. 1910; s. Alfred and Lea (Spiro) S.; e. Französisches Gymnasium (Coll. Français) Berlin 1929; Univ. of Berlin; Univ. of Göttingen Ph.D. 1935; m. Eva Paula d. Hans Goldschmidt 24 Apl. 1946; children: John, Michael, Margaret; PROF. EMERITUS OF MATH. UNIV. OF TORONTO since 1980; Prof. 1959-80; Hon. Research Fellow, Yale Univ. 1940-41; Postdoctoral Asst. Ind. Univ. 1941-43; Instr. to Prof. Univ. of Sask. 1943-59; Visiting Assoc. Prof. Univ. of S. Cal. 1952-53; Visiting Prof. Univ. of Pa. 1956-57; Visiting Prof., Kiel Univ., 1980; author "Foundations of Geometry" 1976; co-author "Rudiments of Plane Affine Geometry" 1975; author some 55 papers; mem. Royal Soc. Can.; Candn. Math. Cong.; Am. Math. Soc.; Anglican; recreations: music, books, gardening, walking; Home: 247 Yonge Blvd., Toronto, Ont. M5M 3J1; Office: Toronto, Ont. M5S 1A1.

SCHIFF, Harold I., M.A., Ph.D., F.C.I.C.; educator, scientist; b. Kitchener, Ont., 24 June 1923; s. Jacob and Lena (Bierstock) S.; e. Univ. of Toronto, B.A. 1945, M.A. 1946, Ph.D. 1948; m. Dorothy Fane Daphne, d. William Line, 30 Dec. 1948; children: Jack Michael, Sherry Lin; Univ. Prof. York Univ.; PRES. UNISEARCH ASSOC. INC.; Dir., Scintrex Limited; National Research Council Fellow, 1948-50; Asst. Prof., McGill Univ., 1950; Prof. 1960-65 and Dir., Upper Atmosphere Group; Prof., Chrmn., Dept. of Chem. and Dir., Natural Science, York Univ. 1964; Dean of Science 1965-72; Consultant, U.S. Dept. of Comm.; Nuffield Fellow, Cambridge, Univ., 1959-60; author (with L. Dotto), "The Ozone War" 1978; Distinguished Author Award, U.S. Dept. of Comm., 1966; author of over 130 research papers; 50 tech. reports and chapters in three scient. books; mem. Ed. Bd. "Planetary & Space Science", "Internat. Journ. Photochem"; reporter, "Laboratory measurements of Aeronomical interest" Div. II, Internat. Assn. Geomagnetism & Aeronomy; Chrmn., Montreal Sec., Chem. Inst. Can. 1953 (Chrmn. Educ. Div. 1962); mem., Extve. Comte., Internat. Conf. on Physics of Elect. & Atomic Collisions; Am. Meteorol. Soc. (Comte. on Meso- and Thermospheres); mem., Comte. on Stratospheric Pollution, Govt. Canada, Scient. Adv. Council, Candn. Soc. Weizmann Inst. Science; U.S. Acad. of Sci. Comm. on Impact of Stratospheric Change; Chrmn., U.S. Acad. of Sci., Panel on Stratospheric Chemistry; Review Panel, Nat. Scient. Balloon Facility;

Candn. Assn. Univ. Teachers; Assoc. Comtes. of Nat. Research Council; Sigma Xi; Home: 60 Donwoods Dr., Toronto, Ont. M4N 2G5.

SCHIOLER, John Pontoppidan, M.A.; diplomat; b. Winnipeg, Manitoba, 8 Jan. 1933; s. Knud and Kirsten (Pontoppidan) S.; e. Univ. of Manitoba, B.A. (Hons.) 1956; Univ. of Rochester, M.A. 1958; Oxford (Rhodes Scholar) B.A. 1959, M.A. 1962; Laval Univ. (French) 1973-74; m. Gail Alexandra Olmsted; one d. Tegan; Permanent Rep. of Can., ICSC, Hanoi 1961-62; Second Secy. Candn. Embassy Rome 1962-64 and to High Comn. Cyprus 1964-65; Extve. Asst. Commonwealth Secretariat, London 1965-66; Counsellor, Candn. High Comn., Lagos 1969-71; Acting Dir. Defence Relations Div., External Affairs 1972 and Dir., Middle East Div. 1972-73; Ambassador to Zaire, Burundi, Rwanda and Congo 1974-76; Dir. Staff Relations and Compensation, Ext. Affs. 1976-78; Policy Adviser, Off. of the Pres. of the Privy Council 1978-80; Dir. Middle East Div., 1980- ; Address: Dept. of External Affairs, Ottawa, Ont. K1A 0G2.

SCHLEEH, Hans, R.C.A.; sculptor; b. Koenigsfeld, Germany, 1928; studied at Lahr under Richard Class; settled in Montreal, Que., 1951; comnd. to do sculptures for several chs. incl. Ste. Anne de Beaupré Basilica; participated in several group exhns. 1953-60; one-man exhns. incl., Dominion Gallery, Montreal, 1960, 65, 66, 68, 69, 70, 74, 76, 79; New Art Centre Gallery, N.Y. 1962; Kunsthalle, Duesseldorf, Germany 1964; group exhns. incl., Salon de la jeune Sculpture, Paris 1966, 67; Stratford, Ont. 1966; Expo, Montreal 1967; Que. Sculptors Assn. 1965-70; Musee d'Art Contemporain, Montreal 1970-71; Musee Rodin, Paris 1970-71; Landesmuseem, Bonn, Germany 1971; IV Exposition Internat. de Sculpture Contemporaine, Paris 1971; Goethe Inst., Toronto 1978; studied in France, Italy, Switzerland and Germany, 1963-64; works in perm. collections in Can., U.S. and Europe incl., Art Gallery of Winnipeg; Vancouver Art Gallery; Sarnia Art Gallery; St. Catharine's and Dist. Arts Council; Univ. of Sherbrooke; Queen's Univ.; Stormking Arts Centre, Mountainville, N.Y.; Christie Manson and Woods, London, Eng.; Nathan Cummings, Chicago; J. A. MacAulay Collection, Winnipeg; Tel Aviv Museum, Israel; Bloomfield Collection, London, Eng.; Toronto-Dominion Bank, Place des Arts, Montreal Trust Co.; Ciba Co., Upper Trafalgar Place, Plaza Cote des Nieges, Montreal Mus. F.A.; and Musée d'Art Contemporain (Montreal); Montreal; Chamber of Comm., Duesseldorf, Germany; Address: 1040 Carson, Dorval, Qué. H9S 1L9.

SCHLOSSER, John Lewis; investment executive; b. Indian Head, Sask., 17 May 1928; e. High School, Estevan, Saskatchewan; University of N. Dakota, 1947, 1948, 1951; Univ. of Alta., 1949-50; m. Kathleen Patricia, d. H. A. Scott; children: Walter Scott, Mary Ann, Arden Patricia; PRESIDENT, TRI-JAY INVESTMENTS LTD.; Pres., Jay-Car Investments Ltd.; Vice Pres., Nu-Alta Developments Ltd.; Vice Pres. and Secy., Princeton Developments Ltd.; Dir., Northwestern Utilities Ltd.; Revelstoke Companies Ltd.; Bank of British Columbia; Alberta Investments Ltd.; mem. of Alta. Adv. Bd., National Trust Co. Ltd.; Chrmn. Bd. Govs., Univ. of Alberta; Bank of British Columbia Realty Trust; former Vice Pres., Northland Utilities Ltd.; Past Pres., The Edmonton Symphony Soc.; Un. Community Fund of Edmonton; Edmonton Art Gallery; Boy Scouts of Can. (Edmonton & Prov.); served as Pilot, 418 Reserve Sqdn. RCAF; recreations: sailing, scuba diving, skiing, fishing, hunting, reading: Home: 105 Westbrook Drive, Edmonton, Alta. T6J 2C8; Office: Room 1200, Petroleum Plaza N. Tower, 9945-108 St., Edmonton, Alta. T5K 2G6.

SCHMIDT, Hon. Dallas Wilbur, M.L.A.; politician; farmer; b. Wetaskiwin, Alta. 9 Aug. 1922; s. Herbert Julius and Gertha (Nilsson) S.; e. Wetaskiwin and Millet, Alta. schs.; m. Christine Norma d. Horrace Palmer Somerville, Endiang, Alta. 19 Apl. 1946; children: Garry Rae, Kenneth Herbert, Lori Elaine; MIN. OF AGRICULTURE, ALTA. 1979- ; Councillor and Reeve City of Wetaskiwin 1960-75; P. Cons. Can. prov. g.e. 1967 def.; el. M.L.A. for Wetaskiwin-Leduc prov. g.e. 1975, re-el. 1979; Min. without Portfolio 1975; Assoc. Min. of Energy & Natural Resources responsible for Pub. Lands 1976; served with RCAF 1941-45, rank Flight Lt., Pilot, DFC & Bar, 1951-56; mem. Royal Candn. Legion; Wetaskiwin Flying Club; P. Conservative; Lutheran; Office: 228 Legislative Bldg., Edmonton, Alta. T5K 2B6.

SCHMIDT, Robert Leo; trust company executive; b. Winnipeg, Man. 17 May 1937; s. Leo and Anne S.; e. Winnipeg, Man.; m. F. Gail d. George and Phoebe Herrod, Lloydminster, Sask. 20 Aug. 1960; three children; Regional Vice Pres. Corporate Services, Guaranty Trust Co. of Canada; Dir., Alta. Theatre Projects Fdn.; Past Chrmn. N.B. Sec. Trust Co's Assn. Can.; Past Pres. Saint John N.B. Lions Club; Past Treas. Kiwanis Club Edmonton Downtown; Dir. and Vice-Chmn., United Way, Calgary, 1981; Fellow Trust Co's Inst.; recreations: curling, golf, reading, gardening; Clubs: Calgary Petroleum; Glencoe; Home: 755 Cedarille Way S.W., Calgary, Alta. T2W 2G9; Office: Ste. 370, 401 — 9th Ave. S.W., Calgary, Alta. T2P 3C5.

SCHMON, Robert McCormick, B.A.; company Chmn. and CEO; b. Glen Ridge, N.J., U.S.A., 2 Dec. 1923; s. of late Arthur Albert and late Celeste (Reynolds) S.; e. Ridley Coll., St. Catharines, Ont.; Princeton Univ., B.A. 1948; m. Galena Netchi, 2 July 1966; two s., Arthur Albert II, Robert McCormick Jr.; CHAIRMAN OF THE BOARD AND CHIEF EXTVE. OFFR., & DIR., THE ONTARIO PAPER CO. LTD.; Q.N.S, Paper Co. Ltd.; Chrmn. of Bd., C.E.O. and Dir., Que. & Ont. Trans. Co. Ltd. Chrmn. of Bd. and Trustee Ontario Paper Co. Foundation; Pres. and Dir. Manicouagan Power Co.; Dir., Tribune Co. (Chicago); Dir., Ritz-Carlton Hotel Co. of Montreal Limited; Niagara Frontier Hockey Corp. (Buffalo Sabres); Great Lakes Waterways Dev. Assn.; Que Labrador Found (Canada) Inc.; mem. Bd. Govs., Ridley Coll., Trustee, Quetico Foundation; joined the companies in Oct. 1948 serving in various capacities at Baie Comeau, Thorold & St. Catharines el. Pres. 1963, Chrmn. 1979; served in 2nd World War with R.C.A.F. as Pilot 1942-45; mem.; Extve. Bd., Candn. Pulp & Paper Assn.; Princeton Alumni Assn. Can. (Extve. Comte.); Anglican; recreations: fishing, golf; Clubs: Mount Royal (Montreal); Mount Bruno Country; The Toronto; Buffalo Country; Niagara Falls Country (Lewiston, N.Y.); Lyford Cay (Nassau); Grande Romaine (Gethsemani, Que.); Carlton; International; St. Catharines; Home: 115 Front St., Niagara-on-the-Lake, Ont. L0S 1J0; Office: P.O. Box 3026, St. Catharines, Ont. L2R 7G2.

SCHNEIDER, Frederick Paul, B.A., M.Com.; executive, food processors; b. Kitchener, Ont., 14 March 1926; s. Frederick Henry and Ella E. (Daniels) S.; e. Kitchener (Ont.) Pub. Schs. and Kitchener-Waterloo Coll. Inst.; McMaster Univ., B.A. 1947; Univ. of Toronto, M.Com. 1949; m. Frances Jane, d. Ervin Cressman, Kitchener, Ont. 11 July 1953; children: Peter Frederick, Daniel John, Thomas Ervin, Anne Cecile, Margaret Ella: CHRMN., THE HERITAGE GROUP INC. (formerly J. M. Schneider Inc.); el. to Bd. of Dirs. 1952, By-Products Mgr. 1961, Vice-Pres. 1963, Extve. Vice-Pres. 1967, Pres. 1968; Chief Extve. Offr. 1969; Chrmn. of Bd. 1970; Past Pres., K-W Symphony Orchestra Assn. Inc.; Past Pres., Candn. Meat Council; Protestant; recreations: skiing, boating, outdoor activities; Home: 344 Old Chicopee Dr., R.R. #3, Kitchener, Ont. N2G 3W6; Office: 175 Columbia St. W., P.O. Box 1620, Waterloo, Ont. N2J 4M3.

SCHNEIDER, William George, O.C. (1976), M.Sc., Ph.D., D.Sc., LL.D., F.R.S.C., F.R.S.; research chemist; b. Wolseley, Sask., 1 June 1915; s. Michael and Phillipina

(Kraushaar) S.; e. Luther Coll., Regina, Sask.; Univ. of Sask., B.Sc. 1937, M.Sc. 1939; McGill Univ., Ph.D. 1941; Acadia, D.Sc. 1976; Harvard Univ. (post-doctoral research) 1941-43; D.Sc. York 1966, Memorial 1968, Sask., Moncton, McMaster, Laval 1969, New Brunswick, Montréal, McGill 1970, Acadian Univ., 1976, Regina Univ., 1976, Ottawa Univ., 1978; LL.D. Alberta 1968; Laurentian 1968; m. Jean Frances, d. Frank Purves Saskatoon, Sask., 2 Sept. 1940; two d. Judith Ann, Joanne Frances; ret. Pres., Nat. Research Council, 1967-80, (Vice-Pres., Scientific 1965-67); joined N.R.C., Pure Chem. Div., 1946; Research Physicist at Oceanographic Inst., Woods Hole, Mass., under contract with OSRD-NDRC and U.S. Navy, 1943-46; Cert. of Merit, U.S. Navy (1946); Publications: Co-author "High Resolution Nuclear Magnetic Resonnance", 1959; over 120 publ. papers in physical chem.; Fellow, Chem. Inst. Can. (Dir. 1956-59, Medal 1961, Montreal Medal 1973); mem., Am. Chem. Soc.; Am. Physical Soc.; rec'd. Henry Marshall Tory Medal of Royal Soc. of Can. 1969; recreations: tennis, skiing; Office: National Research Council, Susssex Dr., Ottawa, Ont..

SCHNELL, Bruce Robert, B.S.P., M.B.A., Ph.D., Ph.C., P.E.B.C.; b. Maymount, Sask., 1 May 1937; s. Leonard William and Nellie (Rankin) S.; e. Univ. of Sask. Coll. of Pharm. B.S.P. 1960; Univ. of Toronto Sch. of Business M.B.A. 1966; Univ. of Wis. Sch. of Pharm. Ph.D. 1971; m. June Gladys d. Everett Johnsson, 9 Oct. 1961; children: Gregory, Sandra; DEAN OF PHARMACY, UNIV. OF SASK. since 1976, joined present Univ. as Asst. Prof. 1966, Assoc. Prof. 1971, Prof. 1976; Chrmn., Edit. Adv. Panel, Compendium of Pharmaceuticals & Specialties; mem. Bd. of Regents, St. Andrew's Coll., Sask. (Extve Comte); Assoc. Ed. Canadian Journal of Hospital Pharmacy; Dir. Candn. Foundation for Advancement of Pharmacy; mem. Pharm. Examining Bd. of Can. (Pres. 1973, Extve. Comte.) Cdn. Foundation for the Advancement of Pharmacy (Exec. Comm.); Amer. Assn. of Coll. of Pharmacy; Assn. of Deans, of Pharm. of Can. (vice pres. 1977, Pres. 1978); Candn. Academy of Hist. of Pharm.; Candn. Society of Hospital Pharmacists; Candn. Pharm. Assn.; Sask. Pharm. Assn.; Medical Research Council; Address: Saskatoon, Sask..

SCHOECK, Richard J., M.A., Ph.D., F.R.H.S., F.R.S.C. (1967); univ. professor and educator; b. New York, N.Y., 10 Oct. 1920; s. Gustav J. and Frances M. (Kuntz) S.; e. McGill Univ., 1937-38; Mil. Service Schs., 1941-45; Princeton Univ., 1946-49, M.A., Ph.D.; m. Reta R., d. late William J. Haberer, June 1945; divorced 1976; children: Eric, Christine, Jennifer; m. 2ndly, Megan S. Lloyd, Feb. 1977; PROF. OF ENGLISH AND HUMANITIES, UNIVERSITY OF COLORADO since 1975; Chrmn., Dept. of Integrated Studies 1976-79; mem. Extve. Comte., Collected Work of Erasmus (First Co-ordinating Ed.), Toronto 1969-71); Works of Richard Hooker; Works of George Buchanan; Am. Journ. Jurisprudence; mem. Ed. Comte., Complete Works of Richard Hooker; mem. Bd. Trustees, Natural Law Forum (Notre Dame); mem. Univ. of Toronto Senate (1964-68); Adv. Bd., Candn.-Am. Inst., Univ. of Windsor; Columbia Univ. Seminar in Legal Hist.; Catholic Comn. on Intellectual & Cultural Affairs (Washington); Gen. Ed., Chicago-Toronto series of Lit. Criticism; Instr., Cornell Univ. 1949-55; Asst. and Assoc. Prof., Univ. of Notre Dame, 1955-61; Prof. of Eng., St. Michael's Coll., Univ. of Toronto 1961-71 and Head of Dept. there 1965-70; Prof. of Vernacular Lit., Pontifical Inst. of Mediaeval Studies, Toronto, 1961-71; Fellow, Yale Univ., 1959-60; Visiting Prof. of Eng., Princeton Univ., 1964; Fellow, Fund for Advanc. of Educ., 1951-52; Director Research Activities, Folger Shakespeare Lib. and Dir. Folger Inst. of Renaissance and 18th Century Studies, Washington, D.C. 1970-74; Adjunct Prof. of Eng., Catholic Univ. of Am. 1972, Univ. of Md. 1972-74; Prof. of Eng. and of Medieval and Renaissance Studies, Univ. of Md. 1974-75; Consultant Nat. Endowment for Humanities since 1972;

served in 2nd World War in Signal Corps and Parachute Troops, U.S. Army; discharged with rank of 1st Lieutenant; Co-editor, "Chaucer Criticism", I and II, 1960-61; "Voices of Literature", I and II 1964; "Legends of the Saints" 1961; Ed. of "Shakespeare Quarterly", 1972-74; numerous articles in learned journals; an Editor, Yale "Complete Works of Sir Thomas More"; ed., "Editing Sixteenth-Century Texts" 1966; "The Legends of the Saints" 1961; Ascham's "Scholemaster" 1966; Contributing Editor, "New Catholic Encyclopedia"; former Associate Editor, "Neo-Latin News" 1955-63; Asst. Ed., "Natural Law Forum", 1958-60; Gen. Ed. "The Confutation of Tyndale" by Sir Thomas More, 3 Vols. 1973; author "The Achievement of Thomas More", 1976; Special ed. and contrib. to "Canada" number of "Review of National Literatures", 1977; has done research on early hist. of Inns of Court (awarded John Simon Guggenheim Mem. Foundation Fellowship 1967); Sr. Fellow, Canada Council; Rep. Modern Language Assn. Am. on Ad Hoc Comte. for Copyright Law Revision 1972-75; Pres and mem., Extve. Comte., Internat. Assn. for Neo-Latin Studies 1976-79; mem., Mediaeval Acad. of America; Renaissance Soc. of Am. (Rep. for legal history on Council); Selden Soc.; Anglo-Norman Text Soc.; Modern Lang. Assn. of Am.; Bibliographical Soc. (London); ACUTE; Humanities Assn. Can. (since 1963); Internat. Assn. of Univ. Prof. of Eng. (I.A.U.P.E.); recreations: skiing, swimming; Clubs: PEN (N.Y.); Office: Dept. of English, University of Colorado, Boulder, Colo. 80309.

SCHOELER, Paul Jean René, B. Arch., F.R.A.I.C. R.C.A.; architect; b. Toronto, Ont. 29 Oct. 1923; s. Gabriel and Anna (Malcoz) S.; e. France 1932-37; St. Leo's Acad. Westmount, Que. 1941; Polytechnique Montreal 1942-43; McGill Univ. B.Arch. 1951, Town Planning 1951-54 (CMHC Scholarship); children: Peter, Robert, Sebastien; PARTNER, SCHOELER & HEATON; private arch. practice since 1958; Design Awards incl. Gold Medal 13th Milan Triennale; First Prize Arch. Competition for Juvenile & Family Court Bldg. Ottawa; Hon. Mention Arch. Competition Ottawa Builders Exchange; Candn. Housing Design Council Design Award 1976 (Sr. Citizens Apt. Bldg. Kanata); various annual design awards Ont. Assn. Archs.; RAIC Festival of Arch. Awards (2) of Merit 1979 (J.W.I. Office Bldg. and Charlebois High Sch. Ottawa); Canadian Architect design awards (2) 1981; served with Candn. Army, First Special Service Force Italy, wounded near Rome 1944; mem. Ont. Assn. Archs.; Order Archs. Quebec.; Royal Arch. Inst. Can.; Royal Canadian Academy; Home: 17 Linden Terrace, Ottawa, Ont.; Office: 148 Bank St., Ottawa, Ont. K1P 5N8.

SCHOENAUER, Norbert, M.Arch., R.C.A.; educator; architect; b. Reghin, Romania 2 Jan. 1923; s. Norbert and Ira (Gergelyffy Mischinger) S.; e. Royal Hungarian Tech. Univ. Budapest B.Arch. 1945; Royal Acad. Fine Arts Copenhagen Cert. in Arch. 1950; McGill Univ. M.Arch. 1959; m. Astrid d. Johannes Christiansen MacDonald; PROF. OF ARCH., McGILL UNIV., Dir. Sch. of Arch. there 1972-75; arch. and planning practice with Maurice Desnoyers 1967-75; Extve. Dir. CMHC Nat. Office 1975-77; Candn. Del to UN Econ. Comn. Europe, Budapest 1976, Ottawa 1977; Consultant to Polservice, Poland 1978; recipient several awards and prizes designs in nat. arch. competitions; author "Introduction to Contemporary Indigenous Housing" 1973; "6,000 Years of Housing" Vols. 1-3 1981; co-author "The Court-Garden House" 1962; "University Housing in Canada" 1966; several mag. articles on Housing and Town Planning; mem. Royal Arch. Inst. Can.; Order Archs. Que.; Corp. Professionnelle des Urbanistes du Qué.; Lutheran; Home: 3220 Ridgewood Ave., Apt. P-2, Montreal, Que. H3V 1B9; Office: 3480 University St., Montreal, Que. H3A 2A7.

SCHOGT, Henry Gilius, M.A., Ph.D., F.R.S.C.; educator; b. Amsterdam, Netherlands 24 May 1927; s. Johannes Herman and Ida Jacoba (van Rijn) S.; e. Barlaeus Gymnasium Amsterdan 1945; Univ. of Amsterdam Dept. Romance Langs. B.A. 1947, M.A. 1952, Dept. Slavic Langs. B.A. 1949, M.A. 1951; Univ. of Utrecht Ph.D. 1960; m. Corrie d. Philip Salomon Frenkel 2 Apl. 1955; children: Barbara, Philibert Johannes, Elida; PROF. OF FRENCH, UNIV. OF TORONTO since 1969; Univ. of Groningen, Docent 1953-63 (Russian); Univ. of Utrecht, Wetenschappelijk hoofdambtenaar 1954-63 (French); Sorbonne, Univ. of Paris, Maître-assistant 1963-64 (Gen. Linguistics); Princeton Univ. Visiting Lectr. 1964-66 (Russian and French); Assoc. Prof. of French Univ. Toronto 1966, Chrmn. Grad. Dept. French 1972-77; author "Les Causes de la double issue de e fermé tonique libre en français" 1960; "De Palm die door het dak breekt" (8 short stories transl. from Russian into Dutch) 1966; "Le Système verbal du français contemporain" 1968 "Sémantique synchronique, synonymie, homonymie, polysémie" 1976; co-author "La Phonologie" 1977; over 30 articles phonology, verbal systems, semantics, diachronic linguistics, various book reviews; recreations: hiking, gardening; Home: 47 Turner Rd., Toronto, Ont. M6G 3H7; Office: Toronto, Ont. M5S 1A1.

SCHOLES, John M., B.Eng., M.B.A.; trust company executive; b. Stretford, England, 27 April 1932; e. McGill Univ. B.Eng.; Harvard Business Sch. M.B.A.; m. Isabel E. Painter; children: Stephen Norman, Robert John, Sandra Jean; PRESIDENT AND CHIEF EXECUTIVE OFFR., ROYAL TRUST CO. LTD. 1982- ; Dir. The Royal Trust Group of Companies; Invest. Clk. Royal Trust, Montreal 1954, Invest. Trust Offr. 1955, Asst. Treas. 1960, Mgr. Invest. Research 1961, Asst. Supvr. Invests./Gen. Supvr. 1962, Asst. Vice Pres. Invests. 1969, Vice Pres. Invests. 1971, Group Vice Pres. Invests. 1973, Group Vice Pres. Regional Operations 1975, Extve. Vice Pres. Operations 1976, Sr. Extve. Vice Pres. 1978, Sr. Extve. Vice Pres. and Chief Operating Offr. 1978, Pres. and Chief Operating Officer 1981, Pres. and Chief Executive Officer 1982; Home: 108 Elm Ave. Toronto, Ont. M4W 1P2; Office: Toronto Dominion Bank Tower, Toronto Dominion Centre, Toronto, Ont. M5W 1P9.

SCHREYER, Right Hon. Edward Richard, C.C., C.M.M., C.D., M.A.; b. Beausejour, Man., 21 Dec. 1935; s. John and Elizabeth (Gottfried) S.; e. Beausejour (Man.) Collegiate; United Coll., Winnipeg, Man.; St. John's Coll., Univ. of Man., B.A., B.Paed., B.Ed., M.A.; m. Lily, d. Jacob Schulz, 30 June 1960; children: Lisa, Karmel, Jason, Toban; GOVERNOR-GENERAL OF CANADA AND COMMANDER IN CHIEF OF CANADA since 1979; Chancellor and Principal Companion of the Ord. of Can.; Chancellor and Cmdr. of the Ord. of Military Merit; first el. to Manitoba Legislature 1958 (youngest mem. of Legislature); re-el. 1959 and 1962; Prof. of Pol. Sc. and Internat'l Relations, St. Paul's Coll., Univ. of Man. 1962-65; el. to H. of C. for Springfield 1965, re-el. 1968 as M.P. for Selkirk; el. Leader of Manitoba N.D.P. June 1969; Premier of Man. 1969-77 (Min. of Dom.-Prov. Relations, Min. of Finance 1972-76, Min. of admin. of Hydro Act 1971-77); Leader of Opposition, Man. Legislature 1977-78; Second Lieut., C.O.T.C.-R.C.A.C., 1954-56; mem., Candn. Assn. of Univ. Teachers; Commonwealth Parlty. Assn.; Inter-Parlty. Union; awarded Vanier Award as outstanding Young Canadian, 1975; N.D.P.; Roman Catholic; recreations: golf, carpentry; Clubs: East St. Paul Curling; East St. Paul Legion; Home: Government House, Ottawa, Ont. K1A 0A1.

SCHROEDER, Horst Wilhelm; executive; b. Schwerin, Germany 5 May 1941; e. Univ. Gottingen, W. Germany, Degree in Econ. & Business Adm. (Diplom-Kaufmann) 1965; came to Can. 1981; PRESIDENT AND CHIEF EXTVE. OFFR., KELLOGG SALADA CANADA INC.; Dir. Tea Council Can.; mem. Grocery Products Mfrs. Can.; Bd. Trade Metrop. Toronto; recreations: tennis, squash; Club: Toronto Cricket Skating & Curling; Office: 6700 Finch Ave. W., Rexdale, Ont. M9W 5P2.

SCHRYVER, (Mary) Louise, B.A., B.L.S., A.M.L.S.; ret. librarian; b. Belleville Ont., 27 Dec. 1914; d. Allan Ross and Stella Mabel (Dyer) Schryver; e. Belleville (Ont.) Coll. Inst.; Victoria Coll., Univ. of Toronto, B.A. 1936; Univ. of Toronto Lib. Sch., B.L.S. 1938; Univ. of Mich., A.M.L.S. 1958; with Midland, Ont., Public Lib., 1938-43; Calgary, Alta., Public Lib., 1943-44; Librarian, Chatham Public Library, 1944-79; rec'd. travel study grant from Ford Foundation Fund for Adult Educ., 1958; Visiting Lecturer at Univ. of Western Ont. 1970; Publication: Blue Print for Library Service in the Kent-Chatham Region, 1958; various writing in prof. journs. and newspapers; Dir., S.W. Ont. Regional Lib. Co-op., 1964-65; mem., Inst. of Prof. Librarians (Pres. 1960-61); Ont. Library Assn. (Pres. 1961-62); Founding mem. and Pres. (1976-77), Administrators of Medium Sized Pub. Libs. Ont.; awarded Centennial Medal 1967; Queen's Jubilee Medal 1977; OLTA Award 1978; Protestant; recreations: music, art, conversation, photography, gardening; Club: University Womens; Home: 454 King St. W., Chatham, Ont. N7M 1G5; .

SCHULTZ, Charles Davies, B.A.Sc.; R.P.F.; P.Eng.; consulting forest eng. and company president; b. Vancouver, B.C., 26 Oct. 1904; s. late His Hon. Judge Samuel Davies and Maude Dunwell (Squarebriggs) S., R.N.; e. Chesterfield Private Sch., Pub. and High Sch., N. Vancouver, B.C.; Univ. of British Columbia, B.A.Sc. (Forest Engineering) 1931; m. Margaret Amy, d. Reginald Beaumont, Vancouver, B.C., 18 June 1947; children: Elizabeth Amy, Beaumont Charles, Margaret Maude; PRESIDENT, CHARLES D. SCHULTZ LTD. TIMBER MANAGEMENT CONSULTANTS since 1944; Pres., C. D. Schultz & Co. Inc., Seattle Washington; Schultz International Ltd.; C. D. Schultz and Co. Ltd., Forest Resource and Engineering Consultants and Resource & Environmental Consultants, 1944-79; jr. positions with B.C. Forest Service and lumber & logging cos., 1922-28; Engr., Pacific Great Eastern Railway Resources Survey, 1929; Chief of Party, Forest Surveys Div., Dept. of Lands & Forests, B.C. Govt., 1930-31 and as Forest Engr., 1931-35; Trader, Seabord Lumber Sales Co. Ltd., Vancouver, B.C. 1935-36; B.C. Timber Commr. to B.W.I. and S. Am., 1936-39; Mgr., West Indies and Caribbean Dept., Seabord Lbr. Sales Co. Ltd., 1939; Resident Engr., Bloedel, Stewart & Welch Ltd., Bloedel, B.C., 1940-44; served with N.P.A.M. as Lieut., R.C.E., 1933-35 and with Jamaica Engn. Corps, Kingston, Jamaica, 1936-39; Lieut., 5th Regt., R.C.A., C.A.S.F., 1939-40 when invalided out of army; mem., Vancouver Bd. Trade; Bd. of Dirs., Candn. Forestry Assn., Vancouver; Assn. of Consulting Engrs. Can. (Chrmn. Comte. on Natural Resources, 1962-65); Assn. of Consulting Engrs. (Dir. 1965-66); Candn. Inst. Forestry; Soc. of Am. Foresters; Engn. Inst. Can.; Forest Products Research Society; Commonwealth Forestry Association (Canadian Rep. Gov. Council); Association of B.C. Foresters (mem. Council 1949); Assn. Prof. Engrs. B.C. (mem. council, 1951-52); Candn. Pulp & Paper Assn.; Assn. of Prof. Engrs. of State of Wash.; Native Sons of B.C.; author of 'Your Forest Estate' (recorded in Canadiana, issued by Nat. Lib.); Hoo-Hoo; Phi Gamma Delta; Freemason; Anglican; recreations: golf, boating, fishing; Clubs: Capilano Golf & Country; Royal Vancouver Yacht; Vancouver Lawn Tennis & Badminton; Union (Victoria); Vancouver; Home: 3050 O'Hara Lane, Crescent Beach, Surrey, B.C. V4A 3E6 Office: 1155 West Georgia St., Vancouver, B.C. V6E 3H4.

SCHULTZ, Erich R.W., B.A., B.D., M.Th., B.L.S.; University Librarian; Archivist; b. Rankin, Ont. 1 June 1930; s. William H. and Martha (Geelhaar) S.; e. Univ. of W. Ont. B.A. 1951; Waterloo Luth. Semy. B.D. 1954; Univ. of Toronto M.Th. 1958, B.L.S. 1959; LIBRARIAN AND ARCHIVIST, WILFRID LAURIER UNIV. (formerly Waterloo Lutheran Seminary) 1960- ; Pastor, St. Paul's Lutheran, Ellice Twp., Ont. 1954-56; Librarian, Waterloo Luth. Semy. 1959-60; ed. and bibliogr, ''Ambulatio Fidei: essays in honour of Otto W. Heick'' 1965; ''Vita Laudanda: essays in memory of Ulrich S. Leopold'' 1975; translator, ''Getting Along with Difficult People'' (by Friederich Schmitt) 1970; mem., Ont. Librarians Assn. (Vice-Pres. 1967-68, Pres. 1968-69); Inst. of Professional Librarians of Ont. (Vice Pres. & Pres. 1969-70); Amer. Theological Library Assn. (Vice Pres. & Pres. 1975-77); Candn. Libr. Assn. (mem. CLA and CACUL Cmtes., Convenor CLA Outstanding Service Award Cmte. 1978-80); OCUL (Chrmn. 1978-80); Assn. of Candn. Archivists; Toronto Area Archivist Grp.; Waterloo Historical Soc. (Vice Pres. 1980-82); Kitchener-Waterloo Commy. Concert Assn. (Bd. of Dir.); Lutheran; recreations: music, golf; Home: 235 Erb St. E., Waterloo, Ont. N2J 1M9; Office: 75 University Ave. W., Waterloo, Ont. N2L 3C4

SCHWARTZ, Gerald Wilfred, B.Com., LL.B., M.B.A.; industrialist; b. Winnipeg, Man. 24 Nov. 1941; s. Andrew O. and Lillian (Arkin) S.; e. Univ. of Man. B.Comm. 1962, LL.B. 1966; Harvard Univ. M.B.A. 1970; children: Carey, Jill; PRES. AND DIR., MEM. EXTVE. COMTE. CANWEST CAPITAL CORP. since 1977; Chrmn. CanWest Investment Corp.; Depy. Chrmn. of Bd. and Chrmn. Extve. Comte, The Monarch Life Assurance Co.; Chrm. Extve. Comte. and Dir., Crown Trust Co.: Chrm. of Bd., MacLeod-Stedman Inc.; Depy. Chmn. of Bd. and Chrmn. Extve. Comte. Na-Churs Plant Food Co.; Vice Chrmn. and Dir. Universal Subscription Television Inc.; Vice Chrmn., Dir. & mem. Extve Comte., Aristar Inc.; John Alden Life Ins. Co.; Vice-Chmn. of Bd., Global Communications Ltd.; Dir., Prosoccer Ltd.; Winnipeg Art Gallery Fdn.; Regional Vice-Chmn. and Dir., Council for Business and the Arts in Canada; called to Bar of Man. 1966; law practice Asper, Freedman & Co. Winnipeg 1966 — 68; Assoc., Corporate Finance, Estabrook & Co. Inc. N.Y. 1970, Vice Pres. Corporate Finance 1971; Sr. Assoc., Bear, Stearns & Co. 1973, Vice Pres. Corporate Finance 1974; Assoc. Prof. (Adj.) N.Y. Univ. Grad. Sch. Business Adm.; Law Lectr. Man. Inst. C.A.'s and Estate Planning Inst. Can.; Jewish; recreations: tennis, sailing; Clubs: Winnipeg Squash Racquet; Glendale Golf & Country; Harvard (N.Y.); Home: 155 Carlton St., Winnipeg, Man. R3C 3H8; Office: One Lakeview Sq., Winnipeg, Man. R3C 3H8.

SCHWARTZ, Harold Simpson, B.Sc.; metallurgist; b. Cape Town, S. Africa 8 June 1928; s. Maurice Schwartz; e. Muizenberg High Sch.; Univ. of Cape Town B.Sc. (Applied & Industrial Chemistry) 1948; m. Bernice Rochelle Benjamin; children: Clive, Jogail, Gary; PRES., CANDN. METALS DIV., HUDSON BAY MINING & SMELTING CO. 1979- ; Mgr. Metall., Anglo American Corp., Zambia until 1973; Mgr., Rio Tinto Zinc, S. Africa 1973-74; Consulting Metall., Anglo American Corp., S. Africa 1975-79; Sr. Vice Pres. Metall. present Co. 1979; mem. Inst. Mining Metall. (U.K.); Soc. of Mining Eng. of A.I.M.E.; candn. Inst. Metall. (Toronto Br.); recreations: squash, golf; Home: 8 Gardiner Rd., Toronto, Ont. M5P 3B3; Office: (P.O. Box 28) Toronto-Dominion Centre, Toronto, Ont. M5K 1B8.

SCHWARZMANN, Maurice, M.A.: b. Malaga, Spain, 21 Dec., 1920; s. Louis and Aurelia (Monterde) s.; Mill-Hill School, London, England; Institut Frilley (Hautes Etudes Commerciales), Paris, France; University of McGill; University of Toronto B.A. (Political Science & Economy); M.A. 1950; m. Patricia D. Finlayson de la Guardia, d. late John Finlayson; October 30, 1975; children: Violet, Robert, Edward, Ronald and Patricia; appt. to Dept. Trade & Commerce, May, 1949; Dir. Intr. Trade Relations Br., 1958; Minister (Econ), Canadian Embassy, Washington D.C. 1959-1964; Assist. Deputy Minister, Trade & Ind. Policy, Ottawa, 1964; participated in Cndn. Ministerial Trade Mission to Latin America, 1952; Trade Agreements with Spain and Portugal, 1954; GATT Review Conf., Geneva, 1954; Commonwealth Finance Ministers Conf., Mt. Tremblant, 1957; Commwth. Trade & Econ. Conf., Montreal, 1958; Canada-U.S., Canada-Japan and other Ministerial Conferences; Chairman Cdn. Delegations to numerous trade & economic negotiations, GATT, OECD, Textiles and Intr. Wheat Agreements; Minister Cdn. Delegation to Kennedy Round Trade Negotiations, Geneva, 1964-1967; Member Ministerial Mission to Latin America, 1968; InterAmerican Development Bank Conf., Quito, Ecuador, 1972; Ambassador to Mexico and concurrently to Guatemala, 1972-75; Ambassador to Venezuela and concurrently Dominican Republic, 1975-77; served in Second World War, 1943-46, with Canadian Army Intelligence Corps, UK and Netherlands, incl. Supreme Headquarters Allied Expeditionary Forces, London, & First Candn. Corps Headquarters, Utrecht; left Govt. Service to enter private activities as Business Consultant in March 1977, now residing in Mexico; Apartado Postal M-2876, Mexico 1, D.F. Mexico.

SCHWEITZER, Eugene Howard; consultant, retired executive; b. Kincardine, Ont. 20 June 1915; s. Edward A. and Jeanette (Ludwig) S.; e. Kincardine High Sch.; Curtiss-Wright Tech. Inst., Los Angeles, Calif., 1940; m. Helen Bernice, d. Charles G. Taillon, St. Lambert, Que., 10 May 1957; Vice-Pres., Computer Operations, Pratt & Whitney Aircraft Of Canada Ltd. to 1981; mem., Canadian Aero. and Space Inst.; Protestant; recreations: gardening, swimming; Home: 722 Casgrain Ave., St. Lambert, Que. J4R 1G7; .

SCHWERDTFEGER, Hans W. E., Ph.D.; mathematician; professor emeritus; b. Göttingen, Germany 9 Dec. 1902; s. Otto Schwerdtfeger; e. Univ. of Leipzig 1926-27; Univ. of Goettingen 1927-32; Univ. of Bonn Ph.D. 1934; m. Hanna d. Max Maeder 30 March 1935; children: Peter S., Roland W. S.; Lectr. in Math. Univ. of Adelaide, Australia 1940-47; Sr. Lectr. Univ. of Melbourne 1948-57; Visiting Prof. Queen's Univ. 1954-55; Assoc. Prof. McGill Univ. 1957-59, Prof. 1959-73, Prof. Emeritus since 1973; author "Fonctions de Matrices" 1938; "Introduction to Linear Algebra and the Theory of Matrices" 1950, 2nd ed. 1961; "Geometry of Complex Numbers" 1962; "Introduction to Group Theory" 1976; coauthor "Grundzuege der Galois'schen Theorie" 1950; numerous research articles Linear Algebra, Numerical Math., Geom. and Group Theory; mem. Am. Math. Soc.; Edinburgh Math. Soc.; Austrian Math. Soc.; Australian Math. Soc.; Math. Assn. Am.; Royal Soc. Can.; Candn. Math. Cong. 1958-74; Office: Dept. of Mathematics, McGill University Montreal, Que. H3A 2K6.

SCOBIE, Stephen Arthur Cross, M.A., Ph.D.; educator; author; b. Carnoustie, Scot. 31 Dec. 1943; s. Arthur Cross S.; e. Univ. of St. Andrews M.A. 1965; Univ. of B.C. Ph.D. 1969; m. Sharon Maureen d. Joseph Melville McHale, Langley, B.C. 6 May 1967; PROF. OF ENGLISH, UNIV. OF VICTORIA 1981- ; joined Univ. of Alta. Dept. Eng. 1969-81, Prof. 1980-81; rec'd Gov. Gen.'s Award for Poetry 1980; author (poetry) "Babylondromat" 1966; "In the Silence of the Year" 1971, reprinted 1973; "The Birken Tree" 1973; "Stone Poems" 1974; "The Rooms We Are" 1975; "Airloom" 1975; "les toiles n'ont peur de rien" 1979; "McAlmon's Chinese Opera" 1980; "A Grand Memory for Forgetting" 1981; co-author "The Pirates of Pen's Chance" 1981; critical study "Leonard Cohen" 1978; over 20 critical articles Candn. lit. and experimental poetry various publs.; short stories; poetry readings across Can. and Twelfth Internat. Sound Poetry Festival, New York 1980; co-ed. "The Maple Laugh Forever: An Anthology of Canadian Comic Poetry" 1981; mem. League of Candn. Poets (Vice Pres.); recreations: movies, opera, golf; Home: 4278 Parkside Cres., Victoria, B.C. V8N 2C3; Office: Victoria, B.C. V8W 2Y2.

SCOFFIELD, Charles Herbert; F.C.I.S.; retired association executive; b. Liverpool, Eng., 24 Apl. 1911; s. Charles Herbert and Isobel (Village) S.; e. Brantford (Ont.) Coll. Inst., 1929; m. Marion Isobel, d. A. W. Van-

Sickle, Onondaga, Ont., 1 May 1937; children: Barbara Ruth, Margaret Isobel, Eric VanSickle, Brian Herbert; former Gen. Mgr. The Canadian Chamber of Commerce, Dir., Canadian Executive Service Overseas; joined Waterous Ltd. 1929; held various positions incl. Purchasing Agt. 1942-46; joined present organ. as Mgr., Membership Dept. 1946; apptd. Asst. Secy. 1947; Asst. Gen. Mgr. 1950; Ald., City of Brantford, 1943-45; Pub. Utilities Commr., 1946; Nat. Vice-Pres., Candn. Jr. Chamber of Comm., 1944-45; Pres., Brantford Optimist Club, 1942; Pres., Young Men's Sec., Brantford Bd. of Trade, 1943; Dean, Candn. Inst. for Organ. Mang., 1954-64; Dir., Jr. Achievement of Canada, 1967-75; mem., Montreal Bd. Trade Assoc.'s; Baptist; Home: 4327 Coolbrook Ave. Montreal, Que. H4A 3G1.

SCOLLARD, Rev. Robert Joseph, B.L.S., A.M. (R.C.); b. Toronto, Ont., 15 Aug. 1908; s. Robert and Lillian (McFadden) S.; e. St. Michael's Coll., Univ. of Toronto, B.A. 1928; Library Sch., B.L.S. 1939; Univ. of Mich., A.M. (Lib. Science) 1942; Secy-Gen. of the Basilian Fathers, 1954-68; Librarian, Pontifical Inst. of Mediaeval Studies, 1932-51, Librarian, St. Basil's Semy., 1951-59, 1968-69; Periodicals Librarian, Univ. of St. Michael's College, 1969-75; archivist 1975; Univ. of Toronto Alumni-Faculty Award, St. Michael's Coll. Constit.; mem., Candn. Lib. Assn.; Ont. Lib. Assn.; Assn. of Candn. Archivists; Toronto Area Archivists Group; Canadian Cath. Hist. Assn. (Secy. 1970-73, Clerk Medal 1975); author of "Dictionary of Basilian Biography", 1969; "A Calendar of the Deceased Bishops and Priests of the Archdiocese of Toronto", 2nd ed. 1975, 3rd 1981; "Footprints in the Sand of Clover Hill, Anniversaries and Notable Events in the History of St. Michael's College, 1852-1977"; "A Register of the Convocations and the Graduates in Theology of the University of St. Michael's College, 1955-79"; and other pamphlets on local history; Contrib. to "New Catholic Encyclopedia"; Ed., "The Basilian Historial Bulletin" since 1970; "The Basilian Annals", 1943-68 and "The Basilian Newsletter", 1961-68; contrib. Dict. Candn. Biog.; Address: 50 St. Joseph St., Toronto, Ont. M5S 1J4.

SCOTT, Andrew Edington, B.Sc., Ph.D., F.C.I.C.; educator (ret.); b. Newport-on-Tay, Scot. 27 Apl. 1919; s. John Colville and Edith (Mathers) S.; e. Madras Coll. St. Andrews, Scot. 1939; Univ. of St. Andrews B.Sc. 1949, Ph.D. 1959; m. Vivien Nelson d. late George Nelson Weekes, London, Ont. 27 July 1946; one d. Vivien Edith Nelson; PROFESSOR EMERITUS, UNIV. OF WESTERN ONT. and Dean, Fac. of Science there 1966-79, and Prof. of Chem. there since 1965; also mem. Bd. of Govs. 1974-78; Research Fellow Ont. Research Foundation Toronto 1950-53, Research Chem. 1956-60; Research Chem. Electric Reduction of Canada Ltd. Toronto 1953-55; Lectr. Bristol Univ. 1960-62; joined present Univ. as Asst. Prof. 1963, Assoc. Prof. 1964, Head Dept. Chem. 1965-66; holds two patents; served with Black Watch 1939-41, RA 1941-46, rank Capt.; author several scient. publs.; Presbyterian; recreations: walking, scottish country dancing; Club: University; Home: 451 Westmount Dr., London, Ont. N6K 1X4.

SCOTT, Angus C., M.A.; educator; b. Hamilton, Ont. 19 Aug. 1925; s. S. W. C. and Marie L. (Morris) S.; e. Ridley Coll., St. Catharines, Ont. (1937-43); Univ. of Toronto, B.A. 1949; Cambridge Univ., B.A. 1952, M.A. 1957; Harvard Univ., 1960-61; m. Lorna P., d. J. G. Hungerford, 25 June 1959; children: Peter J. C., Douglas H., Sally P., Angus M. B., Robert Norman Seagram; HEADMASTER, TRINITY COLL. SCH., since 1962; Teacher, Appleby Coll., Oakville, Ont., 1949-50; Teacher, Trinity Coll. Sch., 1952, Housemaster, 1955, Asst. Headmaster, 1959; served in R.N.V.R. (Fleet Air Arm) 1944-46; mem., Ont. Educ. Assn.; Nat. Council of Teachers of Eng.; Kappa Alpha; Anglican; recreations: camping, squash, skiing; Clubs: University (Toronto); Toronto Racquet; Address: Trinity College School, Port Hope, Ont. L1A 3W2.

SCOTT, Anthony Dalton, B.Com., M.A., Ph.D., LL.D., F.R.S.C. (1969); university professor; economist; b. Vancouver, B.C., 2 Aug. 1923; s. Sydney Dunn and Edith (Dalton) S.; e. Prince of Wales High Sch., Vancouver, 1940; Univ. of B.C., B.Com. 1946, B.A. 1947; Harvard Univ., A.M. 1949; London Sch. of Econ., Ph.D. 1953; Univ. of Guelph, hon. LL.D., 1980; m. Barbara Ruth, d. Chief Justice J. O. Wilson, 1953; two children; PROF. OF ECON., UNIV. OF BRIT. COLUMBIA; joined present Univ. as Lectr., Summer Session 1949; faculty mem. 1953-55 and 1956-present; Acting Head, Dept. of Econ. and Pol. Science, 1962-63; Head, Econ. Dept., 1965-69; Asst. Lectr., London Sch. of Econ., 1950-53; Research Worker, Dept. of Applied Econ., Cambridge Univ., 1949-50, Visitor 1959-60; Staff, Royal Comn. on Can's Econ. Prospects, 1955-56; served with Candn. Army (Armoured Corps) 1943-45; mem., Nat. Adv. Council on Water Resources Research; Senate, Univ. of B.C., 1964-70; Extve., B.C. Natural Resources Conf., 1963; Can. Council Sr. Research Fellow 1959-60; Lilly Faculty Fellow, Univ. of Chicago, 1964-65; Can. Council Killam Award 1972 and 1974; co-author: 'Output, Labour and Capital in the Canadian Economy', 1958; 'Canadian Economic Policy', 1961, rev. ed. 1965; 'Manual of Benefit-Cost Analysis', 1962; 'The Common Wealth in Ocean Fisheries', 1966; 'Efficiency in the Open Economy; Collected Writings on Canadian Economic Problems and Policies', 1969; co-author with Paul A. Samuelson of 'Economics', Cdn. Edition, 1966, 5th ed. 1980; author: 'Natural Resources: The Economics of Conservation', 1954 and 1973; co-author, "The Brain Drain" 1977; ed. and contributor," Natural Resources Revenues: A Test of Federalism" 1976; co-author "The Economic Constitution of Federal States" 1978; "The Design of Federations" 1980; mem. ed. bd. various journals and extve. bds of various professional assns.; Pres. Candn. Pol. Science Assn. 1966-67; Pres., Academy of Humanities and Social Sciences, Roy. Soc. of Can. 1979-80; Commissioner, Cdn. section, Internat. Joint Comm. Can.-U.S. Boundary Waters Treaty 1968-72; Reserve Bank of Australia Fellow, 1977/8; Anniversary Medal, 1978; Home: 3906 W 36th Ave. Vancouver, B.C.V6N 2S8.

SCOTT, Campbell; artist; educator; b. Milngavie, Scotland 5 Oct. 1930; s. Robert and Catherine (Tulloch) s.; came to Can. Sept. 1951; e. Milngavie H.S., Scotland 1945; Glasgow Sch. of Art; Royal Technical Coll., Glasgow; INSTRUCTOR, ST. CATHARINES COLLEGIATE & VOCATIONAL SCHOOL; served five-yr. apprenticeship as woodcarver/joiner 1946-51; carpenter 1951-53; one-man show, Upstairs Gallery, Toronto 1960; student of woodblock printing, Japan 1963; student of graphic design and furniture, Royal Acad. of Art, Copenhagen 1965; student of engraving and etching with S.W. Hayter, Paris 1966; invitation section, First Biennial Internat. Show of Graphics, Krakow, Poland 1966; Internat. Group Show, F.A.A.P. Gravura S'Paulo, Brazil 1968; Internat. Group Show, Norrkoping Museum, Sweden 1968; one-man show, Rodman Hall Art Centre, St. Catharines, Ont. 1968; invitation sect., First British Internat. Print Biennial 1969; selected for travelling exhibition of graphics by Nat. Gallery of Can. 1969; one-man show, Gallery Pascal, Toronto 1969; Fifth Burnaby Print Show, B.C. 1969; Candn. Graphics Show circulated by Gallery of Ont. 1969; Third Internat. Biennial, Krakow 1970; Nat. Exhibition of Amer. colour prints 1970; 4th Amer. Biennial of Engraving, Santiago, Chile 1970; Exhibition of Candn. Graphics, Candn. Embassy, Washington, D.C. 1971; First Internat. Print Exhibition, Gallery Bleu, Phillipines 1972; selected for 'Who's Who in American Art' 1979; represented in the following public collections: Brit. Museum, London; Montreal Mus. of Art (Samuel Bronfman Collection); Hamilton Art Gallery, Hamilton, Ont.; Victoria & Albert Mus., London, England; Bibliotheque National, Paris; Scottish Nat. Gallery of Modern Art; Rodman Hall Art Gallery, St. Catharines, Ont.; Niagara Falls Public Library (Bronze Sculpture); St. Catharines Public Library (Wood Sculpture); Univ. of Guelph Master Print Collec-

tion; mem., Print and Drawing Council of Can.; recreation: sailing; Home: 89 Byron, Niagara-on-the-Lake, Ont. L0S 1J0; Office: Lincoln County Bd. of Educ., 112 Oakdale Ave., St. Catharines, Ont. L2P 3J9

SCOTT, Charles E., B.Sc., M.B.A.; executive; b. Montreal, Que., 6 March 1935; s. George W. and Bess G. (Helliker) S.; e. Leaside (Ont.) High Sch. 1949-54, Univ. of Toronto B.Sc. (Engn.) 1958; McMaster Univ. M.B.A. 1973; m. Barbara J., d. John D. Connell, Toronto, Ont., 20 Feb. 1960; children: David Charles, Jo-Anne Lynn, Jennifer Susan, James Douglas; PRESIDENT AND DIR., DOMINION DAIRIES LTD., since Oct. 1975; began in Tech. Sales with Sun Oil Co. 1958-60; joined Canada Bread (now Corporate Foods) 1960-69 successively Production Mgr., Distribution Mgr., Area Mgr., Sales Mgr. and Labour Relations Mgr.; joined Dominion Dairies as Dist. Mgr. Production & Distribution, Toronto May 1969; promoted Dir. of Operations-Corp. Staff Jan. 1972, Vice Pres. — Operations Oct. 1973; Dir., Nat. Dairy Council; mem. Assn. Prof. Engrs. Ont.; Conservative; Protestant; recreations: tennis, curling; Club: Donalda; Home: 30 Aldenham Crescent, Don Mills, Ont. M3A 1S2; Office: 235 Walmer Road, Toronto, Ont. M5R 2Y1.

SCOTT, Donald Clayton, B.A., F.C.A.; executive; b. Windsor, Ont. 30 July 1927; s. Clayton Carlyle S.; e. Patterson Coll. Inst. Windsor 1945; Univ. of W. Ont. B.A. (Business Adm.) 1949; m. Eileen Isabel d. E. M. Smith, London, Ont. 2 Dec. 1950; children: Christine Lynn, Lauren Jane, Barbara Kaye, Jeffrey Clayton, Gary Stewart, Robert Donald; SR. PARTNER AND CHRMN. EXTVE. COMTE., CLARKSON GORDON. since 1979; Dir. Woods Gordon; The Clarkson Co. Ltd.; joined present firm 1949, Partner 1956, Mang. Partner-Montreal 1963 and Toronto 1967, Chrmn. Mang. Comte. 1972; played prof. football with Toronto Argonauts 1949 — 51; Vice-Pres. and mem. Nat. Extve. Comte. Arthritis Soc.; Adv. Comte. to the School of Business Admin., Univ. of Western Ont.; Fellow, Ont. Inst. C.A.'s; Australian Soc. Accts.; mem. Inst. C.A.'s Ont. (Pres. 1978 — 79, Extve. Comte. 1974 — 79, Council 1972 — 79); Candn. Inst. C.A.'s (Bd. Govs. 1976 — 79); Order C.A.'s Que.; Zeta Psi; United Church; recreations: golf, Nordic skiing, gardening; Clubs: Toronto; Granite; Rosedale Golf; Home: 33 Daneswood Rd., Toronto, Ont. M4N 3J7; Office: (P.O. Box 251) Royal Trust Tower, Toronto Dominion Centre, Toronto, Ont. M5K 1J7.

SCOTT, Donald John, B.L.S.; librarian; b. Florence, Cape Breton, N.S. 17 July 1940; s. William Lawson and Jessie Elizabeth (Grainger) S.; e. Florence Composite Sch. 1956; Sydney Mines High Sch. 1957; Mount Allison Univ. B.A. 1963; McGill Univ. Lib. Sch. B.L.S. 1964; m. Jeanette Anne d. Herbert Fredrick Poole, New Annan, P.E.I. 16 July 1966; two s. Peter William, Jeffery Michael; LIBRARIAN, P.E.I. PROV. LIBRARY; Dir. P.E.I. Prot. Children's Trust; Trustee, Leg. and Pub. Lib.; mem. Atlantic Provs. Lib. Assn. (Past Pres.); Candn. Lib. Assn.; United Church; recreations: outdoor activities, gardening, photography, reading; Home: Tea Hall Cres., R.R. 1, Charlottetown, P.E.I. C1A 7J6; Office: University Ave., Charlottetown, P.E.I. C1A 7N9.

SCOTT, Donald S., M.Sc., Ph.D., F.C.I.C.; P.Eng.; university professor; b. Edmonton, Alta 17 Dec. 1922; s. Robert James and Clara Regina (Allen) S.; e. Univ. of Alta., B.Sc. 1944, M.Sc. 1946; Univ. of Illinois, Ph.D. 1947-49; m. Dorothy Phyllis, d. R. Alexander Hensel, Edmonton, Alta., 17 May 1945; children: Garry Alexander Donald, Jillian Damaris Clare; PROF. OF CHEM. ENGN., UNIV. OF WATERLOO, since 1970; joined Imperial Oil Ltd. N.W.T. 1944; Nat. Research Council of Can., Ottawa, 1946; Asst. and Assoc. Prof. Univ. of Brit. Columbia, 1949; Shell Visiting Prof., Cambridge Univ., 1963; Prof. and Chrmn. Dept. Chem. Engn., Univ. of Waterloo; 1964, Acting Dean, Faculty of Engn. 1969; Assoc. Dean,

Fac. of Eng., 1980; Visiting Fellow, Royal Sch. of Mines, Imperial Coll. London, Eng., 1971; Res. Consultant to various Co's.; author of over 60 research papers, articles, monographs, books, etc.; N.R.C. Fellowship, 1947; Univ. of Illinois Fellowship, 1948, Plummer Medal, Engn. Inst. of Can., 1962; Best Publication 1966, (Can. Journal of Chem. Engn.); Centennial Medal, 1967; Queen's Jubilee Medal, 1977; Sr. Research Fellowship, Brit. Research Council 1971; mem. Comte. for an Independent Can. (Nat. Steering Comte.); Candn. Soc. for Chem. Engn. (Vice Pres. 1970-71, Pres. 1971-72); Am. Inst. Mining & Metall. Engrs. Am. Inst. of Chem Engrs., Fellow; American Chem. Society; Sigma Xi; Phi Lambda Upsilon; Delta Upsilon; Protestant; recreations: golf, skiing, curling; Home: 382 Arden Place, Waterloo, Ont. N2L 2N7; Office: Waterloo, Ont.

SCOTT, Edward A.; investment dealer; b. Hamilton, Ont., 6 July 1928; s. Edward Winfield and Leta Mildred Claressa (Thrower) S.; e. A. M. Cunningham Sch., Hamilton, Ont.; Runnymede Coll. Inst., Toronto, Ont.; McMaster Univ.; m. Joan Alice, d. Norman Edmund and Muriel Lemoine (Cartwright) Kittson, 15 Oct. 1955; one s., Edward James, two d., Karen Leta, Shelley Muriel; PRESIDENT, BELLENDAINE INVESTMENTS LTD. since 1972; entered invest. business as Clerk with Bartlett Cayley & Co. Ltd. 1951; Sales Trainee, Gairdner & Co. Ltd., Toronto 1954, Sales Rep., Hamilton 1954-59; opened and managed Ottawa Br. 1959-63, Montreal Sales Mgr. and el. a Dir. 1965, Nat. Retail Sales Mgr. 1966, Vice-Pres. and Gen. Mgr. 1969; Pres. and Dir., Canadian Security Management Ltd. 1970; Pres., Canadian Gas and Energy Fund Ltd. and Canadian Security Growth Fund Ltd. 1971; Pres. and Dir., Canadian Security Management (Quebec) Ltée 1971; Extve. Vice-Pres. and Dir., CSM Japan Fund Ltd. Vice Pres., Cessland Corp. Ltd.; 1971; recreations: hunting, fishing, boating, skiing, travel; Club, Rideau, Ottawa; Home: R.R. 2, King City, Ont. L0G 1K0; Office: King City, Ont. L0G 1K0.

SCOTT, Most Rev. Edward Walter, C.C., B.A., L.Th., D.D. (Ang.); b. Edmonton, Alta., 30 Apl. 1919; e. Univ. of Brit. Columbia, B.A.; Theol. Col., Vancouver, L.Th., 1942; m. Isabel Florence Brannan, Fort Frances, Ont.; children: Maureen (Mrs. Peter Harris), Patricia Anne (Mrs. Paul Robinson), Douglas, Elizabeth Jean (Bacon); ARCHBISHOP & PRIMATE OF THE ANGLICAN CHURCH OF CANADA, since 1971; Moderator of the World Council of Churches 1975-83; Rector, St. Peter's, Seal Cove, Prince Rupert, B.C., 1942-45; Gen. Secy., Student Christian Movement, Univ. of Man., 1945-49; also part-time lectr. St. John's Coll.; Rector, Ch. of St. John the Baptist, Fort Garry, 1949-55 and St. Jude's, Winnipeg 1955-60; named Dir. of Social Service and Priest-Dir. of Indian Work for Diocese of Rupert's Land, 1960; helped estbd. first Indian-Metis Friendship Centre; joined staff of Ch.'s nat. hdqrs., Toronto, 1964; consecrated Bishop of Kootenay 1966; Address: 600 Jarvis St., Toronto, Ont. M4Y 2J6.

SCOTT, Eric C., B.A.Sc.; executive; b. Picton, Ont.; s. Wilfred Ernest and Ella M. (Bongard) S.; e. Picton Coll. & Vocational Inst.; Univ. of Toronto B.A.Sc. 1949; McGill Univ.; m. Jane d. Dr. Sandford Fleming Goodchild, Toronto, Ont. 16 Sept. 1950; children: David, Sandra, Brian, Glen; EXTVE. VICE PRES. FEDERAL BUSINESS DEVELOPMENT BANK since 1978; Design Engr. Canadian International Paper Co. Ltd. Trois-Rivières 1949-51; Canadian Industries Ltd. 1951-58, Resident Constr. Engr. Shawinigan Falls, served in Ont. and Eng. as Supvr. Polyester Staple Fibre Plant 1954-58; Industrial Development Bank 1958-75, Engr. and Credit Offr. Montreal Br. 1958-61, mgr. personnel adm. 1961-69, Chief Engr. 1970, Dir. Adv. Services 1972; Gen. Mgr. Mang. Services present Bank 1976; served with Candn. Inf. Corps 1944-45; mem. Engn. Inst. Can.; Internat. Council Small Business;

Clubs: St. James's, Mount Stephen; Office: 901 Victoria Sq., Montreal, Que. H2Z 1R1.

SCOTT, F. David D. B.A., M.B.A.; financial executive; b. Toronto, Ont., 6 Nov. 1934; s. late Henry Duke and Lillian Mary (Chapman) S.; e. Upper Can. Coll., Toronto 1953; Bishop's Univ., B.A. 1958; Univ. of W. Ont., M.B.A. 1960; m. Catherine Ann, d. Eivion Owen, Ph.D., 18 Jan. 1958; children: Stephen Owen Duke, Julia Catherine, Bronwen; PRES., CHIEF EXTVE. OFFR. & DIR., BOLTON TREMBLAY FUNDS INC. since 1981; Dir., Tarus Fund Ltd.; Planned Resources Fund Ltd.; joined Candn. Bank of Commerce 1953-55; Dominion Securities Corp. Ltd. 1960-62; RoyNat Ltd. 1962-65 (Ont. Dist. Mgr. 1964-65); Royal Securities Corp. Ltd. 1965-66 (Mgr. Research Dept.); joined Calvin Bullock Ltd. 1966; Financial Analyst 1966-68; Vice Pres. Invest. 1968-71; Extve. Vice Pres. 1972-73; Pres., C.E.O. and Dir., Scotiafund Financial Services Ltd. 1973-81; served with COTC 1956-58; rank 2nd Lieut.; Chrmn. Investment Funds Inst. Can., 1980-82; mem., Montreal Soc. Financial Analysts; Anglican; Clubs: Montreal Badminton and Squash; University (Montreal); National (Toronto); Royal Canadian Yacht (Toronto); Home: 32 Roxborough St. E., Toronto, Ont. M4W 1V6; Office: 1 First Canadian Place, Toronto, Ont. M5X 1B1.

SCOTT, Fordyce Boyd, B.A.; b. Orillia, Ont., 23 Aug. 1915; s. Matthew Brown and Jean Edgar (Johnstone) S.; e. Timmins (Ont.) High Sch., 1933; Univ. of Toronto, B.A. 1937; Univ. of W. Ont., Business Adm. Course 1965; m. Edith Grace, d. late George Howorth, 4 Oct. 1941; children: Leith (Mrs. Donald Knight), Douglas Boys, Robert Bruce; PRESIDENT, GEN. MGR. AND DIR., NORTON CO. OF CANADA LTD. since 1965; joined present Co. 1937; Foreman in Brantford plant, 1938-44; Asst. Prod. Mgr. 1945-48, Prod. Mgr. 1948-52; apptd. Works Mgr., Behr-Manning de France, 1953-56, Gen. Mgr. 1957-59; became Vice-Pres.-Sales, Norton Internat., Worcester, Mass., 1959-63; Gen. Mgr. of present Co. 1963; mem., Candn. Mfrs. Assn.; Tech. Sec., Candn. Pulp & Paper Assn.; Candn. Chamber Comm.; Freemason; United Church; recreations: golf, skiing, gardening; Clubs: Hamilton; Brantford; Hamilton Golf & Country; Home: 10 Auchmar Rd., Hamilton, Ont. L9C 1C6; Office: 3 Beach Rd., Hamilton, Ont. L8L 3Z5.

SCOTT, Frank (Francis Reginald), C.C. (1967), Q.C., B.A., B.Litt., B.C.L., D.C.L., LL.D., D. es Jur., D.Litt., F.R.S.C. (1947); retired educator, poet; b. Quebec, P.Q., 1 Aug. 1899; s. Archdeacon Frederick George and Amy S.; e. Quebec High Sch.; Bishop's Coll., Lennoxville, Que., B.A. 1919; Magdalen Coll. Oxford (Rhodes Scholar) B.A. 1922, B.Litt. 1923; McGill Univ., B.C.L. 1927; LL.D., Dalhousie 1958, Manitoba 1961, Queen's 1964, Brit. Columbia 1965, Saskatchewan 1965, Osgoode Hall 1966, McGill 1967, Laval 1969, York 1976, Carleton 1977, Simon Fraser 1980; D. Litt., Sir George Williams 1966, Toronto 1969; D.C.L., Bishop's 1970, Windsor 1970; D. és Jur., Montréal 1966; m. Marian Mildred Dale 1928; one s.; Teacher, Que. High Sch. 1919, Bishop's Coll. Sch. 1920, Lower Can. Coll. 1923-24; practised law 1927, becoming full-time teacher, McGill Faculty of Law 1928, Dean of Faculty 1961-64; Co-founder (with F. H. Underhill) and Past Pres., League for Social Reconstr.; mem. Nat Extve., Candn. Inst. Internat. Affairs 1935-50; Nat. Chrmn., CCF Party 1942-50; UN Tech. Assistance Res. Rep. to Burma 1952; Chrmn., Candn. Writers Conf. 1955; Pres., Academy II, Roy. Soc. Can. 1960; Adviser to Sask. Govt. at Constitutional Confs. 1950 and 1960; Co-Ed., McGill Fortnightly Review 1925-27, The Canadian Mercury 1928, Canadian Forum 1936-39, Preview 1942-45, Northern Review 1945-47; Chrmn., Legal Research Comte., Candn. Bar Assn. 1954-56; Del. to Brit. Commonwealth Labour Parties Confs., London, Eng. 1944, Toronto 1947; Counsel in several civil liberties cases, Supreme Court Can. 1956-64; Guggenheim Fellow 1940; Hon. Foreign mem.,

Am. Acad. Arts and Sciences 1967; Corresponding Fellow Br. Acad. 1978; mem. Royal Comn. on Bilingualism and Biculturalism 1963-71; Visiting Prof., Univ. of Toronto 1953, Mich. State Univ. 1957, French Studies Programme McGill Univ. 1967-71, Dalhousie 1969-71; poetry books published: 'Overture' 1945; 'Events and Signals' 1954, 'The Eye of the Needle' 1957; 'Poems of Garneau and Hébert' (translation) 1962; 'Signature' 1964; 'Selected Poems' 1966, 'Trouvailles' 1967; 'The Dance Is One', 1973; 'Poems of French Canada' 1977 (translations winner of Can. Council Award); other publications: 'Canada Today, Her National Interests and National Policy' 1938; 'Civil Liberties and Canadian Federalism' 1959; '''Essays on the Constitution'' 1977 (Gov. Gen.'s Award); Co-author of 'Social Planning for Canada' 1935; 'Democracy Needs Socialism' 1938; 'Make This Your Canada' 1943; 'Canada After The War' 1943; 'Quebec States Her Case' 1964; Co-ed. (with A. J. M. Smith) 'New Provinces,Poems of Several Authors' 1936; 'The Blasted Pine, an Anthology of Satire, Irreverent and Disrespectful Verse' 1957; also articles on constitutional law and pol.; Awards incl. Guarantors' Prize, Poetry, Chicago 1944; Que. Lit. Prize 1960 and 1964; Lorne Pierce Medal, Royal Soc. Can. 1964; Molson Award, Can. Council 1967; professor emeritus, McGill 1975; Writer-in-Residence, Concordia Univ. 1979-80; Hon. Life mem. The Writers' Union of Can., 1980; Clubs: Faculty (McGill); University (Montreal); Address: 451 Clarke Ave., Montreal, Que. H3Y 3C5.

SCOTT, George David, M.A., Ph.D., university professor; b. Toronto, Ont., 2 Jan. 1918; s. Charles Geldard and Elizabeth Alice (Faircloth) S.; e. Univ. of Toronto, B.A., 1939, M.A. 1940, Ph.D. 1946; m. Mary Allison, d. George F. Simson, Toronto, 31 May 1948; children: Donna, Nancy, Stephen; PROF. OF PHYSICS, UNIV. OF TORONTO; served in 2nd World War with R.C.N.V.R., 1943-45; Radar Offr., Royal Navy; mem., Candn. Assn. Physicists (Secy. 1960-63); author of over 50 papers in scient. journs.; recreation: cottage; Home: 74 Yorkminister Road, Willowdale, Ont. M2P 1M3.

SCOTT, George H., B.Sc.; executive; b. Philadelphia, Pa., 19 Nov. 1912; e. Lafayette Coll., B.Sc. 1935; m. Jane Segsworth; children: Ruth Ann, George H. Jr., Judith Ethel, David G., W. John, Sharron L.; Dir. and retired Pres., Engelhard Industries of Can. Ltd.; Pres. and Dir., Engelhard Ore and Base Metal Corp. Ltd.; Dir., Dickenson Mines Ltd.; Engelhard Industries International; Vice-Pres., Orthopaedic and Arthritic Hosp.; Past Pres., Candn. Jewellers Assn.; Freemason; United Church; recreations: curling, fishing; Clubs: Caledon Mountain Trout; Rotary (Toronto); Board of Trade; 24 KARAT; Granite (Dir.); Home: 66 Arjay Cres., Willowdale, Ont. M2L 1C7.

SCOTT, H. Brent, B.Sc., P.Eng.; b. Calgary, Alta. 11 June 1925; s. Henry Earl and Isobel (Lang) S.; e. Crescent Heights High Sch., Calgary 1943; Univ. of Alta. B.Sc. (Civil Engn.) 1947; m. Lillian Isobel, d. Richard Swift, 10 May 1947; three s., Richard Brent, James Rowan, Brian Kelly; Pres. And Chief Extve. Offr., Syncrude Canada Ltd. since 1975-81; joined British American Oil (subsequently Gulf Canada) in 1947 serving in various positions Calgary, Moose Jaw, Edmonton, Clarkson; Mgr. Engn. Refining Dept., Toronto; joined present Co. as Vice Pres. and Gen. Mgr. 1972, Extve. Vice Pres. 1974; mem. Adv. Bd. Alta. & Candn. Content, Assn. Prof. Engrs, Geol., & Geophys. of Alta.; Chrmn., Adv. Bd., Co-ordinated Summer Work Program, Eng. Faculty, U. of A.; mem., Bus. Adv. Council Faculty Bus. Admin. and Comm., U. of A.; mem. Engn. Inst. Can.; Assn. Prof. Engrs.; Cdn. Council, Conference Bd. in Can.; Regular mem. Conference Bd. Inc., N.Y.; Chrmn., Ninth Nat. Northern Devel. Conf. (1982); recreations: skiing, sailing; Clubs: Royal Glenora; Edmonton Petroleum; Home: 33 Westbrook Dr., Edmonton, Alta. T6J 2C8;.

SCOTT, Henry James, M.D., D.C.L., F.R.C.S.(C), F.A.C.S., F.A.C.C.P.; surgeon, professor; b. Montreal, Quebec, 16 January 1918; s. Hon. William Bridges and Esther Florence (Aird) S.; e. Selwyn House School 1925-27; Roslyn School 1927-30; Westmount (P.Q.) High Sch. 1930-32; Trinity Coll. Sch. 1932-34; Bishop's Univ. B.A. 1937; McGill Univ. M.D. 1941, Dipl. in Surgery, 1951; F.R.C.S.(C) 1950; m. Pamela Todd, now divorced; children: Susan Jennifer, Christopher William Richard, Charles Farquhar, Mary Lee; 2ndly, Audrey MacKenzie; SR. SURGEON AND DIRECTOR, DIV. OF THORACIC & CARDIOVASCULAR SURGERY, MONTREAL GENERAL HOSPITAL, since 1963; Consultant in Thoracic and Cardiac Surgery, Reddy Mem. Hosp.; Prof. of Surgery, McGill Univ.; interned Montreal General Hosp. 1941-42; apptd. to Surgical Staff, 1951; served in 2nd World War in R.C.A.M.C., in Can. and overseas, No. 17 Candn. Gen. Hosp. 1942-45; mem. of Corp., Bishop's Univ.; mem., Montreal Clinisurgical Soc.; Lafleur Reporting Soc.; McGill-Osler Reporting Soc.; Assn. of Surg., P.Q.; Assn. of Thoracic and Cardiovascular Surg., P.Q.; Candn. Cardiovascular Soc.; Candn. Soc. Clinical Surgeons; Am. Assn. for Thoracic Surg.; Central Surg. Assn.; Hon. D.C.L. Bishop's; Alpha Delta Phi; Anglican; recreations: golf, skiing; Clubs: Royal Montreal Golf; Red Birds Ski; Montreal Badminton & Squash; Home: 611 Sydenham Ave., Westmount, P.Q. H3Y 2Z3; Office: 3550 Cote des Neiges Rd., Montreal, P.Q. H3H 1V4.

SCOTT, J. Michael G.; investment executive; b. Toronto, Ont. 9 Sept. 1927; s. William Pearson and Joan Alix (Grierson) S.; e. Upper Can. Coll. and Univ. of Toronto Schs., Toronto; Univ. of Toronto; m. Janet White, d. Douglas W. Ambridge, 21 Oct. 1950; children: Peter, Tom, Sarah, Geoffrey, Martha, Mary; VICE CHRMN., WOOD GUNDY LTD.; Dir. Simpsons, Ltd.; Bombardier Inc.; Redpath Ind. Ltd.; Dir. Bishop's Coll. Sch.; Toronto Mendelssohn Choir; Montreal Childrens Hosp. Foundation; Montreal Museum of Fine Arts; Gov. Montreal Gen. Hosp. Corp.; Montreal Stock Exchange mem. Invest. Dealers Assn.; Arthritis Soc., Que. Div.; Anglican; recreations: golf, tennis, hunting, fishing; Clubs: Mount Royal; Mount Bruno Golf & Country; Montreal Badminton & Squash; Toronto Golf; Toronto Badminton & Racquet; Vancouver; Vancouver Lawn Tennis & Racquet; Ristigouche Salmon; Home: 324 Kensington Ave., Westmount, Que. H3Z 2H3; Office: One Place Ville Marie, Montreal, Que. H3B 3P7

SCOTT, John Douglass, B.Sc.; company president; b. Port McNicoll, Ont., 29 Apl. 1920; s. Rev. William J. and Helen (Ford) S.; e. Pub. Sch., Owen Sound, Ont.; High Sch., Flesherton and Stirling, Ont.; Queen's Univ., B.Sc. (Mech. Engn.) 1942; m. Jean, d. Dr. R. M. Parker, 18 Aug. 1944; children: Gordon, Brian, Deborah; PRESIDENT AND CHRMN. OF BD. CROWN CORK & SEAL CAN. INC. Dir., Crown Cork & Seal West Indies Ltd.; joined present Co. as Jr. Engr., 1945; Vice-Pres. and Dir. 1950; Extve. Vice-Pres. 1967; served with RCN in N. Atlantic 1942-45; rank Lt.; mem., Soc. Soft Drink Techs.; Master Brewers Assn.; Assn. Prof. Engrs. Ont.; Candn. Mfrs. Assn.; Bd. Trade Metrop. Toronto; United Church; recreations: golf, skiing, boating; Home: 32 HiMount Dr., Willowdale, Ont.; Office: 7900 Keele St., Concord, Ont..

SCOTT, John Wilson, M.A., M.D.; physician; retired university professor; b. Toronto, Ont., 7 July 1915; s. Dr. Paul Lindsay and Mary Agnes (Wilson) S.; e. Oakwood Coll. Inst., Toronto, Ont.; Univ. of Toronto (Victoria), B.A. 1937, M.A. (Physiol.) 1938, M.D. 1941; Post-grad. study, Toronto Gen. Hosp. (1941 and 1946-47), Atomic Energy Project, Chalk River (1947), Montreal Neurol. Inst. (1948). Nat. Hosp., Queen Sq., London, Eng., Nuffield Fellow (1948-49) m. Grace Winnifred, d. late Russell Workman, North Bay, Ont. 7 June 1941; children: Aleda Mary, James Russell; Assoc. Prof. 1956-60, Prof. of Physiology, Univ. of Toronto 1960-78; Dir. of EEG Lab., Toronto Gen. Hosp.; Consultant to Sunnybrook Hosp., D.V.A., Toronto 1951-62; Consultant in Electroencephal. to R.C.A.F. (1956); served in 2nd World War; Surg. Lieut, R.C.N.V.R., May 1942; apptd. to R.C.N. Med. Research Univ, 1942; promoted Surg. Lieut-Commdr. 1945 for duty with Royal Navy; trans. to inactive service Aug. 1946; Dir. and Vice Pres., Associated Medical Serv. since 1976; mem., Acad. Med. Toronto (mem. of Council; Editor of 'Bulletin', 1949-62; Treas. 1966-69; Pres. 1970-71); Candn. Neurol. Soc. (Council 1952-55); Eastern Assn. Electroencephal. (Pres., 1960); Am. E.E.G. Soc. (Council 1958-59); Ont. Med. Assn.; Candn. Med. Assn.; Chrmn., R.C.N. Personnel Research Comte. (1954-65), Surg. Gen. Adv. Comte. (1963); Pres. (1960-62), York Pioneer & Hist. Soc.; mem. Toronto Hist. Bd. since 1968 (Chrmn. 1977-80); author and jt. author of a no. of articles relating to his special field in scient. journs.; United Church: recreations: gardening, painting, medical and local history; Clubs: Arts and Letters; Roy. Candn. Mil. Inst.; Home: Box 142, Bond Head, Ont. L0G 1B0; Office: 101 College St., Toronto, Ont. M5G 1L7.

SCOTT, Marian Dale, R.C.A.; painter; b. Montreal, Que. 26 June 1906; d. Robert J. and Marian (Barclay) Dale; e. The Study Montreal; Art Gallery of Montreal; Ecole des Beaux-Arts Montreal; Monument Nat. Montreal; Slade Sch. of Art Eng.; m. Francis Reginald Scott 28 Feb. 1928; one s. Peter Dale; solo exhns. incl. Grace Horne Galleries Boston 1941; Queen's Univ. 1948; Dom. Gallery Montreal 1954, 1956, 1958; Laing Gallery Toronto 1961; Galerie Camille Hébert Montreal 1964; Galerie Libre Montreal 1967; Galerie L'Atelier Renée Le Sieur Quebec City 1970; McGill Univ. 1978; due exhns.: Montreal Museum of Fine Arts 1949, 1960; Art Gallery of Ont. 1941, 1953; Hart House Univ. of Toronto 1941; rep. in nat. and internat. group shows incl.: N.Y. World's Fair 1939 (watercolour); 50 Yrs. of Candn. Painting Nat. Gallery Can. 1942; Addison Gallery Andover, Mass. (travelling) 1942; Biennale Sao Paulo Brazil 1951, 1953; Devel. Candn. Painting 1665-1945 Nat. Gallery Can., Musée du Qué., Art Assn. Montreal, Art Gallery of Ont.; Master Candn. Painters & Sculptors London, Ont. 1963; "Panorama" Peinture du Qué. 1940-66 Musée d'Art Contemporain; Que. Pavillion Expo '67; Exposition des Créateurs du Qué. Quebec City 1971; Women Painters in Can. Agnes Etherington Art Centre Kingston 1976; Spectrum Can. 1976; Exchange Exhn. Galerie Pleides New York and Conseil de la Peintures du Qué. 1979; Artistes Canadiens à New York Noho Gallery 1980; Contemporary Art Soc. Montreal 1937-48 Edmonton Art Gallery 1980; rep. in various pub., corporate and private colls. incl. Nat. Gallery Can., Montreal Museum of Fine Arts, Musée du Qué., Art Gallery of Ont.; recipient Candn. Group of Painters Exhn. Prize 1966; Purchase Award Thomas More Inst. Montreal 1967; Baxter Purchase Award Ont. Soc. Artists 1969; mem. Candn. Group Painters; Soc. des Artistes en Arts Visuels du Qué.; Royal Candn. Academy of Arts; Address: 451 Clarke Ave., Westmount, Que. H3Y 3C5.

SCOTT, Marianne Florence, B.A., B.L.S.: librarian; b. Toronto, Ont. 4 Dec. 1928; d. Merle Redvers Scott; e. McGill Univ. B.A. 1949, B.L.S. 1952; DIR. OF LIBRARIES, McGILL UNIV. 1975- ; Asst. Lib., Bank of Montreal, 1952-55; Law Lib., McGill Univ. 1955-73, Law Area Lib. 1973-74, Lectr. in Legal Bibliog. 1964-74; rec'd Queen's Silver Jubilee Medal 1977; Co-founder and Ed., "Index to Canadian Legal Periodical Literature" 1963- ; author various articles; mem. Internat. Assn. Law Libraries (mem. of Bd. 1969-71); Am. Assn. Law Libraries (mem. of Comtes. 1973-77); Candn. Assn. Law Libraries (Pres. 1963-69, Extve. Bd. 1973-75), First Hon. mem. 1980-); Que. Lib. Assn. (Pres 1961-62); Corp. Prof. Librarians Que. (Vice Pres. 1975); Candn. Assn. Research Libs. (Pres. 1978-79), Past Pres. 1979-80, Exec. 1980-81); mem. Libs. Sub-Comte., Conf. des Recteurs et des Principaux des Universites du Qué. (Chrmn. 1976-78); UNICAT/-TELECAT Mang. Comte. (Chrmn. 1975-80) Candn. Li-

brary Assn. (First Vice pres., 1980-81; Pres. 1981-82); Internat. Fedn. of Library Assn. (Hon. Comte., 48th Gen. Conference of IFLA, Montreal, 1982); The Centre for Research Libraries (Bd. of Dir. 1980-83); Club: University Women's; Home: 3848 Melrose Ave., Montreal, Que. H4A 2S2; Office: 3459 McTavish St., Montreal, Que. H3A 1Y1.

SCOTT, Robert Alexander, B.Com., LL.B.; Alberta public servant; b. Port Arthur, Ont., 11 May 1930; s. David James and Christina (Ross) S.; e. Daniel McIntyre Coll. Inst., Winnipeg, 1948; Univ. of Man., B. Com. 1951; Univ. of Sask., LL.B. 1957; m. Estelle Margaret Pillar, 18 July 1959; two s., Andrew N., Ian D.; PRES., VANCOUVER STOCK EXCHANGE; called to Bars of Sask. 1958, Alta. 1961; Solr., Francis, Gauley & Hughes, Saskatoon 1958-60; Fenerty & Co., Calgary 1961-69; B.C. Securities Comn. 1970 (Depy. Supt. of Brokers of Comn. 1971-72); Asst. Vice Pres. and Vice Pres., Membership and Compliance, Vancouver Stock Exchange 1973; Chrmn., Alberta Securities Comn. 1974-76; mem. Law Soc. Sask.; Law Soc. Alta.; Candn. Bar Assn.; Home: 216 Rondoval Cr., N. Vancouver, B.C. V7N 2W7; Office: 536 Howe St., Vancouver, B.C. V6C 2E1.

SCOTT, Rev. Robert Balgarnie Young, M.A., B.D., Ph.D., D.D., F.R.S.C.; clergyman; educator; b. Toronto, Ont. 16 July 1899; s. late Rev. John McPherson S. and late Elizabeth (Young) S.; e. Toronto Model Sch.; Univ. of Toronto Schs. 1917; Univ. of Toronto B.A. 1922, M.A. 1924, Ph.D. 1928; Union Coll. (Knox-Victoria) Toronto B.D. 1926; Hon. D.D.: Victoria Univ. Toronto 1945, Union Coll. of B.C. 1957, Univ. of Aberdeen 1968, McGill Univ. 1977; m. (1) Kathleen D. d. late Arthur B. Cordingley 10 Sept. 1924; children: Mary Elizabeth (Mrs. J.V. Poapst), John McPherson, Gavin Robert Wakefield; m. (2) Ruth Trethewey, W. Frank Secord, 28 Nov. 1981; Prof. Emeritus of Religion, Princeton Univ. since 1968; o. 1926; Prof. of Old Testament Lit. Union Coll. of B.C. 1928-1931; Un. Theol. Coll. Montreal 1931-55; Faculty of Divinity, McGill Univ. 1948-55 (Dean 1948-49); Prof. of Religion, Princeton Univ. 1955-68, Chrmn. 1963-65, McCosh Faculty Fellow 1966-67; Annual Prof. Am. Sch. of Oriental Research, Jerusalem 1962-63; served with RNCVR 1917-19, Wireless Operator; RCAF 1943-45, Hon. Flight Lt. and Chaplain; rec'd Prov. of Que. Lit. Prize 1946; Candn. Council Chs. Prize for Centennial Hymn 1967; author 10 hymns (lyrics) publ. in more than 30 hymn books nat. and internat.; ed. and contrib. "Towards the Christian Revolution" 1936; author "The Relevance of the Prophets" 1944 (rev. ed., 1968); "Treasures from Judean Caves" 1955; "Isaiah 1-39 (Interpreter's Bible)" 1956; "The Psalms as Christian Praise" 1958; "Proverbs and Ecclesiastes" 1965; "The Way of Wisdom" 1971; book chapters, contrib. reference works, articles and reviews; Fellow, Am. Council Learned Socs. 1962-63; mem. Soc. Biblical Lit. (Pres. 1960); Candn. Soc. Biblical Studies (Secy.-Treas. 1932-39, Pres. 1972); Soc. Old Testament Study (UK) 1948-74; Internat. Congs. Old Testament Studies 1952-65; United Church; Address: 55 Belmont St., Toronto, Ont. M5R 1R1.

SCOTT-HARSTON, John Charles, Q.C., M.A.; b. Hong Kong, 26 Nov. 1912; s. John and Mabel (Melbourne) S-H.; e. Sherborne Sch., Dorset, Eng.; Magdalen Coll., Oxford Univ., B.A. 1934, M.A.; m. Cloradh, d. James Gaffney, Limerick, Ireland, 18 Oct. 1940; one s. Michael; ASSOC. COUNCIL AND RETIRED PARTNER, CREASE & CO.; admitted as Solr. of Supreme Court in Eng. 1937; called to Bar of B.C. 1949; cr. Q.C. 1967; Commr. for Oaths, Eng., 1946; Gov., Candn. Tax Foundation, 1960-64; served with Brit. Army Overseas 1939-45; author, 'Tax Planned Will Precedents', 1965; Consultant, Law Reform Comm. of B.C. 1982-85; mem., Law Soc., Eng.; Victoria and Candn. Bar Assns.; Law Soc. B.C.; Club: Union, Home: Apt. 202 2340 Oak Bay Ave., Victoria, B.C. V8R 1G9; Office: 1070 Douglas, Victoria, B.C. V8W 2S8.

SCURFIELD, Ralph Thomas, B.Sc.; executive; b. Broadview, Sask. 7 Jan. 1928; s. Ralph and Anne Marie (Parsons) S.; e. Univ. of Man. B.Sc. 1948, Teaching Dipl. 1950; Harvard Univ. Advanced Mang. Program; m. Sonia d. late John C. Onishenko 24 July 1954; 7 children; CHRMN. OF BD. AND CHIEF EXTVE. OFFR., NU-WEST GROUP LTD.; Dir. Nu-West Developments; Voyager Petroleums Ltd.; Nu-West Inc.; Carma Ltd.; TransAlta Utilities Corp.; MICC Investments Ltd.; The Mortgage Insurance Co. of Canada; Alberta Gas Chemicals Ltd.; Allarco Group Ltd.; mem. Conf. Bd. Can.; Gov., Banff Centre; mem. Mang. Adv. Council Univ. of Calgary; Pres. Nu-West Homes Ltd. 1957; Past Pres., N. Calgary Business Assn.; Housing & Urban Devel. Assn. Calgary; Housing & Urban Devel. Assn. Can.; Past Chrmn. Residential Devel. Council HUDAC; United Church; recreations: skiing, golf, fishing; Clubs: Ranchmen's; Silver Springs Golf & County; Calgary Winter; Calgary Petroleum; Home: 1640 Cayuga Dr. N.W., Calgary, Alta. T2L 0N3; Office: (P.O. Box 6958, Stn. D) 3030 - 2 Ave. S.E., Calgary, Alta. T2P 4A6.

SEABORN, James Blair, M.A.; Canadian public servant; b. Toronto, Ont., 18 March 1924; s. Richard and Muriel Kathleen (Reid) S.; e. Normal Model Sch., Toronto, 1936; Univ. of Toronto Schs., 1941, Univ. of Toronto, B.A. (Trinity Coll.) 1947, M.A. 1948; m. Carol Allen, d. Rolph M. Trow, Stratford, Ont., 9 Sept. 1950; children: Geoffrey Blair, Virginia Allen: DEPY. MIN. ENVIRONMENT CANADA, since January 1975; joined Dept. of External Affairs 1948; Third Secy. and Second Secy., The Hague, 1950-54, Ottawa 1955-57; First Secy., Paris, 1957-59; Counsellor, Moscow, 1959-62; Head of E. European Sec., Ottawa, 1962-64; Commr. Candn. Del. to Internat. Comn. for Supervision and Control, Vietnam, 1964-65; Depy. Head of Eastern European Section, Ottawa, 1966-67; Head of Far E. Div., Ottawa, 1967-70; Asst. Depy. Min. (Consumer Affairs) Dept. Consumer & Corporate Affairs 1970-74; served with Canadian Army in Canada and U.K. 1943-46; Anglican; recreations: skiing, tennis; Home: 79 MacKay St., Ottawa, Ont. K1M 2E4; Office: Fontaine Bldg. (Hull) Ottawa, Ont. K1A 0H3.

SEABORN, Right Rev. Robert Lowder, M.A. B.D., D.D., D.C.L., LL.D. (Ang.); b. Toronto, Ont. 9 July 1911; s. Rev. Richard and Muriel Kathleen (Reid) S.; e. Normal Model Sch., Toronto; Univ. of Toronto Schs.; Trinity Coll., Toronto, B.A. 1932, M.A. 1934, B.D. 1938, D.D. 1948; Bishops Univ., D.C.L. 1962; LL.D., Memorial 1972; D.D., Montreal Diocesan Theological Coll. 1980; Oxford Univ., 1936-37; m. Mary Elizabeth, d. George McC. Gilchrist, Toronto, 29 Jan. 1938; children: Richard Gilchrist, John Robert, Elizabeth Jane, Charles Alan, Michael Reid; BISHOP ORDINARY TO CANADIAN ARMED FORCES since 1980; Archbishop and Metropolitan of the Eccl. Prov. of Can. 1975-80; o. Deacon. 1934; Priest, 1935; Asst. Curate, St. Simon's Church, Toronto, 1934-36; St. James' Cath., Toronto 1937-41; Rector, St. Peter's Cobourg, Ont., 1941-48; Dean and Rector, Holy Trinity Cath., Quebec, 1948-57; Rector, St. Mary's Kerrisdale, Vancouver, 1957-58; Asst. Bishop of Nfld., 1958-65; Bishop of Nfld. 1965-75; Archbishop of E. Nfld. and Labrador 1976-80; served with Candn. Chaplain Service, Hon. Capt., 3rd Bn. Q.O.R., 1942-43 in Can.; 1st Bn., Candn Scot. Regt., Eng. and N.W. Europe, 1943-45; awarded Croix de Guerre (France); mem., Royal Candn. Legion; recreations: golf, camping; Address: 247 Lake St., Cobourg, Ont. K9A 1R6

SEABROOK, Victor Melville; barrister and solicitor; b. Ottawa, Ont., 25 June 1928; s. Richard Melville and Marjorie Edith (Crawford) S.; e. Univ. of Toronto, B.A. 1951; Osgoode Hall, Toronto, Ont.; m. Isobel Ruth, d. Alexander Cameron, North Bay, Ont., 27 Dec. 1955; children: Richard Melville, Peter Cameron, Timothy Victor; PARTNER, SEABROOK & ASSOC.; Pres. and Dir., Denver TC, Inc.; Vice-Pres. and Dir., Granada Distributors (Can-

ada) Ltd.; Secy and Dir., Granada TV Rental Ltd.; Bradley Family Holdings Ltd.; Dir. and Secy.-Treas., Quartet Energy Resources Ltd.; International Gold and Minerals Ltd.; Oiltex International Ltd.; Dir., Energy Assets International Corp., Barclays Finance Corp.; Barclays Bank of Canada; read law with McMillan, Binch, Stuart, Berry, Dunn, Corrigan & Howland, Toronto, Ont. called to the Bar of Ont., 1955; mem., St. Andrew's Soc.; P. Conservative; Anglican; recreations: golf, skiing; Clubs: Albany; Canadian (New York); Granite; Toronto Golf; Briars Golf and Country; Home: 126 Forest Hill Road, Toronto, Ont. M4V 2L9 Office: Ste. 3300, P.O. Box 33, First Canadian Place, Toronto, Ont. M5X 1A9.

SEAGRAM, Norman Meredith, B.A.Sc., M.Sc.; b. Toronto, Ont., 10 July 1934; s. Norman Oliver and Constance Beatrice (Mills) S.; e. Trinity Coll. Sch., Port Hope, Ont.; Univ. of Toronto, B.A.Sc. 1958; Univ. of Birmingham (U.K.) M.Sc. 1964; m. Joyce Elizabeth, d. Frederick William McMackon, Victoria, B.C., 21 Aug. 1958; children: Susan Elizabeth; Norman Philip, Joseph Frederick, Samantha; PRES., SEAWAY/MIDWEST LTD., since 1977; Dir., Canlon Investments Limited; commenced as Engr., Production Systems Department, Rootes Limited. Coventry England 1958; Consultant, Associated Industrial Consultants Limited, London, England 1960, Nairobi, Kenya and Salisbury, Rhodesia 1961-63; Consultant, Management Sciences Limited, London, Eng. 1964; Princ., Inbucon Services Ltd., Halifax, N.S. and Toronto, Ont. 1965; Extve. Asst. to Sr. Vice-Pres., Candn. Indust. Group Molson Industries Ltd., Toronto 1968; Mgr., Marketing, Anthes Equipment Ltd., Port Credit, Ont. 1969; Dir., Planning, Molson Breweries of Canada Ltd., Montreal 1970; Vice Pres. Planning & Personnel 1972; Vice Pres. Planning & Industry Affairs 1976; mem. Assn. Prof. Engrs. Ontario; Candn. Operational Research Soc.; N. Am. Soc. for Corp. Planning; Alpha Delta Phi; P. Conservative; Anglican; recreations: tennis, squash, golf, skiing, hockey; Clubs: Toronto Golf; Toronto Badminton & Racquet; Hillside Tennis; Home: 61 Highland Ave., Toronto, Ont. M4W 2A2; Office: 160 Carrier Dr., Rexdale, Ont. M9W 5P7.

SEAGRAM, Norman Oliver, Q.C., B.A.; b. Toronto, Ont., 6 Sept. 1908; s. Norman and Gladys May (Buchanan) S.; e. Trinity Coll. Sch., Port Hope, Ont.; Univ. of Toronto, B.A. 1930; Osgoode Hall, Toronto, Ont.; m. Constance Beatrice Mills, 14 Sept. 1933; children: Norman Meredith, John David, Robert Michael; PARTNER STRATHY, ARCHIBALD, & SEAGRAM; Chrmn. Hogg, Robinson Innes Ins. Brokers Ltd.; read law with Blake, Lash, Anglin and Cassels; called to the Bar of Ontario, 1933; cr. Q.C. 1954; Wing Commander, R.C.A.F. in 2nd World War, 1940-45; mem., Toronto Bd. Trade; Alpha Delta Phi; Conservative; Anglican; recreations: golf, curling, skiing, Clubs: Toronto; Toronto Golf; University; Badminton & Racquet; Toronto Cricket, Skating & Curling; Toronto Lawyers: Royal & Ancient Golf (St. Andrews, Scotland); St. Andrews (Scotland); Home: Granite Place, 63 St. Clair Ave. W., Toronto, Ont. M4V 2Y9; Office: Ste. 3800 Commerce Court West, Toronto, Ont..

SEAMAN, Byron J., B.Sc.; petroleum executive; b. Sask. 1923; e. Univ. of Sask. B.Sc. (Mech. Engn.) 1945; m. Evelyn Virginia, Sept. 1949; children: Karen Gayle, Ronald James, Deborah Joan, Allan Byron; VICE CHRMN. AND DIR., BOW VALLEY INDUSTRIES LTD. 1976-; Chrmn. of Bd. and Dir. Bow Valley Resource Services Ltd.; Dir. Western Rock Bit Co. Ltd.; Fidelity Trust Co.; Fort Garry Trust Co.; Patrician Land Holdings Ltd.; former Instr. in Mech. Engn. Univ. of Sask.; Geophysicist, Carter Oil Co.; Liaison Engr. Constr. Dept. Gulf Oil; Seismograph Operator Western Geophysical; joined brother Seaman Engineering and Drilling Co. Ltd. 1949 (now present co.), Vice Pres. and Dir. Bow Valley 1960, Sr. Vice Pres. 1968, Extve. Vice Pres. 1975, Vice Chrmn. 1976; mem. Calgary Chamber Comm.; Home: 4704 Britania Dr. S.W., Calgary, Alta. Office: 1800, 321 Sixth Ave. S.W., Calgary, Alta. T2P 2V8.

SEAMAN, Daryl K., B.Sc.; petroleum executive; b. Sask. 1925; e. Univ. of Sask. B.Sc. (Mech. Eng.) 1948; CHRMN. OF BD., PRES., CHIEF EXTVE. OFFR. AND DIR., BOW VALLEY INDUSTRIES LTD. (formerly Seaman Engineering & Drilling Co. Ltd., inc. 1949 with 2 brothers); Dir. Crown Trust Co.; Pan-Alberta Gas Ltd.; Revelstoke Companies Ltd.; Marathon Realty Ltd.; Nova; mem. Bd. Regents Athol Murray Coll. of Notre Dame; Club: Calgary Petroleum; Office: 1800, 321 Sixth Ave. S.W., Calgary, Alta. T2P 2V8

SEARLE, James Elmhurst, B.Arch., F.R.A.I.C., Hon. F.A.I.A. architect; b. Winnipeg, 13 June 1929; s. James Winning and Agnes Elizabeth (Graham) S.; e. Univ. of Manitoba, B. Arch. 1951; m. Judith P. Menzies, d. A. Wilfred Menzies, Toronto, March 1973; children of previous marriage: Lauraine, James, Christine, Michael; SR. VICE PRES., GENSTAR CONSTRUCTION LTD INTERNATIONAL DIVISION; 1979- ; Dir., Western Foundry Co. Ltd.; joined staff of firm headed by Smith and Carter on grad.; Assoc., 1954, Partner 1959, firm merging with John B. Parkin, Toronto, firm 1969; Man. Partner, Searle Wilbee Rowland; Partner, Smith Carter Partners; Pres. S.W.R. Consultants Ltd., all 1969-73; Sr. Vice Pres. Abbey Glen Property Corp. 1973-77; Pres., Grenstar Commercial Development Co.; Sr. Vice Pres., Genstar Projects (Middle East) Ltd. 1977-79; F.R.A.I.C. (Pres., 1967-68); mem., (Ont. Assn. Archs; Ordre des architects, Que.; Anglican; Clubs: Manitoba; Winnipeg Squash Racquet (Life mem.); Cambridge Granite; Home: 93 Bedford Rd., Toronto, Ont. M5R 2K4; Office: 123 Edward St., 14th Floor, Toronto M5G 1G5.

SEARLE, Stewart Augustus, B.Com.; executive; b. Winnipeg, Man., 29 Dec. 1923; s. Stewart Augustus and Sally Elizabeth (Appleyard) S.; e. St. John's-Ravenscourt Sch., Winnipeg; Trinity Coll. Sch., Port Hope, Ont.; Queen's Univ., B.Com. 1947; m. Maudie, d. Peter Jessiman, 9 Nov. 1949; children: Stewart A., David J.; CHRMN. OF BD. AND DIR., FEDERAL INDUSTRIES LIMITED: Dir., The White Pass and Yukon Corps. Ltd.; Standard Aero. Ltd; Thunder Bay Terminals Ltd.; mem. Adv. Bd., Royal Trust; Vice Pres., Treas., Searle Grain Co. Ltd.; Vice Pres., Oper., Pres. 1965; Exec. Vice Pres., Fed. Grain Ltd. 1972; mem. Nat. Bd. of Candn. Council of Christians and Jews; served in 2nd World War, Artillery and Infantry 1942-45; rank on discharge Lieutenant; Nat. Bd. mem., Candn. Council Christians and Jews; Anglican; recreations: sailing , electronics, gardening, chess, Clubs: Winnipeg Winter; Winnipeg Squash; Home: 118 Handsart Blvd., Winnipeg, Man.; R3P 0C5; Office: 2400 One Lombard Place, Winnipeg, Man. R3B 0X3.

SEARS, John T., B.Com., M.B.A., D.B.A.; educator; b. Antigonish, N.S., 19 Oct. 1931; s. Cyril Francis and Irene G. (MacDonald) S.; e. St. Francis Xavier Univ., B.Com. 1952; Univ. of Detroit, M.B.A. 1954; Harvard Univ., D.B.A. 1966 m. Mary Ann, d. J. C. Hemeon, Liverpool, N.S. 23 May 1955; children: Stephanie, Meaghan, Mark, (late) Siobhan, Mairi: PROF. OF BUSINESS ADM., ST. FRANCIS XAVIER UNIV. since 1969, Dean of Arts there 1970-81 and Dean of Science 1972-81; Dir., Industrial Estates Ltd. 1970-75; joined present Univ. as Lectr. in Business Adm. 1954, Asst. Prof. 1956-57. Assoc. Prof. 1960-69; Visiting Assoc. Prof. of Business Adm., Univ of W., Ont. 1968-69 and 1978-79; mem., Regional Adv. Council, Fed. Business Devel. Bank 1978-81; Pres., Bd. of Trustees. St. Martha's Hospital, Antigonish, since 1972; Gov., Inst. Canadian Bankers 1971-73; mem., Nova Scotia Region Enterprise Devel. Bd. of Dept. of Industry, Trade and Commerce, 1981- ; author, 'Institutional Financing of Small Business in Nova Scotia'. 1972; mem., Am. Finance Assn.; Financial Mang. Assn.; R. Catholic; recreations:

skiing, golf, fishing; Home: 52 Hawthorne St., Antigonish, N.S. B2G 1A4; Office: Antigonish, N.S..

SEARY, Edgar Ronald, M.A., Ph.D., Litt.D., F.R. Hist.S., F.S.A.; professor; b. Sheffield, England, 17 Jan. 1908; s. Henry and Edith (Brunt) S.; e. Univ. of Sheffield, B.A. (Hons. Eng. Lang. and Lit.) 1929, M.A. 1930, Ph.D. 1933 (Research Scholar and Fellow of University, 1930-32), Litt.D. 1971; Memorial, D.Litt. 1973; m. Agnes Gwendolen, d. late J. R. Crookes, Birley Carr, Yorks, England, 1935; children: John, Peter, Richard; EMERITUS PROFESSOR OF ENGLISH, MEMORIAL UNIV. OF NFLD., 1978; Prof. since 1953 and Head of Dept. of Eng. Lang. & Lit. 1954-70; Henrietta Harvey Prof. 1970; Lect. in Eng., Dolmetscher Institut, Handelshochschule, Mannheim, Germany, 1933; Lect. and subsequently Sr. Lect. in Eng., Rhodes Univ., S. Africa, 1935-51; Prof. of Eng., Coll. of Arts & Science, Baghdad, 1951-53; served in 2nd World War with S.A. Arty. and S.A. Army Educ. Service, 1940-45, with rank of Capt.; Publications: "South African Short Stories", 1947; "Reading English", 1958 (with G. M. Story); "The Avalon Peninsula of Newfoundland", 1968 (with G. M. Story and W. Kirwin); "Place Names of the Avalon Peninsula of the Island of Newfoundland", 1971; "Family Names of the Island of Newfoundland", 1977; contrib. to "Chambers Encyclopaedia", "Cassell's Encyclopaedia of Literature", etc.; awarded Centennial Medal; mem., Candn. Humanities Assn. (1st Pres., St. John's Br.); Candn. Linguistic Assn. (Pres. 1960-62); Assn. of Candn. Univ. Teachers of English (Pres. 1963-64); Anglican; recreations: listening to music, chess, gardening; Home: 537 Topsail Rd., St. John's, Nfld. A1E 2C6.

SEATH, Herbert N., B.Com.; investment counsellor; b. Montreal, Que. 19 May 1932; s. Norman and Laura Benning (Johnson) S.; e. Sir George Williams (Concordia) Univ. B. Com.1961; m. Margaret M. L. d. George Martin 19 Feb. 1953; children: Brian, David, Carol Anne, Rosemary; PRINCIPAL, KNIGHT, BAIN, SEATH & HOLBROOK, CAPITAL MANAGEMENT INC. 1980- ; joined Montreal Trust as Mgr. Pension Invest. 1954-69; Canada Trust Mgr. Invest. 1969-72; Air Canada Dir. Invest. 1972, Treas. 1973, Controller 1975; Canada Trust Sr. Vice-Pres. Finance 1976-9; Vice Pres., Comm. Lending, Can. Permanent Trust 1979-80;Protestant; recreations: squash, tennis, skiing; Clubs: Toronto Racquet; R.C.Y.C.; Home: 5 Coldstream Ave., Toronto, Ont. M5N 1X5; Office: 8 King St. E., Toronto, Ont. M5C 1B5.

SECORD, Donald Neil; labour leader (ret.); b. Kingsville, Ont., 13 July 1911; s. Clarence Allison and Clara (Lynchbury) s.; e. Kingsville (Ont.) Pub. and High Schs., 1928; Windsor (Ont.) Business Coll., grad. 1929; m. Nellie Tomes, d. William Murray, and Nellie (Tomes), Detroit, Mich., 4 May 1935; two s. William Keith Allison, Bryan Campbell; joined Candn. Nat. Rlys., Express Dept., Windsor, 1929; became mem. of present Brotherhood 1929 and Local Chrmn., Local 191, Windsor, 1935; assisted with formation of Windsor Labour Council and served as Vice Pres. for 2 yrs., became Panel mem. of Court of Referees, Unemployment Ins. Comm. until leaving Windsor; on leave of absence from Rly. to W.P.T.B. as Labour Liaison Offr. for Ont., 1944-46; apptd. a rep. of Brotherhood, Toronto, March 1947 and el. Gen. Chrmn., Express Gen. Adjustment Comte., Nov. 1947; el. Vice Chrmn., Jt. Protective Bd. of Brotherhood, 1950; apptd. to Nat. Bd. of Trustees of Brotherhood 1946-52 when apptd. Nat. Secy.-Treas., Ottawa; re-el. to 1976; Nat. Pres., Brotherhood Candn. Railway, Trans. & Gen. Workers, 1970-76 (ret.); Past Pres. and Man. Dir., Mutual Press Ltd.; Past Mem. Exec. Council, C.L.C.; Past Mem. Exec. Bd. of Evangelism and Soc. Ser.; Past Dir., Ont. Fed. of Labour Union Centres; Past Cdn. Rly. Labour Assoc. Co-Op. Ins. Services; Past mem. Exec. Bd. of the International Transport Workers Federation; NDP; United Church; recreations: horticulture, curling, swimming, reading; Club: Granite Curling; Home: Northwest One Apartments, 265 Poulin Ave., Ottawa, Ont. K2B 7X8 Office: 2300 Carling Ave., Ottawa, Ont. K2B 7G1.

SECORD, Lloyd Calvin, B.Sc., F. E. I. C., F.C.A.S.I.; consulting engineer; b. St. Thomas, Ont. 28 Aug. 1923; s. Eleanor Louva (Ward) and late Cortland Lionel S.; e. Queen's Univ., B.Sc. (Hons.) 1945 (Gold Medal for highest standing in Mech. Engn.); m. Lillian Gordon, d. late John Frederick Mutrie, 14 Sept. 1944; one s. Timothy Scott; PRES. & CHIEF EXTVE. OFFR., DSMA ATCON LTD., Consulting Engrs.; Dir., Dilworth, Secord, Meagher & Assoc. Ltd.; Pres., Pengalta Research & Devel. Ltd.; Electric Vehicle Assn. of Can.;mem. Adv. Council, Ryerson Polytech. Inst.; Toronto; Chrmn., Space Comm., AIR Ind. Assoc.; Dir. (Past Pres.) Candn Nuclear Assn.; Reg. Consult. Engr. (Ont.); mem. Assn. Prof. Engrs. Ont.; Soc. Automotive Engrs.; Assn. Consulting Engrs. Can.; Candn. Soc. Mech. Engrs.; author of numerous papers and presentations; holds patents in Can., U.S., U.K. and Europe; Protestant; recreations: golf, sailing; Clubs: The Ontario; St. Georges; Home: 413 The Kingsway Islington, Ont. M9A 3W1; Office: 4195 Dundas St. W., Toronto, Ont. M8X 1Y4.

SEDAWIE, Norman William; television producer-director-writer; b. Vancouver, B.C., 1 Oct. 1928; s. Fred and Jessie Elizabeth (Wood) S.; e. Pub. and High Schs., Vancouver; m. Gayle Ina, d. Jack Gibson and Lola (Pitchford), Bewdley, Ont., 23 June 1956; three s.: Mark, Glen, Grant; Pres., Tel-Pro Entertainment Inc.; writer, ed. Vancouver Sun 1945 and Vancouver Province to 1954; writer, producer, dir., CBC TV, Toronto, 1954-65; numerous TV credits in Hollywood incl. long term contracts with Danny Kaye and Tom Smothers co's; winner of various TV awards; first prize in Montreaux, Switzerland TV festival for co-production with Gayle Gibson Sedawie of Rich Little's Christmas Carol (winner of Internat. Emmy, 1979 for same program); mem., Dirs. Guild Am.; Nat. Acad. TV Arts & Sciences; Writers Guild Am.; ACTRA; recreation: boating, tennis Home: 5352 Topeka Dr., Tarzana, Cal. U.S.A.

SEEBER, Orville Alexander, B.A.; geological consultant; mining executive; b. Ottawa, Ont., 17 Nov. 1913; s. Harrie Cooper and Jean (Alexander) S.; e. Ogdensburg, N.Y. Schs.; Queen's Univ., B.A. (Geol. & Minerol.) 1937; VICE PRES., EXPLORATIONS, QUEBEC STURGEON RIVER MINES LTD.; Dir., Explorations, Anglo-Candn. Exploration (ACE) Ltd.; Exec. Vice Pres. Anglo-Dominion Gold Exploration Ltd.; Vice Pres. Bachelor Lake Gold Mines Inc.; Dir. Hillsborough Exploration Ltd.; York Consolidated Exploration Ltd.; Vice pres. Satellite Metal Mines Ltd.; Coniagas Mines Ltd.; Geol., Falconbridge Nickel Mines Ltd., 1938-45; Chief Field Geol. 1945-54; Chief Geol., M. J. Boylen Engineering Offices, 1954-69; Vice-Pres., Exploration, Northgate Exploration Ltd. 1969 till formed own geol. consultant firm 1972; received C A.O. Dufresne Award, 1981; mem., Candn. Inst. Mining & Metall.; Soc. Econ. Geols.; Geol. Assn. Can.; Bd. Trade Metrop. Toronto; Presbyterian; recreations: fishing, photography; Home: Box 259, Sydenham, Ont. K0H 2T0; Office: Ground Floor, 166 Pearl St. Toronto, Ont. M5H 1L3.

SEELY, Hugh E., B.Sc., P.Eng.; construction executive; b. Edmunston, N.B., 23 Oct. 1925; s. Walter Lee and Kathleen Lillian (Miller) S.; e. Pub. and High Schs., Edmunston and Woodstock, N.B.; Univ. of N.B., B.Sc. (Civil Engn.) 1947; also several mang., marketing and adm. courses; m. Peggy, d. James Stephenson, 8 Oct. 1949; PRESIDENT AND C.E.O., H. H. ROBERTSON CO. since 1981; joined the Co., Sales Office, Montreal 1948, with subsequent marketing service and various appts. in Toronto and Hamilton, Ont.; Pres., Robertson Building Systems Ltd., 1970-81; Dir., 1970- ; served in 2nd World War, R.C.A. 1944-45 as Instr. of Inf., Advanced Training Centre; Past Pres. and Past Dir., Candn.

Sheet Steel Bldg. Inst.; Past Dir., Candn. Steel Industries Constr. Council; mem. Engn. Inst. Can. (Past Chrm. Hamilton Br.); Assn. Prof. Engrs. Ont.; Anglican; recreations: travel, golf, curling; Clubs: Hamilton Golf & Country; Canadian; Home: Office: Ste. 403, The Plaza, 111 Grandview Ave., Pittsburgh PA 15211

SEEMAN, Philip, M.Sc., M.D., Ph.D.; educator; b. Winnipeg, Man. 8 Feb. 1934; s. Jacob and Fanny (Wigdor) S.; e. Baron Byng High Sch. Montreal 1950; McGill Univ. B.Sc. 1955, M.Sc. 1956, M.D. 1960; Rockefeller Univ. Ph.D. 1966; m. Mary Violette d. Alexander Szwarc 30 June 1959; children: Marc, Bob, Neil; PROF. AND CHRMN. OF PHARMACOL. UNIV. OF TORONTO since 1977; Internship, Harper Hosp. Wayne State Univ. Detroit 1960-61; Med. Research Council Can. Fellow, Cambridge Univ. 1966-67; joined present univ. 1967; rec'd Clark Inst. Psychiatry Research Award; Chrmn. Hawthorne Bilingual Sch. Toronto 1976; Ed. 'Frontiers in Neurology and Neuroscience Research' 1974; 'Principles of Medical Pharmacology' 1976; author numerous articles; mem. Soc. Neuroscience; Candn. Pharmacol. Soc.; Am. Coll. Neuropsychopharmacol.; Am. Chem. Soc.; Ont. Coll. Phys. & Surgs.; Home: 32 Parkwood Ave., Toronto M4V 2X1; Office: Medical Sciences Bldg., Toronto, Ont. M5S 1A8.

SEGALL, Harold Nathan, M.D., C.M., F.A.C.P., F.R.S.A.; cardiologist; b. Jassy, Romania, 18 Oct. 1897; s. Fischel and Creina (Solomon) S.; e. McGill Univ., M.D., C.M. 1920; Univ. Coll., London (Dept. of Physiol. 1924-26); McGill Univ. (Path. and Bacter.) 1920-22; Mass. Gen. Hosp. (Research in Thyroid Diseases, 1922-23 and Cardio-Vascular Diseases, 1923-24); m. Dorothy Violet Caplin, 6 Mar. 1934; children: Carol Tova, Jack Oba Caplin; Chief of Dept. of Cardiology, Jewish Gen. Hosp., Montreal, Que.; Sr. Physician there; Assoc. Physician, Montreal Gen. Hosp.; Asst. Prof. of Med., McGill Univ. till 1960; originator of a method of writing symbols to describe heart sounds and murmurs; author of a number of scient. and gen. articles relating to his special field of medicine and history of medicine; mem., Physiol. Soc. of Gt. Brit.; Candn. Heart Assn. (Pres. 1952); Montreal Cardiac Soc. (Pres.); Montreal Clinical Soc. (Pres. 1937); Candn. Heart Foundation (Vice-Pres.; Award of Merit 1972); Pres. (1965-67) Que. Heart Foundation; Chrmn., Louis Gross Mem. Lecture Comte. 1937-64; Hon. Pres. (1971-72 and 1978-79) McGill Osler Soc.; mem. Am. Assn. for Hist. of Medicine; Candn. Soc. for Hist.of Medicine; Montreal Jewish Hist. Soc.; Home: No. 19, 4100 Cote des Neiges Rd., Montreal, Que. H3H 1W8;

SEGUIN, Fernand, O.C., M.Sc.; biochemist; scientific commentator; b. Montreal, Que. 9 June 1922; s. late Emilien and late Blanche (Lahaise) S.; e. Ecole Hippolyte Lafontaine and Ecole Superieure le Plateau, Montreal 1940; Univ. of Montreal L.Sc. 1944, M.Sc. 1945; Northwestern Univ. 1945 (summer); Hon. degree, Sherbrooke Univ., 1975; Concordia Univ. 1979; Univ. of Montreal, 1980; m. Fernande d. late Alexandre Giroux 30 June 1971; children: Isabelle, Sylvie (by former marriage); PRES., LES ENTREPRISES F. SEGUIN, INC (consulting in audio-visual communications); joined French CBC 1947, Radio lectures on Science (over 100) 1947 — 52, Scient. Programs TV (over 150) 1954 — 62, Social Science Programs TV (over 150) 1954 — 62, Social Science Programs TV (over 80) 1962 — 65, one-hour talk shows with personalities (over 100) 1965 — 70, weekly half-hour scient. chronicles for radio (over 300) 1970 — 78 and for TV (5 minutes, over 40) 1974 — 75, 1978; scenario (with G. Thérien) for one-hour documentary on brain Nat. Film Bd. 1977; mem. Council of Univs.; Bd. mem. Montreal Cancer Inst.; Presses Univs. du Qué.; Candn. Mental Health Assn. (Qué. Div.); rec'd Casgrain-Charbonneau Prize for best pharm. research 1945; Archambault Medal for outstanding contrib. to science 1961; journalism Prize Soc. St-Jean Baptiste 1977; U.N.E.S.C.O. Internat. Kalinga Prize for popularization of science; author "Entretiens sur la vie" 1952; co-author "Les chemins de la science" (7 student textbooks, 7 teacher's guides kindergarten to 6th grade) 1970 — 75; "Le monde des plantes" 1959; "Le Sel De La Science", 1980; numerous scient. articles various journs.; mem. Assn. des communicateurs scientifiques; recreations: walking, music, cooking, swimming; Home: 113 Richelieu, St-Charles-sur-Richelieu, Qué. J0H 2G0.

SEGUIN, Robert-Lionel, D.ès L.; ethnologue; auteur; né Rigaud, Qué. 7 mars 1920; é. Univ. de Montréal licencié ès sciences sociales, économiques et politiques 1951; Univ. Laval diplôme d'études supérieures en histoire 1962, docteur ès lettres et histoire 1964; Sorbonne docteur ès lettres et sciences humaines 1972; Univ. Strasbourg docteur ès lettres et ethnologie; ép Huguette Servant; PROFESSEUR, Chercheur invité au CELAT, Faculté des Lettres, Univ. Laval; travaille périodique au Musée national des arts et traditions populaires de Paris; auteur "Le mouvement insurrectionnel dans la presqu'île de Vaudreuil 1837-1838" 1955; "L'équipement de la ferme canadienne aux XVIIe et XVIIIe siècles" 1959; "Les moules du Québec" 1963; "Les granges du Québec" 1963; "La civilisation traditionnelle de l' "habitant" aux 17e et 18e siècles" 1967; "La victoire de Saint-Denis" 1968; "Le costume civil en Nouvelle-France" 1968, "La maison en Nouvelle-France" 1968; "Les divertissements en Nouvelle-France" 1968; "Les jouets anciens du Québec" 1971; "Les ustensiles en Nouvelle-France" 1972; "La vie libertine en Nouvelle-France au XVIIe siècle" 2 vol. 1972; "L'esprit révolutionnaire dans l'art québécois" 1973; L'injure en Nouvelle-France" 1976; "La sorcellerie au Québec du XVIIe au XIXe siècle" 1978; "L' Equipement aratoire et horticole ancien au Québec" 2 vol. 1981; quelque cent cinquante articles (ethno-historiques) publiés dans des cahiers, bulletins et revues du Québec et de France; tous ces travaux traitent de la civilisation traditionnelle du Québec; prix litteraires: Gouverneur général du Can. 1967; Broquette Gonin (Académie française) 1967; France-Québec 1973; Duvernay (Société Saint-Jean-Baptiste) 1976; mem. Soc. d'ethnologie française (Paris); Soc. des Dix (Qué.); Soc. royale du Can.; Catholique; Adresse: Grand-Ligne, Rigaud, Qué.

SEGUIN, Roger Nantel, O.C. (1967), Q.C., B.A., LL.L., LL.D.; b. Ottawa, Ont., 27 Aug. 1913; s. Charles A. and Germaine (Nantel) S.; e. Univ. of Ottawa, B.A. 1935, LL.D. (hon. causa); Univ. of Montreal, LL.L. 1938; m. Estelle, d. Edouard Desormeaux, 14 April 1941; children: Jean-Pierre, André, Suzanne, Adèle; PARTNER, SEGUIN, & LANDRIAULT LAMOUREUX; former Pres., La Caisse Populaire Laurier d'Ottawa Ltée.; former mem. Adv. Bd., Canada Permanent Trust Co.; Chrmn. Bd. Govs., Univ. of Ottawa; former Pres., French Speaking Scouts, Ottawa Region; Hon. mem. Council, Candn. Council on Social Devel.; Hon. Dir., Ottawa Boys Club; former Commr., Ont. Hydro Comn.; former Dir., C.B.C.; mem. Reserve Army, 1932-39; Kt., Order of St. Gregory, 1968; Kt. Wooden Cross of Jerusalem; Medal, Le Conseil de la Vie Française; en Amerique; "Man of the Month" Que. Chamber Comm. 1960; "Man of the Year", Jeune Chambre d'Ottawa et Eastview 1967; called to the Bar of Ont., 1946, Bar of Que., 1938; cr. K.C. 1949; Roman Catholic; recreation: reading; Clubs: Cercle Universitaire.

SELBY, Roger Lowell, B.A.; museum director; b. Philadelphia, Pa. 4 July 1933; s. Willard Lowell Selby; e. Univ. of Md. B.A. 1960; Claremont Grad. Sch. 1960-61; Ind. Univ. 1963-65; m. Claudia Anne d. Gilbert Engel 23 Oct. 1974; one d. Christine; DIR., THE WINNIPEG ART GALLERY 1974-   ; Curator of Educ., Nat. Gallery of Art Washington, D.C. 1961-62; Corcoran Gallery of Art Washington 1965-68; Head of Educ. Wadsworth Atheneum Hartford, Conn. 1968-74; Instr. in Art Hist., Grad. Sch. U.S. Dept. Agric. Washington 1961-63; Corcoran Sch. of Art 1965-68; State Dept. Foreign Service Inst. Washington 1967-68; Hartford Art Sch. Univ. of Hartford

1969-71; Hon. Prof. Univ. of Winnipeg 1978-82; rec'd Queen's Silver Jubilee Medal 1978; Consultant, Govt. Man. Heritage Working Group 1981; Univ. of Winnipeg 1979-   (Museology Program); Aetna Life & Casualty Co. 1973; Juror, 15th Annual All Alaska Art Exhn. 1980; author various publs.; mem. Candn. Art Museum Dirs. Organ. (Pres. 1979-81, Secy. 1976-79); Candn. Museums Assn. (Extve. Comte. 1979-   , Chrmn. Policy, Finance Comtes. 1980-82); Council Associate Museum Dirs.; Assn. Art Museum Dirs.; Home: 134 Wellington Cres., Winnipeg, Man. R3M 0A9; Office: 300 Memorial Blvd., Winnipeg, Man. R3C 1V1.

SELLERS, Edward Alexander, M.D., Ph.D.; university professor; b. Winnipeg, Man., 14 Sept. 1916; s. Henry Eugene and Irene (Maulson) S.; e. Ridley Coll., St. Catharines, Ont.; Univ. of Manitoba, M.D. 1939 (Gold Medal); Univ. of Toronto, Ph.D. 1947; m. Jean Isobel Glen, d. Hugh G., Moncrieff, 9 Oct. 1939; children: Edward Moncrieff, Henry Hugh, Alexander George; Interne, Winnipeg Gen. Hosp., 1938-39; Research Assoc., Banting & Best Dept. of Med. Research, Toronto, 1945; Asst. Prof. of Pharmacol., Univ. of Toronto, 1946-48; Assoc. Prof. of Physiol, there 1948-51, Prof., 1951-58, Prof. and Head of Dept. 1958-66, Assoc. Dean, Faculty of Med. 1965-68; Chief Supt., Defence Research Med. Labs., 1955-58; joined R.C.N.V.R. (N.P.A.M.) 1937; mobilized 1939; Surg. Lieut., Med. Research Divn., 1942; Surg. Lieut. Commdr., R.C.N. (R), Surg. Commdr. 1951; Publications: mostly relative to burn shock, thyroid, environmental physiology, liver diseases; mem., Am. Physiol. Soc.; Am. Assn. Advanc. Science; Candn. Physiol. Soc.; Toronto Biochem. & Biophys. Soc.; Toronto Acad. of Med.; Pharmacol. Soc. of Can. (Pres. 1965); Am. Soc. Pharmacol. & Exper. Therapy; Pi-Epsilon of Zeta Psi; Anglican; recreations: gardening, photography;

SELLERS, George Henry, A.F.C.; company president; b. Winnipeg, Man., 19 Apl. 1914; s. Henry Eugene and Irene (Maulson) S.; e. Ridley Coll., St. Catharines, Ont.; Univ. of Man., Faculty of Law; m. Margaret Anne, d. G. H. Aikins, D.S.O., Q.C., 26 Sept. 1936; children: Dr. David Henry Aikins, Ph.D., M.Sc., P.Eng.; Margaret Anne, Harvey, Joan Irene Audette; PRES: SELLERS-DICKSON SECURITIES LTD. Riverwood Investments Ltd.; Director, Greater Winnipeg Gas Company; Can. Malting Co. Limited; Bank of Montreal; Pilot Investment Fund (Bermuda); mem. Winnipeg Adv. Bd., Royal Trust Co.; Past President, St. John Ambulance Assn.; with Fed. Grain Ltd. 1933-36; Melady, Sellers & Co. Ltd., 1936-39; Dir., Fed. Grain Ltd. 1945; with Melady, Sellers & Co. Ltd., 1945-52; Pres., Central Northern Airways Ltd. 1946-56; Pres., Selburn Oil Co. Ltd., 1948-52; Melady, Sellers Securities & Grain Corp. Ltd., 1952-61; Bailey Selburn Oil & Gas Ltd., 1952-62; Pres. and Chief Extve. Offr. Fed. Grain Ltd. 1963-72; Commd. Pilot Offr. in 112th Auxiliary Sqdn., R.C.A.F., 13 June 1933 and served overseas, 1940-41; served in Can. as Chief Flying Instr. Stn. Commdr. and Sr. Staff Offr.; C.O. 39th Fighter Recce Wing, Tactical Air Force, Europe, 1944-45; trans. to R.C.A.F. Reserve with rank of Group Capt.; awarded A.F.C.; apptd. Hon. A.D.C. to Gov.-Gen. of Can., 1946; Offr. Order of St. John; Zeta Psi; Anglican; recreations: shooting, riding, flying, skiing; Clubs: Manitoba; Ranchmen's (Calgary); Home: 300 Park Blvd., Winnipeg Man. R3P 0G7

SELLS, Bruce Howard, B.Sc., M.A., Ph.D.; educator; b. Ottawa, Ont. 15 Aug. 1930; e. Carleton Univ. B.Sc. 1952; Queen's Univ. M.A. 1954; McGill Univ. Ph.D. 1957; ASSOC. DEAN, DIV. OF BASIC MEDICAL SCIENCES, FACULTY OF MEDICINE MEMORIAL UNIV. OF NFLD. 1979; Demonst. Chem. Labs. McGill Univ. 1954-57; Damon Runyon Research Fellow, Lab. of Animal Morphology, Free Univ. of Brussels 1957-59, Statens Seruminstitut, Copenhagen 1959-60; Cancer Research Scient. Roswell park Mem. Inst. Buffalo 1960-61; Research Assoc. Columbia Univ. 1961-62; Asst. Prof. of Biochem. St. Jude Children's Research Hosp. and Univ. of Tenn. 1962-64, Assoc. Prof. 1964-68, mem. of Hosp. and Assoc. Prof. of Univ. 1968-72; Prof. and Dir. of Molecular Biology, Memorial Univ. 1972-79; Visiting Research Scient. Inst. Animal Genetics, Univ. of Edinburgh 1969-70; Killam Sr. Research Fellow 1978-79, Inst. Research in Molecular Biol. Paris, France; Assoc. Ed. Candn. Journal of Biochemistry, 1974- ; mem. Biochem. Grants Panel, M. R. C., 1973-78; mem. of Council, Medical Research Council of Can., 1980- ; Centennial Fellowship Panel-M.R.C., 1980- ; Pres., Cdn. Biochem. Soc., 1981-82; Scientific Officer, Nat. Cancer Inst., 1979-81 ;Med. Research Council Can. Visiting Scient. Award; Centre Nat. Recherche Scientifique, Exchange Scient. Award; Home: Site 6, Box 1, RR #1, Nfld. Paradise, A1C 2C2; Office: St. John's, Nfld.

SELYE, Hans, C.C. (1968), M.D., Ph.D., D.Sc., LL.D., F.R.S.C.; research scientist; b. Vienna, Austria, 26 January 1907; s. Dr. Hugo and Maria Felicitas (Langbank) S.; e. German University of Prague, Czechoslovakia, M.D., 1929, Ph.D., 1931; Univ. of Paris; Univ. of Rome; McGill Univ., D.Sc., 1942; D.hon. causa, Nat. Univs. of Argentina, 1950; D.Sc., Assumption 1955, Cath. Univ. Chile 1956; Prof. Hon., Univ. of Montevideo, 1956; Hon. degree, Med., Münster (Germany) 1966; Univ. Guelph 1973; M.D. Laval 1975; LL.D. Philadelphia Coll. 1975; Hon. Fellowship, Hebrew Univ. of Jerusalem (Israel) 1977; Hon. Fellowship, Univ. of Haifa (Toronto) 1978; LL.D., Univ. of Alta. (Edmonton) 1978; children: Michel, Jean, Marie, Andre; Pres., Internat. Inst. of Stress, Montreal, since 1976; Pres., Hans Selye Foundation, since 1979; Founding mem., Scient. Council, American Heart Assn.; served as Asst. in Exper. Path., German Univ. of Prague, in charge of Histol. Lab., 1929-31; awarded Rockefeller Research Fellow., Dept. of Biochem. Hygiene, Johns Hopkins Univ. 1931; Dept. of Biochem., McGill Univ. 1932-33; Lectr. in Biochem., McGill Univ., 1933-34, Asst. Prof., 1934-37, Asst. Prof. in Histol., in charge of Research Labs., 1937-41, Assoc. Prof., 1941-45; Expert Consultant to Surg.-Gen., U.S. Army, 1947-57; Prof. and Dir., Inst. de Médecine et de Chirurgie expérimentales, Univ. de Montréal, 1945-76; Prof. Emeritus since 1977; Fellow, Am. Assn. for Advanc. Science; N.Y. Acad. of Sciences; Am. Geriatrics Soc.; Hon. Fellow, Internat. Coll. of Surgs.; mem., Am. Assn. for Cancer Research; Am. Heart Assn.; Am. Physiol. Society; Am. Society for Clinical Investigation; Am. Soc. for Study of Arteriosclerosis; The Endocrine Soc.; Candn. Inter-Am. Assn.; Candn. Physiol. Soc.; Candn. Soc. for Study of Allergy; Montreal Physiol. Soc. (Pres. 1943-44); Soc. de Biol. de Montréal (Pres. 1951-52); Soc. d'Endocrinologie (France); Soc. for Experimental Biol. and Med. (U.S.A.); Founder mem., Soc. for Endocrinology (Eng.); Hon. mem., Aesculapian Soc. of Univ. of Ottawa; Am. Clinical and Climatol. Assn. (U.S.A.); Essex Co. Path. and Anat. Soc. (U.S.A.); Heberden Soc. (Eng.); New Mexico Clin. Soc.; Russian Endocrinological Soc.; Soc. Argentina de Biol.; Soc. de Biol. (Chile); Soc. Médico-Quirurgica del Guayas (Ecuador); Soc. de Endocrinologia, e. Metabologia de Rio de Janeiro; Soc. Endocrinologica Bohemica; Soc. de Path. comparée (France); Svenska Endokrinologföreningen (Sweden); Inst. d'Endocrinologie d'Haiti; Soc. Biol. Montevideo; Soc. Endocrinologia y Metabologia, Mexico; Acad. Med. di Roma; Indian Soc. Endocrinology; Soc. de Médecine de Paris; National Univs. of Argentina; Pan Am. Med. Assn.; corr. mem., Acad. Nacional de Medicina de Buenos Aires; Argentina Medi. Assn.; Real Acad. Nacional de Med. (Spain); Soc. Argentina de Biol.; Soc. Philomathique de Paris; Soc. Biol. Montréal; Internat. Acad. Preventive Med.; Nat. Assn. Preventive Med. (France); etc.; member Editorial Board, "Acta Anatomica" (Switzerland); "Ars Medici" (Belgium); "Excerpta Medica" (Netherlands); "Experimental Medicine and Surgery" (U.S.A.); "Journal de Physiologie" (France); "Medicus" (Pakistan); "American Journal of

Proctology"; "International Archives of Allergy and Applied Immunology" (Sweden); "Angiology" (U.S.A.); "Indian J. of Endocrinology and Metabolism"; awarded Casgrain and Charbonneau Prize for orig. work leading to improvement in the prevention and treatment of disease, 1946; Gordon Wilson Medal, by Am. Clin. and Climatol. Assn., 1948; The Heberden Research Medal, 1950; Medal of Acad. Med. Fisica (Italy), 1950; Semmelweiss Medal, N.Y., 1955; Hon. Citizen of Verona, Italy, 1955; Cert. of Merit, Hokkaido Univ., Japan; Hon. award, W. Soc. of Periodontology, U.S.A.; Can. B'nai B'rith Humanitarian Award; Henderson Gold Medal of Am. Geriatrics Soc.; Lecture Award, Am. Assn. for Advanc. of Science; Amer. Hungarian Studies Foundation George Washington Award 1967; Starr Award 1972; Bell Mem. Lecture, Univ. Minn. 1973; Rennebohm Lecture Univ. Wisc. 1973; Oeuvre Scient. l'Assn. des médecins de langue française (Can.) prize 1974; Distinguished Service Award, Am. Soc. Abdominal Surgeons 1974; Killam Prize 1974; Man of the Year Assn. Assureurs-Vie de Montréal 1974; K.St.J. 1975; Medaille Archambault 1975; Internat'l Kittay Award (U.S.A.) 1976; Achievement in Life Award, Encyclopedia Britannica 1977; Cdn. Authors Assoc. Literary Award for best non-fiction book of 1977 ("The Stress of My Life) 1978; Publications: "Encyc. of Endocrinology" Sec. 1 (4 vols.), classified index of steroid hormones & related compounds, 1943, Sec. 4 (2 vols.); "The Ovary", 1946; "Textbook of Endocrinology", 1947, & 2nd ed. 1949; "Stress (The Physiology and Pathology of Exposure to Stress)", 1950; "On the Experimental Morphology of the Adrenal Cortex" (with H. Stone), 1950; co-author, Five Annual Reports on Stress, 1951-56; "The Story of the Adaptation Syndrome", 1952; "The Stress of Life", 1956 & 2nd ed. 1976; "The Chemical Prevention of Cardiac Necroses", 1958; "Symbolic Shorthand System for Physiology and Medicine" 1964; "The Pluricausal Cardiopathies", 1961; "Calciphylaxis", 1962; "From Dream to Discovery", 1964 & 1975; "The Mast Cells", 1965; "In Vivo", 1967; "Stress Without Distress" 1974; "Stress in Health and Disease" 1976; "The Stress of My Life" 1977 and 1979; "Cancer, Stress and Death" (ed. with J. Taché and S. B. Day) 1979; "Selye's Guide to Stress Research" Vol. I, 1980; "Stress", the Official Journal of the Internat. Inst. of Stress 1:1-4 (1980); "Selye's Guide to Stess Research", Vol. II, 1981; has written and publ. over 1700 scient. papers relating to his research field; Roman Catholic; Home: 659 Milton St., Montreal, Que. H2X 1W6

SESSIONS, Vivian Siemon, M.A., M.S.; educator; librarian; b. Ossining, N.Y. 15 Dec. 1920; d. Israel and Eva (Rabinowitz) Siemon; e. Univ. of Mich. A.B. 1945, M.A. 1948; Columbia Univ. M.S. 1959; m. 1 Jan. 1942; children: Roger, Hilary; PROF AND DIR., GRAD. SCH. OF LIB. SCIENCE, McGILL UNIV. 1976- ; Librarian and Sr. Librarian, Mun. Reference Lib. of N.Y. 1959-65; Project Dir. Research Foundation, City Univ. of N.Y. 1965-69, Dir. and Assoc. Prof. Center for Advanc. of Lib. Information Science there 1969-76; co-author "URBANDOC/A Bibliographic Information System" 3 vols. 1971; ed. "Data Bases in the Social and Behavioral Sciences" 1974; articles various journ. publs.; mem. Am. Soc. Information Science (Chrmn. Special Interest Group in Behavioral & Social Sciences 1975-76, 1980-81); Assn. Am. Lib. Schs.; Assn. pour l'avancement des sciences et des techniques de la documentation; Candn. Assn. for Information Science Continuing Lib. Educ. Network; Corp. Prof. Librarians Que. (Vice Pres. 1979-80); Que. Lib. Assn.; Special Libraries Assoc.; Home: 3460 Peel St., Apt. 814, Montreal, Que. H3A 2M1; Office: 3459 McTavish St., Montreal, Que. H3A 1Y1.

SETTERFIELD, George Ambrose, Ph.D., F.R.S.C.; biologist; educator; b. Halifax, N.S. 29 Aug. 1929; s. Ambrose Charles Setterfield; e. Univ. of B.C. B.A. 1951; Univ. of Wis. Ph.D. 1954; m. Diana Evelyn d. late Hugh Charter 19 May 1951; children: Thomas Neal, David George, Jennifer Ann, Christopher, Wayne; PROF. OF BIOL. CARLETON UNIV. since 1964; Instr. in Biol. Univ. of B.C. 1954-56; Asst. Research Offr. Nat. Research Council Ottawa 1956-58, Assoc. Research Offr. 1958-62; Assoc. Prof. of Biol. Carleton Univ. 1962, Chrmn. of Biol. 1963-68; Sabbatical Leave, Dept. de Biologie, Laval Univ. 1963-68; Nat. Research Council Saskatoon 1977-78; co-ed. "Biochemistry and Physiology of Plant Growth Substances" 1968; author some 50 papers scient. journs.; rec'd Queen's Silver Jubilee Medal; mem. Candn. Soc. Cell Biol. (Pres. 1974-75); Candn. Soc. Plant Physiols. (Pres. 1964-65); Internat. Assn. Plant Tissue Culture; Soc. Devel. Biol.; Candn. Microscopical Soc.; Genetics Soc. Can.; Am. Soc. Cell Biol.; recreations: wilderness canoeing, photography, cross-country skiing; Home: R.R. 3, North Gower, Ont. KOA 2TO; Office: Ottawa, Ont. K1S 5B6.

SEVIER, Gerald Leslie, R.C.A.; artist; b. Hamilton, Ont. 25 Jan. 1934; s. Frank Leslie Sevier; e. Brantford (Ont.) Coll. & Vocational Sch. 1952; Ont. Coll. of Art 1956 (Comm. Advertising Medal); m. Jean Eleanor d. Jack Wratten, Brantford, Ont. 21 Sept. 1956; children: Shawn, Jason, Tim, Theo; PROP., HOTHOUSE (comm. design & illustration); Teacher, Ont. Coll. of Art; solo exhns. incl. Sobot Gallery Toronto 1963, 1964, 1967; Shaw-Rimmington Gallery Toronto 1968; Merton Gallery Toronto 1970, 1973, 1975, 1979, 1980, 1981; Art Gallery of Brantford (retrospect) 1975; Kensington Gallery, Calgary 1981; exhns. Glenhyrst Gardens Brantford 1961, 1968; rep. in many group exhns. since 1961; rep. in various pub., corporate and private colls.; awards incl. Art Dirs. Club Toronto and New York, USA Illustrator Club, Graphics mag. Europe; mem. Ont. Soc. Artists (Pres 1969-72); recreations: baseball, snorkeling, fishing, waterskiing; Club: Arts & Letters; Home: 137 Glengrove Ave. W., Toronto, Ont. M4R 1P1; Office: 25 Wood St., Suite 101, Toronto, Ont. M4Y 2P9.

SEVIGNY, Col. the Hon. Pierre, P.C. (Can. 1959), E.D., B.A., B.Com.; b. Quebec City, 12 Sept. 1917; s. Hon. Albert, P.C. and Jeanne (Lavery) S.; e. Loyola Coll., Montreal, Que.; Laval Univ., B.Com.; Quebec Semy., B.A.; m. Corinne, d. late R. P. Kernan, 22 June 1946; children: Pierrette, Albert, Robert; Gov., Montreal Gen. Hosp.; Dir., The Windsor Hotel; Dir. Horizon Realities; Pres. Horizon Investments Co.; Corenco Energy Corp.; Dieppe Home for Epileptics; formerly active in fields of contr. and real estate; 1st el. to H. of C. for Longueuil in g.e. 1958; re-el. g.e. June 1962; el. Depy. Speaker of H. of C., 1958; apptd. Assoc. Min. of Nat. Defence in Diefenbaker Govt., 1959; resigned his portfolio 9 Feb. 1963; def. g.e. Apl. 1963; served in 2nd World War; enlisted 1939; retired 1946; service in Eng. and W. Front; Polish Virtuti Militari; Belgian Croix de Guerre; Past Pres., Candn. Club of Montreal; Offr. Grand Cross of Order of Lazarus of Jerusalem (Chancellor for Can.); author: "This Game of Politics", 1965; P. Conservative; Roman Catholic; recreations: golf, bridge; Clubs: Rideau; Garrison (Quebec); Home: 370 Wood, Westmount, Que. H3Z 1Z2

SEWELL, Edward John Charles B.A., LL.B.; b. Toronto, Ont. 8 Dec. 1940; s. William S. and Helen (Sanderson) S.; e. Univ. of Toronto B.A. 1961 (Victoria Coll.), LL.B. 1964; one s. Nicholas; Mayor, City of Toronto 1978-80; el. Ald. mun. el. 1969, re-el. until 1980; re-el. again 1981; called to Bar of Ont. 1967; author "Sense of Time and Place" 1972; "Up Against City Hall" 1972; various articles mun. matters newspapers and mags.; mem. Law Soc. Upper Can. Office: City Hall, Toronto, Ont.

SEYMOUR, Lynn (Mrs. Colin Edward Jones); C.B.E.(1976); ballet dancer; b. Wainwright, Alberta, 8 March 1939; d. Edward Victor and Marjorie Isabelle (McIvor) Springbett; e. Public Schs. and Kitsilano High Sch., Vancouver, B.C.; Royal Ballet Sch., London, Eng.; Ballet teachers in Can.: Jean Jepson, Nicholai Svetlanoff; princi-

pal teachers in Eng.: Winnifred Edwards, Barbara Fewster, Pamela May, Erling Sunde, and in U.S.A. Valentina Peryaslanec; created rôles for The Royal Ballet: Adolescent Girl in "The Burrow" (MacMillan), The Bride in "Le Baiser de la Fee" (MacMillan), The Girl in "The Invitation" (MacMillan), Gourouli in "Les Deux Pigeons (Ashton), Principal Figure in "Symphony" (MacMillan), 2 Sonnets in "Images of Love" (MacMillan), Juliet in "Romeo & Juliet" (MacMillan); other principal rôles for Royal Ballet incl.: Odette-Odile in "Swan Lake" (Petipa), Giselle in "Giselle" (Perrot-Coralli), Princess Aurora in "Sleeping Beauty" (Petipa), Cinderella in "Cinderelle" (Ashton), Ophelia in "Hamlet" (Helpmman), The Bride in "Le Fête Etrange" (Howard), The Girl in "Solitaire" (MacMillan), Principal Girl in "Danses Concertante" (MacMillan); Guest artist with Stuttgart Ballet and Nat. Ballet of Canada; left Can. in Sept. 1953 to join Royal Ballet Sch.; joined Royal Ballet in 1956, first created rôle, 1956, first principal rôle 1957, since when has preferred created and modern works to classics; third generation Candn. on both sides of her family; m. 16 July 1963; recreation: cinema.

SHABEN, Hon. Larry R., M.L.A.; politician; b. Hanna, Alta. 30 March 1935; s. Albert Mohammed and Lila (Kazeil) S.; e. Eastwood High Sch. Edmonton 1953; Univ. of Alta. 1954 — 55; m. Alma Amina d. of Rikia Hyder and the late Samuel Saddy 8 July 1960; children: Linda, Carol, Larry, James, Joan; MIN. OF UTILITIES AND TELEPHONES, ALTA.; independent businessman since 1962; mem. High Prairie Town Council 1969 — 74; High Prairie Recreation Bd. 1969 — 74; Pres., Lesser Slave Lake P. Cons. Assn. 1969 — 74; el. M.L.A. for Lesser Slave Lake 1975; Pres., North Peace Sr. Hockey League 1972 — 74; High Prairie Minor Hockey Assn. 1973 — 74; Dir. and Vice Pres. Peace Tourist Assn. 1970 — 72; P. Conservative; Muslim; Club: Optimist (Secy. High Prairie 1967 [78]); Home: (P.O. Box 1050) High Prairie, Alta. T0G 1E0; Office: 403 Legislative Bldg., Edmonton, Alta. T5K 2B6.

SHADBOLT, Douglas, B.Arch., D.Eng., F.R.A.I.C.; architect; educator; b. Victoria, B.C. 18 Apl. 1925; s. Edmund and Alice Mary Maud (Healy) S.; e. Univ. of B.C.; McGill Univ.; Univ. of Ore. B.Arch. 1957; N.S. Tech. Coll. D.Eng. 1969; m.Sidney Osborne Scott; children: Catherine Shand Craig, James Osborne Craig; DIR., SCH. OF ARCH., UNIV. OF B.C. 1979- ; Asst., Assoc. Prof. of Arch. McGill Univ. 1958-61; Prof. and Founding Dir. Sch. Arch. N.S. Tech. Coll. Halifax 1961-68; Prof. and Founding Dir. Sch. Arch. Carleton Univ. Ottawa 1968-79 and Sch. Indust. Design 1973 (Founder); mem. Arch. Inst. B.C.; Home: 4525 Gothard St., Vancouver, B.C. V5R 3K8; Office: 2075 Wesbrook Mall, Vancouver, B.C. V6T 1W5.

SHADBOLT, Jack, O.C. (1972), LL.D.; artist; b. Shoeburyness Eng. 4 Feb. 1909; s. late Edmond and Alice Mary Maude S.; e. Victoria (B.C.) High Sch. 1925; Victoria Coll. 1927; Victoria (B.C.) Normal Sch. 1928; Art Students' League, N.Y.C. 1928; André L'Hote Sch. of Art, Paris 1937; Euston Rd. Art Sch., London, Eng. 1937; Art Student; League, N.Y.C. 1948; LL.D. Univ. of Victoria 1973, Simon Fraser 1978; B.C. 1978; m. Doris Kathleen, d. late Rufus Meisel, 20 Sept. 1945; Former Head, Drawing & Painting Sec., Vancouver Sch. of Art and sometime juror. lectr. and writer; incl. in exhns.: Venice Biennial; Carnegie Internat.; Pittsburgh; Sao Paulo; Tate Gallery, London, Eng.; World Fairs Brussels and Seattle; Warsaw; Toulouse; Mexico City; Chicago; Sydney; oneman shows incl. New York, San Francisco, Seattle, Portland, Montreal, Toronto, Vancouver; Restrospectives; Thirty Yrs. Nat. Gallery, Ottawa and travelling; Ten Yrs. Retrospective, Vancouver Art Gallery; Early watercolours Victoria Art Gallery; Collections (public): Brooklyn, Cleveland, Portland, Seattle and all major Candn. galleries; in many private and corp. collections; Comns. incl. Edmonton Internat. Airport; CBC Bldg., Vancouver;

Confederation Centre, Charlottetown, P.E.I.; Nat. Arts Centre, Ottawa; rec'd Candn. Guggenheim Internat. Award 1957; Candn. Govt. Overseas Fellowship (France, Italy and Greece); Molson Prize 1978; Univ. of Alta. Nat. Painting Award 1969; O.S.A. award 1981; served in 2nd World War; Adm. Offr., Candn. War Artists; author of "In Search of Form" 1968; "Mind's I" (poems) 1973; "Act of Art", 1981; also numerous articles concerning art in various journs.; Address: 5121 Harborview Rd., N. Burnaby, B.C. V5B 1C9

SHAFFNER, Hon. John Elvin, B.A.; executive; b. Lawrencetown Annapolis Co., N.S., 3 March 1911; s. John Elvin and Naomi Winifred (Durling) S.; e. Lawrencetown Public Sch. (1917-27); Acadia Univ., B.A. 1931; m. Nell Margaret, d. Outhit R. Potter, Middleton, N.S., 4 Sept. 1936; children: Susan Burdette (Mrs. W. M. Lewis), Margaret Lynn (Mrs. Geoffrey Leppinns); LIEUTENANT GOVERNOR OF NOVA SCOTIA since 1978; Agent Gen. in U.K. and Europe for Province of Nova Scotia since 1973; Past Chairman, T. P. Calkin Ltd.; Past Vice-Pres., Evangeline Investments Ltd.; Past Dir., Rothmans of Pall Mall Canada Ltd.; Carling O'Keefe Ltd.; Avon Valley Greenhouses Ltd.; Pathfinder Credit Ltd.; Past mem., Halifax Adv. Bd., Can. Perm. Mortgage Corp.; Canada Permanent Trust Co.; Dir., Atlantic Provs. Econ. Council 1957; Past mem. & Vice Chrmn.; Board of Governors, Acadia Univ.; employed by Crowell, Balcom & Co., Chart. Accts., Halifax, N.S. as Jr. Audit Clerk, 1932-34; Mgr. of retail family business at Lawrencetown, N.S., 1934-39; Inspector for N.S. Bd. of Public Utilities, 1940-41; joined staff of M. W. Graves & Co. Ltd. at Bridgetown, N.S., as Acct. 1941; apptd. Mgr. of (subsidiary) Annapolis Valley Cider Co. Ltd., 1942; apptd. Secy.-Treas. of and assoc. beverage co.'s, 1943, at same time assuming full management of beverage co.'s till their sale in 1961; Pres. and Dir. 1950; M. W. Graves & Co. Ltd.; 7-Up Maritimes Ltd.; Canada Foods Ltd.; mem. of Town Council of Bridgetown, Nova Scotia, 1946-48; President, N.S. Liberal Association, 1958-60; President of King's Co. Branch of Canadian Mental Health Association; Candn. Food Processors Assn. 1961-62; mem. of Extve., Candn. Mfrs. Assn., 1961-62; Agent-Gen. of Nova Scotia in U.K. 1973-76; Liberal; Anglican; recreations: golf, fishing; Clubs: Rotary; Ken-Wo Golf & Country; Outport mem., R.N.S.Y.S.; Home: Belcher St., Port Williams, N.S. B0P 1T0

SHAND, Frederick Page, B.A.Sc., P.Eng.; company executive; b. Toronto, 15 Nov. 1919; s. Fred B. and Clara (Ruickbie) S.; e. Runnymede Coll. Inst., Toronto; Univ. of Toronto, B.A.Sc. (Elect. Engn.) 1943; m. Frances J., d. W. Robertson, 23 Oct. 1943; children: Sandra, John; CHRMN. OF THE BD., BUILDING PRODUCTS OF CANADA; joined John Inglis Co. 1946-57; served in various capacities incl. Nat. Sales Mgr., Gen. Mgr.-Ont. Distribution, Nat. Service Mgr.; held various extve. positions in indust. sales and mang., Combined Enterprises Ltd., Toronto, 1958-61; joined present Co. 1962; served as Vice Pres.-Marketing, Vice Pres. and Gen. Mgr.-Bldg. Materials Div., Extve. Vice Pres. and Dir., Pres. and Chief Extve. Offr.; served with Candn. Army 1942-45; rank Capt.; mem., Candn. Standards Assn. (Dir. and 2nd Vice Pres.); HUDAC (Extve. Comte of Mfrs.' Council); P. Conservative; Presbyterian; Clubs: Montreal Rotary; Royal St. Lawrence Yacht; Baie d'Urfe Curling; Carlton (Winnipeg); 79 Farningham Cres., Islington, Ont. M9B 2B7

SHANLY, Coote Nisbitt, B.Com.; manufacturing executive; b. Quebec City, Que. 24 Oct. 1925; s. late Coote Nisbitt and Berys Alleyn Rolt (Sharples) S.; e. St. George's Sch. Quebec; St. Alban's Sch. Brockville; Lower Can. Coll. Montreal; Queen's Univ. B.Com. 1949; m. Nonie Mary d. Arthur Fitzpatrick, Que City 24 June 1950; three s. John James Arthur (deceased), Walter Patrick Francis, Charles Coote Nisbitt (deceased); PRES., DIR., CEO, DY-

NATEL INC. since 1979; Pres. and Dir. Crane Carrier (Canada Ltd. 1977-78; Vice-Pres. and Gen. Mgr. Teledyne Canada Tsp. Group 1974-77; Pres. and Dir., J.S.W. Holdings Ltd.; Vice Pres. and Dir., Queensway Tank Lines Ltd.; Roads Resurfacing Co. Ltd.; Dir., Tandem Mgt. Ltd.; Carefree Travel Ltd.; Kaps Transport Ltd.; Bolster Transport Ltd.; R. R. Dales Const. Co. Ltd.; Norcan Parts and Equip't. Ltd.; Sunnybrook Stables Ltd.; joined Royal Bank of Canada 1944; Industrial Acceptance Corp. Ltd. 1951-74 serving in various positions incl. Vice Pres. and Gen. Mgr. Indust. Financing & Leasing Operations; Reserve Offrs. Training Course; mem. Ont. Trucking Assn.; Am. Trucking Assn.; Nat. Tank Truck Carriers (US); Roads & Transport. Assn. Can.; Nat. Ready Mix Concrete Assn.; Ont. Good Roads Assn.; Bd. Trade Metrop. Toronto; P. Conservative; Anglican; recreation: antique and classic cars; Clubs: Granite; RCYC; Mount Royal (Montreal); Home: Apt. 607, Skymark I, 3303 Don Mills Rd., Willowdale, Ont. M2J 4T6 Office: 3857 Nashua Dr., Mississauga, Ont. L4V 1R3

SHANNON, Gerald Edward, B.J.; diplomat; b. Ottawa, Ont. 8 June 1935; s. Gerald Edmund and Kathleen (Burke) S.; e. Nepean High Sch. Ottawa; Carleton Univ. B.J. 1957; m. Diane Leone d. Thomas Matthew Barnett, Carleton Place, Ont. 21 Dec. 1963; children: Michael Thomas, Steven Patrick; joined Dept. of External Affairs Ottawa 1963, Third Secy. Washington 1964, First Secy. Belgrade 1969, Depy. Dir. Comm. Policy Div. Ottawa 1972 and Dir. 1974, Ambassador to Korea 1977, Min. (Econ.) Washington 1978; served with COTC 1954-57, Pilot Offr.; mem. Prof. Assn. Foreign Service Offrs.; Anglican; recreations: outdoor sports; Office: Lester B. Pearson Bldg., 125 Sussex Dr., Ottawa, Ont. K1A 0G2.

SHANNON, Joy Marianne (Mrs. James Grant Shannon); b. Toronto, Ont., 31 Oct. 1922; d. Charles and Jessica (Lennard) Sedgwick; e. Univ. of Toronto; McGill Univ., Concordia, B.A. B.F.A.; m. James Grant Shannon, 22 May 1946; children: Patricia Ellen, James David; Dir., Montreal Neurological Hosp.; Assoc. Director, Montreal Neurol. Institute; mem. Bd. Dirs., Gov.; McGill Univ.; mem., Canadian College of Health Executives; recreations: music, golf, swimming; Clubs: Faculty (McGill); University (Montreal); Home: P.O. Box 85, South Lancaster, Ont. K0C 2C0

SHANNON, Hon. Melvin Earl, B.A., LL.B.; judge; b. Near Harris, Sask. 22 March 1927; s. Robert Andrew and Beatrice May (Lakey) S.; e. Delisle, Sask.; Univ. of Sask. B.A. (distinction) 1947, LL.B. (distinction) 1949 (Carswell Prize); m. Suzanne Sarah d. late Ernest Arlington McCullough 24 June 1952; children: Sarah Ann, Mel Andrew, Daniel Howard, Kathleen, Stephen Michael, Ann; JUSTICE, COURT OF QUEEN's BENCH OF ALTA. since 1973; read law with R. H. Fenerty, Q.C.; called to Bar of Alta. 1950; cr. Q.C. 1968; Counsel, Mclaws & Co. 1950-53; estbd. Shannon & Cook 1954, Sr. Partner; Ald. City of Calgary 1953-54; def. Lib. Cand. for Calgary S. fed. g.e. 1958; mem. Adv. Bd. C.S.T. Foundation; Trustee Patrons Fund Candn. Lawn Tennis Assn.; Past Pres. Kts. Round Table; mem. Law Soc. Alta. (Bencher 1968-73, Pres. 1973); Candn. Bar Assn.; recreations: tennis, squash, french lang., reading; Clubs: Glencoe (Dir. 1961-71, Pres. 1969-71); L'Alliance Française; Home: 4108 Crestview Rd., Calgary, Alta. T2T 2L4; Office: Court House 611-4th St. S.W., Calgary, Alta. T2P 1T5.

SHANSKI, John; business consultant; b. Warren, Man., 16 April 1909; s. Anton Smerechanski and Dora (Hooley) S.; m. Olga Safneck, 5 Sept., 1936; children: Don, Patricia, R.N., John David, B.A., B.Com.; PRESIDENT, CONIFER ENTERPRISES 1980 LTD.; mem., Candn. Radio Television Comn.; def. cand. for fed. riding of Selkirk in g.e. 1954 and for prov. riding of Inkster in g.e. 1962; Past Pres., N. Winnipeg YMCA; Ukrainian Prof. & Businessmen's Club; N. Winnipeg Lib. Assn.; Past Dir.,

Metrop. YMCA; Winnipeg Football Club; del., Man. Trade Mission to Europe, 1962; Chrmn., Man. Indust. Devel. Bd., 1965; Prov. Chrmn., Man. March of Dimes, 1964-65; Hon. Counsellor and mem., Winnipeg Chamber Comm.; mem., W. Candn. Lumbermen's Assn.; Man. Golden Boys Movement; rec'd "Good Citizen Award", Man. Travel & Conv. Assn.; "Outstanding Citizenship" Award, City of Winnipeg; Liberal; Ukrainian Catholic; Clubs: Manitoba; Winnipeg Rotary (Dir. 1965, 1966); Canadian; Winnipeg Winter; Home: 32 Fairway Place, Winnipeg, Man. R3R 2P3; Office: 56 Myrtle St., Winnipeg, Man. R3E 2R1

SHAPIRO, Bernard J., Ph.D.; academic administrator; b. Montreal, Que. 8 June 1935; s. Maxwell and Mary (Tafler) S.; e. Lower Can. Coll. Montreal; McGill Univ. B.A. 1956 (Univ. Scholar 1953-56, Alan Oliver Gold Medal 1956); Harvard Univ. MAT 1962, Ph.D. 1966; m. Phyllis Pearl d. Maxwell A. Schwartz, Jerusalem, Israel 30 June 1957; children: Marvin Michael, Arlene Rose; DIR., ONT. INST. FOR STUDIES IN EDUCATION 1980- ; Secy.-Treas. William Barbara Corp. and Ruby Foo'ss Ltd., Montreal 1956-61; Prof. of Educ. Boston Univ. 1966-76; Dean of Educ. Univ. of W. Ont. 1976-78, Vice Pres. (Acad.) 1978-80; author "Readings in Educational Psychology" 1976; numerous articles cognitive devel., program evaluation, lang. learning, policy devel. in higher educ.; mem. Candn. Assn. Teacher Educ. (Pres.); Candn. Soc. Studies in Educ.; Psychometric Soc.; Am. Stat. Assn.; Nat. Council Measurement in Educ.; Jewish; recreations: opera, keyboard instruments, walking; Home: 66 Collier St., #5A, Toronto, Ont. M4W 1L9; Office: 252 Bloor St. W., Toronto, Ont. M5S 1V6.

SHARON, William Frederick, M.C., B.Sc., M.E.I.C.; consultaant; b. Red Deer, Alberta, 6 April 1915; s. Hugh and Meda (King) S.; e. Public Sch., Vancouver, B.C.; Royal Mil. Coll., Kingston, Ont. (grad. 1937); Queen's Univ., B.Sc. (Civil Engn.) 1939; m. Mary Euphemia Parsons (widow), d. late Harry Duncan, Leask, Sask., 14 Sept. 1959; children: (by 1st m.) Douglas Gregory, Robert Hugh, Frances Anne; (by 2nd m.) Karin Ruth Parsons, Brian Richard Parsons, Timothy Rippath Sharon; SR. CONSULTANT, BROWNELL DESIGN LTD. 1980; Pres. and Dir., O.K. Construction Ltd., Edmonton, Alta.; Mannix International Inc., Minneapolis, Minn.; La Cie Mannix (Quebec) Ltée.; Supt., Conradi Construction Co. Ltd., N. Ont., 1937-38; Dominion Bridge Co. Ltd., Riverside Iron Works, Calgary, Alta., commencing as Production Engr. and successively as Sales Engr., Contract Engr., and Mgr. of Sales, 1945-51; Chief Engr. and Vice-Pres., Sparling Davis Co. Ltd., Edmonton, Alta., 1951; Vice-Pres. and Gen. Mgr., Sparling Tank & Mfg. Co., Toronto, Ont., 1952-55, and Pres. and Dir., 1956-57; Exec. Vice-Pres. and Dir., Mannix Co. Ltd. 1957-62; consultant to engineering, construction and resource industries 1962-75; C.E.O., Public Utilities Bd., Alta., 1975-80; served in 2nd World War with Candn. Army Corps. of Engrs., 1939-45; M.D. No. 5, Quebec, 1939-41; O.C. 12 Field Co., R.C.E., W. Can., 1942; 7 Field Co., R.C.E. and 9 Field Sqdn., R.C.E., Gt. Brit. and N.W. Europe, 1943-44; attached to Am. Army, S.W. Pac. Theatre (Okinawa) 1945; awarded M.C.; mem., Engn. Inst. Can.; Protestant; recreations: riding, skiing, hunting; Home: 5040 White Mud Rd., Edmonton, Alta.

SHARP, Gen. Frederick Ralph, C.M.M., D.F.C., C.D.; retired officer; b. Moosomin, Sask., 8 Dec. 1915; s. John Andrew and Florence (Black) S.; e. Moosomin High Sch., grad. 1934; Royal Mil. Coll., Kingston, Military Dipl., 1938; Univ. of Western Ont., (Dipl. Business Adm., 1950); m. Elizabeth Lenore Weaver, 27 Sept. 1940; children: John Frederick, Brenda Lee, Richard Ames, Barbara Jane, Elizabeth Killoran; joined RCAF, July 1938; trained as Pilot, becoming Flying Instr., 3 Service Flying Training Sch., Calgary, Alta., 1940; trans. to Instr. Staff, 15 Service Flying Training Sch., Claresholm, Alta. and in 1943 to 2

Flying Instructional Sch., Vulcan, Alta.; posted on course, War Staff Coll., Jan. 1944; overseas Mar. 1944, 408 Bomber Sqdn. of 6 Bomber Group, eventually as Sqdn. Commdr.; awarded D.F.C.; apptd. to Directorate of Postings & Careers A.F. Hdqrs., Ottawa, 1945; O.C., Central Flying Sch., Trenton, Ont. 1947; trans. as Exchange Offr. attached to Directing Staff, RAF Staff Coll., Eng., 1950-53; O.C., RCAF Station, North Bay, Ont., 1953-4; trans. to AFHQ to Directorate of Organ. & Establishments and later the Directorate of Mang. Engn.; apptd. Depy. Commdr. of 25th Region, NORAD, 1960 and Bangor Sector of 26th Region, 1962; apptd. Dir.-Gen., Management Engn. and Automation, Candn. Forces Hdqrs., 1964; Vice Chief of the Defence Staff, 1966-69, Chief 1969-72; Depy. Commdr. in Chief, Norad 1969; promoted Air Vice Marshal, 1965, Air Marshal, 1966, Lt. Gen. 1 Feb. 1968; and subsequently promoted Gen. and apptd. Chief, Defence Staff; Partner, P. S. Ross & Partners, 1972, mem. Mang. Comte., Partner i/c. Ottawa 1972-74, Partner i/c. International Consulting 1974-75; Dir., Internat. Consulting, Touche Ross Internat. N.Y. 1975-78; Consulting Assoc. P.S. Ross 1978; Clubs: Rideau; Royal Ottawa; R.M.C.; R.C.M.I.; Old Port Yacht's Palm Beach; Home: R.R. #2, Carrying Place, Ont.

SHARP, Isadore; hotel executive; b. Toronto, Ont., 8 Oct. 1931; s. Max and Lena (Godfrey) S.; e. Forest Hill Coll. Inst., Toronto; Ryerson Inst. (Medal in Arch. 1954); m. Rosalie, d. Joseph Wise, 6 Sept. 1955; four s. Jordon, Gregory, Anthony; CHAIRMAN, PRESIDENT & C. E. O., FOUR SEASONS HOTELS LTD. since 1960; Pres., Sharps Development (Toronto) Ltd.; Max Sharp & Son Construction Ltd.; (house and subdiv. devel. and apt. constr.); entered hotel constr. 1960, opening Four Seasons Hotel 1961; other Four Seasons Hotels are located in: London, Eng.; Montreal; Ottawa; Belleville; Toronto; Calgary; Edmonton; Vancouver; New York; Dallas; Philadelphia; San Francisco; Chicago; San Antonio; Washington, D.C.; Houston; Seattle; recreations: tennis, skiing; Clubs: Devil's Glen Ski; York Racquets; Home: 26 Forest Glen Cres., Toronto, Ont.; Office: 1100 Eglinton Ave. E., Don Mills, Ont. M3C 1H8

SHARP, John Wemyss; industrialist; b. Montreal, Que., 14 Jan. 1918; s. late Emily (Starke) and the late Otho Rupert S.; e. Selwyn House Sch., Montreal; Ashbury Coll., Ottawa; Univ. of W. Ont. (Management Training); m. Frances V., d. late Charles A. Robinson, 27 Nov. 1943; divorced; m. Lucille S., d. F. Stuart Molson, 27 Aug. 1980; children: John A. V., Sonja V., Cynthia R.; REPRESENTATIVE, F. H. DEACON HODGSON INC.; Dir., Keystone Custodian Funds Inc.; Unimed Pharmaceuticals Ltd.; Unimed, Inc.; with McColl-Frontenac Oil Company Limited (Texaco), 1935-39; Murphy Paint & Thorp-Hambrook Company Ltd., 1945-49; controlling shareholder, Vilas Co. Ltd., 1949-62; Chrmn., Vilas Industries Ltd. 1962-69; Sr. Econ. Counselor Que. Gov't., New York City, 1973-77; served in 2nd World War; 1st Bn. Black Watch (RHR) Canada, Eng., 8th Argyll & Sutherland Highlanders, N. Africa, confirmed rank Major; Mentioned in Despatches; wounded; mem., Bd. Dirs., Pres., Montreal Gen. Hosp. (Centre Bd.); Gov., Douglas Hosp., Montreal; Gov., Dir., Adv. Bd., Bishop's Coll. Sch., Lennoxville, Que.; Gov. Montreal Children's Hosp.; Past Chrmn., Candn. Council of Furniture Manufacturers; Dir. and Past Pres., Que. Furniture Mfrs. Assn.; Past Pres., Nat. Council and now Hon. Vice Pres., Nat. Council & Que. Prov. Council, Boy Scouts of Can.; mem. of Corp., King's Hall, Compton, Que.; Dir., and Past Pres., E. Twps. Forestry Assn.; mem., Que. Forestry Assn.; Anglican; recreations: fishing, hunting, shooting, golf; Clubs: Mount Royal; St. James's; Mount Bruno Country; Montreal Racket; Montreal Skeet; N.Y. Racquet and Tennis; Residence: Apt. 707, 3488 Cote des Neiges, Montreal, Que. H3H 2M6.

SHARP, Hon. Mitchell W., P.C., B.A., D.Sc., LL.D.; b. Winnipeg, Man., 11 May 1911; s. Thomas and Elizabeth S.; e. Univ. of Manitoba, B.A. 1934, LL.D. 1965; London Sch. of Economics 1937; Univ. of Ottawa D.Sc. 1970; Univ. W. Ont. LL.D. 1977; m. late Daisy, d. late John Boyd, Victoria, B.C., 23 April 1938 (Dec.); one s. Noel; m. Jeanette Dugal, 14 April 1976 (resigned from Cabinet 1976); COMMR., NORTHERN PIPELINE AGENCY, since 1978; Appts. incl. Officer, Department of Finance, Ottawa, 1942-51; Director of Economic Policy Division, 1947-51; Associate Deputy Minister of Trade and Commerce, 1951-57; Deputy Minister, 1957-58; Min. of Trade & Comm. 1963-65; Min. of Finance, 1965-68; Secy. State for External Affairs 1968-74; Pres., Privy Council and Leader of Govt., H. of C., 1974-76; resigned from Parlt. May 1, 1978; mem., N. Am. Depy. Chrmn., Trilateral Comm.; Liberal; United Church; Home: 33 Monkland Ave., Ottawa, Ont. K1S 1Y8; Office: P.O. Box 1605, Station B, Ottawa, Ont. K1P 5A0

SHARPE, C. Richard, B.A.; executive; b. St. Catharines, Ont. 11 Feb. 1925; s. J. Walter Sharpe; e. St. Catharines, Ont.; Univ. of W. Ont. B.A. (hons.) (Business Adm.); m. Peggy Pepler; one s., three d.; CHRMN. OF BD., CEO AND DIR., SIMPSONS-SEARS LTD., 1979- ; Dir., Simpsons-Sears Acceptance Co. Ltd.; Allstate Insurance Co. of Canada; Allstate Life Insurance Co. of Canada; Mollenhauer Ltd.; Standard Brands Ltd.; Redpath Industries; Inglis Limited; Nabisco Brands Inc., New York; joined Simpsons Ltd. Toronto 1950 continuing with Simpsons-Sears Ltd. upon formation 1953; held various positions incl. Buyer, Merchandise Mgr., Gen. Merchandise Mgr.; apptd. Vice Pres. Merchandising 1970; Served overseas as pilot with RCAF 1943-46; Jet Flying Reserve 1950-55; Vice-Chmn., Retail Council Can.; Dir., Sir Edmund Hillary Foundation; Candn. Club of Toronto; Gwendolyn Peacher Foundation for Traditional Arts; Vice Pres. Ridley Coll.; Gov., Toronto French Sch.; Member, Advisory Council, School of Business Admin., University of Western Ontario; Member, Ministers Advisory Council Dept. Industry, Trade & Commerce; former mem. Nat. Design Council Ottawa; Business Council on Nat. Issues, Cdn. Amer. Comte.; Bd. Trade Metrop. Toronto; recreations: golf, fishing, skiing; Clubs: Toronto; York; Canadian; Caledon Ski; Toronto Golf; University; Ristigouché Salmon; Home: 759 Cardinal Pl., Mississauga, Ont. L5J 2R8; Office: 222 Jarvis St., Toronto, Ont. M5B 2B8.

SHARROW, Marilyn Jane, B.S., M.A.L.S.; library director; b. Oakland, Cal.; d. Charles Leroy and Helen Evelyn (Yarger) Sharrow; e. Univ. of Mich. B.S. 1967, M.A.L.S. 1969; m. Lawrence John Davis; DIR. OF LIBRARIES, UNIV. OF MAN. 1979- ; librarian, Detroit Pub. Lib. 1968-70; Head, Fine Arts Dept. Syracuse Univ. Libs. 1970-73; Dir., Roseville Pub. Lib., Mich. 1973-75; Asst. Dir. Undergrad. Lib. Services, Univ. of Wash. 1975-78, Assoc. Dir. of Libs. 1978-79; rec'd Alma Josenhans Scholarship, Detroit Pub. Lib. 1968; mem. Univ. of Man. Press Bd.; Am. Lib. Assn.; Man. Lib. Assn.; Candn. Lib. Assn.; Nat. Lib. of Can., Resource Network Comte.; Humanities Assn.; Business and Professional Women's Club of Winnipeg; recreation: painting; Office: Winnipeg, Man. R3T 2N2.

SHARWOOD, Gordon Robertson, B.A., M.A.; investment executive; b. Montreal, Que., 26 Feb. 1932; s. late Robert W. and Joan M. H. Sharwood; e. Selwyn House Sch., Montreal; Bishop's Coll. Sch., Lennoxville, Que.; McGill Univ.; Oxford Univ.; Harvard Univ.; two s., one d.; PRES., SHARWOOD AND CO., merchant bankers and finan. consults.; Dr., Fed. Business Devel. Bank; Dir., Candn. Pacific Transport; Dover Industries; Western Capital Invest. Corp.; Nabob Foods Ltd.; Realequimor Ltd., Real Property Trust of Canada; Marshall Ind.; Metals and Alloys Co. Ltd.; joined The Canadian Bank of Commerce, Montreal, 1956; Assistant Manager, Hamilton, Ont., 1957; Assistant Manager, Vancouver, B.C.,

1958; Manager, Economics Department, Toronto, 1959; Agent, New York, 1960; Asst. Gen. Mgr., Canadian Imperial Bank of Commerce, Toronto 1962; Regional Gen. Mgr., Toronto, 1963; Depy. Chief Gen. Mgr., H.O., 1966; Chief Gen. Mgr. 1968-69; Chrmn. Extve. Comte., Traders Group Ltd., Toronto 1970; Vice Chrmn. and Vice Pres., Guaranty Trust Co. of Can. 1971; el. Pres. 1972 and Chrmn. 1975; ret. as Chrmn. 1976; Pres., Acres Ltd. Dir., The Nat. Youth Orchestra; The Niagara Inst.; Clubs: Toronto; Toronto Golf; Badminton & Racquet; Office: 20 Victoria St., Toronto, Ont. M5C 2N8

SHATNER, William, B.A.; actor; b. Montreal, Que. 22 March 1931; s. Joseph and Anne Shatner; e. McGill Univ. B.A. 1952; m. 1stly Gloria Rand 12 Aug. 1956 (divorced 1969); m. 2ndly Marcy Lafferty 20 Oct. 1973; 3 d.; stage debut 1952; appeared Montreal Playhouse summers 1952, 1953; juvenile roles Candn. Repertory Theatre Ottawa 1952-53, 1953-54; appeared Stratford (Ont.) Festival 1954-56; Broadway appearances incl. "Tamburlaine the Great" 1956; "The World of Suzie Wong" 1958; "A Shot in the Dark" 1961; films incl. "The Brothers Karamazov" 1958; "The Explosive Generation" 1961; "Judgement at Nuremburg" 1961; "The Intruder" 1962; "The Outrage" 1964; "Dead of Night" 1974; "The Devil's Rain" 1975; "Star Trek" 1979; TV movies and appearances incl. "Omnibus", "Studio One", "U.S. Steel Hour"; "Alfred Hitchcock Presents", "Naked City", "Alcoa Premiere", "Twilight Zone", "Bob Hope Chrysler Theatre", "Name of the Game", "Mission Impossible", "Testimony of Two Men", "The Tenth Level", "The Andersonville Trial"; star TV Series "Star Trek" 1966-69, animated series 1973-75; "Barbaray Coast" 1975-76; "The Bastard" 1978; "Disaster on the Coastliner" 1979; rec'd Tyrone Guthrie Award 1956; Theatre World Award 1958; mem. Actors Equity Assn.; A.F.T.R.A.; Screen Actors Guild; A.C.T.A.; Address: c/o William Morris Agency, 151 El Camino, Beverly Hills, Calif. 90212.

SHAVICK, Lenard M., B.A.; retailer; b. Paterson, N.J., 14 Nov. 1921; s. Emanuel and Bess (Goldberg) S.; e. N.Y. Mil. Acad., 1938; Lafayette Coll., B.A. 1942; m. Barbara, d. Alvin J. Walker, Westmount, Que., 26 May 1946; children: Catherine, James, Margaret; CHMN., AND CHIEF EXTVE. OFFR., HOLT, RENFREW & CO. LTD., since 1981; joined present Co. as Trainee, Asst. Buyer, Men's Wear, 1946; Buyer Sportswear, 1947 and Accessories, 1948; Merchandise Mgr., Montreal store, 1949; Dir. of Co. 1955; Gen. Merchandise Mgr. of Co. 1961; Vice-Pres. Mech. 1965; Extve. Vice-Pres., Aug. 1965, Pres. 1967; C.E.O. 1968; served as Ensign with U.S.N.R. during 2nd World War; rec'd Presidential Unit Citation; Trustee, Temple Emanu-El, Westmount, Que.; Dir., Montreal Symphony Orchestra; recreations: golf, tennis; Clubs: Montefiore; Elm Ridge Country; Mt. Royal; Home: 4386 Montrose Ave., Westmount, Que. H3Y 2B1; Office: 1300 Sherbrooke St. W., Montreal, Que. H3G 1H9

SHAW, Allan Cameron, B.Sc., M.B.A.; manufacturer; b. Halifax, N.S. 23 Nov. 1942; s. Ronald Harry S.; e. Queen Elizabeth High Sch. Halifax 1960; Dalhousie Univ. B.Sc. 1964; Harvard Business Sch. M.B.A. 1971; m. Leslie Ann d. Frederick Alexander Baldwin, Halifax, N.S. 30 July 1965; children: Lisa Gabrielle, Sarah Naomi; PRES. GEN. MGR. AND DIR. L. E. SHAW LTD. since 1979; Pres. and Dir. L. E. Shaw Transport Ltd.; Nova Scotia Sand & Gravel Ltd.; Suburban Industries Ltd.; Dir. Clayton Developments Ltd.; held various positions Pyramid Structural Concrete Div. of present co. incl. Mgr. 1964-69, Vice Pres. Mfg. 1971-74; mem. Voluntary Planning Bd. Prov. of N.S., Dir. and Chrmn. Mfg. Sector; Am. Concrete Pipe Assn. (Dir. 1970-73, Chrmn. Candn. Region 1973); Nat. Concrete Producers Assn. (Dir. 1971-77, Pres. 1975); Clay Brick Assn. Can. (Dir. 1972, Pres. 1976-77); Constr. Mang. Labor Bureau Ltd. (Dir. 1975, Chrm. 1978); Unitarian; recreation: tennis; Clubs: Waegwoltic; Burnside

Tennis; Halifax; Home: 6463 Coburg Rd., Halifax, N.S. B3H 2A6; Office: P.O. Box 996, Halifax, N.S. B3J 2X1.

SHAW, Denis Martin, M.A., Ph.D., F.R.S.C. (1961), F.G.S.; geochemist; university professor; b. St. Annes, Lancs., England, 20 Aug. 1923; s. Norman Wade and Alice Jane Sylvia (Shackleton) S.; e. Emmanuel Coll., Cambridge, B.A. 1943, M.A. 1948; Univ. of Chicago (Salisbury Fellow), Ph.D. 1951; m. Doris Pauline, d. Dr. late C. A. Mitchell, Ottawa, Ont., 6 April 1946; divorced; children: Geoffrey, Jill, Peter; m. 2ndly, Susan Louise Evans, d. Dr. E.L.M. Evans, Port Credit, Ont. 9 April 1976; mem. of the Faculty, McMaster Univ. since 1949; Chrmn., Dept. of Geol., 1953-59, 1962-66; Dean of Grad. Studies 1979- ; part-time Geol. Offr. with Ont. Dept. of Mines 1949, 1950, 1958 and with Que. Dept. of Mines 1954-56; Visiting Prof. at Ecole Nat. Supérieur de Géol., Univ. de Nancy, 1959-60, Inst. de Minéralogie, Univ. de Genève, 1966-67; served in 2nd World War in R.A.F. Transport Command, Signals Offr., 1943-46; Publications: about 100 articles in scient. journs.; Ed. "Geochimica et Cosmochimica Acta"; mem. Geochem. Soc.; Mineral. Soc. Can.; Home: 130 St. Joseph's Dr. Hamilton, Ont. L8N 2E8

SHAW, Edgar Albert George, B.Sc., Ph.D., F.R.S.C.; physicist; b. Teddington, Middlesex, Eng. 10 July 1921; s. Albert and Lily Florence (Hill) S.; e. Harrow Co. Sch. Eng. 1937; Acton Tech. Coll. London 1938 — 40; Imp. Coll. Univ. of London 1946 — 50, B.Sc., Ph.D.; m. Millicent Selina d. late Arthur Chandler, New York City, N.Y. and Baltimore, Md. 6 Oct. 1945; children: Jennifer, Kenneth; HEAD, ACOUSTICS SEC., DIV. OF PHYSICS, NAT. RESEARCH COUNCIL since 1975 and Princ. Research Offr. since 1974; Lectr. Univ. of Ottawa since 1958; Tech. Offr. Ministry of Aircraft Production (London) and Brit. Air Comn. (Washington) 1940 — 46; Asst. Research Offr. Div. of Physics, Nat. Research Council 1950, Assc. Research Offr. 1953, Sr. Research Offr. 1960 — 74; inventions incl. Hearing Protector (high-spring constant liquid filled cushion), Improved Earphone (variable effective coupling vol.), Probe Microphone with Horn Coupling; mem. Internat. Comn. on Acoustics 1972 — 78, Chrmn. 1975 — 78; Comte. on Hearing, Bioacoustics & Biomechanics, U.S. Nat. Acad. of Science, mem. since 1965, Extve. council 1973 — 75; author over 50 research papers, book chapters; acoustical waves & vibrations, hearing measurements, hearing protection, physiol. acoustics, urban noise, electroacoustics; Fellow, Royal Soc. of Can.; Fellow, Acoustical Soc. Am. (Vice Pres. 1968 — 70, Pres. 1973 — 74); rec'd Rayleigh Medal awarded by Institute of Acoustics (Gt Britain), 1979; mem. Candn. Assn. Physicists; Inst. of Physics (Brit.); Hon. mem. Candn. Chiefs Police Assn.; Presbyterian; recreations: walking, cross country skiing, gardening, reading; Home: 1391 Wesmar Dr., Ottawa, Ont. K1H 7T4; Office: Ottawa, Ont. K1A 0R6.

SHAW, James M.; manufacturer; b. Maryland, U.S.A., 4 Sept. 1920; s. James Marvin and Emma (Kiehne) S.; came to Canada 1932; e. Public Sch. and North Toronto Collegiate; McGill Univ.; m. Helena; d. late W. H. A. Verweij, Nijmegen, Netherlands; children: Alexandra Nicòle, James Nicholas; PRESIDENT, NOXZEMA CANADA LTD., 1954-78; Hon. Chrmn. 1978; Dir. Noxell Inc. 1966-78; Dir. C. G. Jung Foundation N.Y. 1960-66; Co-founder and Dir., Analytical Psy. Soc. of Ont. 1970, Pres. 1978; co-founder and Pres., West End Productions and West End Studios Ltd. 1974-78; served in 2nd World War Overseas with R.C.A.F., as Pilot; on operations as Flying Offr. with R.A.F. Bomber Sqdn. No. 77 (shot down in Holland, 1944, P.O.W. till 1945); recreations: psychology, history, tennis, sailing, flying; Clubs: R.C.Y.C.; Granite; The Queens (Chart. mem.); Home: 13 Riverside Cres., Toronto, Ont. M6S 1B5; Office: 77 Park Lawn Rd., Toronto, Ont. M8Y 3H7

SHAW, Michael, M.Sc., Ph.D., D.Sc., F.R.S.C.; educator; b. Barbados, W.I., 11 Feb. 1924; s. Anthony and Myra (Perkins) S.; e. Lodge Sch., Barbados, W.I. (1935-43); McGill Univ., B.Sc. (1st Class Hons. Botany), 1946, M.Sc. 1947, Ph.D. 1949; Post doctoral Fellow Bot. Sch., Cambridge, Eng. (1949-50); Ph.D. ad eund. Univ. Sask. 1971; D.Sc. (Honoris causa) McGill Univ. 1975; m. Jean Norah, d. late N. W. Berkinshaw, 16 Oct. 1948; children: Christopher Anthony, Rosemary Ellen, Nicholas Richard, Andrew Lawrence; VICE PRES. (ACAD.) AND PROVOST UNIV. B.C.; Prof. Agric. Botany; formerly Dean, Faculty Agric. Sciences 1967-75; Associate Professor of Biol., University of Saskatchewan, 1950-54; Professor 1954-67 and Head of Dept. 1961-67; Fellow Royal Soc. of Can., 1962; mem. Biol. Council of Can. (Pres. 1972); Am. Soc. Plant Physiols; Am. Phytopath Soc.; Candn. Soc. Plant Physiols. (Pres. 1963); Candn. Phytopath. Soc.; Candn. Bot. Assn. (Pres. 1980); N.Y. Acad. of Sciences; B.C. Inst. of Agrologists; Agric. Inst. of Can.; Science Council Study Group on Agric., 1966-67; Candn. Agric. Svces. Co-ord. Comte., Candn. Dept. of Agric., 1967-75; Adv. Council, Western Coll. of Vet. Med., Univ. of Sask., 1967-75; Sci. Council of Can.; Nat. Scis. and Engn. Res. Council of Can. 1978-80; rec'd. Gold Medal, Candn. Soc. Plant Physiols. 1971; Fellow, Am. Phytopath. Soc. 1973; Flavelle Medal, Roy. Soc. of Can. 1976; Queen's Jubilee Medal 1977; Editor, "Canadian Journal of Botany", 1964-79; Ed. Bd., "Physiological Plant Pathology", 1971-81; author of over 85 papers in sci. journals; recreations: reading, walking, swimming; Home: 1792 Western Parkway, Vancouver, B.C. V6T 1V3

SHAW, Neil M.; company executive; b. Toronto, Ont., 31 May 1929; s. Harold LeRoy and Fabiola Marie (McGowan) S.; e. Knowlton (Que.) High Sch., 1946; Glacier Inst. of Mang., London, Eng., 1966; Am. Foundation Mang. Research, 1968; m. Frances Audrey, d. R. H. Robinson, Knowlton, Que., 7 June 1952; children: David, Michael, Cynthia, Andrea, Toni; VICE-CHMN., REDPATH INDUSTRIES LTD., since 1982 and Dir. since 1971; Group Managing Dir., Tate & Lyle Ltd., London Eng. 1980; Chmn. and Dir., Tate & Lyle Industries Ltd., 1981; Tate and Lyle Holdings Ltd., 1981; Chrmn., Chrmn. & Dir., Redpath Sugars Ltd.; Dir., Texaco Canada Ltd.; Mid Industries & Explorations Ltd.; Daymond Ltd.; CB Packaging Ltd.; Multi Fittings Ltd.; Clerk, Royal Bank of Canada, 1946; Trust Officer, Crown Trust Company, 1948; joined present Co. as Executive Assistant 1954; Merchandising Mgr. 1958; Export Sales Mgr., Tate & Lyle Ltd., London, Eng., 1963; Vice Pres. & Gen. Mgr., Canada & Dominion Sugar Co. Ltd. 1967; Pres., Daymond Ltd. 1969; Anglican; recreations: skiing, golf, sailing; Clubs: Toronto Golf; Toronto; Mount Royal; Office: Tate & Lyle, Ltd., Sugar Quay, Lower Thames St., London Eng.;

SHAW, Robert Fletcher, C.C. (1967), D.Eng., D.Sc.; consulting engineer; b. Montreal, P.Q., 16 February 1910; s. John Fletcher and Edna Mary Baker (Anglin) S.; e. Pub. Schs. in Montreal, Lethbridge, Calgary, Edmonton and Grad., in Revelstoke, B.C., with Gov. Gen's. Medal in 1925; Revelstoke High Sch., 1928; McGill Univ., B.Eng. (Civil) 1933; D.Sc. (Hon. causa) McMaster 1967; D.Eng. (Hon. causa) N.S. Tech. Coll. 1967; m. Johann Alexandra, d. John MacInnes, Toronto, Ont. 24 Dec. 1935; CONSULTANT TO MONTREAL ENGINEERING COMPANY LIMTIED, 1975- ; Consultant to Dept. of Ind. Devel., Gov't of Nfld. and Labrador, 1979-80; Chrmn. Research Policy Advisory Comte., Centre for Cold Ocean Resources Eng. (C. Core), Memorial Univ. of Nfld.; mem. Montreal Adv. Bd., Crown Trust Co.; began learning construction business as Labourer in 1933 serving with the Foundation Co. and its subsidiaries, and with Dominion Bridge Co. Ltd., A. Janin & Co. Ltd., Duranceau & Duranceau and Anglin-Norcross Corp. Ltd., in various capacities; apptd. Asst. to Vice-Pres. of Foundation Co. of Can. Ltd. i/c constr. June 1940; subsequently apptd. Asst. to Pres., i/c Design Dept., 1941, 1942; Mgr.,

Pictou (N.S.) Shipyard Foundation Maritime Ltd., 1943; Asst. to Pres. (Engn.) 1946; Mgr., Engn. Dept., 1949; on loan to Dept. of Defence Production, Ottawa, May 1951-Dec. 1952 as Vice-Pres. and Chief Engr. Defence Construction (1951) Ltd., and as Candn. Rep. on N.A.T.O. Engn. Team on Airfield Constr.; Vice-Pres., The Foundation Co. of Can. Ltd., 1950-58; Extve. Vice Pres., 1958-62, Pres., 1962-63; Depy. Commr.-Gen., Vice Pres. and Dir., Candn. Corp. for the 1967 World Exhibition, (Expo'67) 1963-68; Commr. Gen. and Pres., 1968; Vice Principal, McGill Univ. 1968-71; Chrmn. Bd. and Dir., Foundation of Canada Engineering Corp. Ltd. 1969; Depy. Min. Dept. of the Environment, 1971; Gov., Univ. N.B. 1975, Chmn., 1978-80; Pres., Moneco Pipeline Consultants 1975-78; President, Canadian Assn. for Retarded Children, 1962-65; Pres., Grad. Soc. McGill Univ., 1964-65, Gold Medal 1968; Pres., Corp. of Prof. Engrs. Que., 1953; Pres., Engn. Inst. Can. 1975-76, Fellow 1975; Julian C. Smith Medal 1967; Keefe Medal 1979; mem. Assn. of Prof. Engrs. Ont., Gold Medal 1968; Gold Medal, Cdn. Council of P. Eng. 1979; Sigma Chi; Protestant; recreations: swimming, golf, Clubs: Royal Ottawa Golf; Royal Montreal Golf; Home: C29, 3980 Cote des Neiges Rd., Montreal, Que. H3H 1W2; Office: Montreal Engineering Co. Ltd., P.O. Box 6088, Stn. A, Montreal, Que. H3C 3Z8

SHEARD, Rowland Leslie; banker (retired); b. Leeds, Eng. 4 Nov. 1907; s. Roland and Lily (Cockerham) S.; e. Leeds (Eng.) Modern Sch.; McGill Univ. various courses; m. Evelyn d. Thomas Dunnigan 26 Dec. 1935; one d. Joan (Mrs. C. J. Augustine); Pres. and Dir. Arless Holdings Ltd.; joined Yorkshire Bank, Leeds 1924-28; Bank of Montreal, London, Eng. 1928 serving in various brs. Toronto, Acct. Waterloo, Ont. 1939-40, trans. to Secy's Dept. H.O. Montreal 1940-42, Credit Dept. 1945, Asst. Mgr. Peterborough, Ont. 1945, London (Eng.) 1947, Asst. Supt. W. Div. H.O. 1949, Asst. Chief Inspr. 1951, Sr. Asst. Mgr. Montreal Main Office 1953, Supt. W. Div. 1955, Chief Inspr. 1961, Depy. Gen. Mgr. Ont. Div. 1964, Gen. Mgr. Domestic Banking 1965, Extve. Vice Pres. 1967, Extve. Vice Pres. and Gen. Mgr. 1969, retired 1970; Pres. CEO and Dir. General Appraisal of Canada Ltd. 1971, Chrmn. and CEO 1973; retired 1974; Dir., Peel Condominium Corp. No. 1079; Pres. 1980; served with RCAF 1942-45, rank Flight Lt.; Past Gov. Frontier Coll. Toronto; mem. Finance Comte. Thomas More Inst. Montreal; Assoc. Carleton Univ.; Fellow, Inst. Bankers (Eng.); mem. Bd. Trade Metrop. Toronto; Kts. of Malta; Liberal; R. Catholic; recreations: golf, photography; Clubs: S. Peel Camera (Pres. 1977-78); Markland Wood Country; Home: Apt. 408, Applewood Landmark, 1300 Bloor St., Mississauga, Ont. L4Y 3Z2

SHEARE, Eino Jack, B.A.Sc., P.Eng.; manufacturer; b. Thunder Bay, Ont., 16 Sept. 1906; s. John S.; e. Port Arthur (Ont.) Coll. Inst. (Sr. Matric. 1926); Univ. of Toronto B.A.Sc. (Mech. Engn.) 1931; m. Margaret Sainio 24 Dec. 1937; one d.; Past Chrmn. of Bd., Taylor Instrument Co.'s of Canada Ltd., since 1969; began as Draughtsman with C. D. Howe & Co., Consulting Engrs., Port Arthur, Ont., 1929-30; with Dept. of N. Devel. on survey parties and as Foreman, 1931-33; joined present Co., 1933; apptd. Chief Engr. 1935, Mgr. of Application Engn. 1940, Sales Mgr. 1946; subsequently el. a Dir., then Asst. Mang. Dir. and Mang. Dir., Pres. 1960-69; mem., Candn. Mfrs. Assn.; Candn. Food & Dairy Industry Supply Assn. (Pres. 1966-67); Assn. Prof. Engrs. Ont.; Indust. Instrument Mfrs. Assn. (Past Pres.); Toronto Bd. Trade; Dir., Nat. Dairy Council, Canada, 1966, 67, 68; United Church; recreations: golf, deer-hunting, cottage; Club: Rotary; Home: 545 Blythwood Road, Toronto, Ont. M4N 1B4

SHEARER, Ronald Alexander, M.A., Ph.D.; educator; b. Trail, B.C. 15 June 1932; s. James Boyd Shearer; e. Rossland (B.C.) Primary and High Schs. 1950; Trail (B.C.) High Sch. 1951; Univ. of B.C., B.A. 1954; Ohio State Univ. M.A. 1955, Ph.D. 1959; m. Renate Elizabeth d. late

Ernst Selig, Dayton, Ohio Dec. 1956 (separated); two s. Carl Thomas, Bruce Stephen; PROF. OF ECON., UNIV. OF B.C. 1963- , Head of Econ. 1972-76, Asst. to Vice Pres. (Acad. Devel.) 1978-79; Asst. Prof. of Econ. Univ. of Mich. 1958-62; Research Econ. Royal Comn. Banking & Finance 1962-63; Assoc. Ed. Candn. Pub. Policy 1980- ; co-author "Economics of the Canadian Financial System" 1972; "Money and Banking" 1976; ed. "Exploiting our Economic Potential: Public Policy and the British Columbia Economy" 1968; "Trade Liberalization and a Regional Economy" 1971; articles Candn. monetary hist. and Candn. monetary policy; mem. Candn. Econ. Assn.; Am. Econ. Assn.; Home: 3514 West 36th Ave., Vancouver, B.C.; Office: 997, 1873 East Mall, Vancouver, B.C. V6T 1Y2.

SHEARWOOD, Alexander Perry, P.Eng.; Winner, World Champion Cup, for Maple Syrup at Royal Agricultural Fair, 1981; b. Montreal, Que., 8 July 1908; s. Frederick Perry and Mary (Henderson) S.; e. Prep Sch., Lakefield, Ont.; Westmount High Sch.; McGill Univ., B.A. 1930, B. Eng. 1932; m. Christina Fraser, 1950; children: Perry, Christopher, Diana; with Dominion Bridge Company 1927-28; Candn. Pacific Railway, 1929-30; travelled in Europe, 1931; Engineer, National Steel Car Corpn., Hamilton, Ontario, 1932-33, 1933-1947 at Montreal; apptd. Sales Mgr. 1947 and el. a Dir., 1953; Chrmn. of Bd. and Chief Extve. Offr., 1953-60; Chrmn. of Bd., Pres. and Chief Executive Officer, 1960; Chairman and Chief Executive Offr. 1966; Chrmn. 1974; retired 1977; mem., Engn. Inst. Can.; mem., Corp. Engrs. Quebec; Kappa Alpha; Anglican; recreation: farming; Clubs: Royal St. Lawrence Yacht; Home: 120 Aberdeen Ave., Westmount, Que. H3Y 3A7

SHEBIB, Donald (Everett), M.A.; film director; b. Toronto, Ont., 27 Jan. 1938; s. Moses and Mary Alice (Long) S.; e. De La Salle "Oaklands" 1955; Univ. of Toronto, B.A. 1960; Univ. of Cal. (UCLA), M.A. 1965; PRESIDENT, EVDON FILMS LTD.; Director, "The Duel" (UCLA), 1962; "Surfin" (CBC TV), 1963; "Revival" (UCLA thesis), 1964; awarded 1st prize "best short", Montreal Film Festival and 3rd prize, Kenyon Film Festival, 1966; "Plaza Gang" (CBC TV) and "Satans Choice" (NFB) 1966; "Basketball" (CBC TV), "Search for Learning" (NFB) and "This Land is People" (CTV), 1967; "Haight Ashbury 1967" and "Robert Stanfield" (CBC), 1968; Candn. Film Award for "Good Times Bad Times" (CBC), 1970; "Goin Down the Road", 1970; recreations: golf, surfing, music, football; Address: 300 Winona Dr., Toronto, Ont. M5C 3S9

SHEEHAN, John P., C.A.; executive; b. Cork, Ireland, 1 March 1931; s. John Maurice and Ellen (Russell) S.; e. Our Lady's Mount High Schs. Cork and Cork Schs. of Comm.; (Chart. Secy.); C.A. 1964; CIM (Cert. Indust. Mgr.); m. Bridget Mary, d. Timothy Harrington, 10 Sept. 1953; children: Theresa Mary, Heather Elizabeth, Sonia Frances, Russell John; EXTVE. VICE PRES., BRITISH COLUMBIA HYDRO; mem., Chart Inst. Secys. (Past Chrmn. Toronto Chapter); Vancouver Bd. Trade; R. Catholic; recreation: golf; Club: Hollyburn Country 1117 Gilston Rd., W. Vancouver, B.C. V7S 2E7

SHEEHY, Hon. Gerald Earle, M.L.A., D.V.Sc.; politician; veterinarian; b. Noel, Hants Co., N.S. 24 June 1924; s. Basil Thomas and Iva (Miller) S.; e. elem. and jr. high schs. Upper Kennetcook, N.S.; Windsor (N.S.) Acad.; Ont. Veterinary Coll. Univ. of Toronto D.V.Sc.; m. Emma Grant d. George Davidson, Aberdeen, Scot. 20 Sept. 1945; children: Grant Earle, Patricia Kim, Theresa Georgene; MIN. OF HEALTH, N.S. 1978- and Min. in Charge of Drug Dependency Act, Registrar Gen.; veterinary med. practice Guelph, Ont. 1952-53, Erin, Ont. 1954-58, Middleton, N.S. 1958-78; former Town Councillor and Depy. Mayor, Middleton, N.S.; el. M.L.A. 1970, re-el. since; former Gov., Dalhousie Univ.; Chrmn. Sch.

Bd. Middleton; served with RCAF 1942-46, Navig.-Bomber Command, rank Flying Offr.; mem. Candn. Veterinary Med. Assn.; N.S. Veterinary Med. Assn.; P. Conservative; Anglican; recreations: golf, curling, cross-country skiing, swimming; Clubs: Rotary (Past Pres.); Middleton Curling (Past Pres.); Home: 181 Main St., Middleton, N.S. B0S 1P0; Office: (P.O. Box 488) Halifax, N.S. B3J 2R8.

SHEFFER, Harry, M.A., Ph.D., F.C.I.C.; scientist; b. Toronto, Ont., 23 Aug. 1917; s. Morris and Anne (Davis) S.; e. Univ. of Toronto, B.A. (Physics & Chem.) 1939, M.A. (Phys. Chem.) 1940, Ph.D. (Phys. Chem.) 1942; m. Evelyn Widman, 6 Sept. 1942; children: Andra, Marla; Dir. of Research, Defence Research Chem. Labs., 1949; Sr. Scient. Staff Offr., Special Weapons, Defence Research Bd., 1952; Supt., Defence Research Chem. Labs., 1954-57; Chief Supt. 1957-67; Supt., Defence Research Kingston Lab., 1955-57, Chief Supt. 1957-67; Scient. Asst. to Vice Chief of Defence Staff, CFHQ, 1967-69; Depy. Chrmn. (Scient.) of present Bd., Jan.-July 1969; Vice Chmn., Defence Research Bd. 1969-78; Depy. Head, Operation Oil Task Force on clean-up of "Arrow" oil spill (3 vol. report publ.) 1971; served with Candn. Army 1942-47; rank Maj. on discharge; holds 3 patents; writings incl. numerous articles in scient. journs.; recreations: golf, music, theatre; Club: Rideau View Golf & Country; Home: 956 Parkhurst Blvd., Ottawa, Ont. K2A 3M9

SHEFFIELD, Edward Fletcher, M.A., Ed.D., LL.D., F.R.C.G.S.; educator; b. Calgary, Alta., 20 June 1912; s. late Georgie Alice (Fletcher) and Herbert Tremaine Sheffield; e. Mount Royal Jr. Coll., Calgary, 1933-34; McGill Univ., B.A. 1936, M.A. 1941; New York Univ., Ed.D. 1950; LL.D., Sir George Williams 1969, P.E.I. 1971; m. Nora Young, d. late late Mary (Young) and William Morrison, 2 July 1938; children: Susan, William Herbert; PROF. EMERITUS OF HIGHER EDUC., UNIV. OF TORONTO since 1977; Registrar and Bursar, Sir George Williams Coll. 1936-43; Educ. Specialist, U.N. Dept. of Trusteeship and Information from Non-Self-Governing Terr., N.Y., 1946; Carleton Coll., 1947-54 (Adm. Offr., Registrar and Dir. of Student Personnel Services); Dir., Educ. Div., Dom. Bureau of Stat., Ottawa, 1954-58; Dir. of Research, Assn. of Univs. and Colls. of Can., Ottawa, 1958-66; Extve. Vice-Chrmn., Comte. of Presidents of Univs. of Ont. 1966-68; Prof. of Higher Educ., Univ. of Toronto 1966-77; Chrmn., Higher Educ. Group, Univ. of Toronto 1969-71, 1972-77; served with R.C.N. as Personnel Selection Offr. then Strategic Planning Offr., 1943-46; Adviser, Candn. Del. to Gen. Conf. of UNESCO, Paris, 1958; Chrmn., Scholarship Adv. Panel, External Aid Office, Ottawa, 1959-63; Candn. Observer, UNESCO Conf. on Devel. of Higher Educ. in Africa, Tananarive, 1962; Consultant to Univ. of E. Africa, 1964; Adv. on Higher Educ. to Govt. of P.E.I. 1968-69; Chrmn., P.E.I. Comte. on Post-Secondary Educ. 1969-71; Pres., Candn. Soc. for Study of Higher Educ. 1970-71; Commonwealth Visiting Prof., Univ. of London (Institute of Education) 1971-72; mem., Adv. Acad. Panel, Can. Council 1974-78; author of "Research on Post secdary Education in Canada", 1981; and other pubs. on higher educ.; co-author "Systems of Higher Education: Canada" 1978; Editor, "Canadian Universities and Colleges", 1960-66; "University Affairs", Vols. 1-7; "Agencies for Higher Education in Ontario" 1974; "Teaching in the Universities: No One Way" 1974; rec'd. Cert. of Merit, Royal Candn. Legion, 1948; Coronation Medal; Kappa Delta Pi; Fellow, Inst. Chartered Secretaries and Administrators 1952-77; Fellow, Royal Candn. geogr. Soc., 1956; Hon. mem., Can. Soc. for Study of Higher Educ. 1977; Unitarian; Home: 104 - 1275 Richmond Rd., Ottawa, Ont. K2B 8E3

SHEININ, Rose, F.R.S.C., M.A., Ph.D.; Biochemist, b. Toronto, Ont. 18 May 1930; d. Harry and Anne (Szyber) Shuber; e. Univ. of Toronto B.A. 1951, M.A. 1953, Ph.D. (Biochem.) 1956; m. Joseph Sheinin, Calgary, Alta. 15

July 1951; children: David Matthew Khazanov, Lisa Basya Judith, Rachel Sarah Rebecca; PROF. AND CHRMN. OF MICROBIOL. & PARASITOL., UNIV. OF TORONTO since 1975; Prof. of Med. Biophysics since 1978; Assoc. Prof. of Med. Biophysics 1975-78; Demonst. in Biochem. present Univ. 1951-53, Asst. Prof. of Microbiol. 1964-75, Asst. Prof. of Med. Biophysics 1967-75, mem. Health Sciences Comte.; Visiting Research Assoc. Chem. Microbiol. Cambridge Univ. 1956-57, Nat. Inst. for Med. Research London 1957-58; Research Assoc. Fellow, Ont. Cancer Inst. Div. Biol. Research 1958-67; Scient. Offr. Cancer Grants panel Med. Research Council Can.; mem. Candn. Scient. Del. to People's Repub. of China 1973; mem. Adv. Comte. Prov. Lottery Health Research Awards; rec'd Scholarship in Enzymology 1951-52; Nat. Cancer Inst. Can. Fellowship 1953-56, 1958-61; Brit. Empire Cancer Campaign Fellowship 1956-58; Med. Research Council Can. Visiting Prof. of Biochem. Univ. of Alta. 1971; Queen's Silver Jubilee Medal; Josiah Macy Jr. Faculty Scholar 1981-82; author or co-author numerous publs.; Assoc. Ed. 'Canadian Journal of Biochemistry' 1968-71; 'Virology' 1969-72; Intervirology' since 1974; mem. Ed. Bd. 'Microbiological Reviews' 1977-80; el. Fellow of the Royal Soc. of Canada, 1981; Fellow, Am. Acad. Microbiol.; mem. Candn. Biochem. Soc. (Vice Pres. 1974-75); Candn. Soc. Cell Biol. (Pres. 1975-76); Am. Soc. Microbiols.; Assn. Women in Science; Scitech; Soc. Complex Carbohydrates; Toronto Biochem. & Biophys. Soc. (Vice Pres. 1968-69, Pres. 1960-70, Council 1970-74); Office: 150 College St., Toronto, Ont. M5S 1A1.

SHELLEY, Gabriel Charles, B.S.M.E., M.B.A., P. Eng., C.M.C; management consultant; b. Budapest, Hungary 11 Dec. 1950; s. Charles Ivan Shelley; e. Queen's Univ. B.S.M.E. 1972; York Univ. M.B.A. 1975; m. Jennifer Anne d. Jack Addison Robinson 2 Sept. 1972; children: Paul Andrew; David James; PARTNER, THORNE STEVENSON & KELLOGG, MANAGEMENT CONSULTANTS since 1979; Process Engr. DuPont of Canada, Kingston 1972 — 74; Indust. Engr. Dominion Stores, Toronto 1974 — 75, Mgr. Indust. Engn. 1975 — 76; Associate Kearney: Management Consultants, Toronto 1976 — 77, Mgr. 1978 — 79; rec'd Purchasing Mang. Assn. Can. Bursary; author various publs.; mem. Assn Prof. Engrs. Prov. Ont.; Candn. Assn. Phys. Distribution Mang.; Nat. Council Phys. Distribution Mang.; recreations: photography, writing, tennis, squash; Home: 14711 58th Ave. Edmonton, Alta. T6H 4T3; Office: Suite 1320, Royal Trust Tower, Edmonton Centre, Edmonton, Alta.

SHEMILT, Leslie W., M.Sc., Ph.D., F.C.I.C., F.A.I. Ch.E., F. E. I. C., P.Eng.; b. Souris, Man., 25 Dec. 1919; s. John Henry and Myrtle (Webster) S.; e. Univ. of Toronto, B.A.Sc. 1941, Ph.D. 1947; Univ. of Manitoba, M.Sc. 1946; m. Elizabeth MacKenzie, 25 May 1946; children: Roderick, Roslyn; PROFESSOR OF CHEM. ENGN., McMASTER UNIV., since 1969; Supervisor, Defence Industries Ltd., Winnipeg, 1941-44, Lectr., Univ. of Manitoba, 1944-45; Asst., Univ. of Toronto, 1946-48; Special Lecturer 1946-47; Asst. Prof., Univ. B.C. 1947-49, Assoc. Prof. 1949-57; Prof. 1957-60; Shell Visiting Prof., Univ. Coll. London, 1959-60; Prof. & Head, Dept. Chem. Engn., Univ. N.B. 1960-69; Dean of Engn., McMaster Univ. 1969-79; Prof. invité, Inst. génie chim., Ecole Polytech. Féd. de Lausaunne 1975; Ed., "Candn. Journ. of Chem. Engn." since 1967; Fellow Chem. Inst. of Can.; Engn. Inst. of Can.; Am. Inst. Chem. Eng. mem., Am. Chem. Soc.; Am. Soc. for Engn. Educ.; Assn. of Prof. Eng. of Ont.; Fellow, Nat. Council on Relig. in Higher Educ.; mem., Nat. Research Council Can. 1966-69; Chrmn. N.B. Res. and Prod'y Council 1962-69; Tech. Adv. Comm. A.E.C.L. Waste Mgmt. Program 1979- ; N.D.P.; United Church; Home: 17 Hillcrest Court, Hamilton, Ont. L8P 2X7

SHENSTONE, Michael, B.A., M.A.; diplomat; b. Toronto, Ont. 25 June 1928; s. late Prof. Allen Goodrich,

O.B.E., M.C., F.R.S. and late Mildred Madeline (Chadwick) S.; e. Ashbury Coll., Ottawa 1941-45; Univ. of Toronto, Trinity Coll. B.A. 1949; Cambridge Univ., Trinity Coll., B.A., M.A. 1949-51; Univ. de Paris 1951-52; m. Susan Louise, d. late Archibald Leith Burgess, 8 Sept. 1951; children: Thomas Leith, Barbara Fairweather, Mary; joined Dept. of External Affairs 1952; Jan. 1954 Middle East Centre for Arab Studies, Shemlan, Lebanon; Third, then Second Secy. Candn. Legation, Beirut 1954; Middle East Div., Ottawa, 1957; Second, then First Secy., Candn. Embassy, Cairo, 1960; First Secy., Candn. Embassy, Washington, D.C. 1963, Counsellor 1964; Head, Peacekeeping and Mil. Assistance Div., NATO, then Dir., Defence Relations Div. (both Ottawa) 1967; Royal Coll. Defence Studies, London, 1972; Principal Adv. to Candn. Ambassador, Helsinki, for Multilateral talks on Conf. on Security and Cooperation in Europe, 1972; Ambassador and Head of Candn. del. to C.S.C.E. 1973; Ambassador to Saudi Arabia 1974-76; Dir.-Gen., African and Middle Eastern (Ottawa) 1976-80; Assist. Under-Secy. of State for External Affairs since Oct. 1980; Commandant, Confrerie des Chevaliers du Tastevin, Nuits-Saint-Georges, Côte d'Or, France; Ch. of Eng.; recreations: potterymaking, sailing, stamps, wine; Home: 10 Ellesmere Pl., Rockcliffe, Ottawa K1M 0N9; Office: Bureau of African and Middle Eastern Affairs, Dept. of External Affairs, Ottawa K1A 0G2

SHEPARD, Clarence Day, Q.C., LL.B.; b. Winnipeg, Man., 31 July 1914; s. late Clarence Day and May (Merrill) S.; e. Winnipeg Pub. Schs.; St. John's Coll., Winnipeg, Man.; Appleby Coll., Oakville, Ont. McGill Univ.; Univ. of Manitoba Law Sch., LL.B.; m. Caroline Faith, d. Willis Ware Spring, Duluth, Minn., 23 Apl. 1938; two s., Clarence Day. Jr., Merrill Webster; two d. Caroline Kennedy (Mrs. Hugh Nangle), Sarah; BD. OF DIRS., GULF CANADA LTD. (formerly British American Oil Co. Ltd.), since 1964; Dir., The Toronto-Dominion Bank; former Counsel, Govt. of Manitoba on Transportation; read law with J. Prudhomme, Q.C.; cr. Q.C. 1951; Internal Solr., Grain Insurance Guarantee Co., Winnipeg, Man., 1937-39; Western Supvr., Phoenix Insurance Co. of Hartford Group, Winnipeg, Man. 1939-40; practised law in Winnipeg with firm of Thompson, Shepard, Dilts, Jones & Hall, 1945-57; Chief Commr., Bd. of Transport Commrs., Can. 1957-58; Acting Chrmn., Air Transport Bd. Ottawa, July-Dec. 1958; apptd. Gen. Councel of present Co., 1 Jan. 1959; Vice-Pres. Dir. and Gen. Counsel, Feb. 1960; Fellow, Ins. Inst. Am.; former Bencher, Law Soc. Man.; Lectr., Man. Law Sch., 1946-53; former Pres., Man. Br.; Candn. Red Cross Soc. and apptd. Nat. Campaign Comte. Chrmn., 1958-59, Chrmn., Nat. Budget Comte., 1950-53; Trustee, Hospital for Sick Children, Toronto; mem., Upper Canada Law Soc.; Ont. Alcoholism and Drug Addiction Research Foundation; served in 2nd World War with Candn. Army Overseas with rank of Capt.; Anglican; Clubs: Manitoba (Winnipeg); Rideau (Ottawa); Country (Ottawa); Donalda; Toronto; York.

SHEPHERD, Francis Harold, D.D.S.; retired; b. Shelburne, Ont., 27 Jan. 1902; s. Francis and Emma Elizabeth (Mann) S.; e. Public and High Sch., Shelburne, Ont.; Oakwood and Harbord Co. Inst., Toronto, Ont.; Univ. of Toronto, D.D.S. 1925; m. Jean Holland Ruthven, d. George Thomas Wright, 28 June 1934; children: Ann Elizabeth, Paul Wright; engaged in the general practice of his prof. since 1925; Demonst. on Staff of Faculty of Dent., Univ. of Toronto, 1926-28; Pres., Acad. of Dent., Toronto, Ont., 1947-48; Pres., Ont. Dental Assn., 1957-58; Psi Omega (Depy. Councillor, 1928-30); el. Fellow, Internat. Coll. of Dentists, 1963; Freemason; Conservative; United Church; recreations: fishing, woodworking; Address: Suite 2004, West Tower, 400 Walmer Rd., Toronto, Ont. M5P 2X7

SHEPHERD, Helen Parsons, R.C.A.; artist; b. St. John's, Nfld. 16 Jan. 1923; d. Richard Augustus and Bessie Parsons; e. Bishop Spencer Coll.; Mem. Univ. of Nfld.; Ont. Coll. of Art A.O.C.A. 1948; m. 9 Apl. 1948; one s. R. Scott; Co-Founder and Teacher Nfld. Acad. of Art 1949-61; painted in Europe 1957; solo exhn. Mem. Univ. of Nfld. 1975, exhn. toured Ont. and Atlantic regions 1975-76; rep. in perm. colls. Beaverbrook Gallery, Mem. Univ. Nfld. and many private colls.; portraits incl. Presidents of Mem. Univ. Nfld., Speakers of House of Assembly Nfld., Mayors City of St. John's, official portraits for Govt. House, St. John's; mem. Arts Council Nfld. & Labrador; Anglican; recreations: swimming, sailing, reading; Address: 26 Oxen Pond Rd., St. John's, Nfld. A1B 3J3.

SHEPHERD, John Joseph, M.A.; electronics executive; b. Lancashire, Eng. 20 Feb. 1929; s. William Albert and Angelina (Mulholland) S.; e. Univ. of London B.A. 1954; McMaster Univ. M.A. 1958; m. 19 May 1956; children: William Paul, Andrew Duncan, Adam John, Kristin Hamilton, Victoria Mary, Matthew Thomas; CHMN. LEIGH INSTRUMENTS LTD. Vice Chrmn., Science Council of Can.; Dir., Candn. Inst. for Econ. Policy; Trustee, Forum for Young Candns.; served U.K. and Candn. Civil Service 1947 — 55; Candn. electronics industry 1955 — 61; Founder, Pres. and Chrmn. of Bd. Leigh Instruments 1961 — 75; mem. Adv. Council to Min. of Industry, Trade & Comm. 1969 — 70; Dir. Candn. Patents & Development Ltd. 1970 — 75; — 75; Foreign mem. Royal Swedish Acad. Engn. Sciences; mem. Candn. Inst. Strategic Studies; Extve. Dir. and Vice Chrmn. Science Council of Can. 1972-79; Dir., Candn. Inst. for Ecom. Policy; R. Catholic; Club: Rideau; Home: 90 Kilbarry Rd., Toronto, Ont.; Office: 2680 Queenview Dr., Ottawa, Ont.K2B 8J9

SHEPHERD, Murray C., B.Ed., M.A.; university librarian; b. Saskatoon, Sask. 31 July 1938; s. Gordon R. and Isobel Knowles (Murray) S.; e. Thornton Elem. and Nutana (Sask.) Coll. Inst.; Univ. of Sask. B.Ed. 1963; Univ. of Denver M.A. (Lib. Science) 1968; m. Ruth Maureen Bacon 3 March 1973; two s. Mark C., M. Craig; CHIEF LIBRARIAN, UNIV. OF WATERLOO since 1973; Teacher, Walter Murray Coll. Inst. Saskatoon 1963-64; Asst. Lib. Educ. Lib. Univ. of Sask. (Regina) 1964-67, Head Catalogue Dept. 1967-69; Head Tech. Services present Univ. 1969, Assoc. Lib. 1971-73; mem. Candn. Lib. Assn.; Am. Lib. Assn.; Candn. Assn. Research Libs.; OCUL (Chrmn. 1975, 1976); CACUL; Sask. Assn. Sch. Libs. (Past Chrmn.); U.W. Arts Centre Board; 1979- ; U.W. Faculty Club Exec. Comte 1978-79; ACRL; Nat. Lib. Adv. Bd. Resource Network Comm.; Net Trial and Bibliographic Common Interest Group; Club: Kitchener Waterloo Skating (Dir. 1976-78); Home: 23 Silverspring Cr., Kitchener, Ont. N2M 4P1 Office: Waterloo, Ont. N2L 3G1

SHEPHERD, Reginald, R.C.A., F.I.A.L.; painter; printmaker; b. Nfld. 28 March 1924; s. Robert Wilson and Margaret (Moore) S.; e. Ont. Coll. of Art A.O.C.A. 1949; studied in Europe on Candn. Govt. Fellowship awarded by Royal Soc. Can. 1956-57; m. Helen d. Richard A. Parsons 9 Apl. 1948; one s. Reginald Scott; Dir., Nfld. Acad. of Art 1949-61; Visiting Lectr. in Art Mem. Univ. of Nfld. 1951-61; exhns. incl. 1st Biennial Nat. Gallery Can. 1955; Montreal Museum of Fine Arts 1964, 1968; London and Hamilton Galleries; N.B. Museum; St. Mary's Univ.; Zwickers Gallery; Trinity Coll. Univ. of Toronto 1969; Candn. Printmakers Showcase Carleton Univ. 1974; Gallery Graphics Ottawa; Burnaby Gallery; several exhns. Maritime Art Assn.; Mem. Univ. Nfld. 1972; Ont. Soc. Art Exhn. Toronto 1974; Travelling Print Show Univ. of Ore. 1976; rep. in many pub. and private colls. Can., USA, Europe and Mexico; el. Provincial Vice Pres. R.C.A. 1978; served with RCAF during World War II; Anglican; recreations: sailing, swimming, gardening; Address: 26 Oxen Pond Rd., St. John's, Nfld. A1B 3J3.

SHEPPARD, Claude-Armand, B.A., B.C.L.; b. Ghent, Belgium, 26 May 1935; came to Can. 1950; e. McGill Univ.

B.A. 1955, B.C.L. 1958; m. Claudine Proutat; children: Jean-Pierre, Michel, Marie-Claude, Stephane, Annabelle; PARTNER, ROBINSON CUTLER SHEPPARD BORENSTEIN SHAPIRO LANGLOIS FLAM & GREEN; law lectr. at various acad. insts.; legal commentator for French and Eng. radio and TV networks of CBC; Past Pres., Candn. Civil Liberties Union; Counsel to Parlty. Comte. investigating Co. of Young Candns.; Prosecuting Atty. in Sir George Williams Univ. affair; Atty. for Eng.-speaking parents of St. Leonard since 1968; Dr. Henry Morgentaller's defence counsel; Legal Supvr. and Counsel to Que. Royal Comn. of Inquiry on Situation of French Lang. and on Linguistic Rights in Que. (Gendron Comn.); Fellow on linguistic rights of the UN; called to Bar of Que. 1959; author of numerous legal studies in various legal and other learned journs.; other works incl. reports for various Royal Comns. (Bilingualism & Biculturalism Castonguay Comn.; Gendron Comn.); former mem., Federal Advisory Council on the Status of Women; mem., Bar of Que.; Candn. Bar Assn.; Candn. Inst. for the Adm. of Justice; Soc. des amis de Jean Cocteau; Soc. des amis de Balzac; Chambre de Comm. Française au Can.; Candn. Civil Liberties Assn.; McGill Law Grad. Assn.; Soc. des amis de Montaigne; Soc. des amis de Marcel Proust; Soc. des amis de Colette; Soc. des Amis de François Mauriac; Soc. des Amis de Jacques Rivière et Alain Fournier; Byron Soc.; Musée des Beaux-Arts de Montreal; Museum of Modern Art, N.Y.; Cinémathéque Québecoise, Memphremagog Conservation Inc., Stanstead Historical Soc.; Pres. Ballets Jazz de Montreal; Vice-Pres., Canada Student Exchange Program; Dir., Fondation du Théâtre du Nouveau Monde; Office: 800 Place Victoria 612, Montreal, Que.H4Z 1H6

SHEPPARD, John Gavin; industrialist executive; b. Ottawa, Ont., 2 July 1916; s. Frank E. and Lillie Scott (Macfarlane) S.; e. Delta Coll. Inst. (Hamilton, Ont.); m. Mary Suzanne, d. late William G. Wood, 19 May 1945; children: Gavin W., J. Scott, Blair H., Carol J.; EXTVE. VICE PRES., FINANCIAL AND DIR., DOFASCO INC., LTD., since Oct. 1964; Dir., National Trust Co. Ltd.; Hamilton Group; National Steel Car Corp., Ltd.; Arnaud Railway Co.; Wabush Lake Railway Co.; Simcoe Erie Investors Ltd.; Chmn. and Dir., Prudential Steel, Ltd.; Canada Devel. Corp.; joined present firm June 1935; held various positions in Order Dept., Mill Offices, Sales and Order Dept.; apptd. Asst. to Vice Pres.'s 1950; Vice Pres. and Secy.-Comptroller 1961; Nat. Past Pres. (1949-50) Jr. Chamber of Comm. Can.; Past Chrmn. Hamilton United Appeal; Past Dir. Hamilton United Services; Past Pres. Hamilton Y.M.C.A.; Hamilton Jr. Chamber Comm.; Chrmn. and Dir., Roy. Bot. Gdns. Hamilton; mem. Bd.; Govs., McMaster Univ. mem., Bd. Trustees, Art Gallery of Hamilton (past Pres.); mem., Am. Iron & Steel Inst.; Internat. Iron & Steel Inst.; Financial Extves. Inst. (Pres. Hamilton Chapter 1962; Past Pres. F.E.I. Can. 1967-68); Chamber of Comm. Hamilton; Candn. Mfrs. Assn.; Comm. on Can.-U.S. Relations; United Church; recreations: golf, fishing, bridge, gardening; Clubs: The Hamilton; Hamilton Golf and Country; The Toronto; Tamahaac; Canadian; Home: 399 Queen St. S., Hamilton, Ont. L8P 3T8; Office: 1330 Burlington St. E., P. O. Box 460, Hamilton, Ont. L8N 3J5

SHEPPARD, Norman Thomas; retired executive; b. Toronto, Ont., 17 June 1911; s. Thomas and Mary Alice (Tyler) S.; e. Vaughan Rd. Coll. Inst., Toronto; Univ. of Toronto (Journalism Extension Course); m. Elizabeth, d. Lt.-Col. William Andrewes, 10 Nov. 1939; children: Patrick A., Brian E; joined Manufacturers Life Ins. Co. in 1928, trans. to Field Service Dept. 1936, Mgr. there 1950, trans. to Agency Dept. 1952, Agency Supt., U.S. Div. 1956, Asst. Agency Vice-Pres. 1964, Agency Vice-Pres. 1969; Vice Pres., Public Relations 1972; ret. 1976; United Church; recreations: golf, fishing, photography; Home: 10 Nesbitt Dr., Toronto, Ont. M4W 2G3

SHERBANIUK, Douglas John, B.A., LL.M.; b. Vegreville, Alta., 11 Apl. 1929; s. Dmytro and Ena (Wolshyna) S.; e. Univ. of Alta., B.A. (Hons. Modern Langs.) 1950, LL.B. 1953; Columbia Univ., LL.M. 1962; m. Joyce, d. Enoch Loveseth, 15 Sept. 1958; children: Martha, Kathleen, Douglas; DIR., CANADIAN TAX FOUNDATION, since 1967; Prof. of Law, Univ. of Toronto, since 1965; called to Bar of Alta. 1954, Ont. 1971; Asst. Prof. Law, Univ. Alta., 1955, Assoc. Prof. 1959; Tax Consultant, Edmonton, 1955-65; mem. Research Staff (1963-64) and Sr. Staff (1965-67), Royal Comn. on Taxation; mem. Research Staff Ont. Select Comn. on Co. Law, 1967; mem., Fed. Govt. Task Force, Can. Corp. Act. 1967, and Legal Advisor to Fed. Govt. Task Force on Structure of Canadian Industry, 1967; mem., Mississauga Hydro-Elec. Comm.; mem., Canadian Bar Association; Candn. Assn. Univ. Teachers; Assn. Candn. Law Teachers; Kappa Sigma; United Church; recreations: tennis, skating, bridge; Club: Ontario; Home: 2234 Courrier Lane, Mississauga, Ont. L5C 1V2; Office: P. O. Box 6, Suite 1900, 130 Adelaide St. West, Toronto, Ont. M5H 3P5

SHERBOURNE, Archibald Norbert, M.S., M.A., Ph.D., D.Sc., F.R.S.A., P.Eng., C.Eng. (U.K.); educator; consultant; b. Bombay, India, 8 July 1929; s. Maneckji Nowroji Bulsara and Sarah Agnes S.; e. Univ. of London, B.Sc. 1953, D.Sc. 1969; Lehigh Univ., B.S. 1955, M.S. 1957; Univ. of Cambridge, M.A. 1959, Ph.D. 1960; m. Jean Duncan, d. William Jeffrey Nicol, Comrie, Scot. 15 Aug. 1959; children: Mary Ann, Sarah Elizabeth, Jeffrey Andrew, Nicolas Duncan, Jonathan David, Simon Alexander; PROF. OF CIVIL ENGN., UNIV. OF WATERLOO since 1963; Dean of Engn. there 1966-74; Chrmn., Adv. Comtes. on Engineering Educ.; Partner, Frew & Sherbourne Consultants; Engr., British Rlys., London, 1948-51; Engr. Local Govt., Greater London Council, UK, 1952-54; Instr., Lehigh Univ., 1954-57; Sr. Asst. in Research, Univ. of Cambridge, 1957-61; joined present Univ. as Assoc. Prof. 1961-63, Chrmn. Dept. of Civil Engn., 1964-66, Dean of Engn. 1966-74; Visiting Sr. Lecturer, University Coll., University of London, 1963-64; Visiting OECD-DSIR Fellow, E.T.H. Zurich 1964; CIDA Visiting Professor, University of West Indies, Trinidad, 1969-70 and others; NRC Senior Research Fellow, LNEC Portugal, 1970; Visiting Prof., EPF Lausanne, 1975-77; DAAD Visiting Fellowship, West Germany, 1975; NATO Sr. Scientist Fellowship & Visiting Lectureship, 1975-76; Gledden Visiting Sr. Fellow, Univ. of Western Australia, 1978; Visiting Prof., Michigan Tech. Univ. 1980-81; writings include over 175 papers, articles, reports in technical journals; awarded Engn. Medal, Assn. Prof. Engrs. Ont. 1975; Fellow, Institute Structural Engrs. London; mem., Internat. Assn. Bridge & Structural Engrs. Switzerland; R. Catholic; recreation: travel; Home: "Tigh-Na-Bruadar", 46 Glasgow Rd., N., Conestogo, Ont. N0B 1N0; Office: Waterloo, Ont. N2L 3G1

SHERMAN, Edward David, M.D., C.M., F.A.C.P., F.R.C.P.(C); b. Sydney, N.S., 15 March 1908; s. Frederick and Sara (Epstein) S.; e. Sydney (N.S.) Acad.; McGill Univ., M.D., C.M., 1932; m. Anne Helen Doner, 22 Feb. 1955; 1 s., Neil (by 1st m.); DIR OF RESEARCH EMERTUS, REHABILITATION INST. OF MONTREAL, since 1981 (Prof. since 1962); certified specialist, Internal Med., Coll. of Physicians of Que.; Med. Dir., Jewish Vocational Service; Vice-Pres., Inst. of Gerontology and Lectr. in Geriatrics, Sch. of Rehab., Univ. of Montreal; consultant, Sr. Citizens Programme, Quebec Div. Canadian Red Cross; post graduate studies Women's General Hospital, Montreal and Mount Sinai Hosp., N.Y. 1931-35; practised Internal Med., Sydney, N.S., 1935-46; N.Y. City 1946-55 (N.Y. Hosp.-Cornell Medical Center and Bellevue Hosp.); served with R.C.A.M.C., 1943-44, rank Capt.; mem. Bd. of Dirs., Herzl Dispensary; rec'd Malford W. Thewlis Award for outstanding contribs. to Am. Geriatrics Soc., 1965; Hon. Life mem., St. John's Ambulance Assn.; Hon. Attending Staff, Maimonides Hosp. &

Home for the Aged; Jewish Gen. Hosp.; co-recipient Rabbi Harry Stern Award, Temple Emanu-El 1974; Queen's Jubilee Medal 1977; Abstract Ed., N.S. Medical Bull., 1940-45; scient. contribs. to med. journs. in fields of Aging and Rehab.; Co-ed., "Human Rights for the Physically Handicapped and Aged"; appeared by invitation before Senate Comte. on Aging, 1963 (Chrmn. of Del., Candn. Med. Assn.); Candn. Rep., White House Conf. on Aging, Wash., D.C. Nov. 28-Dec. 2, 1971; Fellow, Am. Geriatrics Soc. (Past Pres. 1963-64; Chrmn. Bd. Dirs. 1964-65; mem. Bd. Dirs.); Fellow; Am. Coll. of Physians; Royal Coll. of Physians of Can.; Fellow, Gerontol. Soc.; Royal Soc. Med.; Internat. Coll. Angiology; Royal Soc. Arts; Am. Coll. Preventive Med.; mem., Nat. Council of Candn. Human Rights Found.; Comte. of Med. Research and Higher Studies, Fac. of Med., Univ. of Montreal; N.Y. Acad. Sciences; Am. Psychosomatic Soc.; Candn. Assn. on Gerontology; Candn. Assn. of Physical Med. & Rehab.; Candn. Med. Assn. (Chrmn., Comte. on Aging; mem. Gen. Council 1963-67; Que. Med. Assn. (Chrmn. Comte. on Aging; mem. Bd. Dirs. 1963-77); Internat. Assn. Gerontology (mem. Council, Hist. Gerontology Comte. 1963-66); International Society of Internal Med.; Extve. Comte., Candn. Conf. on Aging 1964-66; mem., Med. Adv. Bd. Candn. Geriatric Research Soc.; Freemason; Pi Lambda Phi; Sigma Xi; Jewish; recreations: walking, bicycling, golf; Club: St. James Literary Soc.; Address: 4330 Hampton Ave., Montreal, Que. H4A 2L2

SHERMAN, Frank H., B.Sc., P.Eng.; industrialist; b. Bellevue, Pa., 4 Oct. 1916; s. Frank Albert and Anna Mary (Howard) S.; e. Earl Kitchener Pub. Sch. and Westdale Sec. High Sch., Hamilton, Ont.; Queen's Univ.; m. late Catherine Audrey, d. late Charles Drysdale Carpenter, 21 May 1941; children: Frank Drysdale, James Howard; PRES., DIR. AND CHIEF EXTVE. OFFR., DOFASCO INC. since 1964; Dir., Arnaud Railway Co.; Bank of Nova Scotia; Crown Life Insurance Co.; Knoll Lake Minerals Ltd.; National Steel Car Corp. Ltd.; Canadian Pacific Ltd.; Wabush Lake Railway Co. Ltd.; Canron Ltd.; Am. Iron and Steel Inst.; Great Lake Waterways Devel. Assoc.; Council for Canadian Unity; joined present Co. as Metall. Asst., 1939, Asst. Works Mgr., 1945, Works Mgr., 1947, Vice-Pres. and Works Mgr., 1949, Extve. Vice-Pres., 1952, Gen. Mgr. 1957, Pres. 1959; mem. Bd. Govs. McMaster Univ.; Art Gallery of Hamilton; Hamilton Philharmonic Orchestra; mem., Ont. Jockey Club; mem. Nat. Extve. Council, Canadian Mfrs. Assn.; Presbyterian; recreations: golf, photography, boating, fishing, skeet shooting, hunting, thoroughbred horse racing and breeding, tennis; Clubs: Tamahaac; The Hamilton; The Toronto (Ontario); St. James's (Montreal); Caughnawana Fishing & Hunting; Muskoka Lakes Golf & Country Club Ltd.; Caledon Mountain Trout; Hamilton Golf & Country; Hamilton Thistle; York (Toronto); Home: 9 Turner Ave., Hamilton, Ont. L8P 3K4; Office: P.O. Box 460, Hamilton, Ont. L8N 3J5

SHERMAN, John A., D.D.S., F.I.C.D., F.A.C.D.; b. Toronto, Ont., 20 May 1901; s. Jacob and Rose (Taube) S.; e. Jarvis Coll., Toronto, Ont.; Univ. of Toronto, Sch. of Dentistry, L.D.S. 1924, D.D.S.; m. Etta, d. late Philip Taube, 31 July 1928; has practised his prof. since 1924 in Toronto; former Chief of the Dental Dept., New Mt. Sinai Hosp., Toronto, 1953-62; inventor of the air and water spray cooling method for dental drilling, which is now universally used by the prof. throughout the world; Pres., Candn. Sec.; Internat. Coll. of Dentists 1974; Life mem., Candn. Dental Assn.; Ont. Dental Assn. (Gov. 1964-66); Hon. Life mem., Nov. 1979, Acad. of Dent.; Hon. Mem. Pierre Fauchard Acad.; Life mem., Am. Prosthodontic Soc.; Charter mem., Am. Equilibration Soc.; Hon. mem., Israel Dental Assn.; Fellow, Internat. Coll. of Dentists; Am. Coll. of Dentists; Alpha Omega (Nat. Pres., 1958, Nat. Editor 1954-56, Meritorious Award Recipient 1963); a Founder of the Dental Sch. of the Hebrew Univ., Jerusalem; Dir., Alpha Omega Continuing Educ.

Lib.; Dir., Alpha Omega Foundation of Can.; Liberal; Hebrew; recreations: world travel, inventing; Home: 6 Glen Cedar Road, Toronto, Ont. M6C 3G1

SHERMAN, Hon. Louis Ralph, M.L.A., B.A.; politician; b. Quebec City, Que. 24 Dec. 1926; s. Louis Ralph and Carolyn Zerelda (Gillmor) S.; e. Strathcona Boys" Sch. and Central High Sch. Calgary; Kelvin High Sch. Winnipeg; Univ. of Man. B.A.; m. Elizabeth Ann d. Dr. W.G. Beaton, Winnipeg, Man. 28 Dec. 1955; children: Cathy Diane, Christopher Grant, Todd Laurence; MIN. OF HEALTH, MAN. 1977- ; Dir., News & Public Affairs, Channel Seven Television, Winnipeg; served with COTC 1947-49, rank Lt.; el. to H. of C. g.e. 1965, def. g.e. 1968; el. M.L.A. for Fort Garry prov. g.e. 1969, re-el. since; Min. of Health & Social Devel. and Min. Responsible for Corrections & Rehabilitation 1977; Min. of Health & Community Services and Chrmn. Community Services Comn. 1978; P. Conservative; Anglican; Clubs: Winnipeg Squash Racquet; Winnipeg Press; Office: 301 Leglslative Bldg., Winnipeg, Man. R3C 0V8.

SHERMAN, Paddy; newspaper publisher; b. Monmouthshire, Eng., 16 March 1928; came to Canada 1952; m. 1951; 4 children; PUBLISHER, THE VANCOUVER PROVINCE; Vice Pres., Southam Inc.; Dir., VIP Pacific Press Ltd.; Outward Bound (founding Dir.); Chmn., Canadian Section, Internat. Press Inst.; Westwater Research Centre; author of "Cloud Walkers" 1964; "Bennett" 1965; "Expeditions to Nowhere", 1981; recreations: mountain climbing, scuba diving; Clubs: University; Alpine of Canada; Explorers, N. Y.; Home: 556 Newdale Rd., West Vancouver, B.C. V7T 1W6; Office: 2250 Granville St., Vancouver, B.C. V6H 3G2

SHIECK, Ernest O.; insurance executive; b. Lemberg, Sask., 16 June 1918; s. John and Sophia (Oppenheimer) S.; e. Prov. Manitoba Schs.; m. Evelyn, d. Peter McMillan, 15 Feb. 1943; children: Gwendolyn, Gary, Kirby; PRESIDENT AND MANAGING DIR., ANGLO-CANADA INSURANCE CO. AND GIBRALTAR GENERAL INSURANCE CO., since 1970; Dir., Anglo Permanent Corporate Holding Ltd.; Laurier Life Insurance Co.; S.C.D.R. Investments Ltd.; Chief Agent for Can., Societe Commerciale de Reassurance Co.and Amer. Reserve Ins. Co.; began career with N.Y. Underwriters Ins. Co., Toronto, Ont. as Underwriter 1945-49; joined Anglo-Gibraltar Group Toronto as Underwriter 1949-50, Br. Mgr. 1950-57, Asst. Gen. Mgr. 1957-62, Vice Pres. and Mang. Dir. 1962-70; served with R.C.N.R. 1941-45, discharged with rank Petty Offr.; Past Pres., Lions' Club (Tillsonburg); United Church; recreations: golf, curling; Clubs: Tillsonburg Golf & Country (Past Pres.); Charter mem., Charter Secy. and Dir., Tillsonburg Curling; Highland Golf & Country (London, Ont.); London Club Ltd.; Office: 200 Queens Ave., London, Ont. N6A 1J3

SHIH, Hsio-Yen, M.A., Ph.D.; museum director; b. Wachang, Hubei, China 27 July 1933; d. Chao-ying and Fang-jing (WU) S.; Primary and Secondary Schs. Wuchang, Loshan, Ottawa, San Francisco, Vancouver, Philadelphia, Johannesburg, Nanking, Shanghai, Hong Kong, Taipei; Wellesley Coll. B.A. 1955; Univ. of Chicago M.A. 1958; Bryn Mawr Coll. Ph.D. 1961; DIR. NATIONAL GALLERY OF CANADA since 1977; Prof. Dept. East Asian Studies Univ. of Toronto since 1971; Asst. Curator Royal Ont. Museum Far E. Dept. 1961-63, Curator 1968-76; Asst. Prof. Dept. E. Asian Studies Univ. of Toronto 1961-63, Visiting Prof. Trinity Coll. Hartford 1962, Assoc. Prof. and Coordinator for Chinese Studies 1964-68; Faculty of Fine Arts York Univ. Toronto 1970, Dept. Art Univ. Cal. Berkeley 1971; Chrmn. Bd. Studies Fine Arts and Visiting Prof. Inst. Chinese Studies, The Chinese Univ. of Hong Kong 1973-74; author various articles, catalogues and reviews; mem. Coll. Art Assn. Am.; Candn. Soc. Archaeol. Abroad; recreations: cooking, gardening, reading; Office: Elgin St., Ottawa, Ont.

SHIPP, Harold G.; community builder; b. Toronto, Ont., 21 Jan. 1926; s. late Gordon Stanley and Bessie Luella (Breeze) S.; e. Etobicoke (Ontario) Collegiate Inst.; m. June Catharine d. late J. K. Ingram, 30 Sept. 1949; children: Victoria Haviland Shipp-Smith, Catharine Marjorie, Gordon Harold; CHMN. OF BD., PRES. & CHIEF EXTVE. OFFR., SHIPP CORP. LTD.; Shipp Corp. Inc. (Fla.); Pres., Applewood Chevrolet Oldsmobile Ltd.; Chrmn. of Bd., Dominion Mutual Insurance Brokers Limited; joined father in home building business 1945; winner of Candn. Housing Design Council Award 1974; Gov., Queensway Gen. Hosp.; Dir. Friends of Mississauga Hosp. Foundation; Past Pres., Toronto Home Builders Association; Housing and Urban Devel. Assn. Can.; Liaison Director to National Assn. Home Builders U.S.; Trustee, Urban Land Inst. (U.S.); Pres., Kingsway Kiwanis Club, 1960 (Lt. Gov., Div. 4A, Eastern Canada and Caribean Dist., 1964); helped to found Kiwanis Clubs in Caribbean; Gen. Campaign Chrmn., Un. Way Peel Region 1977; Silver Jubilee Medal; United Church; Clubs: Mississaugua Golf & Country; Granite; Port Credit Yacht; Tower (Fort Lauderdale); Home: 500 Comanche Rd., Mississauga, Ont. L5H 1W2; Office: Suite 1100, Mississauga Extve. Centre, 2 Robert Speck Pkwy.

SHIRLEY, Roger John, B.A.; company executive; b. Bathurst, N.B., 7 Aug. 1921; s. Edgar Russell and Lydia (Le Marquand) S.; e. Pub. and High Schs., Bathurst, N.B.; Dalhousie Univ. 1939-41; Univ. of W. Ont., B.A. 1948; m. Janet Armour, d. Strachan Ince, Toronto, Ont., 14 Feb. 1953; children: Anne Lydia, David John, Peter Strachan; PRESIDENT AND DIRECTOR, BOWATER CANADIAN LTD., since 1975; Chrmn. and Dir., Perkins Paper Ltd.; Buchmin Inc.; Pres. and Dir., Vinland Holdings Ltd.; Dir., Bowater Inc.; Bowater Newfoundland Ltd.; Bowater Mersey Paper Co. Ltd.; The Bowater Power Company Ltd.; MPG Investment Corporation Limited; joined J. D. Woods and Gordon, Ltd. as Consultant, 1948; apptd. Dir. 1957; opened Vancouver office 1957 and Calgary office 1960; Administrative Partner 1957-64; Partner, Woods, Gordon & Co., 1962; Administrative Partner, Montreal Office, 1964; Regional Partner, E. Can., 1969; Extve. Vice Pres. and Dir., Canadian International Power Co. Ltd. and Chrmn. Investment Comte. 1972-73; Extve. Vice Pres. and Dir., C.I. Power Services Ltd.; served with R.C.N.V.R. 1941-45; rank Lt. Commdr.; Chairman, Red Feather Foundation; Dir. and Treas., Centraide; Children's Aid Soc. Metrop. Toronto, 1953-57; Un. Community Fund Vancouver, 1957-64; Dir., Vancouver Internat. Festival, 1963-64 (Vice Pres. 1964); Anglican; Clubs: St. James's; Rideau (Ottawa); University (Toronto);

SHISTER, Joseph, Ph.D.; university professor; labour arbitrator; b. Montreal, Que., 27 Nov. 1917; e. Univ. of Montreal, B.S. 1939; Harvard Univ., M.A., Ph.D. 1943; m. Edna Louise Tuch, 28 Dec. 1941; children: Neil Barry, Jane Ellen, Gail Marilyn, Diane Marjorie; PROF. DEPT. OF INDUST. RELATIONS, STATE UNIV. OF NEW YORK since 1950; Teaching Fellow, Harvard Univ., 1940-42; Instr., Cornell Univ., 1942-43; Asst. Prof. and Dir. of Research, Labor and Mang. Center, Yale Univ., 1946-49; Chmn., Dept. of Indust. Relations, State Univ. of New York 1950-78; served with U.S. Army 1943-44; Chrmn. of various Presidential Emergency Labor Dispute Bds.; mem. N.Y. State Bd. of Mediation; Referee in rr. and airlines industs. under Railway Labor Act; Consulting Econ., Nat. War Labor Bd.; mem. Constr. Comn., Nat. Wage Stabilization Bd.; Labor Arbitrator various corps.; mem. Buffalo and N.Y. State Pub. Employment Relations Bds.; Office of Collective Bargaining (N.Y. City); Fed. Mediation & Conciliation Service; Am. Arbitration Assn.; mem. Erie Co. Adv. Comte. on Econ. Devel.; Invitee White House Conference on "National Economic Issues" 1962; Invitee 1972 White House Conf. on the "Industrial World Ahead"; Erie County Grievance Bd.; Pres.'s Comte. for 50th Anniversary U.S. Dept. of Labor; Moderator, Univ. of Buffalo Round Table of the Air; selected as

"one of the outstanding citizens of Western New York" by Buffalo Evening News; author: "Public Policy and Collective Bargaining" 1962; "A Decade of Industrial Relations Research", 1962; "Economics of the Labor Market", 1956; "Labor Economics and Industrial Relations" 1956; "Conflict and Stability in Labor Relations", 1952; "Insights into Labor Issues", 1948; "Job Horizons", 1948; other writings incl. numerous articles on labor econ., indust. and labor relations; mem., Indust. Relations Research Assn. (Extve. Bd. 1959-62); Nat. Acad. Arbitrators; Am. Econ. Assn.; Internat. Indust. Relations Assn.; Am. Assn. Univ. Profs.; Phi Beta Kappa; Beta Gamma Sigma; recreations: travel, sports; Club: Harvard; Home: 310 Brantwood Rd., Snyder, N.Y.; Office: Buffalo, N.Y.

SHOCTOR, Joseph H., C.M., Q.C., B.A., LL.B., LL.D.; b. Edmonton, Alta.; e. Pub. and High Schs. Edmonton; Univ. of Alta, B.A., LL.B.; Hon LL.D., Univ. of Alta. 1981; SR. PARTNER, SHOCTOR, HILL, MOUSSEAU & STARKMAN; Secy., First City Trust Co.; Dir. First City Financial and numerous Alta. Co.s in devel. and service industries; Assoc. Producer on Broadway "Peter Pat" 1965, "Henry Sweet Henry" 1967; Co-Producer Off-Broadway "Hamp" 1966, on Broadway "Billy" 1969, Nicol Williamson's "Hamlet" 1969; Nat. Tour of "Hamlet" 1969; Founder and Pres., Extve. Producer Citadel Theatre, Chrmn. Campaign and Bldg. New Citadel Theatre 1975-77; Gov. Nat. Theatre Sch. Can.; Hon. Gov. Dom. Drama Festival; Panelist CFRN TV "Wide Open" 2 seasons; Producer and Dir. Circle "8" Theatre; Red Cross Entertainment and Travelling N.W. Staging Route; regular Panelist CBC TV "Sports Forum" 1972-74; impressario name bands, entertainers, concert artists Winnipeg to Vancouver early 1950's; originated first entertainment paper Edmonton "Downtown Edmonton", one of Original Founders and first Secy.-Mgr., Bd. mem. 13 yrs. Edmonton Eskimo Football Club; Vice Chrmn. Un. Community Fund 1969, Chrmn. Prof. Div. 1968, Legal Div. 1970, Campaign Chrmn. 1972; Hon. mem. Edmonton Jewish Welfare Bd.; Past Pres. Edmonton Jewish Community Council; Past Nat. Secy. Fed. Zionist Organ. Can.; Past Nat. Vice Pres. Un. Israel Appeal Inc.; Past Bd. mem. Candn. Council Jewish Welfare Funds; named CFRN TV "Man of the Hour" 1966; B'Nai B'rith "Citizen of the Year" 1966; Negev Dinner Honoree Edmonton 1967; City of Edmonton Performing Arts Award 1972; Prov. Alta. "Achievement Award in recognition of Outstanding Service in Theatre Arts"; Queen's Silver Jubilee Med. 1977; C.M. (Order of Canada) 1978; Prime Minister's Med. State of Israel 1978; City of Edmonton 75th Anniversary "Builder of the Community" Award 1979; mem. Edmonton Bar Assn.; Law Soc. Alta.; Candn. Bar Assn.; Edmonton Chamber Comm.; Clubs: Edmonton; Glendale Golf & Country; Home: 9022 Valleyview Dr., Edmonton, Alta. T5R 5T6; Office: 2400, 10123-99th St., Edmonton, Alta. T5J 3J7

SHOEMATE, Charles Richard, B.S., M.B.A.; food company executive; b. La Harpe, Ill. 10 Dec. 1939; s. Richard Osborne and Mary Jane (Gillette) S.; e. W. Ill. Univ. B.S. 1961; Univ. of Chicago M.B.A. 1971; m. Nancy Lee d. Dale E. Gordon, Blandinsville, Ill. 16 Sept. 1962; children: Steven Richard, Jeffrey Dale, Scott Charles; PRES., CANADA STARCH CO. 1981- ; Manufacturing Mgr. CPC International, Argo, Ill. 1962-71, Comptroller Corn Products Unit Englewood Cliffs, N.J. 1971-74, Vice Pres. of Unit 1976-80, Plant Mgr. Corpus Christi, Texas 1974-76; served with U.S. Army Reserve 1957-65; Protestant; recreations: tennis, golf, skiing; Home: 98 Celtic Dr., Beaconsfield, Que. H9W 6A9; Office: 1 Place du Commerce, Montreal, Que. H3E 1A7.

SHOOK, Very Rev. Laurence Kennedy, O.C. (1974), M.A., Ph.D., D.Litt. (R.C.); b. Toronto, Ontario, 6 Nov. 1909; s. Richard Conrad and Mary Ann (Kennedy) S.; e. St. Cecilias Separate Sch.; St. Michael's Coll.; Univ. of Toronto, B.A. 1932, M.A. 1933; Harvard Univ., Ph.D. 1940

(Sheldon Fellow); D.Litt. Univ. Western Mich. 1972, Univ. of Toronto 1977, Univ. of St. Michael's Coll., 1980; o. Priest 1935; Superior and Pres., St. Michael's Coll., Univ. of Toronto, 1952-58; Pres., Pontifical Inst. of Mediaval Studies 1961-73; served in World War, 1943-45 as Flt: Lieut., R.C.A.F.; mem., Basilian Fathers of Toronto; Fellow, Medieval Acad. Am. (Vice Pres. 1967-70; Pres. Fellows 1978-81); Acting Dir., Medieval Acad. of Amer.; Acting Ed., "Speculum", 1980-81; author, some 40 books and articles; mem. Ed. Bd. "Mediaeval Scandanavia"; Address: 59 Queen's Park Crescent, Toronto, Ont. M5S 2C4

SHORT, Rt. Rev. Hedley Vicars Roycraft, B.A., B.D., D.D. (Ang.); bishop; b. Toronto, Ont., 24 Jan. 1914; s. Hedley Vicars and Martha Hallam (Parke) S.; e. Private and Pub. Schs., Toronto; Univ. of Toronto, B.A. 1941; Trinity Coll., L.Th. 1943, B.D. 1945, D.D. 1964; m. Elizabeth Frances Louise, d. Russell Edward and Elsa Louise (Thorning) Shirley, Cochrane, Ont., 14 Apl. 1953; children: Martha Frances (Bowden), Elizabeth Helena (Rodgers), Janet Louise, Margaret Stephane, Desmond James Vicars; BISHOP OF SASKATCHEWAN, since 1970; President of Council, College Emmanuel and St. Chad (Saskatoon), 1974-80; business career 1932-38; o. Deacon 1943; o. Priest 1944; Assistant Curate, St. Michael and All Angels, Toronto, 1943-46; Junior Chaplain, Coventry Cath., Eng., 1946-47; Lectr. and Sr. Tutor, Trinity Coll., Toronto, 1947-51; Dean of Residence 1949-51; Rector, Holy Trinity, Cochrane, Ont., 1951-56; during this period Examining Chaplain to Bishop of Moosonee (Extve. Comte. of Diocese; Prov. Synod; Gen. Synod; Rural Dean of Cochrane); Rector, St. Barnabas' Ch., St. Catharines, Ont., 1956-63; during this period Examining Chaplain to Bishop of Niagara (Extve. Comte. of Diocese; Prov. and Gen. Synods); Canon, Christ's Ch. Cath., Hamilton, Ont., 1962-63; Dean of Sask., Canon Residentiary of St. Alban's Cath., Prince Albert, 1963-70; Archdeacon of Prince Albert 1966-70; Chancellor, Univ. of Emmanuel Coll., 1974-79; Pres. of Council, Coll. of Emmanuel & St Chad, Saskatoon, 1973-80; Hon. Fellow, Univ. of Emmanuel Coll., Saskatoon, 1980; Past Chrmn., High Sch. Bd., Cochrane, Ont.; Past Chrmn. Bd. Govs., Natonum Community Coll., Prince Albert; recreations: music (violin), sketching, reading, travel; Address: Bishopsthorpe, 427 — 21st St. W., Prince Albert, Sask. S6V 4J5

SHORT, Rev. John, M.A., Ph.D., D.D. (Un. Ch.); b. Berwickshire, Scotland, 27 Mar 1896; e. Univ. of Edinburgh, Dipl. in Educ. 1923, M.A. (Hons.) 1924, Ph.D. 1929; Cong. Coll., Edin., Dipl. 1925; St. Andrews Univ., D.D. 1950, McMaster Univ. 1964; m. 1st, 1925; one s. and one d.; 2ndly 1939, two s.; trained for a business career, but turned to the ministry; began study for the church before 1st World War; called to Bathgate E.U. Cong. Ch., 1924; Min., Lyndhurst Rd. Cong. Ch., Hampstead, 1930-37; Richmond Hill Cong. Ch., Bournemouth, 1937-51; Officiating Chaplain to the Forces, 1940-45; former mem. Educ. Comte. (1937-51); former Chrmn. of Cong. Union of Eng. and Wales, 1949-50; Min., St. George's United Ch., Toronto, 1951-64; author of "Triumphant Believing" (sermons), 1952; Exposition of I Corinthians for "Interpreters Bible", Vo. VIII; Freemason (33°; Scot. Rite); recreations: gardening, motoring, reading, travel; Home: 162 Coldstream Ave., Toronto, Ont. M5N 1X9

SHORT, Norman John, M.A.; investment counsel; b. London, Eng., 14 Aug. 1930; s. Rev. John and Rita (Mackinlay) S.; e. Fettes Coll., Edinburgh, Scot.; Worcester Coll., Oxford Univ., M.A. (Econ.) 1953; m. Rosemary, d. Oswald Spencer-Jones, 4 July 1963; one d., Karen Fiona; Chrmn. and Dir., Guardian Capital Investment Counsel Ltd.; Grouped Income Shares Ltd.; President and Dir., Guardian Capital Group Ltd.; Guardian Growth Fund Limited; Dir., Barrick Petroleum Corp.; Tyndall-Guardian Mgmt. Ltd.; Lescarden Ltd.; Chanceller Energy Resources Ltd.; mem., Investment Policy

Comte., Ont. Municipal Employees Retirement System; came to Canada, 1953, joining George Weston Ltd., Toronto; Security Analyst, Confederation Life Assn., Toronto, 1956-60 and Andreae Cole & Co., 1960-62; Candn. Research Mgr., Bache & Co. Inc., 1962-64; joined present firm 1964; served with Brit. Army, Royal Signal Corps, 1948-50; rank 2nd Lt. on discharge; mem., Invest. Counsel Assn.; Toronto Soc. Financial Analysts; Presbyterian; recreations: tennis, skiing, swimming, music; Clubs: Albany; Toronto Lawn Tennis; Home: 4 May St., Toronto, Ont. M4W 2Y1; Office: Suite 500, 48 Yonge Street, Toronto, Ontario M5E 1H3

SHORT, Robert C., B.A.Sc., P.Eng.; association executive; b. Toronto, Ont., 3 Dec. 1925; s. Charles Montague and Gertrude (Algie) S.; e. Pub. Schs., Toronto, Ont. 1937; Univ. of Toronto Schs. (Hons. Jr. and Sr. Matric.) 1943; awarded Nesbit Gold Medal and Bryce Engn. Scholar.; Univ. of Toronto, B.A.Sc. (Hons. Elect. Engn.) 1949; m. Ruth Virginia, d. late N. A. Myra, Sept. 1951; children: Douglas, Jane, David; PRESIDENT, CANADIAN SATELLITE COMMUNICATIONS INC.; with Ferranti Packard Ltd. as Sales Mgr., Que. and Ont. 1949; Pres., Edwards Co. 1960; Pres., Rogers Cable TV Ltd. 1976; Founding Pres., St. Lawrence Coll., Kingston, Ont. 1967; Pres., Candn. Cable TV Rite 1979; Vice-Pres., Selkirk Communications Ltd.; Anglican; recreations: skiing, boating, reading; Clubs: Royal Canadian Yacht; Home: 17 Walmsley Blvd., Toronto Ont. M4V 1X5; Office 45 Charles St. E., Toronto, Ont. M4Y 1S2

SHOULTS, Arthur Milton, B.A., M.B.A.; company executive; b. Winnipeg, Man., 12 Nov. 1915; s. William Arthur and Maud Barton (Cogan) S.; e. Univ. of Manitoba, B.A. 1936; Harvard Sch. of Business, M.B.A. 1938; m. Mary Elaine, d. G. H. Thompson, 1944; children: Thomas Richard, Mary Anne, Joan Elaine; Chmn. CHQT Broadcasting Ltd.; Chmn. Pres., B.R.E. Electric Limited; Dir., Banister Continental Ltd.; Pres. Chester Industrial Tool Supply Ltd.; President (1970-71) Inst. of Candn. Advertising; served in 2nd World War, Lt. R.C.N.V.R.; Protestant; Phi Delta Theta; Office: 5544 - 5th St. S.E., Calgary, Alta. T2H 1L3

SHOYAMA, Thomas Kunito, O.C., B.A., B. Com.; Canadian public servant; b. Kamloops, B.C. 24 Sept. 1916; s. Kunitaro and Kimi (Wakabayashi) S.; e. Pub. and High schs. Kamloops; Univ. of B.C., B.A. 1938, B.Com. 1938; McGill Univ. Post-grad. reading 1948; m. Lorna A. d. Lorne Moore 18 Dec. 1950; one d. Kiyomi A.; VISITING PROF., UNIV. OF VICTORIA; Dir., Petro-Canada Hawker Siddeley Canada Inc.; Bank of Tokyo Canada; Journalist and Publisher 1938 — 45; Candn. Army Intelligence Corps 1945 — 46; Research Econ. Govt. of Sask. 1946 — 48, Econ. Adviser 1950 — 64; Research Econ. Central Mortgage & Housing Corp. Ottawa 1949; Sr. Econ., Econ. Council of Can. 1964 — 67; Asst. Depy. Min. of Finance, Ottawa 1968 — 74, Depy. Min. 1975 — 79; Depy. Min. of Energy, Mines & Resources 1974 — 75; Chrmn. of the Bd., Atomic Energy of Canada Ltd., 1979; Constitutional Advisor, Privy Council Office, 1979; rec'd Outstanding Achievement Award Pub. Service Can. 1978; mem. Candn. Econ. Assn.; Candn. Tax Foundation; Inst. Pub. Adm. Can.; recreations: gardening, fishing, golf, cycling; Home: 272 Cunningham Ave., Ottawa, Ont. K1H 6B4 and 1985 Crescent Rd., Victoria, B.C.; Office: School of Public Administration, Univ. of Victoria, Box 1700, Victoria, B.C. V8W 2Y4

SHROPSHIRE, Robert C., b. N.J., 31 Dec. 1917; s. Robert Campbell and Agnes MacNeil (Brown) S.; e. Bowdoin Coll. Brunswick, Me. 1939; m. Elizabeth Joan d. late William Henry Ross, 15 Dec. 1951; children: Lee Anne, Elizabeth Joan, Robert Campbell III, Scott Fenimore, William Ross; Dir. Glaser Bros. (Los Angeles); Chmn., Gardena Seed and Feeding Inc.; Pres., Inverchair Marketing Inc.; George Weston Ltd. 1969-75; Vice Pres. The Nestlée Co.

USA 1960-65; Vice Pres. and Dir. Beechnut-Lifesavers USA 1965-68; Pres. and Dir. William Neilson Ltd. Toronto 1969-75; chrmn. and CEO, RJR Macdonald Inc. 1975-79 (ret.); served with 1st Bn. Black Watch of Can. 1939-43, RCAF 411 Sqdn. 1943-45; Vice Chrmn. Candn. Tobacco Mfrs.' Council; GPMC 1975 (Dir. Extve. Comte.); Chrmn. Tea Council USA 1964-65; Psi Upsilon; Presbyterian; Recreation: sailing; Clubs: Mount Royal (Montreal); RCYC (Toronto); RTYC (London, Eng.); Indian Harbor Yacht (Greenwich, Conn.); Home: 30 Sighthill Ave., Toronto, Ont. M4T 2G7

SHRUM, Gordon Merritt, O.C. (1967), O.B.E. (1946), M.M. E.D., Ph.D., F.R.S.C.; b. Smithville, Ont., 14 Jan. 1896; s. William Burton and Emma Jane (Merritt) S.; e. Smithville (Ont.) High Sch.; Hamilton (Ont.) Coll. Inst.; Univ. of Toronto, 1913-16, 1919-20, Silver Medal, Maths. 1920, B.A. 1920, M.A. 1921, Ph.D. 1923; Studentship, Nat. Research Council, 1921-22, Fellowship, 1922-24; D.Sc., Univ. of B.C., 1961, McMaster Univ., 1963; LL.D., Simon Fraser 1969; children: Gordon Baillie, Laurna Jane; Dir., Centennial Museum, 1975-76; Chairman and President, International Power and Engineering Consultants Limited; Chairman, B.C. Energy Board; Director, Atomic Energy of Canada Limited; B.C. Bldgs. Corp.; Dean Emeritus and Hon. Prof. Physics, Univ. of B.C.; former Chancellor, Simon Fraser University; Research Asst., University of Toronto, 1923-24; Research Physicist, Corning Glass Works, 1924-25; Asst. Prof., Univ. of Toronto, 1937; Head, Dept. of Physics, 1938-61; Dean, Faculty of Grad. Studies, 1956-61; Pres. and Chief Extve. Offr., B.C. Electric Co. Ltd., 1961-62; Chrmn., B.C. Hydro and Power Authority 1962-73; Project Chmn., Robson Sq. New Courthouse Project 1976-79; Project Chmn., Pacific Rim Trade and Convention Centre 1979; served in 1st World War with C.F.A. C.E.F., 1916-19, Univ. of Toronto 67th, 29th and 36th Battys.; awarded M.M.; O.C. Univ. of B.C. Contingent, C.O.T.C., 1937-46, Hon. Lieut.-Col., 1946-57; Dir., Candn. Nuclear Assn.; Fellow, Royal Soc. Can. (Pres. Sec. III, 1958-59); Candn. Assn. Physicists (Pres., 1953-54); mem., Nat. Research Council Can., 1943-49 and 1950-56, Chrmn., Scholarship Comte., 1958-61; Defence Research Bd., 1947-50 and 1951-54; Acting Dir., B.C. Research Council, 1944-45, 1951-52, Dir., 1952-61; Chrmn., Mil. Studies Comte. of the Nat. Conf. of Candn. Univs., 1946-59; mem., Pacific Science Assn. and Pacific Science Council, 1948-57; Chrmn., Roy. Comn. on B.C. Power Comn., 1958-59; Chrmn., Adv. Comte. on Scient. Research and Devel., Glassco Roy. Comn. on Govt. Organ., 1961; Hon. Secy., B.C. Cancer Foundation, 1938-46; B.C. Chrmn. for Candn. Legion Educ. Services, World War II; Candn. Del., 7th Pacific Science Congress, N.Z., 1949, 8th Congress, Manila, 1953; Hon. Secy., Vancouver Bd. Trade, 1956-57; mem., Candn. Del. to 10th Congress on Refrigeration, Copenhagen, Denmark, 1959; Chrmn., Bd. Examiners, B.C. Dental Techns., 1958-64; Hon. Life mem., Vancouver Museums and Planetarium Assn.; credited with the discovery of the origin of Auroral green line and the liquefaction of helium; Beta Theta Pi; Un. Church; Clubs: Faculty; Electric; Hon. mem., Canada Club (Vancouver); Rotary (Vancouver); Home: 5941 Chancellor Blvd., Vancouver, B.C. V6T 1E6;

SHUMIATCHER, Morris Cyril, O.C. Q.C., B.A., LL.M., Dr. Jur.; b. Calgary, Alta., 20 Sept. 1917; s. A. I., Q.C. and Luba S.; e. Calgary Pub. and High Schs. (Gov. Gen.'s Medal), 1935; Mount Royal Coll., Calgary, 1936; Univ. of Alta., B.A. 1940, LL.B. 1941; Travelling Scholarship to Japan 1940; Univ. of Toronto, LL.M. 1942, Dr. Jur. 1945; m. Jacqueline Clay 1955; called to the Bars of Alta., B.C., Sask., Man. and N.W.T.; K.C. 1948; Law Offr., Dept. of Atty.-Gen., Sask., 1945-49; various positions incl. Counsel to Cabinet of Sask., Personal Advisor and Asst. to Premier, Counsel to Labour Relations Bd. and Econ. Adv. & Planning Bd.; Est. Sask. Air Ambulance Service; author Sask. Bill of Rights, 1947; gen. practice of law in Sask., Alta. and B.C. since 1949; sometime lectr., Adult Educ., Univ. of West. Ont., Dalhousie Univ. Law School; Univ. of Toronto; Law Soc. of Upper Can.; Univ. of Regina; Univ. of Sask. and Touring Guest Speaker & Lecturer to learned societies & service clubs in Can., U.S.A. regular TV lecture series on internat. affairs, criminal law, adm. of justice and leg. policy; CBC lecture series on Indian Affairs, civil liberties, legal problems of farmers, University of the Air; daily radio program "In Touch with Today"; served with RCAF (Air-Gunner) 1943-45; lectr. in mil. law and educ. & vocational guidance; writings incl. "Welfare: Hidden Backlash" 1971, "Man of Law: A Model" 1979 and numerous articles in leading professional journals and magazines; mem., Law Societies Provinces of Alberta, British Columbia, Sask., N.W.T., Man.; Candn. Bar Assn. (Nat. Chairman Civil Liberties Sec.); Internat. Assn. Jurists; Inst. Internat. Affairs (Dir.); Candn. Council of Christians and Jews (Dir.); UN Assn. Can.; Sask. Centre Arts (Dir.); Regina Astron. Assn.; Plains Hist. Museum Soc.; Dom. Drama Festival; Sask. Drama Council; Norman McKenzie Art Gallery Assn. (Past Pres.); Regina Symphony (Past Pres.); John Howard Soc.; Sask. Wild Life Fed.; Sask. Music Festival Assn.; Eng.-Speaking Union Commonwealth in Can. (Pres. Regina Br.); Monarchist League Can. (Hon. Pres. Regina); Polar Bear Club (Founder); Hon. Consul Gen. for Japan at Regina; Dean, Sask. Consular Corps; Candn. Schizophrenia Assn., Bd. of Publs.; Candn. Civil Rights Assn.; Sask. Human Rights Assn.; and other assns. and socs.; Club: Assiniboia; Home: 2520 College Ave., Regina, Sask. S4P 1C9; Office: 2100 Scarth St., Regina, Sask. S4P 2H6

SHUTE, Edward Hugh, transportation executive; b. Winnipeg, Man. 13 Sept. 1916; s. Hugh John and Alice Emily (Birch) S.; e. Winnipeg (Man.) High Sch.; m. Beatrice Mae d. late William B. McKelvey 5 Apl. 1941; children; Marilyn Joan Wright, Jacqueline Marie Reinprecht, Sandra Elinor Olson, Dennis Edward; VICE PRES. OPERATIONS, VIA RAIL CANADA INC. since 1977; joined CP Rail 1939-77, service in Can. and Indonesia; served with RCAF 1940-41; mem. Heritage Park Soc. Calgary; Calgary Exhn. Stampede; Am. Assn. Rr. Supts.; P. Conservative; Protestant; recreation: curling; Office: P.O. Box 8116, Montreal, Que. H3C 3N3.

SHUTE, Wilfred Eugene, B.A., M.D.; physician; b. Berkeley, Ont., 21 Oct. 1907; s. Richard James, M.D., and Elizabeth Jane (Treadgold) S.; e. Coll. Inst., Windsor, Ont.; Univ. of Toronto, B.A. 1929, M.D. 1933; Post-Grad. studies in Chicago and Toronto for five yrs.; CO-FOUNDER EVAN SHUTE FOUNDATION FOR MEDICAL RESEARCH; assoc. with Dr. Evan Shute in clin. investigation of the functions of vitamin E in med. science since 1937; Canada's leading breeder of Doberman Pinschers; Intercoll. Wrestling Champion, Univ. of Toronto, 1932-33; the first "Keeper of the Prints" of the Art Gallery, Hart House; Official Photographer, Hart House Theatre, three yrs.; mem. Ont. Med. Assn.; Candn. Med. Assn.; author of "Vitamin E for Ailing and Healthy Hearts"; has written numerous papers for med. journs.; Reorganized Church of Latter Day Saints; recreations: dog show judging, photography; Home: 1549 Trimble Court, Port Credit, Ont. L5G 3L1; Office: 299 Lakeshore Rd. E., Port Credit, Ont. L5G 1H3

SHUVE, Ainslie St.C.; investment executive; b. Saint John, N.B. 18 Nov. 1922; s. John and Margaret (Moore) S.; e. N.B. Schs.; m. Anne Isobel, d. Arthur H. Washburn, 5 Oct. 1946; children: Dr. Sandra J. Messner, John A.; CONSULTANT, JONES HEWARD & CO. LTD. since 1980; began with Eastern Securities Company Limited, Saint John, M.B. 1947; Investment Mgr. Barclay's Trust Co. Montreal, Que. 1953; joined Crown Trust Co. as Invest. Offr., Montreal 1957, Asst. Treas. 1963, Mgr. Montreal 1965, Asst. Gen. Mgr. and Treas. Toronto 1966; Vice-Pres. Finance 1972; Extve. Vice Pres. 1973; Pres. and CEO

1978-80; Anglican; recreation: golf; Clubs: National; Toronto Hunt, Mount Royal (Montreal); Granite; Home: 1906 Tower Hill West, 355 St. Clair Ave. West, Toronto, Ont. M5P 1N5; Office: Ste. 909, 141 Adelaide St. W., Toronto, Ont. M5H 3L5

SIBLEY, William Maurice, M.A., Ph.D., LL.D.; b. Saskatoon, Sask. 21 June 1919; s. John Cynddylan and Mary Stuart Isabella (Shaw) S.; e. Lord Byng High Sch. Vancouver 1935; Univ. of B.C. B.A. 1939 (Gov. Gen's Gold Medal), M.A. 1940; Brown Univ. Ph.D. 1943; Univ. of Man. LL.D. 1977; m. Margaret Jean d. William A. MacKenzie, Vancouver, B.C. 24 Apl. 1942; children: Robert William, John MacKenzie, Jean Elizabeth, James MacLachlan; CHRMN. SASK. UNIVS. COMN. since 1978; Lectr. Queen's Univ. 1943-46; Asst. Prof. Univ. of Man. 1946, Assoc. Prof. 1947, Prof. and Head of Philos. 1948-69, Dean of Arts & Science 1961-69, Dir. of Planning 1969-70, Vice Pres. 1970-75; Chrmn. Adv. Bd. Educ. Man. 1962-65; Adv. Comte. on Univ. Planning, Assn. Univs. & Colls. Can. 1977; Vice Pres. Mount Allison Univ. 1975-78; Dean Emeritus of Science Univ. Man. 1972 and of Arts 1975; Distinguished Visiting Lectr. Univ. Calgary 1978-79; rec'd Centennial Medal 1967; contributor "Evaluating Institutions For Accountability" 1974; contrib. "International Encyclopedia of Higher Education" 1977; various articles on aspects of univ. planning and adm., accountability and information systems; mem. Candn. Soc. Study Higher Educ. (Pres. 1977-78); Candn. Philos. Assn. (Founding mem.); Assn. Inst. Research; Phi Beta Kappa; United Church; recreations: reading, photography; Home: 98 Baldwin Cres., Saskatoon, Sask. S7H 3M6; Office: 2302 Arlington Ave., Saskatoon, Sask. S7J 3L3.

SIEBNER, Herbert Johannes Josef, R.C.A.; artist; b. Stettin, Germany 16 Apl. 1925; s. Paul Hermann and Margarete Agnes (Resch) S.; e. elem. sch. Stettin 1931-1935; Dr. Schumacher's Private Gymnasium 35-1937; Schiller Real Gymnasium Stettin 37-1941; Atelier Max Richter Stettin 1941-43; Berlin Acad. 1946-69; m. Hannelore d. Willy Roehr 14 Oct. 1950; one d. Angela; came to Can. 1954; Teacher, Studio Group Victoria B.C. 1954-58; Art Gallery Victoria 1958-60; Univ. of B.C. Extension Travelling Lectr.; Visiting Prof. Univ. of Wash. 1963; Univ. of B.C. Summer Sch. Art 1964; Univ. of Alta. Painting Workshop 1966; Univ. of Victoria Graphics Lectr. 1967-68; over 80 solo exhns. Europe, Can. and USA; rep. Candn. Biennale 1959, 1962; Internat. Exhn. Graphics Lugano 1958; Yugoslavia 1959; Brussels World Fair 1957; Seattle World Fair 1962; Victoria Art Gallery Retrospective 1970, Univ. of Victoria 1979; Media Centre Vancouver 1980; recipient Design Award 1952, 1953 Berlin; Reid Award for Graphics Toronto 1956; Sculpture Award B.C. 1957; Seattle Art Museum 1957 Award; Painting Award Winnipeg 1959, Victoria 1960, 1961; Can. Council Sr. Grant 1962; Acad. in Berlin Honour 1963; Internat. Graphic Exhn. Medal 1969; named Hon. Citizen City of Victoria 1973; mural comns. incl. Crown House Victoria 1960; Univ. of Victoria 1964; Prov. Museum Victoria 1968; B.C. Govt. Centre Vancouver 1975 (Media); served with German Army 1943-45, draughtsman, rank Cpl., Russian P.O.W. 1945; co-author "Inscriptions" 1967; "Muse Book" 1972; biog. "Herbert Siebner: 25 Years in B.C." 1979 by R. Skelton; mem. Candn. Group Painters; B.C. Soc. Artists; Limners Soc. Royal Canadian Academy; Home: 270 Meadow Brook Rd., Victoria, B.C. V8X 3X3.

SIFTON, Michael Clifford C.D. publisher and broadcaster; b. Toronto, Ont., 21 Jan. 1931; s. Lieut.-Col. Clifford Sifton, D.S.O., and later Doris Margaret (Greene) S.; e. Public Schs., Toronto, Ont.; Trinity Coll. Sch., Port Hope, Ont.; Thornton Private Sch.; Univ. of Western Ont.; m. Heather Ann McLean, d. Hamilton A. McLean, 8 Sept. 1956; children: Clifford McLean, Michael Gregory, Derek Andrew; PRES., ARMADALE CO. LTD., since 1960; Pres., Armadale Publishers Ltd. (Saskatoon Star-

Phoenix); Regina Leader-Post Ltd.; Armadale Communications Ltd.; Toronto Airways Ltd.; Radio CKCK Regina; Radio CKIT-FM and Radio CKRC and CKWG-FM Winnipeg; CKOC Hamilton; Armadale Enterprises Ltd.; Dir., H. A. McLean Chevrolet-Oldsmobile Ltd.; Phoenix Leasing Ltd.; Eastern Ontario Broadcasting (CFJR); while attending university worked with London Free Press Printing Co. Ltd., London, Ont.; employed with "Peterborough Examiner" summer 1954, later that year joined Sifton family group of Co.'s as Extve. Asst.; served as Offr. with Royal Canadian Armoured Corps. (Militia, Governor Gen. Horse Guards and First Hussars) during 1950's; Hon. Col., 411 Air Reserve Sqdn.; awarded Canadian Forces Decoration; Chmn., Council of Hon. Air Colonels; active Comte. mem.; Royal Winter Fair, Toronto (Dir. 1975); responsible for revival of polo in Toronto after 2nd World War; Dir., Candn. Press; Trustee, Quetico Found.; mem., Toronto Art Gallery; Candn. Daily Newspaper Publ. Assn.; Am. Newspaper Publ. Assn.; Toronto Bd. Trade; Candn. Assn. Broadcasters; Am. Assn. Airport Extves.; Roy. Mil. Inst.; Anglican; recreations: riding, skiing, water-sports; Clubs: Canadian; Empire; Toronto and N. York Hunt (M.F.H., Dir. and Vice-Pres.); Toronto Polo (Pres.); Saskatoon (Sask.); Assiniboia (Regina); The Toronto; Home: Fox Den Farm, R.R.1, Gormley, Ont. L0H 1G0; Office: Toronto-Buttonville Airport, Markham, Ont. L3P 3J9

SILCOX, David Phillips, M.A., F.R.S.A.; art historian; administrator; b. Moose Jaw, Sask. 28 Jan. 1937; s. Albert Phillips Silcox; e. Univ. of Toronto B.A. 1959, M.A. 1966; Courtauld Inst. Univ. of London 1962 — 63; DIR. OF CULTURAL AFFAIRS, MUNICIPALITY OF METROP. TORONTO since 1974; Freelance writer and Broadcaster 1964 — 65; Visual Arts Offr. Can. Council 1965 — 66, Sr. Arts Offr. 1966 — 70; Asst. and subsequently Assoc. Dean of Fine Arts, York Univ. 1970 — 73, Assoc. Prof. 1970 — 77, Chrmn. of Music 1971 — 72, Chrmn. of Visual Arts 1972 — 73; Asst. Dir. Candn. Conf. of Arts 1961, Bd. mem. 1976-81; Organizer, Toronto Outdoor Art Exhn. 1961 (first), Bd. mem. Candn. Film Devel. Corp. Since 1971, Vice Charmn. 1975 — 78; Chmn., 1981; Gov., Massey Hall since 1972; Chrmn. Internat. Sculpture Conf. 1977 — 78; Chmn., CFDC, 1981- ; Bd. mem. Univ. of Toronto Sch. of Continuing Studies; Toronto Theatre Festival 1980-81; Festival of Festivals 1981; past mem. various comtes. Art Gallery of Ont., Ont. Coll. of Arts, 1976-79; Can. Council, Vincent Massey Awards, Stratford Art Gallery; Bd. mem. Assn. Cultural Extves.; Founding mem. Fed. Dept. Pub. Works Fine Arts Comte. 1968 — 70, Chrmn. 1978 — 79; Bd. mem., Stratford Festival, 1981; Toronto Int'l Arts Festival, 1981; Trustee, Jack Bush Estate; art consulting services incl.: Banff Sch. Fine Arts, Mem. Univ. Nfld., Metrop. Toronto, Govt. Alta., Toronto Transit Comn. (Spadina subway), Univ. of Toronto, Fed. Candn. Muns.; Special Advisor to Secy. of State on Fed. Cultural Policy 1978; special lectr. on Candn. art and Candn. Cultural Policy; rec'd Sir Frederick Banting Award 1962; Man of Yr. Globe & Mail 1962; Can. Council Arts Bursary 1962, Research Grant 1973, Research Fellowship 1974 — 75; Arts Award, 1979 — 80; McLean Foundation Research Grant 1970; York Univ. Research Grant 1972; co-author "Tom Thomson: The Silence and the Storm" 1977; Guest Ed. "Canadian Art" 1962; mem. Internat. Ed. Bd., "Studio International" 1968-75; "Christopher Pratt", 1980; mem. of Bd., Koffler Arts Centre; writer/producer/ed. various art catalogues; author various articles, essays and reports art mags. and newspapers; recreations: canoeing, sailing, scuba diving; Home: Apt. 402, 70 Montclair Ave., Toronto M5P 1P7; Office: West Tower, City Hall, Toronto, Ont. M5H 2N1.

SILLCOX, Robert L., B.A.; insurance executive; b. Toronto, Ont. 1931; e. Ridley Coll. St. Catharines, Ont. 1949; Williams Coll. Williamstown, Mass. B.A. 1953; m.; 3 children; VICE PRES. CORPORATE INVESTMENTS, METROPOLITAN LIFE INSURANCE CO. 1979- ; Dir.,

Harris & Partners Ltd. 1956-70; Pres., McDunn, Sillcox & Co. Ltd. 1970-77 and founding Partner, Euro Brokers, Harlow & Co.; Sr. Vice Pres. Investments, Bank of Montreal 1977-79; Bd. of Gov., Ridley Coll. 1981; mem. King Twp. Planning Bd. 1968-72; founding Dir. (Aurora) Blue Hills Acad. Home 1969-71; Co-Chrmn. National Accounts Un. Way (York Region); mem. Financial Adv. Comte. Workmen's Compensation Bd. Ont. 1978-79; Bd. Trade Metrop. Toronto; Financial Extves. Inst. Can.; recreations: horses, shooting, skiing; Clubs: Toronto; University (N.Y.); Muskoka Lakes Golf & Country; Home: Grandview Farm, R.R.3, King, Ont. L0G 1K0; Office: (P.O. Box 160) Royal Bank Plaza, North Tower Suite 790, Toronto, Ont. M5J 2J4.

SIM, David, C.M.G. (1946); b. Glasgow, Scot., 4 May 1899; s. David and Cora Lillian (Angus) S.; e. Haghill Pub. Sch., Glasgow; came to Can. 1911; m. Ada Helen (died 1958), d. Alex Inrig., Toronto, Ont.; children: David Alexander, Doris Winnifred; 2ndly, Winnifred Emily, d. Raymond Lewis Blois, Ottawa, Ont., 1960; with Bank of N.S., Kitchener, Ont., 1919-25; Waterloo Trust & Savings Co. there, as Asst. Secy., 1925-26; Private Secy. to Ministers of Nat. Revenue, 1927-33; Commr. of Excise, Dept. of Nat. Revenue, 1934-43; Depy. Min., Customs and Excise, 1943-Jan. 1965; served overseas with 1st Candn. Inf. Bn., 1916-19; wounded at Passchendaele; Dir., W.P.T.B.; Foreign Exchange Control Bd.; Commodity Prices Stabilization Corpn.; mem., External Trade Advisory Comte.; throughout 2nd World War served as Adm. of Alcoholic Beverages and Adm. of Tobacco, W.P.T.B.; Nat. Joint Council of the Public Service of Can.; mem. Bd., Broadcast Govs.; mem. of Candian del. attending meeting of Prep. Council of Internat. Conf. on Trade and Employment, London, Eng., 1946; del. to 2nd session, Geneva, 1947; awarded King's Jubilee and Coronation Medals; Freemason; Baptist; recreations: reading, music; Clubs: Rotary (Past Pres.); Royal Ottawa Golf; Rideau Curling; Home: 616 - 1833 Riverside Dr., Ottawa, Ont. K1G 0E8

SIMARD, Arthur, Q.C.; company executive; b. Sorel. Que., e. Notre Dame Coll.; Brébeuf Coll., McGill Univ., Univ. of Montreal; Vice-chrmn., Reynolds Aluminium Co. of Canada Ltd.; Sterling Trust; Chrmn Trust General du Canada; Pres., Cie de Charlevoix Ltée; Corpn. Equitable Canadienne; Precision Instruments Inc.; Les Immeubles Dramis Inc.; Vice President, Simcor.; Chrmn. Sherbrooke Trust Co.; Vice-Pres. Voyage Richelieu Inc.; Dir. Prenor Ltd.; mem., Board of Trustees, Diagnostic and Clinical Research Inst. of Montreal; read law with Mathewson, Wilson, Wilson and Smith; admitted to the Bar of Quebec, 1940; cr. Q.C. 1963; Dir., Atlantic Salmon Assn.; recreations: fishing, hunting, yachting; Club: St. Denis, Mount Bruno Country; Home: 47 De la Rive, Ste-Anne de Sorel, Que. J3P 1K1; Office: Sorel, Branch Line, P.O. Box 540 P.Q. J3P 5P4

SIMARD, Hon. Claude, M.N.A., B.Com.; b. Sorel, Que., 22 Oct. 1938; s. J. Edouard and Orise (Brunelle) S.; e. Saint-Joseph de Sorel Coll.; Mont-Jésus-Marie d'Outremont; Ottawa Univ., B.Com. 1962; m. Francine, d. Roland Leroux, Three Rivers, Que., 30 Apl. 1966; one s. Hugues-Edouard; CHRMN. OF BOARD, CLAURÉM-IAND LTÉE. (formerly Pres.); EngineeringProducts of Can. Ltd.; Dir., Sorel Steel and Foundries; Reynolds Aluminium Co. of Canada Ltd.; former Min. of State for Ind. and Comm., Que.; R. Catholic; recreations: swimming, golf, boating; Clubs: Sorel Nautical; Three Rivers Yacht (Dir.); Sorel "Les Dunes" Golf (Dir.); Three Rivers K1-8-EB Golf (Dir.); Home: 801 Laird Blvd., Town of Mount Royal, Que. H3R 1Y7; Office: 1115 Sherbrooke St. W., Montreal, Que.

SIMARD, Hon. Jean-Maurice, M.L.A., B.Com., C.A.; né à Rivière-Bleue, Que., 21 juin 1931; f. J. Evariste et Marie-Anna (Ouellet) S.; é. Univ. d'Ottawa, B.Com. (compt.) 1953; Univ. McGill 1953-55; C.A. dans l'Institut des comptables agréés du Québec 1956; admis à l'Institut des comptables agréés du Nouveau-Brunswick 1958; ép. Francine, f. P. Fréchette 1 août 1959; enfants: Monique, Jean-Marc, Marie-Pierre; Ministre des Finances, Nouveau-Brunswick 1970-74; établit la société des comptables agréés, Simard, Lévesque, Nadeau et Landry, Edmundston, N.B. 1959; s'occupe de la fond. et de l'admin. de plusieurs compagnies de 1952-70; Prés., l'assn. p. conservatrice du N.B., élu nov. 1968 ré-élu jan. 1970; élu député de la Cité d'Edmundston 26 oct. 1970; mem., l'assn. de l'Aviation Royale Candn. d'Edmundston; la Chambre de Comm. d'Edmundston; la Société d'Art Dramatique d'Edmundston; Prés., l'équipe de baseball, "Les Républicains" 1968, 69, 70, 71; Catholique; récréations: golf, bridge; Clubs: Richelieu d'Edmundston; 200 du Collège Saint-Louis; Golf d'Edmundston; Résidence: 64, 48e avenue, Edmundston, N.B. E3U 3C9;

SIMARD, Léon; industrialist; b. Sorel, Que., 21 Nov. 1920; s. Joseph Arthur, O.B.E., and Rose Blanche (Pontbriand) S.; e. Coll. Jean de Brébeuf, Mont Saint Louis, Que.; m. Jacqueline, d. Fernand Levasseur, Montreal, Que., 15 Nov. 1947; one d., Roseanne; PRESIDENT, SIMCOR INC.; Chrmn. Bd., Engineering Products of Canada Ltd.; Dir., Branch Lines Ltd.; Eutectic Canada Ltd.; Electronic Associates of Canada Ltd.; Scott-Lasalle Ltd.; St. Lawrence Diversified Ltd.; Standard Paper Box Mfg.; Sorel Steel Foundries Limited; Simclaire Co. Ltée.; La Cie de Charlevoix Ltée.; Car-Lex; Immeubles Dramis Limited; General Trust Company of Canada; Scott's Restaurants Co. Limited; Canadian Aviation Electronics Ltd.; Scholbeton Que. Inc.; mem. Bd. Trustees, Nat. Museums of Can. 1972-75; mem., Chambre de Commerce de Montréal; Dir., Marie-Enfant Hosp.; Notre-Dame Hosp.; St. John Ambulance; Féd. des Jeunes Chambres du Can.-Français; Greater Montreal Council of the Arts; Olympic Trust of Can.; Inst. Albert-Prévost; Montreal Museum of Fine Arts; Roman Catholic; recreations: golf, hunting, fishing, yachting; Clubs: St. Denis; Montreal Skeet; Montreal Badminton & Racquet; Royal Montreal Golf; Laval-sur-le-Lac; Mount Royal; Surf (Miami); Indian Creek Country (Miami); Home: 3110 Daulac Rd., Montreal, Que. H3Y 1Z9; Office: Room 400, 1405 Peel St., Montreal, Que. H3A 1S5

SIMARD, René, M.D., F.R.C.S.(C); retired physician; university professor; b. Sillery, Que. March 1912; e. Que. Semy.; Laval Univ.; Univ. of Paris; m. Albina Petitclerc, Sorel, P.Q., 1937; children: Geneviève, Jacqueline; Past Prof. of Obstetrics, Laval Univ.; Former Attending Gynecologist, Hôpital du St-Sacrament, mem., Soc. of Obstet. & Gynaecol. Can.; Candn. Med. Assn.; Soc. Méd. de Que.; Assn. des Méd. de Langue Française du Can.; recreations: riding, chess; Club: Cercle Universitaire Laval; Home: 2590 Plaza, Apt. 411, Sillery, Que. G1T 1X2;

SIMINOVITCH, David, M.Sc., Ph.D., F.R.S.C.; research scientist; b. Montreal, Que. 29 May 1916; s. Nathan and Goldie (Wachtman) S.; e. McGill Univ. B.Sc. 1936 (Maj. Hiram Mills Gold Medal in Biol. 1936), M.Sc. 1937 (Nat. Research Council Bursary & Studentship 1937, 1938), Ph.D. 1939; Univ. of Minn. Ph.D. 1946; m. Helen Elizabeth d. late Fred Daubney 4 Sept. 1945; children: David Jonathan, Sara Jane, Michael Jeremy; RESEARCH SCIENT., CHEM. & BIOL. RESEARCH INST., AGRIC. CAN. since 1950, Hon. Research Assoc., 1981; Royal Soc. Can. Travelling Fellowship, Univ. of Minn. 1940-41, Herman Frasch Foundation Research Assoc. and Lectr. 1946-50; rec'd Candn. Soc. Plant Physiols. Gold Medal 1972; author over 40 papers scient. journs. and symposia proceedings; mem. Candn. Soc. Plant Physiols.; Am. Soc. Plant Physiols. (Ed. Bd.); Soc. Cryobiol. (Ed. Bd., Gov.); Hebrew; recreations: swimming, reading, painting, natural history; Home: 1118 Agincourt Rd., Ottawa, Ont. K2C 2H7; Office: K. W. Neatby Bldg., Ottawa, Ont. K1A 0C6.

SIMINOVITCH, Louis, B.Sc., Ph.D., F.R.S.C. (1965), F.R.S. (1980); scientist and professor; b. Montreal, Que., 1 May 1920; s. Nathan and Goldie (Watchman) S.; e. McGill Univ., B.Sc. 1941, Ph.D. 1944; obtained Arts & Science Scholar., 1939-40, Sir. Wm. McDonald Scholar. 1940-41, Anne Molson Prize in Chem. 1941, Nat. Research Council Studentship and Fellowship 1947-49, Nat. Cancer Inst. Can. Fellowships 1953-1955; m. Elinore, d. late Harry Faierman, 2 July 1944; children: Harriet Jean, Katherine Ann, Margaret Ruth; PROF. & CHRMN., DEPT. MEDICAL GENETICS, UNIV. TORONTO, since 1966; Prof. Med. Biophysics since 1960; Assoc. Prof. Pediatrics since 1972; Geneticist-in-chief, Hosp. for Sick Children since 1970; mem., Science Council of Can.; Ed., "Virology"; "Cell"; "Somatic Cell Genetics"; "Journ. Cytogenetics and Cell Genetics"; "Journal of Molecular and Cellular Biology" (1980); with N.R.C. at Ottawa and Chalk River, Ont., 1944-47; Roy. Soc. Fellow, Parsten Inst. 1947-49; employed by Centre Nat. de la Recherche Scient., Paris, France, 1949-53; Connaught Med. Research Labs., Univ. of Toronto, 1953-56; Prof. Microbiol. 1958-67; Head, Div. Biol. Research, Ont. Cancer Inst. 1963-69; Head, Dept. of Med. Cell Biol. 1969-74; Head, Dept. Med. Genetics 1974-79; contrib. over 159 scient. articles to learned journs.; mem., Health Research & Dev. Comte. Ont. Council of Health, 1966- ; (Chrmn. 1974-); Bd. of Dir., Nat. Cancer Inst. of Can., 1975- ; Bid. of Dir., Mount Sinai Inst., Mount Sinai Hosp. (Toronto), 1975- ; mem. of Council, Med. Research Council of Can., 1976- ; (mem. of Extve. 1977-); mem. Adv. Comte. on Genetic Services, Prov. of Ont., 1976- ; Adv. Comte., Nat. Cancer Inst., Nat. Inst. of Health (U.S.A.) 1978- , (Chrmn. 1976-78); mem. of Bd., Ont. Cancer Treatment & Research Foundation, 1979- ; mem. Scientific Adv. Comte. of the Connaught Research Inst., 1980- ; mem. Alfred P. Sloan, Jr., Selection Comte., General Motors Cancer Research Foundation, 1980- ; Hebrew; recreations: tennis, swimming, reading; Home: 106 Wembley Rd., Toronto, Ont. M6C 2G5

SIMMINS, Richard B., M.A.; art consultant; b. Ottawa, Ont. 14 Oct. 1924; s. Marjorie (Beaufort) and late Major R.G.S.; e. Univ. of Toronto, B.A. 1949, M.A. 1952 (Art Hist.); courses at Courtauld Inst., London Univ.; m. Barbara J. d. late Garnet Atkinson D.D.S., Exeter, Ont., 20 May 1950; children: Barbara Zoe, Karen Francesca, Richard Geoffrey, Marjorie Lorraine; Special Lectr. and Curator of Norman Mackenzie Art Gallery, Regina Coll., Univ. of Sask., 1952-57; Dir., Exhibition Extension Services, Nat. Gallery Can., 1957-62; Dir., Vancouver Art Gallery 1963-67, since when Consultant on Visual Arts to Govt., art museums and private industry; mem. (1963), Candn. World's Fair Corp., Fine Art Comte.; Candn. Confed. Centennial Comte. of B.C. (1966-67); Pres. (1965), Candn. Art Museums Dirs. Organ.; Pres. (1965), Candn. Conf. of the Arts; recreation: reading.

SIMMONDS, John Alexander; manufacturer; b. Moncton, N.B., 26 March 1920; s. John Percival and Martha Evangeline (MacDonald) S.; e. Public and High Schs., Charlottetown, P.E.I.; Kings Coll. Sch., Windsor, N.S. (1936-37); Prince of Wales Coll., Charlottetown (1937-40); m. Minnie Lavina, d. Alfred James Watts, Charlottetown, P.E.I., 27 Jan. 1945; children: John Alfred, George William, Donald Watts, James David, Catherine Anne; PRESIDENT, PERFECTION FOODS LTD. (Estbd. 1921); entered the present business at an early age, succeeding his father (the founder) as Pres. in 1951; served in Reserve Army, P.E.I. Lighthorse, 1941-45; mem., Charlottetown Bd. Trade; Immed. Past Chrmn., Nat. Dairy Council; Past Chrmn., Indust. Enterprises Inc.; Past Pres., Atlantic Dairy Council; Rotary Club of Charlottetown; Past Commodore, Charlottetown Yacht Club; Freemason; United Church; recreations: sailing, skiing, swimming; Home: 9 Crestwood Drive, Charlottetown, P.E.I. C1A 3H2; Office: 215 Fitzroy, Charlottetown, P.E.I. C1A 7K2

SIMMONDS, Monty M., Q.C.; b. London, Eng., 8 June 1925; s. Harry and Esther (Pepper) S.; e. Hodgson Pub. Sch. and N. Toronto Coll. Inst.; Univ. of Toronto grad. 1946; Osgoode Hall Law Sch. grad. 1949; m. Judith Leah d. late Samuel B. Godfrey OBE, 23 Dec. 1951; children: Jillian Ruth (Cherniak), Catherine Lea (Perlmutter), Joy Elizabeth (MacAdam), Anne Harriet; PRESIDENT, GODFREY ESTATES LTD.; Pres. York Mutual Investments Ltd.; Dir., John Wood Ltd.; Penberthy Inc.; Life Dir., Mt. Sinai Hospital; Jewish Home for the Aged; Dir., Mt. Sinai Inst.; called to Bar of Ont. 1949; cr. Q.C. 1968; former Vice Pres. and Dir. The Toronto Hospital Steam Corp.; recreations: sailing, skiing, tennis; Clubs: Queen's; Island Yacht; Devil's Glen Country (Pres.); Home: 149 Old Forest Hill Rd., Toronto, Ont. M5N 2N7; Office: 401 Bay St., Toronto, Ont. M5H 2Y4

SIMMONS, Albert Harry; executive; b. Toronto, Ont., 6 May 1915; s. George Henry and Margaret Lillian Agnes (Wright) S.; e. Central Tech. Sch., Toronto (Jr. Matric.); Riverdale Coll., Toronto (Sr. Matric.); Univ. of Toronto, (Extension) Structural Design; m. Lois Mary, d. Alexander Reesor, Markham, Ont., 25 Oct. 1941; children: Nancy (Mrs. Anne Mary Gibbons), Robert George, Penelope Jean Lillian; PRESIDENT AND DIR., BRAUN ELECTRIC CANADA LTD. since 1959; commenced in Brokerage and Securities business 1934; Draughtsman, Dominion Bridge Co. Ltd. 1936-41; Dir., Tech. Services, National Film Bd. 1946; Gen. Sales Mgr.-Gen. Mgr., Gevaert (Canada) Ltd. 1952-58; Pres., Braun Electric America 1961-68; served in 2nd World War with R.C.N. as Offr. i.c. Armament Design Sec. 1941; on loan to R.N. as Tech. Liaison Offr. 1943; Staff Offr., Naval C.inC., Germany 1945; retired with rank Lt.-Commdr. SB(E); mem. (Past Pres. and Dir., Charter mem. 1954) Candn. Photographic Trade Assn.; mem. (Active 25 years) Soc. Motion Picture & TV Engrs.; mem. Master Photo Dealers & Finishers Assn.; Prof. Photographers of Am. & Can.; Bd. Trade Metrop. Toronto; Freemason; Conservative; Anglican; recreations: golf, fishing, photography, movie-making; Clubs: Lions'; Home: 9 Parmalea Cres., Weston, Ont. M9R 2X8; Office: 3269 American Dr., Mississauga, Ont. L4V 1B9

SIMMONS, W. Robert, B.A.Sc., P.Eng.; company executive; b. Toronto, Ont., 29 Nov. 1925; s. William Earl and Grace (Ohlman) S.; e. High School and Univ. of Toronto, Ont., B.A.Sc. 1950; m. Catherine, d. William D'Alesandro 3 May 1952; children: Michael, Stephen, Patricia, Catherine; PRESIDENT AND DIR. ALCHEM LIMITED since Oct. 1970; entire career with Alchem Limited; Tech. Rep. 1950-51, Field Rep. S. Ont. 1951-53 Dist. Engr. Montreal 1953-57, Regional Mgr. East Can. 1957-65 Asst. Field Mgr. 1965-66, Mgr. Indust. Services 1966-70, Vice-Pres. April 1970; served with R.C.N.V.R. 1944-45; mem., Candn. Pulp & Paper Assn.; Am. Mang. Assn.; Candn. Mang. Assn.; recreations: golf, fishing, curling; Club: Burlington Golf & Country; Home: 5103 Bromley Rd., Burlington, Ont. L7L 3E4; Office: 1055 Truman Ave., Burlington, Ont. L7R 3V7

SIMMS, Thomas S.; industrialist;.b. Saint John, N.B.; e. Public Schs., Saint John, N.B.; Stony Brook Acad., Long Island, N.Y. (Grad.); CHAIRMAN, T. S. SIMMS & CO. LTD., Brush Mfrs. (Estbd. 1872); joined the present Co. (of which his father was Pres. till death in 1957) in 1937; later moved to Winnipeg Br., returning to Saint John in 1940; el. a Vice-Pres. of the Co. in 1945 and apptd. Gen. Mgr. in 1947; Pres. 1957; served in 2nd World War for four years with R.C.N.V.R.; Home: 5 Dunedin Rd., East Riverside, St. John, N.B. E2H 1P4; Office: (P.O. Box 820) Saint John, N.B. E2L 4C5

SIMONEAU, Léopold, O.C. (1971), B. ès. A., D.Mus.; singer; educator; b. Quebec, Que., 3 May 1918; s. Joseph and Olivine (Boucher) S.; e. Coll. de Levis, B. ès L.; Laval Univ., B. ès. A.; Columbia Univ., Opera Sch. and Opera Work Shop; Univ. d'Ottawa, D.Mus. 1969; m. Pierrette, d. Sylva Alarie, 1 June 1946; two d., Isabell, Chantal; Teacher, San Francisco Conservatory of Music since 1972; leading singer of Metropolitan Opera; Paris Opera; Opera Comique; La Scala, Milan; Staatsoper, Vienna; Chicago Lyric Opera; guest artist with orchestras of world's capitals; sometime Artistic Dir., Que. Opera; recordings for Columbia, Victor, London, Angel, Deutsche Grammophon, Westminster; rec'd Centennial Medal; Dr. Mus., Laval 1973; Roman Catholic; recreation: golf; Office: Conservatory of Music, San Francisco, Cal. 94122

SIMPSON, C. Norman, B.Sc., LL.D., F.A.S.C.E., P.Eng.; engineering consultant; b. Port Arthur, Ont., 29 Dec. 1917; s. C.N. and Christina (Stocks) S.; e. Public and High Schs., Port Arthur, Ont.; Queen's Univ., B.Sc. Hon Engn. 1940 (Civil Engn. Medal), LL.D. 1970; Post-grad. studies in Hydraulics and Sanitary Engn. (1941); children: Charles, Sarah, Mark; CHRMN. BD., C. NORMAN SIMPSON CONSULTANTS LTD.; Dir., ATCO Industries Ltd.; Chancellor, N.S. Tech. Coll. since 1971; began with Saguenay Power Co., Arvida, Que., 1940, then joined H. G. Acres & Co. Ltd., Niagara Falls, Ont., as Asst. Engr. on numerous projects, 1941-52; Hydraulic Engr., 1952-57, Chief Engr., Hydraulics Div., 1957-59, Vice-Pres. and Gen. Mgr., Engineering, 1959, Extve. Vice-Pres., 1961, Pres., 1962-71; Fellow, Am. Soc. Civil Engrs.; Dir., Candn. Extve. Service Overseas; mem. C.D. Howe Research Inst.; Engn. Inst. Can.; Assn. Prof. Engrs. Ont.; Internat. Assn. for Hydraulic Research; Candn. Assn. Consulting Engrs. Can.; Clubs: Niagara Falls (Canada) Inc.; Empire; Office: 2310 Bellevue Ave., West Vancouver, B.C. V7V 1C8

SIMPSON, Douglas Gordon, C.A.; company executive; b. Glasgow, Scotland, 3 May 1910; s. Fred Gordon and Minnie (Addie) S.; e. Glasgow High Sch. (1918-27), Glasgow Univ., 1929-32; Inst. of Accts. & Actuaries in Glasgow; C.A., Jan. 1933; m. late Annette Harrison, d. H.A. Kidd, Glasgow, Scotland, 28 Nov. 1936; children: Gordon Douglas, Aline Anderson; EXTVE. VICE PRESIDENT, FINANCIAL EXTVES. INST. CANADA, since 1973; Dir., Mid-Canada Development Foundation Inc.; Willson Associates Ltd.; C.A. Apprentice with McFarlane, Hutton and Patrick, Glasgow, Scotland, 1927-32; Accountant to J. Spencer Muirhead, LL.B., Glasgow, 1932-34; with Brown and Company Limited, Engineers and Merchants, Colombo, Ceylon, 1934-47 (Chief Acct., 1934-36; Secretary, 1936-47; Dir., 1946-47); Secy., DeHavilland Propellors Ltd., Bolton, Lancs., Eng.; 1947-52; Financial Dir., DeHavilland Aircraft of Can. Ltd., Toronto, Ont., 1952-54; apptd. Controller and Asst. Treas., TransCanada PipeLines 1954; Mgr. Adm., Northwest Project Group, 1971-73; served in 2nd World War with R.N.V.R. at sea; discharged in Dec. 1945 with rank of Lieut.-Commdr. (in Command); mem., Chart. Accts. of Scotland; Inst. of Chart. Accts. Alta.; Financial Executives Inst.; United Church; recreations: curling, sailing, observing people; Clubs: Granite; Glencoe; Home: Apt. 733, 4000 Yonge St., Toronto, Ont. M4N 2N9; Office: 141 Adelaide St. W., Toronto, Ont. M5H 3L5

SIMPSON, Horace Birch; executive; b. Kelowna, B.C. 17 March 1917; s. Stanley M. and Bertha E. (Birch) S.; e. Kelowna Pub. Schs.; City Park Coll. Inst. Saskatoon; m. Joan K. d. John M. Jennens 17 Nov. 1937; children: Sharron J. Kernaghan, Alan G., G. Stanley; VICE PRES. OKANAGAN HOLDINGS LTD.; Dir. British Columbia Telephone Co.; Inland Natural Gas; Brenda Mines Ltd.; Central Okanagan Foundation (1967-75); Anglican; recreations: golf, fishing; Clubs: Gyro; Kelowna; Home: 4348 Hobson Rd., Kelowna, B.C. V1W 1Y3; Office: 217-1890 Cooper Rd., Kelowna, B.C. V1Y 8B7

SIMPSON, Brig. Gen. James McGarry, C.D., Q.C., LL.M.IDC; b. Winnipeg, Man., 1 Feb. 1923; s. Charles and Margaret (McGarry) S.; e. Norberry Sch. and Glen-

lawn Coll. St. Vital, Man. 1940; Univ. of Man. Arts 1945-47, LL.B. 1951; Harvard Law Sch. LL.M. 1959; Imp. Defence Coll. Idc.1964; m. Shirley A. d. late Nelson Kingsmill, 27 July 1946; children: Paula Anne, Timothy James; SR: LEGAL OFFICER, UNITED NATIONS, since 1976; read law with E. H. Crawford, Q.C. Winnipeg; called to Bar of Man. 1951; cr. Q.C. (fed.) 1971; served with Candn. Army 1940-42 and RCAF (Aircrew Navig.) 1942-45, Europe; rejoined Candn. Armed Forces 1951, Legal Adviser to Candn. Air Div. France and Germany 1953-56 and to first Candn. Contingent to UN Peacekeeping Forces in Middle E. 1956, Dir. of Personnel Adm. (Legal) RCAF Ottawa 1960-61, Asst. Judge Advocate Gen. H.Q. Central Command Oakville 1961-63, Head of Internat. Law Sec. Office of Judge Advocate Gen. Ottawa 1965-68 and Sr. Legal Adviser 1968-69, Depy. Judge Advocate Gen. (Adv.) 1969-72; Judge Adv. Gen. of Candn. Forces 1972-76; mem. Candn. Bar Assn.; Candn. Br. Internat. Law Assn.; Candn. Council on Internat. Law; Man. Law Soc.; Univ. Man. Alumni Assn.; Harvard Law Sch. Alumni; Candn. Forces Staff Coll. Assn.; Ont. Humane Soc., R. Catholic; recreations: golf, swimming, bridge; Clubs: Federal Lawyers (Past Pres.); Harvard (Toronto); Hylands Golf; Home: 9 Doris Dr., Scarsdale, N.Y. 10853 Office: 3440B United Nations, N.Y. 10017

SIMPSON, Jeffrey Carl, B.A., M.Sc.; journalist; b. New York City, N.Y. 17 Feb. 1949; s. Robert Lawrence and Eve Cloud (Matheson) S.; came to Can. 1959; e. Univ. of Toronto Schs. 1967; Queen's Univ. B.A. 1971; London Sch. of Econ. M.Sc. (Internat. Relations) 1972; m. Wendy Elizabeth d. William Everest Bryans, Dundas, Ont. 15 June 1974; one s. Tait Bryans; EUROPEAN CORRESPONDENT, THE GLOBE AND MAIL 1981- ; Parlty . Internship H. of C. Ottawa 1972-73; joined The Globe and Mail 1973; Ottawa Bureau Chief 1979-81; mem. Adv. Council Intergovernmental Affairs Queen's Univ.; author "Discipline of Power: The Conservative Interlude and the Liberal Restoration" 1981 (recipient Gov. Gen.'s Award Non-Fiction 1981); contrib. "Saturday Night"; Anglican; recreations: skiing, tennis, music, reading; Home: 10 Wilbraham Pl., Flat 6, London S.W. 1, Eng.; Office: 164-167 Temple Chambers, Temple Ave., London E.C. 4, Eng.

SIMPSON, Leo James Pascal; writer; exemplary person; b. Limerick, Ireland, 1934; s. Gerald Fitzgerald and Anne (Egan); e. Clongowes Wood College (Winner of Titus Oates Memorial Scholarship), M.A. (Hons.) Pooka McPhellimey Academy, 1954, two years post-grad studies, Acme Correspondence (Ohio), completing epic thesis: "Influences of the *Heimskringla Saga* of Snorri on the lyric poetry of Isabella Valancey Crawford," described by thesis supvr. as "exquisitely pointless"; m. Jacqueline Anne, d. of Jack Murphy, Belleville, 1964; children: one d. Julie, Anne; played viola in Plovdiv Dazduv Quartetz, an emigré Bulgarian string ensemble based in Rome, 1957-58; deported to London, 1959, on suspicion of involvement in Hibbs-Düsskotop plot to "fix" Papal elections of 1958; Foreign Correspondent and Fashion Editor, Putney T&B News, 1960; entered Canada illegally, 1961; Shepherd, Halton Hills, 1961-62; Publicity Dir. and Ed., Macmillan of Canada, 1962-66 (resigned to write full-time); Publications: "Mr. Tiddly and the Big Red Choo-Choo," a brave attempt to match the discipline of the Spenserian stanza (i.e. eight five-foot iambic lines followed by an iambic line of six feet, with a crazy rhyming scheme) to meet requirements of juvenile book market, ages 7-9; "Arkwright" (novel) 1971; "Peacock Papers" (novel) 1973; "The Lady and the Travelling Salesman" (Short stories) 1976; "Kowalski's Last Chance" (novel) 1980; Writer-in-Residence, Univ. of Ottawa, 1973; Univ. of Western Ontario, 1978; mem. Writers' Union; Clubs: Ballynantybeg, Pitch and Toss; Cement (Granite Rejects), Toronto; Residence: Livingstone Street, Madoc, Ont.

SIMPSON, Melvin Oren, Jr., B.Eng.; company president; b. Los Angeles, Cal., 21 Dec. 1926; s. Melvin Oren and Gladys (Star) S.; e. West Hill High Sch., Montreal, Que.; Mass. Inst. of Tech.; McGill Univ., B.Eng.; m. Dorothy Christine, d. late Madison Melville Walter, Montreal, Que., 14 Oct. 1950; five s. Scott Walter, Mark Oren, Madison Melvin, Thomas Jeffrey, David Carl; PRES. AND CHRMN., COMPRO LTD. (formerly Turnbull Elevator Ltd.), and following operating divs.; Hamilton Gear and Machine Co., Eastern Steel Products Ltd., Frink of Canada, since 1967; Dir. Frink Sno-Plows, Inc.; joined Compro Ltd. 1951; Asst. Gen. Mgr., Stuart Bros. Co. Ltd., Montreal, 1951-52; Asst. to Vice-Pres. and Gen. Mgr., Gutta Percha, Toronto, Ont., 1952-54; Extve. Vice-Pres., 1955, Pres. 1957 Chrmn. 1959; Pres., Turnbull Elevator Ltd., 1959-66; Chrmn., Dover Corp. (Canada) Ltd., 1966; served during 2nd World War in U.S.A. Inf., 1945; Corps of Engrs., 1946; Chrmn., Indust. Campaign at time of inauguration of Red Cross Blood Donor Service, 1958; Chrmn., Metrop. Toronto United Appeal Campaign, 1959; Protestant; recreations: golf, skiing, fishing, shooting, boating, flying, photography; Club: York; Office: 365 Evans Ave., Suite 404, Toronto, Ont. M8V 1A5

SIMPSON, Norman MacDougall, Q.C., B.A.; b. Vancouver, B.C., 25 July 1917; s. James Inglis and Jean Kinloch (MacDougall) S.; e. Westmount (Que.) High Sch., Upper Can. Coll., Toronto, grad. 1936; Trinity Coll., Univ. of Toronto, B.A., 1940; Osgoode Hall Law Sch., Toronto; m. Margaret B., d. R. B. Johnston, Q.C. of St. Catharines, Oct. 1948; children: Sandra Jean, James Norman, Elizabeth Margaret, Corey Isobel; PARTNER, BLAKE, CASSELS & GRAYDON; Dir., Marathon Corp. Canada Ltd.; Butterick Canada Ltd.; Rosenthal China (Can.) Ltd.; Cliffs of Canada Ltd.; American Can Canada Inc.; Masoneilan of Canada Ltd.; Standco Can. Ltd.; Transmetro Properties Ltd.; read law with present firm; called to Bar of Ont. 1947; cr. Q.C. 1966; with Imp. Chem. Industries, U.K., 1947-48; Candn. Industries Ltd., 1949-50; rejoined present firm 1951; served in R.C.N., 1941-45; C.O. Corvette H.M.C.S. "Petrolia"; now Lieut. Commdr. (Ret'd.); Councillor, Village of Forest Hill, 1961-64; Chrmn., Extve. Comte. Univ. of Trinity Coll. 1973-75; Dir., Care Canada; Care International; Toronto Trust Cemeteries; The Rotary Foundation (Can.); Past Pres., Naval Offrs. Assns. of Can. (Silver Medal 1970); Centennial Medal 1967; Queen's Jubilee Medal 1977; Alpha Delta Phi; P. Conservative; United Church; recreation: farming; Clubs: National; Granite; Rotary (Pres. 1966-67 Foundation Pres. 1975-); Home: R.R.1, Alliston, Ont. O0M 1A0; Office: Suite 2500, Commerce Court W., Toronto, Ont. M5L 1A9

SIMPSON, William, B.A., F.S.A.; actuary; b. Birch Grove, Cape Breton, N.S., 4 Apl. 1913; s. Robert Alexander and Annabella (Wallace) S.; e. Birch Grove, N.S.; Cumberland Co. Acad., Amherst, N.S.; Mount Allison Univ., B.A. 1930; m. Myrtle Irene, d. late Edward Albert Kosmack, 2 Oct. 1936; children: William Harvey, Margaret S. Winkler, Robina E; joined Sun Life Assurance Co. of Canada as Actuarial Clk., 1930-36; Sec. Head, Profits and Math. Depts., 1937-42; joined Acacia Mutual Life Ins. Co. as Actuarial Asst., 1942-46; Asst. Actuary 1946-50; Assoc. Actuary 1950-56; 2nd Vice Pres. and Assoc. Actuary 1956-61; Vice Pres. and Actuary 1961-74; Sr. Vice Pres. 1974; ret. as Sr. Vice Pres. and Chief Actuary 1978; has served also as Head, Actuarial Dept.; Chrmn., Ins. Devel. Comte., Fed. Income Taxation Group and Mil. Business Subcomte.; Fellow, Actuarial Soc. Am.; Am. Inst. Actuaries; Charter mem., Acad. Actuaries; mem., Life Office Mang. Assn. (Vice Chrmn. Cost Comte. 1954, Chrmn. 1955); Aviation Comte., Soc. Actuaries, 1952-68; Middle Atlantic Actuarial Club; Protestant; Home: 9205 Muskogee Place, Adelphi, Md. 20783; Office: 51 Louisiana Ave., Washington, D.C. 20001

SIMS, Peter Harvey, Q.C.; lawyer; b. Kitchener, 20 Feb. 1933; s. James Kenneth, Q.C. and Mabel A. (Cameron) S.; e. Public Sch., Kitchener, Ont.; Ridley Coll., St. Catharines, Ont.; McGill Univ. 1955; Exchange Student, Univ. of British Columbia 1954; Osgoode Hall Law Sch., Toronto, Ont.; m. Elizabeth, d. Marshall Byers, 22 June 1957; children: Harvey James, Kenneth Marshall, Ellen, Margaret Roos, Alison Cameron; PARTNER, SIMS, McKINNON; Chrmn. and Dir., Chicopee Manufacturing Ltd.; Vice Pres. and Dir., Chicopee Securities Ltd.; Sims Investments Ltd.; Dir., Economical Mutual Insurance Co.; The Missisquoi & Rouville Insurance Co.; Perth Insurance Co.; Waterloo Insurance Co.; called to the Bar of Ont., 1959; mem., Waterloo Co., Bar Assn.; Candn. Bar Assn.; Presbyterian; Liberal; Club: Rotary; Home: 130 Aberdeen Road, Kitchener, Ont. N2M 2Y7; Office: 22 Frederick St., Kitchener, Ont. N2H 6M6

SINCLAIR, Mrs. D. B. (Adelaide), O.C. (1967), O.B.E. (1945), M.A., LL.D., D.Sc.Soc., L.H.D.; b. Toronto, Ont., 16 Jan. 1900; d. Overton F. and Adelaide (Sullivan) Macdonald; e. Havergal Coll., Toronto, Ont., Univ. Coll., Univ. of Toronto, B.A. 1922, M.A. 1925, LL.D. Toronto 1946, Carleton 1967, B.C. 1968; London Sch. of Econ., 1926-27; Univ. of Berlin (Summer Sch.), 1929; Laval Univ., D.Sc.Soc., 1952; Univ. of Rochester, L.H.D. 1956; m. 7 June 1930; former mem. Bd. of Govs., Havergal Coll., Toronto, Ont.; Chrmn. Adam Comte., U.N. Assn. in Can.; mem. of Bd., Candn. Stratford Shakespearean Festival, 1954-55; Lectr. in Econ. and Pol. Science, Univ. of Toronto, 1927-30; Economist, W.P.T.B., Ottawa, 1942; served in 2nd World War as Dir., Women's Roy. Candn. Naval Service, 1943-46, retiring with rank of Capt.; awarded O.B.E. (Mil.); Extve. Asst. to Depy. Min. of Nat. Welfare, Ottawa, Ont., 1946-57; Depy. Extve. Dir., UNICEF 1957-67; sometime Secy., Infants' Homes and York Co. Children's Aid Soc. and Vice-Chrmn., Toronto Welfare Council; Candn. Rep. to U.N. Internat. Children's Emergency Fund (Chrmn. of Programme Comte. 1948-50; Chrmn. of Extve. Bd., 1951 and 1952); mem. Council, Rockliffe Park Village, 1969-74; Chrmn. of Planning Bd., 1975-77; mem., Candn. Conf. on Social Work (Pres. 1952; mem. of Bd. 1954); Alternate Del., Candn. del. to the 9th Gen. Assembly of U.N.; mem. of Candn. del. to UNESCO 1947; Kappa Alpha Theta (Internat. Pres. 1938-42); Anglican; Clubs: Toronto Ladies'; Home: 185 Lakeway Drive, Ottawa, Ont. K1L 5A9

SINCLAIR, Donald Bellamy, D.Sc.; ret. executive; b. Winnipeg, Man., 23 May 1910; s. Coll Claude and Edith Almira (Bellamy) S.; e. Univ. of Man., 1926-29; Mass. Inst. of Technol., B.S. 1931, M.S. 1932, D.Sc. 1935; m. Willona Grace Henderson, 11 July 1932; children: Douglas Coll, Robert Allan, Donald Fraser, Heather Grace; Dir., Liberty Mutual Insurance Co.; Liberty Mutual Fire Ins. Co.; Research Assoc. Mass. Inst. of Technol., 1932-35; Research Assoc. 1935-36; joined General Radio Co. as Engr., 1936-44; Asst. Chief Engr. 1944-50; Chief Engr. 1950-60; Vice President 1954-60, Executive Vice President and Technical Director 1960-63; President 1963-73; Chrmn. 1973-74 Director 1955-74; Technical Rep. U.S. Army Air Force, 1943; Civilian with Office of Scient. Research and Devel., 1944; mem. Div. 5, Nat. Defence Research Council, 1943-45; Consultant, Dept. of Defence, 1954-57 and 1960-61; rec'd. Presidential Cert. of Merit 1948; mem. Corp., Wentworth Inst.; mem. Bd. of Overseers, Boston Symphony Orchestra; Fellow, Inst. Elect. & Electronic Engrs.; Am. Assn. Advanc. Science; mem., Acad. Applied Science; Am. Phys. Soc.; Nat. Acad. Engineering; Sigma Xi; Eta Kappa Nu; Club: St. Boltoph; Home: 250 Beacon St., Boston, Mass. 02116 (Nov.-Apr.); RR3, Port Carling, Ont. P0B 1J0, (May.-Oct.);

SINCLAIR, Douglas Grant; executive; b. Toronto, Ont., 10 April 1921; s. George and Margaret Vance (Thompson) S.; e. Withrow Ave. Pub. Sch., Toronto; Upper Can. Coll., 1941; m. Elizabeth Alice, d. H. S. S. R. Bond, 24 June 1944; children: Michael Douglas, Carol Elizabeth, John David; PRES: AND GEN. MGR., SOMCO STEEL TUBE LTD., a subsidiary of Jannock Ltd.; joined Ed. R.

Lewis Leather Co. Ltd., Toronto, as Jr. Salesman, 1945; with Midland Footwear 1949-51; Sterling Industries; 1951-56; joined Rubbermaid (Canada) Ltd. as Asst. Sales Mgr. 1956, Sales Mgr. 1957, Vice-Pres., Sales, 1959, Pres., Gen. Mgr. and Dir. 1961; Extve. Vice Pres. (Ont.), The Jannock Corp. 1973; served with Candn. Armoured Corps 1941-45; Dir., Rubber Assn. Can.; Ont. Council, Soc. of Plastic Industry; Freemason; Conservative; Anglican; recreations: golf, curling; Clubs: Granite; Rosedale; Home: 100 St. Leonard's Ave., Toronto, Ont. M4N 1K5

SINCLAIR, Eldon M., B.A.Sc.; advertising executive; b. Toronto, Ont., 13 March 1928; s. Charles Eldon and Margaret (McCuaig) S.; e. Upper Canada Coll., Toronto, Ont. (1939-42); Trinity Coll. Sch., Port Hope, Ont. (1942-46); Univ. of Toronto, B.A.Sc. 1950; m. Judith Ellen, d. A.E. Rule, Lorne Park, Ont., 13 Feb. 1970; children: Brenda Louise, Deborah Somers, Tacye Margaret, Joseph Mc Craig; MAN. PARTNER, MULITCOM MARKETING COMMUNICATIONS LTD. Dir., Multicom, London, Eng.; Gov., Trinity Coll. Sch. ; with Lever Bros. Ltd., Internat. Management Trainee (Can. and Eng.) 1950-52; Brand Advertising Mgr., Lipton products, 1952-54; Account Extve. with Leo Burnett Co. of Can. Ltd., Toronto, Ont., 1954-56; Account Extve. with Leo Burnett Inc., Chicago, 1956, and Brand Supervisor 1957; returned to Toronto as Pres., Dir. and Mgr.; Chrmn. Bd. and Mang. Dir., Leo Burnett Advertising Ltd., London, Eng. 1965; Extve. Vice Pres., Leo Burnett Internat. 1970; Alpha Delta Phi; Anglican; recreation: outdoor sports; Office: 52 Picadilly London, W1V 9AA, Eng.

SINCLAIR, George, D.Sc., Ph.D., F.I.E.E.E., F.E.I.C., F.R.S.C. (1973); F.A.A.A.S.; engineer; b. Hamilton, Ont., 5 Nov. 1912; s. late Elizabeth Gilchrist (MacKenzie) and Charles Thomson S.; e. Public and High Schs., Edmonton, Alta.; Univ. of Alberta, B.Sc. 1933, M.Sc. 1935; Ohio State Univ., Ph.D. (Elect. Engn.) 1946, D.Sc. 1973; m. Helen Marie, d. late Thomas Corscadden, 8 Sept. 1951; three d., Andrea Joan, Valerie June, Dorothy Elizabeth; PRES., LASER FUSION LTD., Toronto; Chrmn., Sinclair Radio Labs. Inc., Tonawanda, N.Y.; Sinclair Radio Laboratories Limited, Concord, Ontario; Chrmn., Almax Industries Ltd. (Lindsay Ont.); Director, Antenna Laboratory, The Ohio State University, Columbus, Ohio, 1942-47 (awarded Certificate of Appreciation by U.S. War & Navy Depts.); mem. of Staff, Dept. of Elect. Engn., Univ. of Toronto, 1947-78; Consulting Engr. for Thompson Products Inc., Cleveland, Ohio, 1949-51; mem., Engn. Inst. Can.; Past Internat. Chrmn. of Comn. V1-3 of Union Radio Scientifique Internat.; Past Chrmn., Candn. Inst. of Radio Engrs. Convention, Toronto (one of the first organizers); Dir., Inst. of Radio Engrs., N.Y., 1960-62; Dir., Inst. Elect. & Electronic Engrs., 1964-66, 1974-75; devel. use of scale models for designing and testing aircraft antennas (the techniques are now used by most aircraft companies on this continent); awarded Guggenheim Fellowship, 1958; Fellow Royal Soc. of Canada; McNaughton Award, Inst. of Electrical & Electronic Engineers; Julian C. Smith Medal, Eng. Inst. of Canada; Gamma Alpha; Sigma Xi; Pi Mu Epsilon; Presbyterian; recreations: gardening, photography; Clubs: Kiwanis (West Toronto); Toronto Cricket, Skating and Curling; Lambton Golf and Country; Home: 25 Medalist Road, Willowdale, Ont. M2P 1Y3

SINCLAIR, George G.; retired advertising executive; b. Toronto, Ont., 14 Feb. 1916; s. George Alexander and Bessie (Eesley) S.; m. Margaret Jane, d. Norman McLeod Allan, 31 Jan. 1942; one s. Ian, two d., Nancy, Catriona; PRES., FORKS OF THE CREDIT ESTATES LTD.; since 1965; began in Editorial Department, Toronto (Ontario) Star, 1937; Adv. Dept., Canadian Johns Mansville, Toronto, 1938; Publicity Mgr., Dionne Quintuplets, Callander, Ont., 1939; Public Relations Writer, MacLaren Advertising Ltd., 1940, Copy Writer in Copy Dept., Jan. 1946, Copy Chief, 1951, Creative Dir. 1954, Vice Pres.

and Dir. of Operations, 1957, Asst. Gen. Mgr., 1959, Gen. Mgr., 1963, Pres., 1964, Chrmn. 1965-78; served in 2nd World War with R.C.A.F., AC2, Pilot Offr., Navigator; Overseas as Flight Lieut. with R.A.F., 1943-45; mem., Bd. of Dirs., C.B.C.; Past Pres., Art Gallery of Ont.; Dir., Council for Business and The Arts in Canada; Liberal; Clubs: Caledon Mountain Trout; Metropolitan (New York); R.A.F. (U.K.); Home: R.R.2, Caledon, Ont. L0N 1C0

SINCLAIR, Gordon (Allan), O.C. (1979), F.R.G.S.; journalist; radio commentator; b. Toronto, Ont., 3 June 1900; m. Gladys Prewett, Mount Forest, Ont., May 1926; children: Gordon, Donald, Jean (died 1943) John; formerly Special Writer, "Daily Star", Toronto, Ont.; began as a bank clk., farm hand, and deck hand; mem., Ed. Staff, Toronto "Daily Star", 1922-43; for some months also mem. of staff, MacLaren Advertising Co. Ltd., Toronto 1936; travelled throughout most of the world on special assignments for Toronto "Star" from 1929; author of "Footloose in India", 1932; "Cannibal Quest", 1933; and "Loose Among Devils", 1935; "Khyber Caravan", 1936; "Achievement", 1944; "Bright Paths to Adventure", 1945; "Signpost to Adventure", 1947; "Will the Real Gordon Sinclair Please Stand Up." 1972; "Will Gordon Sinclair Please Sit Down" 1975; various magazine features; did original Candn. TV Broadcast (experimental) with Jessica Dragonette and Jack Dempsey 1938; originated program "Let's Be Personal", C.F.R.B. Toronto, 1942; became panelist on C.B.C.'s "Front Page Challenge" which in 1966 became longest continuing T.V. program in Can.; made Hon. citizen of North Carolina and 12 other states, for C.F.R.B. broadcast "The Americans", 1973, became gold record U.S. and Can., brought Amer. Red Cross several hundred thousand dollars.; Recreations: bird watching, green house, cribbage; Home: 35 Burnhamthorpe Park Blvd., Islington, Ont. M9A 1H8; Office: 2 St. Clair Ave.W., Toronto, Ont. M4V 1L5

SINCLAIR, Gordon Maxwell, B.S.A.; executive; b. Strathclair, Man., 6 Apl. 1931; s. Samuel Gordon and Christine Mary (McRostie) S.; e. Strathclair elem. and high schs. 1948; Univ. of Man. B.S.A. 1952 (Lt. Gov.'s Gold Medal); Co-op Coll. of Can. various short courses; m. Donnie d. Charles Manson, Melfort, Sask., 27 Sept. 1958; two s. Samuel Charles, John Gordon; DIR., PRES. & CHRMN., THE CO-OPERATORS INS. GROUP since 1978; Vice Pres. and Dir. Co-op Insurance Services; Dir. Western Co-operative Fertilizers Ltd.; joined Strathclair Consumers Co-operative 1953, Dir. 1954, Secy. 1955, Pres. 1962-71; el. Dir. Federated Co-operatives Ltd. 1961, Man. Vice Pres. 1964, Vice Pres. 1971; Pre. 1974-80; Trustee Man. Co-operative Promotion Bd. since 1973; served as Pres. and Dir. Co-operative Union of Man. and on Extve. Co-operative Union of Brandon Univ. UN High Sch. Seminar; Freemason; United Church; recreations: flying, antique autos; Home: 26 Eddy Pl., Saskatoon, Sask. S7K 1A1; Office: 1920 College Ave., Regina, Sask.

SINCLAIR, Ian David, B.A., LL.B., LL.D.; b. Winnipeg, Man., 27 Dec. 1913; s. late John David and Lillian S.; e. Pub. Schs., Winnipeg, Man.; Wesley Coll. there; Univ. of Manitoba, B.A. (Econ.) 1937, LL.D. 1967; Manitoba Law Sch., LL.B. 1941; m. Ruth Beatrice Drennan, 1942; two s. and two d.; CHAIRMAN, CHIEF EXTVE. OFFR. AND DIR., CANADIAN PACIFIC ENTERPRISES LIMITED Chairman and Director, Canadian Pacific Air Lines Ltd.; Vice Pres. and Dir., The Royal Bank of Canada; PanCanadian Petroleum Ltd.; Cominco Ltd.; Dir., Canadian Pacific Limited; Candn. Pacific Securities Ltd.; Union Carbide Corp.; Canadian Fund, Inc.; Canadian Pacific (Bermuda) Ltd.; Canadian Pacific Steamships Ltd.; Pacific Forest Products Ltd.; Marathon Realty Co. Ltd.; Soo Line Railroad Co.; Great Lakes Forest Products Ltd.; Canadian Marconi Co.; Canadian Investment Fund Ltd.; Sun Life Assurance Co.; Union Carbide Canada Ltd.; AMCA Internat. Ltd.; AMCA Internat. Corp.; mem., International

Advisory Committee, The Chase Manhattan Bank; read law with Guy Chappel & Co., Winnipeg, Man., 1937-41; called to Bar of Man., 1941; Lectr. in Torts, Univ. of Man., 1942-43; joined Canadian Pacific Law Dept. as Asst. Solr., Winnipeg, Man., 1942, Solr. Montreal, Que., 1946, Asst. to Gen. Counsel, 1951, Gen. Solr., 1953, Vice President & Gen. Counsel Feb. 1960; Vice President, Law, July 1960, Vice President, Dir. and mem. Extve. Comte., 1961, Pres., 1966, Pres. and Chief Extve. Offr. 1969; mem., Candn. Chamber of Comm.; Chmn. and C.E.O. 1972-81; Montreal Bd. of Trade; The Conference Bd. (New York); Presbyterian; Clubs: Canadian Railway; Rideau (Ottawa); Mount Royal; Office: Ste. 1900, Place du Canada, Montreal, Que. H3B 2N2

SINCLAIR, Hon. James, P.C. (Can.) 1952, B.Sc., B.A., M.A.; company chairman; b. Banff, Scot., 26 May 1908; s. James George and Betsy (Ross) S.; e. Univ. of B.C.; Oxford Univ. (Rhodes Schol. 1928); Princeton Univ.; m. Doris Kathleen, d. T. K. Bernard, Hollyburn, B.C., 2 Nov. 1940; children: Heather Louise, Janet Moira, Rosalind, Margaret, Betsy; Chairman, Lafarge Canada Ltd.; Vice Pres. & Dir., Bank of Montreal; Dir., Alcan Aluminium Ltd.; Canada Cement Lafarge Ltd.; 1st el. H. of C. for Vancouver N., g.e. 1940; re-el. 1945, 1949, '53 and '57; apptd. Parlty. Asst. to Min. of Finance, Jan. 1949; Min. of Fisheries 1952-57; Financial Critic for opposition 1957-58; def. g.e. 1958; Liberal; Home: 4364 Rockridge Rd., W. Vancouver, B.C. V7W 1A7; Office: 1051 Main St., Vancouver, B.C. V6A 2V9

SINCLAIR, Lawrence Roy, C.A.; company executive; b. Glenella, Man. 21 Nov. 1930; s. Gregory Wilbert and Tena (Frieze) S.; e. Elem. and High Sch. Winnipeg 1948; Inst. of Chart. Accts. Man., C.A. 1953; Banff Sch. Advanced Mang. 1962; m. Beryl Joy Needham 11 Sept. 1954; children: Susan Daphne, Lawrence Ross, Warren Scott; EXEC. VICE PRES., CHEMICAL SPECIALTIES GROUP, THE MOLSON COMPANIES LTD.; and Chmn., Diversey Corp., Mississauga, Ont.; Dir., Philadelphia Mfctrs. Mutual Ins. Co.; mem. Inst. of Chart. Accts. Man. and Ont.; Financial Extves. Inst.; Clubs: Mississauga Golf & Country; Ontario; Office: 201 City Centre Dr., Mississauga Ont. L5B 2T4

SINCLAIR, Lister, M.A., LL.D., D.Litt., Litt.D.; actor, author, broadcaster; b. Bombay, India, 9 Jan. 1921; s. W. Shedden (Chem. Engr.) and Lillie A. Sinclair; e. Colet Court and St. Paul's, London, Eng.; Univ. of Brit. Columbia, B.A.; Univ. of Toronto, M.A.; LL.D. Mount Allison 1970, B.C. 1972; D.Litt. Waterloo Lutheran 1970; Litt.D. Memorial 1971; m. Alice Mather, Vancouver, B.C., 24 Dec. 1942; one s.; 2ndly m. Margaret Watchman 2 June 1965; one s.; PRES., CANADIAN CONF. OF THE ARTS Vice President, Program Policy & Development, C.B.C. 1975-80 (formerly Executive Vice President 1972); widely known as author, actor (expert at languages and dialects), critic and mathematician; sometime Lect. in Maths., Univ. of Toronto for three yrs.; resigned to devote himself to freelance work, radio play writing and acting, stage play writing and editorial work; is one of the princ. contribs. to C.B.C. radio drama series and has produced a number of successful scripts for other programs, includ. shortwave broadcasts to Europe, institutional documentaries, also film scripts; taught radio writing at Acad. of Radio Arts, Toronto; engaged on Ways of Mankind for the Ford Foundation stage play "Socrates", produced Jupiter Theatre, Toronto, 1952; commissioned to write documentaries for Ford Foundation, 1953; apptd. to the teaching staff of the Royal Conservatory of Music of Toronto, 1952; played cricket and rugby in sch. days; hobby is collecting musical recordings of which he has more than 2,000; author of "A Play on Words and Other Radio Plays", 1948; Office: Suite 707, 141 Laurier Ave. W., Ottawa, Ont. K1P 5J3

SINCLAIR, Robert W., M.A., M.F.A., R.C.A.; artist; educator; b. Saltcoats, Sask. 9 Feb. 1939; s. Lorne Foster and Verita Florabelle (Kettle) S.; e. Univ. of Man. Sch. of Art B.F.A. 1962; State Univ. of Iowa M.A. 1965, M.F.A. 1967; m. Kathryn Anne d. Rev. Russel K. Vickers, Victoria, B.C. 28 Dec. 1961; m. Katharine A. (Ord), Edmonton, Alta.; children: Shaun Kenyon, Andre Foster, Joel Bertrand; PROF. OF ART, UNIV. OF ALTA. 1965- ; Visiting Artist, Univ. of Iowa 1973, Banff Sch. of Fine Arts 1976; solo exhns.: Univ. of Iowa 1965; Univ. of Alta. 1966, 1969; Banff Sch. of Fine Arts 1966; W. Ill. Univ. 1967; Moorhead State Coll. Minn. 1968; maritimes travel exhn. 1968-69; Aggregation Gallery Toronto 1970, 1972, 1976, 1977, 1978, 1979; 1981 Edmonton Art Gallery 1972-73; 1982 Peter Whyte Art Gallery Banff 1973; The Gallery Stratford, Ont. 1976; Art Gallery of Ont. travel exhn. Dec. 1976-77; Chapman Gallery Red Deer 1977-78, 1980, 1982; Equinox Gallery Vancouver 1978, 1980; rep. in over 50 group exhns. Can., USA, Europe and Japan since 1963; rep. in pub., corporate and private colls. incl. Can. Council Art Bank, Alta. Art Foundation, Prov. Alta. Museum; rep. various bibliogs.; Former Dir. and Founding mem. Parkland Acreage Owners Assn.; mem., Royal Cdn. Acad.; Candn. Soc. Painters in Watercolour; Univs. Art Assn.; rec'd Elizabeth Greenshields Mem. Foundation Grant; Protestant; recreations: archery, cross-country skiing, tai chi; Home: 1-18-RR2, Winter Burn, Alta. T0E 2N0; Office: Edmonton, Alta. T6G 2C9.

SINCLAIR, Selby James, D.F.C., C.A.; industrial executive; b. Toronto, Ont., 25 Sept. 1921; s. James Taylor and Elizabeth (Allen) S.; e. C.A. 1948; m. Aileen Patricia Dogherty, 3 May 1953; children: Ann, Gail, Janet, Jane, Peter, John; CHRMN. OF BD. AND CHIEF EXTVE. OFFR., TOROMONT INDUSTRIES LTD.; Chairman, Lewis Refrigeration Company; Dir., CIMCO Ltd. and subsids. Allen Tank Ltd.; Allen Tank (London) Ltd.; Aero Tech. Mfg., Inc.; served with RCAF Bomber Command during World War II; rank Flying Offr.; mem., Candn. Inst. C.A.'s; United Church; recreations: golf, skiing, fishing; Clubs: St. James's (Montreal); Donalda; Granite; Cambridge; Home: 1 Whitney Ave., Toronto, Ont. M4W 2A7; Office: 65 Villiers St., Toronto, Ont. M5A 3S1

SINCLAIR, William Matthew, C.M.; farmer; b. Salem, Ore. 1 Feb. 1895; s. Rev. Lawrence and May Mary (Clarke) S.; came to Can. 1896; e. privately tutored; m. Bertha d. Joseph Mawhiney, Huntsville, 17 Sept. 1917; two d. Alberta Mary Shearer, Ruth Reta Binks; lifetime farmer; regularly shows his potatoes and seed crop in numerous agric. fairs; one of original exhibitors Toronto Royal Agric. Winter Fair since its inception in 1922; has won many prizes for his potato crops; also judges crop competitions throughout Ont. and is active in local agric. groups; Fire Warden, Huntsville; livestock evaluator; served as Pres. Muskoka Lib. Assn. (Prov.); Parry Sound /Muskoka Lib. Assn. (Fed.); Muskoka Soil Improvement Assn.; Councillor, Chaffey Twp.; Trustee, Chaffey Twp. Sch. Bd.; Chrmn., Huntsville Parks Bd.; instrumental in forming Ravenschiffe Telephone Co. 1912 and served as Dir. 22 yrs., Secy.-Treas. 10 yrs.; rec'd Royal Winter Fair 50 Yrs. Award; Agric. Service Dipl.; served with 1st Central Ont. Regt. World War I; mem. N. Muskoka Agric. Soc. (Bd. mem. since 1922); Liberal; Anglican; recreation: philately; Address: R.R. 1, Huntsville, Ont. P0A 1K0.

SIREK, Anna, M.D., Ph.D.; educator; b. Velke Senkvice, Czechoslovakia 12 Jan. 1921; d. Jan and Anna (Subik) Janek; e. Slovak Univ. of Bratislava M.D. 1946; Univ. of Toronto M. A. 1955, Ph.D. 1960; m. 27 July 1946; children: Ann, Jan, Peter, Terese; PROF. OF PHYSIOL. UNIV. OF TORONTO since 1972 and Dir. Div. Teaching Labs. since 1975; Intern, Detskaklinika, Bratislava 1946-47; Research Fellow in Surg., Kronprinsessan Lovisias Barnsjukhus, Stockholm 1947-50 and Hosp. for Sick Children Toronto

1950-54; Research Assoc. Banting & Best Dept. Med. Research present Univ. 1954-60, Lectr. 1960-63, Asst. Prof. of Physiol. Univ. Toronto 1963-66, Assoc. Prof. 1966-72, Asst. Dir. Div. Teaching Labs. 1969-75 rec'd Starr Medal Univ. of Toronto 1960; Centennial Medal 1966 Hoechst Co. Frankfurt/M, Germany; author numerous publs. on metabolic studies in animals, research in diabetes and exper. surg.; mem. Candn. Fed. Biol. Socs.; Am. Assn. Advanc. Science; Candn. Assn. Univ. Teachers; Fed. Med. Women Can; Internat. Diabetes Fed.; Toronto Diabetes Assn.; Candn. Soc. Endocrinol. & Metabolism; Candn. Diabetes Assn. Clinical & Scientific Section; Societa Italiana Di Diabetologia; Cath. Phys. Guild; R. Catholic; recreations: cooking, gardening, music, needlework; Home: 93 Farnham Ave., Toronto, Ont. M4V 1H6; Office: Medical Sciences Bldg., Toronto, Ont. M5S 1A8.

SIRLUCK, Ernest, M.B.E., M.A., Ph.D., LL.D., D. Litt., F.R.S.C.; educationist; b. Winkler, Man., 25 April 1918; s. Isaac and Rose (Nitikman) S.; e. Univ. of Man., B.A. (Hons.) 1940; Univ. of Toronto, M.A. 1941, Ph.D. 1948; m. Lesley Caroline, d. Wm. Carlton McNaught, Toronto, Ont., 10 Aug. 1942; children: Robert, Katherine; President, Univ. of Manitoba 1970-76; Lect., Univ. of Toronto 1946; Asst. Prof., Univ. of Chicago, 1947, Assoc. Prof., 1953, Prof. 1958; Professor English and Assoc. Dean, Sch. of Grad. Studies, Univ. of Toronto 1962, Dean 1964, Vice-Pres. & Grad. Dean 1968; Visiting Prof. of English (part-time) 1977-79; served overseas in France, Belgium, Holland, Germany with Candn. Army 1942-45; discharged with rank of Major; Guggenheim Fellow 1953-54; Fellow, Am. Council Learned Socs. 1958-59; Churchill Coll. Overseas Fellow (Cambridge Univ.) 1966; Chrmn., Interprov. Comte. for Univ. Rationalization 1971; mem., Bd. Dirs., Ass. of Univs. and Colls. of Can. 1971; author of "Complete Prose Works of John Milton" Vol. II 1959; "Paradise Lost: A Deliberate Epic" 1967; Ed. (with others) "Patterns of Literary Criticism" 1965-74; also articles in many prof. journs. in U.S., Can. and U.K. on Milton, Puritan Revolution, Spenser, Shakespeare, Jonson and univ. adm.; Home: 153 Strathallan Blvd., Toronto, Ont. M5N 1S9

SIROIS, Hon. Allyre Louis, M.B.E., B.A., LL.B.; judge; b. Vonda, Sask., 25 Aug. 1923; s. Paul Emile and Bertha (Pion) S.; e. Vonda, Sask., 1928-36, 1939; St. Anthony's Coll., Edmonton, 1937-1938; Radio Coll. of Can., Toronto, 1940-41; Univ. of Sask., B.A. 1948, LL.B. 1950; m. Madeline Anne Marie Ehman, 14 Sept. 1948; children: Valerie, Richard, Guy, Marianne, Lisa, Norman; JUSTICE, COURT OF QUEEN'S BENCH, SASK., since 1964; read law with Culliton & MacLean, Gravelbourg, Sask.; called to Bar of Sask. 1951; practised law Gravelbourg, Sask., 1951-64; served with Candn. Army 1941-45; on loan to War Office (M15) 1943-44; awarded Croix de Guerre avec Palme; Mem. of the Order of the Br. Empire (Mil.); served as Secy.-Treas. of Lib. organs. in local, prov. and fed. constits.; served on Gravelbourg Town Council, Sch. Bd. (Chrmn. for 10 yrs.), Bd. Trade and parish council; Prov. Pres., Assn. Culturelle Franco-Canadienne 1963-64; won scholarship to U.N. summer 1948; mem., Candn. Bar Assn.; K. of C. (Grand Kt.); Royal Candn. Legion; R. Catholic; recreations: reading, sports; Home: 1638 8th Ave. N., Saskatoon, Sask. SK7 2X9; Office: Court House, Saskatoon, Sask.

SIROIS, Raymond, M.Sc.Com.; public utilities administrator; b. St. Epiphane, Que., 26 Jan. 1927; s. Georges-Emile and Bernadette (Levesque) S.; e. Que. Acad. 1945; Laval Univ. M.Sc.Com. 1948; m. Yolande, d. Télesphore Landry, 27 Nov. 1948; children: Michèle, Renée, Marie-Claude, Jean; PRES., CHIEF EXTVE. OFFR., AND CHRMN., QUEBEC TÉLÉPHONE since 1974; Pres. and Chrmn., Bonaventure and Gaspe Telephone Co., Ltd. (subsidiary) since 1974; Dir., General Trust of Canada; Indust. Life Ins. Co.; Radio Stn. CFLP, Rimouski; Chrmn. of Bd., École de technologie supérieure; Gov., Prov.

Chamber of Comm.; Gov., Professional Corp. of Ch. Adminis. of Que.; Laval Univ. Foundation joined Co. in 1948 as Accountant; Asst. Dir. of Traffic Dept. 1964, Dir. of Traffic 1965, Vice Pres. — Operations 1967; el. a Dir. 1969; Gov., Chart. Adms. of Que.; mem. General Council of Industry Que.; K. of C. Rimouski (4th Degree); Catholic; recreations: golf, fishing, hunting; Club: Bic Golf; Home: 241 Jacob St., Rimouski, Que. G5L 6V3; Office: 6 St. Jean, Rimouski, Que. G5L 7E4

SIROIS, Venceslas, B.A., B.Sc.; retired petroleum executive; b. St. Georges de Beauce, Que., 8 June 1920; s. Horace and Maria (Dionne) S.; e. Coll. Brébeuf, Montreal, 1937; Loyola Coll., B.A. 1939; Queen's Univ., B.Sc. (Chem. Engn.) 1943; m. Nancy, d. late C. H. Dickerson, 1943; one d., Anne Marie; DIRECTOR SR. VICE PRES. & DIRECTOR, IMPERIAL OIL LTD.; (ret. Sept. 1980); joined Imperial Oil as Chem. Engr., Montreal E. Refinery, 1943; Process Supvr., Sarnia Refinery, 1952; Process Supt. Chems., Sarnia, 1956; Mang. Asst., Mfg. Dept., Toronto, 1959; Asst. Mgr., Refining Coordination, Toronto, 1961; Refining Advisor, Refining co-ordination, Standard Oil Co. (N.J.), N.Y., 1964; Mgr., Operations coordination, Mfg. Dept., Toronto, 1965; Asst. Gen. Mgr. Supply Logistics Dept., 1969; Vice Pres. and Gen. Mgr., Logistics Dept. 1971; mem. Assn. Prof. Engrs. Prov. Ont.; currently Dir., Federal Pioneer Ltd.; Partek Lavalin Inc.; Chrmn., Bd. of Adv., Concordia Univ., Sch. of Community & Public Affairs (Montreal); R. Catholic; recreations: golf, reading, Club: Donalda; Home: 54 York Rd., North York, Ont. M2L 1H6; Office: Suite 300, 1235 Bay St., Toronto, Ont. M5R 3K4

SIRRS, Robert Douglas, B.A., B.J.; foreign service officer; b. Toronto, Ont., 18 May 1930; s. Robert Raymond and Consuelo (Spangler) S.; e. Am. High Sch., Buenos Aires, Argentina; Pickering Coll., Newmarket, Ont.; Carleton Univ., B.A., B.J.; m. Mary Margaret, d. Dr. A. B. Lucas, London, Ont., 29 Dec. 1956; children: Laurel Margaret, Reid Douglas, Owen Lucas; AMBASSADOR TO COSTA RICA, PANAMA, NICARAGUA, HONDURAS AND EL SALVADOR; 1979 –; Clk., Maclaren Advertising Co., Ottawa, 1950-53; Area Supvr. (Mexico, Colombia and Caribbean), Canadian Coleman Co., 1954-56; apptd. to Trade Commr. Service, Ottawa, 1956; Asst. Comm. Secy., Caracas, 1957-60; Consul and Trade Commr., New York, Defence Production Sharing Liaison Offr., 1960-64; Comm. Secy., Pakistan also accredited to Afghanistan, 1964-66; Chargé d'Affaires, Guatemala, 1966-68; Consul and Sr. Trade Commr., Chicago, 1968-70; Acting Consul General and Trade Commr. 1970-71; Dir., Regional Marketing & Operations — Trade Commissioner 1971-72; Counsellor, (Comm.), Candn. Embassy, Mexico, 1972-76; Dir. European Bureau, Dept. of Industry, Trade & Comm., 1976-79; mem., Prof. Assn. Foreign Service Offrs.; recreations: sailing, tennis, skiing, camping; Clubs: University; Chicago Yacht; Canadian; Office: Canadian Embassy, Apartado 10303, San Jose, Costa Rica

SISAM, John William Bernard, B.Sc.F., M.F., D.Sc., R.P.F.; b. Springhill, N.S., 22 May 1906; s. Rev. Canon William Bernard and Emma Annie (Ancient) S.; e. Prov. Normal Sch., N.B.; Univ. of New Brunswick, B.Sc. (Forestry) 1931; Yale Univ., M.F. 1937; Univ. of New Brunswick, D.Sc. 1956; m. Betty Stewart Neill, 15 Oct. 1932; two s., Peter Neill and John David; Dean Emeritus, Faculty Forestry, Univ. of Toronto; with Dom. Forest Service on forest research 1931-39; Depy. Dir. and Dir., The Commonwealth Forestry Bur. 1939-45; Chrmn. FAO (United Nations) Adv. Comte. on Forestry Educ. 1966-71; Fellow and Past Pres., Canadian Inst. of Forestry; Past Pres., Ontario Prof. Foresters Assn.; Conserv. Council Ontario; Founding Pres., Ont. Forestry Assn.; Chrmn., World Consultation on Forestry Educ. & Training (F.A.O.) Stockholm 1971; Sigma Xi; Anglican; recreations: gardening, tennis; Home: 6 Garland Ave., Toronto, Ont. M4N 2X7

SISLER, Rebecca Jean, R.C.A.; sculptor; author; association executive; b. Mount Forest, Ont. 16 Oct. 1932; d. Byron Cooper and Mildred (Ramsden) Sisler; e. Anne St. Pub. Sch. and Belleville (Ont.) Coll. Inst. 1947; St. Thomas (Ont.) Coll. Inst. 1951; Ont. Coll. of Art 1951-52 (scholarship winner both yrs.); Royal Danish Acad. Fine Arts 1952-54; EXTVE. DIR., ROYAL CANDN. ACAD. OF ARTS 1978- , el. mem. 1973, mem. Nat. Council 1977-78; rec'd Can. Council Grant 1959 to visit Nubian treasures Upper Egypt; various visits Mayan and Incan sites; sculpture comns. incl. "The Minstrels" Centennial Park St. Thomas, Ont. 1967; large walnut cross and candlesticks St. Paul's Ang. Cath. London, Ont. 1968; rep. in many private colls. across Can.; author "The Girls: A Biography of Frances Loring and Florence Wyle" 1972; "Passionate Spirits: A History of the Royal Canadian Academy of Arts" 1880-1980; various essays, articles; mem. Ont. Soc. Artists; Liberal; recreations: reading, gardening, travel; Home: 455 Garafraxa St. N. (P.O. Box 950) Durham, Ont. N0G 1R0; Office: 11 Yorkville Ave., Suite 601, Toronto, Ont. M4W 1L3.

SISSONS, Gordon H., B.Sc.; company president; b. Medicine Hat, Alberta, 27 Jan. 1920; s. Herbert J. and Lissa R. Sissons; e. Public and High Schs., Medicine Hat, Alta.; Univ. of Alberta, B.Sc. (Mining Engn.) 1942; m. Isabelle D., d. Roy E. Newcombe, Medicine Hat, 28 June 1945; children: Wendy R., Clayton H.; PRESIDENT AND GEN. MGR. I-XL INDUSTRIES LTD. and associated Co's.; with International Nickel Co. of Can. Ltd., 1942-43 ; Consol. Mining & Smelting Co. of Can. Ltd., 1944; joined present interests in 1945; Past Pres., Medicine Hat Chamber Comm.; Freemason (Shrine); Presbyterian; recreations: hunting, golf, fishing, skiing; Club: Kiwanis; Home: 320 First St. S.E., Medicine Hat, Alta. T1A 0A6; Office: (P.O. Box 70) Medicine Hat, Alberta T1A 7E7

SIVERTZ, Bent Gestur, O.B.E., B.A.; b. Victoria, B.C., 11 Aug. 1905; s. Christian and Elinborg (Samuelson) S.; e. Public and High Schs., Victoria, B.C.; Univ. of British Columbia, B.A.; Victoria Normal Sch. (Teachers Cert.); m. Barbara Isabel, d. O. B. Prael, Portland, Oregon, 9 July 1948; Seaman and Ships Offr. in Merchant Marine, 1922-32; taught school in B.C., 1936-39; Foreign Service Offr., Dept. of External Affairs, 1946-50; joined Northern Affairs Dept. in 1950 as Staff Offr. in Depy. Minister's Office; apptd. Chief of Arctic Div., 1954; Dir. of N. Adm. Br., Dept. of N. Affairs, 1957-63; Commr. of N.W.T., 1963-67; served in 2nd World War as Lt. Commdr. with R.C.N., 1939-46; awarded O.B.E.; Freemason; Protestant; recreations: art, travel, outdoors, reading; Clubs: Union (Victoria); Thermopylae (Victoria); Home: Box 28 Seacrest, Dorcas Point Rd., Nanoose Bay, B.C. V0R 2R0

SKELTON, Robin, M.A., F.R.S.L. (1966); university professor; poet; b. Easington, E. Yorks., Eng., 12 Oct., 1925; s. Cyril Frederick William and Eliza (Robins) S.; e. Pocklington Grammar Sch., Eng., 1936-43; Christ's Coll., Cambridge Univ., 1943-44 ; Leeds Univ., B.A. (1st Class Hons., Eng. Lang & Lit.) 1950, M.A. 1951; m. Sylvia Mary, d. P. W. Jarrett, Feb. 1957; children: Nicholas John, Alison Jane, Eleanor Brigid; PROF., DEPT. CREATIVE WRITING, UNIV. VICTORIA, Chrmn. 1973-76; Prof. Dept. English 1966-73; Assistant Lecturer, University of Manchester, 1951-54; Lectr. 1954-63; joined present Univ. as Assoc. Prof. 1963; Dir., Creative Writing Programme, 1967; Visiting Centennial Lectr., Univ. of Mass., 1962-63; taught Summer Sch., Victoria Coll., B.C., 1962; Visiting Prof., Univ. of Mich., summer 1967; Examiner in Eng. Lit. for N. Univs. Matric. Bd., Eng., 1954-60 (Chrmn. of Examiners 1958-60); Dir., The Lotus Press 1950-51 and the Pharos Press since 1972; co-founder, Peterloo Group of Poets and Painters, 1957; founding mem. and 1st Hon. Secy., Manchester Inst. of Contemporary Arts, 1960

(Chrmn. Programme Comte. 1960-62); served with RAF in Eng., Pakistan, India and Ceylon, 1944-47; rank Sgt.; Poetry Critic 1956-57 and Theatre Critic 1958-60, "Manchester Guardian"; has done many broadcasts for BBC, CBC and All India Radio; Art Columnist, "Victoria Daily Times", 1964-66; poetry readings given at various univs. in Eng., U.S. and Can.; other activities incl. film making, collage (one-man show in Victoria 1966, 1968, 1980), libretti (composed words for 2 motets and 1 cantata), typography and book design, poetics; author poetry: "Patmos and Other Poems", 1955; "Third Day Lucky", 1958; "Two Ballads of the Muse", 1960; "The Dark Window", 1962; "Valedictory Poem", 1963; "An Irish Gathering", 1964; "A Ballad of Billy Barker", 1965; "Inscriptions", 1967; "The Hold of Our Hands", 1968; "Selected Poems 1947-67", 1968; "Because of This", 1968; "An Irish Album", 1969; "The Selected Poems of Georges Zuk", 1969; "The Hunting Dark", 1971; "Two Hundred Poems from the Greek Anthology", 1971; "Private Speech", 1971; "A Different Mountain", 1971; "Remembering Synge", 1971; "Timelight", 1974; Vol. 2 Georges Zuk - "The Underwear of the Unicorn", 1975; "Callsigns", 1976; "Because of Love", 1977; "Landmarks", 1979; "Collected Shorter Poems 1947-77", 1981; "Limits", 1981; criticism: "John Ruskin: The Final Years", 1955; "The Poetic Pattern", 1956; "Cavalier Poets", 1960; "Poetry", 1963; "The Practice of Poetry ", 1971; "The Writings of J. M. Synge", 1971; "Poet's Calling" 1975; "Poetic Truth" 1978; "Herbert Siebner: A Monograph" 1979; ed., "The Malahat Review"; "J. M. Synge: Translations", 1961; "J. M. Synge: Four Plays and The Aran Islands", 1962; "J. M. Synge: Collected Works", Vol. 1 Poems, 1962; "David Gascoyne: Collected Poems", 1965; "J. M. Synge: Riders to the Sea", 1969; "David Gascoyne: Collected Verse Translations" (with Allan Clodd) 1971; "Synge/Petrarch", 1971; "The Collected Plays of Jack B. Yeats", 1971; anthols.: "Leeds University Poetry 1949", 1950; "Six Irish Poets", 1962; "Five Poets of the Pacific Northwest", 1964; "Poetry of the Thirties", 1964; "Poetry of the Forties", 1968; "Introductions from an Island", 1969, 1971; "Six Poets of British Columbia", 1980; for schs.: "Viewpoint: An Anthology of Poetry", 1962; "Edward Thomas: Selected Poems", 1962; "Selected Poems of Byron", 1964; occult: "Spellcraft", 1978; biography: "J. M. Synge and His World", 1971; social history: "They Call It The Cariboo", 1980; symposia: "The World of W.B. Yeats" (with A. Saddlemyer); "Irish Renaissance" (with D. R. Clark), 1965; "Herbert Read, A Memorial Symposium", 1970; other writings incl. articles on "Rhyme" and "Poetry" in "Encyclopedia Britannica"; also poetry, articles and reviews in various mags.; mem., Writer's Union Can. (Chmn. 1982-83); P.E.N.; League Candn. Poets; Home: 1255 Victoria Ave., Victoria, B.C. V8S 4P3

SKEOCH, Lawrence Alexander, M.A., Ph.D.; university professor; b. Russell, Manitoba, 23 May 1910; s. James and Regina (Hall) S.; e. McMaster Univ., B.A.; Univ. of Toronto, M.A.; Univ. of Calif. (Berkeley), Ph.D.; m. Ragnhildur, d. Halldor Thorsteinsson, Reykjavik, Iceland, 11 Sept. 1943; PROF. OF ECONOMICS, QUEEN'S UNIV., since 1960 (Assoc. Prof. 1958-60); formerly Lectr. in Econ., Univs. of Manitoba, Toronto and Calif.; Sr. Economist, Candn. Wheat Bd. Combines Br. of Dept. of Justice; Rehab. Specialist and Acting Chief UNRRA Mission to the Ukraine; author (with David C. Smith), "Economic Planning: The Relevance of West European Experience for Canada", 1963; "Restrictive Trade Practices in Canada", 1965; "Mergers, Consolidations and Big Business", 1971 and of numerous articles in prof. journs.; mem., Candn. Pol. Science Assn.; Am. Econ. Assn.; Fellow, Royal Econ Soc.; Presbyterian; recreations: duck-shooting, curling; Home: "Glen Ridge", Glenburnie, Ont. K0H 1S0

SKILLING, H. Gordon, A.T.C.M., M.A., Ph.D., F.R.S.C. (1970); university professor; b. Toronto, Ont., 28

Feb. 1912; s. William Watt and Alice (Stevenson) S.; e. Harbord Coll. Inst., Toronto, Ont.; Univ. Coll., Univ. of Toronto, B.A. (Pol. Science and Econ.) 1934; Rhodes Scholar for Ont. 1934; Christ Church, Oxford Univ., 1934-36, B.A., M.A. (Philos., Pol. and Econ.); Sch. of Slavonic and East European Studies, Univ. of London, Ph.D. (European Hist.) 1936-40; M.A. (Hon.) Dartmouth Coll., 1951; m. Sara Conard, d. Horace Bright, 16 Oct. 1937; two s., David Bright, Peter Conard; PROF. OF POL. SCIENCE, UNIV. OF TORONTO, since 1959; Dir., Centre for Russian and E. European Studies there, 1963-75; with Czechoslovak Broadcasting Corp., 1938; B.B.C., 1939-40; Asst., United Coll., Winnipeg, Man., 1940-41; Asst. Prof. Pol. Science, Univ. of Wisconsin, 1941-47; Dept. of Govt., Dartmouth Coll., 1947-51 and Prof. there 1951-59; Sr. Fellow, Russian Inst., Columbia Univ. (on leave) 1949-51 and Visiting Prof. there 1952-53; Internat. Service, C.B.C., Supervisor of Central European Broadcasts, 1944-45 (on leave); U.N. Commentator, C.B.C., 1946 (on leave); Publications: "Canadian Representation Abroad", 1945; "Communism, National and International", 1964; "The Governments of Communist East Europe", 1966; "The Czech Renascence of the Nineteenth Century: Essays in Honour of Otakar Odlozilik", edited by Peter Brock and H. Gordon Skilling, 1970; "Interest Groups in Soviet Politics", edited by H. Gordon Skilling and Franklyn Griffiths, 1971; "Czechoslovakia's Interrupted Revolution", 1976; "Charter 77 and Human Rights in Czechoslovakia", 1981; mem., Cdn. Assoc. of Slavists; Amer. Assoc. for Advancem. of Slavic Studies; Candn. Inst. Internat. Affairs; recreations: swimming, Home: 90 Cheritan Ave., Toronto, Ont. M4R 1S6

SKINNER, Cyril, B.A.; publisher; b. Beverley, Yorks., Eng., 8 March 1920; s. Herbert and Violet (Davison) S.; e. Owen Sound (Ont.) Coll. Inst., 1939; Toronto Teachers' Coll., 1940; Univ. of Toronto, B.A. (Hons. Hist.) 1948; Ont. Coll. of Educ. 1948; m. Sydney Joyce (Woodhouse), 8 Oct. 1949; two s.: Brian and Colin; PRESIDENT, J. M. DENT & SONS (CANADA) LTD.; served with R.C.A.F., 400 Sqdn., 1940-45; with Book Society of Canada, 1948-50; joined present Co. 1951; Anglican; recreations: golf, curling; Clubs: Bowmanville Golf & Country; York Downs Golf & Country; Home: R.R.#5, Bowmanville, Ont.; Office: 100 Scarsdale Road, Don Mills, Ont. M3B 2R8

SLAIGHT, Brian Wright ; newspaper executive; b. Galt, Ont. 30 March 1934; s. John Edgar and Florence Eileen (Wright) S.; e. Dickson Pub. Sch. Galt, Ont.; King George Pub. Sch. and Central High Sch. Moose Jaw, Sask.; Ryerson Inst. of Technol. (Journalism) Toronto; m. Carol Annabel d. John Stewart Gerald 31 Aug. 1967; EXTVE. VICE PRES. AND DIR. THOMSON NEWSPAPERS LTD. 1981- ; Dir. Today Magazine Inc.; Newspaper Marketing Bureau; mem. Candn. Press; Commonwealth Press Union; Reporter, News Ed., Advertising Salesman various newspapers Thomson Newspapers Ltd. 1953-56, Asst. Retail Advertising Mgr. 1956-58; Asst. Gen. Mgr. Timmins Daily Press 1958-59; Ed. and Publisher The Orangeville Banner 1959-61; Gen. Mgr. The Barrie Examiner 1961-63; Asst. Gen. Mgr. (Can.) Thomson Newspapers Ltd. 1963-68, Gen. Mgr. (Can.) 1969-74, Gen. Mgr. 1975-78, Dir. 1975- , Sr. Vice Pres. and Gen. Mgr. 1979; Home 120 Rosedale Valley Rd., Toronto, Ont. M4W 1P8; Office: 65 Queen St. W., Toronto, Ont. M5H 2M8.

SLAIGHT, (Carol) Annabel; book and magazine editor; b. Toronto, Ont. 11 Sept. 1940; d. John Stewart and Carol Elaine (Thompson) Gerald; e. Forest Hill Elem. Sch. and Deer Park Pub. Sch. Toronto 1950; Point Grey Jr. High Sch. Vancouver 1953; Crofton House Sch. Vancouver 1957; Univ. of B.C. 1957-60; m. Brian Wright Slaight 31 Aug. 1967; FOUNDER, GREEY de PENCIER BOOKS (Div. of Key Publishers Ltd.) 1974, Co-Founder, Co-ed. "Owl" mag. 1976- and "Chickadee" mag. 1979- ; Dir., Key Publishers Ltd.; Chmn., The Children's Book Cen-

tre; Pres., The Young Naturalist Foundation; taught elem. sch. Vancouver, B.C. and London, Eng. 1960-64; staff mem. "Architecture Canada" (Journ. of Royal Arch. Inst. Can.) 1964-68, Ed. 1969-73 and of "Building Development Magazine"; rec'd Eve Orpen Award 1979; Can.'s Outstanding Mag. Award for Ed. and Artistic Excellence, "Owl" Mag. 1979; co-ed. "Exploring Toronto" 1973; Co-ed. "Owl's Winter Fun Book", 1980; mem. Assn. Candn. Publishers; Candn. Periodical Publishers Assn.; Home: 120 Rosedale Valley Rd., Toronto, Ont. M4W 1P8; Office: 59 Front St. E., Toronto, Ont. M5E 1B3.

SLAIGHT, (John) Allan; broadcaster; b. Galt, Ont., 19 July 1931; s. John Edgar and Florence Eileen (Wright) S.; e. Dickson Pub. Sch. and Galt (Ont.) Coll. Inst. 1946; Central High Sch. Moose Jaw, Sask. 1946; Univ. of Sask.; m. Ada Winnifred Mitchell, 11 Feb. 1950; children: John Gary, Gregory Allan, Mrs. Jan Tasker; Pres. Dir. and CEO, Radio IWC Ltd.; Pres. and Dir. CFGM Broadcasting Ltd.; CILQ (Q107); Chrmn. Amer. Subscription TV of California Inc.; news reporter/announcer CHAB Radio Moose Jaw, Sask. 1948; news reporter/ed. Radio CFRN Edmonton, Alta. 1950-52 and CJCA Radio 1952-54; News Dir. CHED Radio Edmonton 1954-56, Nat. Sales Mgr. 1956-58; Program Dir. CHUM AM Toronto 1958, Vice Pres. and Gen. Mgr. CHUM AM and FM 1965-66; Pres. and Gen. Mgr. Stephens & Towndrow Co. Ltd. 1967-69; estbd. Slaight Broadcasting Ltd. 1970, merged with IWC Communications Ltd. 1973; Pres. and CEO Global Communications Ltd. 1974-77; former Dir. Candn. Assn. Broadcasters; Past Chrmn. Assn. Independent Metrop. Stns.; Dir., Toronto United Way; Women's Coll. Hospital; Shaw Festival; Protestant; recreations: tennis, skiing; Clubs: Granite; Craigleith Ski; Toronto Lawn & Tennis; Home: 61 St. Clair Ave. W., Toronto, Ont. M4V 2Y8; Office: Suite 3020, 2 Bloor St. E., Toronto, Ont. M4W 1A8

SLATER, David W., M.A., Ph.D., public servant; b. Winnipeg, Man., 17 Oct. 1921; s. William and Jean Proudfoot (Halcrow) S.; e. Univ. of Man., B.Com. 1942; Queen's Univ., B.A. (Hons. Econ.) 1947; Univ. of Chicago, M.A. 1950, Ph.D. 1957; m. Lillian Margaret, d. George C. Bell, Sarnia, Ont., 3 May 1947; children: Barbara Jane, Gail Patricia, Carolyn Louise, Leslie Anne; CHAIRMAN ECON. COUNCIL OF CAN. 1980- ; Instr., in Econ., Queen's Univ., 1946-48; Stanford Univ., 1950-52; Asst. Prof., Queen's 1952-57; Assoc. Prof. 1957-61; Prof. 1961-70; Dean, Sch. of Grad. Studies 1968-70; Pres., York Univ. 1970-73; Dir. and Gen. Dir., Dept. of Finance, Can. 1973-78; Dir., Econ. Council of Can., 1978- ; mem., Research Staff, Royal Commission on Canada's Econ. Prospects, 1955-56; Committee on University Affairs, Prov. of Ont.; served with Candn. Army in N.W. Europe, 1942-45; Mentioned in Despatches; author of "International Trade and Economic Growth." 1968 and special studies for Royal Comn. on Can.'s Econ. Prospects, Candn. Trade Comte. and Econ. Council of Can.; some-time mem. of Extve., Candn. Assn. Univ. Teachers and Social Science Research Council of Can.; some-time mem. CANADA Council, Dir. of Bank of Can., Dir. of Ind. Dev. Bank; Past Pres., Queen's Univ. Faculty Assn.; mem., Candn. Econ. Assn.; Am. Econ. Assn.; United Church; recreations: tennis, squash, golf, skiing; Home: 199 Crocus Ave., Ottawa, Ont. K1H 6E7; Office: 333 River Rd, Ottawa, Ont. J1O 5V6

SLATTERY, Timothy Patrick, M.B.E., Q.C., B.A., B.C.L.; lawyer; author; b. Westmount, Que., 4 Feb. 1911; s. late Timothy Francis and late Rosanna (Lonergan) S.; e. St. Leo's Sch. and Loyola High Sch., Montreal; Loyola Coll., B.A. 1931; McGill Univ., B.C.L. 1934; Univ. of Paris, grad. work in Law 1935; m. Patricia, d. Peter O'Brien, 15 Nov. 1939; children: Mrs. John Durley (Maureen), Brian, Mrs. Barry Hallen (Patricia); SR. PARTNER, SLATTERY, McQUILLAN, & LAFLEUR; read law with H. J. Trihey, Q.C.; called to Bar of Que. 1934; cr. K.C. 1949; Secy. and Solr., Wartime Shipbuilding Ltd. (Crown

Co.); mem. Adv. Bd., Concordia Univ.; former Treas., Bar of Montreal; author "Loyola and Montreal", 1962; "The Assassination of D'Arcy McGee", 1968; "They Got to Find Mee Guilty Yet", 1972; nominee Gov.-Gen.'s Award in Lit., 1968; Edgar Allan Poe Special Award, 1973; Liberal; R. Catholic; recreations: golf, painting, writing; Clubs: Royal Montreal Golf; Montreal Bd. Trade; Home: 4501 Sherbrooke W., Apt. 2E, Westmount, Que. H3Z 1E7; Office: 360 St. James St. W., Montreal, Que. H2Y 1P5

SLEMON, Air Marshal C. Roy, C.B., C.B.E., C.D., B.Sc., LL.D., D.Sc.; b. Winnipeg, Man. 1904; e. Univ. of Man., B.Sc. 1928; Comnd. Lt. in Candn. Offrs. Training Corps. 1922, entering Candn. Air Force 1923; many years exploratory flying in Arctic and Sub-Arctic; R.A.F. Staff Coll., U.K. 1938; involved in coastal operation 1939-41 where rose to command R.C.A.F. on Pacific Coast; subsequently Depy. Commdr. No. 6 Candn. Heavy Bomber Group in U.K and Commdr. for short time before rising to Depy. Air Offr. C. in R. C.A.F. Overseas 1945 with rank of Air Vice-Marshal; after War was mem. Air Council for 4 years and A.O.C. Training Command for 3 years; promoted Air Marshal 1953, Chief of Air Staff 1953-57; Depy. C.inC., N. Am. Air Defence Command (NORAD) 1957-64; retired from R.C.A.F. Aug. 1964; Exec. Vice-Pres., U.S. Air Force Acad. Fdn. Inc. 1964-80; Home: 8 Thayer Rd., Colorado Springs, Colo., U.S.A. 80906

SLEMON, Gordon R., M.A.Sc., Ph.D., D.Sc.; electrical engineer; university professor and dean; b. Bowmanville, Ontario, 15 August 1924; s. Milton Everett and Selena Ethleen (Johns) S.; e. Univ. of Toronto, B.A.Sc. (Elect. Engn.) 1946, M.A.Sc. (Elect. Engn.) 1948; Univ. of London, D.I.C., Ph.D. 1952, D.Sc. 1967; m. Margaret Jean, d. late Rev. Dr. A. Dawson Matheson, 9 July 1949; children: Sally, Stephen, Mark, Jane; Dean, Fac. of Applied Sc. and Engin, Univ. of Toronto since 1979; Chrmn. of Bd., Univ. of Toronto Innovations Foundation, 1980- ; Pres., Elect. Engn. Consociates 1976-79; Head, Dept. of Elect. Engn., Univ. of Toronto 1966-76; Prof. since 1964; Instr. (part-time), Univ. of Toronto, 1946-49; Assoc. Prof. 1955-63; Planning Engr. (part-time), Ont. Hydro, 1946-49; Lectr., Imperial Coll. of Science and Tech., London, Eng., 1949-53; Asst. Prof., N.S. Tech. Coll., Halifax, 1953-55; Tech. Advisor, Candn. Colombo Plan Mangalore, India, to establish new engn. coll. 1963-64; Consultant to various U.S. and Candn. co's. on energy conversion problems, since 1955; rec'd. Western Electric Award, 1965; co-author, "Scientific Basis of Electrical Engineering ", 1961; "Electric Machinery', 1979; author, "Magnetoelectric Devices", 1966; over 100 tech. papers for various learned journs.; Fellow, Inst. Elect. Engrs. (U.K.); Inst. Elect. & Electronic Engrs.; Engn. Inst. of Can.; mem., Am. Soc. for Engn. Educ.; Assn. Prof. Engrs. Ont.; Conf. Internat. des Grands Réseaux Electriques ; United Church; Home: 40 Chatfield Dr., Don Mills, Ont. M3B 1K5

SLOAN, Douglas A., B.Sc., P.Eng.; management consultant; b. Toronto, Ont., 26 June 1920; s. Albert E. and Hazel A. (Townsend) S.; e. Carleton Coll., 1944-45; Queen's Univ., B.Sc. 1949; Urwick Mang. Centre (UK), 1956; m. E. Louise, d. late George B. Thomson, Sept. 1948; children: David A. G., Dianne J.; PARTNER AND DIR., CURRIE, COOPERS & LYBRAND since 1956; also Dir., Mining Services Mang. Partner — Internat. and consultant there; Professor, Univ. of Toronto; Dir., Personnel Appraisal Centre Ltd.; Coopers & Lybrand Assoc. Ltd.; CANAM Rural Services Ltd.; Acct., Canadian Pacific Export Co., 1935-41; Engr., Buffalo Ankerite Mines Ltd., 1947; Metall. Concentrator, Noranda Mines, Ltd., 1948; Engr. Supvr., McIntyre Porcupine Mines Ltd., 1949-50; Supvr., Mang., Falconbridge (Hardy Mine, Falconbridge Mine, Boundary Mine) Mines Ltd., 1950-56; served with Royal Candn. Corps of Signals (Reserve) 1935-39; Kent Regt. (Reserve) 1939; RCAF 1941-45 (Acct. AFHQ); Dir., Candn. Opera Co. (Past Pres.); mem. Adv. Comte., Cambrian Coll.;

mem. Educ. Comte., CIMM; Dir., Candn. Min. & Met. Found.; Fellow, Inst. Mang. Consultants (Pres. Ont 1969; Pres. Can. 1970); mem., Assn. Prof. Engrs. Ont.; Soc. of Mang. Accts.; Brit. Inst. Mang.; Candn. Inst. Mining; Am. Inst. Mining Engrs.; Queen's Jubilee Medal; Citizenship Award of Assoc. P. Eng. Ont., 1979; recreations: skiing, equestrian, scuba, Taekwon Do; Clubs: Eglinton Hunt; Bethany Hills Hunt; Master of Fox Hounds; E. Galway Hunt (Ireland); Bermingham & N. Galway Hunt (Ireland); Faculty; National; Granite; Home: 105 Old Forest Hill Rd., Toronto, Ont. M5P 2R8; Office: 145 King St. W., Toronto, Ont. M5H 1J8

SLOANE, Richard Douglas, B.Sc.; telecommunications executive; b. Stratford, Ont. 6 July 1930; e. Queen's University B.Sc. (Civil Engn.) 1953; VICE PRES. (OPERATIONS PERFORMANCE), BELL CANADA since 1980 joined Bell Canada, Hamilton 1953 holding various line and staff mang. positions Chatham, Toronto, Kitchener and Montreal 1957-62; Staff Engr., American Telephone and Telegraph Co., New York 1963; Engr., Bell Laboratories, Holmdel, N.J. 1966; returned to Bell Canada as Constr. Program Engr., W. Area, Toronto 1966, Area Equipment Engr. 1967, Area Plant Extension & Transmission Engr. 1968, Chief Engr. Toronto 1969, Asst. Vice Pres., Engn. W. Region 1972; Vice Pres., Central Area, Ottawa 1974; Vice Pres. (Operations Staff) Ont. Region, Toronto 1976; Vice-Pres. (Saudi Arabia Project) 1978; Vice Pres. Marketing 1978; mem. Assn. Prof. Engrs. Prov. Ont.; Clubs: Ontario (Toronto); Mississauga Golf and Country; Ottawa Hunt; Le Cercle Universitaire d'Ottawa; Home: 55 Parkland Cres., Ottawa Ont.; Office: 25 Eddy St., Hull, Que.

SLONIM, Rabbi Reuben; b. Winnipeg, Man., 27 Feb. 1914; s. Max and Gisela (Averbook) S.; e. Ill. Inst. of Tech., Chicago, B.S.A.S. 1933; ordained rabbi; teacher and preacher; Jewish Theol. Semy., N.Y. City, M.H.L. 1937; Albany Law Sch., N.Y. 1945-47; m. Rita, d. Jacob Short, Winnipeg Manitoba, 21 June 1936; one daughter, Rena; RABBI, CONG. HABONIM, TORONTO, since 1960; Rabbi of Community Temple, Cleveland, Ohio, 1943-44; Temple Beth El, Troy, N.Y., 1944-47; McCaul St. Synagogue, Toronto, 1937-40 and 1947-54; Jewish Chaplain, N.Y. State Assembly, 1944-47; Rabbi, Beth Tzedec Cong., Toronto, 1954-55; Chairman, Synagogue Council, State of Israel Bonds, 1955-60; Extve. mem., Ont. Zionist Region (1947-60); Candn. Jewish Cong., Ont. Region (1947-60); Nat. Speakers' Bur., Zionist Organ. of Am.; Pres., Min. Assn. of Capitol Dist., N.Y. State, 1946; Pres.; Toronto Zionist Council, 1947-51; Pres., Assembly of Jewish Organs., Toronto, 1947-52; Co-Chrmn., Interfaith Comte. of Metrop. Toronto Community Chest, 1953-55; mem. of World Soc. of Skippers of the Flying Dutchmen; Chaplain, Variety Club, Toronto, 1952-56; mem., Rabbinical Assembly of Am.; Assoc. Editor, "The Telegram", Toronto, 1955-71; author of "In The Steps of Pope Paul", 1965; "Both Sides Now", 1972; "Family Quarrel", 1977; Civilian Chaplain, RCAF 1940-43; Freemason; Home: 625 Roselawn Ave., Toronto, Ont. M5N 1K7

SLYKHUIS, John Timothy, B.S.A., M.Sc., Ph.D., F.R.S.C.; plant pathologist; b. Carlyle, Sask. 7 May 1920; s. William and Emma (Hodgson) S.; e. Mountain Valley Pub. Sch. and Carlyle (Sask.) High Sch. 1938; Univ. of Sask. B.S.A. 1942, M.Sc. 1943; Univ. of Toronto Ph.D. 1947; m. Ruth Enid d. late Russel Leisester Williams 6 July 1946; children: Grace Emma, Margaret Janet, Dorothy Anne, Timothy Arthur, Alan Edward; FRUIT TREE VIROLOGIST, AGRICULTURE CAN. since 1976; Research Plant Pathol. Agric. Can., Harrow, Ont. 1947 — 49, Lethbridge, Alta., 1952 — 57, Ottawa 1957 — 70 (Head, Plant Pathol. Unit 1957 — 60, Head, Plant Virology Sec. 1960 — 70), Cereal Virol. Ottawa Research Stn. 1970 — 76; Research Plant Pathol., S.D. State Coll. 1949 — 52; research discoveries incl.: "spermatosphere" as a region surrounding seeds where soil fungi interact in specific ways 1947; identity of causes of sweet clover failure in Ont. 1947 — 49; wheat striate mosaic virus and its leafhopper vector 1949 — 52; mite vector of wheat streak mosaic virus 1952 — 55; wheat spot mosaic; European wheat striate mosaic virus, its insect vector and unique aspects of virus vector relations, ryegrass mosaic 1956 — 57; Hordeum mosaic virus and Poa semilatent virus in cereal crops, carrier of Agropyron mosaic virus, wheat spindle streak mosaic virus and its transmission by fungus in wheat soils 1957 — 76; author various articles scient. journs.; Fellow, Am. Phytopathol. Soc.; mem. Candn. Phytopathol. Soc. (Past Pres.); Agric. Inst. Can.; N.D.P.; Unitarian; recreations: gardening, hiking, curling, skiing, swimming, handicrafts, violin making, youth group activities; Home: R.R. 1, Bristow Rd., Summerland, B.C. V0H 1Z0; Office: Research Station, Agriculture Can., Summerland, B.C. V0H 1Z0.

SMALL, William D., B.Com., C.A.; C.F.A.; banker; b. Cleveland, Ohio, 28 May 1920; s. Roland B. and Mary W. (Pettet); e. Queen's Univ., B.Com. 1948; C.P.A. (Ont.) 1952; C.A. (Ont.) 1962; Chart. Financial Analyst (U.S.) 1965; m. Margaret C., d. J. Ernest Wright, Picton, Ont., 16 June 1945; children: Donald, Mary Ann, Nancy, Shelley; Vice Pres. Leg. & Govt., Bank of Montreal, 1973-78; joined present Bank, Picton, Ont., 1938-46; Kingston and Westport, Ont., 1947; Securities Dept., H.O., 1948-67; served as Research Analyst, Taxation Offr.; apptd. Asst. Mgr. 1954; Asst. Supt. 1957; Supt. 1959; Supt.-Adm., 1967-68; Vice Pres., Premises and Inspection, 1968-70; Vice Pres., Money Mang. 1970-71; Vice Pres., Investments 1971-73; served with RCAF 1942-45; Lectr. in Taxation (evenings), Sir George Williams Univ., 1951-54; Gov. 1971-73-78; mem. Adv. Bd. Concordia Univ. 1973; mem., Univ. Council, Queen's Univ., 1958-70 (Adv. Council, Sch. of Business, 1960-66; Invest. Comte. since 1964; Pres., Montreal Alumni Assn. 1956-57); author, "Taxation in Canada", 1954; Assoc., Candn. Bankers Assn., 1942; Pres., Montreal Soc. Financial Analysts, 1956-57; Vice Pres., Financial Analysts (U.S.) Fed., 1957-58; mem., Inst. Chart. Financial Analysts (U.S.); Inst. C.A.'s Ont.; Protestant; Home: P.O. Box 10, Picton, Ont. K0K 2T0

SMALLWOOD, Hon. Joseph Roberts, P.C. (1967), D.C.L., LL.D., D.Litt.; b. Gambo, B.B., Nfld.; s. Charles W. and Minnie (Devannah) S.; e. Bishop Feild Coll., St. John's, Nfld.; Labour Temple and Rand Sch. of Social Science, N.Y. City; m. Clara Isobel Oates, 1924; three children: Premier of Newfoundland and Min. of Econ. Devel., 31 March 1949-18 Jan. 1972; re-entered politics Sept. 1975 as Leader, Lib. Reform Party; rejoined Lib. Party Dec. 1976; ret. from seat Twillingate Dist. June 1977; Leader of the Confederation-with-Canada movement, which resulted in Confederation; mem., Nat. Conv. of Nfld.; Secy. of Conventions del. to Ottawa, 1947; formerly Reporter for newspapers in St. John's, Halifax, Boston, New York and London; Ed., several newspapers in Nfld.; has had considerable trade union and co-operative organ. experience; operated largest hog farm in Nfld.; author of "Coaker of Newfoundland", 1926; "The New Newfoundlander", 1932; "The Book of Newfoundland", Vols. I, II 1937, Vols. III, IV, 1967, Vols. V, VI, 1975; "Newfoundland Hand Book, Gazetteer and Almanac", 1940; "Surrogate Robert Carter", 1940; "I Chose Canada", 1973; "The Face of Newfoundland", 1977; "Dr. William Carson", 1978; "Newfoundland Miscellany 1, 1978"; No Apology from Me", 1979; "The Time has Come to Tell", 1979; Liberal; United Church; recreations: reading, research, politics, farming; Address: 119 Portugal Cove Rd., St. John's Nfld. A1B 2N1

SMELLIE, Robert Gordon, Q.C.; b. Russell, Man., 23 Aug. 1923; s. Albert George and Jessie May (Cummings) S.; e. Public and High Schs., Russell, Man., 1942; Royal Mil. Coll., Aldershot, U.K., 1945; Brandon Coll., Univ. of Man., LL.B. 1950; m. Lois Evelyn, d. Robert Stuart Cochrane, 4 July 1946; children: Susan Lynn Kurushima, Carol Ann Gamby, Linda Darlene Gage; m. Jean Patricia (Stallwood) McIntyre, 23 Aug. 1980; PARTNER, AIKINS, MacAULAY & THORVALDSON; read law with Justice J. J. Kelly, K.C. and A. Lorne Campbell; called to Bar of Manitoba 1950; cr. Q.C. 1963; private practice of law, Russell, Manitoba, 1950-63; Smellie and Coppleman, 1963-66; joined present firm 1966; served with Royal Winnipeg Rifles in N.W. Europe during World War II; rank Lt.; def. cand. Man. g.e. 1958; el. Man. g.e. 1959; Min. of Mun. Affairs 1963-66; def. Man. g.e. 1966; Dir., Brandon Coll., 1959-61; Past Pres., Man. Heart Foundation; Chrmn. Local Govt. Boundaries Comn. 1966-70; mem., Man. Bar Assn.; Candn. Bar Assn.; Royal Candn. Legion (Past Dom. Pres.); P. Conservative; United Church; recreations: curling, tennis, woodworking; Home: 100 Eastgate, Winnipeg, Man. R3C 2C3; Office: 333 Broadway, Winnipeg, Man. R3C 0T1

SMETHURST, Robert G., C.D., Q.C., LL.B.; b. Calgary, Alta., 28 May 1929; s. Herbert Guy Humphreys and Muriel Mary (Wilson) S.; e. Magee High Sch., Vancouver; Univ. of B.C.; Univ. of Man. Law Sch., LL.B., 1952; children: Linda Anne, David Guy; PARTNER D'ARCY & DEACON; read law with Albert H. Warner, Q.C.; called to Bar of Man. 1953; cr. Q.C. 1968; Partner, Warner, Billinkoff & Smethurst, Winnipeg, 1954-65; D'Arcy, Irving, Haig & Smethurst 1965-71; Pres., Estate Planning Council of Winnipeg 1970-71; Commr. on Uniform Law Conference of Canada (Pres. 1978-79); drafted leg. for Condominium Act; served as an Offr. with Winnipeg Grenadiers (Militia) 1950-62 (second-in-command of regt. on retirement), Pres., V.O.N. for Man. Inc., 1966-70 and V.O.N. for Can., 1976-79; United Services Institute mem. (Pres. 1961-2), Man. Law Reform Comn.; mem., Man. Bar Assn. (Pres. 1969-70); Candn. Bar Assn. (Pres. of Man. Branch 1971-72); Law Soc. Man.; Phi Delta Theta; P. Conservative; Protestant; Home: 308 Lamont Blvd., Winnipeg, Man.; Office: 300 - 286 Smith St., Winnipeg, Man. R3C 1K6

SMETHURST, Stanley Eric, M.A.; university professor emeritus; b. Manchester, Eng., 19 Jan. 1915; s. Stanley and Anna (Linnert) S.; e. St. John's Coll., Cambridge, B.A. 1937, M.A. 1941; m. Viola Clara, d. Edward Butler, Cambridge, Eng., 22 Aug. 1938; children: Sandra, Anthony; came to Canada 1938; HEAD, DEPT. OF CLASSICS, QUEEN'S UNIV., 1961-1980; Prof. of Classics and Ancient Hist., Univ. of New Brunswick, 1938-47; apptd. Prof. of Classics, Queen's Univ., 1947; mem., Classical Assn.; Am. Philol. Assn.; Unitarian; recreations: writing, photography; Home: 1859 127A Street, Surrey, B.C. V4A 3S6

SMILEY, Donald Victor, M.Ed., M.A., Ph.D., F.R.S.C.; educator; b. Pounce Coupé, B.C. 17 Apl. 1921; s. James Wesley and Eva Victoria (Robeson) S.; e. elem. and high schs. Alta.; Univ. of Alta. B.Ed. 1947, M.Ed. 1948, M.A. 1951; Northwestern Univ. Ph.D. 1954; m. Gwyneth Roberta d. Robert Coote, Leduc, Alta. 30 Apl. 1946; children: Bret, Carol, Patricia, Judith, Alison, Rhondda; PROF. OF POL. SCIENCE, YORK UNIV. since 1976; Teacher of Pol. Science Queen's Univ. 1954-55, Univ. of B.C. 1959-70, Univ. of Toronto 1970-76; served with RCA 1941-45 UK Italy N.W. Europe; author "The Canadian Political Nationality" 1967; "Constitutional Change and Canadian Federalism" 1970; "Canada in Question" 3rd ed. 1980; over 50 acad. papers various aspects Candn. govt.; Ed. "Canadian Public Administration", 1974-79; Vice Pres. Candn. Civil Liberties Assn. 1972; mem. Candn. Pol. Science Assn. (Pres. 1968-69); Inst. Pub. Adm. Can.; United Church; Home: 713 Euclid Ave., Toronto, Ont. M6G 2V1; Office: 4700 Keele St., Downsview, Ont. M3J 1P3.

SMISHEK, Hon. Walter Edmund, M.L.A.; politician; b. Sokal, Poland 21 July 1925; s. Andrew and Mary (Homenuik) S.; m. Ruth Bernice d. Peter Schuck 20 Aug. 1955; children: Mark Edward, Kelly Rae, Erica Kirsten; MIN. OF URBAN AFFAIRS, SASK. 1979- ; Vice Chrmn. Sask. Govt. Ins. Bd. Dirs.; Chrmn. Wascana Centre Authority Bd. Dirs.; Chrmn. of Bd. and Min.-in-Charge of Sask. Housing Corp.; Chrmn. Cabinet Comte. on Social Policy and Min.-in-charge of Social Planning Secretariat; mem. Mun. Financing Corp. Bd. Dirs.; Crown Investments Corp. Bd. Dirs.; came to Can. 1930; Labour Rep., Retail, Wholesale & Dept. Store Union 1949-60, 1964-71; also served on Pol. Educ. Comte. of Candn. Labour Cong. during this period; Extve. Secy. Sask. Fed. of Labour 1960-64; el. M.L.A. for Regina North East 1964, re-el. since; Min. of Health 1971-75; Min. of Finance 1975-79; recreations: skating; jogging, carpentry; Home: 113 20th Ave. E., Regina, Sask. S4N 1J5; Office: 302 Legislative Bldg., Regina, Sask. S4S 0B3.

SMITH, Alexander, Q.C., LL.M., J.S.D., LL.D. (Queen's); b. Hawick, Scot., 22 Feb. 1911; s. Adam and Janet Milne (Scroggie) S.; e. Allan Water Pug. Sch., Hawick, Scot., 1925; Vermilion (Alta.) High Sch., 1934; Univ. of Alta., B.A. 1940, LL.B. 1941; Stanford Univ., LL.M. 1955; J.S.D. 1956; m. Ellen, d. William Cleland, 30 Apl. 1943; one s., Michael Scott Dunedin; read law with George H. Steer, Q.C.; called ot Bar of Alta. 1942; cr. Q.C. 1957; practised law 1941-47; taught law Univ. of Alta. 1942-73; presently Prof. Emeritus; law consultant since 1947; author, "The Commerce Power in Canada and the United States", 1963; also articles in various law periodicals; mem., Candn. Assn. Univ. Teachers; Assn. Candn. Law Teachers; Assn. Acad. Staff Univ. Alta.; Candn. Bar Assn.; Law Soc. Alta.; Edmonton Bar Assn.; Protestant; recreations: hunting, fishing, writing. Office: Law Centre, Univ. of Alberta, Edmonton, Alta.

SMITH, Arnold Cantwell, C.H. (1975), M.A., D.C.L., LL.D.; b. Toronto, Ont., 18 Jan. 1915; s. Victor Arnold and Sarah Cory (Cantwell) S.; e. Upper Can. Coll., Toronto (Head Boy 1932); Lycée Champoléon, Grenoble, France; Univ. of Toronto, B.A. (Pol. Science & Econ.) 1935; Rhodes Scholar for Ont., Christ Church, Oxford, 1935, B.A. (Juris.) 1937, B.C.L. 1938; m. Evelyn Hardwick, d. late Stanley Stewart, Fruitland, Ont., 8 Sept. 1938; children: Alexandra Smith-Gaylord, Stewart Cantwell, Matthew Cantwell; LESTER PEARSON PROF. OF INTERNAT. AFFAIRS, CARLETON UNIV. since 1976; Editor, "The Baltic Times", Tallinn, Estonia, 1939-40; at same time Assoc. Prof. of Pol. Econ., Univ. of Tartu, Estonia; rep. Brit. Council for Estonia, and Press Attaché of Brit. Legation, Tallinn; Attaché, Brit. Embassy, Cairo, Egypt, 1940-41; Special Lectr., Pol. Science and Econ., at Egyptian State Univ., Cairo, 1940-42; Head of Propaganda Divn. of U.K Min. of State for Middle East, 1941-43; Ed.-in-Chief "Akhbar el Harp", "Aera" and "Cephe" (all publ, in Cairo), 1941-43; trans. to Candn. Diplomatic Service and proceeded to Kuibyshev, U.S.S.R., as Secy. Candn. Legation, 1943; Candn. Embassy, Moscow, 1943-45; mem., Econ. Divn., Dept. of External Affairs, Ottawa, 1946-47; Assoc. Dir., Nat. Defence Coll. of Can., Kingston, Ont. 1947-49; served as advisor on various comtes. and councils, rep. Canada at U.N. meetings, becoming Principal Adviser, Perm. Del. of Can. to U.N. and Candn. Del. to U.N. Gen. Assembly, 1949; Alternate Rep. of Can. on U.N. Security Council and Atomic Energy Comn., Lake Success, 1949-50; Counsellor, Candn. Embassy, Brussels and head of Can. Del. to Inter-Allied Reparations Agency, 1950-53; Special Asst. to Secy. of State for External Affairs, 1953-55; Candn. Commr. on Internat. Truce Supervisory Comn. for Cambodia, 1955-56; Candn. Min. to the U.K., 1956-58; Ambassador to the United Arab Republic, 1958-61, to the U.S.S.R., 1961-63; returned to Can. as Asst. Under Secy. of State for External Affairs, 1963-65; elected the first Secy.-Gen. of the Commonwealth, London, Eng. 1965-75; Companion of Honour 1975; Visiting Centennial Prof., Univ. of Toronto 1967; Visiting Cecil and Ada Green Prof., Univ. of B.C.

1978; Chmn. of Bd., Internat'l Peace Academy, New York since 1976; North-South Instit., Ottawa since 1976; Trustee, Hudson Institute, New York; Vice-Pres. (Life) Royal Commonwealth Soc.; Hon. Pres. Royal Commonwealth Soc. of Can.; Hon. Pres., Can.-Med. Institute; mem. Exec. Comte and Council, Duke of Edinburgh's 5th Commonwealth Study Conference, Can. 1980; awarded R. B. Bennett Commonwealth Prize, Royal Soc. Arts 1975; Hon. D.C.L. Michigan 1966, Oxford 1975, Bishop' Univ. 1977; LL.D. Ricker 1964, Queen's 1966, Brit. Columbia, Toronto 1968, N.B. 1969, Leeds 1975, Trent 1979; Zimbabwe Independence Medal 1980; Hon. Fellow, Lady Eaton Coll., Trent Univ.; pub., "Stitches in Time-The Commonwealth in World Politics:", 1981; Beta Theta Pi; Anglican; Clubs: Le Cercle Universitaire, Ottawa; Athenaeum (London); Home: Townhouse Five, 300 Queen Elizabeth Driveway, Ottawa, Ont. K1S 3M6; Office: Norman Paterson School of International Affairs, Carleton Univ., Ottawa, Ont.

SMITH, Arthur J. R., M.A., Ph.D., D.U.C. LL.D.; economist; b. Simcoe, Ont., 7 Jan. 1926; s. Ralph Eugene and Mildred Helen (Johnson) S.; e. Pub. and High Sch. in India and in Simcoe, Ont.; McMaster Univ., B.A. (Math. & Pol. Econ.) 1947, LL.D. 1971; Harvard Univ., M.A. (Econ.) 1949, Ph.D. (Econ.) 1955; Hon. D.U.C., Univ. of Calgary; m. Ruth Frances Elizabeth, d. late H. Stanley Carey, 21 Aug. 1948; three d. Helen Alexandra, Deborah Ann, Barbara Jean; ASSOC., WOODS GORDON since 1981; Dir., The Oshawa Group Ltd.; Teaching Fellow, Harvard University, 1949-50; Econ. successively in Monetary Research Div., Domestic Research Div. and Foreign Research Div., Fed. Reserve Bank of N.Y., 1950-54; Candn. Econ., Nat. Indust. Conf. Bd., Montreal, 1954-57; Lectr., Extension Dept., McGill Univ., 1955-56; Dir. of Research and Secy.-Treas., Private Planning Assn. of Can., Montreal, 1957-63; also Dir. of Research, Candn.-Am. Comte., 1957-63 and Secy., Candn. Trade Comte., 1961-63; Dir., Econ. Council of Can., 1963-67, Chrmn. 1967-71; Pres. Conference Brd. in Can. 1971-76; Vice Pres. Inco 1976-78; Asst. to Chrmn Inco 1978-79; Pres., Nat. Planning Assoc. 1979-81; mem., World Soc. for Ekistics; Cdn.-Am. Comm. 1971-81; Br.-N. Amer. Comm. 1979-81; Comm. on Changing Internat Realities 1979-81; Candn. Econ. Assn.; Am. Econ. Assn.; United Church; Home: 62 Wellesly St. W., Apt. 1906, Toronto, Ont. M5S 1C3; Office: P.O. Box 251, Toronto-Dominion Centre, Toronto, Ont. M5K 1J7

SMITH, Arthur Ryan, D.F.C.; executive; b. Calgary, Alta. 16 May 1919; s. Arthur LeRoy Smith; e. Shawinigan Lake Sch. B.C.; m. Betty Ann d. Bruce Walker 10 May 1964; three children; PRES. AND C.E.O., LAVALIN SERVICES INC.; SINCE 1980 Chrmn. Worldwide Energy Corp.; Dir. DALCO Petroleum Co. Ltd.; Hy's of Canada; Seabord Life Insurance Co.; Petrotech Lavalin Inc.; Drilling Crew, Royalite Oil Co. 1939; Invest. Counsellor, Tanner & Co. Ltd. 1945; Ed. "Oil in Canada" and "Petroleum Exploration Digest" 1952; Asst. to Pres. Anglo American Exploration Ltd. 1953, Pacific Petroleums Ltd. 1957; Pres. Ventures Management Ltd. 1965; Vice Pres. Foster Advertising Ltd. 1970; Pres. Arthur R. Smith & Associates Ltd., Can Trans Services (Malaysia) Ltd. 1973; Vice Pres., Allarco Developments Ltd. 1978; el. Ald. City of Calgary 1953, 1963; M.L.A. 1955; el. to H. of C. 1957, re-el. 1958, 1962; served as Chrmn. various parlty. comtes. 1957 — 63; Advisor, and Candn. Del. to UN 1957, 1959, 1961, 1963; mem. Royal Comn. on Fed. El. Expenses; served as RAF Pathfinder Pilot overseas 1939 — 44; Past Vice Pres. Alta. Chamber Comm.; Past Pres. Calgary Chamber Comm.; former Chrmn. Bd. Alta. Environmental Research Trust; Dir. Calgary Beautification Foundation; Calgary Olympic Devel. Assn.; Gov. RCAF Mem. Fund; Pres. S. Alta. Recreation Devel. Assn.; Hon. Pres. Calgary Jaycees; mem. Chancellor's Club Univ. Calgary; former Dir. Calgary Philharmonic Soc., Calgary Exhn. & Stampede, Un. Services Inst., Stampeder Football Club,

Calgary Community Service Bureau, Theatre Calgary, Gen. Hosp. Bd.; former Chrmn. Calgary Internat. Aviation Conf., Calgary Indust. Comn., Calgary Aviation Comn.; former Pres. Air Cadet League Can., Calgary Booster Club; former Pub. Relations Dir. Candn. Petrol. Assn., Calgary Un. Fund; rec'd Centennial Medal 1967; P. Conservative; Anglican; recreations: golf, tennis; Clubs: Calgary Golf & Country; Glencoe; Calgary Petroleum (Gov.); Home: 1104 Beverley Blvd., Calgary S.W., Alta.; Office: 909-5 Ave. S.W., Calgary, Alta.T2P 3G5

SMITH, Hon. Brian Ray Douglas, M.L.A., M.A., LL.B.; lawyer and politician; b. Victoria, B.C. 7 July 1934; s. Douglas Edgar and E. Eleanor (Parfitt) S.; e. Victoria Coll. B.A.; Queen's Univ. M.A., Univ. of B.C. LL.B.; m. Barbara Claire d. Wallace Courtney, Victoria, B.C. 29 Dec. 1961; children: Claire E., Christopher C.; MIN. OF EDUCATION, B.C. 1979- ; el. M.L.A. for Oak Bay-Gordon Head prov. g.e. 1979; Social Credit; Anglican; Clubs: Union; Victoria Golf; Oak Bay Tennis; Canadian; Victoria Chamber Comm.; Mayor of Oak Bay, B.C. 1974-79; Office: Parliament Bldgs., Victoria, B.C. V8V 1X4.

SMITH, Carlton George, M.D., M.Sc., Ph.D.; university professor; b. Ont., 8 Nov. 1905; s. Charles and Catherine (Wolfe) S.; e. Victoria Coll., Univ. of Toronto, B.A. 1928; Univ. of W. Ont., M.Sc. 1931; Ont. Coll. of Educ. (science specialist) 1932; Univ. of Toronto, M.D. 1935, Ph.D. 1936; m. Marguerite Harland, 1976; PROF. OF ANATOMY, UNIV. of TORONTO; Prof. Emeritus of Anatomy, Univ. of Toronto 1979; Visiting Prof. of Anatomy Uniformed Services Univ. of the Health Sciences 1979-81; served in World War 1939-45 as Surg. Lieut.-Commdr. with R.C.N.V.R.; awarded Reeve Prize for Med. Research; author: "Basic Neuroanatomy" (textbook); "Serial Dissections of the Human Brain" (atlas); mem., Am. Assn. of Anatomists; Candn. Physiol. Soc.; Acad. of Med., Toronto; Candn. Ass. Anats.; Candn. Neurol. Soc.; Alpha Kappa Kappa; United Church; Home: 50 Prince Arthur Ave., Suite 1604, Toronto, Ont. M5R 1B5

SMITH, Charles Franklin, M.Sc.; company executive; b. North Bay, Ont., 2 March 1918; s. Harold William and Charlotte M. (McDole) S.; e. Queen's Univ., B.Sc. 1949, M.Sc. 1950; m. Constance C., d. late George W. Munroe, 18 Aug. 1941; children: Mrs. G. N. Hillmer, Michael G. W.; VICE PRES. — BUSINESS DEVELOPMENT AND GOV'T AFFAIRS, SPERRY VICKERS DIV., SPERRY CORP., Troy, Mich. U.S.A. 1977- ; Vice-Pres., Europe, Sherry Vickers Div. Sperry Ltd., Cobham, Surrey, Eng., 1966-77; Sperry Vickers Div. Sperry Inc., Rexdale, Ont. 1955-66; Vice-Chrmn., Hungarian American Economic Council.; Bulgarian American Economic Council; mem., Assn. Prof. Engrs. Ont; Roy. Inst. of Internat. Affairs; Clubs: Royal Ocean Racing; Home: 3090 Morningview Terrace; Birmingham, MI. 48010; Office: 1401 Crooks Rd., Troy, MI. 48084.

SMITH, Charles Haddon, M.Sc., M.S., Ph.D., P. Eng., F.R.S.C., F.M.S.A.; geologist; b. Dartmouth, N.S. 3 Sept. 1926; s. Albion Benson and Dora Pauline (McGill) S.; e. Dalhousie Univ. B.Sc. and Dipl. in Engn. 1946, M.Sc. 1948; Yale Univ. M.S. 1951, Ph.D. 1952; m. Mary Gertrude d. late Dr. Jabez Ronald Saint 5 Sept. 1949; children: Dr. Charles Douglas, Richard David, Alan Michael, Timothy McGill; SR. ASST. DEPY. MIN. (MINES) DEPT. OF ENERGY, MINES & RESOURCES since 1980; Instr. in Engn. Dalhousie Univ. 1946-48; Geol. Cerro de Pasco Copper Corp. Morococha, Peru 1949; Geol. Survey of Can. Ottawa 1952-64, Chief Petrological Science Div. 1964-67, Chief Crustal Geol. 1967-68; Science Adviser, Science Council of Can. Ottawa 1968-70; Dir. of Planning present Dept. 1970-71, Asst. Depy. Min. (Science & Technol.) 1972-75; Sr. Asst. Depy. Min. 1975-80; author over 45 publs. in earth sciences, energy and mineral fields; mem. Soc. Econ. Geols.; Candn. Inst. Mining & Metall.; Geol. Assn. Can.; Prof. Eng. Prov. of Ont.; mem. Ed. Bd.

'Mineralium Deposita'; United Church; recreations: cycling, biking, flying; Home: 2056 Thistle Cres., Ottawa, Ont. K1H 5P5; Office: 2103 Sir William Logan Bldg., 580 Booth St., Ottawa, Ont. K1A 0E4.

SMITH, Charles Rhodes, M.A., LL.B., B.C.L.; former judge; b. Portage la Prairie, Man., 1896; s. Richard Henry and Marion Sarah S.; e. Pub. Schs., Winnipeg; Univ. Man., B.A., LL.B.; Oxford Univ., M.A., B.C.L.; Univ. of Man., Hon. LL.D. 1968; Univ. of Winnipeg, Hon. LL.D. 1972; m. Luella Gertrude Lick, Davidson, Sask., 24 July 1924; children: Clifford Rhodes, Murray Rhodes; called to Bar of Man. 1923; Q.C. 1940; practised law in Winnipeg with Broad & Smith, 1924-52; Ald., City of Winnipeg, 1935-41; 1st el. to Man. Leg. for City of Winnipeg, g.e. 1941; re-el. g.e. 1945 and 1949; Min. of Labour, Man., 1946-48; Min. of Educ., 1948-50; Attorney-Gen., 1950-52; Chrmn., Restrictive Trade Practices Comn., Ottawa, 1952-62; Chrmn., Can. Labour Relations Bd., 1953-63; apptd. Justice of Court of Queen's Bench, Man., 1963; elevated to Court of Appeal, 1966, Chief Justice of Manitoba 1967-71; Dep. Justice, Federal Court of Can., 1974- ; Chrmn., Royal Comn. Inquiry into The Pas Forestry & Industrial Complex March 1971-Aug. 1974; served in World War 1916-19, Western Univ. Bn. 1916, proceeding overseas; comnd. 1918; Home: 11 K-300 Roslyn Rd., Winnipeg, Man. R3L 0H4

SMITH, David Bruce, B.E., S.M.; company executive; b. Edmonton, Alta., 29 Dec. 1927; s. Sidney Bruce and Doris Gertrude S.; e. Pub. and High Schs., Edmonton, Alta.; McGill Univ., B.E. 1949; Mass. Inst. Tech., S.M. 1952; Banff Sch. of Mgmt., 1964; m. Lorraine Fillmore, d. James C. Tweedell, 5 Apl, 1952; children: Bruce, Kathryn; DIRECTOR—ENERGY RESOURCES, SHERRITT GORDON MINES LTD., 1980- ; joined Sherritt Gordon 1955-59, becoming Head, Eng. Dept.; 1959-73 employed in the natural gas transmission & distribution industry in principal Alta. natural gas distributors as Mgr. of Gas Supply, Dir. & Sr. Vice Pres. (Operations) CWNG and NUL; Vice Pres., Gen. Mgr. & Dir., Pan-Alta. Gas Ltd. (subsidiary of Alta. Gas Trunk Line Co. Ltd.) 1973-74; Dir., Vice Pres. (Industrl. Group), Assoc. Engr. Services Ltd., 1975-76; Pres. David B. Smith Consulting & Mgmt. Ltd. and assoc'd. with Foster Research, Calgary, 1976-80; Dir. Candn. Gas Assn. (Chrmn. of 2nd Nat. Technical Conference); Dir., Campaign Chrmn., United Fund, Calgary; Pres., Calgary Region, Boy Scouts of Can.; Pres., Calgary Br., Candn. Red Cross Soc.; mem., Extve Comte., Calgary Red Cross; dir. & Vice Pres., Alta. Theatre Projects; mem. Alta. Assn. Prof. Engrs., Geol., & Geophys.; mem. Senate, Univ. of Calgary; P. Conservative; Anglican; recreations: home carpentry, swimming, curling; Clubs: Calgary Glencoe; Calgary Ranchman's; Calgary Golf & Country; Home: 7831 Chardie Rd. S.W., Calgary, Alta.; T2V 2T2; Office:

SMITH, David C., M.A., Ph.D., F.R.S.C.; educator; b. Ootacamund, India 12 Aug. 1931; s. Ralph Eugene and Mildred Helen (Johnson) S.; e. McMaster Univ. B.A. 1953; Oxford Univ. M.A. 1955; Harvard Univ. Ph.D. 1959; m. Mary Hilda d. late Kenneth W. Taylor 25 June 1955; children: Monica H., Geoffrey K.C.; PROF. AND HEAD OF ECON. QUEEN'S UNIV. since 1968; Dep. Chrmn., Ont. Econ. Council; Home: 145 King St. W., Kingston, Ont. K7L 2W6; Office: Kingston, Ont. K7L 3N6.

SMITH, David Duncan, M.A., Ph.D.; psychologist; b. Montreal, Que., 8 July 1927; s. Philip Maynard and Mary (Trotter) S.; e. Town of Mount Royal (Que.) High Sch., 1944; High Sch. of Montreal, 1946; Sir George Williams Univ., B.A. 1949; Univ. of Minn., M.A. 1950; McGill Univ., Ph.D. 1957; m. Norma Louise, d. M. A. Metcalf, C.B.E., Montreal, 14 Sept. 1949; children: Philip, Brenda, Valerie, Rosalind, Lorraine; PROF. OF VET. MEDICINE, UNIV. OF PEKTANIAN, MALAYSIA, Research Asst. to

Student Counsellor, Sir George Williams Univ., 1950-51; Student Counsellor and Lectr. in Psychol., 1951-56; Personnel Asst., HQ Personnel Dept., Candn. Nat. Rlys., 1956-58; private practice as Consultant Psychol., 1958-59; Guidance Offr., McGill Univ., 1958-60; Asst. Prof. of Psychol. and Course Dir., Staff Devel. Insts., 1959-60; joined present Univ. as Assoc. Prof. and Head, Dept. of Psychol., 1960-65; Prof. and Head of Dept. 1965-74; Dean, Faculty of Arts, 1969-70; author, "Mammalian Learning and Behaviour", 1965; other writings incl. various articles in psychol. journs.; Gov., Sherbrooke Hosp.; mem., Candn. Psychol. Assn.; Am. Psychol. Assn.; Am. Assn. Advanc. Science; Address: 75 Castle Field Gdns., Sungai Besi Selangor, W. Malaysia

SMITH, David Lawrence Thomson, Ph.D., D.V.M.; b. Regina, Sask., 16 April 1914; s. John Cochrane and Ethel Edna (Waldie) S.; e. Pub. Sch. and Collegiate, Killarney, Man.; Brandon (Man.) Coll.; Ont. Vet. Coll., D.V.M. 1943; post-doctoral studies, Univ. of Toronto, 1947-48; Cornell Univ., Ph.D. 1955; m. Helen Isabel Rundle, 15 Aug. 1942; children: Ian, Brett, Janis; DEAN. COLL. VETERINARY MED., UNIV. OF SASK.; Lectr., Ont. Vet. Coll., 1943-44; studied at Banting Inst., Univ. of Toronto, 1946-48; Assoc. Prof. Ont. Vet. Coll., 1948-51; grad. studies Cornell Univ., 1951-52; Prof. Pathol., 1952-53; Head of Dept. Bacter., Ont. Vet. Coll., till present appt.; served with R.C.A.M.C. as Lt., 1944-46; wrote section of "Diseases of Swine", 1958, Iowa State Coll. Press; Past Pres., Am. Coll. Vet. Pathol.; mem., Sask., Candn. Am. Vet. Med. Assns.; Phi Zeta; Sigma Ix; Un. Church; recreations: golf, curling,

SMITH, Hon. Donald, D.D.S.; senator; b. Liverpool, N.S., 7 July 1905; s. Dr. Jordan Wesley and Alma Enid (Hunt) S.; e. Liverpool High Sch.; Mount Allison Univ., 1921-23; Dalhousie Univ., D.D.S., 1928; m. Florence Elizabeth, d. Rupert F. Morton, 18 Sept. 1929; one s. Donald Morton; mem. of Liverpool, N.S. Town Council, 1935-39; M.P. for Queens-Shelburne, 1949-53; apptd. to the Senate of Can., 28 July 1955; mem., N.S. Dental Assn.; Candn. Dental Assn.; Phi Kappa Pi.; Liberal; United Church; recreation: fishing; Clubs: Liverpool Golf & Country; Liverpool Curling; Address: 50 School St., Liverpool, N.S. B0T 1K0

SMITH, Donald Cameron, M.Sc., M.D., D.P.H., F.R.C.P. (C), F.A.P.H.A.; professor; b. Peterborough, Ont., 2 Feb. 1922; s. James Cameron and Clarice (Leighton) S.; e. Queen's Univ., M.D. 1945; Univ. of Toronto, M.Sc. (Med.) 1948 (Fellow in Physiol.), D.P.H. 1949; m. Ida Jean, d. late Earle Morningstar, 11 Sept. 1946; children: Douglas Frazer, Scott Earle, Donald Ian; Sr. Medical Advisor, Sisters of Mercy Health Corp., Fallington Hills, MI; Vice Pres. for Accreditation, Joint Comm. on Accreditation for Hosps.; Prof. of Psychiatry and Behavorial Sci., Northwestern Univ. Medical Sch.; Internship, Victoria Hosp., London, Ont., 1945-46; Asst. Dir., E. York-Leaside (Ont.) Health Dept. 1949-50; Med. Dir., Kent Co. (Ont.) Health Dept., 1950-51; joined Univ. of Michigan as Commonwealth Fund Fellow in Pediatrics, 1952-55; Asst. Prof. of Maternal and Child Health, 1955-57; Assoc. Prof. 1957-61; Prof. at Maternal and Child Health, Sch. of Public Health, Prof. of Pediatrics, Med. Sch., Univ. of Michigan 1961-78; mem. Extve. Comte.; Inst. for Study of Mental Retardation there; Med. Dir., Mich. Crippled Children Comn., 1962-64; overseas assignments incl. World Health Organ. Study of Child Health and Child Welfare Programs in Middle E., 1957; Review of New Devels. in W. Europe in Provision of Services for Handicapped Children and Youth, 1968; Integration of Maternal and Child Health & Family Planning Services, Repub. of S. Korea, 1969; Chrmn. Forum XI, 1970 White House Conf. on Youth; Chrmn. Dept. Health Devel., Sch. Pub. Health Univ. Mich. 1964-72; Visiting Prof. Harvard Univ. 1969, 70, 71; Princ. Adv. Gov. Milliken (Mich.) Health & Med. Affairs 1972-78; Dir.

Mich. Dept. Mental Health, 1974-78; Chrmn., Health Policy Bd., Mich. Dept. of Corrections since 1976; Team Ldr., Cross-Nat. Study Health Care Services in Europe & Israel (Secy. H.E.W.) 1971; Special consultant, Pres. Comn. Mental Retardation 1968; served with RCN 1946-47; rank Surg. Lt. on discharge; Chrmn., Med. Assistance Adv. Council, Secy. of Health, Educ. and Welfare; Examiner, Am. Bd. Preventive Med., Inc.; writings incl. numerous articles for prof. journs; Fellow, Am. Acad. Pediatrics; mem., Assn. Teachers Maternal & Child Health, Inc. (Secy.); Am. Public Health Assn.; Am. Med. Assn.; Mich. State Med. Soc.; Washtenaw Co. Med. Soc.; Assn. Teachers Preventive Med.; Assn. Ambulatory Pediatric Services; Delta Omega (Pres. 1967); Presbyterian; Home: 1000 Country Club Rd., Aann Arbor, MI 48105

SMITH, Donald Campbell, C.A.; b. Detroit, Mich., 25 July 1922; s. Hugh and Blanche Eleanor (Sainty) S.; e. Daniel Stewarts Coll., Edinburgh, Scot.; Edinburgh Univ.; C.A. Scot. 1948; m. Phyllis Audrey, d. J. H. Miles, Lancs., Eng., 21 May 1952; three children; VICE PRES., FINANCE, BP CANADA INC., since 1970; Dir., BP Oil Ltd.; BP Exploration Canada Ltd.; BP Tanker Finance Canada Ltd.; British Petroleum Investments Canada Ltd.; BP Canada Inc.; B.P. Cdn. Holdings Ltd.; BP Properties Ltd.; BP Minerals Ltd.; BP Oil and Gas Invests. Ltd.; B.C. Oil Lands Ltd.; Sukunka Mines Ltd.; with Finnie, Ross Welch Co., C.A.'s, London, Eng.; 1948-51; Canadian Pacific Railway Co., 1951-52; Canadian Chemical and Cellulose Co. Ltd. 1952-58; joined present Co. as Asst. to Treas., 1958; Asst. Secy. 1958; Asst. Treas. and Asst. Secy. 1962; Secy. and Asst. Treas. 1963; Controller 1966; seconded to British Petroleum, London as Mgr., Systems Development, 1968; Treas. 1970; served with Brit. Army in N. Africa and Italy, 1941-46; rank Acting Maj.; mem., Insts. C.A.'s Que., Alta., Ont. and Scot.; Soc. of Indust. and Cost. Accts.; Protestant; recreations: tennis, golf, skiing; Clubs: National; Royal Canadian Yacht; Home: 20 Browside Ave., Toronto, Ont. M5P 2V1; Office: First Canadian Place, Box 79, Toronto, Ont. M5X 1G8

SMITH, Edward Herbert; trust company executive; b. Saskatoon, Sask. 18 Jan. 1923; s. Herbert and Emily (Baxter) S.; e. City Park Coll. Inst., Saskatoon, Sr. Matric.; Univ. of W. Ont., Mang. Training Course 1972; m. Patricia Margaret, d. late James Powell, 31 Oct. 1944; two s., Richard Edward, Warren James; SR. VICE PRESIDENT, CANADA PERMANENT TRUST CO.; Chmn. and Dir., G. T. Fulford Co. Ltd.; Sr. Vice-Pres., Operations Division, Canada Permanent Trust Co.; served with RCNVR 1941-45; rank Lt.; named Serving Bro., Order of St. John; P. Conservative; Anglican; recreations: photography, music; Clubs: National; Donalda; Home: 52 Apollo Dr., Don Mills, Ont. M3B 2G8; Office: 320 Bay St., Toronto, Ont. M5H 2P6

SMITH, Elvie Lawrence, M.S.; executive; born Eatonia, Sask. 8 Jan. 1926; s. Harry Burton and Laura Mae (Fullerton); e. Nutana Coll. Saskatoon 1943; Univ. of Sask. B.S. 1947; Purdue Univ. M.S. 1949; m. Jacqueline Moy Colleary 15 Dec. 1956; children: Ronald, Paul, David, Marguerite; PRES. & CHIEF EXEC OFFICER, PRATT & WHITNEY AIRCRAFT of Canada Ltd. 1980- ; Chrmn, of the Bd., SCAN Marine Inc.; National Research Council, Ottawa, 1949-56; Pratt & Whitney Aircraft of Canada Ltd. 1957- , V.P. - Operations; has written a number of papers on gas turbine development; recreations: flying aircraft, gliding, skiing; Clubs: Gatineau Gliding, Ottawa; Office: 1000 Blvd. Marie-Victorin, Longueuil, Que. J4K 4X9.

SMITH, Ernest Chalmers, B.Sc., A.M., Ph.D.; retired educator; b. Hillsborough, N.S., 25 Nov. 1912; s. Nathan and Annie Bell (Jackson) S.; e. Acadia Univ., B.Sc. 1936; Harvard Univ., A.M. 1939, Ph.D. 1942; Acadia Univ., D. Sc. 1976; m. Ada Southcott Garland, d. Allan Cameron, 12 Aug. 1939; children: Peter Chalmers, Dorothy Ann Louise; Vice Pres. (Academic), Acadia Univ. 1967-76 and

Dean of Science 1961-76; Prof. of Biol. there 1947-76; Prof. and Head, Dept. of Biol., Memorial Univ. 1944-47; Head, Dept. of Biol. of Acadia Univ. 1955-70; served with RCAF 1943-44, Operational Research Offr.; author of "Flora of Nova Scotia", Vol. I & II, also over 25 scient. papers mainly in fields of cytotaxonomy and plant distribution; mem., Candn. Bot. Assn.; United Church; Home: 54 Westwood Ave., Wolfville, N.S. B0P 1X0

SMITH, Ernest Llewellyn Gibson; executive; b. Goldaming, Eng., 21 June 1918; s. Brig. Armand Armstrong and Evelyn (Gibson) S.; e. Lake Lodge, Grimsby, Ont.; Trinity Coll. Sch., Port Hope, Ont.; Univ. of Bishop's Coll., Lennoxville, Que.; m. Elizabeth Ann, d. Col. Clifford Sifton, Toronto, Ont., 16 June 1945; children: Sharon Evelyn, Daphne June, Llewellyn Sifton; CHRMN. AND CEO, E. D. SMITH & SONS LTD. (estbd. 1882); Dir., Guaranty Trust Co. of Can.; Traders Group Ltd.; served in 2nd World War with Royal Hamilton Light Inf. in Eng., France, Holland, Belgium and Germany as Co. Commdr.; Gov., Past Gov., Hillfield Strathallan Coll.; Hamilton; Past Pres. Candn. Food Processors Assn.; Past Pres., Ont. Food Processors Assn.; mem. Bus. Adv. Council, McMaster Univ.; Founding mem. and Gov., Conservation Found. Hamilton-Wentworth Region; mem., Advis. Council Cdn. Mfg. Assoc.; Conservative; Protestant; recreations: golf, travelling, skiing; Clubs: Toronto; Osler Bluffs; Hamilton Golf; Tamahaac (Hamilton); The Hamilton; Royal Cdn. Mil. Instit., Toronto; Home: "Tree Tops", Winona, Ont.; Office: Highway #8, Winona, Ont. L0R 2L0

SMITH, Fletcher Shuttleworth, B.Comm.; company executive; b. Halifax, N.S., 2 Apl. 1907; s. late Albert and Ethel (Brown) S.; e. Pub. and High Schs. Halifax; Dalhousie Univ., B.Com.; m. Charlotte Tremaine, d. late G. G. Lyall and Jennie Hunter; has one s. and two d.; PRESIDENT, A. M. SMITH & CO. LTD.; Pres., Citadel Investments Ltd.; Parkdale Realties Ltd.; Southern Realties Ltd.; Pres., Fenpark Realties Ltd.; apptd. by Ottawa as a Rep. to Internat. Fisheries Conf., London, Eng., 1939, and on return organized Candn. Atlantic Salt Fish Exporters Assn. and was Pres. for first two yrs. and in 1966-67; Past Vice-Pres., Halifax Y.M.C.A.; Past Dir., Candn. Exporters Assn.; Past mem., Advisory Council of Cdn. Export Credit Corp.; former Alumni Rep. on Bd. of Govs., Dalhousie Univ.; former mem. of Council, Halifax Bd. of Trade; Delta Sigma Phi; Baptist; recreations: golf, swimming; Clubs: Rotary, Waegwoltic; Saraguay; Ashbury Golf; The Halifax; Home: Indian Point, Halifax Co., N.S. B3H 3Z3; Office P.O. Box 8420, Halifax, N.S. B3K 5M1

SMITH, Frank Clifford Goulding; hydrographer; b. Montreal, Que., 15 Oct. 1890; s. Frank Clifford and Ida Lily (Haskett) S.; e. Pub. and High Schs., Montreal, Que.; Engn. Course, Acadia Univ. (Diploma) 1912-14; m. Abbie Marie, d. late Alfred Leslie Danielson, Cambridge, Mass., 16 July 1918; apptd. to Candn. Hydrographic Service, 1914; Dom. Hydrographer, 1952-57; engaged on hydrographic surveys Gulf of St. Lawrence and Labrador Coast, Pacific Coast, Hudson Bay, Great Slave Lake, Hudson Strait and Bay, 1919-35; prepared the 1st edition of Official Vol., "Sailing Directions for the Hudson Bay Route"; charted currents in Montreal Harbour, 1936; survey of Saguenay River, 1937; Supt. of Charts, Candn. Hydrographic Service, 1938; mem. for Can., Internat. Hydrographic Bureau, 1952; author of numerous articles on hydrography of Candn. coastal and inland navig. waters, incl.; "Northward Bound", "A Portal of Empire", in The Blue Peter; "In the Wake of Hudson", "In Chambers Journal", 1940; "Charting Perils of the Sea" in "Candn. Geog. Journ.", 1946; "Charting Northern Seas and Harbours" in "The Candn. Surveyor", 1953, etc.; Fellow, Arctic Inst. of N.Am.; Perm. Comte. on Geog. Names designated the Atlantic Continental-Shelf feature the "Clifford Smith Canyon" 1976 in his honour; served in

1st World War with Candn. Army Overseas (Engrs.) 1915-17; Lieut., R.N.V.R. Hydrographic Service, Brit. Admiralty, 1917-19; United Church; recreations: gardening, woodworking, writing; Home: 643 St. George Street, Annapolis Royal, Nova Scotia B0S 1A0

SMITH, Frederick, Jr., A.B., LL.B., M.P.A.; diplomat; b. Laconia, N.H. 28 June 1929; s. Frederick and Grace Marie (Vohr) S.; e. New Hampton Sch. N.H. 1945; Dartmouth Coll. A.B. 1949; Univ. of Edinburgh 1949; Cornell Law Sch. LL.B. 1952; Harvard Univ. M.P.A. 1973; m. Sharon d. late Orville C. Higbie 4 July 1959; children: Allison, Meredith, Tory, Adam; CONSUL GEN., U.S. CONSULATE GEN. since 1979; called to N.H. Bar 1952; private law practice Concord, N.H. 1952 — 53; Atty.-Adviser, Office of Legal Adviser, U.S. Dept. of State 1957 — 64; Asst. Legal Adviser for Security and Consular Affairs 1964 — 68; Depy. Asst. Secy. of State for Consular Affairs 1968 — 72, 1973 — 75; Consul Gen. Am. Embassy Mexico 1975 — 76; U.S. Foreign Service Inspr. 1976 — 77; Dir. Foreign Service Grievance Staff, Dept. of State 1977 — 79; served with U.S. Navy, Pacific, 1953 — 57, rank Lt. (jg); author law book chapter and articles on consular affairs; mem. N.H. Bar Assn.; Theta Delta Chi; Phi Delta Phi; Protestant; recreations: tennis, golf, skiing; Home: 152 Warren Rd., Toronto, Ont. M4V 2S5; Office: 360 University Ave., Toronto, Ont. M5G 1S4.

SMITH, (George Hayes) Clifford, B.A.Sc., P.Eng.; b. Hamilton, Ont., 3 Apl. 1907; s. George M. and Russell Georgian (Hayes) S.; e. Delta Coll. Inst., Hamilton, Ont.; Univ. of Toronto, B.A.Sc. (Chem. Engn.) 1932; m. (Elizabeth) Wilma, d. W. B. Bate, Toronto, Ont., 15 June 1935; children: Stephen Clifford, Russell Bradnee, Fraser William; CHAIRMAN BD. AND DIR., HYSOL CANADA LTD.; Dir., Bate Equities Ltd; Chrmn. of Bd., Bate Investments Ltd.; Nuodex Products of Canada Ltd.; mem., Assn. Prof. Engrs. Ont.; Lambda Chi Alpha; United Church; recreations: sailing, travel, music, colour-photography; Clubs: Granite; National; Rosedale Golf; Rotary; Home: 39 Strathgowan Crescent, Toronto, Ont. M4N 2Z8; Office: 1210 Sheppard Ave. E., Ste 113, Ont. M2K 1E3

SMITH, Hon. Col. George Isaac, M.B.E., E.D., Q.C., LL.D., D.C.L.; senator; b. Stewiacke, N.S., 6 Apl. 1909; s. John Robert and Susan Ettinger (Colter) S.; e. Stewiacke (N.S.) High Sch., 1923-25; Colchester Co. Acad., Truro, N.S., 1926-28; Dalhousie Law Sch., LL.B. 1932; LL.D.; D.C.L.; m. Sarah Hobart, d. Charles Adams Archibald, Hon. LL.D. and D.C.L., Mt. Allison Univ., St. Mary's Univ., St. Francis Xavier Univ., Acadia Univ., Dalhousie Univ.; Truro, N.S., 17 Nov. 1938; children: John Robert, Ruby Alison, George Isaac Jr.; SR. PARTNER, PATTERSON, SMITH, MATTHEWS AND GRANT; read law with Russell McInnes, Q.C., Halifax, N.S., and with F. H. Patterson, Q.C., Truro, N.S.; called to the Bar of N.S., 1932; cr. K.C. 1951; practised law alone in Truro, N.S., 1932-36, then joined with F. H. Patterson, Truro, N.S., in the firm of Patterson & Smith and successor firms; served in N.P.A.M., 1921-39; served in 2nd World War with Candn. Army (Active), 1939-46, with North Nova Scotia Highlanders and various Headquarters Staffs; M.B.E.; Mentioned in Despatches; Offr.; Order of Orange Nassau; Candn. Army (R), 1946-49 with rank of Lt.-Col.; Town Clerk, Town of Stewiacke, N.S., 1932-48, Town Solr., 1932-56; 1st el. to N.S. Leg. 1949, 1953, 1956, 1960, 1963, 1967, 1970; sworn of the Extve. Council, 20 Nov. 1956, and apptd. Min. of Hwys. Prov. Secy., 1960; Min. i/c Adm., Liquor Control Act, 1956-62; Min. Under Water Act, 1958-62; Premier of Nova Scotia 1967 till govt. def. Oct. 1970; Min. of Finance & Economics, 1962-May 1968; Hon. Col., N.S. Highlanders, 1967-72; Col., 1970; Pres., Candn. Good Roads Assn., 1960-61; summoned to Senate of Can. Aug. 1975; Pres., Nova Scotia Barristors Soc. 1976-77; Chmn., Bd. of Gov., Pine Hill Divinity Hall, 1979-80; mem., N.S. Barristers' Soc.; Candn. Bar Assn.;

Royal Candn. Legion; Conservative; United Church; recreation: photography; Home: 116 Burnyeat St., Truro, N.S. B2N 4R1

SMITH, George T., B.A.Sc.; mining executive; b. Haileybury, Ont., 28 Sept. 1929; s. Terence and Mary (Goodman) S.; e. Pub. and High Schs., Haileybury; Univ. of Toronto, B.A.Sc. 1952; Osgoode Hall Law Sch., Toronto, 1956; m. Margaret Mary, d. Norman H. Kearns, 17 Nov. 1956; children: Mary Elizabeth, George Terence, Ann, Martha Jane; VICE CHRMN., UNITED SISCOE MINES LTD.; Siscoe Metals of Ont. Ltd.; Pres., Camflo Mines Ltd.; LaLuz Mines Ltd.; Pres., Neomar Resources Inc.; Extve. Vice President and Dir., Chesbar Resources Inc.; Vice Pres. and Dir., Consolidated Morrison Explorations Ltd.; Dir., The Granby Mining Co. Ltd.; Rayrock Mines Ltd.; Lacanex Mining Co. Ltd.; Cochenour Willans Gold Mines Ltd.; Granisle Copper Ltd.; International Obaska Mines Ltd.; Silver Eureka Corp.; Westfield Minerals Ltd.; read law with Kilmer, Rumball, Gordon, Davis & Smith, Toronto, 1956; called to Bar of Ont. 1956; joined Northgate Exploration and various mines in Co.'s group as Vice Pres. and Counsel, 1962-70; mem. Bd. of Govs., St. Michael's Coll.; mem., Bd. Trade Metrop. Toronto; Kappa Sigma; R. Catholic; recreations: golf, curling, reading; Clubs: Albany; Granite; Canadian; York Downs Golf & Country; Rosedale Golf; The National Golf; Home: 146 Warren Rd., Toronto, Ont. M4V 2S5;

SMITH, Brig. Gerald Lucian Morgan, C.B.E., C.D., M.A., M.D.; b. Toronto, Ont., 11 June 1909; s. late Dr. Lewis Gerald Smith and Laura Lavinia (Morgan) S.; e. Univ. of Toronto Schs., 1921-26; Trinity Coll., Univ. of Toronto, 1926-30; Med. Faculty, Univ. of Toronto, B.A., M.A., M.D.; m. Edith Emmeline West, 4 May 1936; children: Sarah, Gerald, Deborah; Anglican; Home: "Eblana", Bayfield, Ont. N0M 1G0

SMITH, Gerald Meredith, C.A.; financial consultant; b. St. Johns, Que., 27 Sept. 1911; s. Gerald Meredith, M.Sc., and Helen Johnson (Layton) S.; e. Selwyn House Sch., Montreal; Westhill High Sch.; C.A. 1933; m. Marjorie Helen, d. late Hon. Gordon W. Scott, 28 Sept. 1939; one s. Gordon Scott; Dir. and chrmn., Atlas Copco Canada Ltd.; Dir., BP Canada Inc.; John de Kuyper & Son (Canada) Ltd.; Flakt Canada Ltd.; began with P. S. Ross & Sons, Montreal, Que. (predecessor firm to Touche Ross & Co.) and became a Partner in 1941; Sr. Partner until retirement 1974; during 2nd World War on loan to Atlantic Ferry Organ. as Financial Controller (1940-41) and to W.P.T.B. as Newsprint Adm. (1941-42); served in Candn. Army (Active), Black Watch of Can. with rank of Capt., 1942-45; Hon. Treas., Montreal Museum of Fine Arts, 1951-57; Past Gov., Candn. Tax Foundation; mem., Candn. Inst. Chart. Accts.; Anglican; recreation: golf; Clubs: Royal Ottawa Golf; Mount Royal; Mount Bruno Country; Forest & Stream; Home: 40 Boteler St., Ottawa, Ont. K1N 9C8

SMITH, Gord, R.C.A. (1967); sculptor; b. Montreal, Que., 8 Oct. 1937; s. Cyril John and Mildred Viola (MacCullough) S.; e. Westmount (Que.) Schs.; Sir George Williams Univ., Arch., 1956-59; m. 1stly Wendy Jane, d. Edward Stanley Mathews, Westmount, Que., 1 Oct. 1960; one s. and one d.; 2ndly Jacquelin Diana, d. L. Guy Eon, Ottawa, Ont.; one man shows: The Waddington Galleries, Montreal, 1959, '61, '63, '64, '67, '69; The Isaacs Gallery, Toronto, 1963; Blue Barn Gallery, Ottawa 1969; Waddington Galleries Internat. Exhn. 1971; Mira Godard Galleries Calgary 1980, Toronto 1981; exhns.: Art Gallery of Toronto, 1961; The Montreal Museum of Fine Arts, 1962; Nat. Gallery of Can., 1962; Group shows: First Can. Place, Toronto 1977; Harbourfront Art Gallery, Toronto 1977; Roberts Gallery, Toronto 1979-80; has rec'd. major bronze and steel sculpture comns. incl. McMaster Univ., Internat. Nickel, Dalhousie Univ., Bell Can., A.E. LePage, Can. Embassy, Bonn, W. Germ., Ont. Cancer Inst.,

The Waterloo Trust Co., The Montreal Star, Sault St. Marie Airport, Carling Wood Library, Webb, Zerafa, Menkes, Houston Architects, Weston's Ltd., Pattonia Beach Community Coll., Ottawa and metal screen for Candn. Pavilion, Expo 67; rec'd. Grand Prize, Nat. Fed. of Candn. Univs. for abstract painting "Growth", 1957; Purchase Award for Mural Competition, Que. Hydro, 1961; 1st Prize for Sculpture, Salon de la Jeune Peinture et Sculpture, 1962; 2nd Prize, Fountains and Monuments competition for Expo 67, 1965 and others; Finalist in Save the Children's Fund Fountain Competition, Toronto; Can. Council Grant, 1964; First Prize, Beth Tzedec Art Exhn., Toronto 1968; First Prize (sculpture) Winnipeg Hadassah Art Exhn. 1971; Ontario Soc. of Artists Award 1981; perm. collections, Montreal Museum of Fine Arts, The Nat. Gallery, Sir George Williams Univ., Weston's Texaco Ltd., First National, Vancouver, Musée d'Art Comtemporaire de Montréal, McGill Univ.; mem. Council, R.C.A. 1980-82; Dir., Ont. Soc. of Artists 1980-82, Vice-Pres., 1981- ; mem., Sculptors Soc.; recreations: golf, swimming, squash, running, musician, sailing, water skiing, photography, music; RR1, Ashburn, Ont. L0B 1A0

SMITH, Gordon A., R.C.A., LL.D.; artist; b. Hoveland, 18 June 1919; s. William George and Daisy (Appelbe) S.; came to Canada, 1933; e. Harrow County Sch., Eng.; Vancouver Sch. of Art (Grad.); California Sch. of Fine Arts; Harvard Univ.; LL.S. Simon Fraser 1973; m. Marion Katherine, d. Blair Fleming, White Rock, B.C., 15 Sept. 1941; is Prof. Fine Arts, Univ. of British Columbia; Council mem., R.C.A.; Past Pres., Canadian Group of Painters; member, B.C. Society of Artists; Candn. Society of Painter Etchers; rec'd. 1st Biennial Award, Nat. Gallery of Can.; Baxter Award, Ont. Soc. Artists; Allied Arts Medal, Roy. Arch. Inst. Can. 1978; executed murals, Vancouver Civic Theatre; paintings rep. in Nat. Gallery Can.; Toronto Art Gallery, London Art Museum, Queen's Univ., Hart House, Univ. of Toronto, Univ. of B.C., Vancouver and Victoria Art Galleries, etc.; rec'd. Arts Fellowship from Can. Council, 1960; paintings exhibited in Sao Paulo, Brazil 1961; Warsaw, Poland 1962; Candn. Biennial 1963; World's Fair, Seattle, 1963; (one man show) Agnes Lefort, Montreal, 1963; New Design Gallery, Vancouver, 1964; collab. with Arthur Erickson Osaka Worlds Fair 1970; one man exhns. Toronto, Montreal, Vancouver 1974-75; Art Advis. Comm., The Nat'l Capital Comm., Ottawa, 1977-79; rep. Can., Graphic Arts Portfolio, Prix Nobel, Sweden, 1978; rep. Candn. Sec. Biennials in Yugoslavia, Germany, Spain, France, Norway; works acquired by Museum of Modern Art, N.Y.; Victoria & Albert Museum, London, Eng.; served Overseas with P.P.C.L.I., Intelligence Offr.; wounded Sicily, 1943; Anglican; Home: 5030 The ByWay, West Vancouver, B.C. V7W 1L7

SMITH, Gordon Scott, Ph.D.; Canadian public servant; b. Montreal, Que. 19 July 1941; s. Gerald Meredith and Marjorie Helen (Scott) S.; e. Lower Can. Coll. Montreal; McGill Univ. B.A. 1962; Univ. of Chicago 1962-63; Mass. Inst. of Technol. Ph.D. 1966; separated; children: Derek Scott, Gavin Meredith; DEPT. MINISTER, MIN. OF STATE FOR SOCIAL DEVELOPMENT 1981- ; joined the Defence Research Bd. 1966; transf. to External Affairs 1967; Defence Liaison Div. 1967-68; mem. Candn. Del. to NATO 1968-70; Special Adv. to the Min. of Nat. Defence 1970-72; joined the Privy Council Offc. 1972; Dir. of Planning Devel. 1972-73; Dir. of Gov't. Organization 1973-76; Sr. Assist. Secy. (Machinery of Gov't.) 1976-78; Dep. Secy. to the Cabinet (Plans) 1978-79; returned to External Affairs as Dep. Under-Secy. (Mgmt. & Planning) 1979; Assoc. Secy. to the Cabinet, Privy Council Office, 1980-82; Trustee, Inst. Research Pub. Policy; Dir. Uranium Can. Ltd.; Bd. of Govs., Ashbury Coll.; mem. Internat. Inst. Strategic Studies; Anglican; recreations: tennis, squash, sailing, skiing; Clubs: Five Lakes (Que.); Ottawa Athletic; Rockcliffe Lawn Tennis; Home: 420 Minto Place,

Ottawa, Ont. K1M 0A8; Office: Rm. 1200, Vanguard Bldg., Ottawa, Ont. K1A 1G8

SMITH, Harold Duncan, M.A., Ph.D., D.Sc.; physicist; b. Port Hood, N.S., 30 Aug. 1906; s. Ernest Lynwood and Mary Florence (Wyatt) S.; e. John Oliver High Sch., Vancouver, B.C.; Univ. of B.C., B.A. 1927 (Gov.-Gen. Gold Medal); M.A. 1929 (Maths.); Univ. of Toronto, M.A. 1930 (Physics), Ph.D. 1933; awarded Nat. Research Scholarships, 1929-32; Acadia Univ., D.Sc. 1956; m. Jean Urquhart, d. William Matheson of Vancouver, B.C., 15 Aug. 1934; former Dir., N.S. Research Found. (Pres. 1946-68); mem., Defence Research Bd. Can., 1953-56; Demonst. and Lect. Univ. of Toronto, Dept. of Physics, 1932-35; joined Dept. of Physics, Univ. of B.C., 1938, Prof. 1946; Research Physicist, Nat. Research Council, 1941 and 1942, in radar work; Instr. with U.S. Nave V-12 Program, Notre Dame, 1944, and rocket research 1946 at Johns Hopkins Univ.; mem., Am. Optical Sic.; Am. Physical Soc.; Roy. Astron. Soc. of Can. (Past Pres., Vancouver Br.); B.C. Acad. Sciences (Vice-Pres.); N.S. Inst. Sciences (Pres. 1954-56); Assn. Prof. Engrs. N.S.; Engn. Inst. of Can.; St. Francis Xavier Univ. D.Sc. 1962; United Church; recreations: fishing, hunting, golf. Home: Box 94, Waverley, N.S. BON 2S0.

SMITH, Hon. Horace B., M.L.A.; politician; b. Saint John, N.B. 17 March 1914; s. Herbert H. and Ellen (Fielding) S.; e. Hoyt, N.B. schs.; Saint John Vocational Sch.; Rothesay (N.B.) Coll. Sch.; Fredericton Business Coll.; m. Grace P. d. James Arthurs, Hoyt, N.B. 14 Sept. 1940; MIN. OF MUNICIPAL AFFAIRS, N.B. 1972- ; Sunbury Co. Councillor 1940-55, Co. Secy. 1965-70; Extve. Secy. N.B. P. Cons. Party; Chrmn. Queen Sunbury W. Mem. Hosp.; el. M.L.A. for Sunbury prov. g.e. 1970, re-el. since; Min. without Portfolio 1970-72; Hon. citizen, Republic of Madawaska; received certificate of Commendation from Maritime Municipal Training and Devel. Bd.; P. Conservative; Anglican; Club: Gladstone Curling (hon. mem. and Past Pres.); 700 Forest Hill Rd., Apt. 305, Fredericton, N.B.

SMITH, I. Norman, O.C. (1972), LL.D., D.Litt.; b. Ottawa, Ont., 28 Oct. 1909; s. Ernest Norman and Bessie (Irving) S.; e. Lakefield (Ont.) Prep. Sch. (now Lakefield Coll. Sch.); LL.D., Brock Univ.; D.Litt., Carleton Univ.; m. Mary Frances, d. J. T. O'Neil, Ottawa, 26 May 1936; Pres., Ed. "Ottawa Journal" and The Journal Publishing Co. of Ottawa Ltd., till retired 1972; Pres., The Canadian Press 1970-72; Reporter, "Ottawa Journal", 1928-30; Reporter or Editor with The Candn. Press in Ottawa, Toronto, Winnipeg, Calgary, Vancouver, New York and London, Eng., 1932-38; mem., Press Gallery, Ottawa; former Chrmn., Candn. Sec.; Commonwealth Press Union; mem., N.W.T. Council 1961-64 Chrmn. (1962) Ottawa Community Chest Campaign; Gov., Lakefield College Sch.; Author, "J.F.B. Livesay, A Memoir"; "The Journal Men", 1974; "A Reporter Reports", 1960; also booklets and articles; Ed., "The Diary of E.W. Harrold", 1947; "The Unbelievable Land (Arctic Canada)", 1964; Nat'l Newspaper Award for foreign correspondence, Cdn. Nat'l Press Club, 1955; named mem. of Cdn. News Hall of Fame, 1979; former Pres., Candn. Club, Ottawa; mem. Bd. Govs., Carleton Univ.; Lakefield Sch.; Independent; Anglican; Clubs: Rideau; Royal Ottawa Golf; Ottawa Ski Club; Home: 500 Buena Vista, Rockcliffe, Ottawa, Ont. K1M 0W3

SMITH, Ian Cormack Palmer, M.Sc., Ph.D., F.C.I.C., F.R.S.C.; biophysicist; b. Winnipeg, Man. 23 Sept. 1939; s. Cormack and Grace Mary (Palmer) S.; e. W. Kildonan Coll. Inst. Winnipeg 1956; Univ. of Man. B.Sc. 1961, M.Sc. 1962; Cambridge Univ. Ph.D. 1965; Stanford Univ. postdoctoral study 1966; m. Eva Gunilla d. late Sven Landvik 27 March 1965; children: Brittmarie Siv Grace, Sven Cormack, Duncan Fredrik, Roderick Bjoern; HEAD OF MOLECULAR BIOPHYSICS SEC., NAT. RESEARCH

COUNCIL OF CAN. since 1970; Adjunct Prof. of Chem. Carleton Univ. and Univ. of Ottawa; Research Biophys. Bell Telephone Labs. Murray Hill, N.J. 1966-67; Asst. Research Offr. Nat. Research Council 1967, Assoc. Research Offr. 1970, Sr. Research Offr. since 1974; Trustee, Ottawa mem. Soc. 1969-70, 1980-82; rec'd Merck, Sharp and Dohme Award 1978; Ayerst Award 1978; Barringer Award 1979; author over 200 research papers biophys. and chem.; mem. Candn. Biochem. Soc.; Biophys. Soc.; Chem. Instit. Can.; recreations: tennis, curling; Home: 550 Rivershore Cres., Ottawa, Ont. K1J 7Y7; Office: Ottawa, Ont. K1A 0R6.

SMITH, J. Herbert, M.Sc., D.Sc.; consulting engineer; b. Fredericton, N.B., 21 Nov. 1909; s. Charles Arthur and Amy (Marshall) S.; e. Pub. and High Schs., Fredericton, N.B.; Univ. of New Brunswick, B.Sc. (E.E.) 1932, M.Sc. (E.E.) 1942, D.Sc., 1958; Assumption Univ., D.Sc. 1961; m. Eldred Marian, d. F. J. Shaidle, Waterdown, Ont., 1937; Dir. Emeritus, Canadian Imperial Bank of Commerce; Dir., Sun Life Assurance Co.; Canadian Realty Investors; Acres Consulting Services Ltd.; Pres., Wellesley Hosp. Research Inst., Toronto; joined Canadian General Electric Co. Ltd. test course in 1932 and after experience in engn., hdqrs. and dist. sales work was apptd. Mgr. of Supply Sales for Ont. in 1945; Mgr. of Apparatus Sales for Ont. 1948; Gen. Mgr., Wholesale Divn., 1951, and Vice-Pres. and Gen. Mgr. 1953; Pres. and Chief Extve. Offr. 1957, Chrmn. of Bd. and Chief Extve. Offr. 1970-72; Chrmn. Bd., DeHavilland Aircraft of Can. Ltd. 1974-78; mem., Assn. of Prof. Engrs. of Ont. (Pres. 1953); Fellow, Am. Inst. of Elect. & Electronics Engrs.; mem., Engn. Inst. of Can.; Protestant; Clubs: National; Toronto Hunt; Toronto; York; Home: 44 Charles St. W., Toronto, Ont. M4Y 1R8

SMITH, MRS. J. T. — see: Dumbrille, Dorothy

SMITH, Maj.-Gen. James Desmond Blaise, C.B.E. (1944), D.S.O. (1944), C.D., K.St.J.; Candn. Army (ret.); b. Ottawa, Ont., 7 Oct. 1911; s. William George and Anna Christine (OBrien) S.; e. Univ. of Ottawa, 1925-29; Roy. Mil. Coll., 1929-33; Staff Coll., Camberley, Eng., 1940; Imp. Defence Coll.,London, Eng., 1947; m. Miriam Irene, d. Arthur Stephen Blackburn, London, Ont., 4 Sept. 1937; children: James Desmond, Stephen George; Chrmn. & Chief Extve., Pillar Engineering Ltd.; Dir., RTZ Industries Ltd. and other cos.; joined Royal Candn. Dragoons, 1933; served in World War, 1939-45; twice Mentioned in Despatches; Commandant, Roy. Mil. Coll. 1945-46; Mil. Secretary of the Cabinet Defence Comte., 1948-49; Chrmn., Candn. Jt. Staff and Candn. Mil. Rep. at Supreme Hdqrs., Allied Powers Europe, 1951-54; Commandant, Nat. Defence Coll. Can. 1954-58; Adj. Gen., 1958-62; named (first) Col. of Regt. of Candn. Guards, July 1961-66; awarded Aristion Andrias (Greek); Chevalier, Legion of Hon. (France); Croix de guerre (France); Legion of Merit (U.S.); Order of Republic (Italy); Vice Pres., Engn. Industs. Assn.; Clubs: Carlton; Country; Rideau.

SMITH, James Hamilton, B.Com., C.A.; pulp and paper executive; b. Montreal, Que. 14 July 1931; s. Alexander Laidlaw S.; e. Montreal W. High Sch. 1949; McGill Univ. B.Com. 1953; C.A. 1955; m. Lois Margaret d. late Fred Tanner 2 Oct. 1954; children: Sandra, Terri, Scott; PRES. AND DIR., DOMTAR INC. 1981- ; joined Price Waterhouse & Co. Montreal 1953, Audit Supvr. 1960, Audit Mgr. 1963, Asst. Controller Domtar Inc. Montreal 1966, Controller 1968, Vice Pres. Domtar Pulp & Paper Products 1971, Vice Pres. Finance Domtar Inc. 1974, Extve. Vice Pres. 1978, Pres. Domtar Packaging 1979; Past Dir. Fed. Appeal Greater Montreal; Past Chrmn. Extve. Comte. Combined Health Assn. Greater Montreal; Chrmn. Financial Offrs. Comte. Candn. Pulp & Paper Assn. 1977; mem. Ordre des comptables agréés Qué.; Ont. Inst. C.A.'s; Phi Gamma Delta; Protestant; recreations: golf, skiing, baseball, swimming; Clubs: St. James's; Home: 27 Manresa Court, Beaconsfield, Que. H9W 5H5; Office: (P.O. Box 7210, Montreal, Que. H3C 3M1) 395 de Maisonneuve Blvd. W., Montreal, Que. H3A 1L6.

SMITH, John Forsyth, B.Com.; banker; b. Liverpool, Eng., 24 Sept. 1917; s. late Madge Irene (Cochrane) and late John Forsyth Smith; e. Cannock House Sch., Eltham, Kent, Eng.; Horton Acad., Wolfville, N.S.; Queen's Univ., B.Com. 1949; m. Ruth Audrey, d. L. C. Dennison, Hortonville, N.S., 3 May 1947; one d. Jacalyn Ethel; CHRMN., ROYWEST HOLDINGS LTD.; RoyWest Trust Corp. (Bahamas) Ltd.; RoyWest Invests. Ltd.; Chrmn., Royal Bank of Can. Internat. Ltd.; entered the Royal Bank of Can., Wolfville, N.S., 1935; served in Brs. in N.S. until 1940; H.Q., Montreal, 1949-52; Inspr., Port of Spain, Trinidad, Asst. Mgr., Port of Spain Br. and Mgr., 1952-58; Far Eastern Rep., Hong Kong, 1958-61; Agent, N.Y., 1961-62; Mgr., London, Eng. 1963; Pres., Roy. Bank of Can. Internat Ltd., 1971-78; served with R.C.A.F. 1940-45 as Navig., final rank Flt. Lt.; Mentioned in Despatches 1942; United Church; recreation: golf; Clubs: Overseas Bankers; Hong Kong; Address: P.O. Box N-4889, Nassau, Bahamas

SMITH, John McSwan, B.Com., F.M.C.; management consultant; b. Burbank, Scot., 15 Aug. 1921; s. James Young and Isabella (McSwan) S.; e. Goderich (Ont.) Coll. Inst.; McGill Univ. B.Com. (Lt. Gov.'s Bronze Medal), post-grad. studies Econ. 1950; m. Kathryn Elizabeth d. William A. Corkum, 7 Apl. 1945; children: Shelley, Jeffrey, Graham, Cameron; CHRMN., WOODS, GORDON & CO. since 1969; joined Newsprint Assn. Can. 1948; Special Asst. to Dir. Pulp & Paper Div. Dept. of Defence Production 1951, serving until Div. disbanded 1952; subsequently Econ. and Secy. Pulp Sec. Candn. Pulp & Paper Assn.; served on Staff Royal Comn. on Can's Econ. Prospects 1956; Secy. Comte. on Organ. Govt. in Ont. 1958-59; joined present firm 1957, Partner 1960, Extve. Partner 1967; served with RCNVR during World War II, rank Lt.; Chrmn., Bd. Dirs., St. Joseph's Health Centre; Trustee St. Luke's Un. Ch.; author or co-author various publs.; Queen's Jubilee Medal; mem., Inst. Mang. Consultants Ont.; Dir., Inst. Mang. Consultants of Can.; Protestant; recreation: golf; Clubs: Ontario; Islington Golf (Pres.); Home: 83 Edenvale Cres., Islington, Ont. M9A 4A5; Office: (Box 251) Toronto-Dominion Centre, Toronto, Ont. M5K 1J7

SMITH, John Roxburgh; b. London, Ont. 10 Nov. 1936; s. Hector Hugh Raleigh S.; e. Hillfield Coll. Hamilton 1957; Hamilton Teachers' Coll. 1958; McMaster Univ. B.A.; m. Judith d. George Pollard, Cambridge, Ont. 12 June 1976; children: Hayley Elizabeth, Drew Alexander; COMMR. WORKMEN'S COMPENSATION BD. since 1977; Ald. City of Hamilton 1963-67; MPP for Hamilton Mt. 1967-77, Min. of Correctional Services Ont. 1975-76, Min. of Govt. Service Ont. 1977; rec'd Centennial Medal 1967; Trustee Wycliffe Coll. Toronto; Past Pres. Hamilton Dist. Candn. Bible Soc.; Ont. Hortic. Assn.; Freemason; P. Conservative; Anglican; recreations: gardening, fishing, swimming, travel; Club: Albany; Home: 20 Churchill Ave., Hamilton, Ont. L9A 1J5; Office: 2 Bloor St. E., Toronto, Ont. M4W 3C3.

SMITH, Joseph Percy, Ph.D., D.Litt., LL.D.; b. Canora, Sask., 22 March 1914; s. Rev. Percy and Alice (Hudson) S.; e. Univ. of Sask., B.A. 1940, M.A. 1945; Univ. of Cal., Berkeley, Ph.D. 1949; Carleton Univ., D.Litt. 1970; m. Morine Barbara, d. late Chris Baldwinson, 30 June 1964; children (by previous marriage): Sylvia (Mrs. John Gazsi), Valerie (Mrs. L. Warke), Rhonda, Kevin; EMERITUS PROF. OF DRAMA, UNIV. OF GUELPH, 1981- ; Vice Pres., Academic 1970-76; Prof. of Drama, Univ. of Guelph, 1976-80; Bank of N.S. 1929-37; Instr. in Eng., Univ. of Sask., 1945-46; Asst. Prof. 1948; Assoc. Prof.

1951; Prof. 1958; Teaching Asst., Univ. of Cal., Berkeley, 1946-47; Univ. Fellow in Eng. 1947-48; Visiting Prof. of Dramatic Art, summer 1956; Dir., Shakespearian Seminar, Stratford Shakespearian Festival, summer 1958; Can. Council Sr. Research Fellowship, London, Eng., 1960-61; Extve. Secy., Candn. Assn. Univ. Teachers, 1964-69; Nuffield Travelling Fellowship in Humanities 1969; served with RCAF 1942-45; author, "The Unrepentant Pilgrim: A Study of the Develpment of Bernard Shaw", 1965; also essays and articles for various journs.; Hon. Life mem., Candn. Assn. Univ. Teachers (Milner Mem. Award 1973); LL.D. Univ. Windsor 1974; mem., Humanities Assn. Can.; Assn. Candn. Univ. Teachers Eng.; Candn. Soc. Study Higher Educ.; recreations: reading, music, theatre, gardening; Home: "Bardsey Farm", R.R. 3, Guelph, Ont. N1H 6H9

SMITH, Kenneth Hugo, C.A.; association extve.; b. Winnipeg, Man. 6 May 1917; s. William Alfred and Janie (Hugo) S.; e. Univ. Man.; C.A.; m. Annie Jean d. John Arthur 1943; children: Barry, Roger, Craig, Lynda, Heather; PRES., FINANCIAL EXTVES. INST. OF CAN. 1979- ; Assessor, DNR Taxation, 1946-51; various positions to V.P., Treas., Contr. and Secy., Eddy Forest Products Ltd. (formerly the KVP Co. Ltd.) 1951-69; Secy. (V.P. 1977), George Weston Ltd. 1969-79; Officer and Dir. of many subsidiaries; R.C.A.F. 1942-45; mem. Candn., Ont., Man. Insts. of C.A.'s; Candn. and Ont. Chambrs. of Comm.; Toronto Bd. of Trade; Fin. Extves Inst.; Conservative; Anglican; Club: Ontario; recreations: reading, walking, singing; Home: 1762 Valentine Garden, Mississauga, Ont. L5J 1H5; Office: 141 Adelaide St. W., Toronto, Ont. M5H 3L5

SMITH, Lawrence Napier, B.A.; journalist; b. Toronto, Ont., 17 Mar. 1919; s. Ruth (Langlois) and late Rev. George Napier S.; e. Lafayette High Sch., Buffalo, N.Y.; Ridley Coll., St. Catharines, Ont.; Univ. of Toronto, B.A. (Hon. Hist.) 1941, and John Moss Mem. Scholaras as Best All Round Student; m. Dorothy Joan (died 4 Dec. 1971), 2ndly Briar, d. late E. E. H. Wright, 19 May 1973; children: Sheila, Roger, Priscilla; RETIRED EDITOR-IN-CHIEF, "ST. CATHARINES STANDARD" (Daily newspaper estbd. 1891); 1970-80 (Mang. Ed. l955-70); Dir., The Canadian Press; Editor, "The Varsity", Univ. of Toronto, 1940-41; Reporter for present Newspaper at various intervals, 1938-46 when he became Reporter and Columnist; in U.K., Europe as Winner of Kemsley Empire Journalist Scholarship, 1949-50; promoted to Asst. City Editor, 1950; City Editor, 1952; Mang. Ed. 1955-70; Ed.-in-Chief 1970-80; Winner, W. Ont. Newspaper Award for Spot News, 1957; Pres., Candn. Mang. Editors' Conf., 1959-60; mem. and Chrmn., St. Catharines Public Library Bd. 1952-64; C.O.T.C., Univ. of Toronto, 1940-41; 10th Field Batty. (R), St. Catharines, Ont., 1941-42; 23rd Field Regt. (SP), R.C.A. Overseas, rank of Capt., 1942-46; Chrmn., St. Catharines Chamber Comm. Public Relations Comte.; 1958-60; mem. of Primate's Comte. for new nat. publication for Ang. Ch.; Pres., St. Catharines Rotary Club, 1977-78; Past Vice-Pres., St. Catharines Jr. Chamber Comm.; mem., Bd. of Management, St. George's Ang. Ch., St. Catharines, Ont., Warden, 1962-64; Kappa Alpha (Pres. 1940-41); Anglican; Home: 27 Adelene Cres., St. Catharines, Ont. L2T 3C6; Office: 17 Queen St., St. Catharines, Ont. L2R 5G5

SMITH, Leslie Raymond; retired transportation executive; b. Summerland, B.C., 16 Nov. 1916; s. Harold and Mary E. (Thornthwaite) S.; e. Pub. and High Sch.,Summerland, B.C.; Univ. of W. Ont., Business Adm. Course; Sr. Regional Vice Pres., Pacific Region, Canadian Pacific Rail, since 1974-78; Dir., Pacific Coast Terminals; Pacific Logging Ltd.; Canadian Forestry Assn. B.C.; joined present Co. as Telegrapher and Agent, Revelstoke Div., 1937; assigned to Office of Supt.- Transport, Winnipeg 1943, later becoming Travelling Car Service Agent for W. Lines; Asst. Supt., Lethbridge,

1946, Nelson, B.C., 1948, Cranbrook, 1949; Supt., Penticton, B.C., 1950, Revelstoke, B.C. 1952, Calgary, Alta., 1954, Medicine Hat, Alta., 1955; Gen. Supt., Sask. Dist., Moose Jaw, 1956, B.C. Dist., Vancouver, 1958; Asst. to Pres., Montreal, 1960; Asst. Gen. Mgr., Prairie Region, Winnipeg, 1962; Vice-Pres., Pacific Region, Vancouver, 1963; Vice Pres. Eastern Region, Toronto 1964-74; Past Pres., Bd. Trade Metrop. Toronto; mem. Vancouver Bd. Trade; Candn. Chamber Comm.; Club: The Vancouver; Home: 4330 Salish Dr., Vancouver, B.C. V6N 3M7;

SMITH, Lois Irene; O.C. ballerina; choreographer; b. Vancouver, B.C. 8 Oct. 1929; d. William and Doris (Newbery) Smith; e. Templeton Jr. High Sch. Vancouver; Rosemary Deveson Sch. and Mara McBirney Sch. ballet training, Vancouver; m. David Charles Adams 13 May 1950 (divorced); one d. Janine Dariel Adams; 1 grands. Mark; CHRMN. SCH. OF DANCE, GEORGE BROWN COLL. OF APPLIED ARTS AND TECHNOL. first prof. performance 1945; performed in light operas and musicals Can. and USA 1945-51; joined Nat. Ballet Co. 1951-69, performed as Ballerina 1951-55, became Can.'s First Prima Ballerina 1955-69; among her most acclaimed roles were those of the Swan Queen in Swan Lake and Caroline in Antony Tudor's Lilac Garden; estbd. Lois Smith Sch. of Dance 1969, joined present Coll. 1975; performed various CBC TV Productions 1954-69, Choreographer 3 TV Specials CBC; Choreographer, Candn. Opera Co. Aida and Eugene Onegin 1972, The Merry Widow 1973, Joan of Arc 1978; Alberta Ballet Co. and Winnipeg Opera Co.; Florida Ballet Co. 1975; South West Ballet Co. 1977; Co-Dir. and Choreographer, Candn. Silent Players; many engagements as guest teacher in Can. and elsewhere; guest appearance Nat. Ballet of Can. as Black Queen in Swan Lake (Special Lois Smith Night) 1969; guest artist 1978 as Carabose in Sleeping Beauty; guest artist Nov. 1979 as Queen Mother in Sleeping Beauty; Guest Artist, Nat. Ballet of Can. as Giovanina in Napoli, 1981; Co-choreographer, "The Dancing Circus" (with Earl Kraul) for Dance Co. of Ont., 1979; Artistic Dir., Guest Artist, Nat. Ballet Co. 1981; rec'd Centennial Medal 1967; Internat. Women's Day Bronze Medal 1977; received Order of Canada, Officer, 1980; mem. Candn. Dance Teachers Assn.; Dance in Can. Assn.; A.C.T.R.A-Equity; Toronto Arts Council (Dir.); Hon. mem., Cdn. Dance Members of Amer.; recreations: weaving, designing wall hangings, sewing; Artistic Dir., The Dance Co. of Ont.; Office: P.O. Box 1015, Station B, Toronto, Ont. M5T 2T9.

SMITH, Rev. Michael Joseph, O.M.I., C.M.; Roman Catholic priest; b. Leduc, Alta. 1 Feb. 1911; s. Luke and Victoria (Halwa) S.; e. St. John's Coll. Edmonton 1925; St. Paul's Coll. Winnipeg 1927; Univ. of Alta. 1927-28; St. Charles Semy. North Battleford, Sask. 1933-36, 1938-39; Oblate Semy. Obra, Poland 1936-38; mem. Oblate Fathers of Assumption Prov. (Treas. Corp.); Chrmn. Copernicus Lodge (sr. citizens complex); Dir. Candn. Polish Millenium Fund; Founder (1962-63) and Dir. Queen of Apostles Renewal Centre; co-founder St. Stanislaus St. Casimir's Parish Credit Union 1946; Founder St. Casimir's Parish 1948; Founder of Copernicus Lodge, Sr. Citizens Apts.; K. of C.; R. Catholic; Address: Queen of Apostles Renewal Centre, 1617 Blythe Rd. Mississauga, Ont. L5H 2C3.

SMITH, Peter John, M.A., Ph.D.; educator; b. Rakaia, N.Z. 18 Sept. 1931; s. Sidney Charles and Ethel May (Pettit) S.; e. Ashburton High Sch. N.Z. 1948; Dunedin Teachers' Training Coll. N.Z. Cert. 1950; Univ. of Otago, N.Z. 1949-51; Canterbury Univ. Coll. N.Z. B.A. 1952, M.A. 1953; Univ. of Toronto Dipl. Town & Regional Planning 1959; Univ. of Edinburgh Ph.D. 1964; m. Sheana Mary d. late Alexander James Buchanan Lee, Bridge of Allan, Scot. 30 May 1959; children: Katrina Alison, Hugh Roger; PROF. OF GEOGRAPHY, UNIV. OF ALTA. 1969- ; various teaching positions N.Z. and Gt. Brit. 1952-55; Research Planner City of Calgary 1956-59; joined

present Univ. 1959, Chrmn. of Geog. 1967-75; mem. Science Adv. Comte. Alta. Environment Conserv. Authority 1971-77; Vice Chrmn. and Chrmn. Grants Adv. Comte. Alta. Environment Research Trust; mem. various awards comtes. Social Sciences & Humanities, Research Council Can.; recipient Cert of Distinction Town Planning Inst. Can. 1959; Central Mortgage & Housing Corp., Can. Council and Social Sciences & Humanities Research Council Fellowships; author "Population and Production" 1967; "The Edmonton-Calgary Corridor" 1978; ed. "The Prairie Provinces" 1972; "Edmonton: The Emerging Metropolitan Pattern" 1978; over 50 essays, tech. reports urban planning, pollution, geog. Alta.; mem. Candn. Inst. Planners; Candn. Assn. Geogs. (Councillor 1966-70, Vice Pres., Pres., Past Pres. 1972-75, Ed. "The Canadian Georgrapher" 1978-); Home: 14 Marlboro Rd., Edmonton, Alta. T6J 2C6; Office: Edmonton, Alta. T6G 2H4.

SMITH, Philip Edward Lake, A.M., Ph.D., D.Litt., F.R.S.C.; archaeologist; b. Fortune, Nfld. 12 Aug. 1927; s. late George Frederick and Alice M. (Lake) S.; e. Fortune U.C. High Sch., Acadia Univ. B.A. 1948; Harvard Univ. A.M. 1957, Ph.D. 1962; Thaw Fellow, Harvard, 1954, 56, 60; Univ. de Bordeaux Special Research 1958-59; Mem. Univ. of Nfld. D.Litt. 1976; m. Dr. Fumiko d. late Rev. Dr. Jokei Ikawa, Osaka, Japan 1959; one s. Douglas Philip Edward; PROF. D'ANTHROPOLOGIE, UNIV. DE MONTREAL; served with 401 (Aux.) Fighter Squadron, R.C.A.F.1949-51, rank Aircraftman 1st cl.; Lecturer, Asst. and Assoc. Prof. Univ. of Toronto 1961-66; Assoc. Prof. and Prof., Univ. de Montréal since 1966; Dir., Can. Govt. Arch. Exped. to Egypt, 1962-3 in UNESCO NUBIAN SALVAGE Programme; dir. 7 archaeol. expeditions (Egypt, Iran) since 1962; conducted archaeol. research in Mexico (1954), USA (1955-56), France (1957-59), Iraq (1957), W. Indies (1968, 1977); participant various local and internat. confs. prehistoric archaeol.; occasional consultant; rec'd 1967, Can. Council Research grant 1969, 1971, 1974, 1977, leave grant 1970-71, 1981-82; Centre de Recherches Carribes, Univ. de Montréal (mem. du Conseil, 1977-79); Del. Perm. Council, Internat. Union Anthrop. & Ethnol. Sciences; author "Aboriginal Stone Constructions in the Southern Piedmont" 1962; "Le Solutréen en France" 1966; "Food Production and its Consequences" 1976; contrib. Cambridge History of Africa, Vol. I, 1981; over 60 articles and reports prehistoric archaeol. research; mem. Internat. Union Prehistoric & Protohistoric Sciences Can del. to Perm. Council, 1978- ; Foreign Fellow, Am. Anthrop. Assn.; Am. Assn. Advan. Sci.; The Prehistoric Soc. (Eng.); Current Anthrop. Assoc.; Soc. for Am. Archaeol.; mem. ed Bd., journal Paléorient (Paris); Candn. Soc. Archaeol. Abroad (Vice-Pres.), 1970-71; Pres., 1971-73); Nfld. Hist. Soc.; Royal Society of Canada (elec. 1978); East Coast Archaeological, Marching & Chowder Society; Soc. of Sigma Xi; recreations: walking, reading and idleness; Home: 3955 Ramezay Ave., Montreal, Que. H3Y 3K3; Office: (C.P. 6128, Succ.) Montreal, Que. H3C 3J7.

SMITH, R. Ross, B.Eng., M.B.A., P.Eng.; executive; b. Three Rivers, Que., 28 July 1930; s. Frederick R. Mitchell and Elsie (Anderson) S.; e. Three Rivers (Que.) High Sch., 1947; McGill Univ. B.Eng. 1952; Stanford Univ., M.B.A. 1958; m. Dorothy Grace, d. Julius Milbrath, 18 Aug. 1956; VICE PRES.; ENTERPRISE OPERATIONS, JAMES RICHARDSON & SONS LTD.; Chrmn. Bd., Systems Equipment Ltd.; Vice Pres. and Dir., Pioneer Shipping Ltd.; Pres. and Dir., Enterprise Equipment Ltd.; Marine Pipeline Construction of Canada Ltd.; Dir., Sorel Elevators Ltd.; E. H. Price Limited; Gt. Lakes Waterways Devel. Assn.; Engineer, Production Department, Shell Oil Co., Calgary, 1952-56; Mang. Assistant, Home Oil Co., Calgary 1958, Asst. to Pres. 1960-68; Vice Pres. and Gen. Mgr., Cygnus Corp., 1966-68; mem. Assn. Prof. Engrs. Man.; Delta Kappa Epsilon; Protestant; recreations: golf, cross-country skiing, eonology; Clubs: Manitoba; St. Charles Country; Home: P1-221 Wellington Cres., Winnipeg, Man. R3M 0A1; Office: One Lombard Pl., Winnipeg, Man. R3B 0Y1

SMITH, Robert; executive; b. London, Eng., 16 Apl. 1938; s. Robert George and Hilda Ena (Walder) S.; e. St. Olave's and St. Saviour's Grammar Sch.; m. Olive May, d. George Sims, 5 Oct. 1957; three s., David Robert, Michael John, Andrew Keith, one d. Jennifer Ann; CHRMN., PRES. & DIR., TALCORP ASSOC. LTD. since 1970; Chrmn., CERES Resources Ltd.; Dir., Rogers Cablesystems Inc.; Reichold Ltd.; Bond Industries Inc.; The Genesis Project, N.V.; Sr. Extve., The Thomson Organisation Ltd., London, Eng. 1964-70; mem. Bd. of Govs., Crescent Sch., Toronto; Home: 36 Glenorchy Rd., Don Mills, Ont. M3C 2P9; Office: BOX 351, Toronto-Dominion Centre, Toronto, Ont.

SMITH, Robert Alexander, Q.C., B.A., LL.B.; b. Montreal, Que. 10 June 1928; s. Alexander Guthrie and Agnes (Boyce) S.; e. Westmount (Que.) High Sch.; Dalhousie Univ. B.A., LL.B.; m. Joan Elizabeth d. James Myrden 10 May 1951; three s. Robert Bruce, James Stuart, David Alexander; PARTNER, SMITH, LYONS, TORRANCE, STEVENSON & MAYER; read law with Hon. Gordon S. Cowan; called to Bar of N.S. 1953, Ont. 1953; cr. Q.C. 1964; mem. Law Soc. Upper Can.; N.S. Barristers Soc.; Advocates Soc. Ont. (Dir. 1971-74); Candn. Bar Assn.; Fed. Ins. Counsel; Assoc. mem. Am. Bar Assn.; Co. York Law Assn.; Lawyers Club Toronto; Phi Delta Theta (Pres. 1951); United Church; recreations: skiing, golf, tennis, sailing; Clubs: York Downs Golf & Country (Past Dir., Pres. 1968-69); Osler Bluffs Ski (Past Dir.); Home: 16 Blair Athol Cres., Islington, Ont. M9A 1X5; Office; (P.O. Box 38) Toronto-Dominion Centre, Toronto, Ont. M5K 1C7

SMITH, Robert Neville, C.D.; educator; b. Winnipeg, Man. 3 Sept. 1925; s. William Neville and Caroline (Gowers) S.; e. Royal Roads Victoria Dipl. 1944; Univ. of W. Ont. Dipl. 1965; m. Joan Clark 21 July 1947; children: Julian, Sally; PRES. AND MANAGING DIR. SPROTT-SHAW COLL. OF BUSINESS LTD. 1976- ; Commdr., RCN, Various, 1942-66; Dir. Treasury Bd. Ottawa 1967-71; Dir. Gen. Ministry Urban Affairs 1971-73; Nat. Dir. Educanada 1971-75; Trustee, Greater Victoria Lib. Bd. 1980-82; Dir., Goodwill Industries; former Trustee Greater Victoria Sch. Bd.; former Gov. Glenlyon Sch.; Norfolk House Sch.; mem. Assn. Candn. Career Colls. (Dir. 1978, Vice Pres. 1979, Pres. 1980); Private Career Training Council B.C.; Naval Offrs. Assn. Can.; recreations: skiing, sailing; Clubs: Rotary; Men's Canadian (Vice Pres. 1980, Pres. 1981); Home: 1025 Pentrelew Pl., Victoria, B.C. V8Y 4J5; Office: 1822 Blanshard St., Victoria, B.C. V8T 4J1.

SMITH, Ross; advertising executive; b. St. Lambert, Que. 14 Aug. 1927; s. Henry Earnest and Dorothy Agnes (Ahern) S.; e. Hogg's Private Sch. for Boys; Montreal High Sch.; McGill Univ., Extension Courses; m. Pauline Marie, d. Anarthine Jolicoeur, 5 March 1949; two d., Lynne, Roslyn; PRESIDENT, CROMBIE ADVERTISING LTD. since 1970; joined Stevenson & Scott Ltd., Graphic Arts Dept., Montreal; Radio-TV Dir. 1950; Asst. Mgr. Vancouver Office 1950, Creative Dir., Toronto 1953, Account Mgr. 1958-62, Vice Pres. 1963; merged with present Co. 1964; Vice Pres. Creative 1965, Vice Pres. and Sr. Account Extve. 1966, Extve. Vice Pres. 1968; daily nat. radio series 1966-69; Kiwanis International Ambass. of Goodwill 1967; professional speaker handled by Speakers' Bureau Int'l. and guest lectr. Community Colls.; served with Duke of Connaught Royal Candn. Hussars (R) 1945-49; rank Sgt.; rec'd Royal Humane Soc. Award for Bravery; received Outstanding Service Award from Assn. of Cdn. Advertisers, 1980; mem. Que. Lib. Party; Past Dir., Inst. Can. Advertisers; mem. Que. Soc. Upper Candns.; Past Dir., Quebec Soc. for Crippled Children; Past Pres., St. Bruno Riding Club; Advertising & Sales Extves. Club

Montreal; Presbyterian; recreations: riding, tennis/Chinguacousy Country (Dir.); swimming; 111 Richmond St. W., Toronto, Ont.

SMITH, S. G. Denis, M.A., B.Litt.; professor; b. Edmonton, Alta., 3 Oct. 1932; s. Sidney Bruce and Doris Gertrude (Charlesworth) S.; e. McGill Univ., B.A. 1953; Oxford Univ., B.A. 1955, M.A. 1959, B.Litt. 1959; m. Dawn Louise, d. Sir Donald Banks, K.C.B., D.S.O., M.C., Cadnam, Hampshire, 8 July 1961; PROF. OF POLITICS, TRENT UNIV., Instructor, Department of Pol. Econ., Univ. of Toronto, 1956-57, Lectr., 1957-58; Registrar and Lectr. in Pol. Science, York Univ., 1960-61, Asst. Prof., 1961-63; Chrmn. Dept., Trent Univ. 1966-70; Ed. "Journal of Canadian Studies" 1966-75; "The Canadian Forum", 1975-79; Master, Champlain Coll. 1969-71; author: "Bleeding Hearts, Bleeding Country" 1971; "Gentle Patriot" (Univ. B.C. Medal for Popular Biog.) 1973; mem., Candn. Pol. Science Assn.; Anglican; Home: R.R.#3, Lakefield, Ont. K0L 2H0

SMITH, Sidney Bert, B.Sc.; geologist; b. Long Beach, Cal. 9 Oct. 1928; s. late Bert Cyrus and Lois Eva (Nichols) S.; e. Downey (Cal.) High Sch. 1946; Univ. of Ariz. B.Sc. 1951; m. Luella Prugh d. late Ralph Herndon 11 Apl. 1954; children: Carol, Joanne, Donald; VICE PRES. W. CAN. EXPLORATION, PETRO-CANADA since 1978; joined United States Geol. Survey 1951 — 52; Phillips Petroleum, Gulf Coast Dist. 1954 — 57, Rocky Mountain Dist. 1957 — 66; Staff Geol., Pacific Petroleums Ltd. 1966 — 78, Chief Geol., Exploration Mgr., Vice Pres. Candn. Exploration & Production; served with US Army Corps of Engrs. Terrain Analyst 1952 — 54, Fort Belvoir, Va., Tokyo, Japan; mem. Am. Assn. Petrol. Geols.; Candn. Soc. Petrol. Geols.; Assn. Prof. Engrs., Geols. & Geophysicists Alta.; recreations: winter sports, racquet sports; Clubs: Petroleum; Calgary Chamber of Commerce; Office: P.O. Box 2844, Calgary, Alta. T2P 2M7.

SMITH, Hon. Sidney Bruce, B.A., LL.B., LL.D.; judge; b. Toronto, Ont., 5 Dec. 1899; s. Frederick Howard and Kate M. (Marks) S.; e. Univ. of Alta., B.A. 1919, LL.B. 1922 (Gold Medallist); LL.D., (hon.) Univ. of Alta., 1962; m. Doris Gertrude, d. L. C. Charlesworth, 18 June 1925; two s., David Bruce, M.Sc., Sidney Gerald Denis, B.Litt.; CHIEF JUSTICE OF ALBERTA AND OF COURT OF APPEAL, N.W.T., 1961-74; read law with Hon. Frank Ford; called to Bar of Alta., 1921; cr. K.C. 1939; mem., Smith, Clement, Parlee, Whittaker, Irving, Mustard & Rodney, 1931-59; mem., Edmonton Pub. Sch. Bd., 1937-41; apptd. Chrmn., Bd. Transport Commrs. for Can., 1958; apptd. Judge, Trial Div., Supreme Court of Alta., 1959; mem., Appellate Div., 1960; mem. of Council, Candn. Bar Assn., 1947-59 (mem. Extve., 1957-59, former Vice-Pres. for Alta., and Past Chrmn., Legal Educ. and Training Sec.); Past Pres., Conf. of Gov. Bodies of the Legal Prof. in Can.; Bencher, Law Soc. Alta., 1946-58, (Pres., 1956-58); mem., Edmonton Y.M.C.A. (mem. Bd. Dirs., 1947-59); mem., Bd. of Alcoholism Foundation of Alta. (formerly Hon. Secy. and Vice-Pres.); Past mem., Council of Edmonton Chamber Comm.; Counsel for Edmonton Chamber Comm. and City of Edmonton on numerous freight rate hearings before Bd. of Transport Commrs. of Can.; Chrmn. of Rhodes Scholarship Comte. for Alta., 1959-63; Chancellor, Anglican Diocese of Edmonton, 1959-71; Freemason; Clubs: Edmonton; Faculty; Mayfair; Edmonton Petroleum; Home: Ste. 215 D2 8403 D2 142 St., Edmonton, Alta. T5R 4L3

SMITH, Silas P., B.S.; retired industrial executive; b. West Union, W. Va. 7 Dec. 1912; s. Silas P. and Edith D. (Martin) S.; e. Salem (W. Va.) Coll. 1932; W. Va. Univ. B.S. 1936; m. Katherine d. Charles Riddel, Spencer, W. Va. 26 Sept. 1942; two d. Theresa M., Cecilia L. Lazes; PRESIDENT, CEO AND DIR. PETROSAR LTD.; joined Union Carbide Corp. N.Y. 1936, Dir. Engn., Chem. and Plastics 1962, Vice Pres. Mfg. Chem. and Plastics 1966,

Sr. Vice Pres. Chem. and Plastics 1969-74; joined Petrosor Ltd. 1974; retired as Pres., CEO and Dir., 1978; mem. Am. Inst. Chem. Engrs.; Tau Kappa Epsilon; Protestant; 95 E. 15th St., Avalon, N.J. 08202

SMITH, Stuart Lyon, M.L.A., M.D., F.R.C.P.(C): politician; b. Montreal, Que. 7 May 1938; s. Moe S. and Nettie (Krainer) S.; e. McGill Univ.; m. Patricia Ann d. A.V. Springate, Thornhill Ont. 2 Jan. 1964; children: Tanya, Craig; Leader, Lib. Party of Ont. 1976-82; psychiatrist; el. M.L.A. for Hamilton W. Ont. g.e. 1975, re-el. since; Liberal; Home: 4173 Afton Court, Burlington, Ont. L7I 1J7;

SMITH, Tyrus Raymond, C.D.; company executive; b. Sussex, N.B., 26 June 1918; s. late James Arthur and Hazel Irene (Davis) S.; e. Saint John (N.B.) High Sch.; m. Mary Ellen, d. Paul R. Lawrence, 21 Feb. 1942; children: James Arthur, Barbara Joan (Mrs. Gregory Janz), Mary Jane; CHRMN. OF BD., ARMSTRONG THE MOVER LTD.; Caravan Holdings Ltd.; Leslie's Storage Ltd.; Unicume Storage Co. Ltd.; Armstrong Van and Storage Ltd.; Past Chrmn. and Pres., Allied Van Lines Ltd.; Pres. Better Bus. Bureau, Calgary; served as Banker in various parts of Can. 1934-58 before going into Industry; served with RCAF during 2nd World War and subsequently served in RCAF Auxiliary and Militia, retiring in 1970 with rank of Lt. Col.; Rotarian; Freemason; Shriner; recreations: skiing, sailing; Clubs: Manitoba (Winnipeg); Ranchmen's, Petroleum, Glencoe (Calgary); Home: Canmere-Banff Carrider, Alta.; Office: 1817 - 54 St., S.E., Calgary, Alta. T2B 1N5

SMITH, Victor Gordon, M.Sc.F., Ph.D.; educator; b. Toronto, Ont. 24 May 1927; s. (late) Lewis Gordon and Florence Ione (Wilson) S.; e. John Ross Robertson Pub. Sch. and Lawrence Park Coll. Inst. Toronto 1945; Univ. of Toronto B.Sc.F. 1949, M.Sc.F. 1965; Iowa State Univ. Ph.D. 1972; m. Mary Taylor d. late Benjamin Franklin Avery 22 May 1954; children: Mary Anna, Elizabeth Ruth, Gordon Rymal, Susan Avery; PROF. OF FORESTRY, UNIV. OF TORONTO 1976- , mem. Gov. Council of Univ. 1978- , Presidential Adv. Comtes. on Budget 1979- and Press 1979- ; Forest Engr. The KVP Co. Ltd. Espanola, Ont. 1949-63; Student Lectr. in Forestry present Univ. 1963-65, Assoc. Prof. 1970-76; Instr. Mich. Technol. Univ. 1965-66, Iowa State Univ. 1966-70; Visiting Fellow, Univ. of Canterbury, Christchurch, N.Z. 1977; author or co-author numerous publs.; Tech. Comte. mem. Candn. Standards Assn.; mem. Cdn. Inst. Prof. Foresters' Assn.; Candn. Inst. Forestry; Ont. Forestry Assn.; Biometrics Soc.; Soc. Am. Foresters; Stat. Soc. Can.; Sigma Xi; Gamma Sigma Delta; Xi Sigma Pi; United Church; recreations: curling, camping; Home: 508 Riverside Dr., Toronto, Ont. M6S 4B5; Office: 203 College St., Toronto, Ont. M5S 1A1.

SMITH, W. Dent, LL.D.; e. Univ. of Delaware, Grad. 1922; m. Elizabeth Douglas, d. Dr. Robert P. Fletcher, Easton, Maryland, 23 June 1928; Pres., Wilmington, Delaware, City Council, 1932-33; Secy. of State for Delaware, 1934-35; Presbyterian; Clubs: National; York; Wilmington; Greenville Country; Blue & Gold; Home: Hilltop House, R.R. 1, Claremont, Ont. L0H 1E0

SMITH, Hon. Walter Kirke, B.A., LL.B.; judge; v. Winnipeg, Man., 28 March 1920; s. Walter Thomas and Catherine Edith (Kirke) S.; e. Earl Grey Jr. High and Kelvin High Schs., Winnipeg, 1926; Univ. of Man., B.A. 1940; Univ. of B.C., LL.B. (Gold Medal) 1949; m. Frances Ellen Rudge, Doncaster, Eng. 16 Feb. 1944; children: Richard Kirke, Gail Elizabeth, Terence Brent, Michael Kirke; JUSTICE, SUPREME COURT OF B.C., since 1968; read law with A. Bruce Robertson and K. L. Yule, Q.C.; called to Bar of B.C. 1949; Assoc., Locke, Guild, Lane, Sheppard and Yule, Vancouver, 1949-54; Partner, Andrews, Swinton & Smith, Vancouver, 1954-63 and Paine, Edmonds, Mercer, Smith & Williams, Vancouver, 1963-65; apptd. Judge, Co. Court of Vancouver, 1966; Lectr. in

Law, Univ. of B.C., 1950-62 and Inst of C.A.'s of B.C., 1951-57; Counsel to Royal Comn. on Tree Fruit Industry of B.C., 1957-58; served with Candn. Army 1940-46; retired with rank Capt.; Freemason; Anglican; recreations: curling, skating, fishing; Club: Hollyburn Country; Home: 71 Deep Dene Rd., West Vancouver, B.C. V7S 1A1; Office: Law Courts, 800 Smithe St., Vancouver, B.C. V6Z 2E1

SMITH, Rev. Wilfred Cantwell, M.A., Ph.D., D.D., LL.D., D.Litt., D.H.L., F.R.S.C. (1961); professor; b. Toronto, Ont., 21 July 1916; s. Victor Arnold and Sarah Cory (Cantwell) S.; e. Upper Canada Coll., Toronto, Ont. (Head Boy 1933); Univ. of Toronto, B.A. (with Hons. in Oriental Lang.) 1938; Westminster Coll., Cambridge (Theol.) 1938-40: St. John's Coll., Cambridge (Research Student) 1938-40; Princeton Univ., M.A. 1947 and Ph.D. (Oriental Lang. and Lit.) 1948; m. Muriel, d. Dr. R. Gordon Struthers, Toronto, Ont., 1939; children; Arnold, Julian, Heather, Brian, Rosemary; PROF. OF COMPARATIVE HISTORY OF RELIGION AND CHRMN., STUDY OF RELIGION, HARVARD Univ. since 1978; formerly McCulloch Prof. of Religion, Dalhousie Univ. 1973-78; Prof. of World Religions and Dir., Center for Study of World Religions, Harvard Univ. 1964-73; W. M. Birks Prof. of Comparative Religion, McGill Univ., 1949-63; also Dir. of Islamic Inst. there, 1952-63; Lectr. in Islamic Hist., Forman Christian Coll., Lahore 1941-45; Instr. in Islamic Hist., Univ. of Punjab (Grad. Sch.), 1943-45; Advisory Ed., "Muslim World", Hartford, Conn.; "Religious Studies", Cambridge, Eng.; "Studies in Religion", Toronto; "Dionysius", Halifax; consulting ed., Encyclopaedia Britannica; Visiting Prof., Univ. of London, 1960; Princeton Univ., 1966-67, Univ. of Toronto, 1968, 1981; Chmn., Islamics Sect., Int'l. Congress of Orientalists, 1964; Pres., Am. Soc. for Study of Relig. 1966-69; Pres. Mid. East Studies Assn. of N. Amer. 1977-78; Pres., Cdn. Theological Soc., 1979-80; Pres.-elected Am. Acad. of Religion, 1981; author of "Modern Islam in India, A Social Analysis", 1943 (revised eds., 1947, 1964, 1972); "Islam in Modern History", 1957, 1958, 1959, 1977; "The Faith of Other Men", 1962 (revised ed., 1963, 1964, 1976); "The Meaning and End of Religion", 1963; (rev. ed. 1978); "Questions of Religious Truth", 1967; "Religious Diversity" 1976, 1982; "Belief and History" 1977; "Faith and Belief" 1979; "Towards a World Theology", 1981; "On Understanding Islam", 1981; articles chiefly on Islamic subjects and comparative relig. to various journals; F.R.S.C. (Pres. Humanities & Social Sciences 1972-73); Fellow, Am. Acad. Arts & Sciences; Chaveau Medal, Royal Soc. of Can., 1974; Home: 17 Jason St., Arlington, Mass. Office: 1581 Massachusetts Ave., Cambridge, Mass.

SMITH, Wilfred Irvin, C.D., M.A., Ph.D., D.C.L.; archivist; b. Port La Tour, Nova Scotia, 20 May 1919; s. Albert Claude and Deborah S.; e. Nova Scotia Normal College, Superior 1st Class Teacher's Lic. 1937; Acadia University, B.A. (Honors), 1943, M.A., 1946, D.C.L.; 1975; Univ. of Minnesota, Ph.D. 1968; m. Joan Eileen, d. Frank Capstick, Bebington, Cheshire, Eng., 27 Nov. 1946; children: Gordon Alan, Dorothy Heather, Helen Gail; DOMINION ARCHIVIST, since 1970; Teacher, Schs. in N.S., 1938-40; Lectr., Hist., Univ. of Minnesota, 1948; Instr., Hist., Univ. of Sask., 1948-50; joined Public Archives of Can. 1950; Head, various Secs. and Chief, Manuscript Div., 1963-64; Dir., Hist. Div., 1964-65; Asst. Dom. Archivist 1965, Acting Dom. Archivist 1968; served as Canloan Offr., R.C.I.C., with 4th Bn., Wiltshire Regt., 43 Div., in U.K. and N.W. Europe; Gov. Gen. Foot Guards, 1951-59; Maj. ret'd. list; published articles and book reviews in Prof. journs; Fellow, Soc. Am. Archivists (Chrmn., Comte. on Internat. Archival Affairs 1969, Vice-Pres. 1971-72, Pres. 1972-73); mem. Candn. Hist. Assn. (Ed. Hist. Booklet Series 1964-67, Chrmn. Archives Sec. 1968-69); mem. Historic Sites and Monuments Bd. Can.; Candn. Perm. Comte. on Geog. Names; International Council on Archives (Extve. Comte.; Depy. Secy. Gen.); Assn. Candn. Archivists; Soc. of Archivists (U.K.); British Records Assn.; Canloan Assn.; mem. and Secy. International Comte. on Documentation, Libs. and Archives (UNESCO); mem. Nat. Lib. Adv. Bd.; Am. Antiquarian Soc.; Serving Brother O. St. J.; Hon. Pres., U.E.L. Assn. of Can.; Candn. Heraldry Soc.; Confed. and Jubilee Medals; recreations: gardening, historical research; Home: 655 Weston Dr., Ottawa, Ont. K1G 1V7; Office: 395 Wellington, Ottawa, Ont. K1A 0N3

SMITH, Mt. Rev. William Joseph, D.C.L. (R.C.); b. Greenfield, Ont., 2 Jan. 1897; s. Duncan and Catherine (Grant) S.; e. Ottawa Univ.; St. Augustine's Semy., Toronto; Grand Semy., Montreal; Collegium Angelicum, Rome, D.C.I. 1935; o. Priest 1927; Chancellor, Alexandria Diocese, 1940-45; Bishop of Pembroke 1945-71; Address: 188 Renfrew St., Pembroke, Ont. K8A 5R9

SMITH, William Keith, B. Comm., M.B.A., C.A.; banker; b. Regina Sask., 15 October 1934; s. W. Givens and Grace (Close) S; e. Univ. of Sask. B. Comm. 1955; C.A. Alta. 1958; Univ. of W. Ont. M.B.A. 1960; m. Katherine Adele Woodin Saskatoon, Sask., 19 November 1955; children; Kelly A; SR. VICE PRES. AND COMPTROLLER, BANK OF MONTREAL 1980- ; joined Clarkson Gordon, Calgary 1955-59; Haskins & Sells, New York 1960-64; Vice Pres. Booz, Allen & Hamilton Inc. 1964-71; Extve. Vice Pres., Treas. and Chief Financial Offr. Central National Chicago Corp., Dir., Vice Chrmn. Central National Bank 1971-80; Clubs: Montreal Badminton & Squash, Hillside Tennis, The Chicago Club, Saddle & Cycle (Chicago); Home: 1323 Redpath Crescent Montreal, Que. H3G 1A1; Office: 129 rue St-Jacques, Montreal, Que. H2Y 1L6.

SMITH, William Y., M.A.; university professor; b. Saint John, N.B., 20 June 1920; s. Edward Hermiston and Mary Elizabeth (Young) S.; e. Saint John (N.B.) High Sch., 1937; Univ. of New Brunswick, B.A., 1946; Univ. Coll., Oxford, Eng. (Rhodes Scholar), B.A., 1948, M.A., 1953; m. Mary Joyce, d. late Maurice Edward Firmin, 20 Feb. 1949; children: Elizabeth Jean Young, William Young; HEAD, DEPT. OF ECON. AND POL. SCIENCE, UNIV. OF NEW BRUNSWICK, since 1952; mem., Econ. Council of Can.; Defence Colls. Adv. Bd.; Consulting, Econ. Planning, Dept. of Finance and Econ., Govt. of Nova Scotia, since 1962; Chrmn., Research Adv. Comte., Atlantic Provs. Econ. Council; Lectr. in Econ., St. Lawrence Univ., Canton, N.Y., 1948; Asst. Prof., Univ. of N.B., 1949; Econ. Advisor, Govt. of N.B., 1954-60; Chrmn., Royal Comn., N.B. Coal Mining Industry, 1960; Pres., Atlantic Provs. Econ. Council, 1961-62; named by Fed. Govt. 1st Chrmn. of the (new) Atlantic Devel. Council, May 1969; served with Candn. Inf., Carleton-York Regt. 1940-1943; wounded in N. Africa while attached to Brit. 1st Army, 1943; mem., Candn. Pol. Science Assn.; Royal Econ. Soc.; Anglican; recreations: swimming, walking; Home: 3 Spruce Terrace, Fredericton, N.B. E3B 2S6

SMYTH, Thomas Donald; company executive; b. Trochu, Alta., 15 Aug. 1926; s. Thomas John and Margaret Ruth (Smith) S.; m. Maureen, d. late S. G. Carphin, 15 Oct. 1955; children: Laurie, David; PRES. AND C.E.O., H. J. HEINZ CO. OF CANADA LTD., since 1977; Chmn., Galco Food Products; joined present Co. as Office Asst., Calgary, 1946; apptd. Office Mgr., Edmonton, 1948 and Leamington (Ont.) 1951; Asst. Office Mgr., Toronto, 1953; Office Mgr., Vancouver, 1954; Staff Asst., Vice-Pres., Marketing, 1956; Sales Div., Assignment, Windsor, 1960; Mgr. Distribution, 1961; Gen. Mgr. Services, 1963; Vice Pres. Services, 1965; Serv. Mfg. 1968; Vice Pres., Marketing and Dir. 1969; Extve. Vice Pres. and C.O.O, 1976; Past Pres. and Dir., Leamington Dist. Chamber Comm.; mem., Can.-U.S. Comm. Internat'l. Relations; Freemason; United Church; recreations: squash, golf; Clubs: Essex Golf and Country; Erie Shores Golf & Country; Sunparlour Curling; Royal Canadian

Yacht; Donalda Golf & Country; Home: 40 Restwell Cr., Willowdale, Ont. M2K 2A3; Office: 250 Bloor St. E., Toronto, Ont. M4W 1E6

SNADDON, Andrew William, B.A.; journalist; b. Winnipeg, Man., 28 Apr. 1921; s. William James and Christina Stuart (Scobie) S.; e. Elbow Park Pub. Sch., Rideau Jr. High, Western Can. High, Calgary, Alta.; Univ. of B.C., B.A. (Econ.) 1943; Banff Sch. of Advanced Mang. 1967; m. Jocelyn Winifred, d. late F. L. Sara, 20 March 1948; children: Sara Jane, Elizabeth Andrea; PUBLISHER, THE MEDICINE HAT NEWS; General (1945-51) and Political (1948-51) Reporter, Calgary Herald; Chief, London (Eng.) Bureau, Southam News Services, 1951-53; Writer, Southam Bureau, Press Gallery, Ottawa, 1953-54; Edit. Writer (1954-56), City Editor (1956-57) and Assoc. Editor, (1957-62) Calgary Herald; apptd. Mang. Editor, Edmonton Journal, 1962; served RCNVR, retiring Sub-Lt.; publ. articles in mags.; also engaged in private radio, CBC radio and TV broadcasting; mem., Amer. Newspaper Publisher's Assn.; Canadian Press; Phi Kappa Pi; former mem., Alta. Press Council; recreations: golf, swimming; Club: Cypress; Home: 125 Primrose Dr. S.E., Medicine Hat, Alberta T1B 2C4; Office: 3257 Dunmore Rd. S.E., Medicine Hat, Alta. T1A 7E6

SNELGROVE, Alfred Kitchener, M.Sc., Ph.D.; geologist; b. St. John's Nfld., 7 Apl. 1902; s. Gilbert and Eliza (Smith) S.; e. McGill Univ., B.Sc. 1927, M.Sc. 1928; Princeton Univ., Ph.D. 1930; Memorial Univ. Nfld., D.Sc. 1964; m. Rachel Mary Weaver Betts, 6 June 1936; Leroy Fellow in Geology, McGill Univ. 1928; Asst. in Geol., Instr. and Asst. Prof., Princeton Univ., 1928-40; Nfld. Govt. Geol., 1934-43; Prof. Dept. Geol. Engn., Michigan Technol. Univ. 1940-70; awarded President's Medal, 1928, and Barlow Mem. Prize, 1931, by Candn. Inst. of Mining & Metall.; Visiting Prof., Rutgers Univ., 1945-46; Fullbright Lectr., Univ. of Hong Kong, 1953-54; Univ. of Sind, Hyderabad, West Pakistan, 1961-62; Visiting Prof., Middle E. Tech. Univ., Ankara, Turkey, 1970-71; consultant, U.N. Development Program, Egypt 1972; author of "Mines and Mineral Resources of Newfoundland", 1938; "Opportunities in Geology and Geological Engineering", 1970; "Geohydrology of the Indus River, West Pakistan", 1967; instrumental in inaugurating Geodetic Survey of Nfld. (through grant from Colonial Devel, Fund and co-operation of Geodetic Survey of Can.); mem., Geol. Soc. Am.; Soc. of Econ. Geols.; Mineral. Soc. of Am.; Am. Inst. Mining & Metall. Engrs.; Candn. Inst. Mining & Metall.; Am. Assn. Univ. Prof.; Am. Assn. Advanc. Science; Am. Geophysical Union; Sigma Xi; Psi Upsilon; Theta Tau; United Church; Home: Water's Edge 1100 - 309, 11485 Oakhurst Rd., Largo, Fla. 33540

SNELGROVE, Ralph Trapnell; broadcasting executive; b. Catalina, Nfld., 11 June 1914; s. Charles F. and Susan (Trapnell) C.; e. Pickering Coll., Ont.; Danforth Tech. Sch., Toronto, Ont.; m. Evelyn Alice, d. (d. 1952) d. J. G. Fraser, 26 Aug. 1940; children: Norman Fraser, Ralph Timothy, Evelyn Dorraine; 2ndly, Elsie Val Kidger, 12 May 1954; two d. Elizabeth, Eloise; CHRMN., FOUR SEASONS RADIO LTD.; T-V Stn. CKVR-TV; Pres., Peterborough Broadcasting Co.; Dir., Grey & Bruce Broadcasting Co. Ltd.; CHUM Ltd.; CFRA Limited, served World War, 1942-45, with R.C.N.V.R.; served on H.M.C.S. "Huntsville" as Group Radar Offr. with rank of Lieut.; Past Pres., Barrie Chamber Comm.; Central Can. Broadcasters Assn.; The Radio & Television Extves. Club; Television Bureau of Can. Inc.; mem. Toronto Bd. Trade; Anglican; recreations: fishing, golf; Clubs: Golf and Country; Garrison; Toronto Mens Press; Ontario (Toronto); Toronto Bd. Trade Golf; Home: 3 Theresa St., Barrie, Ont. L4M 1J4; Office: (Box 950), Barrie, Ont. L4M 4V1

SNELL, Rt. Rev. George Boyd, M.A., Ph.D., D.D. (Ang.); b. Toronto, Ont., 17 June 1907; s. John George and Minnie Alice Boyd (Finnie) S.; e. Trinity Coll., Univ. of Toronto, B.A. 1929, M.A. 1930, Ph.D. 1937, D.D. 1948; Oxford Univ., 1933-34; D.D. Wycliffe Coll. 1957, Huron Coll. 1968; m. Esther Mary, d. Robert Hartley, Toronto, Ont., 30 June 1934; o. Deacon 1931; Priest 1932; Asst. Curate, Ch. of St. Michael and All Angels, Toronto, Ont., 1931-39, and Rector there, 1940-48; Rector, St. Marks Port Hope, Ont. 1940; Rector, Cath. Ch. of the Redeemer, Calgary, Alta. and Dean of Calgary, 1948-51; Rector, St. Clements, Toronto, 1951-55; Archdeacon of Toronto, 1953-55; Suffragan Bishop of Toronto, 1955-59; Coadjutor Bishop 1959-66; Bishop 1966-72; mem., St. Georges Soc.; Club: National; Home: 1210 Glen Rd., Mississauga, Ont. L5H 3K8

SNIDER, John Timothy; retired executive; b. Lyon Co., Kansas, 12 Jan. 1916; s. Carl George and Anna (Lyons) S.; e. Elem. Sch., Lyon Co., Kansas; High Sch., Greenwood Co., Kansas; Univ. of Houston; m. Julia Elizabeth, d. Harrold Chambers, March 1945; children: Linda, John Jr.; former Pres., Pinnacle Construction, Anchorage, Alaska; joined Constr. Dept. of Stearns Roger Corp. 1940; trans. to Can. 1956; left the Co. as Mgr., Constr. Dept. 1966; Cofounder, Delta Projects Ltd. 1966 (Co. acquired by Alaska Interstate Co. 1969); moved to Houston, Tex. 1974 to set up office for Pinnacle Construction; Roman Catholic; recreations: golf, fishing; Club: Ft. Bend Country; Home: 806 Foster Dr., Richmond, Tex. 77469

SNOW, Hank (Clarence Eugene); country music performer; b. Brooklyn, N.S. 9 May 1914; s. George Lewis and Marie Alice (Boutlier) S.; m. Minnie Blanche Aalders 2 Sept. 1935; one s. Jimmie Rodgers; star of "Clarence Snow and His Guitar" radio stn. CHNS Halifax 1935; recording star RCA 1936- ; performed as "The Singing Ranger" U.S. and Can. 1946-50; mem. Grand Ole Opry, Nashville 1950- ; owner Hank Snow Music Inc., Hank's Music Inc.; exclusive writer Hill & Range Songs Inc. New York 1948; Entertainer U.S. Armed Forces Korea 1953, Vietnam 1967; Founder, Hank Snow Internat. Foundation Prevention Child Abuse and Neglect of Children Inc. 1978; named Am.'s Favorite Folk Singer, Song Round-Up Mag. Billboard Mag. 1954; Top Country Singer Can. 1940; Songwriter's Hall of Fame 1978; Candn. Hall of Fame 1979; Country Music Hall of Fame 1979; recipient numerous citations, plaques, awards best-selling records; recorded numerous albums incl. "My Early Country Favorites", "Hank Snow Souvenirs", "Hank Snow Sings Your Favorite Country Hits", "Heartbreak Trail", "Gospel Train", "My Nova Scotia Home", "This is My Story", "Cure for the Blues"; numerous singles; Home: 310 E. Marthonna Dr., Madison, Tenn. 37115A8; Office: (P.O. Box 1084) Nashville, Tenn. 37202.

SNOW, Hon. James Wilfred, M.P.P.; contractor; industrialist; politician; b. Esquesing Twp., 12 July 1929; s. Wilfred Oliver and Margaret Florence (Devlin) S.; e. Milton, Ont. pub. and high schs.; m. Barbara Mae Joan, d. Alfred Hughes, 13 Sept. 1952; children: James Douglas, Julie Barbara, Jeffrey Owen, Jennifer Nancy; MIN. OF TRANSPORT & COMMUNICATIONS, ONT. since 1975; Pres., Snow Constr. Ltd. (Georgetown) and Oakville Invests. Ltd.; Chmn., Tube-Fab Ltd. (Streetsville); assumed mang. of family farm, Halton, upon leaving high sch.; estbd. Snow Construction Ltd. (gen. constr.), 1949; has operated beef farm and feed lot, Hornby, Ont., since 1959; el. M.P.P. for Halton E. in prov. g.e. 1967, 1971; elected M.P.P., Oakville, g.e. 1975, 1977, 1981; Dir., Ont. Housing Corp. and Ont. Student Housing Corp., 1970-72; Min. Without Portfolio 1971; Min. of Govt. Serv. 1972-75; rec'd Centennial Medal 1967; Past Pres., Halton Beef Improvement Assn.; Past Dir., Ont. Beef Improvement Association; mem., Chamber Commerce; Candn. Owners' Pilots' Assn.; P. Conservative; United Church; recreations: hunting, fishing, flying; Clubs: Lions (Past Pres. Oakville; Past Dist. Gov. (A-11) Lions Internat.);

Home: R.R. No. 2, Georgetown, Ont. L7G 4S5; Office: Parliament Bldgs., Toronto, Ont.

SNOW, John Harold Thomas, R.C.A.; artist; b. Vancouver, B.C. 12 Dec. 1911; s. Harold and Sophie (Thompson) S.; e. Gordon Sch.; Innisfail High Sch.; Life Drawing under Maxwell Bates 1947-49; m. Kathleen Mary d. Thomas M. Allen 12 July 1963; one s. John Vance Forcade; Banker with Royal Bank of Canada 1928-71; solo exhns. incl. Gallery Pascal Toronto 1968, 1971, 1973, 1975, 1978; Dorothy Cameron Gallery Toronto 1963, 1964; Fleet Gallery Winnipeg 1965, 1972, 1977; Sarnia Pub. Lib. Gallery 1965; Medicine Hat Lib. Gallery 1965; Gallery Allied Arts 1966; Univ. of Calgary 1966, 1967; Pandora's Box Gallery Victoria 1968; Travelling Exhn. Univs. of Maritime Provs. 1967-68; Man. Theatre Centre 1968; Opening Exhn. Gallery Trinity Coll. Sch. Port Hope 1968, 1970; Gallery 96 Ottawa 1970; Univ. of Toronto Erindale Coll. 1970; Godard Multiples Montreal 1971; Calgary Galleries 1972-77; Studio Shop and Gallery Vancouver Opening Show 1973, 1975, 1980; Can. House Gallery London, Eng. 1973; Mendel Art Gallery Saskatoon 1974; Gallery 1640 Montreal 1975; Bau-Xi Gallery Victoria 1975; Attic Gallery Regina 1976; Lefebvre Gallery Edmonton 1976, 1977; Sundance Gallery Calgary 1978-80; rep. in various group exhns. Can., USA, Gt. Brit., Europe, Japan, S. Am., Australia incl. Première Expositions Bienale Internat. de Gravure à Tokio and Osaka 1957; Primera Bienal Interamerica de Pintura Y Grabada Mexico City 1958; 5th Internat. Biennial Colour Lithography Cincinnati 1958; Royal Soc. Brit. Artists London, Eng. 1960, 1962, 1967, 1968, 1969, 1972; Salon Des Beaux Arts Paris 1961, 1963, 1965, 1967, 1969, 1974, 1975; Candn. Print Exhn. Victoria and Albert Museum (travel) 1965; Annuale Italiani d'Arte Grafic Ancona, Italy 1968; rep. various pub., corporate and private colls. incl. Victoria and Albert Museum, Nat. Gallery Can., Art Gallery Ont., CHAR Gallery Puerto Rico, Royal Ont. Museum, Can. Council Art Bank, Can. House London; recipient Candn. Soc. Graphic Art Adrian Sequin Award 1957, 1969, C. W. Jeffreys Award 1961; Winnipeg Show Graphics Award 1961; Calgary Annual Graphics Exhn. Hon. Mention 1962, 1963; Montreal Museum Fine Arts Spring Show Jessie Dow Award 1962; Salon Des Beaux Arts Paris Hon. Mention 1965; Vancouver Print Internat. Purchase Award 1967; Medaglia e Diploma di Segnalzione Internat. Galleria D'Arte Moderna Ancona, Italy 1968; Can. Council comn. special lithograph 1966; cited various publs.; Film: "The Sad Phoenician and Friends," John Snow Sculptures, Robert Kroetsch reading from his works, Quenten Doolittle music, made by Ken Jones (a Clopton Film Production); served with RCAF and RAF as Navig. Gt. Brit., N. Africa, India World War II; Mentioned in Despatches; Fellow, Internat. Inst. Arts & Letters Switzerland; mem. Print & Drawing Council Can.; Address: 915-18th Ave. S.W., Calgary, Alta. T2T 0H2.

SNOW, Michael James Aleck; artist; musician; photographer; film maker; b. Toronto, Ont., 10 Dec. 1929; s. Gerald Bradley and Marie Antoinette Carmen (Levesque) S.; e. Upper Can. Coll., Toronto 1948; Ont. Coll. Art (under John Martin) 1952; LL.D. (Hon.), Brock Univ. 1974; one-man exhns. incl.: Isaacs Gall. 1957, 58, 60, 62, 64, 66, 69, 74; Poindexter Gall., N.Y.C. 1964, 65, 68; "Michael Snow — A Survey", Art Gall. Ont. 1970; XXV Biennale of Venice 1970; Bykert Gall., N.Y. 1970, 72; Cetre for Inter-Am. Relations, N.Y. 1972; "Projected Images", Walker Art Center, Minneapolis 1974; Museum of Fine Art, N.Y. 1976; "Sept Films et Plus Tard", Centre Georges Pompidou, Paris (travelling) 1977-79; one-man film showings: Edinburgh Film Festival 1969, 75; Jewis Museum, N.Y. 1970; Cinemateque Québecoise, Retrospective, Montreal 1975; Museum of Modern Art, N.Y. 1969, 70, 76; Anthology of Film Archives, N.Y. 1975, 76; selected group exhns.: Biennial of Candn. Painting, Nat. Gall. Can. 1957, 59, 65; "Canada 101", Edinburgh Festival 1968; "Art d'Aujourdhui", France, Italy, Holland 1968; "Anti-

Illusion: Procedures and Materials", Whitney Museum, N.Y. 1969; "Another Dimension", Nat. Gall. Can. 1977; performances and group film showings: Cannes Film Festival 1969, 70; Montreux Film Fest., Switz. 1974; London Film Fest. 1973, 75; Edinburgh Film Fest. 1975, 76; "Documenta", Kassel, Germany 1977; CCMC Concert Tours, Europe 1978, 1979, 1980; CCMC Biweekly performances. Music Gallery, Toronto, 1976, 1977, 1978, 1979, 1980; books: "Michael Snow — A Survey", 1970; "Cover to Cover", 1975; records: "The Artists Jazz Band: Live at the Edge", 1977; "Michael Snow: Music for Whistling, Piano, Microphone and Tape Recorder", 1975; CCMC, Vols. 1 to 5; Awards: Sr. Arts Grant, Can. Council 1966, 73, 79; Guggenheim Fellowship 1972; represented in many collections incl.: Museum of Mod. Art; Nat. Gall. Can.; Art Gall. Ont.; Montreal Museum of Fine Arts; Philadelphia Museum of Art; Art Galls. of Vancouver, Edmonton, Winnipeg; represented in many film archives incl.: Osterreichisches Film Museum, Vienna; Museum of Mod. Art; Nat Gall. Can.; Roy. Belgium Film Archive, Brussels; Rijkmuseum, Holland; Centre Pompidou, Musée des Beaux Arts, Paris; Carnegie Inst., Pittsburgh; Home: 137 Summerhill Ave., Toronto, Ont. M4T 1B1; Office: The Isaacs Gallery, 832 Yonge St., Toronto, Ont. M4W 2H1

SNOWDEN, Donald, B.J.; educator; b. Winnipeg, Man., 9 May 1928; s. Ernest Watson and May Isobel (Cameron) S.; e. Lord Roberts and Kelvin High Sch., Winnipeg; Univ. of Man.; Carleton Univ., B.J. 1949; Sr. Govt. Officers Course, Ottawa; children: Nuala-Kathleen, Duncan; Special Adv. to Vice Pres., Memorial University of Newfoundland; mem., Candn. Eskimo Arts Council 1976-80; Chief (first), Industry Division, Department of Northern Affairs and National Resources, 1954-64; organized first Inuit Cooperatives and development of Arctic craft program; consultant on communications in Can., U.S. and India, and on Arctic matters to Alaskan agencies; estbd. N.W.T. Tourist Office; as an advisor to Nat. Film Bd. helped establish Fogo technique of communications; Chrmn., Royal Comn. on Labrador 1972-74; mem., Nat. Film Bd., 1971-77; Adv. to the U.N., Govt. of Venezuela, Caribbean Community Secretariat and Univ. of Guyana on rural devel. and continuing educ., and the use of film and video-tape in rural devel.; Co-director, Nat. Dairy Research Inst. of India, Communications Project, 1979-83; Adviser, Tornga Fishermen's Co-op.; Labrador; Cdn. Arctic Co-operative Fed. Ltd.; Féd. des Co-operatives du Nouveau Qué.; Inuit Devel. Corp.; mem. of Bd., Nat. Council on Developmental Communications, India; recreations: swimming, fishing; Home: 54 Circular Rd., St. John's, Nfld. A1C 2Z1; Office: St, John's, Nfld.

SNYDER, Beverly Wells, B.Sc.; retired extve.; b. Toronto, Ont., 9 June 1908; s. Ross Wilbert and Mabel (Bowering) S.; e. Pub. and High Schs., Calgary, Alta.; Univ. of Alta., B.Sc.; m. 1stly Phyllis Jean (d. 1952), d. William E. Yeo, 15 June 1935; three children; m. 2ndly Jean Dutton d. Frederick D. Weir, Calgary, 21 Nov. 1953; three children; ASSOC. CONSULTANT, FOSTER RESEARCH since 1978 Jr. Engr., City of Calgary 1931; joined Candn. Western Natural Gas Co. Ltd. as Jr. Engr., 1933; Utility Engr. 1936; various engn. appts. with Candn. Western and Northwestern Utilities Ltd.; 1945-56; Tech. Asst. to Pres. 1957; Dir. of Econ. and Rate Engineer 1961; Vice-Pres., Engineering & Rate Adm. 1968, Consultant 1973-76; served with R.C.E. 1939-45 (Overseas 1940-45); Capt. 1942; Staff Offr., 1st Candn. Army HQ, 1942-45; Mentioned in Despatches; Order of Leopold II and Croix de Guerre (Belgium); Order of Orange Nassau (Netherlands); life mem., Engn. Inst. Can.; Assn. Prof. Engrs. Alta.; Pacific Coast Gas Assn.; Candn. Gas Assn. (Past Chrmn., Operating Div.); Candn. Standards Assn. (Past Chrmn., Sectional Comte.); Freemason (P.M.); P. Conservative; United Church; recreations: golf, curling; Clubs: Glencoe; Earl Grey Golf; Home: 1743 Suffolk St. S.W., Calgary, Alberta T3C 2N4;

SNYDER, Hon. Gordon Taylor, M.L.A.; politician; b. Moose Jaw, Sask. 17 Dec. 1924; s. Emrie Delroy and Alta Marie (Taylor) S.; e. Ross Pub. Sch.; Moose Jaw Tech. Sch.; Central Coll. High Sch.; m. Phyllis Anita d. Roy Stanley Copeman 26 Aug. 1950; two s. Randall Taylor, Craig Delroy; MIN. OF LABOUR, SASK.; Vice Chrmn. Sask. Power Corp. Bd.; Min.-in-Charge Minimum Wage Bd.; Labour Relations Bd.; Worker's Comp. Bd., mem. of Treas. Bd.; el. to prov. leg. 1960, re-el. since; apptd. to prov. cabinet 1971 as Min. of Labour, interim appts. as Min. of Welfare; Min. of Govt. Services, Min. of Social Services; served with RCAF 1943-45; rec'd Centennial Medal 1967; mem. Royal Candn. Legion; Elks; NDP; United Church; recreations: badminton, golf; Home: 3406 Wascana St., Regina, Sask.; Office: 128 Legislative Bldg., Regina, Sask.

SNYDER, Harold L., B.Eng.; company president b. Shawinigan Falls, Que., 1 Jan. 1926; s. George Homer and Mary Elizabeth (Wright) S.; e. Shawinigan Falls (Que.) High Sch., 1943; McGill Univ., B.Eng. (Civil) 1950; m. Adele Elizabeth, d. W. T. Greer, Stanstead, Que., 4 July 1953; children: George Gregory, Joyce Elizabeth, Margot Leslie, Christine Mary, Richard William; PRES. & CEO VISTEC RESOURCE SYSTEMS INC. Dir. of Centre for Cold Ocean Resources Engineering, Memorial Univ. Nfld. 1975-81; Prof., Fac. of Eng. & Ap. Sci.; Dir. Brinco Ltd.; Civil Engineer-Surveyor, Shawinigan Engineering Ltd., Que., 1950-51; C. D. Howe Co., Montreal and Chalk River, Ont., 1951-53; City of Kingston, Roads Engr. 1953-55; Constr. Engr., H.C.F. Construction Ltd., Elliot Lake, Ont., 1955-56; Rio Algom Mines Ltd., Elliot Lake and Toronto, Construction Eng., 1957-64; Constr. Mgr., CF(L) Co. 1964; Project Mgr., CF(L) 1968; Extve. Vice Pres. Churchill Falls (Labrador) Corp. Ltd. 1970-74; Vice-Pres. Brinco Ltd. 1971-75; served with Candn. Armoured Corps 1943-45; mem., Engn. Inst. Can.; Candn. Inst. Mining & Metall.; Assn. Engrs. Que.; Assn. Prof. Engrs. Nfld.; Ass. Comte. of Geotechnical Research-Nat. Research Council; Sci. Council of Can.; United Church; recreations: skiing, sailing; Club: Royal Nfld. Yacht; Royal St. Lawrence Yacht; Office: 407 Second St. S.W., Calgary, Alta.

SOBERMAN, Daniel A., B.A., LL.M.; university professor; b. Toronto, Ont., 19 Oct. 1929; s. Joseph Allan and Rose (Offman) S.; e. Kirkland Lake (Ont.) C. & V. I., 1942; Harbord Coll. Inst., Toronto, 1943-45; Queen Elizabeth High Sch., Halifax, 1945-46; Dalhousie Univ., B.A. 1950, LL.B. 1952; Harvard Univ., LL.M. 1955; m. Patricia Margaret, d. Eric Charles Burrage, Morden, Surrey, Eng., 28 July 1958; children: David, Julia, Gail; Dean of Law, Queen's Univ., 1968-77; Assoc. Dean there 1967-68; read law with Robert A. Kanigsberg, Q.C.; called to Bar of N.S. 1952, Ont. 1955; Instr., Dalhousie Univ., 1955-56; Asst. Prof. 1956-57; Asst. Prof., Queen's Univ., 1957-59; Assoc. Prof. 1959-65; Chrmn., Comte. of Faculty Advisors to Overseas Students, Queen's Univ.; former Dir., World Univ. Service of Can. and Candn. Service for Overseas Students and Trainees; Pres., Social Science Research Council of Can. 1971-72; rec'd Sr. Postgrad. Research Fellowship, Univ. of Edinburgh, 1963-64; co-author of "The Law and Business Administration in Canada," 1964; "The Nature of Corporate Personality", in "Studies in Canadian Company Law," 1967; mem., Law Soc. Upper Can.; N.S. Barrister's Soc.; Assn. Candn. Law Teachers (Pres. 1968-69); Candn. Bar Assn.; Am. Soc. Internat. Law; Tau Epsilon Phi (former Chancellor, Tau Iota Chapter); recreations: sailing, photography; Club: Kingston Yacht; Home: 143 Fairway Hills Cres., Kingston, Ont. K7M 2B5

SOBEY, Donald Rae, B.Com.; company president; b. Stellarton, N.S., 23 Oct. 1934; s. Frank H. and Irene (MacDonald) S.; e. Stellarton (N.S.) High Sch.; Queen's Univ., B.Com.; m. Elizabeth, d. George Purvis, Stellarton, N.S., 7 Sept. 1963; children: Robert George, Irene

Elizabeth, Kent Richard; PRESIDENT AND DIR., EMPIRE CO. LTD.; Pres. and Dir., Maritime Theatres Ltd.; Canadian Shopping Centers; Pres., Halifax Developments Ltd.; Foord Housing Ltd.; Gov., Dalhousie Univ., Dir., Sobey Leased Properties Ltd.; Vice Pres. and Dir., Balcolm-Chittick Ltd.; Foord Constr. Ltd.; Empire Theatres Ltd. Jannock Ltd.; Toronto-Dominion Bank; Atlantic Motors Ltd.; Lawtons Drug Stores Ltd.; and others; Sobey Stores Ltd.; Atlantic Shopping Centres; Wajax Ltd.; Tibbetts Paints Ltd.; ICG Scotia Gas Ltd.; Maritime Tel & Tel Ltd.; mem., Lloyds of London; Dir., YMCA; Un. Church; recreations: skiing, boating; Clubs: Saraguay (Halifax); Abercrombie Golf & Country (Trustee); Home: Birch Hill Dr., Stellarton, N.S. B0K 1S0; Office: King St., Stellarton, N.S. B0K 1S0

SOBEY, Frank Hoyse, D.C.L.; retired supermarket merchant and executive; b. Lyons Brook, Pictou Co., N.S.; s. John W. and Eliza (Creighton) S.; D.C.L. King's Coll., Halifax, 1964; D.C.L. St. Jary; Univi, 1979 m. Irene, d. D. W. MacDonald, 1924; children: William M., David F., Donald R., Dianne Sobey; Honorary Chairman, Sobey's Stores Limited,; President, Empire Co. Ltd.; Dir., Sydney Steel Corp.; Halifax Developments Ltd.; Nfld. Amusements Ltd.; Warnock Hersey International Ltd.; Maritime Steel Co. Ltd.; Canadian Shopping Centres Ltd.; Tibbets Paints Ltd.; Mayor of Stellarton, N.S., 1937-59; mem. Royal Bermuda Yacht Squadron; Freemason; Protestant; recreations: golf, fishing, photography; Clubs: Mount Royal (Montreal); The Halifax (N.S.); R.N.S.Y.S. (Halifax); Home: "Crombie", Pictou Co., N.S.; Warwick, Bermuda (Winter); Office: King St., Stellarton, N.S. B0K 1S0

SOBEY, William Macdonald; executive; b. New Glasgow, N.S., 9 June 1927; s. Mr. and Mrs. Frank H. Sobey; e. Stellarton, N.S. schs.; Horton Acad. Wolfville, N.S.; m. Doris Cameron, New Glasgow, N.S.; children: Frank, Karl, Heather, Ann; CHRMN. OF THE BD. SOBEYS STORES LTD.; Chrmn., Gulf Services Ltd.; T.R.A. Foods Ltd.; Foord Construction Ltd.; Dir. Bank of Montreal (Chrmn. Atlantic Provs. Div.); Empire Co. Ltd.; Canadian Shopping Centres Ltd.; Atlantic Shopping Centres Ltd.; Sobeys Holdings Ltd.; T.R.A. Ltd.; Johnson & MacDonald Ltd.; Lumsden Brothers Ltd.; Nfld. Capital Corp.; Eastern Provincial Airways; Mayor Town of Stellarton 5 yrs.; Dir. N.S. Heart Foundation; World Wildlife Fund of Can.; Chmn., Dalhousie Univ., Faculty of Medicine, Research and Development Foundation; mem. Royal Order Jesters; C.D. Howe Research Inst.; Conf. Bd. of U.S.; Newcomen Soc.; Alouette Chapter Young Pres's Assn.; Freemason; Shriner; Protestant; Clubs: Royal N.S. Yacht Sqdn.; Union (Saint John); City (New Glasgow); Abercrombie Country; Halifax; Home: King's Head, Picton Co., N.S.; Office: 115 King St., Stellarton, N.S. B0K 1S0

SODEN, James Arthur, Q.C.; financier; b. Montreal, Que., 20 Oct. 1922; s. late Robert and Violet (McNamara) S.; e. McGill Univ., — grad. with hons. in Law; m. Edna, d. late John McConkey, 30 June 1945; children: Ann, Robert, Margaret, Lesley; CHRMN. SONCO PROPERTY DEVELOPMENT AND SERVICES CORP.; Past C.E.O., Trizec Corp.; Chrmn. Bd. and Dir., Place Bonaventure Inc.; Trizec Equities Ltd.; Place Quebec Inc.; Tristar Western Ltd.; Mobile Home Communities, Inc.; Scarborough Shopping Centre Ltd.; Pres. and Dir., Tristar Developments Inc. (U.S.A.); Scotia Winnipeg Ltd.; Granite Holdings of Canada Ltd.; Vice-President and Director, Covent Canada Corporation Limited; Dir., Real Estate Property Fund; English Property Corporation Ltd.; Canadian Institute Public Real Estate Cos.; called to Bar of Que. 1950; cr. Q.C. 1968; upon grad, joined Montreal law firm of Wainwright, Elder, Laidley, Leslie , Chipman and Bourgeois; became assoc. with firm of Phillips, Bloomfield, Vineberg & Goodman, 1957; former Lectr. in Law at McGill Univ. and Concordia Univ.; served with RCAF during World War II; discharged with rank Sqdn. Leader, 1945; twice

Mentioned in Despatches; Dir., St. Mary's Hospital, Montreal; Honorary Life member York Finch General Hospital; member Quebec and National Councils, Boy Scouts Assn. of Can.; mem., Montreal and Candn. Bar Assns.; R. Catholic; Clubs: Mount Royal; Royal Cdn. Military Inst.; Home: 55A Avenue Rd., W602, Toronto, Ont. M5R 2G3 and Montgomery Centre, Vermont; Office: Suite W602, 55A Avenue Rd., Toronto, Ont. M5R 2G3

SODERSTROM, Ingmar Gustav; executive; b. Hofors, Sweden, 2 Nov. 1920; e. Sweden — Engn. Degree; children: Lars, Monica; CONSUL GENERAL FOR SWEDEN IN TORONTO; joined SKF 1936; Engr., SKF Hofors Steel; Application Engn., SKF Goteborg, 1946; Sales Engr., SKF, Bombay, India, 1949; Regional Mgr., Candn. SKF, 1957, E. Region; Vice Pres. Sales 1964; Pres., 1971-80; Chrmn. of Bd., 1980-1; recreations: fishing, skiing; Club: Scarborough Golf & Country; Office: 2201 Eglinton Ave. E., Scarborough, Ont. M1L 2N4

SOGANICH, John; editor and financial columnist; b. Slovakia, Aug. 3, 1928, came to Canada 1938. e. Ryerson Polytechnical Inst. Toronto, Journalism 1952. s. SR. ED., THE FINANCIAL POST 1977- ; Candn. mining corr. The Financial Times, London, Eng.; contributor. media invest. Marketing, clothing & textile industry invests. Style, Toronto; Ed. Asst. The Northern Miner 1952-60; Asst. Ed. The Financial Post 1960-677; Financial Ed. Investor's Digest of Canada 1972-78; Home: 74 South Dr., Toronto, Ont. M4W 1R5; Office: 481 University Ave., Toronto, Ont. M5W 1A7.

SOKOLOV, David Israel, Q.C., B.A., LL.B.; b. Winnipeg, Man., 11 Dec. 1928; s. Hyman and Rebecca (Rusoff) S.; e. St. John's Tech. High Sch., Winnipeg, 1946 (Valedictorian); Univ. of Man., B.A. 1949; Man. Law Sch., LL.B. 1953; m. Rhoda Lorraine, d. Oscar and Marion Aaron, Vancouver, B.C., 13 Feb. 1960; children: Stephen, Lewis; PARTNER, SOKOLOV, KLEIN & CO.; called to Bar of Man. 1953; cr. Q.C. 1966; Counsel for Man. Mun. Bd., 1961-65 and for Dept. of Mun. Affairs, 1961-69; mem. Ramah Hebrew Sch. Bd., 1968-71 (Secy. 1970-71); Dir., Winnipeg Symphony, 1969-70; mem., P. Conserv. Assn. 1957-69 (Secy. S. Winnipeg Assn. 1960); mem. Law Reform Comte. 1962-65; mem. Comte. to Revise Man. Corp. Act 1977- ; Man. Bar Assn.; Hon. Counsel, Dir. and mem. Extve. Comte.; Rainbow Stage Inc.; Chrmn., Bd. Dirs., Firefighters Burn Fund Inc. 1979- ; recreations: golf, chess; Club: Glendale Country (Dir. 1965-68; Secy. 1968): Office: 1020 - 220 Portage Ave., Winnipeg, Man. R3C 0A5

SOLANDT, Omond McKillop, C.C. (1970), O.B.E. (1946) M.A., M.D., D.Sc., LL.D., D.Eng., F.R.S.C. (1948), F.R.C.P. (Eng.); b. Winnipeg, Man., 2 Sept. 1909; s. Donald McKillop and Edith (Young) S.; e. Univ. of Toronto, B.A., 1931, M.A. 1932, B.Sc. (Med.) 1933, M.D. 1936 (Gold Medal and Ellen Mickle Scholar.); Cambridge Univ. (Lucas Walker Studentship) 1939; Fellow, Trinity Hall 1945; Univ. of Brit. Columbia, D.Sc. 1947, Laval Univ. 1948, Manitoba 1950, McGill 1951; St. Francis Xavier 1956, R.M.C. 1966, Montréal 1967; LL.D. Dalhousie Univ. 1952, Toronto 1954, Sir Geo. Williams 1966, Sask. 1968; D.Eng., Waterloo 1968; m. 1st. Elizabeth (died 1971) d. Dr. Harris McPhedran, Toronto, Ont., Jan. 1941; children: Sigrid, Andrew, Katharine; 2ndly Vaire Pringle, Toronto, Ont. 1972; SR. CONSULTANT, INST. FOR ENVIRONMENTAL STUDIES, UNIVERSITY OF TORONTO since 1976; Vice Chrmn., Internat. Centre for Agric. Research In Dry Areas, Syria 1975-81; mem., Bd. Trustees, Internat. Wheat and Maize Improvement Center, Mexico since 1976; mem. Adv. Bd., Centre for Cold Ocean Resources Engineering, Nfld. 1976-81; mem., Technical Adv. Bd., Urban Transit Dev. Corp., 1974- ; Internat. Senter for Diarrhoeal Diseases Research, Bangladesh since 1979; (Public) Gov., Toronto Stock Exchange 1971-76; Chairman, Ont. Govt. Comn. Inquiry into

Transmission Line Routes 1972-75; Chrmn., Science Council of Can. 1966-72; Dir., Huyck Corp. (Wake Forest, N.C.); Chancellor, University of Toronto, 1965-71; Vice Chrmn. of Bd., ERCO Chemicals Ltd.; Dir., Mitchell Plummer Co. 1971-75; Vice-Pres., Research and Devel., The deHavilland Aircraft of Can. 1963-66; Research in Physiol. under Prof. C. H. Best, Toronto, Ont., 1932-33; Research, Univ. of Cambridge, 1936-37; Interne, Toronto Gen. Hosp. 1937-38; Lecturer, University of Cambridge 1939-46; Director, S.W. London Blood Supply Depot, 1940; Estbd. and Dir. Med. Research Council Physiol. Lab., Armoured Fighting Vehicle Sch., Lulworth, Eng., 1941; Armoured Fighting Vechicle Sec., Army Operational Research Group 1943; joined Candn. Army with rank of Lieut.-Col. Feb. 1944, retaining post of Depy. Supt., Army Operational Research Group, London, Eng.; promoted Supt. with rank of Col. 1944; Dir. Gen. of Defence Research, 1946; Chairman, Defence Research Bd., 1947-56; Vice Pres., Research & Devel., Candn. Nat. Railways 1956-63; Rep. of Can., Geneva Conf. of East-West Atomic Experts, 1958; awarded Medal of Freedom (U.S.) 1947; Gold Medal, Prof. Inst. of Pub. Service of Can., 1956; mem., Candn. Physiol. Soc.; Physiol. Soc. (England); Hon. mem., Engn. Institute Canada; Civic Award of Merit, City of Toronto; United Church; recreations: skiing, canoeing; Home: R.R.1 Bolton, Ont. L0P 1A0

SOLIN, Cecil D., M.A., Ph.D.; e. McGill Univ., B.A. 1937, M.A. 1938; Univ. of Toronto, Ph.D. 1941; PROF. OF MATH. AND DEAN OF STUDENTS, McGILL UNIV., since 1966; after grad. assumed post of Asst. Prof., Univ. of Sask.; since 2nd World War has been teaching at McGill Univ. starting as Lectr. and becoming full Prof. 1960; served as Asst. Dean, Faculty of Arts and Science, 1949-62; Chrmn., Physical Sciences Group, 1962-64; mem. of Senate 1959-62; Lectr., Sch. of Comm. (Evening Div.), since 1958; served with RCAF, Navig. Br., in Can. and overseas, 1941-45; discharged with rank Flt. Lt.; apptd. Commanding Sqdn. Leader of RCAF Univ. Sqdns., 1949; promoted Wing Commdr. 1952; awarded Coronation Medal 1953; mem., Civil Service Comn. Montreal, since 1962; mem. Planning Comte, Ministry of Educ. of Que. on Insts.; Bd. of Govs., Montreal Council of Social Agencies, 1959-64; former mem., Mayor's Adv. Comte., City of Côte St. Luc; mem., Candn. Math. Cong.; Am. Math. Soc.; Home: 6702 Charest Rd., Montreal, Que. H4V 1B5

SOLOMON, Allan Omar, Q.C., C.D., LL.B., B.P.A.; Canadian public servant; b. Winnipeg, Man., 25 Nov. 1914; s. Samuel and Mollie C. (Katz) S.; e. Pub. and High Schs., Dauphin, Man.; Univ. of Man., B.A. 1935, LL.B. 1939; Carleton Univ., B.P.A. 1951; m. Shirley S., d. Mendel Waldman, Vancouver, B.C., 1 Dec. 1940; children: Linda R. McLean, Dr. A. Garry; CHRMN., CANDN. PENSION COMN., since 1971; called to Bar of Man. 1939; practiced law Swan River, Man., 1939-40; joined RCNVR as Sub-Lt. 1942; served in naval postings Nfld., U.K. and Can. during World War II; trans. to RCN with rank Lt. Commdr. 1946, Commdr. 1951, Capt. 1960, retired 1971; Depy. Judge Advocate of the Fleet and Depy. Naval Secy. 1946-48; loaned to USN for special duties 1949; Secy., Candn. Chiefs of Staff Comte., Mil. Secy. to Defence Comte. of Cabinet, 1953-55; Extve. Asst. to Chief of Naval Personnel 1955-57; Liaison Offr. RCN and USN, Washington, 1957-60; Secy., Naval Bd. of Can. and Naval Secy., 1960-64; Judge Advocate of the Fleet and Asst. Chief of Naval Personnel (Adm.) 1964; Dir. of Personnel Legal Services, CFHQ 1964-68; Sr. Legal Adviser (Europe) on defence matters to all Candn. Embassies in Europe and to Candn. Forces there, Bonn, 1968-70; Pres., Candn. Citizenship Court, Europe, 1968-70; Presiding Judge, Special Gen. Courts Martial, 1968-70; Pres., Standing Courts Martial 1968-70; joined present Comn. as Commr., 1970; Dir., Candn. Nat. War Museum, 1960-64; one of Founders, Ottawa Modern Jewish School; Hon. Patron, Jewish War Veterans of Can.; mem., Manitoba

Law Soc.; Royal Canadian Legion; Hon. Life mem., Hong Kong Veterans Assoc.; Hon. mem., War Amputations of Can.; Jewish; Clubs: Rideau View Golf & Country (Past Pres.); Canadian; Home: 692 Highland Ave., Ottawa, Ont. K2A 2K4; Office: Veterans Affairs Bldg., Ottawa, Ont. K1A 0P4

SOLOMON, George Charles, LL.D.; executive; b. Regina, Sask., 10 Apl. 1913; m. Doris Ilene Dean, 26 May 1932; three d. Mrs. Sharon D. Dyksman, Mrs. Vaughn C. Schofield, Mrs. Adrian I. Sterne; PRESIDENT, WESTERN LTD.; Dir. Bank of Montreal; Inter-City Gas Ltd.; Carling O'Keefe Ltd.; International Paints (Canada) Ltd.; Ocelot Industries Ltd.; Potash Corp. of Sask.; Pembina Mountain Clays Ltd.; Westank-Willock; YMCA; Salvation Army; United Church; recreations: boating, swimming; Club: Assiniboia; Home: 2600 — 19th Ave., Regina, Sask. S4T 1X1; Office: Box 1730, 1540 - 10th Ave., Regina, Sask. S4P 3C6

SOLOMON, Hon. John R.; judge; b. Zoria, Manitoba, 30 Apl. 1910; s. Roman and Annie (Drozdowich) S.; e. N. Dauphin (Man.) Coll. Inst.; Univ. of Manitoba, Grad. in Law, 1934; m. Jean Mary, d. Peter Ogryzlo, Fork River, Man., 20 July 1941; children: Patricia, Joan, Holly; JUSTICE, COURT OF QUEEN'S BENCH since 1971; Chrmn.; Adv. Bd., C.N.I.B., Man.; Dir., St. Andrews Coll., Winnioeg, Man.; mem. Adv. Bd., Holy Family Home; after grad. opened office at Selkirk, Man.; joined the firm of Arsenych & Solomon, Winnipeg, Man., 1941; and succeeded as Head of the firm of Solomon, Baryluk, Karasevich & Gingera; el. to Man. Leg. in 1941 and re-el. 1945; re-el. by acclamation in 1949 and re-el. 1953; apptd. Depy. Speaker of Man. Leg., 1953; read law with J. S. Lamont, Q.C. and E. N. McGirr, Q.C.; called to the Bar of Man., 1935; cr. Q.C. 1957; apptd. Judge, E. Judicial Dist., Man. 1957; mem. Order of St. Andrew; mem. of Council, Man. Bar Assn.; before appt. to the Bench was a Dir. of Trident Press, Wildon Hotel Ltd., Prairie Canners Ltd.; Greek Orthodox; recreations: golf, hunting, fishing, curling; Clubs: Carleton; Niakwa Golf; Fellowship C.; Self Reliance League; Home: 142 Seven Oaks, Winnipeg, Man. R2V 0K5; Office: Law Courts, Winnipeg, Man.

SOLOMON, Samuel, M.Sc., Ph.D., F.C.I.C., F.R.S.C.; educator; research scientist; b. Brest, Poland 25 Dec. 1925; s. Nathan and Rachel (Greenberg) S.; e. McGill Univ. B.Sc. 1947, M.Sc. 1951, Ph.D. (Biochem.) 1953; m. Augusta Myers Vineberg 20 July 1974; three s. David, Peter, Jonathan; PROF. DEPTS. BIOCHEM., EXPER. MED. AND OBSTETRICS & GYNECOL., McGILL UNIV., mem. Extve. Comte. Indust. Research Center 1976- ; mem. Bd. Govs. 1974-77, McGill Planning Comn. 1971-75; Secy. Royal Victoria Hosp. Research Inst. 1981- ; Dir. Connaught Research Foundation; Visiting Prof. Univ. of Vt.; mem. Research Comte. St. Mary's Hosp. 1980- ; Pres. Perinatal Research Soc. 1976-77; Chrmn. Endocrine Soc. Employment Service 1972-77, mem. Internat. Affairs Comte. 1972-77; Central Comte. Internat. Soc. Endocrinol. 1964-76; Program Comte. IV Internat. Cong. Endocrinology 1972; co-ed. "Chemical and Biological Aspects of Steroid Conjugation" 1970; over 147 articles endocrinol. of metabolism, maj. journs.; Hebrew; recreations: skiing, tennis; Club: M.A.A.A.; Home: 239 Kensington Ave., Apt. 603, Montreal, Que. H3Z 2H1; Office: Endocrine Laboratory, Royal Victoria Hospital, 687 Pine Ave. W., Montreal, Que. H3A 1A1.

SOLOWAY, Hyman, Q.C., B.A.; b. Russia, 17 Nov. 1913; s. Louis and Annie (Gencher) S.; came to Can., 1924; e. Queen's Univ., B.A.; Sch. Internat. Relations, Switzerland (R. B. Bennett Schol.); Osgoode Hall, Toronto, Ont.; m. Ruth, d. Samuel Spevak, Ottawa, Ont., 5 Dec. 1943; children: Susan, Lawrence; SR. PARTNER, SOLOWAY, WRIGHT, HOUSTON, McKIMM, KILLEEN & GREENBERG; Dir., Shoppers City Ltd. Pure Spring (Can.) Ltd.; M. Loeb Ltd.; mem. Ottawa Adv. Bd., Guaranty Trust Co. of Can.; read law with Luxenburg & Levinter, Toronto; called to Bar of Ont., 1939, cr. Q.C., 1953; assoc. with Berger, Greenberg & Soloway, 1939-41; served in 2nd World War, 1941-45; mem., Nat. Extve., Candn. Jewish Cong.; Pres., Jewish Community Centre, Ottawa; Liberal; Hebrew; recreations: golf, reading; Clubs: Montefiore; Rideauview Golf; Home: 196 Acacia Ave., Ottawa, Ont. K1M 0L5; Office: 170 Metcalfe, Ottawa, Ont. K2P 1P3

SOMERS, Carin Alma, M.A., B.L.S.; librarian; b. Frankfurt/Main, Germany 18 March 1934; d. Josef and Helen Josephine (Badham) Stein; came to Can. 1949; e. Newton (Mass.) Coll. of Sacred Heart B.A. 1955; Dalhousie Univ. M.A. 1956; Univ. of Toronto B.L.S. 1961; m. Frank George Somers 23 Aug. 1958; DIR., N. S. PROV. LIBRARY 1974- ; Registrar then Lectr. in French, St. Mary's Univ. Halifax 1956-60; Halifax City Regional Lib. 1958-64, Librarian Tech. Services 1961-64; Asst. Librarian, Chief Librarian, Halifax Co. Regional Lib. 1964-73; Supvr. Pub. Libs., N.S. Prov. Lib. 1973-74; occasional lectr. Dalhousie Univ. Sch. of Lib. Service; rec'd Gov. Gen.'s Medal 1953; Queen's Silver Jubilee Medal 1977; contrib. to prof. journs.; mem. Candn. Lib. Assn. (2nd Vice Pres. 1974-75); Atlantic Provs. Lib. Assn. (Pres. 1969-70); N.S. Lib. Assn.; N.S. Bird Soc.; Candn. Nature Fed.; R. Catholic; recreations: ornithology, fishing, photography, travel; Club: R.N.S.Y.S.; Home: Armdale P.O. Box 772, Halifax, N.S. B3L 4K5; Office: 5250 Spring Garden Rd., Halifax, N.S. B3J 1E8.

SOMERS, Harry, C.C. (1971), Hon. Doc. in Law (Univ. of Toronto), Hon. Doc. in Letters (York Univ.), Hon. Doc. of Music (Ottawa Univ.); composer; b. Toronto, Ont., 11 Sept. 1925; e. Royal Conserv. Music, Toronto; studied piano with Dorothy Hornfelt, Reginald Godden; theory and composition under John Weinzweig; piano study with Robert Schmitz 1948; composition under Darius Milhaud, Paris 1949; wrote his first String Quartet at age 17; other works incl., opera: "Louis Riel" 1967; Chamber operas: "The Fool" 1953; "Enkidu" 1977; 3 ballet scores; 2 piano concertos; 3 string quartets; 5 piano sonatas and numerous other works for orchestras, chamber groups and soloists and music for T.V. and film; received numerous commissions and awards including companion to the Ord. of Can. and Can. Council Sr. Arts Fellowship 1960; Address: 158 Douglas Dr., Toronto, Ont. M4W 2B7

SOMERS, Msgr. Hugh Joseph, O.C. (1976), M.A., J.C.B., PhD., D. Ed., D.C.L., LL.D., D.Litt., F.R.Hist.S., F.R.S.A. (R.C.); b. Sylvan Valley, Antigonish, N.S., 30 June 1902; s. Thomas and Annie (O'Brien) S.; e. St. Francis Xavier Univ., B.A. 1923; St. Augustine's Semy., Toronto, Ont. 1923-27 (o. 1927); Cath. Univ. of America, M.A. 1928, J.C.B. 1928, Ph.D. 1931; Laval, D.Litt. 1961; D.Ed. St. Anne's Coll. 1965; LL.D. Mount Allison 1965, St. Francis Xavier 1966; St. Dunstan's Univ. 1968; D.C.L. Univ. of King's Coll. 1965; Mem., Maritime Provs. Higher Educ. Comn. 1974-80; Director, Nat. Conference of Canadian Univs., 1958-59; Dir., Candn. Univs.- Foundation, 1958-61; Prof. of Hist., St. Francis Xavier Univ. 1931, Bursar 1933; Vice-Pres. of the Univ. and Secy. Treas. of Bd. of Govs., 1944; Dir. of Public Relations and Finance, 1950; Pres., 1954-64; Extve. Dir., Association of Atlantic Universities 1964-71; served as Commdg. Offr., No. 20 Univ. A.T.S. with rank of Sqdn. Leader, 1943-44; Past Pres. (1942) Candn. Cath. Hist. Soc.; mem., Candn. Cath. Hist. Assn.; N.S. Hist. Soc.; K. of C.; author of "Life and Times of the Honorable and Right Reverend Alexander Macdonell (1762-1840)", 1931; invested Domestic Prelate, 1955; Address: (P.O. Box 178) St. Francis Xavier University, Antigonish, N.S.

SOMERVILLE, Thomas Aymer, B.Eng.; civil engineer; b. Westmount, Que., 16 March 1919; s. late Thomas Aymer and Edna (Webster) S.; e. Westmount High Sch.,

Que.; Royal Mil. Coll., 1939; McGill Univ., B.Eng. 1948; m. Annette Coralie, d. late George Field, 5 Feb. 1949; children: Catherine, Patricia, Bruce, Gordon; DIR., E.G.M. CAPE & COMPANY LIMITED; Dir., Czarnikow (Montreal) Ltd.; Past President, Canadian Constr. Assn., 1963-64; joined present Co. in 1946; served in 2nd World War, 1939-46 with Royal Candn. Engrs.; served in Eng. and N.W. Europe in 1st and 2nd Divs.; Mentioned in Despatches; retired with rank of Major; mem., Order of Engrs. of Que.; Assn. Prof. Engrs. Ont.; Engn. Inst. of Can.; Zeta Psi; Anglican; Clubs: St. James's; Rosedale Golf; Knowlton Golf; Home: Box 622, Knowlton, Que. J0E 1V0; Office: 180 Duncan Mill Rd., Don Mills, Ont. M3B 3K2

SOMERVILLE, William Henry; trust company executive; b. Blanshard Twp., Perth Co., Ont. 25 Apr. 1921; s. John and Mary (Taylor) S.; e. St. Mary's (Ont.) Coll. Inst. 1939; Internat. Accts. Soc. 1953; m. Jean d. Charles Fawcett 16 June 1945; children: John, Karen; PRES., CEO AND DIR., VICTORIA AND GREY TRUSTCO LTD. and Victoria and Grey Mortgage Corp. and Victoria and Grey Trust Dir., E-L Financial Corp.; Empire Life Ins. Co.; Dominion of Canada Gen. Ins. Co.; The Casualty Co. of Canada; Ellis-Don Ltd.; Transohio Financial Corp.; Prop., Drug Store, St. Mary's, Ont. 1946-55; Executive, Drug Trading Co., London 1956-62; Mgr., St. Mary's Br., British Mortgage & Trust Co. 1962; Mgr., St. Mary's Br. president Co. 1965, Stratford Br. 1966, Asst. Gen. Mgr. 1968, Vice Pres. 1973, Vice Pres. - Mortgages 1976, Extve. Vice Pres. 1977; Mayor, Town of St. Mary's 1965-66, Councillor 1962-64; Alderman, City of Stratford 1970-73; Lib. Cand. for Perth Riding Fed. g.e. 1968; Chmn., Corp. Fund Raising, Lib. Party of Canada (Ont.); Councillor Trust Co's Inst.; mem. Extve. Comte. Trust Co's Assn. Can; mem. Bd. of Gov., Stratford Shakespearean Festival; United Church; Clubs: Stratford Country; Ontario, Toronto, Empire, Canadian; Home: 240 Delamere Ave., Stratford, Ont.; Office: 165 University Ave., Toronto, Ont. M5H 2T8 and 1 Ontario St., Stratford, Ont.

SOMERVILLE, William L.; stock exchange executive (ret.); b. New York City, 23 Dec. 1915; s. William Lyon and Evelyn Mary (Gillard) S.; e. Univ. of Toronto Schs. (1934); Univ. of Toronto (1937); Osgoode Hall (1940); m. Frances Fraser, d. late F. W. Scott, 10 Aug. 1945; two d. Anne Fraser, Sarah Jane; Exec. Vice-Pres., Toronto Stock Exchange, 1958-1978; called to the Bar of Ont. 1940; engaged in the practice of law, 1945-49, when joined the Toronto Stock Exchange; served in 2nd World War with R.C.A.F., 1941-45; Liberal; Protestant; Home: 179 Glencairn Ave., Toronto, Ont. M4R 1N9

SOMERVILLE, William L. N., Q.C., B.A., LL.B.; b. Ottawa, Ont., 24 Aug. 1921; s. William Lorne and Olive Triscott (Northmore) S.; e. elem. and high schs., Collingwood, Ont.; Univ. of Toronto, Trinity Coll. B.A. 1943, LL.B. 1948; Osgoode Hall Law Sch. 1949; m. Denise Madeleine, d. late Herbert Thomas Church, 11 June 1948; children: Fred, David, Sarah, William, Nancy; PARTNER, AND CHMN., BORDEN & ELLIOT 1980- ; mem. Candn. Bd., Norwich Union Life Insurance Soc.; Norwich Union Fire Insurance Soc.; read law with Fennell McLean & Davis; called to Bar of Ont. 1949, of Sask. 1972; cr. Q.C. 1960; served with RCA and Royal Candn. Intelligence Corps 1943-46; Can., USA and Japan; mem. Corp., Trinity Coll.; Churchwarden, St. James Cathedral 1977-80; Fellow, Am. Coll. of Trial Lawyers; mem. Candn. Bar Assn. (Chrmn. Ont. Br. 1969-70, Nat. Treas. 1972-73, Vice Pres. 1973-74, Pres. 1974-75); Advocates' Soc. (Past Dir.); Internat. Assn. Ins. Counsel; Zeta Psi (Pres.); Anglican; recreations: tennis, skiing; Clubs: York; National; Osler Bluff Ski; Toronto Hunt; Home: 27 Cluny Dr., Toronto, Ont. M4W 2P9; Office: 250 University Ave., Toronto, Ont. M5H 3E5

SOOD, Vinod Kumar, M.Sc., C.A,; executive; b. India 24 Apl. 1935; e. Agra Univ. B.Sc. 1954; C.A. (India) 1958; Mass. Inst. Technol. M.Sc. 1964 (Sloan Fellow); m. Lata; two s. Vikram, Vivek; PRES., CHIEF OPERATING OFFR. AND DIR., FINNING TRACTOR & EQUIPMENT CO. LTD. 1981- ; Dir. J. P. Morgan of Canada Ltd.; Trustee, European & Pacific Investment Trust, Toronto; various mang. positions Bajaj Electricals Ltd. 1959-67; joined present Co. 1968, Vice Pres. Finance, Dir. and mem. Extve. Comte. 1969, Extve. Vice Pres. 1976; Gov., Employers' Council B.C.; recreations: tennis, jogging; Clubs: Shaughnessy Golf & Country; Vancouver Lawn, Tennis & Badminton; Canadian (Dir.); Home: 2012 Acadia Rd., Vancouver, B.C. V6T 1R5; Office: 555 Great Northern Way, Vancouver, B.C. V5T 1E2.

SOPER, John R.; insurance executive; b. Brantford, Ont. 8 Nov. 1923; m. Jean, 10 April 1946; children: one d. Jennifer; PRESIDENT AND CHIEF EXTVE. OFFR., INA INSURANCE CO. OF CANADA; Dir. INA Canada; mem. Bd. Trade Metrop. Toronto; recreations: squash, skiing, golf; Club: National; Home: 25 Unicorn Ave., Willowdale, Ont. M2K 2L3; Office: 161 Eglinton Ave. E., Toronto, Ont. M4P 1J5.

SOPER, Warren Y., B.A.; investment dealer, b. Montreal, Que., 24 Jan. 1919; s. Harold Warren and Alice (Ross) S.; e. Lower Canada Coll., Montreal, Que.; St. Andrews Coll., Aurora, Ont., McGill Univ., B.A. 1942; m. Lilianne Binard; children: Warren Y., Jr., Jane Isabel; VICE PRES. & DIR., PITFIELD MACKAY ROSS LTD.; Chrmn., Thomas R. Fisher Ltd.; Chrmn. Calmont Leasing Ltd.; Chrmn. Surplus Holdings Ltd.; Dir., Evangeline Savings & Mortgage Corp.; Warnaco of Canada Ltd.; Can. Reynolds Metals Ltd.; with Defence Industries Ltd., 1943-46; joined present firm in 1946; Sub-Lieut. R.C.N.V.R.; Protestant; recreations: fishing, golf; Clubs: St. James's; Mount Bruno Country; Gulfstream Golf (Delray Beach, Fla.); Gulfstream Bath & Tennis; Rideau (Ottawa); Home: 1415 Scarboro Road, Town of Mount Royal, Que. H3P 2S2; Office: Suite 2101, 1 Place Ville Marie, Montreal, Que. H3B 4H5

SOUCCAR, Joseph Edward, B.Sc., M.B.A.; executive; b. Alexandria, Egypt, 2 Dec. 1933; s. Edward and Becca (Bondi) S.; e. Victoria Coll. Alexandria, Egypt 1951; Leeds (Eng.) Univ. B.Sc. (Elect. Engn.) 1954; McGill Univ. Dipl. Business Adm. 1958; Univ. of W. Ont. M.B.A. 1959; m. 1957 (divorced); children: Debbie, Audrey, Diane; PRESIDENT, DOMGLAS INC.; 1976; Dir. Twinpak Ltd.; Diamond Glass; Ampak Ltd.; Systems Engr. and Designer, Northern Electric Co. Ltd. 1954-58; Export Mgr. and Mgr. Marketing Services, Atlas Steels Co. 1959, Sales Mgr.-Atlas UK 1960, Mang. Dir. Atlas Australia 1961 and Atlas Europe 1963, Dir. Marketing 1965; Mang. Consultant P.S. Ross & Partners 1966-69, Vice-Pres., Marketing 1969-76, Evec. Vice-Pres. 1975-76; recreations: tennis, squash, skiing, swimming; Clubs: Donalda Club (Toronto); Home: 44A Maple Ave., Toronto, Ont. M4W 2T7 Office: 2070 Hadwen Rd., Mississauga, Ont. L5K 2C9

SOUCY, Maurice W., B.Sc.; industrialist; b. St-Antonin, Cté. Rivière-du-Loup, Que. 22 Sept. 1922; s. Wilfrid P. and Marie-Louise (Loranger) S.; e. Coll. Ste.-Anne, La Pocatière, Que.; Moncton Univ. B.Sc.; Hautes Etudes Commerciales Montréal; m. Estelle Lapointe 10 Aug. 1946; children: Yves G., Claire (Mme Réjean Parent), Paul, Marc, Josée; Pres. Nap. Dumont Ltée; Nap. Transport Ltée; Loubec Inc.; Quinar Inc.; La Traverse Rivière-du-Loup St-Siméon Ltée; Corp. d'Aménagement Touristique de l'Est du Qué.; Administratuer, Banque Nationale du Canada; Dir., Fondation Bouchard Inc.; Pres. Corp. de Développement Industriel; Corp. de Promotion du Port de Mer de Gros-Cacouna; Dir., Centre des Dirigeants d'Enterprise (Dir. l'exécutif prov.); Past Pres. Chambre de Commerce; Conseil de Développement Témiscouata Grand-Portage; Chevalier de Colomb;

Commandant, Candn. Power Sqdn.; R. Catholic; recreations: yachting, golf, cross-country skiing; Clubs: Richelieu (Ex-Gouverneur); Yacht (Vice-Commodore); Golf St-Patrice (Dir.); Home; 35 St-Louis, Rivière-du-Loup, Qué. G5R 2V3; Office: 37 St-Louis, Rivière-du-Loup, Qué. G5R 2V3

SOURKES, Theodore Lionel, M.Sc., Ph.D., F.R.S.C.; educator; b. Montreal, Que. 21 Feb. 1919; s. Irving and Fanny (Golt) S.; e. McGill Univ. B.Sc. 1939, M.Sc. 1946; Queen's Univ. 1940-41; Cornell Univ. Ph.D. 1948; m. Shena d. Abraham Rosenblatt, Toronto, Ont. 17 Jan. 1943; children: Barbara May, Myra June; PROF. OF BIOCHEM., McGILL UNIV:, Dir. Lab. of Neurochem. Allan Mem. Inst. of Psychiatry; author "Biochemistry of Mental Disease" 1962; "Nobel Prize Winners in Medicine and Physiology" 1966; over 285 scient. articles biochem. of nervous system and mental disease; mem. many biochem., pharmacol. and neuroscience organs.; Home: 4645 Montclair Ave., Montreal, Que. H4B 2J8; Office: 1033 Pine Ave W., Montreal, Que. H3A 1A1.

SOUSTER, Raymond; poet; b. Toronto, Ont. 1921; first works appeared in Montreal mag. "First Statement" 1942 and later in "Unit of Five" 1944; author of, "When We Are Young" 1946; "Go to Sleep, World" 1947; "The Winter of Time", novel pub. under psuedonym of "Raymond Holmes" 1949; "City Hall Street" 1951; "Shake Hands with the Hangman; Poems 1940-52" 1953; "A Dream that is Dying" 1954; "Walking Death" 1955; "For What Time Slays" 1955; "Selected Poems" (ed. by Louis Dudek) 1956; "Crêpe-Hangers Carnival: Selected Poems 1955-58" 1958; "A Local Pride" 1962; "Place of Meeting: Poems 1958-60" 1962; "The Colour of the Times" (Gov. Gen's Award for Poetry in English) 1964; "Ten Elephants on Yonge Street" 1965; "As Is" 1967; "Lost and Found: Uncollected Poems" 1968; "So Far So Good: Poems 1938-68" 1969; "The Years" 1971; "Selected Poems" 1972; "On Target", novel pub. under pseud. of "John Holmes" 1972; "Change-up" 1974; "Double-Header" 1975; "Rain-Check" 1975; "Extra Innings" 1977; "Hanging In: New Poems" 1979; "Collected Poems of Raymond Souster: Vol. One 1940-55", 1980; co-author "From Hell to Breakfast" (with Douglas, Alcorn); Co-ed. mag. "Direction" 1943-46; Ed. mags. "Contact" 1952-54 and "Combustion" 1957-60; Ed. "Poets '56", 1956; "New Wave Canada" anthology 1966; Co-ed. (with Douglas Lochhead) "Made in Canada" anthology 1970; "100 Poems of Nineteenth Century Canada" 1974; "Generation Now" (with Richard Woollatt) an exper. high sch. poetry textbook; "Sights & Sounds" (with R. Woollatt) a jr. poetry text 1972; "These Loved These Hated Lands" 1975; "Vapour and Blue", poetry of W.W. Campbell, selected and introd. by R. Souster; 1978; "Comfort of the Fields", poetry of A. Lampman, selected and introd. by R. Souster 1979; "Poems of A Snow-Eyed Country" (anthology (with R. Woollatt) 1979; "Collected Poems of Raymond Souster, Vol. 2, 1955-1962"; 1981; "Collected Poems of Raymond Sousten Vol. 3, 1962-74", 1982; served in 2nd World War. R.C.A.F.; employed as Asst. Supvr., Securities, Canadian Imperial Bank of Commerce; Chrmn. and a Co-Founder. Candn. League of Poets; Home: 39 Baby Point Rd., Toronto, Ont. M6S 2G2; Office: Canadian Imperial Bank of Commerce, Main Br., Commerce Court, Toronto, Ont.M5L 1G9

SOUTHAM, (Mrs.) Audrey Goodwin, B.A.; school principal (ret.); b. Montreal, Que., 12 Oct. 1919; d. William Carlyle and Ida Charlotte (Walker) Goodwin; e. Long Island, N.Y., 1935-37; McGill Univ., B.A. 1941; Ont. Coll. of Educ., Teaching Cert. 1965; m. 29 Sept. 1945 (divorced); children: Sandra (Mrs. R. S. White), Linda (Mrs. D. W. Tait), Carlyle, Judith, (Mrs. U. G. McMillan) Neal; ASSOC., D. L. IMMES LTD., Realtor, since 1975; served on various Bds. of Jr. League of Hamilton, Art Gallery of Hamilton, Ballet Guild, 1945-64; Teacher of Eng. and Hist., Hillfield-Strathallan Colls., Hamilton, 1946-68; Headmistress 1968-72; Principal, Havergal Coll. 1972-75; served overseas with Candn. Red Cross Corps (V.A.D.) during World War II; loaned to Brit. Red Cross serving in Eng. hosp.; mem., Art Gall. Hamilton; Nat. Ballet Can., Pres Hamilton Branch); Hamilton Art Gallery; Anglican; recreations: swimming, boating, skiing; Club: Address: P.O. Box 18, Ancaster, Ont. L9G 3L3

SOUTHAM, Gordon Hamilton, O.C. (1977), B.A.; civil servant; b. Ottawa, Ont., 19 Dec. 1916; s. of Wilson Mills S.; e. Univ. of Toronto, B.A. 1939; Oxford, 1939 (Modern Hist.); LL.D., Trent 1977; Carlton 1978; DCL King's Coll. 1981; m. 1stly Jacqueline, d. Pierre Lambert-David, Chateau de Ferney-Voltaire, France, 15 April 1940 (divorced); children: Peter, Christopher, Jennifer, Michael; 2ndly Gro Mortensen, Oslo, Norway, 1968; (divorced); children: Henrietta, Gordon; 3rdly Marion Charpentier, Paris, France, 1981; served in 2nd World War; Offr. Cadet, Royal Arty., 1939; Lieut., R.C.A., 1940; served in U.K., Italy, N.W. Europe; discharged, 1945 with rank of Capt.; Mentioned in Despatches; Reporter, "The Times", London, 1945-46; Edit. Writer, "The Citizen", Ottawa, 1946-47; joined Dept. of External Affairs 1948; Third Secy., Stockholm, Aug. 1949; Chargé d'Affaires a.i. Warsaw, March 1959, Ambassador to Poland, 1960-62; Head, Information Div., Dept. External Affairs, 1962; Coordinator, Candn. Centre for the Performing Arts (now National Arts Centre), Feb. 1964; Dir. Gen., Nat. Arts Centre 1967-77; Chrmn., Lively Arts Market Builders; Pres., Cdn. Mediterranean Inst. (Athens, Cairo and Rome); mem. of Bd., Southam Inc.; Nat. Theatre School; Cdn. Opera Co.; Cdn. Film Inst.; 1st Pres., Nat. Gallery Assn.; 1st Pres., Nat. Capital Arts Alliance 1963-64; Chrmn. Organ. Comte., UNESCO Festival and Seminar on Films on Art, Ottawa, 1963; Internat. Theatre Colloquium '67, Montreal 1967; recreations: walking, tennis, sailing, skiing; Clubs: Cercle Universitaire (Ottawa); Reform (London); Anglican; Homes: 9 Rideau Gate, Ottawa, Ont. K1M 1M6 and "Bending Birches", Portland, Ont.

SOUTHAM, Robert Wilson, B.A., M.S.; publisher; b. Ottawa, Ont., 3 Dec. 1914; s. Harry Stevenson and Lilias (Ahearn) S.; e. Ashbury Coll. Sch., Ottawa, 1923-32; Queen's Univ., B.A. 1936; Columbia Univ., M.S. (Journ.) 1937; D.C.L., Univ. of King's Coll. 1937; LL.D., Queen's Univ., 1980; m. Margaret Ann, d. W. R. Creighton, Ottawa, Ont., 2 Nov. 1939; children: Ross, Susan, Richard; former Publisher, Ottawa "Citizen"; Chairman, Board of Trustees, Queen's University 1975-80; served in 2nd World War with Royal Canadian Navy, joining in June 1940 and discharged in Aug. 1945 with rank of Lieut.-Commdr.; Pres., Candn. Daily Newspaper Publishers Assn., 1960-61; Liberal; Anglican; Clubs: Rideau; Royal Ottawa Golf; Home: 10 Crescent Rd., Rockcliffe Park, Ottawa, Ont. K1M 0N3

SOUTHAM, William Watson, B.Sc; retired executive; b. Hamilton, Ontario, 16 April 1908; s. William James and Annie Beatrice (Watson) S.; e. Trinity Coll. Sch., Port Hope, Ont.; McGill Univ., B.Sc. (Elect. Engn.) 1930; m. Katinka Raimondi, d. late Dr. George Young, Colchester, Eng., 10 July 1930; children: Zoë, Peter Young, Patricia Maureen; 2ndly, Joan Evelyn, d. late John T. Wilson, Kenya, Africa, 30 Apl. 1955; children: Michael W., Kenneth W., Brenda W., Brian W.; 3rdly, Katinka Raimondi, d. late Dr. George Young, Colchester, Eng., 23 Oct. 1969; with Vancouver "Daily Province", 1930-45; el. a Dir. Southam Inc. 1950, Vice-President 1954 until retirement; mem., Assn. Prof. Engrs. Ont.; Engn. Inst. Can.; Delta Upsilon; recreations: photography, home workshop; Clubs: Toronto Badminton and Racquet; Home: 30 Glen Elm Ave., Toronto, Ont. M4T 1T7

SOUTHERN, Ronald D., B.Sc., industrial executive; b. Calgary; Alta., 25 July 1930; s. Samuel Donald and Alexandra Cuthill (MacDonald) S.; e. Stanley Jones Sch.

(1936-44) and Crescent Heights High Sc. (1944-48), Calgary, Alta.; Univ. of Alta., B.Sc. 1953; (Hon.,) D., L., Calgary Univ. 1976; m. Margaret Elizabeth, d. Charles Visser, Calgary, Alta., 30 July 1954; children: Nancy Christine, Linda Anne; PRESIDENT AND CHIEF EXTVE. OFFR., ATCO. LTD. Nova An Alta Corp.; Dir., Candn. Pacific Enterprises Ltd.; Canada Cement Lafarge Ltd.; Royal Insurance Co. Ltd.; Scott & Easton Ltd.; Crown Zellerbach Canada Ltd.; Pacific Western Airlines Ltd.; ATCO Ltd., Candn. Utilities Ltd.; mem., Young President's Organ.; Conf. Bd. in Can.; Gov., Olympic Trust Can.; Freemason; Protestant; recreations: horses, tennis, sailing, skiing; Clubs: Calgary Petroleum; Glencoe; Earl Grey Golf; Home: 67 Massey Pl. S.W., Calgary, Alta. T2V 2G7; Office: 1243 McKnight Blvd. Calgary, Alta. T2E 5T2

SOUTHERN, Samuel Donald; mobile home company executive; CHRMN. OF BD., ATCO LTD.; former farmer, trucker, firefighter; served as fire chief and instr. with RCAF during World War II, rank Warrant Offr.; founded Alberta Trailer Hire 1916 becoming Trans-Canada Rent-A-Trailer; founded Alberta Trailer Co. 1949, renamed ATCO; Office: 1243 McKnight Blvd. N.E., Calgary, Alta. T2E 5T2.

SOUTHEY, Hon. James Bonham Strange, B.A.; judge; b. Bowmanville, Ont., 26 Oct. 1926; s. Edmund Charles Clay and Mary Campbell (Strange) S.; e. Bowmanville (Ont.) High Sch.; Trinity Coll. Sch. Port Hope, Ont.; Queen's Univ. B.A. 1948; Osgoode Hall Law Sch. 1951 (Silver Medal); m. Winifred Mary Joyce d. Hugh M. Hughson, Ottawa, Ont., 27 June 1953; children: Sara Joyce, Robert George Hughson, Peter McBean, Edmund Campbell Armstrong, Michael Hugh Strange; JUSTICE OF HIGH COURT, SUPREME COURT OF ONT. since 1975; Read law with C.F.H. Carson, Q.C.; called to Bar of Ont. 1951, Bar of Sask. 1964; cr. Q.C. 1966; practised law with Tilley, Carson & Findlay and predecessor firms Toronto 1951-75; served with Candn. Army 1945; Gov. Trinity Coll. Sch.; Past Pres. Lawyers Club Toronto; mem' Candn. Bar Assn.; Phi Delta Phi; Anglican; recreations: tennis, golf, skiing; Clubs: Toronto Golf; Badminton & Racquet; Home: 143 Rosedale Hts. Dr., Toronto, Ont. M4T 1C7; Office: Osgoode Hall, Toronto, Ont.

SOWARD, Frederic Hubert, M.Litt., LL.D., F.R.S.C.; historian; b. Minden, Ont., 10 Apl. 1899; s. Hubert Edward Thomas and Lou Alberta Victoria S.; e. Univ. of Toronto, B.A. 1921 (First Class Hons. in Modern Hist.); Univ. of Edinburgh 1919; Oxford Univ., M.Litt. 1922; LL.D. Edinburgh 1962; Brit. Columbia 1964; m. Catherine Dey, d. late William Minto, Toronto, 30 Aug. 1922; children: Maurice Millington, Stuart Edward, Catherine Jean; first Riddell Schol., Univ. of Toronto, 1915, and first Kylie Schol. there, 1921; Instr. in Hist., Univ. of B.C., 1922-25; Asst. Prof., 1925-29; Assoc. Prof., 1929-36; Prof. of Hist. 1936-63 (Head of the Dept. 1953-63); Dir. of Internat. Studies, 1946-64; Dean of Grad. Studies, 1961 and Dean Emeritus 1964; attended Inst. of Pac. Relations Conf., 1933, '36, '42 and '50; Brit. Commonwealth Relations Conf., 1938, 1949 and 1965; served in World War, 1917-19, with 15th Bn., 48th Highlrs. of Can.; author of "Moulders of National Destinies", 1938, 2nd ed. 1939; "Twenty-five Troubled Years, 1918-43", 1943; "Canada in World Affairs, 1944-46", "From Normandy to Paris", 1950; "The Changing Commonwealth", 1950; principal author, "Canada in World Affairs — The PreWar Years", 1941; awarded Centennial Medal 1967; Hon. mem., Candn. Hist. Assn. (1972); mem., Am. Hist. Assn. (Pres. Pac. Coast Br., 1961-62); Candn. Inst. Internat. Affairs (Chrmn., Vancouver Bd., 1937-39, 1948-50); mem., Nat. Research Comte.; Special Asst. to the Under-Secy. of State for Extenal Affairs, 1943-46 and summers 1949, '51 and '52; awarded Carnegie Travel and Research Grant, 1950, to study external policies of all commonwealth countries; mem., Candn. del. to 11th Assembly of U.N.,

1956-57; Co-Dir., World Univ. Service Seminar in Japan, summer 1955; guest of the Fed. Republic of Germany for a study tour, Nov.-Dec. 1955; Visiting Prof. Indian Sch. of Internat. Studies, 1959; Pres. of Sec. 2, Roy. Soc. Can. 1965-66; Hon. mem. Candn. Inst. Internat. Affairs; Phi Gamma Delta; Anglican; Home: Apt. 1102, 4620 W. 10th Ave., Vancouver, B.C. V6R 2J5

SOWARD, Reginald Harvey, Q.C.; b. Minden, Ont., 3 June 1907;s. Hubert Edward Thomas and Lue Alberta Victoria (Stinson) S.; e. Univ. of Toronto, B.A. (Mod. Hist.) 1928; Osgoode Hall, Toronto, 1931; m. Lillian Ruth, d. Prof. George A. Cornish, Toronto, 14 Oct. 1931; MEMBER, McLAUGHLIN, SOWARD, MORDEN & BALES, since 1964; Dir. and Vice-Pres., Victoria & Grey Trust Co.; mem. of Council, Wycliffe Coll., Toronto; Chancellor, Diocese of Toronto, 1949-75; Chancellor to the Primate since 1977; Dir., Ang. Foundation of Can.; mem., Gen. Synod of Ang. Ch., since 1943; read law with R. J. McLaughlin, K.C.; began practice with McLaughlin, Johnston, Moorhead & Macaulay, 1931; mem. of firm 1939; mem., N. York Sch. Bd., 1937-40; Lawyers Club of Toronto (Pres. 1943-44); mem., Ruskin Lit. & Debating Soc. 1936- ; Assoc. Ed. of 5th ed., Holmstead and Langton's "Ontario Judicature Act", 1940; Ed., 5th ed., Bicknell & Seager's "Division Court Manual", 1938; has contrib. articles to Candn. Encycl. Digest of Law (Ont.); I.O.F. (Past Chief Ranger); P. Conservative; Anglican; recreations: gardening, travelling, reading; Club: Albany; Home: 6 De Vere Gardens, Toronto, Ont., M5M 3E5; Office: 200 University Ave., Toronto, Ont., M5H 3C6

SPALDING, J. Stuart, C.A.; chartered accountant; b. Edinburgh, Scotland 23 Nov. 1934; came to Can. 1957; e. C.A., Scotland, 1957; C.A., Montreal 1962; m. Louise Bourgeau 7 May 1960; children: Eric, Martin, Elizabeth, Valerie; VICE PRES. AND TREASURER, BELL CANADA since 1979; Treasurer, 1976; Dir.: The Resource Service Group Ltd., Tele-Direct Ltd., Natl. Telephone Dir. Corp.; Maritime Telegraph and Tel. Co. Ltd., Ronalds-Federated Ltd.; mem., Financial Extve. Inst.; Past. Pres. Mtl. Soc. of Financial Analysts; Clubs: St. James, Mtl.; Mt. Bruno Country Club; Hillside Tennis; Home: 35 Thornhill Ave., Westmount, Que. H3Y 2E1; Office: 1050 Beaver Hall Hill, Montreal, Que. H2Z 1S4

SPALDING Thomas Lester, J.D.; airline executive; b. Winnipeg., Man., 12 May 1920; s. late Capt. Lester Luther, M.C., D.C.M. and late Florence Irene (Bunting) S.; e. Univ. of Minn., 1938-39; Sioux Falls Coll., 1939-40; Hamline Univ., 1940-41; Kent Coll. of Law, Ill. Inst. of Technol., J.D. 1951; m. Helen Ruth, d. late William P. Cain, 30 May 1946; one d., Anne Catherine; EXTVE. VICE PRES. & DIR., WARDAIR INTERNAT. LTD.,; Wardair Canada (1975) Ltd.; Internat. Vacations Ltd.; Wardair Equipment Ltd.; Wardair Hawaii Ltd.; Dir., Wardair U.K. Ltd.; Wardair Jamaica Ltd.; Redrock Reinsurance Ltd.; with Liberty Mutual Insurance Co., Boston, 1942-57; held various positions incl. Mgr., Special Claims Div., H.O.; Dir. of Contracts, Comm. Airplane Group, The Boeing Co., Seattle, 1957-70; called to Bar of Ill. 1951; served with U.S.N.R.-M1, U.S. Maritime Service, Med. Corpsman, 1942-43; Chrmn., Air Transport Assn. Can. 1977-78; mem., Ill. State Bar Assn.; Am. Bar Assn.; Phi Delta Phi; Sigma Sigma (Pres. 1939-40); Alpha Sigma Chi; Liberal; Protestant; recreation: fishing; Club: Wings Club, N.Y.; Home: 1502, 11307 99th Ave., Edmonton, Alta., T5K 0H2; Office: 2201 T.D. Tower, Edmonton Centre, Edmonton, Alta. T5J 0K4

SPARKS, Robert (Jack) W.; petroleum executive; b. Amarillo, Texas, 9 Oct. 1918; s. Thomas Charles and Angelina (Wilson) S.; e. Amarillo (Texas) Jr. Coll.; W. Texas State; Texas Technol. Inst.; m. Mary Ann, d. late W. T. Stanberry 15 Jan. 1938; two s. Robert Charles, Stephen Terrence; CHRMN. OF THE BOARD AND CHIEF

EXTVE. OFFR. TEXACO CANADA INC. Dir. Federated Pipelines Co. Texas; trans. to Can. as Mgr. Elect. Logging and Wire Lane Services 1949, Mgr. co. operations in Can. 1952; assigned to Aramco (Saudi Arabia) 1951 as Elect. Logging Engr.; joined present co. (then McColl-Frontenac) as Chief Engr. Producing Dept. 1954, Mgr. Producing Dept. 1959, Asst. to Pres. 1969, Vice Pres. Sales 1971, Vice Pres. W. Can. 1973, Extve. Vice Pres. 1975; became Candn. citizen 1967; licensed pilot; Presbyterian; recreations: golf, skiing, hunting, fishing; Clubs: Toronto Lambton Golf & Country; Calgary Petroleum (Past Pres.); Office: 90 Wynford Dr., Don Mills, Ont. M3C 1K4

SPARLING, Maj.-Gen. H. Alan, C.B.E., D.S.O., C.D.; b. Toronto, Ont., 2 June 1907; s. Lt.-Col. Herbert Cosford, D.S.O., and Mabel Ester (Widner) S.; e. Elem. Schs., Saint John, N.B.; Roy. Mil. Coll., Kingston, Grad. 1929; Dalhousie Univ., 1932; Woolwich, Eng. (Gunnery Staff Course), 1933-34; m. Edith Blanche, d. James Archibald Hunter, Minneapolis, Minn., 30 Nov. 1935, one s.; Regimental Offr., Royal Canadian Horse Arty., 1929-33; Instr. in Gunnery, Winnipeg, 1934-37; 1938 with Nat. Defence Hdqr., Ottawa, as G.S.O. III in Directorate of Mil. Operations; Jan.-Sept. 1939 attended Staff Coll., Camberley, Eng.; G.S.O. II 1939; apptd. Bgde. Maj., 2nd Candn. Div. Arty., and proceeded overseas 1940; Sr. Staff Offr., Directorate of Mil. Training in Can., with rank of Lt.-Col., 1941; Acting Dir., 1942; assumed commd. overseas of 13th Candn. Field Regt., R.C.A., 1942; specially employed in Sicily and later in Italy, 8th Army, and 13th (Br.) Corps, 1943; promoted Brig. in command of Divn. Artillery of 5 Candn. Armoured Divn., Italy; Corps Arty. Commdr., 1st Candn. Corps in Italy; and N.W. Europe, 1945; returned to Can. to command Divn. Arty., of Candn. Army, Pacific Force, 1945, on disbanding of which proceeded overseas as CRA, 3rd Candn. Inf. Divn., Candn. Army Occupation Force in Germany; on return to Can. apptd. Dist. Offr. Commdg. Mil. Dist. No. 2, Toronto; Commdr., W. Ont. Area, 1947-49; attended Imp. Defence Coll., London, 1950; promoted Maj.-Gen. 1950; Vice-Chief of Gen. Staff, Candn. Army, Nov. 1950-Dec. 1955; Chrmn., Candn. Joint Staff, Wash., D.C., 1956-58; G.O.C. Central Command, 1958-62; retired Feb. 1963; apptd. mem., of Ontario Police Comn. 1962-78 retired; Col. Commandant, Roy. Regt. Candn. Arty. 1969-74; degree of officer, U.S. Legion of Merit; Anglican; recreations: golf, curling; Address: 1236 Cumnock Cres., Oakville, Ont., L6J 2N5

SPARROW, Hon. Herbert Orville; senator; b. Saskatoon, Sask., 4 Jan. 1930; s. Abiah Andrew and Olive (Gramson) S.; e. Minnesota Sch. Dist., Sask., 1944; Bedford Rd. Coll., Saskatoon, Sask., 1948; m. Lois Irene, d. William J. Perkins, North Battleford, Sask., 31 Jan. 1951; four s.: Kenneth, Bryan, Robert, Ronald; Pres. and Gen. Mgr., The Ranch House Ltd., Pres., Sparrow Enterprises Ltd.;, Sparlite Ranch Ltd., Westman Contracting Ltd.; Candn. Bank of Commerce, 1948-51; Ald., City of North Battleford, 1957-65; Lib. cand. in Sask. g.e. 1964 and 1967; Pres., Sask. Lib. Assn., 1964-68; summonded to Senate of Can. 1968; Chrmn., Bd. of Trustees, North Battleford Sch. for Retarded Children; mem., North Battleford Hosp.; Pub. Lib. Bd.; and Community Planning Bd.; mem., North Battleford Chamber Comm.; Depy. Chmn., Senate Finance Comte.; Senate Agricultural Comte.; mem., Senate Foreign Affairs Comte.; Senate Transportation and Communication Comte.; Hon. Pres., Candn. Fed. of Amateur Baseball; Freemason; Shriner; Liberal; United Church; Club: Kinsmen (Life mem.); Home: 9113 Walker Dr., North Battleford, Sask. S9A 2Y2

SPARSHOTT, Francis Edward, M.A., F.R.S.C.; educator; poet; b. Chatham, Eng. 19 May 1926; s. Frank Brownley and Gladwys Winifred (Head) S.; e. The King's Sch. Rochester, Eng. 1943; Corpus Christi Coll. Oxford Univ. B.A., M.A. 1950; m. Kathleen Elizabeth d. late W. Stewart Vaughan, Willowdale, Ont. 1953; one d. Pumpkin

Margaret Elizabeth; PROF. OF PHILOSOPHY, VICTORIA COLL. UNIV. OF TORONTO since 1964; joined present Univ. as Lectr. in Philos, 1950, Asst. Prof. 1955, Assoc. Prof. 1962, Chrmn. Victoria Coll. Dept. of Philosophy 1965-70; Visiting Assoc. Prof. of Philos. Northwestern Univ. 1958-59; Visiting Prof. of Philos. Univ. of Ill. 1966; served with Brit. Army Intelligence Corps 1944-47; Killam Sr. Research Scholar 1977; Pres's Medal for best single poem Univ. of W. Ont. 1958; author "An Enquiry into Goodness and Related Concepts" 1958; "The Structure of Aesthetics" 1963; "A Divided Voice" 1965; "The Concept of Criticism" 1967; "A Cardboard Garage" 1968; "Looking for Philosophy" 1972; "The Naming of the Beasts" 1979; "The Rainy Hills" 1979; "The Theory of the Arts", 1982; mem. Candn. Philos. Assn. (Vice Pres. 1974-75, Pres. 1975-76); Am. Soc. Aesthetics (Trustee 1973-75 and 1977-79, Vice Pres. 1979-80, Pres. 1981-82); League of Candn. Poets (Extve. Comte. 1970-76, Pres. 1977-79); Aristotelian Soc.; Am. Philos. Assn.; Classical Assn. Can.; recreation: photography; Home: 50 Crescentwood Rd., Scarborough, Ont., M1N 1E4; Office: 73 Queen's Park Cres. E., Toronto, Ont., M5S 1K7

SPEARS, Borden, B.A.; b. Pine Lake, Alta., 19 Feb. 1913; s. late Thomas John and late Laura Augusta (Weir) S.; e. Pub. and 2ndary Schs., Red Deer, Alta.; Vancouver, B.C.; Tobermory, Owen Sound and London, Ont.; Univ. of W. Ontario, B.A. (Classics) 1936 (Gold Medallist); m. Mary Gracey, d. late T. C. King, 4 May 1944; children: George, Laura, John, Thomas; Commissioner, Royal Commission On Newspapers, 1981; (retired) joined Toronto Star as Reporter, 1939-48; apptd. City Ed., 1948-58; Mang. Ed., Toronto Star, 1959-60; Sr. Ed. (retired 1980); Ed. Consultant, Maclean-Hunter Publishing Co., 1961; Extve. Ed., "Financial Post", 1964; Ed., "Macleans" Magazine 1964-69; Extve. Consultant, Special Senate Comte. on Mass Media 1969-70; served with RCAF during 2nd World War in U.K., Italy, India, Burma, rank Flt. Lt.; United Church; Home: 176 Lawrence Ave. E., Toronto, Ont., M4N 1T1;

SPEIRS, Derek J., B.Com., C.A., M.B.A.; b. Montreal, Que. 21 Dec. 1933; e. McGill Univ. B.Com. 1954, M.B.A. 1959; C.A. 1956; Chart. Secy. 1956; m. Carol Cumming; 15 Dec. 1967; children: Lara, Gregory, Scott; VICE PRES. FINANCE & CORPORATE DEVEL., DOMTAR INC. 1978- ; Controller, Legal Adm., Tax & Gen., Kruger Pulp 1960-65; accounting and offshore assignments Cynamid of Canada 1965-70; Devel. Dir. (Fine Papers) and Accounting Dir. (Corporate) Domtar Ltd. 1970-72; Vice Pres. Finance & Secy., Dir., Consoltex 1972-76; Dir. Corporate Planning Domtar Inc. 1976-78; recreations: travel, skiing; Home: 365 Stanstead, Town of Mount Royal, Qué. H3R 1X6; Office: (P.O. Box 7210 Stn. A) Montréal, Qué. H3C 3M1.

SPENCE, Ernest John Hamilton, O.B.E. (1946), B.A., B.Com., M.B.A., Ph.D.; educator; consultant; extve.; b. Winnipeg, Man., 14 Apl. 1915; s. William John and Mary Alice (Clements) S.; e. Univ. of Man., B.A. 1935; Queen's Univ. B.Com. 1938; Northwestern Univ., Ill., M.B.A. 1939, Ph.D. 1947; m. Mary Jane, d. late C. U. Gotschall, White Rock, B.C., 30 June 1938; children: Michael, Randall, Murray; PRES., TORHAM PACKAGING INC. since 1978 Prof. of Business, Faculty of Adm. Studies, York Univ. since 1966-77; Vice Chairman, Signet Food Systems Inc.1971-77; Dir., Bovis Corp. Ltd.; Reed Paper Ltd.; Lectr., Econ. and Finance, Northwestern Univ., 1939-42; joined W.P.T.B., Ottawa, 1942; Chief, Prices Divn. there, 1945-47; Asst. to Chrmn. 1947; Asst. Gen. Mgr., Fur Trade Dept., Hudson's Bay Co., Winnipeg, 1947-49; apptd. Vice-Pres. of Canadian Food Products Limited, Toronto, Ontario, 1949, General Manager, 1950, President 1951-59; Executive Vice-President, Triarch Corporation Ltd. 1960-65; Visiting Lect., Univ. of W. Ont. 1965-66; Phi Kappa Pi; Beta Gamma Sigma; Protestant; Clubs: National; Granite; Princeton (New York); Home: 115 An-

tibes Dr., Apt. 1006, Willowdale, Ont. Office: 44 Norwood Tererace, Toronto, Ont. M4E 2H1

SPENCE, Hon. Wishart Flett, C.C. O.B.E., LL.D.; s. late Hon. (Senator) James Houston and Margaret (Hackland) S.; e. Univ. of Toronto Schs.; Univ. of Toronto, B.A. (Pol. Science) 1925; Osgoode Hall, Toronto, Ont. (Gold Medal); Harvard Univ., LL.M. 1929; LL.D., York 1974; Toronto 1976; m.; has one s. and one d.; Justice Supreme Court of Can. 1963-78 (ret.); called to the Bar of Ont. 1928; practised law with firm of Starr, Spence & Hall till 1934 and later formed partnership with his father and S. A. Shoemaker; apptd. a Justice, Supreme Court of Ont. 1950; part time Lect. at Osgoode Hall, 1930-46; served during 2nd World War with W.P.T.B. as Enforcement Administrator; Chairman, Royal Comn. on Coastal Trade (apptd. 1955); apptd. by Fed. Govt. to lead probe into Munsinger case, March 1966.

SPENCELEY, Harry Noble; real estate executive and consultant; b. Stratford, Ont. 12 April 1924; s. late Wm. B. and late Grace V. (Noble) S.; e. Univ of Toronto Grad. Sch. Business (AIREA Appraisal I); Stanford Univ. (AIREA Appraisal II); New York City (Appraisal IV); m. Luella, d. John Somerville 23 Sept. 1949; children: Robert, Stephen, Marilee, Patricia; PRES. H. N. SPENCELEY ASSOC LTD. (formerly Landauer Assoc. Ltd.) since 1978; Secty-Treasurer, Foxwick and Foxcroft Corps; Vice-Chrmn & Dir., Republic Management Corp., New York; Vice Pres. James D. Landauer Assocs. Inc. 1965-70 and Gen. Mgr. Corp. Adm. (Real Estate and Real Estate Devel.) Bank of Nova Scotia 1970-73; Vice Pres. Managing Dir., Landower Assoc. Ltd. 1973-78; previously Gen. Mgr. Metropolitan and Provincial Properties Co. (Canada) Ltd.; Vice-Pres. Appraising, Consulting and Special Projects and Co-ord. Vice-Pres. Sales Dept., Alexander Summer Cos., N.J.; sometime owner Spenceley Realty Ltd.; Cert. Sr. Real Estate Analyst; Soc. Real Estate Appraisers 1963; Counselor of Real Estate, Am. Soc. Real Estate Counselors; Fellow Realtor's Inst., Real Estate Inst. of Can.; mem. Appraisal Inst. Can.; Am. Inst. Real Estate Appraisers; Anglican; Clubs: Canadian; Granite; National; Board of Trade; Br. Can. Trade Assoc.; Home: 1166 Bay St., Apt. 405, Toronto, Ont., M5S 2W8; Office: 439 University Ave., Toronto, Ont. M5G 1Y8

SPENCER, Elvins Yuill, M.Sc., Ph.D., F.C.I.C.; research chemist; b. Edmonton, Alta., 28 Oct. 1914; s. Henry Elvins and Harriett Zella (Crowe) S.; e. Univ. of Alta., B.Sc. 1936, M.Sc. 1938; Univ. of Toronto, Ph.D. 1941; m. Hanna, d. Adolf Fischl, 11 July 1942; children: Erica, Martin; Dir., Research Inst., Dept. of Agric., Univ. of W. Ont., 1960-78; (Principal Chemist, 1951-60); Hon. Prof. in Chem., Hon. Lect. in Biochem., Univ. of W. Ont., since 1951; Chief Chem., Fine Chemicals of Can., Toronto, 1941-42; Research Chem., Gelatin Products, Windsor, Ont. (later Detroit, Mich.) 1942-43; Consol. Mining & Smelting Co. Ltd., Trail, B.C.; Prof., of Chem., Univ. of Sask., 1946-51; Co-ordinator of Research, Sask. Research Council, 1949-51; Visiting Prof., Cambridge Univ. 1956-57; Visiting Scholar, Rockefeller Conf. and Study Centre, Bellagio, Italy, spring 1976; Vice-Pres. and Dir. Jr. Un. Farmers of Alta., 1936-38; Consultant to Sask. Dept. of Natural Resources on potash problems, 1950; Ed., "Pesticide Biochem. and Physiol." since 1978; mem., Chem., Inst. Can.; Am. Chem. Soc.; Agric. Inst. Can.; Candn. Biochem. Soc.; Unitarian; recreations: photography, tennis, study of world affairs; Home: 7 Westview Dr., London, Ont., N6A 2Y2

SPENCER, Maj.-Gen. (ret.) George Hylton, O.B.E., C.D., B.Sc., P. Eng.; b. Seaford, Sussex, Eng., 20 Nov. 1916; s. Angus Farquharson and Nora (Taylor) S.; e. Roy. Mil. Coll. Dipl. 1938; Queen's Univ., B.Sc. (civil eng.) 1939; Staff Coll., Camberley, 1943; Imp. Defence Coll., London, 1957; m. Jean Frances, d. M. D. Fitzgerald, Halifax, N.S., 5 Dec. 1939; children: Peter Fitzgerald, Kenneth George, Michael Hylton; MANAGMENT CONSULTANT since 1978; Lieutenant serving at Kingston, Petawawa, Dundurn and Saint John, 1938-39; overseas in England, France, Burma, Belgium, Holland and Germany with R.C.E., 1940-45, in various regimental, command and staff capacities; Candn. Army Pac. Force, June to Sept. 1945; Asst. Dir. of Works and Constr., Army Hdqrs., Ottawa, 1945-46; mem. Dir. Staff, Candn. Army Staff Coll., 1946-49; Deputy Dir. Staff Duties, 1950-51; Dir. of Weapons & Devel., Army Hdqrs., Ottawa, 1951-54; Commdr., Candn. Base Units, Europe, 1954-56; Col. i/c of Adm., Hdqrs. Eastern Command, Halifax, N.S., 1958-61; Commandant, Royal Nilitary College of Canada, Kingston, Ontario, 1962-63; Commander and Chief Engr., Northwest Highway System, 1963-64; Dir. Gen. of Training and Recruiting, Candn. Forces Hdqrs., 1964-67; Asst. Chief of Staff for Plans and Policy, Supreme H.Q. Allied Powers Europe 1967-70; Depy. Comptroller Gen., Candn. Forces Hdqrs. 1970 till retired from Armed Forces 1971; Dir. Metric Conversion, Standards Council of Can. 1972-77; apptd. Col. Commandant, Candn. Military Engrs. 1978; mem., Engn. Inst. Can.; Assoc. Prof. Eng. of N.S.; Military Eng. Assoc. of Can.; Roy. United Services Inst. of N.S.; Anglican; recreations: golf, sailing, trail skiing; Home: Marriott's Cove, N.S. B0J 1K0

SPENCER, John Nugent; retired manufacturer; b. Moncton, N.B., 6 Nov. 1914; s. George O. and Edith A. (Nugent) S.; e. Moncton, (N.B.) Public and High Schs.; Acadia Univ., 1933-35; m. Dorothy L., d. Wm. O. Tudhope, Orillia, Ont., 3 Aug. 1942; children: John Timothy, Gail Edith; Former Pres., Tudhope Specialties Ltd. and Lear Siegler (Can.) Ltd., 1954-72; mem. Adv. Comte., Victoria & Grey Trust Co.; served in 2nd World War R.C.A.F., Jan. 1940-Dec. 1945; retired with rank of Sqdn. Ldr.; Hon. mem. Bd. Govs., Georgian Coll.; Past Pres. Rotary Club of Orillia (1954-55); Past Pres., Orillia Chamber Comm.; mem. Royal Candn. Mil. Inst.; Baptist; recreations: hi-fi music, photography; Club: National (Toronto); Home: 355 Brewery Lane, Orillia, Ont. L3V 3Y7

SPENCER, Mary Eileen, B.A., M.Sc., Ph.D., F.C.I.C.; F.R.S.(C.);biochemist; educator; b. Regina, Sask., 4 Oct. 1923; d. John J., M.A., LL.B. and Etta Christina (Hamren) Stapleton; e. Regina Coll., Assoc. in Arts 1942; Univ. of Sask., B.A. (Chem.) 1945; Bryn Mawr Coll., M.A. (Chem.) 1946; Univ. of Cal. (Berkeley), Ph.D. (Agric. Chem.) 1951; m. Henry Anderson Spencer, 3 July 1946; one d., Susan Mary; PROFESSOR OF PLANT SCIENCE, UNIVERSITY OF ALBERTA since 1964; Secy.-Treasurer, Spencer-Lemaire Industries Ltd.; Chem., Ayerst, McKenna and Harrison Ltd., Montreal, summer 1945, full-time 1946-47; Nat. Canners Assn., San Francisco, 1948; Teaching Fellow, Univ. of Cal. (Berkeley) 1949, Instr. in Food Chem. 1951; joined present Univ. 1953; served as Instr., Asst. and Assoc. Prof., Biochem. Dept., Acting Head, 1961-64, Plant Science Dept. 1962, Prof. 1964; mem. Nat. Research Council of Can. 1970, 1970-73; re-reapptd. 1973-76; mem. Task Force on Post-Secondary Educ., Alta. Govt. Comm. on Educ. Planning, 1970-72; author of book chapters and numerous scient. papers in field of plant biochem.; Chairman, National Advisory Comte. on Biol., Nat. Research Council; Consultative Comte. on I.B.T. Pesticides, 1981; mem. Candn. Soc. Plant Physiols. (Pres. 1971-72); Bd. of Govs., Univ. of Alta 1976-79; Candn. Biochem. Soc.; Am. Soc. Plant Physiols.; Candn. Assn. Univ. Teachers; Japanese Soc. of Plant Physiologists; Internt. Assn. for Plant Tissue Culture; Amer. Assn. for Advancement of Sci.; Growth Regulators Working Group; past mem., Adv. Bd. for Prairie Regional Laboratory; Adv. Bd. for Atlantic Regional Library; Chrmn. (past) NRC ad hoc Visiting Comte. in Forestry Research 1975-76; recipient Queen's Jubilee Medal; Home: 8005 - 137th St., Edmonton, Alta. T5R 0C1; Office: Univ. of Alberta, Edmonton, Alta.

SPICER, Erik J., C.D., B.A., B.L.S., M.A., librarian b. Ottawa, Ont., 9 April 1926; s. Clifford and Violet (Gundersen) S.; e. Model Sch. and Lisgar Collegiate, Ottawa; Kenmore (N.Y.) Sr. High Sch.; "Rehab" Sch., Toronto, Ont.; Victoria Coll., Univ. of Toronto, B.A. 1948; Univ. of Toronto Library Sch., B.L.S. 1949; Dept. of Grad. Studies, Univ. of Toronto, 1949-50; Univ. of Michigan, M.A. (Library Science) 1959; m. Helen, d. late Dr. William Gourlay Blair, 4 July 1953; children: Erika Anne, John Blair; PARLIAMENTARY LIBRARIAN CANADA, since 16 Nov. 1960; Chrmn. Parlty. Libs. Sec., Internat. Fed. of Lib. Assn., The Hague (Voting Del. since 1966); engaged in Circulation and Reference, Ottawa Public Library, 1950-53; Circulation, Gen. Library, Univ. of Mich., 1953-54; Deputy Librarian, Ottawa Public Library, 1954-60; held Library Service Fellowship, Univ. of Mich., 1953-54; Canada Council Fellowship, 1959; served in 2nd World War with R.C.A.F.-R.C.I.C., 1944-45; Gov.-Gens. Foot Guards, 1951-62, Major, retired list; author of various papers in library and parlty. journs.; Founding Pres., Candn. Assn. Parlty. Librarians in Can.; Pres. (1959-60), Inst. of Prof. Librarians; mem., Library Assn. of Ottawa (Pres. 1955-56); Institute of Public Adm. Canada; Candn. Political Science Association; Life mem., Ontario Library Assn. (Pres. 1962-63); Life mem., Candn. Library Assn. (Councillor 1964-67; Pres. 1979-80); Internat. Assn. of Documentalists 1979-80; Dir., Candn. Corr., Internat. Centre for Parlty. Documentation of the Inter-Parlty. Union, Geneva; Trustee, Ottawa Public Lib. Bd. 1970-73; Beta Phi Mu; Phi Kappa Phi; Clubs: Royal Canadian Military Institute; Country; Home: 73 Delaware Ave., Ottawa, Ont., K2P 0Z2; Office: Library of Parliament, Ottawa, Ont. K1A 0A9

SPICER, John H., B.Sc.; retired transportation executive; b. Moose Jaw, Sask., 12 Aug. 1924; s. Ralph Manley and Euphemia Alexander (Gow) S.; e. Greenway & Gen. Wolfe Sch., 1939 and Shellmouth & Daniel MacIntyre Sch., 1942, Winnipeg; Univ. of Man., B.Sc. (Civil Engn.) 1948; m. Irene, d. late Cuthbert Allison, Vancouver, 1 Sept. 1950; EXTVE. VICE PRES., CANADIAN NATIONAL RAILWAYS, since 1976; Director, Northwest Telecommunications, Nfld. Telecommunications; joined present Co. as instrumentman, Winnipeg, 1948; Office Engr., Vancouver, 1949; Asst. Engr., Winnipeg, 1950; Div. Engr., Prince Rupert, 1951; Dist. Engr., Edmonton, 1955 and Montreal, 1956; Asst. Gen. Supvr. of Budgets, Montreal, 1957, Chief Budget Offr. 1958, Chief of Engr. Econ. 1959, Coordinator of Analytical Services 1960; Area Mgr., Toronto, 1961; Asst. Vice Pres., Montreal, 1967; Vice-Pres., Mountain Region, April 1970; System Vice Pres., Planning & Admin. 1974; served with R.C.A.F. 1943-45; mem., Univ. of Man. Alumni Assn.; Protestant; recreations: music, golf, curling; Club: Toronto Railway; Canadian Railway; Kelowna Golf & Country; Kelowna Chamber of Commerce; Home: 13 Alameda Ct., Kelowna, B.C. V1V 1C6; Office: 935 Lagauchetiere St. W., Montreal, Que. H3C 3N4

SPICER, Keith, O.C., Ph.D., LL.D.; journalist; broadcaster; professor b. Toronto, Ont. 6 March 1934; s. George James and Gertrude Grace (McMullen) S.; e. elem. and secondary schs. Toronto; Univ. of Paris Dipl. d'études de civilisation française, degré supérieur Sorbonne 1955, Dipl. de l'Institut d'Etudes Politiques (Internat. Relations) 1958; Univ. of Toronto B.A. 1956, Ph.D. 1962; LL.D. Laurentian Univ. 1973, York Univ. 1974, Univ. Ottawa 1977; children: Dag, Genevieve, Nicolas; Syndicated Columnist, "The Vancouver Sun" since 1977, U.S. Syndication; 1980; Lectr. and Asst. Prof. of Pol. Science Univ. of Ottawa 1961-66; Assoc. Prof. of Pol. Science and Special Lectr. on French Can. Univ. of Toronto 1966-69; Visiting Assoc. Prof. of Pol. Science, Dartmouth Coll. 1967, Glendon Coll. York Univ. 1969-70; Visiting Prof. of Pol. Science Univ. of B.C. 1977-78; Ed. Writer "The Globe and Mail" Toronto 1966-69; Commentator on French TV and Radio networks CBC 1961-69, CBC Internat. Service in French 1968-69, Host and Interviewer CBOFT Ottawa 1965-66; Documentary T.V. Host, CBC. 1979; Host TV Talk Show, "Les invités de Keith Spicer, "Radio-Québec, 1978-80; Staff Researcher on Armed Forces, Royal Comn. Bilingualism and Biculturalism 1964; Special Asst. to Min. of Justice and Pres. Privy Council 1964-65; Founder Candn. Overseas Volunteers 1960-61; Commr. of Official Langs. 1970-77; Dir. Katimavik; Can World Youth; mem. Adv. Comte. Candn. Bilingual Dictionary Project; Comte on Nuclear Issues in the community (Royal Soc. of Canada and Science Council of Canada, 1978-9); Officer, Ordre de la Pleiade, 1980; author "A Samaritan State? External Aid in Canada's Foreign Policy" U. of T. Press, 1966; "Cher péquiste . . . et néanmoins ami: propos pré-référendaires dans un esprit post référendaire," Les Editions La Presse, 1980; "Winging It: Everybody's Guide to Making Speeches Fly Without Notes", 1982; various articles; United Church; Office: Vancouver Sun, 2250 Granville St., Vancouver, B.C.

SPICKETT, Ron, Sr.; painter, sculptor; b. Regina, Sask., 11 Apl. 1926; s. Hubert John and Catherine Georgina (Miller) S.; e. Calgary Prov. Inst. Tech. and Art; Ont. Coll. Art; Instituto Allende, Mexico; m. Anna Barbara Rose, d. late Michael Wingert, 29 June 1950; children: Ronald John, Richard James, Rae Janus; Sessional Instr., Univ. of Calgary, since 1967; Display Artist. Simpson's, Toronto, 1949-51; Hudson's Bay Co., 1951-55; Instr., Alta. Coll. of Art, Calgary 1957-67; has exhibited in Ottawa, Mexico, Montreal, Toronto, Calgary, etc. in special shows; work rep. in coll. Edmonton, Toronto, London, Vancouver, Victoria Art Galleries, Sir Geo. Williams Univ., Rothman Coll., Albert Art Fdn., Can. Council Art Bank Coll., Nat. Gallery, Zack's Coll., C.I.L. Coll., Toronto-Dominion Bank Coll., Shell Oil, Firestone Coll., and others; work includes mural sculpture, free lance comn. work; won O'Keefe Award for Painting, 1951; Baxter Award, O.S.A., 1959; Canada Purchase Award Print, Vancouver, 1961; Can. Council grant for study in Japan, 1962; el. R.C.A. 1968; Arts Fellowship, Can. Council 1969; Sr. Arts Grant, Can. Council 1976; private publ.: "Art as a Mirror of Tathagata Dhyana", 1974; served overseas in 2nd World War with R.C.N.V.R., 1943-46; Home: April Rain, 3427 Elbow Dr., Calgary Alta. T2S 2J5

SPINKS, John William Tranter, C.C. (1970), M.B.E., B.Sc., Ph.D., D.Sc., LL.D., D.M. Sc. F.R.S.C., F.C.I.C.; b. Norfolk, England, 1 January 1908; s. John William and Sarah Jane (Tranter) S.; e. King's College, London Univ., B.Sc.; Ph.D. 1930; Research in Spectroscopy, Darmstadt, Germany, 1933-34; came to Canada 1930; m. Mary Strelioff, 5 June 1939; President, University of Saskatchewan 1959-74 (formerly Dean of Grad. School and Head of Department of Chem. there); mem., Nat. Research Council Can.; Sask. Research Council mem., Sask. Oil & Gas Conservation Bd. since 1952; mem., Defence Research Bd.; The Canada Council; served in World War, 1939-45, as Operational Research Offr., R.C.A.F.; Candn. Atomic Energy Project, 1944-45; mem., Chem. Inst. Can. (Pres. 1953-54); Royal Inst. of Chem.; Faraday Soc.; Am. Chem. Soc.; Inst. of Internat. Affairs; transl. in co-operation with G. Herzberg, "Atomic Spectra", 1937, and "Molecular Spectra", 1939; co-author with R. J. Woods, "Radiation Chemistry"; "Two Blades of Grass", 1980; Anglican; recreations: archaeology, reading; Home: 932 University Dr., Saskatoon, Sask., S7N 0K1

SPIVAK, Sidney, Q.C., b. Winnipeg, Man., 23 May 1928; s. late Malick David, Q.C. and Rose (Portigal) S.; e. Univ. of Man., LL.B. 1951; Harvard Law Sch., LL.M. 1952; m. Mira, d. Sam Steele, 29 May 1955; children: Lori, Harold, Diane; Min. of Industry & Comm., Man. 1966-69; Leader, Man. P. Conservative Party and Leader of Official Opposition, Man., Feb. 1971-5; Min. and co-chrmn. of Task Force on Gov's. Organization and Economy, Man., Oct. 1977-78; Min. Gov. Services, 1978-79; mem. Bd. of Govs., Miamedes Coll.; former Chrmn., Hillel

Foundation Adv. Bd., Univ. of Man.; mem., Candn. Friends of Hebrew Univ.; Past Pres., Rainbow Stage; past Bd. mem., Man. Theatre Centre; Candn. Inst. Internat. Affairs; Man. Hist. Soc.; Harvard Club of Man.; Pres., Central Candn. Council, B'nai B'rith; Co-Chrmn., Mid-Western Adv. Bd., B'nai B'rith Foundation of U.S. and Can.; Chmn., Winnipeg's Refugee Asst. Comm. Inc., 1979; Mem. Bd. of Governors, Univ. of Man.; Bd. of Dir., Citizenship Council of Man.; Hon. Counsellor Wpg. Chamber of Commerce; Mem. Bd. of Dir., Health Sciences Centre Research Foundation, Inc.; St. Boniface Gen. Hosp.; Prairie Theatre Exchange; Man. Opera Foundation Conservative; Hebrew; recreation: tennis; Home: 703 Wellington Cres., Winnipeg, Man. R3M 0A7; Office: 607-386 Broadway, Winnipeg, Man. R3C 3R6

SPLANE, Robert Arthur; banker; b. Athabasca, Alta. 10 July 1935; e. Alta. pub. and secondary schs.; Seattle Pacific Coll. Sciences 1954; Carlton Univ. Sciences 1955-56; Univ. of Alta. Pub. Adm. 1967-70; Banff Sch. of Advanced Mang. 1970; Cert. Gen. Accts. Assn. 1970-74; m. Stella Grace Dafoe 1957; children: Coleen Mavis Taylor, Teresa Louise Buchanan, Patricia Ann, Robert Erwin; PRES. AND DIR. CANADIAN COMMERCIAL BANK 1980- ; Chrmn. and Chief Extve. Offr. CCB Leasing; Dir. Equitable Life Insurance Co. of Canada; Alberta Municipal Finance Corp.; mem. Alta. Teachers'' Retirement Fund Investment Comte.; mem. Students'' Finance Bd. 1970-78; Gen. Mgr. Alberta Municipal Finance Corp. 1975-78; Asst. Depy. Prov. Treas. Prov. Alta. 1975-78; Vice Pres. Canadian Commercial Bank 1978-79, Extve. Vice Pres. and Chief Operating Offr. 1979-80; rec'd Queen's Silver Jubilee Medal 1977; mem. Financial Extves. Inst.; Protestant; recreations: skiing, golf, farming; Clubs: Edmonton Centre; Mayfair Golf & Country; Edmonton; Home: R.R. 1, Sherwood Park, Alta. T8A 3K1; Office: Edmonton, Alta. T5J 2Z1.

SPOONER, Michael Alan, B.A., M.D., M.A.; physician; educator; b. Regina, Sask. 18 March 1937; s. Harold John and Inez L. (Rainer) S.; e. Univ. of Sask. B.A. 1958; Univ. of Toronto M.D. 1963; Mich. State Univ. M.A. 1972; m. Donna Marie Kernaghan d. Ernest A. Rice 17 May 1958; children: Peter Harold, Jane Elizabeth, Melinda Anne, Thomas Beattie; PROF. AND CHRMN. OF FAMILY MED. UNIV. OF SASK. since 1977; Partner, Med. Arts Clinic, Regina 1964-71; Educ. Research Offr. Univ. of Sask. 1972-73, Head of Family Med. Plains Health Centre 1973-77; service CFMS Militia, rank Capt.; mem. Sask. Med. Assn.; Candn. Med. Assn.; Coll. Family Phys. Can. (Past Pres.); Am. Educ. Research Assn.; Presbyterian; recreations: hunting, fishing, tennis; Home: 10 Culliton Cres., Regina, Sask. S4S 4J6; Office: 4500 Wascana Parkway, Regina, Sask. S4S 5W9.

SPRACHMAN, Mandel Charles, B.Arch.; architect; b. Toronto, Ont. 15 Jan. 1925; s. Abraham and Mina (Offenberger) S.; e. Univ. of Toronto B.Arch. 1951; m. Carol Nina d. Carl Frankel, Toronto, Ont. 28 Nov. 1953; children: Benjamin, Robert, Andrew, Barnett; PRINC., MANDEL SPRACHMAN, ARCHITECT; Home: 77 Highland Ave., Toronto, Ont. M4W 2A4; Office: 30 Roden Pl., Toronto, Ont. M5R 1P5.

SPRAGUE, Daniel, F.C.A., b. Winnipeg, Man., 16 Sept. 1908; s. late Frank Edward and late Jacqlin (Moir) S.; e. Kelvin High Sch., Winnipeg, Man.; C.A. 1932; m. Shirley, d. late James Stewart, 26 Dec. 1945; children: Stewart, David, John; Pres., Management Svces. Ltd.; Dir., Budd Can. Inc.; Partner, Laird, Sprague 1938-56 when practice amalg. with Cooper and Lybrand; Pres., Candn. Mfrs. Assn. 1972-73 (Past Chrmn., Man. Div.); Past Chrmn., Industrial Development Bd. of Greater Winnipeg; Pres., Inst. of Chatr. Accts. of Manitoba, 1955-56; Presbyterian; recreations: golf, tree farming; Clubs: Manitoba; St. Charles Country; Royal Poinciani Golf; Florida;

Home: 315 Dromore Ave., Winnipeg, Man. R3M 0J2; Office: 2300 One Lombard Place, Winnipeg, Man.

SPROTT, David Arthur, M.A., Ph.D., F.R.S.C.; educator; b. Toronto, Ont. 31 May 1930; s. Arthur Frederick and Dorothy (Barry) S.; e. Univ. of Toronto B.A. 1952, M.A. 1953, Ph.D. 1955; m. Muriel Doris Vogel 16 Dec. 19; children: Anne Ellen, Jane Barry; PROF. OF STATISTICS, UNIV. OF WATERLOO; co-ed. "Foundations of Statistical Inference" 1971; author numerous tech. papers; Fellow, Royal Photographic Soc.; Am. Stat. Assn.; Inst. Math. Stat.; mem. Internat. Stat. Inst.; Internat. Biometric Soc.; Royal Stat. Soc.; Nat. Assn. Photographic Art; recreation: photography; Home: 295 Ferndale Pl., Waterloo, Ont. N2J 3X8; Office: Waterloo, Ont. N2L 3G1.

SPRUNG, Donald Whitfield, Loyal, B.A., Ph.D., D.Sc.; F.R.S.C.; physicist; university professor; b. Kitchener, Ont. June 1934; s. Lyall McCauley and Doreen Bishop (Price) S.; e. Kitchener Waterloo Coll. and Vocational Sch. 1949-53; Univ. of Toronto B.A. 1957; Univ. of Birmingham, Eng., Ph.D. 1961, D.Sc. 1977; m. Hannah Sueko Nagai 12 Dec. 1958; children: Anne Elizabeth, Carol Hanako; PHYSICIST AND DEAN, FACULTY OF SCIENCE, MCMASTER UNIV. since 1975; Professor since 1971; instr. Cornell Univ., 1961-62; Asst. Prof. McMaster Univ. 1962-66; Researcher Massachusetts Inst. of Tech. 1964-65; Assoc. Prof. McMaster Univ. 1966-71; Visiting Prof. Université de Paris-sud (Orsay) 1969-70; Gäst Prof. Univ. Tubingen, Germany, 1980-81; author of over 70 scientific papers in field of theoretical nuclear physics; Fellow Inst. of Physics (London); Am. Physical Society; Candn. Assn. of Physicists; Lt.-Gov. Silver Medal, 1957; C.D. Howe Memorial Fellow, 1969; Herzberg Medal of the Candn. Assn. of Physicists, 1972; recreations: cabinet making, bicycling, travel; Home: 15 Little John Rd., Dundas, Ont. L9H 4G5; Office: 1280 Main St. W., Hamilton, Ont. L8S 4K1.

SPRUNG, Lyall Macaulay, F.S.A., F.C.I.A.; retired actuary; b. Stratford, Ontario, 15 Nov. 1908; s. Whitfield Lyman and Jessie Thorne (Macaulay) S.; e. Stratford (Ont.) Coll. Inst., 1921-26; Univ. of Toronto, B.Com. 1930; m. Doreene, d. late John Price, Moncton, N.B., 6 May 1932; children: Dr. Donald W. L., Ralph S., J. Peter, Mrs. David Christener (Elizabeth), Mrs. Gary Colmer (Margaret), Michael R.; joined Mutual Life Assnce. Co. of Can. 1931; Group, Valuation, Policy Change, Claims & Underwriting Depts.; apptd. Asst. Actuary 1944; Assoc. Actuary 1954; Actuary 1959; Secy., 1966; Vice-Pres. and Secy. 1968; Vice Pres., Secy. and Chief Extve. Offr. 1969, Sr. Vice Pres. 1973-75; Un. Church; recreations: golf, curling; Club: Gyro; Home: 1005-130 Mount Hope St., Kitchener, Ont. N2G 4M6

SPRY, Maj.-Gen. Daniel Charles, C.B.E. (1945), D.S.O. (1944) C.D.; b. Winnipeg, Man. 4 Feb. 1913; s. Maj.-Gen. Daniel Wm. Bigelow and Ethelyn Alma (Rich) S.; e. Pub. Schs., Calgary and Halifax; Ashford Sch., Eng.; Dalhousie Univ.; m. Elisabeth, d. Roy Fletcher Forbes, Halifax, N.S., 23 Mar. 1939; children: Margot Elisabeth Forbes (Mrs. David Trevor Gowing), Daniel Anthony Forbes; Non-Govermental Organs. Division, Canadian International Development Agency, 1968-76; joined Boy Scouts movement 1923; Chief Executive Commissioner, The Boy Scouts Assn. of Can., 1946-53, when apptd. Dir., Boy Scouts World Bureau, retiring 1965; Ed. Dalhousie "Gazette", 1931-32; served with Candn. Mil., 2nd Lieut., Princess Louise Fusiliers, 1932; Roy. Candn. Regt. (permanent force) 1934, Capt. 1939, Maj. 1940, Lieut.-Col. 1943, Brig. 1943; Maj.-Gen. 1944; retired as Vice-Chief of Gen. Staff, 1946; Commdr., Order of the Crown of Belgium; Croix de Guerre (Belgium); twice Mentioned in Despatches; Col., Royal Candn. Regt. 1965-78; Anglican; recreations: sailing, gardening, fishing, philately; Club: Rideau (Ottawa); Address: 4 Rock Ave., Ottawa, Ont. K1M 1A6

SPRY, Graham, C.C. (1970), M.A., LL.D., F.R.G.S., b. St. Thomas, Ont., 20 Feb. 1900; s. Maj.-Gen. D.W.B., O.B.E., and Ethelyn Alma (Rich) S.; e. various Pub. Schs. in Can., 1905-10; Abbotsford, Folkestone, Kent, Eng. 1915-17; Khaki Univ., Shorncliffe and Witley Camps, 1918; Univ. of Man., B.A. (Gold Medalist) 1922; Univ. Coll. of Oxford (Rhodes Scholar) B.A. 1924; M.A. 1938; Summer Sch. Grenoble Univ. 1923; LL.D. Brock 1968, Sask. (Regina) 1968, York; m. Irene Mary Biss, 30 June 1938; children: Robin G.M., Richard Daniel Evan (deceased), Elizabeth de Gaspe; Reporter and Editorial Writer, Manitoba Free Press, 1920-22; I.L.O., League of Nations, Geneva, 1925-26; National Secretary, Assn. of Candn. Clubs, Ottawa, 1926-32; Publisher, "Farmers' Sun", Toronto, 1932-34; Extve. 1937, Dir. 1940-46, Cal. Standard Oil Co., London, Eng., 1940-46, Dir., British Ethyl Corp., London, Eng., 1937; 1940-46, Dir., Assoc. Ethyl Corp., London, Eng., Ceylon Petroleum Co., Colombo, Ceylon; apptd. Personal Asst. to Rt. Hon. Sir Stafford Cripps, 1942-45; mem., Inter-Dept. Comte. on Civil Aviation, London, 1943; XXth Century Fund Econ. Survey on Turkey, 1946-68; Agent-Gen. for Sask. in U.K. and Europe 1946-68; served in 1st World War, Pte., C.A.S.C. and C.F.A., Eng. 1918; 2nd World War, 1940-45; Sgt. Home Guard, London; War. Corr., Candn. Army, Italy, "Times" London; N.W. Europe, "Citizen" Ottawa; Chrmn., Ont. C.C.F., 1934-36; def. cand. Toronto-Broadview by-el., Sept. 1934; Fed. g.e. Oct. 1935; Extve. Comte. League of Nations Soc., 1927-32; Current Affairs Comte. Eng. Speaking Union, London, 1948-63; Quebec House (Wolfe's Birthplace), Westerham, Surrey, National Trust, London, Eng., 1963; Hon. Ed. "Interdependence" 1927-32; co-author "Social Planning for Canada" 1934; "Canada" 1941; "Turkey: An Economic Appraisal" 1949; various articles on broadcasting policy and briefs to H. of C. Comte., 1930-34, Bd. of Broadcast Govs., 1958-67 and Candn. Radio-Television Comn. 1968-72; among ACTRA Awards (1972) rec'd. John Drainie Award "for distinguished contribution to broadcasting"; Hom. Life mem., Candn. Radio League (Organ & Chrmn., 1930-34 Chrmn. Can. Broadcasting League 1968-73; Vice-Pres., Candn. Chamber Comm. (London); Zeta Psi; Anglican; recreations: reading, history, broadcasting policy; Clubs: Rideau (Ottawa); Travellers; London (Eng.); Home: 446 Cloverdale Road, Ottawa, Ont. K1M 0Y6

SPRY, William Francis; executive; b. Toronto, Ont., 22 June 1898; s. Francis Philip and Mary Anne (Cox) S.; e. Toronto (Ont.) Schs.; m. Dorothea, d. Joseph Harvard, 1919; one d. Vivienne Dorothea; CHRMN. BD. JOHN F. SULLIVAN CO. OF CANADA LTD. since Jan. 1972; Toronto General Insurance Co.; Traders General Insurance Co.; Vice-Pres., mem. Extve. Comte. and Dir., Guaranty Trust Co. of Canada Ltd.; Vice-Pres. and Dir., Canadian Insurance Shares Ltd.; Dir., All Canada Insurance Fed.; Canadian General Insurance Group; Canadian General Insurance Co.; Clk., Accting. Dept., Candn. Surety Co., 1919, later Asst. Mgr., Ont. Br., 1927; Ont. Mgr., Candn. Indemnity Co., 1927-29; joined Candn. Gen. and Toronto Gen. 1929; Ont. Mgr. Apl. 1929; Asst. Gen. Mgr., 1936; Vice-Pres. and Gen. Mgr., 1944 and Pres. and Gen. Mgr., 1956; served in World War, 1918-19, with C.E.F. (S) Signal Corps; Vice-Pres., Wartime Transit Ins. Conf.; Independent Ins. Conf.; mem., Auto. Stat. Adv. Comte.; Supts. of Ins. of Can.; Pres., Ins. Inst. Can. (1958); Chrmn. and Dir., Ins. Bureau of Can.; Freemason; Protestant; recreations: golf, curling; Clubs: Engineers'; St. George's Golf; Home: 415 The Kingsway, Islington, Ont. M9A 3W1; Office: (Box 383) Commerce Court N., Toronto, Ont. M5L 1G3

SQUIRES, Arthur H., M.D., F.R.C.P. (C); physician; university professor; b. Toronto, Ont., 3 Oct. 1909; s. Henry Frank and Catherine (Clark) S.; e. Univ. of Toronto, M.D. 1935; m. Miriam H., d. E. C. Fox, Toronto, Ont., 1 June 1940; three s.; Consultant, Wellesley Hosp.; Sr. Consultant, Princess Margaret Hosp.; Prof. and Special Lecturer, Univ. of Toronto; Chief Physician, The Wellesley Hospital, Toronto and Prof. of Medicine Univ. of Toronto 1955-74; served in 2nd World War, Lieut.-Col., R.C.A.M.C.; served in Eng. and Italy; Fellow, Internat. Soc. of Hematology; AOA; Delta Kappa Epsilon; Protestant; recreations: golf, fishing; Office: 160 Wellesley St. E., Toronto, Ont. M4Y 1J3

SQUIRES, William Austin, B.A., M.Sc., LL.D.; curator emeritus; Fredericton, N.B., 6 Sept. 1905; s. Nathan Chesley and Susan Katherine (Dayton) S.; e. Univ. of N.B., B.A. (Hons. in Natural Science and Chem.) 1927; Ohio State Univ., M.Sc. 1929; LL.D. New Brunswick 1964; m. Helen Georgina, d. Charles Edwin Bird, Fredericton, N.B., 1933; 4 children; Secy. of Bd. and Extve. Comte., N.B. Museum 1941-69 (mem. Bd. since 1972, Pres. 1973-76); Chrmn., New Brunswick Hist., Sites Bd., 1955-60; Asst. in Biol., Univ. of N.B., 1926-28; Instr. in Zool., Ohio State Univ., 1928-30; Teacher, N.B. Pub. Schs., 1930-39; Curator, Natural Science Dept., N.B. Museum 1939-68; Chief Curator, N.B. Museum 1968 and Curator Emeritus and mem. Extve. Comte. since 1969; served in Candn. Mil. with St. John Fusiliers with rank of Capt.; Hon. Trustee, N.B. Museum 1978; elective mem., Am. Ornithol. Union; mem., Ottawa Field-Naturalists Club; Fredericton Field-Naturalists Club (Pres. 1972); N.B. Hist. Soc.; Vice President, York-Sunbury Hist. Soc. 1974-75; member of Executive Council, Canadian Museums Assn., 1947-49, 51-53, 56-58; Publications: "Reversing Falls Portage", 1941; "History and Development of the New Brunswick Museum", 1945; "The Birds of N.B.", 1952, 2nd ed. 1975; "The 104th Regiment of Foot, The New Brunswick Regiment", 1962; "A Naturalist in New Brunswick" 1972; and numerous articles on natural science and history; Award of Merit from Am. Assn. for State & Local Hist., 1963; Sigma Xi; Gamma Alpha; United Church; recreations: camping, bird study; Club: Fortnightly; Home: 621 Regent St., Fredericton, N.B. E3B 3Y2

STABBACK, Jack Garry, B.Sc., P.Eng.; b. Gleichen, Alta., 18 Aug. 1920; s. Robin Maxwell and Jessie Lavina (Eddie) S.; e. Pub. and High Schs., Calgary, Alta.; Univ. of Alta., B.Sc. (Chem. Engn.) 1949; m. Delphy, d. Martin Gronsdahl, Victoria, B.C., 14 Nov. 1959; children: Lynne, Susan, Garry, Cheryl, Lynda, Kent; SENIOR VICE PRES. GLOBAL ENERGY & MINERALS GROUP, THE ROYAL BANK Calgary, 1980- ; joined Alta. Oil and Gas Conservation Board, 1949 and served as Field Engineer, Chief Gas Engineer and Adm. for Gas to 1964; on loan to Nat. Energy Board during 1960 as Acting Chief Engr.; carried out natural gas investigation for S. Australian Govt., 1964; joined Nat. Energy Board as Chief Engineer, 1964; appointed a member 1968; Assoc. Vice Chrmn. 1974; Vice Chrmn. of Bd. 1976; Chrmn. 1978-80; served with the Canadian Army and R.C.A.F. during World War II; mem., Canadian Institute Mining & Metall.; Assoc. of P. Eng. of Ont. and Alta.; Freemason; Shriner; Baptist; recreations: swimming, travelling, gardening; Home: 880 Edgemont Rd., N.W., Calgary, Alta. T3A 2J2; Office: 335-8th Ave. S.W., Calgary, Alta. T2P 1C9

STACEY, Col. Charles Perry, O.C. (1969), O.B.E., C.D., B.A., A.M., Ph.D., LL.D., D.Litt., D. Mil. Sci., F.R.S.C.; historian; b. Toronto, Ont., 30 July 1906; s. Dr. Charles Edward and Pearl (Perry) S.; e. Univ. of Toronto, B.A. 1927; Oxford Univ. (Corpus Christi), B.A. 1929; Princeton Univ., A.M. 1931, Ph.D. 1933; m. late Doris Newton, d. R. T. Shiell, Toronto, 26 Aug. 1939; m. Helen Kathleen Allen, O.C., LL.D., 3 Oct. 1980; served in ranks, Candn. Corps of Signals (N.P.A.M.) 1924; Comnd. 1925; Reserve of Offrs. 1929-40; Hist. Offr., Candn. Mil. Hdqrs., London, 1940-45; Instr. in Hist., Princeton Univ., 1934-39; Asst. Prof., 1939-40; Dir. of Hist. Sec. Gen. Staff, Army Hdqrs., 1945-59 when he retired from Army; Prof. of Hist., University of Toronto; Hon. Secy., Royal Soc. of

Can., 1957-59; mem., Candn. Hist. Assn. (Pres., 1952-53); Am. Hist. Assn.; Pres., Candn. Writers Foundation, 1958-59; author of "Canada and the British Army, 1846-71", 1936; "The Military Problems of Canada", 1940; "Canada's Battle in Normandy", 1946; "The Canadian Army, 1939-45", 1948 (Gov. Gen's. Award for Academic Non-Fiction); "Introduction to the Study of Military History", 4th ed., 1955; "Six Years of War", 1955; "Quebec, 1759", 1959; "Records of the Nile Voyageurs", 1959; "The Victory Campaign", 1960; "Arms, Men and Governments" 1970; "The Arts of War and Peace 1914-45" (Hist. documents of Canada, Vol. V) 1972; "A Very Double Life: The Private World of Mackenzie King" 1976; "Mackenzie King and the Atlantic Triangle" 1977; "Canada and the Age of Conflict", Vol. I 1977; Vol. II: "The Mackenzie King Era," 1981; awarded Tyrrell Medal in Canadian History by Royal Society of Canada, 1955; mem., Royal Candn. Mil. Inst. (Hon. Historian); Dir., Hist. Sec., Candn. Forces Hdqrs., Ottawa (on leave from Univ. of Toronto) 1965-66; Univ. Prof., Univ. of Toronto 1973-75, Special Lectr. 1975-76; Fellow Emeritus, Massey Coll., Hon. Curator, Old Fort York; Anglican; Home: 21 Dale Ave., Apt. 706, Toronto, Ont. M4W 1K3

STACKHOUSE, Reginald Francis, M.A., B.D., Ph.D.; educator; b. Toronto, Ont. 30 Apl. 1925; s. Edward and Emma (McNeill) S.; e. Univ. of Toronto B.A. 1946, M.A. 1951; Wycliffe Coll. Toronto L.Th. 1950, B.D. 1954; Yale Univ. Ph.D. 1962; m. Margaret Eleanor d. Roland Allman, Toronto, Ont. 2 June 1951; children: Mary, Elizabeth, Ruth, John; PRINCIPAL, WYCLIFFE COLL.; Chaplain, Hospitaller Order of St. John of Jerusalem; Chrmn. Bd. of Govs. Centennial Coll. Scarborough 1966-69 (Hon. grad.); mem. Scarborough Pub. Lib. Bd. 1963-64; Scarborough Bd. Educ. 1965-72; Parlt. of Can. 1972-74; Ont. Council of Regents 1969-72; author "Christianity and Politics" 1965; also various articles; P. Conservative; Anglican; recreations: theatre, writing, music, gardening, reading; Club: Empire (Pres. 1980-81); Home: 20 Queens Park Cr. W., Toronto, Ont. M5S 2W2; Office: 5 Hoskin Ave., Toronto, Ont. M5S 1H7

STADELMAN, William Ralph, B.A.Sc., M.B.A.; b. St. Mary's, Ont., 18 July 1919; s. John Joseph and Lillian (Trachsell) S.; e. Univ. of Toronto, B.A.Sc. (Chem. Engn.) 1941; Univ. of Pennsylvania (Wharton Sch. of Finance & Econ.), M.B.A. 1949; m. Jean, d. late Walker McLaren, Nov. 1951; one d. Laren; PRESIDENT, ONT. RESEARCH FOUNDATION, since 1964; joined Defense Industries Ltd., Winnipeg, Man., as Acid Plant Supvr. and Lab. Supvr., 1941-43; apptd. Chief Devel. Engr. becoming Chief Process Engr., Candn. Synthetic Rubber Ltd., Sarnia, Ont., 1943-47; Lectr. in Marketing, Univ. of Pa., 1948-49; joined Pennsylvania Salt, Wyandotte, Mich., as Special Asst. to Mgr.; apptd. Secy.-Treas., Ont. Research Foundation, 1950; mem., Club of Rome; mem., Assn. Prof. Engrs. Ont.; Home: 31 Rykert Cr., Toronto, Ont. M4G 2T1; Office: Sheridan Park, Mississauga, Ont. L5K 1B3

STAINES, David McKenzie, A.M., Ph.D.; educator; b. Toronto, Ont. 8 Aug. 1946; s. Ralph McKenzie and Mary Rita (Hayes) S.; e. St. Michael's Coll. Sch. Toronto 1963; St. Michael's Coll. Univ. of Toronto B.A. 1967; Harvard Univ. A.M. 1968, Ph.D. 1973; VISITING ASSOC. PROFESSOR OF CAN. STUDIES, FIVE COLLEGES, AMHERST, MASS. 1982-4; Assoc. Prof. of English, Univ. of Ottawa 1978- ; Teaching Fellow in Eng. Harvard Univ. 1968-73, Asst. Prof. of Eng. 1973-78, Visiting Assoc. Prof. summers 1980, 1982; Visiting Asst. Prof. of Eng. Univ. of P.E.I. summer 1975; Hon. Research Fellow, Univ. Coll. London 1977-78; recipient Can. Council Doctoral Fellowship 1968-72; Charles Dexter Travelling Scholarship 1971; Nat. Endowment for Humanities Fellowship Independent Study & Research 1977-78; Huntington Lib. Fellowship 1979; Newberry Lib. Fellowship 1980; Ed. "The Canadian Imagination: Dimensions of a Literary Culture"

1977; "Responses and Evaluations: Essays on Canada by E. K. Brown" 1977; "Reappraisals: The Callaghan Symposium" 1981; author "Tennyson's Camelot" 1982; various articles and reviews Arthurian lit., medieval drama & romance, Victorian poetry, Candn. lit.; mem. Medieval Acad. Am. (Chrmn. Comte. on Centers & Regional Assns. 1981-84); Internat. Arthurian Soc.; Modern Lang. Assn.; Assn. Candn. Univ. Teachers Eng.; R. Catholic; recreations: theatre, bridge; Office: Dept. of English, Smith College, Northampton, Mass. 01063

STANBURY, H. Norman, F.C.I.S.; investment counsellor; b. Saint John, N.B., 2 June 1911; s. Harvey Norman MacKenzie and Gertrude Georgina (Rockcliffe-Knight) S.; e. Pub. Schs. and St. Mary's Coll., Halifax, N.S.; m. Amadita Diana, d. Lt.-Col. S. C. Oland, Halifax, 7 July 1938; children: Penelope, Michael, Bruce, Christopher, Lindita, Norman; Vice Pres. and Secy.-Treas., Lindwood Holdings Ltd.; Dir., Oland Investments Ltd.; Culverwell Holdings Ltd.; Tartan Seafoods Ltd.; mem., Board of Govs., Canadian Corps of Commissionaires (N.S. Div.); with Eastern Securities Co. Ltd., Halifax, N.S., 1919-39; estbd. Stanbury & Co. Ltd. 1939, invest. dealers; served with Candn. Mil., N.P.A.M., as Lieut., R.C.A., 1930-40; mem. Bd. Mgrs., Past President and Dir., Halifax Sch. for the Blind; Kt. of Malta; Roman Catholic; Clubs: Halifax; Saraguay; Home: 909 Young Ave., Halifax, N.S. B3H 2V9; Office: Keith Hall, 1475 Hollis St., Halifax, N.S. B3J 1V1

STANBURY, Hon. Richard J., Q.C.; senator; b. Exeter, Ont., 2 May 1923; s. Judge James George Stuart and Jane (Hardy) S.; e. Exeter (Ont.) Pub. Sch., 1935; St. Catharines (Ont.) Coll. Inst., 1940; Univ. of W. Ont., B.A. (Econ. & Pol. Science) 1944; Osgoode Hall Law Sch., 1948; m. Margaret F. M., d. T. F. Walker, Toronto, Ont., 14 Oct. 1944; two d.; Margaret Jane, Sally Barbara; PARTNER, CASSELS BROCK, since 1974; Dir., Rogers Cablesystems Ltd. Rogers Radio Broadcasting Ltd.; Victoria and Grey Trust Co.; Beneficial Finance Co. of Canada; Presbyterian Building Corp.; Candn. Bureau of Internat. Educ.; read law with Aylesworth, Garden & Company; called to the Bar of Ont. 1948; cr. Q.C. 1961; Jr. Solr., Aylesworth & Co. 1948-52; Partner, 1952-54; Partner, Hollingworth and Stanbury 1955-73; Lecturer Osgoode Hall Bar Admission Course, 1959-64; served with Candn. Inf. Corps, 1944-45; rank 2nd Lt.; summoned to Senate of Can., 1968; Pres., York Centre Liberal Assn., 1952-57; Toronto Dist. Lib. Assn., 1961-64; Lib. Fed. of Can., 1968-73; Chrmn., Nat. Policy Comte. Liberal Party 1965-68; Chrmn., of Finance, Ont. Lib. Campaign, 1967; Chrmn., N. York Pub. Library Bd., 1958-63; Metro Special Lib. Comte., 1960-63; Secy., N. York Gen. Hosp. 1963-68; mem. Adm. Council, Presb. Ch. in Can. 1962-79; Secy. Corp. of Synod of Toronto and Kingston, 1959-71; Chrmn, Can. Folk Arts Council; Hon. Dir., Boy Scouts of Can.; mem., Candn. Bar Assn.; York Co. Law Assn.; Freemason; Liberal; Presbyterian; recreations: community work, swimming; Clubs: Ontario; Rotary; Home: 16 Dell Park Ave., Toronto 19, Ont. M6B 2T4; Office: 130 Adelaide St. W. Toronto, Ont. M5H 3C2

STANBURY, Hon. Robert Douglas George, P.C. (Can.) 1969, Q.C. (Fed.), B.A.; lawyer; corporate executive; b. Exeter, Ont. 26 Oct. 1929; s. James George Stuart and Elizabeth Jean (Hardy) S.; e. St. Catharines (Ontario) Collegiate Institute and Vocational School (1947); University of Western Ontario, B.A. (Journalism) 1950; Osgoode Hall Law Sch. 1955; m. Miriam, d. Oliver Voelker, Kitchener, Ont., 21 June 1952; children: Susan (Meloff), Carol (Trought), Ian, Duncan; VICE PRES., GEN. COUNSEL, SECY. AND DIR., FIRESTONE CANADA INC.; Secy. and Dir., Dayton Tire Can. Ltd.; Secy, Yorkminster Investments Ltd.; Dir., NAR Developments Ltd.; read law with Aylesworth & Co., Hollingworth & Stanbury; called to Bar of Ont. 1955; Account Extve., Public & Industrial Relations Ltd., Toronto, 1950-51; Partner, Hollingworth

& Stanbury, Toronto, Ont., 1955-65; Pres., Candn. Univ. Lib. Fed., 1954; Trustee, 1961-64, (Vice-Chrmn. 1962, Chrmn. 1963-64) N. York Bd. of Educ.; mem. Metrop. Toronto Planning Bd., 1963; Metrop. Sch. Bd., Toronto, 1963-64; 1st el. to H. of C., 1965 (L. York-Scarborough), re-elected 1968, 1972, 1974; Chairman, House of Commons Standing Committee on Broadcasting, Films and Assistance to the Arts, 1966-68; Parlty. Secy. to Secy. of State 1968-69; Min. without Portfolio responsible for Citizenship Oct. 1969, additionally for Information Canada Feb. 1970; apptd. Min. Communications 1971; Min. Nat. Revenue 1972; Candn. Del. to U.N. Gen. Assembly 1974-76; Headed Canadian Delegations to U.N. Conf. on Prevention of Crime and Treatment of Offenders, Kyoto, Japan 1970; UNESCO 25th Anniversary Session, Paris 1971; Inter-Am. Devel. Bank annual meeting, Jamaica 1973; U.N. Conf. on Racism, Nigeria 1977; Chrmn., Candn. Group, Inter-Parlty. Union 1974-77; Founding Chrmn. Candn. Parlty. Helsinki Group 1977; Vice Pres. and Dir., Hamilton and District Ch. of Comm.; Hamilton Foundation; Dir., Art Gallery of Hamilton; mem., Amnesty Internat.; Internat. Comm. of Jurists; Law Soc. Upper Canada; Candn. Bar Assn.; Kappa Alpha; Phi Delta Phi; Liberal; Presb.; Home: 246 York Rd., Dundas, Ont. L9H 6L8; Office: Box 400, Hamilton, Ont. L8N 3J1

STANFIELD, Gordon Dawson, B.Eng.; manufacturer; b. Truro, N.S., 23 Nov. 1915; s. Hon. Frank and Sara Emma (Thomas) S.; m. Katherine Margaret, d. late C. W. Stairs, 17 April 1940; children: Gordon, Nancy, Margaret, David; PRES., STARR MANUFACTURING LTD. (Steel and Plastics Products, Estbd. 1864); Dir., Stanfield's Ltd.; Dir., Mutual Life Assurance Co. of Canada; mem., Halifax Adv. Bd., Montreal Trust Co.; Engr. with Dominion Steel & Coal Corp. Ltd. in Sydney, N.S., 1939-40; Chrmn. of Bd., Victoria Gen. Hosp.; Engr. with Trenton Industries Ltd., 1941-45; mem., Engn. Inst. Can.; Assn. Prof Engrs. N.S.; Phi Kappa Pi; Conservative; Anglican; recreations: golfing, gardening, fishing; Clubs: The Halifax, Royal N.S. Yacht Squadron; Ashburn Golf; Saraguay; Home: 1803 Armview Terrace, Halifax, N.S. B3H 4H3; Office: Prince Albert Road, (P.O. Box 500) Dartmouth, N.S. B2Y 3Y8

STANFIELD, Hon. Robert L., P.C. (1967), Q.C., M.P., B.A., LL.D.; legislator; b. Truro, N.S., 11 April 1914; s. Frank and Sarah Emma (Thomas) S.; e. Colchester Acad. Truro, N.S.; Ashbury Coll., Ottawa, Ont.; Dalhousie Univ., B.A. (with high Hons. in Econ. and Pol. Science) 1936, winning Gov. General's Medal; Harvard Univ., LL.B. (with Hons.) 1939; LL.D., Univ. of N.B., 1958, McGill 1967; m. 1st late Nora Joyce, d. late C. Weston Frazee, 5 June 1940; children: Sarah Jamesie, Robert Maxwell, Judith Joyce, Miriam Julia; 2ndly, late Mary Margaret Hall, 1957; 3rdly, Anne Austin, 10 Aug. 1978; called to the Bar of Nova Scotia, 1940; cr. K.C. Dec. 1950; 1st el. to N.S. Leg., g.e. 1949; Leader of the Opposition in Leg., 1949-56; Premier and Min. of Educ. 1956-67; el. to Leader of P. Conservative Party of Can., 9 Sept. 1967; el. to H. of C. for Colchester-Hants. in by-el. 6 Nov. 1967; Leader of H.M. Opposition in H. of C. 15 Nov. 1967-22 Feb. 1976; Special Rep. of Gov't. to Middle East and North Africa July 79-Feb. 80; P. Conservative; Anglican; recreation: gardening; Clubs: Halifax; Albany (Toronto); Home: 136 Acacia Ave., Rockcliffe Park, Ont. K1M 0R1

STANFORD, A. R., B.A.Sc.; company executive, b. Broad Cove, Baie de Vert Dist., Nfld., 20 Nov. 1919; s. Joseph Cooper and Clara Edith (Stanford) S.; e. Mt. Allison Univ.; Queen's Univ., B.A.Sc. (Chem. Engn.), 1948; m. Joyce, d. Peter Bishop, 25 March 1946; children: David Ronald, Donald William, James Reginald; PRES. AND GEN. MGR., NORTH STAR CEMENT LTD.; Dir., Portland Cement Assoc. (Skokie, Ill.); joined Bowaters Newfoundland Pulp & Paper Mills 1948, Vice-Pres. Production 1965-69 when joined present Co.; served in 2nd World War R.C.A.F.; Past Pres., Association of Prof. Engineers of Newfoundland; United Church; recreations: golf, fishing, Clubs: Blomidon Country; Crows Nest (St. John's); Home: 17 Humber Park, Corner Brook, Nfld. A2H 2Z7; Office: (Box 160), Corner Brook, Nfld. A2H 6C7

STANFORD, Joseph Stephen, LL.B.; diplomat; b. Montreal, Que. 7 May 1934; s. Walter Albert and Geraldine (O'Loghlin) S.; e. St. Leo's Acad. Westmount, Que.; St. Mary's High Sch. Calgary, Alta.; Loyola Coll., Univ. of Montreal B.A. 1953; Univ. of Alta. LL.B. 1956; m. Agnes d. late Glen Walker 16 Nov. 1957; children: Kevin, Karen, Michael; AMBASSADOR TO ISRAEL 1979- ; called to Bar of Alta. 1957; private law practice Calgary 1957-60; joined diplomatic service 1960 serving in Paris 1961-64, Kingston, Jamaica 1964-66, Bonn 1970-73; Dir. Legal Adv. Div. Dept. External Affairs 1975-77, Dir. Gen. Bureau of Comm. and Commodity Relations 1977-79; contrib. to learned journs. on treaty law, GATT, internat. nuclear relations, foreign invest. developing countries, application U.S. antitrust law in Can.; mem. Prof. Assn. Foreign Service Offrs.; Candn. Council on Internat. Law; Phi Delta Theta; R. Catholic; recreations: skiing, sailing; Home: Beit Avrahami, Rehov Harishonim, Ramat Hasharon, Israel; Office: 220 Hayarkon St., Tel Aviv, Israel

STANGELAND, Tor Oscar, B.A., B.C.L.; b. Quebec City, Que., 13 June 1929; s. Karl S.; e. McGill Univ. B.A. 1950, B.C.L. 1953; m. Barbara Perry; children: Lynne, Cara, Eric; EXTVE. VICE PRES.-PULP & PAPER, CONSOLIDATED-BATHURST INC. and Dir. several subsidiaries since 1976; joined Legal Dept. Dupont of Canada 1955; Asst. Mgr. Real Estate & Ins. Consolidated Paper Corp. Ltd. 1958, Asst. Secy. and Mgr. Real Estate & Ins. 1959, Dir. Employee and Pub. Relations present Co. 1967, Vice Pres.-Personnel and Secy. 1971; Dir., Sceptre Resources Ltd.; Office Equipment Co. of Can. Ltd.; Dir., Unlimited Skills Inc.; Dir. and Vice-Chmn., Que. Forest Industries Assoc., Ltd.; Bd. of Govs. and Vice Pres. Julius Richardson Convalescent Hosp.; mem. Bar Prov. Que.; recreations: tennis, skiing; Clubs: Mont Bruno Country; Montreal Badminton and Squash; St. James's; Mount Royal; Office: 800 Dorchester Blvd. W., Montreal, Que. H3B 1Y9

STANISZEWSKI, His Hon. Paul Ignace Blaze; judge; b. Montreal, Que., 4 June 1925; s. Julian and Rose (Kawecki) S.; e. St. Anselm Parochial Sch. and D'Arcy McGee High Sch., Montreal, 1943; Loyola Coll. 1943-45; Univ. Coll., Univ. of Toronto, B.A. 1950; Osgoode Hall Law Sch.; m. Wanda Marie (d.), d. late Stanley Bougslawski, 5 June 1949; four d., Gayle Paula, Camille Ellen, Michelle Lila, Andrea Juliane; m. 2ndly, Tevis Marie Bagnell, 3 July 1971; JR. JUDGE OF CO. COURT, ESSEX, since 1967; read law with Bagwell, Stevens, McFarlane & Co.; called to Bar of Ont. 1954; practiced law with above firm; def. Lib. cand. for High Park in prov. g.e. 1959, 1963, and 1967; Pres., Central Polish Candn. Youth Clubs; Polish Students' Club; Candn. Polish Youth Congress; Toronto Br., Candn. Polish Congress (Secy. Nat. Extve.); Vice Pres., Inter-Ethnic Council of Metrop. Toronto; Secy., Polish Welfare Soc., Montreal; Kt. of Malta; mem., Co. York Law Assn. (Civil Justice and Legal Aid Comtes.); Candn. Bar Assn.; Pres., Windsor Friends of the Roman Catholic Univ. of Lublin, Poland; mem., Holy Roman Trinity Church, Windsor and Our Lady of Guadalupe Church, Windsor; recreations: gardening, carpentry, swimming, music; Home: 5420 Riverside Dr. E., Windsor, Ont. N8S 1A4; Office: Court House, Windsor, Ont. N9A 1J2

STANISZKIS, Joanna Katarzyna, B.F.A., R.C.A.; tapestry artist; educator; b. Czestochowa, Poland 10 Apl. 1944; d. Stefan and Amelia (Krukowska) Kiljanski; e. elem. and high schs. Warsaw 1962; Acad. of Fine Arts Warsaw Interior Arch. 1962-64; Chicago Art Inst. (US Dept. State Scholarship) B.F.A. (Interior & Textile Design) 1967; Universidad Catholica Lima, Precolumbian Textiles 1965;

m. Olgierd Thomas Staniszkis 9 Apl. 1968; one s. Michael; ASSOC. PROF. OF DESIGN, SCH. OF HOME ECON., UNIV. OF B.C. 1973- ; Instr.-in-charge of Design Univ. B.C. 1969-73; Acting Head of Textiles Ont. Coll. of Art 1975-76; Vice Pres. Bd. of Trustees Cartwright Street Gallery Vancouver; solo exhns.; Merton Gallery Toronto 1972, 1974, 1976; Mido Gallery Vancouver 1973; Equinox Gallery Vancouver 1978; rep. in numerous group exhns. incl.: Internat. Tapestry Exhn. Jacques Baruch Gallery Chicago 1976; Invitational Internat. Tapestry Exhn. Vevey Switzerland 1977; 2nd Internat. Invitational Tapestry Triennale Lodz, Poland 1977; RCA Centennial Exhn. Toronto 1980; Contemporary Candn. Tapestry Can. House London, Eng., Centre Culturel Canadien Paris and St-Etienne 1980; 3 Candn. Tapestry Artists Windsor (Ont.) Art Gallery 1981 (1 yr. travel exhn. Can. and Europe); maj. colls. and comns. incl.: 2 tapestries Bank of Montreal Bentall III Vancouver; Textile Museum Lodz, Poland; 3 tapestries Alta. Gas Trunk Line Calgary; Canadian Pacific London, Eng.; St. Bernardette Ch. Surrey, B.C.; Mercantile Bank Los Angeles; 1st Prize Competitions: Crown Life Vancouver; Daon Bldg. Vancouver; rep. in numerous pub., corporate and private colls. N.Am. and Europe; Saidye Bronfman Award for excellence in crafts, 1981; Liberal; R. Catholic; recreations: travel, skiing; Home: 6044 Gleneagles Dr., West Vancouver, B.C. V7W 1W2; Studio: 604 Stamps Landing, False Creek, Vancouver, B.C.

STANLEY, David Christopher Hall, B.A., M. Comm.; corporate director; b. Toronto, Ont., 12 July 1927; s. Oswald and Betty Blanche (Diamond) S.; e. Univ. of Toronto Schs., 1939-42; Upper Ca . Coll., Toronto, 1942-45; Univ. of Toronto (B.A. 1949, M. Comm. 1954); m. Colleen Frances, d. Hugh C. Brown, Toronto, 17 Nov. 1950; children: Julia Elizabeth, David Christopher Archibald; Dir., Polysar Ltd.; Thomson Newspapers Ltd.; Wajax Ltd.; Great Lakes Nickel Ltd.; Comshare Inc.; Comshare Ltd.; joined Wood Gundy Ltd. 1949; el. Dir. 1966; Vice-Pres. 1969, ret. 1979; Past Pres. Toronto Soc. Financial Analysts; mem., Nat'l. Council, Candn. Nat. Inst. for Blind (Hon. Treasr. 1973-76, Pres. 1976-79); Dir., Toronto Mendelssohn Choir; Liberal; Anglican; Clubs: Toronto; National; Home: 453 Russell Hill Rd., Toronto, Ont. M5P 2S6;

STANLEY, Eric, Ph.D., D.Sc., F.R.S.A., F.Inst.P., F.I.M.A., F.C.I.C.; educator; b. Liverpool, Eng., 2 Feb. 1924; s. Charles Edgar and Millie (Bailey) S.; e. Univ. of Wales, B.Sc. 1944, B.Sc. (Hons.) 1949, Ph.D. 1952; Univ. of Sask., Ph.D. 1970, D.Sc. 1972; m. Sylvia, d. Samuel Atherton, 26 March 1959; children: Judith, Christopher; PROF. OF PHYSICS, UNIV. OF NEW BRUNSWICK and Dean of Faculty there since 1973; Exper. Offr., RN Scient. Service, 1944-47; Visiting Research Fellow, Univ. of S. Cal., 19552-53; Postdoctoral Research Fellow, NRC, Ottawa, 1953-55; Lectr. in Physics, Univ. of Manchester 1955-64; Prof. of Physics, Univ. of Sask., 1964-72; Dir., of Acad. Services and Planning 1968-72; Past Dir., Sask. Jr. Concert Soc.; Regina Symphony Orchestra; Vice-Pres., Atlantic Symphony Inc.; Saint John Social services Council; Min. of Soc. Services Advis. Council; Cdn. Nat'l Comm. of the Internat'l Union of Crystallography; St. John Y.M.C.A.; Sec. St. John Y's Men Club; New Brunswick Competitive Music Festival; New Brunswick Summer Music Camp; author numerous research publs. generally in field of crystal structure analysis by X-Ray diffraction; Fellow, Inst. Math., Inst. of Physics, Royal Soc. of Arts, Chem. Inst. Can.; mem., Inst. Pub. Adm. Can.; Am. Crystallographic Assn.; New York Acad. of Sciences; Anglican; recreations: golf, music, walking; Home: 3 Seely St., Saint John, N.B. E2K 4B1

STANLEY, George Francis Gillman, O.C. (1976), C. St. J., B.A., M.A., M.Litt., D.Phil., D.es.L., D.Litt., LL.D., D.C.L., F.R.S.C., F.R.Hist.S.; educator; b. Calgary, Alberta, 6 July 1907; s. John Henry and Della Catherine (Lillywhite) S.; e. Univs. of Alta. and Oxford, B.A. 1931, M.Litt. 1933, M.A. 1936, D.Phil. 1936 (Rhodes Scholar 1929, Beit Sr. Research Scholar 1932; Royal Soc. Can. Scholar, 1934); Guggenheim Fellow, 1948; Canada Council Sr. Fellowship 1960; Hon. doctorates, Laval, 1965; Mount Allison, 1967; St. Dunstan's, 1969; Alberta, 1971; R.M.C., 1972; St. Francis Xavier, 1974; New Brunswick, 1975; Dalhousie, 1977; Calgary, 1980; m. Ruth Lynette, d. Alfred H. Hill, St. Lambert, Que., 24 Aug. 1946; children: Della Margaret Maude, Marietta Ruth Ellen, Laurie Catherine Christina; LIEUTENANT GOVERNOR, NEW BRUNSWICK, 1982- ; Emeritus Prof. R.M.C.; Emeritus Prof., Mount Allison Univ. (Dir. Canadian Studies there 1969-75); Gen. Ed., Riel Project, Univ. of Alta., since 1979; Professor of Hist., Mount Allison University, 1936-46 (on military leave, 1940-46); Professor of Cdn. Hist., University of B.C., 1947-49; Dean of Arts, and Head of Hist. Dept., R.M.C., Kingston, 1949-69; served in Candn. Militia (N.B. Rangers), 1938-40, as Lieut.; served in 2nd World War, 1940-46; began as Capt. and retired as Lieut.- Col. and Deputy Dir., Hist. Sec. (Gen. Staff); Overseas 1942-45; Reserve of Offrs., 1947-67; awarded Tyrrell Medal by Royal Soc. Can., 1957, Centennial Medal, 1967; Jubilee Medal, 1977; Croix du Combattant de l'Europe 1979; apptd. Offr., Order of Canada 1976; Commander Order of St. John, 1979; author of ''The Birth of Western Canada'', 1936 (reprinted 1961); ''Canada's Soldiers'' 1954 (rev. 1974); ''In Search of the Magnetic North'', 1955, ''In the Face of Danger'', 1960; ''For Want of a Horse'', 1961; ''Louis Riel'', 1963; ''The Story of Canada's Flag'', 1965; ''New France-The Last Phase 1744-1760'', 1968; ''A Short History of the Canadian Constitution'' 1969; ''Mapping the Frontier'' 1970; ''Canada Invaded 1775-1776'' 1973; ''L'Invasion du Canada 1775-1776'', 1975; ''The Military and Hospitaller Order of Saint Lazarus, a Short History of the Canadian Grand Priory'', 1978; ''Nos Soldats, l'Histoire Militaire du Canada de 1604 à nos jours'', 1980; ed. ''Canadian Universities Today'', 1963 and ''Pioneers of Canadian Science'', 1966; articles in journals and reviews, also in ''Encyclopedia Americana'', ''Canadian Encyclopedia''; Submitted basic design adopted as Canada's flag; Mil. and Hospitaller Order of St. Lazarus of Jerusalem (Kt. Commdr.); Soberana Ordem dos Cavaleiros de Sao Paulo (Brazil) (Comendador); St. John Ambulance Assn. (Pres., N.B. Prov. Council, since 1979); 8th Candn. Hussars Regimental Assn. (Chrmn., Bursary Comte., since 1975); N.B. Army Cadet League (Vice-Pres. since 1978); United Services Inst. (Moncton Br.) Vice-Pres. 1977-81; Maritime Automobile Assoc. (Dir., since 1979); Fellow, Co. of Mil. Historians, 1967 (Gov. 1968-74); mem. Comn. de Planification Academique de l'Univ. de Moncton 1969-72; mem. Candn. Hist. Assn. (President 1955-56); mem. Comte. on Hist. Sites & Monuments, Massey Commission on the Arts, Letters & Sciences, 1950-51; mem. Fed. Gov't. Adv. Bd. on Candn. Mil. Coll. 1973-79; Archaeol. and Hist. Sites Bd. of Ont. 1953-69; Inst. d'Histoire de l'Amérique Francaise; Anglican; Club: Roy. Candn. Mil. Inst. (Toronto); Address: Frosty Hollow, R.R.1, Sackville, N.B. E0A 3C0

STANLEY, James Paul, B.E., P.Eng.; company executive; b. Nontreal, Que., 15 Aug. 1915; s. Paul Garton and Florence May (Tooke) S.; e. Westmount (Que.) High Sch.; McGill Univ. B.E.; m. Anne Seymour, d. late Robert P. Raynsford, 28 May 1949; children: Marie, Susan, James, Sarah; DIRECTOR, RONALDS-FEDERATED LTD.; served in 2nd World War, Engn. Br., rank Sqnd. Ldr. (Act.), 1941-46; mem. Corp. Engrs. Que.; Anglican; recreations: skiing, sailing; Clubs: St. James's; Royal St. Lawrence; Montreal Badminton & Squash; Ste. Marguerite Ski; Home: 799 Wartman Ave., Kingston, Ont. K7M 4M3; Office: 1245 Sherbrooke St. W., Montreal, Quebec, H3G 1G2

STANLEY-PAUL, Norman, C.D., B.A.; company executive; b. Toronto, Ont., 14 Dec. 1926; s. Harold and Jean Conner (Cox) S-P.; e. Westhill High Sch. Montreal, Que.;

N. Toronto Coll.; Univ. of Toronto, B.A.1948; m. Eleanore Vieve, d. Dr. Glenn T. Mitton, Markham, Ont., 5 May 1956; children: Harold Glenn, Maureen Anne; GENERAL MANAGER AND DIRECTOR, MENNEN CANADA INC., since 1977; joined Lever Brothers Ltd. 1948-59 (Brand Mang.); General Foods Ltd., 1959-67 (Product Group Mang.); joined Canvin Products Ltd. as Vice-Pres., Marketing, 1967; promoted to Extve. Vice Pres. and Dir., Pres. 1969-76; served with RCNR 1944-68; rank Lt. Commdr.; Steward Humber Valley United Chruch; mem., Metrop. Toronto Bd. Trade; recreations: golf, photography, carpentry; Clubs: Mississauga Golf & Country; Home: 10 Queensborough Cres., Weston, Ont. M9R 1A2; Office: 6400 Northwest Dr., Mississauga, Ont. L4V 1K1

STANSBURY, Edward James, M.A., ph.D.; university professor; b. Oakville, Ont., 1 Aug. 1927; s. late Leonard Arthur and Isabella McDougall (Purdie) S.; e. Univ. of Toronto, B.A. (Math. & Physics) 1949, M.A. (Physics) 1950, Ph.D. (Physics) 1952; m. Wilda Lee, d. late George Bruce MacQuarrie, 30 Setp. 1952; children: Norma Jean, Douglas Earl; VICE PRINC., PLANNING, McGILL UNIV. since June 1976; Research Assoc. in Molecular Spectroscopy, Dept. of Physics, Univ. of Toronto, 1952-53; mem. Tech. Staff, Semi-conductor Device Devel., Bell Telephone Labs., Murray Hill, N.J., 1953-56; joined present Univ. as Lectr. and Research Assoc. 1956, Asst. Prof. 1957, Assoc. Prof. 1963, Prof. 1969; Assoc. Dean for Student Affairs, Faculty of Arts & Science, 1962-68; Vice Dean of Faculty 1968-69; Dean 1969-71; Dean, Fac. of Science, 1971-76; mem., Candn. Assn. Physicists; Candn. Assn. Univ. Teachers; Home: 11705 Lavigne St., Montreal, Que. H4J 1X4

STAPELLS, Richard Bredin, Q.C., M.A.; b. Toronto, Ont., 13 Aug. 1925; s. late Herbert Gordon, Q.C., and Edith (Bredin) S.; e. St. Andrew's Coll., Aurora, Ont.; Univ. of Toronto, B.A. 1946, M.A. 1949; London Sch. of Economics, 1947; Osgoode Hall, Toronto, Ont. (1950); m. Beverley, d. late Erland S. Echlin, 25 May 1950; children: Victoria Louise, Alexandra Echlin, Elizabeth Bredin; PARTNER, STAPELLS & SEWELL; Dir., Coutts Hallmark Cards; Eddy Match Co.; Floating Floors Inc. (U.S.A.); Pathex (Canada) Ltd.; Canadian Thermos Products Ltd.; Ram Petroleums Ltd.; The Arthur S. Leitch Co. Ltd.; Canadian Canners Ltd.; Ascot Petroleum Corp.; Sweetwater Petroleum Corp.; The Counselling Foundation of Can.; read law with H. G. Stapells, Q.C.; called to the Bar of Ont.; 1950; cr. Q.C. 1961; served in 2nd World War with R.C.A.F., 1944; mem., Candn. Bar Assn.; Past President, Royal Life Saving Society Canada; Vice-President, Royal Life Saving Society (Commonwealth); Past Chrmn., Estate Planning Council of Toronto; Past Gov., Cdn. Tax Fdn.; Beta Theta Pi; Conservative-Independent; Anglican; recreation: gardening; Clubs: National; Albany; R.C.Y.C.; Coral Beach and Tennis (Bermuda); Empire (Past Pres.); Home: 35 Maple Ave., Toronto, Ont. M4W 2T8; Office: Suite 6200, P.O. Box 113, First Canadian Place, Toronto, Ont. M5X 1A4

STAPLETON, Rev. John Francis, B.A., B.L.S. (R.C.); teacher; librarian; pastor; b. Fitzroy Harbour, Ont., 24 Nov. 1921; s. Louis John and Mary Rita (McDermott) S.; e. St. Mary's Separate Sch., Collingwood, Ont. and Collingwood Coll. Inst. there; St. Michael's Coll., Univ. of Toronto, B.A. 1944; St. Basil's Novitiate, Toronto, 1940-41; St. Basil's Semy., Toronto, 1941-43 and 1945-49; Library Sch., Univ. of Toronto, B.L.S. 1950; PASTOR, ST. MARY'S CHURCH, LINWOOD, ONT. since 1976; and Dean of Waterloo since 1979; and Diocesan Consultor since 1979; Asst. Dir. of Studies, Aquinas Inst., Rochester, N.Y., 1944-45; Asst. Librarian, Pontifical Inst. of Mediaeval Studies, 1946-49; Assoc. Lib., 1949-51, Lib. 1951-62; Librarian St. Basil's Seminary 1962-67; lecturer there 1959-72; Pastor St. Mary's Church, Owen Sound 1973-76 mem., Candn. Lib. Assn.; Ont. Lib. Assn.; Address: 15 Isabella St. N., Linwood, Ont. N0B 2A0

STARK, Hon. Alexander; retired judge; b. Toronto, Ont., 15 May 1904; s. late Harry Lorimer and late Annie May (McKay) S.; e. Rosedale Pub. Sch., Toronto; Univ. of Toronto Schs.; Univ. of Toronto, B.A. (Pol. Science; Hons.) 1926, M.A. 1928; Osgoode Hall Law Sch., 1930 (Hons.; winner of Clara Brett Martin Scholarship); m. Helen Bain, d. late William Galer, 7 Sept. 1935; children: Jean (Mrs. Gerald Moore), Susan, Cynthia; retired Justice, Supreme Crt. of Ont.; read law with J. R. L. Starr, K.C.; called to Bar of Ont. 1930; cr. Q.C. 1954; one time Newspaper Reporter for "Whitby Gazette and Chronicle", "Mail and Empire" and "Toronto Daily Star"; commenced practice of law with Starr, Spence & Co., 1930; Gen. Counsel for Toronto Star Ltd. for 27 yrs., also Dir. and Sec.-Treas. for 10 yrs.; as Solr. for late Joseph E. Atkinson arranged legal basis for Atkinson Charitable Foundation and acted as Trustee for many Yrs.; returned to private practice 1957; Psi Upsilon; Pres., Lawyers' Club, Toronto 1944; Pres., Co. of York Law Assn. 1951; Baptist; recreations: music, reading; Clubs: University; Empire (Pres. 1960-61); Homes: 49 St. Clair Ave. W., Apt. 703, Toronto, Ont. and Box 1346, Gravenhurst, Ont. P0C 1G0

STARK, Ethel, C.M., LL.D., F.R.S.A.; conductor; concert violinist; educator; b. Montreal, Que. 25 Aug. 1916; d. Adolph and Laura (Haupt) Stark; e. McGill Conservatory Montreal, Violin studies 5 yrs. (MacDonald Scholarship); Curtis Inst. Philadelphia (1st Candn. winner fellowship grant worldwide competition) studied with Fritz Reiner, Carl Fiesch, Lea Luboshutz, Louis Bailly, Arthur Rodzinski; Concordia Univ. Montreal LL.D. 1980; Founder and Conductor, Montreal Women's Symphony Orchestra (1st Candn. orchestra invited Carnegie Hall, N.Y.), Montreal Women's Symphony Strings, Ethel Stark Symphonietta (men & women), N.Y. Women's Chamber Orchestra, Candn. Chorus (rep. Can. World Festival Song Israel); numerous appearances as guest conductor incl. Tokyo Asahi Philharmonic Orchestra, Nippon Hoso Kyokai Orchestra, Jerusalem Symphony Orchestra, Que. Symphony Orchestra, Toronto Symphony Orchestra, CBC Symphony Orchestra (Radio, TV), Miami Symphony Orchestra; numerous appearances as violin soloist incl. CBC Symphony Orchestra, Curtis Symphony Orchestra, Les Concerts Symphoniques, LesPetits Concerts, Montreal and Toronto Symphony Orchestras; host and soloist radio series on sonata N.Y. City; private recital Prokofieff 1st Violin Concerto Fritz Kreisler; Teacher of Music, Cath. Univ. Washington, D.C. (1st Candn. woman); Prof. of Violin Conservatoire Prov. de Musique, Montreal; mem. Music Faculty Sir George Williams Univ. Montreal; Appointed Mem. of the Order of Canada 1979; el. Fellow of the Royal Sec. of the Arts, Eng., 1980; featured various articles maj. Candn. and Am. mags.; biographical film Nat. Film Bd. Can.; discography, interviews CBC Music Lib. Montreal; Nat. Archives Ottawa; Hon. mem. Musicians' Guild Montreal; Sigma Alpha Iota; Address: 5501 Adalbert Ave., Apt. 1110, Côte St-Luc, Montréal, Qué. H4W 2B1.

STARK, David J., B.Sx., P.Eng.; natural resource executive; b. Calgary, Alta. 23 April 1917; s. Robert Donaldson and Christina Glen (Currie) S.; e. Crescent Heights High Sch. Calgary; Univ. of Oklahoma B.Sc. (Chem. Engn.) 1943; m. Anna, d. Rudolph Seidel; children: Christopher, Glen, Susan Alixe; VICE PRESIDENT ENGN. AND CONSTR., CANADIAN ARCTIC GAS STUDY LTD. since 1975; with Shell Oil Co. of Canada Ltd. Dept. Head, Aviation Gasoline Chief Technol., Catalytic Cracking Dept., Montreal E., Que. 1943-51; Gen. Mgr. Panhandle Eastern pipeline Co. and National Distillers Inc. (jt. venture co.) Tuscola, Ill. 1951-55; Vice-Pres. United Gas Co.; Electric Bond and Share Co., National Research Co. 1955-59; Vice Pres. International Minerals and Chemical

Corp., Skokie, Ill. 1959-65; Pres. Nitrin Inc. 1962-65; various consulting and jt. venture arrangements in natural resources devel., engn. tech., transport. devel. and mang. devel. 1965-74; Gen. Mgr., Candn. Arctic Gas Study Ltd.; mem. Assn. Prof. Engrs. Ont.; Am. Inst. Mining Engrs.; Tau Beta Pi; recreations: golf, hiking, skiing; Clubs: Canadian (N.Y.); New York Athletic; Home: 1919Bayshore Rd., Calgary, Alta. T2V 3M3; Office: 1331 15th St. N., Calgary, Alta. T2M 2B7

STARK, James G., C.A.; executive; b. Montreal, Que. 3 June 1928; s. Thomas John and Marjorie Clare (Dart) S.; e. Que. C.A. 1952; m. Catherine G., d. late John Francis Bulger; children: Norman James, Carol Anne; EXTVE. VICE PRES., FINANCE AND CHIEF FINANCIAL OFFR., NORTHERN TELECOM CO. LTD.; Pres., Nevron Investment, Co. Ltd.; Dir., Data 100 Corp. NT Can. Ltd.; N.T. Inc., BMR Ltd.; Cook Electric Co. Inc.; Analyst. Aluminium Sercurities Ltd. 1953; Treas. and Chief Financial Offr., Alcan Jamaica Ltd. 1958; Dir. and Vice Pres., Alcan Ore Ltd. 1965; Vice Pres. and Treas., Consolidated Edison Co. of New York Inc. 1968; Gen. Partner, Lehman Brothers, New York, Mang. Dir. 1973; mem. Order of C.A.'s of Que.; Anglican; Clubs: Mt. Bruno Country; Mt. Royal; Apawamis (Rye, N.Y.); Wall St. (N.Y.); Home: 1455 Sherbrooke St. W., Apt. 2303, Montreal, Que. H3G 1L2; Office: 1600 Dorchester Blvd. W., Montreal, Que. H3H 1P9

STARNES, John Kennett, B.A., D.C.L.; b. Montreal, P.Q., 5 Feb. 1918; s. Henry Kennett and Altha Ellen (McCrea) S.; e. Selwyn House School, Nontreal (1923-30); Trinity Coll. Sch., Port Hope, Ont. (1931-35); Instit. Sillig, Switzerland (1935-36); Univ. of Munich, 1936; Bishop's Univ., B.A. 1939, D.C.L. 1975; m. Helen Gordon, d. Guy de Lancey Robinson, 10 May 1941; two s., Colin John, Patrick Barclay; joined Department of External Affairs as 3rd Secretary; 1944; Canadian Legation Allied Governments, London, England, 1944-45; Ottawa, 1945-48; Adviser, Canadian Delegation to U.N., 1948-50; Ottawa, 1950-53; Counsellor, Canadian Embassy, Bonn, 1953-56; Deputy Extve. Secy., N. Atlantic Council, Paris, 1956-58; apptd. Acting Asst. Under Secy. of State for External Affairs, 1962; Ambassador to Fed. Republic of Germany and Head of Candn. Mil. Mission, Berlin, 1962-66; Ambassador to Un. Arab Republic and Sudan 1966-67; Asst. Under-Secy. of State for External Affairs, Oct. 1967-70; Dir. Gen. RCMP Security Service 1970-73; since then mem. Council, Internat. Inst. for Strategic Studies, London, Eng.; mem. Adv. Bd., Paterson Centre, Carleton Univ.; served in the 2nd World War, joined Black Watch of Can., 1939; discharged in 1944 with rank of Capt.; author of "Deep Sleepers" (novel) 1981; Anglican; recreation: skiing; Home: Apt. 305, 333 Chapel St., Ottawa, Ont. K1N 8Y8

STARR, Hon. Michael, P.C. (Can.); b. Cooper Cliff, Ont., 14 Nov. 1910; s. Mathew and Mary (Matechuk) m. Anne, d. John Zaritsky, Toronto, Ont., 9 Sept. 1933; children: Robert, Joan; Alderman, City of Oshawa, 1944-49; Mayor of Oshawa, 1949-52; def. candidate for Ont. Legislature, g.e. 1951; el. to H. of C. for Ont., by-el. 26 May 1952; Min of Labour, 1957-63; def. g.e. June 1968; apptd. Presiding Offr. Candn. Citizenship Court, Toronto, Ont. Sept. 1968; Chmn. W.C.B. Ont. 1973; Senator, Jr. Chamber of Commerce; Hon. mem., Rotary Club; Hon. Col., Ontario Regiment; P. Conservative; Home: 25 Olive Ave., Oshawa, Ont. L1H 2N7

STARR, Nathan, C.A.; wholesale distributor; b. Toronto, Ont., 26 Apl. 1927; s. Raphael Storozumnick and Pauline (Greenberg) S.; e. Inst. of C.A.s Ont., C.A. 1950; m. Toby Menkes, 10 De. 1950; children: Robert, Howard, Noreen; PRES., CHIEF EXTVE. AND DIR., ACKLANDS LTD., since 1978; Dir., Selkirk Holdings Ltd.; Trustee, G.H.I. Mortgage Investors; Partner, Starr, Klyman & Co., 1950-56; Freelance Pub. Acct., Toronto, 1956-62;

Partner, Starr Tward & Co., Toronto, 1965-70; joined present Co. as Secy.-Treas. 1962-70; Vice Pres.-Finance 1963-66; Pres. 1976; C.E.O. 1978; Dir., Leonard Wolinsky Foundation; Nat. Treas., Candn. Assn. Retarded Children, 1967, 1968; mem. Bd. Dirs., New Mt. Sinai Hosp. to 1980; Vice Pres., Baycrest Centre for Geriatric Care; mem of Int'l. Bd. of Dir., Shaare Zedek Medical Centre, Jerusalem; Freemason; recreation: golf; Clubs: Primrose; Oakdale Golf & Country; Home: 150 Betty Ann Dr., Willowdale, Ont. M2N 1X4; Office: 100 Norfinch Dr., Downsview, Ont. M3N 1X2

STEACIE, J. Richard, B.E.; electrical engineer; b. Montreal, Que. 22 Jan. 1927; s. Edgar William Richard and Dorothy Catalina (Day) S.; e. King's Sch. Montreal; Lisgar Coll. Inst. Ottawa; McGill Univ. B.E. 1951; m. Pamela Ann d. late Clarence Victor Putman 16 Sept. 1950; children: Pamela, Richard John, Adam Day; J.R.B. STEACIE INVESTMENTS LTD.; Dir., Can. Wire and Cable Ltd.; Bushnell Communications Ltd.; Elect. Engr. Defence Research Bd. Ottawa 1951-56; Computing Devices of Canada 1956-62, Head Instrument Engn.; Co-Founder Leigh Instruments Ltd. 1962, Vice Pres. Engn., Pres. 1974, Chrmn., Pres. and Dir. 1975-79; served with RCNVR 1944-45; mem. Assn. Prof. Engrs. Prov. Ont.; recreations: sailing, golf; Clubs: Rideau; Royal Ottawa Golf Club; Home: 600 Manor Ave., Ottawa, Ont. K1M 0K3; Office: 112 Kent St., Ste. 904, Ottawa, Ont. K1P 5P2

STEAD, Gordon Wilson, D.S.C., B.Com., B.A., LL.D.; b. Vancouver, B.C., 4 Feb. 1913; s. late Frank and Ethel (Ritchie) S.; e. Univ. of British Columbia, B.Com. 1933, B.A. (Hons. in Econ.) 1934, LL.D. 1945; Univ. of California (Econ.) 1946-48; London Sch. of Econ., 1949-50; m. Lucy, d. late Harrison Rodgers Gore and Lucy Sasscer, Upper Marlboro, Md., 24 June 1948; children: Frank Martin, Anne Harriet (Mrs. Raymond Lance); held various positions in accounting, market research, stock brokerage and geodetic surveying, 1933-36; managerial post with McKeen & Wilson Ltd., towboat operators, Vancouver, B.C., 1936-40; Lectr. in Econ., Univ. of Cal. 1946; Teaching Asst. in Accounting Univ. of Cal., 1946-47 and Lectr. 1947; joined Dept. of Finance, Ottawa, 1950; Asst. Secy., Treasury Bd., 1956-58; Dir.-Gen., Marine Services, Dept. of Transport, 1958-60; Asst. Depy. Min., Marine, Dept. of Transport 1960-70; Ldr., Candn. Del. to Intergovernmental Maritime Consultative Organ. 1965-69; Special Adv. (Transport.) Constitutional Review, Privy Council Office 1970-71; Prof. Sch. Community & Regional Planning, Univ. B.C. 1971-76; policy consult., research and writing, since 1973; 2nd Lieutenant B.C. Regiment 1931-33; Lieutenant R.C.N.V.R. 1940; on loan to Royal Navy, 1940-43; served on Northern Patrol, in Eng. Channel and Mediterranean; Lt. Commdr. and Sr. Offr., 3rd Motor Launch Flotilla, 1943; served in H.M.C.S. "Iroquois" in Bay of Biscay, W. Approaches and N. Europe, 1944-45; D.S.C. (Malta, 1942); and Bar (Salerno, 1943); Hon. Commodore, Candn. Coast Guard; Vice Pres. for Can., Inst. of Marine Engrs., 1968-71; Pres., Candn. Port and Harbour Assn. 1964-65; Hakluyt Soc.; Zeta Psi; recreations: hiking, photography, geography, history; Club: Cercle Universitaire d'Ottawa (Pres. 1970-71); Home: 4055 S.W. Marine Dr., Vancouver, B.C. V6N 4A5

STEAD, Robert Allison, B.Com; b. Calgary, Alta., 22 Feb. 1918; s. Robert James and Nettie Mae (Wallace) S.; e. Mutchmor Pub. Sch. and Glebe Coll. Inst., Ottawa, Ont., 1936; Queen's Univ. B.Com. 1939; m. Elizabeth Jane, d. G. S. Paterson, Richmond Hill, Ont., 30 Sept. 1944; children: Susan Gail, Allison Elizabeth, Richard George; ENERGY CONSULTANT, EXECUTIVE CONSULTANTS LTD.; of joined Department of National Defence 1941; Assistant to Financial Superintendent 1941-47; Supt. of Cash Accounts 1947-51; Depy. Naval Secy. (Adm.) 1951-62; Depy. Naval Secy. 1962-64; joined Energy Bd. as Asst. Secy. 1964-65; Secy. of Bd. 1965-72; Secy. of Bd. and Dir.-Gen. Operations 1972-74; Special Advisor to the Chmn.

1974-76; Director-General Operations 1972-74; Special Advisor to the Chmn. 1974-76, Mem., National Energy Bd., 1976-79; former Dir. and District Chairman, Ontario Soc. for Crippled Children; mem., Inst. Pub. Adm. Can.; Inst. Chart. Secys. & Adms.; United Church; Club: Rotary (Past Pres.); Home: 2076 Black Friars Rd., Ottawa, Ont. K2A 3K5; Office: 151 Slater St., Ottawa, Ont. K1P 5H3

STEARN, Colin William, Ph.D., F.R.S.C.; geologist; educator; b. Bishops Stortford, Eng., 16 July 1928; s. Clement Hodgson and Doris L. (Phillips) S.; e. Hillfield Sch., Hamilton, 1934-44; Westdale 2ndary Sch., Hamilton; McMaster Univ., B.Sc. 1949; Yale Univ., Ph.D. (Geol.) 1952; m. Mary Joan, d. Steele C. Mackenzie, Kitchener, Ont., 1953; children: Virginia (Pope), Patricia (Joosse), Andrew; LOGAN PROF. OF GEOL., McGILL UNIV., since June 1968, Chrmn. Dept. Geol. Sciences 1969-74, 1980- ; Asst. Prof. there 1952-58; Asst. Dean, Faculty of Grad. Studies and Research, 1960-63; Assoc. Prof. 1958-66, full Prof. 1966; mem., Geol. Soc. Am.; Geol. Assn. Can.; Paleontol. Soc.; Am. Assn. Petroleum Geols.; Sigma Xi; Baptist; Home: 350 Prince Arthur, Apt. 1811, Montreal, Que. H2X 3R4

STEARNS, Marshal, M.B.E. B.A., LL.B.; stock broker; b. New Canaan, Conn., 22 Jan. 1909; s. Marshal and Charlotte (Shepherd) S.; e. Kent (Conn.) Sch.; Harvard Univ., B.A. 1931; Harvard Univ. Law Sch., LL.B. 1935; m. Helen, d. Thomas Alexander Richardson, Toronto, Ont., 17 Oct. 1936; children: Frances Linda, Nora Richardson, Marshal, Jr.; VICE CHRMN. AND DIR., F. H. DEACON HODGSON, INC. (estbd. 1897); Vice-Chmn. Bd. Trustees, Hosp. for Sick Children, Toronto; Chairman, Board of Governors, Toronto Stock Exchange, 1964-66; President, Canadian Red Cross National Society, 1959-61; Trustee and Chrmn. Extve. Comm., Ont. Hosp. Assn. 1977-81; mem., Extve. Comte and Trustee, Un. Community Fund of Metrop. Toronto, 1958-62; Dir., Social Planning Council of Metrop. Toronto, 1963; called to the Bar of N.Y. State in 1935, and assoc. with the law firm of Duer, Strong & Whitehead, N.Y.C., 1935-37; came to Can. and became a Partner in T. A. Richardson & Co. 1937; served in 2nd World War with 48th Highlanders of Can. and 2nd Candn. Corps; M.B.E.; Mentioned in Despatches; Croix de Guerre 'with palm' (Belgium); Order of Leopold II "with palm" (Belgium); Anglican; recreations: fishing, shooting; Clubs: The Toronto; York; Harvard (New York); Home: 91 Glen Edyth Drive, Toronto, Ont. M4V 2V8; Office: Tenth Floor, 105 Adelaide St. W., Toronto, Ont. M5H 1R4

STECK, Brian Jason, B.Com., M.B.A.; stockbroker; b. Montreal, Que. 26 Dec. 1946; e. Sir Winston Churchill High Sch.; Sir George Williams Univ. B.Com. 1968; Wharton Grad. Sch. of Finance & Comm. M.B.A. 1969; Univ. of Ill. (corr.) Cert. Financial Analyst 1975; m. Ellen Weinstein 22 Aug. 1963; children: one s. Stephen Michel; PRESIDENT, CHIEF OPERATING OFFR. AND DIR., NESBITT, THOMSON INC.; Pres. and Dir. Nesbitt Thomson Bongard Inc.; Nesbitt Thomson Securities Ltd.; Bd. of Gen., Toronto Stork Exchange; Gov., Applied Econ. Research Inst.; Research Analyst, Nesbitt Thomson Securities Ltd. 1969-72, Assoc. mem. Corporate Finance 1972-73; Vice Pres. and Dir. Institutional Sales & Research, Nesbitt Thomson Bongard Inc. 1974-78; Vice Chrmn. Candn. Cancer Soc.; Toronto Fund Raising; mem. Financial Research Inst.; Clubs: Cambridge; Mayfair Tennis; Home: 71 Denlow Blvd., Don Mills, Ont. M3B 1P8; Office: (P.O. Box 35) Toronto Dominion Centre, Toronto, Ont. M5K 1C4.

STEDMAN, Robert William, M.C., B.A.S.C.; consulting engineer; b. Ottawa, Ont., 24 Sept. 1921; s. Air Vice Marshal Ernest Walter, C.B., O.B.E. and Ethel (Studd) S.; e. Ashbury Coll., Ottawa, 1939; Royal Mil. Coll., 1941; Univ. of Toronto, B.A.Sc. 1947; m. Elisabeth, d. late Rt.

Hon. C. D. Howe, 8 June 1946; children: Robin Mary (Mrs. W. MacInnis), Charles E., William R., George F.; PRESIDENT, C. D. HOWE CO. LTD., since 1968; Chrmn., Howe International Ltd.; Dir., Howe India Ltd.; C. D. Howe Western Ltd.; Shoosmith Howe & Partners Ltd. (U.K.); C. D. Howe Est Ltée.; C. D. Howe Central Ltd.; joined present Co. 1947; Vice Pres. 1963; served with Brit. Army in N. Africa and Italy, 1941-45; Reserve Army (Can.) 1947-50; rank Maj. on retirement; mem., Engn. Inst. Can.; Consulting Engrs. Can.; Corp. Engrs. Que.; Assn. Prof. Engrs. Ont.; Anglican; recreation: sailing; Clubs: Rideau (Ottawa); Britannia Yacht (Ottawa); University (Montreal); Baie d'Urfe Yacht (Montreal); Home: 209 Crichton St., Ottawa, Ont.; Office: 77 Metcalfe St., Ottawa, Ont.

STEDMOND, John Mitchell, M.A., Ph.D., F.R.S.C. (1971); university professor; b. Leicester, England, 14 May 1916; s. John Butler and Margaret Hunter (Mitchell) S.; came to Canada, 1924; e. Central Coll.; Moose Jaw, Sask.; Univ. of Sask., B.A. 1950, M.A. 1951; Univ. of Aberdeen, Ph.D. 1953; m. late Nona Fay, d. Ernest C. Horne, Moose Jaw, Sask., 14 Sept. 1940; PROF. OF ENGLISH, QUEEN'S UNIV., since 1965 and Head of the Dept. 1968-77; Emeritus Professor, 1981- ; Assoc. Dir., McGill-Queen's Univ. Pres. 1971-74; Editor, "Queen's Quarterly", 1960-64; Asst. Lectr., Univ. of Aberdeen, 1951-52; Instr. and Asst. Prof. of Eng., Univ. of Sask. 1953-58; served in 2nd World War with R.C.O.C., 1942-45, U.K. and N.W. Europe; author of "The Comic Art of Laurence Sterne", 1967, and numerous articles in scholarly journs.; Ed. "The Winged Skull: Bicentenary Essays on Laurence Sterne" 1971; mem., Humanities Assn. Can. (Vice-Pres. 1958-60, Pres. 1972-73); Humanities Research Council Can. (Chmn. 1972-74); Assn. Candn. Univ. Teachers of Eng.; Modern Lang. Assn.; Candn. Assn. Univ. Teachers; Home: 8 Barclay Road, Kingston, Ont. K7M 2S4

STEELE, Alfred Victor; executive; b. Winnipeg, Man., 20 March 1929; s. Alfred L. and Janet (Bobitt) S.; e. Pub. and High Schs., Montreal, Que.; Univ. of Toronto; m. Lorraine, d. Albert Westcott, 10 July 1954; children: David Victor, Mark Alan, Susan Lorraine; PRESIDENT, FABER-CASTELL CANADA LTD.; Venus Custom Products Ltd.; Venus Promotion Products Ltd.; joined Commercial Credit Corp. Ltd. as Asst. Br. Mgr., Toronto 1951; Dist. Regional Mgr., Redisco of Canada Ltd. 1953; with Allstate Insurance Co. of Canada 1962; Vice-Pres., Gen. Mgr. and Dir., Traders Group Ltd., Interprovincial Building Credits Ltd. 1963; Vice-Pres. and Dir., Traders Mortgage Co. 1966; Sr. Vice-Pres. and Dir. Traders Group Ltd. 1970; mem. Fed. Council Finance Cos.; Salvation Army; recreations: golf, photography, music, theatre; Club: Thornhill Golf & Country; Home: 60 Clarke Haven St., Thornhill, Ont. L4J 2B4; Office: 77 Brown's Line, Toronto, Ont. M8W 4X5

STEELE, Clifford George; executive; b. Vancouver, B.C. 30 March 1929; s. James Elder and Janet (Kinsman) S.; e. Lord Selkirk Sch., Vancouver, B.C.; Vancouver Tech Sch.; m. Margaret, d. Irvine H. Cook, 28 Nov. 1975; PRESIDENT, DIVERSIFIED ELECTRONICS OF CANADA LTD.; commenced as Business Servicer, radio and household appliances 1946; later Relieving Agent and Combination Operator, Dom. Govt. Telephone and Telegraphs; subsequently with Radio Station CKWX Vancouver, then Chief Engr. CKPG, Prince George,B.C.; prior to present position involved in supervisory capacity with tech. and engn. facilities of various sound and intercom equipment developing specialty of buried metal location; equipment and water leak detection svces.; mem. Inst. Elect. and Electronic Engrs.; United Church; recreations: Amateur Radio (VE7LF); fishing; music; Home: 8009 - 17th Ave., Burnaby, B.C. V3N 1M5; Office: 1104 Franklin St., Vancouver, B.C. V6A 1J6

STEELE, Hon. Donald Robert, B.A.Sc.; judge; b. Toronto, Ont., 28 June 1925; s. Harold Learoyd and Gladys Ione (Bateman) S.; e. Upper Can. Coll. 1942; Univ. of Toronto B.A.Sc. 1946; Osgoode Hall Law Sch. 1949; m. Barbara L. d. Carl A. Pollock , 1 Oct. 1955; children: Victoria, Mark, Douglas; JUSTICE, SUPREME COURT OF ONT.; served with RCAF 1944; Lambda Alpha; Theta Delta Chi; Anglican; recreations: golf, skiing; Clubs: Toronto Golf; University; Osler Bluff; Muskoka Lakes Golf; Home: 14 May St. Toronto, Ont. M4W 1Y2; Office: Osgoode Hall, Toronto, Ont.

STEELE, Granville George Ernest, B.A.; b. Windsor, Ont., 11 Jan. 1920; s. Ernest and Ethel Isabel (Fordham) S.; e. High Schs., Montreal, Que. and Toronto, Ont.; Univ. of Toronto, B.A. (Hons. Pol. Science and Econ.) 1949; London Sch. of Econ., 1949-51; m. Edith Clare, d. late Frederick Hamilton Rutherford, Dec. 1948; children: Michael Ernest, Elizabeth Jean, John Peter, Graham Frederick; PRES., CAN. ASSN. OF BROADCASTERS 1978; former Pres., Grocery Products Mfrs. of Can., 1968; mem., Bd. Trustees, Candn. Hunger Foundation; Chrmn. Bd. Govs., Univ. of Ottawa; employed with Toronto Office of Simonds Canada Saw Co. Ltd. as Acct., 1937-41; joined Dept. of Finance, Ottawa, 1951; Asst. Depy. Min. and Secy. of Treasury Bd., 1960-64; Undersecy. of State 1964 till resigned from public service, 1968; served in 2nd World War with R.C.A.F. 1941-45 (Overseas 1943-45); Pres., Candn. Assn. of Broadcasters; mem., Candn. Inst. Public Adm.; Clubs: Canadian; Cercle Universitaire d'Ottawa; Home: 78 Riverdale Ave., Ottawa, Ont.; Office: 165 Sparks St., Box 627, Stn. B.,Ottawa, Ont. K1P 5S2

STEELE, Gray M.; food distribution executive; b. Montreal, Que. 6 June 1916; s. Thomas Archibald and Eliza Jane Patton (Crawford) S.; e. Strathcona Acad. and Guy Drummond Sch. Outremont, Que.; Malvern Coll. Inst. Toronto; Univ. of Toronto Certified Business Grad.; m. Elizabeth Isabella d. William Miller 18 May 1940; children: Susan Elizabeth (Mrs. Robert House), Thomas William, Catherine Anne, Roger Gray; CHRMN. OF THE BD. AND OWNER ST. LAWRENCE FOODS LIMITED; Pres. Gray M. Steele Ltd.; Vice Pres. and Dir. Federated Foods Ltd.; Treas. and Dir. Sunshine Holdings Inc.; Chrmn. of Bd. Toronto E. Gen. Orthapedic Hosp.; served with Candn. Army Reserve 1941-44; RCN 1944-45; rec'd Queen's Silver Jubilee Medal 1977; Pres. Fish & Seafood Assn. Ont. 1955-56; Candn. Frozen Food Assn. 1976-77; Fisheries Council Can. 1977-78; Dir. Nat. Frozen Food Assn. (USA) 1975-77; Elder, Kew Beach Un. Ch.; mem. Bd. Trade Metrop. Toronto; United Church; recreation: cottage; Clubs: Scarboro Golf & Country; Donalda; Boulevard; Toronto Hunt; Office: 70 Denison St., Markham, Ont. L3R 2P5.

STEELE, Robert, M.D., D.P.H., FFCM, F.R.C.P.(C); FAPHA; b. Scotland, 16 Jan. 1929; s. John and Susan Halbert (Hunter) S.; e. Sch. of Med., Royal Colls., Edinburgh Univ., D.P.H. 1956; Univ. of Sask., M.D. 1960; m. Letitia Margaret, d. Robert A. Cuthbertson, Edinburgh, Scot., 30 July 1955; two s., Paul Robert, David Angus; Consultant in Epidemiology, Kingston Gen. Hosp.; mem. Attending Staff, Kingston Gen. and Hotel Dieu Hosps.; joined Dept. of Pub. Health and Social Med., Univ. of Edinburgh as Research Fellow in Epidemiology, 1956; apptd. Hon. Registrar to S.E. Scot. Regional Hosp. Bd., 1957; Asst. Prof., Dept. of Social and Preventive Med., Coll. of Med., Univ. of Sask. 1958; Med. Offr. Hosp. Div. of Scot. Home and Health Dept., Edinburgh, 1962-64; apptd. to Queen's Univ. as Assoc. Prof. of Preventive Med. and Dir. of Research, Child Health Programme, 1964; Prof. and Head, Dept. of Community Health & Epidemiol. 1968; served as Capt. with R.A.M.C. 1953-55; author of numerous articles in med. journs.; mem., Roy. Med. Soc.; Internat. Epidemiology Assn.; Candn. Assn. Teachers Social & Preventive Med.; Assn. Teachers Preventive Med.; recreations: golf, modern lit. and art; Address: Queen's Univ., 25 Union St., Kingston, Ont. K7L 3N6

STEER, Rt. Rev. Stanley Charles, M.A., D.D. (Ang.); retired bishop; b. Aldershot, Hants, England; s. Stanley Edgar and Emma Grace (Comber) S.; e. Margate and Guildford Grammar Schs.; came to Canada 1922; Univ. of Sask., B.A. 1928; Oxford Univ., M.A. 1937; D.D. Wycliffe, 1946, Emmanuel Coll., Saskatoon, 1951, St. Chad's Coll., Regina, 1964; m. Marjorie Slater, 1936; Missy., Vanderhoof, B.C., 1929; Chaplain, St. Mark's Ch., Alexandria 1931; Chaplain, University Coll., Oxford, 1932-33; Tutor, St. John's Hall, Univ. of London, 1933; Vice-Principal there, 1936; Chaplain, The Mercers Company, City of London, 1937; Principal, Emmanuel Coll., Saskatoon, Sask., 1941; Hon. Canon of St. John's Cath., Saskatoon, Sask., 1943; Bishop of Saskatoon 1950-70; served in 1st World War with Imp. Army; 2nd World War, Chaplain, R.O.; Home: 2383 Lincoln Rd., Victoria, B.C. V8R 6A3

STEERS, Barry Connell, B.A.; diplomat; b. London, Ont., 15 Jan. 1927; s. late Connell Gerald and Kathleen Mary (Coles) S.; e. De La Salle Coll., London, Ont.; Univ. of W. Ont., B.A. 1951; m. Marta Molina-Vélez, d. late Arthur Molina, 16 Aug. 1952; children: Connell William, Sara Maria, Gregory Kevin; AMBASSADOR TO JAPAN 1978!; Nat. Research Council of Can., 1951-55; Partner in export/import business, Medellin, Colombia, 1955-57; joined Trade Commr. Service, Ottawa, 1957; Asst. Trade Commr. Singapore, 1958; Second Secy. (Comm.), Athens, 1960; First Secy. (Comm.), Tel Aviv, 1961; Consul and Trade Commr., New York City, 1966; Dir., Internat. Financing Br., Ottawa, 1968; also alternate Dir., Export Devel. Corp., Ottawa; organ. Market Devel. Group, Ottawa and subsequently became Dir., 1970; Ambassador to Brazil 1971; apptd. Consul-Gen., New York, 1976 and concurrently Can.'s first Commr. to Bermuda, 1977; Asst. Dept. Min., Trade Commissioner Service and Int'l Mkting, Dept. Ind., Trade and Commerce, 1979-81; served with COTC, RCAC Militia; Zeta Psi; R. Catholic; recreation: sports; Clubs: Canadian (N.Y.); Canadian Soc. N.Y.; Yacht (Rio de Janeiro); Home: 7 Carr Crescent, Kanata, Ont. K2K 1K5. Office: 235 Queen Street, Ottawa, Ont. K1A OH5

STEEVES, Lea Chapman, M.D., C.M., LL.D., D.Sc., F.R.C.P. (Can.), F.A.C.P.; b. New Westminster, B.C., 4 Nov. 1915; s. Harold Chapman, M.D. and Helen Anna (Lea) S.; e. Pub. and High Schs., New Westminster and Essondale, B.C., Moncton, N.B.; Mount Allison Univ., B.A. (MCL) 1936, LL.D. 1969; McGill Univ., M.D., C.M. 1940; m. Katharine Grace, d. Donald M. Fraser, 19 Feb. 1942; children: Donald Chapman, M.D., Alexander L., M.D., Gordon F., John M., M.D., James I.; ASSOC. DEAN, FACULTY OF MEDICINE, DALHOUSIE UNIV., 1969-81 and Prof. of Med. there; Dir., Div. of Continuing Med. Educ., 1957-72; Assoc. Attending Phys., Victoria Gen. Hosp., Halifax; Med. Specialist, Camp Hill Veterans' Hosp., Halifax; served as Surg.-Lt. with RCNVR 1943-46; mem. Adv. Bd., Candn. Heart Foundation; Bd., N.S. Heart Foundation; Pres.; Med. Council Can. 1969-70; Candn. Assn. Continuing Med. Educ. 1968-69; Med. Soc. N.S. 1969-70; N.S. Div., Candn. Med. Assn.; mem., Halifax Med. Soc.; N.S. Soc. Internal Med.; N.S. Cardiovascular Soc.; Candn. Cardiovascular Soc.; Alpha Omega Alpha; Phi Rho Sigma; rec'd. D.Sc. Memorial Univ. 1974; United Church; recreations: photography, camping, canoeing; Home: 51 Hazelholme Dr., Halifax, N.S. B3M 1M6

STEIGER, Frederic; artist; portrait and abstract landscape painter; b. Solwutz, Austria; s. Michael and Ida (Schaeffer) S.; e. Public Schools, Opava, Czecho-Slovakia, and Olmouc University there; self-taught in art; came to Canada 1922; began painting in Saskatoon, Sask.; in 1937 gave his whole time to painting; opened studio in

Toronto, 1943; made a trip to Nfld. in 1949, where he became much attached to the country and its people; obtained an extended portrait commission from the Nfld. Govt. which enabled a lengthy stay there; began execution of portraits of 26 Speakers of the Leg. Assembly (1832-1949), portraits of 14 Prime Ministers of Nfld. since 1855 (completed 1950-51); portraits of Hon. J. R. Smallwood (1949), Clara Smallwood (1950), Hon. J. R. Chalker (1951), Campbell McPherson (1950), all of Nfld.; among other portraits are those of R.B.C. Noorduyn, Montreal (1944), Dean G. H. Ling, Univ. of Sask. (1945), Sir Chas. G. D. Roberts (1943), Jos. Sedgewick, K.C., Toronto (1947), Boris Hambourg, Toronto (1945), His late Majesty King Peter of Jugoslavia (1974), Hon. William G. Davis, Q.C., Premier of Ont. (1976); comn. by Newfoundland Government (1952) to paint "Signing of Atlantic Charter" for Museum in St. John's; painting trip to France (summer 1952); exhibition of French and Canadian paintings in New York under patronage of Premier J. R. Smallwood of Nfld.; landscape accepted and hung by U.N. Lib., N.Y., 1957; landscapes for new Imperial Oil Bldg., St. John's, Nfld.; sometime Art Consultant, Marketing Research Dept., Imperial Oil Ltd.; has exhibited with Ont. Soc. of Artists; Royal Candn. Acad.; Vancouver Art Gallery; Montreal Museum of Fine Arts; Eaton Centre, 1979-80, Toronto; Galerie Lyson Inc., Toronto, 1980-81; a number of private galleries, etc.; rep. in collection of Govt. of Nfld. and private collections incl. "Cathédrale" 1971 "Study of a Newfoundlander", 1980 (Collection John Norman, St. John's); Collection Paul Emile Rouleau, Montreal and C. A. Denis, Rothmans of Pall Mall, Toronto; Collections: Gerald Gougeon, Min. of Educ., Toronto; Albert J. Wilson, Q.C.; Omer Deslauriers, Brussels; prefers to paint in an impressionistic style relating man to his environment, also semi-abstract and abstract painting; awarded Bronze Medal, Internat. Business Machine Corpn., in its "Contemporary Art of the Western Hemisphere" Exhibition 1941; various paintings since 1961 incl. "Maritime Still Life" (Toronto Pub. Lib.), "Cathedral Spires" (Painters of Can. series); incl. in Spring Exhn. of Candn. art at Cumerford Gallery, N.Y. 1962; "The Fisherman", Mem. Univ., Nfld.; "City Lights" (1964), Hallmark Permanent Coll. of Candn. Art; (portrait) Hon. J. Keiller MacKay; works reproduced by 'Hallmark' cards, 1962-77; Unitarian; recreation: music; Home: 316 The Kingsway, Toronto, Ont. M9A 3V2; Studio: 406 Bloor St. E., Toronto, Ont. M4W 1H4

STEIN, Joseph Charles, Q.C., LL.D.; b. Riviere du Loup, Que., 6 July 1912; s. Hon. Adolphe (former Justice, Superior Court of Que.) and Alice (Hamel) S.; e. Petit Seminaire de Quebec, B.A. 1931; Laval Univ., Ph.L. (summa cum laude) 1932 and LL.L. (summa cum laude) 1934 with Gov. Gen. Gold Medal and other prizes; m. Gabrielle, d. Eugene des Rivieres, 15 Oct. 1938; children: Michel, Claire; PARTNER, LETOURNEAU AND STEIN; read law with Antonio Langlais, K.C., Quebec; called to the Bar of Que. 1934; cr. K.C. 1947; practised his prof. at Quebec City, 1934-38; Jr. Adv. Counsel, Dept. of Justice, Ottawa, 1938, and later Adv. Counsel and Sr. Adv. Counsel; Acting Asst. Depy. Min. of Justice, Sept. 1946; Asst. Depy. Min. of Justice, Feb. 1947 to Jan. 1949; Under Secy. of State & Deputy Registrar Gen. of Can., 1949-61; Roman Catholic; recreations: golf, tennis, jogging, reading; Clubs: Cap-Rouge Golf; Cercle Universitaire (Quebec); Club Tennisport; Home: 4 Jardins de Merici (Apt. 302), Québec, Qué. G1S 4M4; Office: Price House, 65 Ste-Anne St., Québec, Qué. G1R 3X5

STEINBERG, David; comedian, author, actor; b. Winnipeg, Man. 29 Aug. 1942; s. Jacob and Ruth S.; student Hebrew Theol. Coll.; Univ. Chicago; writer, actor "Second City"; actor "Little Murders"; Broadway appearances include: "Carry Me Back to Morningside Heights"; star "Music Scene"; host on Johnny Carson, David Frost, and Dick Cavett shows; appearances on Smothers Bros., Flip Wilson, Glen Campbell shows; author spl. "This is

Sholem Aleichem", "Return of Smothers Bros."; rec. on Elektra," David Steinberg Disguised as a Normal Person; starred in "Something Short of Paradise," 1979; Address: c/o William Morris Agy. Inc., 151 E. Camino, Beverly Hills, CA 90212

STEINBERG, H. Arnold, B.Com., M.B.A.; retail merchant; b. Montreal, Que., 12 May 1933; s. Nathan Annie (Steinberg) S.; e. West Hill (Que.) High Sch.; McGill Univ. B.Com. 1954; Harvard Business Sch., M.B.A. 1957; m. Blema Solomon, 23 June 1957; children: Margot, Donna, Adam; EXTVE. VICE PRES. AND DIR., STEINBERG INC.; Pres. and Dir., Ivanhoe Inc.; Chrmn. Bd., Innocan Investments Ltd.; Dir. Mercantile Bank of Canada; Groupe Prenor Ltée; Sociéte Générale de Financement du Québec; joined Dominion Securities Corp. Limited, 1957-58; joined present Co. 1958; mem. Canada Council; Bd. of Govs. McGill Univ.; mem. Bd. of Mang., Montreal Children's Hosp.; Chrmn. McGill Univ.-Montreal Children's Hosp. Research Inst.; Office: 1500 Atwater, Montreal, Que. H3Z 1Y5

STEINER, Edward Warren; merchant; b. Toronto, Ont., 28 Aug. 1912; s. Ernest Albert and Edith Louise (De La Matter) S.; e. Brown Public Sch. and Oakwood Coll. Inst., Toronto, Ont.; m. Norma Bernice, d. Norman Strong, 20 April 1940; children: Eric Alan, Karen Elizabeth; CHAIRMAN AND DIR., PARSONS-STEINER CANADA LTD. (Mfrs. Agents, Eng. Chinaware, Estbd. 1931) since 1970 (formerly Pres.); Pres., Robwaral Ltd.; with Royal Bank of Canada, 1929-33 when joined the present firm; Liberal; United Church; recreations: golf, fishing; Clubs: Optimist; York Downs Golf & Country; Home: Apt. 601 — 4001 Bayview Ave., Willowdale, Ont. M2M 3Z7; Office: 90 Carnforth Rd., Toronto, Ont. M4A 2L3

STEINER, Jan W., M.D., F.R.C.P.(C); educator; b. Znojmo, Moravia, Czechoslovakia, 27 Dec. 1916; s. Emil and Helena (Blum) S.; e. Charles Univ., Prague and Liverpool Univ., Engl.; Oxford Univ., M.D. 1943; m. Dr. Betty Wilson, d. E. P. Morris, 3 Mar. 1942; PROF. PATH., UNIV. OF TORONTO, and Assoc. Dean of Arts and Sci. 1980; Assoc. Dean, Undergrad. Affairs, 1966-67; served in French Army and Czech regt. of Brit. Army 1939-41; postgrad. training, Univ. of Liverpool (Czech govt. scholarship) 1943; gen. practice, Scunthorpe, Lincolnshire, Engl. 1945; Asst. Path., Mt. Sinai Hosp., Toronto, 1955; Research Assoc., Univ. of Toronto, 1959; Lectr. 1960; Asst. Prof., Dept. of Path., 1961; Visiting Asst. Research Prof., Univ. of Pittsburgh, 1962-65; Assoc. Prof., Dept. of Path., Univ. of Toronto, 1964; Prof., 1965; Visiting Prof., Dept. of Pathol., Chicago Coll. of Osteopathic Med. since 1977; Prof. Lecturer, Univ. of Chicago since 1980; Lecturer in Med., Univ. of Health Sci., Chicago Med. Sch. since 1980; Prof., Clinical Pathology, Northwestern Univ., Chicago 1980; Visiting Prof. Pathology, Rush Medical Coll. Chicago 1980; Lecturer, Sch. Public Health, Univ. of Illinois 1980; received Starr Medal for Med. Research, Univ. of Toronto, 1962; Shovel Award as Best Clinical Teacher 1964, 66; author of over 70 articles in learned journs.; mem. Ed. Bd. "Am. Journ. Pathology," 1964-71; Ed. Consultant "Revue Candnne. de Biologie," 1965; mem. Ed. Bd. "Chemico-Biological Interactions," 1968; Ed. "Virchow Archiv-B Cell Pathology," 1970; Trustee, Candn. Hepatic Foundation; Dir., Ont. Liver Disease Found.; Dir., Ill. Comprehensive Cancer Center; mem., Am. Assn. of Cancer Insts.; Ont. and Candn. Med. Assns.; Am. and Candn. Assns. of Pathol.; Fed. of Am. Biol. Socs.; Internat. Acad. for Study of Liver Diseases; Internat. Acad. of Pathol.; Alpha Omega Alpha; recreations: photography, painting; Home: 65 Castle Frank Cres., Toronto, Ont. M4W 3A2 Office: Sidney Smith Hall, Univ. of Toronto, Toronto, Ont.

STEINHAUER, Hon. Ralph, O.C. (1967); b. Morley, Alta., June 1905; m. Isobel Davidson, 1928; four d., one

s.; former Lieutenant-Governor of Alberta 1974-79; former Councillor (34 yrs.) and Chief (3 yrs.) Saddle Lake Indian Band Alta.; joined Un. Farm Workers of Alta. 1923; co-founder Indian Assn. Alta.; Lib. cand. for Vegreville in fed. el. 1963; mem., Two Hills Chamber of Comm.; Life mem., St. Paul Chamber of Comm.; Past Pres., Alta. Indian Devel. Systems Ltd.; Council mem., N. Alta. Devel. Council; Bd. Alta. Newstart; Centennial Medal 1967.

STEINHOUSE, Herbert, M.A.; author; journalist; public relations; broadcaster; b. Montreal, Que., 15 April 1922; s. Charles Mayer and Ray (Diamond) S.; e. McGill Univ., B.A. 1942; New Sch. for Social Research, New York City, M.A. (Internat. Affairs) 1948; m. Tobie Thelma Davis, artist; two s. Stephan Brock, Adam; DIR. COVERAGE PLANNING, ENG. SERVICES, QUE., CBC served in 2nd World War with R.C.A.F.; three years overseas aircrew with R.A.F. Transport Command; France and Germany with UNRRA, 1945-46; Reuters ed., London, and foreign correspondent, Western Europe, 1948-49; broadcaster with special United Nations Info. mission to S.E. Asia, 1951-52; CBC European Corr. and broadcaster from North Africa and Asia, 1949-52; Information & Radio Consultant to WHO, Geneva, 1950-54; Editor-Producer, UNESCO World Review (a weekly 4-lang. radio programme broadcast in 125 countries), 1952-56; Sr. Producer, CBC Public Affairs, Montreal, 1957-64; Dir. of Eng. Region, CBC Quebec, 1964-66; Dir. Divisional Affairs, CBC French Networks, 1966-73; Dir., Public Relations, CBC English Services, Que., 1973-79; author of "Ten Years After" (U.S. title: "The Time of the Juggernaut"), pol. novel on France and Algeria, 1958; formerly Secy., Fed. of Internat. Civil Servants' Assn., Geneva; Past mem., Nat. Union of Journs. (London); Foreign Correspondents Assn.; N.Y.; mem., Amer. Acad. of Independent Scholars (Denver); Cdn. Communication Assoc.; Candn. Heritage Foundn.; Candn. Pub. Rel. Soc.; Internat. P.E.N.; Authors League of Am.; V.P.; Canadian Club (Montreal); Cdn. Inst. of Int'l Affairs; Trout Unlimited of Can.; Montreal Press Club; Address: 208 Côte St. Antoine Rd., Montreal, Que. H3Y 2J3

STELCK, Charles Richard, M.Sc., Ph.D.; educator; b. Edmonton, Alta. 20 May 1917; s. Robert Ferdinand and Florella Maud Mary (Stanbury) S.; e. Westmount Pub. and Victoria High Schs. Edmonton 1934; Univ. of Alta. B.Sc. 1937, M.Sc. 1941; Stanford Univ. Ph.D. 1951; m. Frances Gertrude d. late Rev. Francis McDowell 24 Apl. 1945; children: David, Brian, Leland, John; PROF. OF GEOL. UNIV. OF ALTA.; Geol. Exploration, Benedum & Trees 1939; Geol., Dept. Mines B.C. 1940-42; Canol Project U.S. Govt. 1942-43; Exploration, Imperial Oil 1943-49; Lectr. Univ. of Alta. 1946; author over 70 scient. articles cretaceous, devonian fossils, W. Can. biostratigraphy, ammonites, arenaceous foraminifera, pelecypods; Fellow Royal Soc. Can.; Assn. Prof. Engrs., Geologists and Geophysicists of Alta.; Can. Soc. Petrol. Geols.; Geol. Soc. Am.; Paleontol. Soc.; Paleontol. Assn. (London); Cushman Foundation Foraminiferal Research; Sigma Xi; P. Conservative; Protestant; recreation: hunting; Home: 11739 - 91 Ave., Edmonton, Alta. T6G 1B1; Office: Edmonton, Alta. T6G 2E3.

STENASON, Walter John, M. Com., Ph.D.; b. Winnipeg, Man., 24 Sept. 1930; s. Walter George and Margaret Rollyns (Smith) S.; e. McGill Univ., B.Com. 1952, M.Com. 1954; Harvard Univ., Ph.D. (Econ.) 1961; m. Letty Trant, d. David Watson, Victoria, B.C., 24 Dec. 1954; children: David, Robert, William; PRESIDENT AND DIRECTOR CANADIAN PACIFIC ENTERPRISES LTD., since 1979; Dir., Canadian Pacific Hotels Ltd.; Cominco Ltd.; Great Lakes Forest Products Ltd.; Processed Minerals Inc.; Mutual Life Assurance Co. of Can.; Canadian Pacific Securities Ltd.; Algoma Steel Corp. Ltd.; Pacific Forest Products Ltd.; PanCanadian Petroleum Limited; Commandant Properties Ltd.; Chateau Insurance Company; AMCA Int'l Ltd.; Canada Trust Co.; Marathon Realty Co. Ltd.; CanPac AgriProducts Ltd.; AMCA Internat. Corp.; Fording Coal Ltd.; Span Holdings; Span Internat.; Com Pacific Enterprises U.S. Inc.; Syracuse China Corp.; Steep Rock Iron Mines Ltd.; Baker Commodities, Inc.; Maple Leaf Mills Ltd.; CIP Inc., with Greenshields Inc., Montreal, 1952; joined C.P. Rly. Co. as Jr. Research Assistant, 1952; Research Econ., 1956, Dir. of Econ. Research, 1958, Asst. to the Pres., 1961, Asst. to the Chrmn. and to the Pres., 1964, Vice-Pres., Co. Services 1966, Vice-Pres., Transport and Ships 1969; Vice Pres. Admin. 1972; Extve. Vice Pres., Cdn. Pacific Investments Ltd. 1974; mem. Lloyd's Candn. Comte.; Am. Econ. Assn.; Am. Stat. Assn.; Candn. Pol. Science Assn.; United Church; recreations: boating, curling; Home: 316 Pinetree Cres., Beaconsfield, Que. H9W 5E1; Office: Suite 1900, Place du Canada, Montreal, Que. H3B 2N2

STEPHEN, George, F.T.C.I. company executive; b. St. Cyrus, Scot., 4 March 1924; s. James Henderson and Katherine Henderson (Lindsay) S.; e. Montrose Acad., Scot., 1929-36; Aberdeen (Scot.) Grammar Sch., 1936-42; Aberdeen Univ., 1942-43; m. Dorothy Lorna, d. Rev. William A. Ross, Toronto, 22 July 1950; two s., Mark Lindsay, Ian Campbell; PRES., AMEDCO PACIFIC LTD. since 1981; joined Montreal Trust Co. 1955, Vice Pres. 1969, Depy. Chrmn. & Mang. Dir., Trust Corp. of Bahamas 1970-73, Vice Pres. Montreal Trust Western Can. 1973-77, Vice Pres. Ont. 1977-81; Dir., Canadian-Scottish Heritage Fdn.; served as Pilot-Air Br., R.N., 1943-50; United Church; recreations: golf, reading; Clubs: Mt. Stephen (Montreal); Royal Montreal Golf; Lyford Cay; Lambton Golf & Country (Toronto); Home: 10 Thelma Ave., Toronto, Ont. M4V 1X9; Office: 130 Adelaide St. W., Toronto, Ont. M5H 3P5

STEPHEN, Hugh Roulston; retired business executive; b. Guildford, Surrey, Eng. 25 Apl. 1913; s. Samuel and Margaret (Scott) S.; e. Bishop's Stortford Coll. Eng.; m. Barbara Leslie d. Richard Clwyd Williams, Victoria, B.C. 16 March 1942; children: Michael Clwyd, Susan Margaret, David Hugh; Dir.; British Columbia Telephone Co.; Canada Trust; Mgr. and Owner New Method Laundries, Victoria 1946-63; Mayor of Victoria 1967-69; Pres. Victoria Chamber Comm. 1957-58; Past Pres. Victoria Art Gallery; Past Chrmn. Brentwood Coll. Bd. Govs.; Chrmn. Univ. of Victoria Bd. Govs.; Trustee, Fraser Inst. Vancouver; Dir. Victoria Br. Candn. Inst. Internat. Affairs; Past Dir. Victoria Foundation; Past Vice Chrmn. Victoria Adv. Planning Comn.; Chrmn. Capital Region Bd. 1969; Gov., Jaycees of Can.; Hon. mem. Community Planning Assn. Can.; Hon. Life mem. Victoria Conserv. of Music; served with 5th B.C. Coast Regt. R.C.A. 1939, subsequently trans. to Candn. Intelligence Corps and served with Psychol. Warfare Div. S.E. Asia Command on attachement to Brit. Forces; rec'd Candn. Centennial Medal 1967; recreations: golf, reading; Clubs: Union; Uplands Golf; Home: 208-1211 Beach Dr., Victoria, B.C. V8S 2N4.

STEPHEN, Kenneth Alexander, B.Com., C.A., F.C.I.S., F.R.I.; real estate executive; b. Toronto, Ont. 29 Aug. 1929; s. late Alexander and Mary J. (Simpson) S.; e. Vaughan Rd. Coll. Inst. 1947; Univ. of Toronto B.Com. 1951; C.A. 1954, A.C.I.S. 1960, F.C.I.S. 1964, F.R.I. 1966; m. Margaret d. late Angus MacTaggart, Toronto, Ont. 19 July 1952; children: Craig Alexander, Heather Margaret, Keith Fraser; PRES., A.E. LePAGE ASSET MANAGEMENT CO., 1980- ; Dir., A.E. LePage Ltd.; Auditor, Clarkson Gordson & Co. 1951-54; Dept. of Nat. Revenue Taxation Corp. Income Tax Assessment 1954-59; Comptroller A.E. LePage Ltd. 1959, Secy.-Treas. 1963, Dir. 1965, Secy. & Vice Pres., Finance, 1967; Sr. Vice Pres. Finance and Secy. 1971, Exec. Vice-Pres., Finance & Admin., 1975; rec'd Nat. and Internat. prizes Chart. Inst. Secy. Course; Claude Leigh Mem. Scholarship Inst. Realtors; Former Treas. and Hon. Life mem. Streetsville Community Centre; Fellow, Real Estate Inst.; Past Chrmn.

Chart. Inst. Secys.; Past Finance Chmn., Cdn. Real Estate Assoc.; P. Conservative; Protestant; recreations: music, theatre, travel, vintage auto racing, golf; Club: Scarboro Golf; Fitness Inst.; Home: 22 Meadowglade Cres., Willowdale, Ont. M2J 1C7; Office: 50 Holly St., Toronto, Ont. M4S 2G1.

STEPHENS, Nigel, B.A.; b. Ottawa, Ont., 10 Dec. 1925; s. Robert G. and Katie R. (Hinge) S.; e. Univ. of Toronto, B.A. 1948; m. Gloria M. Dow, 27 Sept. 1952; children: Nigel D., Timothy M.; PRESIDENT, STEPHENS MANAGEMENT INC.; Founding Dir. and former Vice Pres., Toronto Montessori Schs.; Vice Pres. and dir., Old Can. Investment Corp. Ltd.; Secretary, Investment Counsel Assn. of Can.; Past Pres., Candn. Figure Skating Assn.; former Candn. Singles Skating Champion; Anglican; recreations: skating, skiing; Clubs: Granite; Seigniory (Montebello, Que.); Home: 18 Beechwood Ave., Willowdale, Ont. M2L 1J1; Office: Suite 2517, 401 Bay St., Toronto, Ont. M5H 2Y4

STEPHENS, Vice-Admiral Robert St. George, C.D.; naval officer; b. Esquimalt, B.C., 17 Jan. 1924; s. Rear-Admiral George Leslie and Edna Louise (Woodill) S.; e. Brentwood Coll., Victoria, B.C., 1941; Royal Naval Coll. Dartmouth (Eng.) 1942; Royal Naval Engn. Coll. Plymouth 1945; Royal Naval Coll. Greenwich (Postgrad.-Advanced Engn.) 1948; Imp. Defence Coll. 1965; m. Clotilde Montserrat, d. Prof. Ignatius Gonzalez-LLubera, 26 July 1949; children: Michael St. George, Christopher David, Jeanne Louise, Nicholas Ignatius; joined RCN as Cadet 1941; served during World War II and Korea; Sqdn. Tech. Offr., 5th Candn. Escort Sqdn., 1961-62; Dir., Marine & Elect. Engn., CFHQ, 1962-65; Mgr. Ship Repair HMC Dockyard Halifax 1966; Commdr. Dockyard 1966-67; Chief of Staff Material Command 1967-69; Dir. Gen. Logistic Services 1969; Dir. Gen. Maintenance CFHQ 1969-70; Asst. Chief of Defence Staff, Information Handling Agency, 1970-72; Commdr. Training Command 1972-75; Candn. Mil. Rep. to NATO Mil. Comte. since 1975; Chart. Engr.; mem., Inst. Marine Engrs.; Inst. Mech. Engrs.; Data Processing Inst.; Anglican; recreations: golf, tennis, squash, philately, art;

STEPHENSON, Bette M., M.D. (Mrs. G. Allan Pengelly); physician; b. Aurora, Ont., 31 July 1924; d. Carl Melvin and Clara Mildred (Draper) S.; e. Aurora (Ont.) Pub. Sch.; McKee Ave. Pub. Sch. and Earl Haig Coll. Inst., Willowdale, Ont.; Univ. of Toronto, M.D. 1946; m. Gordon Allan Pengelly, M.D., 1948; children: J. Stephen A., Elizabeth Anne A., C. Christopher A., J. Michael A., P. Timothy A., Mary Katharine A.; MIN. OF EDUC. & MIN. OF COLLS. & UNIVS. since 1978; el. to Ont. Leg. for York Mills, Sept. 1975; re-el. June 1977 and Mar. 1981; Min. of Labour 1975-78; mem. Med. Staff, N. York Gen. Hosp., 1967-76; mem. Med. Staff, Womens Coll. Hosp., since 1950; Chief, and Dir. of Outpatient Dept., Land Dept. of Gen. Practice, 1954-64; Chrmn., Nat. Coordinating Comte. on Educ., Coll. of Family Physicians Canada, 1961-64 and Chrmn., Confs. on Educ. for Gen. Practice, 1961 and 1963; mem. Bd. of N. York Br. V.O.N., 1954-67; mem. Bd., Ont. Med. Foundation; Fellow, Coll. Family Phys. Can.; Fellow, Acad. Med. Toronto; Ont. Med. Assn. (Bd. Dirs. 1964-72; Pres. 1970-71); Candn. Med. Assn. (Bd. Dirs. 1968-75; Pres. 1974-75); Candn. Mental Health Assn.; mem., Art Gallery of Ont.; Royal Ontario Museum; Protestant; Address: 20 McKee Ave., Willowdale, Ont. M2N 4B8

STEPHENSON, Patrick Joseph Thomas, DFC; chartered insurance broker; b. Dublin, Ireland, 25 Aug. 1918; s. Hugh Percival and Gladys Mary (Moloney) S.; e. Schs. France, Switzerland and Belgium; m. Margaret Patricia d. Timothy A. Macauley, 3 Dec. 1949; children: Shane Patrick, Shelagh Mary; CHMN. OF THE BOARD, J. & H. LTD. since 1979; Chrmn. of the Bd. Johnson & Higgins Willis Faber Inc.; Johnson & Higgins Willis Faber (Aviation) Ltd.; Vice Pres. and Dir. Dupuis, Parizeau, Tremblay, Inc.; Vice Pres. Johnson & Higgins (Canada) Ltd. Montreal 1958-63, Pres. 1963-67, Pres. Johnson & Higgins Willis Faber Ltd. 1967-73; Chrmn. Bd., Johnson & Higgins Willis Faber Ltd. 1973-77; Pres., J. & H. Ltd. Bermuda 1977-79; former Pres. Johnson & Higgins Willis Faber Inc.; served with RAF active duty 1939-55, rank Wing Commdr.; rec'd Legion of Honour (France), Croix de Guerre (France), Kt. Sovereign & Mil. Order Malta, Mil. and Hospitaller Order St. Lazarus Jerusalem; R. Catholic; recreations: golf, bridge, skiing; Clubs: Mt. Royal (Montreal); RAF Club (London); Coral Beach and Tennis (Bermuda); Mid-Ocean Club (Bermuda); Home: Marionfield, Warwick, Bermuda; Office: 30 Cedar Ave., P.O. Box 1826, Hamilton 5-24, Bermuda.

STEPHENSON, Thor Eyolfur, M.Sc.; industrialist; b. Winnipeg, Manitoba, 7 Nov. 1919; s. Fredrik and Anna (Olson) S.; e. Pickering Coll., Ont. (Sr. Matric. 1937); Univ. of Toronto, B.A.Sc. (Hons.) 1942; California Inst. of Tech., M.Sc. (Aeronautics) 1946; m. 1stly Aileen Marjory Olson (deceased), 16 Apl. 1943; children: Sigrid Anna, Signy Aileen, Kathryn Thora, Norman Thor; m. 2ndly, Joan Stephanie Jenkins, 11 Jan. 1968; Dir., Eaton's of Canada Ltd.; Jr. Research Engr. to Asst. Dir., Div. of Mech. Engn., Nat. Research Council Can., Ottawa, 1942-52; Asst. Dir. of Aircraft Production, Dept. of Defence Production, Ottawa, 1952-54; Dir. of Aircraft Production, 1954-56; Sales Mgr. of Pratt & Whitney Aircraft of Can. Ltd., 1956-58; apptd. Extve. Vice-Pres. and el. a Dir. 1958; Pres. 1959-75; Chrmn. 1975: Pres., Candn. Aero. Inst. 1956; Dir.; Air Industries Assn. of Can. (Chrmn., 1970-71); Coronation Medal; Phi Delta Theta; Lutheran; Clubs: Mount Royal; St. James's; Home: R.R. 3, Mansonville, Que. J0E 1X0

STEPPLER, Howard Alvey, M.Sc., Ph.D.; university professor; b. Morden, Manitoba, 8 Nov. 1918; s. Alvey Morden and Sophia (Doern) S.; e. Morden Coll. Inst.; Univ. of Manitoba, B.Sc. (Agric.) 1941; McGill Univ., M.Sc. 1948; Iowa State Coll., 1951; McGill Univ., Ph.D. 1955; m. Phyllis, d. H. Parsonage, Burgess Hill, England, 10 May 1945; one s. Glenn; PROF. OF AGRONOMY, and Chrmn. of the Dept., Macdonald Coll.; Lectr., Univ. of Manitoba, 1941-42; Offr. in charge of Forage Work, Dom. Exper. Farm, Brandon, Man., 1948-49; Asst. Prof. of Agron., Macdonald Coll., 1949-51, Assoc. Prof., 1951-57; Prof. since 1957, and Chrmn. of the Dept. 1955-70; Chrmn., Dept. of Plant Sci. 1976-78; Assoc. Dean, Research since 1979; Adviser, Agric., Candn. Internat. Devel. Agency, Ottawa 1970-71; rec'd Nuffield Fellowship, 1955; Sr. Research Fellowship, Internat. Devel. Research Centre 1973-74; served in 2nd World War; joined 1942; served in U.K. and Mediterranean and N.W. Europe with R.C.A., rank Lieut.; discharged with rank of Capt. 1945; Dir., Centro Internac. Agric. Tropical (Cali, Columbia); Trustee, Agric. Dev. Council, N.Y.; Fellow, Agricultural Institute of Canada (President 1964-65); mem., Canadian Soc. of Agron. (Pres. 1957-58); Candn. Seed Growers Assn. Hon. Life mem.; Biometrics Soc.; Agric. Inst. Can. (Que. Dir., 1955-57, Vice-Pres., 1956-57); United Church; recreations: photography, woodworking; Home: Macdonald College P.O., Que.

STERLING, John Ewart Wallace, M.A., Ph.D., D.C.L., LL.D., Litt.D., D.Hu.L.; university chancellor; b. Linwood, Ont. 6 Aug. 1906; s. late Rev. Wm. and Annie (Wallace) S.; e. Ont. Pub. Schs.; Univ. of Toronto, B.A. 1927; Univ. of Alberta, M.A. 1930; Stanford Univ., Ph.D. 1938; LL.D., Pomona 1949, Occidental 1949, San Francisco 1950, Toronto 1950, Brit. Columbia 1958, Northwestern 1958, California 1958, Denver 1961, Loyola 1961, McGill 1961, Columbia 1962, McMaster 1966, Harvard 1968, Alberta 1970; D.C.L., Durham (Eng.) 1953; Litt.D., Caen, (France) 1957; Southn. Cal. 1960; D.Hu.L., St. Mary's 1962, Santa Clara 1963, Mills Coll. 1967, Utah 1968; m. Ann Marie, d. Albert M. Shaver, Ancaster,

Ont., 7 Aug. 1930; children: William Wallace, Susan Hardy, Judith Robinson; CHANCELLOR, STANFORD UNIVERSITY, since Aug. 1968; Dir. (retired), Firemen's Fund Am.; Shell Oil Co.; Kaiser Aluminum and Chemical Corp.; Tridair Corp.; Dean Witter Reynolds; Lectr. in Hist. Regina Coll., Sask., 1927-28; Instr. in Hist., Univ. of Alta., 1928-30; Research Asst., Hoover Institute, Stanford Univ., 1932-37; Instr. in Hist., Stanford Univ., 1935-37; Asst. Prof., Cal. Inst. of Tech., 1937-40; Fellow. Soc. Science Research Council (studied European immigration to Can.), 1939-40; Assoc. Prof. Cal. Inst. of Tech., 1940-42; Secy. of Faculty, 1941-44; Prof. 1942-45; Chrmn. of Faculty, 1944-46; E. S. Harkness Prof. of Hist. and Govt., 1945-48; mem., Resident Civilian Faculty, Nat. War Coll., Washington, D.C., 1947-48; Dir., Huntington Library and Art Gallery, San Marino, Cal., 1948-49; Pres., Stanford Univ., 1949-68; News Analyst, Columbia Broadcasting System, 1942-48; Bd. of Consultants, Nat. War College, Washington, D.C., 1948-52; mem., Comn. of Financing Higher Educ., 1949-52; Vice-Pres., World Affairs Council of N. Cal., 1952 and 1953; Pres., Western Coll. Assn., 1953; mem., Air Univ. Bd. of Visitors, U.S.A.F., 1953; mem., Adv. Bd., Office of Naval Research, 1953; mem. Bd. of Trustees, Thacher Sch., Ojai, Cal., 1954-63; Huntington Library and Art Gallery, San Marino, Cal., 1949-64; Bd. of Visitors, U.S. Naval Acad., 1956-58; Charter mem., Bd. of Dir., Cal. Traffic Safety Foundation, 1956; mem., U.S. Pub. Health Service Nat. Adv. Council on Health Research Facilities, 1956-57; mem., Comte. on Prof. Educ. of Nat. Foundation, 1959-60; mem., U.S. Adv. Comn. on Educ. Exchange, 1960-62; mem., Assn. of Am. Univs. (Pres. 1961-63); mem., Adv. Comte. for Special Awards to Colls. and Univs.; Equitable Life Assurance Soc. of U.S. 1955-72; Trustee, The Asia Foundation, 1958-70; mem., Ford Internat. Fellowship Bd., 1960; mem., Am. Council on Educ.'s Comn. on Educ. and Internat. Affairs, 1960-63; Tulane Univ. Bd. of Visitors 1961-75; mem., Adv. Comte. on Foreign Relations of the U.S., Dept. of State, 1965-68; Chrmn., Comn. on Presidential Scholars, 1965-68; mem., Bd. of Dir., Council for Financial Aid to Educ.; Chrmn., Amer. Revolution Bicentennial Comm. 1969-70 mem., Council on Foreign Relations, Inc.; Publications: Co-ed. of vol. in Hoover Inst. series of publs., 1932-37; Kt. Commdr., Civil Div. of Order of Brit. Empire (by Queen Elizabeth), 1976; Distinguished Citizen Award, Palo Alto Chamber of Comm., 1959; Commdrs. Cross, Order of Merit of Fed. Republic of Germany, 1959; Chev. de la Legion d'Honneur, France, 1960; second Degree of Imp. Order of the Rising Sun, Japan, 1961; awarded Grand Gold Badge of Hon. for Merits to Republic of Austria, May 1965; Herbert Hoover Medal by Stanford Alumnis Assn. 1964; Clark Kerr Award by Acad. Senate, Univ. of Cal., Berkeley; Uncommon Man Award by Stanford Associates 1978; Fellow, Am. Geog. Soc.; mem., Am. Hist. Assn.; Pacific Coast Hist. Assn.; Candn. Inst. of Internat. Affairs; Candn. Hist. Assn.; Candn. Pol. Science Assn.; Protestant; recreation: gardening; Clubs: Commonwealth; Bohemian; Burlingame Country; The Family; University (Palo Alto, San Francisco, New York, Los Angeles); Home: 2220 Stockbridge Ave., Woodside, Cal. 94062; Office: (Box 5096) Stanford, Cal. 94305

STERLING, Thomas Morton, B.A., M.B.A.; brewery executive; b. Calgary, Alta. 30 Aug. 1930; s. John M. and Elfie G. (Thomas) S.; e. Lakefield (Ont.) Coll. Sch. 1949; McGill Univ. 1950; Sorbonne, Univ. of Paris 1951; Bishop's Univ. B.A. 1955; Univ. of W. Ont., M.B.A. 1958; children: Cherylyn, Thomas, Alan, John, Tara; PRES., MOLSON'S WESTERN BREWERIES LTD. 1979- ; Gen. Mgr. Molson's Internat. Sales Div. 1967-69, Vice Pres. Marketing, Molson's Western Breweries Ltd. 1969-72, Pres., Molson Alberta Brewery Ltd. 1972-79; Treasurer, Alta. Chamber Comm.; Chrmn. 4-H Foundation Alberta; P. Conservative; Anglican; recreations: skiing, tennis, Golf, sailing; Clubs: Ranchmen's; Calgary Petroleum; Glencoe; Canyon Meadods Golf & Country; Home: 1031

Prospect Ave. S.W., Calgary, Alta. T2T 0W8; Office: 1040 - 7th Ave. S.W., Calgary, Alta. T2P 3G9.

STERN, Rabbi Harry Joshua, D.D., LL.D., D.Litt.; b. Lithuania, 24 Apr. 1897; s. Morris and Hinda (Markson) S.; e. Pub. Schs., Steubenville, Ohio; Univ. of Cincinnati, B.A. 1920; Hebrew Union Coll., B.H.L. 1919, Rabbi 1922; post-grad. work, Univ. of Chicago, 1926; LL.D. McGill 1938; D.D. Hebrew Union Coll. 1947; D.Litt., Coll. of Steubenville 1970; m. Sylvia Goldstein, 4 July 1937; children: Mrs. H. Stephanie Glaymon, Mrs. Justine A. Bloomfield; Founder of Temple Emanu-El. Inst. on Judaism, 1941, Rabbi Emeritus 1972; el. Secy. of (first) World Jewish Cong., Geneva, 1936; mem., Am. Acad. Pol. & Social Science; Central Conference Am. Rabbis; Union of Am. Hebrew Congs.; Biblical Soc. Can.; Candn. Jewish Cong. (Dom. Extve.); Zionist Organ; Royal Empire Soc.; Life mem., Jewish Chatauqua Soc. of Am.; mem. Legion of Hon., Kiwanis International; Overseer Hebrew Union Coll.-Jewish Inst. of Religion; author of "Jew and Christian," 1927; "Judaism in the War of Ideas;" "The Jewish Spirit Triumphant;" "Martydom And Miracle;" "My Pilgrimage To Israel;" "Europe and Israel Revisited," "Entrusted With Spiritual Leadership", "One World or No World" 1973; and numerous essays and sermon pamphlets; contrib. Ed. to Canadian Jewish Chronicle; Freemason; B'nai B'rith; Phi Lambda Phi; Clubs: Canadian; Kiwanis; recipient B'nai B'rith Humanitarian Award, 1968; Negev Award, Jewish Nat. Fund Can. 1975; named the "Great Montrealer" of the past two decades in the field of religion; recipient, Jobetisky Gold Medal (presented by Menachem Begin, Prime Minister of Israel); Biog. "A Rabbi's Journey", pub. 1981; Office: 4100 Sherbrooke St. W., Montreal, Que. H3Z 1A5

STERN, Max, Ph.D.; art historian; art dealer; b. M. Gladbach, Rhineland, Germany, 18 Apl. 1904; s. Julius and Selma (Heilbron) S.; e. High Sch., Dusseldorf; Bonn Univ., Ph.D. (Hist. of Art; magna cum laude); studied hist. of art. archaeol. and lit. at Univs. of Cologne, Berlin, Vienna and Paris; post-grad. studies in France, Eng. and U.S.; m. late Iris Esther, d. B. O. Westerberg, Malmo, Sweden, 15 Jan. 1946; OWNER, DOMINION GALLERY; entered the Galerie Stern, Dusseldorf, Germany as Mgr. in 1928 (founded by his father and known as one of the leading and largest galleries in Germany; promoted living contemp. artists and dealt in 19th century paintings and old masters); on the death of his father became sole owner in 1934; Founder and Dir. of West's Galleries Ltd. London, Eng. in 1935; on founding of Dom. Gallery, Montreal, in 1942, became Mgr. and Sole Owner (with his wife as Partner) in Jan. 1947; has made important contrib. to the recognition of Candn. painting; among others made the only successful Exhn. of paintings by Emily Carr (1871-1945), during her lifetime and became Agt. for her estate; many of the best contemp. Candn. artists won their reputation through exhns. at his gallery (Archambault; the three Bouchard sisters; Stanley Cosgrove; J. Dallaire, De Tonnancour; Paul. J. Hughes; Henrietta M. May; Goodridge Roberts J.C. de Vilallonga; Lloyd Fitzgerald); specializes in Old Masters; Gov. Montreal Museum of Fine Arts; among others has written articles for the "Thieme Becker Lexikon", a dict. on artists; Clubs: Canadian; Address: 1438 Sherbrooke St. W., Montreal, Que. H3G 1K4

STEVEN, William, B.Sc., Ph.D.; mining executive; b. Glasgow, Scot., 22 Oct. 1917; s. William and Beatrice (Robinson) S.; e. Royal Coll. of Science and Technol., Glasgow, B.Sc. 1939, Ph.D. 1942; m. Margaret Hutchison, 7 July 1940; one s., Gordon Bentley; SR. VICE PRES., CORP. DEVEL. & TECHNOL. AND DIR., INCO LIMITED since 1974; Vice President, International Nickel Co., Inc., N.Y.C.; Metall.; William Jessop & Sons Ltd., Sheffield, Eng., 1942-47; International Nickel Co. (Mond) Ltd., Birmingham, Eng., 1947-59 (Asst. Mgr., Research 1955-57; Mgr., Research 1957-59); trans. to International

Nickel Co., Inc., N.Y.C., 1959, Dir. of Research 1959-62, Mgr., Devel. and Research, 1962-68, Asst. Vice Pres. 1959-66, Vice Pres. 1966; Asst. Vice Pres. of present Co. 1965, Vice-President, Process Technology and Product Development 1968; Vice President, Process Research and Tech. 1969; Sr. Vice President, Corp. Devel. & Tech., 1972; a Gov. Ont. Research Foundation; Fellow, Inst. Metalls. (G. Br.); mem., The Metals Soc. (G. Br.); Am. Soc. Metals; Metall. Soc. of Am. Inst. of Mining; Candn. Inst. Mining & Metall.; Clubs: R.C.Y.C.; The Canadian (New York); University; Home: 78 Forest Grove Dr., Willowdale, Ont. M2K 1Z7; Office: P.O. Box 44, 1 First Canadian Place, Toronto, Ont. M5X 1C4

STEVENS, Charley Herbert, B.Com.; executive; b. Winnipeg, Man. 2 Sept. 1921; s. Albert and Florence (Donnelly) S.; e. Univ. of Sask. B.Com. 1948; B.Com. Advanced Mang. 1966; m. Helen d. late John Koepke 7 Sept. 1946; children: Brian, Charlene; SR. VICE PRES., FINANCE, PanCANADIAN PETROLEUM LTD. since 1976; articled with Rooke Thomas & Co. Regina, Sask. 1948 becoming C.A. 1950; Staff C.A. Clarkson Gordon and Co. Calgary, Alta. 1950-52; Asst. Secy. Treas. Okalta Oils Ltd. 1953-58; Comptroller Canadian Pacific Oil and Gas Ltd. 1958-69; Vice Pres. and Comptroller present Co. 1969-76; Sr. Vice Pres., Finance, PanCanadian Petroleum, 1976-80; served with RCAF 1942-45; mem. Bd. Mang. Grace Hosp.; mem. Financial Extves. Inst.; Inst. C.A.'s Alta.; Inst. C.A.'s Sask.; Protestant; recreations: skiing, golf; Clubs: Ranchmen's; Rotary; Home: 3708 Kerrydale Rd., Calgary, Alta. T3E 4T2; Office: 125 Ninth Ave. S.E., Calgary, Alta.

STEVENS, George Richard, M.A., Ph.D., F.G.S.A.; structural geologist; educator; b. Norfolk, Va. 28 May 1931; s. Glen F. and Maxine Elliott (Hancock) S.; e. Johns Hopkins Univ., A.B. 1951, M.A. 1955, Ph.D. 1960; m. Maeann, d. Oakland Ross Cameron, Findlay, Ohio, Feb. 1952; children: Eric Ross, Laurel Ann, Kirsten Allegra, Astrid Marie; PROF. AND HEAD, DEPT. OF GEOLOGY, ACADIA UNIV. (NOVA SCOTIA) since 1966 and mem. of Univ. Senate; mem. Geol. Dept., Lafayette Coll., Pennsylvania, 1957-66; Visitor, Univ. Bergen, Norway 1973; served with U.S. Army Corps of Engrs. on Active Duty Korean War 1951-53 and Reserve to 1966; rank Capt.; author various prof. papers and consultant reports; mem., Am. Geophys. Union; Am. Assn. Advanc. Science; Fellow, Geol. Soc. America; Geol. Assn. Can.; Sigma Xi; Lutheran; recreation: golf, skiing, antiquarian books, maps; Home: 3 Victoria Ave., Wolfville, N.S. B0P 1X0; Office: Dept. of Geology, Acadian Univ., Wolfville, N.S. B0P 1X0

STEVENS, Hon. Greg Phillip, M.L.A., M.Sc., P. Eng.; politician; b. Toronto, Ont. 24 Nov. 1935; s. Greg and Gladys S.; e. John Franklin Elem. Sch. Toronto; Robert H. Smith Faraday Jr. High Sch. and Isaac Newton High Sch. Winnipeg; Univ. of Man. B.Sc. (Civil Engn.), M.Sc. (City Plng.); m. Patricia Louise d. Thomas and Doris Beeby, Victoria, B.C. 30 Aug. 1958; children: Laura Kim, Thomas Greg, Linda Louise; various City Planning or Town Mang. positions 1962-75; Vice Pres. Alta. Housing Corp. 1975-79; el. M.L.A. for Banff-Cochrane prov. g.e. 1979; served with RCAF 1958-61 Pilot rank Flying Offr.; mem. Assn. Prof. Engrs., Geols & Geophysicists Alta.; P. Conservative; Office: Legislative Bldg., Edmonton, Alta. T5K 2B6.

STEVENS, Homer John; fisherman; union executive; b. Port Guichon, Delta, B.C. 2 Aug. 1923; s. Nicholas Davis and Mary Elizabeth (Sileck) S.; e. Delta (B.C.) Elem. and High Sch.; m. Grace Borchild d. late August Hilland 30 Apl. 1948; children: Ronald Bruce, John Michael, Nicholas Wayne, Barbara Diane; Secy.-Treas. Ladner Local U.F.F.U. 1943-46; Secy. Ladner Fishermen's Co-op Hall 1944; Dir. Un. Fishermen's Co-op Assn. 1945-46, Gen. Organizer 1946-48, Gen. Secy.-Treas. 1948-70, Pres. 1970-

77, Trustee 1977- ; Vice Pres. Fishermen's Co.op Fed. 1945-46; Dir. Delta Credit Union; Gulf & Fraser Fishermen's Credit Union; Ladner Fishermen's Co-op Hall Assn.; fed. and prov. cand. various els.; Govt. Advisor, Law of Sea Conferences in Caracas, 1974, Geneva, 1975, and New York, 1976; Communist; recreations: hunting, fishing, reading, swimming, hockey; Home: 4504 River Rd. W., Port Guichon, Delta, B.C. V4K 1S4; Office: 138 Cordova St. E., Vancouver, B.C.

STEVENS, J. Hugh, B.A., M.A.; manufacturer; b. Chakrata, India, 28 July 1916; s. Col. E. J. Stevens, O.B.E.; e. Cambridge Univ. (Eng.), B.A. (Hons. Mech. Sc.), M.A.; m. Katherine Moulton Guest; CHAIRMAN, CANADA WIRE AND CABLE CO. LIMITED since 1974; Chrmn., Canwirco Inc.; Chrmn., Grandview Indust. Ltd.; Dir.; Noranda Mfg. Ltd.; Industrias Conductores Monterrey, S.A., Monterrey, Mexico; CONELEC S.A., Puebla, Mexico; Fabrica de Alambres Tecnicos, S.A., Bogota, Colombia; Industria de Conductores Electricos C.A., Caracas, Venezuela; Alambres Dominicanos, C. por A, Santo Domingo, Dominican Republic; Tolley Holdings Ltd., Wellington, New Zealand; Sidbec; Sidbec-Dosco; Production Engineer and Supervisor, Research and Devel., Can. Wire & Cable Co. Ltd., 1949; Project Engr., Chief Quality Control Engr. and Chief Plant & Planning Engr. to 1959; apptd. Vice-Pres., Co-ordinating Sales and Engineering 1959, President and Director 1966; commissioned Royal Engrs., 1936, served in 2nd World War with Royal Engineers and R.C.E., served in India, Burma, Malaya, 1943-47; Mentioned in Despatches; retired with rank of Major 1948; mem., Assn. Prof. Engrs. Ont.; Inst. Elect. & Electronics Engrs.; Electrical and Electronic Mfrs. Assn. Can. (Past Pres.); Candn. Electrical Assn. (mem. Extve. Council); Candn. Mfrs. Assn. (Past Pres.; Pres. 1977-78); mem. Economic Council of Can.; Anglican; recreations: golf, sailing; Clubs: University; Toronto; York; Queen's Club; Toronto Golf; Home: 307 Russell Hill Rd., Toronto, Ont. M4V 2T7; Office: 250 Ferrand Dr., Don Mills, Ont. M3C 3J4

STEVENS, Peter Richard; retired manufacturer; b. Toronto, Ont., 8 Aug. 1922; s. Alexander and Charlotte (Tiveron) Stevanato; e. Mimico (Ont.) High Sch.; W. Tech. Sch., Toronto, Ont.; m. Rose Teresa, d. late William Lowe, 23 Sept. 1944; two s., Victor Peter, Anthony Richard; Dir., Thomas Chemicals Ltd.; upon leaving sch. served tool and die apprenticeship at Canadian Acme Screw & Gear Ltd.; purchased Mercury Cycle & Tool, 1949 (name changed to Tonka Corp. (Can.) Ltd. upon purchase of 75% of Co. by Tonka Corp. of Mound, Minn., 1967); Pres., Mgr. and Dir., Tonka Corp. (Can.) Ltd. 1967-79; Pres., Candn. Toy Mfrs. Assn., 1970-72; Past Pres., Tool & Die Mfrs. Assn.; R. Catholic; recreations: hunting, fishing, boating; Home: 18 Ballantyne Court, Islington, Ont. M9A 1W9

STEVENS, Peter Stanley, M.A., Ph.D.; university professor; poet; critic; b. Manchester, Eng., 17 Nov. 1927; s. Stanley Edgar and Elsie (Hill) S.; e. Burnage High Sch., Manchester, 1946; Univ. of Nottingham, B.A. (Eng.), Cert. in Educ., 1951; McMaster Univ., M.A. 1963; Univ. of Sask., Ph.D. 1968; m. June, d. late John Sidebotham, 13 Apl. 1957; children: Gillian, Kirsty, Martin Timothy; Assoc. Prof., Univ. of Windsor, 1969-76; Prof. since 1976; Co-founder and Co-dir., Sesame Press; Teacher, Eng. schs., 1951-57; Hillfield-Strathallan Coll., Hamilton, Ont., 1957-64 (Head of Eng. Dept. 1961-64); Part-time Lectr., McMaster Univ., 1961-64; Lectr. and Asst. Prof., Univ. of Sask., 1964-69; Poetry Ed., Canadian Forum, 1968-73; Ed., The McGill Movement 1969; Co-ed., Forum, 1972; Ed., "The First Day of Spring by Raymond Knister"; author of "Nothing But Spoons", 1969; "A Few Myths", 1971; "Breadcrusts and Glass", 1972; "Family Feelings And Other Poems" 1974; "A Momentary Stay", 1974; "The Dying Sky Like Blood", 1974; "The Bogman Pavese Tactics", 1977 (all poetry), "Modern English-Ca-

nadian Poetry", 1978; "Coming Back", 1981; "Revenge of the Mistresses", 1982; other writings incl. book chapters, articles and reviews in various publs.; regular contributor to "Jazz Radio Canada", (CBC); mem., League Candn. Poets (Prairie Rep. 1968-69; Ont. Rep. 1969-74;) Finalist, Clifford E. Lee Playwriting Competition, 1979; recreations: jazz; canoeing; swimming; Home: 2055 Richmond St., Windsor, Ont. N8Y 1L3

STEVENS, Hon. Sinclair McKnight, P.C., Q.C., M.P., B.A.; b. Esquesing Twp., Ont., 11 Feb. 1927; s. l. Robert Murray and l. Anna Bailey (McKnight) S.; e. Weston (Ont.) Coll. & Vocational Sch.; Oakwood Coll. Inst., Toronto; Univ. of W. Ont., B.A. 1951; Osgoode Hall Law Sch., 1955; m. Noreen Mary, d. Theophil A. Charlebois, 17 May 1958; Partner, Stevens & Stevens; Chmn., York Centre Corp.; Pres., Stevens Securities Ltd.; read law with Fraser & Beatty; called to Bar of Ont. 1955; cr. Q.C. 1971; el. to H. of C. for York-Simcoe in g.e. 1972 1974, 1979, 1980; Apptd. Pres., Treasury Bd., 1979-80; mem., Candn. Bar Assn.; Delta Sigma Phi; Phi Delta Phi; P. Conservative; Protestant; recreations: farming, fishing; Clubs: Albany; Canadian (N.Y.); Home: R.R. 3, King City, Ont. L0G 1K0; Offices: R.R. 3, King City, Ont L0G 1KO and House of Commons, Ottawa, Ont. K1A 0A6 and Ste. 3560-Box 56, Commerce Crt. W., Toronto, Ont. M5L 1B9

STEVENSON, Henry F., B.Arch.; Canadian public servant; b. Winnipeg, Man. 5 Sept. 1911; s. Sydney S. Stevenson; e. Winnipeg schs.; Univ. of Man. B.Arch. 1932; m. Mary R. d. late Dr. Stanley T. Floyd 24 Sept. 1938; children: Cynthia Carsley, Alice Walker, Douglas, Leigh Ann; CHRMN. ENERGY SUPPLIES ALLOCATION BD. CAN. 1980- ; joined Univ. of Toronto 1936-38; Imperial Oil 1938-57 serving as Gen. Operations Mgr.-Marketing and Asst. Gen. Mgr. Marketing; International Petroleum 1957-64, Dir. Marketing/Mfg. Petrochemicals 1957-62, Vice Pres. 1962-64; Standard Oil Co. (N.J.) 1964-71, Depy. Coordinator Europe 1964-65, Chief Extve. Offr. Greece 1965-68, Vice Pres. Esso Europe 1968-71, Pres. Esso Africa 1968-71; Anti-Inflation Bd. Can., Dir. Gen. Prices & Profits 1976-78, Commr. 1978-79; served with U.S. Army Air Force 1942-43, loaned from Imperial Oil; Trustee, Sunnybrook Med. Centre Toronto; mem. Ont. Assn. Archs.; Anglican; recreations: golf, sailing, tennis; Clubs: Lambton Golf & Country; Beaumaris Yacht (Muskoka); Sandy Lane Golf (Barbados); Home: 29 Dunloe Rd., Toronto, Ont. M4V 2W4; Office: 588 Booth St., Ottawa, Ont. K1A 0E4.

STEVENS, (Thomas) Geoffrey (Stewart), B.A.; journalist; b. London, Ont. 30 Jan. 1940; s. Stewart Nicol and Katherine Caroline (Guppy) S.; e. Ryerson Pub. Sch. London, Ont. 1953; Ridley Coll. St. Catharines, Ont. 1958; Univ. of W. Ont. B.A. 1962; NAT. ED., THE GLOBE AND MAIL 1981- ; Reporter, The Globe and Mail, Toronto 1962-65, Ottawa Corr. 1965-68, Queen's Park Bureau Chief Toronto 1969-70, Ottawa Columnist 1973-81, Assoc. Ed. 1975; Ottawa Corr. Time Magazine 1970-73; author "Stanfield" 1973; daily columnist 8 yrs.; Office: 444 Front St. W., Toronto, Ont. M5V 2S9.

STEVENSON, Ian, B.Sc., M.D., C.M.; university professor; b. Montreal, Que., 31 Oct. 1918; s. John Alexander and Ruth Cecilia (Preston) S.; e. Lisgar Coll. Inst., Ottawa, Ont.; Bryanston Sch., Dorset, Eng.; Univ. of St. Andrews, Scotland; McGill Univ., B.Sc. 1941, M.D., C.M. 1943; m. Octavia, d. late Gordon Reynolds, 13 Sept. 1947; CARLSON PROF. OF PSYCHIATRY, UNIV. OF VIRGINIA, SCH. OF MED., since 1967; Interne Royal Victoria Hosp., Montreal, Que., 1944-45; Interne and Resident, St. Joseph's Hosp., Phoenix, Ariz., 1945-46; Fellow in Internal Med., Ochsner Clinic, New Orleans, La., 1946-47; Commonwealth Fellow in Med., Cornell Univ. Med. Coll. 1947-49; Asst. Prof. of Med. and Psychiatry, Louisiana State Univ., 1949-52; Assoc. Prof. 1952-57;

Prof. of Neurol. & Psychiatry, Univ. of Virginia and Chrmn. of Dept. 1957-67; Fellow, Am. Psychiatric Assn.; Am. Soc. for Psychical Research; Am. Psychosomatic Soc.; author of "Medical History-Taking", 1960; "Twenty Cases Suggestive of Reincarnation", 1966, 2nd ed. rev. 1974; "The Psychiatric Examination", 1969; "Telepathic Impressions", 1970; "The Diagnostic Interview" 1971; "Xenoglossy", 1974; "Cases of the Reincarnation Type, Vol. 1 Ten Cases in India", 1975, "Vol. 2 Ten Cases in Sri Lanka", 1977; Vol. 3 "Twelve Cases in Lebanon and Turkey" 1980; recreations: writing, travel, music; Home: Wintergreen, Old Lynchburg Road, Charlottesville, Virginia, 22901.

STEVENSON, John Daniel, Q.C.; b. Cobalt, Ont. 26 March 1929; s. late Carl Stanton and Norma (Cassidy) S.; e. Upper Canada Coll. and Faculty of Law, Univ. of Toronto, B.A., LL.B., m. Joan Elaine d. late Rev. A.P. Gilles, 26 Sept. 1959; one s. John Gillies; two d. Norma Louise, Sarah Joan; read law with late K.B. Palmer, Q.C. 1953; called to Bar of Ont. 1955; cr. Q.C. 1969; PARTNER, SMITH, LYONS, TORRANCE, STEVENSON & MAYER; Dir.; American Express Can. Inc.; Pierson Stéamships Ltd.; Wittington Investments Ltd.; Can. Trust Co.; Fireman's Fund Ins. Co. of Can.; Hayes-Dana Ltd.; George Weston Ltd., Black Clawson Kennedy Ltd.; St. Anne-Nackawic Pulp & Paper Co. Ltd.; Gov. Upper Can. Coll; mem., Cdn. Bar Assn.; Cdn. Tax Fdn.; Anglican; recreations: golf, skiing; Clubs: Toronto; Toronto Golf; Osler Bluff Ski; Royal Canadian Yacht; Home: 166 Forest Hill Rd., Toronto, Ont. M5P 2M9; Office: P.O. Box 420, 2 First Canadian Place, Toronto, Ont. M5X 1E3

STEVENSON, John S., B.A., B.A.Sc., Ph.D., F.G.S.A., F.M.S.A., F.R.S.C.; university professor, consulting geologist; b. New Westminster, B.C., 21 Sept. 1908; s. Benjamin and Emelia Matilda (Johnston) S.; e. Univ. of Brit. Columbia, B.A. 1929, B.A.Sc. 1930; Mass. Inst. of Tech., Ph.D. 1934; m. Louise Francis, d. Edwin B. Stevens, Seattle, Wash., 26 Jan. 1935; children: John Stevens, Robert Francis; CONSULTING GEOLOGIST, since 1977; Dawson Prof. Geol., McGill Univ., 1972-77 (Prof. Mineralogy there 1961, and Chairman, Dept. Geol. Sciences 1966-68); Prof. of Geol., McGill Univ. 1981-82; Consulting Geologist, International Nickel Co. of Canada, Limited, since 1965; Instr. and Asst. in Geol. and Mineral., Mass. Inst. of Tech., 1931-34; with Geol. Survey of Can. as Field Asst., 1927-31, and Asst. Geol., 1932; Engr. in Charge, Longacre Longlac Gold Mines, Ont., 1934-35; Asst. Resident Mining Engr. 1935-36; Associate 1936-41 and Mining Engr. 1941-50 for B.C. Dept. of Mines; Assoc. Prof. of Mineral., McGill Univ., 1950-61; Consultant, Sudbury Basin Research Project, Internat. Nickel Co. of Can. Ltd., since 1952; Specialist in Strategic Materials engaged in war minerals investigations for B.C. Govt., 1939-45; Candn. Fellow, Guggenheim Mem. Foundation, 1947-48; mem., Soc. of Econ. Geol.; Candn. Inst. of Mining & Metall. (Chrmn., Victoria, B.C.; Sec. 1949-50; Councillor, 1950); Royal Candn. Astron. Soc. (Pres. Victoria Centre, 1950); Mineral. Soc. of Am.; Mineral. Soc. (London); Assn. Prof. Engrs. of B.C.; mem., Mineral. Assn. Can. (Pres., 1958, '59 and '60); Fellow, Geol. Assn. Can.; Fellow, Royal Soc. of Can.; Sigma Xi (McGill Chapter, Pres. 1967, Treas. since 1974); United Church; Clubs: Hudson Yacht; Whitlock Golf and Country; Home: 448 Ridge Road, Hudson Heights, Que. J0P 1J0

STEVENSON, Lloyd Grenfell, M.D., Ph.D., author; physician; university professor; b. London, Ont., e. Univ. of Western Ont., B.A., M.D.; Johns Hopkins Univ., Ph.D. (Markle Scholarship in Med. Science, 1950-55); began teaching as Asst. Prof., Univ. of W. Ont.; Assoc. Prof., Hist. of Med., 1954; Dean, Faculty of Med. and Prof. of Hist. of Med.; McGill Univ., 1956-63; Prof. of Hist. of Med. , Dept. of Hist. of Science & Med., Yale Univ. 1963-68; apptd. William H. Welch Prof. of Hist. of

Med. and Dir., Inst. of Hist. of Med., Johns Hopkins Univ., 1968; served in World War with C.A.M.C. as Capt.; author of "Sir Frederick Banting", 1946; "Nobel Prize Winners in Medicine and Physiology", 1953; "The Meaning of Poison", 1959; Home: 11 Wendover Rd.; Baltimore Md. 21218; Office: Johns Hopkins University, Inst. of the History of Medicine, 1900 East Monument St., Baltimore, Md., 21205.

STEVENSON, Hon. Ronald Charles, B.A., LL.B.; judge; b. Fredericton, N.B., 20 Dec. 1929; s. late Osley Vernon and Verna May (Burtt) S.; e. Univ. of N.B., B.A. 1951; Dalhousie Univ., LL.B. 1953; m. Barbara Elizabeth, d. late Dr. J. A. M. Bell, Fredericton, N.B., 20 July 1957; three d., Barbara Christie, Nancy Verna, Sarah Elizabeth; JUSTICE, COURT OF QUEEN'S BENCH OF N.B. since 1979; read law with F. D. Tweedie, Q.C.; called to Bar of N.B. 1953; cr. Q.C. 1972; Justice, Queen's Bench Div., Supreme Crt. of N.B., 1972-79; Home: 260 King's College Rd., Fredericton, N.B. E3B 2E8; Office: Supreme Court Chambers, Justice Bldg., P.O. Box 6000, Fredericton, N.B. E3B 5H1

STEVENSON, William; company executive; b. Belfast, N. Ireland, 14 Nov. 1920; s. Henry and Elizabeth (McMullen) S.; came to Canada 1953; e. Pub. Sch., Belfast, N. Ireland; Coll. of Accts., Glasgow, Scotland, Grad. 1948; m. Jean, d. William Larmour, June 1942; children: Elizabeth Norma, Jennifer Doris, William Larmour; PRESIDENT, MILLBROOK INDUSTRIES LTD. since 1971; Pres. and Dir., Esperar Investments Ltd.; Dir., Benson & Hedges (Canada) Ltd.; with R. R. Brown Printing Co., Belfast, N. Ireland 1948; Mgr., Murphy-Stevenson Co. Ltd., 1950-53; Division Mgr., Candn. Cottons Ltd., 1953-60; Asst. to the Vice-Pres., Can. Wire & Cable Co. Ltd., 1960; Asst. to the Pres., 1961; Vice-Pres., Mfg. and Finance, 1963; Vice-Pres. and Dir., Noranda Mfg. Ltd. 1966; served in 2nd World War with R.A.F., 1941-46; United Church; recreation: golf; Clubs: York Downs; Granite; Home: 51 Coldstream Ave., Toronto, Ont. M5N 1X7; Office: Millbrook, Ont. L0A 1G0

STEVENSON, Hon. William Alexander, B.A., LL.B.; judge; b. Edmonton, Alta. 7 May 1934; s. Alexander Lindsay and Eileen Harriet (Burns) S.; e. Eastwood Sch. Edmonton 1952; Univ. of Alta. B.A. 1956, LL.B. 1957; m. Patricia Ann d. Roland Stevenson, Tadworth, Surrey, U.K. 15 July 1961; children: Catherine, Kevin, Vivian, Jamie; JUDGE, COURT OF APPEAL OF ALTA. since 1980; Judge, Court of Appeal of N.W. Territories since 1980; called to Bar of Alta. 1958; private law practice 1958 — 68, 1970 — 75; Prof. of Law, Univ. of Alta. 1968 — 70, Sessional Lectr. in Law 1963 — 68 and since 1970; apptd. Judge 1975; Depy. Judge, Supreme Courts of N.W.T. and Yukon Territory; Judge, Court of Queen's Bench Alta 1979-80; Dir., Legal Educ. Soc. Alta.; Candn. Inst. Adm. Justice; mem. Candn. Bar Assn.; Candn. Assn. Law Teachers; Anglican; Home: 6312 — 132 St., Edmonton, Alta. T6H 3Y7; Office: Law Courts, Edmonton, Alta. T5J 0R2.

STEWARD, David John, M.B., B.S., F.R.C.P.(C); anaesthesiologist; b. Luton, Eng. 2 Feb. 1934; s. William John and Kathleen (Waterhouse) S.; e. Luton Grammar Sch. 1952; Univ. of London M.B., B.S. 1958; L.R.C.P., M.R.C.S. (Eng) 1958; D.A. (Lond) 1962; Univ. of Toronto 1964-68; F.R.C.P.(C) 1968; Dipl. Anaes. 1968; m. Mary Alexandra Traquair 1 Nov. 1958; children: Jennifer Alexandra (d. 1962), Nigel Robert John; ANAESTHETIST IN CHIEF, THE HOSP. FOR SICK CHILDREN 1971- ; Prof. of Anaesthesia Univ. of Toronto 1975- ; joined Anaesthesia staff present Hosp. 1968; served with RCAF 1960-64 as Med. Offr., rank Flight Lt.; author "Manual of Paediatric Anaesthesia" 1979; ed., "Some Aspects of Psychiatric Anaesthesia", 1981; several book chapters and over 45 articles gen. anaesthesia and paediatric anaesthesia; mem. Malignant Hyperthermia Assn. (Adv. Comte.); Candn.

Med. Assn.; Ont. Med. Assn.; Candn. Anaesthetists Soc. (Past Chrmn. Scient. Comte.); Am. Soc. Anaesthesiols.; Medico Legal Soc. Toronto; Assn. Candn. Univ. Depts. Anaesthesia (Chrmn. Scient. Comte.); Methodist; recreations: photography, collecting antique cameras, sailing; Clubs: Royal Candn. Mil. Inst.; Whitby Yacht; Home: 33 Himount Dr., Willowdale, Ont. M2K 1X3; Office: 555 University Ave., Toronto, Ont. M5G 1X8.

STEWART, Alec Thompson, M.Sc., Ph.D., F.R.S.C., F.A.P.S.; educator; b. Windthorst, Sask., 18 June 1925; s. Arthur and Nelly Blye (Thompson) S.; e. Dalhousie Univ., B.Sc. 1946, M.Sc. 1949; Univ. of Cambridge, Ph.D. 1952; m. Alta Ailene Kennedy, 4 Aug. 1960; children: A. James Kennedy, Hugh Donal, Duncan Roney; PROFESSOR OF PHYSICS, QUEEN'S UNIV. since 1968 (Head of Dept. 1968-74); joined Atomic Energy of Can. Ltd. 1952; Assoc. Prof. Dalhousie Univ., 1957; Assoc. Prof. and Prof., Univ. of N.C., Chapel Hill, 1960-68; author, "Perpetual Motion", 1965; co-ed., "Position Annihilation", 1967; other writings incl. over 70 scient. articles in prof. journs.; mem., Candn. Assn. Physicists (Pres. 1972-73); Office: Kingston, Ont.

STEWART, Andrew, B.S.A., M.A., LL.D., D.Sc. Econ., F.A.I.C., F.R.S.C. (1958); b. Edinburgh, Scotland, 17 Jan. 1904; s. Andrew and Marcia Sabina (Sprot) S.; e. East of Scotland Coll. of Agric., C.D.A. 1924; Univ. of Manitoba, B.S.A. 1931, M.A. 1932; Univ. of Edinburgh, 1933-35; Laval Univ., D.Sc. Econ., 1952; LL.D. Univs. of Manitoba 1951, Melbourne 1955, New Brunswick 1955; m. Jessie Christobel, d. R. A. Borland, Winnipeg, 18 Sept. 1931; children: Robert Andrew, Ian, William, Sabina, Janet, Patrick; former President, Univ. of Alberta; and former Chrmn. of Bd. of Broadcast Govs.; with Univ. of Man. as Lect. in Agric., Econ., 1931-33; Lect. in Pol. Econ., Univ. of Alta., 1935; subsequently apptd. Asst. Prof., Prof. and Head, Dept. of Pol. Econ., Dir.-Gen. of Comm. and Dean of Business Affairs; former mem., Candn. Council on Nutrition; Royal Comm. on Natural Gas (Alta.); apptd. mem. of Roy. Comn. on Canada's Econ. Prospects, 1955; Chrmn., Royal Comn., Price Spreads in Food Products, 1957; Pres., Nat. Conf. on Candn. Univs., 1958; Chrmn., Assn. of Univs. of the Brit. Commonwealth, 1958; mem., Edmonton Pub. Sch. Bd., 1946; mem., Candn. Pol. Science Assn.; Candn. Soc. of Agric. Econs.; Appraisal Inst. of Can.; Fellow, Agric. Inst. of Can.; Chrmn., Candn. Service for Overseas Students and Trainees; United Church. Home: 10435 Allbay Rd., Sidney B.C. V8L 2M8

STEWART, Charles Bruce, retired company president; b. Seaforth, Ont., 9 Oct. 1911; s. late Harry and Mary Matilda (Fitzgerald) S.; e. Seaforth (Ont.) Coll. Inst.; m. Mary Ellen, d. late John O'Brien, Waterford, Ireland, 21 July 1937; children: David Bruce, Brian Edward, Heather Jean; m. 2nd, Katherine Jean Mackay, d. late Rev. A.A. Macleod; Dir., Simpsons, Ltd.; Canada Permanent Trust Co.; Canada Permanent Mortgage Corporation; joined father's retail business, Stewart Bros., Seaforth, Ont., 1929-36; joined The Robert Simpson Co. Ltd. 1936; apptd. Asst. to Gen. Mgr. The Robert Simpson Montreal Limited, 1946; Gen. Mgr., The Robert Simpson Eastern Ltd., Halifax, 1951; European Mgr., The Robert Simpson Co. Ltd., London, Eng., 1954; Gen. Mgr., Toronto, 1960; Vice Pres., Toronto Area, 1964; el. Dir., Simpsons, Ltd. 1961; Executive Vice President, Stores, 1969; Pres. 1970-77 (ret.); Director, The Wellesley Hospital; Presbyterian; Clubs: The Toronto; R.N.S.Y.S.; York; Toronto Hunt; Home: 38 Ardwold Gate, Toronto, Ont. M5R 2W2

STEWART, Chester B., O.C. (1972), C.D., M.D., C.M., Dr. P.H., LL.D., D.Sc., F.R.C.P.(C), F.A.P.H.A.; b. Norboro, P.E.I., 17 Dec. 1910; s. Hugh Alexander and Lucy Ann (Bryant) S.; e. Pub. Sch., Norboro, P.E.I.; Prince of Wales Coll., Charlottetown, P.E.I.; Dalhousie Univ., B.Sc. 1936, M.D., C.M. 1938; Johns Hopkins Univ., M.P.H. 1946, Dr.P.H. 1953; Cert. in Pub. Health, R.C.P.

& S. 1951; Hon. LL.D., Univ. P.E.I., 1971; Dalhousie Univ., 1979; Hon. D.Sc., St. Francis Xavier 1977; m. Kathleen, d. late William French, 20 Apl. 1942; two d., Joan Kathleen (Mrs. Lionel Teed), Moira Anne (Mrs. Thomas Freeman); Assistant Secretary, Assoc. Committee on Medical Research, Nat. Research Council, 1938-40; Prof. of Epidemiology, Dalhousie Univ., 1946-54; Dean of Med. 1954-71; Vice Pres. (Health Sciences) 1971-76; retired but active as consult. and in med. research; served with RCAF Med. Br., 1940-45; RCAF Reserve to 1962; rank Wing Commander; mem., Izaak Walton Killam Hosp. for Children, Halifax; Vice-Pres., Dalhousie Alumni Assn., mem. Bd. of Gov., Dalhousie Univ. (1981); Mt. St. Vincent Univ. (1981); author of numerous articles on aviation med., epidemiology and med. educ.; Pres., Assn. Candn. Med. Colls., 1962-64; mem. Council, Candn. Med. Assn.; Candn. Pub. Health Assn. (President 1968); hon. mem., Cdn. Coll. of Family Physicians (1978); Presbyterian; recreation: med. history; gardening; Clubs: Rotary; Saraguay; Home: 6008 Oakland Road, Halifax, N.S. B3H 1N8

STEWART, Clair C.; industrial designer; b. Kenton, Man., 20 May 1910; s. Rev. Dr. Rupert and Lena (Johnson) S.; e. Pub. Sch., Man.; High Sch., Belleville, Ont.; Ont. Coll. of Art (Grad.); m. Amy, d. J. S. McLean, Toronto, Ont., 7 Sept. 1927; children: Michael, Timothy, John, James, Mary, Andrew; CHAIRMAN, STEWART & MORRISON LTD.; furthered art educ. in Europe, chiefly in Eng., 1932-36; returned to Toronto and engaged in graphic arts 1937-40; joined Rolph-Clark-Stone Ltd., Toronto, Ont., in Creative Dept., 1946; apptd. Creative Dir. 1948; el. a Dir., 1952; formed own firm of Stewart Morrison Ltd., Industrial Engrs., 1960: served in 2nd World War with R.C.A.F.; mem., Roy. Cdn. Academy of Arts; Protestant; recreations: golf, boating, farming; Clubs: Toronto Hunt; Albany; York; Arts & Letters; Home: Highfield, RR1, Caledon E., Ont. LON 1EO; Office: Suite 703, 1300 Yonge St., Toronto, Ont. M4T 1X3

STEWART, David Macdonald, C.M., C.St.J., K.L.J., F.R.S.A., F.H.S.(C), Hon. LL.D. (Acadia); Hon. D.B.A. (McGill), (Moncton); executive; b. Montreal, Que., 16 Sept. 1920; s. Walter Moncrief and May Beatrice Harvey (Sharp) S.; e. Ashbury Coll., Ottawa, Ont.; McGill Univ.; m. Liliane, d. late Albert Spengler, 30 Sept. 1967; four d. and one s. by 1st marriage; one d. by 2nd marriage; DIRECTOR, R.J.R. MACDONALD INC.; President Macdonald Stewart Foundation; Director, Hôtel Dieu Hospital; Life Gov., Chateau Ramezay, Antiq. & Numis. Soc.; Hon. Col., Queen's York Rangers (1st Am. Regt.); Anglican; Clubs: Mount Royal; St. James's; Forest & Stream; Roy. Candn. Mil. Inst. (Toronto); St. Denis; Home: Le Cartier, 1115 Sherbrooke St. W., Montreal, Que. H3A 1H3; Office: 1155 Sherbrooke St. W., Montreal, Que. H3A 2N3

STEWART, Donald Campbell, A.C.R.A.; sculptor; b. Hamilton, Ont. 22 Nov. 1912; s. Joel Williams and Robina (Paterson) S.; e. Westdale Secondary Schs. and Normal Sch., Hamilton, Ont.; McMaster Univ., 1933; Ont. Coll. of Art, Grad. in Sculpture 1937 (Lieut.-Gov's. Medal); m. Anna, d. Rev. A. E. Marshall , 7 September, 1948; divorced 1953; two s. Gordon, Blair; m. 2ndly, Senta, d. Mrs. Anna Pedako; established studio workshop, Toronto, Ontario, 1937; has exhibited sculpture in chief Canadian cities, also New York, Syracuse, Rochester, Minnesota, Boston, Paris; among chief commissions are work for R. S. McLaughlin, Oshawa, Ont., Beck & Eadie (archs.), and Marani & Morris (archs.), Toronto, Ont., Strand Theatre, Kirkland Lake, Ont., Seneca Theatre, Niagara Falls, Ont., coat-of-arms for City Hall, Toronto, Ont., upon occasion of Royal Visit, panels for Bank of Montreal bldg., Toronto, Ont.; Alexander MacKenzie Monument, Fort St. John, B.C.; 1958; Instr. in Three-Dimensional Design, Design Sch., Ont. Coll. of Art, Toronto, Ont., 1945-53; Inst. in Sculpture, Vancouver Sch. of

Art, since 1955 and apptd. Vice-Principal there 1962, Dean 1971, retired 1977; Pres. Fed. of Candn. Artists, B.C. Region, 1957-59; mem., Ont. Sov. of Artists; Candn. Soc. of Graphic Arts; Sculptors' Soc. of Can. (Pres. 1947); Candn. Authors Assn.; Pres. N.W. Inst. of Sculpture, 1961; Hon. Fellow, Oriental Arts Inst. of Hong Kong 1965; has publ. poems in "Contemporary Verse", "Candn. Poetry Mag.", "Candn. Forum", "Parnassus", "New Statement", since 1935; Address: 967 Roslyn Blvd., North Vancouver, B.C. V7G 1P4

STEWART, Donald Henry; real estate executive; b. Montreal, Que., 5 March 1925; s. late Henry John and Irene (Molson) S.; e. Roslyn Elem. and Westmount Sr. High Schs., Montreal; Sir George Williams Univ.; m. Elizabeth Jane, d. late Kendall Lucas, K.C., Toronto, Ont., 3 Oct. 1953; children: James Kendall, Alison Jane; ASSOC. BROKER, A.E. LePAGE COMMERCIAL REALTY CO., 1980- ; Actuarial Asst., Standard Life Assurance Co., Montreal, 1947; Mortgage Mgr., Montreal Trust Co., Montreal 1953; Pres. and Chrmn., Morguard Trust Company, 1966; Vice Pres., Edgecombe investment Services Ltd., 1975-80; served with Candn. Army during World War II; rank Lt.; Past Gov., Mortgage Bankers Assn. Am.; Am. Inst. Real Estate Appraisers; mem. Appraisal Inst. Can.; Soc. Real Estate Appraisers; Am. Soc. Real Estate Counselors; Liberal; Presbyterian; recreation: skiing; Clubs: Montreal Badminton & Squash; Artillery Offrs. Assn. Montreal; Home: 20 Driveway, Ottawa, Ont. K2P 1C8 Office: Suite 1158, 99 Bank St., Ottawa, Ont. K1P 5A3

STEWART, Edward Emslie, M.A., Ed.D.; civil servant; b. Montreal, Que., 11 Sept. 1930; s. Hector Emslie and Alyce Mary (Matthew) S.; e. London (Ont.) Normal Sch.; Univ. of W. Ont., B.A. 1953; Univ. of Michigan, M.A. 1956; Univ. of Toronto, Ed. D. 1969; m. Victoria Elizabeth, d. Charles P. Lavis, Windsor, Ont., 24 Aug. 1956; DEPUTY MINISTER TO THE PREMIER, ONT. since 1974; assumed additional duties as Secy. of Cabinet 1976 and Clerk of Extve. Council 1977; taught in Pub. Schs., Windsor, Ont., 1949-56; on staff of Toronto and Lakeshore Teachers' Colleges, 1956-60; Asst. Supt., Prof. Devel. Br., Ont. Dept. of Educ., 1960-62, Asst. Supt., Curriculum Br., 1963-64; Asst. Depy. Min., Dept. of Univ. Affairs, 1964-67, Depy. Min. 1967-71; Depy. Min. Educ. 1971-73; Phi Delta Kappa; Club: Arts and Letters; Home: 8 Sunnylea Ave. W., Toronto, Ont. M8Y 2J7; Office: Legislative Bldg., Queens Park, Toronto, Ont. M7A 1A1

STEWART, Freeman Kenneth, M.A., M.Ed., LL.D.; educator; b. Stellarton, N.S., 23 May 1913; s. Margaret Belle (Matheson) and late Leonard Charles C.; e. Dalhousie Univ., B.A. 1934; Oxford Univ., B.A. 1937; M.A. 1941; Univ. of Toronto, M.Ed. 1956; Univ. of Alta., LL.D. 1962; m. Thelma Gwendolean, d. late Boyd Langille, 20 Aug. 1939; one d. Diane Elizabeth; Adviser to Atlantic Inst. of Educ.; Consultant to Min. (prov. study on adult educ. 1979-80); Sch. Teacher and Principal in N.S. 1937-41; R.C.A.F. 1941-44; Supt. Candn. Legion Educ. Services, 1944-45; Dir. there, 1945-46; with Candn. Internat. Paper Co., Montreal, 1946-47; Extve. Secy., Candn. Educ. Assn., 1947-77; mem. of various govt. dels. to educ. confs., Geneva, Montevideo, New Delhi, Lagos, Canberra; (leave of absence) Dir., Commonwealth Educ., Liaison Unit, London, Eng., 1963-66, and Secy.-Gen., 3rd Commonwealth Educ. Conf. 1964; author of "Interprovincial Co-operation in Education"; and "The Canadian Education Association, 1957-77"; also numerous articles in prof. journs.; Hon. Life mem., Candn. Assn. for Adult Educ.; Cdn. Educ. Assn.; Cleveland Conf.; Pres., Candn. Foundation for Econ. Educ. 1974-76; United Church; recreations: fishing, golf; Home: Tatamagouche, N.S. B0K 1V0

STEWART, George Calvert, B.A.; ret. investment dealer; b. Toronto, Ont., 27 Feb. 1915; s. late George Shipley and

Anna Christena (Calvert) S.; e. Univ. of Toronto Schs.; Univ. of Toronto, B.A. (Hon.) Pol. Science and Econ., 1937; m. Shirley Pauline, d. Philip T. Lewis, Toronto, Ont., 19 June 1952; children: Susan Noreen, Jane Christena, George Lewis; joined Royal Securities Corp. Limited in 1937; apptd. Mgr. of Toronto Office, 1953, Vice-Pres. 1960, Extve. Vice-Pres. 1969; Pres., Merrill Lynch, Royal Securities Ltd. 1974; el. a mem., Toronto Stock Exchange, 1955; el. a Dir. of Royal Securities Corp. Ltd., Nov. 1955; Vice-Chmn., Merrill Lynch, Royal Securities Ltd. 1978; Vice-Pres. and Dir., Aatco Travel Service (Richmond Street Ltd.) 1978-81; served in 2nd World War; Capt. with Toronto Scottish Regt. overseas (U.K., N.W. Europe) 1940-45; Group Chrmn., Candn. Comte. Investment Bankers Assn. 1969, 71; Gov., Investment Bankers Association 1972; Dir. and Chmn., Investment Comte., Ont. Heart Found.; Theta Delta Chi; Anglican; recreations: golf, sailing, fishing; Clubs: Lambton Golf; Muskoka Lake Golf & Country; Home and Office; 3 Woodmere Court, Islington, Ont. M9A 3J1

STEWART, Harold Brown, M.D., Ph.D.; educator; b. Chatham, Ont., 9 March 1921; s. John Craig and Margaret Gertrude (Brown) S.; e. McKeough Pub. Sch. and Chatham (Ont.) Coll. Inst., 1938; Univ. of Toronto, M.D. 1944, Ph.D. 1950; Univ. of Cambridge, Ph.D. 1955; m. A. Pauline, d. Victor A. Blake, Toronto, Ont., 14 Oct. 1950; one d. Ann Margaret; PROF. OF BIOCHEM., UNIV. OF WESTERN ONT. and Dean, Faculty of Grad. Studies there since 1972; Intern, Toronto W. Hosp., 1944-45; Fellow in Biochem., Univ. of Toronto, 1946; NRC post-doctoral Med. Fellow 1947; Merck post-doctoral Fellow (NRC), Univ. of Cambridge, 1950; Elmore Fellow 1952-53; Med. Research Council Fellow (UK) 1953-55 and Visiting Scient. Dept. of Biochem. 1971-72; joined present univ. as Assoc. Prof. of Biochem. 1955-60; Prof. since 1960; Head of Dept. 1965-72; rec'd Starr Medal, Univ. of Toronto, 1950; served with RCAMC (Student) 1944-45; RCN Surg. 1945-46; rank Lt. Commdr.; author of numerous scient. papers; mem., Candn. Soc. Study Higher Educ.; Biochem. Soc.; Candn. Biochem. Soc.; Candn. Physiol. Soc.; Am.Soc. Biol. Chems.; Alpha Omega Alpha; recreation: gardening; Home: 118 Baseline Rd. E., London, Ont. N6C 2N8

STEWART, Ian Affleck, M.A., Ph.D.; Canadian public servant; b. Toronto, Ont. 6 Aug. 1931; e. Queen's Univ. B.A. 1953, M.A. 1954; Oxford Univ. (Rhodes Scholar) 1954-56; Cornell Univ. Ph.D. 1966; DEPY. MIN. OF FINANCE, CAN. 1980- ; Dir. Atomic Energy of Canada Ltd.; Export Development Corp.; Canada Development Corp.; Petro-Canada Ltd.; Lectr. in Econ. and Asst. Dir. of Banking Courses Queen's Univ. 1956-59; Instr. in Econ. and Asst. Prof. Dartmouth Coll. Hanover, N.H. 1962-66; Research Adviser, Depy. Chief Research Dept. and Assoc. Chief, Bank of Canada 1966-72; Special Adviser Treasury Bd. Secretariat 1972-73; Sr. Econ. Adviser Dept. of Energy, Mines & Resources 1973-75; Asst. Secy. to Cabinet (Econ. Policy) and Econ. Adviser to Privy Council Office 1975-79; Dpy. Min. of Energy, Mines & Resources 1979-80; recipient Reuben Wells Leonard Fellowship Queen's Univ.; Can. Council Grad. Fellowship; Cornell Univ. Grad. Fellowship; Woodrow Wilson Grad. Fellowship; Phi Beta Kappa; Fels Foundation Thesis Fellowship; Ford Foundation Thesis Fellowship; author or co-author various publs.; mem. Candn. Econ. Soc.; Office: Place Bell Canada, Ottawa, Ont. K1A 0G5.

STEWART, Lieut.-Col. J. David, D.S.O., E.D., C.D.; b. Georgetown, P.E.I., 21 August, 1910; s. late James David (Premier of P.E.I., 1923-27 and 1931-33) and Barbara (Westaway) S.; e. West Kent Sch., Charlottetown, P.E.I.; m. Constance Creelman, d. Senator Creelman MacArthur, 16 March 1935; children: (Judith Beattie) Mrs. Mitchell MacLean (Barbara Lois) Mrs. Walter Wolf, (Heather Marion) Mrs. Douglas Ross, Patricia Jane (Mrs. Peter Merrill); President, Northumberland Ferries Limited;

Chmn., Georgetown Shipyards Ltd.; mem. Advisory Board, Canada Permanent Trust Company; served in N.P.A.M. 1928-39; went overseas as Major with North N.S. Highlanders of Can.; Commanded The Argyll & Sutherland Highlanders of Can., N.W. Europe; D.S.O., E.D.; Mentioned in Despatches; Councillor, City of Charlottetown, 1946-51, Mayor 1951-58; el. to Prov. Leg. for 5th Queens, 1959; Prov. Secy., Min. of Tourist Devel. and Min. of Mun. Affairs, 1939 till resignation from Cabinet 1965; Pres., Candn. Fed. of Mayors & Municipalities, 1955-56; Conservative; Presbyterian; recreations: gardening, golf, curling; Clubs: The Charlottetown; The Green Gables Golf; United Services; Home: 12 Crestwood Drive, Charlottetown, P.E.I. C1A 3H3

STEWART, James C. F.; b. Glasgow, Scot., 7 July 1911; s. William and Elizabeth (Rae) S.; e. Dollar Acad., Scot., grad. 1927; trained Glasgow, Scot., deepsea ship broking and chartering, A.I.C.S. Cert. 1929; Tug boat Master's Cert. Can., 1935; Advanced Mang. Cert., Banff, 1956; m. Wyldene, d. William James Mason, 1935; one s. Robert Carlile; CONSULTANT, J: W: STEWART LTD. joined Vancouver Tug Boat Co. Ltd. 1931; advanced through all main phases of the operations of this Co., on merger of Island Tug & Barge Ltd. and Vancouver Tug Boat Co. became Pres., Seaspan Internat. Ltd. 1971-77; mem., Vancouver Bd. Trade; Register Candn. Comte.; recreations: golf, fishing; Clubs: Vancouver; Shaughnessy Golf; Plimsoll (Vancouver); Home: 1708 Western Parkway, Vancouver, B.C. V6T 1V3

STEWART, James F. C., B.Com., M.B.A.; financial executive; e. Univ. of Ottawa B.Com.; McMaster Univ. M.B.A.; PRESIDENT, CHIEF EXTVE. OFFR. AND DIR., TRIARCH CORP. LTD.; Pres. and Chief Extve. Offr. Canadian Venture Capital Corp.; Dir.; Dir. Bakelite Thermosets Ltd.; Triarch Debt Capital Ltd.; Westmills Carpets Ltd.; Alcohol Countermeasure Systems Inc.; Midland Auto Radiator Manufacturing Ltd.; Blue Mountain Pottery Ltd.; Euless Aero Components Inc.; served as Invest. Offr. RoyNat Ltd.; Portfolio Mgr. TD Capital Group, Toronto Dominion Bank; Vice Pres. Triarch Corp. Ltd.; Home: 1578 Old Spar Court, Mississauga, Ont. L5J 1B3.

STEWART, John B., M.A., Ph.D.; b. Antigonish, N.S. 19 Nov. 1924; s. George Harvie and Mary Elizabeth S.; e. Acadia Univ. B.A. (Hons.) 1945, M.A. 1946; Columbia Univ. Ph.D. 1953; unm.; Instr., Acadia Univ. 1945-47; Columbia Univ. 1950-53; Asst. Prof., Barnard College (Columbia Univ.) 1953-59; Consultant, The Rockefeller Foundation, 1953-55 and 1961; Assoc. Prof., Barnard Coll. 1959; Prof., St. Francis Xavier Univ., 1959-62 and 1969-78; Chrmn., Dept. of Govt., Barnard Coll. 1957-59; 1st el. to H. of C. for Antigonish-Guysborough in 1962; re-elect. 1963, 65; Parlty. Secy. to Secy. of State for External Affairs, to Min. of Pub. Works, and to Secy. of State; Leg. Adv. to Pres. of the Privy Council; mem. Adv. Comn. on Parlty. Accommodation; mem. Bd. Govs., Internat. Devel. Research Center; author of "Parliament and Executive in Wartime Canada", "The Moral and Political Thought of David Hume" and "The Canadian House of Commons; Procedure and Reform"; mem., Candn. Pol. Sc. Assn.; The Century Assn. (N.Y.C.); The Halifax; Liberal; Baptist; Home: Bayfield, Antigonish Co., N.S. B0H 1A0

STEWART, John Douglas, B.A., B.L.S., Ph.D.; art historian; educator; b. Kingston, Ont. 28 Jan. 1934; s. Harold Huton and Frances Dunning (Crawford) S.; e. Kingston Coll. & Vocational Inst. 1951; Queen's Univ. B.A. 1955; McGill Univ. B.L.S. 1956; Courtauld Inst. Univ. of London Postgrad. Acad. Dipl. Hist. of Art 1961, Ph.D. 1968; m. Mary d. W. J. Cotterell, Kidderminster, Eng. 1 Sept. 1973; children: Georgiana 1976, Venetia 1978; PROF. OF ART HIST., QUEEN'S UNIV. 1980- ; Librarian, Douglas Lib. Queen's Univ. 1956-58; Cadet Nat. Gallery Can. Museum Training Scheme 1958-59; Lectr. in Fine Art Univ.

of Toronto 1964-65; Asst. Prof. of Art Hist. Queen's Univ. 1965, Assoc. Prof. 1970; served with Princess of Wales Own Regt. (Reserve) 1948-1951, Supplementary Reserve 1952, rank 2nd Lt.; rec'd Can. Council Grants 1958-60, 1968-69, 1973, 1977, Leave Fellowships 1974-75; 1981-2; co-author "Heritage Kingston" 1973 (Best Local Hist. Award Candn. Hist. Assn. 1974); author "Sir Godfrey Kneller and the English Baroque Portrait" 1981; "Sir Godfrey Kneller" (catalogue) 1971; various articles Eng. art, Candn. arch.; mem. Kingston Comte. Arch. Review 1972-73; Dir. Frontenac Foundation 1972-74; mem. Kingston Hist. Soc.; Soc. Study Arch. Can.; P. Conservative; Anglican; Home: 11 Sydenham St., Kingston, Ont.; Office: Kingston, Ont. K7L 3N6.

STEWART, Murray E., B.Sc., M.Com.; transmission company executive; b. Brandon, Manitoba, 30 Sept. 1926; s. William Murray and Elizabeth (Williams) S.; e. Univ. of Alta. B.Sc. (Civil Engn.) 1947; Univ. of Toronto, M.Com. (Bus.Adm.) 1949; m. Muriel Allison, d. Dr. H. M. Young, Moose Jaw, Sask., 28 Dec. 1949; four d. Janet, Arden, Joan, Karen; EXTVE. VICE PRES. AND DIR., FOOTHILLS PIPE LINES (YUKON) LTD. since 1978; joined Northwestern Utilities Ltd. in 1949; apptd. Asst. Gen. Mgr., Jan. 1956 and Gen. Mgr., Dec. 1956; Vice Pres. and Gen. Mgr., 1963; Pres. 1965, and also Pres., Canadian Western Natural Gas Co. Ltd., 1965; Pres. and Dir., General Waterworks Corp. 1968-70; Sr. Vice Pres., IV International Corp., Phila., 1970-72; Pres., Chief Exec. Officer and Dir., C. Brewer & Co. Ltd., Honolulu, 1972-75; Exec. Vice Pres., Alexander & Baldwin, Inc., Honolulu, 1975-78; Protestant; recreation: golf; Clubs: Mayfair Golf & Country (Edmonton Past Pres.); Oahu Country (Honolulu); Waialae (Honolulu); Country Seaview Country (Absecon, N.J.); Suite 1600, 205 Fifth Ave. S.W., Calgary, Alta. T2P 2V7

STEWART, Neil J., B.A., LL.B., petroleum executive; b. Edmonton, Alta., 3 Oct. 1923; s. John N. and Catherine (MacLean) S.; e. Strathcona High Sch. Edmonton 1942; Univ. of Alta. B.A. 1948; Univ. of B.C. LL.B. 1951; Northwestern Univ. Business Adm. 1968; m. Sheila Moyra d. George Mackintosh, Edmonton, Alta., 17 May 1952; children: Ian M., George N., Sandy B.; VICE PRES., MARKETING AND CORPORATE AFFAIRS AND DIR. AMOCO CANADA 1980- ; called to Bar of Alta. 1953; practiced law Edmonton 1952-53; joined Law Dept. present Co. 1953, Head Law Dept. 1956 and Adm. Dept. 1963, Vice Pres.-Finance and Adm. 1968; Assoc. Vice Chrmn. Nat. Energy Bd. 1971-74 Ottawa; Chrmn. Energy Supplies Allocation Bd. 1974-76; Vice Pres., Finance & Admin., and Dir., Amoco Can. 1976-80; Past Pres. Candn. Petroleum Tax Soc.; Past Chrmn. Tax Law Comte. Candn. Petroleum Assn.; Budget Allocation Comte. Calgary Un. Fund; served with Candn. Grenadier Guards as Tank Commdr. N.W. Europe during World War II, piper Band of Calgary Highlanders and Band of 19th Regt. (Calgary) for many yrs.; author various articles on petroleum law and income tax law; P. Conservative; Presbyterian; recreations: jogging, fishing, hiking, snowshoeing; Club: Calgary Petroleum; Home: 828 Madison Ave., Calgary, Alta. T2S 1K3; Office: 444 - 7th Ave., Calgary, Alta. T2P 0X8

STEWART, Peter Beaufort, B.Com., M.B.A.; b. Westmount, Que., 23 Aug. 1923; s. late Harold Beaufort and late Winnifred (Martin) S.; e. Selwyn House Sch., Montreal; McGill Univ., B.Com. 1942; Harvard Univ., M.B.A. 1947; m. Yolande Winifred, d. late William Bleecker Powell, 1955; two s. Thomas, Angus; EXTVE. VICE PRES., ADMINISTRATION, AND DIR., THE MOLSON COS. LTD. since 1975; Dir., The Stewart Group Ltd.; with Building Products Ltd. 1947-62; joined Molson Breweries Ltd. as Dir. of Marketing, 1962; Vice-Pres., Marketing 1965; Pres., Molson's Western Breweries Ltd. 1966, Extve. Vice-Pres., Molson Breweries of Canada Ltd., and subsequently Pres. and Sr. Vice Pres., Brewing Group,

Molson Industries Ltd. 1972-75; served with Candn. Army 1942-45; rank Capt.; Anglican; Clubs: University (Toronto); St. George's Golf & Country; St. James's (Montreal); Montreal Badminton & Squash; Home: 472 Russell Hill Rd., Toronto, Ont. M5P 2S7; Office: 2 International Blvd., Rexdale, Ont. M5W 1A2

STEWART, Peter Malcolm, B.A.; b. Toronto, Ont. 10 Dec. 1931; s. Roy Alexander and Ruth Margaret (Kilbourn) S.; e. Upper Can. Coll., Toronto, 1939-48; Trinity Coll., Univ. of Toronto, B.A. 1952; m. Joan Temple, d. Wilfred Somers, 29 Jan. 1970; (by 1st m.) children: Elizabeth, Pamela, Richard; VICE PRES. & DIR., DOMINION TANNERS SALES CORP. LTD., since 1967; Pres., Wickett & Craig (leather mfrs.) since 1964; joined present Co. after grad.; apptd. Plant Mgr., 1957-60, Vice Pres., 1960-64; Dir., Tanners Assn. Can.; Alpha Delta Phi; Anglican; recreations: tennis, squash, skiing; Clubs: Badminton & Racquet; Caledon Ski; Home: 54 Dunloe Rd., Toronto, Ont. M5P 2T4; Office: 100 Bayview Ave., Toronto, Ont. M5A 3R6

STEWART, Ross, M.A., Ph.D., F.R.S.C.; educator; b. Vancouver, B.C. 16 March 1924; s. Colin and Jessie (Grant) S.; e. Gen. Gordon Sch. and Kitsilano High Sch. Vancouver; Univ. Of B.C. B.A. 1946, M.A. 1948; Univ. of Wash. Ph.D. 1954; m. Greta Marie d. Pearce Morris, Vancouver, B.C. 7 Sept. 1946; children: Cameron Leigh, Ian Hampton; PROF. OF CHEM. UNIV. OF B.C. since 1962; mem. teaching staff Candn. Services Coll., Royal Roads 1949-55; joined Univ. of B.C. 1955; rec'd Lefevre Gold Medal 1946; author "Oxidation Mechanisms" 1964; "Investigation of Organic Reactions" 1966; "Organic Chemistry, Methane to Macromolecules" 1971; over 100 scient. publs.; Pres. B.C. Thoroughbred Breeder's Soc. 1972-74; Vice Pres. Candn. Thoroughbred Horse Soc. 1975-76; Unitarian; recreations: golf, gardening, breeding thoroughbred horses; Club: Point Grey Golf; Home: 4855 Paton St., Vancouver, B.C. V6L 2H9; Office: Vancouver, B.C. V6T 1W5.

STEWART, Sam, B.A.; petroleum executive; e. Univ. of Calif. Los angeles B.A. (Geol.) 1938; SR. VICE PRES., PETRO-CANADA 1978- ; Geol., Richfield Oil Corp. 1937-42, Chief Geol. 1942, Mgr. Candn. Div. 1952, Mgr. Resource Devel. Group Can. 1966, Vice Pres. Atlantic Richfield Canada Ltd. 1971-77; Pres., Petro-Canada Exploration Inc. 1977-78; mem. Candn. Inst. Mining & Metall.; Candn. Soc. Petrol. Geols.; Am. Assn. Petrol. Geols.; Oilman's Golf Tournament; Club: Calgary Petroleum; Office: (P.O. Box 2844) Calgary, Alta. T2P 3E3.

STEWART, William Archibald, O.B.E.; journalist; writer on Quebec affairs; b. Riviere du Loup, Que., 28 Feb. 1914; s. Charles Archibald and Anne Laura (Walsh) S.; e. Coll. St. Patrice, Riviere du Loup; Univ. of Ottawa; m. Katherine Elizabeth, d. Fred A. Young, Winnipeg, Man., 23 Apl. 1946; children: Dugald, Landon, Susan, John, Janet; GENERAL EXECUTIVE, THE CANADIAN PRESS (MONTREAL), 1975-79; joined C.P. 1934 and Corr. at Riviere du Loup, Sydney, N.S., P.E.I. and Quebec City, 1934-38; War Corr., London, Eng., 1941; reported campaigns in Sicily, July-Aug. 1943; Italy, Sept. 1943-Feb. 1944; Normandy invasion and W. European 1944; Southeast Asia 1945; Australian Corr. for CP 1946-47; Chief of Bureau, Quebec City, 1947-52; Chief of Bur. Montreal 1952-75; Roman Catholic; recreations: painting, cartooning; Home: 362 Sanford Ave., St. Lambert, Que. J4P 2X8

STEWART, William G., B.A., C.A.; financial executive; b. Ottawa, Ont. 5 Oct. 1928; s. Herman Alexander and velva edith (Papineau) S.; e. Chatham (Ont.) elem. sch.; Smiths Falls (Ont.) high sch.; Univ. of W. Ont., B.A. 1951; C.A. 1954; m. Dorothy Emily, d. Emerson Harcourt Arnold, Windsor, Ont. 18 Sept. 1950; children: Penelope, Geoffrey, Wendy, Jill; SR. ADVISOR, CORPORATE AF-

FAIRS, RICHARDSON SECURITIES OF CANADA, 1980- ; Pres., CEO and Dir., Union Gas Co., 1974-79; mem. Adv. Comte., Sch. of Bus. Adm., Univ. of W. Ont.; Bd. of Mang., V.O.N., Can.; mem. Candn. Inst. C.A.'s; Candn. Gas Assn.; Ont. Natural Gas Assn. (Pres. 1974-75); United Church; recreations: fishing, boating, collecting antique glass; Club: Toronto; Home: 58 Castle Frank Rd., Toronto, Ont. M4W 2Z8

STIEB, Ernst Walter, M.Sc.Phm., Ph.D.; pharmacist; educator; historian; b. Windsor, Ont., 23 Aug. 1929; s. late Henry and Elizabeth (Freund) S.; e. Univ. of Toronto, B.Sc.Phm. 1952, M.Sc.Phm. 1955; Univ. of Wis., Ph.D. 1959; m. Catharine, d. late Philip Spee, 22 May 1954; children: Susan Anne, David; ASSOC. DEAN, FAC. OF PHARMACY, UNIV. OF TORONTO since 1978; Curator, Niagara Apothecary Museum; Teaching Asst., Univ. of Toronto, 1953; Research Asst., Univ. of Wis., 1955, Instr. 1958, Asst. Prof. 1959, Assoc. Prof. 1964; Prof. of Hist. of Pharm., Univ. of Toronto since 1967 and Inst. for Hist. and Philos. of Sci. and Technol.; Asst. Dean, Fac. of Pharm. 1975-78; Acting Dean, 1978-9; rec'd Edward Kremers Award for "distinguished historical writing", Am. Inst. Hist. of Pharm., 1967; author, "Drug Adulteration: Detection and Control in Nineteenth Century Britain", 1966; "The American College of Apothecaries: The First Quarter Century, 1940-67", 1970; other writings incl. book chapters and papers for various pharm. journs.; Ed., "One Hundred Years of Pharmacy in Canada", 1969; Ed., Faculty of Pharmacy "Newsletter" since 1977; mem., Candn. Acad. Hist. Pharm. (Exec. Dir. since 1968); Am. Inst. Hist. Pharm. (Pres. 1977-79); Assn. Faculties Pharm. Can. (Vice Chrmn. 1972-73, Chrmn. 1973-74); Acad. Med. Toronto; French Soc. Hist. of Pharm.; Brit. Soc. Hist. Pharm.; Candn. Pharm. Assn.; Candn. Soc. Hist. Science; Internat. Acad. Hist. Pharm. (Hon.); Spanish Soc. Hist. Pharm.; Am. Assn. of Colls. of Pharm.; Candn. Soc. for Hist. of Med.; Ont. Museum Assn.; Candn. Museums Assn.; Internat'l Soc. (German) of the Hist. of Pharmacy; Ont. Coll. of Pharmacists (Council, 1978-80); Cdn. Fdn. for the Advancement of Pharmacy (Bd. of Dir. since 1978); Cdn. Conf. on Continuing Educ. in Pharmacy (Council, since 1975); Rho Chi; United Church; recreations: music, gardening, pharmaco-medical philately; Home: 39 Kimbermount Dr., Agincourt, Ont. M1T 2Y1

STIKEMAN, Harry Heward, Q.C.; advocate; b. Montreal, Quebec, 8 July 1913; s. Harry Frederick Cawthorne and Dorothea (Horstmann) S.; e. Chestnut Hill Acad., Phila., Pa.; Selwyn House Sch., Montreal, Que.; Trinity Coll. Sch., Port Hope, Ont.; McGill Univ., B.A. 1935, B.C.L. 1938; Univ. of Dijon, France, Diplome des Francais 1937; m. Virginia Eloise, d. Robert Dunbar Guy, Q.C., Winnipeg, Man., 16 Sept. 1939; children: Virginia Heward, Harry Robert Heward, Ann Heward, Elizabeth Heward; m. 2ndly, Mary Gertrude, d. Dr. M. R. Wilson, Perth, Ont., 14 Oct. 1967; one d. Roben Jane Heward; SR. PARTNER, STIKEMAN, ELLIOTT, TAMAKI, MERCIER & ROBB, MONTREAL, LONDON, ENGLAND, QUEBEC, and HONG KONG and STIKEMAN, ELLIOTT, ROBARTS & BOWMAN, Toronto, Ont.; Dir., CAE Industries Ltd.; Aquila Securities Ltd.; Mercantile Bank of Can.; Federal Commerce & Navigation Ltd.; Dom. Bridge Co. Ltd.; Rawson Trust, Nassau; Past Gov., Candn. Tax Foundation; Chrmn. and Gen. Ed., Richard De Boo Ltd.; collab. for Can., Internat. Bur. of Fiscal Documentation; read law with C. G. Heward, K.C.; called to the Bar of Que. 1938; entered Office of Income Tax Div., Dept. of Nat. Revenue, Ottawa, 1939, as Solr.; became Counsel and Extve. Asst. and finally Asst.Depy. Min. of Nat. Revenue, Legal; worked on all wartime budgets, and asst. in drafting most of the tax leg. during the war; left the Dept. 1946; apptd. Counsel to the Special Comte. of the Senate, investigating taxation; Author and Ed. in Chief, "Canada Tax Cases, Annotated"; Tax Appeal Board Cases"; "Canada Tax Service"; "Canada Tax Manual"; "Stikeman

Canada Tax Acts Consolidated"; "Doing Business in Canada"; has publ. lect. on taxation and articles in Candn. and foreign journs.; Alpha Delta Phi; Conservative; Anglican; recreations: tennis, skiing, sailing, painting; Clubs: Lyford Cay (Nassau); Mount Royal; Rideau (Ottawa); The Toronto (Ont.); Confrerie des Chevaliers du Tastevin; Homes: 3940 Cote des Neiges, Montreal, Que. H3H 1W2, Shefford, Que. and Rideau Ferry, Ont.; Office: 1155 Dorchester Blvd., Montreal, Que. H3B 3V2

STILES, Rev. Frank Bernard, B.A., B.Ed., M.Div.; b. Truro, N.S. 28 Feb. 1935; e. Mount Allison Univ. 1957-62, B.A., B.Ed. (Dean's New Testament Prize; Benjimin Hertz Science Award); Pine Hill Divinity Hall, B.Div. 1964, M.Div. 1974 (Watkins Scholarship Alta.); Laval Univ. 1967-70; m. Louise Elsie Chappell, Amherst, N.S. 1 May 1961; three d. Elizabeth, Patricia Jane; MINISTER, ST. PAUL'S UNITED CHURCH 1970- ; o. Maritime Conf. Un. Ch. Can. 1964; parishes: Cavendish, P.E.I. 1964-67; Trinity, Drummondville, Que. 1967-70; summer work and ministry Mission Fields 1958-64 N. Alta. and N. Sask.; Founder, Nat. Parent Youth Alert Corp. Can. 1969, Dir. Gen. Can. and Chrmn. Nat. Bd. Dirs. 1969-81; Founder and Dir. Companion Program for Alcoholics & Research 1970- ; Protestant Chaplain, Royal Candn. Legion, Huntley Sr. Citizens, Alcoholics Anonymous; author "Drugs, Trips and Tragedies" 1972; rec'd Citations Que. Govt. 1969, City of Drummondville 1970; served with R.O.T.P. and Reserve Army 1954-56; rec'd pilot training precision flying and bush piloting; Inventions: Solid Rocket Fuel, functional (non-commercial) 1945; Automobile Air Conditioner, 1958; Automatic paper-saver dispenser, 1956; Emergency Helicopter Soft Landing System, 1954; Medical Cardio-Vascular blood clot dissolving vacuuming System, 1960; Medical Cardio-Vascular dialiation instrument 1959- ; Automatic heart lung computer (ausculation) analysis, 1961- ; Bionic Hearing Device for persons without inner ear, to include micro computation options, 1961- ; Address: Carp, Ont. (P.O. Box 41) K0A 1L0.

STILES, His Hon. George A. judge; b. Cornwall, Ont., 13 Mar. 1911; s. George Archibald and Mary Elizabeth Ida (Gill) S.; e. Pub. and High Sch., Cornwall; Trinity Coll., Univ. of Toronto, B.A. 1933; Ont. Coll. of Educ., 1934; Osgooed Hall, 1934-37; m. Edith Hope, d. Roland Webster, Victoria, B.C., 2 Nov. 1942; children: Michael J., Julian M., Shirley E.; CO. AND SURROGATE JUDGE,, UN. COS. OF STORMONT, DUNDAS & GLENGARRY since 1971; read law with Lionel Chevrier, K.C.; called to Bar of Ont. 1937; assoc. as Partner with John G. Harkness, K.C.; Harkness & Stiles, 1937-47; practised alone in 1947, thereafter Stiles & McGuire and Stiles & Ross; served in 2nd World War, 1939-45; mem., Stormont, Dundas & Glengarry Highlanders Reserve, until 1940; with R.C.A.F. in Can., Aleutian Islands and Europe; now Flight Lt., Reserve; Anglican; recreations: golf, photography; Home: R.R.1, East Front, Cornwall, Ont. K6H 5R5; Office: Court House, Cornwall, Ont.

STILES, John A., B.Com.; diplomat; b. Fredericton, N.B., 26 Jan. 1918; s. John Alexander and Margaret Campbell (MacVannel) S.; e. Glebe Coll. Inst., Ottawa, Ont.; Univ. of Toronto, B.Com. 1941; m. Margaret Celia, d. Douglas G. Buckley, Ottawa, 5 June 1948; two s. 1 d.; CHIEF INSPECTOR, FOREIGN OPERATIONS, GOV'T OF CANADA, since 1981; joined Trade Commissioner Service 1945; Assistant Trade Commissioner, New York, 1946; Caracas 1948; Asst. Dir., Trade Commissioner Service, Ottawa, 1954; Comm. Counsellor, Bonn, 1957, Sydney 1963; Min. (Comm.), Tokyo, 1967; High Commr. to Guyana 1970-74; Ambassador to Repub. of Korea 1974-77; Foreign Service Visitor 1977-81; served with the Canadian Army in England, France, Belgium, Holland Germany, 1941-45; rank Staff Capt. on discharge; United Church; author: "Developing Canada's Relations Abroad", 1980; Clubs: Royal Ottawa Golf; recreations;

golf, swimming, reading; Address: 299 Roger Rd., Ottawa, Ont. K1H 5C3

STINSON, Ford A., Ph.D; agriculturist; b. Norwood, Ont., 16 Sept. 1909; s. Richard John and Alice (Andrews) S.; e. Ont. Agric. Coll., B.S.A. 1934; Univ. of Toronto, M.S.A., 1938; North Carolina State Coll. of Agric., Ph.D. (Agron.-Soils) 1949; m. Margaret Dexter, d. late James Ross McLachlin, 24 Sept. 1938; children, Richard James, Martha Jane, Donald Andrew; Offr. i/c Dom. Exper. Stn., Delhi, Ont., 1935-49 (devel. of research on flue-cured tobacco); Prof. and Head, Dept. of Soils, Ont. Agric. Coll., 1949-51; (first) Dir., Tobacco Research Bd. of Rhodesia, 1951-56; Farmer, 1956-62; Gen. Mgr., Ont. Flue-cured Tobacco Growers' Mktg. Bd., 1957-58; Head, Field Crops Div., Kemptville Agric. Sch., 1962-66; mem., Ont. Agr. Research Inst., 1962-66; Chmn., Ont. Flue-cured Tobacco Ind. Inquiry Comm., 1962-63; Princ., Kemptville Coll. of Agric. Tech. 1966-74; Prov. Leader, C.I.D.A. Tobacco Mktg. Study, Tanzania 1970; Consult., C.I.D.A. Study Team, Dry Land Agric., India and Sri Lanka 1975; Consult. C.I.D.A. Study Team, Natural Resources Coll., Malawi 1977; Sigma Xi, United Church; Address: Lanark, Ont. K0G 1K0

STINSON, John Floyd, B. Eng.; public utilities executive; b. Montreal, Que., 22 Dec. 1924; s. John Harold and Elsie (Floyd) S.; e. McGill Univ.; B.Eng. (Engn. Physics) 1949, Business Adm. Cert.; m. Helen Frances, d. James Traynor, Scot., 19 Feb. 1955; children: Mark, Monica, Patrice; VICE-PRES., OPERATIONS STAFF, BELL CANADA, since 1972; joined present Co. as Splicer's Helper, Montreal, 1941; served in various engn. capacities in Montreal and Toronto and in various mang. positions until apptd. Area Chief Engr., Toronto, 1968; Asst. Vice Pres. (Engn.) HQ Montreal, 1969; Vice Pres. (Operational Staff) 1970-72; served with RCAF 1943-45; rank Flying Offr.; mem., Assn. Prof. Engrs. Ont.; Club: Royal Candn. Mil. 1nst.; Home: 2 Haddington Ave., Toronto, Ont. M5M 2N7; Office: 393 University Ave., Toronto, Ont. M5G 1W9

STINSON, William W., B.A.; transportation executive; b. Toronto, Ont., 29 Oct. 1933; e. Humewood Sch. Toronto 1946; Univ. of Toronto Schs. 1951; Univ. of Toronto B.A. 1954; Univ. of W. Ont. Dipl. in Business Adm. 1955; m. Eileen Krusic, 29 March 1958; children: Janet, Margo, James; PRES., CANADIAN PACIFIC LTD. 1981- ; joined Canadian Pacific Toronto 1950, held various positions 1950-66;Supt. Toronto Div. 1966, Asst. Gen. Mgr., Ops. and Maint., Pacific Region Vancouver 1969; Gen. Mgr., Oper. and Maintenance Pacific Region 1971 and Eastern Region 1972; Asst. Vice Pres. Operation and Maintenance Montreal 1974; Vice Pres., Oper. and Maint., Montreal, 1976; Exec. Vice-Pres., CP Rail 1979; Dir., CP Ltd.; CP Air Lines Ltd.; CP (Bermuda) Ltd.; CP Express & Transport Ltd.; CP Steamships Ltd.; CNCP Telecommunications, Toronto, Hamilton & Buffalo Railway; Office: Windsor Station, Montreal, Que.H3C 3E4

STIRLING, Geoffrey William; broadcasting and advertising executive; b. St. John's, Nfld. 22 March 1922; s. Edgar Weston and Mary Ethel (Uphill) S.; e. Grammar Sch., Ramsgate, Eng.; Bishop Feild Coll., St. John's, Nfld.; Univ. of Tampa; m. Joyce, d. James Cutler, 1957; children: Scott, Kim, Shawn, S. Greg; Owner, Radio Station CKGM, Montreal (estbd. 1959); Newfoundland Television Ltd., CJCN-TV (estbd. 1955); Newfoundland Broadcasting Co.; President, Newfoundland Sunday Herald; Stirling Restaurant; Weston Enterprises; Newfoundland Enterprises; Newfoundland Television & Advertising Co.; Newfoundland Broadcasting Co. Ltd.; Pres., WWKC Holding Co.; mem. of St. John's Beautification Board; Feildian Educ. Sports Comte.; Candn. Weekly Newspapers Assn.; Assn. of Radio & TV Broadcasters; Broadcast News; founded the Nfld. "Sunday Herald" in 1946 and built it into the paper with the largest circulation in the Prov. within four yrs.; founded Radio Stn. CJON and watched it triple its size within a two yr. period; worked with an alligator firm in Central America; also worked as Freelance Journalist in Mexico, Germany, France, Italy, Portugal, Spain and most other European countries with the prospect of radio, newspaper and TV organization; during 2nd World War worked with Lend-Lease Bd. in Wash., D.C.; Past Pres., St. John's Chamber of Comm.; Nfld. Press Club and Feildian Sports Club; Anglican; recreations: spear-fishing, speedboat racing, water-skiing; Clubs: Bd. of Trade; City (St. John's) Bally Haly Golf (St. John's); Arizona Riding. P.O. Box 2020, St. John's, Nfld. A1C 5S2

STIRLING, Gordon M., C.M., Q.C.; b. St. John's Nfld., 4 Nov. 1907; s. Frederick M., J.P. and Mary Gertrude (Hunt) S.; e. Bishop Feild Coll., St. John's, Nfld.; unm.; PARTNER, STIRLING, RYAN, REID, HARRINGTON, ANDREWS AND LILLY; Master, Supreme Court of Newfoundland; mem. Adv. Bd., Can. Permanent Trust Co.; read law with Charles E. Hunt, C.B.E., Q.C.; called to Bar of Newfoundland 1930; cr. Q.C. 1956; Col. (Hon.) and former C.O., The Church Lads Brigade in Nfld.; Past Pres., Nfld. Br., and Officer of Order of St. John Ambulance; Past Pres., Feildian Athletic Grounds Assn.; Dir., Candn. Scholarship Trust Foundation; Grenfell Assn. of Nfld.; rec'd Centennial Medal 1967; mem. Order of Can., 1980; former Treas., Law Soc. of Nfld.; ex mem. Extve., Candn. Bar Assn.; Pres., Gov. Bodies of Legal Prof. in Can. 1964; Former Regent, Memorial Univ., Nfld.; Former Chancellor, Anglican Diocese of Newfoundland; Past mem. Nat. Council, The Duke of Edinburgh Award in Can.; Anglican; recreations: curling, swimming, gardening, travel; Clubs: Bally Haly Golf & Curling; St. John's Curling; Home: 6 King's Bridge Court, St. John's, Nfld. A1C 2R2; Office: Royal Trust Bldg., Water St., St. John's, Nfld. A1C 5V3

STIRLING, John Bertram, O.C. (1969), C.D., B.A., B.Sc., LL.D., D.Sc.; civil engineer; b. Dundas, Ont., 29 Nov. 1888, s. James Alexander, M.D., and Jessie (Bertram) S.; e. Queen's University, B.A. 1909, B.Sc. 1911 and LL.D. 1951; D.Sc., Royal Military College of Canada 1962, LL.D., Univ. of Toronto 1961, McGill 1963; m. Emily Parker, d. Col. Edward T. Sturdee, 25 April 1928; one d. Jessie Mar; Dir., E.G.M. Cape & Co.; Chancellor Emeritus, Queen's Univ., 1960-74; Past Pres., Better Business Bureau, Montreal; Montreal Bd. of Trade, 1950; served in 1st World War with Candn. Engrs. in France, 1915-19; Past Pres., Engn. Inst. of Can.; Candn. Constr. Assn.; Corps of Prof. Engrs. of Que.; Past Pres., Gen. Alumni Assn., Queen's Univ.; Hon. mem., Engn. Inst. of Can.; Anglican; recreations: country life, sailing, music; Club: St. James's; Home: 10 Richelieu Place, Montreal H3G 1E7 and Ile-aux-noir Que. J0J 1G0 (summer); Office: 180 Duncan Mill Rd., Don Mills, Ont. M3B 3K2

STIRLING, Rear Admiral Michael Grote, C.D. (retired); b. Kelowna, B.C., 29 June 1915; s. Grote and Mabel Katherine (Brigstocke) S.; e. Shawnigan Lake Sch., B.C.; Royal Naval Coll., Greenwich, Eng.; m. Sheelagh Kathleen, d. late Francis Xavier Russell, 3 Aug. 1942; children: Peter, Gillian, Andrew; joined R.C. N. 1933; in R.N. until 1938; specialized in communications in Eng., 1941 and served with Brit. destroyer flotilla; Depy. Dir., Signals Div., Naval Hdqrs., Ottawa, 1942-43; Signals Offr. to Commdr.-in-Chief, Candn. Northwest Atlantic, Halifax, 1943-44; in command H.M.C.S. St. Laurent 1944-45 and HMCS Crusader 1945-46; HMCS Nootka 1947; Staff of Naval mem., Candn. Joint Staff, Washington, 1947; Dir. of Naval Communications, 1949-51; attached to HQ of Supreme Allied Commdr., Atlantic, Norfolk, Va. and promoted to Capt., 1953; Command HMCS Cornwallis, Digby, N.S. 1955; HMCS Crescent and Commdr. 2nd Candn. Escort Sqdn. and Sr. Offr. in Command, 1957; apptd. Naval mem. of Directing Staff, Nat. Defence Coll., Kingston, 1958; promoted to Commodore 1959; apptd.

Sr. Candn. Offr. Afloat (Atlantic) in HMCS Bonaventure, 1961; promoted to Flag rank and Chief of Naval Personnel, 1962; Flag Offr. Pacific Coast and Sr. Off. in Chief Command and Maritime Commdr. Pacific, 1964-66; Dir., Univ. of Victoria Foundation 1967-68; Agent Gen. for B.C. in U.K. & Europe 1968-75; Dir., Schenley Can. Inc., 1980- ; Address: 302-1280 Newport Ave., Victoria, B.C. V8S 5E7

STIRLING, Hon. Rev. R. Laird, M.L.A.; politician; b. Noranda, Que. 22 Aug. 1938; e. McMaster Univ.; Pine Hill Divinity Hall, Halifax; m. Carolyn Wilson; two d. and one s.; MIN. OF SOCIAL SERVICES, N.S. Responsible for co-ordinating native affairs 1979- ; Min. of Consumer Affairs and Min. Responsible for Residential Tenancies Act 1979-80; el. M.L.A. for Dartmouth North prov. g.e. 1978, re-el. 1981; parish minister; hosp. chaplain; Past Pres. Ministerial Assn. Dartmouth and Yarmouth; Past Chrmn. Bd. Dirs. Dartmouth Boys & Girls Club; Past Pres. Rotary Dartmouth; Founder of a Scout Organ N. Sask.; Del. to World Council of Churches, Poverty Conf. 1968, World Lay Cong. Germany, C.P.A., London, Eng. 1979, World Welfare Conf. Hong Kong 1980, World Rehabilitation Conf. 1980; P.C.; United Church; Office: (P.O. Box 696) Johnston Bldg., Prince St., Halifax, N.S. B3J 2T7.

STIVER, Myrtle Pearl, B.S., F.A.P.H.A.: b. Ontario, Can., 9 Nov. 1908; d. Henry and Olga (Smith) S.; e. Toronto Western Hosp. Sch. of Nursing; Univ. of Toronto Sch. of Nursing; Columbia Univ., B.S.; Post-Grad at Toronto Psychiatric Hosp.; unm.; engaged in private nursing for 7 years; with V.O.N., Toronto Br. for a time; then successively, with Dept. of Health, City of Toronto; Dist. Supervisor and Nursing Consultant, Ont. Dept. of Health; Dir. of Public Health, Nursing, City of Ottawa Dept. of Health; Extve. Dir., Candn. Nurses Assn., 1952-63; Charter mem., Bd. Dirs. and Extve. Secy.-Treas., Candn. Nurses Foundation 1963; mem. Nursing Adv. Comte., Candn. Red Cross Soc.; V.O.N. for Can.; Past mem. Nursing Adv. Comte., Priory of Can., Ven. Order St. John of Jerusalem; mem. Dent. and Med. Services Adv. Bd., Govt. Can. 1952-62; mem. Candn. Council on Nutrition 1956-62; mem. Vocational Adv. Comte., Muskoka Bd. Educ.; Royal Soc. of Health; Hon. mem., Ont. Public Health Assn.; Commdr. Order of St. John; Bd. of Dirs., Candn. Citizenship Council; Hon. mem. Candn. Nurses Assn. 1966; Co-owner, "The Croft" (Candn. Handicraft Shop) Baysville, Ont.; co-author "Patient Care in the Home"; rec'd. Centennial Medal 1968; Clubs: Zonta International (Ottawa Club Pres. 1961-63); University Women's (Toronto, Montreal and Orillia); Business and Prof. Women's (Pres., 1970-72, Bracebridge, Ont.); Protestant; Clerk, First Baptist Church (mem. Deacon's Bd. since 1975, Chrmn. 1978), Bracebridge; Home: 360 Wellington St. N., Bracebridge, Ont. P0B 1C0

STOCK, Valentine N., B.A.Sc.; executive; b. Toronto, Ont. 14 May 1923; s. late Valentine F., M.D., F.R.C.P. and Olga Agnes (Wallace) S.; e. Univ. of Toronto Schs.; Univ. of Toronto B.A.Sc.; m. Georgia I. d. late George C. Knowles 1955; children: Michael, Andrew, Barbara; PRESIDENT, C.E.O. AND DIR. CANADA PACKERS, INC.; Dir. Eatonsof Canada; Eaton Acceptance Co.; Consumers Glass Co. Ltd.; Dir. and Chmn., Norwich Union Life and Norwich Union Fire Insurance Societies; Dir., Duplate Can. Ltd.; PPG Industries Can. Ltd.; Gov. and Vice-Chmn., Olympic Trust; served with RCNVR 1944-45, rank Sub-Lt.; mem. Assn. of Professional Engrs.; Trustee, Vice Pres. & mem. Extve. Comte., Art Gallery of Ont.; Gov., Trinity Coll. School; United Church; recreations: tennis, golf, skiing, fishing; Clubs: Toronto Golf; Osler Bluff Ski; Toronto; Badminton & Racquet; Mt. Royal; Home: 189 Forest Hill Rd., Toronto, Ont. M5P 2N3; Office: 95 St. Clair Ave. West, Toronto, Ont. M4V 1P2

STOCKWELL, Clifford Howard, B.A.Sc., Ph.D., F.R.S.C.; geologist; b. Estevan, Sask., 26 Sept. 1897; s. James Robertson and Alfretta Susana (Perry) S.; e. Univ. of British Comumbia, B.A.Sc. 1924; Univ. of Wis., Ph.D. 1930; m. Annette Elizabeth, d. Norman E. Johnston, Vancouver, B.C., 3 June 1935; Geologist, Geol. Survey Can. 1927-68; served in World War as 2nd Lieut., R.A.F., 1917-19; mem. Candn. Inst. Mining & Metall.; Geol. Assn. of Can.; Geol. Soc. of Am.; awarded Willet G. Miller Medal by Royal Soc. of Can., 1953; Logan Medal by Geol. Assn. Can. 1974; Protestant; recreation: amateur photography; Home: 577 Gainsborough Ave., Ottawa, Ont. K2A 2Y6

STODDART, Jack Elliott; publisher; b. Hamilton, Ont. 24 July 1916; s. Henry Elliott and May (Elliott) S.; e. Shelburne Pub. and High Schs.; Westervelt Coll. London; Univ. of Toronto business courses; m. Ruth Elizabeth d. Judge W. T. Robb, Orangeville, Ont. 9 May 1942; children: Jack Elliott, Susan Elizabeth; CHRMN. AND CEO, GENERAL PUBLISHING CO. LTD. Chrmn. and Pres. Stoddart Publishing Ltd.; Chrmn. Musson Book Co.; Chmn. McLeod Publishing; Pres. and Publisher, Paper-Jacks Ltd.; Dir. Nelson, Foster & Scott; Mercor Publishing Ltd.; joined Macmillan Co. of Canada 1936 holding various positions in film production dept. and trade sales subsequently becoming Sales Mgr.; purchased present co. 1957, Musson Book Co. 1967, New Press 1974, Simon & Schuster Canada Ltd. 1976 (become PaperJacks Ltd.); Nelson Foster & Scott Jan. 1, 1978; George J. McLeod Limited Aug. 1, 1978; Candn. Publisher 'Pocket Books'; Publisher/Agt. various US and UK publishers; served with RCAF during World War II; mem. Bd. Trade Metrop. Toronto; P. Conservative; Anglican; recreations: fishing, golf, swimming, Club: Donalda; Home: 54 Bayview Ridge, Willowdale, Ont. M2L 1E6; Office: 30 Lesmill Rd., Don Mills, Ont. M3B 2T6.

STODGELL, John Coatsworth, B.Com.; investment dealer; b. Windsor, Ont., 29 March 1925; s. Simeon John and Edith (Coatsworth) S.; e. Univ. of Toronto, B. Com. 1948; m. late Margaret Abbott, 4 June 1949; children: Jane, Barbara, Robert; CHRMN., WALWYN STODGELL COCHRAN MURRAY LTD.; Pres. & Dir. Walstock Leasing Ltd.; Dir. Walwyn Properties Ltd.; Pres. and Dir., Capital Growth Fund Ltd.; Chrmn., Invest. Dealers Assn. of Can. 1980-81; Hon. Trustee, The Havergal Coll. Foundation; Dir., Ont. Heart Foundation 1964-72; Dir., Children's Aid Soc., Windsor, Ont. 1959-61; served in 2nd World War as Sub.-Lt., R.C.N.V.R., 1943-45; Alpha Delta Phi; Anglican; recreation: golf; Clubs: Toronto Golf; Granite; National; Essex Golf (Windsor); Home: 49 Daneswood Rd., Toronto, Ont. M4N 3J7; Office: 145 King St. W., Suite 1900, Toronto, Ont. M5H 3M1

STOICHEFF, Boris Peter, B.A.Sc., M.A., Ph.D., F.R.S.; F.R.S.C.; university professor; b. Bitol, Yugoslavia, 1 June 1924; s. Peter and Vasilka (Tonna) S.; came to Canada 1931; e. Public and High Schs., Toronto, Ont.; Univ. of Toronto, B.A.Sc., 1947, M.A., 1948, Ph.D., 1950; m. Lillian Joan, d. William G. Ambridge, 15 May 1954; one s. Richard Peter; UNIV. PROF., UNIV. OF TORONTO since 1977 and Prof. of Physics since 1964; Chrmn., Engn. Science 1972-77; Postdoctorate Fellow, Department of Physics, University of Toronto, 1950-51; Div. of Pure Physics, Nat. Research Council, Ottawa, 1951-53, and Research Offr. there 1953-64; Visiting Research Scientist, Dept. of Physics, Mass. Inst. of Tech., 1963-64; Visiting Scholar, Dept. of Physics, Stanford Univ., 1977; apptd. to Nat. Research Council of Can. 1977; served in C.O.T.C.; Univ. of Toronto, 1944-45; author of over 100 publ. papers in prof. journs.; mem. Candn. Assn. of Physicists; Fellow, Optical Soc. of Am. (Pres.-elect 1975; President 1976); Am. Phys. Soc.; Hon. Fellow, Indian Acad. Sciences; awarded Centennial Medal Canada 1967; Gold Medal, Canadian Assn. Physicists 1974; awarded I. W. Killam Mem. Scholarship 1977-79; Sr. Fellow Massey Coll. 1979; Geoffrey Frew Fellow of the Australian Acad.

of Sci., 1980; William F. Meggers Award of Optical Soc. of Am. 1981; discovered generation of sound by light; the inverse Raman effect; prof. interest, lasers, atomic and molecular spectroscopy and structure; Rayleigh, Brillouin and Raman light scattering; stimulated scattering processes and two photon absorption; Home: 66 Collier St., Apt. 6B, Toronto, Ont. M4W 1L9

STOIK, John L., B.E. (Chem); petroleum executive; b. North Battleford, Sask., 5 March 1920; s. late Mike and Barbara (Hoffmann) S.; e. Univ. of Sask. B.E. (Chem. Eng.) 1947; m. Margaret Mary d. late William B. Marshall, New Westminster, B.C., 23 Aug. 1943; two s. John H., Gary L.; PRES. AND C.E.O., GULF CANADA LTD. since 1979; joined present Co. (then B-A Oil) Moose Jaw (Sask.) refinery 1947, Asst. Refinery Mgr.-Moose Jaw 1957 and Clarkson (Ont.) 1961, Mgr. Moose Jaw refinery 1962, Mgr.-Planning and Services H.O. Toronto 1964, Gen. Mgr.-Mfg. H.O. 1965, Vice Pres.-Refining H.O. 1968; Extve. Vice Pres. and Chief Extve. Offr. Korea Oil Corp. Seoul 1970; Sr. Vice Pres. present Co. 1974; Pres. and Chief Operating Offr. Dir., 1976-79; served with RCAF 1942-45; Dir., Candn. Extve. Svce. Overseas; mem. Business and Indust. Adv. Comte. on Energy and Raw Materials to Organ. for Econ. Co-op. and Devel.; Dir., The Toronto-Dominion Bank; Toronto Symphony; mem. Engn. Inst. Can.; Am. Petrol. Inst.; Freemason; P. Conservative; United Church; recreations: golf, curling; Clubs: Granite; Canadian; Toronto; St. George's Golf & Country; Rideau; Engineers'; Home: 79 Rebecca Court, R.R. #2 Maple, Ont. L0J 1E0; Office: 130 Adelaide St. W., Toronto, Ont. M5H 3R6 800 Bay St., Toronto, Ont. M5S 1Y8

STOLLERY, Robert; executive; b. Edmonton, Alta., 1 May 1924; s. William Charles and Kate Elizabeth (Catlin) S.; e. Strathcona High Sch., Edmonton, 1941; Univ. of Alta., Bachelor of Civil Engn. 1949; m. Shirley Jean, d. late William Ernest Hopper, 11 June 1948; children: Carol Wendy, Janet Susan, Douglas Robert; CHRMN. AND C.E.O., PCL CONSTRUCTION LTD., since 1969; Dir., PLC-Braun-Simons Ltd.; Construction Industry Devel. Council Can. Permanent Trust Co.; Can. Permanent Mortgage Corp.; Chembiomed Ltd.; Northern Transportation Ltd.; Technical Service Council; Vice-Chmn., Conference Bd. of Can.; joined present Co. as Engr. 1949-53; Asst. Gen. Supt. 1953-57; Gen. Supt. 1957-60; Mgr., Edmonton, 1960-62; Vice-Pres. and Gen. Mgr. 1962-69; served with RCNVR 1942-45; mem., Assn. Prof. Engrs. Alta.; Engn. Inst. Can.; Edmonton Extve. Assn.; United Church; recreations: golf, fishing, hunting; Home: 99 Westbrook Dr., Edmonton, Alta. T6J 2C8; Office: 5410-99 St., Edmonton, Alta. T6E 3P4

STONE, Arthur Joseph, Q.C., B.A., LL.M.; b. St. Peter's, N.S., 19 Nov. 1929; s. George and Charlotte S.; e. St. Peter's (N.S.) High Sch.; St. Francis Xavier Univ., B.A. (Hons.) 1952; Dalhousie Univ. Law Sch., LL.B. 1955; Harvard Law Sch., LL.M. 1956; m. Anna M. 1956; A SR. PARTNER, McTAGGART, STONE, WINTERS & HERRIDGE; Dir., Ethicon Sutures Ltd.; G.A.V. Properties & Enterprises Ltd.; McNeil Laboratories (Can.) Ltd.; Ortho Pharmaceutical (Can.) Ltd.; Packagemaster Ltd.; 600 Group Equipment Ltd.; Humphreys & Glasgow (Canada) Ltd.; Mead Packaging (Can.) Limited; B-Bar-B (Can.) Ltd.; H. A. Jones Can. Ltd.; Intermarket Can. Ltd.; Marflex Ltd.; Surgikos Canada Inc.; Janssen Pharmaceutical Inc.; read law with Stewart, Smith, McKeen, Halifax, N.S. 1955-56; with Wright and McTaggart, Toronto 1957; called to Bar of N.S. 1956, of Ont. 1958; apptd. Q.C. 1971; Past Pres., Friends of L'Arche (Daybreak), Richmond Hill, Ont.; mem. N.S. Barristers' Soc.; Law Soc. Upper Can.; Candn. Bar Assn. (Past mem. Nat. Extve. Comte.); mem. Bd. Govs. Candn. Tax Foundation; Bd. Trade Metrop. Toronto; Assoc. mem. Assn. Average Adjusters of Can.; Candn. Bd. Marine Underwriters; Candn. Maritime Law Assn. (Pres.); Harvard Law Sch.

Fund (Cdn. Chrmn.); Harvard Law Sch. Assoc. of Ont. (Pres.); Regional Vice Pres., Harvard Law Sch. Assn.; author of several articles on Candn. jurisprudence; Liberal; R. Catholic; recreations: golf, swimming; Clubs: Marine Quay; Granite; Ontario; Home: 80 Weybourne Cres., Toronto, Ont. M4N 2R7; Office: 390 Bay St., Toronto, Ont. M5H 2Y2

STONER (Oliver) Gerald, B.A., LL.D.; public servant; b. London, Ont., 21 Aug. 1922; s. Oliver Christian and Ethel Stoner; e. Wortley Rd. Pub. Sch., London; London, (Ont.) S. Coll., 1933-38; Univ. of W. Ont., 1938-41; Queen's Univ., B.A. (Econ.) 1947; LL.D. (Hon), Univ. of W. Ont. 1980; m. Elizabeth Mary, d. W. G. Allen, Toronto, 1 Sept. 1951; children: Patrick William, Elizabeth Robyn; Chmn., Restrictive Trade Practices Comm. since 1979; former Deputy Min., Dept. Of Industry, Trade & Commerce 1975-77; joined Department of External Affairs 1947; 2nd Secretary, Paris, 1950-54; Dept. of External Affairs, 1954-56 (Responsible for Colombo plan and External Aid); Counsellor, Brussels, 1956 and Chargé d'Affaire, 1958-59; also 1st rep. of Can. to European Econ. Community; in charge of Econ. Affairs, External Affairs, Ottawa, 1959-64; Sr. Asst. Secy. of Cabinet and Asst. Clk. of Privy Council, 1964-67; Deputy Clerk of the P.C. and Deputy Secretary to the Cabinet, 1967-69; Acting Secretary and Acting Clerk 1967-68; Depy. Minister of Transport 1969-75; Vice-Chmn., Bd. of Dir. of Export Devel. Corp. 1975-77; Commissioner, Fed. Royal Comm. on Financial management and Accountability 1977-79; served with the Canadian Armoured Corps, 1941-45; N.W. Europe, 1944-45; discharged with rank A/Maj.; Mentioned in Despatches; Vice-Chmn., Bd. of Dir., De-Havilland Aircraft 1975-77; mem, Bd. of Dir., Cdn. Devel. Corp., Canadair 1975-77; Adv. Council, York Univ. Sch. of Adm.; Protestant; recreations: tennis, reading, amateur hockey; Club: Rockliffe Tennis; Home: 161 Maple Lane, Rockcliffe Pk., Ottawa, Ont. K1M 1G4; Office: 359 Kent St., P. O. Box 336, Station A, Ottawa, Ont. K1N 8V3

STORY, George Morley, D.Phil., F.R.H.S., F.S.A.; educator; author; b. St. John's, Nfld. 13 Oct. 1927; s. George Errington and Dorothy Katharine (White) S.; e. Bishop Feild Coll. St. John's 1946; Mem. Univ. Coll. St. John's 1948; McGill Univ. B.A. 1950; Oriel Coll. Oxford Univ. (Rhodes Scholar) D.Phil. 1954; m. Laura Alice d. J. Ross Stevenson, Pickering, Ont. 16 May 1968; children: Katharine Alice, Lachlan Stevenson, Simon Jonathan; HENRIETTA HARVEY PROF. OF ENG., MEMORIAL UNIV. OF NFLD. 1979- ; Mem. Univ. Lectr. 1950-51, Asst. Prof. 1954, Assoc. Prof. 1959, Prof. 1962- , Secy. of Senate 1965-69, Chrmn. Ed. Adv. Bd. 1979- , Public Orator 1960- ; Chrmn. Prov. Nfld. Task Force on Community Devel. 1972-74; Co-Chrmn. Comte. Fed. Regulations Relating to Seafisheries Nfld. 1973-74; Chrmn. Nfld. and Labrador Arts Council 1980- ; rec'd Molson Prize (Can. Council) 1977; author "Sonnets of William Alabaster" 1959; "Study of English" 1960; "Sermons of Lancelot Andrewes" 1967; "Avalon Peninsula of Newfoundland" 1968; "Christmas Mumming in Newfoundland" 1969; "Dictionary of Newfoundland English" in press; numerous papers and essays Tudor lit., Erasmus & Renaissance humanism, bibliog. & Textual criticism, Nfld. hist., lang. & lit.; mem. Bibliog. Soc. London; Nfld. Hist. Trust (Pres. 1969-71); Nfld. Hist. Soc. (Pres. 1978); United Church; recreations: hunting, fishing, gardening; Home: 335 Southside Rd., St. John's, Nfld. A1E 1A1; Office: St. John's, Nfld. A1C 5S7.

STOTT, Donald Franklin, M.Sc., A.M., Ph.D., F.G.S.A.; geologist; b. Reston, Man. 30 Apl. 1928; s. Franklin Brisbin and Catherine Alice (Parker) S.; e. Univ. of Man. B.Sc. 1953, M.Sc. 1954; Princeton Univ. A.M. 1956, Ph.D. 1958; m. Margaret Elinor Hutton 8 Oct. 1960; three s. Glenn Franklin, David Reed, Donald Alan; RESEARCH SCIENT., INST. SEDIMENTARY AND PETROLEUM GEOL., GEOLOGICAL SURVEY OF CAN.

1980- ; Research Scient. Geol. Survey of Can. 1957-72; Head, Regional Geol. Subdiv. Inst. Sedimentary & Petrol. Geol. 1972-73, Dir. of Inst. 1973-80; author numerous reports Mesozoic Geol. foothills Alta., B.C., Arctic Islands; Fellow, Geol. Assn. Can.; mem. Candn. Soc. Petrol. Geols. (Past Pres.); Soc. Econ. Paleontols. & Minerals.; Sigma Xi; Home: 3398 Breton Close N.W., Calgary, Alta. T2L 1X4; Office: 3303 - 33rd St. N.W., Calgary, Alta. T2L 2A7.

STOVEL, Lieutenant-General Richard Carlton, A.F.C., C.D., Legion of Merit (U.S.A.); b. Winnipeg, Man., 31 March 1921; e. Ravenscourt Sch., Winnipeg; Univ. of Man.; Central Flying Sch., Trenton; R.A.F. Empire Central Flying Sch., 1943; U.S. Army Adjutant Gen.'s Staff Sch., Carlisle Barracks, Pa. and Camp Lee, Va., 1948; Nat. Defence Coll., Kingston, 1962-63; m. Helen M. Govan, Winnipeg, Man.; joined RCAF 1940; rec'd. pilots' wings, Nov. 1940; served for 2 yrs. on flying instructional duties, 2 Service Flying Training Sch., Uplands; Chief Instr., 1943 (completed operational training Mosquito Bombers), following 2nd World War served initially in Personnel Br., Western Air Command HQ, Vancouver; apptd. Staff Offr., Personnel Adm., 1948 and later Staff Offr. Postings and Careers, RCAF Training Command HQ, Trenton; apptd. Air Mem., Air Bd. of NATO Mil. Agency for Standardization, London, Eng. 1951; returned to Can. to become 1st C.O., RCAF Stn. Cold Lake, Alta., 1954; trans. to N.Am. Air Defence Command HQ, Colorado Springs, 1958, as Depy. Dir. of Plans and Policy; assigned to 1 Air Div. HQ, Metz, France as Chief of Staff, 1963; apptd. Dir., Gen. Organization and Manpower Control, CFHQ, 1965; Commander Training Command, Winnipeg 1966-68; Depy. Chief of Personnel, CFHQ 1968-69; Depy. Chief Operations & Reserves, Ottawa 1969-71 when apptd. Cdn. Defence Attaché and Commdr. Candn. Defence Liaison Staff, Wash., D.C.; Depy. Commander in Chief, North Amer. Air Defence Command 1974-76 (ret.); Address: 14 Thayer Rd., Colorado Springs, Colorado 80906

STRAITON, John S., B.A.; company executive; b. Kapuskasing, Ontario; e. Queen's University, B.A. (Psychol.); m.; children: Kenneth, Susan; PRES., STRAITON, PEARSON & MARTIN ADVERTISING since 1975; Chrmn., Ogilvy and Mather (Canada) Ltd. 1973 and subsequently Dir. of Information, Federal Dept. Energy, Mines and Resources; recreations: swimming, painting, movie making; Home: 21 Allan St., Oakville, Ont. L6J 3M7; Office: 10 Adelaide St. E., Toronto, Ont. M5C 1J3

STRAND, Kenneth, B.A., M.S., Ph.D.; university professor; b. Yakima, Washington, 30 June 1931; s. Adolph D. Strand and Margaret Jean Morren Thomson; e. Wash. State Coll., B.A. (Econ.) 1953; Univ. of Wis., M.S. (Econ.) 1956, Ph.D. (Econ.) 1959; m. Elna Karen, d. John Tomaske, 22 Dec. 1960; Prof. Econs., Simon Fraser Univ. (Pres. 1968-74); Instr. and Teaching Asst., Univ. of Wis.; 1956-58; Acting Assistant Professor, Washington State University, 1959-60; Oberlin College, Assistant Professor 1963-65; author: "Jurisdictional Disputes in Construction: The Causes, The Joint Board and the NLRB", 1961; other writings incl. articles for various prof. journs.; mem., Candn. Indust. Relations Assn. Indust. Relations Research Assn.; Am. Econ. Assn.; Internat. Indust. Relations Assn.; Candn. Econ. Assn.; Home: R.R.1, Box 9C, Port Moody, B.C. V3H 3C8

STRANGWAY, David W., M.A., Ph.D., F.R.A.S., F.R.S.C.; geophysicist; b. Simcoe, Ont., 7 June 1934; s. Walter Earl and Alice Kathleen (Skinner) S.; e. Univ. of Toronto, B.A. 1956, M.A. 1958, Ph.D. 1960; m. Alice Norine, d. Omer Gow, Fergus, Ont., 20 Sept. 1957; children: Richard Paul, Susan Kathleen, Patricia Ruth; VICE-PRES. AND PROVOST, UNIV. OF TORONTO 1980- ; former Chrmn., Dept. of Geol., Univ. of Toronto 1972; Assoc. Prof. of Physics 1968-71; Prof. of Physics since 1971; Sr.

Geophysicist, Dominion Gulf Co., May-Oct. 1956; Chief Geophysicist, Ventures Ltd., Toronto, 1956-57 and Consultant 1957-58, 1958-60; Research Geophysicist, Kennecott Copper Corp., Denver, 1960-61; Asst. Prof. of Geol., Univ. of Colo., 1961-64; Asst. Prof. of Geophysics, Mass. Inst. of Technol., 1965-68; Chief, Geophysics Br. NASA, Johnson Space Center, Houston, Texas 1970-72; Chief, Physics Br. 1972-73 and subsequently Acting Chief, Planetary and Earth Sci. Div. and Interim Dir., Lunar Sci. Inst., spring-summer 1973; Visiting Prof., Dept. of Geol., Univ. of Houston, 1971-73; research as principal investigator or co-investigator: magnetic and elect. prooperties of lunar samples; surface elect. properties exper. (S-204) Apollo 17; magnetic and elect. properties of rocks and minerals; geophys. application of ELF and VLF signals; applications of radio frequency interferometry to glacier and permafrost sounding; lab. microwave radar and thermal emission studies of basalt soil in vacuum; continental crust and its min. deposits; audio magnetotelluric sounding; magnetism and stratigraphy in Blake River volcanics; awards: NASA Medal for Exceptional Scientific Achievement, 1972; Virgil Kauffman Gold Medal, Soc. of Explor. Geophys., 1974; Fellow, Roy. Soc. Can., 1974; Pahlavi Lectr., Govt. Iran, 1978; author, "Electromagnetic Scale Modeling in Methods and Techniques in Geophysics", 1966; "The History of the Earth's Magnetic Field", 1970; other writings (as author and co-author) incl. over 100 articles for various scient. journs., papers, book chapters; mem. Ed. Bd., "Geoexploration"; "The Moon"; "Physics and Chemistry of Minerals"; "Geophysical Research Letters"; mem., Soc. Exploration Geophysicists; AGU; EAEG; Soc. of Geomag. and Geoelect.; Geol. Assn. Can.; Candn. Geophys. Union; Am. Assn. Advanc. Sci.; Candn. Explor. Geophys.; Scitec; Hon. mem., Cdn. Soc. of Exploration Geophysicists; United Church; Home: 54A Maple Ave., Toronto, Ont. M4W 2T7; Office: Toronto, Ont. M5S 1A1

STRATAS Teresa (Anastasia Stratakis) O.C., B. Mus; singer; b. Toronto, Ont., 26 May 1938; d. Emanuel and Argero Stratakis; e. studied Voice with Irene Jessner 1956-59; B. Mus; Univ. of Toronto 1959; won Metropolitan Opera Auditions and joined Met. Opera 1959; has sung major roles with every major opera house in world; repetoire includes leading roles in operas "La Boheme", "Eugene Omegin", "Marriage of Figaro", "Pagliacci", "Bartered Bride", "La Traviata", "Rusalka", "Mahogonny", "Lulu"; many recordings and films; Performer of Year Award, Can. Music Council 1979; Address: c/o Metropolitan Opera Co., Lincoln Centre Plaza, New York., N.Y. 10023

STRATE, Grant, B.A., LL.B.; choreographer; b. Cardston, Alta., 7 Dec. 1927; s. Alfred R. and Mabel (Wilson) S.; e. High Sch., Cardston, Alta.; Univ. of Alta., B.A., LL.B.; DIRECTOR, CENTRE FOR THE ARTS, SIMON FRASER UNIVERSITY, 1980- ; read law with Ford, Lindsay, Edmonton; called to Bar of Alta. 1951; choreographer, Nat. Ballet of Can. (20 ballets); 4 ballets, Studio Ballet, Antwerp, Belgium; 1 ballet Julliard Sch. of Dance, N.Y.; 3 ballets, Royal Swedish Ballet, Stockholm; Dir., Programme in Dance and Assoc. Prof., York Univ.; rec'd Centennial Medal 1967; Queen's Jubilee Medal, 1978; mem., Candn. Theatre Centre; Actors Equity Assn.; Assn. Candn. Radio & TV Artists; Dance in Canada Assn.; recreations: reading, swimming, film, music; Home: 738 Hawks Ave., Vancouver, B.C. V5A 3J2; Office: Simon Fraser Univ., Burnaby, B.C. V5A 1S6.

STRATFORD, Philip, B.A., D. de l'U. (Paris); university professor; author; b. Chatham, Ont., 13 Oct. 1927; s. Dr. Reginald Killmaster and Phyllis (Coate) S.; e. Trinity Coll., Sch., Port Hope, Ont., 1945; Univ. of W. Ont., B.A. (Eng.) 1950 (Gold Medal in Eng.); Univ. de Paris, D. de l'U. 1954; m. Jacqueline, d. Vicomte de Puthod, Paris, 27 Sept. 1952; children: John, Catherine, Christopher, Peter, Anne, Marguerite; PROF. TITULAIRE, UNIV. DE

MONTREAL, since 1967 and Dir., Dépt. d'Etudes anglaises, 1969-75; Lectr., Assumption Univ. of Windsor, 1954-56; Asst. Prof., Univ. of W. Ont., 1956-63; Assoc. Prof. 1963-64; joined present Univ. as Prof. Agrégé, 1964-67; Responsable, Programme de Littérature Comparée, 1967-69; Book Ed., "Saturday Night", 1964-65; monthly column on "Quebec Books" for "Globe Magazine", Globe & Mail, Toronto; mem. Ed. Bd., "Journal of Canadian Studies" and "Ellipse"; "English Studies in Canada"; received President's Medal, University of W. Ontario, for "Best Scholarly Article in English", 1964; author, "Faith and Fiction: Creative Process in Greene and Mauriac", 1964; "Marie-Claire Elais", 1971; trans. "Convergence" by Jean Le Moyne, 1966; "In an Iron Glove" by Claire Martin, 1968; "The Madman, the Kite and the Island" by Félix Leclerc, 1976; Ed., "The Viking Portable Graham Greene", 1972; Ed. and transl. "André Laurendeau: Witness for Quebec" 1973; Editor "Stories from Quebec" 1974; Co-ed., "Voices from Québec" 1977; Compiler, "Bibliography of Canadian Books in Translation" 1977; other writings incl. articles for various journs.; mem., Assn. Candn. Univ. Teachers Eng.; Humanities Assn. Can.; Candn. Comparative Lit. Assn.; Founding mem., Lit. Translators' Assn.; Home: 31 Senneville Rd., Senneville, Que. H9X 1B7; Office: C.P. 6128, Montreal, Que. H3C 3J7

STRATHY, Colin Morris Ardagh, E.D., Q.C., B.A.; b. Toronto, Ont., 7 Aug. 1906; s. Gerard Brakenridge, Q.C., LL.D., and Mabel Theodora (Kirkpatrick) S.; e. Crescent Sch., Toronto, Ont. (1913-15); three schs. in England, 1916-19; Trinity Coll. Sch., Port Hope, Ont., 1919-23; Royal Mil. Coll., Kingston, Ont., 1923-27 . (Dipl.); Trinity Coll., Univ. of Toronto, B.A. 1930; Osgoode Hall, Toronto, Ont., 1930-33; m. Ethel Margaret, d. Herbert M. Bate, St. Catharines, Ont. 24 Aug. 1935; two d. Susan Elizabeth Carlisle, Patricia Ann Seton; PARTNER, STRATHY, ARCHIBALD, & SEAGRAM; Dir., Fidelity Insurance Co. of Canada; Canada Permanent Mortgage Corp.; Canada Permanent Trust Co.; read law with Blake, Lash, Anglin & Cassels, Toronto, Ont.; called to the Bar of Ont., 1933; cr. Q.C. 1953; practised law as a Partner of Ingersoll, Pepler & Strathy, St. Catharines, Ont., 1933-39, and after the war joined firm of Strathy, Cowan and Setterington which was estbd. by his father; and became firm Strathy Archibald Seagram & Cole 1969; Lieut. Q.O.R., 1927-33; Lieut. and Capt., Lincoln & Welland Regt., 1933-39; served in 2nd World War; Flying Offr., R.C.A.F., 1940, retired rank of Group Capt., Aug. 1946; was attached to Air Force Hdqrs. as Air Force Rep. on Staff of Judge Advocate Gen. in Ottawa, and successively held appts. as Asst. Judge Advocate Gen. and Deputy Judge Advocate Gen.; served as mem. of Interdept. Comte. Drafting War Crimes Regulations; Lay Del. to Synod Diocese of Toronto; served for five yrs. as Rector's Warden and as People's Warden of St. James Cathedral, Toronto; Kappa Alpha; Conservative; Anglican; recreations: golf, squash; Clubs: Toronto Golf; Toronto; University; Badminton & Racquet, York; Home: Apt. 1903, 20 Avoca Ave., Toronto, Ont. M4T 2B8; Office: 38th Floor, Commerce Crt. West, Box 438, Toronto, Ont. M5L 1J3

STRATTON, Carson Gilmour; banker; b. Valleyfield, Nfld. 17 Dec. 1930; m. Betty M. Davis Oct. 1953; children: Barry, Robert, Pamela, Patricia; mem. Bank of Montreal; Dir. Canadian-Dominion Leasing Corp. Ltd.; recreations: golf, fishing; Clubs: National; Donalda; Granite; Home: 34 Abbeywood Trail, Don Mills, Ont. M3B 3B3; Office: First Canadian Pl., First Bank Tower, Toronto, Ont. M5X 1A1.

STREATCH, Hon. Kenneth, M.L.A.; politician; b. 27 Jan. 1942; e. N.S. Agric. Coll. grad.; m. Barbara Blackburn; 5 children: MIN. OF LABOUR & MANPOWER, N.S.1978- ; Min. of Pub. Works 1978-79; Min. Responsible for Adm. Human Rights 1979; farmer; Past Pres. Fed. Agric.; Co. Councillor 5 yrs.; Past Pres. P. Cons. Cobequid Assn.; el. M.L.A. for Bedford-Musquodoboit Valley prov. g.e. 1978; P. Conservative; Office: (P.O. Box 697) 5151 Terminal Rd., Halifax, N.S. B3J 2T8.

STREET, His Hon. Thomas George, b. Thorold, Ontario, 4 January 1916; s. James Cunard and Marjorie Marie (MacTavish) S.; e. Public and High Sch., Welland, Ont.; Osgoode Hall, Toronto, Ont.; m. Beverly Joan, d. John H. Rolph, Welland, Ont., 27 Dec. 1941; children: Douglas Alan, Linda Marjorie, Thomas George; JUDGE, COUNTY AND DIST. COURTS, ONT., since 1974; read law with John H. Flett; called to the Bar of Ont., Sept. 1939; cr. Q.C. 1960; joined the firm of Macoomb & Macoomb, later Macoomb, Macoomb & Street, Welland, Ont. till 1941, rejoining again after the war till 1948 when apptd. Magistrate for the City of Welland and area; apptd. Deputy Judge of Juvenile and Family Courts, April 1956; Chairman, Nat. Parole Bd. Can. 1959-74; former Chairman, Police Comn. for City of Welland, etc.; former Dir. of Civil Defence, City of Welland; Pres., Jr. Chamber of Comm. and of Welland Badminton Club, 1941; mem. for 17 yrs. and Past Pres., Rotary Club of Welland; served in 2nd World War, 4 yrs. in Candn. Active Army, 3 yrs. Overseas; Saskatoon Light Inf., 1st Div., Sicily, Italy; Air Liaison Offr., Yugoslavia, Greece and Corsica; wounded in Sicily; 48th Highlanders, rank of Capt.; O.C. 170th Batty. of 57th Light anti-aircraft Regt., Welland, Ont., with rank of Major, 1947-52; awarded Centennial Medal, 1967; Hon. Life mem., Ont. Magistrates' Assn. (formerly mem. of Extve.); Pres., Assn. of Paroling Authorities; former Vice Pres., Am. Correctional Assn. and Fed. Lawyer's Club; Fed. Lawyer's Club of Ottawa; Candn. Bar Assn.; Hon. mem., Candn. Assn. of Chiefs of Police; recreations: skiing, golf, tennis; Clubs: London; Royal Ottawa Golf; London Hunt and Country; London; London Tennis; Office: Court House, London, Ont. N6A 2P3

STREIGHT, Harvey Richard Lyle, M.A., Ph.D., D.Sc., F.C.I.C.; chemist and chemical engineer; b. New Westminster, B.C., 31 May 1907; s. Harvey Milton and Alice Maud (Daniels) S.; e. Univ. of B.C., B.A. (Hons.) 1927, M.A. 1929; 1851 Exhibitioner, Birmingham Univ., Ph.D. 1932; Oxford Univ., post-doctoral studies 1932-33; Univ. of Waterloo, D.Sc. 1962; m. late Sina Margaret Burrows; children: Alison Jean, Margaret Catherine; 2ndly Claire Brehaut, 6 Sept. 1975; Extve. Vol., Canadian Extve. Service Overseas since 1974; Science Adv., Candn. Enterprise Devel. Corp. Ltd. 1972-74; Past Principal Research Engr., Du Pont of Canada Ltd. 1968-72; Research Chem., Imperial Chemical Industries, Widnes, Eng., 1933; Group Leader, Heavy Chems. & Chem. Engn., Research Lab., 1935; joined Candn. Industries Ltd. as Devel. Mgr., Windsor Works, 1937; Process Design Engr., Engn. Dept., Montreal, 1939; Sr. Engr., Research & Devel. Depts.; Sr. Eng., Nylon Div., 1952; joined present Co. as Sr. Engr. 1954; Princ. Chem. Engr. 1956; patents held with ICI, CIL and Du Pont in Can., US. and other countries;; rec'd Plummer Medal, Engn. Inst. Can., 1958; Queen's Jubilee Medal 1978; past mem. Fed. Govt.-Student Guidance Comte. (Chem. Engn.); author of "Design of Absorption Towers" and tech. papers publ. in scient. journs. in Can. and Europe; past mem. Ed. Bds., "Chemistry in Canada", "Canadian Journal for Chemical Engineering"; past mem. Indust. Adv. Council, Univ. of Waterloo; Fellow, Royal Chem. Inst. Australia; Chem. Inst. Can.; Am. Inst. Chem. Engrs.; Past Councillor and Pres., Chem. Inst. Can.; Chrmn., Internat. Chem. Engn. Symposium; mem. Candn. Soc. Chem. Engrs.; Corp. Engrs. Que.; Am. Inst. Chem. Engrs.; Phi Delta Theta; Liberal; Protestant; Freemason (Shriner); recreations: travelling, bridge; Home: 4085 Gage Rd., Montreal, Que. H3Y 1R6

STREIT, Mrs. J. Douglas., O.C. (1967), B.A., (Marlene Stewart); amateur golfer; b. Cereal, Alta., 9 Mar. 1934; d. Harold Stewart; e. High Sch.; Rollins, Coll., Winter Park,

Fla., B.A. (Business Adm.) 1956; m. Douglas Streit, 5 April 1957; two d., Darlene Louise, Lynn Elizabeth; began golfing at Lookout Point Golf Club, Fonthill, Ont.; won Ont. Ladies' Championship, 1951, 56, 57, 58, 68, 69, 70, 72, 74, 76, 77; Ont. Jr., 1951; Candn. Ladies' Closed Championship, 1951-57 succesively and 1963; placed 1st in some 10 club tournaments, incl. invitation events in St. Catharines, Oshawa, Kingston, London, Brantford and Toronto, 1951; won Cdn. Ladies Amateur Championship 1951, 1954-56, 1958, 59, 63, 68, 69, 72, 73; semi-finalist in Ont. Ladies' Championship, 1952; won Brit. Ladies Championship, 1953; semi-finalist, 1954; Brit. Women's Amateur at Portcawl, Wales, 1953, 42nd Candn. Ladies' Open Golf at Royal Colwood, Victoria, B.C., 1954, 1955; U.S. Women's Amateur at Meridian Hills Country Club, Indianapolis, 22 Sept. 1956 (first Candn.); U.S. Nat. Intercollegiate, 1956; U.S.N. and S., 1956; Jasper Park, Alta. Totem Pole Tournament, also Medallist, 1956; U.S. Nat. Mixed Foursome with Hobart Manley 1953, with Hillman Robbins 1958, Jack Penrose, 1959 and Hobart Manley, 1963; Nat. Ladies' Two Ball, 1956 with Anne Cassey Johnson; Candn. Commonwealth Team, 1959, 1963, 1967, 1979; Helen Lee Doherty Championship 1959, 60, 61, 65; el. to Can.'s Sports Hall of Fame, 1962; Cdn. Golf Hall of Fame 1974; voted Lou E. Marsh Trophy as Can.'s outstanding athlete, 1951 and 1956; Ont. Sportswriters and Sportscasters Assn., Ont. Outstanding Athlete of the Year, 1951, 1953, 1956; Candn. Woman Athlete of the Year, 1951, 53, 56, 60, 63; tied with Charlotte Whitton in Candn. Press Poll, Woman of the Year, 1953; named Outstanding Female Athlete of the Year in Nat. Poll of Sportswriters, 1951, 52, 53; Low Amateur U.S. Women's Open, 1961; won Australian Women's Amateur, 1963; Women's Amateur of Palm Peach, 1965; mem., Candn. Commonwealth Team, 1959, 63; won (9th) Candn. Women's Amateur Golf title, 1969, (10th) 1972 Candn. Open (Duchess of Connaught Cup); 11th 1973; won North and South Amateur Golf Tournament 1974; Playing Capt. of winning Candn. Team at Commonwealth Golf Tournament, Perth, Australia; Kappa Alpha Theta Sorority; Clubs: York Downs Golf Club; Life mem. Lookout Point Golf; Scarborough Golf; Lambton Golf; Weston Golf; Toronto Ladies Golf; The Toronto Golf; St. George's Golf & Country; Summit Golf & Country; Home: R.R. 4, Stouffville, Ont. L0H 1L0

STRICKLAND, Vernon D'Eyncourt, retired executive; b. Pembroke, Ontario, 18 April 1903; s. Percy D'Eyncourt and Mabel Gertrude (Bright) S.; e. Upper Canada Coll., Toronto, Ont. 1913-20; Univ. of Toronto, B.A.Sc. (Mech. Engn.) 1925; m. Edith Mary, d. Hon. C.J. Burchell, Halifax, N.S., 21 Aug. 1931; remarried Flora C. Feathslontaugh; children: Paul D.,Susan B. (Medland); Dir., Ont. Bd., C.N.I.B.-Eng. Speaking Union; Past Dir., DRG Ltd.; Ercona Adhesives Ltd.; Globe Envelopes Ltd.; Gage Stationery Co.; E.S. & A. Robinson (Can.) Ltd.; Sellotape Can. Ltd.; Kappa Alpha; Anglican; Conservative; recreation: golf; Clubs: University; Caledon; Toronto Golf; Toronto Hunt; Home: 1 Old Forest Hill Road, Toronto, Ont. M5P 2P6

STROM, Harry, M.L.A.; ret. politician; b. Burdett, Alta., 7 July 1914; m. Ruth Johnson, 27 Oct. 1928; children: Howard, Faith, Beverley, Brian, Ronald, Arlene; first el. to Alta. Leg. 1955; apptd. Min. of Agric. Oct. 1962, Min. of Mun. Affairs July 1968; Premier of Alberta 12 Dec. 1968-10 Sept 1971 (Govt. def.); Leader of Opposition in the Leg. Assembly 1971-73; M.L.A. 1955-75; Social Credit; Evangelical Free Church; Home: 11132-54th Ave., Edmonton, Alta. T6H 0V6; Office: Legislative Bldg., Edmonton, Alta.

STRONG, George Gordon, B.A., B.Com., M.B.A., J.D.; retired publisher; b. Vancouver, B.C., 28 Dec. 1913; s. Charles Edmund and Lillian St. Clair (Grant) S.; e. Univ. of B.C., B.Com. 1933, B.A. 1934; Northwestern Univ., M.B.A. 1935; Univ. of Cal., grad. work 1935-36; Univ. of

Toledo, J.D. 1940; m. Jean Boyd, d. Colin McDougall, 7 Aug. 1935; children: George Gordon , Jr.; Jeanne Adele Williams; PRES., OAKLAND TRIBUNE 1977-80; President Thomson-Brush-Moore Newspapers, Inc. 1968-77; Director, Island Press, Bermuda; Dir., Great Lakes Paper Company; Mutual Insurance Co. (Bermuda) 1965-81; Associated Press 1973-79; Mutual Reinsurance Co. 1972-81; Territorial Ins. Co. (Bermuda) 1972-81; called to Bar of Ohio 1940; Gen. Mgr. and Dir., Brush-Moore Newspapers, Inc., 1952-54; Pres. and Gen. Mgr., 1954-64; Pres. and Publisher, 1964-68; Dir., Ohio Broadcasting Co., 1952-68; Pres. and Dir., Pen-Mar Publishing Co. 1958-68; Salisbury (Md.) Times 1959-68; Weirton Newspapers, Inc. 1963-68; Chrmn. and Dir., Thompson Newspapeer, 1972-77; served with Am. Red Cross as Dir. of Accounting & Finance, Mediterranean Theatre, 1943-45; Del. to Repub. Convention, 1956; Trustee, Hiram Coll. 1967-77; Aultman Hosp., Canton, Ohio 1955-79; mem., Ohio Newspaper Assn. (Dir. since 1948-72; Pres. 1956-57); Am. Newspaper Publishers Assn. (Dir. 1956-64; Dir. Research Inst. 1956-64; Dir. Bureau Advertising since 1957; Vice Chrmn. Bd. 1962-64 and Chrmn. 1964-66; Dir. Foundation 1964-66); Inland Daily Press Assn. (Dir. 1958-61); Freemason (Shriner); Beta Gamma Sigma; Beta Alpha Psi; Delta Upsilon; Republican; Presbyterian; recreations: golf, travel; Home: 10 Hillcrest Ct., Oakland, Ca. 94619; Office: 3410 Lakeshore #205, Oakland, Ca. 94610

STRONG, Maurice F., O.C.; business, public and international administrator; b. Oak Lake, Manitoba, 29 Apl. 1929; s. Frederick Milton and Mary (Fyfe) S.; e. Oak Lake (Man.) High Sch.; Hon. degrees from 23 Universities in Can., U.S., & Europe; m. Pauline Olivette, d. Joseph Williams, Sidney, Man., 29 July 1950; div. 1980; m. Hanne Marstrand, 1981; children: Frederick Maurice, Maureen Louise, Mary Anne, Alice, Kenneth Martin; CHRMN., INTERNAT. ENERGY DEV. CORP. Geneza; Switzerland, 1980- ; Chrmn. of Bd. AZL Resources Inc., Phoenix Arizona; Chrmn., Credit Immobilier, Geneva; Vice-Chrmn. Soc. Gén. pour l'Energie et les Ressources, Geneva Switz.; Dir. & Mem. Exec. Comte., Canada Development Corp.; Chrmn., North-South Energy Round Table; Chrmn., Petro Canada 1976-78; Chrmn. Bd. Dirs. Internat Devel. Research centre 1977-78; Pres., Canadian International Devel. Agency since 1966-70; Trustee, Aspen Inst. for Humanistic Studies; Vice Pres., mem. Extve. Comte., World Wildlife Fund, Morges Switzerland; Chrmn., Bureau of the Internat. Union for Conservation of Nature & Natural Resources, Geneva Switz.; mem. Extve. Comte. & Founding Co. Chrmn., Internat. Foundation for Dev. Alternatives, Nyon Switz.; mem. Adv. Bd., Inst. of Ecology, Padjadjaran. Univ., Bandung Indonesia.; mem. Internat. Hon. Comte., Dag Hammarskold Foundation, Uppsala Sweder; mem., Adv. Comte., Centre for Internat. Environment. Information, New York; Accountant, Vincent Mining Corp., Toronto, 1945-47 (helped found New Horizons Explorations Ltd. of which was Dir. and Secy.-Treas) mem. of Secretariat of Un. Nations (N.Y.C.) 1947-48; Securities Analyst, James Richardson & Sons, Winnipeg and Calgary, 1948-51; Asst. to Pres., Dome Exploration (Western) Ltd., 1951-52; Vice-Pres. and Treas., Dome Petroleum Ltd. and assoc. cos., 1954-59; formed M. F. Strong Management Ltd., Calgary, and assumed mang. of Ajax Petroleums Ltd.; reorganizing this co. to form Candn. Indust. Gas Ltd.; became Pres., Power Corp. of Canada Ltd., Montreal, Que., 1964, and Pres. or Dir. of many corporations; Visiting Prof., York Univ., 1969; Montague Burton Prof. Internat. Relations, Univ. Edinburgh 1974; Extve. Dir., U.N. Environment Programme 1973; Tylor Ecology Award 1973; Pahlavi Environment Prize, Govt. Iran 1976; Nat. Audubon Soc. Award, 1975; Mellon Award, 1975; Freedom Festival Award, 1975; Order of Can., 1976; Henri Pittier Order of the Golden Ark (Netherlands) 1979; Past Pres., Nat. Council of YMCAs of Can.; former mem. Extve. Comte. World Alliance of YMCAs; United Church; recreations: swimming, fishing, hiking; riding,

photography; clubs: Calgary Petroleum; Ranchmen's (Calgary); Mount Royal (Montreal); Rideau; Home: 3 Whitehall Court, London SW1, England; Office: 32 St James's St., London SW1A, England.

STRONG, Richard Allen, R.C.A.; landscape architect; b. Chardon, Ohio 26 Sept. 1930; s. Harold Theodore and Hellen (Quiggle) S.; e. Chardon (Ohio) High Sch. 1948; Ohio State Univ. Bachelor Landscape Arch. 1957 (Cert. of Merit; Distinguished Alumnae Award); Harvard Univ. Master Landscape Arch. 1959 (Uriel Crocker Scholarship); m. Georgia Olson d. George John Olson 19 Feb. 1979; children: Greg Allen, ScotAnn, Michael Allen (all by previous marriage); PRES. AND DIR., RICHARD STRONG ASSOCIATES LTD. 1961- ; Dir. Richard Strong Associates, Boseman, Mont.; Pres. and Founder, Sasaki Strong Associates, Toronto; Richard Strong-Steven Moorhead Associates, Toronto; maj. works incl. Expo '67, numerous nat. and prov. parks, maj. housing, indust. and corporate projects; in Can., USA and Australia; Chrmn. and Prof. of Landscape Arch. Univ. of Toronto, estbd. Landscape Arch. Program 1967-77; Visiting Critic or Lectr. Univ. of Guelph, Univ. of Man., Univ. of Calgary, Harvard Univ., Univ. of Mass., Ohio State Univ., Univ. of Mich., Univ. of Minn., Mont. State Univ.; Councilor Twp. of Eromosa, Ont. 1975-77; mem. Planning Bd. Eromosa Twp. 1974-77; Guelph Suburban Planning Bd. 1975-76; recipient Am. Soc. Landscape Archs. Honor Awards; author various articles and projects Candn., USA, UK and Australian prof. journs. and mags.; served with U.S. Army Signal Corps 1951-53, Germany; P. Conservative; Protestant; recreations: flying, fishing, hunting, camping, skiing, swimming, hiking; Home: 1140 15th Ave. S.W., Calgary, Alta. T2R 0S7; Office: 202 10th Ave. S.E., Calgary, Alta. T2G 0W1.

STRUM, Gladys Grace May, B.A., B.Ed., b. Gladstone, Man., 4 Feb. 1906; d. Luther Powell and Sarah Jane (Loggins) Lamb; e. Normal Sch., Moosomin and Regina, Sask.; Univ. of Sask., B.A. and B.Ed. 1962; m. Warner, s. William Strum, Fargo, Md., 16 Nov. 1926; one d. Carol; def. Cand. for Sask. Leg., g.e. 1938 and 1944; M.P. for Qu'Appelle, 1945-49; M.L.A. for Saskatoon 1960-64; 1st woman Pres., C.C.F., Sask., 1944-45 (1st woman to head a pol. organ.); mem., Nat. Council, C.C.F.; mem., I.O.D.E.; N.D.P.; United Church, recreation: interior decorating; Home: 1505 Duncan Ave., Penticton, B.C. V2A 2X7

STRUTH, George Ronald; manufacturer; music publisher; b. Toronto, Ont., 23 June 1931; s. George Alfred and Margery (McComb) S.; m. Muriel Wood; three children; PRESIDENT QUALITY RECORDS LTD.; Dir. Quality Records of America Ltd.; Shediac Music Publishing Ltd.; Quality Music Publishing Ltd.; Past Pres. Candn. Recording Indust. Assn.; Dir. Candn. Acad. Recording Arts & Sciences; Anglican; Home: 24 Windy Ridge Dr., Scarborough, Ont. M1M 1H5; Office: 380 Birchmount Rd., Scarborough, Ont. M1K 1M7

STUART, John L., B. Com.; company executive; b. Kingston, Ont., 30 Aug. 1929; s. John and Hilda B. (Henderson) S.; e. Kelvin Tech. High Sch., Winnipeg, Man., 1947; St. Paul's Coll.; Queen's Univ., B. Com. 1952; m. Shirley Frances, d. Edward Wilson and Edna Conrad, Toronto, Ont., 9 June 1956; children: John William, Shirley Anne; PRESIDENT, STUART HOUSE CANADA LTD.; Stuart House Internat. Ltd.; Protestant; recreation: fishing; Home: 156 Princess Anne Cres., Islington, Ont. M9A 2R6; Office: 22 Lido Rd., Weston, Ont. M9M 1M6

STUART, Ronald Stiles, M.A., Ph.D.; pharmaceutical executive; b. Tingley, N.B., 26 March 1919; s. Frederick Alvah and Flora Margaret (Tingley) S.; e. Univ. of N.B., B.A. 1940; Univ. of Toronto, M.A. 1941, Ph.D. (Organic Chem.) 1944 (Nat. Research Council Can. Scholar); m. Mary Irene, d. Byron Samuel Vanstone, 21 Sept. 1946;

four s., Brian, David, Robert, Craig; DIR., AND EXTVE. DIR. OF RESEARCH, MERCK FROSST LABS., since 1968; Dir., Charles E. Frosst & Co.; Merck Sharp and Dohme Can. Ltd.; Demonst. in Chem., Univ. of Toronto, 1940-42; Research Assoc., Nat. Research Council of Can., 1943-45; Asst. Dir. Research, Dom. Tar & Chem. Co., 1945-48; Mgr., Chem. & Biol. Control, Merck & Co., Ltd., 1948-53, Science Devel. 1953-60, Tech. and Prod. Operations, 1960-62, Research Dir., 1962-65; Pres. (since 1967) and Dir. (since 1961), Montreal Oral Sch. for the Deaf (Educ. Officer 1965-66; President 1967-71 and since Hon. mem. Board); Protestant; recreations: scouting, swimming; Club: University; Home: 2265 rue Cambridge, Ville Mont Royal, Que. H3R 2Y4; Office: 16711 Trans Canada Highway, Kirkland, Que. H9H 3L1

STUART-STUBBS, Basil Frederick, B.A., B.L.S.; librarian; b. Moncton, N.B. 3 Feb. 1930; s. Thomas Edward and Amy (Jefferson) S.; e. Univ. of B.C. B.A. 1952; McGill Univ. B.L.S. 1954; DIR., SCH. OF LIBRARIANSHIP, U. OF B.C., 1981; Univ. Librarian, Univ. of B.C. Lib. 1964-81; Reference Librarian, McGill Univ. Lib. 1954-56; Catalogue Librarian, Univ. of B.C. Lib. 1956, Serials Librarian 1958, Head of Special Collections Div. 1960, Coordinator of Collections 1962-64; Nat. Library Adv. Bd. Bibliographic and Communications Network Comte.; Chmn., C.N.I.B. Library Bd. of Mgt.; B.C. Arts Bd.; Chrmn. Bd., Univ. of B.C. Press; mem. Bd., Vancouver City Archives; Adv. Bd. Scient. & Tech. Information; Bd., Candn. Inst. Hist. Microreproductions; co-author "interlibrary Loan in Canada" 1976; "A Survey and Interpretation of the Literature of Interlibrary Loan" 1976; "The Northpart of America" 1979; numerous articles, papers; mem. Candn. Lib. Assn. (former mem. Council, Chrmn. Copyright Comte.); B.C. Lib. Assn.; Home: 2320 W. 40th Ave., Apt. 321, Vancouver, B.C V6M 4H6; Office: 1956 Main Mall, Univ. of B.C., Vancouver, B.C. V6T 1Y3.

STUBBS, Harold St. George, Q.C.; b. Birtle, Manitoba, 26 Nov. 1912; S. Lewis St. George and Mary (Wilcock) S.; e. Provencher High Sch., St. Boniface, Man., 1927-30; Univ. of Manitoba, 1930-31; Manitoba Law Sch., LL.B. 1936 (Gold Medallist in final year); m. Genevieve Olivine (d. 1964), d. Harrison Dollard, Winnipeg, Man., 18 July 1938; children: Sydney St. George, Maria St. George, Cynthia St. George; m. 2ndly, Eva Wolinsky Koves, 2 Mar. 1965; 1 s., Christopher St. George; PARTNER, STUBBS & STUBBS; Secy. and Treas., Law Soc. of Manitoba; Lectr., Man. Law Sch., since 1955; Pres., Manitoba Bar Assn., 1957-58; mem. of Municipal Council, Fort Garry, Man. (four yrs. on Fort Garry Sch. Bd.); read law with Marcus Hyman, Q.C., and with his father; called to the Bar of Man., 1937; cr. Q.C. 1953; served in 2nd World War with R.C.A.F., 1941-45 as Pilot and Flying Offr.; Liberal; recreations: golf, curling; Clubs: Southwood Golf & Country; Holly Snowshoe; Wildwood Club; Home: 59 Agassiz, Fort Garry, Man. R3T 2K9; Office: 1400, 155 Carlton St., Winnipeg, Man.

STULBERG, Gordon, B.A., LL.B.; motion picture executive; b. Toronto, Ont., 17 Dec. 1923; s. Samuel and Lillian (Newman) S.; e. Univ. of Toronto, B.A. 1946; Cornell Univ., LL.B. 1949; m. Helen, d. Maurice Applebaum, Los Angeles, Cal., 18 March 1953; children: Jac, Scott, Lisa, Tina; PRES. AND C.O.O., POLYGRAM PICTURES CORP., 1980- ; Partner, Mitchell, Silberberg and Knupp 1975-81; Dir., Penn. Corp. Financial; called to Bars of N.Y. and Cal.; Assoc., Pacht, Ross, Warne & Bernhard, 1949-56; Extve. Asst. to Vice Pres., Columbia Pictures Corp., 1956-60; Vice Pres. and Chief Studio Adm. Offr. 1960-67; Pres., Cinema Center Films (div. of CBS), 1967-71; Pres., 20th Century Fox 1971-75; served with RCAF 1942-45; Chrmn., Un. Jewish Welfare Fund 1963-64; Motion Picture Permanent Charities 1962-63; mem. Beverley Hills Bar Assn.; Los Angeles Copyright Soc. (Founder); recreations: swimming, fishing, tennis; Home: 425 Com-

stock Ave., Los Angeles, Cal. 90024; Office: 3940 Overland Ave., Culver City, Cal. 90230

STURDY, Kenneth Gordon; artist; art educator; b. Peny-lan, Wales 19 Apl. 1920; s. Wilfred and Mary Alice (Rushton) S.; e. Holloway Sch. London, Eng.; Loughborough Coll. Eng. D.L.C. (Hons.) 1949; Chelsea Sch. of Art London D.A. (Chelsea) 1953; Nat. Dipl. in Design 1953; m. 1stly Mary d. late William Stephenson 15 March 1942; children: Robin Wilfred, Zoë Helen (Mrs. R. Brownlee), Valentine Kevin; m. 2ndly Frances Una d. Late Neil McLaren Tosh, Gourock, Scot. 20 July 1963; children: Christopher Jeremy Kenneth, Lochinvar, Honey Alice; HEAD, ALBERTA COLL. OF ART; joined Ont. Dept. Educ. 1954; Alta. Coll. of Art 1954-62 and since 1969; Prot. Sch. Bd. Greater Montreal 1963-66; Glasgow Sch. of Art. Scot. 1966-67; Can. Council Award (Italy) 1967-68; served with RN Convoy Escort Vessels and Combined Operations 1941-46, rank Petty Offr.; Chrmn. Calgary Allied Arts Foundation; Bd. mem. Calgary Region Arts. Foundation; Past Pres. Alta. Soc. Artists; mem. Inst. Pub. Adms. Can.; Candn. Inst. Pub. Affairs; Anglican; Home: 1107-15 St. N.W., Calgary, Alta. T2N 2B5; Office: 1301-16 Ave. N.W., Calgary, Alta. T2M 0L4

STURSBERG, Peter; writer and broadcaster; b. Chefoo, China, 31 Aug. 1913; s. Walter Arthur and Mary Ellen (Shaw) S.; e. Royal Oak Pub. Sch., B.C.; Bedford Sch., England; West Hill High Sch., Montreal, P.Q.; McGill Univ.; m. Jessamy, d. late J. H. Anderson Robertson, 5 Oct. 1946; children: Richard Barclay, Judith Mary; began as Reporter with Victoria "Daily Times", 1934-38; Empire Press Union Exchange Reporter, "Daily Herald", London, Eng., 1938-39; Reporter, Vancouver "Daily Province", 1939-40; News Editor, Candn. Broadcasting Corp., Vancouver, B.C., 1941-43; War Corr., C.B.C., 1943-45, first to broadcast on Candns. in action (Sicilian invasion); Roving Foreign Corr., "Daily Herald", London, 1945-50 (travelled extensively in Europe, India, W. Indies, Africa); United Nations Corr., C.B.C., 1950-56; Ottawa Ed., Toronto Daily Star 1956-57; briefly, Research Offr. to Prime Min.; Secy., Candn. Trade Mission to U.K., 1957-58; Ottawa Newscaster, Commentator, CJOH, CTV 1960-73; Instructor, Cdn. Studies, Simon Fraser Univ., 1980- ; author: "Journey Into Victory", 1944; "Agreement in Principle", 1961; "Those Were The Days", 1969; "Mister Broadcasting, The Ernie Bushnell Story", 1971; "Diefenbaker Leadership Gained 1956-62" 1975; "Diefenbaker Leadership Lost 1962-67" 1976; "Lester Pearson and the Dream of Unity" 1978; "Lester Pearson and the American Dilemma" 1980; received Candn. Radio Award 1950; mem. of Bd. of Govs., U.N. Internat. Sch., New York, 1952-55; Vice-Pres., U.N. Corr. Assn., 1955-56; Life mem., Press Gallery, Ottawa; Candn. War Corrs. Assn.; Anglican; recreations: tennis, reading; Club: National Press; Hollyburn Country Home: 5132 Alderfield Pl., W. Vancouver, B.C. V7W 2W7

SUDDICK, Patrick J., B.A.Sc., P.Eng.; company exeuctive; b. London, Ont., 27 Sept. 1923; s. Percy Edward and Mrs. (Jones) S.; e. Univ. of Toronto, B.A.Sc. (Engn. & Business) 1949; m. Mary, d. late Joseph Walsh, 7 July 1951; children: Paul, Peter, Michael, Jane, Mark; VICE PRES. CORP. FIELD MARKETING; DIR, HONEYWELL LTD.; AND Honeywell Holdings Ltd.; Engn. Sales for 2½ yrs., B. F. Goodrich Rubber Co.; joined Honeywell 1953; Sales Rep., Indust. Div., Toronto, 1953; estbd. and headed up Candn. Transport Div., Montreal, 1954; Candn. Rep., Boston Div. (formerly Doelcam), 1955; Head, Candn. Ordinance & Marine Divs., 1956; Asst. Mgr., Service Engn. Dept. Candn. Aeronautical Div., 1957; Comm. Div., Sales, 1958; Gen. Mgr., EDP Div., 1965; Vice Pres., EDP Div., 1968; Vice Pres. & Gen. Mgr., Information Systems 1970; mem., Cdn. NIAG, Delegation to NATO; served with RCA in Can., Eng., Holland and Germany during World War II; Chmn., Bd. Govs., Seneca Coll.; Past Chrmn., Candn. Nat. Business Show,

Data Processing Conf.; mem., Assn. Prof. Engrs. Ont.; Past Pres. Candn. Business Equipment Mfrs. Assn.; Bd. Trade Metrop. Toronto; R. Catholic; recreations: golf, gardening, bridge, squash; Club: Granite; Home: 7 Gossamer Ave., Willowdale, Ont. M2M 2X1 Office: The Honeywell Centre, 155 Gordon Baker Rd., Willowdale, Ont. M2H 3N7

SUEDFELD, Peter, B.A., M.A., Ph.D.; university professor; b. Budapest, Hungary 30 Aug. 1935; came to Can. 1972; s. Leslie John Field and Jolan (Eichenbaum) S.; e. Univ. of the Philippines, 1956-57; Queen's Coll., City Univ. of N.Y., B.A. 1960; Princeton Univ. M.A. 1962, Ph.D. 1963; m. Gabrielle Debra Guterman 11 June 1961; children: Michael Thomas, Joanne Ruth, David Lee; PROF. AND DEPT. HEAD, PSYCHOLOGY, UNIV. OF B.C. since 1972; Research Assoc., Princeton Univ., 1963-64; Visiting Asst. Prof., Univ. of Illinois, 1964-65; Asst. Prof. and Chrmn., Dept. of Psych., Univ. Coll., Rutgers Univ., 1965-72; served with U.S. Army, 1955-58; U.S. Air Force Reserve, 1958-72, discharged 1st Lieut.; Invited Lectr. in inst. and meetings North, Central and South America, Europe, Australia, N.Z., Japan; author of "Social Processes", 1966; "Personality Theory and Information Processing", 1971; "The Behavioral Basis of Design", 1976-77; "Attitude Change: The Competing Views," 1971; "Restricted Environmental Stimulation," 1980; Ed., "Journal of Applied Social Psychology," 1976-82; other writings incl. over 100 scientific articles and book chapters in anthologies on intellectual functioning, decision making, the effects of environmental factors on human behaviour, health maintenance and enhancement, international and political problem solving; mem. of various ed. bds., assn. cmtes.; grant reviewer for US and Candn. govt. agencies; manuscript reviewer for professional jnls. and book publs.; Fellow, Candn. and Am. Psychol. Assns.; mem., Acad. of Behavioral Medicine Research; N.Y. Acad. of Sciences; Interamerican Soc. of Psychol.; Amer. Assn. for the Advancement of Science; Psychonomic Soc.; recreations: skiing, scuba diving, target shooting, fishing; Home: #2005 - 1501 Haro St., Vancouver, V.C. V6G 1G4; Office: Vancouver, B.C. V6T 1W5.

SULATYCKY, Allen, b. Hafford, Saskatchewan, 13 June 1938; s. Dmytro and Polly (Bodnarchuk) S.; m. Marilyn Joyce, d. Irvin Perkins, Calgary, Alta., 17 Feb. 1962; children: Warren, Robert, Annemarie, Donald; PARTNER, PARLEE, IRVING, HENNING, MUSTARD & RODNEY; Dir., Panarctic Oils Ltd.; candn. in fed. by-el. 1967; el. to H. of C. for Rocky Mt., g.e. 1968; apptd. Parlty. Secy. to Min. of Energy, Mines & Resources, 1971; Parlty. Secy. to Min. of Indian Affairs and Northern Devel., 1972; def. g.e. Oct. 1972; Liberal; Greek Orthodox; Office: 2100-300 - 5th Ave. S.W., Calgary Alta. T2P 3C4

SULLIVAN, His Honour Judge Allan, Q.C., B.A., LL.B.; b. New Glasgow, N.S., 23 June 1932; s. Dr. Charles A. and late Florence Fraser (MacNeil) S.; e. Central Sch. and Sydney (N.S.) Acad., 1950; Dalhousie Univ., B.A. 1954. LL.B. 1956; m. Dawn Christina, d. late J. Andrew Simpson, 9 July 1956; children: Lynn, Shauna, Janet, Florie, Allan; JUDGE OF COUNTY COURT FOR DISTRICT 7 AND LOCAL JUDGE OF SUPREME COURT, 1976; read law with John MacNeil, Q.C.; called to Bar of N.S. 1956; practised law with Sullivan, Smith, Campbell and Bourdreau; appointed Minister Welfare and Mines, Minister under the Water Act 1970-72; Min. of Public Works, 1972; Min. Responsible for Civil Service, 1972; Min. of Education, 1973; Attorney Gen. & Min. of Human Rights 1973-75; Min. of Health, 1975; Gov. House Leader, 1971-76; Dir., Bairncroft (child-caring institute); Chmn. Bd. of Gov., College of Cape Breton; Dir., Alexander Graham Bell Inst.; mem., Nova Scotia Barristers' Society; Cape Breton and Canadian Barristers' Associations; Candn. Judges Assn; Freemason; Liberal; Presbyterian; recreation: golf; Clubs: Lingan Country; Royal Cape Bre-

ton Yacht; Home: 53 Lynnbrook Dr., Sydney River, N.S. B1R 1R2; Office: Civic Centre, Sidney, N.S.

SULLIVAN, Arthur Gerald; company executive; b. Montreal, P.Q., 21 April 1908; s. late William and late Elizabeth (McQuillan) S.; e. St. Patrick's Acad., Montreal, P.Q.: m. R. Marguerite, d. late Lawrence A. Cleary, 17 Dec. 1935; children: Marie Elizabeth, Lawrence Arthur; Dir., Eastern Canada Towing Ltd.; Point Tupper Towing Ltd.; Foundation Co. of Canada Ltd.; mem., Atlantic Pilotage Authority; Past President and Director, Foundation Maritime Limited; joined Foundation Co. of Canada Ltd. in Montreal in Purchasing Dept. in 1925; apptd. Purchasing & Traffic Agent at Halifax, N.S., 1928; served in various capacities on constr. projects, 1930-35; apptd. Gen. Purchasing Agt., Montreal, 1936; Asst. to the Pres., 1943, Secretary, 1947, Vice-Pres. and Gen. Mgr., 1950, Pres., 1958; Pres. and Dir.; M.I.L. Tug & Salvage Co. 1968; Pres., Canadian Constr. Assn. 1961-62; Past Pres., Halifax Constr. Assn.; served in Reserve Army 1940; Roman Catholic; Clubs: Halifax, R.N.S.Y.S.; Home: 73 Forestside Crescent, Clayton Park, Halifax, N.S. B3M 1M5

SULLIVAN, Hon. Joseph A., Q.H.S. (1958), M.D., C.M., F.R.C.S.(C), F.R.S.M.; physician; senator; b. Toronto, Ont., 8 Jan. 1902; s. late Edward S.; e. Univ. of Toronto Schs.; Univ. of Toronto, M.D. C.M. 1926; postgrad. work in Univ. of Toronto, New York and several European centres (Otolaryngol.); Dir., Famous Players Canadian Corpn. Ltd.; Consultant in Laryngol. to R.C.A.F. Defence Research Bd., Ottawa; Chief of Dept. of Otolaryngol., St. Michael's Hosp., Toronto, Ont.; Gov., Univ. of Toronto; mem., Ont. Research Foundation; pioneered new tech. for surgical treatment of otosclerosis; as an undergrad. achieved prominence as a hockey player and golfer; mem., Candn. Jr. Hockey Championship Team 1919; Varsity Grads. Hockey Team (Olympic Champions 1928); Vice-Pres. and Chrmn. of E. Sec., Am. Laryngol., Rhinol. & Otol. Soc. (1955); rec'd Award of Merit from Am. Otological Soc. 1970; mem., Candn. Med. Assn.; Internat. Cong. of Otolaryngol., London, Eng.; summoned to the Senate of Can., 12 Oct. 1957; Clubs: York; University; Rosedale Golf; Seigniory; Granite; Rideau (Ottawa): Home: 11 Mason Blvd., Toronto, Ont. M5M 3C6; Office: 1 Medical Place, 20 Wynford Drive, Don Mills, Ont. M3C 1J4

SULLIVAN, Kenneth Howard, B.A.Sc.; b. Toronto, Ont., 21 Aug. 1922; s. Eugene Anthony and Elizabeth (Bonnell) S.; e. St. Michael's Coll. Sch., Toronto; Univ. of Toronto, B.A.Sc. (Hons. Aero. Engn.), 1949; m. Elsie Marian, d. Robert L. Leiterman, 8 Aug. 1949; children: Nancy, Eric, Lee, Scott, Luke, Dwight; VICE-PRES., MARKETING AND DIR., PRATT & WHITNEY AIRCRAFT OF CANADA LTD.; joined the Co., 1951; Sales Engn. Mgr., 1963; Indust. Rep. to Nat. Defence Coll., 1966-67; served with R.C.A.F., 1943-45; mem., Prof. Engrs. Que.; Canadian Aero. and Space Institute; recreations: skiing, curling, fishing; Home: 29 rue de Lombardie, St. Lambert, Que. J4S 1P3; Office: P.O. Box 10, Longueuil, Que. J4H 3W2

SULTAN, Ralph George Martin, B.A.Sc., M.B.A., M.A., Ph.D.; executive; b. Vancouver, B.C. 6 June 1933; s. John Edward Sultan; e. Univ. of B.C. B.A.Sc. 1956; Harvard Business Sch. M.B.A. 1960; Harvard Univ. M.A. 1964, Ph.D. (Econ.) 1965; m. Shirley Anne Steele 1956; children: Nels, Kirsten, Christina, Karla; EXEC. VICE PRES., HUDSON BAY MINING & SMELTING CO. ; Indust. Sales Rep. Union Carbide Corp. 1956 — 58; Teaching Fellow in Econ. Harvard Univ. 1962 — 63, Assoc. Prof. Harvard Grad. Sch. Business Adm. 1964 — 73; Asst. Gen. Mgr., Vice-Pres., Sr. Vice-Pres., Royal Bank of Canada 1973-80; Baker Scholar, Harvard Univ. 1960; Ford Foundation Fellow in Econ. 1962 — 64; Mem. Econ. Council Can.; Harvard Business Sch. Club Montreal; author "Pricing in the Electrical Oligopoly" Vol. I "Competition or Collusion" 1974, Vol. II "Business Strategy" 1975; "Problems in Marketing" 1969; various articles; mem. Assn. Prof. Engrs. Prov. Ont.; l'Assn. des Ingénieurs du Qué.; Assn. Prof. Eng. and Geol., Alta; Am. Econ. Assn.; Candn. Inst. Mining & Metall.; Beta Theta Pi, Sigma Tan Chi; Lutheran; recreations: skiing; Clubs: University (Montreal); Ranchmen's (Calgary); Home: 1102 Talon Avenue S.W. Calgary, Alta. T2T 1G1; Office: Box 28, Toronto Dominion Centre, Toronto, Ont.

SURREY, Philip Henry, R.C.A.; artist; b. Calgary, Alta. 8 Oct. 1910; s. Henry Philip and Kate Alice (de Guérin) S.; e. St Paul's Sch. Darjeeling, India; Avondale Prep. Sch. Clifton, Eng.; Kelvin Tech. High Sch. Winnipeg; Winnipeg Sch. of Art evening classes 1927-29; Vancouver Sch. of Art 1930-35; Art Students' League New York 1936-37; m. Margaret Henrietta Day 22 June 1939; Instr. in Drawing, Concordia Univ. 1965-75; retrospective exhn. of 50 paintings at Musée d'art contemporain de Montréal, entitled Peintre dans la ville, Can. Cultural Centre Paris, 1972; over 20 solo exhns.; rep. in over 80 group exhns.; rep. in various pub., corporate and private colls. incl. Nat. Gallery Can., Montreal Museum of Fine Arts, Musée du Qué., Art Gallery Ont., Bezalel Museum Jerusalem; Hon. D.D.L. (Honoris causa). Concordia Univ., 1981; Founding mem. and Treas. Contemporary Arts Soc. mem. E. Group, Fed. Candn. Artists; Liberal; Anglican; Club: Montreal Press; Home: 478 Grosvenor Ave., Montréal, Qué, H3Y 2S4.

SUSSMAN, Henry B., B.Sc.; real estate broker; b. Toronto, Ont., 21 Jan. 1922; s. David and Rachel (Cohen) S.: e. Pub. and High Schs., Toronto, Ont.; St. John's Mil. Acad., Delafield Wis., Grad. 1941; Coll. of Business Adm., Syracuse Univ., Grad. 1945 B.Sc.; PRES., DELA-FIELD INVESTMENTS LTD.; pres., Henry Sussman Real Estate Ltd.; Jarrow Holdings Ltd.; Westbanc Financial Corp. Ltd.; entered family business, 1946; joined real estate firm of L. G. Candler Associates Ltd., 1954; Partner, 1956; resigned, 1958; formed own firm, H. B. Sussman Associates Ltd., and assumed Presidency, 1958; Pres. and Dir., The Sussman Realty Corp. Ltd. 1962-73; served with U.S. Army; Dir., Mt. Sinai Hosp., Zeta Beta Tau; recreations: golf, tennis, reading; Clubs: Oakdale Golf & Country (Dir.); Primrose; York Raqiets Home: 38 Oriole Rd., Toronto, Ont. M4V 2E8; Office: Penthouse suite, 21 St. Clair Ave., E., Toronto, Ont. M4T 2T7

SUTHERLAND, Daniel Rae, B.Sc.; P. Eng.; consulting engineer; executive; b. Edmonton, Alta. 4 March 1926; s. Daniel Robert and Stella Mary (Boyle) S.; e. Pub. and High schs.; Univ. of Alberta, B.Sc. (Civil Engn) 1948; m. Lorna Phylis Pearce 1 Sept. 1951; children: Terry Ingrid, Kim Joanne, Barbara Gail; CHRMN. CANADIAN ENGINEERING SURVEYS CO. LTD.; Chrmn. Mercantile Ventures Holding Ltd.; Pres., Codavision Dev. Ltd.; Former Chairman, Pay Television Corp.; Mystery Lake Broadcasting Ltd.; ČESM-TV Ltd.; Western Coded Television Ltd.; Smart Management Systems Ltd.; Former Chrmn., now Dir. Western Industrial Research Training Centre; Canadian Rurul Television Network CRTN Ltd.; Former Dir., Unity Bank of Canada; Chrmn., Kiwanis Children's Home; Pres., Windsor Pk. Home & School; mem. Alta. Prof. Engrs. & Geol. Assn.; Canadian Inst. of Surveying; Dom., Alta. & Sask. Land Surveyors; Phi Kappa Pi; Presbyterian, recreations: skiing, golf, swimming, climbing, hiking; Clubs: Kiwanis; Edmonton; Mayfair; Petroleum; Derrick; Home: 85 Westbrook Drive, Edmonton, Alta. T6J 2C8 Office: 10310 Jasper Avenue, Edmonton, Alta. T5J 2W4

SUTHERLAND, Donald, O.C.; actor; b. Saint John, N.B. 17 July 1934; e. Univ. Toronto; m. Shirley Douglas (div.); Theatre appearances incl. "The Male Animal", "The Tempest", "August for People" (London debut), "On a Clear Day You Can See to Canterbury", "The Shewing Up of Blanco Posnet", "The Spoon River

Anthology"; films incl.; "The Castle of the Living Dead", "Dr. Terror's House of Horrors", "The Dirty Dozen", "Oedipus the King", "Interlude", "Joanna", "The Split", "Start the Revolution Without Me", "The Act of the Heart", "MASH", "Kelly's Heroes", "Little Murders", "Alex in Wonderland", "Klute", "Steelyard Blues", "Alien Thunder", "The Master", "Don't Look Now", "Lady Ice", "SPYS", "The Day of the Locust", "Casanova", "The Eagle Has Landed", "The Great Train Robbery", "Murder by Decree", "Invasion of the Body Snatchers", "Animal House", "A Man, A Woman and A Bank", 1981 oscar winning (best picture) "Ordinary People"; TV appearances "Marching to Sea", "The Death of Bessie Smith", "Hamlet at Elsinore", "The Saint", "The Avengers", Gideon's Way", "The Champions"; formerly with London Acad. Music and Dramatic Art, Perth Repertory Theatre, Scotland; also repertory at Nottingham, Chesterfield, Branley, Shieffield; Address: c/o Avco Embassy Pictures, 6601 Romaine St., Los Angeles, CA 90038

SUTHERLAND, James Robert Henry, B.A., LL.B.; retired publisher; editor; b. Westville, N.S. 7 Oct. 1913; s. late John William Henderson and Agnes Isabel (Fraser) S.; e. New Glasgow (N.S.) High Sch.; Dalhousie Univ., B.A. 1934; LL.B. 1936; m. 1st Elisabeth, d. Dr. John Ballem, New Glasgow, N.S., Oct. 1938; children: Elliot, Marcia, Elisabeth, J.R.H. III; 2ndly, Catherine W. Fairbanks; Publisher and Ed., "The Evening News", New Glasgow N.S. 1936-75 and now Ed. contributor; Pres., Canadian Daily Newspaper Publishers' Assn., 1961-62; Pres., The Canadian Press, 1968-70; read law with R. H. MacLeod; called to the Bar of N.S. 1937; Conservative; United Church; recreations: swimming, boating, fishing; Club: Rotary; Home: 371 Forbes St., New Glasgow, N.S. B2H 4R1

SUTTER, Morley Carman, M.D., B.Sc.(Med.), Ph.D.; educator; pharmacologist; b. Redvers, Sask. 18 May 1933; s. Christian Benjamin and Amelia (Duke) S.; e. Redvers (Sask.) High Sch. 1950 (Gov. Gen.'s Medal); Univ. of Man. M.D., B.Sc.(Med.) 1957 (Isbister Scholarship 1952), Ph.D. 1963; m. Virginia F. M. d. Robert Laidlaw, Winnipeg, Man. 29 June 1957; children: Gregory Robert, F. Michelle, Brent Morley; PROF. AND HEAD OF PHARMACOL. UNIV. OF B.C. since 1971; gen. med. practice Souris, Man. 1957-58; Med. Resident Winnipeg Gen. Hosp. 1958-59; Med. Research Council Fellow Univ. of Man. 1959-63; Imperial Chemical Industries Fellow, Cambridge Univ. 1963-65; Asst. Prof. of Pharmacol. Univ. of Toronto 1965-66; Med. Research Scholar Dept. Pharmacol. present univ. 1966-71, Asst. Prof. 1966, Assoc. Prof. 1968; Wellcome Foundation Travel Fellow 1963; mem., Comte. on Ethics of Exper. on Human Subjects Univ. of B.C.; B.C. Med. Assn. Comte. on Pharmacy; author various articles scient. journs.; mem., Pharmacol. Soc. of Can.; Br. Pharmacol. Soc.; Amer. Soc. Pharmac. and Exp. Therapy; Pharmacol. & Exper. Therap.; Candn. Med. Assn.; New York Acad. of Sciences; recreations: reading, music, gardening, baseball, tennis; Office: University of British Columbia, Vancouver, B.C. V6T 1W5,

SUTTIE, Thomas Ronald, F.I.A., F.C.I.A.; insurance executive; b. Clontarf, Ireland, 8 March 1915; s. William Frew and Agnes (Steven) S.; e. Morrisons Acad., Crieff, Scot.; m. Florence Nina, d. late Gilbert Thomas, 29 Oct. 1938; children: Ian Peter, Pamela Wendy Miske; CHRMN. OF BD., EQUITABLE LIFE INSURANCE CO. OF CANADA since 1978; Dir. Waterloo Insurance Co.; Asst. Actuary, Royal London Mutual Insurance Co., London, Eng. 1946; joined present Co. as Actuary 1948; Extve. Vice Pres. 1971; mem. Candn. Inst. of Actuaries, (Past Pres.); Home: 187 Forsyth Dr., Waterloo, Ont. N2L 1A1; Office: One Westmount Rd., Waterloo, Ont. N2J 4C7

SUTTON, Gerald Dudley; economist; b. Uckfield, Sussex, Eng., 23 July 1925; s. John Reginald and Mildred Anne (Lockyer) s.; m. Margaret Lillian, d. James Scally, Kingston, Ont., 15 May 1948; children: Brian Dudley, Malcolm Robert, Christine Mary, Deborah Anne; PRESIDENT, CANDN. ENTERPRISE DEVELOPMENT CORP. LIMITED: Dir., Cassidy's Ltd.; Unican Security Systems Inc.; Mortgage Insurance Company of Canada; Conventures Ltd.; with Bank of Montreal 1943-58; apptd. Asst. Econ. Adviser, 1955; joined Nesbitt, Thomson and Co., Ltd. as Dir. of Research, 1958-64; became Gen. Mgr. of present Co. 1964; Vice Pres. and Gen. Mgr. 1966; served with RCAF 1943-45 as Pilot Offr. (Pilot); past Pres., Child Care & Child Guidance Centres Inc.; Montreal Econs. Assn.; Montreal Jr. Bd. Trade; Que. Assn. for Mentally Retarded Children; Anglican; Clubs: University; National (Toronto); Mount Royal; Home: 230 Morrison Rd., Oakville, Ont. L6J 4J4 Office: 1103, 199 Bay St. Toronto M5J 1L4

SUTTON, Stewart Albert; social worker; b. Coaticook, Que., 19 July 1909; s. Earl Philander and Julia Jane (Gill) S.; e. Univ. of Toronto, Dipl. in Social Science 1933; m. Alice Victoria, d. Frederick Alexander Ritchie, 17 Apl. 1937; children: David Alison, Lawrence Ritchie Stewart, Q.C. Anna Gillian Stewart (Mrs. Peter R.P. Anderson); served YMCA, Toronto and Regina, 1927-30; Asst. Dir., York Co. Children's Aid Soc.,1935-40; Dir., Frontenac. Co. (1940-42) and Toronto (1946-55) Children's Aid Socs.; joined U.N. Children's Fund (UNICEF) as Field Rep., Africa, 1955-56; Dir. for Middle East, 1956-61; Dir. for Africa, 1961-63; Extve. Dir., Internat. Social Service, 1963-65; Secy.-Gen., The Vanier Inst. of the Family, Ottawa 1966-71; Chief Consultant until 1972; subsequently Consultant, New Horizons Programme, Fed. Dept. Health & Welfare and now Extve. Dir., Internat. Soc. Serv. Can.; served with R.C.A.M.C. 1942-46; rank Lt. Col.; Dir. of Social Science, Candn. Army; Stanstead Hist. Soc. (Que.); Past Pres., Candn. Music Assocs.; Protestant; Club: Arts and Letters (Toronto); Home: 377 Maple Lane, Ottawa, Ont. K1M 1H7 and R.R. 5, Orangeville, Ont. L9W 2Z2

SUZUKI, David T., O.C. (1977), Ph.D., LL.D.; F.R.S.C.; scientist; educator; b. Vancouver, B.C., 24 March 1936; s. Kaoru Carr and Setsu Sue (Nakamura) S.; e. Amherst Coll. (Scholarship 1954-58) B.A. 1958; Univ. of Chicago (John M. Prather Fellowship 1960-61) Ph.D. 1961; Univ. of P.E.I., LL.D. 1974; Acadia Univ., D.Sc. 1979; Univ. of Windsor, D. Sc. 1979; Trent Univ. 1981; m. Tara Elizabeth Cullis, Vancouver, B.C. 1972; M. Zindly Joane Sunahara, B.C. 10 Dec. 1972; children: Tamiko Lynda, Troy Takashi, Laura Kimiko, Severn Setsu Elizabeth; PROF. OF ZOOLOGY, UNIV. OF BRITISH COLUMBIA, since 1969; Teaching Asst. Biol. Amherst Coll. 1957; Research Asst. Univ. of Chicago 1958; Teaching Asst. Zool. 1959; Research Assoc. Biol. Div. Oak Ridge (Tenn.) Nat. Lab. 1961; Asst. Prof. Genetis Univ. of Alta. 1962; joined present Univ. as Asst. Prof. Zool. 1963; Assoc. Prof. 1965; Visiting Assoc. Prof. Zool. Univ. of Cal. Los Angeles 1966; Visiting Prof. Univ. of Cal. Berkeley 1969, 1976, 1977; Hon. Prof. Biol. Univ. of Utah 1971-72; Visiting Prof. Biol. Univ. of Puerto Rico 1972; Visiting Prof. Zool., Univ. of Toronto 1978; has rec'd grants Nat. Research Council Can., U.S. Atomic Energy Comn, Nat. Cancer Inst. Can.; Candn. Del. Internat. Congress Genetics The Hague 1963, Chrmn. Tokyo 1968 and Berkeley 1973; NRC Exchange Scientist France 1969; U.S.S.R. 1973; NATO Research Fellow W. Germany 1974; internat. speaker and lectr. various univs. scient. confs. meetings; has served as Host and Moderator on various TV programs and films incl. PEMC "Interface - Science and Society" 1974-75 CBC "Suzuki on Science" 1971-72, "Science Magazine" 1974-79; "Quirks and Quarks" (radio) 1974-79; "Nature of things" since 1979; subject of "Telescope" 1971; E.W.R. Steacie mem. Fellowship (Outstanding Research Scientist in Can.) 1969-72; mem. Grant Comte.

Nat. Research Council Can. 1969-72; named "Outstanding Japanese Canadian of the Year" 1972; Candn. Human Rights Foundation Award 1975; Assoc. Ed. "Genetics" 1976-78; Pres. Candn. Soc. Cell Biol. 1969-70; mem., Sci. Council of Can. 1978-81; Secty., Genetics Soc. of Amer. 1980-82; Hon. Life mem. Univ. of B.C. Alumni Assn; Fellow, Amer. Assoc. for Advancement of Sci. (AAAS) 1980; recreations: scuba diving, skiing, fishing, camping, football; Home: 2477 Point Grey Rd., Vancouver, B.C. V6K 1A1; Office: Dept. of Zoology, Univ. of B.C., Vancouver, B.C. V6T 1W5

SWAN, Conrad Marshall John Fisher, M.V.O. (4th class, 1978), M.A., Ph.D., F.S.A. (1971); b. Duncan, Vancouver Island, B.C., 13 May 1924; s. Henry Peter, M.D., C.M. and Edna Hanson Magdalen (Green) S. Cross of Honour, 'Pro Ecclesia et Pontifice''; 1979; e. Queen Margaret's Sch., Duncan, V.I., B.C.; St. George's Coll., Weybridge, Surrey, Eng.; Univ. of London; Univ. of Western Ont., B.A. 1949, M.A. 1951; Univ. of Cambridge (Peterhouse), Ph.D. 1955; m. The Lady Hilda Susan Mary Northcote, younger d. Earl of Iddesleigh and cousin of H.R.H. the Princess of Wales and Field Marshal the Viscount Montgomery of Alamein, K.G., 28 Dec. 1957; children: Andrew Conrad Henry Joseph, Mary Elizabeth Magdalen Herring, Hilda Juliana Mary, Catherine Sylveria Mary, Anastasia Cecilia Mary; YORK HERALD OF ARMS, since June 1968; Geneologist: Order of the Bath, 1972- ; of Grand Priory, Most Ven. Order of St. John, 1976- ; joined Assumption Univ., Windsor, Ont. as Lectr. in Hist., 1955; Lectr. in Pol. Science, 1955-57; Asst. Prof. of Hist., 1957-61; Univ. Beadle, 1957-61; Guest Lecturer at universities etc. in U.K., Europe, Canada, U.S., Australia, South Am., Iceland, Thailand, Japan; Woodward Lectr., Yale 1964; Confed. Centennial Lectr., Univ. of Sask. 1967; Inaugural Sir Wm. Scott Mem. Lect. (Ulster-Scot Hist. Foundation) 1968; Rouge Dragon Pursuivant of Arms, 1962-68 (Offr. of Arms-in-Ordinary to H.M. the Queen, and as such a mem. of the Royal Household — first Candn. to be so apptd.); on Earl Marshal's Staff for State Funeral of Sir Winston Spencer-Churchill, K.G., 1965; in vestiture of Prince of Wales 1969; attended upon H.R.H. the Prince of Wales, at his Installation as Great Master of the Order of the Bath, 1975; and upon H.M. The Queen at Silver Jubilee Service, St. Paul's Cathedral, 1977; First Herald of Crown to execute duties in Tabard on W. side of Atlantic (Bermuda 1969), in Southern Hemisphere Australia 1977 (Aust. Silver Jubilee tour); to visit New Zealand 1976, and complete round world tour 1970; served in 2nd World War in Europe and the Far East in the Indian Army (Madras Regt.) rank of Capt.; author, "Heraldry: Ulster and North American Connections" 1972; "Canada: Symbols of Sovereignty" 1977; "The Chapel of the Order of Beth, Westminster Abbey" 1978; and a number of monographs and articles (armorial, historical, sigillographic) in various journs.; Kt. of Honour and Devotion of Sovereign and Mil. Order of Malta and Geneal., British Association of that order; Kt. Grand Cross of Sacred and Mil. Order of Constantine St. George; Hon. Citizen of Texas; Freeman of Shreveport, La.; Birmingham, Ala.; Loudoun Co., Virginia; St. George, Bermuda, City of London; Freeman and Liveryman of Gunmakers Company of City of London; Vice-President and Founder mem. of Heraldry Society of Canada; Honorary Vice-Pres., U.E.L. Assn. of Can.; K. St. J. (1976) Roman Catholic; recreations: riding, rearing ornamental pheasants & waterfowl; beagling; Home: Boxford House, Suffolk, C06 5JT Eng.; Office: College of Arms, Queen Victoria St., London, EC4 4BT, England.

SWAN, Rev. Peter Julian Michael, M.A., Ph.D. (R.C.); priest, professor; b. Folkestone, Kent, Eng., 21 May 1919; s. Henry Peter (Major RCAMC and RAMC) and Edna Hanson (Green) S.; e. Queen Margaret's Sch., Duncan, B.C.; Duncan (B.C.) Grammar and High Schs.; St. Michaels Coll., Univ. of Toronto, B.A. 1938; Sch. of Grad. Studies, Univ. of Toronto, M.A. 1942, Ph.D. 1946; St.

Basil's Semy., Toronto. 1940-44; PRES. & VICE CHAN-CELLOR, UNIV. OF ST. MICHAEL'S COLL., since 1978; Vice Pres. 1977-78; o. Priest 1943; Assoc. Prof. of Philos., Assumption Univ. of Windsor, 1946-61, Registrar 1949-61, Acad. Vice Pres. 1958-61 and Secy. and mem. of Bd. of Govs. there 1953-61; Princ. and Prof. of Philos., St. Thomas More Coll., Univ. of Sask., 1961-77; Gen. Councillor, Basilian Fathers, 1970-73; Councillor, Internat. Federation of Catholic Universities, 1980-83; mem. Candn. Philos. Assn.; Am. Cath. Philos. Soc.; Heraldry Soc. Can.; Chaplain Kts. of Malta 1968; recreation: reading; Clubs: Challoner, English-Speaking Union (London, Eng.); Faculty; Address: 81 St. Mary St., Toronto, Ont. M5S 1J4

SWANGARD, Erwin Michael; business consultant; b. Munich, Germany, 11 May 1908; s.late Dr. F.M. and Elizabeth (Wallner) S.; came to Canada, 1930; m. Doris, d. late W. D. Clarke, 14 April 1938; children: Trevor, Graham, Randy; PRESIDENT AND DIRECTOR, PACIFIC NATIONAL EXHIBITION; former Dir. of News, CJOR Radio Station; former Managing Editor, Vancouver Sun and Past Executive Vice-President, Northwest Publications; served one year as Adm., Midwest Newspapers Corp., Benin, Nigeria, under sponsorship of Candn. Extve. Service Overseas; Founder, B.C. Tournament of Soccer Champions; Past Pres. & Member of Kingsway-Burnaby Rotary Club; Hon. mem. B.C. Youth Soccer Assn.; Nat. Fitness & Amateur Sports Council (1967-70); Convocation Founder, Simon Fraser Univ. (Senator 1972-75); Co-Founder, B.C. Lions Football Club; Address: 5105 McKee St., Burnaby, B.C. V5J 2T5

SWANN, Peter Charles; b. London, Eng., 20 Dec. 1921; e. Tottenham Grammar Sch., London, 1939; Oxford Univ., read Chinese (1st Class Hons., Scarborough Scholarship); London Univ., 1942; Leyden Univ., 1947-48; Hon. Doctorate Brock and Queen; Univ.; m. Elizabeth Hayden, 9 Aug. 1952 (now divorced); children: Sebastian Paul, Toby Nicholas, Geron Matthew, Francesca, Claire; Dir., J. E. Seagram and Sons Ltd.; Cadillac-Fairview Corp. Ltd.; Seagram Museum; founder and Pres., Assoc. of Cultural Executives; former Dir., Royal Ont. Museum 1966-June 1972; studied in Japan 1950-51; apptd. to Ashmolean Museum 1952; in charge of Dept. 1956; planned new dept. and made Keeper 1961; served with R.N. 1942-46, destroyer service, Japanese Intelligence, Combined Chiefs of Staff, Washington; author of "Introduction to Japanese Art"; "Hokusai"; "Chinese Painting"; "The Monumental Art of China"; "Japanese Art"; "2,000 of Japanese Art" (with Y. Yashiro); "The Arts of China, Korea and Japan"; "A Concise History of Japanese Art"; Ed., "Oriental Art" 1955-68; transl. "Yün-Kang" (15 vols.); mem., Worshipful Co. or Turners; Exec. Dir. (First) Samuel and Saidye Bronfman Family Foundation; 1916 Tupper St., Montreal, Que. H3H 1N5

SWANSON, A.L., B.A., M.H.A., M.D., C.M., F.A.C.H.A.; b. Red Deer, Alta., 29 Sept. 1918; s. William Frederick and Clara Isabella (Pierce) S.; e. Univ. of British Columbia, B.A., 1940; McGill Univ., M.D., C.M. 1943; Northwestern Univ., Master of Hosp. Adm., 1949; m. Joan Maurine, d. Leslie Stuart Hawkins, Vancouver, B. C., 9 April 1942; children: Stuart, Karen, Wendy, David, Eric, Patricia; Executive Director, Canadian Council on Hospital Accreditation, since 1975; Past President, Saskatchewan Hosp. Assn.; mem. of Med. Staff, Prov. Mental Health Services, B.C., 1946-49; Deputy Med. Supt., 1949-52; Extve. Dir., Candn. Hosp Assn., also Editor of "Canadian Hospital", also Asst. Prof., Dept. of Hosp. Adm., Sch. of Hygiene, Univ. of Toronto, 1952-54; Extve. Dir., Univ. Hosp., Saskatoon, and Asst. Prof., Univ. of Sask., 1954-65; Extve. Dir. Victoria Hosp., London, Ont. 1965-70; Adm., Queen St. Mental Health Centre 1970-75; Capt., Royal Candn. Army Med. Corps. 1944-46; mem. Candn. Med. Assn.; Coll. of Phys. and Surg. of B.C. and Ontario; Fellow,, Am. Coll. of Hosp. Adms. (mem. Bd.

of Govs. 1964-68, Past Pres. 1970); Life mem., Sask. Hosp. Assn., 1966; Founding mem. Candn. Coll. of Health Service Execs., 1974; McGill Undergrad. Soc. 1943; Alpha Kappa Kappa (Pres. 1943); Anglican; recreations: boating, skiing; Address: 1815 Alta Vista Dr., Ottawa, Ont. K1G 3Y6

SWANSON, Alaster Gordon, B.Sc.; executive; b. Theodore, Sask. 22 June 1931; s. William and Marian S.; e. Pub. and High Schs. Theodore, Sask.; Univ. of Sask. B.Sc. (Mech. Engn.); M. Patricia Joan d. Cecil K. Armitstead 1 Sept. 1954; children: Alaster Drew, Patricia Louise, Laurel Faye, Evelyn Jill; PRESIDENT AND C.E.O. DIR. MARLINE OIL CORP.; Pres. and Dir. A. G. Swanson Ltd. since 1976; Atomic Energy of Canada Ltd.; Jr. Engr. Nance Exploration Co. Calgary 1951-54; Engr. Brown Boveri (Canada) Ltd. Calgary, Edmonton, Montreal and Europe 1956-62; Mgr. Special Projects, Dynamic Group, Calgary 1962-72; Vice Pres. Mining, Pan Ocean Oil Ltd. 1972-75, Chrmn. and Dir. 1975-76; Dir. Pan Ocean Oil Corp. 1973-76, Vice Chrmn. 1975-76; mem. Candn. Inst. Mining & Metall.; Am. Inst. Mining, Metall. & Petrol. Engrs.; Canadian Nuclear Assn.; Assn. Prof. Engrs. Alta.; Sask. Mining Assn.; Alta. & N.W. Chamber Mines & Resources; B.C. & Yukon Chamber Mines; Calgary Chamber Comm.; Order St. Lazarus Jerusalem; Clubs: Calgary Petroleum; Ranchmen's; Home: 1234 Lansdowne Ave., S.W. Calgary, Alta. T2S 1A6; Office: 4th Floor, Chevron Plaxa, 500-5th Ave. S.W., Calgary, Alta. T2P 3L5

SWANSON, Ven. Cecil, C.M., B.A., D.D. (Ang.); b. 24 Feb. 1889; s. William George and Sarah Sophia S.; e. Dulwich Coll., London, Eng.; Univ. of Toronto, B.A. 1912; Wycliffe Coll., Toronto, Dipl. 1913, Hon. D.D. 1941; St. John's Coll., Winnipeg, Man., Hon. D.D. 1935; Hon. D.C.V., Univ. of Calgary; m. Enid Maye, d. Harrie Schreiber, Woodham, Erindale, Ont., 3 July 1913; children: Vera Edith, Beatrice Enid, Cecile de Lisle; o. Deacon 1912; Priest 1913; Missy., Little Salmon and Camrocks, Diocese of Yukon, 1912-16; Rector, Christ Ch., Whitehorse, Yukon, 1915-17; Master, Univ. Sch., Victoria, B.C., 1918; Vicar, Metchosin, Vancouver Island, B.C., 1919-21; Curate, Christ Ch., Vancouver, 1921-22; Rector, St. Augustin's Church, Lethbridge, Alta., 1922-23; Rural Dean of Lethbridge, 1922-27; Archdeacon of Lethbridge, 1928-32; Rector, St. Stephen's Ch., and Archdeacon of Calgary, 1932-40; Dean and Rector, Christ Ch. Cath., Vancouver, B.C., 1940-53; Rector, St. Paul's, Toronto, 1953-60 when retired; apptd. Archdeacon of Toronto East, 1956; Chrmn., Lethbridge Sch. Bd., 1925-29; Order of Can., 1979; Conservative; recreations: motoring, golf, tennis, cricket; Home: 3040 Glencoe Rd., Calgary, Alta. T2S 2L8

SWANSON, Frank G., B.A., M.S.; newspaper publisher; b. Edmonton, Alberta, 11 April 1917; s. Frank and Clara (Olson) S.; e. Univ. of Alberta, B.A. 1937; Columbia Univ., M.Sc. 1938; m. Vera, d. Wilson Gowing, Brighton, Eng., 2 Dec. 1944; one s. David; PUBLISHER, "CALGARY HERALD", since 1962; Vice-Pres and Dir., Southam Press Ltd.; Assoc. Dir., Calgary Stampede; London Corr., 1945-48; Press Gallery Corr., Ottawa Citizen, 1948-58; Assoc. Editor, 1958-60, Editor, 1960-61; Asst. Publisher, Calgary Herald, 1961-62; served in 2nd World War with Candn. Army, 1940-45, rank Major; Delta Upsilon; Anglican; recreation: fishing; Clubs: Rideau (Ottawa); Calgary Petroleum; Golf & Country; Glencoe; Ranchmen's; Home: R.R. 2, Old Banff Coach Rd., Calgary, Alta. T2P 2G5; Office: Herald Bldg., Calgary, Alta.

SWEATMAN, Alan, Q.C., B.A., LL.B.; b. Winnipeg, Man., 9 Dec. 1920; s. Travers and Constance Winnifred (Newton) S.; e. Pub. and High Schs., Winnipeg, Man.; Univ. of Manitoba, B.A. 1942, LL.B. 1948; m. Lorraine Mary, d. late David Cluness MacDonald, 26 June 1943; children: Alan Travers, Wynn David, Paul, Margaret

Lisa, Elizabeth, Scott; PARTNER, THOMPSON, DORF-MAN, SWEATMAN; Dir.; Toronto-Dominion Bank; Inter-City Gas Corp.; Br. Am. Bank Note Co. Ltd.; Hudson Bay Mining & Smelting Co. Ltd.; Greyhound Lines of Can. Ltd.; mem. Winnipeg Adv. Bd., Montreal Trust Co.; read law with Isaac Pitbaldo, Q.C.; called to Bar of Man. 1948; cr. Q.C. 1962; served in 2nd World War with RCNVR, 1942-45; discharged with rank of Lieut; Liberal; recreations: golf, sailing, skiing; Club: St. Charles Country; Home: 266 Kingsway Ave., Winnipeg, Man. R3M 0H3; Office: 500 Bank of Canada Bldg., 3 Lombard Place, Winnipeg, Manitoba R3B 1N4

SWEET, John Howard; publisher; b. Emerson, Man., 21 March 1907; s. Henry Charles and Hannah (Mooney) s.; e. Univ. of Man., 1923-26; m. Anne Ethel, d. Ernest Wallace, Smithfield, N.C., 4 Oct. 1940; children: Anthony Howard, Elizabeth Anne; President, U.S. News and World Report, 1959-81 and Chairman of the Board since 1973; Asst. Circulation Mgr., A.M.A., 1926-29; Circulation Mgr., Traffic World, 1929-37; Vice Pres., Poor's Publishing Co., 1937-40; Vice Pres., Dickie Raymond, 1940-42; Circulation Dir. of present mag. 1946-51; Extve. Vice Pres. 1951-59; Publisher 1959-78; served with U.S.N. 1942-45; rank Lt. Commdr.; Republican; Presbyterian; recreations: golf, fishing; Clubs: Metropolitan; Nat. Press; Home: 2124 Bancroft Pl. N.W., Washington, D.C. 20008; Office: 2300 N St. N.W., Washington, D.C. 20037.

SWEETING, Dennis, D.S.O., B.A., M.C.; broadcaster, director, actor; b. Calgary, Alta., 23 Nov. 1915; s. John Findlay and Jessie Craven (Dickens) S.; e. St. Johns Coll. Sch., Winnipeg, Man., 1922-29; Univ. of Manitoba (Arts) 1931-33; B.A., Trent Univ. 1978; m. Margaret Elaine Palmer, 21 July 1962; children: (by previous m.) Derek, Pamela, Barbara, (adopted s.) Christopher; President, Sweeting Management Services independent theatrical producers and consultants; with Hudson's Bay Co., Merchandising and Stat. Depts., Winnipeg, 1933-39 (also free lance actor, dir., radio and theatre); after was Announcer, CJAT, Trail, B.C.; with CBC Vancouver, and other posts before appt. as Extve. Secy., Assn. Candn. Radio and Television Artists and Actors Equity Assn., Toronto, Ont., 1954; Gen. Mgr., Candn. Players Ltd., 1958-60; Producer, Kowartha Festival Foundation since 1970; served in 2nd World War with Queen's Own Cameron Highlanders, Winnipeg, 1939; staff appts. with Air Staff, Candn. Army, returning to unit to conclude war with rank of Major; awarded D.S.O., Czechoslovakian M.C.; Publications: T.V. and radio plays, articles, scripts for CBC radio; first Secy., Candn. Theatre Centre, which devel. the Nat. Theatre Sch. of Can.; Anglican; recreation: boating; Office: Suite 3, 50 Kent St. W., Lindsay, Ont. K9V 2Y2

SWINTON, William Elgin, Ph.D., D.Sc., LL.D., F.R.S.E., F.R.S.C., F.R.G.S., F.R.A.I., F.L.S., F.Z.S., F.S.A. (Scot.); univ. professor; b. Kirkcaldy, Fifeshire, Scotland, 30 Sept. 1900; s. William Wilson and Rachel Hunter (Cargill) S.; e. Whitehill Sch., Glasgow, Scot.; Trinity; Coll., Glenalmond, Scot.; Univ. of Glasgow, B.Sc. 1922 (Strang-Steel Prize), Ph.D. 1930; D.Sc. 1971; Hon. LL.D., Toronto 1975; Hon. D.Litt., Western 1977; unm.; Demonst., Univ. of Glasgow, 1922-24; mem. Scottish Spitsbergen Expedition, 1920 mem. Scient. Staff, Brit. Museum (Nat. Hist.), London, 1924-61; Hon. Assoc., Royal Museum of Central Africa (Belgium), since 1950; Dir., Life Sciences, Royal Ont. Museum, 1961-63; Dir., Royal Ont. Museum, 1963-66; Prof. of Zool., Univ. of Toronto, 1962-66, now Prof. Emeritus; Centennial Prof. (History of Sci.) 1966; Visiting Prof., Prince of Wales Coll., P.E.I., 1967; Visiting Prof., Queen's Univ., Anatomy and Biol. 1977 and 1978; Fellow, Massey Coll., since 1966; served in 2nd World War, 1939-45, with Naval Intelligence, Lieut. Commdr., R.N.V.R.; Publications: "The Dinosaurs", 1934; "Corridor of Life", 1946; "Geology & the Museum", 1941; "Wonderful World of Prehistoric

Animals", 1961; "Animals before Adam", 1961; "Fossils", 1961; "Digging for Dinosaurs", 1962; "Giants", 1966; "The Dinosaurs", 1970; and many Brit. Museum Handbooks; has edited prof. journs. and written articles for "Illustrated London News", "Nature", "New Scientist", etc.; Trustee, Ont. Science Centre; Hon. Trustee, Royal Ont. Museum; Hon. Fellow, Hon. Curator, Acad. Museum and Keeper of Rare Bks., Acad. of Med., Toronto; Pres., Museums Assn. (UK), 1958-60 (Hon. fellow 1981); Hon. Gen. Secy., Brit. Assn. for Advanc. of Science, 1959-61 (Pres. Section X 1953); mem., N.Y. Acad. of Sciences; Corresp. mem. Geol. Soc. of Belgium; Hon. mem. Antwerp Zool. Soc.; Case Mem. Lecturer, Univ. of Michigan, 1966; Sr. Fellow, Hannah Inst. for Hist. of Medicine, 1977-79; hon. mem., Royal Candn. Inst.; Admiral of Nebraska 1957; hon. Fellow, Museum of Arts and Sci., Rochester, N.Y.; Hon. Fellow, Roy. Coll. Phys. & Surg. Can. 1978; Silver Jubilee Medal; Conservative; recreation: golf; Clubs: Athenaeum (London, Eng.); Arts & Letters (ex-Pres.); R.C.Y.C.; Royal Canadian Military Institute; Home: 276 St. George St. (Apts. 604-605), Toronto, Ont. M5R 2P6; Office: Massey College, Toronto, Ont. M5S 2E1

SWITZER, Clayton Macfie, M.S.A., Ph.D.; educator; b. Melbourne, Ont., 17 July 1929; s. Wilford H. and Marion V. (Macfie) S.; e. Ont. Agric. Coll., B.S.A. 1951; Univ. of Toronto, M.S.A. 1953; Iowa State Coll., Ph.D. 1955; m. Dorothy Jean, d. late Roger Allan, Windsor, Ont., 28 July 1951; children: John, Karen, Robert; DEAN, ONT. AGRIC. COLL., UNIV. OF GUELPH, since 1972; joined present Coll. as Lectr. 1955-56; Asst. Prof. 1956-60, Assoc. Prof. 1960-62, Prof. 1963-67, Prof. and Chrmn., Dept. of Bot., 1967-72, Assoc. Dean of Coll. 1971-72; Visiting Prof., Univ. Nat. del Sur, Argentina, 1968; visiting Prof., Hawkesbury Agr. Coll. Australia 1975, 1978; Lincoln Coll., New Zealand 1978; author of over 150 scient. papers, reports and articles; Past Pres., Internat. Turfgrass Soc.; Chrmn., Ont. Weed Comte.; mem., Candn. Bot. Soc.; Candn. Soc. Plant Physiol.; Can. Pest Mgmt. Soc.; Am. Assn. Advance. Science; Weed Science Soc. Am.; Agric. Inst. Can.; Past Pres., Ont. Inst. Agrols.; Science Council Can.; Can. Agric. Research Council; recreations: golf, curling; Clubs: Guelph Country; Guelph Curling; Home: 16 Tamarack Pl., Guelph, Ont. N1E 3Y6

SWORD, John Howe, M.A., LL.D.; educator (retired); b. Saskatoon, Sask., 22 Jan. 1915; s. late Martha (Morrison) and late William Brown S.; e. Pub. and High Schs., Winnipeg, Man.; Univ. of Man., B.A., 1935; Univ. of Toronto, M.A. 1950; LL.D. (Hon.), Man. 1970; m. Constance A., d. late Thomas W. Offen, Rivers, Man.; children: Stephen John, Linda May; began career in educ. as teacher, jr. high and high schs., Man., 1936-42; Secy., Man. Royal Comn. on Adult Educ., 1945-46; Asst. Secy., Sch. of Grad. Studies, Univ. of Toronto, 1947-48, Secy., 1948-60; Extve. Asst. to the Pres., Univ. of Toronto, 1960-65; Vice-Provost, 1965-67; Acting Pres., 1967-68; Extve. Vice Pres. (Academic) and Provost 1968-71, Acting Pres. 1971-72; Vice Pres., Inst. Relations & Planning 1972-74; Special Asst. to Pres. 1974; Chmn. of the Press Board (U. of T. Press) 1977-80; Retired 1980; Acting Dir., School of Continuing Studies, 1980-81; Dir., Univ. of Toronto Oral History Project 1981- ; mem., Prov. of Ont. Addiction Research Fdn. 1981- ; served as Aircrew Instr. R.C.A.F., 1942-45; Home: 8 Wychwood Park, Toronto, Ont. M6G 2V5

SYLVAIN, John, B.Com., F.I.I.C.; insurance executive; b. London, Eng., 7 June 1924; s. John Albert and Alice (Carriere) S.; e. Univ. Ottawa, B.Com. 1950; m. Yolande, d. Ernest Maranger, 22 Dec. 1947; five d., one s.; PRESIDENT, GENERAL MANAGER AND DIRECTOR, THE UNITED PROVINCES INSURANCE CO. since 1975; with The Travelers Insurance Co.; Hartford, Conn. 1950; Montreal, Que. 1951, Br. Mgr. Ottawa 1952, Br. Mgr., E. Can., Montreal 1964; Vice-Pres., Marsh & McLennan,

Montreal 1968; Vice Pres., Pratte, Houle, Methot, Montreal 1968; Vice Pres., Maryland Casualty Co., Baltimore, Md.; Pres., Robert Hampson and Son Ltd. 1970; served in 2nd World War, R.C.A.F. in Europe, Africa and Asia; Dir., Insur. Bureau of Canada and Chmn. Quebec Adv. Committee; Groupement des Assureurs Automobile; Montreal Children's Hospital; recreations: golf, tennis, squash, skiing; Clubs: Beaconsfield Golf; M.A.A.A.; St. James; Home: 335 Berwick Drive, Beaconsfield, Que. H9W 1B8; Office: 2021 Union Ave., Ste 1200 Montreal, Que. H3A 2V1

SYLVAIN, Philippe, M.A., D.ès L., F.R.C.S. (1963); educator; historian; b. St. Elzéar, Co. Beauce, P.Q., 27 June 1915; s. Wilbrod and Rose-Anna (Bélanger) S.; e. Univ. of Montreal, B.A. 1937; Laval Univ., Licence ès Sciences, 1940, M.A. 1943; Univ. of Paris (Sorbonne), D. ès L. 1954; Prof. of Fr. Lit. and Latin, Quebec Acad., 1939-50, 1954-62; Hist. research in rel. hist. in Paris, 1950-52, Rome, 1952-53 and Paris, 1953-54; Univ. of Notre Dame, 1957-58 studying Am. Relig. hist.; apptd. Prof. of Relig. Hist., Laval Univ. 1957; Head, Dept. of Hist. 1967-70; Head, Lab. d'hist. relig. 1972-80; Research on Risorgimento Italiano, Rome, 1959; awarded Medal "Benemerito della Cultura Italiana", 1963; Prix David, P.Q., 1959 and 1962; Prix Kornmann from l'Acad. Française; author of "La vie et l'oeuvre de Henry de Courcy, premier historien de l'Eglise catholique aux Etats-Unis", 1955; "Alessandro Gavazzi", 1962; "Libéralisme et ultramontanisme au Canada français: affrontement idéologique et doctrinal (1840-1865)" in "The Shield of Achilles" ed. W. L. Morton, 1968; mem. Council, Candn. Hist. Assn. 1964-67; Secy., Société des Dix since 1969; Pres., Sec. of Que., Candn. Writers Assn., 1972-73; Sec. 1, Roy. Soc. Can., 1972-73; mem., Nat. Lib. Adv. Bd., 1972-76; Am. Hist. Assn.; Soc. d'Hist. moderne; Istituto per la Storia del Risorgimento Italiano; Roman Catholic; recreations: reading, music, travel; Home: 1289, de la Visitation, Sainte-Foy, Québec G1W 3K5

SYLVESTRE, Jean-Guy, L.Ph., M.A., D.Bibl., D.Litt., LL.D., F.R.S.C.; librarian, writer; b. Sorel, P.Q., 17 May 1918; s. Maxime Arthur and Yvonne (Lapierre) S.; e. Coll. Ste-Marie, Montreal, P.Q.; Univ. of Ottawa, B.A. 1939, L.Ph. 1940, M.A. 1941; D.L.S. (Hons.) Ottawa; D. Litt. (Hons) Mount Allison; LL.D. (Hons) Toronto; LL.D. (Hons.) Prince Edward Island; m. Françoise, d. Eugene Poitevin, Ottawa, Ont., 27 Feb. 1943; one d. Marie, two s. Jean, Paul; NATIONAL LIBRARIAN OF CANADA, since 1968; Private Secy. to Rt. Hon. Louis S. St. Laurent, 1945-50; Book Reviewer, Le Droit, Ottawa, Ont., 1939-48; Assoc. Parlty. Librarian, Lib. of Parliament, 1956-68; Ed., Wartime Information; Past Chrmn. of Comte. for Gov.-Gen. Lit. Awards; Past Chrmn., Candn. Writers Foundation; past Pres., Royal Society of Canada; mem. Académie Canadienne Française; Pres. World Poetry Conf., 1967; Commdr., Ordre internat des Bien public; Cdn. Rep., Intergovernmental Council for General Info. Prog.; Unesco 1979-83; Ordre du mérite de Pologne; Candn. Del. to UNESCO Conferences 1949, 70, 72, 74; Chrmn., Conference of Dirs. of Nat. Libraries, 1974-77; Chrmn. Nat. Libraries Section, IFLA., 1977-81; author of "Louis Francoeur, journaliste", 1941; "Situation de la poésie canadienne", 1942; Anthologie de la poésie canadienne d'expression française", 1943; "Poètes catholiques de la France contemporaine", 1944; "Jules Laforgue", 1945; "Sondages", 1945; "Impressions de théâtre", 1950; "Panorama des lettres canadiennes françaises", 1964; "Canadian Writers/ Ecrivains canadiens", 1964; "Un siècle de littérature canadienne", 1967; Life mem., Candn. Library Assn. (CLA); Assn. des Sci. et Tech. de la Documentation; Hon. Life mem. Ont. Library Assn. (OLA); mem. & First Pres., Candn. Assn. for Information Sci.; Roman Catholic; recreation: Clubs: Cercle Universitaire; Home: 1870 Rideau Garden Drive, Ottawa, Ont. K1S 1G6; Office: National Library of Canada, Ottawa, Ont. K1A 0A9

SYMONS, Thomas H.B., O.C., B.A., M.A., LL.D., D.U., F.R.S.C.; professor and educator; b. Toronto, Ontario, 30 May 1929; s. Harry Lutz and Dorothy Sarah (Bull) S.; e. Upper Can. Coll.; Univ. of Toronto Schs.; Univ. of Toronto, B.A. 1951 (1st Class Hons. Modern Hist.; C.S. MacInnes Scholar, Pol. Science; Maurice Cody Scholar. Candn. Hist., Hist. Prize Trinity Coll.; Univ. Hons. Award 1951; Edward Kylie Award and Massey Fellowship for postgrad. study); Oxford Univ. (Oriel Coll.), B.A. 1953, M.A. 1957; independent studies at Paris, Leyden, Rome 1953; Harvard Univ. 1956; LL.D., Waterloo Lutheran 1971, N.B. 1972, York 1973, Trent 1975, Laurentian 1977, Mount Allison 1979, Concordia 1981; D.U. (Ottawa) 1974; m. Christine, d. late Harvey Frederick Ryerson, 17 August 1963; children: Ryerson, Jeffrey Duncan, Mary Elizabeth Caroline; el. to Cumming Fellowship and apptd. Asst. Dean of Men, Trinity Coll. and Instr., Dept. of Hist., Univ. of Toronto 1953-55; Dean, Devonshire House there 1955-63; Awarded Rockefeller Grant for research in Candn. Hist., Harvard Univ. 1956; mem. Policy and Planning Comte., Univ. of Toronto 1959-63; Univ. of Toronto research grant to study univ. planning and curriculum, U.K., Europe and U.S. 1960; apptd. Pres.-Designate and Chrmn. Acad. Planning Comte., Trent Univ. 1960, Pres. and Vice-Chancellor 1961-72; Chrmn., Comm. on Cdn. Studies since 1972; Visiting Fellow, Calgary Instit. for the Humanities 1977; Vanier Prof., Trent Univ., 1979; Assoc. of Australian Studies Centre, Univ. of Queensland, Australia, 1980; mem. Bd., Celanese Canada Inc.; mem. Bd., Assn. of Univs. and Colls. of Can.; Founding mem., Council of Ont. Univ. 1961-72; mem. Council and Hon. Treas.; Assn. Commonwealth Univ. (Chrmn. 1971-72); Del. to Commonwealth Univ. Confs.: Aust. and N.Z. 1968; Nigeria and Ghana 1971; Can. 1972; U.K. 1973; Hong Kong, Malaysia and Singapore 1975; N.Z. 1976; Malta 1977; Can. 1978; India, 1980; Hong Kong, 1981; Chrmn., Internat'l Bd. of United World Colleges; mem. Bd., Lester B. Pearson Coll. of Pacific; Mem. Adv. Comte. Academic Relations, Dept. of External Affairs, 1978- ; Robert and Mary Stanfield Found.; mem. Bd., Jack Chambers Memorial Fdn.; Bd., Artic Inst. of North Amer.; mem. Bd. Trustees, Oriel Coll., Oxford Univ.; Chrmn., Ont. Human Rights Comn. 1975-78; Chrmn., Min. Comn. on Fr. Lang. Educ. in Ont. 1971-72; mem., Adv. Comte. to Confed. to Prime Min. of Ont. 1965-72; Pres., Candn. Assn. in Support of Native Peoples 1972-73; mem., Adv. Comte. on Land Claims of Native Council of Can. 1972-73; Co-Chrmn., Candn. Conf. on Multiculturalism 1973; Co-Chrmn., Ont. Heritage Congress on Multicult. 1972; mem., Ont. Arts Council 1974-76; Can. Council 1976-78; mem., Nat'l Library Bd., Bd. Cdn. Inst. for Historical Microreproduction; Vice Pres., Soc. Sci. and Humanities Research Council since 1978; Special Adv. on higher educ. to Secy. of State since 1976; mem., Federal Cultural Policy Review Comte. 1979-82; mem., Citizen's Task Force on Soc. Security, Candn. Council on Soc. Devel. 1971-72; Chrmn., Candn. Conf. on Soc. Devel. 1976; Bd., Peterborough Red Cross and Community Fund 1964-72; mem. Bd. Govs., Ont. Med. Found.; Adv. Bd., Lakefield Coll. Sch.; Bd., Upper Can. Coll. since 1969; Corp. of Trinity Coll., Univ. of Toronto 1963-74; mem. Bd. Govs., Sir Sandford Fleming Coll. 1964-69 (chart. mem.); Loyalist Coll. 1964-67 (chart. mem.); Chart. mem., World Univ. Service of Can.; Founding mem., Nat. Comte. for Friendly Relations with Overseas Students (now Candn. Bureau for Internat. Educ.); Bd., Academy Theatre Foundation, Lindsay, Ont. 1967-71; founding mem. Ed. Bd., Journ. of Candn. Studies; Founding mem., Candn. Soc. for Study of Higher Educ.; mem. Candn. Hist. Assn.; Ont. Hist. Soc.; Candn. Pol. Science Assn.; Inst. Pub. Adm. of Can.; Candn. Inst. of Internat. Affairs; Candn. Museums Assn.; Royal Ont. Museum; Heritage Can.; Nat. Trust for Historic Preservation (U.S.); Art Gallery of Ont.; Founding mem., Candn. Civil Liberties Assn.; Candn. Soc. for Abolition of Death Penalty; mem. Nat. Council, Amnesty Internat. (Can.); Past Pres., Canadian

Club of Peterborough; Hon. Pres. Peel Co. Hist. Soc.;
mem. Council, Champlain Soc.; mem. Bd. Trustees, John
Graves Simcoe Mem. Foundation 1972-76; Chrmn., Policy Adv. Committee to Hon. R. L. Stanfield 1968-75;
Chrmn. Programme Comte., Priorities for Can. Nat. Policy Conf., P. Conservative Party 1969; Policy Programme
Comte., 1971 and 1974 P. Conservative Annual Meetings;
rec'd. Candn. Centennial Medal 1967; Civic Award of
Merit, Peterborough 1969; Queen's Jubilee Medal 1977;
O.C. 1977; Hon. Dipl. from Sir Sandford Fleming Coll.
1970; Diplôme d'Etudes Collegiates, Dawson Coll., 1981;
Kt., Mil. and Hospitaller Order of St. Lazarus of Jerusa-
lem 1971; co-author of "Life Together: a Report on Hu-
man Rights in Ontario" 1977; author of "To Know Our-
selves: the Report of the Comn. on Candn. Studies" 1976;
"Report of the Ministerial Comn. on Fr. Lang. Educ. in
Ont." 1972; has contrib. chapters to: "One Hundred
Years of Canada's Artic Islands, , 1880-1980", 1981;
"Britian and Canada", 1980; "Issues in Higher
Education" 1979; "Canadian Confederation Forum" 1978;
"Cartographica" 1979; "A History of Peel County" 1967;
"Peterborough Land of Shining Waters" 1967; "The Confederation Challenge" Vol. I 1967, Vol. II 1970; "Fighting
Men" 1967; "One Country or Two" 1971; "The Dictionary of Canadian Biography" Vol. X 1972; "Native Rights
in Canada" 1970 (mem. Research Comte. comnd. to undertake preparation of this study by Nat. Indian Brotherhood, Candn. Métis Soc. and Indian-Eskimo Assn. Can.)
rev. ed. 1972; various articles, papers and reviews in numerous learned and prof. journs.; Nat. Adv. to the Canadian Encyclopedia 1980- ; Clubs: University (Toronto); Rideau (Ottawa); Athenaeum (London); Home: 361 Park
St. N., Peterborough, Ont. K9H 4P7

SYNAN, Rev. Edward A., M.A., Ph.D. (R.C.); educator;
b. Fall River, Mass. 13 Apl. 1918; s. late Edward A. and
late Mary Frances (McDermott) S.; e. Seton Hall Coll.
South Orange, N.J. B.A. 1938; Coll. Américan Univ. de
Louvain 1938-40; Cath. Univ. Washington, D.C. STL
1942; Pontifical Inst. Mediaeval Studies Toronto MSL
1951; Univ. of Toronto M.A., Ph.D. 1952; Prof. of Mediaeval Studies and Sch. of Grad. Studies Univ. of Toronto, Pres. of Inst. 1973-79; Parish Priest Montclair, N.J.
1942-44; Chrmn. Dept. of Philos. Seton Hall Univ. 1952-
59; served as Chaplain USAAF 1944-48 Zone of Interior
and Overseas; rec'd Can. Council Research Grant 1965;
author "The Popes and the Jews in the Middle Ages"
1965; "The Works of Richard of Campsall" Vol. 1 1968;
"The Fountain of Philosophy" 1972; also various articles
and reviews in learned journs.; Hon. Prelate, 1980; Fellow Royal Soc. of Can., 1980; mem. Mediaeval Acad.
Am.; Am. Cath. Theol. Assn.; Candn. Philos.
Assn.TVEecreations: art, films; Address: 59 Queen's Park
Cres. E., Toronto, Ont. M5S 2C4

SZLAZAK, Anita Christina, B.A.; Canadian public servant; b. Fulmer, Bucks., Eng. 1 Jan. 1943; d. Jan P. and
Christina W. (Matecz) S.; e. Univ. of Toronto B.A. 1963;
Coll. of Europe, Bruges Cert. Advanced European Stud-
ies (Econ.) 1964; Harvard Grad. Sch. of Business Admin;
Boston Advanced Management Program, 1981; COMMR.
PUBLIC SERVICE COMN. OF CAN. since 1976; Re-
search Econ. Devel. Centre, Organ. Econ. Coop. and
Devel. Paris 1964-67; Foreign Service Offr. Dept. of Exter-
nal Affairs Ottawa 1967-72; Depy. Dir. Gen. Internat. Te-
lecommunications, Dept. Communications Ottawa 1972-
73, Dir. Gen. 1973-76; mem. Inst. Pub. Admin. Can.
(Extve. Comte. 1976-80); R. Catholic; Clubs: Rockcliffe
Lawn Tennis; Ottawa Valley Hunt; Home: 60 Belvedere
Cres., Ottawa, Ont. K1M 2G6; Office: 300 Laurier Ave.
W., Ottawa, Ont. K1A 0M7.

T

TAGGART, Hon. John David, LL.B.; judge; b. Regina,
Sask., 20 Sept. 1921; s. James Gordon and Mary (Birkett)
T.; e. Univ. of Sask., 1939-41; Univ. of B.C., LL.B. 1949;
m. late Marian Joyce, d. late Capt. Walter Wingate, 5 Jan.
1946; children: James Lawton, Anne Elizabeth, John
David, Ian Gordon; m., Her Honour Judge Valerie Jean,
d. late V. Manning, 18 June, 1981; JUDGE, COURT OF
APPEAL, B.C., since 1968; read law with Senator J. W.
de B. Farris, Q.C.; called to Bar of B.C. 1949; cr. Q.C.
1964; practiced with Farris & Company, 1949-68 (Partner
from 1958); served with Royal Candn. Engrs. in Can.
1941-42 and with 5 Candn. Armoured Div. in U.K., Italy,
N.W. Europe, 1943-45; Mentioned in Despatches; Pres.,
Vancouver Bar Assn., 1967; mem. B.C. Council, Candn.
Bar Assn.; Protestant; recreations: skiing, sailing; Club:
Royal Vancouver Yacht; Home: 7280 Adera Sr., Vancou-
ver, B.C. V6P 5C4; Office: Law Courts, 800 Smithe St.,
Vancouver, B.C. V6C 1P6

TAGGART, Hon. Valerie Jean, LL.B.; judge; b. Cran-
brook, B.C. 9 Aug. 1926; d. Viril Zenis Manning; e. Univ.
of B.C. LL.B. 1949; m. 1stly 9 July 1949; m. 2ndly Hon.
Mr. Justice J. D. Taggart 18 June 1981; children: Deborah
Jean Meredith, Guy Manning Meredith, Daphne Louise
Meredith; PROVINCIAL COURT JUDGE, B.C.; called to
Bar of B.C. 1949; Acting Dir. Continuing Legal Educ.; Re-
search Dir. Law Foundation of B.C.; served with
W.R.C.N.S. 1945; Past Pres. Vancouver Jr. League;
Gamma Phi Beta; recreations: golf, skiing; Club: Shaugh-
nessy Golf; Home: 7280 Adera, Vancouver, B.C. V6P
5C4; Office: 814 Richards St., Vancouver, B.C.

TAHEDL, Ernestine, R.C.A.; artist; b. Austria 12 Oct.
1940; d. Heinrich and Elisabeth (Leutgeb) Tahedl; e.
Acad. for Applied Art Vienna, Masters Degree in
Graphic Art 1961; m. Richard Ian Ogilvie 9 Oct. 1965;
children: Degen Elisabeth, Lars Ian; Asst. to Prof. of
Graphic Arts Acad. for Applied Arts Vienna 1961-63;
Teacher, Edmonton Art Gallery 1963-64; Univ. of Alta.
Art Extension Courses 1964-65; Stewart Hall Cultural
Center Pointe Claire, Qué. 1968; solo exhns. (paintings)
Edmonton 1963, 1965, 1973, 1977, 1978, 1980, 1982; Cal-
gary 1965; Montreal 1967, 1968, 1970, 1972, 1973, 1976,
1977, 1978, 1980; Toronto 1976, 1978, 1982; Ottawa 1972,
1974, 1977; Vienna Wiener Secession 1971; Ecole des
Beaux-Arts Montpellier, France 1975; Cultural Center
Lower Austria 1975; Vered Internat. Art Gallery E.
Hampton, N.Y. 1979; maj. works in stained glass incl.
Sisters of Holy Cross Edmonton 1964; St. Timotheys
Ang. Ch., McKernan Bapt. Ch. Edmonton 1965; The
Sanctuary, Candn. Pavilion Expo '67; Place Bonaventure
Montreal 1968; Mendel Art Gallery Saskatoon 1970; Care-
free Lodge Toronto 1969, 1971; Fed. Revenue Bldg. Qué.
1971; arch. murals incl. Fed. P.O. Terminal Edmonton
1964-66; W.W. Cross Cancer Clinic Hosp. Edmonton
1969; rep. in pub. galleries Vienna, San Salvador, Mont-
pellier, London (Ont.), Musée du Qué.; cited various
bibliogs.; limited edition portfolio of etchings "Circle of
Energy" published 1981, Artworld International; recipient Austrian Govt. Grad. Prize 1961; Vienna Internat.
Exhn. Painting Bronze Medal 1963; Royal Arch. Inst.
Can. Allied Arts Medal 1966; Concours Artistique du
Qué. Purchase Award 1966; Can. Council Arts Award
1967; el. mem. Council RCA 1980; Societé des Artistes en
Arts Visuels du Québec; Conseil de la Gravure du Qué.;
Address: 1066 Béique, Mont St-Hilaire, Qué, J3G 4S6.

TAIT, A. Neil; trust company executive; b. Croydon,
Surrey, England 25 Feb. 1938 e. Cert. Gen. Acct. 1974; m.
Muriel Frisque 17 Aug. 1963 children: Jacqueline, Ste-
phen; PRES., CHIEF EXTVE. OFFR. AND DIR.,
CROWN TRUST CO. 1981- ; served Bank of Montreal 26
yrs. becoming Sr. Vice Pres. Central Ont. Div. 1979, Sr.
Vice Pres. Alta. Div. 1980-81; Dir. Aristar; Monarch Life

Assurance Co.; Clubs: Cambridge; Ontario; Donalda; Glencoe (Calgary); Home: 58 Old Colony Rd., Willowdale, Ont. M2L 2K1; Office: (P.O. Box 38) 1 First Canadian Place, Toronto, Ont. M5X 1G4.

TAIT, George Edward, B.A., B.Paed., Ed.D.; retired professor; author; b. Sarnia, Ont., 19 July 1910; s. James Edward and Maude Eliza (Harrower) T.; e. Watford (Ont.) High Sch.; London Normal Sch. (Grad. 1931); Univ. of W. Ont. B.A. 1939; Univ. of Toronto, B.Paed., 1945, Ed.D., 1957; m. Reginae Mae, d. Maj. R. H. Stapleford, Watford, Ont., 31 Aug. 1938; one s. Gary Edward Stapleford M.A., B.Ed.; Emeritus Prof. Educ., Faculty of Educ., Univ. of Toronto since 1973; Teacher in London, Ont., Pub. Schs., 1931-41; Dir. of Anglo-Am. Sch., Bogotà, S.A., 1941-44; Inspector of Pub. Schs, Huntsville, Ont., 1944-47; Welland, Ont., 1947-50; mem. of Pub. Library Bd., Welland, Ont. 1947-50; Prof. Educ., Univ. Toronto 1950-73; mem. Senate there 1964-72; accompanied Comnr. N.W.T. on tour of Eskimo Settlements; mem. Franklin Probe II 1974; Publications: "The Saddle of Carlos Perez", 1949; "The Silent Gulls", 1950; "Ideas for Junior Grade Teachers", 1951; "Wake of the West Wind", 1952 (dramatized by C.B.C. in 13 progs.), 1954; "Famous Canadian Stories", 1953 (used as a special prizebook by the I.O.D.E.); "Breastplate and Buckskin", 1953; "The World Was Wide", 1954; "The Upward Trail", 1956; co-author of "100 Types of Primary Seatwork", 1948; "Peach Tree Farm", 1950; "What To Do, Reading Workbook", 1949; "Proud Ages", 1958; "Fair Domain", 1960; "One Dominion", revised ed. 1973; co-ed., "Aldine World Atlas", 1961; "Mathematics Enrichment", 1966; "Young Teacher's Handbook", 1967; "The Eagle and the Snake", 1968; "The Unknown People: Indians of North America", 1974; "Here & There in Teacher Education" (co-author) 1974; awarded the McGraw-Hill Ryerson Special Book Award, to mark the outstanding contribution that his books have made to Canadian education, 1978; miscellaneous articles in educ. mags.; presented to Her Majesty Queen Elizabeth I, Buckingham Palace, 1971; mem., Candn. Educ. Assn.; Candn Authors' Assn. (Pres., Toronto Br., 1954-55; mem., Nat. Extve.); Candn. Assn. Profs. of Educ.; Mem. of Bd., John Graves Simcoe Mem. Foundation, 1975- ; Phi Delta Kappa; Un. Church; recreation: landscape painting; Club: The Arctic Circle (Ottawa); Home: 105 Golfdale Rd., Toronto, Ont. M4N 2B8

TAIT, John W., C.A.; industrialist; b. Moncton, N.B., 15 Oct. 1915; s. John LeMurray and Jean Strang (Smith) T.; e. Pub. Schs., St. Lambert, Que.; McGill Univ., 1932-33 (C.A. course, 1933-38), C.A.; m. Eleanor, d. Charles Franklyn Raymond, 25 Jan. 1941; children: Pamela, John, James, David, Ruth; CHRMN. OF BOARD AND CEO OGILVIE MILLS LTD., since 1977; Dir., Catelli Ltd.; McGavin Toastmaster Ltd.; Ault Foods Ltd.; Industrial Grain Products Ltd.; Comm. Union of Can.; empl. by Creak, Cushing and Hodgson, Chart. Accts., Montreal, Que., 1933-40; joined present firm as Comptroller, 1940; Treas., 1952; Vice-Pres. and Treas., 1956; Sr. Vice-Pres., 1960; Extve. Vice-Pres., 1963; Pres., 1966; served in 2nd World War with R. C. Navy on active service, 1941-45; joined as a Sub-Lieut. and retired with rank of Lieut.-Commdr.; Past Pres., Comptrollers Inst. of N. America (Montreal); United Church; recreations: golf, curling; Clubs: St. James's; Toronto Hunt; Toronto Granite; Royal Montreal Golf; Royal Montreal Curling; Home: 70 Montclair Ave., Apt. 205, Toronto, Ont. M5P 1P7;

TALLIN, Clive Kerslake, Q.C., M.A., LL.B.; b. Petrolia, Ont., 31 March 1907; s. George Henry and Candace Rebecca (Waylett) T.; e. pub. and high schs. Winnipeg, Man.; Univ. of Man. B.A. 1929 (Gold Medal in Classics), M.A., LL.B. 1933; m. Ruth d. late Thomas O'Neill, 1 July 1943; PARTNER, TALLIN AND KRISTJANSSON; read law with Hugh Phillips, K.C.; called to Bar of Man. 1933; cr. K.C. 1949; Lectr. in Law Faculty of Comm. Univ. of Man. 1947-75; served with Cameron Highlanders of Can.

1940-46, Directing Staff RMC, rank Maj.; Sch. Trustee 1961; Mayor Town of Tuxedo 1962-71; Pres. Central YMCA 1953-55; mem. Extve. Winnipeg Chamber Comm. 1956-57; Hon. Life Bencher Law Soc. Man. (Pres. 1967-68); Vice Pres. — Man. Candn. Bar Assn. 1961-62; Protestant; recreation: gardening; Club: Manitoba; Home: 1 Nanton Blvd., Winnipeg, Man. R3P 0M8; Office: 232 Portage Ave., Winnipeg, Man. R3C 0B1

TALLIS, Hon. Calvin F., B.A., LL.B.; judge; b. Borden, Sask., 5 March 1930; s. Ernest Forrester and Beryl Irene T.; e. Borden (Sask.) High Sch. 1946; Saskatoon Normal Sch. 1949; Univ. of Sask. B.A. 1952, LL.B. 1954; m. Dorothy Irene d. L. Poppl, Humboldt, Sask., 24 Dec. 1955; JUSTICE, COURT OF APPEAL FOR SASKATCHEWAN since 1981; Depy. Supreme Crt. Judge of N.W.T. 1981- ; Former Justice, Supreme Crt. of N.W.T., 1976-81; Former Depy. Judge of the Supreme Court of the Yukon Territory; Former Justice of Appeal of the Court of Appeal for the Northwest Territories; Former Justice of Appeal for the Yukon Territory; Lectr. in Civil Procedure Univ. of Sask.; read law with J. M. Goldenberg, Q.C.; called to Bar of Sask. 1955; cr. Q.C. 1968; former partner, Goldenberg, Taylor & Tallis, Saskatoon; former (Vice Chrmn.) Sask. Prov. Police Comn.; mem. Med. Complaints Comte. Coll & Phys. & Surgs. (Sask.); Bencher Law Soc. Sask.; mem. Law Soc. B.C.; mem. Candn. Bar Assn.; Protestant; recreations: hunting big game, upland game and waterfowl; Home: Regina, Sask.; Office: Court House Regina, Sask.

TALLMAN, Frederick Wallace, F.C.I.A., A.S.A., F.L.M.I.; executive; b. Winnipeg, Man. 16 Feb. 1922; s. James Wallace and Emma Jane (Hipple) T.; e. Gladstone Sch., Earl Grey Sch. and Kelvin Tech. High Sch., all Winnipeg 1930-38; Univ. of Man., Winnipeg 1938-43; Alice Selina, d. Rupert E. Noakes, 26 Aug. 1944; children: S. Jane Lockley, Fred R. J., Bruce W., Ross F.; PRES. AND BD. MEM. THE CITADEL LIFE ASSURANCE CO. since 1975; Senior Vice Pres. and Bd. mem. The Citadel General Assurance Co.; Bd. mem., Extve Vice Pres., Winterthur Canada Financial Corp.; Chief Financial Officer, The Citadel Assurance Group; Financial Analyst, Lightcap Securities, Winnipeg 1943-44; Lectr. Maths., Univ. Man. 1944-45; Supv., Monarch Life Assurance Co. 1945-57; Asst. Actuary, present Co. 1957-64, Assoc. Actuary 1964-68, Actuary 1968-70, Vice Pres. and Actuary 1970-74, Sr. Vice Pres. and Actuary 1974-75; Chrmn. (1975) Winnipeg Econ. Devel. Bd.; Premier (1940) Older Boys Parliament Winnipeg; Treas. (1945) Univ. of Man. Alumni Assn.; Treas. (1952) Soc. for Crippled Children Winnipeg; Pres. (1953) Jr. Chamber of Comm. Winnipeg; mem. Extve. Winnipeg Chamber Comm. 1978; Treas. (1972) Candn. Inst. Actuaries; mem. Soc. Actuaries; United Ch.; recreations: fishing, stamp collecting; Clubs: Manitoba; Rotary; St. Charles County; Home: 27 Tanbark Cres., Don Mills, Ont. M3B 1N7; Office: 1075 Bay St., Toronto, Ont.

TALMAN, James John, O.B.E. (1970), C.D., M.A., Ph.D., D.Litt., LL.D., F.R.S.C.; b. Beira, Portuguese East Africa, 15 Sept. 1904; s. Stephen G. and Winifred R. (Ross) T.; U. of W. Ont., B.A. 1925, M.A. 1927, LL.D. 1972; Univ. of Toronto, Ph.D. 1930; D.Litt., Univ. of Waterloo, 1960; m. Ruth Helen, d. George H. Davis of London, Ont., 6 Oct. 1930; children: James D., Richard M.; PROF., HIST & GRAD. STUDIES, UNIV. OF W. ONT., since 1956 (Chief Librarian there 1947-70); Asst. in Ont. Prov. Archives Dept., 1930-34; Prov. Archivist, Ont., 1934-39; Leg. Librarian, Ont., 1935-39; Asst. Librarian, Univ. of W. Ont. 1939-47; C.O.T.C., 1940-54 (C.O. 1947-54); author of "Western — 1878-1953" (with R. D. Talman); Loyalist narratives from Upper Canada and various articles on religious, social and econ. hist. of Ont., in newspapers and journs.; Chrmn., Gov.-Gen. Awards Bd., 1956-59; mem., Ont. Library Assn. (Pres. 1945-46); Ont. Hist. Soc. (Pres. 1939-42; Secy. 1944-47); Candn. Hist. Assn. (Pres. 1954-55); Candn. Library Assn. (Council 1949-51, Treas. 1956-59); Hist. Sites and Monuments Bd., Can. 1961-72; mem. Bd. Trustees, Ont. Hist. Studies Series, since 1971; mem. Candn. Comte. Programme for Loyalist Studies & Publs. since 1968; mem. Conserv. Review Bd. (Ont.) since 1975; Freemason (P.G.S.W.); Anglican; Home: R.R. 2, London, Ont. N6A 4B6

TANENBAUM, Joseph Manuel, B.A.Sc.; P.Eng.; executive; b. Toronto, Ont. 1932; e. Runnymede Pub. Sch., Humberside Coll. Inst. and Forest Hill High Sch. Toronto; Univ. of Toronto B.A.Sc. 19..; m. Toby Hockman 1955; children: Michael, Alan, Martin, Susan, Robert; CHRMN. AND CHIEF EXTVE. OFFR., YORK RUSSEL INC.; Dir. First Calgary Petroleum Ltd.; Kilmer Van Nostrand; Canadian Oxygen Ltd.; Warren Paving & Materials Group Ltd.; joined Runnymede Iron & Steel, Toronto as Labourer 1943; York Steel 1951, Asst. Supt. 1955, Production Mgr. 1957, Vice Pres. & Production Mgr. 1965; Pres. & Chief Extve. Offr. Bridge & Tank, Hamilton 1975; York Steel Construction Ltd. 1978; mem. Old Masters Comte. Art Gallery of Ont.; Chrmn. Comte. of Friends Israel Museum; rec'd Roy A. Phinnemore for Accident Prevention Award; mem. Assn. Prof. Engrs. Prov. Ont.; B'nai B'rith Forest Hill; recreation: collecting 19th century French Art; Club: Beth Tzedec Men's; Home: 4 Dewbourne Ave. Toronto, Ont.; Office: 2 St. Clair Ave. E., Toronto, Ont. M4T 2T5

TANNER, Byron Chester, C.A., S.M.; b. Magrath, Alta., 22 Mar. 1919; s. Byron Franklin, LL.B., and Gwendolyn Hannah (Merrill) T.; e. Lethbridge (Alta.) High Sch., Sr. Matric.; Mount Royal Coll., Calgary, 1936-37; Univ. of Alberta, 1939; C.A. 1947; S.M., Mass. Inst. of Technol., 1957; m. Doris Elsie Frances, d. late Dr. H. C. Mewland, Edmonton, 19 Aug. 1944; one s. James, three d. Susan, Merrill, Laura; Pres., Lassiter Kuma Oils Ltd.; Tanner Arctic Oil Ltd.; served articles with Peat, Marwick, Mitchell & Co., Calgary and Edmonton; opened office for the practice of his prof. 1946; Sloan Fellow, Sloan Extve. Devel. Program, Mass. Inst. of Technol., 1957; during 2nd World War was a member of Militia; discharged due to ill-health; mem., Inst. Chart. Accts., Alta.; Liberal (Alta. Pres. 1971-72); recreations: gardening, shooting, ranching, flying; Clubs: Edmonton Petroleum; Mayfair Golf & Country; Highlands Golf; Home: 11309 University Ave., Edmonton, Alta. T6G 1N8 Office: R.R. 1, South Edmonton, Alta. T6H 4N6

TANNER, Roy F., P.Eng.; executive; b. Chewick, London, Eng., 12 June 1923; e. Plymouth and Davenport Tech. Coll. Eng. HNC and Post Higher Nat. Cert. Mech. Engn.; m. Joan Singleton, d. late Leonard Eng., 1948; children: Richard, Joanne; PRESIDENT, CHIEF EXTVE. OFFR. AND DIR., HAWKER SIDDELEY CANADA INC. 1981- ; Chrmn. Can-Car Inc.; Dosco Overseas Engineering Ltd.; Dir. CGTX Inc.; joined A.V. Roe Canada Ltd. (later Hawker Siddeley Canada Inc.) 1953, Dir. of Operations Orenda Div. 1971, Gen. Mgr. 1974, Vice Pres. 1977, Dir. 1980; Fellow, Inst. Mech. Engrs.; mem. Assn. Prof. Engrs. Prov. Ont.; Home: 3264 Homark Dr., Mississauga, Ont. L4Y 2K4; Office: 7 King St. E., Toronto, Ont. M5C 1A3.

TAPLIN, Frank E., M.B.E., M.A., LL.B.; executive; b. Cleveland, Ohio, 22 June 1915; s. late Frank E. and late Edith Roberta (Smith) T.; e. Princeton Univ., B.A. 1937; Oxford Univ. (Queen's Coll.), M.A. 1939; Yale Law Sch., LL.B. 1941; m. Margaret Adams, d. late Joseph O. Eaton, Cleveland, Ohio, 27 April 1953; children: (Mrs.) J. D. (Jennifer) Dickerman, Mrs. W. H. (Martha) Kelly IV, Mrs. V. (Susan) Panella (step-d.), Mrs. M. (Caroline) Ruschell, Mrs. W. T. (Jennifer) Jerome IV, David F.; former CHRMN., SCURRY — RAINBOW OIL LTD.; Dir., North American Coal Corp., Cleveland, Ohio; practised law, 1946-50; Dir., White Motor Co., 1955-57; Asst. to the Pres. of Princeton Univ. 1957-59; called to the Ohio Bar. 1946; served in 2nd World War with U.S.N.R., dis-

charged as Lieut.-Commdr.; served Samoa, New Zealand, S.W. Pacific; awarded M.B.E.; Naval Commendation Ribbon; Dir. (1961 to date), and presently Pres. and CEO, Metropolitan Opera Assn., and pres. (1961-64) of Metrop. Opera Nat. Council; Chrmn., Sarah Lawrence Coll. (1974-77) and Trustee (1969-77); Pres., Cleveland Orchestra, 1955-57; Cleveland Inst. of Music, 1952-56; former Chrmn., Oliver Wendell Holmes Assn.; former Trustee, Princeton Hosp.; Fellow, Pierpont Morgan Library, since 1963; mem., Am. Bar Assn.; Officer, the Most Venerable Order of the Hospital of St. John of Jerusalem, 1980- ; Phi Beta Kappa; recreations: tennis, skiing; Clubs: Century (N.Y.) University (N.Y.); Union (Cleveland); Pretty Brook (Princeton); Home: 55 Armour Road, Princeton, N.J.; Offices: 1 Palmer Sq., Princeton, N.J. 08540; Metropolitan Opera Association, Lincoln Centre, New York, N.Y. 10023.

TARAN, Danny; manufacturer; b. New York, 8 June 1932; s. Maxwell and Vity (Bidner) T.; m. Liane T., 1965; PRESIDENT, CONSOLTEX INC. AND CONSOLTEX CANADA INC.; Chrmn. of Board, Condelle House Ltd.; Hebrew; recreations: skiing, golf, photography; Club: Cedarbrook Golf & Country; Montefiore; Home: 361 Kenaston Ave., Town of Mount Royal, Que. H3R 1M7; Office: 125 Chabanel St. West, Montreal, Que. H2N 1E4

TARDIF, Hon. Guy, M.N.A., M.A., Ph.D.; politician; b. Montréal, Qué. 30 May 1935; s. Paul and Bernadette (Lefebvre) T.; e. Ecole du Christ-Roi; Coll. André Grasset; Univ. of Ottawa; Univ. of Montreal; Ghyslaine d. Henri Meunier, Montréal 21 June 1958; children: Benoit, François, Charles; MIN. OF HOUSING, QUE AND MIN. OF CONSUMER'S PROTECTION, QUE., 1981- ; criminologist; el. M.N.A. for Crémazie prov. g.e. 1976, re-el. 1981; Min. of Municipal Affairs, Que. 1976-80; mem. Assn. Professionnelle des Criminologues Qué.; Soc. de Criminologie Qué.; Soc. Internationale de Criminologie; author numerous articles, courses and publs. criminology; author, "Police et Politique qu Quebec", 1974; Parti Quebecois; R. Catholic; Office: Edifice G, 1045, rue de Lachevrotière, Québec, Qué.

TARDIF, Jean-Paul, M.S.C.; financier; b. Quebec City, Que., 15 May 1923; s. Alphonse and Maria (Blouin) T.; e. Jesuites Coll. and Acad. of Quebec, Quebec City; Laval Univ., M.Com. 1947; m. Madeleine, d. Napoléon Latraverse, 18 Sept. 1948; children: Paul, Jean, Robert, Simon, Marie; CHRMN. AND PRES., SAVINGS & INVESTMENT GROUP; Chrmn. and Pres., Savings & Investment Trust Co.; Chrmn. of Bd. Aeterna-Life Assurance Co.; Pres., Savings and Investment, Mutual Fund of Canada Ltd.; Savings and Investment American Fund Ltd.; Dir., La St-Maurice, Assurance Co.; Dir., la Compagnie Dohohue Ltée.; Gov. (1964) Candn. Mutual Fund Assn.; mem. Gen. Council of Industry; Que. Chamber of Commerce; Roman Catholic; recreations: golf, tennis; Clubs: Cercle Universitaire; Quebec Garrison; Montcalm Tennis; Home: 1286 Parc Lemoine, Sillery, Que. G1S 1A3; Office: 850 d'Youville Square, Quebec, Que. G1R 3P6.

TARNOPOLSKY, Walter Surma, A.M., LL.M., F.R.S.C.; educator; b. Gronlid, Sask., 1 Aug. 1932; s. Harry and Mary (Surma) T.; e. Univ. of Sask., B.A. 1953, LL.B. 1957; Columbia Univ., A.M. 1955; Univ. of London, LL.M. 1962; m. Joanne Gerdina, d. Dr. Klaas Kramer, Brockport, N.Y., 18 Aug. 1973; children: Mark Andrew, Christina Helen, Alexandra Justine, Michelle Raissa, Gregory Jan; Prof. of Law, and Dir., Human Rights Inst., Faculty of Law, Univ. of Ottawa; read law with Makaroff, Carter & Carter, Saskatoon, Sask.; called to Bar of Sask., 1960; Law Society of Upper Canada, 1970; Lectr., Coll. of Law, Univ. of Sask., 1959-60; Faculty of Common Law, Univ. of Ottawa, 1962-63; Asst. Prof., Coll. of Law, Univ. of Sask., 1963-66, Assoc. Prof., 1966-67; Assoc. Prof., Osgoode Hall Law Sch., Toronto, Ont., 1967-68, Prof., July-Aug. 1968; Dean and Prof. of Law,

Univ. of Windsor, 1968-72 and mem. Bd. of Govs. of the Univ. 1969-72; Vice-Pres. (Acad.) York Univ. 1972; Prof. of Law, Osgoode Hall Law School, 1972-80; comnd. C.O.T.C., 1957; author, "The Canadian Bill of Rights", 1966; 2nd ed., (1975); "Discrimination and the Law in Canada", 1982; articles on civil and human rights for various law reviews; Vice-Pres., Bd. Dirs., Mohyla Ukrainian Inst., 1964-66; Pres., Fed. Candn. Univ. Students, 1957-58; mem. UN Human Rights Comte. 1977-84; Commr. Candn. Human Rights Com. 1978-83; Pres. Candn. Civil Liberties Assn. 1977-81; mem. Candn. Bar Assn.; Assn. Candn. Law Teachers; Candn. Assn. Comparative Law; Candn. Inst. Internat. Affairs; Liberal; Ukrainian Greek Orthodox; Address: Faculty of Law, University of Ottawa, Ottawa, K1N 6N5

TARR, Robert Haggart, B.A., LL.B.; executive (retired); b. Winnipeg, Man., 19 July 1909; s. Edgar Jordan and Kathleen Anderson (Burke) T.; e. Univ. of Man., B.A. 1930, LL.B. 1934; m. Barbara, d. Brig.-Gen. R. W. Paterson, 1 Aug. 1936; children: Beverley, David, Valerie; former Vice-Pres., Canadian National Railways; read law with Messrs. Craig, Tarr, Hughes & Macleod, Winnipeg; called to Bar of Man. 1934; practised law with firm of Craig, Tarr, Hughes & Macleod, Winnipeg, 1934-39; joined Bank of Canada 1939 and loaned to Foreign Exchange Control Bd. on its estab., 1939; Asst. Secy., 1939-41; Secy., 1941-52; joined C.N.R. as Asst. Secy., 1952; Secy., 1954; Vice-Pres., 1958; Zeta Psi; Baptist; Home: 3449 Capilano Rd., North Vancouver, B.C.

TASCHEREAU, Maurice E., B.Eng.; industrialist; b. Noranda, Que. 5 Jan. 1930; s. Rogers H. and Louise (Rolland) T.; e. McGill Univ. B.Eng. 1953; m. Louise Y. d. Frederic Hébert, Montreal, Que. 5 Sept. 1953; children: Denise, Claire, Madeleine, Lucille; PRESIDENT AND CEO, ASBESTOS CORP. LTD.; served Noranda Group 25 yrs. various positions incl. Pres. Gaspé Copper Mines Ltd.; Vice Pres. Brunswick Mining and Smelting Ltd.; mem. Candn. Inst. Mining & Metall.; Am. Inst. Mining & Metall.; Corp. Prof. Engrs. Que.; recreations: golf, swimming, skiing, gardening; Office: 1155 Metcalfe St., Montreal, Que. H3B 2X6

TASCHEREAU, Pierre, Q.C.; b. Quebec City, Que., 13 Jan. 1920; s. late Edouard, Q.C. and Juliette (Carroll) T.; e. Garnier Coll., B.A. 1938; Laval Univ., LL.L. 1941; Univ. of W. Ont., Mang. Training Course, 1952; m. Yseult, d. Laurent Beaudry, LL.D., Montreal, Que., 13 Aug. 1945; children: Paule, Laurent, Francois; Dir., Air Canada; The Royal Trust Co.; read law with late Hon. L. Fournier, Hull, Que.; called to Bar of Que. 1941; cr. Q.C. 1955; Secretary, Que. Prof. Comtes., Department of Justice, Ottawa, 1941-42; Asst. Solr., Solr. & Asst. Gen. Solr., Law Dept., C.N.R., 1946-63; Sr. mem., Geoffrion & Prud'homme, Montreal, 1963-67; Vice Pres., Candn. Transport Comn. 1967-71; joined Candn. National as Vice-Pres. and Gen. Counsel 1971, Extve. Vice Pres.-Corp. Affairs 1972-74; Chrmn., 1974-77; Chmn. of Bd., 1975-81; served in Canada 1942-46, Inf. and permanent Prosecutor; retired with rank of Capt.; Gov., Hôpital Marie Enfant, Montreal and Montréal Gen. Hosp.; mem. of Bd., Montreal Heart Inst. Research Foundation; mem., Que. Bar Assn.; Candn. Bar Assn.; Home: 3788 Grey Ave., Montreal, Que. H4A 3N7

TASCONA, Antonio (Tony), R.C.A.; artist; b. St. Boniface, Man. 16 March 1926; s. Sebastiano and Nunziata (Sanfillipo) T.; e. Winnipeg Sch. of Art 1947-50; Univ. of Man. Sch. of Fine Arts 1948-52; m. May Gilchrist 1 June 1951; children: Lorenzo, Martin, Christopher, Catherine; joined Canadian Aerospace Industries 1953-56; Trans Canada Airlines metal-plating technician 1956-70; solo exhns.: Univ. of Man. 1958; Winnipeg Art Gallery 1960, 1962, 1967, 1974; Allied Arts Centre Brandon 1962; La Gallerie Soixante Montreal 1964; Calgary Allied Arts Centre 1962; Confed. Art Centre Charlottetown 1965; Mem.

Art Centre St. John's, Nfld. 1965; Blue Barn Gallery 1966; Carmen Lamanna Gallery Toronto 1968; Griffith Gallery Vancouver 1969; Grant Gallery 1961 and Yellow Door Gallery Winnipeg 1965; Atlantic Art Circuit, Maritimes 1972-73; Art Gallery of Brant, Brantford 1973-74; La Gallerie Internationale 1976 Ribe, Denmark; Rodman Hall Art Gallery St. Catharines 1976; Art Gallery of Windsor 1976; Kesik Gallery Regina 1979; rep. in numerous group exhns. Can., USA and Europe incl. Nat. Gallery Biennial 1965 and 7th Biennial Exhn. 1968; Candn. Artists Exhn. Habitat Expo '67; Survey 68 Montreal Museum of Fine Arts; Montreal Olympics 1976; Cardiff Commonwealth Arts Festival Wales 1965; Nat. Gallery Exhn. Australia 1967; Travel Exhn. Paris, France 1976-77; Royal Candn. Acad. Centennial Exhn., Winnipeg Art Gallery, 1980; rep. in pub., corporate and private colls. incl. Nat. Gallery Can.; Can. Council Art Bank; Univ. of Man. Tony Tascona Perm. Exhn. cert. by Cultural Property Review Bd. 1978 and 17 works 1949-77; comns. incl. murals Man. Centennial Art Centre 1967, YWCA Bldg. Univ. Man. 1969, and Fletcher Argue Bldg. 1970-71, Windsor, Ont. 1973; Hanging Mobile Freshwater Inst. Univ. Man. 1971-72; 2 murals Centennial Concert Hall Winnipeg 1967; Winnipeg Centennial Lib. sculpture 1977; rec'd Can. Council Grant (Materials) 1967-79, Sr. Arts Award 1972-73; Bethzedec Competition Toronto 1969; Royal Arch. Inst. Arts Medal 1970; Man. Arts Council Sr. Arts Award 1976-77; Queen's Silver Jubilee Medal 1977; Academia Italia Del Arti e Del Lavoro Gold Medal 1980; Gov., Winnipeg Art Gallery; mem. Art Adv. Bd. Man. Dept. Pub. Works Mural Competitions 1975-78; Dir. Univ. Man. Faculty Arch. Endowment Fund 1980; mem. Candn. Artists' Representation; Candn. Conf. of Arts; served with Candn. Army 1944-46; R. Catholic; recreation: walking; Address: 151 Tache Ave., Winnipeg, Man. R2H 1Z4.

TASSE, Jean-Louis; stockbroker; b. Bellevue, Qué., 23 July 1932; s. Louis and Georgette (Plamondon) T.; e. Loyola Coll., Montreal, Qué.; m. Hélène, d. Joseph Cuierrier, 26 May 1956; three s. Louis-Joseph, Jean-Baptiste, Thomas Emmanuel; three d. Héloise, Sophie, Catherine; PRESIDENT, TASSE & ASSOCIES, LIMITEE mem. Montreal (Gov. 1972, 1978, 1979) Toronto and Vancouver Stock Exchanges and Investment Dealers' Assn. Can. (Vice-Pres. 1976, 1977); Pres., La Cie de Transport des Laurentides Ltée; joined Royal Securities Corp. 1951, later with W. C. Pitfield & Co. Ltd. and other nat. and Montreal dealers until 1967 when founded present Co.; Pres. (1972 and 1977) Montreal Bond Traders' Assn.; Past Vice-Pres., Montreal Jr. Chamber Comm.; mem. Chamber Comm. Que.; Catholic; recreations: travel, swimming; Clubs: Canadien; M.A.A.A.; St. Jame's (Montreal); Home: 600 Rabastalière E., St. Bruno, Que. J3V 1Z9; Office: 630 Dorchester Blvd. West, Montreal Qué. H3B 1T4

TASSÉ, Roger, O.C., Q.C., B.A., LL.L.; civil servant; b. Montreal, Que. 5 June 1931; e. Coll. Ste-Marie B.A. 1952; Univ. of Montreal LL.L. 1956; Univ. of Ottawa Dipl. Grad. Studies in Law 1957; U. of Montreal. Dipl. of merit 1978; m. Renée Marcil; 4 children; DEPY. MIN. OF JUSTICE AND DEPY. ATTORNEY GENERAL OF CAN. since 1977; called to Bar of Que. 1956; Yukon Territory Bar 1977; cr. Q.C. 1971; Solr. Civil Law Sec. Dept. of Justice Can. 1957, Supt. of Bankruptcy 1965, Asst. Depy. Min. (Corporate Affairs) Dept. Consumer and Corporate Affairs 1968; Chrmn. Study Comte. on Bankruptcy and Insolvency Leg. Report, June, 1970; Depy. Solr. Gen. of Can. 1972; Chrmn. Comte. on Young offenders, Report "Young Persons in Conflict with the Law." 1975; Lectr. Law Faculty Univ. of Ottawa and Pub. Adm. Law Inst.; Trustee, La Commission Scolaire Outaouais-Hull (Outaouais/Hull Sch. Bd.) 1972-74; Dir. CEGEP de l'Outaouais; Vice Pres., CEGEP de l'Outaouais, 1976-78; Chrmn. Nat'l Council on Administration of Justice in Canada (Cdn. Bar Assn.); mem. Cdn. Law Info. Council; Home: Chelsea, Que. J0X 1N0; Office: Justice Bldg., Ottawa, Ont. K1A 0H8

TATA, Sam Bejan, R.C.A.; photographer; b. Shanghai, China 30 Sept. 1911; s. Bejan Dadabhoy and Naja Tata; e. Shanghai Pub. Sch.; Univ. of Hong Kong 2 yrs.; came to Can. 1956; formerly m. to Marketa Langer; one d. Antonia; as photojournalist has contributed to maj. Candn. mags. since 1956 incl. Time Can.; exhn., National Gallery, "Shanghai 1949", 1981; rep. in exhns. Shanghai, Bombay, Phoenix, George Eastman House Rochester, Boston, Paris, Toronto, Ottawa and Montreal; recipient various Can. Council grants incl. 2 Sr. Arts Grants; Queen's Silver Jubilee Medal 1977; co-author "Montreal" (photographs) with late Frank Lowe 1963; Canadian Fiction Magazine 50 portraits Candn. writers 1958-78, 1979; mem. Royal Photographic Soc. (Eng.); Liberal; Zoroastrian; recreations: classical music, reading; Address: 1750 Crevier, Apt. 7, St. Laurent, Que, H4L 2X5.

TATE, W. Hunter, B.Sc.; executive; b. North Battleford, Sask. 5 June 1920; s. John J. and Mabel (Raines) T.; e. High Sch. North Battleford, Sask.; Univ. of Sask. B.Sc. (Mech. Engn.) 1942; m. Murial, d. Alexander Wilson 11 Dec. 1943; children: Lionel, John, Paul; PRES., DIR. AND CEO., LENNOX INDUSTRIES (CANADA) LTD., since 1970; mem., Bd. of Dir., Lennox Industries (Canada) Ltd.; commenced as Test Engr., Candn. Gen. Electric Co. Ltd., Peterborough, Ont. 1942-43; Engr., Toronto 1943-44, Calgary, Alta. 1944-58; joined present Co., Calgary, Alta. as Comm. Engr., 1958-61, Sales Mgr. 1961-64, apptd. Dir. 1966, Gen. Mgr. W. Div. 1964-69, Vice-Pres. Sales 1969; mem., Engn. Inst. of Can.; United Church; recreations: golf, curling; Clubs: Glencoe (Calgary, Alta.); Earl Grey Golf (Calgary); Home: 2352 Lone Gridlock Dr. S.W., Calgary, Alta. T3E 5H8

TATE, William Charles, C.A. B.Com.; electronics executive; b. Regina, Sask., 12 May 1925; s. Merlin James and Nelda (Wait) T.; e. Queen's Univ., B.Com. 1949; four sons and one daughter; VICE-PRESIDENT, GEN. MGR. AND MANG. DIR., GARRETT MANUFACTURING LTD. since 1962; Dir., Dunham Bush Canada Ltd.; Dir., Electrical and Electronic Manufacturing Association of Canada; Air Industries Assoc. of Can.; gained C.A. with Clarkson, Gordon & Co. 1949-54; joined present Co. as Controller 1954; Asst. to Vice-Pres., Finance, U.S.A. 1959; apptd. Gen. Mgr. 1960, Vice-Pres. 1961; served with R.C.A.F. 1943-46 as Instrument Mech.; mem., Inst. Chartered Accts.; Canadian Aero Space Inst.; Queen's Univ. Alumni; Bd. Trade Club Metrop. Toronto; recreations: golf, swimming, gardening; Home: 1493 Elite Rd., Clarkson, Ont. L5J 3B3; Office: 255 Attwell Dr., Rexdale, Ont. M9W 5B8

TATOSSIAN, Armand, R.C.A.; artist; b. Alexandria, Egypt 26 Sept. 1948; e. Cath. Coll. of St. Marc, Alexandria; Montreal High Sch. 1967; McGill Univ. Art Hist. 1967-69; drawing and sculpture under J. Majzner; pupil of A. S. Scott, R.C.A. 1966-69; Cararra Acad. Bergamo, Italy mural painting 1970; Paris, France 1971; m.; one d. Anais; assisted in restoration of murals Bank of Montreal St. James St. Br. Montreal; Prof. of Art Educ. Concordia Univ. 1971-74; Chrmn. Cultural Comte. Armenian Gen. Benevolent Union Montreal 1976-77; solo exhns. incl. Double Take Art Gallery New York 1968; Galerie Gauvreau Montreal 1968, 1970, 1971; Molesworth Gallery New York 1969; Mount Stephen Club Montreal 1972; Studio des Artistes Canadiens Inc. Quebec City 1973; Galerie Bernard Desroches Montreal 1973, 1975, 1980; Galerie Peintre Québécois Baie St-Paul 1974; Galerie St. Laurent Ottawa 1976; Nat. Gallery of Armenia, Yerevan, U.S.S.R. 1976; A.G.B.U. Gallery New York 1977; Dominion Corinth Ottawa 1978; Kaspar Gallery Toronto 1978, 1979; Menasen Gallery Sherbrooke 1978; Pub. Archives Can. Ottawa 1980; Lindchrist Gallery Windsor, Ont. 1980; rep. various group exhns.; rep. numerous perm. colls. incl. Museum of Fine Arts of Soviet Armenia, Musée de Québec, Nat. Gallery Can.; work cited various publs.; mem. Conseil de la peinture du Québec; recrea-

tions: music, travel, reading; Clubs: Montreal Art; Arts & Letters Toronto; Address: #811, 201 Metcalfe Ave., Montreal, Que. H3Z 2H7.

TAURINS, Alfred, Dr. Chem., F.C.I.C., F.R.S.C.; educator; b. Dauguli, Latvia 20 Aug. 1904; s. Michael and Matilda Elizabeth (Otter) T.; e. Univ. of Latvia, Eng.-Chem. 1930, Dr.Chem. 1936; Kaiser-Wilhelm-Institut für medizinische Forschung, Heidelberg, Research Fellow 1939; m. Milija d. Peter Neimanis 23 June 1930; two d. Egina (Mrs. J. C. Nicholson), Ilze (Mrs. R. B. Dwyer); Instr. in Chem. Univ. of Latvia 1930-38, Privat-Dozent Faculty of Chem. 1938-39; Prof. of Chem. Acad. of Agric. Jelgava, Latvia 1939-44; Prof. UNRRA Univ. Munich, Germany 1946-47; Assoc. Prof. of Organic Chem. McGill Univ. 1949, Macdonald Prof. of Chem. 1963, Prof. Emeritus since 1972; Elder, Trinity Lutheran Ch. Montreal 1949-54; co-author "Special Topics in Heterocyclic Chemistry" 1977; author over 60 research articles organic and heterocyclic chem.; Am. Chem. Soc.; Sigma Xi; Lutheran; recreation: gardening; Home: 1870 Gray St., St.-Bruno, Que. J3V 4G3; Office: 801 Sherbrooke St. W., Montreal, Que. H3A 2K6.

TAVNER, Bruce Henry, P.Eng.; communications executive; b. Toronto, Ont. 10 Sept. 1937; s. Albert Henry and late Eva (Clee) T.; e. Weston (Ont.) Coll. & Vocational Sch. 1954; Ryerson Inst. of Technol. Toronto Dipl. Electronics Technol. 1957; P.Eng. 1966; m. Erita d. late Eric Dik 23 May 1959; children: Laura, Bradley; VICE PRES. (INTERNAT.) BELL CANADA 1981- Chrmn. of Bd. Bell Canada International; Dir. Northern Telecom International Ltd.; joined Bell Canada 1957 serving in numerous engn. and operations assignments Toronto, Montreal, Ottawa, apptd. Asst. Vice Pres. Trans Canada 1972 becoming Asst. Vice Pres. Business Devel. Marketing and Gen. Mgr. Cont. Prov.; mem. Inst. Elect. & Electronic Engrs.; Assn. Prof. Engrs. Prov. Ont.; Protestant; Clubs: Ontario; Mississauga Golf & Country; Home: 1710 Ruscombe Close, Mississauga, Ont. L5J 1Y5; Office: F21, 393 University Ave., Toronto, Ont. M5G 1W9.

TAYLOR, Allan Richard; banking executive; b. Prince Albert, Sask. 14 Sept. 1932; s. Norman and Anna Lydia (Norbeck) T.; m. Shirley d. late Ellis K. Ruston 5 Oct. 1957; children: Rodney Allan, Leslie Ann; EXTVE. VICE PRES., INTL. BANKING, THE ROYAL BANK OF CAN. since 1980; Dir., Orion Royal Bank Ltd., London, Eng.; Dir., RBC Holdings B.V., Amsterdam; Dir., Candn. Council, Intl. Chamber of Commerce; joined the Royal Bank in Prince Albert, 1949; served at other Sask. branches and the Dist. Gen. Mgr's Dept., Regina; Dist. Gen. Mgr.'s Dept., Toronto, 1957; Sr. Asst. Agent New York, 1965; Agent, New York Agency, 1967; Supervisor, Correspondent Banking, Montreal, 1969; Asst. Gen. Mgr., Intl. Div., 1970; Mgr., Toronto Main Branch, 1971; Deputy Gen. Mgr., Intl. Div., Head Office, Montreal, 1974; Extve. Vice Pres. and Gen. Mgr., Intl. Div., Jan. 1977; Anglican; Clubs: Forest and Stream; St. Jame's; Royal Mtl. Golf; Mississauga Golf and Country; National, Toronto; recreations: golf, tennis; Home: 411 Lakeshore Rd., Beaconsfield, Que. H9W 4J2; Office: Box 6001, Montreal, Que. H3C 3A9.

TAYLOR, Charles, B.A., D.Phil.; educator; b. Montreal, Que., 5 Nov. 1931; s. Walter Margrave and Simone (Beaubien) T.; e. Selwyn House Sch. 1946; Trinity Coll. Sch. Port Hope, Ont. 1949; McGill Univ. B.A. 1952; Oxford Univ. B.A. 1955, D.Phil. 1961 (Fellow All Souls' Coll. 1956-61); m. Alba d. Tadeusz Romer, 2 Apl. 1956; children: Karen, Miriam, Wanda, Gabrielle, Gretta; PROF. OF POL. SCIENCE, McGILL UNIV. and of Philos. 1973; joined present Univ. as Asst. Prof. 1961; Prof. of Philos. Univ. de Montréal 1962-71; Visiting Prof. Princeton Univ. 1965, Univ. of Cal. Berkeley 1974; mem., Inst. for Advanced Study, Princeton, 1981-82; el. Chichele Prof. of Pol. and Social Theory, Univ. of Oxford 1976-82; former

Vice Pres., fed. NDP, Pres. Que. NDP; author "Explanation of Behaviour" 1964; "Pattern of Politics" 1970; "Hegel" 1975; "Hegel and Modern Society" 1979; articles fields of philos. and pol. theory in various learned journs. mags.; mem. Candn. Pol. Science Assn.; Candn. Philos. Assn.; Royal Soc. Can.; British Academy; NDP; R. Catholic; recreations: swimming, skiing, hiking; Home: 344 Metcalfe Ave., Montreal, Que. H3Z 2J3

TAYLOR, Claude I., transportation executive; b. Salisbury, N.B., 20 May 1925; s. Martin Luther and Essie (Troope) T.; e. Salisbury (N.B.) High Sch., 1941; Robinson Business Coll., N.B., 1942; McGill Univ. Extension, 1950-53; D.C.L. (Hon.C.) Univ. of N.B., 1980; m. Frances Bernice, d. late Robert Watters, 4 Nov. 1947; children: Peter, Karen; PRESIDENT AND C.E.O. — AIR CANADA since 1976; previously served with Hudson McMackin & Co. (Chart. Accts.) and Robbins Ltd. (Asst. Gen. Mgr.); has served Air Canada as Gen. Mgr. Comm. Planning, Gen. Mgr. Marketing Services, Vice Pres. Strategic Devel., Vice Pres., Govt. & Industry Affairs, Vice Pres. Pub. Affairs; Past Pres. Internat. Air Trans. Assn.; Past Pres. (1972-73), Travel Industry Assn. of Can.; Chrmn. (1975-76) Air Transport Assn. Can. (1979-80); Dir., Guinness Peat Aviation; Gov., Montreal Gen. Hosp.; Commander of the Order of St. John; Vice-Pres., Boy Scouts of Canada; Hon. Chmn. Quebec Assn. for Children Disabilities 1982 Corporate Campaign; mem. Bd. of Directors, Concordia Centre for Management Studies; mem. Adv. Bd., Salvation Army; mem. Gov. Council of Gov. General's First Study Conference, 1983; mem., Exec. Council, Candn Chamber of Comm.; Professional Corp. of Industrial Accountants of Quebec; Hon. Mem. H.R.H. the Duke of Edinburgh's Fifth Commonwealth Study Conf., Can. 1980; rec'd. Gordon R. McGregor Trophy, Royal Candn. Airforce Assn., 1980 Hon. Dir. Aviation Hall of Fame; C.N.E.; Baptist; Clubs: Mount Stephen; Mount Royal, Rideau, (Ottawa,) Wings, (N.Y.) Forest and Stream, (Mtl.); Office: Place Ville Marie, Montreal, Que. H3B 3P7

TAYLOR, Edward Plunket, C.M.G. (1946); LL.D.; industrialist; financier; b. Ottawa, Ont. 29 Jan. 1901; s. the late Lt.-Col. Plunket Bourchier and Florence Gertrude (Magee) T.; e. Ashbury Coll. and Ottawa Coll. Inst., Ottawa, Ont.; McGill Univ., B.Sc. (Mech. Engn.) 1922; m. Winifred Thornton, d. late Charles F. M. Duguid, Ottawa, Ont., 15 June 1927; children: Judith Winifred (Mrs. John N. Mappin), Mary Louise (Mrs. Alan Edwards), Charles P. B.; CHAIRMAN, NEW PROVIDENCE DEVELOPMENT CO. LTD. NASSAU: Chrmn. International Housing Ltd.; Pres. Lyford Cay Co. Ltd.; Windfields Farms Ltd.; Hon. Chrmn., The Ontario Jockey Club; Hon. Chrmn. Jockey Club of Canada; (1st Candn) mem. The Jockey Club N.Y.; became assoc with The Brading Breweries Ltd. as a Dir., 1923; also entered the invest. house of McLeod Young, Weir & Co. Ltd., Ottawa, Ont., 1923; Dir. 1929; resigned 1930, to become President, Canadian Breweries Ltd.; Chrmn. of the Bd. 1944; appt. mem. of Extve. Comte., Dept. of Mun. & Supply, Ottawa, April 1940; apptd. Jt. Dir.-Gen. of Mun. Production, Nov. 1940; apptd. Extve. Asst. to Min. of Mun. & Supply, Feb. 1941; Pres., War Supplies Ltd., Wash., D.C., 1941; apptd. by Prime Min. Churchill, Pres. and Vice-Chrmn. of Brit. Supply Council of N. Am., Sept. 1941; Dir.-Gen., Brit. Min. of Supply Mission, Feb. 1942; Candn. Depy. mem. on the Combined Production and Resources Bd., Nov. 1942; also Candn. Chrmn., Jt. War Aid Comte., U.S.-Canada, Sept. 1943; Hon. Treas., H.R.H. The Duke of Edinburgh's Second Commonwealth Study Conf.; mem. Bd. Govs., Trinity College Sch., Ashbury College; Dir. emeritus, Thoroughbred Racing Assn., Inc. N.Y. Past Nat. Pres., V.O.N. for Can.; awarded first Gold Medal for distinguished service by McGill Univ. Grad. Soc., 1957; maintains a substantial breeding and racing establishment; breeder of 18 Queen's Plate Winners Leading breeder in N.A.-money won 1975-79; breeder and owner

(Windfields Farm) of "Northern Dancer," first Candn. bred to win Kentucky Derby and Queen's Plate, 1964; Delta Upsilon; Anglican; recreations: riding, golf; Clubs: Toronto; York; Rideau (Ottawa); Metropolitan (N.Y.); Buck's (London, Eng.); Turf (England); Lyford Cay (Bahamas); East Hill (Bahamas); Address: Lyford Cay, New Providence, Bahamas.

TAYLOR, Frederick Cleveland; company officer; b. Ottawa, Ont., 12 May 1911; s. Thomas Henry and Margaret Alice T.; e. Kitchener-Waterloo Coll. Inst.; m. Margaret Mathilda, d. A. Polzin, Kitchener, Ont., 15 Sept. 1934; children: Brian Duncan, Karen Lynn; CHAIRMAN BD. AND DIR., WATERLOO MFG. CO. LTD.; Pres., Aylor Investments Ltd.; Pres. and Dir., Maple Heights Ltd.; Freemason; Conservative; Anglican; recreations: hunting, fishing, farming; Clubs: Westmount Golf; Home: 190 Alexandra Ave. W., Waterloo, Ont. N2L 1M5; Office: 263 Phillip St., Waterloo, Ont. N2L 3W8

TAYLOR, Harry William, B.Sc., M.Sc., Ph.D.; university professor; b. Sturgeon Valley, Sask. 28 Sept. 1925; s. Wm. and Gladys Muriel (Evans) T.; e. Univ. of Manitoba B.Sc. 1951, M.Sc. 1952, Ph.D. 1954; m. Wanda Jason 18 June 1949; children: Allison Leslie, Karen Elizabeth; ASSOC. PROF. OF PHYSICS, UNIV. OF TORONTO since 1965; Lectr. Univ. of Manitoba, 1952-53; Post-doctoral Fellow NRC, Ottawa, 1954-55; Lectr., Asst. Prof. Queen's Univ., 1955-61; Assoc. Prof. Univ. of Alta., 1961-65; served with RCNVR, active service, 1944-45; awarded Candn. Volunteer Service Medal, War Medal 1939-45; has written scientific papers with special reference to nuclear spectroscopy, environmental radioactivity; Fellow, Am. Physical Society; Fellow, Inst. of Physics; Fellow, Inst. of Nuclear Engn.; Fellow, Am. Assoc. for Advancement of Science; mem., Candn. Assn. of Univ. Teachers; recreations: military history, tennis; Home: 3525 Grand Forks Road, Mississauga, Ont. L4Y 3N2; Office: Toronto, Ont. M5S 1A7.

TAYLOR, Hugh; insurance executive; b. Edinburgh, Scotland 21 Jan. 1925; e. Glasgow Univ. m. Mary-Lee (Hubbs) T.; children: Jan, Graham, Trudy, Joseph, Kelly-Ann; PRESIDENT FOR CAN., NORWICH UNION LIFE INSURANCE SOC.; Pres. Norgroup Realty Canada Ltd. 1977- ; Dir. Canada Security Assurance Co.; V & G Computer Systems Ltd.; Dir. Canadian-Scottish Philharmonic Foundation; joined Norwich Union Life, Scot. 1941, held various appts. after World War II service UK, Mgr. E. Africa 1956, Asst. Gen. Mgr. Can. 1961, Gen. Mgr. Can. 1977-81; recreations: automobile racing, sports, music; Home: R.R. 5, Bowmanville, Ont. L1C 3K6; Office: 60 Yonge St., Toronto, Ont. M5E 1H5.

TAYLOR, J. Allyn, B.A.; trust and loan company executive; b. Winnipeg, Man., 10 Apl. 1907; s. John and Florence Elizabeth (Poyntz) T.; e. Pub. Schs. and Model Sch., Winnipeg, Man.; St. Michael's Sch., Victoria, B.C., Kelvin High Sch., Winnipeg, Man.; Univ. of Manitoba, B.A. 1928; m. Elizabeth D., d. Hon. Senator John T. Haig, Winnipeg, Man., 15 Oct. 1938; children: Ann, Lynn, John; Hon. CHAIRMAN, THE CANADA TRUST CO. and Canada Trustco Mortgage Co. since 1978; Director and member Extve. Comte., The London Life Insurance Co.; Silverwood Industries Ltd.; Dir., Canadian General Investments Ltd.; Third Candn. Gen. Investments Trust; Hon. Dir., John Labatt Ltd.; Trust Officer, The Royal Trust Co., Winnipeg, Man., 1935-43; Trust Supt., London, Ont. 1943, Trust Extve. 1946; Asst. Gen. Mgr.; 1949; Asst. Gen. Mgr., Canada Trust-Huron & Erie, 1952; Joint Gen. Mgr., 1955; Gen. Mgr., 1957; el. a Dir., 1957; Pres. & Gen. Mgr. 1958; Chrmn. & Pres. 1968; Chrmn. 1973; Past Pres., Trust Co's. Assns. of Can. and Ont.; Past Pres. (1969-70) Candn. Chamber of Comm.; Past Pres., London Health Association (Univ. Hospital); Chrmn., London Foundation; Anglican; recreations: golf, bridge, billiards; Clubs: The London; London Hunt; York (Toronto);

Home: 1117 The Parkway, London, Ont. N6A 2X2; Office: 275 Dundas St., London, Ont.

TAYLOR, J. David, Q.C.; industrialist; b. Toronto, Ont. 13 Oct. 1928; s. John D. and Mabel (Pugh) T.; e. Public and High Schs. Hamilton, Ont.; McMaster Univ., Hons. Pol. Econ.; Osgoode Hall Law Sch., Hons. 1954; m. Jean, d. S. G. Parker 27 Dec. 1954; children: Michael, Caroline, Nancy, David; ANGLO AMERICAN CORP. OF CANADA LTD. since 1974, currently stationed in S. Africa; Dir. Hudson Bay Mining and Smelting Co. Ltd.; Minerals and Resources Corp. Ltd.; Botswana RST Ltd.; alternate Dir., Anglo Amer. Corp. of S. Africa Ltd.; called to Bar Ontario 1954; cr. Q.C. 1967; with Fasken & Calvin 1954, Partner 1959; joined present Co. as Executive Director 1973; C.O.T.C. McMaster Univ.; mem. Candn. Bar Assn.; Mining Assn. Can.; Law Soc. Upper Can.; Baptist; Clubs: Caughnawana Hunting & Fishing; National; Canadian (N.Y.C.); Home: 15 Whitney Ave., Toronto, Ont. M4W 2A7; Office: 44 Main St., Johannesburg, S. Africa

TAYLOR, James Coyne, B.A., F.C.A.; educator; b. St. Thomas, Ont., 22 Sept. 1914; s. late Charles Berkeley and Christine Elliot Bowes (Coyne) T.; e. Pub. and High Schs., St. Thomas, Ont.; Unvi. of Western Ont., (Grad. Business Adm.) 1938; m. Phyllis Brewster, Ph.D.; children: Stephanie, Gillian; SR. PROF. OF BUSINESS ADM., UNIV. OF WESTERN ONTARIO since 1949; with Clarkson, Gordon & Co. (Chart. Accts.) 1938-45; Assoc. Prof., Business Adm., Univ. of British Columbia, 1945-49; apptd. to Faculty of Mang. Devel. Inst., Univ. of Lausanne, Switzerland (leave of absence) 1958-59; Address: London, Ont. N6A 3K7

TAYLOR, John Daniel, B.S.; executive b. Rochester, Ind., 2 Oct. 1922; s. Guy Hubert and Louise T. (Bailey); e. Ind. Univ. B.S. (Business) 1947; m. Margaret Mason Witman, 7 Feb. 1976; children: Jeffrey, Janis Bryant, Daniel, Gail Andrus, William Witman; PRES., CHIEF OPERATING OFFICER AND DIR. SIMPSONS-SEARS LIMITED 1979- ; Pres. and Dir. Simpsons-Sears Acceptance Co. Ltd.; Dir., Allstate Insurance Co. of Canada; Allstate Life Insurance Co. of Canada; Canadian Pacific Hotels Ltd.; DeSoto Coatings Ltd.; Rio Algom Limited; joined Sears, Roebuck & Co. Fort Wayne, Ind. 1947; Asst. Mgr. La Porte (Ind.), Bay City (Mich.) and Lexington (Ky.); Mid-W. Zone Fieldman, (Chicago); Mgr. Springfield (Ohio); Gen. Merchandise Office Nat. HQ Chicago; Group Mgr. Columbus (Ohio); Adm. Asst. to Vice Pres. Mid-W. Territory; Mid-W. Zone Mgr. (Ill. and Mich.); Gen. Mgr. Chicago Group; Pres., Simpsons-Sears Limited, 1976; Pres. and Dir. Boys and Girls Clubs of Can.; Dir. Canadian Special Olympics; served with US Navy during World War II; mem. Bd. Trade Metrop. Toronto; mem. Ont. Business Adv. Council; Protestant; recreations: golf, Clubs: Toronto Hunt; Canadian; Granite; Toronto; York; Home: 15 Cluny Dr., Toronto, Ont. M4W 2P8; Office: 222 Jarvis St., Toronto, Ont. M5B 2B8

TAYLOR, John Howard; executive; b. Gananoque, Ont., 8 Oct. 1913; s. Howard W. and Clara (Reid) T.; e. McGill Univ., B.Eng. 1935; m. Marian, d. Hon. Lorne C. Webster, Montreal, Que., 5 June 1937; children: Howard W., Ann (Mrs. B. Collombin), Sherrill (Mrs. John C. Eaton), Anthony J., Jane (Mrs. James C. Irwin); Chrmn., North American Life Assurance Co.; Slough Estates Canada Ltd.; Cadbury-Schweppes Powell Ltd.; Chrm. Exec. Comm.; Bramalea Ltd.; Dir., Greyhound Lines of Canada Ltd.; Greyhound Computer of Can. Ltd.; Ultramar Canada Ltd.; RoyFund Ltd.; Procor Ltd.; Mercantile Bank of Canada Ltd.; Morton Norwich Products Ltd.; Motor Coach Industries Ltd.; Paul Poque Companies Ltd.; Davie Centre Ltd.; Hamac International Ltd.; began with Weaver Coal Co., 1935; then associated with Liquifuels Ltd. at inception, becoming Pres. and Chief Extve. Offr.; served in 2nd World War, 1943-44, as Lieut. R.C.A. and later (on leave of absence) became Dir. of Bituminous

Coal Supply under Dept. of Mun. & Supply; Past Vice-Pres., Metrop. Toronto Indust. Comn.; Past Pres., Board Trade Metrop. Toronto; Alpha Delta Phi; United Church; Clubs: The Toronto; York (Toronto); Naples Yacht, Royal Poinciana Golf; Moorings Golf & Country; (all Naples, Fla.); Boca Grandé (Fla.); Home: 145 Cumberland, Apt. 1904, Toronto, Ont.; Office: 2815 Thamesgate Dr., Malton, Ont. L4T 1G5

TAYLOR, John McGuire, B.Sc.; consultant; b. Sandgate, Kent, Eng., 6 Nov. 1917; s. James McWilliam and Wenefred (McGuire) T.; e. Solihull (Eng.) Sch.; Univ. of W. Ont., 1938-39; Univ. of Oklahoma, B.Sc. 1947; m. Mary Elizabeth, d. W. A. Shaw, Windsor, Ont., 3 Apl. 1948; children: Michael, Karen, Mark, Geoffrey; PRES., LIQUID AIR ENERGY CORP. and Chmn., Imperial Continental Gas Alberta Ltd.; Chrmn. and Dir., Panarctic Oils Ltd.; Petroleum Engr. and/or consultant various oil companies Alta. 1947-55; joined Canadian Pacific Oil & Gas as Petroleum Engr., 1955; Asst. to Mgr., 1957-58, Mgr., 1958-64, Vice Pres. and Gen. Mgr. 1968, Pres. 1969; Pres. Central Del-Rio Oils Ltd. 1969; Pres. Pan Canadian Petroleum Ltd., to 1980 (retired); member, Association Prof. Engrs., Geols. and Geophysicists Alta.; Assoc. Inst. Mech. Engrs.; Past Pres. Independent Petroleum Assn. Can. 1976-77; served in 2nd World War with R.C.A.F. as Observer; Flt. Lieut., 1940-45, Eng., Middle East; shot down Nov. 1941; P.O.W. till May 1945; recreations: tennis, swimming; Clubs: Calgary Petroleum; Glencoe; Home: 1407, 330-26 Ave S.W., Calgary, Alta. T2S 273; Office: 202-S, 8500 MacLeod Trail, S.E., Calgary, Alta. T2H 2N1

TAYLOR, Kenneth Douglas, O.C., M.B.A., LL.D.; diplomat; b. Calgary, Alta. 5 Oct. 1934; s. Richard Taylor; e. Univ. of Toronto B.A. 1957; Univ. of Cal. Berkeley M.B.A. 1959; Laurentian Univ. LL.D.; m. P. E. Lee 1 Oct. 1960; one s. Douglas; CANDN. CONSUL GEN., N.Y. and Candn. Commr. to Bermuda 1981- ; joined Candn. Foreign Service 1959; Guatemala 1960, Detroit 1963, Karachi 1966, Counsellor London, Eng. 1967, Ottawa 1971 (various assignments incl. Asst. Secy. Interdepartmental Comte. on External Relations, Dir. Finance and Personnel Trade Commr. Service 1972, Dir. Gen. Foreign Trade Service 1973); Candn. Ambassador to Iran 1977; when U.S. Embassy was taken by Iranians in 1979 and its occupants captured, six escaped and were successfully hidden by the Canadian Embassy staff, directed by Mr. Taylor, and later escaped from Iran posing as Canadians; recipient U.S. Congressional Gold Medal; Haas Internat. Award Univ. of Cal. Berkeley; Detroit-Windsor Internat. Freedom Festival Award; Candn. Club N.Y. Gold Medal Award; Am. Acad. Achievement Gold Plate Award; N.Y. Police Dept., St. George's Assn. Golden Rule Award; State of Cal. Medal of Merit; Ave. of Americas Assn. N.Y. Gold Key Award; Key to City of N.Y.; Am. Friendship Medal, Freedoms Foundation Valley Forge, Pa.; Sigma Chi; recreations: tennis, squash, golf; Club: Canadian (N.Y.); Home: 550 Park Ave., New York, N.Y. 10021; Office: 1251 Ave. of the Americas, New York, N.Y. 10020.

TAYLOR, Malcolm Gordon, M.A., Ph.D., LL.D.; b. Alberta, 31 Aug. 1915; s. Charles G. and Ora E. T.; e. Calgary (Alta.) Normal Sch., 1933-34; Univ. of Calif., B.A., M.A., Ph.D. (1949); LL.D. Alberta 1965; children: Deanne Elizabeth, Burke Gordon; PROF. OF PUBLIC POLICY, YORK UNIV.; with Indust. Relations Dept., Henry Kaiser Corp., Calif., 1941-43; subsequently Assoc. Prof. of Pol. Econ., Univ. of Toronto; Principal, Univ. of Alberta (Calgary), 1960-64; Research Consultant, Royal Comm. on Health Services 1961-64; Pres., Univ. of Victoria (B.C.), 1964-68; Pres., Candn. Soc. for Higher Educ. 1974-75; Chrmn., Nat. Manpower Council for Mental Retardation 1972-76; Research Consultant (Hall) Health Services Review, 1978-80; Publications: "Administration of Health Insurance in Canada", 1956; "Financial Aspects of Health Insurance", 1958; "Health Insurance and Canadian Public Policy" 1978; and articles in prof. and learned journs.; Ed., "Canadian Journal of Public Administration", 1958-60; mem., Inst. Public Adm. Can. (Pres., 1959-60); Awarded Roy. Soc. of Canada J.A. Hannah Book Medal, 1980; Hannah Lecturer, 1980-81; Nat. Health Scientist Award 1981; Candn. Pol. Science Assn.; Phi Beta Kappa; Pi Sigma Alpha; United Church; Club: Arts & Letters; Address: York University, Downsview, Ont. M3J 1P3

TAYLOR, Hon. Martin Rapson, LL.B.; judge; b. Harrow, Eng. 18 May 1931; s. Henry Archibald, C.B.E. and Muriel Kathleen (Little) T.; e. Univ. of B.C. LL.B. 1962; m. Carolyn Frances d. Frank W. Harvie, Vancouver, B.C. 1960; children: Michael, Alexandra, Susan; JUDGE, SUPREME COURT OF B.C. since 1978; read law with C. W. Brazier, Q.C.; called to Bar of B.C. 1963; law practice Davis & Co. Vancouver and at Prince George 1963 — 78; Counsel for Atty. Gen. B.C. 1965 — 75; Advisor to Govt. of B.C. on estab. of B.C. Energy Comn. and on other pub. utility and energy matters 1973 — 77; Counsel for B.C. Energy Comn. on Inquiry into B.C. Natural Gas Industry 1973; mem. B.C. Del. to First Mins. Conf. on Energy 1974; Dir. B.C. Petroleum Corp. 1973 — 74, Secy. 1973 — 77; Chrmn. B.C. Motor Carrier Comn. 1973 — 74; Counsel to Royal Comn. on B.C. Rly. 1977 — 78; Chrmn. Univ. of Calgary Faculty Remuneration Arbitration Bd. 1978; mem. Extve. Vancouver Bar Assn. 1976 — 78; Dir. The Lawyers' Inn 1972 — 74; mem. Ed. Bd. "The Advocate" 1971 — 78; Home: 941 Belvedere Dr., North Vancouver, B.C. V7R 2C2; Office: The Court House, Vancouver, B.C. V6C 1P6.

TAYLOR, Richard Allan Hugh, B.A.; company executive; b. New Liskeard, Ont., 13 Jan. 1915; s. William Allan and Louise (Stadelman) T.; e. Pub. and High Schs., New Liskeard, Ont.; Univ. of Toronto (Victoria), B.A. 1937; m. Nonie de Lille, d. Robert S. Robinson, 23 Sept. 1939; children: Robert, Michael, Amanda; CHAIRMAN BD., MORISETTE DIAMOND DRILLING LTD.; Morisette Mfg. Ltd.; Director, Northern Telephone Ltd. and Hudson Bay Mines Ltd.; Temiskaming Printing Co.; Adm. Fabricated Metal, W.P.T.B., 1943-45; el. to Ont. Leg. for Temiskaming (Liberal), g.e. Sept. 1963; Pres. Candn. Wholesale Hardware Assn., 1954-55; United Church; Home: 33 Mary St., New Liskeard, Ont. P0J 1P0; Office: Haileybury, Ont. P0J 1K0

TAYLOR, Richard Gordon, B.A.Sc., M.B.A.; executive; b. Simcoe, Ont., 16 July 1935; s. Harold Charlton and Pearl A. (Haley) T.; e. Pub. and High Schs., Delhi, Ont.; Univ. of Toronto, B.A.Sc. 1957; Univ. of W. Ont., M.B.A. 1960; PRES., DIR. AND CHIEF EXTVE. OFFR., DATACROWN INC. since 1971; with Polymer Corp. as Chem. Engr., 1957-58; Applied Science Rep., IBM Canada Ltd., Toronto 1960, Systems Engn. Supv. 1962, Br. Systems Engn. Mgr. 1963, District Systems Engn. Mgr. 1965, Gen. Mgr., IBM's Expo '67 Exhibit 1967, Mgr. Information Systems 1967; Vice-Pres. and Dir., SDI Associates Ltd. 1969; joined Crown Life Insurance Co. to establish present Co. (a computer services subsidiary) 1971; mem. Assn. Prof. Engrs. Ont.; Candn. Information Processing Soc.; Candn. Operational Research Soc.; Sigma Chi; Anglican; recreations: boating, camping, golf; Clubs: Bayview Golf and Country; National; Office: 650 McNicoll Ave., Willowdale, Ont. M2H 2E1

TAYLOR, Robert Berkeley, B.A., LL.D., F.C.A.; b. St. Thomas, Ont., 22 Sept. 1914, LL.D. 1981; s. late Charles Berkeley and late Christine Elliot Bowes (Coyne) T.; e. St. Thomas (Ont.) Coll. Inst. (Sr. Matric. 1933); Univ. of Western Ont., B.A. 1941; McMaster Univ. LL.D. 1976; m. Marian Elizabeth, d. late Judge A. A. Ingram, St. Thomas, Ont., 13 Feb. 1943; children: Patricia, Margaret, Paul; began as Clerk, Dominion Bank, 1934-37; Faculty, Dept. of Business Adm., Univ. of W. Ont., 1941-42, 1945-49

(rank on leaving Assoc. Prof.); joined The Steel Co. of Canada 1949, Vice-Pres. and Treas. 1959-74; joined Ont. Hydro as Vice-Chrmn. 1974, Chrm. 1975-79; served in 2nd World War with Royal Candn. Navy (Lieut.) 1942-45; Executive-in-Residence, School of Business Administration, Queens Univ., 1979-80; Dir., AGF Funds; Boise Cascade Canada Ltd.; Engineering Interface Ltd.; mem., Ont. Council on University Affairs; past mem. Ont. Econ. Council; Adv. Comte. Sch. of Business Adm., Univ. Western Ont.; Past mem. and Chrmn Bd. Govs. McMaster Univ.; Delta Upsilon; United Church; recreations: golf, skiing, reading, photography; music; Clubs: University (Toronto); Toronto; Lambton Golf and Country; Home: 11 Country Club Drive, Islington, Ont. M9A 3J3

TAYLOR, William E., Jr. A.M., Ph.D., F.R.A.I., F.R.G.S., F.R.S.C., D.U.C.; archaeologist; b. Toronto, Ont., 21 Nov. 1927; s. William E. and Margaret (Patrick) T.; e. Univ. of Toronto, B.A. 1951; Univ. of Ill., A.M. 1952; Univ. of Mich., Ph.D. 1965; Univ. Calgary Hon. Doctorate; m. Joan Doris, d. John Elliott, Scarborough, Ont., 12 Sept. 1952; children: Alison, Beth, William E.; DIRECTOR NATIONAL MUSEUM OF MAN; Director, Candn. Centre for Anthrop. Research; Past Chrmn., Bd. Govs., Candn. War Museum; made several discoveries in Eskimo archaeol. between 1950 and 1966; author of "The Arnapik and Tyara Sites", 1968; other writings incl. over 70 prof. papers in archaeol. mostly of Arctic Am.; Fellow, Am. Anthrop. Assn.; Arctic Inst. N. Am.; Sigma XI; Bd. mem. Museum of Archeology, U. of Western Ont.; Advisory Panel Assoc. of Canadian Studies; mem. Ed. Bd., Journal of Canadian Studies Trent U.; Res. Scholar, School of American Research, Sante Fe, New Mexico, 1977-78; Jury member, Guild of Northwest Coast Artists; Perm. Council mem., Internat. Union Anthrop. and Ethnol. Sciences and Internat. Union Prehist. & Protohist. Sciences; Fellow, Am. Assn. Advanc. Science; Hon. Fellow Society of Antiquaries of Scotland; Unitarian; recreations: skiing, reading; Home: 509 Piccadilly, Ottawa, Ont. K1Y 0H7; Office: McLeod St., Ottawa, Ont.

TCHORZEWSKI, Hon. Ed., M.L.A., B.A.; b. Sask., 22 Apl. 1943; s. Ezydor and Francis (Deptuch) T.; e. Hudson Bay Composite High Sch., 1962; Univ. of Sask., B.A. 1968; m. Shirley Ann, d. Steve Stasiuk, Preeceville, Sask., 4 Aug. 1966; four children; MINISTER OF FINANCE, PROV: OF SASKATCHEWAN June 1979— ; Min. in charge of Public Service Comm., Chmn. of Treasury Bd.; el. M.L.A. for Humboldt g.e. 1971, 1975; Teacher, St. Augustine Sch., Humboldt, 1965-67 and 1968-71; Councillor, Humboldt Br., Sask. Teachers Fed., 1970-71; apptd to Cabinet, 1972, with portfolios of Dept. of Culture and Youth; Dept of Consumer Affairs, Dept. of Prov. Secty.; 1975, Dept. of Consumer Affairs transferred; became Min. of Educ.; Continuing Educ.; Culture and Youth; later, Min. of Health; K. of C.; NDP; R. Catholic, recreations: curling, baseball, football, fishing; Home: 4010 Lakeview Ave., Regina, Sask. S4S 1H9; Office: Legislative Bldgs., Regina, Sask.

TEBBS, Robert J., B.A., LL.D.; retired company executive; b. Hamilton, Ont., 23 May 1916; s. Frederick C. and Rhea Jane (Snoddy) T.; e. Primary and Sec. Schs., Hamilton; McMaster Univ., B.A. (Econ.) 1939; m. Helen Margaret, d. late James S. McCaughey, 29 Nov. 1941; children: Nora Jane (Mrs. Wm. Bondy), James Stewart, Kathryn Evelyn (Mrs. Jos. Elliot); DIR., HIRAM WALKER-GOODERHAM & WORTS LTD.; Dir. Hiram Walker-Consumers Home Ltd., Toronto; Office Mgr., Windsor Br., Burroughs Adding Machine Co., 1940-41; with Hiram Walker — Gooderham & Worts Ltd., and/or its subsidiaries since 1941; served with Essex Scottish Reserve 1940-41; Private R.C.O.C.; Capt., Asst. to Master Gen. Ordance NDHQ 1944-45; United Church; recreations: boating, curling, golf; Clubs: Beach Grove Golf; Grosse Pointe

Yacht; Port Clinton Yacht; Home: 206 Vernon Crescent, Windsor, Ont. N8S 1R4

TEDLIE, Maj.-Gen. Alfred James, D.S.O., K. St. J., C.D.; b. Montreal, Que., March 1916; e. Sir George Williams Univ.; Candn. Army Staff Coll., Kingston, Nat. Defence Coll., Kingston; m. Margaret Mary Brown, Feb. 1940; children: Jane, Judith and Jennifer; enlisted 17th Duke of York's Candn. Hussars, 1939; Royal Montreal Regt. (Machine Gun), 1940; served in Brit. with 32 Reconnaissance Regt., Royal Candn. Armoured Corps, 1941-44; later served in N.W. Europe and commanded 3rd Btn., Cameron Highlanders of Ottawa during occupation of Germany; following war served as Staff Offr., Army H.Q.; Commandant, Fort Churchill, Man., 1948-50; apptd. G.S.O. and Depy. Dir. of Mil. Training Army H.Q. 1950-54; Mil. Adviser, Mil. Component Candn. Del., Indochina, 1954-55; Chief of Staff, Prairie Command, Winnipeg 1956; Commandant, Royal Candn. Armoured Corps Sch., Camp Borden, 1958; Dir. of Armour, Army HQ, 1960; Dir. of Combat Devel., 1961; Commdr., 2nd Candn. Inf. Bgde. Group, Camp Petawawa, 1963; Commdr., Nicosia zone, U.N. Forces in Cyprus, 1964 and 4th Candn. Inf. Bgde. Group, Germany, Dec. 1964; Chief of Staff (Training) and Depy. Commdr., Training Command, 1966-68; Depy. Chief of Defence Staff for Force Devel. 1968-70, for Intelligence & Security for the Armed Forces 1970-Oct. 1971 when retired; B.C. Prov. Commr., St. John Ambulance Bgde. 1973-76, Depy. Chief Commr. for Can. 1976-81; recreations: golf; swimming; Clubs: Glen Meadows Golf & Country; R.U.S.I. of V.I.; Address: 2289 Adela Place, Sidney, B.C. V8L 1R1

TEES, Miriam Hadley, M.L.S.; librarian; educator; b. Montreal, Que. 24 Feb. 1923; d. Frederick James and Beatrice Mary (Armstrong) T.; e. McGill Univ. B.A. 1944, B.L.S. 1951, M.L.S. 1975; ASSOC. PROF., GRAD. SCH. OF LIB. SCIENCE, McGILL UNIV. 1979- ; Lib., McGill Univ. Med. Lib. 1951; Internat. Civil Aviation Organ. 1951-53; Chief Lib. The Royal Bank of Canada 1953-79; mem. Comn. des bibliothèques publiques de la Prov. de Qué. 1974-78; Nat. Comte. on Liturgy Un. Ch. Can.; author various articles librarianship; mem. Special Libs. Assn. (N.Y., Pres. 1975-76); Corp. des Bibliothécaires professionnels du Qué. (Pres. 1971-72); Internat. Fed. Lib. Assns. (Dir. Lib. Schs. Sec.); United Church; recreations: early music, choir, gardening; Home: 24 Holton Ave., Westmount, Que. H3Y 2E8; Office: 3459 McTavish St., Montreal, Que. H3A 1Y1

TEILLET, Hon. Roger, P.C. (Can.); Canadian public service, retired; b. St. Vital, Manitoba, 21 Aug. 1912; s. Camille and Sara (Riel) T.; e. St. Vital and St. Boniface Schs.; St. Boniface Coll.; also with European Univs. through "Internat. Students" while P.O.W. in Germany; m. Jeanne, d. Jean Baptiste Boux, 18 May 1940; two s., Phillippe, Richard; COMMR., CANDN. PENSION COMN., since 1968; M.P. for St. Boniface 1962-68; M.L.A. in Man. 1953-59; served in 2nd World War with R.C.A.F., 1939-45; attached to R.A.F. #35 Sqdn. Bomber Command, no. four Group and Pathfinder Force; shot down over France and P.O.W. in Germany, Oct. 1942-May 1945; discharged with rank of Lt.; Past Pres., St. Boniface Liberal Assn.; Founder, St. Vital Young Liberal Assn.; Past Offr., Man. Liberal Assn.; Winnipeg South Liberal Assn.; mem. P.O.W. Assn. (Air Force Br.); Royal Candn. Legion; K. of C. (4th Degree); Liberal; Roman Catholic; recreations: golf, curling; Home: 1001-1195 Richmond Rd., Ottawa, Ont. K2P 8E4

TELLIER, Lt.-Gen. Henri, D.S.O., C.D.; executive; b. Montreal, Que., 1 Sept. 1918; s. Henry Joseph and Jeanne(St. Cyr) T.; e. St. Leo's Academy, Westmount, Que.; University of Montreal 1935-40; Univ. of Ottawa 1946-47; Candn. Army Staff Coll. 1942-43; Imp. Defence Coll., London, Eng. 1966; Dept. of Defence Computor Inst., Washington, D.C. (Sr. Business Mang. Course), 1968; m.

Virginia Ann Wright, 23 July 1945; children: Pierre, Michele, Suzanne, John, Nicole; Nat. Comnr., Canadian Red Cross Soc. since Nov., 1975; commnd in C.O.T.C. Univ. of Montreal 1940; served with Le Regt. de Joliette, Le Regt. de la Chaudiere, Le Royal 22e Regt., in Can.; U.K., Mediterranean Theatre and N.W. Europe as both Commdr. of troops and staff offr.; awarded D.S.O., C.D., Inhuldigingsmedaille (Netherlands); Commander, Order of Merit, Jt. Intelligence Staff, 1954-57; Mil. Adviser, Mentioned in Despatches; Asst. Secy. to Min. of Nat. Defence 1945-48; C.O. Royal 22e Regt. 1948-51; Instr., Candn. Army Staff Coll. 1951-54; Army mem., Jt. Intelligence Staff, 1954-57; Mil. Adviser, Viet Nam 1957-58; Chief of Staff, Quebec Mil. Dist. 1958-60; Mil. Attaché, Rome, Italy 1960-63; Dir. Mil. Operations and Plans, Army 1963-64; Dir. Internat. Plans, Integrated Armed Forces 1964-65; Commdr. Candn. Contingent, Cyprus 1965-66; Dir. Gen. Plans, 1970-71; Candn. Mil. Rep. to NATO Brussels, 1971-73; retired Nov. 1973; Assoc. Nat. Comnr., Candn. Red Cross Soc. 1973, Nat. Comnr. Jan. 1975; member Mil. co-op Comte. — Can.-U.S. (Chrmn. Candn. Sec.); Commr., Comn. for Strategic and Internat. Studies; mem. Perm. Jt. Bd. on Defence — Can.-U.S.; Candn. Inst. Internat. Affairs; Assn. Roy. 22e Regt.; R. Catholic; recreations: aquatic sports, badminton, cycling; Address: c/o Canadian Red Cross Society, 95 Wellesley St. E., Toronto, Ont. M4Y 1H6

TELLIER, Paul M., Q.C., LL.L., M.A., B.Litt.; Canadian public servant; b. Joliette, Que. 8 May 1939; s. late Maurice and Eva (Bouvier) T.; e. Univ. of Ottawa B.A. 1959, LL.L. 1962; Univ. of Montreal M.A. Law (requirements) 1963; Oxford Univ. B.Litt. 1966; m. Andree d. Jean-Paul Poirier 6 June 1959; children: Claude, Marc; DEPY. MIN. OF INDIAN AND NORTHERN AFFAIRS 1979- ; called to Bar of Que. 1963; Asst. Prof. of Law, Univ. of Montreal 1966-67; Extve. Asst. to Min. of Energy, Mines & Resources Ottawa 1967-68; Privy Council Office. Constitutional Review, Ottawa 1968, Asst. Secy. to Cabinet 1968-70; Depy. Secy. to Cabinet, Extve. Council, Govt. of Que. 1970-72; Dir. Gen. Urban Policy Br. Ministry of State for Urban Affairs, Ottawa 1972-73; Coordinator, Official Langs. Program, Pub. Service Comn. Ottawa 1974, Extve. Dir. Comn. 1975; Sr. Asst. Depy. Min. of Fisheries and the Environment 1976; Depy. Secy. to Cabinet (coordination) Fed.-Prov. Relations Office 1977-79; appointed Queen's Council, 1980; author various articles on pub. adm.; mem. Inst. Pub. Adm.; R. Catholic; recreations: squash, skiing, tennis; Club: Five Lakes Fishing; Home: 2404 Wyndale Cres., Ottawa, Ont. K1H 7A6; Office: 2101 Les Terrasses de la Chaudiere, Ottawa, Ont. K1A 0H4.

TELLIER, Pierre P., B.Com.; pulp and paper executive; b. Montreal, Que. 18 July 1944; s. Florimond and Simone (Doucet) T.; e. Sir George Williams Univ. B.Com.; INSEAD; m. Louise, d. Raymond Perron, 4 Sept. 1965; children: Catherine, Louis-Martin; Chrmn. & C.E.O., Société de Machinisme Agricole MACHINAG Inc.; Société de Machinisme Agricole AGRIMACH Inc.; Dir., AGRIMACH Inc.; MACHINAG Inc.; Ralco Farm Equipment Co. Ltd.; Cie. R.A. Lajoie Ltée.; Cie. J.E. Jutras Inc.; Dir. Acadia Pulp Div. of Jannock Industries Ltd. as Gen. Mgr. 1972-74; Pres. and C.E.O., Acadia Forest Products Ltd., 1974-81; Dir., Assn. des Fabricants de Materiel Agricole du Que. (A.F.M.A.Q.); R. Catholic; recreations: skiing, tennis, golf; Clubs: Mount Stephen; Hillside Tennis; Home: 276 Auclair Cr., Otterburn Park, P.Q. J3H 1P5

TEMPLEMAN, Wilfred, O.B.E. (1948), B.Sc., M.A., PhD., D.Sc., F.R.S.C.; university professor; b. Bonavista, Nfld., 22 Feb. 1908; s. Charles and Sarah (Fisher) T.; e. Memorial Univ. Coll., 1927-28 (Sr. Jub. Scholar); Dalhousie Univ., B.Sc. 1930; Univ. of Toronto, M.A., Ph.D. 1930-33; Memorial Univ. D.Sc. 1976; m. Eileen Eliza, d. William McGrath, Pointe du Chene, N.B., 7 Sept. 1937; children: Margaret Elizabeth, Barbara Eileen, Sheila Joan, Sandra Louise; J. L. PATON PROF. MARINE BIOLOGY & FISHERIES, MEMORIAL UNIV.; Lect. in Zool., McGill

Univ., 1933-36; Assoc. Prof. of Biol., Memorial Univ. Coll., St. John's, Nfld., 1936-43; Prof. 1943-44; Dir., Nfld. Govt. Lab., 1944-49; Dir. Fish. Res. Bd. Canada Biol. Stn., St. John's, Nfld., 1949-72; Visiting Research Prof. Marine Biol., Memorial Univ., 1957-72; mem., Marine Biol. Assn. of U.K.; Am. Fisheries Soc.; Candn. Soc. Zools.; Am. Soc. Ichthyologists & Herpetologists; Publications: papers on groundfish and other fishes, lobster and other invertebrates of the N.W. Atlantic; United Church; Home: 12 Darling St., St. John's, Nfld. A1B 1V6; Office: Queen's College, Prince Philip Dr., St. John's, Nfld. A1B 3R6

TEMPLETON, Carson Howard, O.C., B.Sc.; professional engineer; b. Wainwright, Alberta, 9 Sept. 1917; s. Ellen Florence (Porteous) and late Samuel Howard T.; e. Central Coll. Inst., Calgary, Alta. (Sr. Matric.); Univ. of Alberta, B.Sc. (Applied Science) 1943; Alberta Inst. of Technol. (Dipl.); m. Laurie Jean, d. late Rory MacLachlan, 29 April 1948; children: Colleen, Neil; PRES., C.H. TEMPLETON & ASSOC., (consulting Engrs.); Chrmn., Alaska Hwy. Pipeline Panel; Pres., Northern Environment Foundation; Dir., Winnipeg Children's Hosp. 1958-81; Dir., Canada-West Foundation; Engn. Adv. to Banff Centre and the Coalition of Citizen and Native Organizations on the Beaufort Sea Devel.; Vice Chairman Board of Governors, University of Manitoba 1968-71; Pres. (1968-69) Assn. of Consulting Engrs. of Canada; began engn. experience in the field in Yukon and N.W.T.; subsequently Asst. Chief Engr. of Fraser Valley Dyking Bd., Chief Engr. of Winnipeg Dyking Bd., Dir. (1956) of Greater Winnipeg Flood Protection Comte., then Mgr. of Interior of B.C. Div. of Marwell Construction Co.; mem., Assns. of Prof. Engrs. of B.C., Manitoba, Alta.; Fellow, Engn. Inst. Can.; Candn. Standards Assn.; Protestant; Home: 5265 Santa Clara Ave., Victoria, B.C. V8Y 1W6

TEMPLETON, Charles B., D.D.; broadcaster, author; b. Toronto, Ont., 7 Oct. 1915; s. William Loftus T.; e. Parkdale Coll. Inst., Toronto, Ont., 1927-31; Princeton Theol. Semy., 1948-51; Lafayette Coll., D.D. 1952; m. Madeleine, d. late Leroy DesBrisay Stevens, 21 Dec. 1980; children: Deborah A., Michael D., Bradley S., Tyrone M.; Sports Cartoonist, Toronto "Globe & Mail", 1932-36; o. Ch. of the Nazarene, 1938; Minister, Avenue Rd. Ch., Toronto, Ont., 1941-48; Secy. of Evangelism, Nat. Council of the Churches of Christ, U.S.A., 1952-54; Dir. of Evangelism, Presbyterian Ch. of U.S.A., 1955-56; Performer on CBC Television since 1957; formerly Moderator many CBC, CTV television programs; Managing Editor, "Toronto Star", 1960-64 when resigned & entered politics; contested Liberal Party Leadership in Ont. (def.); Dir. of News & Pub. Affairs CTV Television Network Ltd. 1967-69; Editor, "Macleans Mag." Feb.-Sept. 1969; has had numerous plays performed on CBC, BBC and Aust. Broadcasting Corp.; daily on CKEY Dialogue (with Pierre Berton); author of books: "Life Looks Up" (novel), "Evangelism for Tomorrow", "Jesus", and "The Kidnapping of the President", "Act of God" (novel) "The Temptation", (novel 1980); "The Cosy Tea Room" (play) 1981; mem. Can. Assn. Pub. and Comp. Home: 75 Douglas Cresc., Toronto, Ont. M4W 2E6; Office: R.R. #1, Penetanguishene, Ont.

TEMPLETON, Ian Malcolm, M.A., D.Phil., F.R.S.C., F.Inst.P.; research physicist; b. Rugby, Eng. 31 July 1929; s. late William and late Eleanor Clayton (Butcher) T.; e. Rugby (Eng.) Sch.; Univ. Coll. Oxford Univ. M.A. 1950, D.Phil. 1953; m. Elsa d. late John Victor Wood, Sedbergh, Eng. 11 Aug. 1956; children: Nicola Jean, Jennifer Jane; PRINC. RESEARCH OFFR. NAT. RESEARCH COUNCIL OF CAN. since 1971, Head Electronic Structure & Calorimetry Group since 1976; Chrmn. Candn. Nat. Comte. for Internat. Union of Pure & Applied Physics since 1978; Postdoctoral Fellow, Physics Div. Nat. Research Council of Can. 1953-54, Asst. Research Offr. 1957-60, Assoc. Research Offr. 1960-64; Sr. Research Offr. 1964-71; Jt. Head Metal Physics Group 1969-76; Staff

mem. Research Lab. Associated Electrical Industries, Rugby, Eng. 1955-57; author over 60 scient. papers low temperature metal physics; mem. Candn. Assn. Physicists; Am. Phys. Soc.; Home: 17 Dunvegan Rd., Ottawa, Ont. K1K 3E8; Office: Ottawa, Ont. K1A 0R6.

TEN CATE, Arnold Richard, B.Sc., Ph.D., B.D.S.; educator; b. Accrington, Lancs., Eng. 21 Oct. 1933; s. Gys Johan Ten Cate; e. London Hosp. Med. Coll. Univ. of London B.Sc. 1955; Ph.D. (Anat.) 1957, B.D.S. 1960; m. Alice Annie d. Charles Mitchell, Markham, Ont. 7 Apl. 1956; children: Pauline Ann, Jill Elaine, Ian Richard; DEAN, FACULTY OF DENTISTRY, UNIV. OF TORONTO since 1977; Leverhulme Fellow, Royal Coll. of Surgs. London 1961-63; Sr. Lectr. (Anat.) Guy's Hosp. Univ. of London 1963-68; Prof. Univ. of Toronto 1968, Prof. and Chrmn. Biol. Sciences (Dent.) 1971-77; rec'd Colyer Prize Royal Soc. med. 1962; Milo Hellman Award Am. Assn. Orthodontists 1975; Isaac Schour Mem. Award Internat. Assn. Dental Research 1978; author 'Oral Histology: Development, Structure & Function' 1980; co-author 'Techniques in Photomicroscopy' 1963; 'Advances in Dental Histology' 3rd ed. 1976; over 50 scient. papers, articles and chapters; mem. Internat. Assn. Dental Research; P. Conservative; recreations: gardening, fishing, swimming; Home: 50 Squire Bakers Lane, Markham, Ont. L3P 3G9; Office: 124 Edward St., Toronto, Ont. M5G 1G6.

TENISON, Robert Blake; executive; b. Houston, Texas, 26 Jan. 1924; s. Jack R. and Auban (Blake) T.; e. Univ. of Texas, 1942-46; m. Anna Jo, d. L. B. Romans, Ardmore, Okla., 5 Nov. 1949; children: Robert B. Jr., William B., John Thomas, Susan; PRESIDENT AND CHRMN. OF BD., WORLDWIDE ENERGY CO. LTD., since 1966; Pres. and C.E.O., Worldwide Energy Corp.; Cold Lake Transmission Ltd.; Chrmn. of Bd., Worldwide Energy (U.K.) Ltd.; Operations Mgr. for Independent Oil Operator Texas and Okla., 1947-51; Independent Oil Operator and Drilling Contractor, Texas, Colo., Mont., Wyo. and N. Dak., 1951-59; Vice Pres., Consolidated Oil & Gas, Inc., Denver, 1959-67; joined present co. (then Cold Lake Pipe Line Co. Ltd.), 1965; served with USN 1943-46; rank Lt.-jg; Anglican; recreations: hunting, fishing, skiing, tennis; Clubs: Petroleum; Calgary Golf & Country; Denver Club; Garden of the Gods; Home: 10 Sedgwick,Englewood, Colo. 80110 Office: 1600 Tower Bldg., United Bank Centre, 1700 Broadway, Denver, Colo. 80290

TENNANT, Veronica, O.C. (1975); ballerina; b. London, England, 15 January 1946; d. Harry and Doris (Bassous) T.; e. Bishop Strachan School, Toronto; National Ballet School, Toronto, graduated 1964; m. Dr. John Robert Wright, 11 June 1969; one d. Jessica Robin Wright; joined National Ballet Company as principal dancer 1964; danced "Juliet" in CBC TV production "Romeo and Juliet" 1965 (production rec'd René Bartlélémy Prix de Monte Carlo); danced "Cinderella" in Emmy winning CBC TV production 1967; created leading role in "Kraanerg" by Ronald Petit at opening of Nat. Arts Centre, Ottawa 1969; danced "Juliet" in Osaka at Expo 70; guest artist, Jacob's Pillow Internat. Dance Festival, USA, 1971; danced opposite Rudolf Nureyev in world premiere of his "Sleeping Beauty", Ottawa 1972 (TV production of ballet rec'd Emmy Award 1973); danced premiere performance of "La Sylphide" for princess Anne in London, Eng. (first European engagement for Nat. Ballet Co.); danced opposite Rudolf Nureyev in premiere performance at Metrop. Opera House, N.Y., 1973 (Co.'s N.Y. debut) and throughout N. Am. tour; performed at Newport Music Festival, R.I., summer 1973; 1974 roles incl. "Aurora" in 'The Sleeping Beauty' opposite Rudolf Nureyev and leading roles in "Giselle", "Le Loup" and Erik Bruhn's productions of "Les Sylphides" Swan Lake; "The Dream"; "La Fille Mal Gardée" and "Etudes" and John Neumeier's "Don Juan"; featured on CBC's "Telescope" (1970), "Impressions" (1973) and "Arts

Magazine" (1974); also various TV talk programmes; has lectured on dance, Waterloo and York Univs.; C.B.C./TV production "La Sylphide" July 1974 with Mikhail Baryshnikov (first Western ballerina to dance with him after his defection from Soviet Union); live performance with Baryshnikov at Ontario Place Aug. 1974; cr. role Swanhilda in world premier Erik Bruhn's "Coppelia", O'Keefe Centre, Toronto Feb. 1975; several guest appearances U.S. 1975-76; other lead roles in Balanchine's Serenade; Kettentanz, Dark Elegies, and Brian MacDonald's Newcomers; Danced Role of Teresina to Peter Schaufuss' Gennard in production of August Bournonville's Gallet Napoli, in the National Ballet of Canada's 30th Anniversary Performance, O'Keefe Centre, Toronto, 1981; Officer of the Order of Canada, 1975; danced at opening Stratford Shakespearean Festival 1978; danced at world premiere of "Washington Square", a new Canadian ballet, Toronto 1978; made her stage acting debut at the Young Peoples Theatre, Toronto, in "Hans Christian Andersen", 1978; starred in the film "Mad Shadows" 1979; Starred in "La Sylphide" with Fernando Bjones as guest of American Ballet Theatre. Lincolm Centre, N.Y. 1979; Dancers' Rep. Bd. Dirs. Nat. Ballet Co. 1970-73; author "On Stage Please" 1977; recreations: writing, theatre; Studio: 157 King St. E., Toronto, Ont. M5C 1G9

TERASMAE, Jaan, Ph. D.; educator; b. Estonia 28 May 1926; s. Enn and Virge (Lepik) T.; e. elem. and secondary educ. Estonia and Sweden; Univ. of Uppsala Bachelor's degree 1951; McMaster Univ. Ph.D. 1955; m. Vaike d. Mihkel Jurima, Estonia 31 July 1954; PROF. OF GEOL. SCIENCES, BROCK UNIV. since 1968, Chrmn. of Geol. Sciences 1969-73, 1975-76; Head of Pleistocene Palynology Lab., Mines & Tech. Surveys, Geol. Survey of Can. 1955-67, Head of Paleoecology and Geochronology Sec., Energy, Mines & Resources 1968; author or co-author book chapters and over 100 papers and reports quaternary geol., palynology and paleoecology; Ed. "Quaternary Research in Canada" 8 yrs.; served many nat. and internat. scient. comtes. incl. Nat. Research Council; Candn. del. several internat. confs. and congs.; mem. Am. Assn. Advanc. Science; Am. Assn. Stratigraphic Palynols.; Am. Quaternary Assn.; Arctic Inst. N. Am.; Bot. Soc. Am.; Candn. Assn. Palynols.; Geol. Assn. Can.; Geol. Soc. Am.; Internat. Assn. Gt. Lakes Research; Internat. Glaciol. Soc.; Internat. Peat Soc.; Royal Candn. Geog. Soc.; Royal Soc. Can.; Soc. Environmental Geochem. & Health; Swedish Phytogeog. Soc.; Tree-Ring Soc.; Lutheran; recreations: photography, scuba diving; Home: 196 Woodside Dr., St. Catharines, Ont. L2T 1X6; Office: St. Catharines, Ont. L2S 3A1.

TERON, William; executive; b. Gardenton, Man. 15 Nov. 1932; s. George and Sadie (Sandul) T.; e. St. John's High Sch. Winnipeg; m. Jean Miriam d. Rev. H.K. Woodwark 5 Sept. 1955; children: Christopher John, Kim Allison, William George, Bruce Charles; CHIEF EXTVE OFFICER, TERON INTERERNATIONAL LTD.; Chrmn. of Bd. Central Mortgage & Housing Corp. 1973-76; Chrm. 1976-79; Secy., Ministry of State for Urban Affairs 1976-79; Gov. Lester B. Pearson Coll. of the Pacific; Chief Extve. Offr. William Teron and Associates, Teron Construction Co. Ltd., Carleton Towers Hotels Ltd., Marina City (Kingston) Ltd., Golden Ridge Developments Ltd. (Kanata), 1970-73; Chrmn. of Bd. Commerce Capital Corp., Edelweiss Valley Ltd. 1955-73; Chrmn. of Bd. and Pres. Central Mortgage and Housing Corp. 1973; former Trustee, Nat. Arts Centre, Ottawa Gen. Hosp., Queensway Carleton Hosp.; Past Gov. Carleton Univ.; Past Dir. Candn. Council on Urban & Regional Research, Candn. Housing Design Council, Ashbury Coll., Ottawa Football Club; Past Chrmn. African Students Foundation, Nat. Capital Arts Alliance; rec'd 2 Nat. Awards, 4 Regional Awards and Nat. Award for Community Design (Kanata), Candn. Housing Design Council; Hon. Fellow, Royal Arch. Inst. Can.; recreations: skiing, tennis, walking,

boating; Home: 7 Crescent Rd., Ottawa, Ont. K1M 0N1; Office: 541 Sussex St., Ottawa, Ont. K1N 6Z6

TETLEY, William, Q.C., LL.L., B.A.; b. 10 Feb. 1927; e. Pub. Sch., Montreal; Royal Candn. Naval Coll., 1st Class Cert. and Sword of Honour; McGill Univ., B.A. (Econ. & Pol. Science); Laval Univ., LL.L.; m. Rosslyn M. Abraham; children: Pauline, Jane, Priscilla, William; PROF. OF LAW, McGILL UNIV. since 1976; called to the Bar of Quebec 1952; cr. Q.C. 1968; practised law 18 yrs. with Martineau, Walker, Allison, Beaulieu, Tetley & Phelan, becoming Senior Partner; served with the R.C.N.V.R.; rank Lieutenant; Municipal Councillor, Town of Mount Royal, 1965-68; el. M.N.A. for Notre-Dame-de-Grâce in by-el. 1968, re-el. 1970, 73; apptd. Min. of Revenue, May 1970; Min. of Consumer Affairs Cooperatives & Financial Insts. 5 yrs.; Min. of Pub. Works & Supply 1 yr.; resigned 1976 to become Prof. of Law, McGill Univ.; has taken active interest in Boy Scouts Can. and YMCA; awarded Boy Scout Medal of Hon. 1968; rep. Can. at internat. law conventions; lit. critic, "Montreal Gazette" 1952-65; is editor, and has publ. in internat. law journs. in Italy, Belgium for International Maritime legal writing; U.K., France and U.S.; author, "Marine Cargo Claims", 1966, 2nd ed. 1978, publ. in English, Russian and Japanese; Judge of the Candn. Human Rights Tribunal; Dir., Candn. Human Rights Foundation; Dir., Candn. Maritime Law Assn.; Anglican; Home: 112 Cornwall Ave., Montreal, Que. H3P 1M8; Office: 3644 Peel St., Montreal, Que. H3A 1W9

TETLOW, William Lloyd, M.A., Ph.D.; educator; administrator; b. Philadelphia, Pa. 2 July 1938; s. William Lloyd and Mary (Ferris) T.; e. Cornell Univ. Elect Engn. 1956-60, M.A. 1965, Ph.D. 1973; Univ. of Omaha B.G.E. 1963; m. Amber Jane d. William Ludwig Riederer, Westfield, N.J. 13 June 1964; children: Jennifer Kay, Rebecca Dawn, Derek William; DIR. OFFICE OF INST. ANALYSIS AND PLANNING, UNIV. OF BRIT. COLUMBIA and Assoc. Prof. Educ. Adm.; Pres. International Planning Simulations Inc.; Research Math. Selas Corp. 1961; Adm. Asst. Cornell Univ. 1963-64, Dir. Office Inst. Studies 1966-70; joined present Univ. as Assoc. Dir. Office Acad. Planning and Asst. Prof. Educ. Adm. 1970-75; served with US Army Inf. 1961-63, rec'd Army Commendation Medal 1963; Candn. del. O.E.C.D. Conf. on Inst. Mang. in Higher Educ. Paris 1975; B.C. del. to conf. on Assessing Demand for Post-Secondary Educ. Candn. Council of Mins. Educ. 1975; mem. Univ. of B.C. Evaluation Team for selection adm. trainees 6 B.C. Sch. Dists. 1973-81; Consultant Collective Bargaining in US Colls. and Univs. 1970; Consultant, B.C. Ministry of Education, 1978-79; author several publs. and simulation materials for training newcomers to field of Inst. Research; participant several prof. confs.; mem. Assn. Inst. Research (Secy. 1975-78, Vice Pres 1980, Pres. 1981); Candn. Soc. Study Higher Educ.; Candn. Soc. Study Educ. Adm.; Candn. Assn. Univ. Teacher's; Am. Assn. Higher Educ.; B.C. Forecasting Comte. (Secy. 1971-75) Phi Delta Kappa; Chi Psi; Freemason; recreations: racquetball, skiing, watersports, reading; Home: 962 Pacific Dr., Tsawwassen, Delta, B.C. V4M 2K3; Office: 6328 Memorial, Vancouver, B.C. V6T 1W5

TETREAULT, Robert, B.A., M.Com., C.A.; b. Granby, Que. 1925; s. Leon and Marie-Emma (Valcourt) T.; e. St.-Hyacinthe Semy. B.A. 1947, M.Com. 1955; C.A. 1956; m. Madeleine d. A. Domingue 23 June 1956; Children: Gilles, Julie, Louise; SEN. CONSULTANT, COGEN INC.; Marketing Research Firm; joined Marchands En Quincaillerie 1958; Comptroller Metro Food Stores Ltd. 1966, Gen. Mgr. 1970; former Extve. Vice-Pres., Metro-Richelieu Inc.; R. Catholic; Recreations: golf, swimming, sailing, skiing, cycling; Home: 154 Greenwood, Dollard-Des-Ormeaux, Que. H9A 1E8; Office: 1420 Sherbrooke St. W., Montreal, Que.

THACKRAY, James Carden, B.Sc.; Telecommunications Co. executive; b. Granby, Que., 25 Feb. 1924; s. Carden Cousens and Maud Stewart (Macpherson) T.; e. Westmount (Que.) High Sch., 1939; McGill Univ., B.Sc. 1946; m. Marie Therese, d. Dr. David Stephenson, Scarborough, Yorks., Eng., 6 March 1948; children: David, Anne, Elizabeth, James; PRES. AND DIR., BELL CANADA, since 1976; Dir., Bank of Montreal; Union Carbide Canada Ltd.; Le Conseil du Patronat du Québec; Adv. Bd. of the Salvation Army; Nat. Bd. of Adv. of ALESEC Can. Inc.; Kimberly Clark, U.S.A.; North American Telegraph Co.; Northern Telecom Ltd.; Northern Telecom Inc., U.S.A.; Northern Telecom (Ireland) Ltd.; Extve. Vice Pres. Operations, Bell Canada 1974-76; Served with R.C.N.V.R. N. Atlantic, Mediterranean and Far E., 1942-46; rank Lt.; Past Pres. Can. Safety Council, 1970-72, Past campaign Chrm., Metro Toronto United Way; Chmn., Toronto Redevel. Adv. Council; Trustee, Hosp. for Sick Children; Gov. Montreal Gen. Hosp. Foundation; Anglican; recreations: skiing, golf; Clubs: Toronto; York; Granite; St. James's; Mount Royal; Mount Bruno Country; Home: 61 St Clair Ave. W., Toronto, Ont. M4V 2Y8 Office: 145 King St. W., Fl. 26, Toronto, Ont. M5G 1W9

THAIN, Donald Hammond, D.B.A.; university professor; b. Toronto, Ont., 6 May 1928; s. William Edwards and Lucy May (Marsden) T.; e. Univ. of Toronto Schs.; Univ. of Toronto; Harvard Univ., M.B.A. 1953, D.B.A. 1955; m. Helen Margaret, d. Kenneth Steeves, 28 Aug. 1952; children: Peter Marsden, Carol Ann, John Fraser; PROF. OF BUSINESS ADM., UNIV. OF WESTERN ONT., since 1964; Dir., Silverwoods Industries Ltd.; Charterhouse Canada Ltd.; Cooper Canada Ltd.; Lawson and Jones Ltd.; Pres. A. E. Silverwood Foundation; Account Extve., Spitzer, Mills & Bates Ltd., Toronto, 1948-51; Research Asst., Harvard Business Sch., 1953-54; Instr. 1955-56; joined present Univ. as Asst. Prof. 1956; Assoc. Prof. 1959-64; Prof. of Gen. Mang.; IMEDE (l'Institut pour l'Etude des Methodes de Direction de l'Enterprise), 1965-66; Instr. in Marketing Mang. course for extves. 1957-68, and in Mang. Training for sr. mang. since 1961; has planned and/or taught mang. training programs for various co.'s and assns.; consultant on maj. problems of business policy, government relations, marketing and mang. devel. with numerous Candn. and Am. co.'s; mem., Task Force evaluating internationalization of curriculum of business schs., sponsored by Ford Foundation, 1967-68; mem., Fed. Task Force on Agric. 1968-70; Project Dir. on study of Candn. Aero-Space Indust. for Dept. of Indust., Trade & Comm., 1968-69; mem. Fed. Computer-Communications Industry Task Force 1971-72; Petrochem. Sector Task Force Dept. Indust. Trade & Comm. 1978; Trustee, W. Ont. Therapeutic Hostel Community; author, "Corporate Long Range Planning in Canada", 1963; co-author, "Marketing in Canada", 1959; "How Industry Buys", 1960 (Media-Scope Award); "Business Administration in Canada", 1961; contrib. author, "Internationalizing the Traditional Business Curriculum", 1968; Protestant; recreations: golf, sailing; Home: 80 Sherwood Ave., London, Ont. N6A 2E2

THALL, Burnett M., B.A.Sc., M.A.Sc., Ph.D.; b. Toronto, Ont., 27 Sept. 1922; s. Henry Rosenthal and Selina (Harris) T.; e. Harbord Coll. Inst., Toronto, Ont.; Univ. of Toronto, B.A.Sc. 1945, M.A.Sc. 1947, Ph.D. 1950 (Winner of Ont. Research Council Fellowship, 1948); m. Eleanor, d. M. Langbord, Toronto, Ont., 23 Sept. 1945; two s., Nelson Spencer, Martin Evan; SR. VICE PRES., TORSTAR CORP.; Dir. Toronto Star Newspapers Ltd.; Comac Communications Ltd.; Ont. Cancer Inst.; Gov. Council, Univ. of Toronto; Ont. Cancer Treatment & Research Foundation; Trustee, Atkinson Charitable Foundation; Gov., Women's Coll. Hosp., Toronto; assoc. with Nat. Research Council in Montreal at Univ. of Montreal in 1945 where initial engn. work and research for Can. first atomic reactor was conducted; Research Physicist at

Deep River, Ont., engaged in fundamental research at Chalk River Atomic Energy Plant; apptd. Lectr. in Dept. of Applied Science & Engn., Univ. of Toronto, 1947 and Special Lectr.; joined present interest in 1947 as Consulting Engr. dealing specifically with production problems; el. a Dir., Dec. 1956; mem., Assn. of Prof. Engrs. Ont.; Home: 15 Rosemary Lane, Toronto, Ont. M5P 3E7; Office: One Yonge St., Toronto, Ont. M5E 1E6

THEALL, Donald F., M.A., Ph.D.; educator; b. Mount Vernon, N.Y., 13 Oct. 1928; s. Harold A. and Helen A. (Donaldson) T.; e. A. B. Davis High Sch., Mount Vernon, N.Y., 1946; Yale Univ., B.A. 1950; Univ. of Toronto, M.A., 1951, Ph.D. 1954; m. Joan Ada, d. Frederick Benedict, Staten Island, N.Y., 14 June 1950; children: Thomas, Margaret, John, Harold, Lawrence, Michael; PRES., TRENT UNIV., 1980- ; Molson Professor, Department of English, McGill University, 1972-80; (Chairman Dept. 1966-74, Dir. Grad. Program in Communications 1975-80); Lecturer to Prof., University of Toronto, 1953-65; Chrmn., Jt. Depts. of Eng., 1964-65; Secy. and mem. Culture & Communications Seminar 1953-54; mem. comte. exam. second lang. teaching 1956-59; Eng. Sub-comte., Toronto Bd. Educ. Curriculum Study, 1960-61; Prof. and Chrmn., Dept. of Eng. (Atkinson) and Dir. of Communications, York Univ., 1965-66; Dir., special 16 week seminar "Human Communications: The Structure of Interaction", 1965-66; Dir., project on audio-visual and multi media exhibits, Expo '67, 1967-69; mem. co-op. Educ. TV Bd. of Can. and U.S.; Candn. UNESCO rep., Conf. on Student Participation in Univ. Govt., Dubrovnik, 1970; First Cultural Exchange Professor, People's Republic of China 1974-75; consultant in fields of education, communication; author of "Let's Speak English", 4 volumes (translated into 21 languages), 1962; Educational T.V. Hon. Mention, Ohio State Univ., for "Let's Speak English" series, C.B.C., 1962; Report on the Creation of a Visual Arts Info. Service for Canada, 1968; Report on Cultural Effects of Advertising to Que. Ministry of Communications, 1978; "The Medium is the Rear View Mirror", 1971; Co-ed. "Studies in Canadian Communications" 1975; Chrmn., Ed. Comte., "Arts Canada", 1966-68; Past Vice Pres., Soc. Arts Publs.; Past Dir., Ont. Council Teachers Eng.; Assn. Teachers Eng., Quebec; Founding Chrmn., Candn. Assn. of Chairmen of Eng. 1971-74; mem., Candn. Assn. of Univ. Teachers; Cinémathèque Canadienne; Modern Lang. Assn.; Philol. Soc. Gt. Brit.; Internat. Communications Assn. (Dir. 1978-81); Internat. Inst. Communications', Editorial Bd. of Sci-Fiction Studies, 1976- ; "Jour. Can. Communications." 1979- ; "Cultureand Content" 1979- ; "Jour. Can. Studies." 1980- ; Chrmn. Comte. to Form Candn. Communications Assn. 1978, elected Founding Pres., Can. Communications Assoc., 1979- ; Chmn., Council of Ont. Univ. Comte on the Disabled, 1981- ; Corr. Fellow, Acad. Medicine Toronto; recreations: swimming, films, theatre; Clubs: University (Toronto); McGill Faculty; Yale (Montreal); Peterborough; Home: 1604 Champlain Drive, Peterborough, Ont. K9L 1N6

THEPOT, R. François; artist; b. Landeleau (Finistère), France, 18 Feb. 1925; s. François and Marie Jeanne (Cam) T.; m. M. Magdeleine, d. Ferdinand Piquet, 26 March 1957; one-man exhns. at Galerie Breteau, 1952, Galerie LaRoue, 1954, and Galerie Hautefeuille, 1961, (all Paris); Raaklijn Centre, Bruges, 1963; Galerie La Proue, Brussels, 1963; Roberts Gallery, Toronto, 1965; Moos Gallery, Toronto, 1967; Galerie Casanova, Paris, 1967; has exhibited in group exhns. in various centres of Europe, Can. (Royal Acad. of Can. 1965-66-67; Ont. Soc. of Artists 1965 and 1967), in Havana, Cuba, and Tokyo, Japan; rep. in perm. collections of Nat. Gallery of Can.; Museum of Modern Art, N.Y.; Art Gallery of Ont.; Mendel Art Gallery, Saskatoon; Musée d'Art Moderne, Paris; Musée d'Art Moderne, Céret, France; Musée des Beaux-Arts, St. Etienne, France; Raymond Nacenta, Galerie Charpentier, Paris; Michel Seuphor, Paris; Lucie and Edgar Faure,

Maurice Naessens, Brussels; Samuel and Ayala, Zacks, Toronto, and other private collections in Europe and N. Am.; founding mem. of The Groupe Mesure, Paris; rec'd. Baxter Award, Toronto, 1967; R. Catholic;

THERIAULT, Lt.-Gen. Gerard Charles Edouard, C.M.M., C.D., B.A.; Canadian armed forces; b. Gaspe, Qué. 5 June 1932; e. Sir George Williams Univ. B.A. (Econ.); Flying Instr. Sch. Trenton, Ont. 1957; U.S. Armed Forces Staff Coll. Norfolk, Va. 1966; m. 26 July 1956; two s. Dwight, Pierre; VICE CHIEF OF DEFENCE STAFF 1980-; enrolled as pilot RCAF 1951 and on completion of training assigned to 430 (Fighter) Sqdn. Grostenquin, France; Instr. 2 Advanced Flying Sch. Portage la Prairie, Man. 1958; assigned to Offrs. Selection Unit Centralia, Ont. 1960 becoming Chief Adm. Offr.; promoted to Sqdn. Leader 1962 returning to Grostenquin, France as Acting Offr. Commanding 421 Strike & Attack Sqdn. 1963; C.O. 444 Strike Attack Sqdn. Baden Soellingen, Germany 1966, promoted Wing Commdr.; C.O. Cadet Wing and Vice Commandant Coll. Militaire Royal, St. Jean, Que. 1967, promoted Col. and assumed command of Coll. 1970; Commdr. Candn. Forces Base Bagotville, Que. 1971; promoted Brig.-Gen. and apptd. Commdr. 1 Candn. Air Group Lahr, W. Germany 1973; Chief of Staff Operations Air Command Hdqrs. 1975; promoted Maj.-Gen. and apptd. Commdr. Air Command 1976; Chief of Air Doctrine & Operations, Nat. Defence Hdqrs. 1977; promoted Lt.-Gen. and apptd. Depy. Chief of Defence Staff 1978; recreation: apptd. Depy. Chief of Defence Staff 1978; recreation: sailing; Home: 40 Blenheim Dr., Ottawa, Ont. K1L 5B5; Office: National Defence Hdqrs., Ottawa, Ont. K1A 0K2.

THERIAULT, Yves, O.C. (1975); writer; b. Quebec, Que., 28 Nov. 1916; s. Alcide and Aurore (Nadeau) T.; m. Michelle Blanchet, 21 Apl. 1942; children: Yves-Michel, Marie-José; Publications: "Contes pour un homme seul", 1944; "La Fille Laide", 1950; "Le Dompteur d'ours", 1950; "Les Vendeurs du Temple", 1953; "Aaron", 1954, Paris ed. 1966; "Agaguk", 1958, (German, Italian, Portuguese, Japanese and Spanish trans. 1959); "Ashini" (rec'd. French Lang. Award for Fiction, 1961); mem., Candn. Authors Assn.; Internat. P.E.N. Club: Syndicat Nat. des Ecrivains de France; Soc. des Gens. de Lettres (Paris); Soc. des Ecrivains canadiens; Soc. des Auteurs Dramatiques; Roman Catholic

THÉRIO, Adrien, M.A., Ph.D.; éducateur; auteur; né St-Modeste, Qué. 15 août 1925; f. Charles-Eugène et Eva (Bouchard) T.; é. Univ. d'Ottawa B.A. 1950; Univ. Lavl M.A. 1951, Ph.D. 1952; Harvard Univ. Rockefeller Foundation Fellowship Studies in Am. Lit. 1953-54; Notre Dame Univ. M.A. 1959; Univ. of Toronto Studies in Pol. Science 1959-60; PROFESSEUR DE LETTRES FRANÇAISES, UNIV. D'OTTAWA; dir. de "Lettres Québécoises" depuis 1976; Fondateur et dir. de "Livres et auteurs québécois" 1961-72; Head of French, Royal Mil. Coll. Kingston 1962-69; auteur: "Les brèves années" (roman) 1953; "La soif et le Mirage" (roman) 1958; "Mes Beaux Meurtres" (nouvelles) 1961; "Le Printemps qui pleure" (roman) 1962; "Ceux du Chemin-Taché" (contes) 1962; "Le Mors aux flancs" (récit humoristique) 1965; "Soliloque en hommage à une femme" (roman) 1968; "Un païen chez les pingouins" (récit) 1970; Les Fous d'amour" (roman) 1973; "La Colère du père" (récit) 1974; "La Tête en fête" (histoires) 1975; "C'est ici que le monde a commencé" (récit-reportage) 1978; pour adolescents: "Contes des belles saisons" 1958; "Flamberge au vent" (roman) 1958; études: Jules Fournier, journaliste de combat" 1955; "Mon encrier de Jules Fournier" 1965; "Conteurs canadiens-français" (anthologie) 1968; "L'Humour au Canada français" (anthologie) 1968; théâtre: "Les Renégats" (pièce en trois actes) 1964; "Le Roi d'Aragon" (pièce en 2 actes) 1979; traduction: "Un Yankee au Canada de Henry David Thoreau" 1962; mem. Union des écrivains québécois; Soc. Royale du Can.;

Adresse: Apt. 609, 1100 Dr. Penfield, Montréal, Qué. H3A 1A8 Bureau: Univ. d'Ottawa, Ont. et C.P. 1840 Succ. B, Montréal, Qué. H3B 3L4

THERRIEN, F. Eugène, Q.C.; b. Montreal, Que. 9 Aug. 1906; s. Aldège and Emérentienne (Legault) T.; e. Jardin de l'Enfance; Coll. Ste-Marie; Univ. de Montréal (Grad. in Law); m. late Gilberte, d. Dr. J. W. Tétrault, 14 May 1932; HON. PRESIDENT, SOCIETE NATIONALE DE FIDUCIE; Hon. Dir., L'Economie Mutuelle d'assurance; called to Bar Que. 1930; mem. Royal Comn. on Adm. of Fed. Govt. (Glassco Comn.) 1960-63; Past Pres., Conseil d'Expansion Economique; mem. Que. Bar Assn.; Montreal Bd. Trade; Past Pres., Soc. Saint-Jean-Baptiste de Montréal; R. Catholic; recreations: travelling, hunting, fishing, golf; Clubs: Lavel-sur-le-Lac; Montreal Flying (Past Pres.); Home and Office: 12268 De Serres, Montreal, Que. H4J 2G9

THIBERT, Roger Joseph, B.A., M.S., Ph.D., F.C.I.C.; university professor; b. Tecumseh, Ont., 29 Aug. 1929; s. Charles and Violet (Hebert) T.; e. Assumption High Sch., Windsor, Ont. 1948; Univ. of Western Ont. Assumption Coll., B.A. 1951; Univ. of Detroit, M.S. 1954; Research Fellow. Mich. Heart Assn. (1956-57); Wayne State Univ. Ph.D. 1958 (excellence Prize in Phys. Sc.); m. Audrey M. (R.T., B.A.) d. Robert Orville Wissler, Windsor, Ont. 10 July 1954; children: Mark, Robert; DIR. OF CLIN. CHEM. UNIV. OF WINDSOR since 1973; Prof. Pathol., Wayne State Univ. Sch. Med., since 1972; Assoc. Div. Head, Clin. Chem., Detroit; Receiving Hosp.-University Health Centre since 1974; began career as Quality Control Asst., Green Giant Co. of Can., Tecumseh, Ont., summers 1948-53; Clin. Chem., Grace Hosp., Windsor, Ont., summer 1954; Detroit Mem. Hosp. summer 1955; Lectr. in Chem., Assumption Univ. of Windsor, 1953-57; Asst. Prof. 1957-61, Univ. of Windsor, Assoc. Prof. 1961-67, Prof. since 1967; Assoc. Dean Faculty of Arts and Science 1964-70; Instr. Nursing Chem., Grace Hospital School of Nursing 1954-73; Research Associate, Dept. of Pathology, Wayne Univ. Sch. of Med. 1971-72; rec'd Union Carbide Award of the Chemical Inst. of Canada for Chem. Educ. 1978; rec'd. Smith Kline Clinical Laboratories Award, Am. Assn. for Clinical Chem., for Outstanding Efforts for Educ. & Training, 1980; Publications: various articles in chem. and learned journs.; Fellow, Am. Assn. Advanc. Science; Nat. Acad. Clin. Biochem.; Chem. Inst. of Can.; mem., Am. Chem Soc.; Am. Soc. Biol. Chems.; Am. Assn. Clin. Chem.; Candn. Soc. Clin. Chems.; Candn. Assn. Univ. Teachers; Candn. Biochem. Soc.; Sigma Xi; Roman Catholic; recreation: music (guitar); Home: 445 Randolph St., Windsor, Ont. N9B 2T5

THIESSEN, Abram J.; transportation executive; b. Rosenfeld, Man. 12 Dec. 1910; s. Abram and Susanna (Braun) T.; e. elem. sch. Rosenfeld and high sch. Steinbach, Man.; m. Lenora, d. Bernhard Friesen, 28 July 1935; children: Ronald, Bernard, William, Irvine, Carolyn; CHAIRMAN OF THE BOARD, GOOSE CORP LTD.; Dir. Secy., Grey Goose Bus Lines Ltd.; Dir.; Manitoba Mineral Resources Ltd.; Dir., Laidlaw Transportation; Tantallum Mining Corp.; Yellow Cab Ltd.; Central Disposal Ltd.; Acme Sanitation Ltd.; Ideal Waste Co. (Salt Lake City); elected Underwriting Mem., Lloyd's of London, 1978; with Rosenfeld Trucking 1931-45; Partner, G. H. Fast Automobile & Farm Machinery dealership, Rosenfeld and Altona 1936-59; began bus transport, business 1946; estbd. and became first Pres. and Gen. Mgr., Radio Stn. CFAM, Altona 1957; rec'd Coronation Medal 1953, Centennial Medal 1967; P. Cons. cand. g.e. 1953 and 1962; Past Pres., Man. Assn. Sch. Trustees; Candn. Sch. Trustee Assn.; Rosenfeld Chamber Comm.; mem. Winnipeg Commodity Exchange; Dir., Man. Mennonite Hist. Soc.; Past Chrmn., Bd. Dirs., Mennonite Coll. Inst., Gretna, Man.; P. Conservative; Mennonite; recreations: curling, golf, fishing, reading; Clubs: Manitoba; St. Charles Country; Winnipeg Winter; Home: 517 Shaftesbury Blvd., Winnipeg, Man. R3P 0M3; Office: 301 Burnell St., Winnipeg, Man. R3G 2A6

THIESSEN, George J., M.Sc., Ph.D., F.R.S.C.; research physicist; b. Russia, 7 May 1913; s. Rev. Jacob G. and Sara (Goetz) T.; came to Canada, 1923; e. Saskatoon Normal Sch., Sask.; Univ. of Sask., B.Sc. 1935, M.Sc. 1937; Columbia Univ., Ph.D. 1941; m. Isabel, d. Arthur Clendenan, 12 Aug. 1946; children: Edwin George, Carol Isabel, Randolph Richard; with Nat. Research Council, Can. as visiting, distinguished scientist; part-time private consultant; author of more than 45 scient. papers; Fellow, Acoustical Soc. Am., Fellow. Royal. Soc. of Can.; Home: 242 Roger Road, Ottawa, Ont. K1H 5C6

THODE, Henry George, C.C. (1967), M.B.E. (1946), M.Sc., D.Sc., Ph.D., LL.D., F.R.S. (1954), F.R.S.C. (1943), F.C.I.C. (1948); b. Dundurn, Sask., 10 Sept. 1910; s. Charles Herman and Zelma Ann (Jacoby) T.; e. Univ. Sask., B.Sc. 1930, M.Sc. 1932; Univ. Chicago, Ph.D. 1934; Columbia Univ. (Research) 1936-39; LL.D. Univ. of Sask. 1958; D.Sc., Univ. of Toronto 1955, Brit. Columbia 1960, Acadia 1960, Laval 1963, Royal Mil. Coll. 1964, McGill 1966, Queen's 1967, York 1972, McMaster 1973; m. Sadie Alicia, d. John A. M. Patrick, 1 February 1935; children: John Charles, Henry Patrick, Richard Lee; mem. of Defence Research Board, 1955-61; National Research Council of Canada, 1955-61; Research Consultant, Atomic Energy of Canada 1952-65; Asst. Professor of Chemistry, McMaster Univ., 1939-42, Assoc. Prof. 1942-44, Prof. 1944-79; Dir., of Research, 1947-61; Head of Dept., 1948-52, Vice Pres. of the Univ. 1957-61, (Principal of Hamilton Coll. there 1949-63), Pres. and Vice Chancellor July 1961-30 June 1972, cont. as Prof. Emeritus of Chem.; on leave of absence for War Research with Nat. Research Council of Can. 1943-45; Pres., sec., 111, Roy. Soc. of Can., 1950-51 and Pres. of Soc. 1960; mem. Comn. on Atomic Weights, Inorganic Chem. Div. 1963-79 & mem. Canadian National Committee 1975-79, International Union Pure and Applied Chem.; Dir., Western New York Nuclear Research Centre 1965-73; Atomic Energy of Canada, Ltd.; Stelco Inc.; Equitrust Mortgage & Savings Corp.; Gov., Ontario Research Foundation; Royal Bot. Gardens 1961-73; mem., Chem. Inst. of Can. (Pres. 1951-52, Medal 1957); Am. Chem. Soc.; mem., Ed. Adv. Bds. "Journal of Inorganic & Nuclear Chemistry"; "Earth & Planetary Science Letters"; has written articles relating to separation of isotopes, mass spectrometry, & isotope abundances in terrestrial, meteoritic and lunar materials, etc.; awarded H.M. Tory Medal by Royal Soc. Canada 1959; Nat. Science Foundation Sr. Foreign Scientist Fellowship 1970; Hon. Shell Fellow 1974; Sherman Fairchild Distinguished Scholar, Caltech 1977; awarded Arthur L. Day Medal by Geolog. Soc. of Am., 1980; Sigma Xi; Gamma Alpha; United Church; recreations: swimming, farming; Club: Rotary; Address: McMaster University, Nuclear Research Bldg., 1280 Main St. W., Hamilton, Ont. L8S 4K1

THOM, James Lewis; transportation executive; B. Paterson, N.J., 23 Oct. 1921; s. James Balfour and Florence Roberts (Lewis) T.; e. (came to Canada 1921); Westhill High Sch.; Sir George Williams Coll.; m. Martine Merlevede; children: James Colin, Eugene Graeme; PRESIDENT AND DIR., MONTREAL SHIPPING INC; Vice-Pres. and Dir., Allied Steamship Lines Ltd.; Smit-Lloyd (Canada) Ltd.; Assoc., Inst. of Chart. Shipbrokers (London); mem. C.D. Howe Inst.; Port of Montreal Authority; Protestant; Clubs: Mount Royal; Mount Bruno Golf & Country; Rideau (Ottawa); India House (New York); Home: 467 Mount Stephen Ave., Westmount, Que. H3Y 2X8; Office: 360 Rue Saint-Jacques, Montreal, Que. H2Y 1R2

THOM, Stuart Douglas, Q.C., B.A., LL.B., LL.D.; b. Regina, Sask. 7 Sept. 1906; s. Douglas John and Mabel (Chown) T.; e. Victoria Coll., Univ. of Toronto B.A. 1927; Univ. of Sask. LL.B. 1929; m. Lian, d. Harold Douglas

Stephen 8 Nov. 1935; one s. Stephen; PARTNER, OSLER HOSKIN & HARCOURT; called to the Bar of Sask. 1930, Ont. 1947; c. Q.C. 1957; Legal Asst., Dept. of Nat. Revenue, Taxation 1945-47; joined firm Smith, Rae & Greer, Toronto 1947; present firm 1954; served R.C.N.V.R. 1940-45, convoy duty in N. Atlantic, rank Lt. Commdr.; a Gov. (1953-55) Candn. Tax Foundation (Chrmn. 1959-60); el. a Bencher, Law Soc. Upper Can. 1966, 71 (Chrmn. Admissions Comte. 1968-70, Discipline 1971-74, Treas. 1974); mem. Candn. Bar Assn.; Liberal; recreations: reading, walking; Clubs: National; University; Lawyers; Home: 27 Ridgevalley Cres., Islington, Ont.; Office: First Canadian Place, King St. W., Toronto, Ont. M5X 1B8.

THOMAS, Mrs. Clara McCandless, M.A., Ph.D.; b. Strathroy, Ont., 22 May 1919; d. Basil and Mabel Elizabeth (Sullivan) McCandless; e. Univ. Western Ont., B.A. 1941, M.A. 1944; Univ. of Toronto, Ph.D. 1962; m. Morley Keith, s. Morley Thomas, 23 May 1942; two s. Stephen Morley, John David; Assoc. Prof. in Eng., York Univ., 1961-68, Prof. since 1969; Pres., A.C.U.T.E., 1971-72; Killam Awards Bd., 1978-81; Acad. Adv. Panel, SSHRCC, 1981- ; Ed. Bd., Literary History of Canada, 2nd revision; Journal of Canadian Studies; Journal of Canadian Fiction; Short Stories Series, Univ. of Ottawa; author of "Canadian Novelists 1920-45"; "Love and Work Enough: the life of Anna Jameson"; "Margaret Laurence", "Ryerson of Upper Canada", "Our Nature: Our Voices"; "The Manawaka World of Margaret Laurence"; "William Arthur Deacon; A Canadian Literary Life", with John Lennox, 1982; Charter Secy., Drama Guild of Can.; Protestant; Home: 15 Lewes Crescent, Toronto, Ontario M4N 3J1

THOMAS, David Diplock, F.C.A.; industrialist; b. Winnipeg, Man., 23 July 1924; s. Edgar James and Blanche (Stevens) T.; e. Public and High Schools Winnipeg, Man.; Man. Inst. Chart. Accts., C.A. 1947; m. Eva Johnston, 16 Nov. 1968; children: Nancy Elizabeth, John Edgar, Gordon James, Patricia Ann; PRESIDENT, CHIEF EXTVE. OFFR. AND DIR., SHERRITT GORDON MINES LTD. since 1967; joined Sherritt as Asst. Secy. 1947, Comptroller and Asst. Secy. 1959, Treas. and Dir. 1964; Pres. and Dir., Michipicoten Iron Mines Ltd., Dickstone Copper Mines Ltd.; Dir. other Sherritt subsidiaries; Pres. & Dir., Mining Assn. Can.; Dir., Marinduque Mining & Industrial Corp., Ingersoll-Rand Canada Inc., Centre for Resource Studies - Queen's Univ.; mem. Task Force on Nat. Finance of Bus. Council on Nat. Issues (B.C.N.I.), Nat. Advis. Comte. on the Mining Industry (N.A.C.O.M.I.), Candn. Inst. Mining and Metall., Prospectors and Developers Assn., Candn. Inst. Chart. Accts., Man. Inst. Chart. Accts.; recreations: golf, curling; Clubs: Donalda; Bd. Trade Metrop. Toronto; Home: 52 Lawrence Cres., Toronto, Ont. M4N 1N2; Office: (Box 28) Commerce Court W., Toronto, Ont. M5L 1B1

THOMAS, Gordon W., O.C. (1970), M.D., C.M., D.C.L., F.R.C.S.(C), F.A.C.S.; surgeon; b. Ottawa, Ont., 28 Dec. 1919; s. Russell Henry and Florence Mabel (Waddell) T.; e. Lachine (Que.) High Sch., 1936; McGill Univ., B.A. 1940, M.D., C.M. 1943; Acadia Univ., D.C.L., 1969; Mem. Univ. Nfld., D.Dc. (Hon.) 1979; Dalhousie Univ., LL.D. (Hon.) 1979; Officer of the Order of St. John; m. Thora Patricia, d. late Lawrence E. Lister, 27 May 1944; children: (Mrs.) Patricia Ruth Simpson, Leonard Lister, Pamela Jane; Country Practitioner, Mabou, N.S.; on staff as Surgeon, Inverness County Mem. Hosp.; Surgeon-in-Chief and Extve. Dir., Internat. Grenfell Assn., 1959-78; Clin. Prof. of Surg., Memorial Univ. of Nfld.; Lectr., Dalhousie Sch. Outpost Nurses; Surg., Grenfell Hosp. St. Anthony, 1946-57; Acting Supt. and Surg.-in-Chief, 1957-59; Teaching Fellow Surg. Pathol., McGill Univ., 1953-54; Fellow, Thoracic Clinic Karolinska Inst., Stockholm, 1957-58; Teaching Fellow and Clin. Asst. Cardiovascular Surg., Univ. of Toronto, 1961-62; Clin. Asst. Surg. and Paediatric Surg., Dalhousie Univ., 1965-66; served with

RCAMC 1942-46; rank Capt.; rec'd Centennial Medal 1967; Queen's Jubilee Medal 1976; Royal Bank Award for work in Nfld, and Labrador, 1977; Part-time mem. Candn. Radio & TV Comn. 1967-76; J.P., Nfld.; Dir., Nfld. Hosp. Assn.; Vanier Inst. of the Family; mem. Nfld. Med. Council; Past Chrmn., Grenfell Sch. Bd.; author of various med. papers and articles; Fellow Victoria Inst.; Gov-at-large, Am. Coll. Surgs.; mem. Council, Royal Coll. of Physicians (Can.) & Surgs. (Canada); Can. Cancer Inst.; American Assn. of Thoracic Surg.; Thoracic Soc.; Candn. Thoracic Soc.; Protestant; recreations: riding, fishing, flying; Address: P.O. Box 99, Mabou, N.S. B0E 1X0

THOMAS, John Arthur, B.A., B.Sc., P.Eng.; b. Wellington, Ont., 12 Nov. 1914; s. William Woodman and Lillian Alice (White) T.; e. Picton (Ont.) Coll. Inst.; Queen's Univ., B.A. 1936, B.Sc. 1942; m. Hazel Ethel, d. late Chester Warren McBride, 26 Jan., 1946; children: John Grant, Janet Mary, Donald William; Consultant, The Shawinigan Engineering Co. Ltd.; Asst. Engr., Hydro-Electric Power Comn. of Ont., 1942-46 (less war service); Hydraulic Div., Dom. Engineering Works, 1946-48; Hydraulic Engr., present Co., 1948-56: Chief Engr., Civil Div., 1956-61; Vice President, Engineering and Director, Nov. 1961, Vice President and Director 1964; retired, 1979; served in 2nd World War with R.C.N. as Lieut. (E), 1943-45; co-author "Engineering Aspects of the Peribonka Developments", EIC Annual Meeting, May 1954; "Engineering Features of the Beechwood Development", 1959 (awarded Gzowski Medal); author "Current Trends in Hydro-Electric Practice", 1963; Fellow. Am. Soc. Civil Engrs.; mem., Am. Soc. Mech. Engrs.; Order Engrs. Que.; Engn. Inst. Can.; International Electrotech. Comn.; Internat. Comn. on Large Dams; recreations: curling, hunting; Clubs: Rotary; University; Home: R.R. No. 2, Arundel, Que. J0T 1A0; Office: 620 Dorchester Blvd. W., Montreal, Que. H3B 1N7

THOMAS, (John Warren) Nevil, B.Com., M.A., M.B.A., C.F.A.; executive; financial analyst; b. Toronto, Ont. 7 Feb. 1938; s. late Charles Cleeve Nevil and Margaret Lillian (Jones) T.; e. pub. and private schs. Ont.; Trinity Coll. Univ. of Toronto B.Com.; Queen's Univ. M.A. (Econ.); York Univ. M.B.A.; Univ. of Va. Chart. Financial Analyst; m. Susanne Elizabeth d. F. Claude Passy, Ottawa, Ont. 12 Sept. 1964; children: Rebecca Susanne, Jeremy Christopher Nevill, Julian David Nevill, Ryan John Nevill; PRES. AND DIR., NEVCO INVESTMENT CORP. LTD. since 1970; Chrmn. and Dir. Plumbing Mart Corp. since 1974; Dir. Fidelity Trusco; Autocrown Corp.; Simcoe Erie Investors Ltd.; Reliable Life Insurance Co.; Chatham Intl. Ltd. (Jacquin Distilleries);joined Dominion Securities Ltd. Toronto and London, Eng. 1963 — 65; Pitfield Mackay 1965 — 67; Midland Doherty 1967 — 79; mem. Inst. Chart. Financial Analysts; Assn. Corporate Growth; P. Conservative; Anglican; recreations: sailing, travel; Clubs: University; Canadian (N.Y.); Metropolitan (N.Y.); R.C.Y.C.; Lyford Cay (Bahamas); Home: 110 Sandringham Dr., Downsview, Ont. M3H 1E2; Office: Bedford Rd., Toronto, Ont. L6T 3V1.

THOMAS, Leslie Roderick, B.Sc., D.I.C., F.I. Chem. E.; executive; b. Rhondda, South Wales 12 June 1920; s. Nefydd and Margaretta (Morgan) T.; e. South Wales Sch. of Mines Dipl. Chem. Engn. 1940; Univ. of London B.Sc. 1941, D.I.C. 1947; m. Joyce Evelyn d. Hugh Williams, Llangollen, North Wales 29 Apl. 1950; children: Susan, Jill, Ruth; CHRMN. AND C.E.O., ACRES DAVY McKEE LTD. since 1978; Pres., Acres Davy Ltd.; Vice Pres. Acres Consulting Services Ltd.; Chief Chem. Engr., Monsanto Chemicals (U.K.) 1955 — 56; Pres., Humphreys & Glasgow (Canada) Ltd., 1958-68; Dir. Operations, Humphreys & Glasgow Ltd. (U.K.) 1968-72; Dir., Vice Pres. Operations, Acres Consulting Services Ltd. 1973 — 78; served with Brit. Army 1941 — 46, U.K., India and Burma, rank Capt.; Fellow, Inst. Chem Engrs.; mem. Assn.

Prof. Engrs. Prov. Ont.; Protestant; Club: Royal Candn. Mil. Inst.; Home: 153 Wolfdale Ave., Oakville, Ont.; Office: 21 Voyager Court S., Rexdale, Ont.

THOMAS, Lewis H., Ph.D., LL.D.; b. Saskatoon, Sask., 13 April 1917; s. Rev. Robert Bremner and Margaret (Ross) T.; e. University of Sask., B.A. 1939 and M.A. 1941; University of Minn., Ph.D. 1953; Univ. of Regina, LL.D. 1972; m. Margaret Eleanor, d. J. M. Telford, Regina, Saskatchewan, 14 August 1946; children: Jean Alice, Robert Telford; PROF. OF HISTORY, UNIVERSITY OF ALBERTA, and Chrmn. of the Dept., 1965-68, Professor Emeritus, 1982; Assoc. Prof. of Hist., Univ. of Sask., Regina Campus, 1957-64; Assoc. Prof. of Hist. Univ. of Alta., 1964-65; Prov. Archivist of Sask., 1948-57; Editor, "Saskatchewan History" (Mag.), 1949-57; "Essays in Western History" 1976; "Wm. Aberhart and Social Credit in Alberta" 1977; mem. Hist. Sites & Monuments Bd. Can. 1968-77; mem., Candn. Hist. Assn.; author of "The Struggle for Responsible Government in the North-West Territories", 1956, 2nd ed.; "The Renaissance of Canadian History; A Biography of A. L. Burt" 1975; United Church; "The Making of a Socialist: The Recollections of T.C. Douglas", 1982; recreations: photography; Home: Ste. 101, 102 Gryphons Walk, Regina, Sask. S4S 6X1.

THOMAS, Lionel Arthur John, R.C.A.; artist; b. Toronto, Ont. 3 Apl. 1915; s. Arthur Edward and Ida Mae (Mooney) T.; e. John Russel Sch. Fine Arts Toronto 1933-35; Ont. Coll. Art 1936-37; Karl Godwin Sch. Illustration Toronto 1937; Candn. Coll. Music Dipl. 1930; Hans Hofman Sch. Fine Arts Provincetown, Mass. grad. 1947; Calif. Sch. Fine Arts San Francisco grad. 1949; m. Patricia Simmons 10 Sept 1940; children: Aurora Elyse Stewart, Michael Tristan John, Anthony Brian; former Instr. Vancouver Sch. Art; Instr. Sch. of Arch. Univ. of B.C. 1950-59, Asst. Prof. of Arch. 1959-64, Assoc. Prof. of Fine Arts 1964-80; guest speaker/lectr. 1950-79; Chrmn. Comte on Applied Design B.C. Archives & Centennial Museum Project Victoria 1965-67; maj. exhns. incl. Vancouver Art Gallery 1942, 1948; Univ. of B.C. 1947, 1948, 1951; 200 drawings & paintings Zan Art Gallery Victoria 1973; 136 enamels Spatial Concepts & Origin of Constellations Univ. Calgary 1973; U-Frame-It Gallery Toronto, Exposition Gallery Vancouver and Ward Plaza Gallery Honolulu (88 intaglio etchings) 1976; Students Union Bldg. Univ. B.C. 1977; Northland Plaza Gallery and Southland Gallery Edmonton 1977; Vancouver Planetarium & Museum (226 framed works) 1977; Harrison Galleries Vancouver 1978; Omniplex Museum Oklahoma City 1978; Strasenburgh Planetarium Rochester 1978; Fleischmann Atmospherium Planetarium Univ. Nevada 1978, 1979; Hansen Planetarium Gallery Salt Lake City 1978; Russell C. Davis Planetarium & Science Centre Jackson, Miss. 1978-79; Reading Museum & Art Gallery, Pa. 1979; William Penn State Mem. Museum & Archives Bldg. 1979; 282 framed works, The Pacific Science Centre Foundation, Seattle, Wash., April 4th - May 25th, 1980; rep. in numerous group exhns. and travelling exhns. Can., USA, Europe and S. Am.; rep. in various pub. and private colls. incl. Nat. Gallery Can., Art Gallery Ont., Vancouver Arts Gallery, Univ. Victoria, Fla. S. Coll.; comns. incl. bronze fountain Edmonton City Hall; copper and bronze doors St. Thomas More Coll. Univ. Sask.; diarama carved wood "Nootka Whaling Scene" and door panels B.C. Prov. Museum Victoria; numerous bas relief, murals, sculptures; "The Pacific Rim" mural Student Union Bldg. Univ. B.C.; co-author (illustrations) forthcoming book "Firmaments: The Story of the Constellations"; recipient John Russel Sch. Fine Arts Scholarship 1935; Emily Carr Trust Fund Scholarship 1949-50; Fla. Internat. Art Exhn. Award; Royal Arch. Inst. Can. Allied Arts Medal 1956; Pacific Northwest Artists Exhn. Award 1952; served with Seaforth Highlanders Regt. 1941-44; mem. B.C. Soc. Artists; Candn. Group Painters; Pacific Artists Assn.; Northwest Inst. Sculptors; Royal Astron. Soc.; Soc. Am. Archaeols.; Am. Craftsmen

Council; cited numerous bibliogs.; recreations: swimming, walking Address: 3351 Craigend Rd., West Vancouver, B.C. V7V 3G1.

THOMPSON, Alan; investment dealer; b. Winnipeg, Man. 23 Nov. 1927; s. Henry H. and Gladys R. (Holland) T.; e. Woodsworth Elementary School; Brooklands College; Cecil Rhodes High School, Winnipeg, Man.; m. Doreen E., d. W. B. Gibson, Winnipeg, 3 June 1950; children: Randal J., Derek W.; CHRMN., BRINK HUDSON & LEFEVER LTD.;& Dir., Chrmn. Dir., Morganite Can. Ltd.; Liberian Iron Ore Ltd.; Anthes Industries Ltd.; First Devonian Petroleum Ltd.; J. Henry Schroder and Co. Ltd.; Past Pres. and Chrmn., Investment Dealers' Assn. Can. 1971-72; past Chrmn. (1966) Vancouver Stock Exchange; Conservative; Protestant; recreations: sailing, golf; Clubs: Manitoba; The Vancouver (B.C.); Royal Vancouver Yacht; Royal Lake of the Woods Yacht; Home: 1124 Eyremont Dr., West Vancouver, B.C. V7S 2C2.Office: 400-700 West Pender St., Vancouver, B.C. V6C 1C1

THOMPSON, Hon. Andrew E., M.S.W., B.A.; senator; b. Ireland, 14 Dec. 1924; s. Joseph Stanley and Edith (Magill) T.; e. Monkton Combe Sch., Eng.; Oakwood Collegiate, Toronto Ont., 1940-42; Univ. of Toronto, 1942-43; Queen's Univ., B.A. 1947; Univ. of B.C., M.S.W. 1949; m. Amy, d. Edward Riisna, Toronto, Ont.; Past Chrmn. Transair; Past Chrmn., Canadian Foods Ltd.; Dir. CHIN Radio (Toronto); with Dept. Atty. Gen., B.C. 1949; Candn. Citizenship and Immigration 1951-57; Special Asst. to Hon. L. B. Pearson 1958; Lectr. Univ. Man. 1953; Nat. Program Organizer CBC 1957; el. M.P.P. Dovercourt (Toronto, Ont.) 1959; former consultant Toronto Star; el. Leader, Liberal Party in Ont., 1965; summoned to Senate of Canada April 1967; enlisted in RCNVR, 1943; discharged with rank of Lieut., 1946; mem., Candn. Commonwealth Parlty. Assn.; NATO Parlty. Assn.; Interparlty. Union; World Fed. Parlty. Union; Hon. mem., Ethnic Press Assn. Can.; Baltic Fed. Can.; Homes 12 Ava Cres., Toronto, Ont. M5P 3B1 and Kendal, Ont.L0A 1E0

THOMPSON, Andrew Royden, LL.M., J.S.D.; educator; b. Winnipeg, Man. 23 March 1925; s. Frederick George and Stella (Henderson) T.; e. St. John's Coll., Winnipeg, 1943; Queen's Univ. 1943-44; Univ. of Man. LL.B. 1948; Univ. of Toronto LL.M. 1954; Columbia Univ. (Stone Fellow 1962-63) J.S.D. 1967; m. Agnes, d. John McBeath, 27 Dec. 1948; children: John, David, Paul, Margaret; DIR., WESTWATER RESEARCH CENTRE; U.B.C. Prof. of Law, Univ. of B.C.; Visiting Prof. Univ. of Auckland 1967; mem. International Council on Environmental Law; Comn. on Environmental Law; Comn. on Environmental Policy, Law and Adm.; Internat. Union for Conservation of Nature and Natural Resources; former Chrmn. Candn Arctic Resources Comte.; Hon. Dir. Arctic Internat. Wildlife Range Soc.; Founding mem. Candn. Petrol. Law Foundation (Dir.); mem., Trustees for Alaska; Cdn. Inst. for Econ. Policy (Dir.); Former Comm., West Coast Oil Ports Inquiry; former Chrmn. B.C. Energy Comn.; co-author "Canadian Oil and Gas", 1955; Gen. Ed. Butterworth's Ontario Digest; author Butterworth's; author of numerous articles in various legal journs.; served with Candn. Army 1943-45; rank Lt.; mem. Law Soc. Man., Alta., NWT; Candn. Bar Assn.; Candn. Assn. Univ. Teachers; Assn. Candn. Law Teachers (Pres. 1970-71); Anglican; recreations: skiing, canoeing, camping; Home: 1308 W. 47th Ave., Vancouver, B.C. V6M 2L8.

THOMPSON, Brig. Gen. Charles H. A., C.D.; b. Eng., Oct. 1920; e. Univ. B.C., B.Sc. (Mech. Engn.) 1949; enlisted in RCAF in 1942; grad. as Pilot 1943; served operationally and as an Instr. in Can. till 1945 when trans. to transport duties overseas; served at Vancouver, Edmonton, Air Material Command HQ and Sea Island, B.C. before trans. to Candn. Jt. Air Training Centre, Rivers, Man., as Chief Tech. Offr., 1956; apptd. Staff Offr. for Aero Engn. at Training Command HQ, 1958; Air Trans-port Command HQ, Trenton, 1959; became Dir., Mobile Support Equipment, Air Force HQ. 1963; apptd. Dir., Gen. Maintenance, after integration of CFHQ; Chief of Staff, 1 Air Div. Hdqrs. 1966; attended Imp. Defence Coll., London, Eng. 1970-71; Former Dir.-Gen. Personnel Services, C.F.H.Q.;

THOMPSON, Donald Alexander, Q.C., LL.D.; b. Winnipeg, Man. 12 Feb. 1904; s. Frank W. and Mabel (Summerhayes) T.; e. Regina and Winnipeg Pub. Schs.; St. Johns Coll., Winnipeg, Man.; Manitoba Law Sch., 1924; Univ. of Manitoba, B.L. 1924, LL.D. 1969; D.C.L. St. John's Coll. 1973; m. Lillian Ruby, d. late F. M. Loud, 23 Aug. 1930; children: Bruce, David, Margaret, Donald; PARTNER, THOMPSON, DORFMAN, SWEATMAN; Director, Gordon Hotels (1971) Ltd.; Supercrete Inc.; Chancellor, Eccles. Prov. of Ruperts Land; Registrar and Past Chancellor Diocese of Rupert's Land; Past Chrmn. & mem. Adv. Bd., Misericordia Gen. Hosp., Winnipeg; Past mem. and Chrmn. Finance Comte. Bd. of Govs. Univ. of Man.; Past Pres., Canadian Council, Boy Scouts of Canada; called to the Bar of Man., 1925; cr. K.C. 1951; served in Winnipeg Grenadiers (Reserve Bn.) with rank of Lieut., 1939-36; Anglican; Club: Manitoba; Home: 3 Oakdale Drive., Charleswood, Winnipeg, Man. R3R 0Z3; Office: 3 Lombard Place, Winnipeg, Man. R3B 1N4

THOMPSON, Donald N., B.A., B.Com., M.B.A., Ph.D.; University prof. and management consultant; b. Winnipeg, Man., 11 Apl. 1939; s. Lawrence Ernest and Margaret (Neill) T.; e. Univ. of Man. B.A. 1959, B.Com. (Hon.) 1960; Univ. of Cal. M.B.A. 1962, Ph.D. 1968; PRESIDENT, DONALD N. THOMPSON & ASSOCIATES; Dir. Research, and Chief Economist, Royal Comn. Corporate Concentration; served Procter and Gamble Ltd., Coca Cola Ltd.; Lectr. Univ. of Alta., Long Island Univ., Harvard Univ. and York Univ.; consultant to various business organs. Can. and US and to govts. of Ont., Can., US, Israel, Thailand, Laos; rec'd Research Grants from Can. Council, Nat. Science Foundation; author "Franchise Operations and Antitrust" 1971; "Contractual Marketing Systems" 1971; "The Economics of Environmental Protection" 1973; "Canadian Marketing Problems and Prospects" 1973; "Problems In Canadian Marketing" 1977; "Conglomerate Mergers" 1978; "MACROMARKETING: A Canadian Perspective" 1979; other writings incl. over 50 articles in various prof. journs. newspapers and mags.; mem. Am. Econ. Assn.; Am. Marketing Assn.; recreation: competitive track and field; Clubs: Lucayan, Grand Bahama; Address: 348 Walmer Rd., Toronto, Ont. M5R 2Y4.

THOMPSON, Eldon Dale, B.Sc., P.Eng.; communications executive; b. Fairville, N.B. 24 Apl. 1934; e. Univ. of N.B. B.Sc. (Elect. Engn.) 1957; PRES., TELESAT CANADA 1980- ; mem. TransCanada Telephone System Bd. of Mang.; Dir. and Vice Chrmn. Extve. Comte., Inst. for Research on Pub. Policy; mem. Cabinet Secretariat and Secy. to Treasury Bd. N.B. Govt. 1972; Pres. Trans-Canada Telephone System 1974; Pres. The New Brunswick Telephone Co. Ltd. 1977; Beaverbrook Scholar; Sr. mem. Inst. Elect. & Electronic Engrs.; mem. Assn. Prof. Engrs. Prov. Ont.; Home: 18 Pineglen Cres., Nepean, Ont. K2E 6X9; Office: 333 River Rd., Vanier, Ont. K1L 8B9.

THOMPSON, Elmer Andrew, B.A.Sc.; manufacturer; b. New Westminster, B.C. 11 June 1920; s. Andrew Johnson and Ellen Rebecca T.; e. Univ. of B.C., B.A.Sc. 1940; m. Gwynneth Catherine, d. late George Jones, 20 Dec. 1945; three s., James E., Donald A., Robert G.; CHRMN. OF BOARD AND DIRECTOR, DOMGLAS INC.; Extve. Vice Pres. Packaging, Consolidated-Bathurst Inc.; Dir., Maritime Paper Products Ltd., DGHC Inc., Royersford Pa.; Twinpak Ltd.; Sanvik Canada Corp.; mem. Supervis. Bd., Europa Carton A.G. (W. Germany); with Domtar Limited 1945-67 leaving as Sr. Vice-Pres.; served with

R.C.A.F. during 2nd World War; mem., Order Engrs. Que.; Glass Container Mfrs. Inst. Protestant; recreations: skiing, fishing, tennis; Clubs: St. James's; The National; Mount Royal; Home: 116 Chartwell Rd., Oakville, Ont. L6J 3Z6 Office: 2070 Hawden Rd., Mississauga, Ont. L5K 2C9.

THOMPSON, George Christie, B.Com., LL.B.; transportation executive; b. Halifax, N.S., 8 Sept. 1911; s. George Andrew and Cynthia Matilda (Garroway) T.; e. Chebucto Rd. Sch. and Bloomfield High Sch., Halifax; Dalhousie Univ., B.Com. 1933, LL.B. 1936; m. Lois Vivian, d. late Hugh J. H. Mitchell, 30 Sept. 1970; one step-d., Rhonda Lois; PRESIDENT, ACADIAN LINES LTD. since 1955; Chrmn. of Bd. Gray Line Sight-Seeing Co's Assoc. (Inc.); Vice Pres. and Dir. Rainbow Haven Ltd.; called to Bar of N.S. 1936; Gen. Mgr. Acadian Coach Lines 1938; Dir. responsible for operation Golden ARrow Coaches Ltd., St. John's, Nfld. 1939; Dir. Park Transit Ltd., Halifax 1940; Gen. Mgr. Wagner Tours Ltd., Halifax 1941 (became Acadian Lines Ltd. in 1947); mem. Maritime Div. and Nat. Council, Extve. Comte., Candn. Nat. Inst. for Blind; Dir., N.S. Safety Council; Candn. Motor Coach Assn.; Am. Bus Assn.; N.S. Barristers Soc.; United Church; recreations: golf, dancing; Clubs: Halifax; Ashburn Golf; Saraguay; Home: 1951 Parkwood Terrace, Halifax, N.S. B3H 4G4; Office: 6040 Almon St., Halifax, N.S. B3K 5M1

THOMPSON, Gordon Edward, B.A., LL.B.; lawyer; b. Montreal, Que. 27 Oct. 1943; s. George Carson and Aileen Mary (Dawson) T.; e. elem. and high schs. Montreal; Univ. of Bishop's Coll. B.A. 1964; Queen's Univ. LL.B. 1967; m. Margaret Ann d. Douglas Charles Melville, Toronto, Ont. 30 May 1970; Children: Sara Kerr, Timothy Gordon, Patrick Douglas Carson; PARTNER, BORDEN & ELLIOT; Dir., Rorer Can. Inc.; Armet Industries Corp.; Seibels, Bruce Policy Management Systems Ltd.; Spun Steel Ltd.; Granning Suspensions Ltd.; Change-o-matic of Canada Ltd.; called to Bar of Ont. 1969; publs. incl. "Manual on Legal Citation" 1967; mem. Candn. Inst. for Adm. Justice; Law Soc. Upper Can.; Candn. Bar Assn.; Co. York Law Assn.; Lawyers Club; Liberal; Anglican; recreations: swimming, tennis; Home: 112 Cortleigh Blvd., Toronto, Ont. M4R 1K6; Office: 700 - 250 University Ave., Toronto, Ont. M5H 3E9.

THOMPSON, Harold, B.Com., F.S.A., F.C.I.A.; insurance executive; b. Winnipeg, Man., 18 Aug. 1922; s. Harry and Hrodny (Finson) T.; e. Univ. of Man., B. Com.; m. Beatrice May, d. Henry J. Shipman, Victoria, B.C., 21 Sept. 1946; children: Patricia Lynn, Gordon Douglas; PRESIDENT AND CHIEF EXTVE. OFFR., MONARCH LIFE ASSURANCE CO., since 1971; served with RCAF, Fleet Air Arm-RN, during World War II; Past Pres., Winnipeg Lions Club; Past Pres., Candn. Cancer Soc. (Man. Div.); Dir., Greater Winnipeg Gas Co.; Crown Trust Co.;, Winnipeg Health Sciences Centre; Univ. of Winnipeg; Winnipeg Rh Inst. Inc.; Liberal; Protestant; recreations: curling, Clubs: Winnipeg Winter; Manitoba; Home: 53 Aldershot Blvd., Winnipeg, Man. R3P 0C9; Office: 333 Broadway, Winnipeg, Man. R3C 0S9

THOMPSON, Homer Armstrong, M.A., Ph.D., LL.D., F.R.S.C.; university professor; b. Devlin, Ont., 7 Sept. 1906; s. William James and Sarah Gertrude (Armstrong) T; e. Univ. of Brit. Columbia, B.A. 1925, M.A. 1927, LL.D., 1949; Univ. of Mich., Ph.D. 1929; Hon. Degree; Brit. Columbia 1949, Dartmouth Coll., 1957, Michigan, 1957, Toronto, 1961; Athens 1963, Lyon 1963, Freiburg i. Br. 1966; N.Y. 1972; m. Dorothy, d. Charles Henry Burr, Phila., Pa., 15 Aug. 1934; children: Hope, Hilary, Pamela; staff mem. for the excavation of the Agora at Athens under the auspices of the Am. Sch. of Classical Studies, 1929-39, Field Dir., 1947-67; Asst. Prof. of Archaeol., Univ. of Toronto 1933-42, Assoc. Prof. 1942-45, Prof. 1945-47; Asst. Dir., Roy. Ont. Museum, 1933-47; Prof. of Classical Archaeol., Inst. for Advanced Study, Princeton,

N.J. 1947-1977, Prof. Emeritus since 1977; Eastman Prof., Oxford Univ., 1959-60; Geddes-Harrower Visiting Prof., Univ. of Aberdeen, 1964; Visiting Prof. Univ. of Sydney 1972; served in World War as Lieut. with R.C.N.V.R. (S.B.) 1942-45; Hon. mem., Greek Archaeol. Soc.; Heidelberg Acad.; Göteborg Acad.; Hon. Citizen of Athens; Commdr., Order of the Phoenix; Gold Medalist, Archaeol. Inst. Am., 1972; mem., Class. Assoc. of Canada; Archaeol. Inst. Am. (sometime Vice-Pres.); Am. Numis. Soc.; Soc. Antiquaries, London; Soc. Arch. Historians; Am. Philos. Soc.; Am. Acad. Arts & Sciences; Corr. Fellow, Brit. Acad.; Hon. mem., Soc. for Promotion of Hellenic Studies, Deutsches Archäologisches Institut; For. mem., Academy of Athens; author of various articles and books on topography and monuments of Athens; Presbyterian; recreation: gardening; Home: Princeton, N.J. 08540

THOMPSON, Col. J. Gordon, C.D., LL.D.; b. Aylmer, Ont. 2 Jan. 1894; e. Corunna and London Pub. Schs.; London Coll. Inst.; m. late Essie K. Thompson; children: Col. James G., Mrs. S. C. Bacon; Dir. UOP Manufacturing Ltd., USA; Hon. Dir. Canada Trust Co.; Hon. Chrmn. Adv. Bd. War Mem. Children's Hosp.; Clk., Robinson, Little & Co. 1914; C.E.F. 1914-18; Soldiers' Civil Re-estab. Comn. (Indust. Survey Offr.) 1918-20; organized Canada Vulcanizer & Equipment Co. Ltd. 1920; London Automotive Service Ltd. 1922; incorporated Supertest of Ottawa Ltd., Supertest of Elgin Ltd. and Supertest of Hamilton Ltd. 1923-24; Supertest Ltd. 1924; amalgamation Supertest co's 1925, known as Supertest Petroleum Corp. Ltd.; Partner in organ. of Supersilk Hosiery Mills 1925; during World War II served as Chrmn. Nat. Registration, Nat. War Finance Comte. for W. Ont., Citizens' War Services Comte., P.O.W. Parcels for V.P.; Candn. Red Cross Soc.; Community Chest; Gov., Univ. of W. Ont. 1952-68; recreations: boating, golf, trapshooting; Clubs: Sunningdale Golf (Pres.); London Hunt & Country; London; RCYC; Lago Mar Country and Lauderdale Yacht (Fort Lauderdale, Fla.); Past Gov. Candn. Golf Srs.; mem. Royal Candn. Legion Vimy Br.; Home: 252 Sydenham St., London, Ont. N6A 1W5; Office: P.O. Box 5664, London, Ont. N6A 4L6.

THOMPSON, James Gordon; b. London, Ont., 18 Dec. 1926; s. John Gordon and Essie (McCreery) T.; e. London (Ont.) Pub. Sch.; Ridley Coll., St. Catharines, Ont.; Royal Roads, Victoria, B.C.; Univ. of Toronto, Europe; Univ. of W. Ont., Business Adm.; m. Beverly, d. Dr. H. L. Smith, Windsor, Ont. 26 Nov. 1949; children: Adair, Leslie, Ann, Robin, Gordon; Pres. Corlon Investments Ltd.; (former President, Supertest Petroleum Corp. Limited; Dir., Cities Heating Co. Ltd.); Victoria Hospital; joined General Products Mfg. Corp. Ltd. as Asst. Secy. 1949; and Past Pres., Boy Scouts (London, Ont.); mem. Adv. Bd., War Mem. Children's Hosp.; mem. extve. Bd. Huron College; London Adv. Bd., Salvation Army Anglican; recreations: golf, boating; Clubs: London Hunt; London; Sunningdale Golf; Home: 1674 Louise Blvd., London, Ont. N6G 2R3; Office: (Box 5664) London, Ont. N6A 4L6.

THOMPSON, James Scott, B.A., M.A., M.D.; university professor; b. Saskatoon, Sask. 31 July 1919; s. late Walter Palmer and late Marjorie (Gordon) T.; e. Univ. of Saskatchewan B.A. 1940, M.A. 1941; Univ. of Toronto M.D. 1945; m. Margaret Anne d. late David H. Wilson, 19 Aug. 1944; children: Gordon Moore, David Bruce; PROF. OF ANATOMY, UNIV. OF TORONTO since 1963 (Chrmn. 1966-76); Research Assoc. Univ. of Toronto, 1946-48; Lectr., Asst. Prof. Univ. of W. Ont., 1948-50; Assoc. Prof. and Prof. Univ. of Alta., 1950-62; Extve. Secy. and Asst. Dean, Faculty of Medicine Univ. of Alta., 1955-62; Secy. Treas. of Candn. Assn. of Medical Colleges, 1956-62; mem. Bd. of Dir. Royal Alexandra Hosp., Edmonton, 1961-62; Visiting Investigator Jackson Lab, Bar Harbor, Maine, 1962-63; served with RCAMC, 1943-46; discharged Captain; co-author of "Genetics in Medicine",

1966; author of "Core Textbook of Anatomy", 1977, various articles related to medical education and antherosclerosis; mem., Candn. Assn. of Anatomists (Pres. 1975-76); Am. Assn. of Anatomists; Alpha Kappa Kappa; Alpha Omega Alpha Honor Medical Society; recreations: gardening, photography; Home: 7 Danville Dr., Willowdale, Ont. M5S 1A8; Office; Toronto, Ont. M2P 1H7.

THOMPSON, John D., B.Eng., M.B.A.; financier; b. Montreal Que., 28 Sept. 1934; s. William Douglas and Anne F. (Whebby) T.; e. McGill Univ., B.Eng. (Mining Engn.) 1957; Univ. of W. Ont., M.B.A. 1960; children: Jacqueline, Catherine, Peter; PRESIDENT, CEO AND DIRECTOR, ROYNAT INC.; Dir. J.S. Redpath Ltd., J.S. Redpath Corp., U.S.A.; Dir. Can. Pacific Hotels. Ltd.; Dir. Montreal Children's Hosp. Foundation; St. Mary's Hosp. Corp.; mem., Assn. Prof. Engrs. Ont. and Que.; Montreal Bd. Trade; R. Catholic; recreations: skiing, golf; Clubs: Mount Royal; St. James's; Royal Montreal Golf; Montreal Amateur Athletic Assoc.; Home: 710 Victoria Ave., Longueuil, Que. J4H 2K3; Office: 620 Dorchester Blvd. W., Montreal, Que. H3B 1P2

THOMPSON, Margaret Anne Wilson, B.A., Ph.D.; geneticist; b. Northwich, Cheshire, Eng., 7 Jan. 1920; d. David Heywood and Essie Margaret (Moore) Wilson; e. Univ. of Sask., B.A. 1943; Univ. of Toronto, Ph.D. 1948; m. Dr. James Scott Thompson, 19 Aug. 1944; two s., Gordon Moore, David Bruce; PROF. MED. GENETICS, UNIV. OF TORONTO, and Geneticist, Hosp. for Sick Children, Toronto, since 1963; Faculty mem. Univ. of Toronto 1944-48, Univ. of W. Ont. 1948-50, Univ. of Alta. 1955-62; visiting Investigator, Jackson Lab. Bar Harbor, Me., 1962-63; Hon. Research Associate, Univ. Coll., London, Eng. 1977-78; Saul Lehmann Visiting Prof., SUNY Downstate, Brooklyn, 1981; Fellow, Canadian College of Medical Geneticists; Dir., Muscular Dystrophy Assn. Can. 1963-80; Trustee, Queen Elizabeth II Fund for Research on Diseases of Children, Governing Council, Univ. of Toronto, 1974-77 Eugenics Bd. of Alta. 1959-62; rec'd Ramsay Wright Fellowship in Zoology 1943-44; Muscular Dystrophy Assn. Can. Post-doctoral Fellowship 1962-63; co-author, "Genetics in Medicine", 1966, 2nd ed. 1973, 3rd ed. 1980; other writings incl. scient. publs. in human and med. genetics; mem., Genetics Soc. Can. (Pres. 1972-73); Am. Soc. Human Genetics; Home: 7 Danville Dr., Willowdale, Ont. M2P 1H7; Office: 555 University Ave., Toronto, Ont. M5G 1X8

THOMPSON, Michael David, B.A.,; lawyer; b. Toronto, Ont. 15 March 1929; s. Thomas Clive and Isabel (Cope) T.; e. Trinity Coll. Sch. 1947; Trinity Coll. Univ. of Toronto B.A. 1951; Osgoode Hall Law Sch. 1956; m. Mary Loudd. late Burton W. Emmerson 21 Dec. 1953; children: Suzanne, Judith, Jennifer; LAWYER, ABITIBI-PRICE INC.; called to Bar of Ont., 1956; Apptd. Secy. and Gen. Counsel, June 1975; Past Pres. Rosedale-St. David P. Conservative Assn.; and Moore Park Ratepayer's Assn.; mem., Candn. Bar Assn.; Delta Chil P. Conservative; Anglican; Clubs: Toronto Lawn Tennis; Queen's; Craigleith Ski Club; recreations: tennis, skiing; 'Home: 36 Ridge Dr., Toronto, Ont. M4T 1B7; Office: Toronto-Dominion Centre, Toronto, Ont. M5K 1B3.

THOMPSON, Morley P., A.B., M.B.A., J.D.; financier; b. San Francisco, Cal., 2 Jan. 1927; s. Morley Punshon and Ruth Ethel (Wetmore) T.; e. Stanford Univ. A.B. 1948; Harvard Univ. Grad. Sch. of Business Adm. M.B.A. 1950; Salmon P. Chase Coll. of Law J. D. 1969; m. Patricia Ann d. late George F. Smith, 31 Jan. 1953; children Page Elizabeth, Morley P. Jr.; PRESIDENT, BALDWIN-UNITED CORP.; Chrmn. Canadian International Power Co. Ltd.; Dir. Anchor Hocking Corp.; Cincinnati Bell Inc.; FMC Corp.; The Kroger Co.; Cincinnati Milacron Inc.; served with US Navy Supply Corps 1952-54, rank Lt.; Chrm., Cincinnati Inst. Fine Arts; mem. Am. Bar Assn.; Am. Inst. C.P.A.'s; Beta Theta Pi; Presbyteri-

an; recreations: tennis, swimming, skiing; Clubs: Commercial Cincinnati; Commonwealth; Cincinnati Country; Camargo; Queen City; Home: 8250 Remington Rd., Cincinnati, Ohio; Office: 1801 Gilbert, Cincinnati, Ohio.

THOMSON, Dale C., D.F.C., B.A., D.ès L.; b. Westlock, Alta., 17 June 1923; s. Walter J. C. and Margaret C. (Falkson) T.; e. Fort Assiniboine Pub. Sch., Alta., 1928-38; Barrhead (Alta.) High Sch., 1938-41; Univ. of Alta., B.A. 1948; Univ. de Paris, Dipl., Inst. d'Etudes Pol. 1950, D.ès L. 1951; PROF., POL. SCIENCE, McGILL UNIV. since 1975; Prof. of Pol. Science, Univ. de Montréal 1960-73, Dir. Dept. of Pol. Science 1963-67; Dir. Center Candn. Studies & Prof. Candn. Studies, Johns Hopkins Univ. 1969-73; founding Pres. Assn. Candn. Studies US 1971-73; Vice Princ. (Planning) McGill Univ. 1973-76; served with R.C.A.F. 1941-45 as Pilot, rank Flt. Lt.; participated in D-Day and liberation of W. Europe; Secy. to Prime Min. St. Laurent, 1953-58; def. cand. for Jasper-Edson in g.e. 1958; author of "Alexander Mackenzie Clear Grit", 1960, "Louis St. Laurent: Canadian", "Canadian Foreign Policy: Options and Perspectives" (with Roger F. Swanson); Ed., "Quebec Society & Politics: Views from the Inside" 1973; and numerous articles; mem., Candn. Hist. Assn.; Candn. Pol. Science Assn.; Societe Canadienne de Science Politique; Am. Pol. Science Assn.; Liberal; United Church; recreations: skiing, swimming, scuba diving, squash; Address: McGill University, Montreal, Que.

THOMSON, Douglas Ferguson Scott, M.A.; university professor; b. Renfrewshire, Scot., 13 Oct. 1919; s. James Scott and Louise Ferguson (Pearson) T.; e. Glasgow (Scot.) Acad., 1928-38; Merton Coll. Oxford Univ., B.A., M.A., 1946; m. Eleanor Mary, d. late A. E. Hodgkins, M.C., Tunbridge Wells, Eng., 27 June 1953; children: James Fetherston Scott, Sarah Mary Scott, Jessica Jane Scott; PROF. OF LATIN, UNIV. COLL., UNIV. OF TORONTO, since 1969; Lect. present Coll. 1948-56, Asst. Prof. 1956-62, Assoc. Prof. 1962-69; Nuffield (Travelling) Fellow, London and Oxford, 1959-60; Visiting Prof., Univ. of N.C., 1967-68; Resident Tutor, Univ. Coll. Men's Residence, 1950-53; served with RA (Field and Mtn. Batteries), Europe, Middle East, Burma, 1939-45; rank Capt.; COTC, Univ. of Toronto, 1954-60; rank Maj.; Chrmn., Inter-Univs. Council on Grade 13 Latin (Ont.) 1963-64; author/editor, "Catullus; a critical edition", 1978; co-author, "Erasmus and Cambridge", 1964; other writings incl. articles and book chapters; translator "Collected Works of Erasmus"; Past mem. Ed. Comte. "Phoenix", 1958-71; mem., Am. Philol. Assn.; Soc. Promotion Roman Studies; Classical Assn. Can.; Ont. Classical Assn. (Past Vice Pres.); recreations: reading, music; Home: 116 Manor Rd. E., Toronto, Ont. M4S 1P8

THOMSON, James Wylie, F.C.I.S.; retired industrialist; b. Waterloo, Eng., 18 Oct. 1911; s. Andrew and Mary (Muir) T.; e. Ottawa (Ont.) Tech. Inst.; m. Doris May Ekins, 1940; one s., Douglas Andrew M.; ret. (1972) Dir., Maclaren Power and Paper Company (former Chrmn.); Dir., Chrmn. The James Maclaren Co., Ltd.; Thurso Pulp & Paper Co.; Asst. Secy., Maclaren Companies, 1948-52; Secy. 1952-60; Asst. Gen. Mgr. 1960-65; Gen. Mgr. 1967-68; Pres. and Gen. Mgr. 1968-70; Vice Pres. and Dir., Maclaren Quebec Power Co.; served with RCOC 1941-45; Protestant; recreations: fishing, curling, golf; 18 Angeline St. S., Lindsay, Ont. K9V 3K8.

THOMSON, The Rt. Hon. Lord, of Fleet of Northbridge in the City of Edinburgh; newspaper proprietor; b. Toronto, Ont. 1 Sept. 1923; s. late Rt. Hon. Lord Thomson of Fleet; (Founder of the Thomson Newspapers); e. Upper Can. Coll. Toronto; Univ. of Cambridge B.A., M.A. 1947; m. Nora Marilyn d. A. V. Lavis June 1956; children: David Kenneth Roy, Peter John, Lesley Lynne; CHMN. OF THE BD. AND C.E.O. AND DIR., THOMSON NEWSPAPERS LTD. (Owners of 40 daily newspapers in Canada); CHMN. OF THE BD. AND DIR., INTERNAT.

THOMSON ORGANIZATION LTD.; THE THOMSON CORP. LTD., THE THOMSON ORGANIZATION LTD.; THE WOODBRIDGE CO. LTD.; THOMSON BRITISH HOLDINGS LTD.; THOMSON EQUITABLE CORP. LTD.; THOMSON INVESTMENTS LTD.; THOMSON NEWSPAPERS INC.; (Owners of 76 daily newspapers in the United States); Pres. & Dir. Dominion-Consolidated Holdings Ltd.; Fleet St. Publishers Ltd.; Kenthom Holdings Ltd.; The Standard St. Lawrence Co. Ltd.; Thomfleet Holdings Ltd.; Thomson Internat. Corp. Ltd.; Thomson Mississauga Properties Ltd.; Thomson Works of Art Ltd.; Vice-Pres. & Dir., Cablevue (quinte) Ltd.; Veribest Products Ltd.; Dir., Abitibi-Price Inc.; The Advocate Co. Ltd.; Caribbean Trust Ltd.; Central Canada Insurance Service Ltd.; Dominion-Consolidated Truck Lines Ltd.; Hudson's Bay Co.; Internat. Thomson Holdings Inc.; Load & Go Transport Inc.; McCallum Transport Inc.; Nipa Lodge Co. Ltd.; Orchid Lodge Co. Ltd.; Scottish & York Holdings Ltd.; Simpsons, Ltd.; Thomson Scottish Assoc. Ltd.; Thomson Television Ltd.; The Toronto-Dominion Bank; Began in editorial dept. of Timmins Daily Press, 1947; Advertising Dept. Cambridge (Galt) Reporter, 1948-50; Gen. Mgr., 1950-53; Returned to Toronto Head Office to take over direction of Company's Canadian & Am. operations; Served in 2nd World War with R.C.A.F.; Clubs: York Downs; National; Toronto; York; Granite; Toronto Hunt; Recreation: Collecting antiques and Old Master paintings; Baptist; Residence: 8 Castle Frank Rd., Toronto, Ont. M4W 2Z4; and 8 Kensington Palace Gardens, London W8, England; Office: 65 Queen St. W., Toronto, Ont. M5H 2M8

THOMSON, Nancy Gordon, B.A.; educator; investment executive; b. Toronto, Ont. 26 Apl. 1933; d. Ewart Kenneth and Marjorie (Forbes) Fockler; e. Blythwood Pub. Sch. and Lawrence Park Coll. Inst. Toronto 1951; Univ. of Toronto Victoria Coll. B.A. 1954; Ont. Coll. of Educ. 1955; Ryerson Polytech. Sch. (Econ.); Candn. Securities Course Toronto; m. Thomas Harold Thomson 21 June 1958; children: Lynda Gordon, Laurel Jean, Gregory Harold; PRES., NANCY THOMSON, INVESTING FOR WOMEN 1979- ; Dir. National Trust Co. Ltd.; Secondary Sch. Teacher of Eng., Hist. and Latin 5 years Kitchener, Toronto, Montreal, Boston; Remedial Reading Instr. 2 yrs. Boston, Toronto; author Basic Course-Investing For Women, Course II - Investing For Women; Past Dir. Vancouver Art Gallery; Past Chrmn. of Bd. Festival Singers Can.; mem. Assn. Women Extves.; United Church; recreations: reading, skiing, travel; Club: Granite; Office: 60 St. Clair Ave. E., Suite 702, Toronto, Ont. M4T 1N5.

THOMSON, Peter Nesbitt; financier; b. Westmount, Que. 22 March 1926; s. late Peter Alfred and Lottie (Corey) T.; e. Selwyn House Sch., Westmount, Que.; Westmount High Sch.; Lower Canada Coll.; Sir George Williams Coll.; LL.D. St Thomas Univ. (Fredericton N.B.) 1968; m. Monique, d. Gaston Saintonge, Q.C., Valleyfield, Que., 9 June 1950; one s. and one d.; CHAIRMAN, TIW INDUSTRIES LTD.; Chrmn., Thomcor Holdings Ltd.; Chrmn. & C.E.O. P. Lawson Travel Ltd.; Dir., Bathurst Paper Ltd.; Caribbean Utilities Co. Ltd.; Canbro U.K. Ltd.; Common-wealth Industrial Bank Ltd. (Nassau); Consolidated Bathurst Inc.; Domglas Inc.; Power Corp. of Can.; Radisson Furniture Ltd.; Royal Bank of Can.; Shawinigan Industries Ltd.; Sterling Tankers Ltd.; The Point Farm Inc.; Trans Canada Corp. Funds; West Indies Power Corp. Ltd.; began career with Investment Secretariat Ltd., Montreal, 1944; Clubs: Annabel (London Eng.) Eastern Ionosphere; Lyford Cay (Bahamas); Palm Bay (Florida); Mount Bruno Golf (Quebec); Royal Canadian Yacht (Toronto); Royal St. Lawrence Yatch (Quebec); St James's (Montréal); Homes: Coral Harbour, New Providence Island, Bahamas; and Point Farm, Grand Isle, Vt. 05458 Office: Suite 1100, 90 Sparks St., Ottawa, Ont. K1P 5B4

THOMSON, Richard Murray, B.A.Sc., M.B.A.; banker; b. Winnipeg, Man., 14 Aug. 1933; s. Mr. and Mrs. H. W. Thomson; e. Univ. of Toronto, B.A.Sc. (Engn.) 1955; Harvard Business Sch., M.B.A. 1957; Queen's Univ., Fellows' course in Banking, 1958; CHRMN. AND CEO, DIR. THE TORONTO DOMINION BANK since 1978; Dir., Canadian Gypsum Co. Ltd.; S. C. Johnson and Son Limited; Eaton's of Canada Limited; Texasgulf Inc.; Cadillac Fairview Corp. Ltd.; Union Carbide of Canada; The Prudential Insurance Co. of America; Midland and International Bank Ltd.; entered service of Toronto Dominion Bank at H.O., Toronto, 1957 and served in several Bds. in various positions; Sr. Asst. Mgr., St. James and McGill, Montreal, 1961; Asst. to Pres., H.O., 1963, Chief Gen. Mgr. July 1968, Vice Pres., Chief Gen. Mgr. & Dir. 1971, Pres. 1972, Pres. & CEO 1977, Chrm. and C.E.O. 1978; Vice-Chmn., Bd. of Trustees, Hosp. for Sick Children; Office: P.O. Box 1, Toronto-Dominion Centre, Toronto, Ont. M5K 1A2

THOMSON, Robert, E.D., F.C.I.S.; executive; b. Aberdeen, Scotland, 16 May 1904; s. Robert and Mary (Brodie) T.; came to Canada, 1914; e. William Dawson and Comm. High Sch., Montreal Que.; m. Annabel Scott, d. Robert Doig, Lachute, Que., 30 June 1934; one s. Robert Graham; VICE-PRES. AND DIR., YALE PROPERTIES LTD. since 1969; Dir., First Hamilton Corp.; Ontario & Quebec Railway Co.; Treas. & Dir. Nationwide Capital; Greater Hamilton Developer Ltd.; joined Standard Life Assurance Co. as a Jr. Clerk, 1919; apptd. Secy. for Canada, 1937, Asst. Mgr. 1956, Depy. General Manager 1957 Extve. Dir. 1966; served in 2nd World War, 1940-45 Overseas with 17th Duke of York's Royal Candn. Hussars, Candn. Mil. Hdqrs., Eng.; discharged with rank of Major; Freemason; Conservative; Protestant; recreations: golf, gardening, reading; Clubs: Mount Royal; Saint James's; Kanawaki Golf; Toronto Golf; Home: 4555 Montclair Ave., Montreal, Que. H4B 2J8; Office: 2015 Peel St., Montreal, Que. H3A 1T8

THORBURN, Hugh Garnet, A.M., Ph.D.; university professor b. Toronto, Ont., 8 Feb. 1924; s. Hugh and Delia Amanda (Jacobs) T.; e. N. Toronto Coll. Inst., 1937-42 (silver medal in 1941 and gold medal 1942 for scholarship); Univ. of Toronto, B.A. (Pol. Science & Econ.) 1949; Columbia Univ., A.M. 1950, Cert. of European Inst., 1951, Ph.D. 1958; m. Gwendolyn Alice Montgomery, 8 July 1950; children: Janet, Julie, Hugh A. R., John, Maria, Malcolm; PROF. DEPT. OF POL. STUDIES, QUEEN'S UNIV. (Head of Dept. 1968-71); Lectr. in Pol. Science and Econ., Mount Allison University 1951-52; Assistant Professor 1953; taught, summer session 1953, University of Sask.; apptd. Asst. Prof. (granted 1 yr. leave of absence from Mount Allison), 1954-55; returned Mount Allison 1955-56; joined present Univ. 1956; served with Candn. Army 1943-46; enlisted as Pte. in Inf.; commnd. 2nd Lt. 1944; trans. to Candn Intelligence Corps attached to Candn. Mil. HQ. London; served as Intelligence Offr. in HQ 1st Candn. Army, HQ 2nd Candn. Corps, HQ 30 Brit. Corps; served as Interrogation Offr. and later as Field Security Offr., Holland and Germany; discharged 1946 with rank Capt.; author of "Politics in New Brunswick", 1961; "Party Politics in Canada", 1963 (4th revised ed. 1978); Co-author, "Canadian Anti-Combines Administration 1952-60", 1963; has written numerous articles for various learned journs. and has completed 2 studies for Royal Comn. on Bilingualism and Biculturalism; prepared "Political Science in Canada; Graduate Studies & Research", for Commission on Graduate Studies in Humanities & Social Sciences 1975; awarded grants for research from Canadian Social Science Research Council, Can. Council, Queen's Univ. and French Govt. (Bourse d'Etude 1961); rec'd Centennial Medal 1968; Queen's Jubilee Medal 1978; Mem. Bd. of Dir., Social Science Federation of Canada, 1979-80; Pres., Candn. Pol. Science Assn., 1977-78 (mem. Extve. Comte. 1965-67, Vice Pres. 1968-69); Pres., Social Science Research Council Can., 1967-69 (Chrmn., Publs. Comte., 1965-67); Chrmn., Kingston Br., Candn. Inst. Internat. Affairs, 1965-67; Delta Chi; Home: 194 Johnson St., Kingston, Ont. K7L 1Y1

THORLAKSON, Paul H. T., C.C. (1970), M.D., C.M., M.R.C.S.(Eng.), L.R.C.P. (London)F.R.C.S. (C), F.A.C.S.; surgeon; b. Park River, N. Dak., 5 Oct. 1895; s. Miels S., and Erika (Rynning) T.; e. Univ. of Man., M.D., C.M.; Lon. degrees: LL.D. (Man.), M.D. (Iceland), F.I.C.S., D. Sc.(Brandon) F.A.C.H.A.; LL.D. (Winnipeg); m. Gladys Maree, d. Robert Andrew Henry, 10 Nov. 1920; children: Kenneth, Robert, Tannis Maree; Founder and Hon. Pres., Winnipeg Clinic; Prof. Emeritus of Surg., Univ. of Man.; Commr., Man. Health Services Comn. 1962-70, 1971-74; Chancellor, Univ. of Winnipeg 1969-78; served in World War, 1916-17, with Inf. Bn. in Eng.; awarded Order of the Falcon, Iceland; Past Chrmn., W. Regional Comte., Divn. of Med. Sciences, Nat. Research Council; Founder and Past Pres., Winnipeg Clinic Research Inst.; mem., Am. Surg. Assn.; W. Surg. Soc.; Winnipeg Med. Soc.; Man. Med. Assn.; Candn. Med. Assn.; Candn. Assn. Med. Clin.; World Med. Assn.; Pan-Pacific Surg. Assn.; Past Chrmn. Man. Chapter, Candns for Health Research; Freemason; United Church; Clubs: The Manitoba; St. Charles Country; Home: 1203-99 Wellington Cres., Winnipeg Man. R3M 0A2; Office: 425 St. Mary's Ave., Winnipeg, Man.R3C 0N2

THORNHILL, Hon. Roland John, M.H.A.; politician; stockbroker; b. Grand Bank, Nfld. 3 Sept. 1935; s. Archibald and Ruth (Williams) T.; e. Mem. and Dalhousie Univs.; m. Joyce Marie d. late William Moore, Halifax, N.S. 12 May 1955; two s. Christopher, Jeffrey; MIN. OF DEVELOPMENT AND DEPY. PREMIER, N.S. 1978-; Dir. Sydney Steel Corp.; Industrial Estates Ltd.; Waterfront Development Corp.; Min. responsible for adm. of N.S. Research Foundation Corp. Act; el. to Dartmouth City Council 1961; Mayor 1967, re-el. 1970; el. to N.S. House of Assembly for Dartmouth S. 1974, re-el. 1978; rec'd Vanier Award 1974; P. Conservative; United Church; recreations: reading, curling; Clubs: Kiwanis; Brightwood Golf; Dartmouth Curling; Home: 299 Portland St., Dartmouth, N.S. B2Y 1K3; Office: (P.O. Box 519) Halifax, N.S. B3J 2R7.

THORNTON, Archibald Paton, M.A., D.Phil., F.R.Hist.S., F.R.S.C.; university professor; b. Glasgow, Scotland, 21 Oct. 1921; s. John Joseph and Margaret (Paton) T.; e. Kelvinside Acad., Glasgow, 1929-39; Univ. of Glasgow 1939-41, 1945-47 (M.A. 1947); Univ. of Oxford, Trinity Coll., 1947-50 (D.Phil. 1952); m. Janet Joan, d. late George Thomson Mowat, 30 July 1948; two s.: Roderick Charles Stuart and Andrew Rohan George; PROF. OF HISTORY, UNIV. OF TORONTO since 1960 and Chrmn. of Dept. 1967-72; Capt., E. Riding Yorks. Imp. Yeomanry, 1942-45; Lect. in Modern Hist., Trinity Coll., Oxford 1948-50; Lect. in Imp. Hist., Univ. of Aberdeen 1950-57; Prof. of Hist. and Chrmn. of the Dept., and Dean of Arts, Univ. of W. Indies 1957-60; mem., H.M. Colonial Service Appts. Bd., 1952-57; Commonwealth Fellow of St. John's Coll., Cambridge, 1966; Visiting Smuts Fellow in Commonwealth Studies, Univ. of Cambridge, 1965-66; Fellow of the Royal Society of Canada; author "West-India Policy under the Restoration," 1956; "The Imperial Idea and its Enemies," 1959; "Doctrines of Imperialism," 1965; "The Habit of Authority," 1966; "For the File on Empire," 1968; "Imperialism in the 20th Century" 1978; over 40 articles, reviews in learned journs.; mem. Am. Hist. Assn.; Candn. Hist. Assn.; Hakluyt Soc.; Reform (London); Presbyterian; recreations: golf, chess, theatre; Office: University College, Toronto, Ont. M5S 1A1.

THORSON, Hon. Donald Scarth, b. Winnipeg, Man., 2 Aug. 1925; s. Joseph Thorarrin and Alleen Blanche (Scarth) T.; e. Queen's Univ., B.A., 1946; Osgoode Hall

Law Sch., 1951; m. Jane Elizabeth, d. L. N. Moore, Ottawa, 1957; children: Jennifer Lynn, Rebecca Gail, Stephanie Jane: JUDGE, COURT OF APPEAL ONT. since 1978; read law with Gowling Osborne & Henderson, Ottawa; called to the Bar of Ont. 1951; Dir., Leg. Sec., Dept. Justice 1957; Asst. Depy. Min. Justice 1961; cr. Q.C. 1962; Assoc. Depy. Min. Justice 1967; Depy. Min. of Justice and Depy. Atty. Gen. of Can. 1973-77; Constitutional Advisor to Prime Min. 1977-78; mem. Canadian Bar Assn.; Candn. Inst. for Adm. Justice in Can.; Past Pres., Uniform Law Conf. Can.; Phi Delta Phi (Legal); Phi Kappa Pi; recreations: fishing, hunting, sailing, sculpture; Home: 16 Alderbrook Drive, Don Mills, Ont. M3B 1E4; Office: Osgoode Hall, Queen St., Toronto, Ont. M5H 2N5

THRASHER, Richard Devere, Q.C., B.A.; b. Amherstburg, Ont., 5 March 1922; s. Charles Devere and Irene Agnes (Richard) T.; e. Assumption Coll., B.A. 1948; Osgoode Hall, Toronto, Ont.; m. Norma Jeanne, d. Francis Edwin Whittal, Amherstburg, Ont., 23 Nov. 1940; children: Linda, Heather, Richard, Jr., Bradley, Daniel; read law with McKenzie, Wood & Goodchild, Toronto, Ont.; called to the Bar of Ont., 1951; cr. Q.C., 1962; served in 2nd World War with R.C.A.F. 1942-45, rank Flying Offr.; Past Secy., S. Essex P. Cons. Assn.; el. to H. of C. for Essex S. in g.e. 1957 and re-el. 1958; apptd. Parlty. Secy. to Minister of Labour, Nov. 1959; def. in g.e. June 1962; Special Asst. to Prime Min. of Can. 1962; named Chief Adm. Offr., P. Cons. Party Nat. Hdqrs. and Nat. Dir. of Party, June 1963; def. cand. (Essex S.) to H. of C. in g.e. Nov. 1965; a Magistrate for Windsor, Ont. area 1966-67; mem., Essex Law Assn.; Candn. Bar Assn.; Royal Candn. Legion; K. of C.; P. Conservative; Roman Catholic; Home: 41 Woodbridge Drive, Amherstburg, Ont. N9V 1T9; Office: 300-380 Ouellette Ave., Windsor, Ont. N9A 6X5

THRIFT, Eric W., M.Arch., F.R.A.I.C. (1961)F.C.I.P., A.I.C.P.; educator; b. Winnipeg, Man., 23 Aug. 1912; s. William David and Amy Eveline (Daw) T.; e. St. James (Man.) Pub. and Coll. Inst.; Univ. of Manitoba, B.Arch. 1935 (Gold Medal); Mass Inst. of Technol., M.Arch. 1938; m. Melba Maude, d. Tilley W. Belyea, 22 Aug. 1941; children: Kristin Elizabeth, Murray Eric, William David, Dennis Gordon; currently PROFESSOR EMERITUS, QUEEN'S UNIV. (1981-) and Private Planning Consultant with Hudson's Bay Co. Buildings Office, 1938-42; Lectr. in Arch. & Planning, 1942-50, Univ. of Manitoba; Tech. Adviser on Planning to Postwar Reconstr. Comte., Prov. of Man., 1943-44; Planning Consultant in Alta., Sask., Man., and Ont., 1948-60; Dir., Metrop. Planning Comn. of Greater Winnipeg 1945-60; Gen. Mgr., Nat. Capital Comn. 1960-70; r., Prov. of Man. Planning Service, 1957-60; private Indust. Design Consultant & Arch.; mem. Man. Assn. of Archs. (Pres. 1949); Roy. Arch. Inst. Can.; Am. Inst. Planners; Internat. Fed. for Housing & Planning; Am. Acad. Pol. and Social Science; Roads & Transport. Assn. Can. 1961-71; Urban & Regional Information Systems Assn., 1970-75; Town Planning Inst. Can., (Pres. 1953-54, 1961-62); Am. Soc. of Planning Officials, (Pres. 1964-65); mem. Ottawa Planning Area Bd., 1960-71; Candn. Council on Urban and Regional Research, 1963-66; Pres., Univ. of Man. Alumni Assn., 1950; Pres., Nat. Gallery Assn., 1968-71; rec'd R.A.I.C. Gold Medal, 1935; Centennial Medal of Can., 1967; Queen's Jubilee Medal, 1977; Fellow, Royal Arch. Inst. of Canada, 1961; Canadian Inst. of Planners, 1978; Hon. Life Mem., Am. Planning Assoc. 1978; Charter Mem., American Institute of Certified Planners, 1978; Publications; numerous articles on arch. and planning contrib. to mags; mem. Kiwanis Club, Winnipeg 1952-60, Ottawa 1961-68; United Church; recreations: music; art; books; swimming; Home: 1088 Johnson St., Kingston, Ont. K7M 2N5; Office: Ellis Hall, Queen's Univ., Kingston, Ont.K7L 3N6

THUOT, Julien, E.D., B.A., M.Com.; retired public utilities executive; b. Fall River, Mass., 15 Sept. 1913; s. Hormidas and Helene (Côté) T.; naturalized British Subject, 1935; e. St-Joseph Semy., Rimouski, Que., 1932; Laval Univ., B.A. 1935; Univ. de Montréal, M.Com.; m. Madeleine, d. late Ernest Champoux, 4 Sept. 1937; one d. Marie-Josee; Cost Acct., Montreal Suspenders & Umbrellas Co. Ltd. Montreal, 1935-39; joined Quebec Telephone as Comm. and Traffic Supvr., Rimouski, Que., 1939-40; Dir. of Comm. Affairs 1946-55; Asst. to Pres. 1955-66; Vice Pres.-Revenue Requirements, 1966-69, Finance & Treas. 1969, Vice Pres. Corporate Planning and Treas. 1974-76, First Vice Pres., Vice Pres. Finance and Treas. 1977-78 (ret.); commnd. as Lieutenant in COTC 1934; served with St. Lawrence Fusiliers and Royal 22nd Regt. in Can. and Eng. 1940-45; rank Maj.; trans. to Supplementary Reserve 1945; placed on list of retired officers 1969; Liberal; Roman Catholic; recreations: reading, fishing; Home: 300 St. Georges St. Apt. 509, St. Lambert, Que.;

THUR, Otto E., M.B.A., M.A.; economist; educator; b. Darda, Hungary, 1 Aug. 1928; s. Antal and Ilona (Kapronczay) T.; e. St. Stephen's Coll., Kalocsa, Hungary, B.A. 1947; Univ. of Budapest, 1947-49; Univ. of Louvain, M.B.A. 1952 M.A. (Econ.) 1954; m. Livia M., d. C. Rechnitzer, Benidorm, Spain, 1955; Chrmn., Textile and Clothing Bd.; former Asst. Depy. Min., Dept. Finance; Vice-Chrmn., Econ. Council Can.; Research Asst., Inst. of Econ. & Social Research, Univ. Louvain, Belgium, 1952-56; Dir. of Research, 1956-59; Asst. Prof., Louvain Social Sch., 1954-59; Visiting Prof., Internat. Univ. of Luxembourg, 1959; joined Univ. de Montreal as Asst. Prof. 1959, Assoc. Prof. 1960-66, Prof. and Chairman, Dept. Economics & Assistant Dean, Faculty of Social Sciences 1967-70; Vice Chrmn., Econ. Council Can., 1970-73; Visiting Prof., Laval Univ., 1962-67; Consultant, Ministry of Industry and Comm., Govt. of Que., 1961-68 and Conseil D'Orientation Economique, Que., 1962-64; Econ. Adviser, Candn. Corp for 1967 World Exhn., 1966-68; Ed., "Canadian Economic Outlook — Conjoncture Economique Canadienne"; author of over 120 articles in Candn. and European econ. journs.; mem., Social Science Research Council (Extve. Comte.); Can. Council (Killam Comte.); Candn. Econ. Assn.; Soc. Canadienne de Science Economique; Montreal Econ. Assn.; Roman Catholic. Office: Floor 01W, 235 Queen St., Ottawa, Ont. K1A 0N5

THURSTON, Frank Russel, B.Sc.; b. Chicago, Ill., 5 Dec. 1914; s. Charles William and Emma Louise (Connor) T.; e. Univ. of London, B.Sc. (Physics) 1940; m. Olive, d. Alfred Cullingworth, 23 Nov. 1940; one child: CONSULTANT, NAT. RESEARCH COUNCIL AND DEPT. OF TRANSPORT; since 1959; joined Nat. Phys. Lab., Teddington Eng., 1937-47; joined present Council, Div. of Mech. Engn., 1947; former Dir., Nat. Aeronautical Estab., N.R.C., 1959-79; Dir. of many nat. and internat. comtes. and organs. in field of science and engn.; author of numerous publs. on theory of structures, fatigue of materials and structures, materials research and aerodynamics; mem., Inst. Physics & Phys. Soc.; Candn. Aeronautics & Space Inst.; Adv. Group for Aerospace Research & Devel. (N.A.T.O.); Commonwealth Adv. Aeronautical Research Council; recipient, McCurdy Award; Von Karman Medal; Home: 793 Hemlock Rd., Ottawa, Ont. K1K 0K6; Office: Montreal Rd., Ottawa, Ont. K1A 0R6

THURSTON, Lorne A.; banker; b. Vancouver, B.C. 10 Mar. 1930; e. Univ. of B.C. 1948-50; m. Edith O., Nov. 1953; children: Wendy Ann, Brenda Leslie; SR. VICE PRES. COMM. BANKING, THE BANK OF NOVA SCOTIA 1981- ; with present Bank 30 yrs., Mgr. Vancouver Br. 1969, Asst. Gen. Mgr. Montreal Regional Office 1971, Asst. Gen. Mgr. Corporate Credit 1973, Gen. Mgr. Corporate Credit 1976, Vice Pres. and Gen. Mgr. W. and N. Ont. Regional Office 1977-81; Clubs: Ontario; Ce-

dar Brae Golf & Country; Office: 44 King St. W., Toronto, Ont. M5H 1H1.

TIGER, Lionel, M.A., Ph.D., F.R.A.I.; social scientist; b. Montreal, Que., 5 Feb. 1937; s. Martin and Lillian (Schneider) T.; e. McGill Univ., B.A. 1957 (with Distinction), M.A. (Sociol.) 1959; London Sch. of Econ. Ph.D. (Pol. Sociol.) 1963; m. Virginia Marie, d. Gordon Conner, Toronto, Ont., 19 Aug. 1964; one s., Sebastian Benjamin; PROF.   OF   DIR.   GRAD.   PROGRAMS, ANTHROPOLOGY, RUTGERS UNIVERSITY since 1972; Research Director, H. F. Guggenheim Foundation; Lectr. on Bureaucracy and Adm., Inst. of Pub. Adm., Ghana and Visiting Lectr., Univ. of Ghana, 1961; Asst. Prof. of Sociol., Univ. of B.C., 1963-68; mem. Dean's Comte. study B.A. Degree 1963-64; gave lecture series in Nursing Educ., Vancouver Gen. Hosp., 1964-65; Rep., McGill Univ. Student Soc., World Univ. Senate Study Seminar, W. Africa, 1957; rec'd. Nat. Council of Jewish Women Bursary, 1956; Chester McNaughton Prize for Creative Writing, 1956; McGill Univ. Fellowship 1957; Can. Council Fellowships 1958 and 1960, Grant 1965, Special Award 1966-67 and Killam Bequest Inaugural Award 1968, renewed 1969; I.O.D.E. First World War Mem. Overseas Post-grad. Fellowship for Que., 1959; Comte. on Comparative Bureaucracy of S.S.R.C. Grant-in-aid, 1960; Ford Foundation Foreign Area Training Fellowship 1962; Univ. of B.C. Pres.'s Research Fund Grant 1965; Nat. Research Council of Can. Grant-in-aid 1966-67; John Simon Guggenheim Mem. Foundation Fellowship 1968; Rockefeller Fellowship, The Aspen Inst. for Humanistic Studies, 1979; author, "Men in Groups", 1969, French transl. 1970; "The Imperial Animal" (with Robin Fox) 1971; "Der Mannergruppe" 1972; "Women in the Kibbutz" (with J. Shepher) 1975; "Optimism: The Biology of Hope" 1978; Ed. "Female Hierarchies" 1978; other writings incl. numerous articles in Candn. and foreign journs.; mem. Ed. Bd., "Journal of African Studies in Canada", 1966-68; "Social Science Information"; Fellow, Society for Study of Evolution; American Sociol. Assn.; mem., Committee African Studies in Can.; Candn. Sociol./Anthrop. Assn.; Assn. for Study Animal Behaviour; Am. Assn. Advanc. Science; N.Y. Acad. Science; Am. Anthrop. Assn.; P.E.N., U.S.A., Secy Exec. Bd., 1981- ; Address: Livingston Coll., Rutgers Univ., New Brunswick, N.J. 08903

TILL, Eric Stanley; film director; b. London, Eng. 24 Nov. 1939; s. William George and Daisy Beatrice (Porter) T.; e. Beal Grammar Sch. Oxon. Eng.; Christchurch London, Eng.; Clarkes Coll. London, Eng.; name to Can. 1954; m. Betty Ann d. William Pope, Hope, B.C. 14 June 1957; children: Alison Elizabeth, Douglas William, David Stephen, Justine Carolyn; Assoc. Prof. York Univ.; served BBC London, Eng. Serious Music Productions; Brit. Forces Network Germany, Writer/Producer; Nat. Ballet of Can., Co. Mgr.; CBC TV Toronto, Drama/Music Dir.; MGM London, Eng., Film Dir.; Liberal; Anglican; recreation: music; Address: 62 Chaplin Cres., Toronto, Ont. M5P 1A3.

TILL, James Edgar, M.A., Ph.D., F.R.S.C.; scientist; b. Lloydminster, Sask. 25 Aug. 1931; s. William and Gertrude Ruth (Isaac) T.; e. Univ. of Sask. B.A. 1952, M.A. 1954; Yale Univ. Ph.D. 1957; m. Marion Joyce d. late Alfred Victor Sinclair 6 June 1959; children: David William, Karen Sinclair, Susan Elizabeth; HEAD OF BIOL. RESEARCH, ONT. CANCER INST. since 1969, Biophysicist since 1957; Prof. of Med. Biophysics, Univ. of Toronto since 1965; Postdoctoral Fellow, Connaught Med. Research Labs. Toronto 1956-57; Asst. Prof. Univ. of Toronto 1958, Assoc. Prof. 1962; Assoc. Dean, Life Sciences, School of Grad. Studies, 1981; co-recipient Gairdner Foundation Internat. Award 1969; author or co-author over 150 scient. publs. various aspects biophysics, cell biol., genetics, exper. hematology, immunology and cancer research; mem. Candn. Soc. Cell Biol.; Am. Assn.

Cancer Research; Soc. for Medical Decision-Making Royal Soc. of Canada; Office: 500 Sherbourne St., Toronto, Ont. M4X 1K9.

TILLARD, Rev. Jean-Marie, D.Ph., D.Th.; educator; priest; b. Saint-Pierre-et-Miquelon, France 2 Sept. 1927; s. Ferdinand and Madeleine (Ferron) T.; e. Angelicum, Rome D.Ph.; Le Saulchoir Paris D.Th.; Magisterium in Sacra Theologia Rome; Trinity Coll. and St. Michael's Coll. Univ. of Toronto D.Th.; PROF. OF THEOL. DOMINICAN COLL. OF PHILOSOPHY AND THEOLOGY 1959- , Maitre des Etudes; Vice Chrmn. Faith & Order World Council Chs. Geneva; mem. Ang.-R.C. Internat. Comn.; Orthodox-R.C. Internat. Comn.; Consultor of Vatican for Ecumenical Affairs; mem. Internat. Comn. of Theologians (counselling the Vatican); mem. Bd. Tantur (Jerusalem); invited lectr. Laval Univ., St. Stephen's Oxford Univ., Univ. of Nottingham; visiting prof. Louvain, Brussels; Fribourg 1982; author "L'Eucharistie Pâque de l'Eglise" 1964; "Adaption et Renovation de la Vie Religieuse" 1967; Devant Dieu et Pour le Monde" 1974; "L'evêque de Rome", 1982; various articles; mem. N. Am. Ecumenists; Alcuin Club; Soc. Promotion Religious Studies; R. Catholic; Address: 96 Empress Ave., Ottawa, Ont. K1R 7G2.

TILLEY, Donald Egerton, B.Sc., Ph.D.; educator; physicist b. Flushing, N.Y., 6 July 1925; s. Arthur and Florence Mary (Fortier) T.; came to Can. 1938; e. Mahwah (N.J.) Grammar Sch. 1938; Lakefield Coll. Sch. 1942; McGill Univ., B.Sc. (Hons. Math & Physics) 1948, Ph.D. (Physics) 1951; m. Margaret Elizabeth d. late James Ferrier Torrance, 5 June 1948; children: James Arthur, Margaret Anne, Peter Donald; PRINCIPAL, ROYAL MILITARY COLL. OF CANADA, 1979- ; Research Assoc., McGill Univ. 1951; joined Coll. militaire royal as Asst. Prof. 1952, Assoc. Prof. 1953-57, Prof. of Physics 1957-78, Head Dept. of Physics 1961-71, Dean, Science and Engn. 1969-78; served in 2nd World War Flying Offr., R.C.A.F. 1942-45; mem. Candn. Assn. Physcists; Am. Phys. Soc.; Am. Assn. Physics Teachers; mem. St. Johns Prot. Sch. Bd. 1964-72; rec'd Centennial Medal 1967; has researched in fields of nuclear physics and physics of dielectrics; co-author of, "Physics: A Modern Approach" 1970; "College Physics: A Text with Applications to the Life Sciences" 1971; "Physics in Medicine" 1972; "Physics for College Students" 1974; author "University Physics for Science & Engineering" 1976; "Contemporary College Physics" 1979; United Church; recreation: golf; Clubs: Cataraqui Golf and Country; Home 2 Hewett House, Royal Military College, Kingston, Ont. K7L 2W3 Office: Kingston, Ont. K7L 2W3

TILSTON, Frederick A., V.C., C.St.J., C.D., Phm. B., LL.D; joined Sterling Drug Ltd. 1930, apptd. Vice-Pres. i/c Sales 1946, Pres. 1958, Chrmn. Bd. 1970 till retired; during 2nd World War served in Essex Scottish; awarded V.C. as Co. Commdr.; wounded; awarded Coronation Medal, 1953; named "Man of the Year" by Independent Retail Druggists' Assn., 1965; Home: R.R. 1, Kettleby, Ont. L0G 1J0

TIMBRELL, David Yorke, M.A., F.C.A.; b. London, Eng., 20 June 1928; s. Vincent Yorke and Christine Margaret (Williams) T.; e. Thames Valley Grammar Sch., Eng.; St. John's Coll., Cambridge Univ., B.A. (Eng. & Law) 1950, M.A. 1969; C.A. (Ontario) 1956, F.C.A. 1968; m. E. Joan, d. A. E. R. Westman, Ph.D., Toronto, 28 March 1952; children: Peter Yorke, Jennifer Margaret; PARTNER COOPERS & LYBRAND, since 1959; Dir., Currie, Coopers & Lybrand Limited; Larry Smith & Assoc. Ltd.; mem. Taxation Adv. Comte., Dept. of National Revenue 1969-75; Gov. Candn. Tax Foundation 1979-81; Co-author, "Canadian Estate Planning", 1966; "Taxation of Mining Industry in Canada", 1967; "Canadian Taxation of Foreign Affiliates" 3rd Ed. 1981; "Essays on Tax Avoidance" 1979; mem. Candn. Inst. C.A.'s (Chrmn. Tax

Course 1967-70); Ont. Inst. C.A.'s; Candn. Tax Foundation; Clubs: University; The York; Strollers; Home: 62 Rowanwood Ave., Toronto, Ont. M4W 1Y9; Office: 145 King St. W., Toronto, Ont. M5H 1V8

TIMBRELL, Hon. Dennis Roy, M.P.P.; b. Kingston, Ont., 13 Nov. 1946; s. Walter William Sydney and Beryl (Clark) T.; e. Elem. and High Schs., Kingston and Scarborough, Ont.; Toronto Teacher's Coll.; Atkinson Coll., York Univ.; m. Janet Mary Lees, 1 Feb. 1980; 6 children: Michelle, Melanie, Mia, John, Ryan, Devon; MINISTER OF AGRICULTURE, 1982- ; PROV. OF ONT. taught math. and hist., Don Mills (Ont.) Jr. High Sch. 1967-70; Ald., Borough of N. York, 1969-72; el. M.P.P. prov. g.e. 1971, 1975, 1977 and 1981; Parlty, Asst. to Min. of Colls. and Univs. 1973-74; Min.-without-Portfolio, Ont., responsible for Youth Secretariat, 1974, becoming the youngest Minister in the history of Ont.; apptd. Min. of Energy Jan. 1975; Min. of Health, 1977-82; awarded Vanier Award, one of five Outstanding Young Candns. of 1975 by J. Chamber of Comm. Can., 1976; P. Conservative; Protestant; recreations: squash, tennis; Clubs: Albany; Victoria Village Civitan; Home: 23 Anewen Dr., Toronto, Ont. M4A 1R9; Office: 80 Grosvesnor St., 10th Floor, Hepburn Block, Queen's Park, Toronto, Ontario, M9A 2C4

TIMMIS, Denis William; industrialist; b. Bickley, Eng. 3 Dec. 1919; s. William Udal and Phyllis Irene (Bowater) T.; e. Wellington Coll., Eng.; came to Can. 1947; one s., Mark William; PRESIDENT, CHIEF EXTVE. OFFR. AND DIR. SANDWELL AND CO. LTD. since 1978; Dir., Canadian General Electric Company Ltd.; commenced as Accountant, Peat, Marwick, Mitchell, London, Eng. 1938; Asst. Controller Bowaters Newfoundland, Cornerbrook, Nfld. 1947-49, Corp. Secy. 1950-51; Secy., Bowaters Southern Paper Corp. Ltd., Calhoun, Tenn. 1952; Vice Pres., Bowaters Southern, Bowaters Carolina and Bowaters Board Co., Catawba, S.C. 1957-59; Mang. Dir., Tasman Pulp & Paper Co., Kawerau, N.Z. 1960; Depy. Chrmn. and Gen. Mgr., Bowater United Kingdom Pulp & Paper Co., London, Eng. 1963; Consultant, Sandwell & Co., Vancouver 1964; joined MacMillan Bloedel Ltd. 1964 and served successively as Mgr.-Special Projects, Extve. Asst. to Group Vice Pres.-Pulp and Paper, Group Vice Pres.-Pulp and Paper, Extve. vice Pres.-Operations and Pres. & CEO; served with Brit. and Indian Armies during World War II; active service Burma; rank Maj. on discharge; recreations: golf, bridge, gardening, fishing; Clubs: Vancouver; Shaughnessy Golf & Country; Home: 5005 Pine Cres., Vancouver, B.C. V6M 3P6; Office: 1550 Alberni St., Vancouver, B.C. V6G 1A4

TINGLEY, Rupert James, B.Sc.; transportation executive; b. Petitcodiac, N.B. 12 Jan. 1926; s. late John Lloyd and Hazel Pearl (Lounsbury) T.; e. Petitcodiac High Sch. 1942; Univ. of N.B., B.Sc. (Civil Engn.) 1950; m. Alice Joyce d. late Harold Carter 11 July 1953; children: Mary Ellen, James Carter, Nancy Irene; PRES., GEN. MGR. AND DIR., CN MARINE INC. 1979- ; joined CN 1950 serving in various engn., customer research, marketing and operating positions Atlantic Provs., Ont. and Nat. Hdqrs. Montreal; subsequently became responsible for modernization and mang. CN's Atlantic Ferry Operations; Dir. Moncton Comte. Atlantic Symphony Orchestra; Dir., N.B. Arthritis Soc.; Secy. and Dir. Atlantic Bapt. Sr. Citizens; Pres. FMH Management Ltd.; mem. & Chrmn., Can.'s Marine Transport. Research & Devel. Adv. Bd.; served with RCAF 3 yrs.; mem. Internat. Marine Transit Assn. (Past Pres. and Dir.); Dir., Tourism Industry Assn. of Can.; mem. Candn Comte, Lloyd's Register of Shipping; Pres. and Dir., Coastal Transport; Chmn. and Dir., Lakespan Marine Inc.; mem., Nat. Research Council, Adv. Comte on Artic Vessel and Marine Research; Assn. Prof. Engrs. N.B.; Bds. Trade Atlantic Provs.; Baptist; recreations: gardening, woodworking, travel; Club Rotary; Home: 15 Farview Dr., Moncton,

N.B. E1E 3C5; Office: 100 Cameron St., Moncton, N.B. E1C 5Y6.

TINNING, George Campbell, R.C.A.; artist; b. Saskatoon, Sask. 25 Feb. 1910; s. George Richard and Caroline Georgina (Campbell) T.; e. St. Johns and Earl Grey Schs. Winnipeg; Regina Coll. Inst.; paintings in perm. colls. Nat. Gallery Can., Nat. War Museum Ottawa, Montreal Museum of Fine Arts, Confed. Centre Art Gallery Charlottetown and other pub., corporate and private colls.; served with Can. army World War II Eng., Italy and Holland, War Artist, rank Capt.; el. Royal Canadian Academy, 1954; Anglican; recreation: walking; Address: The Linton, Apt. 52, 1509 Sherbrooke St. W., Montreal, Que. H3G 1M1.

TISDALL, John Charles Woodland; public relations consultant; b. Toronto, Ont., 8 May 1919; s. Frederick Fitz-Gerald Tisdall and Betty Alberta (Woodland) Tisdall Burton; e. St. Andrew's Coll., Aurora, Ont.; m. Diana Gage, d. William Martin Griffith, 29 Sept. 1951; twin d., Martha Gage, Marilee Carmen; MANAGING PARTNER, TISDALL, CLARK AND PARTNERS LIMITED; Ed-Announcer, Radio Stn. CHML, Hamilton, Ont., 1938-39; Dept. of Pub. Information, Ottawa, in charge of Consumer Information Service, 1940; later with Wartime Information Bd. becoming Assoc. Dir. of Indust. Information; scenario writer and Film Dir., J. Arthur Rank Organization, 1947; Dir. of Pub. Relations, Tandy Advertising Agency, Toronto, 1949; with partner formed Tisdall, Clark and Co. (now present firm), 1952; el. Chairman of Board 1967; rec'd Centennial Medal 1967; mem., Candn. Pub. Relations Soc. (Toronto) Inc. Pres. 1956-57; Candn. Pub. Relations Soc. (Accredited men., Nat. Pres. 1963-64 and Chrmn., Nat. Accreditation Bd., 1968-71); Pub. Relations Soc. Am. (Accredited mem.); Foundation for Pub. Relations Research and Educ., N.Y. (Trustee 1965-68); Chrmn. Internat. Accreditation Council; Anglican; recreations: music, reading, art; Home: 64 South Dr., Toronto, Ont. M4W 1R5; Office: 130 Bloor St. W., Toronto, Ont.

TITTEMORE, C. R., B.Sc.; executive; b. Regina, Sask., 13 Aug. 1921; s. E. L. and late Hazel (Robinson) T.; e. Univ. of Sask., B.Sc. (Chem. Engn.) 1942; m. Ruby Onishenko, 6 Aug. 1943; children: Robert, James; PRESIDENT AND DIR., THE PRICE COMPANY LIMITED; Exec. Vice-President & Dir., Abitibi-Price Inc.; with St. Maurice Chemicals Ltd. as Production Supv., Shawinigan, Que. 1942; Production Supv., Canadian Resins & Chemicals Ltd. 1945; Control Supt., Gaspesia Pulp & Paper Ltd., Chandler, Que. 1947, Control & Bleach Plant Supt. 1952; Asst. Gen. Supt., Price (Nfld.) Pulp & Paper Ltd., Grand Falls, Nfld. 1955, Gen. Supt. 1956, Mill Mgr. 1958, Asst. Gen. Mgr. 1960, Gen. Mgr. and Vice-Pres. 1962; headed joint venture for W. Coast Pulp Mill (subsequently dissolved) 1965; joined present Co. as Vice-Pres. 1968, Extve. Vice Pres. 1972; el. Pres., The Price Co. Ltd., 1973; mem. Candn. Pulp & Paper Assn.; Chem. Inst. of Can.; Office: Toronto-Dominion Centre, Toronto, Ont. M5K 1B3

TITUS, Richard Ford, B.Sc., B.E.; construction executive; b. Moncton, N.B., 22 Mar. 1921; s. late Harrison Burrill and Annie Belle (Ford) T.; e. Moncton (N.B.) High Sch. (Grad. 1939); Mount Allison Univ., 1939-40 (course interrupted by war), B.Sc. 1948; N.S. Tech. Coll., 1948-50, B.E. 1950; m. Annabel (Nancy), d. late Alexander S. Donald, 11 July 1942; children: Richard Hugh, Barbara Catherine; PRÉSIDENT, STANDARD PAVING MARITIME LTD., since April 1965; Vice-Pres., Standard Industries Ltd.; Pres., Hillsvale Farms Ltd.; joined Standard Paving Maritime Ltd., Halifax N.S., as Constr. Engr., 1950; apptd. Asst. Mgr., 1955; Mgr., Standard Paving Ltd., Toronto, Ont., 1956; Vice-Pres.-Constr., Standard Paving Maritime Ltd., 1959-65; Lieut, R.C.N.V.R., 1940-45; Lieut., R.C.N.(R), 1949-52; Past Pres, N.S. Road Builders

Assn.; Halifax Metro Centre Ltd.; Past Chrmn. Halifax Metro Centre Comn.; Pres., Nova Scotia Voyageurs (American Hockey League); mem., Assn. Prof. Engrs. Ont. and N.S.; Freemason; United Church; recreations: swimming, yachting, farming; Clubs: Granite (Toronto); Saraguay; Home: 1752 Dunvegan Dr., Halifax, N.S. B3H 4G1; Office: (P.O. Box 2106) Halifax, N.S. B3J 3B7

TIVY, Robert C., C.D., B.Sc., P.Eng.; executive; b. Fenelon Falls, Ont. 16 Oct. 1923; s. Clifford and Meta M. (Moffat) T.; e. Central Pub. and Peterborough (Ont.) Coll. Inst.; Queen's Univ., B.Sc. (Hons., Elec. Engn.) 1951; m. Ethel V., d. Thomas Wilson, Brockville, Ont. 2 June 1945; children: Jane W. (Johnston), Mary E.; CHMN. OF THE BD., BLACK & DECKER CANADA INC. since 1979; Vice Pres., Canadian-Pacific Operations since 1979; Dir. Black & Decker Canada, Australia, New Zealand, McCulloch Australia; Tradesman, Canadian General Electric, Peterborough 1939-42; Product Engr., Phillips Cables, Brockville 1951; Automatic Electric (GTE) 1953-70; joined present Co. as Dir. of Production 1970, Vice Pres. Mfg. 1970, Vice Pres. and Gen. Mgr. 1972; Pres, Gen. Mgr and Dir. 1974; served with Prince of Wales Rangers (Militia) 1939-41; Royal Candn. Inf. Active Service 1942-46; rank Lt; Brockville Rifles (Militia) retired rank Lt. Col., C.O.; mem. Brockville Dist. High Sch. Bd. 1960-64; mem. Assn.; Prof. Engrs. Ont.; Business Council on Nat. Issues; Anglican; recreations: boating, golf; Clubs: Bel Air Country Club, Los Angeles, California; Canadian (Los Angeles); Royal Candn. Mil. Inst.; Brockville Co. (Past Pres.); Home: 2423 Still Forest Rd., Baltimore, MD, 21208; Office: Black & Decker Americas International, Towson, MD, 21204

TOD, Murray Oswald Leslie; grain merchant; b. Walton-on Thames, Surrey, Eng., 5 May 1919; s. William Leslie and Marion Adamson (Mail) T.; e. Private Prep Schs., Eng.; Bradfield Coll., Berks., Eng., grad. 1936; Ecole Supérieure de Comm., Univ. of Neuchâtel French Dipl. 1937; m. Barbara Jean Dudley, d. Charles William Reid, Somerset, Eng., 24 May 1947; m. Vivian Evelyn Harrington (née Toews), 26 Aug. 1976; children: Brian William Leslie, Carol Astrid Susan, Diana Marion Karen; MANAGING DIR.; ANGLO CANADIAN GRAIN CO. LTD., to 1980; Dir., Market Development, Inter-Ocean Grain Co. Ltd. 1981- ; Pres. Redboine Grain Ltd.; Chrmn., Winnipeg Grain Exchange 1965-66; Trainee Dealer, London Metal Exchange, 1937-39; Ministry of Supply, Brit. Disposals Mission, Belgium, 1946-47; E. African High Comn. Kenya, 1948-50; Asst. and later Br. Mgr., Ralli Brothers Ltd., Nairobi, Kenya, 1950-55; Asst. becoming Canadian Mgr., Winnipeg, Man., 1955-62; served with R. A. 1939-46, India 1942-46, rank A/Lt. Col.; mem., Winnipeg Chamber Comm.; Eng. Speaking Union (Past Pres., Winnipeg Br.); Royal Commonwealth Soc. Pres.; Manitoba Br., 1980-); recreations: reading, gardening, golf, swimming; Clubs: Winnipeg Winter; Niakwa Country; Hon. Artillery Co. (London, Eng.); Home: 407 Kelvin Blvd., Winnipeg, Man. R3P 0J3; Office: 704 Grain Exchange Bldg., 167 Lombard Ave., Winnipeg, Man. R3B 0V3

TODD, F. Foster, B.Sc.; company director; b. Crisfield, Md., 7 April 1907; s. late Fred Foster and late Fanny (Pruitt) T.; e. Crisfield High Sch., 1925; Mich. Coll. of Mining and Technol., Engr. of Mines, B.Sc., 1928; came to Canada 1929; (Candn. Citizen 1941); m. Phyllis Webster, d. late David Corlette Fields, 7 April 1934; one d., Mrs. Urla Virginia Scott; Dir., Cochrane-Dunlap Ltd.; joined International Nickel Co. of Canada Limited as Engineer, Frood Mine, Copper Cliff, Ontario, 1929; Safety Engineer, Copper Cliff, 1937; General Foreman, Levack Mine, 1939; Superintendent, Murray Mine, 1942; Garson Mine, 1945; Asst. Supt. of Mines, Copper Cliff, 1952; Asst. Mgr., Man. Div., Thompson, Man., 1957; Gen. Mgr., Man. Div., 1962; Asst. Vice-Pres. and Gen. Mgr., Man. Div., 1964; trans. to N.Y. Office as Asst. Vice-Pres., International Nickel Co. of Canada, Ltd., 1965; Extve.

Vice-Pres., Toronto 1967-71; mem., Candn. Inst. Mining & Metall.; Am. Inst. Mining, Metall, and Petroleum Engrs.; Mid-West Metal Mining Assn. (Pres., 1964); Mining Assn. Can. (Dir., Pres. 1971-72); Mining & Metall. Soc. of Am.; Protestant; recreations: golf, hunting; Clubs: Mississauga Golf & Country; Copper Cliff (Ont.); Royal Poincinia Golf and Country (Florida); Home: 2 Ennisclare Dr., Oakville, Ont. L6J 4N2

TODD, William L., B.Eng.; b. Huntingdon, Que., 3 May 1916; s. Elizabeth Arnton (McEwen) and late William Stewart Todd; e. Elem. and High Schs., Huntingdon, Que.; McGill Univ., B.Eng. (Mech. Engn.) 1941; m. Ruth Katherine Winnifred Loken, 10 July 1948; children: Bruce, Bryan, Kevan, Marilyn Heather; retired Vice President, Stadler Hurter, Ltd. (Consulting Engineers); prior to joining Stadler Hurter, served in various capacities with Canadian Hoosier Engineering Company, Quebec Roads Dept., Malinckrodt Chemical Works, Defence Industries Ltd., St. Lawrence Corp., R. A. Rankin & Co.; served with RCN for 4 yrs. as Engr. offr.; discharged with rank of Lt. Commdr. (E) RCNVR; mem., Assn. Consulting Engrs. Can. Inc.; Candn. Pulp & Paper Assn.; Engn. Inst. Can.; Order of Engrs. Que.; Assn. Prof. Engrs. Ont.; Protestant; Home and Office: 377 Church St., Beaconsfield, Que. H9W 3R3

TOGO, Yukiyasu; executive; PRESIDENT AND DIR., TOYOTA CANADA INC.; Office: 1291 Bellamy Rd. N., Scarborough, Ont. M1H 1H9.

TOLMIE, J. Ross, Q.C., M.A., B.C.L.; b. Hartney, Man., 24 Aug. 1908; s. Dr. J. A. and Maude Emma (Ross) T.; e. Univ. of Brit. Columbia, B.A. 1929; Oxford Univ., B.A. (Juris.) M.A. and B.C.L. 1932; m. Helen Louise, d. Leon J. Ladner, Q.C., Vancouver, B.C. 6 July 1936; two d. and four s.; MEM. HERRIDGE, TOLMIE; called to the Bar of British Columbia 1932, and of Ontario, 1945; cr. Q.C. 1955; Solr. and Counsel to Income Tax Divn., Ottawa, 1935-41; Solr., Dept. of Finance, Ottawa, 1941-46; mem., Law Soc. of B.C.; Law Soc. of Upper Can.; Candn. Bar Assn.; Can.-U.S. Comte. of the Chamber of Comm.; author of "Canadian Tax Service", 1938; Liberal; Presbyterian; recreations: skiing, fishing, hunting; Clubs: Rideau; Cercle Universitaire; Home: 597 Mariposa Ave., Rockcliffe, Ottawa, Ont. K1M 0S3; Office: 116 Albert St., Ottawa, Ont. K1P 5G3

TOMARIN, Harry Paul; executive; b. Russia, 17 Jan. 1916; s. Samuel Paul and Millie (Rudolph) T.; came to Can. 1926; e. St. Catharines, Ont. pub. and high schs.; m. Adelle Eudice d. Maurice Slepkov 22 Nov. 1939; children: Seymour, Larry; CHRMN. AND CHIEF EXTVE. OFFR. NIAGARA STRUCTURAL STEEL (ST. CATHARINES) LTD. since 1977; joined Revzen & Tomarin, St. Catharines, Ont. 1937, estbd. Steel Warehouse br. 1946 and Steel Fabricating Plant 1948; formed Niagara Structural Steel Ltd. 1949 (inc. 1952); subsidiary Northern Steel formed Sept-Iles, Que. 1967; gentleman farmer (Tomarin Acres); served 4 yrs. Lincoln and Welland Regt. (Militia), rank Sgt.; Dir. Brock University; mem. St. Catharines Symphony; Hon. Dir. Shaw Theatre Bd.; mem. Un. Jewish Appeal; Candn. Chamber Comm.; Candn. Inst. Steel Constr. (Dir.); P. Conservative; Jewish; recreations: golf, fishing; Clubs: Lookout Point Golf; Niagara Falls; Canadian; Primrose; St. Catherines; Home: 18 Decew Rd., St. Catharines, Ont.; Office: (P.O. Box 730) 23 Smith St., St. Catharines, Ont. L2R 6Y6

TOMBALAKIAN, Artin S., B.A., M.A.Sc., Ph.D., F.C.I.C.; educator; b. Jerusalem, Palestine, 4 Nov. 1929; s. Sarkis and Mary T.; e. Am. Univ. of Beirut, B.A. 1952; Univ. of Toronto, M.A.Sc. 1954, Ph.D. (Chem. Engn.) 1958; m. Mary, d. Krikor Pandjardjian, 23 Aug. 1959; three d. Lisa Mary, Nora Jane, Celia Margaret; PROF. AND DIR., SCH. OF ENGN., LAURENTIAN UNIV. OF SUDBURY 1968-79, and Prof. of Chem. there; Head,

Dept. of Chem., Univ. of Sudbury, 1958-60 and of Laurentian Univ. of Sudbury, 1960-70; mem. Bd. of Govs., Cambrian Coll. of Applied Arts & Technol. 1971-78; research activities incl. diffusion & mass transfer across ion-exchange membranes, treatment of indust. waste waters, sorption of crude oil derivatives on Arctic terrain, processing of copper & nickel sulphide ores; designated Specialist in Chem. Processes 1973; author of various articles in prof. journs.; mem. Am. Chem. Soc.; Assn. Prof. Engrs. Ont.; Chem. Inst. Can.; CIM Metallurgical Soc., Armenian Apostolic Church; recreations: music, swimming, table tennis, bridge, fishing, hunting; Home: 172 Walford Rd. E., Sudbury, Ont. P3E 2G9

TOMBS, Laurence Chalmers, M.A., D.Sc.P.; transportation executive; b. Quebec City, Que., 23 July 1903; s. late Guy and late Isabella Ethel (Cree) T.; e. Argyle Sch. and Westmount High Sch., Montreal, Que.; McGill Univ., B.A. 1924, M.A. 1926; New Coll., Oxford; Univ. of Geneva, D.Sc.P. 1936; m. Eleanor Jean, B.A. d. late Rev. Professor F. C. Grant, Gwynedd, PA., 20 Sept. 1945; children: Catherine Joan Somma, Guy Matthew, Robert Laurence, George Frederick; one grandchild; CHAIRMAN, GUY TOMBS LTD. freight, shipping and travel agents (estbd. 1921); Consul of Finland, 1950-62, Consul General, 1962-70; President Emeritus, Canadian-Scandinavian Foundation; mem., Am.-Scandinavian Foundation; Life Gov., Montreal Gen. Hosp.; on Editorial Staff, Quebec 'Daily Telegraph', 1921-22; Govs. Grad. Fellow in Econ. and Pol. Science, McGill Univ., 1925-26; Extension Lectr., McGill Univ., 1927-28; with Guy Tombs Limited 1926-30 and since 1939; President of the Company 1964-1980; mem. of Communications and Transit Sec., League of Nations Secretariat, Geneva, 1930-39; entrusted with 22 League Missions in Belgium, Canada, Czechoslovakia, Denmark, France, Hungary, Poland, Portugal, Sweden, Switzerland and U.S.A.; carried out research on internat. organ. in European air transport for Social Science Research Council, N.Y., 1932-34; mem., Internat. Comn. for Asst. of Spanish Child Refugees, Paris, 1939, with missions in France and Ireland; Special Offr., Extve. Council, Que. 1942-44; Consultant, Brit. Overseas Airways Corporation, London, 1943-44; organ. H.O. of Internat. Air Transport Assn., Montreal, Que., 1945-46, as Extve. Secy.; missions in Washington, N.Y., London, Paris, Cairo, Chrmn. World Travel Cong., Paris 1951, Rome, 1953, San Francisco 1954; Del. of Finland, Assembly I.C.A.O., 1950-52; mem., Finnish Del. Expo '67; Chrmn of Internat. conf. at which was estbd. the Universal Organ. of Travel Agents Assns. (UOTAA), N.Y., 1964 and Treas. Montreal H.Q. 1965-67; designated "Ami de Paris" by Munic. Council, Commdr. & Offr., L'Ordre du Mérite Touristique (France); Commdr., Spanish Order Civil Merit; Kt. Commdr., Order of Balboa (Panama); Grand Officer of Merit, Sovereign Mil. Order of Malta; Star of Italian Solidarity (2nd Class); Commander, Finnish Order of the Lion; also rec'd two Mexican Govt. Certs. of Merit; Publications: "The Port of Montreal", 1926; "The Problems of Canadian Transportation," 1927; "International Organization in European Air Transport", 1936; "Early Portuguese Discovery and Exploration in Canada", 1963; mem. Canadian Inst. Travel Counsellors; Chambre de Comm. de la Province de Quebec (former mem. Bd.); Am. Soc. Travel Agts., Pres. 1953-54; Life mem., Candn. Hist. Assn.; Pres. (1954-56) former Candn. Inter-Am. Assn. (now Canadian Assn. for Latin Am.); Anglican; Club: University; Home: 42 Bretagne, St. Lambert, Que. J4S 1A4; Office: 1085 Beaver Hall Hill, Montreal, Que. H2Z 1S5

TOMKINSON, Constance (Lady Weeks); author; b. Canso, N.S., 22 June 1915; d. Rev. Harold Tomkinson, a minister of the Un. Ch. who held leading charges in E. Can., and Grace (Avard) Tomkinson, D.Litt; e. Public Schs. in McAdam and Moncton, N.B., and Yarmouth, N.S.; Yarmouth High Sch., Grad. 1935; attended the

Neighborhood Playhouse, N.Y. as a Scholarship Pupil in 1933 and grad. in 1935; m. Sir Hugh Weeks, Kt., C.M.G. 19 Nov. 1949; one d. Jane Avard Weeks; appeared as an actress on Broadway in the play "Libel" in 1935, and in repertory companies in Maryland and N.Y. state; appeared as a dancer in various shows in Eng., Sweden, France, Germany, Italy and Holland; during the war yrs. was a temporary Civil Servant in charge of the Dir. General's Office of the Brit. Min. of Supply in N.Y.; in 1945 engaged with the S. Command Entertainments Br. entertaining the troops in Eng.; in 1946 became Secy. of the Sadlers Wells Ballet at the Royal Opera House till 1948; in 1949 joined the staff of the Old Vic Theatre, London, and worked with them till 1952; since then has engaged in writing; author of: "Les Girls" (autobiography), 1956, Italian and Spanish eds. 1957; "African Follies", 1959; "What a Performance!" 1962; "Dancing Attendance" 1965; Protestant; recreation: travel; Address: 8 The Grove, Highgate Village, London N. 6, England.

TOMLINSON, George Herbert, Ph.D., F.R.S.C.; b. Fullerton, La., 2 May 1912 (came to Canada 1914); s. late George Herbert and Irene Loretta (Nourse) T.; e. Cornwall (Ont.) Coll. & Vocational Sch., 1928; Bishop's Univ., B.A. 1931 (Gov. Gen.'s and Lt. Gov.'s Medals 1931); McGill Univ., Ph.D. 1935; m. Frances Louise, d. late Samuel S. Fowler, Riondel, B.C., 17 July 1937; children: Peter, David, Susan; SR. RESEARCH ADVISOR DOMTAR INC., since 1977; Research Assoc., Dept. of Indust. & Cellulose Chem., McGill Univ., 1935-36; Chief Chem., Howard Smith Chemicals, 1937-40; Dir. of Research, Howard Smith Paper Mills, 1940-61; joined Domtar Ltd. as Dir. of Research 1961-70, Vice Pres. Research & Environmental Technol. 1970-77; inventor on no. of processes in pulp and paper indust.; mem., Corp., Bishop's University; awarded Weldon Medal 1947; Tappi Medal 1969; mem., Tech. Assn. Pulp & Paper Indust.; Candn. Pulp & Paper Assn. (Tech. Sec. Council); Candn. Inst. Chem.; Am. Chem. Soc.; Am. Assn. Advanc. Science; Delta Sigma Phi; Anglican; recreations: skiing, swimming, canoeing; Home: 920 Perrot Blvd. N., Ile Perrot, Que. J7V 3K1; Office: 395 de Maisonneuve Blvd. W., Montreal, Quebec. H3A 1L6

TONDINO, Gentile, R.C.A.; artist; educator; b. Montreal, Que. 3 Sept. 1923; s. Antonio and Lucia (Liberatore) T.; e. full-time apprenticeship with A. S. Scott 1942-47; Montreal Sch. of Art 1947-48; Montreal Museum of Fine Arts Sch. of Art & Design (under Dr. Arthur Lismer) Dipl. 1950, Art Centre Child and Adult Art Teaching 1952-53; m. Livia Helen d. Mario Martucci 14 Nov. 1945; children: Guido, Tristan, Lisa; ASSOC. PROF. OF DRAWING & PAINTING, FACULTY OF EDUC., McGILL UNIV. 1977- , Sch. of Arch. 1959- and Part-time Instr. in Sketching Summer Sch. 1966- ; Asst. in Adult Teaching Montreal Museum of Fine Arts 1952-53, Instr. in Basic and Advanced Drawing & Painting 1953-67; Instr. in Drawing & Painting McGill Univ. Dept. Fine Arts 1964-69; recipient Montreal Museum of Fine Arts Scholarship 1951; rep. in numerous exhns. since 1940's incl. Art Gallery of Ont., Brussels World Fair, Vancouver Art Gallery, Spring Exhns. Montreal Museum of Fine Arts, Candn. Group of Painters, R.C.A., Candn. Biennial Exhns.; mem. Candn. Group of Painters; Home: 4594 Earnscliffe, Montreal, Que. H3X 2P2; Office: 817 Sherbrooke St. W., Montreal, Que. H3A 2K6.

TOOLE, John L., B.A., C.A.; transportation executive (retired); b. London, Ont., 16 Feb. 1913; s. late Mabel (Leary) and Wade T.; e. Public and High Schs., Guelph, Ont.; Univ. of Toronto, B.A. (Comm. & Finance); C.A., Ont.; m. Elaine Patricia, d. late C.A. Callen, 9 Sept. 1943; Retired (1977) Dir., The Mortgage Insurance Company of Canada; MICC Investments Ltd.; Morguard Mortgage Investment Co. of Canada; Toronto College Street Centre Limited; Seachel Accommodations Ltd.; Markborough

Properties Ltd.; Auditor with Sholto Scott, C.A., 1938-40; Asst. to Group Acct., Canadian Industries Ltd. 1940-42; Asst. Controller, and later Control Mgr., Dominion Rubber Co. Ltd., 1942-49; Asst. Controller, Ford Motor Co. of Canada Ltd., 1949-54; Asst. Comptroller, Canadian Nat. Rlys., 1954-57, and Comptroller, 1957-59; Vice Pres., Acct. & Finance, 1959-68; Vice Pres. & Chrmn. CN Invest. Div. Candn. Nat. Rlys. 1968-77; Past mem. of Assn. of Am. Railroads; Inst. Chart. Accts. of Ont. and Que.; Sigma Chi; United Church; recreations: golf, photography; Home: 1133 Ocean Shore Blvd., Apt. 401, Ormond Beach, Florida 32074.

TOOLEY, James F., C.A.; financial consultant; b. Winnipeg, Manitoba, 9 Sept. 1915; s. Herbert and Hannah Sutherland (MacBeth) T.; e. St. Johns' Coll. Sch., Winnipeg, Man.; Univ. of Manitoba, C.A.; m. Dorothy Bernice, d. Arthur Yates, Victoria, B.C., 16 Sept. 1939; children: Mrs. David Kitteridge (Heather Jane). James Arthur, George; CHRMN., JAYTOWL INC. 1979- ; Chrm. and C.E.O., Nordair Ltd., 1967-79; Dir., Mitchell Holland Ltd., Marine Transport Ltd., Selkirk Navigation Ltd.; joined Canadair Ltd., 1947 as Asst. Comptroller; Comptroller, 1950-54; Vice-Pres. 1954-57; Pres. and C.E.O., CAE Industries Ltd., Montreal, 1957-67; mem., Inst. of Chart. Accts. Man.; United Church: Home: 3185 Delavigne Rd., Montreal, Que. H3Y 2C5; Office: Suite 2425, 1 Place Ville Marie, Montreal, Que. H3B 3M9

TOPPING, Coral Wesley, B.D., M.A., S.T.D., Ph.D.; university professor (emeritus); b. Fitzroy Harbour, Ont., 30 July 1889; s. Rev. Nassau Bolton, D.D., and Catherine (Cooke) T.; e. Queen's Univ., B.A. 1912, B.D. 1919; Wesleyan Theol. Coll., 1920 (Gold Medal); Travelling Fellow, Montreal Theol. Coll., 1920-22; Columbia Univ., M.A. 1921; Union Theol. Semy., S.T.M. 1921; Wesleyan Theol. Coll. S.T.D. 1925; Columbia Univ., Ph.D. 1929; m. Marjorie May, d. Rev. John Dunlop Ellis, D.D., 25 Aug. 1925; children: Ellis William, Helen May; o. London, Eng., 1917; Gov., Kingston Jail, 1918-19; boys' worker, Madison Square Ch. House, 1922; Prof. of Hist. & Sociol., Coll. of Puget Sound, 1923-25, Prof. of Sociol. 1926-29; Assoc. Prof., Dept. of Econ. Pol. Science & Sociol., Univ. of B.C., 1929-45; Prof., 1945-54, since when Emeritus; Prof. of Sociology, United Coll., Univ. of Manitoba 1954-57; Feature writer "Winnipeg Trubune", 1957; Prof. Wisconsin State Coll., 1959; Willamette Univ., 1959-60; has been a Visiting Prof. at numerous univs. in Can. and U.S.; 1941-57; served in World War, 1915-18, with 6th Candn. Field Ambulance; 21st Candn. Inf. Bn.; World War 1939-46, C.O.T.C. (Univ. of B.C.), 2nd in Command; retired as Maj.; mem., John Howard Soc. of B.C. (organ. Bd. mem., sometime Pres.); Un. Nations Soc. of B.C. (sometime Pres.); mem., Am. Social Assn. (Fellow); Pacific Sociol. Assn.; Candn. Correctional Assn.; Pacific N.W. Conf. on Family Relations (Past Pres.); Canadian Anthro. and Soc. Assn.; Elisabeth Fry Soc. (Life mem.); author of "Canadian Penal Institutions", 1929 (U.S. ed. 1930; revised ed. 1943; "Society Under Analysis" (with Elmer Pendell and others), 1942; "The Family and Modern Marriage", 1953, U.S. ed.; 1954; "Crime and You", 1960; "Jewish Flower Child", 1970; "Hot Words with Music", 1971; "Jesus Christ, Rabble Rouser", 1975; "The Jesus Revolution" 1976; "Blood on the Snows" (essays), 1980; articles in Brit., US and Candn. Mags.; Mu Sigma Delta; Pi Gamma Mu; United Church; recreations: gardening, bridge; Home: 4665 West Tenth Ave., Apt. 904, Vancouver, B.C. V6R 2J4

TOPPING, Frederick Victor, B.A.Sc.; company president; b. Toronto, Ont., 13 April 1924; s. Victor, B.A.Sc., M.A., M.Sc. and Agnes (White) Topping, M.B., B.S.; e. Pub. Schs., Toronto; Trinity Coll. Sch., Port Hope, Ont.; Univ. of Toronto (1945-51), B.A.Sc., 1951; m. Doris, d. Fred E. Pearson, Aug. 1947; three s. Christopher, Edward, Douglas; one d. Marilyn; PRESIDENT AND DIR., TOPPING ELECTRONICS LTD. since 1956; Pres. Spectrac Ltd. Holding Co.; Research Enterprises, Toronto, as Radar Inspr. 1940-42; Engineer, Canadian Radio Mfg., Toronto, 1951-54; Project Engr., Radio Condenser Ltd., Toronto, 1954-56; served with R.C.A., Staff Sgt., Radar Instr.; discharged 1945 (C.V.S.M.); mem., Fed. Govt. Electronic Trade Mission to S.E. Asia (1966); mem., Assn. Prof. Engrs. of Ont.; Candn. Mfrs. Assn.; contrib. of articles to mags. and journs. in field of electronics; articles on guns to "American Rifleman"; holder of patents re electronics; Anglican; recreations: boating, target shooting; Homes: 3 Kirkton Rd., Downsview, Ont. and Brocks Beach, Stayner, Ont. M3H 1K6; Office: 1320 Ellesmere Rd., Scarborough, Ont. M1P M2H 1K6

TORNO, Noah, M.B.E.; executive; b. Toronto, Ont., 27 Nov. 1910; s. Fred and Sophie T.; m. Rose Rein (Laine), 10 April 1950; one stepson, Michael Laine; Vice-Chrmn. Consumers Gas Co. Ltd.; Dir., Canada Trust and Canada Trustco; Consumers' Gas Co. Ltd.; 1001 Trust, World Wildlife Fund; Dir., Mount Sinai Hosp.; Treas., Mount Sinai Inst.; Past Chrmn., Royal Ont. Museum; served in 2nd World War with RCN, 1942-45 with rank of Lieut.; Life mem., Art Gallery Ont.; Royal Candn. Inst.; Haida, Inc.; Candn. Guild Crafts; Arch. Conserv. Ont.; Naval Offrs. Assn. Can.; Home: 155 Cumberland St., Toronto, Ont. M5R 1A2; Office: P.O. Box No. 3, Toronto-Dominion Centre Bank Tower, Toronto, Ont. M5K 1A1

TORREY, David L., B.A.; investment dealer; b. Ottawa, Ont., 6 Oct. 1931; s. Arthur Starrat and Josephine E. (Leonard) T.; e. Vermont Acad.; St. Lawrence Univ., B.A. (Econ.) 1953; Univ. of W. Ont., Grad. Sch. of Business Adm. Dipl. 1954; m. 17 Sept. 1955 (divorced); three s., two d.; VICE CHAIRMAN & DIR., PITFIELD MACKAY ROSS LTD.; 1980- ; Director, Canadian Stebbins Engineering & Manufacturing Co. Ltd.; Phillips Cables Ltd.; Total Petroleum (N.Am.) Ltd.; Wajax Ltd.; Pres., Pitfield, Mackay & Co. Inc. (N.Y.), 1963-71; Chrmn., Bd. of Mang., Montreal (Downtown) YMCA, 1972; mem. Council, Montreal Bd. Trade, 1968-70; Trustee, Vermont Acad., 1976-79; Chrmn., Bd. of Govs., Montreal Stock Exchange, 1972; Gov., Securities Indust. Assn. (N.Y.), 1971; Beta Theta Pi; United Church; recreations: sailing, golf; Clubs: St. James's; Royal Montreal Golf; Mount Royal; Home: 389 Carlyle Ave., Montreal, Que. H3R 1T3; Office: Suite 2101, 1 Place Ville Marie, Montreal, Que. H3B 4H5

TORY, John A., Q.C., LL.B.; PRES. & DIR. THE THOMSON CORP. LTD. and Thomson Equitable Corp. Ltd.; Pres. & Dir., The Woodbridge Co. Ltd.; Dep. Chrmn., & Dir., Thomson Newspapers Ltd.; Internat. Thomson Organization Ltd.; Vice-Chmn. and Dir., Thomson Newspapers Inc. (U.S.); Partner, Tory, Tory, DesLauriers & Binnington; Dir., The Royal Bank of Canada; Sun Life Assurance Co. of Canada; The Thomson Organisation Ltd. (U.K.); Rogers Radio Broadcasting Ltd.; Scottish & York Holdings Ltd.; Talcorp Associates Ltd.; Thomson British Holdings Ltd. (U.K.); Abitibi-Price Inc.; Hudson's Bay Co.; Starson Investment Ltd.; Rogers Cablesystems Ltd.; Trustee, Clarke Inst. of Psychiatry; Hon. Solr., Candn. Mental Health Assn.; Home: 41 Glenallan Rd., Toronto, Ont. M4N 1G9; Office: Office: 65 Queen St. W., Toronto, Ont. M5H 2M8

TOSSELL, William Ellwood, M.S.A., Ph.D.; educator; agronomist; b. Binbrook, Ont., 3 Jan. 1926; s. Franklin Edward and Elizabeth (Shannon) T.; e. Ont. Agric. Coll. Univ. of Toronto, B.S.A. 1947, M.S.A. 1948; Univ. of Wis., Ph.D. 1953; m. Jean Anne, d. Wilfrid Laurier Calander, 27 Dec. 1947; children: Karen Jean (Mrs. J. Vandergrift), David William, John Franklin; PROF. OF CROP SCIENCE, UNIV. OF GUELPH since 1953 and Dean of Research there since 1970; joined the Univ. (then Ont. Agric. Coll.) as Lectr. 1948, Asst. Prof. 1950-52, Chrmn., Crop Science Dept., 1961-66, Assoc. Dean of Coll. 1966-70; Visiting Prof. (Nuffield Fellow), Cambridge Univ.,

1973-74; author of over 50 scient. and tech. papers; mem., Candn. Soc. Agron. (Past Pres.); Candn. Assn. Univ. Research Adms. (Past Pres.); Agric. Inst. Can.; Am. Soc. Agron.; Crop Science Soc. Am.; Am. Assn. Advance. Science; Soc. Research Adms.; Candn. Assn. Univ. Teachers; Sigma Xi (Past President, Guelph); SITEC; Baptist; recreations: cottaging, woodwork, antiques; Home: 21 Norwich St.W., Guelph, Ont.

TOTEN, John Ernest, B.A.; economist; banker; b. London, Ont., 4 May 1918; s. Mabel Winifred (Bugler) and late Alfred George T.; e. Univ. of W. Ont., B.A. (Pol. and Econ. Science) 1948; m. Mary R., d. late Andrew Sweeton, Perth County, Ont., 19 Sept. 1942; children: Kenneth, Janet; VICE PRES. BANK OF MONTREAL,; joined Bank of Montreal at London, Ont., 1935 (returned after army service and univ.); apptd. Secy. Asst. to the Pres., 1951; a Br. Mgr. in Montreal, 1953; in 1955 engaged with Royal Comn. on Canada's Econ. Prospects (compiling survey of Candn. Service Industries); Asst. Mgr., Hamilton, Ont. Br. 1956; Asst. Supt. of W. Credit Dept., at H.O., Montreal, 1958; Associate Econ. Adviser, 1959, Econ. Adviser, 1961, Vice President Planning and Econ. 1965-75; Chief Economist 1975-78; served in 2nd World War; enlisted in Royal Candn. Engrs. Sept. 1939; discharged 1945 with rank of Q.M.Sgt.; Vice-Chrmn., Business and Ind. Adv. Comte. to OECD, Paris, France; Anglican; Club: University; Montreal; Home: 2241 All Saints Cres., Oakville, Ont. L6J 5N1; First Bank Tower, First Canadian Place, Toronto, Ont. M5X 1A1.

TOTH, Hon. Thomas; judge; b. Budapest, Hungary, 27 June 1925; s. Nicolas and Claire (Czàjlik) T.; e. Pères Piaristes Coll., Budapest, Baccalauréat classique 1943; Univ. of Budapest (Law and Pol. Science) 1943; Univ. of Fribourg (Post-Grad. studies in Law), Dr. Utriusque Iuris 1949; came to Can. 1950; m. Thérèse, d. Arsène Fournier, Granby, Qué., 3 Aug. 1954; children: Marie-Josée, François; JUSTICE, SUPERIOR COURT QUE.; Pres. (1967-71) Bd. Examiners, Bar of Que.; Pres. (1969-70) Assn. des Avocats du Province de Que.; called to Bar of Que. June 1956; R. Catholic; Office: Court House, Granby, Que.

TOULMIN, Margaret Clarisse, R.C.A.; sculptor; b. Bristol, Eng. 2 Oct. 1916; d. Christopher and Dorothy (Wilkins) Hayes; e. St. Faith's, Weston-super-Mare, Eng.; W. of Eng. Sch. of Art Bristol; m. William Toulmin 2 Nov. 1940; three s. Christopher, Alastair, Nicholas; came to Can. 1953; sculptor in clay, plaster and ceramics; rep. in churches, pub. and private colls.; W.U.K., Can. Iran and Nigeria; rec'd Premier Award 1950 Exhn. Abadan, Iran; Assoc. Royal W. of Eng. Acad. 1939; mem. Community Arts Council, Salt Spring Island, B.C.; Salt Spring Island Lady Lions; Anglican; recreations: gardening, boating, painting; Address: (P.O. Box 369) Ganges, B.C. V0S 1E0.

TOUPIN, Fernand, R.C.A.; artiste; né Montréal, Qué. 12 nov. 1930; f. Anatole et Albertine (Lapointe) T.; é. Mont-Saint-Louis Montréal; Ecole des Beaux-Arts de Montréal 1949; étudie la peinture avec Jean-Paul Jérôme 1949-53; ép. Yolande Labelle 28 août 1950; enfants: Pierre (d.), Ginette Toupin-Benoit; expositions personnelles: à Montréal: Galerie Denyse Delrue 1959; Galerie Agnès Lefort 1962; Galerie Camille Hébert 1965; Musée d'art contemporain 1967 (Quinze ans de peinture de Fernand Toupin), 1974; Galerie Gilles Corbeil 1970; 1980; Galerie Bernard Desroches 1974; 1976; Place des Arts 1977; Les jeunesses musicales du Can. Mont-Orford, Qué. 1977; Claude Gadoury Art Moderne 1979; Galerie Arnaud Paris 1970, 1972 et 1976; Centre Culturel canadien Paris (Rétrospective) 1972; Galerie Frédéric Palardy St-Lambert 1979; expositions de groupe comprenant Musée des Beaux-Arts de Montréal 1958 (Lauréat du 1er prix de cette exposition); Pavillon du Qué. Exposition Universelle d'Osaka 1970; IVe Festival Internat. de Peinture Cagnes-sur-Mer, France 1972 (Lauréat du prix national pour le Can.); Candn. Canvas exposition itinérante de tableaux grands formats dans neuf musées canadiens 1975; Musée d'art contemporain Montréal Jauran et les premiers plasticiens 1977; Internat. Art Exhn. N.Y. 1980; 10 ans de propositions géométriques Musée d'art contemporain 1980; collections publiques comprenant Musée du Qué., Galerie nationale du Can., Musée d'art contemporain, Statische Kuntsgalerie Bochum, Allemagne, Centre national d'art contemporain Paris; création de tapisseries, ateliers Pierre Daquin Paris 1970-72; création d'un décor aux Grands Ballets Canadiens 1974, 1977; sérigraphies: "Errances" album de sept sérigraphies sur des poèmes de Fernand Quellette 1975; "Prochain Episode" livre d'art comprenant quatorze sérigraphies et une gravure sur le roman d'Hubert Aquin 1978; mem. fondateur du groupe Les Plasticiens et co-signataire du manifeste des Plasticienss1955; Dir. des Expositions au Conseil Exécutif de l'Assn. des artistes non-figuratifs de Montréal 1957-58; mem. Assn. des Artistes Professionnels du Qué.; Opimian Soc.; Addresse: 3535 Papineau Ave., app. 1710, Montréal, Qué. H2K 4J9.

TOURILLON, Jules, B.A., B.A.Sc.; b. Montreal, Que., 15 July 1925; s. Théophile and Adéle (Delanoe) T.; e. Coll. Jean de Brébeuf, Montreal, B.A. 1945; Ecole Polytech. de Montréal, B.A.Sc. 1950; m. Thérèse, d. Wilfrid Girouard, 16 April 1945; children: Marie-Dominique, Louis, Danielle, Geneviève, Bernard: PRESIDENT AND GEN. MGR., DAVID LORD LIMITEE (vegetable cannery), since 1964; Treas. Louis Giroux & Associés Ltée; President, Managex Inc.; Dir., Mount Royal Rice Mills Ltd.; Plant Engr., The Solex Co. Ltd., Montreal, 1950-52; Plant Supt., 1952-54; Plant Supt. and Supvrv. Mgr. Engn., 1954-56; Plant Supt., Lido Biscuits Co., 1956-58, Gen. Mgr., 1958-64; mem., Ordre Engrs. Que.; R. Catholic; recreations: skiing, reading; Clubs: St-Denis; Home: 61 Courcelette, Outremont, Que. H2V 3A5; Office: 115-560 Henri-Bourassa Blvd. West, Montreal, Que. H3L 1P4

TOUSIGNANT, Claude, O.C.; artist; b. Montréal, Qué. 23 Dec. 1932; s. Alberic and Gilberte (Hardy-Lacasse) T.; e. Montréal Museum of Fine Arts Sch. of Art & Design 1948-51; m. Judith d. Neville Terry, Wantage, Berks., Eng.; 2 children: Isa and Zoë; rec'd Candn. Inst. Rome Prize 1973-74; Home: 4678 St. André, Montreal, Qué.; Office: 3684 St. Lawrence Blvd., Montréal, Qué.

TOVELL, Vincent Massey, M.A., R.C.A.; television producer; b. Toronto, Ont. 29 July 1922; s. Harold Murchison and Ruth Lillian (Massey) T.; e. Crescent Sch. Toronto; Washington Hall Brussels; Upper Can. Coll. Toronto 1940; Univ. of Toronto Schs. 1941; Univ. Coll. Univ. of Toronto B.A. 1945, M.A. 1946; Columbia Univ. 1948-50; EXTVE. PRODUCER, TV ARTS, MUSIC & SCIENCE, CBC Lectr. in Eng. Univ. Coll. Univ. of Toronto 1946-48; Actor, New Play Soc. Toronto 1946-46, Dir., Hart House Theatre 1947-48; CBC Radio 1942-48; Radio Producer, Writer, U.N.; New York and CBC Radio/TV Producer, Writer 1953-57; Producer, Writer and Performer CBC/TV since 1957; lectr. on TV York Univ., Ont. Inst. for Studies in Educ.; various lectures and panel seminars incl. Couchiching Conf.; Chrmn. 25th Anniversary Internat. Seminar Nat. Ballet Co. of Can. 1976, 20th Anniversary Internat. Seminar Nat. Ballet Sch. 1978; Trustee, Art Gallery of Ont.; Nat. Ballet Sch. of Can.; mem. Nat. Theatre Sch. Montreal; Chrmn. Adv. Arts Panel Can. Council 1966-70; Vice Pres. Royal Candn. Acad. Arts; co-author "Success of a Mission: Lord Durham in Canada" (3 TV scripts) 1960; created and produced "Images of Canada" CBC TV 1970-76; author various theatre reviews, scripts for radio and TV and documentaries; T.V. Producer/Director of "The Masseys" 1978; "The Owl and the Dynamo; The Vision of George Grant", 1980; "Fire & Sand: The Mysteries of GLass", 1981; rec'd Centennial Medal 1967; Queen's Silver Jubilee Medal 1978; mem. Candn. Conf. of Arts (Past Vice Pres.); Club: Arts & Letters; Home: Apt. 701, 190 St. George St., Toronto, Ont.

M5R 2N4; Office: (P.O. Box 500 Terminal A) Toronto, Ont. M5W 1E6.

TOWE, Peter Milburn, M.A.; diplomat; b. London, Ont., 1 Nov. 1922; s. Allen Milburn and Clare (Durdle) T.; e. Univ. of W. Ont., B.A. (Econ.); Queen's Univ. M.A. (Econ.); m. Carol, d. Walter Krumm, Sioux City, Iowa, 2 Aug. 1953; children: Christopher, Fredericka, Jennifer; CHMN., PETRO-CANADA INTERNATIONAL since 1981; served with Dept. of External Affairs since 1947 in Washington, Bonn, Beirut, Paris (Candn. Rep. to Organ. for Econ. Co-op. and Devel.); Depy. Dir. Gen., External Aid Office (now Candn. Internat. Devel. Agency) 1962-67; Min., Candn., Embassy Washington, D.C. 1967; Ambassador and Perm. Rep. to OECD 1972-75; Asst. Under-Secy. of State for External Affairs 1975-77; Ambassador to U.S.A. 1977-81; served overseas as an Offr. with R.C.A.F. Bomber Command, 1942-45; United Church; recreations: golf, fishing; Clubs: Royal Ottawa Golf; Five Lakes Fishing; Chevy Chase (Md.); Office: Ste. 707, 350 Sparks St., Ottawa K1R 7S8

TOWN, Harold Barling, O.C. (1968), Litt.D., A.R.C.A.; painter, sculptor, muralist, print maker; b. Ont., 13 June 1924; s. William Harry and Ellen Noelice (Watson) T.; e. Western Tech. Comm. Sch., Toronto, Ont. (Grad. 1942); Ont. Coll. of Art, Grad. 1944; Litt.D., York Univ. 1966; m. Trudella Carol, d. Eric Tredwell, Toronto, Ont., 3 Sept. 1957; two d. Heather, Shelley; exhibited first in 1956, Venice Biennale, Painters 11, Riverside Museum (N.Y.); since then has continuously exhibited in leading galleries, museums, etc. in chief cities of Can., U.S.A., Europe, S. Am., Mexico, Japan, Australia; Awards: Arno Prize, Sao Paulo Biennale, 1957; Prize Internat. Exhn. of Drawings & Prints, Lugano, Switzerland, 1958; 2nd Candn. Biennial, Nat. Gallery of Can. (2); Can. Council Purchase Award, Montreal Spring Show, 1960; Nat. Sec. (Hon. Mention Can.), Guggenheim, 1960; Baxter Award, Ont. Soc. Artists, 1961; Roy. Candn. Acad Honour Award, 1963; Grand Prix, Albert H. Robinson Award, Spring Show, Montreal Museum, 1963; Fellowship, Institute de Cultura, Hispanica, Arte de America 7 Espana, Madrid, 1963; Women's Comte., Toronto Art Gallery Prize, 1963; Medal Award, Montreal A.D.C., 1963; Primera, Bienal Americana de Grabado, Contemporaneo de La Universidad de Chile, Santiago, 2nd prize, 1964; Award of Merit, City of Toronto, 1979; (galleries) Tate, London, Eng.; Hamilton, Ont.; Edmonton, Alta.; Victoria, B.C.; Oshawa, Ont.; S. S. Kresge Collection, Detroit, Mich.; Allied Art Council, Lethbridge, Alta.; Burnaby (B.C.) Art Assn.; Ont. Govt. Collection, Ont. Place, Toronto; (museums): Modern Art and Metrop. Museum of Fine Art, N.Y.; Stedelijk, Amsterdam; Guggenheim, N.Y.; Brooklyn, N.Y.; Cleveland, Ohio; Modern Art, Sao Paulo; Fine Arts, Montreal; Beaverbrook, Fredericton, N.B.; Museo d'Arte Contemporaneo, Santiago, Chile; Balleria d'Arte di villa Ciani, Lugano; N.B. Museum; Saganaw (Mich.) Museum; (univs.): Hart House, Toronto; Sir George Williams; British Columbia; Queen's; Mount Allison; (major retrospective) opening exhn. Art Gallery of Windsor 1975; (commissions): two part mural and brass screen, Malton Airport, Toronto, 1963-64; Mural and Collage, Lobby, Telegram Building, Toronto, 1963 (since destroyed); Costumes and Decor, "House of Atreus", National Ballet, Toronto, 1963-64; Mural, Queen's Park Complex, Toronto; Toronto-Dominion Centre, Toronto; (design): Banner, Founders College, York Univ., Toronto, 1965; Publications: "Enigmas", text and drawings, plus original lithograph, 1964; original etching and drawings for "Anthology of Love Poetry", 1962; drawings "Love where the Nights are Long", Layton & Town, 1962; "Drawings Harold Town" (with text by Bob Fulford) 1969; "Silent Stars, Sound Stars, Film Stars" 1971; "Albert Franck, Keeper of the Lanes" 1974; co-author "Tom Thomson: The Silence and The Storm" (winner C.B.A. Book Award 1977); limited edition, 20th Anniversary Poster, Canadian Opera Co.; limited gen.

ed., Ontario Place Opening Poster; Film: "Pyramid of Roses" by Christopher Chapman, all drawings from the Vale Variation Suite, (shown Cannes 1980); One-man exhib., "Poets and Other People", Windsor Art Gal., Oct 1980; author, illustration "The Ice Rage of Inugrump" 1979 (Children's storey); Protestant; Home: 9 Castle Frank Cresc., Toronto, Ont. M4W 3A2; Office: Studio 6 and 4, 25 Severn St., Toronto, Ont. M9V 1M7 and Old Orchard Farm, Old Norwood Rd. R.R. 7, Peterborough, Ont. K9J 6X8

TOWNSEND, G. Leigh, B.Com., C.A.; manufacturer; b. Charlottetown, P.E.I. 2 Sept. 1932; s. William Arthur and Edna Jane (Cloutier) T.; e. Sir George Williams Univ., B.Com. 1961, Business Adm. 1962; C.A. 1964; m. Phyllis Earla, d. late Alfred Newbatt, 22 Dec. 1956; children: Bruce, Brian, Cynthia, Barry; GEN. MNG., SOUTH SHORE IND. LTD. 1980- ; Past Pres. Consolidex Inc., 1978-80; Vilas Industries Ltd. 1968-78; Supvr., Dupont of Canada 1954-63; Mgr., McDonald, Currie & Co. 1964, Extve. Vice Pres., Credico 1966; mem. Order C.A.'s Que.; Que. Furniture Mfg. Assn. (Pres.); Conseil du Patronat du Que. (Dir.); recreations: boating, skiing; Home: 93 Place Courcelle, St. Hilaire, Que. J3H 2S6; Office: 145, rue Anger, Ste.-Croix, Co. Lotbinière, Qué. G0S 2H0

TOWNSEND, Stuart R., M.D., C.M., F.R.C.P.(C), F.A.C.P.; physician; b. Montreal, Que. 2 June 1907; s. James Edward and Helen (Robertson) T.; e. High Sch. of Montreal 1925; McGill Univ. B.A. 1929, M.D., C.M. 1933; Harvard Univ. Research Fellow in Med. (Osler Scholarship 1936) 1936-37; m. Catherine L. d. James Anderson 27 March 1943; Consultant in Med., Montreal Gen. Hosp., former Dir. Div. of Hematology, former Sr. Physician, Rotating Jr. Internship 1933-34, Resident in Med. & Pediatrics W. Div. 1934-35, Sr. Resident in Med. Central Div. 1935-36; Asst. in Med. Johns Hopkins Univ. 1937-38; former Prof. of Med. McGill Univ.; Consultant in Med. RCAF 1942-45, rank Wing Commdr.; author over 50 scient. articles various N.Am. med. journs.; Fellow, Internat. Soc. Hematol.; mem. Am. Soc. Hematol.; Candn. Soc. Hematol.; Candn. Soc. Clin. Investigation; Candn. Soc. Immunol.; Montreal Med.-Chirurgical Soc. (Past Pres.); Osler Reporting Soc. (Past Pres.); Lafleur Reporting Soc. (Vice Pres.); Am. Fed. Clin. Research; Candn. Med. Assn.; Protestant; Address: 570 Chester Ave., Town of Mount Royal, Que. H3R 1W9.

TOZER, Edward T., B.A., Ph.D., F.G.S., F.G.S.A., F.R.S.C.; geologist; b. England, 13 Jan. 1928; s. Alfred and Olive Vera (Bicknell) T.; e. Cambridge Univ., B.A. 1948; Univ. of Toronto, Ph.D. 1952; m. Ruth Jane, d. Keith A. B. Wilson, Sussex, Eng., 7 Oct. 1958; children: Paul Alfred, Sally Jane; with Geol. Survey of Can. since 1952; Lectr. in Geol., Univ. of W. Ont., 1948-52; has publ. a no. of scient. reports and papers; Fellow, Arctic Inst. N. Am.; awarded Founders Medal, Royal Geographical Soc., 1969; Willet G. Miller Medal, Royal Soc. of Canada, 1979; recreations: sailing, skiing; Home: 548 Driveway, Ottawa, Ont. K1S 3N4; Office: 601 Booth St., Ottawa, Ont. K1A 0E8

TRABANDT, Joachim, LL.D., B.Sc. (Econ.); executive; b. Ruegenwalde, Germany 14 Dec. 1935; s. Paul and Charlotte (Ziebell) T.; e. Katharineum zu Luebeck (Coll.) 1956; Univ. of Hamburg Law Degree 1962, Faculté Internationale de Droit Comparé, Strasbourg, France, Diplôme de Droit comparé, Doctorate 1971; Univ. of London B.Sc. (Econ.) 1972; m. Hanna M. d. Franz Wulf 6 June 1961; two s. Jorg Joachim, Jan Uwe; PRESIDENT AND DIR., TRAFOR CORPORATION; Apprentice, Feder & Berg Export House, Hamburg 1956; Deutsche Bundesbank, 1963; Asst. to the Bd. Gerling-Konzern Globale, Cologne 1966; Asst. Mgr. Gerling Global Reinsurance Co. Ltd. London, Eng. 1967; Mgr. Gerling Insurance Service Co. Ltd. London 1969; Direktor, Concordia Lebensvers. A. G., Cologne 1970; Gen. Mgr. and Chief

Agt. for Can. Concordia Life Insurance Co. Toronto 1971; Pres., Colonia Life Ins. Co. and Colonia Life Holdings Ltd., 1977; Past Dir., Candn.-German Chamber Indust. & Comm.; German-Candn. Business & Prof. Assn.; mem., Mensa; Schlaraffia; recreations: sports, boating, reading; Office: 24 Ravenscroft Circle, Willowdale, Ont. M2K 1W9

TRACY, Clarence, B.A., Ph.D., D.C.L., F.R.S.C.; retired professor; b. Toronto, Ontario, 9 May 1908; s. Frederick and Charlotte (Haines) T.; e. Pub. & High Schs., Toronto, Ont.; Univ. of Toronto, B.A., 1930; Yale Univ., Ph.D., 1935; m. Minerva, d. D. Jacox, Edmonton, Alta., 20 Aug. 1940; children: Prudence, Nicholas, Sarah; Lectr. (Latin), Queen's Univ., 1930-31; Instr. (Eng.), Cornell Univ., 1934-36; Lectr., Asst. Prof. of Eng., Univ. of Alberta, 1936-47; Assoc. Prof. Univ. of N.B. 1947-50; Prof. Univ. of Sask., 1950-66 (Head of Dept. and Dean of Residence 1964-66); Prof., Univ. of British Columbia 1966-68; Prof. and Head., Dept. Eng., Acadia Univ. 1968-73; Visiting Prof. Univ. Toronto 1973-75; Adj., Univ. of Alta. Contingent, C.O.T.C., 1940-45; author, "The Artificial Bastard", 1953; Ed., "Poetical Works of Richard Savage", 1962; Richard Graves's "The Spiritual Quixote", 1967; Samuel Johnson's "Life of Savage", 1971; "The Rape Observ'd" 1974; many articles & reviews especially in "Queen's Quarterly"; mem., Modern Lang. Assn. Am.; Amer. Soc. for Eighteenth-Century Studies; Internat. Assn. Univ. Prof. of Eng.; Humanities Assn. Can.; Assn. Candn. Univ. Teachers of Eng.; Anglican; recreations: music, travel; Address: Port Maitland, N.S. B0W 2V0

TRAINOR, Hon. Richard Gerald; judge; b. Star City, Sask. 8 July 1930; s. Martin Gerald and Bertha May (McKenna) T.; e. St. Thomas Sch. and Sudbury (Ont.) High Sch. 1950; Univ. of Toronto 1953; Osgoode Hall Law Sch. Toronto 1958; m. Jacqueline St. Denis 24 Sept. 1955; children: Patricia, Therese, Martin, Jackie May, Susan, Jennifer; JUDGE, SUPREME COURT OF ONT.; called to Bar of Ont. 1958; cr. Q.C. 1974; R. Catholic; Home: 8 Echo Valley Rd., Islington, Ont.; Office: Osgoode Hall, Toronto, Ont. M5H 2N5.

TRAINOR, Hon. William Joseph, B.Sc., LL.B.; judge; b. Peace River, Alta. 11 Jan. 1923; e. Peace River Pub. and High Schs. 1939; Vermilion (Alta.) Sch. of Agric. 1939-40; Univ. of Alta. B.Sc. 1943; Univ. of B.C. LL.B. 1950; m. Gwendolyn Elizabeth Williams, Halifax, N.S. 1945; children: Michael, Brian, Monica, Niall, Christine; JUDGE, SUPREME COURT OF B.C. 1977- ; called to Bar of B.C. 1951, NWT 1971; cr. Q.C. 1972; Devel. Engr., Canadian Marconi Co., Montreal 1943-47; law practice Vancouver 1951-63; Police Magistrate and Judge of Juvenile Court - Y.T., Dist. Magistrate of Prov. Court B.C. 1963-68; Sr. Adv. Counsel, Dept. of Justice Ottawa 1968-73; Judge, Co. Court of Vancouver 1973, Sr. Judge 1975; Judge, Court Martial Appeal Court 1979- ; Lib. Cand. Burnaby-Richmond Riding Fed. g.e. 1962, 1963; R. Catholic; Home: 3416 Cedar Cres., Vancouver, B.C. V6J 2R3; Office: Law Courts, 800 Smithe St., Vancouver, B.C. V6Z 2E1.

TRANT, Gerald Ion, B.S.A., M.S., Ph.D.; Canadian civil servant; b. Toronto, Ont. 11 Oct. 1928; s. Frederick and Katherine Frances (Wadson) T.; e. Ont. Agric. Coll. Univ. of Toronto B.S.A. 1951; Mich. State Univ. M.S. 1954, Ph.D. 1959; SR. ASST. DEPY. MIN., POLICY ADVISOR, AGRICULTURE CANADA 1977- ; A.D.M., Farm Income Services Br.; Chrmn. Agric. Stabilization Bd.; Agric. Products Bd.; Dir. Farm Credit Corp.; Research Asst., Lectr. Ont. Agric. Coll. 1951-53, Assoc. Prof. 1958-62; Lectr. Mich. State Univ. 1955-47; Prof. in charge of Production, Univ. of Guelph 1962-66; Visiting Prof. Universidad del Valle, Colombia 1966-71; Dir. Gen. Econ. Br. Agric. Can. Ottawa 1972, Asst. Depy. Min. Econ. 1975-77; Anglican; recreations: skiing, swimming, reading; Office: Sir John Carling Bldg., 930 Carling Ave., Ottawa, Ont. K1A 0C5.

TREAT, Sanford M., Jr., B.A.; executive; b. Flushing, N.Y. 22 Jan. 1923; s. Sanford M. Treat; e. Deerfield Acad. 1942; Dartmouth Coll. B.A. 1949; Internat. Mang. Sch. Geneva 1956-57; widower; children: Cindy Hollister, Leslie, Sanford M., III; PRESIDENT, ALCAN PRODUCTS LTD. 1980- ; Dir. Aluminum Co. of Canada Ltd.; Alcan Aluminum Corp.; Trainee and Sales positions Aluminum Co. of Canada Ltd. 1950-54; Sales Area Mgr. Alcan Sales, Central Am. & Caribbean 1954-56; Pres. Alcan de Venezuela 1957-60; E. Dist. Sales Mgr. Alcan Sales 1961-63; Product & Marketing Mgr. Sheet & Plate, Alcan Sales & Alroll 1964-65; Nat. Sales Mgr. Alcan Aluminum Corp. 1965-71, Vice Pres. Sales Sheet & Plate Div. 1971-73, Vice Pres. & Gen. Mgr. Warren Profit Centre 1973-78, Extve. Vice Pres. Alcan Sheet & Plate 1978-80; recreations: tennis, skiing; Clubs: Ontario; Toronto Law Tennis; Downtown Tennis; Home: 65 Harbour Square, Apt. 3102, Toronto, Ont. M5R 2L4; Office: (P.O. Box 269) Toronto-Dominion Centre, Toronto, Ont. M5K 1K1.

TREDGETT, Roy Gordon, B.A.Sc., P.Eng.; executive; b. Toronto, Ont. 20 July 1925; s. Frank and Lucy (Cruikshank) T.; e. Public and High Schs. Toronto; Univ. of Toronto, B.A.Sc. 1947, Advanced Structural Hons. 1947; m. April, d. George Wilen 12 Oct. 1962; children: David, Judith, Martha, Mark, Jonathan; CONSULTING ENGINEER, DUNFIELD INVESTMENTS; 1980- ; joined Proctor & Redfern Inc., 1947, retired as Dir., Pres. & Gen. Mgr. 1980; mem. Bd. Govs. Ont. Bible Coll.; Am. Water Works Assn.; Candn. Inst. Pollution Control; Assn. Prof. Engrs. Ont.; Assn. Consulting Engrs. Ont.; Knox Presby.; recreations: golf, squash; Clubs: Thornhill Golf & Country; Granite; Home: 82 Highland Cres., Willowdale, Ont. M2L 1G9

TREMAINE, Marie, B.A., D.Litt.; bibliographer; b. Buffalo, N.Y., 23 Feb. 1902; d. William James Smith and Jeanette Elizabeth (Roe) T.; came to Canada, 1911; e. Humberside Coll. Inst., Toronto, Ont.; Univ. of Toronto, 1921-28, B.A. 1926; Univ. of London Sch. of Librarianship, 1929-30; Yale Univ., 1935-37; Trent Univ. D.Litt. 1976; Carnegie Scholar., 1929, Carnegie Fellowship, 1935-36; Reference Lib. and Assoc. Head of Reference Div., Toronto Public Libraries, 1927-47; bibliog., Arctic Inst. of North America, 1947-68; Publications: "Arctic Bibliography", 1953-69; "Bibliography of Canadiana", 1934; "Canadian Book of Printing", 1940; "Canadian Imprints 1751-1800", 1952; "Early Printing in Canada", 1934; various articles in prof. journs.; mem., Arctic Circle; Arctic Inst. N. Am.; Bibliographical Soc. Can.; Candn. Lib. Assn.; Ont. Lib. Assn.; Address: 1551-33rd St., N.W., Washington, D.C. 20007

TREMBLAY, Jean-Marc, B.A., LL.L.; advocate; telecommunications executive; b. Rimouski, Que., 27 Aug. 1932; s. Albert and Jeanne (Dubé) T.; e. Pub. Sch. Rimouski; St. Alexandre Coll., Hull, Que.; Coll. of Rimouski (Univ. Laval B.A. 1954); Univ. of Montreal, LL.L. 1957; m. Germaine, d. Euclide Sinclair, 26 July 1958; children: Pierre, Françoise, Kathleen; VICE PRESIDENT, HUMAN RESOURCES & LEGAL AFFAIRS, SECRETARY, QUEBEC-TELEPHONE; called to the Bar of Quebec 1958; legal practice in Matane, Que. until 1960; joined present Co. as Legal Adviser and Asst. Secy. 1960; Secy. and Gen. Counsel 1969; Vice Pres. Personnel, Gen Counsel and Secy.; K. of C.; R. Catholic; recreations: golf, curling, fishing, hunting; Club: Lions; Home: 145 Côté St., Rimouski, Que. G5L 2Y1; Office: 6 St. Jean St., Rimouski, Que. G5L 7E4

TREMBLAY, Lucien, Q.C., LL.D.; b. Verdun, Que., 25 March 1912; s. Joseph and Marie (Bois) T.; e. Richard Acad., Verdun, 1918-25; Semy. of St-Anthony, Three Rivers, Que., 1925-31; Semy. of Philos., Montreal, B.A. 1933; Univ. of Montreal, LL.M. 1936 and LL.D. 1944; LL.D. Laval Univ.; m. Jeannine, d. Henri Martin, Verdun, Que., 30 May 1939; children: Monique, Pierre, Jean,

François; Counsel, Gilbert, Magnan, Marcotte, Tremblay & Forget since 1978; Prof. Emeritus, Faculty of Law, Univ. of Montreal; read law with Justices E. F. Surveyer, Alphonse Decary and Jos. Blain, Q.C.; called to the Bar of Que. July 1936; cr. K.C. Nov. 1949; practised alone for one year and then in partnership with Raymond Eudes, 1937-44; with Letourneau, Tansey, Monk, de Grandpre, Lippe & Tremblay and Letourneau, Monk, Tremblay, Forest, Godbout & Deschênes, 1944-52; with Tremblay, Monk, Forget, Bruneau & Boivin and Tremblay, Monk, Deschênes, Forget & Boivin, 1952-61; Asst. Prof. of Civil Procedure, Univ. of Montreal, 1950-59; Chief Justice of Que. and Chief Justice Court of Queen's Bench Que. 1961-77; Past Counsellor of the Bar of Montreal and Del. to Gen. Council of the Bar of Que.; Roman Catholic; recreations: reading, fishing; Clubs: Quebec Garrison; Cercle de la Place d'Armes; Home: 209 Habitat '67, Cité du Havre, Montreal, Que. H3C 3R6;

TREMBLAY, Marc-Adélard, O.C., B.A., L.S.A., M.Soc., Ph.D.; anthropologue; né Les Eboulements, Comté de Charlevoix, Qué. 24 avril 1922; f. Willie et Laurette T.; é. Univ. de Montréal B.A. 1944, L.S.A. 1948; Univ. Laval M.Soc. 1950; Cornell Univ. Ph.D. 1954; ép. Jacqueline J. Georges Cyr 27 décembre 1949; enfants: Geneviève, Lorraine, Marc, Colette, Dominique, Suzanne; Dean, Grad. School, Laval Univ. 1971-79, et Prof. d'Anthropologie; Conseiller en recherche, Comn. d'enquête sur la santé et le bien-être Qué. 1967-69; Co-dir. des études sur l'enthnographic de la Cote Nord du Saint-Laurent 1971-76; mem. groupe de recherche en gérontologie 1971-73; Prés., Soc. Royale du Canada, 1981- ; auteur "Initiation à la recherche dans les sciences humaines" 1968; co-auteur "People of Cove and Woodlot: Communities from the Viewpoint of Social Psychiatry" vol. 11 1960; "Etude des conditions de vie, des besoins et des aspirations des familles salariées canadiennes-françaises" 1962; "Les comportements économiques de la famille salariée du Québec" 1964; "Les fondements sociaux de la maturation chez l'enfant" 1965; "Rural Canada in Transition" 1966; "Etude sur les Indiens contemporains du Canada" 1969; "Les changements socio-culturels à Saint-Augustin" 1969; "Famille et parenté en Acadie" 1971 "Changements dans l'organisation économique et sociale à Tête-à-la-Baleine" 1971; "Le jeu des cartes d'identité" (Télé-université) 1976; "The Individual, language and Society in Canada - L'individu, la langue et la Société au Canada" 1977; en collaboration "Une décennie de recherches au Centre d'études nordiques 1961-1970" 1971, éd. "Communities and Culture in French Canada" 1973, "Les Facettes de l'identité amérindienne" 1976; rapports articles, chapitres des livres; mem. Assn. Internat. des Sociologues de langue française; Am. Anthrop. Assn.; Soc. Applied Anthrop.; Soc. Med. Anthrop.; Assn. Can de Sociologie et d'anthropologie; Soc. canadienne d'ethnologie; Assn. des Sociologues et anthropologues de langue française; mem., Académie des Lettres et des Sciences Humaines de la Soc. Royal du Canada; Sec. Acad. des Sciences Morales et Politiques (Montreal); ca tholique; Adresse: 835 Nouvelle Orléans, Sainte Foy Qué. G1X 3J4; Bureau: Québec City, Qué.

TRENHOLME, Margery Wynne, B.A., B.L.S.; librarian b. Columbia, Missouri, 20 April 1913; d. Norman McLaren and Ethel Ida (Hurst) Trenholme; a Canadian citizen; came to Canada, 1921; e. High Sch. for Girls, Montreal, Que. (Grad. 1931); McGill Univ., B.A. 1935 (1st Class Hons. Classic), B.L.S. 1946; CHIEF LIBRARIAN THE FRASER-HICKSON INST., since 1950; teaching and business experience, 1936-45; Cataloguer in Foreign Law Dept., Library of Harvard Law Sch., Cambridge, Mass. 1946-47; McGill Sch. for Grad. Nurses Library, 1947-50; Gov., The Montreal Gen. Hosp.; Chrm., Fellowships Comm.Candn. Fed. Univ. Women; mem. ASTED; Que Lib. Assn.; Candn. Lib. Assn.; Corp. Prof. Librarians o Que.; Kappa Alpha Theta; Protestant; Club: Montrea University Women's (Candn. Fed.); Home: #5, 499

Clanranald, Montreal, Que. H3X 2S2; Office: 4855 Kensington, Montreal, Que. H3X 3S6

TRENT, John Elliot, M.A.; educator; b. Toronto, Ont. 12 May 1936; s. Gordon Chapman and Dorothy Agnes (Bell) T.; e. St. Andrew's Coll. Aurora 1953; Harvard University A.B. 1958; University of Toronto and Ryerson Dipls. in Journalism and Public Relations 1959; Sorbonne and Inst. d'Etudes Politiques 1963-64; Univ. de Montréal M.A. 1968; Queen's Univ. doctoral studies; m. Colette d. Antonio Alepins, Montréal, Qué. 26 June 1965; children: Deborah Marie, Andrew Powell, Patrick Leduc; Executive Director, Social Science Federation of Canada since January 1979, on leave as Asst. Prof. of Pol. Science, Univ. of Ottawa (since 1971); Bank of Toronto and Burns, Bros. & Denton, Toronto 1953-55; Pub. Relations Counsellor, Public and Industrial Relations Ltd. Toronto 1958-62; Lectr. in Pol. & Econ. Science Royal Mil. Coll. Kingston 1969-71; rec'd Govt. of Ont. Fellowship 1966-68; Can. Council Pre-doctoral Fellowship 1966-69; Press, Radio and TV Commentator, guest lectr.; author various articles, papers, reviews, reports; mem. Constitutional Comn Que. Lib. Party 1978-79; Secy.-Gen. Internat. Political Science Association since 1976 (Chrmn. Candn. Organ. Comte. IX World Congress, Montreal 1973); Pol. Science Rep. on International Social Science Council; Secretary-Treasurer, Canadian Political Science Association (1969-1976); Chrmn. Research and Policy Comte., Comte. for Independent Canada (1973-1974); Director Toronto Jr. Bd. Trade 1960-62; Dir., Canadian Political Science Assn. (1966-1968); Soc. Canadienne de science politique (Vice-Président, 1968-1969); Quebec Liberal Party; Club: Cercle Universitaire; Home: (C.P. 165) R.R. 1, Chelsea, Québec, J0X 1N0; Office: 151 Slater Street, Ottawa, Ontario.

TRENTMAN, John Allen, B.A., M.A., Ph.D.; university professor; b. Willmar, Minn. 17 Feb. 1935; came to Can. 1963; s. John Libory and Johannah Marie Violet (Johnson) T.; e. Univ. of Minn. B.A. 1956, M.A. 1958, Ph.D. 1964; Lunds Universitet, Lund, Sweden, 1958-59; Yale Univ. 1960-61; m. Florine Opal d. Oliver B. Tweeten 16 July 1955; children: Anne Elisabeth, Karna Marie, John Stefan Per, Denise Erika; PROF. OF PHILOSOPHY, MCGILL UNIV. since 1971; Gov. Mtl. Diocesan Theol. Coll. 1978- ; Instr. Univ. of Minn., 1961-63; at Huron Coll., Univ. W. Ont., Lectr. 1963-64, Asst. Prof., 1964-67, Acting Head, Dept. of Phil., 1965-67; came to McGill Univ. as Assoc. Prof., 1967-70, Chrmn. Dept. of Phil. 1967-72; Vice Dean, Humanities, Faculty of Arts and Science, 1968-71; Visiting Prof. and Lectr. at Univ. of Minn., 1966; O.I.S.E., Univ. of Toronto, 1972; Institut for Graesk og Latinsk Middelalder-filolgi, Københavns Universitet, 1974; Harvard Univ., 1977; Dir. McGill-Queen's Univ. Press, 1976-77; author of "Vincent Ferrer: Tractatus De Suppositionibus", 1977; "Scholasticism in the Seventeenth Century", Cambridge Hist. of Later Medieval Phil.; "Ferrer, Vincenz", Theologische Realenzyklopädie; other writings incl. contributions to books and professional jnls. on late medieval logic, metaphysics, natural law theory in the late middle ages and renaissance, and critical editions of medieval latin texts; rec'd. undergrad. athletic and academic scholarships; sometime Fellow, American-Scandinavian Foundation; Kent Fellow; Can. Council Leave Fellowship (1974-75); SSHRCC Leave Fellowship (1981-82); Corresponding Mem. HRCC; mem. Société Internationale pour l'Etude de la Phil. Médiévale; Soc. for Medieval and Renaissance Phil.; Soc. of Christian Phil.; Cambridge Bibliographical Soc.; Am. Catholic Phil. Assn.; Candn. Phil. Assn. (Co-Chrmn., Programme Cmte. 1978); Phi Beta Kappa; Anglican; Club: McGill Univ. Faculty (Pres. 1971); recreations: running, music; Home: 212 Kindersley, Mt. Royal, Que. H3R 1R7; Office: 1001 Sherbrooke St. W., Montreal, Que. H3A 1G5.

TRIANTIS, Stephen George, B.A., M.A., LL.B., Ph.D.; educator; b. Patras, Greece 4 Jan. 1918; s. George N. and Stefanie (Stefanou) T.; e. Gymnasium, Patras 1933; Univ. of Athens B.A. (Pol. Science & Econ.), LL.B. 1938; Univ. of Toronto M.A. (Econ.), Ph.D. 1949; m. Danae d. Andrew D. Nicoletopoulos 16 Sept. 1959; two s. George Gregory, Alexander John; PROF. OF ECON., UNIV. OF TORONTO 1964- ; Barrister and Solicitor 1939-44; joined Univ. of Toronto 1947, mem. Governing Council 1978- ; Adviser, Dept. Econ. & Devel. Govt. Ont. 1962, Candn. Internat. Devel. Agency, Government of Canada 1969, Select Comte. Ont. Leg. on Econ. & Cultural Nationalism 1972; Visiting Prof. Univ. of Calif. 1963; Consultant, Smith Comte. on Taxation in Ont. 1964, World Bank 1977; Econ. Adviser to Govt. of Greece 1965, Pres. Univ. of Patras 1965; Dir. Harvard Univ. Devel. Adv. Service in Greece 1966-67; Dir. January Sch. Toronto 1969-70; served with Greek Navy 1939-41, Brit. Army 1944-45; rec'd Athens Acad. Arts & Letters Prize 1944; mem. Ed. Adv. Bd. "International Encyclopedia of the Social Sciences" 1965-67; author "Common Market and Economic Development" 1965; "Cyclical Changes in Trade Balances of Countries Exporting Primary Products 1927-1933: A Comparative Study of Forty-Nine Countries" 1967; numerous contribs. to books and scholarly journs.; mem. Candn. Econ. Assn.; Candn. Inst. Internat. Affairs; Inter-Am. Stat Inst. (Constituent mem. 1965-76); Am. Econ. Assn.; Royal Econ. Soc.; Hellenic-Candn. Cultural Soc. (Vice Pres. 1960-63); Program Comte., Canadian Save the Children Fund; recreations: reading, music, philately; Home: 32 Elmsthorpe Ave., Toronto, Ont. M5P 2L6; Office: 100 St. George St., Toronto, Ont. M5S 1A1.

TRIGG, Eric Austin, B.Com., M.B.A.; industrialist; b. Verdun, Que., 5 Dec. 1923; s. Walter A. L. and Winifred (Tupling) T.; e. McGill Univ., B.Com. 1944; Harvard Business Sch., M.B.A. 1947; m. Marjorie Evelyn, d. John Berry, Dorval, Que., 20 Aug. 1949; children: Linda Joyce, Heather Ann, Eric Bruce, David Michael; SENIOR VICE PRESIDENT, DIRECTOR, ALCAN ALUMINIUM LIMITED; Pres. & Dir. Alcan Asia & South Pacific Ltd.; Dir., Hunter Douglas N.V.; Alcan Queensland Pty. Ltd.; Alcan Australia Ltd.; Alcan New Zealand Ltd.; Indian Aluminium Ltd.; Nippon Light Metal Co. Ltd.; Asst. Treas., Aluminum Co. of Canada, Ltd., 1951-54; Treas. and Chief Financial Offr., Alcan Industries Ltd. (U.K.), 1955-60; Treas. and Planning Officer, Alcan Aluminium Limited (Canada), 1963-64; Pres. and Dir., Alcan Aluminum Corp. 1965-70; Area General Manager (Europe, North Africa and Middle East) 1970-75; Extve. Vice Pres. 1975-81; served as Pilot Officer, R.C.A.F. during the 2nd World War; Protestant; recreations: golf, reading; Clubs: Wentworth (Virginia Water, Eng.); Canada (London, Eng.); University (Montreal and N.Y.); Mt. Royal; Mt. Bruno, Montreal; Home: 57 de Lavigne Rd., Westmount, Que. H3Y 2C3

TRIGGER, Bruce Graham, B.A., Ph.D., F.R.S.C., F.R.A.I.; anthropologist & archaeologist; educator; b. Cambridge (Preston), Ont. 18 June 1937; s. late John Wesley Dodd and Gertrude Elizabeth (Graham) T.; e. Preston (Ont.) and St. Marys (Ont.) Pub. Schs. 1950; St. Marys Coll. Inst. 1951; Stratford (Ont.) Coll. Inst. 1955; Univ. of Toronto B.A. 1959; Yale Univ. Ph.D. 1964; m. Barbara Marian d. Edgar S. Welch, Marlow, Eng. 7 Dec. 1968; children: Isabel Marian, Rosalyn Theodora; PROF. OF ANTHROP. McGILL UNIV. since 1969; Asst. Prof. Northwestern Univ. 1963-64; Asst. Prof. McGill Univ. 1964, Assoc. Prof. 1967, Chrmn. of Anthrop. 1970-75; Chief Archaeol. Pa.-Yale Expdn. to Egypt 1962; Staff Archaeol. Oriental Inst. Sudan Expdn. 1963-64; rec'd Queen's Silver Jubilee Medal; Cornplanter Medal for Iroquois Research, 1979; Riddell Award, 1980; Hoijer Lecturer, UCLA, 1981; Woodrow Wilson Fellowships 1959, 1963; Killam Award 1971; Can. Council Leave Fellowships 1968, 1977; Judge, Ste Marie Prize in Hist. since 1973; Adv. Bd., World Archaeology since 1968; mem. Council of the Inst. of Early Am. Hist. & Culture, 1980-

83; Bd. of Dir., Canadian Inst. in Egypt; McCord Museum, 1980- ; Ed. Bd., Ontario History, 1980- ; author "History and Settlement in Lower Nubia" 1965; "The Late Nubian Settlement at Arminna West" 1967; "Beyond History: The Methods of Prehistory" 1968; "The Huron: Farmers of the North" 1969; "The Meroitic Funerary Inscriptions from Arminna West" 1970; "Cartier's Hochelaga and the Dawson Site" 1972 (co-author); "The Children of Aataentsic: A History of the Huron People to 1660" 2 vols. 1976; "Nubia Under the Pharaohs" 1976; "Time and Traditions: Essays in Archaeological Interpretation" 1978; "Gordon Childe: Revolutions in Archaeology" 1980; vol editor, "Handbook of North American Indians", vol 15, Northeast, 1978; numerous articles ethnohist., African archaeol., Meroitic lang., theory & hist. of archaeol.; Fellow, Sigma Xi; Foreign Fellow, Am. Anthrop. Assn.; Fellow, Royal Anthrop. Inst.; recreations: sandcastles goldfish; Home: Apt. 603, 3495 Mountain St., Montreal, Que. H3G 2A5; Office: 855 Sherbrooke St. W., Montreal, Que. H3A 2T7.

TROPEA, Orland, B.Com.; public utilities executive; b. Toronto, Ont., 15 Feb. 1919; s. Joseph and Mary (Irwin) T.; e. Univ. of Toronto, B.Com. 1942; m. Elizabeth, d. late Percy Kaiser, 11 Dec. 1943; children: Ronald, Robert, Richard, Thomas, Peter, Elizabeth; VICE-CHRMN., BELL CANADA since Jan. 1980; Dir., Bell Canada; N.B. Telephone Co. Ltd.; Northern Telecom Canada Ltd.; Union Bank of Switzerland (Canada); Chrmn., Tele-Direct Ltd.; Ronalds-Federated Ltd.; joined present Co. 1942; held various mang. positions in Toronto and Montreal 1942-60; Accounting Mgr. for Montreal area 1960; Asst. Vice Pres. (Finance) 1961; Operations Mgr., N. Div., W. Area, Toronto, 1962 & 1965; Asst. Vice Pres. (Revenue Requirements), Montreal HQ, 1964; Comptroller, 1966, Vice Pres. (regulatory matters) 1968; Exec. Vice-Pres., (Administration) 1975; Exec. Vice-Pres., (Corporate) Apr. 1979; served as Meteorol. Offr. attached to RCAF 1943-46; Gov. Lakeshore Gen. Hosp.; mem., Telephone Pioneers Am. (Charles Fleetford Sise Chapter); Past Chrm., Can.-U.S. Committee Canadian Chamber of Comm.; past chrmn., extve. comte., Candn. Chamber of Comm.; Protestant; Clubs: Saint James's; Mt. Bruno Golf; Forest & Stream Home: 139 Bathurst, Pointe Claire, Que. H9S 5A2; Office: 1050 Beaver Hall Hill, Montreal, Que. H2Z 1S3

TROST, Walter Raymond, B.Sc., Ph.D., F.C.I.C.; b. Castor, Alta., 2 March 1919; s. Raymond and Hilda (Ulmer) T.; e. Castor (Alta.) High Sch.; Univ. of Alta., B.Sc. 1944; McGill Univ., Ph.D. 1947; Oxford Univ., Postdoctoral Fellow 1948; m. Margaret Grace, d. late Renaldo William Armstrong, 19 Sept. 1947; children: Heidi Helen, Richard Walter, Jennifer Margaret; Postdoctoral Fellow, Nat. Research Council, Ottawa, 1947; Asst. Prof. of Chem., Dalhousie Univ., 1948, Prof. 1960, Dean, Faculty of Grad. Studies 1961-66; apptd. Vice-Pres. (Academic) Univ. of Calgary 1966; with Mines Br., Dept. of Mines and Tech. Surveys, Ottawa and Univ. of Toronto, 1957-58; Chrmn., Div. of Inorganic Chem., Chem. Inst. Can., 1958-59; mem. Bd. Assn. Univs. and Colls. Can. 1962-66; mem. Bd., Defence Research Bd. 1962-68; Pres., LaBorde, Simat & Trost Ltd., Consultants 1969-70; Highridge Associates Ltd.; Chrmn., Alta. Environment Conserv. Authority, 1970-77; Pres., Candn. Assn. of Graduate Schools (CAGS) 1965; Vice Chrmn., Candn. Comte., Interrat, Union for the Conservation of Nature, (CCIUCN), 1977; author of over 60 patents, papers and reports on science education, resource and environment conservation, and other matters; Protestant; recreations: golf, gardening; Home: 3190 Ripon Rd., Victoria, B.C. V8R 6G5

TROTTER, Bernard, M.A.; university officer; b. Palo Alto, Cal., 24 March 1924; s. Reginald George and Prudence Hale (Fisher) T.; e. McMaster Univ. B.A. 1945; Acad. of Radio Arts Toronto 1946-47; Queen's Univ. M.A. 1948; Nat. Defence Coll. Can. Course V 1951-52; m.

Jean Cairns, d. James Findlay, Eng. 16 Sept. 1948; children: Reginald James, Victoria Jane; EXEC. DIR., COMMUNICATIONS AND EXTERNAL LIASON QUEEN'S UNIV.; Dir. Candian Broadcasting Corp. 1975-80; joined CBC as Asst. Talks Producer Winnipeg 1948, rep. at SN 1950-51, Head Eng. Lang. Sec. Internat. Service 1952, European Rep. London 1954, Supervising Producer TV Pub. Affairs Toronto 1957, Gen. Supvr. Pub. Affairs 1960-63; Extve. Asst. to Princ. 1963-68; Head of Academic Planning 1968-81; Queen's Univ.; mem. sub-comte. Comte. of Pres's Ont. Univs. to develop funding system for Ont. univs. 1967; Chrmn. Assn. Univs. and Colls. Can. Adv. Comte. on Univ. Planning 1972-73; Co-Chrmn. Council Ont. Univs. Comte. on Instructional Devel. 1972-75; Past Pres., Kingston Symphony Assoc.; author "Television and Technology in University Teaching" 1970; co-author "Towards 2000: the Future of Post-Secondary Education in Ontario" 1971; "Planning for Planning: Relationships Between Universities and Governments in Canada: Guidelines to Process" 1974; numerous other writings and broadcasts; mem. Candn. Soc. Study Higher Educ.; Assn. Inst. Research; Internat. Inst. Communication; Soc. Coll. & Univ. Planning; Club: Arts & Letters (Toronto); Homes: 320 King St. W., Kingston, Ont. K7L 2X1

TROTTIER, Armand; b. Québec, Qué., 7 Oct. 1923; s. Philippe and Alice (Hamel) T.; e. Coll. St-François d'Assise, Qué.; Séminaire St-Alphonse, Ste-Anne de Beaupré, Que.; Ecole Technique Qué.; m. Janine, d. Edmond Bolduc, 26 June 1946; children: Louise, Claude, Jean-Marc, Hélène, François, Stéphane; PRESIDENT, PHILIPPE TROTTIER INC. (indust. constr.); Past Pres., Candn. Construction Assn. Past Pres. Quebec Urban Community; Commr., Mun. Comn. Que.; R. Catholic; recreations: theatre; swimming; Address: 175 Blvd. Benoit XV, Quebec, Que. G1L 2Y8

TROTTIER, Pierre, B.A., LL.B.; diplomate; né Montréal, Qué. 21 mars 1925; f. Louis et Marie-Rose (Lalumière) T.; é. Coll. Jean-de-Brébeuf B.A. 1942; Univ. de Montréal LL.B. 1945; Harvard Univ. Center Internat. Affairs (Fellow) 1969; ép. Barbara Theis 24 avril 1952; enfants: Anne, Maxime, Jean; AMBASSADEUR ET DÉLÉGUÉ PERM. AUPRÈS DE L'UNESCO depuis 1979; Barreau de Québec 1946; postes diplomatiques à Moscou 1951 — 54, Jakarta 1956 — 57, Londres 1957 — 61; Conseiller culturel à Paris 1964 — 68; Ministre-Conseiller à Moscou 1970 — 73; Ambassadeur à Lima 1973 — 76; ouvrages parus: "Le Combat contre Tristan" 1951; "Poèmes de Russie" 1957; "Les Belles au Bois Dormant" 1960 (Prix David); "Le Retour d'Oedipe" 1962 (Prix de la Soc. des Gens de Lettres 1964); "Mon Babel" 1963; "Retour" 1970; "Sainte-Mémoire" 1972; "Un Pays baroque" 1979; mem. Soc. Royale du Can.; Catholique; récréations: la littérature, le voyage, la marche, la ou les modes (intellectuelles, artistiques, vestimentaires); club: Cercle Universitaire d'Ottawa; adresse: 40, av. Foch, 75116 Paris, France; bureau: 1, rue Miollis, 75015 Paris, France.

TROYER, Warner; journalist; b. Cochrane, Ont. 16 Jan. 1932; s. J. Gordon and Ruth (Warner) T.; m. 2ndly Anita (Gelnys); children: Peggy, Marc, Scott, Jill, Jennifer, John, Peter, Anne; former radio reporter, stringer Canadian Press, Toronto Star and ed. daily newspaper Portage la Prairie, Man.; Reporter, Winnipeg Free Press 1958-61; writer, dir. and producer CBC TV "Inquiry" 1961-64, "This Hour Has Seven Days" 1964-66, Extve. Producer "Public Eye" 1966-68, "W-5" 1968-70, "Fifth Estate" 1973-76, "Sunday Morning" 1977-79; Adjunct Professor (M.A. Course), Dept. of Journalism, U. of Western Ont., 1976-80; organizing nat. TV stn. govt. Sri Lanka 1980- ; author "No Safe Place" 1977; "Divorced Kids" 1979; "200 Days: Joe Clark in Power" 1980; "The Sound and the Fury: An Anecdotal History of canadian Broadcasting" 1980; various articles Candn. newspapers and mags.; rec'd Wilderness Award 1962; Canadian Editors' Guild Award, Documentary Category, 1971;

Assn. Candn. TV & Radio Artists 2 awards 1976; s, 1972; Awarded Ohio State Award for a series of 10 films: "Parts of the Sun", 1977; New York Internat. Film Festival Award; Office: 303 Davenport Rd., Toronto, Ont. M5R 1K5.

TRUDEAU, Clarence E.; b. Springfield, Mass., 8 June 1912; s. Ernest E. and Delia (Gemme) T.; e. Chicopee (Mass.) High Sch. (Grad. 1930); Bay Path. Inst., Springfield, Mass. (Grad. 1932); m. Rosina (d. 1976), d. late Michael Kamrad, 21 Sept. 1937; two d. Mary Rosina Bratty, Jo Anne; M. Margaret d. late James McDevitt 19 Feb. 1977; Auditor, Taylor Bunker & Co., C.P.A.'s Springfield, Mass., 1932-33; R. G. Rankin & Co., C.P.A.'s, New York City, 1933-34; Office Mgr., The Goodyear Tire & Rubber Co., Akron, Ohio, 1934-36; Sales Supv. 1936-39; Sales and Sales Supervision Work, CIT Corp., N.Y.C. 1939-43, Sales Supervisor, 1946-47, Assistant Vice-President, 1947-55; apptd. Vice-President, Canadian Acceptance Corp. Ltd., 1955, President and Director 1961, Chrmn. and Chief Extve. Offr. 1975-77; served in the 2nd World War with U.S. Army, 1943-46; European Theatre of Operations, August, 1944-March 1946; with 29th Inf. Div. as Staff Sgt.; mem., K. of C.; Roman Catholic; recreations: curling, golf; Clubs: Donalda; American; Home: 4 Forest Laneway, Apt. 2903, Willowdale, Ont. M2N 5X8

TRUDEAU, Rt. Hon. Pierre Elliott, P.C., Q.C., LL.D., F.R.S.C.; b. Montreal, Que., 18 Oct. 1919; s. Charles-Emile and Grace (Elliott) T.; e. Querbes Primary Sch., Montreal; Jean de Brébeuf Coll., Montreal, B.A. (Hons.) 1940; Univ. of Montreal, law degree with Hons. 1943; Harvard Univ., M.A. (Pol. Econ.) 1945; Ecole des Sciences Politiques, Paris and London Sch. of Econ., post-grad. studies in law, econ. and pol. science; LL.D. Alberta 1968; Queen's 1968; Hon. LL.D., Berkeley Campus, Univ. of California,1977; m. Margaret, d. Hon. James Sinclair, P.C., W. Vancouver, B.C., 4 March 1971; three sons, Justin Pierre James, Alexandre Emmanuel (Sacha), Michel Charles-Emile; RETURNED AS PRIME MINISTER OF CANADA, Feb. 18, 1980- ; Previously Prime Minister of Canada, 1968-79; called to Bar of Que. 1943; Q.C. 1969; joined P. Council Office, Ottawa, as Econ. and Policy Advisor, 1949; began practice of law specializing in labour law and civil liberties cases in Que., 1951; apptd. Assoc. Prof. of Law, Univ. of Montreal and mem. staff, Institut de Recherches en Droit Pub., 1961; el. to H. of C. for Mount Royal in g.e. 1965; re-el. g.e. 1968, 1972, 1974, 1979, 1980; served on Justice and Legal Affairs, External Affairs, Broadcasting and Assistance to Arts, and Divorce Comtes.; apptd. Parlty. Secy. to Prime Min., 1966, 1967; Min. of Justice and Atty. Gen. of Can., 1967; el. Leader of Lib. Party of Can. 6 Apl. 1968; del. to France-Can. Interparlty. Assn., Paris, 1966; rep. Can. at 21st Session of U.N. Gen. Assembly, 1966; toured French-speaking African states in 1967 on behalf of Prime Min. and Secy. of State for External Affairs; travelled extensively in Europe, Middle East and Asia, 1948-49; attended Internat. Econ. Conf., Moscow, 1952; co-founded, co-directed and major contrib. to "Cité Libre" (monthly review); author of "Federalism and the French Canadians," 1968; "Réponses", 1967; co-author, "Deux Innocents en Chine," 1961; contrib. to "Canadian Dualism/La Dualité Canadienne," 1960; "The Future of Canadian Federalism," 1965; "Politics: Canada," 1966; has written numerous articles and papers in socio-econ. and pol. fields for many publs.; Founding mem., Montreal Civil Liberties Union; recreations: skiing, flying, scuba-diving, canoeing; Office: House of Commons, Ottawa, Ont. K1A 0AZ.

TRUDEL, Marcel, O.C. (1971), Docteur ès lettres; (1967); né St-Narcisse-de-Champlain, Qué., 29 mai 1917; é. Univ. Laval, B.A., 1938; L.ès lettres, 1941; d.ès lettres summa cum laude, 1945; Univ. Harvard, recherches, 1945-47; ép. Anne Chrétien, 11 Juil. 1942; enfants: Jean-

ne, Madeleine, Marc.; ép. Micheline d'Allaire, 27 août 1970; DIR. DEPART. D'HISTOIRE, UNIV. D'OTTAWA de 1966 à 1968; prof. Coll. Bourget, Rigaud, 1941-45; prof. d'hist. du Can., Univ. Laval, 1947-65; Univ. Carleton 1965-66; sec., Inst. d'Hist. et Géog., Laval, 1948-54; dir., 1954-55; dir., Inst. d'Hist., Laval, 1955-64; sec., Fac. des lettres, Laval, 1952-58; dir., Inst. of Candn. Studies, Carleton Univ., 1965-66; conférencier; Inst. Scient.fr.-can., 1957; a la Sorbonne et l'Inst. cath. de Paris, a l'Univ. de Poitiers, France; Gray Lectures, Univ. de Toronto, 1966; président, Candn. Hist. Assn., 1963-64; dir. gén. adj. de vol I "Dict. biogr. du Can."; dir., "Revue canad. d'hist. soc."; dir. de collection, "Hist. de la Nlle-Fr."; dir. adj., "Centre de recherche en hist. relig. du Can."; co-dir. de collect., "Fleur de Lys"; prés., Conseil des Arts de Qué.; membre: Acad. can-fr.; Acad. berrichonne; bur. comm. des Monuments et lieux hist. du Can.; jury, Aff. univ. dans Conseil des Arts du Can.; prix David, 1945 et 1951; prix Casgrain, 1961; prix Concours Litt. du Qué., 1963 et 1966; prix Duvernay, 1966; prix Gouv. Gén., 1967; prix Molson, 1980; Médailles: Léo-Pariseau, 1960; Tyrrell, 1964; ouvrages; L'influence de Voltaire au Can., 1945; Vézine, 1946; Louis XVI, le Congrès amér. et le Canada, 1949; Carte seign. de la Nlle-Fr., 1950; Hist. du Can. par les textes, 1952; La régime milit. dans le Gouvernment des Trois-Riv., 1952; L'affaire Jumonville, 1953; Chiniquy, Les Trois-Riv., 1955; Le régime seigneurial, 1956; Champlain, 1956; L'Eglise can. sous le régime milit. (2 vol) 1956, 1957; L'esclavage au Can.fr., 1960; Atlas hist. du Can.fr., 1961; Hist. de la Nlle-Fr., vol I, 1963; vol. II, 1966; Canada: Unity and Diversity, 1967; Initiation à la Nlle-Fr., 1968; Jacques Cartier, 1968; "Le Terrier du Saint-Laurent en 1663", 1972; "La Population du Canada en 1663" 1973; "The Beginning of New France", 1972; "Les débuts du régime seigneurial au Canada", 1974; "La formation d'une Société: Montréal 1642-1663", 1976; "La révolution américaine" 1976; La seigneurie descent-associés", Kome 1; "Les evenements", 1979; Adresse d'Affaires: Université d'Ottawa, Ottawa, Ont. J9H 1G1

TRUEMAN, Albert William, O.C. (1974), M.A., D.Litt., LL.D., D.S.L.; b. Waverley, Penn., 17 Jan. 1902; s. John Main and Clara Louise (Huff) T.; e. Colchester Acad., Truro, N.S.; Mt. Allison Univ., B.A. 1927 and Hon. D.Litt. 1945; Oxford Univ., M.A. 1932; Univ. of Chicago and Columbia Univ. (summer session); D.Litt., St. Francis Xavier, Windsor; LL.D., Man., New Brunswick, Laval, Dalhousie, Victoria, Memorial, W. Ont.; Waterloo Lutheran; Univ. of Toronto D.S.L.; m. Jean, d. W. A. Miller, Charlottetown, P.E.I., 8 June 1931; children: Peter, Sara; Headmaster, Stanstead Coll., 1927-28; Asst. Prof. of Eng., Mt. Allison Univ., 1930-37, Head of Dept. 1937-42; Supt. of Pub. Sch. System, Saint John, N.B., 1942-45; Pres., Univ. of Manitoba, 1945-48; Pres., Univ. of New Brunswick, 1948-53; Commr., National Film Bd., 1953-57; Dir., The Canada Council 1957-65; Principal and Dean of University Coll., Univ. of W. Ont. 1965-67 when named Chancellor of the Univ.; apptd. Visiting Prof., Dept. of Eng., Carleton Univ., Ottawa, 1967; Dir., Saint John Public Library, 1942-45; Interim Chrmn., Candn. Legion Educ. Services, N.B., 1945; Pres., Assn. of Candn. Clubs, 1952-53; Bd. of Gov., C.B.C., 1944-45; author of "The United Empire Loyalists", 1946; "Candian University of New Brunswick"; United Church; recreations: music, golf, billiards; Club: Rideau; Address: 407 Wood Ave., Rockcliffe, Ottawa, Ont. K1M 1J8

TRUMP, Edwin Martin; b. Vancouver, B.C., 15 June 1926; s. Edwin and Gertrude Mary (Martin) T.; e. Kerrisdale Sch.; Pt. Grey Jr. High Sch. and Magee High Sch., Vancouver, B.C.; Univ. of Brit. Columbia; Queen's Univ.; m. Veronica Irene Wasyliw, 12 May 1953; children: Stephen Anthony, Geoffrey Allan, Christopher Martin; VICE PRESIDENT, HOSPITAL DIVISION, AND DIRECTOR, JOHNSON & JOHNSON INC.; has served with Candn. Electrical Supply Co., Aviation Electric Ltd., Candn. Aviation Electronics (liaison between CAE and

Curtiss-Wright) became Purchasing Agent, Dumont Television Div.; joined present Co. as Dir. of Purchasing; apptd. Vice Pres., Purchasing and Distrib. 1964; served 18 months on Active Service during 2nd World War; Past Dir., Home Owners Assn., Dollard Des Ormeaux; Past Div. Chrmn., Candn. Cancer Soc.; has addressed various trade and prof. groups on purchasing and written no. of articles for trade journs.; Past Nat. Chrmn., (1975-76), Packaging Assn. Can., Past Pres. (1966-67); Purchasing Mang. Assn. Can.; Protestant; recreations: fishing, music; Home: 149 Aspen St., Dollard Des Ormeaux, Que. H9A 2N9; Office: 2155 Pie IX Blvd., Montreal, Que. H1V 2E4

TRYNCHY, Hon. Peter Jr., M.L.A.; businessman, farmer; b. Rochfort Bridge, Alta. 22 Aug. 1931; s. Peter and Anna (Roszko) T.; e. Rochfort Bridge (Alta.) Schs.; m. Lorraine Mary d. Frank Wilkinson Sr., Mayerthorpe, Alta. 29 Oct. 1952; children: Darlene Annette, Marlin Peter; MIN. OF RECREATION AND PARKS, ALTA. since 1979; owner Paddle Farm Equipment, Mayerthorpe Mar. and various farms; served Mayerthorpe Town Council 6 yrs.; first el. M.L.A. Alta. g.e. 1971, re-el. g.e. 1975 and 1979; Past Pres. Mayerthorpe Chamber Comm.; mem. Royal Cndn. Legion; Freemason (P.M.); Kinsman; P. Conservative; United Church; recreations: baseball, curling, golf; Club: Mayerthorpe Curling (Dir.); Home: (P.O. Box 449) Mayerthorpe, Alta. T0E 1N0; Office: 107 Legislative Bldg., Edmonton, Alta. T5K 2B6.

TRYON, Victor Weld, Jr., B.A.; company executive; b. Manhattan, Montana, 2 Feb. 1914; s. Victor W. and Grace (Brown) T.; e. (came to Canada, 1918) Winnipeg (Man.) Pub. and High Schs.; Univ. of Manitoba, B.A. 1933; m. Constance Janet, d. late Travers Sweatman, K.C., 13 Nov. 1943; children: Alix Tremaine, Victor W. 3rd; Vice President, Pratt & Whitney Aircraft of Canada Ltd., 1976-79; after grad. employed by International Petroleum Co. Ltd. and posted to Colombia, S.A.; left in 1946 to join present Co. as Gen. Acct.; promoted to Treas., 1947; el. a Dir., 1960; mem., Montreal Chapter, Financial Extves. Inst. (Past Pres.); Delta Kappa Epsilon; recreation: golf; Clubs: Royal Montreal Golf; Hamilton Golf and Country; Home: 148 Colonial Court, Burlington, Ont.).

TUBBY, Allan, B.Eng., LL.D. (Hon); contractor; b. Saskatoon, Sask., 27 March 1910; s. Harry James and Gertrude (Bowles) T.; e. Pub. Sch. and Nutana Collegiate, Saskatoon, Sask.; Univ. of Sask., B.Eng. (Civil) 1932; Univ. of Sask., LL.D., 1972; m. Margaret McPherson, d. late David W. Mundell, 6 Aug. 1938; two d., Janet Kathleen, Susan Mildred; PRESIDENT, TUBBY & WILKS CONTRACTORS LTD., (Gen. Contractors), Past Chrmn., Bd. of Govs., Univ. of Saskatchewan; Pres., Saskatoon Bd. of Trade, 1962; Past Pres., Assn. of Prof. Engrs. of Sask.; Past Chrmn., Sask. Br., Engn. Inst. of Can.; Vice-Pres. for Sask., Candn. Constr. Assn.; Offr. in charge (Flight Lieut.), No. 3 Training Command, Montreal, 1942-45; Saskatoon B'nai B'rith Lodge, "We Are Proud of You Award", 1977; Freemason (32° Scot. Rite; Shrine); Protestant; recreations: golf, curling; Clubs: Saskatoon City; Riverside Golf & Country; Rotary; Home: 302 Cumberland Ave. N., Saskatoon, Sask. S7N 1M5; Office: 1802 Ontario Ave., Saskatoon, Sask. S7K 1T3

TUCK, John A., Q.C., B.A., LL.B.; executive; b. Niagara Falls, Ont., 12 Feb. 1913; s. Dr. John R. and Elizabeth (Cleghorn) T.; e. Univ. of Alberta, B.A. 1932, LL.B. 1935; m. Dorothy, d. William Reed, Toronto, Ont., 10 Aug. 1938; children: John, David, Margaret, Barbara; Exec. Dir., Arbitrators' Inst. of Can. Inc.; Past. Pres., Toronto Rehab. Centre; Past Chairman, Ins. Law Sec., Candn. Bar Assn.; read law with Woods, Field, Craig & Hyndman, Edmonton, Alta.; called to Bar of Alta., 1936, and to Bar of Ont., 1947; cr. Q.C. 1955; practised law with Woods, Field, Craig & Hyndman, Edmonton, Alta.,

1936-37; joined staff of Candn. Life Ins. Assn. as Legal Asst., Dec. 1937; apptd. Asst. Gen. Counsel 1948, Gen. Counsel 1955, Mang. Dir. & Gen. Counsel 1961, Mang. Dir. 1966; Extve. Dir. 1972-78; Dir., Equitable Life Ins. Co. of Can.; Toronto Rehabilitation Centre; Arbitrators Inst. of Can., Inc.; Delta Upsilon; Un. Church; recreations: golf, curling; Clubs: Rosedale Golf; Toronto Cricket, Skating & Curling; Home: 177 Alexandra Blvd., Toronto, Ont. M4R 1M3;

TUFFIN, George Guild; executive; b. London, Ont., 8 Oct. 1920; s. Francis Arthur and Annie Guild (Turbyne) T.; e. London, Ont.; m. Eunice, d. William F. Chapman, 13 Dec. 1944; two d. Marsha, Janis; CHRMN. OF BD., PRESIDENT, DIR. AND CHIEF EXTVE. OFFR., ESSELTE PENDAFLEX CANADA INC. since 1971; commenced with London Life Insurance Co. as Clerk 1938, rejoining that Co. after war service; in Sales Dept. 1946, Supt., Ont. 1948; Mgr., Philips Industries Ltd., Lighting Div., Toronto 1953, Mgr. Lighting and Philishave Divs. 1957; Asst. to Pres., Eagle Pencil Co. of Canada Ltd. 1959, Vice-Pres., Gen. Mgr. and Dir. 1960; Vice-Pres., North-Rite Ltd. 1965; Pres., Eagle and North-Rite 1967; Pres. and Dir., Berol Corp. of Canada Ltd. 1970; served in 2nd World War, R.C.A.F. 1940-45; served in Middle E., Europe and U.K. with R.A.F.; rank on discharge Flight Lt.; mem. Candn. Chamber Comm.; Candn. Mfrs. Assn.; United Church; Clubs: Granite; Lambton Golf; Rotary; Freemason; Home: 343 Glengrove Ave. W., Toronto, Ont. M5N 1W4; Office: 200 Norseman St., Toronto, Ont. M8Z 5M7

TULLY, John Patrick, M.B.E. (1945), B.Sc., ph.D., F.R.S.C.; oceanographer; research scientist; b. Brandon, Man., 29 Nov. 1906; s. John and Agnes (Mott) T.; e. Winnipeg (Man.) Pub. Schs.; Univ. of Man., B.Sc. 1931; Univ. of Wash., Ph.D. 1948; m. Ethel Lorraine, d. late James Hamilton, 18 Sept. 1938; children: Jean Agnes (Prout), Anne Lorraine (Gill), James Hamilton; Consultant in Oceanography to Chrmn., Fisheries Research Bd.; Secy., Candn. Comte. on Oceanography; joined staff of Biol. Stn., Nanaimo, B.C., upon grad.; led Fisheries Research Bd's oceanographic program on Pacific coast for many yrs.; apptd. Oceanographer-in-Charge, Pacific Oceanographic Group, 1946; seconded to RCN as Scientist, 1942-46; mem., Nanaimo Sch. Bd., 1953-55; Nanaimo Civil Defence, 1940-43; B.C. Research Council, 1960-64; author of many scient. papers in field of oceanography; has rep. Can. at scient. meetings throughout world; rec'd Coronation Medal 1953; Medaille Commemorative de Prince Albert I de Monaco (Manley-Bendall Prize) 1967; Queen's Silver Jubilee Medal 1978; past mem., Inst. Chem.; Candn. Inst. Chem.; mem., Am. Geophys. Union; Am. Soc. Limnology & Oceanography; Am. Assn. Advanc. Science (W.Div.) (Pres. 1963); Sigma Xi; United Church; recreation: swimming; Home: 2740 Fandell Ave., Nanaimo, B.C. V9S 3R3

TULVING, Ruth, R.C.A.; artist; b. Estonia 23 Dec. 1932; d. Edward and Hilda (Martinson) Mikkelsaar; came to Can. 1949; e. Ont. Coll. of Art grad. 1962; California Coll. of Art; Paris, France; m. 1951; children: Elo Ann, Linda; many solo exhns. Can., USA and Europe; rep. in numerous nat. and private colls.; Vice Pres. Ont. Soc. Artists; Club: 21 McGill; Address: 45 Baby Point Cres., Toronto, Ont. M6S 2B7.

TUPPER, Rev. Borden Roger, D.D. (Un. Ch.); b. Round Hill, Annapolis Co., N.S., 2 June 1904; s. Maj. James Howard and Letitia May (McLaughlin) T.; e. Dalhousie Univ., B.A. 1927; Pine Hill Divinity Hall, 1929 (Hon. D.D. 1963); m. Janet Selina, d. William Piggott, Bridgetown, N.S., 25 June 1930; children: Joyce Elizabeth, Anne Marie, James Howard, William Bruce; Pres., Hants Co. Council of Home & Sch., 1941-42; Chrmn., Maritime Conf. Fund, 1942-47; Secy., Bd. of Govs., Halifax Prot. Orphans' Home, 1944-57; Stat. Secy., Halifax Presby.,

1944-54; Pres., N.S. Temperance Fed., 1949; Pres., Halifax Br., Candn. Mental Health Assn., 1955-56; mem., Bd. of Atlantic Christian Training Center, 1954-58 (Secy. 1956-58); mem. Senate, Pine Hill Divinity Hall, 1958-61; Min., Loch Katrine-Lochaber, 1929-39,, Shubenacadie, N.S., 1939-43, Halifax United Mem. Ch., 1943-61 and Sambro United Ch., 1961-69; retired in 1969; recreations: woodwork, gardening; Home: 63 Woodlawn Rd., Dartmouth, N.S. B2W 2S2

TURCOT, Lt.-Gen. G. A., C.M.M., C.D., B.A.; b. Québec, Que., 9 December 1917; s. René and Yvonne (Légaré) T.; e. Laval Univ., B.A.; m. Helen, d. William P. Mitchell; two d.; with N.P.A.M., Les Voltigeurs de Québec, 1935-39 (2nd Lieut., Lieut.); Active Army, Royal 22e Regt., 1939; served in U.K. (1939), Sicily (1943), Italy (1943-44), France, Netherlands, Germany (1945); apptd. C.O., R22eR., 1945; awarded Croix de Guerre; attended Candn. Staff Coll., 1946, Gen. Staff Appt., Army Hdqrs., Ottawa, 1947; re-apptd. C.O., R22eR, 1948-49; Candn. Joint Staff, London, Eng., 1950-52; attended Jt. Services Staff Coll., Eng., 1952; Dir. of Mil. Operations, AHQ Ottawa, 1952-56; attended Nat. Def. Coll., Canada, 1956; Mil. Adviser, Internat. Supervisory Comn., Indo China, 1957-58; Offr. in charge of Adm., Hdqrs. Quebec Command, Montreal, Que., 1958-59; Commdr., 1st Canadian Inf. Brigade Group, Calgary, Alta., 1959-62; Dir.-Gen. of Mil. Training, AHQ Ottawa, 1962-64, G.O.C., E. Command, Halifax 1964-66; Commdr. of Allied Command Europe Mobile Force, 1966-69; Commdr., Mobile Command 1969 till retired 9 Dec. 1972; Capt. 1940, Major 1941, Lieut.-Col. 1943, Col. 1952, Brig. 1959, Maj.-Gen. 1964, Lt.-Gen. 1969; Dir.-Gen. Services, Organising Comte. of Olympic Games Montréal 1976; Past Pres. The Last Post Fund Que. Br. 1978; Roman Catholic; Clubs: United Service; Hermitage; Address: "La Redoute", R.R. 3, Magog, Que. J1X 3W4

TURCOTTE, The Hon. L. Sherman, LL.D.; retired Justice; b. Grand'mere, Que., 10 Oct. 1904; s. Alex and Mary Elizabeth (Kelly) T.; e. Univ. of Alberta, LL.B. (cum laude) 1924; m. late Agnes V. Dinwoodie, 5 Aug. 1940; Supernumerary Justice since 1979; Chancellor (first), Univ. of Lethbridge 1968-72; called to the Bar of Alta., Dec., 1925; practised law at Vegreville, Alta., 1925-29, Cardston, Alta. 1929-36, Lethbridge, Alta., 1936-55; apptd. Dist. Court Judge for Dist. of S. Alta. 1955; Chief Judge Dist. Court S. Alta. 1969-75; Assoc. Chief Judge Dist. Court Alta. 1975; Justice of Court of Queens Bench, June 30, 1979; retired Oct. 10, 1979; mem. of Lethbridge City Council for two yr. terms, 1944 and 1946; re-el. 1949; Mayor of Lethbridge, 1950-53 and Alderman, 1953-55; Liberal cand. for Lethbridge (Fed.) 1945 (def.) and 1949 (def.); rec'd. Hon. LL.D. Lethbridge 1972; recreation: golf; Home: 626 17th St. S., Lethbridge, Alta. T1J 3C6

TURMEL, Antoine; excutive; b. Thetford Mines, Que.; s. Irenée and Claire (Hébert) T.; e. Semy. de Sherbrooke; Alexander Hamilton Inst. (Extension courses); Laval Univ.; Univ. of Sherbrooke Hon. Degree in Business Adm. 1970; children: André, Jean-François, Hélène, Marie-Josée; CHRMN. OF BD. AND CEO, PROVIGO INC. since 1969 and Dir. Provigo's wholly-owned subsidiaries; Chrmn. of Bd., M. Loeb Ltd.; National Drug Ltd.; Horne & Pitfield Foods Ltd.; Market Wholesale Grocery Co. (Cal.); Dir., Nat. Bank of Canada; The Provident Assurance Co.; UAP Inc.; Quebec-Telephone Co.; Canadian General Electric Co. Ltd.; Montreal Heart Inst. Research Fund; Noranda Mines Limited; Shell Can. Ltd.; Gov., Prov. Que. Chamber Comm.; Past Gov. Montreal Stock Exchange; named "Man of the Month" Commerce Review 1963; French Candn. Man of Yr. 1967; "Personality of the Year in the Food Industry" l'Assn. des Détaillants en Alimentation 1977; Hon. Dir. Order St. John, Que. Council 1978; Chrmn. 1972 Pub. Subscription Campaign Univ. Sherbrooke; mem., Can. Chamber of Commerce; Montreal Bd. of Trade; Montreal Chamber of Commerce;

Conseil du Patronat du Qué.; Montreal Corporate Headquarters Committee; Montreal Assn. for Recreational & Cultural Action; Adv. Council, HEC (affiliated to Univ. of Montreal); Liberal; R. Catholic; recreations: golf, bridge; Clubs: Longchamp Golf (Dir. since 1972); Saint James's; Forest and Stream; Home: 32 Surrey Gdns., Westmount, Que. H3Y 1N6; Office: 800 Dorchester Blvd. W. Suite 500, Montreal, Que. H3B 1Y2.

TURMEL, Hon. Gerard, B.A., LL.L.; judge; b. Beauce Co., Que. 26 June 1926; s. Leon and Marie-Ange T.; e. La Verendrye Sch. and Lebrun Sch. Montreal; Ste-Therese Coll.; Ste-Croix Coll. B.A.; Univ. of Montreal LL.L. 1954; m. Suzanne d. late Hon. L. A. Giroux 18 Aug. 1956; children: Helene, Benoit, Lucie, François, Antoine; JUDGE; SUPERIOR COURT OF QUE.; called to Bar of Que. 1954; cr. Q.C. 1969; R. Catholic; Club: Cowansville Country; Home: 116 Pine, Cowansville, Que. J2K 2G6.

TURNBULL, A.M. Gordon, M.A., LL.B., C.A.; financial executive; b. Dumfries, Scot. 29 Dec. 1935; s. Catherine R. and late Rev. R. W. Turnbull, B.D.; e. Univ. of Edinburgh M.A. 1956, LL.B. 1958; Inst. of C. A.'s Scot., C.A. 1960; m. Karen M. d. Fred B. Walker, York, Eng. 1965; children: Candida, Andrew; VICE PRES. & TREASURER, INDAL LTD., 1981- ; joined Price Waterhouse & Co. Paris 1960-62; U.S. Time Corp. (Timex) Besancon, France 1962-63 and Waterbury, Conn. 1963-64; Group Financial Controller, Formica International Ltd., London, Eng. 1965-70; Finance Dir. Donald Macpherson Group Ltd., London 1970-77; Controller & Asst. Treas., Indal Ltd., 1978-81; Office: 4000 Weston Rd., Weston, Ont. M9L 2W8; Home: 2590 Homelands Drive, Mississauga, Ont., L5K 1H6.

TURNER, Edward Kerr; agricultural executive; b. Maymont, Sask., 6 Apl. 1927; e. Sch. of Agric., Univ. of Sask.; m. Patricia Melville Bright, 5 July 1950; three d., Janice, Joy, Jill; PRESIDENT, SASK. WHEAT POOL; Pres., Bd. of Dirs., Candn. Co-o. Wheat Producers Ltd.; Candn. Pool Agencies; Pool Insurance Co.; Bd. mem., Western Co-op. Fertilizers Ltd.; Xcan Grain Ltd.; Can. Grains Council; mem., Agric. Econ. Research Council of Can.; Adv. Comte., Candn. Wheat Bd.; Adv. Council to Min. of Indust., Trade & Comm.; toured India as mem. agric. group to observe agric. production and marketing and Candn. aid programs, 1966; mem. Duke of Edinburgh's Third Commonwealth Conf., Australia, 1968; mem. Candn.-Am. Comte. of Private Planning Assn.; Un. Ch.; recreation: sports; Home: 1527 Parker St., Regina, Sask. S4S 4R9; Office: Albert & Victoria, Regina, Sask.

TURNER, Harold Melvin, Jr., B.A.; advertising executive; b. Toronto, Ont. 20 Jan. 1927; s. Harold Melvin and Esther (Joel) T.; e. Public and High Schs., Toronto, Ont.; Tufts Univ. B.A. 1950; m. Gloria, d. Arthur Coops 30 Sept. 1950; children: Judith, Jeffrey; CHRM., INTERMART INC. and CHRMN. MacLaren Advertising since 1974; with General Electric, Corp. Advertising and Public Relations N.Y. 1950; joined present Co. as Media Space Buyer 1952, Radio and TV Dept. 1953, Acct. Extve. 1954, Acct. Mang. Corp. Devel., Vice-Pres. 1962; Dir. Children's Broadcast Inst.; Chmn., Young Naturalist Fdn.; Dir., Ont. Community Centre for the Deaf; Metropolitan Zoological Soc.; Canadian Business Health Research Inst.; Trustee, Royal Ont. Museum; mem. Toronto Bd. Trade; Inst. Candn. Advertising; Business Council on Nat. Issues; Delta Tau Delta; recreations: tennis, squash, sailing; Clubs: Caledon Mountain Trout; Queen's; Toronto; R.C.Y.C.; University; Toronto; Home: Apt. #608, 61 St. Clair Ave. West, Toronto, Ont. M4V 2Y8; Office: 415 Yonge St., Toronto, Ont. M5B 2E6

TURNER, Hon. John, P.C., Q.C., M.A., B.C.L.; b. Richmond, England 7 June 1929; s. Leonard and Phyllis (Gregory) T.; came to Canada 1932; e. Normal Model Pub. Sch., Ottawa, Ont. 1934-39; Ashbury Coll., 1939-42; St.

Patrick's Coll., 1942-45; Univ. of B.C., B.A. (Pol. Science, Hons.) 1949; Rhodes Scholar, Oxford Univ., B.A. (Juris) 1951, B.C.L. 1952, M.A. 1957; Univ. of Paris 1952-53; m. Geills McCrae Kilgour, 11 May, 1963; one d. Elizabeth; three s. Michael, David, Andrew; Partner, McMillan, Binch; Dir., Bechtel Canada Ltd.; C. P. Ltd.; Candn. Investment Fund Ltd.; Credit Foncier; MacMillan Bloedel Ltd.; Marathon Realty Ltd.; Massey-Ferguson Ltd.; Sandoz(Can.) Ltd.; The Seagram Co. Ltd.; Wander Ltd.; Candn. Council of Christian and Jews; Salvation Army Metro Toronto; Toronto Sch. of Theology; Collegium of St. Michael's College; read law with Stikeman & Elliott, Montreal, Que., and practised with them after being called to English Bar 1953; Bar of Quebec 1954, of Ont. 1968, of B.C. 1969, of Yukon and N.W.T. 1969; cr. Q.C. 1968; el. to H. of C. 1962; resigned, 1976; during parliamentary career held post of Parliamentary Secretary to Min. of Northern Affairs and Nat. Resources; Min. without Portfolio; Registrar General; Min. of Consumer and Corp. Affairs; Sol. Gen; Min. of Justice and Attorney Gen.; Min. of Finance; men. of Eng. Bar, Grey's Inn, London; and bar of Ont., Que., B.C. Yukon, N.W. Territories, Barbados, Trinidad; Liberal; R. Catholic; recreations: tennis, squash, canoeing, skiing; Clubs: St. James's (Montreal); Mt. Royal; Montreal Racquet; Cercle Universitaire d'Ottawa; Queen's; Badminton & Racquet; York (Toronto); Home: 435 Russell Hill Rd., Toronto, Ont. M5P 2S4; Office: P. O. Box 38, Royal Bank Plaza, Toronto, Ont. M5J 2J7

TURNER, Peter Merrick, B.A.Sc., M.B.A.; executive; b. Toronto, Ont., 4 July 1931; s. William Ian MacKenzie and Marjorie Hilda (Merrick) T.; e. Univ. of Toronto, B.A.Sc. 1954; Harvard Univ., M.B.A. 1956; m. Beverley, d. late Harold Miller Brophey, 13 Sept. 1958; children: Peter Merrick Jr., Christopher Harold, David MacKenzie; GROUP VICE-PRES., INTERNATIONAL AND VICE-PRES. CORPORATE PLANNING AND DEVELOPMENT, SEALED POWER CORP. 1978- ; Dir., Grand Trunk Western Railroad Co.; Detroit, Toledo & Ivonton Railroad Co., Grand Trunk Corp.; joined Bridgeport Brass Co., Bridgeport, Conn., 1956; Secy.-Treas., Perkins Paper Products Ltd., Montreal, 1957; Asst. to Mang., Texaco Canada Ltd., 1958, Adm., Marketing Research, 1959, Adm., Planning, 1962, Asst. Treas. 1964, Treas. 1966 also Treas., Montreal Pipeline Co. Ltd. and Treas. and Dir., Public Fuel Transmission Systems Ltd., Ottawa; joined Molson Breweries Ltd. as Budgeting and Planning Dir., Corporate Devel., 1968; Vice Pres., Planning Molson Breweries of Canada Ltd., 1968; Vice-Pres. Corporate Devel., Molson Industries Ltd. 1970; Extve. Vice Pres., Bennett Pump Co. 1972; Pres. 1973-78; Chrmn., Salvation Army Campaign for Montreal, 1969-70; Lectr. in Extension Dept., McGill Univ., 1960-67; Chairman, McGill Assocs., 1969-70; Chrm., Muskegon Area Chamber of Comm. Long Range Planning Comte.; Muskegon Community College Long Range Planning Committee; Lectr. in Extension Dept., Grand Valley State College; mem. of Bd., Hackley Hosp.; West Shore Symphony Orchestra; mem., Assn. Prof. Engrs. Ont.; Zeta Psi; Anglican; recreations: reading, skiing, hiking; Clubs: Mount Royal; Granite; Lake O'Hara Trails; Century (Muskegon, Chrmn. Bd. of Govs.); Rotary; Home: 1001 Moulton Ave., N. Muskegon, Mich. 49445; Office: 100 Terrace Plaza, Muskegon, Mich. 49443

TURNER, R(obert) Edward, M.D., F.R.C.P.(C); psychiatrist; educator; b. Hamilton, Ont. 8 June 1926; s. late Robert William and Alice May (Johnson) T.; e. McMaster Univ. B.A. 1948; Univ. of Toronto M.D. 1952, Dipl. in Psychiatry 1957; Univ. of Bristol postgrad. studies Psychastry 1953-55; m. Gene Anne d. late Robert Boys Stewart 27 Sept. 1952; children: Margaret Anne, John William, Robert Paul; RICHARD JAMES PROF. OF FORENSIC PSYCHIATRY, UNIV. OF TORONTO 1977- ; Dir. and Psychiatrist-in-Charge, Metrop. Toronto Forensic Service (METFORS); Pres., Kenneth G.

Gray Foundation 1971- ; Interneship Hamilton Gen. Hosp. 1952-53; Asst. Prof. of Psychiatry, Univ. of Toronto 1964, Assoc. Prof. 1968, Prof. 1973-77; mem. Centre of Criminology 1977-78; mem. Bd. Clin. Inst. Addiction Research Foundation Ont. 1973- ; Chrmn. Ethics Comte. Research Adv. Comte. Clarke Inst. Psychiatry 1976- ; Adv. Review Bd. Ont. 1976-80, 1980-83; Legal Task Force Comte. Mental Health Services Ont., Ont. Council Health 1978-79; Adv. Council Candn. Inst. Law & Med.; Consultant in Psychiatry Law Reform Comn. Can. 1972- ; co-author "Pedophilia and Exhibitionism" 1964; numerous book chapters, articles Forensic Psychiatry; mem. Council, Medico-Legal Soc. Toronto 1980-82; Pres. Ont. Psychiatric Assn. 1975-76, Council 1972-74; Dir. Candn. Psychiatric Assn. 1974-77; Fellow, Am. Psychiatric Assn.; Royal Coll. Psychiatrists (UK); Anglican; recreations: photography, history, art, music, theatre, travel; Home: 163 Bayview Hts. Dr., Toronto, Ont. M4G 2Y7; Office: METFORS, 1001 Queen St. W., Toronto, Ont. M6J 1H4.

TURNER, Ross J.; company executive; b. Winnipeg, Man., 1 May 1930; s. James Valentine and Gretta H. (Ross) T.; e. Kildonan Coll., Winnipeg; Univ. of Man. Extension, R.I.A. 1951; Banff Sch. of Advanced Mang. 1956; m. Helen Elizabeth, d. Thomas Todd, Winnipeg, Man. 9 June 1950; children: Ralph, Rick, Tracy Lee; PRESIDENT, CEO AND DIR., GENSTAR CORP. since 1976; Dir., Canada Permanent Mortgage Corp.; Crown Zellerbach Canada; Rio Algom Ltd.; The Great Western Life Assurance Co.; Trustee, The Fraser Inst.; Acct. Dominion Bridge Co., Winnipeg, 1951-53; Secretary-Treasurer, Standard Iron and Engineering Works Limited, Alberta, 1954-57; Controller, Dominion Bridge, Alberta Division, Edmonton, 1958; Manager, Accounting Services, H.O. Montreal, 1959-61; Div. Vice President, BACM Industries Ltd., Winnipeg, 1962-63, Treas. and Dir. 1963-64, Extve. Vice Pres. 1965-68; Extve. Vice Pres. Neonex International Ltd. Vancouver 1968-69, Pres. and Chief Operating Offr. 1969-71; Pres. and Chief Operating Offr. Seaspan International Ltd. 1971-72; Pres. and Dir. Genstar Western Ltd. 1973-76; mem. Soc. Mang. Accts. Can.; Protestant; recreation: sports; Clubs: Capilano Golf & Country; The Vancouver; Mount Royal; St. James's (Montreal); World Trade; Peninsula Golf and Country (San Francisco); Toronto; Office: 4 Embarcadero Centre, San Francisco California, 94111

TURNER, William Ian MacKenzie, B.A.Sc., P.Eng.; management and engineering consultant; b. Kenora, Ont., 26 May 1903; s. Herbert E. and Katherine F. (MacKenzie) T.; e. Toronto Pub. Schs.; Univ. of Toronto, B.A.Sc. 1925; Univ. of W. Ont. (Business Mang.) 1948; m. Marjorie Hilda, d. late Walter P. Merrick, 9 Apl. 1928; children: William Ian MacKenzie, Peter Merrick; Hon. Dir., Canadian Controllers Ltd.; with Westinghouse Electric & Mfr. Corpn., Pittsburg, in grad. student course, 1925-26, and as Sales Engr., Power Transformer Sec., Sharon, Pa., 1926-30; joined Railway & Power Engineering Corpn. Ltd.; Toronto, Ont., 1930; Sales Engr. 1930-34, Mgr. Control Apparatus Div. 1934-46, el. a Dir. 1944, Asst. Gen. Mgr. 1946-49; Vice-Pres. & Gen. Mgr., Canadian Controllers Ltd. 1949-53, Pres. and Gen. Mgr. 1953-68; Dir., Toronto Industrial Comn. 1968-75; mem. Senate, Univ. of Toronto, 1960-68; U. of T. Engineering Alumni Council, 1954-80 (Pres. 1960-62); Candn. Elect. Mfrs. Assn. (Pres., 1958-59); Roy. Candn. Inst.; Assn. Prof. Engrs. Ont. Hart House; St. Andrew's Soc. of Toronto (Pres: 1965-67); Phi Kappa Pi; Anglican; recreations: golf, fishing, photography, music; Clubs: Engineers; Granite; Toronto Electric (Pres. 1960-75); Empire; Home: 57 Mason Blvd., Toronto, Ont. M5M 3C6

TURNER, William Ian MacKenzie, Jr., B.A.Sc., M.B.A., P.Eng.; b. Sharon, Pa. (Canadian citizen) 17 Jan. 1929; s. William I. M. Sr.; e. University of Toronto, B.A.Sc. (Hons. Mech. Engn.) 1951; Harvard Business School,

M.B.A. (with Distinction) 1953; m. Ann McCreery: two s. William, James; two d. Julia, Carol; PRESIDENT AND CHIEF EXECUTIVE OFFR., CONSOLIDATED-BA-THURST INC. since 1971; Chrmn. Domglas Inc.; Dir., Power Corp. of Canada Ltd.; Bombardier MLW Ltd.; Axel Johnson Industries Ltd.; Diamond Glass Co.; Celanese Canada Ltd.; Canadian Ingersoll-Rand Co.; J. Henry Schroder Banking Corp.; Internat. Adv. Council, Wells Fargo Bank; Chrmn., British North American Comte., Exec. Comte.; Asst. to Pres., Willys-Overland Export Corp., Toledo, Ohio 1953; Controller, Canadian Ingersoll-Rand Co. 1954; Vice-Pres., Power Corp. of Canada Ltd. 1963, Extve. Vice-Pres. 1964, Pres. 1966; apptd. Pres. of present Co. 1970; Gov., Stratford Shakespearean Festival Fdn.; Vice Chrmn. Bd. Govs., Royal Victoria Hosp.; Trustee, The Conference Bd.; recreations: racquets, squash, reading; Clubs: Brook; Knickerbocker (both New York); National; York (both Toronto); Toronto; Mount Royal; St. James's; Mount Bruno Country; M.A.A.A.; Montreal Racket; Hillside Tennis; Home: 4294 Montrose Ave., Westmount, Que. H3Y 2A5; Office: 800 Dorchester Blvd. W., Montreal, Que. H3B 1Y9

TURTA, Ronald, B.Com., C.A.; b. Saskatoon, Sask.; e. Pub. and High Schs., Saskatoon, Sask.; Univ. of Sask., B.Com. 1948; Inst. of Chart. Accts., Quebec, C.A. 1959; one child: R. Dean; Vice President and Treasurer, Telesat Canada since 1969; Assessor with Treas. Taxation Div. of Income Tax Dept., Saskatoon, Sask., 1948-49; with P. S. Ross & Sons, Chart. Accts., Montreal, Que., 1949-52; apptd. Comptroller of Newfoundland & Labrador Corpn. Ltd. 1952; Secy.-Treas., 1953; Vice-Pres., 1954-57; Comptroller, Nesbitt, Thomson & Co. Ltd., Montreal, 1958-59; apptd. Special Asst., Industrial Devel. Bank 1960; served in 2nd World War with R.C.A.F., 1942-45; mem., Inst. Chart. Accts. Que. and Ont.; recreations: car rallying, reading, skiing; Home: 1833 Riverside Dr., Apt. 1011, Ottawa, Ont. K1G 0E8; Office: 333 River Rd., Ottawa, Ont. K1L 8B9

TURVOLGYI, Bertalan Leslie, B.A.Sc.; executive; b. Nyiregyhaza, Hungary 20 Oct. 1924; e. elem. and high schs. Budapest, Hungary; Univ. of Toronto B.A.Sc. 1953; children: two; SR. VICE PRES. DU PONT CANADA INC. since 1978; joined Du Pont as Tech. Asst. Textile Fibres, Kingston 1953, Foreman 1954, Devel. Engr. 1956, Process Engr., Maitland 1957, Process Supvr. 1958, Chief Supvr.-Devel., Kingston 1959, Process Supt. 1963, Asst. Works Mgr. Kingston 1968, Works Mgr. 1968, Mgr. Strategic Planning H.O. Montreal 1970, Mgr. Corporate Planning Div. 1971, Ass't Mgr. Corporate Devel. Div. 1973, Vice Pres. Corporate Devel. 1973, Vice Pres. Operations 1974, Vice Pres. Marketing 1975, Vice Pres. Operations 1976; mem. Soc. Chem. Indust.; Chem. Inst. Can.; Soc. Plastics Indust.; Clubs: St. James's; St-Denis; Home: Islington, Ont. M9A 4A5; Office: 6700 Century Ave., Mississauga, Ont. L5M 2H3

TUSHINGHAM, A. Douglas, B.A., B.D., Ph.D., F.S.A., F.R.S.C.; b. Toronto, Ontario, 19 Jan. 1914; s. Arthur Douglas and Lottie Elizabeth (Betts) T.; e. Univ. of Toronto, B.A. 1936; Univ. of Chicago, B.D. 1941, Ph.D. 1948; m. Margaret McAndrew, d. Henry Thomson, Toronto, Ont., 9 April 1948; children: Margaret Elizabeth, Ian Douglas David; HEAD, JERUSALEM PROJECT OFFICE, R.O.M. Lecturer, Pine Hill Divinity Hall, Halifax, N.S., 1941-42 and 1946; Lectr., University of Chicago, 1948-51; Annual Prof., American Sch. of Oriental Research, Jerusalem, Jordan, 1951-52, and Dir., 1952-53; Assoc. Prof., Queen's Theol. Coll., Kingston, Ont., 1953-55; Head, Art and Archaeology Div., Royal Ont. Museum, 1955-64; Chief Archaeologist, R.O.M. 1964-79; Prof. Dept. of Near Eastern Studies, Univ. of Toronto, 1955-79; was Asst. Dir. of Excavation of Jericho in 1952, 1953, and 1956; participated in and directed excavations at Dhiban, Jordan, in 1951-53; Assoc. Director, excavations in Jerusalem, Jordan, 1962-67; President (1964-65), Canadian Museums

Association; member of Advisory Council and former Chairman, Toronto Hist. Board; member of the Board of Palestine Archeol. Museum, Jerusalem, Jordan, 1951-53; served in 2nd World War with Royal Candn. Navy 1942-45; Lieut., R.C.N.V.R.; 1st Lieut. of Frigate; Publications: "Masks: the Many Faces of Man", 1959; "The Beardmore Relics: Hoax or History?", 1966; (with V. B. Meen) "The Crown Jewels of Iran", 1968; (with A. Denis Baly) "Atlas of the Biblical World", 1971; "The Excavations at Dibon (Dhibân) in Moab" 1972; "Gold for the Gods" 1976; "Studies in Ancient Peruvian Metalworking" 1979; has contrib. many archaeol. and Old Testament studies to "Nat. Geog. Mag"; "Bull." of Am. Schs. of Oriental Research; "Journ. of Near Eastern Studies"; "Biblical Archaeology"; "Zeitschrift des Deutschen Palästinavereins"; etc.; Fellow, Canadian Museum Assn.; Victoria College; Royal Soc. of Canada; Society of Antiquaries of London; Silver Service Medal of the City of Toronto; Gold Award of Merit of the City of Toronto; Gold Medal presented by Gov't of Iran; Silver Jubilee Medal; mem., American Schools of Oriental Research; Archaeol. Inst. of Am. United Church; Home: 66 Collier St., Toronto, Ont. M4W 1L9; Office: Royal Ontario Museum, Toronto, Ont. M5S 2C6

TUTTE, William Thomas, B.A., M.Sc., Ph.D., F.R.S.C.; educator; b. Newmarket, Eng. 14 May 1917; s. William John Tutte; e. Cambridge and Co. High Sch. Eng. 1935; Trinity Coll. Cambridge Univ. B.A. 1938, M.Sc. 1941, Ph.D. 1948; m. Dorothea Geraldine Mitchell 8 Oct. 1949; PROF. OF MATH. UNIV. OF WATERLOO since 1962; Dept. of Math. Univ. of Toronto 1948-62; author "Connectivity in Graphs" 1966; "Introduction to the Theory of Matroids" 1971; rec'd Tory Medal, Royal Soc. Can. 1975; mem. London Math. Soc.; Cambridge Philosophical Soc.; Am. Math. Soc.; Candn. Math. Soc.; Home 16 Bridge St., W. Montrose, Ont. N0B 2V0, Office: Waterloo, Ont. N2L 3GL.

TUTTLE, George Milledge, B.A., B.D., Th.D., D.D. LL.D. (Un. Ch.); retired clergyman; educator; b. Medicine Hat, Alta. 4 Oct. 1915; s. Aubrey Stephen and Mary Anna (Johnson) T.; e. Garneau Pub. and High Schs. Edmonton; Univ. of Alta. B.A. 1937, B.D. 1949; St. Stephen's Coll. Edmonton, Dipl. 1941; Queen's Univ. grad. studies 1938-40; Emmanuel Coll. Toronto Th.D. 1963; Vancouver Sch. of Theol. D.D.; Mount Allison Univ., D.D. 1979; LL.D., Univ. of Calgary, 1980; m. Helen Robertson d. late David Brodie Mitchell 1 July 1944; children: Julia Margaret Devereux, John Robert; Moderator, United Church Of Canada 1977-80; Princ. St. Stephen's Theol. Coll. Univ. of Alta. 1966-79; Dir. Youth Dept. Bd. of Christian Educ. Un. Ch. Toronto 1941-43; Assoc. Dir. Candn. Youth Comn. Toronto 1943-45; Pastor Un. Ch. Sangudo, Alta. 1945-49; Prof. of Christian Educ. Union Coll. of B.C. Vancouver 1951-66; Visiting Prof. St. Paul's Coll. Limuru, Kenya 1965; author 'Youth and Jobs in Canada' (Part I) 1945; 'Youth Organization in Canada' 1946; 'The Christian as Citizen' 1949; 'Paul Pioneers the Church' (Textbook) 1966; also various articles, book chapters and booklets; mem. Candn. Theol. Soc.; Candn. Assn. Pastoral Educ.; Delta Kappa Epsilon; recreations: camping, canoeing, skiing; Home: 2030 Salem Terrace, R.R. 3, Sidney, B.C. V8L 3X9;

TUZ, Paul John, C.M., C.D., M.B.A., D.B.A., P.Eng.; association executive; b. Vienna, Austria 20 Oct. 1929; came to Can. 1943; e. Univ. of Detroit M.B.A. 1971; Ind. Univ. D.B.A. 1973; PRES. AND DIR., BETTER BUSINESS BUREAU OF METROP. TORONTO INC. 1976- ; held various engn. positions Can. and abroad 1954-58; Controller, Emergency Measures for Muns. of N. York, Leaside and Weston 1958-62; Dir. of Educ., Constr. Safety Assn. Ont. 1962-64; Dir. of Safety & Workmen's Compensation, Chrysler Corp.'s Candn. operations 1964-74; Extve. Vice Pres. and Chief Operating Offr. present Bureau 1975; mem. Bd. on Curriculum Planning in Business Adm. Univ. of Detroit 1972-77, mem. Alumni Council; Columnist "The Toronto Sun" 1975-77; present Columnist "The Oshawa Times"; host MTV "moneywise" 1981; served with militia Royal Candn. Army Service Corps, Royal Candn. Corps of Signals, commanded Essex & Kent Scottish, rank Lt. Col.; invested as mem. of Order of Canada, 1979; former Trustee N.York Liv. Bd.; Past Vice Chrmn. N.York Safety Council; N.York Community Council; Riverview Hosp. Bd.; Past Chrmn. Court of Revision City of Windsor; Essex Co. Div. and Metal Trades Div. Indust. Accident Prevention Assn. Ont.; mem. of Extve., St. John Ambulance, Metropolitan Toronto; Safety Dirs.' Comte. Motor Vehicle Mfrs.' Assn.; Dir. Army Cadet League Can.; Past Gov. Tau Kappa Epsilon; recreations: photography, chess, shooting; Home: 8 Hilltop Rd., Toronto, Ont. M6C 3C6; Office: 321 Bloor St. E., Toronto, Ont. M4W 3K6.

TWAITS, William Osborn, C.C. (1974), F.R.S.A., B.Com., D.C.L., D.B.A., LL.D., F.R.S.A.; b. Galt, Ont. 12 June 1910; s. William and Laura Josephine (Osborn) T.; e. Pub. Schs. Galt and Sarnia, Ont.; Sarnia High Sch. 1928; Univ. of Toronto B.Com. 1933; Acadia Univ. D.C.L.; Univ. of Ottawa D.B.A.; Univ. of Windsor LL.D. 1978; m. Frances Helen d. W. R. Begg, Toronto, Ont. 29 May 1937; childen: Judith F. Allan, Sheryl J. Young; Pres. Sarcalto Ltd.; Vice Pres. and Dir. The Royal Bank of Canada; Dir. Alcan Aluminium Ltd.; New York Life Insurance Co.; TRI Ltd.; joined Imperial Oil Ltd. 1933 Sarnia, el. Dir. 1950, Extve. Vice Pres. 1956, Pres. 1960, Chrmn. 1973-74; Sr. mem., Business Council on Nat. Issues; Hon. Dir., C.D. Howe Inst. (mem. Brit.-N.Am. Comte.); Councillor, The Conf. Bd.; Hon. Assoc. The Conf. Bd. of Can.; Council of Honour, Stanford Research Inst.; Past mem. Governing Council, Univ. of Toronto, Past Chrmn. Mang. Adv. Council Faculty of Mang. Studies, Univ. of Toronto; Hon. Dir. Can.'s Aviation Hall of Fame; Hon. Pres. Arthritis Soc.; mem. Delta Kappa Epsilon; Anglican; recreations: golf, fishing, hunting; Clubs: Augusta National Golf; Rideau (Ottawa); Rosedale Golf; York; Home: 17 Old Forest Hill Rd., Toronto, Ont. M5P 2P6.

TWEEDY, Robert J., B.A., M.B.A.; executive; b. Toronto, Ont. 29 June 1942; s. James Donald and Barbara Margaret (Ault) T.; e. Univ. of Toronto Schs. 1960; Univ. of Toronto Trinity Coll. B.A. 1964 Stanford Univ. M.B.A. 1966; m. Diana Maria d. Humphrey B. Style 27 Aug. 1965; two d. Laura Anne Lisa Diana; PRESIDENT, PCL INDUSTRIES LTD.; Dir. PCL Industries Ltd.; Bata Shoe Co. Inc. (U.S.A.); Fleck Manufacturing Co.; Commercial Finance Corp. Ltd.; J. C. Hallman Ltd.; joined McKinsey and Co. Inc. (mang. consultants) Cleveland, Toronto and Paris 1966-72; Extve. Holderbank Financiere, Glaris, Switzerland 1972-73; Pres. DCP Group, Toronto 1973-77; Pres. Bata Shoe Co. Inc. (U.S.A.) and Regional Co-ordinator, Bata Caribbeau, 1977-80; Chrmn. Prov. Task Force on Reorgan. Ont. Ministry of Indust. and Tourism 1976; mem. Young Pres. Organ.; Am. Marketing Assn.; Delta Kappa Epsilon; Anglican; recreations: tennis, golf, squash, fishing, reading; Club: Missisauga Golf & Country; Home: 155 Rosedale Hts. Dr., Toronto, Ont. M4T 1C7

TYAACK, Franz H., B.S.; manufacturer; b. Elizabeth, N.J. 25 May 1927; s. William and Hedwig M. (Kratschmer) T.; e. Mass. Inst. Technol. B.S. (Elect. Engn.) 1950; m. Lois H. d. Robert M. Hoy, Bellefonte, Pa. 6 Oct. 1951; children: Janet R. Nall, Patti E.; PRES. AND CEO WESTINGHOUSE CANADA LTD. since 1978; Engr. Arma Corp. Long Island, N.Y. 1950-53; Supervisory Engr. Westinghouse Electric Corp. Baltimore Md. 1953-59, Consultant Research Pittsburgh, Pa. 1961, Planning Mgr. 1962, Gen. Mgr. Indust. Plastics Div. 1965, Vice Pres. and Gen. Mgr. Process Equipment & Systems Div. 1972-78; served with US Army Air Corps 1945-46; Christian Reformed; recreation: golf; Home: 1954 Fieldgate Dr., Bur-

lington, Ont. L7P 3H6; Office: Box 510, Hamilton, Ont. L8N 3K2.

TYERMAN, David McIntyre, Q.C., LL.B.; b. Prince Albert, Sask., 14 Nov. 1906; s. Peter David and Jessie (Thompson) T.; e. Pub. and High Schs., Prince Albert, Sask.; Univ. of Sask., LL.B. 1928; m. Emilia Hedwick, 7 July 1945; children: Jane, Peter, Nancy; retired MacPHERSON, LESLIE & TYERMAN (estbd. 1921); Dir., Prairie Oil Royalties Co. Ltd.; Centennial Shopping Centre; read law with M. A. MacPherson, Q.C. and E.C. Leslie, Q.C.; called to the Bar of Saskatchewan 1956; cr. Q.C. 1956; served with RCN 1939-45; rank Commdr. (S); Candn. Extve. Services Overseas; former Gov., Candn. Tax Foundation; Candn. Petroleum Assn.; mem., Candn. Bar Assn.; Sask. Law Soc.; Regina Bar Assn.; Freemason (P.M.); Liberal; United Church; recreations: golf, curling, fishing; Clubs: Assiniboia; Wascana Country; Canadian; Home: 3465 Argyle Rd., Regina, Sask. S4S 2B7; Office: 2161 Scarth St., Regina, Sask., S4P 2V4

TYHURST, James Stewart, B.Sc., M.D., C.M., F.A.P.A.; university professor; b. Victoria, B.C., 24 Feb. 1922; s. Robert John Stewart and Muriel Hope (Milligan) T.; e. Victoria Coll., Univ. of B.C. 1938-39; McGill Univ. (1939-44) B.S., M.D., C.M.; m. Libuse d. Josef Juklicek, Sutton, Que., 14 Apl. 1949; children: Robert Stewart, Catherine Hope, John Stewart; PROF. OF PSYCHIATRY, UNIV. OF B.C., since 1957 and sometime Chrmn. of the Dept. there; successively Asst. Prof., Clinical Psychiatry, Cornell Univ., Asst. Prof., Sociol. and Anthrop., there; Assoc. Prof. Psychiatry, McGill Univ.; mem., Nat. Adv. Comte., Mental Health, Dept. Nat. Health & Welfare, Ottawa; Behavioral Sciences Study Sec., Nat. Inst. of Mental Health, Washington, D.C.; Fellow, Centre for Advanced Study in Behavioral Sciences, Palo Alto, Cal.; Chrmn., Comte. on Mental Services, Candn. Mental Health Assn.; since 1957, Head, Dept. of Psychiatry, Shaughnessy Hosp., Vancouver, B.C. and Head, Dept. of Psychiatry, Vancouver Gen. Hosp.; R.C.A.M.C., 1941-46; R.C.A., 1939-40; Fellow, Am. Assn. Advanc. Science; Am. Psychiatric Assn.; mem., Candn. Psychiatric Assn.; Candn. Med. Assn.; Publications: "More for the Mind", 1963; various articles on clin. psychiatry, change and transition, patterns of patient care, etc., to scient. journs.; specializes in basic studies of effect of change on human personality; nat. survey of patterns of patient care in psychiatry, present and future; Anglican; recreation: sailing; Clubs: Royal Vancouver Yacht; University; Office: 2075 Wesbrook Mall, Vancouver, B.C. V6T 1W5:

TYNKALUK, William G., B.A.; executive; b. Sault Ste Marie, Ont. 7 Dec. 1929; e. Univ. of Toronto B.A. 1953; m. Margaret Brown; children: Gregory W., Gail M.; PRESIDENT, LEON FRAZER & ASSOCIATES LTD.; Vice Pres. Associate Investors Ltd.; Dir. Goldtrust; Goldfund Ltd.; Autocrown Corp. Ltd.; mem. Bd. Trade Metrop. Toronto; Clubs: Gyro; Albany; Home: 46 Palomino Cres., Willowdale, Ont. M2K 1W3; Office: 8 King St. E., Suite 2001, Toronto, Ont. M5C 1B5.

TYRWHITT-DRAKE, His. Hon. Montague Lawrence, LL.B.; judge; b. Victoria, B.C., 14 Oct. 1922; s. Brian Halsey and Constance Laetitia (Lawrence) T-D.; e. Victoria Coll., Victoria, B.C., 1939-40; McGill Univ., 1940-43; Univ. of B.C., LL.B., 1949; m. Nancy Elizabeth, d. Daniel Webster Lang, K.C., 7 June 1946; children: Elizabeth Laetitia (Holovsky), Montague Daniel, Guy Lawrence; JUDGE, COUNTY COURT OF VANCOUVER ISLAND; mem. Pension Appeals Bd.; served in 2nd World War, Black Watch of Canada, 1942-46; discharged with rank of Capt.; Kappa Alpha; recreation: fishing; Clubs: Union of B.C.; Victoria Golf; Home: 404 Lands End Rd., R.R. 4, Sidney, B.C. V8L 4R4; Office: Law Courts, Victoria, B.C.

U

UCHIDA, Irene Ayako, Ph.D.; educator; b. Vancouver, B.C. 8 Apl. 1917; d. Sentaro Uchida; e. Univ. of Toronto Ph.D. 1951; PROF. DEPT. OF PEDIATRICS AND PATHOLOGY McMASTER UNIV. and Dir. Regional Cytogenetics Lab. since 1969; Research Assoc. Hosp. for Sick Children Toronto 1951-59; Rockefeller Fellow, Univ. of Wisc. 1959; Dir. Med. Genetics Children's Hosp. of Winnipeg; 1960-69, Asst. Prof. Pediatrics 1962, Assoc. Prof. 1967-69 Univ. of Man.; mem. Organizing Comte. on Standardization of Human Cytogenetics (Internat.) 1966; Visiting Prof. Univ. of Ala. 1968; Med. Research Council Visiting Scient. Univ. of London and Harwell 1969; mem. Science Council of Can. 1970-73; MRC Genetics Grants Comte. 1970-73; MRC Visiting Prof. Univ. of W. Ont. 1973; Consultant to Internat. Program in Radiation Genetics, NEA of OECD, Paris 1973; Organizing Comte. Candn. Coll. Med. Genetics 1976; Task Force on Cytogenetics for Adv. Comte. on Genetic Services 1977; mem. Adv. Comte. on Genetic Services for Ontario, 1979- ; Task Force on High Tech. Diagnostic Lab. Procedures & Equipment, Ont. Council of Health, 1980; Am. Bd. of Medical Genetics (Consultant) 1980; Mental Retardation Research Comte, Nat. Inst. of Child Health & Human Dev., Nat. Inst. of Health, H.E.W., U.S.A. 1980- ; Ont. Med. Assn. Lab. Proficiency Testing Programme, Genetic Cell Culture Comm. Chmn. 1981- ; Ont. Med. Assn. Lab. Proficiency Testing Programme Steering Comte. 1981- ; author various reports on genetics and cytogenetics in scient. and med. journs. and monographs; mem. Am. Soc. Human Genetics (Pres. 1968); Am. Assn. Advanc. Science; Assn. Genetic Counsellors Ont.; Candn. Coll. Med. Geneticists (Chrmn., Quality Control of Cytogenetics Laboratories, 1979- , Bd. mem. 1980-); Genetics Soc. Can.; Home: 20 North Shore Blvd. W. #1210, Burlington, Ont. L7T 1A1; Office: 1200 Main St. W., Hamilton, Ont. L8S 4J9.

UFFEN, Robert James, B.A.Sc., M.A., Ph.D., D.Sc., F.R.S.C., F.G.S.A., P.Eng.; b. Toronto, Ont., 21 Sept. 1923; s. James Frederick and Elsie May (Harris) U.; e. Univ. of Toronto, B.A.Sc. (Engn. Physics) 1949, M.A. (Geo. physics) 1950; Univ. of Western Ont., Ph.D. (Physics) 1952; D.Sc. Queen's 1967, W. Ont. 1970; R.M.C. 1978; m. Mary Ruth, d. John Ross Paterson, Toronto, Ont., 3 May 1949; children: Joanne Grace, Robert Ross; PROF. OF GEOPHYSICS, QUEEN'S UNIV. 1971- ; Dean, Faculty of Applied Science, 1971-80; Chrmn. Candn. Engn. Manpower Council 1972-74; mem. Fisheries Research Bd. Can. 1975-79; mem. Bd. of Dir., Ont. Hydro 1973-79 (Vice Chrmn. 1975-79); Commissioner Ont. Royal Commission on Asbestos, 1980- ; Ont. Comm. on Truck Safety, 1981- ; Chmn., Exploration Technology Devel. Fund, Ont., 1981- ; joined Univ. of W. Ont. 1953; Princ. Univ. Coll. of Arts & Science U.W.O., 1961-65; Dean, Coll. of Science, 1965-66; mem. Nat. Research Council Can. 1963-66; mem., Defence Research Bd., Can. 1964-69 (Chrmn. 1967-69); mem. N.R.C. Selection Bd., 1962; mem., Science Council Can. 1967-71; Chief Science Adviser to the Cabinet, Privy Council Office, Ottawa, 1969-71; mem. Council of Regents, Colls. Applied Arts & Technol. Ont. 1966-69, 72-75; Visiting Fellow, Sci. Policy Research Unit, Univ. of Sussex 1976-77; Bd. of Dir., Centre for Resource Studies, 1973-77, 1980- ; mem., Comm. of Ont. Deans of Eng. since 1971-80 (Chrmn, 1977-78); N.R.C. Assoc. Comm. on Environment since 1979; mem., Candn. Assn. Physicists; Assn. Prof. Engrs. Ont. (Council mem. 1975-79); Am. Geophys. Union; Soc. Exploration Geophysicists; Geol. Soc. Am. (Fellow 1967); Am. Inst. Mining, Metall. & Petroleum Engrs.; Candn. Inst. Mining & Metall.; Club of Rome (1969-); co-discoverer of Allard Lake titanium deposits, Que.; served in 2nd World War with R.C.A. as Pte., 1942, Lieut. 1943; C.I.C. Lieut., 1944-45; has written numerous articles on geophysics, evolution, science policy and nuclear waste; Sigma Chi; United Church; recreation: painting; Home: 167 Fairway Hill Cresc., Kingston, Ont. K7M 2B5

ULLYATT, Charles Raymond, M.A.; manufacturer; b. Chesterfield, Eng., 4 March 1924; s. George Charles and Eva (Hardy) U.; e. Chesterfield (Eng.) Grammar Sch., 1941; St. Edmund Hall, Oxford Univ., B.A. 1947, M.A. 1949; Univ. of Grenoble, 1947; Univ. of Siena, 1949; m. Janet Susan, d. James H. F. Matthews, Sunninghill, Eng., 11 May 1959; children: Louise Frances, Katharine Susan, John Raymond; PRESIDENT, J. & P. COATS (CANADA) INC., since 1962; Dynacast Ltd.; Jaeger Fashions of Canada Ltd.; Dir., Coats Patons (N. Amer.) Inc.; Menorah Mines Ltd.; joined J. & P. Coats Ltd., Glasgow, 1949; trained Sweden 1950-51, Sales Mgr. Finland 1952, Turkey 1954, Greece 1955, Can. 1956-61; carried out selling /O.R./ Systems assignments in Norway, Iceland, Belgium and Spain 1953, 1955-56; served with Royal Corps of Signals 1943-47, Italy; GHQ Staff Offr.; rank Capt.; Founding mem., Christian & Jewish Dialogue, Montreal; mem., Candn. Textile Inst. (Dir.); Brit. Candn. Trade Associates; Soc. Candn. Slide Fasteners Mfrs.; Candn. Mfrs. Assn.; Bd. Trade Montreal; Montreal Chamber Comm.; District Council and Grp. Comm., Boy Scouts of Can.; Anglican; recreations: music, reading, fishing, snow-shoeing, amateur theatre, astronomy; Home: 432 Strathcona Ave., Westmount, Que. H3Y 2X1; Office: 421 Blvd. Pie IX, Montreal, Que. H1V 2B8

UMBRICO, Judy Loman, harpist; b. Goshen, Ind. 3 Nov. 1936; d. Herschel Gilmour and Sabra Pauline (Waltz) Leatherman; came to Can. 1957; e. Carlos Salzedo, Camden,. Ma. and Curtis Inst. of Music Diploma 1949-56; m. Joseph U. 25 June 1956; children:. Pennie, Linda, Julie, Joey; HARPIST, TORONTO SYMPHONY ORCHESTRA; Adjunct Prof., Univ. of Toronto; Instr., Royal Conservatory of Music; Instr., Fenelon Falls Harp Sch.; harp soloist; has recorded for RCA, CBC, Aquitane and CBS; soloist in Eur., U.S.A., Can. with Tor. Symphony, Shaw Festival, Stratford Festival, CBC Radio and TV; Juno 1979; Grand Prix du Disque 1980; commissioned new works for harp; Home: 38 Burnside Dr., Toronto, Ont. M6G 2M8; Office: 215 Victoria St., Toronto, Ont. M5B 1V1

UNDERHILL, Herbert Stuart; journalist; b. Vancouver, B.C. 20 May 1914; s. Harold John and Helena (Ross) U.; e. elem. and high schs. B.C.; m. Emma Gwendolyn d. late J. T. MacGregor 23 July 1937; childen: Carol, James Stuart; PRESIDENT, VICTORIA PRESS 1978-79; Publisher, Victoria Times and Vice Pres. Victoria Press (Div. of F. P. Publications (Western) Ltd.) 1971-78; Corr. and Ed. The Canadian Press, Vancouver, Toronto, New York and London 1937-50; N. Am. Ed. Reuters (London, Eng.) 1950, Asst. Gen. Mgr. 1958, Mang. Ed. 1965-68, Depy. Gen. Mgr. (N. and S. Am., Caribbean) 1963-70; Asst. Publisher Financial Times of Canada 1970; winner Candn. Newspaper Award for Corr. 1950; Dir. The Candn. Press 1972-78; Candn. Newspaper Publishers Assn. 1972-76; Anglican; Home: 308 Beach Dr., Victoria, B.C. V8S 2M2; Office: 2621 Douglas St., Victoria, B.C. V8W 2N4.

UNRAU, A. M., M.S.A., Ph.D., F.C.I.C.; educator; b. 16 Feb. 1926; Ph.D. (1956) Plant Science; Ph.D. (1959) Biochemistry; m. Irene Cathrine Jane Andersen; 4 s. Albert, Laurence, William, Vincent; CHRMN. BIO-ORGANIC CHEM. DEPT., SIMON FRASER UNIV.; Pres., Prospect Enterprises Ltd.; Asst. Prof., Univ. of Hawaii, 1959; Research Assoc., Univ. of B.C., 1960; Assoc. Prof., Univ. of Man., 1961 and present Univ., 1965; Chrmn., Simon Fraser Awards Comte., 1966-76; author or co-author of over 80 papers in scient. journs.; mem., Am. Chem. Soc.; Chem. Soc. (London); recreations: badminton, skiing, yachting, golf, architecture and house design; Clubs: Vancouver Lawn Tennis & Badminton; Vancouver Golf;

Home: 4635 Prospect Rd. N., Vancouver, B.C. V7N 3M1; Office: Burnaby, B.C.

UPSON, W. Terrell, B.A., M.B.A.; financial executive; b. New Haven, Conn. 4 Sept. 1938; e. Yale University B.A. 1960; New York Univ. M.B.A. 1968; Harvard Grad. Sch. of Business Adm. PMD 1971; m. Katherine Darrow 9 June 1962; children: Daniel, Mary, Martha; PRES. DIR. & CEO LEASING, CHEMICAL BANK OF CANADA 1981- ; Dir. Chemco Canada Inc.; Chemical New York N.V.; served with U.S. Navy 1960-63, rank Lt.; joined Chemical Bank, New York 1964; Vice Pres. 1971-80; Sen. Vice Pres. 1980; recreations: sailing tennis, skiing; Clubs: Empire; Cambridge; Toronto Cricket Skating & Curling; Home: 263 Glencairn Ave., Toronto, Ont. M5N 1T8; Office: 150 York St., Toronto, Ont.

URIE, Hon. John J., B.Com; judge; b. Guelph, Ont., 2 Jan. 1920; s. late Dr. George Norman and Jane A. (Ballantyne) U.; e. Lisgar and Glebe Coll. Insts., Ottawa; Queen's Univ., B.Com. 1941; Osgoode Hall Law Sch. 1948; m. Dorothy Elizabeth, d. late Dr. Ivan W. James, 2 Sept. 1946; children: John David, Janet Elizabeth, Alison Jill; JUSTICE, APPEAL DIV., FEDERAL COURT OF CANADA since 1973; read law with McIlraith & McIlraith, Ottawa; called to Bar of Ont. 1948; cr. Q.C. 1961; assoc. with McIlraith & McIlraith, Ottawa, 1948-50; Ewart, Scott, Kelley & Burke-Robertson, 1950-54; Partner, Burke-Robertson, Urie, Weller & Chadwick, 1954-73; served with Cameron Highlanders of Ottawa, Overseas, 1942-45; mem. Candn. Bar Assn.; Royal Candn. Mil. Inst. (Toronto); Phi Delta Phi; Protestant; recreations: golf, curling, skiing and other sports; Clubs: Rideau; Ottawa Hunt & Golf; Home: 1291 Parkhill Circle Ottawa, Ont. K1H 6K2; Office: Wellington St., Ottawa, Ont.

URQUHART, Malcolm Charles, B.A., F.R.S.C.; educator; b. Islay, Alta. 12 Dec. 1913; s. William Gordon and Mary Louise (Marlow) U.; e. elem. sch. Islay, Alta.; Strathcona High Sch. Edmonton, Alta.; Edmonton Normal Sch. Teacher's Cert. 1932; Univ. of Alta. B.A. 1940; Univ. of Chicago 1940-42, 1948-49 (Invited Fellow); London Sch. of Econ. and Cambridge Univ. 1962-63; Univ. of Cal. (Berkeley) 1969-70; m. Mary Elizabeth d. Howard Paige Rowell 8 June 1969; step-children: Elizabeth Anne Arrowsmith, John David Arrowsmith; SIR JOHN A. MACDONALD PROF. OF ECON. QUEEN'S UNIV.; Instr. Mass. Inst. of Technol. 1942-43; Asst. to Dir. Gen. Econ. Research, Dept. of Finance, Dept. of Reconstruction & Supply 1943-45; Asst. Prof. Queen's Univ. 1945 becoming Assoc. Prof. and Prof. of Econ., Dir. Inst. for Econ. Research 1960-66, Head of Econ. 1964-68, Acting Head of Econ. 1970-71; Adv. on Forecasting Models, Econ. Research Br. Ottawa 1945-47; Adv. to Govt. of Pakistan on 1st Econ. Devel. Program 1954-55; mem. Comte. on Healing Arts Ont. 1966-70; mem. Extve. Comte. Conf. on Research in Income and Wealth, Nat. Bureau of Econ. Research 1967-70; co-founder Conf. on Quantitative Econ. Hist. in Can. 1964; mem. Subcomte. on Research Grants, Comte. on Health Research, Ont. Council of Health 1968-72; Visiting Prof., Centre of Candn. Studies, Univ. of Edinburgh, 1979-80; co-author "Public Investment and Capital Formation: A Study of Public and Private Investment Outlay, Canada, 1926-41" 1945; "Economics" 1959; Mgr. and Contrib. Ed. "Historical Statistics of Canada" 1959-65; author or co-author book chapters, reports, articles, papers; rec'd Gov. Gen.'s Gold Medal Alta. 1940; Pres., Candn. Econ. Assn. 1968-69; Acad. Humanities & Social Sciences, Royal Soc. Can. 1975-76, mem. Gen. Council 1974-77; mem. Art Collection Soc. Kingston (Secy., Pres.); Community Chest Kingston (Chrmn. Budget Comte.); Anglican; recreation: curling; Club: Cataraqui Golf & Country; Home: 94 Beverley St., Kingston, Ont. K7L 3N6; Office: Queen's University, Kingston, Ont. K7L 3N6.

USSELMAN, Anton M.; executive; b. Sask. 9 March 1922; s. Fred and Caroline (Fetch) U.; e. Univ. of Man., Agric.; various business and pub. speaking courses; German and Spanish studies; m. Olive Doreen Donaldson 24 March 1950; one s. Paul; Pres., Logger Lumber& Anton Developments Ltd.; Dir. and Past Chrmn. Carma Developers Ltd.; Appraiser, Prudential of America, Winnipeg 1950-53; Builder and Past Pres. Built-Rite Homes Ltd. 1953-72; Past Chrmn. Alta. Housing Council; Past Pres. Calgary Hudac; served 3½ yrs. RCAF, Air Observer Sch.; recreations: travel, bridge, chess, golf, curling, music; Club: Rotary (Past Pres. N. Hill Charter); Home: 2560 Toronto Cres., Calgary, Alta.; Office: Suite 231, 6715-8th St. N.E., Calgary, Alta.

UTTING, Robert A.; banker; L. Niagara Falls, Ont.; VICE CHRMN. AND DIR., THE ROYAL BANK OF CANADA 1980- ; joined present Bank Niagara Falls, Ont. 1940, various brs. Ont.; Sr. Asst. Mgr. Edmonton Main Br. 1955, Inspr. Candn. Credits H.O. 1958, Foreign Dept. H.O. 1959, Far E. Rep. Hong Kong 1960, Agt. New York 1962, Mang. Dir. RoyWest Banking Corp. Ltd. Nassau 1965, Asst. Gen. Mgr. H.O. 1968, Depy. Gen. Mgr. Internat. Div. 1969, Vice Pres. Europe, London, Eng. 1973, Depy. Chief Gen. Mgr. H.O. 1978, Chief Gen. Mgr. 1978; served with RCAF 1942-46; Office: 1 Place Ville Marie, Montreal, Que. H3B 4A7.

V

VACHON, François, B.A., B.Sc., F.S.A., F.I.C.A.; actuaire; né Montréal, Qué. 8 juillet 1935; f. Irénée et Aimée (Masson) V.; é. Coll. de Saint Laurent B.A. 1953; Univ. de Montréal B.Sc. (Math) 1956; ép Marie Andrée f. Rodrique Lefebvre 9 nov. 1968; enfants: André, Bernard, Pierre; CONTROLEUR COMPAGNIE INTERNATIONALE DE PAPIER DU CANADA depuis 1979; au service de Sun Life du Canada de 1956 à 1979; Chargé de cours, Faculté des Sciences, Univ. de Montréal 1956-59; Trésorier, Confédération des Sports du Qué 1973-75; mem. du Conseil, Inst. Canadien des Actuaires 1973-75; Prés. Club des Actuaires de Montréal 1975-76; Résidence: 323 ave. Stuart, Outremont, Qué. H2V 3G9; Bureau: Edifice Sun Life, Square Dominion, Montreal, Que., H3B 2X1

VACHON, Rt. Rev. Msgr. Louis-Albert, C.C. (1969), D.Th., D.Ph., LL.D., F.R.S.C.; b. St. Frederic (Beauce), Que., 4 Feb. 1912; s. Napoleon and Alexandrine (Gilbert) V.; e. Que. Semy., B.A. 1934; Laval Univ., D.Ph. 1947; Angelicum, Rome, D.Th. 1949; Hon. degrees from Montreal, McGill, Victoria 1964, Guelph 1966, Moncton 1967, Bishop's, Queen's, Strasbourg 1968, Notre Dame 1971, Carleton 1972; Prof. of Philos. Laval Univ., 1941-47; Prof. of Theol. 1949-55; Superior of Grand Seminary of Quebec, 1955-59; Vice Rector of Laval Univ., 1959-60, Rector 1960-72; Supt. gén. séminaire de Québec 1960-77; Auxiliary Bishop of the Diocese of Quebec 1977-81; Archbishop of Quebec and Primate of Canadian Church, 1981- ; Offr. de l'Ordre de la Fidélité française (1963); author of: "Espérance et présomption", 1958; "Verité et Liberté", 1962; "Unité de l'Université", 1962; "Apostolat de l'universitaire catholique", 1963; "Mémorial", 1963; "Communauté universitaire", 1963; "Progrés de l'université et consentement populaire", 1964; "Responsabilité collective des universitaires", 1964; "Les humanités, aujourd'hui", 1966; "Excellence et loyauté des universitaires" 1969; rec'd Centennial Medal 1967; President of "L'Entraide universitaire mondiale du Canada"; "Conf. (1965-68) des recteurs et des Principaux des Universités du Québec"; mem. Assn. des Univ. et Coll. de Can. (Pres. 1965-66); Conseil d'administration de la Fédération Internationale des universités catholiques" (FIUC); Conseil d'adm. de l'Assn. des universités partiellement ou entièrement de langue française (AUPELF); Candn. Educ. Assn.; "Société Canadienne de l'histoire de l'Eglise catholique"; Catholic Theol. Soc. Am.; Société Canadienne pour l'histoire et la philosophie des sciences; Union mondiale des enseignants catholiques; Pres. de l'Association canadienne des éducateurs de langue française (ACELF); Assn. Commonwealth Univs.; Société des écrivains canadiens; Hon. Fellow, Royal Coll. Phys. & Surgs. (Canada) 1972; mem. de la Soc. royale du Canada; Address: Archevêche de Québec, C.P. 459, Haute-Ville, Qué. G1R 4R6

VAILLANCOURT, Louise Brais; b. Montreal, Que. 12 Aug. 1926; d. Hon. F. Philippe Brais, C.C., C.B.E., Q.C., LL.D., and Louisette (Doré) OBE, Brais; e. The Mother House Business Coll. 1946; Couvent du Sacré-Coeur, Sault au Récollets, Montréal 1944; m. Paul Vaillancourt jr. 14 June 1947; children: Michèle (Mme. Jean René de Cotret), Louise (Mme. Pierre-Yves Châtillon), Marie, Paul III; Gov., Hôpital Marie-Enfant; Dir. Bell Canada; Banque Nationale du Canada; Carling O'Keefe Ltd.; F.W. Woolworth Co. Ltd.; Institut Armand Frappier; The Council for Candn. Unity; Past Pres. L'Assn. des Anciennes du Sacré-Coeur; recipient Cross of Merit Order of Malta; R. Catholic; Liberal; recreations: skiing, studying; Home: 75 Ave. Courcelette, Montreal, Que. H2V 3A5

VAILLANCOURT, Paul, Jr., B.A. M. Com.; insurance executive; b. Montreal, Que. 29 Oct. 1921; s. Paul and Madeleine Panet (Raymond) V.; e. Montreal College B.A.; Univ. of Montreal, M.Com.; m. Louise, d. Hon. F. P. Brais, 14 June 1947; children: Michèle, Louise, Marie, Paul III; Dir., J. & E. Hall (Canada) Ltd.; Canada Starch Co. Ltd.; Canadian Reinsurance Co.; Canadian Reassurance Co.; mem. Advisory Board, Guaranty Trust Co. of Canada; Lieut. (Infantry) Reserve; Group Chairman, H.R.H. Prince Philip's II Commonwealth Conference (1st Nat. Chrmn. of Candn. Del. 1956-61); mem., Montreal Chamber of Comm. (Dir. 1957-62); Que. Div., Candn. Red Cross; Past Pres., Assn. of Comm. Faculty of Univ. of Montreal; Chrmn., French-Fed. Charities; R. Catholic; recreation: country sports; Home: 75 ave. Courcelette, Outremont, Que. H2V 3A5;

VALENTINE, Rt. Rev. Barry, M.A., B.D., L.Th., D.D.; bishop (Ang.); b. Shenfield, Essex, Eng., 26 Sept.1927; s. Harry John and Ethel Margaret (Purkiss) V.; e. St. Thomas Ch. Sch. and Brentwood Sch., Eng.; St. John's Coll., Cambridge Univ., B.A. 1949, M.A. 1952; McGill Univ., B.D. 1951; Montreal Diocesan Theol. Coll., L.Th. 1951; St. John's Coll., Winnipeg, D.D. 1969, Montreal Diocesan Theol. Coll. 1970; m. Mary Currell, d. late Roland Earle Hayes, Ottawa, Ont., 4 Oct. 1952; children: John Nugent, Lesley Claire, Guy Richard Neville, Michael Hayes; BISHOP OF RUPERT'S LAND, since 1970; Curate, Christ Ch. Cath., Montreal, 1952; Incumbent, Chateauguay-Beauharnois, 1954; Dir., Religious Educ., Diocese of Montreal, 1957; Rector of St. Lambert, 1961; Extve. Offr., Diocese of Montreal, 1965; Archdeacon of Montreal 1966, Dean of Montreal and Rector of Christ Ch. Cath. 1968; Coadjutor Bishop of Rupert's Land, 1969; Chancellor, St. John's Coll., Winnipeg, 1970; recreations: music, theatre, walking, hockey; Home: Suite 178, 1 Snow, Fort Gary, Man. R3T 2M4

VALLANCE, retired Col. Mary Graham, O.M.M., C.D., A-de-C.; b. Atwood, Ont. 6 Feb. 1924; d. Lloyd Duncan and Anne Campbell (Lochead) V.; e. Sr. Matric. Listowel, Ont. 1942; Westervelt Sch. (Extve. Secretarial Course) London, Ont. 1944; 1st yr. Univ. of Western Ont. (Soc. Sciences); Dir., Women Personnel, Dept. of Nat. Defence 1971-76.; Secy. McCormick's Ltd. London, Ont. 1944; Teacher, Westervelt Sch., London 1949-53; enlisted RCAF 1954 rank Flight Cadet; attended Offrs.' Sch., London, Ont. later becoming Adj. there 1955-57; Adj. Radar & Communications Sch. Clinton, Ont. 1954-55; Recruiting Offr. Regina, Sask. 1957; Personnel Adm. Offr., 3 (F) Wing, Zweibrucken, Germany 1958; served in Personnel Adm. and Training, Parent, Que., St. Jean, Que., Camp

Borden, Ont. and Winnipeg, Man. 1961-67; Personnel Adm. Offr., 4 (F) Wing, Baden Soellingen, Germany 1967; Base Personnel Adm. Offr., CFB Rockcliffe, Ont. 1968 and CFB Toronto-Downsview 1969-71; promoted Col. 1974; Presbyterian; recreations: cycling, skating, reading, rug-making, spectator sports; Clubs: RCAF Assn.; Gloucester St. Offrs. Mess; Home: King St., Atwood, Ont. N0G 1B0.

VALLANCE-JONES, Alister, M.Sc., Ph.D., F.R.S.C.; physicist; b. Christchurch, N.Z. 4 Feb. 1924; s. Frederick Edmund and Nellie Marion (Vallance) J.; e. St. Andrews Coll. Christchurch 1941; Canterbury Coll. Univ. of N.Z. B.Sc. 1945, M.Sc. 1946; Univ. of Cambridge Ph.D. 1950; m. Catherine d. James Fergusson, Farr, Scot. 1 Dec. 1951; children: Elizabeth Marie Villeneuve, Catriona Anne Vallance-Jones, Alasdair Frederick Vallance-Jones; PHYSICIST, NAT. RESEARCH COUNCIL OF CAN.; Post-Doctoral Fellow, Physics Div. Nat. Research Council 1951; Prof. of Physics Univ. of Sask. 1952-68; author "Aurora" 1974; over 77 publs. on research aurora and airglow; Ed. "Canadian Association of Physicists" 1963-66; Protestant; recreations: sailing, skiing; Club: Britannia Yacht; Home: 2145 Fillmore Cres., Ottawa, Ont. K1J 6A1; Office: Herzberg Inst. of Astrophysics, Ottawa, Ont. K1A 0R6.

VALLE, Henry, LL.D.; industrialist; b. Hammerfest, Norway, 23 Nov. 1920; s. Inga (Holmgren) and the late Henry V.; e. High Sch. of Montreal; Univ. of W. Ont. (Mang. Training Course); LL.D. Waterloo Lutheran Univ. 1967; m. Carmel, d. late J. O. Costello, 7 April 1951; children: Grant, Craig; VICE-PRES. CORPORATE DEVELOPMENT, TRANSPORTATION, AND DIR., BOMBARDIER INC. since 1978; Dir., Bombardier Inc.; Dir., Quebec Industrial Relations Institute; Past Pres., Weredale House & Foundation; Past Chrmn. Extve. Council, Candn. Chamber of Comm.; began with present Co. as Apprentice Draftsman, 1939; Mgr., Diesel Service, 1952-56, Marketing, 1957-59, Vice Pres. Marketing, 1960-61, Vice Pres., 1961-62, Pres. and Dir., 1962-72; Vice Chrmn. 1972-74; Chrmn. and Dir., 1974-75; Pres. of MLW Industries, 1975-78; Past Pres., MLW International; served in 2nd World War, 1942-45, with R.C.O.C., Capt.; recreations: golf, fishing, skiing; Clubs: Rotary; Kanawaki Golf; Canadian Railway; Mount Royal; Lac la Raquette Fish & Game; Home: 55 Dufferin Rd., Hampstead, Québec, H3X 2X8 Office: Suite 1520, 800 Dorchester St. W., Montreal, Que. H3B 1X9

VALLEE, Francis Gerald, Ph.D., F.R.S.C.; anthropologist; educator; b. Montreal, Que. 27 July 1918; s. Richard Boulanger and Clara (Dempsey) V.; e. D'Arcy McGee High Sch. Montreal; McGill Univ. B.A. 1950; Univ. of London Ph.D. 1955; m. Anna Mathilde d. Hette Kerst Hylkema, Bilthoven, Holland 2 Aug. 1947; children: Richard Kerst, Frances Margaret, Martine Claire, Paul Nicholas; PROF. OF ANTHROP. CARLETON UNIV.; Lectr. Univ. of Edinburgh 1953-55; Chief, Research Div. Dept. Citizenship & Immigration Ottawa 1955-57; Asst. to Assoc. Prof. McMaster Univ. 1957-64; Assoc. to Full Prof. Carleton Univ. since 1964; Visiting Prof. Univ. of Hawaii 1970-71, Australian Nat. Univ. 1978; mem. N.W.T. Leg. Council 1964-67; rec'd Candn. Centennial Medal 1967; served with RCA 1940-45, 14th Field Regt.; author "Kabloona and Eskimo" 1967; "Survey of the Contemporary Indians of Canada" Vol. II 1967; "Eskimo of the Canadian Arctic" 1968; "Language Use In Canada", 1980; various articles ethnic relations, lang. and soc.; mem. Candn. Ethnol. Soc. (Pres.); Candn. Sociol. & Anthrop. Assn.; Candn. Ethnic Studies Assn.; Am. Anthrop. Assn.; NDP; recreations: music, sports, reading; Home: 2022 Rideau River Dr., Ottawa, Ont. K1S 1V2; Office: Colonel By Dr., Ottawa, Ont. K1S 5B6.

VALLEE, Hon. Gabrielle, LL.L.; judge; b. Quebec City 3 Apl. 1928; d. Ivan E. and Gabrielle (Legendre) V.; e. St-

Dominique Sch. 1942; Ursulines Coll. 1949; Laval Univ. LL.L. 1954; SR. ASSOC. CHIEF JUSTICE QUE. since 1976; called to Bar of Que. 1954; cr. Q.C. 1971; law practice Depeyre, Michaud, Beaudry & Vallée 1954-73; called to Superior Ct. of Que. 1973; mem. Candn. Bar Assn.; Que. Bar Assn.; R. Catholic; recreation: skiing; Clubs: Altrusa; University; Office: Court House, 12 St-Louis St., Quebec City, Que. G1R 4P6.

VALLERAND, Hon. Claude R., B.A., LL.L.; judge; b. Montreal, Que., 1 Sept. 1932; s. René and Claudine (Simard) V.; e. Coll. Stanislas, Montreal, B.A. 1949; Univ. de Montréal, LL.L. 1954; m. Lucie, d. Rolland Rinfret, Montreal, Que., 10 Sept. 1955; children: René, François, Josée; JUSTICE, SUPERIOR COURT OF QUE.; read law with Blain, Piché, Godbout, Emery, Blain & Vallerand; called to Bar of Que. 1955; service with RCAF (Reserve); rank Flying Offr.; appt'd. to the Bench, Dec. 1971; R. Catholic; recreations: skiing, music, theatre; Home: 56 ave. Kelvin, Outremont, Que. H2V 1T3; Office: Court House, Montreal, Que. H2Y 1A2

VAN ALSTYNE, Thelma Selina, R.C.A.; artist; b. Victoria, B.C. 26 Jan. 1913; d. Alpha Thomas and Rosetta Schoch (Cooper) Scribbans; e. Miss Seymours Sch. for Girls Vancouver; Duffus Sch. of Business 1929; Vancouver Sch. of Art 1944-46; Doone Sch. of Art, studied with Jock MacDonald; m. E. Lloyd Van Alstyne 12 June 1953; one step-d.; solo exhns. incl. Pollock Gallery 1960-80; Le Fevre Gallery Edmonton 1981; rep. in numerous group exhns. incl. Candn. Group of Painters Montreal Museum of Fine Arts 1961; Colour and Form Soc. Toronto 1968-70; Bryan Robertson White Gallery London, Eng. (Centennial Purchase) 1967; Art Gallery of Ont. 1968, 1971; Birmingham, Ala. Can. Council Group 1979; rep. in pub., corporate and private colls. incl. Can. Council Art Bank, OISE Coll.; recipient Hadassah Auction Prizes 1972-80; Can. Council Grant 1972; NDP; Buddhist; recreations: gardening, travel, religions; Address: 81 Bramley St. S., Port Hope, Ont. L1A 3K6.

van BRIDGE, Tony; actor; director; writer; b. London, Eng., 28 May 1917; s. Arthur Stanley and Edith Christina (Drane) Bridge; e. Elmhurst Coll., Kingston-on-Thames, Eng.; Royal Acad. of Dramatic Art; m. Elizabeth Adamson Tully (deceased, 11 July 1979); children: Peter, David, Shona Elizabeth; acting career incls. 15 yrs. with Stratford (Ont.) Festival (notably as Falstaff in all 3 plays in which that character appears); Old Vic Co.; 5 yrs. with Shaw Festival, Niagara on the Lake, notably for Capt. Shotover in "Heartbreak House", 1968, and as director of "Man and Superman", 1977; Lincoln Center, N.Y.; Stratford, Conn.; Houston, Texas; TV work in Hollywood; wrote original play "The Old Ones" which appeared on CBC TV and did adaption of "Diary of a Scoundrel"; appears frequently in his one-man show "GKC", based on G.K. Chesterton; served with Brit. Army 1940-46; rank Capt. on discharge; Queen Elizabeth Silver Jubilee Medal; Anglican; Clubs: Arts & Letters, recreations: golf, astronomy; Address: 45 Spadina Rd., Toronto, Ont. M5R 2S9.

VAN CAMP, Hon. Mabel Margaret; judge; b. Blackstock, Ont. 11 May 1920; d. William John Weir and Mary Jane (Smith) Van Camp; e. Blackstock Pub. and High Schs.; Univ. of Toronto, Victoria Coll. B.A. 1941; Osgoode Hall Law Sch. 1947; JUDGE, SUPREME COURT OF ONT. read law with Macdonald & Macintosh; called to Bar of Ont. 1947; cr. Q.C. 1965; joined Gerard Beaudoin law practice 1947 becoming Partner, Beaudoin, Pepper & Van Camp; Pres. YWCA Metrop. Toronto 1965 — 68; del. to World Conf. Australia 1967; former mem. Goal Setting Comte. & Allocations Comte. Un. Community Fund; Past Regent, Fudger House Chapter IODE; Past Pres. Women's Law Assn. Ont.; former Council mem. Candn. Bar Assn.; former Chancellor and Dean, Alpha Mu Chapter of Kappa Beta Pi; Anglican; Clubs: Royal Candn. Mil. Inst.; Women's University; Home: 7 Jackes

Ave., #1608, Toronto, Ont. M4T 1E3 and 1 Church St., Blackstock L0B 1B0; Office: Osgoode Hall, 130 Queen St. W., Toronto,Ont. M5H 2N5.

VANCISE, William John, Q.C., B.A., LL.B.; b. Regina, Sask., 10 Jan. 1938; s. Albert John and Jean Finlayson (Sclater) V.; e. Luther Co., 1956; Univ. of Sask., B.A. 1958, LL.B. 1960; m. Joy Yvonne, d. William Watson, 26 Aug. 1961; children: Robert William, John Allen, Nancy Jean; PARTNER, BALFOUR, MILLIKEN, MOSS, LASCHUK, KYLE, & VANCISE, Dir., CN Railways; Paragon Business Forms (Western); Ltd.; The H. A. Roberts Group Ltd.; Bird Machine Canada Limited; read law with R. M. Balfour, Q.C.; called to Bar of Sask. 1961; assoc. with Balfour & Balfour 1961-62, Balfour MacLeod, MacDonald, Laschuk & Kyle, 1962-63; named Partner of Balfour, MacLeod in 1963; Appointed Q.C. 1980 Dir., YMCA Regina; mem., Regina Bar Assn.; Sask. Law Soc.; Candn. Bar Assn. (Sec. Chrmn.); Luther Coll. Alumni Assn. (Past Pres.); Freemason; Liberal; Protestant; recreations: skiing; Clubs: Rotary (Pres. Eastview 1973-74); Lakeshore Estates Tennis; Assiniboia; Home: 110 Sunset Dr., Regina, Sask. S4S 2R9; Office: 1850 Cornwall, Regina, Sask. S4P 2K3

VAN CLEAVE, Allan Bishop, O.C., M.Sc., Ph.D., F.R.S.C.; retired university dean; b. Medicine Hat, Alta., 19 Aug. 1910; s. Galen Bishop and Emily Mabel (McKeage) Van C.; e. Pub. Sch., Estuary, Sask., 1918-24; High Sch., Empress, Alta., 1924-27; Univ. of Sask., B.Sc. 1931, M.Sc. 1933; McGill Univ., Ph.D. (Chem.) 1935; Cambridge Univ., Ph.D. (Surface Chem.) 1937; m. Dorothy Eleanora, d. late William J. Yeo, 16 Aug. 1934; children: Galen Murray, M. Elaine, Dalton C., Carol M.; Dean, Faculty of Grad. Studies, Univ. of Regina, 1969-76; retired as Prof. Emeritus of Chemistry, 1977; since 1969 and Dean, Univ. Coll. of Grad. Studies, Regina and Saskatoon Campuses, 1970-74; joined Univ. as Asst. Prof. of Chem., 1937-46; Assoc. Prof. 1946-52; Prof. 1952-62; Chrmn., Div. of Natural Sciences, Regina Campus, 1962-68; mem. Defence Research Bd. of Can. 1966-72; Sask. Research Council, 1968-74; rec'd Centennial Medal 1967; Chem. Educ. Award, Chem. Inst. Can. 1968; Order of Canada, 1976; author of over 50 scient. papers; mem., Chem. Inst. Can. (Councillor 1948-51; Chrmn., Chem. Educ. Div. 1952-53 and 1965-66); Protestant; recreations: curling, gardening; Clubs: Kiwanis; Home: 1001 McNiven Ave., Regina, Sask. S4S 3X4

van den BERG, Gijsbertus Johannes; b. The Hague, Holland, 10 April 1917; s. Gijsbertus Johannes and Louisa Francina (Ketelaar) van den B.; e. Mulo and HBS, The Hague, Holland; m. Catharina van Schagen, The Hague Holland, 23 Oct. 1942; children: Bert J. P., Hendrina, L. Frans, Johan H., Fred; Dir., The Mortgage Insurance Co. of Canada; The Investors Group; MICC Investments Ltd.; Fidelity Trust; Trustee, Canadian Realty Investors; joined Royal Dutch/Shell Group 1935; held various positions in Holland and Curacao, N.A.; joined Canadian Pacific Ltd. as Mgr. Pension Fund, 1960; Vice Pres. Finance 1964; retired 1973; Home: 65 Harbour Sq., Suite 3310, Toronto, Ont. M5J 2L4

van den BERGH, Sidney, A.B., M.Sc., Dr.rer.nat.; astronomer; b. Wassenaar, Holland 20 May 1929; s. Sidney J. and S. M. (van den Berg) van den B.; e. Leiden Univ. 1947-48; Princeton Univ. A.B. 1950; Ohio State Univ. M.Sc. 1954; Univ. Göttingen Dr.rer.nat. 1956; children: Peter, Mieke, Sabine; DIR. DOMINION ASTROPHYSICAL OBSERVATORY since 1977; Asst. Prof. Ohio State Univ. 1956-58; Prof. Univ. of Toronto 1958-77; mem. Internat. Astron. Union (Vice Pres.), Dir., Canada-France-Hawaii Telescope Corp.; Royal Soc. Can.; Am. Astron. Soc.; Royal Astron. Soc.; recreations: photography, archaeology; Home: 418 Lands End Rd., Sidney, B.C. V8L 4R4; Office: 5071 W. Saanich Rd., Victoria, B.C. V8X 4M6.

VANDEN BORN, William H., M.Sc., Ph.D.; educator; b. Rhenen, Netherlands, 17 Nov. 1932; came to Canada 1949; e. Univ. of Alta., B.Sc. (Agric.) 1956, M.Sc. 1958; Univ. of Toronto, Ph.D. (Bot.) 1961; m. Edigna Wierenga, 6 June 1958; 5 children; PROF. OF PLANT SCIENCE, UNIV. OF ALBERTA since 1972; joined present Univ. as Asst. Prof. 1961, Assoc. Prof. 1966, Chrmn., Dept. of Plant Science, 1970-75; author of numerous articles in various scient. journs.; Home: 9520 - 145 St. Edmonton, Alta. T5N 2W8; Office: Edmonton, Alta. T6G 2P5

VANDEN BRINK, A. (Tony); industrial executive; born Enschede, Holland; 10 Oct. 1928; e. Enschede, Holland; m. Kathleen Rose Archibald, 18 July 1953; children: Paul B., Stephen R., Sandra J.; PRESIDENT, CHIEF OPERAT-ING OFFR. AND DIR., TRIMAC LTD. 1980- ; came to Can. 1951 serving in drilling industry; Field Supt. Peter Bawden Drilling Ltd. 1958; Operations Mgr. Jennings Drilling 1960; co-founder Petrolia Drilling Co. 1963; merged with Kenting Group 1967; became Vice Pres. Drilling Kenting Ltd. and Dir. 1972; named Pres. Kenting; Group 1973 (co. acquired by Trimac 1977, named Dir. Trimac Ltd. 1976); Director Western Rock Bit Co. Ltd.; Member Calgary Advisory Council of Salvation Army. Home: Calgary, Alta.; Office: (P.O. Box 3500), Calgary, Alta. T2P 2P9.

van der MEULEN, Emiel Georg, B.Sc., R.C.A.; landscape architect; b. Rheden, The Netherlands 6 Oct. 1928; s. Daniel and A.C.E. (Kelling) van der M.; e. High Sch. Zutphen, Netherlands 1947; Mich. State Univ. B.Sc. (Landscape Arch.) 1959, postgrad. Fellowship 1960; Harvard Univ. Master Landscape Arch. 1961; m. Elodie Charlotte Bamford d. Joseph Tomlinson, Nassau, Bahamas 8 Sept. 1979; children: Coral Ann Amanda, Emil George, Rossal Scott Sandford, Paul Ritchie Sandford, Susan Elodie Sandford; PRINC., EVM LTD. LAND-SCAPE ARCHITECTS 1976- ; Pres., VM Landscape Architects, Athens 1981- ; Canlarch 1978- ; Assoc. Prof. in Landscape Arch. Univ. of Toronto 1968-70; Dir. Landscape Arch. Dept. Ryerson Polytech. Inst. Toronto 1972-74; Prof. of Environmental Design King Abdul Aziz Univ. Jeddah, Saudi Arabia 1979-80; Princ., van der Meulen, Zohar, Associates Toronto 1969-76; maj. projects 1970-80 incl. Trent Univ. Landscape; Landscape Consultant to Queen's Univ.; Shaw Festival Theatre; Courtyard York Univ.; First Canadian Place Toronto; Royal Bank Plaza H.O. Toronto; New Massey Hall Toronto; Downtown West, Toronto; Royal Ont. Museum Courtyard; Bank of Canada, Ottawa; mem. Art Adv. Comte. City Hall Toronto 10 yrs.; Design Comte. Nat. Capital Comn. Ottawa, Chrmn. Fine Arts Comte.; Past Councillor Stratford Seminar Civic Design; mem. Royal Ont. Museum; Art Gallery of Ont.; served with Royal Netherlands Marines 1948-49; rec'd Civic Award City of Toronto 1979; Design Awards, Landscape Ont.; author various articles Landscape arch.; Fellow, Candn. Soc. Landscape Archs.; mem. Past Pres., Ont. Assn. Landscape Archs.; Am. Assn. Landscape Archs.; Atlantic Provs. Assn. Landscape Archs.; Beta Alpha Sigma (Past Pres.); recreations: scuba diving, sculpting, archeology; Home: 18 Artemidos, Holargos, Athens, Greece; Office: 77 Mowat Ave., Suite 201, Toronto, Ont. M6K 3E3.

van der MEULEN, Emiel Georg, B.Sc., R.C.A.; landscape architect; b. Rheden, The Netherlands 6 Oct. 1928; s. Daniel and A.C.E. (Kelling) van der M.; e. High Sch. Zutphen, Netherlands 1947; Mich. State Univ. B.Sc. (Landscape Arch.) 1959, postgrad. Fellowship 1960; Harvard Univ. Master Landscape Arch. 1961; children: Coral Ann Amanda, Emil George; PRINC., EVM LTD. LAND-SCAPE ARCHITECTS 1976- ; Pres., VM Ltd., Landscape Architects, Athens 1981- ; Pres., BVM Ltd., Landscape Consultants, Saudi Arabia Canlarch 1978- ; Assoc. Prof. in Landscape Arch. Univ. of Toronto 1968-70; Dir. Landscape Arch. Dept. Ryerson Polytech. Inst. Toronto 1972-73; Prof. of Environmental Design King Abdul Aziz Univ.

Jeddah, Saudi Arabia 1979-80; Princ., van der Meulen, Zohar, Associates Toronto 1969-76; maj. projects 1970-80 incl. Trent Univ. Landscape; Landscape Consultant to Queen's Univ.; Shaw Festival Theatre; Courtyard York Univ.; First Canadian Place Toronto; Royal Bank Plaza H.O. Toronto; New Massey Hall Toronto; Tea Garden, Old City Hall, Toronto; Downtown West, Toronto; Royal Ont. Museum Courtyard; Bank of Canada, Ottawa; mem. Art Adv. Comte. City Hall Toronto 10 yrs.; Design Comte. Nat. Capital Comn. Ottawa, Chrmn. Fine Arts Comte. L-N.C.C., Ottawa; Past Councillor Stratford Seminar Civic Design; mem. Royal Ont. Museum; Art Gallery of Ont.; served with Royal Netherlands Marines 1948-50; rec'd Civic Award City of Toronto 1979; Design Awards, Landscape Ont.; author various articles Landscape arch.; Fellow, Candn. Soc. Landscape Archs.; mem. Past Pres., Ont. Assn. Landscape Archs.; Am. Assn. Landscape Archs.; Atlantic Provs. Assn. Landscape Archs.; Beta Alpha Sigma (Past Pres.); recreations: scuba diving, sculpting; Office: 77 Mowat Ave., Suite 201, Toronto, Ont. M6K 3E3.

VANDERNOOT, Henry J. F.; executive; b. Ghent, Belgium, 17 May 1922; s. Armand and Jenny (Vanderhaeghen) V.; e. Univ. of Ghent, Civil Engn. 1946; m. Luce, d. Adelin Adam, 14 June 1947; children: Kathleen (Mrs. Michel Vinois), Michael, David, Danielle; CHRMN., FRANKI CANADA LTD.; Vice pres. (N. Amer.), Franki Internat.; Dir., Franki Foundation Co., Boston; Chmn., Franki Trinidad Ltd., Port of Spain; joined Electrorail 1946, subsequently stationed in Ghent, Brussels, Cairo and Montreal; joined present Co. as Works Mgr., Montreal 1958, Div. Mgr. 1961, Vice-Pres. 1964, Extve. Vice-Pres. 1972, Pres. 1972; served in 2nd World War, Volunteer, Belgium Army 1944-45; Past Pres., Engn. Inst. Can. (Montreal Br.); Past Vice-Pres., Montreal Constr. Assn.; Dir. & Vice Chmn., Candn. Constr. Assn.; mem. Candn. Geotech. Soc.; Candn. Soc. Civil Engrs.; Ordre des Ingénr. de la Prov. de Qué.; recreations: golf, bridge; Clubs: St-Denis; Royal Montreal Golf; Home: 376 Grenfell Ave., Town of Mount Royal, Que. H3R 1G3; Office: 1320 Graham Blvd., Town of Mount Royal, Que. H3P 3C8

Van der ZALM, Hon. William Nick; politician; b. Noordwykerhout, Holland 29 May 1934; s. Wilhelmus Antonius and Agatha C. (Warmerdam) Van der Z.; e. St. Josephs Noordwykerhout, Holland; Bradner and Mt. Lehman, B.C.; Phillip Sheffield, Abbotsford, B.C.; m. Lillian B. d. John Mihalick, Kelowna, B.C. 27 June 1956; children: Jeffrey, Juanita, Wim, Lucia; MIN. OF HUMAN RESOURCES, B.C. since 1976; Pres. Art Knapp Nurseries Ltd.; Ald. Surrey, B.C. 4 yrs., Mayor 6 yrs.; mem. K. of C.; Chamber Comm.; Social Credit; R. Catholic; recreations: gardening, fishing, soccer; Club: Lions; Home: 19003-88 Ave., Surrey, B.C. V3S 4P1; Office: Parliament Bldgs., Victoria, B.C.

van de WATER, Frank, B.Com., C.A.; executive; b. Amsterdam, The Netherlands 7 June 1941; s. J. H. A. van de Water; came to Can. 1947; e. West Hill High Sch. Montreal 1957; Sir George Williams Univ. B.Com. 1961; C.A. 1963; m. Jean Dulcie d. late Fraser McIntosh, N.Z. 27 Sept. 1975; one d. Melanie; VICE PRES. FINANCE AND SECY., CAE INDUSTRIES LTD. since 1979; Dir. CAE Electronics Ltd.; CAE Metals Ltd.; Canadian Bronze Co. Ltd.; Union Screen Plate Co. Ltd.; CAE Aircraft Ltd.; CAE Machinery Ltd.; Webster Manufacturing (London) Ltd.; Accurcast Die Casting Ltd.; CAE Morse Ltd.; Northwest Industries Ltd.; Welmet Industries Ltd.; CAE Montupet Ltd.; joined Coopers & Lybrand, Montreal and London, Eng. 1957 — 66; Controller, Patino, N.V., Toronto and London, Eng. 1966 — 73; Vice Pres. and Group Controller, Hambro Canada Ltd., Toronto 1973 — 75; Pres., Peel-Elder Developments Ltd. 1974 — 75; Vice Pres. Finance and Treas. Y & R Properties Ltd. 1976 — 79; mem. C.A.'s Inst. Que. and Ont.; Protestant; recreations: squash, skiing; Clubs: RCYC; Ontario; Cambridge;

Home: 99 Otter Cres., Toronto, Ont. M5N 2W9; Office: 3060 Royal Bank Plaza, Toronto, Ont. M5J 2J1.

van GINKEL, Blanche Lemco, B.Arch., M.C.P., F.R.A.I.C., M.C.I.P., R.C.A.; architect; educator; b. London, Eng. 14 Dec. 1923; d. Myer and Claire Lemco; e. McGill Univ. B.Arch. 1945; Harvard Univ. M.C.P. 1950; m. 1956; children: Brenda Renée, Marc Ian; PARTNER, van GINKEL ASSOCIATES 1957- ; Dir. Sch. of Arch. Univ. of Toronto 1977- , and Dean of Arch. & Landscape Arch. 1980- ; Mgr. City Planning Office Regina, Sask. 1946; Arch. Atelier Le Corbusier, Paris 1948; Asst. Prof. Univ. of Pa. 1951-57; mem. Nat. Capital Planning Comte.; Adv. Council Sch. of Arch. Princeton Univ.; recipient Lt. Gov.'s Medal 1945; Massey Medal for Arch. 1962; Candn. Arch. Award for Excellence 1972; Queen's Silver Jubilee Medal 1977; author various articles; Past Offr. Prov. Que. Assn. Archs.; Town Planners Inst. Can.; Corp. Urbanists Que.; Candn. Housing Design Council Can.; Bd. Internat. Film Festivals Montreal; Office: 34 Summerhill Gdns., Toronto; Ont. M4T 1B4.

VANIER, Guy, Q.C., LL.D.; b. Montreal, Que., 22 Dec. 1888; s. Joseph and Sephora (Dandurand) V.; e. St. Mary's Coll., Montreal, Que., B.A. (Medalist) 1908; Univ. of Montreal, LL.D.; m. Irène Grenier, grandd. Hon. Fèlix Gabriel Marchand, formerly Premier of Que.; one d., Lucie (Mrs. Auguste Vincent); SENIOR PARTNER, VANIER & VANIER, which he founded 1926; Vice Pres. and Dir., Gaz Metropolitain Inc.; Pres., Montreal City and District Savings Bank for 18 yrs. (retired); cr. K.C. 1926; practised with Hon. P. B. Migneault until his nomination to Supreme Court of Canada; Prof. Emeritus of Finance and Econ., Univ. of Montreal; mem., Montreal City Council, 1942-60; mem., of Montreal Metrop. Comn. and Pres. of Finance Comte. during many yrs.; known for his philanthropic and social activities and has travelled extensively throughout Europe and Am.; has done considerable lect. and has contrib. various articles to reviews; Roman Catholic; Home: 319 Redfern Ave., Westmount, Que. H3Z 2G4;

VAN IERSSEL, Harry, B.A., C.A.; administrator; b. Breda, The Netherlands, 25 July 1936; s. Harry Cornelis and Josephina Constanza Van I.; e. Holy Heart Pub. Sch., Breda, Holland, 1948; Gymnasium B, Canisius Coll., Nymegan, Holland, 1954; Sch. of Econ., Tilburg, Holland, B.A. (Econ.) 1958; C.A. (Ont.) 1963; m. Christine Ingrid Renata Repsilber, 21 Dec. 1963; children: Marcus, Jacqueline; FINANCIAL ADM., UNIV. OF TORONTO PRESS since 1967; Gen. Mgr., Downsview Div. since 1979; joined Deloitte Haskins & Sells as student-in-accts. Toronto, 1958, trans. to Montreal office 1963 and apptd. Supvr.; Asst. Comptroller, Associated Textiles Ltd., Montreal 1965; joined Clairtone Sound Ltd. to set up accounting system, Stellarton, N.S., 1966, trans. Toronto as Asst. to Vice Pres. Finance and apptd. to Group Comptroller of various Clairtone Co.'s 1967; Treas. (1975-76) Am. Univ. Press Services Inc. and Assn. of Am. Univ. Presses; Treasurer, Assn. of Candn. Publishers, 1978-81; co-author, "Publishing: The Creative Business" 1974; Chrmn., Stat. Comte., Assn. Am. Univ. Presses 1971-73 (mem. Comte. 1974-80); mem. Journals Comm. 1979-81; recreations: tennis, travel; Home: 262 Ridgewood Rd., West Hill, Ont. M1C 2X2; Office: 5201 Dufferin St., Downsview, Ont. M3H 5T8

VANNAN, Harley Benson; insurance executive; b. Schreiber, Ont., 2 Oct. 1920; s. Harley George and Katheryn Ethel (Benson) B.; e. Daniel McIntyre Coll. Inst.; m. Audrey Isabel, d. Robert Wright, Winnipeg, Man., 13 June 1947; children: Harley Wright, Jefferey Robert, Mark Allan, Lisa Katheryn, Gillian Leah; PRESIDENT AND DIR., THE CANADIAN INDEMNITY CO. (estbd. 1895) since 1970; Pres., Panamerican Surety Assoc.; Dir., United Canadian Shares Ltd.; Dir., Centre for Study of Insurance Operations; Underwriters Adjustment Bureau;

joined the Co. as Automobile Underwriter, Winnipeg, Man. 1947, Casualty Mgr. 1954, Vice-Pres., Underwriting 1963, el. a Dir. 1966; served in R.C.N. 1940-45, joining as Ordinary Coder, Leading Coder 1942, Sub-Lt. Extve. Br. 1943; rank on discharge Lt. Extve. Br.; Hon. Fellow, Ins. Inst. Can. (Pres. 1968-69); Assoc. mem. Ins. Inst. N. Am.; Pres., Ind. Ins. Conf. 1969-70; author of many articles on surety; recreations: golf, painting; Clubs: The Manitoba; Donalda; The Ontario; Home: 11 Denlow Blvd., Don Mills, Ont. M3B 1P3; Office: 3130 South Tower, Royal Bank Plaza, Toronto, Ont. M5J 2J1

VAN NEST, Norman Gary, B.Com.; investment dealer; b. Windsor, Ont., 22 July 1936; s. William Norman and Elmira Van N.; e. Patterson Coll., Windsor, Ont.; Univ. of Windsor, B.Com.; m. Joyce Elaine, d. Thomas B. Paterson, 27 July 1957; children: Richard Norman, Alison Joyce; PRESIDENT, HERITAGE SECURITIES CORP., June 1980- ; Pres. & C.E.O., Triarch 1975-1980; Chrmn. Expetro Resources Ltd., Calgary, 1980- ; Dir., Royal Candn. Geographic Soc.; National Business Systems Inc.; Eldorado Nuclear Ltd.; with Richardson Securities of Canada as Trainee, Toronto 1957; Salesman, Royal Securities Corp. Ltd., Montreal 1958, Sales Mgr. 1964, Extve. Asst., Business Devel. 1966; Dir., Wisener and Partners Ltd. 1967, Vice Pres. and Dir. 1969, Pres. and Dir. 1972, Chrmn. Bd. 1974 and Consultant till 1975; recreation: skiing, golf, squash, tennis; Clubs: St. James's (Montreal); Lambton Golf & Country; National; Cambridge; Home: 17 Kingsway Cres., Toronto, Ont. M8X 2P9; Office: 7 King St. East, Ste. 1404, Toronto, Ont. M5C 1A6

van ROGGEN, Hon. George Clifford; senator; b. Vancouver, B.C., 22 July 1921; s. Matthew A. and Margaret (Risteen) van R.; e. Univ. of B.C., ; children: Norman, Trish; called to Bars of B.C. 1947 and Yukon 1949; partner Vancouver legal firm Douglas, Symes and Brissenden until retirement from active practise in 1981; summoned to Senate 4 Nov. 1971; Chrmn., Senate Standing Comte. on Foreign Affairs since 1974; Candn. Co-Chrmn., Candn.-European Parliament Inter-parliamentary Group 1974-78 and Chrmn. 1980; mem., Can.-U.S. Interparliamentary Group 1973-81; mem. Bd. of Trustees of Discovery Foundation; Life Fellow, Foundation for Legal Research in Can.; Dir. Weyerhaeuser Canada Ltd.; Dillingham Corp. Can. Ltd.; Liberal; Clubs: Vancouver; Canadian; Offices: 602-1285 West Pender St., Vancouver, B.C. V6E 4B1; The Senate, Parliament Buildings, Ottawa, Ont. K1A 0A4

VAN ROOYEN, Clennel Evelyn, M.D., Ch.B., D.Sc., F.R.C.P., F.R.C.P.(C); F.R.C.(Path.), F.R.S.C. (1970); university professor; b. Ceylon, 28 Sept. 1907; s. Dr. Charles Ellard and Annie Priscilla V. R.; e. The Roy. Infirmary, Edinburgh; Univ. of Edinburgh, M.B., Ch.B. 1931; M.D. 1934, D.Sc. 1941; F.R.C.P. (Lond.) (awarded Gunning Prizes in med. and Pathol., also Lewis Cameron Prize in Diagnosis of Disease) m. Hilda Mary, d. Albert Price, Londonderry, 3 Aug. 1946; came to Can. 1946; PROF. EMERITUS OF MICROBIOLOGY, DALHOUSIE UNIV. MEDICAL SCHOOL and Consultant to Victoria Gen. Hosp., Halifax, N.S.; Dir., N.S. Div. of Pub. Health Labs.; Consulting Bacteriol., Camp. Hill Hosp., D.V.A.; Childrens Hosps., Halifax; Canadian Forces Hosp., R.C.N., Halifax; former Lect. in Med., Roy. Coll. of Phys. of Can., former Sr. Lect. in Bacteriol., Univ. of Edinburgh; Hon. Extra Bacteriol. to The Roy. Infirmary of Edinburgh; formerly, Sir Halley Stewart Trust, London Research Fellow; served in World War, 1939-45; Pathol., 1st Gen. Hosp., R.A.M.C., B.E.F., Dieppe, France, subsequently, Offr. with special knowledge of virus diseases to Central Lab. of Middle East Force, Egypt; Pathol. to Edinburgh Castle Mil. Hosp., Scot. Command; Mentioned in Despatches; demobilized 1945 with Hon. rank of Maj., R.A.M.C.; awarded Order of Ismail (4th Class, Mil. Div.) Egypt, in recognition of services rendered to study of typhus fever and smallpox; Past Pres., Candn. Soc. of Microbiol.; Queen's Silver Jubilee Medal, 1978; co-author, with Dr. Andrew Rhodes, of "Virus Diseases of Man", 1940; also "A Textbook of Virology for Medical Students", 1968; author of "Muirs Bacteriological Atlas" (2nd ed.) 1937 also contrib. to med. and scient. literature on study of virus diseases of man, bacteriol. and immunology; Presbyterian; recreations: golf, fishing; Home: 1074 Wellington St., Halifax, N.S. B3H 2Z8

VAN SANT, Vernon, Jr.; petroleum executive; b. Morehead, Ky., 27 May 1921; s. Vernon and Jessie Milton (Jones) Van S.; children: Frances Helen, Donna Kathlyn, Jessie Lee, Benjamin Franklin, Rebecca Anne; DIR., CHRMN. OF THE BOARD & C.E.O., FRANCANA OIL & GAS LTD.; Pres., Gen. Mgr. and Dir., Kananaskis Exploration & Development Co. Ltd.; Brazeau Collieries Ltd.; Whitehall Mining Co. Ltd.; Dir. Kananaskis Mines Ltd.; Midhurst Corp.; Camco. Inc.; Hudson Bay Mining and Smelting Co., Ltd.; served with USN, S. Pacific, 1943-46; mem., Candn. Petrol. Assn.; Independent Petrol Assn. Can. (Past Dir. & Treas.; mem. Comte.); Protestant; recreations: outdoor sports, shooting, fishing; Home: 24 Eagle Ridge Dr. S.W., Calgary, Alta. T2V 2V4; Office: 700, 505-5th Street S.W., Calgary, Alta. T2P 3J2

Van SCHAIK, Gerard, M.Sc., M.A.; executive; b. Eindhoven, Holland, 17 Nov. 1930; s. John A. and (Sophia Kraan) Van S.; e. Carnegie Inst. of Technol., B.Sc. (Mech. Engn.) 1957; Ecole Polytechnique, M.Sc. 1959; McGill Univ., Dipl. in Mang. 1964; Univ. of Sherbrooke, M.A. (Econ.) 1967; m. Henriette Christina Helga, d. Gerard Veldhuis, Groningen, Holland 4 Apl. 1959; children: André Louis, Clare Frances; Management Consultant (Self-employed), Toronto, since 1978; Past President, Beloit Canada Ltee/Ltd. 1974-78; Asst. Gen. Mgr., Velan Engineering, Montreal 1960; Vice Pres. of Mfg., B. K. Johl 1963; Production Mgr., Canadian Ingersoll-Rand 1965; Plant Mgr., Canadian Allis Chalmers 1966-69; self employed mang. consultant, Vancouver 1970-74; mem. Assn. of Prof. Engrs. of Ont.; Am. Soc. Mech. Engrs.; R. Catholic; recreations: reading, photography; jogging; Home: 44 Palomino Cres., Willowdale, Ont. M2K 1W3

VAN TIGHEM, Clarence Joseph, B.Com.; diplomat; b. Strathmore, Alta., 12 March 1921; s. Joseph L. and Jane (Kelly) Van T.; e. Queen's Univ.; Univ. of Manitoba, B.Com. 1942; m. Noëlle Mary, d. late George Frederick Waters, 23 April 1949; children: Paul Gregory, Mark David, John Michael; CHIEF OF PROTOCOL, DEPT. OF INDUSTRY, TRADE, AND COMMERCE since 1981; joined Fed. Dept. Trade and Comm. 1945; Comm. Secy., Candn. Embassy, Lima, Peru 1945; Consul and Trade Commr., Sao Paulo, Brazil 1949; Comm. Secy., Rio de Janeiro, Brazil 1954; Comm. Counsellor, Mexico City, Mexico 1956; Dir., Trade Publicity Br., Dept. Trade and Comm., Ottawa 1959; Comm. Counsellor, Vienna, Austria 1962; Depy. Consul. Gen. (Comm.) New York 1964; Min. Comm., Candn. High Comn., London, Eng. 1969; Ambassador to Venezuela and concurrently to Dominican Republic 1972; Consul General, Milan, Italy, 1975; served in R.C.N.V.R., Lt. 1942-45; R. Catholic; recreation: golf; Office: 235 Queen St., Ottawa, Ont. K1A 0H5

VAN VLIET, Maurice Lewis, O.C., M.S., Ph.D., LL.D.; educator; b. Bellingham, Wash., 3 Aug. 1913; s. Frank Davis and Nellie (Booker) V.; e. Univ. of Ore., B.S. 1936, M.S. 1939; Univ. of Cal., Los Angeles, Ph.D. 1950; Univ. of W. Ont., LL.D. 1973; Univ. of Windsor, LL.D. 1978; Univ. of Alta., LL.D. 1979; Dalhousie Univ., LL.D. 1979; Queen's Univ., LL.D. 1980; Univ. of Victoria, LL.D., 1982; m. Virginia, d. Capt. William Peace Gaddis, Cal., 9 Sept. 1936; children: Maury, Victoria, Pieter, Katherine; DEAN, FACULTY OF PHYSICAL EDUC., UNIV. OF ALBERTA since 1962; Dir. of Phys. Educ., Univ. of B.C. 1936-45 and of present Univ. 1945-62; served with Candn. Reserve Forces; rank Maj. on retirement; rec'd

Centennial Award 1967; Premier's award for Excellence 1978; Edmonton's 75th Anniversary Award; Cert. of Meritorious Service, City of Edmonton; Candn. Parks & Recreation Assn. Honor Award; Fed. Scholarship for Advanced Study; Nat. Fitness & Amateur Sport Travel Fellowship; Alumnus of the Yr. (1967), Citrus Coll., Cal.; Pres. XI Commonwealth Games; mem. Edmonton Sportsmen Hall of Fame; author, "Physical Education for Junior and High Schools", 1956; co-author, "Physical Education and Recreation in Europe", 1963; "Physical Education Activities for Secondary Schools", 1967; Ed., "Physical Education in Canada", 1965; Bd. mem., Digital Equipment of Canada; Past Chrmn., Alta. Prov. Recreation Bd.; Fellow, Am. Coll. Sports Med.; Past Pres., B.C. Phys. Educ. Assn.; Alta. Assn. Health, Phys. Educ. & Recreation; W. Candn. Intercoll. Athletic Assn.; Alta. Paraplegic Assn.; Candn. Intercoll. Athletic Union; Candn. Assn. Health, Phys. Educ. & Recreation (Honor Award, Hon. Pres.); Alta. Recreation Assn.; Chrmn., Candn. Wheelchair Sports Assn.; mem., Candn. Assn. Sports Sciences; Am. Assn. Health, Phys. Educ. & Recreation; Nat. Coll. Phys. Assn. Men.; Pres. (1974-75), Candn. Council Univ. Phys. Educ. Adms.; B.C. Sports Hall of Fame, 1981; Kappa Sigma; Protestant; recreations: golf, swimming, cross-country skiing, camping; Club: Edmonton Centre (Chmn. of Bd.); Rotary; Home: RR #1, Gunn, Alta. T0E 1A0; Home: 13910 Stony Plain Rd., Apt. 503, Edmonton, Alta. T5N 3R2

van VOGT, Alfred E., A.B.; professional writer; b. Manitoba, 26 Apl. 1912; s. Henry and Agnetha (Buhr) van V.; e. Pub. Sch., Neville, Sask., and Morden, Man.; Kelvin Tech. High Sch., Winnipeg, Man.; courses at Univs. of Ottawa and California; Hon. A.B. Golden State University, Los Angeles, California; m. late Edna Mayne Hull, Winnipeg, Man., 9 May 1939; 2nd, Lydia Brayman, (Sup. Ct. Interpretor) Oct. 6, 1979; has been writing professionally since 1932, short stories, articles, serials, books and radio plays; rep. in Winnipeg, Man., of business paper of Maclean Publ. Co., Toronto, Ont., 1937-39; mem. of Extve., Candn. Authors' Assn., Toronto, Ont., Br., 1943-44; mem., Authors' Guild; Authors' League of Am.; is a student of gen. semantics, dianetics and hypnosis and has given talks and demonstration on all; Pres., Hubbard Dianetic Auditors Assn. Internat. 1951-52; Pres., Cal. Assn. of Dianetic Auditors, since 1960; Pres., Internat. Dianetic Soc., Inc., since 1957; author of "Slan", 1946; "The Weapon Makers", 1947; "The Book of Ptath", 1947; "Out of the Unknown" (with E. Mayne Hull, short stories), 1948; "The World of A.", 1948; "Masters of Time", 1950; "Away and Beyond" (short stories), 1950; "Voyage of the Space Beagle", 1950; "House That Stood Still", 1950; "Destination: Universe" (short stories), 1951; "Weapon Shops of Isher", 1951; "The Mixed Men", 1952; co-author with psychologist Charles E. Cooke, of "The Hypnotism Handbook", 1956; "Planets for Sale" (with E. Mayne Hull), 1954; "Empire of the Atom", 1956; "The Mind Cage", 1957; "The War Against the Rull", 1959; "The Violent Man", 1962; "The Beast", 1963; "Rogue Ship", 1965; "The Winged Man" (with E. Mayne Hull), 1966; "The Universe Maker", 1953; "The Pawns of Null-A", 1956; "Siege of the Unseen" 1959; "The Wizard of Linn", 1962; "Monsters" (short stories), 1965; "The Far-Out Worlds of A. E. van Vogt" (short stories), 1968; "Quest for the Future", 1970; "Children of Tomorrow", 1970; "The Battle of Forever", 1971; "The Proxy Intelligence and other Mind Benders", 1971; "M-33 in Andromeda", 1971; "The Darkness on Diamondia", 1972; "The Money Personality" (non-fiction) 1972; "The Book of Van Vogt", 1972; "Future Glitter" 1973; "The Secret Galactics" 1974; "The Man with a Thousand Names" 1974; "Reflections of A. E. Van Vogt" (autobiography) 1975; "The Best of A. Van Vogt", 1976; "The Anarchistic Colossus", 1977; "Supermind", 1977; "Pendulum," a collection all new stories, 1978; "Renaissance", novel, 1979; "Cosmic Encounter", novel, 1980; Home: 2850 Belden Dr., Los Angeles, Cal. 90068.

VAN WACHEM, Gerardus J., executive; b. P. Brandan, Indonesia, 15 Oct. 1925; s. Gerardus and Annigje (Verheul) V.; e. High Sch. and Univ. Entrance Holland; Univ. of Alta. Extension Courses (Mang. Devel., Stnary Steam Engn.); children: Gerard, Anne, Yolande, Ron; PRESIDENT AND GEN. MGR. WESTANK INDUSTRIES LTD. since 1969; Dir. Industrial Leaseholds; Ralph MacKay Canada Ltd.; joined CIL as Process Operator; Pres. Edmonton Barrel Co. Ltd. 1962-69; served with Dutch Marines; recreation: sailing; Home: Saskatchewan Beach, Sask.; Office: Park St., Regina, Sask.

VAN ZUIDEN, Thomas, F.C.A.; executive; b. The Netherlands 26 Sept. 1924; s. Louw Van Zuiden; e. Chatham (Ont.) Coll. Inst.; Inst. C.A.'s Ont., C.A. 1948; VICE PRES.-FINANCE, DOFASCO INC.; Dir. May & Baker Canada Inc.; Past Pres. Financial Extves. Inst. Can.; Protestant; recreations: golf, skiing; Clubs: Hamilton; Hamilton Golf & Country; Home: 81 Auchmar Rd., Hamilton, Ont. L9C 1C6; Office: P.O. Box 460, Hamilton, Ont. L8N 3J5.

VARDY, Maxwell Clarence; forestry executive; b. Millertown, Nfld., 5 July 1917; s. George and Lily (Martin) V.; e. Amalg. Sch., Howley; Atlantic Summer Sch. in Advanced Business Adm., King's Coll., Halifax; m. Irene, d. Ernest King, Corner Brook, 12 March 1938; children: (Mrs.) Earle Pollett, Cyril Vardy; DIR. AND WOODLANDS MGR., BOWATERS NEWFOUNDLAND LTD., since 1970; joined Co. in 1933; worked in woods labour for 5 yrs., scaling for 6 yrs.; Camp Foreman, 1946; Dist. Supt., Glenwood, 1948; Gen. Supt., Coastal Operations and Glenwood, 1955; apptd. Asst. Woods Mgr., 1962; Woodlands Mgr. 1967; el. a Dir. 1970; mem., Candn. Inst. of Forestry; Candn. Pulp & Paper Assn. (Woodlands Sec.); Freemason; United Church; recreations: hunting, fishing, curling; Clubs: Lions; Blomidon Country; Gander Airport; Home: 14 Marcelle Avenue, Corner Brook, Nfld. A2H 2V7; Office: Corner Brook, Nfld.

VARSHNI, Yatendra Pal, M.Sc., Ph.D., F.A.P.S., F. Inst. P. F.R.A.S.; educator; b. Allahabad, India 21 May 1932; s. Harpal; e. Univ. of Allahabad B.Sc. 1948, M.Sc. 1952, Ph.D. 1956; PROF. OF PHYSICS, UNIV. OF OTTAWA 1969- ; Asst. Prof. of Physics Univ. Allahabad 1955-60; Postdoctorate Fellow, Nat. Research Council, Ottawa 1960-62; Asst. Prof. present Univ. 1962, Assoc. Prof. 1965; recipient Ward-Vidyant Gold Medal 1952; Univ. Jubilee Silver Medal 1952; author numerous research publs. astrophysics, nuclear structure, molecular structure, solid-state physics; Fellow, Brit. Interplanetary Soc.; Indian Physical Soc.; mem. Candn. Assn. Physicists; Candn. Astron. Soc.; Royal Astron. Soc. Can.; Am. Astron. Soc.; Astron. Soc. Pacific; Am. Assn. Physics Teachers; Am. Assn. Advanc. Science; European Physical Soc.; Hindu; recreations: reading history of science, biographies; Home: Apt. 1102, 333 Chapel St., Ottawa, Ont. K1N 8Y8; Office: 375 Nicholas St., Ottawa, Ont. K1N 6N5.

VAS, Stephen I., M.D., Ph.D.; physician; university professor; b. Budapest, Hungary 4 June 1926; came to Can. 1957; s. Gyula and Ilona (Rosenberg) V.; e. Univ. of Budapest M.D. 1950, Ph.D. 1956; m. Magdalene d. Stephen Raditz 25 April 1953; PHYSICIAN, TORONTO WESTERN HOSP.; PROF., UNIV. OF TORONTO; author of over 60 scientific articles; Home: 96 Princess Margaret Blvd., Etobicoke, Ont. M9B 2Y9; Office: 399 Bathurst St., Toronto, Ont. M5T 2S8.

VAUCLAIR, André S.; real estate investments executive; b. Montreal, Que. 1932; e. Officers Sch. Candn. Army 1949-51; Univ. of Montreal Ecole Polytechnique, Civil Engn. 1956; Real Estate Appraising 1956; m.; 4 children; VICE PRES. REAL ESTATE INVESTMENTS, METROPOLITAN LIFE INSURANCE CO. 1976- ; City Assessor's Dept. Cité de Montréal 1956-62; Coronation Credit Corp.

1962-68; Regional Supvr. Real Estate Financing Office Montreal present Co. 1968, Asst. Vice Pres. Real Estate Financing 1973; served with Régt. de Maisonneuve (Reserve) 1951-60, rank Capt.; Vice Pres. Parents Council 1974-76; Chrmn. Finance Sec. Centraide (Un. Way) Montreal Region 1976-80; mem. Les Vignerons de Saint-Vincent; mem. Order Engrs. Que.; Internat. Council Shopping Centers; Mortgage Bankers Assn.; Montreal Real Estate Bd.; Candn. Real Estate Bd.; recreations: tennis, gourmet cooking; Home: 371 Morrison, Town of Mount Royal, Que. H3R 1K8; Office: 1550 Place du Canada, Montreal, Que. H3B 2N2.

VAUGHAN, David Lisle, Q.C., B.A., LL.B.; b. Vancouver, B.C., 15 Feb. 1922; s. William Randolph and Blanche (Park) V.; e. Lord Byng High Sch., Vancouver; Univ. of B.C., B.A. 1943; LL.B. 1948; m. Mavis Ann, d. Dudley Christopher Carter, Anacortes, Wash., 20 May 1944; children: Michael David, Anna Teresa, Peter Christopher; MEM., ASSOCIATE COUNSEL, VAUGHAN & COMPANY; mem., Assessment Appeal Bd. of B.C.; formerly Sr. Partner, Farris, Vaughan, Wills & Murphy; read law with Mr. Justice E. B. Bull; called to Bar of B.C. 1948; cr. Q.C. 1967; Assoc., Farris, Stultz, Bull & Farris, 1948; Partner 1956; served with Candn. Army 1943-45; rank Lt. on discharge; joined The Brit. Columbia Regt. (DCO) 1946; C.O. 1962; retired 1964; Trustee, B.C. Regiment Assn.; Life mem., The Royal Candn. Armoured Corps Assn. (Cavalry); Chmn. of Bd., Festival Concert Soc., Johannesen Internat. School of Arts; Canada Opera Piccola & Victoria Internat. Festival, 1980-81; mem., Vancouver Art Gallery; Founding mem., Metrop. Co-op Theatre Soc.; mem., Vancouver Bar Assn. (Extve 1954); Candn. Bar Assn.; Liberal; Protestant; recreations: sailing, gardening; Clubs: Vancouver; University; W. Vancouver Yacht; Office: 16th floor, 1100 Melville St., Vancouver, B.C. V6E 4B4

VAUGHAN, Sir G. Edgar, K.B.E. (1963), M.A., F.R.Hist.S.; retired university professor and diplomat; b. Cardiff, Wales, 24 Feb. 1907; s. William John and Kate (Caudle) V.; e. Cheltenham Grammar Sch., 1916-25; Jesus Coll., Oxford Univ., B.A. 1928 (Modern Hist.-1st Class Hons.), 1929 (Philos., Politics & Econ.-1st Class Hons.), M.A. 1935; Laming Travelling Fellow, Queen's Coll., Oxford Univ. 1929-31; m. Elsie Winifred Deubert, 15 July, 1933; two d., one s.; Professor of History, University of Saskatchewan, Regina Campus 1967-74; Dean, Faculty of Arts and Science (Regina Campus), 1969-73; mem. of Brit. Foreign Service serving in Consular and Dipl. posts in Europe, Africa, U.S.A. and Latin Am. (17 yrs.), 1931-66; Brit. Ambassador to Panama, 1960-64 and to Colombia, 1964-66; joined Univ. of Sask. as Special Lectr. in Hist., 1966; named Hon. Fellow of Jesus Coll., Oxford Univ., 1966; mem., Soc. for Latin Am. Studies, England; Hist. Soc. of Guelph, Ontario; recreations: historical research, golf; Club: Travellers' (London, Eng.); Home: 27 Birch Grove, West Acton, London W39S.P.

VAUGHAN, Ralph Thomas, Q.C., LL.B., LL.D.; b. Halifax, N.S., 12 July 1919; s. Francis William and late Lillian Clare (Hemsworth) V.; e. Common Schs., Halifax, N.S.; St. Mary's Univ., B.A. 1940, LL.D. 1969; Dalhousie Univ., LL.B. 1943; m. Elinore Pauline Gavin, 28 Oct. 1950; children: Gavin, Scott, Martha, Patrick; SENIOR VICE. PRES., CORPORATE & LEGAL AFFAIRS, AIR CANADA since 1980; read law with Daley, Phinney and Fielding & O'Hearn; called to Bar of N.S. 1948; News Ed., "Halifax-Herald", 1943-47; Partner, Fielding, OHearn & Vaughan till 1950; Extve. Asst. to Premier Angus L. Macdonald, 1951-54; joined CNR as Special Asst. to the Pres., 1955, Asst. to Pres. 1958, Secy. of Co. subsidiaries and Air Canada, 1962; Vice Pres., Asst. to Chrmn. & Secy. CNR, 1972; in same post Air Canada 1971-73; Pres. Air Canada, 1973-75; Sr. Vice Pres., Corp. Serv. 1976-79; served with Candn. Army, 1944-46, discharged with rank Capt.; mem., N.S. Barristers' Soc.; Candn. Bar Assn.;

Hon. Vice Pres., Que. Prov. Council of Boy Scouts of Can.; Officer, Order of St. John of Jerusalem; R. Catholic; recreation: golf; Clubs: St. James's; Summerlea Golf & Country; Home: 393 Devon Ave., Town of Mount Royal, Que. H3R 1C1; Office: Place Ville Marie, Montreal, Que. H3B 3P7

VAYDA, Eugene, B.S., M.D., F.R.C.P.(C), F.A.C.P., F.A.P.H.A.; educator; b. Cleveland, Ohio 1 Aug. 1925; s. Sol Aren and Sophie (Berman) V.; e. Case Western Reserve Univ. B.S. 1948, M.D. 1951; m. Elaine Ruth d. Philip E. Jacobs, Cleveland, Ohio 18 June 1949; children: Joseph Marc, Paul Andrew; ASSOCIATE DEAN, COMMUNITY HEALTH UNIV. OF TORONTO since 1981 and Prof. of Med.; Intern, Resident and Teaching Fellow Dept. Med. Univ. Hosps. Cleveland 1951-55; Boston Veteran's Hosp. 1953-54; private practice Internal Med. Cleveland 1955-64; Med. Dir. Community Health Foundation Cleveland 1964-69, concurrently Asst. Prof. Depts. Internal Med. and Preventive Med. Case Western Reserve Univ.; Visiting Fellow, Epidemiol. and Pub. Health Yale Univ. 1969-70; Assoc. Prof. and Prof. Depts. Clin. Epidemiol. and Biostats. & Med. McMaster Univ. 1970-76; Prof. and Chmn. Dept. of Health Admin. 1976-81; rec'd Faculty Fellowship Award Milbank Mem. Fund 1966-73; served with US Army 1944-46; Home: 40 Oaklands Ave., Toronto Ont. M4V 2Z3; Office: University of Toronto, McMurrich Bldg., Toronto, Ont. M5S 1A8.

VENIOT, Harvey A., Q.C., M.H.A., B.A., LL.B.; judge; b. Pictou, N.S., 18 Nov. 1915; s. Alexander R. and Gladys (Maclean) V.; e. Pictou (N.S.) Acad., 1934; St. Francis Xavier Univ., B.A. 1936; Dalhousie Law Sch.; Univ. of Sask., LL.B. 1939; m. Rhoda Marion, d. Jack and Nettie MacLeod, Montague, P.E.I., 10 Feb. 1942; children: James Stewart, Susan Rhoda; JUDGE OF PROVINCIAL COURT OF NOVA SCOTIA, 1979- ; read law with J. Welsford MacDonald, Q.C.; called to Bar of N.S. 1940; cr. Q.C. 1960; def. in Prov. g.e. 1953; 1st el. 1956; re-el. since; apptd. Speaker of N.S. Assembly 1961; Min. of Agric. 1968; Min. of Municipal Affairs, 1969; defeated in prov. el. 1974, returned to law practice; appt'd judge Jan 1979; former Solr., Town of Pictou; mem., N.S. Bar Assn.; P. Conservative; R. Catholic; recreations: swimming, golf; Clubs: Pictou Lions (Past Pres.); Pictou; Home: 56 Faulkland St., Pictou, N.S. B0K 1H0

VENNE, Gerard, E.D., F.R.A.I.C., Hon. F.A.I.A.; b. Québec, Qué., 23 Oct. 1910; s Alexandrine (Emond) and late Joseph Venne; e. St. Louis de Gonzague, Que.; Séminaire de Qué., Qué., 1930; Beaux-Arts de Qué., Arch.; m. Florence, d. late Eric Klaus, 17 July 1943; mem. of Extve., Royal Arch. Inst. Can., since 1940 (Vice Pres. 1964-65; Pres. 1965-66; Registrar, Coll. of Fellows, 1962-65); Chancellor, Coll. of Fellows, 1973-75; Vice Pres., Permanent Town Planing Comte., City of Sillery; mem., Structural Group, Revision Comte. on Nat. Bldg. Code, Nat. Research Council, 1959-65; served with Militia, 1931-40 and 1945-62; Active Service 1940-45; R.O. since 1942, rank Lt. Col.; Pres., Jr. Chamber Comm., 1947-48; Que. Press Club 1950-51; Prov. Que. Assn. Archs. 1958; Que. Reform Club 1959; Prov. Que. Curlers Assn. 1960-61 (Trustee since 1962); Que. Central Lions 1956-57 (Zone Chrmn. 1958-59; Dist. Gov. 1964-65; Internat. Counsellor 1965); mem., United Services Inst.; Anciens de Laval; R. Catholic; Clubs: Quebec Winter; Jacques-Cartier Curling; Lorette Golf; Levis Golf; Home and Office: 1531 Gignac, Sillery, Qué. G1T 2M6;

VENNEMA, Alje, O.C. (1967), M.D., C.M., M.P.H.-T.M.; b. Leeuwarden, The Netherlands, 11 Aug. 1932; s. Sytze and Tryntje (Hiemstra) V.; came to Can. 1951; e. Western Reserve Univ., B.A. 1958; McGill Univ., M.D.C.M. 1962; Tulane Univ., M.P.H.-T.M. 1969; Hammersmith Post-grad. Med. Sch., London, Eng., Internal Med. 1969; Welsh Nat. Sch. of Med., Dipl. in Tuberculosis and Chest Diseases (D.T.C.D.) 1970; Med. Offr., Cot-

tage Hosp., Govt. of Nfld., 1963-64; Team Capt., Volunteer Med. Team CARE-MEDICO, Prov. Hosp., Quang-Ngai, S. Vietnam, 1964-65; Tech. Adviser to Govt. of S. Vietnam under Candn. Colombo Plan, assigned to Prov. Hosp., 1965-66; Dir. of Candn. Med. Assistance to S. Vietnam, 1966-68; mem. Faculty of Med., Univ. of Dar es Salaam, Tanzania 1970-72; Univ. London, Sch. Tropical Med. & Hygiene and Sch. Econs., research in demography 1972-74; Dept. Pediatrics, Tulane Univ., New Orleans; now Asst. Prof. Pediatrics, New York Univ. Sch. Med.; Dir., Pediatric Education, N.Y. Infirmary; Director, Bureau of Tuberculosis, N.Y. City Dept. of Health; Medical Dir. (USA), Tom Dooley Heritage Inc. rec'd Order of Merit, Govt. of S. Vietnam, 1965; Distinguished Grad. Award, McGill Univ., 1966; Order of Distinguished Service to Vietnamese People, Govt. of S. Vietnam, 1968; co-author, "Harvest of Death", 1972; "The Viet Cong Massacre at Hue" 1975; author of various articles for prof. journs.; mem., Candn. Med. Assn.; Ont. Med. Assn.; mem. American Thoracic Soc. Home: 2120 Wellington Ave., Burlington, Ont. L7R 1P5

VENNING, Eleanor M. Hill, B.A., M.Sc., Ph.D., F.R.S.C.; retired professor; b. Montreal, Que., 16 March 1900; d. George W. (noted Candn. Sculptor) and Elsie A. (Kent) H.; e. McGill Univ., B.A., 1920, M.Sc. 1921; Ph.D. 1933; m. late Edward A. Venning, 1929; Prof. of Exper. Medicine, McGill Univ. and Research Assoc., Royal Victoria Hosp. (Univ. Clinic) until 1968; primarily interested in clin. research in Endocrinology (fat metabolism, reproductive hormones and adrenal cortical function); mem., Candn. Physiol. Soc. (Pres. 1954-55) Endocrine Soc., (U.S.); Fellow, New York Acad. of Science; mem., Soc. Biol. Chem.; Sigma Xi; Protestant; Home: 250 Clarke Ave., Montreal, Que. H3Z 2E5

VERDIER, Philippe M; educator; b. Lambersart (Nord), France 5 Oct. 1912; e. Ecole Normale Supérieure, France 1933-37; Sorbonne 1929-36; Ecole Française de Rome 1938-39; m. Patricia Cowles 3 July 1954; children: Francesca, Claire-Elisabeth, Caroline, Patrik; PROF. ET DIR. D'HISTOIRE DE L'ART, UNIV. DE MONTREAL since 1966, Professor Emeritus, 1979; Consultant, Menil Foundation Inc. Houston and Paris; served as Prof. Lycée de Bar-le-Duc and Saint-Brieuc, France; French Insts. of Barcelona and Madrid; Fellowship Yale Univ. 1951-52; Visiting Prof. Bryn Mawr Coll. Pa. 1952-53, Yale Univ. 1959, 1961, The Johns Hopkins Univ. 1954-65, Harvard Univ. 1967; Curator, The Walters Art Gallery, Baltimore 1953-65, Museum of Art, Carnegie Inst. 1963-64; mem. Sch. for Advanced Study, Princeton 1964-65; Visiting Prof. Univ. de Poitiers 1964, Univ. de Montréal 1965-66, Carleton Univ. 1972-74; co-organizer "Art and the Courts, France and England from 1254 to 1328" Nat. Gallery of Can. 1972; rec'd Killam Fellowship 1974-76; collab. Marshall Council, Paris 1947-48; Dir., Formes de l'Art, Paris 1948-50; Dir. Internat. Center Medieval Art 1965-68; mem. Conf. des recteurs et des principaux des universités du Qué. 1973-74; Représentant le Can. au Comité internat. d'Histoire de l'Art 1968-74; Curator, The Cleveland Museum of Art, 1979-81; served with French Air Force 1937-38, 1939-40, 1945; rec'd Légion d'Honneur, author "L'Art Religieux" 1956; "Russian Art" 1959; "Arts of the Migration Period" 1961; "The Arts in Europe Around 1400" 1962; "The Painted Enamels of the Renaissance" 1967; "Ancient Bronzes" 1964; "L'Art et la cour, France en Angleterre 1254-1328", "Art and the Courts, France and England from 1254-1328" 1972; "The Role of Women in the Middle Ages" 1975; "La Wallonie Le Pays des Hommes" 1977; "Limoges Painted Enamels" 1977; "Le Couronnement de la Vierge", 1980; "Animals In Ancient Art", 1981; over 200 articles publ. Europe, USA and Can.; mem. Royal Soc. Can.; Liberal; R. Catholic; Address: RFD #1, Haversham, Westerly, Rhode Island 02891.

VERGE, Hon. Lynn, M.H.A.; politician; MIN. OF EDUC., NFLD. 1979- ; el. M.H.A. for Humber East prov.

g.e. 1979; P. Conservative; Office: (P.O. Box 2017) Confederation Bldg., St. John's, Nfld. A1C 5R9.

VERNEY, Douglas V., M.A., Ph.D.; university professor; b. Liverpool, England, 21 Jan. 1924; s. John Henry and Olive Shirley (Barritt) V.; e. Oriel Coll., Oxford, B.A. 1947, M.A. 1948; Liverpool Univ., Ph.D. 1954; m. Diana Mary Read, d. William Robinson, Cheshire, Eng., 24 June 1950 (deceased 1974); two s.; Andrew John Edmund, Jonathan Edward; m. Prof. Francine Ruth Frankel, 28 Nov. 1975; PROF. OF POL. SCIENCE, YORK UNIV.; Chrmn. of the Dept., 1962-67; Lektor, Svenska Handelhogskolan, Helsinki, 1948-49; Asst. Lectr. and Lectr. in Pol. Science, Univ. of Liverpool, 1949-61; Commonwealth Fund Fellow, Columbia Univ., 1953, and Univ. of Cal. (Berkeley), 1954; Visiting Assoc. Prof., Univ. of Florida, 1958-59; Assoc. Prof. of Pol. Science, York Univ., 1961-62; Visiting Grad. Prof., Columbia Univ. 1967; Can. Council Sr. Fellow 1967-68, 1974-75; served as Capt., W. Somerset Yeomanry (R.A.); Publications: "Parliamentary Reform in Sweden 1866-1921" 1957; "Public Enterprise in Sweden", 1959; "The Analysis of Political Systems", 1959; "Political Patterns in Today's World" (with Prof. Sir Denis Brogan) 1963, 1968; "British Government and Politics", 1966, 1971, 1976; and various articles to journs., Editor, "Canadian Public Administration" 1970-74; Dir., Soc. Sci Research Council of Can. 1972-74; mem., Inst. for Advanced Study, Princeton, N.J. 1977-78; mem., Pol. Studies Assn. of U.K.; Am. Pol. Science Assn.; Candn. Pol. Science Assn. (Pres. 1969-70); Internat. Pol. Science Assn.; Inst. Public Adm.; Candn. Inst. Internat. Affairs; Anglican; Club: University; recreations: tennis, squash; Address: 4700 Keele St., Downsview, Ont.

VIAU, Jacques, O.C. Q.C., B.A., LL.L., LL.D.; b. Lachine, Que., 13 May 1919; s. late Joseph-Dalbé (prominent architect. and former Mayor of Lachine) and Mathilde (Lacas) V.; e. Acad. Piché, Lachine, Que.; Brébeuf Coll., Montreal, Univ. of Montreal; Osgoode Hall, Toronto, Ont. (B.A., LL.L.); Dalhousie Univ., Hon. LL.D. 1978; m. Laurette Cadieux; children: Hélène and Jacques Jr.; SR. PARTNER, VIAU, BELANGER, & ASSOCIES; Recorder of City of Lachine and of Town of Dorval, 1947-52; Chrmn., Jr. Bar Sec.; Candn. Bar Assn. 1948-49; Chrmn. Lachine Chamber Comm. 1948-49; Chrmn., Adv. Council on Adm. of Justice 1968-71; Chrmn., Coord. Comm. of School Planning of Montreal Area 1964-66; mem. and Chrm. Lachine School Board 1946-67; Chrmn., Mun. Law Sec., Candn. Bar Assn. 1966-68; Pres., Que. Br., Candn. Bar Assn. 1969-70; Bâtonnier Bar of montreal; Batonnier General (Que.) 1973-74; mem., Exec. Comm., Candn. Bar Assn. 1974-79; Pres., Candn. Bar Assn. 1977-78; Officer of the Order of Canada 1978; Dir. Que. Heart Foundation; mem., Amer. Bar Assn.; Intern. Bar Assn.; Chamber of Comm., Dist. of Montreal; Montreal Museum of Fine Arts; Internat. Union of Local Authorities; Assoc. mem., Nat. Inst. of Municipal Law Offrs. (U.S.); autho of "Education Act of the Province of Quebec", 1957; "Acts and Jurisprudence of cities and town, of the Province of Quebec", 6th ed. 1981, 6th ed. 1980; R. Catholic; recreations: fishing, golfing, travelling; Clubs: Cercle de la Place d'Armes; Mount Stephen; Home: 334 - 43rd Ave., Lachine, Que.; Office: 2810 Stock Exchange Tower, 800 Place Victoria, Montreal, Que.

VICKAR, Hon. Norman, M.L.A.; politician; b. Brooksby, Sask. 21 Feb. 1917; s. Samuel and Gertrude V.; m. Florence Ivy 20 Apl. 1947; children: Larry, Reva Micflikier, Faye Cohen; MIN. OF INDUSTRY & COMM., SASK. 1976- ; Mayor of Melfort; el. M.L.A. for Melfort prov. g.e. 1975, re-el. since; NDP; Hebrew; Office: 306 Legislative Bldg., Regina, Sask. S4S 0B3.

VICKERS, Jon, C.C. (1968), D. Mus., D.C.L., LL.D.; opera singer; b. Prince Albert, Sask., 1926; e. Royal Conservatory Music Toronto (with George Lambert); LL.D.

Sask.; D.C.L. Bishop's; D. Mus. Univ of Western Ont.; Brandon Univ.; Univ. of Guelph Ont; mem. Royal Acad of Music; m. Hetti Outerbridge 1953; five children; operatic debut with Toronto Opera Festival 1952; a winner of Singing Stars of Tomorrow and 1st Prize "Nos Futures Etoiles", Montreal; internat career began 1956; appearances at Festivals of Stratford (Ont.), Bayreuth, Vancouver, Salzburg, Tanglewood, Isreal and Geulph (Ont.); appeared at Opera Companies of Covent Garden, Vienna State, Dallas Civic, Berlin, Paris, Munich, Metropolitan (N.Y.C.), Philadelphia, Florence, Venice, San Francisco, La Scala (Milan), Chicago Lyric, Montreal Expo, Quebec City, Colon Beunos Aires; roles include: Trojans, Tristan and Isolde, Battered Bride, Fidelio, Aida, Masked Ball, Jenufa, Andre Chenier, Parsifal, Don Carlos, Pagliacci, Norma, Benvenuto Cellini, Coranazione de Poppea, Trovatore, Rigoletto, La Traviata, Carmen, die Walkure, Otello, Peter Grimes; films include: Carmen, Fidelio, Tristan and Isolde, Norma, Pagliacci, Otello; numerous recordings, oratorio, concert, symphony and CBC appearances; Address: c/o Metropolitan Opera, New York, N.Y. 10018

VIGER, Raymond, M.Com.; insurance executive; b. Laval, Que. 25 July 1927; s. Joseph Adolphe and Eglantine (Gascon) V.; e. Coll. Laval; Univ. of Montreal M.Com. 1949; m. Huguette d. Philippe Chartrand 26 Aug. 1950; children: Christian-Daniel, Marie-France; GENERAL MANAGER, CANADIAN PROVIDENT GENERAL INSURANCE 1980- ; served present Co. as Treas., Gen. Mgr. 1972, Extve. Vice Pres. 1975; Pres., Prof. Reinsurance Consultants Inc.; Dir., Paragon Ins. Co. of Can.; Vancouver; The Personal Ins. Co. of Can., Toronto; mem. Bd. of Dir. & Extve Comte., Le Groupement des Assureurs Automobiles; Facility & Facility Assn.; Bd. of Dir., Ins. Crime Prevention Bureau; Advr. Bd., I.B.C.; Ligne de Sécurité du Que.; mem. Corp. des Administrateurs Agréés; Financial Analysts Assn.; Am. Mang. Assn.; Montreal Bd. of Trade; Clubs; Canadian; University; R. Catholic; recreation: tennis; Home: 8376 Place Chanceaux, Anjou, Que. H1K 1M7; Office: 801 Sherbrooke St. E., Montreal, Que. H2L 1K7

VINAY, Jean-Paul, M.A., Agr. Univ., D.Litt., F.R.S.C.; b; Paris, France, 18 July 1910; s. Maurice and Blanche (Leconte) V.; e. University of Paris, B.A. 1930; University of London, M.A. (Linguistics and Phonetics) 1937; Agrégé, Univ. of France, 1941, Titular Sch. of Higher Studies, 1945; Officer of the Acad., 1952; D. Lett. Univ. of Ottawa, 1975; Chevalier Légion d'Honneur 1978; m. Marie-Paule, d. Pierre A. du Clos, Marquis de Fontaines, 13 Nov. 1940; children: Marie-Elisabeth, Patrick, François, Marie-Emmanuelle; Former Head, Dept. Linguistics & Dean, Faculty Arts & Science, Univ. Victoria 1968-69, 1972-75; Emeritus Prof. of Linguistics, Univ. of Victoria, 1976; began teaching career, Swansea Grammar School for Boys, 1932; Assoc. Lectr., Dept. of Phonetics, University Coll., London, 1937-39; Prof., Chartres High Sch., 1941-42; Inspector-Gen. Modern Lang., City of Paris, 1942-46; joined staff of Univ. of Montreal in 1946; retired from Univ. as Dir., Dept. of Linguistics; Consultant, I.A.C.O., Montreal, on Internat. Spelling Alphabets, 1948-51; Consultant with I.A.L.A., New York, 1946-48; Publications: "A Basis and Essentials French Reader", 1946; "A Basis and Essentials Welsh Grammar", 1947; "Fluent English", Vol. 1 and 2, "Stylistique comp. français & anglais", 1958; "The Canadian Dictionary" (Editor in Chief) 1962 (new enlarged ed. with support from Donner Foundation, Canada, 1971, and Canada Council, 1975-76); co-author "Le Français international" 1966-71; mem., Internat. Phonetic Assn. (Mem. Council); Internat. Council French Language (Paris); Inst. of Translation, Montreal (Vice-Pres.); Soc. of Translators & Interpreters of Can. (Past Pres.); Past Editor, Translators' Journal; Journ. Candn. Assn. Linguistics; mem., Linguistic Soc. of Am.; Visiting Prof., Univ. of Strasbourg, 1964-65; Conservative; Roman

Catholic; Home: 2620 Margate Ave., Victoria, B.C. V8S 3A5

VINCENT, Arthur J., A.F.C.; grain merchant; b. Toronto, Ont. 3 Dec. 1913; s. Cecil Roy and Zella (Rowat) V.; e. Parkdale Coll. Inst., Toronto, Ont. (Sr. Matric.); m. Patricia Milroy, d. W. A. Murphy, 11 Dec. 1942; children: Kitson, Barry, Paul, Connie, Gerald; PRESIDENT AND DIR., SMITH VINCENT & CO. LTD. (Estbd. 1950); Pres., Roynor Investments Ltd.; Patvin Investments Ltd.; Vice-Pres. and Dir., Futures Investments Ltd.; Pres., W. A. Investments Ltd. The Traders' Building Association Ltd.; served in 2nd World War with R.C.A.F., 1939-46, overseas, 1942-43; discharged with rank of Wing Commdr.; awarded A.F.C.; Freemason (Shrine); Protestant; recreations: golf, photography, boating; Clubs: St. Charles Country; The Manitoba;; Home: 307 Dromore Avenue, Winnipeg, Man. R3M 0J2; Office: Suite 919, 167 Lombard Ave., Winnipeg, Man. R3B 0V3

VINCENT, Jean Denis, B.A.; insurance executive; b. Kapuskasing, Ont. 15 Apl. 1930; s. late Gaston, LL.D., C.R. and Robertine (Gauthier) V.; e. Univ. of Ottawa B.A. 1951; m. Denyse d. Alphonse Ouimet, Pointe Claire, Que. 13 Aug. 1980; children: Denis, Josée; PRES. AND CHIEF OPERATING OFFR., ALLIANCE MUTUAL LIFE INSURANCE CO. 1981- ; Dir. Central Dynamics Ltd., Dir., Trust Gén. du Canada joined Quebec Trust Co. (Fiducie du Québec), Montreal 1964-67, Depy. Gen. Mgr. and Mgr. Le Fonds Desjardins; Saving and Investment Ltd. Quebec 1967-69, Vice Pres. and Dir.; Philips Electronics Ltd. 1969-81, Vice Pres.; service with RCN rank Lt.; Dir. Les Grands Ballets Canadiens; North South Inst. Ottawa; Revue Internationale de Gestion, Montreal; Past Pres. and Dir. Un. Way Can., Ottawa; Past Dir. Fédération des Oeuvres de Charité Canadiennes Françaises, Montréal; Catholic Montréal; R. Catholic; Clubs: Cercle de la Place D'Armes, St. Denis; Laval Sur Le Lac; Home: 237 Ste Claire, Pointe Claire, Que. H9S 4E3; Office: 680 Sherbrooke St. W., Suite 680, Montreal, Que. H3A 2S6.

VINEBERG, Philip Fischel, O.C. (1974), Q.C., M.A., B.C.L., LL.D., F.R.E.S.; b. Mattawa, Ont., 21 July 1914; s. Malcolm and Rebecca (Phillips) V.; McGill Univ., B.A. 1935, M.A. 1936, B.C.L. 1939; Ecole des Sciences Politique Paris, 1935-36; m. Miriam Sylvia, d. Abraham Schachter, Westmount, Que.; children: Robert S., Michael D.; PARTNER, PHILLIPS & VINEBERG; Dir., Cemp Investments Ltd.; The Seagram Company Ltd.; Reitman's (Canada) Ltd.; Edper Investments Ltd.; Nat. Bank of Can.; Cadillac-Fairview Corp. Ltd.; and various other cos.; read law with Sam Jacobs, K.C., M.P., and Lazarus Phillips, O.B.E., Q.C.; called to the Bar of Que. 1939; cr. Q.C. 1959; Lectr. in Econ., Sir. George Williams Coll., Montreal, Que. 1936-39, and McGill Univ., 1939; Asst. to Dir., Sch. of Comm., McGill Univ., 1940; Asst. Prof. of Econs., 1942; Lectr. in Co. Law, Faculty of Law 1957-69; Batonnier, Bar of Montreal 1969-70; Chrmn., Candn. Tax Foundation 1966-67; mem., Internat. Fiscal Assn. (Pres., Candn. Br. 1971-74, Internat. Extve.; Trustee Inst. for Research on Pub. Policy; Pres., Fellows Foundation for Legal Research in Can. 1973-76; mem. Candn. Bar Assn. (Nat. Extve. 1975-76; Pres. Que. Br. 1974-75); Econ. Consultant to W.P.T.B., Ottawa, 1942-46; mem. Fed. Conciliation Bds. dealing with railway wages and working conditions, 1958 and 1960; Fellow, Am. Coll. of Trial Lawyers; Vice Pres. Taxation Comte. World Assn. of Lawyers; Chrmn. Conseil Consultif, Que., Ministry of Revenue; Fellow and Trustee Bar-Ilan Univ.; Gov. Benjamin Cardozo School of Law; tel. to Bd. of Govs., McGill Univ. 1977; Fellow of Brandeis Univ.; Vice-Pres., Candn. Friends of Alliance Israelite Universelle; Dir., Candn. Friends Technion, Hon. Vice Pres. United Talmud Torahs; Hon. Dir. Jewish General Hosp.; Publications: Prentice-Hall, "Income Taxation in Canada" (contr. ed.); "The French Franc and the Gold Standard", 1st ed. 1936, 2nd ed. 1938; chap. on Candn. Banking System in

F. C. James Economics of "Money Credit and Banking" (3rd ed.); chapter on "Tax considerations in Canadian Company Law" and various articles in legal and financial journs.; Liberal; Hebrew; Clubs: Elm Ridge; Montefiore; Mount Royal; St. Denis; University; Home: 32 Summit Crescent, Westmount, Que. H3Y 1B3; Office: Suite 1700, Royal Bank of Canada Bldg., 5 Place Ville Marie, Montreal, Que. H3B 2A5

VINING, Leo Charles, Ph.D., F.C.I.C., F.C.S., F.R.S.C.; microbiologist; educator; b. Whangarei, N.Z. 28 March 1925; s. Charles Hildrup and Ruby Robina (Withers) V.; e. Whangarei (N.Z.) High Sch. 1941; Auckland Univ. B.Sc. 1948, M.Sc. 1949; Cambridge Univ. Ph.D. 1951; Kiel Univ. Germany 1951-52; Rutgers Univ. 1953-54; children: Robert Charles, Michael Taylor, Deborah Lee, Russell James; PROF. OF BIOL. DALHOUSIE UNIV. since 1971; Instr. Rutgers Univ. 1954-55; Research Offr. Prairie Regional Lab. Nat. Research Council Can. 1956-62, Sec. Head Atlantic Regional Lab. Nat. Research Council Can. 1963-71; Merck Sharp and Dohme Lectr. Chem. Inst. Can. 1965; rec'd Harrison Prize in Microbiol. Royal Soc. Can. 1972; CSM Award, Candn. Soc. Microbiol. 1976; served with Royal N.Z. Navy (Fleet Air Arm) 1943-45; author various articles and over 175 research papers chem., biochem. and microbiol. of natural products especially antibiotics produced by fungi and actinomycetes; Bd. Trustees, Internat. Fdn. for Science, 1981- ; Dir. Chem. Inst. Can. 1972-77; mem. Am. Chem. Soc.; Candn. Soc. Microbiols. (Extve. 1972-76); Am. Soc. Microbiol.; Am. Assn. Advanc. Science; N.S. Inst. Science (Pres. 1980-81); Home: 621 Regina., Halifax, N.S. B3H 1N4; Office: Halifax, N.S. B3H 4J1.

VIPOND, James French, D.F.C.; recreation director; b. Southport, Lancs., Eng. 11 July 1916; s. late Rev. Frank and late Jessy (French) V.; came to Can. 1920; e. Streetsville (Ont.) public school; Lake Lodge Boys Sch. Grimsby, Ont.; E. York Coll. Inst. Toronto; Trinity Coll. Sch. Port Hope, Ont.; m. late May Elizabeth d. late John Hollinger, E. York, Ont. 15 Sept. 1942; m. Beverley Sims, Toronto; children: Barbara (Mrs. James Paerg), Christopher; ONT. ATHLETICS COMMR.; Sports Ed., "The Globe and Mail" for 30 yrs.; served with RCAF 1943 — 45, Navig. 434 (Bluenose) Sqdn., rank Flight Lt.; DFC; mem. City of Toronto Civic Awards Comte.; Chrmn. Candn. Sports Hall of Fame Selection Comte.; mem. Candn. Football and Basketball Halls of Fame Selection Comtes. and Lou Marsh Award Comte.; involved in various fund raising projects incl. retarded and crippled children, Conacher Cancer Research Fund; author "Gordie Howe No. 9"; Past Pres. Ont. Sportswriters and Sportcasters Assn.; Life mem. Toronto Men's Press Club; P. Conservative; Anglican; Home: Apt. 1509, 53 Thorncliffe Park Dr., Toronto, Ont. M4H 1L1; Office: Ministry of Community and Social Affairs, Toronto, Ont.

VIPOND, Richard Weatheritt; executive; b. Toronto, Ont. 27 Aug. 1927; s. William Chester and Ellen Kyle (Boyd) V.; e. Runnymede Coll. Toronto 1943; Western Tech. Sch., grad. comm. artist 1945; m. Margaret Jane. d. late Thomas Goodwin Stewart 11 June 1949; children: Christopher Richard, Penelope Lynn; PRES. AND C.E.O., A. C. NIELSEN CO. OF CANADA since 1982; joined the Co. as Artist 1945, in various production positions 1948-56, Service Asst. 1957, Client Service Extve. 1958, Vice-Pres., 1961, Head Sales and Training Devel. 1964, Head Sales and Servicing 1971, Gen. Mgr. & Extve. Vice Pres., Retail Index Div. 1974; Exec. Vice-Pres., 1974-82; Anglican; recreations: watercolour painting, golf, painting and collecting military figurines; Club: Donalda; Home: 7 Hatherton Cres., Don Mills, Ont. M3A 1P6; Office: 160 McNabb St., Markham, Ont. L3R 4B8

VIRTUE, Charles G., Q.C., B.A, LL.B.; b. Lethbridge, Alta., 30 May 1926; s. Abner Gladstone and Marian (Ells) V.; e. McMaster Univ., B.A. 1947; Univ. of Alta., LL.B.

1950; m. Mary Irene, d. Charles Greenwood, 21 June 1952; children: Marni, George, Carol, Jephson, Judson, Marian Jane; Partner, Virtue & Co.; read law with A. Gladstone Virtue; called to Bar of Alta. 1951; cr. Q.C. 1968; mem. Bd. Lethbridge Mun. Hosp. since 1963 (Chrmn. 1968-69); Past Pres., Alta. Hosp. Assn. (mem. Bd. 1966-70); Past Pres., Lethbridge Bar Assn.; mem., Alberta Hosp. Services Comm., (1970-78); Pres., 1975 Canada Winter Games; Bencher, Law Soc. of Alberta; (1978- ;) Chrmm. Alberta Law Foundation 1980- ; Past Pres., Lethbridge YMCA; Prairie Reg. Distr. Gov. of Y Men's Club, 1960-62; Zeta Psi; Liberal; Baptist; recreations: sailing, skiing, golfing; Club: Y Men's; Home 1323 - 15th Ave. S., Lethbridge, Alta.; T1K 0W4; Office: 601 Woodward Tower, Lethbridge, Alta.

VOADEN, Herman Arthur, C.M., M.A., C.D.A., F.R.S.A. (1970); teacher, theatre director, playwright, editor, arts leader; b. London, Ont. 19 Jan. 1903; s. Arthur and Louisa (Bale) V.; e. Queen's Univ. B.A. 1923, M.A. 1926; Yale Univ. Dept. Drama 1930-31; m. Violet d. Joseph Kilpatrick, Dungannon, Ont. 21 June 1935; Dir. Dept. Eng. Central High Sch. Comm. Toronto 1928-64; Teacher Glebe Coll. Inst. Ottawa 1924-26; Head Dept. Eng. Windsor-Walkerville Tech. Sch. 1926-27; Coll. Inst. and Voc. Sch. Sarnia, Ont. 1927-28; pioneered in oral, creative, dramatic English teaching methods; Dir. Toronto Play Workshop 1932-55; Dir. Summer Course Drama and Play Production Queen's Univ. 1934-36; Dir. "Murder in the Cathedral" Queen's Univ. and Massey Hall 1936; rec'd Candn. Drama Award 1937; plays: "Wilderness" 1931 (pub. 1978, re-pub. 1980); Wrote and produced 5 'symphonic' plays: "Rocks" 1932, "Earth Song" 1932 (pub. 1976), "Hill-Land" 1934, "Murder Pattern" 1936 (pub. 1975, re-pub. 1980), "Ascend as the Sun" 1942; dramatization "Maria Chapdelaine" 1938; 2 dance dramas "Dance Chorale" 1935, "Romeo and Juliet" 1936; "Emily Carr" stage biog. with paintings Queen's Univ. 1960, Victoria 1966; libretti "The Prodigal Son" composer Fred K. Jacobi, Toronto performances 1952 and 1954, "Esther" comp. Godfrey Ridout perf. 1952 and 1964; Ed. "Six Canadian Plays" 1930, "A Book of Plays" 1935, "Four Good Plays" 1944, "On Stage" 1945, "Murder in the Cathedral" 1959, "Four Plays of Our Time" 1960, "Drama IV" 1965, "Human Values in Drama" 1966, "Julius Caesar" 1966, "Nobody Waved Good-Bye and Other Plays" 1966; "Look Both Ways" 1975; cand. CCF Trinity Riding Toronto 3 fed. els. one by-el. 1945-54; Pres. (First) Candn. Arts Council 1945-48; mem. Candn. Del. First Gen. Assembly UNESCO Paris 1946; Assoc. Dir., Extve. Dir. Candn. Conf. of Arts 1966-68 (prepared 2 submissions to Royal Comn. on Bilingualism & Biculturalism 1965 and 1966, two vol. report "The Arts and Education" 1967); organized Ste-Adele Seminar 1967 to examine Centennial initiatives and future directions for performing arts in Can.; Pres. Candn. Guild of Crafts 1968-70; Elected Fellow of Royal Society of Arts, 1970; Member of the Order of Canada, 1974; Queen's Jubilee Medal, 1977; Hon. Life mem., Assn. for Candn. Theatre History, 1980; recreations: theatre, travel; Club: Arts and Letters; Address: 8 Bracondale Hill Rd., Toronto, Ont. M6G 3P4

VOGEL, Robert, M.A., Ph.D.; educator; b. Vienna, Austria, 4 Nov. 1929; s. Frederick and Helen V.; e. King Henry VIII's Grammar Sch., Abergavenny, Wales, 1941-45; Cardiff (Wales) High Sch., 1945-48 (Glamorgan Co. Scholarship); Sir George Williams Coll., B.A. 1952 (Lt. Gov. Silver Medal); McGill Univ., M.A. 1954, Ph.D. 1959; m. Sylvia Silverman, 21 Oct. 1953; one s. Peter; DEAN, FACULTY OF ARTS, McGILL UNIV. since 1971; Lectr. in Hist., Sir George Williams Univ., 1955-58; Lectr. in Hist., McGill Univ., 1958-61; Asst. Prof. 1961-64; Assoc. Prof. 1964-69; Prof. since 1969; Chrmn., Dept. of Hist. 1966-71; Secy., Faculty of Arts and Science, 1964-66; Vice-Dean, Social Sciences Div. of Faculty, 1969-71; author, "A Breviate of British Diplomatic Blue Books 1919-39", 1963 and various papers and reviews; mem. Candn. Hist. Assn.; Am. Hist. Assn.; Peace Research Inst.; Home: 4145 Marlowe Ave., Montreal, Que. H4A 3M3 Office: 845 Sherbrooke St. W., Montreal, Que. H3A 2T5

VOGEL-SPROTT, Muriel Doris, M.A., Ph.D.; university professor; b. Waterloo, Ont., 20 Aug. 1934; d. Henry and Anne Ellen (Stroh) Vogel; e. McMaster Univ. B.A. 1955; Univ. of Toronto M.A. 1957, Ph.D. 1960; m. David Arthur Sprott, 16 Dec. 1961; two d. Anne Ellen, Jane Barry; PROF. OF PSYCHOL. UNIV. OF WATERLOO since 1969, mem. of Senate and Bd. of Govs. (Extve.) 1976-78; Acting Dean of Graduate Studies, 1978; Research Assoc. Addiction Research Foundation Toronto 1959-61; Asst. Prof. present Univ. 1961, Assoc. Prof. 1965, Assoc. Dean of Grad. Affairs Arts Faculty 1971-78; Visiting Scholar Pharmacol. Dept. Univ. Coll. and Psychol. Dept. Bedford Coll. London, Eng. 1969-70; mem. Science Council Can. 1973-79; author numerous research papers in prof. journs. and book chapters on topics of human learning, alcoholism and alcohol effects on behaviour; mem. Am. Psychol. Assn.; Fellow, Candn. Psychol. Assn.; Ont. Psychol. Assn. (Registration as Clin. Psychol); Home: 295 Ferndale Pl., Waterloo, Ont. N2J 3X8

VOGT, Erich Wolfgang, O.C. (1976); Ph.D., F.R.S.C.; physicist; b. Steinbach, Man., 12 Nov. 1929; s. Peter Andrew and Susan (Reimer) V.; e. Steinbach (Man.) Pub. and High Schs.; Univ. of Man., B.Sc. 1951 (Gold Medal in Hon. Science), M.Sc. 1952; Princeton Univ., Ph.D. 1955; m. Barbara Mary, d. Edward Herbert Greenfield, Vancouver, B.C., 27 Aug. 1952; children: Edith Susan, Elizabeth Mary, David Eric, Jonathan Michael, Robert Jeremy; Physicist, Univ. Of Brit. Columbia; Vice Pres. (Faculty & Student Affairs) there 1975-81; First Chrmn., Sci. Council of B.C. 1978-80; Chrmn., Bd of Management, TRIUMF Project 1974-80; Dir. since 1980; rec'd Centennial Medal 1967; editor "Advances in Nuclear Physics", Vols. 1-11, 1968-79; other writings incl. over 50 scient. papers; Pres. (1970-71) Candn. Assn. Physicists; Liberal; recreations: hiking, tennis; Club: Canadian; Home: 1816 Wesbrook Cr., Vancouver, B.C. V6T 1W2

VOKES, Maj.-Gen. Christopher, C.B. (1945), C.B.E. (1944), D.S.O. (1943); Canadian Army (retired); b. Armagh, Co. of Armagh, Ireland, 13 April 1904; s. Frederick and Elizabeth (Briens) V.; came to Can. 1910; e. Kingston Coll. Inst., 1921; Royal Mil. Coll., Kingston, Ont., Grad. 1925; McGill Univ. B.Sc. 1927; Staff Coll., Camberley, Eng., 1934-35 (p.s.c.); m. Constance Mary, d. John Calder Waugh, Winnipeg, Man., 30 Jan. 1932; two s., Christopher, Michael; Lieut., R.C.E., 1925; served in World War, 1939-45, in England, Sicily, Italy, N.W. Europe; command and staff appts. incl. A.A. & Q.M.G., G.S.O.1, O.C., P.P.C.L.I., 1st Can. Divn. up to May 1942; Commdr., 2nd Can. Inf. Brigade from June 1942; G.O.C. 1st Can. Divn., Nov. 1943 to Nov. 1944; G.O.C. 4th Can. Armoured Divn., Nov. 1944 to June 1945; G.O.C. of Can. Occupation Force in Germany, 1945-46; G.O.C., Central Command, 1946-50; W. Command, 1950-59; awarded Croix de Guerre with Palm (France); Offr., Legion of Honneur (France); Order of Gallantry (Greece); Commdr., Order of Italy; Can. Forces Decoration; Mentioned twice in Despatches; Anglican; Home: 105 Allan St., Apt. 702, Oakville, Ont. L6J 3N2

VOLKOFF, George Michael, M.B.E. (1946), M.A., Ph.D., D.Sc., F.R.S.C. (1948); retired university professor; b. Moscow, Russia, 23 Feb. 1914; s. Michael and Elizabeth (Titoff) V.; came to Can. 1924; e. Univ. of Brit. Columbia, B.A. 1934, M.A. 1936; D.Sc. (honoris causa) 1945; Univ. of Cal., Ph.D. 1940; Princeton Univ., 1940; m. Olga, d. Joseph Okulitch, Vancouver, 22 June 1940; children: Elizabeth, Alexandra, Olga; PROFESSOR EMERITUS AND DEAN EMERITUS, UNIV. OF B.C., since 1979; mem. Bd. of Trustees, Vancouver Gen. Hosp. 1979- ; mem. Tech. Adv. Comte. to AECL on Nuclear

Fuel Waste Management Program 1979- ; mem., Nat. Research Council Can. 1969-75; Research Physicist i/c of Theoretical Physics Br., Atomic Energy Divn., Nat. Research Council, Chalk River, Ont., 1945-46; Asst. Prof. of Physics, Univ. of B.C., 1940-43; Assoc. Research Physicist, Montreal Lab., Nat. Research Council, 1943-45; Prof. of Physics, Univ. of B.C., 1946 and Head of the Dept. 1961-71; Dean, Fac. of Sci. 1972-79; Editor, "Canadian Journal of Physics", 1950-56; "Soviet Physics-Uspekhi", 1979; Fellow, Am. Phys. Soc.; Am. Assn. Advanc. Science; mem., Am. Assn. of Phys. Teachers; Candn. Assn. of Phys.; Phi Beta Kappa; Sigma Xi; Gamma Alpha; Greek Orthodox; Home: 1776 Western Parkway, Vancouver, B.C. V6T 1V3

von BRENTANI, Mario, B.Sc.; artist-painter, writer, publisher; b. St. Quirico-Genova, Italy, 5 March 1908; s. Adolph and Maria (de Scalini) von B.; e. High Sch. and Univ. of Frankfurt on Main, 1918-31, B.Sc.; m. Ruth, d. late George Luetjens, 10 Oct. 1931; children: Brigitta-Maria von Brentani, Maren von Brentani, Mario von Brentani, Annette-Christiane von Brentani, Anneleen von Brentani, Ulrike von Brentani, Immeruth von Brentani, Heideleen von Brentani, Gittà von Brentani; Founder and Editor in Chief "Montrealer Nachrichten" (German lang. weekly newspaper) 1954-75; author of 20 books, (novels, short stories, essays, etc.); specialized in painting of Candn. Eskimo life; solo exhns. by government invitations, all over world; awarded order of merit (1969), order of peace (1972); Great Star in Gold (1978); German Democratic Rep.; Hon. mem., Candn. Peace Counsel (1974) Cultural Soc. Que.-USSR (1974); Co-founder, Conseil Culturel du Quebec, 1978; biographies "Mario von Brentani the painter of the Candn. Eskimoes" by Prof. Dr. Lea Grundig and Dr. Heinz Israel, Union Publishers, Berlin, Germany; "Mario von Brentani and his Eskimo Paintings" by City Councillor Dr. Ives Desmarais, Montreal, Waigel Publishers Montreal.; "The Eskimo Painter Mario von Brentani", official Biography by Candn. Gov. appointed biographer Nicole Lecours, Montreal.; honoured as Man of the Year (1980) of the Chateauguay County, Quebec; repeatedly honoured by Prime Minister P.E. Trudeau; Royal Gov. Gen. of Canada, Edward Schreyer, 1981; R. Catholic; Address: 210 Chateauguay St., Huntingdon, Que. J0S 1H0

von KARSTEDT, Jock; automotive executive; b. Wismar, Germany, 10 July 1930; s. Baron Wilhelm A. and Countess Maximiliana (Mycielska) von K.; e. High Sch., Arts & Science, West Berlin, Sr. Matric. 1948; Tech. Univ., Indust. Mang. 1948-51, W. Berlin; various special courses in business mang., marketing, langs.; m. Mary Kathryn Jean, d. William Basil George, B.Sc., 15 Jan. 1955; children: Heidi Ann, Angela, Kelly; GEN. SALES AND MARKETING MGR., VOLKSWAGEN DO BRASIL S.A.; joined White Motor Co. of Can. 1951; Industrial Acceptance Corp. Ltd. 1953; Volkswagen Canada Ltd., Toronto 1956-71, Customer Relations 1956, Head of Warranty and Customer Relations Dept. 1957, Dist. Mgr., S.W. Ont., Sask., Alta. 1958, Asst. Regional Mgr., Pacific Region, Vancouver 1962, Regional Mgr., Que. and E. Ont., Montreal 1963, Nat. Sales Mgr. 1967, Gen. Mgr. Operations, 1970; Volkswagen of America, Inc. Englewood Cliffs, N.J. 1971-72; Marketing Coordinator for Can.; Mgr., Business Development, Volkswagen can. Ltd. 1975; founded Candn. Mobile Camping 1977; founded Greenbelt Motors and acquired Volkswagen Audi Franchise 1978; Pres., Intervestcan Ltd.; Internat. Consultant, Dept. of Industry & Tourism, Ont. Gov't. 1982; R. Catholic; recreations: photography, tennis, tree farming, sailing; Clubs: Granite (Toronto); Royal St. Lawrence Yacht (Montreal); Madawaska Ski; Club de Campo; Home: 8 Walmsley Blvd., Toronto, Ont. M4X 1X6 Office: Government of Ont. Can., Min of Industry and Tourism, 900 Bay St., Hearst Block, Queen's Park, Toronto, M7A 2E4.

von PODEWILS, H. E. Count Max;diplomat; b. Munich, Germany 17 Aug. 1919; s. Count Hans and Marie (v. Zwehl) von P.; e. elem. and high schs. Munich; m. Christina d. Rudolf von Miller, Niederpöcking, W. Germany 2 Apl. 1975 (m. 1stly 16 Aug. 1948, widower); 7 children; AMBASSADOR TO VIENNA since 1979; Bavarian Ministry of Econ. Munich 1946; mem. Del. of Bi-Zone, later Fed. Repub. of Germany, to OEEC Paris 1949; Embassy New Delhi 1952, Foreign Office 1957, Embassies Tehran 1960, Tunis 1963, Foreign Office 1968, Ambassador, Dir. of Protocol 1971; Ambassador of the Federal Republic of Germany, 1975-79; served with German Forces 1937-46, rank 1st Lt.; awarded K.C. Order of Merit Fed. Repub. Germany and 21 Foreign Decorations; R. Catholic; recreations: literature, music, sports, sculpture; Home: Heilmannstrasse 45, -D-8000 Munich, W. Germany; Office: 1 Waverley St., Ottawa, Ont. K2P 0T8.

von RICHTHOFEN, Erich B., Dr. Phil. Dr. Habil. F.R.S.C.; university professor; b. Hirschberg, Silesia, 8 May 1913; s. Friedrich-Wilhelm and Sibylla-Dorothea (von Knoblauch) von R.; e. Berlin (High Sch. Cert.); Instituto Interuniversitario, Rome; Ca' Foscari, Venice; Centro de Estudios Históricos, Madrid; Univs. of Hamburg, Berlin, Frankfurt/Main (Dr. Phil 1940, Dr. Habil, 1943); m. Eleanor A., d. Robert-Jacques Gruss 1944; one s., Daniel F.; Prof. Emeritus of Romance Langs. & Lit., Univ. of Toronto, 1964-79; Privatdozent and Ausserplanmässiger Prof. der Romanischen Philologie 1943-56 and Dir., Internat. Summer Sch. 1952-56, Frankfurt; Visiting Prof., Univ. of Chicago, 1954; Assoc. Prof. and Prof. of Romance Studies, Univ. of Alta., 1956-62; Prof., Boston Coll., 1962-64; author of "Alfonso Martínez de Toledo und sein Arcipreste de Talavera", 1941; "Studien zur romanischen Heldensage des Mittelalters", 1944; "Vier altfranzösische Lais der Marie de France; Chievrefueil, Austic, Bisclavret, Guingamor", 1954; "Estudios épicos medievales", 1954; "Veltro und Diana: Dantes mittelalterliche und antike Gleichnisse", 1956; "Commentaire sur "Mon Faust" de Paul Valéry", 1961; "The Spanish toponyms of the British Columbia Coast" 1963; "Nuevos estudios épicos medievales" 1970; "Tradicionalismo épico-novelesco" 1972; "Limitations of literary criticism" 1973; "Límites de la crítica literaria y analectas de filología comparada", 1976; "Sincretismo literario", 1981; has written numerous articles and reviews for various learned journs; mem., Soc. Rencesvals; Soc. Internat. Arthurienne; Dante Soc. of Am.; Internat. Assn. Hispanists; Asociación de Lingüistica Filologia de Am. Latina; Candn. Assn. Hispanists; Cdn. Soc. for Study of Names; Lutheran; Home: 232 Panorama Pl., Lions Bay B.C. V0N 2E0

VOSS, Walter Arthur Geoffrey, , B.Sc., Ph.D., P.Eng., C.Eng. (U.K.); engineer; educator; b. Westcliff-on-Sea, Eng., 4 June 1935; s. Walter Arthur Staehling and Winfred Joyce (Burgess) V.; came to Canada 1959; e. Brentwood Sch., Eng. 1954; B.B.C. Scholar., Univ. of London, Queen Mary Coll., B.Sc. (Hons. Engn.) 1959, Ph.D. 1961; Univ. of Brit. Columbia (NATO Exchange Scholar) 1960-61; m. Carole Jane, d. Victor Dougherty, 13 April 1963; children: Jeremy David, Graham Miles, Shauna Elizabeth; PROF. OF ELECT. ENGN., UNIV. OF ALTA. since 1969; Prof. (formerly Dir.) of Biomedical Engr., Fac. of Medicine; Princ., Geoffrey Voss and Assoc., Div. of Greenfeel Int. Ltd., Consultants in Applied Science and Educ.; joined University of British Columbia as Assistant Prof., Dept. Elect. Engn. 1961; Assoc. Prof., Univ. of Alta. 1964; Private Consultant in practice of Voss Tinga Associates, Vancouver, B.C. 1966; Past Chrmn. and Past mem. Bd. Govs., Internat. Microwave Power Inst.; Ed., Journ. Microwave Power 1966-77; mem. Inst. Electronic & Elect. Engrs.; Inst. Elect Engrs. (U.K.); Assn. Prof. Engrs. B.C. and Alta.; Mem., Soc. for Cryobiology (US); staff instructor, Alta. Soccer Assn; co-author of "Microwave Power Engineering" 1968; contrib. to "Handbuch der Elektrowärme" 1973' and other books; published research papers in biology, physics, and engineering; Anglican; recreations: walking, swimming, squash, soccer; Home: 2601 Dufferin Ave., Victoria B.C. V8R 3L5; Offices: Edmonton, Alta. and Vancouver, B.C.

VUCHNICH, Michael Nickolas, B.Sc.; company executive; b. Southwest Pennsylvania, 23 Oct. 1906; s. George and Martha (Hayden) V.; e. Hurst High Sch.; Kiskimentas Prep. Sch.; Ohio State Univ., B.Sc.; m. Edith Virginia, d. Elmer D. Myers, 6 Apl. 1937; one s.; CHAIRMAN AND C.E.O., LINCOLN ELECTRIC CO. OF CANADA LTD., since 1940; Dir., Almag. Aluminum and Magnesium Ltd.; Student, the Lincoln Electric Co., Cleveland, 1934; Mgr., S. Africa, 1936; presented with the Langton Award which is given annually to the individual who has contributed most to the advancement of foremanship in Canadian industry by the Canadian Council of Foremen's Clubs, 1955; mem., Candn. Chamber of Comm.; Candn. Welding Bur. (Dir.); Am. Soc. for Metals; Am. Welding Soc.; Candn. Welding Soc.; Ohio State Univ. Assn.; Candn. Mfrs. Assn.; Candn. Elect. Mfrs. Assn. (Dir. 1950-53); Dir. and mem. Exec. Comte C.N.E.; Dir. Council for Profit Sharing Ind. Council for Profit Sharing Industries; Am. Management Assn.; rec'd the Langton Award for Outstanding contrib. to Candn. Industry, 1955; Dir., Candn. Nat. Exhn., Toronto, Ont.; Delta Upsilon; recreation: golf; Clubs: Rosedale Golf; Granite; Rotary (Leaside, Ont., Pres. 1947-48); Home: 50 Weybourne Crescent, Toronto, Ont. M4N 2R5; Office: 179 Wickstead Ave., Toronto, Ont. M4G 2B9

W

WACHOWICH, Hon. Mr. Justice Allan H., B.A., B.L.; judge; b. Edmonton, Alta. 8 March 1935; s. Phillip Wachowich; e. Opal, Alta.; St. John's, Grandin and St. Josephs High Schs., Edmonton, Alta.; Univ. of Alta. B.A. 1957, B.L. 1958; m. Elizabeth Louise d. Dr. John Byers, Ponoka, Alta. 8 Aug. 1959; children: David, Patrick, Jane, Nancy; JUSTICE, COURT OF QUEEN'S BENCH ALTA. and Judge, Supreme Court of Y.T. since 1979; called to Bar of Alta. 1959; Partner, Kosowan, Wachowich 1959 — 74; apptd. to Dist. Court of Alta. 1974; Past Pres. in Can. and Chrmn. Bd. Govs. Candn. Cath. Organ. Devel. & Peace; Dir. Un. Community Fund of Edmonton 1968 — 71; Past Pres. Cath. Charities and Alta. Cath. Welfare Assn.; Past Dir. Nat. Cath. Council Social Services; Past Pres. Edmonton E., Fed. Lib. Assn.; mem. Adv. Bd. XI Commonwealth Games Foundation; Past Pres. St. Thomas Moore Lawyers Guild; Pres. of Friars 1974 — 75; Chrmn. Alta. Automobile Ins. Bd.; Bd. Advisors, Edmonton Gen. Hosp.; Pres. Bd. Govs., Alta. (Edmonton) Coll.; Pres. Edmonton Medico-Legal Soc.; Co-Chrm., Edmonton Chapter Candn. Council Christians & Jews; Pres., Friends Univ. Alta.; mem. Hon. Order Blue Goose Internat.; Alta. Aviation Council; YMCA; R. Catholic; Zeta Psi (Past Pres.); Bd. Dir., Citadel Theatre; recreations: golf, hockey, baseball; Clubs: Edmonton; Serra; Highlands Golf; Centre; Home: 11234 — 63 St., Edmonton, Alta. T5W 4E6; Office: The Law Courts, Edmonton, Alta. T5J 0R2.

WADDELL, Ian Gardiner, M.P.; politician; b. Glasgow, Scot. 21 Nov. 1942; s. John and Isabel (Dickie) W.; came to Can. 1947; e. Alderwood Coll. Inst. Toronto 1960; Univ. of Toronto B.A. 1963, LL.B. 1967; Ont. Coll. of Educ. 1964; London Sch. of Econ. LL.M. 1968; called to Bar of B.C. 1969, N.W.T. 1975; Asst. City Prosecutor Vancouver 1969-71; Dir. Storefront Lawyers Vancouver 1971-73; Special Counsel Berger Inquiry Mackenzie Valley Pipeline 1974-77; Partner, De Cario & Waddell 1977-80; el. to H. of C. for Vancouver Kingsway 1979, Energy Critic, NDP; re-el. 1980; Dir. Arts Club Vancouver; S.M.A.L.L.; mem. Candn. and Am. Socs. Internat. Law; NDP; recreations: skiing, yoga, theatre; Home: 1729

Trutch St., Vancouver, B.C.; Office: House of Commons, Ottawa, Ont. K1A 0A6.

WADDINGTON, (Mrs.) Miriam, M.A., M.S.W., D.Litt.; teacher, poet; b. Winnipeg, Man., 23 Dec. 1917; d. Isidore and Mussia (Dobrusin) Dworkin; e. Machray (Winnipeg) Sch. and Jr. High Sch.; Lisgar (Ottawa) Coll. Inst., Univ. of Toronto, B.A., 1939, Sch. of Soc. Work Dipl., 1942, M.A. 1968; Univ. of Pennsylvania, M.S.W., 1945; D.Litt. Lakehead 1975; m. Patrick Donald s. John Frushard W., London, Eng., 1939 (divorced, 1965); children: Marcus, Jonathan; began career in social work as Caseworker, Jewish Family Service, Toronto, 1942-44; Student and Caseworker, Philadelphia Child Guidance Clinic, 1944-45; Assistant Director, Jewish Child Service, Montreal, 1945-46; Lecturer and Supervisor, Fieldwork, McGill School of Social Work, Montreal, 1946-49; Caseworker, Speech Clinic, Montreal Children's Hosp., 1950-52, John Howard Soc., 1955-57, Jewish Family Service, 1957-60; Supv., N. York Family Service, Toronto, 1960-62; Sr. Fellowship in Creative Writing, Canada Council, 1962-63; Can. Council Fellowship in Writing 1971-72; Lectr., Dept. of English, York Univ., 1964, Asst. Prof. 1967, Assoc. Prof. 1969, Prof. 1972; Writer-in-Residence, Univ. Ottawa 1974; Borestone Mountain Prize for Best Poem, 1974; Canada Council Wales Exchange Poet, 1980; Publications: "Green World" 1945; "The Second Silence" 1955; "The Season's Lovers" 1958; "The Glass Trumpet" 1966; "Call Them Canadians" 1968; "Say Yes" 1969; "A. M. Klein" 1970; "The Visitants" 1981; "Summer at Lonely Beach" 1982; ed., "John Sutherland: essays, controversies, poems" 1972, "Driving Home: Poems, New & Selected" 1972, "The Dream Telescope" 1973; "The Price of Gold", 1976; Ed. "The Collected Poems of A. M. Klein" 1974; "Mister Never" 1978; poems and articles in various anthols., and journs.; her manuscripts have been acquired by Public Archives in Ottawa; mem., Modern Lang. Assn.; Montreal Centre, Internat. PEN; Otto Rank Assn.; League of Canadian Poets and ACUTE; Jewish; Home: 32 Yewfield Cres., Don Mills, Ont. M3B 2Y6

WADDS, Jean (Mrs. A. C. Casselman), B.A.; b. Newton Robinson, Ont., 16 Sept. 1920; d. Hon. William Earl and Treva (Lennox) Rowe; e. Newton Robinson Public and Cookstown Cont. Schs.; Barrie (Ont.) High Sch.; Univ. Coll., Univ. of Toronto B.A. 1940; Weller Business Coll.; m. late Arza Clair Casselman, 24 May 1946; children: Nancy, Clair; HIGH COMMISSIONER TO GREAT BRITAIN, 1979- ; Del. to United Nations 1961; Parlty. Secy. to Min. of Nat. Health & Welfare, 1962-63; M.P. for Grenville-Dundas, 1958-68; mem., Ont. Municipal Bd., 1975-79; Kappa Kappa Gamma; P. Conservative; United Church; Clubs: Prescott Golf; Prescott Curling; Address: Sir John A. Macdonald Bldg., 1 Grosvenor Sq., London WIX OAB

WADE, (H) Mason, M.A., LL.D., D.ès.L.; D. Sci. Soc.; D. Litt.; historian; b. New York, 3 July 1913; s. Alfred Byers and Helena (Mein) W.; e. The Choate Sch., Wallingford, Conn.; Harvard Univ.; 1935; McGill Univ. Dem. M.A., 1953; LL.D., Univ. of N.B., 1957; D.ès.L., Ottawa University, 1963, D.Sc. Soc. Laval University, 1973; D. Litt. Univ. of Vermont, 1978; m. Eloise, d. late William S. Bergland, 29 Dec. 1951; 2ndly, Joan, d. late John G. Glassco of Winnipeg, 30 June 1967; 3rdly, Elisabeth, d. late Gordon Macdougall, Montreal, 10 June 1980; Publisher's Editor, Harcourt, Brace & Co., 1935-36, and Little, Brown & Co., 1936-37; Guggenheim Fellow in Candn. Hist., 1943-45; Rockefeller and Carnegie grants in aid, 1946, 1949; Foreign Service Reserve Offr., serving as Public Affairs Offr. U.S. Embassy, Ottawa, Ont., 1951-53; Lectr. (summer sch.), Laval Univ., 1946-48; apptd. Prof. at Catholic Univ. of Am., 1950; Gray Lectr., Univ. of Toronto, 1954; Lectr. (summer sch.) Univ. of B.C., 1954; Visiting Fellow, Inst. of Candn. Studies, Carleton Univ., 1963; Dir. of Candn. Studies, Univ. of Rochester (initiated 1953), 1955-65 and Prof. of Hist. there, 1960-65; Prof. of

Hist., Univ. of W. Ont. 1965-72; Publications: "Margaret Fuller", 1940; "Francis Parkman", 1942; "The French-Canadian Outlook", 1946; "The French Canadians, 1760-1945", 1955, rev. ed. "The French Canadians, 1760-1967" 1968; Editor of "The Writings of Margaret Fuller", 1941; "The Oregon Trail", 1943; "The Journals of Francis Parkman", 1948; "Canadian Dualism", 1960; "Canadian Regionalism 1867-1967" 1969; "The International Megalopolis" 1969; contrib., "Essays on Contemporary Quebec", 1953; "The U.S. and the World Today", 1957; "Tradition, Values, and Socio-Economic Developments"; 1961; "French Canada Today", 1962; "Canada — Success or Failure?", 1962; "Culture of Contemporary Canada", 1957; "Our Living Tradition", 1957; "The United States and Canada", 1964; "Our Living Tradition" (6th series), 1965; many articles and book reviews; mem., Candn. Hist. Assn. (Pres. 1964-65); Candn. Pol. Science Assn.; Authors League; Am. Historical Assn.; Org. of Am. Historians; Democrat; Roman Catholic; recreations: walking, skiing, tennis; Clubs: Rideau (Ottawa); University (Montreal); St. Botolph (Boston); Home: Cornish, New Hampshire 03745

WADSWORTH, Jeffery Page Rein; b. Toronto, Ont., 27 July 1911; s. William Rein and Mildred (Jeffery) W.; e. Lakefield Coll. Sch.; Upper Canada Coll.; m. Elizabeth Cameron, d. John R. Bunting, Toronto, Ont., 21 Sep. 1940; one d.; CHAIRMAN, CONFEDERATION LIFE, since 1977; Director, Candn. Imp. Bank of Commerce, Holt, Renfrew Co. Ltd.; Massey Ferguson Ltd.; MacMillan Bloedel Ltd.; Bayer Foreign Investments Ltd.; Chrmn., Bd. of Govs., Univ. of Waterloo; Bd. of Govs., Lester B. Pearson College of the Pacific; joined The Canadian Bank of Commerce, Port Credit, Ont. 1928; Inspector's Dept., H.O., Toronto 1934; Asst. Mgr., Hamilton, Ont. 1943-45, Toronto 1945-49; Regional Supt., Calgary, Alta. 1950; Asst. Gen. Mgr., H.O., Toronto 1953, Montreal, Que. 1955; Gen. Mgr., H.O. 1956, Vice-Pres. and Dir. 1957; el. Vice-Pres. and Gen. Mgr. at amalg. with Imperial Bank of Canada, June 1961, Pres. 1963, Vice-Chrmn. 1964, Depy. Chrmn. 1970; Depy. Chrmn., Pres. and Chief Extve. Offr. 1971; Chrmn. and C.E.O. 1973; Anglican; recreations: golf, skiing, sailing, fishing; Clubs: The Toronto; York; Mount Royal; Home: Suite 303, 7 Thornwood Rd., Toronto, Ont., M4W 2R8; Office: Suite 4100, Commerce Court West, P.O. Box 211, Toronto, Ont. M5L 1E8

WADSWORTH, John Peter; company executive; b. Ottawa, Ont., 2 Nov. 1939; s. late John Bernard and Catherine Theresa (Kehoe) W.; e. De LaSalle Coll. "Oaklands", Toronto; m. Lynda Edna, d. late James Harold Ferguson, 11 Apl. 1964; children: Lisa Ann, Deborah Lynne, Jeffrey Bernard; PRES., TIREMASTER CORP, since 1976; joined Gen. Tire and Rubber Co. of Canada as a Store Mgr., 1963; held various Sales Mang. positions until apptd. Gen. Mgr. 1970; mem., Rubber Assn. Can. (Dir.); Candn. Mfrs'. Assn. (Regional Dir.); recreations: skiing, golf; Office: 300 Midwest Rd., Scarborough, Ont.

WAGNER, Norman Ernest, Ph.D.; educator; b. Edenwold, Sask. 29 March 1935; s. Robert Eric and Gertrude Margaret (Brandt) W.; e. Luther Coll. Regina 1952-53; Univ. of Sask. 1953-58; Univ. of Toronto 1958-63; m. Catherine Caroline d. Jacob E. Hack, Grenfell, Sask. 16 May 1957; children: Marjorie Dianne, Richard Roger, Janet Marie; PRES. UNIV. OF CALGARY; author "Canadian Biblical Studies" 1967; co-author "The Moyer Site: A Prehistoric Village in Waterloo County" 1974; various articles learned journs.; serves on bd., Hockey Canada; The Alta. Heritage Foundation for Medical Research; Pres. Candn. Soc. Biblical Studies 1976; Extve. Dir. Council on Study Religion 1971-77; mem. Candn. Archaeol. Assn.; Soc. Biblical Lit.; Lutheran; recreations: music, tennis; Home: 1356 Montreal Ave. S.W., Calgary, Alta. T2T 0Z5; Office: 2500 University Dr., N.W., Calgary, Alta. T2N 1N4.

WAGNER, Sydney, Ph.D.; physicist; Canadian public servant; b. Montreal, Que., 1 Nov. 1919; s. late Carl and late Jennie (Herscovitch) W.; e. McGill Univ., Ph.D. (Physics) 1951; m. Marie Flore Madeleine, d. late Charles Edouard Vaillancourt, 11 Nov. 1961; one d., Janet; DIR. GEN., RESEARCH PLANNING, DEPT. OF COMMUNICATIONS, 1980- ; Counselor (Scientific) Canadian Embassy, Paris France; past Gen. Dir., Office of Science and Technol., Dept. of Industry, Trade and Comm.; Prof. of Physics, McGill Univ., 1948-55; Assoc. Dir. Research, RCA Victor Co. Ltd., 1955-62; Pres., Simtec Ltd., 1962-68; served with RCN 1941-46; Sr. mem., Inst. Elect. & Electronic Engrs.; mem., Electrochem. Soc.; Candn. Assn. Physicists; Sigma Xi; Jewish; Home: 1 Chemin Frontenac, Aylmer, Que.

WAHN, Ian Grant, Q.C., LL.B., M.A.; b. Herbert, Sask. 18 April 1916; s. Edgar Valentine and Florence Margaret (Reid) W.; e. Swift Current (Sask.) Pub. Sch. 1922-28; Swift Current Coll. Inst. 1928-32; Univ. of Sask, 1932-37; Queen's Coll., Oxford Univ. 1937-39; Osgoode Hall Law Sch. 1939-42; m. Pearl Helen, d. George Lychak, Aberdeen, Sask., 15 Dec. 1942; children: Ian G. V., Gordon D. A.; ret. 1980 as Counsel, Smith, Lyons, Torrance, Stevenson & Mayer (Estbd. 1962); Dir., Potash Co. of Canada Ltd.; Dir., Candn. Badger Co. Ltd.; Candn. Rhodes Scholar Fdn.; read law with Fraser, Beatty, Palmer & Tucker; called to Bar of Ont. 1942; practised law with Borden, Elliot, Kelley, and Palmer, 1942-61; served in 2nd World War with Queen's Own Rifles in Holland and Germany; mem., H. of Commons for Toronto-St. Paul's 1962-1972; mem., Law Soc. of Upper Can.; recreations: tennis, skating; Clubs: National; Toronto Cricket Skating & Curling; Home: 62 Heath St. W., Toronto, Ont. M4V 1T4; Office:

WAINWRIGHT, Robert Barry, R.C.A.; artist; educator; b. Chilliwack, B.C. 29 June 1935; s. Ralph and Ethel Irene (Kipp) W.; e. Vancouver Sch. of Art 1962; Atelier 17 (with S.W. Haytor), Paris 1962-64; assn. with Atelier Libre des Recherches Graphiques Montréal 1965-67; m. Frances Elizabeth d. Hans Heinsheimer, New York, N.Y. 7 Oct. 1967; children: Carla Elise, Julian Abram; ASSOC. PROF. OF FINE ARTS, CONCORDIA UNIV., Chmn., Dept. of Printmaking; solo exhns. incl. Concordia Univ. 1969, 1976, 1980; Galerie Martal Montreal 1972; Mazelow Gallery Toronto 1977; rep. in numerous nat. and internat. group exhns. incl. Vancouver Print Internat. 1967; Internat. Biennale of Graphic Art Cracow 1968, 1970; Brit. Print Internat., Bradford, Eng. 1970; Premio Internazionale Biella per l'Incisione Italy 1971, 1973, 1976; Creation Que. au Salon Internat. Art 3/72, Basel, Switzerland 1972; III Biennale de Gravure de Paris 1972; Spectrum Can. R.C.A. Tour Exhn. 1976; rep. in pub., corporate and private colls. incl. Nat. Gallery Can., Art Gallery Ont., Musée d'Art Contemporain Montreal; Can. Council Art Bank; Montreal Museum of Fine Arts; recipient Emily Carr Travel Study Scholarship 1962; Leon & Thea Koerner Foundation Grant 1963; Can. Council Grant 1963, 1967; Internat. Exhn. Graphics Montreal Prize 1971; Concours Artistique du Que. 1971; Hadassah Nov. Art Action Prize, 1981; Home: 4248 Hampton Ave., Montreal, Que. H4A 2K9; Office: Dept. of Printmaking, Concordia Univ., 1455 de Maisonneuve Blvd. W., Montreal, Que. H3G 1M8.

WAISGLASS, Harry J., B.Com., M.A.; economist, professor, mediator, arbitrator, industrial relations consultant; b. Toronto, Ont., 19 May 1921; s. Nathan and Tammy (Henechovitch) W.; e. Univ. of Toronto, B.Com. 1944, M.A. 1948, Ph.D. studies 1947-50; m. Mari Joseph, 13 June 1943; children: Elaine, Barry, Karen, David; Prof. of Industrial Relations, Fac. of Business, McMaster Univ., 1976-79, and Dir., Labour Studies Prog. there 1976-81; Vice Chmn., Grievance Settlement Bd., Ont. Public Service, 1980- ; mem. Long Range Planning Advisory Council of the Ont. Educ. Communications Auth;

mediator for Ont. Educ. Rel. Comm. in School Board Teacher, disputes; previously served as Research Consultant to Special Planning Secretariat, Privy Council Office, Ottawa; Research Director (Can.) for United Steelworkers of America; Education and Research Director (Can.) for Amalgamated Clothing Workers of Am.; Lectr. in Indust. Relations and Research Fellow in former Indust. Relations Inst., Univ. of Toronto; Stat. and Researcher, Dept. of Labour and Indust. Production Co-op. Bd., 1944-47; Internat. Labour Office Consultant, Singapore Govt. and trade unions, 1963-64; served on Voluntary Planning Bd. for N.S., 1964-67; Financial Adv. Comte. of Ont. Govt's Devel. Agency, 1963; apptd. Dir. Gen. Research & Devel., Dept. of Labour Can. 1968; Visiting Prof., Indus. Relations, McMaster Univ. 1974-76; Vocational Adv. Comte., Toronto Bd. of Educ.; Bd. of Dir., Cdn. Foundation for Econ. Educ.; numerous bds. of conciliation and arbitration in labour disputes; Chrmn., Leg. Comte., Toronto and Dist. Labour Council for many yrs.; served on several comtes. for Candn. Labour offr. and bd. mem. with local welfare agencies; author, "Towards Equitable Income Distribution: Some Social and Economic Considerations for Union Wage Policies", 1966; contrib. articles to various journals.; Office: 49 Saunders Blvd., Hamilton, Ont. L8S 3J5

WAISMAN, Allan Harvie, B.Arch., F.R.A.I.C. (1968), A.R.I.B.A.; b. Winnipeg, Man., 24 Jan. 1928; s. Rubin and Bessie W.; e. Mulvie and Gordon Bell Schs., Winnipeg, Man.; Univ. of Man., B.Arch. 1950; children: Sheera Joy, Yail, Tully J., Dean; PARTNER, WAISMAN, DEWAR, GROUT, Archs. & Planners, since 1971; Dir. several Candn. cos.; Chmn. of Bd., Intercon. Management Ltd.; Canadian Centres Network; formed Partnership of Waisman, Ross & Assoc. 1953; Waisman Ross Blankstein Coop Gillmor Hanna 1964; mem. B.C., Ont. Minn. and Washington Assn. Archs.; Past Dir., Winnipeg Art Gallery; Industrial Devel. Bd.; Dir., Royal Winnipeg Ballet; Vancouver Playhouse Theatre; Awards incl. Internat. Stainless Steel Design Award; several Massey Medals for Arch.; Royal Arch. Inst. award for high density housing and for Hudson's Bay Dept. Store, Coquitlam Shopping Centre; planning award for Whistler Town Centre; City of Seattle award for Seattle Trade Centre; recreation: boating; Club: Eagle Harbour Yacht; Home: 5590 Gallagher Place, W. Vancouver, B.C. V7W 1N9; Office: 500 Cardero St. on the Water, Vancouver, B.C. V6G 2W6

WAIT, Mrs. Arthur H., B.A.; b. Vancouver, B.C., 1 Aug. 1913; d. late Chief Justice Malcolm Archibald and Ida Lena (Baird) Macdonald; g.d. of the late Senator Geo. T. Baird of Andover, N.B.; niece of the late Senator J. H. King, P.C., former Min. of Public Works, Leader of the Senate, Speaker of the Senate, etc.; e. Royal Victoria Coll., 1930-32; Univ. of British Columbia, B.A. 1934; m. late R. Reginald Arkell, former Vice-Pres. and Gen. Mgr., Kelly, Douglas & Co., Ltd., Vancouver, B.C., 16 Sept. 1939; one d., Elena Angela; 2ndly Arthur H. Wait, Toronto, Ont.; former mem. of Can. Council (apptd. 1957); former Dir., Vancouver Festival Soc.; Community Arts Council; Vancouver Centennial Comte.; Past Pres., Jr. League of Vancouver; Community Arts Council of Vancouver; Past Dir., Vancouver Symphony Soc.; Nat. Ballet Guild of Can.; Community Chest & Council; Volunteer Bureau of Greater Vancouver; Women's Auxiliary of Vancouver Art Gallery; Red Cross Lodge; Friends of Chamber Music; mem., Council of Bureau of Municipal Research (Toronto); Delta Gamma; Liberal; Anglican; recreation: gardening; Home: 7 Cluny Drive, Toronto, Ont. M4W 2P8

WAITE, Peter B., Ph.D., F.R.S.C.; b. Toronto, Ont., 12 July 1922; s. Cyril and Mary (Craig) W.; e. Saint John (N.B.) High Sch., 1937; Univ. of B.C., B.A. 1948, M.A. 1950; Univ. of Toronto, Ph.D. 1954; m. Masha, d. Dr. Ante Gropuzzo, Rijeka, Yugoslavia, 22 Aug. 1958; children: Alice Nina, Anya Mary; PROF. OF HIST., DAL-

HOUSIE UNIV., since 1961 and Head of Dept. there 1960-68; with Dom. Bank 1937-41; served withR.C.N. 1941-45, rank Lt.; apptd. Lectr. in Hist. at present Univ., 1951, Asst. Prof. 1955, Assoc. Prof. 1960; visiting Prof., Univ. W. Ont. 1963-64; Dartmouth Coll., Hanover, U.S. 1967; author of "The Life and times of Confederation, 1864-1867", 1962; "The Confederation debates in the province of Canada, 1865", 1963; "Pre-Confederation" (Vol. II Candn. Hist. Documents), 1965; "Canada 1874-1896: Arduous Destiny" vol. 13 Candn. Centenary Series 1971; "Confederation, 1854-1867", 1972; "Macdonald: his life and world" 1975; Ed., "Candn. Parlty, Debates, 1867-1874" (1867-69 publ.; 1870-74 in prog.); Great-West Life Lecture, Centre for Cdn. Studies, Univ. of Edinburgh, May, 1980; Winthrop Bell Lecture, Mt. Allison Univ., 1981; Chrmn., Macdonald Prize Comte., Candn. Hist. Assn. 1976-80; mem. Canadian Historical Assn. (President 1968-69); Humanities Research Council (Chrmn. 1968-70); mem. Hist. Sites & Monuments Bd. Can. (1968-77); Nat. Archives Appraisal Bd., 1979- ; Home: 960 Ritchie Dr., Halifax, N.S. B3H 3P5

WAITZER, Paul L.; investment executive; b. New York, N.Y. 2 April 1927; came to Can. 1956, citizen 1967; e. Schs., Norfolk, Va.; William & Mary Univ.; m. Valorie Levine 15 March 1953; two s., Edward Michael, one d., Sloane; Pres. The T. Milburn Co. Ltd.; Yorkvest Ltd.; mem., Board of Governors, Toronto Stock Exchange; President Murray Wholesale Drug Corp., Norfolk, Va. 1951; apptd. Pres. The T. Milburn Co. Ltd. 1956; founded and assumed Pres. Chempac Ltd. 1959 until sale in 1967; Vice-Pres. and Dir., E. H. Pooler & Co. (former name of Yorkton Securities Ltd.) 1969; Pres., Yorkton Securities Ltd. 1970; Chrmn. and CEO 1972-76; served in 2nd World War as Hosp. Corpsman, U.S.N.; hon. discharge 1945; mem. Bd. Trade Metrop. Toronto; Jewish (Pres. Temple Sinai Cong.); recreations: sailing, tennis, swimming, bridge, walking; Clubs: Ontario; Island Yacht; Home: 420 Glencairn Ave., Toronto, Ont. M5N 1V5; Office: D Floor, Royal York Hotel, 100 Front St. W., Toronto, Ont. M5J 1E3

WAKEFIELD, Wesley Halpenny; evangelist; b. Vancouver, B.C., 22 Aug. 1929; s. late Pastor William James Elijah and Jane Mitchell (Halpenny) W.; m. Mildred June Shouldice; Calgary, Alta., 24 Oct. 1959; el. Internat. Leader, Bible Holiness Movement since inception 1949; author, "Bible Doctrine"; "Jesus is Lord", 1977; "Foundation of Freedom" 1979; Ed., "Wesleyan Annotated edition Bible" 1980- ; "Truth on Fire" since 1949; "Christian Social Vanguard", 1960-61; "Canadian Church and State" since 1977; Dir., "Bible Broadcast", 1952-56; researcher on effects of marijuana and youth 1969; labour leg. conscience clauses 1973, also religious liberty leg.; Vice Pres., Candns. United for Separation of Church and State; Chrmn., Concerned Christians for Racial Equality; Religious Freedom Conf. 1978-79; Bd. mem., Candn. Council of Japan Evangelistic Band; Nat. Comte mem., Christian Holiness Assn.; Pres., Imperial Security Guard Service Ltd.; Secy., Cumo Resources Ltd.; Mrg., Liberty Press; Evangelistic Book Serv.; Aldersgate Advertising Agency; mem. Anti-Slavery Soc.; Candn. Bible Soc.; Creation Science Assn.; Nat. Assn. Advanc. Coloured People; recreation: model railways; Address: P.O. Box 223, Postal Stn. A., Vancouver, B.C. V6C 2M3

WALDOCK, Peter John, B.A.; book publisher; b. Lincoln, Eng. 26 Feb. 1945; came to Can. 1967; s. Norman Bruce and Norah (Dransfield) W.; e. Glyn Grammar Sch., W. Ewell, Eng., 1956-63; Keele Univ., Staffordshire, Eng., BA 1967; m. Gillian Irene Rigg 23 May 1970; children: Christopher James, Sarah Elizabeth; VICE PRES. AND GEN. MGR./PRES., PENGUIN BOOKS CAN. LTD. since 1974; joined Penguin Books as Sales Dir. and Mgr., 1967; Pres., Candn. Telebook Agency; Extve. Mem., CBPC; Pres., Paperback Group, CBPC; Protestant; recreations: tennis, squash, volleyball; Home: 139 Manor Rd.

E., Toronto, Ont. M4S 1R7; Office: 2801 John St., Markham, Ont. L3R 1B4

WALDON, David George; retired Interprovincial Pipe Line Ltd., chairman; b. Toronto, Ont., 24 Aug. 1916; s. late Ethel (Park) and Charles D. W.; e. North Toronto Coll., 1935; Shaw Business Sch., 1935-37; m. Mary Eileen, d. late Wellington Moore, Toronto, 21 Oct. 1944; one s., Robert David; Dir., National Life Assurance Co. of Canada; Union Gas Ltd.; Royal Trustco.; Canuck Well Servicing Ltd. (Edmonton); Jr. Clerk, Andian National Corp. Ltd. 1935; trans. to operating H.Q., Cartagena, Colombia, S.A., 1936, Asst. Chief Acct., 1941, Asst. to Mgr., 1947; joined (I.P.L.) as Office Auditor, Edmonton, Alta., 1950, Asst. Treas.; 1953; trans. to Toronto, apptd. Treas., 1954; trans. to Edmonton as Asst. Gen. Mgr., 1959, Gen. Mgr., 1964; returned to Toronto as Vice-Pres., el. a Dir., 1966; Pres. 1967; Chrmn and Dir. 1977-78 (ret.); Hon. life mem., Can. Petroleum Assn.; Trust., Toronto Western Hosp.; Clubs: National; York Downs Golf; Home: 469 Oriole Pky., Toronto, Ont. M5P 2H9

WALDRON, Norman V.; insurance executive; b. Montreal, Que., 21 Feb. 1918; s. late Percy and Hannah (Spence Holbrook) W.; e. Strathcona Acad., Outremont, Que. (1935); Ins. Inst. Can., A.I.I.C.; Chart. Ins. Broker; m. Edel, d. late Sigvardt Wennevold;children: Norman Randolph, Timothy Victor, Bonita Lilie; SENIOR VICE-PRES. REED, STENHOUSE LTD.; 5 yrs. with Royal Bank of Canada; 10 yrs. with Northern Assurance Co. Ltd. Asst. Casualty Supt. for Canada; 7 yrs. with Alliance Assurance Co. Ltd., Casualty and Multi-Peril Supt. for Can.; joined Morgan Insurance Services Ltd. as a Dir., 1956; apptd. Dir. of Underwriting, then Vice Pres. 1960, Gen. Mgr. 1962, Extve. Vice-Pres., Gen. Mgr. and Dir. 1963 until merger with present Co.; Hon. Past Pres. Adv. Bd., Ins. Inst. of Que.; mem., Ins. Brokers Assn. Que.; Anglican; recreations: boating, swimming; pub. speaking; Clubs: St. James's; Home: Apt. 712, 3470 Simpson Ave., Montreal, Que. H3G 2J5; Office: 759 Victoria Sq., Montreal, Que. H2Y 2K2

WALFORD, Alfred Ernest, C.B., C.B.E., M.M., E.D., C.A., F.C.I.S.; b. Montreal, Que., 20 Aug. 1896; s. Alfred G. S. and Phoebe Ann (McQuat) W.; e. Westmount Acad., Montreal, Que.; m. Olive M. Dyke, 7 Oct. 1922; one s. A. Harvie D.; Hon. Dir., Canada Trust Co.; Hon. Chrmn. Candn. Nat. Comte., Eng. Speaking Union; mem., Metrop. Adv. Bd., Y.M.C.A.; National Advisory Bd. Salvation Army; Fellow of the Royal Commonwealth Soc.; Past Pres., Montreal Bd. Trade; Past Chrmn., Extve. Devel. Inst.; mem., Nat. Comte., Candn. Boy Scouts (Regional Commr. 1949-62); Gov., McMaster Univ., 1947-64; Partner, Alfred Walford & Sons, Montreal, Que., 1920-32; Controller and Secy.-Treas., Jas. A. Ogilvy's Ltd., 1929-39; Treas. Dir., Henry Morgan & Co. Ltd.; 1946-61; Pres. and Dir., Morgan Trust Co., 1946-63; Chrmn. Bd., Canadian Vickers Ltd. 1958-67; E.G.M. Cape & Co. Ltd. 1965-68; Dir., Mercantile Bank, 1961-70; Canada Trust Co., 1960-72; entered Candn. Army as Pte. 1914, and advanced through grades to Maj-Gen., 1944; served with R.C.A. 1914-39; 1st Candn. Div. and 1st Candn. Corps. 1939-43; Chief Adm. Staff Offr., 1st Candn. Army, 1943-44;Adj.-Gen., Candn. Forces, 1944-46; retired 1946; Hon. A.D.C. to Gov. Gen. of Can., 1946-53; Hon. Col., 3rd Div. Arty., 1946-53; awarded M.M. 1916, C.B.E. 1944, C.B. 1946, Lgion of Merit; (U.S.A.) 1945; Life mem., Order Chart. Accts. Que.; Fellow, Candn. Chart. Inst. Accys. and Administrators; Clubs: St. James's; Forest & Stream; Home: Apt. E90, 1321 Sherbrooke St. W., Montreal, Que. H3G 1J4.

WALFORD, Harvie Dyke, B.Eng., B.A., M.A.; executive; b. Montreal, Que., 25 July 1927; s. A. Ernest and Olive M. (Dyke) W.; e. Westmount (Que.) High Sch., 1944; McGill Univ., B.Eng. 1949; Cambridge Univ., B.A. 1951, M.A. 1956; Centre d'Etudes Industrielles, Geneva,

Cert. 1952; m. Dorice C. Brown, 9 Feb. 1952; children: Robert, Joanne, Alan, Mark; VICE PRES., CORP. PLANNING, CANADAIR LTD., since 1978; Sr. Vice-Pres., Adm., Bank of Montreal, since 1973; Market Mgr.-Packaging, Aluminum Co. of Can., 1961; Sales Mgr., E. Region, 1965; Mgr., Market Research, 1967; Market Mgr., Alcan International, 1968, Asst. to Extve. Vice Pres.-Adm. of Bank, 1969; Vice Pres. Adm. 1970; mem. Order Engrs, Que.; mem. Council, Montreal Bd. of Trade; Awarded Silver Jubilee Medal, 1977; Anglican; recreations: reading, skiing, volunteer work; Club: St. James's; McGill Univ. Faculty; Home: 400 Kensington Ave., Apt. 307, Westmount, Que. H3Y A28; Office: Blvd. Laurentien, St. Laurent, P.O. Box 6087, Montreal, Que. H3C 3G9

WALKER, David Harry, M.B.E., Hon. D. Litt.; author; b. Scotland, 9 Feb. 1911; s. Harry Giles and Elizabeth Bewley (Newsom) W.; e. Shrewsbury Sch., Eng.; Royal Mil. Coll., Sandhurst; Univ. of New Brunswick, Litt.D., 1955; m. Willa, d. Col. Allan A. Magee, Montreal, 27 July 1939; children: Patrick (Deceased), Giles, Barclay, David, Julian; served as Army Offr., The Black Watch 1931-47,India and Sudan, 1932-38; A.D.C. to Gov.-Gen. of Can., 1938-39; with 51st Divn. in France; prisoner of war, 1940-45; Staff Coll., Camberley, 1945-46; Comptroller to Viceroy of India, 1946-47; mem., Royal Company of Archers; author, "The Storm and the Silence", 1949; "Geordie", 1950; "The Pillar", 1952; "Digby", 1953; "Harry Black", 1956; "Sandy was a Soldier's Boy", 1957; "Where The High Winds Blow", 1960; "Storms of Our Journey", 1963; "Dragon Hill", 1963; "Winter of Madness", 1964; "Mallabec", 1965; "Come Back Geordie", 1966; "Devil's Plunge" (USA title "Cab-Intersec"), 1968; "Pirate Rock", 1969; "Big Ben"; 1969; ."The Lord's Pink Ocean", 1972; "Black Dougal", (U.S. 1974); "Ash", 1976; "Pot of Gold", 1977; winner of Gov.-Gen. Awards for fiction, 1952 and 1953; Fellow, Roy. Soc. of Literature; mem. of the Canada Council, 1957-61; Candn. Commr., Roosevelt Campobello Internat. Park Comn., 1965 (Chrmn. 1970-72); Presbyterian; Club: Royal and Ancient Golf (St. Andrews, Scotland); Address: Strathcroix, St. Andrews, N.B. E0G 2X0

WALKER, Hon. David James, P.C. (Can.), Q.C., LL.D.; senator; b. Toronto, Ont., 10 May 1905; s. David James and Margaret (Robertson) W.; e. Winchester Pub. Sch.; Toronto Model Sch.; and Jarvis Coll. Inst., Toronto, Ont.; Univ. of Toronto, B.A. 1928; Osgoode Hall, Toronto, 1928-31; m. Elizabeth Joyce, d. Irving W. Smith, Toronto; Ont., 2 Sept. 1933; children: David James, Margaret Joyce (Mrs. W. D. McKeough), Diane Elizabeth (Mrs. R. B. Walters); Dir., Anglo Canada Fire & General Insurance Co.; Gilbraltar Insurance Co.; former Bencher, Law Soc. of Upper Can.; read law with Tilley, Johnston, Thomson & Parmenter; called to Bar of Ont. 1931; cr. K.C. 1944; Special Crown Prosecutor for Dom. Govt., 1931-35; Secy. of Royal Comn. Investigating H.E.P.C. of Ont., 1932; Past Pres. of following: Macdonald-Cartier Club of Univ. of Toronto; Osgoode Hall Cons. Club; Toronto P. Cons. Business Men's Club; Nominated JOHN DIEFENBAKER for leadership of National P.C. Party, 1942; DIEFENBAKEL campaign Mgr at Leadership Convention, 1948, and his official agent in 1956 when he was elected Leader, and 1957 when he became Prime Minister responsible for initial drafting of Bill of Rights; def. cand. for Rosedale to H. of C., g.e. 1953; el. to H. of C. g.e. 1957 and re-el. 1958; Parlty. Asst. to Min. of Justice, 1957-58; apptd. Min. of Public Works, 20 Aug. 1959, also Min. of Housing and Nat. Capital Comm.; def. g.e. June 1962; summoned to Senate of Can., Feb. 1963; P. Conservative; Anglican; recreations: riding, skiing; Clubs: Albany (Pres. 1949-52); Rideau Club (Ottawa); Toronto Lawyers (Pres. 1951-52); Toronto Hunt; Badminton & Racquet; Advocates Society; Home: 65 Glen Edyth Dr., Toronto, Ont. M4V 2V8; Office: Rm. 568 S, The Senate, Ottawa, Ont. K1A 0A4

WALKER, David Moffatt, B.A., M.S.; broadcasting executive; b. Ottawa, Ont., 18 Dec. 1927; s. Harry James and Olive Kennedy (Moffatt) W.; e. Queen's Univ., Hon. B.A. 1950; Inst. World Affairs, Conn., 1951; Columbia Univ., M.S. 1951; m. Moyra Margaret, d. late John Wilson, Cal., 13 Nov. 1954; children: Stephen, Hilary, Nicholas; Extve. Director, Corporate Affairs, Ontario Educational Communications Authority since 1975; Editor, Yale Reports, Poynter Fellow, Yale Univ., 1966-71; Producer, Radio & TV, C.B.C., 1951-56; Producer, WGBH-TV, Boston and "Of Science and Scientists" for Ford Foundation and Harvard Univ., 1956; Program Organ., C.B.C. Toronto, 1957-61; Supv., Information and Adult Educ., CBC, 1962-66; Dir., Corp. Affairs, O.E.C.A 1971; mem. Nat. Assn. Science Writers (U.S.A.); Dir., Cdn. Assoc. for Adult Educ.; Dir., Cdn. Inst. in Pub. Affairs; recreation: gardening; Home: 2 Rose Park Dr., Toronto, Ont. M4T 1P9

WALKER, Edward Bullock III, M.S.; petroleum executive; b. Norfolk, Va. 10 Jan. 1922; s. Edward Bullock and Mary Rennick (Ray) W.; e. Boston (Mass.) Latin High School, 1940; Mass. Inst. Technol., B.S. (Geol.) 1946, M.S. 1947; m. Katherine Evelyn, d. Nels P. Miller, Medicine Lake, Mont. 5 Sept. 1953; two s. Edward Bullock, Richard Miller; PRES., GULF OIL CORP. 1981- ; 1978 to present; and Dir. since 1974; Exploration Mgr., Mene Grande Oil Co., Venezuela 1947; Exploration Co-ordinator, Gulf Eastern Co., London 1962; Dir., Exploration Div. Gulf Research Development Co., Pittsburgh 1967; Vice Pres., Mene Grande Oil Co. 1967; Pres., Gulf Mineral Resources Co. 1968; apptd. Vice Pres. present Co. 1971; Pres., Gulf Energy & Minerals Co. 1975-78; Exec. Vice-Pres. of Present Company 1971-75; 1978-81; served with US Army 1943-46; awarded Bronze Star with Oak Leaf Cluster; mem., Am. Assn. Petrol. Geols.; Amer. Inst. of Professional Geol.; London Geol. Soc.; Amer. Petroleum Inst. (Dir.); recreations: hiking, backpacking, skiing, fishing; Clubs: Duquesne, Fox Chapel Golf (Pittsburgh, Pa.); Rolling Rock (Ligonier, Pa.); Cherry Hills (Denver Co.); River Oaks, Ramada, Houston Metro. Racquet (Houston, Tex.); Office: Box 4523, Houston, Texas 210

WALKER, Edwin Hodges, B.I.E., LL.D., O.St.J.; b. Hamilton, Ont. 1909; e. General Motors Inst., Flint, Mich. (Indust. Engn.); m. has one s. and one d.; founding mem. Bd. of Govs., York Univ., Toronto and Shaver Hosp. for Chest Diseases, St. Catharines, Ont.; joined the McKinnon Industries Ltd. in 1933 rising through various executive positions to Pres. and Gen. Mgr., 1953; Pres. and Gen. Mgr., General Motors of Canada Ltd., 1957-68; Vice Pres. and mem., Overseas Policy Group 1958-68; Adm. Comte. G.M. Corp. 1963-68; Dir., General Motors of Canada Ltd.; Past Pres., Motor Vehicle Mfrs. Assn.; Past Pres. Soc. of Auto. Engrs.; recreations: golf, fishing, boating; Clubs: York (Toronto); Rosedale Golf (Toronto); St. Catharines Golf & Country; The St. Catharines; Home: 354 Martindale Road, St. Catharines, Ont. L2R 6P9

WALKER, Gordon Arthur Hunter, Ph.D.; educator; b. Kinghorn, Scot. 30 Jan. 1936; s. Frederic Thomas and Mary (Hunter) W.; e. The Edinburgh Acad. 1954; Edinburgh Univ. B.Sc. 1958; Cambridge Univ. Ph.D. 1962; m. Sigrid Helene Fischer 21 Apl. 1962; two s. Nicholas Ian, Eric Gordon Thomas; PROF. OF ASTRONOMY, UNIV. OF B.C. 1972- ; NRC Postdoctoral Fellow, Dom. Astrophysical Observatory, Victoria 1962-64, Research Scient. II 1962-69; Assoc. Prof. present Univ. 1969-72; author over 60 scient. papers astron. prof. journs.; mem. Candn. Astron. Soc. (Pres. 1980-82); Am. Astron. Soc.; Astron. Soc. Pacific; Royal Soc. Can.; recreations: skiing, hiking, tennis; Home: 2499 West 35th Ave., Vancouver, B.C. V6M 1J7; Office: Vancouver, B.C. V6T 1W5.

WALKER, Gordon Wallace, B.Sc., P.Eng.; executive; b. Edmonton, Alta., 16 July 1926; s. George Arthur and Elizabeth (Roulston) W.; e. Univ. of Alberta, B.Sc. (Civil Engn.), 1949; m. Patricia Anne, d. John William Shelton, 27 Aug. 1949; children: Alison Ann, Susan Ruth; CHMN. OF BD., CANUCK ENGINEERING, since 1981; with Imperial Oil Ltd., Canal Project, N.W.T., summer 1943; Northwestern Utilities Ltd., summer 1944-48; Design and Project Engr., Interprovincial Pipe Line Co., Edmonton, 1949-54; Mannix Co. Ltd., Calgary; Mgr., Pipe Line Div., 1955-63; Vice Pres. Engn., Alberta Gas Trunk Line Co. Ltd. 1963-67, Operations 1967-72; Dir. Engn., Canadian Arctic Gas Study Ltd. 1972-74; Pres., Canuk Engineering, 1974-81; mem., Engn. Inst. of Can.; Pipeline Contractors Assn. (Past Pres.); Protestant; recreation: skiing; Home: 15-448 Strathcona Dr., S.W., Calgary, Alta. T3H 1M3; Office: 924A - 17th Ave. S.W., Calgary, Alta.

WALKER, Hon. Gordon Wayne, Q.C., MPP.P., LL.B.; politician; b. St. Thomas, Ont. 10 Sept. 1941; s. Albert Cornwall and Ruby Pearl (Stansell) W.; e. elem. and secondary schs. St. Thomas, Ont. 1961; Univ. of W. Ont. B.A. 1964, LL.B. 1967; m. Harriet Emmeline d. Harold Whitfield Hedley, Woodstock, Ont. 21 Dec. 1968; two d. Wynsom Harriet, Melanie Jennifer; MIN. OF INDUSTRY & TRADE DEVELOPMENT 1982- ; Min. of Consumer & Commercial Relations, 1981-82 and Prov. Secy. for Justice, Ont. 1979-82; called to Bar of Ont. 1969; cr. Q.C. 1979; Partner, Walker & Wood, London, Ont. 1969-71, 1976-77, part-time 1971-75, 1977-78; Ald. City of London 1967-71; el. M.P.P. for London North 1971, def. 1975, re-el. for London South 1977; Min. of Correctional Services 1978-1981; Prov. Secy. for Justice 1979-81; rec'd Centennial Medal 1967; Queen's Silver Jubilee Medal 1977; mem. Law Soc. Upper Can.; P. Conservative; United Church; Home: 385 Ridout St. S., London, Ont. N6C 3Z8; Office: Parliament Bldgs., Queen's Park, Toronto, Ont. M7A 1A1.

WALKER, Graham H.; investment dealer; b. Sask. 24 Aug. 1931; s. George Keys and Anne Viola (Sled) W.; e. High Sch.; children: Michael, Alison, Sandra, Erin; CHMN., C.E.O. AND DIR., HOUSTON, WILLOUGHBY LTD. since 1981; Chmn., and C.E.O. Houston Willoughby Investments Ltd.; Dir., Candn. Commercial Bank; Dir., Cairns Homes Ltd.; Atlantic Council of Can.; B.B. and E.Corp.; Conference Bd. of Canada; Can-Com Management Ltd.; joined present Co. 1955, apptd. Dir. 1965, Vice Pres. Adm. 1967; Pres. 1974; Dir. Morguard Properties Ltd.; Nuwest Group Ltd.; mem. Bd. of Regents, St. Andrews Coll., Saskatoon; Chamber Comm.; Protestant; recreation: squash; Clubs: Optimist; Assiniboia; Home: 15 Hogarth Pl., Regina, Sask. S4S 4J8; Office: 1825 Cornwall St., Regina, Sask. S4P 3C9

WALKER, Ian Lawrence, B.Sc., P.Eng.; b. Plymouth, Eng. 25 May 1937; s. Clifford Lawrence and Lilian (Marwood) W.; came to Canada 1968; e. Clifton Coll., Bristol, Eng. 1955; Woolwich Polytech., London, Eng. 1955-59, 1965, B.Sc. (Mech. Engn.); Brit. Inst. Mang., Dipl. Mang. Studies; m. Beryl Evelyn, d. W. J. Stone, Portsmouth, Eng. April 1970; children: Stephen, Karen, Kevin, Jeremy, Jonathan, Eve; PRES., INTEG-INTERCONTINENTAL ENGINEERING LTD. Dir., CH2M Hill Canada; Dir., Westwood Polygas Ltd.; Dir., Balfour Beatty Power Consultants Canada Ltd.; with General Electric Co. Ltd., U.K. as Operational Service Engr. 1959, Project Mgr. 1960, Test Engr. 1962, Contract Mgr. 1964; Sr. Mech. Engr., Balfour, Beatty & Co. Ltd. 1966; Mgr. Balfour Beatty Power Consultants Canada Ltd., Vancouver, B.C. 1968; apptd. an Extve. Dir. present Co. and Intercontinental Engineering of Alberta Ltd. 1972; mem. Assns. Prof. Engrs. B.C., Alta. and Sask.; Chart. Engrs. Gt. Brit.; Inst. Mech. Engrs. (U.K.); Assoc. mem. Brit. Inst. Mang.; recreations: sailing, scuba diving, travel; Home: 3886 Trenton Place, N. Vancouver, B.C. V7R 3G5; Office: 1155 W. Pender St., Vancouver, B.C. V6E 2P4

WALKER, James Barrett, B.A., F.S.A., F.C.I.A.; retired executive actuary; b. Toronto, Ont., 22 July 1919; s. James Morley George and Mary Ellen (Barrett) W.; e. Oakwood Coll. Inst.; Toronto, 1938; Univ. of Toronto (Victoria Coll.), B.A., 1942; Univ. of W. Ont. (Mang. Training Course), 1965; m. Doris June d. late R. J. Riddell, Cardinal, Ont., 25 Dec. 1944; children: June Anne, Candace Marion, James Barrett; Pres. and Dir., Canada Life Insurance Co. of New York; entire business career spent with present Co. having joined 1946; trans. to Group Ins. Dept. 1953; apptd. Asst. Actuary 1951, Group Actuary 1959, Vice-President and Director of Group 1968; Vice-Pres. and Dir., U.S. Div. 1970; Exec. Vice-Pres. 1977-81; Sub. Lieut., R.C.N.V.R., Feb. 1941; on loan to R.C.N., Dec. 1941 to Feb. 1944; discharged, rank of Lieut. Commdr., Dec. 1945; Mentioned in Despatches, 1944; mem. Internat. Cong. of Actuaries; Conservative; Protestant; recreations: golf, sailing and other summer water sports, music, reading; Clubs: National; Lambton Golf & Country; Empire; Home: 43 Abilene Dr., Islington, Ont. M9A 2N1.

WALKER; John A., B.Sc.; retired executive; b. Saint John, N.B., 3 Feb. 1915; s. Daniel D. and Mary McKenzie (White) W.; e. Lower Can. Coll., Montreal, Que.; McGill Univ., B.Sc.; m. Josephine, d. Everett C. Kirkpatrick, 20 Sept. 1940; children: Lynn, Lee, Jack, Daniel; President, Ayerst McKenna & Harrison Inc. (pharm. mfrs.), 1970-80; Pres., Ayerst Organics Ltd.; served with R.C.N. during 2nd World War as Offr.; Past Pres., Theta Delta Chi; Protestant; recreations: tennis, skiing; Club: Mount Royal; Home: 45 Ainslie Rd., Montreal West, Que. H4X 1K5; Office: P.O. Box 6115, Montreal, Que. H3C 3J1

WALKER, John D., M.A.Sc.; manufacturer; b. Stratford, Ont., March 1928; s. Frank S. and Ray (Rollinson) W.; e. Stratford (Ont.) Pub. and High Schs.; Univ. of Toronto, B.A.Sc. 1950; Mass. Inst. of Technol., M.A.Sc. 1952; m. Gretchen, d. Gordon Ratz, 1952; two children: MANG. DIR., CBSA EUROPE (Cooper-Bessemer (U.K.) Ltd.); after grad. joined Canadian National Railways and apptd. Div. Mgr. 1957; joined Cooper-Bessemer as Sales Engr., Mount Vernon, Ohio, 1960; trans. to Candn. Co. as Sales Engr., Toronto, 1962, Br. Mgr. 1963, Pres. and Dir. 1966; mem., Candn. Machinery Mfrs.' Assn.; Bd. Trade Metrop. Toronto; recreations: golf, curling; Club: Thornhill Golf & Country; Office: 173 Sloane St., London S.W. 1, Eng.

WALKER, Robert Harold Earle, D.S.O., E.D., Q.C., B.C.L.; b. Davos, Switzerland, 2 Feb. 1912; s. James Harold Earle and Hazel Alice (Hart) W.; e. Selwyn House Sch., Montreal; Lower Can. Coll., Montreal 1928; Royal Mil. Coll., Dipl. 1933; McGill Univ. B.C.L. 1936; m. Kathleen Margaret Mary, d. John Raymond Ryan, 10 June 1936; children: Jane Ann (Mrs. Glenn Williams), Christine (Mrs. Graham Bagnall); COUNSEL, MARTINEAU WALKER; Dir., American Express Canada, Inc.; Dominion Electric Protection Co.; Martin-Black Inc.; called to Bar of Que. 1936; cr. K.C. 1949; law practice with present and predecessor firms since 1936, Partner 1946-80; mem. Jt. Comte. on Taxation 1966-70; Special Comtes. on Royal Comn. Report, White Paper on Tax Reform and Tax Reform Bill 1970-72; mem. Taxation Adv. Comte. (apptd. by Dept. of Nat. Revenue); Chrmn. Candn. Tax Foundation, 1974-75; served RCA 1939-45; rank Lt. Col. commdg. 15th Candn. Armoured Field Regt. 1944; mem. Que. Bar Assn.; Candn. Bar Assn. (Chrmn. Taxation Sec. 1969-70, Vice Pres. for Que. 1970-71); Am. Coll. Probate Counsel (Bd. of Regents 1967-72); Delta Upsilon (Pres. McGill Chapter 1936); Protestant; recreations: skiing, tennis; Club: St. James's; Home: 4089 Highland Ave., Montreal, Que. H3Y 1R4; Office: 800 Victoria Sq.; Montreal, Que. H4Z 1E9

WALKER, Victor H. J., B.A.Sc.; director; b. Stratford, Ont., 24 Jan. 1926; s. George Edward and Eva Victoria

(Saunders) W.; e. Univ. of Toronto, B.A.Sc. (Ceramic Engn.) 1950; m. Kathleen Sheila Patricia, d. David Keogh, 8 May 1948; children: Gina, Bruce, Lloyd; DIRECTOR, DOON AND CAMBRIDGE CAMPUSES, CONESTOGA COLLEGE; engn. and supervisory positions with General Steel Wares, London, Ont., 1950-54; Prod. Mgr., 1954; Plant Acct. and Office Mgr., 1960; Chief Inspr., 1957; Dir. Mfg. & Engn., Brantford Washing Machines Co. Ltd., Toronto, 1962; Mgr. of Mfg., Hupp Canada Ltd., L'Assumption, Que., 1965; Mfg. Mgr., John Inglis Co. Ltd., Toronto, 1969; Vice-Pres. Mfg. and Chief Extve. Offr., Brunswick of Canada Ltd. 1970; Vice-Pres. and Dir. Mfg., Sunbeam Corp. (Can) Ltd. 1973; mem. Assn. Prof. Engrs. of Ont.; former Nat. Gov. and Candn. Regional Vice-Pres., Soc. for Advancement of Mang.; recreations: music, travel, photography; Home: 65 Forest Hill Dr., Kitchener, Ont. N2M 4G2; Office: 299 Doon Valley Dr., Kitchener, Ont. N2G 4M4

WALLACE, (Catherine); LL.D., Ph.D.; ret. educator; b. Lawrence, Mass., 10 March 1917; d. Michael and Sarah Alice W.; e. St. Patrick's Elem. and High Schs., Lawrence, Mass.; Dalhousie Univ., B.A. 1939; Saint John's Univ., N.Y., M.A. 1945, Ph.D. 1951; LL.D., Mount Allison 1971; St. Thomas Univ., 1969, LL.D. (Civil), Univ. King's College, 1971; LL.D. Univ. of N.B., 1973; LL.D. Memorial Univ. 1974; LL.D. Dalhousie Univ. 1974; Ph.D., Laval Univ., 1974; LL.D. Univ. of Western Ont. 1975; McMaster 1974; Univ. of Guelph 1980; Dir. Canadian Imperial Bank of Commerce; Maritime Telegraph and Telephone Co. Ltd.; Canada Development Corp.; Teacher, St. Patrick's High Sch., Roxbury, Mass., 1939-40; Our Lady Help of Christians Sch., Brooklyn, 1940-43; Seton Hall Co-Educ. High Sch., N.Y., 1943-53; Principal, First Central High Sch., Vancouver, 1953-59; Prof. Dept. of Eng., Mount Saint Vincent Coll., 1959-65; Pres. Mount St. Vincent Univ. 1966-74; Chrmn. Maritime Provs. Higher Educ. Comn.; R. Catholic; Address: 715 - 700 Forest Hill Rd., Fredericton, N.B. E3B 5X9

WALLACE, Brig. Frederic Campbell, D.S.O., M.C.; industrialist; b. West Ireland; e. Schools of Ireland and England; Dir., Royal Agric. Winter Fair; Pres., Candn. Elect. Mfrs. Assn., 1952-53; formerly Dir. of Radio Div., Nat. Research Council of Can. and Vice-Pres. in charge of Production, Research Enterprises Ltd. (Crown Co.) during 2nd World War; served in 1st World War 1914-18 with Royal Irish Rifles in France and Belgium; retired with rank of Bgde. Major; awarded D.S.O., M.C. and Bar; Croix de Guerre; 2nd World War with Royal Arty.; took part in Dunkirk; later Mil. mem. of Tizard Scient. Mission to N. Am. (information on radar); Home: Rolling Hills Farm, R.R. 5, Georgetown, Ont. L7G 4S8

WALLACE, John Leslie, C.D.; retired insurance executive; b. Regina, Sask. 18 Sept. 1913; s. late William Leslie and Mildred (Ross) W.; e. Regina (Sask.) Central Coll. Inst. 1931; m. Joyce d. late L. C. Thornton, Regina, Sask. June 1944; two s. George Thornton, Brian Ross; joined Northern Assurance Co. Ltd. Winnipeg, Man. 1931; Asst. Br. Mgr. Union Insurance Soc. of Canton Ltd. Winnipeg 1933-40; Partner, Wallace & Milne 1947 Regina; joined Morris & MacKenzie Ltd. 1948, Gen. Mgr. 1954, Vice Pres. 1956, Pres. 1964, Chrmn. and CEO 1972; Chrmn., 1977; served with 17th Field Regt. RCA 1940-43, 5 Candn. Armoured Div. 1943-44, Staff Candn. Army Overseas 1945, Reserve Army 1945-63, rank Lt. Col.; Past Chrmn. Corp. Montreal Children's Hosp. since 1973 (Bd. mem. since 1957, Pres. 1971-72-73, Chrmn. Foundation 1973-75); mem. Ins. Inst. Prov. Que. (Pres. 1963); Montreal Bd. Trade (Council 1971-73); Freemason; United Church; Clubs: St. James's; Royal Montreal Golf; Sunningdale Country; Sugar Mill Golf and Country; New Smyrna; Home: Winter, Sugar Mill Estates, New Smyrna Beach, Florida, Summer 790 Wonderland Rd., London, Ont.

WALLACE, Lawrence James, O.C.(1972), LL.D. B.A., M.Ed., C.St.J.; B.C. civil servant; b. Victoria, B.C., 24 April 1913; s. John and Mary E. B. (Parker) W.; e. Victoria (B.C.) Public and High Schs.; Univ. of Brit. Columbia, B.A. 1938; Univ. of Washington, M.Ed. 1945; m. Lois d. Arthur Leeming, Duncan, B.C., 24 April 1942; children: Marilyn, Gillian, Wendy; Deputy Minister to the Premier of British Columbia 1980-81; in U.K. and Europe 1977-80; joined B.C. Govt. Service 1953 as Dir., Community Programmes Br. and Adult Educ.; Dept. of Educ.; joined R.C.N.V.R. 1941; trained in Extve. Br., Royal Roads; Lt.-Commdr. 1945; Depy. Prov. Secy., B.C. 1959-77 and Depy. to premier, 1969-72; Gen. Chmn four centennial celebrations, marking founding of Crown Colony of B. C. in 1858, union of Crown Colonies of Van. Is. and B.C., 1866, Cdn. Confedn. 1867 and joining into confedn by B.C. in 1871; Past Chmn., Inter-Provincial Lottery Corp., Queen Eùizabeth II Schol. Cttee, and Nancy Greene Schol. Cttee; Hon. Trustee, B.C. Sports Hall of Fame; Dir., Duke of Edinburgh Awards Cttee; BC Forest Museum; Adv. Bd. Salvalation Army; Cdn. Council of Christians and Jews; Named B.C. Man of the Year, 1958, and Greater Vancouver Man of the Year, 1967; Cdn. Centennial Medal, 1967; Comdr Brother, OStJ, 1969; City of Victoria Citizenship Award, 1971; Queen's Jubilee Medal, 1977; Freeman of the City of London 1978; Hon. LLD, Univ. of B.C., 1978; Hon. Mem., BC High Sch. Basketball Assoc; BC Recreation Assoc.; Hon. Chief, Alberni, Gilford and Southern Vancouver Is. Indian Bands; Recreations: gardening, community activities. Address:(A6) 1345 Fairfield Rd., Victoria, B.C. V8S 1E4(A7)(M3)(J8)

WALLACE, Lila Bell Acheson, B.A.; publisher; b. Virden, Man.; d. Rev. T. Davis Acheson and Mary E. (Huston)A.; e. Ward Belmont Coll., Nashville, Tenn.; Univ. of Oregon, B.A. 1917; m. DeWitt, s. Dr. James Wallace, St. Paul, Minn., 15 Oct. 1921; a Founder and Editor, "Reader's Digest," 1921-65 when apptd. Co-Chrmn. of Bd.; retired 1973; Presbyterian; recreations: gardens; horses; Home: "High Winds", Mt. Kisco, N.Y.

WALLACE, Philip Russell, M.A., Ph.D., F.R.S.C.; professor; b. Toronto, Ont., 19 April 1915; s. George Russell and Mildred (Stillwaugh) W.; e. Univ. of Toronto, B.A. 1937, M.A. 1938, Ph.D. 1940; m. Jean Elizabeth, d. late Albert Young, 15 Aug. 1940; children: Michael David, Kathryn Joan, Robert Philip; McDONALD PROFESSOR OF PHYSICS, MCGILL UNIV., since 1977 Founder and first Chrm., Theoretical Physics Div., Candn. Assn. of Physicists; Dir., Inst. of Theoretical Physics 1966-1970; Fellow in Applied Math., Univ. of Toronto, 1937-40; Instr. in Math., Univ. of Cincinnati, 1940-42; Mass. Inst. Tech., 1942; Assoc. Research Physicist, Nat. Research Council Can. (Div. of Atomic Energy), 1943-46; Assoc. Prof. Applied Math.; McGill Univ., 1946-49; visiting prof., Laboratoire de physique des solides, Université Paul Sabatier, Toulouse, 1972-73; Prof., Laboratoire de Physique des Solides, Univ. Paul Sabatier, Toulouse, 1980-81; author of 70 scientific papers on relativity, nuclear and solid state physics; auther, "Mathematical Analysis of Physical Problems' 1972; ed, "Superconductivity (2 vols) 1969; coed, "New Developments in Semiconductors' 1973; mem., Intl. Adv. Comm., Intl. Conference on Narrow Gap Semiconductors, Warsaw 1977; Intl. Adv. Comm., 14th Intl. Conference on Semiconductors, Edinburgh 1978; 15th Intl. Conference on Semiconductors, Kyoto 1980; 16th Intl. Conference on Semiconductors, Montpellier, 1982; Ed., Candn. Journ. Physics; mem., Ed. Adv. Bd., McGill-Queen's Press 1975-78; mem., Commission de l'enseignement supérieur, Conseil de l'éducation du Québec 1970-72; mem., Univ. Grants Comm. for Physics, Nat. Research Coun. of Canada 1972-76; mem., 1967 Centennial Scholarships Comte, NSERC, 1980-83; Comm. on Semiconductors, Intl. Union of Pure and Applied Physics 1981- ; Candn. Assn. Physicists; Am. Physical Soc., Candn. Assn. Univ. Teachers; Am. Assn. Phys-

ics Teachers; Sigma Xi; Home: 125 Spartan Cres., Point Claire, Que. H9R 3R4

WALLACE, Stuart Hubert, LL.B.; photographer; b. Vancouver, B.C., 9 Dec. 1926; s. Hubert Alfred and late Gwladys (Griffiths) W.; e. Univ. of B.C. Arts; Dalhousie Univ. LL.B. 1950; m. Beverly Enolia, d. Harry C. Anderson, Vancouver, B.C. 8 Nov. 1968; children: John S., Christopher S., Timothy C., Georgina S.; called to Bar of B.C. 1950; joined law firm Russell & DuMoulin 1950, Assoc. 1950, Partner 1953-75; Gov. St. George's Sch. for Boys; Dir., Vancouver Maritime Museum; mem. Law Soc. B.C.; Candn. Bar Assn.; Zeta Psi; Liberal; Anglican; recreations: yachting, water-skiing, hunting, tennis; Clubs: Vancouver; Arbutus; Royal Vancouver Yacht; Vancouver Lawn Tennis & Badminton; Shaughnessy Golf & Country; Home: 1588 Wesbrook Cres., Vancouver, B.C. V6T 1V8;

WALLER, Dalton McFarlane; company president; b. Toronto, Ont.; s. Stanley McFarlane and Mary Elizabeth (McCutcheon) W.; e. Lawrence Park Coll., Toronto; Queen's Univ.; m. Margaret Patricia, d. Charles Grover Cleveland, 1945; three s., Grant McFarlane, Garfield Dalton, Andrew Jay; PRESIDENT AND DIRECTOR, DALMAR FOODS LTD., since 1963; Chmn. of Bd., Hospital Dietary Service Ltd.; Pres., R. L. Petty Ltd.; Pres., Walfoods Ltd., Toronto, 1946-61; served in 2nd World War with R.C.N.; Past Pres., Convention and Tourist Bureau Metrop. Toronto; Past Pres., Candn. Restaurant Assn.; Tourist Industry Assn. Can.; mem. Bd. Trade Metrop. Toronto; Freemason; Anglican; recreations: golf, tennis, squash; Clubs: Rosedale Golf; Badminton & Racquet; Home: 61 St. Clair Ave. W., Toronto, Ont. M4V 2Y8; Office: 43 Parliament St., Toronto, Ont. M5A 2Y3

WALLIS, Col. Hugh Macdonell, O.C. (1969), D.S.O., O.B.E.; M.C., V.D., C.D., K.C.L.J., F.R.S.A. (1959); b. San Francisco, Cal. 7 Dec. 1893; s. John McCall W. of "Merino", Peterborough, Ont., and Gertrude T. W. (d. of Lieut.-Col. Samuel Smith Macdonell, Q.C., LL.D., D.C.L., Windsor, Ont.); e. "The Grove", Lakefield, Ont.; Peterborough (Ont.) Coll. Inst.; Univ. of Toronto; m. 1stly Leslie Carson, London, Eng., 1935 (m. dissolved 1953); 2ndly Corinne de Boucherville Desy, June 1969; Pres. and Mang. Dir. Mount Royal Rice Mills Ltd., 1924-53; Pres., Montreal Museum of Fine Arts, 1957-64; Chrmn., Adv. Bd., Candn. Centenary Council (Chrmn. Extve., 1961-64); Gov., Montreal Gen. Hosp.; Montreal Childrens Hosp. (Chrmn. Extve., 1959); mem., Adv. Bd., Lakefield Prep. Sch.; Hon. Sponsor, Trent Univ.; Assoc., McGill Univ.; de l'Université de Montréal; served in 1st World War 1914-19 in France, Belgium and Germany; awarded D.S.O., M.C.; twice Mentioned in Despatches; Col. and Commandant, The Black Watch (RH) of Can., 1930-31 (Hon. Lt. Col. 3rd Bn. 1961-68); Hon. A.D.C. to the Gov. Gen. of Can.; 1931-35; Jubilee Medal, 1935; served in 2nd World War 1940-46 as Col. A.D.A.G.; awarded O.B.E.; with McDonald, Currie & Co., 1919-24; admitted mem., The Inst. of Chart. Accts. of Que., 1923; a founder, 1922 and Pres. of United Services Club, 1925; Pres., St. Andrews Soc. of Montreal, 1936-38; Candn. Citizenship Council, 1951-52; Canadian Club of Montreal, 1954-55; apptd. (1960) mem. and Chrmn. of (7-man) Interim and Organizing Comte. planning Canada's 1967 Centenary Celebrations; given "Outstanding Citizen" award by Montreal Citizenship Council, 1967; Centennial Medal 1967; apptd. Kt. Companion, Order St. Lazarus of Jerusalem 1971; recreations: fine arts, travelling, Canadiana; Clubs: United Services; Canadian; Braeside Golf; Home: 3468 Drummond St., Montreal, Que. H3G 1Y4

WALLOT, Jean-Pierre, L.ès L., M.A., Ph.D.; educator; b. Valleyfield, Qué. 22 May 1935; s. Albert and Adrienne (Thibodeau) W.; e. Univ. de Montréal B.A. 1954, L.ès L. 1957, M.A. 1957, Ph.D. 1965; m. Rita d. Joseph Girard, Melocheville, Qué. 10 Aug. 1957; children: Normand,

Robert, Sylvie; PROF. D'HISTOIRE, UNIV. DE MONT-REAL, Chrmn. d'histoire 1973-75, Vice Dean (Studies) des Arts et des Sciences 1975-78; Vice Dean, Research, Fac. of Arts and Sci. since 1979; el. mem., Univ. Council, 1981-84; mem. Faculty of Arts & Science Council, Univ. of Toronto 1970-71; mem. Can. Council Acad. Panel 1973-76, Negotiated Grants Comte. 1975-1980 (Chrmn. 1978); Dir. de recherche associé Ecole des Hautes Etudes en Sciences sociales, Paris 1975, 1979, 1981; Guest Lectr. Univ. of Sherbrooke 1967, 1968, UQUAM 1972, Univ. of B.C. 1972, Laval Univ. 1973, 1977; Assoc. Prof., Univ. of Toronto 1969-1971, Prof. Concordia U. 1971-73; rec'd yearly research grants Can. Council and Qué. Govt. since 1961; Shawinigan Prize best feature (reportage) Candn. Weeklies Assn. Newspapers 1957-58, 1958-59; Médaille Marie Tremaine Soc. canadienne de bibliog. 1973; author "Intrigues françaises et américaines au Canada (1800-1802)" 1965; "Un Québec qui bougeait" 1973; co-author "Les Imprimes dans le Bas-Canada 1801-1810" 1967; "Patronage et pouvoir dans le Bas-Canada 1794-1812" 1973; Ed. "Mèmoires d'un Bourgeois de Montréal" 1980; mem. various ed. comtes.; author over 50 articles econ. and social hist. Qué.; Ed. "Le Progrès de Valleyfield"; mem., sec., Academy I, Royal Soc. Can.; Candn. Hist. Assn. (Dir. 1970-73, Vice-Pres. 1981-); Inst. d'histoire de l'amérique française (Dir. since 1970, Vice Pres. 1971-73, Pres. 1973-77); 1st vice-pres., Assn. canadienne-française pour l'avancement des sciences; chevaliers de colomb; catholique; recreation: music (drums); Clubs: Rotary; Richelieu; Home: 3455 Melrose, Montréal, Qué. H4A 2R9; Office: (C.P. 6128) Montréal, Qué. H3C 3J7

WALMSLEY, Lewis Calvin, D.Paed.; b. Milford, Prince Edward County, Ont., 3 Dec. 1897; s. James Franklin and Sarah Ann (Welbanks) W.; e. Picton (Ont.) Coll., Grad. 1914; Univ. of Toronto, B.A. 1919; Coll. of Educ., Specialist in Math. and Physics, 1920; Columbia Univ. (summer) 1927; Coll. of Educ., D.Paed., 1945; m. 1stly, late Constance Ellen; d. Dr. Omar L. Kilborn, Chengtu, Sze, China, 9 Aug. 1921; children: Glenn Kilborn, James Omar, Enid Elizabeth, Marion Alfretta; 2ndly, Dorothy Hamilton Brush, 1 Dec. 1962; entered service of Un. Ch. of Can. Overseas Mission Bd. and went to China, 1921, to the Candn. Sch. and served as Princ., 1923-43; returned from China and taught in the Sch. of Chinese Studies, Chinese Hist. and Civilization, 1944-45; sent to India to become Princ. of Woodstock Sch. and Coll.; called back to China in 1947; Assoc. Prof. of E. Asiatic Studies, Univ. of Toronto, 1948-63; served in 1st World War, 1917-18, with C.A.M.C.; Toronto; has collab. on two books: "Poems by Wang Wei"; "Wang Wei, the Painter-Poet", 1975; "Bishop in Honan" 1974; "History of the West China Union Univ." 1975; United Church; recreation: painting; Home: Apt. 2807, No. 1 Massey Square, Toronto, Ont. M4C 5L4

WALSH, Hon. Allison Arthur Mariotti, B.A., B.C.L., judge; b. Montreal, Que., 30 June 1911; s. James Francis and Isabel (Mariotti) W.; e. High Sch. of Montreal, 1929; McGill Univ., B.A. 1933 (Oliver Gold Medal in Econ. & Pol. Science), B.C.L. 1936; Univ. De Grenoble, Cert. d'Etudes Francaises 1936; m. Carol, d. Albert Edward Stevens, 27 Dec. 1939; two d. Julia S. Keleher, Diana Allison Lockwood; PUISNE JUDGE, FEDERAL COURT OF CAN., since 1964; Judge, Court Martial Appeal Court, 1968; read law with late Aubrey H. Elder, Q.C.; called to Bar of Que. 1936; cr. Q.C. 1960; practised law in Montreal with Creelman, Edmison & Beullac, later known as Creelman and Walsh, 1939-54 and with Campbell, Weldon, McFadden & Walsh which became Laidley, Campbell, Walsh & Kisilenko until 1964; has served as Commr. of Senate in connection with Resolutions for Dissolution of Marriage and as Umpire under Unemployment Ins. Act.; Past Pres., Hampstead Mun. Assn.; Hampstead Home & Sch. Assn.; Iverley Community Centre, Montreal; McGill Alumni Inter-Fraternity Council; rec'd Centennial Medal, 1967; Queen's Jubilee Medal, 1976; Hon.

mem. Phi Delta Phi Legal Fraternity; Sigma Chi; Protestant; recreations: golf, billiards, travel; Clubs: Rideau; Royal Ottawa Golf; Kiwanis (Past Dir.); Canadian; University (Montreal); Montreal Badminton & Squash; M.A.A.A. (Life mem.); Home: Apt. 1411 - Ten Driveway, Ottawa, Ont. K2P 1C7; Office: Supreme Court of Can. Bldg., Ottawa, Ont. K1A 0H9

WALSH, Edward P., B.E., pulp and paper executive; b. Quebec City, Que. 7 Sept. 1924; s. Edward Michael and Clara (Bussière) W.; e. St. Patrick's High Sch. Que.; McGill Univ. B.E. (Chem. Engn.); m. Rowena d. E. J. Mercer 16 Oct. 1951; two s, three d.; PRES. AND CHIEF EXTVE. OFFR., DIR., DONOHUE INC. 1967- ; Pres. and Dir. Donohue Charlevoix Inc.; Donohue Malbaie Inc.; Pres. and Dir. Donohue St-Felicien Inc.; Donohue Normick Inc.; J.E. Therrien Inc.; Devel. Engr. Canadian Industries Ltd., Shawinigan Falls, Cornwall 1946-47; Asst. Control Supt. Anglo Newfoundland Development Co. Ltd., Grand Falls, Nfld. 1947-51; Control Supt., Groundwood Supt. and Gen. Supt. Anglo Canadian Pulp and Paper Mill, Quebec 1952-62; Gen. Mgr. Gaspesia Pulp and Paper Co. Ltd., Chandler 1962-67; mem., bd. of Dir., Forintek Canada Corp.; Forest Engineering Research Inst. of Canada; Quebec Forest Industries Assn.; Candn. Pulp & Paper Assn.; mem., Tech. Assn. Pulp & Paper Industry; Prof. Engrs. Que.; Engn. Inst. Can.; Chamber Comm.; R. Catholic; recreations: golf, tennis, skiing, skating; Clubs: Garrison; Mount Royal; Murray Bay Golf; Home: 1264 des Gouverneurs, Sillery, Que. G1T 2G1; Office: 500 Grand Allée E., Quebec, Que. G1R 2J7.

WALSH, Lieut.-Gen. Geoffrey, C.B.E., D.S.O., C.D., B.Eng., D.M.Sc.; b. Brantford, Ont., 19 Aug. 1909; s. late Harris Leamon and late Bertha Ione (Benson) W.; e. St. Catharines (Ont.) Coll. Inst.; Royal Mil. Coll. (Dipl.) 1926-30; Nova Scotia Tech Coll., 1930-31; McGill Univ., B.Eng. (Elect.), 1932, D.M.Sc. 1971; Nat. Defence Coll. 1948; m. Gwynn Abigail, d. late Robert S. Currie, 14 Sept. 1935; one s., Robert Geoffrey; Lieut., R.C.E., 1930; served in 2nd World War, proceeding Overseas in May 1940 and returning in Aug. 1945; served in Spitzbergen, Sicily, Italy, N.W. Europe; Commanded a Field Co.; C.R.E., 1 & 4 Divs.; Chief Engr., 2 Corps; Chief Engr., Candn. Army; awarded C.B.E., D.S.O.; Mentioned in Despatches (twice); Commdr., Order of Orange Nassau (Netherlands); Legion of Merit (U.S.); organ. N.W. Highway System to take over Alaska Rd. from U.S. Army and operated it two yrs.; O.C., Eastern Ont. Area at Kingston, Ont., for three yrs.; Commanded 27th Bgde. on its formation and trained and Commanded it in Germany for one yr.; Dir.-Gen. of Mil. Training 1953-55; Quartermaster General 1955-59; G.O.C. Western Command. 1959-61; Chief of the Gen. Staff, Oct. 1961-Aug. 1964 when apptd. Vice Chief Candn. Defence Staff on integration of 3 services; Col. Commandant, R.C.A. Cadets 1970-74; Anglican; recreations: fishing, golf; Address: 201 Northcote Place, Ottawa, Ont. K1M 0Y7

WALSH, Harry, Q.C., B.A., LL.B.; b. Old Kildonan, Man., 14 Aug. 1913; s. Philip and Fanny (Mastensky) W.; e. King Edward Sch., Isaac Newton Sch. and St. John's Tech. Sch., Winnipeg; Univ. of Man., B.A. 1932, LL.B. 1937; m. Irene, d. Vasily Oleinikov, Belgrade, Yugoslavia, 14 Aug. 1964; children: Paul Victor, Arlene; PARTNER, WALSH, MICAY AND CO. (estbd. 1937); read law with The Hon. Edward James McMurray, P.C., Q.C.; called to Bars of Man. 1937, Ont. 1949, Sask. 1955, B.C. 1963, Alta. 1970, N.W.T. 1972; cr. Q.C. 1953; served with RCA as Lance Bombardier during World War II; Life Bencher, and of Standards Comte. Law Soc. of Man. (Vice-Chrmn., Legal Aid Comte.); Nat. Chrmn., Wills and Bequests, United Israel Appeal of Can. Inc.; Chrmn., Jud. Comm. of Benchers, Law Soc. of Man.; Gov., Ben-Gurion Univ., Negev, Israel; Bd. mem., and Senior Vice-Pres., Candn. Assocs., Ben-Gurion Univ.; Past Pres., Winnipeg N. Lib. Assn.; Hon. Pres., YMHA Community

Centre, Winnipeg; Head of Bar Admission Course in Criminal Law, Law Soc. of Man. and Lectr. in Continuing Legal Educ.; Dir., Legal Aid Services Soc. Man.; former Nat. Chrmn., Criminal Justice Sec., Candn. Bar Assn.; Nat. Chrmn. of Comte. on Evidence and Nat. Chrmn. of Legal Aid Liason Comte., Candn. Bar Assn.; Liberal Hebrew; recreations: reading, cycling, golf; Club: Glendale Golf & Country; Home: 425 Scotia St., Winnipeg, Man. R2V 1W3; Office: 211 Portage, Winnipeg, Man. R3B 2A2

WALTERS, Jack Henry, M.D., F.R.C.S.(C), F.A.C.O.G., D.A.B.O.G., F.R.C.O.G.; obstetrician-gynaecologist; educator; b. Toronto, Ont. 2 Apl. 1925; s. Henry Melville and Josephine Isabella (O'Donnell) W.; e. St. George's Pub. Sch. and London (Ont.) Central Coll. Inst. 1943; Univ. of W. Ont. B.A. 1946, M.D. 1951 (Teaching Fellow in Physiol. 1946-47, Nat. Research Council Fellow 1952-53), Post-grad. Program Obstetrics-Gynaecol. 1951-58; m. Mary Joan d. late Dr. Frank Robert Clegg, London, Ont. 7 Sept. 1949; children: Joan Anne, John Frank, Janet Patricia; PROF. AND CHRMN. OF OBSTETRICS/GYNAECOL. UNIV. OF OTTAWA since 1978; Chief of Obstetrics/Gynaecol. Ottawa Gen. Hosp. since 1978; Prof. of Obstetrics & Gynaecol. Univ. of W. Ont. 1960-73, mem. Senate 1967-68; Prof. and Chrmn. of Obstetrics & Gynecol. Med. Coll. of Ohio 1973-78; Chief of Obstetrics & Gynaecol. St. Joseph's Hosp. 1960-73, Dir. of Cytol. 1958-73; John S. McEachern Mem. Traveling Fellow 1956-58 (Stockholm, Amsterdam, Austria, Eng., Buffalo); mem. Bd. Dirs. London Symphony Orchestra 1970-73; London Art Gallery 1970-73; Film Task Force Ont. Dept. Indust. & Tourism 1972; Chrmn. Ont. Film Festival Comte. 1972; London Music Scholarship Foundation 1971-72; Perinatal Consultant Ohio Dept. Health 1974-78; Consultant Perinatal Units Alta. Hosp. Comn. 1973; Dir. Univ. of W. Ont. Foundation Inc. N.Y.; served with RCAF (Reserve), rank Sqdn. Leader; Co-Chrmn., Comm. on Reproductive Care, Ont. Min. of Health 1979-80; author "Perinatal Problems" 1971; various publs. and papers; Fellow, Am. Coll. Obstetricians & Gynecols.; Internat. Coll. Pediatrics; Mich. Soc. Obstetricians & Gynecols.; diplomate Am. Bd. Obstetricians & Gynecols.; Central Assn. Obstetricians & Gynecols.; Am. Assn. Gynecol. Laparoscopist; N. Am. Gynecol. Soc. (past Pres.); Ont. Med. Assn. (Pres. 1970); Candn. Med. Assn. (Extve. Comte. 1967-70); Chmn., Task Force on Imaging, 1980; Specialized Services, High Technology Comte. 1981; Ont. Council Health; Candn. Cancer Soc. (Dir. Ont. Div. 1970-73); Soc. Obstetricians Gynecols. of Can.; N.Y. Acad. Sciences; Am. Cancer Soc. (Ohio Div. Bd. 1976-78); Laser Soc., and other med. assns.; Alpha Omega Alpha (Pres. Toledo Chapter 1977); Alpha Kappa Kappa; Bayfield Internat. Croquet Assn.; P. Conservative; Anglican; recreations: music, fishing, croquet; Club: London Hunt & Country; Home: 79 Powell St., Ottawa, Ont.; Office: Ottawa Gen. Hosp., 501 Smyth Rd., Ottawa, Ont. K1G 8L6.

WALTERS, James Allan, B.A., M.D., F.R.C.P.(C), F.A.C.P.; neuropsychiatrist; b. Napanee, Ont. 21 July 1906; s. Charles Augustus and Stella Grace (Wagar) W.; e. Napanee Coll. Inst. 1925; Queen's Univ. 1925-26; Univ. of Toronto B.A. 1930, M.D. 1933; Dipl. Psychol. Med., Eng. 1939; post-grad. training in Med., Neurol. and Psychiatry Toronto and London, Eng. 1933-43; m. 1stly Kathleen Jane (d. 1978) d. late Harry Wark 20 June 1936; m. 2ndly Anne Hewitt Thompson, nee Amys, Feb. 8, 1980; presently Special Lectr. Univ. of Toronto and Consultant in Med. & Psychiatry, Wellesley Hosp.; hon. consultant in psychiatry, Toronto Gen. Hosp.; private consulting practice Toronto 1945-77; teaching and research Univ. of Toronto Dept. of Med. 1945-79 and Dept. of Psychiatry 1955-79, Assoc. Prof.; Toronto Gen. Hosp. and Wellesley Hosp. 1945-79, Sr. Phys. and Sr. Psychiatrist; served with Candn. Army overseas 1943-45, maj. specialist in neuropsychiatry, Neurol. & Plastic Surg. Hosp. U.K. N.W. Europe; rec'd Queen's Silver Jubilee Medal 1977; named

Hon. Fellow, Trinity Coll. Toronto 1978; Glenn Sawyer Award, Ont. Med. Assn. 1979; Fox Medal, Napanee Coll. Inst., 1925; Grant Scholar, Queen's Univ., 1925; Moss Scholar, U of Tor., 1930; research incl. Thiopentone Pain Test; author various med. and hist. publs.; mem. Acad. Med.; Ont. and Candn. Med. Assns.; Candn. Neurol. Soc. (Pres.); Am. Neurol. Assn.; Assn. Research Nervous & Mental Disease; Royal Candn. Inst.; Pres.: Univ. of Toronto Hist. Soc.; Toronto Med. Hist. Soc.; Phi Rho Sigma; Sydenham Club; P. Conservative; Anglican; recreations: gardening, Ontario history; Address: 104 Cluny Dr., Toronto, Ont. M4W 2R4.

WALTERS, Peter Ingram, B. Com.; petroleum executive; b. Birmingham, Eng. 11 March 1931; s. late Stephen and Edna Florence (Redgate) W.; e. King Edwards Sch. Birmingham, Eng.; Birmingham Univ. B.Com. 1952; m. Patricia Anne d. late Frederick Tulloch 20 Feb. 1960; two s., one d.;CHRMN., BRITISH PETROLEUM CO. LTD.1981- ; Dir Standard Oil Co.; BP North America Trading Ltd.; BP Chemicals (Americas) Ltd.; Erdölchemie GmbH.; Soc. Industrielle Belge de Petroles; joined British Petroleum 1954; Vice Pres. BP North America 1965-67, Gen. Mgr. Supply Dept. 1969, Regional Dir. W. Hemisphere, Australasia and Far E. 1971, Mang. Dir. 1973; Depy. Chmn., 1980-81; nat. service RASC, rank Lt.; Past Pres., Gen. Council Brit. Shipping; Soc. Chem. Industry; Pres. Inst. Manpower Studies; recreation: golf; Office: Britannic House, Moor Lane, London EC2Y9BU, Eng.

WAMBOLT, Marjorie Grace, Q.C.; b. Halifax, N.S., d. James Peter and Mary Ann (Allen) Wambolt; e. Halifax Pub. Schs.; Halifax Acad.; Dalhousie Univ., B.A. 1923, LL.B. 1925; read law with Mr. Justice Jenks; called to the Bar of N.S. 1925; cr. K.C. 1950; began prof. practice with law firm of Yeoman & Matheson, Halifax, N.S.; later entered partnership with R. F. Yeoman, K.C., as Yeoman & Wambolt, subsequently Yeoman, Wambolt & Graham; in 1940, took over the practice under own name; mem. Bd. of Govs., Dalhousie Univ., 1939-42; Past Pres., Dalhousie Univ. Alumnae Assn.; Past Pres., Halifax Business & Professional Women; mem. of Adv. Bd., Halifax Prot. Infants Foundation; Vice-Chrmn., Alcoholism Research Foundation of N.S. 1962-70; mem., N.S. Barristers Soc. (mem. of Council for two terms, Hon. Pres. 1979-80); Halifax Local Council of Women; Heritage Trust of N.S.; Vice Chancellor Anglican Diocese of Nova Scotia 1968-70; Progressive Conservative; Anglican; recreations: swimming; photography, foreign travel; Club: The Saraguay; Home: Ste. 810, 5959 Springarden Rd., Halifax, N.S.

WANSBROUGH, John Christopher Counsel, B.A., C.F.A.; F.T.C.I.; trust company executive; b. Montreal, Que. 30 Apl. 1932; s. Victor Counsel and Ruth (Fleming) W.; e. St. Andrew's Coll., Aurora, Ont.; Univ. of Toronto B.A. 1955; m. Jean Elizabeth, d. late Harold R. Lawrence, Brampton, Ont. 14 Sept. 1957; three d., Susan, Jane, Ruth; PRES. AND DIR., NATIONAL TRUST CO. LTD.since 1977; Chrmn. Munich Reins Co. of Can.; Munich Holdings Ltd.; The Great Lakes Reins Co.; Dir. Canborough Corp.; Munich-London Mgmt. Corp. Ltd. Invest. Underwriting, Wood Gundy, Toronto 1956-63; joined present co. as Invest. Offr. 1963, Mgr.-Vancouver 1966, Asst. Vice Pres.-Finance Toronto 1970, Vice Pres.-Finance 1972; Extve. Vice-Pres. 1974; Dir., The Arthritis Soc.; Fellow Trust Companies Inst.; mem., Inst. of Chartered Financial Analysts; Kappa Alpha; recreations: tennis, golf; Clubs: Toronto; National; Toronto Golf; Badminton & Racquet; Home: 335 Lytton Blvd., Toronto, Ont. M5N 1R9; Office: 21 King St. E., Toronto, Ont. M5C 1B3

WARD, Arthur G., M.A., F.R.S.C.; physicist; b. Moose Jaw, Sask., 17 Sept. 1914; s. Arthur Maurice and Helena (Gowsell) W.; e. Queen's Univ., B.A. 1935, M.A. 1936; Cambridge Univ., 1937-40; m. Beryl Doreen Norcott, 3 Apl. 1944; three s. Robert, Bill, David; Consultant; Researcher (centimetre radar), Brit. Min. of Aircraft Production, 1940-44; with U.K. Atomic Energy Authority, 1944-51; Physicist, Atomic Energy of Can. Ltd. 1951-74; mem., Candn. Assn. Physicists; Am. Nuclear Soc.; author of many articles on nuclear energy in books and scientific journs; Protestant; recreations: golf; Home: 62 Hillcrest Ave., Deep River, Ont. K0J 1P0

WARD, David Anthony, Q.C., B.Com; b. Calgary, Alta. 24 March 1931; s. late Richard James and Gwendolyn E. W.; e. Queen's Univ. B.Com.; Osgoode Hall Law Sch.; m. Nancy Ruth d. Secord Robinson 12 July 1958; two d. Martha Jane, Mary Ruth; PARTNER, DAVIES, WARD & BECK; Dir., Abitibi-Price Inc.; Brinco Ltd.; called to Bar of Ont. 1958; author "Current Estate Planning" 1969, 2nd ed. 1972; "Current Tax Planning" 1971; former Ed. "Tax and Estate Planning"; mem. Candn. Bar Assn.; Internat. Bar Assn.; Candn. Tax Foundation; Internat. Fiscal Assn.; Delta Chi; Anglican; recreations: skiing, sailing; Clubs: Ontario; Granite; R.C.Y.C.; Georgian Peaks Ski; Home: 28 Daleberry Place, Don Mills, Ont. M3B 2A7; Office: 47th Floor, Commerce Court West, Toronto, Ont.

WARD, James Thomas Laurance, B.Arch.; architect; b. Winnipeg, Manitoba, 20 March 1925; s. James and Mabel (Morgan) W.; e. Pub. and High Schs., W. Kildonan, Man.; St. Johns Coll., Winnipeg; Univ. of Manitoba, B. Arch. 1947; m. Elizabeth Blanche, d. Thomas Hiddleston, 25 June 1954; children: Thomas Michael, James Stephen, Susanne Elizabeth, Laurene Mary; Dir., Whitehall Buildings Ltd.; Functional Buildings Ltd.; began prof. career with Prairie Rural Housing, 1948; with Moody & Moore, Arch., Winnipeg, Man., 1948-49 and later 1949 joined with Edgar Prain forming Prain & Ward, 1951-58; Sr. partner, Ward & Macdonald Architects, 1959-68; Sr. partner, Ward, Macdonald, Cockburn, McLeod & McFeetors, 1969-73; private practice 1974-79; joined Dept. of Education, Prov. of Man., 1980; mem., Royal Arch. Inst. Can.; Man. Assn. of Arch.; Anglican; Home: 2679 Scotia St., Box 13, Group 33, RR-1A Winnipeg, Man. R3C 4A2

WARD, Norman, O.C. (1974), M.A., Ph.D., LL.D., F.R.S.C. (1963); professor; author; radio and television commentator; b. Hamilton, Ont., 10 May 1918; s. Arthur Bramwell and Rachel Brown (McQueen) W.; e. Hamilton Central Coll. Inst.; McMaster Univ. B.A. 1941, LL.D. 1974; Univ. of Toronto, M.A. 1943, Ph.D. 1949; Queen's Univ. LL.D., 1977; m. Betty Edith, d. E. G. Davis, Stratford, Ont., 11 Sept.1943; children: Nora, Nancy, Norman, Donald, Colin, Michael; BRITNELL PROF. OF POL. SCIENCE UNIV. OF SASK.; Vice Chrmn., Sask. Archives Bd.; mem., Comte. on Election Expenses 1965-66; Econ. Asst., Royal Comn. on Prov. Devel. N.S., 1943-44; joined Faculty of Univ. of Sask., 1945 and successively Instr., Asst. Prof., Assoc . Prof. and Prof.; Publications: "The Canadian House of Commons: Representation", 1950; "Government in Canada", 1960; "Mice in the Beer", 1961 (Leacock Medal for Humor, 1960); "The Public Purse", 1962; "The Fully Processed Cheese", 1964; edited 4th ed., R. M. Dawson's "The Government of Canada", 1963, 5th ed., 1970; ed. "A Party Politician: The Memoirs of Chubby Power", 1966; "Politics in Saskatchewan" (with Duff Spafford) 1968; (with D. Hoffman) "Bilingualism and Biculturalism in the Canadian House of Commons" 1970; ed. 4th ed., R. M. Dawson's "Democratic Government in Canada" 1971; Ed. "The Politician" (James Gardiner) 1975; "Her Majesty's Mice", 1977; rec'd. President's Medal, Univ. of W. Ontario for best scholarly article, 1952; Skelton Clark Fellow, Queen's Univ., 1958-59; Killam Award 1974-75; contrib. to Candn. scholarly and popular journs.; mem., Candn. Pol. Science Assn.; mem. and Depy. Chrmn. Electoral Boundaries Comn. for Sask.; mem., The Canada Council 1974-80; Trustee, Forum for Young Canadians; Protestant; recreations: swimming, canoeing; Home: 412 Albert Ave., Saskatoon, Sask. S7N 1G3

WARD, Walter George, B.E.; retired executive b. Peterborough, Ont., 8 Dec. 1914; s. Eldin and Ethel Grace (Forsyth) W.; e. Peterborough, (Ont.) Tech. Sch.; Jarvis Coll. Inst., Toronto, Ont.; McGill Univ.; B.Eng. 1942; m. Myrtle Grace, d. Frederick John Strange, 17 May 1947; children: John, Nancy, Susan, Janet; Chairman, The Algoma Steel Corp. Ltd. 1977-81; Dir., Candn. Gen. Elec. Co. Ltd.; Candn. Appliance Manufacturing Co. Ltd.; Jannock Ltd.; Canadian Imperial Bank of Commerce; Candn. Oxygen Ltd.; Can. Packers Ltd.; Dir., Kawartha Broadcasting Ltd., Algoma Steel Corp.; joined Candn. General Electric Co. 1931; after war held mang. positions in electronic equipment operations; Gen. Mgr., Maj. Appliance Dept., 1952, Appliance Div. 1954, Wholesale Dept., 1957, Apparatus Dept. 1957-64, Vice Pres. 1959; trans. to General Electric and apptd. Gen. Mgr. Area Div., Europe, 1964, Vice Pres., General Eelctric Co., 1965; returned to Can. as Extve. Vice Pres. C.G.E. 1968, Dir. 1968, Pres. 1970; Chrmn. of Bd. and C.E.O., 1972-77; served with RCN during World War II; rank Lt.-Commdr.; Mentioned in Despatches for services during invasion of Normandy; mem. Bd. Govs., Trent Univ., mem. Assn. Prof. Engrs. Ont.; mem. Bd., Council for Business and Arts; Sr. mem., Business Council in Can.; mem., Conference Bd. of New York; recreations: swimming, reading, music; Clubs: York; Toronto; Kawartha Golf & Country; Peterborough; St. Andrews, Florida; Residence: R.R.#2, Cavan, Ont.

WARDER, Anthony K., Ph.D.; university professor; b. London, Eng., 8 Sept. 1924; s. Donald and Margery Dalmer (Payne) W.; e. Univ. of London; B.A. Hons. (Indo-Aryan) 1949, Ph.D. 1954; m. Nargez Rustomji, d. Rustom Vachha, Bombay, 4 Sept. 1954; CHAIRMAN, SANSKRIT AND INDIAN STUDIES, UNIV. OF TORONTO, since 1971, and Prof. of Sanskrit there since 1963; served with Royal Navy 1942-46; Research Fellowship (Ford Foundation Grant) London, working with Pali Text Soc. 1954-55; Lect. and Head of Dept. of Sanskrit, Univ. of Edinburgh, 1955-63 (el. to Senate 1962-63); Chrmn., East Asian Studies, Univ. of Toronto 1966-71; awarded Can. Council Grant to lead research project in Pali, 1966-72; mem. Council of Pali Text Soc.; mem. Senate Univ. of Toronto; mem., Assn. of Univ. Teachers; Dir. Shastri Indo-Candn. Inst.; published eleven books, in fields of Pali, Buddhism, Indian philos. and lit.; articles and reviews in fields of Indian philos., lit. hist., and philol.; recreation: music; Home: 131 Bloor St. West, Toronto, Ont. M5S 1R1

WARDLE, Frederick David; book publisher; b. Belleville, Ont. 18 March 1939; s. Reginald Albert and Catherine (McCallum) W.; e. Cornwall (Ont.) Coll. & Vocational Sch. 1958; Sir George Williams Univ. 1962; m. Maxine d. Max Valiquette (div.); 2ndly Susan Traer, 30 Dec. 1981; children: Jennifer Lesley, Jonathan Frederick; VICE PRES. AND GEN. MGR. METHUEN PUBLICATIONS since 1967; Dir. Carswell Co. Ltd.; joined McGraw-Hill Co. of Canada 1962-66, McGraw-Hill Book Co. (UK) 1966-67; Pres., Candn. Book Publishers Council 1978; Home: 382 Balliol Street, Toronto, Ont. Office: 2330 Midland Ave., Agincourt, Ont. M1S 1P7.

WARING, George Ernest, B.Sc.; company president; b. Saint John, N.B., 29 Apl. 1927; s. George Ramus and Sarah (Martin) W.; e. Univ. of N.B., B.Sc.; m. Ellen Annette Driscoll, 9 Oct. 1948; children: Patricia, Peter, Michael; PRES., OCEAN MAID FOODS LTD., Pres., Star-Kist Canada Inc.; Past Commissioner to Internat. Comn. for Conserv. of Atlantic Tunas and Inter-Am. Tropical Tuna Comn.; mem., Am. Chem. Soc.; Chem. Inst. Can.; Sugar Indust. Technols.; Freemason; Anglo-Catholic; recreations: sailing, reading; Home: 111 Charnwood Rd., Beaconsfield, Que. H9W 4Z4; Office: P.O. Box 2800, 3767 Thimens, St. Laurent, Que. H4R 1W4

WARNER, A. Grant; executive; b. Ottawa, Ont., 30 March 1927; s. Harold Cecil and Gladys Adelaide (Huber)

W.; e. Gen. Motors Inst. Indust. Engn. 1953; m. late Elizabeth Joyce d. John Hatton Berry, C.M.G., O.B.E., London, Ont., 27 Dec. 1952; VICE PRES. AND GEN. MANUFACTURING MGR. GENERAL MOTORS OF CANADA LTD.; mem. Soc. Automotive Engrs.; Anglican; Home: Toronto, Ont.; Office: 215 William St.E., Oshawa, Ont. L1G 1K7

WARNHOFF, Edgar W., Ph.D.; university professor; b. Knoxville, Tenn., 5 May 1929; s. Edgar William and Mabel Catherine (Huth) W.; e. Washington Univ., A.B. 1949; Univ. of Wisc., Ph.D. 1953; m. Patricia Catherine, d. late Samuel Reynolds, 1956; three s. Mark, Andrew, Rolf; PROF. OF CHEM., UNIV. OF WESTERN ONT., since 1966; Postdoctoral Fellow, Birkbeck Coll., London, 1953-54; Asst. Scientist, U.S. Pub. Health Service, 1954-56; Post-doctoral Fellow Faculté de Pharmacie, Paris, 1957-58; Research Assoc., Mass. Inst. of Technol., 1958-59; Asst. Prof., Univ. S. Cal., 1959-62; joined present Univ. as Asst. Prof. 1962; Assoc. Prof. 1963; rec'd Merck Sharp and Dohme Lecture Award of Chem Inst. Can., 1969: co-author, "Molecular Rearrangements", 1964; co-author, "Rearrangements in Ground and Excited States", vol. 1, 1980; other writings incl. over 80 papers in chem. journs.; ed. of the Canadian Journal of Chemistry 1982- ; mem., Chem. Inst. Can.; Chem. Soc. London; Am. Chem. Soc.; Address: London, Ont. N6A 5B7

WARNOCK, Frank McLeod; company executive; b. Scotland 8 March 1925; s. John McLeod and Joan (Connel) W.; e. Eastwood Sch., Glasgow, Scot.; Univ. Coll. Southampton; m. Eleanor L., d. Roy Jackson, 8 Apl. 1950; children: John Robert McLeod, Eleanor Anne McLeod, James Hamish McLeod, Alastair Alexander McLeod; PRESIDENT AND CHIEF EXTVE. OFFR., M. LOEB LTD. since 1976; Pres., M. Loeb Corp. (U.S.A.); Vice-Chmn., IGA Can. Ltd., Dir., Provigo Inc., Mtl.; Nat. Drug and Chem. Co. of Can., Mtl.; Market Wholesale Groc. Co. of Cal.; Sales Mang. and Dir. Marketing, Scott Paper Co. Ltd. 1955-69; joined Dominion Dairies (Sealtest) Ltd. as Vice Pres. Sales and Marketing 1969-72; Pres. and Chief Extve. Offr. 1972-75; served with RAF during World War II; mem., Adv. Council to the School of Business, U. of B.C.; External Adv. Cmte, Trent Univ.; Dep. Chmn., United Way Campaign, Ottawa 1981; Gov., St. Vincent Hosp., Ottawa; Gov. Trent Univ. mem., Ottawa Bd. of Trade; Cdn. Groc. Distributors' Inst.; Presbyterian; recreation: Gulf; Clubs: Royal Ottawa Golf; Laurentian; Rideau; Home: 3681 Revelstoke Dr., Ottawa, Ont. K1V 7C2; Office: 400 Industrial Ave., Ottawa, Ont. K1G 3K8

WARNTZ, William, B.S., A.M., Ph.D., F.R.S.C.; educator; b. Berwick, Pa. 10 Oct. 1922; s. Sterling Adrian and Lillian Mary (Grey) W.; e. Berwick Sch. 1940; Univ. of Pa. B.S. 1949, A.M. 1951, Ph.D. 1955 (Annual Fellowships 1949-55); McGill Univ. (Carnegie Foundation Fellow) 1950; m. A. Minerva d. Richard Mosdell, St. John's, Nfld. 19 June 1947; children: Christopher William, Pamela Mary Elizabeth; PROF. OF GEOG. UNIV. OF W. ONT. since 1971; Instr. to Asst. Prof. Econ. and Geog. Univ. of Pa. 1949-56; Research Assoc. Prof. of Astro-phys. Sciences, Princeton Univ. 1956-66. mem. Adv. Council on Graphics and Engn. Drawing 1965-68; Prof. of Theoretical Geog. and Dir. Lab. for Computer Graphics, Harvard Univ. 1966-71, Ed. Harvard Papers in Theoretical Geog. 1966-77; Visiting Prof. Cambridge Univ. 1976-77; Fellow, 1976-77 and Life Assoc., Clare Hall, Cambridge since 1977; mem. Adv. Council Bureau of Census Washington, D.C. 1956-66; Nat. Science Foundation Consultant 1956-71; Educ. Services Consultant, Cambridge, Mass. 1960-66; Learning Center, Princeton, N.J. 1960-66; Comte. on Earth Sciences, Nat. Acad. of Sciences 1966; Consultant, Brookings Inst., Fed. Science Execs. Policy Program 1960-76; Chrmn. Bd. Dirs. Regional Science Research Inst., Cambridge, Mass. since 1964; served with US Air Force 1943-48, Navig. US Eighth Air Force Combat Operations 1944-45, Mil. Air Transport 1945-47, Air Sea Rescue 1947-

48; rec'd Air Medal with 2 Oak Leaf Clusters, Purple Heart, Distinguished Unit Citation; author "Toward A Geography of Price" 1959; "Geography, Geometry and Graphics" 1963; "Geographers and What They Do" 1964; "Geography Now And Then" 1964; "Macrogeography And Income Fronts" 1965; "Breakthroughs In Geography" 1971; contributed to 16 other books and over 90 journ. articles; Fellow, Am. Assn. Advanc. Science; mem. Candn. Assn. Univ. Teachers; Regional Science Assn. (Pres. 1964-65); Internat. Geog. Union; Council on Social Graphics (Charter mem.); Cambridge Soc.; Fellow, Explorers Club (NYC); Alpha Sigma Phi; Anglican; recreations: music, skiing, squash, walking; Club: University (London, Ont.); Royal Overseas League (London, Eng.); Home: 1433 Wonderland Rd. North, London, Ont. N6G 2C2; Office: 2411 S.S.C., Univ. of Western Ont., London, Ont. N6A 5C2.

WARRACK, Hon. Allan Alexander, B.Sc., M.S., Ph.D.; professor; b. Calgary, Alta. 24 May 1937; s. Alexander Low and Alice Katherine (Christensen) W.; e. Strathmore High Sch. 1955; Olds Sch. of Agric. 1956; Univ. of Alta. B.Sc. (Agric.) 1961; Iowa State Univ. M.S. (Agric. Econ.) 1963, Ph.D. (Econ.) 1967; m. Linda Jean d. Gordon Herbert Rennie, Edmonton, Alta. 18 Aug. 1962; children: Lauren Jean, James Allan, Daniel Gordon Alexander; ASSOCIATE DEAN AND DIRECTOR, MASTER OF PUBLIC MANAGEMENT PROGRAM FACULTY OF BUSINESS ADMINISTRATION AND COMMERCE, UNIV. OF ALTA. 1981- ; operates A & A Farms, Langdon, Alta.; Sales Rep. Upjohn Co. Madison, Wis. 1963-64; Asst. Prof. Univ. Alta. 1967, Assoc. Prof. 1969-71; el. M.L.A. for Three Hills 1971, re-el. 1975, declined re-el. 1979; Min. of Lands and Forests 1971-75; Min. of Utilities and Telephones 1975-79; Prof. of Rural Econ., Univ. of Alta., 1979-81; rec'd Queen's Silver Jubilee Medal 1977; author numerous agric. econ. articles in various tech. and other publs.; mem. Inst. of Public Admin. of Canada; Alta. Inst. Agrology; Candn. Agric. Econ. Soc.; Am. Agric. Econ. Assn.; Internat. Assn. Agric. Econ.; Agric. Inst. Can.; W. Agric. Econ. Assn.; Am. Econ. Assn.; Phi Kappa Phi; Delta Upsilon (Pres., Field Secy.); Gamma Sigma Delta; P. Conservative; United Church; recreations: racquetball, golf, tennis, skiing; Club: Derrick Golf & Winter; Home: 91 Fairway Dr., Edmonton, Alta. T6J 2C2; Office: Faculty of Business Administration and Commerce, Univ. of Alta., Edmonton, Alta. T6G 2G1.

WARREN, Jack H.; banker; b. Howard Township, Ont. 10 Apr. 1921; e. Queen's Univ. BA 1941, LL.D. (Hon.) 1974; m. Hilary J. Titterington, 7 May 1953; children: Hilary Nicolson, Martin, Jennifer, Ian; VICE-CHRMN. AND DIR., BANK OF MONTREAL 1979- ; Chairman and Dir. Bank of Montreal International Ltd.; Dir. Bank of Montreal (Bahamas & Caribbean) Ltd.; Roins Holding Ltd.; Royal Insurance Co. of Canada; The Western Assurance Co.; Trustee, BMRI Realty Investments; served with Royal Canadian Navy 1941-45; public service with Departments of External Affairs, Finance, Trade & Comm., Industry, Trade & Comm.; diplomatic postings Ottawa, London, Washington, Paris, Geneva; Asst. Depy. Min. Dept. of Trade & Comm. 1958; Chrmn. Council of Reps. Gen. Agreement on Tariffs & Trade 1960; Chrmn. Contracting Parties GATT 1962-1964; Depy. Min. Dept. of Trade & Commerce 1964; Depy. Min. Dept. of Industry Trade & Comm. 1969; Candn. High Commr. to U.K. 1971-74; Canadian Ambassador to U.S.A. 1975-77; Ambassador & Co-ordinator for the Multilateral Trade Negotiations 1977-79; rec'd. Outstanding Achievement Award Pub. Service Can. 1975; Home: 1460 rue Docteur Penfield, Montreal, Quebec H3G 1B3 Office: 129 St. James St. W., Montreal, Quebec H2Y 1L6

WARREN, Harry Verney, O.C. (1971), **D.Sc., D.Phil., F.R.S.C., F.G.S.A.**; consulting geological engineer; b. Anacortes, Wash., 27 Aug. 1904; s. Victor Mackenzie and Rosamond Burrell (Campion) W.; e. Univ. of Brit. Columbia, B.A. 1926 (Rhodes Schol. for B.C. 1926-29), B.A.Sc. 1927; Oxford Univ., M.Sc. 1928, D.Phil. 1929 (Commonwealth Fund Fellow 1929-32); Cal. Inst. of Tech. (Research), 1929-32; D.Sc. Univ. Waterloo 1975; Univ. of B.C. 1978; m. Margaret Bessie, d. Charles Edward Tisdall, 14 July 1934; children: Charlotte Louisa Verney, Victor Henry Verney; Pres. B.C. & Yukon Chamber of Mines, 1952-54; mem. Senate, Univ. B.C. 1939-60, 1963-72; Tech. Adviser, Vancouver Stock Exchange, 1938-40; Lectr., Dept. of Geol. & Geog., Univ. of B.C., 1932-35; Asst. Prof., 1935-39; Assoc. Prof. 1939-45, Prof. 1945-73; Hon. Prof. 1973-81; Pres., Third Resources Conf. (B.C.) 1949-50; Pres.; Un. Nations Assn. of Can. (Vancouver Br.) 1955, 1956, 1957; Fellow, Geol. Soc. of Am.; Geol. Soc. of Finland; Fellow Inst. of Mining & Metall. (Gt. Britain); Am. Inst. Mining & Metall. Engrs.; Assn. of Prof. Engrs. B.C.; Soc. of Econ. Geols.; Mineral. Soc. (Gt. Brit.) Walker Mineral Soc.; Pres., Candn. Field Hockey Assn. 1960-64; has written over 180 articles contrib. to scient. journs.; Hon. Fellow, Royal Coll. Gen. Practice (Gt. Brit.) 1973; Founding mem., Assn. Exploration Geochems.; Soc. Environmental Geochem. & Health; mem. Council, Vancouver Bd. Trade variously 1939-81; Sigma Xi; Anglican; recreations: cricket, field hockey; Club: Faculty; Home: 1816 Western Parkway, Vancouver, B.C. V6T 1V4

WARREN, Herbert Hamilton, B.Com., C.A., L.I.A.; textile executive; b. Cobourg, Ont., 25 April 1908; s. late Alice Francis (Rattray) and late Herbert Lawrence Warren; e. Strathcona Acad., Outremount, Que.; McGill Univ., B.Com., 1930, Que. Inst. C.A.'s, C.A. 1931; m. Madeline Y., d. late Wesley Moses, 6 June 1935; children: Diane, Peter; VICE-PRES. AND DIRECTOR, BELDING-CORTICELLI LTD., since 1978; Pres., Century Mutual Building Soc.; Secy.-Treas., Warrendale Shirt Co. Ltd., 1930-50, Vice Pres., 1950-61; joined present Co. as Vice Pres., 1960-61; Pres., 1961; Chrmn. 1977-78; Dir., Candn. Textile Inst.; Freemason; United Church; recreations: fishing, hunting; Club: Montreal Badminton & Squash; Home: Cedar Ridge Farm, R.R. 1, Kanata, Ont. K2H 7E6; Office: 1790 du Canal St., Montreal, Que. K2K 1X7

WARREN, Pierre, P.Eng.; executive; b. La Malbaie, Que., 1 Aug. 1909; s. Philippe and Julia (Danais) W.; e. Acad. de Que.; Univ. of Montrea, L'Ecole Polytechnique, (civil engn.) 1932; m. Marguerite, d. René Dastous, Feb. 1958; one s. Jean Pierre; President Airco Products Ltd.; Industries Warren Inc.; Enamel & Heating Products Ltd.; Founder and former Pres., Structal Quebec; Engr., Pub. Works of Can., Rimouski, 1934-35; Constr. Engr., Quebec City, 1936-39, 1944-62; City Engr. for town of Rouyn, 1939-40; Candn. Arsenals 1940-44; mem., Corp. Engrs. Que.; R. Catholic; recreations: swiming, golf; Clubs: Garrison; Murray Bay Golf; Home: 80 de Bernieres, Quebec, Que. G1K 7Z9; Office: 150 Blvd. du Grand Tronc, Quebec, Que. G1K 7Z9

WARREN, Robert Michael, B.Com.; crown corporation executive; b. Montreal, Que. 10 Apl. 1937; s. late John Edward Leslie and Isabelle Sophie Janie (Dodwell) W.; e. Lower Can. Coll., Selwyn House and Montreal W. High Sch.; Sir George Williams Univ. B.Com. 1956; children: Stephen Gregory, Scott Edward Kenneth, Victoria Claire; PRESIDENT, CHIEF EXTVE. OFFR. AND DIR., CANADA POST CORP. 1981- ; Dir., MDS Health Group Ltd., Toronto; Sales Engr. Lincoln Electric, Toronto 1958-60; Sales Mgr. S. Coorsh & Sons, Toronto 1960-62; Indust. Devel. Offr. Trade & Devel. Govt. Ont., Extve. Asst. to Min. of Labour Ont.; Extve. Dir. Manpower Services Ont., Depy. Prov. Secy. and Depy. Min. of Citizenship Ont., Depy. Solr. Gen. Ont., Depy. Min. of Housing Ont. 1962-75; Pres., R. Michael Warren & Associates Ltd., Consultants 1975; Chief Gen. Mgr. Toronto Transit Comn., Dir. Grey Coach Lines 1975-81; Pres. Candn. Urban Transit Assn. 1980-81; recipient Candn. Centennial Medal 1967; Vice Pres. Am. Pub. Transit Assn. 1978-81; recreations: farming, skiing, squash;

Clubs: Cercle Universitaire d'Ottawa; Ottawa Athletic; Office: Sir Alexander Campbell Bldg., Confederation Heights, Ottawa, Ont. K1A 0B1.

WARREN, Russell A.; CHAIRMAN & C.E.O., SIMMONS LTD.; joined Simmons Ltd. in 1953 as Secy. and Asst. Treasurer, after eighteen yrs. of banking experience; el. a Dir. in 1954 and became Extve. Vice Pres. in 1959; el. Pres. in 1962; Chrmn. and Chief Extve. Offr., 1978; Pres. & Dir., Andrew Malcolm Furniture Co. Ltd.; Dir., Simmons Universal Corp. (New York); Simmons U.S.A. Corp. (Atlanta); Belding-Corticelli Ltd.; served in 2nd World War as a Pilot in R.C.A.F.; Home: Apt. 302-39 Old Mill Rd., Toronto, Ont. M8X 1G6; Office: 6900 Airport Rd., Mississauga, Ont. L4V 1E8

WARREN, Trumbull, O.B.E.; manufacturer; b. Montreal, Que., 1 Aug. 1915; s. Trumbull W. and Marjorie Laura (Braithwaite) Snively; e. Crescent Sch., Toronto, Ont. (1922-24) Upper Canada Coll., Toronto, Ont. (1924-27); Lakefield Coll. (1927-30); Ridley Coll., St. Catharines, Ont. (1930-34); m. Mary, d. Gerald W. Wigle, Hamilton, Ont., 9 Sept. 1939; children: Mary Trumbull (Mrs. David Arkell), Margaret Ann (Mrs. John Lang), Joan Trumbull (Mrs. Grant Fisher); CHRMN. OF THE BD., DIR.; RHEEM CANADA INC. (Mfrs.' of Steel Shipping Containers, Domestic, and Commercial water Heaters, Estbd. 1946); Dir. Phoenix Assurance Co. of Canada; Hendrie & Co.; Acadia Life Ins. Co.; Angus Corp.; Hollinger-Argus Corp. Ltd.; Dominion Stores; mem., Hamilton Adv. Bd., The Royal Trust Co.; joined 48th Highlanders of Can., N.P.A.M., 1934 served in 2nd World War with rank of Lieut.-Col. in Eng., W. Desert, Sicily, Italy, France, Belgium, Holland and Germany; O.B.E.; Mentioned in Despatches; American Bronze Star; Conservative; Anglican; recreation: skeet-shooting and golf; Clubs: Tamahaac; The Toronto (Ont.); University (Toronto); Home: Corwhin Acres, R.R. 1, Puslinch, Ont. N0B 2J0; Office: 128 Barton St. W., Hamilton, Ont. L8R 2H2

WASHBURN, Robert Neil, B.A.; telecommunications executive; b. Chippawa, Ont., 6 June 1922; e. Delta Coll. Inst., Hamilton, Ont.,; McMaster Univ., B.A. (Econ.) 1947; VICE PRES., ADMINISTRATION, ONT. REGION, BELL CANADA, since 1980; Dir., Tele-Direct Ltd.; Nat. Telephone Directory Corp.; Bell Canada Intl. Mgmt. Research and Consulting Ltd.; Capital Telephone Co. Ltd.; Ronalds Federated Ltd.; joined present Co., Hamilton, 1947; served in various mang. pos. in Hamilton, Sudbury, Montreal and Toronto, 1948-64; Regional Marketing Mgr., Ont. Region, 1965; Asst. Vice-Pres. (Marketing) Montreal, 1967; Vice-Pres. (Admin.) Ont. Region, 1970; Vice-Pres, South/West Area, 1976; served with RCN 1941-45; rank Lt.; Dir., Donwood Inst.; Mississauga Golf & Country Club; mem., Bd. Trade Metrop. Toronto; Candn. Chamber Comm.; Royal Hamilton Military Inst.; Bd. of Govs., Univ. of Waterloo; Clubs: Mississauga Golf & Country; National; Home: 1105 Fairbirch Dr., Mississauga, Ont. L5H 1M4; Office: 22F, 393 University Ave., Toronto, Ont. M5G 1W9

WASON, John Stuart Munro, F.F.A.; A.S.A.; ins. executive; b. St. Helen's, Eng., 30 Aug. 1922; s. Thomas Stewart and Mary Ross (Munro) W.; came to Canada 1950; e. The Leys Sch., Cambridge, Eng.; m. Winifred Marjorie, d. Frank Horsfall, Pudsey, Yorks., Eng., 5 June 1948; one s. Stuart; GEN. MGR. SHIELD LIFE INSUR. CO., DUBLIN former President, the Empire Life Insurance Company; joined Standard Life Assurance Co., Edinburgh, Scot. as Actuarial Student 1946; Actuarial Asst., later Secy. and Actuary, Maritime Life Assurance Co., Halifax, N.S. 1950-60; joined Dom. of Can. Gen. Ins. Co. as Actuary, Toronto, Ont. 1961; Assistant General Manager and Actuary 1967, General Manager, Life Insurance and Actuary 1969; served in 2nd World War; enlisted as Gunner and later commissioned in R.H.A. 1941; served Overseas with Surrey & Sussex Yeomanry, N. Africa, Italy and N.W. Europe 1943-45; Staff Offr., Rhine Army 1945-46; retired with rank of Captain; member International Actuarial Association; mem. Candn. Planning Comte., Life Office Mang. Assn. 1964-70; P. Conservative; United Church; recreations: golf, bowling, travel; Clubs: Granite; National (Toronto); Cataraqui Golf & Country (Kingston); Woodbrook Golf (Dublin); Home: 39 Point Cres., Kingston, Ont. K7M 3P2 and 9 Cornelscourt Hill, Foxrock, Dublin 18, Ireland

WASSON, Evans Ernest, Q.C., B.A.; b. Nelson, B.C., 13 July 1905; s. William Ernest and Elizabeth (Lennox) W.; e. Univ. of B.C., B.A.; Osgoode Hall Law Sch.; m. Joan Marion, d. late Harold Thomas Curtis, 17 June 1933; two s., Garth Curtis, Brian William; with law firm of Wasson & Wasson; Dir. of no. private cos.; read law with Brown & Dawson; called to Bar of B.C. 1928; cr. Q.C. 1969; served in Adj. Gen.'s Br. and Judge Advocate Gen.'s Br. in Can. and N.W. Europe during World War II; P. Conservative; Anglican; recreation: sailing; Clubs: The Vancouver; Royal Vancouver Yacht; Home: 225 West Cres., Qualicum Beach, B.C. V0R 2T0; Office: 525 Seymour St., Vancouver, B.C. V6B 3H7

WATERHOUSE, Alan, B.A., M.Sc., Dr.Ing.; educator; planning consultant; b. Sheffield, Eng., 13 Apl. 1936; s. Herbert and Jessie (Whelpton) W.; e. Univ. of Manchester, B.A. (Arch.) 1959; Univ. of Toronto, M.Sc. (Urban & Regional Planning); Univ. of Berlin, Dr. Ing. (City Planning) 1968; m. Karin-Maria, d. Friedrich Seidel, Univ. of Cologne, 3 Jan. 1960; PROF. AND CHRMN., DEPT. URBAN & REGIONAL PLANNING, UNIV. OF TORONTO since 1972; Tech. Consultant, U.N., since 1969; Asst. Arch., London (Eng.) Co. Council, 1959; Arch./Planner, Central Mortgage & Housing Corp., 1961-63; Dir., Planning Dept., Canadian Michell Assoc., 1964-66; joined present Univ. as Lectr. 1965-66, Asst. Prof. and Assoc. Prof. 1969-72; Housing Consultant, Govt. ofEthiopia, 1966-67; Dozent, Technische Universitat Berlin, 1966-67; author, "Terms of Reference for a Proposed Low Income Housing Study" 1967; "Urban Development in Medieval Europe", 1971; "Visual Change in Cities" (Die Reaktion der Bewohner auf die aussere Veranderung der Stadte), 1972; co-author, "A National Housing Program for the Empire of Ethiopia", 1966; other writings incl. papers in prof. journs.; tech. and research reports; several planning reports for communities and agencies in Can., U.S.A., Bahamas, Germany and Africa; Office: 230 College St., Toronto, Ont. M5T 1R2

WATERLAND, Hon. Thomas Manville, M.L.A., B.Sc.; politician; b. Anyox, B.C. 15 Dec. 1933; s. Timothy Waterland; e. Brittania Beach (B.C.) High Sch. 1952; S. Dakota Sch. of Mines B.Sc. 1957; m. Donalda Stewart 18 Aug. 1956; three d. Terry, Patricia, Elizabeth;MIN. OF FORESTS,B.C. 1976- ; operated mines Nfld., Ont. and B.C. 1957-66; Resident Engr. Kamloops, B.C. Dept. Mines 1866-75; and Dept. Mines & Petroleum Resources 1972-75; Princ. and Consulting Engr. Mining Contracting Co. 1969-72; el. M.L.A. for Yale-Lillooet 1975; Min. of Forests and Min. of Mines & Petroleum Resources 1975; mem. Candn. Inst. Mines & Metall.; B.C. Assn. Prof. Engrs.; Freemason; Social Credit; United Church; recreations: skiing, golf, flying; Office: 323 Parliament Bldgs., Victoria, B.C. V8V 1X4.

WATERMAN, Rt. Rev. Robert Harold, D.D. (Ang.); b. Franktown, Ont., 11 Mar. 1894; s. Rev. Robert Barton and Annabella (Hughton) W.; e. Bishop's Univ., B.A. 1914, L.S.T. 1920, B.D. 1932, D.D. 1939; King's Coll., N.S., D.D. 1949; m. Frances Isabel, d. Rev. Norman Bayne, Lennoxville, Que., 30 June 1921; children: Gerald, Marjorie, Harold, Robert, Janice; o. Deacon 1920, Priest 1921; Rector, Bear Brook, Ont., 1920-27; Pembroke, Ont., 1927-33; St. John's, Smiths Falls, Ont., 1933-37; Rector, Christ Ch. Cath., Hamilton; Ont., 1937-48; Dean of Niagara (Ont.) Diocese, 1938-48; el. Coadjutor Bishop of N.S.,

5 Nov. 1947 and consecrated 27 Jan. 1948; succeeded as Bishop, 20 Nov. 1950 and enthroned, 25 Jan. 1951; retired June 1963; served in World War, 1915-19; enlisted as Private, 5th C.M.R.; later Lieut. and Acting Staff Capt.; mem., Bd. of Educ., Pembroke, Ont., 1929-33; Conservative; recreations: golf, carpentering; Connaught Home, North Hatley, Que. J0B 2C0

WATERS, Peter David; banker; b. England 11 Aug. 1935; e. England; m. Charlotte 16 May 1959; children: Caroline, Trevor, Gerry and Beverley; SR. VICE PRES. SPECIAL FINANCING, WORLD CORPORATE BANKING, BANK OF MONTREAL; Home: 1400 Goldthorpe Rd., Mississauga, Ont. L5G 3R3; Office: 1 First Canadian Place, Toronto, Ont. M5X 1A1.

WATSON, Alan Graeme, F.C.A. (1959); b. Toronto, Ont., 6 Aug. 1919; s. late James Graeme and Dorothy (Shannon) W.; e. Upper Canada Coll. (1928-37); McGill Univ. (1937-39); m. Joan Beverley, d. late H. G. (Peter) Davidson, 3 June 1949; children: Peter, Sheila; SECY. GEN. PEAT MARWICK INTERNAT., Partner, Peat, Marwick, Mitchell & Co., since 1952; Dir., E. & S. Currie Ltd.; joined present Co. in Toronto, Sept. 1940 as a student (C.A. 1949 with Gold Medal for highest marks in Can.); trans. to New York Office, 1949, to Montreal Office in 1950, returning to Toronto in 1951; served in 2nd World War, active service R.C.N.V.R., May 1941-Oct. 1945, discharged with rank of Lieut.-Commdr.; Mentioned in Despatches; Past Pres., Toronto Br., Candn. Red Cross Soc.; Past Pres., Child. Aid Soc. of Metrop. Toronto; mem., Inst. Chart. Accts. Ont. (Past Pres.); Alpha Delta Phi; Anglican; recreations: golf, sailing; Clubs: The Toronto; Toronto Golf; Badminton & Racquet; York; Home: 182 Dunvegan Road, Toronto, Ont. M5P 2P2; Office: P.O. Box 261, Commerce Court W., Toronto, Ont. M5L 1J5

WATSON, Alexander Gardner, M.D., F.R.C.S.(C), F.A.C.S.; ophthalmologist; educator; b. Scot. 28 March 1918; s. Capt. John Salter and Lilias (Gardner) W.; m. Patricia Jane Brown d. late Senator Prentiss Brown, St. Ignace, Mich. 30 May 1953; children: John Brown, Alexander Gardner; CHRMN. AND PROF. OF OPHTHALMOL. UNIV. OF OTTAWA since 1969; Head of Ophthalmol. Ottawa Gen. Hosp.; Consultant Ophthalmol. Ottawa Civic Hosp.; Children's Hosp. of E. Ont.; Extve. Dir. Sally Letson Foundation for Eye Research; elected Councillor, Rockcliffe Park Village, 1978; Gov., Ashbury Coll.; served with RCAF Med. Services, rank Wing Commdr.; Mgr. Candn. Olympic Hockey Team 1948; el. to Candn. Armed Services Sports Hall of Fame; mem. Candn. Olympic Assn.; author or co-author numerous publs.; mem. Candn. Ophthal. Soc.; Ottawa Acad. Med.; Internat. Soc. Eye Surgs. (Founding mem.); Ont. Med. Assn.; Candn. Med. Assn.; Royal Coll. Speciality Comte. on Ophthalmol.; Royal Coll. Phys. & Surgs. and mem. various Ophthalmol. comtes.); The Conservation Council of Ont.; Alpha Omega Alpha; Presbyterian; recreations: golf, hockey; Office: 267 O'Connor St., Ottawa, Ont. K2P 1V3.

WATSON, Colin D., B.A.Sc., M.B.A.; broadcasting executive; b. Kettering, Eng. 5 July 1941; s. Harry John W.; e. Public Sch. Kettering, Eng.; High Sch. N. Vancouver, B.C.; Univ. of B.C., B.A.SC. 1963; Univ. of W. Ont. M.B.A. 1970; m. Barbara d. Russel J. Preeter; children (by previous marriage): Christopher, Kevin, Matthew; PRES. AND DIR., ROGERS CABLESYSTEMS INC. (formerly Candn. Cablesystems Ltd.) 1979- ; Pres. and Dir. PTN Pay Television Network Ltd.; Festival of Festivals; Devel. Engr., Polymer Corp., Sarnia, Ont. 1963; Product Mgr. Trane Co. of Canada Ltd. 1964-68; Asst. to Vice-Pres. Industrial Devel., Brascan Ltd. 1970-71; Vice-Pres. Triarch Corp., Treas. Jonlab Investments Ltd. and Pres. Canadian Venture Capital Corp. 1972-74; Pres. and Dir., Metro Cable TV Ltd., 1974-76; Vice Pres., Cdn. Cablesystems Ltd. 1976-79; mem. Assn. Prof. Engrs. Ont.; Anglican; recreations: squash, tennis, sailing, skiing; Clubs: Boulevard; Caledon Ski; Home: 153 Roxborough St., Toronto, Ont. M9W 1V9; Office: Suite 2602, Commercial Union Tower, P.O. Box 249, Toronto-Dominion Centre, Toronto, Ont. M5K 1J5

WATSON, David Barr, M.B.E., E.M., C.D., B.Com; management consultant; b. Swansea, U.K., 5 Sept. 1920; s. Thomas and Winnifred (Davies) W.; e. Haileybury Coll., Eng. (Sr. Matric.) 1938; Univ. of London, B.Com. 1941; London Polytech. (Sales) Dipl. 1946; Univ. of W. Ontario (Mang. Training Course) Dipl. 1953; m. Nancy Roberta, d. R. P. Cretney, Toronto, 3 Nov. 1973; children: Nigel, Ian; PARTNER, WOODS, GORDON & CO. (Management Consultants, estbd. 1932), since 1954; Asst. Export Sales Mgr., Philips Radio, England, 1946-47; with Remington-Rand Ltd., Toronto, Ont., 1947-49; joined present Co. 1949, apptd. Supervisor, 1951, Secy., 1953, Partner, 1954; served with Hon. Arty. Co. (U.K.) 1938-40; served in 2nd World War; Major, Royal Corps of Signals (Airborne), 1940-46; M.B.E., M.I.D.; Lieut.-Col., Royal Candn. Signals (Militia), Toronto, Ont., 1947-62; Hon. Col., 709 Communications Regt.; mem., Inst. Mang. Consultants Ont.; Anglican; Club: National; Home: 27 Lawrence Cres., Toronto, Ont. M4N 1M9; Office: (Box 253) Royal Trust Tower, Toronto-Dominion Centre, Toronto, Ont. M5K 1J7

WATSON, Donald, M.A.; consultant; b. Bristol, Eng., 19 May 1919; s. Herbert Ernest and Violet Gertrude May (Forse) W.; e. Oxford Univ., B.A. (Physics) 1940; m. Mary, d. late J. P. Plenderleith, Belfast, N.I., Dec. 1945; children: Peter, Shirley; with Telecommunications Research Establishment, Eng., 1940-45 and trans. to India, 1945; joined Chalk River, Project, Atomic Energy of Can. Ltd., Canada, 1946; Asst. to Vice-Pres., Research & Devel., 1948-55; Secy., 1956-63; Vice Pres. Adm. 1963-74; Anglican; Home: 2342 Rembrant Rd., Ottawa, Ont. K2B 7P5

WATSON, Donald N.; b. Winnipeg, Man. 21 Sept. 1921; s. Leonard and Maude (Davies) W.; e. St. James Coll. Inst., Man.; m. Doris Pearl, d. Hallen Watkin, 28 Nov. 1942; children: Terry, Sharon; CHMN. OF BD., B.C. RESOURCES INVESTMENT CORP., 1981- ; began aviation career 1937; Co-originator Sask. Govt. Air Ambulance Service, Regina, 1946; Mang. Dir., Ont. Central Airlines, Kenora, Ont. 1949 till joining Pacific Western Airlines 1958; served as Asst. to Pres., Gen. Mgr. Mainline Operations, Vice Pres. Mang. and Tech. Services and Pres. , CEO and Dir.; Brit. Commonwealth Air Training Plan 1940-45; civilian attached to USAF March-Oct. 1945; Dir., Mount Royal Coll.-Aviation Sec., Calgary; Can.'s Aviation Hall of Fame; mem. Order of Icarus and Polaris; Hon. mem., Air Transport Assn. Can.; mem., Candn. Aeronautics & Space Inst.; Am. Inst. Aeronautics & Astronautics; Scot. Rite; Protestant; recreation: farming; Clubs: OX5 Aviation Pioneers; Quarter Century Aviation Can.; Vancouver; Home: 17452 - 18th Ave., Surrey, B.C.; Office: 1176 West Georgia St., Vancouver, B.C.

WATSON, Earle Macbeth, M.D., M.Sc., F.R.C.P. (Edin.) 1930, F.R.C.P.(C) 1929, F.A.C.P. 1948; b. Belmont, Ont., 26 Nov. 1895; s. Reuben and Minnie (Macbeth) W.; e. Univ. of W. Ontario, M.D. with Silver Medal 1919, M.Sc. 1927; post grad. studies in Edinburgh and London, Eng.; m. Zoe Eileen, d. George Addy, Sheffield, Eng., 1 Aug. 1922; children: Celia, Clarice, Barry; sometime Demonst. in Physiol., Univ. of Sheffield, Eng., and Biochem. at the Roy. Infirmary there; subsequently Prof. of Path. Chem. and Sr. Assoc. in Med., Univ. of W. Ont. and now Prof. Emeritus there; mem., Am. Diabetes Assn.; Candn. Soc. Clinical Chemists; Hon. mem., Candn. Soc. Clinical Investig.; AOA Med. Soc.; mem. Clinical and Scient. Sec., Candn. Diabetes Assn.; Delta Upsilon; Protestant; recreations: photography, art; Address: 427 Regent St., London, Ont. N5Y 4H1

WATSON, George Nelson, B.A., F.S.A. (1945), F.C.I.A., M.A.A.A.; actuary; b. Toronto, Ont., 21 Oct. 1914; s. Harold and Alice Florence (Elliott) W.; e. Malvern Coll., Inst., Toronto, Ont.; Victoria Coll., Univ. of Toronto, B.A. 1936 (Hon. Math. and Physics); m. Hylda, d. Samuel Hayhurst, 4 Dec. 1937; one s., Cameron Nelson; PRES., G.N. WATSON LTD., and Fraser, Watson Actuaries Ltd.; Fellow, Candn. Inst. of Actuaries; The Society of Actuaries; mem., Internat. Actuarial Assn.; Am. Acad. of Actuaries; Past Pres., Candn. Assn. Accident and Sickness Insurers (1965-66); Candn. Pension Conf. (1971-73); Chrmn. of Organizing Comte., Pacific Ins. Conf. 1979; Conservative; Protestant; recreation: golf; Clubs: The Ontario Club; The Metro Toronto Bd. of Trade; Home: RR #1, Palgrave, Ont. L0N 1P0; Office: 1 Eva Rd., Ste. 203, Etobicoke, Ont. M9C 4Z5

WATSON, Ian, M.P., B.A., B.C.L.; lawyer; politician; b. Howick, Que., 10 April 1934; s. Wilfred, D.V.M. and late Jean (Whillans) W.; e. Howick (Que.) High Sch.; Bishop's Univ., B.A.; McGill Univ., B.C.L.; m. Monique, d. late Leopold Carle, M.D., 20 Nov. 1965; children: Mark, Chantal, Yannie, Anik; Co-Chrmn., Canada U.S. Interparliamentary Group, 1980-82; Rapporteur, Scient. and Tech. Comtes., North Atlantic Parl. Assembly, 1978-81; called to Bar of Que. 1959, since then in law practice with firm of Cerini, Salmon, Watson, Souaid and Harris; 1st el. to H. of C. for Chateauguay-Huntingdon-Laprairie 1963, re-el. 1965; re-el. for Constit. of Laprairie 1968, 1972 and 1974; re-elect. Const. of Chateauguay, 1979 & 1980; Vice-Chrmn., H. of C. Comte. on Mines, Forest & Waters 1963-64; Parlty. Observer, Candn. Del. to U.N., New York 1965 and 1966; Chrmn., H. of C. Comte. on Citizenship, Immigration, Indian Affairs & Human Rights 1965; Jt. Chrmn., H. of C. and Senate Comte. on Penitentiaries 1966-67; Chrmn. H. of C. Standing Comte. on Indian Affairs and N. Devel. 1968-72, 1976-79; Parlty. Secy. to Min. of Nat. Revenue 1972; Parlty. Secy. to Min. State for Urban Affairs 1973-74; Chrmn., H. of C. Comte. Nat. Resources & Public Works, 1980- ; mem. Que. Bar Assn.; Candn. Bar Assn.; NATO Parlty. Assn.; Liberal; Presbyterian House of Commons, Ottawa, Ont.

WATSON, John Hamilton, B.Com., M.B.A.; insurance executive; b. Toronto, Ont. 15 Nov. 1943; s. Gordon McKay and Kathleen (Hamilton) W.; e. Vaughan Rd. Coll. Inst. Toronto 1962; Univ. of Toronto B.Com. 1966, M.B.A. 1967; Invest. Dealers Assn. Course I 1968; m. Denise Florence d. Thomas A. Humphrey, Thornhill, Ont. 21 Sept. 1968; one s. Andrew Gordon; VICE PRES. INVESTS. CONFEDERATION LIFE INSURANCE CO. since 1977; Dir. Fairbank Lumber Co. Ltd.; Dover Park Development Corp. Ltd; joined present Co. as Invest. Analyst Trainee Bond Dept. 1967, Invest. Analyst Bond Dept. 1969 and Stock Dept. 1970, Invest. Mgr. US Common Stocks 1971, Asst. Vice Pres. Invest. Research 1973; Offr. Investments Unltd.; Fellow Life Mang. Inst.; C.F.A. 1973; mem. Toronto Soc. Financial Analysts; Freemason; United Church; recreations: hockey, golf, bowling, squash; Clubs: Empire; Thornhill Country; Mayfair Racquetball; Home: 22 Nevada Ave., Toronto, Ont. M2M 3N8; Office: 321 Bloor St. E., Toronto, Ont. M4W 1H1

WATSON, Patrick, M.A., O.C.; television journalist; filmmaker; writer; b. Toronto, Ont. 23 Dec. 1929; s. Stanley Alvin and Lucy Lovell (Bate) W.; e. Univ. of Toronto B.A. 1951, M.A. 1953; Univ. of Mich. doctoral studies 1954-55; m. Beverly d. Dr. W. H. Holmes, Toronto, Ont. 11 June 1951 (separated 1977); children: Christopher, Gregory, Andrew; ed., W. J. Gage & Co. Toronto 1953-56; TV Producer CBC Toronto and Ottawa 1956-66 (program series incl. "Close-Up", "Inquiry", "This Hour Has Seven Days"); Adjunct Prof. of Pol. Science Univ. of Waterloo 1966-67; Ed. and Anchorman 'The Fifty-First State" N.Y. Pub. TV 1972-73; documentary films incl. "The Seven Hundred Million", "Search in the Deep" (with Jacques Cousteau); Pres., Patrick Watson Enterprises Ltd., since 1968; Rideau Broadcasting Ltd., since 1979; Vice. Pres. Programming, Bushnell Communications Ltd. 1969-70; Vice Pres. Immedia Inc. 1975-77; Host, "Witness to Yesterday" 1973-75; "Some Honourable Members" 1973-75; "The Watson Report" since 1975; "Titans" 1981; author "Alter Ego" 1978; "Zero to Airtime" 1974; "Fasanella's City" 1973; "Conspirators in Silence" 1969; co-author "Alexander Dolgun's Story" 1975; numerous articles on science, religion, broadcasting, educ.; numerous film and TV scripts; comm. pilot mem. Candn. Owners & Pilots Assn.; Candn. Aeronautics & Space Inst.; Assn. Candn. Radio & TV Artists; Officer of Order of Canada, 1981; recreations: piano, cooking, reading, flying; Address: R.R.6, Smith's Falls, Ont. K7A 4S7.

WATSON, Robert George, M.Sc., P.Eng.; company president; b. Creemore, Ont., 17 Sept. 1917; s. Norman and Ella Jane (Blackburn) W.; e. Queen's Univ., M.Sc.; Harvard Univ.; m. Florence Irene Pearce, 4 Sept. 1948; children: Linda, William, Calvin, Shirley, Nancy; PRESIDENT AND DIRECTOR, R. G. WATSON CO. LTD. since 1956; practised civil engn. in Can. 1947-51; organized own engn. firm, 1951; inc. as R. G. Watson Co. Ltd. 1956; Dir: Burke Canada Inc., Ayers Cliff, P.Q.; mem., Assn. Prof. Engrs. of Ont., B.C. and Alta.; life mem., Soc. Civil Engrs.; Am. Concrete Inst.; recreations: golf, hunting, skiing; Clubs: Rosedale Golf; Granite; Engineers; Muskoka Lakes Golf & Country; Goodwood; Home: 95 Glengowan Rd., Toronto, Ont. M4N 1G5; Office: 1176 Yonge St., Toronto, Ont. M4W 2L9

WATSON, William Heriot, M.A., Ph.D., F.R.S.C. (1937); physicist; educator; b. Edinburgh, Scotland, 12 Dec. 1899; s. Peter and Margaret (Lindsay) W.; e. Edinburgh University, M.A. (1st Class Hons.) 1921, Ph.D. 1925; Cambridge Univ., Ph.D. 1931; m. Marjorie, d. William Sowler, 25 June 1931; children: Peter Heriot, Kenneth; Carnegie Fellowship, Caius Coll., Cambridge, 1928-31; Asst. Prof. of Physics, McGill Univ., 1931-39, Assoc. Prof. 1939-44; Prof. of Math. and Head of Dept., Univ. of Sask., 1944-46; Research Physicist and Head of Theoretical Physics Br., Divn. of Atomic Energy, Nat. Research Council, 1946-50; Asst. Dir., Physics Sub-Divn. there, 1949-50; Head, Dept. of Physics, Univ. of Toronto, 1950-61; Dir., Computation Centre, 1952-62, when resigned; Sr. Consulting Scientist, Lockheed Missiles & Space Co., Palo Alto & Sunnyvale, Cal. 1962-69; served in World War, 1918-19, in Eng.; Pres., Sec. III, Royal Soc. Can., 1956; author of "On Understanding Physics", 1938; "Wave Guide Transmission and Antenna Systems", 1947; "The Effects of Computing Devices on Productivity" (a submission to Gordon Comn.), 1956; "Understanding Physics Today", 1963; liberal; Protestant; recreations: music, garden; Home: 2095 Avondale Rd., Victoria, B.C. V8P 1V5

WATSON, Wreford, Pen-name as poet, James Wreford; M.A., Ph.D., LL.D., F.R.S.C., F.R.S.E.; educator; poet; b. Shensi, China 8 Feb. 1915; s. James and Evelyn (Russell) W.; (Canadian citizen since 1953); e. George Watson's Coll. Edinburgh; Edinburgh Univ. M.A. 1936; Univ. of Toronto Ph.D. 1945; McMaster Univ. LL.D. 1977; Carleton Univ. LL.D. 1979; m. Jessie Wilson herself a lecturer in Geogy, Moray House College of Education, Edinburgh, d. James Black, Galloway, Scot. 24 Aug. 1939; children: Margaret Anne, James McGregor; FOUNDER AND CONVENOR, CENTRE OF CANDN. STUDIES, EDINBURGH UNIV. since 1972; Atlas Consultant, Thos. Nelson of Canada since 1968; Instr. McMaster Univ. 1938-40, first Prof. Dept. Geog. 1945-49; Chief Geog. Can. 1949-54 and Chrmn. Nat. Atlas of Can. Comte.; first Prof. Dept. Geog. Carleton Univ. 1950-54; Prof. of Geog. and Founder-mem. Program of N. Am. Studies present Univ. 1955-76; Visiting Prof. Queen's Univ. 1959-60; Univ. of Man. 1968-69; Simon Fraser Univ. 1976-77; Calgary Univ., 1980-81; Prof. of Geog. various Candn. univ. sum-

mer schs.; rec'd Award of Merit Am. Assn. Geogs. 1952; Gov. Gen.'s (Can.) Award for Poetry 1954; Murcheson Award Royal Geog. Soc. 1962; Research Medal Royal Scot. Geog. Soc. 1964; Special Award, Can. Assoc. Geogrs., 1977; mem. Educ. Comte. Edinburgh Town Council; Bd. Govs. Napier Coll. of Technol. Edinburgh since 1970; author Poetry Pubns., "Of Time and the Lover", 1953, "Countryside Canada", 1979; Academic Pubns., "General Geography" 1953; "North America, Its Countries and Regions" 1968; "Canada, Problems and Prospects" 1970; "A Social Geography of the United States" 1978; "The United States: habitation of hope", 1981- ; co-author/co-ed. "The British Isles, A Systematic Geography" 1964; "Bermuda, A Geography" 1966; "The American Environment, Perceptions and Policies" 1976; (with wife) "The Canadians; How They Live and Work" 1977; mem. Brit. Assn. Candn. Studies (Pres.); Royal Scot. Geog. Soc. (Pres.); Brit. Assn. Advanc. Science (Pres. Geog. Sec. 1968); Candn. Assn. Geogrs. (Organ. Chrmn. 1953); Fellow, Royal Soc. Canada 1954; Fellow, Royal Soc. Edinburgh, 1964; Liberal; Baptist; recreations: photography; travel; Home: "Manotick", 67 Bonaly Rd., Edinburgh, Scotland; Office: 21 George Square, Edinburgh, Scotland.

WATT, Donald Richard, stockbroker; b. Raymore, Sask., 5 Feb. 1912; s. Richard Paul and Minnie Agnes Burns (Lee) W.; e. High Sch., Raymore, Sask. (Grad. 1930); Reliance Sch. of Comm. Regina, Sask.; m. Edna Mae, d. James Tate, 23 May 1935; ACCOUNT, WATT CARMICHAEL SECURITIES LTD. since 1971; Hon. Director, Consolidated Morrison Explorations Ltd.; Salesman, Beatty Washing Machines, Toronto, 1931-32; Manager, Dominion Stores Ltd., Toronto, 1932-34; Manager and Comptroller, Williams, McLean & Bell, Stockbrokers, Toronto, 1934-37; Asst. Comptroller and Manager, H. R. Bain & Co., Stockbrokers, Toronto, 1937-40; Gen. Mgr., Yolles Furniture Co. Ltd., Toronto, 1940-49; Sales Mgr., Wallace Silversmiths, Wallingford, Conn., 1949-53; Special Rep., Newling & Co., Stockbrokers, Toronto, July 1953-Mar. 1954; Pres., G. W. Nicholson & Co. Ltd. 1954-69; Salesman, Grant Johnston Ltd. 1969-71; Chmn. of Bd., Watt Carmichael Securities 1971-81; Protestant; recreations: golf; Clubs: Portmarnoch Golf (Ireland); Rosedale Golf; Calgary Golf; Canadian (New York); Board of Trade; Pine Tree Golf (Fla.); Home: Benvenuto Place, Apt. 605, Toronto, Ont. M4V 2L2; Office: Suite 3470, 1 First Canadian Place, Toronto Ont. M5X 1B1

WATT, Leonard Nelson; financier; b. Scudder, Ont., 6 May 1919; s. James G. W. and Madeline (Rahm) W.; m. Jessie May (Robertson) W.; children: James A., Robert L.; Nancy J., William D.; Barbara M.; PRES., FISCAL CONSULTANTS CANADA LTD.; Dindune Corp. Ltd.; Wellore Resources Ltd.; C.E.O. Fiscon Fund; Dir. Sugar Loaf Ranches Ltd.; Multiple Sclerosis Soc.; World Wild Life Fund; mem. Bd. Trade Metrop. Toronto; United Church; Clubs: Canadian; National; Home: RR #1, Glen Huron Ont. L0M 1L0; Office: Suite 905, 1075 Bay St., Toronto, Ont. M5S 2B1

WATT, Lynn Alexander Keeling, M.S., Ph.D.; educator; b. Winnipeg, Man. 25 Oct. 1924; s. Alexander Robb and Mary Isabelle (Keeling) W.; e. Elem. and High Schs. Winnipeg, Man.; Univ. of Man. B.Sc. 1947; Univ. of Chicago M.S. 1951 (Univ. Fellowship 1947); Univ. of Minn. Ph.D. 1959; m. Pauline Marion d. late Christian Oliver Einarson 18 Aug. 1948; children: Martha Bjorg Isabel (Mrs. J. Jurkovic), Laura Geraldine (Mrs. K. Nyback), Paula Lynn, Graham Alexander Kristinn; DEAN OF GRAD. STUDIES UNIV. OF WATERLOO since 1972 and Prof. of Elect. Engn. since 1966; Lectr. Dept. Physics Univ. of Man. 1948-49, 1951-52; Asst. Research Offr. Atomic Energy of Canada Ltd. Chalk River Nuclear Labs. 1952-55; Research Fellow Dept. Elect. Engn. Univ. of Minn. 1955-59; Asst. Prof. of Elect. Engn. Univ. of Wash. 1959, Assoc. Prof. 1962, Prof. 1966; Chrmn. Ont. Council on Grad. Studies

1976-78; author various research papers on magnetics and semiconductor materials and devices; Pres. Candn. Assn. Grad. Schs. 1977-78 (Vice Pres. 1976-77); mem. Inst. Elect. & Electronics Engrs.; Am. Soc. Engn. Educ.; Am. Phys. Soc.; Candn. Assn. Physicists; Candn. Soc. Higher Educ.; Sigma Xi (Treas. Waterloo); Unitarian; recreations: tennis, cross-country skiing, gardening, reading; Home: 193 Mohawk Ave., Waterloo, Ont. N2L 2T4

WATTS, Ronald Lampman, O.C., M.A., D.Phil.; educator; b. Japan, 10 March 1929; s. Candn. missy. parents; e. Univ. of Toronto, B.A. 1952; Oxford Univ., Oriel Coll. (Rhodes Scholar), B.A. 1954, M.A. 1959, D.Phil. 1962 (Can. Council Fellowships 1959-61); m. 1954; joined Queen's University as Lecturer in Pol. Philosophy 1955, Don, Men's Residence 1955-56, Warden 1956-59, Asst. Prof. of Pol. Studies 1961, Assoc. Prof. 1963, Prof. since 1965; Asst. Dean, Faculty of Arts and Science, 1964-66; Assoc. Dean 1966-69, Dean 1969-74; Principal and Vice Chancellor 1974; Nuffield College, Oxford University (on leave from Queen's) 1959-61; Tutor i.c. Politics teaching Balliol Coll., Oxford 1961; Can. Council Sr. Fellowship for sabbatical leave 1967-68; Candn.-Commonwealth Exchange Scholar to Australia 1968; Visiting Fellow, Australian Nat. Univ., Canberra 1968; Ford Foundation Visiting Prof., Inst. of Adm., Univ. of Ife, Ibadan, Nigeria 1969; Consultant, Uganda Govt. re E. African Fed. 1963; consultant, Dept. of Secy. of State re citizenship in fed. systems 1970-74; consultant, Constit. Planning Comte., Govt. of Papua New Guinea 1974-75; has been active in univ. affairs at prov. and nat. level incl. Chrmn. Council Deans Arts & Science Ont. 1971-73, Ont. Univs. Council on Admissions 1972-74, Special Comte. on Guidelines for Recruiting of Students 1972-73; Ministry of Educ. Liaison Comte. 1972-74; mem. Application Centre Bd. of Mang. 1971-74; Special Comte. on Undergrad. Scholarship Policy 1973-74; Visiting Lectr., Brit., USA, Australia, N.Z., Africa, Asia and Can.; mem., Task Force on Cdn. Unity 1978-79; Chrmn., Council of Ont. Univ. 1979-81; Exec. Assn. of Univ. and Coll. of Can., 1975-77, 1979-81; mem., Seconday Education Review Comte. (Ont.) 1980; Comte. on Future Role of the Universities (Ont.) 1980; Exec. Council for Canadian Unity 1980; Bd. of Gov., Donner Foundation 1979; Officer, Order of Canada 1980; author, "New Federations: Experiments in the Commonwealth" 1966, rev. ed. 1968; "Administration in Federal Systems" 1970; also book chapters, comnd. reports and articles in various learned and prof. journs.; recreation: sailing (Past Vice-Commodore, Kingston Yacht Club; Chief Class Offr., Sailing, Olympics 1976); Home: Summerhill, Queen's University, Kingston, Ont. K7L 3N6; Office: Queen's University, Kingston, Ont.

WAUGH, Douglas Oliver William, M.Sc., Ph.D., M.D.C.M., F.R.C.P.(C); educator; b. Hove, Sussex, Eng., 21 Mar. 1918; s. Oliver S., M.D. and Helen A. (Champion) W.; e. Pub. and High Schs., Winnipeg, Man.; Univ. of Man., 1935-38; McGill Univ., M.D.C.M. 1942, M.Sc. (Path.) 1948, Ph.D. (Path.) 1950; m. Sheila Louise, d. late Dr. G. Lyman Duff, 16 Jan. 1971; EXTVE. DIR., ASSN. CANDN. MED. COLLS., since 1975; Demonst. Path., Asst. in Surg. Path., Path. Inst., McGill Univ., 1946-47; Grad. Med., Research Fellow, N.R.C. of Can.., Dept. of Path., Path. Inst., McGill Univ., 1947-50; Assoc. Prof. of Path., Univ. of Alta., 1950-51; McGill Univ., 1951-58; Assoc. Prof. of Pathol., Queen's Univ., 1958-61, Prof. 1961-64, and Pathol., Hotel Dieu Hosp., Kingston, 1958-64; Prof. and Head, Dept. of Pathol., Dalhousie Univ. and Head V.G. Hosp. N.S., Pathol. Inst. 1964-70; Dean, Faculty of Med., Queen's Univ. 1970-75 Vice Princ., Health Sciences there 1971; served in 2nd World War, 1942-46 with R.C.A.M.C.; service in Can. and N.W. Europe; Dir., Nat. Cancer Inst. (Pres. 1974-76); Candn. Cancer Soc.; Medical Adviser, N.S. Div., Candn. Heart Foundation; Chrmn. (1964-65) Candn. Cytology Council; Chrmn., Medical Research Council Assessment Group for Pathology, 1967-68; mem., Nat. Comte. on Physician Manpower, since

1974; Council Roy. Coll. of Physicians and Surgeons of Can., 1969-70; Que. Assn. of Path.; Candn. Assn. of Pathol.; Am. Assn. of Path. & Bacter.; Internat. Acad. Path.; Am. Soc. for Exper. Path.; Alpha Omega Alpha; Pluto Club; Home: 183 Marlborough Ave., Ottawa, Ont. K1N 8G3; Office: 151 Slater St., Ottawa, K1P 5H3

WAUGH, William Bruce, B.A., F.S.A., F.C.I.A.; actuary; b. Winnipeg, Man., 13 Nov. 1920; s. William Sydney and Jane Morris (Williams) W.; e. Univ. of Toronto Schs., 1934-39; Univ. of Toronto, B.A. 1943; m. Isobel Ruth, d. Leslie Brown Allan, Toronto, Ont., 22 June 1946; children: Allan Bruce, Marilyn Ruth, Gordon William; VICE PRES., CHIEF ACTUARY AND CONTROLLER, CANADA LIFE ASSURANCE CO., since 1981; joined the Co. 1946, Asst. Actuary and Co. Offr., 1951, Assoc. Actuary 1958, Actuary Electronics 1961, Data Processing Extve. 1966, Data Processing Vice Pres. 1968; Adm. Vice-Pres. 1972; Vice-Pres. and Controller, 1973; served with RCN 1943-46; Fellow, Soc. Actuaries, 1949; Candn. Inst. Actuaries; Anglican; recreations: golf, squash, tennis; Clubs: Board of Trade; University; Home: 331 Lytton Blvd., Toronto, Ont. M5N 1R9; Office: 330 University Ave., Toronto, Ont. M5G 1R8

WAXMAN, Albert Samuel, B.A.; actor; director; producer; b. Toronto, Ont. 2 March 1935; s. Aaron and Tobie (Glass) W.; e. Univ. of W. Ont. B.A. 1957; Univ. of Toronto Law Sch.; Neighbourhood Playhouse Sch. of the Theatre, New York; London (Eng.) Sch. of Film Technique; m. Sara d. Manuel Shapiro, Winnipeg, Man. 24 Oct. 1968; children: Tobaron, Adam Collier; PRES., TOBARON PRODUCTIONS LTD.; actor/dir. or writer over 50 TV or feature films, commercials, documentaries and industrials London, New York, Hollywood, Montreal, Toronto, theatre in London and New York; repertory theatre Eng. and summer stock New Eng. and Can.; TV series incl. "King of Kensington" 1975-80; "Circus International with Al Waxman" 1979, 1980; currently "Cagney & Lacey"; recipient Actra awards Best Performance in a Continuing Role 1976, Best Acting Performance in TV (Earle Grey Award) for "The Winnings of Frankie Walls" 1981; Metro Toronto Community Involvement Award 1980; Queen's Silver Jubilee Award 1977; named Spiritual Father of the Yr. 1980 Pioneer Women of Can.; Nat. Campaign Chrmn. Candn. Cancer Soc. 1979-81; Hon. Recruitment Chrmn. B.'nai B'rith Can. 1980-82; Hon. Big Brother, Big Brothers: Variety Club; mem. Dirs. Guild Can.; Candn. Assn. Motion Picture Producers; Acad. Canda. Cinema; Assoc. of Candn. T.V. & Radio Artists; Jewish; recreations: tennis, travel; Address: c/o Prendergasts Talent Co. Ltd., 105 Dupont St., Toronto, Ont. M5R 1V4

WAYGOOD, Ernest Roy, M.S.A., Ph.D., F.C.I.C., F.R.S.C.; educator; b. Bramhall, Cheshire, Eng. 26 Oct. 1918; s. Edward Samuel and Alice (Harrison) W.; e. Macclesfield, Cheshire Mill Hill Elem. Sch. and Cheadle Hulme Secondary Sch. 1935; Reaseheath Agric. Coll. 1936; Ont. Agric. Coll. B.S.A. 1941 (Cheshire Co. Univ. Scholarship in Agric. 1937-41, Whitehead Scout Scholarship 1937-39); Univ. of Toronto M.S.A. 1947, Ph.D. 1949; m. Adorée Magdalyn Woolf-LeBrooy 30 Dec. 1950; one d. Pamela Mimi; PROF. EMERITUS, UNIV. OF MAN. since 1979; Assoc. Dir. Biomass Energy Inst. Winnipeg; Asst. Prof. of Bot. McGill Univ. 1949-52, Assoc. Prof. 1952-54; Research Assoc. Nat. Research Council 1950; Prof. and Head of Bot. Univ. Man. 1954-74; Prof. 1974-79 (ret.); Visiting Prof. of Agron. Univ. of Ill. 1958; Dir. Algal Project (Nat. Research Council Devel. Grant) 1974-77; Lalor Foundation Research Award 1956; served with RCAF 1941-45, Pilot RAF Transport Command 24 Sqdn., 512 Sqdn. Mediterranean & W. Africa Theatres, Ferry Command Dorval, Que.; Assoc. Ed. "The Plant Biochemical Journal" (India) 1974; "Canadian Journal Botany" 1971; over 85 scient. publs.; mem. Candn. Soc. Plant Physiols. (Pres. 1960); Anglican; recreations: farming, swimming; Home: (P.O. Box 144), St. Germain, Man. R0G 2A0 and

9925 Quarry Rd., Chilliwack, B.C. V2P 3M3 Office: Univ. Man. Winnipeg R3T 2N2.

WEATHERSTON, Hon. Francis Stephen; b. Beverly Twp.; Ont., 16 Oct. 1917; s. George and Florence Edith (Millen) W.; e. Dundas High Sch.; Osgoode Hall Law Sch. grad. (Hons.) 1940; m. Mary Helen, d. F. W. Warren, 30 May 1975; children: David, Richard, Martin; JUSTICE COURT OF APPEAL, since 1977; Chrmn., Bd. Govs. Dundas Valley Sch. of Art, 1977-78; called to the Bar of Ont. 1940; cr. Q.C. 1958; Acting City Solr., Hamilton, Ont. 1959; Partner, Weatherston, Bowlby Luchak & Martino until 1974; Justice Supreme Court of Ont., 1974; Gen. Solr., Toronto Hamilton & Buffalo Rly. Co. 1964-74; served with Royal Hamilton Light Inf. 1940-45, staff appts. U.K. and Continent, discharged with rank Capt.; Pres. (1952) Hamilton Lawyers Club; Pres. (1973) Hamilton Law Assn. (Area Dir., Legal Aid Plan 1967-74); Presb.; Freemason; Delta Chi; recreations: golf, fishing; Club: Hamilton Golf & Country; Home: 2329 Otami Trail, Mississauga, Ont. L5H 3N2; Office: Osgoode Hall, Toronto, Ont. M5H 2N6

WEAVER, Arthur Gordon, B.A., F.S.A., F.C.I.A., F.T.C.I.; executive; b. Toronto, Ont., 21 June 1915; s. S. Roy and Edith S. (Pratt) W.; e. Town of Mount Royal (Que.) and Westmount (Que.) High Schs.; McGill Univ., B.A. (Math.) 1936; Harvard Business Sch., Advanced Mang. Course 1959; m. Melba L. Trombley, 27 Sept. 1941; children: David R., Arthur Bruce; Dir. L. FidMor Mortgage Investors Corp.; Exec. Services, Ltd.; HFC Trust Co.; retired Dir., Eaton's of Can. Ltd.; Eaton/Bay Financial Services Ltd.; Eaton/Bay Life Assnce. Co.; Eaton/Bay Funds; Eaton/Bay Ins. Co.; Eaton/Bay Trust Co.; Actuarial Asst., Candn. H.O., Prudential Life Assurance Co. Ltd. of England, 1936-39; Actuarial Assoc., Montreal Life Insurance Co., Montreal, 1945-49; Dir. of Group Research, John Hancock Mutual Life Insurance Co., Boston, 1949-55, Assoc. Group Actuary 1955-56, 2nd Vice Pres. 1956-66, Vice Pres. 1966-70; Pres. & C.E.O., Eaton/Bay Group, 1970-78; served with RCAF 1939-45; Air Navig., rank Flight Lt.; Gov., Soc. Crippled Civilians, 1951-76; mem., Am. Acad. Actuaries; Internat. Actuarial Assn.; Soc. of Actuaries; Candn. Inst. of Actuaries; Bd. Trade Metrop. Toronto; Baptist; recreations: water sports, skiing, reading, chess; Club: National; Home: Box 8, Site E, R.R. 2, Sutton W., Ont. L0E 1R0 and 4223 Bay Beach Lane, Ste. FS, Fort Myers Beach, Florida 33931.

WEBB, Donald Irving, B.A., B.Com., F.C.A.; financial consultant; b. Saskatoon, Sask., 1 Feb. 1920; s. Lewis Charles and Alice (Hyslop) W.; e. Kennedy Coll. Inst., Windsor, Ont.; Queen's Univ., B.A. (Hons. Math. and Econ.) 1943, B.Com., 1946; C.A. (Ont.) 1949; m. Dorothy Isobel, d. Andrew Nesbitt, Kingston, Ont.; 22 May 1943; children: Ian Donald Andrew, Barbara Allison; Dir. Traders Group Ltd.; Director; Guaranty Trust Company of Can.; Capital Growth Fund; Shorcan Intl. Brokers Ltd.; with Clarkson, Gordon & Co., Chart. Accts., Toronto, Ont., 1946-55 latterly as a Partner; Partner, J. H. Crang & Co., Stock Brokers, Toronto, Ont., 1955-59; Pres. Merrill Lynch, Pierce, Fenner & Smith of Canada Ltd. 1969 and subsequently Chrmn., Merrill Lynch Royal Securities Ltd. till 1972 since when a Financial Consultant; served in 2nd World War; R.C.N.V.R., 1942-45 (N. Atlantic); mem., Inst. Chart. Accts. Ont.; recreation: golf; Clubs: National; Granite; Rosedale Golf; Goodwood; Lost Tree (Fla.); Address: 23 Country Lane, Willowdale, Ont. M2L 1E1

WEBB, Peter John, M.R.A.I.C., F.R.I.B.A.; architect; b. Kent, Eng., 17 April 1927; s. Oswald C. and Louise Jane (Weller) W.; e. Private and Sec. Schs., Eng.; Northern Polytechnic Sch. of Arch., London, Eng., grad. 1958 (Hons. Diploma in Arch., with Distinction in design thesis; Interior Design Prize, 1952); m. Nanette, d. J. Lezzerini, 2 March 1957; one s. Justin Peter; PARTNER, WEBB ZER-

AFA MENKES, HOUSDEN; Pres., Uniplan Ltd.; Asst. Arch. in London, Eng. on projects in U.K. and Middle East before coming to Can. in 1957; joined Peter Dickenson & Assoc. in 1958; formed present firm, 1961; firm awarded the Massey Medal, Nat. Design and Nat. Steel Design Awards in 1964; designed and supv. constr. of most major type bldgs, incl. schs. and univs., hotels, commercial offices, shopping, indust. and residential centres and Govt. projects; also projects in Toronto, Montreal, Calgary, Lancaster, N.B., etc.; served with Royal Navy, 1944-48; mem., Ont., Que. and Man. Assns. Archs.; Montreal Soc. Archs. (Toronto Chapter of Ont. Assn. Archs.); recreations: fishing, golf, hunting; Club: Toronto Anglers & Hunters; Office: 99 Yorkville, Toronto, Ont. M5R 3K5

WEBBER, Patrick Neil, M.L.A., B.Sc., B.Ed., M.A., Ph.D.; politician; b. Hanna, Alta. 17 Apl. 1936; s. Charles and Katherine (McAuliffe) W.; e. Univ. of Alta. B.Sc. 1957, B.Ed. 1962, Ph.D. 1973; Univ. of Toronto Meteorol. Office 1962; Univ. of Mont. M.A. 1963; m. Dorothy d. late John Platzer 3 Aug. 1957; children: Barbara, Carol, Len, Lorne, Dianne; Assoc. Min. of Telephones for Prov. of Alta.; Chrmn. Alta. Govt. Telephones Comn.; el. M.L.A. Alta. 1975, re-el. 1979; Past mem. Mount Royal Coll. Bd. Govs.; Candn. Math. Cong.; Assn. Inst. Research; Math. Council Alta. Teachers' Assn.; Nat. Council Teachers Math.; Alta. Assn. Coll. Faculties; Mount Royal Coll. Faculty Assn.; P. Conservative; R. Catholic; recreations: skiing, jogging, tennis, bridge, reading; Home: 4612 Brockington Rd. N.W., Calgary, Alta. T2L 1R6; Office: 132 Legislature Bldg., Edmonton, Alta. T5K 2B6.

WEBBER, William Alexander, M.D., F.R.C.P.; educator; b. Nfld. 8 Apl. 1934; s. William Grant and Hester Mary (Constable) W.; e. Univ. of B.C. M.D. 1958; m. Marilyn Joan d. late William M. Robson 17 May 1958; children: Susan Joyce, Eric Michael, George David; DEAN OF MEDICINE, UNIV. OF B.C. since 1977 and Prof. of Anat. since 1969; Intern, Vancouver Gen. Hosp. 1958-59; Fellow, Cornell Med. Coll. 1959-61; Asst. Prof. of Anat. present Univ. 1961, Assoc. Prof. 1966; author various publs. on structure and function of kidney; mem. Candn. Assn. Anatomists; B.C. Med. Assn.; Candn. Nephrol. Soc.; Am. Assn. Anatomists; recreation: soccer; Office: Vancouver, B.C. V6T 1W5.

WEBER, Johnstone Ainsley, B.Com., F.R.I.; retired executive; b. Edmonton, Alta., 28 Dec. 1914; s. late Lewis Aldred and Matilda Edith (Trapp) W.; e. Pub. and High Schs., Edmonton, Alta.; Univ. of Alberta; Univ. of British Columbia, B.Com. 1937; m. Alice Maxine, d. late Sidne McMillan, 21 Mar. 1942; one d., Keltie Edith; retired Pres., Weber Bros. Realty Ltd.; Past Pres., Candn. Chapter, Internat. Real Estate Fed., 1965-66; Candn. Assn. of Real Estate Bds., 1954-55; Candn. Inst. of Realtors, 1955-56; began with Toronto General Trusts Corp. (Estate Dept.), Vancouver, B.C., May 1937; returned to Edmonton, 1939, to join Edmonton Credit Co. (family Corp. and one of the pioneer auto finance Co's. in W. Can.); in June 1945 purchased the assets of Edmonton Credit Co. Ltd. and acquired ownership of Weber Bros. Agencies Ltd.; served as Lieut., C.O.T.C. and R.C.N.V.R.; Past Pres., Alta. Real Estate Assn.; Edmonton Real Estate Bd.; Edmonton Ins. Agents Assn.; mem., Soc. of Industrial Realtors; Edmonton Chamber of Comm.; Past Regional Pres., Jr. Chamber of Comm. for Alta.; Past Dir., Candn. Nat. Inst. for the Blind; Freemason (Scot. Rite); Protestant; recreations: golf, hunting, curling; Home: 20 Riverside Crescent, Edmonton, Alta. T5N 3M5; Office: 5555 Calgary Trail, Edmonton, Alta. T6H 4J9

WEBER, Kathleen Nichol Murray(Kay), R.C.A.; artist; b. R.R.3, Ayr, Ont. 5 Nov. 1919; d. John and Annie Fulton (Carswell) Murray; e. Ayr Continuation Sch.; Galt Coll. Inst. 1935; Ont. Coll. of Art 1959; Printmaking Monitor

1960-62; Univ. of Calgary summer Lithography workshop 1969; George Brown Coll. Toronto photographic screen workshop 1971-77; m. L. George Weber, D.V.M. 31 Aug. 1946; children: Mark Frederick, Krista Jane; Dir., Visual Arts Ont. 1973-74; organized silk screen workshop and taught serigraphy Centennial Coll. Scarborough 1968-70; serigraphy workshops Ont. Dept. of Culture & Recreation; Visiting Artist Dept. of Art & Environment Fanshawe Coll. London, Ont. 1973; solo exhns. Merton Gallery Toronto 1977; Gallery Moos Toronto 1980; rep. in numerous group exhns. incl. Internat. Graphics Montreal Museum of Fine Arts 1971; Contemporary Candns. Albright-Knox Gallery Buffalo 1971; 9th and 10th Internat. Exhns. Graphic Art Ljubljana, Yugoslavia 1971, 1973; 4th Internat. Print Biennial Cracow, Poland 1972; Survey Contemporary Candn. Prints Pratt Graphic Center N.Y. 1972; The Mall Galleries London, Eng. 6 Candn. Artists with Soc. Wood Engravers & Relief Printers (invitational) 1973; World Print Competition San Francisco Museum 1973; 1st Internat. Biennial Graphic Art & Multiples Segovia, Spain (invitational) 1974; 2nd Vienna Graphic Biennale (invitational) 1975; travel exhn. Ont. 1975-77; exchange Print exhn. Chelsea Sch. Art Eng. and Ont. Coll. Art 1975; 100 Yrs. Evolution Ont. Coll. Art, Art Gallery Ont. 1976; RCA Centennial Contemporary Exhn. 1980; rep. in pub., corporate and private colls. incl. Albertina Art Museum Vienna; Nat. Gallery Can.; Le Service de la Culture du Conseil Municipal de Cracovie, Poland; Ont. Arts Council; Purchase Awards: Internat. Print Biennial Cracow 1972; Graphex I Brantford, Ont. 1973; Toronto-Dominion Bank 1975, 1978; Crown Life Insurance Co. 1978; Dofasco 1978; recipient Metrop. Award Candn. Soc. Graphic Art Robert McLaughlin Gallery Oshawa 1969; Hon. Mention Art Gallery of Brant Annual Exhn. Brantford 1970; Print & Drawing Council Can. Award 'Imprint '76' Montreal 1976; Juror's Award 9th Burnaby (B.C.) Biennial Print Show 1977; Editions Award Graphex 6 Art Gallery of Brant 1978; O.S.A. Award for Mixed Media 1978; Award of Merit "Pressure 79" O.S.A. Print Exhn. Toronto 1979; Collectors Choice Award "Image '79'" St. Catharines, Ont. 1980; mem. Candn. Soc. Graphic Art (Extve. 1964-65, Treas. 1966-67); Candn. Painter-Etchers & Engravers; Print & Drawing Council Can.; O.S.A.; Candn. Artists' Representation; Liberal; Protestant; recreation: photography; Address: 109 Roxborough Dr., Toronto; Ont. M4W 1X5.

WEBSTER, Alexander Robertson (Sandy), B.A.; actor; b. Fort William, Ont. 30 Jan. 1923; s. William and Sarah Jane (Stewart) W.; e. Sr. Matric. Fort William Coll. Inst.; Queen's Univ. B.A. (Hons. Hist., Pol., Eng.) 1949; Grad. Lorne Greene Acad. Radio Arts, Toronto, 1950; m. Ruth Marie, d. Henry S. Fennell, Brantford, Ont. 16 Oct. 1959; children: Bruce, Gail, Craig; an actor in Candn. radio, television and theatre since 1950; leading roles in CBC "Stage Series"; Thomas Craig, Head of Farm Family in CBC Ont. Farm Broadcast; Currently plays Dr. Chisholùm in CBC-TV Drama series, "The Great Detective"; frequent appearances in Candn. regional theatres; mem. both Shaw and Stratford Festival Cos.; served with R.C.A.F. 1942-45; comnd. Air Bombardier, discharged with rank of Flying Offr.; mem. Prof. Council, Candn. Theatre Sch., Montreal; mem. Coun. Candn. Actors. Equity Assn. (former Chrmn, Vice-Pres. 1973-76); Vice Pres. Actors' Fund of Canada; Talent Group, 185 Bloor St. E., Agent; United Church; recreations: curling, swimming, golf; Home: 178 Bingham Ave., Toronto, Ont. M4E 3R3;

WEBSTER, Colin Wesley, B.A.; industrialist; b. Quebec, Que., 29 Nov. 1902; s. Hon. Senator Lorne C. and Muriel (Taylor) W.; e. Lower Canada Coll.; McGill Univ., B.A. 1924; m. Jean, d. Charles E. Frosst, 1 Dec. 1927; children: Lorne Charles, Donald Colin, Beverley Frosst; Chairman of Board, International Paints (Canada) Ltd.; St. Lawrence Stevedoring Co. Ltd.; Director, Stewart Smith (Canada) Ltd.; Montreal Shipping Co. Ltd.; St. Lawrence Stevedoring Co.; Canadian Liquid Air Ltd.; Liquid Air Corp. of N.A.; Little Lon Lac Gold Mines Ltd.; Montship Lines Ltd.; Napierville Junction Railway Co.; St. Lawrence Cement Co.; Toronto, Hamilton & Buffalo Railroad Co.; Ultramar Can. Inc.; Past Pres., Metrop. Bd., Y.M.C.A.; United Church; recreations: golf, hunting, skiing; Clubs: Royal Montreal Golf; Montreal Badminton & Squash; St. James's; Home: 52 Gordon Cres., Westmount, Que. H3Y 1M6; Office: 4999 St. Catherine St. W., Suite 504, Westmount, Que. H3Z 1T3

WEBSTER, Edward Clark, M.A., Ph.D.; university professor; professional psychologist; b. North Battleford, Sask., 13 Jan. 1909; s. Arthur George and Bertha (Carrothers) W.; e. Elem. and High Schs., Edmonton, Alta.; Univ. of Alberta, 1926-28; McGill Univ., B.A. 1931, M.A. 1933, Ph.D. 1936; m. Inez Graham, d. late Hugh M. Patton, 1 July 1938; children: Eleanor, William, Marian; PROF. OF PSYCHOLOGY, McGILL UNIV. and Dir., Centre for Continuing Educ. there; Consulting Psychologist, 1936-42; Pres., Opinions Surveys Ltd., 1940-42; Lectr., Sir. Geo. Williams Coll., 1936-40; Special Lectr. in Indust. Psychol., McGill Univ., 1946-48, and Assoc. Prof. of Psychol. there, 1949-53; Dir., Applied Psychol. Centre, 1952-68 (full Prof. 1958); served in Candn. Army, 1942-45; Major, Research & Information Sec., AG Br., N.D.H.Q.; Publications: "Guidance for the High School Pupil", 1939; "Put Yourself to the Test", 1941; "Decision Making in the Employment Interview", 1964; "The Couchiching Conference", 1967; Pres., Sch. for Handicapped Children (Mental) 1950-52; Fellow, Am. Psychol. Assn.; mem., Candn. Psychol. Assn.; Am. Bd. of Examiners in Prof. Psychol. (Diplomate, Indust. Psychol.); Protestant; Clubs: Faculty; University; Office: 522 Pine Ave. W., Montreal, Que. H2W 1S6

WEBSTER, J.B.; manufacturer; b. London, Ont., 1 Jan. 1918; s. William Gourlay Webster; e. Lord Roberts Pub. Sch., London, Ont.; Central Coll. Inst., London, Ont.; Assumption Coll., Windsor, Ont.; m. Elizabeth Baxter; two s. William, John; CHMN. AND C.E.O., WEBSTER MFG. (LONDON) LTD.; Pres., GunWeb Ltd.; Webster Group Investments Ltd.; Dir., Canadian Curtiss-Wright Ltd.; Webster Air Equipment Ltd.; served in 2nd World War; Lieut., Royal Hamilton Light Inf., 1940-45; captured in Dieppe Raid, 1942; Prisoner of War till 1945; P. Conservative; United Church; Clubs: The London; London Hunt & Country; Canadian; Home: 161 Windermere Rd., London, Ont. N6G 2J4; Office: (P.O. Box 4575, Stn. C) 1161 King St., London, Ont. N5W 5K4

WEBSTER, John Hamilton, M.D., C.M., F.R.C.P.(C); educator; b. Belleville, Ont. 17 Dec. 1928; s. late Frederick John and Katherine Margaret Dorothea (Hamilton) W.; e. elem. and high schs. Picton, Ont. Queen's Univ. M.D., C.M. 1955; m. Doreen Elizabeth Beatrix d. late Prof. A. E. Prince and late Mrs. Beatrix Prince 17 Aug. 1953; children: Diana, Lorna, Patrick, Geoffrey; PROF., DEPT. OF RADIOLOGY, JOINT RADIATION ONCOLOGY CENTRE, UNIV. OF PITTSBURGH; Prof. and Chrmn. of Radiation Oncology, McGill Univ.; Therapeutic Radiol.-in-Chief, Montreal Gen. Hosp., Royal Victoria Hosp., Jewish Gen. Hosp., Montreal Children's Hosp. 1974-79; internship Mem. Hosp. Manchester, Conn. 1955-56; Residency, Therapeutic Radiol. Roswell Park Mem. Inst. Buffalo 1956-59, Sr. Cancer Research Radiol. 1959-62, Assoc. Cancer Research Radiol. 1962-63, Assoc. Chief Cancer Research Radiol. 1963-64, Chief of Therapeutic Radiol. 1964-74; author or co-author numerous med. publs.; mem. Am. Coll. Radiol.; Am. Soc. Therapeutic Radiols.; Royal College of Physicians & Sugeons of Canada; Candn. Oncology Soc.; Internat. Assn. Study Lung Cancer; Soc. Chrmn. Acad. Radiation Oncology Programs; Home: 302 Bank St., Sewickley, P.A. 15143; Office: Joint Radiation, Oncology Centre, 230 Lothrop St., Pittsburgh, P.A. 15213 U.S.A.

WEBSTER, John Malcolm, B.Sc., Ph.D., D.I.C., F.L.S.; educator; b. Wakefield, Eng. 5 May 1936; s. Colin Ernest and Marion (Waterhouse) W.; e. Imp. Coll. Univ. London B.Sc. 1958, Ph.D. 1962, A.R.C.S., D.I.C.; m. Carolyn Ann d. Hon. George Argo McGillivray, Toronto, Ont. 15 May 1970; children: Gordon John, Sandra Jane; ASSOC. VICE-PRES., ACADEMIC, SIMON FRASER UNIV. since 1980; Agric. Research Council Scholar, Imp. Coll. Univ. London 1958-61; Research Scient. Rothamsted Exper. Stn. Eng. 1961-66; Canada Dept. of Agric., Belleville, 1966-67; Assoc. Prof. of Biol. Sciences present univ. 1967, Prof. 1971-, Chrmn. 1974-76, Dean of Science 1976-80; Ed. 'Economic Nematology' 1972; author over 90 publs. in parasitology and nematology; mem. Bd. Mgmt., TRIUMF project; Pres., West. Cdn. Univ. Marine Biol. Station; Vice-Pres., Soc. of Neuratologists; mem. Candn. Soc. Zool.; Candn. Phytopathol. Soc.; European Soc. Nematology; Fellow of the Inst. Biol.; Fellow of the Linnean Soc. of London; and other nat. and foreign socs.; Pres., Arts, Sciences and Technology Centre, Vancouver; Home: 1069 Marigold Pl., North Vancouver, B.C. V7R 2E5; Office: Burnaby, B.C. V5A 1S6.

WEBSTER, Leonard C., manufacturer; b. Sherbrooke, Que., 28 Nov. 1918, s. Ralph and Vera (Channell) W.; e. Bishop's Coll. Sch., Lennoxville, Que., 1937; Bentley Coll. (Mass.), 1939; m. Mary, d. John Pattinson, 16 Aug. 1944; children: Carolyn, Ralph, James; PRESIDENT, DIRECT SELLERS' ASSN 1971-75 Director, Mirror Press Ltd.; Imperial Furniture Mfg. Co. Ltd.; Vice-Pres. and Chief Extve. Offr., O'Cedar of Canada Ltd., 1957-62; Vice-Pres. and Gen. Mgr., Drackett Canada Ltd., 1961, Pres. 1966; joined Bristol-Myers Products (Canada) as Vice-Pres. Adm., 1967; Extve. Vice-Pres., 1970; Vice Pres. Corp. Staff (Assignment Can.) Bristol-Myers Co. 1971; served in 2nd World War, Flight Lt., RCAF; Chrmn., Stratford Gen. Hosp., 1964-68; Co-ordinated Arts Services — Toronto 1967-71; Pres., Stratford Shakespearian Festival, 1961-63; Stratford Rotary Club 1966; Stratford Country Club 1957; Dir., Associated Councils of the Arts (New York); former Dir.; Renison Coll., Univ. of Waterloo; mem.; Candn. Mfrs. Assn.; Bd. of Trade Metrop. Toronto; recreations: golf, curling, boating; Club: Mississauga Country; Home: 250 Dalewood Drive, Oakville, Ont. L6J 4P3; Office: 390 Bay St. Suite 1506. Toronto, Ont. M5H 2Y2

WEBSTER, Lorne C., B.E.; company officer; b. Montreal, Que., 19 Sept. 1928; s. Colin Wesley and Jean (Frosst) W.; e. St. Georges Sch., Westmount, Que.; Lower Canada Coll., Montreal, Que.; McGill Univ., B.E. (Mech.); m. Beverley Meredith Evans, children Adam Wesley; Lorne Howard, Beverley Meredith; by former marriage Feb. 1954, children: Linda Ann, Brenda Alice, Lorne Campbell; PRES., PRENOR GROUP LTD.; Chrmn. Personal Insurance Co. of Canada Ltd.; Can. Provident Gem Inc.; Northern Life Ins. Co. of Canada; Pres. Canabam Ltd.; Cambrelin HOldings Ltd.; Campbell Assets (Dominion) Ltd.; Cartier Towel Ltd.; Vice-Chrmn., Montreal Baseball Club Ltd.; Dir., Bank of Montreal; Murphy Oil Co. Ltd.; Dale-Ross Holdings Ltd.; Domtar Ltd.; Imperial Trust Co.; Canadian Fur Investments Ltd.; Cullman Ventures Inc. (New York); Quebec Inc.; Kativo S.A. (Sam José, Costa Rica) Sallingbury Ltd. (U.K.); Cullman Ventures Inc. (N.Y.); Comindus S.A. (Paris); Quebecair Ltd.; Webster Holdings Ltd.; Taurus Trust Ltd.; Planned Resources Fund, Ltd.; Stadacona Investments Ltd.; Paragon Ins. of Can. Ltd.; R.H. Webster Foundation; Douglas Investments Ltd.; H. B. Fuller Ltd. (St. Paul, Minn.); Helix Investments Limited; Kirkhill Developments Limited; La Preservatric Ltd., (Sydney, Australia); Windsor Hotel; Pres. Julius Richardson Convalescent Hosp.; Chmn., Bd. of Trustees, Stanstead Coll.; Gov. McGill Univ.; United Church; recreations: skiing, squash, racquets, tennis, golf; Clubs: Hillside Tennis; Montreal Badminton & Squash; Montreal Racket; Royal Montreal Golf; The Jesters; University; Mt. Royal; The Brook (N.Y.); Royal Ten-

nis Court, (U.K.); Soc. Sportif de Jeu de Paume et de Racquets, (Paris); Home: 56 Belvedere Circle, Westmount, Que. H3Y 1P8; Office: 801 Sherbrooke St. East, Montreal, Que. H2L 1K7

WEBSTER, (Reginald) Howard, B.A.; industrialist; b. 1910; s. late Hon. Lorne Campbell and Muriel Warren (Taylor) W.; e. Lower Canada Coll., Montreal, Que.; McGill Univ., B.A.; Babson Inst., Boston, Mass.; unm.; Chrmn., The Globe & Mail Ltd.; Quebecair; Windsor Hotel Ltd.; Penobscot Bldg. (Detroit); Pres. Detroit Marine Terminals Inc.; Durand Corp.; Annis Furs (Detroit); Imperial Trust Co.; Dir., Burns Foods Ltd.; Holt, Renfrew & Co. Ltd.; Québecair; Pres., Canadian Fur Investments Ltd.; began with Imperial Trust Co., Montreal, 1933; Home: 19 Southridge, Ile Bizard, Ste. Geneviève, Que. H9E 1B3; Office: Rm. 2912, 1155 Dorchester Blvd. W., Montreal, Que. H3B 3Z4

WEDEPOHL, Leonhard Martin, B.Sc., Ph.D., F.I.E.E., P.Eng.; electrical engineer; educator; b. Pretoria, S. Africa 26 Jan. 1933; s. Martin Willie and Liselotte (Franz) W.; e. Grey Coll. Bloemfontein 1949; Univ. of Witwatersrand B.Sc. 1953; Univ. of Manchester Ph.D. 1957; m. Rosemary Joy d. Ernest Guy Elliot 29 March 1958; two s. Martin, Graham; DEAN, FACULTY OF APPL. SCI., UNIV. OF B.C. 1979-; mem. Science Council, B.C. 1975-79; Dean, Fac. of Engineering, Univ. of Man. 1974-1979; Vice-Chrmn. Manitoba Hydro Electric Bd., Dec. 1978-Aug 1979; Bd. Manitoba Hydro Electric Corp.; Telecommunications Planning Engr. S. African Electricity Supply Comn. 1957-61; Mgr. L. M. Ericcson, Pretoria 1961-62; Sec. Leader Protection Relay R & D Reyrolle, Eng. 1962-64; Elect. Engn. Dept. Univ. of Manchester 1964-74, Prof. Head Power Systems 1967-70, Chrmn. of Dept. 1970-74, Bd. of Govs. 1968-71; mem. N.W. Council for Higher Educ. 1968-72; Gov. Bolton Coll. 1972-74; holds 4 patents on electronic relays for protecting high voltage transmission lines; developed first transistorised protection relay system which went into field service on high voltage transmission line 1958; author numerous papers; mem. Candn. Soc. Elect. Engrs.; Sr. mem. Inst. of Elect. & Electronic Engrs.; Fellow, Inst. of Electrical Engineers, London; Lutheran; recreations: skiing, camping, music; Club: University, Vancouver; Home: 12426-23rd Ave., Surrey, B.C.

WEEKS, Lady — see: Tomkinson, Constance.

WEES, Frances Shelley; author; b. Gresham, Oregon, 29 Apl. 1902; d. Ralph Eaton Johnson and Rose Emily (Shelley) J.; e. Elem. Schs., Ore., Secondary Schs., Saskatoon, Sask.; Edmonton, Alta.; m. Wilfred Rusk, s. Frederick Milton Wees (U.E.L.), 1924; one d., Margarita (Mrs. E. V. Smith); one s., Timothy John; sometime Sch. Teacher, Sask.; Dir., Candn. Chautauquas, 8 seasons; Pub. Relations Counsel, Toronto 3 yrs., Ottawa 2 yrs.; author: "Maestro Murders", 1931; "Detectives Ltd.", 1932; "Mystery of the Creeping Man", 1932; "Romance Island", 1933; "Honeymoon Mountain", 1933; "It Began in Eden", 1936; "Untravelled World", 1936; "Lost House", 1938; "Sally, Baby and Joe", 1938; "Home and Roundabout", 1938; "The Open Door", 1938; "Storyland", 1938; "A Star for Susan", 1940; "Someone Called Maggie Lane", 1947; "Under the Quiet Water", 1948; "Empty the Haunted Air", 1948; "Quarantine", 1949; "Melody Unheard", 1950; "The Mystery of Married Love", 1953; "M'Lord, I Am Not Guilty", 1951; "The Keyes of My Prison", 1956; "Where Is Jenny Now?", 1958; "The Country of the Strangers", 1959; "The Last Concubine", 1962; "The Treasure of Echo Valley", 1964; "Danger in Newfoundland", "The Faceless Enemy", 1965; contrib. poems, stories, articles to journs. in U.K., Can. and U.S.; mem., Mystery Writers Am.; New Eng. Hist. Geneal. Soc.; Nat. Geneal. Soc.; Brit. Soc. Geneal.; Daughters Am. Revolution; Clubs: Heliconian; Media;

Candn. Authors'; Home: R.R. No. 3, Stouffville, Ont. L0H 1L0

WEES, Wilfred Rusk, M.A., M.Ed., Ph.D., LL.D., F.O.T.F., F.O.I.S.E.; b. Bracebridge, Ont., 24 Nov. 1899; s. Frederick Milton and Josephine (Rusk) W.; e. Moose Jaw (Sask.) Coll.; Univ. of Alta., B.A. 1923, M.A. 1925, M.Ed. 1928; Leland Stanford Univ. 1931; Univ. of Toronto, Ph.D. 1935; LL.D. 1961; m. Frances Shelley Johnson, 27 Sept. 1924; children: Margarita Josephine, Timothy John; Prof. Ont. Inst. for Studies in Educ., since 1968; Rural Sch. Teacher, 1916-18; High Sch. Teacher 1919 and 1923-29; Normal Sch. Teacher and Univ. Lectr. (Psychol.) 1929-33; columnist reviewing current events in Edmonton Journal, 1928-29; Ed., W. J. Gage & Co. Ltd., 1935-38, el. a Dir. 1949; Vice-Pres. and Mgr., Textbook Div., 1953; served with R.C.A.F. Reserve 1918; Lieut., C.O.T.C. 1925; on active service 1941; overseas 1944-45 in charge of Personnel Selection at Candn. Mil. Hdqrs. with rank of Lieut.-Col.; Dir. of Educ. and Counselling, Dept. of Veteran's Affairs, Ottawa, 1946-47; Life mem., Ontario Psychol. Assn.; Fellow, Ont. Teachers Fed.; Ont. Assn. for Curriculum Devel.; Ont. Educ. Assn.; Nat. Soc. for Study of Educ.; Comm. Travellers Assn.; Candn. Psychol. Assn.; Candn. Educ. Assn.; Diplomate, Am. Psych. Assn. Fellow, Ont. Inst. for Studies in Education; awarded Centennial Medal; author: "The Way Ahead"; "Nobody Can Teach Anyone Anything"; "Teaching Teachers Teaching"; has contrib. numerous newspaper and journ. articles on education; Protestant; recreation: country activities; Home: R.R. No. 3, Stouffville, Ont. L0H 1L0

WEILBRENNER, Bernard, M.A.; archiviste; né à Verdun, Qué., 3 nov. 1929; f. Wilfrid et Alma (Morency) W.; é. Collège St. Laurent, B.A. 1949; Univ. de Montréal, M.A. (Histoire) 1951; Comm. de la Fonction Publique, Ottawa, Cert., cours en adm. 1958; American Univ., Washington, D.C., cert. en archivistique 1958; ép. Renée Beaulne 4 août 1956; ARCHIVISTE FEDERAL ADJOINT, depuis 1971; Archiviste, Archives Publiques du Canada 1952-63; Dir., Archives Nat. du Qué. 1963-67; Dir., Direction des Archives Historiques, 1967-71; Prof. d'Archivistique, Univ. Laval 1965-67 et Ecole des bibliothécaires, Univ. d'Ottawa 1970-71; Editeur, "Rapport des Archives du Québec" 1964-66; "Etat général des archives publiques et privées", Archives du Québec 1968; "Inventaire des greffes de notaires", Archives du Québec, tomes 19-21; "Table des matières des rapports des Archives du Québec," 1964; biographies dans "Dictionnaire biographique du Canada," tomes I et II; mem., Soc. hist. du Canada (Consel 1961-62, secrétaire de langue française 1962-69, vice-prés. sec. des archives 1969-70, prés. 1970-71); mem., Conseil Internat. des Archives depuis 1959, corr. pour le Canada depuis 1970, membre, comité pour le développement; mem., Soc. of Archivists (U.K.) depuis 1960; Soc. hist. du Québec (vice-prés. 1966-67), Féd. des Soc. hist. du Québec (vice-prés. 1967); Assn. des Archivistes du Qué. (prés. 1981); Assn. of Candn. Archivists; Soc. of Amer. Archivists; prés. comté. des Archives de l'Inst. pan-am. de géog. et d'hist.; catholique; residence: 272 avenue Crocus, Ottawa, Ont. K1H 6E9; Bureau: 395, rue Wellington, Ottawa, Ont. K1A 0N3

WEILER, Hon. Karen Merle Magnuson, B.A., LL.M.; judge; b. Regina, Sask. 13 June 1945; d. Edgar Theodore and Rose Emma (Beliveau) Magnuson; e. Spiritwood, Sask.; Nutana Coll. Saskatoon, Sask. (rec'd Assn. Franco-Canadien Prov. Prize in French Lit. 1960; Sask. Govt. Scholarship 1962); Univ. of Sask. B.A., Law Sch 1964-65; Osgoode Hall Law Sch. Toronto LL.B. 1967, LL.M. 1974; m. Robert David Weiler 29 July 1967; two d. Nancy Elizabeth, Catherine Victoria: CO. COURT JUDGE, COUNTIES & DISTRICTS OF ONT. 1980- ; read law with Blake, Cassels & Graydon; called to Bar of Ont. 1969; law practice Weiler, Weiler & Maloney 1969-72; Lectr. in Business

Law Lakehead Univ. Sch. of Business evening 1970-72; Instr. in Family Law Bar Admission Course 1975-79; Solr. Ministry of Community & Social Services Legal Services Br. 1973-74; Counsel, Policy Devel. Div. Ministry of Atty. Gen. 1974 becoming Sr. Counsel to 1980; Ont. Commr. Uniform Law Conf. 1976, 1977, 1979; Del. 5th Commonwealth Law Conf. 1977; 4th Nat. Conf. on Juvenile Justice 1977; mem. Atty.-Gen's Comte. on Representation of Children 1977; Dir., Family Court Conciliation Project 1976-79; C. M. Hincks Treatment Centre for Adolescents 1975-79; The Thomas More Lawyers' Guild Toronto; Participant Internat. Fed. Women Lawyers Conf. 1975; mem. Alliance Prov. Voluntary Agencies Service to Children 1975; Co-ordinating Council Emotionally Disturbed Children & Youth 1976; Comte. on Enforcement Family Law Orders; Panelist CBC TV and Univ. of Windsor co-prod. "The Law Makers" and "Custody" 1980; Tech. Adviser and Panelist CFTO TV "The Sting" 1979; Panelist and Speaker, Connaught Devel. Confs. 1976, 1977; Law Soc. Upper Can. 2nd Annual Inst. on Continuing Legal Educ. 1977; frequent guest lectr., speaker and commentator; mem. Ont. Status Women Council 1976-77; Ont. Comte. Candn. Council on Children & Youth 1977-79; co-author "Law and Practice Under the Family Law Reform Act (Ontario)"; author or co-author various articles book chapters; Pres. Family Law Sec. Ont. Br. Candn. Bar Assn. 1977-78, Secy. Ont. Extve.; Hon. mem. Phi Delta Phi; mem. Co. & Dist. Judges Assn. Ont.; Candn. Inst. Adm. Justice; R. Catholic; recreations: reading, swimming, biking, skiing; Home: 76 Lascelles Blvd., Toronto, Ont.; Office: 322 Court House, 361 University Ave., Toronto, Ont. M5G 1T3.

WEILER, Paul C., M.A., LL.M.; b. Port Arthur, Ont., 28 Jan. 1939; s. Gerard Bernard and Mary Marcella (Cronin) W.; e. St. Patrick's High Sch., Fort William, Ont., 1956; Univ. of Toronto, B.A. 1960, M.A. 1961; Osgoode Hall Law Sch., LL.B. 1964; Harvard Law Sch., LL.M. 1965; Univ. of Victoria, hon. LL.D.; children: Virginia, John, Kathryn, Charles; MACKENZIE KING PROF. OF CANDN. STUDIES, HARVARD LAW SCH. apptd. Prof. of Law, Osgoode Hall Law Sch., York Univ. 1972; called to Bar of Ont. 1967; joined Faculty Osgoode Hall Law Sch. 1965; Labour Arbitrator 1965-73; Chrmn., Labour Relations Bd. of B.C. 1973-78; Research Consultant, McRuer Royal Comn. on Civil Rights, 1966-67, Woods Task Force on Labour Relations, 1968-69, LeDain Comn. on Drugs, 1971-72, Nat. Law Reform Comn. Project on Criminal Code Study, 1974; Special Counsel to Gov't of Ont. to review Worker's Compensation Law, 1980- ; Chmn., Ont. Joint Comte. on Physicians Compensation, 1980- ; appt. to Public Rev. Bd. of the United Auto Workers; author, "Labour Arbitration and Industrial Change", 1970; "In the Last Resort — A Critical Study of the Supreme Court of Canada", 1974; "Reconcilable Differences: New Directions in Canadian Labour Law," 1980; "Reshaping Workers' Compensation in Ontario", 1980; also numerous articles in law journs.; Co-ed., "Labour Relations Law", 2nd ed. 1974; co-author "Studies in Sentencing" 1974; mem. Candn. Bar Association; Candn. Law Teachers; Candn. Assn. Univ. Teachers; Nat. Acad. Arbitrators; R. Catholic; recreations: golf, skiing, squash; Home: 371 Harvard St., Cambridge, Mass. 02138; Office: Cambridge, Mass. 02138

WEINSTEIN, William, B.Sc., P.Eng.; executive; b. Brooklyn, N.Y., 19 Sept. 1925; s. Harry Louis and Bess Helen (Brodach) W.; e. Univ. of Mo., Sch. of Mines, B.Sc. (Civil Engn.); m. Marilyn, d. Louis Hillman, Brooklyn, N.Y., 22 June 1952; children: Lawrence Mark, Judi Lynne (Liska), Andrea Jo; CHMN. SNC ENGINEERING AND PROJECT MANAGEMENT SERVICES INC. President, SNC/GECO Can. Inc. 1978; Dir., SNC/GECO; Metaltech; DGB; Arctec; Terratech; joined U.S. Dept. of Interior, Alaska, as Engr. (Jr.) 1950; Engr. (Field), F. R. Harris, Inc., N.J., 1951, Engr. (Design), N.Y., 1952; Project Engr., Fenco-Harris, Toronto, 1955; Div. Engr. Transport. of FENCO 1959, Vice Pres. Foreign Operations 1965, Sr. Vice Pres. 1968; Pres. and Dir., Fdn. of Can. Engn. Corp. Ltd. (FENCO), 1974; served with U.S. Army during World War II; rank Staff Sgt.; mem. Assn. Prof. Engrs. Mo.; Assn. Prof. Engrs. Ont. (Past Chrmn. Consulting Engrs. Div.); Engn. Inst. Can.; Assn. of Consulting Engrs. Ont. (Past Dir.); Roads and Transport Assn. Canada (Past Chairman Design Committee, Geom. Design Comte., Tech. Council); Assn. of Consulting Engineers of Canada (Dir.); Bd. Trade Metrop. Toronto; Tau Kappa Epsilon; Theta Tau, Blue Key; recreations: golf, skiing, music; Clubs: Ontario, Empire; Home: 30 Whittaker Cres., Willowdale, Ont. M2K 1K8; Office: 74 Victoria St., Toronto, Ont. M5C 2A5

WEINZWEIG, John, O.C. (1974), D.Mus.; composer; b. Toronto, Ontario, 11 March 1913; s. Joseph and Rose (Burshtyn) W.; e. University of Toronto, Mus.B. 1937; Eastman School of Music, University of Rochester, Mus.M. 1938; D.Mus., Ottawa 1969; m. Helen Tenenbaum, 19 July 1940; children: Paul, Daniel; began as Teacher Composition and Orchestration, Royal Conservatory of Music of Toronto 1939; Professor of Composition, University of Toronto, 1952; Prof. Emeritus 1978; has trained many of the new generation of Canadian composers; Pres., Dir. and Founder (1951), Canadian League of Composers; Founder and Conductor of the University of Toronto Symphony Orchestra, 1934-37; has conducted his own compositions with Toronto Philharmonic, Vancouver Symphony, etc., his compositions broadcast and performed in many countries; comn. by Nat. Film Bd. to write musical scores for 4 films; has written over 100 scores for C.B.C. radio plays; compositions incl. music for Ballet "Red Ear of Corn", sonatas for piano, cello, violin, etc.; won highest award for Chamber Music in Arts Div. of London Olympiad for his "Divertimento" for flute and string orchestra, 1948; Violin Concerto completed 1954 and received first performance 30 May 1955, C.B.C. broadcast; Commissions include: Wine of Peace for soprano and orchestra (CBC) and dedicated to the United Nations, premiered by CBC Symphony 1958; Symphonic Ode (Saskatoon Symphony); Divertimento No. 3 (Saskatoon Festival); Divertimento No. 5 (American Wind Symphony of Pittsburgh); Piano Concerto 1966 (comn. by CBC); Harp Concerto 1967 (comn. by Candn. Centennial Comn.); "Pieces of Five" Brass Quintet (comn. by Canadian Brass) 1976; Dummiyah 1969 (comn. by CBC); Divertimento No. 6 1972 (comn. by Internat. Saxophone Cong.); Riffs 1974 (comn. by New Music Concerts Toronto); Contrasts for solo guitar (comn. by Guitar Soc. of Toronto), 1976; "Anthology" recorded works issued by Radio Canada International, 1978; "Divertimento" No. 7, 1979 (Comm. by Ont. Arts Council); "Divertimento" No. 8, Tuba & Orch., 1980 (Comm for 21st anniv. of Canadian Music Centre); rec'd. Can. Council Sr. Arts Award 1968, 1975; Order of Canada 1974;. Victor M. Lynch-Staunton Award 1975, Medal, Can. Music Council 1978; Molson prize from Canada Council; 1981 ($20,000 for exceptional achievement in music); Dir., Canadian Music Centre; Composers Authors Assn. Can. (Pres. 1973-75); served in 2nd World War in R.C.A.F. 1943-45; Hebrew; Home: 107 Manor Rd. E., Toronto, Ont. M4S 1R3; Office: Edward Johnson Bldg., Univ. of Toronto, Ontario.

WEIR, Stephen James, C.A., M.B.A.; executive; b. Calgary, Alta. 22 March 1940; s. Jack W. and Elizabeth T. (Speirs) W.; e. Univ. of Manitoba C.A. 1962; Univ. of W. Ont. M.B.A. 1967; m. Janet R. d. late James H. Suggitt 8 July 1961; children: James S., Jennifer J.; VICE PRES., ASST. GEN. MANAGER, INTL. DIV., DOMINION TEXTILE INC. since 1981; C.A., Robinson, Green and Co., Winn., 1957-63; Manager Credit and Data Process Control, 3M Co., London, 1963-65; joined Bank of Mtl., Special Projects, Head Off., 1967-69; Planning and Analysis, 1969-70; Asst. Credit Manager (Mtl. Main Branch), 1970-71; Asst. Cr. Manager (Corp. Cr.), 1971-72; joined Do-

minion Textile Inc. as Asst. Treasurer, 1972-73; Treasurer, 1973-77; Corp. Comptroller, 1977-81; mem., Financial Extve. Inst.; Inst. of C.A.; Club: Mtl. Amateur Athletic Assn.; recreations: squash, hockey, golf, skiing, tennis; Office:. 1950 Sherbrooke St. West, Montreal, Que. H3H 1E7.

WEISMAN, Maj.-Gen. Mortimer Lyon Aaron, C.M.M., C.D., B.A.; Canadian Forces; b. North Bay, Ont. 28 June 1927; s. Ellis S. and Mildred (Lefcoe) W.; e. North Bay Coll. Inst. 1945; Univ. of Toronto B.A. 1949; Candn. Army Staff Coll. psc 1961; Jt. Services Staff Coll. U.K. jssc 1965; Nat. Defence Coll. ndc 1974; m. Mary-Ruth d. late Harold Burke 31 May 1957; children: Sarah, Andrew; COMMANDER, CDN. DEFENCE LIAISON STAFF (WASHINGTON) AND DEFENCE ATTACHÉ since 1980; Dir. Gen., Policy Planning, Candn Forces 1979-80; joined Royal Candn. Inf. Corps (Active Force) 1945; comnd. into The Royal Candn. Dragoons (RCD), Camp Petawawa 1949; served with 27 Candn. Inf. Bgde. Group, W. Germany 1951-53; apptd. to staff Prairie Command HQ Winnipeg 1954; rtn'd to RCD Petawawa 1957; Hemer, W. Germany until 1959; assigned 4 Candn. Inf. Bgde. Group, Soest, W. Germany 1961; Sqdn. Commdr. RCD, CFB Gagetown, N.B. 1965. Mobile Command HQ St. Hubert, Que. 1966; promoted Lt. Col. and Sr. Staff Offr. Logistics 1967; promoted Col. and First Base Commdr. CFB Suffield, Alta. 1971; Dir., Continental Plans Coordination, Nat. Defence HQ Ottawa 1974; promoted to Brigadier General and apptd. Dir. Gen., Mil. Plans & Operations 1976; promoted to present rank, 1980; Jewish; Home: 6505 Ursline Ct., McLean, Virginia 22101; Office: 2450 Massachusetts Ave. N.W., Washington, D.C. 20008, U.S.A.

WEISS, (Ephrum) Philip; retired Canadian public servant; designer; b. Montreal, Que., 19 Apl. 1924; s. Hyman and Gertrude (Vogel) W.; e. Central Tech. Sch., Toronto, grad. Comm. Art 1941; Ont. Coll. of Art, Toronto, grad. Fine Art 1947; m. Nancy Johanna, d. late Klaas Raven, 28 Dec. 1945; children: Paul Raymond, Stephen Roy, Karl Raven, Benjamin Ronald; Secy. Gen., Nat. Design Council, 1970-76 Sr. Designer, Candn. Govt. Exhn. Comn., 1947-61; Asst. Dir.; Nat. Design Br., Depts. Trade & Comm. and Indust., Can., 1961-65; Gen. Dir., Office of Design, Depts. of Indust. and Indust. Trade & Comm. 1965-70; Dir., Nat. Design Council, 1961-70; Cdn. Exec. Serv. Overseas volunteer for advancement of ind. design in developing countries; served with Candn. Army (Overseas) in Can. and Europe 1943-46; designer of 10 Candn. postal stamps; contrib. to estab. of Standards Council of Can.; mem. Fed. Govt. Adv. Comtes. for improvement of design and standards in govt. accommodation and constr., procurement and graphics; taught art and design in extension courses, Ottawa Tech. High Sch., Univ. of Toronto, Carleton Coll.; speaker and contrib. to Candn. publs. on subject of design; Hon. mem., Assn. Candn. Indust. Designers; recreations: art, sculpture, camping; Home: R. R. #4, Picton, Ont.

WELCH, Hon. Robert, Q.C., M.P.P., LL.D.; b. St. Catharines, Ont., 13 July 1928; s. John Robert Charles and Edna Rebecca (Groombridge) Kemp-Welch; e. St. Catharines (Ont.) Pub. and High Schs.; McMaster Univ., B.A. 1949; Osgoode Hall Law Sch., grad. 1953; Brock Univ., LL.D. 1971; m. Margaret Emily, d. William James Boston, Montreal, Que., 18 July 1953; children: Robert William Peter, Christine Elizabeth Anne, Willa Mary-Jayne; MINISTER OF ENERGY, ONT., since 1979, and Deputy Premier since 1977; called to Bar of Ont. 1953; cr. Q.C. 1966; Partner, Lancaster Mix Welch Thorsteinson and Edwards, St. Catharines, Ont.; first el. M.P.P. for Lincoln in Prov. g.e. 1963; re-el. since; Pres., Lincoln Co. P. Cons. Assn. 1957-63; served on Select Comte. on Youth 1964-65 and Select Comte. on Co. Law 1965-66; Prov. Secy., Min. of Citizenship and Registrar Gen., 1966-71; mem. Treasury Bd. 1968-71; Govt. House Leader 1969-71; Min. responsible for Civil Service Comn. and Dept. of Civil Service 1969-71; cand. for Leadership of Ont. P. Cons. Party Feb. 1971; Min. of Educ. 1971-72; Prov. Secy. for Social Devel. 1972-74; Min. Housing 1973-74; Prov. Secy. for Justice and Atty. Gen. 1974-75; Govt. House Leader, 1975-79; Min. Culture and Recreation 1975-78; Prov. Secy. for Justice 1978-79; mem., St. Catharines Recreation Comn. 1953-54; St. Catharines Bd. of Educ. 1955-63 (Chrmn. 1958, 1961 and 1962); Campaign Chrmn., Un. Appeal, 1960; Chancellor, Diocese of Niagara, 1965; mem. Niagara Diocesan, Prov. and Gen. Synods, Ang. Ch. of Can.; mem., Lincoln Co. Law Assn.; Candn. Bar Assn.; Club: The St. Catharines; Home: 72 Johnson St., Niagara on the Lake, Ont. L0S 1J0; Office: Parliament Bldgs., Toronto, Ont.

WELD, Charles Beecher, M.A., M.D., LL.D., F.R.S.C.; professor emeritus; b. Vancouver, B.C. 3 Feb. 1899; s. late Octavius and late Esther Beecher (Noyes) W.; e. Univ. of B.C. B.A. 1922, M.A. 1924; Univ. of Toronto M.D. 1929; Dalhousie Univ. LL.D. 1970; m. Catherine Eleanor d. late Dr. R. D. Rudolf, Toronto, Ont. 5 July 1930; children: Caroline Marguerite (Mrs. P. A. Rance), Gordon Beecher, Robert John Rudolf; Lab Tech. Vancouver Gen. Hosp. 1922-24; Research Asst. Connaught lab. 1924-25 and Fisheries Research Lab. (Halifax) 1926-27; Asst. Prof. and Research Assoc., Univ. of Toronto and Hosp. for Sick Children 1930-36; Prof. of Physiol. Dalhousie Univ. 1936-69, Secy. Faculty of Med. 1948-65, Chrmn. Comte. on Cultural Activities 1964-68, Prof. Emeritus since 1969; Visiting Prof. Univ. of B.C. 1969; mem. Assoc. Comte. on Naval Med. Research, Nat. Research Council 1941-45, mem. Med. Div. 1945-50; Asst. Dir. Red Cross Blood Donor Clinic Halifax 1941-45; Dir., N.S. Museum since 1948; Prov. Surg.-Commr.-Pres., St. John Ambulance N.S. 1943-66; Extve., N.S. Soc. Prevention Cruelty 1968-80; served with 5th Candn. Siege Batty. 1917-19, Gunner; named Kt. Order St. John Jerusalem 1961; rec'd Starr Gold Medal (Research) Univ. Toronto 1933; Candn. Centennial Medal 1967; author or co-author 95 papers med. science research; retired mem. Candn. Physiol. Soc. (Past Pres.); Br. Physiol. Soc.; Am. Physiol. Soc.; N.S. Inst. Science (Past Pres.); N.S. Soc. Artists (Past Pres.); Halifax Med. Soc.; A.O.A. Hon. Med. Soc.; Anglican; Club: Waegwoltic (Past Pres.); Home: 6550 Waegwoltic Ave., Halifax, N.S. B3H 2B4.

WELD, Douglas Simpson; printer; publisher; b. London, Ont., 5 May 1896; s. John, well-known pioneer publisher and printer in Ont. and Florence W.; e. Pub. Sch., London; Ridley Coll., St. Catharines; Ont. Agric. Coll.; m. Helen Gordon, d. Thomas Baker, Toronto, Ont., 10 Oct. 1925; one s. John; HONORARY CHRMN. OF THE BOARD OF DIRECTORS, THE BRYANT PRESS LTD., served in 1st World War; went overseas in 1915; served in France as Capt., R.F.C.; prisoner 1917; Anglican; recreations: shooting, fishing; Clubs: Granite; Toronto Hunt; Home: 230 Forest Hill Rd., Toronto, Ont. M5P 2N5; Office: 260 Bartley Dr., Toronto, Ont. M4A 1G5

WELDON, David Black, B.A.; b. London, Ont., 27 June 1925; investment dealer; s. Douglas Black and Margaret (Black) W.; e. Pub. Sch., London, Ont.; Ridley Coll.; Univ. of W. Ontario, B.A. (Hons.), Business Adm.; m. Ina G., d. late Fred Perry, 7 July 1951; two s., three d.; CHRMN. BD., MIDLAND DOHERTY LTD. (Investment Dealers and Stockbrokers); Vice-Pres. and Dir., Goderich Elevators Limited; Dir., Biltmore Industries Ltd.; Guaranty Trust Company; Gould Outdoor (Posters) Limited; Grafton Group Limited; Silverwood Industries Ltd.; Emco Ltd.; Trustee, Toronto General Hospital; Ont. Jockey Club; mem. Advisory Board, U. of Western Ontario Business School, Pres. Royal Agricultural Winter Fair; mem., Board of Govs., Ridley Coll.; started as Clerk with Dominion Securities Corp. Ltd., Montreal, Que., 1947-49; Stat. Clk., Bank of Montreal, Montreal, Que., 1949-50; Securities Trader, Midland Securities Corp. Ltd.,

Toronto, Ont., 1950-51, Securities Salesman, London, Ont., 1951, Dir. and Treas., 1955, Vice-Pres. and Treas., 1959; Extve. Vice-Pres., Midland-Osler Securities Ltd. (merger), 1963, Pres. and Dir. 1966; Pres., Midland Doherty (merged cos.) 1974; served with Canadian Infantry, 1944-45; Pres., P. Cons. Assn., London, Ont., 1963-65; mem., Invest. Dealers Assn. Can.; Conservative; Anglican; recreations: fishing, golf, horses, hunting; Clubs: The London; London Hunt & Country; The Toronto; Toronto Golf; York; Albany; Caledon Mountain Trout; Royal & Ancient Golf of St. Andrews (Scot.); Griffith Island: Ristigouche Salmon; Homes: Prospect Farms, Arva, Ont. N0M 1C0 and Apt. 408, Hazelton Lanes, 18A Hazelton Ave., Toronto, Ont. M5R 2E2; Office: P.O. Box 25, Toronto-Dominion Centre, Toronto, Ont. M5K 1B5

WELDON, Joseph Anthony, M.B.E., M.C., C.A.; b. Chatham, Ont. 28 Nov. 1897; s. Frank and Hattie (O'Donohue) W.; e. Pub. Schs., Winnipeg, Man.; Univ. of Manitoba; m. Gertrude, d. William Whalley, 20 Aug. 1924; one d. Diane (Mrs. R. H. Pitfield); Dir. and Vice-President, Rolland Paper Company Ltd.; Dir., Canada Glazed Papers Ltd.; mem., Advisory Council, St. Mary's Hosp.; joined Price Waterhouse & Co., Winnipeg, Man., in 1920 and trans. to Montreal, Que. in 1924; joined W. C. Pitfield & Co. Ltd. on its formation 1928 as Secy. Treas.; el. a Dir. 1933; Vice-Pres. 1947; Partner, Hugh Mackay & Co., 1952; retired from Pitfield & Mackay 1963; served in 1st World War; enlisted in Western Univ. Br. as Pte. 1915; gaz. Lieut. Apl. 1917 with 78th Bn., Winnipeg Grenadiers; promoted Capt. 1918; M.C.; Mentioned in Despatches; served in 2nd World War in civilian service, R.C.A.F. H.Q., 1941 and as Controller Allied War Supplies Corp. (D.M.S.), 1942-45; M.B.E.; mem., Soc. Chart. Accts. of Man. and Que.; Roman Catholic; recreation: golf; Clubs: St. James's; Montreal Badminton; Beaconsfield Golf (Past Pres.); Home: Chequers Place, Suite 2B, 3033 Sherbrooke St. W., Westmount, Que. H3Z 1A3; Office: Suite 1200, 615 Dorchester Blvd. W., Montreal, Que., H3H 1R5

WELLAND, Rear Adm. Robert Philip, D.S.C.; b. Oxbow, Sask., 7 March 1918; s. Herbert Edward and Mabel Blanche (Amos) W.; e. Sr. Matric, Dauphin, Man.; Royal Naval Coll., Greenwich, Eng.; Banff Sch. Advanced Business Adm., Alta.; m. Ruth Stephanie, d. Gordon Campbell, 7 Nov. 1942; children: Michael, Anthony, Christopher, Gillian; joined RCN as Cadet, 1936; trained with RN until 1940; became Anti-Sub Specialist; Capt. on Destroyer Assiniboine, 1943-44 and Haida 1944-45; 2nd in Command, Royal Roads, Victoria, B.C., 1946-48; Capt., Athabaskan, 1949-51 (Korean War); led Navy Coronation Contingent, 1953; Capt. of Offr. Mch. Venture, 1955-57; Capt. (cruiser) Ontario, 1957-58; Naval Air Stn., Shearwater, N.S., 1958-61 (obtained pilot's qualification); Ship and Weapon Requirements, Ottawa, 1962; Float Commdr. Atlantic Fleet, 1963-64; Vice Chief of Naval Staff, 1964-66; Depy. Chief of Defence Staff (Operations) 1966 till retired; apptd. Sub Ltd. 1939; Lt. 1940; Lt. Commdr. 1943; Commdr., 1949; Capt. 1953; Commodore 1961; Rear Adm. 1964; rec'd D.S.C. and Bar for sub sinking in HMCS St. Laurent 1940; Am. Legion of Merit; twice Mentioned in Despatches; Anglican; recreations: writing; golf; skiing; ocean racing; big game fishing; Clubs: Rideau; Royal Ottawa Golf;

WELLS, Clyde Kirby, Q.C., B.A., LL.B.; b. Buchans Junction, Nfld. 9 Nov. 1937; s. Ralph Pennell and Maude (Kirby) W.; e. All Saints Sch. Stephenville Crossing, Nfld. 1953; Mem. Univ. of Nfld. B.A. 1959; Dalhousie Univ. Law Sch. LL.B. 1962; m. Eleanor d. Arthur B. Bishop, Stephenville Crossing, Nfld. 20 Aug. 1962; children: Mark, Heidi, David; SR. PARTNER, WELLS, MONAGHAN; Dir. Newfoundland Light & Power Co. Ltd.; Shellbird Cable Ltd.; private law practice since 1964; el. M.H.A. 1966, Min. of Labour 1966, resigned from Cabinet 1968 and from House of Assembly 1971; called to

Bar of N.S. 1963, Nfld. 1964; cr. Q.C. 1977; mem. Candn. Bar Assn.; served with COTC 1955-57, Judge Advocate Gen.'s Office 1962-64, rank Capt.; Liberal; Anglican; recreations: skiing, sailing; Clubs: Blomidon Country; Corner Brook Ski; Home: 11 Highland Ave., Corner Brook, Nfld. Office: (P.O. Box 815) 17 West St., Corner Brook, Nfld. A2H 6H9.

WELLS, Dalton Courtright, Q.C., M.A. LL.D.; b. Toronto, Ont., 2 June 1900; s. Dr. John and Dr. Josephine W.; e. Pub. Schs. and Harbord Coll. Inst., Toronto; Univ. of Toronto, B.A., 1922, M.A. 1928; Osgoode Hall, Toronto, Grad. 1925; LL.D., McMaster Univ. 1975; m. Kathleen P., d. Charles W. Irwin, 28 January 1939; children: Caroline Warren, Susan Lount, Irwin; District Judge in Admiralty of Exchequer Court of Canada for Ontario, 1960 until creation of Federal Court; subsequently a Deputy Judge of Federal Court; read law with McLaughlin, Johnston, Moorehead & Macaulay and practised his prof. with that firm 1925-41 and 1944-46; Head, Wartime Prices and Trade Bd., 1941-44; apptd. a Justice of Supreme Court of Ont., 1946; elevated to Court of Appeal, June 1964; Chief Justice, High Court Ontario 1967-75; Visitor at Massey Coll. 1973-78 (first since Vicent Massey); Hon. Sr. Fellow, Massey Coll. 1978; called to the Bar of Ontario, 1925; cr. K.C. 1945; mem. of first Bd. of the Canadian Opera Company; Head of Dominion Drama Festival, 1949; Past Pres., Toronto Lawyers' Club; Registrar of Cdn. Bar Assn. for a number of years, Sec. for Ont. Sec.; Past Chrmn., Wycliffe Coll. Council; Past Pres., Candn. Bible Soc.; 3 times Chrmn. Library Bd. of Toronto; co-author with W. P. M. Kennedy of "The Taxing Power in Canada", 1931; chosen Man of the Year by Toronto Reg. Council B'Nai B'Rith, 1969; Delta Chi; Freemason; Anglican; recreation: sailing; Clubs: University; R.C.Y.C.; Home: Apt. 109, 350 Lonsdale Rd., Toronto, Ont. M5P 1R6

WELLS, Hon. Thomas Leonard, M.P.P.; politician; b. Toronto, Ont., 2 May 1930; s. Leonard and Lillian May (Butler) W.; e. Malvern Coll. Inst., Toronto, Sr. Matric., 1948; Univ. of Toronto, 1949-51; m. Audrey Alice, d. Arthur C. Richardson, 24 April 1954; children: Andrew Thomas, Brenda Elizabeth, Beverley Gail; MINISTER OF INTERGOVERNMENTAL AFFAIRS, ONT. and Gov't House Leader since 1978; Min. of Education 1972-78; Trustee, Scarborough, (Ont.) Bd. of Educ., 7 yrs., (Chrmn. 1961, 1962); Scarborough Rep., Metro. Sch. Bd., 1962, 1963; (Chrmn. Finance Comte., 1963); el. to Ont. Leg. for Scarborough N. in g.e. in 1963; re-el. in g.e. in 1967, 1971, 1973 and 1975; Minister without Portfolio, 1966-69, Minister of Health, 1969-71, of Social & Family Services, 1971-72; Hon. mem., Bd. of Govs., Scarborough Gen. Hosp.; mem., Bd. Dirs., Albany Club of Toronto; P. Conservative; United Church; recreations: golf, photography; Home: 14 Robintide Ct., Agincourt, Ont. M1T 1V1; Office: 6th Floor, Mowat Block, Queen's Park, Toronto, Ont.

WELSH, Harry Lambert, O.C. (1971), M.A., Ph.D., D.Sc., F.R.S., F.R.S.C.; professor; b. Aurora, Ont., 23 March 1910; s. Israel and Harriet Maria (Collingwood) W.; e. Univ. of Toronto, B.A. 1930, M.A. 1931; Univ. of Goettingen, 1931-33; Univ. of Toronto, Ph.D. 1936; m. Marguerite Hazel, d. William Ostrander, Tillsonburg, Ont., 13 June 1942; PROF. EMERITUS OF PHYSICS, UNIV. OF TORONTO, since 1978; Prof. 1954-78 (Chrmn. of the Dept. 1962-68); Asst. Prof. there 1942-48, Assoc. Prof. 1948-54; medal of Candn. Assn. of Physicists, 1965; Tory Medal, Royal Soc. Can. 1963; Hon. D.Sc. Univ. of Windsor, 1964; Hon. D.Sc. Memorial Univ., 1968; Chrmn., Research Bd. Univ. of Toronto, 1971-73; Megger's Medal, Opt. Soc. America, 1974; research concerned with molecular spectroscopy and physics of high pressure gases; has publ. numerous papers on infra-red and Raman spectra of molecules, determination of molecular constants, infra-red absorption in high pressure gas-

es, selective reflection from metallic vapours, influence of intermolecular forces on molecular spectra, etc.; served in 2nd World War; Lt.-Commdr., R.C.N.V.R. (Operational Research at Naval Hdqrs., Ottawa); Fellow, Am. Phys. Soc.; Fellow, Opt. Soc. America; mem., Candn. Assn. of Phys. (Pres., 1973-74); mem., Royal Astron. Soc. of Can.; recreation: music; Home: 8 Tally Lane, Willowdale, Ont. M2K 1V4

WELSH, Sydney Wallis; cablevision executive; b. Vancouver, B.C. 24 Nov. 1913; s. Frederick Wallis and Alice Maude (Robinson) W.; e. Vancouver Tech. Sch.; m. Jeannette Millicent d. late Bert M. Cope, Vancouver, B.C. 2 March 1937; children: Frederick Wallis, Wendy Jeannette Marshall, Barbara Lyne Anderson; DIR., PREMIER CABLESYSTEMS LTD.; Chrmn. of Bd., Fred Welsh Ltd.; Chmn. of Bd., Central Heat Distributors Ltd.; Dir., Rogers Cablesystems Inc.; North West Sports Ltd.; Wester Broadcasting Co. Ltd.; Vandusen Botanical Guardens; Hon. Chmn., Rogers Cablesystems Inc.; former Ald., Dist. of W. Vancouver; Past Chrmn., Town Planning Adv. Comn. W. Vancouver; former Dir. Lions Gate Hosp. N. Vancouver; Dir. Grace Hosp. Vancouver; Commr., Royal Comn. on B.C. Rly. 1977 — 78; Past Pres. World Council Young Men's Service Clubs; Past Pres. and Life mem. Vancouver Bd. Trade; Amalgamated Constr. Assn. B.C.; Past Nat. Pres. and Life mem. Candn. Plumbing & Mech. Contractors Assn.; Past Vice Pres. for B.C., Candn. Constr. Assn.; Freemason; Kinsmen (Past Nat. Pres.); P. Conservative; Anglican; recreations: fishing, horticulture, golf; Clubs: Vancouver; Capilano Golf & Country; Pennask Lake Fish & Game; Rotary; Men's Canadian; Home: 9811 Kearns Rd., Whonnock, B.C. V0M 1S0; Office: 870 — 1100 Melveille St., Vancouver, B.C. V6E 4A6.

WELSH, W. Keith, O.B.E., M.B., F.R.C.S.(E), F.R.C.S.(C), F.A.C.S.; surgeon; b. Norfolk County, Ont., 15 June 1903; s. John and Sarah (Skinner) W.; e. Brantford (Ont.) Coll. Inst.; Univ. of . Toronto, M.B. 1926; m. Ethel Davis, d. James Baxter, Kingston, Ont., 19 July 1932; children: James Keith, Helen Jane; Honourary nsultant, North York Gen. Hosp.; Consulting Surgeon, St. Michael's Hosp.; Emeritus Prof. of Surg., Univ. of Toronto; served in 2nd World War with Royal Candn. Navy for four years; rank Surgeon Commdr.; awarded O.B.E.; mem., Candn. Assn. of Clinical Surgs.; Central Surg. Assn.; Alpha Omega Alpha; Protestant; Club: University; Home: 148 Mildenhall Rd., Toronto, Ont. M4N 3H6; Office: 1100 Sheppard Ave. E., Ste 202, Willowdale, Ont. M2K 2W1

WELWOOD, Ronald Joseph Adrian, B.A., B.L.S.; library director; b. Penticton, B.C. 14 Feb. 1940; s. Joseph Roy and Alice Marie (Bonthoux) W.; e. Univ. of B.C., B.A. 1966, B.L.S. 1967; m. Frances Josephine, d. late Albert Edward Clay, 8 Oct. 1966; children: Gregory Joseph, Michael Edward; DIR., DAVID THOMPSON UNIV. CENTRE LIBRARY; (formerly Notre Dame Univ. Library); Dir., Kootenay-Columbia Arts Council; Kootenay Museum Assn. (1971-73); Nelson Heritage Advisory Comte., 1981- ; Nelson and Dist. Hist. Assn.; Candn. Assn. of Coll. & Univ. Lib. 1971-73; Bd. Mgmt., Mt. St. Francis Hosp.; ed. Union List of Candn. newspapers held by Candn. libs. 1968-69; Nat. Lib. of Can. (acting head, newspaper section 1968-69) 1967-69; ed. "Centennial Issues of Candn. Newspapers", "Kootenainana", 1976; author "Kootenay Inst. Lib. System: A Proposal"; "Flexible working hours", Candn. Lib. Journal (Aug. 1976); "Book budget allocations", Candn. Lib. Journal (June 1977); mem., B.C. Lib. Assn. (Publicity); Kootenay Lib. System Soc. (Dir. Vice Chrmn.); Candn. Lib. Assn.; Educ. Library Adv. Comm.; Roman Catholic; recreations: hiking, photography; Club: Gryo; Home: R.R. #1, Nelson, B.C. V1L 5P4

WENDEBORN, Richard Donald; heavy equipment manufacturer; b. Winnipeg, Man. 16 Sept. 1929; s. Curtis Ernest and Rose Elizabeth (Lysecki) W.; e. Elma (Man.) elem. and high schs.; Univ. of Man. 2 yrs.; Colo. Sch. of Mines, Engr. of Mines 1952, Distinguished Achievement Award 1973; m. Dorothy Ann d. late R.S. Errol Munn 24 Aug. 1957; children: Margaret Gayle, Beverley Jane, Stephen Richard, Peter Donald, Ann Elizabeth; EXTVE. VICE PRES., INGERSOLL-RAND CO. 1976- ; Chrmn. of Bd. Ingersoll-Rand Canada Inc. 1975- ; Dir. Combustion Engineering-Superheater Ltd.; Niject Services Inc.; joined Ingersoll-Rand Canada Inc. as Sales Engr., Sydney, N.S. and St. John's, Nfld. 1952-56, Mgr. Carset Bit Div. Montreal H.O. 1956, Mgr. Rock Drill Div. H.O. 1957, Mgr. Moncton Br. 1959, Mgr. Mining Constr. & Indust. Sales 1961, Mgr. Montreal Br. 1963, Gen. Mgr. Sales H.O. 1965, Vice Pres. and Gen. Mgr. 1968, Pres. and Dir. 1969; mem. Machinery & Equipment Mfrs. Assn. Can.; Internat. Compressed Air & Gas Inst.; US-USSR Trade & Econ. Council; Colo. Sch. Mines Alumni Assn. (Dir.); Tau Beta Pi; recreation: golf; Clubs: St. James's (Montreal); Mount Royal (Montreal); Mining (New York City); Apple Ridge Country (Mahwah, N.J.); Home: 34 Grist Mill Lane, Upper Saddle River, N.J. 07458; Office: 200 Chestnut Ridge Rd., Woodcliff Lake, N.J. 07675.

WEST, Allen Sherman, Jr., B.Sc., Ph.D.; university professor; b. Worcester, Mass., 13 Aug. 1909; s. Allen Sherman and Grace May (Booth) W.; e. Mass. State Coll., B.Sc. 1931; Yale Univ., Ph.D. 1935; m. Mary Lucille, d. Dr. Harry Quinn, 30 Nov. 1946; Mgr. Environmental Policy, Nfld. and Labrador Hydro, 1975-78; Emeritus Prof. of Biology, Queen's Univ., 1974; Prof. of Biology, Queen's Univ., 1949-74; Forest Entomol. with U.S. Dept. Agric., engaged in research and control work in Ariz. and Cal. 1935-39; Prof. of Forest Entomol., Univ. of New Brunswick, 1939-43 (1st chair of forest entomol. in Can.); Assoc. Prof. of Biol., Queen's Univ., 1946-49; served in World War, 1943-46, with Candn. Army in Chem. Warfare Service with rank of Capt.; mem. Entomol. Soc. of Ont.; Entomol. Soc. of Can.; Am. Mosquito Control Assn.; Entomol. Soc. of Am.; United Church; Home: 208 Albert St., Kinston, Ont. K7L 3V3

WEST, Kenneth Albert, M.A., Ph.D.; industrial consultant; b. Edmonton, Alta., 25 Sept. 1916; s. John and Emma (Long) W.; e. Univ. of Brit. Columbia, M.A. 1939; McGill Univ., Ph.D. 1942; m. Irene, d. late Charles Pieper, 21 Dec. 1944; two d., Daphne Ruth, Linda Susan; Pres., Kenneth A. West Co. Ltd.; Dir., Stone & Webster Canada Ltd.; Kondo Enterprises Ltd.; gained experience in the oil industry in Can. and U.S., 1942-51; Chief Process Engr., Candn. Oil Cos. Ltd., 1951-60; apptd. Vice-Pres., 1960; Vice Pres., Shell Canada Ltd., 1963-67; Vice-Pres., Ont. Div., Candn. Cancer Soc.; mem., Assn. Prof. Engrs. Ont.; Chemical Inst. Can.; Am. Inst. Chemical Engrs.; Am. Petroleum Inst.; Engn. Inst. Can.; Extve. Comte., World Petroleum Cong.; Protestant; recreations: golf, Clubs: Rosedale Golf; National; Home: 5 James Foxway, Willowdale, Ont. M2K 2S2

WEST, William Arthur, B.A.Sc., M.B.S.; petroleum executive; b. Toronto, Ont. 19 Oct. 1934; s. Arthur Currie and Ruth Wilhelmina (Frankish) W.; e. Runnymede High Sch. Toronto 1952; Univ. of Toronto B.A.Sc. 1956; Univ. of W. Ont. M.B.S. 1958; m. Judith Rosamund d. James P. Norrie 19 July 1958; children: Jennifer, James, Sharon, Andrew; PRES., ESSO PETROLEUM CANADA, 1981- ; Dir. Interprovincial Pipe Line Ltd.; Trans Mountain Pipeline Ltd.; Portland and Montreal Pipelines; Div. Mgr. Cargo Trading Dept. Exxon International Inc. N.Y. 1970-71; Asst. Gen. Mgr. Logistics Dept. Imperial Oil 1971, Marketing Dept. 1973, Vice Pres. and Gen. Mgr. Marketing Dept. 1974-76; Extve. Asst. to Chrmn. Exxon Corp. N.Y. 1976-77; Sr. Vice Pres. Exxon International Inc. 1977-78; Vice-Pres. and Gen. Mgr. Logistics, Imperial Oil Ltd., 1978-81; Co-Chrmn. Ont. Coll. of Art Fund for the Future; mem. Assn. Prof. Engrs. Prov. Ont.; Bd. Trade Metrop. Toronto; recreations: golf, jogging, reading; Club: St. George's Golf & Country; Home: 248 Warren Rd., Toronto, Ont. M4V 2S8; Office: 558 St. Clair Ave. W., Toronto, Ont. M5W 2J8.

WESTAWAY, James Whitlock, B.Com.; executive; b. Regina, Sask. 21 Nov. 1912; s. late Charles Whitlock Clement and late Jessie Evelyn (Grobb) W.; e. Brantford (Ont.) Coll. Inst.; Univ. of Toronto B.Com. 1934; m. Mary Kathryn d. late Charles Glenholm Ellis Apl. 1937; children: Mary Lynn, James Glenholm, Peter Whitlock; CHRMN., BARBECON INC. 1977- ; Dir. The Excelsior Life Insurance Co.; Aetna Casualty Co. of Canada; Costain Ltd.; UTLAS; Pres., The Excelsior Life Insurance Co. 1967, Chrmn. 1975-77; Dir. Massey Hall; Toronto Mendelssohn Choir; Toronto Mendelssohn Choir Foundation; mem. Delta Upsilon; P. Conservative; United Church; recreations: golf, photography; Clubs: Toronto; University; Toronto Hunt; Toronto Arts & Letters; Tuson National Golf; Home: 30A Oriole Rd., Toronto, Ont. M4V 2E8; Office: 2300 Yonge St., Suite 1900, Toronto, Ont. M4P 1E4.

WESTELL, Anthony; journalist; b. Exeter, Devon, Eng., 27 Jan. 1926; s. John Wescombe and Blanche (Smedley) W.; e. Mount Radford Sch., Exeter, Eng.; m. Jeanne Margaret Collings, 10 Jan. 1950; children: Dan, Tracy; began career as Apprentice Reporter, "Express and Echo", Exeter, Eng., 1942-43, 1945-48; joined "Evening World", Bristol, Eng., 1948-49; Northcliffe Newspaper Group, London, Eng., 1949-55; apptd. Pol. Corr. for Group 1950-55 and occasional Columnist and Ed. Writer, "Sunday Express", London; became Dipl. Corr., "Evening Standard", London, 1955-56; joined "Globe & Mail", Toronto, as Reporter, 1956-59; mem. Ed. Bd., Chief Ed. Writer, Asst. to Ed. 1959-64; Chief, Ottawa Bureau 1964-69; Ottawa Ed., "Toronto Star" 1969-71, 73-74; Ottawa columnist, Ed. Page and Prof. of Journalism, Carleton Univ., 1972-73, 1975- ; Assoc. Ed. (N. Amer.), World Paper, Boston since 1978; Visiting Fellow, Inst. Candn. Studies, Carleton Univ., 1974-75; Senior Associate, Carnegie Endowment for Internat. Peace, N.Y. 1980; author, "Paradox — Trudeau as Prime Minister" 1972; "The New Society", 1977; served in 2nd World War with Royal Navy, 1943-46; mem., Newspaper Guild; recreations: reading, sailing; Clubs: National Press; Home: 81, Somerset St. West, Apt. 4, Ottawa, Ont. K2P 0H3; Office: School of Journalism, Carleton Univ., Colonel By Dr., Ottawa, Ont.

WESTLEY, William A., M.A., Ph.D., F.R.S.A. (1960); university professor; b. Chester, Penna., 17 May 1920; s. William Eyde and Grace (Meilkejohn) W.; e. Cornell Univ. (1938-40); Univ. of Chicago, 1940-42, 1946-51 (B.A. 1947, M.A. (Sociol.) 1948, Ph.D. (Sociol.) 1951); m. Margaret Frances, d. Lamar Weaver, Copperhill, Tenn., 13 Feb. 1943; children: David Neil, Frances Rae, Margaret Grace; DIR., INDUSTRIAL CENTRE McGILL UNIV., since 1966 (formerly Prof. of Sociol. and Anthropol. and Chrmn. of Dept.); Lectr. in Sociol. and Anthropol. and Chrmn. of Dept.); Lectr. in Sociol., Indiana Univ., 1948-50; joined McGill Univ. staff as Associate Professor 1951, Professor 1961; served in 2nd World War; 1st Lieut., U.S. Army Intelligence, 1942-45 (service in India and Burma); author of many articles in tech. journs.; Past Dir., John Howard Soc. of Montreal; Candn. Corrections Assn.; speaker and moderator on numerous Candn. T.V. programs dealing with social problems; Research Consultant to Defence Research Bd. on Crowd Control; recreations: tennis, badminton, swimming, reading. Office: 845 Sherbrooke St. W., Montreal, Que. H3A 2T5

WESTMAN, Albert Ernest Roberts, F.R.S.C. (1961), Ph.D., F.C.I.C.; chemist; b. Ottawa, Ont., 31 May 1900; s. Thomas and Florence Augusta (Collett) W.; e. Univ. of Toronto, B.A. (Chem.) 1921, M.A. (Phys. and Electro-

Chem.) 1922, Ph.D. 1924; m. Agnes Jean, d. Milton Havelock Minore, Bowmanville, Ont., 1925; children: Ellen Joan, Barbara Collett, Sheila Margaret; Research Assoc., Ceramics Engn. Experimental Stn., Illinois, 1924-28; Assoc. Prof., Dept. of Ceramics, Rutgers Univ., 1928-29; Dir., Dept. of Chem., Ont. Research Foundation, 1929-58; and Dir. of Research there, 1958-65; served in World War, 1914-18, as Flight Cadet, R.C.N.A.S., in Eng.; author "Phosphates Ceramics" 1977; Fellow, Am. Ceramic Soc., Inc.; Can. Ceramic Soc.; Soc. Glass Techn.; Am. Stat. Assoc.; Am. Soc. for Quality Control; rec'd. Frank Forrest Award, 1954; United Church; recreations: swimming, piano; Home: 35 Glenayr Rd., Toronto, Ont. M5P 3B9

WESTON, W. Galen, executive; b. Eng., 29 Oct. 1940; s. W. Garfield and Reta Lila (Howard) W.; m. Hilary Mary; Chrmn. George Weston Ltd.; Loblaw Cos. Ltd.; National Tea Co.; Wittington Investments Limited; Brown Thomas Group Ltd.; Dir., Candn. Imperial Bank of Commerce; Fortnum & Mason Limited; Assoc. British Foods Ltd.; Kelly, Douglas & Co., Ltd.; B.C. Packers Ltd.; Loblaws Ltd.; recreations: polo, tennis; Clubs: Granite; York; Toronto; Badminton & Raquet; Toronto Lawn Tennis; Address: Weston Centre, Suite 2001 — 22 St. Clair Ave. E., Toronto, Ont. M4T 2S3

WESTWATER, George Traill, M.A., F.F.A., F.C.I.A., A.S.A.; actuary; b. Hawick, Roxburgshire, Scot., 26 June 1911; s. Alexander and Christina (Henderson) W.; e. Edinburgh Univ., M.A. (1st Class Hons.) 1933; m. Phoebe Mary, d. George E. Moss, St. Helena, 12 Jan. 1944; one d. Judith Margaret; with present Standard Life Assnce. Co., Edinburgh, Scot., 1933-39; Montreal Que., 1946; Gen. Mgr., 1957; apptd. Extve. Dir., 1 Sept. 1966; retired 1976; served in World War, 1939-45, with R.N.V.R., Naval Meteorol. Service; Fellow, Candn. Inst. Actuaries; past Vice Pres., Faculty of Actuaries (Scotland); Anglican; recreation: golf; Clubs: Mt. Royal; Royal Montreal Golf; Home: 14 Willow Ave., Westmount, Que. H3Y 1Y2

WESTWOOD, John C. N., M.B., B.Ch.; b. Sonepur, India, 27 May 1917; s. John David and Ann McDougal (Paulin) W.; e. Trinity Coll., Cambridge Univ., B.A. 1939, M.B., B.Ch. 1942; London Royal Colls., M.R.C.S., L.R.C.P. 1942; Dipl. Bacteriol., London, 1947; m. Ruth Daphne, d. John Allez, Guernsey, Channel Islands, 6 Feb. 1945; children: Elizabeth, Diana Ruth; PROF. OF MICROBIOL., UNIV. OF OTTAWA and Chrmn. of Dept. there since 1966; Medical Microbiologist, Ottawa Gen. Hosp.; Consultant in Virology, Ottawa Civic Hosp.; House Physician to Med. Unit, St. Bartholomew's Hosp., 1942-43; seconded to Dept. of Bacteriol., Univ. Coll. Hosp., London and Sr. Bacteriol., Virus Reference Lab., Central Pub. Health Lab., Colindale, 1946-64; Dir. of Virus Unit with rank Sr. Principal Scient. Offr., 1954-55; Depy. Chief Scient. Offr., Microbiol. Research Estab., Ministry of Supply, Porton, Eng., 1955-63; joined Univ. of Ottawa as Assoc. Prof. of Bacteriol., 1963-65; served with R.A.M.C. 1943-46; has written over 50 scient. papers on virology, tissue cultures and nosocomial infections; Anglican; Home: 21 Briarcliffe Dr., Ottawa, Ont. K1J 6E3

WETMORE, Rt. Rev. James Stuart, B.S.Litt., D.D., bishop (P.Epis.); b. Hampton, N.B., 22 Oct. 1915; s. Charles Talbot and Alberta Mae (McCordic) W.; e. Hampton (N.B.) Consol. Sch.; Sussex (N.B.) High Sch. (Matric.); Univ. of King's Coll., B.A. 1938, L.Th. 1939, B.S.Litt. 1949, D.D. 1960; Yale Divinity Sch. 1947; m. Frances Howard, d. E. Wallace Robinson, Annapolis Royal and Bear River, N.S., 4 July 1940; children: Mrs. J. L. Faulds, Charles Edward, Stuart Andrew, Mrs. J. Bohun, Jane Robin; SUFFRAGAN BISHOP, DIOCESE OF NEW YORK, since 1960; Chaplain, Candn. Soc. of New York; made Deacon, All Saints Cath., Halifax, 1938; Cu-

rate, St. Anne's Parish Ch., Fredericton, N.B., 1939-41; o. Priest, Christ Ch. Cath., Fredericton, 1939; Rector, Westfield, N.B., 1941-43; St. James Ch., Saint John, N.B., 1943-47; Eastern Field Secy., Gen. Bd. of Religious Educ., Ch. of Eng. in Can., 1947-51, and Asst. to the Gen. Secy., 1951-53; Dir., Christian Educ., Epis. Diocese of New York, 1953-60; Canon (Hon.), Cath. of Saint John the Divine, N.Y.C.; el. Suffragan Bishop, Diocese of N.Y., 1959, consecrated, 1960; served in Princess Louise (N.B.) Hussars, 1929-32; King's O.T.C., Co. Commdr. and Adjt., 1933-39; Chaplain, No. 7 Dist. Depot, Fredericton, N.B., 1939-41, Reserve Chaplain, No. 7 Mil. Dist., 1943-47; Pres., Soldier Comfort Assn., Fredericton, 1939-40; mem., Bd. of Trustees, Windham House, N.Y.C., 1955-58; Vice-Pres., Metrop. Chapter, Relig. Educ. Assn., 1958-60; Vice-Pres., Prot. Epis. City Missions Soc., N.Y.; Pres., N.Y. Churchmen's Clericus, 1960; Pres., Richmond Fellowship of America, 1973-78; Convenor, Metrop. Mission Task Force, N.Y. Met. Area; mem., Presiding Bishop's Comte. on Evangelism; St. George's Soc., N.Y.; the Pilgrims of U.S.; Atlantic Union; Dept. Christian Educ. of Nat. Council, Prot. Epis. Ch. (1960-65); Secy., House of Bishops of Second Prov. 1960-1966; Chrmn. Extve. Comm., Internat. Council of Religions; mem., Bd. of Dir., N.Y. State Council of Churches; Prot. Council of N.Y.; mem. Dept. of Ch. Renewal, Nat. Council of Chs.; Secy.-Treas. Assn. for Christian Mission in City of N.Y.; Vice Pres., Ch. Plan Comm. for N.Y. Metrop. Area; Pres. (1958) Friends of Kings Coll., Halifax Inc.; Pres., Episcopal Housing Corp.; Good Shepherd-on-the-Island Corp.; St. Peter's School, Peekskill, N.Y.; Anglican Soc.; Second Province of Episcopal Ch.; Chrmn., House of Bishops Comte. on Educ.; Sub-Prelate, Order St. John Jerusalem (Am. Chapter); Secy., Council of Diocese of N.Y.; Affiliate, Soc. of the Atonement; Pres., U.S. Friends of the Anglican Diocese of the Arctic; Home: 7 Fox Meadow Rd., Scarsdale, N.Y. 10583; Office: Synod House, Cathedral Heights, New York 10025, N.Y.

WETTLAUFER, John J., B.A., M.B.A., LL.D.; educator; b. S. Easthope Twp. Ont. 2 Apl. 1918; s. Jacob W. and late Ida (Schwantz) W.; e. Univ. of W. Ont. B.A. 1950, M.B.A. 1951; Waterloo Lutheran Univ. LL.D. (hon) 1967; University fo Calgary LL.D. (hon) 1979; m. Florence Christine d. late Theodore C. Haberer 20 June 1953; children: John Mark, Anne Christine; PROF. OF BUSINESS ADM. UNIV. OF W. ONT.; Dir. London Life Insurance Co.; Hayes Dana Ltd.; S.C. Johnson Ltd.; Dir. Marketing Mang. Course 1953-63; Dean Sch. of Business Adm. present univ. 1963-78; Dir. Candn. Extve. Service Overseas; London Symphony Orchestra Assoc.; mem. Adv. Council Federal Dept. Indust. Trade & Comm.; Trustee Spencer Hall Foundation; Past Gov. Waterloo Coll.; rec'd Award of Merit Univ. W. Ont. Alumni Assn.; co-author 'Canadian Business Administration' 1957; 'Business Administration in Canada' 1961; Study No. 17, report Task Force on Labour Relations 1968; Hon. Fellow, Inst. Candn. Bankers; Hon. Life mem. London Personnel Assn.; Past Dir. London Chamber Comm.; mem. Acad. Mang.; Indust. Relations Research Assn.; Candn. Assn. Business Schs. (Past Chrmn.); Recreations: swimming, boating and music; Lutheran; Home: 411 Lawson Rd., London, Ont. N6G 1X7; Office: London, Ont. N6A 3K7.

WEVERS, John William, Th.D., D.D., F.R.S.C.; educator; b. Baldwin, Wis. 4 June 1919; s. Ben and Wilemina (Te Grootenhuis) W.; e. Calvin Coll. B.A. 1940; Calvin Semy. Th.B. 1943; Princeton Theol. Semy. and Princeton Univ. Th.D. 1945, post-doctoral work Arabic, Islamic Hist. Indo-European Philol. Sanskrit 1945-47; Dropsie Coll. work in Akkadian, Aramaic Dialects, Ugaritic 1947-48; Knox Coll. D.D. 1973; m. Grace Della d. late Rev. Samuel G. Brondsema 23 May 1942; children: Robert Dick, John William Jr., Harold George, James Merrit; PROF. OF NEAR EASTERN STUDIES, UNIV. OF TORONTO since 1975; Teaching Fellow, Dept. Biblical

Langs. Princeton Theol. Semy. 1944-46, Lectr. in Old Testament and Semitic Langs. 1946-48, Asst. Prof. 1948-51; Asst. Prof. of Oriental Langs. Univ. Coll. Univ. of Toronto 1951 becoming Assoc. Prof. and Prof. of Near E. Studies; Chrmn. Grad. Dept. Near E. Studies 1972-75; Chmn of Dept., Near East Studies, 1975-80; Fellow Rockefeller Foundation studying Modern Arabic Dialects and Modern Islamic Movements in Near East 1954; CBC Teacher series 'Let's Speak English' 1961-62; Site Supvr. Archaeol. Excavations of Jerusalem summers 1962, 1963; Lectr. Theol. Faculty Univ. of Leiden 1954, Lund 1954, Göttingen 1971, Uppsala 1971, Groningen 1972, Madrid 1972; Gov. Central Hosp. Toronto since 1963 (Chrmn. 1967-80); Pres., Central Hosp. Foundation, since 1980; Vice Chrmn. Hosp. Council Metrop. Toronto 1973-74 (Chrmn. 1974-75); Gov., Ont. Hosp. Assn. (Pres. 1978-79); el. Corr. mem. Akademie der Wissenschaften in Göttingen, Philologisch-historische Klasse 1972; el. Fellow, Royal Soc. of Canada 1976; Ed-in-Chief 'Canadian Journal of Linguistics' 1960-67; author 'The Way of the Righteous' 1961; 'A Commentary on the Book of Ezekiel' 1969; 'Genesis, Septuaginta' 1973; 'Text History of the Greek Genesis' 1974; 'Deuteronomium, Septuaginta' 1977; 'Text History of the Greek Deuteronomy' 1978; "Numerii, Septucginta", 1981; co-author 'Let's Speak English' 4 vols. 1960; reviews and articles on linguistics, Hebrew studies, Semitic Grammar, Septuagint in various internat. journs.; mem. Soc. Biblical Lit.; Oriental Club Toronto; Internat. Organ. Septuagint & Cognate Studies (Pres.); Presbyterian; recreation: Scottish country dancing; Club: Arts & Letters; Home: 116 Briar Hill Ave., Toronto, Ont. M4R 1H9; Office: 280 Huron St., Toronto, Ont. M5S 1A1.

WEYANT, Robert George, M.A., Ph.D.; educator; b. Jersey City, N.J., 27 July 1933; s. late Edgar Merrill and late Emma Henrietta (Haberdenk) W.; e. Lafayette Coll., B.A. 1955; Kent State Univ., M.A. 1957; Univ. of Iowa, Ph.D. 1960; m. Doris Joan, d. late John J. Barry, Aug. 1955; two s., Stephen Barry, David Thomas; Prof. of Psychol., Univ. of Calgary since 1970 and mem. Bd. of Govs.; Asst. Prof., St. Lawrence Univ., 1960, Assoc. Prof. 1964-65; Assoc. Prof. present Univ. 1965-70, Asst. Dean present faculty 1967-68, Vice Dean 1968-69, Dean 1972-75; mem. Council, Banff Sch. of Fine Arts; Bd. Dirs., Archives Hist. of Psychol., Univ. of Akron; rec'd Prov. of Alta. Achievement Award in Psychol.; Nat. Science Foundation, Nat. Research Council and Can. Council Grants; Ed. Bd., "The Journal of the History of Behavioral Sciences"; "An Essay on the Origin of Human Knowledge" (by Etienne Bonnot), 1971; author of numerous papers; Fellow, Am. Psychol. Assn.; Candn. Assn. Deans Arts & Science (Chrmn. 1973-74); Am. Assn. Advanc. Science; Hist. of Sci. Soc.; Internat. Soc. Hist. Behavioral & Social Sciences; Psi Chi; Sigma Xi; Bd. of Dirs., Candn Club, Calgary; Home: 2015 7th St. S. W., Calgary Alta, T2T 2X1

WHALLEY, Edward, Ph.D., D.I.C., D.Sc. ; chemist; b. Darwen, U.K. 20 June 1925; s. Edward and Doris (Riding) W.; e. St. Mary's Coll. Blackburn 1941; Blackburn Tech. Coll. 1941-43; Imp. Coll. London B.Sc., A.R.C.S. 1945, Ph.D., D.I.C. 1949, D.Sc. 1963; m. Isabel Elizabeth d. late James Gillespie 25 Aug. 1956; children: Brian, Monica, Kevin; PRINC. RESEARCH OFFR. AND HEAD OF HIGH PRESSURE SEC., DIVISION OF CHEMISTRY, NAT. RESEARCH COUNCIL OF CAN. since 1961; Lectr. Royal Tech. Coll. Salford, U.K. 1948-50; Post-doctoral Fellow, Nat. Research Council Can. Ottawa 1950-52, Asst. Research Offr. 1952, Assoc. Research Offr. 1955, Sr. Research Offr. 1959; Sessional Lectr. Univ. of Ottawa Dept. Chem. Engn. Dept. Chem. 1967, 1969; Visiting Prof. Univ. of W. Ont. 1969; Univ. of Kyoto 1974-75; co-ed. "Physics and Chemistry of Ice" 1973; author or co-author 220 research papers phys. chem. high pressures and related topics; Candn. Ed. "Accidents in North American Mountaineering" 1976-80, mem. Alpine Club Can. (Chrmn. Ottawa Sec. 1970-74, Chrmn. Safety

Comte. 1975-80, Silver Rope 1979 Eastern Vice Pres. 1978-80, Pres. 1980-); mem. Royal Soc. Can. (Assoc. Hon. Treas. 1969-71, Assoc. Hon. Secy. and Chrmn. Awards Comte. 1971-74, Hon. Sec., 1974-77; Ed. Acad. III 1972-74 Chmn., Devel. Comte. 1981-82); Chem. Inst. Can. (Fellow, 1968, Chrmn. Phys. Chem. Div. 1971-72); Internat. Glaciol. Soc.; Am. Phys. Soc.; Internat. Assn. Advanc. High Pressure Science & Technol. (Hon. Treas. since 1975); Internat. Assn. Properties Steam; Candn. Nat. Comte. Properties Steam (Founding mem. and 1st Chrmn. since 1973); Silver Jubilee Medal 1977; R. Catholic; recreations: mountain climbing, skiing; Home: 175 Blenheim Dr., Ottawa, Ont. K1L 5B8; Office: Ottawa, Ont. K1A 0R9.

WHALLEY, George, C.D., M.A., Ph.D., D.Litt., D.C.L., F.R.S.L., F.R.S.C.; university professor; author; poet; critic; b. Kingston, Ont., 25 July 1915; s. Very Rev. Arthur Francis Cecil, M.A., D.D., and Dorothy (Quirk) W.; e. St. Alban's Sch., Brockville, Ont. (1922-30); Bishop's Univ., B.A. 1935, M.A. 1948; Oriel Coll., Oxford, B.A. 1939, M.A. 1945; King's Coll., London, Ph.D. 1950; Carleton Univ., D.Litt., 1977; Univ. Sask., D.Litt. 1979; Bishop's Univ. D.C.L., 1979; m. Elizabeth Cecilia Muriel, d. Capt. A. B. Watts R.N. (retired), Tewkesbury, Eng. 25 July 1944; children: Katharine Cecilia, Christopher Gilbert, Emily Elizabeth; as undergrad., Organist, Bishop's Univ. 1932-35; Schoolmaster, Rothesay Coll. School, N.B., 1935-36, 1939-40; Rhodes Scholar for Quebec 1936; rowed bow in record-breaking Oriel coxwainless IV, Visitors' Cup, Henley Royal Regatta, 1938; Captain of Boats, Oriel Coll., Oxford, 1938-39; trial cap., Oxford Univ. VIII, 1939; Lecturer to Assistant Professor of English, Bishop's University, 1945-58; joined Queen's University as Assistant Prof. of English 1950; Visiting Prof. Univ. of Wisconsin, 1962; James Cappon Prof. English, Queen's Univ. 1962-70, 1977-80 (Head of Dept. 1962-67, 1977-80); Nuffield Travelling Fellowship, 1956-57; John Simon Guggenheim Mem. Foundation Fellowship 1967-68; Killam Sr. Research Scholarship 1973-75; served in 2nd World War; Sub-Lieutenant R.C.N.V.R. June 1940; on loan to R.N. 1940-44 (general service and special duties); Lieutenant-Commander, R.C.N.V.R. 1943; Senior Staff course, R.N.C. Greenwich, 1944; served with R.C.N. April-September 1945; active Reserve till 1956; C.O., H.M.C.S. "Cataraqui" 1952-56; Commdr., R.C.N.(R) 1953; now retired; Royal Humane Soc. Bronze Medal for Saving Life at Sea, 1941; Kingston Symphony Assn. (Pres. 1963-70); Adv. Comte. on Candn. Service Coll. 1962-67; mem., Assn. of Candn. Univ. Teachers of English (Pres., 1958-59); Humanities Assn.; Charles Lamb Soc.; Candn. Federation for the Humanities; Publications: "Poems 1939-1944", 1946; "No Man an Island", 1948; "Poetic Process", 1953, 1967, 1973; "Coleridge and Sara Hutchinson", 1955; "The Legend of John Hornby", 1962, 1977; 1980; Editor, "Selected Poems of George Herbert Clarke", 1954; "Writing in Canada", 1956; "A Place of Liberty", 1964 "Death in the Barren Ground: The Diary of Edgar Christian," 1980; Christopher Pepys, 1914-1974; "Marginalia of S. T. Coleridge" Vol. 1 (of 5), 1980, for "Collected Works of S. T. Coleridge"; numerous articles, essays and reviews, chiefly on S. T. Coleridge and early 19th century literature, poetics and literary criticism; broadcast talks and poetry readings for CBC and BBC; feature scripts for radio and television; Anglican; recreations: music, typography, skiing; Home: R.R. No. 1, Hartington, Ont. K0H 1W0

WHEALY, Hon. Arthur Carrick, LL.B.; judge; b. Toronto, Ont. 30 July 1929; s. Arthur Treloar, D.S.C. and BAR, D.F.C. and Margaret Agnes (Carrick) W.; e. Upper Can. Coll. Toronto 1948; Royal Mil. Coll.; Univ. of Toronto; Dalhousie Law Sch. LL.B. 1958; m. Anna Damasdy 1979; two d. Elisabeth Honore 1959, Victoria Anne Marie 1963; JUDGE, CO. AND DIST. COURTS OF ONT. since 1978; called to Bar of N.S. 1958, Ont. 1961; cr. Q.C. 1975; Sr. Adv. Counsel, Dept. of Justice (Can.) 1958 — 67; private law practice Toronto 1967 — 78; Lieut. with Q.O.R. Reserve 1949 — 51, Active Service 1951 — 54; Lectr. Bar Admission Course Osgoode Hall 1970 — 78; Founding Dir. and Past Pres. Criminal Lawyers Assn.; mem. Advocates Soc. (Dir. 1970 — 71); Home: 310 Oriole Parkway, Toronto, Ont. M5P 2H5; Office: 361 University Ave., Toronto, Ont. M5G 1T3.

WHEELER, John Oliver, B.A.Sc., Ph.D., F.G.S.A., F.R.S.C.; geologist, b. Mussoorie, India 19 Dec. 1924; s. Edward Oliver and Dorothea (Danielsen) W.; e. Shawnigan Lake Sch. Vancouver Island, B.C. 1942; Univ. of B.C. B.A.Sc. (Geol. Engn.) 1947; Columbia Univ. Ph.D. (Geol.) 1956; m. Nora Jean d. late James H. C. Hughes 17 May 1952; two d. Kathleen Anna (Mrs. T.R. Hunter), Jennifer Margaret (Mrs. R.D. Crompton); RESEARCH SCIENTIST, CORD. DIV. GEOL. SURVEY OF CANADA since 1979; Geol., Geol. Survey of Can. Ottawa, 1951-61, Vancouver 1961-65, Research Scient. Vancouver 1965-70, head of Cordilleran & Pacific Margin Sec. 1967-70, Research Mgr. Ottawa 1970-79, Chief of Regional & Econ. Geol. Div. 1970-73; Depy. Dir. Gen. 1973-79; Visiting Prof. Univ. of Toronto 1972; Instr. Mountain Warfare Sch., Pacific Command 1944; rec'd Queen's Silver Jubilee Medal 1977; author various scient. papers, monographs and geol. maps on geol. of Central and S. Yukon, S.E. B.C., glacial geol. S. Yukon, tectonics and structure S. part W. Candn. Cordillera, recent glacial fluctuations in Selkirk Mts.; Fellow, Geol. Assn. Can. (Pres. 1970-71); Dir. Can. Geol. Foundation (Pres. 1975-79); Candn. Geoscience Council (Pres., 1981); mem. Candn. Inst. Mining & Metall.; Alpine Club Can.; Am. Alpine Club; Anglican; recreations: mountaineering, skiing, hiking; Home: 3333 Mathers Ave., W. Vancouver, B.C. V7V 2K6; Office: 6th Floor, 100 West Pender St., Vancouver, B.C. V6B 1R8.

WHEELER, John St. Clair, executive; b. Brackley, Eng. 17 Dec. 1918; s. John and Clara Elizabeth W.; e. Univ. of Mich., Sch. of Engn. 1939-40, 1945-46; Univ. of Toronto, Sch. of Practical Science 1947-49; m. Mary Katherine, d. late Dr. John A. Bothwell, 26 May 1944; children: Peter Alexander, Paul Frederick, Wendy Elizabeth, James Stuart Bothwell; PRESIDENT, SAXONY COURT ESTATES INC.; consultants; served with RCASC 1940-45; Founding Chrmn. and mem. Adv. Bd., St. Georges Coll., Toronto; mem. Am. Soc. for Testing & Materials (Past Pres.); Candn. Standards Assn.; Anglican; recreation: flying, choral musician, guncollector; Clubs: Boulevard; Toronto Lions (Past Pres. Runnymede) Bd. of Trade, Metro Tor.; Address: 1354 Tecumseh Pk. Dr., Mississauga, Ont. L5H 2W6

WHEELER, Lucile, O.C.; skier; b. 1935; m. June 1960; one d., one s.; finished third in Womens Downhill at Cortina d'Ampezzo, Italy 1956, winning Canada's first Olympic Medal for skiing; won Women's Downhill, Hohnekamm Tournament, Kitzbühel, Austria 1957, also combined Title there; World Championship Downhill Title, and Giant Slalom Title, Bad Gastein, Austria, 1958; served on Nat. Fitness Council for 2 years; named Canadian Athlete of the Year, 1958; 1st Canadian to receive Perry Medal awarded by Ski Club of Gt. Britain; 1st skier to win Lou Marsh Trophy (1958); Address: Knowlton, Que. J0E 1V0

WHEELER, Orson Shorey, R.C.A. (1954), D.C.L.; sculptor; b. Barnston, Que., 17 Sept. 1902; s. Fred Hollis and Mary (Moulton) W.; e. Bishop's Univ., B.A.; Roy. Candn. Acad. classes, Montreal, Que.; Cooper Union, N.Y.; Beaux-Arts Inst. of Design, N.Y.; Nat. Acad. of Design, N.Y.; Part Time Lecturer, Fine Arts, Concordia University, Sir. Geo. Williams Campus, 1975- ; Chrmn. of the Permanent Collection, Candn. Handicraft Guild 1944-64; Co-Chairman 1964-68; has executed bust for Canadian Pacific Ltd.; Jacobs Monument, Montreal, Que.; bust of the Rt. Hon. Sir Lyman Duff in Supreme Court Bldg., Ot-

tawa, Ont.; Morrill Memorial, Stanstead, Que.; sculpture in Court House, Montreal, Que.; Montreal Children's Hosp.; King's College, Halifax, N.S.; Bishop's Univ., Sir George Williams Univ.; Prov. Archives, Que.; Dow Chemical of Can. Ltd.; T.V. Film "Quebec Arts '58'', produced by C.B.C.; Monument to Sen. J. T. Hackett, Stanstead, Que.; rep. in Montreal Museum of Fine Arts and in private colls.; has made over 200 scale models of famous bldgs. of the world, to illustrate the hist. of architecture (exhn. of these models, Prot. School Bd. Greater Montreal & McGill Univ. 1971); Lectr. in Fine Arts, Sir George Williams Univ. Montreal 1931-74; Sessional Lectr. in Arch., McGill Univ., Montreal, 1949-75; mem., Sculptor's Soc. of Can. (Treas. 1952-67); awarded Centennial Medal; D.C.L., Bishop's Univ. 1976; Address: 1435 Drummond St., Montreal, Que. H3G 1W4

WHELAN, Hon. Eugene Francis, P.C. (1972), M.P.; poiitician; farmer; b. Amherstberg, Ont., 11 July 1924; s. Charles B. and Francis L. (Kelly) W.; e. Separate Schs., Anderdon Twp., Ont.; Gen. Amherst High Sch., Windsor, Ont.; Walkerville (Ont.) Vocational & Tech. Sch.; m. Elizabeth, d. Frank Pollinger, Kingsville , Ont., 30 Apl. 1960; children: Theresa Ann, Susan Elizabeth, Catherine, Frances; RETURNED AS MIN. OF AGRICULTURE, CAN. Feb. 18, 1980; def. Lib. Cand. for Essex S., Prov. g.e. 1959; el. to H. of C., g.e. 1962 and re-el. since; Parlty. Secy. to Min. of Forestry and to Min. of Fisheries 1968; Min. of Agric. Fed. Gov. 1972-79; Former Reeve; Twp. of Anderdon; Warden, Essex Co., Ont. 1962; Past mem. Bd. Govs., Ont. Fed. of Agric.; Past Pres., Essex Co. Fed. of Agric.; Past Dir., Un. Co-ops. of Ont.; Harrow Farmers Co-op; Ont. Winter Wheat Producers Marketing Bd.; Past mem. Local Sch. Bd.; Kt. of Columbus; Liberal; R. Catholic; Club: Lions; Home: 727 Front Rd. N., Amherstberg, Ont. N9V 2V6; Office: Sir John Carling Bldg., Carling Ave., Ottawa, Ont. K1A 0C5

WHELAN, Harry Joseph, B.Sc.; construction executive; b. Vancouver, B.C. 20 Jan. 1922; s. Patrick J. and Helen D. (McNally) W.; e. Univ. of Sask., B.Sc. (Engn.) 1945; m. Margaret Eileen Hambly, d. Dr. V. T. Mooney, Toronto, Ont. 21 Sept. 1946; children: H. Lee, Tracy Lynn, Vicki Janice; PRES. & DIR., LUMMUS CANADA INC. since 1974; Dir., R & I Ramtite Canada Limited; Rayrock Resources Ltd.; Discovery Mines; Camlaren Mines; Longford Equipment Internat. Ltd.; joined Co. 1960, assignments London, England, Houston, Texas, Montreal, Toronto, apptd. Gen. Mgr. 1963, Vice Pres. 1967; mem. Assn. Prof. Engrs. Ont., Que. and Alta.; Dir. Candn. Nuclear Assn.; Candn. Pulp & Paper Inst.; Candn. Inst. Mining & Metall.; Protestant; recreation: golf; Club: York Downs Golf; Calgary Golf and Country; Home: Apt. 407, 1555 Finch Ave. E., Willowdale, Ont. M2J 4X9; Office: 255 Consumers Rd., Toronto, Ont. M2J 4H4

WHILLANS, Morley Gray, M.D.; b. Man., 22 Aug. 1911; s. Rev. James William and Olive (Dryden) W.; e. Univ. of Liverpool and Univ. of Toronto, M.D. 1935; m. Olive ("Obi"), d. John Noble, Toronto, Ont., 1 July 1939; children: Ian M., Penelope J., Timothy P.; Interne, Hamilton Gen. Hosp., 1935-37; Fellowships, Banting Inst., Univ. of Toronto, Pathology, 1937-38; Neuropathology, 1938-39; Harvard Univ. Neurology, 1939-40; Consultant Neurology, Ont. Dept. of Health, 1940-41; Head, Dept. of Pharmacol., Dalhousie Univ., 1945-48; Dir., Biol. Research, Defence Research Bd., 1948-50; Supt., Defence Research Med. Labs., 1950-55; Prof. Banting & Best Dept. of Med. Research, Univ. of Toronto, 1954-55; Asst. Chief Scientist and Dir. of Biosciences Research, Defence Research Bd., 1955-63; Vice Chrmn., Aerospace Med. Panel AGARD (NATO), 1952-55; Chief, Canadian Defence Research Staff, London (Eng.), 1963-68, Adv. Career Devel., DRB, 1968-72, when retired; served in 2nd World War with R.C.A.F., 1941-45, engaged in aviation med. research; has publ. papers on pathology, aviation med., pharmacology, physiol., survival techniques; Hon. mem., Phi

Rho Sigma; Protestant; recreations: photography, sketching, cabinet making; Exec. Secy., Comte. on Behalf of Colourblind Drivers; Clubs: Union Club of B.C.; Home: c/o R.R. #2, Galiano Island, B.C. V0N 1P0

WHITAKER, William Denis, D.S.O.; company president; b. Calgary, Alta., 27 Feb. 1915; s. Guy S. and Bertha (Moore) W.; e. Univ. of Toronto Schs., grad. 1933; Roy. Mil. Coll. of Can., grad. 1937; comnd. as Lieut., Royal Hamilton Light Inf. (WR); m. Shelagh Dunwoody, 9 Feb. 1980; children: Gail, Clarke, Michael; PRES., W. DENIS WHITAKER & ASSOCIATES LTD.; Dir., William Mara Co. Ltd.; Scintrex Ltd.; Asst. to Supt., Stanley Works of Can., Hamilton, Ont., 1937-39; Extve. Dir., Hamilton Centennial Celebration, 1946; Comm. Mgr., Radio Stn. CHML, 1946-61; Vice-Pres., O'Keefe Brewing Co. Ltd., Toronto, Apl. 1962, Pres., 1962-65; Pres., Radio Sales Bureau, 1965-67; served in 2nd World War, 1939-46; discharged with rank of Brigadier; C.O. Third Infantry Brigade till retired, 1951; Hon. Colonel, Royal Hamilton Light Infantry since 1973; mem., Executive Committee, Dir., Canadian Equestrian Team; Dir., Canadian Olympic Assn.; Dir., Candn. Olympic Trust; Anglican; recreations: hunting, squash, water skiing; Clubs: Hamilton Hunt (Master); Oakville Badminton and Racquet (Toronto); Home: 173 Chartwell Rd., Oakville, Ont. L6J 3Z7; Office: Burns Fry Ltd., Suite 5000, First Canadian Place, P.O. Box 150, Toronto, Ont. M5X 1H3.

WHITE, Adrian M.S., F.C.A.; banker; b. Kent, Eng., 15 Aug. 1940; e. C.A. 1964, F.C.A. 1982; m. Elaine Margaret 10 Sept. 1966; children: Malcolm, Catherine; VICE PRES. CAPITAL FUNDING, BANK OF MONTREAL 1981- ; articled with Coopers & Lybrand 1962-64; Acting Treas. Rothesay Paper Corp. 1965; Asst. Treas. Genstar Ltd. 1967-71; Treas. Brinco Ltd. and Churchill Falls (Labrador) Corp. 1971-75; Treas. Algoma Steel Corp. Ltd. 1975-80; Vice Pres. Finance Little Long Lac Group, Toronto 1980; mem. Ont. Inst. C.A.'s (Council 1977-), Extve. 1979-); Que. Inst. C.A.'s; Financial Extves. Inst. Can.; Prof. Devel. Comte. Financial Extves. Inst. New York; Internat. Fiscal Assn.; Candn. Tax Foundation; Club: Boulevard; United Church; Home: 72 Sir Williams Lane, Islington, Ont. M9A 1V3; Office: 1 First Canadian Place, Toronto, Ont. M5X 1A1

WHITE, Arthur Walter; mine executive and financier; b. Guelph, Ont., 26 Mar. 1911; s. late Arthur Walter and late Elizabeth Ann (Payne) W.; e. Public and High Schs., Hamilton, Ont.; m. Agnes Isobel, d. late Dr. James M. McIntyre, Ottawa, Ont., 25 Oct. 1939; children: Harvey Vance, Nancy Evelyn, Kathleen Lorna; CHRMN OF BD., DICKENSON MINES LTD.; Pres., Langis Silver and Cobalt Mining Co. Ltd.; Tundra Gold Mines Ltd.; Kam-Kotia Mines Limited; Mid-North Engineering Services Ltd.; Nickel Rim Mines Ltd.; and other mining Co's.; Dir., Brewis & White Ltd.; Bishop Building Materials Ltd., etc.; mem., entered into field of mine financing, 1939, after wide experience in the fields of banking and ins.; Pres., Brewis & White Ltd., 1943-60; formed the present firm in 1943 and inc. in 1946, and has been responsible for the opening of four successful mines; Conservative; United Church; recreations: fishing, skating, curling, boating, skiing; Clubs: Engineer's; Canadian (New York) Toronto Board of Trade; Home: RR #1, Mono Centre, Orangeville, Ont. L9W 2Y8; Office: Suite 600, 65 Queen St. W., Toronto, Ont. M5H 2M5

WHITE, Cecil Garfield, B.A., F.S.A., F.C.I.A.; insurance executive; b. Toronto, Ont., 23 November 1919; e. Oakwood Coll. Inst., Toronto; Univ. of Toronto, B.A. (Hons. Math.) 1942; Sr. Offrs. Course in Adm., Civil Service Can.; Advanced Mang. Course, Princeton Univ. (Metrop. Life Ins. Co.); m. Florence Irene Peterkin, 31 Dec. 1944; one d. Patricia Leslie; VICE PRESIDENT, METROPOLITAN LIFE INSURANCE COMPANY, since 1970; Senior Actuary, Fed. Dept. of Ins., 1949-59; joined pres-

ent Co. as Extve. Asst. 1959, Asst. Vice Pres. 1960, Third Vice Pres. 1966, served with R.N. in Brit. Isles, Mediterranean, N. and S. Atlantic and Indian Oceans, 1941-45; rank on discharge Lt.-Commdr.; Pres., Candn. Assn. Accident & Sickness Insurers, 1971-72; Candn. Inst. Actuaries 1974-75; Ottawa Ch., Financial Extves. Inst. 1975-76; Men's Canadian Club of Ottawa, 1976-78; Mem. Bd. of Governors, Soc. of Actuaries, 1975-79; Dir., Financial Executives Inst., 1981-84; Anglican; recreation: music; art; Home: 12 Chinook Cres., Nepean, Ont. K2H 7E1; Office: 99 Bank St., Ottawa, Ont. K1P 5A3

WHITE, Cyril, Q.C., LL.B.; b. Ballymahon, Ireland, 20 Dec. 1921; s. John Dunlop and Anna Louise (Cunningham) W.; e. Elem. and High Schs. Vancouver; B.C. Sch. of Pharm & Science; Prov. Normal Sch.; Univ. of B.C. LL.B. 1949; m. Mildred Mary, d. late Francis Arthur Dobbin, 21 May 1949; two d. Marilyn Louise, Sharon Elizabeth; read law with Henry Smilie; called to Bar of B.C. 1949; cr. Q.C. 1969; PARTNER, BOUGHTON & CO., BARRISTERS, since 1976; Sr. Partner, White, Shore, Davies & Co. 1949-62; Magistrate, City of Vancouver, 1962-68; Chrmn. B.C. Workmen's Compensation Bd. 1968-73; Chief Judge Prov. Court B.C. and Chrmn. Judicial Council for B.C. 1971-73; Pres. and Chief Extve. Offr. Vancouver Stock Exchange 1973-76; served with Candn. Army 1942-47, Candn. Mil. HQ London, Eng.; mem. Vancouver Zoning Bd. Appeal 1959-62; Past Pres. Grandview Br. Royal Candn. Legion; Past Offr. Vancouver E. Lions; Grandview Community Assn.; Grandview Chamber Comm.; Past Dir. Easter Seals; Hon. mem. Indust. First Aid Attendants Assn.; Hon. Vice Pres. St. John's Ambulance Assn.; mem. B.C. Consistory; named Offr. Order St. John Jerusalem 1970; mem. Vancouver Bar Assn.; B.C. Bar Assn.; Candn. Bar Assn.; Law Soc. B.C.; Shriner; Freemason; Protestant; recreations: hunting, fishing, boating; Clubs: Terminal City; Arbutus; Vancouver Gun; Home: 7319 Laburnum, Vancouver, B.C. V6P 5N2; Office: 1100 Melville St., Vancouver, B.C. V6E 4B4

WHITE, Denis Naldrett, M.A., M.D., F.A.C.P., F.R.C.P.; editor, biomedical research; b. Bristol, England, 10 June 1916; s. Dr. Percy Walter and Ethelind Charlotte (Chambers) W.; e. Clifton Coll., England; Gonville and Caius College, Cambridge; London Hosp. Med. Sch.; m. Elizabeth Hogg, d. Dr. Allan Martin, 17 Sept. 1938; children: Dawn Charmaine, Martin Naldrett, Elizabeth Ann, Denis Anthony; Prof. Emeritus, Queen's Univ.; author of "Ultrasonic Encephalography"; "Ultrasound in Medical Diagnosis"; "Ultrasonic Encephalography II"; and over 100 scient. papers on the subject; Ed.-in-chief "Ultrasound in Medicine and Biology" and "Ultrasound in Biomedicine" series; Fellow, Amer Inst. Ultrasound in Med. (former Pres.); hon. mem., Yugoslav Union of Soc. of Ultrasound in Med.; Senior mem., Amer. Neurological Assoc.; Amer. Inst. of Neurology; former Prof. of Medicine (Neurology), Queen's Univ.; Home and Office 230 Alwington Place, Kingston, Ont. K7L 4P8;

WHITE, Donald Allen; manufacturer; b. Toronto, Ont., 7 June 1913; s. Frederick Charles and late Mabel Clair (Griswold) W.; e. Stratford (Ont.) Coll. Inst.; Shaw Business Schs.; m. Zeita Alberta, d. the late James D. Mason, 6 Aug. 1938; children: Donald Richard, Dennis James Frederick; CHMN. OF THE BD., HUNTINGTON LABORATORIES LTD.; Pres., Donald A. Manufacturing Co. Ltd.; former Chrmn., Bd. Govs., Humber Coll. of Applied Arts & Technol.; with C.N. Rlys., 1929-31; engaged in sales work, 1932-34; Clerk and later Dept. Mgr., Standard Tube Co. Ltd., Woodstock, Ont., 1934-39; Gen. Mgr., Metal Fabricators Ltd., Woodstock and Tillsonburg, 1939-49; served in Reserve Army as Capt.; Conservative; United Church; recreation: philately; Clubs: Kiwanis (Kingsway); Ochtawan (Toronto); Home: 58 Riverwood Parkway, Toronto, Ont. M8Y 4E5; Office: 15 Victoria Crescent, Bramalea, Ont. L6T 1E3

WHITE, Evan William; real estate executive; b. Verdun, Que. 3 Sept. 1934; s. Charles Herbert and Gladys Victoria (Lewis) W.; e. Westmount (Que.) High Sch.; m. Maureen Ann Rowell 16 Aug. 1958; children: Jennifer, Joanne, Evan, Jeffrey, David; EXEC. VICE PRES., BUS. DEVEL., A. E. LePAGE LIMITED; since 1977; Dir. A. E. LePage Ltd.; A. E. LePage (Prairies) Ltd.; Canlea Ltd.; Delta Hotels Ltd.; joined Westmount Realties Co. 1950 serving in Appraisal, Property Mang., Invest. and Comm. Leasing Divs. becoming Mgr. Comm. Leasing and Invest. Divs.; Extve. Vice pres. and subsequently Pres. A. E. LePage & Westmount Realties Inc. 1973; mem. Candn. Inst. Realtors; Protestant; recreations: farming, flying, skiing, tennis, golf; Clubs: Cambridge; Knowlton (Que.) Golf; National; Home: Tannery Hill Farm, RE.R. 2, King City, Ont. L0G 1K0; Office: (P.O. Box 100) 3300-Toronto-Dominion Centre, Toronto, Ont. M5K 1G8.

WHITE, Fredrick Thornton, B.A.Sc., M.B.A.; manufacturer; b. Toronto, Ont. 17 March 1935; s. Fredrick Symonds and Mary Patton (Thornton) W.; e. Univ. of Toronto B.A.Sc. 1957, M.B.A. 1962; m. Shirley Ann d. Alfred Charles Gandy 4 May 1957; children: Scott Fredrick, Steven Alfred, Susan Lynn, Robert William, Michael James; PRESIDENT, AMDAHL LTD. since 1976; Dir. TCC Inc. Austin, Texas; Viceroy Manufacturing Co., Toronto; Canadian Equipment Manufacturers Assn.; Research Engr. Canadian Industries Ltd. Brownsburg, Que. 1957-58; held various positions incl. Dist. Mgr. Central and W. Can. Data Processing Div. IBM Canada 1958-68; Extve. Vice Pres. AGT Data Systems Ltd. and Sr. Vice Pres. Multiple Access Ltd. Toronto 1968-76; Trustee Bd. of Educ. Borough of Etobicoke 1967-69; mem. Assn. Prof. Engrs. Prov. Ont.; P. Conservative; Anglican; Home: 15 The Kingsway, Toronto, Ont M8X 2S9; Office: 123 First Canadian Place, Suite 3940, Toronto, Ont. M5X 1A4.

WHITE, John, M.A.; financial executive; b. Chicago, Ill., 16 Aug. 1925; s. Howard Rivers and Margaret Lyell (Johnston) W.; e. Univ. of W. Ont. B.A. 1946, Dipl. Business Adm. 1949, M.A. (Econ.) 1966'; m. Beatrice Elizabeth d. Charles Ivey, Port Dover, Ont., 15 June 1957; two d. Martha Nancy, Emily Barbara; PRESIDENT, CANADIAN DEVELOPMENT CO. LTD.; Dir.; Lavalin Services; Jarmain Communications Inc.; Anglo Can. Gen. Ins. Co.; Gibraltor Gen. Ins. Co.; el. to Ont. Leg. 1959, re-el. 1963, 1967, 1971; Min. of Revenue 1968-71; Min. of Colls. and Univs. 1971-72; Min. of Industry & Tourism 1972-73; Treas. Min. of Econ. & Intergovernmental Affairs 1973-75; former Chrmn. and C.E.O., Candev Financial Services Ltd.; served with RCNVR 1943-45, rank Sub-Lt.; Chrmn. First Candn. Mortage Fud (Bank of Montréal); Chrmn., Inst. for Pol. Involvement; Chmn., Ont. Heritage Foundation; Delta Upsilon (Past Pres.); P. Conservative; Anglican; recreations: travel, reading, gardening; Clubs: Albany (Dir.); London; Home: 119 Base Line E., London, Ont. N6C 2N6; Office: 200 Queen's Ave., Ste. 604, London, Ont. N6A 1J3.

WHITE, John Cecil, B.Sc.; mining executive; b. Margate, Kent, Eng. 10 March 1933; s. Cecil and Lillian (Bushell) W.; e. Royal Sch. of Mines, Imp. Coll. Univ. of London B.Sc. 1954; m. Margaret d. Joseph and Edith Barrow, Retford, Eng. 21 May 1956; children: Andrew, Michael, Philip, Timothy; VICE PRES.-MINES, NORANDA MINES LTD. 1980- ; Dir. Pamour Porcupine Mines Ltd.; Dumagami Mines Ltd.; joined Madsen Red Lake Gold Mines 1954-59; Gaspe Copper Mines 1959-70, Asst. Mgr. 1969-70; Mattabi Mines Ltd. 1970-76, Mgr.; Mines Gaspe 1976-78, Mgr.; Gen. Mgr.-Mines present Co. 1978-80; rec'd Leonard Medal, Engn. Inst. Can. 1968; mem. Assn. Prof. Engrs. Prov. Ont.; Soc. Mining Engrs. A.I.M.E.; Candn. Inst. Mining & Metall.; United Church; recreations: pottery, gardening, golf, skiing; Club: Engineers; Home: 323 Warminster Dr., Oakville, Ont. L6L 4N1; Office: (P.O. Box 45) Commerce Court W., Toronto, Ont. M5L 1B6.

WHITE, Lt. Col. Kenneth Alan, C.D.; b. Toronto, Ont., 5 April 1914; s. Richard H. and Emily (Alexander) W.; e. Frankland Pub. Sch., Toronto; Jarvis Coll. Inst., Toronto; m. Joan Frankish; three children; CHRMN., CHIEF EXEC. OFFR. AND DIR., ROYAL TRUSTCO LIMITED Chmn. and Dir., Royal Trust Corporation of Canada, The Royal Trust Company, and Royal Trust world wide subsidiary companies; since 1970; Dir., Canabam Ltd.; Canadian Pacific Limited; Dominion Textile Inc.; Stelco Inc.; Great Lakes Forest Products Limited; Chrmn. and Dir., Commercial Union Assurance of Can. Ltd. joined present firm as Joint Mgr. Investments, Toronto, 1950, Asst. Supvr. of Invests., Toronto, 1956, Asst. Mgr., Toronto Br., 1957, Supvr. of Invests., Montreal, 1958, Co. Supvr. of Invests., 1961, Asst. Gen. Mgr. and Mgr., Toronto Br., 1963, Vice Pres. and Mgr., Montreal Br., 1964, Extve. Vice Pres. 1965; el. a Dir. 1967; served with Toronto Scottish 1940-46; post-war Reserve Army; mem., Trust Cos. Assn. Can. (Pres. 1975); Anglican; Clubs: The Toronto; The York Club (Ont.); St. James's; Mount Royal; Montreal; Rideau, Ottawa; Home: 67 Barringham Dr., Oakville, Ont. L6J 4B3 Office: 4400 T-D Bank Tower, Toronto-Dominion Centre, Toronto, Ont. M5W 1P9

WHITE, Kerr Lachlan, M.D., F.A.C.P.; educator; physician; b. Winnipeg, Man., 23 Jan. 1917; s. John Alexander Stevenson and Ruth Cecelia (Preston) W.; e. McGill Univ., B.A. (Econ.) 1940, M.D., C.M. 1949; hon. Dr. Med., Univ. of Leuven 1978; Hon. mem., Nat. Acad. of Med. of Argentina, 1980- ; Yale Univ. Grad. Sch., Cert. in Econ. 1941; Univ. of London and London Sch. of Hygiene & Tropical Med., 1959-60; m. Isabel Anne, d. Clarence Pennefather, 26 Nov. 1943; two d., Susan Isabel, Margot Edith; DEPUTY DIRECTOR FOR HEALTH SCIENCES, ROCKEFELLER FOUNDATION since 1978; Interne, Mary Hitchcock Mem. Hosp., Hanover, N.H., 1949-50; Resident in Med., Dartmouth Med. Sch., Mary Hitchcock Mem. Hosp. 1950-52; Hosmer Research Fellow, McGill Univ., Royal Victoria Hosp.; Asst. Prof. of Med. and Preventive Med., Univ. of N.C., 1953-57; Assoc. Prof. 1957-59 and 1960-62; Chrmn. and Prof., Dept. of Epidemiol. and Community Med., Univ. of Vermont 1962-65; Prof.. Dept. of Health Care Organization, John Hopkins Univ. Sch. of Hygiene and Public Health 1965-77 (Chrmn. 1965-72); served with Candn. Army Overseas 1942-44; Consultant: Nat. Center for Health Stat.; World Health Organ.; Dir., Foundation for Child Devel.; mem., Health Adv. Comm., off. of Technology Assessment, U.S. Congress; mem., Visiting Committee, Sch. Public Health, Harvard University; mem. various councils, U.S. Department of Health Education and Welfare; Expert Panel of Organization of Medical Care, World Health Organization; received Oliver Gold Medal, McGill Univ.; author numerous books and scient. papers for various prof. journs.; Fellow, Am. Assn. Advanc. Science; Am. Heart Assn.; Am. Pub. Health Assn. (Gov. Council 1964-68 and 1971); Royal Soc. of Med.; mem., Am. Med. Assn.; Am. Hosp. Assn.; Am. Fed. Clin. Research; Am. Sociol. Assn.; Assn. Am. Med. Colls.; Group Health Assn. Am. Inc.; Internat Hosp. Fed.; N.Y. Acad. Sciences; N.Y. Acad. of Med.; Soc. Epidemiol. Research; Internat. Epidemiol. Assn. (mem. Council; Treas. 1964-71; Pres. 1974-77); Inst. Med., National Acad. Sciences (mem. Council 1973-76); Sigma Xi; Alpha Omega Alpha; recreations: gardening, travel, reading; Clubs: Century Assn. (N.Y. City); Cosmos (Washington D.C.); Home: Rte. #1, Box 285, Stanardsville, Virginia 22973; Office: 1133 Avenue of the Americas, New York, N.Y. 10036

WHITE, Peter G., B.A., M.B.A.; newspaper executive; b. London, Eng., 1 Aug. 1939; s. Cyril Grove Costley and Elizabeth Katherine Mary (Delmore) W.; e. Eton Coll. 1957; Univ. of W. Ont. B.A. 1966, M.B.A. 1970; m. Martha Grace d. W. J. Blackburn, London, Ont., 24 June 1967; children: Richard, Sarah, Annabelle; PRESIDENT THE LONDON FREE PRESS since 1976; Dir. London Free Press Holdings Ltd.; London Free Press Printing Co.

Ltd.; CFPL Broadcasting Ltd.; Wingham Investments Ltd.; Training Asst. Training and Personnel Policy Dept. Aluminum Co. of Canada Ltd. 1961-63, Area Salesman 1966-67, Placement Offr. Staff Personnel 1967, Area Manager Export Sales 1967-68; joined present newspaper as Marketing Services Mgr. 1970, Planning and Devel. Mgr. 1972, Asst. to Pres. and Publisher and Dir. Planning and Devel. 1975; served with 1st Greenjackets UK 1958-60; Dir., Nat. Ballet of Can.; London Symphony Orchestra; recreation: winter and summer sports; Clubs: London Hunt & Country; Ojibway; London Squash; Home: 29 Kingspark Cres., London, Ont. N6H 4C3; Office: (P.O. Box 2280) London, Ont. N6A 4G1

WHITE, Richard Paul, O.B.E., C.M., V.R.D.; Consultant b. Ottawa, Ont., 29 May 1915; s. Louis Talbot and Dorothy Gordon (Brown) W.; e. Normal-Model Sch. (1928) and Lisgar Coll. Inst. (1933), Ottawa, Ont.; Univ. of W. Ont. (Management Training) 1952; m. June Ruth, d. F. W. White, Ottawa, Ont., 6 Apr. 1940; children: Martha Jocelyn, Gordon Paul, Phyllis Jane; CONSULTANT, BRITISH AMERICAN BANK NOTE INC., Dir., Plough Canada Inc.; Skene Boats Ltd.; Occidental Life Insurance Co. of Can.; Schering Canada Inc.; mem., Ottawa Advisory Bd., the Royal Trust Co.; joined present Company, 1933; apptd Plant Mgr, 1948; Gen Mgr., 1951; Vice-Pres.and Gen Mgr, 1953; el. a Dir., 1953; Extve. Vice-Pres., 1965-66; Pres., 1966-76; Vice-Chmn, 1976-81; joined Naval Reserve, 1934; served in 2nd World War on active service, 1939-46; at Sea in N. Atlantic, Mediterranean and Pacific, and Ashore in Can. and U.K.; awarded O.B.E., Hon. Gov. Candn. Corps of Commissionnaires; Dir., The Perley Hosp; Dir., Ottawa Civic Hospital Foundation; Dir. Royal Candn. Naval Benevolent Fund; Capt., R.C.N. (retired); Anglican; recreations: skiing, fishing, golf; Clubs: Rideau; Royal Ottawa Golf and Country; Maganasippi Fish and Game; Home: 480 Cloverdale Rd., Rockcliffe Park, Ottawa, Ont. K1M 0Y6; Office: 975 Gladstone Ave., Ottawa, Ont.

WHITE, William F., B.A.Sc., M.B.A.; investment dealer; b. London, Ont. 24 April 1944; e. Univ. of B.C., B.A.Sc. 1967; Univ. of W. Ont. M.B.A. 1969; m. Gale Rosanne Wilcock, 27 May 1967; children: Vivien, Michael, Kristopher; DIR., BURNS FRY LTD.; Pres. and dir. Energy & Precious Metals Inc. 1979- ; Founder and Dir. Vanguard Trust of Canada Ltd. 1974- ; Dir. Kam-Kotia Mines Ltd. 1980- ; with present Co. 13 yrs.; Vice Chrmn. Market Functions Comte.; Toronto Stock Exchange 1976-77, mem. Market Access Comte. 1980- ; Treas. and mem. Bd. Govs. Montcrest Sch.; The People's Ch.; recreations: tennis, golf, junior hockey, jogging; Home: 6 Galloway Rd., West Hill, Ont. M1E 1W4; Office: (P.O. Box 150) 5000, First Canadian Place, Toronto, Ont. M5X 1H3.

WHITE, William Henry; shipbuilder; b. Plymouth, Eng., 12 July 1920; s. George Hilliard and Hannah (Bath) W.; e. Elem. Schs., Plymouth, Eng. and Bermuda; Warwick (Bermuda) Acad., 1933-35; Royal Naval Tech. Coll., 1935-39; m. Catherine Jean, d. Edward McNally, M.B.E., Prescott, Ont., 12 Jan. 1946; children: Peter William, Edward George; PRES., DAVIE SHIPBUILDING LTD.; Vice Pres. and Dir., Soconav Limitée; Gescomar Limited; D.A.C. Group Ltd.; served with British Admiralty Dockyard, Bermuda till 1944 when trans. to British Admiralty Tech. Mission, Ottawa, Can., as Tech. Mission, Naval Constr. Dept.; joined Davie Shipbuilding Ltd., Lauzon, Que. as Ship Draughtsman 1945; later Chief Hull & Elect. Draughtsman, Asst. Naval Arch., Naval Arch., Asst. to Gen. Mgr., Tech Mgr.; returned to Bermuda 1960 as Gen. Mgr., Bermuda Marine Services Ltd.; concurrently Govt. Marine Surveyor and Dir., Ocean Lines Ltd.; resigned to join Hall Corp. of Can., Montreal, as Marine Supt., 1962; apptd. Mgr. of Operations, 1963; apptd. Gen. Mgr., Saint John Shipbuilding & Dry Dock Co. Ltd. 1965, Vice Pres. and Gen. Mgr. 1966; joined Marine Industry Ltd., Sorel, as Gen. Mgr. Shipbuilding Division 1970; Apptd. Vice-

Pres. & Gen. Mgr., 1974; resigned 1976 to become Vice-Pres., Davie Shipbuilding Ltd.; Dir., Canadian Shipbuilding & Ship Repairing Association (Pres. 1968-69); Fellow, Royal Institute of Naval Archs.; mem. Society of Naval Architects & Marine Engrs.; Standards Council of Canada; Bureau veritas Intl. Cmte; Am. Bureau of Shipping Cmte; Freemason; recreations: golf, swimming; Clubs: Laurentian; Marine Toronto; Home: Bldg. 5, Apt. 103, Jardins Merici, Qué. G1S 1W4; Office: 22 Georges D. Davie St., Lauzon, Que. G6V 3A5

WHITEBONE, James Alexander, M.B.E.; labour executive; b. Saint John, N.B., 31 May 1894; s. Jacob Sander (cigar maker) and Sarah (Pentland) W.; e. High Sch., Saint John, N.B.; m. Lillian Gertrude Lynch; Pres., N.B. Fed Labour; President, Saint John Trades & Labour Council (1926-42) and since 1960; mem., Internat. Alliance of Theatrical Stage Employees & Moving Picture Machine Operators of the U.S. & Can. (A.F.L.), which he joined 1917 (Business Agt. and Secy., Local 440); rep. Trades & Labour Cong. of Can. at Cong. at London, Eng., and World Trade Union Cong., 1945; Labour Rep., I.L.O. Geneva, June 1951; del., I.C.F.T.U., Milan, Italy, July 1951; mem., Saint John City Council, for 16 yrs., Mayor 1960; author of "History of Labour in N.B.", 1927; mem., Candn. Kennel Club and N.B. Kennel Club; Freemason; Anglican; recreations: gardening, woodworking, fishing; Home: 537 Edward Ave., Lancaster, N.B.

WHITEHEAD, Francis Edward Paxton; actor; director; b. Kent, Eng., 17 Oct. 1937; s. Charles Parkin and Louise (Hunt) W.; e. Rugby Sch., Eng.; Webber-Douglas Sch. of Singing and Dramatic Art, 1957; m. Patricia d. Heather Gage; came to Canada 1965; Artistic Dir., Playhouse Theatre, Vancouver, 1971-72; Shaw Festival, 1967-77; theatre work incls. Shaw Festival, Candn. Players, Manitoba Theatre Centre, Citadel and U.S. Regional Theatres, and tours, "You Never Can Tell", "Major Barbara", "Charleys Aunt", "Devils Disciple", "The Bed before Yesterday", "Thark"; and Broadway ("Beyond the Fringe", "The Affair", "Candida"; "Habeas Corpus" and Sherlock Holmes in "Crucifer of Blood"; U.K., USSR with Royal Shakespeare Theatre, Stratford-on-Avon; CBC and BBC TV; co-author "The Chemmy Circle" (play), world premiere 1968; "There's One in Every Marriage" (play), world premiere 1970; Council mem.; Candn. Actors Equity Assn.; Hon. LL.D., Trent Univ., 1978; Anglican; recreations: tennis, skiing; Club: Players (N.Y.); Address: Box 1234, Niagara on the Lake, Ont. L0S 1J0

WHITEHEAD, James Rennie, B.Sc., Ph.D., F.R.S.C., P.Eng.; consultant; b. Barrow (near Clitheroe), Lancashire, England, 4 Aug. 1917; s. William and Beatrice Cora (Fenning) W.; e. Barrow Elem. Sch., Eng.; Clitheroe Royal Grammar Sch., Lancs., Eng.; Univ. of Manchester, B.Sc. (Hons. Physics), 1939; Camb. Univ. (Gonville and Caius), Ph.D. (Physics), 1949; m. Nesta Doone, d. Robert Roberts James, Malvern, Eng., 1 Nov. 1944; children: Valerie Lesley, Michael James Rennie; SR. VICE PRESIDENT, PHILIP A. LAPP LTD. and Consultant on Science Policy and Research since 1975; Scientific Officer, Telecommunications Establishment (TRE), Dundee, Swanage and Malvern, England, 1939-44 (designed airborne radar identification transponder fitted to all allied ships and aircraft); on loan to Brit. Air Comn., Wash., D.C. on Scient. Liaison, 1944-45; Headed Research Div. at TRE Malvern on millimeter waves and pulsed-light radar, 1945-46; on loan to Physics and Chem. of Surfaces Research Group, Univ. of Cambridge as Consultant on Electronics 1946-49; Head Physical Electronics Div., TRE Malvern, 1949-51; came to Canada, 1951; joined Physics Staff, McGill Univ. (Headed experimental work incl. trials, on Mid-Canada Line (McGill Fence) from Jan. 1952 to the start of its implementation in 1955); Dir. of Research RCA Victor Co. Ltd., 1955-65; Princ. Science Adviser, Science Secretariat, Privy Council Office 1965-71; Asst. Secy. Min. of State for

Science and Tech. 1971-73; Special Advisor 1973-75; Cdn. mem. of Science Policy Committees of NATO, OECD, ECE, and Commonwealth during period 1965-75; member-at-large of Cdn. Commission for UNESCO, 1975- ; Senior mem., Institute of Electrical and Electronic Engrs.; Fellow, Royal Soc. of Canada; Fellow, Institution Elect. Engrs.; Inst. of Physics, Canadian Aero and Space Inst.; mem., Candn. Assn. Physicists; Candn. Research Mang. Assn.; Prof. Engrs. Ont.; Club of Rome; Anglican; recreations: automobiles, hi-fi, carpentry, philately, chess, stage management; Clubs: Cercle Universitaire; Royal Auto. of Can.; Home: 1368 Chattaway Ave., Ottawa, Ont K1H 7S3

WHITEHEAD, Michael Anthony, Ph.D., F.R.I.C., F.C.I.C.; educator; b. London, Eng. 30 June 1935; s. Francis Henry and Edith Downes (Rotherham) W.; e. Kilburn Grammar Sch. London, Eng. 1953; Queen Mary Coll. Univ. of London, 1st Class Hons. Degree in Special Chem. 1956, Ph.D. (Chem.) 1960; Univ. of Cincinnati Postdoctoral studies 1960-61; m. Karen Charlotte d. Ernest Eliasen, Montreal, Que. 27 May 1977; one s. Christopher Mark Eliasen; PROF. OF THEORETICAL CHEM., McGILL UNIV. 1974- ; Asst. Lectr. Queen Mary Coll. Univ. of London 1958-60; Asst. Prof. of Chem. Univ. of Cincinnati 1961-62; Asst. Prof. of Chem. present Univ. 1962, Assoc. Prof. 1966, Assoc. Prof. with tenure 1971; Visiting Prof. of Theoretical Chem. Cambridge Univ. 1971-72, Oxford Univ. 1972-74; Visiting Prof. Fellow in Chem. Univ. Coll. of Wales 1980; author over 120 research papers quantum chem. and nuclear quadrupole resonance spectroscopy; mem. Am. Physical Soc.; Am. Chem. Soc.; Candn. Assn. Physicists; Phi Lambda Upsilon, Sigma Xi (Pres. 1970-71, 1981-82); Eng. Speaking Union (Vice Pres. Montreal Br. 1970-72); Anglican; recreation: hill walking; Home: 6 Kenaston Ave., Town of Mount Royal, Que. H3R 1L8; Office: 801 Sherbrooke St. W., Montreal, Que. H3A 2K6.

WHITEHEAD, Robert; theatre producer; b. Montreal, Que.; 3 March 1916; s. William Thomas and Lena Mary (Labatt) W.; e. Lower Can. Coll., Montreal, Que.; Trinity Coll. Sch., Port Hope, Ont. (1927-34); m. late Virginia, d. late Ross Bolen, Colorado, 16 April 1948; 2ndly, Zoe Caldwell; former Producing Dir., Lincoln Centre Repertory Theatre, till resigned, Dec. 1964; Past Pres. and Gov., League of New York Theatres; Dir., Neighborhood Playhouse, N.Y.; Trustee, Shakespeare Festival, Stratford, Conn.; Dir., Shakespeare in Park, N.Y.C.; V.P.; Am. National Theatre & Acad.; produced on Broadway; "Medea" (Judith Anderson), 1947; "Crime & Punishment" (John Gielgud), 1947; "Member of the Wedding" (prize winning play by Carson McCullers), 1949; "Golden Boy" (by Clifford Odetts), 1951; "Desire Under the Elms" (O'Neill), 1951; "Mrs. McThing" (Helen Hayes), 1951; "Time of the Cuckoo" (Shirley Booth), 1952; "Bus Stop" (by Wm. Inge), 1954; "The Remarkable Mr. Pennypacker", 1955; "Separate Tables" (by T. Rattigan), 1956; "Waltz of the Toreadors" (by Jean Anouilh), 1957; "Orpheus Descending" (by Tennessee Williams), 1957; "A Hole in the Head", 1957; "The Visit" (Alfred Lunt, Lynn Fontaine), 1958; "A Touch of the Poet" (by E. O'Neill), 1959; "The Cold Wind and the Warm" (by S. N. Behrman), 1959; "Much Ado About Nothing" (Sir John Gielgud); "A Man for All Seasons" (by Robert Bolt) with Paul Scofield (5 Tony Awards; Drama Critics Award) 1961; "The Price" (by Arthur Miller) 1968; "The Prime of Miss Jean Brodie" (by Jay Allen) 1968; "Sheep on the Runway" (by Art Buchwald) 1970; served in 2nd World War with Am. Field Service attached to Brit. 8th Army in Africa and Italy, 1942-45, and Brit. 14th Army, Burma, 1945; mem., Am. Arbitration Soc.; Anglican; recreation: fishing; Clubs: Players; Century.

WHITELAW, Donald Mackay, B.A., M.D. C.M.; physician; educator; b. Vancouver, B.C., 20 Oct. 1913; s. William Albert and Ann Elizabeth (Mackay) W.; e. Univ. of British Columbia, B.A. 1934; McGill Univ., M.D. C.M. 1939; m. Jean Agnes, d. Wm. A. Berger, Franklin, N.J., 21 Sept. 1940; children: William Albert, John Peter, Bruce Andrew; EMERITUS PROF. OF MED., UNIV. OF BRIT. COLUMBIA, since 1978; Hon. physician, Shaughnessy Hosp. and Cancer Control Agency of B.C.; Physician, B.C. Cancer Inst.; private practice of Med., 1948; Assoc. Prof. of Med., Univ. of British Columbia, 1953, and Prof. 1960-61; subsequently Assoc. Prof. of Med., Univ. of Toronto; Prof. of Med., U.B.C., 1964-77; mem. of Senate, Univ. of B.C., 1959-61; served in 2nd World War with R.C.N.V.R. 1941-46, Surgeon Lieut.-Commander; Fellow, Royal Coll. Phys. of Canada; Internat. Soc. of Hematol.; Zeta Psi.; Conservative; recreation: bird-photography; Home: 6848 Hudson St., Vancouver, B.C. V6P 4K5

WHITELAW, John Coghlan, C.M., Q.C., B.A., LL.B. retired executive; b. Montreal, Que., 16 June 1907; s. John and Norah (Coghlan) W.; e. Loyola Coll., Montreal, B.A.; Univ. of Montreal (law); m. Yolande, d. late C. N. Moisan, Montreal, Que. 1 June 1940; called to the Bar of Que. 1932; cr. K.C. 1946; practised his prof. in Montreal, Que., before becoming Mgr. of CMA's Que. Div. which position he held for 13 yrs. before his appt. as Extve Vice Pres. and Gen. Mgr. in 1953-74 and life member, 1975; retired mem., Candn. Bar Assn.; Order of Canada, 1975; Roman Catholic; Clubs: National; Rotary; Mississauga Golf & Country; Imperial Gold and Country, Naples, Home: Old Mill Towers, 39 Old Mill Rd., Toronto, Ont.

WHITELY, Jack Benson, B.A.; executive; b. Toronto, Ont., 13 April 1930; s. Arthur Cromwell and Margaret Victoria (McLeod) W.; e. Pub. Schs., Toronto; Leaside High Sch., Toronto 1949; Victoria Coll., Univ. of Toronto, B.A. (Pol. Science and Econ.) 1953; m. Eleanor Mae, d. W. B. Trimming, 18 Dec. 1954; one d. Elizabeth Anne, two s. David Benson, Jeffrey Thomas; CHAIRMAN, CHIEF EXTVE. OFFR. AND DIR., CALVERT-DALE ESTATES LTD 1981- ; Chmn. & Dir., Aledo Oil & Gas Co. Ltd; Argyll Resources Ltd.; Pres. & Dir. of J.B. Whitely & Co. Ltd.; Dir., Crown Trust Co.; Sklar Manufacturing Ltd., mem. Adv. Bd., Midland, Doherty Ltd.; Research Assistant, Bank of Canada, Research Department, Ottawa 1954; Account Exec., R.D. Steers & Co. Ltd., Ottawa 1956; Ass't to Treas., Can. Council, Ottawa 1958; Vice-Pres., Gen. Mgr. and Dir., Annett & Co. Ltd. Toronto and Montreal 1959; Vice-Pres., Finance, Canadian Interurban Properties Ltd., Montreal 1968; formed J.B. Whitely & Company Limited (financial consultants) and became Pres. and Dir. 1969; President, Chief Exec. Officer and Dir., Commerce Capital Corp. Ltd. and Chairman, Pres. and Dir. of Commerce Capital Trust 1970; Pres. & Dir. J.B. Whitely & Company Ltd., 1979; President & Chief Exec. Officer, Crown Trust Co. 1980; Chrmn. & C.E.O. Calvert-Dale Estates Ltd., 1981; Pres., Victoria Coll. Union 1952-53; United Church; recreations: tennis, golf; Club: Oakville; Home: 6 Ennisclare Dr., Oakville, Ont. L6J 4N2; Office: Suite 7060, P.O. Box 84, 1 First Canadian Place, Toronto, Ont. M5X 1B1.

WHITHAM, Kenneth, M.A., Ph.D., F.R.S.C. (1969) geophysicist; Canadian public servant; b. Chesterfield, Eng., 6 Nov. 1927; s. Joseph and Evelyn (Murphy) W.; e. Cambridge Univ., B.A. 1948, M.A. 1952; Univ. of Toronto, M.A. 1949, Ph.D. 1951; m. Joan Dorothy Glasspool, 21 Nov. 1953; three d. Melanie Judith, Katherine Hilary, Stephanie Frances; Asst. Dep. Min., Research and Technology, Dept. Energy, Mines & Resources, since 1981; Geophysicist, Dom. Observatory, Ottawa, 1951-59 and 1960-64; U.N. Tech. Asst. Expert, Brit. E. Africa, 1959-60; Chief, Div. Seismology, Earth Physics Br., Dept. Energy, Mines & Resources 1964-73; Dir. Gen., Earth Physics Br., 1973-79; Asst. Depy. Min., Conservation and Non-Petroleum Energy, 1979-81; author or co-author of over 50 technical articles incl. chapters in learned monographs; mem., Candn. Geophys. Union; Fellow, Geol. Assn. Canada; Anglican; recreations: reading, philately; Home:

1367 Morley Blvd., Ottawa, Ont., K2C 1R4; Office: 580 Booth St. Ottawa, Ont., K1A 0E4

WHITLEY, George Everett, Q.C., B.A., LL.B.; lawyer; b. Winnipeg, Man. 22 Feb. 1924; s. Everett Mansfield and Christina (Teskey) W.; e. U.C.C., Toronto 1936-42; Univ. of Toronto, B.A. 1947; Osgoode Hall Law Sch. LL.B. 1950; m. Betty Jean Smith 28 Dec. 1946; children: Everett Michael; LAWYER, VICE PRES., SECY., GEN. COUNSEL., TRADERS GROUP LTD. since 1972; Vice Pres. Guaranty Trust Co. of Can.; Secy., Guaranty Properties Ltd., Trans Can. Credit Corp. Ltd., Aetna Fin. Services Ltd., Trans Can. Credit Realty Ltd., Traders Corp. (1976) Ltd.; called to the Bar of Ont. 1950; cr. Q.C. 1974; legal dept., Ford Motor Co. of Can., 1950-59; joined Traders Group Ltd. (prior to 1966 known as Traders Finance Corp. Ltd.) as Legal Counsel, 1959-61; Asst. Secy. and Legal Counsel, 1961-64; Secy. and Legal Counsel, 1964-72; served with RCAF, 1943-45, flying instr., discharged rank Flying Offr.; mem., Candn. Bar Assn.; Law Soc. of U.C.; Conservative; Protestant; Clubs: Caledon Mt. Trout; Canard Gun; Theta Delta Chi; recreations: duck shooting, fly fishing, golf, snowmobiling, wood cutting; Home: 37 Munro Blvd., Willowdale, Ont. M2P 1C1; Office: 625 Church St., Toronto, Ont. M4Y 2G1.

WHITMORE, Gordon Francis, M.A., Ph.D.; scientist; educator; b. Saskatoon, Sask. 29 June 1931; s. Ernest Francis and Mary Anne (MacLean) W.; e. Univ. of Sask. B.A. 1953, M.A. 1954; Yale Univ. Ph.D. 1956; m. Margaret Dawn d. William D. Stuart, Victoria, B.C. 1 Sept. 1954; children: Christine, Elinor, Meredith; PHYSICIST, PHYSICS DIV. ONT. CANCER INST. since 1956; Prof. and Head of Med. Biophys. Univ. of Toronto since 1971; Asst. Prof. of Med. Biophys. Univ. of Toronto 1958, Assoc. Prof. 1962, Prof. 1965, Assoc. Dean Basic Sciences & Research Faculty of Med. 1974-77; rec'd David-Anderson-Berry Gold Medal Royal Soc. Edinburgh 1966; Failla Award 1978; co-author "Radiobiology of Cultured Mammalian Cells" 1967; numerous works in areas radiation phys., radiation biol., somatic cell genetics, action of chemotherapeutic agts.; mem. Candn. Assn. Phys.; Candn. Assn. Cell Biols.; Biophys. Soc.; Radiation Research Soc.; Am. Assn. Advanc. Science; Protestant; recreations: swimming, skiing, travel; Home: 78 Roxborough St. W., Toronto, Ont. M5R 1T8; Office: 500 Sherbourne St., Toronto. Ont. M4X 1K9.

WHITMORE, Norman E.; investment executive; b. Regina, Sask., 20 Sept. 1907; s. Albert Eugene and Florence Helen (Marsh) W.; e. Regina, (Sask.) Pub. Schs.; Upper Can. Coll., Toronto, 1923-27; McGill Univ., 1927-28; m. Ruth Constant Forrest, 6 Nov. 1946; children: John A., Peter A., Victoria R.; PRESIDENT, WASCANA INVESTMENTS LTD.; Whitmore Farms Ltd.; Regina Land Development Co. Ltd.; Canada Permanent Trust Co.; Canada Permanent Mortgage Corp.; Hon. Dir., The Molson Cos. Ltd.; served with R.C.N.V.R. 1938-45; retired with rank Commdr.; Conservative; Anglican; recreation: golf, Clubs: Assiniboia; Wascana Country; Toronto; Eldorado Country; Marrakesh Country; Home: 59 Academy Park Rd., Regina, Sask. S4S 4T8; Office: 311 Hotel Saskatchewan, Regina, Sask. S4P 0S3

WHITNEY, John Arthur; banking executive; b. Mayo, Y.T. 9 Jan. 1924; s. Frank Arthur and Theos Juliet (Rosman) W.; e. Brentwood Coll., Victoria, B.C. 1941; m. Mary, d. late Ralph Forrester, 5 Oct. 1946; children: Frank Andrew, Ralph Allen, (John) Christopher, Hugh Gordon, Merrill Elizabeth; EXTVE. VICE PRES. AND CHRMN., CREDIT POLICY COMTE., BANK OF MONTREAL since 1976; Pres. and Dir., Pension Fund Soc. of Bank of Montreal; Dir., Bank of Montreal Mortgage Corp.; joined Bank of Montreal, Mayo, Y.T. 1941; held various positions B.C. Div. 1945-62; Asst. Supt. B.C. Div. 1963-65, (various positions, Head Office, Montreal, 1965-69) Vice Pres. Credit H.O. 1970, Sr. Vice Pres.-

Credit 1973, Extve. Vice Pres.-Credit and Invests. 1973; Extve. Vice-Pres. and Chief Gen. Mgr., 1974-76; served with RCA 1944-45; mem. Adv. Council, Sch. of Business, Queen's Univ.; Mem., Bd. of Dir., Royal Victoria Hosp. Foundation; Royal Victoria Hosp. Corp.; United Church; recreations: golf, curling, bridge; Club: St. James's; Home: 102 Willington Blvd., Etobicoke, Ont. M8X Montreal West, Que. H4X 2C1; Office: Bank of Montreal, First Canadian Pl., Toronto, Ont. M5X 1A1

WHITNEY, John Leo, B.A., Q.C., K.C.S.G.; b. Hamilton, Ont., 19 Sept. 1911; s. Joseph James and Anne Victoria (McMahon) W.; e. McMaster Univ., B.A. 1934; Osgoode Hall Law Sch.; m. Ethel Joan Hall; children: Michael, Sharon, Mark, Sheilagh; retired Partner, Whitney, Whitney & Associates; read law with R. M. W. Chitty, Q.C.; called to Bar of Ont. 1937; cr. Q.C. 1956; Mayor of Waterloo, 1956-57; Commr., Ont. Med. Services Enquiry, 1963-64; Founding Dir., Ont. Sch. Trustees Assn.; Pres., Eng. Cath. Educ. Assn. of Ont., 1954-56; mem., Board of Governors, Univ. of Waterloo, 1957-72; P. Conservative; recreation: fishing; Clubs: Waterloo; Westmount Golf & Country; Home: 204 MacDonald Place, Waterloo, Ont. N2L 1L1

WHITTAKER, Herbert William, D.Litt, O.C.; columnist, drama critic; b. Montreal, Que., 20 Sept. 1911; s. George Herbert and Eleanor (Trappitt) W.; e. Strathcona Acad., Outremont, Que.; Ecole des Beaux Arts, Montreal, Que.; D.Litt., York 1971; as Critic; "Globe & Mail", Drama Critic there 1949-75; formerly "The Gazette", Montreal, radio, film and stage critic; has also written criticism for "New York Times", "New York Herald-Tribune", "Christian Science Monitor", etc.; as Director; Montreal Repertory Theatre, Brae Manor Playhouse, Knowlton, Que., Trinity Coll., Univ. of Toronto, Hart House, Univ. Alumnae Dramatic Club, The Crest Theatre, Drama Centre, Univ. of Toronto, Jupiter Theatre; as Designer: Shakespeare Soc. of Montreal, Univ. Alumnae Dramatic Club, Canadian Players, Montreal Festivals; as Adjudicator: Dom. Drama Festivals and regional festivals in B.C., Alta., W. Ont., etc.; twice winner of Louis Jouvet Trophy for direction; Martha Allan Award for Design; Bessborough and Sir Barry Jackson Awards, D.D.F.; also Candn. Drama Award; Publications: "The Stratford Festival 1953-58", "Canada's National Ballet" 1967; special articles for "Encyclopaedia Brittanica", "Encyclopaedia Americana", The Culture of Canada, "The Saturday Review", "Theatre Arts", "The Stage" (London), etc.; Film: "Canada at 8.30" 1971; Bd. of Trustees, Nat. Arts Centre Corp. 1976-82; mem. Extve. Comte., Dom. Drama Festival 1957-68, and Gov. 1949-69; First Chairman, Drama Bench (Toronto) 1972-75; First Chmn., Nat. Bd., Cdn. Theatre Critics Assn., 1980; final judge, Theatre Ont. Playwrights Showcase Competition, 1980; mem., Am. Newspaper Guild; First Life mem., Candn. Actors' Equity Assn. 1976; Advisory Boards, Shaw Festival, Brown Theatre Dept., "Scene Changes"; Danny Grossman Dance Co.; recreation: theatre; Home: 26 Chestnut Park Rd., Toronto, Ont. M4W 1W6

WHITTALL, Fred Richard, B.Com.; stock broker; b. Montreal, Que., 24 April 1922; s. Fred Richard and Jean Wilken (Brankley) W.; e. Bishop's Coll. Sch., Lennoxville, Que.; McGill Univ., B.Com. 1947; m. Marjorie Ruth, d. late Thomas Irving Findley, 21 Sept. 1943; children: John Duncan, Barbara Elizabeth; EXEC. VICE PRES AND DIR., BRAULT, GUY, O'BRIEN INC.; former Pres.and Dir., C. J. Hodgson, Richardson Inc.; Dir. and Vice-Pres., Growth Oil & Gas Investment Fund of Can. Ltd.; mem. Montreal (Chrmn. 1970) and Candn. Stock Exchanges; with Sherwin-Williams Co. of Canada Ltd., 1939-40; served in 2nd World War with R.C.N.V.R. 1940-45; Zeta Psi; Anglican; recreation: golf; Clubs: Royal Montreal Golf; Hermitage Country; St. James's; Home: 627 Main Rd., Hudson, Que. J0P 1H0; Office: 635 Dorchester Blvd. West, Suite 1000, Montreal, Que. H3B 1R8

WHITTALL, Hubert Richard, , D.F.C.; investment dealer; b. Vancouver, B.C., 3 April 1923; s. Norman Reginald and Glen Margaret (McLennan) W.; e. Brentwood Coll., V.I., B.C. (Grad. 1940); m. Jocelyn Hamilton, d. Mr. Justice C. Gerald O'Connor, 29 Oct. 1949; children: Gerald Bruce, Richard O'Connor, Pamela Glen, Virginia Ann; PARTNER, RICHARDSON SECURITIES OF CANADA; Chairman, Grosvenor International Holdings Ltd.; Depy. Chairman, Canada Cement Lafarge Ltd.; Dir., Placer Development Ltd.; B.C. Sugar Refinery Ltd.; Weldwood of Canada Ltd.; British Columbia Television Broadcasting System Ltd.; Brenda Mines Ltd.; Cyprus Anvil Mining Corp.; Inland Natural Gas Company Limited; following military service employed by General Petroleum Co., 1945-46; joined present Co., 1946; served in 2nd World War with R.C.A.F., 1941-45; awarded D.F.C. and Bar; Anglican; recreations: tennis, fishing; Clubs: The Vancouver; Shaughnessy Golf; Home: 3410 Marpole Ave., Vancouver, B.C. V6J 2S1; Office: 500-1066 W. Hastings St., Vancouver, B.C. V6E 3X1

WHITTALL, James William, D.S.C.; insurance broker; b. Vancouver, B.C., 12 Oct. 1914; s. Norman R. and Glen Margaret (McLennan) W.; e. Vernon (B.C.) Prep. Sch.; Shawnigan Lake Sch., Vancouver Is.; m. Gwenneth Anne, d. Keir Clark, Montague, P.E.I., 22 September 1970; children: Degnan, Catherine, Melanie, Mary Jennifer (Mrs. Cecil Planedin); CHRMN. REED STENHOUSE COS. LTD.; Dir., Algoma Central Railway; Internat. Thomson Organ. Ltd.; mem. of Lloyd's; served with R.C.N.V.R. 1940-45; Overseas 1940, on loan to R.N. to 1945; Mentioned in Despatches 1942; D.S.C. 1943; mem. and Assoc., Ins. Inst. Am.; Clubs: The Toronto; The Vancouver (B.C.); Office: P.O. Box 10028, Pacific Centre, Vancouver B.C. V7Y 1B4

WHITTEN, John A., B.A.Sc., P.Eng.; company executive; b. Toronto, Ont., 23 Aug. 1922; s. Alfred R. and Gladys Aileen (Weese) W.; e. Humberside Coll. Inst., Toronto, Ont.; Univ. of Toronto, B.A.Sc. 1947; m. Margaret Jean, d. W. E. Webster, Niagara-on-the-Lake, Ont., 16 June 1951; children: Robin Jill, Janet Ann; SR. VICE-PRES. CHRISTIE, BROWN & CO. LTD.; dir., Christie, Brown; joined Christie Brown and Co. Ltd. 1948 as Plant Engr.; Chief Engr., 1953, Dir. of Production and Engn., 1955, Vice-Pres., Production and Dir., 1958; Vice Pres. and Gen. Mgr., Nabisco Foods Div., 1971-79; served in 2nd World War with Royal Candn. Arty., 1943-45; Past Councillor, World Packaging Organ.; Past Pres., N. Am. Packaging Fed.; Packaging Assn. Can.; Gov., Univ. of Toronto; Conservative; Anglican; recreations: sailing, golf; Clubs: R.C.Y.C.; Oakville (Ont.) Golf; Board of Trade; Home: 1122 Balmoral Place, Oakville, Ont. L6J 2C9; Office: 2150 Lakeshore Blvd. W., Toronto, Ont. M8V 1A3

WHYARD, Florence Esther, B.A., LL.D.; journalist; b. London, Ont. 13 Jan. 1917; d. William Edmund Elliott; e. pub. schs. London, Toronto and Woodstock, Ont.; High Sch. Woodstock, Ont.; Univ. of W. Ont. B.A. 1938; LL.D. 1979; m. James Herbert Whyard 22 July 1944; children: Mary Ellen, Judith (Mrs. John Anton), William Elliott; MAYOR, WHITEHORSE, YUKON TERRITORY, 1981-83; former Assoc. Ed. "Fort Erie Times-Review"; writer, Johnston, Everson & Charlesworth, Toronto; free-lanced for CBC-IS and Cndn. programs, Yellowknife; served on staff of "News of the North" N.W.T., stringer for "Edmonton Journal" etc.; became Ed. "Whitehorse Star" 7 yrs., Candn. Ed. Alaska Northwest Publishing Co. 4 yrs.; resigned when el. M.L.A. for Whitehorse West, Yukon Leg. Assembly 1974; mem. Extve. Comte. Y.T. Govt. 1975 — 78, Mem. responsible for Health, Welfare & Rehabilitation; served with WRCNS Naval Information Br. Ottawa during World War II, rank Lt.; Charter mem., Univ. of Canada North 1971; mem., Yukon Medical Council; Hon. Vice-Pres. Yukon Red Cross; mem., Council for Canadian Unity; Mem., RCN Benevolent Fund;

Hon. Regent, Whitehorse IODE; Hon. Life mem. W.A. Ang. Ch.; Hon. Life mem. Golden Age Soc. Yukon; Charter mem., Univ. Women's Club Whse. Br.; publs. incl.: Canada Ed., Alaska Magazine, 1980; "My Ninety Years" 1976; pamphlets: "Five Pioneer Women in Yukon" 1964; "Kiwi in the Klondike" 1972; Kappa Alpha Theta (Gamma Epsilon Chapter); P. Conservative; Anglican; recreations: reading, travel; Address: 89 Sunset Dr. N., Whitehorse, Y.T. Y1A 3G5.

WICK, Donald, M.A., F.L.A.; librarian; b. Enfield, Eng., 15 Feb. 1928; s. Ernest Charles and Marjorie Joyce (Ridler) W.; e. Enfield (Eng.) Grammar Sch.; Cambridge Univ., B.A. 1952, M.A. 1956; Loughborough Coll., Sch. of Librarianship; children: Adrian, Jonathan, Patricia; UNIV. ARCHIVIST AND ACTING UNIV. LIBRARIAN, UNIV. OF LETHBRIDGE 1975-1979; Br. Librarian, Worthing Pub. Libs., 1954; Interne Librarian, Toronto Pub. Libs., 1955; Bookmobile Librarian, Etobicoke (Ont.) Pub. Libs., 1956, Head of Reference Dept. 1959; Coll. Librarian, Selkirk Coll., Castlegar, B.C., 1965-67; Chief Librarian, Univ. of Lethbridge, 1967-74; served with Royal Elect. and Mech. Engrs. 1948-49; Chrmn., Comte. for Survey of Ont. Reference Services, Ont. Lib. Assn. Workshop, 1964-65; Vice Chrmn., Council of Prairie Univ. Libs., 1972-73; author bibliogs., research papers, articles; mem., Candn. Lib. Assn.; Candn. Assn. Coll. & Univ. Libs. (Chrmn., Mang. Audio Visual Services, 1972); Council, Bibliog. Soc. Can.; recreations: tennis, golf, chess; Home: 1117 - 18th St. S., Lethbridge, Alta. T1K 2A4

WICKENDEN, Robert Thomas Daubigny, M.A., Ph.D., F.R.S.C.; geologist; b. Outremont, Que., 17 July 1901; s. Robert John and Ada Louise (Ahier) W.; e. Brown Univ., Ph.B. 1926; Harvard Univ., M.A. 1929, Ph.D. 1931; m. Lyla Eloise, d. Frederick Rogers, 18 Sept. 1929; one s. John N.; Geologist with Geol. Survey of Canada, 1930-66; now retired; mem., Geol. Soc. of Am.; Canadian Soc. of Petroleum Geols.; Unitarian; recreations: hunting, target-shooting; Home: 1450 Beach Dr., Victoria, B.C. V8S 2N8

WICKENS, George Michael, M.A., F.R.S.C.; educator; b. London, Eng. 7 Aug. 1918; s. George William and Annie (White) W.; e. Holloway Sch. London, Eng. 1929-36; Trinity Coll. Cambridge B.A. 1939, M.A. 1946 (Maj., Sr. & Research Scholar); m. Ruth Joyce d. late William Thomas Lindop 9 Nov. 1940; children: Maxim, Anna, Simon, Clare, Andrew, Giles, Stephen, Paul; PROF. OF MIDDLE E. AND ISLAMIC STUDIES, UNIV. OF TORONTO since 1960; Lectr. Univ. of London 1946-49; Lectr. in Oriental Studies, Cambridge Univ. 1949-57; Assoc. Prof. present Univ. 1957-60, Chrmn. of Middle E. & Islamic Studies 1961-68; appt. Univ Prof., 1980; served with RAPC 1939-41, Intelligence Corps 1941-46 Middle E., rank Capt., Mentioned in Despatches; author "Avicenna: Scientist and Philosopher" 1952; "Booklist on Asia For Canadians" 1961; "The Nasirean Ethics" 1964; "Morals Pointed and Tales Adorned" 1974; "Introduction to Islamic Civilisation" 1976; "Hájí Ághá", 1979; "Arabic Grammar", 1980; numerous articles and reviews in learned journs. on Middle E. lit., thought and hist.; Founding Fellow, Middle E. Studies Assn. Am.; mem. am. Oriental Soc.; Home: 235 St. Clair Ave. W., Ste. 406, Toronto, Ont. M4V 1R4 Office: Toronto, Ont. M5S 1A1.

WIDDRINGTON, Peter Nigel Tinling, M.B.A.; executive; b. Toronto, Ont. 2 June 1930; s. Gerard Nigel Tinling and Margery (MacDonald) W.; e. Pickering Coll. Newmarket, Ont. 1949; Queen's Univ. B.A. 1952; Harvard Business Sch. M.B.A. 1955; m. Betty Ann Lawrence 12 Oct. 1956; two d. Lucinda Ann, Andrea Stacy; PRES. AND C.E.O., JOHN LABATT LTD. 1973- ; Dir. B.P. Canada Inc.; Brascan Ltd.; Canada Trust; Salesman, Labatt's 1955; Asst. Regional Mgr. S. Ont. Region, Labatt's Ontario Breweries Ltd. 1957, Regional Mgr. 1958; Gen. Mgr. Kiewel and Pelissiers, Winnipeg 1961, Labatt's Manitoba

Breweries Ltd. 1962, Labatt's B.C. Breweries Ltd. 1965; Pres. Lucky Breweries Inc. San Francisco 1968; Vice Pres. Corporate Devel. John Labatt Ltd. 1971, Sr. Vice Pres. 1973; Dir. Toronto Blue Jays Baseball Club; Gov. Stratford Shakespearean Festival; P. Conservative; Anglican; recreations: tennis, hockey, golf, swimming, jogging; Clubs: London; London Hunt & Country; Granite (Toronto); Shaughnessey Golf & Country (Vancouver); Olympia (San Francisco); Home: 1 Doncaster Ave., London, Ont. N6G 2A1; Office: 451 Ridout St. N., London, Ont. N6A 4M3.

WIGDOR, Blossom T(emkin), M.A., Ph.D.; psychologist & gerontologist; b. Montreal, Que. 13 June 1924; d. Solomon and Olga (Gilels) Temkin; e. McGill Univ. B.A. 1945, Ph.D. 1952; Univ. of Toronto M.A. 1946; m. Leon Wigdor 31 May 1945; one child Mitchell; DIR.-PROGRAM IN GERONTOLOGY, UNIV. OF TORONTO and Assoc. Prof. of Psychol. since 1979; Editor-in. Chief, Can. Journal on Aging, 1981; joined Dept. of Veterans Affairs 1946, Psychol. Christie St. Hosp. and Sunnybrook Hosp. 1946-47, Ste. Anne de Bellevue and Queen Mary Veterans Hosps. 1947-78; Consultant in Psychol., Maimonides Hosp. and Home for Aged Montreal 1954-68; participated in organ. of Multi disciplinary Geriatric Clinic, Jewish Gen. Hosp. Montreal 1955-56; Sr. Consultant in Psychol. Queen Elizabeth Hosp. Montreal 1963-74; Dir. of Psychol. Services Centre Hospitalier Cote des Neiges (formerly Queen Mary Veteran Hosp.) 1961-79, Dir. Psychiatric-Psychol. Research Unit 1965-78, M.B.O. Advisor (Mang. & Organ. Devel.) 1971-78; Consultant in Psychol. to Asst. Depy. Min. D.V.A. Ottawa 1965-78; Assoc. Prof. of Psychol. McGill Univ. 1972-79; Chrmn. Grad. Faculty Comte. on Aging; mem. Science Council Can., 1973-79; External Consultant, Can. Council and Dept. Nat. Health & Welfare; conducted many seminars med. and grad. students in psychol., nurses and others on topics in clin. psychol. and aging; named Woman of Achievement YWCA Montreal 1975; Editor "Recent Advances in Behaviour Change" 1964; Ed. "Canadian Gerontological Collection I" 1977; Vice-Chmn. & mem. Bd. of Directors, Gerontological Research Council of Ont.; Mem. Bd. of Dir., Baycrest Centre for Geriatric Care; mem. Adv. Comte to Bd. of Governors, West Pk. Hosp.; mem. Ed. Bd. "Psychiatric Journal of the Univ. Ottawa"; author or co-author various articles, papers, reports; Fellow, Candn. Psychol. Assn.; Gerontol. Soc. of America; Soc. Personality Assessment; mem. Candn. Assn. Gerontol. (2nd Vice Pres., 1977-81; Am. Psychol. Assn.; E. Psychol. Assn.; Candn. Assn. Club Rome; recreations: theatre, reading, cross-country skiing; Home: Apt. 708, 21 Dale Ave., University of Toronto, Toronto, Ont. M4W 1K3; Office: Toronto, Ont. M5S 1A1.

WIGGINS, Chris; actor; writer; b. Lancs., Eng., 13 Jan. 1931; s. Walter and May (Ellor) W.; m. Erica Margaret, d. Max Montesole; stage career incls. Stratford (Ont.) Festival, Alley Theatre (Houston), Crest and Museum Theatres (Toronto), Globe Theatre; over 1380 TV roles for CBC, CTV and Nat. Film Bd. in Can.; various networks in U.S.; over 120 film roles incl. Yardley in "Two Solitudes"; King Carroll in "Highballin' "; Lyle Bishop in "Why Shoot the Teacher"; John Sheardown in "Escape from Iran"; over 800 radio roles and over 200 roles in educ. TV; rec'd Telegram Theatre Award for Best Candn. Actor 1964; "Etrog" Candn. Film Award for Best Actor 1969; Ohio State Competition Award for Host-Narrator; Jessie De Rivers Award for Dramatic Writing, Candn. Authors' Assn., 1973; Andrew Allan Award for Best Radio Drama Performance, ACTRA, 1976; author, "Sinbad and the Mermaid" and "Sleeping Beauty" (children's plays), 1965; other writings incl. plays for TV, radio and film incl. "The Ballad Master", "Spaniard's Rock"; "Five Unpleasant Canadian Stories" (radio); "The Subject is the Dog", Radio Internat.; title role "Paul Bernard, Psychiatrist" and Father Robinson, "Swiss Family Robinson" (t.v. series); also educ. series for film, TV and

radio; named Hon. Chief of Stoney Indian Tribe of Alta. under title "Swift-Running Bear Cub"; Home: R.R. 1, Unionville, Ont. L3R 2L6

WIGGS, H. Ross, B.Sc., R.C.A., F.R.I.B.A., F.R.A.I.C.; architect; b. Quebec, Quebec, 28 December 1895; s. Wm. Henry and Emma Clara (Ross) W.; e. Que. High Sch. for Boys, Quebec, Que.; Ridley Coll., St. Catharines, Ont., 1912-15; McGill Univ., 1915-20; Mass. Inst. of Tech., B.Sc. (Arch.) 1922; m. Mildred Jean (Billy), d. Maj.-Gen. Sir David Watson, K.C.B., C.M.G. and Lady Watson, Quebec, Que.,, 28 July 1923; has one d., (Marjorie) Mrs. Keith Gould; practised his prof. in Montreal for many yrs., his commissions covering a wide range of arch. design incl. office bldg., various schs. in Montreal for Pros. Sch. Bd. of Greater Montreal; bldgs. for Dept. of Nat. Defence; Chapel for the Ch. of St. James the Apostle, Montreal; Mont Tremblant Lodge (ski resort); numerous large residences throughout Que. etc.; served in 1st World War, 1917-18, with 10th Candn. Siege Batty. (McGill) in France; mem., Que. Assn. of Arch. (Pres. 1951); Roy. Arch. Inst. of Can.; Ont. Assn. of Arch.; Roy Cdn. Acad. Arts; Phi Kappa Pi; Anglican; recreations: painting, philately; Home: 301-130 St. Joseph's Dr., Hamilton, Ont. L8N 2E8

WIGHTON, Eric Alexander Annan, C.A.; insurance executive; b. Edinburgh, Scot. 21 Jan. 1926; s. Alfred Annan and Martha Brownlie (Yuill) W.; e. Edinburgh Acad. 1943; C.A. Scot. 1951, Can. 1960; m. Carol d. Richard Arnold Whiteside, Jersey, C.I. 3 July 1954; children: Angus Alexander, Lorna Allison, Gillian Christine; VICE PRES. FINANCE, CANADIAN GENERAL INSURANCE CO. since 1976; Vice Pres. Finance, Toronto General Insurance Co.; Traders General Insurance Co.; articled Richard Brown & Co. Edinburgh 1946-51; joined Graham, Smart & Annan, Edinburgh 1951-54; Clarkson Gordon & Co. Toronto 1954; Internal Audit, Traders Group Ltd. 1954, Asst. Treas. 1957, Treas. 1960, Vice Pres. and Treas. 1974; served with RN 1944-46, rank Sub-Lt.; mem. Bd. Trade Metrop. Toronto; P. Conservative; Church of Scotland; recreation: figure skating; Club: Toronto Cricket Skating & Curling; Home: 10 Tanburn Pl., Don Mills, Ont. M3A 1X5; Office: 170 University Ave., Toronto, Ont. M5H 3B5.

WIGLE, William Ward, M.D., C.M.; b. Dryden, Ont., 6 Aug. 1917; s. Russell Gilbert and Henrietta Anna Casey (McMonagle) W.; e. Dryden (Ont.) Public and High Schs.; Success Business Coll., Winnipeg, Man. (1937); Queen's Univ., M.D., C.M. 1943; m. Frances McLean, d. Frank Foulis, 6 May 1944; children: William Foulis, John Frederick, Margaret Anne; Regional Coroner, Kenora Region, 1975; Past Pres., Pharm. Mfrs. Assn. Can.; Dir., Candn. Mental Health Assn.; formerly Dir., Hosp. Med. Records Inst.; Past Pres., Candn. Med. Assn.; Ont. Med. Assn.; Consultant to Candn. Pharm. Mfrs. Assn.; formerly mem., Dryden (Ont.) Public Sch. Bd., Dryden Mun. Council; Student, R.C.A.M.C., 1942-44; Surgeon-Lieut., R.C.N.V.R., 1944-45; Freemason; United Church; recreations: fishing, flying; Past Pres., Dryden Rotary Club; Address: Apt. 4C, 283 Van Horne Ave., Dryden, Ontario P8N 2C7

WILDER, William Price, B.Com., M.B.A.; financier; b. Toronto, Ont., 26 Sept. 1922; s. William Edward and Marjorie Margaret (Murray) W.; e. Elmhouse Sch. 1934; Upper Canada Coll. 1940 (both Toronto, Ont.); McGill Univ., B.Com. 1946; Harvard Univ., M.B.A. 1950; m. Judith Ryrie, d. Edward W. Bickle, Toronto, Ont., 18 Sept. 1953; children: Martha Helen, William Edward, Thomas Bickle, Andrew Murray; PRESIDENT AND C.E.O., HIRAM WALKER RESOURCES LTD. since 1979; Chmn., Consumers Gas Co. Ltd.; Dir., Maclean Hunter Ltd.; Noranda Mines Ltd.; John Labatt Ltd.; Simpsons-Sears Ltd.; Home Oil Co. Ltd., Scurry-Rainbow Oil Ltd.; Canada Life Ass. Co.; Hiram Walker Gooder ham & Worts; The

Royal Bank of Can.; Adv. Bd. and Extve. Comte., Sch. of Business, Univ. of W. Ont.; mem., Bd. of Gov., McGill Univ.; Trustee, Hosp. for Sick Children, Toronto; joined Wood Gundy and Co. Ltd. 1946, Extve. Vice-Pres. and Dir. 1961, Pres. 1967; Chrmn., Candn. Arctic Gas Study Ltd. 1972-77; Extve. Vice Pres., Gulf Can. Ltd. 1977-79; served in 2nd World War; Lt., R.C.N.V.R. on loan to Royal Navy 1941-44; Alpha Delta Phi; United Church; recreations: golf, tennis, skiing, fishing; Clubs: York; The Toronto; Toronto Golf; Badminton & Raquet (Toronto); Cambridge (Toronto); Rideau (Ottawa); Tadenac Fishing; St. James's (Montreal); Queen's (Toronto); Brooks's (London); Home: 401 Russell Hill Rd., Toronto, Ont. M4V 2V3; Office: P.O. Box 90, 1 First Canadian Place, Toronto, Ont. M5X 1C5

WILDMAN, Sally Ann, R.C.A.; painter; b. Tynemouth, Eng. 2 Aug. 1939; d. William Caddy and Norah (Taylor) Wildman; e. Ont. Coll. of Art; Goldsmiths Coll. of Art Univ. of London; came to Can. 1953; mem. Ont. Soc. Artists; rep. in numerous private and pub. colls. Can. and USA; Address: (P.O. Box 97) Claremont, Ont. L0H 1E0.

WILES, David McKeen, M.Sc., Ph.D., F.C.I.C.; research chemist; b. Springhill, N.S. 28 Dec. 1932; s. late Prof. Roy McKeen Wiles; e. McMaster Univ. B.Sc. 1954, M.Sc. (Chem.) 1955; McGill Univ. Ph.D. (Chem.) 1957; Leeds Univ. Sir William Ramsay Postdoctoral Fellow 1957-59; m. Valerie Joan d. late Maj. H. E. Rowlands 8 June 1957; children: Gordon Stuart, Sandra Lorraine; DIR. CHEM. DIV., NAT. RESEARCH COUNCIL OF CAN. 1975- ; Research Offr. Chem. Div. present Council 1959-66, Head, Textile Chem. Sec. 1966- ; mem. Engn. Adv. Council Queen's Univ. 1977-79; SCITEC Extve. Comte. and Council 1974-77; assoc. Grad. Faculty Univ. of Guelph 1967-76; recipient Dunlop Lecture Award 1981; Textile Science Award 1980; Queen's Silver Jubilee Medal 1977; author over 180 publs. incl. 6 book chapters; holds 15 patents polymer and fiber science; Pres. Chem. Inst. Can. 1975-76, Chrmn. of Bd. 1972-74; mem. Inst. Textile Science (Pres. 1973-74); Textile Inst. U.K. (Vice Pres. 1982-83); Candn. High Polymer Forum (Pres. 1967-69); United Church; Home: 1927 Fairmeadow Cres., Ottawa, Ont. K1H 7B8; Office: Ottawa, Ont. K1A 0R9.

WILK, Martin Bradbury, B.E., M.S., Ph.D., F.S.S.; Canadian public servant; statistician; b. Montreal, Que. 18 Dec. 1922; e. Strathcona Acad. Outremont, Que. 1940; McGill Univ. B.E. (Chem. Engn.) 1945; Iowa State Univ. M.S. (Stat.) 1953, Ph.D. (Stat.) 1955; m. 1stly Thora Sugrue (d); m. 2ndly Dorothy Louise Barrett 3 July 1974; children: Bonnie, Rebecca, Carol Nancy Landsman, David Terrence, Teresa Jane, Kathryn Joan Thompson, Kathleen Schade; CHIEF STATISTICIAN OF CANADA 1980- ; Research Chem. Engr. Nat. Research Council of Can. (Atomic Energy Project) 1945-50; Research Assoc., Instr. and Asst. Prof. Iowa State Univ. 1951-55; Research Assoc. and Asst. Dir. Stat. Techniques Group 1955-57; Prof. and Dir. of Research in Stat. 1959-63 Rutgers Univ.; mem. Tech. Staff Stat. Research Bell Telephone Labs. 1956, Head of Stat and Data Analysis Research Dept. 1963, Head of Stat. Models & Methods Research Dept. 1968, Stat. Dir. Mang. Sciences Research 1969-70; joined American Telephone and Telegraph Co. 1970 as Dir.-Corporate Modeling Research, Dir.-Corporate Research 1971, Dir.-Planning 1972, Dir.-Corporate Planning 1973, Asst. Vice Pres.-Dir. of Corporate Planning 1976-80; author or co-author various scient. publs.; rec'd Jack Youden Prize Am. Soc. Quality Control 1972; mem. Census Adv. Comte. 1973-75; Fellow, Am. Stat. Assn. (Chrmn. Sec. on Phys. & Engn. Sciences 1971; Dir. 1973-74, 1980-82; Vice Pres. 1980-82); Inst. Math. Stat. (mem. Council 1956-58; Visiting Lectr. 1969-70); Am. Assn. Advanc. Science; N.Y. Acad. Sciences; mem. Internat. Stat. Inst.; Biometric Soc.; Internat. Assn. Stat. in Phys. Sciences; Classification Soc.; Sigma Xi; Phi Kappa Phi; Pi Mu Epsilon; Assoc. Ed. "Technometrics" 1959-63; Home:

P.O. Box 191, R.R. 3, Stittsville, Ont. K0A 3G0; Office: 26th Floor, R. H. Coats Bldg., Tunney's Pasture, Ottawa, Ont. K1A 0T6.

WILKINS, James Raymond; insurance broker; b. Nipawin, Sask. 27 Nov. 1928; s. Walter Earl and Emma Virginia (de Rosier) W.; e. North Vancouver High Sch. 1946; Ins. Inst. of Am., A.I.A.A. 1952; Ins. Inst. of Can. A.I.I.C. 1956; m. Frances Wilhemein d. William George Tait, Evansburg, Alta. 6 Oct. 1961; children: Matt, Mary-Ellen; EXTVE. VICE PRES. AND DIR., REED STENHOUSE LTD. 1978- ; Pres. Wilkins Investments Ltd.; Chrmn. of Bd. Imperial Lumber Co. Ltd.; Dir. Reed Stenhouse Associates Ltd.; joined present Co. 1946, opened Edmonton Office 1953, Sr. Partner 1968; mem. Bd. Govs. Edmonton Eskimo Football Club, Pres. 1975-76, Dir. 10 yrs.; Past Pres. Western Football Conf.; Past mem. Extve. Candn. Football League; Chrmn. Adv. Comte. to Redemptorist Fathers; mem. Edmonton Sr. Chamber Comm.; P. Conservative; R. Catholic; recreations: golf, hunting, skiing; Clubs: Mayfair Golf & Country; The Centre; Ironwood Golf & Country (Palm Desert, Calif.); Home: 62 Willow Way, Edmonton, Alta. T5T 1C8; Office: 2100 Royal Trust Tower, Edmonton Centre, Edmonton, Alta. T5J 0Y2.

WILKINSON, Bruce William, B.Com., M.A. Ph.D.; educator; economist; b. Vanguard, Sask. 10 Apl. 1933; s. William and Florence Mary (Stewart) W.; e. Univ. of Sask. B.Com. 1953; Univ. of Alta. M.A. 1961; Mass. Inst. Technol. Ph.D. 1964; m. Myrna Ellen d. Lawrence Elmer Plewis 8 Oct. 1960; children: Craig William, Glenda Anne, Myrna Lynn; PROF. OF ECON., UNIV. OF ALTA. since 1971; joined Imperial Oil Ltd. 1953 — 60; Asst. Prof. of Econ. Univ. of Sask. 1964 — 66; Visiting Asst. Prof. of Econ. Univ. of W. Ont. 1966 — 67; Assoc. Prof. Econ. 1967 — 71 Univ. Alta., Chrmn. of Econ. 1972 — 77; Consultant, Econ. Council Can.; C. D. Howe Research Inst.; Dir. Consult. Inst. Econ. Policy; author "Studies in the Economics of Education" 1965; "Canada's International Trade: An Analysis of Recent Trends and Patterns" 1968; "Canada in the Changing World Economy" 1980; co-author "Effective Protection in the Canadian Economy" 1968; "Canada in a Wider Economic Community" 1973; "Effective Protection and the Return to Capital" 1975; various articles econ. of educ., Candn. trade, balance of payments, comm. policy; mem. Candn. Econ. Assn.; Am. Econ. Assn.; Royal Econ. Soc. (Eng.); Anglican; recreations: gardening, swimming, reading; Home: 13320 27th Ave., Edmonton, Alta. T5R 3G5; Office: Edmonton, Alta. T6G 2H4.

WILKINSON, Sir Denys Haigh, Kt. (1974), M.A., Ph.D., Sc.D., D.Sc., Fil.Dr., F.R.S. (1956), F.Inst.P., F.A.P.S.; b. Leeds, Yorkshire, England, 5 Sept. 1922; s. Charles and Hilda (Haigh) W.; e. Cambridge Univ. grad 1943, M.A., Ph.D., Sc.D.; m. 1stly, Christiane Clavier, 23 June 1947; three d.; m. 2ndly, Helen Sommers, 14 June 1967; 2 step-d.; five children; VICE-CHANCELLOR AND PROF. OF PHYSICS, UNIV. OF SUSSEX since 1976; Fellow of Jesus College, Cambridge 1944-59, Hon. Fellow since 1961; Demonst. and Lect. in Physics 1946-57; Prof. of Exper. Physics 1959-76, Nuclear Physics 1957-59; Head, Nuclear Physics Dept., Oxford Univ., 1962-76; Student of Christ Church 1957-76; Hon. Student since 1979; Pres., Inst. of Physics, 1980- ; awards: Tom W. Bonner Prize (Am. Phys. Soc.) 1974; Comte. d'Honneur du Bontemps de Medoc et des Graves 1973; Goodspeed-Richards Mem. (Univ. of Penn.) 1969; Silliman Mem. (Yale Univ.) 1966; Queen's Lecture (Berlin) 1966; Hughes Medallist (Roy. Soc.) 1965; Graham Young (Glasgow) 1964; Rutherford Mem. 1967; Royal Medal (Roy. Soc.) 1980; Scott Lectures (Cambridge Univ.) 1961; Holweck Medallist of Fr. and Brit. Phys. Socs. 1957; Hon. degree University of Saskatchewan; State Univ. of Utah; Uppsala Univ.; Univ. of Guelph; author of "Ionization Chambers and Counters"; ed., "Isospin in Nuclear Physics,"

"Mesons in Nuclei" and some 200 articles in learned journs.; Lauritsen Mem. Lect. (Cal. Tech.) 1976; Schiff Mem. Lect. (Stanford) 1977; Racah Mem. Lect. (Jerusalem) 1977; mem. Brit.-Candn. Atomic Energy Project 1943-46; Cambridge Philos. Soc.; Brit. Ornithol. Union; foreign mem., Royal Swedish Acad. of Sciences; recreations: music, ornithology, ancient art; Clubs: Achilles; Athenaeum; Home: Gayles Orchard, Friston, Eastbourne, E. Sussex, Eng. BN200BA; Office: Falmer, Brighton, Eng. BN1 9RH

WILKINSON, Edward David Hooper, Q.C., B.Com.; b. Port Alberni, B.C., 15 Jan. 1915; s. Thomas Hooper and Margaret (Hardy) W.; e. Univ. of B.C., B.Com. 1937; widower; children: Judith Mary Bowles, Margaret Joan Lamb; PARTNER, RUSSELL & DUMOULIN; Dir., Price Co. Ltd.; Mercantile Bank of Canada; Phillips Cables Ltd.; Trans-Continental Resources Ltd.; called to Bar of B.C. 1941; cr. Q.C. 1971; served with 2nd Armoured Bgde. during World War II; Secy., Nat. Second Century Fund of B.C.; mem., Law Soc. B.C.; Candn. Bar Assn.; Alpha Delta Phi; Anglican; recreations: golf, fishing, hunting; Home: 34-4100 Salish Dr., Vancouver, B.C. V6N 3M2;; Office: 1075 W. Georgia St., Vancouver, B.C. VG2 3C9

WILKINSON, Frank Cameron, B.Com.; industrialist; b. Vancouver, B.C., 2 May 1928; s. Joseph William and Marion McGillivray (Cameron) W.; e. St. George's Sch., Vancouver, B.C.; Univ. of British Columbia, B.Com. 1948; London Sch. of Econ., Univ. of London (Post-Grad. work) 1948-49; m. Teresa Ann (King), 16 Mar. 1955; children: Graeme Cameron, Marion Gail, Virginia Ann; CHMN., C.E.O. AND DIR., WILKINSON CO. LTD. (Steel & Metal Distributors, estbd. 1910); Chmn. and Dir., Wilkinson Metal Industries Ltd.; Exchanger Industries Ltd.; Monarch Steelcraft Ltd.; Square Core Electrode Inc.; Dir., B.C. Sugar Refinery Ltd.; Polysar Ltd.; Crown Zellerbach Canada Ltd.; Grosvenor International Holdings Ltd.; mem. Vancouver Adv. Bd., National Trust Co.; Dir., Cdn. Steel Serv. Centre Inst.; Cdn. Cancer Soc.; Duke of Edinburgh's Award in Can.; Vancouver Playhouse Theatre (hon Life mem. and Past Pres.); Gov., St. George's Sch. for Boys; Alpha Delta Phi; Anglican; recreations: skiing, fishing, riding; Clubs: Shaughnessy Golf; The Vancouver; Vancouver Lawn Tennis; Home: 6389 Macdonald St., Vancouver, B.C. V6N 1E8; Office: Suite 1060, One Bentall Centre, 505 Burrard St., Vancouver, B.C. V7X 1M5

WILL, George R.; company president; b. Toronto, Ont., 23 May 1929; s. George Lewis and Anne (Moore) W.; e. Scarborough (Ont.) Coll. Inst.; Univ. of Toronto; Univ. of Detroit; m. Helen Doreen, d. John Stanley McGlashan, Dunbarton, Ont., 28 June 1952; children: Stephen, Gregory, Jeffrey, Lisa, Karen; PRESIDENT, CANADIAN CONTROLLERS LTD., since 1971; Engr. Trainee, Ont. Hydro, 1953-56; Sales Engr., Railway and Power Engineering, 1956-58; Br. Mgr., Klockner-Moeller, London, Ont., 1958-65; joined present firm as Dist. Mgr., London, Ont., 1965-66, Regional Mgr., Calgary, 1966-68, Dir. of Marketing, Scarborough, 1968-69, Vice Pres. and Gen. Mgr. 1969-71; mem., Candn. Elect. Mfrs. Assn. (Dir.); Anglican; Home: R.R.1, Claremont, Ont. L0H 1E0; Office: 1550 Birchmount Rd., Scarborough, Ont. M1P 2H1

WILLAN, Gordon E., B.A.Sc.; retired chemical engineer and executive; b. Toronto, Ont., 3 Oct. 1914; s. Thomas E. and Unite F. (Kirkegaard) W.; e. Univ. of Toronto, B.A.Sc. 1941; m. 1stly, late Mary E., d. late Michael S. White, 1 Feb. 1947; two d., Grace Anne, Karen Edith; 2ndly, Margery Joan, d. late S. G. Renouf, Regina, Sask., 22 June 1963; Mgr., Agricultural Products Ltd., BASF Canada Inc., 1973-81; Supvr. of Acid Dept., Defence Industries Ltd., Transcona, Man., 1941-43; Process Engr. and later Personnel Mgr., Canadian Synthetic Rubber Co. Ltd., Sarnia, Ont., 1943-45; Plant Supt., Dalglish

Chemicals Ltd., Toronto, Ont., 1945-47; Plant Supt., Niagara Brand Spray Ltd., 1947; apptd. Gen. Mgr. 1953; resigned as Vice-Pres. & Gen. Mgr., Niagara Chemicals, to join present firm, 1973; Del. to Gen. Assembly, Groupement Internat. des Assns. Nationales de Fabricants de Pesticides, 1969-73; mem., Assn. of Prof. Engrs. of Ont.; Candn. Agric. Chemicals Assn. (Pres. 1956-57); Kappa Sigma (G.M.); Protestant; recreations: gardening, home repairs, summer cottage; Club: Lions (Pres. 1967-68); Home: 1287 Fairway Court, Burlington, Ont. L7P 1M5;

WILLEMSEN, Richard Martin, B.A., F.I.I.C.; insurance executive; b. London, Eng., 2 Dec. 1932; s. Verner Rendtorff and Cicely (Jennings) W.; e. Schs. in Eng.; Upper Can. Coll., TorontO, Ont.; Amherst Coll., B.A. (cum laude) 1954; m. Aldona, d. Victor Bulzgis, 14 Jan. 1958; two d. Susan and Cynthia; PRESIDENT AND DIRECTOR, STERLING OFFICES OF CANADA LIMITED, since 1973; Dir., Solar Admin. Systems Ltd.; with Sterling Offices, Paris, France, 1954; Asst. Secy., Toronto, Ont., 1957; Mgr. in Mexico, 1958-60; Secy., Toronto, Ont., 1960, Asst. Vice Pres. 1963, Vice-Pres. 1965, Extve. Vice Pres. and Dir., 1968; former Hon. Consul General of Dominican Republic; Past President, Ins. Institute Canada; Ins. Inst. of Ont.; Psi Upsilon; Anglican; recreations: golf, squash, scuba diving, bridge; Clubs: Granite; York Downs Golf & Country; Ontario; University; Danish (London, Eng.); Home: 12 The Bridle Path, Willowdale, Ont. M2L 1C8; Office: 25 Adelaide St. E., Toronto, Ont. M5C 1Y4

WILLETT, Terence Charles, B.Sc., Ph.D.; educator; b. Warwickshire, Eng., 23 Dec. 1918; s. Charles Joseph and Elsie Jane (Allport) W.; e. Greenmore Coll., Eng., 1939; Staff Coll. Camberley, p.s.c. 1951; Univ. of London, B.Sc. 1957; London Sch. of Econ., Ph.D. 1962; m. Winifred, d. Gilbert Small, Providence, R.I., 12 Dec. 1942; children: Mark, Susan; PROF., DEPT. OF SOCIOLOGY, QUEEN'S UNIV. since 1973; Sr. Lectr. in Sociol., Royal Mil. Acad. Sandhurst, 1958; Lectr. in Sociol., Univ. of Reading, Berks, UK, 1964; joined present Univ. as Assoc. Prof. of Sociol. 1970; served with Royal Regt. of Arty. 1938-58; rank Lt. Col.; awarded T.D.; J.P. for Royal Co. of Berks. 1968-70; Sch. Gov., Camberley (Eng.) Schs.; Visitor, H.M. Borstals; author, "Criminal on the Road", 1964 (runner-up for Denis Carrol Prize, Internat. Soc. Criminol. 1965); "Drivers After Sentence", 1973; also book reviews and various articles on criminol. and sociol. of mil.; mem., Candn. Assn. for the Prevention of Crime; mem., Candn. Soc. Sociol. & Anthrop.; Fellow, Inter-Univ. Seminar on Armed Forces and Soc. 1976; Anglican; recreations: squash, golf; Home: 136 Bagot St., Kingston, Ont. K7L E3S; Office: Kingston, Ont.

WILLIAMS, Bruce MacGillivray, B.A.; diplomat; b. Nipigon, Ont., 31 Jan. 1918; s. Herbert Bruce and Margaret (Hogan) W.; e. Univ. of Toronto, B.A. 1941; EXTVE. VICE PRES., CANDN. INTERNATIONAL DEVELOPMENT AGENCY since 1974; joined the Department of External Affairs in 1946 as a Foreign Service Offr.; served with Candn. del. to the U.N., New York, 1946-48; Depy. Permanent Del. of Can. to European Office of the U.N., Geneva, 1952-53; Counsellor, Office of High Commr., for Can. in India, 1953-56; Candn. Commr. Internat. Supervisory Comn. for Vietnam, 1956-57; High Commr. for Can. in Ghana, 1959-62, and concurrently Ambassador to Togo, Upper Volta, Ivory Coast and Guinea; Ambassador to Turkey, 1962-64; Ass't. Undersecy. of State for External Affairs, 1964-67; Ambassador to Yugoslavia, Bulgaria and Romania 1967-72; High Commr. to India 1972-74; served with Canadian Army in 2nd World War; recreations: golf, bridge; Clubs: Royal Ottawa Golf; Delhi Gymkhana; Address: Jackson Bldg., Bank St., Ottawa, Ont. K1M 2E4

WILLIAMS, (David) Carlton, M.A., Ph.D., LL.D.; retired educator; b. Winnipeg, Man., 7 July 1912; s. John

Andrew and Anna (Carlton) W.; e. Gordon Bell and Kelvin High Schs., Winnipeg, Man.; Univ. of Manitoba, B.A. 1932, LL.D. 1969; Univ. of Toronto, M.A. 1937, Ph.D. 1940, LL.D. 1978; Univ. of Windsor LL.D. 1977; U. Western Ont., LL.D. 1978; m. Margaret Ashwell, d. late William Oliver Carson, 20 Nov. 1943; children: Catherine Ann, David Bruce Carson; Chrmn., Ont. Comm. on Freedom of Information and Individual Privacy 1977-80; Dir. of Research, Toronto Welfare Council, 1940-41; Research Assoc., Nat. Research Council on problems of pilot selection, 1941-42; Special Lectr., Univ. of Toronto 1945-46; Assoc. Prof. of Psychol, Univ. of Manitoba, 1946-48, and Prof. and Head of Dept. of Psychol. there, 1948-49; Prof. of Psychol, Univ. of Toronto, 1949-58; Dir., Divn. of Univ. Extension, 1958-65; Vice Pres., Univ. of Toronto, for Scarborough and Erindale Colls., and Princ. of Erindale Coll., 1965-67, Pres. and Vice Chancellor, Univ. of Western Ont. 1967-77; served in 2nd World War, with Personnel Selection, R.C.A.F. 1942-44, and Aircrew and as Pilot, 1944-45; Consultant, Toronto Juvenile Court Clinic, 1951-58; Dir., Addiction Research Foundation; London Health Assn.; mem., Adv. Comm., Women's Christian Assn.; London Symphony Orchestra; Fellow, Candn. Psychol. Assn. (Pres. 1954); Fellow Am. Psychol. Assn.; Publications: "The Arts as Communication" (ed) 1962; "Public Government for Private People," 1980; Report of Ont. Comm, on Freedom of Information and Individual Privacy (Chmn.); United Church; Clubs: Arts and Letters; York (Toronto); The London; London Hunt & Country; Home 252 Sydenham St., London, Ont. N6A 1W5

WILLIAMS, David Malcolm Lewis, F.R.C.S., F.R.C.S.(C); educator; b. Swansea, Wales 9 June 1932; s. late David Ievan and Gertrude (Jones) W.; e. Gowerton Boys' Grammar Sch. 1951 (Head Boy, Glamorgan Co. Scholarship 1951); Univ. of Sheffield 1951-58; qualified M.R.C.S. Eng., L.R.C.P. London 1958; m. Elizabeth Mary Denise d. late William Thomas Bassett 9 Aug. 1958; children: Paul Bassett, Siân Bassett, Clare Elizabeth; HEAD OF OTOLARYNGOLOGY, QUEEN'S UNIV. and Kingston Gen. Hosp. (also Chrmn. Med. Adv. Comte.-Chief of Staff) since 1969; House Surg. and House. Phys. Royal Infirmary, Sheffield 1958-59; Sr. House Offr. Wharncliffe Hosp. Sheffield 1959; Sr. House Offr. (Otolaryngol.) Gen. Hosp. Bristol 1959-60; Registrar (Otolaryngol.) The United Sheffield Hosps. 1960-62, 1964-6; Demonst. in anat. Univ. of Sheffield 1962-64; Registrar and Sr. Registrar (Otolaryngol.) cardiff Hosps. and Welsh Hosp. Bd. 1965-67; Fellow in Otology, Wayne State Univ. Detroit; author or co-author various med. publs., med. film; mem. Candn. Otolaryngol. Soc. (Educ. Comte., Chrmn. Postgrad. Curriculum Comte.); Kingston Acad. Med.; Candn. Standards Assn.; Ont. Med. Assn.; Am. Acad. Otolaryngol.; recreations: music, carpentry, silversmithing; Club: Kingston Yacht; Home: 61 Kensington Av., Kingston Ont., K7L 4B4; Office: Nickel 2, Kingston Gen. Hosp., Kingston, Ont.

WILLIAMS, David Rogerson, Jr.; Professional engineer; executive; b. Tulsa, Okla., 20 Oct. 1921; s. David Rogerson and Martha Reynolds (Hill) W.; e. Yale Univ. 1943; m. Pauline Bolton, 28 May 1944; children: Pauline Bolton (Mrs. Gerard E. d'Aquin), David Rogerson III, Rachel Katharine; Chrmn. of the Bd. and Pres., The Resources Sciences Corp. (Tulsa); Chmn. and CEO, Holmes & Narver, Inc. (Orange, Calif.); Chmn., Williams Brothers Canada Ltd. (Calgary); Williams Brothers Engineering Co.; Williams Brothers Process Services Inc.; Williams Brothers Urban Ore Inc.; East/West Energy Co.; (all of Tulsa); Alaskan Resource Sciences Corp. (Anchorage); Dir., Burlington Northern Inc. (St. Paul); Great Western Bank & Trust (Tucson); Northern Resources Inc. (Billings, Montana); Patagonia Corporation (Tucson); Pima Savings and Loan Association (Tucson); Western Am. Mortgage Co. (Phoenix); United States Filter Corporation (N.Y.); Filtrol Corporation (Los Angeles); Williams Brothers Engineer-

ing Ltd. (London, U.K.); Williams Brothers Engineering Malaysia Sdn. Bhd. (Tulsa); Constr. Engr., Foreman and Supt. Williams Brothers Corp. 1939, co-founder and Vice Pres. Williams Brothers Co. 1949, Extve. Vice Pres. 1956, Chrmn. Extve. Comte. 1966-70; served with USAAF, UTO 1943-46, rank Capt.; rec'd Air Medal, three Oak Leaf Clusters; Fellow, Am. Soc. Civil Engrs.; mem. Alta. Assn. Prof. Engrs.; Am. Gas Assn.; Am. Petroleum Inst.; Independent Natural Gas Assn.; Roy. Soc. of the Arts (London); Yale Engn. Assn.; Trustee; Desert Research Inst. (Reno); Hudson Inst. (Croton-on-Hudson, N.Y.); National Symphony Orch. (Wash., D.C.); Episcopalian; recreations: fishing, polo, painting, archaeology; Clubs: Ranchmen's (Calgary); Toronto; various US; Home: Oak Bar Ranch, Route 82 (Box 150) Nogales, Ariz. 85621 and Royal Antler Ranch, Invermere, B.C.; Office: 6600 S. Yale Ave., Tulsa, Okla, 74177

WILLIAMS, George Ronald, Ph.D., D.Sc., F.R.S.C.; educator; b. Liverpool, Eng. 4 Jan. 1928; s. George Williams; e. Rawson Rd. Sch. Seaforth 1939; Merchant Taylors' Sch. Crosby 1946; Univ. of Liverpool B.Sc. 1949, Ph.D. 1951, D.Sc. 1969; m. Joyce d. James Mutch 10 May 1952; children: Geoffrey Martin, Glynis Christine, Timothy George; CHRMN., DIV. OF LIFE SCIENCES, SCARBOROUGH COLL. UNIV. OF TORONTO, since 1978; Prof. of Biochem. Univ. of Toronto Med. Sch.; Commonwealth Travelling Scholar Worshipful Co. Goldsmiths, Banting & Best Dept. Med. Research Univ. of Toronto 1952-53, Asst. Prof. 1956-61, Assoc. Prof. of Biochem. 1961-66, Chrmn. of Biochem. 1970-77; Fellow, Johnson Foundation, Univ. of Pa. 1953-55; Med. Research Council appt. Sch. of Pathol. Oxford Univ. 1955-56; Sr. Research Fellow Nat. Research Council Can., Royal N. Shore Hosp. of Sydney, Australia 1967-68; Scient. Offr. Med. Research Council Can. 1969-73; Visiting Prof. of Geochem. Lamont-Doherty Geol. Observatory, Columbia Univ. 1977-78; author over 100 articles various scient. journs.; mem. Candn. Biochem. Soc. (Pres. 1971-72); Candn. Soc. Cell. Biol.; Biochem. Soc.; Am. Soc. Biol. Chems.; Geochem. Soc.; Royal Soc. Can.; United Church; recreations: reading, walking, travel; Home: 15 Bournville Dr., West Hill, Ont. M1E 1C3; Office: West Hill, Ont. M1C 1A4.

WILLIAMS, Gerald Haliburton; manufacturer; b. Chatham, Ont., 8 Nov. 1925; s. late Mr. and Mrs. Margaret (Patterson) W.; e. J. E. Benson Pub. Sch. and W. D. Lowe Vocational Sch., 1943, Windsor, Ont.; m. Ruth Lorraine, d. Walter Leard, Bedeque, P.E.I., 6 Apl. 1946; children: Richard Ernest, Karen Ruth, Jeffrey Leard; PRESIDENT, DeVILBISS CO., since 1976; joined present Co. (then De-Vilbiss Manufacturing Co. Ltd.), Windsor, as Draftsman, 1943, Candn. Sales Correspondent 1948, Toronto Office Sales Clk. 1950, Sales Rep.-W. Ont., 1950, Rep. W. Can., Fort William to Victoria, 1951, Br. Mgr., Windsor, 1953, Mgr., Indust. Sales, H.O., Barrie, Ont., 1960, Dir. of Engn. and Asst. to Pres., 1966, Extve. Vice Pres. 1967; Pres., DeVilbiss (Can.) Ltd. 1968-76; Dir., Champion Spark Plug Co.; served with R.C.N. 1944-46; Ald., Twp. of Sandwich W., 1959-60; City of Barrie, 1966-67; mem., Candn. Mfrs.' Assn.; P. Conservative; United Church; recreations: golf, curling; Clubs: Toledo Club; Toledo Rotary: Inverness (Toledo); Office: 300 Phillips Ave., Toledo, Ohio

WILLIAMS, Harry Leverne, M.Sc., Ph.D., F.R.S.C., F.C.I.C., F.R.S.C. (U.K.); chemist; educator; b. Warwick Twp., Ont. 16 Nov. 1916; s. Harry Young and Rosa Malinda (Brown) W.; e. Univ. of W. Ont. B.A. 1939, M.Sc. 1940; McGill Univ. Ph.D. 1943; m. Mary Eileen d. Samuel Cawson 31 Aug. 1946; children: Jai Joan Mary, Harvey Thomas Leverne; PROF. OF CHEM. ENGN. AND APPLIED CHEM., UNIV. OF TORONTO 1967- ; Dir. Chemical Engineering Research Consultants Ltd.; Research Chem., Group Leader/Supvr., Asst. Mgr./Projects Mgr., Princ. Scient. Research & Devel. Div. Polymer Corp. Ltd. 1946-67; mem. Senate, Univ. of W. Ont. 1955-

67; author "Polymer Engineering" 1975; over 100 scient. papers synthesis, characterization and properties synthetic high polymers; mem. various journ. adv. bds.; Fellow, N.Y. Acad. Sciences; Am. Assn. Advanc. Science; Plastics & Rubber Inst.; mem. (Life), Soc. Chem. Industry; mem. Soc. Plastics Industry; Assn. Chem. Prof. Ont.; Assn. Prof. Engrs. Prov. Ont.; Soc. Plastics Engrs.; Am. Chem. Soc.; Sigma Xi; recreations: music, art; Home: 255 Glenlake Ave., Apt. 2011, Toronto, Ont. M6P 1G2; Office: Toronto, Ont. M5S 1A4.

WILLIAMS, Jack; retired labour executive; b. Bradford, Eng., 26 Feb. 1907; s. John George and Emily Mary (Watts) W.; e. St. Catharines (Ont.) Coll. & Vocational Sch.; m. Carrie, d. R. N. Rymer, St. Catharines, Ont., 1930; children: John Donald, Carolyn Jeanne, Mary Elizabeth; with Edit. Staff, St. Catharines "Standard", 1928-41; Candn. Press Parlty. Staff, Ottawa (specializing in Labour) 1941-46; Public Relations Dir., Candn. Congress of Labour, 1946-56; retired as Public Relations Counsel, Candn Labour Congress; mem., Candn. Public Relations Soc.; N.D.P.; Home: R.R. 1, First Ave., Louth, Vineland Station, Ont. L0R 2E0

WILLIAMS, James Alwin, B.Sc., M.Eng.; petroleum executive; b. Billings, Mont. 8 Oct. 1934; s. William Dudley and Jessica H. (Kramer) W.; e. Lloydminster High Sch. 1953; Mount Royal Coll. 1954; Univ. of Okla. B.Sc. 1956, M.Eng. (Petroleum Engn.) 1958; Stanford Univ. Extve. Program in Business Mang. 1972; m. Kathryn G. d. Mark Rockwell 30 Aug. 1959; children: James J., William R., Stephen R., Patrick A., Laura K.; PRES., DRUMMOND PETROLEUM LTD., 1980- ; Petroleum Eng., Pure Oil Co., Ill., Colo. and Wyo. 1962-64; Dist. Engr., Husky Oil. Lloydminster 1965, Area Supt. 1966, Extve. Asst. to Pres., Calgary 1971, Special Projects Mgr. Denver 1972, Extve. Asst. to Pres., Cody 1973, Mgr. Calif. Project, Cody 1974, Vice Pres. Cody 1975, Sr. Vice Pres. Exploration & Production Cody 1975 and Calgary 1977; Extve. Vice Pres., Husky Oil Operations Ltd., 1979; Chrmn. Recreation Bd. Lloydminster 1969-71; Pres. Lloydminster Hockey Assn. 1967-68; served with U.S. Navy 1958-62, rank Lt.; Past Dir. W. Oil & Gas Assn.; Past mem. Extve. Comte. Rocky Mt. Oil & Gas Assn.; mem. Am. Inst. Mining Engrs.; Life mem. Okla Alumni Assn.; mem. of L.K.O.T.; Past Pres. Delta Kappa Epsilon; Freemason; Protestant; recreations: hunting, fishing, golf, skiing; Clubs: Calgary Petroleum; Glencoe; Pinebrook Golf & Winter; Home: P.O. Box 11, (Site 24, R.R. 12, Calgary, Alta. T3E 6W3; Office: #400 Edinburgh Pl., 900 6th Ave. S.W., Calgary, Alta. T2P 3K2

WILLIAMS, John Francis, C.A., C.M.C.; executive; b. Fort Frances, Ont. 21 Jan. 1935; s. Leonard Francis and Sarah Eileen (Young) W.; e. Fort Frances High Sch. 1953; Inst. C.A.'s Ont.; Queen's Univ. Correspondence/Articling; m. Evelyn Lenore d. late J. Grant Fraser 27 Oct. 1956; children: Barbara, Wendy, Lawrence, Randal;PRES., CHIEF OPERATING OFFR. AND DIR. HEADWAY CORP. LTD.1978- ; Dir. Sunway Financial Services Inc.; Lakehead Developers Ltd.; Secy.-Treas., Jim Mathieu Lumber Ltd. 1963-66; Mang. Consultant, Urwick Currie & Partners 1966-68; Mang. Dir. Quetico Centre 1968-69; Princ., Currie Coopers Lybrand 1969-75; Extve. Vice Pres. and Gen. Mgr. present Co. 1975-78; Dir. and Past Pres. Quetico Centre for Continuing Educ.; Gov. Lakehead Univ.; mem. Inst. C.A.'s Ont.; Inst. Mang. Consultants Ont.; recreations: tennis, curling, reading; Club: Thunder Bay Country; Home: 421 Laurel Court, Thunder Bay, Ont. P7A 7L3; Office291 South Court St., Thunder Bay, Ont. P7B 5G6.

WILLIAMS, Joseph Kenneth; Q.C., B.Com., b. Toronto, Ont., 9 May, 1916; s. Harry B. and Myra M. (Hargreaves) W.; e. Runnymede Coll., Toronto, Ont.; Univ. of Toronto, B.Com. 1938; Osgoode Hall, Toronto, Ont. (1939-42); m. Barbara I., d. late Willis D. McLennan, 8 Sept. 1945;

one s., Rodney M.; Senior Vice Pres., Gen. Counsel & Secy., The National Life Assurance Co. Of Canada, 1967-81; read law with Arnoldi, Parry & Campbell, Toronto, Ont.; Dir., National Life; called to the Bar of Ont., June 1942; cr. Q.C. 1961; with Shell Oil Co. of Can. Ltd., Toronto, Ont., 1946-47; Mgr., Property & Legal Dept., The National Life Assnce. Co. of Can., 1947, Secy. 1952, Gen. Counsel and Secy. 1958-67, Vice-Pres. 1967-79; served in 2nd World War with R.C.A.F. as Meteorol. Offr., 1942-45; mem. Law Soc. Upper Can.; Candn. Bar Assn.; Assn. of Life Ins. Counsel; Phi Delta Phi; Protestant; recreations: golf, skiing; Clubs: Mississaugua Golf & Country; Home: 48 Langmuir Crescent, Toronto, Ont. M6S 2A7;

WILLIAMS, Hon. Louis Allan, Q.C., M.L.A., LL.B.; politician; b. Glenavon, Sask. 22 May 1922; s. Louis Pomerine and Eula Belle (MacPherson) W.; e. primary and secondary schs. Sask.; Univ. of B.C., LL.B.; m. Marjorie Ruth Lake, Vancouver, B.C. 25 June 1948; children: Louis Ryder, Leslie Ruth, Susan Jane;ATTORNEY-GENERAL OF B.C.1979- ; el. M.L.A. for West Vancouver-Howe Sound prov. g.e. 1966, re-el. since; Min. of Labour 1975; served with RCAF, rank Flight Lt.; Social Credit; Protestant; Office: Parliament Bldgs., Victoria, B.C. V8V 1X4.

WILLIAMS, Margaret, B.A., B.L.S.; librarian; b. St. John's, Nfld. 11 Dec. 1931; d. Frank and Alice (Williams) Jarvis; e. Memorial Univ. B.A. 1953; Univ. of Toronto B.L.S. 1961; unm.; UNIVERSITY LIBRARIAN, MEMORIAL UNIVERSITY OF NEWFOUNDLAND LIBRARY since 1980; mem. Nat. Lib. Adv. Bd.1972-78; Cataloguer, Memorial Univ. Lib. 1953-61, Asst. Librarian 1961-68, Asst. Librarian for Tech. Services 1968-75; Assoc. Librarian, 1975-80; author of articles in A.P.L.A. Bulletin; mem. Candn. Lib. Assn.; Candn. Assn. Coll. and Univ. Libs. (Pres. 1973-74); Atlantic Provs. Lib. Assn. (Vice Pres. 1969-70); Nfld. Lib. Assn. (Pres. 1969-71); Bibliographical soc. of Canada Council 1978-81; rec'd. Centennial Medal; Catholic; Home: Apt. 604, 100 Elizabeth Ave., St. John's, Nfld. A1B 1S1; Office: St. John's, Nfld.

WILLIAMS, Marshall MacKenzie, M.Eng.; utilities exec-utive; b. Londonderry, N.S., 11 Dec. 1923; s. late Millard Filmore and late Gladys Christine (MacKenzie) W.; e. N. S. Tech. Coll., B.E. (Civil Engn.) 1947, M.Eng. 1949; Banff Sch. of Advanced Mang. 1955; m. Joan Atlee, d. late G. W. W. Ross, 6 Sept. 1952; children: Peter, Alex, Stephen, Margot; PRESIDENT, & DIRECTOR, TRANSALTA UTILITIES CORP.; Dir., PanCanadian Petroleum Limit-ed; Royal Trust Corp. of Can.; Royal Trustco Ltd.; Candn. Energy Research Inst.; Alberta Research Council; AEC Power Ltd.; Nfld. Light & Power Co. Ltd.; Sun Life Assnce. Co. of Can.; Soc., Environ. & Energy Devel. Studies Fdn.; mem. Adv. Bd., Royal Trust (Calgary); joined Montreal Engineering Company, Limited 1948-54; joined present Co. as Asst. to Gen. Mgr. 1954, Extve. Asst. 1960; Asst. Gen. Mgr. 1966, Extve. Vice Pres. 1968; Dir. 1972; Pres. 1973; Pres. and C.E.O. 1980; Calgary Chamber Comm.; Construction Industry Industrial Rela-tions Council; Assn. Prof. Engrs., Geols. & Geophysicists Alta.; Dir., Candn. Elect. Assn.; N.W. Elect. Light & Power Assn.; Presbyterian; recreations: skiing, fishing, hiking; Club: The Ranchmen's; Home: 1315 — 70th Ave. S.W., Calgary, Alta. T2V 0R2; Office: 110 — 12th Ave. S.W., Calgary Alta. T2R 0G7

WILLIAMS, Michael Allan, B.Com., F.C.A.; petroleum executive; b. Vancouver, B.C. 29 May 1933; s. John Sam-uel and Joyce Winerfred (Cooper) W.; e. Univ. of B.C. B.Com. 1956; m. Daisy Pauline Popoff 18 July 1959; chil-dren: Susan, Jennifer, John; PRES., Sulpetro LTD., Inter-nat. Div. 1980- ; Accounting Clk. Husky Oil & Refining 1956-57; Student and C.A., Peat Marwick Mitchell & Co. 1957-62; various financial and taxation functions Home Oil Co. Ltd. 1962-69; Treas. and Mgr. Accounting present Co. 1969, Vice Pres. Finance & Treas. 1971, Sr. Vice Pres.

and Treas. 1974, Extve. Vice Pres. 1975-80; Gov. Univ. of Calgary; Dir. and Past Pres. Jr. Achievement of S. Alta.; mem. Alta. Inst. C.A.'s; Financial Extves. Inst. Can.; Clubs: Calgary Petroleum; Ranchmen's; Calgary Winter; Home: 18 Varview Pl. N.W., Calgary, Alta. T3A 0G5; Office: 28 Floor, 330 Fifth Ave. S.W., Calgary, Alta. T2P 0L4.

WILLIAMS, Neville Rudyard; retired construction executive; b. Portland, Ore., U.S.A., 12 Jan. 1908; s. Alfred Neville and Alice Anne (Riggall) W.; e. Kelvin Tech. High Sch., Winnipeg, Man.; m. Dorothy Cole, 30 Nov. 1935; three d. Carole Anne, Janice Lynne, Frances Glenda; with father's Co., Williams Engineering Co. Ltd., Winnipeg, Man., on part-time basis. 1924-29; Supt. and Dir., 1935; formed own Co., Maple Leaf Construction Ltd., 1942; estbd. Maple Leaf Distributors Ltd., 1947; mem., Winnipeg Builders' Exchange; Candn. Good Roads Assn.; Winnipeg Chamber of Comm.; Candn. Chamber of Comm.; Candn. Constr. Assn., since 1944 (Vice-Pres., 1963-64; Pres. 1965); Pres., Manitoba Road Builders' Assn., 1949; Prairie Road Builders' Assn., 1955; Protestant; recreations: fishing, music; Club: Carleton; Office: 777 Erin St., Winnipeg, Man. R3G 2W2

WILLIAMS, Rhys John, B.Sc.; engineering executive; b. London, Eng. 17 Feb. 1934; s. late Rees and late Lilian Sarah (Moore) W.; e. Bancroft's Sch. Woodford Green, Eng. 1952; Queen Mary Coll. Univ. of London B.Sc. (Engn.) 1955; Manchester (Eng.) Business Sch. 1967; m. Yvonne Ann d. Joseph George Tatton, London, Eng. 18 Aug. 1956; two s. Gareth, Lloyd; PRES. AND CHIEF EXTVE. OFFR., CANADIAN MARCONI CO. 1977- ; Dir. A. B. Dick Co. of Canada Ltd.; A.E.I. Telecommunications (Canada) Ltd.; Mang. Trainee, The Marconi Co. Ltd. Chelmsford, Eng. 1957, Production Controller 1961, Supplies Mgr. 1965; Mang. Dir. Marconi South Africa Ltd. Johannesburg 1967; Mgr. Radio & Space Communications Div. Marconi Communication Systems Ltd. Eng. 1970, Dir. and Gen. Mgr. 1973; served with Fleet Air Arm of R.N. 1955-57, Sub-Lt. Observer; Anglican; recreations: boating, squash, photography; Club: Forest & Stream; Home: 2 Morgan Rd., Baie d'Urfe, Que. H9X 3A2; Office: 2442 Trenton Ave., Montreal, Que. H3P 1Y9.

WILLIAMS, William Lewis; insurance executive; b. Newport, U.K., 28 Nov. 1918; s. Evan Jones and Rhoda Elizabeth (Brown) W.; e. St. Julians High Sch., U.K., 1930-35; Worcester Coll. (U.K.), Teaching Dip. 1946; m. Winifred Hilda, d. late William Ridd Pope, U.K., 8 Aug. 1941; children: Stuart Ridd, Anne Rosemarie; PRES. C.E.O, AND DIR., COMMERCIAL LIFE ASSURANCE CO. OF CANADA since 1968 & HALIFAX INSURANCE COMPANY, since 1972; Dir., Insurance Bureau of Can.; Insurers Advisory Organization of Canada; Canadian Childrens' Fdn.; Canada/Netherlands Chamber of Commerce; emigrated to N. Am. in 1952; joined Mutual of Omaha Insurance Co. in E. U.S., 1952; served as Rep., Agency Mang., Regional Supvr., Dir. of Sales and Marketing for Can. becoming Vice-Pres., 1967; served with RAF 1939-45; comnd. Burma/India Theatre 1943; rank Flight Lt.; mem., Bd. Trade Metrop. Toronto; Freemason; Protestant; recreations: fishing, boating, golf; Home: King City, Ont. L0G 1K0; Office: 1303 Yonge St., Toronto, Ont. M4T 1W9

WILLIAMSON, Moncrieff, LL.D., O.C.; gallery and museum director; b. East Linton, Scotland, 23 Nov. 1915; s. James Watt, J.P., and Gwendoline Pilkington Jackson W.; e. Loretto Sch., Scotland; Michot Mongenast, Brussels; Edinburgh Coll. of Art; LL.D. P.E.I. 1972; m. Pamela Upton, d. Jocelyn Herbert Fanshawe, 30 Sept. 1948; one s. Timothy Malcolm Moncrieff; DIR. CONFEDERATION ART GALLERY AND MUSEUM, since 1964; Asst. Prof. of Fine Art, Prince of Wales Coll., and Univ. P.E.I. 1966-71; formerly a Dir., Art Exhns. Bureau, London, Eng.; Dir., Art Dept., Glenbow Foundation, Calgary, Alta.; Curator, Art Gallery of Greater Victoria, B.C.; served in

2nd World War, Brit. Army Intelligence Corps in Eng., France, Belgium, Germany; Govt. Communications Dept., Foreign Office; Brit. Air Comn., Washington, D.C.; Publications: "Four Poems", 1945; "Fluid Idol" 1952; "Canadian Fine Crafts", 1967; "Robert Harris 1849-1919; An Unconventional Biography" 1971; "Through Canadian Eyes", 1976; Organiser and Catalogue Author, "Robert Harris" Portraits, Nat. Gallery Can. 1973; numerous articles and poems publ. Eng., Germany, U.S., New Zealand, Canada (Diplôme d'honneur, 1975); President (1971-73) Canadian Art Museum Directors Organ.; Fellow Royal Society of Arts; mem., Candn. Museums Assn.; Internat. Council of Museums, Paris; Am. Art Museum Dirs. Assn.; Consultative Comte., Candn. Conf. of the Arts; Commonwealth Assoc. of Museums, London; Movable Cultural Property Review Bd., Ottawa (1976-80); Fellow, Canadian Museums Assoc. 1980; Council mem., Cdn. Soc. of Decorative Arts, 1981; rec'd Centennial Medal; Silver Jubilee Medal 1977; R.C.A. 1978; Liberal; Anglican; recreations: conversation, reading, swimming; Home: 14 Churchill Ave., Charlottetown, P.E.I. C1A 1Y8; Office: Confederation Centre, Charlottetown, P.E.I.

WILLISTON, Ray Gillis, B.A.; industrialist; b. Victoria, B.C., 17 Jan. 1914; s. Hubert Haines (U.E.L.) and Islay (McCalman) W.; e. high sch. Salmon Arm, B.C., 1932; Normal Sch. Victoria, B.C. (elem. teacher) 1933; Univ. of B.C. B.A. 1940, teaching cert.; m. Gladys Edna d. late Neil McInnes, 7 Apl. 1939; children: Dr. Hubert, Mrs. Sandra Dunn, Mrs. Dianne Pagurut; CHRMN. AND PRES. BRITISH COLUMBIA CELLULOSE CO. since 1976; Chrmn. Ocean Falls Corp.; Dir. Canadian Cellulose Co. Ltd. 1976-80; elem/secondary teacher various B.C. schs. 1934-41; Supervising Princ. Prince George Schs. 1945-49, Supt. of Schs. Peace River, Prince George, Vanderhoof, McBride 1949-53; M.L.A. for Fort George 1953-72, Min. of Educ. 1954-56, Min. of Lands & Forests 1956-62, Min. of Lands, Forests and Water Resources 1962-72; Dir. of B.C. Rly. 1957-72; Dir. B.C. Hydro and mem. Extve. Mang. 1962-72; Chrmn. Candn. Entity Columbia River Devel. 1970-72; Chrmn. Environment and Land Use Comte. 1971-72; Consultant forestry Govt. of N.B., UN Devel. Corp., F.A.O. (Rome), C.I.D.A. 1972-76; Gen. Mgr. N.B. Forest Authority 1973-76; Chrmn. B.C. Columbia River Treaty Negotiations; served with RCAF 1941-45, Ground Instr. and Pilot; Dir., Roy. Cdn. Geog. Soc. since 1978; Victoria YM/YWCA 1960-72; named Brit. Columbian of Yr. Newsmen's Club 1964; Distinguished Current Achievement Forestry Award W. Forestry & Conserv. Assn. 1965; Forestry Achievement Award Candn. Inst. Foresters 1970; Freemason; Shriner; Social Credit; United Church; recreations: sports, photography, trailering; Club: Union; Home: 3922 Cedar Hill Rd., Victoria, B.C. V8P 2N2; Office: 2659 Douglas, Victoria, B.C. V8T 4M3

WILLMOT, Donald Gilpin, B.A.Sc.; executive; b. Toronto, Ont. 7 March 1916; s. Harold Edward and Florence (Gilpin) W.; e. John Fisher Pub. Sch. and N. Toronto Coll. Inst., Toronto; Univ. of Toronto B.A.Sc. 1937; m. Ivy Vivien d. late Leonard Sutcliffe 18 Nov. 1939; children: Michael, Wendy, David; CHRMN. OF BD., THE MOLSON COMPANIES LTD. 1974- ; Vice Pres. and Dir. The Bank of Nova Scotia; Dir. Crown Life Insurance Co.; Hayes-Dana Ltd.; Inco Ltd.; Jannock Ltd.; Engr. Canadian SKF Co. Ltd. Toronto 1937-38; Plant Supt. Anthes Imperial Ltd. St. Catharines 1939-41; Supt., Mgr. Personnel & Pub. Relations, Asst. to Vice Pres., Gen. Mgr. Atlas Steels Ltd. Welland 1942-48; Pres. and Dir. Anthes Imperial Ltd. 1948-68; Pres. and Dir. Molson Industries Ltd. Toronto 1968-73; Depy. Chrmn of Bd. The Molson Companies Ltd. 1973-74; Trustee, Toronto Western Hosp.; Ont. Jockey Club; Past Chrmn. Bd. of Govs. Brock Univ.; mem. Bd. Govs. Ridley Coll. St. Catharines; mem. Adv. Council, Candn. Mfrs.' Assn.; Anglican; recreations: golf, tennis; Clubs: Toronto; York; Rosedale Golf; Mount Royal; Florida Country; Home: Kinghaven Farms, R.R. 2,

King, Ont. L0G 1K0; Office: (P.O. Box 6015) 2 International Blvd., Toronto, Ont. A.M.F., L5P 1B8.

WILLMOTT, Ross Marlton; company director; b. Milton, Ont., 28 Apl. 1910; s. Carleton Ross and Elma Elizabeth Ann Proctor (Marlton) W.; e. North Toronto Coll. Inst., Toronto, Ont.; m. Althea Evangeline, d. Very Rev. C. E. Riley, Toronto, Ont., 18 July 1942; two d. Caroline Althea, Judith Margaret; Trustee, BM-RT Realty Investments; with stockbroking firms 1929-35; joined Traders Finance Corp. Limited as an Accountant, 1935, Internal Audit Department, 1938-49, apptd. Assistant Treasurer, 1949, Treasurer, 1952, el. Dir. 1953, Vice-Pres. and Treas., 1954, Extve. Vice-Pres. and Treas., 1956-60, Pres. and Dir. 1960-70; served in 2nd World War; Flying Offr., R.C.A.F., 1943-45; Navigator (Overseas) 1944-45; Freemason; Conservative; Anglican; recreations: gardening, travelling; Clubs: York; National; Mount Royal (Montreal); Naples Yacht; Homes: Apt. 1805, 61 St. Clair Ave. W., Toronto, Ont. M4V 2Y8

WILLOUGHBY, Bertram Elmore, B.S.A., F.R.I.; real estate broker; b. Georgetown, Ont., 17 July 1917; s. John Armstrong and Florence Elizabeth (Mothersill) W.; e. Pub. Sch. and N. Toronto Coll. Inst. and Northern Vocational (Matric.) Sch., Toronto, Ont.; Ont. Agric. Coll., B.S.A.; m. Evelyn Gertrude, d. Albert H. Boddy, 25 June 1942; children: Diane Lesley, Beverly; DIR., A.E. LEPAGE LTD., Pres., Trans Canada Holdings Ltd.; Gibson Willoughby Ltd.; Gibswill Ltd.; Vice Pres. and Dir., Standard Trust Co.; Dir., Denison Mines Ltd.; Conray Resources Ltd.; Chrmn., A.E. Le Page (Ont.) Ltd.; Toronto Medical Arts Building Co. Ltd.; with Canadian Industries Ltd. as Production Supvr., Shawinigan Falls Works, 1941-45; Past Pres., Ont. Assn. of Real Estate Bds. (1952-53); Toronto Real Estate Bd. (1954-55); Past Pres., Candn. Inst. of Realtors (1960-61); Past Pres., Candn. Assn. of Real Estate Bds. (1964-65); Past Pres., Candn. Chapter, Internat. Real Estate Fed. (1973, 74); mem. Nat. Assn. Realtors; Candn. Real Estate Assn.; Ont. Real Estate Assn.; Toronto Real Estate Bd.; Am. Soc. Real Estate Counselors; Soc. of Residential Appraisers; Anglican; recreations: golf, fishing, all sports; Clubs: Rosedale Golf; Board of Trade; St. Andrews (Fla.); Caledon Mountain Trout; Caledon Riding & Hunt; Bocaraton Hotel & Club (Fla.) Home: c/o Belfountain P.O., Belfountain, Ont. L0N 1B0; Office: 50 Holly St., Toronto, Ont. M4S 2G1

WILLSON, Bruce Franklin, B.Sc.; executive; b. Edmonton, Alta., 1 May 1921; s. Norman Currie and Myrtle Viola (Bragg) W.; e. Garneau Pub. and High Schs., Edmonton, Alta.; Univ. of Alberta, B.Sc. (Civil Engn.); m. Joan Whitman, d. George Heath MacDonald, Edmonton, 29 May 1943; two s., one d.; Dir., Chas. Tennant & Co. (Canada) Ltd.; Prudential Growth Fund Canada Limited; Trustee, Prudential Income Fund; commenced career as Distribution Engineer, Northwestern Utilities Limited, Edmonton 1945; Vice-President, Operations, Northwestern Utilities Ltd. and Canadian Western Natural Gas Company Ltd., Calgary 1956, Extve. Vice-Pres. 1958, Pres. (both Companies) 1962; President, Canadian Bechtel Ltd. 1965-71; President, Union Gas Limited 1971-74; served with 13th Co. Engrs., Service and Works, as Lt. 1943-45; mem. Candn. Gas Assn. (Dir. and Past Pres.); Engn. Inst. Can.; Pacific Coast Gas Assn.; Assns. Prof. Engrs. Ont.; Past Dir., Alta. Heart Foundation; Un. Fund Calgary; Past Nat. Chrmn., Comte. for an Indep. Can.; Alta. Div., Candn. Petroleum Assn.; United Church; recreations: curling, golf; Clubs: National; York Downs Golf & Country; Rosedale Golf (Toronto); Royal and Ancient Golf Club of St. Andrews (Scotland); Edmonton; Home: 32 Quail Valley Drive, Thornhill, Ont. L3T 4R2

WILLSON, Robert Alan; banker and management consultant; b. Toronto, Ont. 7 May 1918; s. Donald Francis and Edna Mackenzie (Reid) W.; e. Humberside Coll. Inst.

Toronto 1934; Univ. of Toronto Extension Courses; m. Florence Margaret d. David Mark Wickett 24 Sept. 1943; children: Roderick Laird, Gary David, Martha Ann; CHRMN. OF THE BD. NORTHLAND BANK since 1976; (formerly Pres. and founding Bd. mem.); Chmn., Willson Associates Ltd. Management Counsel; mem. Bd. of Gov., Exec. Comte., Univ. of Calgary; mem. Bd., Calgary Research and Devel. Authority; Co-Chmn., Canadians for Canada; Sales Analyst Lever Brothers Ltd. 1936-42; Personnel Personnel Mang. Massey-Ferguson Ltd. 1942-46; Conciliation Offr. Fed. Dept. of Labour 1946-48; Dir., Indust. and Pub. Relations Studebaker of Can. 1948-54; Long Range Planning & Corporate Adm. General Foods Ltd. 1954-61; Asst. Prof. Mang. and Asst. Dean Sch. of Business Univ. of Minn. 1963-65; Dean and Extve. Dir. The Banff Sch. of Advanced Mang. 1965-69, presently Chrmn. of Bd.; served with Candn. Armed Forces 1942; Chrmn. Citizens' Comte. on Human Cost of Unemployment for Candn. Senate; Founding Chrmn. Coll./Fed. Agency Univ. of Minn.; Past Pres. Community Welfare Council Hamilton, Ont.; Ont. Welfare Council; Past Bd. mem. Candn. Council for Social Devel.; Big Brother Movement; Past Chrmn. Overseas Inst. Can.; mem. Candn. Chamber Comm.; P. Conservative; United Church; recreations: history, travel, photography, golf; Clubs: Willow Park Golf & Country; Ranchmen's; Rotary; Office: 324 — 8th Ave., S.W., Calgary, Alta.

WILSON, Albert John Greene, Q.C., C.D., M.A., O. St. J., F.S.A. (Scot.); b. Hamilton, Ont., 20 Jan. 1907; s. Henry Dillon and Julia Isabella (Greene) W.; e. Univ. of Toronto, B.A. 1930, M.A. 1933; Osgoode Hall Law Sch., Toronto, Ont.; Univ. of Michigan (Law Sch.); m. late Margaret Eleanor, d. Lawrence Killam, LL.D., 24 Sept. 1938; children: Henry Lawrence Killam, B.A., D.D.S., Ruth Eleanor Killam (Mrs. W.K. Winkler), Margaret Anne Killam (Mrs. Glenn Munro), David Albert Killam, B.A., M.D.; m. 2ndly, Helen Royale Nelson, 7 April 1973; served in 2nd World War, 1941-46, and in Militia with rank of Major; def. (Liberal) cand. in Eglinton for H. of C. in g.e. 1957 and 1958; read law with Bicknell & O'Brien, Toronto, Ont.; called to the Bar of Ont., 1935; cr. Q.C. 1958; Past Pres., Multiple Sclerosis Soc.; Augustan Soc.; Order of St. Sava and Order of the Crown of Yugoslavia; Order of St. Lazarus; Freemason (Scot. Rite); Phi Delta Phi Internt. Legal Frat.; Episcopalian; Home: 57 Lytton Blvd., Toronto, Ont. M4R 1L2

WILSON, Charles Frederick, A.M., Ph.D.; Canadian public service; b. London, Ont., 11 Mar. 1907; s. David Craig and Mary Jane (Mitchell) W.; e. Univ. of W. Ont., B.A. 1928; Harvard Univ., A.M. 1932, Ph.D. 1937; m. Ruth, d. Ralph Tillinghast Barnefield, Pawtucket, R.I., 28 Nov. 1936; children: David Arnold, Hope; Princ., Berbice Boys High Sch., New Amsterdam, Brit. Guiana, 1928-31; Instr. in Econ., wellesley Coll., 1933-35; Brown Univ., 1935-36; Grain Stat., Dom. Bur. of Stat., 1936-40; Chief., Agric. Br. there, 1940-43; Dir., Wheat & Grain Div., Dept. of Trade & Commerce and Secretary/Adviser Cabinet Wheat Comte., 1943-52; Agric. Counsellor, Candn. Embassy, Rome 1952-54; Comm. Counsellor, Candn. Embassy, Copenhagen 1955-60; Consul General of Canada, Chicago 1960-64; Minister-Counsellor, Candn. Embassy, Vienna, 1965-67; in charge of arrangements for establishing the Canada Grains Council 1968-69; mem. Grains Group under Min. i/c of Candn. Wheat Board, 1969-72; author of "Review of Government Grain Policy", "A Century of Candn. Grain: Government Policy to 1951", "Grain Marketing in Canada"; "C.D. Howe: An Optimist's Response to a Surfeit of Grain"; mem., Candn. Del. on negotiation Internat. Wheat Agreement, 1947-62; Chairman, Comte. on Commodity Problems, FAO of UN, Rome, 1958-59; Elder, St. Andrews Ch., Ottawa; Presbyterian; recreations: golf, cabinet-making; Clubs: Royal Ottawa Golf; Address: 200 Mariposa Ave., Rockcliffe Pk., Ottawa, Ont. K1M 0T6

WILSON, Charles Laird, B.Sc., M.D., C.M., F.R.C.S. (Can.); surgeon; b. Ottawa, Ont., 16 Aug. 1916; s. Herbert Ernest and Lynda Bradley (Gamble) W.; e. Montreal (Que.) High Sch., 1933; McGill Univ., B.Sc., M.D., C.M. 1940, Dipl. Surg. 1948; m. Margaret Agnes, d. late Wishart Van Every 23 June 1941; childen: Patricia Margaret, Robert Laird, Brenda Elizabeth; SR. ORTHOPEDIC SURGEON, MONTREAL GEN. HOSP.; Chief of Orthopedic Surg., Reddy Mem. Hosp.; began practice in Montreal 1948; served with RCN 1942-45; Visiting Orthopedic Specialist to Tunisia for Medico, 1968; Djakarta, 1972; awarded Surg. Medal, Royal Coll. of Surgs. of Can., 1951; Am. Nat. Research Fellowship 1941, 1945 and 1946; mem., Candn. Med. Assn.; Candn. Orthopedic Assn.; Internat. Soc. Orthopedics & Traumatology; Que. Soc. Orthopedics & Traumatology; Lafleur Reporting Soc.; Psi Upsilon; Protestant; recreations: golf, skiing, curling, boating; Clubs: Royal Montreal Golf; Mid-Ocean (Bermuda); Bermuda Golf; Ste Marguerite Golf; Thistle Curling; Ste Marguerite Ski; Home: 35 Thurlow Rd., Hampstead, Que. H3X 3G7; Office: 3550 Cote des Neiges Rd., Montreal, Que. H3H 1V3

WILSON, Donald James; insurance executive; b. Halifax, N.S., 21 Sept. 1920; s. Gordon Ross and Mary (O'Hearn) W.; e. Halifax Co. Acad., 1937; m. Isabelle Christine MacFayden, 5 Oct. 1945; children: Ian Ross, late Brian Donald; EXTVE. VICE PRESIDENT AND DIRECTOR, FAMILY LIFE ASSURANCE GROUP, including Sovreign General Ins. Co. since 1978; joined Royal Trust Company, Halifax 1937-41; Acct., Halifax, 1945-47; Partner, Major Adjustments Bureau, 1947-51; Owner, D.J. Wilson Ltd. (loss adjusting), 1951-54; Regional Supvr. then Asst. Gen. Mgr., Interprov. Claims, Montreal, 1954-56; joined present Co. as Regional Mgr., Toronto, 1956-59; Asst. Vice Pres. and Gen. Sales Mgr., Montreal, 1959-64; Vice Pres. and Asst. Gen. Mgr., 1964; Vice Pres. and Mang. Dir., Montreal 1965; served with the R.C.N.V.R. 1941-45, retired with rank Lt. Commdr.; Assoc., Ins. Inst. of Can. 1963 (1963); Dir., Ins. Bur. Can.; mem., Bd. Trade Metrop. Toronto; United Church; recreations: golf, skiing; Clubs: Granite; York Downs Golf; Willow Park Golf (Calgary); Home: 21-3201 Rideau Pl. S.W., Calgary, Alta. T2S 2T1; Office: 300-5th Ave. S.W., Calgary, Alta. T2P 0L3

WILSON, Donald Laurence, M.A., M.D., C.M., F.R.C.P. (C), F.A.C.P.; physician; b. Hamilton, Ont., 2 Oct. 1921; s. Donald Alexander and Laura Louise (Dressel) W.; e. Hamilton (Ont.) Central Coll. (1935-39); Queen's Univ., M.D., C.M. 1944; Fellow in Biochem., Univ. of Toronto (1946-48); M.A. 1948; Fellow in Med., Harvard Med. Sch., 1949-51; m. Mary Isobel, d. late John Wesley Pierce, Peterborough, Ont., 6 Jan. 1945; children: Mary Barbara, Judith Isobel, John Alexander, Peter Pierce, Helen Elizabeth, Donald Bruce; Prof. & Head, Dept. of Medicine, Queen's Univ., 1976- ; (Asst. Prof. 1952-60; Assoc. Prof. 1960-68); Attending Phys., Kingston Gen. Hosp.; Chief of Med., Kingston General Hosp. and Hotel Dieu Hosp., Kingston; Consultant in Medicine, St. Mary's of the Lake Hosp. and Kingston Psychiatric Hosp., Kingston; apptd. to Council of Coll. of Phys. & Surg. Ont., 1960 (Pres. 1965-66); served in Can. with R.C.A.M.C., Feb. 1945-Sept. 1946, discharged with rank of Capt.; Publications: many scient. articles to learned journs.; mem., Kingston Acad. Medicine; Ontario Medical Assn. (Pres. 1973-74); Canadian Medical Assn.(Chrmn. of the Board, 1976-78, Pres., 1979-80); Canadian Physiol. Society; Canadian Society for Clinical Investig.; Endocrine Soc.; Am. Diabetes Assn.; Conservative; United Church; recreations: fishing, hunting; Home: 1601 Harbour Pl., 185 Ontario St., Kingston, Ont. K7L 2Y7; Office: Etherington Hall, Stuart St., Kingston, Ont.

WILSON, Everett Stuart, M.B.A.; company executive; b. Boston, Mass., 1 March 1923; s. Everett B. and Jessie (McDonald) W.; e. Newton (Mass.) High Sch., 1940; Worcester Acad., 1941; Williams Coll., B.A., 1947; Har-

vard Business Sch., M.B.A., 1950; came to Canada 15 July 1955; m. Joan, d. Robert Eastty, N.J., 23 June 1951; children: Richard, Robert, Susan; PRESIDENT AND C.O.B., GTE SYLVANIA CANADA LIMITED, since 1964; served with 35th Inf. Div., U.S. Army, 1942-45; Chi Psi; recreations: golf, tennis, reading; Clubs: Harvard Business School; Home: 10 Queen Mary's Dr., Toronto, Ont. M8X 1S2; Office: 35 Vulcan St., Rexdale, Ont. M9W 1L3

WILSON, George Wilton, B.Com., M.A., Ph.D.; educator; b. Winnipeg, Man., 15 Feb. 1928; s. Walter and Ida Jane (Wilton) W.; e. Carleton Univ., B.Com. 1950; Univ. of Ky., M.A. (Econ.) 1951; Cornell Univ., Ph.D. (Econ.) 1955; Inst. of Basic Math. for Application to Business, Harvard Univ., 1959-60; m. Ina Marie, d. Harold McKinney, Portland, Ont., 6 Sept. 1952; children: Ronald Leslie, Douglas Scott, Suzanne Rita; PROFESSOR ECONS. AND BUSINESS ADM., INDIANA UNIV., since 1973; Dean, Coll. Arts & Sciences there 1970-73; Pres., Transport, Research Forum; Consultant to various pub. and private organs.; Econ., Bd. of Transport Commrs., Ottawa, 1951-52; Teaching Fellow, Cornell Univ., 1952-55; summer session Instr., Carleton Univ., 1955, 1956; Econ., Dept. of Labour, Ottawa, summers 1955, 1956, 1957; Asst. Prof. of Econ., Middlebury (Vt.) Coll., 1955-57; Asst. Prof. of Transport, Ind. Univ., 1957-59, Assoc. Prof. 1959-62; Chrmn. Econ. Dept. there 1966-70; leave of absence to work with Prof. Gunnar Myrdal on S. Asian econ. devel. in Stockholm, 1961; Dir. of study on transport, and econ. devel. for Brookings Inst. and on Can.'s Needs and Resources for Twentieth Century fund; mem. Presidential Task Force on Transport., 1964; mem. Univ. Study Comte., 1965; Dir., study on rail freight rates & devel. W. Can. for Fed.-Prov. Comte. on Western Transport. 1974; author: "Regulation of Rates of Common Carriers, Does It Need Revision?", 1956; "Essays On Some Unsettled Questions in the Economics of Transportation", 1962; "Output and Employment Relationships", 1957; "Classics of Economic Theory", 1964; "An Introduction to Aggregative Economics", Part I, 1962; co-author: "Mathematical Models and Methods in Marketing", 1961; "Road Transportation: History and Economics", Part I, 1962; "Physical Distribution Management", Part I, 1963; "Canada: An Appraisal of Its Needs and Resources", 1965; "Growth and Change at Indiana University", 1966; "The Impact of Highway Investment on Development", 1966; "Asian Drama", 1968; "Transportation on the Prairies", 1968; "Transportation and the Economic Development of Indo China", 5 vols. 1973; "Economic Analysis of Intercity Transportation", 1980; "Inflation: Causes, Consequences and Cures", 1982; numerous articles for various prof. journs.; first recipient A. Davidson Dunton Alumni Award, Carleton Univ. 1975; Awarded Disting. Professorship, Indiana Univ., 1978; mem., Am. Econ. Assn.; recreations: writing, tennis, travel; Home: 2325 Woodstock Pl., Bloomington, Ind. 47401

WILSON, Harry David Bruce, B.Sc., M.S., Ph.D., F.R.S.C.; geologist; university professor; b. Winnipeg. Man., 10 Nov. 1916; s. Frank Ernest and Elizabeth (McFaul) W.; e. Univ. of Man., B.Sc. 1936; California Inst. Tech., M.S. 1939, Ph.D. 1942; m. Marjorie Mae, d. late William H. Singleton, 1 Oct. 1941; children: Terry Ernest, Wendy Ann, Mary Elizabeth; Prof. of Geology Univ. of Manitoba; Pres., Central Geophysics Ltd.; Consulting Geologist, Falconbridge Nickel Mines Ltd., Selco Mining Corp. Ltd.; Geol., Internat. Nickel Co., 1941-47, 1949-51; Asst. Prof., Univ. of Man., 1947-49, Assoc. Prof., 1951, Prof. 1956; mem. of several comtes. in Nat. Research Council and Nat. Adv. Comte. for Research in Geol. Science; awarded Barlow Mem. Medal, Candn. Inst. Mining & Metall., 1959; author of numerous papers in scient. journs.; mem. (1969-72) Nat. Research Council Can.; Fellow, Geol. Soc. of Am.; Geol. Assn. Can. (Councillor, 1962-63, Pres. 1965); mem., Candn. Inst. Mining & Metall. (Chrmn., Geol. Div. 1961-62); Soc. Econ. Geols.

(Pres. 1976); Assn. Prof. Engrs. Man.; United Church; recreations: water sports, curling; Home: 602-255 Wellington Cres., Winnipeg, Man. R3M 3V4

WILSON, J. Carl, B.A.Sc., P.Eng.; manufacturer; b. Toronto, Ont. 13 July 1914; s. Jonathon A. and Jean (Carmichael) w.; e. Annette St. Pub. Sch. and Humberside Coll. Inst., Toronto; Univ. of Toronto, B.A.Sc. (Elect. Engn.); m. Dorothy A., d. Cecil H. Keys, 17 June 1939; children: Donald K., Kenneth C., Norma L., Debbi E.; PRES., CARL WILSON INDUSTRIES LTD.; Chrmn., J. A. Wilson Display Ltd.; mem. Illuminating Engn. Soc. (rec'd Distinguished Service Award); Assn. Prof. Engrs. Ont.; Delta Tau Delta; Protestant; recreations: golf, fishing, boating; Clubs: Rotary; Boulevard; Great Lakes Cruising; Home: 16 Country Club Dr., Islington, Ont. M9A 3J4; Office: 1725 Matheson Blvd., Mississauga, Ont. L4W 1Z1

WILSON, James H.; executive; b. Toronto, Ont., 18 May 1923; s. Harry H. Wilson; e. Withrow Pub. Sch. and Danforth Tech. Sch., Toronto; Shaw's Business Coll., Toronto, 1941; Univ. of W. Ont., Business Mang. Course, 1960; Univ. of Waterloo, Foreign Trade Course, 1962; m. Sarah Edwina, d. Hugh Stuart Lawson, 4 June 1947; children: Ronald James, Paul Hazlett, Catherine Edwina, Barbara Ann; PRESIDENT AND CHIEF EXTVE. OFFR., CEI INDUSTRIES LTD., since 1964; Chrmn. and Mang. Dir., Emtage Electric Co. Ltd. (Barbados); Pres., Principal Heating Co. Ltd.; Penn Metal Products Co. Ltd.; Treas. and Dir., Kerrwil Publications Ltd.; Dir., CECO Industries Ltd. (Trinidad); joined Amalgamated Electric Corp., Toronto, as Sales Engr., 1945; apptd. Product Sales Mgr., 1950; Secy.-Dir. and Gen. Sales Mgr., BullDog Electric Co. (Can.) Ltd., 1954, Vice Pres., 1957; Vice Pres., I.T.E. Circuit Breaker (Can.) Ltd., 1954; served with RCAF 1943-45, rank Flt. Lt.; mem. Bd. Govs., North York Gen. Hosp.; mem., Bd. Trade Metrop. Toronto; Conservative; Baptist; recreations: fishing, curling, golf; Club: Engineers; Home: 8 Riverside Blvd., Thornhill, Ont. L4J 1H3; Office: 59 Penn Drive, Weston, Ont. M9L 2A8

WILSON, John Alexander, B.A.Sc., P.Eng.; manufacturer; b. Hamilton, Ont., 27 Apl. 1913; s. Donald Alexander and Laura Louise (Dressel) w.; e. Univ. of Toronto, B.A.Sc. (Metall. Engn.) 1936; m. Jeanette Agnes, d. late James Alexander Gray, 2 July 1968; children: Mrs. Linda L. Burke, Donald A., Pauline A., R. Malcolm, C. G. James Thomson, Courtland W. Thomson, Mark A. Thomson; PRES., CHIEF EXTVE. OFFR. AND DIR., FAHRALLOY CANADA LTD., since 1969; Pres. and Chief Extve. Offr., Fahralloy-Wisconsin Ltd.; Dir., The Stirling Trusts Corp.; joined present Co. as Engr. 1936-40, Sales Mgr. 1940-55, Extve. Vice Pres. 1955-69; el. a Dir. 1962; served on various local sch. and hosp. bds.; Chrmn., Technol. Adv. Comte., Georgian Coll. of Applied Arts and Technol.; awarded Centennial Medal; mem., Am. Soc. Metals; Candn. Inst. Mining & Metall.; Lambda Chi Alpha; Freemason (Scot. Rite); P. Conservative; United Church; recreations: fishing, golf, curling; Clubs: Engineers (Toronto); The Hamilton (Ont.); Home 51 Brant St. E., Orillia, Ont. L3V 1Z1; Office: Orillia, Ont.

WILSON, John Montgomery, B.A.Sc.; mechanical engineer; executive; b. Toronto, Ont. 3 Nov. 1932; s. John Austin and Edith (Montgomery) W.; e. Univ. of Toronto Schs.; Univ. of Toronto B.A.Sc. (Mech. Engn.) 1955; Centre d'Etudes Industrielles, Geneva 1956; m. Nancy d. Paige Rosell 6 Aug. 1955; children: John, Paige, Kate; VICE PRES. FABRICATING TECHNOLOGY AND DIR. PERSONNEL, ALCAN INTERNATIONAL LTD. 1980- ; Dir. Alcan d'Afrique et du Moyen Orient Ltée; Alcan Laboratories Ltd.; Alcan Research & Development Ltd.; Works Mgr. Alcan Canada Products, Kingston, Ont. 1968-71; Dir. Kingston Research Centre, Alcan International Ltd. 1971, Dir. Research Centres 1976, Vice Pres. Research & Devel. 1978-80; Dir. Chamber Comm. Kingston; Un. Fund Kingston; mem. and Chrmn. Kingston

Indust. Comn.; mem. Bd. Govs. Kingston Gen. Hosp. (former mem. Mang. Comte.); Dir. and Pres. Agnes Hetherington Gallery, Queen's Univ.; Chrmn. Queen's Adv. Council on Engr. 1981-82; Delta Tau Delta (Pres. Toronto Chapter 1954-55); Protestant; Home: 14 Sydenham St., Kingston, Ont. K7L 3G9; Office: (P.O. Box 6090) Montreal, Que. H3C 3H2.

WILSON, John Tuzo, C.C. (1974), O.B.E. (1946), Ph.D., D.Sc. LL.D., D.Univ., F.R.S.C., F.R.S.; educator; b. Ottawa, Ont., 24 Oct. 1908; s. John Armitstead, C.B.E., and Henrietta Loetitia (Tuzo) W.; e. Trinity Coll., Toronto, B.A. 1930 (Massey Fellow to Cambridge, 1930-32) Univ. of Cambridge, B.A. 1932, M.A. 1940, Sc.D., 1958; Princeton Univ., Ph.D. 1936; D.Sc., Univ. of W. Ont., 1958, Acadia 1968, Memorial 1968, McGill 1972, Toronto 1977, Laurentian 1978; Middlebury Coll., 1981; LL.D., Carleton 1958, Simon Fraser 1978; Sc.D., Franklin & Marshall Coll. 1969; D.Univ. Calgary 1973; m. Isabel Jean Dickson, d. late W. M. Linden Terrace, Ottawa, Ont., 29 Oct. 1938; two d., Patricia Isabel, Susan Loetitia Clark; DIRECTOR GENERAL, ONTARIO SCIENCE CENTRE, since 1974; Pres., International Union of Geodesy & Geophysics, 1957-60; mem., Nat. Research Council of Can. 1958-64; Sci. Council Can. 1977-83; Asst. Geol., Geol. Survey of Can., 1936-39; spent summers prospecting and in field geol., 1924-39; served in World War, 1939-46; 2nd Lieut., R.C.E., 1939; Lieut. and Capt., 1st Candn. Tunnelling Co., overseas, 1940-41; Maj. and Lieut.-Col., Candn. Mil. Hdqrs. overseas, 1942-43; Col. and Dir., Operational Research, Nat. Defence Hdqrs., 1943-46; Depy. Dir., Exercise Muskox, 1945-46; Prof. of Geophysics, Univ. of Toronto, 1946-74; Principal, Erindale College there 1967-74; awarded American Legion of Merit; mem., Arctic Inst. of N. Am. (Gov. and Chrmn. 1947); Roy. Candn. Geog. Soc. (Hon. Vice Pres.); Pres., Am. Geophysical Union, 1980-82, admitted Hon. Fellow, Trinity Coll., Toronto, 1962; Fellow, Massey Coll., Toronto, 1963; Overseas Fellow, Churchill Coll., Cambridge, 1965; Visiting Prof. Australian National Univ., 1950 and 1965; Foreign Associate, Nat. Acad. of Sciences (USA), 1967; Publications: "Physics and Geology" (with J. A. Jacobs and R. D. Russell), 2nd ed. 1973; "One Chinese Moon," 1959; "IGY: Year of the New Moons", 1961; "Unglazed China" 1973; Ed., "Continents Adrift" 1972; "Continents Adrift and Continents Aground" 1977; made first ascent of Mt. Hague, Montana (12,328 ft.) 1935; awarded Willet G. Miller Medal, Royal Soc. Canada, 1958; Selwyn G. Blaylock Medal, Candn. Inst. Mining & Metall., 1958; Civic Award of Merit, Toronto, 1960; Logan Medal, Geol. Assn. Canada 1968; Bucher Medal, Am. Geophys. Union, 1968; Penrose Medal, Geol. Society America 1968; named O.C. 1969; J. J. Carty Medal, National Academy Science, 1975; Gold Medal, Roy. Cdn. Geog. Soc. 1978; Wollaston Medal, Geol. Soc. London 1978; Vetlesen Prize, Columbia Univ. 1978; J. Tuzo Wilson Medal, Cdn. Geophys. Union, 1978; Ewing Medal, Am. Geophys. Union, 1980; M. Ewing Medal, The Soc. of Exploration Geophysicists, 1981; A.G. Huntsman Award, Bedford Inst. of Oceanography, 1981; Foreign Hon. mem., Am. Acad. Arts & Sciences 1970; Am. Philos. Soc. 1971; Assoc., Academic Royale de Belgique, 1981; recreations: outdoor exercise, travel, collecting books on Arctic; Home: 27 Pricefield Rd., Toronto, Ont. M4W 1Z8

WILSON, Kenneth Albert, Q.C.; b. Black Lake, Que., 22 May 1899; s. David and Emma (Kinnear) W.; e. Sherbrooke High Sch.; McGill Univ., B.C.L. 1921; m. Helen, d. W. S. Hunter, Montreal, Que., 6 Oct. 1923; children: Hunter Wilson, Barbara Wilson; COUNSEL, LAFLEUR, BROWN, DE GRANDPRE; Dir., Investment Foundation Ltd.; read law with Wells & Lynch, Sherbrooke, Que.; Advocate 1921; cr. K.C. 1932; formerly in the firm of Wells & Lynch, Sherbrooke, Que., until 1923 and then joined Wells, Lynch & Wilson until 1929; Lect. in Bankruptcy Law in McGill Univ. 1930; served in World War, 1917-18, with 7th Siege Batty.; Theta Delta Chi; Conservative; Anglican; recreations: golf, curling; Clubs: United Services; Home: Apt. 302, 2 Westmount Sq., Westmount, Que. H3Z 2S4; Office: Suite 720, 800 Victoria Sq., P.O. Box 214, Montreal, Que. H4Z 1E4

WILSON, Lynton Ronald, M.A.; executive; b. Port Colborne, Ont. 3 Apl. 1940; s. Ronald Alfred and Blanche Evelyn (Matthews) W.; e. Port Colborne High Sch.; McMaster Univ. B.A. 1962; Cornell Univ. M.A. 1967; m. Brenda Jean d. Dr. J. Howard Black 23 Dec. 1968; children: Edward Ronald, Margot Jean, Jennifer Lyn; PRES., CHIEF EXTVE. OFFR. AND DIR., REDPATH INDUSTRIES LTD. 1981- ; Dir. Tate & Lyle Inc., N.Y.; Ontario Energy Corp.; Niagara Inst.; Asst. Comm. Secy. Candn. Embassy Vienna 1963-65; Second Secy. Tokyo 1967-68; Teaching Asst. Cornell Univ. 1968-69; Corporate Econ. John Labatt Ltd., London, Ont. 1969-70, Dir. of Econ. Research 1970-71; Co-ordinator, Indust. R & D Policy, Ministry of State, Science & Technol. Ottawa 1972; Strategic Planning and Devel. MacMillan Bloedel Ltd. Vancouver 1973-74, Vice Pres. and Dir. MacMillan Bloedel Enterprises Inc. Boston, Mass. 1974-77; Extve. Dir. Ministry of Industry & Tourism Ont., Toronto 1977-78, Depy. Min. of Industry & Tourism 1978-81; Dir., Arthritis Soc.; mem. Candn. Econ. Assn.; Presbyterian; recreations: golf, tennis, swimming, skiing; Clubs: Albany Club; Rideau (Ottawa); Cambridge; Home: 769 Cardinal Pl., Mississauga, Ont. L5J 2R8; Office: (P.O. Box 66) Royal Bank Plaza, Toronto, Ont. M5J 2J2.

WILSON, Marie, Q.C., B.A.; b. Toronto, Ont.; d. Marie (Trotter) and the late Albert Edward Wilson; e. Bishop Strachan Sch., Toronto, Ont.; Univ. of Toronto, B.A.; Osgoode Hall Law Sch., Toronto, Ont.; PRESIDENT, A. E. WILSON & CO. LTD. (Insurance Agents, Estbd. 1905); Dir., Standard Trust Co.; Bank of Nova Scotia; Pres. (1960 and 1961) Ont. Br., Candn. Ladies Golf Union; apptd. Vice-Pres. of A. E. Wilson & Co. Ltd. in 1949, Pres. on the death of her father in Nov. 1959; mem. Candn. Ladies Golf Assn., Ont. Br. (Past Pres.); Kappa Alpha Theta; P. Conservative; United Church; recreations: golf, music; Clubs: Granite; Rosedale Golf; Canadian; Home: 89 Binscarth Road, Toronto, Ont. M4W 1Y3; Office: 20 Queen St. W., Toronto, Ont. M5H 3R3

WILSON, Murray P., B.Sc.; company president; b. Winnipeg, Man., 29 Jan. 1927; s. Peter McAuslan and Jessie Dodds (Fyfe) W.; e. Univ. of Manitoba, B.Sc., 1949; m. Gertrude Wilhelmine Ruth, 16 June 1950; children: Peter Murray, Christine Lynne; PRESIDENT HARRISONS & CROSFIELD (CANADA) LTD. since 1972; Harrisons & Crosfield (America) Inc.; Harrisons & Crosfield (Pacific) Inc.; Harcros Inc.; Canada Chrome & Chemicals Limited; Nalor Distrib. Ltd/Lteé; Harcros Ins. Agencies Ltd; Chemist, Burns & Co. Winnipeg, 1949; joined present Co. 1951, successively Manager, Man. and Saskatchewan 1958; Dir. 1965; Vice President 1970; mem. Chemical Institute of Can.; Agric. Inst. of Can.; Ont. Inst. of Agrols.; Protestant; recreations: golf, photography; Clubs: St. Charles Country; Donalda; Home: 18 Swifdale Pl., Don Mills, Ont. M3B 1M4; Office: 4 Banigan.Dr., Toronto, Ont. M4H 1E9

WILSON, Robert J(ames), M.A., M.D., D.P.H., b. Edmonton, Alta., 5 Feb. 1915; s. William Edgar and Hallie May (Banford) W.; e. Univ. of British Columbia, B.A. 1935, M.A. 1937; Univ. of Toronto, M.D. 1942, D.P.H. 1946; m. Madelon Vivian, d. John Rowan, Toronto, Ont., 18 Oct. 1941; children: Raymond Charles, Lynn Sharon; HONOURARY CHMN. AND CONSULTANT TO THE CHRMN., CONNAUGHT LABORATORIES LIMITED 1978; Chrmn. and Scient. Dir., Connaught Lab. Ltd. 1972-78; Banting Research Foundation Grantee, Univ. of B.C. (Bacter. Research) 1936-37; Fellow in Hygiene and Preventive Med., Univ. of Toronto, 1937-46; Research Assoc., Connaugh Med. Research Labs., 1946-56, Research mem., 1956, Asst. Dir. 1957; Assoc. in Hygiene

and Preventive Med., Univ. of Toronto, 1946. Asst. Prof. 1948, Assoc. Prof. Microbiol., Prof. Pub. Health Adm. 1971; Assoc. Dir., Connaught Medical Research Labs. 1970-72; served in 2nd World War with R.C.N. 1942-46 with rank of Surg.-Lieut. Commdr.; mem., Royal Candn. Mil. Inst.; Royal Candn. Inst.; Candn. Pub. Health Assn.; Candn. Medical Assn.; Ont. Med. Assn.; United Church; recreations: photography, fishing, hunting; Home: 16 The Palisades, Toronto, Ont. M6S 2W8; Office: 1755 Steeles Ave. W., Willowdale, Ont. M2N 5T8

WILSON, Robert L., B.Com.; manufacturer; b. Montreal, Que., 30 Jan. 1932; s. Robert and Margaret (Neilson) W.; e. Pub. and High Schs., Montreal, Que.; Sir George Williams Univ., B.Com. 1961; m. Dorothy, d. Charles Herring, 2 Oct. 1954; children: Karen Leslie, Robert Graham; PRESIDENT AND CHIEF EXTVE. OFFR., DOMINION MANUFACTURERS LTD. since 1972; with St. Lawrence Sugar Refineries Ltd. as Vice-Pres., Sales and Marketing, Montreal 1954; Extve. Vice-Pres., and Gen. Mgr., Canadian Electronics Ltd., Edmonton, Alta. 1966; Extve. Asst. to Pres., The Cassidy Group of Cos., Montreal 1967-69; apptd. Gen. Mgr., present Co. 1970; mem. Oakville Chamber Comm.; recreations: golf, music; Clubs: Engineers (Montreal); Board of Trade (Toronto); Home: 2203 Devon Rd., Oakville, Ont. L6J 5M1; Office: P.O. Box 217, 277 Lakeshore Rd. East, Suite 207, Oakville, Ont. L6J 5A2

WILSON, Roger David, Q.C.; b. Toronto, Ont. 3 April 1932; s. J. H. Douglas and Beatrice (Avery) W.; e. Chatham (Ont.) Coll. 1950; Queen's Univ. (Econ. and Pol. Sc.) 1954; Osgoode Hall Law Sch. 1958; m. Margaret, d. Alexander Macnaughton 11 May 1963; children: Martha, David, Duncan; PARTNER, FASKEN & CALVIN; Dir. Canada Permanent Mortgage Corp. Toronto-Dominion Realty Co. Ltd.; MDS Health Group Ltd.; McCain Foods Ltd.; Guardian Capital Group Ltd. and other public and private companies; read law with C. C. Calvin, Q.C.; called to the Bar of Ont. June 1958; joined Fasken & Calvin (then called Fasken, Robertson, Aitchison, Pickup & Calvin) 1958, becoming a Partner 1964; cr. Q.C. 1974; Anglican; P. Conservative; recreations: sailing, skiing, reading; Clubs: Royal Canadian Yacht; Toronto Club; Badminton & Racquet; Alpine Ski (all Toronto); Homes: 109 Cluny Dr., Toronto, Ont. M4W 2R5 and 9 Wyandot Ave., Toronto Island M5J 2E6; Office: 30th Floor, Toronto-Dominion Bank Tower, T-D Centre, Toronto, Ont. M5K 1C1

WILSON, Roland Frederick, Q.C.; b. Hamilton, Ont., 8 Oct. 1901; s. Archdale McDonald and Elizabeth W.; e. Hamilton Coll. Inst.; Univ. of Toronto, LL.B.; Osgoode Hall, Toronto; m. Adelaide Bernice Sill, d. Dr. W. T. Langrill of Hamilton, Ont., 1934; children: Donald Langrill, Frances Elizabeth, Stephen Roland; MEMBER, DAY, WILSON, CAMPBELL; called to the Bar of Ont., 1925; cr. K.C. 1944; specializes in Counsel work; Bencher, Law Soc. of Upper Can.; recreation: golf; Clubs: University; Toronto Hunt; Home: Apt. 605, 44 Jackes Ave., Toronto, Ont. M4T 1E5; Office: 250 University Ave., Toronto, Ont. M5H 3E7

WILSON, (Ronald) York, R.C.A. (1948); artist; painter; b. Toronto, Ont., 6 Dec. 1907; s. William James and Maryanne Maude (York) W.; e. Oakwood Coll. Inst., Toronto, Ont.; Central Technical Sch., Toronto, Ont.; Art Inst., Detroit, Mich.; etc. but mostly self-taught; m. Lela May, d. George Miller, Aurora, Ont., July 1933; one d., Virginia June; el. to Ont. Soc. of Artists, 1942 (Pres. 1946); el. Assoc., Roy. Candn. Acad., 1945; mem. Candn. Group of Painters, Pres. 1967; has exhibited internationally, incl. N.Y. World's Fair, 1939, Museo de Bellas Artes, Tenerife, Spain, Solo, 1952; Carnegie Internat. 1952; Candn. Biennials 1956, 58, 60, 62, Sao Paulo with L'Ecole de Paris 1963, Musée Galliera (Solo, main gallery) Paris 1963-64; ''Confrontation'' (by invitation) Musée de Dijon, France, 1964; L'Art au Canada, Bordeaux, France, 1962; Retrospective: Sarnia Art Gallery, Agnes Etherington Gallery, Kingston, Confederation Art Gallery, P.E.I., Roberts Gallery, Toronto, 1965; Rose Fried Gallery, New York (solo) 1968; Palacio de Bellas Artes, Mexico (solo) 1969; Centro Cultural Ignacio Ramirez, Mexico, (Solo) 1970; Birla Academy Museum & Travelling Exhibitions, India, 1969; Retrospective: Sarnia Art Gallery; Rothmans Art Gallery, Stratford; The Robert McLaughlin Gallery, Oshawa;London Art Museum, 1974-75; more than 40 solo exhibitions; more than 170 Group Exhibitions. Murals: McGill University, 1954; and in Toronto, Salvation Army Prayer Room, 1955; Imperial Oil Bldg., 1957; O'Keefe Centre for Performing Arts, 1959; Bell Canada Bldg. (Mosaics), 1965; Dow Corning Co., 1965; MacDonald Bldg., Ontario Government Complex, 1968; Central Hospital, 1970; Simpsons-Sears (Tapestry); General Hospital, Thunder Bay, 1965; Carleton University, Ottawa 1970 (Mosaics); incl. in permanent collections of Musée National d'Art Moderne, Paris; Musée d'Art de Dijon, France; Birla Academy Museum, India; Museo Moderno de Bellas Artes, Mexico; Museo Eduardo Westerdahl, Spain; Tanaka Museum, Japan; Musée des Beaux Arts, Montreal; Musée d'Art Contemporain, Montreal; Art Gallery of Ontario; National Gallery of Canada; Lord Beaverbrook Gallery, N.B.; Sarnia Art Gallery; London Art Gallery; Tom Thomson Memorial Gallery, Owen Sound; Winnipeg Art Gallery; Calgary Art Gallery; Art Gallery of Windsor; Art Gallery of Nova Scotia; Robert McLaughlin Gallery; McMichael Conservation Gallery; Ontario Heritage Foundation; Algoma Gallery, Sault Ste. Marie; Uffizi Gallery, Florence (self-portrait, 1981); Dept. of External Affairs; Sam & Ayala Zacks Collection; Isabel McLaughlin Collection, Oshawa; Universities: Toronto; Queens; Mount Allison; Laval; Laurentian; Alberta; Western Ontario; St. Mary's; Guelph; Clubs: The National; Ontario; Rosedale; Yorkdowns; Arts and Letters Club; Granite; York;; Banks: Commerce; Royal; Toronto-Dominion; Citicorp and many other Public & Private Collections in Canada; U.S.A.; Eng.; Mexico; France; Italy; Switzerland; Spain; Canary Islands; Hawaii; Hong Kong; Belgium; Israel; India; etc. Does Tapestries and Prints; Films: "Mural" by Crawley Films for Imperial Oil; "York Wilson" by Michael Foyteni for CBC; Limited Ed. book "York Wilson", by Paul Duval, foreword by Marshall McLuhan; Awards: J. W. L. Forster Award for figure painting 1945 & 1951; G. B. R. Award, Winnipeg, 1956; Baxter Foundation Award, 1959; Won Competition for McGill Univ. Mural, 1953; Centennial Medal of Cda., 1967; Won case against International Union & kept artists free, 1959; 1st. prize for Prints, Montreal (lithograph "Mayan") 1978; Studio: 41 Alcina Ave., Toronto, Ont. M6G 2E7

WILSON, William Moore, C.A.; financial executive; b. Glasgow, Scotland 21 May 1937; e. Edinburgh, Scot.; C.A. (Scot.) 1960; m. Margaret Spalding 20 Oct. 1966; children: Andrew, Alyson, Lorna; PRESIDENT AND CHIEF EXTVE. OFFR., REED STENHOUSE COMPANIES LTD.; Group Acct., Stenhouse Holdings Ltd. 1961, Secy. 1964, Finance Dir. 1966; joined present co. 1973, Dir., Vice Pres. Finance, Chief Financial Offr.; Clubs: Royal Scottish Automobile; Caledonian (London, Eng.); R.C.Y.C.; Toronto; Cambridge (Toronto); Home: 1 Cluny Ave., Toronto, Ont. M4W 1S4.

WILSON, William Ray, B.S.A.; retired farmer; b. Haileybury, Ont., 26 Aug. 1911; s. Edward E. and Emily Esther (Sparks) W.; e. York's Corners Pub. Sch.; Kenmore High Sch.; Ont. Agric. Coll., B.S.A. 1934; m. Jean Eleanor, d. Dr. J. H. MacIntosh, Riceville, Ont., 15 July 1944; two s., William MacIntosh, John Edward; long operated Wilsondale farm at Kenmore, Ont., which was established by his father; noted breeder of Holstein-Friesian cattle; Dir., Ottawa Winter Fair; Pres., Holstein-Friesian Assn. of Can.; served with the Dom. Dept. Agric. as a Poultry Inspector and later as a Poultry Products Inspector (part time), 1935-41; retired from farming 1968 since when has been Mgr., Metcalfe (Ont.) Community Cen-

tre; mem., Am. Soc. of Dowsers; rec'd. Master Breeders' Award, Holstein-Friesian Assn. Can. 1968; Freemason; Anglican; recreations: hockey, skating, softball; Address: Metcalfe, Ont. K0A 2P0

WILSON-SMITH, Maj. Gen. Norman George, D.S.O., M.B.E., C.D.; b. St. Catharines, Ont., 4 Oct. 1916; s. George and Margaret (Thompson) W-S.; e. Univ. of Man.; m. Beatrice Claire, d. late Garnet Carmichael, 7 Oct. 1964; one d.; joined Candn. Army 1939; served in various staff and command appts.; during World War II served in Inf.; wounded N.W. Europe; commanded 1st Bn. P.P.C.L.I. (Parachute), Korea, 1952; thereafter various staff appts. in Can.; on NATO staff 1961; Commdr., 3rd Candn. Inf. Bgde., 1962; U.N. Troops, Nicosia, Cyprus, 1965; Mil. Attaché, Washington, 1965-67; apptd. Depy. Chief, Force Devel. 1967; retired, 1969; Mang. Dir., London Office of Gen. Dynamics Inc. and Canadair till 1974; now Pres., Zinder-Neris Inc. International Coal Marketing Consultants; qualified pilot fixed and rotary wing; Anglican; recreations: golf, skiing, flying; Clubs: Bucks (London); Royal Ottawa Golf; Home: Sussex Apts., Ottawa, Ont. and Greenwich, Conn.; Office: 530 Fifth Ave., New York, N.Y.

WINCH, David Monk, Ph.D., F.R.S.C.; educator; b. London, Eng. 22 July 1933; s. late Alexander and Lily Ruth (Monk) W.; e. Co. High Sch. for Boys, Ilford, Eng. 1951; London Sch. of Econ., London Univ. B.Sc. 1954, Ph.D. 1957; Yale Univ. 1955-56; Commonwealth Fellow, St. John's Coll. Cambridge Univ. M.A. 1970; m. Mary Elizabeth d. late Henry Edward Scadding 6 July 1957 (divorced 1973); children: Elizabeth Ann, Alexander David; PROF. OF ECON. McMASTER UNIV. since 1966; mem. Ont. Econ. Council since 1973; Research Assoc. Univ. of Toronto 1957-58, Visiting Prof. of Econ. 1965-66; Special Lectr. in Econ. Univ. of Sask. 1958-60; Asst./Assoc. Prof. of Econ. Univ. of Alta. 1960-66; Chrmn. of Econ. McMaster Univ. 1971-77; rec'd Killam Award 1970; author "The Economics of Highway Planning" 1963; "Analytical Welfare Economics" 1971; various articles on econ. theory learned journs.; mem. Candn. Econ. Assn.; Am. Econ. Assn.; Candn. Assn. Univ. Teachers; Home: 661 Holt Dr., Burlington, Ont. L7T 3N4; Office: Hamilton, Ont. L8S 4M4.

WINCH, Harold Edward, b. Loughton, Essex, Eng., 18 June 1907; s. Ernest Edward, M.L.A., and Linda Marion (Hendy) W.; e. Vancouver, B.C.; m. Dorothy Ada, d. A. Hutchinson, Vancouver, B.C., 11 May 1929; children: Donald Ernest Arthur, Gerald Edward, Shirley Doreen; an electrician by trade; Mang. Ed., B.C. "Clarion" (official organ. of Socialist Party in Can.), 1932-35; awarded King's Jubilee Medal, 1935, which he refused as a protest against govt. inaction in econ. crisis; 1st el. to B.C. Leg. for Vancouver E., g.e. 1933; Parlty. Leader of the C.C.F., 1938-53; Leader of the Opposition in the Leg., 1941-53; resigned seat in Leg., 1953, and el. to H. of C. for Vancouver E. in g.e. 1953, re-el. till 1972; Chrmn., Boag Fdn. Ltd.; Canada West Fdn.; Council of Christians & Jews (Pacific Reg.); mem., Internat. Brotherhood of Electrical Workers; Army, Navy & Air Force Verterans' Unit 100; Royal Candn. Legion (Hon. Pres., Br. 179); Freeman, City of Vancouver; Life mem., Commonwealth Parlty. Assn.; N.D.P.; recreations: books, gardening; Home: 3741 Knight St., Vancouver, B.C. V5N 3L7

WINDSOR, Hon. H. Neil, M.H.A., B.E.; politician; b. St. John's, Nfld. 8 July 1945; s. H. R. Hunter and Rose (Baggs) W.; e. Holloway Sch. and Prince of Wales Coll. St. John's 1962; Mem. Univ. of Nfld. Engn. Dipl. 1968; N.S. Tech. Coll. B.E. (Civil) 1970; m. Judy A. d. Ian Watson, Mount Pearl, Nfld. 9 Sept. 1967; children: Heidi, Devon; MINISTER RESPONSIBLE FOR DEPT. OF MINES AND ENERGY, NFLD. AND LABRADOR, 1981; Min. Of Development, 1980; el. M.H.A. for Mount Pearl 1975, re-el. 1979; Parlty. Asst. to Premier 1975; Min. of Mun. Affairs 1978; Min. of Mun. Affairs & Housing, Pres. of Treasury Bd. 1979; service Royal Nfld. Militia (Reserve); mem. Assn. Prof. Engrs. Nfld.; Delta Beta Sigma; P. Conservative; United Church; recreation: Mount Pearl Minor Hockey Assn.; Club: Rotary; Home: 2 Donovan St., Mount Pearl, Nfld. A1N 2C6; Office: 504 Atlantic Pl., St. John's, Nfld. A1C 5T7.

WINEGARD, William Charles, M.A.Sc., Ph.D.; educator; b. Hamilton, Ont., 17 Sept. 1924; e. Caledonia (Ont.) Pub. and High Schs., 1924-42; Univ. of Toronto, B.A.Sc. (Hons. in Metall. Engn.) 1949, M.A.Sc. (Phys. Metall.) 1950, Ph.D. (Phys. Metall.) 1952; m. Mary Elizabeth Jaques; children: William, Charles, Kathryn; Education and Engineering Consultant; Special Lecturer in Metallurgical Engineering, University of Toronto, 1950, Lecturer 1952, Asst. Professor 1954, Assoc. Prof. 1957, Prof. 1964, Asst. Dean Sch. of Grad. Studies, 1964, Acting Dean 1966; Tech. Consultant to many Candn. and Am. Co.'s 1950-66 and to Ont. Fire Marshal, 1950-60; mem., Nat. Research Council Comte. for Corrosion Research and Prevention, 1955-59; on leave with Dept. of Metall., Cambridge Univ. (research on crystal growth), 1959-60; Lectr., Australian Inst. of Metals, 1965; Pres. & Vice Chancellor, Univ. of Guelph 1967-75; served with R.C.N.V.R. 1942-45; rank Sub-Lt.; rec'd 1967 Alcan Award; Ed.-in-Chief, "Canadian Metallurgical Quarterly," 1965-67; author of "An Introduction To The Solidification of Metals," 1964 (Japanese trans. 1966) and over 80 tech. papers in metall. field; Fellow, Am. Soc. of Metals (Vice Chrmn., Ont. Chapter, 1958-59, Chrmn., Educ. Comte. of Chapter, 1954-64; mem. Transactions Comte., 1957-59); Chrmn., 1st Welding Seminar, Candn. Welding Soc., 1958; mem. Ed. Adv. Bd., Internat. Journ. for Crystal Growth; Anglican; recreations: athletics; community activities

WINESANKER, Michael Max, Mus.Bac., M.A., Ph.D.; university professor; b. Toronto, Ont., 7 Aug. 1913; s. late Samuel and Ida (English) W.; e. Humberside Coll. Inst., Toronto; Univ. of Toronto, Mus.Bac. 1933; Trinity Coll., London, L.Mus. T.C.L. 1940; Univ. of Mich., M.A. 1941; Cornell Univ., Ph.D. 1944; m. Esther, d. late Paul Frumhartz, 12 Dec. 1937; two d., Miriam Ruth, Rebecca Ann; PROF. OF MUSICOLOGY, TEXAS CHRISTIAN UNIV., since 1946 and Chrmn., Dept. of Music, since 1956; private teacher of piano and theory, Toronto, 1933-39; debut as concert pianist, Eaton Auditorium, Toronto, 1937; teacher of piano, Hambourg Conserv., Toronto, 1940-42; Prof. of Music Hist. and Theory, Bayview Summer Coll., Mich., 1945; Prof. of Musicology, Univ. of Texas, 1945-46; mem., Bd., Ft. Worth Symphony Orchestra; Vice-Pres., Van Cliburn Internat. Piano Competition; mem. Board, Youth Orchestra of Greater Ft. Worth; received research grants from American Council Learned Societies, Carnegie Foundation and present University; author, "The Record of English Musical Drama", dissertation, 1944; also introduction to "Foundations of English Opera", "A List of Books on Music", 1977; "Books on Music, a classified List" 1979; and numerous articles in various prof. journs.; mem., Am. Musicol. Soc. (Past Pres., Texas Chapter); Music Teachers Nat. Assn.; Ft. Worth Piano Teachers Forum (Dir.); Nat. Assn. Schs. Music (Chrmn., Lib. Comte.); chosen Piper Prof., 1976; Jewish; Home: 3613 Park Ridge Blvd., Fort Worth, Texas 76109

WINGATE, Henry Smith, B.A., J.D., LL.D., LH.D.; executive; b. Talas, Turkey, 8 Oct. 1905; s. Henry Knowles and Jane Caroline (Smith) W.; e. Carleton Coll. Minnesota, B.A. 1927, LH.D. 1973; Univ. of Mich., J.D. 1929; LL.D., Marshall Univ., W. Va.; Manitoba 1957, York 1967, Laurentian 1968, Colby Coll. 1970; m. Ardis Adeline Swenson, 11 Sept. 1929; children: Henry Knowles, William Peter; former Dir., American Standard Inc.; Bank of Montreal; Canadian Pacific Ltd.; J. P. Morgan & Co. Inc.; Morgan Guaranty Trust Co. of New York; United States Steel Corp.; admitted to Bar of N.Y. 1931; assoc.

with Sullivan & Cromwell, N.Y.C. 1929; Asst. Secy., International Nickel Co. of Canada Ltd. 1935, Secy. 1939, el. a Dir. 1942, Vice-Pres. 1949, Pres. 1954, Chrmn. of Bd. 1960-72, Dir. 1972; mem. Bd. Trustees, Seamen's Bank for Savings, N.Y.; Councils of the Americas; U.S. Council Internat. Chamber Comm.; The Conference Bd. Inc.; mem. Business Council, Washington, D.C.; Candn.-Am. Comte., Nat. Planning Assn., Washington, D.C. and C. D. Howe Research Inst., Montreal; Am. Bureau of Metal Stat.; Candn. Inst. Mining & Metall.; Council on Foreign Relations; Adv. Council, Morgan Guaranty Trust Co. of New York; St. George Soc.; Fdn. for Child Devel.; Economic Club of New York; Assn. of the Bar of City of N.Y.; Mining & Metall. Soc. Am.; Am. Inst. Mining. Metall. & Petroleum Engrs. Inc.; Pilgrims of the U.S.; Canadian Soc., N.Y.; Dir. and Vice Pres., Am. Friends of Can.; Order of Coif; Delta Sigma Rho; Clubs: Lloyd Neck; N.Y. Bath; Huntington Country; Recess; Union; University; Home: 520 E. 86th St., New York, N.Y. 10028; Office: One New York Plaza, New York, N.Y. 10004

WINKLER, Warren Keith, Q.C., LL.M.; lawyer; b. Virden, Man. 10 Dec. 1938; s. Anthony Valentine and Eulalia May (Stephenson) W.; e. Univ. of Man. B.A. 1959; Osgoode Hall Law Sch. LL.B. 1962, LL.M. 1964; m. Ruth Eleanor Killam d. Albert J. G. Wilson, Q.C., Toronto, Ont. 8 July 1967; two d. Julia Christine, Janet Lynn; PARTNER, WINKLER, FILION & WAKELY; Dir. Prepaid Legal Services Program of Can., Faculty of Law, Univ. of Windsor 1979- ; called to Bar of Ont. 1965; cr. Q.C. 1977; author various publs.; mem. Law Soc. Upper Can. (Co-Chrmn. Continuing Educ. Program in Labour Relations Law 1973-); Candn. Bar Assn. (Nat. Extve. 1973-75; Extve. Comte. Ont. Br. 1972-74; Past Chrmn. Nat. Labour Relations Sec. 1969-71, Ont. Labour Relations Sub-Sec. 1965-67; Special Comte. on Judiciary Ont. Br. 1977-79); Advocates' Soc.; recreations: shooting, fishing, farming; Home: 254 Lytton Blvd., Toronto, Ont. M5N 1R6; Office: 390 Bay St., Suite 1800, Toronto, Ont. M5H 2G3.

WINNETT, Rev. Frederick Victor, M.A., Ph.D., F.R.S.C. (1959); (Un. Ch.); educator; b. Oil Springs, Ont., 25 May 1903; s. Frederick Walter and Sarah Jane (Blain) W.; e. Univ. of Toronto (Univ. Coll.), B.A. 1923 and M.A. 1924; Knox Theol. Coll., 1923-27; Univ. of Toronto, Ph.D. 1928; Hartford Theol. Semy. (post grad. studies); m. Margaret Johnstone, B.A., d. Rev. J. T. Taylor, D.D., 15 Sept. 1928; children: William Walter, Jane Marilyn; Prof. Emeritus of Near E. Studies, Univ. of Toronto; Vice Princ., Univ. Coll. 1966-69; Dir. of American Sch. of Oriental Research, Jerusalem, Jordan, 1950-51 and 1958-59; enlisted in Univ. of Toronto Contingent, C.O.T.C., 1942; Commissioned 1943; has made contrib. towards the decipherment of early N. Arabian inscriptions (Lihyanite and Thamudic) and participated in two archael. and epigraphical surveys of North Arabia, 1962-67; author of "A Study of the Lihyanite and Thamudic Inscriptions" 1937; "The Mosaic Tradition", 1949; "Safaitic Inscriptions from Jordan", 1957; "The Excavations at Dibon (Dhiban) in Moab. The First Campaign, 1950-51", 1964; "Ancient Records from North Arabia" (with W. L. Reed) 1970; "Inscription from Fifty Safaitic Cairns" (with G. L. Harding), 1978; mem., Am. Oriental Soc.; Soc. of Biblical Lit.; Home: 56 Otter Crescent, Toronto, Ont. M5N 2W5

WINSPEAR, Francis George, O.C. (1967), LL.D., F.C.A., R.I.A., F.R.S.A.; b. Birmingham, Eng., 30 May 1903; s. William Willan and Anne Jane (Dewes) E.; e. Pub.. and High Schs., Calgary, Alta.; F.C.A., Alta.; Univ. of Alta., Hon. LL.D.; m. late Bessie, d. late Geo. E. Watchorn, Calgary, Alta., 6 Aug. 1927; children: Claude, William; remarried, Harriet Snowball, 26 Mar. 1980; FOUNDING PARTNER WINSPEAR, HAMILTON, ANDERSON & CO. (Chart. Accts. now amalgamated with Deloutte Haskins and Sells); Chrmn. Bd., Coutts Machinery Co. Ltd.; Pres., The Winspear Foundation; Winham

Investments Ltd.; Hon. Dir., Lake Ontario Steel Co. Ltd.; Co-Steel International Ltd.; Sheerness Steel Co. Ltd.; Raritan River Steel Co.; Past President, Canadian Chamber of Commerce; former Professor of Accounting, University of Alberta; former member, Econ. Council Can.; Past Pres., Edmonton Chamber of Comm.; mem., Inst. of Chart. Accts. of Alberta, B.C. and Manitoba; Soc. of Indust. Accts. of Alta.; Candn.-Am. C. D. Howe Research Inst.; Care of Can. (Hon. Dir.); mem. Bd. Govs., Edmonton Opera Assn.; Fellow, Royal Soc. for the Encouragement of Arts, Mfrs. & Comm., London; mem., Nat. Advisers of Y.M.C.A.; Delta Upsilon; Freemason; Liberal; Anglican; recreations: golf, photography; Clubs: The Edmonton; Mayfair Golf & Country; Home: 701 Valleyview Manor, Edmonton, Alta.; Office: 300 Bentall Bldg., Edmonton, Alta.

WINSPEAR, William W., B.Com., C.A.; industrialist; b. Edmonton, Alta., 23 Oct. 1933; s. Francis George and Bessie (Brooks) W.; e. Oliver (Edmonton) Elem. Sch.; Trinity Coll. Sch., Port Hope, Ont., 1950; Univ. of Alta., B.Com. 1954; m. Margot, d. C. M. Macleod, Edmonton, Alta., 30 May 1955; children: Deborah Jean, Donald William, Malcolm George, Barbara Louise, Robert Lloyd; PRESIDENT, CHAPARRAL STEEL CO.; joined Winspear, Hamilton, Anderson & Co. becoming Partner 1958; Pres., Lake Ontario Steel Co. Ltd., 1970-74; Pres. and Dir., TPL Industries Ltd. 1964-69; Vice-Pres., Dallas Civic Opera; Chmn., Admin. Cmte., St. Mark's School of Texas; mem. Inst. of Chart. Accts. of Alta.; Delta Upsilon; Anglican; recreations: golf, tennis; Office: (P.O. Box 1100) Midlothian, Texas 76065.

WINTER, Bruce O., executive; b. Toronto, Ont., 3 June 1921; s. Dr. Ogden Alfred and Gladys M. (Moriarty) W.; e. N. Toronto Coll. Inst.; Univ. of Toronto, B.A.Sc. (Engn. & Business) 1950; m. Helen M. Hart, 7 Oct. 1950; two s., David Bruce, Robert Allan; VICE-PRES. & GEN. MGR., AGRIC. CHEMICALS DIV., C-I-L INC, 1980- ; Pres. and Chief Extve. Offr., Dir., Canadian Hanson Ltd., 1971- ; Consultant, Harvey Spry & Associates Ltd., 1950-52; Indust. Engn. Dept., Canadian Industries Ltd., 1952; subsequently Indust. Engn. Mgr.-Engn. Dept., Control Engn.-Explosives & Ammunitions Div. and Distribution Mgr.-Corporate; served with RCAF 1942-45; S.E. Asia; rank Flying Offr. (Pilot); mem. Assn. Prof. Engrs. Ont.; Dir., Canadian Fertilizer Inst.; Chipman Inc.; Potash & Phosphates Institute since 1976; Clubs: London Club, Sunningdale Golf; Home: 407 Huron St., London, Ont. N5Y 4J2 Office: 171 Queens Ave., London, Ont. N6A 4L6

WINTER, Gerald Marmaduke; executive; b. St. John's, Nfld., 19 Mar. 1917; s. Robert Gordon and Ethel Phyllis W.; e. Bishop Feild Coll., St. John's Nfld.; Rossall Sch., Eng.; m. Phyllis Boyd, d. John Boyd Baird, St. John's, Nfld., 3 Mar. 1941; children: Keith, John, Stephen; CHRMN. OF THE BD., NEWFOUNDLAND BREWERY LTD., since 1966; Dir., T. & M. Winter Ltd.; Standard Mfg. Co. Ltd.; Molson Breweries of Canada Ltd.; served in World War, 1940-45, as Flight Lieut. with R.C.A.F.; rec'd. King's Commendation; Past Vice Pres., Candn. Chamber Comm.; Past Vice Chrmn., Bd. of Govs., Prince of Wales Coll.; mem., St. John's Mem. Stadium Comn.; Dir., Royal Candn. Geog. Soc.; former mem. of The Canada Council; Past Pres., Nfld. Board of Trade; Vice Chrmn., Maritime Transportation Comn.; Hon. mem., St. John's Regatta Comte.; Anglican; recreations: golf, fishing; Clubs: City; Murray's Pond Fishing; Officers' (Crow's Nest); Bally Haly Golf & Country; Royal Canadian Legion Club; Home: 2 Beech Place, St. John's Nfld., A1B 2S7; Office: 55 Belvedere St., St. John's, Nfld., A1C 5W1

WINTER, Hon. Gordon Arnaud, O.C. (1974), LL.D., Kst.J., K.M.L.J.; b. St. John's, Nfld. 6 Oct. 1912; s. Robert Gordon and Ethel Phyllis (Arnaud) W.; e. Bishop Feild Coll., St. John's, Nfld.; Loretto Sch., Musselburgh, Scotland; LL.D., Memorial 1970; m. Millicent, d. Dr. Thomas Anderson, St. John's, Nfld., 2 Sept. 1937; children: Linda, Valda; CHMN., T & M WINTER LIMITED; Lieut. Governor Of Newfoundland 1974-81; Chrmn. T & M Winter Limited; Standard Mfg. Co. Limited; Chairman, Board of Regents, Memorial University of Newfoundland 1968-74; Chairman, St. John's Housing Corpn., 1949-50; Pres., Nfld. Bd. of Trade, 1946; mem. Adv. Bd., Nfld. Savings Bank, 1959-62; Gov., Candn. Broadcasting Corp., 1952-58; apptd. by H.E. the Gov. in Comn., mem., of the Nfld. del. which negotiated and signed on 11 Dec. 1948, the Terms of Union between Nfld. and Can.; apptd. Min of Finance in first Prov. Govt. of Nfld., 1 Apl. 1949; Anglican; recreations: golfing, curling; Clubs: Bally Haly Golf & Curling; Murray's Pond Fishing; St. Joh's Curling; Coral Beach and Tennis (Bermuda); Home: 6 Winter Pl., St. John's, Nfld. A1B 1J6; Office: 51 James Lane, St. John's, Nfld. A1E 3Y3

WINTER, Maurice Walcot; company director; b. St. John's, Nfld., 22 Aug. 1923; s. late Ethel Phyllis (Arnaud) and the late Robert Gordon Winter; e. Bishop Feild Coll., St. John's, Nfld.; Ridley Coll., St. Catharines, Ont.; m. Mary Ethel, d. late Lionel G. Munn, St. John's, Nfld., 29 Sept. 1948; children: Sharon, Susan, Robert; PRESIDENT, T. & M. WINTER LTD.; Dir., Newfoundland Marine Insurance Co. Ltd.; John Howard Soc. of Can. Ltd. (Nfld. Br.); Past Pres., Newfoundland Game Fish Protection Society Limited; Past President, Newfoundland Board of Ins. Underwriters; Councillor, Newfoundland Bd. Trade 1962-64; Dir., Nfld. Transportation Co. Ltd.; Nfld. Containers Ltd.; Newfoundland Marine Holdings Ltd.; Vanguard Paper Box Ltd.; commenced business career with T. & M. Winter, Ltd., 1942; apptd. a Dir., 1959; served in 2nd World War, 1943-46 as Sgt.-Pilot with RCAF; mem., RCAF Assn.; Roy. Candn. Legion; B.P.O. Elks (PDDGER and Past E.R.); Internat. Atlantic Salmon Foundation; Candn. Wildlife Federation; Anglican; recreations: fishing, curling; Clubs: Bally Haly Golf & Curling; Murray Pond Fishing; Home: 168 Elizabeth Ave., Churchill Park, St. John's, Nfld., A1B 1S6; Office: 51 James Lane, St. John's, Nfld., A1E 3Y3

WINTER, William A., R.C.A. (1953), genre painter; b. Winnipeg, Man., 1909; represented in many private and official collections; best known pictures, "Country Bedroom", Art Gallery of Toronto; "Midnight at Charlie's", Vancouver Art Gallery; winner of J. W. L. Forster Prize, 1943; Home and Studio: 15 Pricefield Road, Toronto, Ont., M4W 1Z8

WINTROBE, Maxwell Myer, M.D., D.Sc., Ph.D., M.A.C.P.; physician; b. Halifax, N.S., 27 Oct. 1901; s. Herman and Ethel (Swerling) W.; e. Univ. of Man., B.A. 1921 (Schol. in French and Pol. Econ. 1920; Gold Medals 1921), M.D. 1926 (Schols. of Med. Coll. 1922-25 and Gordon Bell Fellow. in Med. 1926-27), L.M.C.C. 1926, B.Sc. 1928, D.Sc. (Hon.) 1958; Tulane Univ., Ph.D. 1929; Utah, D.Sc. (Hon.) 1967, Wisc. (Hon.) 1974; Athens, Greece, M.D. (Hon.); m. Becky, d. Jacob Zanphir, Winnipeg, Man., 1 Jan. 1928; children: Susan Hope, Paul W. Herman (died); DISTINGUISHED PROFESSOR OF INTERNAL MED., UNIVERSITY OF UTAH, since 1970; Chairman, Scientific Advisory Board, Scripps Clinic and Research Foundation, La Jolla, California, 1964-74; Physician-in-Chief, Salt Lake General Hosp., 1943-65; Univ. of Utah Medical Center, 1965-67; Consultant to U.S. Pub. Health Service; Surg. Gen., U.S. Army; Atomic Energy Comn., U.S.; Veterans' Hosps., U.S.A.; former Chrmn., Med. Adv. Council, Life Insurance Medical Research Fund; formerly Dir., Laboratory for Study of Hereditary & Metabolic Disorders, Univ. of Utah; Am. Soc. of Human Genetics; Interne, King George Hosp., Winnipeg, Man., 1925; Winnipeg Gen. Hosp., 1925-26; Instr. in Med., Tulane Univ. and Asst. Visiting Phys., Charity Hosp., New Orleans, La., 1927-30; Instr. in Med., Johns

Hopkins Univ. 1930-35, Assoc. in Med. there, and Assoc. Phys., Hematologist and Phys.-in-charge, Clinic for Nutritional, Gastrointestinal & Hemopoietic Disorders, Johns Hopkins Hosp., 1935-43; Prof. of Med., Univ. of Utah 1943-70; Advisory Ed., "Tice Practice of Medicine", 1943-56; Fulbright Lecturer, India, 1956; Thayer Lectr., Johns Hopkins Univ., 1966; Lilly Lectr., Roy. Coll. of Phys., London, 1968; Visiting Prof., Johns Hopkins Univ.; Harvard; Vanderbilt; Rochester; New York Univ.; Univ. Calif. (L.A.); Toronto; McGill; Ottawa; U.B.C.; Dalhousie; N. Carolina; Emory; Miami; Tulane; etc.; Chrmn., Comte. Consultant, on Nutritional Anaemias, WHO, Geneva; mem., Council on Drugs, Am. Med. Assn., 1960-66, Vice-Chmn., 1965-66, chmn., cmte on adverse drug reactions; Assoc. Ed., "Blood"; mem. Ed. Bd., "Am. Journ. Med", "Blood", "Journ. of Clinical Nutrition", "Medicine", "Cancer", "Journ. of Clinical Investigation", "Journ. Clin. Path." (British) and others; Mang. Ed. of the "Bulletin", Johns Hopkins, 1941-43; author of "Diseases of the Blood", 1931 (rev. ed. 1936, 1956), in vol. 6 "Tice's Practice of Medicine"; "Polycythemia", in "Handbook of Hematology", 1938, in collab. with G. E. Harrop; "Clinical Hematology", (1st ed. 1942, 8th ed. 1981); Chief Editor, 6th and 7th ed. "Harrison's Principles of Internal Medicine" (1st ed. 1950, 7th ed. 1974); "Blood, Pure and Eloquent" 1980; also over 400 articles and monographs in med. journs; served in C.O.T.C., 1917-18; inventor of the "Wintrobe Hemoglobinometer" and "Wintrobe Hematocrit"; rec'd. Lambie-Dew Oration Medal, Sydney, Australia, 1958; Homenaje, Valparaiso, Chile, 1959; John Phillips Medal for Achievements in Medicine, Am. Coll. of Phys., 1967; Mayo Soley Award 1970; Robert H. Williams Award 1973; Kober Medal, Assn. Am. Phys. 1974; Hon. mem., Squires Club, Toronto 1978; Physician of Excellence Award, Medical Times 1979; el. Nat. Acad. Science (U.S.) 1973; member, Utah Society of History of Medicine. (Pres. 1971-72); Am. Soc. Hematol. (Pres. 1971-72); Am. Soc. Clin. Investigation; Assn. Am. Physicians (Pres. 1965-66); Am. Soc. Exper. Path.; Am. Fed. Clin. Research; American College Physicians (Master); Internat. Soc. Hematol. (President-Elect, 1976-78, Pres. 1978-80); Hon. Fellow Italian, Swiss, German Hematol. Soc.; Past Pres., Western Assn. of Physicians; Pres., Assn. Prof. of Med.; mem., Nat. Adv. Bd., Utah Symphony; founder, mem., Bd. of Dir. (Vice-Pres.), Chamber Music Soc.; Alpha Omega Alpha; Hon. Phi Beta Kappa; Sigma Alpha Mu; Sigma Xi (Founder); Liberal; recreations: tennis, canoeing, fishing, skiing, golf, music (violin); Home: 5882 Brentwood Dr., Salt Lake City, 84121, Utah; Office: Univ. of Utah Medical Center, 50 N. Medical Drive, Salt Lake City, Utah 84132.

WISDOM, John Oulton, B.A., Ph.D.; university educator; b. Dublin, Ireland, 29 Dec. 1908; s. Thomas Hume and Jane Susan Margaret (Oulton) W.; e. Earlsfort House Sch., Dublin, 1926; Trinity Coll., Univ. of Dublin, B.A. 1931, Ph.D. 1933; Cambridge Univ., 1933; m. Clara, d. William Norman Williams, 1970; children: Adrian, Clive, Jane; UNIV. PROFESSOR OF PHILOS. AND SOCIAL SCIENCE, YORK UNIVERSITY, retired; served with Home Guard 1940-43; rank 2nd Lieutenant; awarded Senior Foreign Science Fellowship, National Science Foundation; author, "The Metamorphosis of Philosophy", 1947; "The Unconscious Origin of Berkeley's Philosophy", 1953; "Philosophy and its Place in our Culture" 1975; "Challengeability in Modern Science"; also papers in philos., philos. of science, psychoanalysis, psychosomatic med.; ed. "Philosophy of the Social Sciences"; Past Pres., Soc. Psychosomatic Research (London); recreations: music; Home: Wilmont, Castlebridge Co., Wexford, Irish Republic

WISE, Jack Marlowe, B.F.A., M.Sc., R.C.A.; artist; b. Centerville, Iowa 27 Apl. 1928; s. Ralph Marlowe and Zarilda Jane (Morris) W.; e. New Orleans Sch. of Fine Arts 1949; Wash. Univ. St. Louis B.F.A. 1953; Fla. State

Univ. M.Sc. 1955; m. Mary Beatrice d. Winfield Hubbard 1969; children: Jonathon Marlowe, Maria Zarilda, Tomas Winfield; Trustee, Victoria Coll. Art, Resident Artist; Trustee, Art Gallery Greater Victoria 1978-79; solo exhns. incl. New Design Gallery Vancouver 1965, 1966; Art Gallery Greater Victoria, Rex Evans Gallery Los Angeles, 1966; Bau-Xi Gallery Vancouver 1967, 1968, 1970, 1971, 1972, 1973, 1974, 1975, Toronto 1976; Galerie Godard-Lefort Montreal 1968; Commonwealth Inst. Art Gallery London, Eng., Richard Demarco Gallery Edinburgh 1969; Regina Pub. Lib. Gallery, Univ. of Lethbridge Art Gallery 1970; Mendel Gallery Saskatoon, Polly Friedlander Gallery Seattle 1971; Upstairs Gallery Winnipeg, Univ. of Winnipeg 1973; Wells Gallery Ottawa 1976; Kyle's Gallery Victoria 1979; Ken Heffle Gallery Vancouver 1980; across Can. tour exhn. Jack Wise: A Decade of Work 1977-78; rep. in numerous group exhns. Can., USA, Australia and Mexico since 1959; rep. in pub., corporate and private colls. incl. Scot. Arts Council Edinburgh, Can. Council Art Bank, Archives of Am. Art Smithsonian Inst.; rec'd Can. Council Sr. Fellowship for travel and study of Tibetan art in India 1966 and Sr. Arts Award for residence in Europe 1969; Ed. and Forewood "Mystic Circle" 1973; Phi Kappa Phi; recreations: camping, reading, horseback riding; Address: 1014 Park Blvd., Victoria, B.C. V8V 2T4.

WISE, Hon. John, M.P.; politician; b. St. Thomas, Ont. 12 Dec. 1935; s. Clayton Wesley and Mary (White) W.; e. St. Thomas and Elgin Pub. and High Schs.; Univ. of Guelph grad. 1956; m. Ann Dimora d. George Richardson, St. Thomas, Ont. 18 Oct. 1958; two d. Elizabeth, Susan; MIN. OF AGRIC. CAN. since 1979; el. to H. of C. for Elgin g.e. 1972, re-el. since; apptd. Chrmn. P. Cons. Caucus Comte. on Agric. 1976; fifth generation dairy farmer; Pres. Elgin Jersey Breeders 1957 — 58; Dir. Oxford & Dist. Cattle Breeders Assn. 1960, Pres. 1965; formed Elgin Young P. Cons. Assn. and became Charter Pres. 1958; Councillor, Yarmouth Twp. 1960, Depy. Reeve 1965, Reeve 1968; Warden of Elgin Co. and mem. Elgin Co. Council 1969; mem. Prov. Adv. Comte., Mun. Affairs Mins. Ont. 1969; mem. St. Thomas and Suburban Area Planning Bd. 1969; Vice Chrmn. Central Elgin Planning Bd. 1970, Chrmn. 1971 — 72; Dir. Elgin Co-op. Services 1970; mem. original Talbot Shivaree Comte. 1971; Vice Chrmn. Un. Appeal 1961; mem. St. Thomas Elgin Assn. Retarded Children Residence Comte. 1967; has acted as judge numerous occasions Co. and 4-H Dairy shows; rec'd Rotary Club "Adventure in Citizenship" Award 1954; St. Thomas Jaycees' "Outstanding Young Man Award" 1967; Freemason; Shriner; P. Conservative; Anglican; Home: R.R. 4, St. Thomas, Ont. N5P 3S8; Office: House of Commons, Ottawa, Ont. K1A 0X2.

WISE, Nicholas E. M., C.L.U.; b. Rumania, 4 Oct. 1923; s. Edmund and Helen (Ruben) W.; e. Cambridge Univ., 1941; m. Barbara Golden, 13 July 1945; four children: came to Can., 1947; Pres., Nicholas Insurance Enterprises Ltd.; Gen. Agent and Vice-Pres. North West Life Assnce. Co. of Can. 1976; Agent with London Life Insurance Co., 1947-55; Mgr., Northern Life Assurance Co. of Canada, 1955-58; joined Global Life Insurance Co. as Mgr., 1958-63, apptd. Vice-Pres. and Mgr. 1963; served during 2nd World War with Brit. Army in Middle East; discharged with rank of Capt., 1945; mem., Life Underwriters Assn. Montreal (Past Pres.); Ins. Brokers Assn. Prov. Que.; Qualifying & Life mem., Million Dollar Round Table of U.S.; Five Million Dollar Forum of U.S.; Hebrew; recreations: golf, skiing; Clubs: M.A.A.A.; Lachute Golf & Country; Address: 5902 Macdonald Ave., Hampstead, Que., H3X 2X1

WISE, Sydney Francis, B.L.S., M.A.; b. Toronto, Ont., 1924; s. Francis Evelyn and Marjorie Louise (Hutton) W.; e. Bowmore Rd. and Earl Kitchener Pub. Schs., Toronto; Riverdale Coll. Inst., Toronto; Univ. of Toronto, B.A. (Gold Medalist in Hist.) 1949, B.L.S. 1950; Queen's

Univ., M.A. 1953; m. Verna Isobel, d. Walter Workman Mulholland, Toronto, 5 Sept. 1947; children: John Francis Hutton, Catherine Ellen, Bruce Douglas; DEAN OF GRADUATE STUDIES, CARLETON UNIV., Dir., Inst. of Candn. Studies and Professor of History, Carleton Univ. 1981- ; 1978; Bd. of Gov., 1980- ; Gen. Ed., Carleton Library Series, 1979-81; Lectr. in History, Royal Mil. Coll., 1950-55; with Dept. of Hist., Queen's Univ., 1955-66 (apptd. full Prof. 1964); R. Samuel McLaughlin Research Prof., Queen's Univ., 1964-65, Director, History, Dept. National Defence 1966-73; Visiting Prof., Inst. of Candn. Studies, Carleton Univ., 1964; Prof. of History, 1973; served with R.C.A.F. as Pilot, 1943-45, rank Flying Offr.; co-author of "Men in Arms: a history of the inter-relationships of warfare and western society'', 1956, 2nd ed. 1962, 3rd ed. 1970, 4th ed. 1979; co-author, Task Force Report to Fed. Cabinet on Sport for Canadians 1969; "Canada's Sporting Heroes: Their Lives & Times" 1974; "Canadian Airmen in the First World War", Vol. 1, 1980; and others; has publ. articles and reviews in various journs.; Awarded Cruikshank Gold Medal, Ont. Hist. Soc. ("for outstanding service to the cause of history in Ont."); Pres., Social Science Research Council Canada 1974-75; mem., Canadian Hist. Assn. (Council 1962-65, Pres. 1973-74); U.N. Assn. Can. (Pres. Kingston Bd., 1963-65); Ont. Hist. Soc. (mem. Extve 1964-65, Vice Pres. 1966-68, Pres. 1968-69); Chrmn., Archeol. & Hist. Sites Bd. Ont. 1972-74; Vice-Chmn., Ont. Heritage Fdn., 1975-80; Chrmn., 1980-81, Ont. Heritage Foundation; Chmn., Conservation Review Bd. of Ont. 1981- ; Vice Pres., Champlain Society; Executive mem. SCITEC 1972-73; Anglican; Club: Royal Canadian Military Institute; Home: 562 Lisgar St. Ottawa, Ont.

WISEMAN, Hon. Douglas J., M.P.P.; politician; b. Smiths Falls, Ont. 21 July 1930; s. Walter Robert and Beatrice Viola (Garland) W.; e. pub. and high schs. Smiths Falls; Mang. and Sales courses in Shoe Retailing; Animal Husbandry and Judging courses; m. Bernice Emma d. John Holmes Drummond, Toledo, Ont. 26 June 1951; children: Clifford Douglas, Karen Grace; Robert Drummond; MIN. OF GOVT. SERVICES, ONT. 1979- ; prior to entering politics operated shoe and real estate businesses, private hosp., purebred cattle operation; el. M.P.P. for Lanark 1971, re-el. since; Parlty. Asst. to Min. of Health 1975; Min. without Portfolio 1978; served Perth Pub. Sch. Bd. as mem. then Chrmn. 12 yrs.; former Chrmn. Perth Retail Merchants Assn.; Past Vice Pres. Lanark Co. P. Cons. Assn.; Past Chrmn. E. Ont. Charolais Assn.; mem. of Session and Trustee, St. Paul's Un. Ch. Perth; former mem. Children's Aid Soc.; co-recipient Candn. Shoe Retail Industry Merit Award; rec'd Breeder's Award Candn. Carolais Assn.; P. Conservative; United Church; Home: R.R.5, Perth, Ont. K7H 3C7; Office: 12th Floor Ferguson Block, Parliament Bldgs., Toronto, Ont. M7A 1N3.

WISENER, Robert A., B.Sc.; merchant banker; b. Toronto, Ont., 8 Feb. 1927; s. late Philip A. and Margaret Jeanne (McLaughlin) W.; e. Toronto Pub. Schs.; Crescent Sch., Toronto; Trinity Coll. Sch., Port Hope, Ont.; Royal Candn. Naval Coll., Royal Roads, B.C.; Univ. of Toronto, B.Sc. 1950; m. (3rd) Patricia, d. Patricia King, Glasgow, Scotland; children: Cynthia, Philip, Lee, Robin, Susan, Joanne, James, Timothy; CHAIRMAN, THE MERBANCO GROUP Dir., Northways Gestalt Corp.; Taro Industries Ltd.; Patrician Land Development Corp. Ltd.; Bluesky Oil and Gas Ltd.; Fidelity Trust; mem., Businessmen's Advisory Board for Industry Trade and Commerce; National Advisory Committee on Conservation and Renewable Energy. Anglican; recreations: sailing, squash, skiing; Home: Site 19, Box 36 S.S. #1, Bears Paw Village Calgary, Alta. T2M 4N3 Office: 330, 999 8th Street, Calgary, Alta. T2R 1J5

WISMER, William Miller, Q.C., B.A.; business executive; b. Jordan Station, Ont., 13 Sept. 1913; s. Philip

Henry and Minnie Margaret (Miller) W.; e. St. Catharines Coll. Inst. & Vocational Sch. (Sr. Matric. 1932); Univ. of Toronto (Univ. Coll.), B.A. 1938; Osgoode Hall Law Sch., Toronto, Ont.; m. Margaret Katharine Anna, d. Robert Chalmers, Niagara Falls, Ont., 16 June 1938; one d., Margaret Katharine; PRESIDENT & DIR., BISON PETROLEUM & MINERALS LTD.; Pres. and Dir., Dominion Jubilee Corp. Ltd.; read law with Peter White, K.C.; called to the Bar of Ont., 1941; practised law with the firm of White, Ruel & Bristol, Toronto, Ont., 1941-43; Solr. with Ont. Securities Comn., 1945-48; Extve. Secy. and General Counsel, The Broker-Dealers' Assn. of Ont., 1948-56; Vice Pres., The Toronto Stock Exchange 1956-64; Vice-President and Dir., Draper Dobie & Co. Ltd., 1965-72; Pres., Canadian Javelin Ltd., 1967-74; served in 2nd World War with the R.C.N.V.R. 1943-45 with rank of Lieut.; mem., Toronto Bd. of Trade; Premier of 14th Ont. Older Boys' Parliament, 1934-35; Phi Delta Phi; recreations: reading, walking, golf, fishing; Clubs: Islington Golf; Engineers; Home: Penthouse 1, 50 Prince Arthur Ave., Toronto, Ont., M5R 1B5; Office: Suite 1200, 100 Adelaide St. W., Tor. Ont. M5H 1S3

WITHER, George Malcolm, B.Eng.; executive; b. Winnipeg, Man., 5 Jan. 1916; s. William A. and Jean (Fardell) W.; e. Pub. and High Sch., Winnipeg, Man.; Univ. of Man.; McGill Univ., B.Eng. 1941; m. Marguerite L., d. James Greer, 26 June 1941; children: Jeannie Elizabeth, Janet Alison, Kathleen Mary; former Vice-Pres. And Dir., Alcan Canada Products Limited, Pres; G.M. Wither & Assoc. Ltd. Dir., Supreme Aluminum Industries; Devel. Geol., Hollinger Mines, 1941; Metall., Alcan, Toronto, 1942-45; joined Aluminum Goods Limited as Metall., 1945-53; apptd. Works Manager, 1953-67; President and Director 1967; Past Director, Y.M.C.A.; Secy., Indust. Accident Prevention Assn.; mem., Candn. Mfrs. Assn.; United Church; Clubs: Weston Golf; Home: 6 Cranleigh Court, Islington, Ont., M9A 3Y3;

WITHERS, Gen. Ramsey Muir, CM.M. C.D., B.Sc.; army officer; b. Toronto, Ont., 28 July 1930; s. late William Muir and Alice Hope Smith (Hannah) W.; e. Royal Mil. Coll. Can., Dipl. 1952; Queen's Univ., B.Sc. 1954; Candn. Army Staff Coll., psc 1961; Jt. Services Staff Coll., Eng., jssc 1963; m. Jean Alison, d. S. F. Saunders, Orillia, Ont., 8 May 1954; children: James Scott, Leslie Susan, Deidre Ann; CHIEF OF DEFENSE STAFF, CANADIAN ARMED FORCES; served in Korea, Can., Germany and Eng.; Mobile Command H.Q.; CFHQ; N. Region H.Q. presently mem. Assn. Prof. Engrs. Ont.; Anglican; recreations: boating, curling; Address: Nat. Defence HQ., Ottawa, Ont.

WITHERSPOON, Douglas Charles; executive; b. Toronto, Ont. 8 Sept. 1929; s. Robert James and Hattie Alic (Kelday) W.; e. Bloor Coll. Inst. Toronto 1949; Alexander Hamilton Inst., Business Adm. 1960; Queen's Univ. Business Course 1962; Univ. of W. Ont. Mang. Training Course 1971; m. Barbara June d. Robert Clarke Burns, Toronto, Ont. 15 Sept. 1956; PRES. AND DIR., SCHOLL (CANADA) INC. since 1978; Pres.; Dr. Scholl's Ltd.; Dir. Taylor Soaps-Perfumes Ltd.; Retail Attendant, The Scholl Manufacturing Co. Ltd. Toronto 1949, Sales Rep. Wholesale 1950, Asst. to Mgr.-Retail Div. 1956, Asst. to Sales Mgr. 1958, Asst. to Gen. Mgr. 1960, Gen. Sales Mgr. 1967, Vice Pres.-Marketing 1971, Dir. 1973, Vice Pres. & Gen. Mgr. 1975; Country Gen. Mgr. for Canada, International Consumer Products Div. of Schering-Plough; mem. Comm. Travellers' Assn. Can. (Past Pres.), Dir.; Sales Research Club Toronto (Past Pres.); Vice-Pres., The Proprietary Assn. of Can.; P. Conservative; Protestant; recreations: golf, tennis, swimming, curling, fishing; Clubs: Thornhill Golf & Country; Rotary; Home: 1714 — 45 Wynford Heights Cres., Don Mills, Ont. M3C 1L3; Office: 174 Bartley Dr., Toronto, Ont. M4A 1E3.

WITHROW, William J., C.M., M.A., M.Ed. C.D.; b. Toronto, Ont., 30 Sept. 1926; s. Wilfred Forbes and Evelyn Gertrude W.; e. Univ. of Toronto, B.A. (Art & Archaeol.) 1950; Art Specialist, O.C.E. 1951; B.Ed. 1955, M.Ed. 1958; M.A. (Fine Art) 1961; m. June Roselea Van Ostrom, 1948; three s. and one d.; DIRECTOR, ART GALLERY OF ONTARIO, since 1961; Art. Dept. Head, Earl Haig Coll. 1951-59; Instr. in oil painting and ceramic pottery & sculpture, Adult Night Sch. Programme, 1951-59; Principal and Research Dir., Ont. Dept. of Educ. 1957-59; served during 2nd World War; discharged with rank of Capt.; mem., Candn. Museums Assn.; Assn. Art Museum Dirs.; Past Pres., Canadian Art Museum Dir's. Organ.; Club: University; Home: 7 Malabar Place, Don Mills, Ont., M3B 1A4; Office: 317 Dundas St. W., Toronto, Ont. M5T 1G4

WITTKOWER, Eric David, M.D., F.R.S.M., F.B., Ps.S.; F.R.C.P.(C), C.S.P.Q.; emeritus prof.; b. Berlin, Germany, 4 Apl. 1899; s. Louis and Bertha (Katz) W.; e. Univ. Berlin, M.D. 1924; Univ. Edinburgh, LRCP & S., 1936; Univ. of Glasgow, L.R.F.P.S., 1936; Certification in specialty of Psychiatry, Royal College of Physicians and Surgeons, Canada, 1955; Quebec, 1955; m. Claire Francesca, d. Isidor Weil, 29 July 1931; children: Andrew B., Sylvia Dorothy; Consulting Psychiatrist, Royal Victoria Hosp., Montreal, Que., since 1963; Consulting Psychiatrist to Montreal Gen. Hosp., since 1951; Privat-dozent, Psychosomatic Med., Univ. of Berlin, 1932-33; Research Fellow, Maudsley Hosp., Univ. of London, 1933-35; Sir Halley Stewart Research Fellow, Tavistock Clinic, 1935-40 and Consulting Psychiatrist there 1948-51; Psychiatrist, St. Bartholomew's Hosp., Univ. of London, 1948-51; Lectr., Maudsley Hosp., Univ. of London, 1949-51; Assoc. Prof., Psychiatry McGill, 1953-63; Prof. 1963-72 since when Emeritus Prof.; served in 2nd World War; Major, R.A.M.C., 1940-45 (Army Psychiatrist, Brit. War Office, London); Editor, "Transcultural Psychiatric Review and Newsletter"; Assoc. Ed. "Social Science and Medicine", Journal American Academy of Psychoanalysis, etc.; Publications: "The Pathology of High Altitude Climate", 1937; "A Psychiatrist Looks at Tuberculosis", 1949; "Recent Developments in Psychosomatic Medicine", 1954; "Emotional Factors in Skin Diseases", 1953, "Psychosomatic Medicine: Its Clinical Implications", 1977; "Divergent Views in Psychiatry", and over 200 articles in scient. journs.; Past Pres., Internat. Coll. of Psychosmatic Med.; Life Fellow Am. Psychiatric Assn.; Coll. of Am. Psychiatrists; Life Fellow Candn. Psychoanalytic Soc. (Pres. 1966-67); Am. Psychosomatic Soc. (Pres. 1959-60); Candn. Psychiatric Assn.; Amer. Acad. Psychoanalysis (Pres 1969-70); Cdn. Psychoanalytic Soc. (Pres. 1966-67); Fellow, Royal Coll. of Phys. & Surg., Can.; mem., World Fed. of Mental Health; Founding Fellow, Brit. Coll. Psychiatrists; Home: 363 Clarke Ave., Westmount, Que., H3Z 2E7

WOADDEN, Robert; deputy city clerk; b. Broughton Astley, Eng., 28 Dec. 1922; s. Algernon Francis and Freeda Alathea (Nash) W.; e. Gateway Sch., Leicester; Coll. of Art & Technol., Leicester, Inst. of Linguists Dipl.; Loughborough Coll., Sch. of Librarianship; m. Gladys Joan Truepenny, 13 Jan. 1945; two d., Elizabeth Frances, Christina; DEPUTY CITY CLERK, since 1975; Br. Librarian, Leicester, Eng., 1949-51; Depy. to Town Librarian, Dover, Eng., 1951-56; Registrar, Candn. Jewellers Inst., 1957-60; Dir. of Records and City Archivist, City Clerks Dept., Toronto, 1960-75; served with RN 1942-46 in Caribbean, Middle E., Far E. and Europe; author of various articles on records mang., mun. hist. in prof. mags. and hist. soc. publs.; mem., Soc. Am. Archivists; Candn. Inst. Public Adm.; Assn. Mun. Clerks & Treas., Ont.; Anglican; recreations: golf, swimming, bowling; Clubs: Toronto Press; Bd. of Trade; Home: 10 Council Cres., Downsview, Ont. Office: City Hall, Toronto, Ont. M3J 1J6

WOHLFARTH, Harry, M.F.A., Dr.acad.; artist; university professor; b. Oberstdorf, Germany, 26 April 1921; s. Kurt Walter and Franziska (Gammel) W.; e. Art Acad. Dresden, Kokoschka, Saltzburg; State Univ. of Guanajuato, Mexico, M.F.A. 1968; Roman Acad. Arts and Sciences, Doctoris Academiae 1962; one s., Gunnar; Prof. of Art, Univ. Alta.; one-man exhns. incl.; Banff Sch. Fine Arts 1959; State Univ. Mont. 1960; Univ. of Man. Gallery 1963; Fleet Gallery, Winnipeg, 1964; Jacox Galleries, Edmonton, 1964, 1965; Gallery L'Art de L'Ouest, Montreal, 1968; State Univ. of Guanajuato Gallery, Mexico, 1968; Accademia Tiberina Gallery, Rome, 1970; Environment '71 Calgary; Lefebvre Gallery 1971, 1973 and Latitude 53 Gallery, Edmonton 1975, 1976, 1978; Zurich, Switzerland 1975; Galerie Mauffe, Paris 1976; City Gallerie, Bad Duerrheim 1977; Koenigsfeld 1978; Bad Woerislofen 1978; Gallerie Stern, Villingen (all in Germany), 1978; Burkhardt Academy Gallery, Rome 1980; Friendship Center Gallery, Moscow 1980; paintings and sculptures in permanent collections include: Banff School of Fine Arts, State Museum Kalkar (Germany), Vatican Collection (Rome), Academia Romana di Science ed Arti, Univ. of Alta., State Univ. of Guanajuato, N. Alta., Jubilee Auditorium, Can. House (New Delhi) and in various private colls.; el. mem. German Acad. of Color Sciences, Bonn, 1961, Pres., 1980-85; el. Fellow, Internat. Inst. Arts & Letters, Geneva, 1961; Senator, Roman Acad. of Arts & Sciences, 1962; mem. Tiberian Acad., Rome, 1968; mem. Internat. Acad. Leonardo da Vinci, Rome, 1970; Hon. Causa mem. Internat. Academy of Letters, Arts and Sciences, Rome 1972; Internat. Burkhardt. Acad., Rome (Gold Medal 1978, 1979, Rennaissance Prize 1979); rec'd. Gold Medal, Tiberian Acad., 1970; Alta. Govt. Award 1970; Gold Medal, Internat. Acad. "Leonardo da Vinci" 1971; Cross, Legion d'Oro Honore 1971; Gold Medal, Internat. Acad. Letters, Art & Sciences 1972; Alta. Govt. Achievement Awards 1970, 72, 74; author of over 40 scholastic and research publs.; served with Alpine Corps, German Army 1940-45; wounded in action 4 times in Russia; rec'd. Iron Cross, Hand-to-Hand Combat Medal; recreations: climbing, hiking; Club: Alpine; Home: 11025-82 Ave., Suite 1101, Edmonton, Alta., T6G 0T1

WOJCIECHOWSKI, Jerzy A., L.Ph., Ph.D.; educator; b. Brzesc, Poland, 30 June 1925; s. Roman and Antonina (Widawska) W.; e. Warsaw, Poland (Sr. Matric.) 1942; Warsaw Tech. Univ. (Mech. Engn.); Inst. Superieur de Philos., Univ. de Louvain, B.Ph. 1949; Univ. Laval, L.Ph. 1951, Ph.D. 1953; m. Cécile, d. late Adrien Cloutier, 27 Dec. 1966; children: Maria, Ewa; PROF. OF PHILOSOPHY, UNIV. OF OTTAWA since 1965; came to Can. 1949; Teacher (part-time) Montreal 1952; St. Francis Xavier Univ. 1953; joined present Univ. 1954; served in 2nd World War, Polish Underground Army, Mil. Intelligence Div. 1942-45; Offrs. Sch. 1944, took part in Warsaw Insurrection as Cadet-Offr.; twice wounded and decorated; organized 7th Inter-Am. Cong. of Philos.; Pres., Candn. Philos. Assn., 1969-70; Inter-Univ. Comte. on Candn. Slavs; Vice-Pres., Polish Candn. Cong.; Dir., Survey on Status of Philos. in Can.; Chrmn., Organ. Comte., 1st Ottawa Conf. on Conceptual Basis of Classification of Knowledge 1970; mem. (Hon. Life) Candn. Philos. Assn.; mem. Extve. Council, Humanities Research Council Can., 1970-72; Am. Philos. Assn.; Polish Soc. Arts & Sciences Abroad (U.K.); Polish Inst. Arts & Sciences in Am. (N.Y.); author of "Survey of the Status of Philosophy in Canada", 1970; Ed., "Conceptual Basis of the Classification of Knowledge", 1974; co-ed.; "Polonia of Tomorrow", 1977; and of numerous papers and articles in learned and prof. journs.; R. Catholic; Home: 80 Pleasant Park Rd., Ottawa, Ont., K1H 5L9

WOLFE, Major-Gen. John Patterson, C.D., Q.C., LL.M.; Canadian Forces; b. Winnipeg, Man. 2 May 1924; s. Harold Bertram Wolfe; e. Univ. Alta.; LL.B. 1954 (Gold Medal); King's Coll. London LL.M. 1968; m. Emily Odilla d. late Angelo Borgna 4 Dec. 1976; one s. John Francis, four d. (by previous marriage) Andrea Gail, Catherine Janice, Lorraine Patricia, Leslie Karen; JUDGE ADVOCATE GEN., CANDN. FORCES 1976- ; joined Candn. Army 1942-45, Normandy, wounded in action 1942; rejoined 1951, trans. to Legal Br. 1954; called to Bar 1954; cr. Q.C. 1974; loaned to Tanzanian Govt. to assist in drafting defence leg. 1965-66; Depy Judge Advocate Gen. 1972-75; served 6 months Vietnam as Legal Adviser to Internat. Comn. Control & Supervision; Depy. Head, Canadn. Del. to Diplomatic Conf. on Reaffirmation & Devel. of Humanitarian Law Applicable in Armed Conflicts, Geneva 1973-77 and on Possible Restrictions on Use of Certain Conventional Weapons, Geneva 1979; co-author "Canadian Perspectives on International Law and Organization" 1974; author various journ. articles; mem. Internat. Law Soc.; Candn. Council Internat. Law; Fed. Lawyers' Club; Internat. Soc. Mil. Law & Law of War (Dir.); R. Catholic; recreations: swimming, cross-country skiing; Home: 970 Cahil Dr. W., Ottawa, Ont. K1V 9H8; Office: 101 Colonel By Dr., Ottawa, Ont. K1A 0K2.

WOLFE, Leonhard Scott, M.Sc., Ph.D., M.D., Sc.D., F.R.C.P. & S. (C), F.R.S.C.; educator; physician; b. Auckland N.Z. 25 March 1926; s. Paul George and May (Kelsall) W.; e. Cornwall Park Elem. Sch. and Auckland Grammar Sch. 1943; Longburn Missy. Coll. Palmerston North, N.Z. 1943-45; Canterbury Univ. Coll. Univ. of N.Z. B.Sc. 1947, M.Sc. 1949; Cambridge Univ. Ph.D. 1952, Sc.D. 1976; Univ. of W. Ont. M.D. 1958; m. Jeanne Mary d. James Saunders 4 Aug. 1959; children: Alexander Paul, Elizabeth Anne; PROF. OF NEUROLOGY & NEUROSURGERY, MONTREAL NEUROLOGICAL INST. since 1970 and Prof. of Biochem. McGill Univ., Dir. Donner Lab. of Exper. Neurochem., Chrmn. McGill-Med. Research Council Biomed. Mass Spectrometry Unit; Asst. Prof. Exper. Neurol. and Assoc. Neurochem. present Inst. and Univ. 1960, Assoc. Prof. of Neurol. & Neurosurg. 1965; Biomed. Adv. Dermatol. Research Unit, Royal Victoria Hosp.; Visiting Prof. Centre de Neurochimie CNRS Univ. of Strasbourg, Univ. of W. Ont. Med. Sch., Univ. of Sask. Med. Sch., Univ. of Sask. Med. Sch.; Career Scientist, Med. Research Council; Counselor, Intramural Program, Nat. Inst. of Neurol. Communicable Disorders & Stroke; Adv. to Research Program, Eunice Kennedy Shriver Center for Mental Retardation; co-author "Radiation, Radioactivity and Insects" 1963; over 150 articles and chapters scient. journs. and books; Chmn., Publications Comte., "Journal of Neurochemistry"; mem. ed. bds. various med. journs.; mem. Corp. Phys. & Surgs. Que.; Montreal Physiol. Soc. (Pres.); Candn. Biochem. Soc. (Council); Am. Soc. Neurochem.; Am. Soc. Biol. Chems.; Soc. Neurosciences; Internat. Soc. Neurochem.; Internat. Brain Research Organ.; NDP; recreations: music, sailing, philately; Club: Oxford & Cambridge; NIH Alumni Assn.; Home: 4700 Westmount Ave., Montreal, Que. H3Y 1X4; Office: 3801 University St., Montreal, Que. H3A 2B4.

WOLFE, Ray D., C.M., B.A.; executive; b. Toronto, Ont., 3 Aug. 1917; s. Maurice and Tillie (Manovitz) W.; e. Univ. of Toronto, B.A. 1939; m. Rose, d. late Maurice Senderowitz, 5 July 1940; children: Jonathan Alexander, Leslie Elizabeth; CHRMN. AND PRES., THE OSHAWA GROUP LTD.; Chrmn., IGA Canada Ltd.; Dir., Confederation Life Insurance Co.; Canadian Pacific Ltd.; Bank of Nova Scotia; Food Marketing Inst.; Retail Council of Can.; served in 2nd World War with R.C.A.F., 1943-46; Chrmn., Canada-Israel Chamber Comm.; Pres., Candn. Jewish News; Dir., Baycrest Centre for Geriatric Care; Candn. Council Christians & Jews (Human Relations Award 1958); Gov., Mount Sinai Hospital; mem., Council of Trustees, Inst. for Research on Public Policy; Can. Jewish Congress Exec. Comte.; Hon. Pres., Candn. Friends of Haifa Univ. (Hon. Fellowship 1978); Order of Canada 1980; Ben Sadowski Award of Merit 1975; recreation: golf; Clubs: Primrose; Oakdale; Montefiore; Home: 89 Bay-

view Ridge, Willowdale, Ont., M2L 1E3; Office: 302 The East Mall, Islington, Ont., M9B 6B8

WOLFF, Terrance Alban, B.A., B.Com.; executive; b. Peterborough, Ont. 4 Nov. 1931; s. Alban Cecil and Jean (Thorndyke) W.; e. St. Peters Sch., Peterborough; St. Francis Xavier Univ., B.A. and B.Com. 1954; m. Irene, d. J. M. Lapoint 16 Nov. 1957; children: Byron, Marc, Jeanne; PRESIDENT AND CHIEF EXTVE. OFFR., SCOTIA LEASING LTD. since 1978; joined Bank of Nova Scotia as Asst. Acct. 1954; New Business Mgr. Canadian Acceptance Corp. Ltd. 1956; consecutively Br. Mgr. with IAC Ltd. in Ottawa, Vancouver and Toronto 1957-68, Regional Mgr. H.O. Toronto 1968, Asst. Vice-Pres. 1972; Pres., Dir. and C.E.O., Scotia Toronto-Dominion Leasing Ltd., 1974; mem. and Chrmn. of Extve. Comte., Equipment Lessors Assn. Can.; Candn. Assn. Equipment Distributors; Bd. Trade Metrop. Toronto; recreations: golf, skiing, swimming; Club: Donalda; Home: 27 Boyd Crt., RR #2, Gormley, Ont. L0H 1G0; Office: 44 King St. W., Toronto, Ont., M5H 1H1

WOLFSON, Joseph Laurence, M.Sc., Ph.D.; educator; b. Winnipeg, Man. 22 July 1917; s. Samuel Wolfson; e. Univ. of Man. B.Sc. 1942, M.Sc. 1943; McGill Univ. Ph.D. 1948; m. Beatrice d. late Aaron Chaifetz 6 Aug. 1944; children: Diana Dell, Jon Gordon; PROF. OF PHYSICS, CARLETON UNIV. 1974-   ; Asst. Research Offr. Atomic Energy of Canada Ltd. 1948-55; Radiation Physicist Jewish Gen. Hosp. Montreal 1955-58; Assoc. Research Offr. Nat. Research Council of Can. Ottawa 1958-64; Prof. and Assoc. Dean Univ. of Sask. Regina 1964-74; Dean of Science present Univ. 1974-80; author numerous papers research in physics scient. journs.; mem. Candn. Assn. Physicists; Am. Physical Soc.; Assoc. mem. Sigma Xi; Jewish; recreations: hiking, cross-country skiing; Home: 951 Blythdale Rd., Ottawa, Ont. K2A 3N9; Office: Colonel By Dr., Ottawa, Ont. K1S 5B6.

WONG, Robert C., B.Sc., M.B.A.; stockbroker; b. Fort Erie, Ont. 27 April 1941; e. Univ. of Toronto B.Sc. 1963; York Univ. M.B.A. 1972; Harvard; Univ. of Waterloo; m. Alice Dong 28 Aug. 1971; CHRMN., GOULDING, ROSE & TURNER LTD.; Dir. Multilingual Television Ltd.; mem. Toronto Soc. Financial Analysts; recreation: public affairs; Club: Ontario; Home: 101 Glenrose Ave., Toronto, Ont. M4T 1K7; Office: 11 King St. W., Toronto, Ont. M5H 1A5.

WONNACOTT, Ronald Johnston, Ph.D.; university professor; b. London, Ont., 11 Sept. 1930; s. H. Gordon E. and Muriel Smalley (Johnston) W.; e. Univ. of W. Ont., B.A. 1955 (Pres., Univ. Students' Council, 1954-55); Harvard Univ. A.M. 1957, Ph.D. 1959; m. Frances Eloise, d. Jack C. Howlett, London, Ont., 11 Sept. 1954; children: Douglas, Rob, Cathy Anne; PROF. OF ECON., UNIV. OF WESTERN ONT., since 1965 and Chrmn. of Dept. 1969-72; Teaching Fellow, Econ. Dept. and Law School, Harvard Univ., 1956-58; joined present Univ. as Asst. Prof., 1958-61; Assoc. Prof. 1962-65; Visiting Assoc. Prof., Univ. of Minn., 1961-62; served with R.C.N.R; rank Lt.; mem. Senate, Univ. of W. Ont.; rec'd Woodrow Wilson, Dafoe and Ford Fellowships; also Harvard Univ. Scholarship; author "Canadian-American Dependence", 1962; "Canada's Trade Options" 1975; co=author; "Cost of Capital in Canada", 1962; "Free Trade Between the United States and Canada", 1967; "Introductory Statistics", 1969; "Econometrics", 1970; "Introductory Statistics for Business and Economics", 1972; "Economics" 1979; other writings incl. articles in learned jounrs; mem., Candn. Econ. Assn., Pres., 1981-82; Am. Econ. Assn.; United Church; recreations: golf, skiing, swimming; Clubs: London Hunt; Sunningdale (U.K.); University; Home: 171 Wychwood Park, London, Ont., N6G 1S1

WOOD, Arthur Edgar; publisher; b. Seaham, Co. Durham, Eng. 7 Aug. 1925; s. John and Emeline Julia (Stonehouse) W.; e. Seaham High Sch. 1939; m. Violet Elizabeth d. late John Young 30 June 1948; children: Maureen Barbara (Mrs. Michael Donahoe), Michael John; PUBLISHER, CAMBRIDGE DAILY REPORTER; former Pres. and Publisher, Ottawa Journal joined "The Montreal Star" as Dist. Mgr. Circulation Dept. 1947, Office Mgr.-Can. Wide (syndicate) 1949, Photo Ed. 1952, Asst. Mgr. Ed. 1967, Mang. Ed. 1968, Extve. Ed. 1976, Publisher 1979; joined Brit. Merchant Navy as Radio Offr. 1942, trans. to Brit. Royal Fleet Auxiliary-Convoy duty N. Atlantic 1942 — 45; Protestant; recreations: golf, swimming; Clubs: Galt Country; Office: Cambridge, Ont.

WOOD, James Douglas, B.Sc., Ph.D.; educator; b. Aberdeen, Scot. 25 Jan. 1930; s. James and Hilda (Johnston) W.; e. Robert Gordon's Coll. Aberdeen 1947; Univ. of Aberdeen B.Sc. 1951, Ph.D. 1954; m. Leila Margaret d. Blake Nephew, Finch, Ont. 29 Dec. 1956; children: Roderick James, Robert Gordon, John Stewart; PROF. AND HEAD OF BIOCHEM. UNIV. OF SASK. since 1968; Research Offr. Can. Dept. Agric. Ottawa 1954-57; Sr. Scient. Fisheries Research Bd. of Can., Vancouver 1957-61; Head, Physiol. Chem. Sec. Defence Research Med. Labs. Toronto 1961-68; Asst. Dean of Med. Univ. Sask. 1975-78; mem. Council, Med. Research Council of Can.; author over 80 research papers on biochem. and neurochem.; mem. Candn. Biochem. Soc. (Council 1975-78); Internat. Soc. Neurochem.; Am. Soc. Neurochem.; recreations: curling, golf; Home: 504 Quance Ave., Saskatoon, Sask. S7H 3B4; Office: Saskatoon, Sask. S7N 0W0.

WOOD, John Denison, B.A.Sc., M.S., Ph.D.; civil engineer; b. Calgary, Alta., 28 Sept. 1931; s. Ernest William and Ellen Gartshore (Pender) W.; e. Crescent Heights High Sch., Calgary, 1949; Univ. of B.C., B.A.Sc. (Civil Engn.) 1953; Stanford Univ., M.S. (Civil Engn.-Structures) 1954, Ph.D. (Civil Engn. & Engn. Mech.)1956; m. Christena Isabel, d. Charles Visser, Calgary, Alta., 24 July 1953; one d., Donna M.; PRESIDENT AND C.E.O, ATCO INDUSTRIES N.A. LTD., since 1977 Defence Research Bd., Research Asst. in Civil Engn. and Engn. Mech., Stanford Univ., 1953-56; Assoc. Mgr., Dynamics Dept., Engn. Mech. Lab. (sec. head of missile and aerospace vehicle dynamics), Space Tech. Labs., Inc., Redondo Beach, Calif., 1956-62; Dir. Research and Devel. Programs in connection with U.S. Aerospace & Aircraft Industs.; Pres. and Dir., Mechanics Research Inc., El Segundo, Calif., 1962-68; Sr. Vice Pres., Engn. & Research, Atco Ind. Ltd. 1966-68; Sr. Vice Pres., Eastern Region, 1968-75; Sr. Vice Pres., Planning 1975-77; mem. of bd. Nat. Trust Co. Ltd.; ATCO Ltd.; Co-author, "Ballistic Missile and Space Vehicle Systems," 1961; awarded Athlone Fellowship; mem., Engn. Inst. of Can.; Scientific Research Soc. of Amer.; Am. Soc. Mech. Engrs.; A.I.A.A.; Scient. Soc. Am.; Assn. Prof. Engrs. Alta.; Antarctican Soc.; Tau Beta Pi; Sigma Xi; Baptist; recreations: golf, badminton, skiing; Clubs: Glencoe; Earl Grey; Calgary Petroleum; Home: 1428 Beverley Place, S. W., Calgary, Alta. T2V 2C6 Office: 5115 Crowchild Trail S.W., Calgary, Alta. T3E 1T9

WOOD, Neil Cameron Walker; executive; b. Leeds Eng., 27 June 1930; s. Dr. James Walker and Minnie (Pennington) W.; e. Moorlands Prep Sch., Leeds, Eng., 1935-42; Bootham Sch., Yorks., Eng., 1942-47; Leeds Engn. Coll., 1947-49 and 1951-52; m. Sue, d. Raymond P. Corby; Children: Stuart Cameron Walker, Charles Cameron Walker, Jane Walker, Kate Walker; PRESIDENT, WALKER WOOD LTD., since 1959; Pres., Chmn., The White Cross Group of Companies; Pres., Walker Wood Realty; Past Chmn., Fidelity Trust, Fort Gary Trust; served with Brit. Army, REME attached to Edinburgh Univ., 1949-51; comnd. Queen's Own Cameron Highlanders, Candn. Army Reserve, 1959; Chmn. Financial Adv. Comte., St. John's Cathedral Boys Sch., Selkirk, Man.; Bd. of Trade;

Old York Scholars Assn.; Anglican; recreations: sailing, riding; Clubs: The National; R.V.Y.C.; Home: Walker Wood Farms, R.R. #2, Georgetown, Ont. L7G 4S5; Office: 260 Richmond St. W., Toronto, Ont. M5V 1W8

WOOD, Neil R., B.Com., M.B.A.; executive; b. Winnipeg, Man., 22 Aug. 1931; s. Reginald and Pearl (Beake) W.; e. Pub. and High Schs., Winnipeg, Man.; Univ. of Man., B.Com. 1952; Harvard Univ., M.B.A. 1955; m. Jean, d. John Hume, 10 Aug. 1957; children: Barbara, David, John, Brian; VICE-CHMN. AND DIR., THE CADILLAC FAIRVIEW CORP. LTD., since 1971; Asst. Mgr., Ont. Real Estate Invest. Office, Great-West Life Assurance Co., 1955-59; joined present firm as Gen. Mgr., Ont., 1959-61; Vice-Pres. and Dir. 1963, Extve. Vice-Pres. and Dir. 1968; Pres., Canadianwide Properties Ltd., 1962; mem., Bd. Trustees and Past Pres., Internat. Council Shopping Centres; Assoc. Dir., Can. Nat'l Exhibition Assoc.; Phi Delta Theta; United Church; recreations: golf, skiing, water sports, music; Clubs: Lambton Golf; National; Rosedale; Granite; Craigleith Ski; Beaumaris; Home: 17 Whitney Ave., Toronto, Ont., M4W 2A7; Office: 55 University Ave., Ste. 600, Toronto, Ont., M5J 2H7

WOOD, Peter Gillard, M.A.; banker; b. Wolverhampton, Eng., 22 Aug. 1932; s. late Frederick Daniel and Phyllis Marjorie (Hall) W.; e. Primary Sch., Linton, Eng. 1941; Eccleshall 1942; King Edward VI Sch., Stafford, Eng. 1950 (Sch. Cert. 1946, Higher Sch. Cert. 1949, 1950, Co. Maj. Scholar. 1950, Sch. Leaving Scholar, 1950); Queen's Coll., Oxford Univ., M.A. 1955; came to Canada 1955; m. Patricia Jane Laurie, d. late Eric Burns, Ottawa, 1 Aug. 1958; children: Christopher David Gillard, Elizabeth Ann, Sara Laurie, Judith Marjorie; PRES. & CEO, WELLS FARGO & CO. CANADA LTD., 1981-; Vice President-International Banking, Canadian Commercial and Industrial Bank 1976-81; with J. H. Crang & Co. as Invest. Analyst 1955; Party Chief, ABEM (Canada) Ltd.1956; Coordinator, Systems Dept., Arvida Works and later Sr. Operations Analyst, Montreal, Aluminum Co. of Canada Ltd. 1957; Mgr., Systems Devel., Canadian Ingersoll- Rand 1965; Functional Dir., P. S. Ross & Partners 1967; apptd. Asst. Dir., Inst. Candn. Bankers, March 1969; Assoc. Dir., Nov. 1969; Dir., Inst. of Candn. Bankers 1971 served with Royal Arty. 1950-52; Comnd. 1951, with Terr. Army 1952-55; Chrmn., Council on Prof. and Business Educ.; Inst. Assn. Extves.; mem., German-Cdn. Ch. of Comm.; Cdn. Ch. of Comm.; recreations: golf, tennis, bridge; Clubs: Canadian; University; Royal Canadian Military Inst.; St. James's; Royal Glenora; Edmonton; Univ. of Alta. Faculty; Home: 10335-132 St., Edmonton, Alta; Office: Suite 3106, 425 - 1st St. S.W., Calgary, Alta. T2P 3L8

WOOD, Peter Warburton, M.C., FCA; executive; b. Nottingham, Eng. 22 June 1919; s. late Warburton William and late Lillian Mary (Brettle) W.; m. Jane Stephenson, d. late P. M. Bull, 10 March 1951; children: David Warburton, Allison Mary, Peter Stephenson, Anthony William Percival; EXTVE. VICE PRES., HUDSON'S BAY CO.; Dir. Hudson's Bay Co.; Simpsons Ltd.; Zellers Ltd.; Eaton/Bay Financial Services Ltd.; Eaton/Bay Trust Co.; Eaton/Bay Life Assurance Co.; Eaton/Bay Fund Mgnt. Ltd.; Hudson's Bay & Annings Ltd. (Eng.); Markborough Properties Ltd.; Guardian Ins. Co. of Can.; Nat. Dir., Candn. Cancer Soc.; joined present firm 1947; Treasurer 1962; Vice Pres. Finance 1972; Extve. Vice Pres. 1977; served with Brit. Army 1939-46, awarded Military Cross; Anglican; Clubs: Toronto Manitoba; Home: R.R. 3, Shelburne, Ont., L0N 1S0; Office: 2 Bloor St. E., Toronto, Ont., M4W 3H7

WOOD, W. Donald, Ph.D.; b. Palermo, Ont., 5 April 1920; s. George Stanley and Ethel (Popplewell) W.; e. McMaster Univ., B.A. 1950; Queen's Univ., M.A. 1952; Princeton Univ., A.M., Ph.D. 1955; m. Constance, d. Wm. Leigh, Scotia Junction, Ont., 25 Aug. 1945; children:

Leslie Anne, Sandra Leigh; PROF. OF ECON. AND DIR., INDUST. RELATIONS CENTRE, QUEEN'S UNIV., since 1960; Dir., Indust. Relations Research Div., Imperial Oil Ltd., Toronto, 1955-60; served with R.C.A.F. during 2nd World War; United Church; recreations: sports; public affairs; Home: 54 Edgehill St., Kingston, Ont., K7L 2T5

WOODALL, L. Ronald; bank executive; b. Elmira, Ont. 1 March 1925; s. Leighton C. and Gladys V. (Moyer) W.; e. Willingdon Public Sch., West Hill High Sch., Montreal; m. June D. Panabaker, 25 June 1949; children: Susan J., Gail and Lori; SENIOR VICE-PRESIDENT, CONTINEN-TAL BANK; Sr. Vice Pres., IAC Ltd.; joined Household Finance Corp. of Canada 1947; joined Niagara Finance Co. Ltd., St. Catharines, Ont. 1961; Dir. Supervision, 1966; Asst. Gen. Mgr., 1967; Vice-Pres. 1971; el. a Dir., 1973, Extve. Vice Pres. 1975; Sr. Vice Pres. IAC Limited Oct. 1976; served with R.C.N.V.R. 1942-45; recreations: fishing, tennis; Clubs: National; Toronto Board of Trade; Home: 5 Stoneham Rd., Etobicoke, Ont. M9C 4V7; Office: 130 Adelaide St. W., Toronto, Ontario, M5H 3R2

WOODARD, John Miller; retired transport commissioner; b. Chapleau, Ontario, 8 February 1917; s. Edward and Jessie (Miller) W.; e. Chapleau (Ont.) High Sch., Sr. Matric.; m. Maryann Kay Reid, 25 Apl. 1969; joined CPR, Chapleau, 1937; Locomotive Fireman 1940; Locomotive Engr. 1943; Rd. Foreman of Engines 1949; Local Chrmn., Brotherhood Locomotive Engrs. 1953, Gen. Chrmn., E. Region, Montreal, 1954; Commr., Cdn. Transport Comm. 1959-78 (ret.) I.O.O.F.; mem., Candn. Rr. Hist. Soc.; Protestant; recreations: swimming, fishing, gardening; Club: Candn. Railway; Home: RR #5, Perth, Ont. K7H 3C7

WOODBURY, Leonard (E.), A.M., Ph.D., F.R.S.C.; b. Regina, Saskatchewan, 30 Aug. 1918; s. Ernest Francis and Florence Lashbrook (Crisp) W.; e. Daniel McIntyre Coll. Inst., Winnipeg, Man.; Univ. of Manitoba, B.A. 1940; Harvard Univ., A.M. 1942, Ph.D. 1944; m. late Marjorie Rotzler, d. Edgar Dawson Bell, Pittsburgh, Pa., 13 May 1944; children: Christopher Dawson, Alison Bell; PROF. OF CLASSICS, UNIV. COLL., Univ. of Toronto, since 1959; Head, Dept. of Classics there 1958-66; Lectr. in Classics, Univ. Coll., Univ. of Toronto, 1945-48, Asst. Prof. of Greek, 1948-55, Assoc. Prof. 1955-59; served in Meteorol. Service of Canada, 1944-45; Publications: various articles and reviews on classical subjects in Candn. and Am. journs.; mem., Classical Assn. Can. (Pres. 1974-76); mem., Edit. Bd. "Phoenix" (1947-74); Classical Assn. (Gt. Britain); Am. Philol. Assn.; Pres., (1965-66) Soc. for Ancient Greek Philosophy; Anglican; Home: 21 Otter Cres., Toronto, Ont., M5N 2W3

WOODCOCK, George, LL.D., D.Litt., F.R.G.S.; author; editor; b. Winnipeg, Manitoba, 8 May 1912; s. Samuel Arthur and Margaret Gertrude (Lewis) W.; e. Sir William Borlase's Sch.; Morley Coll., London, England; LL.D., Victoria, Winnipeg; D.Litt., Sir George Williams, Ottawa, U.B.C.; m. Ingeborg Hedwig Elisabeth, d. Otto Linzer, Offenbach, Germany, 10 February 1949; Editor of "Canadian Literature", 1959-77; Broadcaster (has contributed several hundred talks and scripts of plays and documentaries to CBC programs); Editor of "NOW", 1940-47; prof. writer since 1946; first in England to 1949 and afterwards in Can. with interludes of teaching (Univ. of Wash. 1954-55, Univ. of B.C. since 1956, resigning rank of Assoc. Prof. in 1963 to devote more time to writing); has travelled greatly in Europe, S.A., the South Pacific and Asia; Guggenheim Fellowship, 1951-52; Candn. Govt. Overseas Fellowship, 1957-58; Can. Council Travel Grants, 1961, 1963, 1965; Can. Council Killam Fellowship 1970-71; Molson Prize 1973; Can. Council Sen. Art Award, 1978; UBC Medal for Popular Biography, 1971 and 1975; Publications: "The White Island," 1940; "The Centre Cannot Hold," 1943; "William Godwin, A

Biography," 1946; "The Incomparable Aphra: A Life of Mrs. Aphra Behn," 1948; "The Writer and Politics," 1948; "Imagine the South," 1947; "The Paradox of Oscar Wilde," 1950; "A Hundred Years of Revolution: 1848 and After," 1948; "The Letters of Charles Lamb," 1950; "The Anarchist Prince," 1950 (later trans. into French); "Ravens and Prophets: Travels in Western Canada," 1952; "Pierre-Joseph Proudhon," 1956; "To the City of the Dead: Travels in Mexico" 1956; "Incas and Other Men: Travels in Peru", 1959; "Anarchism," 1962; "Faces of India," 1964; "Asia, Gods and Cities," 1966; "The Greeks in India," 1966; "A Choice of Critics," 1966; "The Crystal Spirit," 1966; (Gov. Gen. Award for Eng. Nonfiction); "Kerala", 1967; "Selected Poems", 1967; "The Doukhobors", 1968; "Canada and the Canadians", 1969; "The British in the Far East", 1969; "The Hudson's Bay Company", 1970; "Odysseus Ever Returning", 1970; "Gandhi", 1971; "Dawn and the Darkest Hour: A Study of Aldous Huxley", 1972 "Herbert Read, The Stream & the Source" 1972; "The Rejection of Politics" 1972; "Who Killed the British Empire?" 1974; "Amor de Cosmos" 1974; "Gabriel Dumont", 1975; "Notes on Visitations", 1975; "South Sea Journey", 1976; "Peoples of the Coast", 1977; "Thomas Merton, Monk and Poet", 1978; "The Kestrel and Other Poems", 1978; "Faces from History", 1978; "The Canadians", 1979; "The World of Canadian Writing", 1980; "The George Woodcock Reader", 1980; "The Mountain Road", 1981; "Confederation Betrayed", 1981; "Taking it to the Letter", 1981; Home: 6429 McCleery St., Vancouver, B.C., V6N 1G5

WOODFINE, William Joseph, M.A., Ph.D.; university professor; b. Montreal, Que., 21 May 1930; s. Peter Gerard and Mona (McManus) W.; e. St. Francis Xavier Univ., B.A. 1951; McGill Univ., M.A. 1953; Mass. Inst. of Tech., Ph.D. 1959; m. Helen Mary, d. John Macken, Montreal, Que., 15 Aug. 1953; children: Mary, Peter, Jennifer, Paul, Julie, John, Susan; PROF. OF ECON., ST. FRANCIS XA-VIER UNIV. and Chrmn., Econ. Dept. there; Sr. Fellow, Can. Council, London Sch. of Econ., U.K. 1967-68; mem. Bd. of Broadcast Govs. 1963-67; mem. Task Force, Structure of Candn. Industry, 1967; Chrmn. (1972) N.S. Task Force on Cost of Prescription Drugs; mem., N.S. Health Council; Candn. Econ. Assn.; Am. Econ. Assn.; R. Catholic; Home: Harbour Rd., Antigonish Landing, Antigonish, N.S., B2G 2L5

WOODRUFF, Laurence D., B.A.; petroleum executive; b. Detroit, Mich. 20 Feb. 1924; s. Norris C. and Mabel M. (Fleming) W.; e. Univ. of Toronto B.A.; m. Elizabeth M. Wilcox; PRES. AND DIR., ULTRAMAR CANADA INC.; Dir., Ultramar Co. Ltd., London, Eng.; Home: 4 Hedgewood Rd., Willowdale, Ont. M2L 1L5; Office: 1 Valleybrook Dr., Don Mills, Ont. M3B 2S8.

WOODS, David Mason, B.A.; executive; b. Toronto, Ont., 29 July 1912; s. William B. and Bertha (Mason) W.; e. Upper Canada Coll., Ashbury Coll.; Univ. of Toronto, B.A. 1934; President, Toronto Board of Trade, 1955 = 56; Canadian Retail Fed. 1961-62; Chrmn., Bd. of Govs., Upper Can. Coll. 1967-72; Trent Univ. 1975-80; Dir., Candn. Scholarship Trust; served in 2nd World War in Candn. Armoured Corps and Queen's Own Rifles of Canada with rank of Capt.; Vice Chrmn., Ont. Heart Foundation; mem. R & D comte Ont. Council of Health; United Church; Home: 100 Roxborough St. E., Toronto, Ont. M4W 1W1

WOODS, George W., A.F.C., B.Com., C.A., F.C.A.; executive; b. Montreal, Que. 8 Dec. 1921; s. Norman Parke and Dorothy (Webster) W.; e. McGill Univ., B.Com. 1947; m. Elizabeth Brown 1973; VICE-CHRMN. & C.O.O. DIR., TRANSCANADA PIPELINES; Dir. Great Lakes Gas Transmission Co.; ABN Canada Ltd.; Canada Safety Council; Ontario Chamber of Commerce; Gov., Wilfred Laurier Univ.; served with RCAF 1940-45; Dir., Toronto Symphony; National Club; United Church;

Clubs: National; Granite; Rosedale; Home: 288 Glencairn Ave., Toronto, Ont., M5N 1T9; Office: (P.O. Box 54) Commerce Court W., Toronto, Ont., M5L 1C2

WOODS, Harry D., O.C., M.A., LL.D., F.R.S.C., university professor; b. Welsford, N.B., 16 Jan. 1907; s. Henry Wellington and Hannah Zelda (Goreham) W.; e. Univ. of New Brunswick, B.A. (Hons. Econ. and Philos.), 1930, LL.D. 1964; McGill Univ., M.A. (Econ.), 1931; Univ. of Toronto and London School of Econ., grad. studies; m. Patricia, d. Frederick Parker Burden, 10 May 1934; children: Frederick Douglas, Steven Francis, Mrs. W. A. Parker, Hanford Cedric, Mrs. A. Rider; PROF. OF ECON., McGILL UNIV.; Chrmn., Task Force on Labour Relations, Govt. of Can.; Vice-Pres. and mem. Bd. Dirs., Nat. Acad. of Arbitrators; lectured as Asst., Dept. of Econ., Univ. of Toronto, 1935-37; Asst. and Assoc. Prof., Econ., Un. Coll.; Registrar and Secy., Royal Comn. on Co-ops., 1945; Dir., Sch. of Comm., McGill Univ., 1946-53; estbd. and apptd. Dir., Industrial Relations Centre, McGill Univ., 1948; promoted Prof., 1951, Dean, Faculty of Arts & Sciences 1964-69; apptd. by I.L.O. to serve as expert on Indust. Relations in Manilla, Philippines, 1956; acted for Govt. of Jamaica Labour Dept., 1960; Ford Foundation Fellowship for study of Candn. Labour relations, policy and practice, 1960-61; apptd. Chrmn., Social Sciences Group, McGill Univ., 1962; Consultant, Comte. on Manitoba's Econ. Future, 1962; Chrmn., Joint Lab.-Mang. Comte., Prov. of Man., 1963; served in Royal Candn. Corps of Signals, 1941-42; Directorate of Personnel Selection, 1942-45; Publications: Co-author, "Labour Policy and Labour Economics in Canada," 1962; Ed., "Patterns of Industrial Dispute Settlement"; articles in Candn. and foreign journs. on labour relations; helped estab. Montreal Chapter, Indust. Relations Research Assn., el. 1st Pres., 1961; former mem., Extve. Bd., Indust. Relations Research Assn.; Pres. Nat. Acad. Arbitrators, 1976; mem. Candn. Pol. Science Assn.; Am. Econ. Assn.; Candn. Hist. Assn.; Candn. Indust. Relations Research Assn. (mem., founding group and 1st Pres.); Prof. Emeritus, McGill Univ. since 1968; Consultant on Ind. Relations in Southern N.B. since 1976; visiting lecturer Univ. of N.B. since 1978; Appointed Officer, Order of Canada, 1981; Protestant; Home: 83 Shore St., Fredericton, N.B. E3B 1R3

WOODS, John Hayden, M.A., Ph.D.; University President; b. Barrie, Ont. 16 March 1937; s. late John Frederick and Gertrude Mary (Hayden) W.; e. St. Mary's Sch., St. Joseph's High Sch. and Barrie (Ont.) & Dist. Coll. Inst.; Univ. of Toronto B.A. 1958, M.A. 1959; Univ. of Mich. Ph.D. 1965; m. Carol Gwendolyn d. late Walter Arnold, Toronto, Ont. 13 July 1957; children: Catherine Lynn, Kelly Ann, Michael John; PRES., VICE-CHANCELLOR & PROFESSOR OF PHILOSOPHY, UNIV. OF LETH-BRIDGE, 1979- ; Dean, Faculty of Humanities, Univ. of Calgary and Prof. of Philos. 1976-79; Teaching Asst. Univ. of Toronto 1958-59, Lectr. 1962-64, Asst. Prof. 1964-66 Assoc. Prof. 1966-71 also Assoc. Prof. Centre for Linguistic Studies 1966-71 (Extve. Comte. 1966-67); Toronto and Dist. Rep. Nat. Film Bd. Can. 1958-59; Teaching Fellow, Univ. of Mich. 1959-61, Instr. 1961-62, Assoc. Prof. Summer Inst. of Linguistic Soc. Am. 1967; Visiting Prof. Stanford Univ. summer 1971; Prof. Univ. of Victoria 1971-76, Chrmn. Dept. Philos. 1974-75, Assoc. Dean Faculty of Arts & Science 1975-76; rec'd Horace H. Rackham Univ. Fellowship 1961; Can. Council Research Grants 1968-69, 1971; Humanities Research Council Grants 1974, 1976; author; "Identity and Modality" 1975; "Engineered Death: Abortion, Suicide, Euthanasia, Senecide" 1978 Co-author "Argument, The Logic of the Fallacies" 1981; Co-ed. "Literature and Formal Semantics" 1979; "Humanities in the Present Day" 1979; Ed. "Dialogue: The Canadian Philosophical Review" 1974-81; mem. Ed. Bd. Philos. Research Archives; Cdn. Semiotic Research; Co-ed. "Necessary Truth"1969; author "Proof and Truth" 1974; "The Logic of Fiction: A Philosophical

Sounding of Deviant Logics" 1974; over 70 articles and over 80 philos. addresses; Chmn. of Bd. and C.E.O., The Berczy Group, 1980- ; mem. Candn. Philos. Assn.; Am. Philos. Assn. (Extve. Comte Pacific Div. 1971-74, Chrmn. of same 1972-73); Soc. for Exact Philosophy; Humanities Research Council Can.; Candn. Federation for the Humanities (Extve. Comte. since 1978, Vice-Pres., 1980-81, Pres., 1981-82); Universities Coordinating Council (Alta.), Exec. Comte., Humanities Assn. Can.; Candn. Assn. Univ. Teachers; Adv. Cmte., Intl. Dev. Office, since 1979; Renaissance Soc. of Amer.; Phi Beta Kappa; recreations: alpine hiking; cross-country skiing; Clubs; Chinook; University (Toronto); Home: 1410 20 Ave. S., Lethbridge, Alta. T1K 1E9

WOODS, Hon. Mervyn John, M.B.E., C.D., B.A., LL.M., J.S.D.; judge; b. Regina, Sask. 8 June 1909; s. James Andrew and Florence Lauretta (Dodd) W.; e. Regina and Kincaid, Sask. pub. schs.; Kincaid High Sch. and Moose Jaw Coll.; Moose Jaw Teachers' Coll. 1929; Univ. of Sask. B.A. 1937; N.Y. Univ. LL.M. 1959, J.S.D. 1962; m. Winnifred Agnes Elaine d. Robert Dunne Scott 1 Dec. 1939; children: Mervyn Scott, Lauretta Brown, William Forde, Maureen Shelagh; JUDGE, COURT OF APPEAL, SASK. since 1961; taught pub. sch. 1929 — 34; called to Bar of Sask. 1939; Lectr. in Law Univ. of Sask. 1946 — 56, Prof. of Law 1956 — 61; Pres., P. Cons. Party Sask. 6 yrs.; Nat. Pres. Royal Candn. Legion 1960 — 62; Past Pres. St. John Ambulance Assn. Sask.; Past Commr. St. John Ambulance Bgde. Sask.; served with COTC Sask. 1934 — 37, RCNVR 1937 — 45 (Active Service 1939 — 45), RCNR 1956 — 61; commanded HMCS Longueil 1944 — 45; rank Lt. Commdr.; presently Hon. Col. Regina Rifle Regt.; named Kt. Order St. John Jerusalem; author "Federal Taxation of Income of Cooperative Trading Corporations in the United States and Canada" 1962; numerous articles legal journs.; mem. Sask. Law Soc.; Candn. Bar Assn.; Inst. Judicial Adm.; Freemason (P.G.M. Sask.); United Church; Clubs: United Services; Saskatoon; Kiwanis (former Lt. Gov.); Home: 35 Bryant St., Regina, Sask. S4S 4S7; Office: Court House, 2425 Victoria Ave., Regina, Sask. S4P 3V7.

WOODSIDE, Donald G., B.Sc., D.D.S., M.Sc., F.R.C.D. (C); orthodontist; b. Pittsburgh, Penna; 28 April 1927; s. Marshall Leslie and Eleanor (Murchison) W.; e. Dalhousie Univ., B.Sc. 1948, D.D.S. 1952; Univ. of Toronto, M.Sc. (Dent.) 1956; m. Sheila Margaret, d. Dr. Howard MacDonald, 8 Aug. 1953; three s. Donald Blake, Thane Paul, Scott MacDonald; PROF. AND HEAD, ORTHO-DONTIC DEPT., UNIV. TORONTO since 1963; engaged also in private practice; Hon. Consultant, Ont. Crippled Children's Hosp.; Dept. of Public Health, Gov't. of N.S., 1952-53; Assoc. in Orthodontics, Faculty of Dentistry, Univ. of Toronto, 1956-58, Assoc. Prof., 1958-59, Acting Head of Dept., 1958-59, and 1962; Assoc. Dean, Faculty of Dent. 1970-73; co-author of a manual of Undergrad. Ortho Technicians; mem. Great Lakes Soc. Orths.; Am. Assn. Orths.; Charles Tweed Foundation for Orth. Research; Omicron Kappa Upsilon; recreations: sailing, skiing; Clubs: R.C.Y.C.; Devil's Glen Country; Home: 6 May Tree Road, York Mills Valley, Toronto, Ont., M2P 1V8; Office: 185 St. Clair Ave., West, Toronto, Ont., M4V 1P7

WOODSWORTH, Anne, B.F.A., M.L.S.; librarian; b. Fredericia, Denmark 10 Feb. 1941; d. Thorvald Ernst and Roma Yrsa Lykke Tideman (Jensen) Lindner; came to Can. 1951; e. Univ. of Man. B.F.A. 1962; Univ. of Toronto B.L.S. 1964, M.L.S. 1969; one d. Yrsa Anne; DIR. OF LI-BRARIES, YORK UNIV. 1978- ; Pres., Anni Lindner Ltd. (Inc.); Dir., Population Research Foundation Toronto; Librarian, Faculty of Educ. Univ. of Man. 1964-65; Reference Librarian, Winnipeg Pub. Lib. 1965-67; Science & Med. Reference Librarian, Univ. of Toronto 1967-68, Adm. Asst. and Head of Reference Dept. 1970-74; Med. Librarian, Toronto Western Hosp. 1969-70; Personnel Dir., Toronto Pub. Lib. 1975-78; rec'd Ont. Arts Council

Grant 1974; Can. Council Grant 1974; author "The 'Alternative Press' in Canada" 1973; ed., "Non-Print Media Problems" 1975; various articles and reports; mem. Candn. Lib. Assn. (Councillor 1977-80); Candn. Assn. Research Libs. (Secy. 1979-80 Pres. 1980-81); Candn. Assn. Special Libs. and Information Services (Treas. 1974-75, Chrmn. 1975-76); Home: 1532 Point-O-Woods Rd., Mississauga, Ont. L5G 2X7; Office: 4700 Keele St., Downsview, Ont. M3J 2R2.

WOODWARD, Charles Namby Wynn; department store executive; b. Vancouver, B.C.; e. Univ. of British Columbia; m., two d., two s.; CHRMN. & CHIEF EXECUTIVE OFFICER, WOODWARD STORES LIMITED; President, Douglas Lake Cattle Co. Limited; Dir., Royal Bank of Canada; Westcoast Transmission Co. Limited; British Columbia Molybdenum Ltd.; B.C. Resources Inv. Corp.; quit Univ. as a sophomore and joined Candn. Army serving overseas with 12th Manitoba Dragoons; third generation of his family to attain the presidency of Woodward's; began after the war as Manager of the Park Royal shopping centre in West Vancouver in 1950; then moving on to New Westminster, B.C. to open another centre; succeeded to the post of Pres. on the death of his father; recreations: hunting, fishing; Office: 101 W. Hastings St., Vancouver, B.C., V6B 1H4

WOOLL, Gerald Ray (Gerry); aviation executive; b. Peterborough, Ont., 15 Sept. 1913; s. Charles Godfrey and Effie Esther (Staples) W.; e. Peterborough (Ont.) Coll. Inst. & Vocational Sch., 1933; Univ. of Toronto and Brock Univ. Extension courses; m. Audrey, d. Samuel Whittaker, Peterborough, Ont., 29 May 1943; three d., Lorraine, Mary, Susan; VICE PRES. AND MANG. DIR GENAIRE LTD.; Pres., Amaser Ltd.; with Photographic Survey Corp., 1947-48; Kenting Aviation Ltd., 1948-49; Mang. Dir., Field Aviation Co., 1949-51; Leader, Aircraft Industries Trade Mission to Aust., New Zealand and Japan, 1964; served with RAF 1939-46 and with RCAF 1946-47; rank Sqdn. Leader; flew 85 operational missions then became Test Pilot for Ministry of Aircraft Production; Councillor, Town of Bowmanville, 1950, Town of Niagara, 1953, and 1954; served on Pub. Sch. Bd. 1955-60 (Chrmn. 2 yrs.); Mayor, Town of Niagara, Niagara-on-the-Lake, 1961-64, mem. Planning Bd. for 9 yrs.; Dir., Court House Theatre (Shaw Festival); Pres., Niagara Foundation; chosen "Citizen of the Year" 1965 by Niagara Town and Township Chamber Comm.; mem. Bd. of Dirs., Rotary Internat. Treas. Rotary International an Rotary Found.; Council of Regents, Colls. of Applied Arts & Tech.; Elder, St. Andrew's Presb. Ch.; Assoc. Fellow Royal Aero. Soc.; Assoc. Fellow, Candn. Aero. & Space Inst.; Chrmn., Air Industs. Assn. Can.; Trustee, Brock Univ.; Dir., Town of Niagara Chamber Comm.; Presbyterian; recreations: community affairs, fishing; Clubs: RAF (London, Eng.); Naval & Military (London, Eng.); Canadian; Niagara Peninsula Armed Forces Inst.; Rotary (Past Pres. St. Catharines; Dist. 709 Gov.); Home: 69 Prideaux St., Niagara-on-the-Lake, Ont., L0S 1J0; Office: (Box 84), St. Catharines, Ont., L2R 6R4

WOOLLEY, Douglas Campbell, Q.C., B.A.; b. Toronto, Ont. 28 Jan. 1929; s. Harold E. and Dorothy F. P. (Nichol) W.; e. Runnymede Public Sch. and Humberside Coll. Inst., Toronto, Ont.; Queen's Univ., B.A.; Osgoode Hall Law Sch.; children: Campbell, Mardi, Cori; PARTNER, WOOLLEY DALE & DINGWALL since 1972; Dir. Grafton Group Limited; Leonard Pipeline Contractors Ltd.; Griffin Products Inc.; Koss Limited; Reynolds and Reynolds (Canada) Limited; Russill H. Morin Prods. Ltd.; Network Data Systems Ltd.; Cantherm Heating Ltd.; read law with Daly Thistle Judson & Harvey 1953-54; Assoc. Wm. A. Cobban 1955; Partner, Cobban and Woolley 1957, Cobban Woolley and Dale 1961, Woolley Dale and Stevens 1971; mem. York Co. Law Assn.; Candn. Bar Assn.; Phi Delta Phi; Anglican; recreations: skiing, hunting, tennis; Club: National; Home: Glengate Farm, R.R.3

Milton, Ont., L9T 2X7; Office: Box 65, Toronto-Dominion Centre, Toronto, Ont., M5K 1E7

WOOLLIAMS, Eldon M., Q.C., M.P., B.A., LL.B.; teacher and lawyer; b. Rosetown, Sask., 12 April 1916; s. Frank and Gertrude (Mattison) W.; e. Univ. of Sask., B.A. 1943, LL.B. 1943; m. Erva Leola, d. Aaron Jones, 1 Sept. 1943; children: Elda Lynn, Brian Mattison; read law with Frank Bastedo, Q.C.; called to Bar of Sask. 1944, of Alta. 1952; cr. Q.C. 1964; former partner in law firm of Van Blaricom, Hamilton & Woolliams, Tisdale, Sask.; the present Firm of Woolliams, Korman, Moore & Wittman created in Calgary with subsequent additions; 1st el. to H. of C. g.e. 1958; el. for Constit. Calgary N. 1962, 63, 65, 68, 72, 74; Delegate to Inter-Parliamentary Group U.S. and Canada 1959; Canadian Delegate and Lecturer, U.N. Seminar on Human & Civil Rights, Mexico City 1961; mem. Candn. Del., Inter-Parlty. Union World Conf., Denmark 1964, Lima, Peru 1968; Chrmn. Cons. Caucus on Secy. of State 1963-65; Justice Critic for the Official Opposition since 1968; Justice del. for Can., Conf. on Peace through Law, Yugoslavia 1971, and Washington, D.C. 1975; del. Commonwealth Seminar Conf. London, Eng. 1972; NATO Conf. London, Eng. & Lahr, Germany 1974; Chrmn. P. Cons. caucus comtes. on Secy. State, Justice & Legal Affairs, Manpower & Immigration, and Housing & Urban Affairs; Chmn., Parl. Standing Cmte. on Justice and Legal Affairs, 1978-79; Vice-Pres., Candn. Jr. Chamber Comm. 1948-50; Freemason (32 Shrine); P. Conservative (Past Sask. Vice Pres. and mem. Nat. Extve.); Anglican; recreations: golf, fishing; Clubs: Calgary Petroleum; Calgary Golf and Country Club (Alta.); Albany (Toronto); Home: 114 Scarboro Ave., S.W., Calgary Alta., T3C 2H1; Office: 502 Canada Permanent Bldg., 315-8th Ave. S.W., Calgary, Alta., T2P 1C8

WOOLSEY, Leonard R., B.Sc.; banker; b. Penzance, Sask. 30 Dec. 1922; e. Univ. of Sask. B.Sc. (Mech. Engn.) 19..; m. Alice Dickson 27 June 1947; children: Diane, Douglas, Dixie, Debbie; GEN. MGR. MARKETING, THE BANK OF NOVA SCOTIA; joined Gulf Canada Ltd. 1949-71, Salesman, Dist. Mgr., Operations Mgr., Gen. Mgr. Marketing, Vice Pres. Marketing; joined present Bank 1971; mem. Bd. Trade Metrop. Toronto; N. York YMCA; Clubs: Donalda; Ontario; Canadian Empire; Home: 78 Quail Valley Lane, Thornhill, Ont. L3T 4R3; Office: 44 King St. W., Toronto, Ont. M5H 1H1.

WOROBETZ, Hon. Stephen, M.C., B.Sc., M.D., F.R.C.S. (C); surgeon; b. Krydor, Sask., 26 Dec. 1914; s. Justin and Mary (Boryski) W.; e. Pub. and High Schs., Krydor and Saskatoon, Sask.; Univ. of Sask., B.Sc. 1935; Univ. of Man., M.D. 1940; post grad. work Winnipeg and Philadelphia; m. Michelene, d. late Henry Kindrachuk, 1 May 1949; Gen. Practitioner, Lucky Lake, Sask., 1941-42 and Saskatoon, Sask., 1946-52; Gen. Surg. Saskatoon, 1954-70; Pres., Med. Staff. St. Paul's Hosp., Saskatoon, 1954-55; mem. Clin. Teacher, Univ. of Sask. Med. Sch., 1955-70; Lt.-Gov. of Sask., 1970-76; served with R.C.A.M.C. in Can., Eng., Italy and Holland, 1942-46; rec'd M.C. while Med. Offr. with P.P.C.L.I. in Italy; Trustee, Separate Sch. Saskatoon, 1950-52; Past Chrmn. St. Joseph's Nursing Home, Saskatoon; Past Pres., P.P.C.L.I. Assn. of Saskatchewan; Candn. Club of Sask. 1977-78; Sask. Council for Cdn. Unity; Bd. of Gov., Cdn. Corps of Commissionaires; sen. life mem., Cdn. Med. Assn.; Royal Coll. Phys. and Surgs. Can.; mem. Ukrainian Catholic Brotherhood; K.St.J. (1971); mem. Roy. Candn. Legion; K. of C.; Liberal; Ukrainian Catholic; recreations: fishing, photography, reading; Home: 405 Lake Cres., Saskatoon, Sask., S7H 3A3

WORT, Dennis James, M.Sc., Ph.D.; university professor; b. England, 19 July 1906; s. Dennis James and Florence Ann (Dimmer) W.; e. Prov. (Sask.) Normal Sch., 1924-25; Univ. of Sask., B.Sc. (with Great Distinction) 1932, M.Sc. 1934; Univ. of Chicago, Ph.D. 1940; m. Helen

Nora, d. D. B. Kinnon, Saskatoon, Sask., 23 June 1936; children: Dennis James, Margaret Helen; PROF. EMERITUS OF PLANT PHYSIOLOGY, UNIV. OF BRIT. COLUMBIA, since 1975; Prof. of Plant Physiology, 1947-72; Research Assoc. 1972; mem. of Ed. Board, "Northwest Science", 1950-73; taught high sch. in Sask. for 20 yrs.; Coulter Research Fellow in Botany, Univ. of Chicago, 1939 and 1940; Nuffield Foundation Award, 1959; Lectr. in Botany and Biol., Univ. of Sask., 1943-45; Assoc. Professor in Biology and Botany, University of British Columbia, 1945; Trustee, Northwest Scient. Association 1969-72, Pres. 1973-74, Hon. Life Mem. 1974; author of "Biology Check Charts", 1940; co-author "Diversity in Living Things", 1966; "Physiology and Biochemistry of Herbicides", 1964 "Handbuch der Pflanzenphysiologie", 1961; "Tree Growth" 1962; many important papers, mainly on crop plants, chemical control of plant growth and productivity, and cognate subjects; Fellow, Am. Assn. Advanc. Science; mem., Canadian Society Plant Physiol.; American Society Sugar Beet Technol.; American Society Plant Physiol. (Chairman Western Section 1955); Bot. Soc. of America; B.C. Acad. of Sciences (Pres. 1953); Am. Soc. Agron.; Sigma Xi; Protestant; recreation: choral director; Home: 1540 Wesbrook Crescent, Vancouver, B.C., V6T 1V8

WORTHEN, Charles R., B.A.; executive; b. Beebe, Que., 26 Dec. 1921; s. Homer Ralph and Grace Inez (House) W.; e. Bishops Univ., B.A. 1949; Queen's Univ., Indust. Relations 1950; m. Mary Emily, d. Robert Guy Ward, 19 July 1943; children: Nancy, Ann; PRESIDENT, CANADIAN BANK NOTE CO., LTD., since 1965; in Textile business, Brockville, Ont., 1950-55; joined present Co. 1955; apptd. Asst. to Pres. 1957, Vice Pres. 1964; served with Candn. Inf. Corps in Can., Eng. and N.W. Europe, 1942-46; discharged with rank of Capt.; Anglican; recreations: golf, skiing; Clubs: Royal Ottawa Golf; Home: Apt 2408, 400 Stewart St., Ottawa, Ont., K1N 6L2; Office: 145 Richmond Rd., Ottawa, Ont., K1G 3H8

WORTON, David A., M.A.; Canadian civil servant; b. Leeds, England 1924; e. Univ. of Leeds B.A. 1950; Univ. of Toronto M.A. 1961; m. Joyce Froggatt 1952; children: Elise, Margaret, Patricia, Jane, Katherine, Sarah; ASST. CHIEF STATISTICIAN CAN., LABOUR MARKET ANALYSIS, STATISTICS CANADA; Lectr. and Dept. Head, Ryerson Polytech. Inst. Toronto 1953-62; served with RAF 1942-47; mem. Candn. Econ. Assn.; Am. Econ. Assn.; Royal Econ. Soc.; Internat. Assn. Research Income & Wealth; Home: 347 Island Park Dr., Ottawa, Ont. K1Y 0A6; Office: R. H. Coats Bldg., Tunney's Pasture, Ottawa, Ont. K1A 0T6.

WOTHERSPOON, Brig. Gordon Dorward de Salaberry, D.S.O., E.D., Q.C.; b. Port Hope, Ont., 12 Jan. 1909; s. Hugh C. and Mildred (Cumberland) W.; e. Trinity Coll. Sch., Port Hope, Ont.; Royal Mil. Coll., Kingston, Ont.; Osgoode Hall, Toronto, Ont.; m. Margaret Trumbull Warren, 21 Sept. 1935; three s. and one d.; Chrmn. Eaton Commonwealth Fund Ltd.; Eaton Leverage Fund Limited; Eaton Financial Serivces Limited; Eaton Life Assurance Company; Eaton Viking Fund Limited; Dir., Eaton's of Canada Limited; The Toronto-Dominion Bank; Interprovincial Pipe Line Co.; Aquitaine Company of Canada Ltd.; called to Bar of Ont., June 1933; cr. K.C., Dec. 1952; served with N.P.A.M. 16 years, Gov. Gen Horse Guards (R) and 19th Armoured Bgde. (R); served in 2nd World War with Gov. General's Horse Guards, S. Alberta Regt. and 4th Armoured Bgde. in Can., Eng. and N.W. Europe, 1941-46; Mentioned in Despatches; Bronze Lion (The Netherlands); Kappa Alpha; Anglican; recreations: golf, hunting, fishing; Clubs: The Toronto; Toronto Golf; University; Echo Beach Fishing; Home: 5 Whitney Ave., Toronto, Ont., M4W 2A7; Office: 190 Yonge St., Toronto, Ont., M5B 1N6

WOUK, Arthur, B.S., M.A., Ph.D.; educator; b. New York City, N.Y. 25 March 1924; s. Louis and Sarah (Feldman) W.; e. City Coll. New York B.S. 1943; Johns Hopkins Univ. M.A. 1947, Ph.D. (Math.) 1951; m. Vita Ruth d. Ralph P. Boruchoff, Miami, Fla. 5 Nov. 1944; two d. Nina Grace, Fay Ellen; PROF. OF COMPUTING SCIENCE, UNIV. OF ALTA. 1972- , Chrmn. of Computing Science 1972-77; Instr. in Math. Queens Coll. Flushing, N.Y. 1950-52; Sr. Math., Project Cyclone, Reeves Instrument Corp. New York 1952-54; Sr. Math., Missile Systems Lab., Sylvania Electronic Systems, Waltham, Mass, also Sec. Head Computing Sec. 1954-58, Dept. Mgr. 1958-61 and Sr. Engn. Specialist 1961-62, Math. & Operations Research, Applied Research Lab., 1958-62; Lectr. in Math. Northeastern Univ. Boston 1959-61, Boston Univ. 1960-62; Visiting Prof. Math. Research Center Univ. of Wisc. 1962-63; Visiting Prof. of Math., Northwestern Univ. summers 1961-62, Assoc. Prof. of Math. and Engn. Science 1963-69, Prof. 1969-70, Prof. of Math., Engn. Science and Computer Science 1970-72, Chrmn. Comte. on Applied Math. 1967-72; Visiting Prof. of Computer Science Pa. State Univ. 1980-81; Consultant, Applied Research Lab. Electronic Systems Div. Sylvania 1962-65; Applied Math. Div. Argonne Nat. Labs. 1963-70; served with U.S. Army 1943-46; author "A Course of Applied Functional Analysis" 1979; various papers applied math. and computational methods; assoc. ed. various publs.; mem. Am. Math. Soc.; Soc. Indust. & Applied Math.; Op. Res. Soc. Am.; Assn. Computing Machinery; Candn. Math. Soc.; Jewish; Home: 8711 - 138 St., Edmonton, Alta. T5R 0E2; Office: Edmonton, Alta. T6G 2H1.

WRIGHT, Arthur Robert, M.A.; diplomat; b. Kamloops, B.C. 7 Sept. 1939; s. Late Arthur Edwin and Louise Constance (Nuyens) W.; e. Notre Dame Coll. Nelson, B.C. 1958; St. Francis Xavier Univ. B.A. 1960; Carleton Univ. Dipl. in Pub. Adm., M.A. 1962; Univ. of Pittsburgh Grad. Sch. Pub. & Internat. Affairs 1970-71; m. Sylvia Anne d. Dr. Donald Cameron Bews, Senneville, Que. 26 Dec. 1972; HIGH COMMR. TO BANGLADESH and Ambassador to Burma 1979- ; Finance Offr., Dept. of Finance Ottawa 1960-62; Foreign Service Offr., Dept. of External Affairs Ottawa 1962, Third Secy. Lagos 1964, Second Secy. Kuala Lumpur 1966, Consul Bangkok 1967, U.N. Social & Econ. Affairs Officer, Ottawa 1968-69, Aid & Devel. Officer, Ottawa 1971, Counsellor Dar es Salaam 1972, Counsellor (Devel.) New Delhi 1975, Depy. Dir. Comm. & Gen. Econ. Policy Ottawa 1977-79; author various publs.; mem. Soc. Internat. Devel. Rome; Overseas Devel. Council Washington; Prof. Assn. Foreign Service Offrs.; recreations: sports, photography, conservation, anthropology; Home: 18 Gulshan Ave., Dacca, Bangladesh; Office: (P.O. Box 569) Dacca, Bangladesh.

WRIGHT, Don (Donald John Alexander); musician; composer; arranger; educator; b. Strathroy, Ont. 6 Sept. 1908; s. Ernest Joel and Mary Jean (Clark) W.; e. Strathroy Pub. and High Schs.; Univ. of W. Ont. Honour Classics '33 (G. Howard Ferguson Trophy); Ont. Coll. of Educ. Toronto 1933-34; m. Lillian Mary Laura d. late Rt. Hon. Arthur Meighen 29 June 1935; children: Timothy A. J., Prisicila J. M. (Mrs. Geoff Scott), Patrick O. G.; FOUNDER, DON WRIGHT PRODUCTIONS 1950- ; Dir. Oracabessa Ltd.; Lilmaxted Ltd.; Telimax Ltd.; Teacher of Classics and Hist. Sir Adam Beck Coll. Inst. London 1934; Dir. of Music for London 1940; Mgr. Radio Stn. CFPL 1946, Don Wright Chorus estbd. (10 yrs. on the air); Don Wright Singers estbd. 1957, many TV and radio appearances incl. Chrysler Festivals; composed, arranged and conducted music various films incl. "Trail of '98", "Opening of Seaway", "A Day to Remember", many CBC documentaries; guest speaker many clinics and workshops youthful voices; formed Don Wright Charitable Foundation (1966) Scholarships for Music Students Univ. of W. Ont. and other Candn. univs.; composed "Proudly We Praise" 1966, performed Parlt. Hill 1st July 1967; rec'd Centennial Medal; compiled thesaurus excerpts life's work in music for educ. purposes covering vocal devel. and instrumental arranging 1978-79; donated complete sets "Fifty Years of Music with Don Wright" to Music Dept. Candn. univs. and teachers' colls. 1980; author "Collegiate Choir Series" 1938-39; "Youthful Voices Series" 1940, revised 1964; "Pre-teen Song Settings" 1960; "Don Wright Choral Series"; "Lets Read Music"; served with C.O.T.C. rank Capt., RCAF rank Flying Offr. World War II, wrote music and dir. 12 piece orchestra troop shows; Freemason; mem. ACTRA; Delta Upsilon; P. Conservative; Anglican; recreations: music, travel, walking; Address: 77 Chestnut Park Rd., Toronto, Ont. M4W 1W7.

WRIGHT, Donald John, Q.C., B.A.; b. Toronto, Ont., 5 Oct. 1928; s. Robert Paton and Anita Rosalie (Lyall) W.; e. Univ. of Toronto Schs.; Trinity Coll.; George C. and B.A.; Osgoode Hall Law Sch.; m. Jane Elizabeth, d. David P. Rogers, 19 June 1953; four children; PARTNER, LANG, MICHENER, CRANSTON, FARQUHARSON & WRIGHT since 1964; Dir., Union Gas Limited and other cos.; Counsel, Hayhurst, Dale & Deeth, Patent Attys.; read law with Arnoldi, Parry & Campbell; called to Bar of Ont. 1954; cr. Q.C. 1966; Partner, Blake, Cassels & Graydon 1961; mem. Candn. Bar Assn.; Co. of York Law Assn.; Alpha Delta Phi; Clubs: University; Badminton & Racquet; Devil's Glen Country; Home: 60 Rosedale Heights Dr., Toronto, Ont., M4T 1C5; Office: P.O. Box 10, First Canadian Place, Toronto, Ont. M5X 1A2

WRIGHT, Douglas T., Ph.D., D.Eng., LL.D., D.Sc.; civil engineer; b. Toronto, Ont., 4 Oct. 1927; s. George C. and Etta (Tyndall) W.; e. Univ. of Toronto, B.A.Sc. 1949; Univ. of Ill., M.S. 1952; Cambridge Univ., Ph.D. 1954; Carleton Univ., D.Eng., 1967; Brock Univ., LL.D. 1967; Mem. Univ. of Nfld., D.Sc. 1969; m. Margaret, d. late Dr. W. T. Maxwell, Sydney, Australia, 21 May 1955; children: William M., M. Clyde, Robert T., Sarah Jane, Anna Marie, PRES., UNIV. OF WATERLOO, 1981- ; Structural Designer, Morrison, Hershfield, Millman & Huggins, consulting engrs., Toronto, 1949 and 1952; Research Asst. in Structural Engn., Univ. of Ill., 1949-51; Athlone Fellow, Cambridge Univ., 1952-54; successively Lectr., Asst. Prof., Assoc. Prof., Dept. of Civil Engn., Queens Univ., 1954-58; Prof. of Civil Engn., Univ. of Waterloo, 1958, Chrmn., Dept. of Civil Engn., 1958-63, Dean of Engn. 1959-66; Chrmn., Comte. on Univ. Affairs, Prov. of Ont., 1967-72; Chrmn., Comn. on Post Secondary Educ. in Ont., 1969-72; Depy. Prov. Secy. for Soc. Dev., 1972-79; Depy. Minister of Culture and Recreation 1979-81; Visiting Professor, Instituto de Ingenieria, Universidad Nacional Autonoma de Mexico, 1964, 1966; Université de Sherbrooke 1966-67; Commonwealth Fellow, Australia 1974; consulting engineer on structural problems incl. aseismic design and spaceframe structures; consultant, Netherlands and Mexican Pavilions, Expo 67; Olympic Sports Palace, Mexico City, 1968; Ont. Place Dome and Forum, 1971; mem. or offr. numerous comtes. concerned with tech. standards under Candn. Standards Assn., Nat. Research Council, Nat. Bldg. Code of Can.; devel. comprehensive theories for structural analysis and design of large reticulated shells; author or co-author of numerous papers on structural engn., engn. educ. and higher educ.; Dir., Assn. Univs. and Colls. of Can., 1965-67; Fellow, Am. Soc. Civil Engrs.; Engn. Inst. Can.; mem., Assn. Prof. Engrs. Ontario; Internat. Assn. Bridge & Structural Engn.; Candn. Inst. Pub. Adm.; Candn. Inst. Internat. Affairs; recreations: reading, sailing; Clubs: University; RCYC; Home: 73 George St., Waterloo, Ont. Office: Univ. of Waterloo, Waterloo, Ont., N2L 3G1

WRIGHT, Esther Clark, Ph.D., D.Litt., Ll.D.; historian; b. Fredericton, N.B., 4 May 1895; d. William George (Lt. Gov. N.B. 1940-45) and Harriet Hannah (Richardson) Clark; e. Fredericton (N.B.) High Sch. 1912 (Classics Medal); Acadia Univ. 1916, hon. D.Litt. 1975; Univ. of

Toronto; Oxford Univ., Radcliffe Coll., Ph.D. 1931; Dalhousie Univ., Ll.D. (hon.) 1981; m. Conrad Payling Wright, 31 July 1924; Research Asst. Food Research Inst. Stanford Univ. 1925-26; Asst. to Prof. of Business Hist. Grad. Sch. of Business Adm. Harvard Univ. 1927-28; Lectr. in Econ. and Sociol. Acadia Univ. 1943-47; Vice Pres. Nat. Council of Women 1951-54; Candn. Fed. Univ. Women 1952-55; mem. Wolfville (N.S.) Sch. Bd. 1935-38; Acadia Univ. Senate 1936-54; rec'd Award of Merit Am. Assn. for State & Local Hist. 1968; Silver Jubilee Medal, 1978; Regional History Award, Cdn. Hist. Assn. 1980; author "Alexander Clark, Loyalist" 1940; "The Miramichi" 1944; "The Petitcodiac" 1945; "The Saint John River" 1949; "The Loyalists of New Brunswick" 1955, reprinted 1972 and 1977; "Blomidon Rose" 1957, reprinted 1972 and 1977; "Grandmother's Child" 1959; "Samphire Greens" 1961; "The Steeves Descendants" 1965; "The Saint John River and Its Tributaries" 1966, reprinted 1975; "People and Places New Brunswick" 1973; "The Ships of St. Martins" 1974, reprinted 1979; "Saint John Ships and Their Builders" 1976; "Planters and Pioneers: Nova Scotia 1749 to 1775", 1978; also numerous articles; Fellow Royal Candn. Geog. Soc.; Royal Commonwealth Soc.; Life mem. Candn. Hist. Assn.; Candn. Authors Assn.; N.S. Heritage Trust; Baptist; recreations: canoeing, gardening, travel, swimming; Home: 4 Hillside Ave., Wolfville N.S., B0P 1X0; Office: (P.O. Box 710) Wolfville, N.S., B0P 1X0

WRIGHT, James Osborne; agricultural co-operative executive; b. Tisdale, Sask. 16 Sept. 1925; s. Percy Ellis and Alice Isabel (Dougherty) W.; e. Luther Coll. 1942; Univ. of Sask. Dipl. in Agric. 1948; Banff Sch. of Advanced Mang. 1965; m. Marjorie Rosina d. Albert Wilmer 24 Nov. 1945; children: Barbara, Marjorie, Deborah, Christine, James W.; CORP. SECTY. SASK. WHEAT POOL 1967-; Secy., Candn. Cooperative Wheat Producers; Pres. Standing Comte., Agric. Cooperatives, Internat. Fed. Agric. Producers; Pres. and Dir. Tisdale (Sask.) Co-op Assn. 1952-56; Moosomin (Sask.) Credit Union 1960-62; Dir. Sherwood Credit Union, Regina 1974-76; Commr., Metric Comm. Can. 1972-80; Trustee, Candn. Hunger Foundation 1972-78; served with Regina Rifle Regt. Can., U.K. and N.W. Europe during World War II; United Church; recreations: golf, cross-country skiing; Club: Regina Rotary; Home: 52 Gardiner Ave., Regina, Sask. S4S 4P6; Office: 2625 Victoria Ave., Regina, Sask. S4P 2Y6.

WRIGHT, John Elmer, B.Sc.; executive; b. Leamington, Ont. 12 Jan. 1929; s. Elmer and Dora (Levi) W.; e. Pub. and High Sch., Windsor, Ont.; Queen's Univ., B.Sc. (Mech. Engn.) 1951; m. Donalda, d. Henry Paff, 17 June 1953; children: John, Edward, Mary, Donald, Martha; PRESIDENT AND DIR., TEMPRITE INDUSTRIES LTD. since 1971; Pres. and Dir., Applied Thermal Products Co. Ltd., Ackrite Consultants Inc.; Jackson and Brooks Ltd.; began with American Standard Products (Canada) Ltd., Toronto, as Field Engr. 1951-58; apptd. Vice-Pres., R. C. Black & Co. Ltd., Toronto 1958-61; founded and assumed Presidency, Applied Thermal Products Co. Ltd. 1961; mem., Am. Soc. of Heating, Refrigeration & Air Conditioning Engrs.; Assn. Prof. Engrs. of Ont.; Air Moving & Control Assn.; Cdn. Gas Assn.; Liberal; Anglican; recreations: skiing, golf, tennis, squash; Clubs: Weston Golf & Country (Past Pres.); The Boulevard Homes: 1407 Royal York Rd., Weston, Ont. and R.R.1, Palgrave, Ont.; Office: 6470 Viscount Rd., Mississauga, Ont.M9W 1G1

WRIGHT, Kenneth Osborne, M.A., Ph.D., D.Sc., F.R.S.C.; astronomer; b. Fort George, B.C., 1 Nov. 1911; s. Charles Melville and Agnes Pearl (Osborne) W.; e. Univ. of Toronto Schs., 1923-29; Univ. of Toronto, B.A. 1933, M.A. 1934; Univ. of Mich., Ph.D. 1940; D.Sc. N. Corpernicus Univ., Torun, Poland 1973; m. 1stly Margaret Lindsay, d. Frederick B. Sharp, 25 September 1937 (died 7 June 1969); one d. Nora Louise; 2ndly Jean M.

(MacLachlan) Ellis, 21 March 1970; Hon. Prof. Physics, Univ. Victoria 1965-81, mem. Senate 1973-78, Bd. Govs. 1973-75; Chrmn., National Research Council, Assoc. Comte. on Astron. 1971-74; Assistant in Astronomy, University of Toronto, 1933-34; summer Assistant in Astronomy, University of Michigan, 1936; Astron. Assistant Dom. Astrophysical Observatory, 1936-39 and Astrophysicist, 1940-1960; Ass't Dir. 1960-66; Dir. 1966-76; Guest Investigator, 1976- ; Lect. in Physics, Univ. of Brit. Columbia, 1943-44; Visiting Prof., Toronto 1960-61; Visiting Foreign Prof., Am. Astron. Soc., Amherst-Mt. Holyoke, 1963; Dir., Dominion Astrophysical Observatory, Victoria, 1966-76; Research Assoc., Mt. Wilson & Palomar Observatories 1962; author of over 70 articles in scient. journals; mem., Royal Astron. Soc. of Can. (Pres. 1964-66); Am. Astron. Soc. (Councillor, 1953-56); Astron. Soc. of the Pacific; Internat. Astron. Union; Royal Astron. Soc.; Candn. Astron. Soc.; United Church; Home: 205-2768 Satellite St., Victoria, B.C., V8S 5G8

WRIGHT, Mary Jean, M.A., Ph.D.; psychologist; university professor; b. Strathroy, Ont., 20 May 1915; d. Ernest Joel and Mary Jean (Clark) W.; e. Strathroy (Ont.) Coll. Inst., 1935; Univ. of W. Ont., B.A. 1939; Univ. of Toronto, M.A. 1940, Ph.D. 1949; Brock Univ., LL.D. 1979; Prof. Emeritus, 1980, Prof. of Psychol., and Dir. of Lab. Preschool, Univ. of Western Ont., 1973-80, Chrmn. of Dept. 1960-70; Secy., E. J. Wright Central and Affiliated Co.'s, Strathroy 1956-78; Psychol., Prot. Children's Village, Ottawa, 1941-42 and Mental Health Clinic, Hamilton, 1944-45; Instr., Inst. of Child Study, Univ. of Toronto, 1945-46; joined present Univ. as Asst. Prof. 1946-54, Assoc. Prof. 1955-61; Prof. 1962; served overseas with Candn. Children's Service and as Instr., Garrison Lane Nursery Training Sch., Birmingham, Eng., 1942-44; mem. Adv. Bd., Un. Community Services, 1953-59; Retarded Children's Assn. 1954-57; Children's Psychiatric Research Inst., 1966-70; Dir., Un. Appeal, 1956-59; Family Service Bureau 1954-60; Child Guidance Clinic 1960-63; mem. Ont. Comte. on Children 1958-67 (Vice Pres. 1964-65); Candn. Comte. on Early Childhood since 1961; writings incl. articles for prof. journs.; mem., Adv. Acad. Panel, Canada Council, 1976-78; Soc. Sci. and Hum. Research Council of Can. 1978-79; Ont. Bd. Examiners in Psychol. 1970-75 (Chrmn., 1973-74); Ont. Psychol. Assn. (President 1950-51); Canadian Psychol. Assn. (Director 1959-62; President 1968-69, Hon. President 1975-76); American Psychol. Assn. (Comte. on Internat. Relations, 1976-79); Soc. Research Child Devel.; Eastern Psychol. Assn.; Nursery Educ. Assn. Ont. (Dir. 1956-60; Chrmn., Cert. Bd., 1964-66); Candn. Assn. Univ. Teachers; Gamma Phi Beta; P. Conservative; Anglican; recreations: music, travel; Home: 1032 Western Rd., London, Ont., N6G 1G4

WRIGHT, Hon. Peter, O.B.E., C.D.; retired judge; b. Toronto, Ont., 16 July 1910; s. late Ward W., K.C., and Geraldine (Robinson) W.; e. Univ. of Toronto Schs., 1920-28; St. Andrew's Univ., Scotland, M.A. 1931; Osgoode Hall, Toronto, Ont., 1931-34; m. Cecilia Oxley, 28 June 1969; Justice, Supreme Court of Ont., 1969-80: Delta Chi; Home: 423 Avenue Rd., Toronto, Ont. M4V 2H7

WRIGHT, Raymond C., B.A., B.L.S.; librarian; b. Winnipeg, Man., 4 May 1917; s. Perce Vancouver and Anna Maud (Lipsett) W.; e. Gordon Bell High Sch., Winnipeg, 1935; Univ. Of Man., B.A. 1939; McGill Univ., B.L.S. 1947; m. (Eileen) Patricia, d. late Robert Collins, 22 Aug. 1942; children: Robert Clifford, Terri Eileen; CHIEF LIBRARIAN, UNIV. OF WINNIPEG, since 1967; Documents Librarian, Prov. Lib., Govt. of Man., 1947-55; Asst. Librarian, Man. Extension Lib., Univ. of Man., 1955-61; Chief Librarian, United Coll., 1961-67 when coll. inc. in present Univ.; served with RCAF 1941-45; mem., Man. Lib. Assn. (Secy. 3 yrs., Treas. 2yrs., Pres. 2 yrs.); Secy., Comte. Prairie Univ. Librarians, 1972-73; Chmn., Council of Prairie Univ. Libraries 1981-82 (Secy. 1979-80); Alpha

Delta Epsilon; United Church; recreations: reading, watching sports; Home: 488 Queenston St., Winnipeg, Man., R3N 0X2

WRIGHT, Richard B., B.A.; author; b. Midland, Ont. 4 March 1937; s. Lavern and Laura (Thomas) W.; e. Midland (Ont.) High Sch. 1956; Ryerson Polytech. Inst. Toronto grad. in Radio and TV Arts 1959, B.A. 1972; m. Phyllis Mary d. Irvin Cotton, Brampton, Ont. 2 Sept. 1966; two s. Christopher Stephen, Richard Andrew; Journalist and Radio Copywriter 1959-60; Asst. Ed. Macmillan of Canada 1960-65, Trade Sales Mgr. 1966-68; Sales Rep. Oxford University Press 1969-70; Novelist and Freelance Writer 1970-75; Head of Eng., Ridley Coll. St. Catharines, Ont. 1976-79; author "Andrew Tolliver" (children) 1965; "The Weekend Man" 1970; "In the Middle of a Life" 1973 (Toronto Book Award 1973, Faber Mem. Prize U.K. 1975); "Farthing's Fortunes" 1976; "Final Things" 1980; "The Teacher's Daughter" 1982; recipient Can. Council Jr. and Sr. Fellowships; Ont. Arts Council Fellowship; recreations: walking, reading, music; Address: 52 St. Patrick St., St. Catharines, Ont. L2R 1K3.

WRIGHT, Wilfred J.; company executive; b. Toronto, Ont. 24 Oct. 1928; s. John Edward and Sarah Anne (Wright) W.; e. East York Coll. Inst., Toronto, 1946; Univ. of Toronto Extension in conjunction with Soc. Indust. Accts., R.I.A. 1955; York Univ., Advanced Advertising Mang. Course, 1960; Univ. of W. Ont., Marketing Mang. Course, 1964; m. Ethel Elizabeth, d. Frederick Roy Frey, Toronto, Ont., 26 June 1956; children: Mark, Melody; PRES. AND C.E.O., W.J. Wright Enterprises Ltd., AND PRESIDENT, AND CHIEF EXECUTIVE OFFICER, Muffin Break (Ontario) Inc.; Pres., Chackers Inc.; Gen. Mgr. of Operations, Peoples Church, Toronto; joined Philco Corp. as Accounting Clerk, 1946; Jr. Acct., Shirriff's Ltd.; 1948; Cost Acct. 1950; Asst. to Comptroller 1952; Adm. Asst. to Extve. Vice-Pres., Shirriff-Horsey, 1956; Controller, Shirriff Div., Salada-Shirriff-Horsey, 1957; Adm. Mgr., Shirriff Div., 1958 and Candn. Div., 1959; Product Mgr., Salada Foods, 1960; Mgr., Corporate Planning, 1962; Gen. Mgr., Snack Foods Div., 1964; Mang. Dir., Chief Extve. Offr. and Dir., Peek Frean (Canada) Ltd. and Langley, Harris & Co. Ltd. 1968; Pres., Chief Extve. Offr. & Mang. Dir., 1970; Pres. and C.E.O., Associated Biscuits of Can. Ltd., 1972-80; Pres. & C.E.O. N. Am. Div. Associated Biscuits 1979-80; mem. Bd. of Trade Metrop. Toronto; The Presidents' Assn.; Soc. Management Accts.; P. Conservative; Protestant; Clubs: Empire; Granite; Home: 123 Citation Dr., Willowdale, Ont., M2K 1T3

WRIGHT, William Norman, retired insurance executive; b. Sheffield, Eng. 5 Feb. 1913; s. Samuel and Mary Sarah (Bean) W.; e. King Edward VII Sch. Sheffield, Eng. 1924-29; m. Alice Hildegard Linke 29 Apl. 1935; two s. Stephen, Geoffrey; Dir., Bowring Bros. Ltd.; 9 yrs. service prior to World War II with Royal Insurance Co. Ltd. and affiliated co's in Eng. trans. to Can. 1947 serving in various capacities Toronto, Winnipeg and Montreal incl. Marketing Rep., Asst. Agency Supt., Production Supt., Asst. Br. Mgr., Br. Mgr., Agency Mgr. for Can.; Asst. Gen. Mgr. for Can., Depy. Gen. Mgr. for Can.; Extve. Vice Pres. (Ins. Oper.), retired 1978; Vice Pres. and Chrmn. Pub. Relations Comte. All-Can. Ins. Fed. 1967-69 (now Ins. Bureau Can.); Commnd. W. Yorks. Regt. (Terr.) March 1939; seconded to Roy. W. African Frontier Force 1940; served W. Africa, India, Burma, rank Lt. Col.; Candn. Army Inf. Reserve, rank Maj.; Assoc. Chart. Ins. Inst.; Nat. Secy., Br. Cdn. Trade Assoc.; Councillor, Roy. Commonwealth Soc.; Big Bros. of Can.; Past Pres. St. George's Soc. Toronto; Hon. Commandant, Old Fort York, 1978; mem., Chrmn. Museums Comte. of Toronto Historical Bd.; 1980; mem. exec., Imperial Officers Assn. of Can., 1979; P. Conservative; Anglican; recreations: music, reading; Clubs: Ontario; Roy. Cdn. Mil. Inst.; Arts and Letters (Toronto); Home: Suite 1204, 2010 Islington Ave., Weston, Ont. M9P 3S8

WRINCH, Maj.-Gen. Arthur Egbert, C.B.E. (1945), C.D.; army officer, retired; b. Hazelton, B.C. 13 Nov. 1908; s. Dr. Horace Cooper and Alice Jane (Breckon) W.; e. Univ. of Brit. Columbia, 1926; Roy. Mil. Coll., Dipl. with Hons. 1931; Queen's Univ., B.Sc. (Elect. Engn. with Hons.) 1935; m. late Janet Madalene Wightman; one s., John Arthur; 2ndly Margaret Evelynn, d. Sidney H. R. Howard, 26 Aug. 1972; gazetted Lieutenant, R.C.C.S., 1931; Adj., Candn. Signal Training Centre Camp Borden, Ontario, 1936-37; Dist. Signal Offr., Military Distric No. 5 (Que.) 1937-39; employed in Fortress Communications, East Coast, 1939-40; 5th Candn. Armoured Divn. Signals, 1940-42; proceeded to U.K. 1941; O.C., 1st Candn. Corps Signals, 1942-43; 5th Candn. Armoured Divn. Signals, 1943-45; proceeded to Italy 1943; Chief Signal Offr., 1st Candn. Corps. Jan. to June 1945; to N.W. Europe, Feb. 1945; returned to Can. as Signal Offr., Candn. Army Pac. Force, June 1945; Chief Signal Offr., Candn. Forces in the Netherlands, Sept. 1945; returned to Can. Candn. Dec. 1945; promoted Capt. 1937, Maj. 1940, Lieut.-Col. 1942, Brig. 1945, Maj.-Gen. 1959; twice Mentioned in Despatches; Dir., Roy. Candn. Corps of Signals, 1946-49; Candn. Army Staff course, 1949; Chief of Staff, Candn. Army Staff, Wash, D.C., and Asst. Mil. Attache 1949-51; Depy. Q.M.G. (Design and Development), Ottawa, May 1951-Feb. 1953; Vice-Q.M.G. 1953-54; attended Imp. Defence Coll., London, 1955; Commdr., 1 Candn. Inf. Bgde. Gp., 1956-58; Dir.-Gen. of Army Personnel 1958; Maj.-Gen. Survival 1959; retired to Suppl. Reserve, 1964; Nat. Comnr., Candn. Red Cross, 1963-75; Chrmn., Devel. Prog. Adv. Comte., League of Red Cross Soc., Geneva, 1969-77; Vice Pres., Candn. Red Cross, 1975; Hon. mem., Candn. Red Cross, 1978; mem., Assn. Prof. Engrs. Ont.; Royal Candn. Legion (Fort York Br.); Life mem., Candn. Signals Assn.; Signals Welfare Inc.; mem., Bd. of Trade, Metro. Tor.; mem., R.M.C. Club of Can. (Dir., Toronto Br.); Governor Hillcrest Hosp.; Awarded U.S. Legion of Merit, 1945; Queen's Coronation Medal; Centennial Medal; Queen's Silver Jubilee Medal; Finland Red Cross Silver Medal, 1968; Mexican Red Cross Grand Cross, 1971; Phillipino Nat. Red Cross Sampaguita Medal, 1975; United Church; Home: Apt. 503, 1 Clarendon Ave., Toronto, Ont., M4V 1H8;

WRONG, Dennis Hume, Ph.D.; professor; b. Toronto, Ont., 22 Nov. 1923; s. late Humphrey Hume and Mary Joyce (Hutton) W.; e. Ecole Internationale, Geneva, 1937-39; Upper Can. Coll., Toronto, 1939-41; Univ. of Toronto, B.A. 1945; Columbia Univ., Ph.D. 1956; m. Jacqueline d. late Earl Conrath, Portland, Ore., 26 March 1966; one s. Terence Hume (by previous m.); PROF. OF SOCIOL. NEW YORK UNIV., since 1963; Instr., Princeton Univ. 1949-50 and Rutgers Univ. 1950-51; Research Asst. to Hon. George F. Kennan, Inst. for Advanced Study, Princeton, 1951-52; Lectr., Dept. of Pol. Econ., Univ. of Toronto 1954-56; Asst. and Assoc. Prof., Brown Univ. 1956-61; Assoc. Prof., Grad. Faculty, New Sch. for Social Research, 1961-63; joined present Univ. 1963; Chrmn., Dept. of Sociol., Univ. Coll., 1963-65; Visiting Prof., Univ. of Nevada, 1965-66; author; Visiting Fellow, Nuffield Coll., Oxford, 1978; "American and Canadian Viewpoints ", 1955; "Population", 1956; "Population and Society", 1961, 4th ed. 1977; ed. "Max Weber", 1970; "Sceptical Sociology" 1976; "Power: Its Forms Bases and Uses" 1979; "Class Fertility Trends in Western Nations" (Sociology Dissertation Series), 1980; co-ed., "Readings in Introductory Sociology", 1967 3rd ed. 1977; ed. "Contemporary Sociology": A Journal of Reviews 1972-74"; other writings incl. numerous articles and reviews in various journs.; mem., Am. Sociol. Assn. (Program Comte. 1970, Nominations Comte. 1971-72, Pub. Comte. 1971-74); E. Sociol. Soc. (Extve. Comte. 1964-66); Home: Drakes Corner Rd., Princeton, N.J.

WRONG, Norman NcKinnon, M.D., F.R.C.P. (C.); physician; b. Aylmer, Ont., 12 Nov. 1901; s. James Murray and Cecilia (Arkell) W.; e. Aylmer Pub. Sch. and Coll. Inst. (Matric. 1919); Univ. of Toronto, M.B. 1927 (with Hons.) M.D. 1947; m. Rhona, d. late Wm. A. MacKinnon, 12 Nov. 1932; children: Nancy MacKinnon, Christopher Murray; Graduate Lectr. in Med., Univ. of Toronto, since 1962; Assoc. Prof. of Med. in charge of Dermatology there 1954-62; Sr. Phys., Toronto Gen. Hosp.; Active Consultant, Hosp. for Sick Children, Toronto, Ont.; Consultant in Dermatol., Sunnybrook Hosp., Univ. of Toronto, Toronto, Ont.; hon. Consultant, North York Gen. Hosp.; served in 2nd World War, R.C.A.M.C.; Reserve, 1940-42; Active, 1943-45, Eng. and N.W. Europe with rank of Major; Publications: some 32 scient. articles in Med. lit. since 1932; Fellow, Am. Dermatol. Assn. (Vice. Pres. 1964); Candn. Dermatol. Assn. (Pres. 1955); Am. Acad. of Dermatol. (Vice-Pres. 1958-59); Hon. Mem., Aust. Dermatol. Assn.; Brit. Assn. Dermatol. (1961); Hon. mem., N.Y. Dermatological Soc.; Nu Sigma Nu; Alpha Omega Alpha; Anglican; recreations: golf, gardening; Club: Granite, Thornhill Golf; Home: 128 Buckingham Ave., Toronto, Ont. M4N 1R6

WYATT, Gerard Robert, B.A., Ph.D.; biologist; b. Palo Alto, Ca. 3 Sept. 1925; s. Horace Graham and Mary Aimee (Strickland) W.; came to Can. 1935; e. Univ. of B.C. B.A. 1945; Univ. of Ca. Berkeley 1947; Univ. of Cambridge, England Ph.D. 1950; m. late Sarah Silver d. late Arthur Silver Morton 19 Dec. 1951; children: Eve Morton, Graham Strickland, Diana Silver; PROF., DEPT. OF BIOLOGY, QUEEN'S UNIV., 1973- ; Scientific Officer, Candn. Agricult. Insect Pathology Lab., 1950; Asst. Prof. Biochem., Yale Univ. 1954; Assoc. Prof. Biol. 1960; Prof. Biol. 1964; Prof. and Head of Biol. Dept., Queen's Univ., 1973-75; author many research papers and scholarly reviews in field; mem., Amer. Soc. Biol. Chem.; Amer. Soc. Zoologists; Amer. Entomological Soc.; Candn. Soc. Biol. Chem.; Candn. Soc. Cell. Biol.; Candn. Entomological Soc.; Soc. Developmental Biol.; Royal Soc. Can.; Home: 114 Earl St., Kingston, Ont. K7L 2H1; Office: Kingston, Ont. K7L 3N6

WYATT, Harold Edmund; banker; b. Moose Jaw, Sask., 30 Nov. 1921; s. Edmund Rundle and Zelma Aleta (Turk) W.; e. King George Pub. Sch. and Central Coll. Inst. (Sr. Matric. 1939), Moose Jaw, Sask.; m. Isabel Margaret, d. late Neil John MacDonald, 9 May 1942; children: Andrea Maureen Shumka, David MacDonald, Kathryn Margaret; VICE CHRMN. (WESTERN CANADA) AND DIR., ROYAL BANK OF CANADA joined the Bank in Moose Jaw, Sask.; served in various centres in Prov. incl. Prince Albert, Saskatoon and Regina; apptd. Staff Offr. for Alta. Dist., Calgary, 1951; Asst. to Supvr. of Staff, Montreal, 1954; Supvr. of Staff, 1961; Asst. Gen. Mgr., Toronto 1965, then Depy. Gen. Mgr. Personnel, Montreal, 1968; apptd. Head of Candn. Dists. 1970, Vice Pres. & Gen. Mgr. 1971; Vice Chrmn. and Dir. 1978; served with R.C.A.F. 4½ years during 2nd World War; discharged with rank Flt. Lt.; Immediate Past-Chrmn., Candn. Chamber of Comm.; Gov., Can. Jaycees; Dir., Council for Cdn. Unity; United Church; recreations: golf, swimming; Office: 335-8th Ave. S.W., Calgary, Alta

WYCZNSKI, Paul, L. ès L., D.E.S., Ph.D., D.Lit.; educator; b. Zelgoszcz, Poland 29 June 1921; s. Lucjan and Clara W.; e. Univ. de Lille L. ès L. 1949, D.E.S. 1950; Univ. d'Ottawa Ph.D. 1957; Univ. Laurentienne D.Lit. 1978; m. Régine d. André Delabit, France 11 Sept. 1951; children: Michel, Isabelle, Rita, Bernard, Marc, Monique, Anne; PROF. TITULAIRE DE RECHERCHE, UNIV. D'OTTAWA since 1970, Prof. agrégé 1960, Prof. titulaire 1964, Dir-fondateur du Centre de recherche en littérature canadienne-française 1958 — 73; mem. Royal Comn. on Bilingualism & Biculturalism 1963 — 69; Prof. de l'année Univ. d'Ottawa 1968; fondateur et coordonateur "Archives des lettres canadiennes"; publs. incl. "No

Betlejemska" (théâtre) 1949; "Emile Nelligan: Sources et Originalité de son oeuvre" 1960; "Poésie et Symbole" 1965; François-Xavier Garneau: Aspects littéraires de son eouvre" 1966; "Emile Nelligan" 1967; "François-Xavier Garneau: Voyage en Angleterre et en France dans les années 1831, 1832 35 1833" 1968; "Nelligan et la Musique" 1971; "Albert Laberge — Charles Gill" (catalogue) 1971; "Bibliographie descriptive et critique d'Emile Nelligan" 1973; "Dictionnaire pratique des auteurs québécois" en collaboration 1976; "Francois-Xavier Garneau 1809 — 1866 (catalogue) 1977; "W slonecznej cienni", (poetry) 1981; numerous articles various journs.; mem. Royal Soc. Can.; Assn. de littérature comparée; Soc. des écrivains canadiens-français; Soc. française d'histoire d'outre-mer; Inst. polonais des sciences et lettres en Amérique du Nord; Assn. Candn. Profs.; Home: 156 rue Kehoe, Ottawa, Ont. K2B 6A5; Office: Ottawa, Ont. K1N 6N5.

WYGANT, James Peter; foods executive; b. Montreal West, Que., 31 Oct. 1926; s. Samuel Edwin and Louise (Biersach) W.; e. Montreal West High Sch.; Kennedy Coll., Windsor, Ont.; McGill Univ., 1945-46; Univ. of Syracuse, Grad. Sch. of Sales Mang. and Marketing; m. Ruth Evelyn, d. late David B. and Margaret Mitchell, 11 June 1948; children: Margaret, Patricia, Sally; PRES. AND CHIEF EXTVE. OFFR., GENERAL BAKERIES LTD. since 1974; Dir., Bakery Council of Can.; W. E. Long Co., Chicago; Chmn., Margaret's Fine Foods; Campbell Soup Co., 1948; various assignments in U.S. from 1949-60; Gen. Sales Mgr., 1961; Vice Pres., Standard Brands, 1966; el. a Dir. 1967; Extve. Vice Pres., General Bakeries 1972-74; served with R.C.N., 1944-45 on H.M.C.S. Huron; mem., United Church; recreations: golf, tennis, bridge, music; Home: 29 Rainbow Creekway, Willowdale, Ont. M2K 2T9; Office: 75 The Donway W., Don Mills, Ont. M3C 2E9

WYKES, Edmund Harold, LL.B.; lawyer; corporate secretary; b. Newcastle-on-Tyne, Eng. 19 July 1928; s. late Cyril Edmund and Sylvia (Glover) W.; e. elem. and sec. sch. Durham, Eng.; Durham Univ. LL.B. 1949; m. Joan d. late Thomas Wilfrid Nightingale 16 Oct. 1955; children: Julie Caroline, Christopher John; VICE PRES., GEN. COUNSEL AND SECY., IMPERIAL LIFE ASSURANCE CO. OF CAN.; has held various positions assoc. with legal dept. of Imperial Life since 1957; admitted as Solicitor in Eng. 1953, in Ont. 1958; served with RAF; demobilized with rank of Flying Offr., 1949-51; mem., Eng. Law Soc.; Law Soc. of U.C.; Assn. of Life Assurance Counsel; Am. Soc. of Corp. Secys.; Candn. Bar Assn.; Chrmn. Insurance Law Section, Ont. Br., Candn. Bar Assn., 1979; Anglican; Clubs: University, Toronto; recreations: music, reading; Home: 86 Wimbleton Rd., Islington, Ont. M9A 3S5; Office: 95 St. Clair Ave. W., Toronto, Ont. M4V 1N7.

WYMAN, William Robert, B.Com.; investment dealer; b. Edmonton, Alta. 4 Dec. 1930; s. Robert Andrew and Dora (Joberns) W.; e. Primary Sch. Edmonton, Alta.; Trinity Coll., Port Hope, Ont.; High Schs. Vancouver, Kelowna & Kamloops, B.C.; Univ. of B.C., B.Comm. 1956; m. Dorothy, d. Charles Taylor, 4 Sept. 1954; children: Timothy, Robyn, Leslie; PRESIDENT, CHIEF EXTVE. OFFR. AND DIR., PEMBERTON SECURITIES LTD. since 1975; Dir. Pacific Management Ltd.; Ryan Investment Ltd.; Yorkshire Trust Co.; joined Canada Life Assurance Co., Toronto as Analyst, Invest. Dept. 1956; Analyst, Hall Securities Ltd., Vancouver 1957; Registered Rep., Richardson Securities Canada 1960; Mgr. Research Dept., Pemberton Securities Ltd. 1962, Retail Dept. Mgr. and Dir. 1965, Vice-Pres. 1969, Sr. Vice-Pres. 1971; Past Chrmn. Invest. Dealers Assn. Can.; Chmn., Van. Bd. of Trade; Anglican; recreations: golf, skiing, fishing; Clubs: Capilano Golf & Country; The Vancouver; Home: 3320 Mathers Ave., West Vancouver, B.C. V7V 2K5; Office: (Box 49160) 3 Bentall Centre, Vancouver, B.C. V7X 1K6

WYND, G. Douglas; association executive; b. Montreal, Que., 23 Apl. 1914; s. William Dougal and Jessie D. (Johnston) W.; e. Pub. and High Schs., Montreal; McGill Univ.; Univ. of Toronto; m. Madeline Leslie, 5 Oct. 1940; children: Bruce, Joan, David; CONSULTANT, ATHERTON, MILNER & ASSOC. LTD.; Acct., Elmhurst Dairy Ltd., 1933; Gen. Mgr., Candn. Airways Ltd., 1941; Sr. Auditor, Cost Audit & Investigation Dept., Fed. Govt., 1945; Asst. Gen. Mgr., Asst. to Pres., Remington Rand (Canada) Ltd., Montreal and Toronto, 1946-63; Gen. Mgr. Adm., Pitney Bowes, 1963-65; Gen. Mgr. and Dir., Cdn. Business Equip. Mfrs. Assn. Inc. 1965-79; mem., Inst. Assn. Extves. (Pres.); Am. Soc. Assn. Extves.; Bd. Trade Metrop. Toronto; Freemason (P.M. Sunnylea Lodge); United Church; recreations: music, golf, reading; Club: Islington Golf; Home: 86 Valecrest Dr., Islington, Ont. M9A 4P6; Office: P.O. Box 192, One First Canadian Place, Toronto, Ont. M5X 1A6

WYNDHAM, John Steen; publisher; b. Oakville, Ont., 21 April 1915; s. William B. and Agnes (Steen) W., e. Oakville High Sch., Grad. 1932; Northern Inst. of Tech., Grad. 1942; m. Marjorie Anne, d. Dr. David A. Hopper, Waterdown, Ont., 4 April 1942; PRES., STONE & COX LTD.; Publisher, "Annual Publications"; joined firm of Stone & Cox Ltd., 1934, Pres. since 1956; Ed., year books, 1938; Asst. Ed., Candn. Ins. Law Service, 1938; Ed. of Publs., 1946; served in World War, 1942-45, as Radio Offr. with R.A.F. Ferry Command; Protestant; recreations: golf, curling; Clubs: Oakville Golf; Oakville Curling; Home: 1162 Morrison Heights Drive, Oakville, Ont. L6J 4J1; Office: 100 Simcoe St., Ste. 200, Toronto, Ont. M5H 3G2

WYNNE-EDWARDS, Hugh Robert, B.Sc., M.A., Ph.D., D.Sc., F.R.S.C., P.Eng.; scientist; b. Montreal, Quebec, 19 January 1934; s. Prof. Vero Copner and Jeannie Campbell (Morris) W-E.; e. Montreal (Que.) High Sch., 1938-46; Aberdeen (Scot.) Grammar Sch., 1946-51; Univ. of Aberdeen, B.Sc. 1955; Queen's Univ., M.A. 1957, Ph.D. 1959; D. Sc. (Hon.) Memorial Univ. 1975; children by former marriages: Robin Alexander, Katherine Elizabeth, Renée Elizabeth Lortie, Jeannie Elizabeth, Alexander Vernon; VICE-PRES. AND CHIEF SCIENTIFIC OFFICER, ALCAN INTERNATIONAL, 1980- ; with Geol. Survey of Canada, 1958-59; joined Queen's Univ. as Lectr., 1959-61, Asst. Prof. 1961-64, Assoc. Prof. 1964-68, Secy., Faculty of Arts and Science, 1965-68, Prof. and Head Dept. Geol. Sciences 1968-72; and Prof., Cominco Prof. and Head, Dept. of Geol. Sciences, U.B.C. 1972-77; Asst., Secy., Univ. Branch, Min. of State for Science and Technology, 1977-79; Scientific Dir., Alcan Intl., 1979-80; Visiting Prof., Univ. of Aberdeen, 1965-66; State Guest advising Directorate of Geol. and Mining, Uttar Pradesh, India, 1964; Advisor (1968-72), Grenville Project, Que. Dept. Nat. Resources (Co-ordinator of Project, Geol. Survey of Can. 1964-65); Visiting Prof., Univ. of Witwatersrand, Johannesberg, S. Africa 1972; Spendiarov Prize (24th Internat. Geol. Cong. 1972); Pres., Candn. Geoscience Council, 1973-74; Pres., Scitec, 1977; CBC Science Adv. Comte., 1980- ; Conseil de la politique scientifique du Québec, 1981- ; mem. Geol. Assn. Can.; Am. Assn. Advanc. Science; Geol. Soc. Am.; United Church; recreations: tennis, skiing, carpentry; Address: Alcan International Ltd., 1 Place Ville Marie, Montreal, Que. H3C 3H2; Home: 4319 Montrose Ave., Westmount, Que. H3Y 2A8

WYSZECKI, Gunter Wolfgang, Ph.D.; scientist; b. Tilsit, Germany 8 Nov. 1925; came to Can. 1955; s. Bruno Bernhard and Helene (Goerke) W.; e. Technical Univ. of Berlin Diplom-Ingenieur 1951, Ph.D. Mathematics 1953; m. Ingeborg Christine d. late Karl Rathjens 4 Aug. 1954; children: Wolfgang Michael, Joana Maria; ASST. DIR. OF PHYSICS AND HEAD OF OPTICS, NATL. RESEARCH COUNCIL OF CAN.; Vice Pres., Comn. Internationale De l'éclairage, Adjunct Prof., Sch. of Optometry, Univ. of Waterloo, served with German Navy, 1943-45; author of "Farbsysteme", 1962; co-author, "Color in Business, Science, and Industry", 3rd ed. 1975; "Color Science", 1967; over 80 publs. in the field of color science (color vision, colorimetry, photometry, rediometry); rec'd. Judd Gold Medal of Assn. Internationale de la Couleur, 1979; Godlove Award of Intersociety Color Council, 1979; Bruning Award of Federation of Societies of Coating Technologies, 1979; Fellow, Optical Soc. of Am.; Fellow, Illuminating Engn. Soc.; mem., Candn. Soc. for Color (Pres. 1972-73); Lutheran; Home: 172 Roger Rd., Ottawa, Ont. K1H 5C8; Office: Ottawa, Ont. K1A 0R6.

Y

YAFFE, Leo, B.Sc., M.Sc., Ph.D., D.Litt. F.C.I.C., F.R.S.C., F.A.P.S.; university professor; b. Devil's Lake, N.D., U.S.A., 6 July 1916; s. Samuel and Mary (Cohen) Y.; e. Univ. of Manitoba, B.Sc. 1940, M.Sc. 1941; McGill Univ., Ph.D. 1943; D.Litt., Trent Univ.; m. Betty, d. Abraham Workman, Montreal, Que., 18 March 1945; children: Carla Joy, Mark John; VICE PRINCIPAL (ADM. & PROF. FACULTIES) McGILL UNIV., 1974-81; Macdonald Professor Chem. since 1959 (Chairman Dept. 1965-72); Project Leader, Nuclear Chem. and Tracer Research, Atomic Energy of Canada Ltd., Chalk River, Ont., 1943-52; Special Lectr. and Dir. of Radiochem. Lab., Dept. of Chem., McGill Univ., 1952-54; Assoc. Prof. 1955-59; on leave (1963-65) as Dir., Div. of Research & Labs., Internat. Atomic Energy Agency, Vienna, Austria; author of over 145 articles in the field of radiochem.; Fellow, Royal Society of Canada; Chem. Inst. Can.; Am. Phys. Soc.; Am. Assn. for Adv. of Science; Home: 5777 McAlear Ave., Montreal, Que. H4W 2H2

YALDEN, Maxwell Freeman, M.A., Ph.D.; Canadian public servant; b. Toronto, Ont., 12 Apl. 1930; s. late Frederick George and Helen Marie (Smith) Y.; e. Victoria Coll., Univ. of Toronto, B.A. 1952; Univ. of Mich., M.A. 1954, Ph.D. 1956; m. Janice MacKenzie, d. Colin MacKenzie Shaw, Tunbridge Wells, Eng., 28 Jan. 1952; children: Robert, Cicely; COMMR. OF OFFICIAL LANGUAGES, since 1977; joined Dept. of External Affairs 1956; posted to Moscow 1958; CPMUN Geneva (10 Nation Conf. on Disarmament) 1960; Ottawa 1960-63; First Secy., Paris 1963, becoming Counsellor 1965; Special Asst. for Fed.-Prov. questions Office of Under Secy. of State for External Affairs, Ottawa, 1967; apptd. Asst. Under Secy. of State 1969; Depy. Min. of Communications, 1973; Home: 167 Clemow Ave., Ottawa, Ont. K1S 2B3; Office: 66 Slater St., Ottawa, Ont. K1A 0T8

YAMAMOTO, Lucas Yasokazu, M.D.; educator; b. Shibetzu-Shi, Hokkaido, Japan 19 Jan 1928; s. Torimatsu and Chiyo (Ikeda) Y.; e. Shibetzu Primary Sch. and Nayoro Secondary Sch. Hokkaido, Japan 1945; Hoddaido Univ. 1945 — 48, M.D. 1952; Georgetown Med. Center, Georgetown Univ. Neurosurg. 1954 — 58; Nuclear Med. and Radiation Research, Med. Research Center, Brookhaven Nat. Lab., L.I., N.Y.; m. Jeanine Marilyn d. Joseph Zollner, River Phillip, N.S. 25 Oct. 1958; children: Ann Marie, Grace, Peter; ASSOC. PROF. OF NEUROL. AND NEUROSURG., DIR. OF NEUROISOTOPE LAB., McGILL UNIV. AND MONTREAL NEUROLOGICAL INST.; mem. Med. Council Can.; author over 100 articles nuclear med. various med. journs.; mem. Soc. Nuclear Med.; Montreal Neurol. Soc.; Candn. Med. Assn.; Am. Coll. Nuclear Physicians; Candn. Neurol. Soc.; Candn. Assn. Nuclear Med.; Coll. Phys. & Surgs. Que.; Am. Bd. Nuclear Med.; Cert. Specialist Nuclear Med. Que.; R. Catholic; recreations: swimming, skiing; Home: 4861 Parkinson Blvd., Pierrefonds, Que. H8Y 2Z2; Office: 3801 University, Montreal, Que. H3A 2B4 and Medical Arts Bldg. 814, 1538 Sherbrooke St. W., Montreal, Que.

YANOSIK, Hon. Clarence George, LL.B.; judge; b. Lethbridge, Alta. 20 Apl. 1926; s. George Reginald and Anne (Chollak) Y.; e. St. Basil's Elem. and St. Patrick's High Schs. Lethbridge 1942; Sch. for Veterans Calgary Sr. Matric. 1946; Univ. of B.C. B.A. 1951, LL.B. 1952; m. Cecily Gwyneth d. late Melvin Muir, Vancouver, B.C. 20 Aug. 1954; children: Robert Glen, Larry George, Laurie E. A., Clarence Thomas B. (Tim); JUDGE, COURT OF QUEEN'S BENCH, ALTA. 1979- ; called to Bar of Alta. 1953; Barrister and Solr. 1953-69; Judge, Dist. Court of S. Alta. 1969-75, Dist. Court of Alta. 1975-79; served with RCNVR 1943-45; former Dir. Alta. Lib. Assn.; Past Pres., Lethbridge Lib. Assn.; Lethbridge Bar Assn.; Lib. Cand. Fed. g.e. 1958; mem. Candn. Bar Assn.; Alta. Bar Assn.; R. Catholic; recreations: skiing, golf, fishing, hunting, jogging, weight-lifting; Home: 2818 - 6th Ave. A. South, Lethbridge, Alta. T1J 1H2; Office: Court House, 1010 - 4th Ave. South, Lethbridge, Alta. T1J 4C7.

YAPHE, Wilfred, Ph.D.; educator; b. Lachine, Que. 9 July 1921; s. Sam and Rachel Y.; e. McGill Univ. B.Sc. 1949, Ph.D. 1952; m. Ruth 16 Jan. 1966; children: Arona, Anna, John; PROF. OF MICROBIOLOGY, McGILL UNIV. 1966- ; served with RCAF 1942-46; author various research papers polysaccharides of marine algae; Hebrew; Office: 3775 University, Montreal, Que. H3A 2B4.

YAREMKO, John, Q.C., LL.D.; b. Welland, Ontario, 10 August 1918; e. Hamilton (Ont.) Central Coll. Inst. (Sir John Gibson Scholar, Reuben Wells Leonard Scholar, Carter Scholar, Norman Slater Mem. Scholar, W. H. Ballard Gold Medallist, Valedictorian); Univ. of Toronto, Honour Law B.A. 1941 (Dent McCrea Prizeman, Harold G. Fox Prizeman); Osgoode Hall, Toronto, Ont. (Medallist and Christopher Robinson Mem. Prizeman); LL.D. Sir Wilfrid Laurier Univ. 1968; Honourary Doctorate, De Rerum Politicarum, Ukrainian Free Univ., Munich m. Mary Anne, d. Michael Materyn, Toronto, Ontario, 3 February 1945; CHRMN. COMMERCIAL REGISTRATION APPEAL TRIBUNAL, LIQUOR LICENCE APPEAL TRIBUNAL PROV. ONT. read law with Elliot, Hume, McKague & Hume; called to the Bar of Ont. (proxy 1944) 1946; cr. Q.C. 1953; 1st el. to Ont. Leg. for Bellwoods, g.e. 1951; re-el. 1955, 1959, 1963, 1967, 1971; apptd. Min. without Portfolio; April 1958, Min. of Transport, Dec. 1958-60, Prov. Secy. and Min. of Citizenship, 1960, Min. of Pub. Welfare Nov. 1966 (name changed to Social & Family Services Nov. 1967); Prov. Secy. and Minister of Citizenship 1971; Solicitor General 1972-74; served as 2nd Lieutenant, Canadian Infantry Corps; Dir. St. Alban's Boys Club; Hon. Pres. The Adult Cerebral Palsy Institute of Metro Toronto; mem., Candn. Bar Assn.; York Co. Law Assn.; P. Conservative; Ukrainian Orthodox; recreation: Canadiana collector; Clubs: The Lawyers (Past Pres.); Canadian; Empire; Home: 1 Connable Drive, Toronto, Ont. M5R 1Z7; Office: 1 St. Clair Ave. W., Toronto, Ont. M4V 1K6

YARMON, Elliot N., B.Sc., LL.B.; executive; b. New York, N.Y., 14 July 1919; s. J. M. and Mary (Berman) Y.; e. Coll. of City of New York, B.Sc. (Soc. Science) 1939; Columbia Univ. Law Sch., LL.B. 1946; m. Charlotte, d. S. Simon, Dec. 1941; children: James, Thomas, Mary; PRESIDENT, TANKOOS YARMON LTD.; Dir. State Mutual Investors Ltd.; Executive International Investors Ltd.; served with U.S. Army 1942-46, rank Captain; Dir.; North York General Hospital Foundation; mem., Toronto, Montreal and New York Real Estate Boards; recreations: tennis, skiing; Clubs: Donalda, Queens; Home: 91 Laurentide Dr., Don Mills, Ont. M3A 3E4; Office: 8 King St. E., Toronto, Ont. M5C 1B5

YARNELL, John R., B.Com., M.B.A.; company executive; b. Montreal, Que. 26 July 1928; s. John E. and M. (Robertson) Y.; ed. Pub. Schs., Winnipeg, Man.; Univ. of Manitoba, B. Com. 1949; Harvard Univ. M.B.A. 1952; m. Elizabeth H. d. S. P. Gemmill, 14 June 1952; children:

Sarah, Robert, Ann; CHRMN. AND CHIEF EXTVE., YCL RESOURCES INC., YARNELL COMPANIES LTD., YARNELL/TRUSTY ASSOC. INC. Norren Energy Resources Ltd.; Orion Petroleums Ltd.; Petrotech Inc.; Canadian-Dominion Leasing Corp. Ltd.; Women's College Hosp.; Pearson College; with Gulf Oil Canada 1952-64; Pres. & Chrmn., Inspiration Ltd. 1964-65; Vice Pres., Consolidated-Bathurst Ltd. 1966-73; Arctic Gas Companies, 1973-78; Presbyterian; recreations: golf, tennis, skiing, hunting; Home: 161 Roxborough Dr., Toronto, Ont. M4W 1X7; Office: Ste. 604, 11 Adelaide St. W., Toronto, Ont.

YAROSKY, Harvey W., B.A., B.C.L.; lawyer, b. Montreal, Que., 8 Dec. 1934; s. late Harry and Rhoda (Kom) Y.; e. Baron Byng High Sch. Montreal 1951; McGill Univ. B.A. 1955, B.C.L. 1961; Univ. of Paris (Inst. d'études Politiques) 1955-56; m. Elaine, d. Irving (Auckie) Sanft 3 July 1962; two d. Karen Anne, Lauren Julie; PARTNER, YAROSKY, FISH, ZIGMAN, ISAACS & DAVIAULT; read law with Joseph Cohen, Q.C. and Fred Kaufman, Q.C.; called to Bar of Que. 1962; Lectr. in Criminal Law Univ. of Montreal 1970-71; Univ. of Ottawa 1970-72; McGill Univ. 1971-77; Extve. asst. to Chrmn. Dept. of Justice (Can.) Special Comte. on Hate Propaganda 1965; mem. Govt. of Que. Adv. Council on Justice 1974-78; Counsel to Fed. Comn. of Inquiry (Marin) concerning R.C.M.P. 1974-76; Special Counsel to prov. Comn. of Inquiry on Union activities in Constr. Indust. 1974-75; Dir. John Howard Soc. Que. Inc. 1967-70; mem. Corp. of the Philippe Pinel Inst. of Montreal since 1974; a Gov. of Portage Program for Drug Dependencies Inc. since 1975; author legal articles; mem. Bar of Montreal (Comte. on Lawyer Referral Service 1968-70, mem. 1968-74 and Chrmn. 1971-74 Comte. on Adm. of Criminal Justice); Bar of Que. (Bd. of Examiners 1968-73, Cmte. on Discipline, 1975-, Chrmn. Comte. on Adm. Criminal Justice 1972-74); Candn. Bar Assn. (Chrmn. Criminal Justice Sub-Sec. Que. Br. 1970-72, Treas. 1973-74 and Vice Chrmn. Nat. Criminal Justice Sec., 1974-77); Jewish; recreations: theatre, music, reading; Club: University; Home: 492 Argyle, Westmount, Que. H3Y 3B5; Office: 1255 Phillips Sq., Montreal, Que. H3B 3G1

YARRILL, Eric Herbert, M.A., F.I.A.L.; professor; b. Heston Hounslow, Middlesex, Eng., 28 Dec. 1914; s. Herbert George and Amelia Louise (Blackford) Y.; came to Can. 1926; e. Univ. of Toronto, B.A. (Hons.) 1937, M.A. 1938; various Awards at Toronto, Paris and Chicago; Univ. of Paris, Dipl. 1938; Alliance Française de Paris, Cert. and Dipl.; Univ. of Chicago (grad. courses); PROF. EMERITUS OF MODERN LANGUAGES, BISHOPS UNIV. and with Dept. since 1938; Dir., Que. Dept. of Educ. Fr. Specialists/Summer Sch. for 5 yrs.; Visiting Prof. of Fr., Univ. of New Brunswick Summer Session, for 2 yrs.; numerous publications in Can., U.S. and German periodicals; with Reserve Army C.O.T.C., 1940-43, gaz. 2nd Lieut.; R.C.N.V.R., 1943-45, with Directorate of Naval Intel. as Lieut.; with Admiralty on loan to Royal Navy, 1944; Centennial Medal 1967; Anglican; Address: 11 High St., Lennoxville, Que. J1M 1E6

YATES, Havelock Howard, B.Sc., Ph.D.; metallurgical engineer; b. Cochrane, Ont., 27 Sept. 1918; s. James Gordon and Bertha May (Hall) Y.; e. Springfield Coll., Mass., 1939-41; McGill Univ., B.Sc. 1948, Ph.D. 1952; m. Barbara, d. late Harold B. Wood, 11 Dec. 1943; children: Barbara Lynn, Pamela Joan, Gordon Havelock; EXTVE. VICE CHRMN., ONT. COUNCIL ON GRAD. STUDIES, since 1975; with Standard Oil Development Co. N.J., 1951-52; Asst. Prof., Metall. Engn., McGill Univ., 1952-55, Assoc. Prof. 1955, Prof. 1961, Chrmn. Metall. Engn., 1961-66; Assoc. Dean, Faculty Engn. 1963-71; Vice Pres., Academic, Ryerson Polytechnical Inst. 1971-73; Consultant to the Pres. 1973-75; served in 2nd World War with R.C.A.F. 1941-45; Sigma Xi; mem., Candn. Inst. Mining & Metall.; Bd. of Trustees, Candn. Nat. Sportsmen's

Fund, 1977; Nat. Assn. Corrosion Engrs. (Offr.); recreation; swimming; Home: 39 Creekwood Drive, West Hill, Ont. M1E 4L6

YATES, J. Michael, M.A.; writer, publisher; professor; b. Minto Inlet, Victoria Island, NWT, 10 Apl. 1938; s. Joel Hume and Marjorie Diane (Carmichael) Y.; e. Univ. of Mo., B.A. 1961, M.A. 1962; Univ. of Mich., Ph.D. program in Comparative Lit. 1962-64; m. Mary Jean, d. late John Joseph West, 4 Apl. 1970; Pres., The Sono Nis Press and J. Michael Yates Ltd. since 1968; Nat. Creative & Promotional Dir., Public Radio Corp., 1961-62; Instr. Creative Writing, Ohio Univ., 1964-65; Special Lectr. Creative Writing, Comparative Lit., Univ. of Alaska, 1965-66; Visiting Asst. Prof. of Creative Writing, Univ. of B.C. 1966-67, Asst. Prof. 1967-69, Assoc. Prof. 1969-71; Visiting Prof. of Eng. & Creative Writing, Univ. of Ark. 1972; rec'd Univ. of Kans. City Poetry Prize 1960; Internat. Broadcasting Award 1961, 1962; Maj. Hopwood Award for Poetry and for Drama, 1964; Can. Council Awards 1968, 1969, 1971, Sr. Arts Award 1972-73; The Far Point Contrib. Prize for Poetry 1971; author, "Spiral of Mirrors" 1967; "Hunt in an Unmapped Interior" 1967; "Canticle for Electronic Music" (all poetry), 1967; "Man in the Glass Octopus" (fiction), 1968; "The Great Bear Lake Meditations", 1970; "Parallax" (poetry) 1971; "The Abstract Beast" (fiction & drama), 1971; "Nothing Speaks for the Blue Moraines", (poetry) 1973; "Breath of the Snow Leopard" (poetry) 1974; "The Grand Master Cranker of Racoons" (fiction) 1975; "Quarks" (drama) 1975; Ed., "Contemporary Poetry of British Columbia", Vol. 1, 1970; "Volvox: Poetry from the Unofficial Languages of Canada in English Translation", 1971; Mag. Editing, "Contemporary Literature in Translation"; "Mundus Artium" (Bd.); "Canadian Fiction Magazine" (Bd.); "Prism International" (Acting Ed.-in-Chief 1966-67; Poetry Ed. 1967-71); other writings incl. numerous dramas produced in Europe and N. Am., also CBC Radio; papers, reviews, philos. studies for various publs.; mem., Internat. P.E.N. (London Chapter); League Candn. Poets (Extve. 1970-71); Internat. Platform Assn.; Prof. Photog's Am.; Torch & Scroll; Omicron Delta Kappa; Sigma Tau Delta; Alpha Phi Omega; Tau Kappa Epsilon; recreation: fishing; Office: 1745 Blanshard St., Victoria, B.C. V8W 2J8

YATES, Peter, M.Sc., Ph.D., F.R.S.C., F.C.I.C., F.R.S.C.(C), university professor; b. Wanstead, Essex, England, 26 Aug. 1924; s. Harold Andrew and Kathlyn (Yexley) Y.; e. Bancroft's Sch., Woodford Green, Essex, Eng.; Queen Mary Coll., Univ. of London, B.Sc. (1st Class) 1946; Dalhousie Univ., M.Sc. 1948; Yale Univ., Ph.D. 1951; m. Mary Ann, d. late P. S. Palmer, 9 Sept. 1950; one s. John Anthony; step s. Wm. P. Franklin, Thomas J. Franklin; PROF. OF CHEM., UNIV. OF TORONTO, since 1960; Research Fellow, Harvard Univ. 1950-51; Instr. in Chem., Yale Univ., 1951-52; Harvard Univ., 1952-55 and Asst. Prof. there 1955-60; Sloan Foundation Fellow, 1957-60; Visiting Prof., Yale Univ. 1966; Princeton, 1977; Candn. Govt. Centennial Medalist 1968; Secy., I.U.P.A.C. Organic Chem. Div. 1973-75, Vice-Pres., 1975-77, Pres., 1977-79; mem., Am. Chem. Soc.; Candn. Inst. Chem. (Merck, Sharp and Dohme Lectr. 1963); Home: 351 St. Clair Ave. E., Toronto, Ont. M4T 1P3

YEATES, Allan Burnside, B.A.; advertising executive; b. Hamilton, Ont., 7 March 1926; s. Ralph Howard and Helen B. (Reeves) Y.; e. Westdale Secondary Sch., Hamilton, 1944; Univ. of W. Ont., Sch. of Business Adm., B.A. 1948; m. Charlotte E., d. T. S. Farley, Naples, Fla., 19 May 1948; children: Carolyn Ruth, Jody Helen, Stephen Allan, Peter Gordon, Patricia Charlotte; PRESIDENT AND C.E.O., BAKER LOVICK LTD.; Director, Comcore Communications Ltd.; Dir., Inst. of Cdn. Advertising; Gov., Cdn. Advertising Fdn.; Business writer and analyst, "Financial Post", 1948 and "Toronto Daily Star",

1949-51; Asst. Mgr., Pub. Relations and Advertising Dept., Prudential Insurance Co. of America, 1951, Mgr. 1951-53, Asst. Gen. Mgr. and Dir., Pub. Relations and Advertising, 1954-61; joined Spitzer, Mills & Bates Ltd. as Vice Pres., and Account Supvr., 1961-62, Sr. Vice Pres. and Mang. Rep., 1962-64, Extve. Vice Pres. 1964-69, Pres. and Chief Extve. Offr. 1969-72; Past Pres., Assn. Candn. Advertisers; Past Chrmn., Candn. Advt. Standards Council; Past Pres. Candn. Advt. Adv. Bd.; Past Chrmn., Inst. of Candn. Advt.; Delta Upsilon; United Church; Home: Horshoe Valley, R.R. 1, Barrie, Ont. L4M 4Y8; Office: 60 Bloor St. W., Toronto, Ont. M4W 3B8

YEO, Leslie James; actor; producer; writer; director; adjudicator; b. Swindon, Wilts., Eng., 29 May 1915; s. Frederick James and Sybil Annie (Stride) Y.; e. The Coll., Swindon, Wilts.; m. 1stly late Hilary (actress prof. known as Hilary Vernon), d. late Harold Vernon Pagniez, 11 May 1954; one s. Jamie Donald; m. 2ndly Grete Knudsen, d. late Erling Knudsen, 29 Aug. 1977; performed in over 600 roles on Brit. stage 1939-50; numerous radio, TV and film roles in Can. since 1950 and stage roles at Playhouse, Vancouver; Citadel, Edmonton; M.T.C., Winnipeg; Theatre plus, Toronto; Theatre Aquarius, Hamilton; Alley Theatre, Houston; Meadowbrook Theatre, Detroit; Shaw Festival, Niagara-on-the-Lake, 1966, 1967, 1976, 1978; Stratford Shakespearean Festival, 1975, 1977; role of Alan Brooke in world premiere of "The Soldiers", Theatre Toronto, 1968; first lead in a musical, Pop, Fraser in David Warrack's "Drummer", Banff Centre, 1980; actor-manager of London Theatre Co. in Maritimes for 6 winter seasons, 1951-57 (brought first Brit. stock co. in 30 yrs.); feature film roles: Stan Mountain in "The Luck of Ginger Coffe"; Fred Reeves in "Proper Channels", 1980; Vice Pres., Strand Electric (Can.) Ltd., 1957-61; mem., of Bd. and Extve., Candn. Opera Co., 1959-63; co-producer, "Actually this Autumn", Dell Theatre, Toronto, 1964 and "Ding Dong at the Dell", 1965; adjudicator, Dom. Drama Festival, CODL Regional Finals 1968 and WODL preliminaries 1967; EODL one-act Festival 1969; prod./dir. major industrial musicals and conventions Canada and abroad since 1966; dir. "Mrs. Warren's Profession", Shaw Festival 1976 and five prod. at Alley Theatre, Houston, Texas, 1975-78; Neptune Theatre, Halifax, 1980, 1981; Artistic Dir. Shaw Festival 1978-79; directed, "The Corn is Green"; "Blithe Spirit"; wrote and directed "Cinderella", Hamilton Place, 1980; gave Master classes in comedy technique, Banff Centre, 1980; Univ. of Alta., Edmonton, 1981; Master Class director, "The Guardsman" Banff, 1981; served with RAF in U.K., India and Burma, 1941-46; rank Sgt. on discharge; Treas. ACTRA, 1969-71; Treas. ACTRA Ins. and Retirement Plan and Fraternal Soc.; Treas., Candn. Actors' Rquity Assn., 1976-79; Comus Music Theatre of Can.; mem., Adv. Bd., Theatre Arts Prog., George Brown Coll.; Awarded Silver Jubilee Medal; P. Conservative; Anglican; recreations: golf, riding; Club: Celebrity; Address: 19 Binscarth Rd., Toronto, Ont. M4W 1Y2

YEO, Ronald Frederick, B.L.S.; librarian; b. Woodstock, Ont. 13 Nov. 1923; s. Frederick Thomas and Jugertha Aleda (Vansickle) Y.; e. Univ. of Toronto B.A. 1948, B.L.S. 1967; m. Margaret Elizabeth d. Frederick Horsley 12 Sept. 1953; children: Joanne, Peter; CHIEF LIBRARIAN, REGINA PUBLIC LIBRARY 1972- ; mem. Adv. Bd. Kelsey Inst. Lib. Program; Chrmn. Steering Comte. Project: Progress (future of pub. libs. in Can.); served with RCAF 1942-45; Mgr. Book Dept., American News Co. Toronto 1948-53; Sales Mgr., Dir., British Book Service, Toronto 1953-63; Mgr. Trade Div. Collier-Macmillan Canada Ltd. Toronto 1963-65; Pub. Services Coordinator, North York Pub. Lib. 1966-1971; rec'd Queen's Silver Jubilee Medal 1977; mem. Candn. Lib. Assn. (Pres. 1978-79); Candn. Assn. Pub. Libs. (Chrmn. 1975-76); Administrators of Large Pub. Libs. (Chrmn. 1973-74); Club: Kiwanis; Home: 1453 Parker Ave., Regina, Sask. S4S 4R7; Office: 2311 - 12th Ave., Regina, Sask. S4P 0N3.

YEOMANS, Donald Ralph, B.A.Sc., P.Eng., R.I.A.; federal public servant; b. Toronto, Ont. 25 March 1925; s. Ralph and Louise Margaret (Weismiller) Y.; e. Humbercrest Pub. Sch. and Humberside Coll. Inst. Toronto; Univ. of Toronto B.A.Sc. 1947; Urwick Mang. Centre, Slough, 1960; m. Catharine Simpson d. William F. Williams. Toronto, Ont. 13 May 1950; children: Patricia (Mrs. Danyluk), Nancy (Mrs. Love), Jane; COMMR: OF CORRECTIONS, since 1978; Design Engr. Eastern Steel Products Ltd. Toronto 1947, Sales Engr. 1948; Field Engr. Canadian Comstock Co. Ltd. 1949, Chief Field Engr. 1951. Coordinator of Operations 1952, Area Supt. 1956; joined Urwick Currie Ltd. as Mang. Consultant 1959, Sr. Consultant 1961; Dir. Organ. Research Group, Royal (Glassco) Comn. on Govt. Organ. 1961; joined Cabinet Secretariat to implement Glassco recommendations 1962, Special Adv. Bureau of Govt. Organ. 1963, Asst. to Secy. to Treasury Bd. 1964, Deputy Secy. to Treasury Bd. in charge of Mang. Improvement Br. 1965; responsible for coordinating all interaction between Expo 67, Privy Council Office and Treasury Bd.; Bicultural Program Quebec City 1968; Special Adv. to Chrmn. Comitée Mineau 1969; Asst. Depy. Min. Dept. Supply and Services 1969, named by Auditor Gen. as mem. Steering Comte. to study Financial Mang. and Controls Govt. Can. 1974, Assoc. Extve. Dir. Anti-Inflation Bd. 1975, Special Adv. Royal Comn. Inquiry Financial Organ. and Accountability in Govt. of Can. (Lambert Comn.) 1977; Asst. Depy. Min. Admin., Dept. of Nat. Health and Welfare, 1977; apptd. Lectr. Extension Dept. Carleton Univ. 1964; has served as mem. numerous adv. comtes. various univs.; rec'd Centennial Medal 1967; Jubilee Medal 1977; Dir. Ottawa YM-YWCA 1965; Extve. Comte. Ottawa Red Cross 1967; Dir. Un. Way of Can. 1975; served Un. Ch. of Can. in numerous extve. positions; Fellow, Soc. of Management Accountants of Can. (F.S.M.A.C); mem. Inst. Pub. Adm. Can. (Pres. 1974); Soc. Indust. Accts. Can. (Pres. 1977); Men's Canadian Club of Ottawa (Pres. 1978); mem., Bd. of Gov. Carleton Univ., 1980; Beta Theta Pi; United Church; recreations: skiing, fishing; Clubs: Five Lakes Fishing (Pres. 1975); Home: 310 Clemow Ave., Ottawa, Ont. K1S 2B8; Office: Sir Wilfred Laurier Bldg., Ottawa, Ont.

YOLTON, John W., M.A., D.Phil., LL.D.; educator; b. Birmingham, Ala., 20 Nov. 1921; s. Robert Elgene and Ella Maude (Holmes) Y.; e. Univ. of Cincinnati, B.A. 1945, M.A. (Philos.) 1946; Univ. of Cal. Berkeley, grad. student and teaching asst., 1946-49 (Fellow in Philos. 1949-50); Balliol Coll., Oxford Univ., D. Phil. 1952 (Fulbright Scholar); m. Jean Mary, d. late Joseph Sebastian, 5 Sept. 1945; two d., Karin Frances (Mrs. Bryant Griffith), Pamela Holmes; PROF., DEPT. OF PHILOS., YORK UNIV., since 1968 (Chrmn. Dept. 1963-79 acting Pres. of the Univ. 1973-74); Visiting Lectr. in Philos., The Johns Hopkins Univ., 1952-53; Lectr. Univ. of Baltimore 1952; Asst. Prof., Princeton Univ., 1953-56, 1956-57 and Jonathan Dickinson Preceptor, 1953-56; Assoc. Prof., Kenyon Coll., 1957-60; Prof., Univ. of Md., 1961-63; Acting Dean of Grad. Studies of present Univ., 1967-68; rec'd F. C. S. Schiller Essay Prize 1948; A. S. Eddington Essay Prize 1956; Leonard Nelson Essay Prize 1959; Can. Council Fellowship 1968-69; mem. Ed. Bd. and Consultant, "Studies in the History and Philosophy of Science"; "American Philophical Quarterly"; "Journal of the History of Philosophy"; "Philosophy of the Social Sciences"; "Studi Internazionali di Filosofia"; Ed., "Locke's Essay Concerning Human Understanding", 2 vols. 1961; "Theory of Knowledge", 1965; "John Locke: Problems and Perspectives", 1969; author, "John Locke and the Way of Ideas", 1956; "The Philosophy of Science of A. S. Eddington", 1960; "Thinking and Perceiving: A Study in the Philosophy of Mind", 1962. "Metaphysical Analysis", 1967; "Locke and the Compass of Human Understanding", 1970; "Locke and Education" 1971; other writings incl. numerous articles in 17th Century and modern philos., epistemol. and metaphysics for various journs.; Fellow, Am. Council Learned Soc's, 1960-61; recreation: tennis; Home: 18 Paulson Rd., Toronto, Ont. M6M 2H3

YONGE, Keith A., M.D., C.M., D.P.M., F.R.C.P.(C), F.R.C.P. (U.K.), F.A.C.P.; psychiatrist; educator; b. London, Eng., 22 June 1910; s. Frank Arthur and Alice Maud (Liddle) Y.; e. Tollington Sch., London, Eng., 1928; McGill Univ., M.D., C.M. 1948; Univ. of London, D.P.M. 1952; m. Jane Elizabeth, d. Orval L. Beatty, Victoria, B.C.; 21 June 1948; children: Keith S., Martin B., Devon Anne, Janet E.; Prof. And Chrmn., Dept. Of Psychiatry, Univ. Of Alberta 1957-75; Prof. Emeritus since 1975; Phys., Med. Specialist (Psychiatrist), Univ. Hosp.; Gen. Mgr., Labrador Development Co., 1935-42; Dir., Mental Health Clinic, Moose Jaw, Sask., 1952; Asst. Prof., Dept. Psychiatry, Univ. of Sask., 1954, Assoc. Prof. 1956; rec'd Centennial Medal 1967; author over 40 publs. in prof. and scient. journs.; mem. Alta. Med. Assn.; Candn. Med. scient. journs.; mem. Alta. Med. Assn.; Candn. Med. Assn.; Candn. Psychiatric Assn. (Pres. 1970-71); Am. Psychiatric Assn.; World Psychiatric Assn.; Inter-Am. Council Psychiatric Assn. (Pres. 1973); Candn. Mental Health Assn. (Past Chrmn., Nat. Scient. Planning Council); P. Conservative; Anglican; recreations: hiking, swimming, skiing, tennis, photography; Home: 4345 Kingscote Rd., Cobble Hill, B.C.

YOST, Elwy McMurran, B.A.; television executive producer and host; author; b. Weston, Ont. 10 July 1925; s. Elwy Honderich and Annie Josephine (McMurran) Y.; e. Weston Coll. & Vocational Sch. 1943; Univ. of Toronto B.A. 1948; m. Lila Ragnhild d. Monrad Melby, North Surrey, B.C. 16 June 1951; two s. Christopher, Graham Boz; EXTVE. PRODUCER AND HOST ("Saturday Night at the Movies", "Magic Shadows", "Talking Film") and Exec. Producer of "Rough Cuts" TV ONTARIO 1974- ; joined Circulation Dept. Toronto Star 1948-52; prof. actor in Ont. (summer stock) 1946-53; Human Relations Counselor, Avro Aircraft 1953-59; Eng. Teacher Burnhamthorpe Coll. Inst. 1959-64; TV Producer, Metrop. Educ. TV Assn. Toronto 1964-66, Extve. Dir. 1967-70; Supt. of Regional Liaison, TV Ontario 1970-73; served with Candn. Army 1944-45, writer/actor Candn. Army Show 1945; author "Magic Moments From The Movies" 1978; "Secret of the Lost Empire" 1980; various articles on cinema, TV and educ., radio plays CBC; currently writing children's novel "Billy and the Bubble Ship" and mystery novel "Kreeps"; mem. Ont. Secondary Sch. Teachers Fed.; Assn. Candn. TV & Radio Artists; Protestant; recreations: walking; attending movies, theatres & art galleries, reading, loafing, travelling; Club: Arts & Letters; Sons of the Desert; Home: 15 Sir Williams Lane, Islington, Ont. M9A 1T8; Office: (P.O. Box 200, Stn. Q) 2180 Yonge St., Toronto, Ont. M4T 2T1.

YOUNG, Charles Bellamy, M.A.; financial executive; b. Middletown, Conn. 7 Aug. 1940; s. Harold Buckley and Margaretta (Schaefer) Y.; e. elem. and high schs. Middletown and Watertown, Conn. 1958; Yale Univ. B.A. 1962; Johns Hopkins Univ. Sch. Advanced Internat. Studies M.A. 1964; m. Carol Ann d. late Joseph Claude Lombardi 31 Aug. 1963; two s. Alexander B., Christopher B.; PRES. AND CEO. CITICORP CANADA 1978- ; Sr. Vice Pres., Citibank, N.A.; joined Citibank, N.A. 1964; Bogota, Columbia 1965; Training Dir. Internat. Personnel Unit, N.Y. 1967; Extve. Vice Pres. and CEO, Taiwan First Investment Co. Ltd., Taipei 1971; assigned to N.Y. 1972; Pres. and Dir., General Citibank France 1974; author "A Nation Without Coins" 1965; recreations: travel, art, architecture, sailing; Clubs: Yale (N.Y.); Travellers (Paris); Cambridge (Toronto); Empire: Canadian; Bd. Trade Metrop. Toronto; Home: 470 Russell Hill Rd., Toronto, Ont. M5P 2S7; Office: 3400-First Canadian Pl., 100 King St. W., Toronto, Ont. M5X 1C3.

YOUNG, Hon. Douglas Haig, M.H.A.; politician; b. Upper Island Cove, Nfld. 13 Apl. 1928; s. John and Bertha Y.; e. Upper Island Cove; Mem. Univ. of Nfld.; m. Shirley d. Weston Farrar, Bell Island, Nfld. 8 Aug. 1951; children: Douglas, Marina;MIN. OF PUBLIC WORKS & SERVICES, NFLD.1979- ; funeral dir.; mem. first Town Council Upper Island Cove 1965; Justice of the Peace 1966; el. M.H.A. for Harbour Grace prov. g.e. 1972, re-el. since; Freemason; P. Conservative; Anglican; Office: Confederation Bldg., St. John's, Nfld. A1C 5T7.

YOUNG, Eric Thomas; banker; b. Kent, Eng. 19 Jan. 1920; s. late Vyvyan Leigh and Winifred Constance (Deane) Y.; e. Latymer Upper Coll. London, Eng.; m. Daphne Marguerite d. late Dr. A. R. Dale 19 Aug. 1950; one s. Ian D. V.; SENIOR VICE-PRES., NORTHLAND BANK since 1976; joined National Westminster Bank 1936-76, Mgr. City Office (London) 1968-73, Gen. Mgr. and Dir. Natwest Canada Ltd. (Toronto) 1973-76; served with Brit. Armed Forces 1939-46, Anti Tank Offr., N. Africa Italy Greece and Austria; Assoc. Inst. Bankers; Vice-Pres., Extve. Council Candn. Bankers Assn.; Calgary Chamber Comm.; recreations: golf, cross country skiing, history, travel; Clubs: Glencoe; Petroleum; Pinebrook Golf & Winter; Bayview Country (Toronto); Office: 324-8th Ave., Calgary, Alta. T2P 2Z2.

YOUNG, Hon. Leslie Gordon, M.L.A., B.A., M.Sc.; politician; b. Compton, Que. 19 Aug. 1934; s. Gordon F. and Lena N. (Cairns) Y.; e. Compton, Waterville and Lennoxville schs.; Park Business Coll. Hamilton; Univ. of Montreal B.A.; Univ. of Mass. M.S.; m. Helen G. d. John G. McKirdy, Thunder Bay, Ont. 28 June 1958; two d. Susan L., Mary A.;MIN. OF LABOUR, ALTA.1979- ; econ. and business consultant; el. M.L.A. for Edmonton Jasper Place prov. g.e. 1971, re-el. since; mem. Candn. Inst. Pub. Adm.; Edmonton Chamber Comm.; P. Conservative; Presbyterian; Office: 404 Legislative Bldg., Edmonton, Alta. T5K 2B6.

YOUNG, Neil Percival; musician; b. Toronto, Ont. 12 Nov. 1945; s. Scott Young; first performed with rock band Squires" in Man. and N. Ont. 1962-64; performed with Mynah Birds Toronto coffeehouses and later in Detroit; formed rock group Buffalo Springfield, Los Angeles 1966-68; performed with Crosby Stills Nash and Young 1969-74 and with Stills 1976; solo career began 1968 performing alone or with accompanying group Crazy Horse throughout N. Am., Europe and Japan during 1970's; Inducted into Canadian Hall of Fame 14 April 1982; named Best Male Singer and Best Composer 1971 and album "After the Gold Rush" voted Best Album 1970 by Melody Maker readers; his numerous songs incl. "Expecting to Fly", "Broken Arrow", "I Am a Child", "Country Girl", "Helpless", "Ohio", "Southern Man", "Round and Round", "Everyone Knows This is Nowhere", "Only Love Can Break Your Heart", "Tell Me Why", "Cinnamon Girl", "Heart of Gold", "Lotta Love"; rec'd numerous gold record sales awards for albums 1969-74 and million-selling hit song "Heart of Gold" 1972; various anthols. of songs published; wrote soundtrack autobiographical film "Journey Through the Past"; documentary "Rust Never Sleeps" of Young in concert released 1979;

YOUNG, Scott Alexander, journalist; author; b. Glenboro, Man. 14 Apl. 1918; s. Percy Andrew and Jean Ferguson (Paterson) Y.; e. Kelvin Tech. High Sch. Winnipeg; m. Edna B. Ragland June 1940; two s. Robert, Neil; m. Astrid e. Mead May 1961; two d. Deirdre, Astrid; m. Margaret Hogan, May, 1980; Columnist, Globe and Mail, 1971-80 and 1957-69; Pres. Ascot Productions Ltd.; Journalist, Winnipeg Free Press 1936-40; The Candn. Press 1940-43, 1945, Corr. in London 1942-43; Asst. Ed. Maclean's 1945-48; Sports Ed. Toronto Telegram 1969-71; author 28 books and 75 published short stories; rec'd Nat. Newspaper Award 1959; CBC Wilderness Award for TV script 1962; served with RCNVR 1944-45, Europe, Mediterranean (Italy, Yugoslavia, Greece); Fellow, McLaughlin Coll. York Univ.; mem. Candn. War Corr's Assn.; Writers Union Can.; Protestant; recreations: walking, amateur study flora and fauna; Home and Office: R.R.2, Cavan, Ont. L0A 1C0

YOUNG, William H.; company executive; b. Hamilton, Ont., 21 Dec. 1918; s. James Vernon and Willmot (Holton) Y.; e. Grove Sch., Lakefield, Ont.; Hillfield Sch., Hamilton, Ont.; Royal Mil. Coll.; Univ. of Toronto; m. Joyce, d. Gordon Ferrie, 4 May 1946; children: Gordon Douglas, Catherine Frances, William James; PRESIDENT AND DIR., THE HAMILTON GROUP LTD. since 1960; Dir., Harding Carpets Ltd.; Steel Co. of Canada Ltd.; National Trust Co. Ltd.; Gore Mutual Insurance Company; Gulf Oil Canada Ltd.; worked in textile industry in N.C., 1946-47; joined Hamilton Cotton Co. Ltd., (predecessor firm) 1947; apptd. Gen. Works Mgr., 1951; Dir., 1954; Vice-Pres. and Gen. Mgr., 1956; served in 2nd World War with Candn. Army with rank of Maj., 1939-45; Presbyterian; recreation: golf; Clubs: Hamilton Golf & Country; Home: Sulphur Springs Rd., Ancaster, Ont., Office: 5050 South Service Road, Burlington, Ont. L7L 44Y7

YOUNG, William James, B.A.; company executive; b. Windsor; Ont. 10 May 1927; s. Reginald Sebastien Fruschard and Mary Janet (Grieves) Y.; e. Walkerville Coll., Windsor 1940-45; Univ. of Toronto, Victoria Coll. B.A. (Hons. Pol. Science and Econs., Gold Medal) 1949; m. Betty Jean, d. late Arthur Robert Davidson, 15 Sept. 1951; children: Robert Scott, Susan; SR. VICE PRES. AND DIR., IMPERIAL OIL LTD.; with Ford of Canada 1949-53; Chrysler of Canada 1953-59; The Steel Co. of Canada 1959-61; joined present Co. in 1961; Dir., The Arthritis Soc.; Anglican; recreations: gardening, writing; Clubs: University (Toronto); Manitoba (Winnipeg); Office: 111 St. Clair Ave. W., Toronto, Ont. M5W 1K3

YOUNGER, James Wallace, Q.C., B.A., B. Comm. company executive; b. Ottawa, Ont. 2 Feb. 1924; s. Lloyd Robert and Edith Margaret (Galloway) Y.; e. Univ. of Toronto Victoria Coll. B.A. 1945; Osgoode Hall Law Sch. 1948; Carleton Coll. B.Comm. 1952; m. Phyllis May, d. Stanley A. Boswell, Burlington, Ont. 3 May 1952; three s., Arthur, Douglas, Calvin; VICE PRES., SECY. AND GEN. COUNSEL, STELCO INC. since 1974; read law with McMillan, Binch; called to Bar of Ont. 1948; cr. Q.C. 1970; Partner, May, McMichael & Younger 1948-58; joined Law Dept. present co. 1958, Asst. Secy. 1961, Secy. and Mgr. Law Dept. 1964, Secy. and Gen. Counsel 1970; former Chrmn. Ottawa Rental Reference Bd.; Ottawa Court Revision; Gov. and Vice-Chrm. of the Bd. N. York Gen. Hosp.; Dir., Shaw Industries Ltd.; mem. Candn. Bar Assn.; Law Soc. Upper Can.; Am. Soc. Corp. Secys., Inc.; York Co. Law Assn.; Assn. Candn. Gen. Counsel; Candn. Mfrs.' Assn. Bd. Trade Metrop. Toronto; Am. Iron and Steel Inst.; The Cdn. Chamber of Commerce - Corp. Affairs Cmte.; Delta Chi; P. Conservative; Presbyterian; Clubs: Toronto; Hamilton; Home: 48 Riverview Dr., Toronto, Ontario M4N 3C7; Office: (P.O. Box 205) Toronto-Dominion Centre, Toronto, Ont. M5K 1J4

YUZYK, Hon. Paul, M.A., Ph.D., LL.D; senator; b. Pinto, Sask., 24 June 1913; s. Martin and Katherine (Chaban) Y.; e; Bedford Rd. Coll. Inst., Saskatoon, 1924-32; Saskatoon Normal Sch. 1932-33; Univ. of Saskatchewan, B.A., 1945, B.A.Hon., 1947, M.A. 1948; Univ. of Minnesota, Ph.D. (Hist.) 1958; Univ. of Sask., LL.D. 1977; Fellow, Man. Hist. Soc., 1948; m. Mary, d. John and Irene Bahniuk, Hafford, Sask., 12 July, 1941; children: Evangeline Paulette (Mrs. George Duravetz), Victoria Irene (Mrs. Robert Karpiak), Vera Catherine, Theodore Ronald; Teacher, Sask. Sch. 1933-42; High Sch. 1940-42; Asst. Prof. in Slavic Studies and Hist. at Univ. of Manitoba, 1951-58; Assoc. Prof., 1958-63; Prof., Russian and Soviet Hist. and Candn.-Soviet Relations, Univ. of Ottawa 1966-

78; Mem. Bd. of Dir., Station CHIN, Toronto 1972-78; served in 2nd World War, Candn. Army, N.C.O., 1942-43; summoned to the Senate of Can., 4 Feb. 1963; Observer, Candn. del. to U.N., 18th Gen. Assembly, 1963; Dir., Research, "Statistical Compendium on Ukrainians in Canada 1891-1976"; reports of Senate Standing Comtes. Foreign Affairs, National Finance; Special Comtes. on Science Policy, Mass Media; author: "The Ukrainians in Manitoba: A Social History", 1953, second ed., 1977; "Ukrainian Canadians: Their Place and Role in Canadian Life" (also transl. French) 1967; "Ukrayintsi v Kanadi: Yikh Rozvytok i Dosyahnennia" 1968; "Concern for Canadian Cultural Rights" 1968; "For a Better Canada" 1973; co-ed., "A Statistical Compendium on the Ukrainians in Canada, 1891-1976", 1980; "The Ukrainian Greek Orthodox of Canada, 1918-1951", 1981; also author of numerous articles on Ukrainian and multicultural topics; co-author, "Ukrainian Reader", 1958; contrib. to Encyc. Canadiana, 1958; Candn. Parlty. del. to: Poland Milenium 1966, 18th, 20th, 21st, 22nd, 23rd, 24th, 25th, 26th, 27th North Atlantic Assembly 1972, 74, 75, 76, 77, 78, 79, 80, 81, Consultive Assembly Council Europe 1974; Assembly of Council of Europe (France) 1974; NATO, Denmark 1975, Virginia 1976; France 1977; Portugal 1978; Canada 1979; Helsinki Review Conference, Belgrade, Yugoslavia 1977 and 1978; Helsinki Review Conference, Madrid, Spain, 1980-81; 34th Gen. Assembly of U.N., 1979; also served on numerous Parlty. Comte.; and many articles to prof. journals and magazines; member, Ukrainian National Youth Federation (President 4 terms); Council mem., Ukrainian Candn. Comte., 1951-63; Editor, Trans. of the Man; Hist. Soc., 1953-59; mem., Ed. Bd. of Man. Pageant, since 1958; Vice Chrm., Candn. NATO Parlty. Assn., 1975- ; Candn. Interparlty. Union; Commonwealth Parlty. Assn.; Pres., Ukrainian Cultural and Educ. Centre, Winnipeg, 1955-1971; Pres., Canadian Assn. of Slavists, 1963-64; Pres., Man. Hist. Soc., 1961-63; Director, Canadian Centenary Council (1963); Dir., Candn. Soc. for Abolition of the Death Penalty; Dir., Winnipeg Symphony Orchestra 1962-68; Chrmn., Human Rights Comn., World Cong. Free Ukrainians trans., 1961- ; Chrmn., Can. Folk Arts Comn., 1975-80, President 1980- ; Director, Canadian Council Christians and Jews; Dir., Nat. Bd., Canada's Birthday, Celebrations, Ottawa, 1980; Vice-Chrmn., Candn. Parlty. Helsinki Group, 1977; mem., Ed. Bd. "Studia Ucrainica" (Periodical) 1978- ; Candn. Scholarship Trust Foundation; rec'd Centennial Medal 1967; Taras Shevchenko Gold Medal, Ukrainian Candn. Congress 1968; Man. Centennial Medal 1970; City of Sudbury 1972; Ukrainian Candn. Comte. (Toronto) Gold Medal 1973; Silver Jubilee Medal, 1977; P. Conservative; Ukrainian Catholic; Home: 1839 Camborne Cres., Ottawa, Ont. K1H 7B6; Office: Rm. 207 EB, The Senate, Ottawa, Ont. K1A 0A4

Z

ZACK, Badanna, B.A., M.F.A., R.C.A.; sculptor; b. Montreal, Que. 22 March 1933; d. William and Sophie (Feigelson) Zack; e. Concordia Univ. B.A. 1964; Rutgers Univ. M.F.A. 1967; rep. in exhns. Can., USA and Europe; Home: 28 MacPherson Ave., #206, Toronto, Ont. M5R 1W8; Studio: 9 Davies Ave., 4th Fl., Toronto, Ont.

ZACKS, Mrs. Ayala Fleg, O.C.(1972), LL.D.; art collector; b. Jerusalem, 31 Dec. 1912; d. Samuel and Rache (Berman) Bentovim; e. Schs., Jerusalem; Coll. Feminin de Bouffemont, Paris 1930; The Sorbonne (courses in French Civilization) 1932; London Sch. of Econ. (Social Science and Social Work) 1934; Columbia Univ. and N.Y. Univ. (Art Hist.); Museum of Modern Art, N.Y. (Museum Adm.) 1951-53; LL.D. Toronto 1971; m. late Samuel Jacob Z. (deceased 1970) 1947; active in French Resistance 1940-45; in Eng. 1942 with Free French; landed with Allied Forces, Europe 1944, rank Capt.; Liaison Offr. detached from French Army to Allied H.Q. G5 Displaced Person SHAEF, Frankfurt with assimilated rank of Col. 1945-46; relief work in concentration camps 1946; i/c French Pavillion, Levant Fair, Palestine 1936 and Palestine Pavilion, Internat. Exposition, Paris 1937; came to Canada 1947; Exhns. of the Ayala and Samuel Zacks Collection incl. Art Gallery Ont. and major museums in Can., U.S. and Israel; built with Mr. Zacks the Hazor Archaeol. Museum at Ayelet-Hashachar 1955-57; donated a collection of some 100 Candn. paintings, sculpture and Eskimo art to Queens Univ. 1963 and the Sam and Ayala Zacks Collection to Art Gallery Ont. 1970; Past Pres., Toronto Chapter, Candn. Wizo-Hadassah; Toronto chapter, Friends of Hebrew Univ.; Past Chrmn., Women's Div., State of Israel Bonds; Chrmn., Study of Public Attitudes to Modern Art; Henry Moore Sculpture Comte. Toronto; mem. Bd. Govs., ICOM Foundation; Weizman Inst. Science; Hebrew Univ.; Jerusalem; Hon. Patron, Royal Ont. Museum; mem. Bd., Art Gallery Ont.; Internat. Council Museums; Can.-Israel Cultural Fund; Am.-Israel Cultural Fund; mem. Internat. Bd., Israel Museum, Jerusalem; Internat. Council, Museum Modern Art, N.Y.; Co-Founder and Pres. (1964) Nat. Youth Orchestra Can.; rec'd (first Candn.) Eleanor Roosevelt Humanities Award 1970; portrait painted by J. Zaretski; Jewish; recreations: yoga, golf; Club: Oakdale Golf & Country.

ZARUBY, Walter Stephen, B.A.Sc.; industrialist; b. Vegreville, Alta., 4 March 1930; e. Univ. of Toronto, B.A.Sc. (Engn. and Business) 1952; m. Beth Fargey; children: Stephen, Jeffrey; PRESIDENT, RADIUM HOLDINGS LTD. AND RADIUM RESOURCES LTD. since 1977; Dir., Aberford Resources Ltd.; joined The Shell Oil Co. Ltd., various engn. and field operating assignments, Can. and U.S. 1952-65; organized offshore drilling programs, W. and E. Coast Can., Shell Canada Ltd. 1965; Offshore Project Mgr., W. Coast Drilling Program, Shell Canada Ltd. 1967; Offshore Devel. Mgr. 1969; Sr. Vice Pres., Drilling, Westburne International Industries Ltd. 1970, Pres., 1973-76; Clubs: Calgary Golf & Country; Calgary Petroleum; Glencoe; The Ranchmans; Home: 1012 Bel-Aire Drive S.W., Calgary, Alta. T2V 2B9; Office: 2500 - 144 4 Ave. S.W., Calgary, Alta. T2P 3N4

ZASLOW, Morris, Ph.D.; educator; b. Rosthern, Sask., 22 Dec. 1918; s. Isaac and Bessie (Hardin) Z.; e. Parkdale Pub. Sch., Edmonton, Alta., 1925-32; Eastwood High Sch., Edmonton, Alta., 1932-36; Univ. of Alta., B.A. 1940, Coll. of Educ. Specialist Cert. in Hist. 1941, B.Ed. 1942; Univ. of Toronto, M.A. 1948, Ph.D. 1957; m. Betty Winifred, d. Robert J. Stone, Devon, Eng., 3 Oct. 1945; one s. Jonathan; PROF. OF HIST., SOCIAL SCIENCE CENTRE, UNIVERSITY OF WESTERN ONTARIO, since 1965; High School Teacher, Hillspring (1941-42), Big Valley (1946) and Trochu (1946-47) all in Alberta; Lecturer Carleton College (now Carleton University), 1950-52; Lectr., Univ. of Toronto, 1952-59; Asst. Prof. 1959-64, Assoc. Prof. 1964-65; Visiting Prof. of Can. Studies, Univ. of Calgary, 1979-80; served with RCAF, Radar Mech. Service, in Can. and U.K., 1942-45; author of "The Opening of the Canadian North 1870-1914", 1971; "Reading the Rocks: The Story of the Geological Survey of Canada 1842-1972", 1975; Editor, "The Defended Border: Upper Canada and the War of 1812", 1964; Ed., "A Century of Canada's Arctic Islands, 1880-1980", 1981; "Ontario History", 1956-62; "Issues in Canadian History"; Gen. Ed., Champlain Soc., 1961-71; Adv. Ed., "Encyclopedia Americana"; has written numerous articles mainly upon aspects of Canada's Northern devel.; rec'd Candn. Social Science Research Council Fellowship, 1949; Rockefeller Fund Grants, 1955, 1956; Can. Council Fellowships, 1960, 1966, 1968, 1969; Nuffield Foundation Travelling Fellowship in Humanities, 1960-61; Killam Sr. Research Fellowship 1973-74; Centennial Medal; Cruikshank Medal; member Hist. Advisory Committee, Metrop. Toronto and Region Conservation Authority, 1958-65; mem. Archaeol. and Hist. Sites Bd. Ont.; Pres. (1966-67), Ont.

Hist. Soc.; Vice-Pres., Champlain Soc.; Fellow, Roy. Soc. of Can.; Chmn. and organizer of symposium "A Century of Canada's Arctic Islands, 1880-1980", 1980 (for Royal Soc.); Arctic Inst. of North Am.; mem., Canadian Hist. Association; Royal Commonwealth Soc.; Royal Candn. Geog. Soc.; Hebrew; recreations: stamp collecting; travel; Home: 838 Waterloo St., London, Ont. N6A 3W6

ZEIDLER, Eberhard Heinrich, Dipl. Ing., F.R.A.I.C., R.C.A.; O.A.Q. architect; b. Germany; e. Weimar during Bauhaus revival post 1945; Univ. Karlsruhe, summa cum laude 1949; m. Phyllis Jane, d. Robert Abbott, 26 Jan. 1957; PARTNER, ZEIDLER ROBERTS PARTNERSHIP/ARCHITECTS (formerly Craig Zeidler Strong); Since 1951 has been responsible for the design devel. of all projects of firm; Lectr. in Arch., Univ. of Toronto 1953-55; mem. City of Toronto Planning Bd., 1972-75; Dir., Harbourfront Corp., 1978-79; some major projects: Whitby Gen. Hosp.; Ontario Place, Toronto; McMaster Univ. Health Sciences Centre; called obsolescence-proof by 1969 World Hosp. Congress; Fanshawe Coll. of Applied Arts & Technol., London, Ont.; Physical Sciences Bldg., Univ. of Guelph; Dumont Hosp., Moncton; Chalmers Hosp., Fredericton; Saint John Regional Hosp.; Hotel L'Abri, Mont Ste Marie, Que.; Detroit Gen. Hosp.; Wayne State Univ. Clinic; Eaton Centre, Toronto; Health Sciences Centre, Univ. of Alta., Walter C. McKenzie Health Sciences Centre Edmonton; Young People's Theatre, Toronto; Queen's Quay Terminal, Toronto; Discovery Bay, Hong Kong; Endicott Centre, St. Petersburg, Fla.; Yerba Buena Centre, San Francisco; over 60 nat. and internat. awards incl.: Massey Medals and mentioned for outstanding Candn. arch.; Nat. Design Awards 1962, 67, 72; O.M.R. Council Design Awards 1964, 65, 66, 68, 70, 71, 73; Award of Excellence, "Candn. Arch." 1969, 70, 71, 74; Eedee Award 1971; Prestressed Concrete Inst. Award 1970; Am. Iron & Steel Inst. Award 1973; Progressive Arch. Design Award 1972; l'Orde des Architectes du Québec 1978; Am. Soc. of Interior Designers (ASID) Internat. Design Award (Ont. Place, 1975); Am. Soc. of Landscape Architects (ASLA) Internat. Design Award (Ont. Place, 1975); Ont. Assoc. of Architects, Design Award, 1976; Engineering Soc. of N.Y., Outstanding Achievement Award, 1980; Urban Design Award 1978; Detroit Chapter AIA, Honor Award, 1979; AIA Honor Award, 1980; Urban Design Awards for Excellence, 1980; author of over 200 major articles in leading prof. mags. incl. Domus, Bauen + Wohnen, L'Architecture Aujourd'hui, Candn. and Am. journs.; author of "Healing the Hospital"; "Multi-Use Architecture", served on juries for Candn. Arch. Yearbook Awards 1967; O.M.R. Design Awards 1973; 22nd Progressive Arch. Awards Program 1974; Minnesota Society AIA, Awards Program, 1980; Ohio Chapter AIA Awards Program, 1980; 1981 Louis Sullivan Award; has been Guest Lecturer, Nihon Univ. (Japan); Cornell, U.C.L.A.; Univ. of Munich; Columbia Univ.; Clubs: Badmington & Racquet Club, Toronto; Osler Bluff Ski Club; R.C.Y.C., Toronto; Office: 98 Queen St. E., Toronto, Ont. M5C 1S7

ZEIGLER, Earle Frederick, M.A., Ph.D., LL.D. (Windsor); educator; b. New York, N.Y. 20 August 1919; s. Clarence M. Shinkle and Margaret C. (Beyerkohler) Z.; e. Bates Coll., B.A. (German) 1940; Arnold Coll., Minor Phys. Educ. 1944; Yale Univ. M.A. (German) 1944; Columbia Univ., Grad. Minor Health & Phys. Educ. 1946; Yale Univ., Ph.D. (Educ.) 1951; Univ. of Windsor, Hon. LL.D. 1975; m. Bertha M;, d. Hazen R. Bell 25 June 1941; children: Donald Hazen, Barbara Ann; PROF., FACULTY OF PHYS. EDUC., UNIV. OF WESTERN ONT. since 1971; Assoc. Phys. and Aquatic Dir., YMCA, Bridgeport, Conn. 1941; Instr. in German, Univ. of Conn. 1943-47, in Phys. Educ., Yale Univ. 1943-49; joined present Univ. as Asst. Prof. in Phys., Health & Recreation Educ. and Lectr. in German 1949 (Prof. and Head Dept. Phys., Health & Recreation Educ. 1950-56); Assoc. Prof. of Sch. of Educ. and Supvr. Phys. Educ. & Athletics, Univ. of

Mich. 1956-63 (Chrmn. Dept. Phys. Educ. in Sch. of Educ. 1961-63); Prof., Dept. Phys. Educ. for Men, Coll. Phys. Educ., Univ. of Ill. 1963-72 (Head Dept. 1964-68); re-joined present Univ. as Prof., Phys. Educ. 1971 (Dean of Faculty, 1972-77); Fellow, Am. Acad. Phys. Educ.; Philos. Educ. Soc.; Hon. fellow, Soc. Mun. Recreational Dirs. Ont.; Am. Assn. for Health, Phys. Educ. & Recreation; Coll. Phys. Educ. Assn.; Am. Philos. Assn.; Philos. Soc. for Study of Sport (Pres., 1974); Candn. Assn. Health, Phys. Educ. & Recreation (Vice-Pres. 1952-53); Ont. Recreation Assn. (Vice-Pres., 1955-56); author of 'Administration of Physical Education and Athletics'' 1959; "Philosophical Foundations for Physical, Health, and Recreation Education" 1964; "Physical Education: Progressivism or Essentialism?'' 1966; "Problems in the History and Philosophy of Physical Education and Sport'' 1968; "Research in the History, Philosophy and Comparative Aspects of Physical Education and Sport'' (with Howell and Trekell) 1971; Editor, "A History of Sport and Physical Education to 1900'' 1973 (with M.J. Spaeth) "Administrative Theory and Practice in Physical Education and Athletics'', 1975; "A History of Physical Education and Sport in the United States and Canada'', 1975; Ed., "Professing Physical Education and Sport Philosophy'', 1975; "Physical Education and Sport Philosophy'', 1977; "A History of Physical Education and Sport'' 1979; "Issues in North American Sport and Physical Education" 1979; also over 350 articles in prof. journs., mags. and newspapers; Hon. Award Soc. Municipal Recreation Directives of Ont., 1956; Hon. Award, Candn. Assn. for Health, Phys. & Rec. 1975; Scholar-of-the-Year, Am. Alliance for Health, Phys. Educ. & Rec., 1978; Distinguished Service Award from Int'l Relations Council of Am. Assn. for Health, Phys. Ed., and Recreation, 1979; Pres., Am. Academy of Physical Education, 1981; Hon. Award, Am. Alliance for Health, Phys. Ed., Recreation & Dance, 1981; Delta Phi Alpha; Phi Epsilon Kappa; Unitarian; Liberal; recreations: piano, swimming; Home: 25 Berkshire Court, London, Ont. N6J 3N8; Office: London, Ont.

ZEMAN, Jarold Knox, B.D., D.Theol. (Bapt.); educator; b. Czechoslovakia, 27 Feb. 1926; e. Charles Univ., Philos. Faculty, Prague, grad. 1948; Hus Theol. Faculty, Prague, Th. Cand. 1948; Knox Coll., Univ. of Toronto, B.D. 1952; Univ. of Zurich, D.Theol. 1966; m. Lillian, d. James K. Koncicky, Esterhazy, Sask., 18 June 1951; children: Miriam, Dagman (Mrs. Gary Carter), Timothy, Janice PROF. OF CHURCH HISTORY 1968- , DIR. OF CONTINUING THEOL. EDUC., 1970-81, DIR. OF CONFERENCES, 1981- , ACADIA UNIV. AND ACADIA DIVINITY COLL. Pres., Baptist Federation of Canada, 1979-82; mem., Rel. Advisory Committee, CBC, 1979-83; Chrmn., Atlantic Bapt. Hist. Comte.; Bapt. Min., Toronto, 1949-55, Villa Nova, Ont., 1955-59; Secy., Dept. of Candn. Missions, Bapt. Conv. Ont., and Que., Toronto, 1959-68; Lectr., Bapt. Theol. Semy., Ruschlikon, Switzerland, 1965; Atlantic Sch. of Theology, Halifax, 1974; Mennonite Seminary, Elkhart, Ind; 1976-77; Regent College, Vancouver 1979; Visiting Lectr. to ten univs. since 1963; author, "The Whole World at Our Door", 1963; "God's Mission and Ours", 1964; "Historical Topography of Moravian Anabaptism", 1967; "The Anabaptists and the Czech Brethren" 1969; "Baptists in Canada and Co-operative Christianity", 1972; "The Hussite Movement and the Reformation", 1977; "Baptist Roots and Identity", 1978; "The Believers' Church in Canada", 1979 (co-ed.); "Baptists in Canada", 1980 (ed.); also articles; mem., Candn. Soc. Ch. Hist.; Am. Soc. Ch. Hist.; Am. Acad. Religion; Am. Soc. Ref. Research; Czechoslovak Soc. Arts & Sciences Am.; Address: Wolfville, N.S. B0P 1X0

ZEMANS, Mozah Edith, O.C. (1975), B.A.; b. St. Paul, Minn., 6 June 1913; d. Abraham Henry and Marcia (Calmenson) Goldberg; e. University of Alberta; University of Minnesota, B.A. 1934; m. Newton Irving Zemans, 15 January 1935; children: Frederick Henry, Sarah Gail; Presi-

dent, Vanier Inst. of the Family; mem. Nat. Extve., Candn. Jewish Congress; Past Nat. Pres., Nat. Council of Jewish Women; Dir., Spare of B.C.; Chrmn., First Candn. Conf. of Women's Organs.; Past mem. Adv. Comte. on Preventive Welfare, City of Calgary; First Senate, Univ. of Calgary; has served on numerous nat. and local bds. and comtes. of vol. organs.; rec'd Centennial Medal 1967; Jewish; Home: #1103, 2055 Pendrell St. Vancouver, B.C. V6G 1T9

ZERAFA, Boris Ernest, B.Arch., A.R.I.B.A.; architect; b. Cairo, Egypt, of Brit. parents, 20 June 1933; s. Ivan and Velda (Bertelli) Z.; e. Coll. Ste. Famille, Egypt and France; London Matric. (Eng.) 1950; Kingston Sch. of Arch., Eng., grad. (Sr. Art Award) 1955; m. Beverlev, d. Leslie Orde, Aug. 1954; children: Lian Anthony, Melanie Ann, Samantha Anne; PARTNER, WEBB, ZERAFA MENKES, HOUSDEN; was Chief Asst. Arch. with a firm in Eng., 1955-57; employed on projects in Montreal, Que., 1957-58; joined Peter Dickinson & Assoc. there in 1958; formed present Practice in 1961; firm awarded the Massey Medal, Nat. Design and Nat. Steel Design Awards; designed and supv. constr. of most major type bldgs. incl. schs. and univs., hotels, commercial offices, shopping, indust. and residential centres and Govt. projects; also projects in Toronto, Montreal, Calgary, Vancouver, Edmonton, Halifax, Quebec City, Boston, Dallas, London (Eng.), Paris, N.B., etc.; mem., Roy. Arch. Inst. Can.; Ont. Assn. Archs.; Roy. Candn. Acad.; Roy. Inst. of Brit. Architects; Am. Assn. of Architects; Ordre des architectes du Qué.; Specification Writers Assn. Can.; R. Catholic; recreations: music, travelling, fishing; Club: Bayview Country; Home: 33 Old Younge St., Toronto, Ont.; Office: 99 Yorkville Ave., Toronto, Ont. M5R 1C1

ZIEGLER, Brig. William Smith, C.B.E., D.S.O., E.D.; retired company executive; b. Calgary, Alta., 5 April 1911; s. Wm. Geo. and Mary E. (Smith) Z.; e. Schs. of Calgary and Edmonton, Alta.; Univ. of Alberta; m. Mildred E. Dean of Lake Louise and Edmonton, Alta.; one s., Rodney Christopher; Dir., Canadian Executive Service Overseas; mem. Adv. Bd., Salvation Army; joined Candn. Nat. Railways in 1951 and after a series of promotions through various adm. and extve. positions was apptd. Asst. Vice-Pres.-Personnel in Montreal in May 1955; service with Inland Cement Industries Ltd., Edmonton, 1956-73 as Exec. Vice-Pres., Pres. and Chmn.; served in 2nd World War; joined Candn. Army, 1939, serving Overseas in various theatres in Europe; gaz. Brig. at age 32; awarded D.S.O. (1944), C.B.E. (1945); Golden Aristion Andrias (Greece); Commdr. Order Orange Nassau with Swords (Netherlands); after hostilities served with Brit. Foreign Office (German Sec.) Control Comn. for Germany as Regional Adm. Offr., Land Niedersachsen; mem., Assn. Prof. Engrs. Alta.; Phi Kappa Pi; United Church of Canada; recreations: fishing, shooting, home carpentry; Clubs: Mayfair Golf & Country; Edmonton Petroleum; Home: 13834 Ravine Drive, Edmonton, Alta.

ZIFKIN, Harry; medical technologist, retired; b. Toronto, Ont., 12 Oct. 1913; s. Benjamin and Rose (Chertkoff) Z.; e. High Sch., Sioux City, Iowa; Mount Sinai Hosp., Toronto, Ont. (tech. training in med. tech.); Lic., Candn. Soc. of Lab. Tech. (M.T.); Candn. Soc. of Radiographers (R.T.); m. late Lyl, d. Joseph Pascoe of Winnipeg, Man., 1 Sept. 1940; children: Anita Lois, David Louis; Mgr. and Consultant, Lab-Exp. Ltd.; owner, Lylhar Photographics and Philatelics; Biomedical Resources Ltd.; Pres., Lylhar Holdings Ltd.; Med. Tech. in Mount Sinai Hosp., 1936-46; entered Partnership with Mr. M. A. Starkman, in Starkman Biological Laboratory, 1946; sole owner as of July 1, 1948; estab. branch at Montreal 1948, Winnipeg, 1948, Sydney, N.S., 1953; Vice-Pres., Toronto Acad. of Med. Technol., 1952-53; Vice-Pres. Central Region (1961-62), Zionist Organ. Canada; Pres., Z.O.C. Central Reg., 1964-66; Past Pres. (1960-61), Toronto Zionist Council;

mem. Un. Jewish Welfare Fund; Toronto Camera Club, Photo. Soc. of Am.; Candn. Assn. for Israel Philately (Pres.); Royal Philatelic Society (London); Biol. Photographic Assn.; Candn. Soc. of Lab. Tech.; Candn. Soc. of Radiographers; Pres. (1964), Central Div., Zionist Organ. of Can.; Lic., Candn. Lab. of Med. Technols.; has contrib. articles to Candn. Journ. of Med. Tech.; Liberal; Hebrew; recreations: photography, philately; Home: 608 Vesta Drive, Toronto, Ont. M5N 1H9

ZIMMERMAN, Adam Hartley, Jr., B.A., F.C.A.; company executive; b. Toronto, Ont., 19 Feb. 1927; s. Adam Hartley and Mary Ethelwyn (Ballantyne) Z.; e. Upper Canada Coll., 1938-40; Ridley Coll., 1940-44; Royal Candn. Naval Coll., 1944-46; Trinity Coll., Univ. of Toronto, 1946-50; m. Janet Digby d. John S. Lewis, Toronto, 19 May 1951; children: Barbara, Thomas, Mary, Kate; EXTVE. VICE-PRESIDENT & DIR., NORANDA MINES LIMITED, since 1974; Chrmn. and Dir., Fraser Inc. and Fraser Paper Ltd.; Maclaren Power and Paper Co.; Chrmn., and Dir. Northwood Mills Ltd.; Noranda Metal Indus. Ltd.; Noranda Aluminum Inc.; Vice-Chmn., MacMillan Bloedel Ltd.; Pres., Northwood Pulp and Timber Ltd.; Dir., B.C. Chemicals Ltd.; Royal Insurance Co. of Can. Ltd.; Southam Inc.; Economic Investment Trust Ltd.; Canada Wire & Cable Ltd.; Continental Bank of Canada; Wire Rope Indus. Ltd.; Southam Communications Limited; Canada Packers Inc.; Steetley Industries; C.D. Howe Inst.; Trustee, Hospital for Sick Children (Toronto); mem. Advisory Bd., Branksome Hall School, U. of Toronto, Faculty of Forestry; York U., School of Business, began career as Student-in-Accounts, Clarkson, Gordon & Co., 1950-54; Chart. Acct. 1956; Supv., 1956-58; joined present Co. as Asst. Comptroller, 1958, Comptroller, 1961-66, Vice President and Comptroller 1966-74; served 6 years in R.C.N.(R); mem., Corpn., Trinity Coll.; Fellow, Inst. of Chart. Accts. of Ont. Mining Assn. of Canada; Candn. Pulp & Paper Assn.; Cdn. Am. Cmte.; Zeta Psi; recreations: skiing, sailing, golf; Clubs: York; University; Mount Royal Toronto Golf; Craigleith Ski; Madawaska; Home: 15 Edgar Ave., Toronto, Ontario M4W 2B1; Office: (P.O. Box 45) Commerce Court W., Toronto, Ont. M5L 1B6

ZIMMERMAN, Arthur Maurice, B.A., M.S., Ph.D.; university professor; b. N.Y. City, N.Y., 24 May 1929; s. Frank and Marion (Ellentuck) Z.; e. New York Univ. B.A. 1950, M.S. 1954, Ph.D. 1956; m. Selma, d. Max Blau, 4 Oct. 1953; children: Susan Ann, Beth Leslie, Robert James; PROF. OF ZOOLOGY; Assoc. Dean, Sch. Of Graduate Studies, 1978-81; Acting Dir., Inst. of Immunology, 1980-81; Prof. of Zoology since 1964; Assoc. Chrm., Univ. of Toronto (1975-78); Research Asst. (1953-55) and Assoc. (1955-56), New York Univ., Instr., Newark State Coll., 1956 (rec'd. Lalor Research Award, Marine Biol. Lab., Woods Hole, (Mass.); Research Fellow, Nat. Cancer Inst., Univ. of Cal., Berkeley, 1956-58; Instr. of Pharmacol., State Univ. of N.Y., Downstate Med. Center, N.Y., 1958-60, and Asst. Prof. there 1960-64; Publications: over 100 scient. papers in tech. journs.; Fellow Am. Assn. Advanc. Science; Pres., Candn. Soc. Cell Biols., 1976-77; Treas., Am. Soc. Cell Biols., 1974-80; mem., Candn. Soc. Cell Biols.; Am. Soc. Cell Biols.; Corp. of Marine Biol. Lab.; Home: 8 Barksdale Avenue, Downsview, Ont. M3H 4S3

ZIMMERMAN, Edward Paul; executive; b. Toronto, Ont.; e. Oakwood Coll. Inst., Toronto; Univ. of Toronto; m; three s. one d.; PRES., TORSTAR CORP. 1978- ; has served as Pres., Reader's Digest Assn. (Can.) Ltd.; Mgr., Soap Div., Canada Packers Ltd.; Marketing Mgr. and Mgr., Lamp Div., Candn. Westinghouse Ltd., also Gen. Sales Mgr. and Gen. Mgr., Consumer Products; Dir., Toronto Star Newspapers Ltd.; Harlequin Enterprises Ltd.; Today Magazine Inc., Metrospan Printing & Publishing Ltd.; Torstar Corp.; Canadian Extve. Service Overseas; mem., Candn. Chamber Comm.; Clubs: Rideau; Quay;

Toronto Golf; Office: One Yonge St., Toronto, Ont. M5E 1P9

ZIMMERMAN, G. Douglas, B.A.Sc.; industrialist; b. Toronto, Ont., 8 May 1918; s. Dr. George Foster and Evelyn Pearl (Thompson) Z.; e. Univ. of Toronto, B.A.Sc. (Chem. Engn.) 1943; m. Mary, d. Walter R. McConnell, Toronto, Ont., 28 Aug. 1942; children: Judith Anne, Stephen Michael, Richard Donald, Susan Mary, Virginia Lynn, William Paul; PRESIDENT, VIDITON CORP. LTD.; Chrmn. Ahearn & Soper Ltd.; Instrument Engr., Canadian Synthetic Rubber Ltd., Sarnia, Ont., 1943-45; Field Engr., Fischer & Porter (Can.) Limited, 1949-56, & President, 1956-59; Executive Vice President and Director, Candn. Curtiss-Wright Limited, 1959-60; Pres., Industrial Wire & Cableù Ltd. 1960-74; member, Association of Professional Engrs. of Ontario; Presbyterian; recreations: swimming, riding; Clubs: Toronto Board of Trade; Ont. Jockey Club (Trustee); Home: Domarr Farm, R.R. No. 1, Kleinburg, Ont. L0J 1C0; Office: 100 Woodbine Downs, Rexdale, Ont. M5W 5S6

ZIMMERMAN, John Murr, B.A., D.D.; Lutheran clergyman; b. Milverton, Ont. 25 Dec. 1922; s. late John and late Louise (Murr) Z.; e. Milverton Pub. and High Schs.; Waterloo Coll. (Univ. of W. Ont.) B.A. 1944; Waterloo Lutheran Semy. grad. 1947; Waterloo Lutheran Univ. D.D. 1973; m. Alma Elizabeth d. late William Wolff 8 May 1948; children: Mark, Joel, Thomas, Peter, Paul; EXTVE. SECY., LUTHERAN CHURCH IN AMERICA, CAN. SEC. 1973- ; Parish Pastor, Pembroke, Ont. 1947-59; Kitchener, Ont. 1959-62; Spruce Grove, Alta. 1970-73; Pres. Western Can. Synod, Lutheran Ch. in Am. 1962-70; mem. Pembroke & Dist. High Sch. Bd. 1957-59; Vice Pres. North Etobicoke NDP Riding Assn.; mem. and Pres. Bd. of Govs. Waterloo Lutheran Univ. 1959-62; mem. Extve. Comte. and Gen. Bd. Candn. Council Chs.; Extve. Comte. Taskforce on Chs. and Corporate Responsibility; NDP; Lutheran; recreations: gardening, music; Home: 25 Widdicombe Hill, Apt. 210, Weston, Ont. M9R 1B1; Office: 40 St. Clair Ave. E., Toronto, Ont. M4T 1M9.

ZITZERMAN, Saul B., B.A., LL.B.; business consultant and financier; barrister and solicitor; b. Winnipeg, Man., 16 Feb. 1936; s. Harry and Minnie (Daitchman) Z.; e. Univ. of Manitoba, B.A. 1956; Manitoba Law Sch. LL.B. 1960; m. Zelma, d. late Myer Goldberg, 2 Sept. 1956; children: David, Mira; PRESIDENT, COUNSEL MANAGEMENT LTD.; Chrmn., Orphic Productions Ltd.; Sr. Partner, Buchwald, Asper, Henteleff, Ziterman, Greene & Shead, 1970; Dir., Ben Moss Jewellers Champs Food Systems Ltd.; Northern Messenger Ltd.; A & M Distributors Ltd.;r ead law with late L. S. Matlin, Q.C., called to Bar of Man. 1960; Partner, Matlin, Buchwald, Zitzerman, Kushner & Abbott 1961; Buchwald, Henteleff & Zitzerman 1965; Chrmn. Bd. Trustees, Talmud Torah Foundation; Pres. Bd. Dirs., Winnipeg Hebrew Sch.; Joseph Wolinsky Coll.; Dir., Winnipeg Jewish Community Council; Pres., Jewish Nat. Fund of Canada; Counsel to Bank of Nova Scotia 1970-74; Gen. Counsel to Imperial Group 1960-74, Pres., 1974-79; Past Vice-Pres., Liberal Party of Man.; Past Pres., Univ. Student Libs.; mem. Candn. Bar Assn. (Lect. in Taxation, Man. Sec.); Man. Bar Assn.; Law Soc. of Man.; Medico-Legal Assn.; Internat. Comn. of Jurists; Candn. Tax Foundation; Hebrew; Liberal; Zeta Beta Tau; recreations: golf, bowling, reading; Home: 13 Ramsgate Bay, Tuxedo, Man. R3P OV3; Office: 1900-155 Carlton St., Winnipeg, Man. R3C 3H8

ZOLF, Larry, B.A.; broadcast journalist; b. Winnipeg, Man. 19 July 1934; s. Falek Yoshua and Freda Rachel (Pasternak) Z.; e. Univ. of Man. B.A. 1956; Osgoode Hall Law Sch. Toronto; Univ. of Toronto; m. Patricia Beatrice Legge 29 May 1957; children: David, Rachel; Govt. Archivist Prov. Ont. 1958-59; publicist, speechwriter and pub. relations rep. Toronto Labour Council 1959-61; writer, news and current affairs reporter, producer CBC Toronto

1962- ; Lectr. Carleton Univ.; rec'd Wilderness Award TV journalism 1965; Brussels Internat. Labour Film Festival Prize 1966; essays and articles anthologised "The New Romans" 1968; "The Peaceable Kingdom" 1969; "Watkins to Gordon to You" Columbo Books, ed. Mordecai Richler; under pseudonym Jaded Observer "Dance of the Dialectic" 1973; contrib. various mags. and newspapers; Home: 62 Balsam St., Toronto, Ont. M4E 3B7; Office: CBC, 790 Bay St., Toronto, Ont.

ZUKERMAN, Barry, B.Sc.C.F.A; financial executive; b. 24 Dec. 1941; e. McGill Univ. B.Sc. 1963; Chart. Financial Analyst 1971; m. Helen; children: Aviva, Yona; PRES., ELLIOTT & PAGE LTD.; Vice Pres. HCI Holdings Ltd., Mackenzie & Sarlos; Chrmn. Extve. Comte. and Dir. Cineplex Corporation & Symbol Technologies Inc.; Dir. Mineral Resources International; COHO Resources Ltd.; HCI Holdings Ltd., Corrida Oils Ltd.; Nanisivik Mines Ltd., Amer. Bakeries Co. Invest. & Treasury Analyst CPR 1963-67; Invest. Analyst, Jones Heward & Co. 1967-68; Mgr. Special Research Projects, Draper Dobie 1969-72; Supt. Research & Portfolios, Toronto Dominion Bank 1972-78; Home: 15 The Bridle Path, Willowdale, ont. M2L 1C9; Office: Suite 1120, 120 Adelaide St. W., Toronto, Ont. M5H 1V1.

ZURBRIGG, Homer Franklin, M.Sc.; retired mining executive; b. Markham, Ont., 8 July 1909; s. Albert Henry and Mabel (Hutchinson) Z.; e. Queen.s Univ., B.Sc. 1931, M.Sc. 1933; m. Helen, d. late Alexander McLean, 2 May 1936; children: Mrs. John A. Dove (Janet Elizabeth), John Robert; began as Geol. with International Nickel Co. of Canada Ltd., Copper Cliff, Ont., 1933, Chief Geol. (Creighton Mine) 1935, Geologist then Chief Mines Geologist, 1937-40, Chief Geologist, Ont. Div., 1956 and transf. to Toronto, Ont., 1963; apptd. Asst. Vice Pres. and Chief Geol., 1964; Pres. and Dir., Canadian Nickel Co. 1965; Vice President, Exploration, International Nickel Co. of Canada Ltd. 1968-74; retired 1974; mem. Geol. Soc. of America; Canadian Inst. Miining & Metall.; Am. Inst. Mining, Metall. & Petroleum Engrs., Soc. of Econ. Geol.; Prof. Eng., Prov. of Ontario; Mining & Metall. Soc. of Am.; Protestant; Clubs: Bd. of Trade; Lambton; Home: 21 Valecrest Drive, Islington, Ont. M9A 4P4

ZWAIG, Melvin C., B.Com., C.A.; financial executive; b. Montreal, Que. 8 Dec. 1936; e. Sir George Williams Univ. B.Com. 1959; C.A. Que. 1961, Ont. 1964; PRESIDENT, THORNE RIDDELL INC.; Partner and Nat. Dir. Receivership & Insolvency Div. Thorne Riddell; articled with Riddell Stead; mem. Extve. Comte., Ed. Newsletter, Lectr. Summer Evening Sch., Students' Soc., Que. Order C.A.'s 1962-64; Lectr. Extension Dept. McGill Univ. 1962-68; Chrmn. Bankruptcy Study Group Candn. Inst. C.A.'s 1969-74; mem. Bankruptcy Comte. & Candn. mem'ship Comte. Comm. Law League Am. 1971-74; Insolvency Comte. Montreal Bd. Trade 1971-74; Academic Comte. Inst. Candn. Bankers 1975-77; Assoc. Internat. mem. Inst. Cert. Pub. Accts. Israel; Advisor, Insolvency Leg. Senate Comte. on Banking, Trade & Comm. 1975- ; Gov., Jewish Pub. Lib. Montreal; Dir. Can.-Israel Chamber Comm. & Industry; Montreal Israel Bonds; Pres. Assn. Alumni Sir George Williams Univ. 1972-74; mem. Adv. Bd. Concordia Univ.; Gov., Shaare Zedek Cong.; Jewish People's & Peretz Schs.; Candn. Assn. Ben-Gurion Univ. of Negev (Canadian Pres.); Vice Chairman Executive Committee & Governor, Ben-Gurion Univ.; Treasurer Adventure Place, Toronto; mem. Montreal Bd. Trade; co-author "The Proposed Bankruptcy Act" 1975; "The Proposed Bankruptcy Act" 1978; Clubs: Pinegrove Golf & Country; Montefiore; Ontario; Office: 2400, 630 Dorchester Blvd. W., Montreal, Que. H3B 1W2.

ZWICKER, Sherman Fenwick Homer, B.A.; executive; b. Halifax, N.S., 10 Feb. 1930; s. Fenwick Homer and Marion Louise (Dearborn) Z.; e. Lunenburg Co. Acad., 1935-44; Rothesay (N.B.) Coll. Sch., 1944-47; Dalhousie

Univ. B.A. 1950; (Pres. Students' Council 1949-50); m. Elinor Barbara, d. Dr. Samuel Marcus, Bridgewater, N.S., 30 June 1956; children: Peter Sherman, Lisa Ann, Andrea Barbara; PRES. AND MANG. DIR., ZWICKER & CO. LTD., (Estbd. 1789) since 1960; joined family firm as Secy.-Treas., Exec. Dir. Union of Nova Scotia Municipalities, March 1980- ; 1953; Pres. local Br. of Candn. Red Cross, 1961-63; Secy., Lunenburg Bd. Trade, 1953-56; mem. Bd. of Mang., Lunenburg-Queen's Mental Health Assn., 1962; of Lunenburg 1958-66; Past Dir., Fisheries Council of Can.; Pres., Candn. Atlantic Salt Fish Exporters Assn. 1956-58, 1967-70; Pres. Union of Nova Scotia Municipalities 1977-78; Pres., Lunenburg-Queen's Br. and mem. Prov. Extve., Candn. Mental Health Assn. 1969-70; Councillor, el. Mayor, Town of Lunenburg 1971-79; Dir., Lunenburg Heritage Soc. and Marine Museum Soc.; mem., Atlantic Dir. of Candn. Council of Christians and Jews; Alpha Mu; Zeta Psl; Anglican; Clubs: Bluenose Golf, (Pres. 1958-60); Lunenburg Yacht (Secy. 1958-60, 1967-70); Lunenburg Curling; R.N.S.Y.S.; Home: 150 Brook St., Lunenburg, N.S. B0J 2C0; Office: Suite 134, 1657 Barrington St. Halifax, N.S. B3J 2A1

ZYLAK, Carl John, B.A., M.D., F.R.C.P.(C); radiologist; educator; b. Smeaton, Sask. 30 May 1938; s. John and Joanna (Lipka) Z.; e. Univ. of Sask. B.A. 1958, M.D. 1962; F.R.C.P.(C) 1967; Diplomate Am. Bd. Radiol. 1968; m. Edith Ann d. C. M. McGarry, Fenton, Mich. 30 May 1964; children: Carl, Christopher, Andrew, Karen Ann; PROF. AND CHRMN. OF RADIOLOGY, McMASTER UNIV.; Head of Radiology McMaster Univ. Med. Centre; Internship McLaren Gen. Hosp. Flint, Mich. 1962-63; Henry Ford Hosp. Detroit (Radiol.) 1963-66; Teaching fellow, Univ. of Manitoba, 1966-67; Assoc. Radiol. Winnipeg Gen. Hosp. 1967; Dir. of Radiol. Man. Rehabilitation Hosp. and D. A. Stewart Centre 1970; Active Staff Health Sciences Centre, Gen. Centre, Rehabilitation/Respiratory Centres (Dir.) 1973; Head of Respiratory Radiol. Health Sciences Centre Winnipeg 1975-77; Visiting Prof. Univ. Calgary Med. Sch. 1975; Upstate Med. Center, Syracuse, N.Y. 1978; Univ. of Montreal, 1978; Michigan State Univ., Lansing, 1980; Guest Lecturer, Annual Meeting Royal Australasian Coll. of Radiology, Perth, 1980; Univ. of Monash, Melbourne, 1980; Univ. of Otago, Christchurch, N.Z., 1980; Univ. of Toronto, 1982; Rochester School of Medicine, 1982; mem. Radiol. Soc. N. Am. (Counsellor & mem. Educ. Materials Comte.); Ed. Bd., Chmn., Chest Panel, Radiographics; Royal Coll. Phys. & Surgs. Can. (Examiner Diagnostic Radiol.); Candn. Assn. Radiols. (Alternate Councillor Man. Div. 1971-73, Councillor 1973-75, mem. various comtes.); Man. Med. Assn. (Secy. Sec. Radiol. 1971-73, Pres. of Sec. 1973-75, Hon. Treas. 1974-75); author or co-author numerous scient. publs.; Liberal; R. Catholic; recreations: golf, curling; Clubs: Burlington Golf & country; Hamilton Golf and Country; Home: 1560 Snake Rd., Waterdown, Ont. L0R 2H0; Office: Hamilton; Ont. L8S 4J9.

ZYTARUK, George J., B.Ed., M.A., Ph.D.; educator; b. Edwand, Alta., 6 May 1927; s. John and Doris (Wennick) Z.; e. Smoky Lake (Alta.) High Sch., 1945; Univ. of Alta., B.Ed. 1949, B.A. 1953, M.A. 1958; Univ. of Wash., Ph.D. (Eng.) 1965; m. JoAnn, d. Andrew Korenda, Edmonton, Alta., 12 July 1958; children: Carolyn, John, Maria; PRESIDENT, NIPISSING UNIV. COLL., and Prof. of Eng. there since 1967; Ex-officio mem. Bd. of Govs.; secondary sch. teacher in Alta. 1949-63; Prof. of Eng., Univ. of Alta., 1965-67; served with COTC 1946-49; comnd. 1949; rec'd IODE Overseas Scholarship 1953-54; Can. Council Fellowship 1964-65, Can. Council Leave Fellowship 1975-76; Pres., D. H. Lawrence Soc. of America 1977- ; author, "D. H. Lawrence's Response to Russian Literature", 1971; "The Collected Letters of Jessie Chambers" 1979; Ed., "The Quest for Rananim: D. H. Lawrence's Letters to S. S. Koteliansky", 1970 (selected by Modern Lang. Assn. for Scholar's Lib.); Ed., 'The Letters of D.H. Lawrence", 2. vol. 1981 (in press); other

writings incl. articles in various lit. journs.; Past Pres.,
D.H. Lawrence Soc. of Am.; mem. Assn. of Canadian
Univ. Teachers of Eng. (ACUTE); Modern Lang. Assn.;
Ukrainian Orthodox; recreations: boating, skiing, wood-
work; Club: Rotary; Home: 122 Silver Lady Lane, North
Bay, Ont. P1B 8G4; Office: North Bay, Ont.

ABBREVIATIONS

Short forms of common words, positions, and place-names are used throughout the text where these are free of ambiguity and permit additional information within the space available. However, many other abbreviations, particularly ones relating to academic degrees, honours, and awards, also necessarily appear in the course of the biographies, and the following list of meanings is offered for the convenience of users of the *Canadian Who's Who*.

A.A.A.	Amateur Athletic Association	A.R.I.B.A.	Associate of the Royal Institute of British Architects
A.A.G.	Assistant-Adjutant-General	Arty.	Artillery
A.A.O.N.M.S.	Ancient Arabic Order of the Nobles of the Mystic Shrine	A.S.A.	Associate of the Society of Actuaries
A.A. & Q.M.G.	Assistant Adjutant and Quartermaster General	Atty.	Attorney
A.B.	Bachelor of Arts (U.S.)		
A.C.A.	Associate of the Institute of Chartered Accountants (England)	b.	Born
		B.A.I.	Bachelor of Engineering
Acad.	Academy; Academician; Academic	B.A.O.	Bachelor of Obstetrics
		B.Arch.	Bachelor of Architecture
A.C.C.O.	Associate of the Canadian College of Organists	Bart.	Baronet
		B.A.S.	Bachelor in Agricultural Science
A.C.D.	Archaeologiae Christianae Doctor (See Doct. Arch.)	B.A.Sc.	Bachelor of Applied Science
		Batty.	Battery
A.D.C.	Aide-de-Camp	B.B.A.	Bachelor of Business Administration
Ad eund.	Ad eundem gradum (admitted to the same degree)		
		B.B.C.	British Broadcasting Corporation
Adj (t).	Adjutant	B.C.D.	Bachelier en Chirurgie Dentale
A.D.M.S.	Assistant Director of Medical Services	B.C.L.	Bachelor of Civil (or Common) Law
A.F. & A.M.	Ancient Free and Accepted Masons	B.Ch., B.Chir.	Bachelor of Surgery
		B.Com.	
A.F.C.	Air Force Cross	(B.Comm.)	Bachelor of Commerce
A.F.L.	American Federation of Labour	B.C.S.	Bachelor of Commercial Science
A.F.R.Ae.S.	Associate Fellow Royal Aeronautical Society	B.D.	Bachelor of Divinity
		B.D.C.	Bachelor of Canon Law (Bacc. Droit Canonique)
Ag. de l'U (Paris)	Agrégé de l'Université (Paris)		
Ag. de Phil.	Agrégé de Philosophie	B.E.	Bachelor of Engineering
Agron.	Agronomy; Agronomist	B.Ed.	Bachelor of Education
A.I.A.	Associate of the Institute of Actuaries (England)	Beds.	Bedfordshire
		B.E.E.	Bachelor of Electrical Engineering
A.I.C.E.	Associate of the Institute of Engineers (England)	B.E.F.	British Expeditionary Force
		B. en Ph.	Bachelier en Philosophie
A.I.I.A.	Associate Insurance Institute of America	B.en Sc.Com.	Bachelier en Science Commerciale
A.I.S.A.	Associate of the Incorporated Secretaries' Association	Berks.	Berkshire
		B.ès A.	Bachelier ès Arts
A.L.A.	Associate of the Library Association (England); American Library Association	B.ès L.	Bachelier ès Lettres
		B.ès Sc.	Bachelier ès Science
		B.ès Sc.App.	Bachelier ès Science Appliqué
A.M.	Master of Arts; Albert Medal	B.F.	Bachelor of Forestry
A.M.C.	Army Medical Corps	Bgde.	Brigade
Anat.	Anatomy; Anatomical; Anatomist	B.J.	Bachelor of Journalism
A.O.C.	Air Officer Commanding	B.J.C.	Bachelor in Canon Law
A.O.C.-in-C.	Air Officer Commanding-in-Chief	B.L.	Bachelor in Literature (or of Laws)
A.Q.M.G.	Assistant-Quartermaster-General		
A.R.A.	Associate of the Royal Academy	B.Litt.	Bachelor of Letters (or of Literature)
A.R.A.M.	Associate of the Royal Academy of Music		
		B.L.S.	Bachelor of Library Science
A.R.C.A.	Associate of the Royal Canadian Academy of Arts; Associate Royal College of Art	B.M.	Bachelor of Medicine
		B.Mus.	Bachelor of Music

B.M.V.	Bachelier en Médicine Vetérinaire	**Chev.**	Chevalier
Bn.	Battalion	**Chim.**	Chimie; Chimique; Chimiste
B.N.A.	British North America	**Chirurg.**	Chirurgical; Chirurgien
Bot.	Botany; Botanist; Botanical	**Ch.M.**	Mastery of Surgery
B.Paed.(Péd.)	Bachelor of Pedagogy	**Chrmn.**	Chairman
B.P.A.	Bachelor of Public Administration	**Cie.**	Compagnie
B.P.E.	Bachelor of Physical Education	**C. in C.**	Commander-in-Chief
B.Ph.	Bachelor of Philosophy	**C. of E.**	Church of England
B.P.H.E.	Bachelor of Physical and Health Education	**C.L.C.**	Canadian Labour Congress
Brig.	Brigadier	**C.L.J.**	Commander of the Order of St. Lazarus of Jerusalem
B.S.	Bachelor of Science (U.S.)	**Clin.**	Clinical; Clinic
B.S.A., B.Sc.A.	Bachelor of Science in Agriculture	**Clk.**	Clerk
B.Sc.	Bachelor of Science	**C.L.U.**	Chartered Life Underwriter
B.Sc.Com.	Bachelor of Commercial Science	**C.M.**	Canada Medal; Member of the Order of Canada; Membre de l'Ordre du Canada; Master in Surgery
B.Sc.F.	Bachelor of Science in Forestry		
B.Sc.Soc.	Bachelor of Social Science		
B.S.C.E.	Bachelor of Science in Civil Engineering	**C.M.G.**	Companion of St. Michael and St. George
B.S.Ed.	Bachelor of Science in Education	**C.N.I.B.**	Canadian National Institute for the Blind
B.S.E.E.	Bachelor of Science in Electrical Engineering	**C.N.R.**	Canadian National Railways
		C.O.	Commanding Officer
B.S.F.	Bachelor of Science in Forestry	**Co.**	County; Company
B.S.M.E.	Bachelor of Science in Mechanical Engineering	**C.O.F.**	Canadian Order of Foresters; Catholic Order of Foresters
B.S.P.	Bachelor of Science of Pharmacy	**Coll.**	College; Collegiate
		Cons.	Conservative; Conservateur
B.S.S.	Bachelor of Social Sciences	**C.O.T.C.**	Canadian Officers' Training Corps
B.S.W.	Bachelor of Social Work	**C.P.A.**	Certified Public Accountant
Bt.	Brevet	**Cpl.**	Corporal
B.T., B.Th.	Bachelor of Theology	**C.P.R.**	Canadian Pacific Railway
Bucks.	Buckinghamshire	**C.R.**	Conseil de la reine
B.V.Sc.	Bachelor of Veterinary Science	**cr.**	Created; Crée
B.W.I.	British West Indies	**C.S.I.**	Companion of the Order of the Star of India
		C.St.J.	Commander of the Order of St. John of Jerusalem
(C).	Canada	**C.V.O.**	Companion of the Royal Victorian Order
C.A.	Chartered Accountant		
C.A.D.C.	Canadian Army Dental Corps	**Cytol.**	Cytology; Cytological; Cytologist
Cambs.	Cambridgeshire		
C.A.M.C.	Canadian Army Medical Corps		
Cantab.	Pertaining to Cambridge University, England	**d.**	Daughter; Died
		D.A.	Doctor of Archaeology (Laval)
C.A.P.C.	Canadian Army Pay Corps	**D.A.A.G.**	Deputy Assistant-Adjutant-General
C.A.S.C.	Canadian Army Service Corps		
C.B.	Companion of the Bath; Cape Breton	**D.A.A. & Q.M.G.**	Deputy Assistant-Adjutant and Quartermaster-General
C.B.C.	Canadian Broadcasting Corporation	**D.Adm.**	Doctor of Administration
		D.A.D.M.S.	Deputy Assistant Director of Medical Services
C.B.E.	Commander Order of the British Empire	**D.A.G.**	Deputy Adjutant-General
C.C.	Companion of the Order of Canada; Compagnon de l'Ordre du Canada	**D.A.Q.M.G.**	Deputy Assistant-Quartermaster-General
		D.A.Sc.	Doctor in Agricultural Sciences
C.C.L.	Canadian Congress of Labour	**D.B.A.**	Doctor of Business Administration
C.D.	Canadian Forces Decoration		
C.E.	Civil Engineer	**D.C.L.**	Doctor of Common Law (or Civil Law)
Cer.E.	Ceramic Engineer		
C.E.F.	Canadian Expeditionary Force	**D.C.M.**	Distinguished Conduct Medal
Cert.	Certificate; Certified	**D.C.T.**	Doctor of Christian Theology
C.E.S.	Certificat d'études Secondaires (La Sorbonne)	**D.Cn.L.**	Doctor of Canon Law
C.F.A.	Canadian Field Artillery	**D.D.**	Doctor of Divinity
C.H.	Companion of Honour	**D.D.C.**	Docteur en Droit Canonique
Ch.B.	Bachelor of Surgery		

ABBREVIATIONS

D.de l'Un.	Doctorat de l'Université	**E.**	East; Eastern
D.D.M.S.	Deputy Director of Medical Services	**e.**	Educated; Eldest; Elder
		é.	Eduqué; Education
D.D.S.	Doctor of Dental Surgery	**Ecol.**	Ecology; Ecological; Ecologist
D.D.Sc.	Doctor of Dental Science	**Econ.**	Economy; Economics; Economical; Economist
def.	Defeated; Défaite		
D.Eng.	Doctor of Engineering	**E.D.**	Efficiency Decoration
D.en Méd. Vet.	Docteur en Médicine Vetérinaire	**Ed.D.**	Doctor of Education
D.en Ph.	Docteur en Philosophie	**Ed.M.**	Master of Education (Harvard)
Dent.	Dentist; Dental; Dentistry	**E.E.**	Electrical Engineer
D.ès L.	Docteur ès Lettres (Doctor of Letters)	**el.**	Election; Elected; Electoral
		ép.	Epous; Epouse; Epousé(e)
D.F.A.	Doctor of Fine Arts	**Epis.**	Episcopal; Episcopalian
D.F.C.	Distinguished Flying Cross	**Ethnol.**	Ethnology; Ethnological; Ethnologist
D.F.S.	Doctor in Forest Science (Laval)		
D.F.Sc.	Doctor of Financial Science (Laval)	**f.**	Fils; Fille
D.G.M.	Deputy Grand Master	**F.A.A.A.**	Fellow of the American Academy of Allergy
D.Gén.	Doctorat en Génie	**F.A.A.A.S.**	Fellow of the American Association for the Advancement of Science
D.H.L.	Doctor of Hebrew Literature		
D.Hum.Litt.	Doctor of Humane Letters		
D.I.C.	Diploma of Imperial College		
D.J.C.	Doctor of Canon Law	**F.A.A.S.**	Fellow of the American Academy of Arts and Sciences
D.L.	Doctor in Civil Law		
D.Lit. or D.Litt.	Doctor of Literature; also Letters	**F.A.C.D.**	Fellow of the American College of Dentistry
D.L.S.	Dominion Land Surveyor		
D.Litt.S.	Doctor of Sacred Literature	**F.A.C.H.A.**	Fellow of the American College of Health Administrators
D.M.	Doctorate Médecine		
D.Man.Sc.	Doctor of Management Sciences	**F.A.C.P.**	Fellow of the American College of Physicians
D.Mus.	Doctorat en musique		
D.O.	Doctor of Osteopathy	**F.A.C.S.**	Fellow of the American College of Surgeons
D.O.C.	District Officer Commanding		
Doct.Arch.	Doctor of Christian Archeology (Pontifical Institute, Rome)	**F.A.E.**	Fellow of the Accountants' and Executives' Corporation of Canada
Dom.	Dominion		
D.Paed.(Péd.)	Doctor of Pedagogy	**F.A.G.S.**	Fellow of the American Geographical Society
D.P.H.	Doctor (or Diploma) of Public Health	**F.A.I.A.**	Fellow of the American Institute of Architects
D.Phil., D.Ph.	Doctor of Philosophy		
D.P.Sc.	Doctor of Political, Social and Economic Sciences	**F.A.P.H.A.**	Fellow of the American Public Health Association
Dr.Com.Sc.	Doctor of Commercial Science	**F.A.P.S.**	Fellow of the American Physical Society
Dr. de l'U. (Paris)	Doctor of the University (Paris)	**F.B.A.**	Fellow of the British Academy
Dr. ès Lettres	Doctor of Letters (History of Literature)	**F.B.O.A.**	Fellow of the British Optical Association
Dr.jur.	Doctor Juris	**F.B.O.U.**	Fellow of the British Ornithologists Union
Dr.rer.pol.	Doctor of Political Economy (Dr. Rerum Politicarum)	**F.Brit.I.R.E.**	Fellow of the British Institution of Radio Engineers
D.S.A.	Docteur ès Science Agricole	**F.B.Ps.S.**	Fellow of the British Psychological Society
D.S.C.	Distinguished Service Cross		
D.Sc.	Doctor of Science	**F.B.S.C.**	Fellow of the British Society of Commerce
D.Sc.Adm.	Doctor in Administrative Sciences		
D.Sc.C(om).	Doctor of Commercial Science	**F.C.A.**	Fellow of the Institute of Chartered Accountants
D.Sc.Fin.	Doctor of Financial Science		
D.Sc.Nat.	Doctor of Natural Science	**F.C.A.S.I.**	Fellow of the Canadian Aeronautics and Space Institute
D.Sc.P.	Doctor of Political Science		
D.Sc.Soc.	Doctor of Social Science	**F.C.B.A.**	Fellow of The Canadian Bankers' Association
D.S.O.	Companion of the Distinguished Service Order	**F.C.C.O.**	Fellow of The Canadian College of Organists
D.S.S.	Doctor of Sacred Scripture		
D.Th., D.Theol.	Doctor of Theology	**F.C.I.**	Fellow of the Canadian Credit Institute
D.U.	Docteur d'Université		
D.Univ.(Paris)	Doctor of the University (Paris)	**F.C.I.A.**	Fellow of the Canadian Institute of Actuaries
D.V.M.	Doctor of Veterinary Medicine		
D.V.Sc.	Doctor of Veterinary Science		

F.C.I.C.	Fellow of the Chemical Institute of Canada	**F.R.Ae.S.**	Fellow of the Royal Aeronautical Society
F.C.I.I.	Fellow of the Chartered Insurance Institute	**F.R.A.I.**	Fellow of the Royal Anthropological Institute
F.C.I.S.	Fellow of the Chartered Institute of Secretaries	**F.R.A.I.C.**	Fellow of the Royal Architectural Institute of Canada
F.C.S.	Fellow of the Chemical Society	**F.R.A.M.**	Fellow of the Royal Academy of Music (London)
F.C.W.A.	Fellow of the Institute of Cost and Works Accountants	**F.R.A.S.**	Fellow of the Royal Astronomical Society; also Fellow of the Royal Asiatic Society
F.E.I.C.	Fellow of the Engineering Institute of Canada		
F.E.S.	Fellow of the Entomological Society; Fellow of the Ethnological Society	**F.R.B.S.**	Fellow of the Royal Botanic Society; Fellow of the Royal Society of British Sculptors
F.F.A.	Fellow of the Faculty of Actuaries (Scotland)	**F.R.C.D.(C).**	Fellow of the Royal College of Dentists (Canada)
F.F.P.S.	Fellow of the Royal Faculty of Physicians and Surgeons (Glasgow)	**F.R.C.M.**	Fellow of the Royal College of Music
F.F.R.	Fellow of the Faculty of Radiologists	**F.R.C.O.**	Fellow of the Royal College of Organists
F.G.A.	Fellow of Gemmological Association	**F.R.C.O.G.**	Fellow of the Royal College of Obstetricians and Gynaecologists
F.G.S.	Fellow of the Geological Society	**F.R.C.P.**	Fellow of the Royal College of Physicians
F.G.S.A.	Fellow of the Geological Society of America	**F.R.C.P.(C).**	Fellow of the Royal College of Physicians (Canada)
F.I.A.	Fellow of the Institute of Actuaries (London)	**F.R.C.S.**	Fellow of the Royal College of Surgeons
F.I.A.I.	Fellow of the International Institute of Arts and Letters	**F.R.C.S.(C).**	Fellow of the Royal College of Surgeons (Canada)
F.I.Ae.S.	Fellow of the Institute of Aeronautical Sciences	**F.R.C.V.S.**	Fellow of the Royal College of Veterinary Surgeons
F.I.A.S.	Fellow of the Institute of Aeronautical Sciences (U.S.)	**F.R.E.S.**	Fellow Royal Empire Society; Fellow of the Royal Entomological Society; Fellow of the Royal Economic Society
F.I.C.	Fellow of the Institute of Commerce		
F.I.E.E.	Fellow of the Institute of Electrical Engineers	**F.R.G.S.**	Fellow of the Royal Geographic Society
F.I.I.A.	Fellow of the Institute of Industrial Administration	**F.R.G.S.(C).**	Fellow of the Royal Geographic Society (Canada)
F.I.I.C.	Fellow of the Insurance Institute of Canada	**F.R.H.S., F.R.Hist.S.**	Fellow of the Royal Historical Society
F.I.Inst.	Fellow of the Imperial Institute		
F.I.L.A.	Fellow of the Institute of Landscape Architects	**F.R.Hort.S.**	Fellow of the Royal Horticultural Society
F.I.M.	Fellow of the Institute of Metals	**F.R.I.B.A.**	Fellow of the Royal Institute of British Architects
F.I.M.C.	Fellow of the Institute of Management Consultants	**F.R.I.C.**	Fellow of the Royal Institute of Chemistry
F.Inst.P.	Fellow of Institute of Physics		
F.Inst.Pet.	Fellow of the Institute of Petroleum	**F.R.I.P.H.H.**	Fellow of the Royal Institute of Public Health and Hygiene
F.I.R.E.	Fellow of the Institution of Radio Engineers	**F.R.M.S.**	Fellow of the Royal Microscopical Society
F.I.S.A.	Fellow of the Incorporated Secretaries' Association	**F.R.Met.S.**	Fellow of the Royal Meteorological Society
F.L.A.	Fellow of the Library Association (England)	**F.R.N.S.**	Fellow of the Royal Numismatic Society
F.L.C.M.	Fellow of the London College of Music	**F.R.P.S.L.**	Fellow of the Royal Philatelic Society, London
F.L.S.	Fellow of the Linnean Society	**F.R.S.**	Fellow of the Royal Society
F.M.S.A.	Fellow of the Mineralogical Society of America	**F.R.S.A.**	Fellow of the Royal Society of Arts
F.P.S.	Fellow of Philosophical Society; also Pathological Society of Great Britain	**F.R.S.C.**	Fellow of the Royal Society of Canada
F.Phys.S.	Fellow of the Physical Society	**F.R.S.E.**	Fellow of the Royal Society of Edinburgh

ABBREVIATIONS

F.R.S.H.	Fellow of the Royal Society of Health
F.R.S.L.	Fellow of the Royal Society of Literature
F.R.S.M.	Fellow of the Royal Society of Medicine
F.R.S.T.M.&H.	Fellow of the Royal Society of Tropical Medicine and Hygiene
F.S.A.	Fellow of the Society of Antiquaries; Fellow of the Society of Actuaries (U.S.)
F.S.A.A.	Fellow of the Society of Incorporated Accountants and Auditors
F.S.E.	Fellow of the Society of Engineers
F.S.S.	Fellow of the Royal Statistical Society
F.Z.S.	Fellow of the Zoological Society
Gaz.	Gazetted
G.B.E.	Knight Grand Cross, Order of the British Empire
G.C.	George Cross
G.C.I.E.	Knight Grand Commander of the Indian Empire
G.C.M.G.	Knight Grand Cross of St. Michael and St. George
G.C.S.I.	Knight Grand Commander of the Star of India
G.C.V.O.	Knight Grand Cross of the Royal Victorian Order
g.e.	General Election
Geneal.	Genealogy; Genealogist; Genealogical
Geol.	Geology; Geological; Geologist
G.H.Q.	General Headquarters
Glos.	Gloucestershire
G.M.	George Medal
G.O.C.	General Officer Commanding
G.S.O.	General Staff Officer
H. of C.	House of Commons
Hants.	Hampshire
H.E.	His (or Her) Excellency; His Eminence
Herts.	Hertfordshire
Histol.	Histology; Histological; Histologist
H.M.	His (or Her) Majesty
H.M.C.S.	Her Majesty's Canadian Ship
H.M.S.	Her Majesty's Ship
H.O.	Head Office
Homoeo.	Homoeopathy; Homoeopathic; Homoeopath
Hortic.	Horticulture; Horticultural; Horticulturist
H.Q.	Headquarters
H.R.H.	His (or Her) Royal Highness
Hts.	Heights
Hunts.	Huntingdonshire
i/c	In Charge
I.C.A.O.	International Civil Aviation Organization

I.L.O.	International Labour Office
Inf.	Infantry
Ins.	Insurance
Inspr.	Inspector
Inst.	Institute; Institution; Institut
Inst(r).	Instructor; Instruction
Invest.	Investment; Investissement
Investig.	Investigation
I.O.D.E.	Independent Order Daughters of the Empire
I.O.F.	Independent Order of Foresters
I.O.O.F.	Independent Order of Oddfellows
I.S.O.	Imperial Service Order
J.C.B.	Bachelor of Canon Law
J.C.D.	Juris Canonici Doctor (Doctor of Canon Law)
J.C.L.	Juris Canonici Licentiatus (Licentiate in Canon Law)
J.D.	Doctor of Jurisprudence
J.D.S.	Doctor of Juridical Science
Jos.	Joseph
J.P.	Justice of the Peace
Jt.	Joint
J.U.L.	Licentiate of Law in Utroque (both Civil and Canon Law)
Jur.utr.Dr.	Juris utriusque doctor (equivalent to LL.D.)
K.B.E.	Knight Commander of the British Empire
K.C.	King's Counsel
K.C.B.	Knight Commander of the Bath
K.C.M.G.	Knight Commander of St. Michael and St. George
K.C.S.G.	Knight Commander of St. Gregory
K.C.S.I.	Knight Commander of the Star of India
K.C.V.O.	Knight Commander of the Royal Victorian Order
K.G.	Knight Commander of the Garter
K.St.J.	Knight of Grace, Order of St. John of Jerusalem
K.H.S.	Knight of the Holy Sepulchre
K.St.J.	Knight of Justice, Order of St. John of Jerusalem
K.T.	Knight of the Order of the Thistle; Knight Templar
Kt.	Knight; Knight Bachelor
Lancs.	Lancashire
L.Ch.	Licentiate in Surgery
L.D.C.	Licentiate Droit Canonique
L.Div.	Licentiate in Divinity
Ldr.	Leader
L.D.S.	Licentiate in Dental Surgery
L.ès. D.	Licencié ès Droit
L.ès. L.	Licencié ès Lettres
L.ès. Sc.	Licencié ès Sciences
Lic.	Licentiate; Licencié
Lic.Med.	Licentiate in Medicine
Lit.hum.	Litterae humaniores (classics)
Litt.	Littérateur; Littéraire
Litt.B.	Bachelor of Letters

Litt. D.	Doctor of Letters;	M.M.	Military Medal
	Doctor of Literature	M.N.A.	Member of the National Assembly
L.J.C.	Licentia Juris Canonici	M.P.	Member of Parliament
LL.B.	Bachelor of Laws	M.P.P.	Member of Provincial Parliament
LL.D.	Doctor of Laws	M.S.	Master of Surgery;
LL.L.	Licentiate of Laws		Master of Science (U.S.)
L.L.M.	Master of Laws	M.S.A.	Master of Science in Agriculture
L.M.C.C.	Licentiate of Medical College	M.Sc.Com.	Master in Commercial Sciences
	of Canada	M.Sc.F.	Master of Science in Forestry
L.O.L.	Loyal Orange Lodge	M.S.Ed.	Master of Science in Education
L.Péd.	Licence en Pédagogie		(U.S.)
L.Ph.	Licence en Philosophie	Msgr.	Monseigneur
L.Psych.	Licencié en Psychologie	M.S.S.	Master of Social Science
L.R.A.M.	Licentiate of the Royal Academy	M.S.W.	Master of Social Work
	of Music, London	Mun.	Municipality; Municipal
L.R.C.P.	Licentiate of the Royal College	M.U.Dr.	Medecinae Universae Doctor
	of Physicians		(Prague)
L.R.C.S.	Licentiate of the Royal College		(Dentistry and Medecine)
	of Surgeons	Mus.B(ac).	Bachelor of Music
L.R.C.T.	Licentiate of the Royal	Mus.D(oc).	Doctor of Music
	Conservatory of Toronto	Mus.M.	Master of Music
L.R.C.V.S.	Licentiate of the Royal College	M.V.O.	Member of Royal Victorian Order
	of Veterinary Surgeons	Mycol.	Mycology; Mycological;
L.S.A.	Licentiate in Agricultural Science		Mycologist
L.Sc.Comm.	Licentiate in Commercial Science		
L.S.Sc.	Licentiate in Sacred Scriptures		
L.Sc.Soc.	Licence in Social Science	n.	né(e)
L.Th.	Licentiate in Theology	N.A.T.O.	North Atlantic Treaty
			Organization
		N.D.G.	Notre Dame de Grace
m.	Married; Marié	N.D.P.	New Democratic Party
M.A.	Master of Arts	Neurol.	Neurology; Neurological;
M.A.A.A.	Montreal Amateur Athletic		Neurologist
	Association	No.	Number; Nombre
M.A.I.	Master of Engineering	Notts.	Nottinghamshire
M.A.L.S.	Master of Arts in Library Science	N.P.	Notaire Publique
M.A.N.	Membre de l'Assemblée Nationale	N.P.A.M.	Non Permanent Active Militia
M.A.O.	Master of Obstetric Art	N.S.W.	New South Wales
M.Arch.	Master of Architecture	Numis.	Numismatic
M.A.Sc.	Master of Applied Science	N.Z.	New Zealand
M.B.	Bachelor of Medicine		
M.B.A.	Master in Business		
	Administration	o.	Ordained; Ordiné
M.B.E.	Member of the Order of the	O.B.E.	Officer Order of the British
	British Empire		Empire
M.C.	Military Cross	O.C.	Officer of the Order of Canada;
M.C.E.	Master of Civil Engineering		Officier de l'Ordre du Canada;
M.Ch., M.Chir.	Master in Surgery		Officer Commanding
M.Com.	Master of Commerce	Offr.	Officer
M.D.	Doctor of Medicine	O.F.M.	Franciscan Fathers
	Military District	O.M.	Order of Merit
M.du C.	Canada Medal	O.M.I.	Oblate of Mary Immaculate
M.E.	Mining Engineer; Mechanical	Ophthal(mol).	Ophthalmology; Ophthalmic;
	Engineer		Ophthalmologist
M.Ed.	Master of Education	Organ.	Organization; Organized
Mem.	Memorial	Ornithol.	Ornithology; Ornithological;
M.Eng.	Master of Engineering		Ornithologist
Meth.	Methodist	O.S.A.	Ontario Society of Artists
Metrop.	Metropolitan	O.St.J.	Officer of Order of St. John
M.F.A.	Master of Fine Arts		of Jerusalem
M.H.A.	Member of House Assembly	Otol.	Otology; Otological; Otologist
M.H.L.	Master of Hebrew Letters	Oxon.	Oxfordshire; of Oxford
Mil.	Military; Militia		
Min.	Minister	P.	Progressive
Missy.	Missionary	Pac.	Pacific
M.L.A.	Member of the Legislative	Path(ol).	Pathology; Pathological;
	Assembly		Pathologist

P.C.	Privy Council; Privy Councillor		R.C.E.M.E.	Royal Canadian Electrical and
P.D.D.G.M.	Past District Deputy Grand			Mechanical Engineers
	Master		R.C.F.A.	Royal Canadian Field Artillery
P.Eng.	Professional Engineer		R.C.G.A.	Royal Canadian Garrison
Perm.	Permanent			Artillery
P.G.M.	Past Grand Master		R.C.M.P.	Royal Canadian Mounted Police
P.G.Z.	Past Grand Z		R.C.N.	Royal Canadian Navy
Ph.B.	Bachelor of Philosophy		R.C.N.V.R.	Royal Canadian Naval Volunteer
Ph.C.	Philosopher of Chiropractic			Reserve
Ph.D.	Doctor of Philosophy		R.C.O.C.	Royal Canadian Ordnance Corps
Philol.	Philology; Philological;		R.C.R.	Royal Canadian Regiment
	Philologist		R.C.Y.C.	Royal Canadian Yacht Club
Philos.	Philosophy; Philosophical		R.E.	Royal Engineers
Phm.B.	Bachelor of Pharmacy		Regt.	Regiment
Phys.	Physical; Physician		Res.	Resident
Physiol.	Physiology; Physiological;		R.F.A.	Royal Field Artillery
	Physiologist		R.F.C.	Royal Flying Corps
Phytopath(ol).	Phytopathology; Phytopatho-		Rhinol.	Rhinology; Rhinological;
	logical; Phytopathologist			Rhinologist
P.M.	Past Master		R.I.A.	Registered Industrial and
Pol.	Political			Cost Accountant
Polytech.	Polytechnic; Polytechnique		R.M.C.	Royal Military College (Canada)
Pomol.	Pomology; Pomological;		R.N.	Royal Navy; Registered Nurse
	Pomologist		R.N.S.Y.S.	Royal Nova Scotia Yacht
P.O.W.	Prisoner of War			Squadron
P.P.C.L.I.	Princess Patricia's Canadian		R.O.	Reserve of Officers
	Light Infantry		Röntgenol.	Röntgenology; Röntgenological;
Prep.	Preparatory			Röntgenologist
Presb.	Presbyterian		R.P.F.	Registered Professional Forester
Presby.	Presbytery		R.R.	Rural Route
Prop.	Proprietor; Proprietaire			
Prot.	Protestant		s.	Son
p.s.	Passed School of Instruction		Salop.	Shropshire
	(Officers)		Sask.	Saskatchewan
p.s.a.	Graduate of R.A.F. Staff College		S.B.	Bachelor of Science
p.s.c.	Passed Staff College		S.C.	South Carolina
P.S.G.M.	Past Supreme Grand Master		Sc.D.	Doctor of Science
Psychol.	Psychology; Psychological;		Sc.L.	Licence ès Sciences
	Psychologist		Sc.Soc.B.	Bachelier Science Sociale
Pte.	Private (soldier)		Sc.Soc.D.	Doctor of Social Science
Pty.	Proprietary		Sc.Soc.L.	License in Social Science
P.Z.	Past Z		S.D.	Doctor of Science
			Sec.	Section
Q.C.	Queen's Counsel		Sém.	Seminaire; Seminarien
Q.H.S.	Queen's Honorary Surgeon		Semy.	Seminary
Q.M.	Quartermaster		S.J.	Society of Jesus (Jesuits)
Q.M.G.	Quartermaster-General		S.J.D.	Doctor of Juristic Science
Q.O.R.	Queen's Own Rifles		S.M.	Master of Science
			Soc.	Society; Societé
			Sociol.	Sociology; Sociological;
R.A.	Royal Artillery			Sociologist
	Royal Academician		Solr.	Solicitor
R.A.F.	Royal Air Force		Sqdn.	Squadron
R.A.M.	Royal Academy of Music;		Sr.	Senior
	Royal Arch Mason		S.S.B.	Bachelier en Science Sacrée
R.A.M.C.	Royal Army Medical Corps		S.S.L.	Licentiate in Sacred Scripture
R.B.A.	Royal Society of British		Stat.	Statistical; Statistics; Statistician
	Architects		S.T.B.(S.Th.B.)	Bachelor of Sacred Theology
R.C.A.	Royal Canadian Artillery; Royal		S.T.D.(S.Th.D.)	Doctor of Sacred Theology
	Canadian Academy of Arts		S.T.L.(S.Th.L.)	Licentiate in Sacred Theology
R.C.A.C.	Royal Canadian Armoured Corps		S.T.M.	Master of Sacred Theology
R.C.A.F.	Royal Canadian Air Force			
R.C.A.M.C.	Royal Canadian Army Medical			
	Corps		Th.B.	Bachelor of Theology
R.C.D.	Royal Canadian Dragoons		Theol.	Theology; Theological;
R.C.E.	Royal Canadian Engineers			Theologian

Theos.	Theosophy; Theosophical; Theosophist	**V.C.**	Victoria Cross
		V.D.	Volunteer Officers' Decoration
Th.L.	Theological Licentiate	**Ven.**	Venerable (of an Archdeacon)
Topog.	Topography; Topographical; Topographer	**Very Rev.**	Very Reverend (of a Dean)
		Vet.	Veterinary; Veterinarian
Toxicol.	Toxicology; Toxicologist	**Vol.**	Volunteer; Voluntary; Volume
Twp.	Township	**V.Q.M.G.**	Vice-Quartermaster-General

U.E.L.	United Empire Loyalist	**W.P.T.B.**	Wartime Prices and Trade Board
U.K.	United Kingdom	**W.C.T.U.**	Women's Christian Temperance Union
U.M.W.A.	United Mine Workers of America		
Un.	United; Unis	**W.F.**	White Fathers
U.N.	United Nations	**Wilts.**	Wiltshire
U.N.E.S.C.O.	United Nations Educational, Scientific and Cultural Organization	**W.O.W.**	Woodmen of the World
U.N.I.C.E.F.	United Nations International Chidren's Emergency Fund	**y.**	youngest
unm.	Unmarried	**Y.M.C.A.**	Young Men's Christian Association
U.N.O.	United Nations Organization		
U.N.R.R.A.	United Nations Relief and Rehabilitation Administration	**Y.M.H.A.**	Young Men's Hebrew Association
		Yorks.	Yorkshire
Urol.	Urology; Urological; Urologist	**Y.W.C.A.**	Young Women's Christian Association
U.S.N.	United States Navy